SELECTED COMMERCIAL STATUTES

2016 Edition

Advisory Panel

CAROL L. CHOMSKY
Professor of Law
University of Minnesota Law School

CHRISTINA L. KUNZ
Professor Emerita
Mitchell Hamline School of Law

ELIZABETH R. SCHILTZ
Professor of Law
University of St. Thomas School of Law

CHARLES J. TABB
Mildred Van Voorhis Jones Chair in Law
University of Illinois College of Law

WEST
ACADEMIC
PUBLISHING

The publisher is not engaged in rendering legal or other professional advice, and this publication is not a substitute for the advice of an attorney. If you require legal or other expert advice, you should seek the services of a competent attorney or other professional.

Printed in the United States of America

ISBN: 978-1-63460-749-0

[No claim of copyright is made for official U.S. government statutes, rules or regulations.]

PREFACE

As commercial law professors who use statutory law supplements in our own classes, the four of us on the Advisory Panel welcome the opportunity to continue shaping this mainstay of commercial law teaching to serve the evolving needs of students and teachers. Although the statutes and codes included in the volume are available electronically, we continue to think a one-volume annotatable hard-copy resource remains a valuable tool for teaching and learning the provisions. From our experience updating the compilation each year, we also know the amount of work involved in creating a usable reference tool, making the continued publication of the statutory law supplements a worthwhile endeavor.

In 2016, West Academic Publishing is publishing a comprehensive statutory supplement (a useful tool for students taking more than one commercial law course) as well as abridged volumes appropriate for use in courses on secured transactions, sales and contracts, or payment systems. The materials in each volume reflect changes through the dates noted for each provision.

As we determine what to include or exclude from the comprehensive supplement and how to maximize the usability of the volume, we are constrained by publishing parameters that limit the volume's maximum size, so page thickness, margin size, and font size must be chosen to avoid increasing the size of the comprehensive volume. The price of the book must also stay competitive and within the reach of law students; dividing the comprehensive supplement into multiple volumes to make it less bulky to use (as has been suggested to us) would result in increased cost.

With these constraints in mind and based on our own judgments and discussions with other commercial law professors, we made the following selection decisions:

- The volumes present the UCC as a whole in the form in effect in most jurisdictions and therefore most often taught. For that reason, the compiled UCC (pages 1 to 941) contains the 2001 revision of Article 1 and the version of Article 9 incorporating the 2010 amendments, because those changes have been adopted in a majority of jurisdictions and are therefore likely to be incorporated in most commercial law classes.

- The volumes retain older versions of particular UCC Articles still in transition, to facilitate study of older cases and understanding of the revisions leading to the current version. For that reason, the Appendices to the UCC contain older versions of Articles 1, 3, 4, and 7.

- We have omitted the 2003 Article 2 and 2A amendments, except for those made as part of the Article 7 revisions, because they were withdrawn by the Uniform Law Commission and the ALI in May 2011.

- Professors differ widely on which international sources they teach, if any. We omit some suggested sources (for instance, the ICC's Incoterms) because copyright permission fees would make the book too expensive. Some less frequently used international sources (for instance, UNIDROIT and UNCITRAL material) are readily available online and should be accessed there, to keep the book less expensive and less unwieldy for its users. For online access, see:

    www.uncitral.org
    www.unidroit.org
    www.iccwbo.org

- These statutory supplements cannot include the wide variety of material treated in consumer law classes without becoming too bulky for other use. The supplements will nonetheless be adequate for use with consumer law books that have incorporated much of the non-commercial law material directly into their texts.

- For teachers who cover bankruptcy topics in their commercial law courses, the comprehensive supplement and the secured transactions volume include the bankruptcy statute and rules. For the bankruptcy forms, we refer the user to a site for electronic access, where the forms may be completed electronically and are updated to reflect any changes made in the annual revision cycle.

iii

Our aim has been to meet the needs of the majority of teachers, an aim we think we have realized with the four volumes that West Academic Publishing is publishing this year. We reconsider these decisions each year, so we hope that you will let us know how this version served your needs and those of your students.

Advisory Panel:

Prof. Carol L. Chomsky, University of Minnesota Law School, Minneapolis, MN
Prof. Emerita Christina L. Kunz, Mitchell Hamline School of Law, St. Paul, MN
Prof. Elizabeth R. Schiltz, University of St. Thomas School of Law, Minneapolis, MN
Prof. Charles J. Tabb, University of Illinois College of Law, Champaign, IL

June 2016

STUDENT GUIDE:
HOW TO USE THE UCC

The Uniform Commercial Code (UCC) has been widely enacted throughout the United States for almost 60 years. The UCC is not a static product, however. The Permanent Editorial Board for the Uniform Commercial Code, composed of members from the American Law Institute (ALI) and the Uniform Law Commission (ULC), has worked year after year to update and modernize the UCC. This process is reflected in the italicized notes at the beginning of each Article, as well as in the legislative history notes following the text and comments for many UCC sections.

Additional Articles expanded the UCC's coverage into emerging areas of law (Article 2A on leases of goods in 1987, Article 4A on funds transfers in 1989). Articles were deleted if no longer necessary in light of modern commercial realities (Article 6 on bulk sales in 1989). Articles were revised to modernize the law (Article 3 on negotiable instruments and Article 4 on bank deposits and collections in 1990, Article 8 on investment securities in 1994, Article 5 on letters of credit in 1995, Article 9 on secured transactions in 1998, Article 1 containing definitions and rules applicable throughout the UCC in 2001, Article 7 on documents of title in 2003). Frequent amendments keep the UCC current with new developments in commercial practices, including concerns related to electronic commerce and consumer protection.

While most revisions and amendments are adopted by many or all jurisdictions, not all revisions are successful or lasting. In 2003, a set of amendments to Article 2 (sales) and Article 2A (leases) was approved by ALI and ULC, but the amendments were withdrawn from the Official Text in 2011 after state legislatures did not adopt them.

To effectively use the UCC in this volume, you should be aware of the following choices about the substance and format:

- The American Law Institute (ALI) and the Uniform Law Commission (ULC, formerly known as the National Conference of Commissioners on Uniform State Laws) promulgated the Official Text of the Uniform Commercial Code in a series of enactments and subsequent modifications. When referring to such modifications, we use the terms "amended" or "amendment" to refer to changes in language of individual sections. We use the term "revised" or "revision" to refer to a rewrite of an entire UCC Article.

- This volume contains a "compiled" version of the UCC at pages 1 to 941. All of the Articles contained in that compilation are the current versions, reflecting all amendments and revisions adopted by the ALI and ULC, and thus dated 2016. The table on the next page indicates where other earlier versions of those Articles may be found in the appendices.

- The first page of each Article of the compiled UCC shows where in the appendices to find earlier versions, revisions, and amendments. The historical references there and in the table on the next page enable study of the amendment sequence and a comparison of versions.

- PEB [Permanent Editorial Board of the UCC] Commentaries are included in Appendix E. The sales and contracts volume contains only PEB Commentaries 1 and 10, because the others are not typically covered in either of those courses.

For additional source material on the history of the adoption of UCC sections, see

www.ali.org
www.uniformlaws.org

The Uniform Law Commission website (*www.uniformlaws.org*) contains information on pending legislation and enactments of each Article of the UCC.

UCC Article	Compiled UCC	Other version(s)
Article 1	Current	Appendix A: pre-2001 version
Article 2	Current*	
Article 2A	Current*	
Article 3	Current	Appendix B: pre-1990 version** Appendix C: 2002 amendments**
Article 4	Current	Appendix B: pre-1990 version** Appendix C: 2002 amendments**
Article 4A	Current	
Article 5	Current	
Article 6	Current	
Article 7	Current	Appendix D: pre-2003 version
Article 8	Current	
Article 9	Current	

* Except for conforming amendments made as part of the Article 7 revision process, Articles 2 and 2A do not include the 2003 amendments, which were withdrawn in May 2011.

** Appendices B and C are not included in the sales and contracts volume or secured transactions volume because earlier versions of and amendments to Articles 3 and 4 would not likely be taught in those courses.

TABLE OF CONTENTS

UNIFORM COMMERCIAL CODE*

The American Law Institute
and the
Uniform Law Commission

UNIFORM COMMERCIAL CODE (2016)

ARTICLE 1.   GENERAL PROVISIONS

PART 1.   GENERAL PROVISIONS

PART 2.   GENERAL DEFINITIONS AND PRINCIPLES OF INTERPRETATION

PART 3.   TERRITORIAL APPLICABILITY AND GENERAL RULES

ARTICLE 2.   SALES

PART 1.   SHORT TITLE, GENERAL CONSTRUCTION AND SUBJECT MATTER

PART 2.   FORM, FORMATION AND READJUSTMENT OF CONTRACT

UNIFORM COMMERCIAL CODE

UNIFORM COMMERCIAL CODE

ARTICLE 2A. LEASES

PART 1.   GENERAL PROVISIONS

PART 2.   FORMATION AND CONSTRUCTION OF LEASE CONTRACT

PART 3.   EFFECT OF LEASE CONTRACT

UNIFORM COMMERCIAL CODE

C.   DEFAULT BY LESSEE

ARTICLE 3.   NEGOTIABLE INSTRUMENTS

PART 1.   GENERAL PROVISIONS AND DEFINITIONS

PART 2.   NEGOTIATION, TRANSFER, AND INDORSEMENT

PART 3.   ENFORCEMENT OF INSTRUMENTS

ARTICLE 5.　LETTERS OF CREDIT

ARTICLE 6.　BULK TRANSFERS

ALTERNATIVE A

ALTERNATIVE B

ARTICLE 7.　DOCUMENTS OF TITLE

PART 1.　GENERAL

UNIFORM COMMERCIAL CODE

UNIFORM COMMERCIAL CODE

ARTICLE 8.   INVESTMENT SECURITIES

ARTICLE 9.   SECURED TRANSACTIONS

PART 1.   GENERAL PROVISIONS

[SUBPART 1.   SHORT TITLE, DEFINITIONS, AND GENERAL CONCEPTS]

[SUBPART 2.   APPLICABILITY OF ARTICLE]

UNIFORM COMMERCIAL CODE

PART 2. EFFECTIVENESS OF SECURITY AGREEMENT; ATTACHMENT OF SECURITY INTEREST; RIGHTS OF PARTIES TO SECURITY AGREEMENT

[SUBPART 1. EFFECTIVENESS AND ATTACHMENT]

[SUBPART 2. RIGHTS AND DUTIES]

PART 3. PERFECTION AND PRIORITY

[SUBPART 1. LAW GOVERNING PERFECTION AND PRIORITY]

[SUBPART 2. PERFECTION]

[SUBPART 3. PRIORITY]

[SUBPART 2. DUTIES AND OPERATION OF FILING OFFICE]

PART 6. DEFAULT

[SUBPART 1. DEFAULT AND ENFORCEMENT OF SECURITY INTEREST]

_____

UCC ARTICLE 1 (2016)

GENERAL PROVISIONS

Article 1 was revised in 2001.

PART 1.   GENERAL PROVISIONS

PART 2.   GENERAL DEFINITIONS AND PRINCIPLES OF INTERPRETATION

PART 3.   TERRITORIAL APPLICABILITY AND GENERAL RULES

National Conference of Commissioners on Uniform State Laws

DRAFTING COMMITTEE TO REVISE UNIFORM COMMERCIAL CODE ARTICLE 1—GENERAL PROVISIONS

Boris Auerbach, Wyoming, Ohio, *Chair*
Marion W. Benfield, Jr., New Braunfels, Texas

UNIFORM COMMERCIAL CODE

Article 1 Concordance

Unrevised	Revised
1–101	1–101
1–102(1, 2)	1–103
1–102(3, 4)	1–302
1–102(5)	1–106
1–103	1–103
1–104	1–104
1–105	1–301
1–106	1–305
1–107	1–306
1–108	1–105
1–109	1–107
1–201(25, 26, 27)	1–202
1–201(37)	1–201(b)(35), 1–203
1–201(44)	1–204
1–201 (all other)	1–201
1–202	1–307
1–203	1–304
1–204(1)	1–302
1–204(2, 3)	1–205
1–205	1–303
1–206	deleted
1–207	1–308
1–208	1–309
1–209	1–310

PART 1

GENERAL PROVISIONS

§ 1–101. Short Titles.

(a) This [Act] may be cited as the Uniform Commercial Code.

(b) This article may be cited as Uniform Commercial Code-General Provisions.

Official Comment

Source: Former Section 1–101.

Changes from former law: Subsection (b) is new. It is added in order to make the structure of Article 1 parallel with that of the other articles of the Uniform Commercial Code.

1. Each other article of the Uniform Commercial Code (except Articles 10 and 11) may also be cited by its own short title. See Sections 2–101, 2A–101, 3–101, 4–101, 4A–101, 5–101, 6–101, 7–101, 8–101, and 9–101.

§ 1–102. Scope of Article.

This article applies to a transaction to the extent that it is governed by another article of [the Uniform Commercial Code].

Official Comment

Source: New.

1. This section is intended to resolve confusion that has occasionally arisen as to the applicability of the substantive rules in this article. This section makes clear what has always been the case—the rules in Article 1 apply to transactions to the extent that those transactions are governed by one of the other articles of the Uniform Commercial Code. See also Comment 1 to Section 1–301.

§ 1–103. Construction of [Uniform Commercial Code] to Promote Its Purposes and Policies; Applicability of Supplemental Principles of Law.

(a) [The Uniform Commercial Code] must be liberally construed and applied to promote its underlying purposes and policies, which are:

(1) to simplify, clarify, and modernize the law governing commercial transactions;

(2) to permit the continued expansion of commercial practices through custom, usage, and agreement of the parties; and

(3) to make uniform the law among the various jurisdictions.

(b) Unless displaced by the particular provisions of [the Uniform Commercial Code], the principles of law and equity, including the law merchant and the law relative to capacity to contract, principal and agent, estoppel, fraud, misrepresentation, duress, coercion, mistake, bankruptcy, and other validating or invalidating cause supplement its provisions.

Official Comment

Source: Former Section 1–102 (1)–(2); Former Section 1–103.

Changes from former law: This section is derived from subsections (1) and (2) of former Section 1–102 and from former Section 1–103. Subsection (a) of this section combines subsections (1) and (2) of former Section 1–102. Except for changing the form of reference to the Uniform Commercial Code and minor stylistic changes, its language is the same as subsections (1) and (2) of former Section 1–102. Except for changing the form of reference to the Uniform Commercial Code and minor stylistic changes, subsection (b) of this section is identical to former Section 1–103. The provisions have been combined in this section to reflect the interrelationship between them.

1. The Uniform Commercial Code is drawn to provide flexibility so that, since it is intended to be a semi-permanent and infrequently-amended piece of legislation, it will provide its own machinery for expansion of

commercial practices. It is intended to make it possible for the law embodied in the Uniform Commercial Code to be applied by the courts in the light of unforeseen and new circumstances and practices. The proper construction of the Uniform Commercial Code requires, of course, that its interpretation and application be limited to its reason.

Even prior to the enactment of the Uniform Commercial Code, courts were careful to keep broad acts from being hampered in their effects by later acts of limited scope. See *Pacific Wool Growers v. Draper & Co.*, 158 Or. 1, 73 P.2d 1391 (1937), and compare Section 1–104. The courts have often recognized that the policies embodied in an act are applicable in reason to subject-matter that was not expressly included in the language of the act, *Commercial Nat. Bank of New Orleans v. Canal-Louisiana Bank & Trust Co.*, 239 U.S. 520, 36 S.Ct. 194, 60 L.Ed. 417 (1916) (bona fide purchase policy of Uniform Warehouse Receipts Act extended to case not covered but of equivalent nature), and did the same where reason and policy so required, even where the subject-matter had been intentionally excluded from the act in general. *Agar v. Orda*, 264 N.Y. 248, 190 N.E. 479 (1934) (Uniform Sales Act change in seller's remedies applied to contract for sale of choses in action even though the general coverage of that Act was intentionally limited to goods "other than things in action.") They implemented a statutory policy with liberal and useful remedies not provided in the statutory text. They disregarded a statutory limitation of remedy where the reason of the limitation did not apply. *Fiterman v. J. N. Johnson & Co.*, 156 Minn. 201, 194 N.W. 399 (1923) (requirement of return of the goods as a condition to rescission for breach of warranty; also, partial rescission allowed). Nothing in the Uniform Commercial Code stands in the way of the continuance of such action by the courts.

The Uniform Commercial Code should be construed in accordance with its underlying purposes and policies. The text of each section should be read in the light of the purpose and policy of the rule or principle in question, as also of the Uniform Commercial Code as a whole, and the application of the language should be construed narrowly or broadly, as the case may be, in conformity with the purposes and policies involved.

2. **Applicability of supplemental principles of law.** Subsection (b) states the basic relationship of the Uniform Commercial Code to supplemental bodies of law. The Uniform Commercial Code was drafted against the backdrop of existing bodies of law, including the common law and equity, and relies on those bodies of law to supplement its provisions in many important ways. At the same time, the Uniform Commercial Code is the primary source of commercial law rules in areas that it governs, and its rules represent choices made by its drafters and the enacting legislatures about the appropriate policies to be furthered in the transactions it covers. Therefore, while principles of common law and equity may *supplement* provisions of the Uniform Commercial Code, they may not be used to *supplant* its provisions, or the purposes and policies those provisions reflect, unless a specific provision of the Uniform Commercial Code provides otherwise. In the absence of such a provision, the Uniform Commercial Code preempts principles of common law and equity that are inconsistent with either its provisions or its purposes and policies.

The language of subsection (b) is intended to reflect both the concept of supplementation and the concept of preemption. Some courts, however, had difficulty in applying the identical language of former Section 1–103 to determine when other law appropriately may be applied to supplement the Uniform Commercial Code, and when that law has been displaced by the Code. Some decisions applied other law in situations in which that application, while not inconsistent with the text of any particular provision of the Uniform Commercial Code, clearly was inconsistent with the underlying purposes and policies reflected in the relevant provisions of the Code. *See, e.g.*, *Sheerbonnet, Ltd. v. American Express Bank, Ltd.*, 951 F. Supp. 403 (S.D.N.Y. 1995). In part, this difficulty arose from Comment 1 to former Section 1–103, which stated that "this section indicates the continued applicability to commercial contracts of all supplemental bodies of law except insofar as they are explicitly displaced by this Act." The "explicitly displaced" language of that Comment did not accurately reflect the proper scope of Uniform Commercial Code preemption, which extends to displacement of other law that is inconsistent with the purposes and policies of the Uniform Commercial Code, as well as with its text.

3. **Application of subsection (b) to statutes.** The primary focus of Section 1–103 is on the relationship between the Uniform Commercial Code and principles of common law and equity as developed by the courts. State law, however, increasingly is statutory. Not only are there a growing number of state statutes addressing specific issues that come within the scope of the Uniform Commercial Code, but in some States many general principles of common law and equity have been codified. When the other law relating to a matter within the scope of the Uniform Commercial Code is a statute, the principles of subsection (b) remain relevant to the court's analysis of the relationship between that statute and the Uniform Commercial Code, but other principles of statutory interpretation that specifically address the interrelationship between statutes will be relevant as well. In some situations, the principles of subsection (b) still will be determinative. For example, the mere fact that an equitable principle is stated in statutory form rather than in judicial decisions should not change the court's analysis of

whether the principle can be used to supplement the Uniform Commercial Code—under subsection (b), equitable principles may supplement provisions of the Uniform Commercial Code only if they are consistent with the purposes and policies of the Uniform Commercial Code as well as its text. In other situations, however, other interpretive principles addressing the interrelationship between statutes may lead the court to conclude that the other statute is controlling, even though it conflicts with the Uniform Commercial Code. This, for example, would be the result in a situation where the other statute was specifically intended to provide additional protection to a class of individuals engaging in transactions covered by the Uniform Commercial Code.

4.   **Listing not exclusive.** The list of sources of supplemental law in subsection (b) is intended to be merely illustrative of the other law that may supplement the Uniform Commercial Code, and is not exclusive. No listing could be exhaustive. Further, the fact that a particular section of the Uniform Commercial Code makes express reference to other law is not intended to suggest the negation of the general application of the principles of subsection (b). Note also that the word "bankruptcy" in subsection (b), continuing the use of that word from former Section 1–103, should be understood not as a specific reference to federal bankruptcy law but, rather as a reference to general principles of insolvency, whether under federal or state law.

§ 1–104.   Construction Against Implied Repeal.

[The Uniform Commercial Code] being a general act intended as a unified coverage of its subject matter, no part of it shall be deemed to be impliedly repealed by subsequent legislation if such construction can reasonably be avoided.

Official Comment

Source: Former Section 1–104.

Changes from former law: Except for changing the form of reference to the Uniform Commercial Code, this section is identical to former Section 1–104.

1.   This section embodies the policy that an act that bears evidence of carefully considered permanent regulative intention should not lightly be regarded as impliedly repealed by subsequent legislation. The Uniform Commercial Code, carefully integrated and intended as a uniform codification of permanent character covering an entire "field" of law, is to be regarded as particularly resistant to implied repeal.

§ 1–105.   Severability.

If any provision or clause of [the Uniform Commercial Code] or its application to any person or circumstance is held invalid, the invalidity does not affect other provisions or applications of [the Uniform Commercial Code] which can be given effect without the invalid provision or application, and to this end the provisions of [the Uniform Commercial Code] are severable.

Official Comment

Source: Former Section 1–108.

Changes from former law: Except for changing the form of reference to the Uniform Commercial Code, this section is identical to former Section 1–108.

1.   This is the model severability section recommended by the National Conference of Commissioners on Uniform State Laws for inclusion in all acts of extensive scope.

§ 1–106.   Use of Singular and Plural; Gender.

In [the Uniform Commercial Code], unless the statutory context otherwise requires:

(1)   words in the singular number include the plural, and those in the plural include the singular; and

(2)   words of any gender also refer to any other gender.

Official Comment

Source: Former Section 1–102(5). See also 1 U.S.C. Section 1.

Changes from former law: Other than minor stylistic changes, this section is identical to former Section 1–102(5).

1.   This section makes it clear that the use of singular or plural in the text of the Uniform Commercial Code is generally only a matter of drafting style—singular words may be applied in the plural, and plural words may be applied in the singular. Only when it is clear from the statutory context that the use of the singular or plural does not include the other is this rule inapplicable. *See, e.g.*, Section 9–322.

§ 1–107.   Section Captions.

Section captions are part of [the Uniform Commercial Code].

Official Comment

Source: Former Section 1–109.

Changes from former law: None.

1.   Section captions are a part of the text of the Uniform Commercial Code, and not mere surplusage. This is not the case, however, with respect to subsection headings appearing in Article 9. See Comment 3 to Section 9–101 ("subsection headings are not a part of the official text itself and have not been approved by the sponsors.").

§ 1–108.   Relation to Electronic Signatures in Global and National Commerce Act.

This article modifies, limits, and supersedes the Federal Electronic Signatures in Global and National Commerce Act, 15 U.S.C. § 7001 *et seq.*, except that nothing in this article modifies, limits, or supersedes section 7001(c) of that act or authorizes electronic delivery of any of the notices described in section 7003(b) of that Act.

Official Comment

Source: New

1.   The federal Electronic Signatures in Global and National Commerce Act, 15 U.S.C. Section 7001 *et seq.* became effective in 2000. Section 102(a) of that Act provides that a State statute may modify, limit, or supersede the provisions of section 101 of that Act with respect to state law if such statute, *inter alia*, specifies the alternative procedures or requirements for the use or acceptance (or both) of electronic records or electronic signatures to establish the legal effect, validity, or enforceability of contracts or other records, and (i) such alternative procedures or requirements are consistent with Titles I and II of that Act, (ii) such alternative procedures or requirements do not require, or accord greater legal status or effect to, the implementation or application of a specific technology or technical specification for performing the functions of creating, storing, generating, receiving, communicating, or authenticating electronic records or electronic signatures; and (iii) if enacted or adopted after the date of the enactment of that Act, makes specific reference to that Act. Article 1 fulfills the first two of those three criteria; this Section fulfills the third criterion listed above.

2.   As stated in this section, however, Article 1 does not modify, limit, or supersede Section 101(c) of the Electronic Signatures in Global and National Commerce Act (requiring affirmative consent from a consumer to electronic delivery of transactional disclosures that are required by state law to be in writing); nor does it authorize electronic delivery of any of the notices described in Section 103(b) of that Act.

PART 2

GENERAL DEFINITIONS AND PRINCIPLES OF INTERPRETATION

§ 1–201.   General Definitions.

(a)   Unless the context otherwise requires, words or phrases defined in this section, or in the additional definitions contained in other articles of [the Uniform Commercial Code] that apply to particular articles or parts thereof, have the meanings stated.

(b)   Subject to definitions contained in other articles of [the Uniform Commercial Code] that apply to particular articles or parts thereof:

(1) "Action", in the sense of a judicial proceeding, includes recoupment, counterclaim, set-off, suit in equity, and any other proceeding in which rights are determined.

(2) "Aggrieved party" means a party entitled to pursue a remedy.

(3) "Agreement", as distinguished from "contract", means the bargain of the parties in fact, as found in their language or inferred from other circumstances, including course of performance, course of dealing, or usage of trade as provided in Section 1–303.

(4) "Bank" means a person engaged in the business of banking and includes a savings bank, savings and loan association, credit union, and trust company.

(5) "Bearer" means a person in control of a negotiable electronic document of title or a person in possession of a negotiable instrument, negotiable tangible document of title, or certificated security that is payable to bearer or indorsed in blank.

(6) "Bill of lading" means a document of title evidencing the receipt of goods for shipment issued by a person engaged in the business of directly or indirectly transporting or forwarding goods. The term does not include a warehouse receipt.

(7) "Branch" includes a separately incorporated foreign branch of a bank.

(8) "Burden of establishing" a fact means the burden of persuading the trier of fact that the existence of the fact is more probable than its nonexistence.

(9) "Buyer in ordinary course of business" means a person that buys goods in good faith, without knowledge that the sale violates the rights of another person in the goods, and in the ordinary course from a person, other than a pawnbroker, in the business of selling goods of that kind. A person buys goods in the ordinary course if the sale to the person comports with the usual or customary practices in the kind of business in which the seller is engaged or with the seller's own usual or customary practices. A person that sells oil, gas, or other minerals at the wellhead or minehead is a person in the business of selling goods of that kind. A buyer in ordinary course of business may buy for cash, by exchange of other property, or on secured or unsecured credit, and may acquire goods or documents of title under a preexisting contract for sale. Only a buyer that takes possession of the goods or has a right to recover the goods from the seller under Article 2 may be a buyer in ordinary course of business. "Buyer in ordinary course of business" does not include a person that acquires goods in a transfer in bulk or as security for or in total or partial satisfaction of a money debt.

(10) "Conspicuous", with reference to a term, means so written, displayed, or presented that a reasonable person against which it is to operate ought to have noticed it. Whether a term is "conspicuous" or not is a decision for the court. Conspicuous terms include the following:

    (A) a heading in capitals equal to or greater in size than the surrounding text, or in contrasting type, font, or color to the surrounding text of the same or lesser size; and

    (B) language in the body of a record or display in larger type than the surrounding text, or in contrasting type, font, or color to the surrounding text of the same size, or set off from surrounding text of the same size by symbols or other marks that call attention to the language.

(11) "Consumer" means an individual who enters into a transaction primarily for personal, family, or household purposes.

(12) "Contract", as distinguished from "agreement", means the total legal obligation that results from the parties' agreement as determined by [the Uniform Commercial Code] as supplemented by any other applicable laws.

(13) "Creditor" includes a general creditor, a secured creditor, a lien creditor, and any representative of creditors, including an assignee for the benefit of creditors, a trustee in bankruptcy, a receiver in equity, and an executor or administrator of an insolvent debtor's or assignor's estate.

(14) "Defendant" includes a person in the position of defendant in a counterclaim, cross-claim, or third-party claim.

(15) "Delivery", with respect to an electronic document of title means voluntary transfer of control and with respect to an instrument, a tangible document of title, or chattel paper, means voluntary transfer of possession.

(16) "Document of title" means a record (i) that in the regular course of business or financing is treated as adequately evidencing that the person in possession or control of the record is entitled to receive, control, hold, and dispose of the record and the goods the record covers and (ii) that purports to be issued by or addressed to a bailee and to cover goods in the bailee's possession which are either identified or are fungible portions of an identified mass. The term includes a bill of lading, transport document, dock warrant, dock receipt, warehouse receipt, and order for delivery of goods. An electronic document of title means a document of title evidenced by a record consisting of information stored in an electronic medium. A tangible document of title means a document of title evidenced by a record consisting of information that is inscribed on a tangible medium.

(17) "Fault" means a default, breach, or wrongful act or omission.

(18) "Fungible goods" means:

   (A) goods of which any unit, by nature or usage of trade, is the equivalent of any other like unit; or

   (B) goods that by agreement are treated as equivalent.

(19) "Genuine" means free of forgery or counterfeiting.

(20) "Good faith," except as otherwise provided in Article 5, means honesty in fact and the observance of reasonable commercial standards of fair dealing.

(21) "Holder" means:

   (A) the person in possession of a negotiable instrument that is payable either to bearer or to an identified person that is the person in possession;

   (B) the person in possession of a negotiable tangible document of title if the goods are deliverable either to bearer or to the order of the person in possession; or

   (C) the person in control of a negotiable electronic document of title.

(22) "Insolvency proceeding" includes an assignment for the benefit of creditors or other proceeding intended to liquidate or rehabilitate the estate of the person involved.

(23) "Insolvent" means:

   (A) having generally ceased to pay debts in the ordinary course of business other than as a result of bona fide dispute;

   (B) being unable to pay debts as they become due; or

   (C) being insolvent within the meaning of federal bankruptcy law.

(24) "Money" means a medium of exchange currently authorized or adopted by a domestic or foreign government. The term includes a monetary unit of account established by an intergovernmental organization or by agreement between two or more countries.

(25) "Organization" means a person other than an individual.

(26) "Party", as distinguished from "third party", means a person that has engaged in a transaction or made an agreement subject to [the Uniform Commercial Code].

(27) "Person" means an individual, corporation, business trust, estate, trust, partnership, limited liability company, association, joint venture, government, governmental subdivision, agency, or instrumentality, public corporation, or any other legal or commercial entity.

(28) "Present value" means the amount as of a date certain of one or more sums payable in the future, discounted to the date certain by use of either an interest rate specified by the parties if that rate is not manifestly unreasonable at the time the transaction is entered into or, if an interest rate is not so specified, a commercially reasonable rate that takes into account the facts and circumstances at the time the transaction is entered into.

(29) "Purchase" means taking by sale, lease, discount, negotiation, mortgage, pledge, lien, security interest, issue or reissue, gift, or any other voluntary transaction creating an interest in property.

(30) "Purchaser" means a person that takes by purchase.

(31) "Record" means information that is inscribed on a tangible medium or that is stored in an electronic or other medium and is retrievable in perceivable form.

(32) "Remedy" means any remedial right to which an aggrieved party is entitled with or without resort to a tribunal.

(33) "Representative" means a person empowered to act for another, including an agent, an officer of a corporation or association, and a trustee, executor, or administrator of an estate.

(34) "Right" includes remedy.

(35) "Security interest" means an interest in personal property or fixtures which secures payment or performance of an obligation. "Security interest" includes any interest of a consignor and a buyer of accounts, chattel paper, a payment intangible, or a promissory note in a transaction that is subject to Article 9. "Security interest" does not include the special property interest of a buyer of goods on identification of those goods to a contract for sale under Section 2–401, but a buyer may also acquire a "security interest" by complying with Article 9. Except as otherwise provided in Section 2–505, the right of a seller or lessor of goods under Article 2 or 2A to retain or acquire possession of the goods is not a "security interest", but a seller or lessor may also acquire a "security interest" by complying with Article 9. The retention or reservation of title by a seller of goods notwithstanding shipment or delivery to the buyer under Section 2–401 is limited in effect to a reservation of a "security interest." Whether a transaction in the form of a lease creates a "security interest" is determined pursuant to Section 1–203.

(36) "Send" in connection with a writing, record, or notice means:

(A) to deposit in the mail or deliver for transmission by any other usual means of communication with postage or cost of transmission provided for and properly addressed and, in the case of an instrument, to an address specified thereon or otherwise agreed, or if there be none to any address reasonable under the circumstances; or

(B) in any other way to cause to be received any record or notice within the time it would have arrived if properly sent.

(37) "Signed" includes using any symbol executed or adopted with present intention to adopt or accept a writing.

(38) "State" means a State of the United States, the District of Columbia, Puerto Rico, the United States Virgin Islands, or any territory or insular possession subject to the jurisdiction of the United States.

(39) "Surety" includes a guarantor or other secondary obligor.

(40) "Term" means a portion of an agreement that relates to a particular matter.

(41) "Unauthorized signature" means a signature made without actual, implied, or apparent authority. The term includes a forgery.

(42) "Warehouse receipt" means a document of title issued by a person engaged in the business of storing goods for hire.

(43) "Writing" includes printing, typewriting, or any other intentional reduction to tangible form. "Written" has a corresponding meaning.

As amended in 2003.

Official Comment

Source: Former Section 1–201.

Changes from former law: In order to make it clear that all definitions in the Uniform Commercial Code (not just those appearing in Article 1, as stated in former Section 1–201, but also those appearing in other Articles) do not apply if the context otherwise requires, a new subsection (a) to that effect has been added, and the definitions now appear in subsection (b). The reference in subsection (a) to the "context" is intended to refer to the context in which the defined term is used in the Uniform Commercial Code. In other words, the definition applies whenever the defined term is used unless the context in which the defined term is used in the statute indicates that the term was not used in its defined sense. Consider, for example, Sections 3–103(a)(9)* (defining "promise," in relevant part, as "a written undertaking to pay money signed by the person undertaking to pay") and 3–303(a)(1) (indicating that an instrument is issued or transferred for value if "the instrument is issued or transferred for a promise of performance, to the extent that the promise has been performed"). It is clear from the statutory context of the use of the word "promise" in Section 3–303(a)(1) that the term was not used in the sense of its definition in Section 3–103(a)(9).* Thus, the Section 3–103(a)(9)* definition should not be used to give meaning to the word "promise" in Section 3–303(a).

Some definitions in former Section 1–201 have been reformulated as substantive provisions and have been moved to other sections. See Sections 1–202 (explicating concepts of notice and knowledge formerly addressed in Sections 1–201(25)–(27)), 1–204 (determining when a person gives value for rights, replacing the definition of "value" in former Section 1–201(44)), and 1–206 (addressing the meaning of presumptions, replacing the definitions of "presumption" and "presumed" in former Section 1–201(31)). Similarly, the portion of the definition of "security interest" in former Section 1–201(37) which explained the difference between a security interest and a lease has been relocated to Section 1–203.

Two definitions in former Section 1–201 have been deleted. The definition of "honor" in former Section 1–201(21) has been moved to Section 2–103(1)(b), inasmuch as the definition only applies to the use of the word in Article 2.** The definition of "telegram" in former Section 1–201(41) has been deleted because that word no longer appears in the definition of "conspicuous."

Other than minor stylistic changes and renumbering, the remaining definitions in this section are as in former Article 1 except as noted below.

1.   "Action." Unchanged from former Section 1–201, which was derived from similar definitions in Section 191, Uniform Negotiable Instruments Law; Section 76, Uniform Sales Act; Section 58, Uniform Warehouse Receipts Act; Section 53, Uniform Bills of Lading Act.

2.   "Aggrieved party." Unchanged from former Section 1–201.

3.   "Agreement." Derived from former Section 1–201. As used in the Uniform Commercial Code the word is intended to include full recognition of usage of trade, course of dealing, course of performance and the surrounding circumstances as effective parts thereof, and of any agreement permitted under the provisions of the Uniform Commercial Code to displace a stated rule of law. Whether an agreement has legal consequences is determined by applicable provisions of the Uniform Commercial Code and, to the extent provided in Section 1–103, by the law of contracts.

4.   "Bank." Derived from Section 4A–104.

5.   "Bearer." Unchanged, except in one respect, from former section 1–201, which was derived from Section 191, Uniform Negotiable Instruments Law. The term bearer applies to negotiable documents of title and has been broadened to include a person in control of an electronic negotiable document of title. Control of an electronic document of title is defined in Article 7 (Section 7–106).

6.   "Bill of Lading." Derived from former Section 1–201. The reference to, and definition of, an "airbill" has been deleted as no longer necessary. A bill of lading is one type of document of title as defined in subsection (16). This definition should be read in conjunction with the definition of carrier in Article 7 (Section 7–102).

---

*   *Referring to Article 3 before the 2002 revision.*

**   *This sentence appears to be in error because, although "honor" was deleted from Article 1, no conforming amendment to Section 2–103(1) was made as part of the Article 1 revision.*

7.   "Branch." Unchanged from former Section 1–201.

8.   "Burden of establishing a fact." Unchanged from former Section 1–201.

9.   "Buyer in ordinary course of business." Except for minor stylistic changes, identical to former Section 1–201 (as amended in conjunction with the 1999 revisions to Article 9). The major significance of the phrase lies in Section 2–403 and in the Article on Secured Transactions (Article 9).

The first sentence of paragraph (9) makes clear that a buyer from a pawnbroker cannot be a buyer in ordinary course of business. The second sentence explains what it means to buy "in the ordinary course." The penultimate sentence prevents a buyer that does not have the right to possession as against the seller from being a buyer in ordinary course of business. Concerning when a buyer obtains possessory rights, see Sections 2–502 and 2–716. However, the penultimate sentence is not intended to affect a buyer's status as a buyer in ordinary course of business in cases (such as a "drop shipment") involving delivery by the seller to a person buying from the buyer or a donee from the buyer. The requirement relates to whether *as against the seller* the buyer or one taking through the buyer has possessory rights.

10.   "Conspicuous." Derived from former Section 1–201(10). This definition states the general standard that to be conspicuous a term ought to be noticed by a reasonable person. Whether a term is conspicuous is an issue for the court. Subparagraphs (A) and (B) set out several methods for making a term conspicuous. Requiring that a term be conspicuous blends a notice function (the term ought to be noticed) and a planning function (giving guidance to the party relying on the term regarding how that result can be achieved). Although these paragraphs indicate some of the methods for making a term attention-calling, the test is whether attention can reasonably be expected to be called to it. The statutory language should not be construed to permit a result that is inconsistent with that test.

11.   "Consumer." Derived from Section 9–102(a)(25).

12.   "Contract." Except for minor stylistic changes, identical to former Section 1–201.

13.   "Creditor." Unchanged from former Section 1–201.

14.   "Defendant." Except for minor stylistic changes, identical to former Section 1–201, which was derived from Section 76, Uniform Sales Act.

15.   "Delivery." Derived from former Section 1–201. The reference to certificated securities has been deleted in light of the more specific treatment of the matter in Section 8–301. The definition has been revised to accommodate electronic documents of title. Control of an electronic document of title is defined in Article 7 (Section 7–106).

16.   "Document of title." Derived from former Section 1–201, which was derived from Section 76, Uniform Sales Act. This definition makes explicit that the obligation or designation of a third party as "bailee" is essential to a document of title and clearly rejects any such result as obtained in *Hixson v. Ward*, 254 Ill.App. 505 (1929), which treated a conditional sales contract as a document of title. Also the definition is left open so that new types of documents may be included, including documents which gain commercial recognition in the international arena. See UNCITRAL Draft Instrument on the Carriage of Goods By Sea. It is unforeseeable what documents may one day serve the essential purpose now filled by warehouse receipts and bills of lading. The definition is stated in terms of the function of the documents with the intention that any document which gains commercial recognition as accomplishing the desired result shall be included within its scope. Fungible goods are adequately identified within the language of the definition by identification of the mass of which they are a part.

Dock warrants were within the Sales Act definition of document of title apparently for the purpose of recognizing a valid tender by means of such paper. In current commercial practice a dock warrant or receipt is a kind of interim certificate issued by shipping companies upon delivery of the goods at the dock, entitling a designated person to be issued a bill of lading. The receipt itself is invariably nonnegotiable in form although it may indicate that a negotiable bill is to be forthcoming. Such a document is not within the general compass of the definition, although trade usage may in some cases entitle such paper to be treated as a document of title. If the dock receipt actually represents a storage obligation undertaken by the shipping company, then it is a warehouse receipt within this Section regardless of the name given to the instrument.

The goods must be "described," but the description may be by marks or labels and may be qualified in such a way as to disclaim personal knowledge of the issuer regarding contents or condition. However, baggage and parcel checks and similar "tokens" of storage which identify stored goods only as those received in exchange for the token are not covered by this Article. The definition is broad enough to include an airway bill.

A document of title may be either tangible or electronic. Tangible documents of title should be construed to mean traditional paper documents. Electronic documents of title are documents that are stored in an electronic medium instead of in tangible form. The concept of an electronic medium should be construed liberally to include electronic, digital, magnetic, optical, electromagnetic, or any other current or similar emerging technologies. As to reissuing a document of title in an alternative medium, see Article 7, Section 7–105. Control for electronic documents of title is defined in Article 7 (Section 7–106).

17. "Fault." Derived from former Section 1–201. "Default" has been added to the list of events constituting fault.

18. "Fungible goods." Derived from former Section 1–201. References to securities have been deleted because Article 8 no longer uses the term "fungible" to describe securities. Accordingly, this provision now defines the concept only in the context of goods.

19. "Genuine." Unchanged from former Section 1–201.

20. "Good faith." Former Section 1–201(19) defined "good faith" simply as honesty in fact; the definition contained no element of commercial reasonableness. Initially, that definition applied throughout the Code with only one exception. Former Section 2–103(1)(b) provided that "in that Article . . . good faith in the case of a merchant means honesty in fact and the observance of reasonable commercial standards of fair dealing in the trade." This alternative definition was limited in applicability though, because it applied only to transactions within the scope of Article 2 and it applied only to merchants.

Over time, however, amendments to the Uniform Commercial Code brought the Article 2 merchant concept of good faith (subjective honesty and objective commercial reasonableness) into other Articles. First, Article 2A explicitly incorporated the Article 2 standard. See Section 2A–103(7).[*] Then, other Articles broadened the applicability of that standard by adopting it for all parties rather than just for merchants. *See, e.g.*, Sections 3–103(a)(4),[**] 4A–105(a)(6), 7–102(a)(6), 8–102(a)(10), and 9–102(a)(43). Finally, Articles 2 and 2A were amended so as to apply the standard to non-merchants as well as merchants. See Sections 2–103(1)(j), 2A–103(1)(m).[***] All of these definitions are comprised of two elements—honesty in fact *and* the observance of reasonable commercial standards of fair dealing. Only revised Article 5 defines "good faith" solely in terms of subjective honesty, and only Article 6 (in the few states that have not chosen to delete the Article) is without a definition of good faith. (It should be noted that, while revised Article 6 did not define good faith, Comment 2 to revised Section 6–102 states that "this Article adopts the definition of 'good faith' in Article 1 in all cases, even when the buyer is a merchant.")

Thus, the definition of "good faith" in this section merely confirms what has been the case for a number of years as Articles of the UCC have been amended or revised—the obligation of "good faith," applicable in each Article, is to be interpreted in the context of all Articles except for Article 5 as including both the subjective element of honesty in fact and the objective element of the observance of reasonable commercial standards of fair dealing. As a result, both the subjective and objective elements are part of the standard of "good faith," whether that obligation is specifically referenced in another Article of the Code (other than Article 5) or is provided by this Article.

Of course, as noted in the statutory text, the definition of "good faith" in this section does not apply when the narrower definition of "good faith" in revised Article 5 is applicable.

As noted above, the definition of "good faith" in this section requires not only honesty in fact but also "observance of reasonable commercial standards of fair dealing." Although "fair dealing" is a broad term that must be defined in context, it is clear that it is concerned with the fairness of conduct rather than the care with which an act is performed. This is an entirely different concept than whether a party exercised ordinary care in conducting a transaction. Both concepts are to be determined in the light of reasonable commercial standards, but those standards in each case are directed to different aspects of commercial conduct. See e.g., Sections 3–103(a)(9)[**] and 4–104(c) and Comment 4 to Section 3–103.

21. "Holder." Derived from former Section 1–201. The definition has been reorganized for clarity and amended to provide for electronic negotiable documents of title.

22. "Insolvency proceedings." Unchanged from former Section 1–201.

---

[*]   *Note from West Advisory Panel: This provision appears in § 2A–103(3).*

[**]   *Referring to Article 3 before the 2002 revision.*

[***] *Referring to withdrawn 2003 Amendments to Articles 2 and 2A.*

23. "Insolvent." Derived from former Section 1–201. The three tests of insolvency—"generally ceased to pay debts in the ordinary course of business other than as a result of a bona fide dispute as to them," "unable to pay debts as they become due," and "insolvent within the meaning of the federal bankruptcy law"—are expressly set up as alternative tests and must be approached from a commercial standpoint.

24. "Money." Substantively identical to former Section 1–201. The test is that of sanction of government, whether by authorization before issue or adoption afterward, which recognizes the circulating medium as a part of the official currency of that government. The narrow view that money is limited to legal tender is rejected.

25. "Organization." The former definition of this word has been replaced with the standard definition used in acts prepared by the National Conference of Commissioners on Uniform State Laws.

26. "Party." Substantively identical to former Section 1–201. Mention of a party includes, of course, a person acting through an agent. However, where an agent comes into opposition or contrast to the principal, particular account is taken of that situation.

27. "Person." The former definition of this word has been replaced with the standard definition used in acts prepared by the National Conference of Commissioners on Uniform State Laws.

28. "Present value." This definition was formerly contained within the definition of "security interest" in former Section 1–201(37).

29. "Purchase." Derived from former Section 1–201. The form of definition has been changed from "includes" to "means."

30. "Purchaser." Unchanged from former Section 1–201.

31. "Record." Derived from Section 9–102(a)(69).

32. "Remedy." Unchanged from former Section 1–201. The purpose is to make it clear that both remedy and right (as defined) include those remedial rights of "self help" which are among the most important bodies of rights under the Uniform Commercial Code, remedial rights being those to which an aggrieved party may resort on its own.

33. "Representative." Derived from former Section 1–201. Reorganized, and form changed from "includes" to "means."

34. "Right." Except for minor stylistic changes, identical to former Section 1–201.

35. "Security Interest." The definition is the first paragraph of the definition of "security interest" in former Section 1–201, with minor stylistic changes. The remaining portion of that definition has been moved to Section 1–203. Note that, because of the scope of Article 9, the term includes the interest of certain outright buyers of certain kinds of property.

36. "Send." Derived from former Section 1–201. Compare "notifies".

37. "Signed." Derived from former Section 1–201. Former Section 1–201 referred to "intention to authenticate"; because other articles now use the term "authenticate," the language has been changed to "intention to adopt or accept." The latter formulation is derived from the definition of "authenticate" in Section 9–102(a)(7). This provision refers only to writings, because the term "signed," as used in some articles, refers only to writings. This provision also makes it clear that, as the term "signed" is used in the Uniform Commercial Code, a complete signature is not necessary. The symbol may be printed, stamped or written; it may be by initials or by thumbprint. It may be on any part of the document and in appropriate cases may be found in a billhead or letterhead. No catalog of possible situations can be complete and the court must use common sense and commercial experience in passing upon these matters. The question always is whether the symbol was executed or adopted by the party with present intention to adopt or accept the writing.

38. "State." This is the standard definition of the term used in acts prepared by the National Conference of Commissioners on Uniform State Laws.

39. "Surety." This definition makes it clear that "surety" includes all secondary obligors, not just those whose obligation refers to the person obligated as a surety. As to the nature of secondary obligations generally, see Restatement (Third), Suretyship and Guaranty Section 1 (1996).

40. "Term." Unchanged from former Section 1–201.

41. "Unauthorized signature." Unchanged from former Section 1–201.

42. "Warehouse receipt." Derived from former Section 1–201, which was derived from Section 76(1), Uniform Sales Act; Section 1, Uniform Warehouse Receipts Act. Receipts issued by a field warehouse are included, provided the warehouseman and the depositor of the goods are different persons. The definition makes clear that the receipt must qualify as a document of title under subsection (16).

43. "Written" or "writing." Unchanged from former Section 1–201.

As amended in 2003 and 2005.

§ 1–202.   Notice; Knowledge.

(a)   Subject to subsection (f), a person has "notice" of a fact if the person:

(1)   has actual knowledge of it;

(2)   has received a notice or notification of it; or

(3)   from all the facts and circumstances known to the person at the time in question, has reason to know that it exists.

(b)   "Knowledge" means actual knowledge. "Knows" has a corresponding meaning.

(c)   "Discover", "learn", or words of similar import refer to knowledge rather than to reason to know.

(d)   A person "notifies" or "gives" a notice or notification to another person by taking such steps as may be reasonably required to inform the other person in ordinary course, whether or not the other person actually comes to know of it.

(e)   Subject to subsection (f), a person "receives" a notice or notification when:

(1)   it comes to that person's attention; or

(2)   it is duly delivered in a form reasonable under the circumstances at the place of business through which the contract was made or at another location held out by that person as the place for receipt of such communications.

(f)   Notice, knowledge, or a notice or notification received by an organization is effective for a particular transaction from the time it is brought to the attention of the individual conducting that transaction and, in any event, from the time it would have been brought to the individual's attention if the organization had exercised due diligence. An organization exercises due diligence if it maintains reasonable routines for communicating significant information to the person conducting the transaction and there is reasonable compliance with the routines. Due diligence does not require an individual acting for the organization to communicate information unless the communication is part of the individual's regular duties or the individual has reason to know of the transaction and that the transaction would be materially affected by the information.

Official Comment

Source: Derived from former Section 1–201(25)–(27).

Changes from former law: These provisions are substantive rather than purely definitional. Accordingly, they have been relocated from Section 1–201 to this section. The reference to the "forgotten notice" doctrine has been deleted.

1.   Under subsection (a), a person has notice of a fact when, *inter alia*, the person has received a notification of the fact in question.

2.   As provided in subsection (d), the word "notifies" is used when the essential fact is the proper dispatch of the notice, not its receipt. Compare "Send." When the essential fact is the other party's receipt of the notice, that is stated. Subsection (e) states when a notification is received.

3.   Subsection (f) makes clear that notice, knowledge, or a notification, although "received," for instance, by a clerk in Department A of an organization, is effective for a transaction conducted in Department B only from the time when it was or should have been communicated to the individual conducting that transaction.

§ 1–203.   Lease Distinguished From Security Interest.

(a)   Whether a transaction in the form of a lease creates a lease or security interest is determined by the facts of each case.

(b)   A transaction in the form of a lease creates a security interest if the consideration that the lessee is to pay the lessor for the right to possession and use of the goods is an obligation for the term of the lease and is not subject to termination by the lessee, and:

(1)   the original term of the lease is equal to or greater than the remaining economic life of the goods;

(2)   the lessee is bound to renew the lease for the remaining economic life of the goods or is bound to become the owner of the goods;

(3)   the lessee has an option to renew the lease for the remaining economic life of the goods for no additional consideration or for nominal additional consideration upon compliance with the lease agreement; or

(4)   the lessee has an option to become the owner of the goods for no additional consideration or for nominal additional consideration upon compliance with the lease agreement.

(c)   A transaction in the form of a lease does not create a security interest merely because:

(1)   the present value of the consideration the lessee is obligated to pay the lessor for the right to possession and use of the goods is substantially equal to or is greater than the fair market value of the goods at the time the lease is entered into;

(2)   the lessee assumes risk of loss of the goods;

(3)   the lessee agrees to pay, with respect to the goods, taxes, insurance, filing, recording, or registration fees, or service or maintenance costs;

(4)   the lessee has an option to renew the lease or to become the owner of the goods;

(5)   the lessee has an option to renew the lease for a fixed rent that is equal to or greater than the reasonably predictable fair market rent for the use of the goods for the term of the renewal at the time the option is to be performed; or

(6)   the lessee has an option to become the owner of the goods for a fixed price that is equal to or greater than the reasonably predictable fair market value of the goods at the time the option is to be performed.

(d)   Additional consideration is nominal if it is less than the lessee's reasonably predictable cost of performing under the lease agreement if the option is not exercised. Additional consideration is not nominal if:

(1)   when the option to renew the lease is granted to the lessee, the rent is stated to be the fair market rent for the use of the goods for the term of the renewal determined at the time the option is to be performed; or

(2)   when the option to become the owner of the goods is granted to the lessee, the price is stated to be the fair market value of the goods determined at the time the option is to be performed.

(e)   The "remaining economic life of the goods" and "reasonably predictable" fair market rent, fair market value, or cost of performing under the lease agreement must be determined with reference to the facts and circumstances at the time the transaction is entered into.

Official Comment

Source: Former Section 1–201(37).

Changes from former law: This section is substantively identical to those portions of former Section 1–201(37) that distinguished "true" leases from security interests, except that the definition of "present value" formerly embedded in Section 1–201(37) has been placed in Section 1–201(28).*

1.   An interest in personal property or fixtures which secures payment or performance of an obligation is a "security interest." See Section 1–201(37).* Security interests are sometimes created by transactions in the form of leases. Because it can be difficult to distinguish leases that create security interests from those that do not, this section provides rules that govern the determination of whether a transaction in the form of a lease creates a security interest.

2.   One of the reasons it was decided to codify the law with respect to leases was to resolve an issue that created considerable confusion in the courts: what is a lease? The confusion existed, in part, due to the last two sentences of the definition of security interest in the 1978 Official Text of the Act, Section 1–201(37). The confusion was compounded by the rather considerable change in the federal, state and local tax laws and accounting rules as they relate to leases of goods. The answer is important because the definition of lease determines not only the rights and remedies of the parties to the lease but also those of third parties. If a transaction creates a lease and not a security interest, the lessee's interest in the goods is limited to its leasehold estate; the residual interest in the goods belongs to the lessor. This has significant implications to the lessee's creditors. "On common law theory, the lessor, since he has not parted with title, is entitled to full protection against the lessee's creditors and trustee in bankruptcy. . . ." 1 G. Gilmore, *Security Interests in Personal Property* Section 3.6, at 76 (1965).

Under pre-UCC chattel security law there was generally no requirement that the lessor file the lease, a financing statement, or the like, to enforce the lease agreement against the lessee or any third party; the Article on Secured Transactions (Article 9) did not change the common law in that respect. Coogan, *Leasing and the Uniform Commercial Code*, in Equipment Leasing—Leveraged Leasing 681, 700 n.25, 729 n.80 (2d ed.1980). The Article on Leases (Article 2A) did not change the law in that respect, except for leases of fixtures. Section 2A–309. An examination of the common law will not provide an adequate answer to the question of what is a lease. The definition of security interest in Section 1–201(37) of the 1978 Official Text of the Act provided that the Article on Secured Transactions (Article 9) governs security interests disguised as leases, *i.e.*, leases intended as security; however, the definition became vague and outmoded.

Lease is defined in Article 2A as a transfer of the right to possession and use of goods for a term, in return for consideration. Section 2A–103(1)(j). The definition continues by stating that the retention or creation of a security interest is not a lease. Thus, the task of sharpening the line between true leases and security interests disguised as leases continues to be a function of this Article.

This section begins where Section 1–201(35)** leaves off. It draws a sharper line between leases and security interests disguised as leases to create greater certainty in commercial transactions.

Prior to enactment of the rules now codified in this section, the 1978 Official Text of Section 1–201(37) provided that whether a lease was intended as security (*i.e.*, a security interest disguised as a lease) was to be determined from the facts of each case; however, (a) the inclusion of an option to purchase did not itself make the lease one intended for security, and (b) an agreement that upon compliance with the terms of the lease the lessee would become, or had the option to become, the owner of the property for no additional consideration, or for a nominal consideration, did make the lease one intended for security.

Reference to the intent of the parties to create a lease or security interest led to unfortunate results. In discovering intent, courts relied upon factors that were thought to be more consistent with sales or loans than leases. Most of these criteria, however, were as applicable to true leases as to security interests. Examples include the typical net lease provisions, a purported lessor's lack of storage facilities or its character as a financing party rather than a dealer in goods. Accordingly, this section contains no reference to the parties' intent.

Subsections (a) and (b) were originally taken from Section 1(2) of the Uniform Conditional Sales Act (act withdrawn 1943), modified to reflect current leasing practice. Thus, reference to the case law prior to the incorporation of those concepts in this article will provide a useful source of precedent. Gilmore, *Security Law, Formalism and Article 9*, 47 Neb.L.Rev. 659, 671 (1968). Whether a transaction creates a lease or a security interest continues to be determined by the facts of each case. Subsection (b) further provides that a transaction creates a security interest if the lessee has an obligation to continue paying consideration for the term of the lease, if the obligation is not terminable by the lessee (thus correcting early statutory gloss, *e.g.*, *In re Royer's Bakery*,

---

*   *Referring to unrevised Article 1 (Appendix A).*

**   *Should be 1–201(b)(35).*

Inc., 1 U.C.C. Rep.Serv. (Callaghan) 342 (Bankr.E.D.Pa.1963)) and if one of four additional tests is met. The first of these four tests, subparagraph (1), is that the original lease term is equal to or greater than the remaining economic life of the goods. The second of these tests, subparagraph (2), is that the lessee is either bound to renew the lease for the remaining economic life of the goods or to become the owner of the goods. *In re Gehrke Enters.*, 1 Bankr. 647, 651–52 (Bankr.W.D.Wis.1979). The third of these tests, subparagraph (3), is whether the lessee has an option to renew the lease for the remaining economic life of the goods for no additional consideration or for nominal additional consideration, which is defined later in this section. *In re Celeryvale Transp.*, 44 Bankr. 1007, 1014–15 (Bankr.E.D.Tenn.1984). The fourth of these tests, subparagraph (4), is whether the lessee has an option to become the owner of the goods for no additional consideration or for nominal additional consideration. All of these tests focus on economics, not the intent of the parties. *In re Berge*, 32 Bankr. 370, 371–73 (Bankr.W.D.Wis.1983).

The focus on economics is reinforced by subsection (c). It states that a transaction does not create a security interest merely because the transaction has certain characteristics listed therein. Subparagraph (1) has no statutory derivative; it states that a full payout lease does not *per se* create a security interest. *Rushton v. Shea*, 419 F.Supp. 1349, 1365 (D.Del.1976). Subparagraphs (2) and (3) provide the same regarding the provisions of the typical net lease. *Compare All-States Leasing Co. v. Ochs*, 42 Or.App. 319, 600 P.2d 899 (Ct.App.1979), *with In re Tillery*, 571 F.2d 1361 (5th Cir.1978). Subparagraph (4) restates and expands the provisions of the 1978 Official Text of Section 1–201(37) to make clear that the option can be to buy or renew. Subparagraphs (5) and (6) treat fixed price options and provide that fair market value must be determined at the time the transaction is entered into. *Compare Arnold Mach. Co. v. Balls*, 624 P.2d 678 (Utah 1981), *with Aoki v. Shepherd Mach. Co.*, 665 F.2d 941 (9th Cir.1982).

The relationship of subsection (b) to subsection (c) deserves to be explored. The fixed price purchase option provides a useful example. A fixed price purchase option in a lease does not of itself create a security interest. This is particularly true if the fixed price is equal to or greater than the reasonably predictable fair market value of the goods at the time the option is to be performed. A security interest is created only if the option price is nominal and the conditions stated in the introduction to the second paragraph of this subsection are met. There is a set of purchase options whose fixed price is less than fair market value but greater than nominal that must be determined on the facts of each case to ascertain whether the transaction in which the option is included creates a lease or a security interest.

It was possible to provide for various other permutations and combinations with respect to options to purchase and renew. For example, this section could have stated a rule to govern the facts of *In re Marhoefer Packing Co.*, 674 F.2d 1139 (7th Cir.1982). This was not done because it would unnecessarily complicate the definition. Further development of this rule is left to the courts.

Subsections (d) and (e) provide definitions and rules of construction.

§ 1–204. Value.

Except as otherwise provided in Articles 3, 4, [and] 5, [and 6], a person gives value for rights if the person acquires them:

(1) in return for a binding commitment to extend credit or for the extension of immediately available credit, whether or not drawn upon and whether or not a charge-back is provided for in the event of difficulties in collection;

(2) as security for, or in total or partial satisfaction of, a preexisting claim;

(3) by accepting delivery under a preexisting contract for purchase; or

(4) in return for any consideration sufficient to support a simple contract.

Official Comment

Source: Former Section 1–201(44).

Changes from former law: Unchanged from former Section 1–201, which was derived from Sections 25, 26, 27, 191, Uniform Negotiable Instruments Law; Section 76, Uniform Sales Act; Section 53, Uniform Bills of Lading Act; Section 58, Uniform Warehouse Receipts Act; Section 22(1), Uniform Stock Transfer Act; Section 1, Uniform Trust Receipts Act. These provisions are substantive rather than purely definitional. Accordingly, they have been relocated from former Section 1–201 to this section.

1.   All the Uniform Acts in the commercial law field (except the Uniform Conditional Sales Act) have carried definitions of "value." All those definitions provided that value was any consideration sufficient to support a simple contract, including the taking of property in satisfaction of or as security for a pre-existing claim. Subsections (1), (2), and (4) in substance continue the definitions of "value" in the earlier acts. Subsection (3) makes explicit that "value" is also given in a third situation: where a buyer by taking delivery under a pre-existing contract converts a contingent into a fixed obligation.

This definition is not applicable to Articles 3 and 4, but the express inclusion of immediately available credit as value follows the separate definitions in those Articles. See Sections 4–208, 4–209, 3–303. A bank or other financing agency which in good faith makes advances against property held as collateral becomes a bona fide purchaser of that property even though provision may be made for charge-back in case of trouble. Checking credit is "immediately available" within the meaning of this section if the bank would be subject to an action for slander of credit in case checks drawn against the credit were dishonored, and when a charge-back is not discretionary with the bank, but may only be made when difficulties in collection arise in connection with the specific transaction involved.

§ 1–205.   Reasonable Time; Seasonableness.

(a)   Whether a time for taking an action required by [the Uniform Commercial Code] is reasonable depends on the nature, purpose, and circumstances of the action.

(b)   An action is taken seasonably if it is taken at or within the time agreed or, if no time is agreed, at or within a reasonable time.

Official Comment

Source: Former Section 1–204(2)–(3).

Changes from former law: This section is derived from subsections (2) and (3) of former Section 1–204. Subsection (1) of that section is now incorporated in Section 1–302(b).

1.   Subsection (a) makes it clear that requirements that actions be taken within a "reasonable" time are to be applied in the transactional context of the particular action.

2.   Under subsection (b), the agreement that fixes the time need not be part of the main agreement, but may occur separately. Notice also that under the definition of "agreement" (Section 1–201) the circumstances of the transaction, including course of dealing or usages of trade or course of performance may be material. On the question what is a reasonable time these matters will often be important.

§ 1–206.   Presumptions.

Whenever [the Uniform Commercial Code] creates a "presumption" with respect to a fact, or provides that a fact is "presumed," the trier of fact must find the existence of the fact unless and until evidence is introduced that supports a finding of its nonexistence.

Legislative Note: Former Section 1–206, a Statute of Frauds for sales of "kinds of personal property not otherwise covered," has been deleted. The other articles of the Uniform Commercial Code make individual determinations as to requirements for memorializing transactions within their scope, so that the primary effect of former Section 1–206 was to impose a writing requirement on sales transactions not otherwise governed by the UCC. Deletion of former Section 1–206 does not constitute a recommendation to legislatures as to whether such sales transactions should be covered by a Statute of Frauds; rather, it reflects a determination that there is no need for uniform commercial law to resolve that issue.

Official Comment

Source: Former Section 1–201(31).

Changes from former law. None, other than stylistic changes.

1.   Several sections of the Uniform Commercial Code state that there is a "presumption" as to a certain fact, or that the fact is "presumed." This section, derived from the definition appearing in former Section 1–201(31), indicates the effect of those provisions on the proof process.

PART 3

TERRITORIAL APPLICABILITY AND GENERAL RULES

§ 1–301. Territorial Applicability; Parties' Power to Choose Applicable Law.

(a) Except as otherwise provided in this section, when a transaction bears a reasonable relation to this state and also to another state or nation the parties may agree that the law either of this state or of such other state or nation shall govern their rights and duties.

(b) In the absence of an agreement effective under subsection (a), and except as provided in subsection (c), [the Uniform Commercial Code] applies to transactions bearing an appropriate relation to this state.

(c) If one of the following provisions of [the Uniform Commercial Code] specifies the applicable law, that provision governs and a contrary agreement is effective only to the extent permitted by the law so specified:

(1) Section 2–402;

(2) Sections 2A–105 and 2A–106;

(3) Section 4–102;

(4) Section 4A–507;

(5) Section 5–116;

[(6) Section 6–103;]

(7) Section 8–110;

(8) Sections 9–301 through 9–307.

As amended in 2008.

Official Comment

Source: Former Section 1–105.

Changes from former law: This section is substantively identical to former Section 1–105. Changes in language are stylistic only.

1. Subsection (a) states affirmatively the right of the parties to a multi-state transaction or a transaction involving foreign trade to choose their own law. That right is subject to the firm rules stated in the sections listed in subsection (c), and is limited to jurisdictions to which the transaction bears a "reasonable relation." In general, the test of "reasonable relation" is similar to that laid down by the Supreme Court in *Seeman v. Philadelphia Warehouse Co.*, 274 U.S. 403, 47 S.Ct. 626, 71 L.Ed. 1123 (1927). Ordinarily the law chosen must be that of a jurisdiction where a significant enough portion of the making or performance of the contract is to occur or occurs. But an agreement as to choice of law may sometimes take effect as a shorthand expression of the intent of the parties as to matters governed by their agreement, even though the transaction has no significant contact with the jurisdiction chosen.

2. Where there is no agreement as to the governing law, the Act is applicable to any transaction having an "appropriate" relation to any state which enacts it. Of course, the Act applies to any transaction which takes place in its entirety in a state which has enacted the Act. But the mere fact that suit is brought in a state does not make it appropriate to apply the substantive law of that state. Cases where a relation to the enacting state is not "appropriate" include, for example, those where the parties have clearly contracted on the basis of some other law, as where the law of the place of contracting and the law of the place of contemplated performance are the same and are contrary to the law under the Code.

3. Where a transaction has significant contacts with a state which has enacted the Act and also with other jurisdictions, the question what relation is "appropriate" is left to judicial decision. In deciding that question, the court is not strictly bound by precedents established in other contexts. Thus a conflict-of-laws decision refusing to apply a purely local statute or rule of law to a particular multi-state transaction may not be valid precedent for

39

refusal to apply the Code in an analogous situation. Application of the Code in such circumstances may be justified by its comprehensiveness, by the policy of uniformity, and by the fact that it is in large part a reformulation and restatement of the law merchant and of the understanding of a business community which transcends state and even national boundaries. *Compare Global Commerce Corp. v. Clark-Babbitt Industries, Inc.*, 239 F.2d 716, 719 (2d Cir. 1956). In particular, where a transaction is governed in large part by the Code, application of another law to some detail of performance because of an accident of geography may violate the commercial understanding of the parties.

4. Subsection (c) spells out essential limitations on the parties' right to choose the applicable law. Especially in Article 9 parties taking a security interest or asked to extend credit which may be subject to a security interest must have sure ways to find out whether and where to file and where to look for possible existing filings.

5. Sections 9-301 through 9-307 should be consulted as to the rules for perfection of security interests and agricultural liens and the effect of perfection and nonperfection and priority.

6. This section is subject to Section 1-102, which states the scope of Article 1. As that section indicates, the rules of Article 1, including this section, apply to a transaction to the extent that transaction is governed by one of the other Articles of the Uniform Commercial Code.

As amended in 2008.

§ 1-302.   Variation by Agreement.

(a) Except as otherwise provided in subsection (b) or elsewhere in [the Uniform Commercial Code], the effect of provisions of [the Uniform Commercial Code] may be varied by agreement.

(b) The obligations of good faith, diligence, reasonableness, and care prescribed by [the Uniform Commercial Code] may not be disclaimed by agreement. The parties, by agreement, may determine the standards by which the performance of those obligations is to be measured if those standards are not manifestly unreasonable. Whenever [the Uniform Commercial Code] requires an action to be taken within a reasonable time, a time that is not manifestly unreasonable may be fixed by agreement.

(c) The presence in certain provisions of [the Uniform Commercial Code] of the phrase "unless otherwise agreed", or words of similar import, does not imply that the effect of other provisions may not be varied by agreement under this section.

Official Comment

Source: Former Sections 1-102(3)-(4) and 1-204(1).

Changes: This section combines the rules from subsections (3) and (4) of former Section 1-102 and subsection (1) of former Section 1-204. No substantive changes are made.

1. Subsection (a) states affirmatively at the outset that freedom of contract is a principle of the Uniform Commercial Code: "the effect" of its provisions may be varied by "agreement." The meaning of the statute itself must be found in its text, including its definitions, and in appropriate extrinsic aids; it cannot be varied by agreement. But the Uniform Commercial Code seeks to avoid the type of interference with evolutionary growth found in pre-Code cases such as *Manhattan Co. v. Morgan*, 242 N.Y. 38, 150 N.E. 594 (1926). Thus, private parties cannot make an instrument negotiable within the meaning of Article 3 except as provided in Section 3-104; nor can they change the meaning of such terms as "bona fide purchaser," "holder in due course," or "due negotiation," as used in the Uniform Commercial Code. But an agreement can change the legal consequences that would otherwise flow from the provisions of the Uniform Commercial Code. "Agreement" here includes the effect given to course of dealing, usage of trade and course of performance by Sections 1-201 and 1-303; the effect of an agreement on the rights of third parties is left to specific provisions of the Uniform Commercial Code and to supplementary principles applicable under Section 1-103. The rights of third parties under Section 9-317 when a security interest is unperfected, for example, cannot be destroyed by a clause in the security agreement.

This principle of freedom of contract is subject to specific exceptions found elsewhere in the Uniform Commercial Code and to the general exception stated here. The specific exceptions vary in explicitness: the statute of frauds found in Section 2-201, for example, does not explicitly preclude oral waiver of the requirement of a writing, but a fair reading denies enforcement to such a waiver as part of the "contract" made unenforceable; Section 9-602, on the other hand, is a quite explicit limitation on freedom of contract. Under the exception for "the obligations of good faith, diligence, reasonableness and care prescribed by [the Uniform Commercial Code],"

40

provisions of the Uniform Commercial Code prescribing such obligations are not to be disclaimed. However, the section also recognizes the prevailing practice of having agreements set forth standards by which due diligence is measured and explicitly provides that, in the absence of a showing that the standards manifestly are unreasonable, the agreement controls. In this connection, Section 1–303 incorporating into the agreement prior course of dealing and usages of trade is of particular importance.

Subsection (b) also recognizes that nothing is stronger evidence of a reasonable time than the fixing of such time by a fair agreement between the parties. However, provision is made for disregarding a clause which whether by inadvertence or overreaching fixes a time so unreasonable that it amounts to eliminating all remedy under the contract. The parties are not required to fix the most reasonable time but may fix any time which is not obviously unfair as judged by the time of contracting.

2. An agreement that varies the effect of provisions of the Uniform Commercial Code may do so by stating the rules that will govern in lieu of the provisions varied. Alternatively, the parties may vary the effect of such provisions by stating that their relationship will be governed by recognized bodies of rules or principles applicable to commercial transactions. Such bodies of rules or principles may include, for example, those that are promulgated by intergovernmental authorities such as UNCITRAL or UNIDROIT (*see, e.g.,* UNIDROIT Principles of International Commercial Contracts), or non-legal codes such as trade codes.

3. Subsection (c) is intended to make it clear that, as a matter of drafting, phrases such as "unless otherwise agreed" have been used to avoid controversy as to whether the subject matter of a particular section does or does not fall within the exceptions to subsection (b), but absence of such words contains no negative implication since under subsection (b) the general and residual rule is that the effect of all provisions of the Uniform Commercial Code may be varied by agreement.

§ 1–303. Course of Performance, Course of Dealing, and Usage of Trade.

(a) A "course of performance" is a sequence of conduct between the parties to a particular transaction that exists if:

(1) the agreement of the parties with respect to the transaction involves repeated occasions for performance by a party; and

(2) the other party, with knowledge of the nature of the performance and opportunity for objection to it, accepts the performance or acquiesces in it without objection.

(b) A "course of dealing" is a sequence of conduct concerning previous transactions between the parties to a particular transaction that is fairly to be regarded as establishing a common basis of understanding for interpreting their expressions and other conduct.

(c) A "usage of trade" is any practice or method of dealing having such regularity of observance in a place, vocation, or trade as to justify an expectation that it will be observed with respect to the transaction in question. The existence and scope of such a usage must be proved as facts. If it is established that such a usage is embodied in a trade code or similar record, the interpretation of the record is a question of law.

(d) A course of performance or course of dealing between the parties or usage of trade in the vocation or trade in which they are engaged or of which they are or should be aware is relevant in ascertaining the meaning of the parties' agreement, may give particular meaning to specific terms of the agreement, and may supplement or qualify the terms of the agreement. A usage of trade applicable in the place in which part of the performance under the agreement is to occur may be so utilized as to that part of the performance.

(e) Except as otherwise provided in subsection (f), the express terms of an agreement and any applicable course of performance, course of dealing, or usage of trade must be construed whenever reasonable as consistent with each other. If such a construction is unreasonable:

(1) express terms prevail over course of performance, course of dealing, and usage of trade;

(2) course of performance prevails over course of dealing and usage of trade; and

(3) course of dealing prevails over usage of trade.

(f) Subject to Section 2–209 and Section 2A–208, a course of performance is relevant to show a waiver or modification of any term inconsistent with the course of performance.

(g) Evidence of a relevant usage of trade offered by one party is not admissible unless that party has given the other party notice that the court finds sufficient to prevent unfair surprise to the other party.

Official Comment

Source: Former Sections 1–205, 2–208, and Section 2A–207.

Changes from former law: This section integrates the "course of performance" concept from Articles 2 and 2A into the principles of former Section 1–205, which deals with course of dealing and usage of trade. In so doing, the section slightly modifies the articulation of the course of performance rules to fit more comfortably with the approach and structure of former Section 1–205. There are also slight modifications to be more consistent with the definition of "agreement" in former Section 1–201(3). It should be noted that a course of performance that might otherwise establish a defense to the obligation of a party to a negotiable instrument is not available as a defense against a holder in due course who took the instrument without notice of that course of performance.

1.   The Uniform Commercial Code rejects both the "lay-dictionary" and the "conveyancer's" reading of a commercial agreement. Instead the meaning of the agreement of the parties is to be determined by the language used by them and by their action, read and interpreted in the light of commercial practices and other surrounding circumstances. The measure and background for interpretation are set by the commercial context, which may explain and supplement even the language of a formal or final writing.

2.   "Course of dealing," as defined in subsection (b), is restricted, literally, to a sequence of conduct between the parties previous to the agreement. A sequence of conduct after or under the agreement, however, is a "course of performance." "Course of dealing" may enter the agreement either by explicit provisions of the agreement or by tacit recognition.

3.   The Uniform Commercial Code deals with "usage of trade" as a factor in reaching the commercial meaning of the agreement that the parties have made. The language used is to be interpreted as meaning what it may fairly be expected to mean to parties involved in the particular commercial transaction in a given locality or in a given vocation or trade. By adopting in this context the term "usage of trade," the Uniform Commercial Code expresses its intent to reject those cases which see evidence of "custom" as representing an effort to displace or negate "established rules of law." A distinction is to be drawn between mandatory rules of law such as the Statute of Frauds provisions of Article 2 on Sales whose very office is to control and restrict the actions of the parties, and which cannot be abrogated by agreement, or by a usage of trade, and those rules of law (such as those in Part 3 of Article 2 on Sales) which fill in points which the parties have not considered and in fact agreed upon. The latter rules hold "unless otherwise agreed" but yield to the contrary agreement of the parties. Part of the agreement of the parties to which such rules yield is to be sought for in the usages of trade which furnish the background and give particular meaning to the language used, and are the framework of common understanding controlling any general rules of law which hold only when there is no such understanding.

4.   A usage of trade under subsection (c) must have the "regularity of observance" specified. The ancient English tests for "custom" are abandoned in this connection. Therefore, it is not required that a usage of trade be "ancient or immemorial," "universal," or the like. Under the requirement of subsection (c) full recognition is thus available for new usages and for usages currently observed by the great majority of decent dealers, even though dissidents ready to cut corners do not agree. There is room also for proper recognition of usage agreed upon by merchants in trade codes.

5.   The policies of the Uniform Commercial Code controlling explicit unconscionable contracts and clauses (Sections 1–304, 2–302) apply to implicit clauses that rest on usage of trade and carry forward the policy underlying the ancient requirement that a custom or usage must be "reasonable." However, the emphasis is shifted. The very fact of commercial acceptance makes out a *prima facie* case that the usage is reasonable, and the burden is no longer on the usage to establish itself as being reasonable. But the anciently established policing of usage by the courts is continued to the extent necessary to cope with the situation arising if an unconscionable or dishonest practice should become standard.

6.   Subsection (d), giving the prescribed effect to usages of which the parties "are or should be aware," reinforces the provision of subsection (c) requiring not universality but only the described "regularity of observance" of the practice or method. This subsection also reinforces the point of subsection (c) that such usages may be either general to trade or particular to a special branch of trade.

7.   Although the definition of "agreement" in Section 1–201 includes the elements of course of performance, course of dealing, and usage of trade, the fact that express reference is made in some sections to those elements is not to be construed as carrying a contrary intent or implication elsewhere. Compare Section 1–302(c).

8. In cases of a well established line of usage varying from the general rules of the Uniform Commercial Code where the precise amount of the variation has not been worked out into a single standard, the party relying on the usage is entitled, in any event, to the minimum variation demonstrated. The whole is not to be disregarded because no particular line of detail has been established. In case a dominant pattern has been fairly evidenced, the party relying on the usage is entitled under this section to go to the trier of fact on the question of whether such dominant pattern has been incorporated into the agreement.

9. Subsection (g) is intended to insure that this Act's liberal recognition of the needs of commerce in regard to usage of trade shall not be made into an instrument of abuse.

§ 1–304. Obligation of Good Faith.

Every contract or duty within [the Uniform Commercial Code] imposes an obligation of good faith in its performance and enforcement.

Official Comment

Source: Former Section 1–203.

Changes from former law: Except for changing the form of reference to the Uniform Commercial Code, this section is identical to former Section 1–203.

1. This section sets forth a basic principle running throughout the Uniform Commercial Code. The principle is that in commercial transactions good faith is required in the performance and enforcement of all agreements or duties. While this duty is explicitly stated in some provisions of the Uniform Commercial Code, the applicability of the duty is broader than merely these situations and applies generally, as stated in this section, to the performance or enforcement of every contract or duty within this Act. It is further implemented by Section 1–303 on course of dealing, course of performance, and usage of trade. This section does not support an independent cause of action for failure to perform or enforce in good faith. Rather, this section means that a failure to perform or enforce, in good faith, a specific duty or obligation under the contract, constitutes a breach of that contract or makes unavailable, under the particular circumstances, a remedial right or power. This distinction makes it clear that the doctrine of good faith merely directs a court towards interpreting contracts within the commercial context in which they are created, performed, and enforced, and does not create a separate duty of fairness and reasonableness which can be independently breached.

2. "Performance and enforcement" of contracts and duties within the Uniform Commercial Code include the exercise of rights created by the Uniform Commercial Code.

§ 1–305. Remedies to Be Liberally Administered.

(a) The remedies provided by [the Uniform Commercial Code] must be liberally administered to the end that the aggrieved party may be put in as good a position as if the other party had fully performed but neither consequential or special damages nor penal damages may be had except as specifically provided in [the Uniform Commercial Code] or by other rule of law.

(b) Any right or obligation declared by [the Uniform Commercial Code] is enforceable by action unless the provision declaring it specifies a different and limited effect.

Official Comment

Source: Former Section 1–106.

Changes from former law: Other than changes in the form of reference to the Uniform Commercial Code, this section is identical to former Section 1–106.

1. Subsection (a) is intended to effect three propositions. The first is to negate the possibility of unduly narrow or technical interpretation of remedial provisions by providing that the remedies in the Uniform Commercial Code are to be liberally administered to the end stated in this section. The second is to make it clear that compensatory damages are limited to compensation. They do not include consequential or special damages, or penal damages; and the Uniform Commercial Code elsewhere makes it clear that damages must be minimized. Cf. Sections 1–304, 2–706(1), and 2–712(2). The third purpose of subsection (a) is to reject any doctrine that damages must be calculable with mathematical accuracy. Compensatory damages are often at best approximate:

they have to be proved with whatever definiteness and accuracy the facts permit, but no more. Cf. Section 2–204(3).

2. Under subsection (b), any right or obligation described in the Uniform Commercial Code is enforceable by action, even though no remedy may be expressly provided, unless a particular provision specifies a different and limited effect. Whether specific performance or other equitable relief is available is determined not by this section but by specific provisions and by supplementary principles. Cf. Sections 1–103, 2–716.

3. "Consequential" or "special" damages and "penal" damages are not defined in the Uniform Commercial Code; rather, these terms are used in the sense in which they are used outside the Uniform Commercial Code.

§ 1–306. Waiver or Renunciation of Claim or Right After Breach.

A claim or right arising out of an alleged breach may be discharged in whole or in part without consideration by agreement of the aggrieved party in an authenticated record.

Official Comment

Source: Former Section 1–107.

Changes from former law: This section changes former law in two respects. First, former Section 1–107, requiring the "delivery" of a "written waiver or renunciation" merges the separate concepts of the aggrieved party's agreement to forego rights and the manifestation of that agreement. This section separates those concepts, and explicitly requires *agreement* of the aggrieved party. Second, the revised section reflects developments in electronic commerce by providing for memorialization in an authenticated record. In this context, a party may "authenticate" a record by (i) signing a record that is a writing or (ii) attaching to or logically associating with a record that is not a writing an electronic sound, symbol or process with the present intent to adopt or accept the record. See Sections 1–201(b)(37) and 9–102(a)(7).

1. This section makes consideration unnecessary to the effective renunciation or waiver of rights or claims arising out of an alleged breach of a commercial contract where the agreement effecting such renunciation is memorialized in a record authenticated by the aggrieved party. Its provisions, however, must be read in conjunction with the section imposing an obligation of good faith. (Section 1–304).

§ 1–307. Prima Facie Evidence by Third-Party Documents.

A document in due form purporting to be a bill of lading, policy or certificate of insurance, official weigher's or inspector's certificate, consular invoice, or any other document authorized or required by the contract to be issued by a third party is prima facie evidence of its own authenticity and genuineness and of the facts stated in the document by the third party.

Official Comment

Source: Former Section 1–202.

Changes from former law: Except for minor stylistic changes, this Section is identical to former Section 1–202.

1. This section supplies judicial recognition for documents that are relied upon as trustworthy by commercial parties.

2. This section is concerned only with documents that have been given a preferred status by the parties themselves who have required their procurement in the agreement, and for this reason the applicability of the section is limited to actions arising out of the contract that authorized or required the document. The list of documents is intended to be illustrative and not exclusive.

3. The provisions of this section go no further than establishing the documents in question as prima facie evidence and leave to the court the ultimate determination of the facts where the accuracy or authenticity of the documents is questioned. In this connection the section calls for a commercially reasonable interpretation.

4. Documents governed by this section need not be writings if records in another medium are generally relied upon in the context.

§ 1–308. Performance or Acceptance Under Reservation of Rights.

(a) A party that with explicit reservation of rights performs or promises performance or assents to performance in a manner demanded or offered by the other party does not thereby prejudice the rights reserved. Such words as "without prejudice," "under protest," or the like are sufficient.

(b) Subsection (a) does not apply to an accord and satisfaction.

Official Comment

Source: Former Section 1–207.

Changes from former law: This section is identical to former Section 1–207.

1. This section provides machinery for the continuation of performance along the lines contemplated by the contract despite a pending dispute, by adopting the mercantile device of going ahead with delivery, acceptance, or payment "without prejudice," "under protest," "under reserve," "with reservation of all our rights," and the like. All of these phrases completely reserve all rights within the meaning of this section. The section therefore contemplates that limited as well as general reservations and acceptance by a party may be made "subject to satisfaction of our purchaser," "subject to acceptance by our customers," or the like.

2. This section does not add any new requirement of language of reservation where not already required by law, but merely provides a specific measure on which a party can rely as that party makes or concurs in any interim adjustment in the course of performance. It does not affect or impair the provisions of this Act such as those under which the buyer's remedies for defect survive acceptance without being expressly claimed if notice of the defects is given within a reasonable time. Nor does it disturb the policy of those cases which restrict the effect of a waiver of a defect to reasonable limits under the circumstances, even though no such reservation is expressed.

The section is not addressed to the creation or loss of remedies in the ordinary course of performance but rather to a method of procedure where one party is claiming as of right something which the other believes to be unwarranted.

3. Subsection (b) states that this section does not apply to an accord and satisfaction. Section 3–311 governs if an accord and satisfaction is attempted by tender of a negotiable instrument as stated in that section. If Section 3–311 does not apply, the issue of whether an accord and satisfaction has been effected is determined by the law of contract. Whether or not Section 3–311 applies, this section has no application to an accord and satisfaction.

§ 1–309. Option to Accelerate at Will.

A term providing that one party or that party's successor in interest may accelerate payment or performance or require collateral or additional collateral "at will" or when the party "deems itself insecure," or words of similar import, means that the party has power to do so only if that party in good faith believes that the prospect of payment or performance is impaired. The burden of establishing lack of good faith is on the party against which the power has been exercised.

Official Comment

Source: Former Section 1–208.

Changes from former law: Except for minor stylistic changes, this section is identical to former Section 1–208.

1. The common use of acceleration clauses in many transactions governed by the Uniform Commercial Code, including sales of goods on credit, notes payable at a definite time, and secured transactions, raises an issue as to the effect to be given to a clause that seemingly grants the power to accelerate at the whim and caprice of one party. This section is intended to make clear that despite language that might be so construed and which further might be held to make the agreement void as against public policy or to make the contract illusory or too indefinite for enforcement, the option is to be exercised only in the good faith belief that the prospect of payment or performance is impaired.

Obviously this section has no application to demand instruments or obligations whose very nature permits call at any time with or without reason. This section applies only to an obligation of payment or performance which in the first instance is due at a future date.

§ 1–310.　　Subordinated Obligations.

An obligation may be issued as subordinated to performance of another obligation of the person obligated, or a creditor may subordinate its right to performance of an obligation by agreement with either the person obligated or another creditor of the person obligated. Subordination does not create a security interest as against either the common debtor or a subordinated creditor.

Official Comment

Source: Former Section 1–209.

Changes from former law: This section is substantively identical to former Section 1–209. The language in that section stating that it "shall be construed as declaring the law as it existed prior to the enactment of this section and not as modifying it" has been deleted.

1.　　Billions of dollars of subordinated debt are held by the public and by institutional investors. Commonly, the subordinated debt is subordinated on issue or acquisition and is evidenced by an investment security or by a negotiable or non-negotiable note. Debt is also sometimes subordinated after it arises, either by agreement between the subordinating creditor and the debtor, by agreement between two creditors of the same debtor, or by agreement of all three parties. The subordinated creditor may be a stockholder or other "insider" interested in the common debtor; the subordinated debt may consist of accounts or other rights to payment not evidenced by any instrument. All such cases are included in the terms "subordinated obligation," "subordination," and "subordinated creditor."

2.　　Subordination agreements are enforceable between the parties as contracts; and in the bankruptcy of the common debtor dividends otherwise payable to the subordinated creditor are turned over to the superior creditor. This "turn-over" practice has on occasion been explained in terms of "equitable lien," "equitable assignment," or "constructive trust," but whatever the label the practice is essentially an equitable remedy and does not mean that there is a transaction "that creates a security interest in personal property . . . by contract" or a "sale of accounts, chattel paper, payment intangibles, or promissory notes" within the meaning of Section 9–109. On the other hand, nothing in this section prevents one creditor from assigning his rights to another creditor of the same debtor in such a way as to create a security interest within Article 9, where the parties so intend.

3.　　The enforcement of subordination agreements is largely left to supplementary principles under Section 1–103. If the subordinated debt is evidenced by a certificated security, Section 8–202(a) authorizes enforcement against purchasers on terms stated or referred to on the security certificate. If the fact of subordination is noted on a negotiable instrument, a holder under Sections 3–302 and 3–306 is subject to the term because notice precludes him from taking free of the subordination. Sections 3–302(3)(a),* 3–306, and 8–317** severely limit the rights of levying creditors of a subordinated creditor in such cases.

---

*　　*Referring to unrevised Article 3.*
**　*Referring to unrevised Article 8.*

UCC ARTICLE 2 (2016)

SALES

Set forth below are the text and Official Comments of Article 2 as of 2016. The 2003 and 2005 amendments to Article 2, other than those made as part of the Article 7 revision, were officially withdrawn in May 2011 and therefore are not included.

PART 1

SHORT TITLE, GENERAL CONSTRUCTION AND SUBJECT MATTER

§ 2–101. Short Title.

This Article shall be known and may be cited as Uniform Commercial Code—Sales.

Official Comment

This Article is a complete revision and modernization of the Uniform Sales Act which was promulgated by the National Conference of Commissioners on Uniform State Laws in 1906 and has been adopted in 34 states and Alaska, the District of Columbia and Hawaii.

The coverage of the present Article is much more extensive than that of the old Sales Act and extends to the various bodies of case law which have been developed both outside of and under the latter.

49

The arrangement of the present Article is in terms of contract for sale and the various steps of its performance. The legal consequences are stated as following directly from the contract and action taken under it without resorting to the idea of when property or title passed or was to pass as being the determining factor. The purpose is to avoid making practical issues between practical men turn upon the location of an intangible something, the passing of which no man can prove by evidence and to substitute for such abstractions proof of words and actions of a tangible character.

§ 2–102. Scope; Certain Security and Other Transactions Excluded From This Article.

Unless the context otherwise requires, this Article applies to transactions in goods; it does not apply to any transaction which although in the form of an unconditional contract to sell or present sale is intended to operate only as a security transaction nor does this Article impair or repeal any statute regulating sales to consumers, farmers or other specified classes of buyers.

Official Comment

Prior Uniform Statutory Provision: Section 75, Uniform Sales Act.

Changes: Section 75 has been rephrased.

Purposes of Changes and New Matter: To make it clear that:

The Article leaves substantially unaffected the law relating to purchase money security such as conditional sale or chattel mortgage though it regulates the general sales aspects of such transactions. "Security transaction" is used in the same sense as in the Article on Secured Transactions (Article 9).

Cross Reference:

Article 9.

Definitional Cross References:

"Contract". Section 1–201.
"Contract for sale". Section 2–106.
"Present sale". Section 2–106.
"Sale". Section 2–106.

§ 2–103. Definitions and Index of Definitions.

(1)   In this Article unless the context otherwise requires

(a)   "Buyer" means a person who buys or contracts to buy goods.

(b)   [Reserved.] ["Good faith" in the case of a merchant means honesty in fact and the observance of reasonable commercial standards of fair dealing in the trade.]*

(c)   "Receipt" of goods means taking physical possession of them.

(d)   "Seller" means a person who sells or contracts to sell goods.

(2)   Other definitions applying to this Article or to specified Parts thereof, and the sections in which they appear are:

"Acceptance". Section 2–606.
"Banker's credit". Section 2–325.
"Between merchants". Section 2–104.
"Cancellation". Section 2–106(4).
"Commercial unit". Section 2–105.
"Confirmed credit". Section 2–325.
"Conforming to contract". Section 2–106.
"Contract for sale". Section 2–106.
"Cover". Section 2–712.

---

*   *Note from West Advisory Panel: This subsection will be deleted if the jurisdiction adopts the definition of good faith in revised Article 1 (2001).*

"Entrusting". Section 2–403.
"Financing agency". Section 2–104.
"Future goods". Section 2–105.
"Goods". Section 2–105.
"Identification". Section 2–501.
"Installment contract". Section 2–612.
"Letter of Credit". Section 2–325.
"Lot". Section 2–105.
"Merchant". Section 2–104.
"Overseas". Section 2–323.
"Person in position of seller". Section 2–707.
"Present sale". Section 2–106.
"Sale". Section 2–106.
"Sale on approval". Section 2–326.
"Sale or return". Section 2–326.
"Termination". Section 2–106.

(3)　"Control" as provided in Section 7–106 and the following definitions in other Articles apply to this Article:

"Check". Section 3–104.
"Consignee". Section 7–102.
"Consignor". Section 7–102.
"Consumer goods". Section 9–102.
"Dishonor". Section 3–502.
"Draft". Section 3–104.

(4)　In addition Article 1 contains general definitions and principles of construction and interpretation applicable throughout this Article.

As amended in 1994, 1999, and 2003.

Official Comment

Prior Uniform Statutory Provision: Subsection (1): Section 76, Uniform Sales Act.

Changes:

The definitions of "buyer" and "seller" have been slightly rephrased, the reference in Section 76 of the prior Act to "any legal successor in interest of such person" being omitted. The definition of "receipt" is new.

Purposes of Changes and New Matter:

1.　The phrase "any legal successor in interest of such person" has been eliminated since Section 2–210 of this Article, which limits some types of delegation of performance on assignment of a sales contract, makes it clear that not every such successor can be safely included in the definition. In every ordinary case, however, such successors are as of course included.

2.　"Receipt" must be distinguished from delivery particularly in regard to the problems arising out of shipment of goods, whether or not the contract calls for making delivery by way of documents of title, since the seller may frequently fulfill his obligations to "deliver" even though the buyer may never "receive" the goods. Delivery with respect to documents of title is defined in Article 1 and requires transfer of physical delivery of a tangible document of title and transfer of control of an electronic document of title. Otherwise the many divergent incidents of delivery are handled incident by incident.

Cross References:

Point 1: See Section 2–210 and Comment thereon.
Point 2: Section 1–201.

Definitional Cross Reference:

"Person". Section 1–201.

As amended in 2003.

§ 2–104.   Definitions: "Merchant"; "Between Merchants"; "Financing Agency".

(1)   "Merchant" means a person who deals in goods of the kind or otherwise by his occupation holds himself out as having knowledge or skill peculiar to the practices or goods involved in the transaction or to whom such knowledge or skill may be attributed by his employment of an agent or broker or other intermediary who by his occupation holds himself out as having such knowledge or skill.

(2)   "Financing agency" means a bank, finance company or other person who in the ordinary course of business makes advances against goods or documents of title or who by arrangement with either the seller or the buyer intervenes in ordinary course to make or collect payment due or claimed under the contract for sale, as by purchasing or paying the seller's draft or making advances against it or by merely taking it for collection whether or not documents of title accompany or are associated with the draft. "Financing agency" includes also a bank or other person who similarly intervenes between persons who are in the position of seller and buyer in respect to the goods (Section 2–707).

(3)   "Between merchants" means in any transaction with respect to which both parties are chargeable with the knowledge or skill of merchants.

As amended in 2003.

Official Comment

Prior Uniform Statutory Provision: None. But see Sections 15(2), (5), 16(c), 45(2) and 71, Uniform Sales Act, and Sections 35 and 37, Uniform Bills of Lading Act for examples of the policy expressly provided for in this Article.

Purposes:

1.   This Article assumes that transactions between professionals in a given field require special and clear rules which may not apply to a casual or inexperienced seller or buyer. It thus adopts a policy of expressly stating rules applicable "between merchants" and "as against a merchant", wherever they are needed instead of making them depend upon the circumstances of each case as in the statutes cited above. This section lays the foundation of this policy by defining those who are to be regarded as professionals or "merchants" and by stating when a transaction is deemed to be "between merchants".

2.   The term "merchant" as defined here roots in the "law merchant" concept of a professional in business. The professional status under the definition may be based upon specialized knowledge as to the goods, specialized knowledge as to business practices, or specialized knowledge as to both and which kind of specialized knowledge may be sufficient to establish the merchant status is indicated by the nature of the provisions.

The special provisions as to merchants appear only in this Article and they are of three kinds. Sections 2–201(2), 2–205, 2–207 and 2–209 dealing with the statute of frauds, firm offers, confirmatory memoranda and modification rest on normal business practices which are or ought to be typical of and familiar to any person in business. For purposes of these sections almost every person in business would, therefore, be deemed to be a "merchant" under the language "who . . . by his occupation holds himself out as having knowledge or skill peculiar to the practices . . . involved in the transaction . . ." since the practices involved in the transaction are non-specialized business practices such as answering mail. In this type of provision, banks or even universities, for example, well may be "merchants." But even these sections only apply to a merchant in his mercantile capacity; a lawyer or bank president buying fishing tackle for his own use is not a merchant.

On the other hand, in Section 2–314 on the warranty of merchantability, such warranty is implied only "if the seller is a merchant with respect to goods of that kind." Obviously this qualification restricts the implied warranty to a much smaller group than everyone who is engaged in business and requires a professional status as to particular kinds of goods. The exception in Section 2–402(2) for retention of possession by a merchant-seller falls in the same class; as does Section 2–403(2) on entrusting of possession to a merchant "who deals in goods of that kind".

A third group of sections includes 2–103(1)(b), which provides that in the case of a merchant "good faith" includes observance of reasonable commercial standards of fair dealing in the trade; 2–327(1)(c), 2–603 and 2–605, dealing with responsibilities of merchant buyers to follow seller's instructions, etc.; 2–509 on risk of loss, and 2–609 on adequate assurance of performance. This group of sections applies to persons who are merchants under either the "practices" or the "goods" aspect of the definition of merchant.

3.   The "or to whom such knowledge or skill may be attributed by his employment of an agent or broker . . ." clause of the definition of merchant means that even persons such as universities, for example, can come within the definition of merchant if they have regular purchasing departments or business personnel who are familiar with business practices and who are equipped to take any action required.

Cross References:

Point 1: See Sections 1–102 and 1–203.*
Point 2: See Sections 2–314, 2–315 and 2–320 to 2–325, of this Article, and Article 9.

Definitional Cross References:

"Bank". Section 1–201.
"Buyer". Section 2–103.
"Contract for sale". Section 2–106.
"Document of title". Section 1–201.
"Draft". Section 3–104.
"Goods". Section 2–105.
"Person". Section 1–201.
"Purchase". Section 1–201.
"Seller". Section 2–103.

§ 2–105.   Definitions: Transferability; "Goods"; "Future" Goods; "Lot"; "Commercial Unit".

(1)   "Goods" means all things (including specially manufactured goods) which are movable at the time of identification to the contract for sale other than the money in which the price is to be paid, investment securities (Article 8) and things in action. "Goods" also includes the unborn young of animals and growing crops and other identified things attached to realty as described in the section on goods to be severed from realty (Section 2–107).

(2)   Goods must be both existing and identified before any interest in them can pass. Goods which are not both existing and identified are "future" goods. A purported present sale of future goods or of any interest therein operates as a contract to sell.

(3)   There may be a sale of a part interest in existing identified goods.

(4)   An undivided share in an identified bulk of fungible goods is sufficiently identified to be sold although the quantity of the bulk is not determined. Any agreed proportion of such a bulk or any quantity thereof agreed upon by number, weight or other measure may to the extent of the seller's interest in the bulk be sold to the buyer who then becomes an owner in common.

(5)   "Lot" means a parcel or a single article which is the subject matter of a separate sale or delivery, whether or not it is sufficient to perform the contract.

(6)   "Commercial unit" means such a unit of goods as by commercial usage is a single whole for purposes of sale and division of which materially impairs its character or value on the market or in use. A commercial unit may be a single article (as a machine) or a set of articles (as a suite of furniture or an assortment of sizes) or a quantity (as a bale, gross, or carload) or any other unit treated in use or in the relevant market as a single whole.

Official Comment

Prior Uniform Statutory Provision: Subsections (1), (2), (3) and (4)—Sections 5, 6 and 76, Uniform Sales Act; Subsections (5) and (6)—none.

Changes: Rewritten.

---

*   *Referring to unrevised Article 1 (Appendix A).*

Purposes of Changes and New Matter:

1.   Subsection (1) on "goods": The phraseology of the prior uniform statutory provision has been changed so that:

The definition of goods is based on the concept of movability and the term "chattels personal" is not used. It is not intended to deal with things which are not fairly identifiable as movables before the contract is performed.

Growing crops are included within the definition of goods since they are frequently intended for sale. The concept of "industrial" growing crops has been abandoned, for under modern practices fruit, perennial hay, nursery stock and the like must be brought within the scope of this Article. The young of animals are also included expressly in this definition since they, too, are frequently intended for sale and may be contracted for before birth. The period of gestation of domestic animals is such that the provisions of the section on identification can apply as in the case of crops to be planted. The reason of this definition also leads to the inclusion of a wool crop or the like as "goods" subject to identification under this Article.

The exclusion of "money in which the price is to be paid" from the definition of goods does not mean that foreign currency which is included in the definition of money may not be the subject matter of a sales transaction. Goods is intended to cover the sale of money when money is being treated as a commodity but not to include it when money is the medium of payment.

As to contracts to sell timber, minerals, or structures to be removed from the land Section 2–107(1) (Goods to be severed from Realty: recording) controls.

The use of the word "fixtures" is avoided in view of the diversity of definitions of that term. This Article in including within its scope "things attached to realty" adds the further test that they must be capable of severance without material harm thereto. As between the parties any identified things which fall within that definition become "goods" upon the making of the contract for sale.

"Investment securities" are expressly excluded from the coverage of this Article. It is not intended by this exclusion, however, to prevent the application of a particular section of this Article by analogy to securities (as was done with the Original Sales Act in *Agar v. Orda*, 264 N.Y. 248, 190 N.E. 479, 99 A.L.R. 269 (1934)) when the reason of that section makes such application sensible and the situation involved is not covered by the Article of this Act dealing specifically with such securities (Article 8).

2.   References to the fact that a contract for sale can extend to future or contingent goods and that ownership in common follows the sale of a part interest have been omitted here as obvious without need for expression; hence no inference to negate these principles should be drawn from their omission.

3.   Subsection (4) does not touch the question of how far an appropriation of a bulk of fungible goods may or may not satisfy the contract for sale.

4.   Subsections (5) and (6) on "lot" and "commercial unit" are introduced to aid in the phrasing of later sections.

5.   The question of when an identification of goods takes place is determined by the provisions of Section 2–501 and all that this section says is what kinds of goods may be the subject of a sale.

Cross References:

Point 1: Sections 2–107, 2–201, 2–501 and Article 8.
Point 5: Section 2–501.
See also Section 1–201.

Definitional Cross References:

"Buyer". Section 2–103.
"Contract". Section 1–201.
"Contract for sale". Section 2–106.
"Fungible". Section 1–201.
"Money". Section 1–201.
"Present sale". Section 2–106.
"Sale". Section 2–106.
"Seller". Section 2–103.

§ 2–106. Definitions: "Contract"; "Agreement"; "Contract for Sale"; "Sale"; "Present Sale"; "Conforming" to Contract; "Termination"; "Cancellation".

(1) In this Article unless the context otherwise requires "contract" and "agreement" are limited to those relating to the present or future sale of goods. "Contract for sale" includes both a present sale of goods and a contract to sell goods at a future time. A "sale" consists in the passing of title from the seller to the buyer for a price (Section 2–401). A "present sale" means a sale which is accomplished by the making of the contract.

(2) Goods or conduct including any part of a performance are "conforming" or conform to the contract when they are in accordance with the obligations under the contract.

(3) "Termination" occurs when either party pursuant to a power created by agreement or law puts an end to the contract otherwise than for its breach. On "termination" all obligations which are still executory on both sides are discharged but any right based on prior breach or performance survives.

(4) "Cancellation" occurs when either party puts an end to the contract for breach by the other and its effect is the same as that of "termination" except that the cancelling party also retains any remedy for breach of the whole contract or any unperformed balance.

Official Comment

Prior Uniform Statutory Provision: Subsection (1)—Section 1(1) and (2), Uniform Sales Act; Subsection (2)—none, but subsection generally continues policy of Sections 11, 44 and 69, Uniform Sales Act; Subsections (3) and (4)—none.

Changes: Completely rewritten.

Purposes of Changes and New Matter:

1. Subsection (1): "Contract for sale" is used as a general concept throughout this Article, but the rights of the parties do not vary according to whether the transaction is a present sale or a contract to sell unless the Article expressly so provides.

2. Subsection (2): It is in general intended to continue the policy of requiring exact performance by the seller of his obligations as a condition to his right to require acceptance. However, the seller is in part safeguarded against surprise as a result of sudden technicality on the buyer's part by the provisions of Section 2–508 on seller's cure of improper tender or delivery. Moreover usage of trade frequently permits commercial leeways in performance and the language of the agreement itself must be read in the light of such custom or usage and also, prior course of dealing, and in a long term contract, the course of performance.

3. Subsections (3) and (4): These subsections are intended to make clear the distinction carried forward throughout this Article between termination and cancellation.

Cross References:

Point 2: Sections 1–203*, 1–205,* 2–208 and 2–508.

Definitional Cross References:

"Agreement". Section 1–201.
"Buyer". Section 2–103.
"Contract". Section 1–201.
"Goods". Section 2–105.
"Party". Section 1–201.
"Remedy". Section 1–201.
"Rights". Section 1–201.
"Seller". Section 2–103.

---

*   *Referring to unrevised Article 1 (Appendix A).*

§ 2-107.   Goods to Be Severed From Realty: Recording.

(1)   A contract for the sale of minerals or the like (including oil and gas) or a structure or its materials to be removed from realty is a contract for the sale of goods within this Article if they are to be severed by the seller but until severance a purported present sale thereof which is not effective as a transfer of an interest in land is effective only as a contract to sell.

(2)   A contract for the sale apart from the land of growing crops or other things attached to realty and capable of severance without material harm thereto but not described in subsection (1) or of timber to be cut is a contract for the sale of goods within this Article whether the subject matter is to be severed by the buyer or by the seller even though it forms part of the realty at the time of contracting, and the parties can by identification effect a present sale before severance.

(3)   The provisions of this section are subject to any third party rights provided by the law relating to realty records, and the contract for sale may be executed and recorded as a document transferring an interest in land and shall then constitute notice to third parties of the buyer's rights under the contract for sale.

As amended in 1972.

Official Comment

Prior Uniform Statutory Provision: See Section 76, Uniform Sales Act on prior policy; Section 7, Uniform Conditional Sales Act.

Purposes:

1.   Subsection (1).   Notice that this subsection applies only if the minerals or structures "are to be severed by the seller". If the buyer is to sever, such transactions are considered contracts affecting land and all problems of the Statute of Frauds and of the recording of land rights apply to them. Therefore, the Statute of Frauds section of this Article does not apply to such contracts though they must conform to the Statute of Frauds affecting the transfer of interests in land.

2.   Subsection (2).   "Things attached" to the realty which can be severed without material harm are goods within this Article regardless of who is to effect the severance. The word "fixtures" has been avoided because of the diverse definitions of this term, the test of "severance without material harm" being substituted.

The provision in subsection (3) for recording such contracts is within the purview of this Article since it is a means of preserving the buyer's rights under the contract of sale.

3.   The security phases of things attached to or to become attached to realty are dealt with in the Article on Secured Transactions (Article 9) and it is to be noted that the definition of goods in that Article differs from the definition of goods in this Article.

However, both Articles treat as goods growing crops and also timber to be cut under a contract of severance.

Cross References:

Point 1: Section 2-201.
Point 2: Section 2-105.
Point 3: Article 9 and Section 9-102(a)(44).

Definitional Cross References:

"Buyer". Section 2-103.
"Contract". Section 1-201.
"Contract for sale". Section 2-106.
"Goods". Section 2-105.
"Party". Section 1-201.
"Present sale". Section 2-106.
"Rights". Section 1-201.
"Seller". Section 2-103.

PART 2

FORM, FORMATION AND READJUSTMENT
OF CONTRACT

§ 2–201.   Formal Requirements; Statute of Frauds.

(1)   Except as otherwise provided in this section a contract for the sale of goods for the price of $500 or more is not enforceable by way of action or defense unless there is some writing sufficient to indicate that a contract for sale has been made between the parties and signed by the party against whom enforcement is sought or by his authorized agent or broker. A writing is not insufficient because it omits or incorrectly states a term agreed upon but the contract is not enforceable under this paragraph beyond the quantity of goods shown in such writing.

(2)   Between merchants if within a reasonable time a writing in confirmation of the contract and sufficient against the sender is received and the party receiving it has reason to know its contents, it satisfies the requirements of subsection (1) against such party unless written notice of objection to its contents is given within 10 days after it is received.

(3)   A contract which does not satisfy the requirements of subsection (1) but which is valid in other respects is enforceable

(a)   if the goods are to be specially manufactured for the buyer and are not suitable for sale to others in the ordinary course of the seller's business and the seller, before notice of repudiation is received and under circumstances which reasonably indicate that the goods are for the buyer, has made either a substantial beginning of their manufacture or commitments for their procurement; or

(b)   if the party against whom enforcement is sought admits in his pleading, testimony or otherwise in court that a contract for sale was made, but the contract is not enforceable under this provision beyond the quantity of goods admitted; or

(c)   with respect to goods for which payment has been made and accepted or which have been received and accepted (Section 2–606).

Official Comment

Prior Uniform Statutory Provision: Section 4, Uniform Sales Act (which was based on Section 17 of the Statute of 29 Charles II).

Changes: Completely rephrased; restricted to sale of goods. See also Sections 1–206,* 8–319** and 9–203.

Purposes of Changes: The changed phraseology of this section is intended to make it clear that:

1.   The required writing need not contain all the material terms of the contract and such material terms as are stated need not be precisely stated. All that is required is that the writing afford a basis for believing that the offered oral evidence rests on a real transaction. It may be written in lead pencil on a scratch pad. It need not indicate which party is the buyer and which the seller. The only term which must appear is the quantity term which need not be accurately stated but recovery is limited to the amount stated. The price, time and place of payment or delivery, the general quality of the goods, or any particular warranties may all be omitted.

Special emphasis must be placed on the permissibility of omitting the price term in view of the insistence of some courts on the express inclusion of this term even where the parties have contracted on the basis of a published price list. In many valid contracts for sale the parties do not mention the price in express terms, the buyer being bound to pay and the seller to accept a reasonable price which the trier of the fact may well be trusted to determine. Again, frequently the price is not mentioned since the parties have based their agreement on a price list or catalogue known to both of them and this list serves as an efficient safeguard against perjury. Finally, "market" prices and valuations that are current in the vicinity constitute a similar check. Thus if the price is not stated in

---

*   *Referring to unrevised Article 1 (Appendix A).*
**   *Referring to unrevised Article 8.*

the memorandum it can normally be supplied without danger of fraud. Of course if the "price" consists of goods rather than money the quantity of goods must be stated.

Only three definite and invariable requirements as to the memorandum are made by this subsection. First, it must evidence a contract for the sale of goods; second, it must be "signed", a word which includes any authentication which identifies the party to be charged; and third, it must specify a quantity.

2.   "Partial performance" as a substitute for the required memorandum can validate the contract only for the goods which have been accepted or for which payment has been made and accepted.

Receipt and acceptance either of goods or of the price constitutes an unambiguous overt admission by both parties that a contract actually exists. If the court can make a just apportionment, therefore, the agreed price of any goods actually delivered can be recovered without a writing or, if the price has been paid, the seller can be forced to deliver an apportionable part of the goods. The overt actions of the parties make admissible evidence of the other terms of the contract necessary to a just apportionment. This is true even though the actions of the parties are not in themselves inconsistent with a different transaction such as a consignment for resale or a mere loan of money.

Part performance by the buyer requires the delivery of something by him that is accepted by the seller as such performance. Thus, part payment may be made by money or check, accepted by the seller. If the agreed price consists of goods or services, then they must also have been delivered and accepted.

3.   Between merchants, failure to answer a written confirmation of a contract within ten days of receipt is tantamount to a writing under subsection (2) and is sufficient against both parties under subsection (1). The only effect, however, is to take away from the party who fails to answer the defense of the Statute of Frauds; the burden of persuading the trier of fact that a contract was in fact made orally prior to the written confirmation is unaffected. Compare the effect of a failure to reply under Section 2–207.

4.   Failure to satisfy the requirements of this section does not render the contract void for all purposes, but merely prevents it from being judicially enforced in favor of a party to the contract. For example, a buyer who takes possession of goods as provided in an oral contract which the seller has not meanwhile repudiated, is not a trespasser. Nor would the Statute of Frauds provisions of this section be a defense to a third person who wrongfully induces a party to refuse to perform an oral contract, even though the injured party cannot maintain an action for damages against the party so refusing to perform.

5.   The requirement of "signing" is discussed in the comment to Section 1–201.

6.   It is not necessary that the writing be delivered to anybody. It need not be signed or authenticated by both parties but it is, of course, not sufficient against one who has not signed it. Prior to a dispute no one can determine which party's signing of the memorandum may be necessary but from the time of contracting each party should be aware that to him it is signing by the other which is important.

7.   If the making of a contract is admitted in court, either in a written pleading, by stipulation or by oral statement before the court, no additional writing is necessary for protection against fraud. Under this section it is no longer possible to admit the contract in court and still treat the Statute as a defense. However, the contract is not thus conclusively established. The admission so made by a party is itself evidential against him of the truth of the facts so admitted and of nothing more; as against the other party, it is not evidential at all.

Cross References:

See Sections 1–201, 2–202, 2–207, 2–209 and 2–304.

Definitional Cross References:

"Action". Section 1–201.
"Between merchants". Section 2–104.
"Buyer". Section 2–103.
"Contract". Section 1–201.
"Contract for sale". Section 2–106.
"Goods". Section 2–105.
"Notice". Section 1–201.*

---

*   *Referring to unrevised Article 1 (Appendix A).*

"Party". Section 1–201.
"Reasonable time". Section 1–204.*
"Sale". Section 2–106.
"Seller". Section 2–103.

§ 2–202. Final Written Expression: Parol or Extrinsic Evidence.

Terms with respect to which the confirmatory memoranda of the parties agree or which are otherwise set forth in a writing intended by the parties as a final expression of their agreement with respect to such terms as are included therein may not be contradicted by evidence of any prior agreement or of a contemporaneous oral agreement but may be explained or supplemented

(a) by course of performance, course of dealing, or usage of trade (Section 1–303); and

(b) by evidence of consistent additional terms unless the court finds the writing to have been intended also as a complete and exclusive statement of the terms of the agreement.

Official Comment

Prior Uniform Statutory Provisions: None.

Purposes:

1. This section definitely rejects:

(a) Any assumption that because a writing has been worked out which is final on some matters, it is to be taken as including all the matters agreed upon;

(b) The premise that the language used has the meaning attributable to such language by rules of construction existing in the law rather than the meaning which arises out of the commercial context in which it was used; and

(c) The requirement that a condition precedent to the admissibility of the type of evidence specified in paragraph (a) is an original determination by the court that the language used is ambiguous.

2. Paragraph (a) makes admissible evidence of course of dealing, usage of trade and course of performance to explain or supplement the terms of any writing stating the agreement of the parties in order that the true understanding of the parties as to the agreement may be reached. Such writings are to be read on the assumption that the course of prior dealings between the parties and the usages of trade were taken for granted when the document was phrased. Unless carefully negated they have become an element of the meaning of the words used. Similarly, the course of actual performance by the parties is considered the best indication of what they intended the writing to mean.

3. Under paragraph (b) consistent additional terms, not reduced to writing, may be proved unless the court finds that the writing was intended by both parties as a complete and exclusive statement of all the terms. If the additional terms are such that, if agreed upon, they would certainly have been included in the document in the view of the court, then evidence of their alleged making must be kept from the trier of fact.

Cross References:

Point 3: Sections 1–303, 2–207, 2–302 and 2–316.

Definitional Cross References:

"Agreed" and "agreement". Section 1–201.
"Course of dealing". Section 1–303.
"Course of performance". Section 1–303.
"Party". Section 1–201.
"Term". Section 1–201.
"Usage of trade". Section 1–303.
"Written" and "writing". Section 1–201.

---

* *Referring to unrevised Article 1 (Appendix A).*

§ 2–203.   Seals Inoperative.

The affixing of a seal to a writing evidencing a contract for sale or an offer to buy or sell goods does not constitute the writing a sealed instrument and the law with respect to sealed instruments does not apply to such a contract or offer.

Official Comment

Prior Uniform Statutory Provision: Section 3, Uniform Sales Act.

Changes: Portion pertaining to "seals" rewritten.

Purposes of Changes:

1.   This section makes it clear that every effect of the seal which relates to "sealed instruments" as such is wiped out insofar as contracts for sale are concerned. However, the substantial effects of a seal, except extension of the period of limitations, may be had by appropriate drafting as in the case of firm offers (see Section 2–205).

2.   This section leaves untouched any aspects of a seal which relate merely to signatures or to authentication of execution and the like. Thus, a statute providing that a purported signature gives prima facie evidence of its own authenticity or that a signature gives prima facie evidence of consideration is still applicable to sales transactions even though a seal may be held to be a signature within the meaning of such a statute. Similarly, the authorized affixing of a corporate seal bearing the corporate name to a contractual writing purporting to be made by the corporation may have effect as a signature without any reference to the law of sealed instruments.

Cross Reference:

Point 1: Section 2–205.

Definitional Cross References:

"Contract for sale". Section 2–106.
"Goods". Section 2–105.
"Writing". Section 1–201.

§ 2–204.   Formation in General.

(1)   A contract for sale of goods may be made in any manner sufficient to show agreement, including conduct by both parties which recognizes the existence of such a contract.

(2)   An agreement sufficient to constitute a contract for sale may be found even though the moment of its making is undetermined.

(3)   Even though one or more terms are left open a contract for sale does not fail for indefiniteness if the parties have intended to make a contract and there is a reasonably certain basis for giving an appropriate remedy.

Official Comment

Prior Uniform Statutory Provision: Sections 1 and 3, Uniform Sales Act.

Changes: Completely rewritten by this and other sections of this Article.

Purposes of Changes:

Subsection (1) continues without change the basic policy of recognizing any manner of expression of agreement, oral, written or otherwise. The legal effect of such an agreement is, of course, qualified by other provisions of this Article.

Under subsection (1) appropriate conduct by the parties may be sufficient to establish an agreement. Subsection (2) is directed primarily to the situation where the interchanged correspondence does not disclose the exact point at which the deal was closed, but the actions of the parties indicate that a binding obligation has been undertaken.

Subsection (3) states the principle as to "open terms" underlying later sections of the Article. If the parties intend to enter into a binding agreement, this subsection recognizes that agreement as valid in law, despite missing terms, if there is any reasonably certain basis for granting a remedy. The test is not certainty as to what the parties were to do nor as to the exact amount of damages due the plaintiff. Nor is the fact that one or more terms are left to be agreed upon enough of itself to defeat an otherwise adequate agreement. Rather, commercial standards on the point of "indefiniteness" are intended to be applied, this Act making provision elsewhere for missing terms needed for performance, open price, remedies and the like.

The more terms the parties leave open, the less likely it is that they have intended to conclude a binding agreement, but their actions may be frequently conclusive on the matter despite the omissions.

Cross References:

Subsection (1): Sections 1–103, 2–201 and 2–302.
Subsection (2): Sections 2–205 through 2–209.
Subsection (3): See Part 3.

Definitional Cross References:

"Agreement". Section 1–201.
"Contract". Section 1–201.
"Contract for sale". Section 2–106.
"Goods". Section 2–105.
"Party". Section 1–201.
"Remedy". Section 1–201.
"Term". Section 1–201.

§ 2–205.   Firm Offers.

An offer by a merchant to buy or sell goods in a signed writing which by its terms gives assurance that it will be held open is not revocable, for lack of consideration, during the time stated or if no time is stated for a reasonable time, but in no event may such period of irrevocability exceed three months; but any such term of assurance on a form supplied by the offeree must be separately signed by the offeror.

Official Comment

Prior Uniform Statutory Provision: Sections 1 and 3, Uniform Sales Act.

Changes: Completely rewritten by this and other sections of this Article.

Purposes of Changes:

1.   This section is intended to modify the former rule which required that "firm offers" be sustained by consideration in order to bind, and to require instead that they must merely be characterized as such and expressed in signed writings.

2.   The primary purpose of this section is to give effect to the deliberate intention of a merchant to make a current firm offer binding. The deliberation is shown in the case of an individualized document by the merchant's signature to the offer, and in the case of an offer included on a form supplied by the other party to the transaction by the separate signing of the particular clause which contains the offer. "Signed" here also includes authentication but the reasonableness of the authentication herein allowed must be determined in the light of the purpose of the section. The circumstances surrounding the signing may justify something less than a formal signature or initialing but typically the kind of authentication involved here would consist of a minimum of initialing of the clause involved. A handwritten memorandum on the writer's letterhead purporting in its terms to "confirm" a firm offer already made would be enough to satisfy this section, although not subscribed, since under the circumstances it could not be considered a memorandum of mere negotiation and it would adequately show its own authenticity. Similarly, an authorized telegram will suffice, and this is true even though the original draft contained only a typewritten signature. However, despite settled courses of dealing or usages of the trade whereby firm offers are made by oral communication and relied upon without more evidence, such offers remain revocable under this Article since authentication by a writing is the essence of this section.

3.   This section is intended to apply to current "firm" offers and not to long term options, and an outside time limit of three months during which such offers remain irrevocable has been set. The three month period during which firm offers remain irrevocable under this section need not be stated by days or by date. If the offer

states that it is "guaranteed" or "firm" until the happening of a contingency which will occur within the three month period, it will remain irrevocable until that event. A promise made for a longer period will operate under this section to bind the offeror only for the first three months of the period but may of course be renewed. If supported by consideration it may continue for as long as the parties specify. This section deals only with the offer which is not supported by consideration.

4.   Protection is afforded against the inadvertent signing of a firm offer when contained in a form prepared by the offeree by requiring that such a clause be separately authenticated. If the offer clause is called to the offeror's attention and he separately authenticates it, he will be bound; Section 2–302 may operate, however, to prevent an unconscionable result which otherwise would flow from other terms appearing in the form.

5.   Safeguards are provided to offer relief in the case of material mistake by virtue of the requirement of good faith and the general law of mistake.

Cross References:

> Point 1: Section 1–102.*
> Point 2: Section 1–102.*
> Point 3: Section 2–201.
> Point 5: Section 2–302.

Definitional Cross References:

> "Goods". Section 2–105.
> "Merchant". Section 2–104.
> "Signed". Section 1–201.
> "Writing". Section 1–201.

§ 2–206.   Offer and Acceptance in Formation of Contract.

(1)   Unless otherwise unambiguously indicated by the language or circumstances

(a)   an offer to make a contract shall be construed as inviting acceptance in any manner and by any medium reasonable in the circumstances;

(b)   an order or other offer to buy goods for prompt or current shipment shall be construed as inviting acceptance either by a prompt promise to ship or by the prompt or current shipment of conforming or non-conforming goods, but such a shipment of non-conforming goods does not constitute an acceptance if the seller seasonably notifies the buyer that the shipment is offered only as an accommodation to the buyer.

(2)   Where the beginning of a requested performance is a reasonable mode of acceptance an offeror who is not notified of acceptance within a reasonable time may treat the offer as having lapsed before acceptance.

Official Comment

Prior Uniform Statutory Provision: Sections 1 and 3, Uniform Sales Act.

Changes: Completely rewritten in this and other sections of this Article.

Purposes of Changes: To make it clear that:

1.   Any reasonable manner of acceptance is intended to be regarded as available unless the offeror has made quite clear that it will not be acceptable. Former technical rules as to acceptance, such as requiring that telegraphic offers be accepted by telegraphed acceptance, etc., are rejected and a criterion that the acceptance be "in any manner and by any medium reasonable under the circumstances," is substituted. This section is intended to remain flexible and its applicability to be enlarged as new media of communication develop or as the more time-saving present day media come into general use.

2.   Either shipment or a prompt promise to ship is made a proper means of acceptance of an offer looking to current shipment. In accordance with ordinary commercial understanding the section interprets an order

---

*   *Referring to unrevised Article 1 (Appendix A).*

looking to current shipment as allowing acceptance either by actual shipment or by a prompt promise to ship and rejects the artificial theory that only a single mode of acceptance is normally envisaged by an offer. This is true even though the language of the offer happens to be "ship at once" or the like. "Shipment" is here used in the same sense as in Section 2–504; it does not include the beginning of delivery by the seller's own truck or by messenger. But loading on the seller's own truck might be a beginning of performance under subsection (2).

3.   The beginning of performance by an offeree can be effective as acceptance so as to bind the offeror only if followed within a reasonable time by notice to the offeror. Such a beginning of performance must unambiguously express the offeree's intention to engage himself. For the protection of both parties it is essential that notice follow in due course to constitute acceptance. Nothing in this section however bars the possibility that under the common law performance begun may have an intermediate effect of temporarily barring revocation of the offer, or at the offeror's option, final effect in constituting acceptance.

4.   Subsection (1)(b) deals with the situation where a shipment made following an order is shown by a notification of shipment to be referable to that order but has a defect. Such a non-conforming shipment is normally to be understood as intended to close the bargain, even though it proves to have been at the same time a breach. However, the seller by stating that the shipment is non-conforming and is offered only as an accommodation to the buyer keeps the shipment or notification from operating as an acceptance.

Definitional Cross References:

"Buyer". Section 2–103.
"Conforming". Section 2–106.
"Contract". Section 1–201.
"Goods". Section 2–105.
"Notifies". Section 1–201.*
"Reasonable time". Section 1–204.*

§ 2–207.   Additional Terms in Acceptance or Confirmation.

(1)   A definite and seasonable expression of acceptance or a written confirmation which is sent within a reasonable time operates as an acceptance even though it states terms additional to or different from those offered or agreed upon, unless acceptance is expressly made conditional on assent to the additional or different terms.

(2)   The additional terms are to be construed as proposals for addition to the contract. Between merchants such terms become part of the contract unless:

(a)   the offer expressly limits acceptance to the terms of the offer;

(b)   they materially alter it; or

(c)   notification of objection to them has already been given or is given within a reasonable time after notice of them is received.

(3)   Conduct by both parties which recognizes the existence of a contract is sufficient to establish a contract for sale although the writings of the parties do not otherwise establish a contract. In such case the terms of the particular contract consist of those terms on which the writings of the parties agree, together with any supplementary terms incorporated under any other provisions of this Act.

Official Comment

Prior Uniform Statutory Provision: Sections 1 and 3, Uniform Sales Act.

Changes: Completely rewritten by this and other sections of this Article.

Purposes of Changes:

1.   This section is intended to deal with two typical situations. The one is the written confirmation, where an agreement has been reached either orally or by informal correspondence between the parties and is followed by one or both of the parties sending formal memoranda embodying the terms so far as agreed upon and adding terms not discussed. The other situation is offer and acceptance, in which a wire or letter expressed and intended

---

*   *Referring to unrevised Article 1 (Appendix A).*

as an acceptance or the closing of an agreement adds further minor suggestions or proposals such as "ship by Tuesday," "rush," "ship draft against bill of lading inspection allowed," or the like. A frequent example of the second situation is the exchange of printed purchase order and acceptance (sometimes called "acknowledgment") forms. Because the forms are oriented to the thinking of the respective drafting parties, the terms contained in them often do not correspond. Often the seller's form contains terms different from or additional to those set forth in the buyer's form. Nevertheless, the parties proceed with the transaction. [Comment 1 was amended in 1966.]

2.   Under this Article a proposed deal which in commercial understanding has in fact been closed is recognized as a contract. Therefore, any additional matter contained in the confirmation or in the acceptance falls within subsection (2) and must be regarded as a proposal for an added term unless the acceptance is made conditional on the acceptance of the additional or different terms. [Comment 2 was amended in 1966.]

3.   Whether or not additional or different terms will become part of the agreement depends upon the provisions of subsection (2). If they are such as materially to alter the original bargain, they will not be included unless expressly agreed to by the other party. If, however, they are terms which would not so change the bargain they will be incorporated unless notice of objection to them has already been given or is given within a reasonable time.

4.   Examples of typical clauses which would normally "materially alter" the contract and so result in surprise or hardship if incorporated without express awareness by the other party are: a clause negating such standard warranties as that of merchantability or fitness for a particular purpose in circumstances in which either warranty normally attaches; a clause requiring a guaranty of 90% or 100% deliveries in a case such as a contract by cannery, where the usage of the trade allows greater quantity leeways; a clause reserving to the seller the power to cancel upon the buyer's failure to meet any invoice when due; a clause requiring that complaints be made in a time materially shorter than customary or reasonable.

5.   Examples of clauses which involve no element of unreasonable surprise and which therefore are to be incorporated in the contract unless notice of objection is seasonably given are: a clause setting forth and perhaps enlarging slightly upon the seller's exemption due to supervening causes beyond his control, similar to those covered by the provision of this Article on merchant's excuse by failure of presupposed conditions or a clause fixing in advance any reasonable formula of proration under such circumstances; a clause fixing a reasonable time for complaints within customary limits, or in the case of a purchase for sub-sale, providing for inspection by the sub-purchaser; a clause providing for interest on overdue invoices or fixing the seller's standard credit terms where they are within the range of trade practice and do not limit any credit bargained for; a clause limiting the right of rejection for defects which fall within the customary trade tolerances for acceptance "with adjustment" or otherwise limiting remedy in a reasonable manner (see Sections 2–718 and 2–719).

6.   If no answer is received within a reasonable time after additional terms are proposed, it is both fair and commercially sound to assume that their inclusion has been assented to. Where clauses on confirming forms sent by both parties conflict each party must be assumed to object to a clause of the other conflicting with one on the confirmation sent by himself. As a result the requirement that there be notice of objection which is found in subsection (2) is satisfied and the conflicting terms do not become a part of the contract. The contract then consists of the terms originally expressly agreed to, terms on which the confirmations agree, and terms supplied by this Act, including subsection (2). The written confirmation is also subject to Section 2–201. Under that section a failure to respond permits enforcement of a prior oral agreement; under this section a failure to respond permits additional terms to become part of the agreement. [Comment 6 was amended in 1966.]

7.   In many cases, as where goods are shipped, accepted and paid for before any dispute arises, there is no question whether a contract has been made. In such cases, where the writings of the parties do not establish a contract, it is not necessary to determine which act or document constituted the offer and which the acceptance. See Section 2–204. The only question is what terms are included in the contract, and subsection (3) furnishes the governing rule. [Comment 7 was added in 1966.]

Cross References:

See generally Section 2–302.
Point 5: Sections 2–513, 2–602, 2–607, 2–609, 2–612, 2–614, 2–615, 2–616, 2–718 and 2–719.
Point 6: Sections 1–102* and 2–104.

---

*   *Referring to unrevised Article 1 (Appendix A).*

Definitional Cross References:

   "Between merchants". Section 2–104.
   "Contract". Section 1–201.
   "Notification". Section 1–201.*
   "Reasonable time". Section 1–204.*
   "Seasonably". Section 1–204.*
   "Send". Section 1–201.
   "Term". Section 1–201.
   "Written". Section 1–201.

§ 2–208.   [Reserved.] [Course of Performance or Practical Construction.]**

[(1) Where the contract for sale involves repeated occasions for performance by either party with knowledge of the nature of the performance and opportunity for objection to it by the other, any course of performance accepted or acquiesced in without objection shall be relevant to determine the meaning of the agreement.

(2) The express terms of the agreement and any such course of performance, as well as any course of dealing and usage of trade, shall be construed whenever reasonable as consistent with each other; but when such construction is unreasonable, express terms shall control course of performance and course of performance shall control both course of dealing and usage of trade (Section 1–205).*

(3) Subject to the provisions of the next section on modification and waiver, such course of performance shall be relevant to show a waiver or modification of any term inconsistent with such course of performance.

Official Comment

Prior Uniform Statutory Provision: No such general provision but concept of this section recognized by terms such as "course of dealing", "the circumstances of the case," "the conduct of the parties," etc., in Uniform Sales Act.

Purposes:

1. The parties themselves know best what they have meant by their words of agreement and their action under that agreement is the best indication of what that meaning was. This section thus rounds out the set of factors which determines the meaning of the "agreement" and therefore also of the "unless otherwise agreed" qualification to various provisions of this Article.

2. Under this section a course of performance is always relevant to determine the meaning of the agreement. Express mention of course of performance elsewhere in this Article carries no contrary implication when there is a failure to refer to it in other sections.

3. Where it is difficult to determine whether a particular act merely sheds light on the meaning of the agreement or represents a waiver of a term of the agreement, the preference is in favor of "waiver" whenever such construction, plus the application of the provisions on the reinstatement of rights waived (see Section 2–209), is needed to preserve the flexible character of commercial contracts and to prevent surprise or other hardship.

4. A single occasion of conduct does not fall within the language of this section but other sections such as the ones on silence after acceptance and failure to specify particular defects can affect the parties' rights on a single occasion (see Sections 2–605 and 2–607).]

Cross References:

   Point 1: Section 1–201.
   Point 2: Section 2–202.
   Point 3: Sections 2–209, 2–601 and 2–607.
   Point 4: Sections 2–605 and 2–607.

---

   *   *Referring to unrevised Article 1 (Appendix A).*
   ** *Note from West Advisory Panel: This section will be repealed if the jurisdiction adopts revised Article 1 (2001).*

§ 2–209.   Modification, Rescission and Waiver.

(1)   An agreement modifying a contract within this Article needs no consideration to be binding.

(2)   A signed agreement which excludes modification or rescission except by a signed writing cannot be otherwise modified or rescinded, but except as between merchants such a requirement on a form supplied by the merchant must be separately signed by the other party.

(3)   The requirements of the statute of frauds section of this Article (Section 2–201) must be satisfied if the contract as modified is within its provisions.

(4)   Although an attempt at modification or rescission does not satisfy the requirements of subsection (2) or (3) it can operate as a waiver.

(5)   A party who has made a waiver affecting an executory portion of the contract may retract the waiver by reasonable notification received by the other party that strict performance will be required of any term waived, unless the retraction would be unjust in view of a material change of position in reliance on the waiver.

Official Comment

Prior Uniform Statutory Provision: Subsection (1)—Compare Section 1, Uniform Written Obligations Act; Subsections (2) to (5)—none.

Purposes of Changes and New Matter:

1.   This section seeks to protect and make effective all necessary and desirable modifications of sales contracts without regard to the technicalities which at present hamper such adjustments.

2.   Subsection (1) provides that an agreement modifying a sales contract needs no consideration to be binding.

However, modifications made thereunder must meet the test of good faith imposed by this Act. The effective use of bad faith to escape performance on the original contract terms is barred, and the extortion of a "modification" without legitimate commercial reason is ineffective as a violation of the duty of good faith. Nor can a mere technical consideration support a modification made in bad faith.

The test of "good faith" between merchants or as against merchants includes "observance of reasonable commercial standards of fair dealing in the trade" (Section 2–103), and may in some situations require an objectively demonstrable reason for seeking a modification. But such matters as a market shift which makes performance come to involve a loss may provide such a reason even though there is no such unforeseen difficulty as would make out a legal excuse from performance under Sections 2–615 and 2–616.

3.   Subsections (2) and (3) are intended to protect against false allegations of oral modifications. "Modification or rescission" includes abandonment or other change by mutual consent, contrary to the decision in *Green v. Doniger*, 300 N.Y. 238, 90 N.E.2d 56 (1949); it does not include unilateral "termination" or "cancellation" as defined in Section 2–106.

The Statute of Frauds provisions of this Article are expressly applied to modifications by subsection (3). Under those provisions the "delivery and acceptance" test is limited to the goods which have been accepted, that is, to the past. "Modification" for the future cannot therefore be conjured up by oral testimony if the price involved is $500.00 or more since such modification must be shown at least by an authenticated memo. And since a memo is limited in its effect to the quantity of goods set forth in it there is safeguard against oral evidence.

Subsection (2) permits the parties in effect to make their own Statute of Frauds as regards any future modification of the contract by giving effect to a clause in a signed agreement which expressly requires any modification to be by signed writing. But note that if a consumer is to be held to such a clause on a form supplied by a merchant it must be separately signed.

4.   Subsection (4) is intended, despite the provisions of subsections (2) and (3), to prevent contractual provisions excluding modification except by a signed writing from limiting in other respects the legal effect of the parties' actual later conduct. The effect of such conduct as a waiver is further regulated in subsection (5).

Definitional Cross References:

 "Agreement". Section 1–201.
 "Between merchants". Section 2–104.
 "Contract". Section 1–201.
 "Notification". Section 1–201.*
 "Signed". Section 1–201.
 "Term". Section 1–201.
 "Writing". Section 1–201.

§ 2–210.   Delegation of Performance; Assignment of Rights.

(1)   A party may perform his duty through a delegate unless otherwise agreed or unless the other party has a substantial interest in having his original promisor perform or control the acts required by the contract. No delegation of performance relieves the party delegating of any duty to perform or any liability for breach.

(2)   Except as otherwise provided in Section 9–406, unless otherwise agreed, all rights of either seller or buyer can be assigned except where the assignment would materially change the duty of the other party, or increase materially the burden or risk imposed on him by his contract, or impair materially his chance of obtaining return performance. A right to damages for breach of the whole contract or a right arising out of the assignor's due performance of his entire obligation can be assigned despite agreement otherwise.

(3)   The creation, attachment, perfection, or enforcement of a security interest in the seller's interest under a contract is not a transfer that materially changes the duty of or increases materially the burden or risk imposed on the buyer or impairs materially the buyer's chance of obtaining return performance within the purview of subsection (2) unless, and then only to the extent that, enforcement actually results in a delegation of material performance of the seller. Even in that event, the creation, attachment, perfection, and enforcement of the security interest remain effective, but (i) the seller is liable to the buyer for damages caused by the delegation to the extent that the damages could not reasonably be prevented by the buyer, and (ii) a court having jurisdiction may grant other appropriate relief, including cancellation of the contract for sale or an injunction against enforcement of the security interest or consummation of the enforcement.

(4)   Unless the circumstances indicate the contrary a prohibition of assignment of "the contract" is to be construed as barring only the delegation to the assignee of the assignor's performance.

(5)   An assignment of "the contract" or of "all my rights under the contract" or an assignment in similar general terms is an assignment of rights and unless the language or the circumstances (as in an assignment for security) indicate the contrary, it is a delegation of performance of the duties of the assignor and its acceptance by the assignee constitutes a promise by him to perform those duties. This promise is enforceable by either the assignor or the other party to the original contract.

(6)   The other party may treat any assignment which delegates performance as creating reasonable grounds for insecurity and may without prejudice to his rights against the assignor demand assurances from the assignee (Section 2–609).

As amended in 1999.

Official Comment

Prior Uniform Statutory Provision: None.

---

  *   *Referring to unrevised Article 1 (Appendix A).*

Purposes:

1.   Generally, this section recognizes both delegation of performance and assignability as normal and permissible incidents of a contract for the sale of goods.

2.   Delegation of performance, either in conjunction with an assignment or otherwise, is provided for by subsection (1) where no substantial reason can be shown as to why the delegated performance will not be as satisfactory as personal performance.

3.   Under subsection (2) rights which are no longer executory such as a right to damages for breach may be assigned although the agreement prohibits assignment. In such cases no question of delegation of any performance is involved. Subsection (2) is subject to Section 9–406, which makes rights to payment for goods sold ("accounts"), whether or not earned, freely alienable notwithstanding a contrary agreement or rule of law.

4.   The nature of the contract or the circumstances of the case, however, may bar assignment of the contract even where delegation of performance is not involved. This Article and this section are intended to clarify this problem, particularly in cases dealing with output requirement and exclusive dealing contracts. In the first place the section on requirements and exclusive dealing removes from the construction of the original contract most of the "personal discretion" element by substituting the reasonably objective standard of good faith operation of the plant or business to be supplied. Secondly, the section on insecurity and assurances, which is specifically referred to in subsection (5) of this section, frees the other party from the doubts and uncertainty which may afflict him under an assignment of the character in question by permitting him to demand adequate assurance of due performance without which he may suspend his own performance. Subsection (5) is not in any way intended to limit the effect of the section on insecurity and assurances and the word "performance" includes the giving of orders under a requirements contract. Of course, in any case where a material personal discretion is sought to be transferred, effective assignment is barred by subsection (2).

5.   Subsection (4) lays down a general rule of construction distinguishing between a normal commercial assignment, which substitutes the assignee for the assignor both as to rights and duties, and a financing assignment in which only the assignor's rights are transferred.

This Article takes no position on the possibility of extending some recognition or power to the original parties to work out normal commercial readjustments of the contract in the case of financing assignments even after the original obligor has been notified of the assignment. This question is dealt with in the Article on Secured Transactions (Article 9).

6.   Subsection (5) recognizes that the non-assigning original party has a stake in the reliability of the person with whom he has closed the original contract, and is, therefore, entitled to due assurance that any delegated performance will be properly forthcoming.

7.   This section is not intended as a complete statement of the law of delegation and assignment but is limited to clarifying a few points doubtful under the case law. Particularly, neither this section nor this Article touches directly on such questions as the need or effect of notice of the assignment, the rights of successive assignees, or any question of the form of an assignment, either as between the parties or as against any third parties. Some of these questions are dealt with in Article 9.

Cross References:

Point 3: Articles 5 and 9.

Point 4: Sections 2–306 and 2–609.

Point 5: Article 9, Sections 9–402, 9–404, 9–405, and 9–406.

Point 7: Article 9.

Definitional Cross References:

"Agreement". Section 1–201.

"Buyer". Section 2–103.

"Contract". Section 1–201.

"Party". Section 1–201.

"Rights". Section 1–201.

"Seller". Section 2–103.

"Term". Section 1–201.

As amended in 1999.

PART 3

GENERAL OBLIGATION AND CONSTRUCTION OF CONTRACT

§ 2–301. General Obligations of Parties.

The obligation of the seller is to transfer and deliver and that of the buyer is to accept and pay in accordance with the contract.

Official Comment

Prior Uniform Statutory Provision: Sections 11 and 41, Uniform Sales Act.

Changes: Rewritten.

Purposes of Changes:

This section uses the term "obligation" in contrast to the term "duty" in order to provide for the "condition" aspects of delivery and payment insofar as they are not modified by other sections of this Article such as those on cure of tender. It thus replaces not only the general provisions of the Uniform Sales Act on the parties' duties, but also the general provisions of that Act on the effect of conditions. In order to determine what is "in accordance with the contract" under this Article usage of trade, course of dealing and performance, and the general background of circumstances must be given due consideration in conjunction with the lay meaning of the words used to define the scope of the conditions and duties.

Cross References:

Section 1–106.* See also Sections 1–205,* 2–208, 2–209, 2–508 and 2–612.

Definitional Cross References:

"Buyer". Section 2–103.
"Contract". Section 1–201.
"Party". Section 1–201.
"Seller". Section 2–103.

§ 2–302. Unconscionable Contract or Clause.

(1) If the court as a matter of law finds the contract or any clause of the contract to have been unconscionable at the time it was made the court may refuse to enforce the contract, or it may enforce the remainder of the contract without the unconscionable clause, or it may so limit the application of any unconscionable clause as to avoid any unconscionable result.

(2) When it is claimed or appears to the court that the contract or any clause thereof may be unconscionable the parties shall be afforded a reasonable opportunity to present evidence as to its commercial setting, purpose and effect to aid the court in making the determination.

Official Comment

Prior Uniform Statutory Provision: None.

Purposes:

1. This section is intended to make it possible for the courts to police explicitly against the contracts or clauses which they find to be unconscionable. In the past such policing has been accomplished by adverse construction of language, by manipulation of the rules of offer and acceptance or by determinations that the clause is contrary to public policy or to the dominant purpose of the contract. This section is intended to allow the court to pass directly on the unconscionability of the contract or particular clause therein and to make a conclusion of law as to its unconscionability. The basic test is whether, in the light of the general commercial background and

---

*   *Referring to unrevised Article 1 (Appendix A).*

the commercial needs of the particular trade or case, the clauses involved are so one-sided as to be unconscionable under the circumstances existing at the time of the making of the contract. Subsection (2) makes it clear that it is proper for the court to hear evidence upon these questions. The principle is one of the prevention of oppression and unfair surprise (Cf. *Campbell Soup Co. v. Wentz*, 172 F.2d 80, 3d Cir. 1948) and not of disturbance of allocation of risks because of superior bargaining power. The underlying basis of this section is illustrated by the results in cases such as the following:

Kansas City Wholesale Grocery Co. v. Weber Packing Corporation, 93 Utah 414, 73 P.2d 1272 (1937), where a clause limiting time for complaints was held inapplicable to latent defects in a shipment of catsup which could be discovered only by microscopic analysis; *Hardy v. General Motors Acceptance Corporation*, 38 Ga.App. 463, 144 S.E. 327 (1928), holding that a disclaimer of warranty clause applied only to express warranties, thus letting in a fair implied warranty; *Andrews Bros. v. Singer & Co.* (1934 CA) 1 K.B. 17, holding that where a car with substantial mileage was delivered instead of a "new" car, a disclaimer of warranties, including those "implied," left unaffected an "express obligation" on the description, even though the Sale of Goods Act called such an implied warranty; *New Prague Flouring Mill Co. v. G. A. Spears*, 194 Iowa 417, 189 N.W. 815 (1922), holding that a clause permitting the seller, upon the buyer's failure to supply shipping instructions, to cancel, ship, or allow delivery date to be indefinitely postponed 30 days at a time by the inaction, does not indefinitely postpone the date of measuring damages for the buyer's breach, to the seller's advantage; and *Kansas Flour Mills Co. v. Dirks*, 100 Kan. 376, 164 P. 273 (1917), where under a similar clause in a rising market the court permitted the buyer to measure his damages for non-delivery at the end of only one 30 day postponement; *Green v. Arcos, Ltd.* (1931 CA) 47 T.L.R. 336, where a blanket clause prohibiting rejection of shipments by the buyer was restricted to apply to shipments where discrepancies represented merely mercantile variations; *Meyer v. Packard Cleveland Motor Co.*, 106 Ohio St. 328, 140 N.E. 118 (1922), in which the court held that a "waiver" of all agreements not specified did not preclude implied warranty of fitness of a rebuilt dump truck for ordinary use as a dump truck; *Austin Co. v. J. H. Tillman Co.*, 104 Or. 541, 209 P. 131 (1922), where a clause limiting the buyer's remedy to return was held to be applicable only if the seller had delivered a machine needed for a construction job which reasonably met the contract description; *Bekkevold v. Potts*, 173 Minn. 87, 216 N.W. 790, 59 A.L.R. 1164 (1927), refusing to allow warranty of fitness for purpose imposed by law to be negated by clause excluding all warranties "made" by the seller; *Robert A. Munroe & Co. v. Meyer* (1930) 2 K.B. 312, holding that the warranty of description overrides a clause reading "with all faults and defects" where adulterated meat not up to the contract description was delivered.

    2.   Under this section the court, in its discretion, may refuse to enforce the contract as a whole if it is permeated by the unconscionability, or it may strike any single clause or group of clauses which are so tainted or which are contrary to the essential purpose of the agreement, or it may simply limit unconscionable clauses so as to avoid unconscionable results.

    3.   The present section is addressed to the court, and the decision is to be made by it. The commercial evidence referred to in subsection (2) is for the court's consideration, not the jury's. Only the agreement which results from the court's action on these matters is to be submitted to the general triers of the facts.

Definitional Cross Reference:

    "Contract". Section 1-201.

§ 2-303.   Allocation or Division of Risks.

    Where this Article allocates a risk or a burden as between the parties "unless otherwise agreed", the agreement may not only shift the allocation but may also divide the risk or burden.

Official Comment

Prior Uniform Statutory Provision: None.

Purposes:

    1.   This section is intended to make it clear that the parties may modify or allocate "unless otherwise agreed" risks or burdens imposed by this Article as they desire, always subject, of course, to the provisions on unconscionability.

Compare Section 1–102(4).*

2. The risk or burden may be divided by the express terms of the agreement or by the attending circumstances, since under the definition of "agreement" in this Act the circumstances surrounding the transaction as well as the express language used by the parties enter into the meaning and substance of the agreement.

Cross References:

Point 1: Sections 1–102,* 2–302.
Point 2: Section 1–201.

Definitional Cross References:

"Party". Section 1–201.
"Agreement". Section 1–201.

§ 2–304.   Price Payable in Money, Goods, Realty, or Otherwise.

(1)   The price can be made payable in money or otherwise. If it is payable in whole or in part in goods each party is a seller of the goods which he is to transfer.

(2)   Even though all or part of the price is payable in an interest in realty the transfer of the goods and the seller's obligations with reference to them are subject to this Article, but not the transfer of the interest in realty or the transferor's obligations in connection therewith.

Official Comment

Prior Uniform Statutory Provision: Subsections (2) and (3) of Section 9, Uniform Sales Act.

Changes: Rewritten.

Purposes of Changes:

1.   This section corrects the phrasing of the Uniform Sales Act so as to avoid misconstruction and produce greater accuracy in commercial result. While it continues the essential intent and purpose of the Uniform Sales Act it rejects any purely verbalistic construction in disregard of the underlying reason of the provisions.

2.   Under subsection (1) the provisions of this Article are applicable to transactions where the "price" of goods is payable in something other than money. This does not mean, however, that this whole Article applies automatically and in its entirety simply because an agreed transfer of title to goods is not a gift. The basic purposes and reasons of the Article must always be considered in determining the applicability of any of its provisions.

3.   Subsection (2) lays down the general principle that when goods are to be exchanged for realty, the provisions of this Article apply only to those aspects of the transaction which concern the transfer of title to goods but do not affect the transfer of the realty since the detailed regulation of various particular contracts which fall outside the scope of this Article is left to the courts and other legislation. However, the complexities of these situations may be such that each must be analyzed in the light of the underlying reasons in order to determine the applicable principles. Local statutes dealing with realty are not to be lightly disregarded or altered by language of this Article. In contrast, this Article declares definite policies in regard to certain matters legitimately within its scope though concerned with real property situations, and in those instances the provisions of this Article control.

Cross References:

Point 1: Section 1–102.
Point 3: Sections 1–102,* 1–103, 1–104 and 2–107.

Definitional Cross References:

"Goods". Section 2–105.
"Money". Section 1–201.
"Party". Section 1–201.
"Seller". Section 2–103.

---

*   *Referring to unrevised Article 1 (Appendix A).*

§ 2–305.   Open Price Term.

(1)   The parties if they so intend can conclude a contract for sale even though the price is not settled. In such a case the price is a reasonable price at the time for delivery if

(a)   nothing is said as to price; or

(b)   the price is left to be agreed by the parties and they fail to agree; or

(c)   the price is to be fixed in terms of some agreed market or other standard as set or recorded by a third person or agency and it is not so set or recorded.

(2)   A price to be fixed by the seller or by the buyer means a price for him to fix in good faith.

(3)   When a price left to be fixed otherwise than by agreement of the parties fails to be fixed through fault of one party the other may at his option treat the contract as cancelled or himself fix a reasonable price.

(4)   Where, however, the parties intend not to be bound unless the price be fixed or agreed and it is not fixed or agreed there is no contract. In such a case the buyer must return any goods already received or if unable so to do must pay their reasonable value at the time of delivery and the seller must return any portion of the price paid on account.

Official Comment

Prior Uniform Statutory Provision: Sections 9 and 10, Uniform Sales Act.

Changes: Completely rewritten.

Purposes of Changes:

1.   This section applies when the price term is left open on the making of an agreement which is nevertheless intended by the parties to be a binding agreement. This Article rejects in these instances the formula that "an agreement to agree is unenforceable" if the case falls within subsection (1) of this section, and rejects also defeating such agreements on the ground of "indefiniteness". Instead this Article recognizes the dominant intention of the parties to have the deal continue to be binding upon both. As to future performance, since this Article recognizes remedies such as cover (Section 2–712), resale (Section 2–706) and specific performance (Section 2–716) which go beyond any mere arithmetic as between contract price and market price, there is usually a "reasonably certain basis for granting an appropriate remedy for breach" so that the contract need not fail for indefiniteness.

2.   Under some circumstances the postponement of agreement on price will mean that no deal has really been concluded, and this is made express in the preamble of subsection (1) ("The parties *if they so intend*") and in subsection (4). Whether or not this is so is, in most cases, a question to be determined by the trier of fact.

3.   Subsection (2), dealing with the situation where the price is to be fixed by one party rejects the uncommercial idea that an agreement that the seller may fix the price means that he may fix any price he may wish by the express qualification that the price so fixed must be fixed in good faith. Good faith includes observance of reasonable commercial standards of fair dealing in the trade if the party is a merchant. (Section 2–103). But in the normal case a "posted price" or a future seller's or buyer's "given price," "price in effect," "market price," or the like satisfies the good faith requirement.

4.   The section recognizes that there may be cases in which a particular person's judgment is not chosen merely as a barometer or index of a fair price but is an essential condition to the parties' intent to make any contract at all. For example, the case where a known and trusted expert is to "value" a particular painting for which there is no market standard differs sharply from the situation where a named expert is to determine the grade of cotton, and the difference would support a finding that in the one the parties did not intend to make a binding agreement if that expert were unavailable whereas in the other they did so intend. Other circumstances would of course affect the validity of such a finding.

5.   Under subsection (3), wrongful interference by one party with any agreed machinery for price fixing in the contract may be treated by the other party as a repudiation justifying cancellation, or merely as a failure to take cooperative action thus shifting to the aggrieved party the reasonable leeway in fixing the price.

6. Throughout the entire section, the purpose is to give effect to the agreement which has been made. That effect, however, is always conditioned by the requirement of good faith action which is made an inherent part of all contracts within this Act. (Section 1–203).*

Cross References:

Point 1: Sections 2–204(3), 2–706, 2–712 and 2–716.
Point 3: Section 2–103.
Point 5: Sections 2–311 and 2–610.
Point 6: Section 1–203.*

Definitional Cross References:

"Agreement". Section 1–201.
"Burden of establishing". Section 1–201.
"Buyer". Section 2–103.
"Cancellation". Section 2–106.
"Contract". Section 1–201.
"Contract for sale". Section 2–106.
"Fault". Section 1–201.
"Goods". Section 2–105.
"Party". Section 1–201.
"Receipt of goods". Section 2–103.
"Seller". Section 2–103.
"Term". Section 1–201.

§ 2–306. Output, Requirements and Exclusive Dealings.

(1) A term which measures the quantity by the output of the seller or the requirements of the buyer means such actual output or requirements as may occur in good faith, except that no quantity unreasonably disproportionate to any stated estimate or in the absence of a stated estimate to any normal or otherwise comparable prior output or requirements may be tendered or demanded.

(2) A lawful agreement by either the seller or the buyer for exclusive dealing in the kind of goods concerned imposes unless otherwise agreed an obligation by the seller to use best efforts to supply the goods and by the buyer to use best efforts to promote their sale.

Official Comment

Prior Uniform Statutory Provision: None.

Purposes:

1. Subsection (1) of this section, in regard to output and requirements, applies to this specific problem the general approach of this Act which requires the reading of commercial background and intent into the language of any agreement and demands good faith in the performance of that agreement. It applies to such contracts of nonproducing establishments such as dealers or distributors as well as to manufacturing concerns.

2. Under this Article, a contract for output or requirements is not too indefinite since it is held to mean the actual good faith output or requirements of the particular party. Nor does such a contract lack mutuality of obligation since, under this section, the party who will determine quantity is required to operate his plant or conduct his business in good faith and according to commercial standards of fair dealing in the trade so that his output or requirements will approximate a reasonably foreseeable figure. Reasonable elasticity in the requirements is expressly envisaged by this section and good faith variations from prior requirements are permitted even when the variation may be such as to result in discontinuance. A shut-down by a requirements buyer for lack of orders might be permissible when a shut-down merely to curtail losses would not. The essential test is whether the party is acting in good faith. Similarly, a sudden expansion of the plant by which requirements are to be measured would not be included within the scope of the contract as made but normal expansion undertaken in good faith would be within the scope of this section. One of the factors in an expansion situation

---

*   *Referring to unrevised Article 1 (Appendix A).*

73

would be whether the market price had risen greatly in a case in which the requirements contract contained a fixed price. Reasonable variation of an extreme sort is exemplified in *Southwest Natural Gas Co. v. Oklahoma Portland Cement Co.*, 102 F.2d 630 (C.C.A.10, 1939). This Article takes no position as to whether a requirements contract is a provable claim in bankruptcy.

    3.   If an estimate of output or requirements is included in the agreement, no quantity unreasonably disproportionate to it may be tendered or demanded. Any minimum or maximum set by the agreement shows a clear limit on the intended elasticity. In similar fashion, the agreed estimate is to be regarded as a center around which the parties intend the variation to occur.

    4.   When an enterprise is sold, the question may arise whether the buyer is bound by an existing output or requirements contract. That question is outside the scope of this Article, and is to be determined on other principles of law. Assuming that the contract continues, the output or requirements in the hands of the new owner continue to be measured by the actual good faith output or requirements under the normal operation of the enterprise prior to sale. The sale itself is not grounds for sudden expansion or decrease.

    5.   Subsection (2), on exclusive dealing, makes explicit the commercial rule embodied in this Act under which the parties to such contracts are held to have impliedly, even when not expressly, bound themselves to use reasonable diligence as well as good faith in their performance of the contract. Under such contracts the exclusive agent is required, although no express commitment has been made, to use reasonable effort and due diligence in the expansion of the market or the promotion of the product, as the case may be. The principal is expected under such a contract to refrain from supplying any other dealer or agent within the exclusive territory. An exclusive dealing agreement brings into play all of the good faith aspects of the output and requirement problems of subsection (1). It also raises questions of insecurity and right to adequate assurance under this Article.

Cross References:

    Point 4: Section 2–210.
    Point 5: Sections 1–203* and 2–609.

Definitional Cross References:

    "Agreement". Section 1–201.
    "Buyer". Section 2–103.
    "Contract for sale". Section 2–106.
    "Good faith". Section 1–201.
    "Goods". Section 2–105.
    "Party". Section 1–201.
    "Term". Section 1–201.
    "Seller". Section 2–103.

§ 2–307.   Delivery in Single Lot or Several Lots.

    Unless otherwise agreed all goods called for by a contract for sale must be tendered in a single delivery and payment is due only on such tender but where the circumstances give either party the right to make or demand delivery in lots the price if it can be apportioned may be demanded for each lot.

Official Comment

Prior Uniform Statutory Provision: Section 45(1), Uniform Sales Act.

Changes: Rewritten and expanded.

Purposes of Changes:

    1.   This section applies where the parties have not specifically agreed whether delivery and payment are to be by lots and generally continues the essential intent of original Act, Section 45(1) by assuming that the parties intended delivery to be in a single lot.

---

    *   *Referring to unrevised Article 1 (Appendix A).*

2.   Where the actual agreement or the circumstances do not indicate otherwise, delivery in lots is not permitted under this section and the buyer is properly entitled to reject for a deficiency in the tender, subject to any privilege in the seller to cure the tender.

3.   The "but" clause of this section goes to the case in which it is not commercially feasible to deliver or to receive the goods in a single lot as for example, where a contract calls for the shipment of ten carloads of coal and only three cars are available at a given time. Similarly, in a contract involving brick necessary to build a building the buyer's storage space may be limited so that it would be impossible to receive the entire amount of brick at once, or it may be necessary to assemble the goods as in the case of cattle on the range, or to mine them.

In such cases, a partial delivery is not subject to rejection for the defect in quantity alone, if the circumstances do not indicate a repudiation or default by the seller as to the expected balance or do not give the buyer ground for suspending his performance because of insecurity under the provisions of Section 2–609. However, in such cases the undelivered balance of goods under the contract must be forthcoming within a reasonable time and in a reasonable manner according to the policy of Section 2–503 on manner of tender of delivery. This is reinforced by the express provisions of Section 2–608 that if a lot has been accepted on the reasonable assumption that its nonconformity will be cured, the acceptance may be revoked if the cure does not seasonably occur. The section rejects the rule of *Kelly Construction Co. v. Hackensack Brick Co.*, 91 N.J.L. 585, 103 A. 417, 2 A.L.R. 685 (1918) and approves the result in *Lynn M. Ranger, Inc. v. Gildersleeve*, 106 Conn. 372, 138 A. 142 (1927) in which a contract was made for six carloads of coal then rolling from the mines and consigned to the seller but the seller agreed to divert the carloads to the buyer as soon as the car numbers became known to him. He arranged a diversion of two cars and then notified the buyer who then repudiated the contract. The seller was held to be entitled to his full remedy for the two cars diverted because simultaneous delivery of all of the cars was not contemplated by either party.

4.   Where the circumstances indicate that a party has a right to delivery in lots, the price may be demanded for each lot if it is apportionable.

Cross References:

> Point 1: Section 1–201.
> Point 2: Sections 2–508 and 2–601.
> Point 3: Sections 2–503, 2–608 and 2–609.

Definitional Cross References:

> "Contract for sale". Section 2–106.
> "Goods". Section 2–105.
> "Lot". Section 2–105.
> "Party". Section 1–201.
> "Rights". Section 1–201.

§ 2–308.   Absence of Specified Place for Delivery.

Unless otherwise agreed

(a)   the place for delivery of goods is the seller's place of business or if he has none his residence; but

(b)   in a contract for sale of identified goods which to the knowledge of the parties at the time of contracting are in some other place, that place is the place for their delivery; and

(c)   documents of title may be delivered through customary banking channels.

Official Comment

Prior Uniform Statutory Provision: Paragraphs (a) and (b)—Section 43(1), Uniform Sales Act; Paragraph (c)— none.

Changes: Slight modification in language.

Purposes of Changes and New Matter:

1.   Paragraphs (a) and (b) provide for those noncommercial sales and for those occasional commercial sales where no place or means of delivery has been agreed upon by the parties. Where delivery by carrier is "required

or authorized by the agreement", the seller's duties as to delivery of the goods are governed not by this section but by Section 2–504.

2.   Under paragraph (b) when the identified goods contracted for are known to both parties to be in some location other than the seller's place of business or residence, the parties are presumed to have intended that place to be the place of delivery. This paragraph also applies (unless, as would be normal, the circumstances show that delivery by way of documents is intended) to a bulk of goods in the possession of a bailee. In such a case, however, the seller has the additional obligation to procure the acknowledgment by the bailee of the buyer's right to possession.

3.   Where "customary banking channels" call only for due notification by the banker that the documents are available, leaving the buyer himself to see to the physical receipt of the goods, tender at the buyer's address is not required under paragraph (c). But that paragraph merely eliminates the possibility of a default by the seller if "customary banking channels" have been properly used in giving notice to the buyer. Where the bank has purchased a draft accompanied by or associated with documents or has undertaken its collection on behalf of the seller, Part 5 of Article 4 spells out its duties and relations to its customer. Where the documents move forward under a letter of credit the Article on Letters of Credit spells out the duties and relations between the bank, the seller and the buyer. Delivery in relationship to either tangible or electronic documents of title is defined in Article 1, Section 1–201.

4.   The rules of this section apply only "unless otherwise agreed." The surrounding circumstances, usage of trade, course of dealing and course of performance, as well as the express language of the parties, may constitute an "otherwise agreement".

Cross References:

> Point 1: Sections 2–504 and 2–505.
> Point 2: Section 2–503.
> Point 3: Section 2–512, Articles 4, Part 5, and 5.

Definitional Cross References:

> "Contract for sale". Section 2–106.
> "Delivery". Section 1–201.
> "Document of title". Section 1–201.
> "Goods". Section 2–105.
> "Party". Section 1–201.
> "Seller". Section 2–103.

As amended in 2003.

§ 2–309.   Absence of Specific Time Provisions; Notice of Termination.

(1)   The time for shipment or delivery or any other action under a contract if not provided in this Article or agreed upon shall be a reasonable time.

(2)   Where the contract provides for successive performances but is indefinite in duration it is valid for a reasonable time but unless otherwise agreed may be terminated at any time by either party.

(3)   Termination of a contract by one party except on the happening of an agreed event requires that reasonable notification be received by the other party and an agreement dispensing with notification is invalid if its operation would be unconscionable.

Official Comment

Prior Uniform Statutory Provision: Subsection (1)—see Sections 43(2), 45(2), 47(1) and 48, Uniform Sales Act, for policy continued under this Article; Subsection (2)—none; Subsection (3)—none.

Changes: Completely different in scope.

Purposes of Changes and New Matter:

1.   Subsection (1) requires that all actions taken under a sales contract must be taken within a reasonable time where no time has been agreed upon. The reasonable time under this provision turns on the criteria as to

"reasonable time" and on good faith and commercial standards set forth in Sections 1–203,* 1–204* and 2–103. It thus depends upon what constitutes acceptable commercial conduct in view of the nature, purpose and circumstances of the action to be taken. Agreement as to a definite time, however, may be found in a term implied from the contractual circumstances, usage of trade or course of dealing or performance as well as in an express term. Such cases fall outside of this subsection since in them the time for action is "agreed" by usage.

2. The time for payment, where not agreed upon, is related to the time for delivery; the particular problems which arise in connection with determining the appropriate time of payment and the time for any inspection before payment which is both allowed by law and demanded by the buyer are covered in Section 2–513.

3. The facts in regard to shipment and delivery differ so widely as to make detailed provision for them in the text of this Article impracticable. The applicable principles, however, make it clear that surprise is to be avoided, good faith judgment is to be protected, and notice or negotiation to reduce the uncertainty to certainty is to be favored.

4. When the time for delivery is left open, unreasonably early offers of or demands for delivery are intended to be read under this Article as expressions of desire or intention, requesting the assent or acquiescence of the other party, not as final positions which may amount without more to breach or to create breach by the other side. See Sections 2–207 and 2–609.

5. The obligation of good faith under this Act requires reasonable notification before a contract may be treated as breached because a reasonable time for delivery or demand has expired. This operates both in the case of a contract originally indefinite as to time and of one subsequently made indefinite by waiver.

When both parties let an originally reasonable time go by in silence, the course of conduct under the contract may be viewed as enlarging the reasonable time for tender or demand of performance. The contract may be terminated by abandonment.

6. Parties to a contract are not required in giving reasonable notification to fix, at peril of breach, a time which is in fact reasonable in the unforeseeable judgment of a later trier of fact. Effective communication of a proposed time limit calls for a response, so that failure to reply will make out acquiescence. Where objection is made, however, or if the demand is merely for information as to when goods will be delivered or will be ordered out, demand for assurances on the ground of insecurity may be made under this Article pending further negotiations. Only when a party insists on undue delay or on rejection of the other party's reasonable proposal is there a question of flat breach under the present section.

7. Subsection (2) applies a commercially reasonable view to resolve the conflict which has arisen in the cases as to contracts of indefinite duration. The "reasonable time" of duration appropriate to a given arrangement is limited by the circumstances. When the arrangement has been carried on by the parties over the years, the "reasonable time" can continue indefinitely and the contract will not terminate until notice.

8. Subsection (3) recognizes that the application of principles of good faith and sound commercial practice normally call for such notification of the termination of a going contract relationship as will give the other party reasonable time to seek a substitute arrangement. An agreement dispensing with notification or limiting the time for the seeking of a substitute arrangement is, of course, valid under this subsection unless the results of putting it into operation would be the creation of an unconscionable state of affairs.

9. Justifiable cancellation for breach is a remedy for breach and is not the kind of termination covered by the present subsection.

10. The requirement of notification is dispensed with where the contract provides for termination on the happening of an "agreed event." "Event" is a term chosen here to contrast with "option" or the like.

Cross References:

Point 1: Sections 1–203,* 1–204* and 2–103.
Point 2: Sections 2–320, 2–321, 2–504, and 2–511 through 2–514.
Point 5: Section 1–203.*
Point 6: Section 2–609.
Point 7: Section 2–204.
Point 9: Sections 2–106, 2–318, 2–610 and 2–703.

---

* *Referring to unrevised Article 1 (Appendix A).*

Definitional Cross References:

"Agreement". Section 1–201.

"Contract". Section 1–201.

"Notification". Section 1–201.*

"Party". Section 1–201.

"Reasonable time". Section 1–204.*

"Termination". Section 2–106.

§ 2–310.   Open Time for Payment or Running of Credit; Authority to Ship Under Reservation.

Unless otherwise agreed

(a) payment is due at the time and place at which the buyer is to receive the goods even though the place of shipment is the place of delivery; and

(b) if the seller is authorized to send the goods he may ship them under reservation, and may tender the documents of title, but the buyer may inspect the goods after their arrival before payment is due unless such inspection is inconsistent with the terms of the contract (Section 2–513); and

(c) if delivery is authorized and made by way of documents of title otherwise than by subsection (b) then payment is due regardless of where the goods are received (i) at the time and place at which the buyer is to receive delivery of the tangible documents or (ii) at the time the buyer is to receive delivery of the electronic documents and at the seller's place of business or if none, the seller's residence; and

(d) where the seller is required or authorized to ship the goods on credit the credit period runs from the time of shipment but post-dating the invoice or delaying its dispatch will correspondingly delay the starting of the credit period.

As amended in 2003.

Official Comment

Prior Uniform Statutory Provision: Sections 42 and 47(2), Uniform Sales Act.

Changes: Completely rewritten in this and other sections.

Purposes of Changes: This section is drawn to reflect modern business methods of dealing at a distance rather than face to face. Thus:

1. Paragraph (a) provides that payment is due at the time and place "the buyer is to receive the goods" rather than at the point of delivery except in documentary shipment cases (paragraph (c)). This grants an opportunity for the exercise by the buyer of his preliminary right to inspection before paying even though under the delivery term the risk of loss may have previously passed to him or the running of the credit period has already started.

2. Paragraph (b) while providing for inspection by the buyer before he pays, protects the seller. He is not required to give up possession of the goods until he has received payment, where no credit has been contemplated by the parties. The seller may collect through a bank by a sight draft against an order bill of lading "hold until arrival; inspection allowed." The obligations of the bank under such a provision are set forth in Part 5 of Article 4. Under subsection (c), in the absence of a credit term, the seller is permitted to ship under reservation and if he does payment is then due where and when the buyer is to receive delivery of the tangible documents of title. In the case of an electronic document of title, payment is due when the buyer is to receive delivery of the electronic document and at the seller's place of business, or if none, the seller's residence. Delivery as to documents of title is stated in Article 1, Section 1–201.

3. Unless otherwise agreed, the place for the delivery of the documents and payment is the buyer's city but the time for payment is only after arrival of the goods, since under paragraph (b), and Sections 2–512 and 2–513 the buyer is under no duty to pay prior to inspection. Tender of a document of title requires that the seller be

---

*   *Referring to unrevised Article 1 (Appendix A).*

ready, willing and able to transfer possession of a tangible document of title or control of an electronic document of title to the buyer.

4.   Where the mode of shipment is such that goods must be unloaded immediately upon arrival, too rapidly to permit adequate inspection before receipt, the seller must be guided by the provisions of this Article on inspection which provide that if the seller wishes to demand payment before inspection, he must put an appropriate term into the contract. Even requiring payment against documents will not of itself have this desired result if the documents are to be held until the arrival of the goods. But under (b) and (c) if the terms are C.I.F., C.O.D., or cash against documents payment may be due before inspection.

5.   Paragraph (d) states the common commercial understanding that an agreed credit period runs from the time of shipment or from that dating of the invoice which is commonly recognized as a representation of the time of shipment. The provision concerning any delay in sending forth the invoice is included because such conduct results in depriving the buyer of his full notice and warning as to when he must be prepared to pay.

Cross References:

Generally: Part 5.
Point 1: Section 2–509.
Point 2: Sections 2–505, 2–511, 2–512, 2–513 and Article 4.
Point 3: Sections 2–308(b), 2–512 and 2–513.
Point 4: Section 2–513(3)(b).

Definitional Cross References:

"Buyer". Section 2–103.
"Delivery". Section 1–201.
"Document of title". Section 1–201.
"Goods". Section 2–105.
"Receipt of goods". Section 2–103.
"Seller". Section 2–103.
"Send". Section 1–201.
"Term". Section 1–201.

As amended in 2003.

§ 2–311.   Options and Cooperation Respecting Performance.

(1)   An agreement for sale which is otherwise sufficiently definite (subsection (3) of Section 2–204) to be a contract is not made invalid by the fact that it leaves particulars of performance to be specified by one of the parties. Any such specification must be made in good faith and within limits set by commercial reasonableness.

(2)   Unless otherwise agreed specifications relating to assortment of the goods are at the buyer's option and except as otherwise provided in subsections (1)(c) and (3) of Section 2–319 specifications or arrangements relating to shipment are at the seller's option.

(3)   Where such specification would materially affect the other party's performance but is not seasonably made or where one party's cooperation is necessary to the agreed performance of the other but is not seasonably forthcoming, the other party in addition to all other remedies

(a)   is excused for any resulting delay in his own performance; and

(b)   may also either proceed to perform in any reasonable manner or after the time for a material part of his own performance treat the failure to specify or to cooperate as a breach by failure to deliver or accept the goods.

Official Comment

Prior Uniform Statutory Provision: None.

Purposes:

1. Subsection (1) permits the parties to leave certain detailed particulars of performance to be filled in by either of them without running the risk of having the contract invalidated for indefiniteness. The party to whom the agreement gives power to specify the missing details is required to exercise good faith and to act in accordance with commercial standards so that there is no surprise and the range of permissible variation is limited by what is commercially reasonable. The "agreement" which permits one party so to specify may be found as well in a course of dealing, usage of trade, or implication from circumstances as in explicit language used by the parties.

2. Options as to assortment of goods or shipping arrangements are specifically reserved to the buyer and seller respectively under subsection (2) where no other arrangement has been made. This section rejects the test which mechanically and without regard to usage or the purpose of the option gave the option to the party "first under a duty to move" and applies instead a standard commercial interpretation to these circumstances. The "unless otherwise agreed" provision of this subsection covers not only express terms but the background and circumstances which enter into the agreement.

3. Subsection (3) applies when the exercise of an option or cooperation by one party is necessary to or materially affects the other party's performance, but it is not seasonably forthcoming; the subsection relieves the other party from the necessity for performance or excuses his delay in performance as the case may be. The contract-keeping party may at his option under this subsection proceed to perform in any commercially reasonable manner rather than wait. In addition to the special remedies provided, this subsection also reserves "all other remedies". The remedy of particular importance in this connection is that provided for insecurity. Request may also be made pursuant to the obligation of good faith for a reasonable indication of the time and manner of performance for which a party is to hold himself ready.

4. The remedy provided in subsection (3) is one which does not operate in the situation which falls within the scope of Section 2–614 on substituted performance. Where the failure to cooperate results from circumstances set forth in that Section, the other party is under a duty to proffer or demand (as the case may be) substitute performance as a condition to claiming rights against the noncooperating party.

Cross References:

> Point 1: Sections 1–201, 2–204 and 1–203.*
> Point 3: Sections 1–203* and 2–609.
> Point 4: Section 2–614.

Definitional Cross References:

> "Agreement". Section 1–201.
> "Buyer". Section 2–103.
> "Contract for sale". Section 2–106.
> "Goods". Section 2–105.
> "Party". Section 1–201.
> "Remedy". Section 1–201.
> "Seasonably". Section 1–204.*
> "Seller". Section 2–103.

§ 2–312. Warranty of Title and Against Infringement; Buyer's Obligation Against Infringement.

(1) Subject to subsection (2) there is in a contract for sale a warranty by the seller that

(a) the title conveyed shall be good, and its transfer rightful; and

(b) the goods shall be delivered free from any security interest or other lien or encumbrance of which the buyer at the time of contracting has no knowledge.

(2) A warranty under subsection (1) will be excluded or modified only by specific language or by circumstances which give the buyer reason to know that the person selling does not claim title in himself or that he is purporting to sell only such right or title as he or a third person may have.

---

*   *Referring to unrevised Article 1 (Appendix A).*

(3)   Unless otherwise agreed a seller who is a merchant regularly dealing in goods of the kind warrants that the goods shall be delivered free of the rightful claim of any third person by way of infringement or the like but a buyer who furnishes specifications to the seller must hold the seller harmless against any such claim which arises out of compliance with the specifications.

Official Comment

Prior Uniform Statutory Provision: Section 13, Uniform Sales Act.

Changes: Completely rewritten, the provisions concerning infringement being new.

Purposes of Changes:

1.   Subsection (1) makes provision for a buyer's basic needs in respect to a title which he in good faith expects to acquire by his purchase, namely, that he receive a good, clean title transferred to him also in a rightful manner so that he will not be exposed to a lawsuit in order to protect it.

The warranty extends to a buyer whether or not the seller was in possession of the goods at the time the sale or contract to sell was made.

The warranty of quiet possession is abolished. Disturbance of quiet possession, although not mentioned specifically, is one way, among many, in which the breach of the warranty of title may be established.

The "knowledge" referred to in subsection 1(b) is actual knowledge as distinct from notice.

2.   The provisions of this Article requiring notification to the seller within a reasonable time after the buyer's discovery of a breach apply to notice of a breach of the warranty of title, where the seller's breach was innocent. However, if the seller's breach was in bad faith he cannot be permitted to claim that he has been misled or prejudiced by the delay in giving notice. In such case the "reasonable" time for notice should receive a very liberal interpretation. Whether the breach by the seller is in good or bad faith Section 2–725 provides that the cause of action accrues when the breach occurs. Under the provisions of that section the breach of the warranty of good title occurs when tender of delivery is made since the warranty is not one which extends to "future performance of the goods."

3.   When the goods are part of the seller's normal stock and are sold in his normal course of business, it is his duty to see that no claim of infringement of a patent or trademark by a third party will mar the buyer's title. A sale by a person other than a dealer, however, raises no implication in its circumstances of such a warranty. Nor is there such an implication when the buyer orders goods to be assembled, prepared or manufactured on his own specifications. If, in such a case, the resulting product infringes a patent or trademark, the liability will run from buyer to seller. There is, under such circumstances, a tacit representation on the part of the buyer that the seller will be safe in manufacturing according to the specifications, and the buyer is under an obligation in good faith to indemnify him for any loss suffered.

4.   This section rejects the cases which recognize the principle that infringements violate the warranty of title but deny the buyer a remedy unless he has been expressly prevented from using the goods. Under this Article "eviction" is not a necessary condition to the buyer's remedy since the buyer's remedy arises immediately upon receipt of notice of infringement; it is merely one way of establishing the fact of breach.

5.   Subsection (2) recognizes that sales by sheriffs, executors, certain foreclosing lienors and persons similarly situated may be so out of the ordinary commercial course that their peculiar character is immediately apparent to the buyer and therefore no personal obligation is imposed upon the seller who is purporting to sell only an unknown or limited right. This subsection does not touch upon and leaves open all questions of restitution arising in such cases, when a unique article so sold is reclaimed by a third party as the rightful owner.

Foreclosure sales under Article 9 are another matter. Section 9–610 provides that a disposition of collateral under that section includes warranties such as those imposed by this section on a voluntary disposition of property of the kind involved. Consequently, unless properly excluded under subsection (2) or under the special provisions for exclusion in Section 9–610, a disposition under Section 9–610 of collateral consisting of goods includes the warranties imposed by subsection (1) and, if applicable, subsection (3).

6.   The warranty of subsection (1) is not designated as an "implied" warranty, and hence is not subject to Section 2–316(3). Disclaimer of the warranty of title is governed instead by subsection (2), which requires either specific language or the described circumstances.

Cross References:

> Point 1: Section 2–403.
> Point 2: Sections 2–607 and 2–725.
> Point 3: Section 1–203.*
> Point 4: Sections 2–609 and 2–725.
> Point 6: Section 2–316.

Definitional Cross References:

> "Buyer". Section 2–103.
> "Contract for sale". Section 2–106.
> "Goods". Section 2–105.
> "Person". Section 1–201.
> "Right". Section 1–201.
> "Seller". Section 2–103.

As amended in 1999.

§ 2–313.   Express Warranties by Affirmation, Promise, Description, Sample.

(1)   Express warranties by the seller are created as follows:

(a)   Any affirmation of fact or promise made by the seller to the buyer which relates to the goods and becomes part of the basis of the bargain creates an express warranty that the goods shall conform to the affirmation or promise.

(b)   Any description of the goods which is made part of the basis of the bargain creates an express warranty that the goods shall conform to the description.

(c)   Any sample or model which is made part of the basis of the bargain creates an express warranty that the whole of the goods shall conform to the sample or model.

(2)   It is not necessary to the creation of an express warranty that the seller use formal words such as "warrant" or "guarantee" or that he have a specific intention to make a warranty, but an affirmation merely of the value of the goods or a statement purporting to be merely the seller's opinion or commendation of the goods does not create a warranty.

Official Comment

Prior Uniform Statutory Provision: Sections 12, 14 and 16, Uniform Sales Act.

Changes: Rewritten.

Purposes of Changes: To consolidate and systematize basic principles with the result that:

1.   "Express" warranties rest on "dickered" aspects of the individual bargain, and go so clearly to the essence of that bargain that words of disclaimer in a form are repugnant to the basic dickered terms. "Implied" warranties rest so clearly on a common factual situation or set of conditions that no particular language or action is necessary to evidence them and they will arise in such a situation unless unmistakably negated.

This section reverts to the older case law insofar as the warranties of description and sample are designated "express" rather than "implied".

2.   Although this section is limited in its scope and direct purpose to warranties made by the seller to the buyer as part of a contract for sale, the warranty sections of this Article are not designed in any way to disturb those lines of case law growth which have recognized that warranties need not be confined either to sales contracts or to the direct parties to such a contract. They may arise in other appropriate circumstances such as in the case of bailments for hire, whether such bailment is itself the main contract or is merely a supplying of containers under a contract for the sale of their contents. The provisions of Section 2–318 on third party beneficiaries expressly recognize this case law development within one particular area. Beyond that, the matter is left to the case law with the intention that the policies of this Act may offer useful guidance in dealing with further cases as they arise.

---

*   *Referring to unrevised Article 1 (Appendix A).*

3.   The present section deals with affirmations of fact by the seller, descriptions of the goods or exhibitions of samples, exactly as any other part of a negotiation which ends in a contract is dealt with. No specific intention to make a warranty is necessary if any of these factors is made part of the basis of the bargain. In actual practice affirmations of fact made by the seller about the goods during a bargain are regarded as part of the description of those goods; hence no particular reliance on such statements need be shown in order to weave them into the fabric of the agreement. Rather, any fact which is to take such affirmations, once made, out of the agreement requires clear affirmative proof. The issue normally is one of fact.

4.   In view of the principle that the whole purpose of the law of warranty is to determine what it is that the seller has in essence agreed to sell, the policy is adopted of those cases which refuse except in unusual circumstances to recognize a material deletion of the seller's obligation. Thus, a contract is normally a contract for a sale of something describable and described. A clause generally disclaiming "all warranties, express or implied" cannot reduce the seller's obligation with respect to such description and therefore cannot be given literal effect under Section 2–316.

This is not intended to mean that the parties, if they consciously desire, cannot make their own bargain as they wish. But in determining what they have agreed upon good faith is a factor and consideration should be given to the fact that the probability is small that a real price is intended to be exchanged for a pseudo-obligation.

5.   Paragraph (1)(b) makes specific some of the principles set forth above when a description of the goods is given by the seller.

A description need not be by words. Technical specifications, blueprints and the like can afford more exact description than mere language and if made part of the basis of the bargain goods must conform with them. Past deliveries may set the description of quality, either expressly or impliedly by course of dealing. Of course, all descriptions by merchants must be read against the applicable trade usages with the general rules as to merchantability resolving any doubts.

6.   The basic situation as to statements affecting the true essence of the bargain is no different when a sample or model is involved in the transaction. This section includes both a "sample" actually drawn from the bulk of goods which is the subject matter of the sale, and a "model" which is offered for inspection when the subject matter is not at hand and which has not been drawn from the bulk of the goods.

Although the underlying principles are unchanged, the facts are often ambiguous when something is shown as illustrative, rather than as a straight sample. In general, the presumption is that any sample or model just as any affirmation of fact is intended to become a basis of the bargain. But there is no escape from the question of fact. When the seller exhibits a sample purporting to be drawn from an existing bulk, good faith of course requires that the sample be fairly drawn. But in mercantile experience the mere exhibition of a "sample" does not of itself show whether it is merely intended to "suggest" or to "be" the character of the subject-matter of the contract. The question is whether the seller has so acted with reference to the sample as to make him responsible that the whole shall have at least the values shown by it. The circumstances aid in answering this question. If the sample has been drawn from an existing bulk, it must be regarded as describing values of the goods contracted for unless it is accompanied by an unmistakable denial of such responsibility. If, on the other hand, a model of merchandise not on hand is offered, the mercantile presumption that it has become a literal description of the subject matter is not so strong, and particularly so if modification on the buyer's initiative impairs any feature of the model.

7.   The precise time when words of description or affirmation are made or samples are shown is not material. The sole question is whether the language or samples or models are fairly to be regarded as part of the contract. If language is used after the closing of the deal (as when the buyer when taking delivery asks and receives an additional assurance), the warranty becomes a modification, and need not be supported by consideration if it is otherwise reasonable and in order (Section 2–209).

8.   Concerning affirmations of value or a seller's opinion or commendation under subsection (2), the basic question remains the same: What statements of the seller have in the circumstances and in objective judgment become part of the basis of the bargain? As indicated above, all of the statements of the seller do so unless good reason is shown to the contrary. The provisions of subsection (2) are included, however, since common experience discloses that some statements or predictions cannot fairly be viewed as entering into the bargain. Even as to false statements of value, however, the possibility is left open that a remedy may be provided by the law relating to fraud or misrepresentation.

Cross References:

Point 1: Section 2–316.

Point 2: Sections 1–102(3)* and 2–318.
Point 3: Section 2–316(2)(b).
Point 4: Section 2–316.
Point 5: Sections 1–205(4)* and 2–314.
Point 6: Section 2–316.
Point 7: Section 2–209.
Point 8: Section 1–103.*

Definitional Cross References:

"Buyer". Section 2–103.
"Conforming". Section 2–106.
"Goods". Section 2–105.
"Seller". Section 2–103.

§ 2–314.   Implied Warranty: Merchantability; Usage of Trade.

(1)   Unless excluded or modified (Section 2–316), a warranty that the goods shall be merchantable is implied in a contract for their sale if the seller is a merchant with respect to goods of that kind. Under this section the serving for value of food or drink to be consumed either on the premises or elsewhere is a sale.

(2)   Goods to be merchantable must be at least such as

(a)   pass without objection in the trade under the contract description; and

(b)   in the case of fungible goods, are of fair average quality within the description; and

(c)   are fit for the ordinary purposes for which such goods are used; and

(d)   run, within the variations permitted by the agreement, of even kind, quality and quantity within each unit and among all units involved; and

(e)   are adequately contained, packaged, and labeled as the agreement may require; and

(f)   conform to the promise or affirmations of fact made on the container or label if any.

(3)   Unless excluded or modified (Section 2–316) other implied warranties may arise from course of dealing or usage of trade.

Official Comment

Prior Uniform Statutory Provision: Section 15(2), Uniform Sales Act.

Changes: Completely rewritten.

Purposes of Changes: This section, drawn in view of the steadily developing case law on the subject, is intended to make it clear that:

1.   The seller's obligation applies to present sales as well as to contracts to sell subject to the effects of any examination of specific goods. (Subsection (2) of Section 2–316). Also, the warranty of merchantability applies to sales for use as well as to sales for resale.

2.   The question when the warranty is imposed turns basically on the meaning of the terms of the agreement as recognized in the trade. Goods delivered under an agreement made by a merchant in a given line of trade must be of a quality comparable to that generally acceptable in that line of trade under the description or other designation of the goods used in the agreement. The responsibility imposed rests on any merchant-seller, and the absence of the words "grower or manufacturer or not" which appeared in Section 15(2) of the Uniform Sales Act does not restrict the applicability of this section.

3.   A specific designation of goods by the buyer does not exclude the seller's obligation that they be fit for the general purposes appropriate to such goods. A contract for the sale of second-hand goods, however, involves only such obligation as is appropriate to such goods for that is their contract description. A person making an isolated sale of goods is not a "merchant" within the meaning of the full scope of this section and, thus, no warranty

---

*   *Referring to unrevised Article 1 (Appendix A).*

of merchantability would apply. His knowledge of any defects not apparent on inspection would, however, without need for express agreement and in keeping with the underlying reason of the present section and the provisions on good faith, impose an obligation that known material but hidden defects be fully disclosed.

4. Although a seller may not be a "merchant" as to the goods in question, if he states generally that they are "guaranteed" the provisions of this section may furnish a guide to the content of the resulting express warranty. This has particular significance in the case of second-hand sales, and has further significance in limiting the effect of fine-print disclaimer clauses where their effect would be inconsistent with large-print assertions of "guarantee".

5. The second sentence of subsection (1) covers the warranty with respect to food and drink. Serving food or drink for value is a sale, whether to be consumed on the premises or elsewhere. Cases to the contrary are rejected. The principal warranty is that stated in subsections (1) and (2)(c) of this section.

6. Subsection (2) does not purport to exhaust the meaning of "merchantable" nor to negate any of its attributes not specifically mentioned in the text of the statute, but arising by usage of trade or through case law. The language used is "must be at least such as . . . ," and the intention is to leave open other possible attributes of merchantability.

7. Paragraphs (a) and (b) of subsection (2) are to be read together. Both refer, as indicated above, to the standards of that line of the trade which fits the transaction and the seller's business. "Fair average" is a term directly appropriate to agricultural bulk products and means goods centering around the middle belt of quality, not the least or the worst that can be understood in the particular trade by the designation, but such as can pass "without objection." Of course a fair percentage of the least is permissible but the goods are not "fair average" if they are all of the least or worst quality possible under the description. In cases of doubt as to what quality is intended, the price at which a merchant closes a contract is an excellent index of the nature and scope of his obligation under the present section.

8. Fitness for the ordinary purposes for which goods of the type are used is a fundamental concept of the present section and is covered in paragraph (c). As stated above, merchantability is also a part of the obligation owing to the purchaser for use. Correspondingly, protection, under this aspect of the warranty, of the person buying for resale to the ultimate consumer is equally necessary, and merchantable goods must therefore be "honestly" resalable in the normal course of business because they are what they purport to be.

9. Paragraph (d) on evenness of kind, quality and quantity follows case law. But precautionary language has been added as a remainder of the frequent usages of trade which permit substantial variations both with and without an allowance or an obligation to replace the varying units.

10. Paragraph (e) applies only where the nature of the goods and of the transaction require a certain type of container, package or label. Paragraph (f) applies, on the other hand, wherever there is a label or container on which representations are made, even though the original contract, either by express terms or usage of trade, may not have required either the labelling or the representation. This follows from the general obligation of good faith which requires that a buyer should not be placed in the position of reselling or using goods delivered under false representations appearing on the package or container. No problem of extra consideration arises in this connection since, under this Article, an obligation is imposed by the original contract not to deliver mislabeled articles, and the obligation is imposed where mercantile good faith so requires and without reference to the doctrine of consideration.

11. Exclusion or modification of the warranty of merchantability, or of any part of it, is dealt with in the section to which the text of the present section makes explicit precautionary references. That section must be read with particular reference to its subsection (4) on limitation of remedies. The warranty of merchantability, wherever it is normal, is so commonly taken for granted that its exclusion from the contract is a matter threatening surprise and therefore requiring special precaution.

12. Subsection (3) is to make explicit that usage of trade and course of dealing can create warranties and that they are implied rather than express warranties and thus subject to exclusion or modification under Section 2–316. A typical instance would be the obligation to provide pedigree papers to evidence conformity of the animal to the contract in the case of a pedigreed dog or blooded bull.

13. In an action based on breach of warranty, it is of course necessary to show not only the existence of the warranty but the fact that the warranty was broken and that the breach of the warranty was the proximate cause of the loss sustained. In such an action an affirmative showing by the seller that the loss resulted from some action or event following his own delivery of the goods can operate as a defense. Equally, evidence indicating that the seller exercised care in the manufacture, processing or selection of the goods is relevant to the issue of whether

the warranty was in fact broken. Action by the buyer following an examination of the goods which ought to have indicated the defect complained of can be shown as matter bearing on whether the breach itself was the cause of the injury.

Cross References:

> Point 1: Section 2–316.
> Point 3: Sections 1–203* and 2–104.
> Point 5: Section 2–315.
> Point 11: Section 2–316.
> Point 12: Sections 1–201, 1–205* and 2–316.

Definitional Cross References:

> "Agreement". Section 1–201.
> "Contract". Section 1–201.
> "Contract for sale". Section 2–106.
> "Goods". Section 2–105.
> "Merchant". Section 2–104.
> "Seller". Section 2–103.

§ 2–315.   Implied Warranty: Fitness for Particular Purpose.

Where the seller at the time of contracting has reason to know any particular purpose for which the goods are required and that the buyer is relying on the seller's skill or judgment to select or furnish suitable goods, there is unless excluded or modified under the next section an implied warranty that the goods shall be fit for such purpose.

Official Comment

Prior Uniform Statutory Provision: Section 15(1), (4), (5), Uniform Sales Act.

Changes: Rewritten.

Purposes of Changes:

1.   Whether or not this warranty arises in any individual case is basically a question of fact to be determined by the circumstances of the contracting. Under this section the buyer need not bring home to the seller actual knowledge of the particular purpose for which the goods are intended or of his reliance on the seller's skill and judgment, if the circumstances are such that the seller has reason to realize the purpose intended or that the reliance exists. The buyer, of course, must actually be relying on the seller.

2.   A "particular purpose" differs from the ordinary purpose for which the goods are used in that it envisages a specific use by the buyer which is peculiar to the nature of his business whereas the ordinary purposes for which goods are used are those envisaged in the concept of merchantability and go to uses which are customarily made of the goods in question. For example, shoes are generally used for the purpose of walking upon ordinary ground, but a seller may know that a particular pair was selected to be used for climbing mountains.

A contract may of course include both a warranty of merchantability and one of fitness for a particular purpose.

The provisions of this Article on the cumulation and conflict of express and implied warranties must be considered on the question of inconsistency between or among warranties. In such a case any question of fact as to which warranty was intended by the parties to apply must be resolved in favor of the warranty of fitness for particular purpose as against all other warranties except where the buyer has taken upon himself the responsibility of furnishing the technical specifications.

3.   In connection with the warranty of fitness for a particular purpose the provisions of this Article on the allocation or division of risks are particularly applicable in any transaction in which the purpose for which the goods are to be used combines requirements both as to the quality of the goods themselves and compliance with certain laws or regulations. How the risks are divided is a question of fact to be determined, where not expressly

---

*   *Referring to unrevised Article 1 (Appendix A).*

86

contained in the agreement, from the circumstances of contracting, usage of trade, course of performance and the like, matters which may constitute the "otherwise agreement" of the parties by which they may divide the risk or burden.

4.   The absence from this section of the language used in the Uniform Sales Act in referring to the seller, "whether he be the grower or manufacturer or not," is not intended to impose any requirement that the seller be a grower or manufacturer. Although normally the warranty will arise only where the seller is a merchant with the appropriate "skill or judgment," it can arise as to non-merchants where this is justified by the particular circumstances.

5.   The elimination of the "patent or other trade name" exception constitutes the major extension of the warranty of fitness which has been made by the cases and continued in this Article. Under the present section the existence of a patent or other trade name and the designation of the article by that name, or indeed in any other definite manner, is only one of the facts to be considered on the question of whether the buyer actually relied on the seller, but it is not of itself decisive of the issue. If the buyer himself is insisting on a particular brand he is not relying on the seller's skill and judgment and so no warranty results. But the mere fact that the article purchased has a particular patent or trade name is not sufficient to indicate nonreliance if the article has been recommended by the seller as adequate for the buyer's purposes.

6.   The specific reference forward in the present section to the following section on exclusion or modification of warranties is to call attention to the possibility of eliminating the warranty in any given case. However it must be noted that under the following section the warranty of fitness for a particular purpose must be excluded or modified by a conspicuous writing.

Cross References:

> Point 2: Sections 2–314 and 2–317.
> Point 3: Section 2–303.
> Point 6: Section 2–316.

Definitional Cross References:

> "Buyer". Section 2–103.
> "Goods". Section 2–105.
> "Seller". Section 2–103.

§ 2-316.   Exclusion or Modification of Warranties.

(1)   Words or conduct relevant to the creation of an express warranty and words or conduct tending to negate or limit warranty shall be construed wherever reasonable as consistent with each other; but subject to the provisions of this Article on parol or extrinsic evidence (Section 2–202) negation or limitation is inoperative to the extent that such construction is unreasonable.

(2)   Subject to subsection (3), to exclude or modify the implied warranty of merchantability or any part of it the language must mention merchantability and in case of a writing must be conspicuous, and to exclude or modify any implied warranty of fitness the exclusion must be by a writing and conspicuous. Language to exclude all implied warranties of fitness is sufficient if it states, for example, that "There are no warranties which extend beyond the description on the face hereof."

(3)   Notwithstanding subsection (2)

(a)   unless the circumstances indicate otherwise, all implied warranties are excluded by expressions like "as is", "with all faults" or other language which in common understanding calls the buyer's attention to the exclusion of warranties and makes plain that there is no implied warranty; and

(b)   when the buyer before entering into the contract has examined the goods or the sample or model as fully as he desired or has refused to examine the goods there is no implied warranty with regard to defects which an examination ought in the circumstances to have revealed to him; and

(c)   an implied warranty can also be excluded or modified by course of dealing or course of performance or usage of trade.

(4) Remedies for breach of warranty can be limited in accordance with the provisions of this Article on liquidation or limitation of damages and on contractual modification of remedy (Sections 2–718 and 2–719).

Official Comment

Prior Uniform Statutory Provision: None. See sections 15 and 71, Uniform Sales Act.

Purposes:

1. This section is designed principally to deal with those frequent clauses in sales contracts which seek to exclude "all warranties, express or implied." It seeks to protect a buyer from unexpected and unbargained language of disclaimer by denying effect to such language when inconsistent with language of express warranty and permitting the exclusion of implied warranties only by conspicuous language or other circumstances which protect the buyer from surprise.

2. The seller is protected under this Article against false allegations of oral warranties by its provisions on parol and extrinsic evidence and against unauthorized representations by the customary "lack of authority" clauses. This Article treats the limitation or avoidance of consequential damages as a matter of limiting remedies for breach, separate from the matter of creation of liability under a warranty. If no warranty exists, there is of course no problem of limiting remedies for breach of warranty. Under subsection (4) the question of limitation of remedy is governed by the sections referred to rather than by this section.

3. Disclaimer of the implied warranty of merchantability is permitted under subsection (2), but with the safeguard that such disclaimers must mention merchantability and in case of a writing must be conspicuous.

4. Unlike the implied warranty of merchantability, implied warranties of fitness for a particular purpose may be excluded by general language, but only if it is in writing and conspicuous.

5. Subsection (2) presupposes that the implied warranty in question exists unless excluded or modified. Whether or not language of disclaimer satisfies the requirements of this section, such language may be relevant under other sections to the question whether the warranty was ever in fact created. Thus, unless the provisions of this Article on parol and extrinsic evidence prevent, oral language of disclaimer may raise issues of fact as to whether reliance by the buyer occurred and whether the seller had "reason to know" under the section on implied warranty of fitness for a particular purpose.

6. The exceptions to the general rule set forth in paragraphs (a), (b) and (c) of subsection (3) are common factual situations in which the circumstances surrounding the transaction are in themselves sufficient to call the buyer's attention to the fact that no implied warranties are made or that a certain implied warranty is being excluded.

7. Paragraph (a) of subsection (3) deals with general terms such as "as is," "as they stand," "with all faults," and the like. Such terms in ordinary commercial usage are understood to mean that the buyer takes the entire risk as to the quality of the goods involved. The terms covered by paragraph (a) are in fact merely a particularization of paragraph (c) which provides for exclusion or modification of implied warranties by usage of trade.

8. Under paragraph (b) of subsection (3) warranties may be excluded or modified by the circumstances where the buyer examines the goods or a sample or model of them before entering into the contract. "Examination" as used in this paragraph is not synonymous with inspection before acceptance or at any other time after the contract has been made. It goes rather to the nature of the responsibility assumed by the seller at the time of the making of the contract. Of course if the buyer discovers the defect and uses the goods anyway, or if he unreasonably fails to examine the goods before he uses them, resulting injuries may be found to result from his own action rather than proximately from a breach of warranty. See Sections 2–314 and 2–715 and comments thereto.

In order to bring the transaction within the scope of "refused to examine" in paragraph (b), it is not sufficient that the goods are available for inspection. There must in addition be a demand by the seller that the buyer examine the goods fully. The seller by the demand puts the buyer on notice that he is assuming the risk of defects which the examination ought to reveal. The language "refused to examine" in this paragraph is intended to make clear the necessity for such demand.

Application of the doctrine of "caveat emptor" in all cases where the buyer examines the goods regardless of statements made by the seller is, however, rejected by this Article. Thus, if the offer of examination is accompanied by words as to their merchantability or specific attributes and the buyer indicates clearly that he is relying on those words rather than on his examination, they give rise to an "express" warranty. In such cases the question is one of fact as to whether a warranty of merchantability has been expressly incorporated in the agreement. Disclaimer of such an express warranty is governed by subsection (1) of the present section.

The particular buyer's skill and the normal method of examining goods in the circumstances determine what defects are excluded by the examination. A failure to notice defects which are obvious cannot excuse the buyer. However, an examination under circumstances which do not permit chemical or other testing of the goods would not exclude defects which could be ascertained only by such testing. Nor can latent defects be excluded by a simple examination. A professional buyer examining a product in his field will be held to have assumed the risk as to all defects which a professional in the field ought to observe, while a nonprofessional buyer will be held to have assumed the risk only for such defects as a layman might be expected to observe.

9. The situation in which the buyer gives precise and complete specifications to the seller is not explicitly covered in this section, but this is a frequent circumstance by which the implied warranties may be excluded. The warranty of fitness for a particular purpose would not normally arise since in such a situation there is usually no reliance on the seller by the buyer. The warranty of merchantability in such a transaction, however, must be considered in connection with the next section on the cumulation and conflict of warranties. Under paragraph (c) of that section in case of such an inconsistency the implied warranty of merchantability is displaced by the express warranty that the goods will comply with the specifications. Thus, where the buyer gives detailed specifications as to the goods, neither of the implied warranties as to quality will normally apply to the transaction unless consistent with the specifications.

Cross References:

Point 2: Sections 2–202, 2–718 and 2–719.
Point 7: Sections 1–205* and 2–208.

Definitional Cross References:

"Agreement". Section 1–201.
"Buyer". Section 2–103.
"Contract". Section 1–201.
"Course of dealing". Section 1–205.*
"Goods". Section 2–105.
"Remedy". Section 1–201.
"Seller". Section 2–103.
"Usage of trade". Section 1–205.*

§ 2–317. Cumulation and Conflict of Warranties Express or Implied.

Warranties whether express or implied shall be construed as consistent with each other and as cumulative, but if such construction is unreasonable the intention of the parties shall determine which warranty is dominant. In ascertaining that intention the following rules apply:

(a) Exact or technical specifications displace an inconsistent sample or model or general language of description.

(b) A sample from an existing bulk displaces inconsistent general language of description.

(c) Express warranties displace inconsistent implied warranties other than an implied warranty of fitness for a particular purpose.

Official Comment

Prior Uniform Statutory Provision: On cumulation of warranties see Sections 14, 15, and 16, Uniform Sales Act.

Changes: Completely rewritten into one section.

---

* *Referring to unrevised Article 1 (Appendix A).*

Purposes of Changes:

1.   The present section rests on the basic policy of this Article that no warranty is created except by some conduct (either affirmative action or failure to disclose) on the part of the seller. Therefore, all warranties are made cumulative unless this construction of the contract is impossible or unreasonable.

This Article thus follows the general policy of the Uniform Sales Act except that in case of the sale of an article by its patent or trade name the elimination of the warranty of fitness depends solely on whether the buyer has relied on the seller's skill and judgment; the use of the patent or trade name is but one factor in making this determination.

2.   The rules of this section are designed to aid in determining the intention of the parties as to which of inconsistent warranties which have arisen from the circumstances of their transaction shall prevail. These rules of intention are to be applied only where factors making for an equitable estoppel of the seller do not exist and where he has in perfect good faith made warranties which later turn out to be inconsistent. To the extent that the seller has led the buyer to believe that all of the warranties can be performed, he is estopped from setting up any essential inconsistency as a defense.

3.   The rules in subsections (a), (b) and (c) are designed to ascertain the intention of the parties by reference to the factor which probably claimed the attention of the parties in the first instance. These rules are not absolute but may be changed by evidence showing that the conditions which existed at the time of contracting make the construction called for by the section inconsistent or unreasonable.

Cross Reference:

Point 1: Section 2–315.

Definitional Cross Reference:

"Party". Section 1–201.

§ 2–318.   Third Party Beneficiaries of Warranties Express or Implied.

Note: *If this Act is introduced in the Congress of the United States this section should be omitted. (States to select one alternative.)*

ALTERNATIVE A

A seller's warranty whether express or implied extends to any natural person who is in the family or household of his buyer or who is a guest in his home if it is reasonable to expect that such person may use, consume or be affected by the goods and who is injured in person by breach of the warranty. A seller may not exclude or limit the operation of this section.

ALTERNATIVE B

A seller's warranty whether express or implied extends to any natural person who may reasonably be expected to use, consume or be affected by the goods and who is injured in person by breach of the warranty. A seller may not exclude or limit the operation of this section.

ALTERNATIVE C

A seller's warranty whether express or implied extends to any person who may reasonably be expected to use, consume or be affected by the goods and who is injured by breach of the warranty. A seller may not exclude or limit the operation of this section with respect to injury to the person of an individual to whom the warranty extends.

As amended in 1966.

Official Comment

Prior Uniform Statutory Provision: None.

Purposes:

1.   The last sentence of this section does not mean that a seller is precluded from excluding or disclaiming a warranty which might otherwise arise in connection with the sale provided such exclusion or modification is permitted by Section 2–316. Nor does that sentence preclude the seller from limiting the remedies of his own buyer and of any beneficiaries, in any manner provided in Sections 2–718 or 2–719. To the extent that the contract of

sale contains provisions under which warranties are excluded or modified, or remedies for breach are limited, such provisions are equally operative against beneficiaries of warranties under this section. What this last sentence forbids is exclusion of liability by the seller to the persons to whom the warranties which he has made to his buyer would extend under this section.

2.   The purpose of this section is to give certain beneficiaries the benefit of the same warranty which the buyer received in the contract of sale, thereby freeing any such beneficiaries from any technical rules as to "privity." It seeks to accomplish this purpose without any derogation of any right or remedy resting on negligence. It rests primarily upon the merchant-seller's warranty under this Article that the goods sold are merchantable and fit for the ordinary purposes for which such goods are used rather than the warranty of fitness for a particular purpose. Implicit in the section is that any beneficiary of a warranty may bring a direct action for breach of warranty against the seller whose warranty extends to him [As amended in 1966].

3.   The first alternative expressly includes as beneficiaries within its provisions the family, household and guests of the purchaser. Beyond this, the section in this form is neutral and is not intended to enlarge or restrict the developing case law on whether the seller's warranties, given to his buyer who resells, extend to other persons in the distributive chain.

The second alternative is designed for states where the case law has already developed further and for those that desire to expand the class of beneficiaries. The third alternative goes further, following the trend of modern decisions as indicated by Restatement of Torts 2d § 402A (Tentative Draft No. 10, 1965) in extending the rule beyond injuries to the person [As amended in 1966].

Cross References:

Point 1: Sections 2–316, 2–718 and 2–719.
Point 2: Section 2–314.

Definitional Cross References:

"Buyer". Section 2–103.
"Goods". Section 2–105.
"Seller". Section 2–103.

§ 2–319.   F.O.B. and F.A.S. Terms.

(1)   Unless otherwise agreed the term F.O.B. (which means "free on board") at a named place, even though used only in connection with the stated price, is a delivery term under which

(a)   when the term is F.O.B. the place of shipment, the seller must at that place ship the goods in the manner provided in this Article (Section 2–504) and bear the expense and risk of putting them into the possession of the carrier; or

(b)   when the term is F.O.B. the place of destination, the seller must at his own expense and risk transport the goods to that place and there tender delivery of them in the manner provided in this Article (Section 2–503);

(c)   when under either (a) or (b) the term is also F.O.B. vessel, car or other vehicle, the seller must in addition at his own expense and risk load the goods on board. If the term is F.O.B. vessel the buyer must name the vessel and in an appropriate case the seller must comply with the provisions of this Article on the form of bill of lading (Section 2–323).

(2)   Unless otherwise agreed the term F.A.S. vessel (which means "free alongside") at a named port, even though used only in connection with the stated price, is a delivery term under which the seller must

(a)   at his own expense and risk deliver the goods alongside the vessel in the manner usual in that port or on a dock designated and provided by the buyer; and

(b)   obtain and tender a receipt for the goods in exchange for which the carrier is under a duty to issue a bill of lading.

(3)   Unless otherwise agreed in any case falling within subsection (1)(a) or (c) or subsection (2) the buyer must seasonably give any needed instructions for making delivery, including when the term is F.A.S. or F.O.B. the loading berth of the vessel and in an appropriate case its name and sailing date. The seller

may treat the failure of needed instructions as a failure of cooperation under this Article (Section 2–311). He may also at his option move the goods in any reasonable manner preparatory to delivery or shipment.

(4)   Under the term F.O.B. vessel or F.A.S. unless otherwise agreed the buyer must make payment against tender of the required documents and the seller may not tender nor the buyer demand delivery of the goods in substitution for the documents.

Official Comment

Prior Uniform Statutory Provision: None.

Purposes:

1.   This section is intended to negate the uncommercial line of decision which treats an "F.O.B." term as "merely a price term." The distinctions taken in subsection (1) handle most of the issues which have on occasion led to the unfortunate judicial language just referred to. Other matters which have led to sound results being based on unhappy language in regard to F.O.B. clauses are dealt with in this Act by Section 2–311(2) (seller's option re arrangements relating to shipment) and Sections 2–614 and 2–615 (substituted performance and seller's excuse).

2.   Subsection (1)(c) not only specifies the duties of a seller who engages to deliver "F.O.B. vessel," or the like, but ought to make clear that no agreement is soundly drawn when it looks to reshipment from San Francisco or New York, but speaks merely of "F.O.B." the place.

3.   The buyer's obligations stated in subsection (1)(c) and subsection (3) are, as shown in the text, obligations of cooperation. The last sentence of subsection (3) expressly, though perhaps unnecessarily, authorizes the seller, pending instructions, to go ahead with such preparatory moves as shipment from the interior to the named point of delivery. The sentence presupposes the usual case in which instructions "fail"; a prior repudiation by the buyer, giving notice that breach was intended, would remove the reason for the sentence, and would normally bring into play, instead, the second sentence of Section 2–704, which duly calls for lessening damages.

4.   The treatment of "F.O.B. vessel" in conjunction with F.A.S. fits, in regard to the need for payment against documents, with standard practice and case-law; but "F.O.B. vessel" is a term which by its very language makes express the need for an "on board" document. In this respect, that term is stricter than the ordinary overseas "shipment" contract (C.I.F., etc., Section 2–320).

Cross References:

Sections 2–311(3), 2–323, 2–503 and 2–504.

Definitional Cross References:

"Agreed". Section 1–201.
"Bill of lading". Section 1–201.
"Buyer". Section 2–103.
"Goods". Section 2–105.
"Seasonably". Section 1–204.*
"Seller". Section 2–103.
"Term". Section 1–201.

§ 2–320.   C.I.F. and C. & F. Terms.

(1)   The term C.I.F. means that the price includes in a lump sum the cost of the goods and the insurance and freight to the named destination. The term C. & F. or C.F. means that the price so includes cost and freight to the named destination.

(2)   Unless otherwise agreed and even though used only in connection with the stated price and destination, the term C.I.F. destination or its equivalent requires the seller at his own expense and risk to

(a)   put the goods into the possession of a carrier at the port for shipment and obtain a negotiable bill or bills of lading covering the entire transportation to the named destination; and

---

*   *Referring to unrevised Article 1 (Appendix A).*

(b)   load the goods and obtain a receipt from the carrier (which may be contained in the bill of lading) showing that the freight has been paid or provided for; and

(c)   obtain a policy or certificate of insurance, including any war risk insurance, of a kind and on terms then current at the port of shipment in the usual amount, in the currency of the contract, shown to cover the same goods covered by the bill of lading and providing for payment of loss to the order of the buyer or for the account of whom it may concern; but the seller may add to the price the amount of the premium for any such war risk insurance; and

(d)   prepare an invoice of the goods and procure any other documents required to effect shipment or to comply with the contract; and

(e)   forward and tender with commercial promptness all the documents in due form and with any indorsement necessary to perfect the buyer's rights.

(3)   Unless otherwise agreed the term C. & F. or its equivalent has the same effect and imposes upon the seller the same obligations and risks as a C.I.F. term except the obligation as to insurance.

(4)   Under the term C.I.F. or C. & F. unless otherwise agreed the buyer must make payment against tender of the required documents and the seller may not tender nor the buyer demand delivery of the goods in substitution for the documents.

Official Comment

Prior Uniform Statutory Provisions: None.

Purposes: To make it clear that:

1.   The C.I.F. contract is not a destination but a shipment contract with risk of subsequent loss or damage to the goods passing to the buyer upon shipment if the seller has properly performed all his obligations with respect to the goods. Delivery to the carrier is delivery to the buyer for purposes of risk and "title". Delivery of possession of the goods is accomplished by delivery of the bill of lading, and upon tender of the required documents the buyer must pay the agreed price without awaiting the arrival of the goods and if they have been lost or damaged after proper shipment he must seek his remedy against the carrier or insurer. The buyer has no right of inspection prior to payment or acceptance of the documents.

2.   The seller's obligations remain the same even though the C.I.F. term is "used only in connection with the stated price and destination".

3.   The insurance stipulated by the C.I.F. term is for the buyer's benefit, to protect him against the risk of loss or damage to the goods in transit. A clause in a C.I.F. contract "insurance—for the account of sellers" should be viewed in its ordinary mercantile meaning that the sellers must pay for the insurance and not that it is intended to run to the seller's benefit.

4.   A bill of lading covering the entire transportation from the port of shipment is explicitly required but the provision on this point must be read in the light of its reason to assure the buyer of as full protection as the conditions of shipment reasonably permit, remembering always that this type of contract is designed to move the goods in the channels commercially available. To enable the buyer to deal with the goods while they are afloat the bill of lading must be one that covers only the quantity of goods called for by the contract. The buyer is not required to accept his part of the goods without a bill of lading because the latter covers a larger quantity, nor is he required to accept a bill of lading for the whole quantity under a stipulation to hold the excess for the owner. Although the buyer is not compelled to accept either goods or documents under such circumstances he may of course claim his rights in any goods which have been identified to his contract.

5.   The seller is given the option of paying or providing for the payment of freight. He has no option to ship "freight collect" unless the agreement so provides. The rule of the common law that the buyer need not pay the freight if the goods do not arrive is preserved.

Unless the shipment has been sent "freight collect" the buyer is entitled to receive documentary evidence that he is not obligated to pay the freight; the seller is therefore required to obtain a receipt "showing that the freight has been paid or provided for." The usual notation on the bill of lading that the freight has been prepaid is a sufficient receipt, as at common law. The phrase "provided for" is intended to cover the frequent situation in which the carrier extends credit to a shipper for the freight on successive shipments and receives periodical payments of the accrued freight charges from him.

6.   The requirement that unless otherwise agreed the seller must procure insurance "of a kind and on terms then current at the port for shipment in the usual amount, in the currency of the contract, sufficiently shown to cover the same goods covered by the bill of lading", applies to both marine and war risk insurance. As applied to marine insurance, it means such insurance as is usual or customary at the port for shipment with reference to the particular kind of goods involved, the character and equipment of the vessel, the route of the voyage, the port of destination and any other considerations that affect the risk. It is the substantial equivalent of the ordinary insurance in the particular trade and on the particular voyage and is subject to agreed specifications of type or extent of coverage. The language does not mean that the insurance must be adequate to cover all risks to which the goods may be subject in transit. There are some types of loss or damage that are not covered by the usual marine insurance and are excepted in bills of lading or in applicable statutes from the causes of loss or damage for which the carrier or the vessel is liable. Such risks must be borne by the buyer under this Article.

Insurance secured in compliance with a C.I.F. term must cover the entire transportation of the goods to the named destination.

7.   An additional obligation is imposed upon the seller in requiring him to procure customary war risk insurance at the buyer's expense. This changes the common law on the point. The seller is not required to assume the risk of including in the C.I.F. price the cost of such insurance, since it often fluctuates rapidly, but is required to treat it simply as a necessary for the buyer's account. What war risk insurance is "current" or usual turns on the standard forms of policy or rider in common use.

8.   The C.I.F. contract calls for insurance covering the value of the goods at the time and place of shipment and does not include any increase in market value during transit or any anticipated profit to the buyer on a sale by him.

The contract contemplates that before the goods arrive at their destination they may be sold again and again on C.I.F. terms and that the original policy of insurance and bill of lading will run with the interest in the goods by being transferred to each successive buyer. A buyer who becomes the seller in such an intermediate contract for sale does not thereby, if his sub-buyer knows the circumstances, undertake to insure the goods again at an increased price fixed in the new contract or to cover the increase in price by additional insurance, and his buyer may not reject the documents on the ground that the original policy does not cover such higher price. If such a sub-buyer desires additional insurance he must procure it for himself.

Where the seller exercises an option to ship "freight collect" and to credit the buyer with the freight against the C.I.F. price, the insurance need not cover the freight since the freight is not at the buyer's risk. On the other hand, where the seller prepays the freight upon shipping under a bill of lading requiring prepayment and providing that the freight shall be deemed earned and shall be retained by the carrier "ship and/or cargo lost or not lost," or using words of similar import, he must procure insurance that will cover the freight, because notwithstanding that the goods are lost in transit the buyer is bound to pay the freight as part of the C.I.F. price and will be unable to recover it back from the carrier.

9.   Insurance "for the account of whom it may concern" is usual and sufficient. However, for a valid tender the policy of insurance must be one which can be disposed of together with the bill of lading and so must be "sufficiently shown to cover the same goods covered by the bill of lading". It must cover separately the quantity of goods called for by the buyer's contract and not merely insure his goods as part of a larger quantity in which others are interested, a case provided for in American mercantile practice by the use of negotiable certificates of insurance which are expressly authorized by this section. By usage these certificates are treated as the equivalent of separate policies and are good tender under C.I.F. contracts. The term "certificate of insurance", however, does not of itself include certificates or "cover notes" issued by the insurance broker and stating that the goods are covered by a policy. Their sufficiency as substitutes for policies will depend upon proof of an established usage or course of dealing. The present section rejects the English rule that not only brokers' certificates and "cover notes" but also certain forms of American insurance certificates are not the equivalent of policies and are not good tender under a C.I.F. contract.

The seller's failure to tender a proper insurance document is waived if the buyer refuses to make payment on other and untenable grounds at a time when proper insurance could have been obtained and tendered by the seller if timely objection had been made. Even a failure to insure on shipment may be cured by seasonable tender of a policy retroactive in effect; e.g., one insuring the goods "lost or not lost." The provisions of this Article on cure of improper tender and on waiver of buyer's objections by silence are applicable to insurance tenders under a C.I.F. term. Where there is no waiver by the buyer as described above, however, the fact that the goods arrive safely does not cure the seller's breach of his obligations to insure them and tender to the buyer a proper insurance document.

10. The seller's invoice of the goods shipped under a C.I.F. contract is regarded as a usual and necessary document upon which reliance may properly be placed. It is the document which evidences points of description, quality and the like which do not readily appear in other documents. This Article rejects those statements to the effect that the invoice is a usual but not a necessary document under a C.I.F. term.

11. The buyer needs all of the documents required under a C.I.F. contract, in due form and, if a tangible document of title, with necessary endorsements, so that before the goods arrive he may deal with them by negotiating the documents or may obtain prompt possession of the goods after their arrival. If the goods are lost or damaged in transit the documents are necessary to enable him promptly to assert his remedy against the carrier or insurer. The seller is therefore obligated to do what is mercantilely reasonable in the circumstances and should make every reasonable exertion to send forward the documents as soon as possible after the shipment. The requirement that the documents be forwarded with "commercial promptness" expresses a more urgent need for action than that suggested by the phrase "reasonable time".

12. Under a C.I.F. contract the buyer, as under the common law, must pay the price upon tender of the required documents without first inspecting the goods, but his payment in these circumstances does not constitute an acceptance of the goods nor does it impair his right of subsequent inspection or his options and remedies in the case of improper delivery. All remedies and rights for the seller's breach are reserved to him. The buyer must pay before inspection and assert his remedy against the seller afterward unless the nonconformity of the goods amounts to a real failure of consideration, since the purpose of choosing this form of contract is to give the seller protection against the buyer's unjustifiable rejection of the goods at a distant port of destination which would necessitate taking possession of the goods and suing the buyer there.

13. A valid C.I.F. contract may be made which requires part of the transportation to be made on land and part on the sea, as where the goods are to be brought by rail from an inland point to a seaport and thence transported by vessel to the named destination under a "through" or combination bill of lading issued by the railroad company. In such a case shipment by rail from the inland point within the contract period is a timely shipment notwithstanding that the loading of the goods on the vessel is delayed by causes beyond the seller's control.

14. Although subsection (2) stating the legal effects of the C.I.F. term is an "unless otherwise agreed" provision, the express language used in an agreement is frequently a precautionary, fuller statement of the normal C.I.F. terms and hence not intended as a departure or variation from them. Moreover, the dominant outlines of the C.I.F. term are so well understood commercially that any variation should, whenever reasonably possible, be read as falling within those dominant outlines rather than as destroying the whole meaning of a term which essentially indicates a contract for proper shipment rather than one for delivery at destination. Particularly careful consideration is necessary before a printed form or clause is construed to mean agreement otherwise and where a C.I.F. contract is prepared on a printed form designed for some other type of contract, the C.I.F. terms must prevail over printed clauses repugnant to them.

15. Under subsection (4) the fact that the seller knows at the time of the tender of the documents that the goods have been lost in transit does not affect his rights if he has performed his contractual obligations. Similarly, the seller cannot perform under a C.I.F. term by purchasing and tendering landed goods.

16. Under the C. & F. term, as under the C.I.F. term, title and risk of loss are intended to pass to the buyer on shipment. A stipulation in a C. & F. contract that the seller shall effect insurance on the goods and charge the buyer with the premium (in effect that he shall act as the buyer's agent for that purpose) is entirely in keeping with the pattern. On the other hand, it often happens that the buyer is in a more advantageous position than the seller to effect insurance on the goods or that he has in force an "open" or "floating" policy covering all shipments made by him or to him, in either of which events the C. & F. term is adequate without mention of insurance.

17. It is to be remembered that in a French contract the term "C.A.F." does not mean "Cost and Freight" but has exactly the same meaning as the term "C.I.F." since it is merely the French equivalent of that term. The "A" does not stand for "and" but for "assurance" which means insurance.

Cross References:

Point 4: Section 2–323.
Point 6: Section 2–509(1)(a).
Point 9: Sections 2–508 and 2–605(1)(a).
Point 12: Sections 2–321(3), 2–512 and 2–513(3) and Article 5.

Definitional Cross References:

"Bill of lading". Section 1–201.

"Buyer". Section 2–103.

"Contract". Section 1–201.

"Goods". Section 2–105.

"Rights". Section 1–201.

"Seller". Section 2–103.

"Term". Section 1–201.

As amended in 2003.

§ 2–321.   C.I.F. or C. & F.: "Net Landed Weights"; "Payment on Arrival"; Warranty of Condition on Arrival.

Under a contract containing a term C.I.F. or C. & F.

(1)   Where the price is based on or is to be adjusted according to "net landed weights", "delivered weights", "out turn" quantity or quality or the like, unless otherwise agreed the seller must reasonably estimate the price. The payment due on tender of the documents called for by the contract is the amount so estimated, but after final adjustment of the price a settlement must be made with commercial promptness.

(2)   An agreement described in subsection (1) or any warranty of quality or condition of the goods on arrival places upon the seller the risk of ordinary deterioration, shrinkage and the like in transportation but has no effect on the place or time of identification to the contract for sale or delivery or on the passing of the risk of loss.

(3)   Unless otherwise agreed where the contract provides for payment on or after arrival of the goods the seller must before payment allow such preliminary inspection as is feasible; but if the goods are lost delivery of the documents and payment are due when the goods should have arrived.

Official Comment

Prior Uniform Statutory Provision: None.

Purposes:

This section deals with two variations of the C.I.F. contract which have evolved in mercantile practice but are entirely consistent with the basic C.I.F. pattern. Subsections (1) and (2), which provide for a shift to the seller of the risk of quality and weight deterioration during shipment, are designed to conform the law to the best mercantile practice and usage without changing the legal consequences of the C.I.F. or C. & F. term as to the passing of marine risks to the buyer at the point of shipment. Subsection (3) provides that where under the contract documents are to be presented for payment after arrival of the goods, this amounts merely to a postponement of the payment under the C.I.F. contract and is not to be confused with the "no arrival, no sale" contract. If the goods are lost, delivery of the documents and payment against them are due when the goods should have arrived. The clause for payment on or after arrival is not to be construed as such a condition precedent to payment that if the goods are lost in transit the buyer need never pay and the seller must bear the loss.

Cross Reference:

Section 2–324.

Definitional Cross References:

"Agreement". Section 1–201.

"Contract". Section 1–201.

"Delivery". Section 1–201.

"Goods". Section 2–105.

"Seller". Section 2–103.

"Term". Section 1–201.

§ 2–322.   Delivery "Ex-Ship".

(1)   Unless otherwise agreed a term for delivery of goods "ex-ship" (which means from the carrying vessel) or in equivalent language is not restricted to a particular ship and requires delivery from a ship which has reached a place at the named port of destination where goods of the kind are usually discharged.

(2)   Under such a term unless otherwise agreed

(a)   the seller must discharge all liens arising out of the carriage and furnish the buyer with a direction which puts the carrier under a duty to deliver the goods; and

(b)   the risk of loss does not pass to the buyer until the goods leave the ship's tackle or are otherwise properly unloaded.

Official Comment

Prior Uniform Statutory Provision: None.

Purposes:

1.   The delivery term, "ex-ship", as between seller and buyer, is the reverse of the f.a.s. term covered.

2.   Delivery need not be made from any particular vessel under a clause calling for delivery "ex-ship", even though a vessel on which shipment is to be made originally is named in the contract, unless the agreement by appropriate language, restricts the clause to delivery from a named vessel.

3.   The appropriate place and manner of unloading at the port of destination depend upon the nature of the goods and the facilities and usages of the port.

4.   A contract fixing a price "ex-ship" with payment "cash against documents" calls only for such documents as are appropriate to the contract. Tender of a delivery order and of a receipt for the freight after the arrival of the carrying vessel is adequate. The seller is not required to tender a bill of lading as a document of title nor is he required to insure the goods for the buyer's benefit, as the goods are not at the buyer's risk during the voyage.

Cross Reference:

Point 1: Section 2–319(2).

Definitional Cross References:

"Buyer". Section 2–103.
"Goods". Section 2–105.
"Seller". Section 2–103.
"Term". Section 1–201.

§ 2–323.   Form of Bill of Lading Required in Overseas Shipment; "Overseas".

(1)   Where the contract contemplates overseas shipment and contains a term C.I.F. or C. & F. or F.O.B. vessel, the seller unless otherwise agreed must obtain a negotiable bill of lading stating that the goods have been loaded in board or, in the case of a term C.I.F. or C. & F., received for shipment.

(2)   Where in a case within subsection (1) a tangible bill of lading has been issued in a set of parts, unless otherwise agreed if the documents are not to be sent from abroad the buyer may demand tender of the full set; otherwise only one part of the bill of lading need be tendered. Even if the agreement expressly requires a full set

(a)   due tender of a single part is acceptable within the provisions of this Article on cure of improper delivery (subsection (1) of Section 2–508); and

(b)   even though the full set is demanded, if the documents are sent from abroad the person tendering an incomplete set may nevertheless require payment upon furnishing an indemnity which the buyer in good faith deems adequate.

(3)   A shipment by water or by air or a contract contemplating such shipment is "overseas" insofar as by usage of trade or agreement it is subject to the commercial, financing or shipping practices characteristic of international deep water commerce.

As amended in 2003.

Official Comment

Prior Uniform Statutory Provision: None.

Purposes:

1.   Subsection (1) follows the "American" rule that a regular bill of lading indicating delivery of the goods at the dock for shipment is sufficient, except under a term "F.O.B. vessel." See Section 2–319 and comment thereto.

2.   Subsection (2) deals with the problem of bills of lading covering deep water shipments, issued not as a single bill of lading but in a set of parts, each part referring to the other parts and the entire set constituting in commercial practice and at law a single bill of lading. Commercial practice in international commerce is to accept and pay against presentation of the first part of a set if the part is sent from overseas even though the contract of the buyer requires presentation of a full set of bills of lading provided adequate indemnity for the missing parts is forthcoming. In accord with the amendment to Section 7–304, bills of lading in a set are limited to tangible bills.

This subsection codifies that practice as between buyer and seller. Article 5 (Section 5–113)* authorizes banks presenting drafts under letters of credit to give indemnities against the missing parts, and this subsection means that the buyer must accept and act on such indemnities if he in good faith deems them adequate. But neither this subsection nor Article 5 decides whether a bank which has issued a letter of credit is similarly bound. The issuing bank's obligation under a letter of credit is independent and depends on its own terms. See Article 5.

Cross References:

Sections 2–508(2), 5–113.*

Definitional Cross References:

"Bill of lading". Section 1–201.
"Buyer". Section 2–103.
"Contract". Section 1–201.
"Delivery". Section 1–201.
"Financing agency". Section 2–104.
"Person". Section 1–201.
"Seller". Section 2–103.
"Send". Section 1–201.
"Term". Section 1–201.

As amended in 2003.

§ 2–324.   "No Arrival, No Sale" Term.

Under a term "no arrival, no sale" or terms of like meaning, unless otherwise agreed,

(a)   the seller must properly ship conforming goods and if they arrive by any means he must tender them on arrival but he assumes no obligation that the goods will arrive unless he has caused the non-arrival; and

(b)   where without fault of the seller the goods are in part lost or have so deteriorated as no longer to conform to the contract or arrive after the contract time, the buyer may proceed as if there had been casualty to identified goods (Section 2–613).

Official Comment

Prior Uniform Statutory Provision: None.

Purposes:

1.   The "no arrival, no sale" term in a "destination" overseas contract leaves risk of loss on the seller but gives him an exemption from liability for non-delivery. Both the nature of the case and the duty of good faith require that the seller must not interfere with the arrival of the goods in any way. If the circumstances impose

---

*   *Referring to unrevised Article 5.*

upon him the responsibility for making or arranging the shipment, he must have a shipment made despite the exemption clause. Further, the shipment made must be a conforming one, for the exemption under a "no arrival, no sale" term applies only to the hazards of transportation and the goods must be proper in all other respects.

The reason of this section is that where the seller is reselling goods bought by him as shipped by another and this fact is known to the buyer, so that the seller is not under any obligation to make the shipment himself, the seller is entitled under the "no arrival, no sale" clause to exemption from payment of damages for non-delivery if the goods do not arrive or if the goods which actually arrive are non-conforming. This does not extend to sellers who arrange shipment by their own agents, in which case the clause is limited to casualty due to marine hazards. But sellers who make known that they are contracting only with respect to what will be delivered to them by parties over whom they assume no control are entitled to the full quantum of the exemption.

2. The provisions of this Article on identification must be read together with the present section in order to bring the exemption into application. Until there is some designation of the goods in a particular shipment or on a particular ship as being those to which the contract refers there can be no application of an exemption for their non-arrival.

3. The seller's duty to tender the agreed or declared goods if they do arrive is not impaired because of their delay in arrival or by their arrival after transshipment.

4. The phrase "to arrive" is often employed in the same sense as "no arrival, no sale" and may then be given the same effect. But a "to arrive" term, added to a C.I.F. or C. & F. contract, does not have the full meaning given by this section to "no arrival, no sale". Such a "to arrive" term is usually intended to operate only to the extent that the risks are not covered by the agreed insurance and the loss or casualty is due to such uncovered hazards. In some instances the "to arrive" term may be regarded as a time of payment term, or, in the case of the reselling seller discussed in point 1 above, as negating responsibility for conformity of the goods, if they arrive, to any description which was based on his good faith belief of the quality. Whether this is the intention of the parties is a question of fact based on all the circumstances surrounding the resale and in case of ambiguity the rules of Sections 2–316 and 2–317 apply to preclude dishonor.

5. Paragraph (b) applies where goods arrive impaired by damage or partial loss during transportation and makes the policy of this Article on casualty to identified goods applicable to such a situation. For the term cannot be regarded as intending to give the seller an unforeseen profit through casualty; it is intended only to protect him from loss due to causes beyond his control.

Cross References:

Point 1: Section 1–203.*
Point 2: Section 2–501(a) and (c).
Point 5: Section 2–613.

Definitional Cross References:

"Buyer". Section 2–103.
"Conforming". Section 2–106.
"Contract". Section 1–201.
"Fault". Section 1–201.
"Goods". Section 2–105.
"Sale". Section 2–106.
"Seller". Section 2–103.
"Term". Section 1–201.

§ 2–325. "Letter of Credit" Term; "Confirmed Credit".

(1) Failure of the buyer seasonably to furnish an agreed letter of credit is a breach of the contract for sale.

---

* *Referring to unrevised Article 1 (Appendix A).*

(2)   The delivery to seller of a proper letter of credit suspends the buyer's obligation to pay. If the letter of credit is dishonored, the seller may on seasonable notification to the buyer require payment directly from him.

(3)   Unless otherwise agreed the term "letter of credit" or "banker's credit" in a contract for sale means an irrevocable credit issued by a financing agency of good repute and, where the shipment is overseas, of good international repute. The term "confirmed credit" means that the credit must also carry the direct obligation of such an agency which does business in the seller's financial market.

Official Comment

Prior Uniform Statutory Provision: None.

Purposes: To express the established commercial and banking understanding as to the meaning and effects of terms calling for "letters of credit" or "confirmed credit":

1.   Subsection (2) follows the general policy of this Article and Article 3 (Section 3–802)* on conditional payment, under which payment by check or other short-term instrument is not ordinarily final as between the parties if the recipient duly presents the instrument and honor is refused. Thus the furnishing of a letter of credit does not substitute the financing agency's obligation for the buyer's, but the seller must first give the buyer reasonable notice of his intention to demand direct payment from him.

2.   Subsection (3) requires that the credit be irrevocable and be a prime credit as determined by the standing of the issuer. It is not necessary, unless otherwise agreed, that the credit be a negotiation credit; the seller can finance himself by an assignment of the proceeds under Section 5–116(2).**

3.   The definition of "confirmed credit" is drawn on the supposition that the credit is issued by a bank which is not doing direct business in the seller's financial market; there is no intention to require the obligation of two banks both local to the seller.

Cross References:

Sections 2–403, 2–511(3) and 3–802* and Article 5.

Definitional Cross References:

"Buyer". Section 2–103.
"Contract for sale". Section 2–106.
"Draft". Section 3–104.
"Financing agency". Section 2–104.
"Notifies". Section 1–201.***
"Overseas". Section 2–323.
"Purchaser". Section 1–201.
"Seasonably". Section 1–204.***
"Seller". Section 2–103.
"Term". Section 1–201.

§ 2–326.   Sale on Approval and Sale or Return; Rights of Creditors.

(1)   Unless otherwise agreed, if delivered goods may be returned by the buyer even though they conform to the contract, the transaction is

(a)   a "sale on approval" if the goods are delivered primarily for use, and

(b)   a "sale or return" if the goods are delivered primarily for resale.

(2)   Goods held on approval are not subject to the claims of the buyer's creditors until acceptance; goods held on sale or return are subject to such claims while in the buyer's possession.

---

*   *Referring to unrevised Article 3 (Appendix B).*
**   *Referring to unrevised Article 5.*
*** *Referring to unrevised Article 1 (Appendix A).*

100

(3)   Any "or return" term of a contract for sale is to be treated as a separate contract for sale within the statute of frauds section of this Article (Section 2–201) and as contradicting the sale aspect of the contract within the provisions of this Article on parol or extrinsic evidence (Section 2–202).

As amended in 1999.

Official Comment

Prior Uniform Statutory Provision: Section 19(3), Uniform Sales Act.

Changes: Completely rewritten in this and the succeeding section.

Purposes of Changes: To make it clear that:

1.   Both a "sale on approval" and a "sale or return" should be distinguished from other types of transactions with which they frequently have been confused. A "sale on approval," sometimes also called a sale "on trial" or "on satisfaction," deals with a contract under which the seller undertakes a risk in order to satisfy its prospective buyer with the appearance or performance of the goods that are sold. The goods are delivered to the proposed purchaser but they remain the property of the seller until the buyer accepts them. The price has already been agreed. The buyer's willingness to receive and test the goods is the consideration for the seller's engagement to deliver and sell. A "sale or return," on the other hand, typically is a sale to a merchant whose unwillingness to buy is overcome by the seller's engagement to take back the goods (or any commercial unit of goods) in lieu of payment if they fail to be resold. A sale or return is a present sale of goods which may be undone at the buyer's option. Accordingly, subsection (2) provides that goods delivered on approval are not subject to the prospective buyer's creditors until acceptance, and goods delivered in a sale or return are subject to the buyer's creditors while in the buyer's possession.

These two transactions are so strongly delineated in practice and in general understanding that every presumption runs against a delivery to a consumer being a "sale or return" and against a delivery to a merchant for resale being a "sale on approval."

2.   The right to return goods for failure to conform to the contract of sale does not make the transaction a "sale on approval" or "sale or return" and has nothing to do with this section or Section 2–327. This section is not concerned with remedies for breach of contract. It deals instead with a power given by the contract to turn back the goods even though they are wholly as warranted. This section nevertheless presupposes that a contract for sale is contemplated by the parties, although that contract may be of the particular character that this section addresses (i.e., a sale on approval or a sale or return).

If a buyer's obligation as a buyer is conditioned not on its personal approval but on the article's passing a described objective test, the risk of loss by casualty pending the test is properly the seller's and proper return is at its expense. On the point of "satisfaction" as meaning "reasonable satisfaction" when an industrial machine is involved, this Article takes no position.

3.   Subsection (3) resolves a conflict in the pre-UCC case law by recognizing that an "or return" provision is so definitely at odds with any ordinary contract for sale of goods that if a written agreement is involved the "or return" term must be contained in a written memorandum. The "or return" aspect of a sales contract must be treated as a separate contract under the Statute of Frauds section and as contradicting the sale insofar as questions of parol or extrinsic evidence are concerned.

4.   Certain true consignment transactions were dealt with in former Sections 2–326(3) and 9–114. These provisions have been deleted and have been replaced by new provisions in Article 9. See, e.g., Sections 9–109(a)(4); 9–103(d); 9–319.

Cross References:

Point 2: Article 9.
Point 3: Sections 2–201 and 2–202.

Definitional Cross References:

"Between merchants". Section 2–104.
"Buyer". Section 2–103.
"Conform". Section 2–106.
"Contract for sale". Section 2–106.

"Creditor". Section 1–201.
"Goods". Section 2–105.
"Sale". Section 2–106.
"Seller". Section 2–103.

As amended in 1999 and 2000.

§ 2–327.   Special Incidents of Sale on Approval and Sale or Return.

(1)   Under a sale on approval unless otherwise agreed

(a)   although the goods are identified to the contract the risk of loss and the title do not pass to the buyer until acceptance; and

(b)   use of the goods consistent with the purpose of trial is not acceptance but failure seasonally to notify the seller of election to return the goods is acceptance, and if the goods conform to the contract acceptance of any part is acceptance of the whole; and

(c)   after due notification of election to return, the return is at the seller's risk and expense but a merchant buyer must follow any reasonable instructions.

(2)   Under a sale or return unless otherwise agreed

(a)   the option to return extends to the whole or any commercial unit of the goods while in substantially their original condition, but must be exercised seasonably; and

(b)   the return is at the buyer's risk and expense.

Official Comment

Prior Uniform Statutory Provision: Section 19(3), Uniform Sales Act.

Changes: Completely rewritten in preceding and this section.

Purposes of Changes: To make it clear that:

1.   In the case of a sale on approval:

If all of the goods involved conform to the contract, the buyer's acceptance of part of the goods constitutes acceptance of the whole. Acceptance of part falls outside the normal intent of the parties in the "on approval" situation and the policy of this Article allowing partial acceptance of a defective delivery has no application here. A case where a buyer takes home two dresses to select one commonly involves two distinct contracts; if not, it is covered by the words "unless otherwise agreed".

2.   In the case of a sale or return, the return of any unsold unit merely because it is unsold is the normal intent of the "sale or return" provision, and therefore the right to return for this reason alone is independent of any other action under the contract which would turn on wholly different considerations. On the other hand, where the return of goods is for breach, including return of items resold by the buyer and returned by the ultimate purchasers because of defects, the return procedure is governed not by the present section but by the provisions on the effects and revocation of acceptance.

3.   In the case of a sale on approval the risk rests on the seller until acceptance of the goods by the buyer, while in a sale or return the risk remains throughout on the buyer.

4.   Notice of election to return given by the buyer in a sale on approval is sufficient to relieve him of any further liability. Actual return by the buyer to the seller is required in the case of a sale or return contract. What constitutes due "giving" of notice, as required in "on approval" sales, is governed by the provisions on good faith and notice. "Seasonable" is used here as defined in Section 1–204.* Nevertheless, the provisions of both this Article and of the contract on this point must be read with commercial reason and with full attention to good faith.

Cross References:

Point 1: Sections 2–501, 2–601 and 2–603.

---

*   *Referring to unrevised Article 1 (Appendix A).*

Point 2: Sections 2–607 and 2–608.

Point 4: Sections 1–201 and 1–204.*

Definitional Cross References:

"Agreed". Section 1–201.

"Buyer". Section 2–103.

"Commercial unit". Section 2–105.

"Conform". Section 2–106.

"Contract". Section 1–201.

"Goods". Section 2–105.

"Merchant". Section 2–104.

"Notifies". Section 1–201.*

"Notification". Section 1–201.*

"Sale on approval". Section 2–326.

"Sale or return". Section 2–326.

"Seasonably". Section 1–204.*

"Seller". Section 2–103.

§ 2–328.   Sale by Auction.

(1)   In a sale by auction if goods are put up in lots each lot is the subject of a separate sale.

(2)   A sale by auction is complete when the auctioneer so announces by the fall of the hammer or in other customary manner. Where a bid is made while the hammer is falling in acceptance of a prior bid the auctioneer may in his discretion reopen the bidding or declare the goods sold under the bid on which the hammer was falling.

(3)   Such a sale is with reserve unless the goods are in explicit terms put up without reserve. In an auction with reserve the auctioneer may withdraw the goods at any time until he announces completion of the sale. In an auction without reserve, after the auctioneer calls for bids on an article or lot, that article or lot cannot be withdrawn unless no bid is made within a reasonable time. In either case a bidder may retract his bid until the auctioneer's announcement of completion of the sale, but a bidder's retraction does not revive any previous bid.

(4)   If the auctioneer knowingly receives a bid on the seller's behalf or the seller makes or procures such a bid, and notice has not been given that liberty for such bidding is reserved, the buyer may at his option avoid the sale or take the goods at the price of the last good faith bid prior to the completion of the sale. This subsection shall not apply to any bid at a forced sale.

Official Comment

Prior Uniform Statutory Provision: Section 21, Uniform Sales Act.

Changes: Completely rewritten.

Purposes of Changes: To make it clear that:

1.   The auctioneer may in his discretion either reopen the bidding or close the sale on the bid on which the hammer was falling when a bid is made at that moment. The recognition of a bid of this kind by the auctioneer in his discretion does not mean a closing in favor of such a bidder, but only that the bid has been accepted as a continuation of the bidding. If recognized, such a bid discharges the bid on which the hammer was falling when it was made.

2.   An auction "with reserve" is the normal procedure. The crucial point, however, for determining the nature of an auction is the "putting up" of the goods. This Article accepts the view that the goods may be withdrawn before they are actually "put up," regardless of whether the auction is advertised as one without reserve, without liability on the part of the auction announcer to persons who are present. This is subject to any peculiar facts which might bring the case within the "firm offer" principle of this Article, but an offer to persons generally would

---

*   *Referring to unrevised Article 1 (Appendix A).*

require unmistakable language in order to fall within that section. The prior announcement of the nature of the auction either as with reserve or without reserve will, however, enter as an "explicit term" in the "putting up" of the goods and conduct thereafter must be governed accordingly. The present section continues the prior rule permitting withdrawal of bids in auctions both with and without reserve; and the rule is made explicit that the retraction of a bid does not revive a prior bid.

Cross Reference:

> Point 2: Section 2–205.

Definitional Cross References:

> "Buyer". Section 2–103.
> "Good faith". Section 1–201.
> "Goods". Section 2–105.
> "Lot". Section 2–105.
> "Notice". Section 1–201.*
> "Sale". Section 2–106.
> "Seller". Section 2–103.

PART 4

TITLE, CREDITORS AND GOOD FAITH PURCHASERS

§ 2–401. Passing of Title; Reservation for Security; Limited Application of This Section.

Each provision of this Article with regard to the rights, obligations and remedies of the seller, the buyer, purchasers or other third parties applies irrespective of title to the goods except where the provision refers to such title. Insofar as situations are not covered by the other provisions of this Article and matters concerning title become material the following rules apply:

(1) Title to goods cannot pass under a contract for sale prior to their identification to the contract (Section 2–501), and unless otherwise explicitly agreed the buyer acquires by their identification a special property as limited by this Act. Any retention or reservation by the seller of the title (property) in goods shipped or delivered to the buyer is limited in effect to a reservation of a security interest. Subject to these provisions and to the provisions of the Article on Secured Transactions (Article 9), title to goods passes from the seller to the buyer in any manner and on any conditions explicitly agreed on by the parties.

(2) Unless otherwise explicitly agreed title passes to the buyer at the time and place at which the seller completes his performance with reference to the physical delivery of the goods, despite any reservation of a security interest and even though a document of title is to be delivered at a different time or place; and in particular and despite any reservation of a security interest by the bill of lading

    (a) if the contract requires or authorizes the seller to send the goods to the buyer but does not require him to deliver them at destination, title passes to the buyer at the time and place of shipment; but

    (b) if the contract requires delivery at destination, title passes on tender there.

(3) Unless otherwise explicitly agreed where delivery is to be made without moving the goods,

    (a) if the seller is to deliver a tangible document of title, title passes at the time when and the place where he delivers such documents and if the seller is to deliver an electronic document of title, title passes when the seller delivers the document; or

    (b) if the goods are at the time of contracting already identified and no documents of title are to be delivered, title passes at the time and place of contracting.

---

* *Referring to unrevised Article 1 (Appendix A).*

(4)   A rejection or other refusal by the buyer to receive or retain the goods, whether or not justified, or a justified revocation of acceptance revests title to the goods in the seller. Such revesting occurs by operation of law and is not a "sale".

As amended in 2003.

Official Comment

Prior Uniform Statutory Provision: See generally, Sections 17, 18, 19 and 20, Uniform Sales Act.

Purposes: To make it clear that:

1.   This Article deals with the issues between seller and buyer in terms of step by step performance or non-performance under the contract for sale and not in terms of whether or not "title" to the goods has passed. That the rules of this section in no way alter the rights of either the buyer, seller or third parties declared elsewhere in the Article is made clear by the preamble of this section. This section, however, in no way intends to indicate which line of interpretation should be followed in cases where the applicability of "public" regulation depends upon a "sale" or upon location of "title" without further definition. The basic policy of this Article that known purpose and reason should govern interpretation cannot extend beyond the scope of its own provisions. It is therefore necessary to state what a "sale" is and when title passes under this Article in case the courts deem any public regulation to incorporate the defined term of the "private" law.

2.   "Future" goods cannot be the subject of a present sale. Before title can pass the goods must be identified in the manner set forth in Section 2–501. The parties, however, have full liberty to arrange by specific terms for the passing of title to goods which are existing.

3.   The "special property" of the buyer in goods identified to the contract is excluded from the definition of "security interest"; its incidents are defined in provisions of this Article such as those on the rights of the seller's creditors, on good faith purchase, on the buyer's right to goods on the seller's insolvency, and on the buyer's right to specific performance or replevin.

4.   The factual situations in subsections (2) and (3) upon which passage of title turn actually base the test upon the time when the seller has finally committed himself in regard to specific goods. Thus in a "shipment" contract he commits himself by the act of making the shipment. If shipment is not contemplated subsection (3) turns on the seller's final commitment, i.e. the delivery of documents or the making of the contract. As to delivery of an electronic document of title, see definition of delivery in Article 1, Section 1–201. This Article does not state a rule as to the place of title passage as to goods covered by an electronic document of title.

Cross References:

Point 2: Sections 2–102, 2–501 and 2–502.
Point 3: Sections 1–201, 2–402, 2–403, 2–502 and 2–716.

Definitional Cross References:

"Agreement". Section 1–201.
"Bill of lading". Section 1–201.
"Buyer". Section 2–103.
"Contract". Section 1–201.
"Contract for sale". Section 2–106.
"Delivery". Section 1–201.
"Document of title". Section 1–201.
"Good faith". Section 2–103.
"Goods". Section 2–105.
"Party". Section 1–201.
"Purchaser". Section 1–201.
"Receipt" of goods. Section 2–103.
"Remedy". Section 1–201.
"Rights". Section 1–201.
"Sale". Section 2–106.
"Security interest". Section 1–201.
"Seller". Section 2–103.

"Send". Section 1–201.

As amended in 2003.

§ 2–402.   Rights of Seller's Creditors Against Sold Goods.

(1)   Except as provided in subsections (2) and (3), rights of unsecured creditors of the seller with respect to goods which have been identified to a contract for sale are subject to the buyer's rights to recover the goods under this Article (Sections 2–502 and 2–716).

(2)   A creditor of the seller may treat a sale or an identification of goods to a contract for sale as void if as against him a retention of possession by the seller is fraudulent under any rule of law of the state where the goods are situated, except that retention of possession in good faith and current course of trade by a merchant-seller for a commercially reasonable time after a sale or identification is not fraudulent.

(3)   Nothing in this Article shall be deemed to impair the rights of creditors of the seller

(a)   under the provisions of the Article on Secured Transactions (Article 9); or

(b)   where identification to the contract or delivery is made not in current course of trade but in satisfaction of or as security for a pre-existing claim for money, security or the like and is made under circumstances which under any rule of law of the state where the goods are situated would apart from this Article constitute the transaction a fraudulent transfer or voidable preference.

Official Comment

Prior Uniform Statutory Provision: Subsection (2)—Section 26, Uniform Sales Act; Subsections (1) and (3)—none.

Changes: Rephrased.

Purposes of Changes and New Matter: To avoid confusion on ordinary issues between current sellers and buyers and issues in the field of preference and hindrance by making it clear that:

1.   Local law on questions of hindrance of creditors by the seller's retention of possession of the goods are outside the scope of this Article, but retention of possession in the current course of trade is legitimate. Transactions which fall within the law's policy against improper preferences are reserved from the protection of this Article.

2.   The retention of possession of the goods by a merchant seller for a commercially reasonable time after a sale or identification in current course is exempted from attack as fraudulent. Similarly, the provisions of subsection (3) have no application to identification or delivery made in the current course of trade, as measured against general commercial understanding of what a "current" transaction is.

Definitional Cross References:

"Contract for sale". Section 2–106.
"Creditor". Section 1–201.
"Good faith". Section 2–103.
"Goods". Section 2–105.
"Merchant". Section 2–104.
"Money". Section 1–201.
"Reasonable time". Section 1–204.*
"Rights". Section 1–201.
"Sale". Section 2–106.
"Seller". Section 2–103.

§ 2–403.   Power to Transfer; Good Faith Purchase of Goods; "Entrusting".

(1)   A purchaser of goods acquires all title which his transferor had or had power to transfer except that a purchaser of a limited interest acquires rights only to the extent of the interest purchased. A person

---

*   *Referring to unrevised Article 1 (Appendix A).*

with voidable title has power to transfer a good title to a good faith purchaser for value. When goods have been delivered under a transaction of purchase the purchaser has such power even though

(a)   the transferor was deceived as to the identity of the purchaser, or

(b)   the delivery was in exchange for a check which is later dishonored, or

(c)   it was agreed that the transaction was to be a "cash sale", or

(d)   the delivery was procured through fraud punishable as larcenous under the criminal law.

(2)   Any entrusting of possession of goods to a merchant who deals in goods of that kind gives him power to transfer all rights of the entruster to a buyer in ordinary course of business.

(3)   "Entrusting" includes any delivery and any acquiescence in retention of possession regardless of any condition expressed between the parties to the delivery or acquiescence and regardless of whether the procurement of the entrusting or the possessor's disposition of the goods have been such as to be larcenous under the criminal law.

[Publisher's Editorial Note: If a state adopts the repealer of Article 6—Bulk Transfers (Alternative A), subsec. (4) should read as follows:]

(4)   The rights of other purchasers of goods and of lien creditors are governed by the Articles on Secured Transactions (Article 9) and Documents of Title (Article 7).

[Publisher's Editorial Note: If a state adopts Revised Article 6—Bulk Sales (Alternative B), subsec. (4) should read as follows:]

(4)   The rights of other purchasers of goods and of lien creditors are governed by the Articles on Secured Transactions (Article 9), Bulk Sales (Article 6) and Documents of Title (Article 7).

As amended in 1988.

For material relating to the changes made in text in 1988, see section 3 of Alternative A (Repealer of Article 6—Bulk Transfers) and Conforming Amendment to Section 2–403 following end of Alternative B (Revised Article 6—Bulk Sales).

Official Comment

Prior Uniform Statutory Provision: Sections 20(4), 23, 24, 25, Uniform Sales Act; Section 9, especially 9(2), Uniform Trust Receipts Act; Section 9, Uniform Conditional Sales Act.

Changes: Consolidated and rewritten.

Purposes of Changes: To gather together a series of prior uniform statutory provisions and the case-law thereunder and to state a unified and simplified policy on good faith purchase of goods.

1.   The basic policy of our law allowing transfer of such title as the transferor has is generally continued and expanded under subsection (1). In this respect the provisions of the section are applicable to a person taking by any form of "purchase" as defined by this Act. Moreover the policy of this Act expressly providing for the application of supplementary general principles of law to sales transactions wherever appropriate joins with the present section to continue unimpaired all rights acquired under the law of agency or of apparent agency or ownership or other estoppel, whether based on statutory provisions or on case law principles. The section also leaves unimpaired the powers given to selling factors under the earlier Factors Acts. In addition subsection (1) provides specifically for the protection of the good faith purchaser for value in a number of specific situations which have been troublesome under prior law.

On the other hand, the contract of purchase is of course limited by its own terms as in a case of pledge for a limited amount or of sale of a fractional interest in goods.

2.   The many particular situations in which a buyer in ordinary course of business from a dealer has been protected against reservation of property or other hidden interest are gathered by subsections (2)–(4) into a single principle protecting persons who buy in ordinary course out of inventory. Consignors have no reason to complain, nor have lenders who hold a security interest in the inventory, since the very purpose of goods in inventory is to be turned into cash by sale.

The principle is extended in subsection (3) to fit with the abolition of the old law of "cash sale" by subsection (1)(c). It is also freed from any technicalities depending on the extended law of larceny; such extension of the concept of theft to include trick, particular types of fraud, and the like is for the purpose of helping conviction of the offender; it has no proper application to the long-standing policy of civil protection of buyers from persons guilty of such trick or fraud. Finally, the policy is extended, in the interest of simplicity and sense, to any entrusting by a bailor; this is in consonance with the explicit provisions of Section 7–205 on the powers of a warehouse who is also in the business of buying and selling fungible goods of the kind he stores. As to entrusting by a secured party, subsection (2) is limited by the more specific provisions of Section 9–320, which deny protection to a person buying farm products from a person engaged in farming operations.

3.   The definition of "buyer in ordinary course of business" (Section 1–201) is effective here and preserves the essence of the healthy limitations engrafted by the case-law on the older statutes. The older loose concept of good faith and wide definition of value combined to create apparent good faith purchasers in many situations in which the result outraged common sense; the court's solution was to protect the original title especially by use of "cash sale" or of over-technical construction of the enabling clauses of the statutes. But such rulings then turned into limitations on the proper protection of buyers in the ordinary market. Section 1–201(9)* cuts down the category of buyer in ordinary course in such fashion as to take care of the results of the cases, but with no price either in confusion or in injustice to proper dealings in the normal market.

4.   Except as provided in subsection (1), the rights of purchasers other than buyers in ordinary course are left to the Articles on Secured Transactions, Documents of Title, and Bulk Sales.

Cross References:

Point 1: Sections 1–103* and 1–201.
Point 2: Sections 1–201, 2–402, 7–205 and 9–320.
Points 3 and 4: Sections 1–102,* 1–201, 2–104, 2–707 and Articles 6, 7 and 9.

Definitional Cross References:

"Buyer in ordinary course of business". Section 1–201.
"Good faith". Sections 1–201 and 2–103.
"Goods". Section 2–105.
"Person". Section 1–201.
"Purchaser". Section 1–201.
"Signed". Section 1–201.
"Term". Section 1–201.
"Value". Section 1–201.*

As amended in 2003.

PART 5

PERFORMANCE

§ 2–501.   Insurable Interest in Goods; Manner of Identification of Goods.

(1)   The buyer obtains a special property and an insurable interest in goods by identification of existing goods as goods to which the contract refers even though the goods so identified are non-conforming and he has an option to return or reject them. Such identification can be made at any time and in any manner explicitly agreed to by the parties. In the absence of explicit agreement identification occurs

(a)   when the contract is made if it is for the sale of goods already existing and identified;

(b)   if the contract is for the sale of future goods other than those described in paragraph (c), when goods are shipped, marked or otherwise designated by the seller as goods to which the contract refers;

---

*   *Referring to unrevised Article 1 (Appendix A).*

(c) when the crops are planted or otherwise become growing crops or the young are conceived if the contract is for the sale of unborn young to be born within twelve months after contracting or for the sale of crops to be harvested within twelve months or the next normal harvest season after contracting whichever is longer.

(2) The seller retains an insurable interest in goods so long as title to or any security interest in the goods remains in him and where the identification is by the seller alone he may until default or insolvency or notification to the buyer that the identification is final substitute other goods for those identified.

(3) Nothing in this section impairs any insurable interest recognized under any other statute or rule of law.

Official Comment

Prior Uniform Statutory Provision: See Sections 17 and 19, Uniform Sales Act.

Purposes:

1. The present section deals with the manner of identifying goods to the contract so that an insurable interest in the buyer and the rights set forth in the next section will accrue. Generally speaking, identification may be made in any manner "explicitly agreed to" by the parties. The rules of paragraphs (a), (b) and (c) apply only in the absence of such "explicit agreement".

2. In the ordinary case identification of particular existing goods as goods to which the contract refers is unambiguous and may occur in one of many ways. It is possible, however, for the identification to be tentative or contingent. In view of the limited effect given to identification by this Article, the general policy is to resolve all doubts in favor of identification.

3. The provision of this section as to "explicit agreement" clarifies the present confusion in the law of sales which has arisen from the fact that under prior uniform legislation all rules of presumption with reference to the passing of title or to appropriation (which in turn depended upon identification) were regarded as subject to the contrary intention of the parties or of the party appropriating. Such uncertainty is reduced to a minimum under this section by requiring "explicit agreement" of the parties before the rules of paragraphs (a), (b) and (c) are displaced—as they would be by a term giving the buyer power to select the goods. An "explicit" agreement, however, need not necessarily be found in the terms used in the particular transaction. Thus, where a usage of the trade has previously been made explicit by reduction to a standard set of "rules and regulations" currently incorporated by reference into the contracts of the parties, a relevant provision of those "rules and regulations" is "explicit" within the meaning of this section.

4. In view of the limited function of identification there is no requirement in this section that the goods be in deliverable state or that all of the seller's duties with respect to the processing of the goods be completed in order that identification occur. For example, despite identification the risk of loss remains on the seller under the risk of loss provisions until completion of his duties as to the goods and all of his remedies remain dependent upon his not defaulting under the contract.

5. Undivided shares in an identified fungible bulk, such as grain in an elevator or oil in a storage tank, can be sold. The mere making of the contract with reference to an undivided share in an identified fungible bulk is enough under subsection (a) to effect an identification if there is no explicit agreement otherwise. The seller's duty, however, to segregate and deliver according to the contract is not affected by such an identification but is controlled by other provisions of this Article.

6. Identification of crops under paragraph (c) is made upon planting only if they are to be harvested within the year or within the next normal harvest season. The phrase "next normal harvest season" fairly includes nursery stock raised for normally quick "harvest," but plainly excludes a "timber" crop to which the concept of a harvest "season" is inapplicable.

Paragraph (c) is also applicable to a crop of wool or the young of animals to be born within twelve months after contracting. The product of a lumbering, mining or fishing operation, though seasonal, is not within the concept of "growing". Identification under a contract for all or part of the output of such an operation can be effected early in the operation.

Cross References:

Point 1: Section 2–502.

Point 4: Sections 2–509, 2–510 and 2–703.
Point 5: Sections 2–105, 2–308, 2–503 and 2–509.
Point 6: Sections 2–105(1), 2–107(1) and 2–402.

Definitional Cross References:

"Agreement". Section 1–201.
"Contract". Section 1–201.
"Contract for sale". Section 2–106.
"Future goods". Section 2–105.
"Goods". Section 2–105.
"Notification". Section 1–201.*
"Party". Section 1–201.
"Sale". Section 2–106.
"Security interest". Section 1–201.
"Seller". Section 2–103.

§ 2–502.   Buyer's Right to Goods on Seller's Repudiation, Failure to Deliver, or Insolvency.

(1)   Subject to subsections (2) and (3) and even though the goods have not been shipped a buyer who has paid a part or all of the price of goods in which he has a special property under the provisions of the immediately preceding section may on making and keeping good a tender of any unpaid portion of their price recover them from the seller if:

(a)   in the case of goods bought for personal, family, or household purposes, the seller repudiates or fails to deliver as required by the contract; or

(b)   in all cases, the seller becomes insolvent within ten days after receipt of the first installment on their price.

(2)   The buyer's right to recover the goods under subsection (1)(a) vests upon acquisition of a special property, even if the seller had not then repudiated or failed to deliver.

(3)   If the identification creating his special property has been made by the buyer he acquires the right to recover the goods only if they conform to the contract for sale.

As amended in 1999.

Official Comment

Prior Uniform Statutory Provision: Compare Sections 17, 18 and 19, Uniform Sales Act.

Purposes:

1.   This section gives an additional right to the buyer as a result of identification of the goods to the contract in the manner provided in Section 2–501. The buyer is given a right to recover the goods, conditioned upon making and keeping good a tender of any unpaid portion of the price, in two limited circumstances. First, the buyer may recover goods bought for personal, family, or household purposes if the seller repudiates the contract or fails to deliver the goods. Second, in any case, the buyer may recover the goods if the seller becomes insolvent within 10 days after the seller receives the first installment on their price. The buyer's right to recover the goods under this section is an exception to the usual rule, under which the disappointed buyer must resort to an action to recover damages.

2.   The question of whether the buyer also acquires a security interest in identified goods and has rights to the goods when insolvency takes place after the ten-day period provided in this section depends upon compliance with the provisions of the Article on Secured Transactions (Article 9).

3.   Under subsection (2), the buyer's right to recover consumer goods under subsection (1)(a) vests upon acquisition of a special property, which occurs upon identification of the goods to the contract. See Section 2–501.

---

*   *Referring to unrevised Article 1 (Appendix A).*

Inasmuch as a secured party normally acquires no greater rights in its collateral that its debtor had or had power to convey, see Section 2–403(1) (first sentence), a buyer who acquires a right to recover under this section will take free of a security interest created by the seller if it attaches to the goods after the goods have been identified to the contract. The buyer will take free, even if the buyer does not buy in ordinary course and even if the security interest is perfected. Of course, to the extent that the buyer pays the price after the security interest attaches, the payments will constitute proceeds of the security interest.

4.   Subsection (3) is included to preclude the possibility of unjust enrichment, which would exist if the buyer were permitted to recover goods even though they were greatly superior in quality or quantity to that called for by the contract for sale.

Cross References:

Point 1: Sections 1–201 and 2–702.
Point 2: Article 9.

Definitional Cross References:

"Buyer". Section 2–103.
"Conform". Section 2–106.
"Contract for sale". Section 2–106.
"Goods". Section 2–105.
"Insolvent". Section 1–201.
"Rights". Section 1–201.
"Seller". Section 2–103.

As amended in 1999.

§ 2–503.   Manner of Seller's Tender of Delivery.

(1)   Tender of delivery requires that the seller put and hold conforming goods at the buyer's disposition and give the buyer any notification reasonably necessary to enable him to take delivery. The manner, time and place for tender are determined by the agreement and this Article, and in particular

(a)   tender must be at a reasonable hour, and if it is of goods they must be kept available for the period reasonably necessary to enable the buyer to take possession; but

(b)   unless otherwise agreed the buyer must furnish facilities reasonably suited to the receipt of the goods.

(2)   Where the case is within the next section respecting shipment tender requires that the seller comply with its provisions.

(3)   Where the seller is required to deliver at a particular destination tender requires that he comply with subsection (1) and also in any appropriate case tender documents as described in subsections (4) and (5) of this section.

(4)   Where goods are in the possession of a bailee and are to be delivered without being moved

(a)   tender requires that the seller either tender a negotiable document of title covering such goods or procure acknowledgment by the bailee of the buyer's right to possession of the goods; but

(b)   tender to the buyer of a non-negotiable document of title or of a record directing the bailee to deliver is sufficient tender unless the buyer seasonably objects, and except as otherwise provided in Article 9 receipt by the bailee of notification of the buyer's rights fixes those rights as against the bailee and all third persons; but risk of loss of the goods and of any failure by the bailee to honor the non-negotiable document of title or to obey the direction remains on the seller until the buyer has had a reasonable time to present the document or direction, and a refusal by the bailee to honor the document or to obey the direction defeats the tender.

(5)   Where the contract requires the seller to deliver documents

    (a)   he must tender all such documents in correct form, except as provided in this Article with respect to bills of lading in a set (subsection (2) of Section 2–323); and

    (b)   tender through customary banking channels is sufficient and dishonor of a draft accompanying or associated with the documents constitutes non-acceptance or rejection.

As amended in 2003.

Official Comment

Prior Uniform Statutory Provision: See Sections 11, 19, 20, 43(3) and (4), 46 and 51, Uniform Sales Act.

Changes: The general policy of the above sections is continued and supplemented but subsection (3) changes the rule of prior section 19(5) as to what constitutes a "destination" contract and subsection (4) incorporates a minor correction as to tender of delivery of goods in the possession of a bailee.

Purposes of Changes:

    1.   The major general rules governing the manner of proper or due tender of delivery are gathered in this section. The term "tender" is used in this Article in two different senses. In one sense it refers to "due tender" which contemplates an offer coupled with a present ability to fulfill all the conditions resting on the tendering party and must be followed by actual performance if the other party shows himself ready to proceed. Unless the context unmistakably indicates otherwise this is the meaning of "tender" in this Article and the occasional addition of the word "due" is only for clarity and emphasis. At other times it is used to refer to an offer of goods or documents under a contract as if in fulfillment of its conditions even though there is a defect when measured against the contract obligation. Used in either sense, however, "tender" connotes such performance by the tendering party as puts the other party in default if he fails to proceed in some manner. These concepts of tender would apply to tender of either tangible or electronic documents of title.

    2.   The seller's general duty to tender and deliver is laid down in Section 2–301 and more particularly in Section 2–507. The seller's right to a receipt if he demands one and receipts are customary is governed by Section 1–205.[*] Subsection (1) of the present section proceeds to set forth two primary requirements of tender: first, that the seller "put and hold conforming goods at the buyer's disposition" and, second, that he "give the buyer any notice reasonably necessary to enable him to take delivery."

    In cases in which payment is due and demanded upon delivery the "buyer's disposition" is qualified by the seller's right to retain control of the goods until payment by the provision of this Article on delivery on condition. However, where the seller is demanding payment on delivery he must first allow the buyer to inspect the goods in order to avoid impairing his tender unless the contract for sale is on C.I.F., C.O.D., cash against documents or similar terms negating the privilege of inspection before payment.

    In the case of contracts involving documents the seller can "put and hold conforming goods at the buyer's disposition" under subsection (1) by tendering documents which give the buyer complete control of the goods under the provisions of Article 7 on due negotiation.

    3.   Under paragraph (a) of subsection (1) usage of the trade and the circumstances of the particular case determine what is a reasonable hour for tender and what constitutes a reasonable period of holding the goods available.

    4.   The buyer must furnish reasonable facilities for the receipt of the goods tendered by the seller under subsection (1), paragraph (b). This obligation of the buyer is no part of the seller's tender.

    5.   For the purposes of subsections (2) and (3) there is omitted from this Article the rule under prior uniform legislation that a term requiring the seller to pay the freight or cost of transportation to the buyer is equivalent to an agreement by the seller to deliver to the buyer or at an agreed destination. This omission is with the specific intention of negating the rule, for under this Article the "shipment" contract is regarded as the normal one and the "destination" contract as the variant type. The seller is not obligated to deliver at a named destination and bear the concurrent risk of loss until arrival, unless he has specifically agreed so to deliver or the commercial understanding of the terms used by the parties contemplates such delivery.

    6.   Paragraph (a) of subsection (4) continues the rule of the prior uniform legislation as to acknowledgment by the bailee. Paragraph (b) of subsection (4) adopts the rule that between the buyer and the seller the risk of loss

---

[*]   *Referring to unrevised Article 1 (Appendix A).*

112

remains on the seller during a period reasonable for securing acknowledgment of the transfer from the bailee, while as against all other parties the buyer's rights are fixed as of the time the bailee receives notice of the transfer.

7.　Under subsection (5) documents are never "required" except where there is an express contract term or it is plainly implicit in the peculiar circumstances of the case or in a usage of trade. Documents may, of course, be "authorized" although not required, but such cases are not within the scope of this subsection. When documents are required, there are three main requirements of this subsection: (1) "All": each required document is essential to a proper tender; (2) "Such": the documents must be the ones actually required by the contract in terms of source and substance; (3) "Correct form": All documents must be in correct form. These requirements apply to both tangible and electronic documents of title. When tender is made through customary banking channels, a draft may accompany or be associated with a document of title. The language has been broadened to allow for drafts to be associated with an electronic document of title. Compare Section 2–104(2) definition of financing agency.

When a prescribed document cannot be procured, a question of fact arises under the provision of this Article on substituted performance as to whether the agreed manner of delivery is actually commercially impracticable and whether the substitute is commercially reasonable.

Cross References:

Point 2: Sections 1–205,* 2–301, 2–310, 2–507 and 2–513 and Article 7.
Point 5: Sections 2–308, 2–310 and 2–509.
Point 7: Section 2–614(1).

Specific matters involving tender are covered in many additional sections of this Article. See Sections 1–205,* 2–301, 2–306 to 2–319, 2–321(3), 2–504, 2–507(2), 2–511(1), 2–513, 2–612 and 2–614.

Definitional Cross References:

"Agreement". Section 1–201.
"Bill of lading". Section 1–201.
"Buyer". Section 2–103.
"Conforming". Section 2–106.
"Contract". Section 1–201.
"Delivery". Section 1–201.
"Dishonor". Section 3–508.**
"Document of title". Section 1–201.
"Draft". Section 3–104.
"Goods". Section 2–105.
"Notification". Section 1–201.*
"Reasonable time". Section 1–204.*
"Receipt" of goods. Section 2–103.
"Rights". Section 1–201.
"Seasonably". Section 1–204.*
"Seller". Section 2–103.
"Written". Section 1–201.

As amended in 2003.

§ 2–504.　Shipment by Seller.

Where the seller is required or authorized to send the goods to the buyer and the contract does not require him to deliver them at a particular destination, then unless otherwise agreed he must

(a)　put the goods in the possession of such a carrier and make such a contract for their transportation as may be reasonable having regard to the nature of the goods and other circumstances of the case; and

---

*　*Referring to unrevised Article 1 (Appendix A).*
**　*Referring to unrevised Article 3 (Appendix B).*

(b)   obtain and promptly deliver or tender in due form any document necessary to enable the buyer to obtain possession of the goods or otherwise required by the agreement or by usage of trade; and

(c)   promptly notify the buyer of the shipment.

Failure to notify the buyer under paragraph (c) or to make a proper contract under paragraph (a) is a ground for rejection only if material delay or loss ensues.

Official Comment

Prior Uniform Statutory Provision: Section 46, Uniform Sales Act.

Changes: Rewritten.

Purposes of Changes: To continue the general policy of the prior uniform statutory provision while incorporating certain modifications with respect to the requirement that the contract with the carrier be made expressly on behalf of the buyer and as to the necessity of giving notice of the shipment to the buyer, so that:

1.   The section is limited to "shipment" contracts as contrasted with "destination" contracts or contracts for delivery at the place where the goods are located. The general principles embodied in this section cover the special cases of F.O.B. point of shipment contracts and C.I.F. and C. & F. contracts. Under the preceding section on manner of tender of delivery, due tender by the seller requires that he comply with the requirements of this section in appropriate cases.

2.   The contract to be made with the carrier under paragraph (a) must conform to all express terms of the agreement, subject to any substitution necessary because of failure of agreed facilities as provided in the later provision on substituted performance. However, under the policies of this Article on good faith and commercial standards and on buyer's rights on improper delivery, the requirements of explicit provisions must be read in terms of their commercial and not their literal meaning. This policy is made express with respect to bills of lading in a set in the provision of this Article on form of bills of lading required in overseas shipment.

3.   In the absence of agreement, the provision of this Article on options and cooperation respecting performance gives the seller the choice of any reasonable carrier, routing and other arrangements. Whether or not the shipment is at the buyer's expense the seller must see to any arrangements, reasonable in the circumstances, such as refrigeration, watering of live stock, protection against cold, the sending along of any necessary help, selection of specialized cars and the like for paragraph (a) is intended to cover all necessary arrangements whether made by contract with the carrier or otherwise. There is, however, a proper relaxation of such requirements if the buyer is himself in a position to make the appropriate arrangements and the seller gives him reasonable notice of the need to do so. It is an improper contract under paragraph (a) for the seller to agree with the carrier to a limited valuation below the true value and thus cut off the buyer's opportunity to recover from the carrier in the event of loss, when the risk of shipment is placed on the buyer by his contract with the seller.

4.   Both the language of paragraph (b) and the nature of the situation it concerns indicate that the requirement that the seller must obtain and deliver promptly to the buyer in due form any document necessary to enable him to obtain possession of the goods is intended to cumulate with the other duties of the seller such as those covered in paragraph (a).

In this connection, in the case of pool car shipments a delivery order furnished by the seller on the pool car consignee, or on the carrier for delivery out of a larger quantity, satisfies the requirements of paragraph (b) unless the contract requires some other form of document.

5.   This Article, unlike the prior uniform statutory provision, makes it the seller's duty to notify the buyer of shipment in all cases. The consequences of his failure to do so, however, are limited in that the buyer may reject on this ground only where material delay or loss ensues.

A standard and acceptable manner of notification in open credit shipments is the sending of an invoice and in the case of documentary contracts is the prompt forwarding of the documents as under paragraph (b) of this section. It is also usual to send on a straight bill of lading but this is not necessary to the required notification. However, should such a document prove necessary or convenient to the buyer, as in the case of loss and claim against the carrier, good faith would require the seller to send it on request.

Frequently the agreement expressly requires prompt notification as by wire or cable. Such a term may be of the essence and the final clause of paragraph (c) does not prevent the parties from making this a particular ground for rejection. To have this vital and irreparable effect upon the seller's duties, such a term should be part of the "dickered" terms written in any "form," or should otherwise be called seasonably and sharply to the seller's attention.

6. Generally, under the final sentence of the section, rejection by the buyer is justified only when the seller's dereliction as to any of the requirements of this section in fact is followed by material delay or damage. It rests on the seller, so far as concerns matters not within the peculiar knowledge of the buyer, to establish that his error has not been followed by events which justify rejection.

Cross References:

Point 1: Sections 2–319, 2–320 and 2–503(2).
Point 2: Sections 1–203,* 2–323(2), 2–601 and 2–614(1).
Point 3: Section 2–311(2).
Point 5: Section 1–203.*

Definitional Cross References:

"Agreement". Section 1–201.
"Buyer". Section 2–103.
"Contract". Section 1–201.
"Delivery". Section 1–201.
"Goods". Section 2–105.
"Notifies". Section 1–201.*
"Seller". Section 2–103.
"Send". Section 1–201.
"Usage of trade". Section 1–205.*

§ 2–505. Seller's Shipment Under Reservation.

(1) Where the seller has identified goods to the contract by or before shipment:

(a) his procurement of a negotiable bill of lading to his own order or otherwise reserves in him a security interest in the goods. His procurement of the bill to the order of a financing agency or of the buyer indicates in addition only the seller's expectation of transferring that interest to the person named.

(b) a non-negotiable bill of lading to himself or his nominee reserves possession of the goods as security but except in a case of conditional delivery (subsection (2) of Section 2–507) a non-negotiable bill of lading naming the buyer as consignee reserves no security interest even though the seller retains possession or control of the bill of lading.

(2) When shipment by the seller with reservation of a security interest is in violation of the contract for sale it constitutes an improper contract for transportation within the preceding section but impairs neither the rights given to the buyer by shipment and identification of the goods to the contract nor the seller's powers as a holder of a negotiable document of title.

As amended in 2003.

Official Comment

Prior Uniform Statutory Provision: Section 20(2), (3), (4), Uniform Sales Act.

Changes: Completely rephrased, the "powers" of the parties in cases of reservation being emphasized primarily rather than the "rightfulness" of reservation.

Purposes of Changes: To continue in general the policy of the prior uniform statutory provision with certain modifications of emphasis and language, so that:

1. The security interest reserved to the seller under subsection (1) is restricted to securing payment or performance by the buyer and the seller is strictly limited in his disposition and control of the goods as against the buyer and third parties. Under this Article, the provision as to the passing of interest expressly applies "despite

---

* *Referring to unrevised Article 1 (Appendix A).*

any reservation of security title" and also provides that the "rights, obligations and remedies" of the parties are not altered by the incidence of title generally. The security interest, therefore, must be regarded as a means given to the seller to enforce his rights against the buyer which is unaffected by and in turn does not affect the location of title generally. The rules set forth in subsection (1) are not to be altered by any apparent "contrary intent" of the parties as to passing of title, since the rights and remedies of the parties to the contract of sale, as defined in this Article, rest on the contract and its performance or breach and not on stereotyped presumptions as to the location of title.

This Article does not attempt to regulate local procedure in regard to the effective maintenance of the seller's security interest when the action is in replevin by the buyer against the carrier.

2.   Every shipment of identified goods under a negotiable bill of lading reserves a security interest in the seller under subsection (1) paragraph (a).

It is frequently convenient for the seller to make the bill of lading to the order of a nominee such as his agent at destination, the financing agency to which he expects to negotiate the document or the bank issuing a credit to him. In many instances, also, the buyer is made the order party. This Article does not deal directly with the question as to whether a bill of lading made out by the seller to the order of a nominee gives the carrier notice of any rights which the nominee may have so as to limit its freedom or obligation to honor the bill of lading in the hands of the seller as the original shipper if the expected negotiation fails. This is dealt with in the Article on Documents of Title (Article 7).

3.   A non-negotiable bill of lading taken to a party other than the buyer under subsection (1) paragraph (b) reserves possession of the goods as security in the seller but if he seeks to withhold the goods improperly the buyer can tender payment and recover them.

4.   In the case of a shipment by non-negotiable bill of lading taken to a buyer, the seller, under subsection (1) retains no security interest or possession as against the buyer and by the shipment he *de facto* loses control as against the carrier except where he rightfully and effectively stops delivery in transit. In cases in which the contract gives the seller the right to payment against delivery, the seller, by making an immediate demand for payment, can show that his delivery is conditional, but this does not prevent the buyer's power to transfer full title to a sub-buyer in ordinary course or other purchaser under Section 2–403.

5.   Under subsection (2) an improper reservation by the seller which would constitute a breach in no way impairs such of the buyer's rights as result from identification of the goods. The security title reserved by the seller under subsection (1) does not protect his retaining possession or control of the document or the goods for the purpose of exacting more than is due him under the contract.

Cross References:

> Point 1: Section 1–201.
> Point 2: Article 7.
> Point 3: Sections 2–501(2) and 2–504.
> Point 4: Sections 2–403, 2–507(2) and 2–705.
> Point 5: Sections 2–310, 2–319(4), 2–320(4), 2–501 and 2–502 and Article 7.

Definitional Cross References:

> "Bill of lading". Section 1–201.
> "Buyer". Section 2–103.
> "Consignee". Section 7–102.
> "Contract". Section 1–201.
> "Contract for sale". Section 2–106.
> "Delivery". Section 1–201.
> "Financing agency". Section 2–104.
> "Goods". Section 2–105.
> "Holder". Section 1–201.
> "Person". Section 1–201.
> "Security interest". Section 1–201.
> "Seller". Section 2–103.

As amended in 2003.

§ 2–506.   Rights of Financing Agency.

(1)   A financing agency by paying or purchasing for value a draft which relates to a shipment of goods acquires to the extent of the payment or purchase and in addition to its own rights under the draft and any document of title securing it any rights of the shipper in the goods including the right to stop delivery and the shipper's right to have the draft honored by the buyer.

(2)   The right to reimbursement of a financing agency which has in good faith honored or purchased the draft under commitment to or authority from the buyer is not impaired by subsequent discovery of defects with reference to any relevant document which was apparently regular.

As amended in 2003.

Official Comment

Prior Uniform Statutory Provision: None.

Purposes:

1.   "Financing agency" is broadly defined in this Article to cover every normal instance in which a party aids or intervenes in the financing of a sales transaction. The term as used in subsection (1) is not in any sense intended as a limitation and covers any other appropriate situation which may arise outside the scope of the definition.

2.   "Paying" as used in subsection (1) is typified by the letter of credit, or "authority to pay" situation in which a banker, by arrangement with the buyer or other consignee, pays on his behalf a draft for the price of the goods. It is immaterial whether the draft is formally drawn on the party paying or his principal, whether it is a sight draft paid in cash or a time draft "paid" in the first instance by acceptance, or whether the payment is viewed as absolute or conditional. All of these cases constitute "payment" under this subsection. Similarly, "purchasing for value" is used to indicate the whole area of financing by the seller's banker, and the principle of subsection (1) is applicable without any niceties of distinction between "purchase," "discount," "advance against collection" or the like. But it is important to notice that the only right to have the draft honored that is acquired is that *against the buyer*; if any right against any one else is claimed it will have to be under some separate obligation of that other person. A letter of credit does not necessarily protect *purchasers* of drafts. See Article 5. And for the relations of the parties to documentary drafts see Part 5 of Article 4.

3.   Subsection (1) is made applicable to payments or advances against a draft which "relates to" a shipment of goods and this has been chosen as a term of maximum breadth. In particular the term is intended to cover the case of a draft against an invoice or against a delivery order. Further, it is unnecessary that there be an explicit assignment of the invoice attached to the draft to bring the transaction within the reason of this subsection.

4.   After shipment, "the rights of the shipper in the goods" are merely security rights and are subject to the buyer's right to force delivery upon tender of the price. The rights acquired by the financing agency are similarly limited and, moreover, if the agency fails to procure any outstanding negotiable document of title, it may find its exercise of these rights hampered or even defeated by the seller's disposition of the document to a third party. This section does not attempt to create any new rights in the financing agency against the carrier which would force the latter to honor a stop order from the agency, a stranger to the shipment, or any new rights against a holder to whom a document of title has been duly negotiated under Article 7.

5.   The deletion of the language "on its face" from subsection (2) is designed to accommodate electronic documents of title without changing the requirement of regularity of the document.

Cross References:

Point 1: Section 2–104(2) and Article 4.
Point 2: Part 5 of Article 4, and Article 5.
Point 4: Sections 2–501 and 2–502(1) and Article 7.

Definitional Cross References:

"Buyer". Section 2–103.
"Document of title". Section 1–201.
"Draft". Section 3–104.
"Financing agency". Section 2–104.

"Good faith". Section 2–103.
"Goods". Section 2–105.
"Honor". Section 1–201.*
"Purchase". Section 1–201.
"Rights". Section 1–201.
"Value". Section 1–201.*

As amended in 2003.

§ 2–507.   Effect of Seller's Tender; Delivery on Condition.

(1)   Tender of delivery is a condition to the buyer's duty to accept the goods and, unless otherwise agreed, to his duty to pay for them. Tender entitles the seller to acceptance of the goods and to payment according to the contract.

(2)   Where payment is due and demanded on the delivery to the buyer of goods or documents of title, his right as against the seller to retain or dispose of them is conditional upon his making the payment due.

Official Comment

Prior Uniform Statutory Provision: See Sections 11, 41, 42 and 69, Uniform Sales Act.

Purposes:

1.   Subsection (1) continues the policies of the prior uniform statutory provisions with respect to tender and delivery by the seller. Under this Article the same rules in these matters are applied to present sales and to contracts for sale. But the provisions of this subsection must be read within the framework of the other sections of this Article which bear upon the question of delivery and payment.

2.   The "unless otherwise agreed" provision of subsection (1) is directed primarily to cases in which payment in advance has been promised or a letter of credit term has been included. Payment "according to the contract" contemplates immediate payment, payment at the end of an agreed credit term, payment by a time acceptance or the like. Under this Act, "contract" means the total obligation in law which results from the parties' agreement including the effect of this Article. In this context, therefore, there must be considered the effect in law of such provisions as those on means and manner of payment and on failure of agreed means and manner of payment.

3.   Subsection (2) deals with the effect of a conditional delivery by the seller and in such a situation makes the buyer's "right as against the seller" conditional upon payment. These words are used as words of limitation to conform with the policy set forth in the bona fide purchase sections of this Article. Should the seller after making such a conditional delivery fail to follow up his rights, the condition is waived. This subsection (2) codifies the cash seller's right of reclamation which is in the nature of a lien. There is no specific time limit for a cash seller to exercise the right of reclamation. However, the right will be defeated by delay causing prejudice to the buyer, waiver, estoppel, or ratification of the buyer's right to retain possession. Common law rules and precedents governing such principles are applicable (Section 1–103). If third parties are involved, Section 2–403(1) protects good faith purchasers. See PEB Commentary No. 1, dated March 10, 1990.

Cross References:

Point 1: Sections 2–310, 2–503, 2–511, 2–601 and 2–711 to 2–713.
Point 2: Sections 1–201, 2–511 and 2–614.
Point 3: Sections 2–401, 2–403, and 2–702(1)(b).

Definitional Cross References:

"Buyer". Section 2–103.
"Contract". Section 1–201.
"Delivery". Section 1–201.
"Document of title". Section 1–201.
"Goods". Section 2–105.

---

*   *Referring to unrevised Article 1 (Appendix A).*

"Rights". Section 1–201.
"Seller". Section 2–103.

As amended in 1990.

§ 2–508. Cure by Seller of Improper Tender or Delivery; Replacement.

(1) Where any tender or delivery by the seller is rejected because non-conforming and the time for performance has not yet expired, the seller may seasonably notify the buyer of his intention to cure and may then within the contract time make a conforming delivery.

(2) Where the buyer rejects a non-conforming tender which the seller had reasonable grounds to believe would be acceptable with or without money allowance the seller may if he seasonably notifies the buyer have a further reasonable time to substitute a conforming tender.

Official Comment

Prior Uniform Statutory Provision: None.

Purposes:

1. Subsection (1) permits a seller who has made a non-conforming tender in any case to make a conforming delivery within the contract time upon seasonable notification to the buyer. It applies even where the seller has taken back the non-conforming goods and refunded the purchase price. He may still make a good tender within the contract period. The closer, however, it is to the contract date, the greater is the necessity for extreme promptness on the seller's part in notifying of his intention to cure, if such notification is to be "seasonable" under this subsection.

The rule of this subsection, moreover, is qualified by its underlying reasons. Thus if, after contracting for June delivery, a buyer later makes known to the seller his need for shipment early in the month and the seller ships accordingly, the "contract time" has been cut down by the supervening modification and the time for cure of tender must be referred to this modified time term.

2. Subsection (2) seeks to avoid injustice to the seller by reason of a surprise rejection by the buyer. However, the seller is not protected unless he had "reasonable grounds to believe" that the tender would be acceptable. Such reasonable grounds can lie in prior course of dealing, course of performance or usage of trade as well as in the particular circumstances surrounding the making of the contract. The seller is charged with commercial knowledge of any factors in a particular sales situation which require him to comply strictly with his obligations under the contract as, for example, strict conformity of documents in an overseas shipment or the sale of precision parts or chemicals for use in manufacture. Further, if the buyer gives notice either implicitly, as by a prior course of dealing involving rigorous inspections, or expressly, as by the deliberate inclusion of a "no replacement" clause in the contract, the seller is to be held to rigid compliance. If the clause appears in a "form" contract evidence that it is out of line with trade usage or the prior course of dealing and was not called to the seller's attention may be sufficient to show that the seller had reasonable grounds to believe that the tender would be acceptable.

3. The words "a further reasonable time to substitute a conforming tender" are intended as words of limitation to protect the buyer. What is a "reasonable time" depends upon the attending circumstances. Compare Section 2–511 on the comparable case of a seller's surprise demand for legal tender.

4. Existing trade usages permitting variations without rejection but with price allowance enter into the agreement itself as contractual limitations of remedy and are not covered by this section.

Cross References:

Point 2: Section 2–302.
Point 3: Section 2–511.
Point 4: Sections 1–205* and 2–721.

Definitional Cross References:

"Buyer". Section 2–103.

---

* *Referring to unrevised Article 1 (Appendix A).*

"Conforming". Section 2–106.
"Contract". Section 1–201.
"Money". Section 1–201.
"Notifies". Section 1–201.*
"Reasonable time". Section 1–204.*
"Seasonably". Section 1–204.*
"Seller". Section 2–103.

§ 2–509.   Risk of Loss in the Absence of Breach.

(1)   Where the contract requires or authorizes the seller to ship the goods by carrier

(a)   if it does not require him to deliver them at a particular destination, the risk of loss passes to the buyer when the goods are duly delivered to the carrier even though the shipment is under reservation (Section 2–505); but

(b)   if it does require him to deliver them at a particular destination and the goods are there duly tendered while in the possession of the carrier, the risk of loss passes to the buyer when the goods are there duly so tendered as to enable the buyer to take delivery.

(2)   Where the goods are held by a bailee to be delivered without being moved, the risk of loss passes to the buyer

(a)   on his receipt of possession or control of a negotiable document of title covering the goods; or

(b)   on acknowledgment by the bailee of the buyer's right to possession of the goods; or

(c)   after his receipt of possession or control of a non-negotiable document of title or other direction to deliver in a record, as provided in subsection (4)(b) of Section 2–503.

(3)   In any case not within subsection (1) or (2), the risk of loss passes to the buyer on his receipt of the goods if the seller is a merchant; otherwise the risk passes to the buyer on tender of delivery.

(4)   The provisions of this section are subject to contrary agreement of the parties and to the provisions of this Article on sale on approval (Section 2–327) and on effect of breach on risk of loss (Section 2–510).

As amended in 2003.

Official Comment

Prior Uniform Statutory Provision: Section 22, Uniform Sales Act.

Changes: Rewritten, subsection (3) of this section modifying prior law.

Purposes of Changes: To make it clear that:

1.   The underlying theory of these sections on risk of loss is the adoption of the contractual approach rather than an arbitrary shifting of the risk with the "property" in the goods. The scope of the present section, therefore, is limited strictly to those cases where there has been no breach by the seller. Where for any reason his delivery or tender fails to conform to the contract, the present section does not apply and the situation is governed by the provisions on effect of breach on risk of loss.

2.   The provisions of subsection (1) apply where the contract "requires or authorizes" shipment of the goods. This language is intended to be construed parallel to comparable language in the section on shipment by seller. In order that the goods be "duly delivered to the carrier" under paragraph (a) a contract must be entered into with the carrier which will satisfy the requirements of the section on shipment by the seller and the delivery must be made under circumstances which will enable the seller to take any further steps necessary to a due tender. The underlying reason of this subsection does not require that the shipment be made after contracting, but where, for example, the seller buys the goods afloat and later diverts the shipment to the buyer, he must identify the goods to the contract before the risk of loss can pass. To transfer the risk it is enough that a proper shipment and a proper identification come to apply to the same goods although, aside from special agreement, the risk will not pass retroactively to the time of shipment in such a case.

---

*   *Referring to unrevised Article 1 (Appendix A).*

3.   Whether the contract involves delivery at the seller's place of business or at the situs of the goods, a merchant seller cannot transfer risk of loss and it remains upon him until actual receipt by the buyer, even though full payment has been made and the buyer has been notified that the goods are at his disposal. Protection is afforded him, in the event of breach by the buyer, under the next section.

The underlying theory of this rule is that a merchant who is to make physical delivery at his own place continues meanwhile to control the goods and can be expected to insure his interest in them. The buyer, on the other hand, has no control of the goods and it is extremely unlikely that he will carry insurance on goods not yet in his possession.

4.   Where the agreement provides for delivery of the goods as between the buyer and seller without removal from the physical possession of a bailee, the provisions on manner of tender of delivery apply on the point of transfer of risk. Due delivery of a negotiable document of title covering the goods or acknowledgment by the bailee that he holds for the buyer completes the "delivery" and passes the risk. See definition of delivery in Article 1, Section 1–201 and the definition of control in Article 7, Section 7–106.

5.   The provisions of this section are made subject by subsection (4) to the "contrary agreement" of the parties. This language is intended as the equivalent of the phrase "unless otherwise agreed" used more frequently throughout this Act. "Contrary" is in no way used as a word of limitation and the buyer and seller are left free to readjust their rights and risks as declared by this section in any manner agreeable to them. Contrary agreement can also be found in the circumstances of the case, a trade usage or practice, or a course of dealing or performance.

Cross References:

Point 1: Section 2–510(1).
Point 2: Sections 2–503 and 2–504.
Point 3: Sections 2–104, 2–503 and 2–510.
Point 4: Section 2–503(4).
Point 5: Section 1–201.

Definitional Cross References:

"Agreement". Section 1–201.
"Buyer". Section 2–103.
"Contract". Section 1–201.
"Delivery". Section 1–201.
"Document of title". Section 1–201.
"Goods". Section 2–105.
"Merchant". Section 2–104.
"Party". Section 1–201.
"Receipt" of goods. Section 2–103.
"Sale on approval". Section 2–326.
"Seller". Section 2–103.

As amended in 2003.

§ 2–510.   Effect of Breach on Risk of Loss.

(1)   Where a tender or delivery of goods so fails to conform to the contract as to give a right of rejection the risk of their loss remains on the seller until cure or acceptance.

(2)   Where the buyer rightfully revokes acceptance he may to the extent of any deficiency in his effective insurance coverage treat the risk of loss as having rested on the seller from the beginning.

(3)   Where the buyer as to conforming goods already identified to the contract for sale repudiates or is otherwise in breach before risk of their loss has passed to him, the seller may to the extent of any deficiency in his effective insurance coverage treat the risk of loss as resting on the buyer for a commercially reasonable time.

Official Comment

Prior Uniform Statutory Provision: None.

Purposes: To make clear that:

1.   Under subsection (1) the seller by his individual action cannot shift the risk of loss to the buyer unless his action conforms with all the conditions resting on him under the contract.

2.   The "cure" of defective tenders contemplated by subsection (1) applies only to those situations in which the seller makes changes in goods already tendered, such as repair, partial substitution, sorting out from an improper mixture and the like since "cure" by repossession and new tender has no effect on the risk of loss of the goods originally tendered. The seller's privilege of cure does not shift the risk, however, until the cure is completed.

Where defective documents are involved a cure of the defect by the seller or a waiver of the defects by the buyer will operate to shift the risk under this section. However, if the goods have been destroyed prior to the cure or the buyer is unaware of their destruction at the time he waives the defect in the documents, the risk of the loss must still be borne by the seller, for the risk shifts only at the time of cure, waiver of documentary defects or acceptance of the goods.

3.   In cases where there has been a breach of the contract, if the one in control of the goods is the aggrieved party, whatever loss or damage may prove to be uncovered by his insurance falls upon the contract breaker under subsections (2) and (3) rather than upon him. The word "effective" as applied to insurance coverage in those subsections is used to meet the case of supervening insolvency of the insurer. The "deficiency" referred to in the text means such deficiency in the insurance coverage as exists without subrogation. This section merely distributes the risk of loss as stated and is not intended to be disturbed by any subrogation of an insurer.

Cross Reference:

Section 2–509.

Definitional Cross References:

"Buyer". Section 2–103.
"Conform". Section 2–106.
"Contract for sale". Section 2–106.
"Goods". Section 2–105.
"Seller". Section 2–103.

§ 2–511.   Tender of Payment by Buyer; Payment by Check.

(1)   Unless otherwise agreed tender of payment is a condition to the seller's duty to tender and complete any delivery.

(2)   Tender of payment is sufficient when made by any means or in any manner current in the ordinary course of business unless the seller demands payment in legal tender and gives any extension of time reasonably necessary to procure it.

(3)   Subject to the provisions of this Act on the effect of an instrument on an obligation (Section 3–310), payment by check is conditional and is defeated as between the parties by dishonor of the check on due presentment.

As amended in 1994.

Official Comment

Prior Uniform Statutory Provision: Section 42, Uniform Sales Act.

Changes: Rewritten by this section and Section 2–507.

Purposes of Changes:

1.   The requirement of payment against delivery in subsection (1) is applicable to non-commercial sales generally and to ordinary sales at retail although it has no application to the great body of commercial contracts which carry credit terms. Subsection (1) applies also to documentary contracts in general and to contracts which look to shipment by the seller but contain no term on time and manner of payment, in which situations the payment may, in proper case, be demanded against delivery of appropriate documents.

In the case of specific transactions such as C.O.D. sales or agreements providing for payment against documents, the provisions of this subsection must be considered in conjunction with the special sections of the

Article dealing with such terms. The provision that tender of payment is a condition to the seller's duty to tender and complete "any delivery" integrates this section with the language and policy of the section on delivery in several lots which call for separate payment. Finally, attention should be directed to the provision on right to adequate assurance of performance which recognizes, even before the time for tender, an obligation on the buyer not to impair the seller's expectation of receiving payment in due course.

2.   Unless there is agreement otherwise the concurrence of the conditions as to tender of payment and tender of delivery requires their performance at a single place or time. This Article determines that place and time by determining in various other sections the place and time for tender of delivery under various circumstances and in particular types of transactions. The sections dealing with time and place of delivery together with the section on right to inspection of goods answer the subsidiary question as to when payment may be demanded before inspection by the buyer.

3.   The essence of the principle involved in subsection (2) is avoidance of commercial surprise at the time of performance. The section on substituted performance covers the peculiar case in which legal tender is not available to the commercial community.

4.   Subsection (3) is concerned with the rights and obligations as between the parties to a sales transaction when payment is made by check. This Article recognizes that the taking of a seemingly solvent party's check is commercially normal and proper and, if due diligence is exercised in collection, is not to be penalized in any way. The conditional character of the payment under this section refers only to the effect of the transaction "as between the parties" thereto and does not purport to cut into the law of "absolute" and "conditional" payment as applied to such other problems as the discharge of sureties or the responsibilities of a drawee bank which is at the same time an agent for collection.

The phrase "by check" includes not only the buyer's own but any check which does not effect a discharge under Article 3 (Section 3–802).* Similarly the reason of this subsection should apply and the same result should be reached where the buyer "pays" by sight draft on a commercial firm which is financing him.

5.   Under subsection (3) payment by check is defeated if it is not honored upon due presentment. This corresponds to the provisions of article on Commercial Paper. (Section 3–802).* But if the seller procures certification of the check instead of cashing it, the buyer is discharged. (Section 3–411).*

6.   Where the instrument offered by the buyer is not a payment but a credit instrument such as a note or a check post-dated by even one day, the seller's acceptance of the instrument insofar as third parties are concerned, amounts to a delivery on credit and his remedies are set forth in the section on buyer's insolvency. As between the buyer and the seller, however, the matter turns on the present subsection and the section on conditional delivery and subsequent dishonor of the instrument gives the seller rights on it as well as for breach of the contract for sale.

Cross References:

Point 1: Sections 2–307, 2–310, 2–320, 2–325, 2–503, 2–513 and 2–609.
Point 2: Sections 2–307, 2–310, 2–319, 2–322, 2–503, 2–504 and 2–513.
Point 3: Section 2–614.
Point 5: Article 3, esp. Sections 3–802* and 3–411.*
Point 6: Sections 2–507, 2–702, and Article 3.

Definitional Cross References:

"Buyer". Section 2–103.
"Check". Section 3–104.
"Dishonor". Section 3–508.*
"Party". Section 1–201.
"Reasonable time". Section 1–204.**
"Seller". Section 2–103.

---

*   *Referring to unrevised Article 3 (Appendix B).*
**   *Referring to unrevised Article 1 (Appendix A).*

§ 2–512.   Payment by Buyer Before Inspection.

(1)   Where the contract requires payment before inspection non-conformity of the goods does not excuse the buyer from so making payment unless

(a)   the non-conformity appears without inspection; or

(b)   despite tender of the required documents the circumstances would justify injunction against honor under this Act (Section 5–109(b)).

(2)   Payment pursuant to subsection (1) does not constitute an acceptance of goods or impair the buyer's right to inspect or any of his remedies.

As amended in 1995.

Official Comment

Prior Uniform Statutory Provision: None, but see Sections 47 and 49, Uniform Sales Act.

Purposes:

1.   Subsection (1) of the present section recognizes that the essence of a contract providing for payment before inspection is the intention of the parties to shift to the buyer the risks which would usually rest upon the seller. The basic nature of the transaction is thus preserved and the buyer is in most cases required to pay first and litigate as to any defects later.

2.   "Inspection" under this section is an inspection in a manner reasonable for detecting defects in goods whose surface appearance is satisfactory.

3.   Clause (a) of this subsection states an exception to the general rule based on common sense and normal commercial practice. The apparent non-conformity referred to is one which is evident in the mere process of taking delivery.

4.   Clause (b) is concerned with contracts for payment against documents and incorporates the general clarification and modification of the case law contained in the section on excuse of a financing agency. Section 5–109(b).

5.   Subsection (2) makes explicit the general policy of the Uniform Sales Act that the payment required before inspection in no way impairs the buyer's remedies or rights in the event of a default by the seller. The remedies preserved to the buyer are all of his remedies, which include as a matter of reason the remedy for total non-delivery after payment in advance.

The provision on performance or acceptance under reservation of rights does not apply to the situations contemplated here in which payment is made in due course under the contract and the buyer need not pay "under protest" or the like in order to preserve his rights as to defects discovered upon inspection.

6.   This section applies to cases in which the contract requires payment before inspection either by the express agreement of the parties or by reason of the effect in law of that contract. The present section must therefore be considered in conjunction with the provision on right to inspection of goods which sets forth the instances in which the buyer is not entitled to inspection before payment.

Cross References:

Point 4: Article 5.
Point 5: Section 1–207.*
Point 6: Section 2–513(3).

Definitional Cross References:

"Buyer". Section 2–103.
"Conform". Section 2–106.
"Contract". Section 1–201.
"Financing agency". Section 2–104.

---

*   *Referring to unrevised Article 1 (Appendix A).*

"Goods". Section 2–105.
"Remedy". Section 1–201.
"Rights". Section 1–201.

§ 2–513.   Buyer's Right to Inspection of Goods.

(1)   Unless otherwise agreed and subject to subsection (3), where goods are tendered or delivered or identified to the contract for sale, the buyer has a right before payment or acceptance to inspect them at any reasonable place and time and in any reasonable manner. When the seller is required or authorized to send the goods to the buyer, the inspection may be after their arrival.

(2)   Expenses of inspection must be borne by the buyer but may be recovered from the seller if the goods do not conform and are rejected.

(3)   Unless otherwise agreed and subject to the provisions of this Article on C.I.F. contracts (subsection (3) of Section 2–321), the buyer is not entitled to inspect the goods before payment of the price when the contract provides

(a)   for delivery "C.O.D." or on other like terms; or

(b)   for payment against documents of title, except where such payment is due only after the goods are to become available for inspection.

(4)   A place or method of inspection fixed by the parties is presumed to be exclusive but unless otherwise expressly agreed it does not postpone identification or shift the place for delivery or for passing the risk of loss. If compliance becomes impossible, inspection shall be as provided in this section unless the place or method fixed was clearly intended as an indispensable condition failure of which avoids the contract.

Official Comment

Prior Uniform Statutory Provisions: Section 47(2), (3), Uniform Sales Act.

Changes: Rewritten, Subsections (2) and (3) being new.

Purposes of Changes and New Matter: To correspond in substance with the prior uniform statutory provision and to incorporate in addition some of the results of the better case law so that:

1.   The buyer is entitled to inspect goods as provided in subsection (1) unless it has been otherwise agreed by the parties. The phrase "unless otherwise agreed" is intended principally to cover such situations as those outlined in subsections (3) and (4) and those in which the agreement of the parties negates inspection before tender of delivery. However, no agreement by the parties can displace the entire right of inspection except where the contract is simply for the sale of "this thing." Even in a sale of boxed goods "as is" inspection is a right of the buyer, since if the boxes prove to contain some other merchandise altogether the price can be recovered back; nor do the limitations of the provision on effect of acceptance apply in such a case.

2.   The buyer's right of inspection is available to him upon tender, delivery or appropriation of the goods with notice to him. Since inspection is available to him on tender, where payment is due against delivery he may, unless otherwise agreed, make his inspection before payment of the price. It is also available to him after receipt of the goods and so may be postponed after receipt for a reasonable time. Failure to inspect before payment does not impair the right to inspect after receipt of the goods unless the case falls within subsection (4) on agreed and exclusive inspection provisions. The right to inspect goods which have been appropriated with notice to the buyer holds whether or not the sale was by sample.

3.   The buyer may exercise his right of inspection at any reasonable time or place and in any reasonable manner. It is not necessary that he select the most appropriate time, place or manner to inspect or that his selection be the customary one in the trade or locality. Any reasonable time, place or manner is available to him and the reasonableness will be determined by trade usages, past practices between the parties and the other circumstances of the case.

The last sentence of subsection (1) makes it clear that the place of arrival of shipped goods is a reasonable place for their inspection.

4.   Expenses of an inspection made to satisfy the buyer of the seller's performance must be assumed by the buyer in the first instance. Since the rule provides merely for an allocation of expense there is no policy to

prevent the parties from providing otherwise in the agreement. Where the buyer would normally bear the expenses of the inspection but the goods are rightly rejected because of what the inspection reveals, demonstrable and reasonable costs of the inspection are part of his incidental damage caused by the seller's breach.

5.   In the case of payment against documents, subsection (3) requires payment before inspection, since shipping documents against which payment is to be made will commonly be tendered while the goods are still in transit. This Article recognizes no exception in any peculiar case in which the goods happen to arrive before the documents are tendered. However, where by the agreement payment is to await the arrival of the goods, inspection before payment becomes proper since the goods are then "available for inspection."

Where by the agreement the documents are to be tendered after arrival of the goods the buyer is entitled to inspect before payment since the goods are then "available for inspection". Proof of usage is not necessary to establish this right, but if inspection before payment is disputed the contrary must be established by usage or by an explicit contract term to that effect.

For the same reason, that the goods are available for inspection, a term calling for payment against storage documents or a delivery order does not normally bar the buyer's right to inspection before payment under subsection (3)(b). This result is reinforced by the buyer's right under subsection (1) to inspect goods which have been appropriated with notice to him.

6.   Under subsection (4) an agreed place or method of inspection is generally held to be intended as exclusive. However, where compliance with such an agreed inspection term becomes impossible, the question is basically one of intention. If the parties clearly intend that the method of inspection named is to be a necessary condition without which the entire deal is to fail, the contract is at an end if that method becomes impossible. On the other hand, if the parties merely seek to indicate a convenient and reliable method but do not intend to give up the deal in the event of its failure, any reasonable method of inspection may be substituted under this Article.

Since the purpose of an agreed place of inspection is only to make sure at that point whether or not the goods will be thrown back, the "exclusive" feature of the named place is satisfied under this Article if the buyer's failure to inspect there is held to be an acceptance with the knowledge of such defects as inspection would have revealed within the section on waiver of buyer's objections by failure to particularize. Revocation of the acceptance is limited to the situations stated in the section pertaining to that subject. The reasonable time within which to give notice of defects within the section on notice of breach begins to run from the point of the "acceptance."

7.   Clauses on time of inspection are commonly clauses which limit the time in which the buyer must inspect and give notice of defects. Such clauses are therefore governed by the section of this Article which requires that such a time limitation must be reasonable.

8.   Inspection under this Article is not to be regarded as a "condition precedent to the passing of title" so that risk until inspection remains on the seller. Under subsection (4) such an approach cannot be sustained. Issues between the buyer and seller are settled in this Article almost wholly by special provisions and not by the technical determination of the locus of the title. Thus "inspection as a condition to the passing of title" becomes a concept almost without meaning. However, in peculiar circumstances inspection may still have some of the consequences hitherto sought and obtained under that concept.

9.   "Inspection" under this section has to do with the buyer's check-up on whether the seller's performance is in accordance with a contract previously made and is not to be confused with the "examination" of the goods or of a sample or model of them at the time of contracting which may affect the warranties involved in the contract.

Cross References:

Generally: Sections 2–310(b), 2–321(3) and 2–606(1)(b).
Point 1: Section 2–607.
Point 2: Sections 2–501 and 2–502.
Point 4: Section 2–715.
Point 5: Section 2–321(3).
Point 6: Sections 2–606 to 2–608.
Point 7: Section 1–204.*
Point 8: Comment to Section 2–401.
Point 9: Section 2–316(3)(b).

---

*   *Referring to unrevised Article 1 (Appendix A).*

Definitional Cross References:

"Buyer". Section 2–103.
"Conform". Section 2–106.
"Contract". Section 1–201.
"Contract for sale". Section 2–106.
"Document of title". Section 1–201.
"Goods". Section 2–105.
"Party". Section 1–201.
"Presumed". Section 1–201.*
"Reasonable time". Section 1–204.*
"Rights". Section 1–201.
"Seller". Section 2–103.
"Send". Section 1–201.
"Term". Section 1–201.

As amended in 2003.

§ 2–514.   When Documents Deliverable on Acceptance; When on Payment.

Unless otherwise agreed documents against which a draft is drawn are to be delivered to the drawee on acceptance of the draft if it is payable more than three days after presentment; otherwise, only on payment.

Official Comment

Prior Uniform Statutory Provision: Section 41, Uniform Bills of Lading Act.

Changes: Rewritten.

Purposes of Changes: To make the provision one of general application so that:

1.   It covers any document against which a draft may be drawn, whatever may be the form of the document, and applies to interpret the action of a seller or consignor insofar as it may affect the rights and duties of any buyer, consignee or financing agency concerned with the paper. Supplementary or corresponding provisions are found in Sections 4–503 and 5–112.

2.   An "arrival" draft is a sight draft within the purpose of this section.

Cross References:

Point 1: See Sections 2–502, 2–505(2), 2–507(2), 2–512, 2–513, 2–607 concerning protection of rights of buyer and seller, and 4–503 and 5–112** on delivery of documents.

Definitional Cross References:

"Delivery". Section 1–201.
"Draft". Section 3–104.

§ 2–515.   Preserving Evidence of Goods in Dispute.

In furtherance of the adjustment of any claim or dispute

(a)   either party on reasonable notification to the other and for the purpose of ascertaining the facts and preserving evidence has the right to inspect, test and sample the goods including such of them as may be in the possession or control of the other; and

(b)   the parties may agree to a third party inspection or survey to determine the conformity or condition of the goods and may agree that the findings shall be binding upon them in any subsequent litigation or adjustment.

---

*   *Referring to unrevised Article 1 (Appendix A).*
**   *Referring to unrevised Article 5.*

Official Comment

Prior Uniform Statutory Provision: None.

Purposes:

1.   To meet certain serious problems which arise when there is a dispute as to the quality of the goods and thereby perhaps to aid the parties in reaching a settlement, and to further the use of devices which will promote certainty as to the condition of the goods, or at least aid in preserving evidence of their condition.

2.   Under paragraph (a), to afford either party an opportunity for preserving evidence, whether or not agreement has been reached, and thereby to reduce uncertainty in any litigation and, in turn perhaps, to promote agreement.

Paragraph (a) does not conflict with the provisions on the seller's right to resell rejected goods or the buyer's similar right. Apparent conflict between these provisions which will be suggested in certain circumstances is to be resolved by requiring prompt action by the parties. Nor does paragraph (a) impair the effect of a term for payment before inspection. Short of such defects as amount to fraud or substantial failure of consideration, non-conformity is neither an excuse nor a defense to an action for non-acceptance of documents. Normally, therefore, until the buyer has made payment, inspected and rejected the goods, there is no occasion or use for the rights under paragraph (a).

3.   Under paragraph (b), to provide for third party inspection upon the agreement of the parties, thereby opening the door to amicable adjustments based upon the findings of such third parties.

The use of the phrase "conformity or condition" makes it clear that the parties' agreement may range from a complete settlement of all aspects of the dispute by a third party to the use of a third party merely to determine and record the condition of the goods so that they can be resold or used to reduce the stake in controversy. "Conformity", at one end of the scale of possible issues, includes the whole question of interpretation of the agreement and its legal effect, the state of the goods in regard to quality and condition, whether any defects are due to factors which operate at the risk of the buyer, and the degree of non-conformity where that may be material. "Condition", at the other end of the scale, includes nothing but the degree of damage or deterioration which the goods show. Paragraph (b) is intended to reach any point in the gamut which the parties may agree upon.

The principle of the section on reservation of rights reinforces this paragraph in simplifying such adjustments as the parties wish to make in partial settlement while reserving their rights as to any further points. Paragraph (b) also suggests the use of arbitration, where desired, of any points left open, but nothing in this section is intended to repeal or amend any statute governing arbitration. Where any question arises as to the extent of the parties' agreement under the paragraph, the presumption should be that it was meant to extend only to the relation between the contract description and the goods as delivered, since that is what a craftsman in the trade would normally be expected to report upon. Finally, a written and authenticated report of inspection or tests by a third party, whether or not sampling has been practicable, is entitled to be admitted as evidence under this Act, for it is a third party document.

Cross References:

Point 2: Sections 2–513(3), 2–706 and 2–711(2) and Article 5.
Point 3: Sections 1–202* and 1–207.*

Definitional Cross References:

"Conform". Section 2–106.
"Goods". Section 2–105.
"Notification". Section 1–201.*
"Party". Section 1–201.

---

*   *Referring to unrevised Article 1 (Appendix A).*

PART 6

BREACH, REPUDIATION AND EXCUSE

§ 2–601. Buyer's Rights on Improper Delivery.

Subject to the provisions of this Article on breach in installment contracts (Section 2–612) and unless otherwise agreed under the sections on contractual limitations of remedy (Sections 2–718 and 2–719), if the goods or the tender of delivery fail in any respect to conform to the contract, the buyer may

(a) reject the whole; or

(b) accept the whole; or

(c) accept any commercial unit or units and reject the rest.

Official Comment

Prior Uniform Statutory Provision: No one general equivalent provision but numerous provisions, dealing with situations of non-conformity where buyer may accept or reject, including Sections 11, 44 and 69(1), Uniform Sales Act.

Changes: Partial acceptance in good faith is recognized and the buyer's remedies on the contract for breach of warranty and the like, where the buyer has returned the goods after transfer of title, are no longer barred.

Purposes of Changes: To make it clear that:

1. A buyer accepting a non-conforming tender is not penalized by the loss of any remedy otherwise open to him. This policy extends to cover and regulate the acceptance of a part of any lot improperly tendered in any case where the price can reasonably be apportioned. Partial acceptance is permitted whether the part of the goods accepted conforms or not. The only limitation on partial acceptance is that good faith and commercial reasonableness must be used to avoid undue impairment of the value of the remaining portion of the goods. This is the reason for the insistence on the "commercial unit" in paragraph (c). In this respect, the test is not only what unit has been the basis of contract, but whether the partial acceptance produces so materially adverse an effect on the remainder as to constitute bad faith.

2. Acceptance made with the knowledge of the other party is final. An original refusal to accept may be withdrawn by a later acceptance if the seller has indicated that he is holding the tender open. However, if the buyer attempts to accept, either in whole or in part, after his original rejection has caused the seller to arrange for other disposition of the goods, the buyer must answer for any ensuing damage since the next section provides that any exercise of ownership after rejection is wrongful as against the seller. Further, he is liable even though the seller may choose to treat his action as acceptance rather than conversion, since the damage flows from the misleading notice. Such arrangements for resale or other disposition of the goods by the seller must be viewed as within the normal contemplation of a buyer who has given notice of rejection. However, the buyer's attempts in good faith to dispose of defective goods where the seller has failed to give instructions within a reasonable time are not to be regarded as an acceptance.

Cross References:

Sections 2–602(2)(a), 2–612, 2–718 and 2–719.

Definitional Cross References:

"Buyer". Section 2–103.
"Commercial unit". Section 2–105.
"Conform". Section 2–106.
"Contract". Section 1–201.
"Goods". Section 2–105.
"Installment contract". Section 2–612.
"Rights". Section 1–201.

§ 2–602.   Manner and Effect of Rightful Rejection.

(1)   Rejection of goods must be within a reasonable time after their delivery or tender. It is ineffective unless the buyer seasonably notifies the seller.

(2)   Subject to the provisions of the two following sections on rejected goods (Sections 2–603 and 2–604),

(a)   after rejection any exercise of ownership by the buyer with respect to any commercial unit is wrongful as against the seller; and

(b)   if the buyer has before rejection taken physical possession of goods in which he does not have a security interest under the provisions of this Article (subsection (3) of Section 2–711), he is under a duty after rejection to hold them with reasonable care at the seller's disposition for a time sufficient to permit the seller to remove them; but

(c)   the buyer has no further obligations with regard to goods rightfully rejected.

(3)   The seller's rights with respect to goods wrongfully rejected are governed by the provisions of this Article on Seller's remedies in general (Section 2–703).

Official Comment

Prior Uniform Statutory Provision: Section 50, Uniform Sales Act.

Changes: Rewritten.

Purposes of Changes: To make it clear that:

1.   A tender or delivery of goods made pursuant to a contract of sale, even though wholly non-conforming, requires affirmative action by the buyer to avoid acceptance. Under subsection (1), therefore, the buyer is given a reasonable time to notify the seller of his rejection, but without such seasonable notification his rejection is ineffective. The sections of this Article dealing with inspection of goods must be read in connection with the buyer's reasonable time for action under this subsection. Contract provisions limiting the time for rejection fall within the rule of the section on "Time" and are effective if the time set gives the buyer a reasonable time for discovery of defects. What constitutes a due "notifying" of rejection by the buyer to the seller is defined in Section 1–201.*

2.   Subsection (2) lays down the normal duties of the buyer upon rejection, which flow from the relationship of the parties. Beyond his duty to hold the goods with reasonable care for the buyer's [seller's] disposition, this section continues the policy of prior uniform legislation in generally relieving the buyer from any duties with respect to them, except when the circumstances impose the limited obligation of salvage upon him under the next section.

3.   The present section applies only to rightful rejection by the buyer. If the seller has made a tender which in all respects conforms to the contract, the buyer has a positive duty to accept and his failure to do so constitutes a "wrongful rejection" which gives the seller immediate remedies for breach. Subsection (3) is included here to emphasize the sharp distinction between the rejection of an improper tender and the non-acceptance which is a breach by the buyer.

4.   The provisions of this section are to be appropriately limited or modified when a negotiation is in process.

Cross References:

Point 1: Sections 1–201,* 1–204(1) and (3),* 2–512(2), 2–513(1) and 2–606(1)(b).
Point 2: Section 2–603(1).
Point 3: Section 2–703.

Definitional Cross References:

"Buyer". Section 2–103.
"Commercial unit". Section 2–105.
"Goods". Section 2–105.

---

*   *Referring to unrevised Article 1 (Appendix A).*

"Merchant". Section 2–104.
"Notifies". Section 1–201.*
"Reasonable time". Section 1–204.*
"Remedy". Section 1–201.
"Rights". Section 1–201.
"Seasonably". Section 1–204.*
"Security interest". Section 1–201.
"Seller". Section 2–103.

§ 2–603. Merchant Buyer's Duties as to Rightfully Rejected Goods.

(1) Subject to any security interest in the buyer (subsection (3) of Section 2–711), when the seller has no agent or place of business at the market of rejection a merchant buyer is under a duty after rejection of goods in his possession or control to follow any reasonable instructions received from the seller with respect to the goods and in the absence of such instructions to make reasonable efforts to sell them for the seller's account if they are perishable or threaten to decline in value speedily. Instructions are not reasonable if on demand indemnity for expenses is not forthcoming.

(2) When the buyer sells goods under subsection (1), he is entitled to reimbursement from the seller or out of the proceeds for reasonable expenses of caring for and selling them, and if the expenses include no selling commission then to such commission as is usual in the trade or if there is none to a reasonable sum not exceeding ten per cent on the gross proceeds.

(3) In complying with this section the buyer is held only to good faith and good faith conduct hereunder is neither acceptance nor conversion nor the basis of an action for damages.

Official Comment

Prior Uniform Statutory Provision: None.

Purposes:

1. This section recognizes the duty imposed upon the merchant buyer by good faith and commercial practice to follow any reasonable instructions of the seller as to reshipping, storing, delivery to a third party, reselling or the like. Subsection (1) goes further and extends the duty to include the making of reasonable efforts to effect a salvage sale where the value of the goods is threatened and the seller's instructions do not arrive in time to prevent serious loss.

2. The limitations on the buyer's duty to resell under subsection (1) are to be liberally construed. The buyer's duty to resell under this section arises from commercial necessity and thus is present only when the seller has "no agent or place of business at the market of rejection". A financing agency which is acting in behalf of the seller in handling the documents rejected by the buyer is sufficiently the seller's agent to lift the burden of salvage resale from the buyer. (See provisions of Sections 4–503 and 5–112** on bank's duties with respect to rejected documents.) The buyer's duty to resell is extended only to goods in his "possession or control", but these are intended as words of wide, rather than narrow, import. In effect, the measure of the buyer's "control" is whether he can practically effect control without undue commercial burden.

3. The explicit provisions for reimbursement and compensation to the buyer in subsection (2) are applicable and necessary only where he is not acting under instructions from the seller. As provided in subsection (1) the seller's instructions to be "reasonable" must on demand of the buyer include indemnity for expenses.

4. Since this section makes the resale of perishable goods an affirmative duty in contrast to a mere right to sell as under the case law, subsection (3) makes it clear that the buyer is liable only for the exercise of good faith in determining whether the value of the goods is sufficiently threatened to justify a quick resale or whether he has waited a sufficient length of time for instructions, or what a reasonable means and place of resale is.

5. A buyer who fails to make a salvage sale when his duty to do so under this section has arisen is subject to damages pursuant to the section on liberal administration of remedies.

---

*   *Referring to unrevised Article 1 (Appendix A).*

** *Referring to unrevised Article 5.*

Cross References:

> Point 2: Sections 4–503 and 5–112.[*]
> Point 5: Section 1–106.[**] Compare generally section 2–706.

Definitional Cross References:

> "Buyer". Section 2–103.
> "Good faith". Section 1–201.
> "Goods". Section 2–105.
> "Merchant". Section 2–104.
> "Security interest". Section 1–201.
> "Seller". Section 2–103.

§ 2–604.   Buyer's Options as to Salvage of Rightfully Rejected Goods.

Subject to the provisions of the immediately preceding section on perishables if the seller gives no instructions within a reasonable time after notification of rejection the buyer may store the rejected goods for the seller's account or reship them to him or resell them for the seller's account with reimbursement as provided in the preceding section. Such action is not acceptance or conversion.

Official Comment

Prior Uniform Statutory Provision: None.

Purposes:

The basic purpose of this section is twofold: on the one hand it aims at reducing the stake in dispute and on the other at avoiding the pinning of a technical "acceptance" on a buyer who has taken steps towards realization on or preservation of the goods in good faith. This section is essentially a salvage section and the buyer's right to act under it is conditioned upon (1) non-conformity of the goods, (2) due notification of rejection to the seller under the section on manner of rejection, and (3) the absence of any instructions from the seller which the merchant-buyer has a duty to follow under the preceding section.

This section is designed to accord all reasonable leeway to a rightfully rejecting buyer acting in good faith. The listing of what the buyer may do in the absence of instructions from the seller is intended to be not exhaustive but merely illustrative. This is not a "merchant's" section and the options are pure options given to merchant and nonmerchant buyers alike. The merchant-buyer, however, may in some instances be under a duty rather than an option to resell under the provisions of the preceding section.

Cross References:

> Sections 2–602(1), and 2–603(1) and 2–706.

Definitional Cross References:

> "Buyer". Section 2–103.
> "Notification". Section 1–201.[*]
> "Reasonable time". Section 1–204.[*]
> "Seller". Section 2–103.

§ 2–605.   Waiver of Buyer's Objections by Failure to Particularize.

(1)   The buyer's failure to state in connection with rejection a particular defect which is ascertainable by reasonable inspection precludes him from relying on the unstated defect to justify rejection or to establish breach

    (a)   where the seller could have cured it if stated seasonally; or

---

  [*]   *Referring to unrevised Article 5.*
 [**] *Referring to unrevised Article 1 (Appendix A).*

(b) between merchants when the seller has after rejection made a request in writing for a full and final written statement of all defects on which the buyer proposes to rely.

(2) Payment against documents made without reservation of rights precludes recovery of the payment for defects apparent in the documents.

As amended in 2003.

Official Comment

Prior Uniform Statutory Provision: None.

Purposes:

1. The present section rests upon a policy of permitting the buyer to give a quick and informal notice of defects in a tender without penalizing him for omissions in his statement, while at the same time protecting a seller who is reasonably misled by the buyer's failure to state curable defects.

2. Where the defect in a tender is one which could have been cured by the seller, a buyer who merely rejects the delivery without stating his objections to it is probably acting in commercial bad faith and seeking to get out of a deal which has become unprofitable. Subsection (1)(a), following the general policy of this Article which looks to preserving the deal wherever possible, therefore insists that the seller's right to correct his tender in such circumstances be protected.

3. When the time for cure is past, subsection (1)(b) makes it plain that a seller is entitled upon request to a final statement of objections upon which he can rely. What is needed is that he make clear to the buyer exactly what is being sought. A formal demand under paragraph (b) will be sufficient in the case of a merchant-buyer.

4. Subsection (2) applies to the particular case of documents the same principle which the section on effects of acceptance applies to the case of goods. The matter is dealt with in this section in terms of "waiver" of objections rather than of right to revoke acceptance, partly to avoid any confusion with the problems of acceptance of goods and partly because defects in documents which are not taken as grounds for rejection are generally minor ones. The only defects concerned in the present subsection are defects in the documents which are apparent. This rule applies to both tangible and electronic documents of title. Where payment is required against the documents they must be inspected before payment, and the payment then constitutes acceptance of the documents. Under the section dealing with this problem, such acceptance of the documents does not constitute an acceptance of the goods or impair any options or remedies of the buyer for their improper delivery. Where the documents are delivered without requiring such contemporary action as payment from the buyer, the reason of the next section on what constitutes acceptance of goods, applies. Their acceptance by non-objection is therefore postponed until after a reasonable time for their inspection. In either situation, however, the buyer "waives" only the defects apparent in the documents.

Cross References:

Point 2: Section 2–508.
Point 4: Sections 2–512(2), 2–606(1)(b), 2–607(2).

Definitional Cross References:

"Between merchants". Section 2–104.
"Buyer". Section 2–103.
"Seasonably". Section 1–204.*
"Seller". Section 2–103.
"Writing" and "written". Section 1–201.

As amended in 2003.

§ 2–606.   What Constitutes Acceptance of Goods.

(1) Acceptance of goods occurs when the buyer

---

* *Referring to unrevised Article 1 (Appendix A).*

(a) after a reasonable opportunity to inspect the goods signifies to the seller that the goods are conforming or that he will take or retain them in spite of their non-conformity; or

(b) fails to make an effective rejection (subsection (1) of Section 2–602), but such acceptance does not occur until the buyer has had a reasonable opportunity to inspect them; or

(c) does any act inconsistent with the seller's ownership; but if such act is wrongful as against the seller it is an acceptance only if ratified by him.

(2) Acceptance of a part of any commercial unit is acceptance of that entire unit.

Official Comment

Prior Uniform Statutory Provision: Section 48, Uniform Sales Act.

Changes: Rewritten, the qualification in paragraph (c) and subsection (2) being new; otherwise the general policy of the prior legislation is continued.

Purposes of Changes and New Matter: To make it clear that:

1. Under this Article "acceptance" as applied to goods means that the buyer, pursuant to the contract, takes particular goods which have been appropriated to the contract as his own, whether or not he is obligated to do so, and whether he does so by words, action, or silence when it is time to speak. If the goods conform to the contract, acceptance amounts only to the performance by the buyer of one part of his legal obligation.

2. Under this Article acceptance of goods is always acceptance of identified goods which have been appropriated to the contract or are appropriated by the contract. There is no provision for "acceptance of title" apart from acceptance in general, since acceptance of title is not material under this Article to the detailed rights and duties of the parties. (See Section 2–401). The refinements of the older law between acceptance of goods and of title become unnecessary in view of the provisions of the sections on effect and revocation of acceptance, on effects of identification and on risk of loss, and those sections which free the seller's and buyer's remedies from the complications and confusions caused by the question of whether title has or has not passed to the buyer before breach.

3. Under paragraph (a), payment made after tender is always one circumstance tending to signify acceptance of the goods but in itself it can never be more than one circumstance and is not conclusive. Also, a conditional communication of acceptance always remains subject to its expressed conditions.

4. Under paragraph (c), any action taken by the buyer, which is inconsistent with his claim that he has rejected the goods, constitutes an acceptance. However, the provisions of paragraph (c) are subject to the sections dealing with rejection by the buyer which permit the buyer to take certain actions with respect to the goods pursuant to his options and duties imposed by those sections, without effecting an acceptance of the goods. The second clause of paragraph (c) modifies some of the prior case law and makes it clear that "acceptance" in law based on the wrongful act of the acceptor is acceptance only as against the wrongdoer and then only at the option of the party wronged.

In the same manner in which a buyer can bind himself, despite his insistence that he is rejecting or has rejected the goods, by an act inconsistent with the seller's ownership under paragraph (c), he can obligate himself by a communication of acceptance despite a prior rejection under paragraph (a). However, the sections on buyer's rights on improper delivery and on the effect of rightful rejection, make it clear that after he once rejects a tender, paragraph (a) does not operate in favor of the buyer unless the seller has re-tendered the goods or has taken affirmative action indicating that he is holding the tender open. See also Comment 2 to Section 2–601.

5. Subsection (2) supplements the policy of the section on buyer's rights on improper delivery, recognizing the validity of a partial acceptance but insisting that the buyer exercise this right only as to whole commercial units.

Cross References:

Point 2: Sections 2–401, 2–509, 2–510, 2–607, 2–608 and Part 7.
Point 4: Sections 2–601 through 2–604.
Point 5: Section 2–601.

Definitional Cross References:

"Buyer". Section 2–103.

"Commercial unit". Section 2–105.
"Goods". Section 2–105.
"Seller". Section 2–103.

§ 2–607.   Effect of Acceptance; Notice of Breach; Burden of Establishing Breach After Acceptance; Notice of Claim or Litigation to Person Answerable Over.

(1)   The buyer must pay at the contract rate for any goods accepted.

(2)   Acceptance of goods by the buyer precludes rejection of the goods accepted and if made with knowledge of a non-conformity cannot be revoked because of it unless the acceptance was on the reasonable assumption that the non-conformity would be seasonably cured but acceptance does not of itself impair any other remedy provided by this Article for non-conformity.

(3)   Where a tender has been accepted

(a)   the buyer must within a reasonable time after he discovers or should have discovered any breach notify the seller of breach or be barred from any remedy; and

(b)   if the claim is one for infringement or the like (subsection (3) of Section 2–312) and the buyer is sued as a result of such a breach he must so notify the seller within a reasonable time after he receives notice of the litigation or be barred from any remedy over for liability established by the litigation.

(4)   The burden is on the buyer to establish any breach with respect to the goods accepted.

(5)   Where the buyer is sued for breach of a warranty or other obligation for which his seller is answerable over

(a)   he may give his seller written notice of the litigation. If the notice states that the seller may come in and defend and that if the seller does not do so he will be bound in any action against him by his buyer by any determination of fact common to the two litigations, then unless the seller after seasonable receipt of the notice does come in and defend he is so bound.

(b)   if the claim is one for infringement or the like (subsection (3) of Section 2–312) the original seller may demand in writing that his buyer turn over to him control of the litigation including settlement or else be barred from any remedy over and if he also agrees to bear all expense and to satisfy any adverse judgment, then unless the buyer after seasonable receipt of the demand does turn over control the buyer is so barred.

(6)   The provisions of subsections (3), (4) and (5) apply to any obligation of a buyer to hold the seller harmless against infringement or the like (subsection (3) of Section 2–312).

Official Comment

Prior Uniform Statutory Provision: Subsection (1)—Section 41, Uniform Sales Act; Subsections (2) and (3)—Sections 49 and 69, Uniform Sales Act.

Changes: Rewritten.

Purposes of Changes: To continue the prior basic policies with respect to acceptance of goods while making a number of minor though material changes in the interest of simplicity and commercial convenience so that:

1.   Under subsection (1), once the buyer accepts a tender the seller acquires a right to its price on the contract terms. In cases of partial acceptance, the price of any part accepted is, if possible, to be reasonably apportioned, using the type of apportionment familiar to the courts in quantum valebant cases, to be determined in terms of "the contract rate," which is the rate determined from the bargain in fact (the agreement) after the rules and policies of this Article have been brought to bear.

2.   Under subsection (2) acceptance of goods precludes their subsequent rejection. Any return of the goods thereafter must be by way of revocation of acceptance under the next section. Revocation is unavailable for a non-conformity known to the buyer at the time of acceptance, except where the buyer has accepted on the reasonable assumption that the non-conformity would be seasonably cured.

3.   All other remedies of the buyer remain unimpaired under subsection (2). This is intended to include the buyer's full rights with respect to future installments despite his acceptance of any earlier non-conforming installment.

4.   The time of notification is to be determined by applying commercial standards to a merchant buyer. "A reasonable time" for notification from a retail consumer is to be judged by different standards so that in his case it will be extended, for the rule of requiring notification is designed to defeat commercial bad faith, not to deprive a good faith consumer of his remedy.

The content of the notification need merely be sufficient to let the seller know that the transaction is still troublesome and must be watched. There is no reason to require that the notification which saves the buyer's rights under this section must include a clear statement of all the objections that will be relied on by the buyer, as under the section covering statements of defects upon rejection (Section 2–605). Nor is there reason for requiring the notification to be a claim for damages or of any threatened litigation or other resort to a remedy. The notification which saves the buyer's rights under this Article need only be such as informs the seller that the transaction is claimed to involve a breach, and thus opens the way for normal settlement through negotiation.

5.   Under this Article various beneficiaries are given rights for injuries sustained by them because of the seller's breach of warranty. Such a beneficiary does not fall within the reason of the present section in regard to discovery of defects and the giving of notice within a reasonable time after acceptance, since he has nothing to do with acceptance. However, the reason of this section does extend to requiring the beneficiary to notify the seller that an injury has occurred. What is said above, with regard to the extended time for reasonable notification from the lay consumer after the injury is also applicable here; but even a beneficiary can be properly held to the use of good faith in notifying, once he has had time to become aware of the legal situation.

6.   Subsection (4) unambiguously places the burden of proof to establish breach on the buyer after acceptance. However, this rule becomes one purely of procedure when the tender accepted was non-conforming and the buyer has given the seller notice of breach under subsection (3). For subsection (2) makes it clear that acceptance leaves unimpaired the buyer's right to be made whole, and that right can be exercised by the buyer not only by way of cross-claim for damages, but also by way of recoupment in diminution or extinction of the price.

7.   Subsections (3)(b) and (5)(b) give a warrantor against infringement an opportunity to defend or compromise third-party claims or be relieved of his liability. Subsection (5)(a) codifies for all warranties the practice of voucher to defend. Compare Section 3–803.* Subsection (6) makes these provisions applicable to the buyer's liability for infringement under Section 2–312.

8.   All of the provisions of the present section are subject to any explicit reservation of rights.

Cross References:

Point 1: Section 1–201.
Point 2: Section 2–608.
Point 4: Sections 1–204** and 2–605.
Point 5: Section 2–318.
Point 6: Section 2–717.
Point 7: Sections 2–312 and 3–803.*
Point 8: Section 1–207.**

Definitional Cross References:

"Burden of establishing". Section 1–201.
"Buyer". Section 2–103.
"Conform". Section 2–106.
"Contract". Section 1–201.
"Goods". Section 2–105.
"Notifies". Section 1–201.**
"Reasonable time". Section 1–204.**
"Remedy". Section 1–201.

---

*   *Referring to unrevised Article 3 (Appendix B).*
**   *Referring to unrevised Article 1 (Appendix A).*

"Seasonably". Section 1–204.*

§ 2–608.   Revocation of Acceptance in Whole or in Part.

(1)   The buyer may revoke his acceptance of a lot or commercial unit whose non-conformity substantially impairs its value to him if he has accepted it

(a)   on the reasonable assumption that its non-conformity would be cured and it has not been seasonably cured; or

(b)   without discovery of such non-conformity if his acceptance was reasonably induced either by the difficulty of discovery before acceptance or by the seller's assurances.

(2)   Revocation of acceptance must occur within a reasonable time after the buyer discovers or should have discovered the ground for it and before any substantial change in condition of the goods which is not caused by their own defects. It is not effective until the buyer notifies the seller of it.

(3)   A buyer who so revokes has the same rights and duties with regard to the goods involved as if he had rejected them.

Official Comment

Prior Uniform Statutory Provision: Section 69(1)(d), (3), (4) and (5), Uniform Sales Act.

Changes: Rewritten.

Purposes of Changes: To make it clear that:

1.   Although the prior basic policy is continued, the buyer is no longer required to elect between revocation of acceptance and recovery of damages for breach. Both are now available to him. The non-alternative character of the two remedies is stressed by the terms used in the present section. The section no longer speaks of "rescission," a term capable of ambiguous application either to transfer of title to the goods or to the contract of sale and susceptible also of confusion with cancellation for cause of an executed or executory portion of the contract. The remedy under this section is instead referred to simply as "revocation of acceptance" of goods tendered under a contract for sale and involves no suggestion of "election" of any sort.

2.   Revocation of acceptance is possible only where the non-conformity substantially impairs the value of the goods to the buyer. For this purpose the test is not what the seller had reason to know at the time of contracting; the question is whether the non-conformity is such as will in fact cause a substantial impairment of value to the buyer though the seller had no advance knowledge as to the buyer's particular circumstances.

3.   "Assurances" by the seller under paragraph (b) of subsection (1) can rest as well in the circumstances or in the contract as in explicit language used at the time of delivery. The reason for recognizing such assurances is that they induce the buyer to delay discovery. These are the only assurances involved in paragraph (b). Explicit assurances may be made either in good faith or bad faith. In either case any remedy accorded by this Article is available to the buyer under the section on remedies for fraud.

4.   Subsection (2) requires notification of revocation of acceptance within a reasonable time after discovery of the grounds for such revocation. Since this remedy will be generally resorted to only after attempts at adjustment have failed, the reasonable time period should extend in most cases beyond the time in which notification of breach must be given, beyond the time for discovery of non-conformity after acceptance and beyond the time for rejection after tender. The parties may by their agreement limit the time for notification under this section, but the same sanctions and considerations apply to such agreements as are discussed in the comment on manner and effect of rightful rejection.

5.   The content of the notice under subsection (2) is to be determined in this case as in others by considerations of good faith, prevention of surprise, and reasonable adjustment. More will generally be necessary than the mere notification of breach required under the preceding section. On the other hand the requirements of the section on waiver of buyer's objections do not apply here. The fact that quick notification of trouble is desirable affords good ground for being slow to bind a buyer by his first statement. Following the general policy of this Article, the requirements of the content of notification are less stringent in the case of a non-merchant buyer.

---

*   *Referring to unrevised Article 1 (Appendix A).*

6. Under subsection (2) the prior policy is continued of seeking substantial justice in regard to the condition of goods restored to the seller. Thus the buyer may not revoke his acceptance if the goods have materially deteriorated except by reason of their own defects. Worthless goods, however, need not be offered back and minor defects in the articles reoffered are to be disregarded.

7. The policy of the section allowing partial acceptance is carried over into the present section and the buyer may revoke his acceptance, in appropriate cases, as to the entire lot or any commercial unit thereof.

Cross References:

Point 3: Section 2-721.
Point 4: Sections 1-204,* 2-602 and 2-607.
Point 5: Sections 2-605 and 2-607.
Point 7: Section 2-601.

Definitional Cross References:

"Buyer". Section 2-103.
"Commercial unit". Section 2-105.
"Conform". Section 2-106.
"Goods". Section 2-105.
"Lot". Section 2-105.
"Notifies". Section 1-201.*
"Reasonable time". Section 1-204.*
"Rights". Section 1-201.
"Seasonably". Section 1-204.*
"Seller". Section 2-103.

§ 2-609.   Right to Adequate Assurance of Performance.

(1) A contract for sale imposes an obligation on each party that the other's expectation of receiving due performance will not be impaired. When reasonable grounds for insecurity arise with respect to the performance of either party the other may in writing demand adequate assurance of due performance and until he receives such assurance may if commercially reasonable suspend any performance for which he has not already received the agreed return.

(2) Between merchants the reasonableness of grounds for insecurity and the adequacy of any assurance offered shall be determined according to commercial standards.

(3) Acceptance of any improper delivery or payment does not prejudice the aggrieved party's right to demand adequate assurance of future performance.

(4) After receipt of a justified demand failure to provide within a reasonable time not exceeding thirty days such assurance of due performance as is adequate under the circumstances of the particular case is a repudiation of the contract.

Official Comment

Prior Uniform Statutory Provision: See Sections 53, 54(1)(b), 55 and 63(2), Uniform Sales Act.

Purposes:

1. The section rests on the recognition of the fact that the essential purpose of a contract between commercial men is actual performance and they do not bargain merely for a promise, or for a promise plus the right to win a lawsuit and that a continuing sense of reliance and security that the promised performance will be forthcoming when due, is an important feature of the bargain. If either the willingness or the ability of a party to perform declines materially between the time of contracting and the time for performance, the other party is threatened with the loss of a substantial part of what he has bargained for. A seller needs protection not merely against having to deliver on credit to a shaky buyer, but also against having to procure and manufacture the goods, perhaps turning down other customers. Once he has been given reason to believe that the buyer's performance

---

*   *Referring to unrevised Article 1 (Appendix A).*

has become uncertain, it is an undue hardship to force him to continue his own performance. Similarly, a buyer who believes that the seller's deliveries have become uncertain cannot safely wait for the due date of performance when he has been buying to assure himself of materials for his current manufacturing or to replenish his stock of merchandise.

2. Three measures have been adopted to meet the needs of commercial men in such situations. First, the aggrieved party is permitted to suspend his own performance and any preparation therefor, with excuse for any resulting necessary delay, until the situation has been clarified. "Suspend performance" under this section means to hold up performance pending the outcome of the demand, and includes also the holding up of any preparatory action. This is the same principle which governs the ancient law of stoppage and seller's lien, and also of excuse of a buyer from prepayment if the seller's actions manifest that he cannot or will not perform. (Original Act, Section 63(2).)

Secondly, the aggrieved party is given the right to require adequate assurance that the other party's performance will be duly forthcoming. This principle is reflected in the familiar clauses permitting the seller to curtail deliveries if the buyer's credit becomes impaired, which when held within the limits of reasonableness and good faith actually express no more than the fair business meaning of any commercial contract.

Third, and finally, this section provides the means by which the aggrieved party may treat the contract as broken if his reasonable grounds for insecurity are not cleared up within a reasonable time. This is the principle underlying the law of anticipatory breach, whether by way of defective part performance or by repudiation. The present section merges these three principles of law and commercial practice into a single theory of general application to all sales agreements looking to future performance.

3. Subsection (2) of the present section requires that "reasonable" grounds and "adequate" assurance as used in subsection (1) be defined by commercial rather than legal standards. The express reference to commercial standards carries no connotation that the obligation of good faith is not equally applicable here.

Under commercial standards and in accord with commercial practice, a ground for insecurity need not arise from or be directly related to the contract in question. The law as to "dependence" or "independence" of promises within a single contract does not control the application of the present section.

Thus a buyer who falls behind in "his account" with the seller, even though the items involved have to do with separate and legally distinct contracts, impairs the seller's expectation of due performance. Again, under the same test, a buyer who requires precision parts which he intends to use immediately upon delivery, may have reasonable grounds for insecurity if he discovers that his seller is making defective deliveries of such parts to other buyers with similar needs. Thus, too, in a situation such as arose in *Jay Dreher Corporation v. Delco Appliance Corporation*, 93 F.2d 275 (C.C.A.2, 1937), where a manufacturer gave a dealer an exclusive franchise for the sale of his product but on two or three occasions breached the exclusive dealing clause, although there was no default in orders, deliveries or payments under the separate sales contract between the parties, the aggrieved dealer would be entitled to suspend his performance of the contract for sale under the present section and to demand assurance that the exclusive dealing contract would be lived up to. There is no need for an explicit clause tying the exclusive franchise into the contract for the sale of goods since the situation itself ties the agreements together.

The nature of the sales contract enters also into the question of reasonableness. For example, a report from an apparently trustworthy source that the seller had shipped defective goods or was planning to ship them would normally give the buyer reasonable grounds for insecurity. But when the buyer has assumed the risk of payment before inspection of the goods, as in a sales contract on C.I.F. or similar cash against documents terms, that risk is not to be evaded by a demand for assurance. Therefore no ground for insecurity would exist under this section unless the report went to a ground which would excuse payment by the buyer.

4. What constitutes "adequate" assurance of due performance is subject to the same test of factual conditions. For example, where the buyer can make use of a defective delivery, a mere promise by a seller of good repute that he is giving the matter his attention and that the defect will not be repeated, is normally sufficient. Under the same circumstances, however, a similar statement by a known corner-cutter might well be considered insufficient without the posting of a guaranty or, if so demanded by the buyer, a speedy replacement of the delivery involved. By the same token where a delivery has defects, even though easily curable, which interfere with easy use by the buyer, no verbal assurance can be deemed adequate which is not accompanied by replacement, repair, money-allowance, or other commercially reasonable cure.

A fact situation such as arose in *Corn Products Refining Co. v. Fasola*, 94 N.J.L. 181, 109 A. 505 (1920) offers illustration both of reasonable grounds for insecurity and "adequate" assurance. In that case a contract for the sale of oils on 30 days' credit, 2% off for payment within 10 days, provided that credit was to be extended to the buyer only if his financial responsibility was satisfactory to the seller. The buyer had been in the habit of taking advantage of the discount but at the same time that he failed to make his customary 10 day payment, the seller heard rumors, in fact false, that the buyer's financial condition was shaky. Thereupon, the seller demanded cash before shipment or security satisfactory to him. The buyer sent a good credit report from his banker, expressed willingness to make payments when due on the 30 day terms and insisted on further deliveries under the contract. Under this Article the rumors, although false, were enough to make the buyer's financial condition "unsatisfactory" to the seller under the contract clause. Moreover, the buyer's practice of taking the cash discounts is enough, apart from the contract clause, to lay a commercial foundation for suspicion when the practice is suddenly stopped. These matters, however, go only to the justification of the seller's demand for security, or his "reasonable grounds for insecurity".

The adequacy of the assurance given is not measured as in the type of "satisfaction" situation affected with intangibles, such as in personal service cases, cases involving a third party's judgment as final, or cases in which the whole contract is dependent on one party's satisfaction, as in a sale on approval. Here, the seller must exercise good faith and observe commercial standards. This Article thus approves the statement of the court in *James B. Berry's Sons Co. of Illinois v. Monark Gasoline & Oil Co., Inc.*, 32 F.2d 74 (C.C.A.8, 1929), that the seller's satisfaction under such a clause must be based upon reason and must not be arbitrary or capricious; and rejects the purely personal "good faith" test of the Corn Products Refining Co. case, which held that in the seller's sole judgment, if for *any* reason he was dissatisfied, he was entitled to revoke the credit. In the absence of the buyer's failure to take the 2% discount as was his custom, the banker's report given in that case would have been "adequate" assurance under this Act, regardless of the language of the "satisfaction" clause. However, the seller is reasonably entitled to feel insecure at a sudden expansion of the buyer's use of a credit term, and should be entitled either to security or to a satisfactory explanation.

The entire foregoing discussion as to adequacy of assurance by way of explanation is subject to qualification when repeated occasions for the application of this section arise. This Act recognizes that repeated delinquencies must be viewed as cumulative. On the other hand, commercial sense also requires that if repeated claims for assurance are made under this section, the basis for these claims must be increasingly obvious.

5.   A failure to provide adequate assurance of performance and thereby to re-establish the security of expectation, results in a breach only "by repudiation" under subsection (4). Therefore, the possibility is continued of retraction of the repudiation under the section dealing with that problem, unless the aggrieved party has acted on the breach in some manner.

The thirty day limit on the time to provide assurance is laid down to free the question of reasonable time from uncertainty in later litigation.

6.   Clauses seeking to give the protected party exceedingly wide powers to cancel or readjust the contract when ground for insecurity arises must be read against the fact that good faith is a part of the obligation of the contract and not subject to modification by agreement and includes, in the case of a merchant, the reasonable observance of commercial standards of fair dealing in the trade. Such clauses can thus be effective to enlarge the protection given by the present section to a certain extent, to fix the reasonable time within which requested assurance must be given, or to define adequacy of the assurance in any commercially reasonable fashion. But any clause seeking to set up arbitrary standards for action is ineffective under this Article. Acceleration clauses are treated similarly in the Articles on Commercial Paper and Secured Transactions.

Cross References:

> Point 3: Section 1–203.*
> Point 5: Section 2–611.
> Point 6: Sections 1–203* and 1–208* and Articles 3 and 9.

Definitional Cross References:

> "Aggrieved party". Section 1–201.
> "Between merchants". Section 2–104.
> "Contract". Section 1–201.
> "Contract for sale". Section 2–106.

---

*   *Referring to unrevised Article 1 (Appendix A).*

140

"Party". Section 1–201.
"Reasonable time". Section 1–204.*
"Rights". Section 1–201.
"Writing". Section 1–201.

§ 2–610.   Anticipatory Repudiation.

When either party repudiates the contract with respect to a performance not yet due the loss of which will substantially impair the value of the contract to the other, the aggrieved party may

(a) for a commercially reasonable time await performance by the repudiating party; or

(b) resort to any remedy for breach (Section 2–703 or Section 2–711), even though he has notified the repudiating party that he would await the latter's performance and has urged retraction; and

(c) in either case suspend his own performance or proceed in accordance with the provisions of this Article on the seller's right to identify goods to the contract notwithstanding breach or to salvage unfinished goods (Section 2–704).

Official Comment

Prior Uniform Statutory Provision: See Sections 63(2) and 65, Uniform Sales Act.

Purposes: To make it clear that:

1.   With the problem of insecurity taken care of by the preceding section and with provision being made in this Article as to the effect of a defective delivery under an installment contract, anticipatory repudiation centers upon an overt communication of intention or an action which renders performance impossible or demonstrates a clear determination not to continue with performance.

Under the present section when such a repudiation substantially impairs the value of the contract, the aggrieved party may at any time resort to his remedies for breach, or he may suspend his own performance while he negotiates with, or awaits performance by, the other party. But if he awaits performance beyond a commercially reasonable time he cannot recover resulting damages which he should have avoided.

2.   It is not necessary for repudiation that performance be made literally and utterly impossible. Repudiation can result from action which reasonably indicates a rejection of the continuing obligation. And, a repudiation automatically results under the preceding section on insecurity when a party fails to provide adequate assurance of due future performance within thirty days after a justifiable demand therefor has been made. Under the language of this section, a demand by one or both parties for more than the contract calls for in the way of counter-performance is not in itself a repudiation nor does it invalidate a plain expression of desire for future performance. However, when under a fair reading it amounts to a statement of intention not to perform except on conditions which go beyond the contract, it becomes a repudiation.

3.   The test chosen to justify an aggrieved party's action under this section is the same as that in the section on breach in installment contracts—namely the substantial value of the contract. The most useful test of substantial value is to determine whether material inconvenience or injustice will result if the aggrieved party is forced to wait and receive an ultimate tender minus the part or aspect repudiated.

4.   After repudiation, the aggrieved party may immediately resort to any remedy he chooses provided he moves in good faith (see Section 1–203).* Inaction and silence by the aggrieved party may leave the matter open but it cannot be regarded as misleading the repudiating party. Therefore the aggrieved party is left free to proceed at any time with his options under this section, unless he has taken some positive action which in good faith requires notification to the other party before the remedy is pursued.

Cross References:

Point 1: Sections 2–609 and 2–612.
Point 2: Section 2–609.
Point 3: Section 2–612.
Point 4: Section 1–203.*

---

*   *Referring to unrevised Article 1 (Appendix A).*

Definitional Cross References:

> "Aggrieved party". Section 1–201.
> "Contract". Section 1–201.
> "Party". Section 1–201.
> "Remedy". Section 1–201.

§ 2–611.   Retraction of Anticipatory Repudiation.

(1) Until the repudiating party's next performance is due he can retract his repudiation unless the aggrieved party has since the repudiation cancelled or materially changed his position or otherwise indicated that he considers the repudiation final.

(2) Retraction may be by any method which clearly indicates to the aggrieved party that the repudiating party intends to perform, but must include any assurance justifiably demanded under the provisions of this Article (Section 2–609).

(3) Retraction reinstates the repudiating party's rights under the contract with due excuse and allowance to the aggrieved party for any delay occasioned by the repudiation.

Official Comment

Prior Uniform Statutory Provision: None.

Purposes: To make it clear that:

1. The repudiating party's right to reinstate the contract is entirely dependent upon the action taken by the aggrieved party. If the latter has cancelled the contract or materially changed his position at any time after the repudiation, there can be no retraction under this section.

2. Under subsection (2) an effective retraction must be accompanied by any assurances demanded under the section dealing with right to adequate assurance. A repudiation is of course sufficient to give reasonable ground for insecurity and to warrant a request for assurance as an essential condition of the retraction. However, after a timely and unambiguous expression of retraction, a reasonable time for the assurance to be worked out should be allowed by the aggrieved party before cancellation.

Cross Reference:

> Point 2: Section 2–609.

Definitional Cross References:

> "Aggrieved party". Section 1–201.
> "Cancellation". Section 2–106.
> "Contract". Section 1–201.
> "Party". Section 1–201.
> "Rights". Section 1–201.

§ 2–612.   "Installment Contract"; Breach.

(1) An "installment contract" is one which requires or authorizes the delivery of goods in separate lots to be separately accepted, even though the contract contains a clause "each delivery is a separate contract" or its equivalent.

(2) The buyer may reject any installment which is non-conforming if the non-conformity substantially impairs the value of that installment and cannot be cured or if the non-conformity is a defect in the required documents; but if the non-conformity does not fall within subsection (3) and the seller gives adequate assurance of its cure the buyer must accept that installment.

(3) Whenever non-conformity or default with respect to one or more installments substantially impairs the value of the whole contract there is a breach of the whole. But the aggrieved party reinstates the contract if he accepts a non-conforming installment without seasonably notifying of cancellation or if he brings an action with respect only to past installments or demands performance as to future installments.

Official Comment

Prior Uniform Statutory Provision: Section 45(2), Uniform Sales Act.

Changes: Rewritten.

Purposes of Changes: To continue prior law but to make explicit the more mercantile interpretation of many of the rules involved, so that:

1. The definition of an installment contract is phrased more broadly in this Article so as to cover installment deliveries tacitly authorized by the circumstances or by the option of either party.

2. In regard to the apportionment of the price for separate payment this Article applies the more liberal test of what can be apportioned rather than the test of what is clearly apportioned by the agreement. This Article also recognizes approximate calculation or apportionment of price subject to subsequent adjustment. A provision for separate payment for each lot delivered ordinarily means that the price is at least roughly calculable by units of quantity, but such a provision is not essential to an "installment contract." If separate acceptance of separate deliveries is contemplated, no generalized contrast between wholly "entire" and wholly "divisible" contracts has any standing under this Article.

3. This Article rejects any approach which gives clauses such as "each delivery is a separate contract" their legalistically literal effect. Such contracts nonetheless call for installment deliveries. Even where a clause speaks of "a separate contract for all purposes", a commercial reading of the language under the section on good faith and commercial standards requires that the singleness of the document and the negotiation, together with the sense of the situation, prevail over any uncommercial and legalistic interpretation.

4. One of the requirements for rejection under subsection (2) is non-conformity substantially impairing the value of the installment in question. However, an installment agreement may require accurate conformity in quality as a condition to the right to acceptance if the need for such conformity is made clear either by express provision or by the circumstances. In such a case the effect of the agreement is to define explicitly what amounts to substantial impairment of value impossible to cure. A clause requiring accurate compliance as a condition to the right to acceptance must, however, have some basis in reason, must avoid imposing hardship by surprise and is subject to waiver or to displacement by practical construction.

Substantial impairment of the value of an installment can turn not only on the quality of the goods but also on such factors as time, quantity, assortment, and the like. It must be judged in terms of the normal or specifically known purposes of the contract. The defect in required documents refers to such matters as the absence of insurance documents under a C.I.F. contract, falsity of a bill of lading, or one failing to show shipment within the contract period or to the contract destination. Even in such cases, however, the provisions on cure of tender apply if appropriate documents are readily procurable.

5. Under subsection (2) an installment delivery must be accepted if the non-conformity is curable and the seller gives adequate assurance of cure. Cure of non-conformity of an installment in the first instance can usually be afforded by an allowance against the price, or in the case of reasonable discrepancies in quantity either by a further delivery or a partial rejection. This Article requires reasonable action by a buyer in regard to discrepant delivery and good faith requires that the buyer make any reasonable minor outlay of time or money necessary to cure an overshipment by severing out an acceptable percentage thereof. The seller must take over a cure which involves any material burden; the buyer's obligation reaches only to cooperation. Adequate assurance for purposes of subsection (2) is measured by the same standards as under the section on right to adequate assurance of performance.

6. Subsection (3) is designed to further the continuance of the contract in the absence of an overt cancellation. The question arising when an action is brought as to a single installment only is resolved by making such action waive the right to cancellation. This involves merely a defect in one or more installments, as contrasted with the situation where there is a true repudiation within the section on anticipatory repudiation. Whether the non-conformity in any given installment justifies cancellation as to the future depends, not on whether such non-conformity indicates an intent or likelihood that the future deliveries will also be defective, but whether the non-conformity substantially impairs the value of the whole contract. If only the seller's security in regard to future installments is impaired, he has the right to demand adequate assurances of proper future performance but has not an immediate right to cancel the entire contract. It is clear under this Article, however, that defects in prior installments are cumulative in effect, so that acceptance does not wash out the defect "waived." Prior policy is continued, putting the rule as to buyer's default on the same footing as that in regard to seller's default.

7.   Under the requirement of seasonable notification of cancellation under subsection (3), a buyer who accepts a non-conforming instalment which substantially impairs the value of the entire contract should properly be permitted to withhold his decision as to whether or not to cancel pending a response from the seller as to his claim for cure or adjustment. Similarly, a seller may withhold a delivery pending payment for prior ones, at the same time delaying his decision as to cancellation. A reasonable time for notifying of cancellation, judged by commercial standard under the section on good faith, extends of course to include the time covered by any reasonable negotiation in good faith. However, during this period the defaulting party is entitled, on request, to know whether the contract is still in effect, before he can be required to perform further.

Cross References:

> Point 2: Sections 2–307 and 2–607.
> Point 3: Section 1–203.*
> Point 5: Sections 2–208 and 2–609.
> Point 6: Section 2–610.

Definitional Cross References:

> "Action". Section 1–201.
> "Aggrieved party". Section 1–201.
> "Buyer". Section 2–103.
> "Cancellation". Section 2–106.
> "Conform". Section 2–106.
> "Contract". Section 1–201.
> "Lot". Section 2–105.
> "Notifies". Section 1–201.*
> "Seasonably". Section 1–204.*
> "Seller". Section 2–103.

§ 2–613.   Casualty to Identified Goods.

Where the contract requires for its performance goods identified when the contract is made, and the goods suffer casualty without fault of either party before the risk of loss passes to the buyer, or in a proper case under a "no arrival, no sale" term (Section 2–324) then

(a)   if the loss is total the contract is avoided; and

(b)   if the loss is partial or the goods have so deteriorated as no longer to conform to the contract the buyer may nevertheless demand inspection and at his option either treat the contract as avoided or accept the goods with due allowance from the contract price for the deterioration or the deficiency in quantity but without further right against the seller.

Official Comment

Prior Uniform Statutory Provision: Sections 7 and 8, Uniform Sales Act.

Changes: Rewritten, the basic policy being continued but the test of a "divisible" or "indivisible" sale or contract being abandoned in favor of adjustment in business terms.

Purposes of Changes:

1.   Where goods whose continued existence is presupposed by the agreement are destroyed without fault of either party, the buyer is relieved from his obligation but may at his option take the surviving goods at a fair adjustment. "Fault" is intended to include negligence and not merely wilful wrong. The buyer is expressly given the right to inspect the goods in order to determine whether he wishes to avoid the contract entirely or to take the goods with a price adjustment.

2.   The section applies whether the goods were already destroyed at the time of contracting without the knowledge of either party or whether they are destroyed subsequently but before the risk of loss passes to the buyer. Where under the agreement, including of course usage of trade, the risk has passed to the buyer before the

---

*   *Referring to unrevised Article 1 (Appendix A).*

144

casualty, the section has no application. Beyond this, the essential question in determining whether the rules of this section are to be applied is whether the seller has or has not undertaken the responsibility for the continued existence of the goods in proper condition through the time of agreed or expected delivery.

3. The section on the term "no arrival, no sale" makes clear that delay in arrival, quite as much as physical change in the goods, gives the buyer the options set forth in this section.

Cross Reference:

Point 3: Section 2–324.

Definitional Cross References:

"Buyer". Section 2–103.
"Conform". Section 2–106.
"Contract". Section 1–201.
"Fault". Section 1–201.
"Goods". Section 2–105.
"Party". Section 1–201.
"Rights". Section 1–201.
"Seller". Section 2–103.

§ 2–614. Substituted Performance.

(1) Where without fault of either party the agreed berthing, loading, or unloading facilities fail or an agreed type of carrier becomes unavailable or the agreed manner of delivery otherwise becomes commercially impracticable but a commercially reasonable substitute is available, such substitute performance must be tendered and accepted.

(2) If the agreed means or manner of payment fails because of domestic or foreign governmental regulation, the seller may withhold or stop delivery unless the buyer provides a means or manner of payment which is commercially a substantial equivalent. If delivery has already been taken, payment by the means or in the manner provided by the regulation discharges the buyer's obligation unless the regulation is discriminatory, oppressive or predatory.

Official Comment

Prior Uniform Statutory Provision: None.

Purposes:

1. Subsection (1) requires the tender of a commercially reasonable substituted performance where agreed to facilities have failed or become commercially impracticable. Under this Article, in the absence of specific agreement, the normal or usual facilities enter into the agreement either through the circumstances, usage of trade or prior course of dealing.

This section appears between Section 2–613 on casualty to identified goods and the next section on excuse by failure of presupposed conditions, both of which deal with excuse and complete avoidance of the contract where the occurrence or non-occurrence of a contingency which was a basic assumption of the contract makes the expected performance impossible. The distinction between the present section and those sections lies in whether the failure or impossibility of performance arises in connection with an incidental matter or goes to the very heart of the agreement. The differing lines of solution are contrasted in a comparison of *International Paper Co. v. Rockefeller*, 161 App.Div. 180, 146 N.Y.S. 371 (1914) and *Meyer v. Sullivan*, 40 Cal.App. 723, 181 P. 847 (1919). In the former case a contract for the sale of spruce to be cut from a particular tract of land was involved. When a fire destroyed the trees growing on that tract the seller was held excused since performance was impossible. In the latter case the contract called for delivery of wheat "f.o.b. Kosmos Steamer at Seattle." The war led to cancellation of that line's sailing schedule after space had been duly engaged and the buyer was held entitled to demand substituted delivery at the warehouse on the line's loading dock. Under this Article, of course, the seller would also be entitled, had the market gone the other way, to make a substituted tender in that manner.

There must, however, be a true commercial impracticability to excuse the agreed to performance and justify a substituted performance. When this is the case a reasonable substituted performance tendered by either party should excuse him from strict compliance with contract terms which do not go to the essence of the agreement.

2.   The substitution provided in this section as between buyer and seller does not carry over into the obligation of a financing agency under a letter of credit, since such an agency is entitled to performance which is plainly adequate on its face and without need to look into commercial evidence outside of the documents. See Article 5, especially Sections 5–102, 5–103, 5–109, 5–110, 5–114.*

3.   Under subsection (2) where the contract is still executory on both sides, the seller is permitted to withdraw unless the buyer can provide him with a commercially equivalent return despite the governmental regulation. Where, however, only the debt for the price remains, a larger leeway is permitted. The buyer may pay in the manner provided by the regulation even though this may not be commercially equivalent provided that the regulation is not "discriminatory, oppressive or predatory."

Cross Reference:

Point 2: Article 5.

Definitional Cross References:

"Buyer". Section 2–103.
"Fault". Section 1–201.
"Party". Section 1–201.
"Seller". Section 2–103.

§ 2–615.   Excuse by Failure of Presupposed Conditions.

Except so far as a seller may have assumed a greater obligation and subject to the preceding section on substituted performance:

(a)   Delay in delivery or non-delivery in whole or in part by a seller who complies with paragraphs (b) and (c) is not a breach of his duty under a contract for sale if performance as agreed has been made impracticable by the occurrence of a contingency the non-occurrence of which was a basic assumption on which the contract was made or by compliance in good faith with any applicable foreign or domestic governmental regulation or order whether or not it later proves to be invalid.

(b)   Where the causes mentioned in paragraph (a) affect only a part of the seller's capacity to perform, he must allocate production and deliveries among his customers but may at his option include regular customers not then under contract as well as his own requirements for further manufacture. He may so allocate in any manner which is fair and reasonable.

(c)   The seller must notify the buyer seasonably that there will be delay or non-delivery and, when allocation is required under paragraph (b), of the estimated quota thus made available for the buyer.

Official Comment

Prior Uniform Statutory Provision: None.

Purposes:

1.   This section excuses a seller from timely delivery of goods contracted for, where his performance has become commercially impracticable because of unforeseen supervening circumstances not within the contemplation of the parties at the time of contracting. The destruction of specific goods and the problem of the use of substituted performance on points other than delay or quantity, treated elsewhere in this Article, must be distinguished from the matter covered by this section.

2.   The present section deliberately refrains from any effort at an exhaustive expression of contingencies and is to be interpreted in all cases sought to be brought within its scope in terms of its underlying reason and purpose.

3.   The first test for excuse under this Article in terms of basic assumption is a familiar one. The additional test of commercial impracticability (as contrasted with "impossibility," "frustration of performance" or "frustration

---

*   *All section references are to unrevised Article 5.*

of the venture") has been adopted in order to call attention to the commercial character of the criterion chosen by this Article.

4. Increased cost alone does not excuse performance unless the rise in cost is due to some unforeseen contingency which alters the essential nature of the performance. Neither is a rise or a collapse in the market in itself a justification, for that is exactly the type of business risk which business contracts made at fixed prices are intended to cover. But a severe shortage of raw materials or of supplies due to a contingency such as war, embargo, local crop failure, unforeseen shutdown of major sources of supply or the like, which either causes a marked increase in cost or altogether prevents the seller from securing supplies necessary to his performance, is within the contemplation of this section. (See *Ford & Sons, Ltd., v. Henry Leetham & Sons, Ltd.*, 21 Com.Cas. 55 (1915, K.B.D.).)

5. Where a particular source of supply is exclusive under the agreement and fails through casualty, the present section applies rather than the provision on destruction or deterioration of specific goods. The same holds true where a particular source of supply is shown by the circumstances to have been contemplated or assumed by the parties at the time of contracting. (See *Davis Co. v. Hoffmann-LaRoche Chemical Works*, 178 App.Div. 855, 166 N.Y.S. 179 (1917) and *International Paper Co. v. Rockefeller*, 161 App.Div. 180, 146 N.Y.S. 371 (1914).) There is no excuse under this section, however, unless the seller has employed all due measures to assure himself that his source will not fail. (See *Canadian Industrial Alcohol Co., Ltd., v. Dunbar Molasses Co.*, 258 N.Y. 194, 179 N.E. 383, 80 A.L.R. 1173 (1932) and *Washington Mfg. Co. v. Midland Lumber Co.*, 113 Wash. 593, 194 P. 777 (1921).)

In the case of failure of production by an agreed source for causes beyond the seller's control, the seller should, if possible, be excused since production by an agreed source is without more a basic assumption of the contract. Such excuse should not result in relieving the defaulting supplier from liability nor in dropping into the seller's lap an unearned bonus of damages over. The flexible adjustment machinery of this Article provides the solution under the provision on the obligation of good faith. A condition to his making good the claim of excuse is the turning over to the buyer of his rights against the defaulting source of supply to the extent of the buyer's contract in relation to which excuse is being claimed.

6. In situations in which neither sense nor justice is served by either answer when the issue is posed in flat terms of "excuse" or "no excuse," adjustment under the various provisions of this Article is necessary, especially the sections on good faith, on insecurity and assurance and on the reading of all provisions in the light of their purposes, and the general policy of this Act to use equitable principles in furtherance of commercial standards and good faith.

7. The failure of conditions which go to convenience or collateral values rather than to the commercial practicability of the main performance does not amount to a complete excuse. However, good faith and the reason of the present section and of the preceding one may properly be held to justify and even to require any needed delay involved in a good faith inquiry seeking a readjustment of the contract terms to meet the new conditions.

8. The provisions of this section are made subject to assumption of greater liability by agreement and such agreement is to be found not only in the expressed terms of the contract but in the circumstances surrounding the contracting, in trade usage and the like. Thus the exemptions of this section do not apply when the contingency in question is sufficiently foreshadowed at the time of contracting to be included among the business risks which are fairly to be regarded as part of the dickered terms, either consciously or as a matter of reasonable, commercial interpretation from the circumstances. (See *Madeirense Do Brasil, S.A. v. Stulman-Emrick Lumber Co.*, 147 F.2d 399 (C.C.A., 2 Cir., 1945).) The exemption otherwise present through usage of trade under the present section may also be expressly negated by the language of the agreement. Generally, express agreements as to exemptions designed to enlarge upon or supplant the provisions of this section are to be read in the light of mercantile sense and reason, for this section itself sets up the commercial standard for normal and reasonable interpretation and provides a minimum beyond which agreement may not go.

Agreement can also be made in regard to the consequences of exemption as laid down in paragraphs (b) and (c) and the next section on procedure on notice claiming excuse.

9. The case of a farmer who has contracted to sell crops to be grown on designated land may be regarded as falling either within the section on casualty to identified goods or this section, and he may be excused, when there is a failure of the specific crop, either on the basis of the destruction of identified goods or because of the failure of a basic assumption of the contract.

Exemption of the buyer in the case of a "requirements" contract is covered by the "Output and Requirements" section both as to assumption and allocation of the relevant risks. But when a contract by a manufacturer to buy fuel or raw material makes no specific reference to a particular venture and no such reference may be drawn from the circumstances, commercial understanding views it as a general deal in the general market and not conditioned on any assumption of the continuing operation of the buyer's plant. Even when notice is given by the buyer that the supplies are needed to fill a specific contract of a normal commercial kind, commercial understanding does not see such a supply contract as conditioned on the continuance of the buyer's further contract for outlet. On the other hand, where the buyer's contract is in reasonable commercial understanding conditioned on a definite and specific venture or assumption as, for instance, a war procurement subcontract known to be based on a prime contract which is subject to termination, or a supply contract for a particular construction venture, the reason of the present section may well apply and entitle the buyer to the exemption.

10.　Following its basic policy of using commercial practicability as a test for excuse, this section recognizes as of equal significance either a foreign or domestic regulation and disregards any technical distinctions between "law," "regulation," "order" and the like. Nor does it make the present action of the seller depend upon the eventual judicial determination of the legality of the particular governmental action. The seller's good faith belief in the validity of the regulation is the test under this Article and the best evidence of his good faith is the general commercial acceptance of the regulation. However, governmental interference cannot excuse unless it truly "supervenes" in such a manner as to be beyond the seller's assumption of risk. And any action by the party claiming excuse which causes or colludes in inducing the governmental action preventing his performance would be in breach of good faith and would destroy his exemption.

11.　An excused seller must fulfill his contract to the extent which the supervening contingency permits, and if the situation is such that his customers are generally affected he must take account of all in supplying one. Subsections (a) and (b), therefore, explicitly permit in any proration a fair and reasonable attention to the needs of regular customers who are probably relying on spot orders for supplies. Customers at different stages of the manufacturing process may be fairly treated by including the seller's manufacturing requirements. A fortiori, the seller may also take account of contracts later in date than the one in question. The fact that such spot orders may be closed at an advanced price causes no difficulty, since any allocation which exceeds normal past requirements will not be reasonable. However, good faith requires, when prices have advanced, that the seller exercise real care in making his allocations, and in case of doubt his contract customers should be favored and supplies prorated evenly among them regardless of price. Save for the extra care thus required by changes in the market, this section seeks to leave every reasonable business leeway to the seller.

Cross References:

Point 1: Sections 2–613 and 2–614.
Point 2: Section 1–102.*
Point 5: Sections 1–203* and 2–613.
Point 6: Sections 1–102,* 1–203* and 2–609.
Point 7: Section 2–614.
Point 8: Sections 1–201, 2–302 and 2–616.
Point 9: Sections 1–102,* 2–306 and 2–613.

Definitional Cross References:

"Between merchants". Section 2–104.
"Buyer". Section 2–103.
"Contract". Section 1–201.
"Contract for sale". Section 2–106.
"Good faith". Section 1–201.
"Merchant". Section 2–104.
"Notifies". Section 1–201.*
"Seasonably". Section 1–201.*
"Seller". Section 2–103.

---

*　*Referring to unrevised Article 1 (Appendix A).*

§ 2–616. Procedure on Notice Claiming Excuse.

(1) Where the buyer receives notification of a material or indefinite delay or an allocation justified under the preceding section he may by written notification to the seller as to any delivery concerned, and where the prospective deficiency substantially impairs the value of the whole contract under the provisions of this Article relating to breach of installment contracts (Section 2–612), then also as to the whole,

(a) terminate and thereby discharge any unexecuted portion of the contract; or

(b) modify the contract by agreeing to take his available quota in substitution.

(2) If after receipt of such notification from the seller the buyer fails so to modify the contract within a reasonable time not exceeding thirty days the contract lapses with respect to any deliveries affected.

(3) The provisions of this section may not be negated by agreement except in so far as the seller has assumed a greater obligation under the preceding section.

Official Comment

Prior Uniform Statutory Provision: None.

Purposes:

This section seeks to establish simple and workable machinery for providing certainty as to when a supervening and excusing contingency "excuses" the delay, "discharges" the contract, or may result in a waiver of the delay by the buyer. When the seller notifies, in accordance with the preceding section, claiming excuse, the buyer may acquiesce, in which case the contract is so modified. No consideration is necessary in a case of this kind to support such a modification. If the buyer does not elect so to modify the contract, he may terminate it and under subsection (2) his silence after receiving the seller's claim of excuse operates as such a termination. Subsection (3) denies effect to any contract clause made in advance of trouble which would require the buyer to stand ready to take delivery whenever the seller is excused from delivery by unforeseen circumstances.

Cross References:

Point 1: Sections 2–209 and 2–615.

Definitional Cross References:

"Buyer". Section 2–103.
"Contract". Section 1–201.
"Installment contract". Section 2–612.
"Notification". Section 1–201.*
"Reasonable time". Section 1–204.*
"Seller". Section 2–103.
"Termination". Section 2–106.
"Written". Section 1–201.

PART 7

REMEDIES

§ 2–701. Remedies for Breach of Collateral Contracts Not Impaired.

Remedies for breach of any obligation or promise collateral or ancillary to a contract for sale are not impaired by the provisions of this Article.

Official Comment

Prior Uniform Statutory Provision: None.

---

* *Referring to unrevised Article 1 (Appendix A).*

Purposes:

Whether a claim for breach of an obligation collateral to the contract for sale requires separate trial to avoid confusion of issues is beyond the scope of this Article; but contractual arrangements which as a business matter enter vitally into the contract should be considered a part thereof in so far as cross-claims or defenses are concerned.

Definitional Cross References:

"Contract for sale". Section 2–106.
"Remedy". Section 1–201.

§ 2–702.   Seller's Remedies on Discovery of Buyer's Insolvency.

(1) Where the seller discovers the buyer to be insolvent he may refuse delivery except for cash including payment for all goods theretofore delivered under the contract, and stop delivery under this Article (Section 2–705).

(2) Where the seller discovers that the buyer has received goods on credit while insolvent he may reclaim the goods upon demand made within ten days after the receipt, but if misrepresentation of solvency has been made to the particular seller in writing within three months before delivery the ten day limitation does not apply. Except as provided in this subsection the seller may not base a right to reclaim goods on the buyer's fraudulent or innocent misrepresentation of solvency or of intent to pay.

(3) The seller's right to reclaim under subsection (2) is subject to the rights of a buyer in ordinary course or other good faith purchaser under this Article (Section 2–403). Successful reclamation of goods excludes all other remedies with respect to them.

As amended in 1966.

Official Comment

Prior Uniform Statutory Provision: Subsection (1)—Sections 53(1)(b), 54(1)(c) and 57, Uniform Sales Act; Subsection (2)—none; Subsection (3)—Section 76(3), Uniform Sales Act.

Changes: Rewritten, the protection given to a seller who has sold on credit and has delivered goods to the buyer immediately preceding his insolvency being extended.

Purposes of Changes and New Matter: To make it clear that:

1. The seller's right to withhold the goods or to stop delivery except for cash when he discovers the buyer's insolvency is made explicit in subsection (1) regardless of the passage of title, and the concept of stoppage has been extended to include goods in the possession of any bailee who has not yet attorned to the buyer.

2. Subsection (2) takes as its base line the proposition that any receipt of goods on credit by an insolvent buyer amounts to a tacit business misrepresentation of solvency and therefore is fraudulent as against the particular seller. This Article makes discovery of the buyer's insolvency and demand within a ten day period a condition of the right to reclaim goods on this ground. The ten day limitation period operates from the time of receipt of the goods.

An exception to this time limitation is made when a written misrepresentation of solvency has been made to the particular seller within three months prior to the delivery. To fall within the exception the statement of solvency must be in writing, addressed to the particular seller and dated within three months of the delivery.

3. Because the right of the seller to reclaim goods under this section constitutes preferential treatment as against the buyer's other creditors, subsection (3) provides that such reclamation bars all his other remedies as to the goods involved.

As amended in 1966.

Cross References:

Point 1: Sections 2–401 and 2–705.
Compare Section 2–502.

Definitional Cross References:

"Buyer". Section 2–103.
"Buyer in ordinary course of business". Section 1–201.
"Contract". Section 1–201.
"Good faith". Section 1–201.
"Goods". Section 2–105.
"Insolvent". Section 1–201.
"Person". Section 1–201.
"Purchaser". Section 1–201.
"Receipt" of goods. Section 2–103.
"Remedy". Section 1–201.
"Rights". Section 1–201.
"Seller". Section 2–103.
"Writing". Section 1–201.

§ 2–703. Seller's Remedies in General.

Where the buyer wrongfully rejects or revokes acceptance of goods or fails to make a payment due on or before delivery or repudiates with respect to a part or the whole, then with respect to any goods directly affected and, if the breach is of the whole contract (Section 2–612), then also with respect to the whole undelivered balance, the aggrieved seller may

(a) withhold delivery of such goods;

(b) stop delivery by any bailee as hereafter provided (Section 2–705);

(c) proceed under the next section respecting goods still unidentified to the contract;

(d) resell and recover damages as hereafter provided (Section 2–706);

(e) recover damages for non-acceptance (Section 2–708) or in a proper case the price (Section 2–709);

(f) cancel.

Official Comment

Prior Uniform Statutory Provision: No comparable index section. See Section 53, Uniform Sales Act.

Purposes:

1. This section is an index section which gathers together in one convenient place all of the various remedies open to a seller for any breach by the buyer. This Article rejects any doctrine of election of remedy as a fundamental policy and thus the remedies are essentially cumulative in nature and include all of the available remedies for breach. Whether the pursuit of one remedy bars another depends entirely on the facts of the individual case.

2. The buyer's breach which occasions the use of the remedies under this section may involve only one lot or delivery of goods, or may involve all of the goods which are the subject matter of the particular contract. The right of the seller to pursue a remedy as to all the goods when the breach is as to only one or more lots is covered by the section on breach in installment contracts. The present section deals only with the remedies available after the goods involved in the breach have been determined by that section.

3. In addition to the typical case of refusal to pay or default in payment, the language in the preamble, "fails to make a payment due," is intended to cover the dishonor of a check on due presentment, or the non-acceptance of a draft, and the failure to furnish an agreed letter of credit.

4. It should also be noted that this Act requires its remedies to be liberally administered and provides that any right or obligation which it declares is enforceable by action unless a different effect is specifically prescribed (Section 1–106).*

---

* *Referring to unrevised Article 1 (Appendix A).*

Cross References:

> Point 2: Section 2–612.
> Point 3: Section 2–325.
> Point 4: Section 1–106.*

Definitional Cross References:

> "Aggrieved party". Section 1–201.
> "Buyer". Section 2–103.
> "Cancellation". Section 2–106.
> "Contract". Section 1–201.
> "Goods". Section 2–105.
> "Remedy". Section 1–201.
> "Seller". Section 2–103.

§ 2–704.   Seller's Right to Identify Goods to the Contract Notwithstanding Breach or to Salvage Unfinished Goods.

(1)   An aggrieved seller under the preceding section may

(a)   identify to the contract conforming goods not already identified if at the time he learned of the breach they are in his possession or control;

(b)   treat as the subject of resale goods which have demonstrably been intended for the particular contract even though those goods are unfinished.

(2)   Where the goods are unfinished an aggrieved seller may in the exercise of reasonable commercial judgment for the purposes of avoiding loss and of effective realization either complete the manufacture and wholly identify the goods to the contract or cease manufacture and resell for scrap or salvage value or proceed in any other reasonable manner.

Official Comment

Prior Uniform Statutory Provision: Sections 63(3) and 64(4), Uniform Sales Act.

Changes: Rewritten, the seller's rights being broadened.

Purposes of Changes:

1.   This section gives an aggrieved seller the right at the time of breach to identify to the contract any conforming finished goods, regardless of their resalability, and to use reasonable judgment as to completing unfinished goods. It thus makes the goods available for resale under the resale section, the seller's primary remedy, and in the special case in which resale is not practicable, allows the action for the price which would then be necessary to give the seller the value of his contract.

2.   Under this Article the seller is given express power to complete manufacture or procurement of goods for the contract unless the exercise of reasonable commercial judgment as to the facts as they appear at the time he learns of the breach makes it clear that such action will result in a material increase in damages. The burden is on the buyer to show the commercially unreasonable nature of the seller's action in completing manufacture.

Cross References:

> Sections 2–703 and 2–706.

Definitional Cross References:

> "Aggrieved party". Section 1–201.
> "Conforming". Section 2–106.
> "Contract". Section 1–201.
> "Goods". Section 2–105.
> "Rights". Section 1–201.

---

*   *Referring to unrevised Article 1 (Appendix A).*

"Seller". Section 2–103.

§ 2–705.   Seller's Stoppage of Delivery in Transit or Otherwise.

(1)   The seller may stop delivery of goods in the possession of a carrier or other bailee when he discovers the buyer to be insolvent (Section 2–702) and may stop delivery of carload, truckload, planeload or larger shipments of express or freight when the buyer repudiates or fails to make a payment due before delivery or if for any other reason the seller has a right to withhold or reclaim the goods.

(2)   As against such buyer the seller may stop delivery until

(a)   receipt of the goods by the buyer; or

(b)   acknowledgment to the buyer by any bailee of the goods except a carrier that the bailee holds the goods for the buyer; or

(c)   such acknowledgment to the buyer by a carrier by reshipment or as a warehouseman; or

(d)   negotiation to the buyer of any negotiable document of title covering the goods.

(3)(a)   To stop delivery the seller must so notify as to enable the bailee by reasonable diligence to prevent delivery of the goods.

(b)   After such notification the bailee must hold and deliver the goods according to the directions of the seller but the seller is liable to the bailee for any ensuing charges or damages.

(c)   If a negotiable document of title has been issued for goods the bailee is not obliged to obey a notification to stop until surrender of possession or control of the document.

(d)   A carrier who has issued a non-negotiable bill of lading is not obliged to obey a notification to stop received from a person other than the consignor.

As amended in 2003.

Official Comment

Prior Uniform Statutory Provision: Sections 57–59, Uniform Sales Act; see also Sections 12, 14 and 42, Uniform Bills of Lading Act and Sections 9, 11 and 49, Uniform Warehouse Receipts Act.

Changes: This section continues and develops the above sections of the Uniform Sales Act in the light of the other uniform statutory provisions noted.

Purposes: To make it clear that:

1.   Subsection (1) applies the stoppage principle to other bailees as well as carriers.

It also expands the remedy to cover the situations, in addition to buyer's insolvency, specified in the subsection. But since stoppage is a burden in any case to carriers, and might be a very heavy burden to them if it covered all small shipments in all these situations, the right to stop for reasons other than insolvency is limited to carload, truckload, planeload or larger shipments. The seller shipping to a buyer of doubtful credit can protect himself by shipping C.O.D.

Where stoppage occurs for insecurity it is merely a suspension of performance, and if assurances are duly forthcoming from the buyer the seller is not entitled to resell or divert.

Improper stoppage is a breach by the seller if it effectively interferes with the buyer's right to due tender under the section on manner of tender of delivery. However, if the bailee obeys an unjustified order to stop he may also be liable to the buyer. The measure of his obligation is dependent on the provisions of the Documents of Title Article (Section 7–303). Subsection 3(b) therefore gives him a right of indemnity as against the seller in such a case.

2.   "Receipt by the buyer" includes receipt by the buyer's designated representative, the subpurchaser, when shipment is made direct to him and the buyer himself never receives the goods. It is entirely proper under this Article that the seller, by making such direct shipment to the sub-purchaser, be regarded as acquiescing in the latter's purchase and as thus barred from stoppage of the goods as against him.

As between the buyer and the seller, the latter's right to stop the goods at any time until they reach the place of final delivery is recognized by this section.

Under subsection (3)(c) and (d), the carrier is under no duty to recognize the stop order of a person who is a stranger to the carrier's contract. But the seller's right as against the buyer to stop delivery remains, whether or not the carrier is obligated to recognize the stop order. If the carrier does obey it, the buyer cannot complain merely because of that circumstance; and the seller becomes obligated under subsection (3)(b) to pay the carrier any ensuing damages or charges.

3.   A diversion of a shipment is not a "reshipment" under subsection (2)(c) when it is merely an incident to the original contract of transportation. Nor is the procurement of "exchange bills" of lading which change only the name of the consignee to that of the buyer's local agent but do not alter the destination of a reshipment.

Acknowledgment by the carrier as a "warehouse" within the meaning of this Article requires a contract of a truly different character from the original shipment, a contract not in extension of transit but as a warehouse.

4.   Subsection (3)(c) makes the bailee's obedience of a notification to stop conditional upon the surrender of possession or control of any outstanding negotiable document.

5.   Any charges or losses incurred by the carrier in following the seller's orders, whether or not he was obligated to do so, fall to the seller's charge.

6.   After an effective stoppage under this section the seller's rights in the goods are the same as if he had never made a delivery.

Cross References:

> Sections 2–702 and 2–703.
> Point 1: Sections 2–503 and 2–609, and Article 7.
> Point 2: Section 2–103 and Article 7.

Definitional Cross References:

> "Buyer". Section 2–103.
> "Contract for sale". Section 2–106.
> "Document of title". Section 1–201.
> "Goods". Section 2–105.
> "Insolvent". Section 1–201.
> "Notification". Section 1–201.*
> "Receipt" of goods. Section 2–103.
> "Rights". Section 1–201.
> "Seller". Section 2–103.

As amended in 2003.

§ 2–706.   Seller's Resale Including Contract for Resale.

(1)   Under the conditions stated in Section 2–703 on seller's remedies, the seller may resell the goods concerned or the undelivered balance thereof. Where the resale is made in good faith and in a commercially reasonable manner the seller may recover the difference between the resale price and the contract price together with any incidental damages allowed under the provisions of this Article (Section 2–710), but less expenses saved in consequence of the buyer's breach.

(2)   Except as otherwise provided in subsection (3) or unless otherwise agreed resale may be at public or private sale including sale by way of one or more contracts to sell or of identification to an existing contract of the seller. Sale may be as a unit or in parcels and at any time and place and on any terms but every aspect of the sale including the method, manner, time, place and terms must be commercially reasonable. The resale must be reasonably identified as referring to the broken contract, but it is not necessary that the goods be in existence or that any or all of them have been identified to the contract before the breach.

---

*   *Referring to unrevised Article 1 (Appendix A).*

(3)   Where the resale is at private sale the seller must give the buyer reasonable notification of his intention to resell.

(4)   Where the resale is at public sale

(a)   only identified goods can be sold except where there is a recognized market for a public sale of futures in goods of the kind; and

(b)   it must be made at a usual place or market for public sale if one is reasonably available and except in the case of goods which are perishable or threaten to decline in value speedily the seller must give the buyer reasonable notice of the time and place of the resale; and

(c)   if the goods are not to be within the view of those attending the sale the notification of sale must state the place where the goods are located and provide for their reasonable inspection by prospective bidders; and

(d)   the seller may buy.

(5)   A purchaser who buys in good faith at a resale takes the goods free of any rights of the original buyer even though the seller fails to comply with one or more of the requirements of this section.

(6)   The seller is not accountable to the buyer for any profit made on any resale. A person in the position of a seller (Section 2–707) or a buyer who has rightfully rejected or justifiably revoked acceptance must account for any excess over the amount of his security interest, as hereinafter defined (subsection (3) of Section 2–711).

Official Comment

Prior Uniform Statutory Provision: Section 60, Uniform Sales Act.

Changes: Rewritten.

Purposes of Changes: To simplify the prior statutory provision and to make it clear that:

1.   The only condition precedent to the seller's right of resale under subsection (1) is a breach by the buyer within the section on the seller's remedies in general or insolvency. Other meticulous conditions and restrictions of the prior uniform statutory provision are disapproved by this Article and are replaced by standards of commercial reasonableness. Under this section the seller may resell the goods after any breach by the buyer. Thus, an anticipatory repudiation by the buyer gives rise to any of the seller's remedies for breach, and to the right of resale. This principle is supplemented by subsection (2) which authorizes a resale of goods which are not in existence or were not identified to the contract before the breach.

2.   In order to recover the damages prescribed in subsection (1) the seller must act "in good faith and in a commercially reasonable manner" in making the resale. This standard is intended to be more comprehensive than that of "reasonable care and judgment" established by the prior uniform statutory provision. Failure to act properly under this section deprives the seller of the measure of damages here provided and relegates him to that provided in Section 2–708.

Under this Article the seller resells by authority of law, in his own behalf, for his own benefit and for the purpose of fixing his damages. The theory of a seller's agency is thus rejected.

3.   If the seller complies with the prescribed standard of duty in making the resale, he may recover from the buyer the damages provided for in subsection (1). Evidence of market or current prices at any particular time or place is relevant only on the question of whether the seller acted in a commercially reasonable manner in making the resale.

The distinction drawn by some courts between cases where the title had not passed to the buyer and the seller had resold as owner, and cases where the title had passed and the seller had resold by virtue of his lien on the goods, is rejected.

4.   Subsection (2) frees the remedy of resale from legalistic restrictions and enables the seller to resell in accordance with reasonable commercial practices so as to realize as high a price as possible in the circumstances. By "public" sale is meant a sale by auction. A "private" sale may be effected by solicitation and negotiation conducted either directly or through a broker. In choosing between a public and private sale the character of the goods must be considered and relevant trade practices and usages must be observed.

5. Subsection (2) merely clarifies the common law rule that the time for resale is a reasonable time after the buyer's breach, by using the language "commercially reasonable." What is such a reasonable time depends upon the nature of the goods, the condition of the market and the other circumstances of the case; its length cannot be measured by any legal yardstick or divided into degrees. Where a seller contemplating resale receives a demand from the buyer for inspection under the section of preserving evidence of goods in dispute, the time for resale may be appropriately lengthened.

On the question of the place for resale, subsection (2) goes to the ultimate test, the commercial reasonableness of the seller's choice as to the place for an advantageous resale. This Article rejects the theory that the seller is required to resell at the agreed place for delivery and that a resale elsewhere can be permitted only in exceptional cases.

6. The purpose of subsection (2) being to enable the seller to dispose of the goods to the best advantage, he is permitted in making the resale to depart from the terms and conditions of the original contract for sale to any extent "commercially reasonable" in the circumstances.

7. The provision of subsection (2) that the goods need not be in existence to be resold applies when the buyer is guilty of anticipatory repudiation of a contract for future goods, before the goods or some of them have come into existence. In such a case the seller may exercise the right of resale and fix his damages by "one or more contracts to sell" the quantity of conforming future goods affected by the repudiation. The companion provision of subsection (2) that resale may be made although the goods were not identified to the contract prior to the buyer's breach, likewise contemplates an anticipatory repudiation by the buyer but occurring after the goods are in existence. If the goods so identified conform to the contract, their resale will fix the seller's damages quite as satisfactorily as if they had been identified before the breach.

8. Where the resale is to be by private sale, subsection (3) requires that reasonable notification of the seller's intention to resell must be given to the buyer. The length of notification of a private sale depends upon the urgency of the matter. Notification of the time and place of this type of sale is not required.

Subsection (4)(b) requires that the seller give the buyer reasonable notice of the time and place of a public resale so that he may have an opportunity to bid or to secure the attendance of other bidders. An exception is made in the case of goods "which are perishable or threaten to decline speedily in value."

9. Since there would be no reasonable prospect of competitive bidding elsewhere, subsection (4) requires that a public resale "must be made at a usual place or market for public sale if one is reasonably available;" i.e., a place or market which prospective bidders may reasonably be expected to attend. Such a market may still be "reasonably available" under this subsection, though at a considerable distance from the place where the goods are located. In such a case the expense of transporting the goods for resale is recoverable from the buyer as part of the seller's incidental damages under subsection (1). However, the question of availability is one of commercial reasonableness in the circumstances and if such "usual" place or market is not reasonably available, a duly advertised public resale may be held at another place if it is one which prospective bidders may reasonably be expected to attend, as distinguished from a place where there is no demand whatsoever for goods of the kind.

Paragraph (a) of subsection (4) qualifies the last sentence of subsection (2) with respect to resales of unidentified and future goods at public sale. If conforming goods are in existence the seller may identify them to the contract after the buyer's breach and then resell them at public sale. If the goods have not been identified, however, he may resell them at public sale only as "future" goods and only where there is a recognized market for public sale of futures in goods of the kind.

The provisions of paragraph (c) of subsection (4) are intended to permit intelligent bidding.

The provision of paragraph (d) of subsection (4) permitting the seller to bid and, of course, to become the purchaser, benefits the original buyer by tending to increase the resale price and thus decreasing the damages he will have to pay.

10. This Article departs in subsection (5) from the prior uniform statutory provision in permitting a good faith purchaser at resale to take a good title as against the buyer even though the seller fails to comply with the requirements of this section.

11. Under subsection (6), the seller retains profit, if any, without distinction based on whether or not he had a lien since this Article divorces the question of passage of title to the buyer from the seller's right of resale or the consequences of its exercise. On the other hand, where "a person in the position of a seller" or a buyer acting under the section on buyer's remedies, exercises his right of resale under the present section he does so only for

the limited purpose of obtaining cash for his "security interest" in the goods. Once that purpose has been accomplished any excess in the resale price belongs to the seller to whom an accounting must be made as provided in the last sentence of subsection (6).

Cross References:

Point 1: Sections 2–610, 2–702 and 2–703.
Point 2: Section 1–201.
Point 3: Sections 2–708 and 2–710.
Point 4: Section 2–328.
Point 8: Section 2–104.
Point 9: Section 2–710.
Point 11: Sections 2–401, 2–707 and 2–711(3).

Definitional Cross References:

"Buyer". Section 2–103.
"Contract". Section 1–201.
"Contract for sale". Section 2–106.
"Good faith". Section 2–103.
"Goods". Section 2–105.
"Merchant". Section 2–104.
"Notification". Section 1–201.*
"Person in position of seller". Section 2–707.
"Purchase". Section 1–201.
"Rights". Section 1–201.
"Sale". Section 2–106.
"Security interest". Section 1–201.
"Seller". Section 2–103.

§ 2–707.   "Person in the Position of a Seller".

(1)   A "person in the position of a seller" includes as against a principal an agent who has paid or become responsible for the price of goods on behalf of his principal or anyone who otherwise holds a security interest or other right in goods similar to that of a seller.

(2)   A person in the position of a seller may as provided in this Article withhold or stop delivery (Section 2–705) and resell (Section 2–706) and recover incidental damages (Section 2–710).

Official Comment

Prior Uniform Statutory Provision: Section 52(2), Uniform Sales Act.

Changes: Rewritten.

Purposes of Changes: To make it clear that:

In addition to following in general the prior uniform statutory provision, the case of a financing agency which has acquired documents by honoring a letter of credit for the buyer or by discounting a draft for the seller has been included in the term "a person in the position of a seller."

Cross Reference:

Article 5, Section 2–506.

Definitional Cross References:

"Consignee". Section 7–102.
"Consignor". Section 7–102.
"Goods". Section 2–105.

---

*   *Referring to unrevised Article 1 (Appendix A).*

"Security interest". Section 1–201.
"Seller". Section 2–103.

§ 2–708.   Seller's Damages for Non-acceptance or Repudiation.

(1)   Subject to subsection (2) and to the provisions of this Article with respect to proof of market price (Section 2–723), the measure of damages for non-acceptance or repudiation by the buyer is the difference between the market price at the time and place for tender and the unpaid contract price together with any incidental damages provided in this Article (Section 2–710), but less expenses saved in consequence of the buyer's breach.

(2)   If the measure of damages provided in subsection (1) is inadequate to put the seller in as good a position as performance would have done then the measure of damages is the profit (including reasonable overhead) which the seller would have made from full performance by the buyer, together with any incidental damages provided in this Article (Section 2–710), due allowance for costs reasonably incurred and due credit for payments or proceeds of resale.

Official Comment

Prior Uniform Statutory Provision: Section 64, Uniform Sales Act.

Changes: Rewritten.

Purposes of Changes: To make it clear that:

1.   The prior uniform statutory provision is followed generally in setting the current market price at the time and place for tender as the standard by which damages for non-acceptance are to be determined. The time and place of tender is determined by reference to the section on manner of tender of delivery, and to the sections on the effect of such terms as FOB, FAS, CIF, C. & F., Ex Ship and No Arrival, No Sale.

In the event that there is no evidence available of the current market price at the time and place of tender, proof of a substitute market may be made under the section on determination and proof of market price. Furthermore, the section on the admissibility of market quotations is intended to ease materially the problem of providing competent evidence.

2.   The provision of this section permitting recovery of expected profit including reasonable overhead where the standard measure of damages is inadequate, together with the new requirement that price actions may be sustained only where resale is impractical, are designed to eliminate the unfair and economically wasteful results arising under the older law when fixed price articles were involved. This section permits the recovery of lost profits in all appropriate cases, which would include all standard priced goods. The normal measure there would be list price less cost to the dealer or list price less manufacturing cost to the manufacturer. It is not necessary to a recovery of "profit" to show a history of earnings, especially of a new venture is involved.

3.   In all cases the seller may recover incidental damages.

Cross References:

Point 1: Sections 2–319 through 2–324, 2–503, 2–723 and 2–724.
Point 2: Section 2–709.
Point 3: Section 2–710.

Definitional Cross References:

"Buyer". Section 2–103.
"Contract". Section 1–201.
"Seller". Section 2–103.

§ 2–709.   Action for the Price.

(1)   When the buyer fails to pay the price as it becomes due the seller may recover, together with any incidental damages under the next section, the price

(a)   of goods accepted or of conforming goods lost or damaged within a commercially reasonable time after risk of their loss has passed to the buyer; and

(b) of goods identified to the contract if the seller is unable after reasonable effort to resell them at a reasonable price or the circumstances reasonably indicate that such effort will be unavailing.

(2) Where the seller sues for the price he must hold for the buyer any goods which have been identified to the contract and are still in his control except that if resale becomes possible he may resell them at any time prior to the collection of the judgment. The net proceeds of any such resale must be credited to the buyer and payment of the judgment entitles him to any goods not resold.

(3) After the buyer has wrongfully rejected or revoked acceptance of the goods or has failed to make a payment due or has repudiated (Section 2–610), a seller who is held not entitled to the price under this section shall nevertheless be awarded damages for non-acceptance under the preceding section.

Official Comment

Prior Uniform Statutory Provision: Section 63, Uniform Sales Act.

Changes: Rewritten, important commercially needed changes being incorporated.

Purposes of Changes: To make it clear that:

1.   Neither the passing of title to the goods nor the appointment of a day certain for payment is now material to a price action.

2.   The action for the price is now generally limited to those cases where resale of the goods is impracticable except where the buyer has accepted the goods or where they have been destroyed after risk of loss has passed to the buyer.

3.   This section substitutes an objective test by action for the former "not readily resalable" standard. An action for the price under subsection (1)(b) can be sustained only after a "reasonable effort to resell" the goods "at reasonable price" has actually been made or where the circumstances "reasonably indicate" that such an effort will be unavailing.

4.   If a buyer is in default not with respect to the price, but on an obligation to make an advance, the seller should recover not under this section for the price as such, but for the default in the collateral (though coincident) obligation to finance the seller. If the agreement between the parties contemplates that the buyer will acquire, on making the advance, a security interest in the goods, the buyer on making the advance has such an interest as soon as the seller has rights in the agreed collateral. See Section 9–204.

5.   "Goods accepted" by the buyer under subsection (1)(a) include only goods as to which there has been no justified revocation of acceptance, for such a revocation means that there has been a default by the seller which bars his rights under this section. "Goods lost or damaged" are covered by the section on risk of loss. "Goods identified to the contract" under subsection (1)(b) are covered by the section on identification and the section on identification notwithstanding breach.

6.   This section is intended to be exhaustive in its enumeration of cases where an action for the price lies.

7.   If the action for the price fails, the seller may nonetheless have proved a case entitling him to damages for non-acceptance. In such a situation, subsection (3) permits recovery of those damages in the same action.

Cross References:

    Point 4: Section 1–106.*

    Point 5: Sections 2–501, 2–509, 2–510 and 2–704.

    Point 7: Section 2–708.

Definitional Cross References:

    "Action". Section 1–201.

    "Buyer". Section 2–103.

    "Conforming". Section 2–106.

    "Contract". Section 1–201.

    "Goods". Section 2–105.

    "Seller". Section 2–103.

---

*   *Referring to unrevised Article 1 (Appendix A).*

§ 2–710.   Seller's Incidental Damages.

Incidental damages to an aggrieved seller include any commercially reasonable charges, expenses or commissions incurred in stopping delivery, in the transportation, care and custody of goods after the buyer's breach, in connection with return or resale of the goods or otherwise resulting from the breach.

Official Comment

Prior Uniform Statutory Provision: See Sections 64 and 70, Uniform Sales Act.

Purposes: To authorize reimbursement of the seller for expenses reasonably incurred by him as a result of the buyer's breach. The section sets forth the principal normal and necessary additional elements of damage flowing from the breach but intends to allow all commercially reasonable expenditures made by the seller.

Definitional Cross References:

"Aggrieved party". Section 1–201.
"Buyer". Section 2–103.
"Goods". Section 2–105.
"Seller". Section 2–103.

§ 2–711.   Buyer's Remedies in General; Buyer's Security Interest in Rejected Goods.

(1)   Where the seller fails to make delivery or repudiates or the buyer rightfully rejects or justifiably revokes acceptance then with respect to any goods involved, and with respect to the whole if the breach goes to the whole contract (Section 2–612), the buyer may cancel and whether or not he has done so may in addition to recovering so much of the price as has been paid

(a)   "cover" and have damages under the next section as to all the goods affected whether or not they have been identified to the contract; or

(b)   recover damages for non-delivery as provided in this Article (Section 2–713).

(2)   Where the seller fails to deliver or repudiates the buyer may also

(a)   if the goods have been identified recover them as provided in this Article (Section 2–502); or

(b)   in a proper case obtain specific performance or replevy the goods as provided in this Article (Section 2–716).

(3)   On rightful rejection or justifiable revocation of acceptance a buyer has a security interest in goods in his possession or control for any payments made on their price and any expenses reasonably incurred in their inspection, receipt, transportation, care and custody and may hold such goods and resell them in like manner as an aggrieved seller (Section 2–706).

Official Comment

Prior Uniform Statutory Provision: No comparable index section; Subsection (3)—Section 69(5), Uniform Sales Act.

Changes: The prior uniform statutory provision is generally continued and expanded in Subsection (3).

Purposes of Changes and New Matter:

1.   To index in this section the buyer's remedies, subsection (1) covering those remedies permitting the recovery of money damages, and subsection (2) covering those which permit reaching the goods themselves. The remedies listed here are those available to a buyer who has not accepted the goods or who has justifiably revoked his acceptance. The remedies available to a buyer with regard to goods finally accepted appear in the section dealing with breach in regard to accepted goods. The buyer's right to proceed as to all goods when the breach is as to only some of the goods is determined by the section on breach in installment contracts and by the section on partial acceptance.

Despite the seller's breach, proper retender of delivery under the section on cure of improper tender or replacement can effectively preclude the buyer's remedies under this section, except for any delay involved.

2.   To make it clear in subsection (3) that the buyer may hold and resell rejected goods if he has paid a part of the price or incurred expenses of the type specified. "Paid" as used here includes acceptance of a draft or other time negotiable instrument or the signing of a negotiable note. His freedom of resale is coextensive with that of a seller under this Article except that the buyer may not keep any profit resulting from the resale and is limited to retaining only the amount of the price paid and the costs involved in the inspection and handling of the goods. The buyer's security interest in the goods is intended to be limited to the items listed in subsection (3), and the buyer is not permitted to retain such funds as he might believe adequate for his damages. The buyer's right to cover, or to have damages for non-delivery, is not impaired by his exercise of his right of resale.

3.   It should also be noted that this Act requires its remedies to be liberally administered and provides that any right or obligation which it declares is enforceable by action unless a different effect is specifically prescribed (Section 1–106).*

Cross References:

Point 1: Sections 2–508, 2–601(c), 2–608, 2–612 and 2–714.
Point 2: Section 2–706.
Point 3: Section 1–106.*

Definitional Cross References:

"Aggrieved party". Section 1–201.
"Buyer". Section 2–103.
"Cancellation". Section 2–106.
"Contract". Section 1–201.
"Cover". Section 2–712.
"Goods". Section 2–105.
"Notifies". Section 1–201.*
"Receipt" of goods. Section 2–103.
"Remedy". Section 1–201.
"Security interest". Section 1–201.
"Seller". Section 2–103.

§ 2–712.   "Cover"; Buyer's Procurement of Substitute Goods.

(1)   After a breach within the preceding section the buyer may "cover" by making in good faith and without unreasonable delay any reasonable purchase of or contract to purchase goods in substitution for those due from the seller.

(2)   The buyer may recover from the seller as damages the difference between the cost of cover and the contract price together with any incidental or consequential damages as hereinafter defined (Section 2–715), but less expenses saved in consequence of the seller's breach.

(3)   Failure of the buyer to effect cover within this section does not bar him from any other remedy.

Official Comment

Prior Uniform Statutory Provision: None.

Purposes:

1.   This section provides the buyer with a remedy aimed at enabling him to obtain the goods he needs thus meeting his essential need. This remedy is the buyer's equivalent of the seller's right to resell.

2.   The definition of "cover" under subsection (1) envisages a series of contracts or sales, as well as a single contract or sale; goods not identical with those involved but commercially usable as reasonable substitutes under the circumstances of the particular case; and contracts on credit or delivery terms differing from the contract in breach, but again reasonable under the circumstances. The test of proper cover is whether at the time and place the buyer acted in good faith and in a reasonable manner, and it is immaterial that hindsight may later prove that the method of cover used was not the cheapest or most effective.

---

*   *Referring to unrevised Article 1 (Appendix A).*

The requirement that the buyer must cover "without unreasonable delay" is not intended to limit the time necessary for him to look around and decide as to how he may best effect cover. The test here is similar to that generally used in this Article as to reasonable time and seasonable action.

3.   Subsection (3) expresses the policy that cover is not a mandatory remedy for the buyer. The buyer is always free to choose between cover and damages for non-delivery under the next section.

However, this subsection must be read in conjunction with the section which limits the recovery of consequential damages to such as could not have been obviated by cover. Moreover, the operation of the section on specific performance of contracts for "unique" goods must be considered in this connection for availability of the goods to the particular buyer for his particular needs is the test for that remedy and inability to cover is made an express condition to the right of the buyer to replevy the goods.

4.   This section does not limit cover to merchants, in the first instance. It is the vital and important remedy for the consumer buyer as well. Both are free to use cover: the domestic or non-merchant consumer is required only to act in normal good faith while the merchant buyer must also observe all reasonable commercial standards of fair dealing in the trade, since this falls within the definition of good faith on his part.

Cross References:

Point 1: Section 2-706.
Point 2: Section 1-204.*
Point 3: Sections 2-713, 2-715 and 2-716.
Point 4: Section 1-203.*

Definitional Cross References:

"Buyer". Section 2-103.
"Contract". Section 1-201.
"Good faith". Section 2-103.
"Goods". Section 2-105.
"Purchase". Section 1-201.
"Remedy". Section 1-201.
"Seller". Section 2-103.

§ 2-713.   Buyer's Damages for Non-delivery or Repudiation.

(1)   Subject to the provisions of this Article with respect to proof of market price (Section 2-723), the measure of damages for non-delivery or repudiation by the seller is the difference between the market price at the time when the buyer learned of the breach and the contract price together with any incidental and consequential damages provided in this Article (Section 2-715), but less expenses saved in consequence of the seller's breach.

(2)   Market price is to be determined as of the place for tender or, in cases of rejection after arrival or revocation of acceptance, as of the place of arrival.

Official Comment

Prior Uniform Statutory Provision: Section 67(3), Uniform Sales Act.

Changes: Rewritten.

Purposes of Changes: To clarify the former rule so that:

1.   The general baseline adopted in this section uses as a yardstick the market in which the buyer would have obtained cover had he sought that relief. So the place for measuring damages is the place of tender (or the place of arrival if the goods are rejected or their acceptance is revoked after reaching their destination) and the crucial time is the time at which the buyer learns of the breach.

2.   The market or current price to be used in comparison with the contract price under this section is the price for goods of the same kind and in the same branch of trade.

---

*   *Referring to unrevised Article 1 (Appendix A).*

3.   When the current market price under this section is difficult to prove the section on determination and proof of market price is available to permit a showing of a comparable market price or, where no market price is available, evidence of spot sale prices is proper. Where the unavailability of a market price is caused by a scarcity of goods of the type involved, a good case is normally made for specific performance under this Article. Such scarcity conditions, moreover, indicate that the price has risen and under the section providing for liberal administration of remedies, opinion evidence as to the value of the goods would be admissible in the absence of a market price and a liberal construction of allowable consequential damages should also result.

4.   This section carries forward the standard rule that the buyer must deduct from his damages any expenses saved as a result of the breach.

5.   The present section provides a remedy which is completely alternative to cover under the preceding section and applies only when and to the extent that the buyer has not covered.

Cross References:

Point 3: Sections 1-106,* 2-716 and 2-723.
Point 5: Section 2-712.

Definitional Cross References:

"Buyer". Section 2-103.
"Contract". Section 1-201.
"Seller". Section 2-103.

§ 2-714.   Buyer's Damages for Breach in Regard to Accepted Goods.

(1)   Where the buyer has accepted goods and given notification (subsection (3) of Section 2-607) he may recover as damages for any non-conformity of tender the loss resulting in the ordinary course of events from the seller's breach as determined in any manner which is reasonable.

(2)   The measure of damages for breach of warranty is the difference at the time and place of acceptance between the value of the goods accepted and the value they would have had if they had been as warranted, unless special circumstances show proximate damages of a different amount.

(3)   In a proper case any incidental and consequential damages under the next section may also be recovered.

Official Comment

Prior Uniform Statutory Provision: Section 69(6) and (7), Uniform Sales Act.

Changes: Rewritten.

Purposes of Changes:

1.   This section deals with the remedies available to the buyer after the goods have been accepted and the time for revocation of acceptance has gone by. In general this section adopts the rule of the prior uniform statutory provision for measuring damages where there has been a breach of warranty as to goods accepted, but goes further to lay down an explicit provision as to the time and place for determining the loss.

The section on deduction of damages from price provides an additional remedy for a buyer who still owes part of the purchase price, and frequently the two remedies will be available concurrently. The buyer's failure to notify of his claim under the section on effects of acceptance, however, operates to bar his remedies under either that section or the present section.

2.   The "non-conformity" referred to in subsection (1) includes not only breaches of warranties but also any failure of the seller to perform according to his obligations under the contract. In the case of such non-conformity, the buyer is permitted to recover for his loss "in any manner which is reasonable."

3.   Subsection (2) describes the usual, standard and reasonable method of ascertaining damages in the case of breach of warranty but it is not intended as an exclusive measure. It departs from the measure of damages for non-delivery in utilizing the place of acceptance rather than the place of tender. In some cases the two may

---

*   *Referring to unrevised Article 1 (Appendix A).*

coincide, as where the buyer signifies his acceptance upon the tender. If, however, the non-conformity is such as would justify revocation of acceptance, the time and place of acceptance under this section is determined as of the buyer's decision not to revoke.

4.   The incidental and consequential damages referred to in subsection (3), which will usually accompany an action brought under this section, are discussed in detail in the comment on the next section.

Cross References:

Point 1: Compare Section 2–711; Sections 2–607 and 2–717.
Point 2: Section 2–106.
Point 3: Sections 2–608 and 2–713.
Point 4: Section 2–715.

Definitional Cross References:

"Buyer". Section 2–103.
"Conform". Section 2–106.
"Goods". Section 1–201.*
"Notification". Section 1–201.**
"Seller". Section 2–103.

§ 2–715.   Buyer's Incidental and Consequential Damages.

(1)   Incidental damages resulting from the seller's breach include expenses reasonably incurred in inspection, receipt, transportation and care and custody of goods rightfully rejected, any commercially reasonable charges, expenses or commissions in connection with effecting cover and any other reasonable expense incident to the delay or other breach.

(2)   Consequential damages resulting from the seller's breach include

(a)   any loss resulting from general or particular requirements and needs of which the seller at the time of contracting had reason to know and which could not reasonably be prevented by cover or otherwise; and

(b)   injury to person or property proximately resulting from any breach of warranty.

Official Comment

Prior Uniform Statutory Provisions: Subsection (2)(b)—Sections 69(7) and 70, Uniform Sales Act.

Changes: Rewritten.

Purposes of Changes and New Matter:

1.   Subsection (1) is intended to provide reimbursement for the buyer who incurs reasonable expenses in connection with the handling of rightfully rejected goods or goods whose acceptance may be justifiably revoked, or in connection with effecting cover where the breach of the contract lies in non-conformity or non-delivery of the goods. The incidental damages listed are not intended to be exhaustive but are merely illustrative of the typical kinds of incidental damage.

2.   Subsection (2) operates to allow the buyer, in an appropriate case, any consequential damages which are the result of the seller's breach. The "tacit agreement" test for the recovery of consequential damages is rejected. Although the older rule at common law which made the seller liable for all consequential damages of which he had "reason to know" in advance is followed, the liberality of that rule is modified by refusing to permit recovery unless the buyer could not reasonably have prevented the loss by cover or otherwise. Subparagraph (2) carries forward the provisions of the prior uniform statutory provision as to consequential damages resulting from breach of warranty, but modifies the rule by requiring first that the buyer attempt to minimize his damages in good faith, either by cover or otherwise.

---

*   *Note from West Advisory Panel: This provision appears in § 2–105.*

**   *Referring to unrevised Article 1 (Appendix A).*

3. In the absence of excuse under the section on merchant's excuse by failure of presupposed conditions, the seller is liable for consequential damages in all cases where he had reason to know of the buyer's general or particular requirements at the time of contracting. It is not necessary that there be a conscious acceptance of an insurer's liability on the seller's part, nor is his obligation for consequential damages limited to cases in which he fails to use due effort in good faith.

Particular needs of the buyer must generally be made known to the seller while general needs must rarely be made known to charge the seller with knowledge.

Any seller who does not wish to take the risk of consequential damages has available the section on contractual limitation of remedy.

4. The burden of proving the extent of loss incurred by way of consequential damage is on the buyer, but the section on liberal administration of remedies rejects any doctrine of certainty which requires almost mathematical precision in the proof of loss. Loss may be determined in any manner which is reasonable under the circumstances.

5. Subsection (2)(b) states the usual rule as to breach of warranty, allowing recovery for injuries "proximately" resulting from the breach. Where the injury involved follows the use of goods without discovery of the defect causing the damage, the question of "proximate" cause turns on whether it was reasonable for the buyer to use the goods without such inspection as would have revealed the defects. If it was not reasonable for him to do so, or if he did in fact discover the defect prior to his use, the injury would not proximately result from the breach of warranty.

6. In the case of sale of wares to one in the business of reselling them, resale is one of the requirements of which the seller has reason to know within the meaning of subsection (2)(a).

Cross References:

Point 1: Section 2–608.
Point 3: Sections 1–203,* 2–615 and 2–719.
Point 4: Section 1–106.*

Definitional Cross References:

"Cover". Section 2–712.
"Goods". Section 1–201.**
"Person". Section 1–201.
"Receipt" of goods. Section 2–103.
"Seller". Section 2–103.

§ 2–716. Buyer's Right to Specific Performance or Replevin.

(1) Specific performance may be decreed where the goods are unique or in other proper circumstances.

(2) The decree for specific performance may include such terms and conditions as to payment of the price, damages, or other relief as the court may deem just.

(3) The buyer has a right of replevin for goods identified to the contract if after reasonable effort he is unable to effect cover for such goods or the circumstances reasonably indicate that such effort will be unavailing or if the goods have been shipped under reservation and satisfaction of the security interest in them has been made or tendered. In the case of goods bought for personal, family, or household purposes, the buyer's right of replevin vests upon acquisition of a special property, even if the seller had not then repudiated or failed to deliver.

As amended in 1999.

---

* *Referring to unrevised Article 1 (Appendix A).*
** *Note from West Advisory Panel: This provision appears in § 2–105.*

Prior Uniform Statutory Provision: Section 68, Uniform Sales Act.

Changes: Rephrased.

Purposes of Changes: To make it clear that:

    1.   The present section continues in general prior policy as to specific performance and injunction against breach. However, without intending to impair in any way the exercise of the court's sound discretion in the matter, this Article seeks to further a more liberal attitude than some courts have shown in connection with the specific performance of contracts of sale.

    2.   In view of this Article's emphasis on the commercial feasibility of replacement, a new concept of what are "unique" goods is introduced under this section. Specific performance is no longer limited to goods which are already specific or ascertained at the time of contracting. The test of uniqueness under this section must be made in terms of the total situation which characterizes the contract. Output and requirements contracts involving a particular or peculiarly available source or market present today the typical commercial specific performance situation, as contrasted with contracts for the sale of heirlooms or priceless works of art which were usually involved in the older cases. However, uniqueness is not the sole basis of the remedy under this section for the relief may also be granted "in other proper circumstances" and inability to cover is strong evidence of "other proper circumstances".

    3.   The legal remedy of replevin is given to the buyer in cases in which cover is reasonably unavailable and goods have been identified to the contract. This is in addition to the buyer's right to recover identified goods under Section 2–502. For consumer goods, the buyer's right to replevin vests upon the buyer's acquisition of a special property, which occurs upon identification of the goods to the contract. See Section 2–501. Inasmuch as a secured party normally acquires no greater rights in its collateral that its debtor had or had power to convey, see Section 2–403(1) (first sentence), a buyer who acquires a right of replevin under subsection (3) will take free of a security interest created by the seller if it attaches to the goods after the goods have been identified to the contract. The buyer will take free, even if the buyer does not buy in ordinary course and even if the security interest is perfected. Of course, to the extent that the buyer pays the price after the security interest attaches, the payments will constitute proceeds of the security interest.

    4.   This section is intended to give the buyer rights to the goods comparable to the seller's rights to the price.

    5.   If a negotiable document of title is outstanding, the buyer's right of replevin relates of course to the document not directly to the goods. See Article 7, especially Section 7–602.

Cross References:

    Point 3: Section 2–502.
    Point 4: Section 2–709.
    Point 5: Article 7.

Definitional Cross References:

    "Buyer". Section 2–103.
    "Goods". Section 1–201.*
    "Rights". Section 1–201.

As amended in 1999.

§ 2–717.   Deduction of Damages From the Price.

    The buyer on notifying the seller of his intention to do so may deduct all or any part of the damages resulting from any breach of the contract from any part of the price still due under the same contract.

Prior Uniform Statutory Provision: See Section 69(1)(a), Uniform Sales Act.

---

    *   *Note from West Advisory Panel: This provision appears in § 2–105.*

Purposes:

1.   This section permits the buyer to deduct from the price damages resulting from any breach by the seller and does not limit the relief to cases of breach of warranty as did the prior uniform statutory provision. To bring this provision into application the breach involved must be of the same contract under which the price in question is claimed to have been earned.

2.   The buyer, however, must give notice of his intention to withhold all or part of the price if he wishes to avoid a default within the meaning of the section on insecurity and right to assurances. In conformity with the general policies of this Article, no formality of notice is required and any language which reasonably indicates the buyer's reason for holding up his payment is sufficient.

Cross Reference:

Point 2: Section 2–609.

Definitional Cross References:

"Buyer". Section 2–103.
"Notifies". Section 1–201.*

§ 2–718.   Liquidation or Limitation of Damages; Deposits.

(1)   Damages for breach by either party may be liquidated in the agreement but only at an amount which is reasonable in the light of the anticipated or actual harm caused by the breach, the difficulties of proof of loss, and the inconvenience or nonfeasibility of otherwise obtaining an adequate remedy. A term fixing unreasonably large liquidated damages is void as a penalty.

(2)   Where the seller justifiably withholds delivery of goods because of the buyer's breach, the buyer is entitled to restitution of any amount by which the sum of his payments exceeds

(a)   the amount to which the seller is entitled by virtue of terms liquidating the seller's damages in accordance with subsection (1), or

(b)   in the absence of such terms, twenty per cent of the value of the total performance for which the buyer is obligated under the contract or $500, whichever is smaller.

(3)   The buyer's right to restitution under subsection (2) is subject to offset to the extent that the seller establishes

(a)   a right to recover damages under the provisions of this Article other than subsection (1), and

(b)   the amount or value of any benefits received by the buyer directly or indirectly by reason of the contract.

(4)   Where a seller has received payment in goods their reasonable value or the proceeds of their resale shall be treated as payments for the purposes of subsection (2); but if the seller has notice of the buyer's breach before reselling goods received in part performance, his resale is subject to the conditions laid down in this Article on resale by an aggrieved seller (Section 2–706).

Official Comment

Prior Uniform Statutory Provision: None.

Purposes:

1.   Under subsection (1) liquidated damage clauses are allowed where the amount involved is reasonable in the light of the circumstances of the case. The subsection sets forth explicitly the elements to be considered in determining the reasonableness of a liquidated damage clause. A term fixing unreasonably large liquidated damages is expressly made void as a penalty. An unreasonably small amount would be subject to similar criticism and might be stricken under the section on unconscionable contracts or clauses.

---

*   *Referring to unrevised Article 1 (Appendix A).*

2.   Subsection (2) refuses to recognize a forfeiture unless the amount of the payment so forfeited represents a reasonable liquidation of damages as determined under subsection (1). A special exception is made in the case of small amounts (20% of the price or $500, whichever is smaller) deposited as security. No distinction is made between cases in which the payment is to be applied on the price and those in which it is intended as security for performance. Subsection (2) is applicable to any deposit or down or part payment. In the case of a deposit or turn in of goods resold before the breach, the amount actually received on the resale is to be viewed as the deposit rather than the amount allowed the buyer for the trade in. However, if the seller knows of the breach prior to the resale of the goods turned in, he must make reasonable efforts to realize their true value, and this is assured by requiring him to comply with the conditions laid down in the section on resale by an aggrieved seller.

Cross References:

> Point 1: Section 2–302.
> Point 2: Section 2–706.

Definitional Cross References:

> "Aggrieved party". Section 1–201.
> "Agreement". Section 1–201.
> "Buyer". Section 2–103.
> "Goods". Section 2–105.
> "Notice". Section 1–201.*
> "Party". Section 1–201.
> "Remedy". Section 1–201.
> "Seller". Section 2–103.
> "Term". Section 1–201.

§ 2–719.   Contractual Modification or Limitation of Remedy.

(1)   Subject to the provisions of subsections (2) and (3) of this section and of the preceding section on liquidation and limitation of damages,

(a)   the agreement may provide for remedies in addition to or in substitution for those provided in this Article and may limit or alter the measure of damages recoverable under this Article, as by limiting the buyer's remedies to return of the goods and repayment of the price or to repair and replacement of non-conforming goods or parts; and

(b)   resort to a remedy as provided is optional unless the remedy is expressly agreed to be exclusive, in which case it is the sole remedy.

(2)   Where circumstances cause an exclusive or limited remedy to fail of its essential purpose, remedy may be had as provided in this Act.

(3)   Consequential damages may be limited or excluded unless the limitation or exclusion is unconscionable. Limitation of consequential damages for injury to the person in the case of consumer goods is prima facie unconscionable but limitation of damages where the loss is commercial is not.

Official Comment

Prior Uniform Statutory Provision: None.

Purposes:

1.   Under this section parties are left free to shape their remedies to their particular requirements and reasonable agreements limiting or modifying remedies are to be given effect.

However, it is of the very essence of a sales contract that at least minimum adequate remedies be available. If the parties intend to conclude a contract for sale within this Article they must accept the legal consequence that there be at least a fair quantum of remedy for breach of the obligations or duties outlined in the contract. Thus any clause purporting to modify or limit the remedial provisions of this Article in an unconscionable manner is subject to deletion and in that event the remedies made available by this Article are applicable as if the stricken

---

*   *Referring to unrevised Article 1 (Appendix A).*

clause had never existed. Similarly, under subsection (2), where an apparently fair and reasonable clause because of circumstances fails in its purpose or operates to deprive either party of the substantial value of the bargain, it must give way to the general remedy provisions of this Article.

2.   Subsection (1)(b) creates a presumption that clauses prescribing remedies are cumulative rather than exclusive. If the parties intend the term to describe the sole remedy under the contract, this must be clearly expressed.

3.   Subsection (3) recognizes the validity of clauses limiting or excluding consequential damages but makes it clear that they may not operate in an unconscionable manner. Actually such terms are merely an allocation of unknown or undeterminable risks. The seller in all cases is free to disclaim warranties in the manner provided in Section 2–316.

Cross References:

Point 1: Section 2–302.
Point 3: Section 2–316.

Definitional Cross References:

"Agreement". Section 1–201.
"Buyer". Section 2–103.
"Conforming". Section 2–106.
"Contract". Section 1–201.
"Goods". Section 2–105.
"Remedy". Section 1–201.
"Seller". Section 2–103.

§ 2–720.   Effect of "Cancellation" or "Rescission" on Claims for Antecedent Breach.

Unless the contrary intention clearly appears, expressions of "cancellation" or "rescission" of the contract or the like shall not be construed as a renunciation or discharge of any claim in damages for an antecedent breach.

Official Comment

Prior Uniform Statutory Provision: None.

Purpose:

This section is designed to safeguard a person holding a right of action from any unintentional loss of rights by the ill-advised use of such terms as "cancellation", "rescission", or the like. Once a party's rights have accrued they are not to be lightly impaired by concessions made in business decency and without intention to forego them. Therefore, unless the cancellation of a contract expressly declares that it is "without reservation of rights", or the like, it cannot be considered to be a renunciation under this section.

Cross Reference:

Section 1–107.*

Definitional Cross References:

"Cancellation". Section 2–106.
"Contract". Section 1–201.

§ 2–721.   Remedies for Fraud.

Remedies for material misrepresentation or fraud include all remedies available under this Article for non-fraudulent breach. Neither rescission or a claim for rescission of the contract for sale nor rejection or return of the goods shall bar or be deemed inconsistent with a claim for damages or other remedy.

---

*   *Referring to unrevised Article 1 (Appendix A).*

Official Comment

Prior Uniform Statutory Provision: None.

Purposes: To correct the situation by which remedies for fraud have been more circumscribed than the more modern and mercantile remedies for breach of warranty. Thus the remedies for fraud are extended by this section to coincide in scope with those for non-fraudulent breach. This section thus makes it clear that neither rescission of the contract for fraud nor rejection of the goods bars other remedies unless the circumstances of the case make the remedies incompatible.

Definitional Cross References:

> "Contract for sale". Section 2–106.
> "Goods". Section 1–201.*
> "Remedy". Section 1–201.

§ 2–722.   Who Can Sue Third Parties for Injury to Goods.

Where a third party so deals with goods which have been identified to a contract for sale as to cause actionable injury to a party to that contract

(a)   a right of action against the third party is in either party to the contract for sale who has title to or a security interest or a special property or an insurable interest in the goods; and if the goods have been destroyed or converted a right of action is also in the party who either bore the risk of loss under the contract for sale or has since the injury assumed that risk as against the other;

(b)   if at the time of the injury the party plaintiff did not bear the risk of loss as against the other party to the contract for sale and there is no arrangement between them for disposition of the recovery, his suit or settlement is, subject to his own interest, as a fiduciary for the other party to the contract;

(c)   either party may with the consent of the other sue for the benefit of whom it may concern.

Official Comment

Prior Uniform Statutory Provision: None.

Purposes: To adopt and extend somewhat the principle of the statutes which provide for suit by the real party in interest. The provisions of this section apply only after identification of the goods. Prior to that time only the seller has a right of action. During the period between identification and final acceptance (except in the case of revocation of acceptance) it is possible for both parties to have the right of action. Even after final acceptance both parties may have the right of action if the seller retains possession or otherwise retains an interest.

Definitional Cross References:

> "Action". Section 1–201.
> "Buyer". Section 2–103.
> "Contract for sale". Section 2–106.
> "Goods". Section 2–105.
> "Party". Section 1–201.
> "Rights". Section 1–201.
> "Security interest". Section 1–201.

§ 2–723.   Proof of Market Price: Time and Place.

(1)   If an action based on anticipatory repudiation comes to trial before the time for performance with respect to some or all of the goods, any damages based on market price (Section 2–708 or Section 2–713) shall be determined according to the price of such goods prevailing at the time when the aggrieved party learned of the repudiation.

---

*   *Note from West Advisory Panel: This provision appears in § 2–105.*

(2)   If evidence of a price prevailing at the times or places described in this Article is not readily available the price prevailing within any reasonable time before or after the time described or at any other place which in commercial judgment or under usage of trade would serve as a reasonable substitute for the one described may be used, making any proper allowance for the cost of transporting the goods to or from such other place.

(3)   Evidence of a relevant price prevailing at a time or place other than the one described in this Article offered by one party is not admissible unless and until he has given the other party such notice as the court finds sufficient to prevent unfair surprise.

Official Comment

Prior Uniform Statutory Provision: None.

Purposes: To eliminate the most obvious difficulties arising in connection with the determination of market price, when that is stipulated as a measure of damages by some provision of this Article. Where the appropriate market price is not readily available the court is here granted reasonable leeway in receiving evidence of prices current in other comparable markets or at other times comparable to the one in question. In accordance with the general principle of this Article against surprise, however, a party intending to offer evidence of such a substitute price must give suitable notice to the other party.

This section is not intended to exclude the use of any other reasonable method of determining market price or of measuring damages if the circumstances of the case make this necessary.

Definitional Cross References:

"Action". Section 1–201.
"Aggrieved party". Section 1–201.
"Goods". Section 2–105.
"Notifies". Section 1–201.*
"Party". Section 1–201.
"Reasonable time". Section 1–204.*
"Usage of trade". Section 1–205.*

§ 2–724.   Admissibility of Market Quotations.

Whenever the prevailing price or value of any goods regularly bought and sold in any established commodity market is in issue, reports in official publications or trade journals or in newspapers or periodicals of general circulation published as the reports of such market shall be admissible in evidence. The circumstances of the preparation of such a report may be shown to affect its weight but not its admissibility.

Official Comment

Prior Uniform Statutory Provision: None.

Purposes: To make market quotations admissible in evidence while providing for a challenge of the material by showing the circumstances of its preparation.

No explicit provision as to the weight to be given to market quotations is contained in this section, but such quotations, in the absence of compelling challenge, offer an adequate basis for a verdict.

Market quotations are made admissible when the price or value of goods traded "in any established market" is in issue. The reason of the section does not require that the market be closely organized in the manner of a produce exchange. It is sufficient if transactions in the commodity are frequent and open enough to make a market established by usage in which one price can be expected to affect another and in which an informed report of the range and trend of prices can be assumed to be reasonably accurate.

This section does not in any way intend to limit or negate the application of similar rules of admissibility to other material, whether by action of the courts or by statute. The purpose of the present section is to assure a

---

*   *Referring to unrevised Article 1 (Appendix A).*

minimum of mercantile administration in this important situation and not to limit any liberalizing trend in modern law.

Definitional Cross Reference:

"Goods". Section 2–105.

§ 2–725.   Statute of Limitations in Contracts for Sale.

(1)   An action for breach of any contract for sale must be commenced within four years after the cause of action has accrued. By the original agreement the parties may reduce the period of limitation to not less than one year but may not extend it.

(2)   A cause of action accrues when the breach occurs, regardless of the aggrieved party's lack of knowledge of the breach. A breach of warranty occurs when tender of delivery is made, except that where a warranty explicitly extends to future performance of the goods and discovery of the breach must await the time of such performance the cause of action accrues when the breach is or should have been discovered.

(3)   Where an action commenced within the time limited by subsection (1) is so terminated as to leave available a remedy by another action for the same breach such other action may be commenced after the expiration of the time limited and within six months after the termination of the first action unless the termination resulted from voluntary discontinuance or from dismissal for failure or neglect to prosecute.

(4)   This section does not alter the law on tolling of the statute of limitations nor does it apply to causes of action which have accrued before this Act becomes effective.

Official Comment

Prior Uniform Statutory Provision: None.

Purposes: To introduce a uniform statute of limitations for sales contracts, thus eliminating the jurisdictional variations and providing needed relief for concerns doing business on a nationwide scale whose contracts have heretofore been governed by several different periods of limitation depending upon the state in which the transaction occurred. This Article takes sales contracts out of the general laws limiting the time for commencing contractual actions and selects a four year period as the most appropriate to modern business practice. This is within the normal commercial record keeping period.

Subsection (1) permits the parties to reduce the period of limitation. The minimum period is set at one year. The parties may not, however, extend the statutory period.

Subsection (2), providing that the cause of action accrues when the breach occurs, states an exception where the warranty extends to future performance.

Subsection (3) states the saving provision included in many state statutes and permits an additional short period for bringing new actions, where suits begun within the four year period have been terminated so as to leave a remedy still available for the same breach.

Subsection (4) makes it clear that this Article does not purport to alter or modify in any respect the law on tolling of the Statute of Limitations as it now prevails in the various jurisdictions.

Definitional Cross References:

"Action". Section 1–201.
"Aggrieved party". Section 1–201.
"Agreement". Section 1–201.
"Contract for sale". Section 2–106.
"Goods". Section 2–105.
"Party". Section 1–201.
"Remedy". Section 1–201.
"Term". Section 1–201.
"Termination". Section 2–106.

UCC ARTICLE 2A (2016)

LEASES

Set forth below are the text and Official Comments of Article 2A as of 2016. The 2003 and 2005 amendments to Article 2A, other than those made as part of the Article 7 revisions, were withdrawn in May 2011 and therefore are not included.

ARTICLE 2A (2016)

C. DEFAULT BY LESSEE

National Conference of Commissioners on Uniform State Laws

REPORTER

Ronald DeKoven, New York, New York

DRAFTING COMMITTEE

CHAIRMAN

Edward I. Cutler, Tampa, Florida

MEMBERS

Marion W. Benfield, Jr., Champaign, Illinois

William E. Hogan, New York, New York

Stanley M. Johnston, Springfield, Illinois

Peter F. Langrock, Middlebury, Vermont

Morris W. Macey, Atlanta, Georgia

Frederick H. Miller, Norman, Oklahoma

Donald Osheim, Watertown, South Dakota

Howard J. Swibel, Chicago, Illinois

Phillip Carroll, Little Rock, Arkansas
  President, National Conference (Member Ex Officio)

William J. Pierce, Ann Arbor, Michigan
  Executive Director, National Conference

Harvey Bartle, III, Philadelphia, Pennsylvania
  Chairman, Division C (Member Ex Officio)

ABA ADVISORS

Ronald M. Bayer, Los Angeles, California, Section of Corporation, Banking, and Business Law

William M. Toomajian, Cleveland, Ohio, Section of Taxation

FOREWORD

Article 2A of the Uniform Commercial Code, along with Conforming Amendments to Articles 1 and 9, is presented, upon the recommendation of the Permanent Editorial Board for the Uniform Commercial Code, by the National Conference of Commissioners on Uniform State Laws and the American Law Institute. It represents a major development in commercial law, addressing a type of business transaction, the leasing of personal property, that has long existed. Under present law, transactions of this type are governed partly by common law principles relating to personal property, partly by principles relating to real estate leases, and partly by reference to Articles 2 and 9 of the Uniform Commercial Code, dealing with Sales and Secured Transactions respectively. The legal rules and concepts derived from these sources imperfectly fit a transaction that involves personal property rather than realty, and a lease rather than either a sale or a security interest as such. A statute directly addressing the personal property lease is therefore appropriate.

Such a statute has become especially appropriate with the exponential expansion of the number and scale of personal property lease transactions. Article 2A will apply to transactions involving billions of dollars annually. It will apply to consumer's rental of automobiles or do-it-yourself equipment, on the one hand, and to leases of such items as commercial aircraft (to the extent not preempted by federal law) and industrial machinery, on the other. The text recognizes the differences between consumer and business leasing, while resting upon concepts that apply generally to any personal property lease transactions.

The final product represents an important undertaking of the Conference and the Institute. It has proceeded, following recommendations by the Conference's Study Committee in 1981, through preparation and review by the Conference's Drafting Committee first of a proposed free-standing Uniform Personal Property Leasing Act, which was approved by the Conference, and later of Article 2A, which proceeded through the Permanent Editorial Board, the Executive Committee of the Conference, the Conference, and the Council of the Institute and the Annual Meeting of the members of the Institute. Carrying the text through these several stages has required coordination of somewhat different procedures, and continued patience and mutual forbearance. At the same time, the text has been subjected to analysis and criticism from many points of view and thereby steadily improved.

The resulting product borrows from both Articles 2 and 9. These existing Articles of the Uniform Commercial Code have certain imperfections revealed by the long experience since their adoption. Article 2A cannot overcome those imperfections but seeks to minimize their significance as applied to leases. More fundamentally, there is important conceptual dissonance between Article 2 and Article 9. The formulation of Article 2A takes Articles 2 and 9 as they are for the time being and hence has required careful adjustment to this dissonance.

The drafting task has been complicated both as a matter of substance and as a matter of process. The Reporter, Ronald DeKoven, has been a master of substance and a steady and receptive principal in the process. We join with the Conference and the Institute in expressing our admiration and appreciation for his contribution to this important field of law.

Geoffrey C. Hazard, Jr., *Chairman*
Permanent Editorial
Board for the Uniform
Commercial Code

October 1, 1987

PART 1

GENERAL PROVISIONS

§ 2A–101. Short Title.

This Article shall be known and may be cited as the Uniform Commercial Code—Leases.

Official Comment

Rationale for Codification:

There are several reasons for codifying the law with respect to leases of goods. An analysis of the case law as it applies to leases of goods suggests at least three significant issues to be resolved by codification. First, what is a lease? It is necessary to define lease to determine whether a transaction creates a lease or a security interest disguised as a lease. If the transaction creates a security interest disguised as a lease, the lessor will be required to file a financing statement or take other action to perfect its interest in the goods against third parties. There is no such requirement with respect to leases. Yet the distinction between a lease and a security interest disguised as a lease is not clear. Second, will the lessor be deemed to have made warranties to the lessee? If the transaction is a sale the express and implied warranties of Article 2 of the Uniform Commercial Code apply. However, the warranty law with respect to leases is uncertain. Third, what remedies are available to the lessor upon the lessee's default? If the transaction is a security interest disguised as a lease, the answer is stated in Part 5 of the Article on Secured Transactions (Article 9). There is no clear answer with respect to leases.

There are reasons to codify the law with respect to leases of goods in addition to those suggested by a review of the reported cases. The answer to this important question should not be limited to the issues raised in these cases. Is it not also proper to determine the remedies available to the lessee upon the lessor's default? It is, but that issue is not reached through a review of the reported cases. This is only one of the many issues presented in structuring, negotiating and documenting a lease of goods.

Statutory Analogue:

After it was decided to proceed with the codification project, the drafting committee of the National Conference of Commissioners on Uniform State Laws looked for a statutory analogue, gradually narrowing the focus to the Article on Sales (Article 2) and the Article on Secured Transactions (Article 9). A review of the literature with respect to the sale of goods reveals that Article 2 is predicated upon certain assumptions: Parties to the sales transaction frequently are without counsel; the agreement of the parties often is oral or evidenced by scant writings; obligations between the parties are bilateral; applicable law is influenced by the need to preserve freedom of contract. A review of the literature with respect to personal property security law reveals that Article 9 is predicated upon very different assumptions: Parties to a secured transaction regularly are represented by counsel; the agreement of the parties frequently is reduced to a writing, extensive in scope; the obligations between the parties are essentially unilateral; and applicable law seriously limits freedom of contract.

The lease is closer in spirit and form to the sale of goods than to the creation of a security interest. While parties to a lease are sometimes represented by counsel and their agreement is often reduced to a writing, the obligations of the parties are bilateral and the common law of leasing is dominated by the need to preserve freedom of contract. Thus the drafting committee concluded that Article 2 was the appropriate statutory analogue.

Issues: The drafting committee then identified and resolved several issues critical to codification:

Scope: The scope of the Article was limited to leases (Section 2A–102). There was no need to include leases intended as security, *i.e.,* security interests disguised as leases, as they are adequately treated in Article 9. Further, even if leases intended as security were included, the need to preserve the distinction would remain, as policy suggests treatment significantly different from that accorded leases.

Definition of Lease: Lease was defined to exclude leases intended as security (Section 2A–103(1)(j)). Given the litigation to date a revised definition of security interest was suggested for inclusion in the Act. (Section 1–201(37)*). This revision sharpens the distinction between leases and security interests disguised as leases.

Filing: The lessor was not required to file a financing statement against the lessee or take any other action to protect the lessor's interest in the goods (Section 2A–301). The refined definition of security interest will more clearly signal the need to file to potential lessors of goods. Those lessors who are concerned will file a protective financing statement (Section 9–505).

Warranties: All of the express and implied warranties of the Article on Sales (Article 2) were included (Sections 2A–210 through 2A–216), revised to reflect differences in lease transactions. The lease of goods is sufficiently similar to the sale of goods to justify this decision. Further, many courts have reached the same decision.

Certificate of Title Laws: Many leasing transactions involve goods subject to certificate of title statutes. To avoid conflict with those statutes, this Article is subject to them (Section 2A–104(1)(a)).

Consumer Leases: Many leasing transactions involve parties subject to consumer protection statutes or decisions. To avoid conflict with those laws this Article is subject to them to the extent provided in (Section 2A–104(1)(c) and (2)). Further, certain consumer protections have been incorporated in the Article.

Finance Leases: Certain leasing transactions substitute the supplier of the goods for the lessor as the party responsible to the lessee with respect to warranties and the like. The definition of finance lease (Section 2A–103(1)(g)) was developed to describe these transactions. Various sections of the Article implement the substitution of the supplier for the lessor, including Sections 2A–209 and 2A–407. No attempt was made to

---

* *Referring to unrevised Article 1 (Appendix A).*

fashion a special rule where the finance lessor is an affiliate of the supplier of goods; this is to be developed by the courts, case by case.

Sale and Leaseback: Sale and leaseback transactions are becoming increasingly common. A number of state statutes treat transactions where possession is retained by the seller as fraudulent *per se* or *prima facie* fraudulent. That position is not in accord with modern practice and thus is changed by the Article "if the buyer bought for value and in good faith" (Section 2A-308(3)).

Remedies: The Article has not only provided for lessor's remedies upon default by the lessee (Sections 2A-523 through 2A-531), but also for lessee's remedies upon default by the lessor (Sections 2A-508 through 2A-522). This is a significant departure from Article 9, which provides remedies only for the secured party upon default by the debtor. This difference is compelled by the bilateral nature of the obligations between the parties to a lease.

Damages: Many leasing transactions are predicated on the parties' ability to stipulate an appropriate measure of damages in the event of default. The rule with respect to sales of goods (Section 2-718) is not sufficiently flexible to accommodate this practice. Consistent with the common law emphasis upon freedom to contract, the Article has created a revised rule that allows greater flexibility with respect to leases of goods (Section 2A-504(1)).

History:

This Article is a revision of the Uniform Personal Property Leasing Act, which was approved by the National Conference of Commissioners on Uniform State Laws in August, 1985. However, it was believed that the subject matter of the Uniform Personal Property Leasing Act would be better treated as an article of this Act. Thus, although the Conference promulgated the Uniform Personal Property Leasing Act as a Uniform Law, activity was held in abeyance to allow time to restate the Uniform Personal Property Leasing Act as Article 2A.

In August, 1986 the Conference approved and recommended this Article (including conforming amendments to Article 1 and Article 9) for promulgation as an amendment to this Act. In December, 1986 the Council of the American Law Institute approved and recommended this Article (including conforming amendments to Article 1 and Article 9), with official comments, for promulgation as an amendment to this Act. In March, 1987 the Permanent Editorial Board for the Uniform Commercial Code approved and recommended this Article (including conforming amendments to Article 1 and Article 9), with official comments, for promulgation as an amendment to this Act. In May, 1987 the American Law Institute approved and recommended this Article (including conforming amendments to Article 1 and Article 9), with official comments, for promulgation as an amendment to this Act. In August, 1987 the Conference confirmed its approval of the final text of this Article.

Upon its initial promulgation, Article 2A was rapidly enacted in several states, was introduced in a number of other states, and underwent bar association, law revision commission and legislative study in still further states. In that process debate emerged, principally sparked by the study of Article 2A by the California Bar Association, California's non-uniform amendments to Article 2A, and articles appearing in a symposium on Article 2A published after its promulgation in the Alabama Law Review. The debate chiefly centered on whether Article 2A had struck the proper balance or was clear enough concerning the ability of a lessor to grant a security interest in its leasehold interest and in the residual, priority between a secured party and the lessee, and the lessor's remedy structure under Article 2A.

This debate over issues on which reasonable minds could and did differ began to affect the enactment effort for Article 2A in a deleterious manner. Consequently, the Standby Committee for Article 2A, composed predominantly of the former members of the drafting committee, reviewed the legislative actions and studies in the various states, and opened a dialogue with the principal proponents of the non-uniform amendments. Negotiations were conducted in conjunction with, and were facilitated by, a study of the uniform Article and the non-uniform Amendments by the New York Law Revision Commission. Ultimately, a consensus was reached, which has been approved by the membership of the Conference, the Permanent Editorial Board, and the Council of the Institute. Rapid and uniform enactment of Article 2A is expected as a result of the completed amendments. The Article 2A experience reaffirms the essential viability of the procedures of the Conference and the Institute for creating and updating uniform state law in the commercial law area.

Relationship of Article 2A to Other Articles:

The Article on Sales provided a useful point of reference for codifying the law of leases. Many of the provisions of that Article were carried over, changed to reflect differences in style, leasing terminology or leasing practices. Thus, the official comments to those sections of Article 2 whose provisions were carried over are incorporated by reference in Article 2A, as well; further, any case law interpreting those provisions should be viewed as persuasive but not binding on a court when deciding a similar issue with respect to leases. Any change in the sequence that has been made when carrying over a provision from Article 2 should be viewed as a matter of style, not substance. This is not to suggest that in other instances Article 2A did not also incorporate substantially revised provisions of Article 2, Article 9 or otherwise where the revision was driven by a concern over the substance; but for the lack of a mandate, the drafting committee might well have made the same or a similar change in the statutory analogue. Those sections in Article 2A include Sections 2A–104, 2A–105, 2A–106, 2A–108(2) and (4), 2A–109(2), 2A–208, 2A–214(2) and (3)(a), 2A–216, 2A–303, 2A–306, 2A–503, 2A–504(3)(b), 2A–506(2), and 2A–515. For lack of relevance or significance not all of the provisions of Article 2 were incorporated in Article 2A.

This codification was greatly influenced by the fundamental tenet of the common law as it has developed with respect to leases of goods: freedom of the parties to contract. Note that, like all other Articles of this Act, the principles of construction and interpretation contained in Article 1 are applicable throughout Article 2A (Section 2A–103(4)). These principles include the ability of the parties to vary the effect of the provisions of Article 2A, subject to certain limitations including those that relate to the obligations of good faith, diligence, reasonableness and care (Section 1–102(3)).* Consistent with those principles no negative inference is to be drawn by the episodic use of the phrase "unless otherwise agreed" in certain provisions of Article 2A. Section 1–102(4).* Indeed, the contrary is true, as the general rule in the Act, including this Article, is that the effect of the Act's provisions may be varied by agreement. Section 1–102(3).* This conclusion follows even where the statutory analogue contains the phrase and the correlative provision in Article 2A does not.

§ 2A–102. Scope.

This Article applies to any transaction, regardless of form, that creates a lease.

Official Comment

Uniform Statutory Source: Former Section 9–102(1) (now codified as Section 9–109). Throughout this Article, unless otherwise stated, references to "Section" are to other sections of this Act.

Changes: Substantially revised.

Purposes: This Article governs transactions as diverse as the lease of a hand tool to an individual for a few hours and the leveraged lease of a complex line of industrial equipment to a multi-national organization for a number of years.

To achieve that end it was necessary to provide that this Article applies to any transaction, regardless of form, that creates a lease. Since lease is defined as a transfer of an interest in goods (Section 2A–103(1)(j)) and goods is defined to include fixtures (Section 2A–103(1)(h)), application is limited to the extent the transaction relates to goods, including fixtures. Further, since the definition of lease does not include a sale (Section 2–106(1)) or retention or creation of a security interest (Section 1–201(37)*), application is further limited; sales and security interests are governed by other Articles of this Act.

Finally, in recognition of the diversity of the transactions to be governed, the sophistication of many of the parties to these transactions, and the common law tradition as it applies to the bailment for hire or lease, freedom of contract has been preserved. DeKoven, Proceedings After Default by the Lessee Under a True Lease of Equipment, in 1C P. Coogan, W. Hogan, D. Vagts, *Secured Transactions Under the Uniform Commercial Code*, § 29B.02[2] (1986). Thus, despite the extensive regulatory scheme established by this Article, the parties to a lease will be able to create private rules to govern their transaction. Sections 2A–103(4) and 1–102(3).* However, there are special rules in this Article governing consumer leases, as well as other state and federal statutes, that may further limit freedom of contract with respect to consumer leases.

A court may apply this Article by analogy to any transaction, regardless of form, that creates a lease of personal property other than goods, taking into account the expressed intentions of the parties to the transaction and any differences between a lease of goods and a lease of other property. Such application has precedent as the provisions of the Article on Sales (Article 2) have been applied by analogy to leases of goods. *E.g.,* Hawkland, *The Impact of the Uniform Commercial Code on Equipment Leasing*, 1972 Ill.L.F. 446; Murray, *Under the Spreading Analogy of Article 2 of the Uniform Commercial Code*, 39 Fordham L.Rev. 447 (1971). Whether such application

---

* *Referring to unrevised Article 1 (Appendix A).*

would be appropriate for other bailments of personal property, gratuitous or for hire, should be determined by the facts of each case. *See Mieske v. Bartell Drug Co.*, 92 Wash.2d 40, 46–48, 593 P.2d 1308, 1312 (1979).

Further, parties to a transaction creating a lease of personal property other than goods, or a bailment of personal property may provide by agreement that this Article applies. Upholding the parties' choice is consistent with the spirit of this Article.

Cross References:

Sections 1–102(3),* 1–201(37),* Article 2, esp. Section 2–106(1), and Sections 2A–103(1)(h), 2A–103(1)(j) and 2A–103(4).

Definitional Cross Reference:

"Lease". Section 2A–103(1)(j).

§ 2A–103. Definitions and Index of Definitions.

(1)   In this Article unless the context otherwise requires:

(a)   "Buyer in ordinary course of business" means a person who in good faith and without knowledge that the sale to him [or her] is in violation of the ownership rights or security interest or leasehold interest of a third party in the goods buys in ordinary course from a person in the business of selling goods of that kind but does not include a pawnbroker. "Buying" may be for cash or by exchange of other property or on secured or unsecured credit and includes acquiring goods or documents of title under a pre-existing contract for sale but does not include a transfer in bulk or as security for or in total or partial satisfaction of a money debt.

(b)   "Cancellation" occurs when either party puts an end to the lease contract for default by the other party.

(c)   "Commercial unit" means such a unit of goods as by commercial usage is a single whole for purposes of lease and division of which materially impairs its character or value on the market or in use. A commercial unit may be a single article, as a machine, or a set of articles, as a suite of furniture or a line of machinery, or a quantity, as a gross or carload, or any other unit treated in use or in the relevant market as a single whole.

(d)   "Conforming" goods or performance under a lease contract means goods or performance that are in accordance with the obligations under the lease contract.

(e)   "Consumer lease" means a lease that a lessor regularly engaged in the business of leasing or selling makes to a lessee who is an individual and who takes under the lease primarily for a personal, family, or household purpose[, if the total payments to be made under the lease contract, excluding payments for options to renew or buy, do not exceed $_____].

(f)   "Fault" means wrongful act, omission, breach, or default.

(g)   "Finance lease" means a lease with respect to which:

     (i)   the lessor does not select, manufacture, or supply the goods;

     (ii)   the lessor acquires the goods or the right to possession and use of the goods in connection with the lease; and

     (iii)   one of the following occurs:

         (A)   the lessee receives a copy of the contract by which the lessor acquired the goods or the right to possession and use of the goods before signing the lease contract;

         (B)   the lessee's approval of the contract by which the lessor acquired the goods or the right to possession and use of the goods is a condition to effectiveness of the lease contract;

---

*   *Referring to unrevised Article 1 (Appendix A).*

(C)   the lessee, before signing the lease contract, receives an accurate and complete statement designating the promises and warranties, and any disclaimers of warranties, limitations or modifications of remedies, or liquidated damages, including those of a third party, such as the manufacturer of the goods, provided to the lessor by the person supplying the goods in connection with or as part of the contract by which the lessor acquired the goods or the right to possession and use of the goods; or

(D)   if the lease is not a consumer lease, the lessor, before the lessee signs the lease contract, informs the lessee in writing (a) of the identity of the person supplying the goods to the lessor, unless the lessee has selected that person and directed the lessor to acquire the goods or the right to possession and use of the goods from that person, (b) that the lessee is entitled under this Article to the promises and warranties, including those of any third party, provided to the lessor by the person supplying the goods in connection with or as part of the contract by which the lessor acquired the goods or the right to possession and use of the goods, and (c) that the lessee may communicate with the person supplying the goods to the lessor and receive an accurate and complete statement of those promises and warranties, including any disclaimers and limitations of them or of remedies.

(h)   "Goods" means all things that are movable at the time of identification to the lease contract, or are fixtures (Section 2A–309), but the term does not include money, documents, instruments, accounts, chattel paper, general intangibles, or minerals or the like, including oil and gas, before extraction. The term also includes the unborn young of animals.

(i)   "Installment lease contract" means a lease contract that authorizes or requires the delivery of goods in separate lots to be separately accepted, even though the lease contract contains a clause "each delivery is a separate lease" or its equivalent.

(j)   "Lease" means a transfer of the right to possession and use of goods for a term in return for consideration, but a sale, including a sale on approval or a sale or return, or retention or creation of a security interest is not a lease. Unless the context clearly indicates otherwise, the term includes a sublease.

(k)   "Lease agreement" means the bargain, with respect to the lease, of the lessor and the lessee in fact as found in their language or by implication from other circumstances including course of dealing or usage of trade or course of performance as provided in this Article. Unless the context clearly indicates otherwise, the term includes a sublease agreement.

(*l*)   "Lease contract" means the total legal obligation that results from the lease agreement as affected by this Article and any other applicable rules of law. Unless the context clearly indicates otherwise, the term includes a sublease contract.

(m)   "Leasehold interest" means the interest of the lessor or the lessee under a lease contract.

(n)   "Lessee" means a person who acquires the right to possession and use of goods under a lease. Unless the context clearly indicates otherwise, the term includes a sublessee.

(o)   "Lessee in ordinary course of business" means a person who in good faith and without knowledge that the lease to him [or her] is in violation of the ownership rights or security interest or leasehold interest of a third party in the goods, leases in ordinary course from a person in the business of selling or leasing goods of that kind but does not include a pawnbroker. "Leasing" may be for cash or by exchange of other property or on secured or unsecured credit and includes acquiring goods or documents of title under a pre-existing lease contract but does not include a transfer in bulk or as security for or in total or partial satisfaction of a money debt.

(p)   "Lessor" means a person who transfers the right to possession and use of goods under a lease. Unless the context clearly indicates otherwise, the term includes a sublessor.

(q)   "Lessor's residual interest" means the lessor's interest in the goods after expiration, termination, or cancellation of the lease contract.

(r) "Lien" means a charge against or interest in goods to secure payment of a debt or performance of an obligation, but the term does not include a security interest.

(s) "Lot" means a parcel or a single article that is the subject matter of a separate lease or delivery, whether or not it is sufficient to perform the lease contract.

(t) "Merchant lessee" means a lessee that is a merchant with respect to goods of the kind subject to the lease.

(u) "Present value" means the amount as of a date certain of one or more sums payable in the future, discounted to the date certain. The discount is determined by the interest rate specified by the parties if the rate was not manifestly unreasonable at the time the transaction was entered into; otherwise, the discount is determined by a commercially reasonable rate that takes into account the facts and circumstances of each case at the time the transaction was entered into.*

(v) "Purchase" includes taking by sale, lease, mortgage, security interest, pledge, gift, or any other voluntary transaction creating an interest in goods.

(w) "Sublease" means a lease of goods the right to possession and use of which was acquired by the lessor as a lessee under an existing lease.

(x) "Supplier" means a person from whom a lessor buys or leases goods to be leased under a finance lease.

(y) "Supply contract" means a contract under which a lessor buys or leases goods to be leased.

(z) "Termination" occurs when either party pursuant to a power created by agreement or law puts an end to the lease contract otherwise than for default.

(2) Other definitions applying to this Article and the sections in which they appear are:

"Accessions". Section 2A–310(1).
"Construction mortgage". Section 2A–309(1)(d).
"Encumbrance". Section 2A–309(1)(e).
"Fixtures". Section 2A–309(1)(a).
"Fixture filing". Section 2A–309(1)(b).
"Purchase money lease". Section 2A–309(1)(c).

(3) The following definitions in other Articles apply to this Article:

"Account". Section 9–102(a)(2).
"Between merchants". Section 2–104(3).
"Buyer". Section 2–103(1)(a).
"Chattel paper". Section 9–102(a)(11).
"Consumer goods". Section 9–102(a)(23).
"Document". Section 9–102(a)(30).
"Entrusting". Section 2–403(3).
"General intangible". Section 9–102(a)(42).
["Good Faith". Section 2–103(1)(b).]**
"Instrument". Section 9–102(a)(47).
"Merchant". Section 2–104(1).
"Mortgage". Section 9–102(a)(55).
"Pursuant to commitment". Section 9–102(a)(69).
"Receipt". Section 2–103(1)(c).
"Sale". Section 2–106(1).
"Sale on approval". Section 2–326.
"Sale or return". Section 2–326.

---

* *Note from West Advisory Panel: Revised Article 1 (2001) adds a definition of "present value" in § 1–201(b)(28). The conforming amendments to Article 2A erroneously do not delete this definition.*

** *Note from West Advisory Panel: This cross reference will be deleted if the jurisdiction adopts the definition of good faith in revised Article 1 (2001).*

"Seller". Section 2–103(1)(d).

(4)   In addition Article 1 contains general definitions and principles of construction and interpretation applicable throughout this Article.

As amended in 1990, 1999, 2001, 2003, and 2010.

Official Comment

(a)   "Buyer in ordinary course of business". Section 1–201(b)(9).

(b)   "Cancellation". Section 2–106(4). The effect of a cancellation is provided in Section 2A–505(1).

(c)   "Commercial unit". Section 2–105(6).

(d)   "Conforming". Section 2–106(2).

(e)   "Consumer lease". New. This Article includes a subset of rules that applies only to consumer leases. Sections 2A–106, 2A–108(2), 2A–108(4), 2A–109(2), 2A–221, 2A–309, 2A–406, 2A–407, 2A–504(3)(b), and 2A–516(3)(b).

For a transaction to qualify as a consumer lease it must first qualify as a lease. Section 2A–103(1)(j). Note that this Article regulates the transactional elements of a lease, including a consumer lease; consumer protection statutes, present and future, and existing consumer protection decisions are unaffected by this Article. Section 2A–104(1)(c) and (2). Of course, Article 2A as state law also is subject to federal consumer protection law.

This definition is modeled after the definition of consumer lease in the Consumer Leasing Act, 15 U.S.C. § 1667 (1982), and in the Unif. Consumer Credit Code § 1.301(14), 7A U.L.A. 43 (1974). However, this definition of consumer lease differs from its models in several respects: the lessor can be a person regularly engaged either in the business of leasing or of selling goods, the lease need not be for a term exceeding four months, a lease primarily for an agricultural purpose is not covered, and whether there should be a limitation by dollar amount and its amount is left up to the individual states.

This definition focuses on the parties as well as the transaction. If a lease is within this definition, the lessor must be regularly engaged in the business of leasing or selling, and the lessee must be an individual, not an organization; note that a lease to two or more individuals having a common interest through marriage or the like is not excluded as a lease to an organization under Section 1–201(28).* The lessee must take the interest primarily for a personal, family or household purpose. If required by the enacting state, total payments under the lease contract, excluding payments for options to renew or buy, cannot exceed the figure designated.

(f)   "Fault". Section 1–201(16).*

(g)   "Finance Lease". New. This Article includes a subset of rules that applies only to finance leases. Sections 2A–209, 2A–211(2), 2A–212(1), 2A–213, 2A–219(1), 2A–220(1)(a), 2A–221, 2A–405(c), 2A–407, 2A–516(2) and 2A–517(1)(a) and (2).

For a transaction to qualify as a finance lease it must first qualify as a lease. Section 2A–103(1)(j). Unless the lessor is comfortable that the transaction will qualify as a finance lease, the lease agreement should include provisions giving the lessor the benefits created by the subset of rules applicable to the transaction that qualifies as a finance lease under this Article.

A finance lease is the product of a three party transaction. The supplier manufactures or supplies the goods pursuant to the lessee's specification, perhaps even pursuant to a purchase order, sales agreement or lease agreement between the supplier and the lessee. After the prospective finance lease is negotiated, a purchase order, sales agreement, or lease agreement is entered into by the lessor (as buyer or prime lessee) or an existing order, agreement or lease is assigned by the lessee to the lessor, and the lessor and the lessee then enter into a lease or sublease of the goods. Due to the limited function usually performed by the lessor, the lessee looks almost entirely to the supplier for representations, covenants and warranties. If a manufacturer's warranty carries through, the lessee may also look to that. Yet, this definition does not restrict the lessor's function solely to the supply of funds; if the lessor undertakes or performs other functions, express warranties, covenants and the common law will protect the lessee.

---

*   *Referring to unrevised Article 1 (Appendix A).*

This definition focuses on the transaction, not the status of the parties; to avoid confusion it is important to note that in other contexts, *e.g.*, tax and accounting, the term finance lease has been used to connote different types of lease transactions, including leases that are disguised secured transactions. M. Rice, *Equipment Financing,* 62–71 (1981). A lessor who is a merchant with respect to goods of the kind subject to the lease may be a lessor under a finance lease. Many leases that are leases back to the seller of goods (Section 2A–308(3)) will be finance leases. This conclusion is easily demonstrated by a hypothetical. Assume that B has bought goods from C pursuant to a sales contract. After delivery to and acceptance of the goods by B, B negotiates to sell the goods to A and simultaneously to lease the goods back from A, on terms and conditions that, we assume, will qualify the transaction as a lease. Section 2A–103(1)(j). In documenting the sale and lease back, B assigns the original sales contract between B, as buyer, and C, as seller, to A. A review of these facts leads to the conclusion that the lease from A to B qualifies as a finance lease, as all three conditions of the definition are satisfied. Subparagraph (i) is satisfied as A, the lessor, had nothing to do with the selection, manufacture, or supply of the equipment. Subparagraph (ii) is satisfied as A, the lessor, bought the equipment at the same time that A leased the equipment to B, which certainly is in connection with the lease. Finally, subparagraph (iii)(A) is satisfied as A entered into the sales contract with B at the same time that A leased the equipment back to B. B, the lessee, will have received a copy of the sales contract in a timely fashion.

Subsection (i) requires the lessor to remain outside the selection, manufacture and supply of the goods; that is the rationale for releasing the lessor from most of its traditional liability. The lessor is not prohibited from possession, maintenance or operation of the goods, as policy does not require such prohibition. To insure the lessee's reliance on the supplier, and not on the lessor, subsection (ii) requires that the goods (where the lessor is the buyer of the goods) or that the right to possession and use of the goods (where the lessor is the prime lessee and the sublessor of the goods) be acquired in connection with the lease (or sublease) to qualify as a finance lease. The scope of the phrase "in connection with" is to be developed by the courts, case by case. Finally, as the lessee generally relies almost entirely upon the supplier for representations and covenants, and upon the supplier or a manufacturer, or both, for warranties with respect to the goods, subsection (iii) requires that one of the following occur: (A) the lessee receive a copy of the supply contract before signing the lease contract; (B) the lessee's approval of the supply contract is a condition to the effectiveness of the lease contract; (C) the lessee receive a statement describing the promises and warranties and any limitations relevant to the lessee before signing the lease contract; or (D) before signing the lease contract and except in a consumer lease, the lessee receive a writing identifying the supplier (unless the supplier was selected and required by the lessee) and the rights of the lessee under Section 2A–209, and advising the lessee a statement of promises and warranties is available from the supplier. Thus, even where oral supply orders or computer placed supply orders are compelled by custom and usage the transaction may still qualify as a finance lease if the lessee approves the supply contract before the lease contract is effective and such approval was a condition to the effectiveness of the lease contract. Moreover, where the lessor does not want the lessee to see the entire supply contract, including price information, the lessee may be provided with a separate statement of the terms of the supply contract relevant to the lessee; promises between the supplier and the lessor that do not affect the lessee need not be included. The statement can be a restatement of those terms or a copy of portions of the supply contract with the relevant terms clearly designated. Any implied warranties need not be designated, but a disclaimer or modification of remedy must be designated. A copy of any manufacturer's warranty is sufficient if that is the warranty provided. However, a copy of any Regulation M disclosure given pursuant to 12 C.F.R. § 213.4(g) concerning warranties in itself is not sufficient since those disclosures need only briefly identify express warranties and need not include any disclaimer of warranty.

If a transaction does not qualify as a finance lease, the parties may achieve the same result by agreement; no negative implications are to be drawn if the transaction does not qualify. Further, absent the application of special rules (fraud, duress, and the like), a lease that qualifies as a finance lease and is assigned by the lessor or the lessee to a third party does not lose its status as a finance lease under this Article. Finally, this Article creates no special rule where the lessor is an affiliate of the supplier; whether the transaction qualifies as a finance lease will be determined by the facts of each case.

(h) "Goods". Section 9–102(a)(44). See Section 2A–103(3) for reference to the definition of "Account", "Chattel paper", "Document", "General intangibles" and "Instrument". See Section 2A–217 for determination of the time and manner of identification.

(i) "Installment lease contract". Section 2–612(1).

(j) "Lease". New. There are several reasons to codify the law with respect to leases of goods. An analysis of the case law as it applies to leases of goods suggests at least several significant issues to be resolved by codification. First and foremost is the definition of a lease. It is necessary to define lease to determine whether a transaction creates a lease or a security interest disguised as a lease. If the transaction creates a security interest disguised as a lease, the transaction will be governed by the Article on Secured Transactions (Article 9) and the lessor will be required to file a financing statement or take other action to perfect its interest in the goods against third parties. There is no such requirement with respect to leases under the common law and, except with respect to leases of fixtures (Section 2A–309), this Article imposes no such requirement. Yet the distinction between a lease and a security interest disguised as a lease is not clear from the case law at the time of the promulgation of this Article. DeKoven, *Leases of Equipment: Puritan Leasing Company v. August, A Dangerous Decision,* 12 U.S.F. L.Rev. 257 (1978).

At common law a lease of personal property is a bailment for hire. While there are several definitions of bailment for hire, all require a thing to be let and a price for the letting. Thus, in modern terms and as provided in this definition, a lease is created when the lessee agrees to furnish consideration for the right to the possession and use of goods over a specified period of time. Mooney, *Personal Property Leasing: A Challenge,* 36 Bus.Law. 1605, 1607 (1981). Further, a lease is neither a sale (Section 2–106(1)) nor a retention or creation of a security interest (Sections 1–201(b)(35) and 1–203). Due to extensive litigation to distinguish true leases from security interests, an amendment to former Section 1–201(37) (now codified as Section 1–203) was promulgated with this Article to create a sharper distinction.

This section as well as Section 1–203 must be examined to determine whether the transaction in question creates a lease or a security interest. The following hypotheticals indicate the perimeters of the issue. Assume that A has purchased a number of copying machines, new, for $1,000 each; the machines have an estimated useful economic life of three years. A advertises that the machines are available to rent for a minimum of one month and that the monthly rental is $100.00. A intends to enter into leases where A provides all maintenance, without charge to the lessee. Further, the lessee will rent the machine, month to month, with no obligation to renew. At the end of the lease term the lessee will be obligated to return the machine to A's place of business. This transaction qualifies as a lease under the first half of the definition, for the transaction includes a transfer by A to a prospective lessee of possession and use of the machine for a stated term, month to month. The machines are goods (Section 2A–103(1)(h)). The lessee is obligated to pay consideration in return, $100.00 for each month of the term.

However, the second half of the definition provides that a sale or a security interest is not a lease. Since there is no passing of title, there is no sale. Sections 2A–103(3) and 2–106(1). Under pre-Act security law this transaction would have created a bailment for hire or a true lease and not a conditional sale. *Da Rocha v. Macomber,* 330 Mass. 611, 614–15, 116 N.E.2d 139, 142 (1953). Under Section 1–203, the same result would follow. While the lessee is obligated to pay rent for the one month term of the lease, one of the other four conditions of Section 1–203(b) must be met and none is. The term of the lease is one month and the economic life of the machine is 36 months; thus, Section 1–203(b)(1) is not now satisfied. Considering the amount of the monthly rent, absent economic duress or coercion, the lessee is not bound either to renew the lease for the remaining economic life of the goods or to become the owner. If the lessee did lease the machine for 36 months, the lessee would have paid the lessor $3,600 for a machine that could have been purchased for $1,000; thus, Section 1–203(b)(2) is not satisfied. Finally, there are no options; thus, subparagraphs (3) and (4) of 1–203(b) are not satisfied. This transaction creates a lease, not a security interest. However, with each renewal of the lease the facts and circumstances at the time of each renewal must be examined to determine if that conclusion remains accurate, as it is possible that a transaction that first creates a lease, later creates a security interest.

Assume that the facts are changed and that A requires each lessee to lease the goods for 36 months, with no right to terminate. Under pre-Act security law this transaction would have created a conditional sale, and not a bailment for hire or true lease. *Hervey v. Rhode Island Locomotive Works,* 93 U.S. 664, 672–73 (1876). Under this subsection, and Section 1–203, the same result would follow. The lessee's obligation for the term is not subject to termination by the lessee and the term is equal to the economic life of the machine.

Between these extremes there are many transactions that can be created. Some of the transactions were not properly categorized by the courts in applying the 1978 and earlier Official Texts of former Section 1–201(37). This subsection, together with Section 1–203, draws a brighter line, which should create a clearer signal to the professional lessor and lessee.

(k) "Lease agreement". This definition is derived from Section 1–201(b)(3). Because the definition of lease is broad enough to cover future transfers, lease agreement includes an agreement contemplating a current or subsequent transfer. Thus it was not necessary to make an express reference to an agreement for the future lease of goods (Section 2–106(1)). This concept is also incorporated in the definition of lease contract. Note that the definition of lease does not include transactions in ordinary building materials that are incorporated into an improvement on land. Section 2A–309(2).

The provisions of this Article, if applicable, determine whether a lease agreement has legal consequences; otherwise the law of bailments and other applicable law determine the same. Sections 2A–103(4) and 1–103.

(*l*)   "Lease contract". This definition is derived from the definition of contract in Section 1–201(b)(12). Note that a lease contract may be for the future lease of goods, since this notion is included in the definition of lease.

(m)   "Leasehold interest". New.

(n)   "Lessee". New.

(o)   "Lessee in ordinary course of business". Section 1–201(b)(9).

(p)   "Lessor". New.

(q)   "Lessor's residual interest". New.

(r)   "Lien". New. This term is used in Section 2A–307 (Priority of Liens Arising by Attachment or Levy on, Security Interests in, and Other Claims to Goods).

(s)   "Lot". Section 2–105(5).

(t)   "Merchant lessee". New. This term is used in Section 2A–511 (Merchant Lessee's Duties as to Rightfully Rejected Goods). A person may satisfy the requirement of dealing in goods of the kind subject to the lease as lessor, lessee, seller, or buyer.

[(u)   "Present value". New. Authorities agree that present value should be used to determine fairly the damages payable by the lessor or the lessee on default. *E.g., Taylor v. Commercial Credit Equip. Corp.*, 170 Ga.App. 322, 316 S.E.2d 788 (1984). Present value is defined to mean an amount that represents the discounted value as of a date certain of one or more sums payable in the future. This is a function of the economic principle that a dollar today is more valuable to the holder than a dollar payable in two years. While there is no question as to the principle, reasonable people would differ as to the rate of discount to apply in determining the value of that future dollar today. To minimize litigation, this Article allows the parties to specify the discount or interest rate, if the rate was not manifestly unreasonable at the time the transaction was entered into. In all other cases, the interest rate will be a commercially reasonable rate that takes into account the facts and circumstances of each case, as of the time the transaction was entered into.]*

(v)   "Purchase". Section 1–201(b)(29). This definition omits the reference to lien contained in the definition of purchase in Article 1 (Section 1–201(b)(29)). This should not be construed to exclude consensual liens from the definition of purchase in this Article; the exclusion was mandated by the scope of the definition of lien in Section 2A–103(1)(r). Further, the definition of purchaser in this Article adds a reference to lease; as purchase is defined in Section 1–201(b)(29) to include any other voluntary transaction creating an interest in property, this addition is not substantive.

(w)   "Sublease". New.

(x)   "Supplier". New.

(y)   "Supply contract". New.

(z)   "Termination". Section 2–106(3). The effect of a termination is provided in Section 2A–505(2).

As amended in 1999 and 2001.

§ 2A–104.   Leases Subject to Other Law.

(1)   A lease, although subject to this Article, is also subject to any applicable:

(a)   certificate of title statute of this State: (list any certificate of title statutes covering automobiles, trailers, mobile homes, boats, farm tractors, and the like);

(b)   certificate of title statute of another jurisdiction (Section 2A–105); or

(c)   consumer protection statute of this State, or final consumer protection decision of a court of this State existing on the effective date of this Article.

---

*   *Note from West Advisory Panel: Revised Article 1 (2001) adds a definition of "present value" in § 1–201(b)(28). The conforming amendments to Article 2A delete this comment, but erroneously do not delete the definition itself.*

(2)   In case of conflict between this Article, other than Sections 2A–105, 2A–304(3), and 2A–305(3), and a statute or decision referred to in subsection (1), the statute or decision controls.

(3)   Failure to comply with an applicable law has only the effect specified therein.

As amended in 1990.

Official Comment

Uniform Statutory Source: Former Sections 9–203(4) and 9–302(3)(b) and (c) (now codified as Sections 9–201 and 9–311(a)(2) and (3)).

Changes: Substantially revised.

Purposes:

1.   This Article creates a comprehensive scheme for the regulation of transactions that create leases. Section 2A–102. Thus, the Article supersedes all prior legislation dealing with leases, except to the extent set forth in this Section.

2.   Subsection (1) states the general rule that a lease, although governed by the scheme of this Article, also may be governed by certain other applicable laws. This may occur in the case of a consumer lease. Section 2A–103(1)(e). Those laws may be state statutes existing prior to enactment of Article 2A or passed afterward. In this case, it is desirable for this Article to specify which statute controls. Or the law may be a pre-existing consumer protection decision. This Article preserves such decisions. Or the law may be a statute of the United States. Such a law controls without any statement in this Article under applicable principles of preemption.

An illustration of a statute of the United States that governs consumer leases is the Consumer Leasing Act, 15 U.S.C. §§ 1667–1667(e) (1982) and its implementing regulation, Regulation M, 12 C.F.R. § 213 (1986); the statute mandates disclosures of certain lease terms, delimits the liability of a lessee in leasing personal property, and regulates the advertising of lease terms. An illustration of a state statute that governs consumer leases and which if adopted in the enacting state prevails over this Article is the Unif. Consumer Credit Code, which includes many provisions similar to those of the Consumer Leasing Act, e.g. Unif. Consumer Credit Code §§ 3.202, 3.209, 3.401, 7A U.L.A. 108–09, 115, 125 (1974), as well as provisions in addition to those of the Consumer Leasing Act, e.g., Unif. Consumer Credit Code §§ 5.109–.111, 7A U.L.A. 171–76 (1974) (the right to cure a default). Such statutes may define consumer lease so as to govern transactions within and without the definition of consumer lease under this Article.

3.   Under subsection (2), subject to certain limited exclusions, in case of conflict a statute or a decision described in subsection (1) prevails over this Article. For example, a provision like Unif. Consumer Credit Code § 5.112, 7A U.L.A. 176 (1974), limiting self-help repossession, prevails over Section 2A–525(3). A consumer protection decision rendered after the effective date of this Article may supplement its provisions. For example, in relation to Article 9 a court might conclude that an acceleration clause may not be enforced against an individual debtor after late payments have been accepted unless a prior notice of default is given. To the extent the decision establishes a general principle applicable to transactions other than secured transactions, it may supplement Section 2A–502.

4.   Consumer protection in lease transactions is primarily left to other law. However, several provisions of this Article do contain special rules that may not be varied by agreement in the case of a consumer lease. *E.g.*, Sections 2A–106, 2A–108, and 2A–109(2). Were that not so, the ability of the parties to govern their relationship by agreement together with the position of the lessor in a consumer lease too often could result in a one-sided lease agreement.

5.   In construing this provision the reference to statute should be deemed to include applicable regulations. A consumer protection decision is "final" on the effective date of this Article if it is not subject to appeal on that date or, if subject to appeal, is not later reversed on appeal. Of course, such a decision can be overruled by a later decision or superseded by a later statute.

Cross References:

Sections 2A–103(1)(e), 2A–106, 2A–108, 2A–109(2) and 2A–525(3).

Definitional Cross Reference:

"Lease". Section 2A–103(1)(j).

§ 2A–105.   Territorial Application of Article to Goods Covered by Certificate of Title.

Subject to the provisions of Sections 2A–304(3) and 2A–305(3), with respect to goods covered by a certificate of title issued under a statute of this State or of another jurisdiction, compliance and the effect of compliance or noncompliance with a certificate of title statute are governed by the law (including the conflict of laws rules) of the jurisdiction issuing the certificate until the earlier of (a) surrender of the certificate, or (b) four months after the goods are removed from that jurisdiction and thereafter until a new certificate of title is issued by another jurisdiction.

Official Comment

Uniform Statutory Source: Former Section 9–103(2)(a) and (b) (now codified as Sections 9–303 and 9–316).

Changes: Substantially revised. The provisions of the last sentence of former Section 9–103(2)(b) were not incorporated as they are superfluous in this context. The provisions of former Section 9–103(2)(d) were not incorporated because the problems dealt with are adequately addressed by this section and Sections 2A–304(3) and 305(3).

Purposes: The new certificate referred to in (b) must be permanent, not temporary. Generally, the lessor or creditor whose interest is indicated on the most recently issued certificate of title will prevail over interests indicated on certificates issued previously by other jurisdictions. This provision reflects a policy that it is reasonable to require holders of interests in goods covered by a certificate of title to police the goods or risk losing their interests when a new certificate of title is issued by another jurisdiction.

Cross References:

Sections 2A–304(3) and 2A–305(3); former Sections 9–103(2)(b) and 9–103(2)(d) (now codified as Sections 9–303, 9–316, and 9–337).

Definitional Cross Reference:

"Goods". Section 2A–103(1)(h).

§ 2A–106.   Limitation on Power of Parties to Consumer Lease to Choose Applicable Law and Judicial Forum.

(1)   If the law chosen by the parties to a consumer lease is that of a jurisdiction other than a jurisdiction in which the lessee resides at the time the lease agreement becomes enforceable or within 30 days thereafter or in which the goods are to be used, the choice is not enforceable.

(2)   If the judicial forum chosen by the parties to a consumer lease is a forum that would not otherwise have jurisdiction over the lessee, the choice is not enforceable.

Official Comment

Uniform Statutory Source: Unif. Consumer Credit Code § 1.201(8), 7A U.L.A. 36 (1974).

Changes: Substantially revised.

Purposes: There is a real danger that a lessor may induce a consumer lessee to agree that the applicable law will be a jurisdiction that has little effective consumer protection, or to agree that the applicable forum will be a forum that is inconvenient for the lessee in the event of litigation. As a result, this section invalidates these choice of law or forum clauses, except where the law chosen is that of the state of the consumer's residence or where the goods will be kept, or the forum chosen is one that otherwise would have jurisdiction over the lessee.

Subsection (1) limits potentially abusive choice of law clauses in consumer leases. The 30-day rule in subsection (1) was suggested by former Section 9–103(1)(c). This section has no effect on choice of law clauses in leases that are not consumer leases. Such clauses would be governed by other law.

Subsection (2) prevents enforcement of potentially abusive jurisdictional consent clauses in consumer leases. By using the term judicial forum, this section does not limit selection of a nonjudicial forum, such as arbitration. This section has no effect on choice of forum clauses in leases that are not consumer leases; such clauses are, as a matter of current law, "prima facie valid". *The Bremen v. Zapata Off-Shore Co.*, 407 U.S. 1, 10 (1972). Such clauses would be governed by other law, including the Model Choice of Forum Act (1968).

Cross Reference:

Former Section 9–103(1)(c).

Definitional Cross References:

"Consumer lease". Section 2A–103(1)(e).
"Lease agreement". Section 2A–103(1)(k).
"Lessee". Section 2A–103(1)(n).
"Goods". Section 2A–103(1)(h).
"Party". Section 1–201(29).*

§ 2A–107. Waiver or Renunciation of Claim or Right After Default.

Any claim or right arising out of an alleged default or breach of warranty may be discharged in whole or in part without consideration by a written waiver or renunciation signed and delivered by the aggrieved party.

Official Comment

Uniform Statutory Source: Section 1–107.*

Changes: Revised to reflect leasing practices and terminology. This clause is used throughout the official comments to this Article to indicate the scope of change in the provisions of the Uniform Statutory Source included in the section; these changes range from one extreme, *e.g.*, a significant difference in practice (a warranty as to merchantability is not implied in a finance lease (Section 2A–212)) to the other extreme, *e.g.*, a modest difference in style or terminology (the transaction governed is a lease not a sale (Section 2A–203 2A–103**)).

Cross References:

Sections 2A–203 2A–103** and 2A–212.

Definitional Cross References:

"Aggrieved party". Section 1–201(2).*
"Delivery". Section 1–201(14).*
"Rights". Section 1–201(36).*
"Signed". Section 1–201(39).*
"Written". Section 1–201(46).*

§ 2A–108. Unconscionability.

(1)   If the court as a matter of law finds a lease contract or any clause of a lease contract to have been unconscionable at the time it was made the court may refuse to enforce the lease contract, or it may enforce the remainder of the lease contract without the unconscionable clause, or it may so limit the application of any unconscionable clause as to avoid any unconscionable result.

(2)   With respect to a consumer lease, if the court as a matter of law finds that a lease contract or any clause of a lease contract has been induced by unconscionable conduct or that unconscionable conduct has occurred in the collection of a claim arising from a lease contract, the court may grant appropriate relief.

(3)   Before making a finding of unconscionability under subsection (1) or (2), the court, on its own motion or that of a party, shall afford the parties a reasonable opportunity to present evidence as to the setting, purpose, and effect of the lease contract or clause thereof, or of the conduct.

(4)   In an action in which the lessee claims unconscionability with respect to a consumer lease:

(a)   If the court finds unconscionability under subsection (1) or (2), the court shall award reasonable attorney's fees to the lessee.

---

*   *Referring to unrevised Article 1 (Appendix A).*

**   Previous incorrect cross reference corrected by Permanent Editorial Board action November 1992.

(b)   If the court does not find unconscionability and the lessee claiming unconscionability has brought or maintained an action he [or she] knew to be groundless, the court shall award reasonable attorney's fees to the party against whom the claim is made.

(c)   In determining attorney's fees, the amount of the recovery on behalf of the claimant under subsections (1) and (2) is not controlling.

Official Comment

Uniform Statutory Source: Section 2–302 and Unif. Consumer Credit Code § 5.108, 7A U.L.A. 167–69 (1974).

Changes: Subsection (1) is taken almost verbatim from the provisions of Section 2–302(1). Subsection (2) is suggested by the provisions of Unif. Consumer Credit Code § 5.108(1), (2), 7A U.L.A. 167 (1974). Subsection (3), taken from the provisions of Section 2–302(2), has been expanded to cover unconscionable conduct. Unif. Consumer Credit Code § 5.108(3), 7A U.L.A. 167 (1974). The provision for the award of attorney's fees to consumers, subsection (4), covers unconscionability under subsection (1) as well as (2). Subsection (4) is modeled on the provisions of Unif. Consumer Credit Code § 5.108(6), 7A U.L.A. 169 (1974).

Purposes: Subsections (1) and (3) of this section apply the concept of unconscionability reflected in the provisions of Section 2–302 to leases. *See Dillman & Assocs. v. Capitol Leasing Co.*, 110 Ill.App.3d 335, 342, 442 N.E.2d 311, 316 (App.Ct.1982). Subsection (3) omits the adjective "commercial" found in subsection 2–302(2) because subsection (3) is concerned with all leases and the relevant standard of conduct is determined by the context.

The balance of the section is modeled on the provisions of Unif. Consumer Credit Code § 5.108, 7A U.L.A. 167–69 (1974). Thus subsection (2) recognizes that a consumer lease or a clause in a consumer lease may not itself be unconscionable but that the agreement would never have been entered into if unconscionable means had not been employed to induce the consumer to agree. To make a statement to induce the consumer to lease the goods, in the expectation of invoking an integration clause in the lease to exclude the statement's admissibility in a subsequent dispute, may be unconscionable. Subsection (2) also provides a consumer remedy for unconscionable conduct, such as using or threatening to use force or violence, in the collection of a claim arising from a lease contract. These provisions are not exclusive. The remedies of this section are in addition to remedies otherwise available for the same conduct under other law, for example, an action in tort for abusive debt collection or under another statute of this State for such conduct. The reference to appropriate relief in subsection (2) is intended to foster liberal administration of this remedy. Sections 2A–103(4) and 1–106(1).[*]

Subsection (4) authorizes an award of reasonable attorney's fees if the court finds unconscionability with respect to a consumer lease under subsection (1) or (2). Provision is also made for recovery by the party against whom the claim was made if the court does not find unconscionability and does find that the consumer knew the action to be groundless. Further, subsection (4)(b) is independent of, and thus will not override, a term in the lease agreement that provides for the payment of attorney's fees.

Cross References:

Sections 1–106(1),[*] 2–302 and 2A–103(4).

Definitional Cross References:

"Action". Section 1–201(1).[*]
"Consumer lease". Section 2A–103(1)(e).
"Lease contract". Section 2A–103(1)(*l*).
"Lessee". Section 2A–103(1)(n).
"Party". Section 1–201(29).[*]

§ 2A–109.   Option to Accelerate at Will.

(1)   A term providing that one party or his [or her] successor in interest may accelerate payment or performance or require collateral or additional collateral "at will" or "when he [or she] deems himself [or herself] insecure" or in words of similar import must be construed to mean that he [or she] has power to do so only if he [or she] in good faith believes that the prospect of payment or performance is impaired.

---

[*]   *Referring to unrevised Article 1 (Appendix A).*

(2) With respect to a consumer lease, the burden of establishing good faith under subsection (1) is on the party who exercised the power; otherwise the burden of establishing lack of good faith is on the party against whom the power has been exercised.

Official Comment

Uniform Statutory Source: Section 1–208* and Unif. Consumer Credit Code § 5.109(2), 7A U.L.A. 171 (1974).

Purposes: Subsection (1) reflects modest changes in style to the provisions of the first sentence of Section 1–208.*

Subsection (2), however, reflects a significant change in the provisions of the second sentence of Section 1–208* by creating a new rule with respect to a consumer lease. A lease provision allowing acceleration at the will of the lessor or when the lessor deems itself insecure is of critical importance to the lessee. In a consumer lease it is a provision that is not usually agreed to by the parties but is usually mandated by the lessor. Therefore, where its invocation depends not on specific criteria but on the discretion of the lessor, its use should be regulated to prevent abuse. Subsection (1) imposes a duty of good faith upon its exercise. Subsection (2) shifts the burden of establishing good faith to the lessor in the case of a consumer lease, but not otherwise.

Cross Reference:

Section 1–208.*

Definitional Cross References:

"Burden of establishing". Section 1–201(8).*
"Consumer lease". Section 2A–103(1)(e).
"Good faith". Sections 1–201(19)* and 2–103(1)(b).
"Party". Section 1–201(29).*
"Term". Section 1–201(42).*

PART 2

FORMATION AND CONSTRUCTION OF LEASE CONTRACT

§ 2A–201. Statute of Frauds.

(1) A lease contract is not enforceable by way of action or defense unless:

(a) the total payments to be made under the lease contract, excluding payments for options to renew or buy, are less than $1,000; or

(b) there is a writing, signed by the party against whom enforcement is sought or by that party's authorized agent, sufficient to indicate that a lease contract has been made between the parties and to describe the goods leased and the lease term.

(2) Any description of leased goods or of the lease term is sufficient and satisfies subsection (1)(b), whether or not it is specific, if it reasonably identifies what is described.

(3) A writing is not insufficient because it omits or incorrectly states a term agreed upon, but the lease contract is not enforceable under subsection (1)(b) beyond the lease term and the quantity of goods shown in the writing.

(4) A lease contract that does not satisfy the requirements of subsection (1), but which is valid in other respects, is enforceable:

(a) if the goods are to be specially manufactured or obtained for the lessee and are not suitable for lease or sale to others in the ordinary course of the lessor's business, and the lessor, before notice of repudiation is received and under circumstances that reasonably indicate that the goods are

---

* *Referring to unrevised Article 1 (Appendix A).*

for the lessee, has made either a substantial beginning of their manufacture or commitments for their procurement;

(b)   if the party against whom enforcement is sought admits in that party's pleading, testimony or otherwise in court that a lease contract was made, but the lease contract is not enforceable under this provision beyond the quantity of goods admitted; or

(c)   with respect to goods that have been received and accepted by the lessee.

(5)   The lease term under a lease contract referred to in subsection (4) is:

(a)   if there is a writing signed by the party against whom enforcement is sought or by that party's authorized agent specifying the lease term, the term so specified;

(b)   if the party against whom enforcement is sought admits in that party's pleading, testimony, or otherwise in court a lease term, the term so admitted; or

(c)   a reasonable lease term.

Official Comment

Uniform Statutory Source: Section 2–201; former Sections 9–203(1) and 9–110 (now codified as Sections 9–203(b) and 9–108).

Changes: This section is modeled on Section 2–201, with changes to reflect the differences between a lease contract and a contract for the sale of goods. In particular, subsection (1)(b) adds a requirement that the writing "describe the goods leased and the lease term", borrowing that concept, with revisions, from the provisions of former Section 9–203(1)(a) (now codified as Section 9–203(b)(3)(A)). Subsection (2), relying on the statutory analogue in former Section 9–110 (now codified as Section 9–108), sets forth the minimum criterion for satisfying that requirement.

Purposes: The changes in this section conform the provisions of Section 2–201 to custom and usage in lease transactions. Section 2–201(2), stating a special rule between merchants, was not included in this section as the number of such transactions involving leases, as opposed to sales, was thought to be modest. Subsection (4) creates no exception for transactions where payment has been made and accepted. This represents a departure from the analogue, Section 2–201(3)(c). The rationale for the departure is grounded in the distinction between sales and leases. Unlike a buyer in a sales transaction, the lessee does not tender payment in full for goods delivered, but only payment of rent for one or more months. It was decided that, as a matter of policy, this act of payment is not a sufficient substitute for the required memorandum. Subsection (5) was needed to establish the criteria for supplying the lease term if it is omitted, as the lease contract may still be enforceable under subsection (4).

Cross References:

Sections 2–201, 9–108 and 9–203(b)(3)(A).

Definitional Cross References:

"Action". Section 1–201(1).*
"Agreed". Section 1–201(3).*
"Buying". Section 2A–103(1)(a).
"Goods". Section 2A–103(1)(h).
"Lease". Section 2A–103(1)(j).
"Lease contract". Section 2A–103(1)(*l*).
"Lessee". Section 2A–103(1)(n).
"Lessor". Section 2A–103(1)(p).
"Notice". Section 1–201(25).*
"Party". Section 1–201(29).*
"Sale". Section 2–106(1).
"Signed". Section 1–201(39).*
"Term". Section 1–201(42).*
"Writing". Section 1–201(46).*

---

*   *Referring to unrevised Article 1 (Appendix A).*

§ 2A–202. Final Written Expression: Parol or Extrinsic Evidence.

Terms with respect to which the confirmatory memoranda of the parties agree or which are otherwise set forth in a writing intended by the parties as a final expression of their agreement with respect to such terms as are included therein may not be contradicted by evidence of any prior agreement or of a contemporaneous oral agreement but may be explained or supplemented:

(a)   by course of dealing or usage of trade or by course of performance; and

(b)   by evidence of consistent additional terms unless the court finds the writing to have been intended also as a complete and exclusive statement of the terms of the agreement.

Official Comment

Uniform Statutory Source: Section 2–202.

Definitional Cross References:

"Agreement". Section 1–201(3).*
"Course of dealing". Section 1–205.*
"Party". Section 1–201(29).*
"Term". Section 1–201(42).*
"Usage of trade". Section 1–205.*
"Writing". Section 1–201(46).*

§ 2A–203. Seals Inoperative.

The affixing of a seal to a writing evidencing a lease contract or an offer to enter into a lease contract does not render the writing a sealed instrument and the law with respect to sealed instruments does not apply to the lease contract or offer.

Official Comment

Uniform Statutory Source: Section 2–203.

Changes: Revised to reflect leasing practices and terminology.

Definitional Cross References:

"Lease contract". Section 2A–103(1)(*l*).
"Writing". Section 1–201(46).*

§ 2A–204. Formation in General.

(1)   A lease contract may be made in any manner sufficient to show agreement, including conduct by both parties which recognizes the existence of a lease contract.

(2)   An agreement sufficient to constitute a lease contract may be found although the moment of its making is undetermined.

(3)   Although one or more terms are left open, a lease contract does not fail for indefiniteness if the parties have intended to make a lease contract and there is a reasonably certain basis for giving an appropriate remedy.

Official Comment

Uniform Statutory Source: Section 2–204.

Changes: Revised to reflect leasing practices and terminology.

Definitional Cross References:

"Agreement". Section 1–201(3).*
"Lease contract". Section 2A–103(1)(*l*).

---

*   *Referring to unrevised Article 1 (Appendix A).*

"Party". Section 1–201(29).*
"Remedy". Section 1–201(34).*
"Term". Section 1–201(42).*

§ 2A–205. Firm Offers.

An offer by a merchant to lease goods to or from another person in a signed writing that by its terms gives assurance it will be held open is not revocable, for lack of consideration, during the time stated or, if no time is stated, for a reasonable time, but in no event may the period of irrevocability exceed 3 months. Any such term of assurance on a form supplied by the offeree must be separately signed by the offeror.

Official Comment

Uniform Statutory Source: Section 2–205.

Changes: Revised to reflect leasing practices and terminology.

Definitional Cross References:

"Goods". Section 2A–103(1)(h).
"Lease". Section 2A–103(1)(j).
"Merchant". Section 2–104(1).
"Person". Section 1–201(30).*
"Reasonable time". Section 1–204(1) and (2).*
"Signed". Section 1–201(39).*
"Term". Section 1–201(42).*
"Writing". Section 1–201(46).*

§ 2A–206. Offer and Acceptance in Formation of Lease Contract.

(1)   Unless otherwise unambiguously indicated by the language or circumstances, an offer to make a lease contract must be construed as inviting acceptance in any manner and by any medium reasonable in the circumstances.

(2)   If the beginning of a requested performance is a reasonable mode of acceptance, an offeror who is not notified of acceptance within a reasonable time may treat the offer as having lapsed before acceptance.

Official Comment

Uniform Statutory Source: Section 2–206(1)(a) and (2).

Changes: Revised to reflect leasing practices and terminology.

Definitional Cross References:

"Lease contract". Section 2A–103(1)(*l*).
"Notifies". Section 1–201(26).
"Reasonable time". Section 1–204(1) and (2).*

§ 2A–207. [Reserved.] [Course of Performance or Practical Construction.]**

[(1)   If a lease contract involves repeated occasions for performance by either party with knowledge of the nature of the performance and opportunity for objection to it by the other, any course of performance accepted or acquiesced in without objection is relevant to determine the meaning of the lease agreement.

(2)   The express terms of a lease agreement and any course of performance, as well as any course of dealing and usage of trade, must be construed whenever reasonable as consistent with each other; but if that construction is unreasonable, express terms control course of performance, course of performance controls both course of dealing and usage of trade, and course of dealing controls usage of trade.

---

*   *Referring to unrevised Article 1 (Appendix A).*

**   *Note from West Advisory Panel: This section will be repealed if the jurisdiction adopts revised Article 1.*

(3)   Subject to the provisions of Section 2A–208 on modification and waiver, course of performance is relevant to show a waiver or modification of any term inconsistent with the course of performance.

Official Comment

Uniform Statutory Source: Sections 2–208 and 1–205(4).*

Changes: Revised to reflect leasing practices and terminology, except that subsection (2) was further revised to make the subsection parallel the provisions of Section 1–205(4)* by adding that course of dealing controls usage of trade.

Purposes: The section should be read in conjunction with Section 2A–208. In particular, although a specific term may control over course of performance as a matter of lease construction under subsection (2), subsection (3) allows the same course of dealing to show a waiver or modification, if Section 2A–208 is satisfied.

Cross References:

Sections 1–205(4),* 2–208 and 2A–208.

Definitional Cross References:

"Course of dealing". Section 1–205.*
"Knowledge". Section 1–201(25).*
"Lease agreement". Section 2A–103(1)(k).
"Lease contract". Section 2A–103(1)(*l*).
"Party". Section 1–201(29).*
"Term". Section 1–201(42).*
"Usage of trade". Section 1–205.*]

§ 2A–208.   Modification, Rescission and Waiver.

(1)   An agreement modifying a lease contract needs no consideration to be binding.

(2)   A signed lease agreement that excludes modification or rescission except by a signed writing may not be otherwise modified or rescinded, but, except as between merchants, such a requirement on a form supplied by a merchant must be separately signed by the other party.

(3)   Although an attempt at modification or rescission does not satisfy the requirements of subsection (2), it may operate as a waiver.

(4)   A party who has made a waiver affecting an executory portion of a lease contract may retract the waiver by reasonable notification received by the other party that strict performance will be required of any term waived, unless the retraction would be unjust in view of a material change of position in reliance on the waiver.

Official Comment

Uniform Statutory Source: Section 2–209.

Changes: Revised to reflect leasing practices and terminology, except that the provisions of subsection 2–209(3) were omitted.

Purposes: Section 2–209(3) provides that "the requirements of the statute of frauds section of this Article (Section 2–201) must be satisfied if the contract as modified is within its provisions." This provision was not incorporated as it is unfair to allow an oral modification to make the entire lease contract unenforceable, *e.g.* if the modification takes it a few dollars over the dollar limit. At the same time, the problem could not be solved by providing that the lease contract would still be enforceable in its pre-modification state (if it then satisfied the statute of frauds) since in some cases that might be worse than no enforcement at all. Resolution of the issue is left to the courts based on the facts of each case.

Cross References:

Sections 2–201 and 2–209.

---

*   *Referring to unrevised Article 1 (Appendix A).*

Definitional Cross References:

> "Agreement". Section 1–201(3).*
> "Between merchants". Section 2–104(3).
> "Lease agreement". Section 2A–103(1)(k).
> "Lease contract". Section 2A–103(1)(*l*).
> "Merchant". Section 2–104(1).
> "Notification". Section 1–201(26).*
> "Party". Section 1–201(29).*
> "Signed". Section 1–201(39).*
> "Term". Section 1–201(42).*
> "Writing". Section 1–201(46).

§ 2A–209.   Lessee Under Finance Lease as Beneficiary of Supply Contract.

(1) The benefit of a supplier's promises to the lessor under the supply contract and of all warranties, whether express or implied, including those of any third party provided in connection with or as part of the supply contract, extends to the lessee to the extent of the lessee's leasehold interest under a finance lease related to the supply contract, but is subject to the terms of the warranty and of the supply contract and all defenses or claims arising therefrom.

(2) The extension of the benefit of a supplier's promises and of warranties to the lessee (Section 2A–209(1)) does not: (i) modify the rights and obligations of the parties to the supply contract, whether arising therefrom or otherwise, or (ii) impose any duty or liability under the supply contract on the lessee.

(3) Any modification or rescission of the supply contract by the supplier and the lessor is effective between the supplier and the lessee unless, before the modification or rescission, the supplier has received notice that the lessee has entered into a finance lease related to the supply contract. If the modification or rescission is effective between the supplier and the lessee, the lessor is deemed to have assumed, in addition to the obligations of the lessor to the lessee under the lease contract, promises of the supplier to the lessor and warranties that were so modified or rescinded as they existed and were available to the lessee before modification or rescission.

(4) In addition to the extension of the benefit of the supplier's promises and of warranties to the lessee under subsection (1), the lessee retains all rights that the lessee may have against the supplier which arise from an agreement between the lessee and the supplier or under other law.
As amended in 1990.

Official Comment

Uniform Statutory Source: None.

Changes: This section is modeled on former Section 9–318 (now codified as Sections 9–404 through 9–406), the Restatement (Second) of Contracts §§ 302–315 (1981), and leasing practices. *See Earman Oil Co. v. Burroughs Corp.*, 625 F.2d 1291, 1296–97 (5th Cir.1980).

Purposes:

1. The function performed by the lessor in a finance lease is extremely limited. Section 2A–103(1)(g). The lessee looks to the supplier of the goods for warranties and the like or, in some cases as to warranties, to the manufacturer if a warranty made by that person is passed on. That expectation is reflected in subsection (1), which is self-executing. As a matter of policy, the operation of this provision may not be excluded, modified or limited; however, an exclusion, modification, or limitation of any term of the supply contract or warranty, including any with respect to rights and remedies, and any defense or claim such as a statute of limitations, effective against the lessor as the acquiring party under the supply contract, is also effective against the lessee as the beneficiary designated under this provision. For example, the supplier is not precluded from excluding or modifying an express or implied warranty under a supply contract. Sections 2–312(2) and 2–316, or Section 2A–214. Further, the supplier is not precluded from limiting the rights and remedies of the lessor and from liquidating damages.

---

*   *Referring to unrevised Article 1 (Appendix A).*

Sections 2–718 and 2–719 or Sections 2A–503 and 2A–504. If the supply contract excludes or modifies warranties, limits remedies, or liquidates damages with respect to the lessor, such provisions are enforceable against the lessee as beneficiary. Thus, only selective discrimination against the beneficiaries designated under this section is precluded, i.e., exclusion of the supplier's liability to the lessee with respect to warranties made to the lessor. This section does not affect the development of other law with respect to products liability.

2.   Enforcement of this benefit is by action. Sections 2A–103(4) and 1–106(2).*

3.   The benefit extended by these provisions is not without a price, as this Article also provides in the case of a finance lease that is not a consumer lease that the lessee's promises to the lessor under the lease contract become irrevocable and independent upon the lessee's acceptance of the goods. Section 2A–407.

4.   Subsection (2) limits the effect of subsection (1) on the supplier and the lessor by preserving, notwithstanding the transfer of the benefits of the supply contract to the lessee, all of the supplier's and the lessor's rights and obligations with respect to each other and others; it further absolves the lessee of any duties with respect to the supply contract that might have been inferred from the extension of the benefits thereof.

5.   Subsections (2) and (3) also deal with difficult issues related to modification or rescission of the supply contract. Subsection (2) states a rule that determines the impact of the statutory extension of benefit contained in subsection (1) upon the relationship of the parties to the supply contract and, in a limited respect, upon the lessee. This statutory extension of benefit, like that contained in Sections 2A–216 and 2–318, is not a modification of the supply contract by the parties. Thus, subsection (3) states the rules that apply to a modification or rescission of the supply contract by the parties. Subsection (3) provides that a modification or rescission is not effective between the supplier and the lessee if, before the modification or rescission occurs, the supplier received notice that the lessee has entered into the finance lease. On the other hand, if the modification or rescission is effective, then to the extent of the modification or rescission of the benefit or warranty, the lessor by statutory dictate assumes an obligation to provide to the lessee that which the lessee would otherwise lose. For example, assume a reduction in an express warranty from four years to one year. No prejudice to the lessee may occur if the goods perform as agreed. If, however, there is a breach of the express warranty after one year and before four years pass, the lessor is liable. A remedy for any prejudice to the lessee because of the bifurcation of the lessee's recourse resulting from the action of the supplier and the lessor is left to resolution by the courts based on the facts of each case.

6.   Subsection (4) makes it clear that the rights granted to the lessee by this section do not displace any rights the lessee otherwise may have against the supplier.

Cross References:

Sections 2A–103(1)(g), 2A–407, 9–404, 9–405 and 9–406.

Definitional Cross References:

"Action". Section 1–201(1).*
"Finance lease". Section 2A–103(1)(g).
"Leasehold interest". Section 2A–103(1)(m).
"Lessee". Section 2A–103(1)(n).
"Lessor". Section 2A–103(1)(p).
"Notice". Section 1–201(25).*
"Party". Section 1–201(29).*
"Rights". Section 1–201(36).*
"Supplier". Section 2A–103(1)(x).
"Supply contract". Section 2A–103(1)(y).
"Term". Section 1–201(42).*

§ 2A–210.   Express Warranties.

(1)   Express warranties by the lessor are created as follows:

---

*   *Referring to unrevised Article 1 (Appendix A).*

(a) Any affirmation of fact or promise made by the lessor to the lessee which relates to the goods and becomes part of the basis of the bargain creates an express warranty that the goods will conform to the affirmation or promise.

(b) Any description of the goods which is made part of the basis of the bargain creates an express warranty that the goods will conform to the description.

(c) Any sample or model that is made part of the basis of the bargain creates an express warranty that the whole of the goods will conform to the sample or model.

(2) It is not necessary to the creation of an express warranty that the lessor use formal words, such as "warrant" or "guarantee," or that the lessor have a specific intention to make a warranty, but an affirmation merely of the value of the goods or a statement purporting to be merely the lessor's opinion or commendation of the goods does not create a warranty.

Official Comment

Uniform Statutory Source: Section 2–313.

Changes: Revised to reflect leasing practices and terminology.

Purposes: All of the express and implied warranties of the Article on Sales (Article 2) are included in this Article, revised to reflect the differences between a sale of goods and a lease of goods. Sections 2A–210 through 2A–216. The lease of goods is sufficiently similar to the sale of goods to justify this decision. Hawkland, *The Impact of the Uniform Commercial Code on Equipment Leasing*, 1972 Ill.L.F. 446, 459–60. Many state and federal courts have reached the same conclusion.

Value of the goods, as used in subsection (2), includes rental value.

Cross References:

Article 2, esp. Section 2–313, and Sections 2A–210 through 2A–216.

Definitional Cross References:

"Conforming". Section 2A–103(1)(d).
"Goods". Section 2A–103(1)(h).
"Lessee". Section 2A–103(1)(n).
"Lessor". Section 2A–103(1)(p).
"Value". Section 1–201(44).*

§ 2A–211. Warranties Against Interference and Against Infringement; Lessee's Obligation Against Infringement.

(1) There is in a lease contract a warranty that for the lease term no person holds a claim to or interest in the goods that arose from an act or omission of the lessor, other than a claim by way of infringement or the like, which will interfere with the lessee's enjoyment of its leasehold interest.

(2) Except in a finance lease there is in a lease contract by a lessor who is a merchant regularly dealing in goods of the kind a warranty that the goods are delivered free of the rightful claim of any person by way of infringement or the like.

(3) A lessee who furnishes specifications to a lessor or a supplier shall hold the lessor and the supplier harmless against any claim by way of infringement or the like that arises out of compliance with the specifications.

Official Comment

Uniform Statutory Source: Section 2–312.

Changes: This section is modeled on the provisions of Section 2–312, with modifications to reflect the limited interest transferred by a lease contract and the total interest transferred by a sale. Section 2–312(2), which is

---

*   *Referring to unrevised Article 1 (Appendix A).*

omitted here, is incorporated in Section 2A–214. The warranty of quiet possession was abolished with respect to sales of goods. Section 2–312 official comment 1. Section 2A–211(1) reinstates the warranty of quiet possession with respect to leases. Inherent in the nature of the limited interest transferred by the lease—the right to possession and use of the goods—is the need of the lessee for protection greater than that afforded to the buyer. Since the scope of the protection is limited to claims or interests that arose from acts or omissions of the lessor, the lessor will be in position to evaluate the potential cost, certainly a far better position than that enjoyed by the lessee. Further, to the extent the market will allow, the lessor can attempt to pass on the anticipated additional cost to the lessee in the guise of higher rent.

Purposes: General language was chosen for subsection (1) that expresses the essence of the lessee's expectation: with an exception for infringement and the like, no person holding a claim or interest that arose from an act or omission of the lessor will be able to interfere with the lessee's use and enjoyment of the goods for the lease term. Subsection (2), like other similar provisions in later sections, excludes the finance lessor from extending this warranty; with few exceptions (Sections 2A–210 and 2A–211(1)), the lessee under a finance lease is to look to the supplier for warranties and the like or, in some cases as to warranties, to the manufacturer if a warranty made by that person is passed on. Subsections (2) and (3) are derived from Section 2–312(3). These subsections, as well as the analogue, should be construed so that applicable principles of law and equity supplement their provisions. Sections 2A–103(4) and 1–103.

Cross References:

Sections 2–312, 2–312(1), 2–312(2), 2–312 official comment 1, 2A–210, 2A–211(1) and 2A–214.

Definitional Cross References:

"Delivery". Section 1–201(14).*
"Finance lease". Section 2A–103(1)(g).
"Goods". Section 2A–103(1)(h).
"Lease". Section 2A–103(1)(j).
"Lease contract". Section 2A–103(1)(*l*).
"Leasehold interest". Section 2A–103(1)(m).
"Lessee". Section 2A–103(1)(n).
"Lessor". Section 2A–103(1)(p).
"Merchant". Section 2–104(1).
"Person". Section 1–201(30).*
"Supplier". Section 2A–103(1)(x).

§ 2A–212. Implied Warranty of Merchantability.

(1)   Except in a finance lease, a warranty that the goods will be merchantable is implied in a lease contract if the lessor is a merchant with respect to goods of that kind.

(2)   Goods to be merchantable must be at least such as

(a)   pass without objection in the trade under the description in the lease agreement;

(b)   in the case of fungible goods, are of fair average quality within the description;

(c)   are fit for the ordinary purposes for which goods of that type are used;

(d)   run, within the variation permitted by the lease agreement, of even kind, quality, and quantity within each unit and among all units involved;

(e)   are adequately contained, packaged, and labeled as the lease agreement may require; and

(f)   conform to any promises or affirmations of fact made on the container or label.

(3)   Other implied warranties may arise from course of dealing or usage of trade.

---

*   *Referring to unrevised Article 1 (Appendix A).*

Official Comment

Uniform Statutory Source: Section 2–314.

Changes: Revised to reflect leasing practices and terminology. *E.g., Glenn Dick Equip. Co. v. Galey Constr., Inc.,* 97 Idaho 216, 225, 541 P.2d 1184, 1193 (1975) (implied warranty of merchantability (Article 2) extends to lease transactions).

Definitional Cross References:

"Conforming". Section 2A–103(1)(d).
"Course of dealing". Section 1–205.*
"Finance lease". Section 2A–103(1)(g).
"Fungible". Section 1–201(17).*
"Goods". Section 2A–103(1)(h).
"Lease agreement". Section 2A–103(1)(k).
"Lease contract". Section 2A–103(1)(*l*).
"Lessor". Section 2A–103(1)(p).
"Merchant". Section 2–104(1).
"Usage of trade". Section 1–205.*

§ 2A–213. Implied Warranty of Fitness for Particular Purpose.

Except in a finance lease, if the lessor at the time the lease contract is made has reason to know of any particular purpose for which the goods are required and that the lessee is relying on the lessor's skill or judgment to select or furnish suitable goods, there is in the lease contract an implied warranty that the goods will be fit for that purpose.

Official Comment

Uniform Statutory Source: Section 2–315.

Changes: Revised to reflect leasing practices and terminology. *E.g., All-States Leasing Co. v. Bass,* 96 Idaho 873, 879, 538 P.2d 1177, 1183 (1975) (implied warranty of fitness for a particular purpose (Article 2) extends to lease transactions).

Definitional Cross References:

"Finance lease". Section 2A–103(1)(g).
"Goods". Section 2A–103(1)(h).
"Knows". Section 1–201(25).*
"Lease contract". Section 2A–103(1)(*l*).
"Lessee". Section 2A–103(1)(n).
"Lessor". Section 2A–103(1)(p).

§ 2A–214. Exclusion or Modification of Warranties.

(1)   Words or conduct relevant to the creation of an express warranty and words or conduct tending to negate or limit a warranty must be construed wherever reasonable as consistent with each other; but, subject to the provisions of Section 2A–202 on parol or extrinsic evidence, negation or limitation is inoperative to the extent that the construction is unreasonable.

(2)   Subject to subsection (3), to exclude or modify the implied warranty of merchantability or any part of it the language must mention "merchantability", be by a writing, and be conspicuous. Subject to subsection (3), to exclude or modify any implied warranty of fitness the exclusion must be by a writing and be conspicuous. Language to exclude all implied warranties of fitness is sufficient if it is in writing, is conspicuous and states, for example, "There is no warranty that the goods will be fit for a particular purpose".

---

*   *Referring to unrevised Article 1 (Appendix A).*

(3) Notwithstanding subsection (2), but subject to subsection (4),

(a) unless the circumstances indicate otherwise, all implied warranties are excluded by expressions like "as is," or "with all faults," or by other language that in common understanding calls the lessee's attention to the exclusion of warranties and makes plain that there is no implied warranty, if in writing and conspicuous;

(b) if the lessee before entering into the lease contract has examined the goods or the sample or model as fully as desired or has refused to examine the goods, there is no implied warranty with regard to defects that an examination ought in the circumstances to have revealed; and

(c) an implied warranty may also be excluded or modified by course of dealing, course of performance, or usage of trade.

(4) To exclude or modify a warranty against interference or against infringement (Section 2A–211) or any part of it, the language must be specific, be by a writing, and be conspicuous, unless the circumstances, including course of performance, course of dealing, or usage of trade, give the lessee reason to know that the goods are being leased subject to a claim or interest of any person.

Official Comment

Uniform Statutory Source: Sections 2–316 and 2–312(2).

Changes: Subsection (2) requires that a disclaimer of the warranty of merchantability be conspicuous and in writing as is the case for a disclaimer of the warranty of fitness; this is contrary to the rule stated in Section 2–316(2) with respect to the disclaimer of the warranty of merchantability. This section also provides that to exclude or modify the implied warranty of merchantability, fitness or against interference or infringement the language must be in writing and conspicuous. There are, however, exceptions to the rule. *E.g.,* course of dealing, course of performance, or usage of trade may exclude or modify an implied warranty. Section 2A–214(3)(c). The analogue of Section 2–312(2) has been moved to subsection (4) of this section for a more unified treatment of disclaimers; there is no policy with respect to leases of goods that would justify continuing certain distinctions found in the Article on Sales (Article 2) regarding the treatment of the disclaimer of various warranties. *Compare* Sections 2–312(2) and 2–316(2). Finally, the example of a disclaimer of the implied warranty of fitness stated in subsection (2) differs from the analogue stated in Section 2–316(2); this example should promote a better understanding of the effect of the disclaimer.

Purposes: These changes were made to reflect leasing practices. *E.g., FMC Finance Corp. v. Murphree,* 632 F.2d 413, 418 (5th Cir.1980) (disclaimer of implied warranty under lease transactions must be conspicuous and in writing). The omission of the provisions of Section 2–316(4) was not substantive. Sections 2A–503 and 2A–504.

Cross References:

Article 2, esp. Sections 2–312(2) and 2–316, and Sections 2A–503 and 2A–504.

Definitional Cross References:

"Conspicuous". Section 1–201(10).*
"Course of dealing". Section 1–205.*
"Fault". Section 2A–103(1)(f).
"Goods". Section 2A–103(1)(h).
"Knows". Section 1–201(25).*
"Lease". Section 2A–103(1)(j).
"Lease contract". Section 2A–103(1)(*l*).
"Lessee". Section 2A–103(1)(n).
"Person". Section 1–201(30).*
"Usage of trade". Section 1–205.*
"Writing". Section 1–201(46).*

---

* *Referring to unrevised Article 1 (Appendix A).*

§ 2A–215. Cumulation and Conflict of Warranties Express or Implied.

Warranties, whether express or implied, must be construed as consistent with each other and as cumulative, but if that construction is unreasonable, the intention of the parties determines which warranty is dominant. In ascertaining that intention the following rules apply:

(a) Exact or technical specifications displace an inconsistent sample or model or general language of description.

(b) A sample from an existing bulk displaces inconsistent general language of description.

(c) Express warranties displace inconsistent implied warranties other than an implied warranty of fitness for a particular purpose.

Official Comment

Uniform Statutory Source: Section 2–317.

Definitional Cross Reference:

"Party". Section 1–201(29).*

§ 2A–216. Third-Party Beneficiaries of Express and Implied Warranties.

ALTERNATIVE A

A warranty to or for the benefit of a lessee under this Article, whether express or implied, extends to any natural person who is in the family or household of the lessee or who is a guest in the lessee's home if it is reasonable to expect that such person may use, consume, or be affected by the goods and who is injured in person by breach of the warranty. This section does not displace principles of law and equity that extend a warranty to or for the benefit of a lessee to other persons. The operation of this section may not be excluded, modified, or limited, but an exclusion, modification, or limitation of the warranty, including any with respect to rights and remedies, effective against the lessee is also effective against any beneficiary designated under this section.

ALTERNATIVE B

A warranty to or for the benefit of a lessee under this Article, whether express or implied, extends to any natural person who may reasonably be expected to use, consume, or be affected by the goods and who is injured in person by breach of the warranty. This section does not displace principles of law and equity that extend a warranty to or for the benefit of a lessee to other persons. The operation of this section may not be excluded, modified, or limited, but an exclusion, modification, or limitation of the warranty, including any with respect to rights and remedies, effective against the lessee is also effective against the beneficiary designated under this section.

ALTERNATIVE C

A warranty to or for the benefit of a lessee under this Article, whether express or implied, extends to any person who may reasonably be expected to use, consume, or be affected by the goods and who is injured by breach of the warranty. The operation of this section may not be excluded, modified, or limited with respect to injury to the person of an individual to whom the warranty extends, but an exclusion, modification, or limitation of the warranty, including any with respect to rights and remedies, effective against the lessee is also effective against the beneficiary designated under this section.

Official Comment

Uniform Statutory Source: Section 2–318.

Changes: The provisions of Section 2–318 have been included in this section, modified in two respects: first, to reflect leasing practice, including the special practices of the lessor under a finance lease; second, to reflect and thus codify elements of the official comment to Section 2–318 with respect to the effect of disclaimers and limitations of remedies against third parties.

---

*   *Referring to unrevised Article 1 (Appendix A).*

Purposes: Alternative A is based on the 1962 version of Section 2–318 and is least favorable to the injured person as the doctrine of privity imposed by other law is abrogated to only a limited extent. Alternatives B and C are based on later additions to Section 2–318 and are more favorable to the injured person. In determining which alternative to select, the state legislature should consider making its choice parallel to the choice it made with respect to Section 2–318, as interpreted by the courts.

The last sentence of each of Alternatives A, B and C does not preclude the lessor from excluding or modifying an express or implied warranty under a lease. Section 2A–214. Further, that sentence does not preclude the lessor from limiting the rights and remedies of the lessee and from liquidating damages. Sections 2A–503 and 2A–504. If the lease excludes or modifies warranties, limits remedies for breach, or liquidates damages with respect to the lessee, such provisions are enforceable against the beneficiaries designated under this section. However, this last sentence forbids selective discrimination against the beneficiaries designated under this section, *i.e.*, exclusion of the lessor's liability to the beneficiaries with respect to warranties made by the lessor to the lessee.

Other law, including the Article on Sales (Article 2), may apply in determining the extent to which a warranty to or for the benefit of the lessor extends to the lessee and third parties. This is in part a function of whether the lessor has bought or leased the goods.

This Article does not purport to change the development of the relationship of the common law, with respect to products liability, including strict liability in tort (as restated in Restatement (Second) of Torts, § 402A (1965)), to the provisions of this Act. *Compare Cline v. Prowler Indus. of Maryland*, 418 A.2d 968 (Del.1980) and *Hawkins Constr. Co. v. Matthews Co.*, 190 Neb. 546, 209 N.W.2d 643 (1973) with *Dippel v. Sciano*, 37 Wis.2d 443, 155 N.W.2d 55 (1967).

Cross References:

Article 2, esp. Section 2–318, and Sections 2A–214, 2A–503 and 2A–504.

Definitional Cross References:

"Goods". Section 2A–103(1)(h).
"Lessee". Section 2A–103(1)(n).
"Person". Section 1–201(30).*
"Remedy". Section 1–201(34).*
"Rights". Section 1–201(36).

§ 2A–217. Identification.

Identification of goods as goods to which a lease contract refers may be made at any time and in any manner explicitly agreed to by the parties. In the absence of explicit agreement, identification occurs:

(a) when the lease contract is made if the lease contract is for a lease of goods that are existing and identified;

(b) when the goods are shipped, marked, or otherwise designated by the lessor as goods to which the lease contract refers, if the lease contract is for a lease of goods that are not existing and identified; or

(c) when the young are conceived, if the lease contract is for a lease of unborn young of animals.

Official Comment

Uniform Statutory Source: Section 2–501.

Changes: This section, together with Section 2A–218, is derived from the provisions of Section 2–501, with changes to reflect lease terminology; however, this section omits as irrelevant to leasing practice the treatment of special property.

Purposes: With respect to subsection (b) there is a certain amount of ambiguity in the reference to when goods are designated, *e.g.*, when the lessor is both selling and leasing goods to the same lessee/buyer and has marked goods for delivery but has not distinguished between those related to the lease contract and those related to the sales contract. As in Section 2–501(1)(b), this issue has been left to be resolved by the courts, case by case.

---

*   *Referring to unrevised Article 1 (Appendix A).*

Cross References:

> Sections 2–501 and 2A–218.

Definitional Cross References:

> "Agreement". Section 1–201(3).*
> "Goods". Section 2A–103(1)(h).
> "Lease". Section 2A–103(1)(j).
> "Lease contract". Section 2A–103(1)(*l*).
> "Lessor". Section 2A–103(1)(p).
> "Party". Section 1–201(29).*

§ 2A–218. Insurance and Proceeds.

(1)   A lessee obtains an insurable interest when existing goods are identified to the lease contract even though the goods identified are nonconforming and the lessee has an option to reject them.

(2)   If a lessee has an insurable interest only by reason of the lessor's identification of the goods, the lessor, until default or insolvency or notification to the lessee that identification is final, may substitute other goods for those identified.

(3)   Notwithstanding a lessee's insurable interest under subsections (1) and (2), the lessor retains an insurable interest until an option to buy has been exercised by the lessee and risk of loss has passed to the lessee.

(4)   Nothing in this section impairs any insurable interest recognized under any other statute or rule of law.

(5)   The parties by agreement may determine that one or more parties have an obligation to obtain and pay for insurance covering the goods and by agreement may determine the beneficiary of the proceeds of the insurance.

Official Comment

Uniform Statutory Source: Section 2–501.

Changes: This section, together with Section 2A–217, is derived from the provisions of Section 2–501, with changes and additions to reflect leasing practices and terminology.

Purposes: Subsection (2) states a rule allowing substitution of goods by the lessor under certain circumstances, until default or insolvency of the lessor, or until notification to the lessee that identification is final. Subsection (3) states a rule regarding the lessor's insurable interest that, by virtue of the difference between a sale and a lease, necessarily is different from the rule stated in Section 2–501(2) regarding the seller's insurable interest. For this purpose the option to buy shall be deemed to have been exercised by the lessee when the resulting sale is closed, not when the lessee gives notice to the lessor. Further, subsection (5) is new and reflects the common practice of shifting the responsibility and cost of insuring the goods between the parties to the lease transaction.

Cross References:

> Sections 2–501, 2–501(2) and 2A–217.

Definitional Cross References:

> "Agreement". Section 1–201(3).*
> "Buying". Section 2A–103(1)(a).
> "Conforming". Section 2A–103(1)(d).
> "Goods". Section 2A–103(1)(h).
> "Insolvent". Section 1–201(23).*
> "Lease contract". Section 2A–103(1)(*l*).
> "Lessee". Section 2A–103(1)(n).
> "Lessor". Section 2A–103(1)(p).

---

*   *Referring to unrevised Article 1 (Appendix A).*

"Notification". Section 1–201(26).*
"Party". Section 1–201(29).*

§ 2A–219. Risk of Loss.

(1) Except in the case of a finance lease, risk of loss is retained by the lessor and does not pass to the lessee. In the case of a finance lease, risk of loss passes to the lessee.

(2) Subject to the provisions of this Article on the effect of default on risk of loss (Section 2A–220), if risk of loss is to pass to the lessee and the time of passage is not stated, the following rules apply:

(a) If the lease contract requires or authorizes the goods to be shipped by carrier

(i) and it does not require delivery at a particular destination, the risk of loss passes to the lessee when the goods are duly delivered to the carrier; but

(ii) if it does require delivery at a particular destination and the goods are there duly tendered while in the possession of the carrier, the risk of loss passes to the lessee when the goods are there duly so tendered as to enable the lessee to take delivery.

(b) If the goods are held by a bailee to be delivered without being moved, the risk of loss passes to the lessee on acknowledgment by the bailee of the lessee's right to possession of the goods.

(c) In any case not within subsection (a) or (b), the risk of loss passes to the lessee on the lessee's receipt of the goods if the lessor, or, in the case of a finance lease, the supplier, is a merchant; otherwise the risk passes to the lessee on tender of delivery.

Official Comment

Uniform Statutory Source: Section 2–509(1) through (3).

Changes: Subsection (1) is new. The introduction to subsection (2) is new, but subparagraph (a) incorporates the provisions of Section 2–509(1); subparagraph (b) incorporates the provisions of Section 2–509(2) only in part, reflecting current practice in lease transactions.

Purposes: Subsection (1) states rules related to retention or passage of risk of loss consistent with current practice in lease transactions. The provisions of subsection (4) of Section 2–509 are not incorporated as they are not necessary. This section does not deal with responsibility for loss caused by the wrongful act of either the lessor or the lessee.

Cross References:

Sections 2–509(1), 2–509(2) and 2–509(4).

Definitional Cross References:

"Delivery". Section 1–201(14).*
"Finance lease". Section 2A–103(1)(g).
"Goods". Section 2A–103(1)(h).
"Lease contract". Section 2A–103(1)(*l*).
"Lessee". Section 2A–103(1)(n).
"Lessor". Section 2A–103(1)(p).
"Merchant". Section 2–104(1).
"Receipt". Section 2–103(1)(c).
"Rights". Section 1–201(36).*
"Supplier". Section 2A–103(1)(x).

§ 2A–220. Effect of Default on Risk of Loss.

(1) Where risk of loss is to pass to the lessee and the time of passage is not stated:

---

*   *Referring to unrevised Article 1 (Appendix A).*

   (a)   If a tender or delivery of goods so fails to conform to the lease contract as to give a right of rejection, the risk of their loss remains with the lessor, or, in the case of a finance lease, the supplier, until cure or acceptance.

   (b)   If the lessee rightfully revokes acceptance, he [or she], to the extent of any deficiency in his [or her] effective insurance coverage, may treat the risk of loss as having remained with the lessor from the beginning.

   (2)   Whether or not risk of loss is to pass to the lessee, if the lessee as to conforming goods already identified to a lease contract repudiates or is otherwise in default under the lease contract, the lessor, or, in the case of a finance lease, the supplier, to the extent of any deficiency in his [or her] effective insurance coverage may treat the risk of loss as resting on the lessee for a commercially reasonable time.

Official Comment

Uniform Statutory Source: Section 2–510.

Changes: Revised to reflect leasing practices and terminology. The rule in Section (1)(b) does not allow the lessee under a finance lease to treat the risk of loss as having remained with the supplier from the beginning. This is appropriate given the limited circumstances under which the lessee under a finance lease is allowed to revoke acceptance. Section 2A–517 and Section 2A–516 official comment.

Definitional Cross References:

     "Conforming". Section 2A–103(1)(d).
     "Delivery". Section 1–201(14).*
     "Finance lease". Section 2A–103(1)(g).
     "Goods". Section 2A–103(1)(h).
     "Lease contract". Section 2A–103(1)(*l*).
     "Lessee". Section 2A–103(1)(n).
     "Lessor". Section 2A–103(1)(p).
     "Reasonable time". Section 1–204(1) and (2).*
     "Rights". Section 1–201(36).*
     "Supplier". Section 2A–103(1)(x).

§ 2A–221.   Casualty to Identified Goods.

   If a lease contract requires goods identified when the lease contract is made, and the goods suffer casualty without fault of the lessee, the lessor or the supplier before delivery, or the goods suffer casualty before risk of loss passes to the lessee pursuant to the lease agreement or Section 2A–219, then:

   (a)   if the loss is total, the lease contract is avoided; and

   (b)   if the loss is partial or the goods have so deteriorated as to no longer conform to the lease contract, the lessee may nevertheless demand inspection and at his [or her] option either treat the lease contract as avoided or, except in a finance lease that is not a consumer lease, accept the goods with due allowance from the rent payable for the balance of the lease term for the deterioration or the deficiency in quantity but without further right against the lessor.

Official Comment

Uniform Statutory Source: Section 2–613.

Changes: Revised to reflect leasing practices and terminology.

Purpose: Due to the vagaries of determining the amount of due allowance (Section 2–613(b)), no attempt was made in subsection (b) to treat a problem unique to lease contracts and installment sales contracts: determining how to recapture the allowance, *e.g.*, application to the first or last rent payments or allocation, *pro rata*, to all rent payments.

---

   *   *Referring to unrevised Article 1 (Appendix A).*

Cross References:

Section 2–613.

Definitional Cross References:

"Conforming". Section 2A–103(1)(d).
"Consumer lease". Section 2A–103(1)(e).
"Delivery". Section 1–201(14).*
"Fault". Section 2A–103(1)(f).
"Finance lease". Section 2A–103(1)(g).
"Goods". Section 2A–103(1)(h).
"Lease". Section 2A–103(1)(j).
"Lease agreement". Section 2A–103(1)(k).
"Lease contract". Section 2A–103(1)(*l*).
"Lessee". Section 2A–103(1)(n).
"Lessor". Section 2A–103(1)(p).
"Rights". Section 1–201(36).*
"Supplier". Section 2A–103(1)(x).

PART 3

EFFECT OF LEASE CONTRACT

§ 2A–301.   Enforceability of Lease Contract.

Except as otherwise provided in this Article, a lease contract is effective and enforceable according to its terms between the parties, against purchasers of the goods and against creditors of the parties.

Official Comment

Uniform Statutory Source: Former Section 9–201 (now codified as Section 9–201).

Changes: The first sentence of former Section 9–201 was incorporated, modified to reflect leasing terminology. The second sentence of former Section 9–201 was eliminated as not relevant to leasing practices.

Purposes:

1.   This section establishes a general rule regarding the validity and enforceability of a lease contract. The lease contract is effective and enforceable between the parties and against third parties. Exceptions to this general rule arise where there is a specific rule to the contrary in this Article. Enforceability is, thus, dependent upon the lease contract meeting the requirements of the Statute of Frauds provisions of Section 2A–201. Enforceability is also a function of the lease contract conforming to the principles of construction and interpretation contained in the Article on General Provisions (Article 1). Section 2A–103(4).

2.   The effectiveness or enforceability of the lease contract is not dependent upon the lease contract or any financing statement or the like being filed or recorded; however, the priority of the interest of a lessor of fixtures with respect to the interests of certain third parties in such fixtures is subject to the provisions of the Article on Secured Transactions (Article 9). Section 2A–309. Prior to the adoption of this Article filing or recording was not required with respect to leases, only leases intended as security. The definition of security interest, as amended concurrently with the adoption of this Article, more clearly delineates leases and leases intended as security and thus signals the need to file. Section 1–201(37).* Those lessors who are concerned about whether the transaction creates a lease or a security interest will continue to file a protective financing statement. Section 9–505. Coogan, Leasing and the Uniform Commercial Code, in *Equipment Leasing-Leveraged Leasing* 681, 744–46 (2d ed. 1980).

3.   **Hypothetical:**

(a)   In construing this section it is important to recognize its relationship to other sections in this Article. This is best demonstrated by reference to a hypothetical. Assume that on February 1 A, a manufacturer of combines and other farm equipment, leased a fleet of six combines to B, a corporation

___
*   *Referring to unrevised Article 1 (Appendix A).*

engaged in the business of farming, for a 12 month term. Under the lease agreement between A and B, A agreed to defer B's payment of the first two months' rent to April 1. On March 1 B recognized that it would need only four combines and thus subleased two combines to C for an 11 month term.

(b)   This hypothetical raises a number of issues that are answered by the sections contained in this part. Since lease is defined to include sublease (Section 2A–103(1)(j) and (w)), this section provides that the prime lease between A and B and the sublease between B and C are enforceable in accordance with their terms, except as otherwise provided in this Article; that exception, in this case, is one of considerable scope.

(c)   The separation of ownership, which is in A, and possession, which is in B with respect to four combines and which is in C with respect to two combines, is not relevant. Section 2A–302. A's interest in the six combines cannot be challenged simply because A parted with possession to B, who in turn parted with possession of some of the combines to C. Yet it is important to note that by the terms of Section 2A–302 this conclusion is subject to change if otherwise provided in this Article.

(d)   B's entering the sublease with C raises an issue that is treated by this part. In a dispute over the leased combines A may challenge B's right to sublease. The rule is permissive as to transfers of interests under a lease contract, including subleases. Section 2A–303(2). However, the rule has two significant qualifications. If the prime lease contract between A and B prohibits B from subleasing the combines, or makes such a sublease an event of default, Section 2A–303(2) applies; thus, while B's interest under the prime lease may be transferred under the sublease to C, A may have a remedy pursuant to Section 2A–303(5). Absent a prohibition or default provision in the prime lease contract A might be able to argue that the sublease to C materially increases A's risk; thus, while B's interest under the prime lease may be transferred under the sublease to C, A may have a remedy pursuant to Section 2A–303(5). Section 2A–303(5)(b)(ii).

(e)   Resolution of this issue is also a function of the section dealing with the sublease of goods by a prime lessee (Section 2A–305). Subsection (1) of Section 2A–305, which is subject to the rules of Section 2A–303 stated above, provides that C takes subject to the interest of A under the prime lease between A and B. However, there are two exceptions. First, if B is a merchant (Sections 2A–103(3) and 2–104(1)) dealing in goods of that kind and C is a sublessee in the ordinary course of business (Sections 2A–103(1)(o) and 2A–103(1)(n)), C takes free of the prime lease between A and B. Second, if B has rejected the six combines under the prime lease with A, and B disposes of the goods by sublease to C, C takes free of the prime lease if C can establish good faith. Section 2A–511(4).

(f)   If the facts of this hypothetical are expanded and we assume that the prime lease obligated B to maintain the combines, an additional issue may be presented. Prior to entering the sublease, B, in satisfaction of its maintenance covenant, brought the two combines that it desired to sublease to a local independent dealer of A's. The dealer did the requested work for B. C inspected the combines on the dealer's lot after the work was completed. C signed the sublease with B two days later. C, however, was prevented from taking delivery of the two combines as B refused to pay the dealer's invoice for the repairs. The dealer furnished the repair service to B in the ordinary course of the dealer's business. If under applicable law the dealer has a lien on repaired goods in the dealer's possession, the dealer's lien will take priority over B's and C's interests and also should take priority over A's interest, depending upon the terms of the lease contract and the applicable law. Section 2A–306.

(g)   Now assume that C is in financial straits and one of C's creditors obtains a judgment against C. If the creditor levies on C's subleasehold interest in the two combines, who will prevail? Unless the levying creditor also holds a lien covered by Section 2A–306, discussed above, the judgment creditor will take its interest subject to B's rights under the sublease and A's rights under the prime lease. Section 2A–307(1). The hypothetical becomes more complicated if we assume that B is in financial straits and B's creditor holds the judgment. Here the judgment creditor takes subject to the sublease unless the lien attached to the two combines before the sublease contract became enforceable. Section 2A–307(2)(a). However, B's judgment creditor cannot prime A's interest in the goods because, with respect to A, the judgment creditor is a creditor of B in its capacity as lessee under the prime lease between A and B. Thus, here the judgment creditor's interest is subject to the lease between A and B. Section 2A–307(1).

(h)   Finally, assume that on April 1 B is unable to pay A the deferred rent then due under the prime lease, but that C is current in its payments under the sublease from B. What effect will B's default under the prime lease between A and B have on C's rights under the sublease between B and C? Section 2A–301 provides that a lease contract is effective against the creditors of either party. Since a lease contract includes

208

a sublease contract (Section 2A–103(1)(*l*)), the sublease contract between B and C arguably could be enforceable against A, a prime lessor who has extended unsecured credit to B, the prime lessee/sublessor, if the sublease contract meets the requirements of Section 2A–201. However, the rule stated in Section 2A–301 is subject to other provisions in this Article. Under Section 2A–305, C, as sublessee, would take subject to the prime lease contract in most cases. Thus, B's default under the prime lease will in most cases lead to A's recovery of the goods from C. Section 2A–523. A and C could provide otherwise by agreement. Section 2A–311. C's recourse will be to assert a claim for damages against B. Sections 2A–211(1) and 2A–508.

4. **Relationship Between Sections:**

(a) As the analysis of the hypothetical demonstrates, Part 3 of the Article focuses on issues that relate to the enforceability of the lease contract (Sections 2A–301, 2A–302 and 2A–303) and to the priority of various claims to the goods subject to the lease contract (Sections 2A–304, 2A–305, 2A–306, 2A–307, 2A–308, 2A–309, 2A–310, and 2A–311).

(b) This section states a general rule of enforceability, which is subject to specific rules to the contrary stated elsewhere in the Article. Section 2A–302 negates any notion that the separation of title and possession is fraudulent as a rule of law. Finally, Section 2A–303 states rules with respect to the transfer of the lessor's interest (as well as the residual interest in the goods) or the lessee's interest under the lease contract. Qualifications are imposed as a function of various issues, including whether the transfer is the creation or enforcement of a security interest or one that is material to the other party to the lease contract. In addition, a system of rules is created to deal with the rights and duties among assignor, assignee and the other party to the lease contract.

(c) Sections 2A–304 and 2A–305 are twins that deal with good faith transferees of goods subject to the lease contract. Section 2A–304 creates a set of rules with respect to transfers by the lessor of goods subject to a lease contract; the transferee considered is a subsequent lessee of the goods. The priority dispute covered here is between the subsequent lessee and the original lessee of the goods (or persons claiming through the original lessee). Section 2A–305 creates a set of rules with respect to transfers by the lessee of goods subject to a lease contract; the transferees considered are buyers of the goods or sublessees of the goods. The priority dispute covered here is between the transferee and the lessor of the goods (or persons claiming through the lessor).

(d) Section 2A–306 creates a rule with respect to priority disputes between holders of liens for services or materials furnished with respect to goods subject to a lease contract and the lessor or the lessee under that contract. Section 2A–307 creates a rule with respect to priority disputes between the lessee and creditors of the lessor and priority disputes between the lessor and creditors of the lessee.

(e) Section 2A–308 creates a series of rules relating to allegedly fraudulent transfers and preferences. The most significant rule is that set forth in subsection (3) which validates sale-leaseback transactions if the buyer-lessor can establish that he or she bought for value and in good faith.

(f) Sections 2A–309 and 2A–310 create a series of rules with respect to priority disputes between various third parties and a lessor of fixtures or accessions, respectively, with respect thereto.

(g) Finally, Section 2A–311 allows parties to alter the statutory priorities by agreement.

Cross References:

Article 1, especially Section 1–201(37),* and Sections 2–104(1), 2A–103(1)(j), 2A–103(1)(*l*), 2A–103(1)(n), 2A–103(1)(*o*) and 2A–103(1)(w), 2A–103(3), 2A–103(4), 2A–201, 2A–301 through 2A–303, 2A–303(2), 2A–303(5), 2A–304 through 2A–307, 2A–307(1), 2A–307(2)(a), 2A–308 through 2A–311, 2A–508, 2A–511(4), 2A–523, Article 9, especially Sections 9–201 and 9–505.

Definitional Cross References:

"Creditor". Section 1–201(12).*
"Goods". Section 2A–103(1)(h).
"Lease contract". Section 2A–103(1)(*l*).
"Party". Section 1–201(29).*
"Purchaser". Section 1–201(33).*

---

* *Referring to unrevised Article 1 (Appendix A).*

"Term". Section 1–201(42).*

§ 2A–302. Title to and Possession of Goods.

Except as otherwise provided in this Article, each provision of this Article applies whether the lessor or a third party has title to the goods, and whether the lessor, the lessee, or a third party has possession of the goods, notwithstanding any statute or rule of law that possession or the absence of possession is fraudulent.

Official Comment

Uniform Statutory Source: Former Section 9–202 (now codified as Section 9–202).

Changes: Former Section 9–202 was modified to reflect leasing terminology and to clarify the law of leases with respect to fraudulent conveyances or transfers.

Purposes: The separation of ownership and possession of goods between the lessor and the lessee (or a third party) has created problems under certain fraudulent conveyance statutes. *See, e.g., In re Ludlum Enters.*, 510 F.2d 996 (5th Cir. 1975); *Suburbia Fed. Sav. & Loan Ass'n v. Bel-Air Conditioning Co.*, 385 So.2d 1151 (Fla.Dist.Ct.App.1980). This section provides, among other things, that separation of ownership and possession *per se* does not affect the enforceability of the lease contract. Sections 2A–301 and 2A–308.

Cross References:

Sections 2A–301, 2A–308 and 9–202.

Definitional Cross References:

"Goods". Section 2A–103(1)(h).
"Lessee". Section 2A–103(1)(n).
"Lessor". Section 2A–103(1)(p).

§ 2A–303. Alienability of Party's Interest Under Lease Contract or of Lessor's Residual Interest in Goods; Delegation of Performance; Transfer of Rights.

(1)   As used in this section, "creation of a security interest" includes the sale of a lease contract that is subject to Article 9, Secured Transactions, by reason of Section 9–109(a)(3).

(2)   Except as provided in subsection (3) and Section 9–407, a provision in a lease agreement which (i) prohibits the voluntary or involuntary transfer, including a transfer by sale, sublease, creation or enforcement of a security interest, or attachment, levy, or other judicial process, of an interest of a party under the lease contract or of the lessor's residual interest in the goods, or (ii) makes such a transfer an event of default, gives rise to the rights and remedies provided in subsection (4), but a transfer that is prohibited or is an event of default under the lease agreement is otherwise effective.

(3)   A provision in a lease agreement which (i) prohibits a transfer of a right to damages for default with respect to the whole lease contract or of a right to payment arising out of the transferor's due performance of the transferor's entire obligation, or (ii) makes such a transfer an event of default, is not enforceable, and such a transfer is not a transfer that materially impairs the prospect of obtaining return performance by, materially changes the duty of, or materially increases the burden or risk imposed on, the other party to the lease contract within the purview of subsection (4).

(4)   Subject to subsection (3) and Section 9–407:

(a)   if a transfer is made which is made an event of default under a lease agreement, the party to the lease contract not making the transfer, unless that party waives the default or otherwise agrees, has the rights and remedies described in Section 2A–501(2);

(b)   if paragraph (a) is not applicable and if a transfer is made that (i) is prohibited under a lease agreement or (ii) materially impairs the prospect of obtaining return performance by, materially changes the duty of, or materially increases the burden or risk imposed on, the other party to the

---

*   *Referring to unrevised Article 1 (Appendix A).*

lease contract, unless the party not making the transfer agrees at any time to the transfer in the lease contract or otherwise, then, except as limited by contract, (i) the transferor is liable to the party not making the transfer for damages caused by the transfer to the extent that the damages could not reasonably be prevented by the party not making the transfer and (ii) a court having jurisdiction may grant other appropriate relief, including cancellation of the lease contract or an injunction against the transfer.

(5)　A transfer of "the lease" or of "all my rights under the lease", or a transfer in similar general terms, is a transfer of rights and, unless the language or the circumstances, as in a transfer for security, indicate the contrary, the transfer is a delegation of duties by the transferor to the transferee. Acceptance by the transferee constitutes a promise by the transferee to perform those duties. The promise is enforceable by either the transferor or the other party to the lease contract.

(6)　Unless otherwise agreed by the lessor and the lessee, a delegation of performance does not relieve the transferor as against the other party of any duty to perform or of any liability for default.

(7)　In a consumer lease, to prohibit the transfer of an interest of a party under the lease contract or to make a transfer an event of default, the language must be specific, by a writing, and conspicuous.

As amended in 1990 and 1999.

Official Comment

Uniform Statutory Source: Section 2–210; former Section 9–311 (now codified as Section 9–401).

Changes: The provisions of Section 2–210 and former Section 9–311 were incorporated in this section, with substantial modifications to reflect leasing terminology and practice and to harmonize the principles of the respective provisions, i.e. limitations on delegation of performance on the one hand and alienability of rights on the other. In addition, unlike Section 2–210 which deals only with voluntary transfers, this section deals with involuntary as well as voluntary transfers. Moreover, the principle of former Section 9–318(4) (now codified as Section 9–406) denying effectiveness to contractual terms prohibiting assignments of receivables due and to become due also is implemented.

Purposes:

1.　Subsection (2) states a rule, consistent with Section 9–401(b), that voluntary and involuntary transfers of an interest of a party under the lease contract or of the lessor's residual interest, including by way of the creation or enforcement of a security interest, are effective, notwithstanding a provision in the lease agreement prohibiting the transfer or making the transfer an event of default. Although the transfers are effective, the provision in the lease agreement is nevertheless enforceable, but only as provided in subsection (4). Under subsection (4) the prejudiced party is limited to the remedies on "default under the lease contract" in this Article and, except as limited by this Article, as provided in the lease agreement, if the transfer has been made an event of default. Section 2A–501(2). Usually, there will be a specific provision to this effect or a general provision making a breach of a covenant an event of default. In those cases where the transfer is prohibited, but not made an event of default, the prejudiced party may recover damages; or, if the damage remedy would be ineffective adequately to protect that party, the court can order cancellation of the lease contract or enjoin the transfer. This rule that such provisions generally are enforceable is subject to subsection (3) and Section 9–407, which make such provisions unenforceable in certain instances.

2.　Under Section 9–407, a provision in a lease agreement which prohibits the creation or enforcement of a security interest, including sales of lease contracts subject to Article 9 (Section 9–109(a)(3)), or makes it an event of default is generally not enforceable, reflecting the policy of Section 9–406 and former Section 9–318(4).

3.　Subsection (3) is based upon Section 2–210(2) and Section 9–406. It makes unenforceable a prohibition against transfers of certain rights to payment or a provision making the transfer an event of default. It also provides that such transfers do not materially impair the prospect of obtaining return performance by, materially change the duty of, or materially increase the burden or risk imposed on, the other party to the lease contract so as to give rise to the rights and remedies stated in subsection (4). Accordingly, a transfer of a right to payment cannot be prohibited or made an event of default, or be one that materially impairs performance, changes duties or increases risk, if the right is already due or will become due without further performance being required by the party to receive payment. Thus, a lessor can transfer the right to future payments under the lease contract, including by way of a grant of a security interest, and the transfer will not give rise to the rights and remedies stated in subsection (4) if the lessor has no remaining performance under the lease contract. The mere fact that the lessor is obligated to allow the lessee to remain in possession and to use the goods as long as the lessee is not in default does not mean that there is remaining performance on the part of the lessor. Likewise, the fact that the lessor has potential liability under a "non-operating" lease contract for breaches of warranty does not mean that there is remaining performance. In contrast, the lessor would have remaining performance under a lease contract requiring the lessor to regularly maintain and service the goods or to provide "upgrades" of the equipment on a periodic basis in order to avoid obsolescence. The basic distinction is between a mere potential duty to respond which is not remaining performance, and an affirmative duty to render stipulated performance. Although the distinction may be difficult to draw in some cases, it is instructive to focus on the difference between "operating" and "non-operating" leases as generally understood in the marketplace. Even if there is remaining performance under a lease contract, a transfer for security of a right to payment that is made an event of default or that is in violation of a prohibition against transfer does not give rise to the rights and remedies under subsection (4) if it does not constitute an actual delegation of a material performance under Section 9–407.

4.   The application of either the rule of Section 9–407 or the rule of subsection (3) to the grant by the lessor of a security interest in the lessor's right to future payment under the lease contract may produce the same result. Both provisions generally protect security transfers by the lessor in particular because the creation by the lessor of a security interest or the enforcement of that interest generally will not prejudice the lessee's rights if it does not result in a delegation of the lessor's duties. To the contrary, the receipt of loan proceeds or relief from the enforcement of an antecedent debt normally should enhance the lessor's ability to perform its duties under the lease contract. Nevertheless, there are circumstances where relief might be justified. For example, if ownership of the goods is transferred pursuant to enforcement of a security interest to a party whose ownership would prevent the lessee from continuing to possess the goods, relief might be warranted. See 49 U.S.C. § 1401(a) and (b) which places limitations on the operation of aircraft in the United States based on the citizenship or corporate qualification of the registrant.

5.   Relief on the ground of material prejudice when the lease agreement does not prohibit the transfer or make it an event of default should be afforded only in extreme circumstances, considering the fact that the party asserting material prejudice did not insist upon a provision in the lease agreement that would protect against such a transfer.

6.   Subsection (4) implements the rule of subsection (2). Subsection (2) provides that, even though a transfer is effective, a provision in the lease agreement prohibiting it or making it an event of default may be enforceable as provided in subsection (4). See *Brummund v. First National Bank of Clovis*, 656 P.2d 884, 35 U.C.C. Rep.Serv. (Callaghan) 1311 (N.Mex.1983), stating the analogous rule for Section 9–311. If the transfer prohibited by the lease agreement is made an event of default, then, under subsection (4)(a), unless the default is waived or there is an agreement otherwise, the aggrieved party has the rights and remedies referred to in Section 2A–501(2), viz. those in this Article and, except as limited in the Article, those provided in the lease agreement. In the unlikely circumstance that the lease agreement prohibits the transfer without making a violation of the prohibition an event of default or, even if there is no prohibition against the transfer, and the transfer is one that materially impairs performance, changes duties, or increases risk (for example, a sublease or assignment to a party using the goods improperly or for an illegal purpose), then subsection (4)(b) is applicable. In that circumstance, unless the party aggrieved by the transfer has otherwise agreed in the lease contract, such as by assenting to a particular transfer or to transfers in general, or agrees in some other manner, the aggrieved party has the right to recover damages from the transferor and a court may, in appropriate circumstances, grant other relief, such as cancellation of the lease contract or an injunction against the transfer.

7.   If a transfer gives rise to the rights and remedies provided in subsection (4), the transferee as an alternative may propose, and the other party may accept, adequate cure or compensation for past defaults and adequate assurance of future due performance under the lease contract. Subsection (4) does not preclude any other relief that may be available to a party to the lease contract aggrieved by a transfer subject to an enforceable prohibition, such as an action for interference with contractual relations.

8.   Subsection (7) requires that a provision in a consumer lease prohibiting a transfer, or making it an event of default, must be specific, written and conspicuous. See Section 1–201(10).* This assists in protecting a consumer lessee against surprise assertions of default.

9.   Subsection (5) is taken almost verbatim from the provisions of Section 2–210(5). The subsection states a rule of construction that distinguishes a commercial assignment, which substitutes the assignee for the assignor

---

*   *Referring to unrevised Article 1 (Appendix A).*

as to rights and duties, and an assignment for security or financing assignment, which substitutes the assignee for the assignor only as to rights. Note that the assignment for security or financing assignment is a subset of all security interests. Security interest is defined to include "any interest of a buyer of . . . chattel paper". Section 1–201(37).* Chattel paper is defined to include a lease. Section 9–102. Thus, a buyer of leases is the holder of a security interest in the leases. That conclusion should not influence this issue, as the policy is quite different. Whether a buyer of leases is the holder of a commercial assignment, or an assignment for security or financing assignment should be determined by the language of the assignment or the circumstances of the assignment.

Cross References:

Sections 1–201(11),* 1–201(37),* 2–210, 2A–401, 9–102(a)(11), 9–109(a)(3), 9–406, and 9–407.

Definitional Cross References:

"Agreed" and "Agreement". Section 1–201(3).*
"Conspicuous". Section 1–201(10).*
"Goods". Section 2A–103(1)(h).
"Lease". Section 2A–103(1)(j).
"Lease contract". Section 2A–103(1)(*l*).
"Lessee". Section 2A–103(1)(n).
"Lessor". Section 2A–103(1)(p).
"Lessor's residual interest". Section 2A–103(1)(q).
"Notice". Section 1–201(25).*
"Party". Section 1–201(29).*
"Person". Section 1–201(30).*
"Reasonable time". Section 1–204(1) and (2).*
"Rights". Section 1–201(36).*
"Term". Section 1–201(42).*
"Writing". Section 1–201(46).*

As amended in 1999.

§ 2A–304. Subsequent Lease of Goods by Lessor.

(1)   Subject to Section 2A–303, a subsequent lessee from a lessor of goods under an existing lease contract obtains, to the extent of the leasehold interest transferred, the leasehold interest in the goods that the lessor had or had power to transfer, and except as provided in subsection (2) and Section 2A–527(4), takes subject to the existing lease contract. A lessor with voidable title has power to transfer a good leasehold interest to a good faith subsequent lessee for value, but only to the extent set forth in the preceding sentence. If goods have been delivered under a transaction of purchase, the lessor has that power even though:

(a)   the lessor's transferor was deceived as to the identity of the lessor;

(b)   the delivery was in exchange for a check which is later dishonored;

(c)   it was agreed that the transaction was to be a "cash sale"; or

(d)   the delivery was procured through fraud punishable as larcenous under the criminal law.

(2)   A subsequent lessee in the ordinary course of business from a lessor who is a merchant dealing in goods of that kind to whom the goods were entrusted by the existing lessee of that lessor before the interest of the subsequent lessee became enforceable against that lessor obtains, to the extent of the leasehold interest transferred, all of that lessor's and the existing lessee's rights to the goods, and takes free of the existing lease contract.

(3)   A subsequent lessee from the lessor of goods that are subject to an existing lease contract and are covered by a certificate of title issued under a statute of this State or of another jurisdiction takes no greater rights than those provided both by this section and by the certificate of title statute.

---

*   *Referring to unrevised Article 1 (Appendix A).*

As amended in 1990.

Official Comment

Uniform Statutory Source: Section 2–403.

Changes: While Section 2–403 was used as a model for this section, the provisions of Section 2–403 were significantly revised to reflect leasing practices and to integrate this Article with certificate of title statutes.

Purposes:

1.   This section must be read in conjunction with, as it is subject to, the provisions of Section 2A–303, which govern voluntary and involuntary transfers of rights and duties under a lease contract, including the lessor's residual interest in the goods.

2.   This section must also be read in conjunction with Section 2–403. This section and Section 2A–305 are derived from Section 2–403, which states a unified policy on good faith purchases of goods. Given the scope of the definition of purchaser (Section 1–201(33)*), a person who bought goods to lease as well as a person who bought goods subject to an existing lease from a lessor will take pursuant to Section 2–403. Further, a person who leases such goods from the person who bought them should also be protected under Section 2–403, first because the lessee's rights are derivative and second because the definition of purchaser should be interpreted to include one who takes by lease; no negative implication should be drawn from the inclusion of lease in the definition of purchase in this Article. Section 2A–103(1)(v).

3.   There are hypotheticals that relate to an entrustee's unauthorized lease of entrusted goods to a third party that are outside the provisions of Sections 2–403, 2A–304 and 2A–305. Consider a sale of goods by M, a merchant, to B, a buyer. After paying for the goods B allows M to retain possession of the goods as B is short of storage. Before B calls for the goods M leases the goods to L, a lessee. This transaction is not governed by Section 2–403(2) as L is not a buyer in the ordinary course of business. Section 1–201(9).* Further, this transaction is not governed by Section 2A–304(2) as B is not an existing lessee. Finally, this transaction is not governed by Section 2A–305(2) as B is not M's lessor. Section 2A–307(2) resolves the potential dispute between B, M and L. By virtue of B's entrustment of the goods to M and M's lease of the goods to L, B has a cause of action against M under the common law. Sections 2A–103(4) and 1–103. See, e.g., Restatement (Second) of Torts §§ 222A–243. Thus, B is a creditor of M. Sections 2A–103(4) and 1–201(12).* Section 2A–307(2) provides that B, as M's creditor, takes subject to M's lease to L. Thus, if L does not default under the lease, L's enjoyment and possession of the goods should be undisturbed. However, B is not without recourse. B's action should result in a judgment against M providing, among other things, a turnover of all proceeds arising from M's lease to L, as well as a transfer of all of M's right, title and interest as lessor under M's lease to L, including M's residual interest in the goods. Section 2A–103(1)(q).

4.   Subsection (1) states a rule with respect to the leasehold interest obtained by a subsequent lessee from a lessor of goods under an existing lease contract. The interest will include such leasehold interest as the lessor has in the goods as well as the leasehold interest that the lessor had the power to transfer. Thus, the subsequent lessee obtains unimpaired all rights acquired under the law of agency, apparent agency, ownership or other estoppel, whether based upon statutory provisions or upon case law principles. Sections 2A–103(4) and 1–103. In general, the subsequent lessee takes subject to the existing lease contract, including the existing lessee's rights thereunder. Furthermore, the subsequent lease contract is, of course, limited by its own terms, and the subsequent lessee takes only to the extent of the leasehold interest transferred thereunder.

5.   Subsection (1) further provides that a lessor with voidable title has power to transfer a good leasehold interest to a good faith subsequent lessee for value. In addition, subsections (1)(a) through (d) provide specifically for the protection of the good faith subsequent lessee for value in a number of specific situations which have been troublesome under prior law.

6.   The position of an existing lessee who entrusts leased goods to its lessor is not distinguishable from the position of other entrusters. Thus, subsection (2) provides that the subsequent lessee in the ordinary course of business takes free of the existing lease contract between the lessor entruster and the lessee entruster, if the lessor is a merchant dealing in goods of that kind. Further, the subsequent lessee obtains all of the lessor entrustee's and the lessee entruster's rights to the goods, but only to the extent of the leasehold interest transferred by the lessor entrustee. Thus, the lessor entrustee retains the residual interest in the goods. Section 2A–103(1)(q). However, entrustment by the existing lessee must have occurred before the interest of the subsequent lessee

---

*   *Referring to unrevised Article 1 (Appendix A).*

became enforceable against the lessor. Entrusting is defined in Section 2–403(3) and that definition applies here. Section 2A–103(3).

7. Subsection (3) states a rule with respect to a transfer of goods from a lessor to a subsequent lessee where the goods are subject to an existing lease and covered by a certificate of title. The subsequent lessee's rights are no greater than those provided by this section and the applicable certificate of title statute, including any applicable case law construing such statute. Where the relationship between the certificate of title statute and Section 2–403, the statutory analogue to this section, has been construed by a court, that construction is incorporated here. Sections 2A–103(4) and 1–102(1)* and (2).* The better rule is that the certificate of title statutes are in harmony with Section 2–403 and thus would be in harmony with this section. *E.g., Atwood Chevrolet-Olds v. Aberdeen Mun. School Dist.*, 431 So.2d 926, 928 (Miss.1983); *Godfrey v. Gilsdorf*, 476 P.2d 3, 6, 86 Nev. 714, 718 (1970); *Martin v. Nager*, 192 N.J.Super. 189, 197–98, 469 A.2d 519, 523 (Super.Ct.Ch.Div.1983). Where the certificate of title statute is silent on this issue of transfer, this section will control.

Cross References:

Sections 1–102,* 1–103, 1–201(33),* 2–403, 2A–103(1)(v), 2A–103(3), 2A–103(4), 2A–303 and 2A–305.

Definitional Cross References:

"Agreed". Section 1–201(3).*
"Delivery". Section 1–201(14).*
"Entrusting". Section 2–403(3).
"Good faith". Sections 1–201(19)* and 2–103(1)(b).
"Goods". Section 2A–103(1)(h).
"Lease". Section 2A–103(1)(j).
"Lease contract". Section 2A–103(1)(*l*).
"Leasehold interest". Section 2A–103(1)(m).
"Lessee". Section 2A–103(1)(n).
"Lessee in the ordinary course of business". Section 2A–103(1)(*o*).
"Lessor". Section 2A–103(1)(p).
"Merchant". Section 2–104(1).
"Purchase". Section 2A–103(1)(v).
"Rights". Section 1–201(36).*
"Value". Section 1–201(44).*

§ 2A–305. Sale or Sublease of Goods by Lessee.

(1) Subject to the provisions of Section 2A–303, a buyer or sublessee from the lessee of goods under an existing lease contract obtains, to the extent of the interest transferred, the leasehold interest in the goods that the lessee had or had power to transfer, and except as provided in subsection (2) and Section 2A–511(4), takes subject to the existing lease contract. A lessee with a voidable leasehold interest has power to transfer a good leasehold interest to a good faith buyer for value or a good faith sublessee for value, but only to the extent set forth in the preceding sentence. When goods have been delivered under a transaction of lease the lessee has that power even though:

(a) the lessor was deceived as to the identity of the lessee;

(b) the delivery was in exchange for a check which is later dishonored; or

(c) the delivery was procured through fraud punishable as larcenous under the criminal law.

(2) A buyer in the ordinary course of business or a sublessee in the ordinary course of business from a lessee who is a merchant dealing in goods of that kind to whom the goods were entrusted by the lessor obtains, to the extent of the interest transferred, all of the lessor's and lessee's rights to the goods, and takes free of the existing lease contract.

---

* *Referring to unrevised Article 1 (Appendix A).*

(3)   A buyer or sublessee from the lessee of goods that are subject to an existing lease contract and are covered by a certificate of title issued under a statute of this State or of another jurisdiction takes no greater rights than those provided both by this section and by the certificate of title statute.

Official Comment

Uniform Statutory Source: Section 2–403.

Changes: While Section 2–403 was used as a model for this section, the provisions of Section 2–403 were significantly revised to reflect leasing practice and to integrate this Article with certificate of title statutes.

Purposes: This section, a companion to Section 2A–304, states the rule with respect to the leasehold interest obtained by a buyer or sublessee from a lessee of goods under an existing lease contract. *Cf.* Section 2A–304 official comment. Note that this provision is consistent with existing case law, which prohibits the bailee's transfer of title to a good faith purchaser for value under Section 2–403(1). *Rohweder v. Aberdeen Product. Credit Ass'n*, 765 F.2d 109 (8th Cir. 1985).

Subsection (2) is also consistent with existing case law. *American Standard Credit, Inc. v. National Cement Co.*, 643 F.2d 248, 269–70 (5th Cir. 1981); *but cf. Exxon Co., U.S.A. v. TLW Computer Indus.*, 37 U.C.C.Rep.Serv. (Callaghan) 1052, 1057–58 (D.Mass.1983). Unlike Section 2A–304(2), this subsection does not contain any requirement with respect to the time that the goods were entrusted to the merchant. In Section 2A–304(2) the competition is between two customers of the merchant lessor; the time of entrusting was added as a criterion to create additional protection to the customer who was first in time: the existing lessee. In subsection (2) the equities between the competing interests were viewed as balanced.

There appears to be some overlap between Section 2–403(2) and Section 2A–305(2) with respect to a buyer in the ordinary course of business. However, an examination of this Article's definition of buyer in the ordinary course of business (Section 2A–103(1)(a)) makes clear that this reference was necessary to treat entrusting in the context of a lease.

Subsection (3) states a rule of construction with respect to a transfer of goods from a lessee to a buyer or sublessee, where the goods are subject to an existing lease and covered by a certificate of title. *Cf.* Section 2A–304 official comment.

Cross References:

    Sections 2–403, 2A–103(1)(a), 2A–304 and 2A–305(2).

Definitional Cross References:

    "Buyer". Section 2–103(1)(a).
    "Buyer in the ordinary course of business". Section 2A–103(1)(a).
    "Delivery". Section 1–201(14).*
    "Entrusting". Section 2–403(3).
    "Good faith". Sections 1–201(19)* and 2–103(1)(b).
    "Goods". Section 2A–103(1)(h).
    "Lease". Section 2A–103(1)(j).
    "Lease contract". Section 2A–103(1)(*l*).
    "Leasehold interest." Section 2A–103(1)(m).
    "Lessee". Section 2A–103(1)(n).
    "Lessee in the ordinary course of business". Section 2A–103(1)(o).
    "Lessor". Section 2A–103(1)(p).
    "Merchant". Section 2–104(1).
    "Rights". Section 1–201(36).*
    "Sale". Section 2–106(1).
    "Sublease". Section 2A–103(1)(w).
    "Value". Section 1–201(44).*

---

   *   *Referring to unrevised Article 1 (Appendix A).*

§ 2A-306.   Priority of Certain Liens Arising by Operation of Law.

If a person in the ordinary course of his [or her] business furnishes services or materials with respect to goods subject to a lease contract, a lien upon those goods in the possession of that person given by statute or rule of law for those materials or services takes priority over any interest of the lessor or lessee under the lease contract or this Article unless the lien is created by statute and the statute provides otherwise or unless the lien is created by rule of law and the rule of law provides otherwise.

Official Comment

Uniform Statutory Source: Former Section 9–310 (now codified as Section 9–333).

Changes: The approach reflected in the provisions of former Section 9–310 was included, but revised to conform to leasing terminology and to expand the exception to the special priority granted to protected liens to cover liens created by rule of law as well as those created by statute.

Purposes: This section should be interpreted to allow a qualified lessor or a qualified lessee to be the competing lienholder if the statute or rule of law so provides. The reference to statute includes applicable regulations and cases; these sources must be reviewed in resolving a priority dispute under this section.

Cross Reference:

Section 9–333.

Definitional Cross References:

"Goods". Section 2A–103(1)(h).
"Lease contract". Section 2A–103(1)(*l*).
"Lessee". Section 2A–103(1)(n).
"Lessor". Section 2A–103(1)(p).
"Lien". Section 2A–103(1)(r).
"Person". Section 1–201(30).*

§ 2A-307.   Priority of Liens Arising by Attachment or Levy on, Security Interests in, and Other Claims to Goods.

(1)   Except as otherwise provided in Section 2A–306, a creditor of a lessee takes subject to the lease contract.

(2)   Except as otherwise provided in subsection (3) and in Sections 2A–306 and 2A–308, a creditor of a lessor takes subject to the lease contract unless the creditor holds a lien that attached to the goods before the lease contract became enforceable.

(3)   Except as otherwise provided in Sections 9–317, 9–321, and 9–323, a lessee takes a leasehold interest subject to a security interest held by a creditor of the lessor.

As amended in 1990 and 1999.

Official Comment

Uniform Statutory Source: None for subsection (1). The remainder of the Section was derived from former Sections 9–301 (now codified as Section 9–317) and 9–307(1) and (3) (now codified as Sections 9–320(a) and 9–323), respectively, and was substantially rewritten in conjunction with the 1998 revisions of Article 9.

Changes: The provisions of former Sections 9–301 and 9–307(1) and (3) were incorporated, and modified to reflect leasing terminology and the basic concepts reflected in this Article.

1998 Changes: Many of the substantive provisions of this Section were moved to Article 9 in conjunction with the 1998 revisions of Article 9.

Purposes:

1.   Subsection (1) states a general rule of priority that a creditor of the lessee takes subject to the lease contract. The term lessee (Section 2A–103(1)(n)) includes sublessee. Therefore, this subsection not only covers

---

*   *Referring to unrevised Article 1 (Appendix A).*

disputes between the prime lessor and a creditor of the prime lessee but also disputes between the prime lessor, or the sublessor, and a creditor of the sublessee. Section 2A–301 official comment 3(g). Further, by using the term creditor (Section 1–201(12)),* this subsection will cover disputes with a general creditor, a secured creditor, a lien creditor and any representative of creditors. Section 2A–103(4).

2.   Subsection (2) states a general rule of priority that a creditor of a lessor takes subject to the lease contract. Note the discussion above with regard to the scope of these rules. Section 2A–301 official comment 3(g). Thus, the section will not only cover disputes between the prime lessee and a creditor of the prime lessor but also disputes between the prime lessee, or the sublessee, and a creditor of the sublessor.

3.   To take priority over the lease contract, and the interests derived therefrom, the creditor must come within the exception stated in subsection (2) or within one of the provisions of Article 9 mentioned in subsection (3). Subsection (2) provides that where the creditor holds a lien (Section 2A–103(1)(r)) that attached before the lease contract became enforceable (Section 2A–301), the creditor does not take subject to the lease. Subsection (3) provides that a lessee takes its leasehold interest subject to a security interest except as otherwise provided in Sections 9–317, 9–321, or 9–323.

4.   The rules of this section operate in favor of whichever party to the lease contract may enforce it, even if one party perhaps may not, e.g., under Section 2A–201(1)(b).

Cross References:

Sections 1–201(12),* 1–201(25),* 1–201(37),* 1–201(44),* 2A–103(1)(n), 2A–103(1)(o), 2A–103(1)(r), 2A–103(4), 2A–201(1)(b), 2A–301 official comment 3(g), Article 9, especially Sections 9–317, 9–321 and 9–323.

Definitional Cross References:

"Creditor". Section 1–201(12).*
"Goods". Section 2A–103(1)(h).
"Knowledge" and "Knows". Section 1–201(25).*
"Lease". Section 2A–103(1)(j).
"Lease contract". Section 2A–103(1)(*l*).
"Leasehold interest". Section 2A–103(1)(m).
"Lessee". Section 2A–103(1)(n).
"Lessee in the ordinary course of business". Section 2A–103(1)(o).
"Lessor". Section 2A–103(1)(p).
"Lien". Section 2A–103(1)(r).
"Party". Section 1–201(29).*
"Pursuant to commitment". Section 2A–103(3).
"Security interest". Section 1–201(37).*

As amended in 1999.

§ 2A–308. Special Rights of Creditors.

(1)   A creditor of a lessor in possession of goods subject to a lease contract may treat the lease contract as void if as against the creditor retention of possession by the lessor is fraudulent under any statute or rule of law, but retention of possession in good faith and current course of trade by the lessor for a commercially reasonable time after the lease contract becomes enforceable is not fraudulent.

(2)   Nothing in this Article impairs the rights of creditors of a lessor if the lease contract (a) becomes enforceable, not in current course of trade but in satisfaction of or as security for a pre-existing claim for money, security, or the like, and (b) is made under circumstances which under any statute or rule of law apart from this Article would constitute the transaction a fraudulent transfer or voidable preference.

(3)   A creditor of a seller may treat a sale or an identification of goods to a contract for sale as void if as against the creditor retention of possession by the seller is fraudulent under any statute or rule of law, but retention of possession of the goods pursuant to a lease contract entered into by the seller as lessee and

---

*   *Referring to unrevised Article 1 (Appendix A).*

the buyer as lessor in connection with the sale or identification of the goods is not fraudulent if the buyer bought for value and in good faith.

Official Comment

Uniform Statutory Source: Section 2–402(2) and (3)(b).

Changes: Rephrased and new material added to conform to leasing terminology and practice.

Purposes: Subsection (1) states a general rule of avoidance where the lessor has retained possession of goods if such retention is fraudulent under any statute or rule of law. However, the subsection creates an exception under certain circumstances for retention of possession of goods for a commercially reasonable time after the lease contract becomes enforceable.

Subsection (2) also preserves the possibility of an attack on the lease by creditors of the lessor if the lease was made in satisfaction of or as security for a pre-existing claim, and would constitute a fraudulent transfer or voidable preference under other law.

Finally, subsection (3) states a new rule with respect to sale-leaseback transactions, *i.e.*, transactions where the seller sells goods to a buyer but possession of the goods is retained by the seller pursuant to a lease contract between the buyer as lessor and the seller as lessee. Notwithstanding any statute or rule of law that would treat such retention as fraud, whether *per se, prima facie,* or otherwise, the retention is not fraudulent if the buyer bought for value (Section 1–201(44)[*]) and in good faith (Sections 1–201(19)[*] and 2–103(1)(b)). Section 2A–103(3) and (4). This provision overrides Section 2–402(2) to the extent it would otherwise apply to a sale-leaseback transaction.

Cross References:

Sections 1–201(19),[*] 1–201(44),[*] 2–402(2) and 2A–103(4).

Definitional Cross References:

"Buyer". Section 2–103(1)(a).
"Contract". Section 1–201(11).[*]
"Creditor". Section 1–201(12).[*]
"Good faith". Sections 1–201(19)[*] and 2–103(1)(b).
"Goods". Section 2A–103(1)(h).
"Lease contract". Section 2A–103(1)(*l*).
"Lessee". Section 2A–103(1)(n).
"Lessor". Section 2A–103(1)(p).
"Money". Section 1–201(24).[*]
"Reasonable time". Section 1–204(1) and (2).[*]
"Rights". Section 1–201(36).[*]
"Sale". Section 2–106(1).
"Seller". Section 2–103(1)(d).
"Value". Section 1–201(44).[*]

§ 2A–309. Lessor's and Lessee's Rights When Goods Become Fixtures.

(1) In this section:

(a) goods are "fixtures" when they become so related to particular real estate that an interest in them arises under real estate law;

(b) a "fixture filing" is the filing, in the office where a record of a mortgage on the real estate would be filed or recorded, of a financing statement covering goods that are or are to become fixtures and conforming to the requirements of Section 9–502(a) and (b);

(c) a lease is a "purchase money lease" unless the lessee has possession or use of the goods or the right to possession or use of the goods before the lease agreement is enforceable;

---

[*] *Referring to unrevised Article 1 (Appendix A).*

(d)   a mortgage is a "construction mortgage" to the extent it secures an obligation incurred for the construction of an improvement on land including the acquisition cost of the land, if the recorded writing so indicates; and

(e)   "encumbrance" includes real estate mortgages and other liens on real estate and all other rights in real estate that are not ownership interests.

(2)   Under this Article a lease may be of goods that are fixtures or may continue in goods that become fixtures, but no lease exists under this Article of ordinary building materials incorporated into an improvement on land.

(3)   This Article does not prevent creation of a lease of fixtures pursuant to real estate law.

(4)   The perfected interest of a lessor of fixtures has priority over a conflicting interest of an encumbrancer or owner of the real estate if:

(a)   the lease is a purchase money lease, the conflicting interest of the encumbrancer or owner arises before the goods become fixtures, the interest of the lessor is perfected by a fixture filing before the goods become fixtures or within ten days thereafter, and the lessee has an interest of record in the real estate or is in possession of the real estate; or

(b)   the interest of the lessor is perfected by a fixture filing before the interest of the encumbrancer or owner is of record, the lessor's interest has priority over any conflicting interest of a predecessor in title of the encumbrancer or owner, and the lessee has an interest of record in the real estate or is in possession of the real estate.

(5)   The interest of a lessor of fixtures, whether or not perfected, has priority over the conflicting interest of an encumbrancer or owner of the real estate if:

(a)   the fixtures are readily removable factory or office machines, readily removable equipment that is not primarily used or leased for use in the operation of the real estate, or readily removable replacements of domestic appliances that are goods subject to a consumer lease, and before the goods become fixtures the lease contract is enforceable; or

(b)   the conflicting interest is a lien on the real estate obtained by legal or equitable proceedings after the lease contract is enforceable; or

(c)   the encumbrancer or owner has consented in writing to the lease or has disclaimed an interest in the goods as fixtures; or

(d)   the lessee has a right to remove the goods as against the encumbrancer or owner. If the lessee's right to remove terminates, the priority of the interest of the lessor continues for a reasonable time.

(6)   Notwithstanding subsection (4)(a) but otherwise subject to subsections (4) and (5), the interest of a lessor of fixtures, including the lessor's residual interest, is subordinate to the conflicting interest of an encumbrancer of the real estate under a construction mortgage recorded before the goods become fixtures if the goods become fixtures before the completion of the construction. To the extent given to refinance a construction mortgage, the conflicting interest of an encumbrancer of the real estate under a mortgage has this priority to the same extent as the encumbrancer of the real estate under the construction mortgage.

(7)   In cases not within the preceding subsections, priority between the interest of a lessor of fixtures, including the lessor's residual interest, and the conflicting interest of an encumbrancer or owner of the real estate who is not the lessee is determined by the priority rules governing conflicting interests in real estate.

(8)   If the interest of a lessor of fixtures, including the lessor's residual interest, has priority over all conflicting interests of all owners and encumbrancers of the real estate, the lessor or the lessee may (i) on default, expiration, termination, or cancellation of the lease agreement but subject to the agreement and this Article, or (ii) if necessary to enforce other rights and remedies of the lessor or lessee under this Article, remove the goods from the real estate, free and clear of all conflicting interests of all owners and encumbrancers of the real estate, but the lessor or lessee must reimburse any encumbrancer or owner of the real estate who is not the lessee and who has not otherwise agreed for the cost of repair of any physical

injury, but not for any diminution in value of the real estate caused by the absence of the goods removed or by any necessity of replacing them. A person entitled to reimbursement may refuse permission to remove until the party seeking removal gives adequate security for the performance of this obligation.

(9)   Even though the lease agreement does not create a security interest, the interest of a lessor of fixtures, including the lessor's residual interest, is perfected by filing a financing statement as a fixture filing for leased goods that are or are to become fixtures in accordance with the relevant provisions of the Article on Secured Transactions (Article 9).

As amended in 1990 and 1999.

Official Comment

Uniform Statutory Source: Former Section 9–313.

Changes: Revised to reflect leasing terminology and to add new material.

Purposes:

1.   While former Section 9–313 (now codified as Sections 9–334 and 9–604) provided a model for this section, certain provisions were substantially revised.

2.   Section 2A–309(1)(c), which is new, defines purchase money lease to exclude leases where the lessee had possession or use of the goods or the right thereof before the lease agreement became enforceable. This term is used in subsection (4)(a) as one of the conditions that must be satisfied to obtain priority over the conflicting interest of an encumbrancer or owner of the real estate.

3.   Section 2A–309(4), which states one of several priority rules found in this section, deletes reference to office machines and the like (former Section 9–313(4)(c) (now codified as Section 9–334(e)(2)(A))) as well as certain liens (former Section 9–313(4)(d) (now codified as Section 9–334(e)(3))). However, these items are included in subsection (5), another priority rule that is more permissive than the rule found in subsection (4) as it applies whether or not the interest of the lessor is perfected. In addition, subsection (5)(a) expands the scope of the provisions of former Section 9–313(4)(c) (now codified as Section 9–334(e)(2)(A)) to include readily removable equipment not primarily used or leased for use in the operation of real estate; the qualifier is intended to exclude from the expanded rule equipment integral to the operation of real estate, *e.g.*, heating and air conditioning equipment.

4.   The rule stated in subsection (7) is more liberal than the rule stated in former Section 9–313(7) (now codified as Section 9–334(c)) in that issues of priority not otherwise resolved in this subsection are left for resolution by the priority rules governing conflicting interests in real estate, as opposed to the former Section 9–313(7) (now codified as Section 9–334(c)) automatic subordination of the security interest in fixtures. Note that, for the purpose of this section, where the interest of an encumbrancer or owner of the real estate is paramount to the interest of the lessor, the latter term includes the residual interest of the lessor.

5.   The rule stated in subsection (8) is more liberal than the rule stated in former Section 9–313(8) (now codified as Section 9–604) in that the right of removal is extended to both the lessor and the lessee and the occasion for removal includes expiration, termination or cancellation of the lease agreement, and enforcement of rights and remedies under this Article, as well as default. The new language also provides that upon removal the goods are free and clear of conflicting interests of owners and encumbrancers of the real estate.

6.   Finally, subsection (9) provides a mechanism for the lessor of fixtures to perfect its interest by filing a financing statement under the provisions of the Article on Secured Transactions (Article 9), even though the lease agreement does not create a security interest. Section 1–201(37).* The relevant provisions of Article 9 must be interpreted permissively to give effect to this mechanism as it implicitly expands the scope of Article 9 so that its filing provisions apply to transactions that create a lease of fixtures, even though the lease agreement does not create a security interest. This mechanism is similar to that provided in Section 2–326(3)(c) for the seller of goods on consignment, even though the consignment is not "intended as security". Section 1–201(37).* Given the lack of litigation with respect to the mechanism created for consignment sales, this new mechanism should prove effective.

---

*   *Referring to unrevised Article 1 (Appendix A).*

Cross References:

Sections 1–201(37),* 2A–309(1)(c), 2A–309(4), Article 9, especially Sections 9–334, 9–604 and 9–505.

Definitional Cross References:

"Agreed". Section 1–201(3).
"Cancellation". Section 2A–103(1)(b).
"Conforming". Section 2A–103(1)(d).
"Consumer lease". Section 2A–103(1)(e).
"Goods". Section 2A–103(1)(h).
"Lease". Section 2A–103(1)(j).
"Lease agreement". Section 2A–103(1)(k).
"Lease contract". Section 2A–103(1)(*l*).
"Lessee". Section 2A–103(1)(n).
"Lessor". Section 2A–103(1)(p).
"Lien". Section 2A–103(1)(r).
"Mortgage". Section 9–102(a)(55).
"Party". Section 1–201(29).*
"Person". Section 1–201(30).*
"Reasonable time". Section 1–204(1) and (2).*
"Remedy". Section 1–201(34).*
"Rights". Section 1–201(36).*
"Security interest". Section 1–201(37).*
"Termination". Section 2A–103(1)(z).
"Value". Section 1–201(44).*
"Writing". Section 1–201(46).*

§ 2A–310.　Lessor's and Lessee's Rights When Goods Become Accessions.

(1)　Goods are "accessions" when they are installed in or affixed to other goods.

(2)　The interest of a lessor or a lessee under a lease contract entered into before the goods became accessions is superior to all interests in the whole except as stated in subsection (4).

(3)　The interest of a lessor or a lessee under a lease contract entered into at the time or after the goods became accessions is superior to all subsequently acquired interests in the whole except as stated in subsection (4) but is subordinate to interests in the whole existing at the time the lease contract was made unless the holders of such interests in the whole have in writing consented to the lease or disclaimed an interest in the goods as part of the whole.

(4)　The interest of a lessor or a lessee under a lease contract described in subsection (2) or (3) is subordinate to the interest of

(a)　a buyer in the ordinary course of business or a lessee in the ordinary course of business of any interest in the whole acquired after the goods became accessions; or

(b)　a creditor with a security interest in the whole perfected before the lease contract was made to the extent that the creditor makes subsequent advances without knowledge of the lease contract.

(5)　When under subsections (2) or (3) and (4) a lessor or a lessee of accessions holds an interest that is superior to all interests in the whole, the lessor or the lessee may (a) on default, expiration, termination, or cancellation of the lease contract by the other party but subject to the provisions of the lease contract and this Article, or (b) if necessary to enforce his [or her] other rights and remedies under this Article, remove the goods from the whole, free and clear of all interests in the whole, but he [or she] must reimburse any holder of an interest in the whole who is not the lessee and who has not otherwise agreed for the cost of repair of any physical injury but not for any diminution in value of the whole caused by the absence of the

---

　*　*Referring to unrevised Article 1 (Appendix A).*

goods removed or by any necessity for replacing them. A person entitled to reimbursement may refuse permission to remove until the party seeking removal gives adequate security for the performance of this obligation.

Official Comment

Uniform Statutory Source: Former Section 9–314 (now codified as Section 9–335).

Changes: Revised to reflect leasing terminology and to add new material.

Purposes: Subsection (1) defines "accessions." Subsection (2) adds leasing terminology to the priority rule that applies when the lease is entered into before the goods become accessions. Subsection (3) adds leasing terminology to the priority rule that applies when the lease is entered into on or after the goods become accessions.

Subsection (4) creates two exceptions to the priority rules stated in subsections (2) and (3).

Finally, subsection (5) is modeled on the provisions of former Section 9–314(4) (now codified as Section 9–335(d) and (e)) with respect to removal of accessions, restated to reflect the parallel changes in Section 2A–309(8).

Neither this section nor Section 9–335 governs where the accession to the goods is not subject to the interest of a lessor or a lessee under a lease contract and is not subject to the interest of a secured party under a security agreement. This issue is to be resolved by the courts, case by case.

Cross References:

Sections 2A–309(8), 9–102(a)(1), 9–335.

Definitional Cross References:

"Agreed". Section 1–201(3).*
"Buyer in the ordinary course of business". Section 2A–103(1)(a).
"Cancellation". Section 2A–103(1)(b).
"Creditor". Section 1–201(12).*
"Goods". Section 2A–103(1)(h).
"Holder". Section 1–201(20).*
"Knowledge". Section 1–201(25).*
"Lease". Section 2A–103(1)(j).
"Lease contract". Section 2A–103(1)(*l*).
"Lessee". Section 2A–103(1)(n).
"Lessee in the ordinary course of business". Section 2A–103(1)(o).
"Lessor". Section 2A–103(1)(p).
"Party". Section 1–201(29).*
"Person". Section 1–201(30).*
"Remedy". Section 1–201(34).*
"Rights". Section 1–201(36).*
"Security interest". Section 1–201(37).*
"Termination". Section 2A–103(1)(z).
"Value". Section 1–201(44).*
"Writing". Section 1–201(46).

§ 2A–311. Priority Subject to Subordination.

Nothing in this Article prevents subordination by agreement by any person entitled to priority. As added in 1990.

Official Comment

Uniform Statutory Source: Former Section 9–316 (now codified as Section 9–339).

---

*   *Referring to unrevised Article 1 (Appendix A).*

Purposes: The several preceding sections deal with questions of priority. This section is inserted to make it entirely clear that a person entitled to priority may effectively agree to subordinate the claim. Only the person entitled to priority may make such an agreement: the rights of such a person cannot be adversely affected by an agreement to which that person is not a party.

Cross References:

Sections 1–102* and 2A–304 through 2A–310.

Definitional Cross References:

"Agreement". Section 1–201(3).*
"Person". Section 1–201(30).*

PART 4

PERFORMANCE OF LEASE CONTRACT: REPUDIATED, SUBSTITUTED AND EXCUSED

§ 2A–401. Insecurity: Adequate Assurance of Performance.

(1)   A lease contract imposes an obligation on each party that the other's expectation of receiving due performance will not be impaired.

(2)   If reasonable grounds for insecurity arise with respect to the performance of either party, the insecure party may demand in writing adequate assurance of due performance. Until the insecure party receives that assurance, if commercially reasonable the insecure party may suspend any performance for which he [or she] has not already received the agreed return.

(3)   A repudiation of the lease contract occurs if assurance of due performance adequate under the circumstances of the particular case is not provided to the insecure party within a reasonable time, not to exceed 30 days after receipt of a demand by the other party.

(4)   Between merchants, the reasonableness of grounds for insecurity and the adequacy of any assurance offered must be determined according to commercial standards.

(5)   Acceptance of any nonconforming delivery or payment does not prejudice the aggrieved party's right to demand adequate assurance of future performance.

Official Comment

Uniform Statutory Source: Section 2–609.

Changes: Revised to reflect leasing practices and terminology. Note that in the analogue to subsection (3) (Section 2–609(4)), the adjective "justified" modifies demand. The adjective was deleted here as unnecessary, implying no substantive change.

Definitional Cross References:

"Aggrieved party". Section 1–201(2).*
"Agreed". Section 1–201(3).*
"Between merchants". Section 2–104(3).
"Conforming". Section 2A–103(1)(d).
"Delivery". Section 1–201(14).*
"Lease contract". Section 2A–103(1)(*l*).
"Party". Section 1–201(29).*
"Reasonable time". Section 1–204(1) and (2).*
"Receipt". Section 2–103(1)(c).
"Rights". Section 1–201(36).*
"Writing". Section 1–201(46).*

---

*   *Referring to unrevised Article 1 (Appendix A).*

§ 2A–402. Anticipatory Repudiation.

If either party repudiates a lease contract with respect to a performance not yet due under the lease contract, the loss of which performance will substantially impair the value of the lease contract to the other, the aggrieved party may:

(a) for a commercially reasonable time, await retraction of repudiation and performance by the repudiating party;

(b) make demand pursuant to Section 2A–401 and await assurance of future performance adequate under the circumstances of the particular case; or

(c) resort to any right or remedy upon default under the lease contract or this Article, even though the aggrieved party has notified the repudiating party that the aggrieved party would await the repudiating party's performance and assurance and has urged retraction. In addition, whether or not the aggrieved party is pursuing one of the foregoing remedies, the aggrieved party may suspend performance or, if the aggrieved party is the lessor, proceed in accordance with the provisions of this Article on the lessor's right to identify goods to the lease contract notwithstanding default or to salvage unfinished goods (Section 2A–524).

Official Comment

Uniform Statutory Source: Section 2–610.

Changes: Revised to reflect leasing practices and terminology.

Definitional Cross References:

"Aggrieved party". Section 1–201(2).*
"Goods". Section 2A–103(1)(h).
"Lease contract". Section 2A–103(1)(*l*).
"Lessor". Section 2A–103(1)(p).
"Notifies". Section 1–201(26).*
"Party". Section 1–201(29).*
"Reasonable time". Section 1–204(1) and (2).*
"Remedy". Section 1–201(34).*
"Rights". Section 1–201(36).*
"Value". Section 1–201(44).*

§ 2A–403. Retraction of Anticipatory Repudiation.

(1) Until the repudiating party's next performance is due, the repudiating party can retract the repudiation unless, since the repudiation, the aggrieved party has cancelled the lease contract or materially changed the aggrieved party's position or otherwise indicated that the aggrieved party considers the repudiation final.

(2) Retraction may be by any method that clearly indicates to the aggrieved party that the repudiating party intends to perform under the lease contract and includes any assurance demanded under Section 2A–401.

(3) Retraction reinstates a repudiating party's rights under a lease contract with due excuse and allowance to the aggrieved party for any delay occasioned by the repudiation.

Official Comment

Uniform Statutory Source: Section 2–611.

Changes: Revised to reflect leasing practices and terminology. Note that in the analogue to subsection (2) (Section 2–611(2)) the adjective "justifiably" modifies demanded. The adjective was deleted here (as it was in Section 2A–401) as unnecessary, implying no substantive change.

---

* *Referring to unrevised Article 1 (Appendix A).*

Definitional Cross References:

> "Aggrieved party". Section 1–201(2).*
> "Cancellation". Section 2A–103(1)(b).
> "Lease contract". Section 2A–103(1)(*l*).
> "Party". Section 1–201(29).*
> "Rights". Section 1–201(36).*

§ 2A–404. Substituted Performance.

(1) If without fault of the lessee, the lessor and the supplier, the agreed berthing, loading, or unloading facilities fail or the agreed type of carrier becomes unavailable or the agreed manner of delivery otherwise becomes commercially impracticable, but a commercially reasonable substitute is available, the substitute performance must be tendered and accepted.

(2) If the agreed means or manner of payment fails because of domestic or foreign governmental regulation:

- (a) the lessor may withhold or stop delivery or cause the supplier to withhold or stop delivery unless the lessee provides a means or manner of payment that is commercially a substantial equivalent; and

- (b) if delivery has already been taken, payment by the means or in the manner provided by the regulation discharges the lessee's obligation unless the regulation is discriminatory, oppressive, or predatory.

Official Comment

Uniform Statutory Source: Section 2–614.

Changes: Revised to reflect leasing practices and terminology.

Definitional Cross References:

> "Agreed". Section 1–201(3).*
> "Delivery". Section 1–201(14).*
> "Fault". Section 2A–103(1)(f).
> "Lessee". Section 2A–103(1)(n).
> "Lessor". Section 2A–103(1)(p).
> "Supplier". Section 2A–103(1)(x).

§ 2A–405. Excused Performance.

Subject to Section 2A–404 on substituted performance, the following rules apply:

- (a) Delay in delivery or nondelivery in whole or in part by a lessor or a supplier who complies with paragraphs (b) and (c) is not a default under the lease contract if performance as agreed has been made impracticable by the occurrence of a contingency the nonoccurrence of which was a basic assumption on which the lease contract was made or by compliance in good faith with any applicable foreign or domestic governmental regulation or order, whether or not the regulation or order later proves to be invalid.

- (b) If the causes mentioned in paragraph (a) affect only part of the lessor's or the supplier's capacity to perform, he [or she] shall allocate production and deliveries among his [or her] customers but at his [or her] option may include regular customers not then under contract for sale or lease as well as his [or her] own requirements for further manufacture. He [or she] may so allocate in any manner that is fair and reasonable.

- (c) The lessor seasonably shall notify the lessee and in the case of a finance lease the supplier seasonably shall notify the lessor and the lessee, if known, that there will be delay or nondelivery

---

* *Referring to unrevised Article 1 (Appendix A).*

and, if allocation is required under paragraph (b), of the estimated quota thus made available for the lessee.

Official Comment

Uniform Statutory Source: Section 2–615.

Changes: Revised to reflect leasing practices and terminology.

Definitional Cross References:

"Agreed". Section 1–201(3).*
"Contract". Section 1–201(11).*
"Delivery". Section 1–201(14).*
"Finance lease". Section 2A–103(1)(g).
"Good faith". Sections 1–201(19)* and 2–103(1)(b).
"Knows". Section 1–201(25).*
"Lease". Section 2A–103(1)(j).
"Lease contract". Section 2A–103(1)(*l*).
"Lessee". Section 2A–103(1)(n).
"Lessor". Section 2A–103(1)(p).
"Notifies". Section 1–201(26).*
"Sale". Section 2–106(1).
"Seasonably". Section 1–204(3).*
"Supplier". Section 2A–103(1)(x).

§ 2A–406. Procedure on Excused Performance.

(1) If the lessee receives notification of a material or indefinite delay or an allocation justified under Section 2A–405, the lessee may by written notification to the lessor as to any goods involved, and with respect to all of the goods if under an installment lease contract the value of the whole lease contract is substantially impaired (Section 2A–510):

(a) terminate the lease contract (Section 2A–505(2)); or

(b) except in a finance lease that is not a consumer lease, modify the lease contract by accepting the available quota in substitution, with due allowance from the rent payable for the balance of the lease term for the deficiency but without further right against the lessor.

(2) If, after receipt of a notification from the lessor under Section 2A–405, the lessee fails so to modify the lease agreement within a reasonable time not exceeding 30 days, the lease contract lapses with respect to any deliveries affected.

Official Comment

Uniform Statutory Source: Section 2–616(1) and (2).

Changes: Revised to reflect leasing practices and terminology. Note that subsection 1(a) allows the lessee under a lease, including a finance lease, the right to terminate the lease for excused performance (Sections 2A–404 and 2A–405). However, subsection 1(b), which allows the lessee the right to modify the lease for excused performance, excludes a finance lease that is not a consumer lease. This exclusion is compelled by the same policy that led to codification of provisions with respect to irrevocable promises. Section 2A–407.

Definitional Cross References:

"Consumer lease". Section 2A–103(1)(e).
"Delivery". Section 1–201(14).*
"Finance lease". Section 2A–103(1)(g).
"Goods". Section 2A–103(1)(h).
"Installment lease contract". Section 2A–103(1)(i).

---

*   *Referring to unrevised Article 1 (Appendix A).*

"Lease agreement". Section 2A–103(1)(k).
"Lease contract". Section 2A–103(1)(*l*).
"Lessee". Section 2A–103(1)(n).
"Lessor". Section 2A–103(1)(p).
"Notice". Section 1–201(25).*
"Reasonable time". Section 1–204(1) and (2).*
"Receipt". Section 2–103(1)(c).
"Rights". Section 1–201(36).*
"Termination". Section 2A–103(1)(z).
"Value". Section 1–201(44).*
"Written". Section 1–201(46).*

§ 2A–407. Irrevocable Promises: Finance Leases.

(1)   In the case of a finance lease that is not a consumer lease the lessee's promises under the lease contract become irrevocable and independent upon the lessee's acceptance of the goods.

(2)   A promise that has become irrevocable and independent under subsection (1):

(a)   is effective and enforceable between the parties, and by or against third parties including assignees of the parties; and

(b)   is not subject to cancellation, termination, modification, repudiation, excuse, or substitution without the consent of the party to whom the promise runs.

(3)   This section does not affect the validity under any other law of a covenant in any lease contract making the lessee's promises irrevocable and independent upon the lessee's acceptance of the goods.

As amended in 1990.

Official Comment

Uniform Statutory Source: None.

Purposes:

1.   This section extends the benefits of the classic "hell or high water" clause to a finance lease that is not a consumer lease. This section is self-executing; no special provision need be added to the contract. This section makes covenants in a finance lease irrevocable and independent due to the function of the finance lessor in a three party relationship: the lessee is looking to the supplier to perform the essential covenants and warranties. Section 2A–209. Thus, upon the lessee's acceptance of the goods the lessee's promises to the lessor under the lease contract become irrevocable and independent. The provisions of this section remain subject to the obligation of good faith (Sections 2A–103(4) and 1–203*), and the lessee's revocation of acceptance (Section 2A–517).

2.   The section requires the lessee to perform even if the lessor's performance after the lessee's acceptance is not in accordance with the lease contract; the lessee may, however, have and pursue a cause of action against the lessor, e.g., breach of certain limited warranties (Sections 2A–210 and 2A–211(1)). This is appropriate because the benefit of the supplier's promises and warranties to the lessor under the supply contract and, in some cases, the warranty of a manufacturer who is not the supplier, is extended to the lessee under the finance lease. Section 2A–209. Despite this balance, this section excludes a finance lease that is a consumer lease. That a consumer be obligated to pay notwithstanding defective goods or the like is a principle that is not tenable under case law (*Unico v. Owen*, 50 N.J. 101, 232 A.2d 405 (1967)), state statute (Unif.Consumer Credit Code §§ 3.403–.405, 7A U.L.A. 126–31 (1974)), or federal statute (15 U.S.C. § 1666i (1982)).

3.   The relationship of the three parties to a transaction that qualifies as a finance lease is best demonstrated by a hypothetical. A, the potential lessor, has been contacted by B, the potential lessee, to discuss the lease of an expensive line of equipment that B has recently placed an order for with C, the manufacturer of such goods. The negotiation is completed and A, as lessor, and B, as lessee, sign a lease of the line of equipment

---

* *Referring to unrevised Article 1 (Appendix A).*

for a 60-month term. B, as buyer, assigns the purchase order with C to A. If this transaction creates a lease (Section 2A–103(1)(j)), this transaction should qualify as a finance lease. Section 2A–103(1)(g).

4. The line of equipment is delivered by C to B's place of business. After installation by C and testing by B, B accepts the goods by signing a certificate of delivery and acceptance, a copy of which is sent by B to A and C. One year later the line of equipment malfunctions and B falls behind in its manufacturing schedule.

5. Under this Article, because the lease is a finance lease, no warranty of fitness or merchantability is extended by A to B. Sections 2A–212(1) and 2A–213. Absent an express provision in the lease agreement, application of Section 2A–210 or Section 2A–211(1), or application of the principles of law and equity, including the law with respect to fraud, duress, or the like (Sections 2A–103(4) and 1–103), B has no claim against A. B's obligation to pay rent to A continues as the obligation became irrevocable and independent when B accepted the line of equipment (Section 2A–407(1)). B has no right of set-off with respect to any part of the rent still due under the lease. Section 2A–508(6). However, B may have another remedy. Despite the lack of privity between B and C (the purchase order with C having been assigned by B to A), B may have a claim against C. Section 2A–209(1).

6. This section does not address whether a "hell or high water" clause, *i.e.*, a clause that is to the effect of this section, is enforceable if included in a finance lease that is a consumer lease or a lease that is not a finance lease. That issue will continue to be determined by the facts of each case and other law which this section does not affect. Sections 2A–104, 2A–103(4), 9–403 and 9–404. However, with respect to finance leases that are not consumer leases courts have enforced "hell or high water" clauses. *In re O.P.M. Leasing Servs.*, 21 Bankr. 993, 1006 (Bankr.S.D.N.Y.1982).

7. Subsection (2) further provides that a promise that has become irrevocable and independent under subsection (1) is enforceable not only between the parties but also against third parties. Thus, the finance lease can be transferred or assigned without disturbing enforceability. Further, subsection (2) also provides that the promise cannot, among other things, be cancelled or terminated without the consent of the lessor.

Cross References:

Sections 1–103, 1–203,* 2A–103(1)(g), 2A–103(1)(j), 2A–103(4), 2A–104, 2A–209, 2A–209(1), 2A–210, 2A–211(1), 2A–212(1), 2A–213, 2A–517(1)(b), 9–403 and 9–404.

Definitional Cross References:

"Cancellation". Section 2A–103(1)(b).
"Consumer lease". Section 2A–103(1)(e).
"Finance lease". Section 2A–103(1)(g).
"Goods". Section 2A–103(1)(h).
"Lease contract". Section 2A–103(1)(*l*).
"Lessee". Section 2A–103(1)(n).
"Party". Section 1–201(29).*
"Termination". Section 2A–103(1)(z).

PART 5

DEFAULT

A. IN GENERAL

§ 2A–501. Default: Procedure.

(1) Whether the lessor or the lessee is in default under a lease contract is determined by the lease agreement and this Article.

(2) If the lessor or the lessee is in default under the lease contract, the party seeking enforcement has rights and remedies as provided in this Article and, except as limited by this Article, as provided in the lease agreement.

---

*   *Referring to unrevised Article 1 (Appendix A).*

(3) If the lessor or the lessee is in default under the lease contract, the party seeking enforcement may reduce the party's claim to judgment, or otherwise enforce the lease contract by self-help or any available judicial procedure or nonjudicial procedure, including administrative proceeding, arbitration, or the like, in accordance with this Article.

(4) Except as otherwise provided in Section 1–305(a) or this Article or the lease agreement, the rights and remedies referred to in subsections (2) and (3) are cumulative.

(5) If the lease agreement covers both real property and goods, the party seeking enforcement may proceed under this Part as to the goods, or under other applicable law as to both the real property and the goods in accordance with that party's rights and remedies in respect of the real property, in which case this Part does not apply.

As amended in 1990 and 2001.

Official Comment

Uniform Statutory Source: Former Section 9–501 (now codified as Sections 9–601 through 9–604).

Changes: Substantially revised.

Purposes:

1. Subsection (1) is new and represents a departure from the Article on Secured Transactions (Article 9) as the subsection makes clear that whether a party to the lease agreement is in default is determined by this Article as well as the agreement. Sections 2A–508 and 2A–523. It further departs from Article 9 in recognizing the potential default of either party, a function of the bilateral nature of the obligations between the parties to the lease contract.

2. Subsection (2) is a version of the first sentence of Section 9–601(a), revised to reflect leasing terminology.

3. Subsection (3), an expansive version of the second sentence of Section 9–601(a), lists the procedures that may be followed by the party seeking enforcement; in effect, the scope of the procedures listed in subsection (3) is consistent with the scope of the procedures available to the foreclosing secured party.

4. Subsection (4) establishes that the parties' rights and remedies are cumulative. DeKoven, *Leases of Equipment: Puritan Leasing Company v. August, A Dangerous Decision*, 12 U.S.F.L.Rev. 257, 276–80 (1978). Cumulation, and largely unrestricted selection, of remedies is allowed in furtherance of the general policy of the Commercial Code, stated in Section 1–305, that remedies be liberally administered to put the aggrieved party in as good a position as if the other party had fully performed. Therefore, cumulation of, or selection among, remedies is available to the extent necessary to put the aggrieved party in as good a position as it would have been in had there been full performance. However, cumulation of, or selection among, remedies is not available to the extent that the cumulation or selection would put the aggrieved party in a better position than it would have been in had there been full performance by the other party.

5. Section 9–602, which, among other things, states that certain rules, to the extent they give rights to the debtor and impose duties on the secured party, may not be waived or varied, is not incorporated in this Article. Given the significance of freedom of contract in the development of the common law as it applies to bailments for hire and the lessee's lack of an equity of redemption, there is no reason to impose that restraint.

Cross References:

Sections 1–305, 2A–508, 2A–523, Article 9, especially Sections 9–601 and 9–602.

Definitional Cross References:

"Goods". Section 2A–103(1)(h).
"Lease agreement". Section 2A–103(1)(k).
"Lease contract". Section 2A–103(1)(*l*).
"Lessee". Section 2A–103(1)(n).
"Lessor". Section 2A–103(1)(p).
"Party". Section 1–201(b)(26).
"Remedy". Section 1–201(b)(32).

"Rights". Section 1–201(b)(34).

As amended in 2001.

§ 2A–502. Notice After Default.

Except as otherwise provided in this Article or the lease agreement, the lessor or lessee in default under the lease contract is not entitled to notice of default or notice of enforcement from the other party to the lease agreement.

Official Comment

Uniform Statutory Source: None.

Purposes: This section makes clear that absent agreement to the contrary or provision in this Article to the contrary, *e.g.*, Section 2A–516(3)(a), the party in default is not entitled to notice of default or enforcement. While a review of Part 5 of Article 9 leads to the same conclusion with respect to giving notice of default to the debtor, it is never stated. Although Article 9 requires notice of disposition and strict foreclosure, the different scheme of lessors' and lessees' rights and remedies developed under the common law, and codified by this Article, generally does not require notice of enforcement; furthermore, such notice is not mandated by due process requirements. However, certain sections of this Article do require notice. *E.g.*, Section 2A–517(2) 2A–517(4)*.

Cross References:

Sections 2A–516(3)(a), 2A–517(2) 2A–517(4)*, and Article 9, esp. Part 5.

Definitional Cross References:

"Lease agreement". Section 2A–103(1)(k).

"Lease contract". Section 2A–103(1)(*l*).

"Lessee". Section 2A–103(1)(n).

"Lessor". Section 2A–103(1)(p).

"Notice". Section 1–201(25).**

"Party". Section 1–201(29).*

§ 2A–503. Modification or Impairment of Rights and Remedies.

(1) Except as otherwise provided in this Article, the lease agreement may include rights and remedies for default in addition to or in substitution for those provided in this Article and may limit or alter the measure of damages recoverable under this Article.

(2) Resort to a remedy provided under this Article or in the lease agreement is optional unless the remedy is expressly agreed to be exclusive. If circumstances cause an exclusive or limited remedy to fail of its essential purpose, or provision for an exclusive remedy is unconscionable, remedy may be had as provided in this Article.

(3) Consequential damages may be liquidated under Section 2A–504, or may otherwise be limited, altered, or excluded unless the limitation, alteration, or exclusion is unconscionable. Limitation, alteration, or exclusion of consequential damages for injury to the person in the case of consumer goods is prima facie unconscionable but limitation, alteration, or exclusion of damages where the loss is commercial is not prima facie unconscionable.

(4) Rights and remedies on default by the lessor or the lessee with respect to any obligation or promise collateral or ancillary to the lease contract are not impaired by this Article.

As amended in 1990.

---

*   Previous incorrect cross reference corrected by Permanent Editorial Board action, November 1992.

**   *Referring to unrevised Article 1 (Appendix A).*

Official Comment

Uniform Statutory Source: Sections 2–719 and 2–701.

Changes: Rewritten to reflect lease terminology and to clarify the relationship between this section and Section 2A–504.

Purposes:

1.   A significant purpose of this Part is to provide rights and remedies for those parties to a lease who fail to provide them by agreement or whose rights and remedies fail of their essential purpose or are unenforceable. However, it is important to note that this implies no restriction on freedom to contract. Sections 2A–103(4) and 1–102(3).* Thus, subsection (1), a revised version of the provisions of Section 2–719(1), allows the parties to the lease agreement freedom to provide for rights and remedies in addition to or in substitution for those provided in this Article and to alter or limit the measure of damages recoverable under this Article. Except to the extent otherwise provided in this Article (*e.g.*, Sections 2A–105, 106 and 108(1) and (2)), this Part shall be construed neither to restrict the parties' ability to provide for rights and remedies or to limit or alter the measure of damages by agreement, nor to imply disapproval of rights and remedy schemes other than those set forth in this Part.

2.   Subsection (2) makes explicit with respect to this Article what is implicit in Section 2–719 with respect to the Article on Sales (Article 2): if an exclusive remedy is held to be unconscionable, remedies under this Article are available. Section 2–719 official comment 1.

3.   Subsection (3), a revision of Section 2–719(3), makes clear that consequential damages may also be liquidated. Section 2A–504(1).

4.   Subsection (4) is a revision of the provisions of Section 2–701. This subsection leaves the treatment of default with respect to obligations or promises collateral or ancillary to the lease contract to other law. Sections 2A–103(4) and 1–103. An example of such an obligation would be that of the lessor to the secured creditor which has provided the funds to leverage the lessor's lease transaction; an example of such a promise would be that of the lessee, as seller, to the lessor, as buyer, in a sale-leaseback transaction.

Cross References:

Sections 1–102(3),* 1–103, Article 2, especially Sections 2–701, 2–719, 2–719(1), 2–719(3), 2–719 official comment 1, and Sections 2A–103(4), 2A–105, 2A–106, 2A–108(1), 2A–108(2), and 2A–504.

Definitional Cross References:

"Agreed". Section 1–201(3).*
"Consumer goods". Section 9–102(a)(23).
"Lease agreement". Section 2A–103(1)(k).
"Lease contract". Section 2A–103(1)(*l*).
"Lessee". Section 2A–103(1)(n).
"Lessor". Section 2A–103(1)(p).
"Person". Section 1–201(30).*
"Remedy". Section 1–201(34).*
"Rights". Section 1–201(36).*

§ 2A–504.   Liquidation of Damages.

(1)   Damages payable by either party for default, or any other act or omission, including indemnity for loss or diminution of anticipated tax benefits or loss or damage to lessor's residual interest, may be liquidated in the lease agreement but only at an amount or by a formula that is reasonable in light of the then anticipated harm caused by the default or other act or omission.

(2)   If the lease agreement provides for liquidation of damages, and such provision does not comply with subsection (1), or such provision is an exclusive or limited remedy that circumstances cause to fail of its essential purpose, remedy may be had as provided in this Article.

---

   *   *Referring to unrevised Article 1 (Appendix A).*

(3)   If the lessor justifiably withholds or stops delivery of goods because of the lessee's default or insolvency (Section 2A–525 or 2A–526), the lessee is entitled to restitution of any amount by which the sum of his [or her] payments exceeds:

(a)   the amount to which the lessor is entitled by virtue of terms liquidating the lessor's damages in accordance with subsection (1); or

(b)   in the absence of those terms, 20 percent of the then present value of the total rent the lessee was obligated to pay for the balance of the lease term, or, in the case of a consumer lease, the lesser of such amount or $500.

(4)   A lessee's right to restitution under subsection (3) is subject to offset to the extent the lessor establishes:

(a)   a right to recover damages under the provisions of this Article other than subsection (1); and

(b)   the amount or value of any benefits received by the lessee directly or indirectly by reason of the lease contract.

Official Comment

Uniform Statutory Source: Sections 2–718(1), (2), (3) and 2–719(2).

Changes: Substantially rewritten.

Purposes: Many leasing transactions are predicated on the parties' ability to agree to an appropriate amount of damages or formula for damages in the event of default or other act or omission. The rule with respect to sales of goods (Section 2–718) may not be sufficiently flexible to accommodate this practice. Thus, consistent with the common law emphasis upon freedom to contract with respect to bailments for hire, this section has created a revised rule that allows greater flexibility with respect to leases of goods.

Subsection (1), a significantly modified version of the provisions of Section 2–718(1), provides for liquidation of damages in the lease agreement at an amount or by a formula. Section 2–718(1) does not by its express terms include liquidation by a formula; this change was compelled by modern leasing practice. Subsection (1), in a further expansion of Section 2–718(1), provides for liquidation of damages for default as well as any other act or omission.

A liquidated damages formula that is common in leasing practice provides that the sum of lease payments past due, accelerated future lease payments, and the lessor's estimated residual interest, less the net proceeds of disposition (whether by sale or re-lease) of the leased goods is the lessor's damages. Tax indemnities, costs, interest and attorney's fees are also added to determine the lessor's damages. Another common liquidated damages formula utilizes a periodic depreciation allocation as a credit to the aforesaid amount in mitigation of a lessor's damages. A third formula provides for a fixed number of periodic payments as a means of liquidating damages. Stipulated loss or stipulated damage schedules are also common. Whether these formulae are enforceable will be determined in the context of each case by applying a standard of reasonableness in light of the harm anticipated when the formula was agreed to. Whether the inclusion of these formulae will affect the classification of the transaction as a lease or a security interest is to be determined by the facts of each case. Section 1–201(37).[*] *E.g., In re Noack*, 44 Bankr. 172, 174–75 (Bankr.E.D.Wis.1984).

This section does not incorporate two other tests that under sales law determine enforceability of liquidated damages, *i.e.*, difficulties of proof of loss and inconvenience or nonfeasibility of otherwise obtaining an adequate remedy. The ability to liquidate damages is critical to modern leasing practice; given the parties' freedom to contract at common law, the policy behind retaining these two additional requirements here was thought to be outweighed. Further, given the expansion of subsection (1) to enable the parties to liquidate the amount payable with respect to an indemnity for loss or diminution of anticipated tax benefits resulted in another change: the last sentence of Section 2–718(1), providing that a term fixing unreasonably large liquidated damages is void as a penalty, was also not incorporated. The impact of local, state and federal tax laws on a leasing transaction can result in an amount payable with respect to the tax indemnity many times greater than the original purchase price of the goods. By deleting the reference to unreasonably large liquidated damages the parties are free to negotiate a formula, restrained by the rule of reasonableness in this section. These changes should invite the parties to liquidate damages. Peters, *Remedies for Breach of Contracts Relating to the Sale of Goods Under the Uniform Commercial Code: A Roadmap for Article Two*, 73 Yale L.J. 199, 278 (1963).

---

[*]   *Referring to unrevised Article 1 (Appendix A).*

Subsection (2), a revised version of Section 2–719(2), provides that if the liquidated damages provision is not enforceable or fails of its essential purpose, remedy may be had as provided in this Article.

Subsection (3)(b) of this section differs from subsection (2)(b) of Section 2–718; in the absence of a valid liquidated damages amount or formula the lessor is permitted to retain 20 percent of the present value of the total rent payable under the lease. The alternative limitation of $500 contained in Section 2–718 is deleted as unrealistically low with respect to a lease other than a consumer lease.

Cross References:

Sections 1–201(37),* 2–718, 2–718(1), 2–718(2)(b) and 2–719(2).

Definitional Cross References:

"Consumer lease". Section 2A–103(1)(e).
"Delivery". Section 1–201(14).*
"Goods". Section 2A–103(1)(h).
"Insolvent". Section 1–201(23).*
"Lease agreement". Section 2A–103(1)(k).
"Lease contract". Section 2A–103(1)(*l*).
"Lessee". Section 2A–103(1)(n).
"Lessor". Section 2A–103(1)(p).
"Lessor's residual interest". Section 2A–103(1)(q).
"Party". Section 1–201(29).*
"Present value". Section 2A–103(1)(u).
"Remedy". Section 1–201(34).*
"Rights". Section 1–201(36).*
"Term". Section 1–201(42).*
"Value". Section 1–201(44).*

§ 2A–505. Cancellation and Termination and Effect of Cancellation, Termination, Rescission, or Fraud on Rights and Remedies.

(1)   On cancellation of the lease contract, all obligations that are still executory on both sides are discharged, but any right based on prior default or performance survives, and the cancelling party also retains any remedy for default of the whole lease contract or any unperformed balance.

(2)   On termination of the lease contract, all obligations that are still executory on both sides are discharged but any right based on prior default or performance survives.

(3)   Unless the contrary intention clearly appears, expressions of "cancellation," "rescission," or the like of the lease contract may not be construed as a renunciation or discharge of any claim in damages for an antecedent default.

(4)   Rights and remedies for material misrepresentation or fraud include all rights and remedies available under this Article for default.

(5)   Neither rescission nor a claim for rescission of the lease contract nor rejection or return of the goods may bar or be deemed inconsistent with a claim for damages or other right or remedy.

Official Comment

Uniform Statutory Source: Sections 2–106(3) and (4), 2–720 and 2–721.

Changes: Revised to reflect leasing practices and terminology.

Definitional Cross References:

"Cancellation". Section 2A–103(1)(b).
"Goods". Section 2A–103(1)(h).

---

*   *Referring to unrevised Article 1 (Appendix A).*

"Lease contract". Section 2A–103(1)(*l*).
"Party". Section 1–201(29).*
"Remedy". Section 1–201(34).*
"Rights". Section 1–201(36).*
"Termination". Section 2A–103(1)(z).

§ 2A–506. Statute of Limitations.

(1)   An action for default under a lease contract, including breach of warranty or indemnity, must be commenced within 4 years after the cause of action accrued. By the original lease contract the parties may reduce the period of limitation to not less than one year.

(2)   A cause of action for default accrues when the act or omission on which the default or breach of warranty is based is or should have been discovered by the aggrieved party, or when the default occurs, whichever is later. A cause of action for indemnity accrues when the act or omission on which the claim for indemnity is based is or should have been discovered by the indemnified party, whichever is later.

(3)   If an action commenced within the time limited by subsection (1) is so terminated as to leave available a remedy by another action for the same default or breach of warranty or indemnity, the other action may be commenced after the expiration of the time limited and within 6 months after the termination of the first action unless the termination resulted from voluntary discontinuance or from dismissal for failure or neglect to prosecute.

(4)   This section does not alter the law on tolling of the statute of limitations nor does it apply to causes of action that have accrued before this Article becomes effective.

Official Comment

Uniform Statutory Source: Section 2–725.

Changes: Substantially rewritten.

Purposes: Subsection (1) does not incorporate the limitation found in Section 2–725(1) prohibiting the parties from extending the period of limitation. Breach of warranty and indemnity claims often arise in a lease transaction; with the passage of time such claims often diminish or are eliminated. To encourage the parties to commence litigation under these circumstances makes little sense.

Subsection (2) states two rules for determining when a cause of action accrues. With respect to default, the rule of Section 2–725(2) is not incorporated in favor of a more liberal rule of the later of the date when the default occurs or when the act or omission on which it is based is or should have been discovered. With respect to indemnity, a similarly liberal rule is adopted.

Cross References:

Sections 2–725(1) and 2–725(2).

Definitional Cross References:

"Action". Section 1–201(1).*
"Aggrieved party". Section 1–201(2).*
"Lease contract". Section 2A–103(1)(*l*).
"Party". Section 1–201(29).*
"Remedy". Section 1–201(34).*
"Termination". Section 2A–103(1)(z).

§ 2A–507. Proof of Market Rent: Time and Place.

(1)   Damages based on market rent (Section 2A–519 or 2A–528) are determined according to the rent for the use of the goods concerned for a lease term identical to the remaining lease term of the original lease agreement and prevailing at the times specified in Sections 2A–519 and 2A–528.

---

*   *Referring to unrevised Article 1 (Appendix A).*

(2)   If evidence of rent for the use of the goods concerned for a lease term identical to the remaining lease term of the original lease agreement and prevailing at the times or places described in this Article is not readily available, the rent prevailing within any reasonable time before or after the time described or at any other place or for a different lease term which in commercial judgment or under usage of trade would serve as a reasonable substitute for the one described may be used, making any proper allowance for the difference, including the cost of transporting the goods to or from the other place.

(3)   Evidence of a relevant rent prevailing at a time or place or for a lease term other than the one described in this Article offered by one party is not admissible unless and until he [or she] has given the other party notice the court finds sufficient to prevent unfair surprise.

(4)   If the prevailing rent or value of any goods regularly leased in any established market is in issue, reports in official publications or trade journals or in newspapers or periodicals of general circulation published as the reports of that market are admissible in evidence. The circumstances of the preparation of the report may be shown to affect its weight but not its admissibility.

As amended in 1990.

Official Comment

Uniform Statutory Source: Sections 2–723 and 2–724.

Changes: Revised to reflect leasing practices and terminology. Sections 2A–519 and 2A–528 specify the times as of which market rent is to be determined.

Definitional Cross References:

"Goods". Section 2A–103(1)(h).

"Lease". Section 2A–103(1)(j).

"Lease agreement". Section 2A–103(1)(k).

"Notice". Section 1–201(25).*

"Party". Section 1–201(29).*

"Reasonable time". Section 1–204(1) and (2).*

"Usage of trade". Section 1–205.*

"Value". Section 1–201(44).*

B.   DEFAULT BY LESSOR

§ 2A–508.   Lessee's Remedies.

(1)   If a lessor fails to deliver the goods in conformity to the lease contract (Section 2A–509) or repudiates the lease contract (Section 2A–402), or a lessee rightfully rejects the goods (Section 2A–509) or justifiably revokes acceptance of the goods (Section 2A–517), then with respect to any goods involved, and with respect to all of the goods if under an installment lease contract the value of the whole lease contract is substantially impaired (Section 2A–510), the lessor is in default under the lease contract and the lessee may:

(a)   cancel the lease contract (Section 2A–505(1));

(b)   recover so much of the rent and security as has been paid and is just under the circumstances;

(c)   cover and recover damages as to all goods affected whether or not they have been identified to the lease contract (Sections 2A–518 and 2A–520), or recover damages for nondelivery (Sections 2A–519 and 2A–520);

(d)   exercise any other rights or pursue any other remedies provided in the lease contract.

(2)   If a lessor fails to deliver the goods in conformity to the lease contract or repudiates the lease contract, the lessee may also:

(a)   if the goods have been identified, recover them (Section 2A–522); or

---

*   *Referring to unrevised Article 1 (Appendix A).*

(b)   in a proper case, obtain specific performance or replevy the goods (Section 2A–521).

(3)   If a lessor is otherwise in default under a lease contract, the lessee may exercise the rights and pursue the remedies provided in the lease contract, which may include a right to cancel the lease, and in Section 2A–519(3).

(4)   If a lessor has breached a warranty, whether express or implied, the lessee may recover damages (Section 2A–519(4)).

(5)   On rightful rejection or justifiable revocation of acceptance, a lessee has a security interest in goods in the lessee's possession or control for any rent and security that has been paid and any expenses reasonably incurred in their inspection, receipt, transportation, and care and custody and may hold those goods and dispose of them in good faith and in a commercially reasonable manner, subject to Section 2A–527(5).

(6)   Subject to the provisions of Section 2A–407, a lessee, on notifying the lessor of the lessee's intention to do so, may deduct all or any part of the damages resulting from any default under the lease contract from any part of the rent still due under the same lease contract.

As amended in 1990.

Official Comment

Uniform Statutory Source: Sections 2–711 and 2–717.

Changes: Substantially rewritten.

Purposes:

1.   This section is an index to Sections 2A–509 through 522 which set out the lessee's rights and remedies after the lessor's default. The lessor and the lessee can agree to modify the rights and remedies available under this Article; they can, among other things, provide that for defaults other than those specified in subsection (1) the lessee can exercise the rights and remedies referred to in subsection (1); and they can create a new scheme of rights and remedies triggered by the occurrence of the default. Sections 2A–103(4) and 1–102(3).*

2.   Subsection (1), a substantially rewritten version of the provisions of Section 2–711(1), lists three cumulative remedies of the lessee where the lessor has failed to deliver conforming goods or has repudiated the contract, or the lessee has rightfully rejected or justifiably revoked. Sections 2A–501(2) and (4). Subsection (1) also allows the lessee to exercise any contractual remedy. This Article rejects any general doctrine of election of remedy. To determine if one remedy bars another in a particular case is a function of whether the lessee has been put in as good a position as if the lessor had fully performed the lease agreement. Use of multiple remedies is barred only if the effect is to put the lessee in a better position than it would have been in had the lessor fully performed under the lease. Sections 2A–103(4), 2A–501(4), and 1–106(1).* Subsection (1)(b), in recognition that no bright line can be created that would operate fairly in all installment lease cases and in recognition of the fact that a lessee may be able to cancel the lease (revoke acceptance of the goods) after the goods have been in use for some period of time, does not require that all lease payments made by the lessee under the lease be returned upon cancellation. Rather, only such portion as is just of the rent and security payments made may be recovered. If a defect in the goods is discovered immediately upon tender to the lessee and the goods are rejected immediately, then the lessee should recover all payments made. If, however, for example, a 36-month equipment lease is terminated in the 12th month because the lessor has materially breached the contract by failing to perform its maintenance obligations, it may be just to return only a small part or none of the rental payments already made.

3.   Subsection (2), a version of the provisions of Section 2–711(2) revised to reflect leasing terminology, lists two alternative remedies for the recovery of the goods by the lessee; however, each of these remedies is cumulative with respect to those listed in subsection (1).

4.   Subsection (3) is new. It covers defaults which do not deprive the lessee of the goods and which are not so serious as to justify rejection or revocation of acceptance under subsection (1). It also covers defaults for which the lessee could have rejected or revoked acceptance of the goods but elects not to do so and retains the goods. In either case, a lessee which retains the goods is entitled to recover damages as stated in Section 2A–519(3). That measure of damages is "the loss resulting in the ordinary course of events from the lessor's default as determined

---

*   *Referring to unrevised Article 1 (Appendix A).*

237

in any manner that is reasonable together with incidental and consequential damages, less expenses saved in consequence of the lessor's breach."

    5.   Subsection (1)(d) and subsection (3) recognize that the lease agreement may provide rights and remedies in addition to or different from those which Article 2A provides. In particular, subsection (3) provides that the lease agreement may give the remedy of cancellation of the lease for defaults by the lessor that would not otherwise be material defaults which would justify cancellation under subsection (1). If there is a right to cancel, there is, of course, a right to reject or revoke acceptance of the goods.

    6.   Subsection (4) is new and merely adds to the completeness of the index by including a reference to the lessee's recovery of damages upon the lessor's breach of warranty; such breach may not rise to the level of a default by the lessor justifying revocation of acceptance. If the lessee properly rejects or revokes acceptance of the goods because of a breach of warranty, the rights and remedies are those provided in subsection (1) rather than those in Section 2A–519(4).

    7.   Subsection (5), a revised version of the provisions of Section 2–711(3), recognizes, on rightful rejection or justifiable revocation, the lessee's security interest in goods in its possession and control. Former Section 9–113 (now codified as Section 9–110), which recognized security interests arising under the Article on Sales (Article 2), was amended with the adoption of this Article to reflect the security interests arising under this Article. Pursuant to Section 2A–511(4), a purchaser who purchases goods from the lessee in good faith takes free of any rights of the lessor, or in the case of a finance lease, the supplier. Such goods, however, must have been rightfully rejected and disposed of pursuant to Section 2A–511 or 2A–512. However, Section 2A–517(5) provides that the lessee will have the same rights and duties with respect to goods where acceptance has been revoked as with respect to goods rejected. Thus, Section 2A–511(4) will apply to the lessee's disposition of such goods.

    8.   Pursuant to Section 2A–527(5), the lessee must account to the lessor for the excess proceeds of such disposition, after satisfaction of the claim secured by the lessee's security interest.

    9.   Subsection (6), a slightly revised version of the provisions of Section 2–717, sanctions a right of set-off by the lessee, subject to the rule of Section 2A–407 with respect to irrevocable promises in a finance lease that is not a consumer lease, and further subject to an enforceable "hell or high water" clause in the lease agreement. Section 2A–407 official comment. No attempt is made to state how the set-off should occur; this is to be determined by the facts of each case.

    10.   There is no special treatment of the finance lease in this section. Absent supplemental principles of law and equity to the contrary, in the case of most finance leases, following the lessee's acceptance of the goods, the lessee will have no rights or remedies against the lessor, because the lessor's obligations to the lessee are minimal. Sections 2A–210 and 2A–211(1). Since the lessee will look to the supplier for performance, this is appropriate. Section 2A–209.

Cross References:

     Sections 1–102(3),* 1–103, 1–106(1),* Article 2, especially Sections 2–711, 2–717 and Sections 2A–103(4), 2A–209, 2A–210, 2A–211(1), 2A–407, 2A–501(2), 2A–501(4), 2A–509 through 2A–522, 2A–511(3), 2A–517(5), 2A–527(5) and Section 9–110.

Definitional Cross References:

     "Conforming". Section 2A–103(1)(d).

     "Delivery". Section 1–201(14).*

     "Good faith". Sections 1–201(19)* and 2–103(1)(b).

     "Goods". Section 2A–103(1)(h).

     "Installment lease contract". Section 2A–103(1)(i).

     "Lease contract". Section 2A–103(1)(l).

     "Lessee". Section 2A–103(1)(n).

     "Lessor". Section 2A–103(1)(p).

     "Notifies". Section 1–201(26).*

     "Receipt". Section 2–103(1)(c).

     "Remedy". Section 1–201(34).*

---

  *   *Referring to unrevised Article 1 (Appendix A).*

"Rights". Section 1–201(36).*

"Security interest". Section 1–201(37).*

"Value". Section 1–201(44).*

§ 2A–509. Lessee's Rights on Improper Delivery; Rightful Rejection.

(1)   Subject to the provisions of Section 2A–510 on default in installment lease contracts, if the goods or the tender or delivery fail in any respect to conform to the lease contract, the lessee may reject or accept the goods or accept any commercial unit or units and reject the rest of the goods.

(2)   Rejection of goods is ineffective unless it is within a reasonable time after tender or delivery of the goods and the lessee seasonably notifies the lessor.

Official Comment

Uniform Statutory Source: Sections 2–601 and 2–602(1).

Changes: Revised to reflect leasing practices and terminology.

Definitional Cross References:

"Commercial unit". Section 2A–103(1)(c).

"Conforming". Section 2A–103(1)(d).

"Delivery". Section 1–201(14).*

"Goods". Section 2A–103(1)(h).

"Installment lease contract". Section 2A–103(1)(i).

"Lease contract". Section 2A–103(1)(l).

"Lessee". Section 2A–103(1)(n).

"Lessor". Section 2A–103(1)(p).

"Notifies". Section 1–201(26).*

"Reasonable time". Section 1–204(1) and (2).*

"Rights". Section 1–201(36).*

"Seasonably". Section 1–204(3).*

§ 2A–510. Installment Lease Contracts: Rejection and Default.

(1)   Under an installment lease contract a lessee may reject any delivery that is nonconforming if the nonconformity substantially impairs the value of that delivery and cannot be cured or the nonconformity is a defect in the required documents; but if the nonconformity does not fall within subsection (2) and the lessor or the supplier gives adequate assurance of its cure, the lessee must accept that delivery.

(2)   Whenever nonconformity or default with respect to one or more deliveries substantially impairs the value of the installment lease contract as a whole there is a default with respect to the whole. But, the aggrieved party reinstates the installment lease contract as a whole if the aggrieved party accepts a nonconforming delivery without seasonably notifying of cancellation or brings an action with respect only to past deliveries or demands performance as to future deliveries.

Official Comment

Uniform Statutory Source: Section 2–612.

Changes: Revised to reflect leasing practices and terminology.

Definitional Cross References:

"Action". Section 1–201(1).*

"Aggrieved party". Section 1–201(2).*

"Cancellation". Section 2A–103(1)(b).

"Conforming". Section 2A–103(1)(d).

"Delivery". Section 1–201(14).*

---

*   *Referring to unrevised Article 1 (Appendix A).*

"Installment lease contract". Section 2A–103(1)(i).
"Lessee". Section 2A–103(1)(n).
"Lessor". Section 2A–103(1)(p).
"Notifies". Section 1–201(26).*
"Seasonably". Section 1–204(3).*
"Supplier". Section 2A–103(1)(x).
"Value". Section 1–201(44).*

§ 2A–511. Merchant Lessee's Duties as to Rightfully Rejected Goods.

(1)   Subject to any security interest of a lessee (Section 2A–508(5)), if a lessor or a supplier has no agent or place of business at the market of rejection, a merchant lessee, after rejection of goods in his [or her] possession or control, shall follow any reasonable instructions received from the lessor or the supplier with respect to the goods. In the absence of those instructions, a merchant lessee shall make reasonable efforts to sell, lease, or otherwise dispose of the goods for the lessor's account if they threaten to decline in value speedily. Instructions are not reasonable if on demand indemnity for expenses is not forthcoming.

(2)   If a merchant lessee (subsection (1)) or any other lessee (Section 2A–512) disposes of goods, he [or she] is entitled to reimbursement either from the lessor or the supplier or out of the proceeds for reasonable expenses of caring for and disposing of the goods and, if the expenses include no disposition commission, to such commission as is usual in the trade, or if there is none, to a reasonable sum not exceeding 10 percent of the gross proceeds.

(3)   In complying with this section or Section 2A–512, the lessee is held only to good faith. Good faith conduct hereunder is neither acceptance or conversion nor the basis of an action for damages.

(4)   A purchaser who purchases in good faith from a lessee pursuant to this section or Section 2A–512 takes the goods free of any rights of the lessor and the supplier even though the lessee fails to comply with one or more of the requirements of this Article.

Official Comment

Uniform Statutory Source: Sections 2–603 and 2–706(5).

Changes: Revised to reflect leasing practices and terminology. This section, by its terms, applies to merchants as well as others. Thus, in construing the section it is important to note that under this Act the term good faith is defined differently for merchants (Section 2–103(1)(b)) than for others (Section 1–201(19)*). Section 2A–103(3) and (4).

Definitional Cross References:

"Action". Section 1–201(1).*
"Good faith". Sections 1–201(19)* and 2–103(1)(b).
"Goods". Section 2A–103(1)(h).
"Lease". Section 2A–103(1)(j).
"Lessee". Section 2A–103(1)(n).
"Lessor". Section 2A–103(1)(p).
"Merchant lessee". Section 2A–103(1)(t).
"Purchaser". Section 1–201(33).*
"Rights". Section 1–201(36).*
"Security interest". Section 1–201(37).*
"Supplier". Section 2A–103(1)(x).
"Value". Section 1–201(44).*

---

*   *Referring to unrevised Article 1 (Appendix A).*

§ 2A–512. Lessee's Duties as to Rightfully Rejected Goods.

(1) Except as otherwise provided with respect to goods that threaten to decline in value speedily (Section 2A–511) and subject to any security interest of a lessee (Section 2A–508(5)):

(a) the lessee, after rejection of goods in the lessee's possession, shall hold them with reasonable care at the lessor's or the supplier's disposition for a reasonable time after the lessee's seasonable notification of rejection;

(b) if the lessor or the supplier gives no instructions within a reasonable time after notification of rejection, the lessee may store the rejected goods for the lessor's or the supplier's account or ship them to the lessor or the supplier or dispose of them for the lessor's or the supplier's account with reimbursement in the manner provided in Section 2A–511; but

(c) the lessee has no further obligations with regard to goods rightfully rejected.

(2) Action by the lessee pursuant to subsection (1) is not acceptance or conversion.

Official Comment

Uniform Statutory Source: Sections 2–602(2)(b) and (c) and 2–604.

Changes: Substantially rewritten.

Purposes: The introduction to subsection (1) references goods that threaten to decline in value speedily and not perishables, the reference in Section 2–604, the statutory analogue. This is a change in style, not substance, as the first phrase includes the second. Subparagraphs (a) and (c) are revised versions of the provisions of Section 2–602(2)(b) and (c). Subparagraph (a) states the rule with respect to the lessee's treatment of goods in its possession following rejection; subparagraph (b) states the rule regarding such goods if the lessor or supplier then fails to give instructions to the lessee. If the lessee performs in a fashion consistent with subparagraphs (a) and (b), subparagraph (c) exonerates the lessee.

Cross References:

Sections 2–602(2)(b), 2–602(2)(c) and 2–604.

Definitional Cross References:

"Action". Section 1–201(1).*
"Goods". Section 2A–103(1)(h).
"Lessee". Section 2A–103(1)(n).
"Lessor". Section 2A–103(1)(p).
"Notification". Section 1–201(26).*
"Reasonable time". Section 1–204(1) and (2).*
"Seasonably". Section 1–204(3).*
"Security interest". Section 1–201(37).*
"Supplier". Section 2A–103(1)(x).
"Value". Section 1–201(44).*

§ 2A–513. Cure by Lessor of Improper Tender or Delivery; Replacement.

(1) If any tender or delivery by the lessor or the supplier is rejected because nonconforming and the time for performance has not yet expired, the lessor or the supplier may seasonably notify the lessee of the lessor's or the supplier's intention to cure and may then make a conforming delivery within the time provided in the lease contract.

(2) If the lessee rejects a nonconforming tender that the lessor or the supplier had reasonable grounds to believe would be acceptable with or without money allowance, the lessor or the supplier may have a further reasonable time to substitute a conforming tender if he [or she] seasonably notifies the lessee.

---

* *Referring to unrevised Article 1 (Appendix A).*

Official Comment

Uniform Statutory Source: Section 2–508.

Changes: Revised to reflect leasing practices and terminology.

Definitional Cross References:

"Conforming". Section 2A–103(1)(d).
"Delivery". Section 1–201(14).*
"Lease contract". Section 2A–103(1)(*l*).
"Lessee". Section 2A–103(1)(n).
"Lessor". Section 2A–103(1)(p).
"Money". Section 1–201(24).*
"Notifies". Section 1–201(26).*
"Reasonable time". Section 1–204(1) and (2).*
"Seasonably". Section 1–204(3).*
"Supplier". Section 2A–103(1)(x).

§ 2A–514. Waiver of Lessee's Objections.

(1)   In rejecting goods, a lessee's failure to state a particular defect that is ascertainable by reasonable inspection precludes the lessee from relying on the defect to justify rejection or to establish default:

(a)   if, stated seasonably, the lessor or the supplier could have cured it (Section 2A–513); or

(b)   between merchants if the lessor or the supplier after rejection has made a request in writing for a full and final written statement of all defects on which the lessee proposes to rely.

(2)   A lessee's failure to reserve rights when paying rent or other consideration against documents precludes recovery of the payment for defects apparent in the documents.

As amended in 2003.

Official Comment

Uniform Statutory Source: Section 2–605.

Changes: Revised to reflect leasing practices and terminology.

Purposes: The principles applicable to the commercial practice of payment against documents (subsection 2) are explained in official comment 4 to Section 2–605, the statutory analogue to this section.

Cross Reference:

Section 2–605 official comment 4.

Definitional Cross References:

"Between merchants". Section 2–104(3).
"Goods". Section 2A–103(1)(h).
"Lessee". Section 2A–103(1)(n).
"Lessor". Section 2A–103(1)(p).
"Rights". Section 1–201(36).*
"Seasonably". Section 1–204(3).*
"Supplier". Section 2A–103(1)(x).
"Writing". Section 1–201(46).*

---

*   *Referring to unrevised Article 1 (Appendix A).*

§ 2A–515. Acceptance of Goods.

(1) Acceptance of goods occurs after the lessee has had a reasonable opportunity to inspect the goods and

    (a) the lessee signifies or acts with respect to the goods in a manner that signifies to the lessor or the supplier that the goods are conforming or that the lessee will take or retain them in spite of their nonconformity; or

    (b) the lessee fails to make an effective rejection of the goods (Section 2A–509(2)).

(2) Acceptance of a part of any commercial unit is acceptance of that entire unit.

Official Comment

Uniform Statutory Source: Section 2–606.

Changes: The provisions of Section 2–606(1)(a) were substantially rewritten to provide that the lessee's conduct may signify acceptance. Further, the provisions of Section 2–606(1)(c) were not incorporated as irrelevant given the lessee's possession and use of the leased goods.

Cross References:

    Sections 2–606(1)(a) and 2–606(1)(c).

Definitional Cross References:

    "Commercial unit". Section 2A–103(1)(c).
    "Conforming". Section 2A–103(1)(d).
    "Goods". Section 2A–103(1)(h).
    "Lessee". Section 2A–103(1)(n).
    "Lessor". Section 2A–103(1)(p).
    "Supplier". Section 2A–103(1)(x).

§ 2A–516. Effect of Acceptance of Goods; Notice of Default; Burden of Establishing Default After Acceptance; Notice of Claim or Litigation to Person Answerable Over.

(1) A lessee must pay rent for any goods accepted in accordance with the lease contract, with due allowance for goods rightfully rejected or not delivered.

(2) A lessee's acceptance of goods precludes rejection of the goods accepted. In the case of a finance lease, if made with knowledge of a nonconformity, acceptance cannot be revoked because of it. In any other case, if made with knowledge of a nonconformity, acceptance cannot be revoked because of it unless the acceptance was on the reasonable assumption that the nonconformity would be seasonably cured. Acceptance does not of itself impair any other remedy provided by this Article or the lease agreement for nonconformity.

(3) If a tender has been accepted:

    (a) within a reasonable time after the lessee discovers or should have discovered any default, the lessee shall notify the lessor and the supplier, if any, or be barred from any remedy against the party not notified;

    (b) except in the case of a consumer lease, within a reasonable time after the lessee receives notice of litigation for infringement or the like (Section 2A–211) the lessee shall notify the lessor or be barred from any remedy over for liability established by the litigation; and

    (c) the burden is on the lessee to establish any default.

(4) If a lessee is sued for breach of a warranty or other obligation for which a lessor or a supplier is answerable over the following apply:

    (a) The lessee may give the lessor or the supplier, or both, written notice of the litigation. If the notice states that the person notified may come in and defend and that if the person notified does not do so that person will be bound in any action against that person by the lessee by any determination of fact common to the two litigations, then unless the person notified after seasonable receipt of the notice does come in and defend that person is so bound.

(b)   The lessor or the supplier may demand in writing that the lessee turn over control of the litigation including settlement if the claim is one for infringement or the like (Section 2A–211) or else be barred from any remedy over. If the demand states that the lessor or the supplier agrees to bear all expense and to satisfy any adverse judgment, then unless the lessee after seasonable receipt of the demand does turn over control the lessee is so barred.

(5)   Subsections (3) and (4) apply to any obligation of a lessee to hold the lessor or the supplier harmless against infringement or the like (Section 2A–211).

As amended in 1990.

Official Comment

Uniform Statutory Source: Section 2–607.

Changes: Substantially revised.

Purposes:

1.   Subsection (2) creates a special rule for finance leases, precluding revocation if acceptance is made with knowledge of nonconformity with respect to the lease agreement, as opposed to the supply agreement; this is not inequitable as the lessee has a direct claim against the supplier. Section 2A–209(1). Revocation of acceptance of a finance lease is permitted if the lessee's acceptance was without discovery of the nonconformity (with respect to the lease agreement, not the supply agreement) and was reasonably induced by the lessor's assurances. Section 2A–517(1)(b). Absent exclusion or modification, the lessor under a finance lease makes certain warranties to the lessee. Sections 2A–210 and 2A–211(1). Revocation of acceptance is not prohibited even after the lessee's promise has become irrevocable and independent. Section 2A–407 official comment. Where the finance lease creates a security interest, the rule may be to the contrary. *General Elec. Credit Corp. of Tennessee v. Ger-Beck Mach. Co.*, 806 F.2d 1207 (3rd Cir. 1986).

2.   Subsection (3)(a) requires the lessee to give notice of default, within a reasonable time after the lessee discovered or should have discovered the default. In a finance lease, notice may be given either to the supplier, the lessor, or both, but remedy is barred against the party not notified. In a finance lease, the lessor is usually not liable for defects in the goods and the essential notice is to the supplier. While notice to the finance lessor will often not give any additional rights to the lessee, it would be good practice to give the notice since the finance lessor has an interest in the goods. Subsection (3)(a) does not use the term finance lease, but the definition of supplier is a person from whom a lessor buys or leases goods to be leased under a finance lease. Section 2A–103(1)(x). Therefore, there can be a "supplier" only in a finance lease. Subsection (4) applies similar notice rules as to lessors and suppliers if a lessee is sued for a breach of warranty or other obligation for which a lessor or supplier is answerable over.

3.   Subsection (3)(b) requires the lessee to give the lessor notice of litigation for infringement or the like. There is an exception created in the case of a consumer lease. While such an exception was considered for a finance lease, it was not created because it was not necessary—the lessor in a finance lease does not give a warranty against infringement. Section 2A–211(2). Even though not required under subsection (3)(b), the lessee who takes under a finance lease should consider giving notice of litigation for infringement or the like to the supplier, because the lessee obtains the benefit of the suppliers' promises subject to the suppliers' defenses or claims. Sections 2A–209(1) and 2–607(3)(b).

Cross References:

Sections 2–607(3)(b), 2A–103(1)(x), 2A–209(1), 2A–210, 2A–211(1), 2A–211(2), 2A–407 official comment and 2A–517(1)(b).

Definitional Cross References:

"Action". Section 1–201(1).*
"Agreement". Section 1–201(3).*

---

*   *Referring to unrevised Article 1 (Appendix A).*

"Burden of establishing". Section 1–201(8).*
"Conforming". Section 2A–103(1)(d).
"Consumer lease". Section 2A–103(1)(e).
"Delivery". Section 1–201(14).*
"Discover". Section 1–201(25).*
"Finance lease". Section 2A–103(1)(g).
"Goods". Section 2A–103(1)(h).
"Knowledge". Section 1–201(25).*
"Lease agreement". Section 2A–103(1)(k).
"Lease contract". Section 2A–103(1)(l).
"Lessee". Section 2A–103(1)(n).
"Lessor". Section 2A–103(1)(p).
"Notice". Section 1–201(25).*
"Notifies". Section 1–201(26).*
"Person". Section 1–201(30).*
"Reasonable time". Section 1–204(1) and (2).*
"Receipt". Section 2–103(1)(c).
"Remedy". Section 1–201(34).*
"Seasonably". Section 1–204(3).*
"Supplier". Section 2A–103(1)(x).
"Written". Section 1–201(46).*

§ 2A–517. Revocation of Acceptance of Goods.

(1)   A lessee may revoke acceptance of a lot or commercial unit whose nonconformity substantially impairs its value to the lessee if the lessee has accepted it:

(a)   except in the case of a finance lease, on the reasonable assumption that its nonconformity would be cured and it has not been seasonably cured; or

(b)   without discovery of the nonconformity if the lessee's acceptance was reasonably induced either by the lessor's assurances or, except in the case of a finance lease, by the difficulty of discovery before acceptance.

(2)   Except in the case of a finance lease that is not a consumer lease, a lessee may revoke acceptance of a lot or commercial unit if the lessor defaults under the lease contract and the default substantially impairs the value of that lot or commercial unit to the lessee.

(3)   If the lease agreement so provides, the lessee may revoke acceptance of a lot or commercial unit because of other defaults by the lessor.

(4)   Revocation of acceptance must occur within a reasonable time after the lessee discovers or should have discovered the ground for it and before any substantial change in condition of the goods which is not caused by the nonconformity. Revocation is not effective until the lessee notifies the lessor.

(5)   A lessee who so revokes has the same rights and duties with regard to the goods involved as if the lessee had rejected them.

As amended in 1990.

Official Comment

Uniform Statutory Source: Section 2–608.

Changes: Revised to reflect leasing practices and terminology. Note that in the case of a finance lease the lessee retains a limited right to revoke acceptance. Sections 2A–517(1)(b) and 2A–516 official comment. New subsections (2) and (3) added.

---

*   *Referring to unrevised Article 1 (Appendix A).*

Purposes:

1.   The section states the situations under which the lessee may return the goods to the lessor and cancel the lease. Subsection (2) recognizes that the lessor may have continuing obligations under the lease and that a default as to those obligations may be sufficiently material to justify revocation of acceptance of the leased items and cancellation of the lease by the lessee. For example, a failure by the lessor to fulfill its obligation to maintain leased equipment or to supply other goods which are necessary for the operation of the leased equipment may justify revocation of acceptance and cancellation of the lease.

2.   Subsection (3) specifically provides that the lease agreement may provide that the lessee can revoke acceptance for defaults by the lessor which in the absence of such an agreement might not be considered sufficiently serious to justify revocation. That is, the parties are free to contract on the question of what defaults are so material that the lessee can cancel the lease.

Cross Reference:

Section 2A–516 official comment.

Definitional Cross References:

"Commercial unit". Section 2A–103(1)(c).
"Conforming". Section 2A–103(1)(d).
"Discover". Section 1–201(25).*
"Finance lease". Section 2A–103(1)(g).
"Goods". Section 2A–103(1)(h).
"Lessee". Section 2A–103(1)(n).
"Lessor". Section 2A–103(1)(p).
"Lot". Section 2A–103(1)(s).
"Notifies". Section 1–201(26).*
"Reasonable time". Section 1–204(1) and (2).*
"Rights". Section 1–201(36).*
"Seasonably". Section 1–204(3).*
"Value". Section 1–201(44).*

§ 2A–518.   Cover; Substitute Goods.

(1)   After a default by a lessor under the lease contract of the type described in Section 2A–508(1), or, if agreed, after other default by the lessor, the lessee may cover by making any purchase or lease of or contract to purchase or lease goods in substitution for those due from the lessor.

(2)   Except as otherwise provided with respect to damages liquidated in the lease agreement (Section 2A–504) or otherwise determined pursuant to agreement of the parties (Sections 1–302 and 2A–503), if a lessee's cover is by a lease agreement substantially similar to the original lease agreement and the new lease agreement is made in good faith and in a commercially reasonable manner, the lessee may recover from the lessor as damages (i) the present value, as of the date of the commencement of the term of the new lease agreement, of the rent under the new lease agreement applicable to that period of the new lease term which is comparable to the then remaining term of the original lease agreement minus the present value as of the same date of the total rent for the then remaining lease term of the original lease agreement, and (ii) any incidental or consequential damages, less expenses saved in consequence of the lessor's default.

(3)   If a lessee's cover is by lease agreement that for any reason does not qualify for treatment under subsection (2), or is by purchase or otherwise, the lessee may recover from the lessor as if the lessee had elected not to cover and Section 2A–519 governs.

As amended in 1990 and 2001.

Official Comment

Uniform Statutory Source: Section 2–712.

---

*   *Referring to unrevised Article 1 (Appendix A).*

Changes: Substantially revised.

Purposes:

1.   Subsection (1) allows the lessee to take action to fix its damages after default by the lessor. Such action may consist of the lease of goods. The decision to cover is a function of commercial judgment, not a statutory mandate replete with sanctions for failure to comply. *Cf.* Section 9–625.

2.   Subsection (2) states a rule for determining the amount of lessee's damages provided that there is no agreement to the contrary. The lessee's damages will be established using the new lease agreement as a measure if the following three criteria are met: (i) the lessee's cover is by lease agreement, (ii) the lease agreement is substantially similar to the original lease agreement, and (iii) such cover was effected in good faith, and in a commercially reasonable manner. Thus, the lessee will be entitled to recover from the lessor the present value, as of the date of commencement of the term of the new lease agreement, of the rent under the new lease agreement applicable to that period which is comparable to the then remaining term of the original lease agreement less the present value of the rent reserved for the remaining term under the original lease, together with incidental or consequential damages less expenses saved in consequence of the lessor's default. Consequential damages may include loss suffered by the lessee because of deprivation of the use of the goods during the period between the default and the acquisition of the goods under the new lease agreement. If the lessee's cover does not satisfy the criteria of subsection (2), Section 2A–519 governs.

3.   Two of the three criteria to be met by the lessee are familiar, but the concept of the new lease agreement being substantially similar to the original lease agreement is not. Given the many variables facing a party who intends to lease goods and the rapidity of change in the market place, the policy decision was made not to draft with specificity. It was thought unwise to seek to establish certainty at the cost of fairness. Thus, the decision of whether the new lease agreement is substantially similar to the original will be determined case by case.

4.   While the section does not draw a bright line, it is possible to describe some of the factors that should be considered in finding that a new lease agreement is substantially similar to the original. First, the goods subject to the new lease agreement should be examined. For example, in a lease of computer equipment the new lease might be for more modern equipment. However, it may be that at the time of the lessor's breach it was not possible to obtain the same type of goods in the market place. Because the lessee's remedy under Section 2A–519 is intended to place the lessee in essentially the same position as if he had covered, if goods similar to those to have been delivered under the original lease are not available, then the computer equipment in this hypothetical should qualify as a commercially reasonable substitute. *See* Section 2–712(1).

5.   Second, the various elements of the new lease agreement should also be examined. Those elements include the presence or absence of options to purchase or release; the lessor's representations, warranties and covenants to the lessee, as well as those to be provided by the lessee to the lessor; and the services, if any, to be provided by the lessor or by the lessee. All of these factors allocate cost and risk between the lessor and the lessee and thus affect the amount of rent to be paid. If the differences between the original lease and the new lease can be easily valued, it would be appropriate for a court to adjust the difference in rental to take account of the difference between the two leases, find that the new lease is substantially similar to the old lease, and award cover damages under this section. If, for example, the new lease requires the lessor to insure the goods in the hands of the lessee, while the original lease required the lessee to insure, the usual cost of such insurance could be deducted from the rent due under the new lease before determining the difference in rental between the two leases.

6.   Having examined the goods and the agreement, the test to be applied is whether, in light of these comparisons, the new lease agreement is substantially similar to the original lease agreement. These findings should not be made with scientific precision, as they are a function of economics, nor should they be made independently with respect to the goods and each element of the agreement, as it is important that a sense of commercial judgment pervade the finding. To establish the new lease as a proper measure of damage under subsection (2), these factors, taken as a whole, must result in a finding that the new lease agreement is substantially similar to the original.

7.   A new lease can be substantially similar to the original lease even though its term extends beyond the remaining term of the original lease, so long as both (a) the lease terms are commercially comparable (e.g., it is highly unlikely that a one-month rental and a five-year lease would reflect similar commercial realities), and (b) the court can fairly apportion a part of the rental payments under the new lease to that part of the term of the new lease which is comparable to the remaining lease term under the original lease. Also, the lease term of the new lease may be comparable to the term of the original lease even though the beginning and ending dates of the two leases are not the same. For example, a two-month lease of agricultural equipment for the months of August

and September may be comparable to a two-month lease running from the 15th of August to the 15th of October if in the particular location two-month leases beginning on August 15th are basically interchangeable with two-month leases beginning August 1st. Similarly, the term of a one-year truck lease beginning on the 15th of January may be comparable to the term of a one-year truck lease beginning January 2d. If the lease terms are found to be comparable, the court may base cover damages on the entire difference between the costs under the two leases.

Cross References:

Sections 2–712(1), 2A–519 and 9–625.

Definitional Cross References:

"Agreement". Section 1–201(b)(3).

"Contract". Section 1–201(b)(12).

"Good faith". Section 1–201(b)(20).

"Goods". Section 2A–103(1)(h).

"Lease". Section 2A–103(1)(j).

"Lease agreement". Section 2A–103(1)(k).

"Lease contract". Section 2A–103(1)(*l*).

"Lessee". Section 2A–103(1)(n).

"Lessor". Section 2A–103(1)(p).

"Party". Section 1–201(b)(26).

"Present value". Section 2A–103(1)(u).*

"Purchase". Section 2A–103(1)(v).

As amended in 2001.

§ 2A-519. Lessee's Damages for Non-delivery, Repudiation, Default, and Breach of Warranty in Regard to Accepted Goods.

(1)   Except as otherwise provided with respect to damages liquidated in the lease agreement (Section 2A–504) or otherwise determined pursuant to agreement of the parties (Sections 1–302 and 2A–503), if a lessee elects not to cover or a lessee elects to cover and the cover is by lease agreement that for any reason does not qualify for treatment under Section 2A–518(2), or is by purchase or otherwise, the measure of damages for non-delivery or repudiation by the lessor or for rejection or revocation of acceptance by the lessee is the present value, as of the date of the default, of the then market rent minus the present value as of the same date of the original rent, computed for the remaining lease term of the original lease agreement, together with incidental and consequential damages, less expenses saved in consequence of the lessor's default.

(2)   Market rent is to be determined as of the place for tender or, in cases of rejection after arrival or revocation of acceptance, as of the place of arrival.

(3)   Except as otherwise agreed, if the lessee has accepted goods and given notification (Section 2A–516(3)), the measure of damages for non-conforming tender or delivery or other default by a lessor is the loss resulting in the ordinary course of events from the lessor's default as determined in any manner that is reasonable together with incidental and consequential damages, less expenses saved in consequence of the lessor's default.

(4)   Except as otherwise agreed, the measure of damages for breach of warranty is the present value at the time and place of acceptance of the difference between the value of the use of the goods accepted and the value if they had been as warranted for the lease term, unless special circumstances show proximate

---

*   *Note from West Advisory Panel: Revised Article 1 (2001) defines "present value" in § 1–201(b)(28) for jurisdictions that adopt that version of Article 1. The conforming amendments to Article 2A delete the comment to the Article 2A definition of "present value" but erroneously do not delete the definition itself.*

damages of a different amount, together with incidental and consequential damages, less expenses saved in consequence of the lessor's default or breach of warranty.

As amended in 1990 and 2001.

Official Comment

Uniform Statutory Source: Sections 2–713 and 2–714.

Changes: Substantially revised.

Purposes:

1.   Subsection (1), a revised version of the provisions of Section 2–713(1), states the basic rule governing the measure of lessee's damages for non-delivery or repudiation by the lessor or for rightful rejection or revocation of acceptance by the lessee. This measure will apply, absent agreement to the contrary, if the lessee does not cover or if the cover does not qualify under Section 2A–518. There is no sanction for cover that does not qualify.

2.   The measure of damage is the present value, as of the date of default, of the market rent for the remaining term of the lease less the present value of the original rent for the remaining term of the lease, plus incidental and consequential damages less expenses saved in consequence of the default. Note that the reference in Section 2A–519(1) is to the date of default not to the date of an event of default. An event of default under a lease agreement becomes a default under a lease agreement only after the expiration of any relevant period of grace and compliance with any notice requirements under this Article and the lease agreement. American Bar Foundation, *Commentaries on Indentures,* § 5–1, at 216–217 (1971). Section 2A–501(1). This conclusion is also a function of whether, as a matter of fact or law, the event of default has been waived, suspended or cured. Sections 2A–103(4) and 1–103.

3.   Subsection (2), a revised version of the provisions of Section 2–713(2), states the rule with respect to determining market rent.

4.   Subsection (3), a revised version of the provisions of Section 2–714(1) and (3), states the measure of damages where goods have been accepted and acceptance is not revoked. The subsection applies both to defaults which occur at the inception of the lease and to defaults which occur subsequently, such as failure to comply with an obligation to maintain the leased goods. The measure in essence is the loss, in the ordinary course of events, flowing from the default.

5.   Subsection (4), a revised version of the provisions of Section 2–714(2), states the measure of damages for breach of warranty. The measure in essence is the present value of the difference between the value of the goods accepted and of the goods if they had been as warranted.

6.   Subsections (1), (3) and (4) specifically state that the parties may by contract vary the damages rules stated in those subsections.

Cross References:

Sections 2–713(1), 2–713(2), 2–714 and Section 2A–518.

Definitional Cross References:

"Conforming". Section 2A–103(1)(d).
"Delivery". Section 1–201(b)(15).
"Goods". Section 2A–103(1)(h).
"Lease". Section 2A–103(1)(j).
"Lease agreement". Section 2A–103(1)(k).
"Lessee". Section 2A–103(1)(n).
"Lessor". Section 2A–103(1)(p).
"Notification". Section 1–202.
"Present value". Section 2A–103(1)(u).*
"Value". Section 1–204.

---

*   *Note from West Advisory Panel: Revised Article 1 (2001) defines "present value" in § 1–201(b)(28) for jurisdictions that adopt that version of Article 1. The conforming amendments to Article 2A delete the comment to the Article 2A definition of "present value" but erroneously do not delete the definition itself.*

As amended in 2001.

§ 2A–520. Lessee's Incidental and Consequential Damages.

(1) Incidental damages resulting from a lessor's default include expenses reasonably incurred in inspection, receipt, transportation, and care and custody of goods rightfully rejected or goods the acceptance of which is justifiably revoked, any commercially reasonable charges, expenses or commissions in connection with effecting cover, and any other reasonable expense incident to the default.

(2) Consequential damages resulting from a lessor's default include:

(a) any loss resulting from general or particular requirements and needs of which the lessor at the time of contracting had reason to know and which could not reasonably be prevented by cover or otherwise; and

(b) injury to person or property proximately resulting from any breach of warranty.

Official Comment

Uniform Statutory Source: Section 2–715.

Changes: Revised to reflect leasing terminology and practices.

Purposes: Subsection (1), a revised version of the provisions of Section 2–715(1), lists some examples of incidental damages resulting from a lessor's default; the list is not exhaustive. Subsection (1) makes clear that it applies not only to rightful rejection, but also to justifiable revocation.

Subsection (2), a revised version of the provisions of Section 2–715(2), lists some examples of consequential damages resulting from a lessor's default; the list is not exhaustive.

Cross References:

Section 2–715.

Definitional Cross References:

"Goods". Section 2A–103(1)(h).
"Knows". Section 1–201(25).*
"Lessee". Section 2A–103(1)(n).
"Lessor". Section 2A–103(1)(p).
"Person". Section 1–201(30).*
"Receipt". Section 2–103(1)(c).

§ 2A–521. Lessee's Right to Specific Performance or Replevin.

(1) Specific performance may be decreed if the goods are unique or in other proper circumstances.

(2) A decree for specific performance may include any terms and conditions as to payment of the rent, damages, or other relief that the court deems just.

(3) A lessee has a right of replevin, detinue, sequestration, claim and delivery, or the like for goods identified to the lease contract if after reasonable effort the lessee is unable to effect cover for those goods or the circumstances reasonably indicate that the effort will be unavailing.

Official Comment

Uniform Statutory Source: Section 2–716.

Changes: Revised to reflect leasing practices and terminology, and to expand the reference to the right of replevin in subsection (3) to include other similar rights of the lessee.

Definitional Cross References:

"Delivery". Section 1–201(14).*

---

    *   *Referring to unrevised Article 1 (Appendix A).*

"Goods". Section 2A–103(1)(h).
"Lease contract". Section 2A–103(1)(*l*).
"Lessee". Section 2A–103(1)(n).
"Rights". Section 1–201(36).*
"Term". Section 1–201(42).*

§ 2A–522. Lessee's Right to Goods on Lessor's Insolvency.

(1) Subject to subsection (2) and even though the goods have not been shipped, a lessee who has paid a part or all of the rent and security for goods identified to a lease contract (Section 2A–217) on making and keeping good a tender of any unpaid portion of the rent and security due under the lease contract may recover the goods identified from the lessor if the lessor becomes insolvent within 10 days after receipt of the first installment of rent and security.

(2) A lessee acquires the right to recover goods identified to a lease contract only if they conform to the lease contract.

Official Comment

Uniform Statutory Source: Section 2–502.

Changes: Revised to reflect leasing practices and terminology.

Definitional Cross References:

"Conforming". Section 2A–103(1)(d).
"Goods". Section 2A–103(1)(h).
"Insolvent". Section 1–201(23).*
"Lease contract". Section 2A–103(1)(*l*).
"Lessee". Section 2A–103(1)(n).
"Lessor". Section 2A–103(1)(p).
"Receipt". Section 2–103(1)(c).
"Rights". Section 1–201(36).*

C. DEFAULT BY LESSEE

§ 2A–523. Lessor's Remedies.

(1) If a lessee wrongfully rejects or revokes acceptance of goods or fails to make a payment when due or repudiates with respect to a part or the whole, then, with respect to any goods involved, and with respect to all of the goods if under an installment lease contract the value of the whole lease contract is substantially impaired (Section 2A–510), the lessee is in default under the lease contract and the lessor may:

(a) cancel the lease contract (Section 2A–505(1));

(b) proceed respecting goods not identified to the lease contract (Section 2A–524);

(c) withhold delivery of the goods and take possession of goods previously delivered (Section 2A–525);

(d) stop delivery of the goods by any bailee (Section 2A–526);

(e) dispose of the goods and recover damages (Section 2A–527), or retain the goods and recover damages (Section 2A–528), or in a proper case recover rent (Section 2A–529);

(f) exercise any other rights or pursue any other remedies provided in the lease contract.

(2) If a lessor does not fully exercise a right or obtain a remedy to which the lessor is entitled under subsection (1), the lessor may recover the loss resulting in the ordinary course of events from the lessee's default as determined in any reasonable manner, together with incidental damages, less expenses saved in consequence of the lessee's default.

---

* *Referring to unrevised Article 1 (Appendix A).*

(3)   If a lessee is otherwise in default under a lease contract, the lessor may exercise the rights and pursue the remedies provided in the lease contract, which may include a right to cancel the lease. In addition, unless otherwise provided in the lease contract:

(a)   if the default substantially impairs the value of the lease contract to the lessor, the lessor may exercise the rights and pursue the remedies provided in subsections (1) or (2); or

(b)   if the default does not substantially impair the value of the lease contract to the lessor, the lessor may recover as provided in subsection (2).

As amended in 1990.

Official Comment

Uniform Statutory Source: Section 2–703.

Changes: Substantially revised.

Purposes:

1.   Subsection (1) is an index to Sections 2A–524 through 2A–531 and states that the remedies provided in those sections are available for the defaults referred to in subsection (1): wrongful rejection or revocation of acceptance, failure to make a payment when due, or repudiation. In addition, remedies provided in the lease contract are available. Subsection (2) sets out a remedy if the lessor does not pursue to completion a right or actually obtain a remedy available under subsection (1), and subsection (3) sets out statutory remedies for defaults not specifically referred to in subsection (1). Subsection (3) provides that, if any default by the lessee other than those specifically referred to in subsection (1) is material, the lessor can exercise the remedies provided in subsection (1) or (2); otherwise the available remedy is as provided in subsection (3). A lessor who has brought an action seeking or has nonjudicially pursued one or more of the remedies available under subsection (1) may amend so as to claim or may nonjudicially pursue a remedy under subsection (2) unless the right or remedy first chosen has been pursued to an extent actually inconsistent with the new course of action. The intent of the provision is to reject the doctrine of election of remedies and to permit an alteration of course by the lessor unless such alteration would actually have an effect on the lessee that would be unreasonable under the circumstances. Further, the lessor may pursue remedies under both subsections (1) and (2) unless doing so would put the lessor in a better position than it would have been in had the lessee fully performed.

2.   The lessor and the lessee can agree to modify the rights and remedies available under the Article; they can, among other things, provide that for defaults other than those specified in subsection (1) the lessor can exercise the rights and remedies referred to in subsection (1), whether or not the default would otherwise be held to substantially impair the value of the lease contract to the lessor; they can also create a new scheme of rights and remedies triggered by the occurrence of the default. Sections 2A–103(4) and 1–102(3).*

3.   Subsection (1), a substantially rewritten version of Section 2–703, lists various cumulative remedies of the lessor where the lessee wrongfully rejects or revokes acceptance, fails to make a payment when due, or repudiates. Section 2A–501(2) and (4). The subsection also allows the lessor to exercise any contractual remedy.

4.   This Article rejects any general doctrine of election of remedy. Whether, in a particular case, one remedy bars another, is a function of whether lessor has been put in as good a position as if the lessee had fully performed the lease contract. Multiple remedies are barred only if the effect is to put the lessor in a better position than it would have been in had the lessee fully performed under the lease. Sections 2A–103(4), 2A–501(4), and 1–106(1).*

5.   **Hypothetical:** To better understand the application of subparagraphs (a) through (e), it is useful to review a hypothetical. Assume that A is a merchant in the business of selling and leasing new bicycles of various types. B is about to engage in the business of subleasing bicycles to summer residents of and visitors to an island resort. A, as lessor, has agreed to lease 60 bicycles to B. While there is one master lease, deliveries and terms are staggered. 20 bicycles are to be delivered by A to B's island location on June 1; the term of the lease of these bicycles is four months. 20 bicycles are to be delivered by A to B's island location on July 1; the term of the lease of these bicycles is three months. Finally, 20 bicycles are to be delivered by A to B's island location on August 1; the term of the lease of these bicycles is two months. B is obligated to pay rent to A on the 15th day of each month during the term for the lease. Rent is $50 per month, per bicycle. B has no option to purchase or release and must

_____
*   *Referring to unrevised Article 1 (Appendix A).*

252

return the bicycles to A at the end of the term, in good condition, reasonable wear and tear excepted. Since the retail price of each bicycle is $400 and bicycles used in the retail rental business have a useful economic life of 36 months, this transaction creates a lease. Sections 2A–103(1)(j) and 1–201(37).*

6. A's current inventory of bicycles is not large. Thus, upon signing the lease with B in February, A agreed to purchase 60 new bicycles from A's principal manufacturer, with special instructions to drop ship the bicycles to B's island location in accordance with the delivery schedule set forth in the lease.

7. The first shipment of 20 bicycles was received by B on May 21. B inspected the bicycles, accepted the same as conforming to the lease and signed a receipt of delivery and acceptance. However, due to poor weather that summer, business was terrible and B was unable to pay the rent due on June 15. Pursuant to the lease A sent B notice of default and proceeded to enforce his rights and remedies against B.

8. A's counsel first advised A that under Section 2A–510(2) and the terms of the lease B's failure to pay was a default with respect to the whole. Thus, to minimize A's continued exposure, A was advised to take possession of the bicycles. If A had possession of the goods A could refuse to deliver. Section 2A–525(1). However, the facts here are different. With respect to the bicycles in B's possession, A has the right to take possession of the bicycles, without breach of the peace. Section 2A–525(2). If B refuses to allow A access to the bicycles, A can proceed by action, including replevin or injunctive relief.

9. With respect to the 40 bicycles that have not been delivered, this Article provides various alternatives. First, assume that 20 of the remaining 40 bicycles have been manufactured and delivered by the manufacturer to a carrier for shipment to B. Given the size of the shipment, the carrier was using a small truck for the delivery and the truck had not yet reached the island ferry when the manufacturer (at the request of A) instructed the carrier to divert the shipment to A's place of business. A's right to stop delivery is recognized under these circumstances. Section 2A–526(1). Second, assume that the 20 remaining bicycles were in the process of manufacture when B defaulted. A retains the right (as between A as lessor and B as lessee) to exercise reasonable commercial judgment whether to complete manufacture or to dispose of the unfinished goods for scrap. Since A is not the manufacturer and A has a binding contract to buy the bicycles, A elected to allow the manufacturer to complete the manufacture of the bicycles, but instructed the manufacturer to deliver the completed bicycles to A's place of business. Section 2A–524(2).

10. Thus, so far A has elected to exercise the remedies referred to in subparagraphs (b) through (d) in subsection (1). None of these remedies bars any of the others because A's election and enforcement merely resulted in A's possession of the bicycles. Had B performed A would have recovered possession of the bicycles. Thus A is in the process of obtaining the benefit of his bargain. Note that A could exercise any other rights or pursue any other remedies provided in the lease contract (Section 2A–523(1)(f)), or elect to recover his loss due to the lessee's default under Section 2A–523(2).

11. A's counsel next would determine what action, if any, should be taken with respect to the goods. As stated in subparagraph (e) and as discussed fully in Section 2A–527(1) the lessor may, but has no obligation to, dispose of the goods by a substantially similar lease (indeed, the lessor has no obligation whatsoever to dispose of the goods at all) and recover damages based on that action, but lessor will not be able to recover damages which put it in a better position than performance would have done, nor will it be able to recover damages for losses which it could have reasonably avoided. In this case, since A is in the business of leasing and selling bicycles, A will probably inventory the 60 bicycles for its retail trade.

12. A's counsel then will determine which of the various means of ascertaining A's damages against B are available. Subparagraph (e) catalogues each relevant section. First, under Section 2A–527(2) the amount of A's claim is computed by comparing the original lease between A and B with any subsequent lease of the bicycles but only if the subsequent lease is substantially similar to the original lease contract. While the section does not define this term, the official comment does establish some parameters. If, however, A elects to lease the bicycles to his retail trade, it is unlikely that the resulting lease will be substantially similar to the original, as leases to retail customers are considerably different from leases to wholesale customers like B. If, however, the leases were substantially similar, the damage claim is for accrued and unpaid rent to the beginning of the new lease, plus the present value as of the same date, of the rent reserved under the original lease for the balance of its term less the present value as of the same date of the rent reserved under the replacement lease for a term comparable to the balance of the term of the original lease, together with incidental damages less expenses saved in consequence of the lessee's default.

---

* *Referring to unrevised Article 1 (Appendix A).*

13.   If the new lease is not substantially similar or if A elects to sell the bicycles or to hold the bicycles, damages are computed under Section 2A–528 or 2A–529.

14.   If A elects to pursue his claim under Section 2A–528(1) the damage rule is the same as that stated in Section 2A–528(2) except that damages are measured from default if the lessee never took possession of the goods or from the time when the lessor did or could have regained possession and that the standard of comparison is not the rent reserved under a substantially similar lease entered into by the lessor but a market rent, as defined in Section 2A–507. Further, if the facts of this hypothetical were more elaborate A may be able to establish that the measure of damage under subsection (1) is inadequate to put him in the same position that B's performance would have, in which case A can claim the present value of his lost profits.

15.   Yet another alternative for computing A's damage claim against B which will be available in some situations is recovery of the present value, as of entry of judgment, of the rent for the then remaining lease term under Section 2A–529. However, this formulation is not available if the goods have been repossessed or tendered back to A. For the 20 bicycles repossessed and the remaining 40 bicycles, A will be able to recover the present value of the rent only if A is unable to dispose of them, or circumstances indicate the effort will be unavailing. If A has prevailed in an action for the rent, at any time up to collection of a judgment by A against B, A might dispose of the bicycles. In such case A's claim for damages against B is governed by Section 2A–527 or 2A–528. Section 2A–529(3). The resulting recalculation of claim should reduce the amount recoverable by A against B and the lessor is required to cause an appropriate credit to be entered against the earlier judgment. However, the nature of the post-judgment proceedings to resolve this issue, and the sanctions for a failure to comply, if any, will be determined by other law.

16.   Finally, if the lease agreement had so provided pursuant to subparagraph (f), A's claim against B would not be determined under any of these statutory formulae, but pursuant to a liquidated damages clause. Section 2A–504(1).

17.   These various methods of computing A's damage claim against B are alternatives subject to Section 2A–501(4). However, the pursuit of any one of these alternatives is not a bar to, nor has it been barred by, A's earlier action to obtain possession of the 60 bicycles. These formulae, which vary as a function of an overt or implied mitigation of damage theory, focus on allowing A a recovery of the benefit of his bargain with B. Had B performed, A would have received the rent as well as the return of the 60 bicycles at the end of the term.

18.   Finally, A's counsel should also advise A of his right to cancel the lease contract under subparagraph (a). Section 2A–505(1). Cancellation will discharge all existing obligations but preserve A's rights and remedies.

19.   Subsection (2) recognizes that a lessor who is entitled to exercise the rights or to obtain a remedy granted by subsection (1) may choose not to do so. In such cases, the lessor can recover damages as provided in subsection (2). For example, for non-payment of rent, the lessor may decide not to take possession of the goods and cancel the lease, but rather to merely sue for the unpaid rent as it comes due plus lost interest or other damages "determined in any reasonable manner." Subsection (2) also negates any loss of alternative rights and remedies by reason of having invoked or commenced the exercise or pursuit of any one or more rights or remedies.

20.   Subsection (3) allows the lessor access to a remedy scheme provided in this Article as well as that contained in the lease contract if the lessee is in default for reasons other than those stated in subsection (1). Note that the reference to this Article includes supplementary principles of law and equity, *e.g.*, fraud, misrepresentation and duress. Sections 2A–103(4) and 1–103.

21.   There is no special treatment of the finance lease in this section. Absent supplementary principles of law to the contrary, in most cases the supplier will have no rights or remedies against the defaulting lessee. Section 2A–209(2)(ii). Given that the supplier will look to the lessor for payment, this is appropriate. However, there is a specific exception to this rule with respect to the right to identify goods to the lease contract. Section 2A–524(2). The parties are free to create a different result in a particular case. Sections 2A–103(4) and 1–102(3).*

Cross References:

Sections 1–102(3),* 1–103, 1–106(1),* 1–201(37),* 2–703, 2A–103(1)(j), 2A–103(4), 2A–209(2)(ii), 2A–501(4), 2A–504(1), 2A–505(1), 2A–507, 2A–510(2), 2A–524 through 2A–531, 2A–524(2), 2A–525(1), 2A–525(2), 2A–526(1), 2A–527(1), 2A–527(2), 2A–528(1) and 2A–529(3).

---

   *   *Referring to unrevised Article 1 (Appendix A).*

Definitional Cross References:

"Delivery". Section 1–201(14).*
"Goods". Section 2A–103(1)(h).
"Installment lease contract". Section 2A–103(1)(i).
"Lease contract". Section 2A–103(1)(*l*).
"Lessee". Section 2A–103(1)(n).
"Lessor". Section 2A–103(1)(p).
"Remedy". Section 1–201(34).*
"Rights". Section 1–201(36).*
"Value". Section 1–201(44).*

§ 2A–524.   Lessor's Right to Identify Goods to Lease Contract.

(1)   After default by the lessee under the lease contract of the type described in Section 2A–523(1) or 2A–523(3)(a) or, if agreed, after other default by the lessee, the lessor may:

(a)   identify to the lease contract conforming goods not already identified if at the time the lessor learned of the default they were in the lessor's or the supplier's possession or control; and

(b)   dispose of goods (Section 2A–527(1)) that demonstrably have been intended for the particular lease contract even though those goods are unfinished.

(2)   If the goods are unfinished, in the exercise of reasonable commercial judgment for the purposes of avoiding loss and of effective realization, an aggrieved lessor or the supplier may either complete manufacture and wholly identify the goods to the lease contract or cease manufacture and lease, sell, or otherwise dispose of the goods for scrap or salvage value or proceed in any other reasonable manner.

As amended in 1990.

Official Comment

Uniform Statutory Source: Section 2–704.

Changes: Revised to reflect leasing practices and terminology.

Purposes: The remedies provided by this section are available to the lessor (i) if there has been a default by the lessee which falls within Section 2A–523(1) or 2A–523(3)(a), or (ii) if there has been any other default for which the lease contract gives the lessor the remedies provided by this section. Under "(ii)", the lease contract may give the lessor the remedies of identification and disposition provided by this section in various ways. For example, a lease provision might specifically refer to the remedies of identification and disposition, or it might refer to this section by number (*i.e.*, 2A–524), or it might do so by a more general reference such as "all rights and remedies provided by Article 2A for default by the lessee."

Definitional Cross References:

"Aggrieved party". Section 1–201(2).*
"Conforming". Section 2A–103(1)(d).
"Goods". Section 2A–103(1)(h).
"Learn". Section 1–201(25).*
"Lease". Section 2A–103(1)(j).
"Lease contract". Section 2A–103(1)(*l*).
"Lessor". Section 2A–103(1)(p).
"Rights". Section 1–201(36).*
"Supplier". Section 2A–103(1)(x).
"Value". Section 1–201(44).*

---

*   *Referring to unrevised Article 1 (Appendix A).*

§ 2A–525. Lessor's Right to Possession of Goods.

(1)   If a lessor discovers the lessee to be insolvent, the lessor may refuse to deliver the goods.

(2)   After a default by the lessee under the lease contract of the type described in Section 2A–523(1) or 2A–523(3)(a) or, if agreed, after other default by the lessee, the lessor has the right to take possession of the goods. If the lease contract so provides, the lessor may require the lessee to assemble the goods and make them available to the lessor at a place to be designated by the lessor which is reasonably convenient to both parties. Without removal, the lessor may render unusable any goods employed in trade or business, and may dispose of goods on the lessee's premises (Section 2A–527).

(3)   The lessor may proceed under subsection (2) without judicial process if it can be done without breach of the peace or the lessor may proceed by action.

As amended in 1990.

Official Comment

Uniform Statutory Source: Section 2–702(1) and former Section 9–503 (now codified as Section 9–609).

Changes: Substantially revised.

Purposes:

1.   Subsection (1), a revised version of the provisions of Section 2–702(1), allows the lessor to refuse to deliver goods if the lessee is insolvent. Note that the provisions of Section 2–702(2), granting the unpaid seller certain rights of reclamation, were not incorporated in this section. Subsection (2) made this unnecessary.

2.   Subsection (2), a revised version of the provisions of former Section 9–503 (now codified as Section 9–609), allows the lessor, on a Section 2A–523(1) or 2A–523(3)(a) default by the lessee, the right to take possession of or reclaim the goods. Also, the lessor can contract for the right to take possession of the goods for other defaults by the lessee. Therefore, since the lessee's insolvency is an event of default in a standard lease agreement, subsection (2) is the functional equivalent of Section 2–702(2). Further, subsection (2) sanctions the classic crate and delivery clause obligating the lessee to assemble the goods and to make them available to the lessor. Finally, the lessor may leave the goods in place, render them unusable (if they are goods employed in trade or business), and dispose of them on the lessee's premises.

3.   Subsection (3), a revised version of the provisions of former Section 9–503 (now codified as Section 9–609), allows the lessor to proceed under subsection (2) without judicial process, absent breach of the peace, or by action. Sections 2A–501(3), 2A–103(4) and 1–201(1).* In the appropriate case action includes injunctive relief. *Clark Equip. Co. v. Armstrong Equip. Co.,* 431 F.2d 54 (5th Cir.1970), *cert. denied,* 402 U.S. 909 (1971). This Section, as well as a number of other Sections in this Part, are included in the Article to codify the lessor's common law right to protect the lessor's reversionary interest in the goods. Section 2A–103(1)(q). These Sections are intended to supplement and not displace principles of law and equity with respect to the protection of such interest. Sections 2A–103(4) and 1–103. Such principles apply in many instances, *e.g.,* loss or damage to goods if risk of loss passes to the lessee, failure of the lessee to return goods to the lessor in the condition stipulated in the lease, and refusal of the lessee to return goods to the lessor after termination or cancellation of the lease. See also Section 2A–532.

Cross References:

Sections 1–106(2),* 2–702(1), 2–702(2), 2A–103(4), 2A–501(3), 2A–532 and 9–609.

Definitional Cross References:

"Action". Section 1–201(1).*
"Delivery". Section 1–201(14).*
"Discover". Section 1–201(25).*
"Goods". Section 2A–103(1)(h).
"Insolvent". Section 1–201(23).*
"Lease contract". Section 2A–103(1)(*l*).
"Lessee". Section 2A–103(1)(n).

---

*   *Referring to unrevised Article 1 (Appendix A).*

"Lessor". Section 2A–103(1)(p).
"Party". Section 1–201(29).*
"Rights". Section 1–201(36).*

§ 2A–526. Lessor's Stoppage of Delivery in Transit or Otherwise.

(1)   A lessor may stop delivery of goods in the possession of a carrier or other bailee if the lessor discovers the lessee to be insolvent and may stop delivery of carload, truckload, planeload, or larger shipments of express or freight if the lessee repudiates or fails to make a payment due before delivery, whether for rent, security or otherwise under the lease contract, or for any other reason the lessor has a right to withhold or take possession of the goods.

(2)   In pursuing its remedies under subsection (1), the lessor may stop delivery until

(a)   receipt of the goods by the lessee;

(b)   acknowledgment to the lessee by any bailee of the goods, except a carrier, that the bailee holds the goods for the lessee; or

(c)   such an acknowledgment to the lessee by a carrier via reshipment or as a warehouse.

(3)(a)   To stop delivery, a lessor shall so notify as to enable the bailee by reasonable diligence to prevent delivery of the goods.

(b)   After notification, the bailee shall hold and deliver the goods according to the directions of the lessor, but the lessor is liable to the bailee for any ensuing charges or damages.

(c)   A carrier who has issued a nonnegotiable bill of lading is not obliged to obey a notification to stop received from a person other than the consignor.

As amended in 2003.

Official Comment

Uniform Statutory Source: Section 2–705.

Changes: Revised to reflect leasing practices and terminology.

Definitional Cross References:

"Bill of lading". Section 1–201(6).*
"Delivery". Section 1–201(14).*
"Discover". Section 1–201(25).*
"Goods". Section 2A–103(1)(h).
"Insolvent". Section 1–201(23).*
"Lease contract". Section 2A–103(1)(*l*).
"Lessee". Section 2A–103(1)(n).
"Lessor". Section 2A–103(1)(p).
"Notifies" and "Notification". Section 1–201(26).*
"Person". Section 1–201(30).*
"Receipt". Section 2–103(1)(c).
"Remedy". Section 1–201(34).*
"Rights". Section 1–201(36).*

§ 2A–527. Lessor's Rights to Dispose of Goods.

(1)   After a default by a lessee under the lease contract of the type described in Section 2A–523(1) or 2A–523(3)(a) or after the lessor refuses to deliver or takes possession of goods (Section 2A–525 or 2A–526), or, if agreed, after other default by a lessee, the lessor may dispose of the goods concerned or the undelivered balance thereof by lease, sale, or otherwise.

---

*   *Referring to unrevised Article 1 (Appendix A).*

(2)   Except as otherwise provided with respect to damages liquidated in the lease agreement (Section 2A–504) or otherwise determined pursuant to agreement of the parties (Sections 1–302 and 2A–503), if the disposition is by lease agreement substantially similar to the original lease agreement and the new lease agreement is made in good faith and in a commercially reasonable manner, the lessor may recover from the lessee as damages (i) accrued and unpaid rent as of the date of the commencement of the term of the new lease agreement, (ii) the present value, as of the same date, of the total rent for the then remaining lease term of the original lease agreement minus the present value, as of the same date, of the rent under the new lease agreement applicable to that period of the new lease term which is comparable to the then remaining term of the original lease agreement, and (iii) any incidental damages allowed under Section 2A–530, less expenses saved in consequence of the lessee's default.

(3)   If the lessor's disposition is by lease agreement that for any reason does not qualify for treatment under subsection (2), or is by sale or otherwise, the lessor may recover from the lessee as if the lessor had elected not to dispose of the goods and Section 2A–528 governs.

(4)   A subsequent buyer or lessee who buys or leases from the lessor in good faith for value as a result of a disposition under this section takes the goods free of the original lease contract and any rights of the original lessee even though the lessor fails to comply with one or more of the requirements of this Article.

(5)   The lessor is not accountable to the lessee for any profit made on any disposition. A lessee who has rightfully rejected or justifiably revoked acceptance shall account to the lessor for any excess over the amount of the lessee's security interest (Section 2A–508(5)).

As amended in 1990 and 2001.

Official Comment

Uniform Statutory Source: Section 2–706(1), (5) and (6).

Changes: Substantially revised.

Purposes:

1.   Subsection (1), a revised version of the first sentence of subsection 2–706(1), allows the lessor the right to dispose of goods after a statutory or other material default by the lessee (even if the goods remain in the lessee's possession—Section 2A–525(2)), after the lessor refuses to deliver or takes possession of the goods, or, if agreed, after other contractual default. The lessor's decision to exercise this right is a function of a commercial judgment, not a statutory mandate replete with sanctions for failure to comply. Cf. Section 9–625. As the owner of the goods, in the case of a lessor, or as the prime lessee of the goods, in the case of a sublessor, compulsory disposition of the goods is inconsistent with the nature of the interest held by the lessor or the sublessor and is not necessary because the interest held by the lessee or the sublessee is not protected by a right of redemption under the common law or this Article. Subsection 2A–527(5).

2.   The rule for determining the measure of damages recoverable by the lessor against the lessee is a function of several variables. If the lessor has elected to effect disposition under subsection (1) and such disposition is by lease that qualifies under subsection (2), the measure of damages set forth in subsection (2) will apply, absent agreement to the contrary. Sections 2A–504, 2A–103(4) and 1–302.

3.   The lessor's damages will be established using the new lease agreement as a measure if the following three criteria are satisfied: (i) the lessor disposed of the goods by lease, (ii) the lease agreement is substantially similar to the original lease agreement, and (iii) such disposition was in good faith, and in a commercially reasonable manner. Thus, the lessor will be entitled to recover from the lessee the accrued and unpaid rent as of the date of commencement of the term of the new lease, and the present value, as of the same date, of the rent, under the original lease for the then remaining term less the present value as of the same date of the rent under the new lease agreement applicable to the period of the new lease comparable to the remaining term under the original lease, together with incidental damages less expenses saved in consequence of the lessee's default. If the lessor's disposition does not satisfy the criteria of subsection (2), the lessor may calculate its claim against the lessee pursuant to Section 2A–528. Section 2A–523(1)(e).

4.   Two of the three criteria to be met by the lessor are familiar, but the concept of the new lease agreement that is substantially similar to the original lease agreement is not. Given the many variables facing a party who intends to lease goods and the rapidity of change in the market place, the policy decision was made not to draft

258

with specificity. It was thought unwise to seek to establish certainty at the cost of fairness. The decision of whether the new lease agreement is substantially similar to the original will be determined case by case.

5.   While the section does not draw a bright line, it is possible to describe some of the factors that should be considered in a finding that a new lease agreement is substantially similar to the original. The various elements of the new lease agreement should be examined. Those elements include the options to purchase or release; the lessor's representations, warranties and covenants to the lessee as well as those to be provided by the lessee to the lessor; and the services, if any, to be provided by the lessor or by the lessee. All of these factors allocate cost and risk between the lessor and the lessee and thus affect the amount of rent to be paid. These findings should not be made with scientific precision, as they are a function of economics, nor should they be made independently, as it is important that a sense of commercial judgment pervade the finding. See Section 2A–507(2). To establish the new lease as a proper measure of damage under subsection (2), these various factors, taken as a whole, must result in a finding that the new lease agreement is substantially similar to the original. If the differences between the original lease and the new lease can be easily valued, it would be appropriate for a court to find that the new lease is substantially similar to the old lease, adjust the difference in the rent between the two leases to take account of the differences, and award damages under this section. If, for example, the new lease requires the lessor to insure the goods in the hands of the lessee, while the original lease required the lessee to insure, the usual cost of such insurance could be deducted from rent due under the new lease before the difference in rental between the two leases is determined.

6.   The following hypothetical illustrates the difficulty of providing a bright line. Assume that A buys a jumbo tractor for $1 million and then leases the tractor to B for a term of 36 months. The tractor is delivered to and is accepted by B on May 1. On June 1 B fails to pay the monthly rent to A. B returns the tractor to A, who immediately releases the tractor to C for a term identical to the term remaining under the lease between A and B. All terms and conditions under the lease between A and C are identical to those under the original lease between A and B, except that C does not provide any property damage or other insurance coverage, and B agreed to provide complete coverage. Coverage is expensive and difficult to obtain. It is a question of fact whether it is so difficult to adjust the recovery to take account of the difference between the two leases as to insurance that the second lease is not substantially similar to the original.

7.   A new lease can be substantially similar to the original lease even though its term extends beyond the remaining term of the original lease, so long as both (a) the lease terms are commercially comparable (e.g., it is highly unlikely that a one-month rental and a five-year lease would reflect similar realities), and (b) the court can fairly apportion a part of the rental payments under the new lease to that part of the term of the new lease which is comparable to the remaining lease term under the original lease. Also, the lease term of the new lease may be comparable to the remaining term of the original lease even though the beginning and ending dates of the two leases are not the same. For example, a two-month lease of agricultural equipment for the months of August and September may be comparable to a two-month lease running from the 15th of August to the 15th of October if in the particular location two-month leases beginning on August 15th are basically interchangeable with two-month leases beginning August 1st. Similarly, the term of a one-year truck lease beginning on the 15th of January may be comparable to the term of a one-year truck lease beginning January 2d. If the lease terms are found to be comparable, the court may base cover damages on the entire difference between the costs under the two leases.

8.   Subsection (3), which is new, provides that if the lessor's disposition is by lease that does not qualify under subsection (2), or is by sale or otherwise, Section 2A–528 governs.

9.   Subsection (4), a revised version of subsection 2–706(5), applies to protect a subsequent buyer or lessee who buys or leases from the lessor in good faith and for value, pursuant to a disposition under this section. Note that by its terms, the rule in subsection 2A–304(1), which provides that the subsequent lessee takes subject to the original lease contract, is controlled by the rule stated in this subsection.

10.   Subsection (5), a revised version of subsection 2–706(6), provides that the lessor is not accountable to the lessee for any profit made by the lessor on a disposition. This rule follows from the fundamental premise of the bailment for hire that the lessee under a lease of goods has no equity of redemption to protect.

Cross References:

Sections 1–302, 2–706(1), 2–706(5), 2–706(6), 2A–103(4), 2A–304(1), 2A–504, 2A–507(2), 2A–523(1)(e), 2A–525(2), 2A–527(5), 2A–528 and 9–625.

Definitional Cross References:

"Buyer" and "Buying". Section 2–103(1)(a).

"Delivery". Section 1–201(b)(15).
"Good faith". Section 1–201(b)(20).
"Goods". Section 2A–103(1)(h).
"Lease". Section 2A–103(1)(j).
"Lease contract". Section 2A–103(1)(*l*).
"Lessee". Section 2A–103(1)(n).
"Lessor". Section 2A–103(1)(p).
"Present value". Section 2A–103(1)(u).*
"Right". Section 1–201(b)(34).
"Sale". Section 2–106(1).
"Security interest". Sections 1–201(b)(35) and 1–203.
"Value". Section 1–204.

As amended in 2001.

§ 2A–528. Lessor's Damages for Non-acceptance, Failure to Pay, Repudiation, or Other Default.

(1) Except as otherwise provided with respect to damages liquidated in the lease agreement (Section 2A–504) or otherwise determined pursuant to agreement of the parties (Sections 1–302 and 2A–503), if a lessor elects to retain the goods or a lessor elects to dispose of the goods and the disposition is by lease agreement that for any reason does not qualify for treatment under Section 2A–527(2), or is by sale or otherwise, the lessor may recover from the lessee as damages for a default of the type described in Section 2A–523(1) or 2A–523(3)(a), or, if agreed, for other default of the lessee, (i) accrued and unpaid rent as of the date of default if the lessee has never taken possession of the goods, or, if the lessee has taken possession of the goods, as of the date the lessor repossesses the goods or an earlier date on which the lessee makes a tender of the goods to the lessor, (ii) the present value as of the date determined under clause (i) of the total rent for the then remaining lease term of the original lease agreement minus the present value as of the same date of the market rent at the place where the goods are located computed for the same lease term, and (iii) any incidental damages allowed under Section 2A–530, less expenses saved in consequence of the lessee's default.

(2) If the measure of damages provided in subsection (1) is inadequate to put a lessor in as good a position as performance would have, the measure of damages is the present value of the profit, including reasonable overhead, the lessor would have made from full performance by the lessee, together with any incidental damages allowed under Section 2A–530, due allowance for costs reasonably incurred and due credit for payments or proceeds of disposition.

As amended in 1990 and 2001.

Official Comment

Uniform Statutory Source: Section 2–708.

Changes: Substantially revised.

Purposes:

1. Subsection (1), a substantially revised version of Section 2–708(1), states the basic rule governing the measure of lessor's damages for a default described in Section 2A–523(1) or (3)(a), and, if agreed, for a contractual default. This measure will apply if the lessor elects to retain the goods (whether undelivered, returned by the lessee, or repossessed by the lessor after acceptance and default by the lessee) or if the lessor's disposition does not qualify under subsection 2A–527(2). Section 2A–527(3). Note that under some of these conditions, the lessor may recover damages from the lessee pursuant to the rule set forth in Section 2A–529. There is no sanction for

---

*   *Note from West Advisory Panel: Revised Article 1 (2001) defines "present value" in § 1–201(b)(28) for jurisdictions that adopt that version of Article 1. The conforming amendments to Article 2A delete the comment to the Article 2A definition of "present value" but erroneously do not delete the definition itself.*

disposition that does not qualify under subsection 2A–527(2). Application of the rule set forth in this section is subject to agreement to the contrary. Sections 2A–504, 2A–103(4) and 1–302.

2.   If the lessee has never taken possession of the goods, the measure of damage is the accrued and unpaid rent as of the date of default together with the present value, as of the date of default, of the original rent for the remaining term of the lease less the present value as of the same date of market rent, and incidental damages, less expenses saved in consequence of the default. Note that the reference in Section 2A–528(1)(i) and (ii) is to the date of default not to the date of an event of default. An event of default under a lease agreement becomes a default under a lease agreement only after the expiration of any relevant period of grace and compliance with any notice requirements under this Article and the lease agreement. American Bar Foundation, *Commentaries on Indentures,* § 5–1, at 216–217 (1971). Section 2A–501(1). This conclusion is also a function of whether, as a matter of fact or law, the event of default has been waived, suspended or cured. Sections 2A–103(4) and 1–103. If the lessee has taken possession of the goods, the measure of damages is the accrued and unpaid rent as of the earlier of the time the lessor repossesses the goods or the time the lessee tenders the goods to the lessor plus the difference between the present value, as of the same time, of the rent under the lease for the remaining lease term and the present value, as of the same time, of the market rent.

3.   Market rent will be computed pursuant to Section 2A–507.

4.   Subsection (2), a somewhat revised version of the provisions of subsection 2–708(2), states a measure of damages which applies if the measure of damages in subsection (1) is inadequate to put the lessor in as good a position as performance would have. The measure of damage is the lessor's profit, including overhead, together with incidental damages, with allowance for costs reasonably incurred and credit for payments or proceeds of disposition. In determining the amount of due credit with respect to proceeds of disposition a proper value should be attributed to the lessor's residual interest in the goods. Sections 2A–103(1)(q) and 2A–507(4).

5.   In calculating profit, a court should include any expected appreciation of the goods, *e.g.* the foal of a leased brood mare. Because this subsection is intended to give the lessor the benefit of the bargain, a court should consider any reasonable benefit or profit expected by the lessor from the performance of the lease agreement. *See Honeywell, Inc. v. Lithonia Lighting, Inc.*, 317 F.Supp. 406, 413 (N.D.Ga.1970); *Locks v. Wade*, 36 N.J.Super. 128, 131, 114 A.2d 875, 877 (Super.Ct.App.Div.1955). Further, in calculating profit the concept of present value must be given effect. *Taylor v. Commercial Credit Equip. Corp.*, 170 Ga.App. 322, 316 S.E.2d 788 (Ct.App.1984). *See generally* Section 2A–103(1)(u).

Cross References:

Sections 1–302, 2–708, 2A–103(1)(u), 2A–402, 2A–504, 2A–507, 2A–527(2) and 2A–529.

Definitional Cross References:

"Agreement". Section 1–201(b)(3).
"Goods". Section 2A–103(1)(h).
"Lease". Section 2A–103(1)(j).
"Lease agreement". Section 2A–103(1)(k).
"Lessee". Section 2A–103(1)(n).
"Lessor". Section 2A–103(1)(p).
"Party". Section 1–201(b)(26).
"Present value". Section 2A–103(1)(u).*
"Sale". Section 2–106(1).

As amended in 2001.

§ 2A–529.   Lessor's Action for the Rent.

(1)   After default by the lessee under the lease contract of the type described in Section 2A–523(1) or 2A–523(3)(a) or, if agreed, after other default by the lessee, if the lessor complies with subsection (2), the lessor may recover from the lessee as damages:

---

*   Note from West Advisory Panel: Revised Article 1 (2001) defines "present value" in § 1–201(b)(28) for jurisdictions that adopt that version of Article 1. The conforming amendments to Article 2A delete the comment to the Article 2A definition of "present value" but erroneously do not delete the definition itself.*

(a) for goods accepted by the lessee and not repossessed by or tendered to the lessor, and for conforming goods lost or damaged within a commercially reasonable time after risk of loss passes to the lessee (Section 2A–219), (i) accrued and unpaid rent as of the date of entry of judgment in favor of the lessor, (ii) the present value as of the same date of the rent for the then remaining lease term of the lease agreement, and (iii) any incidental damages allowed under Section 2A–530, less expenses saved in consequence of the lessee's default; and

(b) for goods identified to the lease contract if the lessor is unable after reasonable effort to dispose of them at a reasonable price or the circumstances reasonably indicate that effort will be unavailing, (i) accrued and unpaid rent as of the date of entry of judgment in favor of the lessor, (ii) the present value as of the same date of the rent for the then remaining lease term of the lease agreement, and (iii) any incidental damages allowed under Section 2A–530, less expenses saved in consequence of the lessee's default.

(2) Except as provided in subsection (3), the lessor shall hold for the lessee for the remaining lease term of the lease agreement any goods that have been identified to the lease contract and are in the lessor's control.

(3) The lessor may dispose of the goods at any time before collection of the judgment for damages obtained pursuant to subsection (1). If the disposition is before the end of the remaining lease term of the lease agreement, the lessor's recovery against the lessee for damages is governed by Section 2A–527 or Section 2A–528, and the lessor will cause an appropriate credit to be provided against a judgment for damages to the extent that the amount of the judgment exceeds the recovery available pursuant to Section 2A–527 or 2A–528.

(4) Payment of the judgment for damages obtained pursuant to subsection (1) entitles the lessee to the use and possession of the goods not then disposed of for the remaining lease term of and in accordance with the lease agreement.

(5) After default by the lessee under the lease contract of the type described in Section 2A–523(1) or Section 2A–523(3)(a) or, if agreed, after other default by the lessee, a lessor who is held not entitled to rent under this section must nevertheless be awarded damages for non-acceptance under Section 2A–527 or Section 2A–528.

As amended in 1990.

Official Comment

Uniform Statutory Source: Section 2–709.

Changes: Substantially revised.

Purposes:

1. Absent a lease contract provision to the contrary, an action for the full unpaid rent (discounted to present value as of the time of entry of judgment as to rent due after that time) is available as to goods not lost or damaged only if the lessee retains possession of the goods or the lessor is or apparently will be unable to dispose of them at a reasonable price after reasonable effort. There is no general right in a lessor to recover the full rent from the lessee upon holding the goods for the lessee. If the lessee tenders goods back to the lessor, and the lessor refuses to accept the tender, the lessor will be limited to the damages it would have suffered had it taken back the goods. The rule in Article 2 that the seller can recover the price of accepted goods is rejected here. In a lease, the lessor always has a residual interest in the goods which the lessor usually realizes upon at the end of a lease term by either sale or a new lease. Therefore, it is not a substantial imposition on the lessor to require it to take back and dispose of the goods if the lessee chooses to tender them back before the end of the lease term: the lessor will merely do earlier what it would have done anyway, sell or relet the goods. Further, the lessee will frequently encounter substantial difficulties if the lessee attempts to sublet the goods for the remainder of the lease term. In contrast to the buyer who owns the entire interest in goods and can easily dispose of them, the lessee is selling only the right to use the goods under the terms of the lease and the sublessee must assume a relationship with the lessor. In that situation, it is usually more efficient to eliminate the original lessee as a middleman by allowing the lessee to return the goods to the lessor who can then redispose of them.

2.   In some situations even where possession of the goods is reacquired, a lessor will be able to recover as damages the present value of the full rent due, not under this section, but under 2A–528(2) which allows a lost profit recovery if necessary to put the lessor in the position it would have been in had the lessee performed. Following is an example of such a case. A is a lessor of construction equipment and maintains a substantial inventory. B leases from A a backhoe for a period of two weeks at a rental of $1,000. After three days, B returns the backhoe and refuses to pay the rent. A has five backhoes in inventory, including the one returned by B. During the next 11 days after the return by B of the backhoe, A rents no more than three backhoes at any one time and, therefore, always has two on hand. If B had kept the backhoe for the full rental period, A would have earned the full rental on that backhoe, plus the rental on the other backhoes it actually did rent during that period. Getting this backhoe back before the end of the lease term did not enable A to make any leases it would not otherwise have made. The only way to put A in the position it would have been in had the lessee fully performed is to give the lessor the full rentals. A realized no savings at all because the backhoe was returned early and might even have incurred additional expense if it was paying for parking space for equipment in inventory. A has no obligation to relet the backhoe for the benefit of B rather than leasing that backhoe or any other in inventory for its own benefit. Further, it is probably not reasonable to expect A to dispose of the backhoe by sale when it is returned in an effort to reduce damages suffered by B. Ordinarily, the loss of a two-week rental would not require A to reduce the size of its backhoe inventory. Whether A would similarly be entitled to full rentals as lost profit in a one-year lease of a backhoe is a question of fact: in any event the lessor, subject to mitigation of damages rules, is entitled to be put in as good a position as it would have been had the lessee fully performed the lease contract.

3.   Under subsection (2) a lessor who is able and elects to sue for the rent due under a lease must hold goods not lost or damaged for the lessee. Subsection (3) creates an exception to the subsection (2) requirement. If the lessor disposes of those goods prior to collection of the judgment (whether as a matter of law or agreement), the lessor's recovery is governed by the measure of damages in Section 2A–527 if the disposition is by lease that is substantially similar to the original lease, or otherwise by the measure of damages in Section 2A–528. Section 2A–523 official comment.

4.   Subsection (4), which is new, further reinforces the requisites of Subsection (2). In the event the judgment for damages obtained by the lessor against the lessee pursuant to subsection (1) is satisfied, the lessee regains the right to use and possession of the remaining goods for the balance of the original lease term; a partial satisfaction of the judgment creates no right in the lessee to use and possession of the goods.

5.   The relationship between subsections (2) and (4) is important to understand. Subsection (2) requires the lessor to hold for the lessee identified goods in the lessor's possession. Absent agreement to the contrary, whether in the lease or otherwise, under most circumstances the requirement that the lessor hold the goods for the lessee for the term will mean that the lessor is not allowed to use them. Sections 2A–103(4) and 1–203. Further, the lessor's use of the goods could be viewed as a disposition of the goods that would bar the lessor from recovery under this section, remitting the lessor to the two preceding sections for a determination of the lessor's claim for damages against the lessee.

6.   Subsection (5), the analogue of subsection 2–709(3), further reinforces the thrust of subsection (3) by stating that a lessor who is held not entitled to rent under this section has not elected a remedy; the lessor must be awarded damages under Sections 2A–527 and 2A–528. This is a function of two significant policies of this Article—that resort to a remedy is optional, unless expressly agreed to be exclusive (Section 2A–503(2)) and that rights and remedies provided in this Article generally are cumulative. (Section 2A–501(2) and (4)).

Cross References:

Sections 1–203, 2–709, 2–709(3), 2A–103(4), 2A–501(2), 2A–501(4), 2A–503(2), 2A–504, 2A–523(1)(e), 2A–525(2), 2A–527, 2A–528 and 2A–529(2).

Definitional Cross References:

"Action". Section 1–201(1).*
"Conforming". Section 2A–103(1)(d).
"Goods". Section 2A–103(1)(h).
"Lease". Section 2A–103(1)(j).
"Lease agreement". Section 2A–103(1)(k).
"Lease contract". Section 2A–103(1)(l).

---

*   Referring to unrevised Article 1 (Appendix A).

"Lessee". Section 2A–103(1)(n).
"Lessor". Section 2A–103(1)(p).
"Present value". Section 2A–103(1)(u).*
"Reasonable time". Section 1–204(1) and (2).**

§ 2A–530. Lessor's Incidental Damages.

Incidental damages to an aggrieved lessor include any commercially reasonable charges, expenses, or commissions incurred in stopping delivery, in the transportation, care and custody of goods after the lessee's default, in connection with return or disposition of the goods, or otherwise resulting from the default.

Official Comment

Uniform Statutory Source: Section 2–710.

Changes: Revised to reflect leasing practices and terminology.

Definitional Cross References:

"Aggrieved party". Section 1–201(2).**
"Delivery". Section 1–201(14).**
"Goods". Section 2A–103(1)(h).
"Lessee". Section 2A–103(1)(n).
"Lessor". Section 2A–103(1)(p).

§ 2A–531. Standing to Sue Third Parties for Injury to Goods.

(1)   If a third party so deals with goods that have been identified to a lease contract as to cause actionable injury to a party to the lease contract (a) the lessor has a right of action against the third party, and (b) the lessee also has a right of action against the third party if the lessee:

    (i)   has a security interest in the goods;

    (ii)   has an insurable interest in the goods; or

    (iii)   bears the risk of loss under the lease contract or has since the injury assumed that risk as against the lessor and the goods have been converted or destroyed.

(2)   If at the time of the injury the party plaintiff did not bear the risk of loss as against the other party to the lease contract and there is no arrangement between them for disposition of the recovery, his [or her] suit or settlement, subject to his [or her] own interest, is as a fiduciary for the other party to the lease contract.

(3)   Either party with the consent of the other may sue for the benefit of whom it may concern.

Official Comment

Uniform Statutory Source: Section 2–722.

Changes: Revised to reflect leasing practices and terminology.

Definitional Cross References:

"Action". Section 1–201(1).**
"Goods". Section 2A–103(1)(h).
"Lease contract". Section 2A–103(1)(*l*).
"Lessee". Section 2A–103(1)(n).
"Lessor". Section 2A–103(1)(p).
"Party". Section 1–201(29).**

---

*   *Note from West Advisory Panel: Revised Article 1 (2001) defines "present value" in § 1–201(b)(28) for jurisdictions that adopt that version of Article 1. The conforming amendments to Article 2A delete the comment to the Article 2A definition of "present value" but erroneously do not delete the definition itself.*

**   *Referring to unrevised Article 1 (Appendix A).*

"Rights". Section 1–201(36).*
"Security interest". Section 1–201(37).*

§ 2A–532. Lessor's Rights to Residual Interest.

In addition to any other recovery permitted by this Article or other law, the lessor may recover from the lessee an amount that will fully compensate the lessor for any loss of or damage to the lessor's residual interest in the goods caused by the default of the lessee.

As added in 1990.

Official Comment

Uniform Statutory Source: None.

Purposes: This section recognizes the right of the lessor to recover under this Article (as well as under other law) from the lessee for failure to comply with the lease obligations as to the condition of leased goods when returned to the lessor, for failure to return the goods at the end of the lease, or for any other default which causes loss or injury to the lessor's residual interest in the goods.

---

* *Referring to unrevised Article 1 (Appendix A).*

UCC ARTICLE 3 (2016)

NEGOTIABLE INSTRUMENTS

Article 3 was revised in 1990 and amended in 2002.

PART 1.   GENERAL PROVISIONS AND DEFINITIONS

PART 2.   NEGOTIATION, TRANSFER, AND INDORSEMENT

PART 3.   ENFORCEMENT OF INSTRUMENTS

UNIFORM COMMERCIAL CODE

National Conference of Commissioners on Uniform State Laws (1990)

REPORTERS

Robert L. Jordan, Los Angeles, California
William D. Warren, Los Angeles, California

ARTICLE 3 (2016)

DRAFTING COMMITTEE

CO-CHAIRMEN

Robert Haydock, Jr., Boston, Massachusetts
Carlyle C. Ring, Jr., Alexandria, Virginia

MEMBERS

Boris Auerbach, Cincinnati, Ohio
William M. Burke, Los Angeles, California
William E. Hogan, New York, New York
Charles W. Joiner, Ann Arbor, Michigan
Frederick H. Miller, Norman, Oklahoma
Donald J. Rapson, Livingston, New Jersey, *The American Law Institute Representative*
Lawrence J. Bugge, Madison, Wisconsin, *President (Member Ex Officio)*
Neal Ossen, Hartford, Connecticut, *Chairman, Division C (Member Ex Officio)*

REVIEW COMMITTEE

CHAIRMAN

Frank F. Jestrab, Chevy Chase, Maryland

MEMBERS

Rupert R. Bullivant, Portland, Oregon
Michael Franck, Lansing, Michigan

CONSULTANT

Fairfax Leary, Jr., Villanova, Pennsylvania

ADVISORS

Thomas C. Baxter, Jr., *Federal Reserve Bank of New York*
Roland E. Brandel, *American Bar Association*
Leon P. Ciferni, *National Westminster Bank USA*
William B. Davenport, *American Bar Association, Section of Business Law, Ad Hoc Committee on Payment Systems*
Carl Felsenfeld, *Association of the Bar of the City of New York*
Thomas J. Greco, *American Bankers Association*
Oliver I. Ireland, *Board of Governors of Federal Reserve System*
John R.H. Kimball, *Federal Reserve Bank of Boston*
John F. Lee, *New York Clearing House Association*
Norman R. Nelson, *New York Clearing House Association*
Ernest T. Patrikis, *Federal Reserve Bank of New York*
Anne B. Pope, *National Corporate Cash Management Association*
Paul S. Turner, *Occidental Petroleum Corporation and National Corporate Cash Management Association*
Stanley M. Walker, *Exxon Company, U.S.A. and National Corporate Cash Management Association*

ADDITIONAL PARTICIPANTS

Henry N. Dyhouse, *U.S. Central Credit Union*
Robert Egan, *Chemical Bank*
Paul T. Even, *National Gypsum Company*
James Foorman, *First Chicago Corporation*
J. Kevin French, *Exxon Company, U.S.A.*
Richard M. Gottlieb, *Manufacturers Hanover Trust Company*
Douglas E. Harris, *Morgan Guaranty Trust Company of New York*
Arthur L. Herold, *National Corporate Cash Management Association*
Shirley Holder, *Atlantic Richfield Company*

269

UNIFORM COMMERCIAL CODE

Paul E. Homrighausen, *Bankers Clearing House Association and National Automated Clearing House Association*

Gail M. Inaba, *Morgan Guaranty Trust Company of New York*

Richard P. Kessler, Jr., *Credit Union National Association*

James W. Kopp, *Shell Oil Company*

Donald R. Lawrence, *Citibank N.A.*

Robert M. MacAllister, *Chase Manhattan Bank NA*

Thomas E. Montgomery, *California Bankers Association*

W. Robert Moore, *American Bankers Association*

Samuel Newman, *Manufacturers Hanover Trust Company*

Nena Nodge, *National Corporate Cash Management Association*

Robert J. Pisapia, *Occidental Petroleum Corporation*

Deborah S. Prutzman, *Arnold & Porter*

James S. Rogers, Professor of Law, Newton, Massachusetts

Robert M. Rosenblith, *Manufacturers Hanover Trust Company*

Jamileh Soufan, *American General Corporation*

Irma Villarreal, *Aon Corporation*

PREFATORY NOTE

Revised Article 3 (with miscellaneous and conforming amendments to Articles 1 and 4) is a companion undertaking to Article 4A on funds transfers. Both efforts were undertaken for the purpose of accommodating modern technologies and practices in payment systems and with respect to negotiable instruments. Both efforts were drafted by the same committee over essentially the same period of time. The work on Article 4A was accorded priority and completed in 1989, and revised Article 3 was completed in 1990.

Revised Article 3 may, not inappropriately, be regarded as the latest effort in the progressive codification of the common law of negotiable instruments that began with the English Bills of Exchange Act enacted by Parliament in 1882. The Uniform Negotiable Instruments Law was promulgated by the Conference in 1896, and it in turn was reorganized and modernized by original Article 3—Commercial Paper as part of the Uniform Commercial Code jointly promulgated in 1952 by the Conference and the American Law Institute. Revised Article 3 in 1990 modernizes, reorganizes and clarifies the law.

Purpose of Drafting Effort

The original Articles 3 and 4 and their predecessors were based upon a paper payment system. Literally, there has been an explosion in the volume of paper to process since Articles 3 and 4 were first promulgated. In the early '50s, around 7 billion checks were processed annually. Correctly anticipating an increase in check volume as the result of a retail approach taken by bankers at that time, the American Bankers Association in 1954 placed a team on a research and development project to identify the most efficient method of processing checks mechanically. The eminently successful MICR line technology was the result. Upon its implementation, checks were processed at high rates of speed. In major part as a result of this technology, a seven-fold explosion in check volume has occurred between the '50s and 1988. In 1988, the Federal Reserve estimated check volume at 48 billion written annually. In 1987, Congress enacted the Expedited Funds Availability Act, and the Federal Reserve Board implemented it in 1988 with Regulation CC. Regulation CC covers many aspects of the forward check collection process and all aspects of the return process.

Present Articles 3 and 4, written for a paper-based system, do not adequately address the issues of responsibility and liability as they relate to modern technologies now employed and the procedures required by the current volume of checks and by the "Expedited Funds Availability Act" and Regulation CC. While agreements among parties to particular transactions have provided some relief, such stop-gap measures are no longer adequate.

In addition, practices have developed which are not easily accommodated within existing Article 3. For example, variable rate notes were unknown when Article 3 first was promulgated; they are common today. Questions about the "cash equivalency" of cashier's checks and money orders have arisen as banks have sought to raise defenses to the payment of these instruments.

ARTICLE 3 (2016)

The revision of Article 3 and Article 4 to update, improve and maintain the viability of it is necessary to accommodate these changing practices and modern technologies, the needs of a rapidly expanding national and international economy, the requirement for more rapid funds availability, and the need for more clarity and certainty. Absent such an update, further Federal preemption of state law may likely occur.

Uniformity is Essential

Traditionally, the legal structures for payments have been regulated by state law through the Uniform Commercial Code. In recent years, however, the Federal government has established regulations for credit and debit cards, and for the availability of funds in a way that regulates much of the check collection process.

With respect to wholesale funds transfers, on an average day two trillion dollars is transferred. Article 4A of the UCC promulgated in 1989 provides the governing comprehensive rules. In 1990, 12 states enacted Article 4A including California, New York and Illinois. In 1991, Article 4A has been introduced in the legislatures of most of the other states, and it is anticipated that most, if not all, will enact Article 4A uniformly. Within a short time, perhaps by 1992, the law of wholesale funds transfers should be uniform throughout the 50 states.

The law for payments through checks and which governs other negotiable instruments similarly should be uniform and up-to-date, either through state enactments or Federal preemption. Otherwise, checks as a viable payment system in international and national transactions will be severely hampered and the utility of other negotiable instruments impaired.

Process of Achieving Uniformity

The essence of uniform law revision is to obtain a sufficient consensus and balance among the interests of the various participants so that universal and uniform adoption by the legislatures of all 50 states may be achieved. As is the practice of the Conference, announcement of the drafting undertaking for Articles 3, 4 and 4A was widely circulated in 1985. Anyone who so requested, received notice of all meetings and was invited to attend. Upon request, names were put on a mailing list to receive copies of drafts as they progressed. In addition, the American Bar Association Ad Hoc Committee on Payments Systems closely followed the work of the Conference and widely circulated the drafts.

The Drafting Committee had 3 or 4 meetings each year and, by August 1990, had held 20 meetings. The drafting meetings began on Friday morning and ended on Sunday at noon. All the meetings were well attended, and the average attendance was 50 or more. The discussion of the drafts was open for comment by all those who attended. In addition, the reporters received a substantial amount of comment and suggestions by written and other communications between meetings of the drafting committee. The work product was read line for line at the annual meetings of the Conference three different years. In addition, the American Law Institute circulated the drafts two or three times to its entire membership. The ALI consultative group also held a meeting to comment and make suggestions on the draft. In addition, progress reports were published annually in *The Business Lawyer* from 1985 through 1990.

The consensus, balance and quality achieved in this lengthy deliberative process is a product not only of the fine work of the reporters and the drafting committee, but also the faithful and energetic participation of the advisors and participants in the drafting meetings. The advisors representing a variety of interests were:

Thomas C. Baxter, Jr., Federal Reserve Bank of New York
Roland E. Brandel, American Bar Association
Leon P. Ciferni, National Westminster Bank USA
William B. Davenport, American Bar Association, Section of Business Law, Ad Hoc Committee on Payment Systems
Carl Felsenfeld, Association of the Bar of the City of New York
Thomas J. Greco, American Bankers Association
Oliver I. Ireland, Board of Governors of Federal Reserve System
John R. H. Kimball, Federal Reserve Bank of Boston
John F. Lee, New York Clearing House Association
Norman R. Nelson, New York Clearing House Association
Ernest T. Patrikis, Federal Reserve Bank of New York

271

UNIFORM COMMERCIAL CODE

Anne B. Pope, National Corporate Cash Management Association

Paul S. Turner, Occidental Petroleum Corporation and National Corporate Cash Management Association

Stanley M. Walker, Exxon Company, U.S.A. and National Corporate Cash Management Association

Other participants who regularly attended drafting meetings were:

Henry N. Dyhouse, U.S. Central Credit Union
Robert Egan, Chemical Bank
Paul T. Even, National Gypsum Corporation
James Foorman, First Chicago Corporation
J. Kevin French, Exxon Company, U.S.A.
Richard M. Gottlieb, Manufacturers Hanover Trust Company
Douglas E. Harris, National Corporate Cash Management Association
Arthur L. Herold, National Corporate Cash Management Association
Shirley Holder, Atlantic Richfield Company
Paul E. Homrighausen, Bankers Clearing House Association
Gail M. Inaba, Morgan Guaranty Trust Company of New York
Richard P. Kessler, Jr., Credit Union National Association
James W. Kopp, Shell Oil Company
Donald R. Lawrence, Citibank, N.A.
Robert M. McAllister, Chase Manhattan Bank, N.A.
Thomas E. Montgomery, California Bankers Association
W. Robert Moore, American Bankers Association
Samuel Newman, Manufacturers Hanover Trust Company
Nena Nodge, National Corporate Cash Management Association
Robert J. Pisapia, Occidental Petroleum Corporation
Deborah S. Prutzman, Arnold & Porter
James S. Rogers, Professor of Law, Newton, Massachusetts
Robert M. Rosenblith, Manufacturers Hanover Trust Company
Jamileh Soufan, American General Corporation
Irma Villarreal, Aon Corporation

Balance Achieved

The consensus reflected in Revised Article 3 and in the conforming amendments to Articles 1 and 4 is supported by the participants from the banking community, the users, and the Federal regulators because it reflects a balance that each interest can reasonably embrace. Some of the benefits of the Revision include:

A. Benefits in the Public Interest

Certainty—Revised Articles 3 and 4 remove numerous uncertainties that exist in the current provisions and thus reduce risk to the payment system and allow appropriate planning by its users and operators.

Speed and Reliability—The Revision removes impediments to the use of automation, and better conforms to Regulation CC to expedite the availability of funds to customers and to reduce risks to banks.

Lower Costs—The Revision by providing for modern technologies, lowers costs to banks and thus to their customers.

Reduced Litigation—By clarification of troublesome issues, and by the provisions of Sections 3–404 through 3–406 which reform rules for allocation of loss from forgeries and alterations, the Revision should significantly reduce litigation.

B. Benefits to Users

"Good Faith"—The definition of good faith under Sections 3–103(a)(4) and 4–104(c) is expanded to include observance of reasonable commercial standards of fair dealing. This objective standard for good faith applies to the performance of all duties and obligations established under Articles 3 and 4.

272

ARTICLE 3 (2016)

Fiduciary Provisions—Section 3–307 protects drawers and persons owed a fiduciary responsibility by imposing stricter standards for obtaining holder in due course rights by a person dealing with the defaulting agent or fiduciary. It also spells out the circumstances under which a person receiving funds has notice of a breach of fiduciary duty, and resulting liability.

Accord and Satisfaction—Under Section 3–311 payees can avoid the unintentional accord and satisfaction by returning the funds or by giving a notice that requires checks to be sent to a particular office where such proposals can be handled. On the other hand, the drawer of a full settlement check is protected from the instrument being indorsed with protest and thus losing the money and being liable on the balance of the claim.

Cashier's Checks—Section 3–411 and related provisions considerably improve the acceptability of bank obligations like cashier's checks as cash equivalents by providing disincentives to wrongful dishonor, such as the possible recovery of consequential damages.

Indorser Liability—Section 3–415 gives more time to hold a check before the user loses indorser liability.

Reporting Forgeries—Section 4–406 increases the outside time a customer has to report forged checks or alterations to thirty days. It also requires a bank truncating checks to retain the item or the capacity to furnish legible copies for seven years.

Individual Agent and Corporate Liability—Section 3–402, as to corporate instruments signed by agents without adequate indication and representation, (except as against a holder in due course), allows a representative to show the parties did not intend individual liability. It affords full protection to the agent that signs a corporate check, even though the check does not show representative status. Also, Section 3–403(b) makes it clear that a signature of an organization is considered unauthorized if more than one signature is required and it is missing.

Direct Suits—Section 3–420 allows a person whose indorsement is forged to sue the depositary bank directly, rather than each drawee of the checks involved.

C. Benefits to the Banking Community

Certainty—Section 3–104 and related provisions clarify what types of contracts are within Article 3 and how they are to be treated, thus promoting certainty of legal rules and reducing litigation costs and risks. Checks that may omit "words of negotiability" are included as fully negotiable; confusion over travelers checks is eliminated; variable rate instruments are included; and there is clarification of the impact of the FTC "Holder" Rule, clarification of the ability of parties to an instrument that is not included in Article 3 to contract for the application of its rules to their contract; and clarification of ordinary money orders as checks rather than bank obligations.

"Ordinary Care"—In Sections 3–103(a)(7) and 4–104(c), ordinary care is defined, making clear that financial institutions taking checks for processing or for payment by automated means need not manually handle each instrument if that is consistent with the institution's procedures and the procedures used do not vary unreasonably from the general usage of banks. This clarification is designed to accommodate and facilitate efficiency, thus lowering costs and lowering expedited funds availability risks. The definition of ordinary care relates to those specific instances in the Code where the standard of ordinary care is set forth.

Statute of Limitations—Sections 3–118 and 4–111 include statutory periods of limitations which will make the law uniform rather than leaving the topic to widely varying state laws.

Employee Fraud—Section 3–405 expands a per se negligence rule to the case of an indorsement forged by an employee whose duties involve handling checks. It also covers that of a faithless employee who supplies a name and then forges the indorsement, but does not require a precise match between the name of the payee and the indorsement.

Bank Definition—The definition of bank is expanded for the purposes of Articles 3 and 4 to clearly include savings and loans and credit unions so that their checks are directly governed by the Code. Section 4–104 clarifies that checks drawn on credit lines are subject to the rules for checks drawn on deposit accounts.

273

Truncation—Section 4–110 authorizes electronic presentment of items and related provisions remove impediments to truncation. Truncation will reduce risks from mandated funds availability and improve the check collection process. Section 4–406 allows an institution the benefit of its provisions even though it does not return the checks due to truncation. If both the customer and the institution fail to use ordinary care, a comparative negligence standard is used rather than placing the full loss on the institution.

Table of Disposition of Sections in Former Article 3

The reference to a section in Revised Article 3 is to the section that refers to the issue addressed by the section in Former Article 3. If there is no comparable section in Revised Article 3 to a section in Former Article 3, that fact is indicated by the word "Omitted."

PART 1

GENERAL PROVISIONS AND DEFINITIONS

§ 3–101.   Short Title.

This Article may be cited as Uniform Commercial Code—Negotiable Instruments.

§ 3–102.   Subject Matter.

(a)   This Article applies to negotiable instruments. It does not apply to money, to payment orders governed by Article 4A, or to securities governed by Article 8.

(b)   If there is conflict between this Article and Article 4 or 9, Articles 4 and 9 govern.

(c)   Regulations of the Board of Governors of the Federal Reserve System and operating circulars of the Federal Reserve Banks supersede any inconsistent provision of this Article to the extent of the inconsistency.

Official Comment

1.   Former Article 3 had no provision affirmatively stating its scope. Former Section 3–103 was a limitation on scope. In revised Article 3, Section 3–102 states that Article 3 applies to "negotiable instruments," defined in Section 3–104. Section 3–104(b) also defines the term "instrument" as a synonym for "negotiable instrument." In most places Article 3 uses the shorter term "instrument." This follows the convention used in former Article 3.

2.   The reference in former Section 3–103(1) to "documents of title" is omitted as superfluous because these documents contain no promise to pay money. The definition of "payment order" in Section 4A–103(a)(1)(iii) excludes drafts which are governed by Article 3. Section 3–102(a) makes clear that a payment order governed by Article 4A is not governed by Article 3. Thus, Article 3 and Article 4A are mutually exclusive.

Article 8 states in Section 8–103(d) that "A writing that is a security certificate is governed by this Article and not by Article 3, even though it also meets the requirements of that Article." Section 3–102(a) conforms to this provision. With respect to some promises or orders to pay money, there may be a question whether the promise or order is an instrument under Section 3–104(a) or a certificated security under Section 8–102(a)(4) and (15). Whether a writing is covered by Article 3 or Article 8 has important consequences. Among other things, under Section 8–207, the issuer of a certificated security may treat the registered owner as the owner for all purposes until the presentment for registration of a transfer. The issuer of a negotiable instrument, on the other hand, may discharge its obligation to pay the instrument only by paying a person entitled to enforce under Section 3–301.

There are also important consequences to an indorser. An indorser of a security does not undertake the issuer's obligation or make any warranty that the issuer will honor the underlying obligation, while an indorser of a negotiable instrument becomes secondarily liable on the underlying obligation.

Ordinarily the distinction between instruments and certificated securities in non-bearer form should be relatively clear. A certificated security under Article 8 must be in registered form (Section 8–102(a)(13)) so that it can be registered on the issuer's records. By contrast, registration plays no part in Article 3. The distinction between an instrument and a certificated security in bearer form may be somewhat more difficult and will generally lie in the economic functions of the two writings. Ordinarily, negotiable instruments under Article 3 will be separate and distinct instruments, while certificated securities under Article 8 will be either one of a class or series or by their terms divisible into a class or series (Section 8–102(a)(15)(ii)). Thus, a promissory note in bearer form could come under either Article 3 if it were simply an individual note, or under Article 8 if it were one of a series of notes or divisible into a series. An additional distinction is whether the instrument is of the type commonly dealt in on securities exchanges or markets or commonly recognized as a medium for investment (Section 8–102(a)(15)(iii)). Thus, a check written in bearer form (i.e., a check made payable to "cash") would not be a certificated security within Article 8 of the Uniform Commercial Code.

Occasionally, a particular writing may fit the definition of both a negotiable instrument under Article 3 and of an investment security under Article 8. In such cases, the instrument is subject exclusively to the requirements of Article 8. Section 8–103(d) and Section 3–102(a).

3.   Although the terms of Article 3 apply to transactions by Federal Reserve Banks, federal preemption would make ineffective any Article 3 provision that conflicts with federal law. The activities of the Federal Reserve Banks are governed by regulations of the Federal Reserve Board and by operating circulars issued by the Reserve Banks themselves. In some instances, the operating circulars are issued pursuant to a Federal Reserve Board regulation. In other cases, the Reserve Bank issues the operating circular under its own authority under the Federal Reserve Act, subject to review by the Federal Reserve Board. Section 3–102(c) states that Federal Reserve Board regulations and operating circulars of the Federal Reserve Banks supersede any inconsistent provision of Article 3 to the extent of the inconsistency. Federal Reserve Board regulations, being valid exercises of regulatory authority pursuant to a federal statute, take precedence over state law if there is an inconsistency. *Childs v. Federal Reserve Bank of Dallas*, 719 F.2d 812 (5th Cir.1983), reh. den. 724 F.2d 127 (5th Cir.1984). Section 3–102(c) treats operating circulars as having the same effect whether issued under the Reserve Bank's own authority or under a Federal Reserve Board regulation. Federal statutes may also preempt Article 3. For example, the Expedited Funds Availability Act, 12 U.S.C. § 4001 et seq., provides that the Act and the regulations issued pursuant to the Act supersede any inconsistent provisions of the UCC. 12 U.S.C. § 4007(b).

4.   In *Clearfield Trust Co. v. United States*, 318 U.S. 363 (1943), the Court held that if the United States is a party to an instrument, its rights and duties are governed by federal common law in the absence of a specific federal statute or regulation. In *United States v. Kimbell Foods, Inc.*, 440 U.S. 715 (1979), the Court stated a three-pronged test to ascertain whether the federal common-law rule should follow the state rule. In most instances courts under the *Kimbell* test have shown a willingness to adopt UCC rules in formulating federal common law on the subject. In *Kimbell* the Court adopted the priorities rules of Article 9.

5.   In 1989 the United Nations Commission on International Trade Law completed a Convention on International Bills of Exchange and International Promissory Notes. If the United States becomes a party to this Convention, the Convention will preempt state law with respect to international bills and notes governed by the Convention. Thus, an international bill of exchange or promissory note that meets the definition of instrument in Section 3–104 will not be governed by Article 3 if it is governed by the Convention. That Convention applies only to bills and notes that indicate on their face that they involve cross-border transactions. It does not apply at all to checks. Convention Articles 1(3), 2(1), 2(2). Moreover, because it applies only if the bill or note specifically calls for application of the Convention, Convention Article 1, there is little chance that the Convention will apply accidentally to a transaction that the parties intended to be governed by this Article.

As amended in 1995 and 2002.

§ 3–103.   Definitions.

(a)   In this Article:

(1)   "Acceptor" means a drawee who has accepted a draft.

(2) "Consumer account" means an account established by an individual primarily for personal, family, or household purposes.

(3) "Consumer transaction" means a transaction in which an individual incurs an obligation primarily for personal, family, or household purposes.

(4) "Drawee" means a person ordered in a draft to make payment.

(5) "Drawer" means a person who signs or is identified in a draft as a person ordering payment.

(6) ["Good faith" means honesty in fact and the observance of reasonable commercial standards of fair dealing.]*

(7) "Maker" means a person who signs or is identified in a note as a person undertaking to pay.

(8) "Order" means a written instruction to pay money signed by the person giving the instruction. The instruction may be addressed to any person, including the person giving the instruction, or to one or more persons jointly or in the alternative but not in succession. An authorization to pay is not an order unless the person authorized to pay is also instructed to pay.

(9) "Ordinary care" in the case of a person engaged in business means observance of reasonable commercial standards, prevailing in the area in which the person is located, with respect to the business in which the person is engaged. In the case of a bank that takes an instrument for processing for collection or payment by automated means, reasonable commercial standards do not require the bank to examine the instrument if the failure to examine does not violate the bank's prescribed procedures and the bank's procedures do not vary unreasonably from general banking usage not disapproved by this Article or Article 4.

(10) "Party" means a party to an instrument.

(11) "Principal obligor," with respect to an instrument, means the accommodated party or any other party to the instrument against whom a secondary obligor has recourse under this article.

(12) "Promise" means a written undertaking to pay money signed by the person undertaking to pay. An acknowledgment of an obligation by the obligor is not a promise unless the obligor also undertakes to pay the obligation.

(13) "Prove" with respect to a fact means to meet the burden of establishing the fact (Section 1–201(b)(8)).

(14) ["Record" means information that is inscribed on a tangible medium or that is stored in an electronic or other medium and is retrievable in perceivable form.]

(15) "Remitter" means a person who purchases an instrument from its issuer if the instrument is payable to an identified person other than the purchaser.

(16) "Remotely-created consumer item" means an item drawn on a consumer account, which is not created by the payor bank and does not bear a handwritten signature purporting to be the signature of the drawer.

(17) "Secondary obligor," with respect to an instrument, means (a) an indorser or an accommodation party, (b) a drawer having the obligation described in Section 3–414(d), or (c) any other party to the instrument that has recourse against another party to the instrument pursuant to Section 3–116(b).

(b) Other definitions applying to this Article and the sections in which they appear are:

"Acceptance" Section 3–409
"Accommodated party" Section 3–419
"Accommodation party" Section 3–419
"Account" Section 4–104

---

* *Note from West Advisory Panel: This subsection will be deleted if the jurisdiction adopts the definition of good faith in revised Article 1 (2001).*

"Alteration" Section 3–407

"Anomalous indorsement" Section 3–205

"Blank indorsement" Section 3–205

"Cashier's check" Section 3–104

"Certificate of deposit" Section 3–104

"Certified check" Section 3–409

"Check" Section 3–104

"Consideration" Section 3–303

"Draft" Section 3–104

"Holder in due course" Section 3–302

"Incomplete instrument" Section 3–115

"Indorsement" Section 3–204

"Indorser" Section 3–204

"Instrument" Section 3–104

"Issue" Section 3–105

"Issuer" Section 3–105

"Negotiable instrument" Section 3–104

"Negotiation" Section 3–201

"Note" Section 3–104

"Payable at a definite time" Section 3–108

"Payable on demand" Section 3–108

"Payable to bearer" Section 3–109

"Payable to order" Section 3–109

"Payment" Section 3–602

"Person entitled to enforce" Section 3–301

"Presentment" Section 3–501

"Reacquisition" Section 3–207

"Special indorsement" Section 3–205

"Teller's check" Section 3–104

"Transfer of instrument" Section 3–203

"Traveler's check" Section 3–104

"Value" Section 3–303

(c)   The following definitions in other Articles apply to this Article:

"Banking day" Section 4–104

"Clearing house" Section 4–104

"Collecting bank" Section 4–105

"Depositary bank" Section 4–105

"Documentary draft" Section 4–104

"Intermediary bank" Section 4–105

"Item" Section 4–104

"Payor bank" Section 4–105

"Suspends payments" Section 4–104

(d)   In addition, Article 1 contains general definitions and principles of construction and interpretation applicable throughout this Article.

Legislative Note. A jurisdiction that enacts this statute that has not yet enacted the revised version of UCC Article 1 should add to Section 3–103 the definition of "good faith" that appears in the official version of Section 1–201(b)(20) and the definition of "record" that appears in the official version of Section 1–201(b)(31). Sections 3–103(a)(6) and (14) are reserved for that purpose. A jurisdiction that already has adopted or simultaneously adopts the revised Article 1 should not add those definitions, but should leave those numbers "reserved." If jurisdictions follow the numbering suggested here, the subsections will have the same numbering in all jurisdictions that have adopted these amendments (whether they have or have not adopted the revised version of UCC Article 1).

As amended in 2001 and 2002.

Official Comment

1. Subsection (a) defines some common terms used throughout the Article that were not defined by former Article 3 and adds the definitions of "order" and "promise" found in former Section 3–102(1)(b) and (c).

2. The definition of "order" includes an instruction given by the signer to itself. The most common example of this kind of order is a cashier's check: a draft with respect to which the drawer and drawee are the same bank or branches of the same bank. Former Section 3–118(a) treated a cashier's check as a note. It stated "a draft drawn on the drawer is effective as a note." Although it is technically more correct to treat a cashier's check as a promise by the issuing bank to pay rather than an order to pay, a cashier's check is in the form of a check and it is normally referred to as a check. Thus, revised Article 3 follows banking practice in referring to a cashier's check as both a draft and a check rather than a note. Some insurance companies also follow the practice of issuing drafts in which the drawer draws on itself and makes the draft payable at or through a bank. These instruments are also treated as drafts. The obligation of the drawer of a cashier's check or other draft drawn on the drawer is stated in Section 3–412.

An order may be addressed to more than one person as drawee either jointly or in the alternative. The authorization of alternative drawees follows former Section 3–102(1)(b) and recognizes the practice of drawers, such as corporations issuing dividend checks, who for commercial convenience name a number of drawees, usually in different parts of the country. Section 3–501(b)(1) provides that presentment may be made to any one of multiple drawees. Drawees in succession are not permitted because the holder should not be required to make more than one presentment. Dishonor by any drawee named in the draft entitles the holder to rights of recourse against the drawer or indorsers.

3. The last sentence of subsection (a)(12) is intended to make it clear that an I.O.U. or other written acknowledgment of indebtedness is not a note unless there is also an undertaking to pay the obligation.

4. This Article now uses the broadened definition of good faith in revised Article 1. The definition requires not only honesty in fact but also "observance of reasonable commercial standards of fair dealing." Although fair dealing is a broad term that must be defined in context, it is clear that it is concerned with the fairness of conduct rather than the care with which an act is performed. Failure to exercise ordinary care in conducting a transaction is an entirely different concept than failure to deal fairly in conducting the transaction. Both fair dealing and ordinary care, which is defined in Section 3–103(a)(9), are to be judged in the light of reasonable commercial standards, but those standards in each case are directed to different aspects of commercial conduct.

5. Subsection (a)(9) is a definition of ordinary care which is applicable not only to Article 3 but to Article 4 as well. See Section 4–104(c). The general rule is stated in the first sentence of subsection (a)(9) and it applies both to banks and to persons engaged in businesses other than banking. Ordinary care means observance of reasonable commercial standards of the relevant businesses prevailing in the area in which the person is located. The second sentence of subsection (a)(9) is a particular rule limited to the duty of a bank to examine an instrument taken by a bank for processing for collection or payment by automated means. This particular rule applies primarily to Section 4–406 and it is discussed in Comment 4 to that section. Nothing in Section 3–103(a)(9) is intended to prevent a customer from proving that the procedures followed by a bank are unreasonable, arbitrary, or unfair.

6. The definition of consumer account includes a joint account established by more than one individual. See Section 1–106(1).*

As amended in 2001 and 2002.

§ 3–104. Negotiable Instrument.

(a) Except as provided in subsections (c) and (d), "negotiable instrument" means an unconditional promise or order to pay a fixed amount of money, with or without interest or other charges described in the promise or order, if it:

(1) is payable to bearer or to order at the time it is issued or first comes into possession of a holder;

(2) is payable on demand or at a definite time; and

---

* *Referring to unrevised Article 1 (Appendix A).*

(3)   does not state any other undertaking or instruction by the person promising or ordering payment to do any act in addition to the payment of money, but the promise or order may contain (i) an undertaking or power to give, maintain, or protect collateral to secure payment, (ii) an authorization or power to the holder to confess judgment or realize on or dispose of collateral, or (iii) a waiver of the benefit of any law intended for the advantage or protection of an obligor.

(b)   "Instrument" means a negotiable instrument.

(c)   An order that meets all of the requirements of subsection (a), except paragraph (1), and otherwise falls within the definition of "check" in subsection (f) is a negotiable instrument and a check.

(d)   A promise or order other than a check is not an instrument if, at the time it is issued or first comes into possession of a holder, it contains a conspicuous statement, however expressed, to the effect that the promise or order is not negotiable or is not an instrument governed by this Article.

(e)   An instrument is a "note" if it is a promise and is a "draft" if it is an order. If an instrument falls within the definition of both "note" and "draft," a person entitled to enforce the instrument may treat it as either.

(f)   "Check" means (i) a draft, other than a documentary draft, payable on demand and drawn on a bank or (ii) a cashier's check or teller's check. An instrument may be a check even though it is described on its face by another term, such as "money order."

(g)   "Cashier's check" means a draft with respect to which the drawer and drawee are the same bank or branches of the same bank.

(h)   "Teller's check" means a draft drawn by a bank (i) on another bank, or (ii) payable at or through a bank.

(i)   "Traveler's check" means an instrument that (i) is payable on demand, (ii) is drawn on or payable at or through a bank, (iii) is designated by the term "traveler's check" or by a substantially similar term, and (iv) requires, as a condition to payment, a countersignature by a person whose specimen signature appears on the instrument.

(j)   "Certificate of deposit" means an instrument containing an acknowledgment by a bank that a sum of money has been received by the bank and a promise by the bank to repay the sum of money. A certificate of deposit is a note of the bank.

Official Comment

1.   The definition of "negotiable instrument" defines the scope of Article 3 since Section 3–102 states: "This Article applies to negotiable instruments." The definition in Section 3–104(a) incorporates other definitions in Article 3. An instrument is either a "promise," defined in Section 3–103(a)(12), or "order," defined in Section 3–103(a)(8). A promise is a written undertaking to pay money signed by the person undertaking to pay. An order is a written instruction to pay money signed by the person giving the instruction. Thus, the term "negotiable instrument" is limited to a signed writing that orders or promises payment of money. "Money" is defined in Section 1–201(24)* and is not limited to United States dollars. It also includes a medium of exchange established by a foreign government or monetary units of account established by an intergovernmental organization or by agreement between two or more nations. Five other requirements are stated in Section 3–104(a): First, the promise or order must be "unconditional." The quoted term is explained in Section 3–106. Second, the amount of money must be "a fixed amount . . . with or without interest or other charges described in the promise or order." Section 3–112(b) relates to "interest." Third, the promise or order must be "payable to bearer or to order." The quoted phrase is explained in Section 3–109. An exception to this requirement is stated in subsection (c). Fourth, the promise or order must be payable "on demand or at a definite time." The quoted phrase is explained in Section 3–108. Fifth, the promise or order may not state "any other undertaking or instruction by the person promising or ordering payment to do any act in addition to the payment of money" with three exceptions. The quoted phrase is based on the first sentence of N.I.L. Section 5 which is the precursor of "no other promise, order, obligation or power given by the maker or drawer" appearing in former Section 3–104(1)(b). The words "instruction" and "undertaking" are used instead of "order" and "promise" that are used in the N.I.L. formulation because the latter words are defined terms that include only orders or promises to pay money. The three exceptions stated in Section

*   *Referring to unrevised Article 1 (Appendix A).*

3–104(a)(3) are based on and are intended to have the same meaning as former Section 3–112(1)(b), (c), (d), and (e), as well as N.I.L. § 5(1), (2), and (3). Subsection (b) states that "instrument" means a "negotiable instrument." This follows former Section 3–102(1)(e) which treated the two terms as synonymous.

2. Unless subsection (c) applies, the effect of subsection (a)(1) and Section 3–102(a) is to exclude from Article 3 any promise or order that is not payable to bearer or to order. There is no provision in revised Article 3 that is comparable to former Section 3–805. The comment to former Section 3–805 states that the typical example of a writing covered by that section is a check reading "Pay John Doe." Such a check was governed by former Article 3 but there could not be a holder in due course of the check. Under Section 3–104(c) such a check is governed by revised Article 3 and there can be a holder in due course of the check. But subsection (c) applies only to checks. The comment to former Section 3–805 does not state any example other than the check to illustrate that section. Subsection (c) is based on the belief that it is good policy to treat checks, which are payment instruments, as negotiable instruments whether or not they contain the words "to the order of". These words are almost always pre-printed on the check form. Occasionally the drawer of a check may strike out these words before issuing the check. In the past some credit unions used check forms that did not contain the quoted words. Such check forms may still be in use but they are no longer common. Absence of the quoted words can easily be overlooked and should not affect the rights of holders who may pay money or give credit for a check without being aware that it is not in the conventional form.

Total exclusion from Article 3 of other promises or orders that are not payable to bearer or to order serves a useful purpose. It provides a simple device to clearly exclude a writing that does not fit the pattern of typical negotiable instruments and which is not intended to be a negotiable instrument. If a writing could be an instrument despite the absence of "to order" or "to bearer" language and a dispute arises with respect to the writing, it might be argued that the writing is a negotiable instrument because the other requirements of subsection (a) are somehow met. Even if the argument is eventually found to be without merit it can be used as a litigation ploy. Words making a promise or order payable to bearer or to order are the most distinguishing feature of a negotiable instrument and such words are frequently referred to as "words of negotiability." Article 3 is not meant to apply to contracts for the sale of goods or services or the sale or lease of real property or similar writings that may contain a promise to pay money. The use of words of negotiability in such contracts would be an aberration. Absence of the words precludes any argument that such contracts might be negotiable instruments.

An order or promise that is excluded from Article 3 because of the requirements of Section 3–104(a) may nevertheless be similar to a negotiable instrument in many respects. Although such a writing cannot be made a negotiable instrument within Article 3 by contract or conduct of its parties, nothing in Section 3–104 or in Section 3–102 is intended to mean that in a particular case involving such a writing a court could not arrive at a result similar to the result that would follow if the writing were a negotiable instrument. For example, a court might find that the obligor with respect to a promise that does not fall within Section 3–104(a) is precluded from asserting a defense against a bona fide purchaser. The preclusion could be based on estoppel or ordinary principles of contract. It does not depend upon the law of negotiable instruments. An example is stated in the paragraph following Case # 2 in Comment 4 to Section 3–302.

Moreover, consistent with the principle stated in Section 1–102(2)(b),* the immediate parties to an order or promise that is not an instrument may provide by agreement that one or more of the provisions of Article 3 determine their rights and obligations under the writing. Upholding the parties' choice is not inconsistent with Article 3. Such an agreement may bind a transferee of the writing if the transferee has notice of it or the agreement arises from usage of trade and the agreement does not violate other law or public policy. An example of such an agreement is a provision that a transferee of the writing has the rights of a holder in due course stated in Article 3 if the transferee took rights under the writing in good faith, for value, and without notice of a claim or defense.

Even without an agreement of the parties to an order or promise that is not an instrument, it may be appropriate, consistent with the principles stated in Section 1–102(2),* for a court to apply one or more provisions of Article 3 to the writing by analogy, taking into account the expectations of the parties and the differences between the writing and an instrument governed by Article 3. Whether such application is appropriate depends upon the facts of each case.

3. Subsection (d) allows exclusion from Article 3 of a writing that would otherwise be an instrument under subsection (a) by a statement to the effect that the writing is not negotiable or is not governed by Article 3. For example, a promissory note can be stamped with the legend NOT NEGOTIABLE. The effect under subsection (d) is not only to negate the possibility of a holder in due course, but to prevent the writing from being a negotiable

---

* *Referring to unrevised Article 1 (Appendix A).*

instrument for any purpose. Subsection (d) does not, however, apply to a check. If a writing is excluded from Article 3 by subsection (d), a court could, nevertheless, apply Article 3 principles to it by analogy as stated in Comment 2.

4. Instruments are divided into two general categories: drafts and notes. A draft is an instrument that is an order. A note is an instrument that is a promise. Section 3–104(e). The term "bill of exchange" is not used in Article 3. It is generally understood to be a synonym for the term "draft." Subsections (f) through (j) define particular instruments that fall within the categories of draft and note. The term "draft," defined in subsection (e), includes a "check" which is defined in subsection (f). "Check" includes a share draft drawn on a credit union payable through a bank because the definition of bank (Section 4–105) includes credit unions. However, a draft drawn on an insurance company payable through a bank is not a check because it is not drawn on a bank. "Money orders" are sold both by banks and non-banks. They vary in form and their form determines how they are treated in Article 3. The most common form of money order sold by banks is that of an ordinary check drawn by the purchaser except that the amount is machine impressed. That kind of money order is a check under Article 3 and is subject to a stop order by the purchaser-drawer as in the case of ordinary checks. The seller bank is the drawee and has no obligation to a holder to pay the money order. If a money order falls within the definition of a teller's check, the rules applicable to teller's checks apply. Postal money orders are subject to federal law. "Teller's check" is separately defined in subsection (h). A teller's check is always drawn by a bank and is usually drawn on another bank. In some cases a teller's check is drawn on a nonbank but is made payable at or through a bank. Article 3 treats both types of teller's check identically, and both are included in the definition of "check." A cashier's check, defined in subsection (g), is also included in the definition of "check." Traveler's checks are issued both by banks and nonbanks and may be in the form of a note or draft. Subsection (i) states the essential characteristics of a traveler's check. The requirement that the instrument be "drawn on or payable at or through a bank" may be satisfied without words on the instrument that identify a bank as drawee or paying agent so long as the instrument bears an appropriate routing number that identifies a bank as paying agent.

The definitions in Regulation CC § 229.2 of the terms "check," "cashier's check," "teller's check," and "traveler's check" are different from the definitions of those terms in Article 3.

Certificates of deposit are treated in former Article 3 as a separate type of instrument. In revised Article 3, Section 3–104(j) treats them as notes.

5. There are some differences between the requirements of Article 3 and the requirements included in Article 3 of the Convention on International Bills of Exchange and International Promissory Notes. Most obviously, the Convention does not include the limitation on extraneous undertakings set forth in Section 3–104(a)(3), and does not permit documents payable to bearer that would be permissible under Section 3–104(a)(1) and Section 3–109. See Convention Article 3. In most respects, however, the requirements of Section 3–104 and Article 3 of the Convention are quite similar.

As amended in 2002.

§ 3–105.   Issue of Instrument.

(a) "Issue" means the first delivery of an instrument by the maker or drawer, whether to a holder or nonholder, for the purpose of giving rights on the instrument to any person.

(b) An unissued instrument, or an unissued incomplete instrument that is completed, is binding on the maker or drawer, but nonissuance is a defense. An instrument that is conditionally issued or is issued for a special purpose is binding on the maker or drawer, but failure of the condition or special purpose to be fulfilled is a defense.

(c) "Issuer" applies to issued and unissued instruments and means a maker or drawer of an instrument.

Official Comment

1. Under former Section 3–102(1)(a) "issue" was defined as the first delivery to a "holder or a remitter" but the term "remitter" was neither defined nor otherwise used. In revised Article 3, Section 3–105(a) defines "issue" more broadly to include the first delivery to anyone by the drawer or maker for the purpose of giving rights

to anyone on the instrument. "Delivery" with respect to instruments is defined in Section 1–201(14)* as meaning "voluntary transfer of possession."

2.   Subsection (b) continues the rule that nonissuance, conditional issuance or issuance for a special purpose is a defense of the maker or drawer of an instrument. Thus, the defense can be asserted against a person other than a holder in due course. The same rule applies to nonissuance of an incomplete instrument later completed.

3.   Subsection (c) defines "issuer" to include the signer of an unissued instrument for convenience of reference in the statute.

§ 3–106.   Unconditional Promise or Order.

(a)   Except as provided in this section, for the purposes of Section 3–104(a), a promise or order is unconditional unless it states (i) an express condition to payment, (ii) that the promise or order is subject to or governed by another record, or (iii) that rights or obligations with respect to the promise or order are stated in another record. A reference to another record does not of itself make the promise or order conditional.

(b)   A promise or order is not made conditional (i) by a reference to another record for a statement of rights with respect to collateral, prepayment, or acceleration, or (ii) because payment is limited to resort to a particular fund or source.

(c)   If a promise or order requires, as a condition to payment, a countersignature by a person whose specimen signature appears on the promise or order, the condition does not make the promise or order conditional for the purposes of Section 3–104(a). If the person whose specimen signature appears on an instrument fails to countersign the instrument, the failure to countersign is a defense to the obligation of the issuer, but the failure does not prevent a transferee of the instrument from becoming a holder of the instrument.

(d)   If a promise or order at the time it is issued or first comes into possession of a holder contains a statement, required by applicable statutory or administrative law, to the effect that the rights of a holder or transferee are subject to claims or defenses that the issuer could assert against the original payee, the promise or order is not thereby made conditional for the purposes of Section 3–104(a); but if the promise or order is an instrument, there cannot be a holder in due course of the instrument.

As amended in 2002.

Official Comment

1.   This provision replaces former Section 3–105. Its purpose is to define when a promise or order fulfills the requirement in Section 3–104(a) that it be an "unconditional" promise or order to pay. Under Section 3–106(a) a promise or order is deemed to be unconditional unless one of the two tests of the subsection make the promise or order conditional. If the promise or order states an express condition to payment, the promise or order is not an instrument. For example, a promise states, "I promise to pay $100,000 to the order of John Doe if he conveys title to Blackacre to me." The promise is not an instrument because there is an express condition to payment. However, suppose a promise states, "In consideration of John Doe's promise to convey title to Blackacre I promise to pay $100,000 to the order of John Doe." That promise can be an instrument if Section 3–104 is otherwise satisfied. Although the recital of the executory promise of Doe to convey Blackacre might be read as an implied condition that the promise be performed, the condition is not an express condition as required by Section 3–106(a)(i). This result is consistent with former Section 3–105(1)(a) and (b). Former Section 3–105(1)(b) is not repeated in Section 3–106 because it is not necessary. It is an example of an implied condition. Former Section 3–105(1)(d), (e), and (f) and the first clause of former Section 3–105(1)(c) are other examples of implied conditions. They are not repeated in Section 3–106 because they are not necessary. The law is not changed.

Section 3–106(a)(ii) and (iii) carry forward the substance of former Section 3–105(2)(a). The only change is the use of "writing" instead of "agreement" and a broadening of the language that can result in conditionality. For example, a promissory note is not an instrument defined by Section 3–104 if it contains any of the following statements: 1. "This note is subject to a contract of sale dated April 1, 1990 between the payee and maker of this

---

*   *Referring to unrevised Article 1 (Appendix A).*

note." 2. "This note is subject to a loan and security agreement dated April 1, 1990 between the payee and maker of this note." 3. "Rights and obligations of the parties with respect to this note are stated in an agreement dated April 1, 1990 between the payee and maker of this note." It is not relevant whether any condition to payment is or is not stated in the writing to which reference is made. The rationale is that the holder of a negotiable instrument should not be required to examine another document to determine rights with respect to payment. But subsection (b)(i) permits reference to a separate writing for information with respect to collateral, prepayment, or acceleration.

Many notes issued in commercial transactions are secured by collateral, are subject to acceleration in the event of default, or are subject to prepayment. A statement of rights and obligations concerning collateral, prepayment, or acceleration does not prevent the note from being an instrument if the statement is in the note itself. See Section 3–104(a)(3) and Section 3–108(b). In some cases it may be convenient not to include a statement concerning collateral, prepayment, or acceleration in the note, but rather to refer to an accompanying loan agreement, security agreement or mortgage for that statement. Subsection (b)(i) allows a reference to the appropriate writing for a statement of these rights. For example, a note would not be made conditional by the following statement: "This note is secured by a security interest in collateral described in a security agreement dated April 1, 1990 between the payee and maker of this note. Rights and obligations with respect to the collateral are [stated in] [governed by] the security agreement." The bracketed words are alternatives, either of which complies.

Subsection (b)(ii) addresses the issues covered by former Section 3–105(1)(f), (g), and (h) and Section 3–105(2)(b). Under Section 3–106(a) a promise or order is not made conditional because payment is limited to payment from a particular source or fund. This reverses the result of former Section 3–105(2)(b). There is no cogent reason why the general credit of a legal entity must be pledged to have a negotiable instrument. Market forces determine the marketability of instruments of this kind. If potential buyers don't want promises or orders that are payable only from a particular source or fund, they won't take them, but Article 3 should apply.

2. Subsection (c) applies to traveler's checks or other instruments that may require a countersignature. Although the requirement of a countersignature is a condition to the obligation to pay, traveler's checks are treated in the commercial world as money substitutes and therefore should be governed by Article 3. The first sentence of subsection (c) allows a traveler's check to meet the definition of instrument by stating that the countersignature condition does not make it conditional for the purposes of Section 3–104. The second sentence states the effect of a failure to meet the condition. Suppose a thief steals a traveler's check and cashes it by skillfully imitating the specimen signature so that the countersignature appears to be authentic. The countersignature is for the purpose of identification of the owner of the instrument. It is not an indorsement. Subsection (c) provides that the failure of the owner to countersign does not prevent a transferee from becoming a holder. Thus, the merchant or bank that cashed the traveler's check becomes a holder when the traveler's check is taken. The forged countersignature is a defense to the obligation of the issuer to pay the instrument, and is included in defenses under Section 3–305(a)(2). These defenses may not be asserted against a holder in due course. Whether a holder has notice of the defense is a factual question. If the countersignature is a very bad forgery, there may be notice. But if the merchant or bank cashed a traveler's check and the countersignature appeared to be similar to the specimen signature, there might not be notice that the countersignature was forged. Thus, the merchant or bank could be a holder in due course.

3. Subsection (d) concerns the effect of a statement to the effect that the rights of a holder or transferee are subject to claims and defenses that the issuer could assert against the original payee. The subsection applies only if the statement is required by statutory or administrative law. The prime example is the Federal Trade Commission Rule (16 C.F.R. Part 433) preserving consumers' claims and defenses in consumer credit sales. The intent of the FTC rule is to make it impossible for there to be a holder in due course of a note bearing the FTC legend and undoubtedly that is the result. But, under former Article 3, the legend may also have had the unintended effect of making the note conditional, thus excluding the note from former Article 3 altogether. Subsection (d) is designed to make it possible to preclude the possibility of a holder in due course without excluding the instrument from Article 3. Most of the provisions of Article 3 are not affected by the holder-in-due-course doctrine and there is no reason why Article 3 should not apply to a note bearing the FTC legend if holder-in-due-course rights are not involved. Under subsection (d) the statement does not make the note conditional. If the note otherwise meets the requirements of Section 3–104(a) it is a negotiable instrument for all purposes except that there cannot be a holder in due course of the note. No particular form of legend or statement is required by subsection (d). The form of a particular legend or statement may be determined by the other statute or administrative law. For example, the FTC legend required in a note taken by the seller in a consumer sale of goods or services is tailored to that particular transaction and therefore uses language that is somewhat different from

that stated in subsection (d), but the difference in expression does not affect the essential similarity of the message conveyed. The effect of the FTC legend is to make the rights of a holder or transferee subject to claims or defenses that the issuer could assert against the original payee of the note.

§ 3–107.   Instrument Payable in Foreign Money.

Unless the instrument otherwise provides, an instrument that states the amount payable in foreign money may be paid in the foreign money or in an equivalent amount in dollars calculated by using the current bank-offered spot rate at the place of payment for the purchase of dollars on the day on which the instrument is paid.

Official Comment

The definition of instrument in Section 3–104 requires that the promise or order be payable in "money." That term is defined in Section 1–201(24)* and is not limited to United States dollars. Section 3–107 states than an instrument payable in foreign money may be paid in dollars if the instrument does not prohibit it. It also states a conversion rate which applies in the absence of a different conversion rate stated in the instrument. The reference in former Section 3–107(1) to instruments payable in "currency" or "current funds" has been dropped as superfluous.

§ 3–108.   Payable on Demand or at Definite Time.

(a)   A promise or order is "payable on demand" if it (i) states that it is payable on demand or at sight, or otherwise indicates that it is payable at the will of the holder, or (ii) does not state any time of payment.

(b)   A promise or order is "payable at a definite time" if it is payable on elapse of a definite period of time after sight or acceptance or at a fixed date or dates or at a time or times readily ascertainable at the time the promise or order is issued, subject to rights of (i) prepayment, (ii) acceleration, (iii) extension at the option of the holder, or (iv) extension to a further definite time at the option of the maker or acceptor or automatically upon or after a specified act or event.

(c)   If an instrument, payable at a fixed date, is also payable upon demand made before the fixed date, the instrument is payable on demand until the fixed date and, if demand for payment is not made before that date, becomes payable at a definite time on the fixed date.

Official Comment

This section is a restatement of former Section 3–108 and Section 3–109. Subsection (b) broadens former Section 3–109 somewhat by providing that a definite time includes a time readily ascertainable at the time the promise or order is issued. Subsection (b)(iii) and (iv) restates former Section 3–109(1)(d). It adopts the generally accepted rule that a clause providing for extension at the option of the holder, even without a time limit, does not affect negotiability since the holder is given only a right which the holder would have without the clause. If the extension is to be at the option of the maker or acceptor or is to be automatic, a definite time limit must be stated or the time of payment remains uncertain and the order or promise is not a negotiable instrument. If a definite time limit is stated, the effect upon certainty of time of payment is the same as if the instrument were made payable at the ultimate date with a term providing for acceleration.

§ 3–109.   Payable to Bearer or to Order.

(a)   A promise or order is payable to bearer if it:

(1)   states that it is payable to bearer or to the order of bearer or otherwise indicates that the person in possession of the promise or order is entitled to payment;

(2)   does not state a payee; or

(3)   states that it is payable to or to the order of cash or otherwise indicates that it is not payable to an identified person.

---

*   *Referring to unrevised Article 1 (Appendix A).*

(b)   A promise or order that is not payable to bearer is payable to order if it is payable (i) to the order of an identified person or (ii) to an identified person or order. A promise or order that is payable to order is payable to the identified person.

(c)   An instrument payable to bearer may become payable to an identified person if it is specially indorsed pursuant to Section 3–205(a). An instrument payable to an identified person may become payable to bearer if it is indorsed in blank pursuant to Section 3–205(b).

Official Comment

1.   Under Section 3–104(a), a promise or order cannot be an instrument unless the instrument is payable to bearer or to order when it is issued or unless Section 3–104(c) applies. The terms "payable to bearer" and "payable to order" are defined in Section 3–109. The quoted terms are also relevant in determining how an instrument is negotiated. If the instrument is payable to bearer it can be negotiated by delivery alone. Section 3–201(b). An instrument that is payable to an identified person cannot be negotiated without the indorsement of the identified person. Section 3–201(b). An instrument payable to order is payable to an identified person. Section 3–109(b). Thus, an instrument payable to order requires the indorsement of the person to whose order the instrument is payable.

2.   Subsection (a) states when an instrument is payable to bearer. An instrument is payable to bearer if it states that it is payable to bearer, but some instruments use ambiguous terms. For example, check forms usually have the words "to the order of" printed at the beginning of the line to be filled in for the name of the payee. If the drawer writes in the word "bearer" or "cash," the check reads "to the order of bearer" or "to the order of cash." In each case the check is payable to bearer. Sometimes the drawer will write the name of the payee "John Doe" but will add the words "or bearer." In that case the check is payable to bearer. Subsection (a). Under subsection (b), if an instrument is payable to bearer it can't be payable to order. This is different from former Section 3–110(3). An instrument that purports to be payable both to order and bearer states contradictory terms. A transferee of the instrument should be able to rely on the bearer term and acquire rights as a holder without obtaining the indorsement of the identified payee. An instrument is also payable to bearer if it does not state a payee. Instruments that do not state a payee are in most cases incomplete instruments. In some cases the drawer of a check may deliver or mail it to the person to be paid without filling in the line for the name of the payee. Under subsection (a) the check is payable to bearer when it is sent or delivered. It is also an incomplete instrument. This case is discussed in Comment 2 to Section 3–115. Subsection (a)(3) contains the words "otherwise indicates that it is not payable to an identified person." The quoted words are meant to cover uncommon cases in which an instrument indicates that it is not meant to be payable to a specific person. Such an instrument is treated like a check payable to "cash." The quoted words are not meant to apply to an instrument stating that it is payable to an identified person such as "ABC Corporation" if ABC Corporation is a nonexistent company. Although the holder of the check cannot be the nonexistent company, the instrument is not payable to bearer. Negotiation of such an instrument is governed by Section 3–404(b).

§ 3–110.   Identification of Person to Whom Instrument Is Payable.

(a)   The person to whom an instrument is initially payable is determined by the intent of the person, whether or not authorized, signing as, or in the name or behalf of, the issuer of the instrument. The instrument is payable to the person intended by the signer even if that person is identified in the instrument by a name or other identification that is not that of the intended person. If more than one person signs in the name or behalf of the issuer of an instrument and all the signers do not intend the same person as payee, the instrument is payable to any person intended by one or more of the signers.

(b)   If the signature of the issuer of an instrument is made by automated means, such as a check-writing machine, the payee of the instrument is determined by the intent of the person who supplied the name or identification of the payee, whether or not authorized to do so.

(c)   A person to whom an instrument is payable may be identified in any way, including by name, identifying number, office, or account number. For the purpose of determining the holder of an instrument, the following rules apply:

(1)   If an instrument is payable to an account and the account is identified only by number, the instrument is payable to the person to whom the account is payable. If an instrument is payable

to an account identified by number and by the name of a person, the instrument is payable to the named person, whether or not that person is the owner of the account identified by number.

(2) If an instrument is payable to:

(i) a trust, an estate, or a person described as trustee or representative of a trust or estate, the instrument is payable to the trustee, the representative, or a successor of either, whether or not the beneficiary or estate is also named;

(ii) a person described as agent or similar representative of a named or identified person, the instrument is payable to the represented person, the representative, or a successor of the representative;

(iii) a fund or organization that is not a legal entity, the instrument is payable to a representative of the members of the fund or organization; or

(iv) an office or to a person described as holding an office, the instrument is payable to the named person, the incumbent of the office, or a successor to the incumbent.

(d) If an instrument is payable to two or more persons alternatively, it is payable to any of them and may be negotiated, discharged, or enforced by any or all of them in possession of the instrument. If an instrument is payable to two or more persons not alternatively, it is payable to all of them and may be negotiated, discharged, or enforced only by all of them. If an instrument payable to two or more persons is ambiguous as to whether it is payable to the persons alternatively, the instrument is payable to the persons alternatively.

Official Comment

1. Section 3–110 states rules for determining the identity of the person to whom an instrument is initially payable if the instrument is payable to an identified person. This issue usually arises in a dispute over the validity of an indorsement in the name of the payee. Subsection (a) states the general rule that the person to whom an instrument is payable is determined by the intent of "the person, whether or not authorized, signing as, or in the name or behalf of, the issuer of the instrument." "Issuer" means the maker or drawer of the instrument. Section 3–105(c). If X signs a check as drawer of a check on X's account, the intent of X controls. If X, as President of Corporation, signs a check as President in behalf of Corporation as drawer, the intent of X controls. If X forges Y's signature as drawer of a check, the intent of X also controls. Under Section 3–103(a)(5), Y is referred to as the drawer of the check because the signing of Y's name identifies Y as the drawer. But since Y's signature was forged Y has no liability as drawer (Section 3–403(a)) unless some other provision of Article 3 or Article 4 makes Y liable. Since X, even though unauthorized, signed in the name of Y as issuer, the intent of X determines to whom the check is payable.

In the case of a check payable to "John Smith," since there are many people in the world named "John Smith" it is not possible to identify the payee of the check unless there is some further identification or the intention of the drawer is determined. Name alone is sufficient under subsection (a), but the intention of the drawer determines which John Smith is the person to whom the check is payable. The same issue is presented in cases of misdescriptions of the payee. The drawer intends to pay a person known to the drawer as John Smith. In fact that person's name is James Smith or John Jones or some other entirely different name. If the check identifies the payee as John Smith, it is nevertheless payable to the person intended by the drawer. That person may indorse the check in either the name John Smith or the person's correct name or in both names. Section 3–204(d). The intent of the drawer is also controlling in fictitious payee cases. Section 3–404(b). The last sentence of subsection (a) refers to rare cases in which the signature of an organization requires more than one signature and the persons signing on behalf of the organization do not all intend the same person as payee. Any person intended by a signer for the organization is the payee and an indorsement by that person is an effective indorsement.

Subsection (b) recognizes the fact that in a large number of cases there is no human signer of an instrument because the instrument, usually a check, is produced by automated means such as a check-writing machine. In that case, the relevant intent is that of the person who supplied the name of the payee. In most cases that person is an employee of the drawer, but in some cases the person could be an outsider who is committing a fraud by introducing names of payees of checks into the system that produces the checks. A check-writing machine is likely to be operated by means of a computer in which is stored information as to name and address of the payee and the amount of the check. Access to the computer may allow production of fraudulent checks without knowledge of the organization that is the issuer of the check. Section 3–404(b) is also concerned with this issue. See Case # 4 in Comment 2 to Section 3–404.

2. Subsection (c) allows the payee to be identified in any way including the various ways stated. Subsection (c)(1) relates to instruments payable to bank accounts. In some cases the account might be identified by name and number, and the name and number might refer to different persons. For example, a check is payable to "X Corporation Account No. 12345 in Bank of Podunk." Under the last sentence of subsection (c)(1), this check is payable to X Corporation and can be negotiated by X Corporation even if Account No. 12345 is some other person's account or the check is not deposited in that account. In other cases the payee is identified by an account number and the name of the owner of the account is not stated. For example, Debtor pays Creditor by issuing a check drawn on Payor Bank. The check is payable to a bank account owned by Creditor but identified only by number. Under the first sentence of subsection (c)(1) the check is payable to Creditor and, under Section 1–201(20),* Creditor becomes the holder when the check is delivered. Under Section 3–201(b), further negotiation of the check requires the indorsement of Creditor. But under Section 4–205(a), if the check is taken by a depositary bank for collection, the bank may become a holder without the indorsement. Under Section 3–102(b), provisions of Article 4 prevail over those of Article 3. The depositary bank warrants that the amount of the check was credited to the payee's account.

3. Subsection (c)(2) replaces former Section 3–117 and subsection (1)(e), (f), and (g) of former Section 3–110. This provision merely determines who can deal with an instrument as a holder. It does not determine ownership of the instrument or its proceeds. Subsection (c)(2)(i) covers trusts and estates. If the instrument is payable to the trust or estate or to the trustee or representative of the trust or estate, the instrument is payable to the trustee or representative or any successor. Under subsection (c)(2)(ii), if the instrument states that it is payable to Doe, President of X Corporation, either Doe or X Corporation can be holder of the instrument. Subsection (c)(2)(iii) concerns informal organizations that are not legal entities such as unincorporated clubs and the like. Any representative of the members of the organization can act as holder. Subsection (c)(2)(iv) applies principally to instruments payable to public offices such as a check payable to County Tax Collector.

4. Subsection (d) replaces former Section 3–116. An instrument payable to X or Y is governed by the first sentence of subsection (d). An instrument payable to X and Y is governed by the second sentence of subsection (d). If an instrument is payable to X or Y, either is the payee and if either is in possession that person is the holder and the person entitled to enforce the instrument. Section 3–301. If an instrument is payable to X and Y, neither X nor Y acting alone is the person to whom the instrument is payable. Neither person, acting alone, can be the holder of the instrument. The instrument is "payable to an identified person." The "identified person" is X and Y acting jointly. Section 3–109(b) and Section 1–102(5)(a).* Thus, under Section 1–201(20)* X or Y, acting alone, cannot be the holder or the person entitled to enforce or negotiate the instrument because neither, acting alone, is the identified person stated in the instrument.

The third sentence of subsection (d) is directed to cases in which it is not clear whether an instrument is payable to multiple payees alternatively. In the case of ambiguity persons dealing with the instrument should be able to rely on the indorsement of a single payee. For example, an instrument payable to X and/or Y is treated like an instrument payable to X or Y.

§ 3–111.　　Place of Payment.

Except as otherwise provided for items in Article 4, an instrument is payable at the place of payment stated in the instrument. If no place of payment is stated, an instrument is payable at the address of the drawee or maker stated in the instrument. If no address is stated, the place of payment is the place of business of the drawee or maker. If a drawee or maker has more than one place of business, the place of payment is any place of business of the drawee or maker chosen by the person entitled to enforce the instrument. If the drawee or maker has no place of business, the place of payment is the residence of the drawee or maker.

Official Comment

If an instrument is payable at a bank in the United States, Section 3–501(b)(1) states that presentment must be made at the place of payment, i.e. the bank. The place of presentment of a check is governed by Regulation CC § 229.36.

---

*　*Referring to unrevised Article 1 (Appendix A).*

§ 3–112.   Interest.

(a)   Unless otherwise provided in the instrument, (i) an instrument is not payable with interest, and (ii) interest on an interest-bearing instrument is payable from the date of the instrument.

(b)   Interest may be stated in an instrument as a fixed or variable amount of money or it may be expressed as a fixed or variable rate or rates. The amount or rate of interest may be stated or described in the instrument in any manner and may require reference to information not contained in the instrument. If an instrument provides for interest, but the amount of interest payable cannot be ascertained from the description, interest is payable at the judgment rate in effect at the place of payment of the instrument and at the time interest first accrues.

Official Comment

1.   Under Section 3–104(a) the requirement of a "fixed amount" applies only to principal. The amount of interest payable is that described in the instrument. If the description of interest in the instrument does not allow for the amount of interest to be ascertained, interest is payable at the judgment rate. Hence, if an instrument calls for interest, the amount of interest will always be determinable. If a variable rate of interest is prescribed, the amount of interest is ascertainable by reference to the formula or index described or referred to in the instrument. The last sentence of subsection (b) replaces subsection (d) of former Section 3–118.

2.   The purpose of subsection (b) is to clarify the meaning of "interest" in the introductory clause of Section 3–104(a). It is not intended to validate a provision for interest in an instrument if that provision violates other law.

§ 3–113.   Date of Instrument.

(a)   An instrument may be antedated or postdated. The date stated determines the time of payment if the instrument is payable at a fixed period after date. Except as provided in Section 4–401(c), an instrument payable on demand is not payable before the date of the instrument.

(b)   If an instrument is undated, its date is the date of its issue or, in the case of an unissued instrument, the date it first comes into possession of a holder.

Official Comment

This section replaces former Section 3–114. Subsections (1) and (3) of former Section 3–114 are deleted as unnecessary. Section 3–113(a) is based in part on subsection (2) of former Section 3–114. The rule that a demand instrument is not payable before the date of the instrument is subject to Section 4–401(c) which allows the payor bank to pay a postdated check unless the drawer has notified the bank of the postdating pursuant to a procedure prescribed in that subsection. With respect to an undated instrument, the date is the date of issue.

§ 3–114.   Contradictory Terms of Instrument.

If an instrument contains contradictory terms, typewritten terms prevail over printed terms, handwritten terms prevail over both, and words prevail over numbers.

Official Comment

Section 3–114 replaces subsections (b) and (c) of former Section 3–118.

§ 3–115.   Incomplete Instrument.

(a)   "Incomplete instrument" means a signed writing, whether or not issued by the signer, the contents of which show at the time of signing that it is incomplete but that the signer intended it to be completed by the addition of words or numbers.

(b)   Subject to subsection (c), if an incomplete instrument is an instrument under Section 3–104, it may be enforced according to its terms if it is not completed, or according to its terms as augmented by completion. If an incomplete instrument is not an instrument under Section 3–104, but, after completion, the requirements of Section 3–104 are met, the instrument may be enforced according to its terms as augmented by completion.

(c)   If words or numbers are added to an incomplete instrument without authority of the signer, there is an alteration of the incomplete instrument under Section 3–407.

(d)   The burden of establishing that words or numbers were added to an incomplete instrument without authority of the signer is on the person asserting the lack of authority.

Official Comment

1.   This section generally carries forward the rules set out in former Section 3–115. The term "incomplete instrument" applies both to an "instrument," i.e. a writing meeting all the requirements of Section 3–104, and to a writing intended to be an instrument that is signed but lacks some element of an instrument. The test in both cases is whether the contents show that it is incomplete and that the signer intended that additional words or numbers be added.

2.   If an incomplete instrument meets the requirements of Section 3–104 and is not completed it may be enforced in accordance with its terms. Suppose, in the following two cases, that a note delivered to the payee is incomplete solely because a space on the pre-printed note form for the due date is not filled in:

Case # 1. If the incomplete instrument is never completed, the note is payable on demand. Section 3–108(a)(ii). However, if the payee and the maker agreed to a due date, the maker may have a defense under Section 3–117 if demand for payment is made before the due date agreed to by the parties.

Case # 2. If the payee completes the note by filling in the due date agreed to by the parties, the note is payable on the due date stated. However, if the due date filled in was not the date agreed to by the parties there is an alteration of the note. Section 3–407 governs the case.

Suppose Debtor pays Creditor by giving Creditor a check on which the space for the name of the payee is left blank. The check is an instrument but it is incomplete. The check is enforceable in its incomplete form and it is payable to bearer because it does not state a payee. Section 3–109(a)(2). Thus, Creditor is a holder of the check. Normally in this kind of case Creditor would simply fill in the space with Creditor's name. When that occurs the check becomes payable to the Creditor.

3.   In some cases the incomplete instrument does not meet the requirements of Section 3–104. An example is a check with the amount not filled in. The check cannot be enforced until the amount is filled in. If the payee fills in an amount authorized by the drawer the check meets the requirements of Section 3–104 and is enforceable as completed. If the payee fills in an unauthorized amount there is an alteration of the check and Section 3–407 applies.

4.   Section 3–302(a)(1) also bears on the problem of incomplete instruments. Under that section a person cannot be a holder in due course of the instrument if it is so incomplete as to call into question its validity. Subsection (d) of Section 3–115 is based on the last clause of subsection (2) of former Section 3–115.

§ 3–116.   Joint and Several Liability; Contribution.

(a)   Except as otherwise provided in the instrument, two or more persons who have the same liability on an instrument as makers, drawers, acceptors, indorsers who indorse as joint payees, or anomalous indorsers are jointly and severally liable in the capacity in which they sign.

(b)   Except as provided in Section 3–419(f) or by agreement of the affected parties, a party having joint and several liability who pays the instrument is entitled to receive from any party having the same joint and several liability contribution in accordance with applicable law.

As amended in 2002.

Official Comment

1.   Subsection (a) replaces subsection (e) of former Section 3–118. Subsection (b) states contribution rights of parties with joint and several liability by referring to applicable law. But subsection (b) is subject to Section 3–419(f). If one of the parties with joint and several liability is an accommodation party and the other is the accommodated party, Section 3–419(f) applies. Because one of the joint and several obligors may have recourse against the other joint and several obligor under subsection (b), each party that is jointly and severally liable under subsection (a) is a secondary obligor in part and a principal obligor in part, as those terms are defined in Section 3–103(a). Accordingly, Section 3–605 determines the effect of a release, an extension of time, or a modification of

the obligation of one of the joint and several obligors, as well as the effect of an impairment of collateral provided by one of those obligors.

2.   Indorsers normally do not have joint and several liability. Rather, an earlier indorser has liability to a later indorser. But indorsers can have joint and several liability in two cases. If an instrument is payable to two payees jointly, both payees must indorse. The indorsement is a joint indorsement and the indorsers have joint and several liability and subsection (b) applies. The other case is that of two or more anomalous indorsers. The term is defined in Section 3–205(d). An anomalous indorsement normally indicates that the indorser signed as an accommodation party. If more than one accommodation party indorses a note as an accommodation to the maker, the indorsers have joint and several liability and subsection (b) applies.

As amended in 2002.

§ 3–117.   Other Agreements Affecting Instrument.

Subject to applicable law regarding exclusion of proof of contemporaneous or previous agreements, the obligation of a party to an instrument to pay the instrument may be modified, supplemented, or nullified by a separate agreement of the obligor and a person entitled to enforce the instrument, if the instrument is issued or the obligation is incurred in reliance on the agreement or as part of the same transaction giving rise to the agreement. To the extent an obligation is modified, supplemented, or nullified by an agreement under this section, the agreement is a defense to the obligation.

Official Comment

1.   The separate agreement might be a security agreement or mortgage or it might be an agreement that contradicts the terms of the instrument. For example, a person may be induced to sign an instrument under an agreement that the signer will not be liable on the instrument unless certain conditions are met. Suppose X requested credit from Creditor who is willing to give the credit only if an acceptable accommodation party will sign the note of X as co-maker. Y agrees to sign as co-maker on the condition that Creditor also obtain the signature of Z as co-maker. Creditor agrees and Y signs as co-maker with X. Creditor fails to obtain the signature of Z on the note. Under Sections 3–412 and 3–419(b), Y is obliged to pay the note, but Section 3–117 applies. In this case, the agreement modifies the terms of the note by stating a condition to the obligation of Y to pay the note. This case is essentially similar to a case in which a maker of a note is induced to sign the note by fraud of the holder. Although the agreement that Y not be liable on the note unless Z also signs may not have been fraudulently made, a subsequent attempt by Creditor to require Y to pay the note in violation of the agreement is a bad faith act. Section 3–117, in treating the agreement as a defense, allows Y to assert the agreement against Creditor, but the defense would not be good against a subsequent holder in due course of the note that took it without notice of the agreement. If there cannot be a holder in due course because of Section 3–106(d), a subsequent holder that took the note in good faith, for value and without knowledge of the agreement would not be able to enforce the liability of Y. This result is consistent with the risk that a holder not in due course takes with respect to fraud in inducing issuance of an instrument.

2.   The effect of merger or integration clauses to the effect that a writing is intended to be the complete and exclusive statement of the terms of the agreement or that the agreement is not subject to conditions is left to the supplementary law of the jurisdiction pursuant to Section 1–103. Thus, in the case discussed in Comment 1, whether Y is permitted to prove the condition to Y's obligation to pay the note is determined by that law. Moreover, nothing in this section is intended to validate an agreement which is fraudulent or void as against public policy, as in the case of a note given to deceive a bank examiner.

§ 3–118.   Statute of Limitations.

(a)   Except as provided in subsection (e), an action to enforce the obligation of a party to pay a note payable at a definite time must be commenced within six years after the due date or dates stated in the note or, if a due date is accelerated, within six years after the accelerated due date.

(b)   Except as provided in subsection (d) or (e), if demand for payment is made to the maker of a note payable on demand, an action to enforce the obligation of a party to pay the note must be commenced within six years after the demand. If no demand for payment is made to the maker, an action to enforce the note is barred if neither principal nor interest on the note has been paid for a continuous period of 10 years.

(c)   Except as provided in subsection (d), an action to enforce the obligation of a party to an unaccepted draft to pay the draft must be commenced within three years after dishonor of the draft or 10 years after the date of the draft, whichever period expires first.

(d)   An action to enforce the obligation of the acceptor of a certified check or the issuer of a teller's check, cashier's check, or traveler's check must be commenced within three years after demand for payment is made to the acceptor or issuer, as the case may be.

(e)   An action to enforce the obligation of a party to a certificate of deposit to pay the instrument must be commenced within six years after demand for payment is made to the maker, but if the instrument states a due date and the maker is not required to pay before that date, the six-year period begins when a demand for payment is in effect and the due date has passed.

(f)   An action to enforce the obligation of a party to pay an accepted draft, other than a certified check, must be commenced (i) within six years after the due date or dates stated in the draft or acceptance if the obligation of the acceptor is payable at a definite time, or (ii) within six years after the date of the acceptance if the obligation of the acceptor is payable on demand.

(g)   Unless governed by other law regarding claims for indemnity or contribution, an action (i) for conversion of an instrument, for money had and received, or like action based on conversion, (ii) for breach of warranty, or (iii) to enforce an obligation, duty, or right arising under this Article and not governed by this section must be commenced within three years after the [cause of action] accrues.

Official Comment

1.   Section 3–118 differs from former Section 3–122, which states when a cause of action accrues on an instrument. Section 3–118 does not define when a cause of action accrues. Accrual of a cause of action is stated in other sections of Article 3 such as those that state the various obligations of parties to an instrument. The only purpose of Section 3–118 is to define the time within which an action to enforce an obligation, duty, or right arising under Article 3 must be commenced. Section 3–118 does not attempt to state all rules with respect to a statute of limitations. For example, the circumstances under which the running of a limitations period may be tolled is left to other law pursuant to Section 1–103.

2.   The first six subsections apply to actions to enforce an obligation of any party to an instrument to pay the instrument. This changes present law in that indorsers who may become liable on an instrument after issue are subject to a period of limitations running from the same date as that of the maker or drawer. Subsections (a) and (b) apply to notes. If the note is payable at a definite time, a six-year limitations period starts at the due date of the note, subject to prior acceleration. If the note is payable on demand, there are two limitations periods. Although a note payable on demand could theoretically be called a day after it was issued, the normal expectation of the parties is that the note will remain outstanding until there is some reason to call it. If the law provides that the limitations period does not start until demand is made, the cause of action to enforce it may never be barred. On the other hand, if the limitations period starts when demand for payment may be made, i.e. at any time after the note was issued, the payee of a note on which interest or portions of principal are being paid could lose the right to enforce the note even though it was treated as a continuing obligation by the parties. Some demand notes are not enforced because the payee has forgiven the debt. This is particularly true in family and other noncommercial transactions. A demand note found after the death of the payee may be presented for payment many years after it was issued. The maker may be a relative and it may be difficult to determine whether the note represents a real or a forgiven debt. Subsection (b) is designed to bar notes that no longer represent a claim to payment and to require reasonably prompt action to enforce notes on which there is default. If a demand for payment is made to the maker, a six-year limitations period starts to run when demand is made. The second sentence of subsection (b) bars an action to enforce a demand note if no demand has been made on the note and no payment of interest or principal has been made for a continuous period of 10 years. This covers the case of a note that does not bear interest or a case in which interest due on the note has not been paid. This kind of case is likely to be a family transaction in which a failure to demand payment may indicate that the holder did not intend to enforce the obligation but neglected to destroy the note. A limitations period that bars stale claims in this kind of case is appropriate if the period is relatively long.

3.   Subsection (c) applies primarily to personal uncertified checks. Checks are payment instruments rather than credit instruments. The limitations period expires three years after the date of dishonor or 10 years after the date of the check, whichever is earlier. Teller's checks, cashier's checks, certified checks, and traveler's checks are treated differently under subsection (d) because they are commonly treated as cash equivalents. A great delay in

presenting a cashier's check for payment in most cases will occur because the check was mislaid during that period. The person to whom traveler's checks are issued may hold them indefinitely as a safe form of cash for use in an emergency. There is no compelling reason for barring the claim of the owner of the cashier's check or traveler's check. Under subsection (d) the claim is never barred because the three-year limitations period does not start to run until demand for payment is made. The limitations period in subsection (d) in effect applies only to cases in which there is a dispute about the legitimacy of the claim of the person demanding payment.

4.   Subsection (e) covers certificates of deposit. The limitations period of six years doesn't start to run until the depositor demands payment. Most certificates of deposit are payable on demand even if they state a due date. The effect of a demand for payment before maturity is usually that the bank will pay, but that a penalty will be assessed against the depositor in the form of a reduction in the amount of interest that is paid. Subsection (e) also provides for cases in which the bank has no obligation to pay until the due date. In that case the limitations period doesn't start to run until there is a demand for payment in effect and the due date has passed.

5.   Subsection (f) applies to accepted drafts other than certified checks. When a draft is accepted it is in effect turned into a note of the acceptor. In almost all cases the acceptor will agree to pay at a definite time. Subsection (f) states that in that case the six-year limitations period starts to run on the due date. In the rare case in which the obligation of the acceptor is payable on demand, the six-year limitations period starts to run at the date of the acceptance.

6.   Subsection (g) covers warranty and conversion cases and other actions to enforce obligations or rights arising under Article 3. A three-year period is stated and subsection (g) follows general law in stating that the period runs from the time the cause of action accrues. Since the traditional term "cause of action" may have been replaced in some states by "claim for relief" or some equivalent term, the words "cause of action" have been bracketed to indicate that the words may be replaced by an appropriate substitute to conform to local practice.

7.   One of the most significant differences between this Article and the Convention on International Bills of Exchange and International Promissory Notes is that the statute of limitation under the Convention generally is only four years, rather than the six years provided by this section. See Convention Article 84.

As amended in 2002.

§ 3–119.   Notice of Right to Defend Action.

In an action for breach of an obligation for which a third person is answerable over pursuant to this Article or Article 4, the defendant may give the third person notice of the litigation in a record, and the person notified may then give similar notice to any other person who is answerable over. If the notice states (i) that the person notified may come in and defend and (ii) that failure to do so will bind the person notified in an action later brought by the person giving the notice as to any determination of fact common to the two litigations, the person notified is so bound unless after seasonable receipt of the notice the person notified does come in and defend.

As amended in 2002.

Official Comment

This section is a restatement of former Section 3–803.

PART 2

NEGOTIATION, TRANSFER, AND INDORSEMENT

§ 3–201.   Negotiation.

(a)   "Negotiation" means a transfer of possession, whether voluntary or involuntary, of an instrument by a person other than the issuer to a person who thereby becomes its holder.

(b)   Except for negotiation by a remitter, if an instrument is payable to an identified person, negotiation requires transfer of possession of the instrument and its indorsement by the holder. If an instrument is payable to bearer, it may be negotiated by transfer of possession alone.

Official Comment

1.   Subsections (a) and (b) are based in part on subsection (1) of former Section 3–202. A person can become holder of an instrument when the instrument is issued to that person, or the status of holder can arise as the result of an event that occurs after issuance. "Negotiation" is the term used in Article 3 to describe this post-issuance event. Normally, negotiation occurs as the result of a voluntary transfer of possession of an instrument by a holder to another person who becomes the holder as a result of the transfer. Negotiation always requires a change in possession of the instrument because nobody can be a holder without possessing the instrument, either directly or through an agent. But in some cases the transfer of possession is involuntary and in some cases the person transferring possession is not a holder. In defining "negotiation" former Section 3–202(1) used the word "transfer," an undefined term, and "delivery," defined in Section 1–201(14)* to mean voluntary change of possession. Instead, subsections (a) and (b) use the term "transfer of possession" and, subsection (a) states that negotiation can occur by an involuntary transfer of possession. For example, if an instrument is payable to bearer and it is stolen by Thief or is found by Finder, Thief or Finder becomes the holder of the instrument when possession is obtained. In this case there is an involuntary transfer of possession that results in negotiation to Thief or Finder.

2.   In most cases negotiation occurs by a transfer of possession by a holder or remitter. Remitter transactions usually involve a cashier's or teller's check. For example, Buyer buys goods from Seller and pays for them with a cashier's check of Bank that Buyer buys from Bank. The check is issued by Bank when it is delivered to Buyer, regardless of whether the check is payable to Buyer or to Seller. Section 3–105(a). If the check is payable to Buyer, negotiation to Seller is done by delivery of the check to Seller after it is indorsed by Buyer. It is more common, however, that the check when issued will be payable to Seller. In that case Buyer is referred to as the "remitter." Section 3–103(a)(15). The remitter, although not a party to the check, is the owner of the check until ownership is transferred to Seller by delivery. This transfer is a negotiation because Seller becomes the holder of the check when Seller obtains possession. In some cases Seller may have acted fraudulently in obtaining possession of the check. In those cases Buyer may be entitled to rescind the transfer to Seller because of the fraud and assert a claim of ownership to the check under Section 3–306 against Seller or a subsequent transferee of the check. Section 3–202(b) provides for rescission of negotiation, and that provision applies to rescission by a remitter as well as by a holder.

3.   Other sections of Article 3 may modify the rule stated in the first sentence of subsection (b). See for example, Sections 3–404, 3–405 and 3–406.

§ 3–202.   Negotiation Subject to Rescission.

(a)   Negotiation is effective even if obtained (i) from an infant, a corporation exceeding its powers, or a person without capacity, (ii) by fraud, duress, or mistake, or (iii) in breach of duty or as part of an illegal transaction.

(b)   To the extent permitted by other law, negotiation may be rescinded or may be subject to other remedies, but those remedies may not be asserted against a subsequent holder in due course or a person paying the instrument in good faith and without knowledge of facts that are a basis for rescission or other remedy.

Official Comment

1.   This section is based on former Section 3–207. Subsection (2) of former Section 3–207 prohibited rescission of a negotiation against holders in due course. Subsection (b) of Section 3–202 extends this protection to payor banks.

2.   Subsection (a) applies even though the lack of capacity or the illegality, is of a character which goes to the essence of the transaction and makes it entirely void. It is inherent in the character of negotiable instruments that any person in possession of an instrument which by its terms is payable to that person or to bearer is a holder and may be dealt with by anyone as a holder. The principle finds its most extreme application in the well settled rule that a holder in due course may take the instrument even from a thief and be protected against the claim of the rightful owner. The policy of subsection (a) is that any person to whom an instrument is negotiated is a holder until the instrument has been recovered from that person's possession. The remedy of a person with a claim to an instrument is to recover the instrument by replevin or otherwise; to impound it or to enjoin its enforcement,

_____

*   *Referring to unrevised Article 1 (Appendix A).*

collection or negotiation; to recover its proceeds from the holder; or to intervene in any action brought by the holder against the obligor. As provided in Section 3–305(c), the claim of the claimant is not a defense to the obligor unless the claimant defends the action.

3. There can be no rescission or other remedy against a holder in due course or a person who pays in good faith and without notice, even though the prior negotiation may have been fraudulent or illegal in its essence and entirely void. As against any other party the claimant may have any remedy permitted by law. This section is not intended to specify what that remedy may be, or to prevent any court from imposing conditions or limitations such as prompt action or return of the consideration received. All such questions are left to the law of the particular jurisdiction. Section 3–202 gives no right that would not otherwise exist. The section is intended to mean that any remedies afforded by other law are cut off only by a holder in due course.

§ 3–203. Transfer of Instrument; Rights Acquired by Transfer.

(a) An instrument is transferred when it is delivered by a person other than its issuer for the purpose of giving to the person receiving delivery the right to enforce the instrument.

(b) Transfer of an instrument, whether or not the transfer is a negotiation, vests in the transferee any right of the transferor to enforce the instrument, including any right as a holder in due course, but the transferee cannot acquire rights of a holder in due course by a transfer, directly or indirectly, from a holder in due course if the transferee engaged in fraud or illegality affecting the instrument.

(c) Unless otherwise agreed, if an instrument is transferred for value and the transferee does not become a holder because of lack of indorsement by the transferor, the transferee has a specifically enforceable right to the unqualified indorsement of the transferor, but negotiation of the instrument does not occur until the indorsement is made.

(d) If a transferor purports to transfer less than the entire instrument, negotiation of the instrument does not occur. The transferee obtains no rights under this Article and has only the rights of a partial assignee.

Official Comment

1. Section 3–203 is based on former Section 3–201 which stated that a transferee received such rights as the transferor had. The former section was confusing because some rights of the transferor are not vested in the transferee unless the transfer is a negotiation. For example, a transferee that did not become the holder could not negotiate the instrument, a right that the transferor had. Former Section 3–201 did not define "transfer." Subsection (a) defines transfer by limiting it to cases in which possession of the instrument is delivered for the purpose of giving to the person receiving delivery the right to enforce the instrument.

Although transfer of an instrument might mean in a particular case that title to the instrument passes to the transferee, that result does not follow in all cases. The right to enforce an instrument and ownership of the instrument are two different concepts. A thief who steals a check payable to bearer becomes the holder of the check and a person entitled to enforce it, but does not become the owner of the check. If the thief transfers the check to a purchaser the transferee obtains the right to enforce the check. If the purchaser is not a holder in due course, the owner's claim to the check may be asserted against the purchaser. Ownership rights in instruments may be determined by principles of the law of property, independent of Article 3, which do not depend upon whether the instrument was transferred under Section 3–203. Moreover, a person who has an ownership right in an instrument might not be a person entitled to enforce the instrument. For example, suppose X is the owner and holder of an instrument payable to X. X sells the instrument to Y but is unable to deliver immediate possession to Y. Instead, X signs a document conveying all of X's right, title, and interest in the instrument to Y. Although the document may be effective to give Y a claim to ownership of the instrument, Y is not a person entitled to enforce the instrument until Y obtains possession of the instrument. No transfer of the instrument occurs under Section 3–203(a) until it is delivered to Y.

An instrument is a reified right to payment. The right is represented by the instrument itself. The right to payment is transferred by delivery of possession of the instrument "by a person other than its issuer for the purpose of giving to the person receiving delivery the right to enforce the instrument." The quoted phrase excludes issue of an instrument, defined in Section 3–105, and cases in which a delivery of possession is for some purpose other than transfer of the right to enforce. For example, if a check is presented for payment by delivering the check to the drawee, no transfer of the check to the drawee occurs because there is no intent to give the drawee the right to enforce the check.

2.   Subsection (b) states that transfer vests in the transferee any right of the transferor to enforce the instrument "including any right as a holder in due course." If the transferee is not a holder because the transferor did not indorse, the transferee is nevertheless a person entitled to enforce the instrument under Section 3–301 if the transferor was a holder at the time of transfer. Although the transferee is not a holder, under subsection (b) the transferee obtained the rights of the transferor as holder. Because the transferee's rights are derivative of the transferor's rights, those rights must be proved. Because the transferee is not a holder, there is no presumption under Section 3–308 that the transferee, by producing the instrument, is entitled to payment. The instrument, by its terms, is not payable to the transferee and the transferee must account for possession of the unindorsed instrument by proving the transaction through which the transferee acquired it. Proof of a transfer to the transferee by a holder is proof that the transferee has acquired the rights of a holder. At that point the transferee is entitled to the presumption under Section 3–308.

Under subsection (b) a holder in due course that transfers an instrument transfers those rights as a holder in due course to the purchaser. The policy is to assure the holder in due course a free market for the instrument. There is one exception to this rule stated in the concluding clause of subsection (b). A person who is party to fraud or illegality affecting the instrument is not permitted to wash the instrument clean by passing it into the hands of a holder in due course and then repurchasing it.

3.   Subsection (c) applies only to a transfer for value. It applies only if the instrument is payable to order or specially indorsed to the transferor. The transferee acquires, in the absence of a contrary agreement, the specifically enforceable right to the indorsement of the transferor. Unless otherwise agreed, it is a right to the general indorsement of the transferor with full liability as indorser, rather than to an indorsement without recourse. The question may arise if the transferee has paid in advance and the indorsement is omitted fraudulently or through oversight. A transferor who is willing to indorse only without recourse or unwilling to indorse at all should make those intentions clear before transfer. The agreement of the transferee to take less than an unqualified indorsement need not be an express one, and the understanding may be implied from conduct, from past practice, or from the circumstances of the transaction. Subsection (c) provides that there is no negotiation of the instrument until the indorsement by the transferor is made. Until that time the transferee does not become a holder, and if earlier notice of a defense or claim is received, the transferee does not qualify as a holder in due course under Section 3–302.

4.   The operation of Section 3–203 is illustrated by the following cases. In each case Payee, by fraud, induced Maker to issue a note to Payee. The fraud is a defense to the obligation of Maker to pay the note under Section 3–305(a)(2).

Case # 1. Payee negotiated the note to X who took as a holder in due course. After the instrument became overdue X negotiated the note to Y who had notice of the fraud. Y succeeds to X's rights as a holder in due course and takes free of Maker's defense of fraud.

Case # 2. Payee negotiated the note to X who took as a holder in due course. Payee then repurchased the note from X. Payee does not succeed to X's rights as a holder in due course and is subject to Maker's defense of fraud.

Case # 3. Payee negotiated the note to X who took as a holder in due course. X sold the note to Purchaser who received possession. The note, however, was indorsed to X and X failed to indorse it. Purchaser is a person entitled to enforce the instrument under Section 3–301 and succeeds to the rights of X as holder in due course. Purchaser is not a holder, however, and under Section 3–308 Purchaser will have to prove the transaction with X under which the rights of X as holder in due course were acquired.

Case # 4. Payee sold the note to Purchaser who took for value, in good faith and without notice of the defense of Maker. Purchaser received possession of the note but Payee neglected to indorse it. Purchaser became a person entitled to enforce the instrument but did not become the holder because of the missing indorsement. If Purchaser received notice of the defense of Maker before obtaining the indorsement of Payee, Purchaser cannot become a holder in due course because at the time notice was received the note had not been negotiated to Purchaser. If indorsement by Payee was made after Purchaser received notice, Purchaser had notice of the defense when it became the holder.

5.   Subsection (d) restates former Section 3–202(3). The cause of action on an instrument cannot be split. Any indorsement which purports to convey to any party less than the entire amount of the instrument is not

effective for negotiation. This is true of either "Pay A one-half," or "Pay A two-thirds and B one-third." Neither A nor B becomes a holder. On the other hand an indorsement reading merely "Pay A and B" is effective, since it transfers the entire cause of action to A and B as tenants in common. An indorsement purporting to convey less than the entire instrument does, however, operate as a partial assignment of the cause of action. Subsection (d) makes no attempt to state the legal effect of such an assignment, which is left to other law. A partial assignee of an instrument has rights only to the extent the applicable law gives rights, either at law or in equity, to a partial assignee.

6.   The rules for transferring instruments set out in this section are similar to the rules in Article 13 of the Convention on International Bills of Exchange and International Promissory Notes.

As amended in 2002.

§ 3–204.   Indorsement.

(a)   "Indorsement" means a signature, other than that of a signer as maker, drawer, or acceptor, that alone or accompanied by other words is made on an instrument for the purpose of (i) negotiating the instrument, (ii) restricting payment of the instrument, or (iii) incurring indorser's liability on the instrument, but regardless of the intent of the signer, a signature and its accompanying words is an indorsement unless the accompanying words, terms of the instrument, place of the signature, or other circumstances unambiguously indicate that the signature was made for a purpose other than indorsement. For the purpose of determining whether a signature is made on an instrument, a paper affixed to the instrument is a part of the instrument.

(b)   "Indorser" means a person who makes an indorsement.

(c)   For the purpose of determining whether the transferee of an instrument is a holder, an indorsement that transfers a security interest in the instrument is effective as an unqualified indorsement of the instrument.

(d)   If an instrument is payable to a holder under a name that is not the name of the holder, indorsement may be made by the holder in the name stated in the instrument or in the holder's name or both, but signature in both names may be required by a person paying or taking the instrument for value or collection.

Official Comment

1.   Subsection (a) is a definition of "indorsement," a term which was not defined in former Article 3. Indorsement is defined in terms of the purpose of the signature. If a blank or special indorsement is made to give rights as a holder to a transferee the indorsement is made for the purpose of negotiating the instrument. Subsection (a)(i). If the holder of a check has an account in the drawee bank and wants to be sure that payment of the check will be made by credit to the holder's account, the holder can indorse the check by signing the holder's name with the accompanying words "for deposit only" before presenting the check for payment to the drawee bank. In that case the purpose of the quoted words is to restrict payment of the instrument. Subsection (a)(ii). If X wants to guarantee payment of a note signed by Y as maker, X can do so by signing X's name to the back of the note as an indorsement. This indorsement is known as an anomalous indorsement (Section 3–205(d)) and is made for the purpose of incurring indorser's liability on the note. Subsection (a)(iii). In some cases an indorsement may serve more than one purpose. For example, if the holder of a check deposits it to the holder's account in a depositary bank for collection and indorses the check by signing the holder's name with the accompanying words "for deposit only" the purpose of the indorsement is both to negotiate the check to the depositary bank and to restrict payment of the check.

The "but" clause of the first sentence of subsection (a) elaborates on former Section 3–402. In some cases it may not be clear whether a signature was meant to be that of an indorser, a party to the instrument in some other capacity such as drawer, maker or acceptor, or a person who was not signing as a party. The general rule is that a signature is an indorsement if the instrument does not indicate an unambiguous intent of the signer not to sign as an indorser. Intent may be determined by words accompanying the signature, the place of signature, or other circumstances. For example, suppose a depositary bank gives cash for a check properly indorsed by the payee. The bank requires the payee's employee to sign the back of the check as evidence that the employee received the cash. If the signature consists only of the initials of the employee it is not reasonable to assume that it was meant to be an indorsement. If there was a full signature but accompanying words indicated that it was meant as a receipt for the cash given for the check, it is not an indorsement. If the signature is not qualified in any way and appears in the place normally used for indorsements, it may be an indorsement even though the signer intended the signature to be a receipt. To take another example, suppose the drawee of a draft signs the draft on the back in the space usually used for indorsements. No words accompany the signature. Since the drawee has no reason to sign a draft unless the intent is to accept the draft, the signature is effective as an acceptance. Custom and usage may be used to determine intent. For example, by long-established custom and usage, a signature in the lower right hand corner of an instrument indicates an intent to sign as the maker of a note or the drawer of a draft. Any similar clear indication of an intent to sign in some other capacity or for some other purpose may establish that a signature is not an indorsement. For example, if the owner of a traveler's check countersigns the check in the process of negotiating it, the countersignature is not an indorsement. The countersignature is a condition to the issuer's obligation to pay and its purpose is to provide a means of verifying the identify of the person negotiating the traveler's check by allowing comparison of the specimen signature and the countersignature. The countersignature is not necessary for negotiation and the signer does not incur indorser's liability. See Comment 2 to Section 3–106.

The last sentence of subsection (a) is based on subsection (2) of former Section 3–202. An indorsement on an allonge is valid even though there is sufficient space on the instrument for an indorsement.

2.   Assume that Payee indorses a note to Creditor as security for a debt. Under subsection (b) of Section 3–203 Creditor takes Payee's rights to enforce or transfer the instrument subject to the limitations imposed by Article 9. Subsection (c) of Section 3–204 makes clear that Payee's indorsement to Creditor, even though it mentions creation of a security interest, is an unqualified indorsement that gives to Creditor the right to enforce the note as its holder.

3.   Subsection (d) is a restatement of former Section 3–203. Section 3–110(a) states that an instrument is payable to the person intended by the person signing as or in the name or behalf of the issuer even if that person is identified by a name that is not the true name of the person. In some cases the name used in the instrument is a misspelling of the correct name and in some cases the two names may be entirely different. The payee may indorse in the name used in the instrument, in the payee's correct name, or in both. In each case the indorsement is effective. But because an indorsement in a name different from that used in the instrument may raise a question about its validity and an indorsement in a name that is not the correct name of the payee may raise a problem of identifying the indorser, the accepted commercial practice is to indorse in both names. Subsection (d) allows a person paying or taking the instrument for value or collection to require indorsement in both names.

§ 3–205.   Special Indorsement; Blank Indorsement; Anomalous Indorsement.

(a)   If an indorsement is made by the holder of an instrument, whether payable to an identified person or payable to bearer, and the indorsement identifies a person to whom it makes the instrument payable, it is a "special indorsement." When specially indorsed, an instrument becomes payable to the identified person and may be negotiated only by the indorsement of that person. The principles stated in Section 3–110 apply to special indorsements.

(b)   If an indorsement is made by the holder of an instrument and it is not a special indorsement, it is a "blank indorsement." When indorsed in blank, an instrument becomes payable to bearer and may be negotiated by transfer of possession alone until specially indorsed.

(c)   The holder may convert a blank indorsement that consists only of a signature into a special indorsement by writing, above the signature of the indorser, words identifying the person to whom the instrument is made payable.

(d)   "Anomalous indorsement" means an indorsement made by a person who is not the holder of the instrument. An anomalous indorsement does not affect the manner in which the instrument may be negotiated.

Official Comment

1.   Subsection (a) is based on subsection (1) of former Section 3–204. It states the test of a special indorsement to be whether the indorsement identifies a person to whom the instrument is payable. Section 3–110 states rules for identifying the payee of an instrument. Section 3–205(a) incorporates the principles stated in Section 3–110 in identifying an indorsee. The language of Section 3–110 refers to language used by the issuer of the instrument. When that section is used with respect to an indorsement, Section 3–110 must be read as referring to the language used by the indorser.

2. Subsection (b) is based on subsection (2) of former Section 3–204. An indorsement made by the holder is either a special or blank indorsement. If the indorsement is made by a holder and is not a special indorsement, it is a blank indorsement. For example, the holder of an instrument, intending to make a special indorsement, writes the words "Pay to the order of" without completing the indorsement by writing the name of the indorsee. The holder's signature appears under the quoted words. The indorsement is not a special indorsement because it does not identify a person to whom it makes the instrument payable. Since it is not a special indorsement it is a blank indorsement and the instrument is payable to bearer. The result is analogous to that of a check in which the name of the payee is left blank by the drawer. In that case the check is payable to bearer. See the last paragraphs of Comment 2 to Section 3–115.

A blank indorsement is usually the signature of the indorser on the back of the instrument without other words. Subsection (c) is based on subsection (3) of former Section 3–204. A "restrictive indorsement" described in Section 3–206 can be either a blank indorsement or a special indorsement. "Pay to T, in trust for B" is a restrictive indorsement. It is also a special indorsement because it identifies T as the person to whom the instrument is payable. "For deposit only" followed by the signature of the payee of a check is a restrictive indorsement. It is also a blank indorsement because it does not identify the person to whom the instrument is payable.

3. The only effect of an "anomalous indorsement," defined in subsection (d), is to make the signer liable on the instrument as an indorser. Such an indorsement is normally made by an accommodation party. Section 3–419.

4. Articles 14 and 16 of the Convention on International Bills of Exchange and International Promissory Notes includes similar rules for blank and special indorsements.

As amended in 2002.

§ 3–206.   Restrictive Indorsement.

(a) An indorsement limiting payment to a particular person or otherwise prohibiting further transfer or negotiation of the instrument is not effective to prevent further transfer or negotiation of the instrument.

(b) An indorsement stating a condition to the right of the indorsee to receive payment does not affect the right of the indorsee to enforce the instrument. A person paying the instrument or taking it for value or collection may disregard the condition, and the rights and liabilities of that person are not affected by whether the condition has been fulfilled.

(c) If an instrument bears an indorsement (i) described in Section 4–201(b), or (ii) in blank or to a particular bank using the words "for deposit," "for collection," or other words indicating a purpose of having the instrument collected by a bank for the indorser or for a particular account, the following rules apply:

(1) A person, other than a bank, who purchases the instrument when so indorsed converts the instrument unless the amount paid for the instrument is received by the indorser or applied consistently with the indorsement.

(2) A depositary bank that purchases the instrument or takes it for collection when so indorsed converts the instrument unless the amount paid by the bank with respect to the instrument is received by the indorser or applied consistently with the indorsement.

(3) A payor bank that is also the depositary bank or that takes the instrument for immediate payment over the counter from a person other than a collecting bank converts the instrument unless the proceeds of the instrument are received by the indorser or applied consistently with the indorsement.

(4) Except as otherwise provided in paragraph (3), a payor bank or intermediary bank may disregard the indorsement and is not liable if the proceeds of the instrument are not received by the indorser or applied consistently with the indorsement.

(d) Except for an indorsement covered by subsection (c), if an instrument bears an indorsement using words to the effect that payment is to be made to the indorsee as agent, trustee, or other fiduciary for the benefit of the indorser or another person, the following rules apply:

(1) Unless there is notice of breach of fiduciary duty as provided in Section 3–307, a person who purchases the instrument from the indorsee or takes the instrument from the indorsee for

collection or payment may pay the proceeds of payment or the value given for the instrument to the indorsee without regard to whether the indorsee violates a fiduciary duty to the indorser.

(2)   A subsequent transferee of the instrument or person who pays the instrument is neither given notice nor otherwise affected by the restriction in the indorsement unless the transferee or payor knows that the fiduciary dealt with the instrument or its proceeds in breach of fiduciary duty.

(e)   The presence on an instrument of an indorsement to which this section applies does not prevent a purchaser of the instrument from becoming a holder in due course of the instrument unless the purchaser is a converter under subsection (c) or has notice or knowledge of breach of fiduciary duty as stated in subsection (d).

(f)   In an action to enforce the obligation of a party to pay the instrument, the obligor has a defense if payment would violate an indorsement to which this section applies and the payment is not permitted by this section.

Official Comment

1.   This section replaces former Sections 3–205 and 3–206 and clarifies the law of restrictive indorsements.

2.   Subsection (a) provides that an indorsement that purports to limit further transfer or negotiation is ineffective to prevent further transfer or negotiation. If a payee indorses "Pay A only," A may negotiate the instrument to subsequent holders who may ignore the restriction on the indorsement. Subsection (b) provides that an indorsement that states a condition to the right of a holder to receive payment is ineffective to condition payment. Thus if a payee indorses "Pay A if A ships goods complying with our contract," the right of A to enforce the instrument is not affected by the condition. In the case of a note, the obligation of the maker to pay A is not affected by the indorsement. In the case of a check, the drawee can pay A without regard to the condition, and if the check is dishonored the drawer is liable to pay A. If the check was negotiated by the payee to A in return for a promise to perform a contract and the promise was not kept, the payee would have a defense or counterclaim against A if the check were dishonored and A sued the payee as indorser, but the payee would have that defense or counterclaim whether or not the condition to the right of A was expressed in the indorsement. Former Section 3–206 treated a conditional indorsement like indorsements for deposit or collection. In revised Article 3, Section 3–206(b) rejects that approach and makes the conditional indorsement ineffective with respect to parties other than the indorser and indorsee. Since the indorsements referred to in subsections (a) and (b) are not effective as restrictive indorsements, they are no longer described as restrictive indorsements.

3.   The great majority of restrictive indorsements are those that fall within subsection (c) which continues previous law. The depositary bank or the payor bank, if it takes the check for immediate payment over the counter, must act consistently with the indorsement, but an intermediary bank or payor bank that takes the check from a collecting bank is not affected by the indorsement. Any other person is also bound by the indorsement. For example, suppose a check is payable to X, who indorses in blank but writes above the signature the words "For deposit only." The check is stolen and is cashed at a grocery store by the thief. The grocery store indorses the check and deposits it in Depositary Bank. The account of the grocery store is credited and the check is forwarded to Payor Bank which pays the check. Under subsection (c), the grocery store and Depositary Bank are converters of the check because X did not receive the amount paid for the check. Payor Bank and any intermediary bank in the collection process are not liable to X. This Article does not displace the law of waiver as it may apply to restrictive indorsements. The circumstances under which a restrictive indorsement may be waived by the person who made it is not determined by this Article.

4.   Subsection (d) replaces subsection (4) of former Section 3–206. Suppose Payee indorses a check "Pay to T in trust for B." T indorses in blank and delivers it to (a) Holder for value; (b) Depositary Bank for collection; or (c) Payor Bank for payment. In each case these takers can safely pay T so long as they have no notice under Section 3–307 of any breach of fiduciary duty that T may be committing. For example, under subsection (b)* of Section 3–307 these takers have notice of a breach of trust if the check was taken in any transaction known by the taker to be for T's personal benefit. Subsequent transferees of the check from Holder or Depositary Bank are not affected by the restriction unless they have knowledge that T dealt with the check in breach of trust.

5.   Subsection (f) allows a restrictive indorsement to be used as a defense by a person obliged to pay the instrument if that person would be liable for paying in violation of the indorsement.

---

*   Previous incorrect cross reference corrected by Permanent Editorial Board action November 1992.

§ 3–207. Reacquisition.

Reacquisition of an instrument occurs if it is transferred to a former holder, by negotiation or otherwise. A former holder who reacquires the instrument may cancel indorsements made after the reacquirer first became a holder of the instrument. If the cancellation causes the instrument to be payable to the reacquirer or to bearer, the reacquirer may negotiate the instrument. An indorser whose indorsement is canceled is discharged, and the discharge is effective against any subsequent holder.

Official Comment

Section 3–207 restates former Section 3–208. Reacquisition refers to cases in which a former holder reacquires the instrument either by negotiation from the present holder or by a transfer other than negotiation. If the reacquisition is by negotiation, the former holder reacquires the status of holder. Although Section 3–207 allows the holder to cancel all indorsements made after the holder first acquired holder status, cancellation is not necessary. Status of holder is not affected whether or not cancellation is made. But if the reacquisition is not the result of negotiation the former holder can obtain holder status only by striking the former holder's indorsement and any subsequent indorsements. The latter case is an exception to the general rule that if an instrument is payable to an identified person, the indorsement of that person is necessary to allow a subsequent transferee to obtain the status of holder. Reacquisition without indorsement by the person to whom the instrument is payable is illustrated by two examples:

Case # 1. X, a former holder, buys the instrument from Y, the present holder. Y delivers the instrument to X but fails to indorse it. Negotiation does not occur because the transfer of possession did not result in X's becoming holder. Section 3–201(a). The instrument by its terms is payable to Y, not to X. But X can obtain the status of holder by striking X's indorsement and all subsequent indorsements. When these indorsements are struck, the instrument by its terms is payable either to X or to bearer, depending upon how X originally became holder. In either case X becomes holder. Section 1–201(20).*

Case # 2. X, the holder of an instrument payable to X, negotiates it to Y by special indorsement. The negotiation is part of an underlying transaction between X and Y. The underlying transaction is rescinded by agreement of X and Y, and Y returns the instrument without Y's indorsement. The analysis is the same as that in Case # 1. X can obtain holder status by cancelling X's indorsement to Y.

In Case # 1 and Case # 2, X acquired ownership of the instrument after reacquisition, but X's title was clouded because the instrument by its terms was not payable to X. Normally, X can remedy the problem by obtaining Y's indorsement, but in some cases X may not be able to conveniently obtain that indorsement. Section 3–207 is a rule of convenience which relieves X of the burden of obtaining an indorsement that serves no substantive purpose. The effect of cancellation of any indorsement under Section 3–207 is to nullify it. Thus, the person whose indorsement is canceled is relieved of indorser's liability. Since cancellation is notice of discharge, discharge is effective even with respect to the rights of a holder in due course. Sections 3–601 and 3–604.

PART 3

ENFORCEMENT OF INSTRUMENTS

§ 3–301. Person Entitled to Enforce Instrument.

"Person entitled to enforce" an instrument means (i) the holder of the instrument, (ii) a nonholder in possession of the instrument who has the rights of a holder, or (iii) a person not in possession of the instrument who is entitled to enforce the instrument pursuant to Section 3–309 or 3–418(d). A person may be a person entitled to enforce the instrument even though the person is not the owner of the instrument or is in wrongful possession of the instrument.

Official Comment

This section replaces former Section 3–301 that stated the rights of a holder. The rights stated in former Section 3–301 to transfer, negotiate, enforce, or discharge an instrument are stated in other sections of Article 3. In revised Article 3, Section 3–301 defines "person entitled to enforce" an instrument. The definition recognizes that enforcement is not limited to holders. The quoted phrase includes a person enforcing a lost or stolen

---

* *Referring to unrevised Article 1 (Appendix A).*

instrument. Section 3–309. It also includes a person in possession of an instrument who is not a holder. A nonholder in possession of an instrument includes a person that acquired rights of a holder by subrogation or under Section 3–203(a). It also includes both a remitter that has received an instrument from the issuer but has not yet transferred or negotiated the instrument to another person and also any other person who under applicable law is a successor to the holder or otherwise acquires the holder's rights.

As amended in 2002.

§ 3–302.   Holder in Due Course.

(a)   Subject to subsection (c) and Section 3–106(d), "holder in due course" means the holder of an instrument if:

(1)   the instrument when issued or negotiated to the holder does not bear such apparent evidence of forgery or alteration or is not otherwise so irregular or incomplete as to call into question its authenticity; and

(2)   the holder took the instrument (i) for value, (ii) in good faith, (iii) without notice that the instrument is overdue or has been dishonored or that there is an uncured default with respect to payment of another instrument issued as part of the same series, (iv) without notice that the instrument contains an unauthorized signature or has been altered, (v) without notice of any claim to the instrument described in Section 3–306, and (vi) without notice that any party has a defense or claim in recoupment described in Section 3–305(a).

(b)   Notice of discharge of a party, other than discharge in an insolvency proceeding, is not notice of a defense under subsection (a), but discharge is effective against a person who became a holder in due course with notice of the discharge. Public filing or recording of a document does not of itself constitute notice of a defense, claim in recoupment, or claim to the instrument.

(c)   Except to the extent a transferor or predecessor in interest has rights as a holder in due course, a person does not acquire rights of a holder in due course of an instrument taken (i) by legal process or by purchase in an execution, bankruptcy, or creditor's sale or similar proceeding, (ii) by purchase as part of a bulk transaction not in ordinary course of business of the transferor, or (iii) as the successor in interest to an estate or other organization.

(d)   If, under Section 3–303(a)(1), the promise of performance that is the consideration for an instrument has been partially performed, the holder may assert rights as a holder in due course of the instrument only to the fraction of the amount payable under the instrument equal to the value of the partial performance divided by the value of the promised performance.

(e)   If (i) the person entitled to enforce an instrument has only a security interest in the instrument and (ii) the person obliged to pay the instrument has a defense, claim in recoupment, or claim to the instrument that may be asserted against the person who granted the security interest, the person entitled to enforce the instrument may assert rights as a holder in due course only to an amount payable under the instrument which, at the time of enforcement of the instrument, does not exceed the amount of the unpaid obligation secured.

(f)   To be effective, notice must be received at a time and in a manner that gives a reasonable opportunity to act on it.

(g)   This section is subject to any law limiting status as a holder in due course in particular classes of transactions.

Official Comment

1.   Subsection (a)(1) is a return to the N.I.L. rule that the taker of an irregular or incomplete instrument is not a person the law should protect against defenses of the obligor or claims of prior owners. This reflects a policy choice against extending the holder in due course doctrine to an instrument that is so incomplete or irregular "as to call into question its authenticity." The term "authenticity" is used to make it clear that the irregularity or incompleteness must indicate that the instrument may not be what it purports to be. Persons who purchase or pay such instruments should do so at their own risk. Under subsection (1) of former Section 3–304, irregularity or incompleteness gave a purchaser notice of a claim or defense. But it was not clear from that provision whether the

claim or defense had to be related to the irregularity or incomplete aspect of the instrument. This ambiguity is not present in subsection (a)(1).

2.   Subsection (a)(2) restates subsection (1) of former Section 3–302. Section 3–305(a) makes a distinction between defenses to the obligation to pay an instrument and claims in recoupment by the maker or drawer that may be asserted to reduce the amount payable on the instrument. Because of this distinction, which was not made in former Article 3, the reference in subsection (a)(2)(vi) is to both a defense and a claim in recoupment. Notice of forgery or alteration is stated separately because forgery and alteration are not technically defenses under subsection (a) of Section 3–305.

3.   Discharge is also separately treated in the first sentence of subsection (b). Except for discharge in an insolvency proceeding, which is specifically stated to be a real defense in Section 3–305(a)(1), discharge is not expressed in Article 3 as a defense and is not included in Section 3–305(a)(2). Discharge is effective against anybody except a person having rights of a holder in due course who took the instrument without notice of the discharge. Notice of discharge does not disqualify a person from becoming a holder in due course. For example, a check certified after it is negotiated by the payee may subsequently be negotiated to a holder. If the holder had notice that the certification occurred after negotiation by the payee, the holder necessarily had notice of the discharge of the payee as indorser. Section 3–415(d). Notice of that discharge does not prevent the holder from becoming a holder in due course, but the discharge is effective against the holder. Section 3–601(b). Notice of a defense under Section 3–305(a)(1) of a maker, drawer or acceptor based on a bankruptcy discharge is different. There is no reason to give holder in due course status to a person with notice of that defense. The second sentence of subsection (b) is from former Section 3–304(5).

4.   Professor Britton in his treatise *Bills and Notes* 309 (1961) stated: "A substantial number of decisions before the [N.I.L.] indicates that at common law there was nothing in the position of the payee as such which made it impossible for him to be a holder in due course." The courts were divided, however, about whether the payee of an instrument could be a holder in due course under the N.I.L. Some courts read N.I.L. § 52(4) to mean that a person could be a holder in due course only if the instrument was "negotiated" to that person. N.I.L. § 30 stated that "an instrument is negotiated when it is transferred from one person to another in such manner as to constitute the transferee the holder thereof." Normally, an instrument is "issued" to the payee; it is not transferred to the payee. N.I.L. § 191 defined "issue" as the "first delivery of the instrument * * * to a person who takes it as a holder." Thus, some courts concluded that the payee never could be a holder in due course. Other courts concluded that there was no evidence that the N.I.L. was intended to change the common law rule that the payee could be a holder in due course. Professor Britton states on p. 318: "The typical situations which raise the [issue] are those where the defense of a maker is interposed because of fraud by a [maker who is] principal debtor * * * against a surety co-maker, or where the defense of fraud by a purchasing remitter is interposed by the drawer of the instrument against the good faith purchasing payee."

Former Section 3–302(2) stated: "A payee may be a holder in due course." This provision was intended to resolve the split of authority under the N.I.L. It made clear that there was no intent to change the common-law rule that allowed a payee to become a holder in due course. See Comment 2 to former Section 3–302. But there was no need to put subsection (2) in former Section 3–302 because the split in authority under the N.I.L. was caused by the particular wording of N.I.L. § 52(4). The troublesome language in that section was not repeated in former Article 3 nor is it repeated in revised Article 3. Former Section 3–302(2) has been omitted in revised Article 3 because it is surplusage and may be misleading. The payee of an instrument can be a holder in due course, but use of the holder-in-due-course doctrine by the payee of an instrument is not the normal situation.

The primary importance of the concept of holder in due course is with respect to assertion of defenses or claims in recoupment (Section 3–305) and of claims to the instrument (Section 3–306). The holder-in-due-course doctrine assumes the following case as typical. Obligor issues a note or check to Obligee. Obligor is the maker of the note or drawer of the check. Obligee is the payee. Obligor has some defense to Obligor's obligation to pay the instrument. For example, Obligor issued the instrument for goods that Obligee promised to deliver. Obligee never delivered the goods. The failure of Obligee to deliver the goods is a defense. Section 3–303(b). Although Obligor has a defense against Obligee, if the instrument is negotiated to Holder and the requirements of subsection (a) are met, Holder may enforce the instrument against Obligor free of the defense. Section 3–305(b). In the typical case the holder in due course is not the payee of the instrument. Rather, the holder in due course is an immediate or remote transferee of the payee. If Obligor in our example is the only obligor on the check or note, the holder-in-due-course doctrine is irrelevant in determining rights between Obligor and Obligee with respect to the instrument.

But in a small percentage of cases it is appropriate to allow the payee of an instrument to assert rights as a holder in due course. The cases are like those referred to in the quotation from Professor Britton referred to above, or other cases in which conduct of some third party is the basis of the defense of the issuer of the instrument. The following are examples:

Case # 1. Buyer pays for goods bought from Seller by giving to Seller a cashier's check bought from Bank. Bank has a defense to its obligation to pay the check because Buyer bought the check from Bank with a check known to be drawn on an account with insufficient funds to cover the check. If Bank issued the check to Buyer as payee and Buyer indorsed it over to Seller, it is clear that Seller can be a holder in due course taking free of the defense if Seller had no notice of the defense. Seller is a transferee of the check. There is no good reason why Seller's position should be any different if Bank drew the check to the order of Seller as payee. In that case, when Buyer took delivery of the check from Bank, Buyer became the owner of the check even though Buyer was not the holder. Buyer was a remitter. Section 3–103(a)(15). At that point nobody was the holder. When Buyer delivered the check to Seller, ownership of the check was transferred to Seller who also became the holder. This is a negotiation. Section 3–201. The rights of Seller should not be affected by the fact that in one case the negotiation to Seller was by a holder and in the other case the negotiation was by a remitter. Moreover, it should be irrelevant whether Bank delivered the check to Buyer and Buyer delivered it to Seller or whether Bank delivered it directly to Seller. In either case Seller can be a holder in due course that takes free of Bank's defense.

Case # 2. X fraudulently induces Y to join X in a spurious venture to purchase a business. The purchase is to be financed by a bank loan for part of the price. Bank lends money to X and Y by deposit in a joint account of X and Y who sign a note payable to Bank for the amount of the loan. X then withdraws the money from the joint account and absconds. Bank acted in good faith and without notice of the fraud of X against Y. Bank is payee of the note executed by Y, but its right to enforce the note against Y should not be affected by the fact that Y was induced to execute the note by the fraud of X. Bank can be a holder in due course that takes free of the defense of Y. Case # 2 is similar to Case # 1. In each case the payee of the instrument has given value to the person committing the fraud in exchange for the obligation of the person against whom the fraud was committed. In each case the payee was not party to the fraud and had no notice of it.

Suppose in Case # 2 that the note does not meet the requirements of Section 3–104(a) and thus is not a negotiable instrument covered by Article 3. In that case, Bank cannot be a holder in due course but the result should be the same. Bank's rights are determined by general principles of contract law. Restatement Second, Contracts § 164(2) governs the case. If Y is induced to enter into a contract with Bank by a fraudulent misrepresentation by X, the contract is voidable by Y unless Bank "in good faith and without reason to know of the misrepresentation either gives value or relies materially on the transaction." Comment e to § 164(2) states:

"This is the same principle that protects an innocent person who purchases goods or commercial paper in good faith, without notice and for value from one who obtained them from the original owner by a misrepresentation. See Uniform Commercial Code §§ 2–403(1), 3–305. In the cases that fall within [§ 164(2)], however, the innocent person deals directly with the recipient of the misrepresentation, which is made by one not a party to the contract."

The same result follows in Case # 2 if Y had been induced to sign the note as an accommodation party (Section 3–419). If Y signs as co-maker of a note for the benefit of X, Y is a surety with respect to the obligation of X to pay the note but is liable as maker of the note to pay Bank. Section 3–419(b). If Bank is a holder in due course, the fraud of X cannot be asserted against Bank under Section 3–305(b). But the result is the same without resort to holder-in-due-course doctrine. If the note is not a negotiable instrument governed by Article 3, general rules of suretyship apply. Restatement, Security § 119 states that the surety (Y) cannot assert a defense against the creditor (Bank) based on the fraud of the principal (X) if the creditor "without knowledge of the fraud * * * extended credit to the principal on the security of the surety's promise * * *." The underlying principle of § 119 is the same as that of § 164(2) of Restatement Second, Contracts.

Case # 3. Corporation draws a check payable to Bank. The check is given to an officer of Corporation who is instructed to deliver it to Bank in payment of a debt owed by Corporation to Bank. Instead, the officer, intending to defraud Corporation, delivers the check to Bank in payment of the officer's personal debt, or the check is delivered to Bank for deposit to the officer's personal account. If Bank obtains payment of the check, Bank has received funds of Corporation which have been used for the personal benefit of the officer. Corporation in this case will assert a claim to the proceeds of the check against Bank. If Bank was a holder in due course of the check it took the check free of Corporation's claim. Section 3–306. The issue in this case is whether Bank had notice of the claim when it took the check. If Bank knew that the officer was a fiduciary with respect to the check, the issue is governed by Section 3–307.

Case # 4. Employer, who owed money to X, signed a blank check and delivered it to Secretary with instructions to complete the check by typing in X's name and the amount owed to X. Secretary fraudulently completed the check by typing in the name of Y, a creditor to whom Secretary owed money. Secretary then delivered the check to Y in payment of Secretary's debt. Y obtained payment of the check. This case is similar to Case # 3. Since Secretary was authorized to complete the check, Employer is bound by Secretary's act in making the check payable to Y. The drawee bank properly paid the check. Y received funds of Employer which were used for the personal benefit of Secretary. Employer asserts a claim to these funds against Y. If Y is a holder in due course, Y takes free of the claim. Whether Y is a holder in due course depends upon whether Y had notice of Employer's claim.

5. Subsection (c) is based on former Section 3–302(3). Like former Section 3–302(3), subsection (c) is intended to state existing case law. It covers a few situations in which the purchaser takes an instrument under unusual circumstances. The purchaser is treated as a successor in interest to the prior holder and can acquire no better rights. But if the prior holder was a holder in due course, the purchaser obtains rights of a holder in due course.

Subsection (c) applies to a purchaser in an execution sale or sale in bankruptcy. It applies equally to an attaching creditor or any other person who acquires the instrument by legal process or to a representative, such as an executor, administrator, receiver or assignee for the benefit of creditors, who takes the instrument as part of an estate. Subsection (c) applies to bulk purchases lying outside of the ordinary course of business of the seller. For example, it applies to the purchase by one bank of a substantial part of the paper held by another bank which is threatened with insolvency and seeking to liquidate its assets. Subsection (c) would also apply when a new partnership takes over for value all of the assets of an old one after a new member has entered the firm, or to a reorganized or consolidated corporation taking over the assets of a predecessor.

In the absence of controlling state law to the contrary, subsection (c) applies to a sale by a state bank commissioner of the assets of an insolvent bank. However, subsection (c) may be preempted by federal law if the Federal Deposit Insurance Corporation takes over an insolvent bank. Under the governing federal law, the FDIC and similar financial institution insurers are given holder in due course status and that status is also acquired by their assignees under the shelter doctrine.

6. Subsections (d) and (e) clarify two matters not specifically addressed by former Article 3:

Case # 5. Payee negotiates a $1,000 note to Holder who agrees to pay $900 for it. After paying $500, Holder learns that Payee defrauded Maker in the transaction giving rise to the note. Under subsection (d) Holder may assert rights as a holder in due course to the extent of $555.55 ($500 ÷ $900 = .555 × $1,000 = $555.55). This formula rewards Holder with a ratable portion of the bargained for profit.

Case # 6. Payee negotiates a note of Maker for $1,000 to Holder as security for payment of Payee's debt to Holder of $600. Maker has a defense which is good against Payee but of which Holder has no notice. Subsection (e) applies. Holder may assert rights as a holder in due course only to the extent of $600. Payee does not get the benefit of the holder-in-due-course status of Holder. With respect to $400 of the note, Maker may assert any rights that Maker has against Payee. A different result follows if the payee of a note negotiated it to a person who took it as a holder in due course and that person pledged the note as security for a debt. Because the defense cannot be asserted against the pledgor, the pledgee can assert rights as a holder in due course for the full amount of the note for the benefit of both the pledgor and the pledgee.

7. There is a large body of state statutory and case law restricting the use of the holder in due course doctrine in consumer transactions as well as some business transactions that raise similar issues. Subsection (g) subordinates Article 3 to that law and any other similar law that may evolve in the future. Section 3–106(d) also relates to statutory or administrative law intended to restrict use of the holder-in-due-course doctrine. See Comment 3 to Section 3–106.

8. The status of holder in due course resembles the status of protected holder under Article 29 of the Convention on International Bills of Exchange and International Promissory Notes. The requirements for being a protected holder under Article 29 generally track those of Section 3–302.

As amended in 2002.

§ 3–303.   Value and Consideration.

(a)   An instrument is issued or transferred for value if:

(1)   the instrument is issued or transferred for a promise of performance, to the extent the promise has been performed;

(2)   the transferee acquires a security interest or other lien in the instrument other than a lien obtained by judicial proceeding;

(3)   the instrument is issued or transferred as payment of, or as security for, an antecedent claim against any person, whether or not the claim is due;

(4)   the instrument is issued or transferred in exchange for a negotiable instrument; or

(5)   the instrument is issued or transferred in exchange for the incurring of an irrevocable obligation to a third party by the person taking the instrument.

(b)   "Consideration" means any consideration sufficient to support a simple contract. The drawer or maker of an instrument has a defense if the instrument is issued without consideration. If an instrument is issued for a promise of performance, the issuer has a defense to the extent performance of the promise is due and the promise has not been performed. If an instrument is issued for value as stated in subsection (a), the instrument is also issued for consideration.

Official Comment

1.   Subsection (a) is a restatement of former Section 3–303 and subsection (b) replaces former Section 3–408. The distinction between value and consideration in Article 3 is a very fine one. Whether an instrument is taken for value is relevant to the issue of whether a holder is a holder in due course. If an instrument is not issued for consideration the issuer has a defense to the obligation to pay the instrument. Consideration is defined in subsection (b) as "any consideration sufficient to support a simple contract." The definition of value in Section 1–201(44),* which doesn't apply to Article 3, includes "any consideration sufficient to support a simple contract." Thus, outside Article 3, anything that is consideration is also value. A different rule applies in Article 3. Subsection (b) of Section 3–303 states that if an instrument is issued for value it is also issued for consideration.

Case # 1. X owes Y $1,000. The debt is not represented by a note. Later X issues a note to Y for the debt. Under subsection (a)(3) X's note is issued for value. Under subsection (b) the note is also issued for consideration whether or not, under contract law, Y is deemed to have given consideration for the note.

Case # 2. X issues a check to Y in consideration of Y's promise to perform services in the future. Although the executory promise is consideration for issuance of the check it is value only to the extent the promise is performed. Subsection (a)(1).

Case # 3. X issues a note to Y in consideration of Y's promise to perform services. If at the due date of the note Y's performance is not yet due, Y may enforce the note because it was issued for consideration. But if at the due date of the note, Y's performance is due and has not been performed, X has a defense. Subsection (b).

2.   Subsection (a), which defines value, has primary importance in cases in which the issue is whether the holder of an instrument is a holder in due course and particularly to cases in which the issuer of the instrument has a defense to the instrument. Suppose Buyer and Seller signed a contract on April 1 for the sale of goods to be delivered on May 1. Payment of 50% of the price of the goods was due upon signing of the contract. On April 1 Buyer delivered to Seller a check in the amount due under the contract. The check was drawn by X to Buyer as payee and was indorsed to Seller. When the check was presented for payment to the drawee on April 2, it was dishonored because X had stopped payment. At that time Seller had not taken any action to perform the contract with Buyer. If X has a defense on the check, the defense can be asserted against Seller who is not a holder in due course because Seller did not give value for the check. Subsection (a)(1). The policy basis for subsection (a)(1) is that the holder who gives an executory promise of performance will not suffer an out-of-pocket loss to the extent the executory promise is unperformed at the time the holder learns of dishonor of the instrument. When Seller took delivery of the check on April 1, Buyer's obligation to pay 50% of the price on that date was suspended, but when the check was dishonored on April 2 the obligation revived. Section 3–310(b). If payment for goods is due at

---

*   *Referring to unrevised Article 1 (Appendix A).*

or before delivery and the buyer fails to make the payment, the seller is excused from performing the promise to deliver the goods. Section 2–703. Thus, Seller is protected from an out-of-pocket loss even if the check is not enforceable. Holder-in-due-course status is not necessary to protect Seller.

3.   Subsection (a)(2) equates value with the obtaining of a security interest or a nonjudicial lien in the instrument. The term "security interest" covers Article 9 cases in which an instrument is taken as collateral as well as bank collection cases in which a bank acquires a security interest under Section 4–210. The acquisition of a common-law or statutory banker's lien is also value under subsection (a)(2). An attaching creditor or other person who acquires a lien by judicial proceedings does not give value for the purposes of subsection (a)(2).

4.   Subsection (a)(3) follows former Section 3–303(b) in providing that the holder takes for value if the instrument is taken in payment of or as security for an antecedent claim, even though there is no extension of time or other concession, and whether or not the claim is due. Subsection (a)(3) applies to any claim against any person; there is no requirement that the claim arise out of contract. In particular the provision is intended to apply to an instrument given in payment of or as security for the debt of a third person, even though no concession is made in return.

5.   Subsection (a)(4) and (5) restate former Section 3–303(c). They state generally recognized exceptions to the rule that an executory promise is not value. A negotiable instrument is value because it carries the possibility of negotiation to a holder in due course, after which the party who gives it is obliged to pay. The same reasoning applies to any irrevocable commitment to a third person, such as a letter of credit issued when an instrument is taken.

6.   The term "promise" in paragraph (a)(1) is used in the phrase "promise of performance" and for that reason does not have the specialized meaning given that term in Section 3–103(a)(12). See Section 1–201 ("Changes from Former Law"). No inference should be drawn from the decision to use the phrase "promise of performance," although the phrase does include the word "promise," which has the specialized definition set forth in Section 3–103. Indeed, that is true even though "undertaking" is used instead of "promise" in Section 3–104(a)(3). See Section 3–104 comment 1 (explaining the use of the term "undertaking" in Section 3–104 to avoid use of the defined term "promise").

As amended in 2002.

§ 3–304.   Overdue Instrument.

(a)   An instrument payable on demand becomes overdue at the earliest of the following times:

(1)   on the day after the day demand for payment is duly made;

(2)   if the instrument is a check, 90 days after its date; or

(3)   if the instrument is not a check, when the instrument has been outstanding for a period of time after its date which is unreasonably long under the circumstances of the particular case in light of the nature of the instrument and usage of the trade.

(b)   With respect to an instrument payable at a definite time the following rules apply:

(1)   If the principal is payable in installments and a due date has not been accelerated, the instrument becomes overdue upon default under the instrument for nonpayment of an installment, and the instrument remains overdue until the default is cured.

(2)   If the principal is not payable in installments and the due date has not been accelerated, the instrument becomes overdue on the day after the due date.

(3)   If a due date with respect to principal has been accelerated, the instrument becomes overdue on the day after the accelerated due date.

(c)   Unless the due date of principal has been accelerated, an instrument does not become overdue if there is default in payment of interest but no default in payment of principal.

Official Comment

1.   To be a holder in due course, one must take without notice that an instrument is overdue. Section 3–302(a)(2)(iii). Section 3–304 replaces subsection (3) of former Section 3–304. For the sake of clarity it treats demand

and time instruments separately. Subsection (a) applies to demand instruments. A check becomes stale after 90 days.

Under former Section 3–304(3)(c), a holder that took a demand note had notice that it was overdue if it was taken "more than a reasonable length of time after its issue." In substitution for this test, subsection (a)(3) requires the trier of fact to look at both the circumstances of the particular case and the nature of the instrument and trade usage. Whether a demand note is stale may vary a great deal depending on the facts of the particular case.

2.   Subsections (b) and (c) cover time instruments. They follow the distinction made under former Article 3 between defaults in payment of principal and interest. In subsection (b) installment instruments and single payment instruments are treated separately. If an installment is late, the instrument is overdue until the default is cured.

§ 3–305.   Defenses and Claims in Recoupment.

(a)   Except as otherwise provided in this section, the right to enforce the obligation of a party to pay an instrument is subject to the following:

(1)   a defense of the obligor based on (i) infancy of the obligor to the extent it is a defense to a simple contract, (ii) duress, lack of legal capacity, or illegality of the transaction which, under other law, nullifies the obligation of the obligor, (iii) fraud that induced the obligor to sign the instrument with neither knowledge nor reasonable opportunity to learn of its character or its essential terms, or (iv) discharge of the obligor in insolvency proceedings;

(2)   a defense of the obligor stated in another section of this Article or a defense of the obligor that would be available if the person entitled to enforce the instrument were enforcing a right to payment under a simple contract; and

(3)   a claim in recoupment of the obligor against the original payee of the instrument if the claim arose from the transaction that gave rise to the instrument; but the claim of the obligor may be asserted against a transferee of the instrument only to reduce the amount owing on the instrument at the time the action is brought.

(b)   The right of a holder in due course to enforce the obligation of a party to pay the instrument is subject to defenses of the obligor stated in subsection (a)(1), but is not subject to defenses of the obligor stated in subsection (a)(2) or claims in recoupment stated in subsection (a)(3) against a person other than the holder.

(c)   Except as stated in subsection (d), in an action to enforce the obligation of a party to pay the instrument, the obligor may not assert against the person entitled to enforce the instrument a defense, claim in recoupment, or claim to the instrument (Section 3–306) of another person, but the other person's claim to the instrument may be asserted by the obligor if the other person is joined in the action and personally asserts the claim against the person entitled to enforce the instrument. An obligor is not obliged to pay the instrument if the person seeking enforcement of the instrument does not have rights of a holder in due course and the obligor proves that the instrument is a lost or stolen instrument.

(d)   In an action to enforce the obligation of an accommodation party to pay an instrument, the accommodation party may assert against the person entitled to enforce the instrument any defense or claim in recoupment under subsection (a) that the accommodated party could assert against the person entitled to enforce the instrument, except the defenses of discharge in insolvency proceedings, infancy, and lack of legal capacity.

(e)   In a consumer transaction, if law other than this article requires that an instrument include a statement to the effect that the rights of a holder or transferee are subject to a claim or defense that the issuer could assert against the original payee, and the instrument does not include such a statement:

(1)   the instrument has the same effect as if the instrument included such a statement;

(2)   the issuer may assert against the holder or transferee all claims and defenses that would have been available if the instrument included such a statement; and

(3)   the extent to which claims may be asserted against the holder or transferee is determined as if the instrument included such a statement.

(f)   This section is subject to law other than this article that establishes a different rule for consumer transactions.

Legislative Note: If a consumer protection law in this state addresses the same issue as subsection (g),* it should be examined for consistency with subsection (g)* and, if inconsistent, should be amended.

As amended in 2002.

Official Comment

1.   Subsection (a) states the defenses to the obligation of a party to pay the instrument. Subsection (a)(1) states the "real defenses" that may be asserted against any person entitled to enforce the instrument.

Subsection (a)(1)(i) allows assertion of the defense of infancy against a holder in due course, even though the effect of the defense is to render the instrument voidable but not void. The policy is one of protection of the infant even at the expense of occasional loss to an innocent purchaser. No attempt is made to state when infancy is available as a defense or the conditions under which it may be asserted. In some jurisdictions it is held that an infant cannot rescind the transaction or set up the defense unless the holder is restored to the position held before the instrument was taken which, in the case of a holder in due course, is normally impossible. In other states an infant who has misrepresented age may be estopped to assert infancy. Such questions are left to other law, as an integral part of the policy of each state as to the protection of infants.

Subsection (a)(1)(ii) covers mental incompetence, guardianship, ultra vires acts or lack of corporate capacity to do business, or any other incapacity apart from infancy. Such incapacity is largely statutory. Its existence and effect is left to the law of each state. If under the state law the effect is to render the obligation of the instrument entirely null and void, the defense may be asserted against a holder in due course. If the effect is merely to render the obligation voidable at the election of the obligor, the defense is cut off.

Duress, which is also covered by subsection (a)(ii), is a matter of degree. An instrument signed at the point of a gun is void, even in the hands of a holder in due course. One signed under threat to prosecute the son of the maker for theft may be merely voidable, so that the defense is cut off. Illegality is most frequently a matter of gambling or usury, but may arise in other forms under a variety of statutes. The statutes differ in their provisions and the interpretations given them. They are primarily a matter of local concern and local policy. All such matters are therefore left to the local law. If under that law the effect of the duress or the illegality is to make the obligation entirely null and void, the defense may be asserted against a holder in due course. Otherwise it is cut off.

Subsection (a)(1)(iii) refers to "real" or "essential" fraud, sometimes called fraud in the essence or fraud in the factum, as effective against a holder in due course. The common illustration is that of the maker who is tricked into signing a note in the belief that it is merely a receipt or some other document. The theory of the defense is that the signature on the instrument is ineffective because the signer did not intend to sign such an instrument at all. Under this provision the defense extends to an instrument signed with knowledge that it is a negotiable instrument, but without knowledge of its essential terms. The test of the defense is that of excusable ignorance of the contents of the writing signed. The party must not only have been in ignorance, but must also have had no reasonable opportunity to obtain knowledge. In determining what is a reasonable opportunity all relevant factors are to be taken into account, including the intelligence, education, business experience, and ability to read or understand English of the signer. Also relevant is the nature of the representations that were made, whether the signer had good reason to rely on the representations or to have confidence in the person making them, the presence or absence of any third person who might read or explain the instrument to the signer, or any other possibility of obtaining independent information, and the apparent necessity, or lack of it, for acting without delay. Unless the misrepresentation meets this test, the defense is cut off by a holder in due course.

Subsection (a)(1)(iv) states specifically that the defense of discharge in insolvency proceedings is not cut off when the instrument is purchased by a holder in due course. "Insolvency proceedings" is defined in Section 1–201(22)** and it includes bankruptcy whether or not the debtor is insolvent. Subsection (2)(e) of former Section 3–305 is omitted. The substance of that provision is stated in Section 3–601(b).

---

*   *Note from West Advisory Panel: So in original; should be (e).*
**   *Referring to unrevised Article 1 (Appendix A).*

2.   Subsection (a)(2) states other defenses that, pursuant to subsection (b), are cut off by a holder in due course. These defenses comprise those specifically stated in Article 3 and those based on common law contract principles. Article 3 defenses are nonissuance of the instrument, conditional issuance, and issuance for a special purpose (Section 3–105(b)); failure to countersign a traveler's check (Section 3–106(c)); modification of the obligation by a separate agreement (Section 3–117); payment that violates a restrictive indorsement (Section 3–206(f)); instruments issued without consideration or for which promised performance has not been given (Section 3–303(b)), and breach of warranty when a draft is accepted (Section 3–417(b)). The most prevalent common law defenses are fraud, misrepresentation or mistake in the issuance of the instrument. In most cases the holder in due course will be an immediate or remote transferee of the payee of the instrument. In most cases the holder-in-due-course doctrine is irrelevant if defenses are being asserted against the payee of the instrument, but in a small number of cases the payee of the instrument may be a holder in due course. Those cases are discussed in Comment 4 to Section 3–302.

Assume Buyer issues a note to Seller in payment of the price of goods that Seller fraudulently promises to deliver but which are never delivered. Seller negotiates the note to Holder who has no notice of the fraud. If Holder is a holder in due course, Holder is not subject to Buyer's defense of fraud. But in some cases an original party to the instrument is a holder in due course. For example, Buyer fraudulently induces Bank to issue a cashier's check to the order of Seller. The check is delivered by Bank to Seller, who has no notice of the fraud. Seller can be a holder in due course and can take the check free of Bank's defense of fraud. This case is discussed as Case # 1 in Comment 4 to Section 3–302. Former Section 3–305 stated that a holder in due course takes free of defenses of "any party to the instrument with whom the holder has not dealt." The meaning of this language was not at all clear and if read literally could have produced the wrong result. In the hypothetical case, it could be argued that Seller "dealt" with Bank because Bank delivered the check to Seller. But it is clear that Seller should take free of Bank's defense against Buyer regardless of whether Seller took delivery of the check from Buyer or from Bank. The quoted language is not included in Section 3–305. It is not necessary. If Buyer issues an instrument to Seller and Buyer has a defense against Seller, that defense can obviously be asserted. Buyer and Seller are the only people involved. The holder-in-due-course doctrine has no relevance. The doctrine applies only to cases in which more than two parties are involved. Its essence is that the holder in due course does not have to suffer the consequences of a defense of the obligor on the instrument that arose from an occurrence with a third party.

3.   Subsection (a)(3) is concerned with claims in recoupment which can be illustrated by the following example. Buyer issues a note to the order of Seller in exchange for a promise of Seller to deliver specified equipment. If Seller fails to deliver the equipment or delivers equipment that is rightfully rejected, Buyer has a defense to the note because the performance that was the consideration for the note was not rendered. Section 3–303(b). This defense is included in Section 3–305(a)(2). That defense can always be asserted against Seller. This result is the same as that reached under former Section 3–408.

But suppose Seller delivered the promised equipment and it was accepted by Buyer. The equipment, however, was defective. Buyer retained the equipment and incurred expenses with respect to its repair. In this case, Buyer does not have a defense under Section 3–303(b). Seller delivered the equipment and the equipment was accepted. Under Article 2, Buyer is obliged to pay the price of the equipment which is represented by the note. But Buyer may have a claim against Seller for breach of warranty. If Buyer has a warranty claim, the claim may be asserted against Seller as a counterclaim or as a claim in recoupment to reduce the amount owing on the note. It is not relevant whether Seller is or is not a holder in due course of the note or whether Seller knew or had notice that Buyer had the warranty claim. It is obvious that holder-in-due-course doctrine cannot be used to allow Seller to cut off a warranty claim that Buyer has against Seller. Subsection (b) specifically covers this point by stating that a holder in due course is not subject to a "claim in recoupment . . . against a person other than the holder."

Suppose Seller negotiates the note to Holder. If Holder had notice of Buyer's warranty claim at the time the note was negotiated to Holder, Holder is not a holder in due course (Section 3–302(a)(2)(iv)) and Buyer may assert the claim against Holder (Section 3–305(a)(3)) but only as a claim in recoupment, i.e. to reduce the amount owed on the note. If the warranty claim is $1,000 and the unpaid note is $10,000, Buyer owes $9,000 to Holder. If the warranty claim is more than the unpaid amount of the note, Buyer owes nothing to Holder, but Buyer cannot recover the unpaid amount of the warranty claim from Holder. If Buyer had already partially paid the note, Buyer is not entitled to recover the amounts paid. The claim can be used only as an offset to amounts owing on the note. If Holder had no notice of Buyer's claim and otherwise qualifies as a holder in due course, Buyer may not assert the claim against Holder. Section 3–305(b).

The result under Section 3–305 is consistent with the result reached under former Article 3, but the rules for reaching the result are stated differently. Under former Article 3 Buyer could assert rights against Holder only if Holder was not a holder in due course, and Holder's status depended upon whether Holder had notice of a defense by Buyer. Courts have held that Holder had that notice if Holder had notice of Buyer's warranty claim. The rationale under former Article 3 was "failure of consideration." This rationale does not distinguish between cases in which the seller fails to perform and those in which the buyer accepts the performance of seller but makes a claim against the seller because the performance is faulty. The term "failure of consideration" is subject to varying interpretations and is not used in Article 3. The use of the term "claim in recoupment" in Section 3–305(a)(3) is a more precise statement of the nature of Buyer's right against Holder. The use of the term does not change the law because the treatment of a defense under subsection (a)(2) and a claim in recoupment under subsection (a)(3) is essentially the same.

Under former Article 3, case law was divided on the issue of the extent to which an obligor on a note could assert against a transferee who is not a holder in due course a debt or other claim that the obligor had against the original payee of the instrument. Some courts limited claims to those that arose in the transaction that gave rise to the note. This is the approach taken in Section 3–305(a)(3). Other courts allowed the obligor on the note to use any debt or other claim, no matter how unrelated to the note, to offset the amount owed on the note. Under current judicial authority and non-UCC statutory law, there will be many cases in which a transferee of a note arising from a sale transaction will not qualify as a holder in due course. For example, applicable law may require the use of a note to which there cannot be a holder in due course. See Section 3–106(d) and Comment 3 to Section 3–106. It is reasonable to provide that the buyer should not be denied the right to assert claims arising out of the sale transaction. Subsection (a)(3) is based on the belief that it is not reasonable to require the transferee to bear the risk that wholly unrelated claims may also be asserted. The determination of whether a claim arose from the transaction that gave rise to the instrument is determined by law other than this Article and thus may vary as local law varies.

4.   Subsection (c) concerns claims and defenses of a person other than the obligor on the instrument. It applies principally to cases in which an obligation is paid with the instrument of a third person. For example, Buyer buys goods from Seller and negotiates to Seller a cashier's check issued by Bank in payment of the price. Shortly after delivering the check to Seller, Buyer learns that Seller had defrauded Buyer in the sale transaction. Seller may enforce the check against Bank even though Seller is not a holder in due course. Bank has no defense to its obligation to pay the check and it may not assert defenses, claims in recoupment, or claims to the instrument of Buyer, except to the extent permitted by the "but" clause of the first sentence of subsection (c). Buyer may have a claim to the instrument under Section 3–306 based on a right to rescind the negotiation to Seller because of Seller's fraud. Section 3–202(b) and Comment 2 to Section 3–201. Bank cannot assert that claim unless Buyer is joined in the action in which Seller is trying to enforce payment of the check. In that case Bank may pay the amount of the check into court and the court will decide whether that amount belongs to Buyer or Seller. The last sentence of subsection (c) allows the issuer of an instrument such as a cashier's check to refuse payment in the rare case in which the issuer can prove that the instrument is a lost or stolen instrument and the person seeking enforcement does not have rights of a holder in due course.

5.   Subsection (d) applies to instruments signed for accommodation (Section 3–419) and this subsection equates the obligation of the accommodation party to that of the accommodated party. The accommodation party can assert whatever defense or claim the accommodated party had against the person enforcing the instrument. The only exceptions are discharge in bankruptcy, infancy and lack of capacity. The same rule does not apply to an indorsement by a holder of the instrument in negotiating the instrument. The indorser, as transferor, makes a warranty to the indorsee, as transferee, that no defense or claim in recoupment is good against the indorser. Section 3–416(a)(4). Thus, if the indorsee sues the indorser because of dishonor of the instrument, the indorser may not assert the defense or claim in recoupment of the maker or drawer against the indorsee.

Section 3–305(d) must be read in conjunction with Section 3–605, which provides rules (usually referred to as suretyship defenses) for determining when the obligation of an accommodation party is discharged, in whole or in part, because of some act or omission of a person entitled to enforce the instrument. To the extent a rule stated in Section 3–605 is inconsistent with Section 3–305(d), the Section 3–605 rule governs. For example, Section 3–605(a) provides rules for determining when and to what extent a discharge of the accommodated party under Section 3–604 will discharge the accommodation party. As explained in Comment 2 to Section 3–605, discharge of the accommodated party is normally part of a settlement under which the holder of a note accepts partial payment from an accommodated party who is financially unable to pay the entire amount of the note. If the holder then brings an action against the accommodation party to recover the remaining unpaid amount of the note, the accommodation party cannot use Section 3–305(d) to nullify Section 3–605(a) by asserting the discharge of the accommodated party as a defense. On the other hand, suppose the accommodated party is a buyer of goods who issued the note to the seller who took the note for the buyer's obligation to pay for the goods. Suppose the buyer has a claim for breach of warranty with respect to the goods against the seller and the warranty claim may be asserted against the holder of the note. The warranty claim is a claim in recoupment. If the holder and the accommodated party reach a settlement under which the holder accepts payment less than the amount of the note in full satisfaction of the note and the warranty claim, the accommodation party could defend an action on the note by the holder by asserting the accord and satisfaction under Section 3–305(d). There is no conflict with Section 3–605(a) because that provision is not intended to apply to settlement of disputed claims.

6.   Subsection (e) is added to clarify the treatment of an instrument that omits the notice currently required by the Federal Trade Commission Rule related to certain consumer credit sales and consumer purchase money loans (16 C.F.R. Part 433). This subsection adopts the view that the instrument should be treated as if the language required by the FTC Rule were present. It is based on the language describing that rule in Section 3–106(d) and the analogous provision in Section 9–404(d).

7.   Subsection (f) is modeled on Sections 9–403(e) and 9–404(c). It ensures that Section 3–305 is interpreted to accommodate relevant consumer-protection laws. The absence of such a provision from other sections in Article 3 should not justify any inference about the meaning of those sections.

8.   Articles 28 and 30 of the Convention on International Bills of Exchange and International Promissory Notes includes a similar dichotomy, with a narrower group of defenses available against a protected holder under Articles 28(1) and 30 than are available under Article 28(2) against a holder that is not a protected holder.

As amended in 1994 and 2002.

§ 3–306.   Claims to an Instrument.

A person taking an instrument, other than a person having rights of a holder in due course, is subject to a claim of a property or possessory right in the instrument or its proceeds, including a claim to rescind a negotiation and to recover the instrument or its proceeds. A person having rights of a holder in due course takes free of the claim to the instrument.

Official Comment

This section expands on the reference to "claims to" the instrument mentioned in former Sections 3–305 and 3–306. Claims covered by the section include not only claims to ownership but also any other claim of a property or possessory right. It includes the claim to a lien or the claim of a person in rightful possession of an instrument who was wrongfully deprived of possession. Also included is a claim based on Section 3–202(b) for rescission of a negotiation of the instrument by the claimant. Claims to an instrument under Section 3–306 are different from claims in recoupment referred to in Section 3–305(a)(3). The rule of this section is similar to the rule of Article 30(2) of the Convention on International Bills of Exchange and International Promissory Notes.

As amended in 2002.

§ 3–307.   Notice of Breach of Fiduciary Duty.

(a)   In this section:

(1)   "Fiduciary" means an agent, trustee, partner, corporate officer or director, or other representative owing a fiduciary duty with respect to an instrument.

(2)   "Represented person" means the principal, beneficiary, partnership, corporation, or other person to whom the duty stated in paragraph (1) is owed.

(b)   If (i) an instrument is taken from a fiduciary for payment or collection or for value, (ii) the taker has knowledge of the fiduciary status of the fiduciary, and (iii) the represented person makes a claim to the instrument or its proceeds on the basis that the transaction of the fiduciary is a breach of fiduciary duty, the following rules apply:

(1)   Notice of breach of fiduciary duty by the fiduciary is notice of the claim of the represented person.

(2)   In the case of an instrument payable to the represented person or the fiduciary as such, the taker has notice of the breach of fiduciary duty if the instrument is (i) taken in payment of or as security for a debt known by the taker to be the personal debt of the fiduciary, (ii) taken in a transaction

316

known by the taker to be for the personal benefit of the fiduciary, or (iii) deposited to an account other than an account of the fiduciary, as such, or an account of the represented person.

(3) If an instrument is issued by the represented person or the fiduciary as such, and made payable to the fiduciary personally, the taker does not have notice of the breach of fiduciary duty unless the taker knows of the breach of fiduciary duty.

(4) If an instrument is issued by the represented person or the fiduciary as such, to the taker as payee, the taker has notice of the breach of fiduciary duty if the instrument is (i) taken in payment of or as security for a debt known by the taker to be the personal debt of the fiduciary, (ii) taken in a transaction known by the taker to be for the personal benefit of the fiduciary, or (iii) deposited to an account other than an account of the fiduciary, as such, or an account of the represented person.

Official Comment

1. This section states rules for determining when a person who has taken an instrument from a fiduciary has notice of a breach of fiduciary duty that occurs as a result of the transaction with the fiduciary. Former Section 3–304(2) and (4)(e) related to this issue, but those provisions were unclear in their meaning. Section 3–307 is intended to clarify the law by stating rules that comprehensively cover the issue of when the taker of an instrument has notice of breach of a fiduciary duty and thus notice of a claim to the instrument or its proceeds.

2. Subsection (a) defines the terms "fiduciary" and "represented person" and the introductory paragraph of subsection (b) describes the transaction to which the section applies. The basic scenario is one in which the fiduciary in effect embezzles money of the represented person by applying the proceeds of an instrument that belongs to the represented person to the personal use of the fiduciary. The person dealing with the fiduciary may be a depositary bank that takes the instrument for collection or a bank or other person that pays value for the instrument. The section also covers a transaction in which an instrument is presented for payment to a payor bank that pays the instrument by giving value to the fiduciary. Subsections (b)(2), (3), and (4) state rules for determining when the person dealing with the fiduciary has notice of breach of fiduciary duty. Subsection (b)(1) states that notice of breach of fiduciary duty is notice of the represented person's claim to the instrument or its proceeds.

Under Section 3–306, a person taking an instrument is subject to a claim to the instrument or its proceeds, unless the taker has rights of a holder in due course. Under Section 3–302(a)(2)(v), the taker cannot be a holder in due course if the instrument was taken with notice of a claim under Section 3–306. Section 3–307 applies to cases in which a represented person is asserting a claim because a breach of fiduciary duty resulted in a misapplication of the proceeds of an instrument. The claim of the represented person is a claim described in Section 3–306. Section 3–307 states rules for determining when a person taking an instrument has notice of the claim which will prevent assertion of rights as a holder in due course. It also states rules for determining when a payor bank pays an instrument with notice of breach of fiduciary duty.

Section 3–307(b) applies only if the person dealing with the fiduciary "has knowledge of the fiduciary status of the fiduciary." Notice which does not amount to knowledge is not enough to cause Section 3–307 to apply. "Knowledge" is defined in Section 1–201(25).* In most cases, the "taker" referred to in Section 3–307 will be a bank or other organization. Knowledge of an organization is determined by the rules stated in Section 1–201(27).* In many cases, the individual who receives and processes an instrument on behalf of the organization that is the taker of the instrument "for payment or collection or for value" is a clerk who has no knowledge of any fiduciary status of the person from whom the instrument is received. In such cases, Section 3–307 doesn't apply because, under Section 1–201(27),* knowledge of the organization is determined by the knowledge of the "individual conducting that transaction," i.e. the clerk who receives and processes the instrument. Furthermore, paragraphs (2) and (4) each require that the person acting for the organization have knowledge of facts that indicate a breach of fiduciary duty. In the case of an instrument taken for deposit to an account, the knowledge is found in the fact that the deposit is made to an account other than that of the represented person or a fiduciary account for benefit of that person. In other cases the person acting for the organization must know that the instrument is taken in payment or as security for a personal debt of the fiduciary or for the personal benefit of the fiduciary. For example, if the instrument is being used to buy goods or services, the person acting for the organization must know that the goods or services are for the personal benefit of the fiduciary. The requirement that the taker have knowledge rather than notice is meant to limit Section 3–307 to relatively uncommon cases in which the person who deals

---

* _Referring to unrevised Article 1 (Appendix A)._

with the fiduciary knows all the relevant facts: the fiduciary status and that the proceeds of the instrument are being used for the personal debt or benefit of the fiduciary or are being paid to an account that is not an account of the represented person or of the fiduciary, as such. Mere notice of these facts is not enough to put the taker on notice of the breach of fiduciary duty and does not give rise to any duty of investigation by the taker.

3.   Subsection (b)(2) applies to instruments payable to the represented person or the fiduciary as such. For example, a check payable to Corporation is indorsed in the name of Corporation by Doe as its President. Doe gives the check to Bank as partial repayment of a personal loan that Bank had made to Doe. The check was indorsed either in blank or to Bank. Bank collects the check and applies the proceeds to reduce the amount owed on Doe's loan. If the person acting for Bank in the transaction knows that Doe is a fiduciary and that the check is being used to pay a personal obligation of Doe, subsection (b)(2) applies. If Corporation has a claim to the proceeds of the check because the use of the check by Doe was a breach of fiduciary duty, Bank has notice of the claim and did not take the check as a holder in due course. The same result follows if Doe had indorsed the check to himself before giving it to Bank. Subsection (b)(2) follows Uniform Fiduciaries Act § 4 in providing that if the instrument is payable to the fiduciary, as such, or to the represented person, the taker has notice of a claim if the instrument is negotiated for the fiduciary's personal debt. If fiduciary funds are deposited to a personal account of the fiduciary or to an account that is not an account of the represented person or of the fiduciary, as such, there is a split of authority concerning whether the bank is on notice of a breach of fiduciary duty. Subsection (b)(2)(iii) states that the bank is given notice of breach of fiduciary duty because of the deposit. The Uniform Fiduciaries Act § 9 states that the bank is not on notice unless it has knowledge of facts that makes its receipt of the deposit an act of bad faith.

The rationale of subsection (b)(2) is that it is not normal for an instrument payable to the represented person or the fiduciary, as such, to be used for the personal benefit of the fiduciary. It is likely that such use reflects an unlawful use of the proceeds of the instrument. If the fiduciary is entitled to compensation from the represented person for services rendered or for expenses incurred by the fiduciary the normal mode of payment is by a check drawn on the fiduciary account to the order of the fiduciary.

4.   Subsection (b)(3) is based on Uniform Fiduciaries Act § 6 and applies when the instrument is drawn by the represented person or the fiduciary as such to the fiduciary personally. The term "personally" is used as it is used in the Uniform Fiduciaries Act to mean that the instrument is payable to the payee as an individual and not as a fiduciary. For example, Doe as President of Corporation writes a check on Corporation's account to the order of Doe personally. The check is then indorsed over to Bank as in Comment 3. In this case there is no notice of breach of fiduciary duty because there is nothing unusual about the transaction. Corporation may have owed Doe money for salary, reimbursement for expenses incurred for the benefit of Corporation, or for any other reason. If Doe is authorized to write checks on behalf of Corporation to pay debts of Corporation, the check is a normal way of paying a debt owed to Doe. Bank may assume that Doe may use the instrument for his personal benefit.

5.   Subsection (b)(4) can be illustrated by a hypothetical case. Corporation draws a check payable to an organization. X, an officer or employee of Corporation, delivers the check to a person acting for the organization. The person signing the check on behalf of Corporation is X or another person. If the person acting for the organization in the transaction knows that X is a fiduciary, the organization is on notice of a claim by Corporation if it takes the instrument under the same circumstances stated in subsection (b)(2). If the organization is a bank and the check is taken in repayment of a personal loan of the bank to X, the case is like the case discussed in Comment 3. It is unusual for Corporation, the represented person, to pay a personal debt of Doe by issuing a check to the bank. It is more likely that the use of the check by Doe reflects an unlawful use of the proceeds of the check. The same analysis applies if the check is made payable to an organization in payment of goods or services. If the person acting for the organization knew of the fiduciary status of X and that the goods or services were for X's personal benefit, the organization is on notice of a claim by Corporation to the proceeds of the check. See the discussion in the last paragraph of Comment 2.

§ 3-308.   Proof of Signatures and Status as Holder in Due Course.

(a)   In an action with respect to an instrument, the authenticity of, and authority to make, each signature on the instrument is admitted unless specifically denied in the pleadings. If the validity of a signature is denied in the pleadings, the burden of establishing validity is on the person claiming validity, but the signature is presumed to be authentic and authorized unless the action is to enforce the liability of the purported signer and the signer is dead or incompetent at the time of trial of the issue of validity of the signature. If an action to enforce the instrument is brought against a person as the undisclosed principal of a person who signed the instrument as a party to the instrument, the plaintiff has the burden of establishing that the defendant is liable on the instrument as a represented person under Section 3–402(a).

(b)   If the validity of signatures is admitted or proved and there is compliance with subsection (a), a plaintiff producing the instrument is entitled to payment if the plaintiff proves entitlement to enforce the instrument under Section 3–301, unless the defendant proves a defense or claim in recoupment. If a defense or claim in recoupment is proved, the right to payment of the plaintiff is subject to the defense or claim, except to the extent the plaintiff proves that the plaintiff has rights of a holder in due course which are not subject to the defense or claim.

Official Comment

1.   Section 3–308 is a modification of former Section 3–307. The first two sentences of subsection (a) are a restatement of former Section 3–307(1). The purpose of the requirement of a specific denial in the pleadings is to give the plaintiff notice of the defendant's claim of forgery or lack of authority as to the particular signature, and to afford the plaintiff an opportunity to investigate and obtain evidence. If local rules of pleading permit, the denial may be on information and belief, or it may be a denial of knowledge or information sufficient to form a belief. It need not be under oath unless the local statutes or rules require verification. In the absence of such specific denial the signature stands admitted, and is not in issue. Nothing in this section is intended, however, to prevent amendment of the pleading in a proper case.

The question of the burden of establishing the signature arises only when it has been put in issue by specific denial. "Burden of establishing" is defined in Section 1–201. The burden is on the party claiming under the signature, but the signature is presumed to be authentic and authorized except as stated in the second sentence of subsection (a). "Presumed" is defined in Section 1–201* and means that until some evidence is introduced which would support a finding that the signature is forged or unauthorized, the plaintiff is not required to prove that it is valid. The presumption rests upon the fact that in ordinary experience forged or unauthorized signatures are very uncommon, and normally any evidence is within the control of, or more accessible to, the defendant. The defendant is therefore required to make some sufficient showing of the grounds for the denial before the plaintiff is required to introduce evidence. The defendant's evidence need not be sufficient to require a directed verdict, but it must be enough to support the denial by permitting a finding in the defendant's favor. Until introduction of such evidence the presumption requires a finding for the plaintiff. Once such evidence is introduced the burden of establishing the signature by a preponderance of the total evidence is on the plaintiff. The presumption does not arise if the action is to enforce the obligation of a purported signer who has died or become incompetent before the evidence is required, and so is disabled from obtaining or introducing it. "Action" is defined in Section 1–201 and includes a claim asserted against the estate of a deceased or an incompetent.

The last sentence of subsection (a) is a new provision that is necessary to take into account Section 3–402(a) that allows an undisclosed principal to be liable on an instrument signed by an authorized representative. In that case the person enforcing the instrument must prove that the undisclosed principal is liable.

2.   Subsection (b) restates former Section 3–307(2) and (3). Once signatures are proved or admitted a holder, by mere production of the instrument, proves "entitlement to enforce the instrument" because under Section 3–301 a holder is a person entitled to enforce the instrument. Any other person in possession of an instrument may recover only if that person has the rights of a holder. Section 3–301. That person must prove a transfer giving that person such rights under Section 3–203(b) or that such rights were obtained by subrogation or succession.

If a plaintiff producing the instrument proves entitlement to enforce the instrument, either as a holder or a person with rights of a holder, the plaintiff is entitled to recovery unless the defendant proves a defense or claim in recoupment. Until proof of a defense or claim in recoupment is made, the issue as to whether the plaintiff has rights of a holder in due course does not arise. In the absence of a defense or claim in recoupment, any person entitled to enforce the instrument is entitled to recover. If a defense or claim in recoupment is proved, the plaintiff may seek to cut off the defense or claim in recoupment by proving that the plaintiff is a holder in due course or that the plaintiff has rights of a holder in due course under Section 3–203(b) or by subrogation or succession. All elements of Section 3–302(a) must be proved.

Nothing in this section is intended to say that the plaintiff must necessarily prove rights as a holder in due course. The plaintiff may elect to introduce no further evidence, in which case a verdict may be directed for the

---

*   *Referring to unrevised Article 1 (Appendix A).*

plaintiff or the defendant, or the issue of the defense or claim in recoupment may be left to the trier of fact, according to the weight and sufficiency of the defendant's evidence. The plaintiff may elect to rebut the defense or claim in recoupment by proof to the contrary, in which case a verdict may be directed for either party or the issue may be for the trier of fact. Subsection (b) means only that if the plaintiff claims the rights of a holder in due course against the defense or claim in recoupment, the plaintiff has the burden of proof on that issue.

§ 3–309.   Enforcement of Lost, Destroyed, or Stolen Instrument.

(a)   A person not in possession of an instrument is entitled to enforce the instrument if:

(1)   the person seeking to enforce the instrument:

(A)   was entitled to enforce the instrument when loss of possession occurred; or

(B)   has directly or indirectly acquired ownership of the instrument from a person who was entitled to enforce the instrument when loss of possession occurred;

(2)   the loss of possession was not the result of a transfer by the person or a lawful seizure; and

(3)   the person cannot reasonably obtain possession of the instrument because the instrument was destroyed, its whereabouts cannot be determined, or it is in the wrongful possession of an unknown person or a person that cannot be found or is not amenable to service of process.

(b)   A person seeking enforcement of an instrument under subsection (a) must prove the terms of the instrument and the person's right to enforce the instrument. If that proof is made, Section 3–308 applies to the case as if the person seeking enforcement had produced the instrument. The court may not enter judgment in favor of the person seeking enforcement unless it finds that the person required to pay the instrument is adequately protected against loss that might occur by reason of a claim by another person to enforce the instrument. Adequate protection may be provided by any reasonable means.

As amended in 2002.

Official Comment

1.   Section 3–309 is a modification of former Section 3–804. The rights stated are those of "a person entitled to enforce the instrument" at the time of loss rather than those of an "owner" as in former Section 3–804. Under subsection (b), judgment to enforce the instrument cannot be given unless the court finds that the defendant will be adequately protected against a claim to the instrument by a holder that may appear at some later time. The court is given discretion in determining how adequate protection is to be assured. Former Section 3–804 allowed the court to "require security indemnifying the defendant against loss." Under Section 3–309 adequate protection is a flexible concept. For example, there is substantial risk that a holder in due course may make a demand for payment if the instrument was payable to bearer when it was lost or stolen. On the other hand if the instrument was payable to the person who lost the instrument and that person did not indorse the instrument, no other person could be a holder of the instrument. In some cases there is risk of loss only if there is doubt about whether the facts alleged by the person who lost the instrument are true. Thus, the type of adequate protection that is reasonable in the circumstances may depend on the degree of certainty about the facts in the case.

2.   Subsection (a) is intended to reject the result in *Dennis Joslin Co. v. Robinson Broadcasting Corp.*, 977 F. Supp. 491 (D.D.C. 1997). A transferee of a lost instrument need prove only that its transferor was entitled to enforce, not that the transferee was in possession at the time the instrument was lost. The protections of subsection (a) should also be available when instruments are lost during transit, because whatever the precise status of ownership at the point of loss, either the sender or the receiver ordinarily would have been entitled to enforce the instrument during the course of transit. The amendments to subsection (a) are not intended to alter in any way the rules that apply to the preservation of checks in connection with truncation or any other expedited method of check collection or processing.

3.   A security interest may attach to the right of a person not in possession of an instrument to enforce the instrument. Although the secured party may not be the owner of the instrument, the secured party may nevertheless be entitled to exercise its debtor's right to enforce the instrument by resorting to its collection rights under the circumstances described in Section 9–607. This section does not address whether the person required to pay the instrument owes any duty to a secured party that is not itself the owner of the instrument.

As amended in 2002.

§ 3–310. Effect of Instrument on Obligation for Which Taken.

(a) Unless otherwise agreed, if a certified check, cashier's check, or teller's check is taken for an obligation, the obligation is discharged to the same extent discharge would result if an amount of money equal to the amount of the instrument were taken in payment of the obligation. Discharge of the obligation does not affect any liability that the obligor may have as an indorser of the instrument.

(b) Unless otherwise agreed and except as provided in subsection (a), if a note or an uncertified check is taken for an obligation, the obligation is suspended to the same extent the obligation would be discharged if an amount of money equal to the amount of the instrument were taken, and the following rules apply:

(1) In the case of an uncertified check, suspension of the obligation continues until dishonor of the check or until it is paid or certified. Payment or certification of the check results in discharge of the obligation to the extent of the amount of the check.

(2) In the case of a note, suspension of the obligation continues until dishonor of the note or until it is paid. Payment of the note results in discharge of the obligation to the extent of the payment.

(3) Except as provided in paragraph (4), if the check or note is dishonored and the obligee of the obligation for which the instrument was taken is the person entitled to enforce the instrument, the obligee may enforce either the instrument or the obligation. In the case of an instrument of a third person which is negotiated to the obligee by the obligor, discharge of the obligor on the instrument also discharges the obligation.

(4) If the person entitled to enforce the instrument taken for an obligation is a person other than the obligee, the obligee may not enforce the obligation to the extent the obligation is suspended. If the obligee is the person entitled to enforce the instrument but no longer has possession of it because it was lost, stolen, or destroyed, the obligation may not be enforced to the extent of the amount payable on the instrument, and to that extent the obligee's rights against the obligor are limited to enforcement of the instrument.

(c) If an instrument other than one described in subsection (a) or (b) is taken for an obligation, the effect is (i) that stated in subsection (a) if the instrument is one on which a bank is liable as maker or acceptor, or (ii) that stated in subsection (b) in any other case.

Official Comment

1. Section 3–310 is a modification of former Section 3–802. As a practical matter, application of former Section 3–802 was limited to cases in which a check or a note was given for an obligation. Subsections (a) and (b) of Section 3–310 are therefore stated in terms of checks and notes in the interests of clarity. Subsection (c) covers the rare cases in which some other instrument is given to pay an obligation.

2. Subsection (a) deals with the case in which a certified check, cashier's check or teller's check is given in payment of an obligation. In that case the obligation is discharged unless there is an agreement to the contrary. Subsection (a) drops the exception in former Section 3–802 for cases in which there is a right of recourse on the instrument against the obligor. Under former Section 3–802(1)(a) the obligation was not discharged if there was a right of recourse on the instrument against the obligor. Subsection (a) changes this result. The underlying obligation is discharged, but any right of recourse on the instrument is preserved.

3. Subsection (b) concerns cases in which an uncertified check or a note is taken for an obligation. The typical case is that in which a buyer pays for goods or services by giving the seller the buyer's personal check, or in which the buyer signs a note for the purchase price. Subsection (b) also applies to the uncommon cases in which a check or note of a third person is given in payment of the obligation. Subsection (b) preserves the rule under former Section 3–802(1)(b) that the buyer's obligation to pay the price is suspended, but subsection (b) spells out the effect more precisely. If the check or note is dishonored, the seller may sue on either the dishonored instrument or the contract of sale if the seller has possession of the instrument and is the person entitled to enforce it. If the right to enforce the instrument is held by somebody other than the seller, the seller can't enforce the right to payment of the price under the sales contract because that right is represented by the instrument which is enforceable by somebody else. Thus, if the seller sold the note or the check to a holder and has not reacquired it after dishonor, the only right that survives is the right to enforce the instrument. What that means is that even though the suspension of the obligation may end upon dishonor under paragraph (b)(1), the obligation is not revived in the circumstances described in paragraph (b)(4).

The last sentence of subsection (b)(3) applies to cases in which an instrument of another person is indorsed over to the obligee in payment of the obligation. For example, Buyer delivers an uncertified personal check of X payable to the order of Buyer to Seller in payment of the price of goods. Buyer indorses the check over to Seller. Buyer is liable on the check as indorser. If Seller neglects to present the check for payment or to deposit it for collection within 30 days of the indorsement, Buyer's liability as indorser is discharged. Section 3–415(e). Under the last sentence of Section 3–310(b)(3) Buyer is also discharged on the obligation to pay for the goods.

4. There was uncertainty concerning the applicability of former Section 3–802 to the case in which the check given for the obligation was stolen from the payee, the payee's signature was forged, and the forger obtained payment. The last sentence of subsection (b)(4) addresses this issue. If the payor bank pays a holder, the drawer is discharged on the underlying obligation because the check was paid. Subsection (b)(1). If the payor bank pays a person not entitled to enforce the instrument, as in the hypothetical case, the suspension of the underlying obligation continues because the check has not been paid. Section 3–602(a). The payee's cause of action is against the depositary bank or payor bank in conversion under Section 3–420 or against the drawer under Section 3–309. In the latter case, the drawer's obligation under Section 3–414(b) is triggered by dishonor which occurs because the check is unpaid. Presentment for payment to the drawee is excused under Section 3–504(a)(i) and, under Section 3–502(e), dishonor occurs without presentment if the check is not paid. The payee cannot merely ignore the instrument and sue the drawer on the underlying contract. This would impose on the drawer the risk that the check when stolen was indorsed in blank or to bearer.

A similar analysis applies with respect to lost instruments that have not been paid. If a creditor takes a check of the debtor in payment of an obligation, the obligation is suspended under the introductory paragraph of subsection (b). If the creditor then loses the check, what are the creditor's rights? The creditor can request the debtor to issue a new check and in many cases, the debtor will issue a replacement check after stopping payment on the lost check. In that case both the debtor and creditor are protected. But the debtor is not obliged to issue a new check. If the debtor refuses to issue a replacement check, the last sentence of subsection (b)(4) applies. The creditor may not enforce the obligation of debtor for which the check was taken. The creditor may assert only rights on the check. The creditor can proceed under Section 3–309 to enforce the obligation of the debtor, as drawer, to pay the check.

5. Subsection (c) deals with rare cases in which other instruments are taken for obligations. If a bank is the obligor on the instrument, subsection (a) applies and the obligation is discharged. In any other case subsection (b) applies.

As amended in 2002.

§ 3–311. Accord and Satisfaction by Use of Instrument.

(a) If a person against whom a claim is asserted proves that (i) that person in good faith tendered an instrument to the claimant as full satisfaction of the claim, (ii) the amount of the claim was unliquidated or subject to a bona fide dispute, and (iii) the claimant obtained payment of the instrument, the following subsections apply.

(b) Unless subsection (c) applies, the claim is discharged if the person against whom the claim is asserted proves that the instrument or an accompanying written communication contained a conspicuous statement to the effect that the instrument was tendered as full satisfaction of the claim.

(c) Subject to subsection (d), a claim is not discharged under subsection (b) if either of the following applies:

(1) The claimant, if an organization, proves that (i) within a reasonable time before the tender, the claimant sent a conspicuous statement to the person against whom the claim is asserted that communications concerning disputed debts, including an instrument tendered as full satisfaction of a debt, are to be sent to a designated person, office, or place, and (ii) the instrument or accompanying communication was not received by that designated person, office, or place.

(2) The claimant, whether or not an organization, proves that within 90 days after payment of the instrument, the claimant tendered repayment of the amount of the instrument to the person against whom the claim is asserted. This paragraph does not apply if the claimant is an organization that sent a statement complying with paragraph (1)(i).

(d) A claim is discharged if the person against whom the claim is asserted proves that within a reasonable time before collection of the instrument was initiated, the claimant, or an agent of the claimant having direct responsibility with respect to the disputed obligation, knew that the instrument was tendered in full satisfaction of the claim.

Official Comment

1. This section deals with an informal method of dispute resolution carried out by use of a negotiable instrument. In the typical case there is a dispute concerning the amount that is owed on a claim.

Case # 1. The claim is for the price of goods or services sold to a consumer who asserts that he or she is not obliged to pay the full price for which the consumer was billed because of a defect or breach of warranty with respect to the goods or services.

Case # 2. A claim is made on an insurance policy. The insurance company alleges that it is not liable under the policy for the amount of the claim.

In either case the person against whom the claim is asserted may attempt an accord and satisfaction of the disputed claim by tendering a check to the claimant for some amount less than the full amount claimed by the claimant. A statement will be included on the check or in a communication accompanying the check to the effect that the check is offered as full payment or full satisfaction of the claim. Frequently, there is also a statement to the effect that obtaining payment of the check is an agreement by the claimant to a settlement of the dispute for the amount tendered. Before enactment of revised Article 3, the case law was in conflict over the question of whether obtaining payment of the check had the effect of an agreement to the settlement proposed by the debtor. This issue was governed by a common law rule, but some courts hold that the common law was modified by former Section 1–207 which they interpreted as applying to full settlement checks.

2. Comment d. to Restatement of Contracts, Section 281 discusses the full satisfaction check and the applicable common law rule. In a case like Case # 1, the buyer can propose a settlement of the disputed bill by a clear notation on the check indicating that the check is tendered as full satisfaction of the bill. Under the common law rule the seller, by obtaining payment of the check accepts the offer of compromise by the buyer. The result is the same if the seller adds a notation to the check indicating that the check is accepted under protest or in only partial satisfaction of the claim. Under the common law rule the seller can refuse the check or can accept it subject to the condition stated by the buyer, but the seller can't accept the check and refuse to be bound by the condition. The rule applies only to an unliquidated claim or a claim disputed in good faith by the buyer. The dispute in the courts was whether Section 1–207* changed the common law rule. The Restatement states that section "need not be read as changing this well-established rule."

3. As part of the revision of Article 3, Section 1–207* has been amended to add subsection (2) stating that Section 1–207* "does not apply to an accord and satisfaction." Because of that amendment and revised Article 3, Section 3–311 governs full satisfaction checks. Section 3–311 follows the common law rule with some minor variations to reflect modern business conditions. In cases covered by Section 3–311 there will often be an individual on one side of the dispute and a business organization on the other. This section is not designed to favor either the individual or the business organization. In Case # 1 the person seeking the accord and satisfaction is an individual. In Case # 2 the person seeking the accord and satisfaction is an insurance company. Section 3–311 is based on a belief that the common law rule produces a fair result and that informal dispute resolution by full satisfaction checks should be encouraged.

4. Subsection (a) states three requirements for application of Section 3–311. "Good faith" in subsection (a)(i) is defined in Section 3–103(a)(6) as not only honesty in fact, but the observance of reasonable commercial standards of fair dealing. The meaning of "fair dealing" will depend upon the facts in the particular case. For example, suppose an insurer tenders a check in settlement of a claim for personal injury in an accident clearly covered by the insurance policy. The claimant is necessitous and the amount of the check is very small in relationship to the extent of the injury and the amount recoverable under the policy. If the trier of fact determines that the insurer was taking unfair advantage of the claimant, an accord and satisfaction would not result from payment of the check because of the absence of good faith by the insurer in making the tender. Another example of lack of good faith is found in the practice of some business debtors in routinely printing full satisfaction language on their check stocks so that all or a large part of the debts of the debtor are paid by checks bearing the full satisfaction language, whether or not there is any dispute with the creditor. Under such a practice the claimant

_____
* *Referring to unrevised Article 1 (Appendix A).*

cannot be sure whether a tender in full satisfaction is or is not being made. Use of a check on which full satisfaction language was affixed routinely pursuant to such a business practice may prevent an accord and satisfaction on the ground that the check was not tendered in good faith under subsection (a)(i).

Section 3–311 does not apply to cases in which the debt is a liquidated amount and not subject to a bona fide dispute. Subsection (a)(ii). Other law applies to cases in which a debtor is seeking discharge of such a debt by paying less than the amount owed. For the purpose of subsection (a)(iii) obtaining acceptance of a check is considered to be obtaining payment of the check.

The person seeking the accord and satisfaction must prove that the requirements of subsection (a) are met. If that person also proves that the statement required by subsection (b) was given, the claim is discharged unless subsection (c) applies. Normally the statement required by subsection (b) is written on the check. Thus, the canceled check can be used to prove the statement as well as the fact that the claimant obtained payment of the check. Subsection (b) requires a "conspicuous" statement that the instrument was tendered in full satisfaction of the claim. "Conspicuous" is defined in Section 1–201(10).* The statement is conspicuous if "it is so written that a reasonable person against whom it is to operate ought to have noticed it." If the claimant can reasonably be expected to examine the check, almost any statement on the check should be noticed and is therefore conspicuous. In cases in which the claimant is an individual the claimant will receive the check and will normally indorse it. Since the statement concerning tender in full satisfaction normally will appear above the space provided for the claimant's indorsement of the check, the claimant "ought to have noticed" the statement.

5.   Subsection (c)(1) is a limitation on subsection (b) in cases in which the claimant is an organization. It is designed to protect the claimant against inadvertent accord and satisfaction. If the claimant is an organization payment of the check might be obtained without notice to the personnel of the organization concerned with the disputed claim. Some business organizations have claims against very large numbers of customers. Examples are department stores, public utilities and the like. These claims are normally paid by checks sent by customers to a designated office at which clerks employed by the claimant or a bank acting for the claimant process the checks and record the amounts paid. If the processing office is not designed to deal with communications extraneous to recording the amount of the check and the account number of the customer, payment of a full satisfaction check can easily be obtained without knowledge by the claimant of the existence of the full satisfaction statement. This is particularly true if the statement is written on the reverse side of the check in the area in which indorsements are usually written. Normally, the clerks of the claimant have no reason to look at the reverse side of checks. Indorsement by the claimant normally is done by mechanical means or there may be no indorsement at all. Section 4–205(a). Subsection (c)(1) allows the claimant to protect itself by advising customers by a conspicuous statement that communications regarding disputed debts must be sent to a particular person, office, or place. The statement must be given to the customer within a reasonable time before the tender is made. This requirement is designed to assure that the customer has reasonable notice that the full satisfaction check must be sent to a particular place. The reasonable time requirement could be satisfied by a notice on the billing statement sent to the customer. If the full satisfaction check is sent to the designated destination and the check is paid, the claim is discharged. If the claimant proves that the check was not received at the designated destination the claim is not discharged unless subsection (d) applies.

6.   Subsection (c)(2) is also designed to prevent inadvertent accord and satisfaction. It can be used by a claimant other than an organization or by a claimant as an alternative to subsection (c)(1). Some organizations may be reluctant to use subsection (c)(1) because it may result in confusion of customers that causes checks to be routinely sent to the special designated person, office, or place. Thus, much of the benefit of rapid processing of checks may be lost. An organization that chooses not to send a notice complying with subsection (c)(1)(i) may prevent an inadvertent accord and satisfaction by complying with subsection (c)(2). If the claimant discovers that it has obtained payment of a full satisfaction check, it may prevent an accord and satisfaction if, within 90 days of the payment of the check, the claimant tenders repayment of the amount of the check to the person against whom the claim is asserted.

7.   Subsection (c) is subject to subsection (d). If a person against whom a claim is asserted proves that the claimant obtained payment of a check known to have been tendered in full satisfaction of the claim by "the claimant or an agent of the claimant having direct responsibility with respect to the disputed obligation," the claim is discharged even if (i) the check was not sent to the person, office, or place required by a notice complying with subsection (c)(1), or (ii) the claimant tendered repayment of the amount of the check in compliance with subsection (c)(2).

---

*   *Referring to unrevised Article 1 (Appendix A).*

A claimant knows that a check was tendered in full satisfaction of a claim when the claimant "has actual knowledge" of that fact. Section 1–201(25).* Under Section 1–201(27),* if the claimant is an organization, it has knowledge that a check was tendered in full satisfaction of the claim when that fact is

"brought to the attention of the individual conducting that transaction, and in any event when it would have been brought to his attention if the organization had exercised due diligence. An organization exercises due diligence if it maintains reasonable routines for communicating significant information to the person conducting the transaction and there is reasonable compliance with the routines. Due diligence does not require an individual acting for the organization to communicate information unless such communication is part of his regular duties or unless he has reason to know of the transaction and that the transaction would be materially affected by the information."

With respect to an attempted accord and satisfaction the "individual conducting that transaction" is an employee or other agent of the organization having direct responsibility with respect to the dispute. For example, if the check and communication are received by a collection agency acting for the claimant to collect the disputed claim, obtaining payment of the check will result in an accord and satisfaction even if the claimant gave notice, pursuant to subsection (c)(1), that full satisfaction checks be sent to some other office. Similarly, if a customer asserting a claim for breach of warranty with respect to defective goods purchased in a retail outlet of a large chain store delivers the full satisfaction check to the manager of the retail outlet at which the goods were purchased, obtaining payment of the check will also result in an accord and satisfaction. On the other hand, if the check is mailed to the chief executive officer of the chain store subsection (d) would probably not be satisfied. The chief executive officer of a large corporation may have general responsibility for operations of the company, but does not normally have direct responsibility for resolving a small disputed bill to a customer. A check for a relatively small amount mailed to a high executive officer of a large organization is not likely to receive the executive's personal attention. Rather, the check would normally be routinely sent to the appropriate office for deposit and credit to the customer's account. If the check does receive the personal attention of the high executive officer and the officer is aware of the full-satisfaction language, collection of the check will result in an accord and satisfaction because subsection (d) applies. In this case the officer has assumed direct responsibility with respect to the disputed transaction.

If a full satisfaction check is sent to a lock box or other office processing checks sent to the claimant, it is irrelevant whether the clerk processing the check did or did not see the statement that the check was tendered as full satisfaction of the claim. Knowledge of the clerk is not imputed to the organization because the clerk has no responsibility with respect to an accord and satisfaction. Moreover, there is no failure of "due diligence" under Section 1–201(27)* if the claimant does not require its clerks to look for full satisfaction statements on checks or accompanying communications. Nor is there any duty of the claimant to assign that duty to its clerks. Section 3–311(c) is intended to allow a claimant to avoid an inadvertent accord and satisfaction by complying with either subsection (c)(1) or (2) without burdening the check-processing operation with extraneous and wasteful additional duties.

8. In some cases the disputed claim may have been assigned to a finance company or bank as part of a financing arrangement with respect to accounts receivable. If the account debtor was notified of the assignment, the claimant is the assignee of the account receivable and the "agent of the claimant" in subsection (d) refers to an agent of the assignee.

§ 3–312. Lost, Destroyed, or Stolen Cashier's Check, Teller's Check, or Certified Check.

(a) In this section:

(1) "Check" means a cashier's check, teller's check, or certified check.

(2) "Claimant" means a person who claims the right to receive the amount of a cashier's check, teller's check, or certified check that was lost, destroyed, or stolen.

(3) "Declaration of loss" means a statement, made in a record under penalty of perjury, to the effect that (i) the declarer lost possession of a check, (ii) the declarer is the drawer or payee of the check, in the case of a certified check, or the remitter or payee of the check, in the case of a cashier's check or teller's check, (iii) the loss of possession was not the result of a transfer by the declarer or a lawful seizure, and (iv) the declarer cannot reasonably obtain possession of the check because

---

* *Referring to unrevised Article 1 (Appendix A).*

the check was destroyed, its whereabouts cannot be determined, or it is in the wrongful possession of an unknown person or a person that cannot be found or is not amenable to service of process.

(4)   "Obligated bank" means the issuer of a cashier's check or teller's check or the acceptor of a certified check.

(b)   A claimant may assert a claim to the amount of a check by a communication to the obligated bank describing the check with reasonable certainty and requesting payment of the amount of the check, if (i) the claimant is the drawer or payee of a certified check or the remitter or payee of a cashier's check or teller's check, (ii) the communication contains or is accompanied by a declaration of loss of the claimant with respect to the check, (iii) the communication is received at a time and in a manner affording the bank a reasonable time to act on it before the check is paid, and (iv) the claimant provides reasonable identification if requested by the obligated bank. Delivery of a declaration of loss is a warranty of the truth of the statements made in the declaration. If a claim is asserted in compliance with this subsection, the following rules apply:

(1)   The claim becomes enforceable at the later of (i) the time the claim is asserted, or (ii) the 90th day following the date of the check, in the case of a cashier's check or teller's check, or the 90th day following the date of the acceptance, in the case of a certified check.

(2)   Until the claim becomes enforceable, it has no legal effect and the obligated bank may pay the check or, in the case of a teller's check, may permit the drawee to pay the check. Payment to a person entitled to enforce the check discharges all liability of the obligated bank with respect to the check.

(3)   If the claim becomes enforceable before the check is presented for payment, the obligated bank is not obliged to pay the check.

(4)   When the claim becomes enforceable, the obligated bank becomes obliged to pay the amount of the check to the claimant if payment of the check has not been made to a person entitled to enforce the check. Subject to Section 4–302(a)(1), payment to the claimant discharges all liability of the obligated bank with respect to the check.

(c)   If the obligated bank pays the amount of a check to a claimant under subsection (b)(4) and the check is presented for payment by a person having rights of a holder in due course, the claimant is obliged to (i) refund the payment to the obligated bank if the check is paid, or (ii) pay the amount of the check to the person having rights of a holder in due course if the check is dishonored.

(d)   If a claimant has the right to assert a claim under subsection (b) and is also a person entitled to enforce a cashier's check, teller's check, or certified check which is lost, destroyed, or stolen, the claimant may assert rights with respect to the check either under this section or Section 3–309.

As added in 1991 and amended in 2002.

Official Comment

1.   This section applies to cases in which a cashier's check, teller's check, or certified check is lost, destroyed, or stolen. In one typical case a customer of a bank closes his or her account and takes a cashier's check or teller's check of the bank as payment of the amount of the account. The customer may be moving to a new area and the check is to be used to open a bank account in that area. In such a case the check will normally be payable to the customer. In another typical case a cashier's check or teller's check is bought from a bank for the purpose of paying some obligation of the buyer of the check. In such a case the check may be made payable to the customer and then negotiated to the creditor by indorsement. But often, the payee of the check is the creditor. In the latter case the customer is a remitter. The section covers loss of the check by either the remitter or the payee. The section also covers loss of a certified check by either the drawer or payee.

Under Section 3–309 a person seeking to enforce a lost, destroyed, or stolen cashier's check or teller's check may be required by the court to give adequate protection to the issuing bank against loss that might occur by reason of the claim by another person to enforce the check. This might require the posting of an expensive bond for the amount of the check. The purpose of Section 3–312 is to offer a person who loses such a check a means of getting refund of the amount of the check within a reasonable period of time without the expense of posting a bond and with full protection of the obligated bank.

2.   A claim to the amount of a lost, destroyed, or stolen cashier's check, teller's check, or certified check may be made under subsection (b) if the following requirements of that subsection are met. First, a claim may be asserted only by the drawer or payee of a certified check or the remitter or payee of a cashier's check or teller's check. An indorsee of a check is not covered because the indorsee is not an original party to the check or a remitter. Limitation to an original party or remitter gives the obligated bank the ability to determine, at the time it becomes obligated on the check, the identity of the person or persons who can assert a claim with respect to the check. The bank is not faced with having to determine the rights of some person who was not a party to the check at that time or with whom the bank had not dealt. If a cashier's check is issued to the order of the person who purchased it from the bank and that person indorses it over to a third person who loses the check, the third person may assert rights to enforce the check under Section 3–309 but has no rights under Section 3–312.

Second, the claim must be asserted by a communication to the obligated bank describing the check with reasonable certainty and requesting payment of the amount of the check. "Obligated bank" is defined in subsection (a)(4). Third, the communication must be received in time to allow the obligated bank to act on the claim before the check is paid, and the claimant must provide reasonable identification if requested. Subsections (b)(iii) and (iv). Fourth, the communication must contain or be accompanied by a declaration of loss described in subsection (b). This declaration is an affidavit or other writing made under penalty of perjury alleging the loss, destruction, or theft of the check and stating that the declarer is a person entitled to assert a claim, i.e. the drawer or payee of a certified check or the remitter or payee of a cashier's check or teller's check.

A claimant who delivers a declaration of loss makes a warranty of the truth of the statements made in the declaration. The warranty is made to the obligated bank and anybody who has a right to enforce the check. If the declaration of loss falsely alleges loss of a cashier's check that did not in fact occur, a holder of the check who was unable to obtain payment because subsection (b)(3) and (4) caused the obligated bank to dishonor the check would have a cause of action against the declarer for breach of warranty.

The obligated bank may not impose additional requirements on the claimant to assert a claim under subsection (b). For example, the obligated bank may not require the posting of a bond or other form of security. Section 3–312(b) states the procedure for asserting claims covered by the section. Thus, procedures that may be stated in other law for stating claims to property do not apply and are displaced within the meaning of Section 1–103.

3.   A claim asserted under subsection (b) does not have any legal effect, however, until the date it becomes enforceable, which cannot be earlier than 90 days after the date of a cashier's check or teller's check or 90 days after the date of acceptance of a certified check. Thus, if a lost check is presented for payment within the 90-day period, the bank may pay a person entitled to enforce the check without regard to the claim and is discharged of all liability with respect to the check. This ensures the continued utility of cashier's checks, teller's checks, and certified checks as cash equivalents. Virtually all such checks are presented for payment within 90 days.

If the claim becomes enforceable and payment has not been made to a person entitled to enforce the check, the bank becomes obligated to pay the amount of the check to the claimant. Subsection (b)(4). When the bank becomes obligated to pay the amount of the check to the claimant, the bank is relieved of its obligation to pay the check. Subsection (b)(3). Thus, any person entitled to enforce the check, including even a holder in due course, loses the right to enforce the check after a claim under subsection (b) becomes enforceable.

If the obligated bank pays the claimant under subsection (b)(4), the bank is discharged of all liability with respect to the check. The only exception is the unlikely case in which the obligated bank subsequently incurs liability under Section 4–302(a)(1) with respect to the check. For example, Obligated Bank is the issuer of a cashier's check and, after a claim becomes enforceable, it pays the claimant under subsection (b)(4). Later the check is presented to Obligated Bank for payment over the counter. Under subsection (b)(3), Obligated Bank is not obliged to pay the check and may dishonor the check by returning it to the person who presented it for payment. But the normal rules of check collection are not affected by Section 3–312. If Obligated Bank retains the check beyond midnight of the day of presentment without settling for it, it becomes accountable for the amount of the check under Section 4–302(a)(1) even though it had no obligation to pay the check.

An obligated bank that pays the amount of a check to a claimant under subsection (b)(4) is discharged of all liability on the check so long as the assertion of the claim meets the requirements of subsection (b) discussed in Comment 2. This is important in cases of fraudulent declarations of loss. For example, if the claimant falsely alleges a loss that in fact did not occur, the bank, subject to Section 1–203,* may rely on the declaration of loss. On

*   *Referring to unrevised Article 1 (Appendix A).*

327

the other hand, a claim may be asserted only by a person described in subsection (b)(i). Thus, the bank is discharged under subsection (a)(4) only if it pays such a person. Although it is highly unlikely, it is possible that more than one person could assert a claim under subsection (b) to the amount of a check. Such a case could occur if one of the claimants makes a false declaration of loss. The obligated bank is not required to determine whether a claimant who complies with subsection (b) is acting wrongfully. The bank may utilize procedures outside this Article, such as interpleader, under which the conflicting claims may be adjudicated.

Although it is unlikely that a lost check would be presented for payment after the claimant was paid by the bank under subsection (b)(4), it is possible for it to happen. Suppose the declaration of loss by the claimant fraudulently alleged a loss that in fact did not occur. If the claimant negotiated the check, presentment for payment would occur shortly after negotiation in almost all cases. Thus, a fraudulent declaration of loss is not likely to occur unless the check is negotiated after the 90-day period has already expired or shortly before expiration. In such a case the holder of the check, who may not have noticed the date of the check, is not entitled to payment from the obligated bank if the check is presented for payment after the claim becomes enforceable. Subsection (b)(3). The remedy of the holder who is denied payment in that case is an action against the claimant under subsection (c) if the holder is a holder in due course, or for breach of warranty under subsection (b). The holder would also have common law remedies against the claimant under the law of restitution or fraud.

4.   The following cases illustrate the operation of Section 3–312:

Case # 1. Obligated Bank (OB) certified a check drawn by its customer, Drawer (D), payable to Payee (P). Two days after the check was certified, D lost the check and then asserted a claim pursuant to subsection (b). The check had not been presented for payment when D's claim became enforceable 90 days after the check was certified. Under subsection (b)(4), at the time D's claim became enforceable OB became obliged to pay D the amount of the check. If the check is later presented for payment, OB may refuse to pay the check and has no obligation to anyone to pay the check. Any obligation owed by D to P, for which the check was intended as payment, is unaffected because the check was never delivered to P.

Case # 2. Obligated Bank (OB) issued a teller's check to Remitter (R) payable to Payee (P). R delivered the check to P in payment of an obligation. P lost the check and then asserted a claim pursuant to subsection (b). To carry out P's order, OB issued an order pursuant to Section 4–403(a) to the drawee of the teller's check to stop payment of the check effective on the 90th day after the date of the teller's check. The check was not presented for payment. On the 90th day after the date of the teller's check P's claim becomes enforceable and OB becomes obliged to pay P the amount of the check. As in Case # 1, OB has no further liability with respect to the check to anyone. When R delivered the check to P, R's underlying obligation to P was discharged under Section 3–310. Thus, R suffered no loss. Since P received the amount of the check, P also suffered no loss except with respect to the delay in receiving the amount of the check.

Case # 3. Obligated Bank (OB) issued a cashier's check to its customer, Payee (P). Two days after issue, the check was stolen from P who then asserted a claim pursuant to subsection (b). Ten days after issue, the check was deposited by X in an account in Depositary Bank (DB). X had found the check and forged the indorsement of P. DB promptly presented the check to OB and obtained payment on behalf of X. On the 90th day after the date of the check P's claim becomes enforceable and P is entitled to receive the amount of the check from OB. Subsection (b)(4). Although the check was presented for payment before P's claim becomes enforceable, OB is not discharged. Because of the forged indorsement X was not a holder and neither was DB. Thus, neither is a person entitled to enforce the check (Section 3–301) and OB is not discharged under Section 3–602(a). Thus, under subsection (b)(4), because OB did not pay a person entitled to enforce the check, OB must pay P. OB's remedy is against DB for breach of warranty under Section 4–208(a)(1). As an alternative to the remedy under Section 3–312, P could recover from DB for conversion under Section 3–420(a).

Case # 4. Obligated Bank (OB) issued a cashier's check to its customer, Payee (P). P made an unrestricted blank indorsement of the check and mailed the check to P's bank for deposit to P's account. The check was never received by P's bank. When P discovered the loss, P asserted a claim pursuant to subsection (b). X found the check and deposited it in X's account in Depositary Bank (DB) after indorsing the check. DB presented the check for payment before the end of the 90-day period after its date. OB paid the check. Because of the unrestricted blank indorsement by P, X became a holder of the check. DB also became a holder. Since the check was paid before P's claim became enforceable and payment was made to a person entitled to enforce the check, OB is discharged of all liability with respect to the check. Subsection (b)(2). Thus, P is not entitled to payment from OB. Subsection (b)(4) doesn't apply.

Case # 5. Obligated Bank (OB) issued a cashier's check to its customer, Payee (P). P made an unrestricted blank indorsement of the check and mailed the check to P's bank for deposit to P's account. The check was never received by P's bank. When P discovered the loss, P asserted a claim pursuant to subsection (b). At the end of the 90-day period after the date of the check, OB paid the amount of the check to P under subsection (b)(4). X then found the check and deposited it to X's account in Depositary Bank (DB). DB presented the check to OB for payment. OB is not obliged to pay the check. Subsection (b)(4). If OB dishonors the check, DB's remedy is to charge back X's account. Section 4–214(a). Although P, as an indorser, would normally have liability to DB under Section 3–415(a) because the check was dishonored, P is released from that liability under Section 3–415(e) because collection of the check was initiated more than 30 days after the indorsement. DB has a remedy only against X. A depositary bank that takes a cashier's check that cannot be presented for payment before expiration of the 90-day period after its date is on notice that the check might not be paid because of the possibility of a claim asserted under subsection (b) which would excuse the issuer of the check from paying the check. Thus, the depositary bank cannot safely release funds with respect to the check until it has assurance that the check has been paid. DB cannot be a holder in due course of the check because it took the check when the check was overdue. Section 3–304(a)(2). Thus, DB has no action against P under subsection (c).

Case # 6. Obligated Bank (OB) issued a cashier's check payable to bearer and delivered it to its customer, Remitter (R). R held the check for 90 days and then wrongfully asserted a claim to the amount of the check under subsection (b). The declaration of loss fraudulently stated that the check was lost. R received payment from OB under subsection (b)(4). R then negotiated the check to X for value. X presented the check to OB for payment. Although OB, under subsection (b)(2), was not obliged to pay the check, OB paid X by mistake. OB's teller did not notice that the check was more than 90 days old and was not aware that OB was not obliged to pay the check. If X took the check in good faith, OB may not recover from X. Section 3–418(c). OB's remedy is to recover from R for fraud or for breach of warranty in making a false declaration of loss. Subsection (b).

As amended in 2004.

PART 4

LIABILITY OF PARTIES

§ 3–401.   Signature.

(a)   A person is not liable on an instrument unless (i) the person signed the instrument, or (ii) the person is represented by an agent or representative who signed the instrument and the signature is binding on the represented person under Section 3–402.

(b)   A signature may be made (i) manually or by means of a device or machine, and (ii) by the use of any name, including a trade or assumed name, or by a word, mark, or symbol executed or adopted by a person with present intention to authenticate a writing.

Official Comment

1.   Obligation on an instrument depends on a signature that is binding on the obligor. The signature may be made by the obligor personally or by an agent authorized to act for the obligor. Signature by agents is covered by Section 3–402. It is not necessary that the name of the obligor appear on the instrument, so long as there is a signature that binds the obligor. Signature includes an indorsement.

2.   A signature may be handwritten, typed, printed or made in any other manner. It need not be subscribed, and may appear in the body of the instrument, as in the case of "I, John Doe, promise to pay * * * " without any other signature. It may be made by mark, or even by thumbprint. It may be made in any name, including any trade name or assumed name, however false and fictitious, which is adopted for the purpose. Parol evidence is admissible to identify the signer, and when the signer is identified the signature is effective. Indorsement in a name other than that of the indorser is governed by Section 3–204(d).

This section is not intended to affect any other law requiring a signature by mark to be witnessed, or any signature to be otherwise authenticated, or requiring any form of proof.

§ 3–402.   Signature by Representative.

(a)   If a person acting, or purporting to act, as a representative signs an instrument by signing either the name of the represented person or the name of the signer, the represented person is bound by the signature to the same extent the represented person would be bound if the signature were on a simple contract. If the represented person is bound, the signature of the representative is the "authorized signature of the represented person" and the represented person is liable on the instrument, whether or not identified in the instrument.

(b)   If a representative signs the name of the representative to an instrument and the signature is an authorized signature of the represented person, the following rules apply:

(1)   If the form of the signature shows unambiguously that the signature is made on behalf of the represented person who is identified in the instrument, the representative is not liable on the instrument.

(2)   Subject to subsection (c), if (i) the form of the signature does not show unambiguously that the signature is made in a representative capacity or (ii) the represented person is not identified in the instrument, the representative is liable on the instrument to a holder in due course that took the instrument without notice that the representative was not intended to be liable on the instrument. With respect to any other person, the representative is liable on the instrument unless the representative proves that the original parties did not intend the representative to be liable on the instrument.

(c)   If a representative signs the name of the representative as drawer of a check without indication of the representative status and the check is payable from an account of the represented person who is identified on the check, the signer is not liable on the check if the signature is an authorized signature of the represented person.

Official Comment

1.   Subsection (a) states when the represented person is bound on an instrument if the instrument is signed by a representative. If under the law of agency the represented person would be bound by the act of the representative in signing either the name of the represented person or that of the representative, the signature is the authorized signature of the represented person. Former Section 3–401(1) stated that "no person is liable on an instrument unless his signature appears thereon." This was interpreted as meaning that an undisclosed principal is not liable on an instrument. This interpretation provided an exception to ordinary agency law that binds an undisclosed principal on a simple contract.

It is questionable whether this exception was justified by the language of former Article 3 and there is no apparent policy justification for it. The exception is rejected by subsection (a) which returns to ordinary rules of agency. If P, the principal, authorized A, the agent, to borrow money on P's behalf and A signed A's name to a note without disclosing that the signature was on behalf of P, A is liable on the instrument. But if the person entitled to enforce the note can also prove that P authorized A to sign on P's behalf, why shouldn't P also be liable on the instrument? To recognize the liability of P takes nothing away from the utility of negotiable instruments. Furthermore, imposing liability on P has the merit of making it impossible to have an instrument on which nobody is liable even though it was authorized by P. That result could occur under former Section 3–401(1) if an authorized agent signed "as agent" but the note did not identify the principal. If the dispute was between the agent and the payee of the note, the agent could escape liability on the note by proving that the agent and the payee did not intend that the agent be liable on the note when the note was issued. Former Section 3–403(2)(b). Under the prevailing interpretation of former Section 3–401(1), the principal was not liable on the note under former 3–401(1) because the principal's name did not appear on the note. Thus, nobody was liable on the note even though all parties knew that the note was signed by the agent on behalf of the principal. Under Section 3–402(a) the principal would be liable on the note.

2.   Subsection (b) concerns the question of when an agent who signs an instrument on behalf of a principal is bound on the instrument. The approach followed by former Section 3–403 was to specify the form of signature that imposed or avoided liability. This approach was unsatisfactory. There are many ways in which there can be ambiguity about a signature. It is better to state a general rule. Subsection (b)(1) states that if the form of the signature unambiguously shows that it is made on behalf of an identified represented person (for example, "P, by A, Treasurer") the agent is not liable. This is a workable standard for a court to apply. Subsection (b)(2) partly

changes former Section 3–403(2). Subsection (b)(2) relates to cases in which the agent signs on behalf of a principal but the form of the signature does not fall within subsection (b)(1). The following cases are illustrative. In each case John Doe is the authorized agent of Richard Roe and John Doe signs a note on behalf of Richard Roe. In each case the intention of the original parties to the instrument is that Roe is to be liable on the instrument but Doe is not to be liable.

Case # 1. Doe signs "John Doe" without indicating in the note that Doe is signing as agent. The note does not identify Richard Roe as the represented person.

Case # 2. Doe signs "John Doe, Agent" but the note does not identify Richard Roe as the represented person.

Case # 3. The name "Richard Roe" is written on the note and immediately below that name Doe signs "John Doe" without indicating that Doe signed as agent.

In each case Doe is liable on the instrument to a holder in due course without notice that Doe was not intended to be liable. In none of the cases does Doe's signature unambiguously show that Doe was signing as agent for an identified principal. A holder in due course should be able to resolve any ambiguity against Doe.

But the situation is different if a holder in due course is not involved. In each case Roe is liable on the note. Subsection (a). If the original parties to the note did not intend that Doe also be liable, imposing liability on Doe is a windfall to the person enforcing the note. Under subsection (b)(2) Doe is prima facie liable because his signature appears on the note and the form of the signature does not unambiguously refute personal liability. But Doe can escape liability by proving that the original parties did not intend that he be liable on the note. This is a change from former Section 3–403(2)(a).

A number of cases under former Article 3 involved situations in which an agent signed the agent's name to a note, without qualification and without naming the person represented, intending to bind the principal but not the agent. The agent attempted to prove that the other party had the same intention. Some of these cases involved mistake, and in some there was evidence that the agent may have been deceived into signing in that manner. In some of the cases the court refused to allow proof of the intention of the parties and imposed liability on the agent based on former Section 3–403(2)(a) even though both parties to the instrument may have intended that the agent not be liable. Subsection (b)(2) changes the result of those cases, and is consistent with Section 3–117 which allows oral or written agreements to modify or nullify apparent obligations on the instrument.

Former Section 3–403 spoke of the represented person being "named" in the instrument. Section 3–402 speaks of the represented person being "identified" in the instrument. This change in terminology is intended to reject decisions under former Section 3–403(2) requiring that the instrument state the legal name of the represented person.

3. Subsection (c) is directed at the check cases. It states that if the check identifies the represented person the agent who signs on the signature line does not have to indicate agency status. Virtually all checks used today are in personalized form which identify the person on whose account the check is drawn. In this case, nobody is deceived into thinking that the person signing the check is meant to be liable. This subsection is meant to overrule cases decided under former Article 3 such as Griffin v. Ellinger, 538 S.W.2d 97 (Texas 1976).

§ 3–403. Unauthorized Signature.

(a) Unless otherwise provided in this Article or Article 4, an unauthorized signature is ineffective except as the signature of the unauthorized signer in favor of a person who in good faith pays the instrument or takes it for value. An unauthorized signature may be ratified for all purposes of this Article.

(b) If the signature of more than one person is required to constitute the authorized signature of an organization, the signature of the organization is unauthorized if one of the required signatures is lacking.

(c) The civil or criminal liability of a person who makes an unauthorized signature is not affected by any provision of this Article which makes the unauthorized signature effective for the purposes of this Article.

Official Comment

1.   "Unauthorized" signature is defined in Section 1–201(43)* as one that includes a forgery as well as a signature made by one exceeding actual or apparent authority. Former Section 3–404(1) stated that an unauthorized signature was inoperative as the signature of the person whose name was signed unless that person "is precluded from denying it." Under former Section 3–406 if negligence by the person whose name was signed contributed to an unauthorized signature, that person "is precluded from asserting the . . . lack of authority." Both of these sections were applied to cases in which a forged signature appeared on an instrument and the person asserting rights on the instrument alleged that the negligence of the purported signer contributed to the forgery. Since the standards for liability between the two sections differ, the overlap between the sections caused confusion. Section 3–403(a) deals with the problem by removing the preclusion language that appeared in former Section 3–404.

2.   The except clause of the first sentence of subsection (a) states the generally accepted rule that the unauthorized signature, while it is wholly inoperative as that of the person whose name is signed, is effective to impose liability upon the signer or to transfer any rights that the signer may have in the instrument. The signer's liability is not in damages for breach of warranty of authority, but is full liability on the instrument in the capacity in which the signer signed. It is, however, limited to parties who take or pay the instrument in good faith; and one who knows that the signature is unauthorized cannot recover from the signer on the instrument.

3.   The last sentence of subsection (a) allows an unauthorized signature to be ratified. Ratification is a retroactive adoption of the unauthorized signature by the person whose name is signed and may be found from conduct as well as from express statements. For example, it may be found from the retention of benefits received in the transaction with knowledge of the unauthorized signature. Although the forger is not an agent, ratification is governed by the rules and principles applicable to ratification of unauthorized acts of an agent.

Ratification is effective for all purposes of this Article. The unauthorized signature becomes valid so far as its effect as a signature is concerned. Although the ratification may relieve the signer of liability on the instrument, it does not of itself relieve the signer of liability to the person whose name is signed. It does not in any way affect the criminal law. No policy of the criminal law prevents a person whose name is forged to assume liability to others on the instrument by ratifying the forgery, but the ratification cannot affect the rights of the state. While the ratification may be taken into account with other relevant facts in determining punishment, it does not relieve the signer of criminal liability.

4.   Subsection (b) clarifies the meaning of "unauthorized" in cases in which an instrument contains less than all of the signatures that are required as authority to pay a check. Judicial authority was split on the issue whether the one-year notice period under former Section 4–406(4) (now Section 4–406(f)) barred a customer's suit against a payor bank that paid a check containing less than all of the signatures required by the customer to authorize payment of the check. Some cases took the view that if a customer required that a check contain the signatures of both A and B to authorize payment and only A signed, there was no unauthorized signature within the meaning of that term in former Section 4–406(4) because A's signature was neither unauthorized nor forged. The other cases correctly pointed out that it was the customer's signature at issue and not that of A; hence, the customer's signature was unauthorized if all signatures required to authorize payment of the check were not on the check. Subsection (b) follows the latter line of cases. The same analysis applies if A forged the signature of B. Because the forgery is not effective as a signature of B, the required signature of B is lacking.

Subsection (b) refers to "the authorized signature of an organization." The definition of "organization" in Section 1–201(28)* is very broad. It covers not only commercial entities but also "two or more persons having a joint or common interest." Hence subsection (b) would apply when a husband and wife are both required to sign an instrument.

§ 3–404.   Impostors; Fictitious Payees.

(a)   If an impostor, by use of the mails or otherwise, induces the issuer of an instrument to issue the instrument to the impostor, or to a person acting in concert with the impostor, by impersonating the payee of the instrument or a person authorized to act for the payee, an indorsement of the instrument by any person in the name of the payee is effective as the indorsement of the payee in favor of a person who, in good faith, pays the instrument or takes it for value or for collection.

---

*   *Referring to unrevised Article 1 (Appendix A).*

(b) If (i) a person whose intent determines to whom an instrument is payable (Section 3–110(a) or (b)) does not intend the person identified as payee to have any interest in the instrument, or (ii) the person identified as payee of an instrument is a fictitious person, the following rules apply until the instrument is negotiated by special indorsement:

(1) Any person in possession of the instrument is its holder.

(2) An indorsement by any person in the name of the payee stated in the instrument is effective as the indorsement of the payee in favor of a person who, in good faith, pays the instrument or takes it for value or for collection.

(c) Under subsection (a) or (b), an indorsement is made in the name of a payee if (i) it is made in a name substantially similar to that of the payee or (ii) the instrument, whether or not indorsed, is deposited in a depositary bank to an account in a name substantially similar to that of the payee.

(d) With respect to an instrument to which subsection (a) or (b) applies, if a person paying the instrument or taking it for value or for collection fails to exercise ordinary care in paying or taking the instrument and that failure substantially contributes to loss resulting from payment of the instrument, the person bearing the loss may recover from the person failing to exercise ordinary care to the extent the failure to exercise ordinary care contributed to the loss.

Official Comment

1. Under former Article 3, the impostor cases were governed by former Section 3–405(1)(a) and the fictitious payee cases were governed by Section 3–405(1)(b). Section 3–404 replaces former Section 3–405(1)(a) and (b) and modifies the previous law in some respects. Former Section 3–405 was read by some courts to require that the indorsement be in the exact name of the named payee. Revised Article 3 rejects this result. Section 3–404(c) requires only that the indorsement be made in a name "substantially similar" to that of the payee. Subsection (c) also recognizes the fact that checks may be deposited without indorsement. Section 4–205(a).

Subsection (a) changes the former law in a case in which the impostor is impersonating an agent. Under former Section 3–405(1)(a), if Impostor impersonated Smith and induced the drawer to draw a check to the order of Smith, Impostor could negotiate the check. If Impostor impersonated Smith, the president of Smith Corporation, and the check was payable to the order of Smith Corporation, the section did not apply. See the last paragraph of Comment 2 to former Section 3–405. In revised Article 3, Section 3–404(a) gives Impostor the power to negotiate the check in both cases.

2. Subsection (b) is based in part on former Section 3–405(1)(b) and in part on N.I.L. § 9(3). It covers cases in which an instrument is payable to a fictitious or nonexisting person and to cases in which the payee is a real person but the drawer or maker does not intend the payee to have any interest in the instrument. Subsection (b) applies to any instrument, but its primary importance is with respect to checks of corporations and other organizations. It also applies to forged check cases. The following cases illustrate subsection (b):

Case # 1. Treasurer is authorized to draw checks in behalf of Corporation. Treasurer fraudulently draws a check of Corporation payable to Supplier Co., a non-existent company. Subsection (b) applies because Supplier Co. is a fictitious person and because Treasurer did not intend Supplier Co. to have any interest in the check. Under subsection (b)(1) Treasurer, as the person in possession of the check, becomes the holder of the check. Treasurer indorses the check in the name "Supplier Co." and deposits it in Depositary Bank. Under subsection (b)(2) and (c)(i), the indorsement is effective to make Depositary Bank the holder and therefore a person entitled to enforce the instrument. Section 3–301.

Case # 2. Same facts as Case # 1 except that Supplier Co. is an actual company that does business with Corporation. If Treasurer intended to steal the check when the check was drawn, the result in Case # 2 is the same as the result in Case # 1. Subsection (b) applies because Treasurer did not intend Supplier Co. to have any interest in the check. It does not make any difference whether Supplier Co. was or was not a creditor of Corporation when the check was drawn. If Treasurer did not decide to steal the check until after the check was drawn, the case is covered by Section 3–405 rather than Section 3–404(b), but the result is the same. See Case # 6 in Comment 3 to Section 3–405.

Case # 3. Checks of Corporation must be signed by two officers. President and Treasurer both sign a check of Corporation payable to Supplier Co., a company that does business with Corporation from time to time but to which Corporation does not owe any money. Treasurer knows that no money is owed to Supplier

Co. and does not intend that Supplier Co. have any interest in the check. President believes that money is owed to Supplier Co. Treasurer obtains possession of the check after it is signed. Subsection (b) applies because Treasurer is "a person whose intent determines to whom an instrument is payable" and Treasurer does not intend Supplier Co. to have any interest in the check. Treasurer becomes the holder of the check and may negotiate it by indorsing it in the name "Supplier Co."

Case # 4. Checks of Corporation are signed by a check-writing machine. Names of payees of checks produced by the machine are determined by information entered into the computer that operates the machine. Thief, a person who is not an employee or other agent of Corporation, obtains access to the computer and causes the check-writing machine to produce a check payable to Supplier Co., a non-existent company. Subsection (b)(ii) applies. Thief then obtains possession of the check. At that point Thief becomes the holder of the check because Thief is the person in possession of the instrument. Subsection (b)(1). Under Section 3–301 Thief, as holder, is the "person entitled to enforce the instrument" even though Thief does not have title to the check and is in wrongful possession of it. Thief indorses the check in the name "Supplier Co." and deposits it in an account in Depositary Bank which Thief opened in the name "Supplier Co." Depositary Bank takes the check in good faith and credits the "Supplier Co." account. Under subsection (b)(2) and (c)(i), the indorsement is effective. Depositary Bank becomes the holder and the person entitled to enforce the check. The check is presented to the drawee bank for payment and payment is made. Thief then withdraws the credit to the account. Although the check was issued without authority given by Corporation, the drawee bank is entitled to pay the check and charge Corporation's account if there was an agreement with Corporation allowing the bank to debit Corporation's account for payment of checks produced by the check-writing machine whether or not authorized. The indorsement is also effective if Supplier Co. is a real person. In that case subsection (b)(i) applies. Under Section 3–110(b) Thief is the person whose intent determines to whom the check is payable, and Thief did not intend Supplier Co. to have any interest in the check. When the drawee bank pays the check, there is no breach of warranty under Section 3–417(a)(1) or 4–208(a)(1) because Depositary Bank was a person entitled to enforce the check when it was forwarded for payment.

Case # 5. Thief, who is not an employee or agent of Corporation, steals check forms of Corporation. John Doe is president of Corporation and is authorized to sign checks on behalf of Corporation as drawer. Thief draws a check in the name of Corporation as drawer by forging the signature of Doe. Thief makes the check payable to the order of Supplier Co. with the intention of stealing it. Whether Supplier Co. is a fictitious person or a real person, Thief becomes the holder of the check and the person entitled to enforce it. The analysis is the same as that in Case # 4. Thief deposits the check in an account in Depositary Bank which Thief opened in the name "Supplier Co." Thief either indorses the check in a name other than "Supplier Co." or does not indorse the check at all. Under Section 4–205(a) a depositary bank may become holder of a check deposited to the account of a customer if the customer was a holder, whether or not the customer indorses. Subsection (c)(ii) treats deposit to an account in a name substantially similar to that of the payee as the equivalent of indorsement in the name of the payee. Thus, the deposit is an effective indorsement of the check. Depositary Bank becomes the holder of the check and the person entitled to enforce the check. If the check is paid by the drawee bank, there is no breach of warranty under Section 3–417(a)(1) or 4–208(a)(1) because Depositary Bank was a person entitled to enforce the check when it was forwarded for payment and, unless Depositary Bank knew about the forgery of Doe's signature, there is no breach of warranty under Section 3–417(a)(3) or 4–208(a)(3). Because the check was a forged check the drawee bank is not entitled to charge Corporation's account unless Section 3–406 or Section 4–406 applies.

3. In cases governed by subsection (a) the dispute will normally be between the drawer of the check that was obtained by the impostor and the drawee bank that paid it. The drawer is precluded from obtaining recredit of the drawer's account by arguing that the check was paid on a forged indorsement so long as the drawee bank acted in good faith in paying the check. Cases governed by subsection (b) are illustrated by Cases # 1 through # 5 in Comment 2. In Cases # 1, # 2, and # 3 there is no forgery of the check, thus the drawer of the check takes the loss if there is no lack of good faith by the banks involved. Cases # 4 and # 5 are forged check cases. Depositary Bank is entitled to retain the proceeds of the check if it didn't know about the forgery. Under Section 3–418 the drawee bank is not entitled to recover from Depositary Bank on the basis of payment by mistake because Depositary Bank took the check in good faith and gave value for the check when the credit given for the check was withdrawn. And there is no breach of warranty under Section 3–417(a)(1) or (3) or 4–208(a)(1) or (3). Unless Section 3–406 applies the loss is taken by the drawee bank if a forged check is paid, and that is the result in Case # 5. In Case # 4 the loss is taken by Corporation, the drawer, because an agreement between Corporation and the drawee bank allowed the bank to debit Corporation's account despite the unauthorized use of the check-writing machine.

If a check payable to an impostor, fictitious payee, or payee not intended to have an interest in the check is paid, the effect of subsections (a) and (b) is to place the loss on the drawer of the check rather than on the drawee or the depositary bank that took the check for collection. Cases governed by subsection (a) always involve fraud, and fraud is almost always involved in cases governed by subsection (b). The drawer is in the best position to avoid the fraud and thus should take the loss. This is true in Case # 1, Case # 2, and Case # 3. But in some cases the person taking the check might have detected the fraud and thus have prevented the loss by the exercise of ordinary care. In those cases, if that person failed to exercise ordinary care, it is reasonable that that person bear loss to the extent the failure contributed to the loss. Subsection (d) is intended to reach that result. It allows the person who suffers loss as a result of payment of the check to recover from the person who failed to exercise ordinary care. In Case # 1, Case # 2, and Case # 3, the person suffering the loss is Corporation, the drawer of the check. In each case the most likely defendant is the depositary bank that took the check and failed to exercise ordinary care. In those cases, the drawer has a cause of action against the offending bank to recover a portion of the loss. The amount of loss to be allocated to each party is left to the trier of fact. Ordinary care is defined in Section 3–103(a)(9). An example of the type of conduct by a depositary bank that could give rise to recovery under subsection (d) is discussed in Comment 4 to Section 3–405. That comment addresses the last sentence of Section 3–405(b) which is similar to Section 3–404(d).

In Case # 1, Case # 2, and Case # 3, there was no forgery of the drawer's signature. But cases involving checks payable to a fictitious payee or a payee not intended to have an interest in the check are often forged check cases as well. Examples are Case # 4 and Case # 5. Normally, the loss in forged check cases is on the drawee bank that paid the check. Case # 5 is an example. In Case # 4 the risk with respect to the forgery is shifted to the drawer because of the agreement between the drawer and the drawee bank. The doctrine that prevents a drawee bank from recovering payment with respect to a forged check if the payment was made to a person who took the check for value and in good faith is incorporated into Section 3–418 and Sections 3–417(a)(3) and 4–208(a)(3). This doctrine is based on the assumption that the depositary bank normally has no way of detecting the forgery because the drawer is not that bank's customer. On the other hand, the drawee bank, at least in some cases, may be able to detect the forgery by comparing the signature on the check with the specimen signature that the drawee has on file. But in some forged check cases the depositary bank is in a position to detect the fraud. Those cases typically involve a check payable to a fictitious payee or a payee not intended to have an interest in the check. Subsection (d) applies to those cases. If the depositary bank failed to exercise ordinary care and the failure substantially contributed to the loss, the drawer in Case # 4 or the drawee bank in Case # 5 has a cause of action against the depositary bank under subsection (d). Comment 4 to Section 3–405 can be used as a guide to the type of conduct that could give rise to recovery under Section 3–404(d).

§ 3–405. Employer's Responsibility for Fraudulent Indorsement by Employee.

(a) In this section:

(1) "Employee" includes an independent contractor and employee of an independent contractor retained by the employer.

(2) "Fraudulent indorsement" means (i) in the case of an instrument payable to the employer, a forged indorsement purporting to be that of the employer, or (ii) in the case of an instrument with respect to which the employer is the issuer, a forged indorsement purporting to be that of the person identified as payee.

(3) "Responsibility" with respect to instruments means authority (i) to sign or indorse instruments on behalf of the employer, (ii) to process instruments received by the employer for bookkeeping purposes, for deposit to an account, or for other disposition, (iii) to prepare or process instruments for issue in the name of the employer, (iv) to supply information determining the names or addresses of payees of instruments to be issued in the name of the employer, (v) to control the disposition of instruments to be issued in the name of the employer, or (vi) to act otherwise with respect to instruments in a responsible capacity. "Responsibility" does not include authority that merely allows an employee to have access to instruments or blank or incomplete instrument forms that are being stored or transported or are part of incoming or outgoing mail, or similar access.

(b) For the purpose of determining the rights and liabilities of a person who, in good faith, pays an instrument or takes it for value or for collection, if an employer entrusted an employee with responsibility with respect to the instrument and the employee or a person acting in concert with the employee makes a fraudulent indorsement of the instrument, the indorsement is effective as the indorsement of the person to whom the instrument is payable if it is made in the name of that person. If the person paying the instrument or taking it for value or for collection fails to exercise ordinary care in paying or taking the instrument and that failure substantially contributes to loss resulting from the fraud, the person bearing the loss may recover from the person failing to exercise ordinary care to the extent the failure to exercise ordinary care contributed to the loss.

(c)   Under subsection (b), an indorsement is made in the name of the person to whom an instrument is payable if (i) it is made in a name substantially similar to the name of that person or (ii) the instrument, whether or not indorsed, is deposited in a depositary bank to an account in a name substantially similar to the name of that person.

Official Comment

1.   Section 3–405 is addressed to fraudulent indorsements made by an employee with respect to instruments with respect to which the employer has given responsibility to the employee. It covers two categories of fraudulent indorsements: indorsements made in the name of the employer to instruments payable to the employer and indorsements made in the name of payees of instruments issued by the employer. This section applies to instruments generally but normally the instrument will be a check. Section 3–405 adopts the principle that the risk of loss for fraudulent indorsements by employees who are entrusted with responsibility with respect to checks should fall on the employer rather than the bank that takes the check or pays it, if the bank was not negligent in the transaction. Section 3–405 is based on the belief that the employer is in a far better position to avoid the loss by care in choosing employees, in supervising them, and in adopting other measures to prevent forged indorsements on instruments payable to the employer or fraud in the issuance of instruments in the name of the employer. If the bank failed to exercise ordinary care, subsection (b) allows the employer to shift loss to the bank to the extent the bank's failure to exercise ordinary care contributed to the loss. "Ordinary care" is defined in Section 3–103(a)(9). The provision applies regardless of whether the employer is negligent.

The first category of cases governed by Section 3–405 are those involving indorsements made in the name of payees of instruments issued by the employer. In this category, Section 3–405 includes cases that were covered by former Section 3–405(1)(c). The scope of Section 3–405 in revised Article 3 is, however, somewhat wider. It covers some cases not covered by former Section 3–405(1)(c) in which the entrusted employee makes a forged indorsement to a check drawn by the employer. An example is Case # 6 in Comment 3. Moreover, a larger group of employees is included in revised Section 3–405. The key provision is the definition of "responsibility" in subsection (a)(1) which identifies the kind of responsibility delegated to an employee which will cause the employer to take responsibility for the fraudulent acts of that employee. An employer can insure this risk by employee fidelity bonds.

The second category of cases governed by Section 3–405—fraudulent indorsements of the name of the employer to instruments payable to the employer—were covered in former Article 3 by Section 3–406. Under former Section 3–406, the employer took the loss only if negligence of the employer could be proved. Under revised Article 3, Section 3–406 need not be used with respect to forgeries of the employer's indorsement. Section 3–405 imposes the loss on the employer without proof of negligence.

2.   With respect to cases governed by former Section 3–405(1)(c), Section 3–405 is more favorable to employers in one respect. The bank was entitled to the preclusion provided by former Section 3–405(1)(c) if it took the check in good faith. The fact that the bank acted negligently did not shift the loss to the bank so long as the bank acted in good faith. Under revised Section 3–405 the loss may be recovered from the bank to the extent the failure of the bank to exercise ordinary care contributed to the loss.

3.   Section 3–404(b) and Section 3–405 both apply to cases of employee fraud. Section 3–404(b) is not limited to cases of employee fraud, but most of the cases to which it applies will be cases of employee fraud. The following cases illustrate the application of Section 3–405. In each case it is assumed that the bank that took the check acted in good faith and was not negligent.

Case # 1. Janitor, an employee of Employer, steals a check for a very large amount payable to Employer after finding it on a desk in one of Employer's offices. Janitor forges Employer's indorsement on the check and obtains payment. Since Janitor was not entrusted with "responsibility" with respect to the check, Section 3–405 does not apply. Section 3–406 might apply to this case. The issue would be whether Employer was negligent in safeguarding the check. If not, Employer could assert that the indorsement was forged and bring an action for conversion against the depositary or payor bank under Section 3–420.

Case # 2. X is Treasurer of Corporation and is authorized to write checks on behalf of Corporation by signing X's name as Treasurer. X draws a check in the name of Corporation and signs X's name as Treasurer. The check is made payable to X. X then indorses the check and obtains payment. Assume that Corporation did not owe any money to X and did not authorize X to write the check. Although the writing of the check was not authorized, Corporation is bound as drawer of the check because X had authority to sign checks on behalf of Corporation. This result follows from agency law and Section 3–402(a). Section 3–405 does not apply in this case because there is no forged indorsement. X was payee of the check so the indorsement is valid. Section 3–110(a).

Case # 3. The duties of Employee, a bookkeeper, include posting the amounts of checks payable to Employer to the accounts of the drawers of the checks. Employee steals a check payable to Employer which was entrusted to Employee and forges Employer's indorsement. The check is deposited by Employee to an account in Depositary Bank which Employee opened in the same name as Employer, and the check is honored by the drawee bank. The indorsement is effective as Employer's indorsement because Employee's duties include processing checks for bookkeeping purposes. Thus, Employee is entrusted with "responsibility" with respect to the check. Neither Depositary Bank nor the drawee bank is liable to Employer for conversion of the check. The same result follows if Employee deposited the check in the account in Depositary Bank without indorsement. Section 4–205(a). Under subsection (c) deposit in a depositary bank in an account in a name substantially similar to that of Employer is the equivalent of an indorsement in the name of Employer.

Case # 4. Employee's duties include stamping Employer's unrestricted blank indorsement on checks received by Employer and depositing them in Employer's bank account. After stamping Employer's unrestricted blank indorsement on a check, Employee steals the check and deposits it in Employee's personal bank account. Section 3–405 doesn't apply because there is no forged indorsement. Employee is authorized by Employer to indorse Employer's checks. The fraud by Employee is not the indorsement but rather the theft of the indorsed check. Whether Employer has a cause of action against the bank in which the check was deposited is determined by whether the bank had notice of the breach of fiduciary duty by Employee. The issue is determined under Section 3–307.

Case # 5. The computer that controls Employer's check-writing machine was programmed to cause a check to be issued to Supplier Co. to which money was owed by Employer. The address of Supplier Co. was included in the information in the computer. Employee is an accounts payable clerk whose duties include entering information into the computer. Employee fraudulently changed the address of Supplier Co. in the computer data bank to an address of Employee. The check was subsequently produced by the check-writing machine and mailed to the address that Employee had entered into the computer. Employee obtained possession of the check, indorsed it in the name of Supplier Co, and deposited it to an account in Depositary Bank which Employee opened in the name "Supplier Co." The check was honored by the drawee bank. The indorsement is effective under Section 3–405(b) because Employee's duties allowed Employee to supply information determining the address of the payee of the check. An employee that is entrusted with duties that enable the employee to determine the address to which a check is to be sent controls the disposition of the check and facilitates forgery of the indorsement. The employer is held responsible. The drawee may debit the account of Employer for the amount of the check. There is no breach of warranty by Depositary Bank under Section 3–417(a)(1) or 4–208(a)(1).

Case # 6. Treasurer is authorized to draw checks in behalf of Corporation. Treasurer draws a check of Corporation payable to Supplier Co., a company that sold goods to Corporation. The check was issued to pay the price of these goods. At the time the check was signed Treasurer had no intention of stealing the check. Later, Treasurer stole the check, indorsed it in the name "Supplier Co." and obtained payment by depositing it to an account in Depositary Bank which Treasurer opened in the name "Supplier Co.". The indorsement is effective under Section 3–405(b). Section 3–404(b) does not apply to this case.

Case # 7. Checks of Corporation are signed by Treasurer in behalf of Corporation as drawer. Clerk's duties include the preparation of checks for issue by Corporation. Clerk prepares a check payable to the order of Supplier Co. for Treasurer's signature. Clerk fraudulently informs Treasurer that the check is needed to pay a debt owed to Supplier Co, a company that does business with Corporation. No money is owed to Supplier Co. and Clerk intends to steal the check. Treasurer signs it and returns it to Clerk for mailing. Clerk does not indorse the check but deposits it to an account in Depositary Bank which Clerk opened in the name "Supplier Co.". The check is honored by the drawee bank. Section 3–404(b)(i) does not apply to this case because Clerk, under Section 3–110(a), is not the person whose intent determines to whom the check is payable. But Section 3–405 does apply and it treats the deposit by Clerk as an effective indorsement by Clerk because Clerk was entrusted with responsibility with respect to the check. If Supplier Co. is a fictitious person Section 3–404(b)(ii) applies. But the result is the same. Clerk's deposit is treated as an effective indorsement of the check whether Supplier Co. is a fictitious or a real person or whether money was or was not owing to Supplier Co. The drawee bank may debit the account of Corporation for the amount of the check and there is no breach of warranty by Depositary Bank under Section 3–417(1)(a).

4.   The last sentence of subsection (b) is similar to subsection (d) of Section 3–404 which is discussed in Comment 3 to Section 3–404. In Case # 5, Case # 6, or Case # 7 the depositary bank may have failed to exercise ordinary care when it allowed the employee to open an account in the name "Supplier Co.," to deposit checks payable to "Supplier Co." in that account, or to withdraw funds from that account that were proceeds of checks payable to Supplier Co. Failure to exercise ordinary care is to be determined in the context of all the facts relating to the bank's conduct with respect to the bank's collection of the check. If the trier of fact finds that there was such a failure and that the failure substantially contributed to loss, it could find the depositary bank liable to the extent the failure contributed to the loss. The last sentence of subsection (b) can be illustrated by an example. Suppose in Case # 5 that the check is not payable to an obscure "Supplier Co." but rather to a well-known national corporation. In addition, the check is for a very large amount of money. Before depositing the check, Employee opens an account in Depositary Bank in the name of the corporation and states to the person conducting the transaction for the bank that Employee is manager of a new office being opened by the corporation. Depositary Bank opens the account without requiring Employee to produce any resolutions of the corporation's board of directors or other evidence of authorization of Employee to act for the corporation. A few days later, the check is deposited, the account is credited, and the check is presented for payment. After Depositary Bank receives payment, it allows Employee to withdraw the credit by a wire transfer to an account in a bank in a foreign country. The trier of fact could find that Depositary Bank did not exercise ordinary care and that the failure to exercise ordinary care contributed to the loss suffered by Employer. The trier of fact could allow recovery by Employer from Depositary Bank for all or part of the loss suffered by Employer.

As amended in 2005.

§ 3–406.   Negligence Contributing to Forged Signature or Alteration of Instrument.

(a)   A person whose failure to exercise ordinary care substantially contributes to an alteration of an instrument or to the making of a forged signature on an instrument is precluded from asserting the alteration or the forgery against a person who, in good faith, pays the instrument or takes it for value or for collection.

(b)   Under subsection (a), if the person asserting the preclusion fails to exercise ordinary care in paying or taking the instrument and that failure substantially contributes to loss, the loss is allocated between the person precluded and the person asserting the preclusion according to the extent to which the failure of each to exercise ordinary care contributed to the loss.

(c)   Under subsection (a), the burden of proving failure to exercise ordinary care is on the person asserting the preclusion. Under subsection (b), the burden of proving failure to exercise ordinary care is on the person precluded.

Official Comment

1.   Section 3–406(a) is based on former Section 3–406. With respect to alteration, Section 3–406 adopts the doctrine of *Young v. Grote*, 4 Bing. 253 (1827), which held that a drawer who so negligently draws an instrument as to facilitate its material alteration is liable to a drawee who pays the altered instrument in good faith. Under Section 3–406 the doctrine is expanded to apply not only to drafts but to all instruments. It includes in the protected class any "person who, in good faith, pays the instrument or takes it for value or for collection." Section 3–406 rejects decisions holding that the maker of a note owes no duty of care to the holder because at the time the instrument is issued there is no contract between them. By issuing the instrument and "setting it afloat upon a sea of strangers" the maker or drawer voluntarily enters into a relation with later holders which justifies imposition of a duty of care. In this respect an instrument so negligently drawn as to facilitate alteration does not differ in principle from an instrument containing blanks which may be filled. Under Section 3–407 a person paying an altered instrument or taking it for value, in good faith and without notice of the alteration may enforce rights with respect to the instrument according to its original terms. If negligence of the obligor substantially contributes to an alteration, this section gives the holder or the payor the alternative right to treat the altered instrument as though it had been issued in the altered form.

No attempt is made to define particular conduct that will constitute "failure to exercise ordinary care [that] substantially contributes to an alteration." Rather, "ordinary care" is defined in Section 3–103(a)(9) in general terms. The question is left to the court or the jury for decision in the light of the circumstances in the particular case including reasonable commercial standards that may apply.

Section 3–406 does not make the negligent party liable in tort for damages resulting from the alteration. If the negligent party is estopped from asserting the alteration the person taking the instrument is fully protected because the taker can treat the instrument as having been issued in the altered form.

2.   Section 3–406 applies equally to a failure to exercise ordinary care that substantially contributes to the making of a forged signature on an instrument. Section 3–406 refers to "forged signature" rather than "unauthorized signature" that appeared in former Section 3–406 because it more accurately describes the scope of the provision. Unauthorized signature is a broader concept that includes not only forgery but also the signature of an agent which does not bind the principal under the law of agency. The agency cases are resolved independently under agency law. Section 3–406 is not necessary in those cases.

The "substantially contributes" test of former Section 3–406 is continued in this section in preference to a "direct and proximate cause" test. The "substantially contributes" test is meant to be less stringent than a "direct and proximate cause" test. Under the less stringent test the preclusion should be easier to establish. Conduct "substantially contributes" to a material alteration or forged signature if it is a contributing cause of the alteration or signature and a substantial factor in bringing it about. The analysis of "substantially contributes" in former Section 3–406 by the court in *Thompson Maple Products v. Citizens National Bank of Corry*, 234 A.2d 32 (Pa.Super.Ct.1967), states what is intended by the use of the same words in revised Section 3–406(b). Since Section 3–404(d) and Section 3–405(b) also use the words "substantially contributes" the analysis of these words also applies to those provisions.

3.   The following cases illustrate the kind of conduct that can be the basis of a preclusion under Section 3–406(a):

Case # 1. Employer signs checks drawn on Employer's account by use of a rubber stamp of Employer's signature. Employer keeps the rubber stamp along with Employer's personalized blank check forms in an unlocked desk drawer. An unauthorized person fraudulently uses the check forms to write checks on Employer's account. The checks are signed by use of the rubber stamp. If Employer demands that Employer's account in the drawee bank be recredited because the forged check was not properly payable, the drawee bank may defend by asserting that Employer is precluded from asserting the forgery. The trier of fact could find that Employer failed to exercise ordinary care to safeguard the rubber stamp and the check forms and that the failure substantially contributed to the forgery of Employer's signature by the unauthorized use of the rubber stamp.

Case # 2. An insurance company draws a check to the order of Sarah Smith in payment of a claim of a policyholder, Sarah Smith, who lives in Alabama. The insurance company also has a policyholder with the same name who lives in Illinois. By mistake, the insurance company mails the check to the Illinois Sarah Smith who indorses the check and obtains payment. Because the payee of the check is the Alabama Sarah Smith, the indorsement by the Illinois Sarah Smith is a forged indorsement. Section 3–110(a). The trier of fact could find that the insurance company failed to exercise ordinary care when it mailed the check to the wrong person and that the failure substantially contributed to the making of the forged indorsement. In that event the insurance company could be precluded from asserting the forged indorsement against the drawee bank that honored the check.

Case # 3. A company writes a check for $10. The figure "10" and the word "ten" are typewritten in the appropriate spaces on the check form. A large blank space is left after the figure and the word. The payee of the check, using a typewriter with a typeface similar to that used on the check, writes the word "thousand" after the word "ten" and a comma and three zeros after the figure "10". The drawee bank in good faith pays $10,000 when the check is presented for payment and debits the account of the drawer in that amount. The trier of fact could find that the drawer failed to exercise ordinary care in writing the check and that the failure substantially contributed to the alteration. In that case the drawer is precluded from asserting the alteration against the drawee if the check was paid in good faith.

4.   Subsection (b) differs from former Section 3–406 in that it adopts a concept of comparative negligence. If the person precluded under subsection (a) proves that the person asserting the preclusion failed to exercise ordinary care and that failure substantially contributed to the loss, the loss may be allocated between the two parties on a comparative negligence basis. In the case of a forged indorsement the litigation is usually between

the payee of the check and the depositary bank that took the check for collection. An example is a case like Case # 1 of Comment 3 to Section 3–405. If the trier of fact finds that Employer failed to exercise ordinary care in safeguarding the check and that the failure substantially contributed to the making of the forged indorsement, subsection (a) of Section 3–406 applies. If Employer brings an action for conversion against the depositary bank that took the checks from the forger, the depositary bank could assert the preclusion under subsection (a). But suppose the forger opened an account in the depositary bank in a name identical to that of Employer, the payee of the check, and then deposited the check in the account. Subsection (b) may apply. There may be an issue whether the depositary bank should have been alerted to possible fraud when a new account was opened for a corporation shortly before a very large check payable to a payee with the same name is deposited. Circumstances surrounding the opening of the account may have suggested that the corporation to which the check was payable may not be the same as the corporation for which the account was opened. If the trier of fact finds that collecting the check under these circumstances was a failure to exercise ordinary care, it could allocate the loss between the depositary bank and Employer, the payee.

§ 3–407.   Alteration.

(a)   "Alteration" means (i) an unauthorized change in an instrument that purports to modify in any respect the obligation of a party, or (ii) an unauthorized addition of words or numbers or other change to an incomplete instrument relating to the obligation of a party.

(b)   Except as provided in subsection (c), an alteration fraudulently made discharges a party whose obligation is affected by the alteration unless that party assents or is precluded from asserting the alteration. No other alteration discharges a party, and the instrument may be enforced according to its original terms.

(c)   A payor bank or drawee paying a fraudulently altered instrument or a person taking it for value, in good faith and without notice of the alteration, may enforce rights with respect to the instrument (i) according to its original terms, or (ii) in the case of an incomplete instrument altered by unauthorized completion, according to its terms as completed.

Official Comment

1.   This provision restates former Section 3–407. Former Section 3–407 defined a "material" alteration as any alteration that changes the contract of the parties in any respect. Revised Section 3–407 refers to such a change as an alteration. As under subsection (2) of former Section 3–407, discharge because of alteration occurs only in the case of an alteration fraudulently made. There is no discharge if a blank is filled in the honest belief that it is authorized or if a change is made with a benevolent motive such as a desire to give the obligor the benefit of a lower interest rate. Changes favorable to the obligor are unlikely to be made with any fraudulent intent, but if such an intent is found the alteration may operate as a discharge.

Discharge is a personal defense of the party whose obligation is modified and anyone whose obligation is not affected is not discharged. But if an alteration discharges a party there is also discharge of any party having a right of recourse against the discharged party because the obligation of the party with the right of recourse is affected by the alteration. Assent to the alteration given before or after it is made will prevent the party from asserting the discharge. The phrase "or is precluded from asserting the alteration" in subsection (b) recognizes the possibility of an estoppel or other ground barring the defense which does not rest on assent.

2.   Under subsection (c) a person paying a fraudulently altered instrument or taking it for value, in good faith and without notice of the alteration, is not affected by a discharge under subsection (b). The person paying or taking the instrument may assert rights with respect to the instrument according to its original terms or, in the case of an incomplete instrument that is altered by unauthorized completion, according to its terms as completed. If blanks are filled or an incomplete instrument is otherwise completed, subsection (c) places the loss upon the party who left the instrument incomplete by permitting enforcement in its completed form. This result is intended even though the instrument was stolen from the issuer and completed after the theft.

§ 3–408.   Drawee Not Liable on Unaccepted Draft.

A check or other draft does not of itself operate as an assignment of funds in the hands of the drawee available for its payment, and the drawee is not liable on the instrument until the drawee accepts it.

Official Comment

1. This section is a restatement of former Section 3–409(1). Subsection (2) of former Section 3–409 is deleted as misleading and superfluous. Comment 3 says of subsection (2): "It is intended to make it clear that this section does not in any way affect any liability which may arise apart from the instrument." In reality subsection (2) did not make anything clear and was a source of confusion. If all it meant was that a bank that has not certified a check may engage in other conduct that might make it liable to a holder, it stated the obvious and was superfluous. Section 1–103 is adequate to cover those cases.

2. Liability with respect to drafts may arise under other law. For example, Section 4–302 imposes liability on a payor bank for late return of an item.

§ 3–409. Acceptance of Draft; Certified Check.

(a) "Acceptance" means the drawee's signed agreement to pay a draft as presented. It must be written on the draft and may consist of the drawee's signature alone. Acceptance may be made at any time and becomes effective when notification pursuant to instructions is given or the accepted draft is delivered for the purpose of giving rights on the acceptance to any person.

(b) A draft may be accepted although it has not been signed by the drawer, is otherwise incomplete, is overdue, or has been dishonored.

(c) If a draft is payable at a fixed period after sight and the acceptor fails to date the acceptance, the holder may complete the acceptance by supplying a date in good faith.

(d) "Certified check" means a check accepted by the bank on which it is drawn. Acceptance may be made as stated in subsection (a) or by a writing on the check which indicates that the check is certified. The drawee of a check has no obligation to certify the check, and refusal to certify is not dishonor of the check.

Official Comment

1. The first three subsections of Section 3–409 are a restatement of former Section 3–410. Subsection (d) adds a definition of certified check which is a type of accepted draft.

2. Subsection (a) states the generally recognized rule that the mere signature of the drawee on the instrument is a sufficient acceptance. Customarily the signature is written vertically across the face of the instrument, but since the drawee has no reason to sign for any other purpose a signature in any other place, even on the back of the instrument, is sufficient. It need not be accompanied by such words as "Accepted," "Certified," or "Good." It must not, however, bear any words indicating an intent to refuse to honor the draft. The last sentence of subsection (a) states the generally recognized rule that an acceptance written on the draft takes effect when the drawee notifies the holder or gives notice according to instructions.

3. The purpose of subsection (c) is to provide a definite date of payment if none appears on the instrument. An undated acceptance of a draft payable "thirty days after sight" is incomplete. Unless the acceptor writes in a different date the holder is authorized to complete the acceptance according to the terms of the draft by supplying a date of acceptance. Any date supplied by the holder is effective if made in good faith.

4. The last sentence of subsection (d) states the generally recognized rule that in the absence of agreement a bank is under no obligation to certify a check. A check is a demand instrument calling for payment rather than acceptance. The bank may be liable for breach of any agreement with the drawer, the holder, or any other person by which it undertakes to certify. Its liability is not on the instrument, since the drawee is not so liable until acceptance. Section 3–408. Any liability is for breach of the separate agreement.

§ 3–410. Acceptance Varying Draft.

(a) If the terms of a drawee's acceptance vary from the terms of the draft as presented, the holder may refuse the acceptance and treat the draft as dishonored. In that case, the drawee may cancel the acceptance.

(b) The terms of a draft are not varied by an acceptance to pay at a particular bank or place in the United States, unless the acceptance states that the draft is to be paid only at that bank or place.

(c)   If the holder assents to an acceptance varying the terms of a draft, the obligation of each drawer and indorser that does not expressly assent to the acceptance is discharged.

Official Comment

1.   This section is a restatement of former Section 3–412. It applies to conditional acceptances, acceptances for part of the amount, acceptances to pay at a different time from that required by the draft, or to the acceptance of less than all of the drawees. It applies to any other engagement changing the essential terms of the draft. If the drawee makes a varied acceptance the holder may either reject it or assent to it. The holder may reject by insisting on acceptance of the draft as presented. Refusal by the drawee to accept the draft as presented is dishonor. In that event the drawee is not bound by the varied acceptance and is entitled to have it canceled.

If the holder assents to the varied acceptance, the drawee's obligation as acceptor is according to the terms of the varied acceptance. Under subsection (c) the effect of the holder's assent is to discharge any drawer or indorser who does not also assent. The assent of the drawer or indorser must be affirmatively expressed. Mere failure to object within a reasonable time is not assent which will prevent the discharge.

2.   Under subsection (b) an acceptance does not vary from the terms of the draft if it provides for payment at any particular bank or place in the United States unless the acceptance states that the draft is to be paid only at such bank or place. Section 3–501(b)(1) states that if an instrument is payable at a bank in the United States presentment must be made at the place of payment (Section 3–111) which in this case is at the designated bank.

§ 3–411.   Refusal to Pay Cashier's Checks, Teller's Checks, and Certified Checks.

(a)   In this section, "obligated bank" means the acceptor of a certified check or the issuer of a cashier's check or teller's check bought from the issuer.

(b)   If the obligated bank wrongfully (i) refuses to pay a cashier's check or certified check, (ii) stops payment of a teller's check, or (iii) refuses to pay a dishonored teller's check, the person asserting the right to enforce the check is entitled to compensation for expenses and loss of interest resulting from the nonpayment and may recover consequential damages if the obligated bank refuses to pay after receiving notice of particular circumstances giving rise to the damages.

(c)   Expenses or consequential damages under subsection (b) are not recoverable if the refusal of the obligated bank to pay occurs because (i) the bank suspends payments, (ii) the obligated bank asserts a claim or defense of the bank that it has reasonable grounds to believe is available against the person entitled to enforce the instrument, (iii) the obligated bank has a reasonable doubt whether the person demanding payment is the person entitled to enforce the instrument, or (iv) payment is prohibited by law.

Official Comment

1.   In some cases a creditor may require that the debt be paid by an obligation of a bank. The debtor may comply by obtaining certification of the debtor's check, but more frequently the debtor buys from a bank a cashier's check or teller's check payable to the creditor. The check is taken by the creditor as a cash equivalent on the assumption that the bank will pay the check. Sometimes, the debtor wants to retract payment by inducing the obligated bank not to pay. The typical case involves a dispute between the parties to the transaction in which the check is given in payment. In the case of a certified check or cashier's check, the bank can safely pay the holder of the check despite notice that there may be an adverse claim to the check (Section 3–602). It is also clear that the bank that sells a teller's check has no duty to order the bank on which it is drawn not to pay it. A debtor using any of these types of checks has no right to stop payment. Nevertheless, some banks will refuse payment as an accommodation to a customer. Section 3–411 is designed to discourage this practice.

2.   The term "obligated bank" refers to the issuer of the cashier's check or teller's check and the acceptor of the certified check. If the obligated bank wrongfully refuses to pay, it is liable to pay for expenses and loss of interest resulting from the refusal to pay. There is no express provision for attorney's fees, but attorney's fees are not meant to be necessarily excluded. They could be granted because they fit within the language "expenses * * * resulting from the nonpayment." In addition the bank may be liable to pay consequential damages if it has notice of the particular circumstances giving rise to the damages.

3.   Subsection (c) provides that expenses or consequential damages are not recoverable if the refusal to pay is because of the reasons stated. The purpose is to limit that recovery to cases in which the bank refuses to pay even though its obligation to pay is clear and it is able to pay. Subsection (b) applies only if the refusal to honor

the check is wrongful. If the bank is not obliged to pay there is no recovery. The bank may assert any claim or defense that it has, but normally the bank would not have a claim or defense. In the usual case it is a remitter that is asserting a claim to the check on the basis of a rescission of negotiation to the payee under Section 3–202. See Comment 2 to Section 3–201. The bank can assert that claim if there is compliance with Section 3–305(c), but the bank is not protected from damages under subsection (b) if the claim of the remitter is not upheld. In that case, the bank is insulated from damages only if payment is enjoined under Section 3–602(b)(1). Subsection (c)(iii) refers to cases in which the bank may have a reasonable doubt about the identity of the person demanding payment. For example, a cashier's check is payable to "Supplier Co." The person in possession of the check presents it for payment over the counter and claims to be an officer of Supplier Co. The bank may refuse payment until it has been given adequate proof that the presentment in fact is being made for Supplier Co., the person entitled to enforce the check.

§ 3–412.   Obligation of Issuer of Note or Cashier's Check.

The issuer of a note or cashier's check or other draft drawn on the drawer is obliged to pay the instrument (i) according to its terms at the time it was issued or, if not issued, at the time it first came into possession of a holder, or (ii) if the issuer signed an incomplete instrument, according to its terms when completed, to the extent stated in Sections 3–115 and 3–407. The obligation is owed to a person entitled to enforce the instrument or to an indorser who paid the instrument under Section 3–415.

Official Comment

1.   The obligations of the maker, acceptor, drawer, and indorser are stated in four separate sections. Section 3–412 states the obligation of the maker of a note and is consistent with former Section 3–413(1). Section 3–412 also applies to the issuer of a cashier's check or other draft drawn on the drawer. Under former Section 3–118(a), since a cashier's check or other draft drawn on the drawer was "effective as a note," the drawer was liable under former Section 3–413(1) as a maker. Under Sections 3–103(a)(8) and 3–104(f) a cashier's check or other draft drawn on the drawer is treated as a draft to reflect common commercial usage, but the liability of the drawer is stated by Section 3–412 as being the same as that of the maker of a note rather than that of the drawer of a draft. Thus, Section 3–412 does not in substance change former law.

2.   Under Section 3–105(b) nonissuance of either a complete or incomplete instrument is a defense by a maker or drawer against a person that is not a holder in due course.

3.   The obligation of the maker may be modified in the case of alteration if, under Section 3–406, the maker is precluded from asserting the alteration.

4.   The rule of this section is similar to the rule of Article 39 of the Convention on International Bills of Exchange and International Promissory Notes.

As amended in 2002.

§ 3–413.   Obligation of Acceptor.

(a)   The acceptor of a draft is obliged to pay the draft (i) according to its terms at the time it was accepted, even though the acceptance states that the draft is payable "as originally drawn" or equivalent terms, (ii) if the acceptance varies the terms of the draft, according to the terms of the draft as varied, or (iii) if the acceptance is of a draft that is an incomplete instrument, according to its terms when completed, to the extent stated in Sections 3–115 and 3–407. The obligation is owed to a person entitled to enforce the draft or to the drawer or an indorser who paid the draft under Section 3–414 or 3–415.

(b)   If the certification of a check or other acceptance of a draft states the amount certified or accepted, the obligation of the acceptor is that amount. If (i) the certification or acceptance does not state an amount, (ii) the amount of the instrument is subsequently raised, and (iii) the instrument is then negotiated to a holder in due course, the obligation of the acceptor is the amount of the instrument at the time it was taken by the holder in due course.

Official Comment

Subsection (a) is consistent with former Section 3–413(1). Subsection (b) has primary importance with respect to certified checks. It protects the holder in due course of a certified check that was altered after certification and before negotiation to the holder in due course. A bank can avoid liability for the altered amount by stating on the check the amount the bank agrees to pay. The subsection applies to other accepted drafts as well. The rule of this section is similar to the rule of Articles 41 of the Convention on International Bills of Exchange and International Promissory Notes. Articles 42 and 43 of the Convention include more detailed rules that in many respects do not have parallels in this Article.

As amended in 2002.

§ 3–414.   Obligation of Drawer.

(a)   This section does not apply to cashier's checks or other drafts drawn on the drawer.

(b)   If an unaccepted draft is dishonored, the drawer is obliged to pay the draft (i) according to its terms at the time it was issued or, if not issued, at the time it first came into possession of a holder, or (ii) if the drawer signed an incomplete instrument, according to its terms when completed, to the extent stated in Sections 3–115 and 3–407. The obligation is owed to a person entitled to enforce the draft or to an indorser who paid the draft under Section 3–415.

(c)   If a draft is accepted by a bank, the drawer is discharged, regardless of when or by whom acceptance was obtained.

(d)   If a draft is accepted and the acceptor is not a bank, the obligation of the drawer to pay the draft if the draft is dishonored by the acceptor is the same as the obligation of an indorser under Section 3–415(a) and (c).

(e)   If a draft states that it is drawn "without recourse" or otherwise disclaims liability of the drawer to pay the draft, the drawer is not liable under subsection (b) to pay the draft if the draft is not a check. A disclaimer of the liability stated in subsection (b) is not effective if the draft is a check.

(f)   If (i) a check is not presented for payment or given to a depositary bank for collection within 30 days after its date, (ii) the drawee suspends payments after expiration of the 30-day period without paying the check, and (iii) because of the suspension of payments, the drawer is deprived of funds maintained with the drawee to cover payment of the check, the drawer to the extent deprived of funds may discharge its obligation to pay the check by assigning to the person entitled to enforce the check the rights of the drawer against the drawee with respect to the funds.

Official Comment

1.   Subsection (a) excludes cashier's checks because the obligation of the issuer of a cashier's check is stated in Section 3–412.

2.   Subsection (b) states the obligation of the drawer on an unaccepted draft. It replaces former Section 3–413(2). The requirement under former Article 3 of notice of dishonor or protest has been eliminated. Under revised Article 3, notice of dishonor is necessary only with respect to indorser's liability. The liability of the drawer of an unaccepted draft is treated as a primary liability. Under former Section 3–102(1)(d) the term "secondary party" was used to refer to a drawer or indorser. The quoted term is not used in revised Article 3. The effect of a draft drawn without recourse is stated in subsection (e).

3.   Under subsection (c) the drawer is discharged of liability on a draft accepted by a bank regardless of when acceptance was obtained. This changes former Section 3–411(1) which provided that the drawer is discharged only if the holder obtains acceptance. Holders that have a bank obligation do not normally rely on the drawer to guarantee the bank's solvency. A holder can obtain protection against the insolvency of a bank acceptor by a specific guaranty of payment by the drawer or by obtaining an indorsement by the drawer. Section 3–205(d).

4.   Subsection (d) states the liability of the drawer if a draft is accepted by a drawee other than a bank and the acceptor dishonors. The drawer of an unaccepted draft is the only party liable on the instrument. The drawee has no liability on the draft. Section 3–408. When the draft is accepted, the obligations change. The drawee, as acceptor, becomes primarily liable and the drawer's liability is that of a person secondarily liable as a guarantor of payment. The drawer's liability is identical to that of an indorser, and subsection (d) states the drawer's liability that way. The drawer is liable to pay the person entitled to enforce the draft or any indorser that pays pursuant to Section 3–415. The drawer in this case is discharged if notice of dishonor is required by Section 3–503 and is not given in compliance with that section. A drawer that pays has a right of recourse against the acceptor. Section 3–413(a).

5. Subsection (e) does not permit the drawer of a check to avoid liability under subsection (b) by drawing the check without recourse. There is no legitimate purpose served by issuing a check on which nobody is liable. Drawing without recourse is effective to disclaim liability of the drawer if the draft is not a check. Suppose, in a documentary sale, Seller draws a draft on Buyer for the price of goods shipped to Buyer. The draft is payable upon delivery to the drawee of an order bill of lading covering the goods. Seller delivers the draft with the bill of lading to Finance Company that is named as payee of the draft. If Seller draws without recourse Finance Company takes the risk that Buyer will dishonor. If Buyer dishonors, Finance Company has no recourse against Seller but it can obtain reimbursement by selling the goods which it controls through the bill of lading.

6. Subsection (f) is derived from former Section 3–502(1)(b). It is designed to protect the drawer of a check against loss resulting from suspension of payments by the drawee bank when the holder of the check delays collection of the check. For example, X writes a check payable to Y for $1,000. The check is covered by funds in X's account in the drawee bank. Y delays initiation of collection of the check for more than 30 days after the date of the check. The drawee bank suspends payments after the 30-day period and before the check is presented for payment. If the $1,000 of funds in X's account have not been withdrawn, X has a claim for those funds against the drawee bank and, if subsection (e) were not in effect, X would be liable to Y on the check because the check was dishonored. Section 3–502(e). If the suspension of payments by the drawee bank will result in payment to X of less than the full amount of the $1,000 in the account or if there is a significant delay in payment to X, X will suffer a loss which would not have been suffered if Y had promptly initiated collection of the check. In most cases, X will not suffer any loss because of the existence of federal bank deposit insurance that covers accounts up to $100,000. Thus, subsection (e) has relatively little importance. There might be some cases, however, in which the account is not fully insured because it exceeds $100,000 or because the account doesn't qualify for deposit insurance. Subsection (f) retains the phrase "deprived of funds maintained with the drawee" appearing in former Section 3–502(1)(b). The quoted phrase applies if the suspension of payments by the drawee prevents the drawer from receiving the benefit of funds which would have paid the check if the holder had been timely in initiating collection. Thus, any significant delay in obtaining full payment of the funds is a deprivation of funds. The drawer can discharge drawer's liability by assigning rights against the drawee with respect to the funds to the holder.

7. The obligation of the drawer under this section is similar to the obligation of the drawer under Article 38 of the Convention on International Bills of Exchange and International Promissory Notes.

As amended in 2002.

§ 3–415.   Obligation of Indorser.

(a) Subject to subsections (b), (c), (d), (e) and to Section 3–419(d), if an instrument is dishonored, an indorser is obliged to pay the amount due on the instrument (i) according to the terms of the instrument at the time it was indorsed, or (ii) if the indorser indorsed an incomplete instrument, according to its terms when completed, to the extent stated in Sections 3–115 and 3–407. The obligation of the indorser is owed to a person entitled to enforce the instrument or to a subsequent indorser who paid the instrument under this section.

(b) If an indorsement states that it is made "without recourse" or otherwise disclaims liability of the indorser, the indorser is not liable under subsection (a) to pay the instrument.

(c) If notice of dishonor of an instrument is required by Section 3–503 and notice of dishonor complying with that section is not given to an indorser, the liability of the indorser under subsection (a) is discharged.

(d) If a draft is accepted by a bank after an indorsement is made, the liability of the indorser under subsection (a) is discharged.

(e) If an indorser of a check is liable under subsection (a) and the check is not presented for payment, or given to a depositary bank for collection, within 30 days after the day the indorsement was made, the liability of the indorser under subsection (a) is discharged.

As amended in 1993.

Official Comment

1. Subsections (a) and (b) restate the substance of former Section 3–414(1). Subsection (2) of former Section 3–414 has been dropped because it is superfluous. Although notice of dishonor is not mentioned in

subsection (a), it must be given in some cases to charge an indorser. It is covered in subsection (c). Regulation CC § 229.35(b) provides that a bank handling a check for collection or return is liable to a bank that subsequently handles the check to the extent the latter bank does not receive payment for the check. This liability applies whether or not the bank incurring the liability indorsed the check.

2.   Section 3–503 states when notice of dishonor is required and how it must be given. If required notice of dishonor is not given in compliance with Section 3–503, subsection (c) of Section 3–415 states that the effect is to discharge the indorser's obligation.

3.   Subsection (d) is similar in effect to Section 3–414(c) if the draft is accepted by a bank after the indorsement is made. See Comment 3 to Section 3–414. If a draft is accepted by a bank before the indorsement is made, the indorser incurs the obligation stated in subsection (a).

4.   Subsection (e) modifies former Sections 3–503(2)(b) and 3–502(1)(a) by stating a 30-day rather than a seven-day period, and stating it as an absolute rather than a presumptive period.

5.   As stated in subsection (a), the obligation of an indorser to pay the amount due on the instrument is generally owed not only to a person entitled to enforce the instrument but also to a subsequent indorser who paid the instrument. But if the prior indorser and the subsequent indorser are both anomalous indorsers, this rule does not apply. In that case, Section 3–116 applies. Under Section 3–116(a), the anomalous indorsers are jointly and severally liable and if either pays the instrument the indorser who pays has a right of contribution against the other. Section 3–116(b). The right to contribution in Section 3–116(b) is subject to "agreement of the affected parties." Suppose the subsequent indorser can prove an agreement with the prior indorser under which the prior indorser agreed to treat the subsequent indorser as a guarantor of the obligation of the prior indorser. Rights of the two indorsers between themselves would be governed by the agreement. Under suretyship law, the subsequent indorser under such an agreement is referred to as a sub-surety. Under the agreement, if the subsequent indorser pays the instrument there is a right to reimbursement from the prior indorser; if the prior indorser pays the instrument, there is no right of recourse against the subsequent indorser. See PEB Commentary No. 11, dated February 10, 1994.

6.   The rule of this section is similar to the rule of Article 44 of the Convention on International Bills of Exchange and International Promissory Notes.

As amended in 1994 and 2002.

§ 3–416.   Transfer Warranties.

(a)   A person who transfers an instrument for consideration warrants to the transferee and, if the transfer is by indorsement, to any subsequent transferee that:

(1)   the warrantor is a person entitled to enforce the instrument;

(2)   all signatures on the instrument are authentic and authorized;

(3)   the instrument has not been altered;

(4)   the instrument is not subject to a defense or claim in recoupment of any party which can be asserted against the warrantor;

(5)   the warrantor has no knowledge of any insolvency proceeding commenced with respect to the maker or acceptor or, in the case of an unaccepted draft, the drawer; and

(6)   with respect to a remotely-created consumer item, that the person on whose account the item is drawn authorized the issuance of the item in the amount for which the item is drawn.

(b)   A person to whom the warranties under subsection (a) are made and who took the instrument in good faith may recover from the warrantor as damages for breach of warranty an amount equal to the loss suffered as a result of the breach, but not more than the amount of the instrument plus expenses and loss of interest incurred as a result of the breach.

(c)   The warranties stated in subsection (a) cannot be disclaimed with respect to checks. Unless notice of a claim for breach of warranty is given to the warrantor within 30 days after the claimant has reason to know of the breach and the identity of the warrantor, the liability of the warrantor under subsection (b) is discharged to the extent of any loss caused by the delay in giving notice of the claim.

(d)   A [cause of action] for breach of warranty under this section accrues when the claimant has reason to know of the breach.

As amended in 2002.

Official Comment

1.   Subsection (a) is taken from subsection (2) of former Section 3–417. Subsections (3) and (4) of former Section 3–417 are deleted. Warranties under subsection (a) in favor of the immediate transferee apply to all persons who transfer an instrument for consideration whether or not the transfer is accompanied by indorsement. Any consideration sufficient to support a simple contract will support those warranties. If there is an indorsement the warranty runs with the instrument and the remote holder may sue the indorser-warrantor directly and thus avoid a multiplicity of suits.

2.   Since the purpose of transfer (Section 3–203(a)) is to give the transferee the right to enforce the instrument, subsection (a)(1) is a warranty that the transferor is a person entitled to enforce the instrument (Section 3–301). Under Section 3–203(b) transfer gives the transferee any right of the transferor to enforce the instrument. Subsection (a)(1) is in effect a warranty that there are no unauthorized or missing indorsements that prevent the transferor from making the transferee a person entitled to enforce the instrument.

3.   The rationale of subsection (a)(4) is that the transferee does not undertake to buy an instrument that is not enforceable in whole or in part, unless there is a contrary agreement. Even if the transferee takes as a holder in due course who takes free of the defense or claim in recoupment, the warranty gives the transferee the option of proceeding against the transferor rather than litigating with the obligor on the instrument the issue of the holder-in-due-course status of the transferee. Subsection (3) of former Section 3–417 which limits this warranty is deleted. The rationale is that while the purpose of a "no recourse" indorsement is to avoid a guaranty of payment, the indorsement does not clearly indicate an intent to disclaim warranties.

4.   Under subsection (a)(5) the transferor does not warrant against difficulties of collection, impairment of the credit of the obligor or even insolvency. The transferee is expected to determine such questions before taking the obligation. If insolvency proceedings as defined in Section 1–201(22)* have been instituted against the party who is expected to pay and the transferor knows it, the concealment of that fact amounts to a fraud upon the transferee, and the warranty against knowledge of such proceedings is provided accordingly.

5.   Transfer warranties may be disclaimed with respect to any instrument except a check. Between the immediate parties disclaimer may be made by agreement. In the case of an indorser, disclaimer of transferor's liability, to be effective, must appear in the indorsement with words such as "without warranties" or some other specific reference to warranties. But in the case of a check, subsection (c) of Section 3–416 provides that transfer warranties cannot be disclaimed at all. In the check collection process the banking system relies on these warranties.

6.   Subsection (b) states the measure of damages for breach of warranty. There is no express provision for attorney's fees, but attorney's fees are not meant to be necessarily excluded. They could be granted because they fit within the phrase "expenses . . . incurred as a result of the breach." The intention is to leave to other state law the issue as to when attorney's fees are recoverable.

7.   Since the traditional term "cause of action" may have been replaced in some states by "claim for relief" or some equivalent term, the words "cause of action" in subsection (d) have been bracketed to indicate that the words may be replaced by an appropriate substitute to conform to local practice.

8.   Subsection (a)(6) is based on a number of nonuniform amendments designed to address concerns about certain kinds of check fraud. The provision implements a limited rejection of *Price v. Neal*, 97 Eng. Rep. 871 (K.B. 1762), so that in certain circumstances (those involving remotely-created consumer items) the payor bank can use a warranty claim to absolve itself of responsibility for honoring an unauthorized item. The provision rests on the premise that monitoring by depositary banks can control this type of fraud more effectively than any practices readily available to payor banks. The provision expressly includes both the case in which the consumer does not authorize the item at all and also the case in which the consumer authorizes the item but in an amount different from the amount in which the item is drawn. Similar provisions appear in Sections 3–417, 4–207, and 4–208.

The provision supplements applicable federal law, which requires telemarketers who submit instruments for payment to obtain the customer's "express verifiable authorization," which may be either in writing or tape

---

*   *Referring to unrevised Article 1 (Appendix A).*

recorded and must be made available upon request to the customer's bank. Federal Trade Commission's Telemarketing Sales Rule, 16 C.F.R. § 310.3(a)(3), implementing the Telemarketing and Consumer Fraud and Abuse Prevention Act, 15 U.S.C. §§ 6101–6108. Some states also have consumer-protection laws governing authorization of instruments in telemarketing transactions. *See, e.g.*, 9 Vt. Stat. Ann. § 2464.

9.   Article 45 of the Convention on International Bills of Exchange and International Promissory Notes includes warranties that are similar (except for the warranty in subsection (a)(6)).

As amended in 2002.

§ 3–417.   Presentment Warranties.

(a)   If an unaccepted draft is presented to the drawee for payment or acceptance and the drawee pays or accepts the draft, (i) the person obtaining payment or acceptance, at the time of presentment, and (ii) a previous transferor of the draft, at the time of transfer, warrant to the drawee making payment or accepting the draft in good faith that:

(1)   the warrantor is, or was, at the time the warrantor transferred the draft, a person entitled to enforce the draft or authorized to obtain payment or acceptance of the draft on behalf of a person entitled to enforce the draft;

(2)   the draft has not been altered;

(3)   the warrantor has no knowledge that the signature of the drawer of the draft is unauthorized; and

(4)   with respect to any remotely-created consumer item, that the person on whose account the item is drawn authorized the issuance of the item in the amount for which the item is drawn.

(b)   A drawee making payment may recover from any warrantor damages for breach of warranty equal to the amount paid by the drawee less the amount the drawee received or is entitled to receive from the drawer because of the payment. In addition, the drawee is entitled to compensation for expenses and loss of interest resulting from the breach. The right of the drawee to recover damages under this subsection is not affected by any failure of the drawee to exercise ordinary care in making payment. If the drawee accepts the draft, breach of warranty is a defense to the obligation of the acceptor. If the acceptor makes payment with respect to the draft, the acceptor is entitled to recover from any warrantor for breach of warranty the amounts stated in this subsection.

(c)   If a drawee asserts a claim for breach of warranty under subsection (a) based on an unauthorized indorsement of the draft or an alteration of the draft, the warrantor may defend by proving that the indorsement is effective under Section 3–404 or 3–405 or the drawer is precluded under Section 3–406 or 4–406 from asserting against the drawee the unauthorized indorsement or alteration.

(d)   If (i) a dishonored draft is presented for payment to the drawer or an indorser or (ii) any other instrument is presented for payment to a party obliged to pay the instrument, and (iii) payment is received, the following rules apply:

(1)   The person obtaining payment and a prior transferor of the instrument warrant to the person making payment in good faith that the warrantor is, or was, at the time the warrantor transferred the instrument, a person entitled to enforce the instrument or authorized to obtain payment on behalf of a person entitled to enforce the instrument.

(2)   The person making payment may recover from any warrantor for breach of warranty an amount equal to the amount paid plus expenses and loss of interest resulting from the breach.

(e)   The warranties stated in subsections (a) and (d) cannot be disclaimed with respect to checks. Unless notice of a claim for breach of warranty is given to the warrantor within 30 days after the claimant has reason to know of the breach and the identity of the warrantor, the liability of the warrantor under subsection (b) or (d) is discharged to the extent of any loss caused by the delay in giving notice of the claim.

(f)   A [cause of action] for breach of warranty under this section accrues when the claimant has reason to know of the breach.

As amended in 2002.

Official Comment

1. This section replaces subsection (1) of former Section 3–417. The former provision was difficult to understand because it purported to state in one subsection all warranties given to any person paying any instrument. The result was a provision replete with exceptions that could not be readily understood except after close scrutiny of the language. In revised Section 3–417, presentment warranties made to drawees of uncertified checks and other unaccepted drafts are stated in subsection (a). All other presentment warranties are stated in subsection (d).

2. Subsection (a) states three warranties. Subsection (a)(1) in effect is a warranty that there are no unauthorized or missing indorsements. "Person entitled to enforce" is defined in Section 3–301. Subsection (a)(2) is a warranty that there is no alteration. Subsection (a)(3) is a warranty of no knowledge that there is a forged drawer's signature. Subsection (a) states that the warranties are made to the drawee and subsections (b) and (c) identify the drawee as the person entitled to recover for breach of warranty. There is no warranty made to the drawer under subsection (a) when presentment is made to the drawee. Warranty to the drawer is governed by subsection (d) and that applies only when presentment for payment is made to the drawer with respect to a dishonored draft. In *Sun 'N Sand, Inc. v. United California Bank*, 582 P.2d 920 (Cal.1978), the court held that under former Section 3–417(1) a warranty was made to the drawer of a check when the check was presented to the drawee for payment. The result in that case is rejected.

3. Subsection (a)(1) retains the rule that the drawee does not admit the authenticity of indorsements and subsection (a)(3) retains the rule of *Price v. Neal*, 3 Burr. 1354 (1762), that the drawee takes the risk that the drawer's signature is unauthorized unless the person presenting the draft has knowledge that the drawer's signature is unauthorized. Under subsection (a)(3) the warranty of no knowledge that the drawer's signature is unauthorized is also given by prior transferors of the draft.

4. Subsection (d) applies to presentment for payment in all cases not covered by subsection (a). It applies to presentment of notes and accepted drafts to any party obliged to pay the instrument, including an indorser, and to presentment of dishonored drafts if made to the drawer or an indorser. In cases covered by subsection (d), there is only one warranty and it is the same as that stated in subsection (a)(1). There are no warranties comparable to subsections (a)(2) and (a)(3) because they are appropriate only in the case of presentment to the drawee of an unaccepted draft. With respect to presentment of an accepted draft to the acceptor, there is no warranty with respect to alteration or knowledge that the signature of the drawer is unauthorized. Those warranties were made to the drawee when the draft was presented for acceptance (Section 3–417(a)(2) and (3)) and breach of that warranty is a defense to the obligation of the drawee as acceptor to pay the draft. If the drawee pays the accepted draft the drawee may recover the payment from any warrantor who was in breach of warranty when the draft was accepted. Section 3–417(b). Thus, there is no necessity for these warranties to be repeated when the accepted draft is presented for payment. Former Section 3–417(1)(b)(iii) and (c)(iii) are not included in revised Section 3–417 because they are unnecessary. Former Section 3–417(1)(c)(iv) is not included because it is also unnecessary. The acceptor should know what the terms of the draft were at the time acceptance was made.

If presentment is made to the drawer or maker, there is no necessity for a warranty concerning the signature of that person or with respect to alteration. If presentment is made to an indorser, the indorser had itself warranted authenticity of signatures and that the instrument was not altered. Section 3–416(a)(2) and (3).

5. The measure of damages for breach of warranty under subsection (a) is stated in subsection (b). There is no express provision for attorney's fees, but attorney's fees are not meant to be necessarily excluded. They could be granted because they fit within the language "expenses . . . resulting from the breach." Subsection (b) provides that the right of the drawee to recover for breach of warranty is not affected by a failure of the drawee to exercise ordinary care in paying the draft. This provision follows the result reached under former Article 3 in *Hartford Accident & Indemnity Co. v. First Pennsylvania Bank*, 859 F.2d 295 (3d Cir.1988).

6. Subsection (c) applies to checks and other unaccepted drafts. It gives to the warrantor the benefit of rights that the drawee has against the drawer under Section 3–404, 3–405, 3–406, or 4–406. If the drawer's conduct contributed to a loss from forgery or alteration, the drawee should not be allowed to shift the loss from the drawer to the warrantor.

7. The first sentence of subsection (e) recognizes that checks are normally paid by automated means and that payor banks rely on warranties in making payment. Thus, it is not appropriate to allow disclaimer or warranties appearing on checks that normally will not be examined by the payor bank. The second sentence

349

requires a breach of warranty claim to be asserted within 30 days after the drawee learns of the breach and the identity of the warrantor.

8.   Since the traditional term "cause of action" may have been replaced in some states by "claim for relief" or some equivalent term, the words "cause of action" in subsection (f) have been bracketed to indicate that the words may be replaced by an appropriate substitute to conform to local practice.

9.   For discussion of subsection (a)(4), see Comment 8 to Section 3–416.

As amended in 2002.

§ 3–418.   Payment or Acceptance by Mistake.

(a)   Except as provided in subsection (c), if the drawee of a draft pays or accepts the draft and the drawee acted on the mistaken belief that (i) payment of the draft had not been stopped pursuant to Section 4–403 or (ii) the signature of the drawer of the draft was authorized, the drawee may recover the amount of the draft from the person to whom or for whose benefit payment was made or, in the case of acceptance, may revoke the acceptance. Rights of the drawee under this subsection are not affected by failure of the drawee to exercise ordinary care in paying or accepting the draft.

(b)   Except as provided in subsection (c), if an instrument has been paid or accepted by mistake and the case is not covered by subsection (a), the person paying or accepting may, to the extent permitted by the law governing mistake and restitution, (i) recover the payment from the person to whom or for whose benefit payment was made or (ii) in the case of acceptance, may revoke the acceptance.

(c)   The remedies provided by subsection (a) or (b) may not be asserted against a person who took the instrument in good faith and for value or who in good faith changed position in reliance on the payment or acceptance. This subsection does not limit remedies provided by Section 3–417 or 4–407.

(d)   Notwithstanding Section 4–215, if an instrument is paid or accepted by mistake and the payor or acceptor recovers payment or revokes acceptance under subsection (a) or (b), the instrument is deemed not to have been paid or accepted and is treated as dishonored, and the person from whom payment is recovered has rights as a person entitled to enforce the dishonored instrument.

Official Comment

1.   This section covers payment or acceptance by mistake and replaces former Section 3–418. Under former Article 3, the remedy of a drawee that paid or accepted a draft by mistake was based on the law of mistake and restitution, but that remedy was not specifically stated. It was provided by Section 1–103. Former Section 3–418 was simply a limitation on the unstated remedy under the law of mistake and restitution. Under revised Article 3, Section 3–418 specifically states the right of restitution in subsections (a) and (b). Subsection (a) allows restitution in the two most common cases in which the problem is presented: payment or acceptance of forged checks and checks on which the drawer has stopped payment. If the drawee acted under a mistaken belief that the check was not forged or had not been stopped, the drawee is entitled to recover the funds paid or to revoke the acceptance whether or not the drawee acted negligently. But in each case, by virtue of subsection (c), the drawee loses the remedy if the person receiving payment or acceptance was a person who took the check in good faith and for value or who in good faith changed position in reliance on the payment or acceptance. Subsections (a) and (c) are consistent with former Section 3–418 and the rule of *Price v. Neal*. The result in the two cases covered by subsection (a) is that the drawee in most cases will not have a remedy against the person paid because there is usually a person who took the check in good faith and for value or who in good faith changed position in reliance on the payment or acceptance.

2.   If a check has been paid by mistake and the payee receiving payment did not give value for the check or did not change position in reliance on the payment, the drawee bank is entitled to recover the amount of the check under subsection (a) regardless of how the check was paid. The drawee bank normally pays a check by a credit to an account of the collecting bank that presents the check for payment. The payee of the check normally receives the payment by a credit to the payee's account in the depositary bank. But in some cases the payee of the check may have received payment directly from the drawee bank by presenting the check for payment over the counter. In those cases the payee is entitled to receive cash, but the payee may prefer another form of payment such as a cashier's check or teller's check issued by the drawee bank. Suppose Seller contracted to sell goods to Buyer. The contract provided for immediate payment by Buyer and delivery of the goods 20 days after payment.

350

Buyer paid by mailing a check for $10,000 drawn on Bank payable to Seller. The next day Buyer gave a stop payment order to Bank with respect to the check Buyer had mailed to Seller. A few days later Seller presented Buyer's check to Bank for payment over the counter and requested a cashier's check as payment. Bank issued and delivered a cashier's check for $10,000 payable to Seller. The teller failed to discover Buyer's stop order. The next day Bank discovered the mistake and immediately advised Seller of the facts. Seller refused to return the cashier's check and did not deliver any goods to Buyer.

Under Section 4–215, Buyer's check was paid by Bank at the time it delivered its cashier's check to Seller. See Comment 3 to Section 4–215. Bank is obliged to pay the cashier's check and has no defense to that obligation. The cashier's check was issued for consideration because it was issued in payment of Buyer's check. Although Bank has no defense on its cashier's check it may have a right to recover $10,000, the amount of Buyer's check, from Seller under Section 3–418(a). Bank paid Buyer's check by mistake. Seller did not give value for Buyer's check because the promise to deliver goods to Buyer was never performed. Section 3–303(a)(1). And, on these facts, Seller did not change position in reliance on the payment of Buyer's check. Thus, the first sentence of Section 3–418(c) does not apply and Seller is obliged to return $10,000 to Bank. Bank is obliged to pay the cashier's check but it has a counterclaim against Seller based on its rights under Section 3–418(a). This claim can be asserted against Seller, but it cannot be asserted against some other person with rights of a holder in due course of the cashier's check. A person without rights of a holder in due course of the cashier's check would take subject to Bank's claim against Seller because it is a claim in recoupment. Section 3–305(a)(3).

If Bank recovers from Seller under Section 3–418(a), the payment of Buyer's check is treated as unpaid and dishonored. Section 3–418(d). One consequence is that Seller may enforce Buyer's obligation as drawer to pay the check. Section 3–414. Another consequence is that Seller's rights against Buyer on the contract of sale are also preserved. Under Section 3–310(b) Buyer's obligation to pay for the goods was suspended when Seller took Buyer's check and remains suspended until the check is either dishonored or paid. Under Section 3–310(b)(2) 3–310(b)(1)* the obligation is discharged when the check is paid. Since Section 3–418(d) treats Buyer's check as unpaid and dishonored, Buyer's obligation is not discharged and suspension of the obligation terminates. Under Section 3–310(b)(3), Seller may enforce either the contract of sale or the check subject to defenses and claims of Buyer.

If Seller had released the goods to Buyer before learning about the stop order, Bank would have no recovery against Seller under Section 3–418(a) because Seller in that case gave value for Buyer's check. Section 3–418(c). In this case Bank's sole remedy is under Section 4–407 by subrogation.

3. Subsection (b) covers cases of payment or acceptance by mistake that are not covered by subsection (a). It directs courts to deal with those cases under the law governing mistake and restitution. Perhaps the most important class of cases that falls under subsection (b), because it is not covered by subsection (a), is that of payment by the drawee bank of a check with respect to which the bank has no duty to the drawer to pay either because the drawer has no account with the bank or because available funds in the drawer's account are not sufficient to cover the amount of the check. With respect to such a case, under Restatement of Restitution § 29, if the bank paid because of a mistaken belief that there were available funds in the drawer's account sufficient to cover the amount of the check, the bank is entitled to restitution. But § 29 is subject to Restatement of Restitution § 33 which denies restitution if the holder of the check receiving payment paid value in good faith for the check and had no reason to know that the check was paid by mistake when payment was received.

The result in some cases is clear. For example, suppose Father gives Daughter a check for $10,000 as a birthday gift. The check is drawn on Bank in which both Father and Daughter have accounts. Daughter deposits the check in her account in Bank. An employee of Bank, acting under the belief that there were available funds in Father's account to cover the check, caused Daughter's account to be credited for $10,000. In fact, Father's account was overdrawn and Father did not have overdraft privileges. Since Daughter received the check gratuitously there is clear unjust enrichment if she is allowed to keep the $10,000 and Bank is unable to obtain reimbursement from Father. Thus, Bank should be permitted to reverse the credit to Daughter's account. But this case is not typical. In most cases the remedy of restitution will not be available because the person receiving payment of the check will have given value for it in good faith.

In some cases, however, it may not be clear whether a drawee bank should have a right of restitution. For example, a check-kiting scheme may involve a large number of checks drawn on a number of different banks in which the drawer's credit balances are based on uncollected funds represented by fraudulently drawn checks. No attempt is made in Section 3–418 to state rules for determining the conflicting claims of the various banks that

---

* Previous incorrect cross reference corrected by Permanent Editorial Board action November 1992.

may be victimized by such a scheme. Rather, such cases are better resolved on the basis of general principles of law and the particular facts presented in the litigation.

4.   The right of the drawee to recover a payment or to revoke an acceptance under Section 3–418 is not affected by the rules under Article 4 that determine when an item is paid. Even though a payor bank may have paid an item under Section 4–215, it may have a right to recover the payment under Section 3–418. *National Savings & Trust Co. v. Park Corp.*, 722 F.2d 1303 (6th Cir.1983), cert. denied, 466 U.S. 939 (1984), correctly states the law on the issue under former Article 3. Revised Article 3 does not change the previous law.

§ 3–419.   Instruments Signed for Accommodation.

(a)   If an instrument is issued for value given for the benefit of a party to the instrument ("accommodated party") and another party to the instrument ("accommodation party") signs the instrument for the purpose of incurring liability on the instrument without being a direct beneficiary of the value given for the instrument, the instrument is signed by the accommodation party "for accommodation."

(b)   An accommodation party may sign the instrument as maker, drawer, acceptor, or indorser and, subject to subsection (d), is obliged to pay the instrument in the capacity in which the accommodation party signs. The obligation of an accommodation party may be enforced notwithstanding any statute of frauds and whether or not the accommodation party receives consideration for the accommodation.

(c)   A person signing an instrument is presumed to be an accommodation party and there is notice that the instrument is signed for accommodation if the signature is an anomalous indorsement or is accompanied by words indicating that the signer is acting as surety or guarantor with respect to the obligation of another party to the instrument. Except as provided in Section 3–605, the obligation of an accommodation party to pay the instrument is not affected by the fact that the person enforcing the obligation had notice when the instrument was taken by that person that the accommodation party signed the instrument for accommodation.

(d)   If the signature of a party to an instrument is accompanied by words indicating unambiguously that the party is guaranteeing collection rather than payment of the obligation of another party to the instrument, the signer is obliged to pay the amount due on the instrument to a person entitled to enforce the instrument only if (i) execution of judgment against the other party has been returned unsatisfied, (ii) the other party is insolvent or in an insolvency proceeding, (iii) the other party cannot be served with process, or (iv) it is otherwise apparent that payment cannot be obtained from the other party.

(e)   If the signature of a party to an instrument is accompanied by words indicating that the party guarantees payment or the signer signs the instrument as an accommodation party in some other manner that does not unambiguously indicate an intention to guarantee collection rather than payment, the signer is obliged to pay the amount due on the instrument to a person entitled to enforce the instrument in the same circumstances as the accommodated party would be obliged, without prior resort to the accommodated party by the person entitled to enforce the instrument.

(f)   An accommodation party who pays the instrument is entitled to reimbursement from the accommodated party and is entitled to enforce the instrument against the accommodated party. In proper circumstances, an accommodation party may obtain relief that requires the accommodated party to perform its obligations on the instrument. An accommodated party that pays the instrument has no right of recourse against, and is not entitled to contribution from, an accommodation party.

As amended in 2002.

Official Comment

1.   Section 3–419 replaces former Section 3–415 and 3–416. An accommodation party is a person who signs an instrument to benefit the accommodated party either by signing at the time value is obtained by the accommodated party or later, and who is not a direct beneficiary of the value obtained. An accommodation party will usually be a co-maker or anomalous indorser. Subsection (a) distinguishes between direct and indirect benefit. For example, if X cosigns a note of Corporation that is given for a loan to Corporation, X is an accommodation party if no part of the loan was paid to X or for X's direct benefit. This is true even though X may receive indirect benefit from the loan because X is employed by Corporation or is a stockholder of Corporation, or even if X is the sole stockholder so long as Corporation and X are recognized as separate entities.

2.   It does not matter whether an accommodation party signs gratuitously either at the time the instrument is issued or after the instrument is in the possession of a holder. Subsection (b) of Section 3–419 takes the view stated in Comment 3 to former Section 3–415 that there need be no consideration running to the accommodation party: "The obligation of the accommodation party is supported by any consideration for which the instrument is taken before it is due. Subsection (2) is intended to change occasional decisions holding that there is no sufficient consideration where an accommodation party signs a note after it is in the hands of a holder who has given value. The [accommodation] party is liable to the holder in such a case even though there is no extension of time or other concession."

3.   As stated in Comment 1, whether a person is an accommodation party is a question of fact. But it is almost always the case that a co-maker who signs with words of guaranty after the signature is an accommodation party. The same is true of an anomalous indorser. In either case a person taking the instrument is put on notice of the accommodation status of the co-maker or indorser. This is relevant to Section 3–605(e). But, under subsection (c), signing with words of guaranty or as an anomalous indorser also creates a presumption that the signer is an accommodation party. A party challenging accommodation party status would have to rebut this presumption by producing evidence that the signer was in fact a direct beneficiary of the value given for the instrument.

An accommodation party is always a surety. A surety who is not a party to the instrument, however, is not an accommodation party. For example, if M issues a note payable to the order of P, and S signs a separate contract in which S agrees to pay P the amount of the instrument if it is dishonored, S is a surety but is not an accommodation party. In such a case, S's rights and duties are determined under the general law of suretyship. In unusual cases two parties to an instrument may have a surety relationship that is not governed by Article 3 because the requirements of Section 3–419(a) are not met. In those cases the general law of suretyship applies to the relationship. See PEB Commentary No. 11, dated February 10, 1994.

4.   Subsection (b) states that an accommodation party is liable on the instrument in the capacity in which the party signed the instrument. In most cases that capacity will be either that of a maker or indorser of a note. But subsection (d) provides a limitation on subsection (b). If the signature of the accommodation party is accompanied by words indicating unambiguously that the party is guaranteeing collection rather than payment of the instrument, liability is limited to that stated in subsection (d), which is based on former Section 3–416(2).

Former Article 3 was confusing because the obligation of a guarantor was covered both in Section 3–415 and in Section 3–416. The latter section suggested that a signature accompanied by words of guaranty created an obligation distinct from that of an accommodation party. Revised Article 3 eliminates that confusion by stating in Section 3–419 the obligation of a person who uses words of guaranty. Portions of former Section 3–416 are preserved. Former Section 3–416(2) is reflected in Section 3–419(d) and former Section 3–416(4) is reflected in Section 3–419(c). Words added to an anomalous indorsement indicating that payment of the instrument is guaranteed by the indorser do not change the liability of the indorser as stated in Section 3–415. This is a change from former Section 3–416(5). See PEB Commentary No. 11, dated February 10, 1994.

5.   Subsection (e) like former Section 3–415(5), provides that an accommodation party that pays the instrument is entitled to enforce the instrument against the accommodated party. Since the accommodation party that pays the instrument is entitled to enforce the instrument against the accommodated party, the accommodation party also obtains rights to any security interest or other collateral that secures payment of the instrument. Subsection (e) also provides that an accommodation party that pays the instrument is entitled to reimbursement from the accommodated party. See PEB Commentary No. 11, dated February 10, 1994.

6.   In occasional cases, the accommodation party might pay the instrument even though the accommodated party had a defense to its obligation that was available to the accommodation party under Section 3–305(d). In such cases, the accommodation party's right to reimbursement may conflict with the accommodated party's right to raise its defense. For example, suppose the accommodation party pays the instrument without being aware of the defense. In that case the accommodation party should be entitled to reimbursement. Suppose the accommodation party paid the instrument with knowledge of the defense. In that case, to the extent of the defense, reimbursement ordinarily would not be justified, but under some circumstances reimbursement may be justified depending upon the facts of the case. The resolution of this conflict is left to the general law of suretyship. Section 1–103. See PEB Commentary No. 11, dated February 10, 1994.

7.   Section 3–419, along with Section 3–116(a) and (b), Section 3–305(d) and Section 3–605, provides rules governing the rights of accommodation parties. In addition, except to the extent that it is displaced by provisions

of this Article, the general law of suretyship also applies to the rights of accommodation parties. Section 1–103. See PEB Commentary No. 11, dated February 10, 1994.

As amended in 1994 and 2002.

§ 3–420.   Conversion of Instrument.

(a)   The law applicable to conversion of personal property applies to instruments. An instrument is also converted if it is taken by transfer, other than a negotiation, from a person not entitled to enforce the instrument or a bank makes or obtains payment with respect to the instrument for a person not entitled to enforce the instrument or receive payment. An action for conversion of an instrument may not be brought by (i) the issuer or acceptor of the instrument or (ii) a payee or indorsee who did not receive delivery of the instrument either directly or through delivery to an agent or a co-payee.

(b)   In an action under subsection (a), the measure of liability is presumed to be the amount payable on the instrument, but recovery may not exceed the amount of the plaintiff's interest in the instrument.

(c)   A representative, other than a depositary bank, who has in good faith dealt with an instrument or its proceeds on behalf of one who was not the person entitled to enforce the instrument is not liable in conversion to that person beyond the amount of any proceeds that it has not paid out.

Official Comment

1.   Section 3–420 is a modification of former Section 3–419. The first sentence of Section 3–420(a) states a general rule that the law of conversion applicable to personal property also applies to instruments. Paragraphs (a) and (b) of former Section 3–419(1) are deleted as inappropriate in cases of noncash items that may be delivered for acceptance or payment in collection letters that contain varying instructions as to what to do in the event of nonpayment on the day of delivery. It is better to allow such cases to be governed by the general law of conversion that would address the issue of when, under the circumstances prevailing, the presenter's right to possession has been denied. The second sentence of Section 3–420(a) states that an instrument is converted if it is taken by transfer other than a negotiation from a person not entitled to enforce the instrument or taken for collection or payment from a person not entitled to enforce the instrument or receive payment. This covers cases in which a depositary or payor bank takes an instrument bearing a forged indorsement. It also covers cases in which an instrument is payable to two persons and the two persons are not alternative payees, e.g. a check payable to John and Jane Doe. Under Section 3–110(d) the check can be negotiated or enforced only by both persons acting jointly. Thus, neither payee acting without the consent of the other, is a person entitled to enforce the instrument. If John indorses the check and Jane does not, the indorsement is not effective to allow negotiation of the check. If Depositary Bank takes the check for deposit to John's account, Depositary Bank is liable to Jane for conversion of the check if she did not consent to the transaction. John, acting alone, is not the person entitled to enforce the check because John is not the holder of the check. Section 3–110(d) and Comment 4 to Section 3–110. Depositary Bank does not get any greater rights under Section 4–205(1). If it acted for John as its customer, it did not become holder of the check under that provision because John, its customer, was not a holder.

Under former Article 3, the cases were divided on the issue of whether the drawer of a check with a forged indorsement can assert rights against a depositary bank that took the check. The last sentence of Section 3–420(a) resolves the conflict by following the rule stated in *Stone & Webster Engineering Corp. v. First National Bank & Trust Co.*, 184 N.E.2d 358 (Mass.1962). There is no reason why a drawer should have an action in conversion. The check represents an obligation of the drawer rather than property of the drawer. The drawer has an adequate remedy against the payor bank for recredit of the drawer's account for unauthorized payment of the check.

There was also a split of authority under former Article 3 on the issue of whether a payee who never received the instrument is a proper plaintiff in a conversion action. The typical case was one in which a check was stolen from the drawer or in which the check was mailed to an address different from that of the payee and was stolen after it arrived at that address. The thief forged the indorsement of the payee and obtained payment by depositing the check to an account in a depositary bank. The issue was whether the payee could bring an action in conversion against the depositary bank or the drawee bank. In revised Article 3, under the last sentence of Section 3–420(a), the payee has no conversion action because the check was never delivered to the payee. Until delivery, the payee does not have any interest in the check. The payee never became the holder of the check nor a person entitled to enforce the check. Section 3–301. Nor is the payee injured by the fraud. Normally the drawer of a check intends to pay an obligation owed to the payee. But if the check is never delivered to the payee, the obligation owed to the payee is not affected. If the check falls into the hands of a thief who obtains payment after forging the signature of the payee as an indorsement, the obligation owed to the payee continues to exist after the thief receives payment. Since the payee's right to enforce the underlying obligation is unaffected by the fraud of the thief, there is no reason to give any additional remedy to the payee. The drawer of the check has no conversion remedy, but the drawee is not entitled to charge the drawer's account when the drawee wrongfully honored the check. The remedy of the drawee is against the depositary bank for breach of warranty under Section 3–417(a)(1) or 4–208(a)(1). The loss will fall on the person who gave value to the thief for the check.

The situation is different if the check is delivered to the payee. If the check is taken for an obligation owed to the payee, the last sentence of Section 3–310(b)(4) provides that the obligation may not be enforced to the extent of the amount of the check. The payee's rights are restricted to enforcement of the payee's rights in the instrument. In this event the payee is injured by the theft and has a cause of action for conversion.

The payee receives delivery when the check comes into the payee's possession, as for example when it is put into the payee's mailbox. Delivery to an agent is delivery to the payee. If a check is payable to more than one payee, delivery to one of the payees is deemed to be delivery to all of the payees. Occasionally, the person asserting a conversion cause of action is an indorsee rather than the original payee. If the check is stolen before the check can be delivered to the indorsee and the indorsee's indorsement is forged, the analysis is similar. For example, a check is payable to the order of A. A indorses it to B and puts it into an envelope addressed to B. The envelope is never delivered to B. Rather, Thief steals the envelope, forges B's indorsement to the check and obtains payment. Because the check was never delivered to B, the indorsee, B has no cause of action for conversion, but A does have such an action. A is the owner of the check. B never obtained rights in the check. If A intended to negotiate the check to B in payment of an obligation, that obligation was not affected by the conduct of Thief. B can enforce that obligation. Thief stole A's property not B's.

2. Subsection (2) of former Section 3–419 is amended because it is not clear why the former law distinguished between the liability of the drawee and that of other converters. Why should there be a conclusive presumption that the liability is face amount if a drawee refuses to pay or return an instrument or makes payment on a forged indorsement, while the liability of a maker who does the same thing is only presumed to be the face amount? Moreover, it was not clear under former Section 3–419(2) what face amount meant. If a note for $10,000 is payable in a year at 10% interest, it is common to refer to $10,000 as the face amount, but if the note is converted the loss to the owner also includes the loss of interest. In revised Article 3, Section 3–420(b), by referring to "amount payable on the instrument," allows the full amount due under the instrument to be recovered.

The "but" clause in subsection (b) addresses the problem of conversion actions in multiple payee checks. Section 3–110(d) states that an instrument cannot be enforced unless all payees join in the action. But an action for conversion might be brought by a payee having no interest or a limited interest in the proceeds of the check. This clause prevents such a plaintiff from receiving a windfall. An example is a check payable to a building contractor and a supplier of building material. The check is not payable to the payees alternatively. Section 3–110(d). The check is delivered to the contractor by the owner of the building. Suppose the contractor forges supplier's signature as an indorsement of the check and receives the entire proceeds of the check. The supplier should not, without qualification, be able to recover the entire amount of the check from the bank that converted the check. Depending upon the contract between the contractor and the supplier, the amount of the check may be due entirely to the contractor, in which case there should be no recovery, entirely to the supplier, in which case recovery should be for the entire amount, or part may be due to one and the rest to the other, in which case recovery should be limited to the amount due to the supplier.

3. Subsection (3) of former Section 3–419 drew criticism from the courts, that saw no reason why a depositary bank should have the defense stated in the subsection. See *Knesz v. Central Jersey Bank & Trust Co.,* 477 A.2d 806 (N.J.1984). The depositary bank is ultimately liable in the case of a forged indorsement check because of its warranty to the payor bank under Section 4–208(a)(1) and it is usually the most convenient defendant in cases involving multiple checks drawn on different banks. There is no basis for requiring the owner of the check to bring multiple actions against the various payor banks and to require those banks to assert warranty rights against the depositary bank. In revised Article 3, the defense provided by Section 3–420(c) is limited to collecting banks other than the depositary bank. If suit is brought against both the payor bank and the depositary bank, the owner, of course, is entitled to but one recovery.

PART 5

DISHONOR

§ 3–501.   Presentment.

(a) "Presentment" means a demand made by or on behalf of a person entitled to enforce an instrument (i) to pay the instrument made to the drawee or a party obliged to pay the instrument or, in the case of a note or accepted draft payable at a bank, to the bank, or (ii) to accept a draft made to the drawee.

(b) The following rules are subject to Article 4, agreement of the parties, and clearing-house rules and the like:

(1) Presentment may be made at the place of payment of the instrument and must be made at the place of payment if the instrument is payable at a bank in the United States; may be made by any commercially reasonable means, including an oral, written, or electronic communication; is effective when the demand for payment or acceptance is received by the person to whom presentment is made; and is effective if made to any one of two or more makers, acceptors, drawees, or other payors.

(2) Upon demand of the person to whom presentment is made, the person making presentment must (i) exhibit the instrument, (ii) give reasonable identification and, if presentment is made on behalf of another person, reasonable evidence of authority to do so, and (iii) sign a receipt on the instrument for any payment made or surrender the instrument if full payment is made.

(3) Without dishonoring the instrument, the party to whom presentment is made may (i) return the instrument for lack of a necessary indorsement, or (ii) refuse payment or acceptance for failure of the presentment to comply with the terms of the instrument, an agreement of the parties, or other applicable law or rule.

(4) The party to whom presentment is made may treat presentment as occurring on the next business day after the day of presentment if the party to whom presentment is made has established a cut-off hour not earlier than 2 p.m. for the receipt and processing of instruments presented for payment or acceptance and presentment is made after the cut-off hour.

Official Comment

Subsection (a) defines presentment. Subsection (b)(1) states the place and manner of presentment. Electronic presentment is authorized. The communication of the demand for payment or acceptance is effective when received. Subsection (b)(2) restates former Section 3–505. Subsection (b)(2)(i) allows the person to whom presentment is made to require exhibition of the instrument, unless the parties have agreed otherwise as in an electronic presentment agreement. Former Section 3–507(3) is the antecedent of subsection (b)(3)(i). Since a payor must decide whether to pay or accept on the day of presentment, subsection (b)(4) allows the payor to set a cut-off hour for receipt of instruments presented.

§ 3–502.   Dishonor.

(a) Dishonor of a note is governed by the following rules:

(1) If the note is payable on demand, the note is dishonored if presentment is duly made to the maker and the note is not paid on the day of presentment.

(2) If the note is not payable on demand and is payable at or through a bank or the terms of the note require presentment, the note is dishonored if presentment is duly made and the note is not paid on the day it becomes payable or the day of presentment, whichever is later.

(3) If the note is not payable on demand and paragraph (2) does not apply, the note is dishonored if it is not paid on the day it becomes payable.

(b) Dishonor of an unaccepted draft other than a documentary draft is governed by the following rules:

356

(1) If a check is duly presented for payment to the payor bank otherwise than for immediate payment over the counter, the check is dishonored if the payor bank makes timely return of the check or sends timely notice of dishonor or nonpayment under Section 4–301 or 4–302, or becomes accountable for the amount of the check under Section 4–302.

(2) If a draft is payable on demand and paragraph (1) does not apply, the draft is dishonored if presentment for payment is duly made to the drawee and the draft is not paid on the day of presentment.

(3) If a draft is payable on a date stated in the draft, the draft is dishonored if (i) presentment for payment is duly made to the drawee and payment is not made on the day the draft becomes payable or the day of presentment, whichever is later, or (ii) presentment for acceptance is duly made before the day the draft becomes payable and the draft is not accepted on the day of presentment.

(4) If a draft is payable on elapse of a period of time after sight or acceptance, the draft is dishonored if presentment for acceptance is duly made and the draft is not accepted on the day of presentment.

(c) Dishonor of an unaccepted documentary draft occurs according to the rules stated in subsection (b)(2), (3), and (4), except that payment or acceptance may be delayed without dishonor until no later than the close of the third business day of the drawee following the day on which payment or acceptance is required by those paragraphs.

(d) Dishonor of an accepted draft is governed by the following rules:

(1) If the draft is payable on demand, the draft is dishonored if presentment for payment is duly made to the acceptor and the draft is not paid on the day of presentment.

(2) If the draft is not payable on demand, the draft is dishonored if presentment for payment is duly made to the acceptor and payment is not made on the day it becomes payable or the day of presentment, whichever is later.

(e) In any case in which presentment is otherwise required for dishonor under this section and presentment is excused under Section 3–504, dishonor occurs without presentment if the instrument is not duly accepted or paid.

(f) If a draft is dishonored because timely acceptance of the draft was not made and the person entitled to demand acceptance consents to a late acceptance, from the time of acceptance the draft is treated as never having been dishonored.

Official Comment

1. Section 3–415 provides that an indorser is obliged to pay an instrument if the instrument is dishonored and is discharged if the indorser is entitled to notice of dishonor and notice is not given. Under Section 3–414, the drawer is obliged to pay an unaccepted draft if it is dishonored. The drawer, however, is not entitled to notice of dishonor except to the extent required in a case governed by Section 3–414(d). Part 5 tells when an instrument is dishonored (Section 3–502) and what it means to give notice of dishonor (Section 3–503). Often dishonor does not occur until presentment (Section 3–501), and frequently presentment and notice of dishonor are excused (Section 3–504).

2. In the great majority of cases presentment and notice of dishonor are waived with respect to notes. In most cases a formal demand for payment to the maker of the note is not contemplated. Rather, the maker is expected to send payment to the holder of the note on the date or dates on which payment is due. If payment is not made when due, the holder usually makes a demand for payment, but in the normal case in which presentment is waived, demand is irrelevant and the holder can proceed against indorsers when payment is not received. Under former Article 3, in the small minority of cases in which presentment and dishonor were not waived with respect to notes, the indorser was discharged from liability (former Section 3–502(1)(a)) unless the holder made presentment to the maker on the exact day the note was due (former Section 3–503(1)(c)) and gave notice of dishonor to the indorser before midnight of the third business day after dishonor (former Section 3–508(2)). These provisions are omitted from Revised Article 3 as inconsistent with practice which seldom involves face-to-face dealings.

3.　　Subsection (a) applies to notes. Subsection (a)(1) applies to notes payable on demand. Dishonor requires presentment, and dishonor occurs if payment is not made on the day of presentment. There is no change from previous Article 3. Subsection (a)(2) applies to notes payable at a definite time if the note is payable at or through a bank or, by its terms, presentment is required. Dishonor requires presentment, and dishonor occurs if payment is not made on the due date or the day of presentment if presentment is made after the due date. Subsection (a)(3) applies to all other notes. If the note is not paid on its due date it is dishonored. This allows holders to collect notes in ways that make sense commercially without having to be concerned about a formal presentment on a given day.

4.　　Subsection (b) applies to unaccepted drafts other than documentary drafts. Subsection (b)(1) applies to checks. Except for checks presented for immediate payment over the counter, which are covered by subsection (b)(2), dishonor occurs according to rules stated in Article 4. Those rules contemplate four separate situations that warrant discussion. The first two situations arise in the normal course of affairs, in which the drawee bank makes settlement for the amount of the check to the presenting bank. In the first situation, the drawee bank under Section 4–301 recovers this settlement if it returns the check by its midnight deadline (Section 4–104). In that case the check is not paid and dishonor occurs under Section 3–502(b)(1). The second situation arises if the drawee bank has made such a settlement and does not return the check or give notice of dishonor or nonpayment within the midnight deadline. In that case, the settlement becomes final payment of the check under Section 4–215. Because the drawee bank already has paid such an item, it cannot be "accountable" for the item under the terms of Section 4–302(a)(1). Thus, no dishonor occurs regardless of whether the drawee bank retains the check indefinitely or for some reason returns the check after its midnight deadline.

The third and fourth situations arise less commonly, in cases in which the drawee bank does not settle for the check when it is received. Under Section 4–302 if the drawee bank is not also the depositary bank and retains the check without settling for it beyond midnight of the day it is presented for payment, the bank at that point becomes "accountable" for the amount of the check, i.e., it is obliged to pay the amount of the check. If the drawee bank is also the depositary bank, the bank becomes accountable for the amount of the check if the bank does not pay the check or return it or send notice of dishonor by its midnight deadline. Hence, if the drawee bank is also the depositary bank and does not either settle for the check when it is received (a settlement that would ripen into final payment if the drawee bank failed to take action to recover the settlement by its midnight deadline) or return the check or an appropriate notice by its midnight deadline, the drawee bank will become accountable for the amount of the check under Section 4–302. Thus, in all cases in which the drawee bank becomes accountable under Section 4–302, the check has not been paid (either by a settlement that became unrecoverable or otherwise) and thus, under Section 3–502(b)(1), the check is dishonored.

The fact that a bank that is accountable for the amount of the check under Section 4–302 is obliged to pay the check does not mean that the check has been paid. Indeed, because each of the paragraphs of Section 4–302(b) is limited by its terms to situations in which a bank has not paid the item, a drawee bank will be accountable under Section 4–302 only in situations in which it has not previously paid the check. Section 3–502(b)(1) reflects the view that a person presenting a check is entitled to payment, not just the ability to hold the drawee accountable under Section 4–302. If that payment is not made in a timely manner, the check is dishonored.

Regulation CC Section 229.36(d) provides that settlement between banks for the forward collection of checks is final. The relationship of that section to Articles 3 and 4 is discussed in the Commentary to that section.

Subsection (b)(2) applies to demand drafts other than those governed by subsection (b)(1). It covers checks presented for immediate payment over the counter and demand drafts other than checks. Dishonor occurs if presentment for payment is made and payment is not made on the day of presentment.

Subsection (b)(3) and (4) applies to time drafts. An unaccepted time draft differs from a time note. The maker of a note knows that the note has been issued, but the drawee of a draft may not know that a draft has been drawn on it. Thus, with respect to drafts, presentment for payment or acceptance is required. Subsection (b)(3) applies to drafts payable on a date stated in the draft. Dishonor occurs if presentment for payment is made and payment is not made on the day the draft becomes payable or the day of presentment if presentment is made after the due date. The holder of an unaccepted draft payable on a stated date has the option of presenting the draft for acceptance before the day the draft becomes payable to establish whether the drawee is willing to assume liability by accepting. Under subsection (b)(3)(ii) dishonor occurs when the draft is presented and not accepted. Subsection (b)(4) applies to unaccepted drafts payable on elapse of a period of time after sight or acceptance. If the draft is payable 30 days after sight, the draft must be presented for acceptance to start the running of the 30-day period. Dishonor occurs if it is not accepted. The rules in subsection (b)(3) and (4) follow former Section 3–501(1)(a).

5. Subsection (c) gives drawees an extended period to pay documentary drafts because of the time that may be needed to examine the documents. The period prescribed is that given by Section 5–112 in cases in which a letter of credit is involved.

6. Subsection (d) governs accepted drafts. If the acceptor's obligation is to pay on demand the rule, stated in subsection (d)(1), is the same as for that of a demand note stated in subsection (a)(1). If the acceptor's obligation is to pay at a definite time the rule, stated in subsection (d)(2), is the same as that of a time note payable at a bank stated in subsection (b)(2).

7. Subsection (e) is a limitation on subsection (a)(1) and (2), subsection (b), subsection (c), and subsection (d). Each of those provisions states dishonor as occurring after presentment. If presentment is excused under Section 3–504, dishonor occurs under those provisions without presentment if the instrument is not duly accepted or paid.

8. Under subsection (b)(3)(ii) and (4) if a draft is presented for acceptance and the draft is not accepted on the day of presentment, there is dishonor. But after dishonor, the holder may consent to late acceptance. In that case, under subsection (f), the late acceptance cures the dishonor. The draft is treated as never having been dishonored. If the draft is subsequently presented for payment and payment is refused dishonor occurs at that time.

As amended in 2002.

§ 3–503.   Notice of Dishonor.

(a)   The obligation of an indorser stated in Section 3–415(a) and the obligation of a drawer stated in Section 3–414(d) may not be enforced unless (i) the indorser or drawer is given notice of dishonor of the instrument complying with this section or (ii) notice of dishonor is excused under Section 3–504(b).

(b)   Notice of dishonor may be given by any person; may be given by any commercially reasonable means, including an oral, written, or electronic communication; and is sufficient if it reasonably identifies the instrument and indicates that the instrument has been dishonored or has not been paid or accepted. Return of an instrument given to a bank for collection is sufficient notice of dishonor.

(c)   Subject to Section 3–504(c), with respect to an instrument taken for collection by a collecting bank, notice of dishonor must be given (i) by the bank before midnight of the next banking day following the banking day on which the bank receives notice of dishonor of the instrument, or (ii) by any other person within 30 days following the day on which the person receives notice of dishonor. With respect to any other instrument, notice of dishonor must be given within 30 days following the day on which dishonor occurs.

Official Comment

1. Subsection (a) is consistent with former Section 3–501(2)(a), but notice of dishonor is no longer relevant to the liability of a drawer except for the case of a draft accepted by an acceptor other than a bank. Comments 2 and 4 to Section 3–414. There is no reason why drawers should be discharged on instruments they draw until payment or acceptance. They are entitled to have the instrument presented to the drawee and dishonored (Section 3–414(b)) before they are liable to pay, but no notice of dishonor need be made to them as a condition of liability. Subsection (b), which states how notice of dishonor is given, is based on former Section 3–508(3).

2. Subsection (c) replaces former Section 3–508(2). It differs from that section in that it provides a 30-day period for a person other than a collecting bank to give notice of dishonor rather than the three-day period allowed in former Article 3. Delay in giving notice of dishonor may be excused under Section 3–504(c).

§ 3–504.   Excused Presentment and Notice of Dishonor.

(a)   Presentment for payment or acceptance of an instrument is excused if (i) the person entitled to present the instrument cannot with reasonable diligence make presentment, (ii) the maker or acceptor has repudiated an obligation to pay the instrument or is dead or in insolvency proceedings, (iii) by the terms of the instrument presentment is not necessary to enforce the obligation of indorsers or the drawer, (iv) the drawer or indorser whose obligation is being enforced has waived presentment or otherwise has no reason to expect or right to require that the instrument be paid or accepted, or (v) the drawer instructed the drawee not to pay or accept the draft or the drawee was not obligated to the drawer to pay the draft.

(b)　Notice of dishonor is excused if (i) by the terms of the instrument notice of dishonor is not necessary to enforce the obligation of a party to pay the instrument, or (ii) the party whose obligation is being enforced waived notice of dishonor. A waiver of presentment is also a waiver of notice of dishonor.

(c)　Delay in giving notice of dishonor is excused if the delay was caused by circumstances beyond the control of the person giving the notice and the person giving the notice exercised reasonable diligence after the cause of the delay ceased to operate.

Official Comment

Section 3–504 is largely a restatement of former Section 3–511. Subsection (4) of former Section 3–511 is replaced by Section 3–502(f).

§ 3–505.　　Evidence of Dishonor.

(a)　The following are admissible as evidence and create a presumption of dishonor and of any notice of dishonor stated:

(1)　a document regular in form as provided in subsection (b) which purports to be a protest;

(2)　a purported stamp or writing of the drawee, payor bank, or presenting bank on or accompanying the instrument stating that acceptance or payment has been refused unless reasons for the refusal are stated and the reasons are not consistent with dishonor;

(3)　a book or record of the drawee, payor bank, or collecting bank, kept in the usual course of business which shows dishonor, even if there is no evidence of who made the entry.

(b)　A protest is a certificate of dishonor made by a United States consul or vice consul, or a notary public or other person authorized to administer oaths by the law of the place where dishonor occurs. It may be made upon information satisfactory to that person. The protest must identify the instrument and certify either that presentment has been made or, if not made, the reason why it was not made, and that the instrument has been dishonored by nonacceptance or nonpayment. The protest may also certify that notice of dishonor has been given to some or all parties.

Official Comment

Protest is no longer mandatory and must be requested by the holder. Even if requested, protest is not a condition to the liability of indorsers or drawers. Protest is a service provided by the banking system to establish that dishonor has occurred. Like other services provided by the banking system, it will be available if market incentives, inter-bank agreements, or governmental regulations require it, but liabilities of parties no longer rest on it. Protest may be a requirement for liability on international drafts governed by foreign law which this Article cannot affect.

PART 6

DISCHARGE AND PAYMENT

§ 3–601.　　Discharge and Effect of Discharge.

(a)　The obligation of a party to pay the instrument is discharged as stated in this Article or by an act or agreement with the party which would discharge an obligation to pay money under a simple contract.

(b)　Discharge of the obligation of a party is not effective against a person acquiring rights of a holder in due course of the instrument without notice of the discharge.

Official Comment

Subsection (a) replaces subsections (1) and (2) of former Section 3–601. Subsection (b) restates former Section 3–602. Notice of discharge is not treated as notice of a defense that prevents holder in due course status. Section 3–302(b). Discharge is effective against a holder in due course only if the holder had notice of the discharge when holder in due course status was acquired. For example, if an instrument bearing a canceled indorsement is taken by a holder, the holder has notice that the indorser has been discharged. Thus, the discharge is effective against the holder even if the holder is a holder in due course.

§ 3–602.   Payment.

(a)   Subject to subsection (e), an instrument is paid to the extent payment is made by or on behalf of a party obliged to pay the instrument, and to a person entitled to enforce the instrument.

(b)   Subject to subsection (e), a note is paid to the extent payment is made by or on behalf of a party obliged to pay the note to a person that formerly was entitled to enforce the note only if at the time of the payment the party obliged to pay has not received adequate notification that the note has been transferred and that payment is to be made to the transferee. A notification is adequate only if it is signed by the transferor or the transferee; reasonably identifies the transferred note; and provides an address at which payments subsequently are to be made. Upon request, a transferee shall seasonably furnish reasonable proof that the note has been transferred. Unless the transferee complies with the request, a payment to the person that formerly was entitled to enforce the note is effective for purposes of subsection (c) even if the party obliged to pay the note has received a notification under this paragraph.

(c)   Subject to subsection (e), to the extent of a payment under subsections (a) and (b), the obligation of the party obliged to pay the instrument is discharged even though payment is made with knowledge of a claim to the instrument under Section 3–306 by another person.

(d)   Subject to subsection (e), a transferee, or any party that has acquired rights in the instrument directly or indirectly from a transferee, including any such party that has rights as a holder in due course, is deemed to have notice of any payment that is made under subsection (b) after the date that the note is transferred to the transferee but before the party obliged to pay the note receives adequate notification of the transfer.

(e)   The obligation of a party to pay the instrument is not discharged under subsections (a) through (d) if:

(1)   a claim to the instrument under Section 3–306 is enforceable against the party receiving payment and (i) payment is made with knowledge by the payor that payment is prohibited by injunction or similar process of a court of competent jurisdiction, or (ii) in the case of an instrument other than a cashier's check, teller's check, or certified check, the party making payment accepted, from the person having a claim to the instrument, indemnity against loss resulting from refusal to pay the person entitled to enforce the instrument; or

(2)   the person making payment knows that the instrument is a stolen instrument and pays a person it knows is in wrongful possession of the instrument.

(f)   As used in this section, "signed," with respect to a record that is not a writing, includes the attachment to or logical association with the record of an electronic symbol, sound, or process with the present intent to adopt or accept the record.

As amended in 2002.

Official Comment

1.   This section replaces former Section 3–603(1). The phrase "claim to the instrument" in subsection (a) means, by reference to Section 3–306, a claim of ownership or possession and not a claim in recoupment. Subsection (e)(1)(ii) is added to conform to Section 3–411. Section 3–411 is intended to discourage an obligated bank from refusing payment of a cashier's check, certified check or dishonored teller's check at the request of a claimant to the check who provided the bank with indemnity against loss. See Comment 1 to Section 3–411. An obligated bank that refuses payment under those circumstances not only remains liable on the check but may also be liable to the holder of the check for consequential damages. Section 3–602(e)(1)(ii) and Section 3–411, read together, change the rule of former Section 3–603(1) with respect to the obligation of the obligated bank on the check. Payment to the holder of a cashier's check, teller's check, or certified check discharges the obligation of the obligated bank on the check to both the holder and the claimant even though indemnity has been given by the person asserting the claim. If the obligated bank pays the check in violation of an agreement with the claimant in connection with the indemnity agreement, any liability that the bank may have for violation of the agreement is not governed by Article 3, but is left to other law. This section continues the rule that the obligor is not discharged on the instrument if payment is made in violation of an injunction against payment. See Section 3–411(c)(iv).

2.   Subsection (a) covers payments made in a traditional manner, to the person entitled to enforce the instrument. Subsection (b), which provides an alternative method of payment, deals with the situation in which a person entitled to enforce the instrument transfers the instrument without giving notice to parties obligated to pay the instrument. If that happens and one of those parties subsequently makes a payment to the transferor, the payment is effective even though it is not made to the person entitled to enforce the instrument. Unlike the earlier version of Section 3–602, this rule is consistent with Section 9–406(a), Restatement of Mortgages § 5.5, and Restatement of Contracts § 338(1).

3.   In determining the party to whom a payment is made for purposes of this section, courts should look to traditional rules of agency. Thus, if the original payee of a note transfers ownership of the note to a third party but continues to service the obligation, the law of agency might treat payments made to the original payee as payments made to the third party.

4.   Subsection (d) assures that the discharge provided by subsection (c) is effective against the transferee and those whose rights derive from the transferee. By deeming those persons to have notice of any payment made under subsection (b), subsection (d) gives those persons "notice of the discharge" within the meaning of Section 3–302(b). Accordingly, the discharge is effective against those persons, even if any of them has the rights of a holder in due course. Compare Section 3–601(b). The deemed notice provided by subsection (d) does not, however, prevent a person from becoming or acquiring the rights of, a holder in due course. See Section 3–302(b). Thus, such a person does not become subject to other defenses described in Section 3–305(a)(2), claims in recoupment described in Section 3–305(a)(3), or claims to the instrument under Section 3–306. A transferee can prevent payment to the transferor from discharging the obligation on the note by assuring that each person who is obligated on the note receives adequate notification pursuant to subsection (b) prior to making a payment.

As amended in 2002 and 2003.

§ 3–603.   Tender of Payment.

(a)   If tender of payment of an obligation to pay an instrument is made to a person entitled to enforce the instrument, the effect of tender is governed by principles of law applicable to tender of payment under a simple contract.

(b)   If tender of payment of an obligation to pay an instrument is made to a person entitled to enforce the instrument and the tender is refused, there is discharge, to the extent of the amount of the tender, of the obligation of an indorser or accommodation party having a right of recourse with respect to the obligation to which the tender relates.

(c)   If tender of payment of an amount due on an instrument is made to a person entitled to enforce the instrument, the obligation of the obligor to pay interest after the due date on the amount tendered is discharged. If presentment is required with respect to an instrument and the obligor is able and ready to pay on the due date at every place of payment stated in the instrument, the obligor is deemed to have made tender of payment on the due date to the person entitled to enforce the instrument.

Official Comment

Section 3–603 replaces former Section 3–604. Subsection (a) generally incorporates the law of tender of payment applicable to simple contracts. Subsections (b) and (c) state particular rules. Subsection (b) replaces former Section 3–604(2). Under subsection (b) refusal of a tender of payment discharges any indorser or accommodation party having a right of recourse against the party making the tender. Subsection (c) replaces former Section 3–604(1) and (3).

§ 3–604.   Discharge by Cancellation or Renunciation.

(a)   A person entitled to enforce an instrument, with or without consideration, may discharge the obligation of a party to pay the instrument (i) by an intentional voluntary act, such as surrender of the instrument to the party, destruction, mutilation, or cancellation of the instrument, cancellation or striking out of the party's signature, or the addition of words to the instrument indicating discharge, or (ii) by agreeing not to sue or otherwise renouncing rights against the party by a signed record.

(b)   Cancellation or striking out of an indorsement pursuant to subsection (a) does not affect the status and rights of a party derived from the indorsement.

(c)   In this section, "signed," with respect to a record that is not a writing, includes the attachment to or logical association with the record of an electronic symbol, sound, or process with the present intent to adopt or accept the record.

As amended in 2002.

Official Comment

Section 3–604 replaces former Section 3–605.

§ 3–605.   Discharge of Secondary Obligors.

(a)   If a person entitled to enforce an instrument releases the obligation of a principal obligor in whole or in part, and another party to the instrument is a secondary obligor with respect to the obligation of that principal obligor, the following rules apply:

(1)   Any obligations of the principal obligor to the secondary obligor with respect to any previous payment by the secondary obligor are not affected. Unless the terms of the release preserve the secondary obligor's recourse, the principal obligor is discharged, to the extent of the release, from any other duties to the secondary obligor under this article.

(2)   Unless the terms of the release provide that the person entitled to enforce the instrument retains the right to enforce the instrument against the secondary obligor, the secondary obligor is discharged to the same extent as the principal obligor from any unperformed portion of its obligation on the instrument. If the instrument is a check and the obligation of the secondary obligor is based on an indorsement of the check, the secondary obligor is discharged without regard to the language or circumstances of the discharge or other release.

(3)   If the secondary obligor is not discharged under paragraph (2), the secondary obligor is discharged to the extent of the value of the consideration for the release, and to the extent that the release would otherwise cause the secondary obligor a loss.

(b)   If a person entitled to enforce an instrument grants a principal obligor an extension of the time at which one or more payments are due on the instrument and another party to the instrument is a secondary obligor with respect to the obligation of that principal obligor, the following rules apply:

(1)   Any obligations of the principal obligor to the secondary obligor with respect to any previous payment by the secondary obligor are not affected. Unless the terms of the extension preserve the secondary obligor's recourse, the extension correspondingly extends the time for performance of any other duties owed to the secondary obligor by the principal obligor under this article.

(2)   The secondary obligor is discharged to the extent that the extension would otherwise cause the secondary obligor a loss.

(3)   To the extent that the secondary obligor is not discharged under paragraph (2), the secondary obligor may perform its obligations to a person entitled to enforce the instrument as if the time for payment had not been extended or, unless the terms of the extension provide that the person entitled to enforce the instrument retains the right to enforce the instrument against the secondary obligor as if the time for payment had not been extended, treat the time for performance of its obligations as having been extended correspondingly.

(c)   If a person entitled to enforce an instrument agrees, with or without consideration, to a modification of the obligation of a principal obligor other than a complete or partial release or an extension of the due date and another party to the instrument is a secondary obligor with respect to the obligation of that principal obligor, the following rules apply:

(1)   Any obligations of the principal obligor to the secondary obligor with respect to any previous payment by the secondary obligor are not affected. The modification correspondingly modifies any other duties owed to the secondary obligor by the principal obligor under this article.

(2)   The secondary obligor is discharged from any unperformed portion of its obligation to the extent that the modification would otherwise cause the secondary obligor a loss.

(3)   To the extent that the secondary obligor is not discharged under paragraph (2), the secondary obligor may satisfy its obligation on the instrument as if the modification had not occurred, or treat its obligation on the instrument as having been modified correspondingly.

(d)   If the obligation of a principal obligor is secured by an interest in collateral, another party to the instrument is a secondary obligor with respect to that obligation, and a person entitled to enforce the instrument impairs the value of the interest in collateral, the obligation of the secondary obligor is discharged to the extent of the impairment. The value of an interest in collateral is impaired to the extent the value of the interest is reduced to an amount less than the amount of the recourse of the secondary obligor, or the reduction in value of the interest causes an increase in the amount by which the amount of the recourse exceeds the value of the interest. For purposes of this subsection, impairing the value of an interest in collateral includes failure to obtain or maintain perfection or recordation of the interest in collateral, release of collateral without substitution of collateral of equal value or equivalent reduction of the underlying obligation, failure to perform a duty to preserve the value of collateral owed, under Article 9 or other law, to a debtor or other person secondarily liable, and failure to comply with applicable law in disposing of or otherwise enforcing the interest in collateral.

(e)   A secondary obligor is not discharged under subsections (a)(3), (b), (c), or (d) unless the person entitled to enforce the instrument knows that the person is a secondary obligor or has notice under Section 3–419(c) that the instrument was signed for accommodation.

(f)   A secondary obligor is not discharged under this section if the secondary obligor consents to the event or conduct that is the basis of the discharge, or the instrument or a separate agreement of the party provides for waiver of discharge under this section specifically or by general language indicating that parties waive defenses based on suretyship or impairment of collateral. Unless the circumstances indicate otherwise, consent by the principal obligor to an act that would lead to a discharge under this section constitutes consent to that act by the secondary obligor if the secondary obligor controls the principal obligor or deals with the person entitled to enforce the instrument on behalf of the principal obligor.

(g)   A release or extension preserves a secondary obligor's recourse if the terms of the release or extension provide that:

(1)   the person entitled to enforce the instrument retains the right to enforce the instrument against the secondary obligor; and

(2)   the recourse of the secondary obligor continues as if the release or extension had not been granted.

(h)   Except as otherwise provided in subsection (i), a secondary obligor asserting discharge under this section has the burden of persuasion both with respect to the occurrence of the acts alleged to harm the secondary obligor and loss or prejudice caused by those acts.

(i)   If the secondary obligor demonstrates prejudice caused by an impairment of its recourse, and the circumstances of the case indicate that the amount of loss is not reasonably susceptible of calculation or requires proof of facts that are not ascertainable, it is presumed that the act impairing recourse caused a loss or impairment equal to the liability of the secondary obligor on the instrument. In that event, the burden of persuasion as to any lesser amount of the loss is on the person entitled to enforce the instrument.

As amended in 2002.

Official Comment

1.   This section contains rules that are applicable when a secondary obligor (as defined in Section 3–103(a)(17)) is a party to an instrument. These rules essentially parallel modern interpretations of the law of suretyship and guaranty that apply when a secondary obligor is not a party to an instrument. See generally Restatement of the Law, Third, Suretyship and Guaranty (1996). Of course, the rules in this section do not resolve all possible issues concerning the rights and duties of the parties. In the event that a situation is presented that is not resolved by this section (or the other related sections of this Article), the resolution may be provided by the general law of suretyship because, pursuant to Section 1–103, that law is applicable unless displaced by provisions of this Act.

2.   Like the law of suretyship and guaranty, Section 3–605 provides secondary obligors with defenses that are not available to other parties to instruments. The general operation of Section 3–605, and its relationship to

the law of suretyship and guaranty, can be illustrated by an example. Bank agrees to lend $10,000 to Borrower, but only if Backer also is liable for repayment of the loan. The parties could consummate that transaction in three different ways. First, if Borrower and Backer incurred those obligations with contracts not governed by this Article (such as a note that is not an instrument for purposes of this Article), the general law of suretyship and guaranty would be applicable. Under modern nomenclature, Bank is the "obligee," Borrower is the "principal obligor," and Backer is the "secondary obligor." See Restatement of Suretyship and Guaranty § 1. Then assume that Bank and Borrower agree to a modification of their rights and obligations after the note is signed. For example, they might agree that Borrower may repay the loan at some date after the due date, or that Borrower may discharge its repayment obligation by paying Bank $3,000 rather than $10,000. Alternatively, suppose that Bank releases collateral that Borrower has given to secure the loan. Under the law of suretyship and guaranty, the secondary obligor may be discharged under certain circumstances if these modifications of the obligations between Bank (the obligee) and Borrower (the principal obligor) are made without the consent of Backer (the secondary obligor). The rights that the secondary obligor has to a discharge of its liability in such cases commonly are referred to as suretyship defenses. The extent of the discharge depends upon the particular circumstances. See Restatement of Suretyship and Guaranty §§ 37, 39–44.

A second possibility is that the parties might decide to evidence the loan by a negotiable instrument. In that scenario, Borrower signs a note under which Borrower is obliged to pay $10,000 to the order of Bank on a due date stated in the note. Backer becomes liable for the repayment obligation by signing the note as a co-maker or indorser. In either case the note is signed for accommodation, Backer is an accommodation party, and Borrower is the accommodated party. See Section 3–419 (describing the obligations of accommodation parties). For purposes of Section 3–605, Backer is also a "secondary obligor" and Borrower is a "principal obligor," as those terms are defined in Section 3–103. Because Backer is a party to the instrument, its rights to a discharge based on any modification of obligations between Bank and Borrower are governed by Section 3–605 rather than by the general law of suretyship and guaranty. Within Section 3–605, subsection (a) describes the consequences of a release of Borrower, subsection (b) describes the consequences of an extension of time, and subsection (c) describes the consequences of other modifications.

The third possibility is that Borrower would use an instrument governed by this Article to evidence its repayment obligation, but Backer's obligation would be created in some way other than by becoming party to that instrument. In that case, Backer's rights are determined by suretyship and guaranty law rather than by this Article. See Comment 3 to Section 3–419.

A person also can acquire secondary liability without having been a secondary obligor at the time that the principal obligation was created. For example, a transferee of real or personal property that assumes the obligation of the transferor as maker of a note secured by the property becomes by operation of law a principal obligor, with the transferor becoming a secondary obligor. Restatement of Suretyship and Guaranty § 2(e); Restatement of Mortgages § 5.1. Article 3 does not determine the effect of the release of the transferee in that case because the assuming transferee is not a "party" to the instrument as defined in Section 3–103(a)(10). Section 3–605(a) does not apply then because the holder has not discharged the obligation of a "principal obligor," a term defined in Section 3–103(a)(11). Thus, the resolution of that question is governed by the law of suretyship. See Restatement of Suretyship and Guaranty § 39.

3.   Section 3–605 is not, however, limited to the conventional situation of the accommodation party discussed in Comment 2. It also applies in four other situations. First, it applies to indorsers of notes who are not accommodation parties. Unless an indorser signs without recourse, the indorser's liability under Section 3–415(a) is functionally similar to that of a guarantor of payment. For example, if Bank in the second hypothetical discussed in Comment 2 indorsed the note and transferred it to Second Bank, Bank is liable to Second Bank in the event of dishonor of the note by Borrower. Section 3–415(a). Because of that secondary liability as indorser, Bank qualifies as a "secondary obligor" under Section 3–103(a)(17) and has the same rights under Section 3–605 as an accommodation party.

Second, a similar analysis applies to the drawer of a draft that is accepted by a party that is not a bank. Under Section 3–414(d), that drawer has liability on the same terms as an indorser under Section 3–415(a). Thus, the drawer in that case is a "secondary obligor" under Section 3–103(a)(17) and has rights under Section 3–605 to that extent.

Third, a similar principle justifies application of Section 3–605 to persons who indorse a check. Assume that Drawer draws a check to the order of Payee. Payee then indorses the check and transfers it to Transferee. If Transferee presents the check and it is dishonored, Transferee may recover from Drawer under Section 3–414 or Payee under Section 3–415. Because of that secondary liability as an indorser, Payee is a secondary obligor under

Section 3–103(a)(17). Drawer is a "principal obligor" under Section 3–103(a)(11). As noted in Comment 4, below, however, Section 3–605(a)(3) will discharge indorsers of checks in some cases in which other secondary obligors will not be discharged by this section.

Fourth, this section also deals with the rights of co-makers of instruments, even when those co-makers do not qualify as accommodation parties. The co-makers' rights of contribution under Section 3–116 make each co-maker a secondary obligor to the extent of that right of contribution.

4.   Subsection (a) is based on Restatement of Suretyship and Guaranty § 39. It addresses the effects of a release of the principal obligor by the person entitled to enforce the instrument. Paragraph (a)(1) governs the effect of that release on the principal obligor's duties to the secondary obligor; paragraphs (a)(2) and (a)(3) govern the effect of that release on the secondary obligor's duties to the person entitled to enforce the instrument.

With respect to the duties of the principal obligor, the release of course cannot affect obligations of the principal obligor with respect to payments that the secondary obligor already has made. But with respect to future payments by the secondary obligor, paragraph (a)(1) (based on Restatement of Suretyship and Guaranty § 39(a)) provides that the principal obligor is discharged, to the extent of the release, from any other duties to the secondary obligor. That rule is appropriate because otherwise the discharge granted to the principal obligor would be illusory: it would have obtained a release from a person entitled to enforce that instrument, but it would be directly liable for the same sum to the secondary obligor if the secondary obligor later complied with its secondary obligation to pay the instrument. This discharge does not occur, though, if the terms of the release effect a "preservation of recourse" as described in subsection (g). See Comment 10, below.

The discharge under paragraph (a)(1) of the principal obligor's duties to the secondary obligor is broad, applying to all duties under this article. This includes not only the principal obligor's liability as a party to an instrument (as a maker, drawer or indorser under Sections 3–412 through 3–415) but also obligations under Sections 3–116 and 3–419.

Paragraph (a)(2) is based closely on Restatement of Suretyship and Guaranty § 39(b). It articulates a default rule that the release of a principal obligor also discharges the secondary obligor, to the extent of the release granted to the principal obligor, from any unperformed portion of its obligation on the instrument. The discharge of the secondary obligor under paragraph (a)(2) is phrased more narrowly than the discharge of the principal obligor is phrased under paragraph (a)(1) because, unlike principal obligors, the only obligations of secondary obligors in Article 3 are "on the instrument" as makers or indorsers.

The parties can opt out of that rule by including a contrary statement in the terms of the release. The provision does not contemplate that any "magic words" are necessary. Thus, discharge of the secondary obligor under paragraph (a)(2) is avoided not only if the terms of the release track the statutory language (e.g., the person entitled to enforce the instrument "retains the right to enforce the instrument" against the secondary obligor), or if the terms of the release effect a preservation of recourse under subsection (g), but also if the terms of the release include a simple statement that the parties intend to "release the principal obligor but not the secondary obligor" or that the person entitled to enforce the instrument "reserves its rights" against the secondary obligor. At the same time, because paragraph (a)(2) refers to the "terms of the release," extrinsic circumstances cannot be used to establish that the parties intended the secondary obligor to remain obligated. If a release of the principal obligor includes such a provision, the secondary obligor is, nonetheless, discharged to the extent of the consideration that is paid for the release; that consideration is treated as a payment in partial satisfaction of the instrument.

Notwithstanding language in the release that prevents discharge of the secondary obligor under paragraph (a)(2), paragraph (a)(3) discharges the secondary obligor from its obligation to a person entitled to enforce the instrument to the extent that the release otherwise would cause the secondary obligor a loss. The rationale for that provision is that a release of the principal obligor changes the economic risk for which the secondary obligor contracted. This risk may be increased in two ways. First, by releasing the principal obligor, the person entitled to enforce the instrument has eliminated the likelihood of future payments by the principal obligor that would lessen the obligation of the secondary obligor. Second, unless the release effects a preservation of the secondary obligor's recourse, the release eliminates the secondary obligor's claims against the principal obligor with respect to any future payment by the secondary obligor. The discharge provided by this paragraph prevents that increased risk from causing the secondary obligor a loss. Moreover, permitting releases to be negotiated between the principal obligor and the person entitled to enforce the instrument without regard to the consequences to the secondary obligor would create an undue risk of opportunistic behavior by the obligee and principal obligor. That concern is lessened, and the discharge is not provided by paragraph (a)(3), if the secondary obligor has consented to the release or is deemed to have consented to it under subsection (f) (which presumes consent by a secondary obligor to actions taken by a principal obligor if the secondary obligor controls the principal obligor or deals with the person entitled to enforce the instrument on behalf of the principal obligor). See Comment 9, below.

Subsection (a) (and Restatement Section 39(b), the concepts of which it follows quite closely) is designed to facilitate negotiated workouts between a creditor and a principal obligor, so long as they are not at the expense of a secondary obligor who has not consented to the arrangement (either specifically or by waiving its rights to discharge under this section). Thus, for example, the provision facilitates an arrangement in which the principal obligor pays some portion of a guaranteed obligation, the person entitled to enforce the instrument grants a release to the principal obligor in exchange for that payment, and the person entitled to enforce the instrument pursues the secondary obligor for the remainder of the obligation. Under paragraph (a)(2), the person entitled to enforce the instrument may pursue the secondary obligor despite the release of the principal obligor so long as the terms of the release provide for this result. Under paragraph (a)(3), though, the secondary obligor will be protected against any loss it might suffer by reason of that release (if the secondary obligor has not waived discharge under subsection (f)). It should be noted that the obligee may be able to minimize the risk of such loss (and, thus, of the secondary obligor's discharge) by giving the secondary obligor prompt notice of the release even though such notice is not required.

The foregoing principles are illustrated by the following cases:

Case 1. D borrows $1000 from C. The repayment obligation is evidenced by a note issued by D, payable to the order of C. S is an accommodation indorser of the note. As the due date of the note approaches, it becomes obvious that D cannot pay the full amount of the note and may soon be facing bankruptcy. C, in order to collect as much as possible from D and lessen the need to seek recovery from S, agrees to release D from its obligation under the note in exchange for $100 in cash. The agreement to release D is silent as to the effect of the release on S. Pursuant to Section 3–605(a)(2), the release of D discharges S from its obligations to C on the note.

Case 2. Same facts as Case 1, except that the terms of the release provide that C retains its rights to enforce the instrument against S. D is discharged from its obligations to S pursuant to Section 3–605(a)(1), but S is not discharged from its obligations to C pursuant to Section 3–605(a)(2). However, if S could have recovered from D any sum it paid to C (had D not been discharged from its obligation to S), S has been harmed by the release and is discharged pursuant to Section 3–605(a)(3) to the extent of that harm.

Case 3. Same facts as Case 1, except that the terms of the release provide that C retains its rights to enforce the instrument against S and that S retains its recourse against D. Under subsection (g), the release effects a preservation of recourse. Thus, S is not discharged from its obligations to C pursuant to Section 3–605(a)(2) and D is not discharged from its obligations to S pursuant to Section 3–605(a)(1). Because S's claims against D are preserved, S will not suffer the kind of loss described in Case 2. If no other loss is suffered by S as a result of the release, S is not discharged pursuant to this section.

Case 4. Same facts as Case 3, except that D had made arrangements to work at a second job in order to earn the money to fulfill its obligations on the note. When C released D, however, D canceled the plans for the second job. While S still retains its recourse against D, S may be discharged from its obligation under the instrument to the extent that D's decision to forgo the second job causes S a loss because forgoing the job renders D unable to fulfill its obligations to S under Section 3–419.

Subsection (a) reflects a change from former Section 3–605(b), which provided categorically that the release of a principal obligor by the person entitled to enforce the instrument did not discharge a secondary obligor's obligation on the instrument and assumed that the release also did not discharge the principal obligor's obligations to the secondary obligor under Section 3–419. The rule under subsection (a) is much closer to the policy of the Restatement of Suretyship and Guaranty than was former Section 3–605(b). The change, however, is likely to affect only a narrow category of cases. First, as discussed above, Section 3–605 applies only to transactions in which the payment obligation is represented by a negotiable instrument, and, within that set of transactions, only to those transactions in which the secondary obligation is incurred by indorsement or cosigning, not to transactions that involve a separate document of guaranty. See Comment 2, above. Second, as provided in subsection (f), secondary obligors cannot obtain a discharge under subsection (a) in any transaction in which they have consented to the challenged conduct. Thus, subsection (a) will not apply to any transaction that includes a provision waiving suretyship defenses (a provision that is almost universally included in commercial loan documentation) or to any transaction in which the creditor obtains the consent of the secondary obligor at the time of the release.

The principal way in which subsection (a) goes beyond the policy of Restatement § 39 is with respect to the liability of indorsers of checks. Specifically, the last sentence of paragraph (a)(2) provides that a release of a principal obligor grants a complete discharge to the indorser of a check, without requiring the indorser to prove harm. In that particular context, it seems likely that continuing responsibility for the indorser often would be so inconsistent with the expectations of the parties as to create a windfall for the creditor and an unfair surprise for the indorser. Thus, the statute implements a simple rule that grants a complete discharge. The creditor, of course, can avoid that rule by contracting with the secondary obligor for a different result at the time that the creditor grants the release to the principal obligor.

5.   Subsection (b) is based on Restatement of Suretyship and Guaranty § 40 and relates to extensions of the due date of the instrument. An extension of time to pay a note is often beneficial to the secondary obligor because the additional time may enable the principal obligor to obtain the funds to pay the instrument. In some cases, however, the extension may cause loss to the secondary obligor, particularly if deterioration of the financial condition of the principal obligor reduces the amount that the secondary obligor is able to recover on its right of recourse when default occurs. For example, suppose that the instrument is an installment note and the principal debtor is temporarily short of funds to pay a monthly installment. The payee agrees to extend the due date of the installment for a month or two to allow the debtor to pay when funds are available. Paragraph (b)(2) provides that an extension of time results in a discharge of the secondary obligor, but only to the extent that the secondary obligor proves that the extension caused loss. See subsection (h) (discussing the burden of proof under Section 3–605). Thus, if the extension is for a long period, the secondary obligor might be able to prove that during the period of extension the principal obligor became insolvent, reducing the value of the right of recourse of the secondary obligor. In such a case, paragraph (b)(2) discharges the secondary obligor to the extent of that harm. Although not required to notify the secondary obligor of the extension, the payee can minimize the risk of loss by the secondary obligor by giving the secondary obligor prompt notice of the extension; prompt notice can enhance the likelihood that the secondary obligor's right of recourse can remain valuable, and thus can limit the likelihood that the secondary obligor will suffer a loss because of the extension. See Restatement of Suretyship and Guaranty Section 38 comment b.

If the secondary obligor is not discharged under paragraph (b)(2) (either because it would not suffer a loss by reason of the extension or because it has waived its right to discharge pursuant to subsection (f)), it is important to understand the effect of the extension on the rights and obligations of the secondary obligor. Consider the following cases:

Case 5. A borrows money from Lender and issues a note payable to the order of Lender that is due on April 1, 2002. B signs the note for accommodation at the request of Lender. B signed the note either as co-maker or as an anomalous indorser. In either case Lender subsequently makes an agreement with A extending the due date of A's obligation to pay the note to July 1, 2002. In either case B did not agree to the extension, and the extension did not address Lender's rights against B. Under paragraph (b)(1), A's obligations to B under this article are also extended to July 1, 2002. Under paragraph (b)(3), if B is not discharged, B may treat its obligations to Lender as also extended, or may pay the instrument on the original due date.

Case 6. Same facts as Case 5, except that the extension agreement includes a statement that the Lender retains its right to enforce the note against B on its original terms. Under paragraph (b)(3), B is liable on the original due date, but under paragraph (b)(1), A's obligations to B under Section 3–419 are not due until July 1, 2002.

Case 7. Same facts as Case 5, except that the extension agreement includes a statement that the Lender retains its right to enforce the note against B on its original terms and B retains its recourse against A as though no extension had been granted. Under paragraph (b)(3), B is liable on the original due date. Under paragraph (b)(1), A's obligations to B under Section 3–419 are not extended.

Under section 3–605(b), the results in Case 5 and Case 7 are identical to the results that follow from the law of suretyship and guaranty. See Restatement of Suretyship and Guaranty § 40. The situation in Case 6 is not specifically addressed in the Restatement, but the resolution in this Section is consistent with the concepts of suretyship and guaranty law as reflected in the Restatement. If the secondary obligor is called upon to pay on the due date, it may be difficult to quantify the extent to which the extension has impaired the right of recourse of the secondary obligor at that time. Still, the secondary obligor does have a right to make a claim against the obligee at that time. As a practical matter a suit making such a claim should establish the facts relevant to the extent of the impairment. See Restatement of Suretyship and Guaranty § 37(4).

As a practical matter, an extension of the due date will normally occur only when the principal obligor is unable to pay on the due date. The interest of the secondary obligor normally is to acquiesce in the willingness of the person entitled to enforce the instrument to wait for payment from the principal obligor rather than to pay right away and rely on an action against the principal obligor that may have little or no value. But in unusual cases the secondary obligor may prefer to pay the holder on the original due date so as to avoid continuing accrual of interest. In such cases, the secondary obligor may do so. See paragraph (b)(3). If the terms of the extension provide that the person entitled to enforce the instrument retains its right to enforce the instrument against the secondary obligor on the original due date, though, those terms are effective and the secondary obligor may not delay payment until the extended due date. Unless the extension agreement effects a preservation of recourse, however, the secondary obligor may not proceed against the principal obligor under Section 3–419 until the extended due date. See paragraph (b)(1). To the extent that delay causes loss to the secondary obligor it is discharged under paragraph (b)(2).

Even in those cases in which a secondary obligor does not have a duty to pay the instrument on the original due date, it always has the right to pay the instrument on that date, and perhaps minimize its loss by doing so. The secondary obligor is not precluded, however, from asserting its rights to discharge under Section 3–605(b)(2) if it does not exercise that option. The critical issue is whether the extension caused the secondary obligor a loss by increasing the difference between its cost of performing its obligation on the instrument and the amount recoverable from the principal obligor under this Article. The decision by the secondary obligor not to exercise its option to pay on the original due date may, under the circumstances, be a factor to be considered in the determination of that issue, especially if the secondary obligor has been given prompt notice of the extension (as discussed above).

6.   Subsection (c) is based on Restatement of Suretyship and Guaranty § 41. It is a residual provision, which applies to modifications of the obligation of the principal obligor that are not covered by subsections (a) and (b). Under subsection (c)(1), a modification of the obligation of the principal obligor on the instrument (other than a release covered by subsection (a) or an extension of the due date covered by subsection (b)), will correspondingly modify the duties of the principal obligor to the secondary obligor. Under subsection (c)(2), such a modification also will result in discharge of the secondary obligor to the extent the modification causes loss to the secondary obligor. To the extent that the secondary obligor is not discharged and the obligation changes the amount of money payable on the instrument, or the timing of such payment, subsection (c)(3) provides the secondary obligor with a choice: it may satisfy its obligation on the instrument as if the modification had not occurred, or it may treat its obligation to pay the instrument as having been modified in a manner corresponding to the modification of the principal obligor's obligation.

The following cases illustrate the application of subsection (c):

Case 8. Corporation borrows money from Lender and issues a note payable to Lender. X signs the note as an accommodation party for Corporation. The note refers to a loan agreement under which the note was issued, which states various events of default that allow Lender to accelerate the due date of the note. Among the events of default are breach of covenants not to incur debt beyond specified limits and not to engage in any line of business substantially different from that currently carried on by Corporation. Without consent of X, Lender agrees to modify the covenants to allow Corporation to enter into a new line of business that X considers to be risky, and to incur debt beyond the limits specified in the loan agreement to finance the new venture. This modification discharges X to the extent that the modification otherwise would cause X a loss.

Case 9. Corporation borrows money from Lender and issues a note payable to Lender in the amount of $100,000. X signs the note as an accommodation party for Corporation. The note calls for 60 equal monthly payments of interest and principal. Before the first payment is made, Corporation and Lender agree to modify the note by changing the repayment schedule to require four annual payments of interest only, followed by a fifth payment of interest and the entire $100,000 principal balance. To the extent that the modification does not discharge X, X has the option of fulfilling its obligation on the note in accordance with the original terms or the modified terms.

7.   Subsection (d) is based on Restatement of Suretyship and Guaranty § 42 and deals with the discharge of secondary obligors by impairment of collateral. The last sentence of subsection (d) states four common examples of what is meant by impairment. Because it uses the term "includes," the provision allows a court to find impairment in other cases as well. There is extensive case law on impairment of collateral. The secondary obligor is discharged to the extent that the secondary obligor proves that impairment was caused by a person entitled to enforce the instrument. For example, assume that the payee of a secured note fails to perfect the security interest. The collateral is owned by the principal obligor who subsequently files in bankruptcy. As a result of the failure to perfect, the security interest is not enforceable in bankruptcy. If the payee were to obtain payment from the secondary obligor, the secondary obligor would be subrogated to the payee's security interest in the collateral

under Section 3–419 and general principles of suretyship law. See Restatement of Suretyship and Guaranty § 28(1)(c). In this situation, though, the value of the security interest is impaired completely because the security interest is unenforceable. Thus, the secondary obligor is discharged from its obligation on the note to the extent of that impairment. If the value of the collateral impaired is as much or more than the amount of the note, and if there will be no recovery on the note as an unsecured claim, there is a complete discharge. Subsection (d) applies whether the collateral is personalty or realty, whenever the obligation in question is in the form of a negotiable instrument.

8.   Subsection (e) is based on the former Section 3–605(h). The requirement of knowledge in the first clause is consistent with Section 9–628. The requirement of notice in the second clause is consistent with Section 3–419(c).

9.   The importance of the suretyship defenses provided in Section 3–605 is greatly diminished by the fact that the right to discharge can be waived as provided in subsection (f). The waiver can be effectuated by a provision in the instrument or in a separate agreement. It is standard practice to include such a waiver of suretyship defenses in notes prepared by financial institutions or other commercial creditors. Thus, Section 3–605 will result in the discharge of an accommodation party on a note only in the occasional case in which the note does not include such a waiver clause and the person entitled to enforce the note nevertheless takes actions that would give rise to a discharge under this section without obtaining the consent of the secondary obligor.

Because subsection (f) by its terms applies only to a discharge "under this section," subsection (f) does not operate to waive a defense created by other law (such as the law governing enforcement of security interests under Article 9) that cannot be waived under that law. See, e.g., Section 9–602.

The last sentence of subsection (f) creates an inference of consent on the part of the secondary obligor whenever the secondary obligor controls the principal obligor or deals with the creditor on behalf of the principal obligor. That sentence is based on Restatement of Suretyship and Guaranty § 48(2).

10.   Subsection (g) explains the criteria for determining whether the terms of a release or extension preserve the secondary obligor's recourse, a concept of importance in the application of subsections (a) and (b). First, the terms of the release or extension must provide that the person entitled to enforce the instrument retains the right to enforce the instrument against the secondary obligor. Second, the terms of the release or extension must provide that the recourse of the secondary obligor against the principal obligor continues as though the release or extension had not been granted. Those requirements are drawn from Restatement of Suretyship and Guaranty § 38.

11.   Subsections (h) and (i) articulate rules for the burden of persuasion under Section 3–605. Those rules are based on Restatement of Suretyship and Guaranty § 49.

As amended in 2002.

UCC ARTICLE 4 (2016)

BANK DEPOSITS AND COLLECTIONS

Article 4 was amended in 1990 and 2002 by the same drafting committees that promulgated the 1990 and 2002 amendments to UCC Article 3.

PART 1.   GENERAL PROVISIONS AND DEFINITIONS

PART 2.   COLLECTION OF ITEMS: DEPOSITARY AND COLLECTING BANKS

PART 3.   COLLECTION OF ITEMS: PAYOR BANKS

PART 1

GENERAL PROVISIONS AND DEFINITIONS

§ 4–101.   Short Title.

This Article may be cited as Uniform Commercial Code—Bank Deposits and Collections.

As amended in 1990.

Official Comment

1.   The great number of checks handled by banks and the country-wide nature of the bank collection process require uniformity in the law of bank collections. There is needed a uniform statement of the principal rules of the bank collection process with ample provision for flexibility to meet the needs of the large volume handled and the changing needs and conditions that are bound to come with the years. This Article meets that need.

2.   In 1950 at the time Article 4 was drafted, 6.7 billion checks were written annually. By the time of the 1990 revision of Article 4 annual volume was estimated by the American Bankers Association to be about 50 billion checks. The banking system could not have coped with this increase in check volume had it not developed in the late 1950s and early 1960s an automated system for check collection based on encoding checks with machine-readable information by Magnetic Ink Character Recognition (MICR). An important goal of the 1990 revision of Article 4 is to promote the efficiency of the check collection process by making the provisions of Article 4 more compatible with the needs of an automated system and, by doing so, increase the speed and lower the cost of check collection for those who write and receive checks. An additional goal of the 1990 revision of Article 4 is to remove any statutory barriers in the Article to the ultimate adoption of programs allowing the presentment of checks to payor banks by electronic transmission of information captured from the MICR line on the checks. The potential of these programs for saving the time and expense of transporting the huge volume of checks from depositary to payor banks is evident.

3.   Article 4 defines rights between parties with respect to bank deposits and collections. It is not a regulatory statute. It does not regulate the terms of the bank-customer agreement, nor does it prescribe what constraints different jurisdictions may wish to impose on that relationship in the interest of consumer protection. The revisions in Article 4 are intended to create a legal framework that accommodates automation and truncation

for the benefit of all bank customers. This may raise consumer problems which enacting jurisdictions may wish to address in individual legislation. For example, with respect to Section 4–401(c), jurisdictions may wish to examine their unfair and deceptive practices laws to determine whether they are adequate to protect drawers who postdate checks from unscrupulous practices that may arise on the part of persons who induce drawers to issue postdated checks in the erroneous belief that the checks will not be immediately payable. Another example arises from the fact that under various truncation plans customers will no longer receive their cancelled checks and will no longer have the cancelled check to prove payment. Individual legislation might provide that a copy of a bank statement along with a copy of the check is prima facie evidence of payment.

§ 4–102. Applicability.

(a) To the extent that items within this Article are also within Articles 3 and 8, they are subject to those Articles. If there is conflict, this Article governs Article 3, but Article 8 governs this Article.

(b) The liability of a bank for action or non-action with respect to an item handled by it for purposes of presentment, payment, or collection is governed by the law of the place where the bank is located. In the case of action or non-action by or at a branch or separate office of a bank, its liability is governed by the law of the place where the branch or separate office is located.

As amended in 1990.

Official Comment

1. The rules of Article 3 governing negotiable instruments, their transfer, and the contracts of the parties thereto apply to the items collected through banking channels wherever no specific provision is found in this Article. In the case of conflict, this Article governs. See Section 3–102(b).

Bonds and like instruments constituting investment securities under Article 8 may also be handled by banks for collection purposes. Various sections of Article 8 prescribe rules of transfer some of which (see ~~Sections 8–304 and 8–306~~ Sections 8–108 and 8–304)* may conflict with provisions of this Article (Sections 4–205, 4–207, and 4–208). In the case of conflict, Article 8 governs.

Section 4–210 deals specifically with overlapping problems and possible conflicts between this Article and Article 9. However, similar reconciling provisions are not necessary in the case of Articles 5 and 7. Sections 4–301 and 4–302 are consistent with Section 5–112.** In the case of Article 7 documents of title frequently accompany items but they are not themselves items. See Section 4–104(a)(9).

In *Clearfield Trust Co. v. United States*, 318 U.S. 363 (1943), the Court held that if the United States is a party to an instrument, its rights and duties are governed by federal common law in the absence of a specific federal statute or regulation. In *United States v. Kimbell Foods, Inc.*, 440 U.S. 715 (1979), the Court stated a three-pronged test to ascertain whether the federal common-law rule should follow the state rule. In most instances courts under the *Kimbell* test have shown a willingness to adopt UCC rules in formulating federal common law on the subject. In *Kimbell* the Court adopted the priorities rules of Article 9.

In addition, applicable federal law may supersede provisions of this Article. One federal law that does so is the Expedited Funds Availability Act, 12 U.S.C. § 4001 et seq., and its implementing Regulation CC, 12 CFR Pt. 229. In some instances this law is alluded to in the statute, e.g., Section 4–215(e) and (f). In other instances, although not referred to in this Article, the provisions of the EFAA and Regulation CC control with respect to checks. For example, except between the depositary bank and its customer, all settlements are final and not provisional (Regulation CC, Section 229.36(d)), and the midnight deadline may be extended (Regulation CC, Section 229.30(c)). The comments to this Article suggest in most instances the relevant Regulation CC provisions.

2. Subsection (b) is designed to state a workable rule for the solution of otherwise vexatious problems of the conflicts of laws:

a. The routine and mechanical nature of bank collections makes it imperative that one law govern the activities of one office of a bank. The requirement found in some cases that to hold an indorser notice must be given in accordance with the law of the place of indorsement, since that method of notice became an implied term of the indorser's contract, is more theoretical than practical.

---

* Amendments approved by the Permanent Editorial Board for Uniform Commercial Code November 4, 1995.
** *Referring to unrevised Article 5.*

b.   Adoption of what is in essence a tort theory of the conflict of laws is consistent with the general theory of this Article that the basic duty of a collecting bank is one of good faith and the exercise of ordinary care. Justification lies in the fact that, in using an ambulatory instrument, the drawer, payee, and indorsers must know that action will be taken with respect to it in other jurisdictions. This is especially pertinent with respect to the law of the place of payment.

c.   The phrase "action or non-action with respect to any item handled by it for purposes of presentment, payment, or collection" is intended to make the conflicts rule of subsection (b) apply from the inception of the collection process of an item through all phases of deposit, forwarding, presentment, payment and remittance or credit of proceeds. Specifically the subsection applies to the initial act of a depositary bank in receiving an item and to the incidents of such receipt. The conflicts rule of *Weissman v. Banque De Bruxelles*, 254 N.Y. 488, 173 N.E. 835 (1930), is rejected. The subsection applies to questions of possible vicarious liability of a bank for action or non-action of sub-agents (see Section 4–202(c)), and tests these questions by the law of the state of the location of the bank which uses the sub-agent. The conflicts rule of *St. Nicholas Bank of New York v. State Nat. Bank*, 128 N.Y. 26, 27 N.E. 849, 13 L.R.A. 241 (1891), is rejected. The subsection applies to action or non-action of a payor bank in connection with handling an item (see Sections 4–215(a), 4–301, 4–302, 4–303) as well as action or non-action of a collecting bank (Sections 4–201 through 4–216); to action or non-action of a bank which suspends payment or is affected by another bank suspending payment (Section 4–216); to action or non-action of a bank with respect to an item under the rule of Part 4 of Article 4.

d.   In a case in which subsection (b) makes this Article applicable, Section 4–103(a) leaves open the possibility of an agreement with respect to applicable law. This freedom of agreement follows the general policy of Section 1–105.*

§ 4–103.   Variation by Agreement; Measure of Damages; Action Constituting Ordinary Care.

(a)   The effect of the provisions of this Article may be varied by agreement, but the parties to the agreement cannot disclaim a bank's responsibility for its lack of good faith or failure to exercise ordinary care or limit the measure of damages for the lack or failure. However, the parties may determine by agreement the standards by which the bank's responsibility is to be measured if those standards are not manifestly unreasonable.

(b)   Federal Reserve regulations and operating circulars, clearing-house rules, and the like have the effect of agreements under subsection (a), whether or not specifically assented to by all parties interested in items handled.

(c)   Action or non-action approved by this Article or pursuant to Federal Reserve regulations or operating circulars is the exercise of ordinary care and, in the absence of special instructions, action or non-action consistent with clearing-house rules and the like or with a general banking usage not disapproved by this Article, is prima facie the exercise of ordinary care.

(d)   The specification or approval of certain procedures by this Article is not disapproval of other procedures that may be reasonable under the circumstances.

(e)   The measure of damages for failure to exercise ordinary care in handling an item is the amount of the item reduced by an amount that could not have been realized by the exercise of ordinary care. If there is also bad faith it includes any other damages the party suffered as a proximate consequence.

As amended in 1990.

Official Comment

1.   Section 1–102 states the general principles and rules for variation of the effect of this Act by agreement and the limitations to this power. Section 4–103 states the specific rules for variation of Article 4 by agreement and also certain standards of ordinary care. In view of the technical complexity of the field of bank collections, the enormous number of items handled by banks, the certainty that there will be variations from the normal in each day's work in each bank, the certainty of changing conditions and the possibility of developing improved methods of collection to speed the process, it would be unwise to freeze present methods of operation by mandatory statutory

---

*   *Referring to unrevised Article 1 (Appendix A).*

rules. This section, therefore, permits within wide limits variation of the effect of provisions of the Article by agreement.

2. Subsection (a) confers blanket power to vary all provisions of the Article by agreements of the ordinary kind. The agreements may not disclaim a bank's responsibility for its own lack of good faith or failure to exercise ordinary care and may not limit the measure of damages for the lack or failure, but this subsection like Section 1–102(3)* approves the practice of parties determining by agreement the standards by which the responsibility is to be measured. In the absence of a showing that the standards manifestly are unreasonable, the agreement controls. Owners of items and other interested parties are not affected by agreements under this subsection unless they are parties to the agreement or are bound by adoption, ratification, estoppel or the like.

As here used "agreement" has the meaning given to it by Section 1–201(3).* The agreement may be direct, as between the owner and the depositary bank; or indirect, as in the case in which the owner authorizes a particular type of procedure and any bank in the collection chain acts pursuant to such authorization. It may be with respect to a single item; or to all items handled for a particular customer, e.g., a general agreement between the depositary bank and the customer at the time a deposit account is opened. Legends on deposit tickets, collection letters and acknowledgments of items, coupled with action by the affected party constituting acceptance, adoption, ratification, estoppel or the like, are agreements if they meet the tests of the definition of "agreement." See Section 1–201(3).* *First Nat. Bank of Denver v. Federal Reserve Bank*, 6 F.2d 339 (8th Cir.1925) (deposit slip); *Jefferson County Bldg. Ass'n v. Southern Bank & Trust Co.*, 225 Ala. 25, 142 So. 66 (1932) (signature card and deposit slip); *Semingson v. Stock Yards Nat. Bank*, 162 Minn. 424, 203 N.W. 412 (1925) (passbook); *Farmers State Bank v. Union Nat. Bank*, 42 N.D. 449, 454, 173 N.W. 789, 790 (1919) (acknowledgment of receipt of item).

3. Subsection (a) (subject to its limitations with respect to good faith and ordinary care) goes far to meet the requirements of flexibility. However, it does not by itself confer fully effective flexibility. Since it is recognized that banks handle a great number of items every business day and that the parties interested in each item include the owner of the item, the drawer (if it is a check), all nonbank indorsers, the payor bank and from one to five or more collecting banks, it is obvious that it is impossible, practically, to obtain direct agreements from all of these parties on all items. In total, the interested parties constitute virtually every adult person and business organization in the United States. On the other hand they may become bound to agreements on the principle that collecting banks acting as agents have authority to make binding agreements with respect to items being handled. This conclusion was assumed but was not flatly decided in *Federal Reserve Bank of Richmond v. Malloy*, 264 U.S. 160, at 167, 44 S.Ct. 296, at 298, 68 L.Ed. 617, 31 A.L.R. 1261 (1924).

To meet this problem subsection (b) provides that official or quasi-official rules of collection, that is Federal Reserve regulations and operating circulars, clearing-house rules, and the like, have the effect of agreements under subsection (a), whether or not specifically assented to by all parties interested in items handled. Consequently, such official or quasi-official rules may, standing by themselves but subject to the good faith and ordinary care limitations, vary the effect of the provisions of Article 4.

Federal Reserve regulations. Various sections of the Federal Reserve Act (12 U.S.C. § 221 et seq.) authorize the Board of Governors of the Federal Reserve System to direct the Federal Reserve banks to exercise bank collection functions. For example, Section 16 (12 U.S.C. § 248(*o*)) authorizes the Board to require each Federal Reserve bank to exercise the functions of a clearing house for its members and Section 13 (12 U.S.C. § 342) authorizes each Federal Reserve bank to receive deposits from nonmember banks solely for the purposes of exchange or of collection. Under this statutory authorization the Board has issued Regulation J (Subpart A—Collection of Checks and Other Items). Under the supremacy clause of the Constitution, federal regulations prevail over state statutes. Moreover, the Expedited Funds Availability Act, 12 U.S.C. Section 4007(b) provides that the Act and Regulation CC, 12 CFR 229, supersede "any provision of the law of any State, including the Uniform Commercial Code as in effect in such State, which is inconsistent with this chapter or such regulations." See Comment 1 to Section 4–102.

Federal Reserve operating circulars. The regulations of the Federal Reserve Board authorize the Federal Reserve banks to promulgate operating circulars covering operating details. Regulation J, for example, provides that "Each Reserve Bank shall receive and handle items in accordance with this subpart, and shall issue operating circulars governing the details of its handling of items and other matters deemed appropriate by the Reserve Bank." This Article recognizes that "operating circulars" issued pursuant to the regulations and concerned with operating details as appropriate may, within their proper sphere, vary the effect of the Article.

---

* *Referring to unrevised Article 1 (Appendix A).*

Clearing-House Rules. Local clearing houses have long issued rules governing the details of clearing; hours of clearing, media of remittance, time for return of mis-sent items and the like. The case law has recognized these rules, within their proper sphere, as binding on affected parties and as appropriate sources for the courts to look to in filling out details of bank collection law. Subsection (b) in recognizing clearing-house rules as a means of preserving flexibility continues the sensible approach indicated in the cases. Included in the term "clearing houses" are county and regional clearing houses as well as those within a single city or town. There is, of course, no intention of authorizing a local clearing house or a group of clearing houses to rewrite the basic law generally. The term "clearing-house rules" should be understood in the light of functions the clearing houses have exercised in the past.

And the like. This phrase is to be construed in the light of the foregoing. "Federal Reserve regulations and operating circulars" cover rules and regulations issued by public or quasi-public agencies under statutory authority. "Clearing-house rules" cover rules issued by a group of banks which have associated themselves to perform through a clearing house some of their collection, payment and clearing functions. Other agencies or associations of this kind may be established in the future whose rules and regulations could be appropriately looked on as constituting means of avoiding absolute statutory rigidity. The phrase "and the like" leaves open possibilities for future development. An agreement between a number of banks or even all the banks in an area simply because they are banks, would not of itself, by virtue of the phrase "and the like," meet the purposes and objectives of subsection (b).

4.   Under this Article banks come under the general obligations of the use of good faith and the exercise of ordinary care. "Good faith" is defined in Section 1–201(b)(20). The term "ordinary care" is defined in Section 3–103(a)(9). These definitions are made to apply to Article 4 by Section 4–104(c). Section 4–202 states respects in which collecting banks must use ordinary care. Subsection (c) of Section 4–103 provides that action or non-action approved by the Article or pursuant to Federal Reserve regulations or operating circulars constitutes the exercise of ordinary care. Federal Reserve regulations and operating circulars constitute an affirmative standard of ordinary care equally with the provisions of Article 4 itself.

Subsection (c) further provides that, absent special instructions, action or non-action consistent with clearing-house rules and the like or with a general banking usage not disapproved by the Article, prima facie constitutes the exercise of ordinary care. Clearing-house rules and the phrase "and the like" have the significance set forth above in these Comments. The term "general banking usage" is not defined but should be taken to mean a general usage common to banks in the area concerned. See Section 1–205(2).[*] In a case in which the adjective "general" is used, the intention is to require a usage broader than a mere practice between two or three banks but it is not intended to require a usage broader than a mere practice between two or three banks but it is not intended to require anything as broad as a country-wide usage. A usage followed generally throughout a state, a substantial portion of a state, a metropolitan area or the like would certainly be sufficient. Consistently with the principle of Section 1–205(3),[*] action or non-action consistent with clearing-house rules or the like or with banking usages prima facie constitutes the exercise of ordinary care. However, the phrase "in the absence of special instructions" affords owners of items an opportunity to prescribe other standards and although there may be no direct supervision or control of clearing houses or banking usages by official supervisory authorities, the confirmation of ordinary care by compliance with these standards is prima facie only, thus conferring on the courts the ultimate power to determine ordinary care in any case in which it should appear desirable to do so. The prima facie rule does, however, impose on the party contesting the standards to establish that they are unreasonable, arbitrary or unfair as used by the particular bank.

5.   Subsection (d), in line with the flexible approach required for the bank collection process is designed to make clear that a novel procedure adopted by a bank is not to be considered unreasonable merely because that procedure is not specifically contemplated by this Article or by agreement, or because it has not yet been generally accepted as a bank usage. Changing conditions constantly call for new procedures and someone has to use the new procedure first. If this procedure is found to be reasonable under the circumstances, provided, of course, that it is not inconsistent with any provision of the Article or other law or agreement, the bank which has followed the new procedure should not be found to have failed in the exercise of ordinary care.

6.   Subsection (e) sets forth a rule for determining the measure of damages for failure to exercise ordinary care which, under subsection (a), cannot be limited by agreement. In the absence of bad faith the maximum recovery is the amount of the item concerned. The term "bad faith" is not defined; the connotation is the absence of good faith (Section 3–103). When it is established that some part or all of the item could not have been collected

---

[*]   *Referring to unrevised Article 1 (Appendix A).*

even by the use of ordinary care the recovery is reduced by the amount that would have been in any event uncollectible. This limitation on recovery follows the case law. Finally, if bad faith is established the rule opens to allow the recovery of other damages, whose "proximateness" is to be tested by the ordinary rules applied in comparable cases. Of course, it continues to be as necessary under subsection (e) as it has been under ordinary common law principles that, before the damage rule of the subsection becomes operative, liability of the bank and some loss to the customer or owner must be established.

As amended in 2002.

§ 4–104. Definitions and Index of Definitions.

(a)   In this Article, unless the context otherwise requires:

(1)   "Account" means any deposit or credit account with a bank, including a demand, time, savings, passbook, share draft, or like account, other than an account evidenced by a certificate of deposit;

(2)   "Afternoon" means the period of a day between noon and midnight;

(3)   "Banking day" means the part of a day on which a bank is open to the public for carrying on substantially all of its banking functions;

(4)   "Clearing house" means an association of banks or other payors regularly clearing items;

(5)   "Customer" means a person having an account with a bank or for whom a bank has agreed to collect items, including a bank that maintains an account at another bank;

(6)   "Documentary draft" means a draft to be presented for acceptance or payment if specified documents, certificated securities (Section 8–102) or instructions for uncertificated securities (Section 8–102), or other certificates, statements, or the like are to be received by the drawee or other payor before acceptance or payment of the draft;

(7)   "Draft" means a draft as defined in Section 3–104 or an item, other than an instrument, that is an order;

(8)   "Drawee" means a person ordered in a draft to make payment;

(9)   "Item" means an instrument or a promise or order to pay money handled by a bank for collection or payment. The term does not include a payment order governed by Article 4A or a credit or debit card slip;

(10)   "Midnight deadline" with respect to a bank is midnight on its next banking day following the banking day on which it receives the relevant item or notice or from which the time for taking action commences to run, whichever is later;

(11)   "Settle" means to pay in cash, by clearing-house settlement, in a charge or credit or by remittance, or otherwise as agreed. A settlement may be either provisional or final;

(12)   "Suspends payments" with respect to a bank means that it has been closed by order of the supervisory authorities, that a public officer has been appointed to take it over, or that it ceases or refuses to make payments in the ordinary course of business.

(b)   Other definitions applying to this Article and the sections in which they appear are:

"Agreement for electronic presentment" Section 4–110.
"Collecting bank" Section 4–105.
"Depositary bank" Section 4–105.
"Intermediary bank" Section 4–105.
"Payor bank" Section 4–105.
"Presenting bank" Section 4–105.
"Presentment notice" Section 4–110.

(c)   "Control" as provided in Section 7–106 and the following definitions in other Articles apply to this Article:

"Acceptance" Section 3–409.

377

"Alteration" Section 3–407.
"Cashier's check" Section 3–104.
"Certificate of deposit" Section 3–104.
"Certified check" Section 3–409.
"Check" Section 3–104.
["Good Faith" Section 3–103.]*
"Holder in due course" Section 3–302.
"Instrument" Section 3–104.
"Notice of dishonor" Section 3–503.
"Order" Section 3–103.
"Ordinary care" Section 3–103.
"Person entitled to enforce" Section 3–301.
"Presentment" Section 3–501.
"Promise" Section 3–103.
"Prove" Section 3–103.
"Record" Section 3–103.
"Remotely-Created consumer item" Section 3–103.
"Teller's check" Section 3–104.
"Unauthorized signature" Section 3–403.

(d) In addition, Article 1 contains general definitions and principles of construction and interpretation applicable throughout this Article.

As amended in 1990, 1994, 2001, 2002 and 2003.

Official Comment

1.   Paragraph (a)(1): "Account" is defined to include both asset accounts in which a customer has deposited money and accounts from which a customer may draw on a line of credit. The limiting factor is that the account must be in a bank.

2.   Paragraph (a)(3): "Banking day." Under this definition that part of a business day when a bank is open only for limited functions, e.g., to receive deposits and cash checks, but with loan, bookkeeping and other departments closed, is not part of a banking day.

3.   Paragraph (a)(4): "Clearing house." Occasionally express companies, governmental agencies and other nonbanks deal directly with a clearing house; hence the definition does not limit the term to an association of banks.

4.   Paragraph (a)(5): "Customer." It is to be noted that this term includes a bank carrying an account with another bank as well as the more typical nonbank customer or depositor.

5.   Paragraph (a)(6): "Documentary draft" applies even though the documents do not accompany the draft but are to be received by the drawee or other payor before acceptance or payment of the draft. Documents may be either in electronic or tangible form. See Article 5, Section 5–102, Comment 2 and Article 1, Section 1–201 (definition of "document of title").

6.   Paragraph (a)(7): "Draft" is defined in Section 3–104 as a form of instrument. Since Article 4 applies to items that may not fall within the definition of instrument, the term is defined here to include an item that is a written order to pay money, even though the item may not qualify as an instrument. The term "order" is defined in Section 3–103.

7.   Paragraph (a)(8): "Drawee" is defined in Section 3–103 in terms of an Article 3 draft which is a form of instrument. Here "drawee" is defined in terms of an Article 4 draft which includes items that may not be instruments.

8.   Paragraph (a)(9): "Item" is defined broadly to include an instrument, as defined in Section 3–104, as well as promises or orders that may not be within the definition of "instrument." The terms "promise" and "order" are defined in Section 3–103. A promise is a written undertaking to pay money. An order is a written instruction

---

*   *Note from West Advisory Panel: The definition of good faith in § 3–103 will be deleted if the jurisdiction adopts the definition of good faith in revised Article 1.*

to pay money. But see Section 4–110(c). Since bonds and other investment securities under Article 8 may be within the term "instrument" or "promise," they are items and when handled by banks for collection are subject to this Article. See Comment 1 to Section 4–102. The functional limitation on the meaning of this term is the willingness of the banking system to handle the instrument, undertaking or instruction for collection or payment.

9.   Paragraph (a)(10): "Midnight deadline." The use of this phrase is an example of the more mechanical approach used in this Article. Midnight is selected as a termination point or time limit to obtain greater uniformity and definiteness than would be possible from other possible terminating points, such as the close of the banking day or business day.

10.   Paragraph (a)(11): The term "settle" has substantial importance throughout Article 4. In the American Bankers Association Bank Collection Code, in deferred posting statutes, in Federal Reserve regulations and operating circulars, in clearing-house rules, in agreements between banks and customers and in legends on deposit tickets and collection letters, there is repeated reference to "conditional" or "provisional" credits or payments. Tied in with this concept of creditors or payments being in some way tentative, has been a related but somewhat different problem as to when an item is "paid" or "finally paid" either to determine the relative priority of the item as against attachments, stop-payment orders and the like or in insolvency situations. There has been extensive litigation in the various states on these problems. To a substantial extent the confusion, the litigation and even the resulting court decisions fail to take into account that in the collection process some debits or credits are provisional or tentative and others are final and that very many debits or credits are provisional or tentative for awhile but later become final. Similarly, some cases fail to recognize that within a single bank, particularly a payor bank, each item goes through a series of processes and that in a payor bank most of these processes are preliminary to the basic act of payment or "final payment."

The term "settle" is used as a convenient term to characterize a broad variety of conditional, provisional, tentative and also final payments of items. Such a comprehensive term is needed because it is frequently difficult or unnecessary to determine whether a particular action is tentative or final or when a particular credit shifts from the tentative class to the final class. Therefore, its use throughout the Article indicates that in that particular context it is unnecessary or unwise to determine whether the debit or the credit or the payment is tentative or final. However, if qualified by the adjective "provisional" its tentative nature is intended, and if qualified by the adjective "final" its permanent nature is intended.

Examples of the various types of settlement contemplated by the term include payments in cash; the efficient but somewhat complicated process of payment through the adjustment and offsetting of balances through clearing houses; debit or credit entries in accounts between banks; the forwarding of various types of remittance instruments, sometimes to cover a particular item but more frequently to cover an entire group of items received on a particular day.

11.   Paragraph (a)(12): "Suspends payments." This term is designed to afford an objective test to determine when a bank is no longer operating as a part of the banking system.

As amended in 2003.

§ 4–105.   Definitions of Types of Banks.

In this Article:

(1)   ["Bank" means a person engaged in the business of banking, including a savings bank, savings and loan association, credit union, or trust company;]

(2)   "Depositary bank" means the first bank to take an item even though it is also the payor bank, unless the item is presented for immediate payment over the counter;

(3)   "Payor bank" means a bank that is the drawee of a draft;

(4)   "Intermediary bank" means a bank to which an item is transferred in course of collection except the depositary or payor bank;

(5)   "Collecting bank" means a bank handling an item for collection except the payor bank;

(6)   "Presenting bank" means a bank presenting an item except a payor bank.

Legislative Note: A jurisdiction that enacts this statute that has not yet enacted the revised version of UCC Article 1 should leave the definition of "Bank" in Section 4–105(1). Section 4–105(1) is reserved for that purpose. A jurisdiction that has adopted or simultaneously adopts the revised Article 1 should delete the definition of "Bank" from Section 4–105(1), but should leave those numbers "reserved." If jurisdictions follow the numbering suggested here, the subsections will have the same numbering in all jurisdictions that have adopted these amendments (whether they have or have not adopted the revised version of UCC Article 1). In either case, they should change the title of the section, as indicated in these revisions, so that all jurisdictions will have the same title for the section.

As amended in 1990 and 2002.

Official Comment

1.   The definitions in general exclude a bank to which an item is issued, as this bank does not take by transfer except in the particular case covered in which the item is issued to a payee for collection, as in the case in which a corporation is transferring balances from one account to another. Thus, the definition of "depositary bank" does not include the bank to which a check is made payable if a check is given in payment of a mortgage. This bank has the status of a payee under Article 3 on Negotiable Instruments and not that of a collecting bank.

2.   Paragraph (1): "Bank" is defined in Section 1–201(4)* as meaning "any person engaged in the business of banking." The definition in paragraph (1) makes clear that "bank" includes savings banks, savings and loan associations, credit unions and trust companies, in addition to the commercial banks commonly denoted by use of the term "bank."

3.   Paragraph (2): A bank that takes an "on us" item for collection, for application to a customer's loan, or first handles the item for other reasons is a depositary bank even though it is also the payor bank. However, if the holder presents the item for immediate payment over the counter, the payor bank is not a depositary bank.

4.   Paragraph (3): The definition of "payor bank" is clarified by use of the term "drawee." That term is defined in Section 4–104 as meaning "a person ordered in a draft to make payment." An "order" is defined in Section 3–103 as meaning "a written instruction to pay money. . . . An authorization to pay is not an order unless the person authorized to pay is also instructed to pay." The definition of order is incorporated into Article 4 by Section 4–104(c). Thus a payor bank is one instructed to pay in the item. A bank does not become a payor bank by being merely authorized to pay or by being given an instruction to pay not contained in the item.

5.   Paragraph (4): The term "intermediary bank" includes the last bank in the collection process if the drawee is not a bank. Usually the last bank is also a presenting bank.

§ 4–106.   Payable Through or Payable at Bank: Collecting Bank.

(a)   If an item states that it is "payable through" a bank identified in the item, (i) the item designates the bank as a collecting bank and does not by itself authorize the bank to pay the item, and (ii) the item may be presented for payment only by or through the bank.

ALTERNATIVE A

(b)   If an item states that it is "payable at" a bank identified in the item, the item is equivalent to a draft drawn on the bank.

ALTERNATIVE B

(b)   If an item states that it is "payable at" a bank identified in the item, (i) the item designates the bank as a collecting bank and does not by itself authorize the bank to pay the item, and (ii) the item may be presented for payment only by or through the bank.

(c)   If a draft names a nonbank drawee and it is unclear whether a bank named in the draft is a co-drawee or a collecting bank, the bank is a collecting bank.

As added in 1990.

Official Comment

1.   This section replaces former Sections 3–120 and 3–121. Some items are made "payable through" a particular bank. Subsection (a) states that such language makes the bank a collecting bank and not a payor bank.

---

*   *Referring to unrevised Article 1 (Appendix A).*

An item identifying a "payable through" bank can be presented for payment to the drawee only by the "payable through" bank. The item cannot be presented to the drawee over the counter for immediate payment or by a collecting bank other than the "payable through" bank.

2.   Subsection (b) retains the alternative approach of the present law. Under Alternative A a note payable at a bank is the equivalent of a draft drawn on the bank and the midnight deadline provisions of Sections 4–301 and 4–302 apply. Under Alternative B a "payable at" bank is in the same position as a "payable through" bank under subsection (a).

3.   Subsection (c) rejects the view of some cases that a bank named below the name of a drawee is itself a drawee. The commercial understanding is that this bank is a collecting bank and is not accountable under Section 4–302 for holding an item beyond its deadline. The liability of the bank is governed by Sections 4–202(a) and 4–103(e).

§ 4–107.   Separate Office of Bank.

A branch or separate office of a bank is a separate bank for the purpose of computing the time within which and determining the place at or to which action may be taken or notices or orders shall be given under this Article and under Article 3.

As amended in 1962 and 1990.

Official Comment

1.   A rule with respect to the status of a branch or separate office of a bank as a part of any statute on bank collections is highly desirable if not absolutely necessary. However, practices in the operations of branches and separate offices vary substantially in the different states and it has not been possible to find any single rule that is logically correct, fair in all situations and workable under all different types of practices. The decision not to draft the section with greater specificity leaves to the courts the resolution of the issues arising under this section on the basis of the facts of each case.

2.   In many states and for many purposes a branch or separate office of the bank should be treated as a separate bank. Many branches function as separate banks in the handling and payment of items and require time for doing so similar to that of a separate bank. This is particularly true if branch banking is permitted throughout a state or in different towns and cities. Similarly, if there is this separate functioning a particular branch or separate office is the only proper place for various types of action to be taken or orders or notices to be given. Examples include the drawing of a check on a particular branch by a customer whose account is carried at that branch; the presentment of that same check at that branch; the issuance of an order to the branch to stop payment on the check.

3.   Section 1 of the American Bankers Association Bank Collection Code provided simply: "A branch or office of any such bank shall be deemed a bank." Although this rule appears to be brief and simple, as applied to particular sections of the ABA Code it produces illogical and, in some cases, unreasonable results. For example, under Section 11 of the ABA Code it seems anomalous for one branch of a bank to have charged an item to the account of the drawer and another branch to have the power to elect to treat the item as dishonored. Similar logical problems would flow from applying the same rule to Article 4. Warranties by one branch to another branch under Sections 4–207 and 4–208 (each considered a separate bank) do not make sense.

4.   Assuming that it is not desirable to make each branch a separate bank for all purposes, this section provides that a branch or separate office is a separate bank for certain purposes. In so doing the single legal entity of the bank as a whole is preserved, thereby carrying with it the liability of the institution as a whole on such obligations as it may be under. On the other hand, in cases in which the Article provides a number of time limits for different types of action by banks, if a branch functions as a separate bank, it should have the time limits available to a separate bank. Similarly if in its relations to customers a branch functions as a separate bank, notices and orders with respect to accounts of customers of the branch should be given at the branch. For example, whether a branch has notice sufficient to affect its status as a holder in due course of an item taken by it should depend upon what notice that branch has received with respect to the item. Similarly the receipt of a stop-payment order at one branch should not be notice to another branch so as to impair the right of the second branch to be a holder in due course of the item, although in circumstances in which ordinary care requires the communication of

a notice or order to the proper branch of a bank, the notice or order would be effective at the proper branch from the time it was or should have been received. See Section 1–201(27).*

5. The bracketed language ("maintaining its own deposit ledger") in former Section 4–106 is deleted. Today banks keep records on customer accounts by electronic data storage. This has led most banks with branches to centralize to some degree their record keeping. The place where records are kept has little meaning if the information is electronically stored and is instantly retrievable at all branches of the bank. Hence, the inference to be drawn from the deletion of the bracketed language is that where record keeping is done is no longer an important factor in determining whether a branch is a separate bank.

§ 4–108.   Time of Receipt of Items.

(a) For the purpose of allowing time to process items, prove balances, and make the necessary entries on its books to determine its position for the day, a bank may fix an afternoon hour of 2 P.M. or later as a cutoff hour for the handling of money and items and the making of entries on its books.

(b) An item or deposit of money received on any day after a cutoff hour so fixed or after the close of the banking day may be treated as being received at the opening of the next banking day.

As amended in 1990.

Official Comment

1. Each of the huge volume of checks processed each day must go through a series of accounting procedures that consume time. Many banks have found it necessary to establish a cutoff hour to allow time for these procedures to be completed within the time limits imposed by Article 4. Subsection (a) approves a cutoff hour of this type provided it is not earlier than 2 P.M. Subsection (b) provides that if such a cutoff hour is fixed, items received after the cutoff hour may be treated as being received at the opening of the next banking day. If the number of items received either through the mail or over the counter tends to taper off radically as the afternoon hours progress, a 2 P.M. cutoff hour does not involve a large portion of the items received but at the same time permits a bank using such a cutoff hour to leave its doors open later in the afternoon without forcing into the evening the completion of its settling and proving process.

2. The provision in subsection (b) that items or deposits received after the close of the banking day may be treated as received at the opening of the next banking day is important in cases in which a bank closes at twelve or one o'clock, e.g., on a Saturday, but continues to receive some items by mail or over the counter if, for example, it opens Saturday evening for the limited purpose of receiving deposits and cashing checks.

§ 4–109.   Delays.

(a) Unless otherwise instructed, a collecting bank in a good faith effort to secure payment of a specific item drawn on a payor other than a bank, and with or without the approval of any person involved, may waive, modify, or extend time limits imposed or permitted by this [Act] for a period not exceeding two additional banking days without discharge of drawers or indorsers or liability to its transferor or a prior party.

(b) Delay by a collecting bank or payor bank beyond time limits prescribed or permitted by this [Act] or by instructions is excused if (i) the delay is caused by interruption of communication or computer facilities, suspension of payments by another bank, war, emergency conditions, failure of equipment, or other circumstances beyond the control of the bank, and (ii) the bank exercises such diligence as the circumstances require.

As amended in 1990.

Official Comment

1. Sections 4–202(b), 4–214, 4–301, and 4–302 prescribe various time limits for the handling of items. These are the limits of time within which a bank, in fulfillment of its obligation to exercise ordinary care, must handle items entrusted to it for collection or payment. Under Section 4–103 they may be varied by agreement or by Federal Reserve regulations or operating circular, clearing-house rules, or the like. Subsection (a) permits a

---

*   *Referring to unrevised Article 1 (Appendix A).*

very limited extension of these time limits. It authorizes a collecting bank to take additional time in attempting to collect drafts drawn on nonbank payors with or without the approval of any interested party. The right of a collecting bank to waive time limits under subsection (a) does not apply to checks. The two-day extension can only be granted in a good faith effort to secure payment and only with respect to specific items. It cannot be exercised if the customer instructs otherwise. Thus limited the escape provision should afford a limited degree of flexibility in special cases but should not interfere with the overall requirement and objective of speedy collections.

2. An extension granted under subsection (a) is without discharge of drawers or indorsers. It therefore extends the times for presentment or payment as specified in Article 3.

3. Subsection (b) is another escape clause from time limits. This clause operates not only with respect to time limits imposed by the Article itself but also time limits imposed by special instructions, by agreement or by Federal regulations or operating circulars, clearing-house rules or the like. The latter time limits are "permitted" by the Code. For example, a payor bank that fails to make timely return of a dishonored item may be accountable for the amount of the item. Subsection (b) excuses a bank from this liability when its failure to meet its midnight deadline resulted from, for example, a computer breakdown that was beyond the control of the bank, so long as the bank exercised the degree of diligence that the circumstances required. In *Port City State Bank v. American National Bank*, 486 F.2d 196 (10th Cir.1973), the court held that a bank exercised sufficient diligence to be excused under this subsection. If delay is sought to be excused under this subsection, the bank has the burden of proof on the issue of whether it exercised "such diligence as the circumstances require." The subsection is consistent with Regulation CC, Section 229.38(e).

§ 4–110. Electronic Presentment.

(a) "Agreement for electronic presentment" means an agreement, clearing-house rule, or Federal Reserve regulation or operating circular, providing that presentment of an item may be made by transmission of an image of an item or information describing the item ("presentment notice") rather than delivery of the item itself. The agreement may provide for procedures governing retention, presentment, payment, dishonor, and other matters concerning items subject to the agreement.

(b) Presentment of an item pursuant to an agreement for presentment is made when the presentment notice is received.

(c) If presentment is made by presentment notice, a reference to "item" or "check" in this Article means the presentment notice unless the context otherwise indicates.

As added in 1990.

Official Comment

1. "An agreement for electronic presentment" refers to an agreement under which presentment may be made to a payor bank by a presentment notice rather than by presentment of the item. Under imaging technology now under development, the presentment notice might be an image of the item. The electronic presentment agreement may provide that the item may be retained by a depositary bank, other collecting bank, or even a customer of the depositary bank, or it may provide that the item will follow the presentment notice. The identifying characteristic of an electronic presentment agreement is that presentment occurs when the presentment notice is received. "An agreement for electronic presentment" does not refer to the common case of retention of items by payor banks because the item itself is presented to the payor bank in these cases. Payor bank check retention is a matter of agreement between payor banks and their customers. Provisions on payor bank check retention are found in Section 4–406(b).

2. The assumptions under which the electronic presentment amendments are based are as follows: No bank will participate in an electronic presentment program without an agreement. These agreements may be either bilateral (Section 4–103(a)), under which two banks that frequently do business with each other may agree to depositary bank check retention, or multilateral (Section 4–103(b)), in which large segments of the banking industry may participate in such a program. In the latter case, federal or other uniform regulatory standards would likely supply the substance of the electronic presentment agreement, the application of which could be triggered by the use of some form of identifier on the item. Regulation CC, Section 229.36(c) authorizes truncation agreements but forbids them from extending return times or otherwise varying requirements of the part of Regulation CC governing check collection without the agreement of all parties interested in the check. For instance, an extension of return time could damage a depositary bank which must make funds available to its

customers under mandatory availability schedules. The Expedited Funds Availability Act, 12 U.S.C. Section 4008(b)(2), directs the Federal Reserve Board to consider requiring that banks provide for check truncation.

3.   The parties affected by an agreement for electronic presentment, with the exception of the customer, can be expected to protect themselves. For example, the payor bank can probably be expected to limit its risk of loss from drawer forgery by limiting the dollar amount of eligible items (Federal Reserve program), by reconcilement agreements (ABA Safekeeping program), by insurance (credit union share draft program), or by other means. Because agreements will exist, only minimal amendments are needed to make clear that the UCC does not prohibit electronic presentment.

§ 4–111.   Statute of Limitations.

An action to enforce an obligation, duty, or right arising under this Article must be commenced within three years after the [cause of action] accrues.

As added in 1990.

Official Comment

This section conforms to the period of limitations set by Section 3–118(g) for actions for breach of warranty and to enforce other obligations, duties or rights arising under Article 3. Bracketing "cause of action" recognizes that some states use a different term, such as "claim for relief."

PART 2

COLLECTION OF ITEMS: DEPOSITARY AND COLLECTING BANKS

§ 4–201.   Status of Collecting Bank as Agent and Provisional Status of Credits; Applicability of Article; Item Indorsed "Pay Any Bank".

(a)   Unless a contrary intent clearly appears and before the time that a settlement given by a collecting bank for an item is or becomes final, the bank, with respect to an item, is an agent or sub-agent of the owner of the item and any settlement given for the item is provisional. This provision applies regardless of the form of indorsement or lack of indorsement and even though credit given for the item is subject to immediate withdrawal as of right or is in fact withdrawn; but the continuance of ownership of an item by its owner and any rights of the owner to proceeds of the item are subject to rights of a collecting bank, such as those resulting from outstanding advances on the item and rights of recoupment or setoff. If an item is handled by banks for purposes of presentment, payment, collection, or return, the relevant provisions of this Article apply even though action of the parties clearly establishes that a particular bank has purchased the item and is the owner of it.

(b)   After an item has been indorsed with the words "pay any bank" or the like, only a bank may acquire the rights of a holder until the item has been:

(1)   returned to the customer initiating collection; or

(2)   specially indorsed by a bank to a person who is not a bank.

As amended in 1990.

Official Comment

1.   This section states certain basic rules of the bank collection process. One basic rule, appearing in the last sentence of subsection (a), is that, to the extent applicable, the provisions of the Article govern without regard to whether a bank handling an item owns the item or is an agent for collection. Historically, much time has been spent and effort expended in determining or attempting to determine whether a bank was a purchaser of an item or merely an agent for collection. See discussion of this subject and cases cited in 11 A.L.R. 1043, 16 A.L.R. 1084, 42 A.L.R. 492, 68 A.L.R. 725, 99 A.L.R. 486. See also Section 4 of the American Bankers Association Bank Collection Code. The general approach of Article 4, similar to that of other articles, is to provide, within reasonable limits, rules or answers to major problems known to exist in the bank collection process without regard to questions

of status and ownership but to keep general principles such as status and ownership available to cover residual areas not covered by specific rules. In line with this approach, the last sentence of subsection (a) says in effect that Article 4 applies to practically every item moving through banks for the purpose of presentment, payment or collection.

2.   Within this general rule of broad coverage, the first two sentences of subsection (a) state a rule of agency status. "Unless a contrary intent clearly appears" the status of a collecting bank is that of an agent or sub-agent for the owner of the item. Although as indicated in Comment 1 it is much less important under Article 4 to determine status than has been the case heretofore, status may have importance in some residual areas not covered by specific rules. Further, since status has been considered so important in the past, to omit all reference to it might cause confusion. The status of agency "applies regardless of the form of indorsement or lack of indorsement and even though credit given for the item is subject to immediate withdrawal as of right or is in fact withdrawn." Thus questions heretofore litigated as to whether ordinary indorsements "for deposit," "for collection" or in blank have the effect of creating an agency status or a purchase, no longer have significance in varying the prima facie rule of agency. Similarly, the nature of the credit given for an item or whether it is subject to immediate withdrawal as of right or is in fact withdrawn, does not alter the agency status. See A.L.R. references supra in Comment 1.

A contrary intent can change agency status but this must be clear. An example of a clear contrary intent would be if collateral papers established or the item bore a legend stating that the item was sold absolutely to the depositary bank.

3.   The prima facie agency status of collecting banks is consistent with prevailing law and practice today. Section 2 of the American Bankers Association Bank Collection Code so provided. Legends on deposit tickets, collection letters and acknowledgments of items and Federal Reserve operating circulars consistently so provide. The status is consistent with rights of charge-back (Section 4–214 and Section 11 of the ABA Code) and risk of loss in the event of insolvency (Section 4–216 and Section 13 of the ABA Code). The right of charge-back with respect to checks is limited by Regulation CC, Section 226.36(d).

4.   Affirmative statement of a prima facie agency status for collecting banks requires certain limitations and qualifications. Under current practices substantially all bank collections sooner or later merge into bank credits, at least if collection is effected. Usually, this takes place within a few days of the initiation of collection. An intermediary bank receives final collection and evidences the result of its collection by a "credit" on its books to the depositary bank. The depositary bank evidences the results of its collection by a "credit" in the account of its customer. As used in these instances the term "credit" clearly indicates a debtor-creditor relationship. At some stage in the bank collection process the agency status of a collecting bank changes to that of debtor, a debtor of its customer. Usually at about the same time it also becomes a creditor for the amount of the item, a creditor of some intermediary, payor or other bank. Thus the collection is completed, all agency aspects are terminated and the identity of the item has become completely merged in bank accounts, that of the customer with the depositary bank and that of one bank with another.

Although Section 4–215(a) provides that an item is finally paid when the payor bank takes or fails to take certain action with respect to the item, the final payment of the item may or may not result in the simultaneous final settlement for the item in the case of all prior parties. If a series of provisional debits and credits for the item have been entered in accounts between banks, the final payment of the item by the payor bank may result in the automatic firming up of all these provisional debits and credits under Section 4–215(c), and the consequent receipt of final settlement for the item by each collecting bank and the customer of the depositary bank simultaneously with such action of the payor bank. However, if the payor bank or some intermediary bank accounts for the item with a remittance draft, the next prior bank usually does not receive final settlement for the item until the remittance draft finally clears. See Section 4–213(c). The first sentence of subsection (a) provides that the agency status of a collecting bank (whether intermediary or depositary) continues until the settlement given by it for the item is or becomes final. In the case of the series of provisional credits covered by Section 4–215(c), this could be simultaneously with the final payment of the item by the payor bank. In cases in which remittance drafts are used or in straight noncash collections, this would not be until the times specified in Sections 4–213(c) and 4–215(d). With respect to checks Regulation CC Sections 229.31(c), 229.32(b) and 229.36(d) provide that all settlements between banks are final in both the forward collection and return of checks.

Under Section 4–213(a) settlements for items may be made by any means agreed to by the parties. Since it is impossible to contemplate all the kinds of settlements that will be utilized, no attempt is made in Article 4 to provide when settlement is final in all cases. The guiding principle is that settlements should be final when the presenting person has received usable funds. Section 4–213(c) and (d) and Section 4–215(c) provide when final settlement occurs with respect to certain kinds of settlement, but these provisions are not intended to be exclusive.

A number of practical results flow from the rule continuing the agency status of a collecting bank until its settlement for the item is or becomes final, some of which are specifically set forth in this Article. One is that risk of loss continues in the owner of the item rather than the agent bank. See Section 4–214. Offsetting rights favorable to the owner are that pending such final settlement, the owner has the preference rights of Section 4–216 and the direct rights of Section 4–302 against the payor bank. It also follows from this rule that the dollar limitations of Federal Deposit Insurance are measured by the claim of the owner of the item rather than that of the collecting bank. With respect to checks, rights of the parties in insolvency are determined by Regulation CC Section 229.39 and the liability of a bank handling a check to a subsequent bank that does not receive payment because of suspension of payments by another bank is stated in Regulation CC Section 229.35(b).

5.   In those cases in which some period of time elapses between the final payment of the item by the payor bank and the time that the settlement of the collecting bank is or becomes final, e.g., if the payor bank or an intermediary bank accounts for the item with a remittance draft or in straight noncash collections, the continuance of the agency status of the collecting bank necessarily carries with it the continuance of the owner's status as principal. The second sentence of subsection (a) provides that whatever rights the owner has to proceeds of the item are subject to the rights of collecting banks for outstanding advances on the item and other valid rights, if any. The rule provides a sound rule to govern cases of attempted attachment of proceeds of a non-cash item in the hands of the payor bank as property of the absent owner. If a collecting bank has made an advance on an item which is still outstanding, its right to obtain reimbursement for this advance should be superior to the rights of the owner to the proceeds or to the rights of a creditor of the owner. An intentional crediting of proceeds of an item to the account of a prior bank known to be insolvent, for the purpose of acquiring a right of setoff, would not produce a valid setoff. See 8 Zollman, *Banks and Banking* (1936) Sec. 5443.

6.   This section and Article 4 as a whole represent an intentional abandonment of the approach to bank collection problems appearing in Section 4 of the American Bankers Association Bank Collection Code. Because the tremendous volume of items handled makes impossible the examination by all banks of all indorsements on all items and thus in fact this examination is not made, except perhaps by depositary banks, it is unrealistic to base the rights and duties of all banks in the collection chain on variations in the form of indorsements. It is anomalous to provide throughout the ABA Code that the prima facie status of collecting banks is that of agent or sub-agent but in Section 4 to provide that subsequent holders (sub-agents) shall have the right to rely on the presumption that the bank of deposit (the primary agent) is the owner of the item. It is unrealistic, particularly in this background, to base rights and duties on status of agent or owner. Thus Section 4–201 makes the pertinent provisions of Article 4 applicable to substantially all items handled by banks for presentment, payment or collection, recognizes the prima facie status of most banks as agents, and then seeks to state appropriate limits and some attributes to the general rules so expressed.

7.   Subsection (b) protects the ownership rights with respect to an item indorsed "pay any bank or banker" or in similar terms of a customer initiating collection or of any bank acquiring a security interest under Section 4–210, in the event the item is subsequently acquired under improper circumstances by a person who is not a bank and transferred by that person to another person, whether or not a bank. Upon return to the customer initiating collection of an item so indorsed, the indorsement may be cancelled (Section 3–207). A bank holding an item so indorsed may transfer the item out of banking channels by special indorsement; however, under Section 4–103(e), the bank would be liable to the owner of the item for any loss resulting therefrom if the transfer had been made in bad faith or with lack of ordinary care. If briefer and more simple forms of bank indorsements are developed under Section 4–206 (e.g., the use of bank transit numbers in lieu of present lengthy forms of bank indorsements), a depositary bank having the transit number "X100" could make subsection (b) operative by indorsements such as "Pay any bank—X100." Regulation CC Section 229.35(c) states the effect of an indorsement on a check by a bank.

§ 4–202.   Responsibility for Collection or Return; When Action Timely.

(a)   A collecting bank must exercise ordinary care in:

(1)   presenting an item or sending it for presentment;

(2)   sending notice of dishonor or nonpayment or returning an item other than a documentary draft to the bank's transferor after learning that the item has not been paid or accepted, as the case may be;

(3)   settling for an item when the bank receives final settlement; and

(4)   notifying its transferor of any loss or delay in transit within a reasonable time after discovery thereof.

(b)   A collecting bank exercises ordinary care under subsection (a) by taking proper action before its midnight deadline following receipt of an item, notice, or settlement. Taking proper action within a reasonably longer time may constitute the exercise of ordinary care, but the bank has the burden of establishing timeliness.

(c)   Subject to subsection (a)(1), a bank is not liable for the insolvency, neglect, misconduct, mistake, or default of another bank or person or for loss or destruction of an item in the possession of others or in transit.

As amended in 1990.

Official Comment

1.   Subsection (a) states the basic responsibilities of a collecting bank. Of course, under Section 1–203* a collecting bank is subject to the standard requirement of good faith. By subsection (a) it must also use ordinary care in the exercise of its basic collection tasks. By Section 4–103(a) neither requirement may be disclaimed.

2.   If the bank makes presentment itself, subsection (a)(1) requires ordinary care with respect both to the time and manner of presentment. (Sections 3–501 and 4–212.) If it forwards the item to be presented the subsection requires ordinary care with respect to routing (Section 4–204), and also in the selection of intermediary banks or other agents.

3.   Subsection (a) describes types of basic action with respect to which a collecting bank must use ordinary care. Subsection (b) deals with the time for taking action. It first prescribes the general standard for timely action, namely, for items received on Monday, proper action (such as forwarding or presenting) on Monday or Tuesday is timely. Although under current "production line" operations banks customarily move items along on regular schedules substantially briefer than two days, the subsection states an outside time within which a bank may know it has taken timely action. To provide flexibility from this standard norm, the subsection further states that action within a reasonably longer time may be timely but the bank has the burden of proof. In the case of time items, action after the midnight deadline, but sufficiently in advance of maturity for proper presentation, is a clear example of a "reasonably longer time" that is timely. The standard of requiring action not later than Tuesday in the case of Monday items is also subject to possibilities of variation under the general provisions of Section 4–103, or under the special provisions regarding time of receipt of items (Section 4–108), and regarding delays (Section 4–109). This subsection (b) deals only with collecting banks. The time limits applicable to payor banks appear in Sections 4–301 and 4–302.

4.   At common law the so-called New York collection rule subjected the initial collecting bank to liability for the actions of subsequent banks in the collection chain; the so-called Massachusetts rule was that each bank, subject to the duty of selecting proper intermediaries, was liable only for its own negligence. Subsection (c) adopts the Massachusetts rule. But since this is stated to be subject to subsection (a)(1) a collecting bank remains responsible for using ordinary care in selecting properly qualified intermediary banks and agents and in giving proper instructions to them. Regulation CC Section 229.36(d) states the liability of a bank during the forward collection of checks.

§ 4–203.   Effect of Instructions.

Subject to Article 3 concerning conversion of instruments (Section 3–420) and restrictive indorsements (Section 3–206), only a collecting bank's transferor can give instructions that affect the bank or constitute notice to it, and a collecting bank is not liable to prior parties for any action taken pursuant to the instructions or in accordance with any agreement with its transferor.

As amended in 1990.

---

*   *Referring to unrevised Article 1 (Appendix A).*

Official Comment

This section adopts a "chain of command" theory which renders it unnecessary for an intermediary or collecting bank to determine whether its transferor is "authorized" to give the instructions. Equally the bank is not put on notice of any "revocation of authority" or "lack of authority" by notice received from any other person. The desirability of speed in the collection process and the fact that, by reason of advances made, the transferor may have the paramount interest in the item requires the rule.

The section is made subject to the provisions of Article 3 concerning conversion of instruments (Section 3–420) and restrictive indorsements (Section 3–206). Of course instructions from or an agreement with its transferor does not relieve a collecting bank of its general obligation to exercise good faith and ordinary care. See Section 4–103(a). If in any particular case a bank has exercised good faith and ordinary care and is relieved of responsibility by reason of instructions of or an agreement with its transferor, the owner of the item may still have a remedy for loss against the transferor (another bank) if such transferor has given wrongful instructions.

The rules of the section are applied only to collecting banks. Payor banks always have the problem of making proper payment of an item; whether such payment is proper should be based upon all of the rules of Articles 3 and 4 and all of the facts of any particular case, and should not be dependent exclusively upon instructions from or an agreement with a person presenting the item.

§ 4–204.   Methods of Sending and Presenting; Sending Directly to Payor Bank.

(a) A collecting bank shall send items by a reasonably prompt method, taking into consideration relevant instructions, the nature of the item, the number of those items on hand, the cost of collection involved, and the method generally used by it or others to present those items.

(b) A collecting bank may send:

(1) an item directly to the payor bank;

(2) an item to a nonbank payor if authorized by its transferor; and

(3) an item other than documentary drafts to a nonbank payor, if authorized by Federal Reserve regulation or operating circular, clearing-house rule, or the like.

(c) Presentment may be made by a presenting bank at a place where the payor bank or other payor has requested that presentment be made.

As amended in 1962 and 1990.

Official Comment

1. Subsection (a) prescribes the general standards applicable to proper sending or forwarding of items. Because of the many types of methods available and the desirability of preserving flexibility any attempt to prescribe limited or precise methods is avoided.

2. Subsection (b)(1) codifies the practice of direct mail, express, messenger or like presentment to payor banks. The practice is now country-wide and is justified by the need for speed, the general responsibility of banks, Federal Deposit Insurance protection and other reasons.

3. Full approval of the practice of direct sending is limited to cases in which a bank is a payor. Since nonbank drawees or payors may be of unknown responsibility, substantial risks may be attached to placing in their hands the instruments calling for payments from them. This is obviously so in the case of documentary drafts. However, in some cities practices have long existed under clearing-house procedures to forward certain types of items to certain nonbank payors. Examples include insurance loss drafts drawn by field agents on home offices. For the purpose of leaving the door open to legitimate practices of this kind, subsection (b)(3) affirmatively approves direct sending of any item other than documentary drafts to any nonbank payor, if authorized by Federal Reserve regulation or operating circular, clearing-house rule or the like.

On the other hand subsection (b)(2) approves sending any item directly to a nonbank payor if authorized by a collecting bank's transferor. This permits special instructions or agreements out of the norm and is consistent with the "chain of command" theory of Section 4–203. However, if a transferor other than the owner of the item, e.g., a prior collecting bank, authorizes a direct sending to a nonbank payor, such transferor assumes responsibility for the propriety or impropriety of such authorization.

4. Section 3–501(b) provides where presentment may be made. This provision is expressly subject to Article 4. Section 4–204(c) specifically approves presentment by a presenting bank at any place requested by the payor bank or other payor. The time when a check is received by a payor bank for presentment is governed by Regulation CC Section 229.36(b).

§ 4–205. Depositary Bank Holder of Unindorsed Item.

If a customer delivers an item to a depositary bank for collection:

(1) the depositary bank becomes a holder of the item at the time it receives the item for collection if the customer at the time of delivery was a holder of the item, whether or not the customer indorses the item, and, if the bank satisfies the other requirements of Section 3–302, it is a holder in due course; and

(2) the depositary bank warrants to collecting banks, the payor bank or other payor, and the drawer that the amount of the item was paid to the customer or deposited to the customer's account.

As amended in 1990.

Official Comment

Section 3–201(b) provides that negotiation of an instrument payable to order requires indorsement by the holder. The rule of former Section 4–205(1) was that the depositary bank may supply a missing indorsement of its customer unless the item contains the words "payee's indorsement required" or the like. The cases have differed on the status of the depositary bank as a holder if it fails to supply its customer's indorsement. *Marine Midland Bank, N.A. v. Price, Miller, Evans & Flowers*, 446 N.Y.S.2d 797 (N.Y.App.Div. 4th Dept.1981), *rev'd*, 455 N.Y.S.2d 565 (N.Y.1982). It is common practice for depositary banks to receive unindorsed checks under so-called "lock-box" agreements from customers who receive a high volume of checks. No function would be served by requiring a depositary bank to run these items through a machine that would supply the customer's indorsement except to afford the drawer and the subsequent banks evidence that the proceeds of the item reached the customer's account. Paragraph (1) provides that the depositary bank becomes a holder when it takes the item for deposit if the depositor is a holder. Whether it supplies the customer's indorsement is immaterial. Paragraph (2) satisfies the need for a receipt of funds by the depositary bank by imposing on that bank a warranty that it paid the customer or deposited the item to the customer's account. This warranty runs not only to collecting banks and to the payor bank or nonbank drawee but also to the drawer, affording protection to these parties that the depositary bank received the item and applied it to the benefit of the holder.

§ 4–206. Transfer Between Banks.

Any agreed method that identifies the transferor bank is sufficient for the item's further transfer to another bank.

As amended in 1990.

Official Comment

This section is designed to permit the simplest possible form of transfer from one bank to another, once an item gets in the bank collection chain, provided only identity of the transferor bank is preserved. This is important for tracing purposes and if recourse is necessary. However, since the responsibilities of the various banks appear in the Article it becomes unnecessary to have liability or responsibility depend on more formal indorsements. Simplicity in the form of transfer is conducive to speed. If the transfer is between banks, this section takes the place of the more formal requirements of Section 3–201.

§ 4–207. Transfer Warranties.

(a) A customer or collecting bank that transfers an item and receives a settlement or other consideration warrants to the transferee and to any subsequent collecting bank that:

(1) the warrantor is a person entitled to enforce the item;

(2) all signatures on the item are authentic and authorized;

(3) the item has not been altered;

(4)   the item is not subject to a defense or claim in recoupment (Section 3–305(a)) of any party that can be asserted against the warrantor;

(5)   the warrantor has no knowledge of any insolvency proceeding commenced with respect to the maker or acceptor or, in the case of an unaccepted draft, the drawer; and

(6)   with respect to any remotely-created consumer item, that the person on whose account the item is drawn authorized the issuance of the item in the amount for which the item is drawn.

(b)   If an item is dishonored, a customer or collecting bank transferring the item and receiving settlement or other consideration is obliged to pay the amount due on the item (i) according to the terms of the item at the time it was transferred, or (ii) if the transfer was of an incomplete item, according to its terms when completed as stated in Sections 3–115 and 3–407. The obligation of a transferor is owed to the transferee and to any subsequent collecting bank that takes the item in good faith. A transferor cannot disclaim its obligation under this subsection by an indorsement stating that it is made "without recourse" or otherwise disclaiming liability.

(c)   A person to whom the warranties under subsection (a) are made and who took the item in good faith may recover from the warrantor as damages for breach of warranty an amount equal to the loss suffered as a result of the breach, but not more than the amount of the item plus expenses and loss of interest incurred as a result of the breach.

(d)   The warranties stated in subsection (a) cannot be disclaimed with respect to checks. Unless notice of a claim for breach of warranty is given to the warrantor within 30 days after the claimant has reason to know of the breach and the identity of the warrantor, the warrantor is discharged to the extent of any loss caused by the delay in giving notice of the claim.

(e)   A cause of action for breach of warranty under this section accrues when the claimant has reason to know of the breach.

As added in 1990 and amended in 2002.

Official Comment

1.   Except for subsection (b), this section conforms to Section 3–416 and extends its coverage to items. The substance of this section is discussed in the Comment to Section 3–416. Subsection (b) provides that customers or collecting banks that transfer items, whether by indorsement or not, undertake to pay the item if the item is dishonored. This obligation cannot be disclaimed by a "without recourse" indorsement or otherwise. With respect to checks, Regulation CC Section 229.34 states the warranties made by paying and returning banks.

2.   For an explanation of subsection (a)(6), see comment 8 to Section 3–416.

As amended in 2002.

§ 4–208.   Presentment Warranties.

(a)   If an unaccepted draft is presented to the drawee for payment or acceptance and the drawee pays or accepts the draft, (i) the person obtaining payment or acceptance, at the time of presentment, and (ii) a previous transferor of the draft, at the time of transfer, warrant to the drawee that pays or accepts the draft in good faith that:

(1)   the warrantor is, or was, at the time the warrantor transferred the draft, a person entitled to enforce the draft or authorized to obtain payment or acceptance of the draft on behalf of a person entitled to enforce the draft;

(2)   the draft has not been altered;

(3)   the warrantor has no knowledge that the signature of the purported drawer of the draft is unauthorized; and

(4)   with respect to any remotely-created consumer item, that the person on whose account the item is drawn authorized the issuance of the item in the amount for which the item is drawn.

(b)   A drawee making payment may recover from a warrantor damages for breach of warranty equal to the amount paid by the drawee less the amount the drawee received or is entitled to receive from the drawer because of the payment. In addition, the drawee is entitled to compensation for expenses and loss of interest resulting from the breach. The right of the drawee to recover damages under this subsection is not affected by any failure of the drawee to exercise ordinary care in making payment. If the drawee accepts the draft (i) breach of warranty is a defense to the obligation of the acceptor, and (ii) if the acceptor makes payment with respect to the draft, the acceptor is entitled to recover from a warrantor for breach of warranty the amounts stated in this subsection.

(c)   If a drawee asserts a claim for breach of warranty under subsection (a) based on an unauthorized indorsement of the draft or an alteration of the draft, the warrantor may defend by proving that the indorsement is effective under Section 3–404 or 3–405 or the drawer is precluded under Section 3–406 or 4–406 from asserting against the drawee the unauthorized indorsement or alteration.

(d)   If (i) a dishonored draft is presented for payment to the drawer or an indorser or (ii) any other item is presented for payment to a party obliged to pay the item, and the item is paid, the person obtaining payment and a prior transferor of the item warrant to the person making payment in good faith that the warrantor is, or was, at the time the warrantor transferred the item, a person entitled to enforce the item or authorized to obtain payment on behalf of a person entitled to enforce the item. The person making payment may recover from any warrantor for breach of warranty an amount equal to the amount paid plus expenses and loss of interest resulting from the breach.

(e)   The warranties stated in subsections (a) and (d) cannot be disclaimed with respect to checks. Unless notice of a claim for breach of warranty is given to the warrantor within 30 days after the claimant has reason to know of the breach and the identity of the warrantor, the warrantor is discharged to the extent of any loss caused by the delay in giving notice of the claim.

(f)   A cause of action for breach of warranty under this section accrues when the claimant has reason to know of the breach.

As added in 1990 and amended in 2002.

Official Comment

1.   This section conforms to Section 3–417 and extends its coverage to items. The substance of this section is discussed in the Comment to Section 3–417. "Draft" is defined in Section 4–104 as including an item that is an order to pay so as to make clear that the term "draft" in Article 4 may include items that are not instruments within Section 3–104.

2.   For an explanation of subsection (a)(4), see comment 8 to Section 3–416.

As amended in 2002.

§ 4–209.   Encoding and Retention Warranties.

(a)   A person who encodes information on or with respect to an item after issue warrants to any subsequent collecting bank and to the payor bank or other payor that the information is correctly encoded. If the customer of a depositary bank encodes, that bank also makes the warranty.

(b)   A person who undertakes to retain an item pursuant to an agreement for electronic presentment warrants to any subsequent collecting bank and to the payor bank or other payor that retention and presentment of the item comply with the agreement. If a customer of a depositary bank undertakes to retain an item, that bank also makes this warranty.

(c)   A person to whom warranties are made under this section and who took the item in good faith may recover from the warrantor as damages for breach of warranty an amount equal to the loss suffered as a result of the breach, plus expenses and loss of interest incurred as a result of the breach.

As added in 1990.

Official Comment

1.   Encoding and retention warranties are included in Article 4 because they are unique to the bank collection process. These warranties are breached only by the person doing the encoding or retaining the item and not by subsequent banks handling the item. Encoding and check retention may be done by customers who are payees of a large volume of checks; hence, this section imposes warranties on customers as well as banks. If a customer encodes or retains, the depositary bank is also liable for any breach of this warranty.

2.   A misencoding of the amount on the MICR line is not an alteration under Section 3–407(a) which defines alteration as changing the contract of the parties. If a drawer wrote a check for $2,500 and the depositary bank encoded $25,000 on the MICR line, the payor bank could debit the drawer's account for only $2,500. This subsection would allow the payor bank to hold the depositary bank liable for the amount paid out over $2,500 without first pursuing the person who received payment. Intervening collecting banks would not be liable to the payor bank for the depositary bank's error. If a drawer wrote a check for $25,000 and the depositary bank encoded $2,500, the payor bank becomes liable for the full amount of the check. The payor bank's rights against the depositary bank depend on whether the payor bank has suffered a loss. Since the payor bank can debit the drawer's account for $25,000, the payor bank has a loss only to the extent that the drawer's account is less than the full amount of the check. There is no requirement that the payor bank pursue collection against the drawer beyond the amount in the drawer's account as a condition to the payor bank's action against the depositary bank for breach of warranty. See *Georgia Railroad Bank & Trust Co. v. First National Bank & Trust*, 229 S.E.2d 482 (Ga.App.1976), aff'd, 235 S.E.2d 1 (Ga.1977), and *First National Bank of Boston v. Fidelity Bank, National Association*, 724 F.Supp. 1168 (E.D.Pa.1989).

3.   A person retaining items under an electronic presentment agreement (Section 4–110) warrants that it has complied with the terms of the agreement regarding its possession of the item and its sending a proper presentment notice. If the keeper is a customer, its depositary bank also makes this warranty.

§ 4–210.   Security Interest of Collecting Bank in Items, Accompanying Documents and Proceeds.

(a)   A collecting bank has a security interest in an item and any accompanying documents or the proceeds of either:

(1)   in case of an item deposited in an account, to the extent to which credit given for the item has been withdrawn or applied;

(2)   in case of an item for which it has given credit available for withdrawal as of right, to the extent of the credit given, whether or not the credit is drawn upon or there is a right of charge-back; or

(3)   if it makes an advance on or against the item.

(b)   If credit given for several items received at one time or pursuant to a single agreement is withdrawn or applied in part, the security interest remains upon all the items, any accompanying documents or the proceeds of either. For the purpose of this section, credits first given are first withdrawn.

(c)   Receipt by a collecting bank of a final settlement for an item is a realization on its security interest in the item, accompanying documents, and proceeds. So long as the bank does not receive final settlement for the item or give up possession of the item or possession or control of the accompanying documents for purposes other than collection, the security interest continues to that extent and is subject to Article 9, but:

(1)   no security agreement is necessary to make the security interest enforceable (Section 9–203(b)(3)(A));

(2)   no filing is required to perfect the security interest; and

(3)   the security interest has priority over conflicting perfected security interests in the item, accompanying documents, or proceeds.

As amended in 1999 and 2003.

Official Comment

1.   Subsection (a) states a rational rule for the interest of a bank in an item. The customer of the depositary bank is normally the owner of the item and the several collecting banks are agents of the customer (Section 4–

201). A collecting agent may properly make advances on the security of paper held for collection, and acquires at common law a possessory lien for these advances. Subsection (a) applies an analogous principle to a bank in the collection chain which extends credit on items in the course of collection. The bank has a security interest to the extent stated in this section. To the extent of its security interest it is a holder for value (Sections 3–303, 4–211) and a holder in due course if it satisfies the other requirements for that status (Section 3–302). Subsection (a) does not derogate from the banker's general common law lien or right of setoff against indebtedness owing in deposit accounts. See Section 1–103. Rather subsection (a) specifically implements and extends the principle as a part of the bank collection process.

2.   Subsection (b) spreads the security interest of the bank over all items in a single deposit or received under a single agreement and a single giving of credit. It also adopts the "first-in, first-out" rule.

3.   Collection statistics establish that the vast majority of items handled for collection are in fact collected. The first sentence of subsection (c) reflects the fact that in the normal case the bank's security interest is self-liquidating. The remainder of the subsection correlates the security interest with the provisions of Article 9, particularly for use in the cases of noncollection in which the security interest may be important.

§ 4–211.   When Bank Gives Value for Purposes of Holder in Due Course.

For purposes of determining its status as a holder in due course, a bank has given value to the extent it has a security interest in an item, if the bank otherwise complies with the requirements of Section 3–302 on what constitutes a holder in due course.

As amended in 1990.

Official Comment

The section completes the thought of the previous section and makes clear that a security interest in an item is "value" for the purpose of determining the holder's status as a holder in due course. The provision is in accord with the prior law (N.I.L. Section 27) and with Article 3 (Section 3–303). The section does not prescribe a security interest under Section 4–210 as a test of "value" generally because the meaning of "value" under other Articles is adequately defined in Section 1–201.*

§ 4–212.   Presentment by Notice of Item Not Payable by, Through, or at Bank; Liability of Drawer or Indorser.

(a)   Unless otherwise instructed, a collecting bank may present an item not payable by, through, or at a bank by sending to the party to accept or pay a record providing notice that the bank holds the item for acceptance or payment. The notice must be sent in time to be received on or before the day when presentment is due and the bank must meet any requirement of the party to accept or pay under Section 3–501 by the close of the bank's next banking day after it knows of the requirement.

(b)   If presentment is made by notice and payment, acceptance, or request for compliance with a requirement under Section 3–501 is not received by the close of business on the day after maturity or, in the case of demand items, by the close of business on the third banking day after notice was sent, the presenting bank may treat the item as dishonored and charge any drawer or indorser by sending it notice of the facts.

As amended in 1990 and 2002.

Official Comment

1.   This section codifies a practice extensively followed in presentation of trade acceptances and documentary and other drafts drawn on nonbank payors. It imposes a duty on the payor to respond to the notice of the item if the item is not to be considered dishonored. Notice of such a dishonor charges drawers and indorsers. Presentment under this section is good presentment under Article 3. See Section 3–501.

2.   A drawee not receiving notice is not, of course, liable to the drawer for wrongful dishonor.

3.   A bank so presenting an instrument must be sufficiently close to the drawee to be able to exhibit the instrument on the day it is requested to do so or the next business day at the latest.

---

   *   *Referring to unrevised Article 1 (Appendix A).*

§ 4–213.   Medium and Time of Settlement by Bank.

(a)   With respect to settlement by a bank, the medium and time of settlement may be prescribed by Federal Reserve regulations or circulars, clearing-house rules, and the like, or agreement. In the absence of such prescription:

(1)   the medium of settlement is cash or credit to an account in a Federal Reserve bank of or specified by the person to receive settlement; and

(2)   the time of settlement, is:

   (i)   with respect to tender of settlement by cash, a cashier's check, or teller's check, when the cash or check is sent or delivered;

   (ii)   with respect to tender of settlement by credit in an account in a Federal Reserve Bank, when the credit is made;

   (iii)   with respect to tender of settlement by a credit or debit to an account in a bank, when the credit or debit is made or, in the case of tender of settlement by authority to charge an account, when the authority is sent or delivered; or

   (iv)   with respect to tender of settlement by a funds transfer, when payment is made pursuant to Section 4A–406(a) to the person receiving settlement.

(b)   If the tender of settlement is not by a medium authorized by subsection (a) or the time of settlement is not fixed by subsection (a), no settlement occurs until the tender of settlement is accepted by the person receiving settlement.

(c)   If settlement for an item is made by cashier's check or teller's check and the person receiving settlement, before its midnight deadline:

(1)   presents or forwards the check for collection, settlement is final when the check is finally paid; or

(2)   fails to present or forward the check for collection, settlement is final at the midnight deadline of the person receiving settlement.

(d)   If settlement for an item is made by giving authority to charge the account of the bank giving settlement in the bank receiving settlement, settlement is final when the charge is made by the bank receiving settlement if there are funds available in the account for the amount of the item.

As amended in 1990.

Official Comment

1.   Subsection (a) sets forth the medium of settlement that the person receiving settlement must accept. In nearly all cases the medium of settlement will be determined by agreement or by Federal Reserve regulations and circulars, clearing-house rules, and the like. In the absence of regulations, rules or agreement, the person receiving settlement may demand cash or credit in a Federal Reserve bank. If the person receiving settlement does not have an account in a Federal Reserve bank, it may specify the account of another bank in a Federal Reserve bank. In the unusual case in which there is no agreement on the medium of settlement and the bank making settlement tenders settlement other than cash or Federal Reserve bank credit, no settlement has occurred under subsection (b) unless the person receiving settlement accepts the settlement tendered. For example, if a payor bank, without agreement, tenders a teller's check, the bank receiving the settlement may reject the check and return it to the payor bank or it may accept the check as settlement.

2.   In several provisions of Article 4 the time that a settlement occurs is relevant. Subsection (a) sets out a general rule that the time of settlement, like the means of settlement, may be prescribed by agreement. In the absence of agreement, the time of settlement for tender of the common agreed media of settlement is that set out in subsection (a)(2). The time of settlement by cash, cashier's or teller's check or authority to charge an account is the time the cash, check or authority is sent, unless presentment is over the counter in which case settlement occurs upon delivery to the presenter. If there is no agreement on the time of settlement and the tender of settlement is not made by one of the media set out in subsection (a), under subsection (b) the time of settlement is the time the settlement is accepted by the person receiving settlement.

3.   Subsections (c) and (d) are special provisions for settlement by remittance drafts and authority to charge an account in the bank receiving settlement. The relationship between final settlement and final payment under Section 4–215 is addressed in subsection (b) of Section 4–215. With respect to settlement by cashier's checks or teller's checks, other than in response to over-the-counter presentment, the bank receiving settlement can keep the risk that the check will not be paid on the bank tendering the check in settlement by acting to initiate collection of the check within the midnight deadline of the bank receiving settlement. If the bank fails to initiate settlement before its midnight deadline, final settlement occurs at the midnight deadline, and the bank receiving settlement assumes the risk that the check will not be paid. If there is no agreement that permits the bank tendering settlement to tender a cashier's or teller's check, subsection (b) allows the bank receiving the check to reject it, and, if it does, no settlement occurs. However, if the bank accepts the check, settlement occurs and the time of final settlement is governed by subsection (c).

With respect to settlement by tender of authority to charge the account of the bank making settlement in the bank receiving settlement, subsection (d) provides that final settlement does not take place until the account charged has available funds to cover the amount of the item. If there is no agreement that permits the bank tendering settlement to tender an authority to charge an account as settlement, subsection (b) allows the bank receiving the tender to reject it. However, if the bank accepts the authority, settlement occurs and the time of final settlement is governed by subsection (d).

§ 4–214.   Right of Charge-Back or Refund; Liability of Collecting Bank: Return of Item.

(a)   If a collecting bank has made provisional settlement with its customer for an item and fails by reason of dishonor, suspension of payments by a bank, or otherwise to receive settlement for the item which is or becomes final, the bank may revoke the settlement given by it, charge back the amount of any credit given for the item to its customer's account, or obtain refund from its customer, whether or not it is able to return the item, if by its midnight deadline or within a longer reasonable time after it learns the facts it returns the item or sends notification of the facts. If the return or notice is delayed beyond the bank's midnight deadline or a longer reasonable time after it learns the facts, the bank may revoke the settlement, charge back the credit, or obtain refund from its customer, but it is liable for any loss resulting from the delay. These rights to revoke, charge back, and obtain refund terminate if and when a settlement for the item received by the bank is or becomes final.

(b)   A collecting bank returns an item when it is sent or delivered to the bank's customer or transferor or pursuant to its instructions.

(c)   A depositary bank that is also the payor may charge back the amount of an item to its customer's account or obtain refund in accordance with the section governing return of an item received by a payor bank for credit on its books (Section 4–301).

(d)   The right to charge back is not affected by:

(1)   previous use of a credit given for the item; or

(2)   failure by any bank to exercise ordinary care with respect to the item, but a bank so failing remains liable.

(e)   A failure to charge back or claim refund does not affect other rights of the bank against the customer or any other party.

(f)   If credit is given in dollars as the equivalent of the value of an item payable in foreign money, the dollar amount of any charge-back or refund must be calculated on the basis of the bank-offered spot rate for the foreign money prevailing on the day when the person entitled to the charge-back or refund learns that it will not receive payment in ordinary course.

As amended in 1990.

Official Comment

1.   Under current bank practice, in a major portion of cases banks make provisional settlement for items when they are first received and then await subsequent determination of whether the item will be finally paid. This is the principal characteristic of what are referred to in banking parlance as "cash items." Statistically, this practice of settling provisionally first and then awaiting final payment is justified because the vast majority of

such cash items are finally paid, with the result that in this great preponderance of cases it becomes unnecessary for the banks making the provisional settlements to make any further entries. In due course the provisional settlements become final simply with the lapse of time. However, in those cases in which the item being collected is not finally paid or if for various reasons the bank making the provisional settlement does not itself receive final payment, provision is made in subsection (a) for the reversal of the provisional settlements, charge-back of provisional credits and the right to obtain refund.

2.   Various causes of a bank's not receiving final payment, with the resulting right of charge-back or refund, are stated or suggested in subsection (a). These include dishonor of the original item; dishonor of a remittance instrument given for it; reversal of a provisional credit for the item; suspension of payments by another bank. The causes stated are illustrative; the right of charge-back or refund is stated to exist whether the failure to receive final payment in ordinary course arises through one of them "or otherwise."

3.   The right of charge-back or refund exists if a collecting bank has made a provisional settlement for an item with its customer but terminates if and when a settlement received by the bank for the item is or becomes final. If the bank fails to receive such a final settlement the right of charge-back or refund must be exercised promptly after the bank learns the facts. The right exists (if so promptly exercised) whether or not the bank is able to return the item. The second sentence of subsection (a) adopts the view of *Appliance Buyers Credit Corp. v. Prospect National Bank*, 708 F.2d 290 (7th Cir.1983), that if the midnight deadline for returning an item or giving notice is not met, a collecting bank loses its rights only to the extent of damages for any loss resulting from the delay.

4.   Subsection (b) states when an item is returned by a collecting bank. Regulation CC, Section 229.31 preempts this subsection with respect to checks by allowing direct return to the depositary bank. Because a returned check may follow a different path than in forward collection, settlement given for the check is final and not provisional except as between the depositary bank and its customer. Regulation CC Section 229.36(d). See also Regulations CC Sections 229.31(c) and 229.32(b). Thus owing to the federal preemption, this subsection applies only to noncheck items.

5.   The rule of subsection (d) relating to charge-back (as distinguished from claim for refund) applies irrespective of the cause of the nonpayment, and of the person ultimately liable for nonpayment. Thus charge-back is permitted even if nonpayment results from the depositary bank's own negligence. Any other rule would result in litigation based upon a claim for wrongful dishonor of other checks of the customer, with potential damages far in excess of the amount of the item. Any other rule would require a bank to determine difficult questions of fact. The customer's protection is found in the general obligation of good faith (Sections 1–203* and 4–103). If bad faith is established the customer's recovery "includes other damages, if any, suffered by the party as a proximate consequence" (Section 4–103(e); see also Section 4–402).

6.   It is clear that the charge-back does not relieve the bank from any liability for failure to exercise ordinary care in handling the item. The measure of damages for such failure is stated in Section 4–103(e).

7.   Subsection (f) states a rule fixing the time for determining the rate of exchange if there is a charge-back or refund of a credit given in dollars for an item payable in a foreign currency. Compare Section 3–107. Fixing such a rule is desirable to avoid disputes. If in any case the parties wish to fix a different time for determining the rate of exchange, they may do so by agreement.

§ 4–215.   Final Payment of Item by Payor Bank; When Provisional Debits and Credits Become Final; When Certain Credits Become Available for Withdrawal.

(a)   An item is finally paid by a payor bank when the bank has first done any of the following:

(1)   paid the item in cash;

(2)   settled for the item without having a right to revoke the settlement under statute, clearing-house rule, or agreement; or

(3)   made a provisional settlement for the item and failed to revoke the settlement in the time and manner permitted by statute, clearing-house rule, or agreement.

(b)   If provisional settlement for an item does not become final, the item is not finally paid.

---

*   *Referring to unrevised Article 1 (Appendix A).*

(c)   If provisional settlement for an item between the presenting and payor banks is made through a clearing house or by debits or credits in an account between them, then to the extent that provisional debits or credits for the item are entered in accounts between the presenting and payor banks or between the presenting and successive prior collecting banks seriatim, they become final upon final payment of the item by the payor bank.

(d)   If a collecting bank receives a settlement for an item which is or becomes final, the bank is accountable to its customer for the amount of the item and any provisional credit given for the item in an account with its customer becomes final.

(e)   Subject to (i) applicable law stating a time for availability of funds and (ii) any right of the bank to apply the credit to an obligation of the customer, credit given by a bank for an item in a customer's account becomes available for withdrawal as of right:

(1)   if the bank has received a provisional settlement for the item, when the settlement becomes final and the bank has had a reasonable time to receive return of the item and the item has not been received within that time;

(2)   if the bank is both the depositary bank and the payor bank, and the item is finally paid, at the opening of the bank's second banking day following receipt of the item.

(f)   Subject to applicable law stating a time for availability of funds and any right of a bank to apply a deposit to an obligation of the depositor, a deposit of money becomes available for withdrawal as of right at the opening of the bank's next banking day after receipt of the deposit.

As amended in 1990.

Official Comment

1.   By the definition and use of the term "settle" (Section 4–104(a)(11)) this Article recognizes that various debits or credits, remittances, settlements or payments given for an item may be either provisional or final, that settlements sometimes are provisional and sometimes are final and sometimes are provisional for awhile but later become final. Subsection (a) defines when settlement for an item constitutes final payment.

Final payment of an item is important for a number of reasons. It is one of several factors determining the relative priorities between items and notices, stop-payment orders, legal process and setoffs (Section 4–303). It is the "end of the line" in the collection process and the "turn around" point commencing the return flow of proceeds. It is the point at which many provisional settlements become final. See Section 4–215(c). Final payment of an item by the payor bank fixes preferential rights under Section 4–216.

2.   If an item being collected moves through several states, e.g., is deposited for collection in California, moves through two or three California banks to the Federal Reserve Bank of San Francisco, to the Federal Reserve Bank of Boston, to a payor bank in Maine, the collection process involves the eastward journey of the item from California to Maine and the westward journey of the proceeds from Maine to California. Subsection (a) recognizes that final payment does not take place, in this hypothetical case, on the journey of the item eastward. It also adopts the view that neither does final payment occur on the journey westward because what in fact is journeying westward are *proceeds* of the item.

3.   Traditionally and under various decisions payment in cash of an item by a payor bank has been considered final payment. Subsection (a)(1) recognizes and provides that payment of an item in cash by a payor bank is final payment.

4.   Section 4–104(a)(11) defines "settle" as meaning "to pay in cash, by clearing-house settlement, in a charge or credit or by remittance, or otherwise as agreed. A settlement may be either provisional or final." Subsection (a)(2) of Section 4–215 provides that an item is finally paid by a payor bank when the bank has "settled for the item without having a right to revoke the settlement under statute, clearing-house rule or agreement." Former subsection (1)(b) is modified by subsection (a)(2) to make clear that a payor bank cannot make settlement provisional by unilaterally reserving a right to revoke the settlement. The right must come from a statute (e.g., Section 4–301), clearing-house rule or other agreement. Subsection (a)(2) provides in effect that if the payor bank finally settles for an item this constitutes final payment of the item. The subsection operates if nothing has occurred and no situation exists making the settlement provisional. If under statute, clearing-house rule or agreement, a right of revocation of the settlement exists, the settlement is provisional. Conversely, if there is an

absence of a right to revoke under statute, clearing-house rule or agreement, the settlement is final and such final settlement constitutes final payment of the item.

A primary example of a statutory right on the part of the payor bank to revoke a settlement is the right to revoke conferred by Section 4–301. The underlying theory and reason for deferred posting statutes (Section 4–301) is to require a settlement on the date of receipt of an item but to keep that settlement provisional with the right to revoke prior to the midnight deadline. In any case in which Section 4–301 is applicable, any settlement by the payor bank is provisional solely by virtue of the statute, subsection (a)(2) of Section 4–215 does not operate, and such provisional settlement does not constitute final payment of the item. With respect to checks, Regulation CC Section 229.36(d) provides that settlement between banks for the forward collection of checks is final. The relationship of this provision to Article 4 is discussed in the Commentary to that section.

A second important example of a right to revoke a settlement is that arising under clearing-house rules. It is very common for clearing-house rules to provide that items exchanged and settled for in a clearing (e.g., before 10:00 a.m. on Monday) may be returned and the settlements revoked up to but not later than 2:00 p.m. on the same day (Monday) or under deferred posting at some hour on the next business day (e.g., 2:00 p.m. Tuesday). Under this type of rule the Monday morning settlement is provisional and being provisional does not constitute a final payment of the item.

An example of an agreement allowing the payor bank to revoke a settlement is a case in which the payor bank is also the depositary bank and has signed a receipt or duplicate deposit ticket or has made an entry in a passbook acknowledging receipt, for credit to the account of A, of a check drawn on it by B. If the receipt, deposit ticket, passbook or other agreement with A is to the effect that any credit so entered is provisional and may be revoked pending the time required by the payor bank to process the item to determine if it is in good form and there are funds to cover it, the agreement keeps the receipt or credit provisional and avoids its being either final settlement or final payment.

The most important application of subsection (a)(2) is that in which presentment of an item has been made over the counter for immediate payment. In this case Section 4–301(a) does not apply to make the settlement provisional, and final payment has occurred unless a rule or agreement provides otherwise.

5.   Former Section 4–213(1)(c) provided that final payment occurred when the payor bank completed the "process of posting." The term was defined in former Section 4–109. In the present Article, Section 4–109 has been deleted and the process-of-posting test has been abandoned in Section 4–215(a) for determining when final payment is made. Difficulties in determining when the events described in former Section 4–109 take place make the process-of-posting test unsuitable for a system of automated check collection or electronic presentment.

6.   The last sentence of former Section 4–213(1) is deleted as an unnecessary source of confusion. Initially the view that payor bank may be accountable for, that is, liable for the amount of, an item that it has already paid seems incongruous. This is particularly true in the light of the language formerly found in Section 4–302 stating that the payor bank can defend against liability for accountability by showing that it has already settled for the item. But, at least with respect to former Section 4–213(1)(c), such a provision was needed because under the process-of-posting test a payor bank may have paid an item without settling for it. Now that Article 4 has abandoned the process-of-posting test, the sentence is no longer needed. If the payor bank has neither paid the item nor returned it within its midnight deadline, the payor bank is accountable under Section 4–302.

7.   Subsection (a)(3) covers the situation in which the payor bank makes a provisional settlement for an item, and this settlement becomes final at a later time by reason of the failure of the payor bank to revoke it in the time and manner permitted by statute, clearing-house rule or agreement. An example of this type of situation is the clearing-house settlement referred to in Comment 4. In the illustration there given if the time limit for the return of items received in the Monday morning clearing is 2:00 p.m. on Tuesday and the provisional settlement has not been revoked at that time in a manner permitted by the clearing-house rules, the provisional settlement made on Monday morning becomes final at 2:00 p.m. on Tuesday. Subsection (a)(3) provides specifically that in this situation the item is finally paid at 2:00 p.m. Tuesday. If on the other hand a payor bank receives an item in the mail on Monday and makes some provisional settlement for the item on Monday, it has until midnight on Tuesday to return the item or give notice and revoke any settlement under Section 4–301. In this situation subsection (a)(3) of Section 4–215 provides that if the provisional settlement made on Monday is not revoked before midnight on Tuesday as permitted by Section 4–301, the item is finally paid at midnight on Tuesday. With respect to checks, Regulation CC Section 229.30(c) allows an extension of the midnight deadline under certain circumstances. If a bank does not expeditiously return a check liability may accrue under Regulation CC Section

229.38. For the relationship of that liability to responsibility under this Article, see Regulation CC Sections 229.30 and 229.38.

8.   Subsection (b) relates final settlement to final payment under Section 4–215. For example, if a payor bank makes provisional settlement for an item by sending a cashier's or teller's check and that settlement fails to become final under Section 4–213(c), subsection (b) provides that final payment has not occurred. If the item is not paid, the drawer remains liable, and under Section 4–302(a) the payor bank is accountable unless it has returned the item before its midnight deadline. In this regard, subsection (b) is an exception to subsection (a)(3). Even if the payor bank has not returned an item by its midnight deadline there is still no final payment if provisional settlement had been made and settlement failed to become final. However, if presentment of the item was over the counter for immediate payment, final payment has occurred under Section 4–215(a)(2). Subsection (b) does not apply because the settlement was not provisional. Section 4–301(a). In this case the presenting person, often the payee of the item, has the right to demand cash or the cash equivalent of federal reserve credit. If the presenting person accepts another medium of settlement such as a cashier's or teller's check, the presenting person takes the risk that the payor bank may fail to pay a cashier's check because of insolvency or that the drawee of a teller's check may dishonor it.

9.   Subsection (c) states the country-wide usage that when the item is finally paid by the payor bank under subsection (a) this final payment automatically without further action "firms up" other provisional settlements made for it. However, the subsection makes clear that this "firming up" occurs only if the settlement between the presenting and payor banks was made either through a clearing house or by debits and credits in accounts between them. It does not take place if the payor bank remits for the item by sending some form of remittance instrument. Further, the "firming up" continues only to the extent that provisional debits and credits are entered seriatim in accounts between banks which are successive to the presenting bank. The automatic "firming up" is broken at any time that any collecting bank remits for the item by sending a remittance draft, because final payment to the remittee then usually depends upon final payment of the remittance draft.

10.   Subsection (d) states the general rule that if a collecting bank receives settlement for an item which is or becomes final, the bank is accountable to its customer for the amount of the item. One means of accounting is to remit to its customer the amount it has received on the item. If previously it gave to its customer a provisional credit for the item in an account its receipt of final settlement for the item "firms up" this provisional credit and makes it final. When this credit given by it so becomes final, in the usual case its agency status terminates and it becomes a debtor to its customer for the amount of the item. See Section 4–201(a). If the accounting is by a remittance instrument or authorization to charge further time will usually be required to complete its accounting (Section 4–213).

11.   Subsection (e) states when certain credits given by a bank to its customer become available for withdrawal as of right. Subsection (e)(1) deals with the situation in which a bank has given a credit (usually provisional) for an item to its customer and in turn has received a provisional settlement for the item from an intermediary or payor bank to which it has forwarded the item. In this situation before the provisional credit entered by the collecting bank in the account of its customer becomes available for withdrawal as of right, it is not only necessary that the provisional settlement received by the bank for the item becomes final but also that the collecting bank has a reasonable time to receive return of the item and the item has not been received within that time. How much time is "reasonable" for these purposes will of course depend on the distance the item has to travel and the number of banks through which it must pass (having in mind not only travel time by regular lines of transmission but also the successive midnight deadlines of the several banks) and other pertinent facts. Also, if the provisional settlement received is some form of a remittance instrument or authorization to charge, the "reasonable" time depends on the identity and location of the payor of the remittance instrument, the means for clearing such instrument, and other pertinent facts. With respect to checks Regulation CC Sections 229.10–229.13 or similar applicable state law (Section 229.20) control. This is also time for the situation described in Comment 12.

12.   Subsection (e)(2) deals with the situation of a bank that is both a depositary bank and a payor bank. The subsection recognizes that if A and B are both customers of a depositary-payor bank and A deposits B's check on the depositary-payor in A's account on Monday, time must be allowed to permit the check under the deferred posting rules of Section 4–301 to reach the bookkeeper for B's account at some time on Tuesday, and, if there are insufficient funds in B's account, to reverse or charge back the provisional credit in A's account. Consequently this provisional credit in A's account does not become available for withdrawal as of right until the opening of business on Wednesday. If it is determined on Tuesday that there are insufficient funds in B's account to pay the check, the credit to A's account can be reversed on Tuesday. On the other hand if the item is in fact paid on Tuesday, the rule

of subsection (e)(2) is desirable to avoid uncertainty and possible disputes between the bank and its customer as to exactly what hour within the day the credit is available.

§ 4–216.   Insolvency and Preference.

(a)   If an item is in or comes into the possession of a payor or collecting bank that suspends payment and the item has not been finally paid, the item must be returned by the receiver, trustee, or agent in charge of the closed bank to the presenting bank or the closed bank's customer.

(b)   If a payor bank finally pays an item and suspends payments without making a settlement for the item with its customer or the presenting bank which settlement is or becomes final, the owner of the item has a preferred claim against the payor bank.

(c)   If a payor bank gives or a collecting bank gives or receives a provisional settlement for an item and thereafter suspends payments, the suspension does not prevent or interfere with the settlement's becoming final if the finality occurs automatically upon the lapse of certain time or the happening of certain events.

(d)   If a collecting bank receives from subsequent parties settlement for an item, which settlement is or becomes final and the bank suspends payments without making a settlement for the item with its customer which settlement is or becomes final, the owner of the item has a preferred claim against the collecting bank.

As amended in 1990.

Official Comment

1.   The underlying purpose of the provisions of this section is not to confer upon banks, holders of items or anyone else preferential positions in the event of bank failures over general depositors or any other creditors of the failed banks. The purpose is to fix as definitely as possible the cut-off point of time for the completion or cessation of the collection process in the case of items that happen to be in the process at the time a particular bank suspends payments. It must be remembered that in bank collections as a whole and in the handling of items by an individual bank, items go through a whole series of processes. It must also be remembered that at any particular point of time a particular bank (at least one of any size) is functioning as a depositary bank for some items, as an intermediary bank for others, as a presenting bank for still others and as a payor bank for still others, and that when it suspends payments it will have close to its normal load of items working through its various processes. For the convenience of receivers, owners of items, banks, and in fact substantially everyone concerned, it is recognized that at the particular moment of time that a bank suspends payment, a certain portion of the items being handled by it have progressed far enough in the bank collection process that it is preferable to permit them to continue the remaining distance, rather than to send them back and reverse the many entries that have been made or the steps that have been taken with respect to them. Therefore, having this background and these purposes in mind, the section states what items must be turned backward at the moment suspension intervenes and what items have progressed far enough that the collection process with respect to them continues, with the resulting necessary statement of rights of various parties flowing from this prescription of the cut-off time.

2.   The rules stated are similar to those stated in the American Bankers Association Bank Collection Code, but with the abandonment of any theory of trust. On the other hand, some law previous to this Act may be relevant. See Note, *Uniform Commercial Code: Stopping Payment of an Item Deposited with an Insolvent Depositary Bank,* 40 Okla.L.Rev. 689 (1987). Although for practical purposes Federal Deposit Insurance affects materially the result of bank failures on holders of items and banks, no attempt is made to vary the rules of the section by reason of such insurance.

3.   It is recognized that in view of *Jennings v. United States Fidelity & Guaranty Co.,* 294 U.S. 216, 55 S.Ct. 394, 79 L.Ed. 869, 99 A.L.R. 1248 (1935), amendment of the National Bank Act would be necessary to have this section apply to national banks. But there is no reason why it should not apply to others. See Section 1–108.*

---

*   *Referring to unrevised Article 1 (Appendix A).*

PART 3

COLLECTION OF ITEMS: PAYOR BANKS

§ 4–301.   Deferred Posting; Recovery of Payment by Return of Items; Time of Dishonor; Return of Items by Payor Bank.

(a)   If a payor bank settles for a demand item other than a documentary draft presented otherwise than for immediate payment over the counter before midnight of the banking day of receipt, the payor bank may revoke the settlement and recover the settlement if, before it has made final payment and before its midnight deadline, it

(1)   returns the item;

(2)   returns an image of the item, if the party to which the return is made has entered into an agreement to accept an image as a return of the item and the image is returned in accordance with that agreement; or

(3)   sends a record providing notice of dishonor or nonpayment if the item is unavailable for return.

(b)   If a demand item is received by a payor bank for credit on its books, it may return the item or send notice of dishonor and may revoke any credit given or recover the amount thereof withdrawn by its customer, if it acts within the time limit and in the manner specified in subsection (a).

(c)   Unless previous notice of dishonor has been sent, an item is dishonored at the time when for purposes of dishonor it is returned or notice sent in accordance with this section.

(d)   An item is returned:

(1)   as to an item presented through a clearing house, when it is delivered to the presenting or last collecting bank or to the clearing house or is sent or delivered in accordance with clearing-house rules; or

(2)   in all other cases, when it is sent or delivered to the bank's customer or transferor or pursuant to instructions.

As amended in 1990 and 2002.

Official Comment

1.   The term "deferred posting" appears in the caption of Section 4–301. This refers to the practice permitted by statute in most of the states before the UCC under which a payor bank receives items on one day but does not post the items to the customer's account until the next day. Items dishonored were then returned after the posting on the day after receipt. Under Section 4–301 the concept of "deferred posting" merely allows a payor bank that has settled for an item on the day of receipt to return a dishonored item on the next day before its midnight deadline, without regard to when the item was actually posted. With respect to checks Regulation CC Section 229.30(c) extends the midnight deadline under the UCC under certain circumstances. See the Commentary to Regulation CC Section 229.38(d) on the relationship between the UCC and Regulation CC on settlement.

2.   The function of this section is to provide the circumstances under which a payor bank that has made timely settlement for an item may return the item and revoke the settlement so that it may recover any settlement made. These circumstances are: (1) the item must be a demand item other than a documentary draft; (2) the item must be presented otherwise than for immediate payment over the counter; and (3) the payor bank must return the item (or give notice if the item is unavailable for return) before its midnight deadline and before it has paid the item. With respect to checks, see Regulation CC Section 229.31(f) on notice in lieu of return and Regulation CC Section 229.33 as to the different requirement of notice of nonpayment. An instance of when an item may be unavailable for return arises under a collecting bank check retention plan under which presentment is made by a presentment notice and the item is retained by the collecting bank. Section 4–215(a)(2) provides that final payment occurs if the payor bank has settled for an item without a right to revoke the settlement under statute, clearing-house rule or agreement. In any case in which Section 4–301(a) is applicable, the payor bank has a right to revoke the settlement by statute; therefore, Section 4–215(a)(2) is inoperable, and the settlement is provisional. Hence, if

the settlement is not over the counter and the payor bank settles in a manner that does not constitute final payment, the payor bank can revoke the settlement by returning the item before its midnight deadline.

3.   The relationship of Section 4–301(a) to final settlement and final payment under Section 4–215 is illustrated by the following case. Depositary Bank sends by mail an item to Payor Bank with instructions to settle by remitting a teller's check drawn on a bank in the city where Depositary Bank is located. Payor Bank sends the teller's check on the day the item was presented. Having made timely settlement, under the deferred posting provisions of Section 4–301(a), Payor Bank may revoke that settlement by returning the item before its midnight deadline. If it fails to return the item before its midnight deadline, it has finally paid the item if the bank on which the teller's check was drawn honors the check. But if the teller's check is dishonored there has been no final settlement under Section 4–213(c) and no final payment under Section 4–215(b). Since the Payor Bank has neither paid the item nor made timely return, it is accountable for the item under Section 4–302(a).

4.   The time limits for action imposed by subsection (a) are adopted by subsection (b) for cases in which the payor bank is also the depositary bank, but in this case the requirement of a settlement on the day of receipt is omitted.

5.   Subsection (c) fixes a base point from which to measure the time within which notice of dishonor must be given. See Section 3–503.

6.   Subsection (d) leaves banks free to agree upon the manner of returning items but establishes a precise time when an item is "returned." For definition of "sent" as used in paragraphs (1) and (2) see Section 1–201(38).[*] Obviously the subsection assumes that the item has not been "finally paid" under Section 4–215(a). If it has been, this provision has no operation.

7.   The fact that an item has been paid under proposed Section 4–215 does not preclude the payor bank from asserting rights of restitution or revocation under Section 3–418. *National Savings and Trust Co. v. Park Corp.*, 722 F.2d 1303 (6th Cir.1983), cert. denied, 466 U.S. 939 (1984), is the correct interpretation of the present law on this issue.

8.   Paragraph (a)(2) is designed to facilitate electronic check-processing by authorizing the payor bank to return an image of the item instead of the actual item. It applies only when the payor bank and the party to which the return has been made have agreed that the payor bank can make such a return and when the return complies with the agreement. The purpose of the paragraph is to prevent third parties (such as the depositor of the check) from contending that the payor bank missed its midnight deadline because it failed to return the actual item in a timely manner. If the payor bank missed its midnight deadline, payment would have become final under Section 4–215 and the depositary bank would have lost its right of chargeback under Section 4–214. Of course, the depositary bank might enter into an agreement with its depositor to resolve that problem, but it is not clear that agreements by banks with their customers can resolve all such issues. In any event, paragraph (a)(2) should eliminate the need for such agreements. The provision rests on the premise that it is inappropriate to penalize a payor bank simply because it returns the actual item a few business days after the midnight deadline of the payor bank sent notice before that deadline to a collecting bank that had agreed to accept such notices.

Nothing in paragraph (a)(2) authorizes the payor bank to destroy the check.

As amended in 2002.

§ 4–302.   Payor Bank's Responsibility for Late Return of Item.

(a)   If an item is presented to and received by a payor bank, the bank is accountable for the amount of:

(1)   a demand item, other than a documentary draft, whether properly payable or not, if the bank, in any case in which it is not also the depositary bank, retains the item beyond midnight of the banking day of receipt without settling for it or, whether or not it is also the depositary bank, does not pay or return the item or send notice of dishonor until after its midnight deadline; or

(2)   any other properly payable item unless, within the time allowed for acceptance or payment of that item, the bank either accepts or pays the item or returns it and accompanying documents.

---

[*]   *Referring to unrevised Article 1 (Appendix A).*

(b) The liability of a payor bank to pay an item pursuant to subsection (a) is subject to defenses based on breach of a presentment warranty (Section 4–208) or proof that the person seeking enforcement of the liability presented or transferred the item for the purpose of defrauding the payor bank.

As amended in 1990.

Official Comment

1. Subsection (a)(1) continues the former law distinguishing between cases in which the payor bank is not also the depositary bank and those in which the payor bank is also the depositary bank ("on us" items). For "on us" items the payor bank is accountable if it retains the item beyond its midnight deadline without settling for it. If the payor bank is not the depositary bank it is accountable if it retains the item beyond midnight of the banking day of receipt without settling for it. It may avoid accountability either by settling for the item on the day of receipt and returning the item before its midnight deadline under Section 4–301 or by returning the item on the day of receipt. This rule is consistent with the deferred posting practice authorized by Section 4–301 which allows the payor bank to make provisional settlement for an item on the day of receipt and to revoke that settlement by returning the item on the next day. With respect to checks, Regulation CC Section 229.36(d) provides that settlements between banks for forward collection of checks are final when made. See the Commentary on that provision for its effect on the UCC.

2. If the settlement given by the payor bank does not become final, there has been no payment under Section 4–215(b), and the payor bank giving the failed settlement is accountable under subsection (a)(1) of Section 4–302. For instance, the payor bank makes provisional settlement by sending a teller's check that is dishonored. In such a case settlement is not final under Section 4–213(c) and no payment occurs under Section 4–215(b). Payor bank is accountable on the item. The general principle is that unless settlement provides the presenting bank with usable funds, settlement has failed and the payor bank is accountable for the amount of the item. On the other hand, if the payor bank makes a settlement for the item that becomes final under Section 4–215, the item has been paid and thus the payor bank is not accountable for the item under this Section.

3. Subsection (b) is an elaboration of the deleted introductory language of former Section 4–302: "In the absence of a valid defense such as breach of a presentment warranty (subsection (1) of Section 4–207), settlement effected or the like. . . ." A payor bank can defend an action against it based on accountability by showing that the item contained a forged indorsement or a fraudulent alteration. Subsection (b) drops the ambiguous "or the like" language and provides that the payor bank may also raise the defense of fraud. Decisions that hold an accountable bank's liability to be "absolute" are rejected. A payor bank that makes a late return of an item should not be liable to a defrauder operating a check kiting scheme. In *Bank of Leumi Trust Co. v. Bally's Park Place Inc.*, 528 F.Supp. 349 (S.D.N.Y.1981), and *American National Bank v. Foodbasket*, 497 P.2d 546 (Wyo.1972), banks that were accountable under Section 4–302 for missing their midnight deadline were successful in defending against parties who initiated collection knowing that the check would not be paid. The "settlement effected" language is deleted as unnecessary. If a payor bank is accountable for an item it is liable to pay it. If it has made final payment for an item, it is no longer accountable for the item.

As amended in 2002.

§ 4–303. When Items Subject to Notice, Stop-Payment Order, Legal Process, or Setoff; Order in Which Items May Be Charged or Certified.

(a) Any knowledge, notice, or stop-payment order received by, legal process served upon, or setoff exercised by a payor bank comes too late to terminate, suspend, or modify the bank's right or duty to pay an item or to charge its customer's account for the item if the knowledge, notice, stop-payment order, or legal process is received or served and a reasonable time for the bank to act thereon expires or the setoff is exercised after the earliest of the following:

(1) the bank accepts or certifies the item;

(2) the bank pays the item in cash;

(3) the bank settles for the item without having a right to revoke the settlement under statute, clearing-house rule, or agreement;

(4) the bank becomes accountable for the amount of the item under Section 4–302 dealing with the payor bank's responsibility for late return of items; or

(5) with respect to checks, a cutoff hour no earlier than one hour after the opening of the next banking day after the banking day on which the bank received the check and no later than the close of that next banking day or, if no cutoff hour is fixed, the close of the next banking day after the banking day on which the bank received the check.

(b)   Subject to subsection (a), items may be accepted, paid, certified, or charged to the indicated account of its customer in any order.

As amended in 1990.

Official Comment

1.   While a payor bank is processing an item presented for payment, it may receive knowledge or a legal notice affecting the item, such as knowledge or a notice that the drawer has filed a petition in bankruptcy or made an assignment for the benefit of creditors; may receive an order of the drawer stopping payment on the item; may have served on it an attachment of the account of the drawer; or the bank itself may exercise a right of setoff against the drawer's account. Each of these events affects the account of the drawer and may eliminate or freeze all or part of whatever balance is available to pay the item. Subsection (a) states the rule for determining the relative priorities between these various legal events and the item.

2.   The rule is that if any one of several things has been done to the item or if it has reached any one of several stages in its processing at the time the knowledge, notice, stop-payment order or legal process is received or served and a reasonable time for the bank to act thereon expires or the setoff is exercised, the knowledge, notice, stop-payment order, legal process or setoff comes too late, the item has priority and a charge to the customer's account may be made and is effective. With respect to the effect of the customer's bankruptcy, the bank's rights are governed by Bankruptcy Code Section 542(c) which codifies the result of *Bank of Marin v. England*, 385 U.S. 99 (1966). Section 4–405 applies to the death or incompetence of the customer.

3.   Once a payor bank has accepted or certified an item or has paid the item in cash, the event has occurred that determines priorities between the item and the various legal events usually described as the "four legals." Paragraphs (1) and (2) of subsection (a) so provide. If a payor bank settles for an item presented over the counter for immediate payment by a cashier's check or teller's check which the presenting person agrees to accept, paragraph (3) of subsection (a) would control and the event determining priority has occurred. Because presentment was over the counter, Section 4–301(a) does not apply to give the payor bank the statutory right to revoke the settlement. Thus the requirements of paragraph (3) have been met unless a clearing-house rule or agreement of the parties provides otherwise.

4.   In the usual case settlement for checks is by entries in bank accounts. Since the process-of-posting test has been abandoned as inappropriate for automated check collection, the determining event for priorities is a given hour on the day after the item is received. (Paragraph (5) of subsection (a).) The hour may be fixed by the bank no earlier than one hour after the opening on the next banking day after the bank received the check and no later than the close of that banking day. If an item is received after the payor bank's regular Section 4–108 cutoff hour, it is treated as received the next banking day. If a bank receives an item after its regular cutoff hour on Monday and an attachment is levied at noon on Tuesday, the attachment is prior to the item if the bank had not before that hour taken the action described in paragraphs (1), (2), and (3) of subsection (a). The Commentary to Regulation CC Section 229.36(d) explains that even though settlement by a paying bank for a check is final for Regulation CC purposes, the paying bank's right to return the check before its midnight deadline under the UCC is not affected.

5.   Another event conferring priority for an item and a charge to the customer's account based upon the item is stated by the language "become accountable for the amount of the item under Section 4–302 dealing with the payor bank's responsibility for late return of items." Expiration of the deadline under Section 4–302 with resulting accountability by the payor bank for the amount of the item, establishes priority of the item over notices, stop-payment orders, legal process or setoff.

6.   In the case of knowledge, notice, stop-payment orders and legal process the effective time for determining whether they were received too late to affect the payment of an item and a charge to the customer's account by reason of such payment, is receipt plus a reasonable time for the bank to act on any of these communications. Usually a relatively short time is required to communicate to the accounting department advice

of one of these events but certainly some time is necessary. Compare Sections 1–201(27)* and 4–403. In the case of setoff the effective time is when the setoff is actually made.

7. As between one item and another no priority rule is stated. This is justified because of the impossibility of stating a rule that would be fair in all cases, having in mind the almost infinite number of combinations of large and small checks in relation to the available balance on hand in the drawer's account; the possible methods of receipt; and other variables. Further, the drawer has drawn all the checks, the drawer should have funds available to meet all of them and has no basis for urging one should be paid before another; and the holders have no direct right against the payor bank in any event, unless of course, the bank has accepted, certified or finally paid a particular item, or has become liable for it under Section 4–302. Under subsection (b) the bank has the right to pay items for which it is itself liable ahead of those for which it is not.

PART 4

RELATIONSHIP BETWEEN PAYOR BANK AND ITS CUSTOMER

§ 4–401. When Bank May Charge Customer's Account.

(a) A bank may charge against the account of a customer an item that is properly payable from the account even though the charge creates an overdraft. An item is properly payable if it is authorized by the customer and is in accordance with any agreement between the customer and bank.

(b) A customer is not liable for the amount of an overdraft if the customer neither signed the item nor benefited from the proceeds of the item.

(c) A bank may charge against the account of a customer a check that is otherwise properly payable from the account, even though payment was made before the date of the check, unless the customer has given notice to the bank of the postdating describing the check with reasonable certainty. The notice is effective for the period stated in Section 4–403(b) for stop-payment orders, and must be received at such time and in such manner as to afford the bank a reasonable opportunity to act on it before the bank takes any action with respect to the check described in Section 4–303. If a bank charges against the account of a customer a check before the date stated in the notice of postdating, the bank is liable for damages for the loss resulting from its act. The loss may include damages for dishonor of subsequent items under Section 4–402.

(d) A bank that in good faith makes payment to a holder may charge the indicated account of its customer according to:

(1) the original terms of the altered item; or

(2) the terms of the completed item, even though the bank knows the item has been completed unless the bank has notice that the completion was improper.

As amended in 1990.

Official Comment

1. An item is properly payable from a customer's account if the customer has authorized the payment and the payment does not violate any agreement that may exist between the bank and its customer. For an example of a payment held to violate an agreement with a customer, see *Torrance National Bank v. Enesco Federal Credit Union*, 285 P.2d 737 (Cal.App.1955). An item drawn for more than the amount of a customer's account may be properly payable. Thus under subsection (a) a bank may charge the customer's account for an item even though payment results in an overdraft. An item containing a forged drawer's signature or forged indorsement is not properly payable. Concern has arisen whether a bank may require a customer to execute a stop-payment order when the customer notifies the bank of the loss of an unindorsed or specially indorsed check. Since such a check cannot be properly payable from the customer's account, it is inappropriate for a bank to require stop-payment order in such a case.

---

* *Referring to unrevised Article 1 (Appendix A).*

2.   Subsection (b) adopts the view of case authority holding that if there is more than one customer who can draw on an account, the nonsigning customer is not liable for an overdraft unless that person benefits from the proceeds of the item.

3.   Subsection (c) is added because the automated check collection system cannot accommodate postdated checks. A check is usually paid upon presentment without respect to the date of the check. Under the former law, if a payor bank paid a postdated check before its stated date, it could not charge the customer's account because the check was not "properly payable." Hence, the bank might have been liable for wrongfully dishonoring subsequent checks of the drawer that would have been paid had the postdated check not been prematurely paid. Under subsection (c) a customer wishing to postdate a check must notify the payor bank of its postdating in time to allow the bank to act on the customer's notice before the bank has to commit itself to pay the check. If the bank fails to act on the customer's timely notice, it may be liable for damages for the resulting loss which may include damages for dishonor of subsequent items. This Act does not regulate fees that banks charge their customers for a notice of postdating or other services covered by the Act, but under principles of law such as unconscionability or good faith and fair dealing, courts have reviewed fees and the bank's exercise of a discretion to set fees. *Perdue v. Crocker National Bank*, 38 Cal.3d 913 (1985) (unconscionability); *Best v. United Bank of Oregon*, 739 P.2d 554, 562–566 (1987) (good faith and fair dealing). In addition, Section 1–203* provides that every contract or duty within this Act imposes an obligation of good faith in its performance or enforcement.

4.   Section 3–407(c) states that a payor bank or drawee which pays a fraudulently altered instrument in good faith and without notice of the alteration may enforce rights with respect to the instrument according to its original terms or, in the case of an incomplete instrument altered by unauthorized completion, according to its terms as completed. Section 4–401(d) follows the rule stated in Section 3–407(c) by applying it to an altered item and allows the bank to enforce rights with respect to the altered item by charging the customer's account.

§ 4–402.   Bank's Liability to Customer for Wrongful Dishonor; Time of Determining Insufficiency of Account.

(a)   Except as otherwise provided in this Article, a payor bank wrongfully dishonors an item if it dishonors an item that is properly payable, but a bank may dishonor an item that would create an overdraft unless it has agreed to pay the overdraft.

(b)   A payor bank is liable to its customer for damages proximately caused by the wrongful dishonor of an item. Liability is limited to actual damages proved and may include damages for an arrest or prosecution of the customer or other consequential damages. Whether any consequential damages are proximately caused by the wrongful dishonor is a question of fact to be determined in each case.

(c)   A payor bank's determination of the customer's account balance on which a decision to dishonor for insufficiency of available funds is based may be made at any time between the time the item is received by the payor bank and the time that the payor bank returns the item or gives notice in lieu of return, and no more than one determination need be made. If, at the election of the payor bank, a subsequent balance determination is made for the purpose of reevaluating the bank's decision to dishonor the item, the account balance at that time is determinative of whether a dishonor for insufficiency of available funds is wrongful.

As amended in 1990.

Official Comment

1.   Subsection (a) states positively what has been assumed under the original Article: that if a bank fails to honor a properly payable item it may be liable to its customer for wrongful dishonor. Under subsection (b) the payor bank's wrongful dishonor of an item gives rise to a statutory cause of action. Damages may include consequential damages. Confusion has resulted from the attempts of courts to reconcile the first and second sentences of former Section 4–402. The second sentence implied that the bank was liable for some form of damages other than those proximately caused by the dishonor if the dishonor was other than by mistake. But nothing in the section described what these noncompensatory damages might be. Some courts have held that in distinguishing between mistaken dishonors and nonmistaken dishonors, the so-called "trader" rule has been retained that allowed a "merchant or trader" to recover substantial damages for wrongful dishonor without proof of damages actually suffered. Comment 3 to former Section 4–402 indicated that this was not the intent of the drafters. White & Summers, Uniform Commercial Code, Section 18–4 (1988), states: "The negative implication is

---

*   *Referring to unrevised Article 1 (Appendix A).*

that when wrongful dishonors occur not 'through mistake' but willfully, the court may impose damages greater than 'actual damages'. . . . Certainly the reference to 'mistake' in the second sentence of 4–402 invites a court to adopt the relevant pre-Code distinction." Subsection (b) by deleting the reference to mistake in the second sentence precludes any inference that Section 4–402 retains the "trader" rule. Whether a bank is liable for noncompensatory damages, such as punitive damages, must be decided by Section 1–103 and Section 1–106* ("by other rule of law").

2. Wrongful dishonor is different from "failure to exercise ordinary care in handling an item," and the measure of damages is that stated in this section, not that stated in Section 4–103(e). By the same token, if a dishonor comes within this section, the measure of damages of this section applies and not another measure of damages. If the wrongful refusal of the beneficiary's bank to make funds available from a funds transfer causes the beneficiary's check to be dishonored, no specific guidance is given as to whether recovery is under this section or Article 4A. In each case this issue must be viewed in its factual context, and it was thought unwise to seek to establish certainty at the cost of fairness.

3. The second and third sentences of subsection (b) reject decisions holding that as a matter of law the dishonor of a check is not the "proximate cause" of the arrest and prosecution of the customer and leave to determination in each case as a question of fact whether the dishonor is or may be the "proximate cause."

4. Banks commonly determine whether there are sufficient funds in an account to pay an item after the close of banking hours on the day of presentment when they post debit and credit items to the account. The determination is made on the basis of credits available for withdrawal as of right or made available for withdrawal by the bank as an accommodation to its customer. When it is determined that payment of the item would overdraw the account, the item may be returned at any time before the bank's midnight deadline the following day. Before the item is returned new credits that are withdrawable as of right may have been added to the account. Subsection (c) eliminates uncertainty under Article 4 as to whether the failure to make a second determination before the item is returned on the day following presentment is a wrongful dishonor if new credits were added to the account on that day that would have covered the amount of the check.

5. Section 4–402 has been construed to preclude an action for wrongful dishonor by a plaintiff other than the bank's customer. *Loucks v. Albuquerque National Bank*, 418 P.2d 191 (N.Mex.1966). Some courts have allowed a plaintiff other than the customer to sue when the customer is a business entity that is one and the same with the individual or individuals operating it. *Murdaugh Volkswagen, Inc. v. First National Bank*, 801 F.2d 719 (4th Cir.1986) and *Karsh v. American City Bank*, 113 Cal.App.3d 419, 169 Cal.Rptr. 851 (1980). However, where the wrongful dishonor impugns the reputation of an operator of the business, the issue is not merely, as the court in *Koger v. East First National Bank*, 443 So.2d 141 (Fla.App.1983), put it, one of a literal versus a liberal interpretation of Section 4–402. Rather the issue is whether the statutory cause of action in Section 4–402 displaces, in accordance with Section 1–103, any cause of action that existed at common law in a person who is not the customer whose reputation was damaged. See *Marcum v. Security Trust and Savings Co.*, 221 Ala. 419, 129 So. 74 (1930). While Section 4–402 should not be interpreted to displace the latter cause of action, the section itself gives no cause of action to other than a "customer," however that definition is construed, and thus confers no cause of action on the holder of a dishonored item. *First American National Bank v. Commerce Union Bank*, 692 S.W.2d 642 (Tenn.App.1985).

§ 4–403. Customer's Right to Stop Payment; Burden of Proof of Loss.

(a) A customer or any person authorized to draw on the account if there is more than one person may stop payment of any item drawn on the customer's account or close the account by an order to the bank describing the item or account with reasonable certainty received at a time and in a manner that affords the bank a reasonable opportunity to act on it before any action by the bank with respect to the item described in Section 4–303. If the signature of more than one person is required to draw on an account, any of these persons may stop payment or close the account.

(b) A stop-payment order is effective for six months, but it lapses after 14 calendar days if the original order was oral and was not confirmed in a record within that period. A stop-payment order may be renewed for additional six-month periods by a record given to the bank within a period during which the stop-payment order is effective.

(c) The burden of establishing the fact and amount of loss resulting from the payment of an item contrary to a stop-payment order or order to close an account is on the customer. The loss from payment of an item contrary to a stop-payment order may include damages for dishonor of subsequent items under Section 4–402.

As amended in 1990 and 2002.

Official Comment

1.   The position taken by this section is that stopping payment or closing an account is a service which depositors expect and are entitled to receive from banks notwithstanding its difficulty, inconvenience and expense. The inevitable occasional losses through failure to stop or close should be borne by the banks as a cost of the business of banking.

2.   Subsection (a) follows the decisions holding that a payee or indorsee has no right to stop payment. This is consistent with the provision governing payment or satisfaction. See Section 3–602. The sole exception to this rule is found in Section 4–405 on payment after notice of death, by which any person claiming an interest in the account can stop payment.

3.   Payment is commonly stopped only on checks; but the right to stop payment is not limited to checks, and extends to any item payable by any bank. If the maker of a note payable at a bank is in a position analogous to that of a drawer (Section 4–106) the maker may stop payment of the note. By analogy the rule extends to drawees other than banks.

4.   A cashier's check or teller's check purchased by a customer whose account is debited in payment for the check is not a check drawn on the customer's account within the meaning of subsection (a); hence, a customer purchasing a cashier's check or teller's check has no right to stop payment of such a check under subsection (a). If a bank issuing a cashier's check or teller's check refuses to pay the check as an accommodation to its customer or for other reasons, its liability on the check is governed by Section 3–411. There is no right to stop payment after certification of a check or other acceptance of a draft, and this is true no matter who procures the certification. See Sections 3–411 and 4–303. The acceptance is the drawee's own engagement to pay, and it is not required to impair its credit by refusing payment for the convenience of the drawer.

5.   Subsection (a) makes clear that if there is more than one person authorized to draw on a customer's account any one of them can stop payment of any check drawn on the account or can order the account closed. Moreover, if there is a customer, such as a corporation, that requires its checks to bear the signatures of more than one person, any of these persons may stop payment on a check. In describing the item, the customer, in the absence of a contrary agreement, must meet the standard of what information allows the bank under the technology then existing to identify the item with reasonable certainty.

6.   Under subsection (b), a stop-payment order is effective after the order, whether written or oral, is received by the bank and the bank has a reasonable opportunity to act on it. If the order is written it remains in effect for six months from that time. If the order is oral it lapses after 14 days unless there is written confirmation. If there is written confirmation within the 14-day period, the six-month period dates from the giving of the oral order. A stop-payment order may be renewed any number of times by written notice given during a six-month period while a stop order is in effect. A new stop-payment order may be given after a six-month period expires, but such a notice takes effect from the date given. When a stop-payment order expires it is as though the order had never been given, and the payor bank may pay the item in good faith under Section 4–404 even though a stop-payment order had once been given.

7.   A payment in violation of an effective direction to stop payment is an improper payment, even though it is made by mistake or inadvertence. Any agreement to the contrary is invalid under Section 4–103(a) if in paying the item over the stop-payment order the bank has failed to exercise ordinary care. An agreement to the contrary which is imposed upon a customer as part of a standard form contract would have to be evaluated in the light of the general obligation of good faith. Sections 1–203* and 4–104(c). The drawee is, however, entitled to subrogation to prevent unjust enrichment (Section 4–407); retains common law defenses, e.g., that by conduct in recognizing the payment the customer has ratified the bank's action in paying over a stop-payment order (Section 1–103); and retains common law rights, e.g., to recover money paid under a mistake under Section 3–418. It has sometimes been said that payment cannot be stopped against a holder in due course, but the statement is inaccurate. The payment can be stopped but the drawer remains liable on the instrument to the holder in due course (Sections 3–305, 3–414) and the drawee, if it pays, becomes subrogated to the rights of the holder in due course against the drawer. Section 4–407. The relationship between Sections 4–403 and 4–407 is discussed in the comments to

---

*   *Referring to unrevised Article 1 (Appendix A).*

Section 4–407. Any defenses available against a holder in due course remain available to the drawer, but other defenses are cut off to the same extent as if the holder were bringing the action.

§ 4–404.   Bank Not Obliged to Pay Check More Than Six Months Old.

A bank is under no obligation to a customer having a checking account to pay a check, other than a certified check, which is presented more than six months after its date, but it may charge its customer's account for a payment made thereafter in good faith.

Official Comment

This section incorporates a type of statute that had been adopted in 26 jurisdictions before the Code. The time limit is set at six months because banking and commercial practice regards a check outstanding for longer than that period as stale, and a bank will normally not pay such a check without consulting the depositor. It is therefore not required to do so, but is given the option to pay because it may be in a position to know, as in the case of dividend checks, that the drawer wants payment made.

Certified checks are excluded from the section because they are the primary obligation of the certifying bank (Sections 3–409 and 3–413). The obligation runs directly to the holder of the check. The customer's account was presumably charged when the check was certified.

§ 4–405.   Death or Incompetence of Customer.

(a)   A payor or collecting bank's authority to accept, pay, or collect an item or to account for proceeds of its collection, if otherwise effective, is not rendered ineffective by incompetence of a customer of either bank existing at the time the item is issued or its collection is undertaken if the bank does not know of an adjudication of incompetence. Neither death nor incompetence of a customer revokes the authority to accept, pay, collect, or account until the bank knows of the fact of death or of an adjudication of incompetence and has reasonable opportunity to act on it.

(b)   Even with knowledge, a bank may for 10 days after the date of death pay or certify checks drawn on or before that date unless ordered to stop payment by a person claiming an interest in the account.

As amended in 1990.

Official Comment

1.   Subsection (a) follows existing decisions holding that a drawee (payor) bank is not liable for the payment of a check before it has notice of the death or incompetence of the drawer. The justice and necessity of the rule are obvious. A check is an order to pay which the bank must obey under penalty of possible liability for dishonor. Further, with the tremendous volume of items handled any rule that required banks to verify the continued life and competency of drawers would be completely unworkable.

One or both of these same reasons apply to other phases of the bank collection and payment process and the rule is made wide enough to apply to these other phases. It applies to all kinds of "items"; to "customers" who own items as well as "customers" who draw or make them; to the function of collecting items as well as the function of accepting or paying them; to the carrying out of instructions to account for proceeds even though these may involve transfers to third parties; to depositary and intermediary banks as well as payor banks; and to incompetency existing at the time of the issuance of an item or the commencement of the collection or payment process as well as to incompetency occurring thereafter. Further, the requirement of actual knowledge makes inapplicable the rule of some cases that an adjudication of incompetency is constructive notice to all the world because obviously it is as impossible for banks to keep posted on such adjudications (in the absence of actual knowledge) as it is to keep posted as to death of immediate or remote customers.

2.   Subsection (b) provides a limited period after death during which a bank may continue to pay checks (as distinguished from other items) even though it has notice. The purpose of the provision, as of the existing statutes, is to permit holders of checks drawn and issued shortly before death to cash them without the necessity of filing a claim in probate. The justification is that these checks normally are given in immediate payment of an obligation, that there is almost never any reason why they should not be paid, and that filing in probate is a useless formality, burdensome to the holder, the executor, the court and the bank.

This section does not prevent an executor or administrator from recovering the payment from the holder of the check. It is not intended to affect the validity of any gift causa mortis or other transfer in contemplation of death, but merely to relieve the bank of liability for the payment.

3.   Any surviving relative, creditor or other person who claims an interest in the account may give a direction to the bank not to pay checks, or not to pay a particular check. Such notice has the same effect as a direction to stop payment. The bank has no responsibility to determine the validity of the claim or even whether it is "colorable." But obviously anyone who has an interest in the estate, including the person named as executor in a will, even if the will has not yet been admitted to probate, is entitled to claim an interest in the account.

§ 4–406.   Customer's Duty to Discover and Report Unauthorized Signature or Alteration.

(a)   A bank that sends or makes available to a customer a statement of account showing payment of items for the account shall either return or make available to the customer the items paid or provide information in the statement of account sufficient to allow the customer reasonably to identify the items paid. The statement of account provides sufficient information if the item is described by item number, amount, and date of payment.

(b)   If the items are not returned to the customer, the person retaining the items shall either retain the items or, if the items are destroyed, maintain the capacity to furnish legible copies of the items until the expiration of seven years after receipt of the items. A customer may request an item from the bank that paid the item, and that bank must provide in a reasonable time either the item or, if the item has been destroyed or is not otherwise obtainable, a legible copy of the item.

(c)   If a bank sends or makes available a statement of account or items pursuant to subsection (a), the customer must exercise reasonable promptness in examining the statement or the items to determine whether any payment was not authorized because of an alteration of an item or because a purported signature by or on behalf of the customer was not authorized. If, based on the statement or items provided, the customer should reasonably have discovered the unauthorized payment, the customer must promptly notify the bank of the relevant facts.

(d)   If the bank proves that the customer failed, with respect to an item, to comply with the duties imposed on the customer by subsection (c), the customer is precluded from asserting against the bank:

(1)   the customer's unauthorized signature or any alteration on the item, if the bank also proves that it suffered a loss by reason of the failure; and

(2)   the customer's unauthorized signature or alteration by the same wrongdoer on any other item paid in good faith by the bank if the payment was made before the bank received notice from the customer of the unauthorized signature or alteration and after the customer had been afforded a reasonable period of time, not exceeding 30 days, in which to examine the item or statement of account and notify the bank.

(e)   If subsection (d) applies and the customer proves that the bank failed to exercise ordinary care in paying the item and that the failure substantially contributed to loss, the loss is allocated between the customer precluded and the bank asserting the preclusion according to the extent to which the failure of the customer to comply with subsection (c) and the failure of the bank to exercise ordinary care contributed to the loss. If the customer proves that the bank did not pay the item in good faith, the preclusion under subsection (d) does not apply.

(f)   Without regard to care or lack of care of either the customer or the bank, a customer who does not within one year after the statement or items are made available to the customer (subsection (a)) discover and report the customer's unauthorized signature on or any alteration on the item is precluded from asserting against the bank the unauthorized signature or alteration. If there is a preclusion under this subsection, the payor bank may not recover for breach of warranty under Section 4–208 with respect to the unauthorized signature or alteration to which the preclusion applies.

As amended in 1990.

Revised Official Comment

1.   Under subsection (a), if a bank that has paid a check or other item for the account of a customer makes available to the customer a statement of account showing payment of the item, the bank must either return the item to the customer or provide a description of the item sufficient to allow the customer to identify it. Under subsection (c), the customer has a duty to exercise reasonable promptness in examining the statement or the returned item to discover any unauthorized signature of the customer or any alteration and to promptly notify the bank if the customer should reasonably have discovered the unauthorized signature or alteration.

The duty stated in subsection (c) becomes operative only if the "bank sends or makes available a statement of account or items pursuant to subsection (a)." A bank is not under a duty to send a statement of account or the paid items to the customer; but, if it does not do so, the customer does not have any duties under subsection (c).

Under subsection (a), a statement of account must provide information "sufficient to allow the customer reasonably to identify the items paid." If the bank supplies its customer with an image of the paid item, it complies with this standard. But a safe harbor rule is provided. The bank complies with the standard of providing "sufficient information" if "the item is described by item number, amount, and date of payment." This means that the customer's duties under subsection (c) are triggered if the bank sends a statement of account complying with the safe harbor rule without returning the paid items. A bank does not have to return the paid items unless it has agreed with the customer to do so. Whether there is such an agreement depends upon the particular circumstances. See Section 1–201(3).* If the bank elects to provide the minimum information that is "sufficient" under subsection (a) and, as a consequence, the customer could not "reasonably have discovered the unauthorized payment," there is no preclusion under subsection (d). If the customer made a record of the issued checks on the check stub or carbonized copies furnished by the bank in the checkbook, the customer should usually be able to verify the paid items shown on the statement of account and discover any unauthorized or altered checks. But there could be exceptional circumstances. For example, if a check is altered by changing the name of the payee, the customer could not normally detect the fraud unless the customer is given the paid check or the statement of account discloses the name of the payee of the altered check. If the customer could not "reasonably have discovered the unauthorized payment" under subsection (c) there would not be a preclusion under subsection (d).

The safe harbor provided by subsection (a) serves to permit a bank, based on the state of existing technology, to trigger the customer's duties under subsection (c) by providing a "statement of account showing payment of items" without having to return the paid items, in any case in which the bank has not agreed with the customer to return the paid items. The safe harbor does not, however, preclude a customer under subsection (d) from asserting its unauthorized signature or an alteration against a bank in those circumstances in which under subsection (c) the customer should not "reasonably have discovered the unauthorized payment." Whether the customer has failed to comply with its duties under subsection (c) is determined on a case-by-case basis.

The provision in subsection (a) that a statement of account contains "sufficient information if the item is described by item number, amount, and date of payment" is based upon the existing state of technology. This information was chosen because it can be obtained by the bank's computer from the check's MICR line without examination of the items involved. The other two items of information that the customer would normally want to know—the name of the payee and the date of the item—cannot currently be obtained from the MICR line. The safe harbor rule is important in determining the feasibility of payor or collecting bank check retention plans. A customer who keeps a record of checks written, e.g., on the check stubs or carbonized copies of the checks supplied by the bank in the checkbook, will usually have sufficient information to identify the items on the basis of item number, amount, and date of payment. But customers who do not utilize these record-keeping methods may not. The policy decision is that accommodating customers who do not keep adequate records is not as desirable as accommodating customers who keep more careful records. This policy results in less cost to the check collection system and thus to all customers of the system. It is expected that technological advances such as image processing may make it possible for banks to give customers more information in the future in a manner that is fully compatible with automation or truncation systems. At that time the Permanent Editorial Board may wish to make recommendations for an amendment revising the safe harbor requirements in the light of those advances.

2.   Subsection (d) states the consequences of a failure by the customer to perform its duty under subsection (c) to report an alteration or the customer's unauthorized signature. Subsection (d)(1) applies to the unauthorized payment of the item to which the duty to report under subsection (c) applies. If the bank proves that the customer "should reasonably have discovered the unauthorized payment" (See Comment 1) and did not notify the bank, the customer is precluded from asserting against the bank the alteration or the customer's unauthorized signature if

---

*   *Referring to unrevised Article 1 (Appendix A).*

the bank proves that it suffered a loss as a result of the failure of the customer to perform its subsection (c) duty. Subsection (d)(2) applies to cases in which the customer fails to report an unauthorized signature or alteration with respect to an item in breach of the subsection (c) duty (See Comment 1) and the bank subsequently pays other items of the customer with respect to which there is an alteration or unauthorized signature of the customer and the same wrongdoer is involved. If the payment of the subsequent items occurred after the customer has had a reasonable time (not exceeding 30 days) to report with respect to the first item and before the bank received notice of the unauthorized signature or alteration of the first item, the customer is precluded from asserting the alteration or unauthorized signature with respect to the subsequent items.

If the customer is precluded in a single or multiple item unauthorized payment situation under subsection (d), but the customer proves that the bank failed to exercise ordinary care in paying the item or items and that the failure substantially contributed to the loss, subsection (e) provides a comparative negligence test for allocating loss between the customer and the bank. Subsection (e) also states that, if the customer proves that the bank did not pay the item in good faith, the preclusion under subsection (d) does not apply.

Subsection (d)(2) changes former subsection (2)(b) by adopting a 30-day period in place of a 14-day period. Although the 14-day period may have been sufficient when the original version of Article 4 was drafted in the 1950s, given the much greater volume of checks at the time of the revision, a longer period was viewed as more appropriate. The rule of subsection (d)(2) follows pre-Code case law that payment of an additional item or items bearing an unauthorized signature or alteration by the same wrongdoer is a loss suffered by the bank traceable to the customer's failure to exercise reasonable care (See Comment 1) in examining the statement and notifying the bank of objections to it. One of the most serious consequences of failure of the customer to comply with the requirements of subsection (c) is the opportunity presented to the wrongdoer to repeat the misdeeds. Conversely, one of the best ways to keep down losses in this type of situation is for the customer to promptly examine the statement and notify the bank of an unauthorized signature or alteration so that the bank will be alerted to stop paying further items. Hence, the rule of subsection (d)(2) is prescribed, and to avoid dispute a specific time limit, 30 days, is designated for cases to which the subsection applies. These considerations are not present if there are no losses resulting from the payment of additional items. In these circumstances, a reasonable period for the customer to comply with its duties under subsection (c) would depend on the circumstances (Section 1–204(2))* and the subsection (d)(2) time limit should not be imported by analogy into subsection (c).

3.   Subsection (b) applies if the items are not returned to the customer. Check retention plans may include a simple payor bank check retention plan or the kind of check retention plan that would be authorized by a truncation agreement in which a collecting bank or the payee may retain the items. Even after agreeing to a check retention plan, a customer may need to see one or more checks for litigation or other purposes. The customer's request for the check may always be made to the payor bank. Under subsection (b) retaining banks may destroy items but must maintain the capacity to furnish legible copies for seven years. A legible copy may include an image of an item. This Act does not define the length of the reasonable period of time for a bank to provide the check or copy of the check. What is reasonable depends on the capacity of the bank and the needs of the customer. This Act does not specify sanctions for failure to retain or furnish the items or legible copies; this is left to other laws regulating banks. See Comment 3 to Section 4–101. Moreover, this Act does not regulate fees that banks charge their customers for furnishing items or copies or other services covered by the Act, but under principles of law such as unconscionability or good faith and fair dealing, courts have reviewed fees and the bank's exercise of a discretion to set fees. *Perdue v. Crocker National Bank*, 38 Cal.3d 913 (1985) (unconscionability); *Best v. United Bank of Oregon*, 739 P.2d 554, 562–566 (1987) (good faith and fair dealing). In addition, Section 1–203* provides that every contract or duty within this Act imposes an obligation of good faith in its performance or enforcement.

4.   Subsection (e) replaces former subsection (3) and poses a modified comparative negligence test for determining liability. See the discussion on this point in the Comments to Sections 3–404, 3–405, and 3–406. The term "good faith" is defined in Section 1–201(b)(20) as including "observance of reasonable commercial standards of fair dealing." The connotation of this standard is fairness and not absence of negligence.

The term "ordinary care" used in subsection (e) is defined in Section 3–103(a)(7), made applicable to Article 4 by Section 4–104(c), to provide that sight examination by a payor bank is not required if its procedure is reasonable and is commonly followed by other comparable banks in the area. The case law is divided on this issue. The definition of "ordinary care" in Section 3–103 rejects those authorities that hold, in effect, that failure to use sight examination is negligence as a matter of law. The effect of the definition of "ordinary care" on Section 4–406 is only to provide that in the small percentage of cases in which a customer's failure to examine its statement or

---

*   *Referring to unrevised Article 1 (Appendix A).*

returned items has led to loss under subsection (d) a bank should not have to share that loss solely because it has adopted an automated collection or payment procedure in order to deal with the great volume of items at a lower cost to all customers.

5.   Several changes are made in former Section 4–406(5). First, former subsection (5) is deleted and its substance is made applicable only to the one-year notice preclusion in former subsection (4) (subsection (f)). Thus if a drawer has not notified the payor bank of an unauthorized check or material alteration within the one-year period, the payor bank may not choose to recredit the drawer's account and pass the loss to the collecting banks on the theory of breach of warranty. Second, the reference in former subsection (4) to unauthorized indorsements is deleted. Section 4–406 imposes no duties on the drawer to look for unauthorized indorsements. Section 4–111 sets out a statute of limitations allowing a customer a three-year period to seek a credit to an account improperly charged by payment of an item bearing an unauthorized indorsement. Third, subsection (c) is added to Section 4–208 to assure that if a depositary bank is sued for breach of a presentment warranty, it can defend by showing that the drawer is precluded by Section 3–406 or Section 4–406(c) and (d).

As amended in 1991 and 2002.

§ 4–407.   Payor Bank's Right to Subrogation on Improper Payment.

If a payor bank has paid an item over the order of the drawer or maker to stop payment, or after an account has been closed, or otherwise under circumstances giving a basis for objection by the drawer or maker, to prevent unjust enrichment and only to the extent necessary to prevent loss to the bank by reason of its payment of the item, the payor bank is subrogated to the rights

(1)   of any holder in due course on the item against the drawer or maker;

(2)   of the payee or any other holder of the item against the drawer or maker either on the item or under the transaction out of which the item arose; and

(3)   of the drawer or maker against the payee or any other holder of the item with respect to the transaction out of which the item arose.

As amended in 1990.

Official Comment

1.   Section 4–403 states that a stop-payment order or an order to close an account is binding on a bank. If a bank pays an item over such an order it is prima facie liable, but under subsection (c) of Section 4–403 the burden of establishing the fact and amount of loss from such payment is on the customer. A defense frequently interposed by a bank in an action against it for wrongful payment over a stop-payment order is that the drawer or maker suffered no loss because it would have been liable to a holder in due course in any event. On this argument some cases have held that payment cannot be stopped against a holder in due course. Payment can be stopped, but if it is, the drawer or maker is liable and the sound rule is that the bank is subrogated to the rights of the holder in due course. The preamble and paragraph (1) of this section state this rule.

2.   Paragraph (2) also subrogates the bank to the rights of the payee or other holder against the drawer or maker either on the item or under the transaction out of which it arose. It may well be that the payee is not a holder in due course but still has good rights against the drawer. These may be on the check but also may not be as, for example, where the drawer buys goods from the payee and the goods are partially defective so that the payee is not entitled to the full price, but the goods are still worth a portion of the contract price. If the drawer retains the goods it is obligated to pay a part of the agreed price. If the bank has paid the check it should be subrogated to this claim of the payee against the drawer.

3.   Paragraph (3) subrogates the bank to the rights of the drawer or maker against the payee or other holder with respect to the transaction out of which the item arose. If, for example, the payee was a fraudulent salesman inducing the drawer to issue a check for defective securities, and the bank pays the check over a stop-payment order but reimburses the drawer for such payment, the bank should have a basis for getting the money back from the fraudulent salesman.

4.   The limitations of the preamble prevent the bank itself from getting any double recovery or benefits out of its subrogation rights conferred by the section.

5.　The spelling out of the affirmative rights of the bank in this section does not destroy other existing rights (Section 1–103). Among others these may include the defense of a payor bank that by conduct in recognizing the payment a customer has ratified the bank's action in paying in disregard of a stop-payment order or right to recover money paid under a mistake.

PART 5

COLLECTION OF DOCUMENTARY DRAFTS

§ 4–501.　　Handling of Documentary Drafts; Duty to Send for Presentment and to Notify Customer of Dishonor.

A bank that takes a documentary draft for collection shall present or send the draft and accompanying documents for presentment and, upon learning that the draft has not been paid or accepted in due course, shall seasonably notify its customer of the fact even though it may have discounted or bought the draft or extended credit available for withdrawal as of right.

As amended in 1990.

Official Comment

This section states the duty of a bank handling a documentary draft for a customer. "Documentary draft" is defined in Section 4–104. The duty stated exists even if the bank has bought the draft. This is because to the customer the draft normally represents an underlying commercial transaction, and if that is not going through as planned the customer should know it promptly. An electronic document of title may be presented through allowing access to the document or delivery of the document. Article 1, Section 1–201 (definition of "delivery").

As amended in 2003.

§ 4–502.　　Presentment of "On Arrival" Drafts.

If a draft or the relevant instructions require presentment "on arrival", "when goods arrive" or the like, the collecting bank need not present until in its judgment a reasonable time for arrival of the goods has expired. Refusal to pay or accept because the goods have not arrived is not dishonor; the bank must notify its transferor of the refusal but need not present the draft again until it is instructed to do so or learns of the arrival of the goods.

As amended in 1990.

Official Comment

The section is designed to establish a definite rule for "on arrival" drafts. The term includes not only drafts drawn payable "on arrival" but also drafts forwarded with instructions to present "on arrival." The term refers to the arrival of the relevant goods. Unless a bank has actual knowledge of the arrival of the goods, as for example, when it is the "notify" party on the bill of lading, the section only requires the exercise of such judgment in estimating time as a bank may be expected to have. Commonly the buyer-drawee will want the goods and will therefore call for the documents and take up the draft when they do arrive.

§ 4–503.　　Responsibility of Presenting Bank for Documents and Goods; Report of Reasons for Dishonor; Referee in Case of Need.

Unless otherwise instructed and except as provided in Article 5, a bank presenting a documentary draft:

(1)　must deliver the documents to the drawee on acceptance of the draft if it is payable more than three days after presentment; otherwise, only on payment; and

(2)　upon dishonor, either in the case of presentment for acceptance or presentment for payment, may seek and follow instructions from any referee in case of need designated in the draft or, if the presenting bank does not choose to utilize the referee's services, it must use diligence and good faith to ascertain the reason for dishonor, must notify its transferor of the dishonor and of the results of its effort to ascertain the reasons therefor, and must request instructions.

However the presenting bank is under no obligation with respect to goods represented by the documents except to follow any reasonable instructions seasonably received; it has a right to reimbursement for any expense incurred in following instructions and to prepayment of or indemnity for those expenses.

As amended in 1990.

Official Comment

1. This section states the rules governing, in the absence of instructions, the duty of the presenting bank in case either of honor or of dishonor of a documentary draft. The section should be read in connection with Section 2–514 on when documents are deliverable on acceptance, when on payment. In the case of a dishonor of the draft, the bank, subject to Section 4–504, must return possession or control of the documents to its principal.

2. If the draft is drawn under a letter of credit, Article 5 controls. See Sections 5–109 through 5–114.*

As amended in 2003.

§ 4–504.   Privilege of Presenting Bank to Deal With Goods; Security Interest for Expenses.

(a) A presenting bank that, following the dishonor of a documentary draft, has seasonably requested instructions but does not receive them within a reasonable time may store, sell, or otherwise deal with the goods in any reasonable manner.

(b) For its reasonable expenses incurred by action under subsection (a) the presenting bank has a lien upon the goods or their proceeds, which may be foreclosed in the same manner as an unpaid seller's lien.

As amended in 1990.

Official Comment

The section gives the presenting bank, after dishonor, a privilege to deal with the goods in any commercially reasonable manner pending instructions from its transferor and, if still unable to communicate with its principal after a reasonable time, a right to realize its expenditures as if foreclosing on an unpaid seller's lien (Section 2–706). The provision includes situations in which storage of goods or other action becomes commercially necessary pending receipt of any requested instructions, even if the requested instructions are later received.

The "reasonable manner" referred to means one reasonable in the light of business factors and the judgment of a business man.

---

* *Referring to unrevised Article 5.*

UCC ARTICLE 4A (2016)

FUNDS TRANSFERS

Article 4A was promulgated in 1989.

UNIFORM COMMERCIAL CODE

PART 5. MISCELLANEOUS PROVISIONS

National Conference of Commissioners on Uniform State Laws

REPORTER

Robert L. Jordan, Los Angeles, California

William D. Warren, Los Angeles, California

DRAFTING COMMITTEE

CO-CHAIRMEN

Carlyle C. Ring, Jr., Alexandria, Virginia

Robert Haydock, Jr., Boston, Massachusetts

MEMBERS

Boris Auerbach, Cincinnati, Ohio

Richard F. Dole, Jr., Houston, Texas

William E. Hogan, New York, New York

Charles W. Joiner, Ann Arbor, Michigan

Frederick H. Miller, Norman, Oklahoma

Donald J. Rapson, Livingston, New Jersey, *The American Law Institute Representative*

Michael P. Sullivan, Minneapolis, Minnesota, *President, (Member Ex Officio)*

Neal Ossen, Hartford, Connecticut, *Chairman, Division C, (Member Ex Officio)*

REVIEW COMMITTEE

CHAIRMAN

Frank F. Jestrab, Chevy Chase, Maryland

MEMBERS

Rupert R. Bullivant, Portland, Oregon

Michael Franck, Lansing, Michigan

CONSULTANT

Fairfax Leary, Jr., Villanova, Pennsylvania

ADVISORS

Thomas C. Baxter, Jr., *Federal Reserve Bank of New York*

Roland E. Brandel, *American Bar Association*

Leon P. Ciferni, *National Westminster Bank, U.S.A.*

William B. Davenport, *American Bar Association, Section of Business Law, Ad Hoc Committee on Payment Systems*

Carl Felsenfeld, *Association of the Bar of the City of New York*

J. Kevin French, *Exxon Company, U.S.A.*

Thomas J. Greco, *American Bankers Association*

ARTICLE 4A (2016)

Arthur L. Herold, *National Corporate Cash Management Association*
John R. H. Kimball, *Federal Reserve Bank of Boston*
John F. Lee, *New York Clearing House Association*
W. Robert Moore, *American Bankers Association*
Ernest T. Patrikis, *Federal Reserve Bank of New York*
Richard B. Wagner, *General Motors Corporation*

ADDITIONAL PARTICIPANTS

Dean Bitner, *Sears, Roebuck & Company*
Henry N. Dyhouse, *U.S. Central Credit Union*
James Foorman, *First Chicago Corporation*
Richard M. Gottlieb, *Manufacturers Hanover Trust Company*
Shirley Holder, *Atlantic Richfield Company*
Paul E. Homrighausen, *Bankers Clearing House Association and National Automated Clearing House Association*
Gail M. Inaba, *Morgan Guaranty Trust Company of New York*
Oliver I. Ireland, *Board of Governors of Federal Reserve System*
Richard P. Kessler, Jr., *Credit Union National Association*
James W. Kopp, *Shell Oil Company*
Robert M. MacAllister, *Chase Manhattan Bank NA*
Thomas E. Montgomery, *California Bankers Association*
Norman R. Nelson, *New York Clearing House Association*
Samuel Newman, *Manufacturers Hanover Trust Company*
Nena Nodge, *National Corporate Cash Management Association*
Robert J. Pisapia, *Occidental Petroleum Corporation*
Deborah S. Prutzman, *Arnold & Porter*
Robert M. Rosenblith, *Manufacturers Hanover Trust Company*
Paul S. Turner, *Occidental Petroleum Corporation*
Irma Villarreal, *Aon Corporation*
Suzanne Weakley, *Atlantic Richfield Company*

PREFATORY NOTE

The National Conference of Commissioners on Uniform State laws and The American Law Institute have approved a new Article 4A to the Uniform Commercial Code. Comments that follow each of the sections of the statute are intended as official comments. They explain in detail the purpose and meaning of the various sections and the policy considerations on which they are based.

Description of transaction covered by Article 4A.

There are a number of mechanisms for making payments through the banking system. Most of these mechanisms are covered in whole or part by state or federal statutes. In terms of number of transactions, payments made by check or credit card are the most common payment methods. Payment by check is covered by Articles 3 and 4 of the UCC and some aspects of payment by credit card are covered by federal law. In recent years electronic funds transfers have been increasingly common in consumer transactions. For example, in some cases a retail customer can pay for purchases by use of an access or debit card inserted in a terminal at the retail store that allows the bank account of the customer to be instantly debited. Some aspects of these point-of-sale transactions and other consumer payments that are effected electronically are covered by a federal statute, the Electronic Fund Transfer Act (EFTA). If any part of a funds transfer is covered by EFTA, the entire funds transfer is excluded from Article 4A.

Another type of payment, commonly referred to as a wholesale wire transfer, is the primary focus of Article 4A. Payments that are covered by Article 4A are overwhelmingly between business or financial institutions. The dollar volume of payments made by wire transfer far exceeds the dollar volume of payments made by other means. The volume of payments by wire transfer over the two principal wire payment systems—the Federal Reserve wire transfer network (Fedwire) and the New York Clearing House Interbank

419

Payments Systems (CHIPS)—exceeds one trillion dollars per day. Most payments carried out by use of automated clearing houses are consumer payments covered by EFTA and therefore not covered by Article 4A. There is, however, a significant volume of nonconsumer ACH payments that closely resemble wholesale wire transfers. These payments are also covered by Article 4A.

There is some resemblance between payments made by wire transfer and payments made by other means such as paper-based checks and credit cards or electronically-based consumer payments, but there are also many differences. Article 4A excludes from its coverage these other payment mechanisms. Article 4A follows a policy of treating the transaction that it covers—a "funds transfer"—as a unique method of payment that is governed by unique principles of law that address the operational and policy issues presented by this kind of payment.

The funds transfer that is covered by Article 4A is not a complex transaction and can be illustrated by the following example which is used throughout the Prefatory Note as a basis for discussion. X, a debtor, wants to pay an obligation owed to Y. Instead of delivering to Y a negotiable instrument such as a check or some other writing such as a credit card slip that enables Y to obtain payment from a bank, X transmits an instruction to X's bank to credit a sum of money to the bank account of Y. In most cases X's bank and Y's bank are different banks. X's bank may carry out X's instruction by instructing Y's bank to credit Y's account in the amount that X requested. The instruction that X issues to its bank is a "payment order." X is the "sender" of the payment order and X's bank is the "receiving bank" with respect to X's order. Y is the "beneficiary" of X's order. When X's bank issues an instruction to Y's bank to carry out X's payment order, X's bank "executes" X's order. The instruction of X's bank to Y's bank is also a payment order. With respect to that order, X's bank is the sender, Y's bank is the receiving bank, and Y is the beneficiary. The entire series of transactions by which X pays Y is knows as the "funds transfer." With respect to the funds transfer, X is the "originator," X's bank is the "originator's bank," Y is the "beneficiary" and Y's bank is the "beneficiary's bank." In more complex transactions there are one or more additional banks known as "intermediary banks" between X's bank and Y's bank. In the funds transfer the instruction contained in the payment order of X to its bank is carried out by a series of payment orders by each bank in the transmission chain to the next bank in the chain until Y's bank receives a payment order to make the credit to Y's account. In most cases, the payment order of each bank to the next bank in the chain is transmitted electronically, and often the payment order of X to its bank is also transmitted electronically, but the means of transmission does not have any legal significance. A payment order may be transmitted by any means, and in some cases the payment order is transmitted by a slow means such as first class mail. To reflect this fact, the broader term "funds transfer" rather than the narrower term "wire transfer" is used in Article 4A to describe the overall payment transaction.

Funds transfers are divided into two categories determined by whether the instruction to pay is given by the person making payment or the person receiving payment. If the instruction is given by the person making the payment, the transfer is commonly referred to as a "credit transfer." If the instruction is given by the person receiving payment, the transfer is commonly referred to as a "debit transfer." Article 4A governs credit transfers and excludes debit transfers.

Why is Article 4A needed?

There is no comprehensive body of law that defines the rights and obligations that arise from wire transfers. Some aspects of wire transfers are governed by rules of the principal transfer systems. Transfers made by Fedwire are governed by Federal Reserve Regulation J and transfers over CHIPS are governed by the CHIPS rules. Transfers made by means of automated clearing houses are governed by uniform rules adopted by various associations of banks in various parts of the nation or by Federal Reserve rules or operating circulars. But the various funds transfer system rules apply to only limited aspects of wire transfer transactions. The resolution of the many issues that are not covered by funds transfer system rules depends on contracts of the parties, to the extent that they exist, or principles of law applicable to other payment mechanisms that might be applied by analogy. The result is a great deal of uncertainty. There is no consensus about the juridical nature of a wire transfer and consequently of the rights and obligations that are created. Article 4A is intended to provide the comprehensive body of law that we do not have today.

ARTICLE 4A (2016)

Characteristics of a funds transfer.

There are a number of characteristics of funds transfers covered by Article 4A that have influenced the drafting of the statute. The typical funds transfer involves a large amount of money. Multimillion dollar transactions are commonplace. The originator of the transfer and the beneficiary are typically sophisticated business or financial organizations. High speed is another predominant characteristic. Most funds transfers are completed on the same day, even in complex transactions in which there are several intermediary banks in the transmission chain. A funds transfer is a highly efficient substitute for payments made by the delivery of paper instruments. Another characteristic is extremely low cost. A transfer that involves many millions of dollars can be made for a price of a few dollars. Price does not normally vary very much or at all with the amount of the transfer. This system of pricing may not be feasible if the bank is exposed to very large liabilities in connection with the transaction. The pricing system assumes that the price reflects primarily the cost of the mechanical operation performed by the bank, but in fact, a bank may have more or less potential liability with respect to a funds transfer depending upon the amount of the transfer. Risk of loss to banks carrying out a funds transfer may arise from a variety of causes. In some funds transfers, there may be extensions of very large amounts of credit for short periods of time by the banks that carry out a funds transfer. If a payment order is issued to the beneficiary's bank, it is normal for the bank to release funds to the beneficiary immediately. Sometimes, payment to the beneficiary's bank by the bank that issued the order to the beneficiary's bank is delayed until the end of the day. If that payment is not received because of the insolvency of the bank that is obliged to pay, the beneficiary's bank may suffer a loss. There is also risk of loss if a bank fails to execute the payment order of a customer, or if the order is executed late. There also may be an error in the payment order issued by a bank that is executing the payment order of its customer. For example, the error might relate to the amount to be paid or to the identity of the person to be paid. Because the dollar amounts involved in funds transfers are so large, the risk of loss if something goes wrong in a transaction may also be very large. A major policy issue in the drafting of Article 4A is that of determining how risk of loss is to be allocated given the price structure in the industry.

Concept of acceptance and effect of acceptance by the beneficiary's bank.

Rights and obligations under Article 4A arise as the result of "acceptance" of a payment order by the bank to which the order is addressed. Section 4A–209. The effect of acceptance varies depending upon whether the payment order is issued to the beneficiary's bank or to a bank other than the beneficiary's bank. Acceptance by the beneficiary's bank is particularly important because it defines when the beneficiary's bank becomes obligated to the beneficiary to pay the amount of the payment order. Although Article 4A follows convention in using the term "funds transfer" to identify the payment from X to Y that is described above, no money or property right of X is actually transferred to Y. X pays Y by causing Y's bank to become indebted to Y in the amount of the payment. This debt arises when Y's bank accepts the payment order that X's bank issued to Y's bank to execute X's order. If the funds transfer was carried out by use of one or more intermediary banks between X's bank and Y's bank, Y's bank becomes indebted to Y when Y's bank accepts the payment order issued to it by an intermediary bank. The funds transfer is completed when this debt is incurred. Acceptance, the event that determines when the debt of Y's bank to Y arises, occurs (i) when Y's bank pays Y or notifies Y of receipt of the payment order, or (ii) when Y's bank receives payment from the bank that issued a payment order to Y's bank.

The only obligation of the beneficiary's bank that results from acceptance of a payment order is to pay the amount of the order to the beneficiary. No obligation is owed to either the sender of the payment order accepted by the beneficiary's bank or to the originator of the funds transfer. The obligation created by acceptance by the beneficiary's bank is for the benefit of the beneficiary. The purpose of the sender's payment order is to effect payment by the originator to the beneficiary and that purpose is achieved when the beneficiary's bank accepts the payment order. Section 4A–405 states rules for determining when the obligation of the beneficiary's bank to the beneficiary has been paid.

Acceptance by a bank other than the beneficiary's bank.

In the funds transfer described above, what is the obligation of X's bank when it receives X's payment order? Funds transfers by a bank on behalf of its customer are made pursuant to an agreement or arrangement that may or may not be reduced to a formal document signed by the parties. It is probably true that in most cases there is either no express agreement or the agreement addresses only some aspects of

421

the transaction. Substantial risk is involved in funds transfers and a bank may not be willing to give this service to all customers, and may not be willing to offer it to any customer unless certain safeguards against loss such as security procedures are in effect. Funds transfers often involve the giving of credit by the receiving bank to the customer, and that also may involve an agreement. These considerations are reflected in Article 4A by the principle that, in the absence of a contrary agreement, a receiving bank does not incur liability with respect to a payment order until it accepts it. If X and X's bank in the hypothetical case had an agreement that obliged the bank to act on X's payment orders and the bank failed to comply with the agreement, the bank can be held liable for breach of the agreement. But apart from any obligation arising by agreement, the bank does not incur any liability with respect to X's payment order until the bank accepts the order. X's payment order is treated by Article 4A as a request by X to the bank to take action that will cause X's payment order to be carried out. That request can be accepted by X's bank by "executing" X's payment order. Execution occurs when X's bank sends a payment order to Y's bank intended by X's bank to carry out the payment order of X. X's bank could also execute X's payment order by issuing a payment order to an intermediary bank instructing the intermediary bank to instruct Y's bank to make the credit to Y's account. In that case execution and acceptance of X's order occur when the payment order of X's bank is sent to the intermediary bank. When X's bank executes X's payment order the bank is entitled to receive payment from X and may debit an authorized account of X. If X's bank does not execute X's order and the amount of the order is covered by a withdrawable credit balance in X's authorized account, the bank must pay X interest on the money represented by X's order unless X is given prompt notice of rejection of the order. Section 4A–210(b).

Bank error in funds transfers.

If a bank, other than the beneficiary's bank, accepts a payment order, the obligations and liabilities are owed to the originator of the funds transfer. Assume in the example stated above, that X's bank executes X's payment order by issuing a payment order to an intermediary bank that executes the order of X's bank by issuing a payment order to Y's bank. The obligations of X's bank with respect to execution are owed to X. The obligations of the intermediary bank with respect to execution are also owed to X. Section 4A–302 states standards with respect to the time and manner of execution of payment orders. Section 4A–305 states the measure of damages for improper execution. It also states that a receiving bank is liable for damages if it fails to execute a payment order that it was obliged by express agreement to execute. In each case consequential damages are not recoverable unless an express agreement of the receiving bank provides for them. The policy basis for this limitation is discussed in Comment 2 to Section 4A–305.

Error in the consummation of a funds transfer is not uncommon. There may be a discrepancy in the amount that the originator orders to be paid to the beneficiary and the amount that the beneficiary's bank is ordered to pay. For example, if the originator's payment order instructs payment of $100,000 and the payment order of the originator's bank instructs payment of $1,000,000, the originator's bank is entitled to receive only $100,000 from the originator and has the burden of recovering the additional $900,000 paid to the beneficiary by mistake. In some cases the originator's bank or an intermediary bank instructs payment to a beneficiary other than the beneficiary stated in the originator's payment order. If the wrong beneficiary is paid the bank that issued the erroneous payment order is not entitled to receive payment of the payment order that it executed and has the burden of recovering the mistaken payment. The originator is not obliged to pay its payment order. Section 4A–303 and Section 4A–207 state rules for determining the rights and obligations of the various parties to the funds transfer in these cases and in other typical cases in which error is made.

Pursuant to Section 4A–402(c) the originator is excused from the obligation to pay the originator's bank if the funds transfer is not completed, i.e. payment by the originator to the beneficiary is not made. Payment by the originator to the beneficiary occurs when the beneficiary's bank accepts a payment order for the benefit of the beneficiary of the originator's payment order. Section 4A–406. If for any reason that acceptance does not occur, the originator is not required to pay the payment order that it issued or, if it already paid, is entitled to refund of the payment with interest. This "money-back guarantee" is an important protection of the originator of a funds transfer. The same rule applies to any other sender in the funds transfer. Each sender's obligation to pay is excused if the beneficiary's bank does not accept a payment order for the benefit of the beneficiary of that sender's order. There is an important exception to this rule. It is common practice for the originator of a funds transfer to designate the intermediary bank or banks through which the funds transfer is to be routed. The originator's bank is required by Section 4A–302 to follow the instruction of the originator with respect to intermediary banks. If the originator's bank sends a payment order to the intermediary bank designated in the originator's order and the intermediary bank causes the funds transfer to miscarry by failing to execute the payment order or by instructing payment to the wrong beneficiary, the originator's bank is not required to pay its payment order and if it has already paid it is entitled to recover payment from the intermediary bank. This remedy is normally adequate, but if the originator's bank already paid its order and the intermediary bank has suspended payments or is not permitted by law to refund payment, the originator's bank will suffer a loss. Since the originator required the originator's bank to use the failed intermediary bank, Section 4A–402(e) provides that in this case the originator is obliged to pay its payment order and has a claim against the intermediary bank for the amount of the order. The same principle applies to any other sender that designates a subsequent intermediary bank.

Unauthorized payment orders.

An important issue addressed in Section 4A–202 and Section 4A–203 is how the risk of loss from unauthorized payment orders is to be allocated. In a large percentage of cases, the payment order of the originator of the funds transfer is transmitted electronically to the originator's bank. In these cases it may not be possible for the bank to know whether the electronic message has been authorized by its customer. To ensure that no unauthorized person is transmitting messages to the bank, the normal practice is to establish security procedures that usually involve the use of codes or identifying numbers or words. If the bank accepts a payment order that purports to be that of its customer after verifying its authenticity by complying with a security procedure agreed to by the customer and the bank, the customer is bound to pay the order even if it was not authorized. But there is an important limitation on this rule. The bank is entitled to payment in the case of an unauthorized order only if the court finds that the security procedure was a commercially reasonable method of providing security against unauthorized payment orders. The customer can also avoid liability if it can prove that the unauthorized order was not initiated by an employee or other agent of the customer having access to confidential security information or by a person who obtained that information from a source controlled by the customer. The policy issues are discussed in the comments following Section 4A–203. If the bank accepts an unauthorized payment order without verifying it in compliance with a security procedure, the loss falls on the bank.

Security procedures are also important in cases of error in the transmission of payment orders. There may be an error by the sender in the amount of the order, or a sender may transmit a payment order and then erroneously transmit a duplicate of the order. Normally, the sender is bound by the payment order even if it is issued by mistake. But in some cases an error of this kind can be detected by a security procedure. Although the receiving bank is not obliged to provide a security procedure for the detection of error, if such a procedure is agreed to by the bank Section 4A–205 provides that if the error is not detected because the receiving bank does not comply with the procedure, any resulting loss is borne by the bank failing to comply with the security procedure.

Insolvency losses.

Some payment orders do not involve the granting of credit to the sender by the receiving bank. In those cases, the receiving bank accepts the sender's order at the same time the bank receives payment of the order. This is true of a transfer of funds by Fedwire or of cases in which the receiving bank can debit a funded account of the sender. But in some cases the granting of credit is the norm. This is true of a payment order over CHIPS. In a CHIPS transaction the receiving bank usually will accept the order before receiving payment from the sending bank. Payment is delayed until the end of the day when settlement is made through the Federal Reserve System. If the receiving bank is an intermediary bank, it will accept by issuing a payment order to another bank and the intermediary bank is obliged to pay that payment order. If the receiving bank is the beneficiary's bank, the bank usually will accept by releasing funds to the beneficiary before the bank has received payment. If a sending bank suspends payments before settling its liabilities at the end of the day, the financial stability of banks that are net creditors of the insolvent bank may also be put into jeopardy, because the dollar volume of funds transfers between the banks may be extremely large. With respect to two banks that are dealing with each other in a series of transactions in which each bank is sometimes a receiving bank and sometimes a sender, the risk of insolvency can be managed if amounts payable as a sender and amounts receivable as a receiving bank are roughly equal. But if these amounts are significantly out of balance, a net creditor bank may have a very significant credit risk during the day before settlement occurs. The Federal Reserve System and the banking community are greatly concerned with this risk, and various measures have been instituted to reduce this credit exposure. Article 4A also addresses this problem. A receiving bank can always avoid this risk by delaying acceptance of a payment order until after the bank has received payment. For example, if the beneficiary's bank credits the beneficiary's account it can avoid acceptance by not notifying the beneficiary of the receipt of the order or by notifying the beneficiary that the credit may not be withdrawn until the beneficiary's bank receives payment. But if the beneficiary's bank releases funds to the beneficiary before receiving settlement, the result in a funds transfer other than a transfer by means of an automated clearing house or similar provisional settlement system is that the beneficiary's bank may not recover the funds if it fails to receive settlement. This rule encourages the banking system to impose credit limitations on banks that issue payment orders. These limitations are already in effect. CHIPS has also proposed a loss-sharing plan to be adopted for implementation in the second half of 1990 under which CHIPS participants will be required to provide funds necessary to complete settlement of the obligations of one or more participants that are unable to meet settlement obligations. Under this plan, it will be a virtual certainty that there will be settlement on CHIPS in the event of failure by a single bank. Section 4A–403(b) and (c) are also addressed to reducing risks of insolvency. Under these provisions the amount owed by a failed bank with respect to payment orders it issued is the net amount owing after setting off amounts owed to the failed bank with respect to payment orders it received. This rule allows credit exposure to be managed by limitations on the net debit position of a bank.

International transfers.

The major international legal document dealing with the subject of electronic funds transfers is the Model Law on International Credit Transfers adopted in 1992 by the United Nations Commission on International Trade Law. It covers basically the same type of transaction as does Article 4A, although it requires the funds transferred to have an international component. The Model Law and Article 4A basically live together in harmony, but to the extent there are differences they must be recognized and, to the extent possible, avoided or adjusted by agreement. See PEB Commentary No. 13, dated February 16, 1994.

PART 1

SUBJECT MATTER AND DEFINITIONS

§ 4A–101. Short Title.

This Article may be cited as Uniform Commercial Code—Funds Transfers.

§ 4A–102. Subject Matter.

Except as otherwise provided in Section 4A–108, this Article applies to funds transfers defined in Section 4A–104.

Official Comment

Article 4A governs a specialized method of payment referred to in the Article as a funds transfer but also commonly referred to in the commercial community as a wholesale wire transfer. A funds transfer is made by means of one or more payment orders. The scope of Article 4A is determined by the definitions of "payment order" and "funds transfer" found in Section 4A–103 and Section 4A–104.

The funds transfer governed by Article 4A is in large part a product of recent and developing technological changes. Before this Article was drafted there was no comprehensive body of law—statutory or judicial—that defined the juridical nature of a funds transfer or the rights and obligations flowing from payment orders. Judicial authority with respect to funds transfers is sparse, undeveloped and not uniform. Judges have had to resolve disputes by referring to general principles of common law or equity, or they have sought guidance in statutes such as Article 4 which are applicable to other payment methods. But attempts to define rights and obligations in funds transfers by general principles or by analogy to rights and obligations in negotiable instrument law or the law of check collection have not been satisfactory.

In the drafting of Article 4A, a deliberate decision was made to write on a clean slate and to treat a funds transfer as a unique method of payment to be governed by unique rules that address the particular issues raised by this method of payment. A deliberate decision was also made to use precise and detailed rules to assign responsibility, define behavioral norms, allocate risks and establish limits on liability, rather than to rely on broadly stated, flexible principles. In the drafting of these rules, a critical consideration was that the various parties to funds transfers need to be able to predict risk with certainty, to insure against risk, to adjust operational and security procedures, and to price funds transfer services appropriately. This consideration is particularly important given the very large amounts of money that are involved in funds transfers.

Funds transfers involve competing interests—those of the banks that provide funds transfer services and the commercial and financial organizations that use the services, as well as the public interest. These competing interests were represented in the drafting process and they were thoroughly considered. The rules that emerged represent a careful and delicate balancing of those interests and are intended to be the exclusive means of determining the rights, duties and liabilities of the affected parties in any situation covered by particular provisions of the Article. Consequently, resort to principles of law or equity outside of Article 4A is not appropriate to create rights, duties and liabilities inconsistent with those stated in this Article.

§ 4A–103. Payment Order—Definitions.

(a)   In this Article:

(1)   "Payment order" means an instruction of a sender to a receiving bank, transmitted orally, electronically, or in writing, to pay, or to cause another bank to pay, a fixed or determinable amount of money to a beneficiary if:

(i)   the instruction does not state a condition to payment to the beneficiary other than time of payment,

(ii)   the receiving bank is to be reimbursed by debiting an account of, or otherwise receiving payment from, the sender, and

(iii)   the instruction is transmitted by the sender directly to the receiving bank or to an agent, funds-transfer system, or communication system for transmittal to the receiving bank.

(2)   "Beneficiary" means the person to be paid by the beneficiary's bank.

(3)   "Beneficiary's bank" means the bank identified in a payment order in which an account of the beneficiary is to be credited pursuant to the order or which otherwise is to make payment to the beneficiary if the order does not provide for payment to an account.

(4)   "Receiving bank" means the bank to which the sender's instruction is addressed.

(5)   "Sender" means the person giving the instruction to the receiving bank.

(b)   If an instruction complying with subsection (a)(1) is to make more than one payment to a beneficiary, the instruction is a separate payment order with respect to each payment.

(c)   A payment order is issued when it is sent to the receiving bank.

Official Comment

This section is discussed in the Comment following Section 4A–104.

§ 4A–104. Funds Transfer—Definitions.

In this Article:

(a)   "Funds transfer" means the series of transactions, beginning with the originator's payment order, made for the purpose of making payment to the beneficiary of the order. The term includes any payment order issued by the originator's bank or an intermediary bank intended to carry out the originator's payment order. A funds transfer is completed by acceptance by the beneficiary's bank of a payment order for the benefit of the beneficiary of the originator's payment order.

(b) "Intermediary bank" means a receiving bank other than the originator's bank or the beneficiary's bank.

(c) "Originator" means the sender of the first payment order in a funds transfer.

(d) "Originator's bank" means (i) the receiving bank to which the payment order of the originator is issued if the originator is not a bank, or (ii) the originator if the originator is a bank.

Official Comment

1.   Article 4A governs a method of payment in which the person making payment (the "originator") directly transmits an instruction to a bank either to make payment to the person receiving payment (the "beneficiary") or to instruct some other bank to make payment to the beneficiary. The payment from the originator to the beneficiary occurs when the bank that is to pay the beneficiary becomes obligated to pay the beneficiary. There are two basic definitions: "Payment order" stated in Section 4A–103 and "Funds transfer" stated in Section 4A–104. These definitions, other related definitions, and the scope of Article 4A can best be understood in the context of specific fact situations. Consider the following cases:

Case #1.   X, which has an account in Bank A, instructs that bank to pay $1,000,000 to Y's account in Bank A. Bank A carries out X's instruction by making a credit of $1,000,000 to Y's account and notifying Y that the credit is available for immediate withdrawal. The instruction by X to Bank A is a "payment order" which was issued when it was sent to Bank A. Section 4A–103(a)(1) and (c). X is the "sender" of the payment order and Bank A is the "receiving bank." Section 4A–103(a)(5) and (a)(4). Y is the "beneficiary" of the payment order and Bank A is the "beneficiary's bank." Section 4A–103(a)(2) and (a)(3). When Bank A notified Y of receipt of the payment order, Bank A "accepted" the payment order. Section 4A–209(b)(1). When Bank A accepted the order it incurred an obligation to Y to pay the amount of the order. Section 4A–404(a). When Bank A accepted X's order, X incurred an obligation to pay Bank A the amount of the order. Section 4A–402(b). Payment from X to Bank A would normally be made by a debit to X's account in Bank A. Section 4A–403(a)(3). At the time Bank A incurred the obligation to pay Y, payment of $1,000,000 by X to Y was also made. Section 4A–406(a). Bank A paid Y when it gave notice to Y of a withdrawable credit of $1,000,000 to Y's account. Section 4A–405(a). The overall transaction, which comprises the acts of X and Bank A, in which the payment by X to Y is accomplished is referred to as the "funds transfer." Section 4A–104(a). In this case only one payment order was involved in the funds transfer. A one-payment-order funds transfer is usually referred to as a "book transfer" because the payment is accomplished by the receiving bank's debiting the account of the sender and crediting the account of the beneficiary in the same bank. X, in addition to being the sender of the payment order to Bank A, is the "originator" of the funds transfer. Section 4A–104(c). Bank A is the "originator's bank" in the funds transfer as well as the beneficiary's bank. Section 4A–104(d).

Case #2.   Assume the same facts as in Case #1 except that X instructs Bank A to pay $1,000,000 to Y's account in Bank B. With respect to this payment order, X is the sender, Y is the beneficiary, and Bank A is the receiving bank. Bank A carries out X's order by instructing Bank B to pay $1,000,000 to Y's account. This instruction is a payment order in which Bank A is the sender, Bank B is the receiving bank, and Y is the beneficiary. When Bank A issued its payment order to Bank B, Bank A "executed" X's order. Section 4A–301(a). In the funds transfer, X is the originator, Bank A is the originator's bank, and Bank B is the beneficiary's bank. When Bank A executed X's order, X incurred an obligation to pay Bank A the amount of the order. Section 4A–402(c). When Bank B accepts the payment order issued to it by Bank A, Bank B incurs an obligation to Y to pay the amount of the order (Section 4A–404(a)) and Bank A incurs an obligation to pay Bank B. Section 4A–402(b). Acceptance by Bank B also results in payment of $1,000,000 by X to Y. Section 4A–406(a). In this case two payment orders are involved in the funds transfer.

Case #3.   Assume the same facts as in Case #2 except that Bank A does not execute X's payment order by issuing a payment order to Bank B. One bank will not normally act to carry out a funds transfer for another bank unless there is a preexisting arrangement between the banks for transmittal of payment orders and settlement of accounts. For example, if Bank B is a foreign bank with which Bank A has no relationship, Bank A can utilize a bank that is a correspondent of both Bank A and Bank B. Assume Bank A issues a payment order to Bank C to pay $1,000,000 to Y's account in Bank B. With respect to this order, Bank A is the sender, Bank C is the receiving bank, and Y is the beneficiary. Bank C will execute the payment order of Bank A by issuing a payment order to Bank B to pay $1,000,000 to Y's account in Bank B. With respect to Bank C's payment order, Bank C is the sender, Bank B is the receiving bank, and Y is the beneficiary. Payment of $1,000,000 by X to Y occurs when Bank B accepts the payment order issued to it by Bank C. In this case the funds transfer involves three payment orders. In the funds transfer, X is the originator, Bank A is the originator's bank, Bank B is the beneficiary's bank, and

Bank C is an "intermediary bank." Section 4A–104(b). In some cases there may be more than one intermediary bank, and in those cases each intermediary bank is treated like Bank C in Case #3.

As the three cases demonstrate, a payment under Article 4A involves an overall transaction, the funds transfer, in which the originator, X, is making payment to the beneficiary, Y, but the funds transfer may encompass a series of payment orders that are issued in order to effect the payment initiated by the originator's payment order.

In some cases the originator and the beneficiary may be the same person. This will occur, for example, when a corporation orders a bank to transfer funds from an account of the corporation in that bank to another account of the corporation in that bank or in some other bank. In some funds transfers the first bank to issue a payment order is a bank that is executing a payment order of a customer that is not a bank. In this case the customer is the originator. In other cases, the first bank to issue a payment order is not acting for a customer, but is making a payment for its own account. In that event the first bank to issue a payment order is the originator as well as the originator's bank.

2. "Payment order" is defined in Section 4A–103(a)(1) as an instruction to a bank to pay, or to cause another bank to pay, a fixed or determinable amount of money. The bank to which the instruction is addressed is known as the "receiving bank." Section 4A–103(a)(4). "Bank" is defined in Section 4A–105(a)(2). The effect of this definition is to limit Article 4A to payments made through the banking system. A transfer of funds made by an entity outside the banking system is excluded. A transfer of funds through an entity other than a bank is usually a consumer transaction involving relatively small amounts of money and a single contract carried out by transfers of cash or a cash equivalent such as a check. Typically, the transferor delivers cash or a check to the company making the transfer, which agrees to pay a like amount to a person designated by the transferor. Transactions covered by Article 4A typically involve very large amounts of money in which several transactions involving several banks may be necessary to carry out the payment. Payments are normally made by debits or credits to bank accounts. Originators and beneficiaries are almost always business organizations and the transfers are usually made to pay obligations. Moreover, these transactions are frequently done on the basis of very short-term credit granted by the receiving bank to the sender of the payment order. Wholesale wire transfers involve policy questions that are distinct from those involved in consumer-based transactions by nonbanks.

3. Further limitations on the scope of Article 4A are found in the three requirements found in subparagraphs (i), (ii), and (iii) of Section 4A–103(a)(1). Subparagraph (i) states that the instruction to pay is a payment order only if it "does not state a condition to payment to the beneficiary other than time of payment." An instruction to pay a beneficiary sometimes is subject to a requirement that the beneficiary perform some act such as delivery of documents. For example, a New York bank may have issued a letter of credit in favor of X, a California seller of goods to be shipped to the New York bank's customer in New York. The terms of the letter of credit provide for payment to X if documents are presented to prove shipment of the goods. Instead of providing for presentment of the documents to the New York bank, the letter of credit states that they may be presented to a California bank that acts as an agent for payment. The New York bank sends an instruction to the California bank to pay X upon presentation of the required documents. The instruction is not covered by Article 4A because payment to the beneficiary is conditional upon receipt of shipping documents. The function of banks in a funds transfer under Article 4A is comparable to the role of banks in the collection and payment of checks in that it is essentially mechanical in nature. The low price and high speed that characterize funds transfers reflect this fact. Conditions to payment by the California bank other than time of payment impose responsibilities on that bank that go beyond those in Article 4A funds transfers. Although the payment by the New York bank to X under the letter of credit is not covered by Article 4A, if X is paid by the California bank, payment of the obligation of the New York bank to reimburse the California bank could be made by an Article 4A funds transfer. In such a case there is a distinction between the payment by the New York bank to X under the letter of credit and the payment by the New York bank to the California bank. For example, if the New York bank pays its reimbursement obligation to the California bank by a Fedwire naming the California bank as beneficiary (see Comment 1 to Section 4A–107), payment is made to the California bank rather than to X. That payment is governed by Article 4A and it could be made either before or after payment by the California bank to X. The payment by the New York bank to X under the letter of credit is not governed by Article 4A and it occurs when the California bank, as agent of the New York bank, pays X. No payment order was involved in that transaction. In this example, if the New York bank had erroneously sent an instruction to the California bank unconditionally instructing payment to X, the instruction would have been an Article 4A payment order. If the payment order was accepted (Section 4A–209(b)) by the California bank, a payment by the New York bank to X would have resulted (Section 4A–406(a)). But Article 4A would not prevent recovery of funds from X on the basis that X was not entitled to retain the funds under the law of mistake and restitution, letter of credit law or other applicable law.

4.   Transfers of funds made through the banking system are commonly referred to as either "credit" transfers or "debit" transfers. In a credit transfer the instruction to pay is given by the person making payment. In a debit transfer the instruction to pay is given by the person receiving payment. The purpose of subparagraph (ii) of subsection (a)(1) of Section 4A–103 is to include credit transfers in Article 4A and to exclude debit transfers. All of the instructions to pay in the three cases described in Comment 1 fall within subparagraph (ii). Take Case #2 as an example. With respect to X's instruction given to Bank A, Bank A will be reimbursed by debiting X's account or otherwise receiving payment from X. With respect to Bank A's instruction to Bank B, Bank B will be reimbursed by receiving payment from Bank A. In a debit transfer, a creditor, pursuant to authority from the debtor, is enabled to draw on the debtor's bank account by issuing an instruction to pay to the debtor's bank. If the debtor's bank pays, it will be reimbursed by the debtor rather than by the person giving the instruction. For example, the holder of an insurance policy may pay premiums by authorizing the insurance company to order the policyholder's bank to pay the insurance company. The order to pay may be in the form of a draft covered by Article 3, or it might be an instruction to pay that is not an instrument under that Article. The bank receives reimbursement by debiting the policyholder's account. Or, a subsidiary corporation may make payments to its parent by authorizing the parent to order the subsidiary's bank to pay the parent from the subsidiary's account. These transactions are not covered by Article 4A because subparagraph (2) is not satisfied. Article 4A is limited to transactions in which the account to be debited by the receiving bank is that of the person in whose name the instruction is given.

If the beneficiary of a funds transfer is the originator of the transfer, the transfer is governed by Article 4A if it is a credit transfer in form. If it is in the form of a debit transfer it is not governed by Article 4A. For example, Corporation has accounts in Bank A and Bank B. Corporation instructs Bank A to pay to Corporation's account in Bank B. The funds transfer is governed by Article 4A. Sometimes, Corporation will authorize Bank B to draw on Corporation's account in Bank A for the purpose of transferring funds into Corporation's account in Bank B. If Corporation also makes an agreement with Bank A under which Bank A is authorized to follow instructions of Bank B, as agent of Corporation, to transfer funds from Customer's account in Bank A, the instruction of Bank B is a payment order of Customer and is governed by Article 4A. This kind of transaction is known in the wire-transfer business as a "drawdown transfer." If Corporation does not make such an agreement with Bank A and Bank B instructs Bank A to make the transfer, the order is in form a debit transfer and is not governed by Article 4A. These debit transfers are normally ACH transactions in which Bank A relies on Bank B's warranties pursuant to ACH rules, including the warranty that the transfer is authorized.

5.   The principal effect of subparagraph (iii) of subsection (a) of Section 4A–103 is to exclude from Article 4A payments made by check or credit card. In those cases the instruction of the debtor to the bank on which the check is drawn or to which the credit card slip is to be presented is contained in the check or credit card slip signed by the debtor. The instruction is not transmitted by the debtor directly to the debtor's bank. Rather, the instruction is delivered or otherwise transmitted by the debtor to the creditor who then presents it to the bank either directly or through bank collection channels. These payments are governed by Articles 3 and 4 and federal law. There are, however, limited instances in which the paper on which a check is printed can be used as the means of transmitting a payment order that is covered by Article 4A. Assume that Originator instructs Originator's Bank to pay $10,000 to the account of Beneficiary in Beneficiary's Bank. Since the amount of Originator's payment order is small, if Originator's Bank and Beneficiary's Bank do not have an account relationship, Originator's Bank may execute Originator's order by issuing a teller's check payable to Beneficiary's Bank for $10,000 along with instructions to credit Beneficiary's account in that amount. The instruction to Beneficiary's Bank to credit Beneficiary's account is a payment order. The check is the means by which Originator's Bank pays its obligation as sender of the payment order. The instruction of Originator's Bank to Beneficiary's Bank might be given in a letter accompanying the check or it may be written on the check itself. In either case the instruction to Beneficiary's Bank is a payment order but the check itself (which is an order to pay addressed to the drawee rather than to Beneficiary's Bank) is an instrument under Article 3 and is not a payment order. The check can be both the means by which Originator's Bank pays its obligation under § 4A–402(b) to Beneficiary's Bank and the means by which the instruction to Beneficiary's Bank is transmitted.

6.   Most payments covered by Article 4A are commonly referred to as wire transfers and usually involve some kind of electronic transmission, but the applicability of Article 4A does not depend upon the means used to transmit the instruction of the sender. Transmission may be by letter or other written communication, oral communication or electronic communication. An oral communication is normally given by telephone. Frequently the message is recorded by the receiving bank to provide evidence of the transaction, but apart from problems of proof there is no need to record the oral instruction. Transmission of an instruction may be a direct communication between the sender and the receiving bank or through an intermediary such as an agent of the sender, a

communication system such as international cable, or a funds transfer system such as CHIPS, SWIFT or an automated clearing house.

§ 4A–105. Other Definitions.

(a) In this Article:

(1) "Authorized account" means a deposit account of a customer in a bank designated by the customer as a source of payment of payment orders issued by the customer to the bank. If a customer does not so designate an account, any account of the customer is an authorized account if payment of a payment order from that account is not inconsistent with a restriction on the use of that account.

(2) "Bank" means a person engaged in the business of banking and includes a savings bank, savings and loan association, credit union, and trust company. A branch or separate office of a bank is a separate bank for purposes of this Article.

(3) "Customer" means a person, including a bank, having an account with a bank or from whom a bank has agreed to receive payment orders.

(4) "Funds-transfer business day" of a receiving bank means the part of a day during which the receiving bank is open for the receipt, processing, and transmittal of payment orders and cancellations and amendments of payment orders.

(5) "Funds-transfer system" means a wire transfer network, automated clearing house, or other communication system of a clearing house or other association of banks through which a payment order by a bank may be transmitted to the bank to which the order is addressed.

(6) [reserved] ["Good faith" means honesty in fact and the observance of reasonable commercial standards of fair dealing.]*

(7) "Prove" with respect to a fact means to meet the burden of establishing the fact (Section 1–201(b)(8)).

(b) Other definitions applying to this Article and the sections in which they appear are:

"Acceptance" Section 4A–209
"Beneficiary" Section 4A–103
"Beneficiary's bank" Section 4A–103
"Executed" Section 4A–301
"Execution date" Section 4A–301
"Funds transfer" Section 4A–104
"Funds-transfer system rule" Section 4A–501
"Intermediary bank" Section 4A–104
"Originator" Section 4A–104
"Originator's bank" Section 4A–104
"Payment by beneficiary's bank to beneficiary" Section 4A–405
"Payment by originator to beneficiary" Section 4A–406
"Payment by sender to receiving bank" Section 4A–403
"Payment date" Section 4A–401
"Payment order" Section 4A–103
"Receiving bank" Section 4A–103
"Security procedure" Section 4A–201
"Sender" Section 4A–103

(c) The following definitions in Article 4 apply to this Article:

"Clearing house" Section 4–104
"Item" Section 4–104

---

* Note from West Advisory Panel: This subsection will be deleted if the jurisdiction adopts the definition of good faith in revised Article 1.

"Suspends payments" Section 4–104

(d)   In addition Article 1 contains general definitions and principles of construction and interpretation applicable throughout this Article.

As amended in 2001.

Official Comment

1.   The definition of "bank" in subsection (a)(2) includes some institutions that are not commercial banks. The definition reflects the fact that many financial institutions now perform functions previously restricted to commercial banks, including acting on behalf of customers in funds transfers. Since many funds transfers involve payment orders to or from foreign countries the definition also covers foreign banks. The definition also includes Federal Reserve Banks. Funds transfers carried out by Federal Reserve Banks are described in Comments 1 and 2 to Section 4A–107.

2.   Funds transfer business is frequently transacted by banks outside of general banking hours. Thus, the definition of banking day in Section 4–104(1)(c) cannot be used to describe when a bank is open for funds transfer business. Subsection (a)(4) defines a new term, "funds transfer business day," which is applicable to Article 4A. The definition states, "is open for the receipt, processing, and transmittal of payment orders and cancellations and amendments of payment orders." In some cases it is possible to electronically transmit payment orders and other communications to a receiving bank at any time. If the receiving bank is not open for the processing of an order when it is received, the communication is stored in the receiving bank's computer for retrieval when the receiving bank is open for processing. The use of the conjunctive makes clear that the defined term is limited to the period during which all functions of the receiving bank can be performed, i.e., receipt, processing, and transmittal of payment orders, cancellations and amendments.

3.   Subsection (a)(5) defines "funds transfer system." The term includes a system such as CHIPS which provides for transmission of a payment order as well as settlement of the obligation of the sender to pay the order. It also includes automated clearing houses, operated by a clearing house or other association of banks, which process and transmit payment orders of banks to other banks. In addition the term includes organizations that provide only transmission services such as SWIFT. The definition also includes the wire transfer network and automated clearing houses of Federal Reserve Banks. Systems of the Federal Reserve Banks, however, are treated differently from systems of other associations of banks. Funds transfer systems other than systems of the Federal Reserve Banks are treated in Article 4A as a means of communication of payment orders between participating banks. Section 4A–206. The Comment to that section and the Comment to Section 4A–107 explain how Federal Reserve Banks function under Article 4A. Funds transfer systems are also able to promulgate rules binding on participating banks that, under Section 4A–501, may supplement or in some cases may even override provisions of Article 4A.

4.   Subsection (d) incorporates definitions stated in Article 1 as well as principles of construction and interpretation stated in that Article. Included is Section 1–103. The last paragraph of the Comment to Section 4A–102 is addressed to the issue of the extent to which general principles of law and equity should apply to situations covered by provisions of Article 4A.

§ 4A–106. Time Payment Order Is Received.

(a)   The time of receipt of a payment order or communication cancelling or amending a payment order is determined by the rules applicable to receipt of a notice stated in Section 1–202. A receiving bank may fix a cut-off time or times on a funds-transfer business day for the receipt and processing of payment orders and communications cancelling or amending payment orders. Different cut-off times may apply to payment orders, cancellations, or amendments, or to different categories of payment orders, cancellations, or amendments. A cut-off time may apply to senders generally or different cut-off times may apply to different senders or categories of payment orders. If a payment order or communication cancelling or amending a payment order is received after the close of a funds-transfer business day or after the appropriate cut-off time on a funds-transfer business day, the receiving bank may treat the payment order or communication as received at the opening of the next funds-transfer business day.

(b)   If this Article refers to an execution date or payment date or states a day on which a receiving bank is required to take action, and the date or day does not fall on a funds-transfer business day, the next day that is a funds-transfer business day is treated as the date or day stated, unless the contrary is stated in this Article.

As amended in 2001.

Official Comment

The time that a payment order is received by a receiving bank usually defines the payment date or the execution date of a payment order. Section 4A–401 and Section 4A–301. The time of receipt of a payment order, or communication cancelling or amending a payment order is defined in subsection (a) by reference to the rules stated in Section 1–202. Thus, time of receipt is determined by the same rules that determine when a notice is received. Time of receipt, however, may be altered by a cut-off time.

As amended in 2001.

§ 4A–107. Federal Reserve Regulations and Operating Circulars.

Regulations of the Board of Governors of the Federal Reserve System and operating circulars of the Federal Reserve Banks supersede any inconsistent provision of this Article to the extent of the inconsistency.

Official Comment

1.   Funds transfers under Article 4A may be made, in whole or in part, by payment orders through a Federal Reserve Bank in what is usually referred to as a transfer by Fedwire. If Bank A, which has an account in Federal Reserve Bank X, wants to pay $1,000,000 to Bank B, which has an account in Federal Reserve Bank Y, Bank A can issue an instruction to Reserve Bank X requesting a debit of $1,000,000 to Bank A's Reserve account and an equal credit to Bank B's Reserve account. Reserve Bank X will debit Bank A's account and will credit the account of Reserve Bank Y. Reserve Bank X will issue an instruction to Reserve Bank Y requesting a debit of $1,000,000 to the account of Reserve Bank X and an equal credit to Bank B's account in Reserve Bank Y. Reserve Bank Y will make the requested debit and credit and will give Bank B an advice of credit. The definition of "bank" in Section 4A–105(a)(2) includes both Reserve Bank X and Reserve Bank Y. Bank A's instruction to Reserve Bank X to pay money to Bank B is a payment order under Section 4A–103(a)(1). Bank A is the sender and Reserve Bank X is the receiving bank. Bank B is the beneficiary of Bank A's order and of the funds transfer. Bank A is the originator of the funds transfer and is also the originator's bank. Section 4A–104(c) and (d). Reserve Bank X, an intermediary bank under Section 4A–104(b), executes Bank A's order by sending a payment order to Reserve Bank Y instructing that bank to credit the Federal Reserve account of Bank B. Reserve Bank Y is the beneficiary's bank.

Suppose the transfer of funds from Bank A to Bank B is part of a larger transaction in which Originator, a customer of Bank A, wants to pay Beneficiary, a customer of Bank B. Originator issues a payment order to Bank A to pay $1,000,000 to the account of Beneficiary in Bank B. Bank A may execute Originator's order by means of Fedwire which simultaneously transfers $1,000,000 from Bank A to Bank B and carries a message instructing Bank B to pay $1,000,000 to the account of Y. The Fedwire transfer is carried out as described in the previous paragraph, except that the beneficiary of the funds transfer is Beneficiary rather than Bank B. Reserve Bank X and Reserve Bank Y are intermediary banks. When Reserve Bank Y advises Bank B of the credit to its Federal Reserve account it will also instruct Bank B to pay to the account of Beneficiary. The instruction is a payment order to Bank B which is the beneficiary's bank. When Reserve Bank Y advises Bank B of the credit to its Federal Reserve account Bank B receives payment of the payment order issued to it by Reserve Bank Y. Section 4A–403(a)(1). The payment order is automatically accepted by Bank B at the time it receives the payment order of Reserve Bank Y. Section 4A–209(b)(2). At the time of acceptance by Bank B payment by Originator to Beneficiary also occurs. Thus, in a Fedwire transfer, payment to the beneficiary's bank, acceptance by the beneficiary's bank and payment by the originator to the beneficiary all occur simultaneously by operation of law at the time the payment order to the beneficiary's bank is received.

If Originator orders payment to the account of Beneficiary in Bank C rather than Bank B, the analysis is somewhat modified. Bank A may not have any relationship with Bank C and may not be able to make payment directly to Bank C. In that case, Bank A could send a Fedwire instructing Bank B to instruct Bank C to pay Beneficiary. The analysis is the same as the previous case except that Bank B is an intermediary bank and Bank C is the beneficiary's bank.

2.   A funds transfer can also be made through a Federal Reserve Bank in an automated clearing house transaction. In a typical case, Originator instructs Originator's Bank to pay to the account of Beneficiary in

Beneficiary's Bank. Originator's instruction to pay a particular beneficiary is transmitted to Originator's Bank along with many other instructions for payment to other beneficiaries by many different beneficiary's banks. All of these instructions are contained in a magnetic tape or other electronic device. Transmission of instructions to the various beneficiary's banks requires that Originator's instructions be processed and repackaged with instructions of other originators so that all instructions to a particular beneficiary's bank are transmitted together to that bank. The repackaging is done in processing centers usually referred to as automated clearing houses. Automated clearing houses are operated either by Federal Reserve Banks or by other associations of banks. If Originator's Bank chooses to execute Originator's instructions by transmitting them to a Federal Reserve Bank for processing by the Federal Reserve Bank, the transmission to the Federal Reserve Bank results in the issuance of payment orders by Originator's Bank to the Federal Reserve Bank, which is an intermediary bank. Processing by the Federal Reserve Bank will result in the issuance of payment orders by the Federal Reserve Bank to Beneficiary's Bank as well as payment orders to other beneficiary's banks making payments to carry out Originator's instructions.

3.   Although the terms of Article 4A apply to funds transfers involving Federal Reserve Banks, federal preemption would make ineffective any Article 4A provision that conflicts with federal law. The payments activities of the Federal Reserve Banks are governed by regulations of the Federal Reserve Board and by operating circulars issued by the Reserve Banks themselves. In some instances, the operating circulars are issued pursuant to a Federal Reserve Board regulation. In other cases, the Reserve Bank issues the operating circular under its own authority under the Federal Reserve Act, subject to review by the Federal Reserve Board. Section 4A–107 states that Federal Reserve Board regulations and operating circulars of the Federal Reserve Banks supersede any inconsistent provision of Article 4A to the extent of the inconsistency. Federal Reserve Board regulations, being valid exercises of regulatory authority pursuant to a federal statute, take precedence over state law if there is an inconsistency. *Childs v. Federal Reserve Bank of Dallas,* 719 F.2d 812 (5th Cir.1983), reh. den. 724 F.2d 127 (5th Cir.1984). Section 4A–107 treats operating circulars as having the same effect whether issued under the Reserve Bank's own authority or under a Federal Reserve Board regulation.

§ 4A–108.   Relationship to Electronic Fund Transfer Act.

(a)   Except as provided in subsection (b), this Article does not apply to a funds transfer any part of which is governed by the Electronic Fund Transfer Act of 1978 (Title XX, Public Law 95–630, 92 Stat. 3728, 15 U.S.C. sec. 1693 et. seq.) as amended from time to time.

(b)   This Article applies to a funds transfer that is a remittance transfer as defined in the Electronic Fund Transfer Act (15 U.S.C. sec. 1693o–1) as amended from time to time, unless the remittance transfer is an electronic fund transfer as defined in the Electronic Fund Transfer Act (15 U.S.C. sec. 1693a) as amended from time to time.

(c)   In a funds transfer to which this Article applies, in the event of an inconsistency between an applicable provision of this Article and an applicable provision of the Electronic Fund Transfer Act, the provision of the Electronic Fund Transfer Act governs to the extent of the inconsistency.

As amended in 2013.

Official Comment

1.   The Electronic Fund Transfer Act (EFTA), implemented by Regulation E, 12 C.F.R. Part 1005, is a federal statute that covers aspects of electronic fund transfers involving consumers. EFTA also governs remittance transfers, defined in 15 U.S.C. sec. 1693o–1, which involve transfers of funds through electronic means by consumers to recipients in another country through persons or financial institutions that provide such transfers in the normal course of their business. Not all "remittance transfers" as defined in EFTA, however, qualify as "electronic fund transfers" as defined under the EFTA, 15 U.S.C. sec. 1693a(7). While Section 4A–108(a) broadly states that Article 4A does not apply to any funds transfer that is governed in any part by EFTA, subsection (b) provides an exception. The purpose of Section 4A–108(b) is to allow this Article to apply to a funds transfer as defined in Section 4A–104(a) (see Section 4A–102) that also is a remittance transfer as defined in EFTA, so long as that remittance transfer is not an electronic fund transfer as defined in EFTA. If the resulting application of this Article to an EFTA-defined "remittance transfer" that is not an EFTA-defined "electronic fund transfer" creates an inconsistency between an applicable provision of this Article and an applicable provision of EFTA, then, as a matter of federal supremacy, the provision of EFTA governs to the extent of the inconsistency. Section 4A–108(c). Of course, in the case of a funds transfer that also relates to another jurisdiction, the forum's conflict of

laws principles determine whether it will apply the law in effect in this State (including this Article and EFTA) or the law of another jurisdiction to all or any part of the funds transfer. See Section 4A–507.

2.   The following cases illustrate the relationship between EFTA and this Article pursuant to Section 4A–108.

Case #1. A commercial customer of Bank A sends a payment order to Bank A, instructing Bank A to transfer funds from its account at Bank A to the account of a consumer at Bank B. The funds transfer is executed by a payment order from Bank A to an intermediary bank and is executed by the intermediary bank by means of an automated clearinghouse credit entry to the consumer's account at Bank B (the beneficiary's bank). The transfer into the consumer's account is an "electronic fund transfer" as defined in 15 U.S.C. sec. 1693a(7). Pursuant to Section 4A–108(a), Article 4A does not apply to any part of the funds transfer because EFTA governs part of the funds transfer. The transfer is not a "remittance transfer" as defined in 15 U.S.C. sec. 1693o–1 because the originator is not a consumer customer. Thus Section 4A–108(b) does not apply.

A court might, however, apply appropriate principles from Article 4A by analogy in analyzing any part of the funds transfer that is not subject to the provisions of EFTA or other law, such as the obligation of the intermediary bank to execute the payment order of the originator's bank (Section 4A–302), or whether the payment order of the commercial customer to Bank A is authorized or verified (Sections 4A–202 and 4A–203).

Case #2. A consumer originates a payment order that is a remittance transfer as defined in 15 U.S.C. sec. 1693o–1 and provides the remittance transfer provider (Bank A) with cash in the amount of the transfer plus any relevant fees. The funds transfer is routed through an intermediary bank for final credit to the designated recipient's account at Bank B. Bank A's payment order identifies the designated recipient by both name and account number in Bank B, but the name and number provided identify different persons. This remittance transfer is not an "electronic fund transfer" as defined in 15 U.S.C. sec. 1693a(7) because it is not initiated by electronic means from a consumer's account, but does qualify as a "funds transfer" as defined in Section 4A–104. Both Article 4A and EFTA apply to the funds transfer. Sections 4A–102, 4A–108(a), (b). Article 4A's provision on mistakes in identifying the designated beneficiary, Section 4A–207, would apply as long as not inconsistent with the governing EFTA provisions. See 15 U.S.C. Sec. *1693o–1*(d), Section 4A–108(c). See Comment 1 to this Section.

Case #3. A consumer originates a payment order from the consumer's account at Bank A to the designated recipient's account at Bank B located outside the United States. Bank A uses the CHIPS system to execute that payment order. The funds transfer is a "remittance transfer" as defined in 15 U.S.C. sec. 1693o–1. This transfer is not an "electronic fund transfer" as defined in 15 U.S.C. Sec. 1693a(7) because of the exclusion for transfers through systems such as CHIPS in 15 U.S.C. Sec. 1693a(7)(B), but qualifies as a "funds transfer" as defined in Section 4A–104. Under Sections 4A–102 and 4A–108(b), both Article 4A and EFTA apply to the funds transfer. The EFTA will prevail to the extent of any inconsistency between EFTA and Article 4A. Section 4A–108(c). See Comment 1 to this Section. For example, if the consumer subsequently exercises a right under EFTA to cancel the remittance transfer and obtain a refund, Bank A would be required to comply with the EFTA rule even if Article 4A prevents Bank A from cancelling or reversing the payment order that Bank A sent to its receiving bank. Section 4A–211.

Case #4. A person fraudulently originates an unauthorized payment order from a consumer's account through use of an online banking interface and the payment order is executed using a system that qualifies the transaction as an "electronic fund transfer" under EFTA. The funds transfer that results from execution of the unauthorized payment order is not governed by Article 4A. Section 4A–108(a). Whether the funds transfer also qualifies as a "remittance transfer" under EFTA has no bearing on the application of Article 4A.

Case #5. A person fraudulently originates an unauthorized payment order from a consumer's account at Bank A through forging written documents that are provided in person to an employee of Bank A. This transaction is not an "electronic fund transfer" as defined in 15 U.S.C. Sec. 1693a(7) because it was not initiated by electronic means, but qualifies as a "funds transfer" as defined in Section 4A–104. Article 4A applies regardless of whether the funds transfer also qualifies as a "remittance transfer" under 15 U.S.C. sec. 1693o–1. If the funds transfer is not a remittance transfer, the provisions of Section 4A–108 are not implicated because the funds transfer does not fall under EFTA, and the general scope provision of Article 4A governs. Section 4A–102. If the funds transfer is a remittance transfer, and thus governed by EFTA,

Section 4A–108(b) provides that Article 4A also applies. The provisions of Article 4A allocate the loss arising from the unauthorized payment order as long as those provisions are not inconsistent with the provisions of the EFTA applicable to remittance transfers. See 15 U.S.C. Sec. 1693o–1, Section 4A–108(c). See Comment 1 to this Section.

3.   Regulation J, 12 C.F.R. Part 210, of the Federal Reserve Board addresses the application of that regulation and EFTA to fund transfers made through Fedwire. Fedwire transfers are further described in Official Comments 1 and 2 to Section 4A–107. In addition, funds transfer system rules may be applicable pursuant to Section 4A–501.

Legislative Note: The reference to EFTA "as amended from time to time" means that the operation of this section at any particular time after enactment may depend on federal legislative action occurring after enactment. In states in which such an arrangement may constitute improper delegation, the language "as amended from time to time" may be deleted. In that case, however, the legislature should consider other mechanisms to assure that this section continues to operate harmoniously with EFTA as it may be subsequently amended.

PART 2

ISSUE AND ACCEPTANCE OF PAYMENT ORDER

§ 4A–201. Security Procedure.

"Security procedure" means a procedure established by agreement of a customer and a receiving bank for the purpose of (i) verifying that a payment order or communication amending or cancelling a payment order is that of the customer, or (ii) detecting error in the transmission or the content of the payment order or communication. A security procedure may require the use of algorithms or other codes, identifying words or numbers, encryption, callback procedures, or similar security devices. Comparison of a signature on a payment order or communication with an authorized specimen signature of the customer is not by itself a security procedure.

Official Comment

A large percentage of payment orders and communications amending or cancelling payment orders are transmitted electronically and it is standard practice to use security procedures that are designed to assure the authenticity of the message. Security procedures can also be used to detect error in the content of messages or to detect payment orders that are transmitted by mistake as in the case of multiple transmission of the same payment order. Security procedures might also apply to communications that are transmitted by telephone or in writing. Section 4A–201 defines these security procedures. The definition of security procedure limits the term to a procedure "established by agreement of a customer and a receiving bank." The term does not apply to procedures that the receiving bank may follow unilaterally in processing payment orders. The question of whether loss that may result from the transmission of a spurious or erroneous payment order will be borne by the receiving bank or the sender or purported sender is affected by whether a security procedure was or was not in effect and whether there was or was not compliance with the procedure. Security procedures are referred to in Sections 4A–202 and 4A–203, which deal with authorized and verified payment orders, and Section 4A–205, which deals with erroneous payment orders.

§ 4A–202. Authorized and Verified Payment Orders.

(a)   A payment order received by the receiving bank is the authorized order of the person identified as sender if that person authorized the order or is otherwise bound by it under the law of agency.

(b)   If a bank and its customer have agreed that the authenticity of payment orders issued to the bank in the name of the customer as sender will be verified pursuant to a security procedure, a payment order received by the receiving bank is effective as the order of the customer, whether or not authorized, if (i) the security procedure is a commercially reasonable method of providing security against unauthorized payment orders, and (ii) the bank proves that it accepted the payment order in good faith and in compliance with the security procedure and any written agreement or instruction of the customer restricting acceptance of payment orders issued in the name of the customer. The bank is not required to follow an instruction that violates a written agreement with the customer or notice of which is not received at a time and in a manner affording the bank a reasonable opportunity to act on it before the payment order is accepted.

(c)   Commercial reasonableness of a security procedure is a question of law to be determined by considering the wishes of the customer expressed to the bank, the circumstances of the customer known to the bank, including the size, type, and frequency of payment orders normally issued by the customer to the bank, alternative security procedures offered to the customer, and security procedures in general use by customers and receiving banks similarly situated. A security procedure is deemed to be commercially reasonable if (i) the security procedure was chosen by the customer after the bank offered, and the customer refused, a security procedure that was commercially reasonable for that customer, and (ii) the customer expressly agreed in writing to be bound by any payment order, whether or not authorized, issued in its name and accepted by the bank in compliance with the security procedure chosen by the customer.

(d)　The term "sender" in this Article includes the customer in whose name a payment order is issued if the order is the authorized order of the customer under subsection (a), or it is effective as the order of the customer under subsection (b).

(e)　This section applies to amendments and cancellations of payment orders to the same extent it applies to payment orders.

(f)　Except as provided in this section and in Section 4A–203(a)(1), rights and obligations arising under this section or Section 4A–203 may not be varied by agreement.

Official Comment

This section is discussed in the Comment following Section 4A–203.

§ 4A–203. Unenforceability of Certain Verified Payment Orders.

(a)　If an accepted payment order is not, under Section 4A–202(a), an authorized order of a customer identified as sender, but is effective as an order of the customer pursuant to Section 4A–202(b), the following rules apply:

(1)　By express written agreement, the receiving bank may limit the extent to which it is entitled to enforce or retain payment of the payment order.

(2)　The receiving bank is not entitled to enforce or retain payment of the payment order if the customer proves that the order was not caused, directly or indirectly, by a person (i) entrusted at any time with duties to act for the customer with respect to payment orders or the security procedure, or (ii) who obtained access to transmitting facilities of the customer or who obtained, from a source controlled by the customer and without authority of the receiving bank, information facilitating breach of the security procedure, regardless of how the information was obtained or whether the customer was at fault. Information includes any access device, computer software, or the like.

(b)　This section applies to amendments of payment orders to the same extent it applies to payment orders.

Official Comment

1.　Some person will always be identified as the sender of a payment order. Acceptance of the order by the receiving bank is based on a belief by the bank that the order was authorized by the person identified as the sender. If the receiving bank is the beneficiary's bank acceptance means that the receiving bank is obliged to pay the beneficiary. If the receiving bank is not the beneficiary's bank, acceptance means that the receiving bank has executed the sender's order and is obliged to pay the bank that accepted the order issued in execution of the sender's order. In either case the receiving bank may suffer a loss unless it is entitled to enforce payment of the payment order that it accepted. If the person identified as the sender of the order refuses to pay on the ground that the order was not authorized by that person, what are the rights of the receiving bank? In the absence of a statute or agreement that specifically addresses the issue, the question usually will be resolved by the law of agency. In some cases, the law of agency works well. For example, suppose the receiving bank executes a payment order given by means of a letter apparently written by a corporation that is a customer of the bank and apparently signed by an officer of the corporation. If the receiving bank acts solely on the basis of the letter, the corporation is not bound as the sender of the payment order unless the signature was that of the officer and the officer was authorized to act for the corporation in the issuance of payment orders, or some other agency doctrine such as apparent authority or estoppel causes the corporation to be bound. Estoppel can be illustrated by the following example. Suppose P is aware that A, who is unauthorized to act for P, has fraudulently misrepresented to T that A is authorized to act for P. T believes A and is about to rely on the misrepresentation. If P does not notify T of the true facts although P could easily do so, P may be estopped from denying A's lack of authority. A similar result could follow if the failure to notify T is the result of negligence rather than a deliberate decision. Restatement, Second, Agency § 8B. Other equitable principles such as subrogation or restitution might also allow a receiving bank to recover with respect to an unauthorized payment order that it accepted. In *Gatoil (U.S.A.), Inc. v. Forest Hill State Bank*, 1 U.C.C.Rep.Serv.2d 171 (D.Md.1986), a joint venturer not authorized to order payments from the account of the joint venture, ordered a funds transfer from the account. The transfer paid a bona fide debt of the joint venture. Although the transfer was unauthorized the court refused to require recredit of the account because the joint venture suffered no loss. The result can be rationalized on the basis of subrogation of the receiving bank to the right of the beneficiary of the funds transfer to receive the payment from the joint venture.

But in most cases these legal principles give the receiving bank very little protection in the case of an authorized payment order. Cases like those just discussed are not typical of the way that most payment orders are transmitted and accepted, and such cases are likely to become even less common. Given the large amount of the typical payment order, a prudent receiving bank will be unwilling to accept a payment order unless it has assurance that the order is what it purports to be. This assurance is normally provided by security procedures described in Section 4A–201.

In a very large percentage of cases covered by Article 4A, transmission of the payment order is made electronically. The receiving bank may be required to act on the basis of a message that appears on a computer screen. Common law concepts of authority of agent to bind principal are not helpful. There is no way of determining the identity or the authority of the person who caused the message to be sent. The receiving bank is not relying on the authority of any particular person to act for the purported sender. The case is not comparable to payment of a check by the drawee bank on the basis of a signature that is forged. Rather, the receiving bank relies on a security procedure pursuant to which the authenticity of the message can be "tested" by various devices which are designed to provide certainty that the message is that of the sender identified in the payment order. In the wire transfer business the concept of "authorized" is different from that found in agency law. In that business a payment order is treated as the order of the person in whose name it is issued if it is properly tested pursuant to a security procedure and the order passes the test.

Section 4A–202 reflects the reality of the wire transfer business. A person in whose name a payment order is issued is considered to be the sender of the order if the order is "authorized" as stated in subsection (a) or if the order is "verified" pursuant to a security procedure in compliance with subsection (b). If subsection (b) does not apply, the question of whether the customer is responsible for the order is determined by the law of agency. The issue is one of actual or apparent authority of the person who caused the order to be issued in the name of the customer. In some cases the law of agency might allow the customer to be bound by an unauthorized order if conduct of the customer can be used to find an estoppel against the customer to deny that the order was unauthorized. If the customer is bound by the order under any of these agency doctrines, subsection (a) treats the order as authorized and thus the customer is deemed to be the sender of the order. In most cases, however, subsection (b) will apply. In that event there is no need to make an agency law analysis to determine authority. Under Section 4A–202, the issue of liability of the purported sender of the payment order will be determined by agency law only if the receiving bank did not comply with subsection (b).

2. The scope of Section 4A–202 can be illustrated by the following cases. *Case #1.* A payment order purporting to be that of Customer is received by Receiving Bank but the order was fraudulently transmitted by a person who had no authority to act for Customer. *Case #2.* An authentic payment order was sent by Customer, but before the order was received by Receiving Bank the order was fraudulently altered by an unauthorized person to change the beneficiary. *Case #3.* An authentic payment order was received by Receiving Bank, but before the order was executed by Receiving Bank a person who had no authority to act for Customer fraudulently sent a communication purporting to amend the order by changing the beneficiary. In each case Receiving Bank acted on the fraudulent communication by accepting the payment order. These cases are all essentially similar and they are treated identically by Section 4A–202. In each case Receiving Bank acted on a communication that it thought was authorized by Customer when in fact the communication was fraudulent. No distinction is made between Case #1 in which Customer took no part at all in the transaction and Case #2 and Case #3 in which an authentic order was fraudulently altered or amended by an unauthorized person. If subsection (b) does not apply, each case is governed by subsection (a). If there are no additional facts on which an estoppel might be found, Customer is not responsible in Case #1 for the fraudulently issued payment order, in Case #2 for the fraudulent alteration or in Case #3 for the fraudulent amendment. Thus, in each case Customer is not liable to pay the order and Receiving Bank takes the loss. The only remedy of Receiving Bank is to seek recovery from the person who received payment as beneficiary of the fraudulent order. If there was verification in compliance with subsection (b), Customer will take the loss unless Section 4A–203 applies.

3.   Subsection (b) of Section 4A–202 is based on the assumption that losses due to fraudulent payment orders can best be avoided by the use of commercially reasonable security procedures, and that the use of such procedures should be encouraged. The subsection is designed to protect both the customer and the receiving bank. A receiving bank needs to be able to rely on objective criteria to determine whether it can safely act on a payment order. Employees of the bank can be trained to "test" a payment order according to the various steps specified in the security procedure. The bank is responsible for the acts of these employees. Subsection (b)(ii) requires the bank to prove that it accepted the payment order in good faith and "in compliance with the security procedure." If the fraud was not detected because the bank's employee did not perform the acts required by the security procedure, the bank has not complied. Subsection (b)(ii) also requires the bank to prove that it complied with any agreement or instruction that restricts acceptance of payment orders issued in the name of the customer. A customer may want to protect itself by imposing limitations on acceptance of payment orders by the bank. For example, the customer may prohibit the bank from accepting a payment order that is not payable from an authorized account, that exceeds the credit balance in specified accounts of the customer, or that exceeds some other amount. Another limitation may relate to the beneficiary. The customer may provide the bank with a list of authorized beneficiaries and prohibit acceptance of any payment order to a beneficiary not appearing on the list. Such limitations may be incorporated into the security procedure itself or they may be covered by a separate agreement or instruction. In either case, the bank must comply with the limitations if the conditions stated in subsection (b) are met. Normally limitations on acceptance would be incorporated into an agreement between the customer and the receiving bank, but in some cases the instruction might be unilaterally given by the customer. If standing instructions or an agreement state limitations on the ability of the receiving bank to act, provision must be made for later modification of the limitations. Normally this would be done by an agreement that specifies particular procedures to be followed. Thus, subsection (b) states that the receiving bank is not required to follow an instruction that violates a written agreement. The receiving bank is not bound by an instruction unless it has adequate notice of it. Subsections (25), (26) and (27) of Section 1–201* apply.

Subsection (b)(i) assures that the interests of the customer will be protected by providing an incentive to a bank to make available to the customer a security procedure that is commercially reasonable. If a commercially reasonable security procedure is not made available to the customer, subsection (b) does not apply. The result is that subsection (a) applies and the bank acts at its peril in accepting a payment order that may be unauthorized. Prudent banking practice may require that security procedures be utilized in virtually all cases except for those in which personal contact between the customer and the bank eliminates the possibility of an unauthorized order. The burden of making available commercially reasonable security procedures is imposed on receiving banks because they generally determine what security procedures can be used and are in the best position to evaluate the efficacy of procedures offered to customers to combat fraud. The burden on the customer is to supervise its employees to assure compliance with the security procedure and to safeguard confidential security information and access to transmitting facilities so that the security procedure cannot be breached.

4.   The principal issue that is likely to arise in litigation involving subsection (b) is whether the security procedure in effect when a fraudulent payment order was accepted was commercially reasonable. The concept of what is commercially reasonable in a given case is flexible. Verification entails labor and equipment costs that can vary greatly depending upon the degree of security that is sought. A customer that transmits very large numbers of payment orders in very large amounts may desire and may reasonably expect to be provided with state-of-the-art procedures that provide maximum security. But the expense involved may make use of a state-of-the-art procedure infeasible for a customer that normally transmits payment orders infrequently or in relatively low amounts. Another variable is the type of receiving bank. It is reasonable to require large money center banks to make available state-of-the-art security procedures. On the other hand, the same requirement may not be reasonable for a small country bank. A receiving bank might have several security procedures that are designed to meet the varying needs of different customers. The type of payment order is another variable. For example, in a wholesale wire transfer, each payment order is normally transmitted electronically and individually. A testing procedure will be individually applied to each payment order. In funds transfers to be made by means of an automated clearing house many payment orders are incorporated into an electronic device such as a magnetic tape that is physically delivered. Testing of the individual payment orders is not feasible. Thus, a different kind of security procedure must be adopted to take into account the different mode of transmission.

The issue of whether a particular security procedure is commercially reasonable is a question of law. Whether the receiving bank complied with the procedure is a question of fact. It is appropriate to make the finding concerning commercial reasonability a matter of law because security procedures are likely to be standardized in

---

*   *Referring to unrevised Article 1 (Appendix A).*

437

the banking industry and a question of law standard leads to more predictability concerning the level of security that a bank must offer to its customers. The purpose of subsection (b) is to encourage banks to institute reasonable safeguards against fraud but not to make them insurers against fraud. A security procedure is not commercially unreasonable simply because another procedure might have been better or because the judge deciding the question would have opted for a more stringent procedure. The standard is not whether the security procedure is the best available. Rather it is whether the procedure is reasonable for the particular customer and the particular bank, which is a lower standard. On the other hand, a security procedure that fails to meet prevailing standards of good banking practice applicable to the particular bank should not be held to be commercially reasonable. Subsection (c) states factors to be considered by the judge in making the determination of commercial reasonableness. Sometimes an informed customer refuses a security procedure that is commercially reasonable and suitable for that customer and insists on using a higher-risk procedure because it is more convenient or cheaper. In that case, under the last sentence of subsection (c), the customer has voluntarily assumed the risk of failure of the procedure and cannot shift the loss to the bank. But this result follows only if the customer expressly agrees in writing to assume that risk. It is implicit in the last sentence of subsection (c) that a bank that accedes to the wishes of its customer in this regard is not acting in bad faith by so doing so long as the customer is made aware of the risk. In all cases, however, a receiving bank cannot get the benefit of subsection (b) unless it has made available to the customer a security procedure that is commercially reasonable and suitable for use by that customer. In most cases, the mutual interest of bank and customer to protect against fraud should lead to agreement to a security procedure which is commercially reasonable.

5.   The effect of Section 4A–202(b) is to place the risk of loss on the customer if an unauthorized payment order is accepted by the receiving bank after verification by the bank in compliance with a commercially reasonable security procedure. An exception to this result is provided by Section 4A–203(a)(2). The customer may avoid the loss resulting from such a payment order if the customer can prove that the fraud was not committed by a person described in that subsection. Breach of a commercially reasonable security procedure requires that the person committing the fraud have knowledge of how the procedure works and knowledge of codes, identifying devices, and the like. That person may also need access to transmitting facilities through an access device or other software in order to breach the security procedure. This confidential information must be obtained either from a source controlled by the customer or from a source controlled by the receiving bank. If the customer can prove that the person committing the fraud did not obtain the confidential information from an agent or former agent of the customer or from a source controlled by the customer, the loss is shifted to the bank. "Prove" is defined in Section 4A–105(a)(7). Because of bank regulation requirements, in this kind of case there will always be a criminal investigation as well as an internal investigation of the bank to determine the probable explanation for the breach of security. Because a funds transfer fraud usually will involve a very large amount of money, both the criminal investigation and the internal investigation are likely to be thorough. In some cases there may be an investigation by bank examiners as well. Frequently, these investigations will develop evidence of who is at fault and the cause of the loss. The customer will have access to evidence developed in these investigations and that evidence can be used by the customer in meeting its burden of proof.

6.   The effect of Section 4A–202(b) may also be changed by an agreement meeting the requirements of Section 4A–203(a)(1). Some customers may be unwilling to take all or part of the risk of loss with respect to unauthorized payment orders even if all of the requirements of Section 4A–202(b) are met. By virtue of Section 4A–203(a)(1), a receiving bank may assume all of the risk of loss with respect to unauthorized payment orders or the customer and bank may agree that losses from unauthorized payment orders are to be divided as provided in the agreement.

7.   In a large majority of cases the sender of a payment order is a bank. In many cases in which there is a bank sender, both the sender and the receiving bank will be members of a funds transfer system over which the payment order is transmitted. Since Section 4A–202(f) does not prohibit a funds transfer system rule from varying rights and obligations under Section 4A–202, a rule of the funds transfer system can determine how loss due to an unauthorized payment order from a participating bank to another participating bank is to be allocated. A funds transfer system rule, however, cannot change the rights of a customer that is not a participating bank. § 4A–501(b). Section 4A–202(f) also prevents variation by agreement except to the extent stated.

§ 4A–204. Refund of Payment and Duty of Customer to Report With Respect to Unauthorized Payment Order.

(a)   If a receiving bank accepts a payment order issued in the name of its customer as sender which is (i) not authorized and not effective as the order of the customer under Section 4A–202, or (ii) not enforceable, in whole or in part, against the customer under Section 4A–203, the bank shall refund any payment of the payment order received from the customer to the extent the bank is not entitled to enforce payment and shall pay interest on the refundable amount calculated from the date the bank received payment to the date of the refund. However, the customer is not entitled to interest from the bank on the amount to be refunded if the customer fails to exercise ordinary care to determine that the order was not authorized by the customer and to notify the bank of the relevant facts within a reasonable time not exceeding 90 days after the date the customer received notification from the bank that the order was accepted or that the customer's account was debited with respect to the order. The bank is not entitled to any recovery from the customer on account of a failure by the customer to give notification as stated in this section.

(b) Reasonable time under subsection (a) may be fixed by agreement as stated in Section 1–302(b), but the obligation of a receiving bank to refund payment as stated in subsection (a) may not otherwise be varied by agreement.

As amended in 2001.

Official Comment

1. With respect to unauthorized payment orders, in a very large percentage of cases a commercially reasonable security procedure will be in effect. Section 4A–204 applies only to cases in which (i) no commercially reasonable security procedure is in effect, (ii) the bank did not comply with a commercially reasonable security procedure that was in effect, (iii) the sender can prove, pursuant to Section 4A–203(a)(2), that the culprit did not obtain confidential security information controlled by the customer, or (iv) the bank, pursuant to Section 4A–203(a)(1) agreed to take all or part of the loss resulting from an unauthorized payment order. In each of these cases the bank takes the risk of loss with respect to an unauthorized payment order because the bank is not entitled to payment from the customer with respect to the order. The bank normally debits the customer's account or otherwise receives payment from the customer shortly after acceptance of the payment order. Subsection (a) of Section 4A–204 states that the bank must recredit the account or refund payment to the extent the bank is not entitled to enforce payment.

2. Section 4A–204 is designed to encourage a customer to promptly notify the receiving bank that it has accepted an unauthorized payment order. Since cases of unauthorized payment orders will almost always involve fraud, the bank's remedy is normally to recover from the beneficiary of the unauthorized order if the beneficiary was party to the fraud. This remedy may not be worth very much and it may not make any difference whether or not the bank promptly learns about the fraud. But in some cases prompt notification may make it easier for the bank to recover some part of its loss from the culprit. The customer will routinely be notified of the debit to its account with respect to an unauthorized order or will otherwise be notified of acceptance of the order. The customer has a duty to exercise ordinary care to determine that the order was unauthorized after it has received notification from the bank, and to advise the bank of the relevant facts within a reasonable time not exceeding 90 days after receipt of notification. Reasonable time is not defined and it may depend on the facts of the particular case. If a payment order for $1,000,000 is wholly unauthorized, the customer should normally discover it in far less than 90 days. If a $1,000,000 payment order was authorized but the name of the beneficiary was fraudulently changed, a much longer period may be necessary to discover the fraud. But in any event, if the customer delays more than 90 days the customer's duty has not been met. The only consequence of a failure of the customer to perform this duty is a loss of interest on the refund payable by the bank. A customer that acts promptly is entitled to interest from the time the customer's account was debited or the customer otherwise made payment. The rate of interest is stated in Section 4A–506. If the customer fails to perform the duty, no interest is recoverable for any part of the period before the bank learns that it accepted an unauthorized order. But the bank is not entitled to any recovery from the customer based on negligence for failure to inform the bank. Loss of interest is in the nature of a penalty on the customer designed to provide an incentive for the customer to police its account. There is no intention to impose a duty on the customer that might result in shifting loss from the unauthorized order to the customer.

§ 4A–205. Erroneous Payment Orders.

(a) If an accepted payment order was transmitted pursuant to a security procedure for the detection of error and the payment order (i) erroneously instructed payment to a beneficiary not intended by the sender, (ii) erroneously instructed payment in an amount greater than the amount intended by the sender, or (iii) was an erroneously transmitted duplicate of a payment order previously sent by the sender, the following rules apply:

(1) If the sender proves that the sender or a person acting on behalf of the sender pursuant to Section 4A–206 complied with the security procedure and that the error would have been detected if the receiving bank had also complied, the sender is not obliged to pay the order to the extent stated in paragraphs (2) and (3).

(2) If the funds transfer is completed on the basis of an erroneous payment order described in clause (i) or (iii) of subsection (a), the sender is not obliged to pay the order and the receiving bank is entitled to recover from the beneficiary any amount paid to the beneficiary to the extent allowed by the law governing mistake and restitution.

(3) If the funds transfer is completed on the basis of a payment order described in clause (ii) of subsection (a), the sender is not obliged to pay the order to the extent the amount received by the beneficiary is greater than the amount intended by the sender. In that case, the receiving bank is entitled to recover from the beneficiary the excess amount received to the extent allowed by the law governing mistake and restitution.

(b) If (i) the sender of an erroneous payment order described in subsection (a) is not obliged to pay all or part of the order, and (ii) the sender receives notification from the receiving bank that the order was accepted by the bank or that the sender's account was debited with respect to the order, the sender has a duty to exercise ordinary care, on the basis of information available to the sender, to discover the error with respect to the order and to advise the bank of the relevant facts within a reasonable time, not exceeding 90 days, after the bank's notification was received by the sender. If the bank proves that the sender failed to perform that duty, the sender is liable to the bank for the loss the bank proves it incurred as a result of the failure, but the liability of the sender may not exceed the amount of the sender's order.

(c) This section applies to amendments to payment orders to the same extent it applies to payment orders.

Official Comment

1. This section concerns error in the content or in the transmission of payment orders. It deals with three kinds of error. *Case #1*. The order identifies a beneficiary not intended by the sender. For example, Sender intends to wire funds to a beneficiary identified only by an account number. The wrong account number is stated in the order. *Case #2*. The error is in the amount of the order. For example, Sender intends to wire $1,000 to Beneficiary. Through error, the payment order instructs payment of $1,000,000. *Case #3*. A payment order is sent to the receiving bank and then, by mistake, the same payment order is sent to the receiving bank again. In Case #3, the receiving bank may have no way of knowing whether the second order is a duplicate of the first or is another order. Similarly, in Case #1 and Case #2, the receiving bank may have no way of knowing that the error exists. In each case, if this section does not apply and the funds transfer is completed, Sender is obliged to pay the order. Section 4A–402. Sender's remedy, based on payment by mistake, is to recover from the beneficiary that received payment.

Sometimes, however, transmission of payment orders of the sender to the receiving bank is made pursuant to a security procedure designed to detect one or more of the errors described above. Since "security procedure" is defined by Section 4A–201 as "a procedure established by agreement of a customer and a receiving bank for the purpose of . . . detecting error . . . ," Section 4A–205 does not apply if the receiving bank and the customer did not agree to the establishment of a procedure for detecting error. A security procedure may be designed to detect an account number that is not one to which Sender normally makes payment. In that case, the security procedure may require a special verification that payment to the stated account number was intended. In the case of dollar amounts, the security procedure may require different codes for different dollar amounts. If a $1,000,000 payment order contains a code that is inappropriate for that amount, the error in amount should be detected. In the case of duplicate orders, the security procedure may require that each payment order be identified by a number or code that applies to no other order. If the number or code of each payment order received is registered in a computer base, the receiving bank can quickly identify a duplicate order. The three cases covered by this section are essentially similar. In each, if the error is not detected, some beneficiary will receive funds that the beneficiary was not intended to receive. If this section applies, the risk of loss with respect to the error of the sender is shifted to the bank which has the burden of recovering the funds from the beneficiary. The risk of loss is shifted to the bank only if the sender proves that the error would have been detected if there had been compliance with the procedure and that the sender (or an agent under Section 4A–206) complied. In the case of a duplicate order or a wrong beneficiary, the sender doesn't have to pay the order. In the case of an overpayment, the sender does not have to pay the order to the extent of the overpayment. If subsection (a)(1) applies, the position of the receiving bank is comparable to that of a receiving bank that erroneously executes a payment order as stated in Section 4A–303. However, failure of the sender to timely report the error is covered by Section 4A–205(b) rather than by Section 4A–304 which applies only to erroneous execution under Section 4A–303. A receiving bank to which the risk of loss is shifted by subsection (a)(1) or (2) is entitled to recover the amount erroneously paid to the beneficiary to the extent allowed by the law of mistake and restitution. Rights of the receiving bank against the beneficiary are similar to those of a receiving bank that erroneously executes a payment order as stated in Section 4A–303. Those rights are discussed in Comment 2 to Section 4A–303.

2. A security procedure established for the purpose of detecting error is not effective unless both sender and receiving bank comply with the procedure. Thus, the bank undertakes a duty of complying with the procedure for the benefit of the sender. This duty is recognized in subsection (a)(1). The loss with respect to the sender's error is shifted to the bank if the bank fails to comply with the procedure and the sender (or an agent under Section 4A–206) does comply. Although the customer may have been negligent in transmitting the erroneous payment order, the loss is put on the bank on a last-clear-chance theory. A similar analysis applies to subsection (b). If the loss with respect to an error is shifted to the receiving bank and the sender is notified by the bank that the erroneous payment order was accepted, the sender has a duty to exercise ordinary care to discover the error and notify the bank of the relevant facts within a reasonable time not exceeding 90 days. If the bank can prove that the sender failed in this duty it is entitled to compensation for the loss incurred as a result of the failure. Whether the bank is entitled to recover from the sender depends upon whether the failure to give timely notice would have made any difference. If the bank could not have recovered from the beneficiary that received payment under the erroneous payment order even if timely notice had been given, the sender's failure to notify did not cause any loss of the bank.

3. Section 4A–205 is subject to variation by agreement under Section 4A–501. Thus, if a receiving bank and its customer have agreed to a security procedure for detection of error, the liability of the receiving bank for failing to detect an error of the customer as provided in Section 4A–205 may be varied as provided in an agreement of the bank and the customer.

§ 4A–206. Transmission of Payment Order Through Funds-Transfer or Other Communication System.

(a) If a payment order addressed to a receiving bank is transmitted to a funds-transfer system or other third-party communication system for transmittal to the bank, the system is deemed to be an agent of the sender for the purpose of transmitting the payment order to the bank. If there is a discrepancy between the terms of the payment order transmitted to the system and the terms of the payment order transmitted by the system to the bank, the terms of the payment order of the sender are those transmitted by the system. This section does not apply to a funds-transfer system of the Federal Reserve Banks.

(b) This section applies to cancellations and amendments of payment orders to the same extent it applies to payment orders.

Official Comment

1. A payment order may be issued to a receiving bank directly by delivery of a writing or electronic device or by an oral or electronic communication. If an agent of the sender is employed to transmit orders on behalf of the sender, the sender is bound by the order transmitted by the agent on the basis of agency law. Section 4A–206 is an application of that principle to cases in which a funds transfer or communication system acts as an intermediary in transmitting the sender's order to the receiving bank. The intermediary is deemed to be an agent of the sender for the purpose of transmitting payment orders and related messages for the sender. Section 4A–206 deals with error by the intermediary.

2. Transmission by an automated clearing house of an association of banks other than the Federal Reserve Banks is an example of a transaction covered by Section 4A–206. Suppose Originator orders Originator's Bank to cause a large number of payments to be made to many accounts in banks in various parts of the country. These payment orders are electronically transmitted to Originator's Bank and stored in an electronic device that is held by Originator's Bank. Or, transmission of the various payment orders is made by delivery to Originator's Bank of an electronic device containing the instruction to the bank. In either case the terms of the various payment orders by Originator are determined by the information contained in the electronic device. In order to execute the various orders, the information in the electronic device must be processed. For example, if some of the orders are for payments to accounts in Bank X and some to accounts in Bank Y, Originator's Bank will execute these orders of Originator by issuing a series of payment orders to Bank X covering all payments to accounts in that bank, and

by issuing a series of payment orders to Bank Y covering all payments to accounts in that bank. The orders to Bank X may be transmitted together by means of an electronic device, and those to Bank Y may be included in another electronic device. Typically, this processing is done by an automated clearing house acting for a group of banks including Originator's Bank. The automated clearing house is a funds transfer system. Section 4A–105(a)(5). Originator's Bank delivers Originator's electronic device or transmits the information contained in the device to the funds transfer system for processing into payment orders of Originator's Bank to the appropriate beneficiary's banks. The processing may result in an erroneous payment order. Originator's Bank, by use of Originator's electronic device, may have given information to the funds transfer system instructing payment of $100,000 to an account in Bank X, but because of human error or an equipment malfunction the processing may have converted that instruction into an instruction to Bank X to make a payment of $1,000,000. Under Section 4A–206, Originator's Bank issued a payment order for $1,000,000 to Bank X when the erroneous information was sent to Bank X. Originator's Bank is responsible for the error of the automated clearing house. The liability of the funds transfer system that made the error is not governed by Article 4A. It is left to the law of contract, a funds transfer system rule, or other applicable law.

In the hypothetical case just discussed, if the automated clearing house is operated by a Federal Reserve Bank, the analysis is different. Section 4A–206 does not apply. Originator's Bank will execute Originator's payment orders by delivery or transmission of the electronic information to the Federal Reserve Bank for processing. The result is that Originator's Bank has issued payment orders to the Federal Reserve Bank which, in this case, is acting as an intermediary bank. When the Federal Reserve Bank has processed the information given to it by Originator's Bank it will issue payment orders to the various beneficiary's banks. If the processing results in an erroneous payment order, the Federal Reserve Bank has erroneously executed the payment order of Originator's Bank and the case is governed by Section 4A–303.

§ 4A–207. Misdescription of Beneficiary.

    (a)   Subject to subsection (b), if, in a payment order received by the beneficiary's bank, the name, bank account number, or other identification of the beneficiary refers to a nonexistent or unidentifiable person or account, no person has rights as a beneficiary of the order and acceptance of the order cannot occur.

    (b)   If a payment order received by the beneficiary's bank identifies the beneficiary both by name and by an identifying or bank account number and the name and number identify different persons, the following rules apply:

        (1)   Except as otherwise provided in subsection (c), if the beneficiary's bank does not know that the name and number refer to different persons, it may rely on the number as the proper identification of the beneficiary of the order. The beneficiary's bank need not determine whether the name and number refer to the same person.

        (2)   If the beneficiary's bank pays the person identified by name or knows that the name and number identify different persons, no person has rights as beneficiary except the person paid by the beneficiary's bank if that person was entitled to receive payment from the originator of the funds transfer. If no person has rights as beneficiary, acceptance of the order cannot occur.

    (c)   If (i) a payment order described in subsection (b) is accepted, (ii) the originator's payment order described the beneficiary inconsistently by name and number, and (iii) the beneficiary's bank pays the person identified by number as permitted by subsection (b)(1), the following rules apply:

        (1)   If the originator is a bank, the originator is obliged to pay its order.

        (2)   If the originator is not a bank and proves that the person identified by number was not entitled to receive payment from the originator, the originator is not obliged to pay its order unless the originator's bank proves that the originator, before acceptance of the originator's order, had notice that payment of a payment order issued by the originator might be made by the beneficiary's bank on the basis of an identifying or bank account number even if it identifies a person different from the named beneficiary. Proof of notice may be made by any admissible evidence. The originator's bank satisfies the burden of proof if it proves that the originator, before the payment order was accepted, signed a writing stating the information to which the notice relates.

(d)   In a case governed by subsection (b)(1), if the beneficiary's bank rightfully pays the person identified by number and that person was not entitled to receive payment from the originator, the amount paid may be recovered from that person to the extent allowed by the law governing mistake and restitution as follows:

(1)   If the originator is obliged to pay its payment order as stated in subsection (c), the originator has the right to recover.

(2)   If the originator is not a bank and is not obliged to pay its payment order, the originator's bank has the right to recover.

Official Comment

1.   Subsection (a) deals with the problem of payment orders issued to the beneficiary's bank for payment to nonexistent or unidentifiable persons or accounts. Since it is not possible in that case for the funds transfer to be completed, subsection (a) states that the order cannot be accepted. Under Section 4A–402(c), a sender of a payment order is not obliged to pay its order unless the beneficiary's bank accepts a payment order instructing payment to the beneficiary of that sender's order. Thus, if the beneficiary of a funds transfer is nonexistent or unidentifiable, each sender in the funds transfer that has paid its payment order is entitled to get its money back.

2.   Subsection (b), which takes precedence over subsection (a), deals with the problem of payment orders in which the description of the beneficiary does not allow identification of the beneficiary because the beneficiary is described by name and by an identifying number or an account number and the name and number refer to different persons. A very large percentage of payment orders issued to the beneficiary's bank by another bank are processed by automated means using machines capable of reading orders on standard formats that identify the beneficiary by an identifying number or the number of a bank account. The processing of the order by the beneficiary's bank and the crediting of the beneficiary's account are done by use of the identifying or bank account number without human reading of the payment order itself. The process is comparable to that used in automated payment of checks. The standard format, however, may also allow the inclusion of the name of the beneficiary and other information which can be useful to the beneficiary's bank and the beneficiary but which plays no part in the process of payment. If the beneficiary's bank has both the account number and name of the beneficiary supplied by the originator of the funds transfer, it is possible for the beneficiary's bank to determine whether the name and number refer to the same person, but if a duty to make that determination is imposed on the beneficiary's bank the benefits of automated payment are lost. Manual handling of payment orders is both expensive and subject to human error. If payment orders can be handled on an automated basis there are substantial economies of operation and the possibility of clerical error is reduced. Subsection (b) allows banks to utilize automated processing by allowing banks to act on the basis of the number without regard to the name if the bank does not know that the name and number refer to different persons. "Know" is defined in Section 1–201(25)* to mean actual knowledge, and Section 1–201(27)* states rules for determining when an organization has knowledge of information received by the organization. The time of payment is the pertinent time at which knowledge or lack of knowledge must be determined.

Although the clear trend is for beneficiary's banks to process payment orders by automated means, Section 4A–207 is not limited to cases in which processing is done by automated means. A bank that processes by semi-automated means or even manually may rely on number as stated in Section 4A–207.

In cases covered by subsection (b) the erroneous identification would in virtually all cases be the identifying or bank account number. In the typical case the error is made by the originator of the funds transfer. The originator should know the name of the person who is to receive payment and can further identify that person by an address that would normally be known to the originator. It is not unlikely, however, that the originator may not be sure whether the identifying or account number refers to the person the originator intends to pay. Subsection (b)(1) deals with the typical case in which the beneficiary's bank pays on the basis of the account number and is not aware at the time of payment that the named beneficiary is not the holder of the account which was paid. In some cases the false number will be the result of error by the originator. In other cases fraud is involved. For example, Doe is the holder of shares in Mutual Fund. Thief, impersonating Doe, requests redemption of the shares and directs Mutual Fund to wire the redemption proceeds to Doe's account #12345 in Beneficiary's Bank. Mutual Fund originates a funds transfer by issuing a payment order to Originator's Bank to make the payment to Doe's account #12345 in Beneficiary's Bank. Originator's Bank executes the order by issuing a conforming payment order to Beneficiary's Bank which makes payment to account #12345. That account is the account of Roe rather than Doe.

---

*   *Referring to unrevised Article 1 (Appendix A).*

Roe might be a person acting in concert with Thief or Roe might be an innocent third party. Assume that Roe is a gem merchant that agreed to sell gems to Thief who agreed to wire the purchase price to Roe's account in Beneficiary's Bank. Roe believed that the credit to Roe's account was a transfer of funds from Thief and released the gems to Thief in good faith in reliance on the payment. The case law is unclear on the responsibility of a beneficiary's bank in carrying out a payment order in which the identification of the beneficiary by name and number is conflicting. See *Securities Fund Services, Inc. v. American National Bank*, 542 F.Supp. 323 (N.D.Ill.1982) and *Bradford Trust Co. v. Texas American Bank*, 790 F.2d 407 (5th Cir.1986). Section 4A–207 resolves the issue.

If Beneficiary's Bank did not know about the conflict between the name and number, subsection (b)(1) applies. Beneficiary's Bank has no duty to determine whether there is a conflict and it may rely on the number as the proper identification of the beneficiary of the order. When it accepts the order, it is entitled to payment from Originator's Bank. Section 4A–402(b). On the other hand, if Beneficiary's Bank knew about the conflict between the name and number and nevertheless paid Roe, subsection (b)(2) applies. Under that provision, acceptance of the payment order of Originator's Bank did not occur because there is no beneficiary of that order. Since acceptance did not occur Originator's Bank is not obliged to pay Beneficiary's Bank. Section 4A–402(b). Similarly, Mutual Fund is excused from its obligation to pay Originator's Bank. Section 4A–402(c). Thus, Beneficiary's Bank takes the loss. Its only cause of action is against Thief. Roe is not obliged to return the payment to the beneficiary's bank because Roe received the payment in good faith and for value. Article 4A makes irrelevant the issue of whether Mutual Fund was or was not negligent in issuing its payment order.

3.   Normally, subsection (b)(1) will apply to the hypothetical case discussed in Comment 2. Beneficiary's Bank will pay on the basis of the number without knowledge of the conflict. In that case subsection (c) places the loss on either Mutual Fund or Originator's Bank. It is not unfair to assign the loss to Mutual Fund because it is the person who dealt with the imposter and it supplied the wrong account number. It could have avoided the loss if it had not used an account number that it was not sure was that of Doe. Mutual Fund, however, may not have been aware of the risk involved in giving both name and number. Subsection (c) is designed to protect the originator, Mutual Fund, in this case. Under that subsection, the originator is responsible for the inconsistent description of the beneficiary if it had notice that the order might be paid by the beneficiary's bank on the basis of the number. If the originator is a bank, the originator always has that responsibility. The rationale is that any bank should know how payment orders are processed and paid. If the originator is not a bank, the originator's bank must prove that its customer, the originator, had notice. Notice can be proved by any admissible evidence, but the bank can always prove notice by providing the customer with a written statement of the required information and obtaining the customer's signature to the statement. That statement will then apply to any payment order accepted by the bank thereafter. The information need not be supplied more than once.

In the hypothetical case if Originator's Bank made the disclosure stated in the last sentence of subsection (c)(2), Mutual Fund must pay Originator's Bank. Under subsection (d)(1), Mutual Fund has an action to recover from Roe if recovery from Roe is permitted by the law governing mistake and restitution. Under the assumed facts Roe should be entitled to keep the money as a person who took it in good faith and for value since it was taken as payment for the gems. In that case, Mutual Fund's only remedy is against Thief. If Roe was not acting in good faith, Roe has to return the money to Mutual Fund. If Originator's Bank does not prove that Mutual Fund had notice as stated in subsection (c)(2), Mutual Fund is not required to pay Originator's Bank. Thus, the risk of loss falls on Originator's Bank whose remedy is against Roe or Thief as stated above. Subsection (d)(2).

§ 4A–208. Misdescription of Intermediary Bank or Beneficiary's Bank.

(a)   This subsection applies to a payment order identifying an intermediary bank or the beneficiary's bank only by an identifying number.

(1)   The receiving bank may rely on the number as the proper identification of the intermediary or beneficiary's bank and need not determine whether the number identifies a bank.

(2)   The sender is obliged to compensate the receiving bank for any loss and expenses incurred by the receiving bank as a result of its reliance on the number in executing or attempting to execute the order.

(b)   This subsection applies to a payment order identifying an intermediary bank or the beneficiary's bank both by name and an identifying number if the name and number identify different persons.

(1) If the sender is a bank, the receiving bank may rely on the number as the proper identification of the intermediary or beneficiary's bank if the receiving bank, when it executes the sender's order, does not know that the name and number identify different persons. The receiving bank need not determine whether the name and number refer to the same person or whether the number refers to a bank. The sender is obliged to compensate the receiving bank for any loss and expenses incurred by the receiving bank as a result of its reliance on the number in executing or attempting to execute the order.

(2) If the sender is not a bank and the receiving bank proves that the sender, before the payment order was accepted, had notice that the receiving bank might rely on the number as the proper identification of the intermediary or beneficiary's bank even if it identifies a person different from the bank identified by name, the rights and obligations of the sender and the receiving bank are governed by subsection (b)(1), as though the sender were a bank. Proof of notice may be made by any admissible evidence. The receiving bank satisfies the burden of proof if it proves that the sender, before the payment order was accepted, signed a writing stating the information to which the notice relates.

(3) Regardless of whether the sender is a bank, the receiving bank may rely on the name as the proper identification of the intermediary or beneficiary's bank if the receiving bank, at the time it executes the sender's order, does not know that the name and number identify different persons. The receiving bank need not determine whether the name and number refer to the same person.

(4) If the receiving bank knows that the name and number identify different persons, reliance on either the name or the number in executing the sender's payment order is a breach of the obligation stated in Section 4A–302(a)(1).

Official Comment

1. This section addresses an issue similar to that addressed by Section 4A–207. Because of automation in the processing of payment orders, a payment order may identify the beneficiary's bank or an intermediary bank by an identifying number. The bank identified by number might or might not also be identified by name. The following two cases illustrate Section 4A–208(a) and (b):

Case #1. Originator's payment order to Originator's Bank identifies the beneficiary's bank as Bank A and instructs payment to Account #12345 in that bank. Originator's Bank executes Originator's order by issuing a payment order to Intermediary Bank. In the payment order of Originator's Bank the beneficiary's bank is identified as Bank A but is also identified by number, #67890. The identifying number refers to Bank B rather than Bank A. If processing by Intermediary Bank of the payment order of Originator's Bank is done by automated means, Intermediary Bank, in executing the order, will rely on the identifying number and will issue a payment order to Bank B rather than Bank A. If there is an Account #12345 in Bank B, the payment order of Intermediary Bank would normally be accepted and payment would be made to a person not intended by Originator. In this case, Section 4A–208(b)(1) puts the risk of loss on Originator's Bank. Intermediary Bank may rely on the number #67890 as the proper identification of the beneficiary's bank. Intermediary Bank has properly executed the payment order of Originator's Bank. By using the wrong number to describe the beneficiary's bank, Originator's Bank has improperly executed Originator's payment order because the payment order of Originator's Bank provides for payment to the wrong beneficiary, the holder of Account #12345 in Bank B rather than the holder of Account #12345 in Bank A. Section 4A–302(a)(1) and Section 4A–303(c). Originator's Bank is not entitled to payment from Originator but is required to pay Intermediary Bank. Section 4A–303(c) and Section 4A–402(c). Intermediary Bank is also entitled to compensation for any loss and expenses resulting from the error by Originator's Bank.

If there is no Account #12345 in Bank B, the result is that there is no beneficiary of the payment order issued by Originator's Bank and the funds transfer will not be completed. Originator's Bank is not entitled to payment from Originator and Intermediary Bank is not entitled to payment from Originator's Bank. Section 4A–402(c). Since Originator's Bank improperly executed Originator's payment order it may be liable for damages under Section 4A–305. As stated above, Intermediary Bank is entitled to compensation for loss and expenses resulting from the error by Originator's Bank.

Case #2. Suppose the same payment order by Originator to Originator's Bank as in Case #1. In executing the payment order Originator's Bank issues a payment order to Intermediary Bank in which the beneficiary's bank is identified only by number, #67890. That number does not refer to Bank A. Rather, it identifies a person that is not a bank. If processing by Intermediary Bank of the payment order of Originator's Bank is done by automated means, Intermediary Bank will rely on the number #67890 to identify the beneficiary's bank. Intermediary Bank has no duty to determine whether the number identifies a bank. The funds transfer cannot be completed in this case because no bank is identified as the beneficiary's bank. Subsection (a) puts the risk of loss on Originator's Bank. Originator's Bank is not entitled to payment from Originator. Section 4A–402(c). Originator's Bank has improperly executed Originator's payment order and may be liable for damages under Section 4A–305. Originator's Bank is obliged to compensate Intermediary Bank for loss and expenses resulting from the error by Originator's Bank.

Subsection (a) also applies if #67890 identifies a bank, but the bank is not Bank A. Intermediary Bank may rely on the number as the proper identification of the beneficiary's bank. If the bank to which Intermediary Bank sends its payment order accepts the order, Intermediary Bank is entitled to payment from Originator's Bank, but Originator's Bank is not entitled to payment from Originator. The analysis is similar to that in Case #1.

2. Subsection (b)(2) of Section 4A–208 addresses cases in which an erroneous identification of a beneficiary's bank or intermediary bank by name and number is made in a payment order of a sender that is not a bank. Suppose Originator issues a payment order to Originator's Bank that instructs that bank to use an intermediary bank identified as Bank A and by an identifying number, #67890. The identifying number refers to Bank B. Originator intended to identify Bank A as intermediary bank. If Originator's Bank relied on the number and issued a payment order to Bank B the rights of Originator's Bank depend upon whether the proof of notice stated in subsection (b)(2) is made by Originator's Bank. If proof is made, Originator's Bank's rights are governed by subsection (b)(1) of Section 4A–208. Originator's Bank is not liable for breach of Section 4A–302(a)(1) and is entitled to compensation from Originator for any loss and expenses resulting from Originator's error. If notice is not proved, Originator's Bank may not rely on the number in executing Originator's payment order. Since Originator's Bank does not get the benefit of subsection (b)(1) in that case, Originator's Bank improperly executed Originator's payment order and is in breach of the obligation stated in Section 4A–302(a)(1). If notice is not given, Originator's Bank can rely on the name if it is not aware of the conflict in name and number. Subsection (b)(3).

3. Although the principal purpose of Section 4A–208 is to accommodate automated processing of payment orders, Section 4A–208 applies regardless of whether processing is done by automation, semiautomated means or manually.

§ 4A–209. Acceptance of Payment Order.

(a) Subject to subsection (d), a receiving bank other than the beneficiary's bank accepts a payment order when it executes the order.

(b) Subject to subsections (c) and (d), a beneficiary's bank accepts a payment order at the earliest of the following times:

(1) when the bank (i) pays the beneficiary as stated in Section 4A–405(a) or 4A–405(b), or (ii) notifies the beneficiary of receipt of the order or that the account of the beneficiary has been credited with respect to the order unless the notice indicates that the bank is rejecting the order or that funds with respect to the order may not be withdrawn or used until receipt of payment from the sender of the order;

(2) when the bank receives payment of the entire amount of the sender's order pursuant to Section 4A–403(a)(1) or 4A–403(a)(2); or

(3) the opening of the next funds-transfer business day of the bank following the payment date of the order if, at that time, the amount of the sender's order is fully covered by a withdrawable credit balance in an authorized account of the sender or the bank has otherwise received full payment from the sender, unless the order was rejected before that time or is rejected within (i) one hour after that time, or (ii) one hour after the opening of the next business day of the sender following the payment date if that time is later. If notice of rejection is received by the sender after the payment date and the authorized account of the sender does not bear interest, the bank is obliged to pay interest to the sender on the amount of the order for the number of days elapsing after the payment date to the day the sender receives notice or learns that the order was not accepted, counting that day as an elapsed day. If the withdrawable credit balance during that period falls below the amount of the order, the amount of interest payable is reduced accordingly.

(c)   Acceptance of a payment order cannot occur before the order is received by the receiving bank. Acceptance does not occur under subsection (b)(2) or (b)(3) if the beneficiary of the payment order does not have an account with the receiving bank, the account has been closed, or the receiving bank is not permitted by law to receive credits for the beneficiary's account.

(d)   A payment order issued to the originator's bank cannot be accepted until the payment date if the bank is the beneficiary's bank, or the execution date if the bank is not the beneficiary's bank. If the originator's bank executes the originator's payment order before the execution date or pays the beneficiary of the originator's payment order before the payment date and the payment order is subsequently canceled pursuant to Section 4A–211(b), the bank may recover from the beneficiary any payment received to the extent allowed by the law governing mistake and restitution.

Official Comment

1.   This section treats the sender's payment order as a request by the sender to the receiving bank to execute or pay the order and that request can be accepted or rejected by the receiving bank. Section 4A–209 defines when acceptance occurs. Section 4A–210 covers rejection. Acceptance of the payment order imposes an obligation on the receiving bank to the sender if the receiving bank is not the beneficiary's bank, or to the beneficiary if the receiving bank is the beneficiary's bank. These obligations are stated in Section 4A–302 and Section 4A–404.

2.   Acceptance by a receiving bank other than the beneficiary's bank is defined in Section 4A–209(a). That subsection states the only way that a bank other than the beneficiary's bank can accept a payment order. A payment order to a bank other than the beneficiary's bank is, in effect, a request that the receiving bank execute the sender's order by issuing a payment order to the beneficiary's bank or to an intermediary bank. Normally, acceptance occurs at the time of execution, but there is an exception stated in subsection (d) and discussed in Comment 9. Execution occurs when the receiving bank "issues a payment order intended to carry out" the sender's order. Section 4A–301(a). In some cases the payment order issued by the receiving bank may not conform to the sender's order. For example, the receiving bank might make a mistake in the amount of its order, or the order might be issued to the wrong beneficiary's bank or for the benefit of the wrong beneficiary. In all of these cases there is acceptance of the sender's order by the bank when the receiving bank issues its order intended to carry out the sender's order, even though the bank's payment order does not in fact carry out the instruction of the sender. Improper execution of the sender's order may lead to liability to the sender for damages or it may mean that the sender is not obliged to pay its payment order. These matters are covered in Section 4A–303, Section 4A–305, and Section 4A–402.

3.   A receiving bank has no duty to accept a payment order unless the bank makes an agreement, either before or after issuance of the payment order, to accept it, or acceptance is required by a funds transfer system rule. If the bank makes such an agreement it incurs a contractual obligation based on the agreement and may be held liable for breach of contract if a failure to execute violates the agreement. In many cases a bank will enter into an agreement with its customer to govern the rights and obligations of the parties with respect to payment orders issued to the bank by the customer or, in cases in which the sender is also a bank, there may be a funds transfer system rule that governs the obligations of a receiving bank with respect to payment orders transmitted over the system. Such agreements or rules can specify the circumstances under which a receiving bank is obliged to execute a payment order and can define the extent of liability of the receiving bank for breach of the agreement or rule. Section 4A–305(d) states the liability for breach of an agreement to execute a payment order.

4.   In the case of a payment order issued to the beneficiary's bank, acceptance is defined in Section 4A–209(b). The function of a beneficiary's bank that receives a payment order is different from that of a receiving bank that receives a payment order for execution. In the typical case, the beneficiary's bank simply receives payment from the sender of the order, credits the account of the beneficiary and notifies the beneficiary of the credit. Acceptance by the beneficiary's bank does not create any obligation to the sender. Acceptance by the beneficiary's bank means that the bank is liable to the beneficiary for the amount of the order. Section 4A–404(a). There are three ways in which the beneficiary's bank can accept a payment order which are described in the following comments.

5.   Under Section 4A–209(b)(1), the beneficiary's bank can accept a payment order by paying the beneficiary. In the normal case of crediting an account of the beneficiary, payment occurs when the beneficiary is given notice of the right to withdraw the credit, the credit is applied to a debt of the beneficiary, or "funds with respect to the order" are otherwise made available to the beneficiary. Section 4A–405(a). The quoted phrase covers cases in which funds are made available to the beneficiary as a result of receipt of a payment order for the benefit of the beneficiary but the release of funds is not expressed as payment of the order. For example, the beneficiary's

bank might express a release of funds equal to the amount of the order as a "loan" that will be automatically repaid when the beneficiary's bank receives payment by the sender of the order. If the release of funds is designated as a loan pursuant to a routine practice of the bank, the release is conditional payment of the order rather than a loan, particularly if normal incidents of a loan such as the signing of a loan agreement or note and the payment of interest are not present. Such a release of funds is payment to the beneficiary under Section 4A–405(a). Under Section 4A–405(c) the bank cannot recover the money from the beneficiary if the bank does not receive payment from the sender of the payment order that it accepted. Exceptions to this rule are stated in § 4A–405(d) and (e). The beneficiary's bank may also accept by notifying the beneficiary that the order has been received. "Notifies" is defined in Section 1–201(26).* In some cases a beneficiary's bank will receive a payment order during the day but settlement of the sender's obligation to pay the order will not occur until the end of the day. If the beneficiary's bank wants to defer incurring liability to the beneficiary until the beneficiary's bank receives payment, it can do so. The beneficiary's bank incurs no liability to the beneficiary with respect to a payment order that it receives until it accepts the order. If the bank does not accept pursuant to subsection (b)(1), acceptance does not occur until the end of the day when the beneficiary's bank receives settlement. If the sender settles, the payment order will be accepted under subsection (b)(2) and the funds will be released to the beneficiary the next morning. If the sender doesn't settle, no acceptance occurs. In either case the beneficiary's bank suffers no loss.

6.   In most cases the beneficiary's bank will receive a payment order from another bank. If the sender is a bank and the beneficiary's bank receives payment from the sender by final settlement through the Federal Reserve System or a funds transfer system (Section 4A–403(a)(1)) or, less commonly, through credit to an account of the beneficiary's bank with the sender or another bank (Section 4A–403(a)(2)), acceptance by the beneficiary's bank occurs at the time payment is made. Section 4A–209(b)(2). A minor exception to this rule is stated in Section 4A–209(c). Section 4A–209(b)(2) results in automatic acceptance of payment orders issued to a beneficiary's bank by means of Fedwire because the Federal Reserve account of the beneficiary's bank is credited and final payment is made to that bank when the payment order is received.

Subsection (b)(2) would also apply to cases in which the beneficiary's bank mistakenly pays a person who is not the beneficiary of the payment order issued to the beneficiary's bank. For example, suppose the payment order provides for immediate payment to Account #12345. The beneficiary's bank erroneously credits Account #12346 and notifies the holder of that account of the credit. No acceptance occurs in this case under subsection (b)(1) because the beneficiary of the order has not been paid or notified. The holder of Account #12345 is the beneficiary of the order issued to the beneficiary's bank. But acceptance will normally occur if the beneficiary's bank takes no other action, because the bank will normally receive settlement with respect to the payment order. At that time the bank has accepted because the sender paid its payment order. The bank is liable to pay the holder of Account #12345. The bank has paid the holder of Account #12346 by mistake, and has a right to recover the payment if the credit is withdrawn, to the extent provided in the law governing mistake and restitution.

7.   Subsection (b)(3) covers cases of inaction by the beneficiary's bank. It applies whether or not the sender is a bank and covers a case in which the sender and the beneficiary both have accounts with the receiving bank and payment will be made by debiting the account of the sender and crediting the account of the beneficiary. Subsection (b)(3) is similar to subsection (b)(2) in that it bases acceptance by the beneficiary's bank on payment by the sender. Payment by the sender is effected by a debit to the sender's account if the account balance is sufficient to cover the amount of the order. On the payment date (Section 4A–401) of the order the beneficiary's bank will normally credit the beneficiary's account and notify the beneficiary of receipt of the order if it is satisfied that the sender's account balance covers the order or is willing to give credit to the sender. In some cases, however, the bank may not be willing to give credit to the sender and it may not be possible for the bank to determine until the end of the day on the payment date whether there are sufficient good funds in the sender's account. There may be various transactions during the day involving funds going into and out of the account. Some of these transactions may occur late in the day or after the close of the banking day. To accommodate this situation, subsection (b)(3) provides that the status of the account is determined at the opening of the next funds transfer business day of the beneficiary's bank after the payment date of the order. If the sender's account balance is sufficient to cover the order, the beneficiary's bank has a source of payment and the result in almost all cases is that the bank accepts the order at that time if it did not previously accept under subsection (b)(1). In rare cases, a bank may want to avoid acceptance under subsection (b)(3) by rejecting the order as discussed in Comment 8.

8.   Section 4A–209 is based on a general principle that a receiving bank is not obliged to accept a payment order unless it has agreed or is bound by a funds transfer system rule to do so. Thus, provision is made to allow the receiving bank to prevent acceptance of the order. This principle is consistently followed if the receiving bank

---

*   *Referring to unrevised Article 1 (Appendix A).*

is not the beneficiary's bank. If the receiving bank is not the beneficiary's bank, acceptance is in the control of the receiving bank because it occurs only if the order is executed. But in the case of the beneficiary's bank acceptance can occur by passive receipt of payment under subsection (b)(2) or (3). In the case of a payment made by Fedwire acceptance cannot be prevented. In other cases the beneficiary's bank can prevent acceptance by giving notice of rejection to the sender before payment occurs under Section 4A–403(a)(1) or (2). A minor exception to the ability of the beneficiary's bank to reject is stated in Section 4A–502(c)(3).

Under subsection (b)(3) acceptance occurs at the opening of the next funds transfer business day of the beneficiary's bank following the payment date unless the bank rejected the order before that time or it rejects within one hour after that time. In some cases the sender and the beneficiary's bank may not be in the same time zone or the beginning of the business day of the sender and the funds transfer business day of the beneficiary's bank may not coincide. For example, the sender may be located in California and the beneficiary's bank in New York. Since in most cases notice of rejection would be communicated electronically or by telephone, it might not be feasible for the bank to give notice before one hour after the opening of the funds transfer business day in New York because at that hour, the sender's business day may not have started in California. For that reason, there are alternative deadlines stated in subsection (b)(3). In the case stated, the bank acts in time if it gives notice within one hour after the opening of the business day of the sender. But if the notice of rejection is received by the sender after the payment date, the bank is obliged to pay interest to the sender if the sender's account does not bear interest. In that case the bank had the use of funds of the sender that the sender could reasonably assume would be used to pay the beneficiary. The rate of interest is stated in Section 4A–506. If the sender receives notice on the day after the payment date the sender is entitled to one day's interest. If receipt of notice is delayed for more than one day, the sender is entitled to interest for each additional day of delay.

9. Subsection (d) applies only to a payment order by the originator of a funds transfer to the originator's bank and it refers to the following situation. On April 1, Originator instructs Bank A to make a payment on April 15 to the account of Beneficiary in Bank B. By mistake, on April 1, Bank A executes Originator's payment order by issuing a payment order to Bank B instructing immediate payment to Beneficiary. Bank B credited Beneficiary's account and immediately released the funds to Beneficiary. Under subsection (d) no acceptance by Bank A occurred on April 1 when Originator's payment order was executed because acceptance cannot occur before the execution date which in this case would be April 15 or shortly before that date. Section 4A–301(b). Under Section 4A–402(c), Originator is not obliged to pay Bank A until the order is accepted and that can't occur until the execution date. But Bank A is required to pay Bank B when Bank B accepted Bank A's order on April 1. Unless Originator and Beneficiary are the same person, in almost all cases Originator is paying a debt owed to Beneficiary and early payment does not injure Originator because Originator does not have to pay Bank A until the execution date. Section 4A–402(c). Bank A takes the interest loss. But suppose that on April 3, Originator concludes that no debt was owed to Beneficiary or that the debt was less than the amount of the payment order. Under Section 4A–211(b) Originator can cancel its payment order if Bank A has not accepted. If early execution of Originator's payment order is acceptance, Originator can suffer a loss because cancellation after acceptance is not possible without the consent of Bank A and Bank B. Section 4A–211(c). If Originator has to pay Bank A, Originator would be required to seek recovery of the money from Beneficiary. Subsection (d) prevents this result and puts the risk of loss on Bank A by providing that the early execution does not result in acceptance until the execution date. Since on April 3 Originator's order was not yet accepted, Originator can cancel it under Section 4A–211(b). The result is that Bank A is not entitled to payment from Originator but is obliged to pay Bank B. Bank A has paid Beneficiary by mistake. If Originator's payment order is cancelled, Bank A becomes the originator of an erroneous funds transfer to Beneficiary. Bank A has the burden of recovering payment from Beneficiary on the basis of a payment by mistake. If Beneficiary received the money in good faith in payment of a debt owed to Beneficiary by Originator, the law of mistake and restitution may allow Beneficiary to keep all or part of the money received. If Originator owed money to Beneficiary, Bank A has paid Originator's debt and, under the law of restitution, which applies pursuant to Section 1–103, Bank A is subrogated to Beneficiary's rights against Originator on the debt.

If Bank A is the Beneficiary's bank and Bank A credited Beneficiary's account and released the funds to Beneficiary on April 1, the analysis is similar. If Originator's order is cancelled, Bank A has paid Beneficiary by mistake. The right of Bank A to recover the payment from Beneficiary is similar to Bank A's rights in the preceding paragraph.

§ 4A–210. Rejection of Payment Order.

(a) A payment order is rejected by the receiving bank by a notice of rejection transmitted to the sender orally, electronically, or in writing. A notice of rejection need not use any particular words and is sufficient if it indicates that the receiving bank is rejecting the order or will not execute or pay the order. Rejection is effective when the notice is given if transmission is by a means that is reasonable in the circumstances. If notice of rejection is given by a means that is not reasonable, rejection is effective when the notice is received. If an agreement of the sender and receiving bank establishes the means to be used to reject a payment order, (i) any means complying with the agreement is reasonable and (ii) any means not complying is not reasonable unless no significant delay in receipt of the notice resulted from the use of the noncomplying means.

(b) This subsection applies if a receiving bank other than the beneficiary's bank fails to execute a payment order despite the existence on the execution date of a withdrawable credit balance in an authorized account of the sender sufficient to cover the order. If the sender does not receive notice of rejection of the order on the execution date and the authorized account of the sender does not bear interest, the bank is obliged to pay interest to the sender on the amount of the order for the number of days elapsing after the execution date to the earlier of the day the order is canceled pursuant to Section 4A–211(d) or the day the sender receives notice or learns that the order was not executed, counting the final day of the period as an elapsed day. If the withdrawable credit balance during that period falls below the amount of the order, the amount of interest is reduced accordingly.

(c) If a receiving bank suspends payments, all unaccepted payment orders issued to it are deemed rejected at the time the bank suspends payments.

(d) Acceptance of a payment order precludes a later rejection of the order. Rejection of a payment order precludes a later acceptance of the order.

Official Comment

1. With respect to payment orders issued to a receiving bank other than the beneficiary's bank, notice of rejection is not necessary to prevent acceptance of the order. Acceptance can occur only if the receiving bank executes the order. Section 4A–209(a). But notice of rejection will routinely be given by such a bank in cases in which the bank cannot or is not willing to execute the order for some reason. There are many reasons why a bank doesn't execute an order. The payment order may not clearly instruct the receiving bank because of some ambiguity in the order or an internal inconsistency. In some cases, the receiving bank may not be able to carry out the instruction because of equipment failure, credit limitations on the receiving bank, or some other factor which makes proper execution of the order infeasible. In those cases notice of rejection is a means of informing the sender of the facts so that a corrected payment order can be transmitted or the sender can seek alternate means of completing the funds transfer. The other major reason for not executing an order is that the sender's account is insufficient to cover the order and the receiving bank is not willing to give credit to the sender. If the sender's account is sufficient to cover the order and the receiving bank chooses not to execute the order, notice of rejection is necessary to prevent liability to pay interest to the sender if the case falls within Section 4A–210(b) which is discussed in Comment 3.

2. A payment order to the beneficiary's bank can be accepted by inaction of the bank. Section 4A–209(b)(2) and (3). To prevent acceptance under those provisions it is necessary for the receiving bank to send notice of rejection before acceptance occurs. Subsection (a) of Section 4A–210 states the rule that rejection is accomplished by giving notice of rejection. This incorporates the definitions in Section 1–201(26).* Rejection is effective when notice is given if it is given by a means that is reasonable in the circumstances. Otherwise, it is effective when the notice is received. The question of when rejection is effective is important only in the relatively few cases under subsection (b)(2) and (3) in which a notice of rejection is necessary to prevent acceptance. The question of whether a particular means is reasonable depends on the facts in a particular case. In a very large percentage of cases the sender and the receiving bank will be in direct electronic contact with each other and in those cases a notice of rejection can be transmitted instantaneously. Since time is of the essence in a large proportion of funds transfers, some quick means of transmission would usually be required, but this is not always the case. The parties may specify by agreement the means by which communication between the parties is to be made.

3. Subsection (b) deals with cases in which a sender does not learn until after the execution date that the sender's order has not been executed. It applies only to cases in which the receiving bank was assured of payment because the sender's account was sufficient to cover the order. Normally, the receiving bank will accept the sender's order if it is assured of payment, but there may be some cases in which the bank chooses to reject. Unless the

---

* *Referring to unrevised Article 1 (Appendix A).*

receiving bank had obligated itself by agreement to accept, the failure to accept is not wrongful. There is no duty of the receiving bank to accept the payment order unless it is obliged to accept by express agreement. Section 4A–212. But even if the bank has not acted wrongfully, the receiving bank had the use of the sender's money that the sender could reasonably assume was to be the source of payment of the funds transfer. Until the sender learns that the order was not accepted the sender is denied the use of that money. Subsection (b) obliges the receiving bank to pay interest to the sender as restitution unless the sender receives notice of rejection on the execution date. The time of receipt of notice is determined pursuant to § 1–201(27).* The rate of interest is stated in Section 4A–506. If the sender receives notice on the day after the execution date, the sender is entitled to one day's interest. If receipt of notice is delayed for more than one day, the sender is entitled to interest for each additional day of delay.

4. Subsection (d) treats acceptance and rejection as mutually exclusive. If a payment order has been accepted, rejection of that order becomes impossible. If a payment order has been rejected it cannot be accepted later by the receiving bank. Once notice of rejection has been given, the sender may have acted on the notice by making the payment through other channels. If the receiving bank wants to act on a payment order that it has rejected it has to obtain the consent of the sender. In that case the consent of the sender would amount to the giving of a second payment order that substitutes for the rejected first order. If the receiving bank suspends payments (Section 4–104(1)(k)), subsection (c) provides that unaccepted payment orders are deemed rejected at the time suspension of payments occurs. This prevents acceptance by passage of time under Section 4A–209(b)(3).

§ 4A–211. Cancellation and Amendment of Payment Order.

(a) A communication of the sender of a payment order cancelling or amending the order may be transmitted to the receiving bank orally, electronically, or in writing. If a security procedure is in effect between the sender and the receiving bank, the communication is not effective to cancel or amend the order unless the communication is verified pursuant to the security procedure or the bank agrees to the cancellation or amendment.

(b) Subject to subsection (a), a communication by the sender cancelling or amending a payment order is effective to cancel or amend the order if notice of the communication is received at a time and in a manner affording the receiving bank a reasonable opportunity to act on the communication before the bank accepts the payment order.

(c) After a payment order has been accepted, cancellation or amendment of the order is not effective unless the receiving bank agrees or a funds-transfer system rule allows cancellation or amendment without agreement of the bank.

(1) With respect to a payment order accepted by a receiving bank other than the beneficiary's bank, cancellation or amendment is not effective unless a conforming cancellation or amendment of the payment order issued by the receiving bank is also made.

(2) With respect to a payment order accepted by the beneficiary's bank, cancellation or amendment is not effective unless the order was issued in execution of an unauthorized payment order, or because of a mistake by a sender in the funds transfer which resulted in the issuance of a payment order (i) that is a duplicate of a payment order previously issued by the sender, (ii) that orders payment to a beneficiary not entitled to receive payment from the originator, or (iii) that orders payment in an amount greater than the amount the beneficiary was entitled to receive from the originator. If the payment order is canceled or amended, the beneficiary's bank is entitled to recover from the beneficiary any amount paid to the beneficiary to the extent allowed by the law governing mistake and restitution.

(d) An unaccepted payment order is canceled by operation of law at the close of the fifth funds-transfer business day of the receiving bank after the execution date or payment date of the order.

(e) A canceled payment order cannot be accepted. If an accepted payment order is canceled, the acceptance is nullified and no person has any right or obligation based on the acceptance. Amendment of a

---

* *Referring to unrevised Article 1 (Appendix A).*

payment order is deemed to be cancellation of the original order at the time of amendment and issue of a new payment order in the amended form at the same time.

(f)   Unless otherwise provided in an agreement of the parties or in a funds-transfer system rule, if the receiving bank, after accepting a payment order, agrees to cancellation or amendment of the order by the sender or is bound by a funds-transfer system rule allowing cancellation or amendment without the bank's agreement, the sender, whether or not cancellation or amendment is effective, is liable to the bank for any loss and expenses, including reasonable attorney's fees, incurred by the bank as a result of the cancellation or amendment or attempted cancellation or amendment.

(g)   A payment order is not revoked by the death or legal incapacity of the sender unless the receiving bank knows of the death or of an adjudication of incapacity by a court of competent jurisdiction and has reasonable opportunity to act before acceptance of the order.

(h)   A funds-transfer system rule is not effective to the extent it conflicts with subsection (c)(2).

Official Comment

1.   This section deals with cancellation and amendment of payment orders. It states the conditions under which cancellation or amendment is both effective and rightful. There is no concept of wrongful cancellation or amendment of a payment order. If the conditions stated in this section are not met the attempted cancellation or amendment is not effective. If the stated conditions are met the cancellation or amendment is effective and rightful. The sender of a payment order may want to withdraw or change the order because the sender has had a change of mind about the transaction or because the payment order was erroneously issued or for any other reason. One common situation is that of multiple transmission of the same order. The sender that mistakenly transmits the same order twice wants to correct the mistake by cancelling the duplicate order. Or, a sender may have intended to order a payment of $1,000,000 but mistakenly issued an order to pay $10,000,000. In this case the sender might try to correct the mistake by cancelling the order and issuing another order in the proper amount. Or, the mistake could be corrected by amending the order to change it to the proper amount. Whether the error is corrected by amendment or cancellation and reissue the net result is the same. This result is stated in the last sentence of subsection (e).

2.   Subsection (a) allows a cancellation or amendment of a payment order to be communicated to the receiving bank "orally, electronically, or in writing." The quoted phrase is consistent with the language of Section 4A–103(a) applicable to payment orders. Cancellations and amendments are normally subject to verification pursuant to security procedures to the same extent as payment orders. Subsection (a) recognizes this fact by providing that in cases in which there is a security procedure in effect between the sender and the receiving bank the bank is not bound by a communication cancelling or amending an order unless verification has been made. This is necessary to protect the bank because under subsection (b) a cancellation or amendment can be effective by unilateral action of the sender. Without verification the bank cannot be sure whether the communication was or was not effective to cancel or amend a previously verified payment order.

3.   If the receiving bank has not yet accepted the order, there is no reason why the sender should not be able to cancel or amend the order unilaterally so long as the requirements of subsections (a) and (b) are met. If the receiving bank has accepted the order, it is possible to cancel or amend but only if the requirements of subsection (c) are met.

First consider the case of a receiving bank other than the beneficiary's bank. If the bank has not yet accepted the order, the sender can unilaterally cancel or amend. The communication amending or cancelling the payment order must be received in time to allow the bank to act on it before the bank issues its payment order in execution of the sender's order. The time that the sender's communication is received is governed by Section 4A–106. If a payment order does not specify a delayed payment date or execution date, the order will normally be executed shortly after receipt. Thus, as a practical matter, the sender will have very little time in which to instruct cancellation or amendment before acceptance. In addition, a receiving bank will normally have cut-off times for receipt of such communications, and the receiving bank is not obliged to act on communications received after the cut-off hour. Cancellation by the sender after execution of the order by the receiving bank requires the agreement of the bank unless a funds transfer rule otherwise provides. Subsection (c). Although execution of the sender's order by the receiving bank does not itself impose liability on the receiving bank (under Section 4A–402 no liability is incurred by the receiving bank to pay its order until it is accepted), it would commonly be the case that acceptance follows shortly after issuance. Thus, as a practical matter, a receiving bank that has executed a payment order will incur a liability to the next bank in the chain before it would be able to act on the cancellation request of its customer. It is unreasonable to impose on the receiving bank a risk of loss with respect to a cancellation request without the consent of the receiving bank.

The statute does not state how or when the agreement of the receiving bank must be obtained for cancellation after execution. The receiving bank's consent could be obtained at the time cancellation occurs or it could be based on a preexisting agreement. Or, a funds transfer system rule could provide that cancellation can be made unilaterally by the sender. By virtue of that rule any receiving bank covered by the rule is bound. Section 4A–501. If the receiving bank has already executed the sender's order, the bank would not consent to cancellation unless the bank to which the receiving bank has issued its payment order consents to cancellation of that order. It makes no sense to allow cancellation of a payment order unless all subsequent payment orders in the funds transfer that were issued because of the cancelled payment order are also cancelled. Under subsection (c)(1), if a receiving bank consents to cancellation of the payment order after it has executed, the cancellation is not effective unless the receiving bank also cancels the payment order issued by the bank.

4. With respect to a payment order issued to the beneficiary's bank, acceptance is particularly important because it creates liability to pay the beneficiary, it defines when the originator pays its obligation to the beneficiary, and it defines when any obligation for which the payment is made is discharged. Since acceptance affects the rights of the originator and the beneficiary it is not appropriate to allow the beneficiary's bank to agree to cancellation or amendment except in unusual cases. Except as provided in subsection (c)(2), cancellation or amendment after acceptance by the beneficiary's bank is not possible unless all parties affected by the order agree. Under subsection (c)(2), cancellation or amendment is possible only in the four cases stated. The following examples illustrate subsection (c)(2):

Case #1. Originator's Bank executed a payment order issued in the name of its customer as sender. The order was not authorized by the customer and was fraudulently issued. Beneficiary's Bank accepted the payment order issued by Originator's Bank. Under subsection (c)(2) Originator's Bank can cancel the order if Beneficiary's Bank consents. It doesn't make any difference whether the payment order that Originator's Bank accepted was or was not enforceable against the customer under Section 4A–202(b). Verification under that provision is important in determining whether Originator's Bank or the customer has the risk of loss, but it has no relevance under Section 4A–211(c)(2). Whether or not verified, the payment order was not authorized by the customer. Cancellation of the payment order to Beneficiary's Bank causes the acceptance of Beneficiary's Bank to be nullified. Subsection (e). Beneficiary's Bank is entitled to recover payment from the beneficiary to the extent allowed by the law of mistake and restitution. In this kind of case the beneficiary is usually a party to the fraud who has no right to receive or retain payment of the order.

Case #2. Originator owed Beneficiary $1,000,000 and ordered Bank A to pay that amount to the account of Beneficiary in Bank B. Bank A issued a complying order to Bank B, but by mistake issued a duplicate order as well. Bank B accepted both orders. Under subsection (c)(2)(i) cancellation of the duplicate order could be made by Bank A with the consent of Bank B. Beneficiary has no right to receive or retain payment of the duplicate payment order if only $1,000,000 was owed by Originator to Beneficiary. If Originator owed $2,000,000 to Beneficiary, the law of restitution might allow Beneficiary to retain the $1,000,000 paid by Bank B on the duplicate order. In that case Bank B is entitled to reimbursement from Bank A under subsection (f).

Case #3. Originator owed $1,000,000 to X. Intending to pay X, Originator ordered Bank A to pay $1,000,000 to Y's account in Bank B. Bank A issued a complying payment order to Bank B which Bank B accepted by releasing the $1,000,000 to Y. Under subsection (c)(2)(ii) Bank A can cancel its payment order to Bank B with the consent of Bank B if Y was not entitled to receive payment from Originator. Originator can also cancel its order to Bank A with Bank A's consent. Subsection (c)(1). Bank B may recover the $1,000,000 from Y unless the law of mistake and restitution allows Y to retain some or all of the amount paid. If no debt was owed to Y, Bank B should have a right of recovery.

Case #4. Originator owed Beneficiary $10,000. By mistake Originator ordered Bank A to pay $1,000,000 to the account of Beneficiary in Bank B. Bank A issued a complying order to Bank B which accepted by notifying Beneficiary of its right to withdraw $1,000,000. Cancellation is permitted in this case under subsection (c)(2)(iii). If Bank B paid Beneficiary it is entitled to recover the payment except to the extent the law of mistake and restitution allows Beneficiary to retain payment. In this case Beneficiary might be entitled to retain $10,000, the amount of the debt owed to Beneficiary. If Beneficiary may retain $10,000, Bank B would be entitled to $10,000 from Bank A pursuant to subsection (f). In this case Originator also cancelled its order. Thus Bank A would be entitled to $10,000 from Originator pursuant to subsection (f).

5.   Unless constrained by a funds transfer system rule, a receiving bank may agree to cancellation or amendment of the payment order under subsection (c) but is not required to do so regardless of the circumstances. If the receiving bank has incurred liability as a result of its acceptance of the sender's order, there are substantial risks in agreeing to cancellation or amendment. This is particularly true for a beneficiary's bank. Cancellation or amendment after acceptance by the beneficiary's bank can be made only in the four cases stated and the beneficiary's bank may not have any way of knowing whether the requirements of subsection (c) have been met or whether it will be able to recover payment from the beneficiary that received payment. Even with indemnity the beneficiary's bank may be reluctant to alienate its customer, the beneficiary, by denying the customer the funds. Subsection (c) leaves the decision to the beneficiary's bank unless the consent of the beneficiary's bank is not required under a funds transfer system rule or other interbank agreement. If a receiving bank agrees to cancellation or amendment under subsection (c)(1) or (2), it is automatically entitled to indemnification from the sender under subsection (f). The indemnification provision recognizes that a sender has no right to cancel a payment order after it is accepted by the receiving bank. If the receiving bank agrees to cancellation, it is doing so as an accommodation to the sender and it should not incur a risk of loss in doing so.

6.   Acceptance by the receiving bank of a payment order issued by the sender is comparable to acceptance of an offer under the law of contracts. Under that law the death or legal incapacity of an offeror terminates the offer even though the offeree has no notice of the death or incapacity. Restatement Second, Contracts § 48. Comment a. to that section states that the "rule seems to be a relic of the obsolete view that a contract requires a 'meeting of minds,' and it is out of harmony with the modern doctrine that a manifestation of assent is effective without regard to actual mental assent." Subsection (g), which reverses the Restatement rule in the case of a payment order, is similar to Section 4–405(1) which applies to checks. Subsection (g) does not address the effect of the bankruptcy of the sender of a payment order before the order is accepted, but the principle of subsection (g) has been recognized in *Bank of Marin v. England*, 385 U.S. 99 (1966). Although Bankruptcy Code Section 542(c) may not have been drafted with wire transfers in mind, its language can be read to allow the receiving bank to charge the sender's account for the amount of the payment order if the receiving bank executed it in ignorance of the bankruptcy.

7.   Subsection (d) deals with stale payment orders. Payment orders normally are executed on the execution date or the day after. An order issued to the beneficiary's bank is normally accepted on the payment date or the day after. If a payment order is not accepted on its execution or payment date or shortly thereafter, it is probable that there was some problem with the terms of the order or the sender did not have sufficient funds or credit to cover the amount of the order. Delayed acceptance of such an order is normally not contemplated, but the order may not have been cancelled by the sender. Subsection (d) provides for cancellation by operation of law to prevent an unexpected delayed acceptance.

8.   A funds transfer system rule can govern rights and obligations between banks that are parties to payment orders transmitted over the system even if the rule conflicts with Article 4A. In some cases, however, a rule governing a transaction between two banks can affect a third party in an unacceptable way. Subsection (h) deals with such a case. A funds transfer system rule cannot allow cancellation of a payment order accepted by the beneficiary's bank if the rule conflicts with subsection (c)(2). Because rights of the beneficiary and the originator are directly affected by acceptance, subsection (c)(2) severely limits cancellation. These limitations cannot be altered by funds transfer system rule.

§ 4A–212.   Liability and Duty of Receiving Bank Regarding Unaccepted Payment Order.

If a receiving bank fails to accept a payment order that it is obliged by express agreement to accept, the bank is liable for breach of the agreement to the extent provided in the agreement or in this Article, but does not otherwise have any duty to accept a payment order or, before acceptance, to take any action, or refrain from taking action, with respect to the order except as provided in this Article or by express agreement. Liability based on acceptance arises only when acceptance occurs as stated in Section 4A–209, and liability is limited to that provided in this Article. A receiving bank is not the agent of the sender or beneficiary of the payment order it accepts, or of any other party to the funds transfer, and the bank owes no duty to any party to the funds transfer except as provided in this Article or by express agreement.

Official Comment

With limited exceptions stated in this Article, the duties and obligations of receiving banks that carry out a funds transfer arise only as a result of acceptance of payment orders or of agreements made by receiving banks. Exceptions are stated in Section 4A–209(b)(3) and Section 4A–210(b). A receiving bank is not like a collecting bank under Article 4. No receiving bank, whether it be an originator's bank, an intermediary bank or a beneficiary's bank, is an agent for any other party in the funds transfer.

PART 3

EXECUTION OF SENDER'S PAYMENT ORDER BY RECEIVING BANK

§ 4A–301. Execution and Execution Date.

(a) A payment order is "executed" by the receiving bank when it issues a payment order intended to carry out the payment order received by the bank. A payment order received by the beneficiary's bank can be accepted but cannot be executed.

(b) "Execution date" of a payment order means the day on which the receiving bank may properly issue a payment order in execution of the sender's order. The execution date may be determined by instruction of the sender but cannot be earlier than the day the order is received and, unless otherwise determined, is the day the order is received. If the sender's instruction states a payment date, the execution date is the payment date or an earlier date on which execution is reasonably necessary to allow payment to the beneficiary on the payment date.

Official Comment

1. The terms "executed," "execution" and "execution date" are used only with respect to a payment order to a receiving bank other than the beneficiary's bank. The beneficiary's bank can accept the payment order that it receives, but it does not execute the order. Execution refers to the act of the receiving bank in issuing a payment order "intended to carry out" the payment order that the bank received. A receiving bank has executed an order even if the order issued by the bank does not carry out the order received by the bank. For example, the bank may have erroneously issued an order to the wrong beneficiary, or in the wrong amount or to the wrong beneficiary's bank. In each of these cases execution has occurred but the execution is erroneous. Erroneous execution is covered in Section 4A–303.

2. "Execution date" refers to the time a payment order should be executed rather than the day it is actually executed. Normally the sender will not specify an execution date, but most payment orders are meant to be executed immediately. Thus, the execution date is normally the day the order is received by the receiving bank. It is common for the sender to specify a "payment date" which is defined in Section 4A–401 as "the day on which the amount of the order is payable to the beneficiary by the beneficiary's bank." Except for automated clearing house transfers, if a funds transfer is entirely within the United States and the payment is to be carried out electronically, the execution date is the payment date unless the order is received after the payment date. If the payment is to be carried out through an automated clearing house, execution may occur before the payment date. In an ACH transfer the beneficiary is usually paid one or two days after issue of the originator's payment order. The execution date is determined by the stated payment date and is a day before the payment date on which execution is reasonably necessary to allow payment on the payment date. A funds transfer system rule could also determine the execution date of orders received by the receiving bank if both the sender and the receiving bank are participants in the funds transfer system. The execution date can be determined by the payment order itself or by separate instructions of the sender or an agreement of the sender and the receiving bank. The second sentence of subsection (b) must be read in the light of Section 4A–106 which states that if a payment order is received after the cut-off time of the receiving bank it may be treated by the bank as received at the opening of the next funds transfer business day.

3. Execution on the execution date is timely, but the order can be executed before or after the execution date. Section 4A–209(d) and Section 4A–402(c) state the consequences of early execution and Section 4A–305(a) states the consequences of late execution.

§ 4A–302. Obligations of Receiving Bank in Execution of Payment Order.

(a) Except as provided in subsections (b) through (d), if the receiving bank accepts a payment order pursuant to Section 4A–209(a), the bank has the following obligations in executing the order:

(1) The receiving bank is obliged to issue, on the execution date, a payment order complying with the sender's order and to follow the sender's instructions concerning (i) any intermediary bank or funds-transfer system to be used in carrying out the funds transfer, or (ii) the means by which payment orders are to be transmitted in the funds transfer. If the originator's bank issues a payment order to an intermediary bank, the originator's bank is obliged to instruct the intermediary bank according to the instruction of the originator. An intermediary bank in the funds transfer is similarly bound by an instruction given to it by the sender of the payment order it accepts.

(2) If the sender's instruction states that the funds transfer is to be carried out telephonically or by wire transfer or otherwise indicates that the funds transfer is to be carried out by the most expeditious means, the receiving bank is obliged to transmit its payment order by the most expeditious available means, and to instruct any intermediary bank accordingly. If a sender's instruction states a payment date, the receiving bank is obliged to transmit its payment order at a time and by means reasonably necessary to allow payment to the beneficiary on the payment date or as soon thereafter as is feasible.

(b) Unless otherwise instructed, a receiving bank executing a payment order may (i) use any funds-transfer system if use of that system is reasonable in the circumstances, and (ii) issue a payment order to the beneficiary's bank or to an intermediary bank through which a payment order conforming to the sender's order can expeditiously be issued to the beneficiary's bank if the receiving bank exercises ordinary care in the selection of the intermediary bank. A receiving bank is not required to follow an instruction of the sender designating a funds-transfer system to be used in carrying out the funds transfer if the receiving bank, in good faith, determines that it is not feasible to follow the instruction or that following the instruction would unduly delay completion of the funds transfer.

(c) Unless subsection (a)(2) applies or the receiving bank is otherwise instructed, the bank may execute a payment order by transmitting its payment order by first class mail or by any means reasonable in the circumstances. If the receiving bank is instructed to execute the sender's order by transmitting its payment order by a particular means, the receiving bank may issue its payment order by the means stated or by any means as expeditious as the means stated.

(d) Unless instructed by the sender, (i) the receiving bank may not obtain payment of its charges for services and expenses in connection with the execution of the sender's order by issuing a payment order in an amount equal to the amount of the sender's order less the amount of the charges, and (ii) may not instruct a subsequent receiving bank to obtain payment of its charges in the same manner.

Official Comment

1. In the absence of agreement, the receiving bank is not obliged to execute an order of the sender. Section 4A–212. Section 4A–302 states the manner in which the receiving bank may execute the sender's order if execution occurs. Subsection (a)(1) states the residual rule. The payment order issued by the receiving bank must comply with the sender's order and, unless some other rule is stated in the section, the receiving bank is obliged to follow any instruction of the sender concerning which funds transfer system is to be used, which intermediary banks are to be used, and what means of transmission is to be used. The instruction of the sender may be incorporated in the payment order itself or may be given separately. For example, there may be a master agreement between the sender and receiving bank containing instructions governing payment orders to be issued from time to time by the sender to the receiving bank. In most funds transfers, speed is a paramount consideration. A sender that wants assurance that the funds transfer will be expeditiously completed can specify the means to be used. The receiving bank can follow the instructions literally or it can use an equivalent means. For example, if the sender instructs the receiving bank to transmit by telex, the receiving bank could use telephone instead. Subsection (c). In most cases the sender will not specify a particular means but will use a general term such as "by wire" or "wire transfer" or "as soon as possible." These words signify that the sender wants a same-day transfer. In these cases the receiving bank is required to use a telephonic or electronic communication to transmit its order and is also required to instruct any intermediary bank to which it issues its order to transmit by similar means. Subsection (a)(2). In other cases, such as an automated clearing house transfer, a same-day transfer is not contemplated. Normally the sender's instruction or the context in which the payment order is received makes clear the type of funds transfer that is appropriate. If the sender states a payment date with respect to the payment order, the receiving bank is obliged to execute the order at a time and in a manner to meet the payment date if that is feasible. Subsection

(a)(2). This provision would apply to many ACH transfers made to pay recurring debts of the sender. In other cases, involving relatively small amounts, time may not be an important factor and cost may be a more important element. Fast means, such as telephone or electronic transmission, are more expensive than slow means such as mailing. Subsection (c) states that in the absence of instructions the receiving bank is given discretion to decide. It may issue its payment order by first class mail or by any means reasonable in the circumstances. Section 4A–305 states the liability of a receiving bank for breach of the obligations stated in Section 4A–302.

2.   Subsection (b) concerns the choice of intermediary banks to be used in completing the funds transfer, and the funds transfer system to be used. If the receiving bank is not instructed about the matter, it can issue an order directly to the beneficiary's bank or can issue an order to an intermediary bank. The receiving bank also has discretion concerning use of a funds transfer system. In some cases it may be reasonable to use either an automated clearing house system or a wire transfer system such as Fedwire or CHIPS. Normally, the receiving bank will follow the instruction of the sender in these matters, but in some cases it may be prudent for the bank not to follow instructions. The sender may have designated a funds transfer system to be used in carrying out the funds transfer, but it may not be feasible to use the designated system because of some impediment such as a computer breakdown which prevents prompt execution of the order. The receiving bank is permitted to use an alternate means of transmittal in a good faith effort to execute the order expeditiously. The same leeway is not given to the receiving bank if the sender designates an intermediary bank through which the funds transfer is to be routed. The sender's designation of that intermediary bank may mean that the beneficiary's bank is expecting to obtain a credit from that intermediary bank and may have relied on that anticipated credit. If the receiving bank uses another intermediary bank the expectations of the beneficiary's bank may not be realized. The receiving bank could choose to route the transfer to another intermediary bank and then to the designated intermediary bank if there were some reason such as a lack of a correspondent-bank relationship or a bilateral credit limitation, but the designated intermediary bank cannot be circumvented. To do so violates the sender's instructions.

3.   The normal rule, under subsection (a)(1), is that the receiving bank, in executing a payment order, is required to issue a payment order that complies as to amount with that of the sender's order. In most cases the receiving bank issues an order equal to the amount of the sender's order and makes a separate charge for services and expenses in executing the sender's order. In some cases, particularly if it is an intermediary bank that is executing an order, charges are collected by deducting them from the amount of the payment order issued by the executing bank. If that is done, the amount of the payment order accepted by the beneficiary's bank will be slightly less than the amount of the originator's payment order. For example, Originator, in order to pay an obligation of $1,000,000 owed to Beneficiary, issues a payment order to Originator's Bank to pay $1,000,000 to the account of Beneficiary in Beneficiary's Bank. Originator's Bank issues a payment order to Intermediary Bank for $1,000,000 and debits Originator's account for $1,000,010. The extra $10 is the fee of Originator's Bank. Intermediary Bank executes the payment order of Originator's Bank by issuing a payment order to Beneficiary's Bank for $999,990, but under § 4A–402(c) is entitled to receive $1,000,000 from Originator's Bank. The $10 difference is the fee of Intermediary Bank. Beneficiary's Bank credits Beneficiary's account for $999,990. When Beneficiary's Bank accepts the payment order of Intermediary Bank the result is a payment of $999,990 from Originator to Beneficiary. Section 4A–406(a). If that payment discharges the $1,000,000 debt, the effect is that Beneficiary has paid the charges of Intermediary Bank and Originator has paid the charges of Originator's Bank. Subsection (d) of Section 4A–302 allows Intermediary Bank to collect its charges by deducting them from the amount of the payment order, but only if instructed to do so by Originator's Bank. Originator's Bank is not authorized to give that instruction to Intermediary Bank unless Originator authorized the instruction. Thus, Originator can control how the charges of Originator's Bank and Intermediary Bank are to be paid. Subsection (d) does not apply to charges of Beneficiary's Bank to Beneficiary.

In the case discussed in the preceding paragraph the $10 charge is trivial in relation to the amount of the payment and it may not be important to Beneficiary how the charge is paid. But it may be very important if the $1,000,000 obligation represented the price of exercising a right such as an option favorable to Originator and unfavorable to Beneficiary. Beneficiary might well argue that it was entitled to receive $1,000,000. If the option was exercised shortly before its expiration date, the result could be loss of the option benefit because the required payment of $1,000,000 was not made before the option expired. Section 4A–406(c) allows Originator to preserve the option benefit. The amount received by Beneficiary is deemed to be $1,000,000 unless Beneficiary demands the $10 and Originator does not pay it.

§ 4A–303. Erroneous Execution of Payment Order.

(a)   A receiving bank that (i) executes the payment order of the sender by issuing a payment order in an amount greater than the amount of the sender's order, or (ii) issues a payment order in execution of the sender's order and then issues a duplicate order, is entitled to payment of the amount of the sender's order under Section 4A–402(c) if that subsection is otherwise satisfied. The bank is entitled to recover from the beneficiary of the erroneous order the excess payment received to the extent allowed by the law governing mistake and restitution.

(b)   A receiving bank that executes the payment order of the sender by issuing a payment order in an amount less than the amount of the sender's order is entitled to payment of the amount of the sender's order under Section 4A–402(c) if (i) that subsection is otherwise satisfied and (ii) the bank corrects its mistake by issuing an additional payment order for the benefit of the beneficiary of the sender's order. If the error is not corrected, the issuer of the erroneous order is entitled to receive or retain payment from the sender of the order it accepted only to the extent of the amount of the erroneous order. This subsection does not apply if the receiving bank executes the sender's payment order by issuing a payment order in an amount less than the amount of the sender's order for the purpose of obtaining payment of its charges for services and expenses pursuant to instruction of the sender.

(c)   If a receiving bank executes the payment order of the sender by issuing a payment order to a beneficiary different from the beneficiary of the sender's order and the funds transfer is completed on the basis of that error, the sender of the payment order that was erroneously executed and all previous senders in the funds transfer are not obliged to pay the payment orders they issued. The issuer of the erroneous order is entitled to recover from the beneficiary of the order the payment received to the extent allowed by the law governing mistake and restitution.

Official Comment

1.   Section 4A–303 states the effect of erroneous execution of a payment order by the receiving bank. Under Section 4A–402(c) the sender of a payment order is obliged to pay the amount of the order to the receiving bank if the bank executes the order, but the obligation to pay is excused if the beneficiary's bank does not accept a payment order instructing payment to the beneficiary of the sender's order. If erroneous execution of the sender's order causes the wrong beneficiary to be paid, the sender is not required to pay. If erroneous execution causes the wrong amount to be paid the sender is not obliged to pay the receiving bank an amount in excess of the amount of the sender's order. Section 4A–303 takes precedence over Section 4A–402(c) and states the liability of the sender and the rights of the receiving bank in various cases of erroneous execution.

2.   Subsections (a) and (b) deal with cases in which the receiving bank executes by issuing a payment order in the wrong amount. If Originator ordered Originator's Bank to pay $1,000,000 to the account of Beneficiary in Beneficiary's Bank, but Originator's Bank erroneously instructed Beneficiary's Bank to pay $2,000,000 to Beneficiary's account, subsection (a) applies. If Beneficiary's Bank accepts the order of Originator's Bank, Beneficiary's Bank is entitled to receive $2,000,000 from Originator's Bank, but Originator's Bank is entitled to receive only $1,000,000 from Originator. Originator's Bank is entitled to recover the overpayment from Beneficiary to the extent allowed by the law governing mistake and restitution. Originator's Bank would normally have a right to recover the overpayment from Beneficiary, but in unusual cases the law of restitution might allow Beneficiary to keep all or part of the overpayment. For example, if Originator owed $2,000,000 to Beneficiary and Beneficiary received the extra $1,000,000 in good faith in discharge of the debt, Beneficiary may be allowed to keep it. In this case Originator's Bank has paid an obligation of Originator and under the law of restitution, which applies through Section 1–103, Originator's Bank would be subrogated to Beneficiary's rights against Originator on the obligation paid by Originator's Bank.

If Originator's Bank erroneously executed Originator's order by instructing Beneficiary's Bank to pay less than $1,000,000, subsection (b) applies. If Originator's Bank corrects its error by issuing another payment order to Beneficiary's Bank that results in payment of $1,000,000 to Beneficiary, Originator's Bank is entitled to payment of $1,000,000 from Originator. If the mistake is not corrected, Originator's Bank is entitled to payment from Originator only in the amount of the order issued by Originator's Bank.

3.   Subsection (a) also applies to duplicate payment orders. Assume Originator's Bank properly executes Originator's $1,000,000 payment order and then by mistake issues a second $1,000,000 payment order in execution of Originator's order. If Beneficiary's Bank accepts both orders issued by Originator's Bank, Beneficiary's Bank is

entitled to receive $2,000,000 from Originator's Bank but Originator's Bank is entitled to receive only $1,000,000 from Originator. The remedy of Originator's Bank is the same as that of a receiving bank that executes by issuing an order in an amount greater than the sender's order. It may recover the overpayment from Beneficiary to the extent allowed by the law governing mistake and restitution and in a proper case as stated in Comment 2 may have subrogation rights if it is not entitled to recover from Beneficiary.

4. Suppose Originator instructs Originator's Bank to pay $1,000,000 to Account #12345 in Beneficiary's Bank. Originator's Bank erroneously instructs Beneficiary's Bank to pay $1,000,000 to Account #12346 and Beneficiary's Bank accepted. Subsection (c) covers this case. Originator is not obliged to pay its payment order, but Originator's Bank is required to pay $1,000,000 to Beneficiary's Bank. The remedy of Originator's Bank is to recover $1,000,000 from the holder of Account #12346 that received payment by mistake. Recovery based on the law of mistake and restitution is described in Comment 2.

§ 4A–304. Duty of Sender to Report Erroneously Executed Payment Order.

If the sender of a payment order that is erroneously executed as stated in Section 4A–303 receives notification from the receiving bank that the order was executed or that the sender's account was debited with respect to the order, the sender has a duty to exercise ordinary care to determine, on the basis of information available to the sender, that the order was erroneously executed and to notify the bank of the relevant facts within a reasonable time not exceeding 90 days after the notification from the bank was received by the sender. If the sender fails to perform that duty, the bank is not obliged to pay interest on any amount refundable to the sender under Section 4A–402(d) for the period before the bank learns of the execution error. The bank is not entitled to any recovery from the sender on account of a failure by the sender to perform the duty stated in this section.

Official Comment

This section is identical in effect to Section 4A–204 which applies to unauthorized orders issued in the name of a customer of the receiving bank. The rationale is stated in Comment 2 to Section 4A–204.

§ 4A–305. Liability for Late or Improper Execution or Failure to Execute Payment Order.

(a) If a funds transfer is completed but execution of a payment order by the receiving bank in breach of Section 4A–302 results in delay in payment to the beneficiary, the bank is obliged to pay interest to either the originator or the beneficiary of the funds transfer for the period of delay caused by the improper execution. Except as provided in subsection (c), additional damages are not recoverable.

(b) If execution of a payment order by a receiving bank in breach of Section 4A–302 results in (i) noncompletion of the funds transfer, (ii) failure to use an intermediary bank designated by the originator, or (iii) issuance of a payment order that does not comply with the terms of the payment order of the originator, the bank is liable to the originator for its expenses in the funds transfer and for incidental expenses and interest losses, to the extent not covered by subsection (a), resulting from the improper execution. Except as provided in subsection (c), additional damages are not recoverable.

(c) In addition to the amounts payable under subsections (a) and (b), damages, including consequential damages, are recoverable to the extent provided in an express written agreement of the receiving bank.

(d) If a receiving bank fails to execute a payment order it was obliged by express agreement to execute, the receiving bank is liable to the sender for its expenses in the transaction and for incidental expenses and interest losses resulting from the failure to execute. Additional damages, including consequential damages, are recoverable to the extent provided in an express written agreement of the receiving bank, but are not otherwise recoverable.

(e) Reasonable attorney's fees are recoverable if demand for compensation under subsection (a) or (b) is made and refused before an action is brought on the claim. If a claim is made for breach of an agreement under subsection (d) and the agreement does not provide for damages, reasonable attorney's fees are recoverable if demand for compensation under subsection (d) is made and refused before an action is brought on the claim.

(f)   Except as stated in this section, the liability of a receiving bank under subsections (a) and (b) may not be varied by agreement.

Official Comment

1.   Subsection (a) covers cases of delay in completion of a funds transfer resulting from an execution by a receiving bank in breach of Section 4A–302(a). The receiving bank is obliged to pay interest on the amount of the order for the period of the delay. The rate of interest is stated in Section 4A–506. With respect to wire transfers (other than ACH transactions) within the United States, the expectation is that the funds transfer will be completed the same day. In those cases, the originator can reasonably expect that the originator's account will be debited on the same day as the beneficiary's account is credited. If the funds transfer is delayed, compensation can be paid either to the originator or to the beneficiary. The normal practice is to compensate the beneficiary's bank to allow that bank to compensate the beneficiary by back-valuing the payment by the number of days of delay. Thus, the beneficiary is in the same position that it would have been in if the funds transfer had been completed on the same day. Assume on Day 1, Originator's Bank issues its payment order to Intermediary Bank which is received on that day. Intermediary Bank does not execute that order until Day 2 when it issues an order to Beneficiary's Bank which is accepted on that day. Intermediary Bank complies with subsection (a) by paying one day's interest to Beneficiary's Bank for the account of Beneficiary.

2.   Subsection (b) applies to cases of breach of Section 4A–302 involving more than mere delay. In those cases the bank is liable for damages for improper execution but they are limited to compensation for interest losses and incidental expenses of the sender resulting from the breach, the expenses of the sender in the funds transfer and attorney's fees. This subsection reflects the judgment that imposition of consequential damages on a bank for commission of an error is not justified.

The leading common law case on the subject of consequential damages is *Evra Corp. v. Swiss Bank Corp.*, 673 F.2d 951 (7th Cir.1982), in which Swiss Bank, an intermediary bank, failed to execute a payment order. Because the beneficiary did not receive timely payment the originator lost a valuable ship charter. The lower court awarded the originator $2.1 million for lost profits even though the amount of the payment order was only $27,000. The Seventh Circuit reversed, in part on the basis of the common law rule of *Hadley v. Baxendale* that consequential damages may not be awarded unless the defendant is put on notice of the special circumstances giving rise to them. Swiss Bank may have known that the originator was paying the shipowner for the hire of a vessel but did not know that a favorable charter would be lost if the payment was delayed. "Electronic payments are not so unusual as to automatically place a bank on notice of extraordinary consequences if such a transfer goes awry. Swiss Bank did not have enough information to infer that if it lost a $27,000 payment order it would face liability in excess of $2 million." 673 F.2d at 956.

If *Evra* means that consequential damages can be imposed if the culpable bank has notice of particular circumstances giving rise to the damages, it does not provide an acceptable solution to the problem of bank liability for consequential damages. In the typical case transmission of the payment order is made electronically. Personnel of the receiving bank that process payment orders are not the appropriate people to evaluate the risk of liability for consequential damages in relation to the price charged for the wire transfer service. Even if notice is received by higher level management personnel who could make an appropriate decision whether the risk is justified by the price, liability based on notice would require evaluation of payment orders on an individual basis. This kind of evaluation is inconsistent with the high-speed, low-price, mechanical nature of the processing system that characterizes wire transfers. Moreover, in *Evra* the culpable bank was an intermediary bank with which the originator did not deal. Notice to the originator's bank would not bind the intermediary bank, and it seems impractical for the originator's bank to convey notice of this kind to intermediary banks in the funds transfer. The success of the wholesale wire transfer industry has largely been based on its ability to effect payment at low cost and great speed. Both of these essential aspects of the modern wire transfer system would be adversely affected by a rule that imposed on banks liability for consequential damages. A banking industry amicus brief in *Evra* stated: "Whether banks can continue to make EFT services available on a widespread basis, by charging reasonable rates, depends on whether they can do so without incurring unlimited consequential risks. Certainly, no bank would handle for $3.25 a transaction entailing potential liability in the millions of dollars."

As the court in *Evra* also noted, the originator of the funds transfer is in the best position to evaluate the risk that a funds transfer will not be made on time and to manage that risk by issuing a payment order in time to allow monitoring of the transaction. The originator, by asking the beneficiary, can quickly determine if the funds transfer has been completed. If the originator has sent the payment order at a time that allows a reasonable margin for correcting error, no loss is likely to result if the transaction is monitored. The other published cases on this issue reach the *Evra* result. *Central Coordinates, Inc. v. Morgan Guaranty Trust Co.*, 40 U.C.C.Rep.Serv. 1340 (N.Y.Sup.Ct.1985), and *Gatoil (U.S.A.), Inc. v. Forest Hill State Bank*, 1 U.C.C.Rep.Serv.2d 171 (D.Md.1986).

Subsection (c) allows the measure of damages in subsection (b) to be increased by an express written agreement of the receiving bank. An originator's bank might be willing to assume additional responsibilities and incur additional liability in exchange for a higher fee.

3. Subsection (d) governs cases in which a receiving bank has obligated itself by express agreement to accept payment orders of a sender. In the absence of such an agreement there is no obligation by a receiving bank to accept a payment order. Section 4A–212. The measure of damages for breach of an agreement to accept a payment order is the same as that stated in subsection (b). As in the case of subsection (b), additional damages, including consequential damages, may be recovered to the extent stated in an express written agreement of the receiving bank.

4. Reasonable attorney's fees are recoverable only in cases in which damages are limited to statutory damages stated in subsections (a), (b) and (d). If additional damages are recoverable because provided for by an express written agreement, attorney's fees are not recoverable. The rationale is that there is no need for statutory attorney's fees in the latter case, because the parties have agreed to a measure of damages which may or may not provide for attorney's fees.

5. The effect of subsection (f) is to prevent reduction of a receiving bank's liability under Section 4A–305.

PART 4

PAYMENT

§ 4A–401. Payment Date.

"Payment date" of a payment order means the day on which the amount of the order is payable to the beneficiary by the beneficiary's bank. The payment date may be determined by instruction of the sender but cannot be earlier than the day the order is received by the beneficiary's bank and, unless otherwise determined, is the day the order is received by the beneficiary's bank.

Official Comment

"Payment date" refers to the day the beneficiary's bank is to pay the beneficiary. The payment date may be expressed in various ways so long as it indicates the day the beneficiary is to receive payment. For example, in ACH transfers the payment date is the equivalent of "settlement date" or "effective date." Payment date applies to the payment order issued to the beneficiary's bank, but a payment order issued to a receiving bank other than the beneficiary's bank may also state a date for payment to the beneficiary. In the latter case, the statement of a payment date is to instruct the receiving bank concerning time of execution of the sender's order. Section 4A–301(b).

§ 4A–402. Obligation of Sender to Pay Receiving Bank.

(a) This section is subject to Sections 4A–205 and 4A–207.

(b) With respect to a payment order issued to the beneficiary's bank, acceptance of the order by the bank obliges the sender to pay the bank the amount of the order, but payment is not due until the payment date of the order.

(c) This subsection is subject to subsection (e) and to Section 4A–303. With respect to a payment order issued to a receiving bank other than the beneficiary's bank, acceptance of the order by the receiving bank obliges the sender to pay the bank the amount of the sender's order. Payment by the sender is not due until the execution date of the sender's order. The obligation of that sender to pay its payment order is excused if the funds transfer is not completed by acceptance by the beneficiary's bank of a payment order instructing payment to the beneficiary of that sender's payment order.

(d) If the sender of a payment order pays the order and was not obliged to pay all or part of the amount paid, the bank receiving payment is obliged to refund payment to the extent the sender was not obliged to pay. Except as provided in Sections 4A–204 and 4A–304, interest is payable on the refundable amount from the date of payment.

(e)   If a funds transfer is not completed as stated in subsection (c) and an intermediary bank is obliged to refund payment as stated in subsection (d) but is unable to do so because not permitted by applicable law or because the bank suspends payments, a sender in the funds transfer that executed a payment order in compliance with an instruction, as stated in Section 4A–302(a)(1), to route the funds transfer through that intermediary bank is entitled to receive or retain payment from the sender of the payment order that it accepted. The first sender in the funds transfer that issued an instruction requiring routing through that intermediary bank is subrogated to the right of the bank that paid the intermediary bank to refund as stated in subsection (d).

(f)   The right of the sender of a payment order to be excused from the obligation to pay the order as stated in subsection (c) or to receive refund under subsection (d) may not be varied by agreement.

Official Comment

1.   Subsection (b) states that the sender of a payment order to the beneficiary's bank must pay the order when the beneficiary's bank accepts the order. At that point the beneficiary's bank is obliged to pay the beneficiary. Section 4A–404(a). The last clause of subsection (b) covers a case of premature acceptance by the beneficiary's bank. In some funds transfers, notably automated clearing house transfers, a beneficiary's bank may receive a payment order with a payment date after the day the order is received. The beneficiary's bank might accept the order before the payment date by notifying the beneficiary of receipt of the order. Although the acceptance obliges the beneficiary's bank to pay the beneficiary, payment is not due until the payment date. The last clause of subsection (b) is consistent with that result. The beneficiary's bank is also not entitled to payment from the sender until the payment date.

2.   Assume that Originator instructs Bank A to order immediate payment to the account of Beneficiary in Bank B. Execution of Originator's payment ordered by Bank A is acceptance under Section 4A–209(a). Under the second sentence of Section 4A–402(c) the acceptance creates an obligation of Originator to pay Bank A the amount of the order. The last clause of that sentence deals with attempted funds transfers that are not completed. In that event the obligation of the sender to pay its payment order is excused. Originator makes payment to Beneficiary when Bank B, the beneficiary's bank, accepts a payment order for the benefit of Beneficiary. Section 4A–406(a). If that acceptance by Bank B does not occur, the funds transfer has miscarried because Originator has not paid Beneficiary. Originator doesn't have to pay its payment order, and if it has already paid it is entitled to refund of the payment with interest. The rate of interest is stated in Section 4A–506. This "money-back guarantee" is an important protection of Originator. Originator is assured that it will not lose its money if something goes wrong in the transfer. For example, risk of loss resulting from payment to the wrong beneficiary is borne by some bank, not by Originator. The most likely reason for noncompletion is a failure to execute or an erroneous execution of a payment order by Bank A or an intermediary bank. Bank A may have issued its payment order to the wrong bank or it may have identified the wrong beneficiary in its order. The money-back guarantee is particularly important to Originator if noncompletion of the funds transfer is due to the fault of an intermediary bank rather than Bank A. In that case Bank A must refund payment to Originator, and Bank A has the burden of obtaining refund from the intermediary bank that it paid.

Subsection (c) can result in loss if an intermediary bank suspends payments. Suppose Originator instructs Bank A to pay to Beneficiary's account in Bank B and to use Bank C as an intermediary bank. Bank A executes Originator's order by issuing a payment order to Bank C. Bank A pays Bank C. Bank C fails to execute the order of Bank A and suspends payments. Under subsections (c) and (d), Originator is not obliged to pay Bank A and is entitled to refund from Bank A of any payment that it may have made. Bank A is entitled to a refund from Bank C, but Bank C is insolvent. Subsection (e) deals with this case. Bank A was required to issue its payment order to Bank C because Bank C was designated as an intermediary bank by Originator. Section 4A–302(a)(1). In this case Originator takes the risk of insolvency of Bank C. Under subsection (e), Bank A is entitled to payment from Originator and Originator is subrogated to the right of Bank A under subsection (d) to refund of payment from Bank C.

3.   A payment order is not like a negotiable instrument on which the drawer or maker has liability. Acceptance of the order by the receiving bank creates an obligation of the sender to pay the receiving bank the amount of the order. That is the extent of the sender's liability to the receiving bank and no other person has any rights against the sender with respect to the sender's order.

§ 4A–403.   Payment by Sender to Receiving Bank.

(a)   Payment of the sender's obligation under Section 4A–402 to pay the receiving bank occurs as follows:

(1)   If the sender is a bank, payment occurs when the receiving bank receives final settlement of the obligation through a Federal Reserve Bank or through a funds-transfer system.

(2)   If the sender is a bank and the sender (i) credited an account of the receiving bank with the sender, or (ii) caused an account of the receiving bank in another bank to be credited, payment occurs when the credit is withdrawn or, if not withdrawn, at midnight of the day on which the credit is withdrawable and the receiving bank learns of that fact.

(3)   If the receiving bank debits an account of the sender with the receiving bank, payment occurs when the debit is made to the extent the debit is covered by a withdrawable credit balance in the account.

(b)   If the sender and receiving bank are members of a funds-transfer system that nets obligations multilaterally among participants, the receiving bank receives final settlement when settlement is complete in accordance with the rules of the system. The obligation of the sender to pay the amount of a payment order transmitted through the funds-transfer system may be satisfied, to the extent permitted by the rules of the system, by setting off and applying against the sender's obligation the right of the sender to receive payment from the receiving bank of the amount of any other payment order transmitted to the sender by the receiving bank through the funds-transfer system. The aggregate balance of obligations owed by each sender to each receiving bank in the funds-transfer system may be satisfied, to the extent permitted by the rules of the system, by setting off and applying against that balance the aggregate balance of obligations owed to the sender by other members of the system. The aggregate balance is determined after the right of setoff stated in the second sentence of this subsection has been exercised.

(c)   If two banks transmit payment orders to each other under an agreement that settlement of the obligations of each bank to the other under Section 4A–402 will be made at the end of the day or other period, the total amount owed with respect to all orders transmitted by one bank shall be set off against the total amount owed with respect to all orders transmitted by the other bank. To the extent of the setoff, each bank has made payment to the other.

(d)   In a case not covered by subsection (a), the time when payment of the sender's obligation under Section 4A–402(b) or 4A–402(c) occurs is governed by applicable principles of law that determine when an obligation is satisfied.

Official Comment

1.   This section defines when a sender pays the obligation stated in Section 4A–402. If a group of two or more banks engage in funds transfers with each other, the participating banks will sometimes be senders and sometimes receiving banks. With respect to payment orders other than Fedwires, the amounts of the various payment orders may be credited and debited to accounts of one bank with another or to a clearing house account of each bank and amounts owed and amounts due are netted. Settlement is made through a Federal Reserve Bank by charges to the Federal Reserve accounts of the net debtor banks and credits to the Federal Reserve accounts of the net creditor banks. In the case of Fedwires the sender's obligation is settled by a debit to the Federal Reserve account of the sender and a credit to the Federal Reserve account of the receiving bank at the time the receiving bank receives the payment order. Both of these cases are covered by subsection (a)(1). When the Federal Reserve settlement becomes final the obligation of the sender under Section 4A–402 is paid.

2.   In some cases a bank does not settle an obligation owed to another bank through a Federal Reserve Bank. This is the case if one of the banks is a foreign bank without access to the Federal Reserve payment system. In this kind of case, payment is usually made by credits or debits to accounts of the two banks with each other or to accounts of the two banks in a third bank. Suppose Bank B has an account in Bank A. Bank A advises Bank B that its account in Bank A has been credited $1,000,000 and that the credit is immediately withdrawable. Bank A also instructs Bank B to pay $1,000,000 to the account of Beneficiary in Bank B. This case is covered by subsection (a)(2). Bank B may want to immediately withdraw this credit. For example, it might do so by instructing Bank A to debit the account and pay some third party. Payment by Bank A to Bank B of Bank A's payment order occurs when the withdrawal is made. Suppose Bank B does not withdraw the credit. Since Bank B is the beneficiary's

bank, one of the effects of receipt of payment by Bank B is that acceptance of Bank A's payment order automatically occurs at the time of payment. Section 4A–209(b)(2). Acceptance means that Bank B is obliged to pay $1,000,000 to Beneficiary. Section 4A–404(a). Subsection (a)(2) of Section 4A–403 states that payment does not occur until midnight if the credit is not withdrawn. This allows Bank B an opportunity to reject the order if it does not have time to withdraw the credit to its account and it is not willing to incur the liability to Beneficiary before it has use of the funds represented by the credit.

    3.   Subsection (a)(3) applies to a case in which the sender (bank or nonbank) has a funded account in the receiving bank. If Sender has an account in Bank and issues a payment order to Bank, Bank can obtain payment from Sender by debiting the account of Sender, which pays its Section 4A–402 obligation to Bank when the debit is made.

    4.   Subsection (b) deals with multilateral settlements made through a funds transfer system and is based on the CHIPS settlement system. In a funds transfer system such as CHIPS, which allows the various banks that transmit payment orders over the system to settle obligations at the end of each day, settlement is not based on individual payment orders. Each bank using the system engages in funds transfers with many other banks using the system. Settlement for any participant is based on the net credit or debit position of that participant with all other banks using the system. Subsection (b) is designed to make clear that the obligations of any sender are paid when the net position of that sender is settled in accordance with the rules of the funds transfer system. This provision is intended to invalidate any argument, based on common-law principles, that multilateral netting is not valid because mutuality of obligation is not present. Subsection (b) dispenses with any mutuality of obligation requirements. Subsection (c) applies to cases in which two banks send payment orders to each other during the day and settle with each other at the end of the day or at the end of some other period. It is similar to subsection (b) in that it recognizes that a sender's obligation to pay a payment order is satisfied by a setoff. The obligations of each bank as sender to the other as receiving bank are obligations of the bank itself and not as representative of customers. These two sections are important in the case of insolvency of a bank. They make clear that liability under Section 4A–402 is based on the net position of the insolvent bank after setoff.

    5.   Subsection (d) relates to the uncommon case in which the sender doesn't have an account relationship with the receiving bank and doesn't settle through a Federal Reserve Bank. An example would be a customer that pays over the counter for a payment order that the customer issues to the receiving bank. Payment would normally be by cash, check or bank obligation. When payment occurs is determined by law outside Article 4A.

§ 4A–404. Obligation of Beneficiary's Bank to Pay and Give Notice to Beneficiary.

    (a)   Subject to Sections 4A–211(e), 4A–405(d), and 4A–405(e), if a beneficiary's bank accepts a payment order, the bank is obliged to pay the amount of the order to the beneficiary of the order. Payment is due on the payment date of the order, but if acceptance occurs on the payment date after the close of the funds-transfer business day of the bank, payment is due on the next funds-transfer business day. If the bank refuses to pay after demand by the beneficiary and receipt of notice of particular circumstances that will give rise to consequential damages as a result of nonpayment, the beneficiary may recover damages resulting from the refusal to pay to the extent the bank had notice of the damages, unless the bank proves that it did not pay because of a reasonable doubt concerning the right of the beneficiary to payment.

    (b)   If a payment order accepted by the beneficiary's bank instructs payment to an account of the beneficiary, the bank is obliged to notify the beneficiary of receipt of the order before midnight of the next funds-transfer business day following the payment date. If the payment order does not instruct payment to an account of the beneficiary, the bank is required to notify the beneficiary only if notice is required by the order. Notice may be given by first class mail or any other means reasonable in the circumstances. If the bank fails to give the required notice, the bank is obliged to pay interest to the beneficiary on the amount of the payment order from the day notice should have been given until the day the beneficiary learned of receipt of the payment order by the bank. No other damages are recoverable. Reasonable attorney's fees are also recoverable if demand for interest is made and refused before an action is brought on the claim.

    (c)   The right of a beneficiary to receive payment and damages as stated in subsection (a) may not be varied by agreement or a funds-transfer system rule. The right of a beneficiary to be notified as stated in subsection (b) may be varied by agreement of the beneficiary or by a funds-transfer system rule if the beneficiary is notified of the rule before initiation of the funds transfer.

Official Comment

1. The first sentence of subsection (a) states the time when the obligation of the beneficiary's bank arises. The second and third sentences state when the beneficiary's bank must make funds available to the beneficiary. They also state the measure of damages for failure, after demand, to comply. Since the Expedited Funds Availability Act, 12 U.S.C. 4001 et seq., also governs funds availability in a funds transfer, the second and third sentences of subsection (a) may be subject to preemption by that Act.

2. Subsection (a) provides that the beneficiary of an accepted payment order may recover consequential damages if the beneficiary's bank refuses to pay the order after demand by the beneficiary if the bank at that time had notice of the particular circumstances giving rise to the damages. Such damages are recoverable only to the extent the bank had "notice of the damages." The quoted phrase requires that the bank have notice of the general type or nature of the damages that will be suffered as a result of the refusal to pay and their general magnitude. There is no requirement that the bank have notice of the exact or even the approximate amount of the damages, but if the amount of damages is extraordinary the bank is entitled to notice of that fact. For example, in *Evra Corp. v. Swiss Bank Corp.*, 673 F.2d 951 (7th Cir.1982), failure to complete a funds transfer of only $27,000 required to retain rights to a very favorable ship charter resulted in a claim for more than $2,000,000 of consequential damages. Since it is not reasonably foreseeable that a failure to make a relatively small payment will result in damages of this magnitude, notice is not sufficient if the beneficiary's bank has notice only that the $27,000 is necessary to retain rights on a ship charter. The bank is entitled to notice that an exceptional amount of damages will result as well. For example, there would be adequate notice if the bank had been made aware that damages of $1,000,000 or more might result.

3. Under the last clause of subsection (a) the beneficiary's bank is not liable for damages if its refusal to pay was "because of a reasonable doubt concerning the right of the beneficiary to payment." Normally there will not be any question about the right of the beneficiary to receive payment. Normally, the bank should be able to determine whether it has accepted the payment order and, if it has been accepted, the first sentence of subsection (a) states that the bank is obliged to pay. There may be uncommon cases, however, in which there is doubt whether acceptance occurred. For example, if acceptance is based on receipt of payment by the beneficiary's bank under Section 4A–403(a)(1) or (2), there may be cases in which the bank is not certain that payment has been received. There may also be cases in which there is doubt about whether the person demanding payment is the person identified in the payment order as beneficiary of the order.

The last clause of subsection (a) does not apply to cases in which a funds transfer is being used to pay an obligation and a dispute arises between the originator and the beneficiary concerning whether the obligation is in fact owed. For example, the originator may try to prevent payment to the beneficiary by the beneficiary's bank by alleging that the beneficiary is not entitled to payment because of fraud against the originator or a breach of contract relating to the obligation. The fraud or breach of contract claim of the originator may be grounds for recovery by the originator from the beneficiary after the beneficiary is paid, but it does not affect the obligation of the beneficiary's bank to pay the beneficiary. Unless the payment order has been cancelled pursuant to Section 4A–211(c), there is no excuse for refusing to pay the beneficiary and, in a proper case, the refusal may result in consequential damages. Except in the case of a book transfer, in which the beneficiary's bank is also the originator's bank, the originator of a funds transfer cannot cancel a payment order to the beneficiary's bank, with or without the consent of that bank, because the originator is not the sender of that order. Thus, the beneficiary's bank may safely ignore any instruction by the originator to withhold payment to the beneficiary.

4. Subsection (b) states the duty of the beneficiary's bank to notify the beneficiary of receipt of the order. If acceptance occurs under Section 4A–209(b)(1) the beneficiary is normally notified. Thus, subsection (b) applies primarily to cases in which acceptance occurs under Section 4A–209(b)(2) or (3). Notice under subsection (b) is not required if the person entitled to the notice agrees or a funds transfer system rule provides that notice is not required and the beneficiary is given notice of the rule. In ACH transactions the normal practice is not to give notice to the beneficiary unless notice is requested by the beneficiary. This practice can be continued by adoption of a funds transfer system rule. Subsection (a) is not subject to variation by agreement or by a funds transfer system rule.

§ 4A–405. Payment by Beneficiary's Bank to Beneficiary.

(a) If the beneficiary's bank credits an account of the beneficiary of a payment order, payment of the bank's obligation under Section 4A–404(a) occurs when and to the extent (i) the beneficiary is notified of the right to withdraw the credit, (ii) the bank lawfully applies the credit to a debt of the beneficiary, or (iii) funds with respect to the order are otherwise made available to the beneficiary by the bank.

(b)   If the beneficiary's bank does not credit an account of the beneficiary of a payment order, the time when payment of the bank's obligation under Section 4A–404(a) occurs is governed by principles of law that determine when an obligation is satisfied.

(c)   Except as stated in subsections (d) and (e), if the beneficiary's bank pays the beneficiary of a payment order under a condition to payment or agreement of the beneficiary giving the bank the right to recover payment from the beneficiary if the bank does not receive payment of the order, the condition to payment or agreement is not enforceable.

(d)   A funds-transfer system rule may provide that payments made to beneficiaries of funds transfers made through the system are provisional until receipt of payment by the beneficiary's bank of the payment order it accepted. A beneficiary's bank that makes a payment that is provisional under the rule is entitled to refund from the beneficiary if (i) the rule requires that both the beneficiary and the originator be given notice of the provisional nature of the payment before the funds transfer is initiated, (ii) the beneficiary, the beneficiary's bank and the originator's bank agreed to be bound by the rule, and (iii) the beneficiary's bank did not receive payment of the payment order that it accepted. If the beneficiary is obliged to refund payment to the beneficiary's bank, acceptance of the payment order by the beneficiary's bank is nullified and no payment by the originator of the funds transfer to the beneficiary occurs under Section 4A–406.

(e)   This subsection applies to a funds transfer that includes a payment order transmitted over a funds-transfer system that (i) nets obligations multilaterally among participants, and (ii) has in effect a loss-sharing agreement among participants for the purpose of providing funds necessary to complete settlement of the obligations of one or more participants that do not meet their settlement obligations. If the beneficiary's bank in the funds transfer accepts a payment order and the system fails to complete settlement pursuant to its rules with respect to any payment order in the funds transfer, (i) the acceptance by the beneficiary's bank is nullified and no person has any right or obligation based on the acceptance, (ii) the beneficiary's bank is entitled to recover payment from the beneficiary, (iii) no payment by the originator to the beneficiary occurs under Section 4A–406, and (iv) subject to Section 4A–402(e), each sender in the funds transfer is excused from its obligation to pay its payment order under Section 4A–402(c) because the funds transfer has not been completed.

Official Comment

1.   This section defines when the beneficiary's bank pays the beneficiary and when the obligation of the beneficiary's bank under Section 4A–404 to pay the beneficiary is satisfied. In almost all cases the bank will credit an account of the beneficiary when it receives a payment order. In the typical case the beneficiary is paid when the beneficiary is given notice of the right to withdraw the credit. Subsection (a)(i). In some cases payment might be made to the beneficiary not by releasing funds to the beneficiary, but by applying the credit to a debt of the beneficiary. Subsection (a)(ii). In this case the beneficiary gets the benefit of the payment order because a debt of the beneficiary has been satisfied. The two principal cases in which payment will occur in this manner are setoff by the beneficiary's bank and payment of the proceeds of the payment order to a garnishing creditor of the beneficiary. These cases are discussed in Comment 2 to Section 4A–502.

2.   If a beneficiary's bank releases funds to the beneficiary before it receives payment from the sender of the payment order, it assumes the risk that the sender may not pay the sender's order because of suspension of payments or other reason. Subsection (c). As stated in Comment 5 to Section 4A–209, the beneficiary's bank can protect itself against this risk by delaying acceptance. But if the bank accepts the order it is obliged to pay the beneficiary. If the beneficiary's bank has given the beneficiary notice of the right to withdraw a credit made to the beneficiary's account, the beneficiary has received payment from the bank. Once payment has been made to the beneficiary with respect to an obligation incurred by the bank under Section 4A–404(a), the payment cannot be recovered by the beneficiary's bank unless subsection (d) or (e) applies. Thus, a right to withdraw a credit cannot be revoked if the right to withdraw constituted payment of the bank's obligation. This principle applies even if funds were released as a "loan" (see Comment 5 to Section 4A–209), or were released subject to a condition that they would be repaid in the event the bank does not receive payment from the sender of the payment order, or the beneficiary agreed to return the payment if the bank did not receive payment from the sender.

3. Subsection (c) is subject to an exception stated in subsection (d) which is intended to apply to automated clearing house transfers. ACH transfers are made in batches. A beneficiary's bank will normally accept, at the same time and as part of a single batch, payment orders with respect to many different originator's banks. Comment 2 to Section 4A-206. The custom in ACH transactions is to release funds to the beneficiary early on the payment date even though settlement to the beneficiary's bank does not occur until later in the day. The understanding is that payments to beneficiaries are provisional until the beneficiary's bank receives settlement. This practice is similar to what happens when a depositary bank releases funds with respect to a check forwarded for collection. If the check is dishonored the bank is entitled to recover the funds from the customer. ACH transfers are widely perceived as check substitutes. Section 4A-405(d) allows the funds transfer system to adopt a rule making payments to beneficiaries provisional. If such a rule is adopted, a beneficiary's bank that releases funds to the beneficiary will be able to recover the payment if it doesn't receive payment of the payment order that it accepted. There are two requirements with respect to the funds transfer system rule. The beneficiary, the beneficiary's bank and the originator's bank must all agree to be bound by the rule and the rule must require that both the beneficiary and the originator be given notice of the provisional nature of the payment before the funds transfer is initiated. There is no requirement that the notice be given with respect to a particular funds transfer. Once notice of the provisional nature of the payment has been given, the notice is effective for all subsequent payments to or from the person to whom the notice was given. Subsection (d) provides only that the funds transfer system rule must require notice to the beneficiary and the originator. The beneficiary's bank will know what the rule requires, but it has no way of knowing whether the originator's bank complied with the rule. Subsection (d) does not require proof that the originator received notice. If the originator's bank failed to give the required notice and the originator suffered as a result, the appropriate remedy is an action by the originator against the originator's bank based on that failure. But the beneficiary's bank will not be able to get the benefit of subsection (d) unless the beneficiary had notice of the provisional nature of the payment because subsection (d) requires an agreement by the beneficiary to be bound by the rule. Implicit in an agreement to be bound by a rule that makes a payment provisional is a requirement that notice be given of what the rule provides. The notice can be part of the agreement or separately given. For example, notice can be given by providing a copy of the system's operating rules.

With respect to ACH transfers made through a Federal Reserve Bank acting as an intermediary bank, the Federal Reserve Bank is obliged under Section 4A-402(b) to pay a beneficiary's bank that accepts the payment order. Unlike Fedwire transfers, under current ACH practice a Federal Reserve Bank that processes a payment order does not obligate itself to pay if the originator's bank fails to pay the Federal Reserve Bank. It is assumed that the Federal Reserve will use its right of preemption which is recognized in Section 4A-107 to disclaim the Section 4A-402(b) obligation in ACH transactions if it decides to retain the provisional payment rule.

4. Subsection (e) is another exception to subsection (c). It refers to funds transfer systems having loss-sharing rules described in the subsection. CHIPS has proposed a rule that fits the description. Under the CHIPS loss-sharing rule the CHIPS banks will have agreed to contribute funds to allow the system to settle for payment orders sent over the system during the day in the event that one or more banks are unable to meet their settlement obligations. Subsection (e) applies only if CHIPS fails to settle despite the loss-sharing rule. Since funds under the loss-sharing rule will be instantly available to CHIPS and will be in an amount sufficient to cover any failure that can be reasonably anticipated, it is extremely unlikely that CHIPS would ever fail to settle. Thus, subsection (e) addresses an event that should never occur. If that event were to occur, all payment orders made over the system would be cancelled under the CHIPS rule. Thus, no bank would receive settlement, whether or not a failed bank was involved in a particular funds transfer. Subsection (e) provides that each funds transfer in which there is a payment order with respect to which there is a settlement failure is unwound. Acceptance by the beneficiary's bank in each funds transfer is nullified. The consequences of nullification are that the beneficiary has no right to receive or retain payment by the beneficiary's bank, no payment is made by the originator to the beneficiary and each sender in the funds transfer is, subject to Section 4A-402(e), not obliged to pay its payment order and is entitled to refund under Section 4A-402(d) if it has already paid.

§ 4A-406. Payment by Originator to Beneficiary; Discharge of Underlying Obligation.

(a) Subject to Sections 4A-211(e), 4A-405(d), and 4A-405(e), the originator of a funds transfer pays the beneficiary of the originator's payment order (i) at the time a payment order for the benefit of the beneficiary is accepted by the beneficiary's bank in the funds transfer and (ii) in an amount equal to the amount of the order accepted by the beneficiary's bank, but not more than the amount of the originator's order.

(b)   If payment under subsection (a) is made to satisfy an obligation, the obligation is discharged to the same extent discharge would result from payment to the beneficiary of the same amount in money, unless (i) the payment under subsection (a) was made by a means prohibited by the contract of the beneficiary with respect to the obligation, (ii) the beneficiary, within a reasonable time after receiving notice of receipt of the order by the beneficiary's bank, notified the originator of the beneficiary's refusal of the payment, (iii) funds with respect to the order were not withdrawn by the beneficiary or applied to a debt of the beneficiary, and (iv) the beneficiary would suffer a loss that could reasonably have been avoided if payment had been made by a means complying with the contract. If payment by the originator does not result in discharge under this section, the originator is subrogated to the rights of the beneficiary to receive payment from the beneficiary's bank under Section 4A–404(a).

(c)   For the purpose of determining whether discharge of an obligation occurs under subsection (b), if the beneficiary's bank accepts a payment order in an amount equal to the amount of the originator's payment order less charges of one or more receiving banks in the funds transfer, payment to the beneficiary is deemed to be in the amount of the originator's order unless upon demand by the beneficiary the originator does not pay the beneficiary the amount of the deducted charges.

(d)   Rights of the originator or of the beneficiary of a funds transfer under this section may be varied only by agreement of the originator and the beneficiary.

Official Comment

1.   Subsection (a) states the fundamental rule of Article 4A that payment by the originator to the beneficiary is accomplished by providing to the beneficiary the obligation of the beneficiary's bank to pay. Since this obligation arises when the beneficiary's bank accepts a payment order, the originator pays the beneficiary at the time of acceptance and in the amount of the payment order accepted.

2.   In a large percentage of funds transfers, the transfer is made to pay an obligation of the originator. Subsection (a) states that the beneficiary is paid by the originator when the beneficiary's bank accepts a payment order for the benefit of the beneficiary. When that happens the effect under subsection (b) is to substitute the obligation of the beneficiary's bank for the obligation of the originator. The effect is similar to that under Article 3 if a cashier's check payable to the beneficiary had been taken by the beneficiary. Normally, payment by funds transfer is sought by the beneficiary because it puts money into the hands of the beneficiary more quickly. As a practical matter the beneficiary and the originator will nearly always agree to the funds transfer in advance. Under subsection (b) acceptance by the beneficiary's bank will result in discharge of the obligation for which payment was made unless the beneficiary had made a contract with respect to the obligation which did not permit payment by the means used. Thus, if there is no contract of the beneficiary with respect to the means of payment of the obligation, acceptance by the beneficiary's bank of a payment order to the account of the beneficiary can result in discharge.

3.   Suppose Beneficiary's contract stated that payment of an obligation owed by Originator was to be made by a cashier's check of Bank A. Instead, Originator paid by a funds transfer to Beneficiary's account in Bank B. Bank B accepted a payment order for the benefit of Beneficiary by immediately notifying Beneficiary that the funds were available for withdrawal. Before Beneficiary had a reasonable opportunity to withdraw the funds Bank B suspended payments. Under the unless clause of subsection (b) Beneficiary is not required to accept the payment as discharging the obligation owed by Originator to Beneficiary if Beneficiary's contract means that Beneficiary was not required to accept payment by wire transfer. Beneficiary could refuse the funds transfer as payment of the obligation and could resort to rights under the underlying contract to enforce the obligation. The rationale is that Originator cannot impose the risk of Bank B's insolvency on Beneficiary if Beneficiary had specified another means of payment that did not entail that risk. If Beneficiary is required to accept Originator's payment, Beneficiary would suffer a loss that would not have occurred if payment had been made by a cashier's check on Bank A, and Bank A has not suspended payments. In this case Originator will have to pay twice. It is obliged to pay the amount of its payment order to the bank that accepted it and has to pay the obligation it owes to Beneficiary which has not been discharged. Under the last sentence of subsection (b) Originator is subrogated to Beneficiary's right to receive payment from Bank B under Section 4A–404(a).

4.   Suppose Beneficiary's contract called for payment by a Fedwire transfer to Bank B, but the payment order accepted by Bank B was not a Fedwire transfer. Before the funds were withdrawn by Beneficiary, Bank B suspended payments. The sender of the payment order to Bank B paid the amount of the order to Bank B. In this case the payment by Originator did not comply with Beneficiary's contract, but the noncompliance did not result

in a loss to Beneficiary as required by subsection (b)(iv). A Fedwire transfer avoids the risk of insolvency of the sender of the payment order to Bank B, but it does not affect the risk that Bank B will suspend payments before withdrawal of the funds by Beneficiary. Thus, the unless clause of subsection (b) is not applicable and the obligation owed to Beneficiary is discharged.

5.   Charges of receiving banks in a funds transfer normally are nominal in relationship to the amount being paid by the originator to the beneficiary. Wire transfers are normally agreed to in advance and the parties may agree concerning how these charges are to be divided between the parties. Subsection (c) states a rule that applies in the absence of agreement. In some funds transfers charges of banks that execute payment orders are collected by deducting the charges from the amount of the payment order issued by the bank, i.e. the bank issues a payment order that is slightly less than the amount of the payment order that is being executed. The process is described in Comment 3 to Section 4A–302. The result in such a case is that the payment order accepted by the beneficiary's bank will be slightly less than the amount of the originator's order. Subsection (c) recognizes the principle that a beneficiary is entitled to full payment of a debt paid by wire transfer as a condition to discharge. On the other hand, subsection (c) prevents a beneficiary from denying the originator the benefit of the payment by asserting that discharge did not occur because deduction of bank charges resulted in less than full payment. The typical case is one in which the payment is made to exercise a valuable right such as an option which is unfavorable to the beneficiary. Subsection (c) allows discharge notwithstanding the deduction unless the originator fails to reimburse the beneficiary for the deducted charges after demand by the beneficiary.

PART 5

MISCELLANEOUS PROVISIONS

§ 4A–501.   Variation by Agreement and Effect of Funds-Transfer System Rule.

(a)   Except as otherwise provided in this Article, the rights and obligations of a party to a funds transfer may be varied by agreement of the affected party.

(b)   "Funds-transfer system rule" means a rule of an association of banks (i) governing transmission of payment orders by means of a funds-transfer system of the association or rights and obligations with respect to those orders, or (ii) to the extent the rule governs rights and obligations between banks that are parties to a funds transfer in which a Federal Reserve Bank, acting as an intermediary bank, sends a payment order to the beneficiary's bank. Except as otherwise provided in this Article, a funds-transfer system rule governing rights and obligations between participating banks using the system may be effective even if the rule conflicts with this Article and indirectly affects another party to the funds transfer who does not consent to the rule. A funds-transfer system rule may also govern rights and obligations of parties other than participating banks using the system to the extent stated in Sections 4A–404(c), 4A–405(d), and 4A–507(c).

Official Comment

1.   This section is designed to give some flexibility to Article 4A. Funds transfer system rules govern rights and obligations between banks that use the system. They may cover a wide variety of matters such as form and content of payment orders, security procedures, cancellation rights and procedures, indemnity rights, compensation rules for delays in completion of a funds transfer, time and method of settlement, credit restrictions with respect to senders of payment orders and risk allocation with respect to suspension of payments by a participating bank. Funds transfer system rules can be very effective in supplementing the provisions of Article 4A and in filling gaps that may be present in Article 4A. To the extent they do not conflict with Article 4A there is no problem with respect to their effectiveness. In that case they merely supplement Article 4A. Section 4A–501 goes further. It states that unless the contrary is stated, funds transfer system rules can override provisions of Article 4A. Thus, rights and obligations of a sender bank and a receiving bank with respect to each other can be different from that stated in Article 4A to the extent a funds transfer system rule applies. Since funds transfer system rules are defined as those governing the relationship between participating banks, a rule can have a direct effect only on participating banks. But a rule that affects the conduct of a participating bank may indirectly affect the rights of nonparticipants such as the originator or beneficiary of a funds transfer, and such a rule can be effective even though it may affect nonparticipants without their consent. For example, a rule might prevent execution of a payment order or might allow cancellation of a payment order with the result that a funds transfer is not completed or is delayed. But a rule purporting to define rights and obligations of nonparticipants in the

system would not be effective to alter Article 4A rights because the rule is not within the definition of funds transfer system rule. Rights and obligations arising under Article 4A may also be varied by agreement of the affected parties, except to the extent Article 4A otherwise provides. Rights and obligations arising under Article 4A can also be changed by Federal Reserve regulations and operating circulars of Federal Reserve Banks. Section 4A–107.

2.   Subsection (b)(ii) refers to ACH transfers. Whether an ACH transfer is made through an automated clearing house of a Federal Reserve Bank or through an automated clearing house of another association of banks, the rights and obligations of the originator's bank and the beneficiary's bank are governed by uniform rules adopted by various associations of banks in various parts of the nation. With respect to transfers in which a Federal Reserve Bank acts as intermediary bank these rules may be incorporated, in whole or in part, in operating circulars of the Federal Reserve Bank. Even if not so incorporated these rules can still be binding on the association banks. If a transfer is made through a Federal Reserve Bank, the rules are effective under subsection (b)(ii). If the transfer is not made through a Federal Reserve Bank, the association rules are effective under subsection (b)(i).

§ 4A–502.   Creditor Process Served on Receiving Bank; Setoff by Beneficiary's Bank.

(a)   As used in this section, "creditor process" means levy, attachment, garnishment, notice of lien, sequestration, or similar process issued by or on behalf of a creditor or other claimant with respect to an account.

(b)   This subsection applies to creditor process with respect to an authorized account of the sender of a payment order if the creditor process is served on the receiving bank. For the purpose of determining rights with respect to the creditor process, if the receiving bank accepts the payment order the balance in the authorized account is deemed to be reduced by the amount of the payment order to the extent the bank did not otherwise receive payment of the order, unless the creditor process is served at a time and in a manner affording the bank a reasonable opportunity to act on it before the bank accepts the payment order.

(c)   If a beneficiary's bank has received a payment order for payment to the beneficiary's account in the bank, the following rules apply:

(1)   The bank may credit the beneficiary's account. The amount credited may be set off against an obligation owed by the beneficiary to the bank or may be applied to satisfy creditor process served on the bank with respect to the account.

(2)   The bank may credit the beneficiary's account and allow withdrawal of the amount credited unless creditor process with respect to the account is served at a time and in a manner affording the bank a reasonable opportunity to act to prevent withdrawal.

(3)   If creditor process with respect to the beneficiary's account has been served and the bank has had a reasonable opportunity to act on it, the bank may not reject the payment order except for a reason unrelated to the service of process.

(d)   Creditor process with respect to a payment by the originator to the beneficiary pursuant to a funds transfer may be served only on the beneficiary's bank with respect to the debt owed by that bank to the beneficiary. Any other bank served with the creditor process is not obliged to act with respect to the process.

Official Comment

1.   When a receiving bank accepts a payment order, the bank normally receives payment from the sender by debiting an authorized account of the sender. In accepting the sender's order the bank may be relying on a credit balance in the account. If creditor process is served on the bank with respect to the account before the bank accepts the order but the bank employee responsible for the acceptance was not aware of the creditor process at the time the acceptance occurred, it is unjust to the bank to allow the creditor process to take the credit balance on which the bank may have relied. Subsection (b) allows the bank to obtain payment from the sender's account in this case. Under that provision, the balance in the sender's account to which the creditor process applies is deemed to be reduced by the amount of the payment order unless there was sufficient time for notice of the service of creditor process to be received by personnel of the bank responsible for the acceptance.

2.   Subsection (c) deals with payment orders issued to the beneficiary's bank. The bank may credit the beneficiary's account when the order is received, but under Section 4A–404(a) the bank incurs no obligation to pay

the beneficiary until the order is accepted pursuant to Section 4A–209(b). Thus, before acceptance, the credit to the beneficiary's account is provisional. But under Section 4A–209(b) acceptance occurs if the beneficiary's bank pays the beneficiary pursuant to Section 4A–405(a). Under that provision, payment occurs if the credit to the beneficiary's account is applied to a debt of the beneficiary. Subsection (c)(1) allows the bank to credit the beneficiary's account with respect to a payment order and to accept the order by setting off the credit against an obligation owed to the bank or applying the credit to creditor process with respect to the account.

Suppose a beneficiary's bank receives a payment order for the benefit of a customer. Before the bank accepts the order, the bank learns that creditor process has been served on the bank with respect to the customer's account. Normally there is no reason for a beneficiary's bank to reject a payment order, but if the beneficiary's account is garnished, the bank may be faced with a difficult choice. If it rejects the order, the garnishing creditor's potential recovery of funds of the beneficiary is frustrated. It may be faced with a claim by the creditor that the rejection was a wrong to the creditor. If the bank accepts the order, the effect is to allow the creditor to seize funds of its customer, the beneficiary. Subsection (c)(3) gives the bank no choice in this case. It provides that it may not favor its customer over the creditor by rejecting the order. The beneficiary's bank may rightfully reject only if there is an independent basis for rejection.

3. Subsection (c)(2) is similar to subsection (b). Normally the beneficiary's bank will release funds to the beneficiary shortly after acceptance or it will accept by releasing funds. Since the bank is bound by a garnishment order served before funds are released to the beneficiary, the bank might suffer a loss if funds were released without knowledge that a garnishment order had been served. Subsection (c)(2) protects the bank if it did not have adequate notice of the garnishment when the funds were released.

4. A creditor may want to reach funds involved in a funds transfer. The creditor may try to do so by serving process on the originator's bank, an intermediary bank or the beneficiary's bank. The purpose of subsection (d) is to guide the creditor and the court as to the proper method of reaching the funds involved in a funds transfer. A creditor of the originator can levy on the account of the originator in the originator's bank before the funds transfer is initiated, but that levy is subject to the limitations stated in subsection (b). The creditor of the originator cannot reach any other funds because no property of the originator is being transferred. A creditor of the beneficiary cannot levy on property of the originator and until the funds transfer is completed by acceptance by the beneficiary's bank of a payment order for the benefit of the beneficiary, the beneficiary has no property interest in the funds transfer which the beneficiary's creditor can reach. A creditor of the beneficiary that wants to reach the funds to be received by the beneficiary must serve creditor process on the beneficiary's bank to reach the obligation of the beneficiary's bank to pay the beneficiary which arises upon acceptance by the beneficiary's bank under Section 4A–404(a).

5. "Creditor process" is defined in subsection (a) to cover a variety of devices by which a creditor of the holder of a bank account or a claimant to a bank account can seize the account. Procedure and nomenclature varies widely from state to state. The term used in Section 4A–502 is a generic term.

§ 4A–503. Injunction or Restraining Order With Respect to Funds Transfer.

For proper cause and in compliance with applicable law, a court may restrain (i) a person from issuing a payment order to initiate a funds transfer, (ii) an originator's bank from executing the payment order of the originator, or (iii) the beneficiary's bank from releasing funds to the beneficiary or the beneficiary from withdrawing the funds. A court may not otherwise restrain a person from issuing a payment order, paying or receiving payment of a payment order, or otherwise acting with respect to a funds transfer.

Official Comment

This section is related to Section 4A–502(d) and to Comment 4 to Section 4A–502. It is designed to prevent interruption of a funds transfer after it has been set in motion. The initiation of a funds transfer can be prevented by enjoining the originator or the originator's bank from issuing a payment order. After the funds transfer is completed by acceptance of a payment order by the beneficiary's bank, that bank can be enjoined from releasing funds to the beneficiary or the beneficiary can be enjoined from withdrawing the funds. No other injunction is permitted. In particular, intermediary banks are protected, and injunctions against the originator and the originator's bank are limited to issuance of a payment order. Except for the beneficiary's bank, nobody can be enjoined from paying a payment order, and no receiving bank can be enjoined from receiving payment from the sender of the order that it accepted.

§ 4A–504. Order in Which Items and Payment Orders May Be Charged to Account; Order of Withdrawals From Account.

(a) If a receiving bank has received more than one payment order of the sender or one or more payment orders and other items that are payable from the sender's account, the bank may charge the sender's account with respect to the various orders and items in any sequence.

(b) In determining whether a credit to an account has been withdrawn by the holder of the account or applied to a debt of the holder of the account, credits first made to the account are first withdrawn or applied.

Official Comment

1.   Subsection (a) concerns priority among various obligations that are to be paid from the same account. A customer may have written checks on its account with the receiving bank and may have issued one or more payment orders payable from the same account. If the account balance is not sufficient to cover all of the checks and payment orders, some checks may be dishonored and some payment orders may not be accepted. Although there is no concept of wrongful dishonor of a payment order in Article 4A in the absence of an agreement to honor by the receiving bank, some rights and obligations may depend on the amount in the customer's account. Section 4A–209(b)(3) and Section 4A–210(b). Whether dishonor of a check is wrongful also may depend upon the balance in the customer's account. Under subsection (a), the bank is not required to consider the competing items and payment orders in any particular order. Rather it may charge the customer's account for the various items and orders in any order. Suppose there is $12,000 in the customer's account. If a check for $5,000 is presented for payment and the bank receives a $10,000 payment order from the customer, the bank could dishonor the check and accept the payment order. Dishonor of the check is not wrongful because the account balance was less than the amount of the check after the bank charged the account $10,000 on account of the payment order. Or, the bank could pay the check and not execute the payment order because the amount of the order is not covered by the balance in the account.

2.   Subsection (b) follows Section 4–208(b) in using the first-in-first-out rule for determining the order in which credits to an account are withdrawn.

§ 4A–505. Preclusion of Objection to Debit of Customer's Account.

If a receiving bank has received payment from its customer with respect to a payment order issued in the name of the customer as sender and accepted by the bank, and the customer received notification reasonably identifying the order, the customer is precluded from asserting that the bank is not entitled to retain the payment unless the customer notifies the bank of the customer's objection to the payment within one year after the notification was received by the customer.

Official Comment

This section is in the nature of a statute of repose for objecting to debits made to the customer's account. A receiving bank that executes payment orders of a customer may have received payment from the customer by debiting the customer's account with respect to a payment order that the customer was not required to pay. For example, the payment order may not have been authorized or verified pursuant to Section 4A–202 or the funds transfer may not have been completed. In either case the receiving bank is obliged to refund the payment to the customer and this obligation to refund payment cannot be varied by agreement. Section 4A–204 and Section 4A–402. Refund may also be required if the receiving bank is not entitled to payment from the customer because the bank erroneously executed a payment order. Section 4A–303. A similar analysis applies to that case. Section 4A–402(d) and (f) require refund and the obligation to refund may not be varied by agreement. Under 4A–505, however, the obligation to refund may not be asserted by the customer if the customer has not objected to the debiting of the account within one year after the customer received notification of the debit.

§ 4A–506. Rate of Interest.

(a) If, under this Article, a receiving bank is obliged to pay interest with respect to a payment order issued to the bank, the amount payable may be determined (i) by agreement of the sender and receiving bank, or (ii) by a funds-transfer system rule if the payment order is transmitted through a funds-transfer system.

(b)   If the amount of interest is not determined by an agreement or rule as stated in subsection (a), the amount is calculated by multiplying the applicable Federal Funds rate by the amount on which interest is payable, and then multiplying the product by the number of days for which interest is payable. The applicable Federal Funds rate is the average of the Federal Funds rates published by the Federal Reserve Bank of New York for each of the days for which interest is payable divided by 360. The Federal Funds rate for any day on which a published rate is not available is the same as the published rate for the next preceding day for which there is a published rate. If a receiving bank that accepted a payment order is required to refund payment to the sender of the order because the funds transfer was not completed, but the failure to complete was not due to any fault by the bank, the interest payable is reduced by a percentage equal to the reserve requirement on deposits of the receiving bank.

Official Comment

1.   A receiving bank is required to pay interest on the amount of a payment order received by the bank in a number of situations. Sometimes the interest is payable to the sender and in other cases it is payable to either the originator or the beneficiary of the funds transfer. The relevant provisions are Section 4A–204(a), Section 4A–209(b)(3), Section 4A–210(b), Section 4A–305(a), Section 4A–402(d) and Section 4A–404(b). The rate of interest may be governed by a funds transfer system rule or by agreement as stated in subsection (a). If subsection (a) doesn't apply, the rate is determined under subsection (b). Subsection (b) is illustrated by the following example. A bank is obliged to pay interest on $1,000,000 for three days, July 3, July 4, and July 5. The published Fed Funds rate is .082 for July 3 and .081 for July 5. There is no published rate for July 4 because that day is not a banking day. The rate for July 3 applies to July 4. The applicable Fed Funds rate is .08167 (the average of .082, .082, and .081) divided by 360 which equals .0002268. The amount of interest payable is $1,000,000 × .0002268 × 3 = $680.40.

2.   In some cases, interest is payable in spite of the fact that there is no fault by the receiving bank. The last sentence of subsection (b) applies to those cases. For example, a funds transfer might not be completed because the beneficiary's bank rejected the payment order issued to it by the originator's bank or an intermediary bank. Section 4A–402(c) provides that the originator is not obliged to pay its payment order and Section 4A–402(d) provides that the originator's bank must refund any payment received plus interest. The requirement to pay interest in this case is not based on fault by the originator's bank. Rather, it is based on restitution. Since the originator's bank had the use of the originator's money, it is required to pay the originator for the value of that use. The value of that use is not determined by multiplying the interest rate by the refundable amount because the originator's bank is required to deposit with the Federal Reserve a percentage of the bank's deposits as a reserve requirement. Since that deposit does not bear interest, the bank had use of the refundable amount reduced by a percentage equal to the reserve requirement. If the reserve requirement is 12%, the amount of interest payable by the bank under the formula stated in subsection (b) is reduced by 12%.

§ 4A–507.   Choice of Law.

(a)   The following rules apply unless the affected parties otherwise agree or subsection (c) applies:

(1)   The rights and obligations between the sender of a payment order and the receiving bank are governed by the law of the jurisdiction in which the receiving bank is located.

(2)   The rights and obligations between the beneficiary's bank and the beneficiary are governed by the law of the jurisdiction in which the beneficiary's bank is located.

(3)   The issue of when payment is made pursuant to a funds transfer by the originator to the beneficiary is governed by the law of the jurisdiction in which the beneficiary's bank is located.

(b)   If the parties described in each paragraph of subsection (a) have made an agreement selecting the law of a particular jurisdiction to govern rights and obligations between each other, the law of that jurisdiction governs those rights and obligations, whether or not the payment order or the funds transfer bears a reasonable relation to that jurisdiction.

(c)   A funds-transfer system rule may select the law of a particular jurisdiction to govern (i) rights and obligations between participating banks with respect to payment orders transmitted or processed through the system, or (ii) the rights and obligations of some or all parties to a funds transfer any part of which is carried out by means of the system. A choice of law made pursuant to clause (i) is binding on participating banks. A choice of law made pursuant to clause (ii) is binding on the originator, other sender, or a receiving bank having notice that the funds-transfer system might be used in the funds transfer and of the choice of law by the system when the originator, other sender, or receiving bank issued or accepted a payment order. The beneficiary of a funds transfer is bound by the choice of law if, when the funds transfer is initiated, the beneficiary has notice that the funds-transfer system might be used in the funds transfer and of the choice of law by the system. The law of a jurisdiction selected pursuant to this subsection may govern, whether or not that law bears a reasonable relation to the matter in issue.

(d)   In the event of inconsistency between an agreement under subsection (b) and a choice-of-law rule under subsection (c), the agreement under subsection (b) prevails.

(e)   If a funds transfer is made by use of more than one funds-transfer system and there is inconsistency between choice-of-law rules of the systems, the matter in issue is governed by the law of the selected jurisdiction that has the most significant relationship to the matter in issue.

Official Comment

1.   Funds transfers are typically interstate or international in character. If part of a funds transfer is governed by Article 4A and another part is governed by other law, the rights and obligations of parties to the funds transfer may be unclear because there is no clear consensus in various jurisdictions concerning the juridical nature of the transaction. Unless all of a funds transfer is governed by a single law it may be very difficult to predict the result if something goes wrong in the transfer. Section 4A–507 deals with this problem. Subsection (b) allows parties to a funds transfer to make a choice-of-law agreement. Subsection (c) allows a funds transfer system to select the law of a particular jurisdiction to govern funds transfers carried out by means of the system. Subsection (a) states residual rules if no choice of law has occurred under subsection (b) or subsection (c).

2.   Subsection (a) deals with three sets of relationships. Rights and obligations between the sender of a payment order and the receiving bank are governed by the law of the jurisdiction in which the receiving bank is located. If the receiving bank is the beneficiary's bank the rights and obligations of the beneficiary are also governed by the law of the jurisdiction in which the receiving bank is located. Suppose Originator, located in Canada, sends a payment order to Originator's Bank located in a state in which Article 4A has been enacted. The order is for payment to an account of Beneficiary in a bank in England. Under subsection (a)(1), the rights and obligations of Originator and Originator's Bank toward each other are governed by Article 4A if an action is brought in a court in the Article 4A state. If an action is brought in a Canadian court, the conflict of laws issue will be determined by Canadian law which might or might not apply the law of the state in which Originator's Bank is located. If that law is applied, the execution of Originator's order will be governed by Article 4A, but with respect to the payment order of Originator's Bank to the English bank, Article 4A may or may not be applied with respect to the rights and obligations between the two banks. The result may depend upon whether action is brought in a court in the state in which Originator's Bank is located or in an English court. Article 4A is binding only on a court in a state that enacts it. It can have extraterritorial effect only to the extent courts of another jurisdiction are willing to apply it. Subsection (c) also bears on the issues discussed in this Comment.

Under Section 4A–406 payment by the originator to the beneficiary of the funds transfer occurs when the beneficiary's bank accepts a payment order for the benefit of the beneficiary. A jurisdiction in which Article 4A is not in effect may follow a different rule or it may not have a clear rule. Under Section 4A–507(a)(3) the issue is governed by the law of the jurisdiction in which the beneficiary's bank is located. Since the payment to the beneficiary is made through the beneficiary's bank it is reasonable that the issue of when payment occurs be governed by the law of the jurisdiction in which the bank is located. Since it is difficult in many cases to determine where a beneficiary is located, the location of the beneficiary's bank provides a more certain rule.

3.   Subsection (b) deals with choice-of-law agreements and it gives maximum freedom of choice. Since the law of funds transfers is not highly developed in the case law there may be a strong incentive to choose the law of a jurisdiction in which Article 4A is in effect because it provides a greater degree of certainty with respect to the rights of various parties. With respect to commercial transactions, it is often said that "[u]niformity and predictability based upon commercial convenience are the prime considerations in making the choice of governing law . . . ." R. Leflar, *American Conflicts Law*, § 185 (1977). Subsection (b) is derived in part from recently enacted choice-of-law rules in the States of New York and California. N.Y.Gen. Obligations Law 5–1401 (McKinney's 1989 Supp.) and California Civil Code § 1646.5. This broad endorsement of freedom of contract is an enhancement of the approach taken by Restatement (Second) of Conflict of Laws § 187(b) (1971). The Restatement recognizes the basic right of freedom of contract, but the freedom granted the parties may be more limited than the freedom granted here. Under the formulation of the Restatement, if there is no substantial relationship to the jurisdiction whose law is selected and there is no "other" reasonable basis for the parties' choice, then the selection of the

parties need not be honored by a court. Further, if the choice is violative of a fundamental policy of a state which has a materially greater interest than the chosen state, the selection could be disregarded by a court. Those limitations are not found in subsection (b).

4. Subsection (c) may be the most important provision in regard to creating uniformity of law in funds transfers. Most rights stated in Article 4A regard parties who are in privity of contract such as originator and beneficiary, sender and receiving bank, and beneficiary's bank and beneficiary. Since they are in privity they can make a choice of law by agreement. But that is not always the case. For example, an intermediary bank that improperly executes a payment order is not in privity with either the originator or the beneficiary. The ability of a funds transfer system to make a choice of law by rule is a convenient way of dispensing with individual agreements and to cover cases in which agreements are not feasible. It is probable that funds transfer systems will adopt a governing law to increase the certainty of commercial transactions that are effected over such systems. A system rule might adopt the law of an Article 4A state to govern transfers on the system in order to provide a consistent, unitary, law governing all transfers made on the system. To the extent such system rules develop, individual choice-of-law agreements become unnecessary.

Subsection (c) has broad application. A system choice of law applies not only to rights and obligations between banks that use the system, but may also apply to other parties to the funds transfer so long as some part of the transfer was carried out over the system. The originator and any other sender or receiving bank in the funds transfer is bound if at the time it issues or accepts a payment order it had notice that the funds transfer involved use of the system and that the system chose the law of a particular jurisdiction. Under Section 4A–107, the Federal Reserve by regulation could make a similar choice of law to govern funds transfers carried out by use of Federal Reserve Banks. Subsection (d) is a limitation on subsection (c). If parties have made a choice-of-law agreement that conflicts with a choice of law made under subsection (c), the agreement prevails.

5. Subsection (e) addresses the case in which a funds transfer involves more than one funds transfer system and the systems adopt conflicting choice-of-law rules. The rule that has the most significant relationship to the matter at issue prevails. For example, each system should be able to make a choice of law governing payment orders transmitted over that system with regard to a choice of law made by another system.

UCC ARTICLE 5 (2016)

LETTERS OF CREDIT

Article 5 was revised in 1995.

National Conference of Commissioners on Uniform State Laws

REPORTER

James J. White, Ann Arbor, Michigan

DRAFTING COMMITTEE

CHAIRMAN

Carlyle C. Ring, Jr., Vienna, Virginia

MEMBERS

Marion W. Benfield, Jr., Winston-Salem, North Carolina
John P. Burton, Santa Fe, New Mexico, *National Conference Representative and The American Law Institute Representative*
Bruce A. Coggeshall, Portland, Maine
William C. Hillman, Boston, Massachusetts
Edwin E. Huddleson, III, Washington, District of Columbia, *The American Law Institute Representative*
Jeremiah Marsh, Chicago, Illinois
Richard L. Morningstar, Washington, District of Columbia
Edwin E. Smith, Boston, Massachusetts
Sandra S. Stern, Scarsdale, New York
Richard C. Hite, Wichita, Kansas, *President (Member Ex Officio)*
Neal Ossen, Hartford, Connecticut, *Chairman, Division C (Member Ex Officio)*

UNIFORM COMMERCIAL CODE

REVIEW COMMITTEE
CHAIRMAN

William M. Burke, Los Angeles, California

MEMBERS

Boris Auerbach, Wyoming, Ohio
Robert J. Desiderio, Albuquerque, New Mexico

PREFATORY NOTE
Reason for Revision

When the original Article 5 was drafted 40 years ago, it was written for paper transactions and before many innovations in letters of credit. Now electronic and other media are used extensively. Since the 50's, standby letters of credit have developed and now nearly $500 billion standby letters of credit are issued annually worldwide, of which $250 billion are issued in the United States. The use of deferred payment letters of credit has also greatly increased. The customs and practices for letters of credit have evolved and are reflected in the Uniform Customs and Practice (UCP), usually incorporated into letters of credit, particularly international letters of credit, which have seen four revisions since the 1950's; the current version became effective in 1994 (UCP 500). Lastly, in a number of areas, court decisions have resulted in conflicting rules.

Prior to the appointment of a drafting committee, the ABA UCC Committee appointed a Task Force composed of knowledgeable practitioners and academics. The ABA Task Force studied the case law, evolving technologies and the changes in customs and practices. The Task Force identified a large number of issues which they discussed at some length, and made recommendations for revisions to Article 5. The Task Force stated in a foreword:

"As a result of these increases and changes in usage, practice, players, and pressure, it comes as no surprise that there has been a sizable increase in litigation. Indeed, the approximately 62 cases reported in the United States in 1987 constituted double the cumulative reported cases up to 1965. . . .

Moreover, almost forty years of hard use have revealed weaknesses, gaps and errors in the original statute which compromise its relevance. U.C.C. Article 5 was one of the few areas of the Uniform Commercial Code which did not benefit from prior codification and it should come as no surprise that it may require some revision. . . .

Measured in terms of these areas which are vital to any system of commercial law, the current combination of statute and case law is found wanting in major respects both as to predictability and certainty. What is at issue here are not matters of sophistry but important issues of substance which have not been resolved by the current case law/code method and which admit of little likelihood of such resolution." (45 Bus. Lawyer 1521, at 1532, 1535–6)[1]

The Drafting Committee began its deliberations with the Task Force Report in hand. The final work of the Drafting Committee varies from many of the suggestions of the Task Force.

Need for Uniformity

Letters of Credit are a major instrument in international trade, as well as domestic transactions. To facilitate its usefulness and competitiveness, it is essential that U.S. law be in harmony with international rules and practices, as well as flexible enough to accommodate changes in technology and practices that have, and are, evolving. Not only should the rules be consistent within the United States, but they need to be substantively and procedurally consistent with international practices.

---

[1] The Task Force members were: Professor James E. Byrne (George Mason University School of Law) Chair; Professor Boris Kozolchyk (University of Arizona College of Law); Michael Evan Avidon (Moses & Singer); James G. Barnes (Baker & McKenzie); Arthur G. Lloyd (Citibank N.A.); Janis S. Penton (Rosen, Wachtell & Gilbert); Richard F. Purcell (Connell, Rice & Sugar Co.); Alan L. Bloodgood (Morgan Guaranty Trust Co.); Charles del Busto (Manufacturers Hanover Trust Co.); Vincent Maulella (Manufacturers Hanover Trust Co.).

Thus, the goals of the drafting effort were:

- conforming the Article 5 rules to current customs and practices;

- accommodating new forms of Letters of Credit, changes in customs and practices, and evolving technology, particularly the use of electronic media;

- maintaining Letters of Credit as an inexpensive and efficient instrument facilitating trade; and

- resolving conflicts among reported decisions.

Process of Achieving Uniformity

The essence of uniform law revision is to obtain a sufficient consensus and balance among the interests of the various participants so that universal and uniform enactment by the various States may be achieved.

In part this is accomplished by extensive consultation on and broad circulation of the drafts from 1990, when the project began, until approval of the final draft by the American law Institute (ALI) and the National Conference of Commissioners on Uniform State Laws (NCCUSL).

Hundreds of groups were invited to participate in the drafting process. Twenty Advisors were appointed, representing a cross-section of interested parties. In addition 20 Observers regularly attended drafting meetings and over 100 were on the mailing list to receive all drafts of the revision.

The Drafting Committee meetings were open and all those who attended were afforded full opportunity to express their views and participate in the dialogue. The Advisors and Observers were a balanced group with ten representatives of users (Beneficiaries and Applicants); five representatives of governmental agencies; five representatives of the U.S. Council on International Banking (USCIB); seven from major banks in letter of credit transactions; eight from regional banks; and seven law professors who teach and write on Letters of Credit.

Nine Drafting Committee meetings were held that began Friday morning and ended Sunday noon. In addition, the draft was twice debated in full by NCCUSL, once by the ALI Council, once considered by the ALI Consultative Group and once by an ad hoc Committee of the Council; and reviewed and discussed by the ABA Subcommittee on Letters of Credit semi-annually and by several state and city bar association committees.

The drafts were regularly reviewed and discussed in *The Business Lawyer*, *Letter of Credit Update*, and in other publications.

The consensus, balance and quality achieved in this lengthy deliberative process is a product of not only its Reporter and the Drafting Committee, but also the faithful and energetic participation of the following Advisors and active participants:

Advisors

Professor Gerald T. McLaughlin, *Loyola Law School, ABA, Section of Business Law*
James G. Barnes, *Baker & McKenzie/U.S. Council on International Banking, Inc.*
Harold S. Burman, *U.S. Department of State*
James E. Byrne, *George Mason University, Institute of International Banking Law and Practice Inc.*
Professor John Dolan, *original ABA Advisor*
Henry N. Dyhouse, *U.S. Central Credit Union*
David P. Goch, *Treasury Management Association*
Thomas J. Greco, *American Bankers Association*
Henry Harfield, *Shearman & Sterling*
Oliver I. Ireland, *Board of Governors of Federal Reserve Board*
James W. Kopp, *Shell Oil Company/Treasury Management Association*
Professor Boris Kozolchyk, *University of Arizona/National Law Center for Inter-American Free Trade, U.S. Council on International Banking, Inc.*
Vincent M. Maulella, *Manufacturers Hanover Trust Co./U.S.Council on International Banking, Inc.*
Robert M. Rosenblith, *National Westminster Bank*
Bradley K. Sabel, *Federal Reserve Bank of New York*

UNIFORM COMMERCIAL CODE

Joseph H. Sommer, *Federal Reserve Bank of New York*
Jamileh Soufan, *American General Corporation/Treasury Management Association*
Dan Taylor, *U.S. Council on International Banking, Inc.*
William H. Thornton, *Security Pacific National Bank/California Bankers Association*
Paul S. Turner, *Occidental Petroleum Corporation/Treasury Management Association*
Stanley M. Walker, *Exxon Company U.S.A./Treasury Management Association*

Active Participants

Michael E. Avidon, *Moses & Singer/N.Y. State Bar Association, Banking Law Committee, Subcommittee on Letters of Credit*
Walter B. Baker, *ABN AMRO Bank, N.V.*
Thomas C. Baxter, Jr., *Federal Reserve Bank of New York*
Professor Amelia H. Boss, *Pennsylvania Bar Association, Section of Corporation, Banking & Business Law, Commercial Law Committee*
Maria A. Chanco, *Bank of America, N.T. & S.A.*
Frank P. Curran, *Treasury Management Association*
Carol R. Dennis, *Office of Federal Procurement Policy, OFMB*
Albert J. Givray, *Oklahoma Bar Association, Section of Banking & Commercial Law*
Sidney S. Goldstein, *New York State Bar Association*
Professor Egon Guttman, *The American University*
George A. Hisert, *State Bar of California, Section of Business Law, Committee on UCC, Subcommittee on Letters of Credit*
Larry J. Jones, *Mobil Oil Credit Corporation*
Carter H. Klein, *Jenner & Block*
Arthur G. Lloyd, *ABA, Section of Business Law, Committee on UCC, Subcommittee on Letters of Credit, Working Group on UCC Article 5 Revision*
Rebecca S. McCulloch, *ABN AMRO Bank, N.V.*
Dennis L. Noah, *First National Bank of Maryland/U.S. Council on International Banking, Inc.*
James Purvis, *The Bank of California*
James E. Roselle, *First National Bank of Chicago*
R. David Whitaker, *ABA, Section of Business Law, Committee on UCC, Subcommittee on ECP, Working Group on EDC*
Brooke Wunnicke, *ABA, Section of Business Law, Committee on UCC, Subcommittee on Letters of Credit*

Balance of Benefits

Uniform laws can be enacted only if there is a consensus that the benefits achieved advance the public interest in a manner that can be embraced by all users of the law. It appears that as drafted, Revised Article 5 will enjoy substantial support by the participating interests in letter of credit transactions.

Benefits of Revised Article 5 in General

Independence Principle. Revised Article 5 clearly and forcefully states the independence of the letter of credit obligations from the underlying transactions that was unexpressed in, but was a fundamental predicate for, the original Article 5 (Sections 5–103(d) and 5–108(f)). Certainty of payment, independent of other claims, setoffs or other causes of action, is a core element of the commercial utility of letters of credit.

Clarifications. The revision authorizes the use of electronic technology (Sections 5–102(a)(14) and 5–104); expressly permits deferred payment letters of credit (Section 5–102(a)(8)) and two party letters of credit (Section 5–102(a)(10)); provides rules for unstated expiry dates (Section 5–106(c)), perpetual letters of credit (Section 5–106(d)), and non-documentary conditions (Section 5–108(g)); clarifies and establishes rules for successors by operation of law (Sections 5–102(a)(15) and 5–113); conforms to existing practice for assignment of proceeds (Section 5–114); and clarifies the rules where decisions have been in conflict (Section 5–106, Comment 1; Section 5–108, Comments 1, 3, 4, 7, and 9; Section 5–109, Comments 1 and 3; Section 5–113, Comment 1; and Section 5–117, Comment 1).

480

ARTICLE 5 (2016)

Harmonizes with International Practice

The UCP is used in most international letters of credit and in many domestic letters of credit. These international practices are well known and employed by the major issuers and users of letters of credit. Revisions have been made to Article 5 to coordinate the Article 5 rules with current international practice (e.g., deferred payment obligations, reasonable time to examine documents, preclusion, non-documentary conditions, return of documents, and irrevocable unless stated to be revocable).

Benefits of Revised Article 5 to Issuers

Consequential Damages. Section 5–111 precludes consequential and punitive damages. It, however, provides strong incentives for Issuers to honor, including provisions for attorneys fees and expenses of litigation, interest, and specific performance. If consequential and punitive damages were allowed, the cost of letters of credit could rise substantially.

Statute of Limitation. Section 5–115 establishes a one year statute of limitation from the expiration date or from accrual of the cause of action, whichever occurs later. Because it is usually obvious to all when there has been a breach, a short limitation period is fair to potential plaintiffs.

Choice of Law. Section 5–116 permits the issuer (or nominated party or adviser) to choose the law of the jurisdiction that will govern even if that law bears no relation to the transaction. Absent agreement, Section 5–116 states choice of law rules.

Assignment of Proceeds. Section 5–114 conforms more fully to existing practice and provides an orderly procedure for recording and accommodating assignments by consent of the issuer (or nominated party).

Subrogation. Section 5–117 clarifies the subrogation rights of an Issuer who has honored a letter of credit. These rights of subrogation also extend to an applicant who reimburses and a nominated party who pays or gives value.

Recognition of UCP. Section 5–116(c) expressly recognizes that if the UCP is incorporated by reference into the letter of credit, the agreement varies the provisions of Article 5 with which it may conflict except for the non-variable provisions of Article 5.

Benefits of Revised Article 5 to Applicants

Warranties. Section 5–110 specifies the warranties made by a beneficiary. It gives the applicant on a letter of credit which has been honored a direct cause of action if a drawing is fraudulent or forged or if a drawing violates any agreement augmented by a letter of credit.

Strict Compliance. Absent agreement to the contrary, the issuer must dishonor a presentation that does not strictly comply under standard practice with the terms and conditions of the letter of credit (Section 5–108).

Subrogation. New Section 5–117 clarifies the parties' rights of subrogation if the letter of credit is honored.

Limitations on General Disclaimers and Waivers. Section 5–103(c) limits the effect of general disclaimers and waivers in a letter of credit, or reimbursement or other agreement.

Benefits of Revised Article 5 to Beneficiaries

Irrevocable. A letter of credit is irrevocable unless the letter of credit expressly provides it is revocable (Section 5–106(a)).

Preclusion. Section 5–108(c) now provides that the Issuer is precluded from asserting any discrepancy not stated in its notice timely given, except for fraud, forgery or expiration.

Timely Examination. Section 5–108(b) requires examination and notice of any discrepancies within a reasonable time not to exceed the 7th business day after presentation of the documents.

Transfers by Operation of Law. New Section 5–113 allows a successor to a beneficiary by operation of law to make presentation and receive payment or acceptance.

UNIFORM COMMERCIAL CODE

Damages. The damages provided are expanded and clarified. They include attorneys fees and expenses of litigation and payment of the full amount of the wrongfully dishonored or repudiated demand, with interest, without an obligation of the beneficiary to mitigate damages (Section 5–111).

Revisions for Article 9 and Transition Provisions

The draft includes suggested revisions to conform Article 9 to the Article 5 changes. Article 9 itself is under revision and the interface with Revised Article 5 will be more fully examined by the Article 9 drafting committee, as well, in light of changes to Article 9. The Article 9 revisions will probably not be completed until 1998–9. Revised Article 8 (1994) also makes changes to Article 9 so care should be taken to coordinate the changes of both Revised Articles 5 and 8 within each State.

The draft also includes transition provisions and some cross reference changes in other Articles of the UCC.

Lastly, there follows a table showing the changes from the original Article 5 made by the revisions to Article 5.

Table of Disposition of Sections in Former Article 5

The reference to a section in revised Article 5 is to the section that refers to the issue addressed by the section in former Article 5. If there is no comparable section in Revised Article 5 to a section in former Article 5, that fact is indicated by the word "Omitted" and a reason is stated.

Former Article 5 Section	Revised Article 5 Section
5–101	5–101
5–102(1)	5–103(a)
5–102(2)	Omitted (inherent in 5–103(a) and definitions)
5–103(3)	(first sentence omitted) 5–103(b)
5–103(1)(a)	5–102(a)(10); 5–106(a); 5–102(a)(8)
5–103(1)(b)	5–102(a)(6)("Document"), and 5–102(a)(14)("Record"); "Documentary" draft or demand not used
5–103(1)(c)	5–102(a)(9)
5–103(1)(d)	5–102(a)(3)
5–103(1)(e)	5–102(a)(1)
5–103(1)(f)	5–102(a)(4)
5–103(1)(g)	("Applicant" rather than "Customer") 5–102(a)(2)
5–103(2)	Omitted as not applicable
5–103(3)	5–102(b)
5–103(4)	5–102(c)
5–104	5–104 and 5–102(6) and (14)
5–105	5–105
5–106(1)	5–106(a)
5–106(2)	5–106(b)
5–106(3)	5–106(b)
5–106(4)	5–106(b)
5–107(1)	5–107(c)
5–107(2)	5–107(a)
5–107(3)	5–107(c)
5–107(4)	Omitted as inadvisable default rule
5–108	Omitted (as outdated)

ARTICLE 5 (2016)

Table of New Provisions

(Provisions which were not included in former Article 5 and subjects not addressed in former Article 5.)

---

§ 5–101.   Short Title.

This article may be cited as Uniform Commercial Code—Letters of Credit.

Official Comment

The Official Comment to the original Section 5–101 was a remarkably brief inaugural address. Noting that letters of credit had not been the subject of statutory enactment and that the law concerning them had been developed in the cases, the Comment stated that Article 5 was intended "within its limited scope" to set an independent theoretical frame for the further development of letters of credit. That statement addressed accurately conditions as they existed when the statement was made, nearly half a century ago. Since Article 5 was originally drafted, the use of letters of credit has expanded and developed, and the case law concerning these developments is, in some respects, discordant.

Revision of Article 5 therefore has required reappraisal both of the statutory goals and of the extent to which particular statutory provisions further or adversely affect achievement of those goals.

The statutory goal of Article 5 was originally stated to be: (1) to set a substantive theoretical frame that describes the function and legal nature of letters of credit; and (2) to preserve procedural flexibility in order to accommodate further development of the efficient use of letters of credit. A letter of credit is an idiosyncratic form of undertaking that supports performance of an obligation incurred in a separate financial, mercantile, or other transaction or arrangement. The objectives of the original and revised Article 5 are best achieved (1) by defining the peculiar characteristics of a letter of credit that distinguish it and the legal consequences of its use from other forms of assurance such as secondary guarantees, performance bonds, and insurance policies, and from ordinary contracts, fiduciary engagements, and escrow arrangements; and (2) by preserving flexibility through variation by agreement in order to respond to and accommodate developments in custom and usage that are not inconsistent with the essential definitions and substantive mandates of the statute. No statute can, however, prescribe the manner in which such substantive rights and duties are to be enforced or imposed without risking stultification of wholesome developments in the letter of credit mechanism. Letter of credit law should remain responsive to commercial reality and in particular to the customs and expectations of the international banking and mercantile community. Courts should read the terms of this article in a manner consistent with these customs and expectations.

The subject matter in Article 5, letters of credit, may also be governed by an international convention that is now being drafted by UNCITRAL, the draft Convention on Independent Guarantees and Standby Letters of Credit. The Uniform Customs and Practice is an international body of trade practice that is commonly adopted by international and domestic letters of credit and as such is the "law of the transaction" by agreement of the parties. Article 5 is consistent with and was influenced by the rules in the existing version of the UCP. In addition to the UCP and the international convention, other bodies of law apply to letters of credit. For example, the federal bankruptcy law applies to letters of credit with respect to applicants and beneficiaries that are in bankruptcy; regulations of the Federal Reserve Board and the Comptroller of the Currency lay out requirements for banks that issue letters of credit and describe how letters of credit are to be treated for calculating asset risk and for the purpose of loan limitations. In addition there is an array of anti-boycott and other similar laws that may affect the issuance and performance of letters of credit. All of these laws are beyond the scope of Article 5, but in certain circumstances they will override Article 5.

§ 5–102.   Definitions.

(a)   In this article:

(1)   "Adviser" means a person who, at the request of the issuer, a confirmer, or another adviser, notifies or requests another adviser to notify the beneficiary that a letter of credit has been issued, confirmed, or amended.

(2)   "Applicant" means a person at whose request or for whose account a letter of credit is issued. The term includes a person who requests an issuer to issue a letter of credit on behalf of another if the person making the request undertakes an obligation to reimburse the issuer.

(3)   "Beneficiary" means a person who under the terms of a letter of credit is entitled to have its complying presentation honored. The term includes a person to whom drawing rights have been transferred under a transferable letter of credit.

(4) "Confirmer" means a nominated person who undertakes, at the request or with the consent of the issuer, to honor a presentation under a letter of credit issued by another.

(5) "Dishonor" of a letter of credit means failure timely to honor or to take an interim action, such as acceptance of a draft, that may be required by the letter of credit.

(6) "Document" means a draft or other demand, document of title, investment security, certificate, invoice, or other record, statement, or representation of fact, law, right, or opinion (i) which is presented in a written or other medium permitted by the letter of credit or, unless prohibited by the letter of credit, by the standard practice referred to in Section 5–108(e) and (ii) which is capable of being examined for compliance with the terms and conditions of the letter of credit. A document may not be oral.

(7) "Good faith" means honesty in fact in the conduct or transaction concerned.

(8) "Honor" of a letter of credit means performance of the issuer's undertaking in the letter of credit to pay or deliver an item of value. Unless the letter of credit otherwise provides, "honor" occurs

    (i)   upon payment,

    (ii)   if the letter of credit provides for acceptance, upon acceptance of a draft and, at maturity, its payment, or

    (iii) if the letter of credit provides for incurring a deferred obligation, upon incurring the obligation and, at maturity, its performance.

(9) "Issuer" means a bank or other person that issues a letter of credit, but does not include an individual who makes an engagement for personal, family, or household purposes.

(10) "Letter of credit" means a definite undertaking that satisfies the requirements of Section 5–104 by an issuer to a beneficiary at the request or for the account of an applicant or, in the case of a financial institution, to itself or for its own account, to honor a documentary presentation by payment or delivery of an item of value.

(11) "Nominated person" means a person whom the issuer (i) designates or authorizes to pay, accept, negotiate, or otherwise give value under a letter of credit and (ii) undertakes by agreement or custom and practice to reimburse.

(12) "Presentation" means delivery of a document to an issuer or nominated person for honor or giving of value under a letter of credit.

(13) "Presenter" means a person making a presentation as or on behalf of a beneficiary or nominated person.

(14) "Record" means information that is inscribed on a tangible medium, or that is stored in an electronic or other medium and is retrievable in perceivable form.

(15) "Successor of a beneficiary" means a person who succeeds to substantially all of the rights of a beneficiary by operation of law, including a corporation with or into which the beneficiary has been merged or consolidated, an administrator, executor, personal representative, trustee in bankruptcy, debtor in possession, liquidator, and receiver.

(b) Definitions in other Articles applying to this article and the sections in which they appear are:

"Accept" or "Acceptance" Section 3–409

"Value" Sections 3–303, 4–211

(c) Article 1 contains certain additional general definitions and principles of construction and interpretation applicable throughout this article.

Official Comment

1. Since no one can be a confirmer unless that person is a nominated person as defined in Section 5–102(a)(11), those who agree to "confirm" without the designation or authorization of the issuer are not confirmers under Article 5. Nonetheless, the undertakings to the beneficiary of such persons may be enforceable by the

beneficiary as letters of credit issued by the "confirmer" for its own account or as guarantees or contracts outside of Article 5.

2.　　The definition of "document" contemplates and facilitates the growing recognition of electronic and other nonpaper media as "documents," however, for the time being, data in those media constitute documents only in certain circumstances. For example, a facsimile received by an issuer would be a document only if the letter of credit explicitly permitted it, if the standard practice authorized it and the letter did not prohibit it, or the agreement of the issuer and beneficiary permitted it. The fact that data transmitted in a nonpaper (unwritten) medium can be recorded on paper by a recipient's computer printer, facsimile machine, or the like does not under current practice render the data so transmitted a "document." A facsimile or S.W.I.F.T. message received directly by the issuer is in an electronic medium when it crosses the boundary of the issuer's place of business. One wishing to make a presentation by facsimile (an electronic medium) will have to procure the explicit agreement of the issuer (assuming that the standard practice does not authorize it). Article 5 contemplates that electronic documents may be presented under a letter of credit and the provisions of this Article should be read to apply to electronic documents as well as tangible documents. An electronic document of title is delivered through the voluntary transfer of control. Article 1, Section 1–201 (definition of "delivery"). See Article 7, Section 7–106 on control of an electronic document. Where electronic transmissions are authorized neither by the letter of credit nor by the practice, the beneficiary may transmit the data electronically to its agent who may be able to put it in written form and make a conforming presentation. Cf. Article 7, Section 7–105 on reissuing an electronic document in a tangible medium.

3.　　"Good faith" continues in revised Article 5 to be defined as "honesty in fact." "Observance of reasonable standards of fair dealing" has not been added to the definition. The narrower definition of "honesty in fact" reinforces the "independence principle" in the treatment of "fraud," "strict compliance," "preclusion," and other tests affecting the performance of obligations that are unique to letters of credit. This narrower definition—which does not include "fair dealing"—is appropriate to the decision to honor or dishonor a presentation of documents specified in a letter of credit. The narrower definition is also appropriate for other parts of revised Article 5 where greater certainty of obligations is necessary and is consistent with the goals of speed and low cost. It is important that U.S. letters of credit have continuing vitality and competitiveness in international transactions.

For example, it would be inconsistent with the "independence" principle if any of the following occurred: (i) the beneficiary's failure to adhere to the standard of "fair dealing" in the underlying transaction or otherwise in presenting documents were to provide applicants and issuers with an "unfairness" defense to dishonor even when the documents complied with the terms of the letter of credit; (ii) the issuer's obligation to honor in "strict compliance in accordance with standard practice" were changed to "reasonable compliance" by use of the "fair dealing" standard, or (iii) the preclusion against the issuer (Section 5–108(d)) were modified under the "fair dealing" standard to enable the issuer later to raise additional deficiencies in the presentation. The rights and obligations arising from presentation, honor, dishonor and reimbursement, are independent and strict, and thus "honesty in fact" is an appropriate standard.

The contract between the applicant and beneficiary is not governed by Article 5, but by applicable contract law, such as Article 2 or the general law of contracts. "Good faith" in that contract is defined by other law, such as Section 2–103(1)(b)* or Restatement of Contracts 2d, § 205, which incorporate the principle of "fair dealing" in most cases, or a State's common law or other statutory provisions that may apply to that contract.

The contract between the applicant and the issuer (sometimes called the "reimbursement" agreement) is governed in part by this article (e.g., Sections 5–108(i), 5–111(b), and 5–103(c)) and partly by other law (e.g., the general law of contracts). The definition of good faith in Section 5–102(a)(7) applies only to the extent that the reimbursement contract is governed by provisions in this article; for other purposes good faith is defined by other law.

4.　　Payment and acceptance are familiar modes of honor. A third mode of honor, incurring an unconditional obligation, has legal effects similar to an acceptance of a time draft but does not technically constitute an acceptance. The practice of making letters of credit available by "deferred payment undertaking" as now provided in UCP 500 has grown up in other countries and spread to the United States. The definition of "honor" will accommodate that practice.

---

*　　*The definition of good faith in 2–103(1)(b) will be deleted if the jurisdiction adopts the definition of good faith in revised Article 1.*

5.   The exclusion of consumers from the definition of "issuer" is to keep creditors from using a letter of credit in consumer transactions in which the consumer might be made the issuer and the creditor would be the beneficiary. If that transaction were recognized under Article 5, the effect would be to leave the consumer without defenses against the creditor. That outcome would violate the policy behind the Federal Trade Commission Rule in 16 CFR Part 433. In a consumer transaction, an individual cannot be an issuer where that person would otherwise be either the principal debtor or a guarantor.

6.   The label on a document is not conclusive; certain documents labelled "guarantees" in accordance with European (and occasionally, American) practice are letters of credit. On the other hand, even documents that are labelled "letter of credit" may not constitute letters of credit under the definition in Section 5–102(a). When a document labelled a letter of credit requires the issuer to pay not upon the presentation of documents, but upon the determination of an extrinsic fact such as applicant's failure to perform a construction contract, and where that condition appears on its face to be fundamental and would, if ignored, leave no obligation to the issuer under the document labelled letter of credit, the issuer's undertaking is not a letter of credit. It is probably some form of suretyship or other contractual arrangement and may be enforceable as such. See Sections 5–102(a)(10) and 5–103(d). Therefore, undertakings whose fundamental term requires an issuer to look beyond documents and beyond conventional reference to the clock, calendar, and practices concerning the form of various documents are not governed by Article 5. Although Section 5–108(g) recognizes that certain nondocumentary conditions can be included in a letter of credit without denying the undertaking the status of letter of credit, that section does not apply to cases where the nondocumentary condition is fundamental to the issuer's obligation. The rules in Sections 5–102(a)(10), 5–103(d), and 5–108(g) approve the conclusion in *Wichita Eagle & Beacon Publishing Co. v. Pacific Nat. Bank*, 493 F.2d 1285 (9th Cir.1974).

The adjective "definite" is taken from the UCP. It approves cases that deny letter of credit status to documents that are unduly vague or incomplete. See, e.g., *Transparent Products Corp. v. Paysaver Credit Union*, 864 F.2d 60 (7th Cir.1988). Note, however, that no particular phrase or label is necessary to establish a letter of credit. It is sufficient if the undertaking of the issuer shows that it is intended to be a letter of credit. In most cases the parties' intention will be indicated by a label on the undertaking itself indicating that it is a "letter of credit," but no such language is necessary.

A financial institution may be both the issuer and the applicant or the issuer and the beneficiary. Such letters are sometimes issued by a bank in support of the bank's own lease obligations or on behalf of one of its divisions as an applicant or to one of its divisions as beneficiary, such as an overseas branch. Because wide use of letters of credit in which the issuer and the applicant or the issuer and the beneficiary are the same would endanger the unique status of letters of credit, only financial institutions are authorized to issue them.

In almost all cases the ultimate performance of the issuer under a letter of credit is the payment of money. In rare cases the issuer's obligation is to deliver stock certificates or the like. The definition of letter of credit in Section 5–102(a)(10) contemplates those cases.

7.   Under the UCP any bank is a nominated bank where the letter of credit is "freely negotiable." A letter of credit might also nominate by the following: "We hereby engage with the drawer, indorsers, and bona fide holders of drafts drawn under and in compliance with the terms of this credit that the same will be duly honored on due presentation" or "available with any bank by negotiation." A restricted negotiation credit might be "available with x bank by negotiation" or the like.

Several legal consequences may attach to the status of nominated person. First, when the issuer nominates a person, it is authorizing that person to pay or give value and is authorizing the beneficiary to make presentation to that person. Unless the letter of credit provides otherwise, the beneficiary need not present the documents to the issuer before the letter of credit expires; it need only present those documents to the nominated person. Secondly, a nominated person that gives value in good faith has a right to payment from the issuer despite fraud. Section 5–109(a)(1).

8.   A "record" must be in or capable of being converted to a perceivable form. For example, an electronic message recorded in a computer memory that could be printed from that memory could constitute a record. Similarly, a tape recording of an oral conversation could be a record.

9.   Absent a specific agreement to the contrary, documents of a beneficiary delivered to an issuer or nominated person are considered to be presented under the letter of credit to which they refer, and any payment or value given for them is considered to be made under that letter of credit. As the court held in *Alaska Textile Co. v. Chase Manhattan Bank, N.A.*, 982 F.2d 813, 820 (2d Cir.1992), it takes a "significant showing" to make the presentation of a beneficiary's documents for "collection only" or otherwise outside letter of credit law and practice.

10.   Although a successor of a beneficiary is one who succeeds "by operation of law," some of the successions contemplated by Section 5–102(a)(15) will have resulted from voluntary action of the beneficiary such as merger of a corporation. Any merger makes the successor corporation the "successor of a beneficiary" even though the transfer occurs partly by operation of law and partly by the voluntary action of the parties. The definition excludes certain transfers, where no part of the transfer is "by operation of law"—such as the sale of assets by one company to another.

11.   "Draft" in Article 5 does not have the same meaning it has in Article 3. For example, a document may be a draft under Article 5 even though it would not be a negotiable instrument, and therefore would not qualify as a draft under Section 3–104(e).

As amended in 2003.

§ 5–103.   Scope.

(a)   This article applies to letters of credit and to certain rights and obligations arising out of transactions involving letters of credit.

(b)   The statement of a rule in this article does not by itself require, imply, or negate application of the same or a different rule to a situation not provided for, or to a person not specified, in this article.

(c)   With the exception of this subsection, subsections (a) and (d), Sections 5–102(a)(9) and (10), 5–106(d), and 5–114(d), and except to the extent prohibited in Sections 1–302 and 5–117(d), the effect of this article may be varied by agreement or by a provision stated or incorporated by reference in an undertaking. A term in an agreement or undertaking generally excusing liability or generally limiting remedies for failure to perform obligations is not sufficient to vary obligations prescribed by this article.

(d)   Rights and obligations of an issuer to a beneficiary or a nominated person under a letter of credit are independent of the existence, performance, or nonperformance of a contract or arrangement out of which the letter of credit arises or which underlies it, including contracts or arrangements between the issuer and the applicant and between the applicant and the beneficiary.

As amended in 2001.

Official Comment

1.   Sections 5–102(a)(10) and 5–103 are the principal limits on the scope of Article 5. Many undertakings in commerce and contract are similar, but not identical to the letter of credit. Principal among those are "secondary," "accessory," or "suretyship" guarantees. Although the word "guarantee" is sometimes used to describe an independent obligation like that of the issuer of a letter of credit (most often in the case of European bank undertakings but occasionally in the case of undertakings of American banks), in the United States the word "guarantee" is more typically used to describe a suretyship transaction in which the "guarantor" is only secondarily liable and has the right to assert the underlying debtor's defenses. This article does not apply to secondary or accessory guarantees and it is important to recognize the distinction between letters of credit and those guarantees. It is often a defense to a secondary or accessory guarantor's liability that the underlying debt has been discharged or that the debtor has other defenses to the underlying liability. In letter of credit law, on the other hand, the independence principle recognized throughout Article 5 states that the issuer's liability is independent of the underlying obligation. That the beneficiary may have breached the underlying contract and thus have given a good defense on that contract to the applicant against the beneficiary is no defense for the issuer's refusal to honor. Only staunch recognition of this principle by the issuers and the courts will give letters of credit the continuing vitality that arises from the certainty and speed of payment under letters of credit. To that end, it is important that the law not carry into letter of credit transactions rules that properly apply only to secondary guarantees or to other forms of engagement.

2.   Like all of the provisions of the Uniform Commercial Code, Article 5 is supplemented by Section 1–103 and, through it, by many rules of statutory and common law. Because this article is quite short and has no rules on many issues that will affect liability with respect to a letter of credit transaction, law beyond Article 5 will often determine rights and liabilities in letter of credit transactions. Even within letter of credit law, the article is far from comprehensive; it deals only with "certain" rights of the parties. Particularly with respect to the standards of performance that are set out in Section 5–108, it is appropriate for the parties and the courts to turn to customs and practice such as the Uniform Customs and Practice for Documentary Credits, currently published by the

International Chamber of Commerce as I.C.C. Pub. No. 500 (hereafter UCP). Many letters of credit specifically adopt the UCP as applicable to the particular transaction. Where the UCP are adopted but conflict with Article 5 and except where variation is prohibited, the UCP terms are permissible contractual modifications under Sections 1–302 and 5–103(c). See Section 5–116(c). Normally Article 5 should not be considered to conflict with practice except when a rule explicitly stated in the UCP or other practice is different from a rule explicitly stated in Article 5.

Except by choosing the law of a jurisdiction that has not adopted the Uniform Commercial Code, it is not possible entirely to escape the Uniform Commercial Code. Since incorporation of the UCP avoids only "conflicting" Article 5 rules, parties who do not wish to be governed by the nonconflicting provisions of Article 5 must normally either adopt the law of a jurisdiction other than a State of the United States or state explicitly the rule that is to govern. When rules of custom and practice are incorporated by reference, they are considered to be explicit terms of the agreement or undertaking.

Neither the obligation of an issuer under Section 5–108 nor that of an adviser under Section 5–107 is an obligation of the kind that is invariable under Section 1–102(3).* Section 5–103(c) and Comment 1 to Section 5–108 make it clear that the applicant and the issuer may agree to almost any provision establishing the obligations of the issuer to the applicant. The last sentence of subsection (c) limits the power of the issuer to achieve that result by a nonnegotiated disclaimer or limitation of remedy.

What the issuer could achieve by an explicit agreement with its applicant or by a term that explicitly defines its duty, it cannot accomplish by a general disclaimer. The restriction on disclaimers in the last sentence of subsection (c) is based more on procedural than on substantive unfairness. Where, for example, the reimbursement agreement provides explicitly that the issuer need not examine any documents, the applicant understands the risk it has undertaken. A term in a reimbursement agreement which states generally that an issuer will not be liable unless it has acted in "bad faith" or committed "gross negligence" is ineffective under Section 5–103(c). On the other hand, less general terms such as terms that permit issuer reliance on an oral or electronic message believed in good faith to have been received from the applicant or terms that entitle an issuer to reimbursement when it honors a "substantially" though not "strictly" complying presentation, are effective. In each case the question is whether the disclaimer or limitation is sufficiently clear and explicit in reallocating a liability or risk that is allocated differently under a variable Article 5 provision.

Of course, no term in a letter of credit, whether incorporated by reference to practice rules or stated specifically, can free an issuer from a conflicting contractual obligation to its applicant. If, for example, an issuer promised its applicant that it would pay only against an inspection certificate of a particular company but failed to require such a certificate in its letter of credit or made the requirement only a nondocumentary condition that had to be disregarded, the issuer might be obliged to pay the beneficiary even though its payment might violate its contract with its applicant.

3. Parties should generally avoid modifying the definitions in Section 5–102. The effect of such an agreement is almost inevitably unclear. To say that something is a "guarantee" in the typical domestic transaction is to say that the parties intend that particular legal rules apply to it. By acknowledging that something is a guarantee, but asserting that it is to be treated as a "letter of credit," the parties leave a court uncertain about where the rules on guarantees stop and those concerning letters of credit begin.

4. Section 5–102(2) and (3) of Article 5 are omitted as unneeded; the omission does not change the law.

As amended in 2001.

§ 5–104. Formal Requirements.

A letter of credit, confirmation, advice, transfer, amendment, or cancellation may be issued in any form that is a record and is authenticated (i) by a signature or (ii) in accordance with the agreement of the parties or the standard practice referred to in Section 5–108(e).

Official Comment

1. Neither Section 5–104 nor the definition of letter of credit in Section 5–102(a)(10) requires inclusion of all the terms that are normally contained in a letter of credit in order for an undertaking to be recognized as a letter of credit under Article 5. For example, a letter of credit will typically specify the amount available, the

---

* *Referring to unrevised Article 1 (Appendix A).*

expiration date, the place where presentation should be made, and the documents that must be presented to entitle a person to honor. Undertakings that have the formalities required by Section 5–104 and meet the conditions specified in Section 5–102(a)(10) will be recognized as letters of credit even though they omit one or more of the items usually contained in a letter of credit.

2.   The authentication specified in this section is authentication only of the identity of the issuer, confirmer, or adviser.

An authentication agreement may be by system rule, by standard practice, or by direct agreement between the parties. The reference to practice is intended to incorporate future developments in the UCP and other practice rules as well as those that may arise spontaneously in commercial practice.

3.   Many banking transactions, including the issuance of many letters of credit, are now conducted mostly by electronic means. For example, S.W.I.F.T. is currently used to transmit letters of credit from issuing to advising banks. The letter of credit text so transmitted may be printed at the advising bank, stamped "original" and provided to the beneficiary in that form. The printed document may then be used as a way of controlling and recording payments and of recording and authorizing assignments of proceeds or transfers of rights under the letter of credit. Nothing in this section should be construed to conflict with that practice.

To be a record sufficient to serve as a letter of credit or other undertaking under this section, data must have a durability consistent with that function. Because consideration is not required for a binding letter of credit or similar undertaking (Section 5–105) yet those undertakings are to be strictly construed (Section 5–108), parties to a letter of credit transaction are especially dependent on the continued availability of the terms and conditions of the letter of credit or other undertaking. By declining to specify any particular medium in which the letter of credit must be established or communicated, Section 5–104 leaves room for future developments.

§ 5–105.   Consideration.

Consideration is not required to issue, amend, transfer, or cancel a letter of credit, advice, or confirmation.

Official Comment

It is not to be expected that any issuer will issue its letter of credit without some form of remuneration. But it is not expected that the beneficiary will know what the issuer's remuneration was or whether in fact there was any identifiable remuneration in a given case. And it might be difficult for the beneficiary to prove the issuer's remuneration. This section dispenses with this proof and is consistent with the position of Lord Mansfield in *Pillans v. Van Mierop,* 97 Eng.Rep. 1035 (K.B. 1765) in making consideration irrelevant.

§ 5–106.   Issuance, Amendment, Cancellation, and Duration.

(a)   A letter of credit is issued and becomes enforceable according to its terms against the issuer when the issuer sends or otherwise transmits it to the person requested to advise or to the beneficiary. A letter of credit is revocable only if it so provides.

(b)   After a letter of credit is issued, rights and obligations of a beneficiary, applicant, confirmer, and issuer are not affected by an amendment or cancellation to which that person has not consented except to the extent the letter of credit provides that it is revocable or that the issuer may amend or cancel the letter of credit without that consent.

(c)   If there is no stated expiration date or other provision that determines its duration, a letter of credit expires one year after its stated date of issuance or, if none is stated, after the date on which it is issued.

(d)   A letter of credit that states that it is perpetual expires five years after its stated date of issuance, or if none is stated, after the date on which it is issued.

Official Comment

1.   This section adopts the position taken by several courts, namely that letters of credit that are silent as to revocability are irrevocable. See, e.g., *Weyerhaeuser Co. v. First Nat. Bank,* 27 UCC Rep.Serv. 777 (S.D. Iowa 1979); *West Va. Hous. Dev. Fund v. Sroka,* 415 F.Supp. 1107 (W.D.Pa.1976). This is the position of the current

UCP (500). Given the usual commercial understanding and purpose of letters of credit, revocable letters of credit offer unhappy possibilities for misleading the parties who deal with them.

2. A person can consent to an amendment by implication. For example, a beneficiary that tenders documents for honor that conform to an amended letter of credit but not to the original letter of credit has probably consented to the amendment. By the same token an applicant that has procured the issuance of a transferable letter of credit has consented to its transfer and to performance under the letter of credit by a person to whom the beneficiary's rights are duly transferred. If some, but not all of the persons involved in a letter of credit transaction consent to performance that does not strictly conform to the original letter of credit, those persons assume the risk that other nonconsenting persons may insist on strict compliance with the original letter of credit. Under subsection (b) those not consenting are not bound. For example, an issuer might agree to amend its letter of credit or honor documents presented after the expiration date in the belief that the applicant has consented or will consent to the amendment or will waive presentation after the original expiration date. If that belief is mistaken, the issuer is bound to the beneficiary by the terms of the letter of credit as amended or waived, even though it may be unable to recover from the applicant.

In general, the rights of a recognized transferee beneficiary cannot be altered without the transferee's consent, but the same is not true of the rights of assignees of proceeds from the beneficiary. When the beneficiary makes a complete transfer of its interest that is effective under the terms for transfer established by the issuer, adviser, or other party controlling transfers, the beneficiary no longer has an interest in the letter of credit, and the transferee steps into the shoes of the beneficiary as the one with rights under the letter of credit. Section 5–102(a)(3). When there is a partial transfer, both the original beneficiary and the transferee beneficiary have an interest in performance of the letter of credit and each expects that its rights will not be altered by amendment unless it consents.

The assignee of proceeds under a letter of credit from the beneficiary enjoys no such expectation. Notwithstanding an assignee's notice to the issuer of the assignment of proceeds, the assignee is not a person protected by subsection (b). An assignee of proceeds should understand that its rights can be changed or completely extinguished by amendment or cancellation of the letter of credit. An assignee's claim is precarious, for it depends entirely upon the continued existence of the letter of credit and upon the beneficiary's preparation and presentation of documents that would entitle the beneficiary to honor under Section 5–108.

3. The issuer's right to cancel a revocable letter of credit does not free it from a duty to reimburse a nominated person who has honored, accepted, or undertaken a deferred obligation prior to receiving notice of the amendment or cancellation. Compare UCP Article 8.

4. Although all letters of credit should specify the date on which the issuer's engagement expires, the failure to specify an expiration date does not invalidate the letter of credit, or diminish or relieve the obligation of any party with respect to the letter of credit. A letter of credit that may be revoked or terminated at the discretion of the issuer by notice to the beneficiary is not "perpetual."

§ 5–107. Confirmer, Nominated Person, and Adviser.

(a) A confirmer is directly obligated on a letter of credit and has the rights and obligations of an issuer to the extent of its confirmation. The confirmer also has rights against and obligations to the issuer as if the issuer were an applicant and the confirmer had issued the letter of credit at the request and for the account of the issuer.

(b) A nominated person who is not a confirmer is not obligated to honor or otherwise give value for a presentation.

(c) A person requested to advise may decline to act as an adviser. An adviser that is not a confirmer is not obligated to honor or give value for a presentation. An adviser undertakes to the issuer and to the beneficiary accurately to advise the terms of the letter of credit, confirmation, amendment, or advice received by that person and undertakes to the beneficiary to check the apparent authenticity of the request to advise. Even if the advice is inaccurate, the letter of credit, confirmation, or amendment is enforceable as issued.

(d) A person who notifies a transferee beneficiary of the terms of a letter of credit, confirmation, amendment, or advice has the rights and obligations of an adviser under subsection (c). The terms in the notice to the transferee beneficiary may differ from the terms in any notice to the transferor beneficiary to the extent permitted by the letter of credit, confirmation, amendment, or advice received by the person who so notifies.

Official Comment

1.   A confirmer has the rights and obligations identified in Section 5–108. Accordingly, unless the context otherwise requires, the terms "confirmer" and "confirmation" should be read into this article wherever the terms "issuer" and "letter of credit" appear.

A confirmer that has paid in accordance with the terms and conditions of the letter of credit is entitled to reimbursement by the issuer even if the beneficiary committed fraud (see Section 5–109(a)(1)(ii)) and, in that sense, has greater rights against the issuer than the beneficiary has. To be entitled to reimbursement from the issuer under the typical confirmed letter of credit, the confirmer must submit conforming documents, but the confirmer's presentation to the issuer need not be made before the expiration date of the letter of credit.

A letter of credit confirmation has been analogized to a guarantee of issuer performance, to a parallel letter of credit issued by the confirmer for the account of the issuer or the letter of credit applicant or both, and to a back-to-back letter of credit in which the confirmer is a kind of beneficiary of the original issuer's letter of credit. Like letter of credit undertakings, confirmations are both unique and flexible, so that no one of these analogies is perfect, but unless otherwise indicated in the letter of credit or confirmation, a confirmer should be viewed by the letter of credit issuer and the beneficiary as an issuer of a parallel letter of credit for the account of the original letter of credit issuer. Absent a direct agreement between the applicant and a confirmer, normally the obligations of a confirmer are to the issuer not the applicant, but the applicant might have a right to injunction against a confirmer under Section 5–109 or warranty claim under Section 5–110, and either might have claims against the other under Section 5–117.

2.   No one has a duty to advise until that person agrees to be an adviser or undertakes to act in accordance with the instructions of the issuer. Except where there is a prior agreement to serve or where the silence of the adviser would be an acceptance of an offer to contract, a person's failure to respond to a request to advise a letter of credit does not in and of itself create any liability, nor does it establish a relationship of issuer and adviser between the two. Since there is no duty to advise a letter of credit in the absence of a prior agreement, there can be no duty to advise it timely or at any particular time. When the adviser manifests its agreement to advise by actually doing so (as is normally the case), the adviser cannot have violated any duty to advise in a timely way. This analysis is consistent with the result of *Sound of Market Street v. Continental Bank International*, 819 F.2d 384 (3d Cir.1987) which held that there is no such duty. This section takes no position on the reasoning of that case, but does not overrule the result. By advising or agreeing to advise a letter of credit, the adviser assumes a duty to the issuer and to the beneficiary accurately to report what it has received from the issuer, but, beyond determining the apparent authenticity of the letter, an adviser has no duty to investigate the accuracy of the message it has received from the issuer. "Checking" the apparent authenticity of the request to advise means only that the prospective adviser must attempt to authenticate the message (e.g., by "testing" the telex that comes from the purported issuer), and if it is unable to authenticate the message must report that fact to the issuer and, if it chooses to advise the message, to the beneficiary. By proper agreement, an adviser may disclaim its obligation under this section.

3.   An issuer may issue a letter of credit which the adviser may advise with different terms. The issuer may then believe that it has undertaken a certain engagement, yet the text in the hands of the beneficiary will contain different terms, and the beneficiary would not be entitled to honor if the documents it submitted did not comply with the terms of the letter of credit as originally issued. On the other hand, if the adviser also confirmed the letter of credit, then as a confirmer it will be independently liable on the letter of credit as advised and confirmed. If in that situation the beneficiary's ultimate presentation entitled it to honor under the terms of the confirmation but not under those in the original letter of credit, the confirmer would have to honor but might not be entitled to reimbursement from the issuer.

4.   When the issuer nominates another person to "pay," "negotiate," or otherwise to take up the documents and give value, there can be confusion about the legal status of the nominated person. In rare cases the person might actually be an agent of the issuer and its act might be the act of the issuer itself. In most cases the nominated person is not an agent of the issuer and has no authority to act on the issuer's behalf. Its "nomination" allows the beneficiary to present to it and earns it certain rights to payment under Section 5–109 that others do not enjoy. For example, when an issuer issues a "freely negotiable credit," it contemplates that banks or others might take up documents under that credit and advance value against them, and it is agreeing to pay those persons but only if the presentation to the issuer made by the nominated person complies with the credit. Usually there will be no

492

agreement to pay, negotiate, or to serve in any other capacity by the nominated person, therefore the nominated person will have the right to decline to take the documents. It may return them or agree merely to act as a forwarding agent for the documents but without giving value against them or taking any responsibility for their conformity to the letter of credit.

§ 5-108. Issuer's Rights and Obligations.

(a) Except as otherwise provided in Section 5-109, an issuer shall honor a presentation that, as determined by the standard practice referred to in subsection (e), appears on its face strictly to comply with the terms and conditions of the letter of credit. Except as otherwise provided in Section 5-113 and unless otherwise agreed with the applicant, an issuer shall dishonor a presentation that does not appear so to comply.

(b) An issuer has a reasonable time after presentation, but not beyond the end of the seventh business day of the issuer after the day of its receipt of documents:

(1) to honor,

(2) if the letter of credit provides for honor to be completed more than seven business days after presentation, to accept a draft or incur a deferred obligation, or

(3) to give notice to the presenter of discrepancies in the presentation.

(c) Except as otherwise provided in subsection (d), an issuer is precluded from asserting as a basis for dishonor any discrepancy if timely notice is not given, or any discrepancy not stated in the notice if timely notice is given.

(d) Failure to give the notice specified in subsection (b) or to mention fraud, forgery, or expiration in the notice does not preclude the issuer from asserting as a basis for dishonor fraud or forgery as described in Section 5-109(a) or expiration of the letter of credit before presentation.

(e) An issuer shall observe standard practice of financial institutions that regularly issue letters of credit. Determination of the issuer's observance of the standard practice is a matter of interpretation for the court. The court shall offer the parties a reasonable opportunity to present evidence of the standard practice.

(f) An issuer is not responsible for:

(1) the performance or nonperformance of the underlying contract, arrangement, or transaction,

(2) an act or omission of others, or

(3) observance or knowledge of the usage of a particular trade other than the standard practice referred to in subsection (e).

(g) If an undertaking constituting a letter of credit under Section 5-102(a)(10) contains nondocumentary conditions, an issuer shall disregard the nondocumentary conditions and treat them as if they were not stated.

(h) An issuer that has dishonored a presentation shall return the documents or hold them at the disposal of, and send advice to that effect to, the presenter.

(i) An issuer that has honored a presentation as permitted or required by this article:

(1) is entitled to be reimbursed by the applicant in immediately available funds not later than the date of its payment of funds;

(2) takes the documents free of claims of the beneficiary or presenter;

(3) is precluded from asserting a right of recourse on a draft under Sections 3-414 and 3-415;

(4) except as otherwise provided in Sections 5-110 and 5-117, is precluded from restitution of money paid or other value given by mistake to the extent the mistake concerns discrepancies in the documents or tender which are apparent on the face of the presentation; and

(5)   is discharged to the extent of its performance under the letter of credit unless the issuer honored a presentation in which a required signature of a beneficiary was forged.

Official Comment

1.   This section combines some of the duties previously included in Sections 5–114 and 5–109. Because a confirmer has the rights and duties of an issuer, this section applies equally to a confirmer and an issuer. See Section 5–107(a).

The standard of strict compliance governs the issuer's obligation to the beneficiary and to the applicant. By requiring that a "presentation" appear strictly to comply, the section requires not only that the documents themselves appear on their face strictly to comply, but also that the other terms of the letter of credit such as those dealing with the time and place of presentation are strictly complied with. Typically, a letter of credit will provide that presentation is timely if made to the issuer, confirmer, or any other nominated person prior to expiration of the letter of credit. Accordingly, a nominated person that has honored a demand or otherwise given value before expiration will have a right to reimbursement from the issuer even though presentation to the issuer is made after the expiration of the letter of credit. Conversely, where the beneficiary negotiates documents to one who is not a nominated person, the beneficiary or that person acting on behalf of the beneficiary must make presentation to a nominated person, confirmer, or issuer prior to the expiration date.

This section does not impose a bifurcated standard under which an issuer's right to reimbursement might be broader than a beneficiary's right to honor. However, the explicit deference to standard practice in Section 5–108(a) and (e) and elsewhere expands issuers' rights of reimbursement where that practice so provides. Also, issuers can and often do contract with their applicants for expanded rights of reimbursement. Where that is done, the beneficiary will have to meet a more stringent standard of compliance as to the issuer than the issuer will have to meet as to the applicant. Similarly, a nominated person may have reimbursement and other rights against the issuer based on this article, the UCP, bank-to-bank reimbursement rules, or other agreement or undertaking of the issuer. These rights may allow the nominated person to recover from the issuer even when the nominated person would have no right to obtain honor under the letter of credit.

The section adopts strict compliance, rather than the standard that commentators have called "substantial compliance," the standard arguably applied in *Banco Español de Credito v. State Street Bank and Trust Company,* 385 F.2d 230 (1st Cir.1967) and *Flagship Cruises Ltd. v. New England Merchants Nat. Bank,* 569 F.2d 699 (1st Cir.1978). Strict compliance does not mean slavish conformity to the terms of the letter of credit. For example, standard practice (what issuers do) may recognize certain presentations as complying that an unschooled layman would regard as discrepant. By adopting standard practice as a way of measuring strict compliance, this article indorses the conclusion of the court in *New Braunfels Nat. Bank v. Odiorne,* 780 S.W.2d 313 (Tex.Ct.App. 1989) (beneficiary could collect when draft requested payment on "Letter of Credit No. 86–122–5" and letter of credit specified "Letter of Credit No. 86–122–S" holding strict compliance does not demand oppressive perfectionism). The section also indorses the result in *Tosco Corp. v. Federal Deposit Insurance Corp.,* 723 F.2d 1242 (6th Cir.1983). The letter of credit in that case called for "drafts Drawn under Bank of Clarksville Letter of Credit Number 105." The draft presented stated "drawn under Bank of Clarksville, Clarksville, Tennessee letter of Credit No. 105." The court correctly found that despite the change of upper case "L" to a lower case "l" and the use of the word "No." instead of "Number," and despite the addition of the words "Clarksville, Tennessee," the presentation conformed. Similarly a document addressed by a foreign person to General Motors as "Jeneral Motors" would strictly conform in the absence of other defects.

Identifying and determining compliance with standard practice are matters of interpretation for the court, not for the jury. As with similar rules in Sections 4A–202(c) and 2–302, it is hoped that there will be more consistency in the outcomes and speedier resolution of disputes if the responsibility for determining the nature and scope of standard practice is granted to the court, not to a jury. Granting the court authority to make these decisions will also encourage the salutary practice of courts' granting summary judgment in circumstances where there are no significant factual disputes. The statute encourages outcomes such as *American Coleman Co. v. Intrawest Bank,* 887 F.2d 1382 (10th Cir.1989), where summary judgment was granted.

In some circumstances standards may be established between the issuer and the applicant by agreement or by custom that would free the issuer from liability that it might otherwise have. For example, an applicant might agree that the issuer would have no duty whatsoever to examine documents on certain presentations (e.g., those below a certain dollar amount). Where the transaction depended upon the issuer's payment in a very short time period (e.g., on the same day or within a few hours of presentation), the issuer and the applicant might agree to reduce the issuer's responsibility for failure to discover discrepancies. By the same token, an agreement between the applicant and the issuer might permit the issuer to examine documents exclusively by electronic or electro-optical means. Neither those agreements nor others like them explicitly made by issuers and applicants violate the terms of Section 5–108(a) or (b) or Section 5–103(c).

2.   Section 5–108(a) balances the need of the issuer for time to examine the documents against the possibility that the examiner (at the urging of the applicant or for fear that it will not be reimbursed) will take excessive time to search for defects. What is a "reasonable time" is not extended to accommodate an issuer's procuring a waiver from the applicant. See Article 14c of the UCP.

Under both the UCC and the UCP the issuer has a reasonable time to honor or give notice. The outside limit of that time is measured in business days under the UCC and in banking days under the UCP, a difference that will rarely be significant. Neither business nor banking days are defined in Article 5, but a court may find useful analogies in Regulation CC, 12 CFR 229.2, in state law outside of the Uniform Commercial Code, and in Article 4.

Examiners must note that the seven-day period is not a safe harbor. The time within which the issuer must give notice is the lesser of a reasonable time or seven business days. Where there are few documents (as, for example, with the mine run standby letter of credit), the reasonable time would be less than seven days. If more than a reasonable time is consumed in examination, no timely notice is possible. What is a "reasonable time" is to be determined by examining the behavior of those in the business of examining documents, mostly banks. Absent prior agreement of the issuer, one could not expect a bank issuer to examine documents while the beneficiary waited in the lobby if the normal practice was to give the documents to a person who had the opportunity to examine those together with many others in an orderly process. That the applicant has not yet paid the issuer or that the applicant's account with the issuer is insufficient to cover the amount of the draft is not a basis for extension of the time period.

This section does not preclude the issuer from contacting the applicant during its examination; however, the decision to honor rests with the issuer, and it has no duty to seek a waiver from the applicant or to notify the applicant of receipt of the documents. If the issuer dishonors a conforming presentation, the beneficiary will be entitled to the remedies under Section 5–111, irrespective of the applicant's views.

Even though the person to whom presentation is made cannot conduct a reasonable examination of documents within the time after presentation and before the expiration date, presentation establishes the parties' rights. The beneficiary's right to honor or the issuer's right to dishonor arises upon presentation at the place provided in the letter of credit even though it might take the person to whom presentation has been made several days to determine whether honor or dishonor is the proper course. The issuer's time for honor or giving notice of dishonor may be extended or shortened by a term in the letter of credit. The time for the issuer's performance may be otherwise modified or waived in accordance with Section 5–106.

The issuer's time to inspect runs from the time of its "receipt of documents." Documents are considered to be received only when they are received at the place specified for presentation by the issuer or other party to whom presentation is made. "Receipt of documents" when documents of title are presented must be read in light of the definition of "delivery" in Article 1, Section 1–201 and the definition of "presentment" in Section 5–102(a)(12).

Failure of the issuer to act within the time permitted by subsection (b) constitutes dishonor. Because of the preclusion in subsection (c) and the liability that the issuer may incur under Section 5–111 for wrongful dishonor, the effect of such a silent dishonor may ultimately be the same as though the issuer had honored, i.e., it may owe damages in the amount drawn but unpaid under the letter of credit.

3.   The requirement that the issuer send notice of the discrepancies or be precluded from asserting discrepancies is new to Article 5. It is taken from the similar provision in the UCP and is intended to promote certainty and finality.

The section thus substitutes a strict preclusion principle for the doctrines of waiver and estoppel that might otherwise apply under Section 1–103. It rejects the reasoning in *Flagship Cruises Ltd. v. New England Merchants' Nat. Bank,* 569 F.2d 699 (1st Cir.1978) and *Wing On Bank Ltd. v. American Nat. Bank & Trust Co.,* 457 F.2d 328 (5th Cir.1972) where the issuer was held to be estopped only if the beneficiary relied on the issuer's failure to give notice.

Assume, for example, that the beneficiary presented documents to the issuer shortly before the letter of credit expired, in circumstances in which the beneficiary could not have cured any discrepancy before expiration. Under the reasoning of *Flagship* and *Wing On,* the beneficiary's inability to cure, even if it had received notice, would absolve the issuer of its failure to give notice. The virtue of the preclusion obligation adopted in this section is that it forecloses litigation about reliance and detriment.

Even though issuers typically give notice of the discrepancy of tardy presentation when presentation is made after the expiration of a credit, they are not required to give that notice and the section permits them to raise late presentation as a defect despite their failure to give that notice.

4.   To act within a reasonable time, the issuer must normally give notice without delay after the examining party makes its decision. If the examiner decides to dishonor on the first day, it would be obliged to notify the beneficiary shortly thereafter, perhaps on the same business day. This rule accepts the reasoning in cases such as *Datapoint Corp. v. M & I Bank*, 665 F.Supp. 722 (W.D.Wis.1987) and *Esso Petroleum Canada, Div. of Imperial Oil, Ltd. v. Security Pacific Bank*, 710 F.Supp. 275 (D.Or.1989).

The section deprives the examining party of the right simply to sit on a presentation that is made within seven days of expiration. The section requires the examiner to examine the documents and make a decision and, having made a decision to dishonor, to communicate promptly with the presenter. Nevertheless, a beneficiary who presents documents shortly before the expiration of a letter of credit runs the risk that it will never have the opportunity to cure any discrepancies.

5.   Confirmers, other nominated persons, and collecting banks acting for beneficiaries can be presenters and, when so, are entitled to the notice provided in subsection (b). Even nominated persons who have honored or given value against an earlier presentation of the beneficiary and are themselves seeking reimbursement or honor need notice of discrepancies in the hope that they may be able to procure complying documents. The issuer has the obligations imposed by this section whether the issuer's performance is characterized as "reimbursement" of a nominated person or as "honor."

6.   In many cases a letter of credit authorizes presentation by the beneficiary to someone other than the issuer. Sometimes that person is identified as a "payor" or "paying bank," or as an "acceptor" or "accepting bank," in other cases as a "negotiating bank," and in other cases there will be no specific designation. The section does not impose any duties on a person other than the issuer or confirmer, however a nominated person or other person may have liability under this article or at common law if it fails to perform an express or implied agreement with the beneficiary.

7.   The issuer's obligation to honor runs not only to the beneficiary but also to the applicant. It is possible that an applicant who has made a favorable contract with the beneficiary will be injured by the issuer's wrongful dishonor. Except to the extent that the contract between the issuer and the applicant limits that liability, the issuer will have liability to the applicant for wrongful dishonor under Section 5–111 as a matter of contract law. A good faith extension of the time in Section 5–108(b) by agreement between the issuer and beneficiary binds the applicant even if the applicant is not consulted or does not consent to the extension.

The issuer's obligation to dishonor when there is no apparent compliance with the letter of credit runs only to the applicant. No other party to the transaction can complain if the applicant waives compliance with terms or conditions of the letter of credit or agrees to a less stringent standard for compliance than that supplied by this article. Except as otherwise agreed with the applicant, an issuer may dishonor a noncomplying presentation despite an applicant's waiver.

Waiver of discrepancies by an issuer or an applicant in one or more presentations does not waive similar discrepancies in a future presentation. Neither the issuer nor the beneficiary can reasonably rely upon honor over past waivers as a basis for concluding that a future defective presentation will justify honor. The reasoning of *Courtaulds of North America Inc. v. North Carolina Nat. Bank*, 528 F.2d 802 (4th Cir.1975) is accepted and that expressed in *Schweibish v. Pontchartrain State Bank*, 389 So.2d 731 (La.App.1980) and *Titanium Metals Corp. v. Space Metals, Inc.*, 529 P.2d 431 (Utah 1974) is rejected.

8.   The standard practice referred to in subsection (e) includes (i) international practice set forth in or referenced by the Uniform Customs and Practice, (ii) other practice rules published by associations of financial institutions, and (iii) local and regional practice. It is possible that standard practice will vary from one place to another. Where there are conflicting practices, the parties should indicate which practice governs their rights. A practice may be overridden by agreement or course of dealing. See Section 1–205(4).*

9.   The responsibility of the issuer under a letter of credit is to examine documents and to make a prompt decision to honor or dishonor based upon that examination. Nondocumentary conditions have no place in this regime and are better accommodated under contract or suretyship law and practice. In requiring that nondocumentary conditions in letters of credit be ignored as surplusage, Article 5 remains aligned with the UCP

---

*   *Referring to unrevised Article 1 (Appendix A).*

(see UCP 500 Article 13c), approves cases like *Pringle-Associated Mortgage Corp. v. Southern National Bank,* 571 F.2d 871, 874 (5th Cir.1978), and rejects the reasoning in cases such as *Sherwood & Roberts, Inc. v. First Security Bank,* 682 P.2d 149 (Mont. 1984).

Subsection (g) recognizes that letters of credit sometimes contain nondocumentary terms or conditions. Conditions such as a term prohibiting "shipment on vessels more than 15 years old," are to be disregarded and treated as surplusage. Similarly, a requirement that there be an award by a "duly appointed arbitrator" would not require the issuer to determine whether the arbitrator had been "duly appointed." Likewise a term in a standby letter of credit that provided for differing forms of certification depending upon the particular type of default does not oblige the issuer independently to determine which kind of default has occurred. These conditions must be disregarded by the issuer. Where the nondocumentary conditions are central and fundamental to the issuer's obligation (as for example a condition that would require the issuer to determine in fact whether the beneficiary had performed the underlying contract or whether the applicant had defaulted) their inclusion may remove the undertaking from the scope of Article 5 entirely. See Section 5–102(a)(10) and Comment 6 to Section 5–102.

Subsection (g) would not permit the beneficiary or the issuer to disregard terms in the letter of credit such as place, time, and mode of presentation. The rule in subsection (g) is intended to prevent an issuer from deciding or even investigating extrinsic facts, but not from consulting the clock, the calendar, the relevant law and practice, or its own general knowledge of documentation or transactions of the type underlying a particular letter of credit.

Even though nondocumentary conditions must be disregarded in determining compliance of a presentation (and thus in determining the issuer's duty to the beneficiary), an issuer that has promised its applicant that it will honor only on the occurrence of those nondocumentary conditions may have liability to its applicant for disregarding the conditions.

10. Subsection (f) condones an issuer's ignorance of "any usage of a particular trade"; that trade is the trade of the applicant, beneficiary, or others who may be involved in the underlying transaction. The issuer is expected to know usage that is commonly encountered in the course of document examination. For example, an issuer should know the common usage with respect to documents in the maritime shipping trade but would not be expected to understand synonyms used in a particular trade for product descriptions appearing in a letter of credit or an invoice.

11. Where the issuer's performance is the delivery of an item of value other than money, the applicant's reimbursement obligation would be to make the "item of value" available to the issuer.

12. An issuer is entitled to reimbursement from the applicant after honor of a forged or fraudulent drawing if honor was permitted under Section 5–109(a).

13. The last clause of Section 5–108(i)(5) deals with a special case in which the fraud is not committed by the beneficiary, but is committed by a stranger to the transaction who forges the beneficiary's signature. If the issuer pays against documents on which a required signature of the beneficiary is forged, it remains liable to the true beneficiary. This principle is applicable to both electronic and tangible documents.

As amended in 2003.

§ 5–109. Fraud and Forgery.

(a) If a presentation is made that appears on its face strictly to comply with the terms and conditions of the letter of credit, but a required document is forged or materially fraudulent, or honor of the presentation would facilitate a material fraud by the beneficiary on the issuer or applicant:

(1) the issuer shall honor the presentation, if honor is demanded by (i) a nominated person who has given value in good faith and without notice of forgery or material fraud, (ii) a confirmer who has honored its confirmation in good faith, (iii) a holder in due course of a draft drawn under the letter of credit which was taken after acceptance by the issuer or nominated person, or (iv) an assignee of the issuer's or nominated person's deferred obligation that was taken for value and without notice of forgery or material fraud after the obligation was incurred by the issuer or nominated person; and

(2) the issuer, acting in good faith, may honor or dishonor the presentation in any other case.

(b) If an applicant claims that a required document is forged or materially fraudulent or that honor of the presentation would facilitate a material fraud by the beneficiary on the issuer or applicant, a court of competent jurisdiction may temporarily or permanently enjoin the issuer from honoring a presentation or grant similar relief against the issuer or other persons only if the court finds that:

(1) the relief is not prohibited under the law applicable to an accepted draft or deferred obligation incurred by the issuer;

(2) a beneficiary, issuer, or nominated person who may be adversely affected is adequately protected against loss that it may suffer because the relief is granted;

(3) all of the conditions to entitle a person to the relief under the law of this State have been met; and

(4) on the basis of the information submitted to the court, the applicant is more likely than not to succeed under its claim of forgery or material fraud and the person demanding honor does not qualify for protection under subsection (a)(1).

Official Comment

1.   This recodification makes clear that fraud must be found either in the documents or must have been committed by the beneficiary on the issuer or applicant. See *Cromwell v. Commerce & Energy Bank,* 464 So.2d 721 (La.1985).

Secondly, it makes clear that fraud must be "material." Necessarily courts must decide the breadth and width of "materiality." The use of the word requires that the fraudulent aspect of a document be material to a purchaser of that document or that the fraudulent act be significant to the participants in the underlying transaction. Assume, for example, that the beneficiary has a contract to deliver 1,000 barrels of salad oil. Knowing that it has delivered only 998, the beneficiary nevertheless submits an invoice showing 1,000 barrels. If two barrels in a 1,000 barrel shipment would be an insubstantial and immaterial breach of the underlying contract, the beneficiary's act, though possibly fraudulent, is not materially so and would not justify an injunction. Conversely, the knowing submission of those invoices upon delivery of only five barrels would be materially fraudulent. The courts must examine the underlying transaction when there is an allegation of material fraud, for only by examining that transaction can one determine whether a document is fraudulent or the beneficiary has committed fraud and, if so, whether the fraud was material.

Material fraud by the beneficiary occurs only when the beneficiary has no colorable right to expect honor and where there is no basis in fact to support such a right to honor. The section indorses articulations such as those stated in *Intraworld Indus. v. Girard Trust Bank,* 336 A.2d 316 (Pa.1975), *Roman Ceramics Corp. v. People's Nat. Bank,* 714 F.2d 1207 (3d Cir.1983), and similar decisions and embraces certain decisions under Section 5–114 that relied upon the phrase "fraud in the transaction." Some of these decisions have been summarized as follows in *Ground Air Transfer v. Westate's Airlines,* 899 F.2d 1269, 1272–73 (1st Cir.1990):

> We have said throughout that courts may not "*normally*" issue an injunction because of an important exception to the general "no injunction" rule. The exception, as we also explained in *Itek,* 730 F.2d at 24–25, concerns "fraud" so serious as to make it obviously pointless and unjust to permit the beneficiary to obtain the money. Where the circumstances "*plainly*" show that the underlying contract forbids the beneficiary to call a letter of credit, *Itek,* 730 F.2d at 24; where they show that the contract deprives the beneficiary of even a "*colorable*" right to do so, id., at 25; where the contract and circumstances reveal that the beneficiary's demand for payment has "absolutely no basis in fact," id.; see *Dynamics Corp. of America,* 356 F.Supp. at 999; where the beneficiary's conduct has "so vitiated the entire transaction that the legitimate purposes of the independence of the issuer's obligation would no longer be served," Itek, 730 F.2d at 25 (quoting *Roman Ceramics Corp. v. Peoples National Bank,* 714 F.2d 1207, 1212 n.12, 1215 (3d Cir.1983)(quoting Intraworld Indus., 336 A.2d at 324–25)); *then* a court may enjoin payment.

2.   Subsection (a)(2) makes clear that the issuer may honor in the face of the applicant's claim of fraud. The subsection also makes clear what was not stated in former Section 5–114, that the issuer may dishonor and defend that dishonor by showing fraud or forgery of the kind stated in subsection (a). Because issuers may be liable for wrongful dishonor if they are unable to prove forgery or material fraud, presumably most issuers will choose to honor despite applicant's claims of fraud or forgery unless the applicant procures an injunction. Merely because the issuer has a right to dishonor and to defend that dishonor by showing forgery or material fraud does not mean it has a duty to the applicant to dishonor. The applicant's normal recourse is to procure an injunction, if the applicant is unable to procure an injunction, it will have a claim against the issuer only in the rare case in which it can show that the issuer did not honor in good faith.

3. Whether a beneficiary can commit fraud by presenting a draft under a clean letter of credit (one calling only for a draft and no other documents) has been much debated. Under the current formulation it would be possible but difficult for there to be fraud in such a presentation. If the applicant were able to show that the beneficiary were committing material fraud on the applicant in the underlying transaction, then payment would facilitate a material fraud by the beneficiary on the applicant and honor could be enjoined. The courts should be skeptical of claims of fraud by one who has signed a "suicide" or clean credit and thus granted a beneficiary the right to draw by mere presentation of a draft.

4. The standard for injunctive relief is high, and the burden remains on the applicant to show, by evidence and not by mere allegation, that such relief is warranted. Some courts have enjoined payments on letters of credit on insufficient showing by the applicant. For example, in *Griffin Cos. v. First Nat. Bank,* 374 N.W.2d 768 (Minn.App.1985), the court enjoined payment under a standby letter of credit, basing its decision on plaintiff's allegation, rather than competent evidence, of fraud.

There are at least two ways to prohibit injunctions against honor under this section after acceptance of a draft by the issuer. First is to define honor (see Section 5–102(a)(8)) in the particular letter of credit to occur upon acceptance and without regard to later payment of the acceptance. Second is explicitly to agree that the applicant has no right to an injunction after acceptance—whether or not the acceptance constitutes honor.

5. Although the statute deals principally with injunctions against honor, it also cautions against granting "similar relief" and the same principles apply when the applicant or issuer attempts to achieve the same legal outcome by injunction against presentation (see *Ground Air Transfer Inc. v. Westates Airlines, Inc.,* 899 F.2d 1269 (1st Cir.1990)), interpleader, declaratory judgment, or attachment. These attempts should face the same obstacles that face efforts to enjoin the issuer from paying. Expanded use of any of these devices could threaten the independence principle just as much as injunctions against honor. For that reason courts should have the same hostility to them and place the same restrictions on their use as would be applied to injunctions against honor. Courts should not allow the "sacred cow of equity to trample the tender vines of letter of credit law."

6. Section 5–109(a)(1) also protects specified third parties against the risk of fraud. By issuing a letter of credit that nominates a person to negotiate or pay, the issuer (ultimately the applicant) induces that nominated person to give value and thereby assumes the risk that a draft drawn under the letter of credit will be transferred to one with a status like that of a holder in due course who deserves to be protected against a fraud defense.

7. The "loss" to be protected against—by bond or otherwise under subsection (b)(2)—includes incidental damages. Among those are legal fees that might be incurred by the beneficiary or issuer in defending against an injunction action.

§ 5–110. Warranties.

(a) If its presentation is honored, the beneficiary warrants:

(1) to the issuer, any other person to whom presentation is made, and the applicant that there is no fraud or forgery of the kind described in Section 5–109(a); and

(2) to the applicant that the drawing does not violate any agreement between the applicant and beneficiary or any other agreement intended by them to be augmented by the letter of credit.

(b) The warranties in subsection (a) are in addition to warranties arising under Article 3, 4, 7, and 8 because of the presentation or transfer of documents covered by any of those articles.

Official Comment

1. Since the warranties in subsection (a) are not given unless a letter of credit has been honored, no breach of warranty under this subsection can be a defense to dishonor by the issuer. Any defense must be based on Section 5–108 or 5–109 and not on this section. Also, breach of the warranties by the beneficiary in subsection (a) cannot excuse the applicant's duty to reimburse.

2. The warranty in Section 5–110(a)(2) assumes that payment under the letter of credit is final. It does not run to the issuer, only to the applicant. In most cases the applicant will have a direct cause of action for breach of the underlying contract. This warranty has primary application in standby letters of credit or other circumstances where the applicant is not a party to an underlying contract with the beneficiary. It is not a warranty that the statements made on the presentation of the documents presented are truthful nor is it a warranty that the documents strictly comply under Section 5–108(a). It is a warranty that the beneficiary has

performed all the acts expressly and implicitly necessary under any underlying agreement to entitle the beneficiary to honor. If, for example, an underlying sales contract authorized the beneficiary to draw only upon "due performance" and the beneficiary drew even though it had breached the underlying contract by delivering defective goods, honor of its draw would break the warranty. By the same token, if the underlying contract authorized the beneficiary to draw only upon actual default or upon its or a third party's determination of default by the applicant and if the beneficiary drew in violation of its authorization, then upon honor of its draw the warranty would be breached. In many cases, therefore, the documents presented to the issuer will contain inaccurate statements (concerning the goods delivered or concerning default or other matters), but the breach of warranty arises not because the statements are untrue but because the beneficiary's drawing violated its express or implied obligations in the underlying transaction.

3.   The damages for breach of warranty are not specified in Section 5–111. Courts may find damage analogies in Section 2–714 in Article 2 and in warranty decisions under Articles 3 and 4.

Unlike wrongful dishonor cases—where the damages usually equal the amount of the draw—the damages for breach of warranty will often be much less than the amount of the draw, sometimes zero. Assume a seller entitled to draw only on proper performance of its sales contract. Assume it breaches the sales contract in a way that gives the buyer a right to damages but no right to reject. The applicant's damages for breach of the warranty in subsection (a)(2) are limited to the damages it could recover for breach of the contract of sale. Alternatively assume an underlying agreement that authorizes a beneficiary to draw only the "amount in default." Assume a default of $200,000 and a draw of $500,000. The damages for breach of warranty would be no more than $300,000.

§ 5–111.   Remedies.

(a)   If an issuer wrongfully dishonors or repudiates its obligation to pay money under a letter of credit before presentation, the beneficiary, successor, or nominated person presenting on its own behalf may recover from the issuer the amount that is the subject of the dishonor or repudiation. If the issuer's obligation under the letter of credit is not for the payment of money, the claimant may obtain specific performance or, at the claimant's election, recover an amount equal to the value of performance from the issuer. In either case, the claimant may also recover incidental but not consequential damages. The claimant is not obligated to take action to avoid damages that might be due from the issuer under this subsection. If, although not obligated to do so, the claimant avoids damages, the claimant's recovery from the issuer must be reduced by the amount of damages avoided. The issuer has the burden of proving the amount of damages avoided. In the case of repudiation the claimant need not present any document.

(b)   If an issuer wrongfully dishonors a draft or demand presented under a letter of credit or honors a draft or demand in breach of its obligation to the applicant, the applicant may recover damages resulting from the breach, including incidental but not consequential damages, less any amount saved as a result of the breach.

(c)   If an adviser or nominated person other than a confirmer breaches an obligation under this article or an issuer breaches an obligation not covered in subsection (a) or (b), a person to whom the obligation is owed may recover damages resulting from the breach, including incidental but not consequential damages, less any amount saved as a result of the breach. To the extent of the confirmation, a confirmer has the liability of an issuer specified in this subsection and subsections (a) and (b).

(d)   An issuer, nominated person, or adviser who is found liable under subsection (a), (b), or (c) shall pay interest on the amount owed thereunder from the date of wrongful dishonor or other appropriate date.

(e)   Reasonable attorney's fees and other expenses of litigation must be awarded to the prevailing party in an action in which a remedy is sought under this article.

(f)   Damages that would otherwise be payable by a party for breach of an obligation under this article may be liquidated by agreement or undertaking, but only in an amount or by a formula that is reasonable in light of the harm anticipated.

Official Comment

1.   The right to specific performance is new. The express limitation on the duty of the beneficiary to mitigate damages adopts the position of certain courts and commentators. Because the letter of credit depends upon speed and certainty of payment, it is important that the issuer not be given an incentive to dishonor. The

issuer might have an incentive to dishonor if it could rely on the burden of mitigation falling on the beneficiary, (to sell goods and sue only for the difference between the price of the goods sold and the amount due under the letter of credit). Under the scheme contemplated by Section 5–111(a), the beneficiary would present the documents to the issuer. If the issuer wrongfully dishonored, the beneficiary would have no further duty to the issuer with respect to the goods covered by documents that the issuer dishonored and returned. The issuer thus takes the risk that the beneficiary will let the goods rot or be destroyed. Of course the beneficiary may have a duty of mitigation to the applicant arising from the underlying agreement, but the issuer would not have the right to assert that duty by way of defense or setoff. See Section 5–117(d). If the beneficiary sells the goods covered by dishonored documents or if the beneficiary sells a draft after acceptance but before dishonor by the issuer, the net amount so gained should be subtracted from the amount of the beneficiary's damages—at least where the damage claim against the issuer equals or exceeds the damage suffered by the beneficiary. If, on the other hand, the beneficiary suffers damages in an underlying transaction in an amount that exceeds the amount of the wrongfully dishonored demand (e.g., where the letter of credit does not cover 100 percent of the underlying obligation), the damages avoided should not necessarily be deducted from the beneficiary's claim against the issuer. In such a case, the damages would be the lesser of (i) the amount recoverable in the absence of mitigation (that is, the amount that is subject to the dishonor or repudiation plus any incidental damages) and (ii) the damages remaining after deduction for the amount of damages actually avoided.

A beneficiary need not present documents as a condition of suit for anticipatory repudiation, but if a beneficiary could never have obtained documents necessary for a presentation conforming to the letter of credit, the beneficiary cannot recover for anticipatory repudiation of the letter of credit. *Doelger v. Battery Park Bank,* 201 A.D. 515, 194 N.Y.S. 582 (1922) and *Decor by Nikkei Int'l, Inc. v. Federal Republic of Nigeria,* 497 F.Supp. 893 (S.D.N.Y.1980), *aff'd,* 647 F.2d 300 (2d Cir.1981), *cert. denied,* 454 U.S. 1148 (1982). The last sentence of subsection (c) does not expand the liability of a confirmer to persons to whom the confirmer would not otherwise be liable under Section 5–107.

Almost all letters of credit, including those that call for an acceptance, are "obligations to pay money" as that term is used in Section 5–111(a).

2.   What damages "result" from improper honor is for the courts to decide. Even though an issuer pays a beneficiary in violation of Section 5–108(a) or of its contract with the applicant, it may have no liability to an applicant. If the underlying contract has been fully performed, the applicant may not have been damaged by the issuer's breach. Such a case would occur when A contracts for goods at $100 per ton, but, upon delivery, the market value of conforming goods has decreased to $25 per ton. If the issuer pays over discrepancies, there should be no recovery by A for the price differential if the issuer's breach did not alter the applicant's obligation under the underlying contract, i.e., to pay $100 per ton for goods now worth $25 per ton. On the other hand, if the applicant intends to resell the goods and must itself satisfy the strict compliance requirements under a second letter of credit in connection with its sale, the applicant may be damaged by the issuer's payment despite discrepancies because the applicant itself may then be unable to procure honor on the letter of credit where it is the beneficiary, and may be unable to mitigate its damages by enforcing its rights against others in the underlying transaction. Note that an issuer found liable to its applicant may have recourse under Section 5–117 by subrogation to the applicant's claim against the beneficiary or other persons.

One who inaccurately advises a letter of credit breaches its obligation to the beneficiary, but may cause no damage. If the beneficiary knows the terms of the letter of credit and understands the advice to be inaccurate, the beneficiary will have suffered no damage as a result of the adviser's breach.

3.   Since the confirmer has the rights and duties of an issuer, in general it has an issuer's liability, see subsection (c). The confirmer is usually a confirming bank. A confirming bank often also plays the role of an adviser. If it breaks its obligation to the beneficiary, the confirming bank may have liability as an issuer or, depending upon the obligation that was broken, as an adviser. For example, a wrongful dishonor would give it liability as an issuer under Section 5–111(a). On the other hand a confirming bank that broke its obligation to advise the credit but did not commit wrongful dishonor would be treated under Section 5–111(c).

4.   Consequential damages for breach of obligations under this article are excluded in the belief that these damages can best be avoided by the beneficiary or the applicant and out of the fear that imposing consequential damages on issuers would raise the cost of the letter of credit to a level that might render it uneconomic. *A fortiori* punitive and exemplary damages are excluded, however, this section does not bar recovery of consequential or even punitive damages for breach of statutory or common law duties arising outside of this article.

5.   The section does not specify a rate of interest. It leaves the setting of the rate to the court. It would be appropriate for a court to use the rate that would normally apply in that court in other situations where interest is imposed by law.

6.   The court must award attorney's fees to the prevailing party, whether that party is an applicant, a beneficiary, an issuer, a nominated person, or adviser. Since the issuer may be entitled to recover its legal fees and costs from the applicant under the reimbursement agreement, allowing the issuer to recover those fees from a losing beneficiary may also protect the applicant against undeserved losses. The party entitled to attorneys' fees has been described as the "prevailing party." Sometimes it will be unclear which party "prevailed," for example, where there are multiple issues and one party wins on some and the other party wins on others. Determining which is the prevailing party is in the discretion of the court. Subsection (e) authorizes attorney's fees in all actions where a remedy is sought "under this article." It applies even when the remedy might be an injunction under Section 5–109 or when the claimed remedy is otherwise outside of Section 5–111. Neither an issuer nor a confirmer should be treated as a "losing" party when an injunction is granted to the applicant over the objection of the issuer or confirmer; accordingly neither should be liable for fees and expenses in that case.

"Expenses of litigation" is intended to be broader than "costs." For example, expense of litigation would include travel expenses of witnesses, fees for expert witnesses, and expenses associated with taking depositions.

7.   For the purposes of Section 5–111(f) "harm anticipated" must be anticipated at the time when the agreement that includes the liquidated damage clause is executed or at the time when the undertaking that includes the clause is issued. See Section 2A–504.

§ 5–112.   Transfer of Letter of Credit.

(a)   Except as otherwise provided in Section 5–113, unless a letter of credit provides that it is transferable, the right of a beneficiary to draw or otherwise demand performance under a letter of credit may not be transferred.

(b)   Even if a letter of credit provides that it is transferable, the issuer may refuse to recognize or carry out a transfer if:

(1)   the transfer would violate applicable law; or

(2)   the transferor or transferee has failed to comply with any requirement stated in the letter of credit or any other requirement relating to transfer imposed by the issuer which is within the standard practice referred to in Section 5–108(e) or is otherwise reasonable under the circumstances.

Official Comment

1.   In order to protect the applicant's reliance on the designated beneficiary, letter of credit law traditionally has forbidden the beneficiary to convey to third parties its right to draw or demand payment under the letter of credit. Subsection (a) codifies that rule. The term "transfer" refers to the beneficiary's conveyance of that right. Absent incorporation of the UCP (which make elaborate provision for partial transfer of a commercial letter of credit) or similar trade practice and absent other express indication in the letter of credit that the term is used to mean something else, a term in the letter of credit indicating that the beneficiary has the right to transfer should be taken to mean that the beneficiary may convey to a third party its right to draw or demand payment. Even in that case, the issuer or other person controlling the transfer may make the beneficiary's right to transfer subject to conditions, such as timely notification, payment of a fee, delivery of the letter of credit to the issuer or other person controlling the transfer, or execution of appropriate forms to document the transfer. A nominated person who is not a confirmer has no obligation to recognize a transfer.

The power to establish "requirements" does not include the right absolutely to refuse to recognize transfers under a transferable letter of credit. An issuer who wishes to retain the right to deny all transfers should not issue transferable letters of credit or should incorporate the UCP. By stating its requirements in the letter of credit an issuer may impose any requirement without regard to its conformity to practice or reasonableness. Transfer requirements of issuers and nominated persons must be made known to potential transferors and transferees to enable those parties to comply with the requirements. A common method of making such requirements known is to use a form that indicates the information that must be provided and the instructions that must be given to enable the issuer or nominated person to comply with a request to transfer.

2.   The issuance of a transferable letter of credit with the concurrence of the applicant is *ipso facto* an agreement by the issuer and applicant to permit a beneficiary to transfer its drawing right and permit a nominated

person to recognize and carry out that transfer without further notice to them. In international commerce, transferable letters of credit are often issued under circumstances in which a nominated person or adviser is expected to facilitate the transfer from the original beneficiary to a transferee and to deal with that transferee. In those circumstances it is the responsibility of the nominated person or adviser to establish procedures satisfactory to protect itself against double presentation or dispute about the right to draw under the letter of credit. Commonly such a person will control the transfer by requiring that the original letter of credit be given to it or by causing a paper copy marked as an original to be issued where the original letter of credit was electronic. By keeping possession of the original letter of credit the nominated person or adviser can minimize or entirely exclude the possibility that the original beneficiary could properly procure payment from another bank. If the letter of credit requires presentation of the original letter of credit itself, no other payment could be procured. In addition to imposing whatever requirements it considers appropriate to protect itself against double payment the person that is facilitating the transfer has a right to charge an appropriate fee for its activity.

"Transfer" of a letter of credit should be distinguished from "assignment of proceeds." The former is analogous to a novation or a substitution of beneficiaries. It contemplates not merely payment to but also performance by the transferee. For example, under the typical terms of transfer for a commercial letter of credit, a transferee could comply with a letter of credit transferred to it by signing and presenting its own draft and invoice. An assignee of proceeds, on the other hand, is wholly dependent on the presentation of a draft and invoice signed by the beneficiary.

By agreeing to the issuance of a transferable letter of credit, which is not qualified or limited, the applicant may lose control over the identity of the person whose performance will earn payment under the letter of credit.

§ 5–113.   Transfer by Operation of Law.

(a)   A successor of a beneficiary may consent to amendments, sign and present documents, and receive payment or other items of value in the name of the beneficiary without disclosing its status as a successor.

(b)   A successor of a beneficiary may consent to amendments, sign and present documents, and receive payment or other items of value in its own name as the disclosed successor of the beneficiary. Except as otherwise provided in subsection (e), an issuer shall recognize a disclosed successor of a beneficiary as beneficiary in full substitution for its predecessor upon compliance with the requirements for recognition by the issuer of a transfer of drawing rights by operation of law under the standard practice referred to in Section 5–108(e) or, in the absence of such a practice, compliance with other reasonable procedures sufficient to protect the issuer.

(c)   An issuer is not obliged to determine whether a purported successor is a successor of a beneficiary or whether the signature of a purported successor is genuine or authorized.

(d)   Honor of a purported successor's apparently complying presentation under subsection (a) or (b) has the consequences specified in Section 5–108(i) even if the purported successor is not the successor of a beneficiary. Documents signed in the name of the beneficiary or of a disclosed successor by a person who is neither the beneficiary nor the successor of the beneficiary are forged documents for the purposes of Section 5–109.

(e)   An issuer whose rights of reimbursement are not covered by subsection (d) or substantially similar law and any confirmer or nominated person may decline to recognize a presentation under subsection (b).

(f)   A beneficiary whose name is changed after the issuance of a letter of credit has the same rights and obligations as a successor of a beneficiary under this section.

Official Comment

This section affirms the result in *Pastor v. Nat. Republic Bank of Chicago,* 76 Ill.2d 139, 390 N.E.2d 894 (Ill.1979) and *Federal Deposit Insurance Co. v. Bank of Boulder,* 911 F.2d 1466 (10th Cir.1990). Both electronic and tangible documents may be signed.

An issuer's requirements for recognition of a successor's status might include presentation of a certificate of merger, a court order appointing a bankruptcy trustee or receiver, a certificate of appointment as bankruptcy trustee, or the like. The issuer is entitled to rely upon such documents which on their face demonstrate that presentation is made by a successor of a beneficiary. It is not obliged to make an independent investigation to determine the fact of succession.

As amended in 2003.

§ 5–114.   Assignment of Proceeds.

(a)   In this section, "proceeds of a letter of credit" means the cash, check, accepted draft, or other item of value paid or delivered upon honor or giving of value by the issuer or any nominated person under the letter of credit. The term does not include a beneficiary's drawing rights or documents presented by the beneficiary.

(b)   A beneficiary may assign its right to part or all of the proceeds of a letter of credit. The beneficiary may do so before presentation as a present assignment of its right to receive proceeds contingent upon its compliance with the terms and conditions of the letter of credit.

(c)   An issuer or nominated person need not recognize an assignment of proceeds of a letter of credit until it consents to the assignment.

(d)   An issuer or nominated person has no obligation to give or withhold its consent to an assignment of proceeds of a letter of credit, but consent may not be unreasonably withheld if the assignee possesses and exhibits the letter of credit and presentation of the letter of credit is a condition to honor.

(e)   Rights of a transferee beneficiary or nominated person are independent of the beneficiary's assignment of the proceeds of a letter of credit and are superior to the assignee's right to the proceeds.

(f)   Neither the rights recognized by this section between an assignee and an issuer, transferee beneficiary, or nominated person nor the issuer's or nominated person's payment of proceeds to an assignee or a third person affect the rights between the assignee and any person other than the issuer, transferee beneficiary, or nominated person. The mode of creating and perfecting a security interest in or granting an assignment of a beneficiary's rights to proceeds is governed by Article 9 or other law. Against persons other than the issuer, transferee beneficiary, or nominated person, the rights and obligations arising upon the creation of a security interest or other assignment of a beneficiary's right to proceeds and its perfection are governed by Article 9 or other law.

Official Comment

1.   Subsection (b) expressly validates the beneficiary's present assignment of letter of credit proceeds if made after the credit is established but before the proceeds are realized. This section adopts the prevailing usage— "assignment of proceeds"—to an assignee. That terminology carries with it no implication, however, that an assignee acquires no interest until the proceeds are paid by the issuer. For example, an "assignment of the right to proceeds" of a letter of credit for purposes of security that meets the requirements of Section 9–203(b) would constitute the present creation of a security interest in a "letter-of-credit right." This security interest can be perfected by control (Section 9–107). Although subsection (a) explains the meaning of " 'proceeds' of a letter of credit," it should be emphasized that those proceeds also may be Article 9 proceeds of other collateral. For example, if a seller of inventory receives a letter of credit to support the account that arises upon the sale, payments made under the letter of credit are Article 9 proceeds of the inventory, account, and any document of title covering the inventory. Thus, the secured party who had a perfected security interest in that inventory, account, or document has a perfected security interest in the proceeds collected under the letter of credit, so long as they are identifiable cash proceeds (Section 9–315(a), (d)). This perfection is continuous, regardless of whether the secured party perfected a security interest in the right to letter of credit proceeds.

2.   An assignee's rights to enforce an assignment of proceeds against an issuer and the priority of the assignee's rights against a nominated person or transferee beneficiary are governed by Article 5. Those rights and that priority are stated in subsections (c), (d), and (e). Note also that Section 4–210 gives first priority to a collecting bank that has given value for a documentary draft.

3.   By requiring that an issuer or nominated person consent to the assignment of proceeds of a letter of credit, subsections (c) and (d) follow more closely recognized national and international letter of credit practices than did prior law. In most circumstances, it has always been advisable for the assignee to obtain the consent of the issuer in order better to safeguard its right to the proceeds. When notice of an assignment has been received, issuers normally have required signatures on a consent form. This practice is reflected in the revision. By

unconditionally consenting to such an assignment, the issuer or nominated person becomes bound, subject to the rights of the superior parties specified in subsection (e), to pay to the assignee the assigned letter of credit proceeds that the issuer or nominated person would otherwise pay to the beneficiary or another assignee.

Where the letter of credit must be presented as a condition to honor and the assignee holds and exhibits the letter of credit to the issuer or nominated person, the risk to the issuer or nominated person of having to pay twice is minimized. In such a situation, subsection (d) provides that the issuer or nominated person may not unreasonably withhold its consent to the assignment.

§ 5–115.　Statute of Limitations.

An action to enforce a right or obligation arising under this article must be commenced within one year after the expiration date of the relevant letter of credit or one year after the [claim for relief] [cause of action] accrues, whichever occurs later. A [claim for relief] [cause of action] accrues when the breach occurs, regardless of the aggrieved party's lack of knowledge of the breach.

Official Comment

1.　This section is based upon Sections 4–111 and 2–725(2).

2.　This section applies to all claims for which there are remedies under Section 5–111 and to other claims made under this article, such as claims for breach of warranty under Section 5–110. Because it covers all claims under Section 5–111, the statute of limitations applies not only to wrongful dishonor claims against the issuer but also to claims between the issuer and the applicant arising from the reimbursement agreement. These might be for reimbursement (issuer v. applicant) or for breach of the reimbursement contract by wrongful honor (applicant v. issuer).

3.　The statute of limitations, like the rest of the statute, applies only to a letter of credit issued on or after the effective date and only to transactions, events, obligations, or duties arising out of or associated with such a letter. If a letter of credit was issued before the effective date and an obligation on that letter of credit was breached after the effective date, the complaining party could bring its suit within the time that would have been permitted prior to the adoption of Section 5–115 and would not be limited by the terms of Section 5–115.

§ 5–116.　Choice of Law and Forum.

(a)　The liability of an issuer, nominated person, or adviser for action or omission is governed by the law of the jurisdiction chosen by an agreement in the form of a record signed or otherwise authenticated by the affected parties in the manner provided in Section 5–104 or by a provision in the person's letter of credit, confirmation, or other undertaking. The jurisdiction whose law is chosen need not bear any relation to the transaction.

(b)　Unless subsection (a) applies, the liability of an issuer, nominated person, or adviser for action or omission is governed by the law of the jurisdiction in which the person is located. The person is considered to be located at the address indicated in the person's undertaking. If more than one address is indicated, the person is considered to be located at the address from which the person's undertaking was issued. For the purpose of jurisdiction, choice of law, and recognition of interbranch letters of credit, but not enforcement of a judgment, all branches of a bank are considered separate juridical entities and a bank is considered to be located at the place where its relevant branch is considered to be located under this subsection.

(c)　Except as otherwise provided in this subsection, the liability of an issuer, nominated person, or adviser is governed by any rules of custom or practice, such as the Uniform Customs and Practice for Documentary Credits, to which the letter of credit, confirmation, or other undertaking is expressly made subject. If (i) this article would govern the liability of an issuer, nominated person, or adviser under subsection (a) or (b), (ii) the relevant undertaking incorporates rules of custom or practice, and (iii) there is conflict between this article and those rules as applied to that undertaking, those rules govern except to the extent of any conflict with the nonvariable provisions specified in Section 5–103(c).

(d)　If there is conflict between this article and Article 3, 4, 4A, or 9, this article governs.

(e)   The forum for settling disputes arising out of an undertaking within this article may be chosen in the manner and with the binding effect that governing law may be chosen in accordance with subsection (a).

Official Comment

1.   Although it would be possible for the parties to agree otherwise, the law normally chosen by agreement under subsection (a) and that provided in the absence of agreement under subsection (b) is the substantive law of a particular jurisdiction not including the choice of law principles of that jurisdiction. Thus, two parties, an issuer and an applicant, both located in Oklahoma might choose the law of New York. Unless they agree otherwise, the section anticipates that they wish the substantive law of New York to apply to their transaction and they do not intend that a New York choice of law principle might direct a court to Oklahoma law. By the same token, the liability of an issuer located in New York is governed by New York substantive law—in the absence of agreement—even in circumstances in which choice of law principles found in the common law of New York might direct one to the law of another State. Subsection (b) states the relevant choice of law principles and it should not be subordinated to some other choice of law rule. Within the States of the United States *renvoi* will not be a problem once every jurisdiction has enacted Section 5–116 because every jurisdiction will then have the same choice of law rule and in a particular case all choice of law rules will point to the same substantive law.

Subsection (b) does not state a choice of law rule for the "liability of an applicant." However, subsection (b) does state a choice of law rule for the liability of an issuer, nominated person, or adviser, and since some of the issues in suits by applicants against those persons involve the "liability of an issuer, nominated person, or adviser," subsection (b) states the choice of law rule for those issues. Because an issuer may have liability to a confirmer both as an issuer (Section 5–108(a), Comment 5 to Section 5–108) and as an applicant (Section 5–107(a), Comment 1 to Section 5–107, Section 5–108(i)), subsection (b) may state the choice of law rule for some but not all of the issuer's liability in a suit by a confirmer.

2.   Because the confirmer or other nominated person may choose different law from that chosen by the issuer or may be located in a different jurisdiction and fail to choose law, it is possible that a confirmer or nominated person may be obligated to pay (under their law) but will not be entitled to payment from the issuer (under its law). Similarly, the rights of an unreimbursed issuer, confirmer, or nominated person against a beneficiary under Section 5–109, 5–110, or 5–117, will not necessarily be governed by the same law that applies to the issuer's or confirmer's obligation upon presentation. Because the UCP and other practice are incorporated in most international letters of credit, disputes arising from different legal obligations to honor have not been frequent. Since Section 5–108 incorporates standard practice, these problems should be further minimized—at least to the extent that the same practice is and continues to be widely followed.

3.   This section does not permit what is now authorized by the nonuniform Section 5–102(4) in New York. Under the current law in New York a letter of credit that incorporates the UCP is not governed in any respect by Article 5. Under revised Section 5–116 letters of credit that incorporate the UCP or similar practice will still be subject to Article 5 in certain respects. First, incorporation of the UCP or other practice does not override the nonvariable terms of Article 5. Second, where there is no conflict between Article 5 and the relevant provision of the UCP or other practice, both apply. Third, practice provisions incorporated in a letter of credit will not be effective if they fail to comply with Section 5–103(c). Assume, for example, that a practice provision purported to free a party from any liability unless it were "grossly negligent" or that the practice generally limited the remedies that one party might have against another. Depending upon the circumstances, that disclaimer or limitation of liability might be ineffective because of Section 5–103(c).

Even though Article 5 is generally consistent with UCP 500, it is not necessarily consistent with other rules or with versions of the UCP that may be adopted after Article 5's revision, or with other practices that may develop. Rules of practice incorporated in the letter of credit or other undertaking are those in effect when the letter of credit or other undertaking is issued. Except in the unusual cases discussed in the immediately preceding paragraph, practice adopted in a letter of credit will override the rules of Article 5 and the parties to letter of credit transactions must be familiar with practice (such as future versions of the UCP) that is explicitly adopted in letters of credit.

4.   In several ways Article 5 conflicts with and overrides similar matters governed by Articles 3 and 4. For example, "draft" is more broadly defined in letter of credit practice than under Section 3–104. The time allowed for honor and the required notification of reasons for dishonor are different in letter of credit practice than in the handling of documentary and other drafts under Articles 3 and 4.

5.   Subsection (e) must be read in conjunction with existing law governing subject matter jurisdiction. If the local law restricts a court to certain subject matter jurisdiction not including letter of credit disputes, subsection (e) does not authorize parties to choose that forum. For example, the parties' agreement under Section 5–116(e) would not confer jurisdiction on a probate court to decide a letter of credit case.

If the parties choose a forum under subsection (e) and if—because of other law—that forum will not take jurisdiction, the parties' agreement or undertaking should then be construed (for the purpose of forum selection) as though it did not contain a clause choosing a particular forum. That result is necessary to avoid sentencing the parties to eternal purgatory where neither the chosen State nor the State which would have jurisdiction but for the clause will take jurisdiction—the former in disregard of the clause and the latter in honor of the clause.

§ 5–117.   Subrogation of Issuer, Applicant, and Nominated Person.

(a)   An issuer that honors a beneficiary's presentation is subrogated to the rights of the beneficiary to the same extent as if the issuer were a secondary obligor of the underlying obligation owed to the beneficiary and of the applicant to the same extent as if the issuer were the secondary obligor of the underlying obligation owed to the applicant.

(b)   An applicant that reimburses an issuer is subrogated to the rights of the issuer against any beneficiary, presenter, or nominated person to the same extent as if the applicant were the secondary obligor of the obligations owed to the issuer and has the rights of subrogation of the issuer to the rights of the beneficiary stated in subsection (a).

(c)   A nominated person who pays or gives value against a draft or demand presented under a letter of credit is subrogated to the rights of:

(1)   the issuer against the applicant to the same extent as if the nominated person were a secondary obligor of the obligation owed to the issuer by the applicant;

(2)   the beneficiary to the same extent as if the nominated person were a secondary obligor of the underlying obligation owed to the beneficiary; and

(3)   the applicant to same extent as if the nominated person were a secondary obligor of the underlying obligation owed to the applicant.

(d)   Notwithstanding any agreement or term to the contrary, the rights of subrogation stated in subsections (a) and (b) do not arise until the issuer honors the letter of credit or otherwise pays and the rights in subsection (c) do not arise until the nominated person pays or otherwise gives value. Until then, the issuer, nominated person, and the applicant do not derive under this section present or prospective rights forming the basis of a claim, defense, or excuse.

Official Comment

1.   By itself this section does not grant any right of subrogation. It grants only the right that would exist if the person seeking subrogation "were a secondary obligor." (The term "secondary obligor" refers to a surety, guarantor, or other person against whom or whose property an obligee has recourse with respect to the obligation of a third party. See Restatement of the Law Third, Suretyship and Guaranty § 1 (1996).) If the secondary obligor would not have a right to subrogation in the circumstances in which one is claimed under this section, none is granted by this section. In effect, the section does no more than to remove an impediment that some courts have found to subrogation because they conclude that the issuer's or other claimant's rights are "independent" of the underlying obligation. If, for example, a secondary obligor would not have a subrogation right because its payment did not fully satisfy the underlying obligation, none would be available under this section. The section indorses the position of Judge Becker in *Tudor Development Group, Inc. v. United States Fidelity and Guaranty,* 968 F.2d 357 (3rd Cir.1991).

2.   To preserve the independence of the letter of credit obligation and to insure that subrogation not be used as an offensive weapon by an issuer or others, the admonition in subsection (d) must be carefully observed. Only one who has completed its performance in a letter of credit transaction can have a right to subrogation. For example, an issuer may not dishonor and then defend its dishonor or assert a setoff on the ground that it is subrogated to another person's rights. Nor may the issuer complain after honor that its subrogation rights have been impaired by any good faith dealings between the beneficiary and the applicant or any other person. Assume, for example, that the beneficiary under a standby letter of credit is a mortgagee. If the mortgagee were obliged to

issue a release of the mortgage upon payment of the underlying debt (by the issuer under the letter of credit), that release might impair the issuer's rights of subrogation, but the beneficiary would have no liability to the issuer for having granted that release.

§ 5–118.   Security Interest of Issuer or Nominated Person.

(a)   An issuer or nominated person has a security interest in a document presented under a letter of credit to the extent that the issuer or nominated person honors or gives value for the presentation.

(b)   So long as and to the extent that an issuer or nominated person has not been reimbursed or has not otherwise recovered the value given with respect to a security interest in a document under subsection (a), the security interest continues and is subject to Article 9, but:

(1)   a security agreement is not necessary to make the security interest enforceable under Section 9–203(b)(3);

(2)   if the document is presented in a medium other than a written or other tangible medium, the security interest is perfected; and

(3)   if the document is presented in a written or other tangible medium and is not a certificated security, chattel paper, a document of title, an instrument, or a letter of credit, the security interest is perfected and has priority over a conflicting security interest in the document so long as the debtor does not have possession of the document.

As added in 1999.

Official Comment

1.   This section gives the issuer of a letter of credit or a nominated person thereunder an automatic perfected security interest in a "document" (as that term is defined in Section 5–102(a)(6)). The security interest arises only if the document is presented to the issuer or nominated person under the letter of credit and only to the extent of the value that is given. This security interest is analogous to that awarded to a collecting bank under Section 4–210. Subsection (b) contains special rules governing the security interest arising under this section. In all other respects, a security interest arising under this section is subject to Article 9. See Section 9–109. Thus, for example, a security interest arising under this section may give rise to a security interest in proceeds under Section 9–315.

2.   Subsection (b)(1) makes a security agreement unnecessary to the creation of a security interest under this section. Under subsection (b)(2), a security interest arising under this section is perfected if the document is presented in a medium other than a written or tangible medium. Documents that are written and that are not an otherwise-defined type of collateral under Article 9 (e.g., an invoice or inspection certificate) may be goods, in which an issuer or nominated person could perfect its security interest by possession. Because the definition of document in Section 5–102(a)(6) includes records (e.g., electronic records) that may not be goods, subsection (b)(2) provides for automatic perfection (i.e., without filing or possession).

Under subsection (b)(3), if the document (i) is in a written or tangible medium, (ii) is not a certificated security, chattel paper, a document of title, an instrument, or a letter of credit, and (iii) is not in the debtor's possession, the security interest is perfected and has priority over a conflicting security interest. If the document is a type of tangible collateral that subsection (b)(3) excludes from its perfection and priority rules, the issuer or nominated person must comply with the normal method of perfection (e.g., possession of an instrument) and is subject to the applicable Article 9 priority rules. Documents to which subsection (b)(3) applies may be important to an issuer or nominated person. For example, a confirmer who pays the beneficiary must be assured that its rights to all documents are not impaired. It will find it necessary to present all of the required documents to the issuer in order to be reimbursed. Moreover, when a nominated person sends documents to an issuer in connection with the nominated person's reimbursement, that activity is not a collection, enforcement, or disposition of collateral under Article 9.

One purpose of this section is to protect an issuer or nominated person from claims of a beneficiary's creditors. It is a fallback provision inasmuch as issuers and nominated persons frequently may obtain and perfect security interests under the usual Article 9 rules, and, in many cases, the documents will be owned by the issuer, nominated person, or applicant.

As added in 1999.

UCC ARTICLE 6 (2016)

ALTERNATIVE A: REPEALER OF ARTICLE 6—
BULK TRANSFERS

ALTERNATIVE B: [REVISED] ARTICLE 6—
BULK SALES

(States To Select One Alternative)

Article 6 was revised in 1989.

ALTERNATIVE A

ALTERNATIVE B

National Conference of Commissioners on Uniform State Laws

CO-REPORTERS

Steven L. Harris, Champaign, Illinois
William D. Hawkland, Baton Rouge, Louisiana

DRAFTING COMMITTEE

CHAIRMAN

Gerald L. Bepko, Indianapolis, Indiana

MEMBERS

William C. Hillman, Providence, Rhode Island
Frederick H. Miller, Norman, Oklahoma
Raymond P. Pepe, Harrisburg, Pennsylvania

UNIFORM COMMERCIAL CODE

Donald J. Rapson, Livingston, New Jersey, *The American Law Institute Representative*
Curtis R. Reitz, Philadelphia, Pennsylvania
Millard H. Ruud, Austin, Texas, *Drafting Liaison*
Hiroshi Sakai, Honolulu, Hawaii
Michael P. Sullivan, Minneapolis, Minnesota, *President (Member Ex Officio)*
Neal Ossen, Hartford, Connecticut, *Chairman, Division C (Member Ex Officio)*

REVIEW COMMITTEE

CHAIRMAN

John A. Chanin, Honolulu, Hawaii

MEMBERS

Stephen E. Cicilline, Providence, Rhode Island
Morris W. Macey, Atlanta, Georgia
Robert G. Pugh, Shreveport, Louisiana

ABA ADVISOR, SECTION OF CORPORATION, BANKING, AND BUSINESS LAW

Howard Ruda, New York, New York

ADDITIONAL ADVISORS

Don L. Baker, *Commercial Law League of America*
William Z. Fox, *National Auctioneers Association*
Thomas J. Greco, *American Bankers Association*
Frank R. Kennedy, *National Bankruptcy Conference*
James E. Snider, *National Association of Credit Management*
Douglas H. Williams, *National Commercial Finance Association*

PREFATORY NOTE

Background. Bulk sale legislation originally was enacted in response to a fraud perceived to be common around the turn of the century: a merchant would acquire his stock in trade on credit, then sell his entire inventory ("in bulk") and abscond with the proceeds, leaving creditors unpaid. The creditors had a right to sue the merchant on the unpaid debts, but that right often was of little practical value. Even if the merchant-debtor was found, in personam jurisdiction over him might not have been readily available. Those creditors who succeeded in obtaining a judgment often were unable to satisfy it because the defrauding seller had spent or hidden the sale proceeds. Nor did the creditors ordinarily have recourse to the merchandise sold. The transfer of the inventory to an innocent buyer effectively immunized the goods from the reach of the seller's creditors. The creditors of a bulk seller thus might be left without a means to satisfy their claims.

To a limited extent, the law of fraudulent conveyances ameliorated the creditors' plight. When the buyer in bulk was in league with the seller or paid less than full value for the inventory, fraudulent conveyance law enabled the defrauded creditors to avoid the sale and apply the transferred inventory toward the satisfaction of their claims against the seller. But fraudulent conveyance law provided no remedy against persons who bought in good faith, without reason to know of the seller's intention to pocket the proceeds and disappear, and for adequate value. In those cases, the only remedy for the seller's creditors was to attempt to recover from the absconding seller.

State legislatures responded to this perceived "bulk sale risk" with a variety of legislative enactments. Common to these statutes was the imposition of a duty on the buyer in bulk to notify the seller's creditors of the impending sale. The buyer's failure to comply with these and any other statutory duties generally afforded the seller's creditors a remedy analogous to the remedy for fraudulent conveyances: the creditors acquired the right to set aside the sale and reach the transferred inventory in the hands of the buyer.

510

ARTICLE 6 (2016)

Like its predecessors, Article 6 (1987 Official Text) is remarkable in that it obligates buyers in bulk to incur costs to protect the interests of the seller's creditors, with whom they usually have no relationship. Even more striking is that Article 6 affords creditors a remedy against a good faith purchaser for full value without notice of any wrongdoing on the part of the seller. The Article thereby impedes normal business transactions, many of which can be expected to benefit the seller's creditors. For this reason, Article 6 has been subjected to serious criticism. See, e.g., Rapson, *U.C.C. Article 6: Should It Be Revised or "Deep-Sixed"?* 38 Bus.Law. 1753 (1983).

In the legal context in which Article 6 (1987 Official Text) and its nonuniform predecessors were enacted, the benefits to creditors appeared to justify the costs of interfering with good faith transactions. Today, however, creditors are better able than ever to make informed decisions about whether to extend credit. Changes in technology have enabled credit reporting services to provide fast, accurate, and more complete credit histories at relatively little cost. A search of the public real estate and personal property records will disclose most encumbrances on a debtor's property with little inconvenience.

In addition, changes in the law now afford creditors greater opportunities to collect their debts. The development of "minimum contacts" with the forum state as a basis for *in personam* jurisdiction and the universal promulgation of state long-arm statutes and rules have greatly improved the possibility of obtaining personal jurisdiction over a debtor who flees to another state. Widespread enactment of the Uniform Enforcement of Foreign Judgments Act has facilitated nation-wide collection of judgments. And to the extent that a bulk sale is fraudulent and the buyer is a party to fraud, aggrieved creditors have a remedy under the Uniform Fraudulent Transfer Act. Moreover, creditors of a merchant no longer face the choice of extending unsecured credit or no credit at all. Retaining an interest in inventory to secure its price has become relatively simple and inexpensive under Article 9.

Finally, there is no evidence that, in today's economy, fraudulent bulk sales are frequent enough, or engender credit losses significant enough, to require regulation of all bulk sales, including the vast majority that are conducted in good faith. Indeed, the experience of the Canadian Province of British Columbia, which repealed its Sale of Goods in Bulk Act in 1985, and of the United Kingdom, which never has enacted bulk sales legislation, suggests that regulation of bulk sales no longer is necessary.

Recommendation. The National Conference of Commissioners on Uniform State Laws and the American Law Institute believe that changes in the business and legal contexts in which sales are conducted have made regulation of bulk sales unnecessary. The Conference and the Institute therefore withdraw their support for Article 6 of the Uniform Commercial Code and encourage those states that have enacted the Article to repeal it.

The Conference and the Institute recognize that bulk sales may present a particular problem in some states and that some legislatures may wish to continue to regulate bulk sales. They believe that existing Article 6 has become inadequate for that purpose. For those states that are disinclined to repeal Article 6, they have promulgated a revised version of Article 6. The revised Article is designed to afford better protection to creditors while minimizing the impediments to good-faith transactions.

The Official Comment to Section 6–101 explains the rationale underlying the revisions and highlights the major substantive changes reflected in them. Of particular interest is Section 6–103(1)(a), which limits the application of the revised Article to bulk sales by sellers whose principal business is the sale of inventory from stock. In approving this provision, the Conference and the Institute were mindful that some states have expanded the coverage of existing Article 6 to include bulk sales conducted by sellers whose principal business is the operation of a restaurant or tavern. Expansion of the scope of revised Article 6 is inconsistent with the recommendation that Article 6 be repealed. Nevertheless, the inclusion of restaurants and taverns within the scope of the revised Article as it is enacted in particular jurisdictions would not disturb the internal logic and structure of the revised Article.

———————

[ALTERNATIVE A]

1. Repeal.
2. Amendment.
3. Amendment.
4. Savings Clause.

_____

§ 1.   Repeal.

Article 6 and Section 9–111* of the Uniform Commercial Code are hereby repealed, effective _____.

§ 2.   Amendment.

Section 1–105(2)** of the Uniform Commercial Code is hereby amended to read as follows:

(2)   Where one of the following provisions of this Act specifies the applicable law, that provision governs and a contrary agreement is effective only to the extent permitted by the law (including the conflict of laws rules) so specified:

Rights of creditors against sold goods. Section 2–402.

Applicability of the Article on Leases. Sections 2A–105 and 2A–106.

Applicability of the Article on Bank Deposits and Collections. Section 4–102.

~~Bulk transfers subject to the Article on Bulk Transfers. Section 6–102.~~

Applicability of the Article on Investment Securities. Section 8–106.***

Perfection provisions of the Article on Secured Transactions. Section 9–103.*

§ 3.   Amendment.

Section 2–403(4) of the Uniform Commercial Code is hereby amended to read as follows:

(4)   The rights of other purchasers of goods and of lien creditors are governed by the Articles on Secured Transactions (Article 9)~~, Bulk Transfers (Article 6)~~ and Documents of Title (Article 7).

§ 4.   Savings Clause.

Rights and obligations that arose under Article 6 and Section 9–111* of the Uniform Commercial Code before their repeal remain valid and may be enforced as though those statutes had not been repealed.]

Legislative Note: To take account of differences between former Article 9 and revised Article 9, a State that repeals Article 6 after revised Article 9 takes effect must make the following changes to Alternative A. First, inasmuch as revised Article 9 contains no counterpart of former Section 9–111, the reference to that section in Section 1 of the repealer should be deleted, and Section 4 of the repeal bill should allude to former Section 9–111. Second, the last entry in Section 1–105(2)** should be amended as shown above in this Appendix.

[END OF ALTERNATIVE A]

_____

*   _Referring to unrevised Article 9._

**   _Referring to unrevised Article 1 (Appendix A)._

***   _Referring to unrevised Article 8._

[ALTERNATIVE B]

---

§ 6–101.   Short Title.

This Article shall be known and may be cited as Uniform Commercial Code—Bulk Sales.

Official Comment

Prior Uniform Statutory Provision: Section 6–101 (1987 Official Text).

Change: This Article applies only to sales, as defined in Section 2–103(1), and not to other transfers.

Purpose of Change: Transfers other than sales, *e.g.*, grants of security interests, do not present risks to creditors necessitating advance notice in accordance with the provisions of this Article. The Uniform Fraudulent Transfer Act affords a remedy to creditors who are injured by donative transfers.

Rationale for Revision of the Article:

Article 6 (1987 Official Text) imposes upon transferees in bulk several duties toward creditors of the transferor. These duties include the duty to notify the creditors of the impending bulk transfer and, in those jurisdictions that have adopted optional Section 6–106, the duty to assure that the new consideration for the transfer is applied to pay debts of the transferor.

Compliance with the provisions of Article 6 can be burdensome, particularly when the transferor has a large number of creditors. When the transferor is actively engaged in business at a number of locations, assembling a current list of creditors may not be possible. Mailing a notice to each creditor may prove costly. When the goods that are the subject of the transfer are located in several jurisdictions, the transferor may be obligated to comply with Article 6 as enacted in each jurisdiction. The widespread enactment of nonuniform amendments makes compliance with Article 6 in multiple-state transactions problematic. Moreover, the Article requires compliance even when there is no reason to believe that the transferor is conducting a fraudulent transfer, *e.g.*, when the transferor is scaling down the business but remaining available to creditors.

Article 6 imposes strict liability for noncompliance. Failure to comply with the provisions of the Article renders the transfer ineffective, even when the transferor has attempted compliance in good faith, and even when no creditor has been injured by the noncompliance. The potential liability for minor noncompliance may be high. If the transferor should enter bankruptcy before the expiration of the limitation period, Bankruptcy Code §§ 544(b), 550(a), 11 U.S.C. §§ 544(b), 550(a), may enable the transferor's bankruptcy trustee to set aside the entire transaction and recover from the noncomplying transferee all the goods transferred or their value. The trustee has this power even though the noncompliance was with respect to only a single creditor holding a small claim.

The benefits that compliance affords to creditors do not justify the substantial burdens and risks that the Article imposes upon good faith purchasers of business assets. The Article requires that notice be sent only ten days before the transferee takes possession of the goods or pays for them, whichever happens first. Given the delay between sending the notice and its receipt, creditors have scant opportunity to avail themselves of a judicial or nonjudicial remedy before the transfer has been consummated.

In some cases Article 6 may have the unintended effect of injuring, rather than aiding, creditors of the transferor. Those transferees who recognize the burdens and risks that Article 6 imposes upon them sometimes

513

agree to purchase only at a reduced price. Others refuse to purchase at all, leaving the creditors to realize only the liquidation value, rather than the going concern value, of the business goods.

As a response to these inadequacies and others, the National Conference of Commissioners on Uniform State Laws has completely revised Article 6. This revision is designed to reduce the burdens and risks imposed upon good-faith buyers of business assets while increasing the protection afforded to creditors. Among the major changes it makes are the following:

—this Article applies only when the buyer has notice, or after reasonable inquiry would have had notice, that the seller will not continue to operate the same or a similar kind of business after the sale (Section 6–102(1)(c)).

—this Article does not apply to sales in which the value of the property otherwise available to creditors is less than $10,000 or those in which the value of the property is greater than $25,000,000 (Section 6–103(3)(*l*)).

—the choice-of-law provision (Sections 6–103(1)(b) and 6–103(2)) limits the applicable law to that of one jurisdiction.

—when the seller is indebted to a large number of persons, the buyer need neither obtain a list of those persons nor send individual notices to each person but instead may give notice by filing (Sections 6–105(2) and 6–104(2)).

—the notice period is increased from 10 days to 45 days (Section 6–105(5)), and the statute of limitations is extended from six months to one year (Section 6–110).

—the notice must include a copy of a "schedule of distribution," which sets forth how the net contract price is to be distributed (Sections 6–105(3) and 6–106(1)).

—a buyer who makes a good faith effort to comply with the requirements of this Article or to exclude the sale from the application of this Article, or who acts on the good faith belief that this Article does not apply to the sale, is not liable for noncompliance (Section 6–107(3)).

—a buyer's noncompliance does not render the sale ineffective or otherwise affect the buyer's title to the goods; rather, the liability of a noncomplying buyer is for damages caused by the noncompliance (Sections 6–107(1) and 6–107(8)).

In addition to making these and other major substantive changes, revised Article 6 resolves the ambiguities that three decades of law practice, judicial construction, and scholarly inquiry have disclosed.

§ 6–102.   Definitions and Index of Definitions.

(1)   In this Article, unless the context otherwise requires:

(a)   "Assets" means the inventory that is the subject of a bulk sale and any tangible and intangible personal property used or held for use primarily in, or arising from, the seller's business and sold in connection with that inventory, but the term does not include:

     (i)   fixtures (section 9–102(a)(41)) other than readily removable factory and office machines;

     (ii)   the lessee's interest in a lease of real property; or

     (iii)   property to the extent it is generally exempt from creditor process under nonbankruptcy law.

(b)   "Auctioneer" means a person whom the seller engages to direct, conduct, control, or be responsible for a sale by auction.

(c)   "Bulk sale" means:

     (i)   in the case of a sale by auction or a sale or series of sales conducted by a liquidator on the seller's behalf, a sale or series of sales not in the ordinary course of the seller's business of more than half of the seller's inventory, as measured by value on the date of the bulk-sale agreement, if on that date the auctioneer or liquidator has notice, or after reasonable inquiry would have had notice, that the seller will not continue to operate the same or a similar kind of business after the sale or series of sales; and

(ii) in all other cases, a sale not in the ordinary course of the seller's business of more than half the seller's inventory, as measured by value on the date of the bulk-sale agreement, if on that date the buyer has notice, or after reasonable inquiry would have had notice, that the seller will not continue to operate the same or a similar kind of business after the sale.

(d) "Claim" means a right to payment from the seller, whether or not the right is reduced to judgment, liquidated, fixed, matured, disputed, secured, legal, or equitable. The term includes costs of collection and attorney's fees only to the extent that the laws of this state permit the holder of the claim to recover them in an action against the obligor.

(e) "Claimant" means a person holding a claim incurred in the seller's business other than:

(i) an unsecured and unmatured claim for employment compensation and benefits, including commissions and vacation, severance, and sick-leave pay;

(ii) a claim for injury to an individual or to property, or for breach of warranty, unless:

(A) a right of action for the claim has accrued;

(B) the claim has been asserted against the seller; and

(C) the seller knows the identity of the person asserting the claim and the basis upon which the person has asserted it; and

(States To Select One Alternative)

[ALTERNATIVE A]

[(iii) a claim for taxes owing to a governmental unit.]

[ALTERNATIVE B]

[(iii) a claim for taxes owing to a governmental unit, if:

(A) a statute governing the enforcement of the claim permits or requires notice of the bulk sale to be given to the governmental unit in a manner other than by compliance with the requirements of this Article; and

(B) notice is given in accordance with the statute.]

(f) "Creditor" means a claimant or other person holding a claim.

(g) (i) "Date of the bulk sale" means:

(A) if the sale is by auction or is conducted by a liquidator on the seller's behalf, the date on which more than ten percent of the net proceeds is paid to or for the benefit of the seller; and

(B) in all other cases, the later of the date on which:

(I) more than ten percent of the net contract price is paid to or for the benefit of the seller; or

(II) more than ten percent of the assets, as measured by value, are transferred to the buyer.

(ii) For purposes of this subsection:

(A) Delivery of a negotiable instrument (Section 3–104(1)*) to or for the benefit of the seller in exchange for assets constitutes payment of the contract price pro tanto;

(B) To the extent that the contract price is deposited in an escrow, the contract price is paid to or for the benefit of the seller when the seller acquires the unconditional right to receive the deposit or when the deposit is delivered to the seller or for the benefit of the seller, whichever is earlier; and

---

* *Referring to unrevised Article 3 (Appendix B).*

(C) An asset is transferred when a person holding an unsecured claim can no longer obtain through judicial proceedings rights to the asset that are superior to those of the buyer arising as a result of the bulk sale. A person holding an unsecured claim can obtain those superior rights to a tangible asset at least until the buyer has an unconditional right, under the bulk-sale agreement, to possess the asset, and a person holding an unsecured claim can obtain those superior rights to an intangible asset at least until the buyer has an unconditional right, under the bulk-sale agreement, to use the asset.

(h) "Date of the bulk-sale agreement" means:

 (i) in the case of a sale by auction or conducted by a liquidator (subsection (c)(i)), the date on which the seller engages the auctioneer or liquidator; and

 (ii) in all other cases, the date on which a bulk-sale agreement becomes enforceable between the buyer and the seller.

(i) "Debt" means liability on a claim.

(j) "Liquidator" means a person who is regularly engaged in the business of disposing of assets for businesses contemplating liquidation or dissolution.

(k) "Net contract price" means the new consideration the buyer is obligated to pay for the assets less:

 (i) the amount of any proceeds of the sale of an asset, to the extent the proceeds are applied in partial or total satisfaction of a debt secured by the asset; and

 (ii) the amount of any debt to the extent it is secured by a security interest or lien that is enforceable against the asset before and after it has been sold to a buyer. If a debt is secured by an asset and other property of the seller, the amount of the debt secured by a security interest or lien that is enforceable against the asset is determined by multiplying the debt by a fraction, the numerator of which is the value of the new consideration for the asset on the date of the bulk sale and the denominator of which is the value of all property securing the debt on the date of the bulk sale.

(l) "Net proceeds" means the new consideration received for assets sold at a sale by auction or a sale conducted by a liquidator on the seller's behalf less:

 (i) commissions and reasonable expenses of the sale;

 (ii) the amount of any proceeds of the sale of an asset, to the extent the proceeds are applied in partial or total satisfaction of a debt secured by the asset; and

 (iii) the amount of any debt to the extent it is secured by a security interest or lien that is enforceable against the asset before and after it has been sold to a buyer. If a debt is secured by an asset and other property of the seller, the amount of the debt secured by a security interest or lien that is enforceable against the asset is determined by multiplying the debt by a fraction, the numerator of which is the value of the new consideration for the asset on the date of the bulk sale and the denominator of which is the value of all property securing the debt on the date of the bulk sale.

(m) A sale is "in the ordinary course of the seller's business" if the sale comports with usual or customary practices in the kind of business in which the seller is engaged or with the seller's own usual or customary practices.

(n) "United States" includes its territories and possessions and the Commonwealth of Puerto Rico.

(o) "Value" means fair market value.

(p) "Verified" means signed and sworn to or affirmed.

(2) The following definitions in other Articles apply to this Article:

(a) "Buyer." Section 2–103(1)(a).

(b) "Equipment." Section 9–102(a)(33).

(c) "Inventory." Section 9–102(a)(48).

(d) "Sale." Section 2–106(1).

(e) "Seller." Section 2–103(1)(d).

(3) In addition, Article 1 contains general definitions and principles of construction and interpretation applicable throughout this Article.

As amended in 1999.

Official Comment

1. (a) "Assets". New. The term generally includes only "personal property." Whether particular property is "personal property" is to be determined by law outside this Article; however, for purposes of this Article, (i) the term includes "readily removable factory and office machines" (compare Section 9–334(e)(2)(A)), even if they are covered by applicable real estate law and thus are "fixtures" as defined in Section 9–102(a)(41); (ii) the term does not include the lessee's interest in a lease of real property, even if that interest is considered to be personal property under other applicable law; and (iii) the term does not include property to the extent that it is "generally exempt from creditor process under nonbankruptcy law."

(b) "Auctioneer". Compare Section 6–108(3) (1987 Official Text).

(c) "Bulk Sale". Bulk sales are of two kinds. Subsection (1)(c)(i) describes bulk sales conducted by a professional intermediary (i.e., an auctioneer or liquidator), as to which sales Section 6–108 applies. If these indirect sales occur as a series of related sales, then the entire series is treated as a single "bulk sale" and the term applies to the sales in the aggregate. Sales made directly by the seller to the buyer, described in subsection (1)(c)(ii), include sales conducted by an auctioneer or liquidator for its own account.

The elements of both direct and indirect sales are the same. Some of these elements have been borrowed from the 1987 Official Text of Article 6 and restated. For example, the term includes only sales that are not "in the ordinary course of the seller's business" (subsection (1)(m)). The sale must be of "more than half of the seller's inventory, as measured by value [subsection (1)(o)] on the date of the bulk-sale agreement [subsection (1)(h)]." All inventory owned by the seller should be included in the calculation, regardless of where it is located. Inventory that is encumbered by a security interest or lien should be counted at its gross value, although the fact that it is encumbered may affect the applicability of this Article to the sale.

The determination whether a sale is a "bulk sale" and thus subject to this Article is not affected by whether other types of property are sold in connection with inventory. However, other provisions of this Article take account of the fact that other property may be sold in connection with inventory. For example, the availability of the exclusion in Section 6–103(3)(l) turns on the value of all the "assets," not just the inventory. Similarly, the notice required by Section 6–105 must describe the "assets," not just the inventory. And Section 6–107(4) measures the buyer's maximum cumulative liability for noncompliance by the value of the inventory and equipment sold in the bulk sale.

In an effort to limit its coverage to sales posing the greatest risks to creditors, this Article adds an additional element to the definition of "bulk sale." A sale is not a "bulk sale" unless the buyer, auctioneer, or liquidator has notice, or after a reasonable inquiry would have had notice, that the seller will not continue to operate the same or a similar kind of business after the sale. Whether a person has "notice" depends upon what the person knows and what the person would have known had the person conducted a reasonable inquiry. The issue of whether a transaction was a bulk sale is likely to be litigated only when the seller has absconded with the sale proceeds. This Article requires that the matters as to which the buyer, auctioneer, or liquidator had notice be determined only by reference to facts that the person knew or would have known at the date of the bulk-sale agreement. Reference to what actually occurred is inappropriate.

Whether an inquiry is "reasonable" depends on the facts and circumstances of each case. These facts and circumstances may include the identities of the buyer and seller and the type of assets being sold. In some cases, a reasonable inquiry may consist of no inquiry at all concerning the seller's future.

Not every change in business operations poses a substantial enough risk to creditors to justify the costs of compliance with this Article. Thus, in determining whether post-sale business is of a kind that is "the same" or "similar" to the business conducted before the sale, a court should consider whether, viewed from the perspective of the creditors of the seller, the change poses extraordinary risks or whether the change is a normal risk that creditors can be assumed to take. In particular, when the post-bulk sale business differs from the pre-bulk sale business only in the size of the business conducted, the seller should be considered to be continuing in the same or a similar kind of business and the sale should not be considered a bulk sale.

The seller must "continue to operate" the same or a similar kind of business as owner. If the owner sells the business assets to a buyer and continues to manage the business as an employee of the buyer, the seller is not continuing to operate the business within the meaning of this Article.

(d)　"Claim". New. The first sentence derives from Bankruptcy Code § 101(4), 11 U.S.C. § 101(4). Changes, including the deletion of Section 101(4)(B), were made for stylistic purposes only.

(e)　"Claimant". New. This term defines the category of claim holders who are the primary beneficiaries of the duties that this Article imposes. Compare "Creditor" (subsection (1)(f)).

States that choose not to afford taxing authorities the benefits of this Article should adopt Alternative A. Adoption of Alternative B would afford the benefits of this Article to taxing authorities except with respect to those taxes as to which there has been compliance with another statute requiring that notice of the bulk sale be given to the taxing authority.

(f)　"Creditor". New. The term includes all holders of claims against the seller, even holders of claims arising from consumer transactions. Compare "Claimant" (subsection (1)(e)).

(g)　"Date of the bulk sale". New. The parties are able to control the date of the bulk sale in several ways. They can keep the proceeds of the sale in escrow, thereby delaying the date of payment, or they can specifically agree that the assets remain subject to the reach of the seller's creditors, thereby delaying the date that the assets are transferred. By adjusting the time that the buyer acquires an unconditional right to possess tangible assets and the time the buyer acquires an unconditional right to use intangible assets, the parties may affect the substantive rights of creditors and thereby control the date the assets are transferred.

The connection between the time of transfer and the buyer's rights under the bulk-sale agreement appears only for purposes of sales to which this Article applies. Subsection (1)(g) does not purport to affect the rights of creditors of a seller of property for other purposes or under other circumstances.

(h)　"Date of the bulk-sale agreement". New. Law outside this Article, including the provisions of Article 2, determines when an agreement for a bulk sale becomes enforceable between the buyer and the seller and when an auctioneer or liquidator is engaged.

(i)　"Debt". New. This subsection is borrowed from Bankruptcy Code Section 101(11).

(j)　"Liquidator". New. Although the definition of "liquidator" is quite broad, the term is used with respect to sales that are "conducted" by a liquidator on behalf of the seller. See subsection (1)(c)(i). Thus only those liquidators that "conduct" sales will be affected by this Article.

(k)　"Net contract price". New. Consideration is not "new consideration" to the extent that it consists of the partial or total satisfaction of an antecedent debt owed to the buyer by the seller. When the buyer buys assets along with property other than assets, the "net contract price" is that portion of the new consideration allocable to the assets.

(l)　"Net proceeds". New. The term appears, without definition, in Section 6–108 (1987 Official Text).

(m)　"In the ordinary course of the seller's business". New.

(n)　"United States". New. This subsection derives from former Section 9–103(3)(c).

(o)　"Value". New. The definition in Section 1–201(44)* is not appropriate in the context of this Article.

(p)　"Verified". New.

2.　"Good faith". This Article adopts the definition of "good faith" in Article 1 in all cases, even when the buyer is a merchant.

Cross-References:

Point 1(a): Sections 9–102, 9–334.

Point 1(c): Sections 1–201 and 6–103.

Point 1(g): Article 2 generally.

----

*　*Referring to unrevised Article 1 (Appendix A).*

Point 1(h): Section 2–201 and Article 2 generally.

As amended in 1999.

§ 6–103.   Applicability of Article.

(1)   Except as otherwise provided in subsection (3), this Article applies to a bulk sale if:

(a)   the seller's principal business is the sale of inventory from stock; and

(b)   on the date of the bulk-sale agreement the seller is located in this state or, if the seller is located in a jurisdiction that is not a part of the United States, the seller's major executive office in the United States is in this state.

(2)   A seller is deemed to be located at his [or her] place of business. If a seller has more than one place of business, the seller is deemed located at his [or her] chief executive office.

(3)   This Article does not apply to:

(a)   a transfer made to secure payment or performance of an obligation;

(b)   a transfer of collateral to a secured party pursuant to Section 9–609;

(c)   a disposition of collateral pursuant to Section 9–610;

(d)   retention of collateral pursuant to Section 9–620;

(e)   a sale of an asset encumbered by a security interest or lien if (i) all the proceeds of the sale are applied in partial or total satisfaction of the debt secured by the security interest or lien or (ii) the security interest or lien is enforceable against the asset after it has been sold to the buyer and the net contract price is zero;

(f)   a general assignment for the benefit of creditors or to a subsequent transfer by the assignee;

(g)   a sale by an executor, administrator, receiver, trustee in bankruptcy, or any public officer under judicial process;

(h)   a sale made in the course of judicial or administrative proceedings for the dissolution or reorganization of an organization;

(i)   a sale to a buyer whose principal place of business is in the United States and who:

    (i)   not earlier than 21 days before the date of the bulk sale, (A) obtains from the seller a verified and dated list of claimants of whom the seller has notice three days before the seller sends or delivers the list to the buyer or (B) conducts a reasonable inquiry to discover the claimants;

    (ii)   assumes in full the debts owed to claimants of whom the buyer has knowledge on the date the buyer receives the list of claimants from the seller or on the date the buyer completes the reasonable inquiry, as the case may be;

    (iii)   is not insolvent after the assumption; and

    (iv)   gives written notice of the assumption not later than 30 days after the date of the bulk sale by sending or delivering a notice to the claimants identified in subparagraph (ii) or by filing a notice in the office of the [Secretary of State];

(j)   a sale to a buyer whose principal place of business is in the United States and who:

    (i)   assumes in full the debts that were incurred in the seller's business before the date of the bulk sale;

    (ii)   is not insolvent after the assumption; and

    (iii)   gives written notice of the assumption not later than 30 days after the date of the bulk sale by sending or delivering a notice to each creditor whose debt is assumed or by filing a notice in the office of the [Secretary of State];

(k)   a sale to a new organization that is organized to take over and continue the business of the seller and that has its principal place of business in the United States if:

     (i)   the buyer assumes in full the debts that were incurred in the seller's business before the date of the bulk sale;

     (ii)   the seller receives nothing from the sale except an interest in the new organization that is subordinate to the claims against the organization arising from the assumption; and

     (iii)   the buyer gives written notice of the assumption not later than 30 days after the date of the bulk sale by sending or delivering a notice to each creditor whose debt is assumed or by filing a notice in the office of the [Secretary of State];

(l)   a sale of assets having:

     (i)   a value, net of liens and security interests, of less than $10,000. If a debt is secured by assets and other property of the seller, the net value of the assets is determined by subtracting from their value an amount equal to the product of the debt multiplied by a fraction, the numerator of which is the value of the assets on the date of the bulk sale and the denominator of which is the value of all property securing the debt on the date of the bulk sale; or

     (ii)   a value of more than $25,000,000 on the date of the bulk-sale agreement; or

(m)   a sale required by, and made pursuant to, statute.

(4)   The notice under subsection (3)(i)(iv) must state: (i) that a sale that may constitute a bulk sale has been or will be made; (ii) the date or prospective date of the bulk sale; (iii) the individual, partnership, or corporate names and the addresses of the seller and buyer; (iv) the address to which inquiries about the sale may be made, if different from the seller's address; and (v) that the buyer has assumed or will assume in full the debts owed to claimants of whom the buyer has knowledge on the date the buyer receives the list of claimants from the seller or completes a reasonable inquiry to discover the claimants.

(5)   The notice under subsections (3)(j)(iii) and (3)(k)(iii) must state: (i) that a sale that may constitute a bulk sale has been or will be made; (ii) the date or prospective date of the bulk sale; (iii) the individual, partnership, or corporate names and the addresses of the seller and buyer; (iv) the address to which inquiries about the sale may be made, if different from the seller's address; and (v) that the buyer has assumed or will assume the debts that were incurred in the seller's business before the date of the bulk sale.

(6)   For purposes of subsection (3)(l), the value of assets is presumed to be equal to the price the buyer agrees to pay for the assets. However, in a sale by auction or a sale conducted by a liquidator on the seller's behalf, the value of assets is presumed to be the amount the auctioneer or liquidator reasonably estimates the assets will bring at auction or upon liquidation.

As amended in 1999.

Official Comment

Prior Uniform Statutory Provision: Sections 6–102 and 6–103 (1987 Official Text).

Changes: New choice-of-law provision; exclusions from the Article clarified, revised, and expanded.

Purposes of Changes and New Matter:

1.   Subsection (1)(a) follows Section 6–102(3) of the 1987 Official Text and makes Article 6 applicable only when the seller's principal business is the sale of inventory from stock. This Article does not apply to a sale by a seller whose principal business is the sale of goods other than inventory, e.g., a farmer, is the sale of inventory not from stock, e.g., a manufacturer who produces goods to order, or is the sale of services, e.g., a dry cleaner, barber, or operator of a hotel, tavern, or restaurant.

2.   The choice-of-law rule in subsections (1)(b) and (2) derives from former Section 9–103(3) (now codified as Sections 9–301 and 9–307). Any agreement between the buyer and the seller with regard to the law governing a bulk sale does not affect the choice-of-law rule in this Article.

3. Some of the transactions excluded by subsection (3), e.g., those excluded by subsection (3)(a), may not be bulk sales. This Article nevertheless specifically excludes them in order to allay any doubts about the Article's applicability. Certain transactions, e.g., the sale of fully encumbered inventory that remains subject to a security interest, may be excluded by more than one subsection.

4. Subsections (3)(a), (b), (c), (d), and (e) derive from subsections (1) and (3) of Section 6–103 (1987 Official Text).

5. Subsections (3)(f), (g), and (h) restate subsections (2), (4), and (5) of Section 6–103 with minor changes.

6. Subsections (3)(i), (j), and (k) relate to sales in which the buyer assumes specified debts of the seller. A bulk sale does not fall within any of these subsections unless the buyer's assumption of debts is binding and irrevocable.

Subsection (3)(j) derives from subsection (6) of Section 6–103 (1987 Official Text) and is available to buyers who are not insolvent (as defined in Section 1–201(23)),* assume all the seller's business debts in full, and give notice of the assumption. Subsection (3)(k) derives from subsection (7) of Section 6–103 (1987 Official Text) and excludes transactions in which the risks to creditors are minimal. Like subsection (3)(j), this subsection applies only if the buyer assumes all the seller's business debts in full and gives notice of the assumption. In addition, the buyer must be a new organization that is organized to take over and continue the seller's business, the seller must receive nothing from the sale other than an interest in the new organization, and the seller's interest must be subordinate to the claims arising from the assumption. Sales that may qualify for the exclusion include the incorporation of a partnership or sole proprietorship.

Buyers often are reluctant to assume debts of which they have no knowledge. Subsection (3)(i), which is new, permits a qualifying buyer to exclude a sale from this Article by assuming only those debts owed to claimants of whom the buyer has knowledge after the buyer either conducts a reasonable inquiry to discover claimants or obtains a list of claimants from the seller. A buyer who takes a verified list from the seller is held to have knowledge of the claimants on the list and is entitled to rely in good faith on the list without making further inquiry. The protection afforded by the assumption of these debts, while not perfect, is sufficiently great to eliminate the need for compliance with Article 6.

7. Subsection (3)(l) is new. Although the bulk sale of even a very small business may be of concern to some creditors, losses to creditors from sales of assets in which the seller's equity is less than $10,000 are not likely to justify the costs of complying with this Article. Sales of assets having a value of more than $25,000,000 have not presented serious risks to creditors. Publicity normally attends sales of that magnitude, and the sellers are unlikely to be able successfully to remove the proceeds from the reach of creditors. As used in this subsection, "price" includes all consideration for the assets, not only new consideration. Compare "Net contract price" (Section 6–102(1)(k)). If the auctioneer or liquidator does not make an estimation, then no presumption arises.

8. Subsection (3)(m) is new. This Article assumes that creditors are aware of statutes that may require their debtors to conduct bulk sales under specified circumstances, e.g., upon the termination of a franchise or of a contract between a dealer and supplier, and are able to take account of any risk that those sales may impose.

Cross-References:

Point 1: Sections 9–102(a)(23), (33), (34), (44), (48).
Point 2: Sections 1–105,* 9–301, and 9–307.
Point 3: Section 6–102.
Point 4: Sections 9–609, 9–610, and 9–620.
Point 6: Sections 1–201 and 1–203.*
Point 7: Section 6–102.

Definitional Cross-References:

"Asset". Section 6–102.
"Auctioneer". Section 6–102.
"Bulk sale". Section 6–102.
"Buyer". Section 2–103.
"Claimant". Section 6–102.

---

* *Referring to unrevised Article 1 (Appendix A).*

"Collateral". Section 9–102(a)(12).

"Date of the bulk sale". Section 6–102.

"Date of the bulk-sale agreement". Section 6–102.

"Debt". Section 6–102.

"Insolvent". Section 1–201.*

"Inventory". Section 9–102(a)(48).

"Knowledge". Section 1–201.*

"Liquidator". Section 6–102.

"Net contract price". Section 6–102.

"Notice". Section 1–201.*

"Organization". Section 1–201.

"Presumed". Section 1–201.*

"Proceeds". Section 9–102(a)(64).

"Sale". Section 2–106.

"Secured party". Section 9–102(a)(72).

"Security interest". Section 1–201.

"Seller". Section 2–103.

"Send". Section 1–201.

"United States". Section 6–102.

"Value". Section 6–102.

"Verified". Section 6–102.

As amended in 1999.

§ 6–104.   Obligations of Buyer.

(1)   In a bulk sale as defined in Section 6–102(1)(c)(ii) the buyer shall:

(a)   obtain from the seller a list of all business names and addresses used by the seller within three years before the date the list is sent or delivered to the buyer;

(b)   unless excused under subsection (2), obtain from the seller a verified and dated list of claimants of whom the seller has notice three days before the seller sends or delivers the list to the buyer and including, to the extent known by the seller, the address of and the amount claimed by each claimant;

(c)   obtain from the seller or prepare a schedule of distribution (Section 6–106(1));

(d)   give notice of the bulk sale in accordance with Section 6–105;

(e)   unless excused under Section 6–106(4), distribute the net contract price in accordance with the undertakings of the buyer in the schedule of distribution; and

(f)   unless excused under subsection (2), make available the list of claimants (subsection (1)(b)) by:

(i)   promptly sending or delivering a copy of the list without charge to any claimant whose written request is received by the buyer no later than six months after the date of the bulk sale;

(ii)   permitting any claimant to inspect and copy the list at any reasonable hour upon request received by the buyer no later than six months after the date of the bulk sale; or

(iii)   filing a copy of the list in the office of the [Secretary of State] no later than the time for giving a notice of the bulk sale (Section 6–105(5)). A list filed in accordance with this subparagraph must state the individual, partnership, or corporate name and a mailing address of the seller.

---

*   *Referring to unrevised Article 1 (Appendix A).*

(2)   A buyer who gives notice in accordance with Section 6–105(2) is excused from complying with the requirements of subsections (1)(b) and (1)(f).

Official Comment

Prior Uniform Statutory Provision: Section 6–104 (1987 Official Text).

Changes: Revised and rewritten.

Purposes of Changes and New Matter:

1.   Subsection (1) sets forth the buyer's duties in a bulk sale conducted by the seller. The buyer's failure to perform these duties may result in liability under Section 6–107. An auctioneer in a bulk sale by auction and a liquidator in a bulk sale that the liquidator conducts on the seller's behalf have similar duties but may face somewhat different liability. See Section 6–108(1). The buyer's duties are designed to afford the seller's claimants the opportunity to learn of the bulk sale before the seller has removed the assets from their reach and has received payment that is easily secreted.

2.   Section 6–104(3) (1987 Official Text) provides that "[r]esponsibility for the completeness and accuracy of the list of creditors rests on the transferor, and the transfer is not rendered ineffective by errors or omissions therein unless the transferee is shown to have had knowledge." This sentence has been deleted as superfluous. Nothing in this Article suggests that the buyer is responsible for the completeness or accuracy of the list of claimants. The buyer's only obligations with respect to the list are to obtain it from the seller and to make it available. A buyer who sends or delivers notice of the bulk sale in accordance with Section 6–105(1) may rely in good faith on the list supplied by the seller unless, at the time the notice is sent or delivered, the buyer has knowledge of a claimant not on the list. A buyer who knows of a claimant not on the list is obligated to send notice of the bulk sale to that claimant.

3.   The buyer's only obligation with respect to the net contract price is to comply with the schedule of distribution. The schedule may provide for the buyer to pay the entire net contract price to the seller. If so, the buyer complies with the requirements of Section 6–104(1)(e) by paying the entire net contract price to the seller.

4.   The purpose of the list of claimants is to enable the buyer to give claimants notice of the bulk sale. If the buyer gives notice by filing in a public office (Section 6–105(2)), then the buyer need not obtain or preserve a list of the seller's claimants.

Cross-References:

Point 1: Sections 6–107 and 6–108.
Point 2: Sections 6–105 and 1–203.
Point 3: Section 6–106.
Point 4: Section 6–105.

Definitional Cross-References:

"Buyer". Section 2–103.
"Bulk sale". Section 6–102.
"Claimant". Section 6–102.
"Date of the bulk sale". Section 6–102.
"Net contract price". Section 6–102.
"Notice". Section 1–201.*
"Seller". Section 2–103.
"Verified". Section 6–102.

§ 6–105.   Notice to Claimants.

(1)   Except as otherwise provided in subsection (2), to comply with Section 6–104(1)(d), the buyer shall send or deliver a written notice of the bulk sale to each claimant on the list of claimants (Section 6–104(1)(b)) and to any other claimant of whom the buyer has knowledge at the time the notice of the bulk sale is sent or delivered.

---

*   *Referring to unrevised Article 1 (Appendix A).*

(2) A buyer may comply with Section 6–104(1)(d) by filing a written notice of the bulk sale in the office of the [Secretary of State] if:

(a) on the date of the bulk-sale agreement the seller has 200 or more claimants, exclusive of claimants holding secured or matured claims for employment compensation and benefits, including commissions and vacation, severance, and sick-leave pay; or

(b) the buyer has received a verified statement from the seller stating that, as of the date of the bulk-sale agreement, the number of claimants, exclusive of claimants holding secured or matured claims for employment compensation and benefits, including commissions and vacation, severance, and sick-leave pay, is 200 or more.

(3) The written notice of the bulk sale must be accompanied by a copy of the schedule of distribution (Section 6–106(1)) and state at least:

(a) that the seller and buyer have entered into an agreement for a sale that may constitute a bulk sale under the laws of the State of _____;

(b) the date of the agreement;

(c) the date on or after which more than ten percent of the assets were or will be transferred;

(d) the date on or after which more than ten percent of the net contract price was or will be paid, if the date is not stated in the schedule of distribution;

(e) the name and a mailing address of the seller;

(f) any other business name and address listed by the seller pursuant to Section 6–104(1)(a);

(g) the name of the buyer and an address of the buyer from which information concerning the sale can be obtained;

(h) a statement indicating the type of assets or describing the assets item by item;

(i) the manner in which the buyer will make available the list of claimants (Section 6–104(1)(f)), if applicable; and

(j) if the sale is in total or partial satisfaction of an antecedent debt owed by the seller, the amount of the debt to be satisfied and the name of the person to whom it is owed.

(4) For purposes of subsections (3)(e) and (3)(g), the name of a person is the person's individual, partnership, or corporate name.

(5) The buyer shall give notice of the bulk sale not less than 45 days before the date of the bulk sale and, if the buyer gives notice in accordance with subsection (1), not more than 30 days after obtaining the list of claimants.

(6) A written notice substantially complying with the requirements of subsection (3) is effective even though it contains minor errors that are not seriously misleading.

(7) A form substantially as follows is sufficient to comply with subsection (3):

Notice of Sale

(1) _____, whose address is _____, is described in this notice as the "seller."

(2) _____, whose address is _____, is described in this notice as the "buyer."

(3) The seller has disclosed to the buyer that within the past three years the seller has used other business names, operated at other addresses, or both, as follows: _____.

(4) The seller and the buyer have entered into an agreement dated _____, for a sale that may constitute a bulk sale under the laws of the state of _____.

(5) The date on or after which more than ten percent of the assets that are the subject of the sale were or will be transferred is _____, and [if not stated in the schedule of distribution] the date on or after which more than ten percent of the net contract price was or will be paid is _____.

(6)   The following assets are the subject of the sale: _____.

(7)   [If applicable] The buyer will make available to claimants of the seller a list of the seller's claimants in the following manner: _____.

(8)   [If applicable] The sale is to satisfy $_____ of an antecedent debt owed by the seller to _____.

(9)   A copy of the schedule of distribution of the net contract price accompanies this notice.

[End of Notice]

Official Comment

Prior Uniform Statutory Provision: Sections 6–105 and 6–107 (1987 Official Text).

Changes: Revised, alternative method of giving notice added, and form of notice added.

Purposes of Changes and New Matter:

1.   Subsection (1) sets forth the method by which the buyer may discharge the duty to notify the seller's claimants of the impending sale. The buyer "has knowledge" of a claimant only if the buyer has actual knowledge sufficient to enable the buyer to send a notice to the claimant. A buyer who knows only that the seller has other, unidentified claimants complies with this subsection by giving notice to the claimants on the seller's list.

2.   Subsection (2) is new. It affords the buyer the opportunity to publish notice in cases in which the number of claimants—and thus the costs of compliance and risk of inadvertent noncompliance—are large. Although a filed notice will not inform every claimant of the impending sale, a filed notice is expected to inform a sufficient number of claimants (perhaps through credit reporting services) to enable them to stop an unfair or fraudulent transaction before it occurs.

The buyer may give notice by filing if the seller actually has 200 or more claimants or if the buyer receives a verified statement that the seller has 200 or more claimants. Claimants who hold secured or matured claims for employment compensation and benefits are not counted in determining the number of claimants for this purpose; however, they are entitled to receive notice of the bulk sale.

The duty to give notice must be performed in good faith. A buyer who receives a verified statement from the seller but knows the statement to be false does not act in good faith and thus does not comply with subsection (2)(b).

3.   Subsection (3) prescribes the contents of the notice. The contents are the same regardless of whether notice is sent to each claimant or filed, except that the information in subsection (3)(i) is required only when notice is sent. The requirements of subsection (3) are the minimum; a notice that includes additional information is effective. The requirement in subsection (3)(h) for the description of assets is modeled on former Section 9–402(1) (now codified as Sections 9–108, 9–502, and 9–504). Neither the identification of assets by serial number nor an item-by-item list of assets is required.

Subsection (3)(j) applies when the sale satisfies a debt owed by the seller to the buyer or to a third party. Section 6–103(3) excludes certain sales of this kind from the application of this Article.

4.   Subsection (4) requires that a notice give the proper name of the seller and the buyer. A trade name is insufficient. See Section 9–503(c). However, subsection (3)(f) requires that trade names be added when the seller has provided them to the buyer. The list need not include trade names or other names that the seller has used but not listed, even if the buyer knows of the names.

5.   Subsection (5) requires that notice be given not less than 45 days before the date of the bulk sale. The period was extended from the 10 days afforded by the 1987 Official Text to provide ample time for claimants to receive or discover the notice and to take any action that the law permits to collect their claims from the seller. For example, depending upon the facts of each case and upon applicable law, claimants might seek to enjoin the sale, acquire a judicial lien on the assets or the proceeds, threaten to refuse to deal with the buyer unless the seller's debt is paid, or file an involuntary bankruptcy petition against the seller. The "date of the bulk sale" is defined in such a way as to permit the seller to transfer the assets to the buyer or the buyer to pay the price to the seller (but not both) before or during the 45 days.

6.   Subsection (6) derives from former Section 9–402(8) (now codified as Section 9–506). The purpose of filing is to give notice to claimants. Whether an error in the seller's name is seriously misleading should depend upon whether a claimant searching under the seller's correct name could have found the filing. Whether an error

525

other than in the seller's name is seriously misleading should depend upon whether the error prejudiced the ability of claimants to assert their rights.

Cross-References:

Point 1: Sections 1–201* and 6–104.
Point 2: Sections 1–203* and 6–104.
Point 3: Sections 6–102, 6–104, 9–108, 9–502 and 9–504.
Point 4: Sections 6–104 and 9–503.
Point 5: Sections 6–102.
Point 6: Sections 6–107 and 9–506.

Definitional Cross-References:

"Asset". Section 6–102.
"Bulk sale". Section 6–102.
"Buyer". Section 2–103.
"Claim". Section 6–102.
"Claimant". Section 6–102.
"Date of the bulk sale". Section 6–102.
"Date of the bulk-sale agreement". Section 6–102.
"Debt". Section 6–102.
"Knowledge". Section 1–201.*
"Net contract price". Section 6–102.
"Seller". Section 2–103.
"Send". Section 1–201.
"Verified". Section 6–102.
"Written". Section 1–201.

As amended in 1999.

§ 6–106. Schedule of Distribution.

(1) The seller and buyer shall agree on how the net contract price is to be distributed and set forth their agreement in a written schedule of distribution.

(2) The schedule of distribution may provide for distribution to any person at any time, including distribution of the entire net contract price to the seller.

(3) The buyer's undertakings in the schedule of distribution run only to the seller. However, a buyer who fails to distribute the net contract price in accordance with the buyer's undertakings in the schedule of distribution is liable to a creditor only as provided in Section 6–107(1).

(4) If the buyer undertakes in the schedule of distribution to distribute any part of the net contract price to a person other than the seller, and, after the buyer has given notice in accordance with Section 6–105, some or all of the anticipated net contract price is or becomes unavailable for distribution as a consequence of the buyer's or seller's having complied with an order of court, legal process, statute, or rule of law, the buyer is excused from any obligation arising under this Article or under any contract with the seller to distribute the net contract price in accordance with the buyer's undertakings in the schedule if the buyer:

(a) distributes the net contract price remaining available in accordance with any priorities for payment stated in the schedule of distribution and, to the extent that the price is insufficient to pay all the debts having a given priority, distributes the price pro rata among those debts shown in the schedule as having the same priority;

(b) distributes the net contract price remaining available in accordance with an order of court;

---

* *Referring to unrevised Article 1 (Appendix A).*

(c)   commences a proceeding for interpleader in a court of competent jurisdiction and is discharged from the proceeding; or

(d)   reaches a new agreement with the seller for the distribution of the net contract price remaining available, sets forth the new agreement in an amended schedule of distribution, gives notice of the amended schedule, and distributes the net contract price remaining available in accordance with the buyer's undertakings in the amended schedule.

(5)   The notice under subsection (4)(d) must identify the buyer and the seller, state the filing number, if any, of the original notice, set forth the amended schedule, and be given in accordance with subsection (1) or (2) of Section 6–105, whichever is applicable, at least 14 days before the buyer distributes any part of the net contract price remaining available.

(6)   If the seller undertakes in the schedule of distribution to distribute any part of the net contract price, and, after the buyer has given notice in accordance with Section 6–105, some or all of the anticipated net contract price is or becomes unavailable for distribution as a consequence of the buyer's or seller's having complied with an order of court, legal process, statute, or rule of law, the seller and any person in control of the seller are excused from any obligation arising under this Article or under any agreement with the buyer to distribute the net contract price in accordance with the seller's undertakings in the schedule if the seller:

(a)   distributes the net contract price remaining available in accordance with any priorities for payment stated in the schedule of distribution and, to the extent that the price is insufficient to pay all the debts having a given priority, distributes the price pro rata among those debts shown in the schedule as having the same priority;

(b)   distributes the net contract price remaining available in accordance with an order of court;

(c)   commences a proceeding for interpleader in a court of competent jurisdiction and is discharged from the proceeding; or

(d)   prepares a written amended schedule of distribution of the net contract price remaining available for distribution, gives notice of the amended schedule, and distributes the net contract price remaining available in accordance with the amended schedule.

(7)   The notice under subsection (6)(d) must identify the buyer and the seller, state the filing number, if any, of the original notice, set forth the amended schedule, and be given in accordance with subsection (1) or (2) of Section 6–105, whichever is applicable, at least 14 days before the seller distributes any part of the net contract price remaining available.

Official Comment

Purposes:

1.   A principal purpose of bulk sales legislation has been to impair the ability of a seller to liquidate inventory and abscond with the proceeds, leaving creditors unpaid. Toward this end, a significant minority of jurisdictions adopted optional Section 6–106 (1987 Official Text), which imposes upon a transferee in bulk the duty to apply the new consideration for the transfer to the debts of the transferor pro rata. When one or more of these debts is unliquidated, disputed, or allegedly secured, making a pro rata distribution may prove quite difficult and distribution of the consideration may be delayed considerably. In addition, since preferences generally are permitted under state law, the appropriateness of mandating a pro rata distribution is questionable. Accordingly, this Article does not require the buyer to apply the consideration to payment of the seller's debts.

This Article recognizes, however, that the seller's claimants have an interest in learning what will happen to the net contract price. If the contemplated distribution is objectionable, claimants should be able to avail themselves of whatever remedies state law or federal law allows to prevent the sale or tie up the price. On the other hand, if the price is to be distributed in a manner that is favorable to creditors, then advance knowledge of that fact will facilitate the sale by obviating any need for claimants to interfere with it.

To afford advance notice of the intended distribution of the contract price, Section 6–105(3) requires the buyer to include with the notice of the sale a copy of the "schedule of distribution"—i.e., of the agreement between the buyer and the seller on how the net contract price is to be distributed.

2. This Article does not require the net contract price to be applied in any particular fashion. Rather, the buyer and the seller may agree to whatever they wish. They must, however, disclose their agreement in ample time before the date of the bulk sale. See Section 6–105(5). The terms of the schedule of distribution in any given sale will be a function of the negotiations between buyer and seller as affected by any applicable non-Code law (e.g., corporate dissolution statutes) imposing distribution requirements in sales of the kind conducted.

In formulating the schedule, the parties may be well advised to consider the likely reaction of claimants to the schedule. For example, a schedule that contemplates the distribution of the entire net contract price to the seller or to a single creditor may prompt the filing of an involuntary bankruptcy petition. A schedule that contemplates paying the net contract price into an escrow established for the benefit of the seller's claimants may be more favorably received.

The seller may incur additional debt between the time the schedule is published and the time the net contract price is paid. The schedule may provide for payment of those debts from the net contract price.

3. Unless otherwise agreed, the buyer's only liability to creditors for failure to comply with his undertakings in the schedule of distribution is set forth in Section 6–107(1). A creditor named in the schedule may not rely on the creation or publication of the schedule as the basis for imposing liability against the buyer on any other theory, including that of estoppel or third-party beneficiary.

The seller may wish to undertake to pay some of the price to creditors. The seller may, but need not, include this undertaking in the schedule of distribution. The buyer is not responsible for performance of the seller's undertakings. Thus, if the seller makes an undertaking with respect to payment of the net contract price and fails to perform in accordance with it, the buyer faces no liability. However, certain persons in control of the seller may be liable under those circumstances. See Section 6–107(11).

4. In some cases, the precise amount of the net contract price may be unknown at the time that the schedule of distribution is formulated and notice of the bulk sale is given. In other cases, the net contract price may prove to be less than originally anticipated. Parties who fail to provide for these contingencies in the schedule of distribution and are unable to abide by the original schedule may be required to give a new notice with a new schedule.

The inability to abide by the schedule may be due to an external legal event, e.g., the suffering of a garnishment lien on the net contract price, the filing of a bankruptcy petition, or compliance with a corporate dissolution statute. If so, subsection (4), which applies to the extent that the net contract price is within the control of the buyer, may afford relief to the buyer, and subsection (6), which applies to the extent the net contract price is within the control of the seller, may afford relief to a person in control of the seller. Although this Article imposes no obligation on sellers with respect to distribution of the net contract price (or otherwise), a seller may incur an obligation of this kind by agreement with the buyer. Accordingly, subsection (6) provides the means by which the seller as well as a person in control of the seller may be excused from any such obligation.

Subsections (4)(a) and (6)(a) permit the buyer or seller respectively to distribute the net contract price remaining available in accordance with any priorities for payment. A schedule need not afford priority to particular debts. If the schedule contains no priorities, then the debts are treated as if they are all of the same priority, and the buyer or seller, as the case may be, may distribute the price pro rata in partial satisfaction of the debts set forth in the schedule. Law other than this Article determines whether a court order or a proceeding for interpleader is available for purposes of subsections (4)(b), (4)(c), (6)(b), and (6)(c).

Cross-References:

    Point 1: Sections 6–104 and 6–105.

    Point 2: Sections 6–105.

    Point 3: Sections 1–102* and 6–107.

Definitional Cross-References:

    "Buyer". Section 2–103.

    "Contract". Section 1–201.

    "Creditor". Section 1–201.

    "Debt". Section 6–102.

---

*   *Referring to unrevised Article 1 (Appendix A).*

"Net contract price". Section 6–102.
"Person". Section 1–201.
"Seller". Section 2–103.
"Written". Section 1–201.

§ 6–107. Liability for Noncompliance.

(1) Except as provided in subsection (3), and subject to the limitation in subsection (4):

(a) a buyer who fails to comply with the requirements of Section 6–104(1)(e) with respect to a creditor is liable to the creditor for damages in the amount of the claim, reduced by any amount that the creditor would not have realized if the buyer had complied; and

(b) a buyer who fails to comply with the requirements of any other subsection of Section 6–104 with respect to a claimant is liable to the claimant for damages in the amount of the claim, reduced by any amount that the claimant would not have realized if the buyer had complied.

(2) In an action under subsection (1), the creditor has the burden of establishing the validity and amount of the claim, and the buyer has the burden of establishing the amount that the creditor would not have realized if the buyer had complied.

(3) A buyer who:

(a) made a good faith and commercially reasonable effort to comply with the requirements of Section 6–104(1) or to exclude the sale from the application of this Article under Section 6–103(3); or

(b) on or after the date of the bulk-sale agreement, but before the date of the bulk sale, held a good faith and commercially reasonable belief that this Article does not apply to the particular sale is not liable to creditors for failure to comply with the requirements of Section 6–104. The buyer has the burden of establishing the good faith and commercial reasonableness of the effort or belief.

(4) In a single bulk sale the cumulative liability of the buyer for failure to comply with the requirements of Section 6–104(1) may not exceed an amount equal to:

(a) if the assets consist only of inventory and equipment, twice the net contract price, less the amount of any part of the net contract price paid to or applied for the benefit of the seller or a creditor; or

(b) if the assets include property other than inventory and equipment, twice the net value of the inventory and equipment less the amount of the portion of any part of the net contract price paid to or applied for the benefit of the seller or a creditor which is allocable to the inventory and equipment.

(5) For the purposes of subsection (4)(b), the "net value" of an asset is the value of the asset less (i) the amount of any proceeds of the sale of an asset, to the extent the proceeds are applied in partial or total satisfaction of a debt secured by the asset and (ii) the amount of any debt to the extent it is secured by a security interest or lien that is enforceable against the asset before and after it has been sold to a buyer. If a debt is secured by an asset and other property of the seller, the amount of the debt secured by a security interest or lien that is enforceable against the asset is determined by multiplying the debt by a fraction, the numerator of which is the value of the asset on the date of the bulk sale and the denominator of which is the value of all property securing the debt on the date of the bulk sale. The portion of a part of the net contract price paid to or applied for the benefit of the seller or a creditor that is "allocable to the inventory and equipment" is the portion that bears the same ratio to that part of the net contract price as the net value of the inventory and equipment bears to the net value of all of the assets.

(6) A payment made by the buyer to a person to whom the buyer is, or believes he [or she] is, liable under subsection (1) reduces pro tanto the buyer's cumulative liability under subsection (4).

(7) No action may be brought under subsection (1)(b) by or on behalf of a claimant whose claim is unliquidated or contingent.

(8) A buyer's failure to comply with the requirements of Section 6–104(1) does not (i) impair the buyer's rights in or title to the assets, (ii) render the sale ineffective, void, or voidable, (iii) entitle a creditor

to more than a single satisfaction of his [or her] claim, or (iv) create liability other than as provided in this Article.

(9) Payment of the buyer's liability under subsection (1) discharges pro tanto the seller's debt to the creditor.

(10) Unless otherwise agreed, a buyer has an immediate right of reimbursement from the seller for any amount paid to a creditor in partial or total satisfaction of the buyer's liability under subsection (1).

(11) If the seller is an organization, a person who is in direct or indirect control of the seller, and who knowingly, intentionally, and without legal justification fails, or causes the seller to fail, to distribute the net contract price in accordance with the schedule of distribution is liable to any creditor to whom the seller undertook to make payment under the schedule for damages caused by the failure.

Official Comment

Prior Uniform Statutory Provision: None.

Purposes:

1. This section sets forth the consequences of noncompliance with the requirements of Section 6–104. Although other legal consequences may result from a bulk sale—*e.g.*, the buyer may be liable to the seller under Article 2 or to the seller's creditors under the Uniform Fraudulent Transfer Act—no other consequences may be imposed by reason of the buyer's failure to comply with the requirements of this Article.

The two subsections of Section 6–107(1) reflect the duties set forth in Section 6–104. The duties generally run only to claimants, but the duty to distribute the net contract price in accordance with the schedule of distribution (Section 6–104(1)(e)) may run also to certain creditors.

2. Article 6 (1987 Official Text), like many of its nonuniform predecessors, makes a noncomplying transfer ineffective against aggrieved creditors. In contrast, noncompliance with this Article neither renders the sale ineffective nor otherwise affects the buyer's rights in or title to the assets.

Liability under this Article is for breach of a statutory duty. The buyer's only liability is personal (*in personam*) liability. Aggrieved creditors may only recover money damages. *In rem* remedies, which are available upon noncompliance with Article 6 (1987 Official Text), are not available under this Article. Thus, aggrieved creditors no longer may treat the sale as if it had not occurred and use the judicial process to apply assets purchased by the buyer toward the satisfaction of their claims against the seller.

The change in the theory of liability and in the available remedy should be of particular significance if the seller enters bankruptcy after the sale is consummated. When an aggrieved creditor of the transferor has a nonbankruptcy right to avoid a transfer in whole or in part, as may be the case under Article 6 (1987 Official Text), the transferor's bankruptcy trustee may avoid the entire transfer. See Bankruptcy Code § 544(b), 11 U.S.C. § 544(b). Under this Article, a person who is aggrieved by the buyer's noncompliance may not avoid the sale. Rather, the person is entitled only to recover damages as provided in this section. Because no creditor has the right to avoid the transaction or to assert a remedy that is the functional equivalent of avoidance, the seller's bankruptcy trustee likewise should be unable to do so.

3. This Article makes explicit what is implicit in Article 6 (1987 Official Text): only those persons as to whom there has been noncompliance are entitled to a remedy. For example, if notices are sent to each claimant other than claimant A, claimant B cannot recover. Similarly, a creditor who acquires a claim after notice is given has no remedy unless the buyer undertakes in the schedule of distribution to pay that creditor and the buyer fails to meet the obligation.

4. Unlike Article 6 (1987 Official Text), which imposes strict liability upon a noncomplying transferee, this Article imposes liability for noncompliance only when the failure to comply actually has injured a creditor and only to the extent of the injury. Each creditor's damages are measured by the injury that the particular creditor sustained as a consequence of the buyer's failure to comply. This measure is stated as the amount of the debt reduced by any amount that the person would not have realized if the buyer had complied. Compare Section 4–103(5).

5. A buyer is liable only for the buyer's own noncompliance with the requirements of Section 6–104. Under that section, the only step the buyer must take to discover the identity of the seller's claimants is to obtain a list

of claimants from the seller. If the seller's list is incomplete and the buyer lacks knowledge of claimant C, then claimant C has no remedy under subsection (1)(b) of this section.

6.   The creditor has the burden of establishing the validity and amount of the debt owed by the seller as well as the fact of the buyer's noncompliance. In contesting the allegation of noncompliance, the buyer may introduce evidence tending to show either that the sale was not a bulk sale or that the sale was a bulk sale to which this Article does not apply. In contesting the validity and amount of the debt, the buyer may introduce evidence tending to show that the seller had a defense to the debt. The buyer has the burden of establishing the amount that the creditor would not have realized even if the buyer had complied. Implicit in subsection (2) is that certain failures to comply with the requirements of this Article will cause no injury and thus result in no liability.

The following examples illustrate the operation of subsection (2):

Example 1: The buyer fails to give notice of the bulk sale. Claimant D, who appears on seller's list of claimants, admits to having had actual knowledge of the impending sale two months before it occurred. The buyer is likely to be able to meet the burden of establishing that even had the buyer given notice of the sale, claimant D would not have recovered any more than the claimant actually recovered.

Example 2: The buyer failed to obtain a list of seller's business names (Section 6–104(1)(a)) or to make available the list of claimants (Section 6–104(1)(f)). In many cases, the buyer may be able to meet the burden of establishing that compliance with those subsections would not have enabled claimants to recover any more than they actually recovered.

7.   Subsection (3) may afford a complete defense to a noncomplying buyer. This defense is available to buyers who establish that they made a good faith effort to comply with the requirements of this Article or made a good faith effort to exclude the sale from the application of this Article (e.g., by assuming debts and attempting to comply with the notice requirements of Section 6–103(3)(i), (j), or (k)). When a buyer makes a good faith effort to comply with this Article or to exclude the transaction from its coverage, the injury caused by noncompliance is likely to be *de minimis*. In any event, the primary responsibility for satisfying claims rests with the creditors, and this Article imposes no greater duty upon buyers who attempt to comply with this Article or to exclude a sale from its application than to make a good faith effort to do so.

The defense of subsection (3) also is available to buyers who act on the good faith belief that this Article does not apply to the sale (e.g., because the sale is not a bulk sale or is excluded under Section 6–103). The good-faith-belief defense is an acknowledgement that reasonable people may disagree over whether a given transaction is or is not a bulk sale and over whether Section 6–103 excludes a particular transaction. A buyer acting in good faith should be protected from the liability that this Article otherwise would impose on buyers who may be completely innocent of wrongdoing. A buyer who is unaware of the requirements of this Article holds no belief concerning the applicability of the Article and so may not use the defense.

8.   Even a buyer who completely fails to comply with this Article may not be liable in an amount equal to sum of the seller's debts. Subsection (4) limits the aggregate recovery for "any one bulk sale," which term includes a series of sales by a liquidator. The maximum cumulative liability for noncompliance with this Article parallels the maximum recovery generally available to creditors under the 1987 Official Text of Article 6. Under that Article, the noncomplying transferee may have to "pay twice" for the goods. First, the transferee may pay the purchase price to the transferor; then, the transferee may lose the goods to aggrieved creditors.

Under this Article, the maximum cumulative liability is an amount equal to twice the net contract price of the inventory and equipment (i.e., twice the amount that would be available to unsecured creditors from the inventory and equipment), less the amount of any portion of that net contract price paid to or applied for the benefit of the seller or a creditor of the seller. Unless the buyer receives credit for amounts paid to the seller (which amounts the creditors have a right to apply to payment of their claims), the buyer might wind up paying an amount equal to the net contract price three times (once to the seller and twice to aggrieved creditors). The grant of credit for amounts paid to the seller's creditors recognizes that ordinarily the seller has no obligation to pay creditors pro rata.

When the assets sold consist of only inventory and equipment, calculation of the maximum cumulative liability is relatively simple. But when the assets sold include property in addition to inventory and equipment, the calculation becomes more difficult. When inventory or equipment secures a debt that also is secured by other collateral and the aggregate value of the collateral exceeds the secured debt, a determination of the amount in clause (ii) of subsection (5) may require an allocation of the collateral to the debt in accordance with the statutory formula. In addition, one may need to determine which portion of payments of the net contract price is allocable to inventory and equipment. Subsection (5) directs that this allocation be made by multiplying the part of the net contract price paid to or applied for the benefit of the seller or a creditor by a fraction whose nominator is the net value of the inventory and equipment and whose denominator is the net value of all the assets.

Sometimes the seller may receive the net contract price and pay some or all of it to one or more creditors. In determining whether a payment to a creditor was made from the net contract price or from another source, courts are free to employ tracing rules. Amounts paid to secured parties usually are taken into account in determining the net contract price; if so, the buyer should not receive credit for them.

9. The buyer need not wait for judgment to be entered before paying a person believed to be a creditor of the seller. Indeed, the buyer is entitled to credit for amounts paid to persons who in fact may not be creditors of the seller, as long as the buyer acts with the belief that the seller is so indebted. As is the case with respect to all obligations under the Code, the buyer's belief must be held in good faith.

10. Any amounts paid by the buyer in satisfaction of the liability created by Section 6–107(1) reduce the seller's liability to the recipient pro tanto. Consequently, the buyer is entitled to immediate reimbursement of those amounts from the seller. The right of reimbursement is available only for amounts paid to actual creditors. Amounts paid to those whom the buyer incorrectly believes to be creditors ordinarily are not recoverable from the seller, although the buyer is entitled to credit for those amounts against the aggregate liability in subsection (4). Of course, the buyer and seller may vary the seller's reimbursement obligation by agreement.

11. Because of the difficulty in valuing claims that are unliquidated or contingent, persons holding claims of that kind may not bring an action under subsection (1)(b). If the claim remains unliquidated or contingent throughout the limitation period in Section 6–110, then these creditors have no remedy for noncompliance under that subsection. They may, however, be entitled to a remedy under subsection (1)(a) of (11) for failure to distribute the net contract price in accordance with the schedule of distribution.

12. In certain circumstances, subsection (11) imposes liability on a person in direct or indirect control of a seller that is an organization. Excuse under Section 6–106(6) is a "legal justification" that prevents liability from attaching under subsection (11). No special provision applies to the seller who fails to comply with the schedule. The seller already owes the debt to the creditor, and other law governs the consequences of a debtor who fails to pay a debt when promised.

Cross-References:

Point 1: Section 6–104.

Point 4: Section 4–103.

Point 5: Sections 6–104 and 6–105.

Point 6: Sections 1–201,* 6–102, 6–103, and 6–104.

Point 7: Sections 1–102,* 1–201,* 6–102 and 6–103.

Point 8: Section 6–102.

Point 9: Section 1–203.*

Point 10: Section 1–102.*

Point 11: Sections 6–102 and 6–110.

Point 12: Section 6–106.

Definitional Cross-References:

"Assets". Section 6–102.

"Bulk sale". Section 6–102.

"Burden of establishing". Section 1–201.

"Buyer". Section 2–103.

"Claim". Section 6–102.

"Claimant". Section 6–102.

"Creditor". Section 6–102.

"Date of the bulk sale". Section 6–102.

"Equipment". Section 6–102.

"Good faith". Section 6–102.

---

* *Referring to unrevised Article 1 (Appendix A).*

"Inventory". Section 9–102(a)(48).
"Net contract price". Section 6–102.
"Organization". Section 1–201.
"Person". Section 1–201.
"Proceeds". Section 9–102(a)(64).
"Security interest". Section 1–201.
"Seller". Section 2–103.
"Written". Section 1–201.

As amended in 1999.

§ 6–108.   Bulk Sales by Auction; Bulk Sales Conducted by Liquidator.

(1)   Sections 6–104, 6–105, 6–106, and 6–107 apply to a bulk sale by auction and a bulk sale conducted by a liquidator on the seller's behalf with the following modifications:

(a)   "buyer" refers to auctioneer or liquidator, as the case may be;

(b)   "net contract price" refers to net proceeds of the auction or net proceeds of the sale, as the case may be;

(c)   the written notice required under Section 6–105(3) must be accompanied by a copy of the schedule of distribution (Section 6–106(1)) and state at least:

   (i)   that the seller and the auctioneer or liquidator have entered into an agreement for auction or liquidation services that may constitute an agreement to make a bulk sale under the laws of the State of _____;

   (ii)   the date of the agreement;

   (iii)   the date on or after which the auction began or will begin or the date on or after which the liquidator began or will begin to sell assets on the seller's behalf;

   (iv)   the date on or after which more than ten percent of the net proceeds of the sale were or will be paid, if the date is not stated in the schedule of distribution;

   (v)   the name and a mailing address of the seller;

   (vi)   any other business name and address listed by the seller pursuant to Section 6–104(1)(a);

   (vii)   the name of the auctioneer or liquidator and an address of the auctioneer or liquidator from which information concerning the sale can be obtained;

   (viii) a statement indicating the type of assets or describing the assets item by item;

   (ix)   the manner in which the auctioneer or liquidator will make available the list of claimants (Section 6–104(1)(f)), if applicable; and

   (x)   if the sale is in total or partial satisfaction of an antecedent debt owed by the seller, the amount of the debt to be satisfied and the name of the person to whom it is owed; and

(d)   in a single bulk sale the cumulative liability of the auctioneer or liquidator for failure to comply with the requirements of this section may not exceed the amount of the net proceeds of the sale allocable to inventory and equipment sold less the amount of the portion of any part of the net proceeds paid to or applied for the benefit of a creditor which is allocable to the inventory and equipment.

(2)   A payment made by the auctioneer or liquidator to a person to whom the auctioneer or liquidator is, or believes he [or she] is, liable under this section reduces pro tanto the auctioneer's or liquidator's cumulative liability under subsection (1)(d).

(3)   A form substantially as follows is sufficient to comply with subsection (1)(c):

Notice of Sale

(1)   _____, whose address is _____, is described in this notice as the "seller."

(2)   _____, whose address is _____, is described in this notice as the "auctioneer" or "liquidator."

(3)   The seller has disclosed to the auctioneer or liquidator that within the past three years the seller has used other business names, operated at other addresses, or both, as follows: _____.

(4)   The seller and the auctioneer or liquidator have entered into an agreement dated _____ for auction or liquidation services that may constitute an agreement to make a bulk sale under the laws of the State of _____.

(5)   The date on or after which the auction began or will begin or the date on or after which the liquidator began or will begin to sell assets on the seller's behalf is _____, and [if not stated in the schedule of distribution] the date on or after which more than ten percent of the net proceeds of the sale were or will be paid is _____.

(6)   The following assets are the subject of the sale: _____.

(7)   [If applicable] The auctioneer or liquidator will make available to claimants of the seller a list of the seller's claimants in the following manner: _____.

(8)   [If applicable] The sale is to satisfy $_____ of an antecedent debt owed by the seller to _____.

(9)   A copy of the schedule of distribution of the net proceeds accompanies this notice.

[End of Notice]

(4)   A person who buys at a bulk sale by auction or conducted by a liquidator need not comply with the requirements of Section 6–104(1) and is not liable for the failure of an auctioneer or liquidator to comply with the requirements of this section.

Official Comment

Prior Uniform Statutory Provision: Section 6–108.

Changes: Revised, expanded to include sales conducted by a liquidator on the seller's behalf, and form of notice added.

Purposes of Changes and New Matter:

1.   This section applies only to bulk sales by auction or conducted by a liquidator on the seller's behalf, as defined in Section 6–102(1)(c). Bulk sales conducted by an auctioneer or liquidator on its own behalf are treated as ordinary bulk sales and are not subject to this section.

2.   Regardless of whether the assets are sold directly from the seller to the buyer, are sold to a variety of buyers at auction, or are sold on the seller's behalf by a liquidator to one or more buyers, a going-out-of-business sale of inventory presents similar risks to claimants. Auctioneers and liquidators are likely to be in a better position to ascertain whether the sale they are conducting is, or is part of, a bulk sale than are their customers. Accordingly, buyers at auctions and from liquidators selling assets of others need not be concerned with complying with this Article. Instead, this section imposes upon auctioneers and liquidators duties and liabilities that are similar, but not always identical, to those of a buyer under Sections 6–104(1) and 6–107. Except to the extent that this section treats bulk sales by auctioneers and liquidators differently from those conducted by the seller on its own behalf, the Official Comments to Sections 6–104(1) and 6–107, as well as the Comments to Sections 6–105 and 6–106, which those sections incorporate by reference, are applicable to sales to which this section applies.

3.   Subsection (1)(d) sets forth the maximum cumulative liability for auctioneers and liquidators "in any one bulk sale," which term includes a series of sales by a liquidator. This liability is to be calculated in a manner similar to that set forth in Sections 6–107(4) and 6–107(5). The term "net proceeds of the auction or sale allocable to inventory and equipment" is analogous to the term "net value of the inventory and equipment"; however, the former takes into account the reasonable expenses of the auction or sale whereas the latter does not. Also, the latter is doubled whereas the former is not. The "amount of the portion of any part of the net proceeds paid to or applied for the benefit of a creditor which is allocable to inventory and equipment" is determined by multiplying the part of the net proceeds paid to or applied for the benefit of a creditor by a fraction whose numerator is the net proceeds of the sale allocable to inventory and equipment and whose denominator is the total net proceeds of the

auction or sale. Because the amount of the net proceeds allocable to inventory and equipment is not doubled, the auctioneer or liquidator is not entitled to credit for payments made to the seller.

4.   Section 6–107(3) applies to all bulk sales. Accordingly, an auctioneer or liquidator who makes a good faith effort to comply with the requirements of this Article or to exclude the sale from this Article or who acts under a good faith belief that this Article does not apply to the sale faces no liability whatsoever.

Cross-References:

Point 1: Section 6–102.
Point 2: Sections 6–102, 6–104, 6–105, 6–106, and 6–107.
Point 3: Sections 6–102 and 6–107.
Point 4: Section 6–107.

Definitional Cross-References:

"Assets". Section 6–102.
"Auctioneer". Section 6–102.
"Bulk sale". Section 6–102.
"Claimants". Section 6–102.
"Creditor". Section 6–102.
"Debt". Section 6–102.
"Equipment". Section 9–102(a)(33).
"Inventory". Section 9–102(a)(48).
"Liquidator". Section 6–102.
"Net proceeds". Section 6–102.
"Person". Section 1–201.
"Seller". Section 2–103.
"Written". Section 1–201.

As amended in 1999.

§ 6–109.   What Constitutes Filing; Duties of Filing Officer; Information From Filing Officer.

(1)   Presentation of a notice or list of claimants for filing and tender of the filing fee or acceptance of the notice or list by the filing officer constitutes filing under this Article.

(2)   The filing officer shall:

(a)   mark each notice or list with a file number and with the date and hour of filing;

(b)   hold the notice or list or a copy for public inspection;

(c)   index the notice or list according to each name given for the seller and for the buyer; and

(d)   note in the index the file number and the addresses of the seller and buyer given in the notice or list.

(3)   If the person filing a notice or list furnishes the filing officer with a copy, the filing officer upon request shall note upon the copy the file number and date and hour of the filing of the original and send or deliver the copy to the person.

(4)   The fee for filing and indexing and for stamping a copy furnished by the person filing to show the date and place of filing is $_____ for the first page and $_____ for each additional page. The fee for indexing each name more than two is $_____.

(5)   Upon request of any person, the filing officer shall issue a certificate showing whether any notice or list with respect to a particular seller or buyer is on file on the date and hour stated in the certificate. If a notice or list is on file, the certificate must give the date and hour of filing of each notice or list and the name and address of each seller, buyer, auctioneer, or liquidator. The fee for the certificate is $_____ if the request for the certificate is in the standard form prescribed by the [Secretary of State] and otherwise

is $_____. Upon request of any person, the filing officer shall furnish a copy of any filed notice or list for a fee of $_____.

(6)   The filing officer shall keep each notice or list for two years after it is filed.

Official Comment

Prior Uniform Statutory Provision: None.

Purposes of New Matter:

This Article contemplates public filing of bulk sale notices and lists of claimants in a single filing office in each state. This section, which derives substantially from former Sections 9–403 and 9–407 (now codified as Sections 9–515, 9–516, 9–519, 9–522, 9–523, and 9–525), governs filing. The filing system is designed to enable one seeking information about a sale to discover any filed notices or lists by searching under either the seller's or the buyer's (but not the auctioneer's or liquidator's) individual, partnership, or corporate name.

Cross-References:

Sections 6–103, 6–105, 9–403,* and 9–407.*

Definitional Cross-References:

"Auctioneer". Section 6–102.
"Buyer". Section 2–103.
"Liquidator". Section 6–102.
"Person". Section 1–201.
"Seller". Section 2–103.
"Send". Section 1–201.

As amended in 1999.

§ 6–110.   Limitation of Actions.

(1)   Except as provided in subsection (2), an action under this Article against a buyer, auctioneer, or liquidator must be commenced within one year after the date of the bulk sale.

(2)   If the buyer, auctioneer, or liquidator conceals the fact that the sale has occurred, the limitation is tolled and an action under this Article may be commenced within the earlier of (i) one year after the person bringing the action discovers that the sale has occurred or (ii) one year after the person bringing the action should have discovered that the sale has occurred, but no later than two years after the date of the bulk sale. Complete noncompliance with the requirements of this Article does not of itself constitute concealment.

(3)   An action under Section 6–107(11) must be commenced within one year after the alleged violation occurs.

Official Comment

Prior Uniform Statutory Provision: Section 6–111 (1987 Official Text).

Changes: Statute of limitations extended and clarified.

Purposes of Changes and New Matter:

1.   This Article imposes liability upon only those who do not make a good faith and commercially reasonable effort to comply with the requirements of the Article or to exclude the sale from the application of the Article and who do not hold a good faith and commercially reasonable belief that the Article is inapplicable to the sale. Consequently, it extends the six-month limitation period of the 1987 Official Text, which applies to good faith transferees as well as those not in good faith, to one year. The period commences with the date of the bulk sale.

_____
*   *Referring to unrevised Article 9.*

2.   Cases decided under the 1987 Official Text of Article 6 disagree over whether the complete failure to comply with the requirements of that Article constitutes a concealment that tolls the limitation. This Article adopts the view that noncompliance does not of itself constitute concealment.

3.   This Article does not contemplate tolling the limitation for actions against a person in control of the seller who fails to distribute the net contract price in accordance with the schedule of distribution. Those actions must be commenced within one year after the alleged violation occurs.

Cross-References:

Point 1: Sections 1–201, 6–102, 6–107 and 6–108.
Point 3: Section 6–107.

Definitional Cross-References:

"Action". Section 1–201.
"Auctioneer". Section 6–102.
"Buyer". Section 2–103.
"Date of the bulk sale". Section 6–102.
"Liquidator". Section 6–102.

[END OF ALTERNATIVE B]

CONFORMING AMENDMENT TO SECTION 1–105*

States adopting Alternative B should amend Section 1–105(2)* of the Uniform Commercial Code to read as follows:

(2)   Where one of the following provisions of this Act specifies the applicable law, that provision governs and a contrary agreement is effective only to the extent permitted by the law (including the conflict of laws rules) so specified:

Rights of creditors against sold goods. Section 2–402.

Applicability of the Article on Leases. Sections 2A–105 and 2A–106.

Applicability of the Article on Bank Deposits and Collections. Section 4–102.

Bulk ~~transfers~~ sales subject to the Article on Bulk ~~Transfers~~ Sales. Section ~~6–102~~ 6–103.

Applicability of the Article on Investment Securities. Section 8–106.**

Perfection provisions of the Article on Secured Transactions. Section 9–103.***

CONFORMING AMENDMENT TO SECTION 2–403

States adopting Alternative B should amend Section 2–403(4) of the Uniform Commercial Code to read as follows:

(4)   The rights of other purchasers of goods and of lien creditors are governed by the Articles on Secured Transactions (Article 9), Bulk ~~Transfers~~ Sales (Article 6) and Documents of Title (Article 7).

---

*   *Referring to unrevised Article 1 (Appendix A).*
**   *Referring to unrevised Article 8.*
***   *Referring to unrevised Article 9.*

UCC ARTICLE 7 (2016)

DOCUMENTS OF TITLE

Article 7 was revised in 2003.

PART 1. GENERAL

PART 2. WAREHOUSE RECEIPTS: SPECIAL PROVISIONS

PART 3. BILLS OF LADING: SPECIAL PROVISIONS

PART 4. WAREHOUSE RECEIPTS AND BILLS OF LADING: GENERAL OBLIGATIONS

UNIFORM COMMERCIAL CODE

National Conference of Commissioners on Uniform State Laws
DRAFTING COMMITTEE

Henry Deeb Gabriel, Jr., New Orleans, Louisiana, *Chair*
Edward V. Cattell, Jr., Philadelphia, Pennsylvania, *The American Law Institute Representative*
Patricia Brumfield Fry, Columbia, Missouri
Sandra S. Stern, New York, New York
Neal Ossen, Hartford, Connecticut, *Enactment Plan Coordinator*
Drew Kershen, Norman, Oklahoma, *Co-Reporter*
Linda J. Rusch, St. Paul, Minnesota, *The American Law Institute Representative and Co-Reporter*

EX OFFICIO

K. King Burnett, Salisbury, Maryland, *President*
Joseph P. Mazurek, Helena, Montana, *Division Chair*

AMERICAN BAR ASSOCIATION ADVISOR

William H. Towle, Missoula, Montana

EXECUTIVE DIRECTOR

William H. Henning, Tuscaloosa, Alabama, *Executive Director*
William J. Pierce, Ann Arbor, Michigan, *Executive Director Emeritus*

PREFATORY NOTE

Article 7 is the last of the articles of the Uniform Commercial Code to be revised. The genesis of this project is twofold: to provide a framework for the further development of electronic documents of title and to update the article for modern times in light of state, federal and international developments. Each section has been reviewed to determine its suitability given modern practice, the need for medium and gender neutrality, and modern statutory drafting.

To provide for electronic documents of title, several definitions in Article 1 were revised including "bearer," "bill of lading," "delivery," "document of title," "holder," and "warehouse receipt." The concept of an electronic document of title allows for commercial practice to determine whether records issued by bailees are "in the regular course of business or financing" and are "treated as adequately evidencing that the person in possession or control of the record is entitled to receive, control, hold, and dispose of the record and the goods the record covers." Rev. Section 1–201(b)(16). Such records in electronic form are electronic documents of title and in tangible form are tangible documents of title. Conforming amendments to other Articles of the UCC are also necessary to fully integrate electronic documents of title into the UCC. Conforming amendments to other Articles of the UCC are contained in Appendix I.[*]

Key to the integration of the electronic document of title scheme is the concept of "control" defined in Section 7–106. This definition is adapted from the Uniform Electronic Transactions Act § 16 on Transferrable Records and from Uniform Commercial Code § 9–105 concerning control of electronic chattel paper. Control of an electronic document of title is the conceptual equivalent to possession and indorsement of a tangible document of title. Of equal importance is the acknowledgment that parties may desire to substitute an electronic document of title for an already-issued paper document and vice versa. Section 7–105 sets forth the minimum requirements that need to be fulfilled in order to give effect to the substitute document issued in the alternate medium. To the extent possible, the rules for electronic documents of title are the same or as similar as possible to the rules for tangible documents of title. If a rule is meant to be limited to one medium or the other, that is clearly stated. Rules that reference documents of title, warehouse receipts, or bills of lading without a designation to "electronic" or "tangible" apply to documents of title in either medium. As with tangible negotiable documents of title, electronic negotiable documents of title may be negotiated and duly negotiated. Section 7–501.

Other changes that have been made are:

1.   New definitions of "carrier," "good faith," "record", "sign" and "shipper" in Section 7–102.

2.   Deletion of references to tariffs or filed classifications given the deregulation of the affected industries. See e.g. section 7–103 and 7–309.

3.   Clarifying the rules regarding when a document is nonnegotiable. Section 7–104.

4.   Making clear when rules apply just to warehouse receipts or bills of lading, thus eliminating the need for former section 7–105.

5.   Clarifying that particular terms need not be included in order to have a valid warehouse receipt. Section 7–202.

6.   Broadening the ability of the warehouse to make an effective limitation of liability in its warehouse receipt or storage agreement in accord with commercial practice. Section 7–204.

7.   Allowing a warehouse to have a lien on goods covered by a storage agreement and clarifying the priority rules regarding the claim of a warehouse lien as against other interests. Section 7–209.

8.   Conforming language usage to modern shipping practice. Sections 7–301 and 7–302.

9.   Clarifying the extent of the carrier's lien. Section 7–307.

10.   Adding references to Article 2A when appropriate. See e.g. Sections 7–503, 7–504, 7–509.

11.   Clarifying that the warranty made by negotiation or delivery of a document of title should apply only in the case of a voluntary transfer of possession or control of the document. Section 7–507.

12.   Providing greater flexibility to a court regarding adequate protection against loss when ordering delivery of the goods or issuance of a substitute document. Section 7–601.

---

[*]   *Note from West Advisory Panel: Article 7 conforming amendments are incorporated in the affected sections so the referenced appendix is not included in this volume.*

13. Providing conforming amendments to the other Articles of the Uniform Commercial Code to accommodate electronic documents of title.

Legislative Note: All cross-references in this draft to Article 1 are to Revised Article 1 (2001). In the event a state has not enacted Revised Article 1, the cross-references should be changed to refer to the relevant sections in former Article 1.

PART 1

GENERAL

§ 7–101.   Short Title.

This article may be cited as Uniform Commercial Code-Documents of Title.

Official Comment

Prior Uniform Statutory Provision: Former Section 7–101.

Changes: Revised for style only.

This Article is a revision of the 1962 Official Text with Comments as amended since 1962. The 1962 Official Text was a consolidation and revision of the Uniform Warehouse Receipts Act and the Uniform Bills of Lading Act, and embraced the provisions of the Uniform Sales Act relating to negotiation of documents of title.

This Article does not contain the substantive criminal provisions found in the Uniform Warehouse Receipts and Bills of Lading Acts. These criminal provisions are inappropriate to a Commercial Code, and for the most part duplicate portions of the ordinary criminal law relating to frauds. This revision deletes the former Section 7–105 that provided that courts could apply a rule from Parts 2 and 3 by analogy to a situation not explicitly covered in the provisions on warehouse receipts or bills of lading when it was appropriate. This is, of course, an unexceptional proposition and need not be stated explicitly in the statute. Thus former Section 7–105 has been deleted. Whether applying a rule by analogy to a situation is appropriate depends upon the facts of each case.

The Article does not attempt to define the tort liability of bailees, except to hold certain classes of bailees to a minimum standard of reasonable care. For important classes of bailees, liabilities in case of loss, damages or destruction, as well as other legal questions associated with particular documents of title, are governed by federal statutes, international treaties, and in some cases regulatory state laws, which supersede the provisions of this Article in case of inconsistency. See Section 7–103.

§ 7–102.   Definitions and Index of Definitions.

(a)   In this article, unless the context otherwise requires:

(1)   "Bailee" means a person that by a warehouse receipt, bill of lading, or other document of title acknowledges possession of goods and contracts to deliver them.

(2)   "Carrier" means a person that issues a bill of lading.

(3)   "Consignee" means a person named in a bill of lading to which or to whose order the bill promises delivery.

(4)   "Consignor" means a person named in a bill of lading as the person from which the goods have been received for shipment.

(5)   "Delivery order" means a record that contains an order to deliver goods directed to a warehouse, carrier, or other person that in the ordinary course of business issues warehouse receipts or bills of lading.

(6)   "Good faith" means honesty in fact and the observance of reasonable commercial standards of fair dealing.

(7)   "Goods" means all things that are treated as movable for the purposes of a contract for storage or transportation.

(8)   "Issuer" means a bailee that issues a document of title or, in the case of an unaccepted delivery order, the person that orders the possessor of goods to deliver. The term includes a person for which an agent or employee purports to act in issuing a document if the agent or employee has real or apparent authority to issue documents, even if the issuer did not receive any goods, the goods were misdescribed, or in any other respect the agent or employee violated the issuer's instructions.

(9)   "Person entitled under the document" means the holder, in the case of a negotiable document of title, or the person to which delivery of the goods is to be made by the terms of, or pursuant to instructions in a record under, a nonnegotiable document of title.

(10) "Record" means information that is inscribed on a tangible medium or that is stored in an electronic or other medium and is retrievable in perceivable form.

(11) "Sign" means, with present intent to authenticate or adopt a record:

(A)   to execute or adopt a tangible symbol; or

(B)   to attach to or logically associate with the record an electronic sound, symbol, or process.

(12) "Shipper" means a person that enters into a contract of transportation with a carrier.

(13) "Warehouse" means a person engaged in the business of storing goods for hire.

(b)   Definitions in other articles applying to this article and the sections in which they appear are:

(1)   "Contract for sale", Section 2–106.

(2)   "Lessee in ordinary course", Section 2A–103.

(3)   "Receipt" of goods, Section 2–103.

(c)   In addition, Article 1 contains general definitions and principles of construction and interpretation applicable throughout this article.

Legislative Note: If the state has enacted Revised Article 1, the definitions of "good faith" in subsection (a)(6) and "record" in (a)(10) need not be enacted in this section as they are contained in Article 1, Section 1–201. These subsections should be marked as "reserved" in order to provide for uniform numbering of subsections.

Official Comment

Prior Uniform Statutory Provision: Former Section 7–102.

Changes: New definitions of "carrier," "good faith," "record," "sign," and "shipper." Other definitions revised to accommodate electronic mediums.

Purposes:

1.   "Bailee" is used in this Article as a blanket term to designate carriers, warehousemen and others who normally issue documents of title on the basis of goods which they have received. The definition does not, however, require actual possession of the goods. If a bailee acknowledges possession when it does not have possession, the bailee is bound by sections of this Article which declare the "bailee's" obligations. (See definition of "Issuer" in this section and Sections 7–203 and 7–301 on liability in case of non-receipt.) A "carrier" is one type of bailee and is defined as a person that issues a bill of lading. A "shipper" is a person who enters into the contract of transportation with the carrier. The definitions of "bailee," "consignee," "consignor," "goods", and "issuer", are unchanged in substance from prior law. "Document of title" is defined in Article 1, and may be in either tangible or electronic form.

2.   The definition of warehouse receipt contained in the general definitions section of this Act (Section 1–201) does not require that the issuing warehouse be "lawfully engaged" in business or for profit. The warehouse's compliance with applicable state regulations such as the filing of a bond has no bearing on the substantive issues dealt with in this Article. Certainly the issuer's violations of law should not diminish its responsibility on

documents the issuer has put in commercial circulation. But it is still essential that the business be storing goods "for hire" (Section 1–201 and this section). A person does not become a warehouse by storing its own goods.

3.   When a delivery order has been accepted by the bailee it is for practical purposes indistinguishable from a warehouse receipt. Prior to such acceptance there is no basis for imposing obligations on the bailee other than the ordinary obligation of contract which the bailee may have assumed to the depositor of the goods. Delivery orders may be either electronic or tangible documents of title. See definition of "document of title" in Section 1–201.

4.   The obligation of good faith imposed by this Article and by Article 1, Section 1–304 includes the observance of reasonable commercial standards of fair dealing.

5.   The definitions of "record" and "sign" are included to facilitate electronic mediums. See comment 9 to Section 9–102 discussing "record" and the comment to amended Section 2–103 discussing "sign."*

6.   "Person entitled under the document" is moved from former Section 7–403.

7.   These definitions apply in this Article unless the context otherwise requires. The "context" is intended to refer to the context in which the defined term is used in the Uniform Commercial Code. The definition applies whenever the defined term is used unless the context in which the defined term is used in the statute indicates that the term was not used in its defined sense. See comment to Section 1–201.

Cross References:

Point 1: Sections 1–201, 7–203 and 7–301.
Point 2: Sections 1–201 and 7–203.
Point 3: Section 1–201.
Point 4: Section 1–304.
Point 5: Section 9–102 and 2–103.
See general comment to document of title in Section 1–201.

Definitional Cross References:

"Bill of lading". Section 1–201.
"Contract". Section 1–201.
"Contract for sale". Section 2–106.
"Delivery". Section 1–201.
"Document of title". Section 1–201.
"Person". Section 1–201.
"Purchase". Section 1–201.
"Receipt of goods". Section 2–103.
"Right". Section 1–201.
"Warehouse receipt". Section 1–201.

§ 7–103.   Relation of Article to Treaty or Statute.

(a)   This article is subject to any treaty or statute of the United States or regulatory statute of this state to the extent the treaty, statute, or regulatory statute is applicable.

(b)   This article does not modify or repeal any law prescribing the form or content of a document of title or the services or facilities to be afforded by a bailee, or otherwise regulating a bailee's business in respects not specifically treated in this article. However, violation of such a law does not affect the status of a document of title that otherwise is within the definition of a document of title.

(c)   This [act] modifies, limits, and supersedes the federal Electronic Signatures in Global and National Commerce Act (15 U.S.C. Section 7001, et. seq.) but does not modify, limit, or supersede Section 101(c) of that act (15 U.S.C. Section 7001(c)) or authorize electronic delivery of any of the notices described in Section 103(b) of that act (15 U.S.C. Section 7003(b)).

---

*   *Referring to the 2003 amendments to Article 2, withdrawn in 2011.*

(d) To the extent there is a conflict between [the Uniform Electronic Transactions Act] and this article, this article governs.

Legislative Note: In states that have not enacted the Uniform Electronic Transactions Act in some form, states should consider their own state laws to determine whether there is a conflict between the provisions of this article and those laws particularly as those other laws may affect electronic documents of title.

Official Comment

Prior Uniform Statutory Provision: Former Sections 7–103 and 10–104.

Changes: Deletion of references to tariffs and classifications; incorporation of former Section 10–104 into subsection (b), provide for intersection with federal and state law governing electronic transactions.

Purposes:

1. To make clear what would of course be true without the Section, that applicable Federal law is paramount.

2. To make clear also that regulatory state statutes (such as those fixing or authorizing a commission to fix rates and prescribe services, authorizing different charges for goods of different values, and limiting liability for loss to the declared value on which the charge was based) are not affected by the Article and are controlling on the matters which they cover unless preempted by federal law. The reference in former Section 7–103 to tariffs, classifications, and regulations filed or issued pursuant to regulatory state statutes has been deleted as inappropriate in the modern era of diminished regulation of carriers and warehouses. If a regulatory scheme requires a carrier or warehouse to issue a tariff or classification, that tariff or classification would be given effect via the state regulatory scheme that this Article recognizes as controlling. Permissive tariffs or classifications would not displace the provisions of this act, pursuant to this section, but may be given effect through the ability of parties to incorporate those terms by reference into their agreement.

3. The document of title provisions of this act supplement the federal law and regulatory state law governing bailees. This Article focuses on the commercial importance and usage of documents of title. *State ex. rel Public Service Commission v. Gunkelman & Sons, Inc.*, 219 N.W.2d 853 (N.D. 1974).

4. Subsection (c) is included to make clear the interrelationship between the federal Electronic Signatures in Global and National Commerce Act and this article and the conforming amendments to other articles of the Uniform Commercial Code promulgated as part of the revision of this article. Section 102 of the federal act allows a State statute to modify, limit, or supersede the provisions of Section 101 of the federal act. See the comments to Revised Article 1, Section 1–108.

5. Subsection (d) makes clear that once this article is in effect, its provisions regarding electronic commerce and regarding electronic documents of title control in the event there is a conflict with the provisions of the Uniform Electronic Transactions Act or other applicable state law governing electronic transactions.

Cross References:

Sections 1–108, 7–201, 7–202, 7–204, 7–206, 7–309, 7–401, 7–403.

Definitional Cross Reference:

"Bill of lading". Section 1–201.

§ 7–104. Negotiable and Nonnegotiable Document of Title.

(a) Except as otherwise provided in subsection (c), a document of title is negotiable if by its terms the goods are to be delivered to bearer or to the order of a named person.

(b) A document of title other than one described in subsection (a) is nonnegotiable. A bill of lading that states that the goods are consigned to a named person is not made negotiable by a provision that the goods are to be delivered only against an order in a record signed by the same or another named person.

(c) A document of title is nonnegotiable if, at the time it is issued, the document has a conspicuous legend, however expressed, that it is nonnegotiable.

Official Comment

Prior Uniform Statutory Provision: Former Section 7–104.

Changes: Subsection (a) is revised to reflect modern style and trade practice. Subsection (b) is revised for style and medium neutrality. Subsection (c) is new.

Purposes:

1.   This Article deals with a class of commercial paper representing commodities in storage or transportation. This "commodity paper" is to be distinguished from what might be called "money paper" dealt with in the Article of this Act on Commercial Paper (Article 3) and "investment paper" dealt with in the Article of this Act on Investment Securities (Article 8). The class of "commodity paper" is designated "document of title" following the terminology of the Uniform Sales Act Section 76. Section 1–201. The distinctions between negotiable and nonnegotiable documents in this section makes the most important subclassification employed in the Article, in that the holder of negotiable documents may acquire more rights than its transferor had (See Section 7–502). The former Section 7–104, which provided that a document of title was negotiable if it runs to a named person or assigns if such designation was recognized in overseas trade, has been deleted as not necessary in light of current commercial practice.

A document of title is negotiable only if it satisfies this section. "Deliverable on proper indorsement and surrender of this receipt" will not render a document negotiable. Bailees often include such provisions as a means of insuring return of nonnegotiable receipts for record purposes. Such language may be regarded as insistence by the bailee upon a particular kind of receipt in connection with delivery of the goods. Subsection (a) makes it clear that a document is not negotiable which provides for delivery to order or bearer only if written instructions to that effect are given by a named person. Either tangible or electronic documents of title may be negotiable if the document meets the requirement of this section.

2.   Subsection (c) is derived from Section 3–104(d). Prior to issuance of the document of title, an issuer may stamp or otherwise provide by a notation on the document that it is nonnegotiable even if the document would otherwise comply with the requirement of subsection (a). Once issued as a negotiable document of title, the document cannot be changed from a negotiable document to a nonnegotiable document. A document of title that is nonnegotiable cannot be made negotiable by stamping or providing a notation that the document is negotiable. The only way to make a document of title negotiable is to comply with subsection (a). A negotiable document of title may fail to be duly negotiated if the negotiation does not comply with the requirements for "due negotiation" stated in Section 7–501.

Cross Reference:

Sections 7–501 and 7–502.

Definitional Cross References:

"Bearer". Section 1–201.
"Bill of lading". Section 1–201.
"Delivery". Section 1–201.
"Document of title". Section 1–201.
"Person". Section 1–201.
"Sign". Section 7–102
"Warehouse receipt". Section 1–201.

§ 7–105.   Reissuance in Alternative Medium.

(a)   Upon request of a person entitled under an electronic document of title, the issuer of the electronic document may issue a tangible document of title as a substitute for the electronic document if:

(1)   the person entitled under the electronic document surrenders control of the document to the issuer; and

(2)   the tangible document when issued contains a statement that it is issued in substitution for the electronic document.

(b)   Upon issuance of a tangible document of title in substitution for an electronic document of title in accordance with subsection (a):

(1)   the electronic document ceases to have any effect or validity; and

(2)   the person that procured issuance of the tangible document warrants to all subsequent persons entitled under the tangible document that the warrantor was a person entitled under the electronic document when the warrantor surrendered control of the electronic document to the issuer.

(c)   Upon request of a person entitled under a tangible document of title, the issuer of the tangible document may issue an electronic document of title as a substitute for the tangible document if:

(1)   the person entitled under the tangible document surrenders possession of the document to the issuer; and

(2)   the electronic document when issued contains a statement that it is issued in substitution for the tangible document.

(d)   Upon issuance of an electronic document of title in substitution for a tangible document of title in accordance with subsection (c):

(1)   the tangible document ceases to have any effect or validity; and

(2)   the person that procured issuance of the electronic document warrants to all subsequent persons entitled under the electronic document that the warrantor was a person entitled under the tangible document when the warrantor surrendered possession of the tangible document to the issuer.

Official Comment

Prior Uniform Statutory Provisions: None.

Other relevant law: UNCITRAL Draft Instrument on the Carriage of Goods by Sea Transport Law.

Purpose:

1.   This section allows for documents of title issued in one medium to be reissued in another medium. This section applies to both negotiable and nonnegotiable documents. This section sets forth minimum requirements for giving the reissued document effect and validity. The issuer is not required to issue a document in an alternative medium and if the issuer chooses to do so, it may impose additional requirements. Because a document of title imposes obligations on the issuer of the document, it is imperative for the issuer to be the one who issues the substitute document in order for the substitute document to be effective and valid.

2.   The request must be made to the issuer by the person entitled to enforce the document of title (Section 7–102(a)(9)) and that person must surrender possession or control of the original document to the issuer. The reissued document must have a notation that it has been issued as a substitute for the original document. These minimum requirements must be met in order to give the substitute document effect and validity. If these minimum requirements are not met for issuance of a substitute document of title, the original document of title continues to be effective and valid. Section 7–402. However, if the minimum requirements imposed by this section are met, in addition to any other requirements that the issuer may impose, the substitute document will be the document that is effective and valid.

3.   To protect parties who subsequently take the substitute document of title, the person who procured issuance of the substitute document warrants that it was a person entitled under the original document at the time it surrendered possession or control of the original document to the issuer. This warranty is modeled after the warranty found in Section 4–209.

Cross Reference:

Sections 7–106, 7–402 and 7–601.

Definitional Cross Reference:

"Person entitled to enforce". Section 7–102.

§ 7–106.   Control of Electronic Document of Title.

(a)   A person has control of an electronic document of title if a system employed for evidencing the transfer of interests in the electronic document reliably establishes that person as the person to which the electronic document was issued or transferred.

(b)   A system satisfies subsection (a), and a person is deemed to have control of an electronic document of title, if the document is created, stored, and assigned in such a manner that:

(1)   a single authoritative copy of the document exists which is unique, identifiable, and, except as otherwise provided in paragraphs (4), (5), and (6), unalterable;

(2)   the authoritative copy identifies the person asserting control as:

(A)   the person to which the document was issued; or

(B)   if the authoritative copy indicates that the document has been transferred, the person to which the document was most recently transferred;

(3)   the authoritative copy is communicated to and maintained by the person asserting control or its designated custodian;

(4)   copies or amendments that add or change an identified assignee of the authoritative copy can be made only with the consent of the person asserting control;

(5)   each copy of the authoritative copy and any copy of a copy is readily identifiable as a copy that is not the authoritative copy; and

(6)   any amendment of the authoritative copy is readily identifiable as authorized or unauthorized.

Official Comment

Prior Uniform Statutory Provision: Uniform Electronic Transactions Act Section 16.

Purpose:

1.   The section defines "control" for electronic documents of title and derives its rules from the Uniform Electronic Transactions Act § 16 on transferrable records. Unlike UETA § 16, however, a document of title may be reissued in an alternative medium pursuant to Section 7–105. At any point in time in which a document of title is in electronic form, the control concept of this section is relevant. As under UETA § 16, the control concept embodied in this section provides the legal framework for developing systems for electronic documents of title.

2.   Control of an electronic document of title substitutes for the concept of indorsement and possession in the tangible document of title context. See Section 7–501. A person with a tangible document of title delivers the document by voluntarily transferring possession and a person with an electronic document of title delivers the document by voluntarily transferring control. (Delivery is defined in Section 1–201).

3.   Subsection (a) sets forth the general rule that the "system employed for evidencing the transfer of interests in the electronic document reliably establishes that person as the person to which the electronic document was issued or transferred." The key to having a system that satisfies this test is that identity of *the* person to which the document was issued or transferred must be reliably established. Of great importance to the functioning of the control concept is to be able to demonstrate, at any point in time, *the person* entitled under the electronic document. For example, a carrier may issue an electronic bill of lading by having the required information in a database that is encrypted and accessible by virtue of a password. If the computer system in which the required information is maintained identifies the person as *the* person to which the electronic bill of lading was issued or transferred, that person has control of the electronic document of title. That identification may be by virtue of passwords or other encryption methods. Registry systems may satisfy this test. For example, see the electronic warehouse receipt system established pursuant to 7 C.F.R. Part 735. This Article leaves to the market place the development of sufficient technologies and business practices that will meet the test.

An electronic document of title is evidenced by a record consisting of information stored in an electronic medium. Section 1–201. For example, a record in a computer database could be an electronic document of title assuming that it otherwise meets the definition of document of title. To the extent that third parties wish to deal in paper mediums, Section 7–105 provides a mechanism for exiting the electronic environment by having the issuer reissue the document of title in a tangible medium. Thus if a person entitled to enforce an electronic document of title causes the information in the record to be printed onto paper without the issuer's involvement in issuing the document of title pursuant to Section 7–105, that paper is not a document of title.

4. Subsection (a) sets forth the general test for control. Subsection (b) sets forth a safe harbor test that if satisfied, results in control under the general test in subsection (a). The test in subsection (b) is also used in Section 9–105 although Section 9–105 does not include the general test of subsection (a).* Under subsection (b), at any point in time, a party should be able to identify the single authoritative copy which is unique and identifiable as the authoritative copy. This does not mean that once created that the authoritative copy need be static and never moved or copied from its original location. To the extent that backup systems exist which result in multiple copies, the key to this idea is that at any point in time, the one authoritative copy needs to be unique and identifiable.

Parties may not by contract provide that control exists. The test for control is a factual test that depends upon whether the general test in subsection (a) or the safe harbor in subsection (b) is satisfied.

5. Article 7 has historically provided for rights under documents of title and rights of transferees of documents of title as those rights relate to the goods covered by the document. Third parties may possess or have control of documents of title. While misfeasance or negligence in failure to transfer or misdelivery of the document by those third parties may create serious issues, this Article has never dealt with those issues as it relates to tangible documents of title, preferring to leave those issues to the law of contracts, agency and tort law. In the electronic document of title regime, third party registry systems are just beginning to develop. It is very difficult to write rules regulating those third parties without some definitive sense of how the third party registry systems will be structured. Systems that are evolving to date tend to be "closed" systems in which all participants must sign on to the master agreement which provides for rights as against the registry system as well as rights among the members. In those closed systems, the document of title never leaves the system so the parties rely upon the master agreement as to rights against the registry for its failures in dealing with the document. This article contemplates that those "closed" systems will continue to evolve and that the control mechanism in this statute provides a method for the participants in the closed system to achieve the benefits of obtaining control allowed by this article.

This article also contemplates that parties will evolve open systems where parties need not be subject to a master agreement. In an open system a party that is expecting to obtain rights through an electronic document may not be a party to the master agreement. To the extent that open systems evolve by use of the control concept contained in this section, the law of contracts, agency, and torts as it applies to the registry's misfeasance or negligence concerning the transfer of control of the electronic document will allocate the risks and liabilities of the parties as that other law now does so for third parties who hold tangible documents and fail to deliver the documents.

Cross Reference:

Sections 7–105 and 7–501.

Definitional Cross References:

"Delivery". 1–201.
"Document of title". 1–201.

PART 2

WAREHOUSE RECEIPTS: SPECIAL PROVISIONS

§ 7–201. Person That May Issue a Warehouse Receipt; Storage Under Bond.

(a) A warehouse receipt may be issued by any warehouse.

(b) If goods, including distilled spirits and agricultural commodities, are stored under a statute requiring a bond against withdrawal or a license for the issuance of receipts in the nature of warehouse receipts, a receipt issued for the goods is deemed to be a warehouse receipt even if issued by a person that is the owner of the goods and is not a warehouse.

---

* *Referring to Article 9 prior to the 2010 amendments.*

Prior Uniform Statutory Provision: Former Section 7–201.

Changes: Update for style only.

Purposes:

It is not intended by re-enactment of subsection (a) to repeal any provisions of special licensing or other statutes regulating who may become a warehouse. Limitations on the transfer of the receipts and criminal sanctions for violation of such limitations are not impaired. Section 7–103. Compare Section 7–401(4) on the liability of the issuer in such cases. Subsection (b) covers receipts issued by the owner for whiskey or other goods stored in bonded warehouses under such statutes as 26 U.S.C. Chapter 51.

Cross References:

Sections 7–103, 7–401.

Definitional Cross References:

"Warehouse receipt". Section 1–201.
"Warehouse". Section 7–102.

§ 7–202. Form of Warehouse Receipt; Effect of Omission.

(a)   A warehouse receipt need not be in any particular form.

(b)   Unless a warehouse receipt provides for each of the following, the warehouse is liable for damages caused to a person injured by its omission:

(1)   a statement of the location of the warehouse facility where the goods are stored;

(2)   the date of issue of the receipt;

(3)   the unique identification code of the receipt;

(4)   a statement whether the goods received will be delivered to the bearer, to a named person, or to a named person or its order;

(5)   the rate of storage and handling charges, unless goods are stored under a field warehousing arrangement, in which case a statement of that fact is sufficient on a nonnegotiable receipt;

(6)   a description of the goods or the packages containing them;

(7)   the signature of the warehouse or its agent;

(8)   if the receipt is issued for goods that the warehouse owns, either solely, jointly, or in common with others, a statement of the fact of that ownership; and

(9)   a statement of the amount of advances made and of liabilities incurred for which the warehouse claims a lien or security interest, unless the precise amount of advances made or liabilities incurred, at the time of the issue of the receipt, is unknown to the warehouse or to its agent that issued the receipt, in which case a statement of the fact that advances have been made or liabilities incurred and the purpose of the advances or liabilities is sufficient.

(c)   A warehouse may insert in its receipt any terms that are not contrary to [the Uniform Commercial Code] and do not impair its obligation of delivery under Section 7–403 or its duty of care under Section 7–204. Any contrary provision is ineffective.

Prior Uniform Statutory Provision: Former Section 7–202.

Changes: Language is updated to accommodate electronic commerce and to reflect modern style.

Purposes:

1.   This section does not displace any particular legislation that requires other terms in a warehouse receipt or that may require a particular form of a warehouse receipt. This section does not require that a warehouse

receipt be issued. A warehouse receipt that is issued need not contain any of the terms listed in subsection (b) in order to qualify as a warehouse receipt as long as the receipt falls within the definition of "warehouse receipt" in Article 1. Thus the title has been changed to eliminate the phrase "essential terms" as provided in prior law. The only consequence of a warehouse receipt not containing any term listed in subsection (b) is that a person injured by a term's omission has a right as against the warehouse for harm caused by the omission. Cases, such as *In re Celotex Corp.*, 134 B. R. 993 (Bankr. M.D. Fla. 1991), that held that in order to have a valid warehouse receipt all of the terms listed in this section must be contained in the receipt, are disapproved.

2. The unique identification code referred to in subsection (b)(3) can include any combination of letters, number, signs, and/or symbols that provide a unique identification. Whether an electronic or tangible warehouse receipt contains a signature will be resolved with the definition of sign in Section 7–102.

Cross References:

Sections 7–103 and 7–401.

Definitional Cross References:

"Bearer". Section 1–201.
"Delivery". Section 1–201.
"Goods". Section 7–102.
"Person". Section 1–201.
"Security interest". Section 1–201.
"Sign". Section 7–102.
"Term". Section 1–201.
"Warehouse receipt". Section 1–201.
"Warehouse". Section 7–102.

§ 7–203.   Liability for Nonreceipt or Misdescription.

A party to or purchaser for value in good faith of a document of title, other than a bill of lading, that relies upon the description of the goods in the document may recover from the issuer damages caused by the nonreceipt or misdescription of the goods, except to the extent that:

(1) the document conspicuously indicates that the issuer does not know whether all or part of the goods in fact were received or conform to the description, such as a case in which the description is in terms of marks or labels or kind, quantity, or condition, or the receipt or description is qualified by "contents, condition, and quality unknown", "said to contain", or words of similar import, if the indication is true; or

(2) the party or purchaser otherwise has notice of the nonreceipt or misdescription.

Official Comment

Prior Uniform Statutory Provision: Former Section 7–203.

Changes: Changes to this section are for style only.

Purpose:

This section is a simplified restatement of existing law as to the method by which a bailee may avoid responsibility for the accuracy of descriptions which are made by or in reliance upon information furnished by the depositor. The issuer is liable on documents issued by an agent, contrary to instructions of its principal, without receiving goods. No disclaimer of the latter liability is permitted.

Cross Reference:

Section 7–301.

Definitional Cross References:

"Conspicuous". Section 1–201.
"Document of title". Section 1–201.
"Goods". Section 7–102.
"Good Faith". Section 1–201. [7–102]

"Issuer". Section 7–102.
"Notice". Section 1–202.
"Party". Section 1–201.
"Purchaser". Section 1–201.
"Receipt of goods". Section 2–103.
"Value". Section 1–204.

§ 7–204.   Duty Of Care; Contractual Limitation of Warehouse's Liability.

(a)   A warehouse is liable for damages for loss of or injury to the goods caused by its failure to exercise care with regard to the goods that a reasonably careful person would exercise under similar circumstances. Unless otherwise agreed, the warehouse is not liable for damages that could not have been avoided by the exercise of that care.

(b)   Damages may be limited by a term in the warehouse receipt or storage agreement limiting the amount of liability in case of loss or damage beyond which the warehouse is not liable. Such a limitation is not effective with respect to the warehouse's liability for conversion to its own use. On request of the bailor in a record at the time of signing the storage agreement or within a reasonable time after receipt of the warehouse receipt, the warehouse's liability may be increased on part or all of the goods covered by the storage agreement or the warehouse receipt. In this event, increased rates may be charged based on an increased valuation of the goods.

(c)   Reasonable provisions as to the time and manner of presenting claims and commencing actions based on the bailment may be included in the warehouse receipt or storage agreement.

[(d)   This section does not modify or repeal [Insert reference to any statute that imposes a higher responsibility upon the warehouse or invalidates a contractual limitation that would be permissible under this Article].]

Legislative Note: Insert in subsection (d) a reference to any statute which imposes a higher responsibility upon the warehouse or invalidates a contractual limitation that would be permissible under this Article. If no such statutes exist, this section should be deleted.

Official Comment

Prior Uniform Statutory Provision: Former Section 7–204.

Changes: Updated to reflect modern, standard commercial practices.

Purposes of Changes:

1.   Subsection (a) continues the rule without change from former Section 7–204 on the warehouse's obligation to exercise reasonable care.

2.   Former Section 7–204(2) required that the term limiting damages do so by setting forth a specific liability per article or item or of a value per unit of weight. This requirement has been deleted as out of step with modern industry practice. Under subsection (b) a warehouse may limit its liability for damages for loss of or damage to the goods by a term in the warehouse receipt or storage agreement without the term constituting an impermissible disclaimer of the obligation of reasonable care. The parties cannot disclaim by contract the warehouse's obligation of care. Section 1–302. For example, limitations based upon per unit of weight, per package, per occurrence, or per receipt as well as limitations based upon a multiple of the storage rate may be commercially appropriate. As subsection (d) makes clear, the states or the federal government may supplement this section with more rigid standards of responsibility for some or all bailees.

3.   Former Section 7–204(2) also provided that an increased rate can not be charged if contrary to a tariff. That language has been deleted. If a tariff is required under state or federal law, pursuant to Section 7–103(a), the tariff would control over the rule of this section allowing an increased rate. The provisions of a non-mandatory tariff may be incorporated by reference in the parties' agreement. See Comment 2 to Section 7–103. Subsection (c) deletes the reference to tariffs for the same reason that the reference has been omitted in subsection (b).

4.   As under former Section 7–204(2), subsection (b) provides that a limitation of damages is ineffective if the warehouse has converted the goods to its own use. A mere failure to redeliver the goods is not conversion to the warehouse's own use. See *Adams v. Ryan & Christie Storage, Inc.*, 563 F. Supp. 409 (E.D. Pa. 1983) aff'd 725

F.2d 666 (3rd Cir. 1983). Cases such as *I.C.C. Metals Inc. v. Municipal Warehouse Co.*, 409 N.E.2d 849 (N.Y. Ct. App. 1980) holding that mere failure to redeliver results in a presumption of conversion to the warehouse's own use are disapproved. "Conversion to its own use" is narrower than the idea of conversion generally. Cases such as *Lipman v. Peterson*, 575 P.2d 19 (Kan. 1978) holding to the contrary are disapproved.

5. Storage agreements commonly establish the contractual relationship between warehouses and depositors who have an on-going relationship. The storage agreement may allow for the movement of goods into and out of a warehouse without the necessity of issuing or amending a warehouse receipt upon each entry or exit of goods from the warehouse.

Cross References:

Sections 1–302, 7–103, 7–309 and 7–403.

Definitional Cross References:

"Goods". Section 7–102.
"Reasonable time". Section 1–204.
"Sign". Section 7–102.
"Term". Section 1–201.
"Value". Section 1–204.
"Warehouse receipt". Section 1–201.
"Warehouse". Section 7–102.

§ 7–205.   Title Under Warehouse Receipt Defeated in Certain Cases.

A buyer in ordinary course of business of fungible goods sold and delivered by a warehouse that is also in the business of buying and selling such goods takes the goods free of any claim under a warehouse receipt even if the receipt is negotiable and has been duly negotiated.

Official Comment

Prior Uniform Statutory Provision: Former Section 7–205.

Changes: Changes for style only.

Purposes:

1. The typical case covered by this section is that of the warehouse-dealer in grain, and the substantive question at issue is whether in case the warehouse becomes insolvent the receipt holders shall be able to trace and recover grain shipped to farmers and other purchasers from the elevator. This was possible under the old acts, although courts were eager to find estoppels to prevent it. The practical difficulty of tracing fungible grain means that the preservation of this theoretical right adds little to the commercial acceptability of negotiable grain receipts, which really circulate on the credit of the warehouse. Moreover, on default of the warehouse, the receipt holders at least share in what grain remains, whereas retaking the grain from a good faith cash purchaser reduces the purchaser completely to the status of general creditor in a situation where there was very little the purchaser could do to guard against the loss. Compare 15 U.S.C. Section 714p enacted in 1955.

2. This provision applies to both negotiable and nonnegotiable warehouse receipts. The concept of due negotiation is provided for in 7–501. The definition of "buyer in ordinary course" is in Article 1 and provides, among other things, that a buyer must either have possession or a right to obtain the goods under Article 2 in order to be a buyer in ordinary course. This section requires actual delivery of the fungible goods to the buyer in ordinary course. Delivery requires voluntary transfer of possession of the fungible goods to the buyer. See amended Section 2–103.* This section is not satisfied by the delivery of the document of title to the buyer in ordinary course.

Cross References:

Sections 2–403 and 9–320.

Definitional Cross References:

"Buyer in ordinary course of business". Section 1–201.
"Delivery". Section 1–201.

---

*   *Referring to the 2003 amendments to Article 2, withdrawn in 2011.*

"Duly negotiate". Section 7–501.
"Fungible" goods. Section 1–201.
"Goods". Section 7–102.
"Value". Section 1–204.
"Warehouse receipt". Section 1–201.
"Warehouse". Section 7–102.

§ 7–206.   Termination of Storage at Warehouse's Option.

(a)   A warehouse, by giving notice to the person on whose account the goods are held and any other person known to claim an interest in the goods, may require payment of any charges and removal of the goods from the warehouse at the termination of the period of storage fixed by the document of title or, if a period is not fixed, within a stated period not less than 30 days after the warehouse gives notice. If the goods are not removed before the date specified in the notice, the warehouse may sell them pursuant to Section 7–210.

(b)   If a warehouse in good faith believes that goods are about to deteriorate or decline in value to less than the amount of its lien within the time provided in subsection (a) and Section 7–210, the warehouse may specify in the notice given under subsection (a) any reasonable shorter time for removal of the goods and, if the goods are not removed, may sell them at public sale held not less than one week after a single advertisement or posting.

(c)   If, as a result of a quality or condition of the goods of which the warehouse did not have notice at the time of deposit, the goods are a hazard to other property, the warehouse facilities, or other persons, the warehouse may sell the goods at public or private sale without advertisement or posting on reasonable notification to all persons known to claim an interest in the goods. If the warehouse, after a reasonable effort, is unable to sell the goods, it may dispose of them in any lawful manner and does not incur liability by reason of that disposition.

(d)   A warehouse shall deliver the goods to any person entitled to them under this article upon due demand made at any time before sale or other disposition under this section.

(e)   A warehouse may satisfy its lien from the proceeds of any sale or disposition under this section but shall hold the balance for delivery on the demand of any person to which the warehouse would have been bound to deliver the goods.

Official Comment

Prior Uniform Statutory Provision: Former Section 7–206.

Changes: Changes for style.

Purposes:

1.   This section provides for three situations in which the warehouse may terminate storage for reasons other then enforcement of its lien as permitted by Section 7–210. Most warehousing is for an indefinite term, the bailor being entitled to delivery on reasonable demand. It is necessary to define the warehouse's power to terminate the bailment, since it would be commercially intolerable to allow warehouses to order removal of the goods on short notice. The thirty day period provided where the document does not carry its own period of termination corresponds to commercial practice of computing rates on a monthly basis. The right to terminate under subsection (a) includes a right to require payment of "any charges", but does not depend on the existence of unpaid charges.

2.   In permitting expeditious disposition of perishable and hazardous goods the pre-Code Uniform Warehouse Receipts Act, Section 34, made no distinction between cases where the warehouse knowingly undertook to store such goods and cases where the goods were discovered to be of that character subsequent to storage. The former situation presents no such emergency as justifies the summary power of removal and sale. Subsections (b) and (c) distinguish between the two situations. The reason of this section should apply if the goods become hazardous during the course of storage. The process for selling the goods described in Section 7–210 governs the sale of goods under this section except as provided in subsections (b) and (c) for the situations described in those subsections respectively.

3.   Protection of its lien is the only interest which the warehouse has to justify summary sale of perishable goods which are not hazardous. This same interest must be recognized when the stored goods, although not perishable, decline in market value to a point which threatens the warehouse's security.

4.   The right to order removal of stored goods is subject to provisions of the public warehousing laws of some states forbidding warehouses from discriminating among customers. Nor does the section relieve the warehouse of any obligation under the state laws to secure the approval of a public official before disposing of deteriorating goods. Such regulatory statutes and the regulations under them remain in force and operative. Section 7–103.

Cross References:

Sections 7–103 and 7–403.

Definitional Cross References:

"Delivery". Section 1–201.
"Document of title". Section 1–102.
"Good faith". Section 1–201 [7–102].
"Goods". Section 7–102.
"Notice". Section 1–202.
"Notification". Section 1–202.
"Person". Section 1–201.
"Reasonable time". Section 1–205.
"Value". Section 1–204.
"Warehouse". Section 7–102.

§ 7–207.   Goods Must Be Kept Separate; Fungible Goods.

(a)   Unless the warehouse receipt provides otherwise, a warehouse shall keep separate the goods covered by each receipt so as to permit at all times identification and delivery of those goods. However, different lots of fungible goods may be commingled.

(b)   If different lots of fungible goods are commingled, the goods are owned in common by the persons entitled thereto and the warehouse is severally liable to each owner for that owner's share. If, because of overissue, a mass of fungible goods is insufficient to meet all the receipts the warehouse has issued against it, the persons entitled include all holders to which overissued receipts have been duly negotiated.

Official Comment

Prior Uniform Statutory Provision: Former Section 7–207.

Changes: Changes for style only.

Purposes:

No change of substance is made from former Section 7–207. Holders to whom overissued receipts have been duly negotiated shall share in a mass of fungible goods. Where individual ownership interests are merged into claims on a common fund, as is necessarily the case with fungible goods, there is no policy reason for discriminating between successive purchasers of similar claims.

Definitional Cross References:

"Delivery". Section 1–201.
"Duly negotiate". Section 7–501.
"Fungible goods". Section 1–201.
"Goods". Section 7–102.
"Holder". Section 1–201.
"Person". Section 1–201.
"Warehouse receipt". Section 1–201.
"Warehouse". Section 7–102.

§ 7–208.   Altered Warehouse Receipts.

If a blank in a negotiable tangible warehouse receipt has been filled in without authority, a good-faith purchaser for value and without notice of the lack of authority may treat the insertion as authorized. Any other unauthorized alteration leaves any tangible or electronic warehouse receipt enforceable against the issuer according to its original tenor.

Official Comment

Prior Uniform Statutory Provision: Former Section 7–208.

Changes: To accommodate electronic documents of title.

Purpose:

1.   The execution of tangible warehouse receipts in blank is a dangerous practice. As between the issuer and an innocent purchaser the risks should clearly fall on the former. The purchaser must have purchased the tangible negotiable warehouse receipt in good faith and for value to be protected under the rule of the first sentence which is a limited exception to the general rule in the second sentence. Electronic document of title systems should have protection against unauthorized access and unauthorized changes. See 7–106. Thus the protection for good faith purchasers found in the first sentence is not necessary in the context of electronic documents.

2.   Under the second sentence of this section, an unauthorized alteration whether made with or without fraudulent intent does not relieve the issuer of its liability on the warehouse receipt as originally executed. The unauthorized alteration itself is of course ineffective against the warehouse. The rule stated in the second sentence applies to both tangible and electronic warehouse receipts.

Definitional Cross References:

"Good faith". Section 1–201 [7–102].
"Issuer". Section 7–102.
"Notice". Section 1–202.
"Purchaser". Section 1–201.
"Value". Section 1–204.
"Warehouse receipt". Section 1–201.

§ 7–209.   Lien of Warehouse.

(a)   A warehouse has a lien against the bailor on the goods covered by a warehouse receipt or storage agreement or on the proceeds thereof in its possession for charges for storage or transportation, including demurrage and terminal charges, insurance, labor, or other charges, present or future, in relation to the goods, and for expenses necessary for preservation of the goods or reasonably incurred in their sale pursuant to law. If the person on whose account the goods are held is liable for similar charges or expenses in relation to other goods whenever deposited and it is stated in the warehouse receipt or storage agreement that a lien is claimed for charges and expenses in relation to other goods, the warehouse also has a lien against the goods covered by the warehouse receipt or storage agreement or on the proceeds thereof in its possession for those charges and expenses, whether or not the other goods have been delivered by the warehouse. However, as against a person to which a negotiable warehouse receipt is duly negotiated, a warehouse's lien is limited to charges in an amount or at a rate specified in the warehouse receipt or, if no charges are so specified, to a reasonable charge for storage of the specific goods covered by the receipt subsequent to the date of the receipt.

(b)   A warehouse may also reserve a security interest against the bailor for the maximum amount specified on the receipt for charges other than those specified in subsection (a), such as for money advanced and interest. The security interest is governed by Article 9.

(c)   A warehouse's lien for charges and expenses under subsection (a) or a security interest under subsection (b) is also effective against any person that so entrusted the bailor with possession of the goods that a pledge of them by the bailor to a good-faith purchaser for value would have been valid. However, the lien or security interest is not effective against a person that before issuance of a document of title had a legal interest or a perfected security interest in the goods and that did not:

(1) deliver or entrust the goods or any document of title covering the goods to the bailor or the bailor's nominee with:

    (A) actual or apparent authority to ship, store, or sell;

    (B) power to obtain delivery under Section 7–403; or

    (C) power of disposition under Sections 2–403, 2A–304(2), 2A–305(2), 9–320, or 9–321(c) or other statute or rule of law; or

(2) acquiesce in the procurement by the bailor or its nominee of any document.

(d) A warehouse's lien on household goods for charges and expenses in relation to the goods under subsection (a) is also effective against all persons if the depositor was the legal possessor of the goods at the time of deposit. In this subsection, "household goods" means furniture, furnishings, or personal effects used by the depositor in a dwelling.

(e) A warehouse loses its lien on any goods that it voluntarily delivers or unjustifiably refuses to deliver.

Official Comment

Prior Uniform Statutory Provision: Former Sections 7–209 and 7–503.

Changes: Expanded to recognize warehouse lien when a warehouse receipt is not issued but goods are covered by a storage agreement.

Purposes:

1. Subsection (a) defines the warehouse's statutory lien. Other than allowing a warehouse to claim a lien under this section when there is a storage agreement and not a warehouse receipt, this section remains unchanged in substance from former Section 7–209(1). Under the first sentence, a specific lien attaches automatically without express notation on the receipt or storage agreement with regard to goods stored under the receipt or the storage agreement. That lien is limited to the usual charges arising out of a storage transaction.

    Example 1: Bailor stored goods with a warehouse and the warehouse issued a warehouse receipt. A lien against those goods arose as set forth in subsection (a), the first sentence, for the charges for storage and the other expenses of those goods. The warehouse may enforce its lien under Section 7–210 as against the bailor. Whether the warehouse receipt is negotiable or nonnegotiable is not important to the warehouse's rights as against the bailor.

Under the second sentence, by notation on the receipt or storage agreement, the lien can be made a general lien extending to like charges in relation to other goods. Both the specific lien and general lien are as to goods in the possession of the warehouse and extend to proceeds from the goods as long as the proceeds are in the possession of the warehouse. The same rules apply whether the receipt is negotiable or non-negotiable.

    Example 2: Bailor stored goods (lot A) with a warehouse and the warehouse issued a warehouse receipt for those goods. In the warehouse receipt it is stated that the warehouse will also have a lien on goods covered by the warehouse receipt for storage charges and the other expenses for any other goods that are stored with the warehouse by the bailor. The statement about the lien on other goods does not specify an amount or a rate. Bailor then stored other goods (lot B) with the warehouse. Under subsection (a), first sentence, the warehouse has a lien on the specific goods (lot A) covered by the warehouse receipt. Under subsection (a), second sentence, the warehouse has a lien on the goods in lot A for the storage charges and the other expenses arising from the goods in lot B. That lien is enforceable as against the bailor regardless of whether the receipt is negotiable or nonnegotiable.

Under the third sentence, if the warehouse receipt is negotiable, the lien as against a holder of that receipt by due negotiation is limited to the amount or rate specified on the receipt for the specific lien or the general lien, or, if none is specified, to a reasonable charge for storage of the specific goods covered by the receipt for storage after the date of the receipt.

    Example 3: Same facts as Example 1 except that the warehouse receipt is negotiable and has been duly negotiated (Section 7–501) to a person other than the bailor. Under the last sentence of subsection (a), the warehouse may enforce its lien against the bailor's goods stored in the warehouse as against the person to whom the negotiable warehouse receipt has been duly negotiated. Section 7–502. That lien is limited to the charges or rates specified in the receipt or a reasonable charge for storage as stated in the last sentence of subsection (a).

Example 4: Same facts as Example 2 except that the warehouse receipt is negotiable and has been duly negotiated (Section 7–501) to a person other than the bailor. Under the last sentence of subsection (a), the lien on lot A goods for the storage charges and the other expenses arising from storage of lot B goods is not enforceable as against the person to whom the receipt has been duly negotiated. Without a statement of a specified amount or rate for the general lien, the warehouse's general lien is not enforceable as against the person to whom the negotiable document has been duly negotiated. However, the warehouse lien for charges and expenses related to storage of lot A goods is still enforceable as against the person to whom the receipt was duly negotiated.

Example 5. Same facts as Examples 2 and 4 except the warehouse had stated on the negotiable warehouse receipt a specified amount or rate for the general lien on other goods (lot B). Under the last sentence of subsection (a), the general lien on lot A goods for the storage charges and the other expenses arising from storage of lot B goods is enforceable as against the person to whom the receipt has been duly negotiated.

2. Subsection (b) provides for a security interest based upon agreement. Such a security interest arises out of relations between the parties other than bailment for storage or transportation, as where the bailee assumes the role of financier or performs a manufacturing operation, extending credit in reliance upon the goods covered by the receipt. Such a security interest is not a statutory lien. Compare Sections 9–109 and 9–333. It is governed in all respects by Article 9, except that subsection (b) requires that the receipt specify a maximum amount and limits the security interest to the amount specified. A warehouse could also take a security interest to secure its charges for storage and the other expenses listed in subsection (a) to protect these claims upon the loss of the statutory possessory warehouse lien if the warehouse loses possession of the goods as provided in subsection (e).

Example 6: Bailor stores goods with a warehouse and the warehouse issues a warehouse receipt that states that the warehouse is taking a security interest in the bailed goods for charges of storage, expenses, for money advanced, for manufacturing services rendered, and all other obligations that the bailor may owe the warehouse. That is a security interest covered in all respects by Article 9. Subsection (b). As allowed by this section, a warehouse may rely upon its statutory possessory lien to protect its charges for storage and the other expenses related to storage. For those storage charges covered by the statutory possessory lien, the warehouse is not required to use a security interest under subsection (b).

3. Subsections (a) and (b) validate the lien and security interest "against the bailor." Under basic principles of derivative rights as provided in Section 7–504, the warehouse lien is also valid as against parties who obtain their rights from the bailor except as otherwise provided in subsection (a), third sentence, or subsection (c).

Example 7: Bailor stores goods with a warehouse and the warehouse issues a nonnegotiable warehouse receipt that also claims a general lien in other goods stored with the warehouse. A lien on the bailed goods for the charges for storage and the other expenses arises under subsection (a). Bailor notifies the warehouse that the goods have been sold to Buyer and the bailee acknowledges that fact to the Buyer. Section 2–503. The warehouse lien for storage of those goods is effective against Buyer for both the specific lien and the general lien. Section 7–504.

Example 8: Bailor stores goods with a warehouse and the warehouse issues a nonnegotiable warehouse receipt. A lien on the bailed goods for the charges for storage and the other expenses arises under subsection (a). Bailor grants a security interest in the goods while the goods are in the warehouse's possession to Secured Party (SP) who properly perfects a security interest in the goods. See Revised 9–312(d). The warehouse lien is superior in priority over SP's security interest. See Revised 9–203(b)(2) (debtor can grant a security interest to the extent of debtor's rights in the collateral).

Example 9: Bailor stores goods with a warehouse and the warehouse issues a negotiable warehouse receipt. A lien on the bailed goods for the charges for storage and the other expenses arises under subsection (a). Bailor grants a security interest in the negotiable document to SP. SP properly perfects its interest in the negotiable document by taking possession through a "due negotiation." Revised 9–312(c). SP's security interest is subordinate to the warehouse lien. Section 7–209(a), third sentence. Given that bailor's rights are subject to the warehouse lien, the bailor cannot grant to the SP greater rights than the bailor has under Section 9–203(b)(2), perfection of the security interest in the negotiable document and the goods covered by the document through SP's filing of a financing statement should not give a different result.

As against third parties who have interests in the goods prior to the storage with the warehouse, subsection (c) continues the rule under the prior uniform statutory provision that to validate the lien or security interest of the warehouse, the owner must have entrusted the goods to the depositor, and that the circumstances must be such that a pledge by the depositor to a good faith purchaser for value would have been valid. Thus the owner's interest will not be subjected to a lien or security interest arising out of a deposit of its goods by a thief. The warehouse may be protected because of the actual, implied or apparent authority of the depositor, because of a Factor's Act, or because of other circumstances which would protect a bona fide pledgee, unless those circumstances are denied effect under the second sentence of subsection (c). The language of Section 7–503 is brought into subsection (c) for purposes of clarity. The comments to Section 7–503 are helpful in interpreting delivery, entrustment or acquiescence.

Where the third party is the holder of a security interest, obtained prior to the issuance of a negotiable warehouse receipt, the rights of the warehouse depend on the priority given to a hypothetical bona fide pledgee by Article 9, particularly Section 9–322. Thus the special priority granted to statutory liens by Section 9–333 does not apply to liens under subsection (a) of this section, since subsection (c), second sentence, "expressly provides otherwise" within the meaning of Section 9–333.

As to household goods, however, subsection (d) makes the warehouse's lien "for charges and expenses in relation to the goods" effective against all persons if the depositor was the legal possessor. The purpose of the exception is to permit the warehouse to accept household goods for storage in sole reliance on the value of the goods themselves, especially in situations of family emergency.

Example 10: Bailor grants a perfected security interest in the goods to SP prior to storage of the goods with the warehouse. Bailor then stores goods with the warehouse and the warehouse issues a warehouse receipt for the goods. A warehouse lien on the bailed goods for the charges for storage or other expenses arises under subsection (a). The warehouse lien is not effective as against SP unless SP entrusted the goods to the bailor with actual or apparent authority to ship store, or sell the goods or with power of disposition under subsection (c)(1) or acquiesced in the bailor's procurement of a document of title under subsection (c)(2). This result obtains whether the receipt is negotiable or nonnegotiable.

Example 11: Sheriff who had lawfully repossessed household goods in an eviction action stored the goods with a warehouse. A lien on the bailed goods arises under subsection (a). The lien is effective as against the owner of the goods. Subsection (d).

4. As under previous law, this section creates a statutory possessory lien in favor of the warehouse on the goods stored with the warehouse or on the proceeds of the goods. The warehouse loses its lien if it loses possession of the goods or the proceeds. Subsection (e).

5. Where goods have been stored under a non-negotiable warehouse receipt and are sold by the person to whom the receipt has been issued, frequently the goods are not withdrawn by the new owner. The obligations of the seller of the goods in this situation are set forth in Section 2–503(4) on tender of delivery and include procurement of an acknowledgment by the bailee of the buyer's right to possession of the goods. If a new receipt is requested, such an acknowledgment can be withheld until storage charges have been paid or provided for. The statutory lien for charges on the goods sold, granted by the first sentence of subsection (a), continues valid unless the bailee gives it up. See Section 7–403. But once a new receipt is issued to the buyer, the buyer becomes "the person on whose account the goods are held" under the second sentence of subsection (a); unless the buyer undertakes liability for charges in relation to other goods stored by the seller, there is no general lien against the buyer for such charges. Of course, the bailee may preserve the general lien in such a case either by an arrangement by which the buyer "is liable for" such charges, or by reserving a security interest under subsection (b).

6. A possessory warehouse lien arises as provided under subsection (a) if the parties to the bailment have a storage agreement or a warehouse receipt is issued. In the modern warehouse, the bailor and the bailee may enter into a master contract governing the bailment with the bailee and bailor keeping track of the goods stored pursuant to the master contract by notation on their respective books and records and the parties send notification via electronic communication as to what goods are covered by the master contract. Warehouse receipts are not issued. See Comment 4 to Section 7–204. There is no particular form for a warehouse receipt and failure to contain any of the terms listed in Section 7–202 does not deprive the warehouse of its lien that arises under subsection (a). See the comment to Section 7–202.

Cross References:

Point 1: Sections 7–501 and 7–502.

Point 2: Sections 9–109 and 9–333.
Point 3: Sections 2–503, 7–503, 7–504, 9–203, 9–312, and 9–322.
Point 4: Sections 2–503, 7–501, 7–502, 7–504, 9–312, 9–331, 9–333, 9–401.
Point 5: Sections 2–503 and 7–403.
Point 6: Sections 7–202 and 7–204.

Definitional Cross References:

"Delivery". Section 1–201.
"Document of Title". Section 1–201
"Goods". Section 7–102.
"Money". Section 1–201.
"Person". Section 1–201.
"Purchaser". Section 1–201.
"Right". Section 1–201.
"Security interest". Section 1–201.
"Value". Section 1–204.
"Warehouse receipt". Section 1–201.
"Warehouse". Section 7–102.

§ 7–210. Enforcement of Warehouse's Lien.

(a) Except as otherwise provided in subsection (b), a warehouse's lien may be enforced by public or private sale of the goods, in bulk or in packages, at any time or place and on any terms that are commercially reasonable, after notifying all persons known to claim an interest in the goods. The notification must include a statement of the amount due, the nature of the proposed sale, and the time and place of any public sale. The fact that a better price could have been obtained by a sale at a different time or in a method different from that selected by the warehouse is not of itself sufficient to establish that the sale was not made in a commercially reasonable manner. The warehouse sells in a commercially reasonable manner if the warehouse sells the goods in the usual manner in any recognized market therefor, sells at the price current in that market at the time of the sale, or otherwise sells in conformity with commercially reasonable practices among dealers in the type of goods sold. A sale of more goods than apparently necessary to be offered to ensure satisfaction of the obligation is not commercially reasonable, except in cases covered by the preceding sentence.

(b) A warehouse may enforce its lien on goods, other than goods stored by a merchant in the course of its business, only if the following requirements are satisfied:

(1) All persons known to claim an interest in the goods must be notified.

(2) The notification must include an itemized statement of the claim, a description of the goods subject to the lien, a demand for payment within a specified time not less than 10 days after receipt of the notification, and a conspicuous statement that unless the claim is paid within that time the goods will be advertised for sale and sold by auction at a specified time and place.

(3) The sale must conform to the terms of the notification.

(4) The sale must be held at the nearest suitable place to where the goods are held or stored.

(5) After the expiration of the time given in the notification, an advertisement of the sale must be published once a week for two weeks consecutively in a newspaper of general circulation where the sale is to be held. The advertisement must include a description of the goods, the name of the person on whose account the goods are being held, and the time and place of the sale. The sale must take place at least 15 days after the first publication. If there is no newspaper of general circulation where the sale is to be held, the advertisement must be posted at least 10 days before the sale in not fewer than six conspicuous places in the neighborhood of the proposed sale.

(c) Before any sale pursuant to this section, any person claiming a right in the goods may pay the amount necessary to satisfy the lien and the reasonable expenses incurred in complying with this section.

In that event, the goods may not be sold but must be retained by the warehouse subject to the terms of the receipt and this article.

(d)   A warehouse may buy at any public sale held pursuant to this section.

(e)   A purchaser in good faith of goods sold to enforce a warehouse's lien takes the goods free of any rights of persons against which the lien was valid, despite the warehouse's noncompliance with this section.

(f)   A warehouse may satisfy its lien from the proceeds of any sale pursuant to this section but shall hold the balance, if any, for delivery on demand to any person to which the warehouse would have been bound to deliver the goods.

(g)   The rights provided by this section are in addition to all other rights allowed by law to a creditor against a debtor.

(h)   If a lien is on goods stored by a merchant in the course of its business, the lien may be enforced in accordance with subsection (a) or (b).

(i)   A warehouse is liable for damages caused by failure to comply with the requirements for sale under this section and, in case of willful violation, is liable for conversion.

Official Comment

Prior Uniform Statutory Provision: Former Section 7–210.

Changes: Update to accommodate electronic commerce and for style.

Purposes:

1.   Subsection (a) makes "commercial reasonableness" the standard for foreclosure proceedings in all cases except non-commercial storage with a warehouse. The latter category embraces principally storage of household goods by private owners; and for such cases the detailed provisions as to notification, publication and public sale are retained in subsection (b) with one change. The requirement in former Section 7–210(2)(b) that the notification must be sent in person or by registered or certified mail has been deleted. Notification may be sent by any reasonable means as provided in Section 1–202. The swifter, more flexible procedure of subsection (a) is appropriate to commercial storage. Compare seller's power of resale on breach by buyer under the provisions of the Article on Sales (Section 2–706). Commercial reasonableness is a flexible concept that allows for a wide variety of actions to satisfy the rule of this section, including electronic means of posting and sale.

2.   The provisions of subsections (d) and (e) permitting the bailee to bid at public sales and confirming the title of purchasers at foreclosure sales are designed to secure more bidding and better prices and remain unchanged from former Section 7–210.

3.   A warehouses may have recourse to an interpleader action in appropriate circumstances. See Section 7–603.

4.   If a warehouse has both a warehouse lien and a security interest, the warehouse may enforce both the lien and the security interest simultaneously by using the procedures of Article 9. Section 7–210 adopts as its touchstone "commercial reasonableness" for the enforcement of a warehouse lien. Following the procedures of Article 9 satisfies "commercial reasonableness."

Cross Reference:

Sections 2–706, 7–403, 7–603 and Part 6 of Article 9.

Definitional Cross References:

"Bill of lading". Section 1–201.
"Conspicuous". Section 1–201.
"Creditor". Section 1–201.
"Delivery". Section 1–201.
"Document of title". Section 1–201.
"Good faith". Section 1–201 [7–102].
"Goods". Section 7–102.
"Notification". Section 1–202.

"Notifies". Section 1–202.
"Person". Section 1–201.
"Purchaser". Section 1–201.
"Rights". Section 1–201.
"Term". Section 1–201.
"Warehouse". Section 7–102.

PART 3

BILLS OF LADING: SPECIAL PROVISIONS

§ 7–301.   Liability for Nonreceipt or Misdescription; "Said to Contain"; "Shipper's Weight, Load, and Count"; Improper Handling.

(a)   A consignee of a nonnegotiable bill of lading which has given value in good faith, or a holder to which a negotiable bill has been duly negotiated, relying upon the description of the goods in the bill or upon the date shown in the bill, may recover from the issuer damages caused by the misdating of the bill or the nonreceipt or misdescription of the goods, except to the extent that the bill indicates that the issuer does not know whether any part or all of the goods in fact were received or conform to the description, such as in a case in which the description is in terms of marks or labels or kind, quantity, or condition or the receipt or description is qualified by "contents or condition of contents of packages unknown", "said to contain", "shipper's weight, load, and count," or words of similar import, if that indication is true.

(b)   If goods are loaded by the issuer of a bill of lading;

(1)   the issuer shall count the packages of goods if shipped in packages and ascertain the kind and quantity if shipped in bulk; and

(2)   words such as "shipper's weight, load, and count," or words of similar import indicating that the description was made by the shipper are ineffective except as to goods concealed in packages.

(c)   If bulk goods are loaded by a shipper that makes available to the issuer of a bill of lading adequate facilities for weighing those goods, the issuer shall ascertain the kind and quantity within a reasonable time after receiving the shipper's request in a record to do so. In that case, "shipper's weight" or words of similar import are ineffective.

(d)   The issuer of a bill of lading, by including in the bill the words "shipper's weight, load, and count," or words of similar import, may indicate that the goods were loaded by the shipper, and, if that statement is true, the issuer is not liable for damages caused by the improper loading. However, omission of such words does not imply liability for damages caused by improper loading.

(e)   A shipper guarantees to an issuer the accuracy at the time of shipment of the description, marks, labels, number, kind, quantity, condition, and weight, as furnished by the shipper, and the shipper shall indemnify the issuer against damage caused by inaccuracies in those particulars. This right of indemnity does not limit the issuer's responsibility or liability under the contract of carriage to any person other than the shipper.

Official Comment

Prior Uniform Statutory Provision: Former Section 7–301.

Changes: Changes for clarity, style and to recognize deregulation in the transportation industry.

Purposes:

1.   This section continues the rules from former Section 7–301 with one substantive change. The obligations of the issuer of the bill of lading under former subsections (2) and (3) were limited to issuers who were common carriers. Subsections (b) and (c) apply the same rules to all issuers not just common carriers. This section is compatible with the policies stated in the federal Bills of Lading Act, 49 U.S.C. § 80113 (2000).

2.   The language of the pre-Code Uniform Bills of Lading Act suggested that a carrier is ordinarily liable for damage caused by improper loading, but may relieve itself of liability by disclosing on the bill that shipper actually loaded. A more accurate statement of the law is that the carrier is not liable for losses caused by act or default of the shipper, which would include improper loading. *D. H. Overmyer Co. v. Nelson Brantley Glass Co.*, 168 S.E.2d 176 (Ga. Ct. App. 1969). There was some question whether under pre-Code law a carrier was liable even to a good faith purchaser of a negotiable bill for such losses, if the shipper's faulty loading in fact caused the loss. Subsection (d) permits the carrier to bar, by disclosure of shipper's loading, liability to a good faith purchaser. There is no implication that decisions such as *Modern Tool Corp. v. Pennsylvania R. Co.*, 100 F.Supp. 595 (D.N.J.1951), are disapproved.

3.   This section is a restatement of existing law as to the method by which a bailee may avoid responsibility for the accuracy of descriptions which are made by or in reliance upon information furnished by the depositor or shipper. The wording in this section—"contents or condition of contents of packages unknown" or "shipper's weight, load and count"—to indicate that the shipper loaded the goods or that the carrier does not know the description, condition, or contents of the loaded packages continues to be appropriate as commonly understood in the transportation industry. The reasons for this wording are as important in 2002 as when the prior section initially was approved. The issuer is liable on documents issued by an agent, contrary to instructions of his principal, without receiving goods. No disclaimer of this liability is permitted since it is not a matter either of the care of the goods or their description.

4.   The shipper's erroneous report to the carrier concerning the goods may cause damage to the carrier. Subsection (e) therefore provides appropriate indemnity.

5.   The word "freight" in the former Section 7–301 has been changed to "goods" to conform to international and domestic land transport usage in which "freight" means the price paid for carriage of the goods and not the goods themselves. Hence, changing the word "freight" to the word "goods" is a clarifying change that fits both international and domestic practice.

Cross References:

Sections 7–203, 7–309 and 7–501.

Definitional Cross References:

"Bill of lading". Section 1–201.

"Consignee". Section 7–102.

"Document of title". Section 1–201.

"Duly negotiate". Section 7–501.

"Good faith". Section 1–201. [7–102].

"Goods". Section 7–102.

"Holder". Section 1–201.

"Issuer". Section 7–102.

"Notice". Section 1–202.

"Party". Section 1–201.

"Purchaser." Section 1–201.

"Receipt of goods". Section 2–103.

"Value". Section 1–204.

§ 7–302.   Through Bills of Lading and Similar Documents of Title.

(a)   The issuer of a through bill of lading, or other document of title embodying an undertaking to be performed in part by a person acting as its agent or by a performing carrier, is liable to any person entitled to recover on the bill or other document for any breach by the other person or the performing carrier of its obligation under the bill or other document. However, to the extent that the bill or other document covers an undertaking to be performed overseas or in territory not contiguous to the continental United States or an undertaking including matters other than transportation, this liability for breach by the other person or the performing carrier may be varied by agreement of the parties.

(b)   If goods covered by a through bill of lading or other document of title embodying an undertaking to be performed in part by a person other than the issuer are received by that person, the person is subject, with respect to its own performance while the goods are in its possession, to the obligation of the issuer. The person's obligation is discharged by delivery of the goods to another person pursuant to the bill or other document and does not include liability for breach by any other person or by the issuer.

(c)   The issuer of a through bill of lading or other document of title described in subsection (a) is entitled to recover from the performing carrier, or other person in possession of the goods when the breach of the obligation under the bill or other document occurred:

(1)   the amount it may be required to pay to any person entitled to recover on the bill or other document for the breach, as may be evidenced by any receipt, judgment, or transcript of judgment; and

(2)   the amount of any expense reasonably incurred by the issuer in defending any action commenced by any person entitled to recover on the bill or other document for the breach.

Official Comment

Prior Uniform Statutory Provision: Former Section 7–302.

Changes: To conform to current terminology and for style.

Purposes:

1.   This section continues the rules from former Section 7–302 without substantive change. The term "performing carrier" is substituted for the term "connecting carrier" to conform the terminology of this section with terminology used in recent UNCITRAL and OAS proposals concerning transportation and through bills of lading. This change in terminology is not substantive. This section is compatible with liability on carriers under federal law. See 49 U.S.C. §§ 11706, 14706 and 15906.

The purpose of this section is to subject the initial carrier under a through bill to suit for breach of the contract of carriage by any performing carrier and to make it clear that any such performing carrier holds the goods on terms which are defined by the document of title even though such performing carrier did not issue the document. Since the performing carrier does hold the goods on the terms of the document, it must honor a proper demand for delivery or a diversion order just as the original bailee would have to. Similarly it has the benefits of the excuses for non-delivery and limitations of liability provided for the original bailee who issued the bill. Unlike the original bailee-issuer, the performing carrier's responsibility is limited to the period while the goods are in its possession. The section does not impose any obligation to issue through bills.

2.   The reference to documents other than through bills looks to the possibility that multi-purpose documents may come into use, e.g., combination warehouse receipts and bills of lading. As electronic documents of title come into common usage, storage documents (e.g. warehouse receipts) and transportation documents (e.g. bills of lading) may merge seamlessly into one electronic document that can serve both the storage and transportation segments of the movement of goods.

3.   Under subsection (a) the issuer of a through bill of lading may become liable for the fault of another person. Subsection (c) gives the issuer appropriate rights of recourse.

4.   Despite the broad language of subsection (a), Section 7–302 is subject to preemption by federal laws and treaties. Section 7–103. The precise scope of federal preemption in the transportation sector is a question determined under federal law.

Cross reference:

Section 7–103.

Definitional Cross References:

"Agreement". Section 1–201.
"Bailee". Section 7–102.
"Bill of lading". Section 1–201.
"Delivery". Section 1–201.
"Document of title". Section 1–201.
"Goods". Section 7–102.

"Issuer". Section 7–102.

"Party". Section 1–201.

"Person". Section 1–201.

§ 7–303.   Diversion; Reconsignment; Change of Instructions.

(a)   Unless the bill of lading otherwise provides, a carrier may deliver the goods to a person or destination other than that stated in the bill or may otherwise dispose of the goods, without liability for misdelivery, on instructions from:

(1)   the holder of a negotiable bill;

(2)   the consignor on a nonnegotiable bill, even if the consignee has given contrary instructions;

(3)   the consignee on a nonnegotiable bill in the absence of contrary instructions from the consignor, if the goods have arrived at the billed destination or if the consignee is in possession of the tangible bill or in control of the electronic bill; or

(4)   the consignee on a nonnegotiable bill, if the consignee is entitled as against the consignor to dispose of the goods.

(b)   Unless instructions described in subsection (a) are included in a negotiable bill of lading, a person to which the bill is duly negotiated may hold the bailee according to the original terms.

Official Comment

Prior Uniform Statutory Provision: Former Section 7–303.

Changes: To accommodate electronic documents and for style.

Purposes:

1.   Diversion is a very common commercial practice which defeats delivery to the consignee originally named in a bill of lading. This section continues former Section 7–303's safe harbor rules for carriers in situations involving diversion and adapts those rules to electronic documents of title. This section works compatibly with Section 2–705. Carriers may as a business matter be willing to accept instructions from consignees in which case the carrier will be liable for misdelivery if the consignee was not the owner or otherwise empowered to dispose of the goods under subsection (a)(4). The section imposes no duty on carriers to undertake diversion. The carrier is of course subject to the provisions of mandatory filed tariffs as provided in Section 7–103.

2.   It should be noted that the section provides only an immunity for carriers against liability for "misdelivery." It does not, for example, defeat the title to the goods which the consignee-buyer may have acquired from the consignor-seller upon delivery of the goods to the carrier under a non-negotiable bill of lading. Thus if the carrier, upon instructions from the consignor, returns the goods to the consignor, the consignee may recover the goods from the consignor or the consignor's insolvent estate. However, under certain circumstances, the consignee's title may be defeated by diversion of the goods in transit to a different consignee. The rights that arise between the consignor-seller and the consignee-buyer out of a contract for the sale of goods are governed by Article 2.

Cross References:

Point 1: Sections 2–705 and 7–103.

Point 2: Article 2, Sections 7–403 and 7–504(3).

Definitional Cross References:

"Bailee". Section 7–102.

"Bill of lading". Section 1–201.

"Carrier". Section 7–102

"Consignee". Section 7–102.

"Consignor". Section 7–102.

"Delivery". Section 1–201.

"Goods". Section 7–102.

"Holder". Section 1–201.
"Notice". Section 1–202.
"Person". Section 1–201.
"Purchaser". Section 1–201.
"Term". Section 1–201.

§ 7–304.   Tangible Bills of Lading in a Set.

(a) Except as customary in international transportation, a tangible bill of lading may not be issued in a set of parts. The issuer is liable for damages caused by violation of this subsection.

(b) If a tangible bill of lading is lawfully issued in a set of parts, each of which contains an identification code and is expressed to be valid only if the goods have not been delivered against any other part, the whole of the parts constitutes one bill.

(c) If a tangible negotiable bill of lading is lawfully issued in a set of parts and different parts are negotiated to different persons, the title of the holder to which the first due negotiation is made prevails as to both the document of title and the goods even if any later holder may have received the goods from the carrier in good faith and discharged the carrier's obligation by surrendering its part.

(d) A person that negotiates or transfers a single part of a tangible bill of lading issued in a set is liable to holders of that part as if it were the whole set.

(e) The bailee shall deliver in accordance with Part 4 against the first presented part of a tangible bill of lading lawfully issued in a set. Delivery in this manner discharges the bailee's obligation on the whole bill.

Official Comment

Prior Uniform Statutory Provision: Former Section 7–304.

Changes: To limit bills in a set to tangible bills of lading and to use terminology more consistent with modern usage.

Purposes:

1. Tangible bills of lading in a set are still used in some nations in international trade. Consequently, a tangible bill of lading part of a set could be at issue in a lawsuit that might come within Article 7. The statement of the legal effect of a lawfully issued set is in accord with existing commercial law relating to maritime and other international tangible bills of lading. This law has been codified in the Hague and Warsaw Conventions and in the Carriage of Goods by Sea Act, the provisions of which would ordinarily govern in situations where bills in a set are recognized by this Article. Tangible bills of lading in a set are prohibited in domestic trade.

2. Electronic bills of lading in domestic or international trade will not be issued in a set given the requirements of control necessary to deliver the bill to another person. An electronic bill of lading will be a single, authoritative copy. Section 7–106. Hence, this section differentiates between electronic bills of lading and tangible bills of lading. This section does not prohibit electronic data messages about goods in transit because these electronic data messages are not the issued bill of lading. Electronic data messages contain information for the carrier's management and handling of the cargo but this information for the carrier's use is not the issued bill of lading.

Cross Reference:

Section 7–103, 7–303 and 7–106.

Definitional Cross References:

"Bailee". Section 7–102.
"Bill of lading". Section 1–201.
"Delivery". Section 1–201.
"Document of title". Section 1–201.
"Duly negotiate". Section 7–501.
"Good faith". Section 1–201. [7–102].

"Goods". Section 7–102.
"Holder". Section 1–201.
"Issuer". Section 7–102.
"Person". Section 1–201.
"Receipt of goods". Section 2–103.

§ 7–305.   Destination Bills.

(a)   Instead of issuing a bill of lading to the consignor at the place of shipment, a carrier, at the request of the consignor, may procure the bill to be issued at destination or at any other place designated in the request.

(b)   Upon request of any person entitled as against a carrier to control the goods while in transit and on surrender of possession or control of any outstanding bill of lading or other receipt covering the goods, the issuer, subject to Section 7–105, may procure a substitute bill to be issued at any place designated in the request.

Official Comment

Prior Uniform Statutory Provision: Former Section 7–305.

Changes: To accommodate electronic bills of lading and for style.

Purposes:

1.   Subsection (a) continues the rules of former Section 7–305(1) without substantive change. This proposal is designed to facilitate the use of order bills in connection with fast shipments. Use of order bills on high speed shipments is impeded by the fact that the goods may arrive at destination before the documents, so that no one is ready to take delivery from the carrier. This is especially inconvenient for carriers by truck and air, who do not have terminal facilities where shipments can be held to await the consignee's appearance. Order bills would be useful to take advantage of bank collection. This may be preferable to C.O.D. shipment in which the carrier, e.g. a truck driver, is the collecting and remitting agent. Financing of shipments under this plan would be handled as follows: seller at San Francisco delivers the goods to an airline with instructions to issue a bill in New York to a named bank. Seller receives a receipt embodying this undertaking to issue a destination bill. Airline wires its New York freight agent to issue the bill as instructed by the seller. Seller wires the New York bank a draft on buyer. New York bank indorses the bill to buyer when the buyer honors the draft. Normally seller would act through its own bank in San Francisco, which would extend credit in reliance on the airline's contract to deliver a bill to the order of its New York correspondent. This section is entirely permissive; it imposes no duty to issue such bills. Whether a performing carrier will act as issuing agent is left to agreement between carriers.

2.   Subsection (b) continues the rule from former Section 7–305(2) with accommodation for electronic bills of lading. If the substitute bill changes from an electronic to a tangible medium or vice versa, the issuance of the substitute bill must comply with Section 7–105 to give the substitute bill validity and effect.

Cross Reference:

Section 7–105.

Definitional Cross References:

"Bill of lading". Section 1–201.
"Consignor". Section 7–102.
"Goods". Section 7–102.
"Issuer". Section 7–102.
"Receipt of goods". Section 2–103.

§ 7–306.   Altered Bills of Lading.

An unauthorized alteration or filling in of a blank in a bill of lading leaves the bill enforceable according to its original tenor.

Official Comment

Prior Uniform Statutory Provision: Former Section 7–306.

Changes: None

Purposes:

An unauthorized alteration or filling in of a blank, whether made with or without fraudulent intent, does not relieve the issuer of its liability on the document as originally executed. This section applies to both tangible and electronic bills of lading, applying the same rule to both types of bills of lading. The control concept of Section 7–106 requires that any changes to the electronic document of title be readily identifiable as authorized or unauthorized. Section 7–306 should be compared to Section 7–208 where a different rule applies to the unauthorized filling in of a blank for tangible warehouse receipts.

Cross Reference:

Sections 7–106 and 7–208.

Definitional Cross References:

"Bill of lading". Section 1–201.
"Issuer". Section 7–102.

§ 7–307.   Lien of Carrier.

(a)   A carrier has a lien on the goods covered by a bill of lading or on the proceeds thereof in its possession for charges after the date of the carrier's receipt of the goods for storage or transportation, including demurrage and terminal charges, and for expenses necessary for preservation of the goods incident to their transportation or reasonably incurred in their sale pursuant to law. However, against a purchaser for value of a negotiable bill of lading, a carrier's lien is limited to charges stated in the bill or the applicable tariffs or, if no charges are stated, a reasonable charge.

(b)   A lien for charges and expenses under subsection (a) on goods that the carrier was required by law to receive for transportation is effective against the consignor or any person entitled to the goods unless the carrier had notice that the consignor lacked authority to subject the goods to those charges and expenses. Any other lien under subsection (a) is effective against the consignor and any person that permitted the bailor to have control or possession of the goods unless the carrier had notice that the bailor lacked authority.

(c)   A carrier loses its lien on any goods that it voluntarily delivers or unjustifiably refuses to deliver.

Official Comment

Prior Uniform Statutory Provision: Former Section 7–307.

Changes: Expanded to cover proceeds of the goods transported.

Purposes:

1.   The section is intended to give carriers a specific statutory lien for charges and expenses similar to that given to warehouses by the first sentence of Section 7–209(a) and extends that lien to the proceeds of the goods as long as the carrier has possession of the proceeds. But because carriers do not commonly claim a lien for charges in relation to other goods or lend money on the security of goods in their hands, provisions for a general lien or a security interest similar to those in Section 7–209(a) and (b) are omitted. Carriers may utilize Article 9 to obtain a security interest and become a secured party or a carrier may agree to limit its lien rights in a transportation agreement with the shipper. As the lien given by this section is specific, and the storage or transportation often preserves or increases the value of the goods, subsection (b) validates the lien against anyone who permitted the bailor to have possession of the goods. Where the carrier is required to receive the goods for transportation, the owner's interest may be subjected to charges and expenses arising out of deposit of his goods by a thief. The crucial mental element is the carrier's knowledge or reason to know of the bailor's lack of authority. If the carrier does not know or have reason to know of the bailor's lack of authority, the carrier has a lien under this section against any person so long as the conditions of subsection (b) are satisfied. In light of the crucial mental element, Sections 7–307 and 9–333 combine to give priority to a carrier's lien over security interests in the goods. In this regard, the judicial decision in *In re Sharon Steel Corp.*, 25 U.C.C. Rep.2d 503, 176 B.R. 384 (W.D. Pa. 1995) is correct and is the controlling precedent.

2.   The reference to charges in this section means charges relating to the bailment relationship for transportation. Charges does not mean that the bill of lading must state a specific rate or a specific amount.

However, failure to state a specific rate or a specific amount has legal consequences under the second sentence of subsection (a).

3. The carrier's specific lien under this section is a possessory lien. See subsection (c). Part 3 of Article 7 does not require any particular form for a bill of lading. The carrier's lien arises when the carrier has issued a bill of lading.

Cross References:

Point 1: Sections 7–209, 9–109 and 9–333.
Point 3. Section 7–202 and 7–209.

Definitional Cross References:

"Bill of lading". Section 1–201.
"Carrier". Section 7–102.
"Consignor". Section 7–102.
"Delivery". Section 1–201.
"Goods". Section 7–102.
"Person". Section 1–201.
"Purchaser". Section 1–201.
"Value". Section 1–204.

§ 7–308.   Enforcement of Carrier's Lien.

(a)   A carrier's lien on goods may be enforced by public or private sale of the goods, in bulk or in packages, at any time or place and on any terms that are commercially reasonable, after notifying all persons known to claim an interest in the goods. The notification must include a statement of the amount due, the nature of the proposed sale, and the time and place of any public sale. The fact that a better price could have been obtained by a sale at a different time or in a method different from that selected by the carrier is not of itself sufficient to establish that the sale was not made in a commercially reasonable manner. The carrier sells goods in a commercially reasonable manner if the carrier sells the goods in the usual manner in any recognized market therefor, sells at the price current in that market at the time of the sale, or otherwise sells in conformity with commercially reasonable practices among dealers in the type of goods sold. A sale of more goods than apparently necessary to be offered to ensure satisfaction of the obligation is not commercially reasonable, except in cases covered by the preceding sentence.

(b)   Before any sale pursuant to this section, any person claiming a right in the goods may pay the amount necessary to satisfy the lien and the reasonable expenses incurred in complying with this section. In that event, the goods may not be sold but must be retained by the carrier, subject to the terms of the bill of lading and this article.

(c)   A carrier may buy at any public sale pursuant to this section.

(d)   A purchaser in good faith of goods sold to enforce a carrier's lien takes the goods free of any rights of persons against which the lien was valid, despite the carrier's noncompliance with this section.

(e)   A carrier may satisfy its lien from the proceeds of any sale pursuant to this section but shall hold the balance, if any, for delivery on demand to any person to which the carrier would have been bound to deliver the goods.

(f)   The rights provided by this section are in addition to all other rights allowed by law to a creditor against a debtor.

(g)   A carrier's lien may be enforced pursuant to either subsection (a) or the procedure set forth in Section 7–210(b).

(h)   A carrier is liable for damages caused by failure to comply with the requirements for sale under this section and, in case of willful violation, is liable for conversion.

Official Comment

Prior Uniform Statutory Provision: Former Section 7–308.

Changes: To conform language to modern usage and for style.

Purposes:

This section is intended to give the carrier an enforcement procedure of its lien coextensive with that given the warehouse in cases other than those covering noncommercial storage by the warehouse. See Section 7–210 and comments.

Cross Reference:

Section 7–210.

Definitional Cross References:

"Bill of lading". Section 1–201.
"Carrier". Section 7–102.
"Creditor". Section 1–201.
"Delivery". Section 1–201.
"Good faith". Section 1–201. [7–102]
"Goods". Section 7–102.
"Notification". Section 1–202.
"Notifies". Section 1–202.
"Person". Section 1–201.
"Purchaser". Section 1–201.
"Rights". Section 1–201.
"Term". Section 1–201.

§ 7–309. Duty of Care; Contractual Limitation of Carrier's Liability.

(a) A carrier that issues a bill of lading, whether negotiable or nonnegotiable, shall exercise the degree of care in relation to the goods which a reasonably careful person would exercise under similar circumstances. This subsection does not affect any statute, regulation, or rule of law that imposes liability upon a common carrier for damages not caused by its negligence.

(b) Damages may be limited by a term in the bill of lading or in a transportation agreement that the carrier's liability may not exceed a value stated in the bill or transportation agreement if the carrier's rates are dependent upon value and the consignor is afforded an opportunity to declare a higher value and the consignor is advised of the opportunity. However, such a limitation is not effective with respect to the carrier's liability for conversion to its own use.

(c) Reasonable provisions as to the time and manner of presenting claims and commencing actions based on the shipment may be included in a bill of lading or a transportation agreement.

Official Comment

Prior Uniform Statutory Provision: Former Section 7–309.

Changes: References to tariffs eliminated because of deregulation, adding reference to transportation agreements, and for style.

Purposes:

1. A bill of lading may also serve as the contract between the carrier and the bailor. Parties in their contract should be able to limit the amount of damages for breach of that contract including breach of the duty to take reasonable care of the goods. The parties cannot disclaim by contract the carrier's obligation of care. Section 1–302.

Federal statutes and treaties for air, maritime and rail transport may alter the standard of care. These federal statutes and treaties preempt this section when applicable. Section 7–103. Subsection (a) does not impair any rule of law imposing the liability of an insurer on a common carrier in intrastate commerce. Subsection (b), however, applies to the common carrier's liability as an insurer as well as to liability based on negligence. Subsection (b) allows the term limiting damages to appear either in the bill of lading or in the parties' transportation agreement. Compare 7–204(b). Subsection (c) allows the parties to agree to provisions regarding time and manner of presenting claims or commencing actions if the provisions are either in the bill of lading or the transportation agreement. Compare 7–204(c). Transportation agreements are commonly used to establish agreed terms between carriers and shippers that have an on-going relationship.

2.   References to public tariffs in former Section 7–309(2) and (3) have been deleted in light of the modern era of deregulation. See Comment 2 to Section 7–103. If a tariff is required under state or federal law, pursuant to Section 7–103(a), the tariff would control over the rule of this section. As governed by contract law, parties may incorporate by reference the limits on the amount of damages or the reasonable provisions as to the time and manner of presenting claims set forth in applicable tariffs, e.g. a maximum unit value beyond which goods are not taken or a disclaimer of responsibility for undeclared articles of extraordinary value.

3.   As under former Section 7–309(2), subsection (b) provides that a limitation of damages is ineffective if the carrier has converted the goods to its own use. A mere failure to redeliver the goods is not conversion to the carrier's own use. "Conversion to its own use" is narrower than the idea of conversion generally. *Art Masters Associates, Ltd. v. United Parcel Service*, 77 N.Y.2d 200, 567 N.E.2d 226 (1990); *See, Kemper Ins. Co. v. Fed. Ex. Corp.*, 252 F.3d 509 (1st Cir.), *cert. denied* 534 U.S. 1020 (2001) (opinion interpreting federal law).

4.   As used in this section, damages may include damages arising from delay in delivery. Delivery dates and times are often specified in the parties' contract. See Section 7–403.

Cross Reference:

Sections 1–302, 7–103, 7–204, 7–403.

Definitional Cross References:

"Action". Section 1–201.
"Bill of lading". Section 1–201.
"Carrier". Section 7–102.
"Consignor". Section 7–102.
"Document of title". Section 1–201.
"Goods". Section 7–102.
"Value". Section 1–204.

PART 4

WAREHOUSE RECEIPTS AND BILLS OF LADING: GENERAL OBLIGATIONS

§ 7–401.   Irregularities in Issue of Receipt or Bill or Conduct of Issuer.

The obligations imposed by this article on an issuer apply to a document of title even if:

(1)   the document does not comply with the requirements of this article or of any other statute, rule, or regulation regarding its issuance, form, or content;

(2)   the issuer violated laws regulating the conduct of its business;

(3)   the goods covered by the document were owned by the bailee when the document was issued; or

(4)   the person issuing the document is not a warehouse but the document purports to be a warehouse receipt.

Official Comment

Prior Uniform Statutory Provision: Former Section 7–401.

Changes: Changes for style only.

Purposes:

The bailee's liability on its document despite non-receipt or misdescription of the goods is affirmed in Sections 7–203 and 7–301. The purpose of this section is to make it clear that regardless of irregularities a document which falls within the definition of document of title imposes on the issuer the obligations stated in this Article. For example, a bailee will not be permitted to avoid its obligation to deliver the goods (Section 7–403) or its obligation of due care with respect to them (Sections 7–204 and 7–309) by taking the position that no valid "document" was issued because it failed to file a statutory bond or did not pay stamp taxes or did not disclose the place of storage in the document. *Tate v. Action Moving & Storage, Inc.*, 383 S.E.2d 229 (N.C. App. 1989), rev. denied 389 S.E.2d 104 (N.C. 1990). Sanctions against violations of statutory or administrative duties with respect to documents should be limited to revocation of license or other measures prescribed by the regulation imposing the duty. See Section 7–103.

Cross References:

Sections 7–103, 7–203, 7–204, 7–301, 7–309.

Definitional Cross References:

"Bailee". Section 7–102.
"Document of title". Section 1–201.
"Goods". Section 7–102.
"Issuer". Section 7–102.
"Person". Section 1–201.
"Warehouse receipt". Section 1–201.
"Warehouse". Section 7–102.

§ 7–402. Duplicate Document of Title; Overissue.

A duplicate or any other document of title purporting to cover goods already represented by an outstanding document of the same issuer does not confer any right in the goods, except as provided in the case of tangible bills of lading in a set of parts, overissue of documents for fungible goods, substitutes for lost, stolen, or destroyed documents, or substitute documents issued pursuant to Section 7–105. The issuer is liable for damages caused by its overissue or failure to identify a duplicate document by a conspicuous notation.

Official Comment

Prior Uniform Statutory Provision: Former Section 7–402.

Changes: Changes to accommodate electronic documents.

Purposes:

1.   This section treats a duplicate which is not properly identified as a duplicate like any other overissue of documents: a purchaser of such a document acquires no title but only a cause of action for damages against the person that made the deception possible, except in the cases noted in the section. But parts of a tangible bill lawfully issued in a set of parts are not "overissue" (Section 7–304). Of course, if the issuer has clearly indicated that a document is a duplicate so that no one can be deceived by it, and in fact the duplicate is a correct copy of the original, the issuer is not liable for preparing and delivering such a duplicate copy.

Section 7–105 allows documents of title to be reissued in another medium. Re-issuance of a document in an alternative medium under Section 7–105 requires that the original document be surrendered to the issuer in order to make the substitute document the effective document. If the substitute document is not issued in compliance with section 7–105, then the document should be treated as a duplicate under this section.

2.   The section applies to nonnegotiable documents to the extent of providing an action for damages for one who acquires an unmarked duplicate from a transferor who knew the facts and would therefore have had no cause of action against the issuer of the duplicate. Ordinarily the transferee of a nonnegotiable document acquires only the rights of its transferor.

3.   Overissue is defined so as to exclude the common situation where two valid documents of different issuers are outstanding for the same goods at the same time. Thus freight forwarders commonly issue bills of lading to their customers for small shipments to be combined into carload shipments for which the railroad will

issue a bill of lading to the forwarder. So also a warehouse receipt may be outstanding against goods, and the holder of the receipt may issue delivery orders against the same goods. In these cases dealings with the subsequently issued documents may be effective to transfer title; e.g. negotiation of a delivery order will effectively transfer title in the ordinary case where no dishonesty has occurred and the goods are available to satisfy the orders. Section 7–503 provides for cases of conflict between documents of different issuers.

Cross References:

> Point 1: Sections 7–105, 7–207, 7–304, and 7–601.
> Point 3: Section 7–503.

Definitional Cross References:

> "Bill of lading". Section 1–201.
> "Conspicuous". Section 1–201.
> "Document of title". Section 1–201.
> "Fungible goods." Section 1–201.
> "Goods". Section 7–102.
> "Issuer". Section 7–102.
> "Right". Section 1–201.

§ 7–403.   Obligation of Bailee to Deliver; Excuse.

(a)   A bailee shall deliver the goods to a person entitled under a document of title if the person complies with subsections (b) and (c), unless and to the extent that the bailee establishes any of the following:

(1)   delivery of the goods to a person whose receipt was rightful as against the claimant;

(2)   damage to or delay, loss, or destruction of the goods for which the bailee is not liable;

(3)   previous sale or other disposition of the goods in lawful enforcement of a lien or on a warehouse's lawful termination of storage;

(4)   the exercise by a seller of its right to stop delivery pursuant to Section 2–705 or by a lessor of its right to stop delivery pursuant to Section 2A–526;

(5)   a diversion, reconsignment, or other disposition pursuant to Section 7–303;

(6)   release, satisfaction, or any other personal defense against the claimant; or

(7)   any other lawful excuse.

(b)   A person claiming goods covered by a document of title shall satisfy the bailee's lien if the bailee so requests or if the bailee is prohibited by law from delivering the goods until the charges are paid.

(c)   Unless a person claiming the goods is a person against which the document of title does not confer a right under Section 7–503(a):

(1)   the person claiming under a document shall surrender possession or control of any outstanding negotiable document covering the goods for cancellation or indication of partial deliveries; and

(2)   the bailee shall cancel the document or conspicuously indicate in the document the partial delivery or the bailee is liable to any person to which the document is duly negotiated.

Official Comment

Prior Uniform Statutory Provision: Former Section 7–403.

Changes: Definition in former Section 7–403(4) moved to Section 7–102; bracketed language in former Section 7–403(1)(b) deleted; added cross reference to Section 2A–526; changes for style.

Purposes:

1. The present section, following former Section 7–403, is constructed on the basis of stating what previous deliveries or other circumstances operate to excuse the bailee's normal obligation on the document. Accordingly, "justified" deliveries under the pre-Code uniform acts now find their place as "excuse" under subsection (a).

2. The principal case covered by subsection (a)(1) is delivery to a person whose title is paramount to the rights represented by the document. For example, if a thief deposits stolen goods in a warehouse facility and takes a negotiable receipt, the warehouse is not liable on the receipt if it has surrendered the goods to the true owner, even though the receipt is held by a good faith purchaser. See Section 7–503(a). However, if the owner entrusted the goods to a person with power of disposition, and that person deposited the goods and took a negotiable document, the owner receiving delivery would not be rightful as against a holder to whom the negotiable document was duly negotiated, and delivery to the owner would not give the bailee a defense against such a holder. See Sections 7–502(a)(2), 7–503(a)(1).

3. Subsection (a)(2) amounts to a cross reference to all the tort law that determines the varying responsibilities and standards of care applicable to commercial bailees. A restatement of this tort law would be beyond the scope of this Act. Much of the applicable law as to responsibility of bailees for the preservation of the goods and limitation of liability in case of loss has been codified for particular classes of bailees in interstate and foreign commerce by federal legislation and treaty and for intrastate carriers and other bailees by the regulatory state laws preserved by Section 7–103. In the absence of governing legislation the common law will prevail subject to the minimum standard of reasonable care prescribed by Sections 7–204 and 7–309 of this Article.

The bracketed language found in former Section 7–403(1)(b) has been deleted thereby leaving the allocations of the burden of going forward with the evidence and the burden of proof to the procedural law of the various states.

Subsection (a)(4) contains a cross reference to both the seller's and the lessor's rights to stop delivery under Article 2 and Article 2A respectively.

4. As under former Section 7–403, there is no requirement that a request for delivery must be accompanied by a formal tender of the amount of the charges due. Rather, the bailee must request payment of the amount of its lien when asked to deliver, and only in case this request is refused is it justified in declining to deliver because of nonpayment of charges. Where delivery without payment is forbidden by law, the request is treated as implicit. Such a prohibition reflects a policy of uniformity to prevent discrimination by failure to request payment in particular cases. Subsection (b) must be read in conjunction with the priorities given to the warehouse lien and the carrier lien under Section 7–209 and 7–307, respectively. If the parties are in dispute about whether the request for payment of the lien is legally proper, the bailee may have recourse to interpleader. See Section 7–603.

5. Subsection (c) states the obvious duty of a bailee to take up a negotiable document or note partial deliveries conspicuously thereon, and the result of failure in that duty. It is subject to only one exception, that stated in subsection (a)(1) of this section and in Section 7–503(a). Subsection (c) is limited to cases of delivery to a claimant; it has no application, for example, where goods held under a negotiable document are lawfully sold to enforce the bailee's lien.

6. When courts are considering subsection (a)(7), "any other lawful excuse," among others, refers to compliance with court orders under Sections 7–601, 7–602 and 7–603.

Cross References:

Point 2: Sections 7–502 and 7–503.
Point 3: Sections 2–705, 2A–526, 7–103, 7–204, and 7–309 and 10–103.
Point 4: Sections 7–209, 7–307 and 7–603.
Point 5: Section 7–503(1).
Point 6: Sections 7–601, 7–602, and 7–603.

Definitional Cross References:

"Bailee". Section 7–102.
"Conspicuous". Section 1–201.
"Delivery". Section 1–201.
"Document of title". Section 1–201.

"Duly negotiate". Section 7–501.
"Goods". Section 7–102.
"Lessor". Section 2A–103.
"Person". Section 1–201.
"Receipt of goods". Section 2–103.
"Right". Section 1–201.
"Terms". Section 1–201.
"Warehouse". Section 7–102.

§ 7–404.   No Liability for Good-Faith Delivery Pursuant to Document of Title.

A bailee that in good faith has received goods and delivered or otherwise disposed of the goods according to the terms of a document of title or pursuant to this article is not liable for the goods even if:

(1)   the person from which the bailee received the goods did not have authority to procure the document or to dispose of the goods; or

(2)   the person to which the bailee delivered the goods did not have authority to receive the goods.

Official Comment

Prior Uniform Statutory Provision: Former Section 7–404.

Changes: Changes reflect the definition of good faith in Section 1–201 [7–102] and for style.

Purposes:

This section uses the test of good faith, as defined in Section 1–201 [7–102], to continue the policy of former Section 7–404. Good faith now means "honesty in fact and the observance of reasonable commercial standards of fair dealing." The section states explicitly that the common law rule of "innocent conversion" by unauthorized "intermeddling" with another's property is inapplicable to the operations of commercial carriers and warehousemen that in good faith perform obligations that they have assumed and that generally they are under a legal compulsion to assume. The section applies to delivery to a fraudulent holder of a valid document as well as to delivery to the holder of an invalid document. Of course, in appropriate circumstances, a bailee may use interpleader or other dispute resolution process. See Section 7–603.

Cross Reference:

Section 7–603.

Definitional Cross References:

"Bailee". Section 7–102.
"Delivery". Section 1–201.
"Document of title". Section 1–201.
"Good faith". Section 1–201. [7–102].
"Goods". Section 7–102.
"Person". Section 1–201.
"Receipt of goods". Section 2–103.
"Term". Section 1–201.

PART 5

WAREHOUSE RECEIPTS AND BILLS OF LADING: NEGOTIATION AND TRANSFER

§ 7–501.   Form of Negotiation and Requirements of Due Negotiation.

(a)   The following rules apply to a negotiable tangible document of title:

(1) If the document's original terms run to the order of a named person, the document is negotiated by the named person's indorsement and delivery. After the named person's indorsement in blank or to bearer, any person may negotiate the document by delivery alone.

(2) If the document's original terms run to bearer, it is negotiated by delivery alone.

(3) If the document's original terms run to the order of a named person and it is delivered to the named person, the effect is the same as if the document had been negotiated.

(4) Negotiation of the document after it has been indorsed to a named person requires indorsement by the named person and delivery.

(5) A document is duly negotiated if it is negotiated in the manner stated in this subsection to a holder that purchases it in good faith, without notice of any defense against or claim to it on the part of any person, and for value, unless it is established that the negotiation is not in the regular course of business or financing or involves receiving the document in settlement or payment of a monetary obligation.

(b) The following rules apply to a negotiable electronic document of title:

(1) If the document's original terms run to the order of a named person or to bearer, the document is negotiated by delivery of the document to another person. Indorsement by the named person is not required to negotiate the document.

(2) If the document's original terms run to the order of a named person and the named person has control of the document, the effect is the same as if the document had been negotiated.

(3) A document is duly negotiated if it is negotiated in the manner stated in this subsection to a holder that purchases it in good faith, without notice of any defense against or claim to it on the part of any person, and for value, unless it is established that the negotiation is not in the regular course of business or financing or involves taking delivery of the document in settlement or payment of a monetary obligation.

(c) Indorsement of a nonnegotiable document of title neither makes it negotiable nor adds to the transferee's rights.

(d) The naming in a negotiable bill of lading of a person to be notified of the arrival of the goods does not limit the negotiability of the bill or constitute notice to a purchaser of the bill of any interest of that person in the goods.

Official Comment

Prior Uniform Statutory Provision: Former Section 7–501.

Changes: To accommodate negotiable electronic documents of title.

Purpose:

1. Subsection (a) has been limited to tangible negotiable documents of title but otherwise remains unchanged in substance from the rules in former Section 7–501. Subsection (b) is new and applies to negotiable electronic documents of title. Delivery of a negotiable electronic document is through voluntary transfer of control. Section 1–201 definition of "delivery." The control concept as applied to negotiable electronic documents of title is the substitute for both possession and indorsement as applied to negotiable tangible documents of title. Section 7–106.

Article 7 does not separately define the term "duly negotiated." However, the elements of "duly negotiated" are set forth in subsection (a)(5) for tangible documents and (b)(3) for electronic documents. As under former Section 7–501, in order to effect a "due negotiation" the negotiation must be in the "regular course of business or financing" in order to transfer greater rights than those held by the person negotiating. The foundation of the mercantile doctrine of good faith purchase for value has always been, as shown by the case situations, the furtherance and protection of the regular course of trade. The reason for allowing a person, in bad faith or in error, to convey away rights which are not its own has from the beginning been to make possible the speedy handling of that great run of commercial transactions which are patently usual and normal.

There are two aspects to the usual and normal course of mercantile dealings, namely, the person making the transfer and the nature of the transaction itself. The first question which arises is: Is the transferor a person with whom it is reasonable to deal as having full powers? In regard to documents of title the only holder whose possession or control appears, commercially, to be in order is almost invariably a person in the trade. No commercial purpose is served by allowing a tramp or a professor to "duly negotiate" an order bill of lading for hides or cotton not their own, and since such a transfer is obviously not in the regular course of business, it is excluded from the scope of the protection of subsections (a)(5) or (b)(3).

The second question posed by the "regular course" qualification is: Is the transaction one which is normally proper to pass full rights without inquiry, even though the transferor itself may not have such rights to pass, and even though the transferor may be acting in breach of duty? In raising this question the "regular course" criterion has the further advantage of limiting, the effective wrongful disposition to transactions whose protection will really further trade. Obviously, the snapping up of goods for quick resale at a price suspiciously below the market deserves no protection as a matter of policy: it is also clearly outside the range of regular course.

Any notice on the document sufficient to put a merchant on inquiry as to the "regular course" quality of the transaction will frustrate a "due negotiation". Thus irregularity of the document or unexplained staleness of a bill of lading may appropriately be recognized as negating a negotiation in "regular" course.

A pre-existing claim constitutes value, and "due negotiation" does not require "new value." A usual and ordinary transaction in which documents are received as security for credit previously extended may be in "regular" course, even though there is a demand for additional collateral because the creditor "deems himself insecure." But the matter has moved out of the regular course of financing if the debtor is thought to be insolvent, the credit previously extended is in effect cancelled, and the creditor snatches a plank in the shipwreck under the guise of a demand for additional collateral. Where a money debt is "paid" in commodity paper, any question of "regular" course disappears, as the case is explicitly excepted from "due negotiation".

2.   Negotiation under this section may be made by any holder no matter how the holder acquired possession or control of the document.

3.   Subsections (a)(3) and (b)(2) make explicit a matter upon which the intent of the pre-Code law was clear but the language somewhat obscure: a negotiation results from a delivery to a banker or buyer to whose order the document has been taken by the person making the bailment. There is no presumption of irregularity in such a negotiation; it may very well be in "regular course."

4.   This Article does not contain any provision creating a presumption of due negotiation to, and full rights in, a holder of a document of title akin to that created by Uniform Commercial Code Article 3. But the reason of the provisions of this Act (Section 1–307) on the prima facie authenticity and accuracy of third party documents, joins with the reason of the present section to work such a presumption in favor of any person who has power to make a due negotiation. It would not make sense for this Act to authorize a purchaser to indulge the presumption of regularity if the courts were not also called upon to do so. Allocations of the burden of going forward with the evidence and the burden of proof are left to the procedural law of the various states.

5.   Subsections (c) and (d) are unchanged from prior law and apply to both tangible and electronic documents of title.

Cross References:

Sections 1–307, 7–502 and 7–503.

Definitional Cross References:

"Bearer". Section 1–201.
"Control". Section 7–106.
"Delivery". Section 1–201.
"Document of title". Section 1–201.
"Good faith". Section 1–201 [7–102].
"Holder". Section 1–201.
"Notice". Section 1–202.
"Person". Section 1–201.
"Purchase". Section 1–201.
"Rights". Section 1–201.

"Term". Section 1–201.
"Value". Section 1–204.

§ 7–502.   Rights Acquired by Due Negotiation.

(a)   Subject to Sections 7–205 and 7–503, a holder to which a negotiable document of title has been duly negotiated acquires thereby:

(1)   title to the document;

(2)   title to the goods;

(3)   all rights accruing under the law of agency or estoppel, including rights to goods delivered to the bailee after the document was issued; and

(4)   the direct obligation of the issuer to hold or deliver the goods according to the terms of the document free of any defense or claim by the issuer except those arising under the terms of the document or under this article, but in the case of a delivery order, the bailee's obligation accrues only upon the bailee's acceptance of the delivery order and the obligation acquired by the holder is that the issuer and any indorser will procure the acceptance of the bailee.

(b)   Subject to Section 7–503, title and rights acquired by due negotiation are not defeated by any stoppage of the goods represented by the document of title or by surrender of the goods by the bailee and are not impaired even if:

(1)   the due negotiation or any prior due negotiation constituted a breach of duty;

(2)   any person has been deprived of possession of a negotiable tangible document or control of a negotiable electronic document by misrepresentation, fraud, accident, mistake, duress, loss, theft, or conversion; or

(3)   a previous sale or other transfer of the goods or document has been made to a third person.

Official Comment

Prior Uniform Statutory Provision: Former Section 7–502.

Changes: To accommodate electronic documents of title and for style.

Purpose:

1.   This section applies to both tangible and electronic documents of title. The elements of duly negotiated, which constitutes a due negotiation, are set forth in Section 7–501. The several necessary qualifications of the broad principle that the holder of a document acquired in a due negotiation is the owner of the document and the goods have been brought together in the next section (Section 7–503).

2.   Subsection (a)(3) covers the case of "feeding" of a duly negotiated document by subsequent delivery to the bailee of such goods as the document falsely purported to cover; the bailee in such case is estopped as against the holder of the document.

3.   The explicit statement in subsection (a)(4) of the bailee's direct obligation to the holder precludes the defense that the document in question was "spent" after the carrier had delivered the goods to a previous holder. But the holder is subject to such defenses as non-negligent destruction even though not apparent on the document. The sentence on delivery orders applies only to delivery orders in negotiable form which have been duly negotiated. On delivery orders, see also Section 7–503(b) and Comment.

4.   Subsection (b) continues the law which gave full effect to the issuance or due negotiation of a negotiable document. The subsection adds nothing to the effect of the rules stated in subsection (a), but it has been included since such explicit reference was provided under former Section 7–502 to preserve the right of a purchaser by due negotiation. The listing is not exhaustive. The language "any stoppage" is included lest an inference be drawn that a stoppage of the goods before or after transit might cut off or otherwise impair the purchaser's rights.

Cross References:

Sections 7–103, 7–205, 7–403, 7–501, and 7–503.

Definitional Cross References:

"Bailee". Section 7–102.
"Control". Section 7–106.
"Delivery". Section 1–201.
"Delivery order". Section 7–102.
"Document of title". Section 1–201.
"Duly negotiate". Section 7–501.
"Fungible". Section 1–201.
"Goods". Section 7–102.
"Holder". Section 1–201.
"Issuer". Section 7–102.
"Person". Section 1–201.
"Rights". Section 1–201.
"Term". Section 1–201.
"Warehouse receipt". Section 1–201.

§ 7–503.   Document of Title to Goods Defeated in Certain Cases.

(a)   A document of title confers no right in goods against a person who that before issuance of the document had a legal interest or a perfected security interest in the goods and that did not:

(1)   deliver or entrust the goods or any document of title covering the goods to the bailor or the bailor's nominee with:

(A)   actual or apparent authority to ship, store, or sell;

(B)   power to obtain delivery under Section 7–403; or

(C)   power of disposition under Section 2–403, 2A–304(2), 2A–305(2), 9–320, or 9–321(c) or other statute or rule of law; or

(2)   acquiesce in the procurement by the bailor or its nominee of any document.

(b)   Title to goods based upon an unaccepted delivery order is subject to the rights of any person to which a negotiable warehouse receipt or bill of lading covering the goods has been duly negotiated. That title may be defeated under Section 7–504 to the same extent as the rights of the issuer or a transferee from the issuer.

(c)   Title to goods based upon a bill of lading issued to a freight forwarder is subject to the rights of any person to which a bill issued by the freight forwarder is duly negotiated. However, delivery by the carrier in accordance with Part 4 pursuant to its own bill of lading discharges the carrier's obligation to deliver.

Official Comment

Prior Uniform Statutory Provision: Former Section 7–503.

Changes: Changes to cross-reference to Article 2A and for style.

Purposes:

1.   In general it may be said that the title of a purchaser by due negotiation prevails over almost any interest in the goods which existed prior to the procurement of the document of title if the possession of the goods by the person obtaining the document derived from any action by the prior claimant which introduced the goods into the stream of commerce or carried them along that stream. A thief of the goods cannot indeed by shipping or storing them to the thief's own order acquire power to transfer them to a good faith purchaser. Nor can a tenant or mortgagor defeat any rights of a landlord or mortgagee which have been perfected under the local law merely by wrongfully shipping or storing a portion of the crop or other goods. However, "acquiescence" by the landlord or mortgagee does not require active consent under subsection (a)(2) and knowledge of the likelihood of storage or shipment with no objection or effort to control it is sufficient to defeat the landlord's or the mortgagee's rights as against one who takes by due negotiation of a negotiable document. *In re Sharon Steel*, 176 B.R. 384 (Bankr. W.D.

Pa. 1995); *In re R.V. Segars Co*, 54 B.R. 170 (Bankr. S.C. 1985); *In re Jamestown Elevators, Inc.*, 49 B.R. 661 (Bankr. N.D. 1985).

On the other hand, where goods are delivered to a factor for sale, even though the factor has made no advances and is limited in its duty to sell for cash, the goods are "entrusted" to the factor "with actual . . . authority . . . to sell" under subsection (a)(1), and if the factor procures a negotiable document of title it can transfer the owner's interest to a purchaser by due negotiation. Further, where the factor is in the business of selling, goods entrusted to it simply for safekeeping or storage may be entrusted under circumstances which give the factor "apparent authority to ship, store or sell" under subsection (a)(1), or power of disposition under Section 2–403, 2A–304(2), 2A–305(2), 7–205, 9–320, or 9–321(c) or under a statute such as the earlier Factors Acts, or under a rule of law giving effect to apparent ownership. See Section 1–103.

Persons having an interest in goods also frequently deliver or entrust them to agents or servants other than factors for the purpose of shipping or warehousing or under circumstances reasonably contemplating such action. This Act is clear that such persons assume full risk that the agent to whom the goods are so delivered may ship or store in breach of duty, take a document to the agent's own order and then proceed to misappropriate the negotiable document of title that embodies the goods. This Act makes no distinction between possession or mere custody in such situations and finds no exception in the case of larceny by a bailee or the like. The safeguard in such situations lies in the requirement that a due negotiation can occur only "in the regular course of business or financing" and that the purchase be in good faith and without notice. See Section 7–501. Documents of title have no market among the commercially inexperienced and the commercially experienced do not take them without inquiry from persons known to be truck drivers or petty clerks even though such persons purport to be operating in their own names.

Again, where the seller allows a buyer to receive goods under a contract for sale, though as a "conditional delivery" or under "cash sale" terms and on explicit agreement for immediate payment, the buyer thereby acquires power to defeat the seller's interest by transfer of the goods to certain good faith purchasers. See Section 2–403. Both in policy and under the language of subsection (a)(1) that same power must be extended to accomplish the same result if the buyer procures a negotiable document of title to the goods and duly negotiates it.

This comment 1 should be considered in interpreting delivery, entrustment or acquiescence in application of Section 7–209.

2.   Under subsection (a) a delivery order issued by a person having no right in or power over the goods is ineffective unless the owner acts as provided in subsection (a)(1) or (2). Thus the rights of a transferee of a non-negotiable warehouse receipt can be defeated by a delivery order subsequently issued by the transferor only if the transferee "delivers or entrusts" to the "person procuring" the delivery order or "acquiesces" in that person's procurement. Similarly, a second delivery order issued by the same issuer for the same goods will ordinarily be subject to the first, both under this section and under Section 7–402. After a delivery order is validly issued but before it is accepted, it may nevertheless be defeated under subsection (b) in much the same way that the rights of a transferee may be defeated under Section 7–504. For example, a buyer in ordinary course from the issuer may defeat the rights of the holder of a prior delivery order if the bailee receives notification of the buyer's rights before notification of the holder's rights. Section 7–504(b)(2). But an accepted delivery order has the same effect as a document issued by the bailee.

3.   Under subsection (c) a bill of lading issued to a freight forwarder is subordinated to the freight forwarder's document of title, since the bill on its face gives notice of the fact that a freight forwarder is in the picture and the freight forwarder has in all probability issued a document of title. But the carrier is protected in following the terms of its own bill of lading.

Cross References:

Point 1: Sections 1–103, 2–403, 2A–304(2), 2A–305(2), 7–205, 7–209, 7–501, 9–320, 9–321(c), and 9–331.
Point 2: Sections 7–402 and 7–504.
Point 3: Sections 7–402, 7–403 and 7–404.

Definitional Cross References:

"Bill of lading". Section 1–201.
"Contract for sale". Section 2–106.
"Delivery". Section 1–201.
"Delivery order". Section 7–102.

"Document of title". Section 1–201.
"Duly negotiate". Section 7–501.
"Goods". Section 7–102.
"Person". Section 1–201.
"Right". Section 1–201.
"Warehouse receipt". Section 1–201.

§ 7–504. Rights Acquired in Absence of Due Negotiation; Effect of Diversion; Stoppage of Delivery.

(a) A transferee of a document of title, whether negotiable or nonnegotiable, to which the document has been delivered but not duly negotiated, acquires the title and rights that its transferor had or had actual authority to convey.

(b) In the case of a transfer of a nonnegotiable document of title, until but not after the bailee receives notice of the transfer, the rights of the transferee may be defeated:

(1) by those creditors of the transferor which could treat the transfer as void under Section 2–402 or 2A–308;

(2) by a buyer from the transferor in ordinary course of business if the bailee has delivered the goods to the buyer or received notification of the buyer's rights;

(3) by a lessee from the transferor in ordinary course of business if the bailee has delivered the goods to the lessee or received notification of the lessee's rights; or

(4) as against the bailee, by good-faith dealings of the bailee with the transferor.

(c) A diversion or other change of shipping instructions by the consignor in a nonnegotiable bill of lading which causes the bailee not to deliver the goods to the consignee defeats the consignee's title to the goods if the goods have been delivered to a buyer in ordinary course of business or a lessee in ordinary course of business and, in any event, defeats the consignee's rights against the bailee.

(d) Delivery of the goods pursuant to a nonnegotiable document of title may be stopped by a seller under Section 2–705 or a lessor under Section 2A–526, subject to the requirements of due notification in those sections. A bailee that honors the seller's or lessor's instructions is entitled to be indemnified by the seller or lessor against any resulting loss or expense.

Official Comment

Prior Uniform Statutory Provision: Former Section 7–504.

Changes: To include cross-references to Article 2A and for style.

Purposes:

1. Under the general principles controlling negotiable documents, it is clear that in the absence of due negotiation a transferor cannot convey greater rights than the transferor has, even when the negotiation is formally perfect. This section recognizes the transferor's power to transfer rights which the transferor has or has "actual authority to convey." Thus, where a negotiable document of title is being transferred the operation of the principle of estoppel is not recognized, as contrasted with situations involving the transfer of the goods themselves. (Compare Section 2–403 on good faith purchase of goods.) This section applies to both tangible and electronic documents of title.

A necessary part of the price for the protection of regular dealings with negotiable documents of title is an insistence that no dealing which is in any way irregular shall be recognized as a good faith purchase of the document or of any rights pertaining to it. So, where the transfer of a negotiable document fails as a negotiation because a requisite indorsement is forged or otherwise missing, the purchaser in good faith and for value may be in the anomalous position of having less rights, in part, than if the purchaser had purchased the goods themselves. True, the purchaser's rights are not subject to defeat by attachment of the goods or surrender of them to the purchaser's transferor (contrast subsection (b)); but on the other hand, the purchaser cannot acquire enforceable rights to control or receive the goods over the bailee's objection merely by giving notice to the bailee. Similarly, a

581

consignee who makes payment to its consignor against a straight bill of lading can thereby acquire the position of a good faith purchaser of goods under provisions of the Article of this Act on Sales (Section 2–403), whereas the same payment made in good faith against an unendorsed order bill would not have such effect. The appropriate remedy of a purchaser in such a situation is to regularize its status by compelling indorsement of the document (see Section 7–506).

2.   As in the case of transfer—as opposed to "due negotiation"—of negotiable documents, subsection (a) empowers the transferor of a nonnegotiable document to transfer only such rights as the transferor has or has "actual authority" to convey. In contrast to situations involving the goods themselves the operation of estoppel or agency principles is not here recognized to enable the transferor to convey greater rights than the transferor actually has. Subsection (b) makes it clear, however, that the transferee of a nonnegotiable document may acquire rights greater in some respects than those of his transferor by giving notice of the transfer to the bailee. New subsection (b)(3) provides for the rights of a lessee in the ordinary course.

Subsection (b)(2) & (3) require delivery of the goods. Delivery of the goods means the voluntary transfer of physical possession of the goods. See amended 2–103.*

3.   Subsection (c) is in part a reiteration of the carrier's immunity from liability if it honors instructions of the consignor to divert, but there is added a provision protecting the title of the substituted consignee if the latter is a buyer in ordinary course of business. A typical situation would be where a manufacturer, having shipped a lot of standardized goods to A on nonnegotiable bill of lading, diverts the goods to customer B who pays for them. Under pre-Code passage-of-title-by-appropriation doctrine A might reclaim the goods from B. However, no consideration of commercial policy supports this involvement of an innocent third party in the default of the manufacturer on his contract to A; and the common commercial practice of diverting goods in transit suggests a trade understanding in accordance with this subsection. The same result should obtain if the substituted consignee is a lessee in ordinary course. The extent of the lessee's interest in the goods is less than a buyer's interest in the goods. However, as against the first consignee and the lessee in ordinary course as the substituted consignee, the lessee's rights in the goods as granted under the lease are superior to the first consignee's rights.

4.   Subsection (d) gives the carrier an express right to indemnity where the carrier honors a seller's request to stop delivery.

5.   Section 1–202 gives the bailee protection, if due diligence is exercised where the bailee's organization has not had time to act on a notification.

Cross References:

> Point 1: Sections 2–403 and 7–506.
> Point 2: Sections 2–403 and 2A–304.
> Point 3: Sections 7–303, 7–403(a)(5) and 7–404.
> Point 4: Sections 2–705 and 7–403(a)(4).
> Point 5: Section 1–202.

Definitional Cross References:

> "Bailee". Section 7–102.
> "Bill of lading". Section 1–201.
> "Buyer in ordinary course of business". Section 1–201.
> "Consignee". Section 7–102.
> "Consignor". Section 7–102.
> "Creditor". Section 1–201.
> "Delivery". Section 1–201.
> "Document of title". Section 1–201.
> "Duly negotiate". Section 7–501.
> "Good faith". Section 1–201. [7–102].
> "Goods". Section 7–102.
> "Honor". Section 1–201.
> "Lessee in ordinary course". Section 2A–103.

---

*   *Referring to the 2003 amendments to Article 2, withdrawn in 2011.*

"Notification" Section 1–202.
"Purchaser". Section 1–201.
"Rights". Section 1–201.

§ 7–505.   Indorser not Guarantor for Other Parties.

The indorsement of a tangible document of title issued by a bailee does not make the indorser liable for any default by the bailee or previous indorsers.

Official Comment

Prior Uniform Statutory Provision: Former Section 7–505.

Changes: Limited to tangible documents of title.

Purposes:

This section is limited to tangible documents of title as the concept of indorsement is irrelevant to electronic documents of title. Electronic documents of title will be transferred by delivery of control. Section 7–106. The indorsement of a tangible document of title is generally understood to be directed towards perfecting the transferee's rights rather than towards assuming additional obligations. The language of the present section, however, does not preclude the one case in which an indorsement given for value guarantees future action, namely, that in which the bailee has not yet become liable upon the document at the time of the indorsement. Under such circumstances the indorser, of course, engages that appropriate honor of the document by the bailee will occur. See Section 7–502(a)(4) as to negotiable delivery orders. However, even in such a case, once the bailee attorns to the transferee, the indorser's obligation has been fulfilled and the policy of this section excludes any continuing obligation on the part of the indorser for the bailee's ultimate actual performance.

Cross Reference:

Sections 7–106 and 7–502.

Definitional Cross References:

"Bailee". Section 7–102.
"Document of title". Section 1–201.
"Party". Section 1–201.

§ 7–506.   Delivery Without Indorsement: Right to Compel Indorsement.

The transferee of a negotiable tangible document of title has a specifically enforceable right to have its transferor supply any necessary indorsement, but the transfer becomes a negotiation only as of the time the indorsement is supplied.

Official Comment

Prior Uniform Statutory Provision: Former Section 7–506.

Changes: Limited to tangible documents of title.

Purposes:

1.   This section is limited to tangible documents of title as the concept of indorsement is irrelevant to electronic documents of title. Electronic documents of title will be transferred by delivery of control. Section 7–106. From a commercial point of view the intention to transfer a tangible negotiable document of title which requires an indorsement for its transfer, is incompatible with an intention to withhold such indorsement and so defeat the effective use of the document. Further, the preceding section and the Comment thereto make it clear that an indorsement generally imposes no responsibility on the indorser.

2.   Although this section provides that delivery of a tangible document of title without the necessary indorsement is effective as a transfer, the transferee, of course, has not regularized its position until such indorsement is supplied. Until this is done the transferee cannot claim rights under due negotiation within the requirements of this Article (Section 7–501(a)(5)) on "due negotiation". Similarly, despite the transfer to the transferee of the transferor's title, the transferee cannot demand the goods from the bailee until the negotiation has been completed and the document is in proper form for surrender. See Section 7–403(c).

Cross References:

> Point 1: Sections 7–106 and 7–505.
> Point 2: Sections 7–501(a)(5) and 7–403(c).

Definitional Cross References:

> "Document of title". Section 1–201.
> "Rights". Section 1–201.

§ 7–507.   Warranties on Negotiation or Delivery of Document of Title.

If a person negotiates or delivers a document of title for value, otherwise than as a mere intermediary under Section 7–508, unless otherwise agreed, the transferor, in addition to any warranty made in selling or leasing the goods, warrants to its immediate purchaser only that:

(1)   the document is genuine;

(2)   the transferor does not have knowledge of any fact that would impair the document's validity or worth; and

(3)   the negotiation or delivery is rightful and fully effective with respect to the title to the document and the goods it represents.

Official Comment

Prior Uniform Statutory Provision: Former Section 7–507.

Changes: Substitution of the word "delivery" for the word "transfer," reference leasing transactions and style.

Purposes:

1.   Delivery of goods by use of a document of title does not limit or displace the ordinary obligations of a seller or lessor as to any warranties regarding the goods that arises under other law. If the transfer of documents attends or follows the making of a contract for the sale or lease of goods, the general obligations on warranties as to the goods (Sections 2–312 through 2–318 and Sections 2A–210 through 2A–316) are brought to bear as well as the special warranties under this section.

2.   The limited warranties of a delivering or collecting intermediary, including a collecting bank, are stated in Section 7–508.

Cross References:

> Point 1: Sections 2–312 through 2–318 and 2A–310 through 2A–316.
> Point 2: Section 7–508.

Definitional Cross References:

> "Delivery". Section 1–201.
> "Document of title". Section 1–201.
> "Genuine". Section 1–201.
> "Goods". Section 7–102.
> "Person". Section 1–201.
> "Purchaser". Section 1–201.
> "Value". Section 1–204.

§ 7–508.   Warranties of Collecting Bank as to Documents of Title.

A collecting bank or other intermediary known to be entrusted with documents of title on behalf of another or with collection of a draft or other claim against delivery of documents warrants by the delivery of the documents only its own good faith and authority even if the collecting bank or other intermediary has purchased or made advances against the claim or draft to be collected.

Official Comment

Prior Uniform Statutory Provision: Former Section 7–508.

Changes: Changes for style only.

Purposes:

    1. To state the limited warranties given with respect to the documents accompanying a documentary draft.

    2. In warranting its authority a collecting bank or other intermediary only warrants its authority from its transferor. See Section 4–203. It does not warrant the genuineness or effectiveness of the document. Compare Section 7–507.

    3. Other duties and rights of banks handling documentary drafts for collection are stated in Article 4, Part 5. On the meaning of draft, see Section 4–104 and Section 5–102, comment 11.

Cross References:

    Sections 4–104, 4–203, 4–501 through 4–504, 5–102, and 7–507.

Definitional Cross References:

    "Collecting bank". Section 4–105.
    "Delivery". Section 1–201.
    "Document of title". Section 1–102.
    "Documentary draft". Section 4–104.
    "Intermediary bank". Section 4–105.
    "Good faith". Section 1–201 [7–102.]

§ 7–509. Adequate Compliance with Commercial Contract.

Whether a document of title is adequate to fulfill the obligations of a contract for sale, a contract for lease, or the conditions of a letter of credit is determined by Article 2, 2A, or 5.

Official Comment

Prior Uniform Statutory Provision: Former Section 7–509.

Changes: To reference Article 2A.

Purposes:

To cross-refer to the Articles of this Act which deal with the substantive issues of the type of document of title required under the contract entered into by the parties.

Cross References:

    Articles 2, 2A and 5.

Definitional Cross References:

    "Contract for sale". Section 2–106.
    "Document of title". Section 1–201.
    "Lease". Section 2A–103.

PART 6

WAREHOUSE RECEIPTS AND BILLS OF LADING: MISCELLANEOUS PROVISIONS

§ 7–601. Lost, Stolen, or Destroyed Documents of Title.

    (a) If a document of title is lost, stolen, or destroyed, a court may order delivery of the goods or issuance of a substitute document and the bailee may without liability to any person comply with the order. If the document was negotiable, a court may not order delivery of the goods or issuance of a substitute document without the claimant's posting security unless it finds that any person that may suffer loss as a result of nonsurrender of possession or control of the document is adequately protected against the loss. If the document was nonnegotiable, the court may require security. The court may also order payment of the bailee's reasonable costs and attorney's fees in any action under this subsection.

(b)   A bailee that, without a court order, delivers goods to a person claiming under a missing negotiable document of title is liable to any person injured thereby. If the delivery is not in good faith, the bailee is liable for conversion. Delivery in good faith is not conversion if the claimant posts security with the bailee in an amount at least double the value of the goods at the time of posting to indemnify any person injured by the delivery which files a notice of claim within one year after the delivery.

Official Comment

Prior Uniform Statutory Provision: Former Section 7–601.

Changes: To accommodate electronic documents; to provide flexibility to courts similar to the flexibility in Section 3–309; to update to the modern era of deregulation; and for style.

Purposes:

1.   Subsection (a) authorizes courts to order compulsory delivery of the goods or compulsory issuance of a substitute document. Compare Section 7–402. Using language similar to that found in Section 3–309, courts are given discretion as to what is adequate protection when the lost, stolen or destroyed document was negotiable or whether security should be required when the lost, stolen or destroyed document was nonnegotiable. In determining whether a party is adequately protected against loss in the case of a negotiable document, the court should consider the likelihood that the party will suffer a loss. The court is also given discretion as to the bailee's costs and attorney fees. The rights and obligations of a bailee under this section depend upon whether the document of title is lost, stolen or destroyed and is in addition to the ability of the bailee to bring an action for interpleader. See Section 7–603.

2.   Courts have the authority under this section to order a substitute document for either tangible or electronic documents. If the substitute document will be in a different medium than the original document, the court should fashion its order in light of the requirements of Section 7–105.

3.   Subsection (b) follows prior Section 7–601 in recognizing the legality of the well established commercial practice of bailees making delivery in good faith when they are satisfied that the claimant is the person entitled under a missing (i.e. lost, stolen, or destroyed) negotiable document. Acting without a court order, the bailee remains liable on the original negotiable document and, to avoid conversion liability, the bailee may insist that the claimant provide an indemnity bond. Cf. Section 7–403.

4.   Claimants on non-negotiable instruments are permitted to avail themselves of the subsection (a) procedure because straight (non-negotiable) bills of lading sometimes contain provisions that the goods shall not be delivered except upon production of the bill. If the carrier should choose to insist upon production of the bill, the consignee should have some means of compelling delivery on satisfactory proof of entitlement. Without a court order, a bailee may deliver, subject to Section 7–403, to a person claiming goods under a non-negotiable document that the same person claims is lost, stolen, or destroyed.

5.   The bailee's lien should be protected when a court orders delivery of the goods pursuant to this section.

Cross References:

> Point 1: Sections 3–309, 7–402 and 7–603.
> Point 2: Section 7–105.
> Point 3: Section 7–403.
> Point 4: Section 7–403.
> Point 5: Sections 7–209 and 7–307.

Definitional Cross References:

> "Bailee". Section 7–102.
> "Delivery". Section 1–201.
> "Document of title". Section 1–201.
> "Good faith". Section 1–201 [7–102].
> "Goods". Section 7–102.
> "Person". Section 1–201.

§ 7–602.   Judicial Process Against Goods Covered by Negotiable Document of Title.

Unless a document of title was originally issued upon delivery of the goods by a person that did not have power to dispose of them, a lien does not attach by virtue of any judicial process to goods in the possession of a bailee for which a negotiable document of title is outstanding unless possession or control of the document is first surrendered to the bailee or the document's negotiation is enjoined. The bailee may not be compelled to deliver the goods pursuant to process until possession or control of the document is surrendered to the bailee or to the court. A purchaser of the document for value without notice of the process or injunction takes free of the lien imposed by judicial process.

Official Comment

Prior Uniform Statutory Provisions: Former Section 7–602.

Changes: Changes to accommodate electronic documents of title and for style.

Purposes:

1.   The purpose of the section is to protect the bailee from conflicting claims of the document of title holder and the judgment creditors of the person who deposited the goods. The rights of the former prevail unless, in effect, the judgment creditors immobilize the negotiable document of title through the surrender of possession of a tangible document or control of an electronic document. However, if the document of title was issued upon deposit of the goods by a person who had no power to dispose of the goods so that the document is ineffective to pass title, judgment liens are valid to the extent of the debtor's interest in the goods.

2.   The last sentence covers the possibility that the holder of a document who has been enjoined from negotiating it will violate the injunction by negotiating to an innocent purchaser for value. In such case the lien will be defeated.

Cross Reference:

Sections 7–106 and 7–501 through 7–503.

Definitional Cross References:

"Bailee". Section 7–102.
"Delivery". Section 1–201.
"Document of title". Section 1–201.
"Goods". Section 7–102.
"Notice". Section 1–202.
"Person". Section 1–201.
"Purchase". Section 1–201.
"Value". Section 1–204.

§ 7–603.   Conflicting Claims; Interpleader.

If more than one person claims title to or possession of the goods, the bailee is excused from delivery until the bailee has a reasonable time to ascertain the validity of the adverse claims or to commence an action for interpleader. The bailee may assert an interpleader either in defending an action for nondelivery of the goods or by original action.

Official Comment

Prior Uniform Statutory Provisions: Former Section 7–603.

Changes: Changes for style only.

Purposes:

1.   The section enables a bailee faced with conflicting claims to the goods to compel the claimants to litigate their claims with each other rather than with the bailee. The bailee is protected from legal liability when the bailee complies with court orders from the interpleader. *See e.g. Northwestern National Sales, Inc. v. Commercial Cold Storage, Inc.*, 162 Ga. App. 741, 293 S.E.2d. 30 (1982).

2.   This section allows the bailee to bring an interpleader action but does not provide an exclusive basis for allowing interpleader. If either state or federal procedural rules allow an interpleader in other situations, the bailee may commence an interpleader under those rules. Even in an interpleader to which this section applies, the state or federal process of interpleader applies to the bailee's action for interpleader. For example, state or federal interpleader statutes or rules may permit a bailee to protect its lien or to seek attorney's fees and costs in the interpleader action.

Cross reference:

Point 1: Section 7–403.

Definitional Cross References:

"Action". Section 1–201.
"Bailee". Section 7–102.
"Delivery". Section 1–201.
"Goods". Section 7–102.
"Person". Section 1–201.
"Reasonable time". Section 1–205.

PART 7
MISCELLANEOUS PROVISIONS

Legislative Note: The following provisions should be used to apply to both the Article 7 provisions and the conforming amendments to other articles of the Uniform Commercial Code.

§ 7–701.   Effective Date.

This [Act] takes effect on [ ].

§ 7–702.   Repeals.

[Existing Article 7] and [Section 10–104 of the Uniform Commercial Code] are repealed.

Official Comment

A state should repeal its prior version of Uniform Commercial Code Article 7 on documents of title and Uniform Commercial Code section 10–204. The substance of Section 10–104 has been incorporated into Section 7–103(b).

§ 7–703.   Applicability.

This [Act] applies to a document of title that is issued or a bailment that arises on or after the effective date of this [Act]. This [Act] does not apply to a document of title that is issued or a bailment that arises before the effective date of this [Act] even if the document of title or bailment would be subject to this [Act] if the document of title had been issued or bailment had arisen on or after the effective date of this [Act]. This [Act] does not apply to a right of action that has accrued before the effective date of this [Act].

Official Comment

This Act will apply prospectively only to documents of title issued or bailments that arise after the effective date of the Act.

§ 7–704.   Savings Clause.

A document of title issued or a bailment that arises before the effective date of this [Act] and the rights, obligations, and interests flowing from that document or bailment are governed by any statute or other rule amended or repealed by this [Act] as if amendment or repeal had not occurred and may be terminated, completed, consummated, or enforced under that statute or other rule.

Official Comment

This Act will apply prospectively only to documents of title issued or bailments that arise after the effective date of the Act. To the extent that issues arise based upon documents of title or rights or obligations that arise prior to the effective date of this Act, prior law will apply to resolve those issues.

UCC ARTICLE 8 (2016)

INVESTMENT SECURITIES

Article 8 was revised in 1994.

PART 1.   SHORT TITLE AND GENERAL MATTERS

PART 2.   ISSUE AND ISSUER

PART 3.   TRANSFER OF CERTIFICATED AND UNCERTIFICATED SECURITIES

UNIFORM COMMERCIAL CODE

PART 4. REGISTRATION

PART 5. SECURITY ENTITLEMENTS

National Conference of Commissioners on Uniform State Laws

REPORTER

James Steven Rogers, Newton, Massachusetts

DRAFTING COMMITTEE

CHAIRMAN

Curtis R. Reitz, Philadelphia, Pennsylvania

MEMBERS

Ann E. Conaway Anker, Wilmington, Delaware

John Fox Arnold, St. Louis, Missouri

Robert J. Desiderio, Albuquerque, New Mexico

Egon Guttman, Washington, District of Columbia, *The American Law Institute Representative*

Howard T. Rosen, Millburn, New Jersey

Richard B. Smith, New York, New York, *The American Law Institute Representative* and *American Bar Association Advisor*

Howard J. Swibel, Chicago, Illinois

Justin L. Vigdor, Rochester, New York

Richard C. Hite, Wichita, Kansas, *President (Member Ex Officio)*

K. King Burnett, Salisbury, Maryland, *Chairman, Division A (Member Ex Officio)*

REVIEW COMMITTEE

CHAIRMAN

Michael P. Sullivan, Minneapolis, Minnesota

ARTICLE 8 (2016)

MEMBERS

Gerald L. Bepko, Indianapolis, Indiana
Reed L. Martineau, Salt Lake City, Utah

ADVISORS

Charles W. Mooney, Jr., *American Bar Association, Section of Business Law*
Thomas J. Greco, *American Bankers Association*

CONSULTANTS

Jonathan Kallman, *United States Securities and Exchange Commission*
Calvin Ninomiya and Cynthia E. Reese, *United States Department of the Treasury*
Lawranne Stewart, *Board of Governors, Federal Reserve System*
Debra W. Cook and MarySue Fisher, *Federal Reserve Bank of New York*

PREFATORY NOTE

The present version of Article 8 is the product of a major revision made necessary by the fact that the prior version of Article 8 did not adequately deal with the system of securities holding through securities intermediaries that has developed in the past few decades. Although the prior version of Article 8 did contain some provisions dealing with securities holding through securities intermediaries, these were engrafted onto a structure designed for securities practices of earlier times. The resulting legal uncertainties adversely affected all participants. The revision is intended to eliminate these uncertainties by providing a modern legal structure for current securities holding practices.

I. EVOLUTION OF SECURITIES HOLDING SYSTEMS

A. The Traditional Securities Holding System

The original version of Article 8, drafted in the 1940s and 1950s, was based on the assumption that possession and delivery of physical certificates are the key elements in the securities holding system. Ownership of securities was traditionally evidenced by possession of the certificates, and changes were accomplished by delivery of the certificates.

Transfer of securities in the traditional certificate-based system was a complicated, labor-intensive process. Each time securities were traded, the physical certificates had to be delivered from the seller to the buyer, and in the case of registered securities the certificates had to be surrendered to the issuer or its transfer agent for registration of transfer. As is well known, the mechanical problems of processing the paperwork for securities transfers reached crisis proportions in the late 1960s, leading to calls for the elimination of the physical certificate and development of modern electronic systems for recording ownership of securities and transfers of ownership. That was the focus of the revision effort that led to the promulgation of the 1978 amendments to Article 8 concerning uncertificated securities.

B. The Uncertificated Securities System Envisioned by the 1978 Amendments

In 1978, amendments to Article 8 were approved to establish the commercial law rules that were thought necessary to permit the evolution of a system in which issuers would no longer issue certificates. The Drafting Committee that produced the 1978 amendments was given a fairly limited charge. It was to draft the revisions that would be needed for uncertificated securities, but otherwise leave the Article 8 rules unchanged. Accordingly, the 1978 amendments primarily took the form of adding parallel provisions dealing with uncertificated securities to the existing rules of Article 8 on certificated securities.

The system of securities holding contemplated by the 1978 amendments differed from the traditional system only in that ownership of securities would not be evidenced by physical certificates. It was contemplated that changes in ownership would continue to be reflected by changes in the records of the issuer. The main difference would be that instead of surrendering an indorsed certificate for registration of transfer, an instruction would be sent to the issuer directing it to register the transfer. Although a system of the sort contemplated by the 1978 amendments may well develop in the coming decades, this has not yet happened for most categories of securities. Mutual funds shares have long been issued in uncertificated

593

form, but virtually all other forms of publicly traded corporate securities are still issued in certificated form. Individual investors who wish to be recorded as registered owners on the issuers' books still obtain and hold physical certificates. The certificates representing the largest portion of the shares of publicly traded companies, however, are not held by the beneficial owners, but by clearing corporations. Settlement of securities trading occurs not by delivery of certificates or by registration of transfer on the records of the issuers or their transfer agents, but by computer entries in the records of clearing corporations and securities intermediaries. That is quite different from the system envisioned by the 1978 amendments.

C. Evolution of the Indirect Holding System

At the time of the "paperwork crunch" in the late 1960s, the trading volume on the New York Stock Exchange that so seriously strained the capacities of the clearance and settlement system was in the range of 10 million shares per day. Today, the system can easily handle trading volume on routine days of hundreds of millions of shares. This processing capacity could have been achieved only by the application of modern electronic information processing systems. Yet the legal rules under which the system operates are *not* the uncertificated securities provisions of Article 8. To understand why this is so, one must delve at least a bit deeper into the operations of the current system.

If one examines the shareholder records of large corporations whose shares are publicly traded on the exchanges or in the over the counter market, one would find that one entity—Cede & Co.—is listed as the shareholder of record of somewhere in the range of sixty to eighty per cent of the outstanding shares of all publicly traded companies. Cede & Co. is the nominee name used by The Depository Trust Company ("DTC"), a limited purpose trust company organized under New York law for the purpose of acting as a depository to hold securities for the benefit of its participants, some 600 or so broker-dealers and banks. Essentially all of the trading in publicly held companies is executed through the broker-dealers who are participants in DTC, and the great bulk of public securities—the sixty to eighty per cent figure noted above— are held by these broker-dealers and banks on behalf of their customers. If all of these broker-dealers and banks held physical certificates, then as trades were executed each day it would be necessary to deliver the certificates back and forth among these broker-dealers and banks. By handing all of their securities over to a common depository all of these deliveries can be eliminated. Transfers can be accomplished by adjustments to the participants' DTC accounts.

Although the use of a common depository eliminates the needs for physical deliveries, an enormous number of entries would still have to be made on DTC's books if each transaction between its participants were recorded one by one on DTC's books. Any two major broker-dealers may have executed numerous trades with each other in a given security on a single day. Significant processing efficiency has been achieved by netting all of the transactions among the participants that occur each day, so that entries need be made on the depository's books only for the net changes in the positions of each participant at the end of each day. This clearance and netting function might well be performed by the securities exchanges or by the same institution that acts as the depository, as is the case in many other securities markets around the world. In the United States, however, this clearance and netting function is carried out by a separate corporation, National Securities Clearing Corporation ("NSCC"). All that needs to be done to settle each day's trading is for NSCC to compute the net receive and deliver obligations and to instruct DTC to make the corresponding adjustments in the participants' accounts.

The broker-dealers and banks who are participants in the DTC-NSCC system in turn provide analogous clearance and settlement functions to their own customers. If Customer A buys 100 shares of XYZ Co. through Broker, and Customer B sells 100 shares of XYZ Co. through the same Broker, the trade can be settled by entries on Broker's books. Neither DTC's books showing Broker's total position in XYZ Co., nor XYZ Co.'s books showing DTC's total position in XYZ Co., need be changed to reflect the settlement of this trade. One can readily appreciate the significance of the settlement function performed at this level if one considers that a single major bank may be acting as securities custodian for hundreds or thousands of mutual funds, pension funds, and other institutional investors. On any given day, the customers of that bank may have entered into an enormous number of trades, yet it is possible that relatively little of this trading activity will result in any net change in the custodian bank's positions on the books of DTC.

Settlement of market trading in most of the major U.S. securities markets is now effected primarily through some form of netted clearance and depository system. Virtually all publicly traded corporate equity securities, corporate debt securities, and municipal debt securities are now eligible for deposit in the DTC system. Recently, DTC has implemented a similar depository settlement system for the commercial paper market, and could, but for limitations in present Article 8, handle other forms of short-term money market securities such as bankers' acceptances. For trading in mortgage-backed securities, such as Ginnie Mae's, a similar depository settlement system has been developed by Participants Trust Company. For trading in U.S. Treasury securities, a somewhat analogous book-entry system is operated under Treasury rules by the Federal Reserve System.

D. Need for Different Legal Rules for the Direct and Indirect Holding Systems

Both the traditional paper-based system, and the uncertificated system contemplated by the 1978 amendments, can be described as "direct" securities holding systems; that is, the beneficial owners of securities have a direct relationship with the issuer of the securities. For securities in bearer form, whoever has possession of the certificate thereby has a direct claim against the issuer. For registered securities, the registered owner, whether of certificated or uncertificated securities, has a direct relationship with the issuer by virtue of being recorded as the owner on the records maintained by the issuer or its transfer agent.

By contrast, the DTC depository system for corporate equity and debt securities can be described as an "indirect holding" system, that is, the issuer's records do not show the identity of all of the beneficial owners. Instead, a large portion of the outstanding securities of any given issue are recorded on the issuer's records as belonging to a depository. The depository's records in turn show the identity of the banks or brokers who are its members, and the records of those securities intermediaries show the identity of their customers.

Even after the 1978 amendments, the rules of Article 8 did not deal effectively with the indirect holding system. The rules of the 1978 version of Article 8 were based on the assumption that changes in ownership of securities would still be effected either by delivery of physical certificates or by registration of transfer on the books of the issuer. Yet in the indirect holding system, settlement of the vast majority of securities trades does not involve either of these events. For most, if not all, of the securities held through DTC, physical certificates representing DTC's total position do exist. These "jumbo certificates," however, are never delivered from person to person. Just as nothing ever happens to these certificates, virtually nothing happens to the official registry of stockholders maintained by the issuers or their transfer agents to reflect the great bulk of the changes in ownership of shares that occur each day.

The principal mechanism through which securities trades are settled today is not delivery of certificates or registration of transfers on the issuer's books, but netted settlement arrangements and accounting entries on the books of a multi-tiered pyramid of securities intermediaries. Herein is the basic problem. Virtually all of the rules of the prior version of Article 8 specifying how changes in ownership of securities are effected, and what happens if something goes awry in the process, were keyed to the concepts of a transfer of physical certificates or registration of transfers on the books of the issuers, yet that is not how changes in ownership are actually reflected in the modern securities holding system.

II. BRIEF OVERVIEW OF REVISED ARTICLE 8

A. Drafting Approach—Neutrality Principle

One of the objectives of the revision of Article 8 is to devise a structure of commercial law rules for investment securities that will be sufficiently flexible to respond to changes in practice over the next few decades. If it were possible to predict with confidence how the securities holding and trading system would develop, one could produce a statute designed specifically for the system envisioned. Recent experience, however, shows the danger of that approach. The 1978 amendments to Article 8 were based on the assumption that the solution to the problems that plagued the paper-based securities trading system of the 1960s would be the development of uncertificated securities. Instead, the solution thus far has been the development of the indirect holding system.

If one thought that the indirect holding system would come to dominate securities holding, one might draft Article 8 rules designed primarily for the indirect holding system, giving limited attention to the traditional direct holding system of security certificates or any uncertificated version of a direct holding system that might develop in the future. It is, however, by no means clear whether the long-term evolution will be toward decreased or increased use of direct holdings. At present, investors in most equity securities can either hold their securities through brokers or request that certificates be issued in their own name. For the immediate future it seems likely that that situation will continue. One can imagine many plausible scenarios for future evolution. Direct holding might become less and less common as investors become more familiar and comfortable with book-entry systems and/or as market or regulatory pressures develop that discourage direct holding. One might note, for example, that major brokerage firms are beginning to impose fees for having certificates issued and that some observers have suggested that acceleration of the cycle for settlement of securities trades might be facilitated by discouraging customers from obtaining certificates. On the other hand, other observers feel that it is important for investors to retain the option of holding securities in certificated form, or at least in some form that gives them a direct relationship with the issuer and does not require them to hold through brokers or other securities intermediaries. Some groups within the securities industry are beginning to work on development of uncertificated systems that would preserve this option.

Revised Article 8 takes a neutral position on the evolution of securities holding practices. The revision was based on the assumption that the path of development will be determined by market and regulatory forces and that the Article 8 rules should not seek to influence that development in any specific direction. Although various drafting approaches were considered, it became apparent early in the revision process that the differences between the direct holding system and the indirect holding system are sufficiently significant that it is best to treat them as separate systems requiring different legal concepts. Accordingly, while the rules of the prior version of Article 8 have, in large measure, been retained for the direct holding system, a new Part 5 has been added, setting out the commercial law rules for the indirect securities holding system. The principle of neutrality does carry some implications for the design of specific Article 8 rules. At the very least, the Article 8 rules for all securities holding systems should be sufficiently clear and predictable that uncertainty about the governing law does not itself operate as a constraint on market developments. In addition, an effort has been made to identify and eliminate any Article 8 rules that might act as impediments to any of the foreseeable paths of development.

B. Direct Holding System

With respect to securities held directly, Revised Article 8 retains the basic conceptual structure and rules of present law. Part 2, which is largely unchanged from former law, deals with certain aspects of the obligations of issuers. The primary purpose of the rules of Part 2 is to apply to investment securities the principles of negotiable instruments law that preclude the issuers of negotiable instruments from asserting defenses against subsequent purchasers. Part 3 deals with transfer for securities held directly. One of its principal purposes is to apply to investment securities the principles of negotiable instruments law that protect purchasers of negotiable instruments against adverse claims. Part 4 deals with the process of registration of transfer by the issuer or transfer agent.

Although the basic concepts of the direct holding system rules have been retained, there are significant changes in terminology, organization, and statement of the rules. Some of the major changes are as follows:

Simplification of Part 3. The addition of the new Part 5 on the indirect holding system makes unnecessary the rather elaborate provisions of former law, such as those in Section 8–313, that sought to fit the indirect holding system into the conceptual structure of the direct holding system. Thus, Part 3 of Revised Article 8 is, in many respects, more similar to the original version of Article 8 than to the 1978 version.

Protected purchaser. The prior version of Article 8 used the term "bona fide purchaser" to refer to those purchasers who took free from adverse claims, and it used the phrase "good faith" in stating the requirements for such status. In order to promote clarity, Revised Article 8 states the rules that protect purchasers against adverse claims without using the phrase "good faith" and uses the new term "protected purchaser" to refer to purchasers in the direct holding system who are protected against adverse claims. See Sections 8–105 and 8–303.

Certificated versus uncertificated securities. The rules of the 1978 version of Article 8 concerning uncertificated securities have been simplified considerably. The 1978 version added provisions on uncertificated securities parallel to the provisions of the original version of Article 8 dealing with securities represented by certificates. Thus, virtually every section had one set of rules on "certificated securities" and another on "uncertificated securities." The constant juxtaposition of "certificated securities" and "uncertificated securities" has probably led readers to overemphasize the differences. Revised Article 8 has a unitary definition of "security" in Section 8–102(a)(15) which refers to the underlying intangible interest or obligation. In Revised Article 8, the difference between certificated and uncertificated is treated not as an inherent attribute of the security but as a difference in the means by which ownership is evidenced. The terms "certificated" and "uncertificated" security are used in those sections where it is important to distinguish between these two means of evidencing ownership. Revised Article 8 also deletes the provisions of the 1978 version concerning "transaction statements" and "registered pledges." These changes are explained in the Revision Notes 3, 4, and 5, below.

Scope of Parts 2, 3, and 4. The rules of Parts 2, 3, and 4 deal only with the rights of persons who hold securities directly. In typical securities holding arrangements in the modern depository system, only the clearing corporation would be a direct holder of the securities. Thus, while the rules of Parts 2, 3, and 4 would apply to the relationship between the issuer and the clearing corporation, they have no application to relationships below the clearing corporation level. Under Revised Article 8, a person who holds a security through a broker or securities custodian has a security entitlement governed by the Part 5 rules but is not the direct holder of the security. Thus, the rules of Revised Section 8–303 on the rights of "protected purchasers," which are the analog of the bona fide purchaser rules of former Article 8, do not apply to persons who hold securities through brokers or securities custodians. Instead, Part 5 contains its own rules to protect investors in the indirect holding system against adverse claims. See Revised Section 8–502.

C.   Indirect Holding System

Although the Revised Article 8 provisions for the indirect holding system are somewhat complex, the basic approach taken can be summarized rather briefly. Revised Article 8 abandons the attempt to describe all of the complex relationships in the indirect holding system using the simple concepts of the traditional direct holding system. Instead, new rules specifically designed for the indirect holding system are added as Part 5 of Article 8. In a nutshell, the approach is to describe the core of the package of rights of a person who holds a security through a securities intermediary and then give that package of rights a name.

The starting point of Revised Article 8's treatment of the indirect holding system is the concept of "security entitlement." The term is defined in Section 8–102(a)(17) as "the rights and property interest of an entitlement holder with respect to a financial asset specified in Part 5." Like many legal concepts, however, the meaning of "security entitlement" is to be found less in any specific definition than in the matrix of rules that use the term. In a sense, then, the entirety of Part 5 is the definition of "security entitlement" because the Part 5 rules specify the rights and property interest that comprise a security entitlement.

Part 5 begins by specifying, in Section 8–501, when an entitlement holder acquires a security entitlement. The basic rule is very simple. A person acquires a security entitlement when the securities intermediary credits the financial asset to the person's account. The remaining sections of Part 5 specify the content of the security entitlement concept. Section 8–504 provides that a securities intermediary must maintain a sufficient quantity of financial assets to satisfy the claims of all of its entitlement holders. Section 8–503 provides that these financial assets are held by the intermediary for the entitlement holders, are not the property of the securities intermediary, and are not subject to claims of the intermediary's general creditors. Thus, a security entitlement is itself a form of property interest not merely an *in personam* claim against the intermediary. The concept of a security entitlement does, however, include a package of *in personam* rights against the intermediary. Other Part 5 rules identify the core of this package of rights, subject to specification by agreement and regulatory law. See Sections 8–505 through 8–509.

To illustrate the basic features of the new rules, consider a simple example of two investors, John and Mary, each of whom owns 1000 shares of Acme, Inc., a publicly traded company. John has a certificate representing his 1000 shares and is registered on the books maintained by Acme's transfer agent as the holder of record of those 1000 shares. Accordingly, he has a direct claim against the issuer, he receives dividends and distributions directly from the issuer, and he receives proxies directly from the issuer for purposes of voting his shares. Mary has chosen to hold her securities through her broker. She does not have a certificate and is not registered on Acme's stock books as a holder of record. She enjoys the economic and corporate benefits of ownership but does so through her broker and any other intermediaries in the chain back to the issuer. John's interest in Acme common stock would be described under Revised Article 8 as a direct interest in a "security." Thus, if John grants a security interest in his investment position, the collateral would be described as a "security." Mary's interest in Acme common stock would be described under Revised Article 8 as a "security entitlement." Thus, if Mary grants a security interest in her investment position, the collateral would be described as a "security entitlement."

For many purposes, there is no need to differentiate among the various ways that an investor might hold securities. For example, for purposes of financial accounting, John and Mary would each be described as the owner of 1000 shares of Acme common stock. For those purposes it is irrelevant that John is the registered owner and has physical possession of a certificate, while Mary holds her position through an intermediary. Revised Article 8 recognizes this point in Section 8–104 which provides that acquiring a security entitlement and acquiring a security certificate are different ways of acquiring an interest in the underlying security.

D.   Security Interests

Along with the revision of Article 8, significant changes have been made in the rules concerning security interests in securities. The revision returns to the pre-1978 structure in which the rules on security interests in investment securities are set out in Article 9, rather than in Article 8. The changes in Article 9 are, in part, conforming changes to adapt Article 9 to the new concept of a security entitlement. The Article 9 changes, however, go beyond that to establish a simplified structure for the creation and perfection of security interests in investment securities, whether held directly or indirectly.

The Revised Article 9 rules continue the long-established principle that a security interest in a security represented by a certificate can be perfected by a possessory pledge. The revised rules, however, do not require that all security interests in investment securities be implemented by procedures based on the conceptual structure of the common law pledge. Under the revised Article 9 rules, a security interest in securities can be created pursuant to Section 9–203 in the same fashion as a security interest in any other form of property, that is, by agreement between the debtor and secured party. There is no requirement of a "transfer," "delivery," or any similar action, physical or metaphysical, for the creation of an effective security interest. A security interest in securities is, of course, a form of property interest, but the only requirements for creation of this form of property interest are those set out in Section 9–203.

The perfection methods for security interests in investment securities are set out in Sections 9–309, 9–312, 9–313, and 9–314. The basic rule is that a security interest may be perfected by "control." The concept of control, defined in Section 8–106, plays an important role in both Article 8 and Article 9. In general, obtaining control means taking the steps necessary to place the lender in a position where it can have the collateral sold off without the further cooperation of the debtor. Thus, for certificated securities, a lender obtains control by taking possession of the certificate with any necessary indorsement. For securities held through a securities intermediary, the lender can obtain control in two ways. First, the lender obtains control if it becomes the entitlement holder; that is, has the securities positions transferred to an account in its own name. Second, the lender obtains control if the securities intermediary agrees to act on instructions from the secured party to dispose of the positions, even though the debtor remains the entitlement holder. Such an arrangement suffices to give the lender control even though the debtor retains the right to trade and exercise other ordinary rights of an entitlement holder.

Except where the debtor is itself a securities firm, filing of an ordinary Article 9 financing statement is also a permissible alternative method of perfection. However, filing with respect to investment property does not assure the lender the same protections as for other forms of collateral, since the priority rules provide that a secured party who obtains control has priority over a secured party who does not obtain control.

The details of the new rules on security interests, as applied both to the retail level and to arrangements for secured financing of securities dealers, are explained in the Official Comments to Sections 9–309, 9–312, 9–313, and 9–314.

ARTICLE 8 (2016)

III. SCOPE AND APPLICATION OF ARTICLE 8

A. Terminology

To understand the scope and application of the rules of Revised Article 8, and the related security interest rules of Article 9, it is necessary to understand some of the key defined terms:

Security, defined in Section 8–102(a)(15), has essentially the same meaning as under the prior version of Article 8. The difference in Revised Article 8 is that the definition of security does not determine the coverage of all of Article 8. Although the direct holding system rules in Parts 2, 3, and 4 apply only to securities, the indirect holding system rules of Part 5 apply to the broader category of "financial assets."

Financial asset, defined in Section 8–103(a)(9), is the term used to describe the forms of property to which the indirect holding system rules of Part 5 apply. The term includes not only "securities," but also other interests, obligations, or property that are held through securities accounts. The best illustration of the broader scope of the term financial asset is the treatment of money market instruments, discussed below.

Security entitlement, defined in Section 8–103(a)(17), is the term used to describe the property interest of a person who holds a security or other financial asset through a securities intermediary.

Securities intermediary, defined in Section 8–103(a)(14), is the term used for those who hold securities for others in the indirect holding system. It covers clearing corporations, banks acting as securities custodians, and brokers holding securities for their customers.

Entitlement holder, defined in Section 8–103(a)(7), is the term used for those who hold securities through intermediaries.

Securities account, defined in Section 8–501(a), describes the form of arrangement between a securities intermediary and an entitlement holder that gives rise to a security entitlement. As explained below, the definition of securities account plays a key role in setting the scope of the indirect holding system rules of Part 5.

Investment property, defined in Section 9–102(a)(49), determines the application of the new Article 9 rules for secured transactions. In addition to securities and security entitlements, the Article 9 term "investment property" is defined to include "securities account" in order to simplify the drafting of the Article 9 rules that permit debtors to grant security interests either in specific security entitlements or in an entire securities account. The other difference between the coverage of the Article 8 and Article 9 terms is that commodity futures contracts are excluded from Article 8, but are included within the Article 9 definition of "investment property." Thus, the new Article 9 rules apply to security interests in commodity futures positions as well as security interests in securities positions.

B. Notes on Scope of Article 8

Article 8 is in no sense a comprehensive codification of the law governing securities or transactions in securities. Although Article 8 deals with some aspects of the rights of securities holders against issuers, most of that relationship is governed not by Article 8, but by corporation, securities, and contract law. Although Article 8 deals with some aspects of the rights and duties of parties who transfer securities, it is not a codification of the law of contracts for the purchase or sale of securities. (The prior version of Article 8 did include a few miscellaneous rules on contracts for the sale of securities, but these have not been included in Revised Article 8). Although the new indirect holding system rules of Part 5 deal with some aspects of the relationship between brokers or other securities professionals and their customers, Article 8 is still not in any sense a comprehensive code of the law governing the relationship between broker-dealers or other securities intermediaries and their customers. Most of the law governing that relationship is the common law of contract and agency, supplemented or supplanted by regulatory law.

The distinction between the aspects of the broker-customer relationship that are and are not dealt with in this Article may be illuminated by considering the differing roles of the broker in a typical securities transaction, in which the broker acts as agent for the customer. When a customer directs a broker to buy or sell securities for the customer, and the broker executes that trade on a securities exchange or in the over the counter market, the broker is entering into a contract for the purchase or sale of the securities as agent of the customer. The rules of the exchange, practices of the market, or regulatory law will specify when and how that contract is to be performed. For example, today the terms of the standard contract for trades in most corporate securities require the seller to deliver the securities, and the buyer to pay for them, five business days after the date that the contract was made, although the SEC has recently promulgated a rule that will accelerate the cycle to require settlement in three business days. In the common speech of the industry, the transaction in which the broker enters into a contract for the purchase or sale of the securities is referred to as executing the trade, and the transaction in which the securities are delivered and paid for is referred to as settlement. Thus, the current settlement cycle is known as T+5, that is, settlement is required on the fifth business day after the date of the trade, and the new SEC rule will change it to T+3. One must be careful in moving from the jargon of the securities industry to the jargon of the legal profession. For most practical economic purposes, the trade date is the date that counts, because that is the time at which the price is set, the risk of price changes shifts, and the parties become bound to perform. For purposes of precise legal analysis, however, the securities phrase "trade" or "execute a trade" means enter into a contract for the purchase or sale of the securities. The transfer of property interests occurs not at the time the contract is made but at the time it is performed, that is, at settlement.

The distinction between trade and settlement is important in understanding the scope of Article 8. Article 8 deals with the settlement phase of securities transactions. It deals with the mechanisms by which interests in securities are transferred, and the rights and duties of those who are involved in the transfer process. It does not deal with the process of entering into contracts for the transfer of securities or regulate the rights and duties of those involved in the contracting process. To use securities parlance, Article 8 deals not with the trade, but with settlement of the trade. Indeed, Article 8 does not even deal with all aspects of settlement. In a netted clearance and settlement system such as the NSCC-DTC system, individual trades are not settled one-by-one by corresponding entries on the books of any depository. Rather, settlement of the individual trades occurs through the clearing arrangements, in accordance with the rules and agreements that govern those arrangements.

In the rules dealing with the indirect holding system, one must be particularly careful to bear in mind the distinction between trade and settlement. Under Revised Article 8, the property interest of a person who holds securities through an intermediary is described as a "security entitlement," which is defined in Revised Section 8–102(a)(17) as the package of rights and property interest of an entitlement holder specified in Part 5. Saying that the security entitlement is a package of rights against the broker does not mean that all of the customer's rights against the broker are part of the security entitlement and hence part of the subject matter of Article 8. The distinction between trade and settlement remains fundamental. The rules of this Article on the indirect holding system deal with brokers and other intermediaries as media through which investors hold their financial assets. Brokers are also media through which investors buy and sell their financial assets, but that aspect of their role is not the subject of this Article.

The principal goal of the Article 8 revision project is to provide a satisfactory framework for analysis of the indirect holding system. The technique used in Revised Article 8 is to acknowledge explicitly that the relationship between a securities intermediary and its entitlement holders is *sui generis*, and to state the applicable commercial law rules directly, rather than by inference from a categorization of the relationship based on legal concepts of a different era. One of the consequences of this drafting technique is that in order to provide content to the concept of security entitlement it becomes necessary to identify the core of the package of rights that make up a security entitlement. Sections 8–504 through 8–508 cover such basic matters as the duty of the securities intermediary to maintain a sufficient quantity of securities to satisfy all of its entitlement holders, the duty of the securities intermediary to pass through to entitlement holder the economic and corporate law rights of ownership of the security, and the duty of the securities intermediary to comply with authorized entitlement orders originated by the entitlement holder. These sections are best thought of as definitional; that is, a relationship which does not include these rights is not the kind of relationship that Revised Article 8 deals with. Because these sections take the form of statements of the duties of an intermediary toward its entitlement holders, one must be careful to avoid a distorted perspective on what Revised Article 8 is and is not designed to do. Revised Article 8 is not, and should not be, a comprehensive body of private law governing the relationship between brokers and their customers, nor a body of regulatory law to police against improper conduct by brokers or other intermediaries. Many, if not most, aspects of the relationship between brokers and customers are governed by the common law of contract and agency, supplemented or supplanted by federal and state regulatory law. Revised Article 8 does not take the place of this body of private and regulatory law. If there are gaps in the regulatory law, they should be dealt with as such; Article 8 is not the place to address them. Article 8 deals with how interests in securities are evidenced and how they are transferred. By way of a rough analogy, one might think of Article 8 as playing the role for the securities markets that real estate recording acts play for the real estate markets. Real estate recording acts do not regulate the conduct of parties to real estate transactions; Article 8 does not regulate the conduct of parties to securities transactions.

C. Application of Revised Articles 8 and 9 to Common Investments and Investment Arrangements

It may aid understanding to sketch briefly the treatment under Revised Articles 8 and 9 of a variety of relatively common products and arrangements.

1. Publicly traded stocks and bonds.

"Security" is defined in Revised Section 8–102(a)(15) in substantially the same terms as in the prior version of Article 8. It covers the ordinary publicly traded investment securities, such as corporate stocks and bonds. Parts 2, 3, and 4 govern the interests of persons who hold securities directly, and Part 5 governs the interest of those who hold securities indirectly.

Ordinary publicly traded securities provide a good illustration of the relationship between the direct and indirect holding system rules. The distinction between the direct and indirect holding systems is not an attribute of the securities themselves but of the way in which a particular person holds the securities. Thus, whether one looks to the direct holding system rules of Parts 2, 3, and 4 or the indirect holding system rules of Part 5 will depend on the level in the securities holding system being analyzed.

Consider, for example, corporate stock which is held through a depository, such as DTC. The clearing corporation, or its nominee, is the registered owner of all of the securities it holds on behalf of all of its participants. Thus the rules of Parts 2, 3, and 4 of Revised Article 8 apply to the relationship between the issuer and the clearing corporation. If, as is typically the case today, the securities are still represented by certificates, the clearing corporation will be the holder of the security certificate or certificates representing its total holdings. So far as Article 8 is concerned, the relationship between the issuer and the clearing corporation is no different from the relationship between the issuer and any other registered owner.

The relationship between the clearing corporation and its participants is governed by the indirect holding system rules of Part 5. At that level, the clearing corporation is the securities intermediary and the participant is the entitlement holder. If the participant is itself a securities intermediary, such as a broker holding for its customers or a bank acting as a securities custodian, the Part 5 rules apply to its relationship to its own customers. At that level the broker or bank custodian is the securities intermediary and the customer is the entitlement holder. Note that the broker or bank custodian is both an entitlement holder and a securities intermediary—but is so with respect to different security entitlements. For purposes of Article 8 analysis, the customer's security entitlement against the broker or bank custodian is a different item of property from the security entitlement of the broker or bank custodian against the clearing corporation.

For investors who hold their securities directly, it makes no difference that some other investors hold their interests indirectly. Many investors today choose to hold their securities directly, becoming the registered owners on the books of the issuer and obtaining certificates registered in their names. For such investors, the addition of the new indirect holding system rules to Article 8 is entirely irrelevant. They will continue to deal directly with the issuers, or their transfer agents, under essentially the same rules as in the prior version of Article 8.

The securities holding options available to investors in a particular form of security may depend on the terms of the security. For example, direct holding is frequently not available for new issues of state and local government bonds. At one time, state and local government bonds were commonly issued in bearer form. Today, however, new issues of state and local government bonds must be in registered form and most are issued in what is known as "book-entry only" form; that is, the issuer specifies that the only person it will directly register as the registered owner is a clearing corporation. Thus, one of the inherent terms of the security is that investors can hold only in the indirect holding system.

2.   Treasury securities.

U.S. government securities fall within the definition of security in Article 8 and therefore are governed by Article 8 in the same fashion as any other publicly held debt security, except insofar as Article 8 is preempted by applicable federal law or regulation.

New Treasury securities are no longer issued in certificated form; they can be held only through the book-entry systems established by the Treasury and Federal Reserve Banks. The Treasury offers a book-entry system, known as "Treasury Direct" which enables individual investors to have their positions recorded directly on the books of a Federal Reserve Bank, in a fashion somewhat similar to the uncertificated direct holding system contemplated by the 1978 version of Article 8. The governing law for the Treasury Direct system, however, is set out in the applicable Treasury regulations. The Treasury Direct system is not designed for active trading.

The great bulk of Treasury securities are held not through the Treasury Direct system but through a multi-tiered indirect holding system. The Federal Reserve Banks, acting as fiscal agent for the Treasury, maintain records of the holdings of member banks of the Federal Reserve System, and those banks in turn maintain records showing the extent to which they are holding for themselves or their own customers, including government securities dealers, institutional investors, or smaller banks who in turn may act as custodians for investors. The indirect holding system for Treasury securities was established under federal regulations promulgated in the 1970s. In the 1980s, Treasury released the proposed TRADES regulations that would have established a more comprehensive body of federal commercial law for the Treasury holding system. During the Article 8 revision process, Treasury withdrew these regulations, anticipating that once Revised Article 8 is enacted, it will be possible to base the law for the Treasury system on the new Article 8 rules.

3.   Broker-customer relationships.

Whether the relationship between a broker and its customer is governed by the Article 8 Part 5 rules depends on the nature of the services that the broker performs for the customer.

Some investors use brokers only to purchase and sell securities. These customers take delivery of certificates representing the securities they purchase and hold them in their own names. When they wish to sell, they deliver the certificates to the brokers. The Article 8 Part 5 rules would not affect such customers, because the Part 5 rules deal with arrangements in which investors hold securities through securities intermediaries. The transaction between the customer and broker might be the traditional agency arrangement in which the broker buys or sells on behalf of the customer as agent for an undisclosed principal, or it might be a dealer transaction in which the "broker" as principal buys from or sells to the customer. In either case, if the customer takes delivery and holds the securities directly, she will become the "purchaser" of a "security" whose interest therein is governed by the rules of Parts 2, 3, and 4 of Article 8. If the customer meets the other requirements of Section 8–303(a), the customer who takes delivery can qualify as a "protected purchaser" who takes free from any adverse claims under Section 8–303(b). The broker's role in such transactions is primarily governed by non-Article 8 law. There are only a few provisions of Article 8 that affect the relationship between the customer and broker in such cases. See Section 8–108 (broker makes to the customer the warranties of a transferor) and 8–115 (broker not liable in conversion if customer was acting wrongfully against a third party in selling securities).

Many investors use brokers not only to purchase and sell securities, but also as the custodians through whom they hold their securities. The indirect holding system rules of Part 5 apply to the custodial aspect of this relationship. If a customer purchases a security through a broker and directs the broker to hold the security in an account for the customer, the customer will never become a "purchaser" of a "security" whose interest therein is governed by the rules of Parts 2, 3, and 4 of Article 8. Accordingly, the customer does not become a "protected purchaser" under Section 8–303. Rather, the customer becomes an "entitlement holder" who has a "security entitlement" to the security against the broker as "securities intermediary." See Section 8–501. It would make no sense to say that the customer in such a case takes an interest in the security free from all other claims, since the nature of the relationship is that the customer has an interest in common with other customers who hold positions in the same security through the same broker. Section 8–502, however, does protect an entitlement holder against adverse claims, in the sense that once the entitlement holder has acquired the package of rights that comprise a security entitlement no one else can take that package of rights away by arguing that the transaction that resulted in the customer's acquisition of the security entitlement was the traceable product of a transfer or transaction that was wrongful as against the claimant.

4. Bank deposit accounts; brokerage asset management accounts.

An ordinary bank deposit account would not fall within the definition of "security" in Section 8–102(a)(15), so the rules of Parts 2, 3, and 4 of Article 8 do not apply to deposit accounts. Nor would the relationship between a bank and its depositors be governed by the rules of Part 5 of Article 8. The Part 5 rules apply to "security entitlements." Section 8–501(b) provides that a person has a security entitlement when a securities intermediary credits a financial asset to the person's "securities account." "Securities account" is defined in Section 8–501(a) as "an account to which a financial asset is or may be credited in accordance with an agreement under which the person maintaining the account undertakes to treat the person for whom the account is maintained as entitled to exercise the rights that comprise the financial asset." The definition of securities account plays a key role in setting the scope of Part 5 of Article 8. A person has a security entitlement governed by Part 5 only if the relationship in question falls within the definition of "securities account." The definition of securities account in Section 8–501(a) excludes deposit accounts from the Part 5 rules of Article 8. One of the basic elements of the relationship between a securities intermediary and an entitlement holder is that the securities intermediary has the duty to hold exactly the quantity of securities that it carries for the account of its customers. See Section 8–504. The assets that a securities intermediary holds for its entitlement holder are not assets that the securities intermediary can use in its own proprietary business. See Section 8–503. A deposit account is an entirely different arrangement. A bank is not required to hold in its vaults or in deposit accounts with other banks a sum of money equal to the claims of all of its depositors. Banks are permitted to use depositors' funds in their ordinary lending business; indeed, that is a primary function of banks. A deposit account, unlike a securities account, is simply a debtor-creditor relationship. Thus a bank or other financial institution maintaining deposit accounts is not covered by Part 5 of Article 8.

Today, it is common for brokers to maintain securities accounts for their customers which include arrangements for the customers to hold liquid "cash" assets in the form of money market mutual fund shares. Insofar as the broker is holding money market mutual fund shares for its customer, the customer has a security entitlement to the money market mutual fund shares. It is also common for brokers to offer their customers an arrangement in which the customer has access to those liquid assets via a deposit account with a bank, whereby shares of the money market fund are redeemed to cover checks drawn on the account. Article 8 applies only to the securities account; the linked bank account remains an account covered by other law. Thus the rights and duties of the customer and the bank are governed not by Article 8, but by the relevant payment system law, such as Article 4 or Article 4A.

5. Trusts.

The indirect holding system rules of Part 5 of Article 8 are not intended to govern all relationships in which one person holds securities "on behalf of" another. Rather, the Part 5 rules come into play only if the relationship in question falls within the definition of securities account in Section 8–501(a). The definition of securities account serves the important function of ensuring that ordinary trust arrangements are not inadvertently swept into Part 5 of Article 8. Suppose that Bank serves as trustee of a trust for the benefit of Beneficiary. The corpus of the trust is invested in securities and other financial assets. Although Bank is, in some senses, holding securities for Beneficiary, the arrangement would not fall within the definition of securities account. Bank, as trustee, has not undertaken to treat Beneficiary as entitled to exercise all of the rights that comprise the portfolio securities. For instance, although Beneficiary receives the economic benefit of the portfolio securities, Beneficiary does not have the right to direct dispositions of individual trust assets or to exercise voting or other corporate law rights with respect to the individual securities. Thus Bank's obligations to Beneficiary as trustee are governed by ordinary trust law, not by Part 5 of Article 8. Of course, if Bank, as trustee, holds the securities through an intermediary, Part 5 of Revised Article 8 would govern the relationship between Bank, as entitlement holder, and the intermediary through which Bank holds the securities. It is also possible that a different department of Bank acts as the intermediary through which Bank, as trustee, holds the securities. Bank, *qua* securities custodian, might be holding securities for a large number of customers, including Bank's own trust department. Insofar as Bank may be regarded as acting in different capacities, Part 5 of Article 8 may be relevant to the relationship between the two sides of Bank's business. However, the relationship between Bank as trustee and the beneficiaries of the trust would remain governed by trust law, not Article 8.

6. Mutual fund shares.

Shares of mutual funds are Article 8 securities, whether the fund is organized as a corporation, business trust, or other form of entity. See Sections 8–102(a)(15) and 8–103(b). Mutual funds commonly do not issue certificates. Thus, mutual fund shares are typically uncertificated securities under Article 8.

Although a mutual fund is, in a colloquial sense, holding the portfolio securities on behalf of the fund's shareholders, the indirect holding system rules of Part 5 do not apply to the relationship between the fund and its shareholders. The Part 5 rules apply to "security entitlements." Section 8–501(e) provides that issuance of a security is not establishment of a security entitlement. Thus, because mutual funds shares do fit within the Article 8 definition of security, the relationship between the fund and its shareholders is automatically excluded from the Part 5 rules.

Of course, a person might hold shares in a mutual fund through a brokerage account. Because mutual fund shares are securities, they automatically fall within the broader term "financial asset," so the Part 5 indirect holding system rules apply to mutual fund shares that are held through securities accounts. That is, a person who holds mutual fund shares through a brokerage account could have a security entitlement to the mutual fund shares, just as the person would have a security entitlement to any other security carried in the brokerage account.

7. Stock of closely held corporations.

Ordinary corporate stock falls within the Article 8 definition of security, whether or not it is publicly traded. See Sections 8–102(a)(15) and 8–103(a). There is nothing in the new indirect holding system rules of Article 8 that would preclude their application to shares of companies that are not publicly traded. The indirect holding system rules, however, would come into play only if the shares were in fact held through a securities account with a securities intermediary. Since that is typically not the case with respect to shares of closely held corporations, transactions involving those shares will continue to be governed by the traditional rules, as amended, that are set out in Parts 2, 3, and 4 of Article 8, and the corresponding provisions of Article 9. The simplification of the Article 8 rules on uncertificated securities may, however, make the alternative of dispensing with certificates more attractive for closely held corporations.

8. Partnership interests and limited liability company shares.

Interests in partnerships or shares of limited liability companies are not Article 8 securities unless they are in fact dealt in or traded on securities exchanges or in securities markets. See Section 8–103(c). The issuers, however, may if they wish explicitly "opt-in" by specifying that the interests or shares are securities governed by Article 8. Even though interests in partnerships or shares of limited liability companies do not generally fall within the category of "security" in Article 8, they would fall within the broader term "financial asset." Accordingly, if such interests are held through a securities account with a securities intermediary, the indirect holding system rules of Part 5 apply, and the interest of a person who holds them through such an account is a security entitlement.

9. Bankers' acceptances, commercial paper, and other money market instruments.

Money market instruments, such as commercial paper, bankers' acceptances, and certificates of deposit, are good examples of a form of property that may fall within the definition of "financial asset," even though they may not fall within the definition of "security." Section 8–103(d) provides that a writing that meets the definition of security certificate under Section 8–102(a)(15) is governed by Article 8, even though it also fits within the definition of "negotiable instrument" in Article 3.

Some forms of short term money market instruments may meet the requirements of an Article 8 security, while others may not. For example, the Article 8 definition of security requires that the obligation be in registered or bearer form. Bankers' acceptances are typically payable "to order," and thus do not qualify as Article 8 securities. Thus, the obligations of the immediate parties to a bankers' acceptance are governed by Article 3, rather than Article 8. That is an entirely appropriate classification, even for those bankers' acceptance that are handled as investment media in the securities markets, because Article 8, unlike Article 3, does not contain rules specifying the standardized obligations of parties to instruments. For example, the

Article 3 rules on the obligations of acceptors and drawers of drafts are necessary to specify the obligations represented by bankers' acceptances, but Article 8 contains no provisions dealing with these issues.

Immobilization through a depository system is, however, just as important for money market instruments as for traditional securities. Under the prior version of Article 8, the rules on the depository system, set out in Section 8–320, applied only to Article 8 securities. Although some forms of money market instruments could be fitted within the language of the Article 8 definition of "security," this is not true for bankers' acceptances. Accordingly, it was not thought feasible to make bankers' acceptances eligible for deposit in clearing corporations under the prior version of Article 8. Revised Article 8 solves this problem by separating the coverage of the Part 5 rules from the definition of security. Even though a bankers' acceptance or other money market instrument is an Article 3 negotiable instrument rather than an Article 8 security, it would still fall within the definition of financial asset in Section 8–102(a)(9). Accordingly, if the instrument is held through a clearing corporation or other securities intermediary, the rules of Part 5 of Article 8 apply.

10. Repurchase agreement transactions.

Repurchase agreements are an important form of transaction in the securities business, particularly in connection with government securities. Repos and reverse repos can be used for a variety of purposes. The one that is of particular concern for purposes of commercial law rules is the use of repurchase agreements as a form of financing transaction for government securities dealers. Government securities dealers typically obtain intra-day financing from their clearing banks, and then at the end of the trading day seek overnight financing from other sources to repay that day's advances from the clearing bank. Repos are the principal source of this financing. The dealer ("repo seller") sells securities to the financing source ("repo buyer") for cash, and at the same time agrees to repurchase the same or like securities the following day, or at some other brief interval. The sources of the financing include a variety of entities seeking short term investments for surplus cash, such as pension funds, business corporations, money market funds, and banks. The pricing may be computed in various ways, but in essence the price at which the dealer agrees to repurchase the securities exceeds the price paid to the dealer by an amount equivalent to interest on the funds.

The transfer of the securities from a securities dealer as repo seller to a provider of funds as repo buyer can be effected in a variety of ways. The repo buyer might be willing to allow the repo seller to keep the securities "in its hands," relying on the dealer's representation that it will hold them on behalf of the repo buyer. In the jargon of the trade, these are known as "hold-in-custody repos" or "HIC repos." At the other extreme, the repo buyer might insist that the dealer "hand over" the securities so that in the event that the dealer fails and is unable to perform its obligation to repurchase them, the repo buyer will have the securities "in its hands." The jargon for these is "delivered-out repos." A wide variety of arrangements between these two extremes might be devised, in which the securities are "handed over" to a third party with powers concerning their disposition allocated between the repo seller and repo buyer in a variety of ways.

Specification of the rights of repo buyers is complicated by the fact that the transfer of the interest in securities from the repo seller to the repo buyer might be characterized as an outright sale or as the creation of a security interest. Article 8 does not attempt to specify any categorical rules on that issue.

Article 8 sets out rules on the rights of parties who have implemented securities transactions in certain ways. It does not, however, deal with the legal characterization of the transactions that are implemented through the Article 8 mechanisms. Rather, the Article 8 rules apply without regard to the characterization of transactions for other purposes. For example, the Article 8 rules for the direct holding system provide that a person who takes delivery of a duly indorsed security certificate for value and without notice of adverse claims takes free from any adverse claims. That rule applies without regard to the character of the transaction in which the security certificate was delivered. It applies both to delivery upon original issue and to delivery upon transfer. It applies to transfers in settlement of sales and to transfers in pledge. Similarly, the Article 8 indirect holding system rules, such as the adverse claim cut-off rules in Sections 8–502 and 8–510, apply to the transactions that fall within their terms, whether those transactions were sales, secured transactions, or something else.

Repos involve transfers of interests in securities. The Article 8 rules apply to transfers of securities in repos, just as they apply to transfers of securities in any other form of transaction. The transfer of the interest in securities from the repo seller to the repo buyer might be characterized as an outright sale or as the creation of a security interest. Article 8 does not determine that question. The rules of Revised Article 8 have, however, been drafted to minimize the possibility that disputes over the characterization of the transfer in a repo would affect substantive questions that are governed by Article 8. See, e.g., Section 8–510 and Comment 4 thereto.

11. Securities lending transactions.

In a typical securities lending transaction, the owner of securities lends them to another person who needs the securities to satisfy a delivery obligation. For example, when a customer of a broker sells a security short, the broker executes an ordinary trade as seller and so must deliver the securities at settlement. The customer is "short" against the broker because the customer has an open obligation to deliver the securities to the broker, which the customer hopes to be able to satisfy by buying in the securities at a lower price. If the short seller's broker does not have the securities in its own inventory, the broker will borrow them from someone else. The securities lender delivers the securities to the borrowing broker, and the borrowing broker becomes contractually obligated to redeliver a like quantity of the same security. Securities borrowers are required to provide collateral, usually government securities, to assure performance of their redelivery obligation.

The securities lender does not retain any property interest in the securities that are delivered to the borrower. The transaction is an outright transfer in which the borrower obtains full title. The whole point of securities lending is that the borrower needs the securities to transfer them to someone else. It would make no sense to say that the lender retains any property interest in the securities it has lent. Accordingly, even if the securities borrower defaults on its redelivery obligation, the securities lender has no property interest in the original securities that could be asserted against any person to whom the securities borrower may have transferred them. One need not look to adverse claim cut-off rules to reach that result; the securities lender never had an adverse claim. The securities borrower's default is no different from any other breach of contract. The securities lender's protection is its right to foreclose on the collateral given to secure the borrower's redelivery obligation. Perhaps the best way to understand securities lending is to note that the word "loan" in securities lending transactions is used in the sense it carries in loans of money, as distinguished from loans of specific identifiable chattels. Someone who lends money does not retain any property interest in the money that is handed over to the borrower. To use civil law terminology, securities lending is *mutuum,* rather than *commodatum.* See Story on Bailments, §§ 6 and 47.

12. Traded stock options.

Stock options issued and cleared through the Options Clearing Corporation ("OCC") are a good example of a form of investment vehicle that is treated as a financial asset to which the Part 5 rules apply, but not as an Article 8 security to which Parts 2, 3, and 4 apply. OCC carries on its books the options positions of the brokerage firms which are clearing members of OCC. The clearing members in turn carry on their books the options positions of their customers. The arrangements are structurally similar to the securities depository system. In the options structure, however, there is no issuer separate from the clearing corporation. The financial assets held through the system are standardized contracts entitling the holder to purchase or sell a certain security at a set price. Rather than being an interest in or obligation of a separate issuer, an option is a contractual right against the counter-party. In order to assure performance of the options, OCC interposes itself as counter-party to each options trade. The rules of Parts 2, 3, and 4 of this Article, however, do not well describe the obligations and rights of OCC. On the other hand, the rules of Part 5, and the related Article 9 rules on security interests and priorities, do provide a workable legal framework for the commercial law analysis of the rights of the participants in the options market. Accordingly, publicly traded securities options are included within the definition of "financial asset," but not "security." See Section 8–103(e). Thus, although OCC would not be an issuer of a security for purposes of this Article, it would be a clearing corporation, against whom its clearing members have security entitlements to the options positions. Similarly, the clearing members' customers have security entitlements against the clearing members. Traded stock options are also a good illustration of the point that the classification issues under Article 8 are very different from classification under other law, such as the federal securities laws. See Section 8–102(d). Stock options are treated as securities for purposes of federal securities laws, but not for purposes of Article 8.

13. Commodity futures.

Section 8–103(f) provides that a "commodity contract" is not a security or a financial asset. Section 9–102(a)(15) defines commodity contract to include commodity futures contracts, commodity options, and options on commodity futures contracts that are traded on or subject to the rules of a board of trade that has been designated as a contract market for that contract pursuant to the federal commodities laws. Thus, commodity contracts themselves are not Article 8 securities to which the rules of Parts 2, 3, and 4 apply, nor is the relationship between a customer and a commodity futures commission merchant governed by the Part 5 rules of Article 8. Commodity contracts, however, are included within the Article 9 definition of "investment property." Thus security interests in commodity positions are governed by essentially the same set of rules as security interests in security entitlements.

14. "Whatever else they have or may devise."

The classification question posed by the above-captioned category of investment products and arrangements is among the most difficult—and important—issue raised by the Article 8 revision process. Rapid innovation is perhaps the only constant characteristic of the securities and financial markets. The rules of Revised Article 8 are intended to be sufficiently flexible to accommodate new developments.

A common mechanism by which new financial instruments are devised is that a financial institution that holds some security, financial instrument, or pool thereof, creates interests in that asset or pool which are sold to others. It is not possible to answer in the abstract the question of how such interests are treated under Article 8, because the variety of such products is limited only by human imagination and current regulatory structures. At this general level, however, one can note that there are at least three possible treatments under Article 8 of the relationship between the institution which creates the interests and the persons who hold them. (Again, it must be borne in mind that the Article 8 classification issue may be different from the classification question posed by federal securities law or other regulation.) First, creation of the new interests in the underlying assets may constitute issuance of a new Article 8 security. In that case the relationship between the institution that created the interest and the persons who hold them is not governed by the Part 5 rules, but by the rules of Parts 2, 3, and 4. See Section 8–501(e). That, for example, is the structure of issuance of mutual fund shares. Second, the relationship between the entity creating the interests and those holding them may fit within the Part 5 rules, so that the persons are treating as having security entitlements against the institution with respect to the underlying assets. That, for example, is the structure used for stock options. Third, it may be that the creation of the new interests in the underlying assets does not constitute issuance of a new Article 8 security, nor does the relationship between the entity creating the interests and those holding them fit within the Part 5 rules. In that case, the relationship is governed by other law, as in the case of ordinary trusts.

The first of these three possibilities—that the creation of the new interest is issuance of a new security for Article 8 purposes—is a fairly common pattern. For example, an American depositary receipt facility does not maintain securities accounts but issues securities called ADRs in respect of foreign securities deposited in such facility. Similarly, custodians of government securities which issue receipts, certificates, or the like representing direct interests in those securities (sometimes interests split between principal and income) do not maintain securities accounts but issue securities representing those interests. Trusts holding assets, in a variety of structured and securitized transactions, which issue certificates or the like representing "pass-through" or undivided beneficial interests in the trust assets, do not maintain securities accounts but issue securities representing those interests.

In analyzing these classification questions, courts should take care to avoid mechanical jurisprudence based solely upon exegesis of the wording of definitions in Article 8. The result of classification questions is that different sets of rules come into play. In order to decide the classification question it is necessary to understand fully the commercial setting and consider which set of rules best fits the transaction. Rather than letting the choice of rules turn on interpretation of the words of the definitions, the interpretation of the words of the definitions should turn on the suitability of the application of the substantive rules.

UNIFORM COMMERCIAL CODE

IV.   CHANGES FROM PRIOR (1978) VERSION OF ARTICLE 8

A.   Table of Disposition of Sections in Prior Version

Article 8 (1978)	Revised Articles 8 and 9
8–101	8–101
8–102(1)(a)	8–102(a)(4) & (15)
8–102(1)(b)	8–102(a)(15) & (18)
8–102(1)(c)	8–102(a)(15)
8–102(1)(d)	8–102(a)(13)
8–102(1)(e)	8–102(a)(2)
8–102(2)	8–202(b)(1)
8–102(3)	8–102(a)(5)
8–102(4)	omitted, see Revision Note 1
8–102(5)	8–102(b)
8–102(6)	8–102(c)
8–103	8–209
8–104	8–210
8–105(1)	omitted, see Revision Note 8
8–105(2)	omitted, see Revision Note 4
8–105(3)	8–114
8–106	8–110
8–107	omitted, see Revision Note 8
8–108	omitted, see Revision Note 5
8–201	8–201
8–202	8–202; transaction statement provisions omitted, see Revision Note 4
8–203	8–203
8–204	8–204; transaction statement provisions omitted, see Revision Note 4
8–205	8–205; transaction statement provisions omitted, see Revision Note 4
8–206	8–206; transaction statement provisions omitted, see Revision Note 4
8–207	8–207; registered pledge provisions omitted, see Revision Note 5
8–208	8–208; transaction statement provisions omitted, see Revision Note 4
8–301	8–302(a) & (b)
8–302(1)	8–303(a)
8–302(2)	8–102(a)(1)
8–302(3)	8–303(b)
8–302(4)	8–302(c)
8–303	8–102(a)(3)
8–304(1)	8–105(d)
8–304(2)	omitted, see Revision Note 4
8–304(3)	8–105(b)
8–305	8–105(c)
8–306(1)	8–108(f)
8–306(2)	8–108(a)
8–306(3)	8–108(g)

B.   Revision Notes

1.   Provisions of former Article 8 on clearing corporations.

The keystone of the treatment of the indirect holding system in the prior version of Article 8 was the special provision on clearing corporations in Section 8–320. Section 8–320 was added to Article 8 in 1962, at the very end of the process that culminated in promulgation and enactment of the original version of the Code. The key concepts of the original version of Article 8 were "bona fide purchaser" and "delivery." Under Section 8–302 (1962) one could qualify as a "bona fide purchaser" only if one had taken delivery of a security, and Section 8–313 (1962) specified what counted as a delivery.

Section 8–320 was added to take account of the development of the system in which trades can be settled by netted book-entry movements at a depository without physical deliveries of certificates. Rather than reworking the basic concepts, however, Section 8–320 brought the depository system within Article 8 by definitional fiat. Subsection (a) of Section 8–320 (1962) stated that a transfer or pledge could be effected by entries on the books of a central depository, and subsection (b) stated that such an entry "has the effect of a delivery of a security in bearer form or duly indorsed in blank." In 1978, Section 8–320 was revised to conform it to the general substitution of the concept of "transfer" for "delivery," but the basic structure remained the same. Under the 1978 version of Article 8, the only book-entry transfers that qualified the transferee for bona fide purchaser rights were those made on the books of a clearing corporation. See Sections 8–302(1)(c), 8–313(1)(g), and 8–320. Thus, for practical purposes, the indirect holding system rules of the prior version of Article 8 required that the securities be held by a clearing corporation in accordance with the central depository rules of Section 8–320.

Some of the definitional provisions concerning clearing corporation in the prior version of Article 8 seem to have conflated the commercial law rules on the effect of book-entry transactions with issues about the regulation of entities that are acting as clearing corporations. For example, the Section 8–320 rules that gave effect to book-entry transfers applied only if the security was "in the custody of the clearing corporation, another clearing corporation, [or] a custodian bank." "Custodian bank" was defined in Section 8–102(4) as "a bank or trust company that is supervised and examined by state or federal authority having supervision over banks and is acting as custodian for a clearing corporation." Although this was probably inadvertent, these definitional provisions have operated as an obstacle to the development of clearing arrangements for global trading, since they effectively precluded clearing corporations from using foreign banks as custodians.

Revised Article 8 is based on the view that Article 8 is not the proper place for regulatory decisions about whether certain sorts of financial institutions should or should not be permitted to engage in a particular aspect of the securities business, such as acting as a clearing corporation, or how they should be permitted to conduct that business. Rather, Article 8 should deal only with the commercial law questions of what duties and rights flow from doing business as a clearing corporation, leaving it to other regulatory law to decide which entities should be permitted to act as clearing corporations, and to regulate their activities. Federal securities laws now establish a detailed regulatory structure for clearing corporations; there is no need for Article 8 to duplicate parts of that structure. Revised Article 8 deletes all provision of the prior version which had the effect of specifying how clearing corporations should conduct their operations. For example, Revised Article 8 deletes the definition of "custodian bank," which operated in the prior version only as a regulatory restriction on how clearing corporations could hold securities.

In general, the structure of Revised Article 8 is such that there is relatively little need for special provisions on clearing corporations. Book-entry transactions effected through clearing corporations are treated under the same rules in Part 5 as book-entry transactions effected through any other securities intermediary. Accordingly, Revised Article 8 has no direct analog of the special provisions in Section 8–320 on transfers on the books of clearing corporations.

2. Former Section 8–313—"Transfer."

Section 8–313 of the 1978 version of Article was extremely complicated, because it attempted to cover many different issues. The following account of the evolution of Section 8–313 may assist in understanding why a different approach is taken in Revised Article 8. This explanation is, however, intended not as an actual account of historical events, but as a conceptual reconstruction, devised from the perspective of, and with the benefit of, hindsight.

The original objective of Article 8 was to ensure that certificates representing investment securities would be "negotiable" in the sense that purchasers would be protected by the bona fide purchaser rules. The requirements for bona fide purchaser status were that the purchaser had to (i) take delivery of the security and (ii) give value in good faith and without notice of adverse claims. Section 8–313 specified what counted as a "delivery," and Section 8–302 specified the other requirements.

The 1978 amendments added provisions on uncertificated securities, but the basic organizational pattern was retained. Section 8–302 continued to state the requirements of value, good faith, and lack of notice for good faith purchase, and Section 8–313 stated the mechanism by which the purchase had to be implemented. Delivery as defined in the original version of Section 8–313 had a meaning similar to the concept known in colloquial securities jargon as "good delivery"; that is, physical delivery with any necessary indorsement. Although the word "delivery" has now come to be used in securities parlance in a broader sense than physical delivery, when the provisions for uncertificated securities were added it was thought preferable to use another word. Thus, the word "transfer" was substituted for "delivery" in Section 8–313.

The 1978 amendments also moved the rules governing security interests in securities from Article 9 to Article 8, though the basic conceptual structure of the common law of pledge was retained. Since a pledge required a delivery, and since the term transfer had been substituted for delivery, the 1978 amendments provided that in order to create a security interest there must be a "transfer," in the defined Article 8 sense, from the debtor to the secured party. Accordingly, provisions had to be added to Section 8–313 so that any of the steps that should suffice to create a perfected security interest would be deemed to constitute a "transfer" within the meaning of Section 8–313. Thus, the Section 8–313 rules on "transfer," which had in the previous version dealt only with what counted as a delivery that qualified one for bona fide purchaser status, became the statutory locus for all of the rules on creation and perfection of security interests in securities. Accordingly the rather elaborate rules of subsections (1)(h), (1)(i), and (1)(j) were added.

Having expanded Section 8–313 to the point that it served as the rule specifying the formal requirements for transfer of all significant forms of interests in securities, it must have seemed only logical to take the next step and make the Section 8–313 rules the exclusive means of transferring interests in securities. Thus, while the prior version had stated that "Delivery to a purchaser occurs when . . .", the 1978 version stated that "Transfer of a security or a limited interest (including a security interest) therein to a purchaser occurs *only* . . . ." Having taken that step, however, it then became necessary to ensure that anyone who should be regarded as having an interest in a security would be covered by some provision of Section 8–313. Thus, the provisions of subsection (1)(d)(ii) and (iii) were added to make it possible to say that the customers of a securities intermediary who hold interests in securities held by the intermediary in fungible bulk received "transfers."

Section 8–313(1)(d) was the key provision in the 1978 version dealing with the indirect holding system at the level below securities depositories. It operated in essentially the same fashion as Section 8–320; that is, it stated that when a broker or bank holding securities in fungible bulk makes entries on its books identifying a quantity of the fungible bulk as belonging to the customer, that action is treated as a "transfer"—in the special Section 8–313 sense—of an interest in the security from the intermediary to the customer.

Revised Article 8 has no direct analog of the 1978 version of Section 8–313. The rules on secured transactions have been returned to Article 9, so subsections of Section 8–313 (1978) dealing with security interests are deleted from Article 8. Insofar as portions of Section 8–313 (1978) were designed to specify the formal requirements for transferees to qualify for protection against adverse claims, their place is taken by Revised Section 8–301, which defines "delivery," in a fashion somewhat akin to the pre-1978 version of Section 8–313. The descendant of the provisions of Section 8–313 (1978) dealing with the indirect holding system is Revised Section 8–501 which specifies when a person acquires a security entitlement. Section 8–501, however, is based on a different analysis of the transaction in which a customer acquires a position in the indirect holding system. The transaction is not described as a "transfer" of an interest in some portion of a fungible bulk of securities held by the securities intermediary but as the creation of a security entitlement. Accordingly, just as Revised Article 8 has no direct analog of the Section 8–320 rules on clearing corporation transfers, it has no direct analog of the Section 8–313(1) rules on "transfers" of interests in securities held in fungible bulk.

3. Uncertificated securities provisions.

Given the way that securities holding practices have evolved, the sharp distinction that the 1978 version of Article 8 drew between certificated securities and uncertificated securities has become somewhat misleading. Since many provisions of the 1978 version had separate subsections dealing first with certificated securities and then with uncertificated securities, and since people intuitively realize that the volume of trading in the modern securities markets could not possibly be handled by pushing around certificates, it was only natural for a reader of the statute to conclude that the uncertificated securities provisions of Article 8 were the basis of the book-entry system. That, however, is not the case. Although physical delivery of certificates plays little role in the settlement system, most publicly traded securities are still, in legal theory, certificated securities. To use clearance and settlement jargon, the book-entry securities holding system has used "immobilization" rather than "dematerialization."

The important legal and practical difference is between the direct holding system, in which the beneficial owners have a direct relationship with the issuer, and the indirect holding system, in which securities are held through tiers of securities intermediaries. Accordingly, in Revised Article 8 the contrast between certificated securities and uncertificated securities has been minimized or eliminated as much as possible in stating the substantive provisions.

4. Transaction statements.

Although the 1978 provisions on uncertificated securities contemplated a system in which there would be no definitive certificates as reifications of the underlying interests or obligations, the 1978 amendments did not really dispense with all requirements of paper evidence of securities holding. The 1978 amendments required issuers of uncertificated securities to send paper "transaction statements" upon registration of transfer. Section 8–408 regulated the content and format of these transaction statements in considerable detail. The statements had to be in writing, include specific information, and contain a conspicuous legend stating that "This statement is merely a record of the rights of the addressee as of the time of its issuance. Delivery of this statement, of itself, confers no rights on the recipient. This statement is neither a negotiable instrument nor a security." Issuers were required to send statements when any transfer was registered (known as "initial transaction statements") and also were required to send periodic statements at least annually and also upon any security holder's reasonable request. Fees were regulated to some extent, in that Section 8–408(8) specified that if periodic statements were sent at least quarterly, the issuer could charge for statements requested by security holders at other times.

The detailed specification of reporting requirements for issuers of uncertificated securities was quite different from the treatment of securities intermediaries. Though the prior version of Article 8 did require non-clearing corporation securities intermediaries to send confirmations of transfers—a requirement deleted in Revised Article 8—it did not regulate their content or format. Article 8 has never imposed periodic reporting requirements on securities intermediaries. Thus, reporting requirements for the indirect holding system were left to agreements and regulatory authorities, while reporting requirements for a book-entry direct holding system were imposed by statute.

Securities holding systems based on transaction statements of the sort contemplated by the 1978 amendments have not yet evolved to any major extent—indeed, the statutory specification of the details of the information system may itself have acted as an impediment to the evolution of a book-entry direct system. Accordingly, Revised Article 8 drops the statutory requirements concerning transaction statements.

The record keeping and reporting obligations of issuers of uncertificated securities would be left to agreement and other law, as is the case today for securities intermediaries.

In the 1978 version, the Part 2 rules concerning transfer restrictions, issuers' defenses, and the like were based on the assumption that transaction statements would be used in a fashion analogous to traditional security certificates. For example, Sections 8–202 and 8–204 specified that the terms of a security, or any restrictions on transfer imposed by the issuer, had to be noted on the transaction statement. Revised Article 8 deletes all such references to transaction statements. The terms of securities, or of restrictions of transfer, would be governed by whatever law or agreement specifies these matters, just as is the case for various other forms of business entities, such as partnerships, that have never issued certificates representing interests. Other Part 2 rules, such as Sections 8–205, 8–206, and 8–208, attempted to state rules on forgery and related matters for transactions statements. Since Revised Article 8 does not specify the format for information systems for uncertificated securities, there is no point in attempting to state rules on the consequences of wrongful information transmission in the particular format of written statements authenticated by signatures.

5. Deletion of provisions on registered pledges.

The 1978 version of Article 8 also added detailed provisions concerning "registered pledges" of uncertificated securities. Revised Article 8 adopts a new system of rules for security interests in securities, for both the direct and indirect holding systems that make it unnecessary to have special statutory provisions for registered pledges of uncertificated securities.

The reason that the 1978 version of Article 8 created this concept was that if the only means of creating security interests was the pledge, it seemed necessary to provide some substitute for the pledge in the absence of a certificate. The point of the registered pledge was, presumably, that it permitted a debtor to grant a perfected security interest in securities, yet still keep the securities in the debtor's own name for purposes of dividends, voting, and the like. The concept of registered pledge has, however, been thought troublesome by many legal commentators and securities industry participants. For example, in Massachusetts where many mutual funds have their headquarters, a non-uniform amendment was enacted to permit the issuer of an uncertificated security to refuse to register a pledge and instead issue a certificate to the owner that the owner could then pledge by ordinary means.

Under the 1978 version of Article 8, if an issuer chose to issue securities in uncertificated form, it was also required by statute to offer a registered pledge program. Revised Articles 8 and 9 take a different approach. All of the provisions dealing with registered pledges have been deleted. This does not mean, however, that issuers cannot offer such a service. The control rules of Revised Section 8–106 and the related priority provisions in Article 9 establish a structure that permits issuers to develop systems akin to the registered pledge device, without mandating that they do so, or legislating the details of the system. In essence, the registered pledge or control device amounts to a record keeping service. A debtor can always transfer securities to its lender. In a registered pledge or control agreement arrangement, the issuer keeps track of which securities the secured party holds for its own account outright, and which securities it holds in pledge from its debtors.

Under the rules of Revised Articles 8 and 9, the registered pledge issue can easily be left to resolution by the market. The concept of control is defined in such fashion that if an issuer or securities intermediary wishes to offer a service akin to the registered pledge device it can do so. The issuer or securities intermediary would offer to enter into agreements with the debtor and secured party under which it would hold the securities for the account of the debtor, but subject to instructions from the secured party. The secured party would thereby obtain control assuring perfection and priority of its lien.

Even if such arrangements are not offered by issuers, persons who hold uncertificated securities will have several options for using them as collateral for secured loans. Under the new rules, filing is a permissible method of perfection, for debtors other than securities firms. A secured party who relies on filing is, of course, exposed to the risk that the debtor will double finance and grant a later secured lender a security interest under circumstances that give that lender control and hence priority. If the lender is unwilling to run that risk, the debtor can transfer the securities outright to the lender on the books of the issuer, though between the parties the debtor would be the owner and the lender only a secured party. That, of course, requires that the debtor trust the secured party not to dispose of the collateral wrongfully, and the debtor may also need to make arrangements with the secured party to exercise benefits of ownership such as voting and receiving distributions.

It may well be that both lenders and borrowers would prefer to have some arrangement, such as the registered pledge device of current law, that permits the debtor to remain as the registered owner entitled to vote and receive dividends but gives the lender exclusive power to order their disposition. The approach taken in this revision is that if there is a genuine demand for such arrangements, it can be met by the market. The difficulty with the approach of present Article 8 is that it mandates that any issuer that wishes to issue securities in uncertificated form must also offer this record keeping service. That obligation may well have acted as a disincentive to the development of uncertificated securities. Thus, the deletion of the mandated registered pledge provisions is consistent with the principle of neutrality toward the evolution of securities holding practices.

6.   Former Section 8–403—Issuer's Duty as to Adverse Claims.

Section 8–403 of the prior version of Article 8 dealt with the obligations of issuers to adverse claimants. The starting point of American law on issuers' liability in such circumstances is the old case of *Lowry v. Commercial & Farmers' Bank,* 15 F.Cas. 1040 (C.C.D.Md.1848) (No. 8551), under which issuers could be held liable for registering a transfer at the direction of a registered owner who was acting wrongfully as against a third person in making the transfer. The *Lowry* principle imposed onerous liability on issuers, particularly in the case of transfers by fiduciaries, such as executors and trustees. To protect against risk of such liability, issuers developed the practice of requiring extensive documentation for fiduciary stock transfers to assure themselves that the fiduciaries were acting rightfully. As a result, fiduciary stock transfers were cumbersome and time consuming.

In the present century, American law has gradually moved away from the *Lowry* principle. Statutes such as the Uniform Fiduciaries Act, the Model Fiduciary Stock Transfer Act, and the Uniform Act for the Simplification of Fiduciary Security Transfers sought to avoid the delays in stock transfers that could result from issuers' demands for documentation by limiting the issuer's responsibility for transfers in breach of the registered owner's duty to others. Although these statutes provided that issuers had no duty of inquiry to determine whether a fiduciary was acting rightfully, they all provided that an issuer could be liable if the issuer acted with notice of third party claims.

The prior version of Article 8 followed the same approach as the various fiduciary transfer statutes. Issuers were not required to seek out information from which they could determine whether a fiduciary was acting properly, but they were liable if they registered a transfer with notice that the fiduciary was acting improperly. Former Section 8–308(11) said that the failure of a fiduciary to comply with a controlling instrument or failure to obtain a court approval required under local law did not render the indorsement or instruction unauthorized. However, if a fiduciary was in fact acting improperly, then the beneficiary would be treated as an adverse claimant. See Section 8–302(2) (1978) and Comment 4. Former Section 8–403 specified that if written notice of an adverse claim had been sent to the issuer, the issuer "shall inquire into the adverse claim" before registering a transfer on the indorsement or instruction of the registered owner. The issuer could "discharge any duty of inquiry by any reasonable means," including by notifying the adverse claimant that the transfer would be registered unless the adverse claimant obtained a court order or gave an indemnity bond.

Revised Article 8 rejects the *Lowry* principle altogether. It provides that an issuer is not liable for wrongful registration if it acts on an effective indorsement or instruction, even though the issuer may have notice of adverse claims, so long as the issuer has not been served with legal process and is not acting in collusion with the wrongdoer in registering the transfer. See Revised Section 8–404 and Comments thereto. The provisions of prior Section 8–403 specifying that issuers had a duty to investigate adverse claims of which they had notice are deleted.

Revised Article 8 also deletes the provisions set out in Section 8–403(3) of prior law specifying that issuers did not have a duty to inquire into the rightfulness of transfers by fiduciaries. The omission of the rules formerly in Section 8–403(3) does not, of course, mean that issuers would be liable for acting on the instruction of fiduciaries in the circumstances covered by former Section 8–403(3). Former Section 8–403(3) assumed that issuers would be liable if they registered a transfer with notice of an adverse claim. Former Section 8–403(3) was necessary only to negate any inference that knowledge that a transfer was initiated by a fiduciary might give constructive notice of adverse claims. Under Section 8–404 of Revised Article 8, mere notice of adverse claims does not impose duties on the issuer. Accordingly the provisions included in former Section 8–403(3) are unnecessary.

Although the prior version of Article 8 included provisions similar or identical to those set out in the Uniform Act for the Simplification of Fiduciary Security Transfers and similar statutes, most states retained these statutes at the time the Uniform Commercial Code was adopted. These statutes are based on a premise different from Revised Article 8. The fiduciary simplification acts are predicated on the assumption that an issuer would be liable to an adverse claimant if the issuer had notice. These statutes seek only to preclude any inference that issuers have such notice when they register transfers on the instructions of a fiduciary. Revised Article 8 is based on the view that a third party should not be able to interfere with the relationship between an issuer and its registered shareholders unless the claimant obtains legal process. Since notice of an adverse claim does not impose duties on an issuer under Revised Article 8, the Uniform Act for the Simplification of Fiduciary Security Transfers, or similar statutes, should be repealed upon enactment of Revised Article 8.

7. Former Section 8–319—Statute of Frauds.

Revised Article 8 deletes the special statute of frauds provision for securities contracts that was set out in former Section 8–319. See Revised Section 8–113. Most of the litigation involving the statute of frauds rule of the prior version of Article 8 involved informal transactions, rather than transactions on the organized securities markets. Typical cases were those in which an employee or former employee of a small enterprise sued to enforce an alleged promise that he or she would receive an equity interest in the business. The usual commercial policies relating to writings in contracts for the sale of personal property are at most tangentially implicated in such cases. There was a rather large and complex body of case law dealing with the applicability of Section 8–319 to cases of this sort. It seems doubtful that the cost of litigating these issues was warranted by whatever protections the statute of frauds offered against fraudulent claims.

Subsection (c) of former Section 8–319 provided that the statute of frauds bar did not apply if a written confirmation was sent and the recipient did not seasonably send an objection. That provision, however, presumably would not have had the effect of binding a broker's customer to the terms of a trade for which confirmation had been sent though the customer had not objected within 10 days. In the first place, the relationship between a broker and customer is ordinarily that of agent and principal; thus the broker is not seeking to enforce a contract for sale of a security, but to bind its principal for action taken by the broker as agent. Former Section 8–319 did not by its terms apply to the agency relationship. Moreover, even if former Section 8–319(c) applied, it is doubtful that it, of its own force, had the effect of precluding the customer from disputing whether there was a contract or what the terms of the contract were. Former Section 8–319(c) only removed the statute of frauds as a bar to enforcement; it did not say that there was a contract or that the confirmation had the effect of excluding other evidence of its terms. Thus, deletion of former Section 8–319 does not change the law one way or the other on whether a customer who fails to object to a written confirmation is precluded from denying the trade described in the confirmation, because that issue was never governed by former Section 8–319(c).

8. Miscellaneous.

Prior Section 8–105. Revised Article 8 deletes the statement found in Section 8–105(1) of the prior version that certificated securities "are negotiable instruments." This provision was added very late in the drafting process of the original Uniform Commercial Code. Apparently the thought was that it might be useful in dealing with potential transition problems arising out of the fact that bonds were then treated as negotiable instruments under the Uniform Negotiable Instruments Law. During that era, many other statutes, such as those specifying permissible categories of investments for regulated entities, might have used such phrases as "negotiable securities" or "negotiable instruments." Section 8–105 seems to have been included in the original version of Article 8 to avoid unfortunate interpretations of those other statutes once securities were moved from the Uniform Negotiable Instruments Law to UCC Article 8. Whether or not Section 8–105 was necessary at that time, it has surely outlived its purpose. The statement that securities "are negotiable instruments" is very confusing. As used in the Uniform Commercial Code, the term "negotiable instrument" means an instrument that is governed by Article 3; yet Article 8 securities are not governed by Article 3. Courts have occasionally cited Section 8–105(1) of prior law for the proposition that the rules that are generally thought of as characteristic of negotiability, such as the rule that bona fide purchasers take free from adverse claims, apply to certificated securities. Section 8–105(1), however, is unnecessary for that purpose, since the relevant rules are set out in specific provisions of Article 8.

Prior Sections 8–107 and 8–314. Article 8 has never been, and should not be, a comprehensive codification of the law of contracts for the purchase and sale of securities. The prior version of Article 8 did contain, however, a number of provisions dealing with miscellaneous aspects of the law of contracts as applied to contracts for the sale of securities. Section 8–107 dealt with one remedy for breach, and Section 8–314 dealt with certain aspects of performance. Revised Article 8 deletes these on the theory that inclusion of a few sections on issues of contract law is likely to cause more harm than good since inferences might be drawn from the failure to cover related issues. The deletion of these sections is not, however, intended as a rejection of the rules of contract law and interpretation that they expressed.

Prior Section 8–315. It is not entirely clear what the function of Section 8–315 of prior law was. The section specified that the owner of a security could recover it from a person to whom it had been transferred, if the transferee did not qualify as a bona fide purchaser. It seems to have been intended only to recognize that securities, like any other form of personal property, are governed by the general principle of property law that an owner can recover property from a person to whom it has been transferred under circumstances that did not cut off the owner's claim. Although many other Articles of the UCC deal with cut-off rules, Article 8 was the only one that included an affirmative statement of the rights of an owner to recover her property. It seems wiser to adopt the same approach as in Articles 2, 3, 7, and 9, and leave this point to other law. Accordingly, Section 8–315 is deleted in Revised Article 8, without, of course, implying rejection of the nearly self-evident rule that it sought to express.

Prior Section 8–407. This section, entitled "Exchangeability of Securities," seemed to say that holders of securities had the right to cause issuers to convert them back and forth from certificated to uncertificated form. The provision, however, applied only if the issuer "regularly maintains a system for issuing the class of securities involved under which both certificated and uncertificated securities are regularly issued to the category of owners, which includes the person in whose name the new security is to be registered." The provision seems unnecessary, since it applied only if the issuer decided that it should. The matter can be covered by agreement or corporate charter or by-laws.

V.   ACKNOWLEDGMENTS

On behalf of the National Conference of Commissioners on Uniform State Laws and the American Law Institute, the Drafting Committee and the Reporter acknowledge with deep appreciation the dedicated and helpful assistance of a great many individuals and organizations. Among the large number of individuals who participated in the development of Revised Article 8, special mention should be made of a few whose contributions were extraordinary.

Preceding the preparation of Revised Article 8, the topic was carefully studied by the Advisory Committee on Settlement of Market Transactions of the American Bar Association Section of Business Law, under the chairmanship of Robert Haydock, Jr., of Boston, MA. Martin Aronstein, of Philadelphia, PA, reporter for the 1977 revision of Article 8, served on the Haydock Committee and continued to advise the Drafting Committee. Robert C. Mendelson, New York, NY, who also served on the Haydock Committee, is chair of the Market Transactions Advisory Committee set up by the Securities and Exchange Commission; Bob Mendelson's considerable contribution to the preparation of Revised Article 8 was most important. Other members of the Haydock Committee had continuing roles either as members of the Drafting Committee or as sources of valuable advice to that committee.

The revision of Article 8 is the culmination of a successful federal-state collaboration among the American Law Institute and the National Conference of Commissioners on Uniform State Laws, sponsors of the Uniform Commercial Code, and representatives of the United States Department of the Treasury, the Securities and Exchange Commission, the Federal Reserve System, and other federal bodies. The product reflects the assistance of many people, and particularly of Jonathan Kallman and Ari Burstein on behalf of the SEC, Calvin Ninomiya, Cynthia E. Reese, and Virginia S. Rutledge of Treasury, Lawranne Stewart of the Board of Governors of the Federal Reserve System, Debra W. Cook and MarySue Fisher of the Federal Reserve Bank of New York, and George Wilder and Carla Behnfeldt of the Commodity Futures Trading Commission.

Representatives of organizations in the securities and banking industry and their counsel gave generously of their time and knowledge. Special mention should be made of Norman R. Nelson, New York Clearing House, R. May Lee, Public Securities Association, Robert J. Woldow and Karen Saperstein, National Securities Clearing Corporation, Leopold S. Rassnick, Participants Trust Company, Robert Wittie and Patricia Louie, Investment Company Institute, Thomas A. Williams, Richard B. Nesson and Carl Urist, Depository Trust Company, Dennis A. Dutterer, Board of Trade Clearing Corporation, Evalyn Lipton Fishbein, State Street Bank and Trust Company, Robert P. DeGregorie, Chemical Bank, Gail M. Inaba, Morgan Guaranty Trust Company of New York, Anthony J. Leitner, Goldman, Sachs & Company, Robert M. MacAllister, The Chase Manhattan Bank, N.A., Kevin J. Moynihan, Merrill Lynch, Pierce, Fenner & Smith Inc., Lois J. Radisch, J.P. Morgan & Co., James J. Volpe, First Chicago Trust Company of New York, and Richard E. Smith, Securities Transfer Association.

Many lawyers and law professors contributed to the work of the Drafting Committee. Special appreciation is due to Sandra M. Rocks, New York, NY, who participated on behalf of the ABA UCC Investment Securities Subcommittee and ABA Task Force on TRADES Regulations. Others who participated included Steven Harris and James R. McDaniel, Chicago, IL, Kenneth B. Davis, Jr., Madison, WI, David M. Huggins and Bradley Y. Smith, New York, NY, David J. Schraa, Brussels, Belgium, and Randall D. Guynn, London, England. The Reporter and Drafting Committee also received assistance from the dedicated work of lawyers, not themselves experts in securities law, who reviewed and commented upon drafts and participated in the revision process through meetings of the Members Consultative Group of the American Law Institute and at various national, state, and local bar association programs.

PART 1

SHORT TITLE AND GENERAL MATTERS

§ 8–101.   Short Title.

This Article may be cited as Uniform Commercial Code—Investment Securities.

§ 8–102.   Definitions.

(a)   In this Article:

(1)   "Adverse claim" means a claim that a claimant has a property interest in a financial asset and that it is a violation of the rights of the claimant for another person to hold, transfer, or deal with the financial asset.

(2)   "Bearer form," as applied to a certificated security, means a form in which the security is payable to the bearer of the security certificate according to its terms but not by reason of an indorsement.

(3)   "Broker" means a person defined as a broker or dealer under the federal securities laws, but without excluding a bank acting in that capacity.

(4)   "Certificated security" means a security that is represented by a certificate.

(5)   "Clearing corporation" means:

     (i)   a person that is registered as a "clearing agency" under the federal securities laws;

     (ii)   a federal reserve bank; or

     (iii)   any other person that provides clearance or settlement services with respect to financial assets that would require it to register as a clearing agency under the federal securities laws but for an exclusion or exemption from the registration requirement, if its activities as a clearing corporation, including promulgation of rules, are subject to regulation by a federal or state governmental authority.

(6) "Communicate" means to:

    (i) send a signed writing; or

    (ii) transmit information by any mechanism agreed upon by the persons transmitting and receiving the information.

(7) "Entitlement holder" means a person identified in the records of a securities intermediary as the person having a security entitlement against the securities intermediary. If a person acquires a security entitlement by virtue of Section 8–501(b)(2) or (3), that person is the entitlement holder.

(8) "Entitlement order" means a notification communicated to a securities intermediary directing transfer or redemption of a financial asset to which the entitlement holder has a security entitlement.

(9) "Financial asset," except as otherwise provided in Section 8–103, means:

    (i) a security;

    (ii) an obligation of a person or a share, participation, or other interest in a person or in property or an enterprise of a person, which is, or is of a type, dealt in or traded on financial markets, or which is recognized in any area in which it is issued or dealt in as a medium for investment; or

    (iii) any property that is held by a securities intermediary for another person in a securities account if the securities intermediary has expressly agreed with the other person that the property is to be treated as a financial asset under this Article.

As context requires, the term means either the interest itself or the means by which a person's claim to it is evidenced, including a certificated or uncertificated security, a security certificate, or a security entitlement.

(10) [Reserved] ["Good faith," for purposes of the obligation of good faith in the performance or enforcement of contracts or duties within this Article, means honesty in fact and the observance of reasonable commercial standards of fair dealing.]*

(11) "Indorsement" means a signature that alone or accompanied by other words is made on a security certificate in registered form or on a separate document for the purpose of assigning, transferring, or redeeming the security or granting a power to assign, transfer, or redeem it.

(12) "Instruction" means a notification communicated to the issuer of an uncertificated security which directs that the transfer of the security be registered or that the security be redeemed.

(13) "Registered form," as applied to a certificated security, means a form in which:

    (i) the security certificate specifies a person entitled to the security; and

    (ii) a transfer of the security may be registered upon books maintained for that purpose by or on behalf of the issuer, or the security certificate so states.

(14) "Securities intermediary" means:

    (i) a clearing corporation; or

    (ii) a person, including a bank or broker, that in the ordinary course of its business maintains securities accounts for others and is acting in that capacity.

(15) "Security," except as otherwise provided in Section 8–103, means an obligation of an issuer or a share, participation, or other interest in an issuer or in property or an enterprise of an issuer:

---

* *Note from West Advisory Panel: This subsection will be deleted if the jurisdiction adopts the definition of good faith in revised Article 1.*

   (i)   which is represented by a security certificate in bearer or registered form, or the transfer of which may be registered upon books maintained for that purpose by or on behalf of the issuer;

   (ii)   which is one of a class or series or by its terms is divisible into a class or series of shares, participations, interests, or obligations; and

   (iii)   which:

      (A)   is, or is of a type, dealt in or traded on securities exchanges or securities markets; or

      (B)   is a medium for investment and by its terms expressly provides that it is a security governed by this Article.

(16) "Security certificate" means a certificate representing a security.

(17) "Security entitlement" means the rights and property interest of an entitlement holder with respect to a financial asset specified in Part 5.

(18) "Uncertificated security" means a security that is not represented by a certificate.

(b)   Other definitions applying to this Article and the sections in which they appear are:

"Appropriate person Section". 8–107.
"Control Section". 8–106.
"Delivery Section". 8–301.
"Investment company security". Section 8–103.
"Issuer Section". 8–201.
"Overissue Section". 8–210.
"Protected purchaser". Section 8–303.
"Securities account". Section 8–501.

(c)   In addition, Article 1 contains general definitions and principles of construction and interpretation applicable throughout this Article.

(d)   The characterization of a person, business, or transaction for purposes of this Article does not determine the characterization of the person, business, or transaction for purposes of any other law, regulation, or rule.

As amended in 2001.

Official Comment

1.   "Adverse claim." The definition of the term "adverse claim" has two components. First, the term refers only to property interests. Second, the term means not merely that a person has a property interest in a financial asset but that it is a violation of the claimant's property interest for the other person to hold or transfer the security or other financial asset.

The term adverse claim is not, of course, limited to ownership rights, but extends to other property interests established by other law. A security interest, for example, would be an adverse claim with respect to a transferee from the debtor since any effort by the secured party to enforce the security interest against the property would be an interference with the transferee's interest.

The definition of adverse claim in the prior version of Article 8 might have been read to suggest that any wrongful action concerning a security, even a simple breach of contract, gave rise to an adverse claim. Insofar as such cases as *Fallon v. Wall Street Clearing Corp.*, 586 N.Y.S.2d 953, 182 A.D.2d 245 (1992) and *Pentech Intl. v. Wall St. Clearing Co.*, 983 F.2d 441 (2d Cir.1993), were based on that view, they are rejected by the new definition which explicitly limits the term adverse claim to property interests. Suppose, for example, that A contracts to sell or deliver securities to B, but fails to do so and instead sells or pledges the securities to C. B, the promisee, has an action against A for breach of contract, but absent unusual circumstances the action for breach would not give rise to a property interest in the securities. Accordingly, B does not have an adverse claim. An adverse claim might, however, be based upon principles of equitable remedies that give rise to property claims. It would, for example, cover a right established by other law to rescind a transaction in which securities were transferred. Suppose, for example, that A holds securities and is induced by B's fraud to transfer them to B. Under the law of contract or restitution, A may have a right to rescind the transfer, which gives A a property claim to the securities. If so, A has an adverse claim to the securities in B's hands. By contrast, if B had committed no fraud, but had merely committed a breach of contract in connection with the transfer from A to B, A may have only a right to damages for breach, not a right to rescind. In that case, A would not have an adverse claim to the securities in B's hands.

2. "Bearer form." The definition of "bearer form" has remained substantially unchanged since the early drafts of the original version of Article 8. The requirement that the certificate be payable to bearer by its terms rather than by an indorsement has the effect of preventing instruments governed by other law, such as chattel paper or Article 3 negotiable instruments, from being inadvertently swept into the Article 8 definition of security merely by virtue of blank indorsements. Although the other elements of the definition of security in Section 8–102(a)(14) probably suffice for that purpose in any event, the language used in the prior version of Article 8 has been retained.

3. "Broker." Broker is defined by reference to the definitions of broker and dealer in the federal securities laws. The only difference is that banks, which are excluded from the federal securities law definition, are included in the Article 8 definition when they perform functions that would bring them within the federal securities law definition if it did not have the clause excluding banks. The definition covers both those who act as agents ("brokers" in securities parlance) and those who act as principals ("dealers" in securities parlance). Since the definition refers to persons "defined" as brokers or dealers under the federal securities law, rather than to persons required to "register" as brokers or dealers under the federal securities law, it covers not only registered brokers and dealers but also those exempt from the registration requirement, such as purely intrastate brokers. The only substantive rules that turn on the defined term broker are one provision of the section on warranties, Section 8–108(i), and the special perfection rule in Article 9 for security interests granted by brokers or securities intermediaries, Section 9–309(10).

4. "Certificated security." The term "certificated security" means a security that is represented by a security certificate.

5. "Clearing corporation." The definition of clearing corporation limits its application to entities that are subject to a rigorous regulatory framework. Accordingly, the definition includes only federal reserve banks, persons who are registered as "clearing agencies" under the federal securities laws (which impose a comprehensive system of regulation of the activities and rules of clearing agencies), and other entities subject to a comparable system of regulatory oversight.

6. "Communicate." The term "communicate" assures that the Article 8 rules will be sufficiently flexible to adapt to changes in information technology. Sending a signed writing always suffices as a communication, but the parties can agree that a different means of transmitting information is to be used. Agreement is defined in Section 1–201(3)* as "the bargain of the parties in fact as found in their language or by implication from other circumstances including course of dealing or usage of trade or course of performance." Thus, use of an information transmission method might be found to be authorized by agreement, even though the parties have not explicitly so specified in a formal agreement. The term communicate is used in Sections 8–102(a)(7) (definition of entitlement order), 8–102(a)(11) (definition of instruction), and 8–403 (demand that issuer not register transfer).

7. "Entitlement holder." This term designates those who hold financial assets through intermediaries in the indirect holding system. Because many of the rules of Part 5 impose duties on securities intermediaries in favor of entitlement holders, the definition of entitlement holder is, in most cases, limited to the person specifically designated as such on the records of the intermediary. The last sentence of the definition covers the relatively unusual cases where a person may acquire a security entitlement under Section 8–501 even though the person may not be specifically designated as an entitlement holder on the records of the securities intermediary.

A person may have an interest in a security entitlement, and may even have the right to give entitlement orders to the securities intermediary with respect to it, even though the person is not the entitlement holder. For example, a person who holds securities through a securities account in its own name may have given discretionary trading authority to another person, such as an investment adviser. Similarly, the control provisions in Section 8–106 and the related provisions in Article 9 are designed to facilitate transactions in which a person who holds securities through a securities account uses them as collateral in an arrangement where the securities intermediary has agreed that if the secured party so directs the intermediary will dispose of the positions. In such arrangements, the debtor remains the entitlement holder but has agreed that the secured party can initiate entitlement orders. Moreover, an entitlement holder may be acting for another person as a nominee, agent, trustee,

---

* *Referring to unrevised Article 1 (Appendix A).*

or in another capacity. Unless the entitlement holder is itself acting as a securities intermediary for the other person, in which case the other person would be an entitlement holder with respect to the securities entitlement, the relationship between an entitlement holder and another person for whose benefit the entitlement holder holds a securities entitlement is governed by other law.

8. "Entitlement order." This term is defined as a notification communicated to a securities intermediary directing transfer or redemption of the financial asset to which an entitlement holder has a security entitlement. The term is used in the rules for the indirect holding system in a fashion analogous to the use of the terms "indorsement" and "instruction" in the rules for the direct holding system. If a person directly holds a certificated security in registered form and wishes to transfer it, the means of transfer is an indorsement. If a person directly holds an uncertificated security and wishes to transfer it, the means of transfer is an instruction. If a person holds a security entitlement, the means of disposition is an entitlement order. An entitlement order includes a direction under Section 8–508 to the securities intermediary to transfer a financial asset to the account of the entitlement holder at another financial intermediary or to cause the financial asset to be transferred to the entitlement holder in the direct holding system (e.g., the delivery of a securities certificate registered in the name of the former entitlement holder). As noted in Comment 7, an entitlement order need not be initiated by the entitlement holder in order to be effective, so long as the entitlement holder has authorized the other party to initiate entitlement orders. See Section 8–107(b).

9. "Financial asset." The definition of "financial asset," in conjunction with the definition of "securities account" in Section 8–501, sets the scope of the indirect holding system rules of Part 5 of Revised Article 8. The Part 5 rules apply not only to securities held through intermediaries, but also to other financial assets held through intermediaries. The term financial asset is defined to include not only securities but also a broader category of obligations, shares, participations, and interests.

Having separate definitions of security and financial asset makes it possible to separate the question of the proper scope of the traditional Article 8 rules from the question of the proper scope of the new indirect holding system rules. Some forms of financial assets should be covered by the indirect holding system rules of Part 5, but not by the rules of Parts 2, 3, and 4. The term financial asset is used to cover such property. Because the term security entitlement is defined in terms of financial assets rather than securities, the rules concerning security entitlements set out in Part 5 of Article 8 and in Revised Article 9 apply to the broader class of financial assets.

The fact that something does or could fall within the definition of financial asset does not, without more, trigger Article 8 coverage. The indirect holding system rules of Revised Article 8 apply only if the financial asset is in fact held in a securities account, so that the interest of the person who holds the financial asset through the securities account is a security entitlement. Thus, questions of the scope of the indirect holding system rules cannot be framed as "Is such-and-such a 'financial asset' under Article 8?" Rather, one must analyze whether the relationship between an institution and a person on whose behalf the institution holds an asset falls within the scope of the term securities account as defined in Section 8–501. That question turns in large measure on whether it makes sense to apply the Part 5 rules to the relationship.

The term financial asset is used to refer both to the underlying asset and the particular means by which ownership of that asset is evidenced. Thus, with respect to a certificated security, the term financial asset may, as context requires, refer either to the interest or obligation of the issuer or to the security certificate representing that interest or obligation. Similarly, if a person holds a security or other financial asset through a securities account, the term financial asset may, as context requires, refer either to the underlying asset or to the person's security entitlement.

10. "Good faith." Section 1–203* provides that "Every contract or duty within [the Uniform Commercial Code] imposes an obligation of good faith in its performance or enforcement." Section 1–201(b)(20) defines "good faith" as "honesty in fact and the observance of reasonable commercial standards of fair dealing." The reference to commercial standards makes clear that assessments of conduct are to be made in light of the commercial setting. The substantive rules of Article 8 have been drafted to take account of the commercial circumstances of the securities holding and processing system. For example, Section 8–115 provides that a securities intermediary acting on an effective entitlement order, or a broker or other agent acting as a conduit in a securities transaction, is not liable to an adverse claimant, unless the claimant obtained legal process or the intermediary acted in collusion with the wrongdoer. This, and other similar provisions, see Sections 8–404 and 8–503(e), do not depend on notice of adverse claims, because it would impair rather than advance the interest of investors in having a sound and efficient securities clearance and settlement system to require intermediaries to investigate the

---

* *Referring to unrevised Article 1 (Appendix A).*

propriety of the transactions they are processing. The good faith obligation does not supplant the standards of conduct established in provisions of this kind.

In Revised Article 8, the definition of good faith is not germane to the question whether a purchaser takes free from adverse claims. The rules on such questions as whether a purchaser who takes in suspicious circumstances is disqualified from protected purchaser status are treated not as an aspect of good faith but directly in the rules of Section 8–105 on notice of adverse claims.

11. "Indorsement" is defined as a signature made on a security certificate or separate document for purposes of transferring or redeeming the security. The definition is adapted from the language of Section 8–308(1) of the prior version and from the definition of indorsement in the Negotiable Instruments Article, see Section 3–204(a). The definition of indorsement does not include the requirement that the signature be made by an appropriate person or be authorized. Those questions are treated in the separate substantive provision on whether the indorsement is effective, rather than in the definition of indorsement. See Section 8–107.

12. "Instruction" is defined as a notification communicated to the issuer of an uncertificated security directing that transfer be registered or that the security be redeemed. Instructions are the analog for uncertificated securities of indorsements of certificated securities.

13. "Registered form." The definition of "registered form" is substantially the same as in the prior version of Article 8. Like the definition of bearer form, it serves primarily to distinguish Article 8 securities from instruments governed by other law, such as Article 3.

Contrary to the holding in *Highland Capital Management LP v. Schneider*, 8 N.Y.3d 406 (2007), the registrability requirement in the definition of "registered form," and its parallel in the definition of "security," are satisfied only if books are maintained by or on behalf of the issuer for the purpose of registration of transfer, including the determination of rights under Section 8–207(a) (or if, in the case of a certificated security, the security certificate so states). It is not sufficient that the issuer records ownership, or records transfers thereof, for other purposes. Nor is it sufficient that the issuer, while not in fact maintaining books for the purpose of registration of transfer, could do so, for such is always the case.

14. "Securities intermediary." A "securities intermediary" is a person that in the ordinary course of its business maintains securities accounts for others and is acting in that capacity. The most common examples of securities intermediaries would be clearing corporations holding securities for their participants, banks acting as securities custodians, and brokers holding securities on behalf of their customers. Clearing corporations are listed separately as a category of securities intermediary in subparagraph (i) even though in most circumstances they would fall within the general definition in subparagraph (ii). The reason is to simplify the analysis of arrangements such as the NSCC-DTC system in which NSCC performs the comparison, clearance, and netting function, while DTC acts as the depository. Because NSCC is a registered clearing agency under the federal securities laws, it is a clearing corporation and hence a securities intermediary under Article 8, regardless of whether it is at any particular time or in any particular aspect of its operations holding securities on behalf of its participants.

The terms securities intermediary and broker have different meanings. Broker means a person engaged in the business of buying and selling securities, as agent for others or as principal. Securities intermediary means a person maintaining securities accounts for others. A stockbroker, in the colloquial sense, may or may not be acting as a securities intermediary.

The definition of securities intermediary includes the requirement that the person in question is "acting in the capacity" of maintaining securities accounts for others. This is to take account of the fact that a particular entity, such as a bank, may act in many different capacities in securities transactions. A bank may act as a transfer agent for issuers, as a securities custodian for institutional investors and private investors, as a dealer in government securities, as a lender taking securities as collateral, and as a provider of general payment and collection services that might be used in connection with securities transactions. A bank that maintains securities accounts for its customers would be a securities intermediary with respect to those accounts; but if it takes a pledge of securities from a borrower to secure a loan, it is not thereby acting as a securities intermediary with respect to the pledged securities, since it holds them for its own account rather than for a customer. In other circumstances, those two functions might be combined. For example, if the bank is a government securities dealer it may maintain securities accounts for customers and also provide the customers with margin credit to purchase or carry the securities, in much the same way that brokers provide margin loans to their customers.

15. "Security." The definition of "security" has three components. First, there is the subparagraph (i) test that the interest or obligation be fully transferable, in the sense that the issuer either maintains transfer books or

the obligation or interest is represented by a certificate in bearer or registered form. Second, there is the subparagraph (ii) test that the interest or obligation be divisible, that is, one of a class or series, as distinguished from individual obligations of the sort governed by ordinary contract law or by Article 3. Third, there is the subparagraph (iii) functional test, which generally turns on whether the interest or obligation is, or is of a type, dealt in or traded on securities markets or securities exchanges. There is, however, an "opt-in" provision in subparagraph (iii) which permits the issuer of any interest or obligation that is "a medium of investment" to specify that it is a security governed by Article 8.

The divisibility test of subparagraph (ii) applies to the security—that is, the underlying intangible interest—not the means by which that interest is evidenced. Thus, securities issued in book-entry only form meet the divisibility test because the underlying intangible interest is divisible via the mechanism of the indirect holding system. This is so even though the clearing corporation is the only eligible direct holder of the security.

The third component, the functional test in subparagraph (iii), provides flexibility while ensuring that the Article 8 rules do not apply to interests or obligations in circumstances so unconnected with the securities markets that parties are unlikely to have thought of the possibility that Article 8 might apply. Subparagraph (iii)(A) covers interests or obligations that either are dealt in or traded on securities exchanges or securities markets, or are of a type dealt in or traded on securities exchanges or securities markets. The "is dealt in or traded on" phrase eliminates problems in the characterization of new forms of securities which are to be traded in the markets, even though no similar type has previously been dealt in or traded in the markets. Subparagraph (iii)(B) covers the broader category of media for investment, but it applies only if the terms of the interest or obligation specify that it is an Article 8 security. This opt-in provision allows for deliberate expansion of the scope of Article 8.

Section 8–103 contains additional rules on the treatment of particular interests as securities or financial assets.

16. "Security certificate." The term "security" refers to the underlying asset, e.g., 1000 shares of common stock of Acme, Inc. The term "security certificate" refers to the paper certificates that have traditionally been used to embody the underlying intangible interest.

17. "Security entitlement" means the rights and property interest of a person who holds securities or other financial assets through a securities intermediary. A security entitlement is both a package of personal rights against the securities intermediary and an interest in the property held by the securities intermediary. A security entitlement is not, however, a specific property interest in any financial asset held by the securities intermediary or by the clearing corporation through which the securities intermediary holds the financial asset. See Sections 8–104(c) and 8–503. The formal definition of security entitlement set out in subsection (a)(16) of this section is a cross-reference to the rules of Part 5. In a sense, then, the entirety of Part 5 is the definition of security entitlement. The Part 5 rules specify the rights and property interest that comprise a security entitlement.

18. "Uncertificated security." The term "uncertificated security" means a security that is not represented by a security certificate. For uncertificated securities, there is no need to draw any distinction between the underlying asset and the means by which a direct holder's interest in that asset is evidenced. Compare "certificated security" and "security certificate."

Definitional Cross References:

"Agreement". Section 1–201(b)(3).
"Bank". Section 1–201(b)(4).
"Person". Section 1–201(b)(27).
"Send". Section 1–201(b)(36).
"Signed". Section 1–201(b)(37).
"Writing". Section 1–201(b)(43).

As amended in 1999, 2001 and 2010.

§ 8–103. Rules for Determining Whether Certain Obligations and Interests are Securities or Financial Assets.

(a) A share or similar equity interest issued by a corporation, business trust, joint stock company, or similar entity is a security.

(b)   An "investment company security" is a security. "Investment company security" means a share or similar equity interest issued by an entity that is registered as an investment company under the federal investment company laws, an interest in a unit investment trust that is so registered, or a face-amount certificate issued by a face-amount certificate company that is so registered. Investment company security does not include an insurance policy or endowment policy or annuity contract issued by an insurance company.

(c)   An interest in a partnership or limited liability company is not a security unless it is dealt in or traded on securities exchanges or in securities markets, its terms expressly provide that it is a security governed by this Article, or it is an investment company security. However, an interest in a partnership or limited liability company is a financial asset if it is held in a securities account.

(d)   A writing that is a security certificate is governed by this Article and not by Article 3, even though it also meets the requirements of that Article. However, a negotiable instrument governed by Article 3 is a financial asset if it is held in a securities account.

(e)   An option or similar obligation issued by a clearing corporation to its participants is not a security, but is a financial asset.

(f)   A commodity contract, as defined in Section 9–102(a)(15), is not a security or a financial asset.

(g)   A document of title is not a financial asset unless Section 8–102(a)(9)(iii) applies.

As amended in 1999 and 2003.

Official Comment

1.   This section contains rules that supplement the definitions of "financial asset" and "security" in Section 8–102. The Section 8–102 definitions are worded in general terms, because they must be sufficiently comprehensive and flexible to cover the wide variety of investment products that now exist or may develop. The rules in this section are intended to foreclose interpretive issues concerning the application of the general definitions to several specific investment products. No implication is made about the application of the Section 8–102 definitions to investment products not covered by this section.

2.   Subsection (a) establishes an unconditional rule that ordinary corporate stock is a security. That is so whether or not the particular issue is dealt in or traded on securities exchanges or in securities markets. Thus, shares of closely held corporations are Article 8 securities.

3.   Subsection (b) establishes that the Article 8 term "security" includes the various forms of the investment vehicles offered to the public by investment companies registered as such under the federal Investment Company Act of 1940, as amended. This clarification is prompted principally by the fact that the typical transaction in shares of open-end investment companies is an issuance or redemption, rather than a transfer of shares from one person to another as is the case with ordinary corporate stock. For similar reasons, the definitions of indorsement, instruction, and entitlement order in Section 8–102 refer to "redemptions" as well as "transfers," to ensure that the Article 8 rules on such matters as signature guaranties, Section 8–306, assurances, Sections 8–402 and 8–507, and effectiveness, Section 8–107, apply to directions to redeem mutual fund shares. The exclusion of insurance products is needed because some insurance company separate accounts are registered under the Investment Company Act of 1940, but these are not traded under the usual Article 8 mechanics.

4.   Subsection (c) is designed to foreclose interpretive questions that might otherwise be raised by the application of the "of a type" language of Section 8–102(a)(15)(iii) to partnership interests. Subsection (c) establishes the general rule that partnership interests or shares of limited liability companies are not Article 8 securities unless they are in fact dealt in or traded on securities exchanges or in securities markets. The issuer, however, may explicitly "opt-in" by specifying that the interests or shares are securities governed by Article 8. Partnership interests or shares of limited liability companies are included in the broader term "financial asset." Thus, if they are held through a securities account, the indirect holding system rules of Part 5 apply, and the interest of a person who holds them through such an account is a security entitlement.

5.   Subsection (d) deals with the line between Article 3 negotiable instruments and Article 8 investment securities. It continues the rule of the prior version of Article 8 that a writing that meets the Article 8 definition is covered by Article 8 rather than Article 3, even though it also meets the definition of negotiable instrument. However, subsection (d) provides that an Article 3 negotiable instrument is a "financial asset" so that the indirect

holding system rules apply if the instrument is held through a securities intermediary. This facilitates making items such as money market instruments eligible for deposit in clearing corporations.

6. Subsection (e) is included to clarify the treatment of investment products such as traded stock options, which are treated as financial assets but not securities. Thus, the indirect holding system rules of Part 5 apply, but the direct holding system rules of Parts 2, 3, and 4 do not.

7. Subsection (f) excludes commodity contracts from all of Article 8. However, under Article 9, commodity contracts are included in the definition of "investment property." Therefore, the Article 9 rules on security interests in investment property do apply to security interests in commodity positions. See Section 9–102 and Comment 6 thereto. "Commodity contract" is defined in Section 9–102(a)(15).

8. Subsection (g) allows a document of title to be a financial asset and thus subject to the indirect holding system rules of Part 5 only to the extent that the intermediary and the person entitled under the document agree to do so. This is to prevent the inadvertent application of the Part 5 rules to intermediaries who may hold either electronic or tangible documents of title.

Definitional Cross References:

"Clearing corporation". Section 8–102(a)(5).
"Commodity contract". Section 9–102(a)(15).
"Financial asset". Section 8–102(a)(9).
"Security". Section 8–102(a)(15).
"Security certificate". Section 8–102(a)(16).

As amended in 2003.

§ 8–104. Acquisition of Security or Financial Asset or Interest Therein.

(a) A person acquires a security or an interest therein, under this Article, if:

(1) the person is a purchaser to whom a security is delivered pursuant to Section 8–301; or

(2) the person acquires a security entitlement to the security pursuant to Section 8–501.

(b) A person acquires a financial asset, other than a security, or an interest therein, under this Article, if the person acquires a security entitlement to the financial asset.

(c) A person who acquires a security entitlement to a security or other financial asset has the rights specified in Part 5, but is a purchaser of any security, security entitlement, or other financial asset held by the securities intermediary only to the extent provided in Section 8–503.

(d) Unless the context shows that a different meaning is intended, a person who is required by other law, regulation, rule, or agreement to transfer, deliver, present, surrender, exchange, or otherwise put in the possession of another person a security or financial asset satisfies that requirement by causing the other person to acquire an interest in the security or financial asset pursuant to subsection (a) or (b).

Official Comment

1. This section lists the ways in which interests in securities and other financial assets are acquired under Article 8. In that sense, it describes the scope of Article 8. Subsection (a) describes the two ways that a person may acquire a security or interest therein under this Article: (1) by delivery (Section 8–301), and (2) by acquiring a security entitlement. Each of these methods is described in detail in the relevant substantive provisions of this Article. Part 3, beginning with the definition of "delivery" in Section 8–301, describes how interests in securities are acquired in the direct holding system. Part 5, beginning with the rules of Section 8–501 on how security entitlements are acquired, describes how interests in securities are acquired in the indirect holding system.

Subsection (b) specifies how a person may acquire an interest under Article 8 in a financial asset other than a security. This Article deals with financial assets other than securities only insofar as they are held in the indirect holding system. For example, a bankers' acceptance falls within the definition of "financial asset," so if it is held through a securities account the entitlement holder's right to it is a security entitlement governed by Part 5. The bankers' acceptance itself, however, is a negotiable instrument governed by Article 3, not by Article 8. Thus, the provisions of Parts 2, 3, and 4 of this Article that deal with the rights of direct holders of securities are not applicable. Article 3, not Article 8, specifies how one acquires a direct interest in a bankers' acceptance. If a bankers' acceptance is delivered to a clearing corporation to be held for the account of the clearing corporation's participants, the clearing corporation becomes the holder of the bankers' acceptance under the Article 3 rules specifying how negotiable instruments are transferred. The rights of the clearing corporation's participants, however, are governed by Part 5 of this Article.

2.   The distinction in usage in Article 8 between the term "security" (and its correlatives "security certificate" and "uncertificated security") on the one hand, and "security entitlement" on the other, corresponds to the distinction between the direct and indirect holding systems. For example, with respect to certificated securities that can be held either directly or through intermediaries, obtaining possession of a security certificate and acquiring a security entitlement are both means of holding the underlying security. For many other purposes, there is no need to draw a distinction between the means of holding. For purposes of commercial law analysis, however, the form of holding may make a difference. Where an item of property can be held in different ways, the rules on how one deals with it, including how one transfers it or how one grants a security interest in it, differ depending on the form of holding.

Although a security entitlement is means of holding the underlying security or other financial asset, a person who has a security entitlement does not have any direct claim to a specific asset in the possession of the securities intermediary. Subsection (c) provides explicitly that a person who acquires a security entitlement is a "purchaser" of any security, security entitlement, or other financial asset held by the securities intermediary only in the sense that under Section 8–503 a security entitlement is treated as a *sui generis* form of property interest.

3.   Subsection (d) is designed to ensure that parties will retain their expected legal rights and duties under Revised Article 8. One of the major changes made by the revision is that the rules for the indirect holding system are stated in terms of the "security entitlements" held by investors, rather than speaking of them as holding direct interests in securities. Subsection (d) is designed as a translation rule to eliminate problems of co-ordination of terminology, and facilitate the continued use of systems for the efficient handling of securities and financial assets through securities intermediaries and clearing corporations. The efficiencies of a securities intermediary or clearing corporation are, in part, dependent on the ability to transfer securities credited to securities accounts in the intermediary or clearing corporation to the account of an issuer, its agent, or other person by book entry in a manner that permits exchanges, redemptions, conversions, and other transactions (which may be governed by pre-existing or new agreements, constitutional documents, or other instruments) to occur and to avoid the need to withdraw from immobilization in an intermediary or clearing corporation physical securities in order to deliver them for such purposes. Existing corporate charters, indentures and like documents may require the "presentation," "surrender," "delivery," or "transfer" of securities or security certificates for purposes of exchange, redemption, conversion or other reason. Likewise, documents may use a wide variety of terminology to describe, in the context for example of a tender or exchange offer, the means of putting the offeror or the issuer or its agent in possession of the security. Subsection (d) takes the place of provisions of prior law which could be used to reach the legal conclusion that book-entry transfers are equivalent to physical delivery to the person to whose account the book entry is credited.

Definitional Cross References:

"Delivery". Section 8–301.

"Financial asset". Section 8–102(a)(9).

"Person". Section 1–201(30).*

"Purchaser". Sections 1–201(33)* & 8–116.

"Security". Section 8–102(a)(15).

"Security entitlement". Section 8–102(a)(17).

§ 8–105.   Notice of Adverse Claim.

(a)   A person has notice of an adverse claim if:

(1)   the person knows of the adverse claim;

(2)   the person is aware of facts sufficient to indicate that there is a significant probability that the adverse claim exists and deliberately avoids information that would establish the existence of the adverse claim; or

---

*   *Referring to unrevised Article 1 (Appendix A).*

(3)   the person has a duty, imposed by statute or regulation, to investigate whether an adverse claim exists, and the investigation so required would establish the existence of the adverse claim.

(b)   Having knowledge that a financial asset or interest therein is or has been transferred by a representative imposes no duty of inquiry into the rightfulness of a transaction and is not notice of an adverse claim. However, a person who knows that a representative has transferred a financial asset or interest therein in a transaction that is, or whose proceeds are being used, for the individual benefit of the representative or otherwise in breach of duty has notice of an adverse claim.

(c)   An act or event that creates a right to immediate performance of the principal obligation represented by a security certificate or sets a date on or after which the certificate is to be presented or surrendered for redemption or exchange does not itself constitute notice of an adverse claim except in the case of a transfer more than:

(1)   one year after a date set for presentment or surrender for redemption or exchange; or

(2)   six months after a date set for payment of money against presentation or surrender of the certificate, if money was available for payment on that date.

(d)   A purchaser of a certificated security has notice of an adverse claim if the security certificate:

(1)   whether in bearer or registered form, has been indorsed "for collection" or "for surrender" or for some other purpose not involving transfer; or

(2)   is in bearer form and has on it an unambiguous statement that it is the property of a person other than the transferor, but the mere writing of a name on the certificate is not such a statement.

(e)   Filing of a financing statement under Article 9 is not notice of an adverse claim to a financial asset.

Official Comment

1.   The rules specifying whether adverse claims can be asserted against persons who acquire securities or security entitlements, Sections 8–303, 8–502, and 8–510, provide that one is protected against an adverse claim only if one takes without notice of the claim. This section defines notice of an adverse claim.

The general Article 1 definition of "notice" in Section 1–201(25)*—which provides that a person has notice of a fact if "from all the facts and circumstances known to him at the time in question he has reason to know that it exists"—does not apply to the interpretation of "notice of adverse claims." The Section 1–201(25)* definition of "notice" does, however, apply to usages of that term and its cognates in Article 8 in contexts other than notice of adverse claims.

2.   This section must be interpreted in light of the definition of "adverse claim" in Section 8–102(a)(1). "Adverse claim" does not include all circumstances in which a third party has a property interest in securities, but only those situations where a security is transferred in violation of the claimant's property interest. Therefore, awareness that someone other than the transferor has a property interest is not notice of an adverse claim. The transferee must be aware that the transfer violates the other party's property interest. If A holds securities in which B has some form of property interest, and A transfers the securities to C, C may know that B has an interest, but infer that A is acting in accordance with A's obligations to B. The mere fact that C knew that B had a property interest does not mean that C had notice of an adverse claim. Whether C had notice of an adverse claim depends on whether C had sufficient awareness that A was acting in violation of B's property rights. The rule in subsection (b) is a particularization of this general principle.

3.   Paragraph (a)(1) provides that a person has notice of an adverse claim if the person has knowledge of the adverse claim. Knowledge is defined in Section 1–201(25)* as actual knowledge.

4.   Paragraph (a)(2) provides that a person has notice of an adverse claim if the person is aware of a significant probability that an adverse claim exists and deliberately avoids information that might establish the existence of the adverse claim. This is intended to codify the "willful blindness" test that has been applied in such cases. See *May v. Chapman,* 16 M. & W. 355, 153 Eng.Rep. 1225 (1847); *Goodman v. Simonds,* 61 U.S. 343 (1857).

---

*   *Referring to unrevised Article 1 (Appendix A).*

The first prong of the willful blindness test of paragraph (a)(2) turns on whether the person is aware facts sufficient to indicate that there is a significant probability that an adverse claim exists. The "awareness" aspect necessarily turns on the actor's state of mind. Whether facts known to a person make the person aware of a "significant probability" that an adverse claim exists turns on facts about the world and the conclusions that would be drawn from those facts, taking account of the experience and position of the person in question. A particular set of facts might indicate a significant probability of an adverse claim to a professional with considerable experience in the usual methods and procedures by which securities transactions are conducted, even though the same facts would not indicate a significant probability of an adverse claim to a non-professional.

The second prong of the willful blindness test of paragraph (a)(2) turns on whether the person "deliberately avoids information" that would establish the existence of the adverse claim. The test is the character of the person's response to the information the person has. The question is whether the person deliberately failed to seek further information because of concern that suspicions would be confirmed.

Application of the "deliberate avoidance" test to a transaction by an organization focuses on the knowledge and the actions of the individual or individuals conducting the transaction on behalf of the organization. Thus, an organization that purchases a security is not willfully blind to an adverse claim unless the officers or agents who conducted that purchase transaction are willfully blind to the adverse claim. Under the two prongs of the willful blindness test, the individual or individuals conducting a transaction must know of facts indicating a substantial probability that the adverse claim exists and deliberately fail to seek further information that might confirm or refute the indication. For this purpose, information known to individuals within an organization who are not conducting or aware of a transaction, but not forwarded to the individuals conducting the transaction, is not pertinent in determining whether the individuals conducting the transaction had knowledge of a substantial probability of the existence of the adverse claim. Cf. Section 1–201(27).* An organization may also "deliberately avoid information" if it acts to preclude or inhibit transmission of pertinent information to those individuals responsible for the conduct of purchase transactions.

5.   Paragraph (a)(3) provides that a person has notice of an adverse claim if the person would have learned of the adverse claim by conducting an investigation that is required by other statute or regulation. This rule applies only if there is some other statute or regulation that explicitly requires persons dealing with securities to conduct some investigation. The federal securities laws require that brokers and banks, in certain specified circumstances, check with a stolen securities registry to determine whether securities offered for sale or pledge have been reported as stolen. If securities that were listed as stolen in the registry are taken by an institution that failed to comply with requirement to check the registry, the institution would be held to have notice of the fact that they were stolen under paragraph (a)(3). Accordingly, the institution could not qualify as a protected purchaser under Section 8–303. The same result has been reached under the prior version of Article 8. See *First Nat'l Bank of Cicero v. Lewco Securities,* 860 F.2d 1407 (7th Cir.1988).

6.   Subsection (b) provides explicitly for some situations involving purchase from one described or identifiable as a representative. Knowledge of the existence of the representative relation is not enough in itself to constitute "notice of an adverse claim" that would disqualify the purchaser from protected purchaser status. A purchaser may take a security on the inference that the representative is acting properly. Knowledge that a security is being transferred to an individual account of the representative or that the proceeds of the transaction will be paid into that account is not sufficient to constitute "notice of an adverse claim," but knowledge that the proceeds will be applied to the personal indebtedness of the representative is. See *State Bank of Binghamton v. Bache,* 162 Misc. 128, 293 N.Y.S. 667 (1937).

7.   Subsection (c) specifies whether a purchaser of a "stale" security is charged with notice of adverse claims, and therefore disqualified from protected purchaser status under Section 8–303. The fact of "staleness" is viewed as notice of certain defects after the lapse of stated periods, but the maturity of the security does not operate automatically to affect holders' rights. The periods of time here stated are shorter than those appearing in the provisions of this Article on staleness as notice of defects or defenses of an issuer (Section 8–203) since a purchaser who takes a security after funds or other securities are available for its redemption has more reason to suspect claims of ownership than issuer's defenses. An owner will normally turn in a security rather than transfer it at such a time. Of itself, a default never constitutes notice of a possible adverse claim. To provide otherwise would not tend to drive defaulted securities home and would serve only to disrupt current financial markets where many defaulted securities are actively traded. Unpaid or overdue coupons attached to a bond do not bring it within the operation of this subsection, though they may be relevant under the general test of notice of adverse claims in subsection (a).

8. Subsection (d) provides the owner of a certificated security with a means of protection while a security certificate is being sent in for redemption or exchange. The owner may endorse it "for collection" or "for surrender," and this constitutes notice of the owner's claims, under subsection (d).

Definitional Cross References:

"Adverse claim". Section 8–102(a)(1).
"Bearer form". Section 8–102(a)(2).
"Certificated security". Section 8–102(a)(4).
"Financial asset". Section 8–102(a)(9).
"Knowledge". Section 1–201(25).*
"Person". Section 1–201(30).*
"Purchaser". Sections 1–201(33)* & 8–116.
"Registered form". Section 8–102(a)(13).
"Representative". Section 1–201(35).*
"Security certificate". Section 8–102(a)(16).

§ 8–106.   Control.

(a) A purchaser has "control" of a certificated security in bearer form if the certificated security is delivered to the purchaser.

(b) A purchaser has "control" of a certificated security in registered form if the certificated security is delivered to the purchaser, and:

(1) the certificate is indorsed to the purchaser or in blank by an effective indorsement; or

(2) the certificate is registered in the name of the purchaser, upon original issue or registration of transfer by the issuer.

(c) A purchaser has "control" of an uncertificated security if:

(1) the uncertificated security is delivered to the purchaser; or

(2) the issuer has agreed that it will comply with instructions originated by the purchaser without further consent by the registered owner.

(d) A purchaser has "control" of a security entitlement if:

(1) the purchaser becomes the entitlement holder;

(2) the securities intermediary has agreed that it will comply with entitlement orders originated by the purchaser without further consent by the entitlement holder; or

(3) another person has control of the security entitlement on behalf of the purchaser or, having previously acquired control of the security entitlement, acknowledges that it has control on behalf of the purchaser.

(e) If an interest in a security entitlement is granted by the entitlement holder to the entitlement holder's own securities intermediary, the securities intermediary has control.

(f) A purchaser who has satisfied the requirements of subsection (c) or (d) has control, even if the registered owner in the case of subsection (c) or the entitlement holder in the case of subsection (d) retains the right to make substitutions for the uncertificated security or security entitlement, to originate instructions or entitlement orders to the issuer or securities intermediary, or otherwise to deal with the uncertificated security or security entitlement.

(g) An issuer or a securities intermediary may not enter into an agreement of the kind described in subsection (c)(2) or (d)(2) without the consent of the registered owner or entitlement holder, but an issuer or a securities intermediary is not required to enter into such an agreement even though the registered owner or entitlement holder so directs. An issuer or securities intermediary that has entered into such an

---

* *Referring to unrevised Article 1 (Appendix A).*

agreement is not required to confirm the existence of the agreement to another party unless requested to do so by the registered owner or entitlement holder.

As amended in 1999.

Official Comment

1.   The concept of "control" plays a key role in various provisions dealing with the rights of purchasers, including secured parties. See Sections 8–303 (protected purchasers); 8–503(e) (purchasers from securities intermediaries); 8–510 (purchasers of security entitlements from entitlement holders); 9–314 (perfection of security interests); 9–328 (priorities among conflicting security interests).

Obtaining "control" means that the purchaser has taken whatever steps are necessary, given the manner in which the securities are held, to place itself in a position where it can have the securities sold, without further action by the owner.

2.   Subsection (a) provides that a purchaser obtains "control" with respect to a certificated security in bearer form by taking "delivery," as defined in Section 8–301. Subsection (b) provides that a purchaser obtains "control" with respect to a certificated security in registered form by taking "delivery," as defined in Section 8–301, provided that the security certificate has been indorsed to the purchaser or in blank. Section 8–301 provides that delivery of a certificated security occurs when the purchaser obtains possession of the security certificate, or when an agent for the purchaser (other than a securities intermediary) either acquires possession or acknowledges that the agent holds for the purchaser.

3.   Subsection (c) specifies the means by which a purchaser can obtain control over uncertificated securities which the transferor holds directly. Two mechanisms are possible.

Under subsection (c)(1), securities can be "delivered" to a purchaser. Section 8–301(b) provides that "delivery" of an uncertificated security occurs when the purchaser becomes the registered holder. So far as the issuer is concerned, the purchaser would then be entitled to exercise all rights of ownership. See Section 8–207. As between the parties to a purchase transaction, however, the rights of the purchaser are determined by their contract. Cf. Section 9–202. Arrangements covered by this paragraph are analogous to arrangements in which bearer certificates are delivered to a secured party—so far as the issuer or any other parties are concerned, the secured party appears to be the outright owner, although it is in fact holding as collateral property that belongs to the debtor.

Under subsection (c)(2), a purchaser has control if the issuer has agreed to act on the instructions of the purchaser, even though the owner remains listed as the registered owner. The issuer, of course, would be acting wrongfully against the registered owner if it entered into such an agreement without the consent of the registered owner. Subsection (g) makes this point explicit. The subsection (c)(2) provision makes it possible for issuers to offer a service akin to the registered pledge device of the 1978 version of Article 8, without mandating that all issuers offer that service.

4.   Subsection (d) specifies the means by which a purchaser can obtain control of a security entitlement. Three mechanisms are possible, analogous to those provided in subsection (c) for uncertificated securities. Under subsection (d)(1), a purchaser has control if it is the entitlement holder. This subsection would apply whether the purchaser holds through the same intermediary that the debtor used, or has the securities position transferred to its own intermediary. Subsection (d)(2) provides that a purchaser has control if the securities intermediary has agreed to act on entitlement orders originated by the purchaser if no further consent by the entitlement holder is required. Under subsection (d)(2), control may be achieved even though the original entitlement holder remains as the entitlement holder. Finally, a purchaser may obtain control under subsection (d)(3) if another person has control and the person acknowledges that it has control on the purchaser's behalf. Control under subsection (d)(3) parallels the delivery of certificated securities and uncertificated securities under Section 8–301. Of course, the acknowledging person cannot be the debtor.

This section specifies only the minimum requirements that such an arrangement must meet to confer "control"; the details of the arrangement can be specified by agreement. The arrangement might cover all of the positions in a particular account or subaccount, or only specified positions. There is no requirement that the control party's right to give entitlement orders be exclusive. The arrangement might provide that only the control party can give entitlement orders, or that either the entitlement holder or the control party can give entitlement orders. See subsection (f).

The following examples illustrate the application of subsection (d):

Example 1. Debtor grants Alpha Bank a security interest in a security entitlement that includes 1000 shares of XYZ Co. stock that Debtor holds through an account with Able & Co. Alpha also has an account with Able. Debtor instructs Able to transfer the shares to Alpha, and Able does so by crediting the shares to Alpha's account. Alpha has control of the 1000 shares under subsection (d)(1). Although Debtor may have become the beneficial owner of the new securities entitlement, as between Debtor and Alpha, Able has agreed to act on Alpha's entitlement orders because, as between Able and Alpha, Alpha has become the entitlement holder. See Section 8–506.

Example 2. Debtor grants Alpha Bank a security interest in a security entitlement that includes 1000 shares of XYZ Co. stock that Debtor holds through an account with Able & Co. Alpha does not have an account with Able. Alpha uses Beta as its securities custodian. Debtor instructs Able to transfer the shares to Beta, for the account of Alpha, and Able does so. Alpha has control of the 1000 shares under subsection (d)(1). As in Example 1, although Debtor may have become the beneficial owner of the new securities entitlement, as between Debtor and Alpha, Beta has agreed to act on Alpha's entitlement orders because, as between Beta and Alpha, Alpha has become the entitlement holder.

Example 3. Debtor grants Alpha Bank a security interest in a security entitlement that includes 1000 shares of XYZ Co. stock that Debtor holds through an account with Able & Co. Debtor, Able, and Alpha enter into an agreement under which Debtor will continue to receive dividends and distributions, and will continue to have the right to direct dispositions, but Alpha also has the right to direct dispositions. Alpha has control of the 1000 shares under subsection (d)(2).

Example 4. Able & Co., a securities dealer, grants Alpha Bank a security interest in a security entitlement that includes 1000 shares of XYZ Co. stock that Able holds through an account with Clearing Corporation. Able causes Clearing Corporation to transfer the shares into Alpha's account at Clearing Corporation. As in Example 1, Alpha has control of the 1000 shares under subsection (d)(1).

Example 5. Able & Co., a securities dealer, grants Alpha Bank a security interest in a security entitlement that includes 1000 shares of XYZ Co. stock that Able holds through an account with Clearing Corporation. Alpha does not have an account with Clearing Corporation. It holds its securities through Beta Bank, which does have an account with Clearing Corporation. Able causes Clearing Corporation to transfer the shares into Beta's account at Clearing Corporation. Beta credits the position to Alpha's account with Beta. As in Example 2, Alpha has control of the 1000 shares under subsection (d)(1).

Example 6. Able & Co., a securities dealer, grants Alpha Bank a security interest in a security entitlement that includes 1000 shares of XYZ Co. stock that Able holds through an account with Clearing Corporation. Able causes Clearing Corporation to transfer the shares into a pledge account, pursuant to an agreement under which Able will continue to receive dividends, distributions, and the like, but Alpha has the right to direct dispositions. As in Example 3, Alpha has control of the 1000 shares under subsection (d)(2).

Example 7. Able & Co., a securities dealer, grants Alpha Bank a security interest in a security entitlement that includes 1000 shares of XYZ Co. stock that Able holds through an account with Clearing Corporation. Able, Alpha, and Clearing Corporation enter into an agreement under which Clearing Corporation will act on instructions from Alpha with respect to the XYZ Co. stock carried in Able's account, but Able will continue to receive dividends, distributions, and the like, and will also have the right to direct dispositions. As in Example 3, Alpha has control of the 1000 shares under subsection (d)(2).

Example 8. Able & Co., a securities dealer, holds a wide range of securities through its account at Clearing Corporation. Able enters into an arrangement with Alpha Bank pursuant to which Alpha provides financing to Able secured by securities identified as the collateral on lists provided by Able to Alpha on a daily or other periodic basis. Able, Alpha, and Clearing Corporation enter into an agreement under which Clearing Corporation agrees that if at any time Alpha directs Clearing Corporation to do so, Clearing Corporation will transfer any securities from Able's account at Alpha's instructions. Because Clearing Corporation has agreed to act on Alpha's instructions with respect to any securities carried in Able's account, at the moment that Alpha's security interest attaches to securities listed by Able, Alpha obtains control of those securities under subsection (d)(2). There is no requirement that Clearing Corporation be informed of which securities Able has pledged to Alpha.

Example 9. Debtor grants Alpha Bank a security interest in a security entitlement that includes 1000 shares of XYZ Co. stock that Debtor holds through an account with Able & Co. Beta Bank agrees with Alpha to act as Alpha's collateral agent with respect to the security entitlement. Debtor, Able, and Beta enter into an agreement under which Debtor will continue to receive dividends and distributions, and will continue to have the right to direct dispositions, but Beta also has the right to direct dispositions. Because Able has agreed that it will comply with entitlement orders originated by Beta without further consent by Debtor, Beta has control of the security entitlement (see Example 3). Because Beta has control on behalf of Alpha, Alpha also has control under subsection (d)(3). It is not necessary for Able to enter into an agreement directly with Alpha or for Able to be aware of Beta's agency relationship with Alpha.

5.   For a purchaser to have "control" under subsection (c)(2) or (d)(2), it is essential that the issuer or securities intermediary, as the case may be, actually be a party to the agreement. If a debtor gives a secured party a power of attorney authorizing the secured party to act in the name of the debtor, but the issuer or securities intermediary does not specifically agree to this arrangement, the secured party does not have "control" within the meaning of subsection (c)(2) or (d)(2) because the issuer or securities intermediary is not a party to the agreement. The secured party does not have control under subsection (c)(1) or (d)(1) because, although the power of attorney might give the secured party authority to act on the debtor's behalf as an agent, the secured party has not actually become the registered owner or entitlement holder.

6.   Subsection (e) provides that if an interest in a security entitlement is granted by an entitlement holder to the securities intermediary through which the security entitlement is maintained, the securities intermediary has control. A common transaction covered by this provision is a margin loan from a broker to its customer.

7.   The term "control" is used in a particular defined sense. The requirements for obtaining control are set out in this section. The concept is not to be interpreted by reference to similar concepts in other bodies of law. In particular, the requirements for "possession" derived from the common law of pledge are not to be used as a basis for interpreting subsection (c)(2) or (d)(2). Those provisions are designed to supplant the concepts of "constructive possession" and the like. A principal purpose of the "control" concept is to eliminate the uncertainty and confusion that results from attempting to apply common law possession concepts to modern securities holding practices.

The key to the control concept is that the purchaser has the ability to have the securities sold or transferred without further action by the transferor. There is no requirement that the powers held by the purchaser be exclusive. For example, in a secured lending arrangement, if the secured party wishes, it can allow the debtor to retain the right to make substitutions, to direct the disposition of the uncertificated security or security entitlement, or otherwise to give instructions or entitlement orders. (As explained in Section 8–102, Comment 8, an entitlement order includes a direction under Section 8–508 to the securities intermediary to transfer a financial asset to the account of the entitlement holder at another financial intermediary or to cause the financial asset to be transferred to the entitlement holder in the direct holding system (e.g., by delivery of a securities certificate registered in the name of the former entitlement holder).) Subsection (f) is included to make clear the general point stated in subsections (c) and (d) that the test of control is whether the purchaser has obtained the requisite power, not whether the debtor has retained other powers. There is no implication that retention by the debtor of powers other than those mentioned in subsection (f) is inconsistent with the purchaser having control. Nor is there a requirement that the purchaser's powers be unconditional, provided that further consent of the entitlement holder is not a condition.

Example 10. Debtor grants to Alpha Bank and to Beta Bank a security interest in a security entitlement that includes 1000 shares of XYZ Co. stock that Debtor holds through an account with Able & Co. By agreement among the parties, Alpha's security interest is senior and Beta's is junior. Able agrees to act on the entitlement orders of either Alpha or Beta. Alpha and Beta each has control under subsection (d)(2). Moreover, Beta has control notwithstanding a term of Able's agreement to the effect that Able's obligation to act on Beta's entitlement orders is conditioned on Alpha's consent. The crucial distinction is that Able's agreement to act on Beta's entitlement orders is not conditioned on Debtor's further consent.

Example 11. Debtor grants to Alpha Bank a security interest in a security entitlement that includes 1000 shares of XYZ Co. stock that Debtor holds through an account with Able & Co. Able agrees to act on the entitlement orders of Alpha, but Alpha's right to give entitlement orders to the securities intermediary is conditioned on the Debtor's default. Alternatively, Alpha's right to give entitlement orders is conditioned upon Alpha's statement to Able that Debtor is in default. Because Able's agreement to act on ~~Beta's~~ Alpha's* entitlement orders is not conditioned on Debtor's further consent, Alpha has control of the securities entitlement under either alternative.

---

*   Amendments in italics approved by the Permanent Editorial Board for Uniform Commercial Code January 15, 2000.

In many situations, it will be better practice for both the securities intermediary and the purchaser to insist that any conditions relating in any way to the entitlement holder be effective only as between the purchaser and the entitlement holder. That practice would avoid the risk that the securities intermediary could be caught between conflicting assertions of the entitlement holder and the purchaser as to whether the conditions in fact have been met. Nonetheless, the existence of unfulfilled conditions effective against the intermediary would not preclude the purchaser from having control.

Definitional Cross References:

"Bearer form". Section 8–102(a)(2).

"Certificated security". Section 8–102(a)(4).

"Delivery". Section 8–301.

"Effective". Section 8–107.

"Entitlement holder". Section 8–102(a)(7).

"Entitlement order". Section 8–102(a)(8).

"Indorsement". Section 8–102(a)(11).

"Instruction". Section 8–102(a)(12).

"Purchaser". Sections 1–201(33)* & 8–116.

"Registered form". Section 8–102(a)(13).

"Securities intermediary". Section 8–102(a)(14).

"Security entitlement". Section 8–102(a)(17).

"Uncertificated security". Section 8–102(a)(18).

As amended in 1999 and 2000.

§ 8–107. Whether Indorsement, Instruction, or Entitlement Order is Effective.

(a) "Appropriate person" means:

(1) with respect to an indorsement, the person specified by a security certificate or by an effective special indorsement to be entitled to the security;

(2) with respect to an instruction, the registered owner of an uncertificated security;

(3) with respect to an entitlement order, the entitlement holder;

(4) if the person designated in paragraph (1), (2), or (3) is deceased, the designated person's successor taking under other law or the designated person's personal representative acting for the estate of the decedent; or

(5) if the person designated in paragraph (1), (2), or (3) lacks capacity, the designated person's guardian, conservator, or other similar representative who has power under other law to transfer the security or financial asset.

(b) An indorsement, instruction, or entitlement order is effective if:

(1) it is made by the appropriate person;

(2) it is made by a person who has power under the law of agency to transfer the security or financial asset on behalf of the appropriate person, including, in the case of an instruction or entitlement order, a person who has control under Section 8–106(c)(2) or (d)(2); or

(3) the appropriate person has ratified it or is otherwise precluded from asserting its ineffectiveness.

(c) An indorsement, instruction, or entitlement order made by a representative is effective even if:

(1) the representative has failed to comply with a controlling instrument or with the law of the State having jurisdiction of the representative relationship, including any law requiring the representative to obtain court approval of the transaction; or

---

* *Referring to unrevised Article 1 (Appendix A).*

(2)   the representative's action in making the indorsement, instruction, or entitlement order or using the proceeds of the transaction is otherwise a breach of duty.

(d)   If a security is registered in the name of or specially indorsed to a person described as a representative, or if a securities account is maintained in the name of a person described as a representative, an indorsement, instruction, or entitlement order made by the person is effective even though the person is no longer serving in the described capacity.

(e)   Effectiveness of an indorsement, instruction, or entitlement order is determined as of the date the indorsement, instruction, or entitlement order is made, and an indorsement, instruction, or entitlement order does not become ineffective by reason of any later change of circumstances.

Official Comment

1.   This section defines two concepts, "appropriate person" and "effective." Effectiveness is a broader concept than appropriate person. For example, if a security or securities account is registered in the name of Mary Roe, Mary Roe is the "appropriate person," but an indorsement, instruction, or entitlement order made by John Doe is "effective" if, under agency or other law, Mary Roe is precluded from denying Doe's authority. Treating these two concepts separately facilitates statement of the rules of Article 8 that state the legal effect of an indorsement, instruction, or entitlement order. For example, a securities intermediary is protected against liability if it acts on an effective entitlement order, but has a duty to comply with an entitlement order only if it is originated by an appropriate person. See Sections 8–115 and 8–507.

One important application of the "effectiveness" concept is in the direct holding system rules on the rights of purchasers. A purchaser of a certificated security in registered form can qualify as a protected purchaser who takes free from adverse claims under Section 8–303 only if the purchaser obtains "control." Section 8–106 provides that a purchaser of a certificated security in registered form obtains control if there has been an "effective" indorsement.

2.   Subsection (a) provides that the term "appropriate person" covers two categories: (1) the person who is actually designated as the person entitled to the security or security entitlement, and (2) the successor or legal representative of that person if that person has died or otherwise lacks capacity. Other law determines who has power to transfer a security on behalf of a person who lacks capacity. For example, if securities are registered in the name of more than one person and one of the designated persons dies, whether the survivor is the appropriate person depends on the form of tenancy. If the two were registered joint tenants with right of survivorship, the survivor would have that power under other law and thus would be the "appropriate person." If securities are registered in the name of an individual and the individual dies, the law of decedents' estates determines who has power to transfer the decedent's securities. That would ordinarily be the executor or administrator, but if a "small estate statute" permits a widow to transfer a decedent's securities without administration proceedings, she would be the appropriate person. If the registration of a security or a securities account contains a designation of a death beneficiary under the Uniform Transfer on Death Security Registration Act or comparable legislation, the designated beneficiary would, under that law, have power to transfer upon the person's death and so would be the appropriate person. Article 8 does not contain a list of such representatives, because any list is likely to become outdated by developments in other law.

3.   Subsection (b) sets out the general rule that an indorsement, instruction, or entitlement order is effective if it is made by the appropriate person or by a person who has power to transfer under agency law or if the appropriate person is precluded from denying its effectiveness. The control rules in Section 8–106 provide for arrangements where a person who holds securities through a securities intermediary, or holds uncertificated securities directly, enters into a control agreement giving the secured party the right to initiate entitlement orders of instructions. Paragraph 2 of subsection (b) states explicitly that an entitlement order or instruction initiated by a person who has obtained such a control agreement is "effective."

Subsections (c), (d), and (e) supplement the general rule of subsection (b) on effectiveness. The term "representative," used in subsections (c) and (d), is defined in Section 1–201(35).*

4.   Subsection (c) provides that an indorsement, instruction, or entitlement order made by a representative is effective even though the representative's action is a violation of duties. The following example illustrates this subsection:

---

*   *Referring to unrevised Article 1 (Appendix A).*

Example 1. Certificated securities are registered in the name of John Doe. Doe dies and Mary Roe is appointed executor. Roe indorses the security certificate and transfers it to a purchaser in a transaction that is a violation of her duties as executor.

Roe's indorsement is effective, because Roe is the appropriate person under subsection (a)(4). This is so even though Roe's transfer violated her obligations as executor. The policies of free transferability of securities that underlie Article 8 dictate that neither a purchaser to whom Roe transfers the securities nor the issuer who registers transfer should be required to investigate the terms of the will to determine whether Roe is acting properly. Although Roe's indorsement is effective under this section, her breach of duty may be such that her beneficiary has an adverse claim to the securities that Roe transferred. The question whether that adverse claim can be asserted against purchasers is governed not by this section but by Section 8–303. Under Section 8–404, the issuer has no duties to an adverse claimant unless the claimant obtains legal process enjoining the issuer from registering transfer.

5. Subsection (d) deals with cases where a security or a securities account is registered in the name of a person specifically designated as a representative. The following example illustrates this subsection:

Example 2. Certificated securities are registered in the name of "John Jones, trustee of the Smith Family Trust." John Jones is removed as trustee and Martha Moe is appointed successor trustee. The securities, however, are not reregistered, but remain registered in the name of "John Jones, trustee of the Smith Family Trust." Jones indorses the security certificate and transfers it to a purchaser.

Subsection (d) provides that an indorsement by John Jones as trustee is effective even though Jones is no longer serving in that capacity. Since the securities were registered in the name of "John Jones, trustee of the Smith Family Trust," a purchaser, or the issuer when called upon to register transfer, should be entitled to assume without further inquiry that Jones has the power to act as trustee for the Smith Family Trust.

Note that subsection (d) does not apply to a case where the security or securities account is registered in the name of principal rather than the representative as such. The following example illustrates this point:

Example 3. Certificated securities are registered in the name of John Doe. John Doe dies and Mary Roe is appointed executor. The securities are not reregistered in the name of Mary Roe as executor. Later, Mary Roe is removed as executor and Martha Moe is appointed as her successor. After being removed, Mary Roe indorses the security certificate that is registered in the name of John Doe and transfers it to a purchaser.

Mary Roe's indorsement is not made effective by subsection (d), because the securities were not registered in the name of Mary Roe as representative. A purchaser or the issuer registering transfer should be required to determine whether Roe has power to act for John Doe. Purchasers and issuers can protect themselves in such cases by requiring signature guaranties. See Section 8–306.

6. Subsection (e) provides that the effectiveness of an indorsement, instruction, or entitlement order is determined as of the date it is made. The following example illustrates this subsection:

Example 4. Certificated securities are registered in the name of John Doe. John Doe dies and Mary Roe is appointed executor. Mary Roe indorses the security certificate that is registered in the name of John Doe and transfers it to a purchaser. After the indorsement and transfer, but before the security certificate is presented to the issuer for registration of transfer, Mary Roe is removed as executor and Martha Moe is appointed as her successor.

Mary Roe's indorsement is effective, because at the time Roe indorsed she was the appropriate person under subsection (a)(4). Her later removal as executor does not render the indorsement ineffective. Accordingly, the issuer would not be liable for registering the transfer. See Section 8–404.

Definitional Cross References:

"Entitlement order". Section 8–102(a)(8).
"Financial asset". Section 8–102(a)(9).
"Indorsement". Section 8–102(a)(11).
"Instruction". Section 8–102(a)(12).
"Representative". Section 1–201(35).*
"Securities account". Section 8–501.

---

* *Referring to unrevised Article 1 (Appendix A).*

"Security". Section 8–102(a)(15).

"Security certificate". Section 8–102(a)(16).

"Security entitlement". Section 8–102(a)(17).

"Uncertificated security". Section 8–102(a)(18).

§ 8–108.   Warranties in Direct Holding.

(a)   A person who transfers a certificated security to a purchaser for value warrants to the purchaser, and an indorser, if the transfer is by indorsement, warrants to any subsequent purchaser, that:

(1)   the certificate is genuine and has not been materially altered;

(2)   the transferor or indorser does not know of any fact that might impair the validity of the security;

(3)   there is no adverse claim to the security;

(4)   the transfer does not violate any restriction on transfer;

(5)   if the transfer is by indorsement, the indorsement is made by an appropriate person, or if the indorsement is by an agent, the agent has actual authority to act on behalf of the appropriate person; and

(6)   the transfer is otherwise effective and rightful.

(b)   A person who originates an instruction for registration of transfer of an uncertificated security to a purchaser for value warrants to the purchaser that:

(1)   the instruction is made by an appropriate person, or if the instruction is by an agent, the agent has actual authority to act on behalf of the appropriate person;

(2)   the security is valid;

(3)   there is no adverse claim to the security; and

(4)   at the time the instruction is presented to the issuer:

(i)   the purchaser will be entitled to the registration of transfer;

(ii)   the transfer will be registered by the issuer free from all liens, security interests, restrictions, and claims other than those specified in the instruction;

(iii)   the transfer will not violate any restriction on transfer; and

(iv)   the requested transfer will otherwise be effective and rightful.

(c)   A person who transfers an uncertificated security to a purchaser for value and does not originate an instruction in connection with the transfer warrants that:

(1)   the uncertificated security is valid;

(2)   there is no adverse claim to the security;

(3)   the transfer does not violate any restriction on transfer; and

(4)   the transfer is otherwise effective and rightful.

(d)   A person who indorses a security certificate warrants to the issuer that:

(1)   there is no adverse claim to the security; and

(2)   the indorsement is effective.

(e)   A person who originates an instruction for registration of transfer of an uncertificated security warrants to the issuer that:

(1)   the instruction is effective; and

(2) at the time the instruction is presented to the issuer the purchaser will be entitled to the registration of transfer.

(f) A person who presents a certificated security for registration of transfer or for payment or exchange warrants to the issuer that the person is entitled to the registration, payment, or exchange, but a purchaser for value and without notice of adverse claims to whom transfer is registered warrants only that the person has no knowledge of any unauthorized signature in a necessary indorsement.

(g) If a person acts as agent of another in delivering a certificated security to a purchaser, the identity of the principal was known to the person to whom the certificate was delivered, and the certificate delivered by the agent was received by the agent from the principal or received by the agent from another person at the direction of the principal, the person delivering the security certificate warrants only that the delivering person has authority to act for the principal and does not know of any adverse claim to the certificated security.

(h) A secured party who redelivers a security certificate received, or after payment and on order of the debtor delivers the security certificate to another person, makes only the warranties of an agent under subsection (g).

(i) Except as otherwise provided in subsection (g), a broker acting for a customer makes to the issuer and a purchaser the warranties provided in subsections (a) through (f). A broker that delivers a security certificate to its customer, or causes its customer to be registered as the owner of an uncertificated security, makes to the customer the warranties provided in subsection (a) or (b), and has the rights and privileges of a purchaser under this section. The warranties of and in favor of the broker acting as an agent are in addition to applicable warranties given by and in favor of the customer.

Official Comment

1. Subsections (a), (b), and (c) deal with warranties by security transferors to purchasers. Subsections (d) and (e) deal with warranties by security transferors to issuers. Subsection (f) deals with presentment warranties.

2. Subsection (a) specifies the warranties made by a person who transfers a certificated security to a purchaser for value. Paragraphs (3), (4), and (5) make explicit several key points that are implicit in the general warranty of paragraph (6) that the transfer is effective and rightful. Subsection (b) sets forth the warranties made to a purchaser for value by one who originates an instruction. These warranties are quite similar to those made by one transferring a certificated security, subsection (a), the principal difference being the absolute warranty of validity. If upon receipt of the instruction the issuer should dispute the validity of the security, the burden of proving validity is upon the transferor. Subsection (c) provides for the limited circumstances in which an uncertificated security could be transferred without an instruction, see Section 8–301(b)(2). Subsections (d) and (e) give the issuer the benefit of the warranties of an indorser or originator on those matters not within the issuer's knowledge.

3. Subsection (f) limits the warranties made by a purchaser for value without notice whose presentation of a security certificate is defective in some way but to whom the issuer does register transfer. The effect is to deny the issuer a remedy against such a person unless at the time of presentment the person had knowledge of an unauthorized signature in a necessary indorsement. The issuer can protect itself by refusing to make the transfer or, if it registers the transfer before it discovers the defect, by pursuing its remedy against a signature guarantor.

4. Subsection (g) eliminates all substantive warranties in the relatively unusual case of a delivery of certificated security by an agent of a disclosed principal where the agent delivers the exact certificate that it received from or for the principal. Subsection (h) limits the warranties given by a secured party who redelivers a certificate. Subsection (i) specifies the warranties of brokers in the more common scenarios.

5. Under Section 1–102(3)* the warranty provisions apply "unless otherwise agreed" and the parties may enter into express agreements to allocate the risks of possible defects. Usual estoppel principles apply with respect to transfers of both certificated and uncertificated securities whenever the purchaser has knowledge of the defect, and these warranties will not be breached in such a case.

Definitional Cross References:

"Adverse claim". Section 8–102(a)(1).

---

* *Referring to unrevised Article 1 (Appendix A).*

"Appropriate person". Section 8–107.

"Broker". Section 8–102(a)(3).

"Certificated security". Section 8–102(a)(4).

"Indorsement". Section 8–102(a)(11).

"Instruction". Section 8–102(a)(12).

"Issuer". Section 8–201.

"Person". Section 1–201(30).*

"Purchaser". Sections 1–201(33)* & 8–116.

"Secured party". Section 9–102(a)(72).**

"Security". Section 8–102(a)(15).

"Security certificate". Section 8–102(a)(16).

"Uncertificated security". Section 8–102(a)(18).

"Value". Sections 1–201(44)* & 8–116.

§ 8–109.   Warranties in Indirect Holding.

(a)   A person who originates an entitlement order to a securities intermediary warrants to the securities intermediary that:

(1)   the entitlement order is made by an appropriate person, or if the entitlement order is by an agent, the agent has actual authority to act on behalf of the appropriate person; and

(2)   there is no adverse claim to the security entitlement.

(b)   A person who delivers a security certificate to a securities intermediary for credit to a securities account or originates an instruction with respect to an uncertificated security directing that the uncertificated security be credited to a securities account makes to the securities intermediary the warranties specified in Section 8–108(a) or (b).

(c)   If a securities intermediary delivers a security certificate to its entitlement holder or causes its entitlement holder to be registered as the owner of an uncertificated security, the securities intermediary makes to the entitlement holder the warranties specified in Section 8–108(a) or (b).

Official Comment

1.   Subsection (a) provides that a person who originates an entitlement order warrants to the securities intermediary that the order is authorized, and warrants the absence of adverse claims. Subsection (b) specifies the warranties that are given when a person who holds securities directly has the holding converted into indirect form. A person who delivers a certificate to a securities intermediary or originates an instruction for an uncertificated security gives to the securities intermediary the transfer warranties under Section 8–108. If the securities intermediary in turn delivers the certificate to a higher level securities intermediary, it gives the same warranties.

2.   Subsection (c) states the warranties that a securities intermediary gives when a customer who has been holding securities in an account with the securities intermediary requests that certificates be delivered or that uncertificated securities be registered in the customer's name. The warranties are the same as those that brokers make with respect to securities that the brokers sell to or buy on behalf of the customers. See Section 8–108(i).

3.   As with the Section 8–108 warranties, the warranties specified in this section may be modified by agreement under Section 1–102(3).*

Definitional Cross References:

"Adverse claim". Section 8–102(a)(1).

"Appropriate person". Section 8–107.

"Entitlement holder". Section 8–102(a)(7).

"Entitlement order". Section 8–102(a)(8).

---

*   *Referring to unrevised Article 1 (Appendix A).*

**   *Referring to Article 9 before the 2010 Amendments.*

"Instruction". Section 8–102(a)(12).
"Person". Section 1–201(30).*
"Securities account". Section 8–501.
"Securities intermediary". Section 8–102(a)(14).
"Security certificate". Section 8–102(a)(16).
"Uncertificated security". Section 8–102(a)(18).

§ 8–110. Applicability; Choice of Law.

(a) The local law of the issuer's jurisdiction, as specified in subsection (d), governs:

(1) the validity of a security;

(2) the rights and duties of the issuer with respect to registration of transfer;

(3) the effectiveness of registration of transfer by the issuer;

(4) whether the issuer owes any duties to an adverse claimant to a security; and

(5) whether an adverse claim can be asserted against a person to whom transfer of a certificated or uncertificated security is registered or a person who obtains control of an uncertificated security.

(b) The local law of the securities intermediary's jurisdiction, as specified in subsection (e), governs:

(1) acquisition of a security entitlement from the securities intermediary;

(2) the rights and duties of the securities intermediary and entitlement holder arising out of a security entitlement;

(3) whether the securities intermediary owes any duties to an adverse claimant to a security entitlement; and

(4) whether an adverse claim can be asserted against a person who acquires a security entitlement from the securities intermediary or a person who purchases a security entitlement or interest therein from an entitlement holder.

(c) The local law of the jurisdiction in which a security certificate is located at the time of delivery governs whether an adverse claim can be asserted against a person to whom the security certificate is delivered.

(d) "Issuer's jurisdiction" means the jurisdiction under which the issuer of the security is organized or, if permitted by the law of that jurisdiction, the law of another jurisdiction specified by the issuer. An issuer organized under the law of this State may specify the law of another jurisdiction as the law governing the matters specified in subsection (a)(2) through (5).

(e) The following rules determine a "securities intermediary's jurisdiction" for purposes of this section:

(1) If an agreement between the securities intermediary and its entitlement holder governing the securities account expressly provides that a particular jurisdiction is the securities intermediary's jurisdiction for purposes of this part, this article, or this [Act], that jurisdiction is the securities intermediary's jurisdiction.

(2) If paragraph (1) does not apply and an agreement between the securities intermediary and its entitlement holder governing the securities account expressly provides that the agreement is governed by the law of a particular jurisdiction, that jurisdiction is the securities intermediary's jurisdiction.

(3) If neither paragraph (1) nor paragraph (2) applies and an agreement between the securities intermediary and its entitlement holder governing the securities account expressly provides that

---

* *Referring to unrevised Article 1 (Appendix A).*

the securities account is maintained at an office in a particular jurisdiction, that jurisdiction is the securities intermediary's jurisdiction.

(4)   If none of the preceding paragraphs applies, the securities intermediary's jurisdiction is the jurisdiction in which the office identified in an account statement as the office serving the entitlement holder's account is located.

(5)   If none of the preceding paragraphs applies, the securities intermediary's jurisdiction is the jurisdiction in which the chief executive office of the securities intermediary is located.

(f)   A securities intermediary's jurisdiction is not determined by the physical location of certificates representing financial assets, or by the jurisdiction in which is organized the issuer of the financial asset with respect to which an entitlement holder has a security entitlement, or by the location of facilities for data processing or other record keeping concerning the account.

As amended in 1999.

Official Comment

1.   This section deals with applicability and choice of law issues concerning Article 8. The distinction between the direct and indirect holding systems plays a significant role in determining the governing law. An investor in the direct holding system is registered on the books of the issuer and/or has possession of a security certificate. Accordingly, the jurisdiction of incorporation of the issuer or location of the certificate determine the applicable law. By contrast, an investor in the indirect holding system has a security entitlement, which is a bundle of rights against the securities intermediary with respect to a security, rather than a direct interest in the underlying security. Accordingly, in the rules for the indirect holding system, the jurisdiction of incorporation of the issuer of the underlying security or the location of any certificates that might be held by the intermediary or a higher tier intermediary, do not determine the applicable law.

The phrase "local law" refers to the law of a jurisdiction other than its conflict of laws rules. See Restatement (Second) of Conflict of Laws § 4.

2.   Subsection (a) provides that the law of an issuer's jurisdiction governs certain issues where the substantive rules of Article 8 determine the issuer's rights and duties. Paragraph (1) of subsection (a) provides that the law of the issuer's jurisdiction governs the validity of the security. This ensures that a single body of law will govern the questions addressed in Part 2 of Article 8, concerning the circumstances in which an issuer can and cannot assert invalidity as a defense against purchasers. Similarly, paragraphs (2), (3), and (4) of subsection (a) ensure that the issuer will be able to look to a single body of law on the questions addressed in Part 4 of Article 8, concerning the issuer's duties and liabilities with respect to registration of transfer.

Paragraph (5) of subsection (a) applies the law of an issuer's jurisdiction to the question whether an adverse claim can be asserted against a purchaser to whom transfer has been registered, or who has obtained control over an uncertificated security. Although this issue deals with the rights of persons other than the issuer, the law of the issuer's jurisdiction applies because the purchasers to whom the provision applies are those whose protection against adverse claims depends on the fact that their interests have been recorded on the books of the issuer.

The principal policy reflected in the choice of law rules in subsection (a) is that an issuer and others should be able to look to a single body of law on the matters specified in subsection (a), rather than having to look to the law of all of the different jurisdictions in which security holders may reside. The choice of law policies reflected in this subsection do not require that the body of law governing all of the matters specified in subsection (a) be that of the jurisdiction in which the issuer is incorporated. Thus, subsection (d) provides that the term "issuer's jurisdiction" means the jurisdiction in which the issuer is organized, or, if permitted by that law, the law of another jurisdiction selected by the issuer. Subsection (d) also provides that issuers organized under the law of a State which adopts this Article may make such a selection, except as to the validity issue specified in paragraph (1). The question whether an issuer can assert the defense of invalidity may implicate significant policies of the issuer's jurisdiction of incorporation. See, e.g., Section 8–202 and Comments thereto.

Although subsection (a) provides that the issuer's rights and duties concerning registration of transfer are governed by the law of the issuer's jurisdiction, other matters related to registration of transfer, such as appointment of a guardian for a registered owner or the existence of agency relationships, might be governed by another jurisdiction's law. Neither this section nor Section 1–105[*] deals with what law governs the appointment of the administrator or executor; that question is determined under generally applicable choice of law rules.

3.   Subsection (b) provides that the law of the securities intermediary's jurisdiction governs the issues concerning the indirect holding system that are dealt with in Article 8. Paragraphs (1) and (2) cover the matters dealt with in the Article 8 rules defining the concept of security entitlement and specifying the duties of securities intermediaries. Paragraph (3) provides that the law of the security intermediary's jurisdiction determines whether the intermediary owes any duties to an adverse claimant. Paragraph (4) provides that the law of the security intermediary's jurisdiction determines whether adverse claims can be asserted against entitlement holders and others.

Subsection (e) determines what is a "securities intermediary's jurisdiction." The policy of subsection (b) is to ensure that a securities intermediary and all of its entitlement holders can look to a single, readily-identifiable body of law to determine their rights and duties. Accordingly, subsection (e) sets out a sequential series of tests to facilitate identification of that body of law. Paragraph (1) of subsection (e) permits specification of the securities intermediary's jurisdiction by agreement. In the absence of such a specification, the law chosen by the parties to govern the securities account determines the securities intermediary's jurisdiction. See paragraph (2). Because the policy of this section is to enable parties to determine, in advance and with certainty, what law will apply to transactions governed by this Article, the validation of the parties' selection of governing law by agreement is not conditioned upon a determination that the jurisdiction whose law is chosen bear a "reasonable relation" to the transaction. See Section 4A–507; compare Section 1–105(1).[*] That is also true with respect to the similar provisions in subsection (d) of this section and in Section 9–305. The remaining paragraphs in subsection (e) contain additional default rules for determining the securities intermediary's jurisdiction.

Subsection (f) makes explicit a point that is implicit in the Article 8 description of a security entitlement as a bundle of rights against the intermediary with respect to a security or other financial asset, rather than as a direct interest in the underlying security or other financial asset. The governing law for relationships in the indirect holding system is not determined by such matters as the jurisdiction of incorporation of the issuer of the securities held through the intermediary, or the location of any physical certificates held by the intermediary or a higher tier intermediary.

4.   Subsection (c) provides a choice of law rule for adverse claim issues that may arise in connection with delivery of security certificates in the direct holding system. It applies the law of the place of delivery. If a certificated security issued by an Idaho corporation is sold, and the sale is settled by physical delivery of the certificate from Seller to Buyer in New York, under subsection (c), New York law determines whether Buyer takes free from adverse claims. The domicile of Seller, Buyer, and any adverse claimant is irrelevant.

5.   The following examples illustrate how a court in a jurisdiction which has enacted this section would determine the governing law:

Example 1. John Doe, a resident of Kansas, maintains a securities account with Able & Co. Able is incorporated in Delaware. Its chief executive offices are located in Illinois. The office where Doe transacts business with Able is located in Missouri. The agreement between Doe and Able specifies that Illinois is the securities intermediary's (Able's) jurisdiction. Through the account, Doe holds securities of a Colorado corporation, which Able holds through Clearing Corporation. The rules of Clearing Corporation provide that the rights and duties of Clearing Corporation and its participants are governed by New York law. Subsection (a) specifies that a controversy concerning the rights and duties as between the issuer and Clearing Corporation is governed by Colorado law. Subsections (b) and (e) specify that a controversy concerning the rights and duties as between the Clearing Corporation and Able is governed by New York law, and that a controversy concerning the rights and duties as between Able and Doe is governed by Illinois law.

Example 2. Same facts as to Doe and Able as in Example 1. Through the account, Doe holds securities of a Senegalese corporation, which Able holds through Clearing Corporation. Clearing Corporation's operations are located in Belgium, and its rules and agreements with its participants provide that they are governed by Belgian law. Clearing Corporation holds the securities through a custodial account at the Paris branch office of Global Bank, which is organized under English law. The agreement between Clearing Corporation and Global Bank provides that it is governed by French law. Subsection (a) specifies that a controversy concerning the rights and duties as between the issuer and Global Bank is governed by Senegalese law. Subsections (b) and (e) specify that a controversy concerning the rights and duties as

---

[*]   *Referring to unrevised Article 1 (Appendix A).*

between Global Bank and Clearing Corporation is governed by French law, that a controversy concerning the rights and duties as between Clearing Corporation and Able is governed by Belgian law, and that a controversy concerning the rights and duties as between Able and Doe is governed by Illinois law.

6.   To the extent that this section does not specify the governing law, general choice of law rules apply. For example, suppose that in either of the examples in the preceding Comment, Doe enters into an agreement with Roe, also a resident of Kansas, in which Doe agrees to transfer all of his interests in the securities held through Able to Roe. Article 8 does not deal with whether such an agreement is enforceable or whether it gives Roe some interest in Doe's security entitlement. This section specifies what jurisdiction's law governs the issues that are dealt with in Article 8. Article 8, however, does specify that securities intermediaries have only limited duties with respect to adverse claims. See Section 8–115. Subsection (b)(3) of this section provides that Illinois law governs whether Able owes any duties to an adverse claimant. Thus, if Illinois has adopted Revised Article 8, Section 8–115 as enacted in Illinois determines whether Roe has any rights against Able.

7.   The choice of law provisions concerning security interests in securities and security entitlements are set out in Section 9–305.

Definitional Cross References:

"Adverse claim". Section 8–102(a)(1).
"Agreement". Section 1–201(3).*
"Certificated security". Section 8–102(a)(4).
"Entitlement holder". Section 8–102(a)(7).
"Financial asset". Section 8–102(a)(9).
"Issuer". Section 8–201.
"Person". Section 1–201(30).*
"Purchase". Section 1–201(32).*
"Securities intermediary". Section 8–102(a)(14).
"Security". Section 8–102(a)(15).
"Security certificate". Section 8–102(a)(16).
"Security entitlement". Section 8–102(a)(17).
"Uncertificated security". Section 8–102(a)(18).

As amended in 1999.

§ 8–111.   Clearing Corporation Rules.

A rule adopted by a clearing corporation governing rights and obligations among the clearing corporation and its participants in the clearing corporation is effective even if the rule conflicts with this [Act] and affects another party who does not consent to the rule.

Official Comment

1.   The experience of the past few decades shows that securities holding and settlement practices may develop rapidly, and in unforeseeable directions. Accordingly, it is desirable that the rules of Article 8 be adaptable both to ensure that commercial law can conform to changing practices and to ensure that commercial law does not operate as an obstacle to developments in securities practice. Even if practices were unchanging, it would not be possible in a general statute to specify in detail the rules needed to provide certainty in the operations of the clearance and settlement system.

The provisions of this Article and Article 1 on the effect of agreements provide considerable flexibility in the specification of the details of the rights and obligations of participants in the securities holding system by agreement. See Sections 8–504 through 8–509, and Section 1–102(3)* and (4).* Given the magnitude of the exposures involved in securities transactions, however, it may not be possible for the parties in developing practices to rely solely on private agreements, particularly with respect to matters that might affect others, such as creditors. For example, in order to be fully effective, rules of clearing corporations on the finality or reversibility of securities settlements must not only bind the participants in the clearing corporation but also be effective against their creditors. Section 8–111 provides that clearing corporation rules are effective even if they indirectly affect third parties, such as creditors of a participant. This provision does not, however, permit rules to be adopted

---

*   *Referring to unrevised Article 1 (Appendix A).*

that would govern the rights and obligations of third parties other than as a consequence of rules that specify the rights and obligations of the clearing corporation and its participants.

2. The definition of clearing corporation in Section 8–102 covers only federal reserve banks, entities registered as clearing agencies under the federal securities laws, and others subject to comparable regulation. The rules of registered clearing agencies are subject to regulatory oversight under the federal securities laws.

Definitional Cross References:

"Clearing corporation". Section 8–102(a)(5).

§ 8–112. Creditor's Legal Process.

(a) The interest of a debtor in a certificated security may be reached by a creditor only by actual seizure of the security certificate by the officer making the attachment or levy, except as otherwise provided in subsection (d). However, a certificated security for which the certificate has been surrendered to the issuer may be reached by a creditor by legal process upon the issuer.

(b) The interest of a debtor in an uncertificated security may be reached by a creditor only by legal process upon the issuer at its chief executive office in the United States, except as otherwise provided in subsection (d).

(c) The interest of a debtor in a security entitlement may be reached by a creditor only by legal process upon the securities intermediary with whom the debtor's securities account is maintained, except as otherwise provided in subsection (d).

(d) The interest of a debtor in a certificated security for which the certificate is in the possession of a secured party, or in an uncertificated security registered in the name of a secured party, or a security entitlement maintained in the name of a secured party, may be reached by a creditor by legal process upon the secured party.

(e) A creditor whose debtor is the owner of a certificated security, uncertificated security, or security entitlement is entitled to aid from a court of competent jurisdiction, by injunction or otherwise, in reaching the certificated security, uncertificated security, or security entitlement or in satisfying the claim by means allowed at law or in equity in regard to property that cannot readily be reached by other legal process.

Official Comment

1. In dealing with certificated securities the instrument itself is the vital thing, and therefore a valid levy cannot be made unless all possibility of the certificate's wrongfully finding its way into a transferee's hands has been removed. This can be accomplished only when the certificate is in the possession of a public officer, the issuer, or an independent third party. A debtor who has been enjoined can still transfer the security in contempt of court. See *Overlock v. Jerome-Portland Copper Mining Co.*, 29 Ariz. 560, 243 P. 400 (1926). Therefore, although injunctive relief is provided in subsection (e) so that creditors may use this method to gain control of the certificated security, the security certificate itself must be reached to constitute a proper levy whenever the debtor has possession.

2. Subsection (b) provides that when the security is uncertificated and registered in the debtor's name, the debtor's interest can be reached only by legal process upon the issuer. The most logical place to serve the issuer would be the place where the transfer records are maintained, but that location might be difficult to identify, especially when the separate elements of a computer network might be situated in different places. The chief executive office is selected as the appropriate place by analogy to Section 9–307(b)(3). See Comment 2 to that section. This section indicates only how attachment is to be made, not when it is legally justified. For that reason there is no conflict between this section and *Shaffer v. Heitner,* 433 U.S. 186 (1977).

3. Subsection (c) provides that a security entitlement can be reached only by legal process upon the debtor's security intermediary. Process is effective only if directed to the debtor's own security intermediary. If Debtor holds securities through Broker, and Broker in turn holds through Clearing Corporation, Debtor's property interest is a security entitlement against Broker. Accordingly, Debtor's creditor cannot reach Debtor's interest by legal process directed to the Clearing Corporation. See also Section 8–115.

4. Subsection (d) provides that when a certificated security, an uncertificated security, or a security entitlement is controlled by a secured party, the debtor's interest can be reached by legal process upon the secured

party. This section does not attempt to provide for rights as between the creditor and the secured party, as, for example, whether or when the secured party must liquidate the security.

Definitional Cross References:

"Certificated security". Section 8–102(a)(4).
"Issuer". Section 8–201.
"Secured party". Section 9–102(a)(72).*
"Securities intermediary". Section 8–102(a)(14).
"Security certificate". Section 8–102(a)(16).
"Security entitlement". Section 8–102(a)(17).
"Uncertificated security". Section 8–102(a)(18).

§ 8–113.   Statute of Frauds Inapplicable.

A contract or modification of a contract for the sale or purchase of a security is enforceable whether or not there is a writing signed or record authenticated by a party against whom enforcement is sought, even if the contract or modification is not capable of performance within one year of its making.

Official Comment

This section provides that the statute of frauds does not apply to contracts for the sale of securities, reversing prior law which had a special statute of frauds in Section 8–319 (1978). With the increasing use of electronic means of communication, the statute of frauds is unsuited to the realities of the securities business. For securities transactions, whatever benefits a statute of frauds may play in filtering out fraudulent claims are outweighed by the obstacles it places in the development of modern commercial practices in the securities business.

Definitional Cross References:

"Action". Section 1–201(1).**
"Contract". Section 1–201(11).**
"Writing". Section 1–201(46).**

§ 8–114.   Evidentiary Rules Concerning Certificated Securities.

The following rules apply in an action on a certificated security against the issuer:

(1)   Unless specifically denied in the pleadings, each signature on a security certificate or in a necessary indorsement is admitted.

(2)   If the effectiveness of a signature is put in issue, the burden of establishing effectiveness is on the party claiming under the signature, but the signature is presumed to be genuine or authorized.

(3)   If signatures on a security certificate are admitted or established, production of the certificate entitles a holder to recover on it unless the defendant establishes a defense or a defect going to the validity of the security.

(4)   If it is shown that a defense or defect exists, the plaintiff has the burden of establishing that the plaintiff or some person under whom the plaintiff claims is a person against whom the defense or defect cannot be asserted.

Official Comment

This section adapts the rules of negotiable instruments law concerning procedure in actions on instruments, see Section 3–308, to actions on certificated securities governed by this Article. An "action on a security" includes any action or proceeding brought against the issuer to enforce a right or interest that is part of the security, such as an action to collect principal or interest or a dividend, or to establish a right to vote or to receive a new security under an exchange offer or plan of reorganization. This section applies only to certificated securities; actions on uncertificated securities are governed by general evidentiary principles.

---

*   *Referring to Article 9 before the 2010 Amendments.*
**   *Referring to unrevised Article 1 (Appendix A).*

Definitional Cross References:

"Action". Section 1–201(1).[*]
"Burden of establishing". Section 1–201(8).[*]
"Certificated security". Section 8–102(a)(4).
"Indorsement". Section 8–102(a)(11).
"Issuer". Section 8–201.
"Presumed". Section 1–201(31).[*]
"Security". Section 8–102(a)(15).
"Security certificate". Section 8–102(a)(16).

§ 8–115. Securities Intermediary and Others Not Liable to Adverse Claimant.

A securities intermediary that has transferred a financial asset pursuant to an effective entitlement order, or a broker or other agent or bailee that has dealt with a financial asset at the direction of its customer or principal, is not liable to a person having an adverse claim to the financial asset, unless the securities intermediary, or broker or other agent or bailee:

(1) took the action after it had been served with an injunction, restraining order, or other legal process enjoining it from doing so, issued by a court of competent jurisdiction, and had a reasonable opportunity to act on the injunction, restraining order, or other legal process; or

(2) acted in collusion with the wrongdoer in violating the rights of the adverse claimant; or

(3) in the case of a security certificate that has been stolen, acted with notice of the adverse claim.

Official Comment

1. Other provisions of Article 8 protect certain purchasers against adverse claims, both for the direct holding system and the indirect holding system. See Sections 8–303 and 8–502. This section deals with the related question of the possible liability of a person who acted as the "conduit" for a securities transaction. It covers both securities intermediaries—the "conduits" in the indirect holding system—and brokers or other agents or bailees—the "conduits" in the direct holding system. The following examples illustrate its operation:

Example 1. John Doe is a customer of the brokerage firm of Able & Co. Doe delivers to Able a certificate for 100 shares of XYZ Co. common stock, registered in Doe's name and properly indorsed, and asks the firm to sell it for him. Able does so. Later, John Doe's spouse Mary Doe brings an action against Able asserting that Able's action was wrongful against her because the XYZ Co. stock was marital property in which she had an interest, and John Doe was acting wrongfully against her in transferring the securities.

Example 2. Mary Roe is a customer of the brokerage firm of Baker & Co. and holds her securities through a securities account with Baker. Roe instructs Baker to sell 100 shares of XYZ Co. common stock that she carried in her account. Baker does so. Later, Mary Roe's spouse John Roe brings an action against Baker asserting that Baker's action was wrongful against him because the XYZ Co. stock was marital property in which he had an interest, and Mary Roe was acting wrongfully against him in transferring the securities.

Under common law conversion principles, Mary Doe might be able to assert that Able & Co. is liable to her in Example 1 for exercising dominion over property inconsistent with her rights in it. On that or some similar theory John Roe might assert that Baker is liable to him in Example 2. Section 8–115 protects both Able and Baker from liability.

2. The policy of this section is similar to that of many other rules of law that protect agents and bailees from liability as innocent converters. If a thief steals property and ships it by mail, express service, or carrier, to another person, the recipient of the property does not obtain good title, even though the recipient may have given value to the thief and had no notice or knowledge that the property was stolen. Accordingly, the true owner can recover the property from the recipient or obtain damages in a conversion or similar action. An action against the postal service, express company, or carrier presents entirely different policy considerations. Accordingly, general

---

[*] *Referring to unrevised Article 1 (Appendix A).*

tort law protects agents or bailees who act on the instructions of their principals or bailors. See Restatement (Second) of Torts § 235. See also UCC Section 7–404.

3.   Except as provided in paragraph 3, this section applies even though the securities intermediary, or the broker or other agent or bailee, had notice or knowledge that another person asserts a claim to the securities. Consider the following examples:

> Example 3. Same facts as in Example 1, except that before John Doe brought the XYZ Co. security certificate to Able for sale, Mary Doe telephoned or wrote to the firm asserting that she had an interest in all of John Doe's securities and demanding that they not trade for him.

> Example 4. Same facts as in Example 2, except that before Mary Roe gave an entitlement order to Baker to sell the XYZ Co. securities from her account, John Doe telephoned or wrote to the firm asserting that he had an interest in all of Mary Roe's securities and demanding that they not trade for her.

Section 8–115 protects Able and Baker from liability. The protections of Section 8–115 do not depend on the presence or absence of notice of adverse claims. It is essential to the securities settlement system that brokers and securities intermediaries be able to act promptly on the directions of their customers. Even though a firm has notice that someone asserts a claim to a customer's securities or security entitlements, the firm should not be placed in the position of having to make a legal judgment about the validity of the claim at the risk of liability either to its customer or to the third party for guessing wrong. Under this section, the broker or securities intermediary is privileged to act on the instructions of its customer or entitlement holder, unless it has been served with a restraining order or other legal process enjoining it from doing so. This is already the law in many jurisdictions. For example a section of the New York Banking Law provides that banks need not recognize any adverse claim to funds or securities on deposit with them unless they have been served with legal process. N.Y. Banking Law § 134. Other sections of the UCC embody a similar policy. See Sections 3–602, 5–114(2)(b).[*]

Paragraph (1) of this section refers only to a court order enjoining the securities intermediary or the broker or other agent or bailee from acting at the instructions of the customer. It does not apply to cases where the adverse claimant tells the intermediary or broker that the customer has been enjoined, or shows the intermediary or broker a copy of a court order binding the customer.

Paragraph (3) takes a different approach in one limited class of cases, those where a customer sells stolen certificated securities through a securities firm. Here the policies that lead to protection of securities firms against assertions of other sorts of claims must be weighed against the desirability of having securities firms guard against the disposition of stolen securities. Accordingly, paragraph (3) denies protection to a broker, custodian, or other agent or bailee who receives a stolen security certificate from its customer, if the broker, custodian, or other agent or bailee had notice of adverse claims. The circumstances that give notice of adverse claims are specified in Section 8–105. The result is that brokers, custodians, and other agents and bailees face the same liability for selling stolen certificated securities that purchasers face for buying them.

4.   As applied to securities intermediaries, this section embodies one of the fundamental principles of the Article 8 indirect holding system rules—that a securities intermediary owes duties only to its own entitlement holders. The following examples illustrate the operation of this section in the multi-tiered indirect holding system:

> Example 5. Able & Co., a broker-dealer, holds 50,000 shares of XYZ Co. stock in its account at Clearing Corporation. Able acquired the XYZ shares from another firm, Baker & Co., in a transaction that Baker contends was tainted by fraud, giving Baker a right to rescind the transaction and recover the XYZ shares from Able. Baker sends notice to Clearing Corporation stating that Baker has a claim to the 50,000 shares of XYZ Co. in Able's account. Able then initiates an entitlement order directing Clearing Corporation to transfer the 50,000 shares of XYZ Co. to another firm in settlement of a trade. Under Section 8–115, Clearing Corporation is privileged to comply with Able's entitlement order, without fear of liability to Baker. This is so even though Clearing Corporation has notice of Baker's claim, unless Baker obtains a court order enjoining Clearing Corporation from acting on Able's entitlement order.

> Example 6. Able & Co., a broker-dealer, holds 50,000 shares of XYZ Co. stock in its account at Clearing Corporation. Able initiates an entitlement order directing Clearing Corporation to transfer the 50,000 shares of XYZ Co. to another firm in settlement of a trade. That trade was made by Able for its own account, and the proceeds were devoted to its own use. Able becomes insolvent, and it is discovered that Able has a shortfall in the shares of XYZ Co. stock that it should have been carrying for its customers. Able's customers

---

[*]   *Referring to unrevised Article 5.*

bring an action against Clearing Corporation asserting that Clearing Corporation acted wrongfully in transferring the XYZ shares on Able's order because those were shares that should have been held by Able for its customers. Under Section 8–115, Clearing Corporation is not liable to Able's customers, because Clearing Corporation acted on an effective entitlement order of its own entitlement holder, Able. Clearing Corporation's protection against liability does not depend on the presence or absence of notice or knowledge of the claim by Clearing Corporation.

5.   If the conduct of a securities intermediary or a broker or other agent or bailee rises to a level of complicity in the wrongdoing of its customer or principal, the policies that favor protection against liability do not apply. Accordingly, paragraph (2) provides that the protections of this section do not apply if the securities intermediary or broker or other agent or bailee acted in collusion with the customer or principal in violating the rights of another person. The collusion test is intended to adopt a standard akin to the tort rules that determine whether a person is liable as an aider or abettor for the tortious conduct of a third party. See Restatement (Second) of Torts § 876.

Knowledge that the action of the customer is wrongful is a necessary but not sufficient condition of the collusion test. The aspect of the role of securities intermediaries and brokers that Article 8 deals with is the clerical or ministerial role of implementing and recording the securities transactions that their customers conduct. Faithful performance of this role consists of following the instructions of the customer. It is not the role of the record-keeper to police whether the transactions recorded are appropriate, so mere awareness that the customer may be acting wrongfully does not itself constitute collusion. That, of course, does not insulate an intermediary or broker from responsibility in egregious cases where its action goes beyond the ordinary standards of the business of implementing and recording transactions, and reaches a level of affirmative misconduct in assisting the customer in the commission of a wrong.

Definitional Cross References:

"Broker". Section 8–102(a)(3).

"Effective". Section 8–107.

"Entitlement order". Section 8–102(a)(8).

"Financial asset". Section 8–102(a)(9).

"Securities intermediary". Section 8–102(a)(14).

"Security certificate". Section 8–102(a)(16).

§ 8–116.   Securities Intermediary as Purchaser for Value.

A securities intermediary that receives a financial asset and establishes a security entitlement to the financial asset in favor of an entitlement holder is a purchaser for value of the financial asset. A securities intermediary that acquires a security entitlement to a financial asset from another securities intermediary acquires the security entitlement for value if the securities intermediary acquiring the security entitlement establishes a security entitlement to the financial asset in favor of an entitlement holder.

Official Comment

1.   This section is intended to make explicit two points that, while implicit in other provisions, are of sufficient importance to the operation of the indirect holding system that they warrant explicit statement. First, it makes clear that a securities intermediary that receives a financial asset and establishes a security entitlement in respect thereof in favor of an entitlement holder is a "purchaser" of the financial asset that the securities intermediary received. Second, it makes clear that by establishing a security entitlement in favor of an entitlement holder a securities intermediary gives value for any corresponding financial asset that the securities intermediary receives or acquires from another party, whether the intermediary holds directly or indirectly.

In many cases a securities intermediary that receives a financial asset will also be transferring value to the person from whom the financial asset was received. That, however, is not always the case. Payment may occur through a different system than settlement of the securities side of the transaction, or the securities might be transferred without a corresponding payment, as when a person moves an account from one securities intermediary to another. Even though the securities intermediary does not give value to the transferor, it does give value by incurring obligations to its own entitlement holder. Although the general definition of value in Section 1–201(44)(d)* should be interpreted to cover the point, this section is included to make this point explicit.

2.   The following examples illustrate the effect of this section:

Example 1. Buyer buys 1000 shares of XYZ Co. common stock through Buyer's broker Able & Co. to be held in Buyer's securities account. In settlement of the trade, the selling broker delivers to Able a security certificate in street name, indorsed in blank, for 1000 shares XYZ Co. stock, which Able holds in its vault. Able credits Buyer's account for securities in that amount. Section 8–116 specifies that Able is a purchaser of the XYZ Co. stock certificate, and gave value for it. Thus, Able can obtain the benefit of Section 8–303, which protects purchasers for value, if it satisfies the other requirements of that section.

Example 2. Buyer buys 1000 shares XYZ Co. common stock through Buyer's broker Able & Co. to be held in Buyer's securities account. The trade is settled by crediting 1000 shares XYZ Co. stock to Able's account at Clearing Corporation. Able credits Buyer's account for securities in that amount. When Clearing Corporation credits Able's account, Able acquires a security entitlement under Section 8–501. Section 8–116 specifies that Able acquired this security entitlement for value. Thus, Able can obtain the benefit of Section 8–502, which protects persons who acquire security entitlements for value, if it satisfies the other requirements of that section.

Example 3. Thief steals a certificated bearer bond from Owner. Thief sends the certificate to his broker Able & Co. to be held in his securities account, and Able credits Thief's account for the bond. Section 8–116 specifies that Able is a purchaser of the bond and gave value for it. Thus, Able can obtain the benefit of Section 8–303, which protects purchasers for value, if it satisfies the other requirements of that section.

Definitional Cross References:

"Financial asset". Section 8–102(a)(9).
"Securities intermediary". Section 8–102(a)(14).
"Security entitlement". Section 8–102(a)(17).
"Entitlement holder". Section 8–102(a)(7).

PART 2

ISSUE AND ISSUER

§ 8–201.   Issuer.

(a)   With respect to an obligation on or a defense to a security, an "issuer" includes a person that:

(1)   places or authorizes the placing of its name on a security certificate, other than as authenticating trustee, registrar, transfer agent, or the like, to evidence a share, participation, or other interest in its property or in an enterprise, or to evidence its duty to perform an obligation represented by the certificate;

(2)   creates a share, participation, or other interest in its property or in an enterprise, or undertakes an obligation, that is an uncertificated security;

(3)   directly or indirectly creates a fractional interest in its rights or property, if the fractional interest is represented by a security certificate; or

(4)   becomes responsible for, or in place of, another person described as an issuer in this section.

(b)   With respect to an obligation on or defense to a security, a guarantor is an issuer to the extent of its guaranty, whether or not its obligation is noted on a security certificate.

(c)   With respect to a registration of a transfer, issuer means a person on whose behalf transfer books are maintained.

---

*   *Referring to unrevised Article 1 (Appendix A).*

Official Comment

1.   The definition of "issuer" in this section functions primarily to describe the persons whose defenses may be cut off under the rules in Part 2. In large measure it simply tracks the language of the definition of security in Section 8–102(a)(15).

2.   Subsection (b) distinguishes the obligations of a guarantor as issuer from those of the principal obligor. However, it does not exempt the guarantor from the impact of subsection (d) of Section 8–202. Whether or not the obligation of the guarantor is noted on the security is immaterial. Typically, guarantors are parent corporations, or stand in some similar relationship to the principal obligor. If that relationship existed at the time the security was originally issued the guaranty would probably have been noted on the security. However, if the relationship arose afterward, e.g., through a purchase of stock or properties, or through merger or consolidation, probably the notation would not have been made. Nonetheless, the holder of the security is entitled to the benefit of the obligation of the guarantor.

3.   Subsection (c) narrows the definition of "issuer" for purposes of Part 4 of this Article (registration of transfer). It is supplemented by Section 8–407.

Definitional Cross References:

"Person". Section 1–201(30).[*]
"Security". Section 8–102(a)(15).
"Security certificate". Section 8–102(a)(16).
"Uncertificated security". Section 8–102(a)(18).

§ 8–202.   Issuer's Responsibility and Defenses; Notice of Defect or Defense.

(a)   Even against a purchaser for value and without notice, the terms of a certificated security include terms stated on the certificate and terms made part of the security by reference on the certificate to another instrument, indenture, or document or to a constitution, statute, ordinance, rule, regulation, order, or the like, to the extent the terms referred to do not conflict with terms stated on the certificate. A reference under this subsection does not of itself charge a purchaser for value with notice of a defect going to the validity of the security, even if the certificate expressly states that a person accepting it admits notice. The terms of an uncertificated security include those stated in any instrument, indenture, or document or in a constitution, statute, ordinance, rule, regulation, order, or the like, pursuant to which the security is issued.

(b)   The following rules apply if an issuer asserts that a security is not valid:

(1)   A security other than one issued by a government or governmental subdivision, agency, or instrumentality, even though issued with a defect going to its validity, is valid in the hands of a purchaser for value and without notice of the particular defect unless the defect involves a violation of a constitutional provision. In that case, the security is valid in the hands of a purchaser for value and without notice of the defect, other than one who takes by original issue.

(2)   Paragraph (1) applies to an issuer that is a government or governmental subdivision, agency, or instrumentality only if there has been substantial compliance with the legal requirements governing the issue or the issuer has received a substantial consideration for the issue as a whole or for the particular security and a stated purpose of the issue is one for which the issuer has power to borrow money or issue the security.

(c)   Except as otherwise provided in Section 8–205, lack of genuineness of a certificated security is a complete defense, even against a purchaser for value and without notice.

(d)   All other defenses of the issuer of a security, including nondelivery and conditional delivery of a certificated security, are ineffective against a purchaser for value who has taken the certificated security without notice of the particular defense.

(e)   This section does not affect the right of a party to cancel a contract for a security "when, as and if issued" or "when distributed" in the event of a material change in the character of the security that is the

---

[*]   *Referring to unrevised Article 1 (Appendix A).*

subject of the contract or in the plan or arrangement pursuant to which the security is to be issued or distributed.

(f)   If a security is held by a securities intermediary against whom an entitlement holder has a security entitlement with respect to the security, the issuer may not assert any defense that the issuer could not assert if the entitlement holder held the security directly.

Official Comment

1.   In this Article the rights of the purchaser for value without notice are divided into two aspects, those against the issuer, and those against other claimants to the security. Part 2 of this Article, and especially this section, deal with rights against the issuer.

Subsection (a) states, in accordance with the prevailing case law, the right of the issuer (who prepares the text of the security) to include terms incorporated by adequate reference to an extrinsic source, so long as the terms so incorporated do not conflict with the stated terms. Thus, the standard practice of referring in a bond or debenture to the trust indenture under which it is issued without spelling out its necessarily complex and lengthy provisions is approved. Every stock certificate refers in some manner to the charter or articles of incorporation of the issuer. At least where there is more than one class of stock authorized applicable corporation codes specifically require a statement or summary as to preferences, voting powers and the like. References to constitutions, statutes, ordinances, rules, regulations or orders are not so common, except in the obligations of governments or governmental agencies or units; but where appropriate they fit into the rule here stated.

Courts have generally held that an issuer is estopped from denying representations made in the text of a security. *Delaware-New Jersey Ferry Co. v. Leeds,* 21 Del.Ch. 279, 186 A. 913 (1936). Nor is a defect in form or the invalidity of a security normally available to the issuer as a defense. *Bonini v. Family Theatre Corporation,* 327 Pa. 273, 194 A. 498 (1937); *First National Bank of Fairbanks v. Alaska Airmotive,* 119 F.2d 267 (C.C.A.Alaska 1941).

2.   The rule in subsection (a) requiring that the terms of a security be noted or referred to on the certificate is based on practices and expectations in the direct holding system for certificated securities. This rule does not express a general rule or policy that the terms of a security are effective only if they are communicated to beneficial owners in some particular fashion. Rather, subsection (a) is based on the principle that a purchaser who does obtain a certificate is entitled to assume that the terms of the security have been noted or referred to on the certificate. That policy does not come into play in a securities holding system in which purchasers do not take delivery of certificates.

The provisions of subsection (a) concerning notation of terms on security certificates are necessary only because paper certificates play such an important role for certificated securities that a purchaser should be protected against assertion of any defenses or rights that are not noted on the certificate. No similar problem exists with respect to uncertificated securities. The last sentence of subsection (a) is, strictly speaking, unnecessary, since it only recognizes the fact that the terms of an uncertificated security are determined by whatever other law or agreement governs the security. It is included only to preclude any inference that uncertificated securities are subject to any requirement analogous to the requirement of notation of terms on security certificates.

The rule of subsection (a) applies to the indirect holding system only in the sense that if a certificated security has been delivered to the clearing corporation or other securities intermediary, the terms of the security should be noted or referred to on the certificate. If the security is uncertificated, that principle does not apply even at the issuer-clearing corporation level. The beneficial owners who hold securities through the clearing corporation are bound by the terms of the security, even though they do not actually see the certificate. Since entitlement holders in an indirect holding system have not taken delivery of certificates, the policy of subsection (a) does not apply.

3.   The penultimate sentence of subsection (a) and all of subsection (b) embody the concept that it is the duty of the issuer, not of the purchaser, to make sure that the security complies with the law governing its issue. The penultimate sentence of subsection (a) makes clear that the issuer cannot, by incorporating a reference to a statute or other document, charge the purchaser with notice of the security's invalidity. Subsection (b) gives to a purchaser for value without notice of the defect the right to enforce the security against the issuer despite the presence of a defect that otherwise would render the security invalid. There are three circumstances in which a purchaser does not gain such rights: first, if the defect involves a violation of constitutional provisions, these rights accrue only to a subsequent purchaser, that is, one who takes other than by original issue. This Article leaves to the law of each particular State the rights of a purchaser on original issue of a security with a constitutional defect. No negative implication is intended by the explicit grant of rights to a subsequent purchaser.

Second, governmental issuers are distinguished in subsection (b) from other issuers as a matter of public policy, and additional safeguards are imposed before governmental issues are validated. Governmental issuers are estopped from asserting defenses only if there has been substantial compliance with the legal requirements governing the issue or if substantial consideration has been received and a stated purpose of the issue is one for which the issuer has power to borrow money or issue the security. The purpose of the substantial compliance requirement is to make certain that a mere technicality as, e.g., in the manner of publishing election notices, shall not be a ground for depriving an innocent purchaser of rights in the security. The policy is here adopted of such cases as *Tommie v. City of Gadsden,* 229 Ala. 521, 158 So. 763 (1935), in which minor discrepancies in the form of the election ballot used were overlooked and the bonds were declared valid since there had been substantial compliance with the statute.

A long and well established line of federal cases recognizes the principle of estoppel in favor of purchasers for value without notices where municipalities issue bonds containing recitals of compliance with governing constitutional and statutory provisions, made by the municipal authorities entrusted with determining such compliance. *Chaffee County v. Potter,* 142 U.S. 355 (1892); *Oregon v. Jennings,* 119 U.S. 74 (1886); *Gunnison County Commissioners v. Rollins,* 173 U.S. 255 (1898). This rule has been qualified, however, by requiring that the municipality have power to issue the security. *Anthony v. County of Jasper,* 101 U.S. 693 (1879); *Town of South Ottawa v. Perkins,* 94 U.S. 260 (1876). This section follows the case law trend, simplifying the rule by setting up two conditions for an estoppel against a governmental issuer: (1) substantial consideration given, and (2) power in the issuer to borrow money or issue the security for the stated purpose. As a practical matter the problem of policing governmental issuers has been alleviated by the present practice of requiring legal opinions as to the validity of the issue. The bulk of the case law on this point is nearly 100 years old and it may be assumed that the question now seldom arises.

Section 8–210, regarding overissue, provides the third exception to the rule that an innocent purchase for value takes a valid security despite the presence of a defect that would otherwise give rise to invalidity. See that section and its Comment for further explanation.

4. Subsection (e) is included to make clear that this section does not affect the presently recognized right of either party to a "when, as and if" or "when distributed" contract to cancel the contract on substantial change.

5. Subsection (f) has been added because the introduction of the security entitlement concept requires some adaptation of the Part 2 rules, particularly those that distinguish between purchasers who take by original issue and subsequent purchasers. The basic concept of Part 2 is to apply to investment securities the principle of negotiable instruments law that an obligor is precluded from asserting most defenses against purchasers for value without notice. Section 8–202 describes in some detail which defenses issuers can raise against purchasers for value and subsequent purchasers for value. Because these rules were drafted with the direct holding system in mind, some interpretive problems might be presented in applying them to the indirect holding. For example, if a municipality issues a bond in book-entry only form, the only direct "purchaser" of that bond would be the clearing corporation. The policy of precluding the issuer from asserting defenses is, however, equally applicable. Subsection (f) is designed to ensure that the defense preclusion rules developed for the direct holding system will also apply to the indirect holding system.

Definitional Cross References:

"Certificated security". Section 8–102(a)(4).
"Notice". Section 1–201(25).*
"Purchaser". Sections 1–201(33)* & 8–116.
"Security". Section 8–102(a)(15).
"Uncertificated security". Section 8–102(a)(18).
"Value". Sections 1–201(44)* & 8–116.

§ 8–203.   Staleness as Notice of Defect or Defense.

After an act or event, other than a call that has been revoked, creating a right to immediate performance of the principal obligation represented by a certificated security or setting a date on or after which the security is to be presented or surrendered for redemption or exchange, a purchaser is charged with notice of any defect in its issue or defense of the issuer, if the act or event:

---

* *Referring to unrevised Article 1 (Appendix A).*

(1) requires the payment of money, the delivery of a certificated security, the registration of transfer of an uncertificated security, or any of them on presentation or surrender of the security certificate, the money or security is available on the date set for payment or exchange, and the purchaser takes the security more than one year after that date; or

(2) is not covered by paragraph (1) and the purchaser takes the security more than two years after the date set for surrender or presentation or the date on which performance became due.

Official Comment

1. The problem of matured or called securities is here dealt with in terms of the effect of such events in giving notice of the issuer's defenses and not in terms of "negotiability". The substance of this section applies only to certificated securities because certificates may be transferred to a purchaser by delivery after the security has matured, been called, or become redeemable or exchangeable. It is contemplated that uncertificated securities which have matured or been called will merely be canceled on the books of the issuer and the proceeds sent to the registered owner. Uncertificated securities which have become redeemable or exchangeable, at the option of the owner, may be transferred to a purchaser, but the transfer is effectuated only by registration of transfer, thus necessitating communication with the issuer. If defects or defenses in such securities exist, the issuer will necessarily have the opportunity to bring them to the attention of the purchaser.

2. The fact that a security certificate is in circulation long after it has been called for redemption or exchange must give rise to the question in a purchaser's mind as to why it has not been surrendered. After the lapse of a reasonable period of time a purchaser can no longer claim "no reason to know" of any defects or irregularities in its issue. Where funds are available for the redemption the security certificate is normally turned in more promptly and a shorter time is set as the "reasonable period" than is set where funds are not available.

Defaulted certificated securities may be traded on financial markets in the same manner as unmatured and undefaulted instruments and a purchaser might not be placed upon notice of irregularity by the mere fact of default. An issuer, however, should at some point be placed in a position to determine definitely its liability on an invalid or improper issue, and for this purpose a security under this section becomes "stale" two years after the default. A different rule applies when the question is notice not of issuer's defenses but of claims of ownership. Section 8–105 and Comment.

3. Nothing in this section is designed to extend the life of preferred stocks called for redemption as "shares of stock" beyond the redemption date. After such a call, the security represents only a right to the funds set aside for redemption.

Definitional Cross References:

"Certificated security". Section 8–102(a)(4).

"Notice". Section 1–201(25).*

"Purchaser". Sections 1–201(33)* & 8–116.

"Security". Section 8–102(a)(15).

"Security certificate". Section 8–102(a)(16).

"Uncertificated security". Section 8–102(a)(18).

§ 8–204. Effect of Issuer's Restriction on Transfer.

A restriction on transfer of a security imposed by the issuer, even if otherwise lawful, is ineffective against a person without knowledge of the restriction unless:

(1) the security is certificated and the restriction is noted conspicuously on the security certificate; or

(2) the security is uncertificated and the registered owner has been notified of the restriction.

Official Comment

1. Restrictions on transfer of securities are imposed by issuers in a variety of circumstances and for a variety of purposes, such as to retain control of a close corporation or to ensure compliance with federal securities

---

* *Referring to unrevised Article 1 (Appendix A).*

laws. Other law determines whether such restrictions are permissible. This section deals only with the consequences of failure to note the restriction on a security certificate.

This section imposes no bar to enforcement of a restriction on transfer against a person who has actual knowledge of it.

2. A restriction on transfer of a certificated security is ineffective against a person without knowledge of the restriction unless the restriction is noted conspicuously on the certificate. The word "noted" is used to make clear that the restriction need not be set forth in full text. Refusal by an issuer to register a transfer on the basis of an unnoted restriction would be a violation of the issuer's duty to register under Section 8–401.

3. The policy of this section is the same as in Section 8–202. A purchaser who takes delivery of a certificated security is entitled to rely on the terms stated on the certificate. That policy obviously does not apply to uncertificated securities. For uncertificated securities, this section requires only that the registered owner has been notified of the restriction. Suppose, for example, that A is the registered owner of an uncertificated security, and that the issuer has notified A of a restriction on transfer. A agrees to sell the security to B, in violation of the restriction. A completes a written instruction directing the issuer to register transfer to B, and B pays A for the security at the time A delivers the instruction to B. A does not inform B of the restriction, and B does not otherwise have notice or knowledge of it at the time B pays and receives the instruction. B presents the instruction to the issuer, but the issuer refuses to register the transfer on the grounds that it would violate the restriction. The issuer has complied with this section, because it did notify the registered owner A of the restriction. The issuer's refusal to register transfer is not wrongful. B has an action against A for breach of transfer warranty, see Section 8–108(b)(4)(iii). B's mistake was treating an uncertificated security transaction in the fashion appropriate only for a certificated security. The mechanism for transfer of uncertificated securities is registration of transfer on the books of the issuer; handing over an instruction only initiates the process. The purchaser should make arrangements to ensure that the price is not paid until it knows that the issuer has or will register transfer.

4. In the indirect holding system, investors neither take physical delivery of security certificates nor have uncertificated securities registered in their names. So long as the requirements of this section have been satisfied at the level of the relationship between the issuer and the securities intermediary that is a direct holder, this section does not preclude the issuer from enforcing a restriction on transfer. See Section 8–202(a) and Comment 2 thereto.

5. This section deals only with restrictions imposed by the issuer. Restrictions imposed by statute are not affected. See *Quiner v. Marblehead Social Co.,* 10 Mass. 476 (1813); *Madison Bank v. Price,* 79 Kan. 289, 100 P. 280 (1909); *Healey v. Steele Center Creamery Ass'n,* 115 Minn. 451, 133 N.W. 69 (1911). Nor does it deal with private agreements between stockholders containing restrictive covenants as to the sale of the security.

Definitional Cross References:

"Certificated security". Section 8–102(a)(4).

"Conspicuous". Section 1–201(10).*

"Issuer". Section 8–201.

"Knowledge". Section 1–201(25).*

"Notify". Section 1–201(25).*

"Purchaser". Sections 1–201(33)* & 8–116.

"Security". Section 8–102(a)(15).

"Security certificate". Section 8–102(a)(16).

"Uncertificated security". Section 8–102(a)(18).

§ 8–205. Effect of Unauthorized Signature on Security Certificate.

An unauthorized signature placed on a security certificate before or in the course of issue is ineffective, but the signature is effective in favor of a purchaser for value of the certificated security if the purchaser is without notice of the lack of authority and the signing has been done by:

---

* *Referring to unrevised Article 1 (Appendix A).*

(1)   an authenticating trustee, registrar, transfer agent, or other person entrusted by the issuer with the signing of the security certificate or of similar security certificates, or the immediate preparation for signing of any of them; or

(2)   an employee of the issuer, or of any of the persons listed in paragraph (1), entrusted with responsible handling of the security certificate.

Official Comment

1.   The problem of forged or unauthorized signatures may arise where an employee of the issuer, transfer agent, or registrar has access to securities which the employee is required to prepare for issue by affixing the corporate seal or by adding a signature necessary for issue. This section is based upon the issuer's duty to avoid the negligent entrusting of securities to such persons. Issuers have long been held responsible for signatures placed upon securities by parties whom they have held out to the public as authorized to prepare such securities. See *Fifth Avenue Bank of New York v. The Forty-Second & Grand Street Ferry Railroad Co.,* 137 N.Y. 231, 33 N.E. 378, 19 L.R.A. 331, 33 Am.St.Rep. 712 (1893); *Jarvis v. Manhattan Beach Co.,* 148 N.Y. 652, 43 N.E. 68, 31 L.R.A. 776, 51 Am.St.Rep. 727 (1896). The "apparent authority" concept of some of the case-law, however, is here extended and this section expressly rejects the technical distinction, made by courts reluctant to recognize forged signatures, between cases where forgers sign signatures they are authorized to sign under proper circumstances and those in which they sign signatures they are never authorized to sign. *Citizens' & Southern National Bank v. Trust Co. of Georgia,* 50 Ga.App. 681, 179 S.E. 278 (1935). Normally the purchaser is not in a position to determine which signature a forger, entrusted with the preparation of securities, has "apparent authority" to sign. The issuer, on the other hand, can protect itself against such fraud by the careful selection and bonding of agents and employees, or by action over against transfer agents and registrars who in turn may bond their personnel.

2.   The issuer cannot be held liable for the honesty of employees not entrusted, directly or indirectly, with the signing, preparation, or responsible handling of similar securities and whose possible commission of forgery it has no reason to anticipate. The result in such cases as *Hudson Trust Co. v. American Linseed Co.,* 232 N.Y. 350, 134 N.E. 178 (1922), and *Dollar Savings Fund & Trust Co. v. Pittsburgh Plate Glass Co.,* 213 Pa. 307, 62 A. 916, 5 Ann.Cas. 248 (1906) is here adopted.

3.   This section is not concerned with forged or unauthorized indorsements, but only with unauthorized signatures of issuers, transfer agents, etc., placed upon security certificates during the course of their issue. The protection here stated is available to all purchasers for value without notice and not merely to subsequent purchasers.

Definitional Cross References:

"Certificated security". Section 8–102(a)(4).

"Issuer". Section 8–201.

"Notice". Section 1–201(25).*

"Purchaser". Sections 1–201(33)* & 8–116.

"Security certificate". Section 8–102(a)(14).

"Unauthorized signature". Section 1–201(43).*

§ 8–206.   Completion of Alteration of Security Certificate.

(a)   If a security certificate contains the signatures necessary to its issue or transfer but is incomplete in any other respect:

(1)   any person may complete it by filling in the blanks as authorized; and

(2)   even if the blanks are incorrectly filled in, the security certificate as completed is enforceable by a purchaser who took it for value and without notice of the incorrectness.

(b)   A complete security certificate that has been improperly altered, even if fraudulently, remains enforceable, but only according to its original terms.

---

*   *Referring to unrevised Article 1 (Appendix A).*

Official Comment

1.   The problem of forged or unauthorized signatures necessary for the issue or transfer of a security is not involved here, and a person in possession of a blank certificate is not, by this section, given authority to fill in blanks with such signatures. Completion of blanks left in a transfer instruction is dealt with elsewhere (Section 8–305(a)).

2.   Blanks left upon issue of a security certificate are the only ones dealt with here, and a purchaser for value without notice is protected. A purchaser is not in a good position to determine whether blanks were completed by the issuer or by some person not authorized to complete them. On the other hand the issuer can protect itself by not placing its signature on the writing until the blanks are completed or, if it does sign before all blanks are completed, by carefully selecting the agents and employees to whom it entrusts the writing after authentication. With respect to a security certificate that is completed by the issuer but later is altered, the issuer has done everything it can to protect the purchaser and thus is not charged with the terms as altered. However, it is charged according to the original terms, since it is not thereby prejudiced. If the completion or alteration is obviously irregular, the purchaser may not qualify as a purchaser who took without notice under this section.

3.   Only the purchaser who physically takes the certificate is directly protected. However, a transferee may receive protection indirectly through Section 8–302(a).

4.   The protection granted a purchaser for value without notice under this section is modified to the extent that an overissue may result where an incorrect amount is inserted into a blank (Section 8–210).

Definitional Cross References:

"Notice". Section 1–201(25).*
"Purchaser". Sections 1–201(33)* & 8–116.
"Security certificate". Section 8–102(a)(16).
"Unauthorized signature". Section 1–201(43).*
"Value". Sections 1–201(44)* & 8–116.

§ 8–207.   Rights and Duties of Issuer with Respect to Registered Owners.

(a)   Before due presentment for registration of transfer of a certificated security in registered form or of an instruction requesting registration of transfer of an uncertificated security, the issuer or indenture trustee may treat the registered owner as the person exclusively entitled to vote, receive notifications, and otherwise exercise all the rights and powers of an owner.

(b)   This Article does not affect the liability of the registered owner of a security for a call, assessment, or the like.

Official Comment

1.   Subsection (a) states the issuer's right to treat the registered owner of a security as the person entitled to exercise all the rights of an owner. This right of the issuer is limited by the provisions of Part 4 of this article. Once there has been due presentation for registration of transfer, the issuer has a duty to register ownership in the name of the transferee. Section 8–401. Thus its right to treat the old registered owner as exclusively entitled to the rights of ownership must cease.

The issuer may under this section make distributions of money or securities to the registered owners of securities without requiring further proof of ownership, provided that such distributions are distributable to the owners of all securities of the same issue and the terms of the security do not require surrender of a security certificate as a condition of payment or exchange. Any such distribution shall constitute a defense against a claim for the same distribution by a person, even if that person is in possession of the security certificate and is a protected purchaser of the security. See PEB Commentary No. 4, dated March 10, 1990.

2.   Subsection (a) is permissive and does not require that the issuer deal exclusively with the registered owner. It is free to require proof of ownership before paying out dividends or the like if it chooses to. *Barbato v. Breeze Corporation,* 128 N.J.L. 309, 26 A.2d 53 (1942).

---

      *   *Referring to unrevised Article 1 (Appendix A).*

3.   This section does not operate to determine who is finally entitled to exercise voting and other rights or to receive payments and distributions. The parties are still free to incorporate their own arrangements as to these matters in seller-purchaser agreements which may be definitive as between them.

4.   No change in existing state laws as to the liability of registered owners for calls and assessments is here intended; nor is anything in this section designed to estop record holders from denying ownership when assessments are levied if they are otherwise entitled to do so under state law. See *State ex rel. Squire v. Murfey, Blosson & Co.,* 131 Ohio St. 289, 2 N.E.2d 866 (1936); *Willing v. Delaplaine,* 23 F.Supp. 579 (1937).

5.   No interference is intended with the common practice of closing the transfer books or taking a record date for dividend, voting, and other purposes, as provided for in by-laws, charters, and statutes.

Definitional Cross References:

"Certificated security". Section 8–102(a)(4).
"Instruction". Section 8–102(a)(12).
"Issuer". Section 8–201.
"Registered form". Section 8–102(a)(13).
"Security". Section 8–102(a)(15).
"Uncertificated security". Section 8–102(a)(18).

§ 8–208.   Effect of Signature of Authenticating Trustee, Registrar, or Transfer Agent.

(a)   A person signing a security certificate as authenticating trustee, registrar, transfer agent, or the like, warrants to a purchaser for value of the certificated security, if the purchaser is without notice of a particular defect, that:

(1)   the certificate is genuine;

(2)   the person's own participation in the issue of the security is within the person's capacity and within the scope of the authority received by the person from the issuer; and

(3)   the person has reasonable grounds to believe that the certificated security is in the form and within the amount the issuer is authorized to issue.

(b)   Unless otherwise agreed, a person signing under subsection (a) does not assume responsibility for the validity of the security in other respects.

Official Comment

1.   The warranties here stated express the current understanding and prevailing case law as to the effect of the signatures of authenticating trustees, transfer agents, and registrars. See *Jarvis v. Manhattan Beach Co.,* 148 N.Y. 652, 43 N.E. 68, 31 L.R.A. 776, 51 Am.St.Rep. 727 (1896). Although it has generally been regarded as the particular obligation of the transfer agent to determine whether securities are in proper form as provided by the by-laws and Articles of Incorporation, neither a registrar nor an authenticating trustee should properly place a signature upon a certificate without determining whether it is at least regular on its face. The obligations of these parties in this respect have therefore been made explicit in terms of due care. See *Feldmeier v. Mortgage Securities, Inc.,* 34 Cal.App.2d 201, 93 P.2d 593 (1939).

2.   Those cases which hold that an authenticating trustee is not liable for any defect in the mortgage or property which secures the bond or for any fraudulent misrepresentations made by the issuer are not here affected since these matters do not involve the genuineness or proper form of the security. *Ainsa v. Mercantile Trust Co.,* 174 Cal. 504, 163 P. 898 (1917); *Tschetinian v. City Trust Co.,* 186 N.Y. 432, 79 N.E. 401 (1906); *Davidge v. Guardian Trust Co. of New York,* 203 N.Y. 331, 96 N.E. 751 (1911).

3.   The charter or an applicable statute may affect the capacity of a bank or other corporation undertaking to act as an authenticating trustee, registrar, or transfer agent. See, for example, the Federal Reserve Act (U.S.C.A., Title 12, Banks and Banking, Section 248) under which the Board of Governors of the Federal Reserve Bank is authorized to grant special permits to National Banks permitting them to act as trustees. Such corporations are therefore held to certify as to their legal capacity to act as well as to their authority.

4.   Authenticating trustees, registrars, and transfer agents have normally been held liable for an issue in excess of the authorized amount. *Jarvis v. Manhattan Beach Co.,* supra; *Mullen v. Eastern Trust & Banking Co.,*

108 Me. 498, 81 A. 948 (1911). In imposing upon these parties a duty of due care with respect to the amount they are authorized to help issue, this section does not necessarily validate the security, but merely holds persons responsible for the excess issue liable in damages for any loss suffered by the purchaser.

5.   Aside from questions of genuineness and excess issue, these parties are not held to certify as to the validity of the security unless they specifically undertake to do so. The case law which has recognized a unique responsibility on the transfer agent's part to testify as to the validity of any security which it countersigns is rejected.

6.   This provision does not prevent a transfer agent or issuer from agreeing with a registrar of stock to protect the registrar in respect of the genuineness and proper form of a security certificate signed by the issuer or the transfer agent or both. Nor does it interfere with proper indemnity arrangements between the issuer and trustees, transfer agents, registrars, and the like.

7.   An unauthorized signature is a signature for purposes of this section if and only if it is made effective by Section 8–205.

Definitional Cross References:

"Certificated security". Section 8–102(a)(4).
"Genuine". Section 1–201(18).*
"Issuer". Section 8–201.
"Notice". Section 1–201(25).*
"Purchaser". Sections 1–201(33)* & 8–116.
"Security". Section 8–102(a)(15).
"Security certificate". Section 8–102(a)(16).
"Uncertificated security". Section 8–102(a)(18).
"Value". Sections 1–201(44)* & 8–116.

§ 8–209.   Issuer's Lien.

A lien in favor of an issuer upon a certificated security is valid against a purchaser only if the right of the issuer to the lien is noted conspicuously on the security certificate.

Official Comment

This section is similar to Sections 8–202 and 8–204 which require that the terms of a certificated security and any restriction on transfer imposed by the issuer be noted on the security certificate. This section differs from those two sections in that the purchaser's knowledge of the issuer's claim is irrelevant. "Noted" makes clear that the text of the lien provisions need not be set forth in full. However, this would not override a provision of an applicable corporation code requiring statement in haec verba. This section does not apply to uncertificated securities. It applies to the indirect holding system in the same fashion as Sections 8–202 and 8–204, see Comment 2 to Section 8–202.

Definitional Cross References:

"Certificated security". Section 8–102(a)(4).
"Issuer". Section 8–201.
"Purchaser". Sections 1–201(33)* & 8–116.
"Security". Section 8–102(a)(15).
"Security certificate". Section 8–102(a)(16).

§ 8–210.   Overissue.

(a)   In this section, "overissue" means the issue of securities in excess of the amount the issuer has corporate power to issue, but an overissue does not occur if appropriate action has cured the overissue.

---

*   *Referring to unrevised Article 1 (Appendix A).*

(b)   Except as otherwise provided in subsections (c) and (d), the provisions of this Article which validate a security or compel its issue or reissue do not apply to the extent that validation, issue, or reissue would result in overissue.

(c)   If an identical security not constituting an overissue is reasonably available for purchase, a person entitled to issue or validation may compel the issuer to purchase the security and deliver it if certificated or register its transfer if uncertificated, against surrender of any security certificate the person holds.

(d)   If a security is not reasonably available for purchase, a person entitled to issue or validation may recover from the issuer the price the person or the last purchaser for value paid for it with interest from the date of the person's demand.

Official Comment

1.   Deeply embedded in corporation law is the conception that "corporate power" to issue securities stems from the statute, either general or special, under which the corporation is organized. Corporation codes universally require that the charter or articles of incorporation state, at least as to capital shares, maximum limits in terms of number of shares or total dollar capital. Historically, special incorporation statutes are similarly drawn and sometimes similarly limit the face amount of authorized debt securities. The theory is that issue of securities in excess of the authorized amounts is prohibited. See, for example, *McWilliams v. Geddes & Moss Undertaking Co.,* 169 So. 894 (1936, La.); *Crawford v. Twin City Oil Co.,* 216 Ala. 216, 113 So. 61 (1927); *New York and New Haven R.R. Co. v. Schuyler,* 34 N.Y. 30 (1865). This conception persists despite modern corporation codes under which, by action of directors and stockholders, additional shares can be authorized by charter amendment and thereafter issued. This section does not give a person entitled to validation, issue, or reissue of a security, the right to compel amendment of the charter to authorize additional shares. Therefore, in a case where issue of an additional security would require charter amendment, the plaintiff is limited to the two alternate remedies set forth in subsections (c) and (d). The last clause of subsection (a), which is added in Revised Article 8, does, however, recognize that under modern conditions, overissue may be a relatively minor technical problem that can be cured by appropriate action under governing corporate law.

2.   Where an identical security is reasonably available for purchase, whether because traded on an organized market, or because one or more security owners may be willing to sell at a not unreasonable price, the issuer, although unable to issue additional shares, will be able to purchase them and may be compelled to follow that procedure. *West v. Tintic Standard Mining Co.,* 71 Utah 158, 263 P. 490 (1928).

3.   The right to recover damages from an issuer who has permitted an overissue to occur is well settled. *New York and New Haven R.R. Co. v. Schuyler,* 34 N.Y. 30 (1865). The measure of such damages, however, has been open to question, some courts basing them upon the value of stock at the time registration is refused; some upon the value at the time of trial; and some upon the highest value between the time of refusal and the time of trial. *Allen v. South Boston Railroad,* 150 Mass. 200, 22 N.E. 917, 5 L.R.A. 716, 15 Am.St.Rep. 185 (1889); *Commercial Bank v. Kortright,* 22 Wend. (N.Y.) 348 (1839). The purchase price of the security to the last purchaser who gave value for it is here adopted as being the fairest means of reducing the possibility of speculation by the purchaser. Interest may be recovered by the best available measure of compensation for delay.

Definitional Cross References:

"Issuer". Section 8–201.
"Security". Section 8–102(a)(15).
"Security certificate". Section 8–102(a)(16).
"Uncertificated security". Section 8–102(a)(18).

PART 3

TRANSFER OF CERTIFICATED AND UNCERTIFICATED SECURITIES

§ 8–301.   Delivery.

(a)   Delivery of a certificated security to a purchaser occurs when:

(1)   the purchaser acquires possession of the security certificate;

(2) another person, other than a securities intermediary, either acquires possession of the security certificate on behalf of the purchaser or, having previously acquired possession of the certificate, acknowledges that it holds for the purchaser; or

(3) a securities intermediary acting on behalf of the purchaser acquires possession of the security certificate, only if the certificate is in registered form and is (i) registered in the name of the purchaser, (ii) payable to the order of the purchaser, or (iii) specially indorsed to the purchaser by an effective indorsement and has not been indorsed to the securities intermediary or in blank.

(b) Delivery of an uncertificated security to a purchaser occurs when:

(1) the issuer registers the purchaser as the registered owner, upon original issue or registration of transfer; or

(2) another person, other than a securities intermediary, either becomes the registered owner of the uncertificated security on behalf of the purchaser or, having previously become the registered owner, acknowledges that it holds for the purchaser.

As amended in 1999.

Official Comment

1. This section specifies the requirements for "delivery" of securities. Delivery is used in Article 8 to describe the formal steps necessary for a purchaser to acquire a direct interest in a security under this Article. The concept of delivery refers to the implementation of a transaction, not the legal categorization of the transaction which is consummated by delivery. Issuance and transfer are different kinds of transaction, though both may be implemented by delivery. Sale and pledge are different kinds of transfers, but both may be implemented by delivery.

2. Subsection (a) defines delivery with respect to certificated securities. Paragraph (1) deals with simple cases where purchasers themselves acquire physical possession of certificates. Paragraphs (2) and (3) of subsection (a) specify the circumstances in which delivery to a purchaser can occur although the certificate is in the possession of a person other than the purchaser. Paragraph (2) contains the general rule that a purchaser can take delivery through another person, so long as the other person is actually acting on behalf of the purchaser or acknowledges that it is holding on behalf of the purchaser. Paragraph (2) does not apply to acquisition of possession by a securities intermediary, because a person who holds securities through a securities account acquires a security entitlement, rather than having a direct interest. See Section 8–501. Subsection (a)(3) specifies the limited circumstances in which delivery of security certificates to a securities intermediary is treated as a delivery to the customer. Note that delivery is a method of perfecting a security interest in a certificated security. See Section 9–313(a), (e).

3. Subsection (b) defines delivery with respect to uncertificated securities. Use of the term "delivery" with respect to uncertificated securities, does, at least on first hearing, seem a bit solecistic. The word "delivery" is, however, routinely used in the securities business in a broader sense than manual tradition. For example, settlement by entries on the books of a clearing corporation is commonly called "delivery," as in the expression "delivery versus payment." The diction of this section has the advantage of using the same term for uncertificated securities as for certificated securities, for which delivery is conventional usage. Paragraph (1) of subsection (b) provides that delivery occurs when the purchaser becomes the registered owner of an uncertificated security, either upon original issue or registration of transfer. Paragraph (2) provides for delivery of an uncertificated security through a third person, in a fashion analogous to subsection (a)(2).

Definitional Cross References:

"Certificated security". Section 8–102(a)(4).
"Effective". Section 8–107.
"Issuer". Section 8–201.
"Purchaser". Sections 1–201(33)* & 8–116.
"Registered form". Section 8–102(a)(13).
"Securities intermediary". Section 8–102(a)(14).
"Security certificate". Section 8–102(a)(16).

---

* *Referring to unrevised Article 1 (Appendix A).*

"Special indorsement". Section 8–304(a).

"Uncertificated security". Section 8–102(a)(18).

As amended in 1999.

§ 8–302.   Rights of Purchaser.

(a)   Except as otherwise provided in subsections (b) and (c), a purchaser of a certificated or uncertificated security acquires all rights in the security that the transferor had or had power to transfer.

(b)   A purchaser of a limited interest acquires rights only to the extent of the interest purchased.

(c)   A purchaser of a certificated security who as a previous holder had notice of an adverse claim does not improve its position by taking from a protected purchaser.

As amended in 1999.

Official Comment

1.   Subsection (a) provides that a purchaser of a certificated or uncertificated security acquires all rights that the transferor had or had power to transfer. This statement of the familiar "shelter" principle is qualified by the exceptions that a purchaser of a limited interest acquires only that interest, subsection (b), and that a person who does not qualify as a protected purchaser cannot improve its position by taking from a subsequent protected purchaser, subsection (c).

2.   Although this section provides that a purchaser acquires a property interest in a certificated or uncertificated security, it does not state that a person can acquire an interest in a security only by purchase. Article 8 also is not a comprehensive codification of all of the law governing the creation or transfer of interests in securities *by purchase*.[*] For example, the grant of a security interest is a transfer of a property interest, but the formal steps necessary to effectuate such a transfer are governed by Article 9, not by Article 8. Under the Article 9 rules, a security interest in a certificated or uncertificated security can be created by execution of a security agreement under Section 9–203 and can be perfected by filing. A transfer of an Article 9 security interest can be implemented by an Article 8 delivery, but need not be.

Similarly, Article 8 does not determine whether a property interest in certificated or uncertificated security is acquired under other law, such as the law of gifts, trusts, or equitable remedies. Nor does Article 8 deal with transfers by operation of law. For example, transfers from decedent to administrator, from ward to guardian, and from bankrupt to trustee in bankruptcy are governed by other law as to both the time they occur and the substance of the transfer. The Article 8 rules do, however, determine whether the issuer is obligated to recognize the rights that a third party, such as a transferee, may acquire under other law. See Sections 8–207, 8–401, and 8–404.

Definitional Cross References:

"Certificated security". Section 8–102(a)(4).

"Notice of adverse claim". Section 8–105.

"Protected purchaser". Section 8–303.

"Purchaser". Sections 1–201(33)[**] & 8–116.

"Uncertificated security". Section 8–102(a)(18).

"Delivery". Section 8–301.

As amended in 1999 and 2000.

§ 8–303.   Protected Purchaser.

(a)   "Protected purchaser" means a purchaser of a certificated or uncertificated security, or of an interest therein, who:

(1)   gives value;

---

[*]   Amendments in italics approved by the Permanent Editorial Board for Uniform Commercial Code January 15, 2000.

[**]   *Referring to unrevised Article 1 (Appendix A).*

(2)   does not have notice of any adverse claim to the security; and

(3)   obtains control of the certificated or uncertificated security.

(b)   In addition to acquiring the rights of a purchaser, a protected purchaser also acquires its interest in the security free of any adverse claim.

Official Comment

1.   Subsection (a) lists the requirements that a purchaser must meet to qualify as a "protected purchaser." Subsection (b) provides that a protected purchaser takes its interest free from adverse claims. "Purchaser" is defined broadly in Section 1–201. A secured party as well as an outright buyer can qualify as a protected purchaser. Also, "purchase" includes taking by issue, so a person to whom a security is originally issued can qualify as a protected purchaser.

2.   To qualify as a protected purchaser, a purchaser must give value, take without notice of any adverse claim, and obtain control. Value is used in the broad sense defined in Section 1–201(44).* See also Section 8–116 (securities intermediary as purchaser for value). Adverse claim is defined in Section 8–102(a)(1). Section 8–105 specifies whether a purchaser has notice of an adverse claim. Control is defined in Section 8–106. To qualify as a protected purchaser there must be a time at which all of the requirements are satisfied. Thus if a purchaser obtains notice of an adverse claim before giving value or satisfying the requirements for control, the purchaser cannot be a protected purchaser. See also Section 8–304(d).

The requirement that a protected purchaser obtain control expresses the point that to qualify for the adverse claim cut-off rule a purchaser must take through a transaction that is implemented by the appropriate mechanism. By contrast, the rules in Part 2 provide that any purchaser for value of a security without notice of a defense may take free of the issuer's defense based on that defense. See Section 8–202.

3.   The requirements for control differ depending on the form of the security. For securities represented by bearer certificates, a purchaser obtains control by delivery. See Sections 8–106(a) and 8–301(a). For securities represented by certificates in registered form, the requirements for control are: (1) delivery as defined in Section 8–301(b), plus (2) either an effective indorsement or registration of transfer by the issuer. See Section 8–106(b). Thus, a person who takes through a forged indorsement does not qualify as a protected purchaser by virtue of the delivery alone. If, however, the purchaser presents the certificate to the issuer for registration of transfer, and the issuer registers transfer over the forged indorsement, the purchaser can qualify as a protected purchaser of the new certificate. If the issuer registers transfer on a forged indorsement, the true owner will be able to recover from the issuer for wrongful registration, see Section 8–404, unless the owner's delay in notifying the issuer of a loss or theft of the certificate results in preclusion under Section 8–406.

For uncertificated securities, a purchaser can obtain control either by delivery, see Sections 8–106(c)(1) and 8–301(b), or by obtaining an agreement pursuant to which the issuer agrees to act on instructions from the purchaser without further consent from the registered owner, see Section 8–106(c)(2). The control agreement device of Section 8–106(c)(2) takes the place of the "registered pledge" concept of the 1978 version of Article 8. A secured lender who obtains a control agreement under Section 8–106(c)(2) can qualify as a protected purchaser of an uncertificated security.

4.   This section states directly the rules determining whether one takes free from adverse claims without using the phrase "good faith." Whether a person who takes under suspicious circumstances is disqualified is determined by the rules of Section 8–105 on notice of adverse claims. The term "protected purchaser," which replaces the term "bona fide purchaser" used in the prior version of Article 8, is derived from the term "protected holder" used in the Convention on International Bills and Notes prepared by the United Nations Commission on International Trade Law ("UNCITRAL").

Definitional Cross References:

"Adverse claim". Section 8–102(a)(1).

"Certificated security". Section 8–102(a)(4).

"Control". Section 8–106.

"Notice of adverse claim". Section 8–105.

"Purchaser". Sections 1–201(33)* & 8–116.

---

*   *Referring to unrevised Article 1 (Appendix A).*

"Uncertificated security". Section 8–102(a)(18).

"Value". Sections 1–201(44)* & 8–116.

§ 8–304.   Indorsement.

(a)   An indorsement may be in blank or special. An indorsement in blank includes an indorsement to bearer. A special indorsement specifies to whom a security is to be transferred or who has power to transfer it. A holder may convert a blank indorsement to a special indorsement.

(b)   An indorsement purporting to be only of part of a security certificate representing units intended by the issuer to be separately transferable is effective to the extent of the indorsement.

(c)   An indorsement, whether special or in blank, does not constitute a transfer until delivery of the certificate on which it appears or, if the indorsement is on a separate document, until delivery of both the document and the certificate.

(d)   If a security certificate in registered form has been delivered to a purchaser without a necessary indorsement, the purchaser may become a protected purchaser only when the indorsement is supplied. However, against a transferor, a transfer is complete upon delivery and the purchaser has a specifically enforceable right to have any necessary indorsement supplied.

(e)   An indorsement of a security certificate in bearer form may give notice of an adverse claim to the certificate, but it does not otherwise affect a right to registration that the holder possesses.

(f)   Unless otherwise agreed, a person making an indorsement assumes only the obligations provided in Section 8–108 and not an obligation that the security will be honored by the issuer.

Official Comment

1.   By virtue of the definition of indorsement in Section 8–102 and the rules of this section, the simplified method of indorsing certificated securities previously set forth in the Uniform Stock Transfer Act is continued. Although more than one special indorsement on a given security certificate is possible, the desire for dividends or interest, as the case may be, should operate to bring the certificate home for registration of transfer within a reasonable period of time. The usual form of assignment which appears on the back of a stock certificate or in a separate "power" may be filled up either in the form of an assignment, a power of attorney to transfer, or both. If it is not filled up at all but merely signed, the indorsement is in blank. If filled up either as an assignment or as a power of attorney to transfer, the indorsement is special.

2.   Subsection (b) recognizes the validity of a "partial" indorsement, e.g., as to fifty shares of the one hundred represented by a single certificate. The rights of a transferee under a partial indorsement to the status of a protected purchaser are left to the case law.

3.   Subsection (c) deals with the effect of an indorsement without delivery. There must be a voluntary parting with control in order to effect a valid transfer of a certificated security as between the parties. *Levey v. Nason,* 279 Mass. 268, 181 N.E. 193 (1932), and *National Surety Co. v. Indemnity Insurance Co. of North America,* 237 App.Div. 485, 261 N.Y.S. 605 (1933). The provision in Section 10 of the Uniform Stock Transfer Act that an attempted transfer without delivery amounts to a promise to transfer is omitted. Even under that Act the effect of such a promise was left to the applicable law of contracts, and this Article by making no reference to such situations intends to achieve a similar result. With respect to delivery there is no counterpart to subsection (d) on right to compel indorsement, such as is envisaged in *Johnson v. Johnson,* 300 Mass. 24, 13 N.E.2d 788 (1938), where the transferee under a written assignment was given the right to compel a transfer of the certificate.

4.   Subsection (d) deals with the effect of delivery without indorsement. As between the parties the transfer is made complete upon delivery, but the transferee cannot become a protected purchaser until indorsement is made. The indorsement does not operate retroactively, and notice may intervene between delivery and indorsement so as to prevent the transferee from becoming a protected purchaser. Although a purchaser taking without a necessary indorsement may be subject to claims of ownership, any issuer's defense of which the purchaser had no notice at the time of delivery will be cut off, since the provisions of this Article protect all purchasers for value without notice (Section 8–202).

---

*   *Referring to unrevised Article 1 (Appendix A).*

The transferee's right to compel an indorsement where a security certificate has been delivered with intent to transfer is recognized in the case law. See *Coats v. Guaranty Bank & Trust Co.*, 170 La. 871, 129 So. 513 (1930). A proper indorsement is one of the requisites of transfer which a purchaser of a certificated security has a right to obtain (Section 8–307). A purchaser may not only compel an indorsement under that section but may also recover for any reasonable expense incurred by the transferor's failure to respond to the demand for an indorsement.

5.   Subsection (e) deals with the significance of an indorsement on a security certificate in bearer form. The concept of indorsement applies only to registered securities. A purported indorsement of bearer paper is normally of no effect. An indorsement "for collection," "for surrender" or the like, charges a purchaser with notice of adverse claims (Section 8–105(d)) but does not operate beyond this to interfere with any right the holder may otherwise possess to have the security registered.

6.   Subsection (f) makes clear that the indorser of a security certificate does not warrant that the issuer will honor the underlying obligation. In view of the nature of investment securities and the circumstances under which they are normally transferred, a transferor cannot be held to warrant as to the issuer's actions. As a transferor the indorser, of course, remains liable for breach of the warranties set forth in this Article (Section 8–108).

Definitional Cross References:

"Bearer form". Section 8–102(a)(2).
"Certificated security". Section 8–102(a)(4).
"Indorsement". Section 8–102(a)(11).
"Purchaser". Sections 1–201(33)* & 8–116.
"Registered form". Section 8–102(a)(13).
"Security certificate". Section 8–102(a)(16).

§ 8–305.   Instruction.

(a)   If an instruction has been originated by an appropriate person but is incomplete in any other respect, any person may complete it as authorized and the issuer may rely on it as completed, even though it has been completed incorrectly.

(b)   Unless otherwise agreed, a person initiating an instruction assumes only the obligations imposed by Section 8–108 and not an obligation that the security will be honored by the issuer.

Official Comment

1.   The term instruction is defined in Section 8–102(a)(12) as a notification communicated to the issuer of an uncertificated security directing that transfer be registered. Section 8–107 specifies who may initiate an effective instruction.

Functionally, presentation of an instruction is quite similar to the presentation of an indorsed certificate for registration. Note that instruction is defined in terms of "communicate," see Section 8–102(a)(6). Thus, the instruction may be in the form of a writing signed by the registered owner or in any other form agreed upon by the issuer and the registered owner. Allowing nonwritten forms of instructions will permit the development and employment of means of transmitting instructions electronically.

When a person who originates an instruction leaves a blank and the blank later is completed, subsection (a) gives the issuer the same rights it would have had against the originating person had that person completed the blank. This is true regardless of whether the person completing the instruction had authority to complete it. Compare Section 8–206 and its Comment, dealing with blanks left upon issue.

2.   Subsection (b) makes clear that the originator of an instruction, like the indorser of a security certificate, does not warrant that the issuer will honor the underlying obligation, but does make warranties as a transferor under Section 8–108.

Definitional Cross References:

"Appropriate person". Section 8–107.
"Instruction". Section 8–102(a)(12).

---

*   *Referring to unrevised Article 1 (Appendix A).*

"Issuer". Section 8–201.

§ 8–306.　Effect of Guaranteeing Signature, Indorsement, or Instruction.

(a)　A person who guarantees a signature of an indorser of a security certificate warrants that at the time of signing:

(1)　the signature was genuine;

(2)　the signer was an appropriate person to indorse, or if the signature is by an agent, the agent had actual authority to act on behalf of the appropriate person; and

(3)　the signer had legal capacity to sign.

(b)　A person who guarantees a signature of the originator of an instruction warrants that at the time of signing:

(1)　the signature was genuine;

(2)　the signer was an appropriate person to originate the instruction, or if the signature is by an agent, the agent had actual authority to act on behalf of the appropriate person, if the person specified in the instruction as the registered owner was, in fact, the registered owner, as to which fact the signature guarantor does not make a warranty; and

(3)　the signer had legal capacity to sign.

(c)　A person who specially guarantees the signature of an originator of an instruction makes the warranties of a signature guarantor under subsection (b) and also warrants that at the time the instruction is presented to the issuer:

(1)　the person specified in the instruction as the registered owner of the uncertificated security will be the registered owner; and

(2)　the transfer of the uncertificated security requested in the instruction will be registered by the issuer free from all liens, security interests, restrictions, and claims other than those specified in the instruction.

(d)　A guarantor under subsections (a) and (b) or a special guarantor under subsection (c) does not otherwise warrant the rightfulness of the transfer.

(e)　A person who guarantees an indorsement of a security certificate makes the warranties of a signature guarantor under subsection (a) and also warrants the rightfulness of the transfer in all respects.

(f)　A person who guarantees an instruction requesting the transfer of an uncertificated security makes the warranties of a special signature guarantor under subsection (c) and also warrants the rightfulness of the transfer in all respects.

(g)　An issuer may not require a special guaranty of signature, a guaranty of indorsement, or a guaranty of instruction as a condition to registration of transfer.

(h)　The warranties under this section are made to a person taking or dealing with the security in reliance on the guaranty, and the guarantor is liable to the person for loss resulting from their breach. An indorser or originator of an instruction whose signature, indorsement, or instruction has been guaranteed is liable to a guarantor for any loss suffered by the guarantor as a result of breach of the warranties of the guarantor.

Official Comment

1.　Subsection (a) provides that a guarantor of the signature of the indorser of a security certificate warrants that the signature is genuine, that the signer is an appropriate person or has actual authority to indorse on behalf of the appropriate person, and that the signer has legal capacity. Subsection (b) provides similar, though not identical, warranties for the guarantor of a signature of the originator of an instruction for transfer of an uncertificated security.

Appropriate person is defined in Section 8–107(a) to include a successor or person who has power under other law to act for a person who is deceased or lacks capacity. Thus if a certificate registered in the name of Mary Roe is indorsed by Jane Doe as executor of Mary Roe, a guarantor of the signature of Jane Doe warrants that she has power to act as executor.

Although the definition of appropriate person in Section 8–107(a) does not itself include an agent, an indorsement by an agent is effective under Section 8–107(b) if the agent has authority to act for the appropriate person. Accordingly, this section provides an explicit warranty of authority for agents.

2.   The rationale of the principle that a signature guarantor warrants the authority of the signer, rather than simply the genuineness of the signature, was explained in the leading case of *Jennie Clarkson Home for Children v. Missouri, K. & T.R. Co.,* 182 N.Y. 47, 74 N.E. 571, 70 A.L.R. 787 (1905), which dealt with a guaranty of the signature of a person indorsing on behalf of a corporation. "If stock is held by an individual who is executing a power of attorney for its transfer, the member of the exchange who signs as a witness thereto guaranties not only the genuineness of the signature affixed to the power of attorney, but that the person signing is the individual in whose name the stock stands. With reference to stock standing in the name of a corporation, which can only sign a power of attorney through its authorized officers or agents, a different situation is presented. If the witnessing of the signature of the corporation is only that of the signature of a person who signs for the corporation, then the guaranty is of no value, and there is nothing to protect purchasers or the companies who are called upon to issue new stock in the place of that transferred from the frauds of persons who have signed the names of corporations without authority. If such is the only effect of the guaranty, purchasers and transfer agents must first go to the corporation in whose name the stock stands and ascertain whether the individual who signed the power of attorney had authority to do so. This will require time, and in many cases will necessitate the postponement of the completion of the purchase by the payment of the money until the facts can be ascertained. The broker who is acting for the owner has an opportunity to become acquainted with his customer, and may readily before sale ascertain, in case of a corporation, the name of the officer who is authorized to execute the power of attorney. It was therefore, we think, the purpose of the rule to cast upon the broker who witnesses the signature the duty of ascertaining whether the person signing the name of the corporation had authority to do so, and making the witness a guarantor that it is the signature of the corporation in whose name the stock stands."

3.   Subsection (b) sets forth the warranties that can reasonably be expected from the guarantor of the signature of the originator of an instruction, who, though familiar with the signer, does not have any evidence that the purported owner is in fact the owner of the subject uncertificated security. This is in contrast to the position of the person guaranteeing a signature on a certificate who can see a certificate in the signer's possession in the name of or indorsed to the signer or in blank. Thus, the warranty in paragraph (2) of subsection (b) is expressly conditioned on the actual registration's conforming to that represented by the originator. If the signer purports to be the owner, the guarantor under paragraph (2), warrants only the identity of the signer. If, however, the signer is acting in a representative capacity, the guarantor warrants both the signer's identity and authority to act for the purported owner. The issuer needs no warranty as to the facts of registration because those facts can be ascertained from the issuer's own records.

4.   Subsection (c) sets forth a "special guaranty of signature" under which the guarantor additionally warrants both registered ownership and freedom from undisclosed defects of record. The guarantor of the signature of an indorser of a security certificate effectively makes these warranties to a purchaser for value on the evidence of a clean certificate issued in the name of the indorser, indorsed to the indorser or indorsed in blank. By specially guaranteeing under subsection (c), the guarantor warrants that the instruction will, when presented to the issuer, result in the requested registration free from defects not specified.

5.   Subsection (d) makes clear that the warranties of a signature guarantor are limited to those specified in this section and do not include a general warranty of rightfulness. On the other hand subsections (e) and (f) provide that a person guaranteeing an indorsement or an instruction does warrant that the transfer is rightful in all respects.

6.   Subsection (g) makes clear what can be inferred from the combination of Sections 8–401 and 8–402, that the issuer may not require as a condition to transfer a guaranty of the indorsement or instruction nor may it require a special signature guaranty.

7.   Subsection (h) specifies to whom the warranties in this section run, and also provides that a person who gives a guaranty under this section has an action against the indorser or originator for any loss suffered by the guarantor.

Definitional Cross References:

"Appropriate person". Section 8–107.
"Genuine". Section 1–201(18).*
"Indorsement". Section 8–102(a)(11).
"Instruction". Section 8–102(a)(12).
"Issuer". Section 8–201.
"Security certificate". Section 8–102(a)(16).
"Uncertificated security". Section 8–102(a)(18).

§ 8–307. Purchaser's Right to Requisites for Registration of Transfer.

Unless otherwise agreed, the transferor of a security on due demand shall supply the purchaser with proof of authority to transfer or with any other requisite necessary to obtain registration of the transfer of the security, but if the transfer is not for value, a transferor need not comply unless the purchaser pays the necessary expenses. If the transferor fails within a reasonable time to comply with the demand, the purchaser may reject or rescind the transfer.

Official Comment

1.   Because registration of the transfer of a security is a matter of vital importance, a purchaser is here provided with the means of obtaining such formal requirements for registration as signature guaranties, proof of authority, transfer tax stamps and the like. The transferor is the one in a position to supply most conveniently whatever documentation may be requisite for registration of transfer, and the duty to do so upon demand within a reasonable time is here stated affirmatively. If an essential item is peculiarly within the province of the transferor so that the transferor is the only one who can obtain it, the purchaser may specifically enforce the right to obtain it. Compare Section 8–304(d). If a transfer is not for value the transferor need not pay expenses.

2.   If the transferor's duty is not performed the transferee may reject or rescind the contract to transfer. The transferee is not bound to do so. An action for damages for breach of contract may be preferred.

Definitional Cross References:

"Purchaser". Sections 1–201(33)* & 8–116.
"Security". Section 8–102(a)(15).
"Value". Sections 1–201(44)* & 8–116.

PART 4

REGISTRATION

§ 8–401. Duty of Issuer to Register Transfer.

(a)   If a certificated security in registered form is presented to an issuer with a request to register transfer or an instruction is presented to an issuer with a request to register transfer of an uncertificated security, the issuer shall register the transfer as requested if:

(1)   under the terms of the security the person seeking registration of transfer is eligible to have the security registered in its name;

(2)   the indorsement or instruction is made by the appropriate person or by an agent who has actual authority to act on behalf of the appropriate person;

(3)   reasonable assurance is given that the indorsement or instruction is genuine and authorized (Section 8–402);

(4)   any applicable law relating to the collection of taxes has been complied with;

---

*   *Referring to unrevised Article 1 (Appendix A).*

666

(5)   the transfer does not violate any restriction on transfer imposed by the issuer in accordance with Section 8–204;

(6)   a demand that the issuer not register transfer has not become effective under Section 8–403, or the issuer has complied with Section 8–403(b) but no legal process or indemnity bond is obtained as provided in Section 8–403(d); and

(7)   the transfer is in fact rightful or is to a protected purchaser.

(b)   If an issuer is under a duty to register a transfer of a security, the issuer is liable to a person presenting a certificated security or an instruction for registration or to the person's principal for loss resulting from unreasonable delay in registration or failure or refusal to register the transfer.

Official Comment

1.   This section states the duty of the issuer to register transfers. A duty exists only if certain preconditions exist. If any of the preconditions do not exist, there is no duty to register transfer. If an indorsement on a security certificate is a forgery, there is no duty. If an instruction to transfer an uncertificated security is not originated by an appropriate person, there is no duty. If there has not been compliance with applicable tax laws, there is no duty. If a security certificate is properly indorsed but nevertheless the transfer is in fact wrongful, there is no duty unless the transfer is to a protected purchaser (and the other preconditions exist).

This section does not constitute a mandate that the issuer must establish that all preconditions are met before the issuer registers a transfer. The issuer may waive the reasonable assurances specified in paragraph (a)(3). If it has confidence in the responsibility of the persons requesting transfer, it may ignore questions of compliance with tax laws. Although an issuer has no duty if the transfer is wrongful, the issuer has no duty to inquire into adverse claims, see Section 8–404.

2.   By subsection (b) the person entitled to registration may not only compel it but may hold the issuer liable in damages for unreasonable delay.

3.   Section 8–201(c) provides that with respect to registration of transfer, "issuer" means the person on whose behalf transfer books are maintained. Transfer agents, registrars or the like within the scope of their respective functions have rights and duties under this Part similar to those of the issuer. See Section 8–407.

Definitional Cross References:

"Appropriate person". Section 8–107.
"Certificated security". Section 8–102(a)(4).
"Genuine". Section 1–201(18).*
"Indorsement". Section 8–102(a)(11).
"Instruction". Section 8–102(a)(12).
"Issuer". Section 8–201.
"Protected purchaser". Section 8–303.
"Registered form". Section 8–102(a)(13).
"Uncertificated security". Section 8–102(a)(18).

§ 8–402.   Assurance that Indorsement or Instruction is Effective.

(a)   An issuer may require the following assurance that each necessary indorsement or each instruction is genuine and authorized:

(1)   in all cases, a guaranty of the signature of the person making an indorsement or originating an instruction including, in the case of an instruction, reasonable assurance of identity;

(2)   if the indorsement is made or the instruction is originated by an agent, appropriate assurance of actual authority to sign;

(3)   if the indorsement is made or the instruction is originated by a fiduciary pursuant to Section 8–107(a)(4) or (a)(5), appropriate evidence of appointment or incumbency;

---

*   *Referring to unrevised Article 1 (Appendix A).*

(4)   if there is more than one fiduciary, reasonable assurance that all who are required to sign have done so; and

(5)   if the indorsement is made or the instruction is originated by a person not covered by another provision of this subsection, assurance appropriate to the case corresponding as nearly as may be to the provisions of this subsection.

(b)   An issuer may elect to require reasonable assurance beyond that specified in this section.

(c)   In this section:

(1)   "Guaranty of the signature" means a guaranty signed by or on behalf of a person reasonably believed by the issuer to be responsible. An issuer may adopt standards with respect to responsibility if they are not manifestly unreasonable.

(2)   "Appropriate evidence of appointment or incumbency" means:

     (i)   in the case of a fiduciary appointed or qualified by a court, a certificate issued by or under the direction or supervision of the court or an officer thereof and dated within 60 days before the date of presentation for transfer; or

     (ii)   in any other case, a copy of a document showing the appointment or a certificate issued by or on behalf of a person reasonably believed by an issuer to be responsible or, in the absence of that document or certificate, other evidence the issuer reasonably considers appropriate.

Official Comment

1.   An issuer is absolutely liable for wrongful registration of transfer if the indorsement or instruction is ineffective. See Section 8–404. Accordingly, an issuer is entitled to require such assurance as is reasonable under the circumstances that all necessary indorsements are effective, and thus to minimize its risk. This section establishes the requirements the issuer may make in terms of documentation which, except in the rarest of instances, should be easily furnished. Subsection (b) provides that an issuer may require additional assurances if that requirement is reasonable under the circumstances, but if the issuer demands more than reasonable assurance that the instruction or the necessary indorsements are genuine and authorized, the presenter may refuse the demand and sue for improper refusal to register. Section 8–401(b).

2.   Under subsection (a)(1), the issuer may require in all cases a guaranty of signature. See Section 8–306. When an instruction is presented the issuer always may require reasonable assurance as to the identity of the originator. Subsection (c) allows the issuer to require that the person making these guaranties be one reasonably believed to be responsible, and the issuer may adopt standards of responsibility which are not manifestly unreasonable. Regulations under the federal securities laws, however, place limits on the requirements transfer agents may impose concerning the responsibility of eligible signature guarantors. See 17 CFR 240.17Ad–15.

3.   This section, by paragraphs (2) through (5) of subsection (a), permits the issuer to seek confirmation that the indorsement or instruction is genuine and authorized. The permitted methods act as a double check on matters which are within the warranties of the signature guarantor. See Section 8–306. Thus, an agent may be required to submit a power of attorney, a corporation to submit a certified resolution evidencing the authority of its signing officer to sign, an executor or administrator to submit the usual "shortform certificate," etc. But failure of a fiduciary to obtain court approval of the transfer or to comply with other requirements does not make the fiduciary's signature ineffective. Section 8–107(c). Hence court orders and other controlling instruments are omitted from subsection (a).

Subsection (a)(3) authorizes the issuer to require "appropriate evidence" of appointment or incumbency, and subsection (c) indicates what evidence will be "appropriate". In the case of a fiduciary appointed or qualified by a court that evidence will be a court certificate dated within sixty days before the date of presentation, subsection (c)(2)(i). Where the fiduciary is not appointed or qualified by a court, as in the case of a successor trustee, subsection (c)(2)(ii) applies. In that case, the issuer may require a copy of a trust instrument or other document showing the appointment, or it may require the certificate of a responsible person. In the absence of such a document or certificate, it may require other appropriate evidence. If the security is registered in the name of the fiduciary as such, the person's signature is effective even though the person is no longer serving in that capacity, see Section 8–107(d), hence no evidence of incumbency is needed.

4.   Circumstances may indicate that a necessary signature was unauthorized or was not that of an appropriate person. Such circumstances would be ignored at risk of absolute liability. To minimize that risk the issuer may properly exercise the option given by subsection (b) to require assurance beyond that specified in subsection (a). On the other hand, the facts at hand may reflect only on the rightfulness of the transfer. Such facts do not create a duty of inquiry, because the issuer is not liable to an adverse claimant unless the claimant obtains legal process. See Section 8–404.

Definitional Cross References:

"Appropriate person". Section 8–107.
"Genuine". Section 1–201(18).*
"Indorsement". Section 8–102(a)(11).
"Instruction". Section 8–102(a)(12).
"Issuer". Section 8–201.

§ 8–403.   Demand that Issuer Not Register Transfer.

(a)   A person who is an appropriate person to make an indorsement or originate an instruction may demand that the issuer not register transfer of a security by communicating to the issuer a notification that identifies the registered owner and the issue of which the security is a part and provides an address for communications directed to the person making the demand. The demand is effective only if it is received by the issuer at a time and in a manner affording the issuer reasonable opportunity to act on it.

(b)   If a certificated security in registered form is presented to an issuer with a request to register transfer or an instruction is presented to an issuer with a request to register transfer of an uncertificated security after a demand that the issuer not register transfer has become effective, the issuer shall promptly communicate to (i) the person who initiated the demand at the address provided in the demand and (ii) the person who presented the security for registration of transfer or initiated the instruction requesting registration of transfer a notification stating that:

(1)   the certificated security has been presented for registration of transfer or the instruction for registration of transfer of the uncertificated security has been received;

(2)   a demand that the issuer not register transfer had previously been received; and

(3)   the issuer will withhold registration of transfer for a period of time stated in the notification in order to provide the person who initiated the demand an opportunity to obtain legal process or an indemnity bond.

(c)   The period described in subsection (b)(3) may not exceed 30 days after the date of communication of the notification. A shorter period may be specified by the issuer if it is not manifestly unreasonable.

(d)   An issuer is not liable to a person who initiated a demand that the issuer not register transfer for any loss the person suffers as a result of registration of a transfer pursuant to an effective indorsement or instruction if the person who initiated the demand does not, within the time stated in the issuer's communication, either:

(1)   obtain an appropriate restraining order, injunction, or other process from a court of competent jurisdiction enjoining the issuer from registering the transfer; or

(2)   file with the issuer an indemnity bond, sufficient in the issuer's judgment to protect the issuer and any transfer agent, registrar, or other agent of the issuer involved from any loss it or they may suffer by refusing to register the transfer.

(e)   This section does not relieve an issuer from liability for registering transfer pursuant to an indorsement or instruction that was not effective.

Official Comment

1.   The general rule under this Article is that if there has been an effective indorsement or instruction, a person who contends that registration of the transfer would be wrongful should not be able to interfere with the

---

*   *Referring to unrevised Article 1 (Appendix A).*

registration process merely by sending notice of the assertion to the issuer. Rather, the claimant must obtain legal process. See Section 8–404. Section 8–403 is an exception to this general rule. It permits the registered owner—but not third parties—to demand that the issuer not register a transfer.

2.   This section is intended to alleviate the problems faced by registered owners of certificated securities who lose or misplace their certificates. A registered owner who realizes that a certificate may have been lost or stolen should promptly report that fact to the issuer, lest the owner be precluded from asserting a claim for wrongful registration. See Section 8–406. The usual practice of issuers and transfer agents is that when a certificate is reported as lost, the owner is notified that a replacement can be obtained if the owner provides an indemnity bond. See Section 8–405. If the registered owner does not plan to transfer the securities, the owner might choose not to obtain a replacement, particularly if the owner suspects that the certificate has merely been misplaced.

Under this section, the owner's notification that the certificate has been lost would constitute a demand that the issuer not register transfer. No indemnity bond or legal process is necessary. If the original certificate is presented for registration of transfer, the issuer is required to notify the registered owner of that fact, and defer registration of transfer for a stated period. In order to prevent undue delay in the process of registration, the stated period may not exceed thirty days. This gives the registered owner an opportunity to either obtain legal process or post an indemnity bond and thereby prevent the issuer from registering transfer.

3.   Subsection (e) makes clear that this section does not relieve an issuer from liability for registering a transfer pursuant to an ineffective indorsement. An issuer's liability for wrongful registration in such cases does not depend on the presence or absence of notice that the indorsement was ineffective. Registered owners who are confident that they neither indorsed the certificates, nor did anything that would preclude them from denying the effectiveness of another's indorsement, see Sections 8–107(b) and 8–406, might prefer to pursue their rights against the issuer for wrongful registration rather than take advantage of the opportunity to post a bond or seek a restraining order when notified by the issuer under this section that their lost certificates have been presented for registration in apparently good order.

Definitional Cross References:

"Appropriate person". Section 8–107.
"Certificated security". Section 8–102(a)(4).
"Communicate". Section 8–102(a)(6).
"Effective". Section 8–107.
"Indorsement". Section 8–102(a)(11).
"Instruction". Section 8–102(a)(12).
"Issuer". Section 8–201.
"Registered form". Section 8–102(a)(13).
"Uncertificated security". Section 8–102(a)(18).

§ 8–404.   Wrongful Registration.

(a)   Except as otherwise provided in Section 8–406, an issuer is liable for wrongful registration of transfer if the issuer has registered a transfer of a security to a person not entitled to it, and the transfer was registered:

(1)   pursuant to an ineffective indorsement or instruction;

(2)   after a demand that the issuer not register transfer became effective under Section 8–403(a) and the issuer did not comply with Section 8–403(b);

(3)   after the issuer had been served with an injunction, restraining order, or other legal process enjoining it from registering the transfer, issued by a court of competent jurisdiction, and the issuer had a reasonable opportunity to act on the injunction, restraining order, or other legal process; or

(4)   by an issuer acting in collusion with the wrongdoer.

(b)   An issuer that is liable for wrongful registration of transfer under subsection (a) on demand shall provide the person entitled to the security with a like certificated or uncertificated security, and any payments or distributions that the person did not receive as a result of the wrongful registration. If an overissue would result, the issuer's liability to provide the person with a like security is governed by Section 8–210.

(c)   Except as otherwise provided in subsection (a) or in a law relating to the collection of taxes, an issuer is not liable to an owner or other person suffering loss as a result of the registration of a transfer of a security if registration was made pursuant to an effective indorsement or instruction.

Official Comment

1.   Subsection (a)(1) provides that an issuer is liable if it registers transfer pursuant to an indorsement or instruction that was not effective. For example, an issuer that registers transfer on a forged indorsement is liable to the registered owner. The fact that the issuer had no reason to suspect that the indorsement was forged or that the issuer obtained the ordinary assurances under Section 8–402 does not relieve the issuer from liability. The reason that issuers obtain signature guaranties and other assurances is that they are liable for wrongful registration.

Subsection (b) specifies the remedy for wrongful registration. Pre-Code cases established the registered owner's right to receive a new security where the issuer had wrongfully registered a transfer, but some cases also allowed the registered owner to elect between an equitable action to compel issue of a new security and an action for damages. Cf. *Casper v. Kalt-Zimmers Mfg. Co.,* 159 Wis. 517, 149 N.W. 754 (1914). Article 8 does not allow such election. The true owner of a certificated security is required to take a new security except where an overissue would result and a similar security is not reasonably available for purchase. See Section 8–210. The true owner of an uncertificated security is entitled and required to take restoration of the records to their proper state, with a similar exception for overissue.

2.   Read together, subsections (c) and (a) have the effect of providing that an issuer has no duties to an adverse claimant unless the claimant serves legal process on the issuer to enjoin registration. Issuers, or their transfer agents, perform a record-keeping function for the direct holding system that is analogous to the functions performed by clearing corporations and securities intermediaries in the indirect holding system. This section applies to the record-keepers for the direct holding system the same standard that Section 8–115 applies to the record-keepers for the indirect holding system. Thus, issuers are not liable to adverse claimants merely on the basis of notice. As in the case of the analogous rules for the indirect holding system, the policy of this section is to protect the right of investors to have their securities transfers processed without the disruption or delay that might result if the record-keepers risked liability to third parties. It would be undesirable to apply different standards to the direct and indirect holding systems, since doing so might operate as a disincentive to the development of a book-entry direct holding system.

3.   This section changes prior law under which an issuer could be held liable, even though it registered transfer on an effective indorsement or instruction, if the issuer had in some fashion been notified that the transfer might be wrongful against a third party, and the issuer did not appropriately discharge its duty to inquire into the adverse claim. See Section 8–403 (1978).

The rule of former Section 8–403 was anomalous inasmuch as Section 8–207 provides that the issuer is entitled to "treat the registered owner as the person exclusively entitled to vote, receive notifications, and otherwise exercise all the rights and powers of an owner." Under Section 8–207, the fact that a third person notifies the issuer of a claim does not preclude the issuer from treating the registered owner as the person entitled to the security. See *Kerrigan v. American Orthodontics Corp.,* 960 F.2d 43 (7th Cir.1992). The change made in the present version of Section 8–404 ensures that the rights of registered owners and the duties of issuers with respect to registration of transfer will be protected against third-party interference in the same fashion as other rights of registered ownership.

Definitional Cross References:

"Certificated security". Section 8–102(a)(4).
"Effective". Section 8–107.
"Indorsement". Section 8–102(a)(11).
"Instruction". Section 8–102(a)(12).
"Issuer". Section 8–201.
"Security". Section 8–102(a)(15).
"Uncertificated security". Section 8–102(a)(18).

§ 8–405.   Replacement of Lost, Destroyed, or Wrongfully Taken Security Certificate.

(a)   If an owner of a certificated security, whether in registered or bearer form, claims that the certificate has been lost, destroyed, or wrongfully taken, the issuer shall issue a new certificate if the owner:

(1)   so requests before the issuer has notice that the certificate has been acquired by a protected purchaser;

(2)   files with the issuer a sufficient indemnity bond; and

(3)   satisfies other reasonable requirements imposed by the issuer.

(b)   If, after the issue of a new security certificate, a protected purchaser of the original certificate presents it for registration of transfer, the issuer shall register the transfer unless an overissue would result. In that case, the issuer's liability is governed by Section 8–210. In addition to any rights on the indemnity bond, an issuer may recover the new certificate from a person to whom it was issued or any person taking under that person, except a protected purchaser.

Official Comment

1.   This section enables the owner to obtain a replacement of a lost, destroyed or stolen certificate, provided that reasonable requirements are satisfied and a sufficient indemnity bond supplied.

2.   Where an "original" security certificate has reached the hands of a protected purchaser, the registered owner—who was in the best position to prevent the loss, destruction or theft of the security certificate—is now deprived of the new security certificate issued as a replacement. This changes the pre-UCC law under which the original certificate was ineffective after the issue of a replacement except insofar as it might represent an action for damages in the hands of a purchaser for value without notice. *Keller v. Eureka Brick Mach. Mfg. Co.,* 43 Mo.App. 84, 11 L.R.A. 472 (1890). Where both the original and the new certificate have reached protected purchasers the issuer is required to honor both certificates unless an overissue would result and the security is not reasonably available for purchase. See Section 8–210. In the latter case alone, the protected purchaser of the original certificate is relegated to an action for damages. In either case, the issuer itself may recover on the indemnity bond.

Definitional Cross References:

"Bearer form". Section 8–102(a)(2).
"Certificated security". Section 8–102(a)(4).
"Issuer". Section 8–201.
"Notice". Section 1–201(25).*
"Overissue". Section 8–210.
"Protected purchaser". Section 8–303.
"Registered form". Section 8–102(a)(13).
"Security certificate". Section 8–102(a)(16).

§ 8–406.   Obligation to Notify Issuer of Lost, Destroyed, or Wrongfully Taken Security Certificate.

If a security certificate has been lost, apparently destroyed, or wrongfully taken, and the owner fails to notify the issuer of that fact within a reasonable time after the owner has notice of it and the issuer registers a transfer of the security before receiving notification, the owner may not assert against the issuer a claim for registering the transfer under Section 8–404 or a claim to a new security certificate under Section 8–405.

Official Comment

An owner who fails to notify the issuer within a reasonable time after the owner knows or has reason to know of the loss or theft of a security certificate is estopped from asserting the ineffectiveness of a forged or unauthorized indorsement and the wrongfulness of the registration of the transfer. If the lost certificate was indorsed by the

---

*   *Referring to unrevised Article 1 (Appendix A).*

owner, then the registration of the transfer was not wrongful under Section 8–404, unless the owner made an effective demand that the issuer not register transfer under Section 8–403.

Definitional Cross References:

"Issuer". Section 8–201.
"Notify". Section 1–201(25).*
"Security certificate". Section 8–102(a)(16).

§ 8–407. Authenticating Trustee, Transfer Agent, and Registrar.

A person acting as authenticating trustee, transfer agent, registrar, or other agent for an issuer in the registration of a transfer of its securities, in the issue of new security certificates or uncertificated securities, or in the cancellation of surrendered security certificates has the same obligation to the holder or owner of a certificated or uncertificated security with regard to the particular functions performed as the issuer has in regard to those functions.

Official Comment

1. Transfer agents, registrars, and the like are here expressly held liable both to the issuer and to the owner for wrongful refusal to register a transfer as well as for wrongful registration of a transfer in any case within the scope of their respective functions where the issuer would itself be liable. Those cases which have regarded these parties solely as agents of the issuer and have therefore refused to recognize their liability to the owner for mere nonfeasance, i.e., refusal to register a transfer, are rejected. *Hulse v. Consolidated Quicksilver Mining Corp.,* 65 Idaho 768, 154 P.2d 149 (1944); *Nicholson v. Morgan,* 119 Misc. 309, 196 N.Y.Supp. 147 (1922); *Lewis v. Hargadine-McKittrick Dry Goods Co.,* 305 Mo. 396, 274 S.W. 1041 (1924).

2. The practice frequently followed by authenticating trustees of issuing certificates of indebtedness rather than authenticating duplicate certificates where securities have been lost or stolen became obsolete in view of the provisions of Section 8–405, which makes express provision for the issue of substitute securities. It is not a breach of trust or lack of due diligence for trustees to authenticate new securities. Cf. *Switzerland General Ins. Co. v. N.Y.C. & H.R.R. Co.,* 152 App.Div. 70, 136 N.Y.S. 726 (1912).

Definitional Cross References:

"Certificated security". Section 8–102(a)(4).
"Issuer". Section 8–201.
"Security". Section 8–102(a)(15).
"Security certificate". Section 8–102(a)(16).
"Uncertificated security". Section 8–102(a)(18).

PART 5

SECURITY ENTITLEMENTS

§ 8–501. Securities Account; Acquisition of Security Entitlement from Securities Intermediary.

(a) "Securities account" means an account to which a financial asset is or may be credited in accordance with an agreement under which the person maintaining the account undertakes to treat the person for whom the account is maintained as entitled to exercise the rights that comprise the financial asset.

(b) Except as otherwise provided in subsections (d) and (e), a person acquires a security entitlement if a securities intermediary:

(1) indicates by book entry that a financial asset has been credited to the person's securities account;

---

* *Referring to unrevised Article 1 (Appendix A).*

(2)   receives a financial asset from the person or acquires a financial asset for the person and, in either case, accepts it for credit to the person's securities account; or

(3)   becomes obligated under other law, regulation, or rule to credit a financial asset to the person's securities account.

(c)   If a condition of subsection (b) has been met, a person has a security entitlement even though the securities intermediary does not itself hold the financial asset.

(d)   If a securities intermediary holds a financial asset for another person, and the financial asset is registered in the name of, payable to the order of, or specially indorsed to the other person, and has not been indorsed to the securities intermediary or in blank, the other person is treated as holding the financial asset directly rather than as having a security entitlement with respect to the financial asset.

(e)   Issuance of a security is not establishment of a security entitlement.

Official Comment

1.   Part 5 rules apply to security entitlements, and Section 8–501(b) provides that a person has a security entitlement when a financial asset has been credited to a "securities account." Thus, the term "securities account" specifies the type of arrangements between institutions and their customers that are covered by Part 5. A securities account is a consensual arrangement in which the intermediary undertakes to treat the customer as entitled to exercise the rights that comprise the financial asset. The consensual aspect is covered by the requirement that the account be established pursuant to agreement. The term agreement is used in the broad sense defined in Section 1–201(3).* There is no requirement that a formal or written agreement be signed.

As the securities business is presently conducted, several significant relationships clearly fall within the definition of a securities account, including the relationship between a clearing corporation and its participants, a broker and customers who leave securities with the broker, and a bank acting as securities custodian and its custodial customers. Given the enormous variety of arrangements concerning securities that exist today, and the certainty that new arrangements will evolve in the future, it is not possible to specify all of the arrangements to which the term does and does not apply.

Whether an arrangement between a firm and another person concerning a security or other financial asset is a "securities account" under this Article depends on whether the firm has undertaken to treat the other person as entitled to exercise the rights that comprise the security or other financial asset. Section 1–102,* however, states the fundamental principle of interpretation that the Code provisions should be construed and applied to promote their underlying purposes and policies. Thus, the question whether a given arrangement is a securities account should be decided not by dictionary analysis of the words of the definition taken out of context, but by considering whether it promotes the objectives of Article 8 to include the arrangement within the term securities account.

The effect of concluding that an arrangement is a securities account is that the rules of Part 5 apply. Accordingly, the definition of "securities account" must be interpreted in light of the substantive provisions in Part 5, which describe the core features of the type of relationship for which the commercial law rules of Revised Article 8 concerning security entitlements were designed. There are many arrangements between institutions and other persons concerning securities or other financial assets which do not fall within the definition of "securities account" because the institutions have not undertaken to treat the other persons as entitled to exercise the ordinary rights of an entitlement holder specified in the Part 5 rules. For example, the term securities account does not cover the relationship between a bank and its depositors or the relationship between a trustee and the beneficiary of an ordinary trust, because those are not relationships in which the holder of a financial asset has undertaken to treat the other as entitled to exercise the rights that comprise the financial asset in the fashion contemplated by the Part 5 rules.

In short, the primary factor in deciding whether an arrangement is a securities account is whether application of the Part 5 rules is consistent with the expectations of the parties to the relationship. Relationships not governed by Part 5 may be governed by other parts of Article 8 if the relationship gives rise to a new security, or may be governed by other law entirely.

2.   Subsection (b) of this section specifies what circumstances give rise to security entitlements. Paragraph (1) of subsection (b) sets out the most important rule. It turns on the intermediary's conduct, reflecting a basic operating assumption of the indirect holding system that once a securities intermediary has acknowledged that it

---

*   *Referring to unrevised Article 1 (Appendix A).*

is carrying a position in a financial asset for its customer or participant, the intermediary is obligated to treat the customer or participant as entitled to the financial asset. Paragraph (1) does not attempt to specify exactly what accounting, record-keeping, or information transmission steps suffice to indicate that the intermediary has credited the account. That is left to agreement, trade practice, or rule in order to provide the flexibility necessary to accommodate varying or changing accounting and information processing systems. The point of paragraph (1) is that once an intermediary has acknowledged that it is carrying a position for the customer or participant, the customer or participant has a security entitlement. The precise form in which the intermediary manifests that acknowledgment is left to private ordering.

Paragraph (2) of subsection (b) sets out a different operational test, turning not on the intermediary's accounting system but on the facts that accounting systems are supposed to represent. Under paragraph (b)(2) a person has a security entitlement if the intermediary has received and accepted a financial asset for credit to the account of its customer or participant. For example, if a customer of a broker or bank custodian delivers a security certificate in proper form to the broker or bank to be held in the customer's account, the customer acquires a security entitlement. Paragraph (b)(2) also covers circumstances in which the intermediary receives a financial asset from a third person for credit to the account of the customer or participant. Paragraph (b)(2) is not limited to circumstances in which the intermediary receives security certificates or other financial assets in physical form. Paragraph (b)(2) also covers circumstances in which the intermediary acquires a security entitlement with respect to a financial asset which is to be credited to the account of the intermediary's own customer. For example, if a customer transfers her account from Broker A to Broker B, she acquires security entitlements against Broker B once the clearing corporation has credited the positions to Broker B's account. It should be noted, however, that paragraph (b)(2) provides that a person acquires a security entitlement when the intermediary not only receives but also accepts the financial asset for credit to the account. This limitation is included to take account of the fact that there may be circumstances in which an intermediary has received a financial asset but is not willing to undertake the obligations that flow from establishing a security entitlement. For example, a security certificate which is sent to an intermediary may not be in proper form, or may represent a type of financial asset which the intermediary is not willing to carry for others. It should be noted that in all but extremely unusual cases, the circumstances covered by paragraph (2) will also be covered by paragraph (1), because the intermediary will have credited the positions to the customer's account.

Paragraph (3) of subsection (b) sets out a residual test, to avoid any implication that the failure of an intermediary to make the appropriate entries to credit a position to a customer's securities account would prevent the customer from acquiring the rights of an entitlement holder under Part 5. As is the case with the paragraph (2) test, the paragraph (3) test would not be needed for the ordinary cases, since they are covered by paragraph (1).

3.   In a sense, Section 8–501(b) is analogous to the rules set out in the provisions of Sections 8–313(1)(d) and 8–320 of the prior version of Article 8 that specified what acts by a securities intermediary or clearing corporation sufficed as a transfer of securities held in fungible bulk. Unlike the prior version of Article 8, however, this section is not based on the idea that an entitlement holder acquires rights only by virtue of a "transfer" from the securities intermediary to the entitlement holder. In the indirect holding system, the significant fact is that the securities intermediary has undertaken to treat the customer as entitled to the financial asset. It is up to the securities intermediary to take the necessary steps to ensure that it will be able to perform its undertaking. It is, for example, entirely possible that a securities intermediary might make entries in a customer's account reflecting that customer's acquisition of a certain security at a time when the securities intermediary did not itself happen to hold any units of that security. The person from whom the securities intermediary bought the security might have failed to deliver and it might have taken some time to clear up the problem, or there may have been an operational gap in time between the crediting of a customer's account and the receipt of securities from another securities intermediary. The entitlement holder's rights against the securities intermediary do not depend on whether or when the securities intermediary acquired its interests. Subsection (c) is intended to make this point clear. Subsection (c) does not mean that the intermediary is free to create security entitlements without itself holding sufficient financial assets to satisfy its entitlement holders. The duty of a securities intermediary to maintain sufficient assets is governed by Section 8–504 and regulatory law. Subsection (c) is included only to make it clear the question whether a person has acquired a security entitlement does not depend on whether the intermediary has complied with that duty.

4.   Part 5 of Article 8 sets out a carefully designed system of rules for the indirect holding system. Persons who hold securities through brokers or custodians have security entitlements that are governed by Part 5, rather than being treated as the direct holders of securities. Subsection (d) specifies the limited circumstance in which a

customer who leaves a financial asset with a broker or other securities intermediary has a direct interest in the financial asset, rather than a security entitlement.

The customer can be a direct holder only if the security certificate, or other financial asset, is registered in the name of, payable to the order of, or specially indorsed to the customer, and has not been indorsed by the customer to the securities intermediary or in blank. The distinction between those circumstances where the customer can be treated as direct owner and those where the customer has a security entitlement is essentially the same as the distinction drawn under the federal bankruptcy code between customer name securities and customer property. The distinction does not turn on any form of physical identification or segregation. A customer who delivers certificates to a broker with blank indorsements or stock powers is not a direct holder but has a security entitlement, even though the broker holds those certificates in some form of separate safe-keeping arrangement for that particular customer. The customer remains the direct holder only if there is no indorsement or stock power so that further action by the customer is required to place the certificates in a form where they can be transferred by the broker.

The rule of subsection (d) corresponds to the rule set out in Section 8–301(a)(3) specifying when acquisition of possession of a certificate by a securities intermediary counts as "delivery" to the customer.

5.   Subsection (e) is intended to make clear that Part 5 does not apply to an arrangement in which a security is issued representing an interest in underlying assets, as distinguished from arrangements in which the underlying assets are carried in a securities account. A common mechanism by which new financial instruments are devised is that a financial institution that holds some security, financial instrument, or pool thereof, creates interests in that asset or pool which are sold to others. In many such cases, the interests so created will fall within the definition of "security" in Section 8–102(a)(15). If so, then by virtue of subsection (e) of Section 8–501, the relationship between the institution that creates the interests and the persons who hold them is not a security entitlement to which the Part 5 rules apply. Accordingly, an arrangement such as an American depositary receipt facility which creates freely transferable interests in underlying securities will be issuance of a security under Article 8 rather than establishment of a security entitlement to the underlying securities.

The subsection (e) rule can be regarded as an aspect of the definitional rules specifying the meaning of securities account and security entitlement. Among the key components of the definition of security in Section 8–102(a)(15) are the "transferability" and "divisibility" tests. Securities, in the Article 8 sense, are fungible interests or obligations that are intended to be tradable. The concept of security entitlement under Part 5 is quite different. A security entitlement is the package of rights that a person has against the person's own intermediary with respect to the positions carried in the person's securities account. That package of rights is not, as such, something that is traded. When a customer sells a security that she had held through a securities account, her security entitlement is terminated; when she buys a security that she will hold through her securities account, she acquires a security entitlement. In most cases, settlement of a securities trade will involve termination of one person's security entitlement and acquisition of a security entitlement by another person. That transaction, however, is not a "transfer" of the same entitlement from one person to another. That is not to say that an entitlement holder cannot transfer an interest in her security entitlement as such; granting a security interest in a security entitlement is such a transfer. On the other hand, the nature of a security entitlement is that the intermediary is undertaking duties only to the person identified as the entitlement holder.

Definitional Cross References:

"Financial asset". Section 8–102(a)(9).

"Indorsement". Section 8–102(a)(11).

"Securities intermediary". Section 8–102(a)(14).

"Security". Section 8–102(a)(15).

"Security entitlement". Section 8–102(a)(17).

§ 8–502.   Assertion of Adverse Claim Against Entitlement Holder.

An action based on an adverse claim to a financial asset, whether framed in conversion, replevin, constructive trust, equitable lien, or other theory, may not be asserted against a person who acquires a security entitlement under Section 8–501 for value and without notice of the adverse claim.

Official Comment

1.   The section provides investors in the indirect holding system with protection against adverse claims by specifying that no adverse claim can be asserted against a person who acquires a security entitlement under Section 8–501 for value and without notice of the adverse claim. It plays a role in the indirect holding system analogous to the rule of the direct holding system that protected purchasers take free from adverse claims (Section 8–303).

This section does not use the locution "takes free from adverse claims" because that could be confusing as applied to the indirect holding system. The nature of indirect holding system is that an entitlement holder has an interest in common with others who hold positions in the same financial asset through the same intermediary. Thus, a particular entitlement holder's interest in the financial assets held by its intermediary is necessarily "subject to" the interests of others. See Section 8–503. The rule stated in this section might have been expressed by saying that a person who acquires a security entitlement under Section 8–501 for value and without notice of adverse claims takes "that security entitlement" free from adverse claims. That formulation has not been used, however, for fear that it would be misinterpreted as suggesting that the person acquires a right to the underlying financial assets that could not be affected by the competing rights of others claiming through common or higher tier intermediaries. A security entitlement is a complex bundle of rights. This section does not deal with the question of what rights are in the bundle. Rather, this section provides that once a person has acquired the bundle, someone else cannot take it away on the basis of assertion that the transaction in which the security entitlement was created involved a violation of the claimant's rights.

2.   Because securities trades are typically settled on a net basis by book-entry movements, it would ordinarily be impossible for anyone to trace the path of any particular security, no matter how the interest of parties who hold through intermediaries is described. Suppose, for example, that S has a 1000 share position in XYZ common stock through an account with a broker, Able & Co. S's identical twin impersonates S and directs Able to sell the securities. That same day, B places an order with Baker & Co., to buy 1000 shares of XYZ common stock. Later, S discovers the wrongful act and seeks to recover "her shares." Even if S can show that, at the stage of the trade, her sell order was matched with B's buy order, that would not suffice to show that "her shares" went to B. Settlement between Able and Baker occurs on a net basis for all trades in XYZ that day; indeed Able's net position may have been such that it received rather than delivered shares in XYZ through the settlement system.

In the unlikely event that this was the only trade in XYZ common stock executed in the market that day, one could follow the shares from S's account to B's account. The plaintiff in an action in conversion or similar legal action to enforce a property interest must show that the defendant has an item of property that belongs to the plaintiff. In this example, B's security entitlement is not the same item of property that formerly was held by S, it is a new package of rights that B acquired against Baker under Section 8–501. Principles of equitable remedies might, however, provide S with a basis for contending that if the position B received was the traceable product of the wrongful taking of S's property by S's twin, a constructive trust should be imposed on B's property in favor of S. See G. Palmer, The Law of Restitution § 2.14. Section 8–502 ensures that no such claims can be asserted against a person, such as B in this example, who acquires a security entitlement under Section 8–501 for value and without notice, regardless of what theory of law or equity is used to describe the basis of the assertion of the adverse claim.

In the above example, S would ordinarily have no reason to pursue B unless Able is insolvent and S's claim will not be satisfied in the insolvency proceedings. Because S did not give an entitlement order for the disposition of her security entitlement, Able must recredit her account for the 1000 shares of XYZ common stock. See Section 8–507(b).

3.   The following examples illustrate the operation of Section 8–502.

Example 1. Thief steals bearer bonds from Owner. Thief delivers the bonds to Broker for credit to Thief's securities account, thereby acquiring a security entitlement under Section 8–501(b). Under other law, Owner may have a claim to have a constructive trust imposed on the security entitlement as the traceable product of the bonds that Thief misappropriated. Because Thief was himself the wrongdoer, Thief obviously had notice of Owner's adverse claim. Accordingly, Section 8–502 does not preclude Owner from asserting an adverse claim against Thief.

Example 2. Thief steals bearer bonds from Owner. Thief owes a personal debt to Creditor. Creditor has a securities account with Broker. Thief agrees to transfer the bonds to Creditor as security for or in satisfaction of his debt to Creditor. Thief does so by sending the bonds to Broker for credit to Creditor's securities account. Creditor thereby acquires a security entitlement under Section 8–501(b). Under other law, Owner may have a claim to have a constructive trust imposed on the security entitlement as the traceable product of the bonds that Thief misappropriated. Creditor acquired the security entitlement for value, since Creditor acquired it as security for or in satisfaction of Thief's debt to Creditor. See Section 1–201(44).* If Creditor did not have notice of Owner's claim, Section 8–502 precludes any action by Owner against Creditor, whether framed in constructive trust or other theory. Section 8–105 specifies what counts as notice of an adverse claim.

Example 3. Father, as trustee for Son, holds XYZ Co. shares in a securities account with Able & Co. In violation of his fiduciary duties, Father sells the XYZ Co. shares and uses the proceeds for personal purposes. Father dies, and his estate is insolvent. Assume—implausibly—that Son is able to trace the XYZ Co. shares and show that the "same shares" ended up in Buyer's securities account with Baker & Co. Section 8–502 precludes any action by Son against Buyer, whether framed in constructive trust or other theory, provided that Buyer acquired the security entitlement for value and without notice of adverse claims.

Example 4. Debtor holds XYZ Co. shares in a securities account with Able & Co. As collateral for a loan from Bank, Debtor grants Bank a security interest in the security entitlement to the XYZ Co. shares. Bank perfects by a method which leaves Debtor with the ability to dispose of the shares. See Section 9–312. In violation of the security agreement, Debtor sells the XYZ Co. shares and absconds with the proceeds. Assume—implausibly—that Bank is able to trace the XYZ Co. shares and show that the "same shares" ended up in Buyer's securities account with Baker & Co. Section 8–502 precludes any action by Bank against Buyer, whether framed in constructive trust or other theory, provided that Buyer acquired the security entitlement for value and without notice of adverse claims.

Example 5. Debtor owns controlling interests in various public companies, including Acme and Ajax. Acme owns 60% of the stock of another public company, Beta. Debtor causes the Beta stock to be pledged to Lending Bank as collateral for Ajax's debt. Acme holds the Beta stock through an account with a securities custodian, C Bank, which in turn holds through Clearing Corporation. Lending Bank is also a Clearing Corporation participant. The pledge of the Beta stock is implemented by Acme instructing C Bank to instruct Clearing Corporation to debit C Bank's account and credit Lending Bank's account. Acme and Ajax both become insolvent. The Beta stock is still valuable. Acme's liquidator asserts that the pledge of the Beta stock for Ajax's debt was wrongful as against Acme and seeks to recover the Beta stock from Lending Bank. Because the pledge was implemented by an outright transfer into Lending Bank's account at Clearing Corporation, Lending Bank acquired a security entitlement to the Beta stock under Section 8–501. Lending Bank acquired the security entitlement for value, since it acquired it as security for a debt. See Section 1–201(44).* If Lending Bank did not have notice of Acme's claim, Section 8–502 will preclude any action by Acme against Lending Bank, whether framed in constructive trust or other theory.

Example 6. Debtor grants Alpha Co. a security interest in a security entitlement that includes 1000 shares of XYZ Co. stock that Debtor holds through an account with Able & Co. Alpha also has an account with Able. Debtor instructs Able to transfer the shares to Alpha, and Able does so by crediting the shares to Alpha's account. Alpha has control of the 1000 shares under Section 8–106(d). (The facts to this point are identical to those in Section 8–106, Comment 4, Example 1, except that Alpha Co. was Alpha Bank.) Alpha next grants Beta Co. a security interest in the 1000 shares included in Alpha's security entitlement. See Section 9–207(c)(3). Alpha instructs Able to transfer the shares to Gamma Co., Beta's custodian. Able does so, and Gamma credits the 1000 shares to Beta's account. Beta now has control under Section 8–106(d). By virtue of Debtor's explicit permission or by virtue of the permission inherent in Debtor's creation of a security interest in favor of Alpha and Alpha's resulting power to grant a security interest under Section 9–207, Debtor has no adverse claim to assert against Beta, assuming implausibly that Debtor could "trace" an interest to the Gamma account. Moreover, even if Debtor did hold an adverse claim, if Beta did not have notice of Debtor's claim, Section 8–502 will preclude any action by Debtor against Beta, whether framed in constructive trust or other theory.

4.　　Although this section protects entitlement holders against adverse claims, it does not protect them against the risk that their securities intermediary will not itself have sufficient financial assets to satisfy the claims of all of its entitlement holders. Suppose that Customer A holds 1000 shares of XYZ Co. stock in an account with her broker, Able & Co. Able in turn holds 1000 shares of XYZ Co. through its account with Clearing Corporation, but has no other positions in

XYZ Co. shares, either for other customers or for its own proprietary account. Customer B places an order with Able for the purchase of 1000 shares of XYZ Co. stock, and pays the purchase price. Able credits B's account

---

　*　*Referring to unrevised Article 1 (Appendix A).*

with a 1000 share position in XYZ Co. stock, but Able does not itself buy any additional XYZ Co. shares. Able fails, having only 1000 shares to satisfy the claims of A and B. Unless other insolvency law establishes a different distributional rule, A and B would share the 1000 shares held by Able pro rata, without regard to the time that their respective entitlements were established. See Section 8–503(b). Section 8–502 protects entitlement holders, such as A and B, against adverse claimants. In this case, however, the problem that A and B face is not that someone is trying to take away their entitlements, but that the entitlements are not worth what they thought. The only role that Section 8–502 plays in this case is to preclude any assertion that A has some form of claim against B by virtue of the fact that Able's establishment of an entitlement in favor of B diluted A's rights to the limited assets held by Able.

Definitional Cross References:

"Adverse claim". Section 8–102(a)(1).
"Financial asset". Section 8–102(a)(9).
"Notice of adverse claim". Section 8–105.
"Security entitlement". Section 8–102(a)(17).
"Value". Sections 1–201(44)* & 8–116.

As amended in 1999.

§ 8–503. Property Interest of Entitlement Holder in Financial Asset Held By Securities Intermediary.

(a)   To the extent necessary for a securities intermediary to satisfy all security entitlements with respect to a particular financial asset, all interests in that financial asset held by the securities intermediary are held by the securities intermediary for the entitlement holders, are not property of the securities intermediary, and are not subject to claims of creditors of the securities intermediary, except as otherwise provided in Section 8–511.

(b)   An entitlement holder's property interest with respect to a particular financial asset under subsection (a) is a pro rata property interest in all interests in that financial asset held by the securities intermediary, without regard to the time the entitlement holder acquired the security entitlement or the time the securities intermediary acquired the interest in that financial asset.

(c)   An entitlement holder's property interest with respect to a particular financial asset under subsection (a) may be enforced against the securities intermediary only by exercise of the entitlement holder's rights under Sections 8–505 through 8–508.

(d)   An entitlement holder's property interest with respect to a particular financial asset under subsection (a) may be enforced against a purchaser of the financial asset or interest therein only if:

(1)   insolvency proceedings have been initiated by or against the securities intermediary;

(2)   the securities intermediary does not have sufficient interests in the financial asset to satisfy the security entitlements of all of its entitlement holders to that financial asset;

(3)   the securities intermediary violated its obligations under Section 8–504 by transferring the financial asset or interest therein to the purchaser; and

(4)   the purchaser is not protected under subsection (e).

The trustee or other liquidator, acting on behalf of all entitlement holders having security entitlements with respect to a particular financial asset, may recover the financial asset, or interest therein, from the purchaser. If the trustee or other liquidator elects not to pursue that right, an entitlement holder whose security entitlement remains unsatisfied has the right to recover its interest in the financial asset from the purchaser.

(e)   An action based on the entitlement holder's property interest with respect to a particular financial asset under subsection (a), whether framed in conversion, replevin, constructive trust, equitable lien, or other theory, may not be asserted against any purchaser of a financial asset or interest therein who gives

---

*   *Referring to unrevised Article 1 (Appendix A).*

value, obtains control, and does not act in collusion with the securities intermediary in violating the securities intermediary's obligations under Section 8–504.

Official Comment

1.   This section specifies the sense in which a security entitlement is an interest in the property held by the securities intermediary. It expresses the ordinary understanding that securities that a firm holds for its customers are not general assets of the firm subject to the claims of creditors. Since securities intermediaries generally do not segregate securities in such fashion that one could identify particular securities as the ones held for customers, it would not be realistic for this section to state that "customers' securities" are not subject to creditors' claims. Rather subsection (a) provides that to the extent necessary to satisfy all customer claims, all units of that security held by the firm are held for the entitlement holders, are not property of the securities intermediary, and are not subject to creditors' claims, except as otherwise provided in Section 8–511.

An entitlement holder's property interest under this section is an interest with respect to a specific issue of securities or financial assets. For example, customers of a firm who have positions in XYZ common stock have security entitlements with respect to the XYZ common stock held by the intermediary, while other customers who have positions in ABC common stock have security entitlements with respect to the ABC common stock held by the intermediary.

Subsection (b) makes clear that the property interest described in subsection (a) is an interest held in common by all entitlement holders who have entitlements to a particular security or other financial asset. Temporal factors are irrelevant. One entitlement holder cannot claim that its rights to the assets held by the intermediary are superior to the rights of another entitlement holder by virtue of having acquired those rights before, or after, the other entitlement holder. Nor does it matter whether the intermediary had sufficient assets to satisfy all entitlement holders' claims at one point, but no longer does. Rather, all entitlement holders have a pro rata interest in whatever positions in that financial asset the intermediary holds.

Although this section describes the property interest of entitlement holders in the assets held by the intermediary, it does not necessarily determine how property held by a failed intermediary will be distributed in insolvency proceedings. If the intermediary fails and its affairs are being administered in an insolvency proceeding, the applicable insolvency law governs how the various parties having claims against the firm are treated. For example, the distributional rules for stockbroker liquidation proceedings under the Bankruptcy Code and Securities Investor Protection Act ("SIPA") provide that all customer property is distributed pro rata among all customers in proportion to the dollar value of their total positions, rather than dividing the property on an issue by issue basis. For intermediaries that are not subject to the Bankruptcy Code and SIPA, other insolvency law would determine what distributional rule is applied.

2.   Although this section recognizes that the entitlement holders of a securities intermediary have a property interest in the financial assets held by the intermediary, the incidents of this property interest are established by the rules of Article 8, not by common law property concepts. The traditional Article 8 rules on certificated securities were based on the idea that a paper certificate could be regarded as a nearly complete reification of the underlying right. The rules on transfer and the consequences of wrongful transfer could then be written using the same basic concepts as the rules for physical chattels. A person's claim of ownership of a certificated security is a right to a specific identifiable physical object, and that right can be asserted against any person who ends up in possession of that physical certificate, unless cut off by the rules protecting purchasers for value without notice. Those concepts do not work for the indirect holding system. A security entitlement is not a claim to a specific identifiable thing; it is a package of rights and interests that a person has against the person's securities intermediary and the property held by the intermediary. The idea that discrete objects might be traced through the hands of different persons has no place in the Revised Article 8 rules for the indirect holding system. The fundamental principles of the indirect holding system rules are that an entitlement holder's own intermediary has the obligation to see to it that the entitlement holder receives all of the economic and corporate rights that comprise the financial asset, and that the entitlement holder can look only to that intermediary for performance of the obligations. The entitlement holder cannot assert rights directly against other persons, such as other intermediaries through whom the intermediary holds the positions, or third parties to whom the intermediary may have wrongfully transferred interests, except in extremely unusual circumstances where the third party was itself a participant in the wrongdoing. Subsections (c) through (e) reflect these fundamental principles.

Subsection (c) provides that an entitlement holder's property interest can be enforced against the intermediary only by exercise of the entitlement holder's rights under Sections 8–505 through 8–508. These are the provisions that set out the duty of an intermediary to see to it that the entitlement holder receives all of the

680

economic and corporate rights that comprise the security. If the intermediary is in insolvency proceedings and can no longer perform in accordance with the ordinary Part 5 rules, the applicable insolvency law will determine how the intermediary's assets are to be distributed.

Subsections (d) and (e) specify the limited circumstances in which an entitlement holder's property interest can be asserted against a third person to whom the intermediary transferred a financial asset that was subject to the entitlement holder's claim when held by the intermediary. Subsection (d) provides that the property interest of entitlement holders cannot be asserted against any transferee except in the circumstances therein specified. So long as the intermediary is solvent, the entitlement holders must look to the intermediary to satisfy their claims. If the intermediary does not hold financial assets corresponding to the entitlement holders' claims, the intermediary has the duty to acquire them. See Section 8–504. Thus, paragraphs (1), (2), and (3) of subsection (d) specify that the only occasion in which the entitlement holders can pursue transferees is when the intermediary is unable to perform its obligation, and the transfer to the transferee was a violation of those obligations. Even in that case, a transferee who gave value and obtained control is protected by virtue of the rule in subsection (e), unless the transferee acted in collusion with the intermediary.

Subsections (d) and (e) have the effect of protecting transferees from an intermediary against adverse claims arising out of assertions by the intermediary's entitlement holders that the intermediary acted wrongfully in transferring the financial assets. These rules, however, operate in a slightly different fashion than traditional adverse claim cut-off rules. Rather than specifying that a certain class of transferee takes free from all claims, subsections (d) and (e) specify the circumstances in which this particular form of claim can be asserted against a transferee. Revised Article 8 also contains general adverse claim cut-off rules for the indirect holding system. See Sections 8–502 and 8–510. The rule of subsections (d) and (e) takes precedence over the general cut-off rules of those sections, because Section 8–503 itself defines and sets limits on the assertion of the property interest of entitlement holders. Thus, the question whether entitlement holders' property interest can be asserted as an adverse claim against a transferee from the intermediary is governed by the collusion test of Section 8–503(e), rather than by the "without notice" test of Sections 8–502 and 8–510.

3. The limitations that subsections (c) through (e) place on the ability of customers of a failed intermediary to recover securities or other financial assets from transferees are consistent with the fundamental policies of investor protection that underlie this Article and other bodies of law governing the securities business. The commercial law rules for the securities holding and transfer system must be assessed from the forward-looking perspective of their impact on the vast number of transactions in which no wrongful conduct occurred or will occur, rather than from the *post hoc* perspective of what rule might be most advantageous to a particular class of persons in litigation that might arise out of the occasional case in which someone has acted wrongfully. Although one can devise hypothetical scenarios where particular customers might find it advantageous to be able to assert rights against someone other than the customers' own intermediary, commercial law rules that permitted customers to do so would impair rather than promote the interest of investors and the safe and efficient operation of the clearance and settlement system. Suppose, for example, that Intermediary A transfers securities to B, that Intermediary A acted wrongfully as against its customers in so doing, and that after the transaction Intermediary A did not have sufficient securities to satisfy its obligations to its entitlement holders. Viewed solely from the standpoint of the customers of Intermediary A, it would seem that permitting the property to be recovered from B, would be good for investors. That, however, is not the case. B may itself be an intermediary with its own customers, or may be some other institution through which individuals invest, such as a pension fund or investment company. There is no reason to think that rules permitting customers of an intermediary to trace and recover securities that their intermediary wrongfully transferred work to the advantage of investors in general. To the contrary, application of such rules would often merely shift losses from one set of investors to another. The uncertainties that would result from rules permitting such recoveries would work to the disadvantage of all participants in the securities markets.

The use of the collusion test in Section 8–503(e) furthers the interests of investors generally in the sound and efficient operation of the securities holding and settlement system. The effect of the choice of this standard is that customers of a failed intermediary must show that the transferee from whom they seek to recover was affirmatively engaged in wrongful conduct, rather than casting on the transferee any burden of showing that the transferee had no awareness of wrongful conduct by the failed intermediary. The rule of Section 8–503(e) is based on the long-standing policy that it is undesirable to impose upon purchasers of securities any duty to investigate whether their sellers may be acting wrongfully.

Rather than imposing duties to investigate, the general policy of the commercial law of the securities holding and transfer system has been to eliminate legal rules that might induce participants to conduct investigations of the authority of persons transferring securities on behalf of others for fear that they might be held liable for participating in a wrongful transfer. The rules in Part 4 of Article 8 concerning transfers by fiduciaries provide a good example. Under *Lowry v. Commercial & Farmers' Bank,* 15 F.Cas. 1040 (C.C.D.Md.1848) (No. 8581), an issuer could be held liable for wrongful transfer if it registered transfer of securities by a fiduciary under circumstances where it had any reason to believe that the fiduciary may have been acting improperly. In one sense that seems to be advantageous for beneficiaries who might be harmed by wrongful conduct by fiduciaries. The consequence of the *Lowry* rule, however, was that in order to protect against risk of such liability, issuers developed the practice of requiring extensive documentation for fiduciary stock transfers, making such transfers cumbersome and time consuming. Accordingly, the rules in Part 4 of Article 8, and in the prior fiduciary transfer statutes, were designed to discourage transfer agents from conducting investigations into the rightfulness of transfers by fiduciaries.

The rules of Revised Article 8 implement for the indirect holding system the same policies that the rules on protected purchasers and registration of transfer adopt for the direct holding system. A securities intermediary is, by definition, a person who is holding securities on behalf of other persons. There is nothing unusual or suspicious about a transaction in which a securities intermediary sells securities that it was holding for its customers. That is exactly what securities intermediaries are in business to do. The interests of customers of securities intermediaries would not be served by a rule that required counterparties to transfers from securities intermediaries to investigate whether the intermediary was acting wrongfully against its customers. Quite the contrary, such a rule would impair the ability of securities intermediaries to perform the function that customers want.

The rules of Section 8–503(c) through (e) apply to transferees generally, including pledgees. The reasons for treating pledgees in the same fashion as other transferees are discussed in the Comments to Section 8–511. The statement in subsection (a) that an intermediary holds financial assets for customers and not as its own property does not, of course, mean that the intermediary lacks power to transfer the financial assets to others. For example, although Article 9 provides that for a security interest to attach the debtor must either have "rights" in the collateral or the power to transfer "rights" in the collateral to a secured party, see Section 9–203, the fact that an intermediary is holding a financial asset in a form that permits ready transfer means that it has such rights, even if the intermediary is acting wrongfully against its entitlement holders in granting the security interest. The question whether the secured party takes subject to the entitlement holder's claim in such a case is governed by Section 8–511, which is an application to secured transactions of the general principles expressed in subsections (d) and (e) of this section.

Definitional Cross References:

> "Control". Section 8–106.
>
> "Entitlement holder". Section 8–102(a)(7).
>
> "Financial asset". Section 8–102(a)(9).
>
> "Insolvency proceedings". Section 1–201(22).*
>
> "Purchaser". Sections 1–201(33)* & 8–116.
>
> "Securities intermediary". Section 8–102(a)(14).
>
> "Security entitlement". Section 8–102(a)(17).
>
> "Value". Sections 1–201(44)* & 8–116.

§ 8–504.   Duty of Securities Intermediary to Maintain Financial Asset.

(a)   A securities intermediary shall promptly obtain and thereafter maintain a financial asset in a quantity corresponding to the aggregate of all security entitlements it has established in favor of its entitlement holders with respect to that financial asset. The securities intermediary may maintain those financial assets directly or through one or more other securities intermediaries.

(b)   Except to the extent otherwise agreed by its entitlement holder, a securities intermediary may not grant any security interests in a financial asset it is obligated to maintain pursuant to subsection (a).

(c)   A securities intermediary satisfies the duty in subsection (a) if:

---

*   *Referring to unrevised Article 1 (Appendix A).*

(1) the securities intermediary acts with respect to the duty as agreed upon by the entitlement holder and the securities intermediary; or

(2) in the absence of agreement, the securities intermediary exercises due care in accordance with reasonable commercial standards to obtain and maintain the financial asset.

(d) This section does not apply to a clearing corporation that is itself the obligor of an option or similar obligation to which its entitlement holders have security entitlements.

Official Comment

1. This section expresses one of the core elements of the relationships for which the Part 5 rules were designed, to wit, that a securities intermediary undertakes to hold financial assets corresponding to the security entitlements of its entitlement holders. The locution "shall promptly obtain and shall thereafter maintain" is taken from the corresponding regulation under federal securities law, 17 C.F.R. § 240.15c3–3. This section recognizes the reality that as the securities business is conducted today, it is not possible to identify particular securities as belonging to customers as distinguished from other particular securities that are the firm's own property. Securities firms typically keep all securities in fungible form, and may maintain their inventory of a particular security in various locations and forms, including physical securities held in vaults or in transit to transfer agents, and book entry positions at one or more clearing corporations. Accordingly, this section states that a securities intermediary shall maintain a quantity of financial assets corresponding to the aggregate of all security entitlements it has established. The last sentence of subsection (a) provides explicitly that the securities intermediary may hold directly or indirectly. That point is implicit in the use of the term "financial asset," inasmuch as Section 8–102(a)(9) provides that the term "financial asset" may refer either to the underlying asset or the means by which it is held, including both security certificates and security entitlements.

2. Subsection (b) states explicitly a point that is implicit in the notion that a securities intermediary must maintain financial assets corresponding to the security entitlements of its entitlement holders, to wit, that it is wrongful for a securities intermediary to grant security interests in positions that it needs to satisfy customers' claims, except as authorized by the customers. This statement does not determine the rights of a secured party to whom a securities intermediary wrongfully grants a security interest; that issue is governed by Sections 8–503 and 8–511.

Margin accounts are common examples of arrangements in which an entitlement holder authorizes the securities intermediary to grant security interests in the positions held for the entitlement holder. Securities firms commonly obtain the funds needed to provide margin loans to their customers by "rehypothecating" the customers' securities. In order to facilitate rehypothecation, agreements between margin customers and their brokers commonly authorize the broker to commingle securities of all margin customers for rehypothecation to the lender who provides the financing. Brokers commonly rehypothecate customer securities having a value somewhat greater than the amount of the loan made to the customer, since the lenders who provide the necessary financing to the broker need some cushion of protection against the risk of decline in the value of the rehypothecated securities. The extent and manner in which a firm may rehypothecate customers' securities are determined by the agreement between the intermediary and the entitlement holder and by applicable regulatory law. Current regulations under the federal securities laws require that brokers obtain the explicit consent of customers before pledging customer securities or commingling different customers' securities for pledge. Federal regulations also limit the extent to which a broker may rehypothecate customer securities to 110% of the aggregate amount of the borrowings of all customers.

3. The statement in this section that an intermediary must obtain and maintain financial assets corresponding to the aggregate of all security entitlements it has established is intended only to capture the general point that one of the key elements that distinguishes securities accounts from other relationships, such as deposit accounts, is that the intermediary undertakes to maintain a direct correspondence between the positions it holds and the claims of its customers. This section is not intended as a detailed specification of precisely how the intermediary is to perform this duty, nor whether there may be special circumstances in which an intermediary's general duty is excused. Accordingly, the general statement of the duties of a securities intermediary in this and the following sections is supplemented by two other provisions. First, each of Sections 8–504 through 8–508 contains an "agreement/due care" provision. Second, Section 8–509 sets out general qualifications on the duties stated in these sections, including the important point that compliance with corresponding regulatory provisions constitutes compliance with the Article 8 duties.

4.   The "agreement/due care" provision in subsection (c) of this section is necessary to provide sufficient flexibility to accommodate the general duty stated in subsection (a) to the wide variety of circumstances that may be encountered in the modern securities holding system. For the most common forms of publicly traded securities, the modern depository-based indirect holding system has made the likelihood of an actual loss of securities remote, though correctable errors in accounting or temporary interruptions of data processing facilities may occur. Indeed, one of the reasons for the evolution of book-entry systems is to eliminate the risk of loss or destruction of physical certificates. There are, however, some forms of securities and other financial assets which must still be held in physical certificated form, with the attendant risk of loss or destruction. Risk of loss or delay may be a more significant consideration in connection with foreign securities. An American securities intermediary may well be willing to hold a foreign security in a securities account for its customer, but the intermediary may have relatively little choice of or control over foreign intermediaries through which the security must in turn be held. Accordingly, it is common for American securities intermediaries to disclaim responsibility for custodial risk of holding through foreign intermediaries.

Subsection (c)(1) provides that a securities intermediary satisfies the duty stated in subsection (a) if the intermediary acts with respect to that duty in accordance with the agreement between the intermediary and the entitlement holder. Subsection (c)(2) provides that if there is no agreement on the matter, the intermediary satisfies the subsection (a) duty if the intermediary exercises due care in accordance with reasonable commercial standards to obtain and maintain the financial asset in question. This formulation does not state that the intermediary has a universally applicable statutory duty of due care. Section 1–102(3)* provides that statutory duties of due care cannot be disclaimed by agreement, but the "agreement/due care" formula contemplates that there may be particular circumstances where the parties do not wish to create a specific duty of due care, for example, with respect to foreign securities. Under subsection (c)(1), compliance with the agreement constitutes satisfaction of the subsection (a) duty, whether or not the agreement provides that the intermediary will exercise due care.

In each of the sections where the "agreement/due care" formula is used, it provides that entering into an agreement and performing in accordance with that agreement is a method by which the securities intermediary may satisfy the statutory duty stated in that section. Accordingly, the general obligation of good faith performance of statutory and contract duties, see Sections 1–203* and 8–102(a)(10), would apply to such an agreement. It would not be consistent with the obligation of good faith performance for an agreement to purport to establish the usual sort of arrangement between an intermediary and entitlement holder, yet disclaim altogether one of the basic elements that define that relationship. For example, an agreement stating that an intermediary assumes no responsibilities whatsoever for the safekeeping any of the entitlement holder's securities positions would not be consistent with good faith performance of the intermediary's duty to obtain and maintain financial assets corresponding to the entitlement holder's security entitlements.

To the extent that no agreement under subsection (c)(1) has specified the details of the intermediary's performance of the subsection (a) duty, subsection (c)(2) provides that the intermediary satisfies that duty if it exercises due care in accordance with reasonable commercial standards. The duty of care includes both care in the intermediary's own operations and care in the selection of other intermediaries through whom the intermediary holds the assets in question. The statement of the obligation of due care is meant to incorporate the principles of the common law under which the specific actions or precautions necessary to meet the obligation of care are determined by such factors as the nature and value of the property, the customs and practices of the business, and the like.

5.   This section necessarily states the duty of a securities intermediary to obtain and maintain financial assets only at the very general and abstract level. For the most part, these matters are specified in great detail by regulatory law. Broker-dealers registered under the federal securities laws are subject to detailed regulation concerning the safeguarding of customer securities. See 17 C.F.R. § 240.15c3–3. Section 8–509(a) provides explicitly that if a securities intermediary complies with such regulatory law, that constitutes compliance with Section 8–503. In certain circumstances, these rules permit a firm to be in a position where it temporarily lacks a sufficient quantity of financial assets to satisfy all customer claims. For example, if another firm has failed to make a delivery to the firm in settlement of a trade, the firm is permitted a certain period of time to clear up the problem before it is obligated to obtain the necessary securities from some other source.

6.   Subsection (d) is intended to recognize that there are some circumstances, where the duty to maintain a sufficient quantity of financial assets does not apply because the intermediary is not holding anything on behalf

---

*   *Referring to unrevised Article 1 (Appendix A).*

684

of others. For example, the Options Clearing Corporation is treated as a "securities intermediary" under this Article, although it does not itself hold options on behalf of its participants. Rather, it becomes the issuer of the options, by virtue of guaranteeing the obligations of participants in the clearing corporation who have written or purchased the options cleared through it. See Section 8–103(e). Accordingly, the general duty of an intermediary under subsection (a) does not apply, nor would other provisions of Part 5 that depend upon the existence of a requirement that the securities intermediary hold financial assets, such as Sections 8–503 and 8–508.

Definitional Cross References:

"Agreement". Section 1–201(3).*
"Clearing corporation". Section 8–102(a)(5).
"Entitlement holder". Section 8–102(a)(7).
"Financial asset". Section 8–102(a)(9).
"Securities intermediary". Section 8–102(a)(14).
"Security entitlement". Section 8–102(a)(17).

§ 8–505. Duty of Securities Intermediary with Respect to Payments and Distributions.

(a) A securities intermediary shall take action to obtain a payment or distribution made by the issuer of a financial asset. A securities intermediary satisfies the duty if:

(1) the securities intermediary acts with respect to the duty as agreed upon by the entitlement holder and the securities intermediary; or

(2) in the absence of agreement, the securities intermediary exercises due care in accordance with reasonable commercial standards to attempt to obtain the payment or distribution.

(b) A securities intermediary is obligated to its entitlement holder for a payment or distribution made by the issuer of a financial asset if the payment or distribution is received by the securities intermediary.

Official Comment

1. One of the core elements of the securities account relationships for which the Part 5 rules were designed is that the securities intermediary passes through to the entitlement holders the economic benefit of ownership of the financial asset, such as payments and distributions made by the issuer. Subsection (a) expresses the ordinary understanding that a securities intermediary will take appropriate action to see to it that any payments or distributions made by the issuer are received. One of the main reasons that investors make use of securities intermediaries is to obtain the services of a professional in performing the record-keeping and other functions necessary to ensure that payments and other distributions are received.

2. Subsection (a) incorporates the same "agreement/due care" formula as the other provisions of Part 5 dealing with the duties of a securities intermediary. See Comment 4 to Section 8–504. This formulation permits the parties to specify by agreement what action, if any, the intermediary is to take with respect to the duty to obtain payments and distributions. In the absence of specification by agreement, the intermediary satisfies the duty if the intermediary exercises due care in accordance with reasonable commercial standards. The provisions of Section 8–509 also apply to the Section 8–505 duty, so that compliance with applicable regulatory requirements constitutes compliance with the Section 8–505 duty.

3. Subsection (b) provides that a securities intermediary is obligated to its entitlement holder for those payments or distributions made by the issuer that are in fact received by the intermediary. It does not deal with the details of the time and manner of payment. Moreover, as with any other monetary obligation, the obligation to pay may be subject to other rights of the obligor, by way of set-off counterclaim or the like. Section 8–509(c) makes this point explicit.

Definitional Cross References:

"Agreement". Section 1–201(3).*
"Entitlement holder". Section 8–102(a)(7).
"Financial asset". Section 8–102(a)(9).
"Securities intermediary". Section 8–102(a)(14).

---

*   *Referring to unrevised Article 1 (Appendix A).*

"Security entitlement". Section 8–102(a)(17).

§ 8–506. Duty of Securities Intermediary to Exercise Rights as Directed by Entitlement Holder.

A securities intermediary shall exercise rights with respect to a financial asset if directed to do so by an entitlement holder. A securities intermediary satisfies the duty if:

(1) the securities intermediary acts with respect to the duty as agreed upon by the entitlement holder and the securities intermediary; or

(2) in the absence of agreement, the securities intermediary either places the entitlement holder in a position to exercise the rights directly or exercises due care in accordance with reasonable commercial standards to follow the direction of the entitlement holder.

Official Comment

1. Another of the core elements of the securities account relationships for which the Part 5 rules were designed is that although the intermediary may, by virtue of the structure of the indirect holding system, be the party who has the power to exercise the corporate and other rights that come from holding the security, the intermediary exercises these powers as representative of the entitlement holder rather than at its own discretion. This characteristic is one of the things that distinguishes a securities account from other arrangements where one person holds securities "on behalf of" another, such as the relationship between a mutual fund and its shareholders or a trustee and its beneficiary.

2. The fact that the intermediary exercises the rights of security holding as representative of the entitlement holder does not, of course, preclude the entitlement holder from conferring discretionary authority upon the intermediary. Arrangements are not uncommon in which investors do not wish to have their intermediaries forward proxy materials or other information. Thus, this section provides that the intermediary shall exercise corporate and other rights "if directed to do so" by the entitlement holder. Moreover, as with the other Part 5 duties, the "agreement/due care" formulation is used in stating how the intermediary is to perform this duty. This section also provides that the intermediary satisfies the duty if it places the entitlement holder in a position to exercise the rights directly. This is to take account of the fact that some of the rights attendant upon ownership of the security, such as rights to bring derivative and other litigation, are far removed from the matters that intermediaries are expected to perform.

3. This section, and the two that follow, deal with the aspects of securities holding that are related to investment decisions. For example, one of the rights of holding a particular security that would fall within the purview of this section would be the right to exercise a conversion right for a convertible security. It is quite common for investors to confer discretionary authority upon another person, such as an investment adviser, with respect to these rights and other investment decisions. Because this section, and the other sections of Part 5, all specify that a securities intermediary satisfies the Part 5 duties if it acts in accordance with the entitlement holder's agreement, there is no inconsistency between the statement of duties of a securities intermediary and these common arrangements.

4. Section 8–509 also applies to the Section 8–506 duty, so that compliance with applicable regulatory requirements constitutes compliance with this duty. This is quite important in this context, since the federal securities laws establish a comprehensive system of regulation of the distribution of proxy materials and exercise of voting rights with respect to securities held through brokers and other intermediaries. By virtue of Section 8–509(a), compliance with such regulatory requirement constitutes compliance with the Section 8–506 duty.

Definitional Cross References:

"Agreement". Section 1–201(3).*
"Entitlement holder". Section 8–102(a)(7).
"Financial asset". Section 8–102(a)(9).
"Securities intermediary". Section 8–102(a)(14).
"Security entitlement". Section 8–102(a)(17).

---

*　Referring to unrevised Article 1 (Appendix A).

§ 8–507.   Duty of Securities Intermediary to Comply With Entitlement Order.

(a)   A securities intermediary shall comply with an entitlement order if the entitlement order is originated by the appropriate person, the securities intermediary has had reasonable opportunity to assure itself that the entitlement order is genuine and authorized, and the securities intermediary has had reasonable opportunity to comply with the entitlement order. A securities intermediary satisfies the duty if:

(1)   the securities intermediary acts with respect to the duty as agreed upon by the entitlement holder and the securities intermediary; or

(2)   in the absence of agreement, the securities intermediary exercises due care in accordance with reasonable commercial standards to comply with the entitlement order.

(b)   If a securities intermediary transfers a financial asset pursuant to an ineffective entitlement order, the securities intermediary shall reestablish a security entitlement in favor of the person entitled to it, and pay or credit any payments or distributions that the person did not receive as a result of the wrongful transfer. If the securities intermediary does not reestablish a security entitlement, the securities intermediary is liable to the entitlement holder for damages.

Official Comment

1.   Subsection (a) of this section states another aspect of duties of securities intermediaries that make up security entitlements—the securities intermediary's duty to comply with entitlement orders. One of the main reasons for holding securities through securities intermediaries is to enable rapid transfer in settlement of trades. Thus the right to have one's orders for disposition of the security entitlement honored is an inherent part of the relationship. Subsection (b) states the correlative liability of a securities intermediary for transferring a financial asset from an entitlement holder's account pursuant to an entitlement order that was not effective.

2.   The duty to comply with entitlement orders is subject to several qualifications. The intermediary has a duty only with respect to an entitlement order that is in fact originated by the appropriate person. Moreover, the intermediary has a duty only if it has had reasonable opportunity to assure itself that the order is genuine and authorized, and reasonable opportunity to comply with the order. The same "agreement/due care" formula is used in this section as in the other Part 5 sections on the duties of intermediaries, and the rules of Section 8–509 apply to the Section 8–507 duty.

3.   Appropriate person is defined in Section 8–107. In the usual case, the appropriate person is the entitlement holder, see Section 8–107(a)(3). Entitlement holder is defined in Section 8–102(a)(7) as the person "identified in the records of a securities intermediary as the person having a security entitlement." Thus, the general rule is that an intermediary's duty with respect to entitlement orders runs only to the person with whom the intermediary has established a relationship. One of the basic principles of the indirect holding system is that securities intermediaries owe duties only to their own customers. See also Section 8–115. The only situation in which a securities intermediary has a duty to comply with entitlement orders originated by a person other than the person with whom the intermediary established a relationship is covered by Section 8–107(a)(4) and (a)(5), which provide that the term "appropriate person" includes the successor or personal representative of a decedent, or the custodian or guardian of a person who lacks capacity. If the entitlement holder is competent, another person does not fall within the defined term "appropriate person" merely by virtue of having power to act as an agent for the entitlement holder. Thus, an intermediary is not required to determine at its peril whether a person who purports to be authorized to act for an entitlement holder is in fact authorized to do so. If an entitlement holder wishes to be able to act through agents, the entitlement holder can establish appropriate arrangements in advance with the securities intermediary.

One important application of this principle is that if an entitlement holder grants a security interest in its security entitlements to a third-party lender, the intermediary owes no duties to the secured party, unless the intermediary has entered into a "control" agreement in which it agrees to act on entitlement orders originated by the secured party. See Section 8–106. Even though the security agreement or some other document may give the secured party authority to act as agent for the debtor, that would not make the secured party an "appropriate person" to whom the security intermediary owes duties. If the entitlement holder and securities intermediary have agreed to such a control arrangement, then the intermediary's action in following instructions from the secured party would satisfy the subsection (a) duty. Although an agent, such as the secured party in this example, is not an "appropriate person," an entitlement order is "effective" if originated by an authorized person. See Section 8–

107(a) and (b). Moreover, Section 8–507(a) provides that the intermediary satisfies its duty if it acts in accordance with the entitlement holder's agreement.

4.   Subsection (b) provides that an intermediary is liable for a wrongful transfer if the entitlement order was "ineffective." Section 8–107 specifies whether an entitlement order is effective. An "effective entitlement order" is different from an "entitlement order originated by an appropriate person." An entitlement order is effective under Section 8–107(b) if it is made by the appropriate person, or by a person who has power to act for the appropriate person under the law of agency, or if the appropriate person has ratified the entitlement order or is precluded from denying its effectiveness. Thus, although a securities intermediary does not have a duty to act on an entitlement order originated by the entitlement holder's agent, the intermediary is not liable for wrongful transfer if it does so.

Subsection (b), together with Section 8–107, has the effect of leaving to other law most of the questions of the sort dealt with by Article 4A for wire transfers of funds, such as allocation between the securities intermediary and the entitlement holder of the risk of fraudulent entitlement orders.

5.   The term entitlement order does not cover all directions that a customer might give a broker concerning securities held through the broker. Article 8 is not a codification of all of the law of customers and stockbrokers. Article 8 deals with the settlement of securities trades, not the trades. The term entitlement order does not refer to instructions to a broker to make trades, that is, enter into contracts for the purchase or sale of securities. Rather, the entitlement order is the mechanism of transfer for securities held through intermediaries, just as indorsements and instructions are the mechanism for securities held directly. In the ordinary case the customer's direction to the broker to deliver the securities at settlement is implicit in the customer's instruction to the broker to sell. The distinction is, however, significant in that this section has no application to the relationship between the customer and broker with respect to the trade itself. For example, assertions by a customer that it was damaged by a broker's failure to execute a trading order sufficiently rapidly or in the proper manner are not governed by this Article.

Definitional Cross References:

"Agreement". Section 1–201(3).*

"Appropriate person". Section 8–107.

"Effective". Section 8–107.

"Entitlement holder". Section 8–102(a)(7).

"Entitlement order". Section 8–102(a)(8).

"Financial asset". Section 8–102(a)(9).

"Securities intermediary". Section 8–102(a)(14).

"Security entitlement". Section 8–102(a)(17).

§ 8–508.   Duty of Securities Intermediary to Change Entitlement Holder's Position to Other Form of Security Holding.

A securities intermediary shall act at the direction of an entitlement holder to change a security entitlement into another available form of holding for which the entitlement holder is eligible, or to cause the financial asset to be transferred to a securities account of the entitlement holder with another securities intermediary. A securities intermediary satisfies the duty if:

(1)   the securities intermediary acts as agreed upon by the entitlement holder and the securities intermediary; or

(2)   in the absence of agreement, the securities intermediary exercises due care in accordance with reasonable commercial standards to follow the direction of the entitlement holder.

Official Comment

1.   This section states another aspect of the duties of securities intermediaries that make up security entitlements—the obligation of the securities intermediary to change an entitlement holder's position into any other form of holding for which the entitlement holder is eligible or to transfer the entitlement holder's position to an account at another intermediary. This section does not state unconditionally that the securities intermediary is obligated to turn over a certificate to the customer or to cause the customer to be registered on the books of the

---

*   *Referring to unrevised Article 1 (Appendix A).*

issuer, because the customer may not be eligible to hold the security directly. For example, municipal bonds are now commonly issued in "book-entry only" form, in which the only entity that the issuer will register on its own books is a depository.

If security certificates in registered form are issued for the security, and individuals are eligible to have the security registered in their own name, the entitlement holder can request that the intermediary deliver or cause to be delivered to the entitlement holder a certificate registered in the name of the entitlement holder or a certificate indorsed in blank or specially indorsed to the entitlement holder. If security certificates in bearer form are issued for the security, the entitlement holder can request that the intermediary deliver or cause to be delivered a certificate in bearer form. If the security can be held by individuals directly in uncertificated form, the entitlement holder can request that the security be registered in its name. The specification of this duty does not determine the pricing terms of the agreement in which the duty arises.

2. The same "agreement/due care" formula is used in this section as in the other Part 5 sections on the duties of intermediaries. So too, the rules of Section 8–509 apply to the Section 8–508 duty.

Definitional Cross References:

"Agreement". Section 1–201(3).*
"Entitlement holder". Section 8–102(a)(7).
"Financial asset". Section 8–102(a)(9).
"Securities intermediary". Section 8–102(a)(14).
"Security entitlement". Section 8–102(a)(17).

§ 8–509. Specification of Duties of Securities Intermediary by Other Statute or Regulation; Manner of Performance of Duties of Securities Intermediary and Exercise of Rights of Entitlement Holder.

(a) If the substance of a duty imposed upon a securities intermediary by Sections 8–504 through 8–508 is the subject of other statute, regulation, or rule, compliance with that statute, regulation, or rule satisfies the duty.

(b) To the extent that specific standards for the performance of the duties of a securities intermediary or the exercise of the rights of an entitlement holder are not specified by other statute, regulation, or rule or by agreement between the securities intermediary and entitlement holder, the securities intermediary shall perform its duties and the entitlement holder shall exercise its rights in a commercially reasonable manner.

(c) The obligation of a securities intermediary to perform the duties imposed by Sections 8–504 through 8–508 is subject to:

(1) rights of the securities intermediary arising out of a security interest under a security agreement with the entitlement holder or otherwise; and

(2) rights of the securities intermediary under other law, regulation, rule, or agreement to withhold performance of its duties as a result of unfulfilled obligations of the entitlement holder to the securities intermediary.

(d) Sections 8–504 through 8–508 do not require a securities intermediary to take any action that is prohibited by other statute, regulation, or rule.

Official Comment

This Article is not a comprehensive statement of the law governing the relationship between broker-dealers or other securities intermediaries and their customers. Most of the law governing that relationship is the common law of contract and agency, supplemented or supplanted by regulatory law. This Article deals only with the most basic commercial/property law principles governing the relationship. Although Sections 8–504 through 8–508 specify certain duties of securities intermediaries to entitlement holders, the point of these sections is to identify what it means to have a security entitlement, not to specify the details of performance of these duties.

---

* *Referring to unrevised Article 1 (Appendix A).*

For many intermediaries, regulatory law specifies in great detail the intermediary's obligations on such matters as safekeeping of customer property, distribution of proxy materials, and the like. To avoid any conflict between the general statement of duties in this Article and the specific statement of intermediaries' obligations in such regulatory schemes, subsection (a) provides that compliance with applicable regulation constitutes compliance with the duties specified in Sections 8–504 through 8–508.

Definitional Cross References:

"Agreement". Section 1–201(3).[*]

"Entitlement holder". Section 8–102(a)(7).

"Securities intermediary". Section 8–102(a)(14).

"Security agreement". Section 9–102(a)(73).

"Security interest". Section 1–201(37).[*]

§ 8–510. Rights of Purchaser of Security Entitlement from Entitlement Holder.

(a) In a case not covered by the priority rules in Article 9 or the rules stated in subsection (c), an action based on an adverse claim to a financial asset or security entitlement, whether framed in conversion, replevin, constructive trust, equitable lien, or other theory, may not be asserted against a person who purchases a security entitlement, or an interest therein, from an entitlement holder if the purchaser gives value, does not have notice of the adverse claim, and obtains control.

(b) If an adverse claim could not have been asserted against an entitlement holder under Section 8–502, the adverse claim cannot be asserted against a person who purchases a security entitlement, or an interest therein, from the entitlement holder.

(c) In a case not covered by the priority rules in Article 9, a purchaser for value of a security entitlement, or an interest therein, who obtains control has priority over a purchaser of a security entitlement, or an interest therein, who does not obtain control. Except as otherwise provided in subsection (d), purchasers who have control rank according to priority in time of:

(1) the purchaser's becoming the person for whom the securities account, in which the security entitlement is carried, is maintained, if the purchaser obtained control under Section 8–106(d)(1);

(2) the securities intermediary's agreement to comply with the purchaser's entitlement orders with respect to security entitlements carried or to be carried in the securities account in which the security entitlement is carried, if the purchaser obtained control under Section 8–106(d)(2); or

(3) if the purchaser obtained control through another person under Section 8–106(d)(3), the time on which priority would be based under this subsection if the other person were the secured party.

(d) A securities intermediary as purchaser has priority over a conflicting purchaser who has control unless otherwise agreed by the securities intermediary.

As amended in 1999.

Official Comment

1. This section specifies certain rules concerning the rights of persons who purchase interests in security entitlements from entitlement holders. The rules of this section are provided to take account of cases where the purchaser's rights are derivative from the rights of another person who is and continues to be the entitlement holder.

2. Subsection (a) provides that no adverse claim can be asserted against a purchaser of an interest in a security entitlement if the purchaser gives value, obtains control, and does not have notice of the adverse claim. The primary purpose of this rule is to give adverse claim protection to persons who take security interests in security entitlements and obtain control, but do not themselves become entitlement holders.

The following examples illustrate subsection (a):

---

[*]   *Referring to unrevised Article 1 (Appendix A).*

Example 1. X steals a certificated bearer bond from Owner. X delivers the certificate to Able & Co. for credit to X's securities account. Later, X borrows from Bank and grants bank a security interest in the security entitlement. Bank obtains control under Section 8–106(d)(2) by virtue of an agreement in which Able agrees to comply with entitlement orders originated by Bank. X absconds.

Example 2. Same facts as in Example 1, except that Bank does not obtain a control agreement. Instead, Bank perfects by filing a financing statement.

In both of these examples, when X deposited the bonds X acquired a security entitlement under Section 8–501. Under other law, Owner may be able to have a constructive trust imposed on the security entitlement as the traceable product of the bonds that X misappropriated. X granted a security interest in that entitlement to Bank. Bank was a purchaser of an interest in the security entitlement from X. In Example 1, although Bank was not a person who acquired a security entitlement from the intermediary, Bank did obtain control. If Bank did not have notice of Owner's claim, Section 8–510(a) precludes Owner from asserting an adverse claim against Bank. In Example 2, Bank had a perfected security interest, but did not obtain control. Accordingly, Section 8–510(a) does not preclude Owner from asserting its adverse claim against Bank.

3.   Subsection (b) applies to the indirect holding system a limited version of the "shelter principle." The following example illustrates the relatively limited class of cases for which it may be needed:

Example 3. Thief steals a certificated bearer bond from Owner. Thief delivers the certificate to Able & Co. for credit to Thief's securities account. Able forwards the certificate to a clearing corporation for credit to Able's account. Later Thief instructs Able to sell the positions in the bonds. Able sells to Baker & Co., acting as broker for Buyer. The trade is settled by book-entries in the accounts of Able and Baker at the clearing corporation, and in the accounts of Thief and Buyer at Able and Baker respectively. Owner may be able to reconstruct the trade records to show that settlement occurred in such fashion that the "same bonds" that were carried in Thief's account at Able are traceable into Buyer's account at Baker. Buyer later decides to donate the bonds to Alma Mater University and executes an assignment of its rights as entitlement holder to Alma Mater.

Buyer had a position in the bonds, which Buyer held in the form of a security entitlement against Baker. Buyer then made a gift of the position to Alma Mater. Although Alma Mater is a purchaser, Section 1–201(33),* it did not give value. Thus, Alma Mater is a person who purchased a security entitlement, or an interest therein, from an entitlement holder (Buyer). Buyer was protected against Owner's adverse claim by the Section 8–502 rule. Thus, by virtue of Section 8–510(b), Owner is also precluded from asserting an adverse claim against Alma Mater.

4.   Subsection (c) specifies a priority rule for cases where an entitlement holder transfers conflicting interests in the same security entitlement to different purchasers. It follows the same principle as the Article 9 priority rule for investment property, that is, control trumps non-control. Indeed, the most significant category of conflicting "purchasers" may be secured parties. Priority questions for security interests, however, are governed by the rules in Article 9. Subsection (c) applies only to cases not covered by the Article 9 rules. It is intended primarily for disputes over conflicting claims arising out of repurchase agreement transactions that are not covered by the other rules set out in Articles 8 and 9.

The following example illustrates subsection (c):

Example 4. Dealer holds securities through an account at Alpha Bank. Alpha Bank in turns holds through a clearing corporation account. Dealer transfers securities to RP1 in a "hold in custody" repo transaction. Dealer then transfers the same securities to RP2 in another repo transaction. The repo to RP2 is implemented by transferring the securities from Dealer's regular account at Alpha Bank to a special account maintained by Alpha Bank for Dealer and RP2. The agreement among Dealer, RP2, and Alpha Bank provides that Dealer can make substitutions for the securities but RP2 can direct Alpha Bank to sell any securities held in the special account. Dealer becomes insolvent. RP1 claims a prior interest in the securities transferred to RP2.

In this example Dealer remained the entitlement holder but agreed that RP2 could initiate entitlement orders to Dealer's security intermediary, Alpha Bank. If RP2 had become the entitlement holder, the adverse claim rule of Section 8–502 would apply. Even if RP2 does not become the entitlement holder, the arrangement among Dealer, Alpha Bank, and RP2 does suffice to give RP2 control. Thus, under Section 8–510(c), RP2 has priority over RP1, because RP2 is a purchaser who obtained control, and RP1 is a purchaser who did not obtain control. The

---

*   *Referring to unrevised Article 1 (Appendix A).*

same result could be reached under Section 8–510(a) which provides that RP1's earlier in time interest cannot be asserted as an adverse claim against RP2. The same result would follow under the Article 9 priority rules if the interests of RP1 and RP2 are characterized as "security interests," see Section 9–328(1).* The main point of the rules of Section 8–510(c) is to ensure that there will be clear rules to cover the conflicting claims of RP1 and RP2 without characterizing their interests as Article 9 security interests.

The priority rules in Article 9 for conflicting security interests also include a default temporal priority rule for cases where multiple secured parties have obtained control but omitted to specify their respective rights by agreement. See Section 9–328(2)* and Comment 5 to Section 9–328.* Because the purchaser priority rule in Section 8–510(c) is intended to track the Article 9 priority rules, it too has a temporal priority rule for cases where multiple non-secured party purchasers have obtained control but omitted to specify their respective rights by agreement. The rule is patterned on Section 9–328(2).*

5.   If a securities intermediary itself is a purchaser, subsection (d) provides that it has priority over the interest of another purchaser who has control. Article 9 contains a similar rule. See Section 9–328(3).*

Definitional Cross References:

"Adverse claim". Section 8–102(a)(1).
"Control". Section 8–106.
"Entitlement holder". Section 8–102(a)(7).
"Notice of adverse claim". Section 8–105.
"Purchase". Section 1–201(32).**
"Purchaser". Sections 1–201(33)** & 8–116.
"Securities intermediary". Section 8–102(a)(14).
"Security entitlement". Section 8–102(a)(17).
"Value". Sections 1–201(44)** & 8–116.

As amended in 1999.

§ 8–511.   Priority Among Security Interests and Entitlement Holders.

(a)   Except as otherwise provided in subsections (b) and (c), if a securities intermediary does not have sufficient interests in a particular financial asset to satisfy both its obligations to entitlement holders who have security entitlements to that financial asset and its obligation to a creditor of the securities intermediary who has a security interest in that financial asset, the claims of entitlement holders, other than the creditor, have priority over the claim of the creditor.

(b)   A claim of a creditor of a securities intermediary who has a security interest in a financial asset held by a securities intermediary has priority over claims of the securities intermediary's entitlement holders who have security entitlements with respect to that financial asset if the creditor has control over the financial asset.

(c)   If a clearing corporation does not have sufficient financial assets to satisfy both its obligations to entitlement holders who have security entitlements with respect to a financial asset and its obligation to a creditor of the clearing corporation who has a security interest in that financial asset, the claim of the creditor has priority over the claims of entitlement holders.

Official Comment

1.   This section sets out priority rules for circumstances in which a securities intermediary fails leaving an insufficient quantity of securities or other financial assets to satisfy the claims of its entitlement holders and the claims of creditors to whom it has granted security interests in financial assets held by it. Subsection (a) provides that entitlement holders' claims have priority except as otherwise provided in subsection (b), and subsection (b) provides that the secured creditor's claim has priority if the secured creditor obtains control, as defined in Section 8–106. The following examples illustrate the operation of these rules.

---

*   *Referring to Article 9 before the 2010 Amendments.*
**   *Referring to unrevised Article 1 (Appendix A).*

Example 1. Able & Co., a broker, borrows from Alpha Bank and grants Alpha Bank a security interest pursuant to a written agreement which identifies certain securities that are to be collateral for the loan, either specifically or by category. Able holds these securities in a clearing corporation account. Able becomes insolvent and it is discovered that Able holds insufficient securities to satisfy the claims of customers who have paid for securities that they held in accounts with Able and the collateral claims of Alpha Bank. Alpha Bank's security interest in the security entitlements that Able holds through the clearing corporation account may be perfected under the automatic perfection rule of Section 9–309(10), but Alpha Bank did not obtain control under Section 8–106. Thus, under Section 8–511(a) the entitlement holders' claims have priority over Alpha Bank's claim.

Example 2. Able & Co., a broker, borrows from Beta Bank and grants Beta Bank a security interest in securities that Able holds in a clearing corporation account. Pursuant to the security agreement, the securities are debited from Alpha's account and credited to Beta's account in the clearing corporation account. Able becomes insolvent and it is discovered that Able holds insufficient securities to satisfy the claims of customers who have paid for securities that they held in accounts with Able and the collateral claims of Alpha Bank. Although the transaction between Able and Beta took the form of an outright transfer on the clearing corporation's books, as between Able and Beta, Able remains the owner and Beta has a security interest. In that respect the situation is no different than if Able had delivered bearer bonds to Beta in pledge to secure a loan. Beta's security interest is perfected, and Beta obtained control. See Sections 8–106 and 9–314. Under Section 8–511(b), Beta Bank's security interest has priority over claims of Able's customers.

The result in Example 2 is an application to this particular setting of the general principle expressed in Section 8–503, and explained in the Comments thereto, that the entitlement holders of a securities intermediary cannot assert rights against third parties to whom the intermediary has wrongfully transferred interests, except in extremely unusual circumstances where the third party was itself a participant in the transferor's wrongdoing. Under subsection (b) the claim of a secured creditor of a securities intermediary has priority over the claims of entitlement holders if the secured creditor has obtained control. If, however, the secured creditor acted in collusion with the intermediary in violating the intermediary's obligation to its entitlement holders, then under Section 8–503(e), the entitlement holders, through their representative in insolvency proceedings, could recover the interest from the secured creditor, that is, set aside the security interest.

2. The risk that investors who hold through an intermediary will suffer a loss as a result of a wrongful pledge by the intermediary is no different than the risk that the intermediary might fail and not have the securities that it was supposed to be holding on behalf of its customers, either because the securities were never acquired by the intermediary or because the intermediary wrongfully sold securities that should have been kept to satisfy customers' claims. Investors are protected against that risk by the regulatory regimes under which securities intermediaries operate. Intermediaries are required to maintain custody, through clearing corporation accounts or in other approved locations, of their customers' securities and are prohibited from using customers' securities in their own business activities. Securities firms who are carrying both customer and proprietary positions are not permitted to grant blanket liens to lenders covering all securities which they hold, for their own account or for their customers. Rather, securities firms designate specifically which positions they are pledging. Under SEC Rules 8c–1 and 15c2–1, customers' securities can be pledged only to fund loans to customers, and only with the consent of the customers. Customers' securities cannot be pledged for loans for the firm's proprietary business; only proprietary positions can be pledged for proprietary loans. SEC Rule 15c3–3 implements these prohibitions in a fashion tailored to modern securities firm accounting systems by requiring brokers to maintain a sufficient inventory of securities, free from any liens, to satisfy the claims of all of their customers for fully paid and excess margin securities. Revised Article 8 mirrors that requirement, specifying in Section 8–504 that a securities intermediary must maintain a sufficient quantity of investment property to satisfy all security entitlements, and may not grant security interests in the positions it is required to hold for customers, except as authorized by the customers.

If a failed brokerage has violated the customer protection regulations and does not have sufficient securities to satisfy customers' claims, its customers are protected against loss from a shortfall by the Securities Investor Protection Act ("SIPA"). Securities firms required to register as brokers or dealers are also required to become members of the Securities Investor Protection Corporation ("SIPC"), which provides their customers with protection somewhat similar to that provided by FDIC and other deposit insurance programs for bank depositors. When a member firm fails, SIPC is authorized to initiate a liquidation proceeding under the provisions of SIPA. If the assets of the securities firm are insufficient to satisfy all customer claims, SIPA makes contributions to the estate from a fund financed by assessments on its members to protect customers against losses up to $500,000 for cash and securities held at member firms.

Article 8 is premised on the view that the important policy of protecting investors against the risk of wrongful conduct by their intermediaries is sufficiently treated by other law.

3.   Subsection (c) sets out a special rule for secured financing provided to enable clearing corporations to complete settlement. In order to permit clearing corporations to establish liquidity facilities where necessary to ensure completion of settlement, subsection (c) provides a priority for secured lenders to such clearing corporations. Subsection (c) does not turn on control because the clearing corporation may be the top tier securities intermediary for the securities pledged, so that there may be no practicable method for conferring control on the lender.

Definitional Cross References:

"Clearing corporation". Section 8–102(a)(5).

"Control". Section 8–106.

"Entitlement holder". Section 8–102(a)(7).

"Financial asset". Section 8–102(a)(9).

"Securities intermediary". Section 8–102(a)(14).

"Security entitlement". Section 8–102(a)(17).

"Security interest". Section 1–201(37).*

"Value". Sections 1–201(44)* & 8–116.

---

*   *Referring to unrevised Article 1 (Appendix A).*

694

UCC ARTICLE 9 (2016)

SECURED TRANSACTIONS

Article 9 was revised in 1999, with a delayed uniform effective
date of 2001. Additional amendments were promulgated in 2010,
with a delayed uniform effective date of 2013.

PART 1.   GENERAL PROVISIONS

[SUBPART 1.   SHORT TITLE, DEFINITIONS, AND GENERAL CONCEPTS]

[SUBPART 2.   APPLICABILITY OF ARTICLE]

PART 2.   EFFECTIVENESS OF SECURITY AGREEMENT; ATTACHMENT OF SECURITY INTEREST; RIGHTS OF PARTIES TO SECURITY AGREEMENT

[SUBPART 1.   EFFECTIVENESS AND ATTACHMENT]

[SUBPART 2.   RIGHTS AND DUTIES]

PART 3.   PERFECTION AND PRIORITY

[SUBPART 1.   LAW GOVERNING PERFECTION AND PRIORITY]

ARTICLE 9 (2016)

ARTICLE 9 (2016)

9–809.   Priority.

National Conference of Commissioners on Uniform State Laws
DRAFTING COMMITTEE TO REVISE UNIFORM COMMERCIAL CODE
ARTICLE 9—SECURED TRANSACTIONS

William M. Burke, Hong Kong, China, *Chair*
Marion W. Benfield, Jr., New Braunfels, Texas
Neil B. Cohen, Brooklyn, New York, *The American Law Institute Representative*
Dale G. Higer, Boise, Idaho
William C. Hillman, Boston, Massachusetts
Michael Houghton, Wilmington, Delaware
Randal C. Picker, Chicago, Illinois
Donald J. Rapson, Livingston, New Jersey, *The American Law Institute Representative*
Harry C. Sigman, Los Angeles, California, *The American Law Institute Representative*
Bradley Y. Smith, New York, New York, *The American Law Institute Representative*
Edwin E. Smith, Boston, Massachusetts
Sandra S. Stern, New York, New York
Steven L. Harris, Chicago, Illinois, *Co-Reporter*
Charles W. Mooney, Jr., Philadelphia, Pennsylvania, *Co-Reporter*

EX OFFICIO

Gene N. Lebrun, Rapid City, South Dakota, *President*
Henry M. Kittleson, Lakeland, Florida, *Division Chair*

AMERICAN BAR ASSOCIATION ADVISORS

Robert Bauer, Arlington, Virginia, *Intellectual Property Law Section Advisor*
Richard E. Cherin, Newark, New Jersey, *Business Law Section Advisor*
Richard R. Goldberg, Philadelphia, Pennsylvania, *Real Property, Probate & Trust Law Section Advisor*
Lawrence A. Manzanares, Denver, Colorado, *Judicial Administration Division, National Conference of Special Court Judges Advisor*
Steven O. Weise, Los Angeles, California, *Advisor*

EXECUTIVE DIRECTOR

Fred H. Miller, Norman, Oklahoma, *Executive Director*
William J. Pierce, Ann Arbor, Michigan, *Executive Director Emeritus*

DRAFTING COMMITTEE ON 2010 AMENDMENTS TO
UNIFORM COMMERCIAL CODE ARTICLE 9

Edwin Smith, Boston, Massachusetts, *Chair*
E. Carolan Berkley, Philadelphia, Pennsylvania, *ALI Representative*
Carl S. Bjerre, Eugene, Oregon
Thomas J. Buiteweg, Ann Arbor, Michigan
Gail K. Hillebrand, San Francisco, California, *ALI Representative*
John T. McGarvey, Louisville, Kentucky
Charles W. Mooney, Jr., Philadelphia, Pennsylvania, *ALI Representative*
Harry C. Sigman, Los Angeles, California, *ALI Representative*
Sandra S. Stern, New York, New York
Steven O. Weise, Los Angeles, California, *ALI Representative*
James J. White, Ann Arbor, Michigan
Steven L. Harris, Chicago, Illinois, *Reporter*

PART 1

GENERAL PROVISIONS

[SUBPART 1. SHORT TITLE, DEFINITIONS, AND GENERAL CONCEPTS]

§ 9–101.   Short Title.

This article may be cited as Uniform Commercial Code-Secured Transactions.

Official Comment

1.   **Source.** This Article supersedes former Uniform Commercial Code (UCC) Article 9. As did its predecessor, it provides a comprehensive scheme for the regulation of security interests in personal property and fixtures. For the most part this Article follows the general approach and retains much of the terminology of former Article 9. In addition to describing many aspects of the operation and interpretation of this Article, these Comments explain the material changes that this Article makes to former Article 9. Former Article 9 superseded the wide variety of pre-UCC security devices. Unlike the Comments to former Article 9, however, these Comments dwell very little on the pre-UCC state of the law. For that reason, the Comments to former Article 9 will remain of substantial historical value and interest. They also will remain useful in understanding the background and general conceptual approach of this Article.

Citations to "Bankruptcy Code Section ____" in these Comments are to Title 11 of the United States Code as in effect on July 1, 2010.

2.   **Background and History.** In 1990, the Permanent Editorial Board for the UCC with the support of its sponsors, The American Law Institute and the National Conference of Commissioners on Uniform State Laws, established a committee to study Article 9 of the UCC. The study committee issued its report as of December 1, 1992, recommending the creation of a drafting committee for the revision of Article 9 and also recommending numerous specific changes to Article 9. Organized in 1993, a drafting committee met fifteen times from 1993 to 1998. This Article was approved by its sponsors in 1998. This Article was conformed to revised Article 1 in 2001 and to amendments to Article 7 in 2003. The sponsors approved amendments to selected sections of this Article in 2010.

3.   **Reorganization and Renumbering; Captions; Style.** This Article reflects a substantial reorganization of former Article 9 and renumbering of most sections. New Part 4 deals with several aspects of third-party rights and duties that are unrelated to perfection and priority. Some of these were covered by Part 3 of former Article 9. Part 5 deals with filing (covered by former Part 4) and Part 6 deals with default and enforcement (covered by former Part 5). Appendix I contains conforming revisions to other articles of the UCC, and Appendix II contains model provisions for production-money priority.*

This Article also includes headings for the subsections as an aid to readers. Unlike section captions, which are part of the UCC, see Section 1–107, subsection headings are not a part of the official text itself and have not

---

*   *Note from West Advisory Panel: Appendices I and II are omitted from this volume.*

been approved by the sponsors. Each jurisdiction in which this Article is introduced may consider whether to adopt the headings as a part of the statute and whether to adopt a provision clarifying the effect, if any, to be given to the headings. This Article also has been conformed to current style conventions.

4. **Summary of Revisions.** Following is a brief summary of some of the more significant revisions of Article 9 that are included in the 1998 revision of this Article.

a. **Scope of Article 9.** This Article expands the scope of Article 9 in several respects.

Deposit accounts. Section 9–109 includes within this Article's scope deposit accounts as original collateral, except in consumer transactions. Former Article 9 dealt with deposit accounts only as proceeds of other collateral.

Sales of payment intangibles and promissory notes. Section 9–109 also includes within the scope of this Article most sales of "payment intangibles" (defined in Section 9–102 as general intangibles under which an account debtor's principal obligation is monetary) and "promissory notes" (also defined in Section 9–102). Former Article 9 included sales of accounts and chattel paper, but not sales of payment intangibles or promissory notes. In its inclusion of sales of payment intangibles and promissory notes, this Article continues the drafting convention found in former Article 9; it provides that the sale of accounts, chattel paper, payment intangibles, or promissory notes creates a "security interest." The definition of "account" in Section 9–102 also has been expanded to include various rights to payment that were general intangibles under former Article 9.

Health-care-insurance receivables. Section 9–109 narrows Article 9's exclusion of transfers of interests in insurance policies by carving out of the exclusion "health-care-insurance receivables" (defined in Section 9–102). A health-care-insurance receivable is included within the definition of "account" in Section 9–102.

Nonpossessory statutory agricultural liens. Section 9–109 also brings nonpossessory statutory agricultural liens within the scope of Article 9.

Consignments. Section 9–109 provides that "true" consignments-bailments for the purpose of sale by the bailee are security interests covered by Article 9, with certain exceptions. See Section 9–102 (defining "consignment"). Currently, many consignments are subject to Article 9's filing requirements by operation of former Section 2–326.

Supporting obligations and property securing rights to payment. This Article also addresses explicitly (i) obligations, such as guaranties and letters of credit, that support payment or performance of collateral such as accounts, chattel paper, and payment intangibles, and (ii) any property (including real property) that secures a right to payment or performance that is subject to an Article 9 security interest. See Sections 9–203, 9–308.

Commercial tort claims. Section 9–109 expands the scope of Article 9 to include the assignment of commercial tort claims by narrowing the exclusion of tort claims generally. However, this Article continues to exclude tort claims for bodily injury and other non-business tort claims of a natural person. See Section 9–102 (defining "commercial tort claim").

Transfers by States and governmental units of States. Section 9–109 narrows the exclusion of transfers by States and their governmental units. It excludes only transfers covered by another statute (other than a statute generally applicable to security interests) to the extent the statute governs the creation, perfection, priority, or enforcement of security interests.

Nonassignable general intangibles, promissory notes, health-care-insurance receivables, and letter-of-credit rights. This Article enables a security interest to attach to letter-of-credit rights, health-care-insurance receivables, promissory notes, and general intangibles, including contracts, permits, licenses, and franchises, notwithstanding a contractual or statutory prohibition against or limitation on assignment. This Article explicitly protects third parties against any adverse effect of the creation or attempted enforcement of the security interest. See Sections 9–408, 9–409.

Subject to Sections 9–408 and 9–409 and two other exceptions (Sections 9–406, concerning accounts, chattel paper, and payment intangibles, and 9–407, concerning interests in leased goods), Section 9–401 establishes a baseline rule that the inclusion of transactions and collateral within the scope of Article 9 has no effect on non-Article 9 law dealing with the alienability or inalienability of property. For example, if a commercial tort claim is nonassignable under other applicable law, the fact that a security interest in the claim is within the scope of Article 9 does not override the other applicable law's effective prohibition of assignment.

b. **Duties of Secured Party.** This Article provides for expanded duties of secured parties.

Release of control. Section 9–208 imposes upon a secured party having control of a deposit account, investment property, or a letter-of-credit right the duty to release control when there is no secured obligation and no commitment to give value. Section 9–209 contains analogous provisions when an account debtor has been notified to pay a secured party.

Information. Section 9–210 expands a secured party's duties to provide the debtor with information concerning collateral and the obligations that it secures.

Default and enforcement. Part 6 also includes some additional duties of secured parties in connection with default and enforcement. See, e.g., Section 9–616 (duty to explain calculation of deficiency or surplus in a consumer-goods transaction).

c. **Choice of Law.** The choice-of-law rules for the law governing perfection, the effect of perfection or nonperfection, and priority are found in Part 3, Subpart 1 (Sections 9–301 through 9–307). See also Section 9–316.

Where to file: Location of debtor. This Article changes the choice-of-law rule governing perfection (i.e., where to file) for most collateral to the law of the jurisdiction where the debtor is located. See Section 9–301. Under former Article 9, the jurisdiction of the debtor's location governed only perfection and priority of a security interest in accounts, general intangibles, mobile goods, and, for purposes of perfection by filing, chattel paper and investment property.

Determining debtor's location. As a baseline rule, Section 9–307 follows former Section 9–103, under which the location of the debtor is the debtor's place of business (or chief executive office, if the debtor has more than one place of business). Section 9–307 contains three major exceptions. First, a "registered organization," such as a corporation or limited liability company, is located in the State under whose law the debtor is organized, e.g., a corporate debtor's State of incorporation. Second, an individual debtor is located at his or her principal residence. Third, there are special rules for determining the location of the United States and registered organizations organized under the law of the United States.

Location of non-U.S. debtors. If, applying the foregoing rules, a debtor is located in a jurisdiction whose law does not require public notice as a condition of perfection of a nonpossessory security interest, the entity is deemed located in the District of Columbia. See Section 9–307. Thus, to the extent that this Article applies to non-U.S. debtors, perfection could be accomplished in many cases by a domestic filing.

Priority. For tangible collateral such as goods and instruments, Section 9–301 provides that the law applicable to priority and the effect of perfection or nonperfection will remain the law of the jurisdiction where the collateral is located, as under former Section 9–103 (but without the confusing "last event" test). For intangible collateral, such as accounts, the applicable law for priority will be that of the jurisdiction in which the debtor is located.

Possessory security interests; agricultural liens. Perfection, the effect of perfection or nonperfection, and priority of a possessory security interest or an agricultural lien are governed by the law of the jurisdiction where the collateral subject to the security interest or lien is located. See Sections 9–301, 9–302.

Goods covered by certificates of title; deposit accounts; letter-of-credit rights; investment property. This Article includes several refinements to the treatment of choice-of-law matters for goods covered by certificates of title. See Section 9–303. It also provides special choice-of-law rules, similar to those for investment property under current Articles 8 and 9, for deposit accounts (Section 9–304), investment property (Section 9–305), and letter-of-credit rights (Section 9–306).

Change in applicable law. Section 9–316 addresses perfection following a change in applicable law.

d. **Perfection.** The rules governing perfection of security interests and agricultural liens are found in Part 3, Subpart 2 (Sections 9–308 through 9–316).

Deposit accounts; letter-of-credit rights. With certain exceptions, this Article provides that a security interest in a deposit account or a letter-of-credit right may be perfected *only* by the secured party's acquiring "control" of the deposit account or letter-of-credit right. See Sections 9–312, 9–314. Under Section 9–104, a secured party has "control" of a deposit account when, with the consent of the debtor, the secured party obtains the depositary bank's agreement to act on the secured party's instructions (including when the secured party becomes the account holder) or when the secured party is itself the depositary bank. The control requirements are patterned on Section 8–106, which specifies the requirements for control of investment property. Under Section 9–107, "control" of a letter-of-credit right occurs when the issuer or nominated person consents to an assignment of proceeds under Section 5–114.

Electronic chattel paper. Section 9–102 includes a new defined term: "electronic chattel paper." Electronic chattel paper is a record or records consisting of information stored in an electronic medium (i.e., it is not written). Perfection of a security interest in electronic chattel paper may be by control or filing. See Sections 9–105 (*sui generis* definition of control of electronic chattel paper), 9–312 (perfection by filing), 9–314 (perfection by control).

Investment property. The perfection requirements for "investment property" (defined in Section 9–102), including perfection by control under Section 9–106, remain substantially unchanged. However, a new provision in Section 9–314 is designed to ensure that a secured party retains control in "repledge" transactions that are typical in the securities markets.

Instruments, agricultural liens, and commercial tort claims. This Article expands the types of collateral in which a security interest may be perfected by filing to include instruments. See Section 9–312. Agricultural liens and security interests in commercial tort claims also are perfected by filing, under this Article. See Sections 9–308, 9–310.

Sales of payment intangibles and promissory notes. Although former Article 9 covered the outright sale of accounts and chattel paper, sales of most other types of receivables also are financing transactions to which Article 9 should apply. Accordingly, Section 9–102 expands the definition of "account" to include many types of receivables (including "health-care-insurance receivables," defined in Section 9–102) that former Article 9 classified as "general intangibles." It thereby subjects to Article 9's filing system sales of more types of receivables than did former Article 9. Certain sales of payment intangibles—primarily bank loan participation transactions—should not be subject to the Article 9 filing rules. These transactions fall in a residual category of collateral, "payment intangibles" (general intangibles under which the account debtor's principal obligation is monetary), the sale of which is exempt from the filing requirements of Article 9. See Sections 9–102, 9–109, 9–309 (perfection upon attachment). The perfection rules for sales of promissory notes are the same as those for sales of payment intangibles.

Possessory security interests. Several provisions of this Article address aspects of security interests involving a secured party or a third party who is in possession of the collateral. In particular, Section 9–313 resolves a number of uncertainties under former Section 9–305. It provides that a security interest in collateral in the possession of a third party is perfected when the third party acknowledges in an authenticated record that it holds for the secured party's benefit. Section 9–313 also provides that a third party need not so acknowledge and that its acknowledgment does not impose any duties on it, unless it otherwise agrees. A special rule in Section 9–313 provides that if a secured party already is in possession of collateral, its security interest remains perfected by possession if it delivers the collateral to a third party and the collateral is accompanied by instructions to hold it for the secured party or to redeliver it to the secured party. Section 9–313 also clarifies the limited circumstances under which a security interest in goods covered by a certificate of title may be perfected by the secured party's taking possession.

Automatic perfection. Section 9–309 lists various types of security interests as to which no public-notice step is required for perfection (e.g., purchase-money security interests in consumer goods other than automobiles). This automatic perfection also extends to a transfer of a health-care-insurance receivable *to* a health-care provider. Those transfers normally will be made by natural persons who receive health-care services; there is little value in requiring filing for perfection in that context. Automatic perfection also applies to security interests created by sales of payment intangibles and promissory notes. Section 9–308 provides that a perfected security interest in collateral supported by a "supporting obligation" (such as an account supported by a guaranty) also is a perfected security interest in the supporting obligation, and that a perfected security interest in an obligation secured by a security interest or lien on property (e.g., a real-property mortgage) also is a perfected security interest in the security interest or lien.

e. **Priority; Special Rules for Banks and Deposit Accounts.** The rules governing priority of security interests and agricultural liens are found in Part 3, Subpart 3 (Sections 9–317 through 9–342). This Article includes several new priority rules and some special rules relating to banks and deposit accounts (Sections 9–340 through 9–342).

Purchase-money security interests: General; consumer-goods transactions; inventory. Section 9–103 substantially rewrites the definition of purchase-money security interest (PMSI) (although the term is not formally "defined"). The substantive changes, however, apply only to non-consumer-goods transactions. (Consumer transactions and consumer-goods transactions are discussed below in Comment 4.j.) For non-consumer-goods transactions, Section 9–103 makes clear that a security interest in collateral may be (to some extent) both a PMSI as well as a non-PMSI, in accord with the "dual status" rule applied by some courts under former Article 9 (thereby rejecting the "transformation" rule). The definition provides an even broader conception of a PMSI in inventory, yielding a result that accords with private agreements entered into in response to the uncertainty under former Article 9. It also treats consignments as purchase-money security interests in inventory. Section 9–324 revises the PMSI priority rules, but for the most part without material change in substance. Section 9–324 also clarifies the priority rules for competing PMSIs in the same collateral.

Purchase-money security interests in livestock; agricultural liens. Section 9–324 provides a special PMSI priority, similar to the inventory PMSI priority rule, for livestock. Section 9–322 (which contains the baseline first-to-file-or-perfect priority rule) also recognizes special non-Article 9 priority rules for agricultural liens, which can override the baseline first-in-time rule.

Purchase-money security interests in software. Section 9–324 contains a new priority rule for a software purchase-money security interest. (Section 9–102 includes a definition of "software.") Under Section 9–103, a software PMSI includes a PMSI in software that is used in goods that are also subject to a PMSI. (Note also that the definition of "chattel paper" has been expanded to include records that evidence a monetary obligation and a security interest in specific goods and software used in the goods.)

Investment property. The priority rules for investment property are substantially similar to the priority rules found in former Section 9–115, which was added in conjunction with the 1994 revisions to UCC Article 8. Under Section 9–328, if a secured party has control of investment property (Sections 8–106, 9–106), its security interest is senior to a security interest perfected in another manner (e.g., by filing). Also under Section 9–328, security interests perfected by control generally rank according to the time that control is obtained or, in the case of a security entitlement or a commodity contract carried in a commodity account, the time when the control arrangement is entered into. This is a change from former Section 9–115, under which the security interests ranked equally. However, as between a securities intermediary's security interest in a security entitlement that it maintains for the debtor and a security interest held by another secured party, the securities intermediary's security interest is senior.

Deposit accounts. This Article's priority rules applicable to deposit accounts are found in Section 9–327. They are patterned on and are similar to those for investment property in former Section 9–115 and Section 9–328 of this Article. Under Section 9–327, if a secured party has control of a deposit account, its security interest is senior to a security interest perfected in another manner (i.e., as cash proceeds). Also under Section 9–327, security interests perfected by control rank according to the time that control is obtained, but as between a depositary bank's security interest and one held by another secured party, the depositary bank's security interest is senior. A corresponding rule in Section 9–340 makes a depositary bank's right of set-off generally senior to a security interest held by another secured party. However, if the other secured party becomes the depositary bank's customer with respect to the deposit account, then its security interest is senior to the depositary bank's security interest and right of set-off. Sections 9–327, 9–340.

Letter-of-credit rights. The priority rules for security interests in letter-of-credit rights are found in Section 9–329. They are somewhat analogous to those for deposit accounts. A security interest perfected by control has priority over one perfected in another manner (i.e., as a supporting obligation for the collateral in which a security interest is perfected). Security interests in a letter-of-credit right perfected by control rank according to the time that control is obtained. However, the rights of a transferee beneficiary or a nominated person are independent and superior to the extent provided in Section 5–114. See Section 9–109(c)(4).

Chattel paper and instruments. Section 9–330 is the successor to former Section 9–308. As under former Section 9–308, differing priority rules apply to purchasers of chattel paper who give new value and take possession (or, in the case of electronic chattel paper, obtain control) of the collateral depending on whether a conflicting security interest in the collateral is claimed merely as proceeds. The principal change relates to the role of knowledge and the effect of an indication of a previous assignment of the collateral. Section 9–330 also affords priority to purchasers of instruments who take possession in good faith and without knowledge that the purchase violates the rights of the competing secured party. In addition, to qualify for priority, purchasers of chattel paper, but not of instruments, must purchase in the ordinary course of business.

Proceeds. Section 9–322 contains new priority rules that clarify when a special priority of a security interest in collateral continues or does not continue with respect to proceeds of the collateral. Other refinements to the priority rules for proceeds are included in Sections 9–324 (purchase-money security interest priority) and 9–330 (priority of certain purchasers of chattel paper and instruments).

Miscellaneous priority provisions. This Article also includes (i) clarifications of selected good-faith-purchase and similar issues (Sections 9–317, 9–331); (ii) new priority rules to deal with the "double debtor" problem arising when a debtor creates a security interest in collateral acquired by the debtor subject to a security interest created by another person (Section 9–325); (iii) new priority rules to deal with the problems created when a change in corporate structure or the like results in a new entity that has become bound by the original debtor's after-acquired property agreement (Section 9–326); (iv) a provision enabling most transferees of funds from a deposit account or money to take free of a security interest (Section 9–332); (v) substantially rewritten and refined priority rules dealing with accessions and commingled goods (Sections 9–335, 9–336); (vi) revised priority rules for security interests in goods covered by a certificate of title (Section 9–337); and (vii) provisions designed to ensure that security interests in deposit accounts will not extend to most transferees of funds on deposit or payees from deposit accounts and will not otherwise "clog" the payments system (Sections 9–341, 9–342).

Model provisions relating to production-money security interests. Appendix II* to this Article contains model definitions and priority rules relating to "production-money security interests" held by secured parties who give new value used in the production of crops. Because no consensus emerged on the wisdom of these provisions during the drafting process, the sponsors make no recommendation on whether these model provisions should be enacted.

f.   **Proceeds.** Section 9–102 contains an expanded definition of "proceeds" of collateral which includes additional rights and property that arise out of collateral, such as distributions on account of collateral and claims arising out of the loss or nonconformity of, defects in, or damage to collateral. The term also includes collections on account of "supporting obligations," such as guarantees.

g.   **Part 4: Additional Provisions Relating to Third-Party Rights.** New Part 4 contains several provisions relating to the relationships between certain third parties and the parties to secured transactions. It contains new Sections 9–401 (replacing former Section 9–311) (alienability of debtor's rights), 9–402 (replacing former Section 9–317) (secured party not obligated on debtor's contracts), 9–403 (replacing former Section 9–206) (agreement not to assert defenses against assignee), 9–404, 9–405, and 9–406 (replacing former Section 9–318) (rights acquired by assignee, modification of assigned contract, discharge of account debtor, restrictions on assignment of account, chattel paper, promissory note, or payment intangible ineffective), 9–407 (replacing some provisions of former Section 2A–303) (restrictions on creation or enforcement of security interest in leasehold interest or lessor's residual interest ineffective). It also contains new Sections 9–408 (restrictions on assignment of promissory notes, health-care-insurance receivables ineffective, and certain general intangibles ineffective) and 9–409 (restrictions on assignment of letter-of-credit rights ineffective), which are discussed above.

h.   **Filing.** Part 5 (formerly Part 4) of Article 9 has been substantially rewritten to simplify the statutory text and to deal with numerous problems of interpretation and implementation that have arisen over the years.

Medium-neutrality. This Article is "medium-neutral"; that is, it makes clear that parties may file and otherwise communicate with a filing office by means of records communicated and stored in media other than on paper.

Identity of person who files a record; authorization. Part 5 is largely indifferent as to the person who effects a filing. Instead, it addresses whose authorization is necessary for a person to file a record with a filing office. The filing scheme does not contemplate that the identity of a "filer" will be a part of the searchable records. This approach is consistent with, and a necessary aspect of, eliminating signatures or other evidence of authorization from the system (except to the extent that filing offices may choose to employ authentication procedures in connection with electronic communications). As long as the appropriate person authorizes the filing, or, in the case of a termination statement, the debtor is entitled to the termination, it is largely insignificant whether the secured party or another person files any given record.

Section 9–509 collects in one place most of the rules that determine when a record may be filed. In general, the debtor's authorization is required for the filing of an initial financing statement or an amendment that adds collateral. With one further exception, a secured party of record's authorization is required for the filing of other amendments. The exception arises if a secured party has failed to provide a termination statement that is required because there is no outstanding secured obligation or commitment to give value. In that situation, a debtor is authorized to file a termination statement indicating that it has been filed by the debtor.

Financing statement formal requisites. The formal requisites for a financing statement are set out in Section 9–502. A financing statement must provide the name of the debtor and the secured party and an indication of the collateral that it covers. Sections 9–503 and 9–506 address the sufficiency of a name provided on a financing statement and clarify when a debtor's name is correct and when an incorrect name is insufficient. Section 9–504 addresses the indication of collateral covered. Under Section 9–504, a super-generic description (e.g.,"all assets"

---

*   *Note from West Advisory Panel: Appendix II is omitted from this volume.*

or "all personal property") in a financing statement is a sufficient indication of the collateral. (Note, however, that a super-generic description is inadequate for purposes of a security agreement. See Sections 9–108, 9–203.) To facilitate electronic filing, this Article does not require that the debtor's signature or other authorization appear on a financing statement. Instead, it prohibits the filing of unauthorized financing statements and imposes liability upon those who violate the prohibition. See Sections 9–509, 9–626.

Filing-office operations. Part 5 contains several provisions governing filing operations. First, it prohibits the filing office from rejecting an initial financing statement or other record for a reason other than one of the few that are specified. See Sections 9–520, 9–516. Second, the filing office is obliged to link all subsequent records (e.g., assignments, continuation statements, etc.) to the initial financing statement to which they relate. See Section 9–519. Third, the filing office may delete a financing statement and related records from the files no earlier than one year after lapse (lapse normally is five years after the filing date), and then only if a continuation statement has not been filed. See Sections 9–515, 9–519, 9–522. Thus, a financing statement and related records would be discovered by a search of the files even after the filing of a termination statement. This approach helps eliminate filing-office discretion and also eases problems associated with multiple secured parties and multiple partial assignments. Fourth, Part 5 mandates performance standards for filing offices. See Sections 9–519, 9–520, 9–523. Fifth, it provides for the promulgation of filing-office rules to deal with details best left out of the statute and requires the filing office to submit periodic reports. See Sections 9–526, 9–527.

Defaulting or missing secured parties and fraudulent filings. In some areas of the country, serious problems have arisen from fraudulent financing statements that are filed against public officials and other persons. This Article addresses the fraud problem by providing the opportunity for a debtor to file a termination statement when a secured party wrongfully refuses or fails to provide a termination statement. See Section 9–509. This opportunity also addresses the problem of secured parties that simply disappear through mergers or liquidations. In addition, Section 9–518 affords a statutory method by which a debtor who believes that a filed record is inaccurate or was wrongfully filed may indicate that fact in the files, albeit without affecting the efficacy, if any, of the challenged record.

Extended period of effectiveness for certain financing statements. Section 9–515 contains an exception to the usual rule that financing statements are effective for five years unless a continuation statement is filed to continue the effectiveness for another five years. Under that section, an initial financing statement filed in connection with a "public-finance transaction" or a "manufactured-home transaction" (terms defined in Section 9–102) is effective for 30 years.

National form of financing statement and related forms. Section 9–521 provides for uniform, national written forms of financing statements and related written records that must be accepted by a filing office that accepts written records.

i.   **Default and Enforcement.** Part 6 of Article 9 extensively revises former Part 5. Provisions relating to enforcement of consumer-goods transactions and consumer transactions are discussed in Comment 4.j.

Debtor, secondary obligor; waiver. Section 9–602 clarifies the identity of persons who have rights and persons to whom a secured party owes specified duties under Part 6. Under that section, the rights and duties are enjoyed by and run to the "debtor," defined in Section 9–102 to mean any person with a non-lien property interest in collateral, and to any "obligor." However, with one exception (Section 9–616, as it relates to a consumer obligor), the rights and duties concerned affect non-debtor obligors only if they are "secondary obligors." "Secondary obligor" is defined in Section 9–102 to include one who is secondarily obligated on the secured obligation, e.g., a guarantor, or one who has a right of recourse against the debtor or another obligor with respect to an obligation secured by collateral. However, under Section 9–628, the secured party is relieved from any duty or liability to any person unless the secured party knows that the person is a debtor or obligor. Resolving an issue on which courts disagreed under former Article 9, this Article generally prohibits waiver by a secondary obligor of its rights and a secured party's duties under Part 6. See Section 9–602. However, Section 9–624 permits a secondary obligor or debtor to waive the right to notification of disposition of collateral and, in a non-consumer transaction, the right to redeem collateral, if the secondary obligor or debtor agrees to do so after default.

Rights of collection and enforcement of collateral. Section 9–607 explains in greater detail than former 9–502 the rights of a secured party who seeks to collect or enforce collateral, including accounts, chattel paper, and payment intangibles. It also sets forth the enforcement rights of a depositary bank holding a security interest in a deposit account maintained with the depositary bank. Section 9–607 relates solely to the rights of a secured party vis-a-vis a debtor with respect to collections and enforcement. It does not affect the rights or duties of third parties, such as account debtors on collateral, which are addressed elsewhere (e.g., Section 9–406). Section 9–608 clarifies the manner in which proceeds of collection or enforcement are to be applied.

Disposition of collateral: Warranties of title. Section 9–610 imposes on a secured party who disposes of collateral the warranties of title, quiet possession, and the like that are otherwise applicable under other law. It also provides rules for the exclusion or modification of those warranties.

Disposition of collateral: Notification, application of proceeds, surplus and deficiency, other effects. Section 9–611 requires a secured party to give notification of a disposition of collateral to other secured parties and lienholders who have filed financing statements against the debtor covering the collateral. (That duty was eliminated by the 1972 revisions to Article 9.) However, that section relieves the secured party from that duty when the secured party undertakes a search of the records and a report of the results is unreasonably delayed. Section 9–613, which applies only to non-consumer transactions, specifies the contents of a sufficient notification of disposition and provides that a notification sent 10 days or more before the earliest time for disposition is sent within a reasonable time. Section 9–615 addresses the application of proceeds of disposition, the entitlement of a debtor to any surplus, and the liability of an obligor for any deficiency. Section 9–619 clarifies the effects of a disposition by a secured party, including the rights of transferees of the collateral.

Rights and duties of secondary obligor. Section 9–618 provides that a secondary obligor obtains the rights and assumes the duties of a secured party if the secondary obligor receives an assignment of a secured obligation, agrees to assume the secured party's rights and duties upon a transfer to it of collateral, or becomes subrogated to the rights of the secured party with respect to the collateral. The assumption, transfer, or subrogation is not a disposition of collateral under Section 9–610, but it does relieve the former secured party of further duties. Former Section 9–504(5) did not address whether a secured party was relieved of its duties in this situation.

Transfer of record or legal title. Section 9–619 contains a new provision making clear that a transfer of record or legal title to a secured party is not of itself a disposition under Part 6. This rule applies regardless of the circumstances under which the transfer of title occurs.

Strict foreclosure. Section 9–620, unlike former Section 9–505, permits a secured party to accept collateral in partial satisfaction, as well as full satisfaction, of the obligations secured. This right of strict foreclosure extends to intangible as well as tangible property. Section 9–622 clarifies the effects of an acceptance of collateral on the rights of junior claimants. It rejects the approach taken by some courts—deeming a secured party to have constructively retained collateral in satisfaction of the secured obligations—in the case of a secured party's unreasonable delay in the disposition of collateral. Instead, unreasonable delay is relevant when determining whether a disposition under Section 9–610 is commercially reasonable.

Effect of noncompliance: "Rebuttable presumption" test. Section 9–626 adopts the "rebuttable presumption" test for the failure of a secured party to proceed in accordance with certain provisions of Part 6. (As discussed in Comment 4.j., the test does not necessarily apply to consumer transactions.) Under this approach, the deficiency claim of a noncomplying secured party is calculated by crediting the obligor with the greater of the actual net proceeds of a disposition and the amount of net proceeds that would have been realized if the disposition had been conducted in accordance with Part 6 (e.g., in a commercially reasonable manner). For non-consumer transactions, Section 9–626 rejects the "absolute bar" test that some courts have imposed; that approach bars a noncomplying secured party from recovering any deficiency, regardless of the loss (if any) the debtor suffered as a consequence of the noncompliance.

"Low-price" dispositions: Calculation of deficiency and surplus. Section 9–615(f) addresses the problem of procedurally regular dispositions that fetch a low price. Subsection (f) provides a special method for calculating a deficiency if the proceeds of a disposition of collateral to a secured party, a person related to the secured party, or a secondary obligor are "significantly below the range of proceeds that a complying disposition to a person other than the secured party, a person related to the secured party, or a secondary obligor would have brought." ("Person related to" is defined in Section 9–102.) In these situations there is reason to suspect that there may be inadequate incentives to obtain a better price. Consequently, instead of calculating a deficiency (or surplus) based on the actual net proceeds, the deficiency (or surplus) would be calculated based on the proceeds that would have been received in a disposition to a person other than the secured party, a person related to the secured party, or a secondary obligor.

j. **Consumer Goods, Consumer-Goods Transactions, and Consumer Transactions.** This Article (including the accompanying conforming revisions (see Appendix I)) includes several special rules for "consumer goods," "consumer transactions," and "consumer-goods transactions." Each term is defined in Section 9–102.

(i)   Revised Sections 2–502 and 2–716 provide a buyer of consumer goods with enhanced rights to possession of the goods, thereby accelerating the opportunity to achieve "buyer in ordinary course of business" status under Section 1–201.

(ii)   Section 9–103(e) (allocation of payments for determining extent of purchase-money status), (f) (purchase-money status not affected by cross-collateralization, refinancing, restructuring, or the like), and (g) (secured party has burden of establishing extent of purchase-money status) do not apply to consumer-goods transactions. Sections 9–103 also provides that the limitation of those provisions to transactions other than consumer-goods transactions leaves to the courts the proper rules for consumer-goods transactions and prohibits the courts from drawing inferences from that limitation.

(iii)   Section 9–108 provides that in a consumer transaction a description of consumer goods, a security entitlement, securities account, or commodity account "only by [UCC-defined] type of collateral" is not a sufficient collateral description in a security agreement.

(iv)   Sections 9–403 and 9–404 make effective the Federal Trade Commission's anti-holder-in-due-course rule (when applicable), 16 C.F.R. Part 433, even in the absence of the required legend.

(v)   The 10-day safe-harbor for notification of a disposition provided by Section 9–612 does not apply in a consumer transaction.

(vi)   Section 9–613 (contents and form of notice of disposition) does not apply to a consumer-goods transaction.

(vii)   Section 9–614 contains special requirements for the contents of a notification of disposition and a safe-harbor, "plain English" form of notification, for consumer-goods transactions.

(viii)   Section 9–616 requires a secured party in a consumer-goods transaction to provide a debtor with a notification of how it calculated a deficiency at the time it first undertakes to collect a deficiency.

(ix)   Section 9–620 prohibits partial strict foreclosure with respect to consumer goods collateral and, unless the debtor agrees to waive the requirement in an authenticated record after default, in certain cases requires the secured party to dispose of consumer goods collateral which has been repossessed.

(x)   Section 9–626 ("rebuttable presumption" rule) does not apply to a consumer transaction. Section 9–626 also provides that its limitation to transactions other than consumer transactions leaves to the courts the proper rules for consumer transactions and prohibits the courts from drawing inferences from that limitation.

k.   **Good Faith.** Section 9–102 contains a new definition of "good faith" that includes not only "honesty in fact" but also "the observance of reasonable commercial standards of fair dealing." The definition is similar to the ones adopted in connection with other, recently completed revisions of the UCC.

l.   **Transition Provisions.** Part 7 (Sections 9–701 through 9–709) contains transition provisions. Transition from former Article 9 to this Article will be particularly challenging in view of its expanded scope, its modification of choice-of-law rules for perfection and priority, and its expansion of the methods of perfection.

m.   **Conforming and Related Amendments to Other UCC Articles.** Appendix I contains several proposed revisions to the provisions and Comments of other UCC articles. For the most part the revisions are explained in the Comments to the proposed revisions. Cross-references in other UCC articles to sections of Article 9 also have been revised.

Article 1. Revised Section 1–201 contains revisions to the definitions of "buyer in ordinary course of business," "purchaser," and "security interest."

Articles 2 and 2A. Sections 2–210, 2–326, 2–502, 2–716, 2A–303, and 2A–307 have been revised to address the intersection between Articles 2 and 2A and Article 9.

Article 5. New Section 5–118 is patterned on Section 4–210. It provides for a security interest in documents presented under a letter of credit in favor of the issuer and a nominated person on the letter of credit.

Article 8. Revisions to Section 8–106, which deals with "control" of securities and security entitlements, conform it to Section 8–302, which deals with "delivery." Revisions to Section 8–110, which deals with a "securities intermediary's jurisdiction," conform it to the revised treatment of a "commodity intermediary's jurisdiction" in Section 9–305. Sections 8–301 and 8–302 have been revised for clarification. Section 8–510 has been revised to conform it to the revised priority rules of Section 9–328. Several Comments in Article 8 also have been revised.

As amended in 2010.

§ 9–102.   Definitions and Index of Definitions.

(a) **[Article 9 definitions.]** In this article:

(1) "Accession" means goods that are physically united with other goods in such a manner that the identity of the original goods is not lost.

(2) "Account", except as used in "account for", means a right to payment of a monetary obligation, whether or not earned by performance, (i) for property that has been or is to be sold, leased, licensed, assigned, or otherwise disposed of, (ii) for services rendered or to be rendered, (iii) for a policy of insurance issued or to be issued, (iv) for a secondary obligation incurred or to be incurred, (v) for energy provided or to be provided, (vi) for the use or hire of a vessel under a charter or other contract, (vii) arising out of the use of a credit or charge card or information contained on or for use with the card, or (viii) as winnings in a lottery or other game of chance operated or sponsored by a State, governmental unit of a State, or person licensed or authorized to operate the game by a State or governmental unit of a State. The term includes health-care-insurance receivables. The term does not include (i) rights to payment evidenced by chattel paper or an instrument, (ii) commercial tort claims, (iii) deposit accounts, (iv) investment property, (v) letter-of-credit rights or letters of credit, or (vi) rights to payment for money or funds advanced or sold, other than rights arising out of the use of a credit or charge card or information contained on or for use with the card.

(3) "Account debtor" means a person obligated on an account, chattel paper, or general intangible. The term does not include persons obligated to pay a negotiable instrument, even if the instrument constitutes part of chattel paper.

(4) "Accounting", except as used in "accounting for", means a record:

(A) authenticated by a secured party;

(B) indicating the aggregate unpaid secured obligations as of a date not more than 35 days earlier or 35 days later than the date of the record; and

(C) identifying the components of the obligations in reasonable detail.

(5) "Agricultural lien" means an interest in farm products:

(A) which secures payment or performance of an obligation for:

(i) goods or services furnished in connection with a debtor's farming operation; or

(ii) rent on real property leased by a debtor in connection with its farming operation;

(B) which is created by statute in favor of a person that:

(i) in the ordinary course of its business furnished goods or services to a debtor in connection with a debtor's farming operation; or

(ii) leased real property to a debtor in connection with the debtor's farming operation; and

(C) whose effectiveness does not depend on the person's possession of the personal property.

(6) "As-extracted collateral" means:

(A) oil, gas, or other minerals that are subject to a security interest that:

(i) is created by a debtor having an interest in the minerals before extraction; and

(ii) attaches to the minerals as extracted; or

(B) accounts arising out of the sale at the wellhead or minehead of oil, gas, or other minerals in which the debtor had an interest before extraction.

(7) "Authenticate" means:

    (A) to sign; or

    (B) with present intent to adopt or accept a record, to attach to or logically associate with the record an electronic sound, symbol, or process.

(8) "Bank" means an organization that is engaged in the business of banking. The term includes savings banks, savings and loan associations, credit unions, and trust companies.

(9) "Cash proceeds" means proceeds that are money, checks, deposit accounts, or the like.

(10) "Certificate of title" means a certificate of title with respect to which a statute provides for the security interest in question to be indicated on the certificate as a condition or result of the security interest's obtaining priority over the rights of a lien creditor with respect to the collateral. The term includes another record maintained as an alternative to a certificate of title by the governmental unit that issues certificates of title if a statute permits the security interest in question to be indicated on the record as a condition or result of the security interest's obtaining priority over the rights of a lien creditor with respect to the collateral.

(11) "Chattel paper" means a record or records that evidence both a monetary obligation and a security interest in specific goods, a security interest in specific goods and software used in the goods, a security interest in specific goods and license of software used in the goods, a lease of specific goods, or a lease of specific goods and license of software used in the goods. In this paragraph, "monetary obligation" means a monetary obligation secured by the goods or owed under a lease of the goods and includes a monetary obligation with respect to software used in the goods. The term does not include (i) charters or other contracts involving the use or hire of a vessel or (ii) records that evidence a right to payment arising out of the use of a credit or charge card or information contained on or for use with the card. If a transaction is evidenced by records that include an instrument or series of instruments, the group of records taken together constitutes chattel paper.

(12) "Collateral" means the property subject to a security interest or agricultural lien. The term includes:

    (A) proceeds to which a security interest attaches;

    (B) accounts, chattel paper, payment intangibles, and promissory notes that have been sold; and

    (C) goods that are the subject of a consignment.

(13) "Commercial tort claim" means a claim arising in tort with respect to which:

    (A) the claimant is an organization; or

    (B) the claimant is an individual and the claim:

        (i) arose in the course of the claimant's business or profession; and

        (ii) does not include damages arising out of personal injury to or the death of an individual.

(14) "Commodity account" means an account maintained by a commodity intermediary in which a commodity contract is carried for a commodity customer.

(15) "Commodity contract" means a commodity futures contract, an option on a commodity futures contract, a commodity option, or another contract if the contract or option is:

    (A) traded on or subject to the rules of a board of trade that has been designated as a contract market for such a contract pursuant to federal commodities laws; or

    (B) traded on a foreign commodity board of trade, exchange, or market, and is carried on the books of a commodity intermediary for a commodity customer.

(16) "Commodity customer" means a person for which a commodity intermediary carries a commodity contract on its books.

(17) "Commodity intermediary" means a person that:

    (A) is registered as a futures commission merchant under federal commodities law; or

    (B) in the ordinary course of its business provides clearance or settlement services for a board of trade that has been designated as a contract market pursuant to federal commodities law.

(18) "Communicate" means:

    (A) to send a written or other tangible record;

    (B) to transmit a record by any means agreed upon by the persons sending and receiving the record; or

    (C) in the case of transmission of a record to or by a filing office, to transmit a record by any means prescribed by filing-office rule.

(19) "Consignee" means a merchant to which goods are delivered in a consignment.

(20) "Consignment" means a transaction, regardless of its form, in which a person delivers goods to a merchant for the purpose of sale and:

    (A) the merchant:

        (i) deals in goods of that kind under a name other than the name of the person making delivery;

        (ii) is not an auctioneer; and

        (iii) is not generally known by its creditors to be substantially engaged in selling the goods of others;

    (B) with respect to each delivery, the aggregate value of the goods is $1,000 or more at the time of delivery;

    (C) the goods are not consumer goods immediately before delivery; and

    (D) the transaction does not create a security interest that secures an obligation.

(21) "Consignor" means a person that delivers goods to a consignee in a consignment.

(22) "Consumer debtor" means a debtor in a consumer transaction.

(23) "Consumer goods" means goods that are used or bought for use primarily for personal, family, or household purposes.

(24) "Consumer-goods transaction" means a consumer transaction in which:

    (A) an individual incurs an obligation primarily for personal, family, or household purposes; and

    (B) a security interest in consumer goods secures the obligation.

(25) "Consumer obligor" means an obligor who is an individual and who incurred the obligation as part of a transaction entered into primarily for personal, family, or household purposes.

(26) "Consumer transaction" means a transaction in which (i) an individual incurs an obligation primarily for personal, family, or household purposes, (ii) a security interest secures the obligation, and (iii) the collateral is held or acquired primarily for personal, family, or household purposes. The term includes consumer-goods transactions.

(27) "Continuation statement" means an amendment of a financing statement which:

    (A) identifies, by its file number, the initial financing statement to which it relates; and

    (B) indicates that it is a continuation statement for, or that it is filed to continue the effectiveness of, the identified financing statement.

(28) "Debtor" means:

  (A) a person having an interest, other than a security interest or other lien, in the collateral, whether or not the person is an obligor;

  (B) a seller of accounts, chattel paper, payment intangibles, or promissory notes; or

  (C) a consignee.

(29) "Deposit account" means a demand, time, savings, passbook, or similar account maintained with a bank. The term does not include investment property or accounts evidenced by an instrument.

(30) "Document" means a document of title or a receipt of the type described in Section 7–201(b).

(31) "Electronic chattel paper" means chattel paper evidenced by a record or records consisting of information stored in an electronic medium.

(32) "Encumbrance" means a right, other than an ownership interest, in real property. The term includes mortgages and other liens on real property.

(33) "Equipment" means goods other than inventory, farm products, or consumer goods.

(34) "Farm products" means goods, other than standing timber, with respect to which the debtor is engaged in a farming operation and which are:

  (A) crops grown, growing, or to be grown, including:

    (i)   crops produced on trees, vines, and bushes; and

    (ii) aquatic goods produced in aquacultural operations;

  (B) livestock, born or unborn, including aquatic goods produced in aquacultural operations;

  (C) supplies used or produced in a farming operation; or

  (D) products of crops or livestock in their unmanufactured states.

(35) "Farming operation" means raising, cultivating, propagating, fattening, grazing, or any other farming, livestock, or aquacultural operation.

(36) "File number" means the number assigned to an initial financing statement pursuant to Section 9–519(a).

(37) "Filing office" means an office designated in Section 9–501 as the place to file a financing statement.

(38) "Filing-office rule" means a rule adopted pursuant to Section 9–526.

(39) "Financing statement" means a record or records composed of an initial financing statement and any filed record relating to the initial financing statement.

(40) "Fixture filing" means the filing of a financing statement covering goods that are or are to become fixtures and satisfying Section 9–502(a) and (b). The term includes the filing of a financing statement covering goods of a transmitting utility which are or are to become fixtures.

(41) "Fixtures" means goods that have become so related to particular real property that an interest in them arises under real property law.

(42) "General intangible" means any personal property, including things in action, other than accounts, chattel paper, commercial tort claims, deposit accounts, documents, goods, instruments, investment property, letter-of-credit rights, letters of credit, money, and oil, gas, or other minerals before extraction. The term includes payment intangibles and software.

(43) [Reserved] ["Good faith" means honesty in fact and the observance of reasonable commercial standards of fair dealing.]*

(44) "Goods" means all things that are movable when a security interest attaches. The term includes (i) fixtures, (ii) standing timber that is to be cut and removed under a conveyance or contract for sale, (iii) the unborn young of animals, (iv) crops grown, growing, or to be grown, even if the crops are produced on trees, vines, or bushes, and (v) manufactured homes. The term also includes a computer program embedded in goods and any supporting information provided in connection with a transaction relating to the program if (i) the program is associated with the goods in such a manner that it customarily is considered part of the goods, or (ii) by becoming the owner of the goods, a person acquires a right to use the program in connection with the goods. The term does not include a computer program embedded in goods that consist solely of the medium in which the program is embedded. The term also does not include accounts, chattel paper, commercial tort claims, deposit accounts, documents, general intangibles, instruments, investment property, letter-of-credit rights, letters of credit, money, or oil, gas, or other minerals before extraction.

(45) "Governmental unit" means a subdivision, agency, department, county, parish, municipality, or other unit of the government of the United States, a State, or a foreign country. The term includes an organization having a separate corporate existence if the organization is eligible to issue debt on which interest is exempt from income taxation under the laws of the United States.

(46) "Health-care-insurance receivable" means an interest in or claim under a policy of insurance which is a right to payment of a monetary obligation for health-care goods or services provided or to be provided.

(47) "Instrument" means a negotiable instrument or any other writing that evidences a right to the payment of a monetary obligation, is not itself a security agreement or lease, and is of a type that in ordinary course of business is transferred by delivery with any necessary indorsement or assignment. The term does not include (i) investment property, (ii) letters of credit, or (iii) writings that evidence a right to payment arising out of the use of a credit or charge card or information contained on or for use with the card.

(48) "Inventory" means goods, other than farm products, which:

    (A)   are leased by a person as lessor;

    (B)   are held by a person for sale or lease or to be furnished under a contract of service;

    (C)   are furnished by a person under a contract of service; or

    (D)   consist of raw materials, work in process, or materials used or consumed in a business.

(49) "Investment property" means a security, whether certificated or uncertificated, security entitlement, securities account, commodity contract, or commodity account.

(50) "Jurisdiction of organization", with respect to a registered organization, means the jurisdiction under whose law the organization is formed or organized.

(51) "Letter-of-credit right" means a right to payment or performance under a letter of credit, whether or not the beneficiary has demanded or is at the time entitled to demand payment or performance. The term does not include the right of a beneficiary to demand payment or performance under a letter of credit.

(52) "Lien creditor" means:

    (A)   a creditor that has acquired a lien on the property involved by attachment, levy, or the like;

    (B)   an assignee for benefit of creditors from the time of assignment;

    (C)   a trustee in bankruptcy from the date of the filing of the petition; or

---

*   *Note from West Advisory Panel: This subsection will be deleted if the jurisdiction adopts the definition of good faith in revised Article 1 (2001).*

(D)   a receiver in equity from the time of appointment.

(53) "Manufactured home" means a structure, transportable in one or more sections, which, in the traveling mode, is eight body feet or more in width or 40 body feet or more in length, or, when erected on site, is 320 or more square feet, and which is built on a permanent chassis and designed to be used as a dwelling with or without a permanent foundation when connected to the required utilities, and includes the plumbing, heating, air-conditioning, and electrical systems contained therein. The term includes any structure that meets all of the requirements of this paragraph except the size requirements and with respect to which the manufacturer voluntarily files a certification required by the United States Secretary of Housing and Urban Development and complies with the standards established under Title 42 of the United States Code.

(54) "Manufactured-home transaction" means a secured transaction:

(A)   that creates a purchase-money security interest in a manufactured home, other than a manufactured home held as inventory; or

(B)   in which a manufactured home, other than a manufactured home held as inventory, is the primary collateral.

(55) "Mortgage" means a consensual interest in real property, including fixtures, which secures payment or performance of an obligation.

(56) "New debtor" means a person that becomes bound as debtor under Section 9–203(d) by a security agreement previously entered into by another person.

(57) "New value" means (i) money, (ii) money's worth in property, services, or new credit, or (iii) release by a transferee of an interest in property previously transferred to the transferee. The term does not include an obligation substituted for another obligation.

(58) "Noncash proceeds" means proceeds other than cash proceeds.

(59) "Obligor" means a person that, with respect to an obligation secured by a security interest in or an agricultural lien on the collateral, (i) owes payment or other performance of the obligation, (ii) has provided property other than the collateral to secure payment or other performance of the obligation, or (iii) is otherwise accountable in whole or in part for payment or other performance of the obligation. The term does not include issuers or nominated persons under a letter of credit.

(60) "Original debtor", except as used in Section 9–310(c), means a person that, as debtor, entered into a security agreement to which a new debtor has become bound under Section 9–203(d).

(61) "Payment intangible" means a general intangible under which the account debtor's principal obligation is a monetary obligation.

(62) "Person related to", with respect to an individual, means:

(A)   the spouse of the individual;

(B)   a brother, brother-in-law, sister, or sister-in-law of the individual;

(C)   an ancestor or lineal descendant of the individual or the individual's spouse; or

(D)   any other relative, by blood or marriage, of the individual or the individual's spouse who shares the same home with the individual.

(63) "Person related to", with respect to an organization, means:

(A)   a person directly or indirectly controlling, controlled by, or under common control with the organization;

(B)   an officer or director of, or a person performing similar functions with respect to, the organization;

(C)   an officer or director of, or a person performing similar functions with respect to, a person described in subparagraph (A);

(D) the spouse of an individual described in subparagraph (A), (B), or (C); or

(E) an individual who is related by blood or marriage to an individual described in subparagraph (A), (B), (C), or (D) and shares the same home with the individual.

(64) "Proceeds", except as used in Section 9–609(b), means the following property:

(A) whatever is acquired upon the sale, lease, license, exchange, or other disposition of collateral;

(B) whatever is collected on, or distributed on account of, collateral;

(C) rights arising out of collateral;

(D) to the extent of the value of collateral, claims arising out of the loss, nonconformity, or interference with the use of, defects or infringement of rights in, or damage to, the collateral; or

(E) to the extent of the value of collateral and to the extent payable to the debtor or the secured party, insurance payable by reason of the loss or nonconformity of, defects or infringement of rights in, or damage to, the collateral.

(65) "Promissory note" means an instrument that evidences a promise to pay a monetary obligation, does not evidence an order to pay, and does not contain an acknowledgment by a bank that the bank has received for deposit a sum of money or funds.

(66) "Proposal" means a record authenticated by a secured party which includes the terms on which the secured party is willing to accept collateral in full or partial satisfaction of the obligation it secures pursuant to Sections 9–620, 9–621, and 9–622.

(67) "Public-finance transaction" means a secured transaction in connection with which:

(A) debt securities are issued;

(B) all or a portion of the securities issued have an initial stated maturity of at least 20 years; and

(C) the debtor, obligor, secured party, account debtor or other person obligated on collateral, assignor or assignee of a secured obligation, or assignor or assignee of a security interest is a State or a governmental unit of a State.

(68) "Public organic record" means a record that is available to the public for inspection and is:

(A) a record consisting of the record initially filed with or issued by a State or the United States to form or organize an organization and any record filed with or issued by the State or the United States which amends or restates the initial record;

(B) an organic record of a business trust consisting of the record initially filed with a State and any record filed with the State which amends or restates the initial record, if a statute of the State governing business trusts requires that the record be filed with the State; or

(C) a record consisting of legislation enacted by the legislature of a State or the Congress of the United States which forms or organizes an organization, any record amending the legislation, and any record filed with or issued by the State or the United States which amends or restates the name of the organization.

(69) "Pursuant to commitment", with respect to an advance made or other value given by a secured party, means pursuant to the secured party's obligation, whether or not a subsequent event of default or other event not within the secured party's control has relieved or may relieve the secured party from its obligation.

(70) "Record", except as used in "for record", "of record", "record or legal title", and "record owner", means information that is inscribed on a tangible medium or which is stored in an electronic or other medium and is retrievable in perceivable form.

(71) "Registered organization" means an organization formed or organized solely under the law of a single State or the United States by the filing of a public organic record with, the issuance of a public organic record by, or the enactment of legislation by the State or the United States. The term includes a business trust that is formed or organized under the law of a single State if a statute of the State governing business trusts requires that the business trust's organic record be filed with the State.

(72) "Secondary obligor" means an obligor to the extent that:

    (A) the obligor's obligation is secondary; or

    (B) the obligor has a right of recourse with respect to an obligation secured by collateral against the debtor, another obligor, or property of either.

(73) "Secured party" means:

    (A) a person in whose favor a security interest is created or provided for under a security agreement, whether or not any obligation to be secured is outstanding;

    (B) a person that holds an agricultural lien;

    (C) a consignor;

    (D) a person to which accounts, chattel paper, payment intangibles, or promissory notes have been sold;

    (E) a trustee, indenture trustee, agent, collateral agent, or other representative in whose favor a security interest or agricultural lien is created or provided for; or

    (F) a person that holds a security interest arising under Section 2–401, 2–505, 2–711(3), 2A–508(5), 4–210, or 5–118.

(74) "Security agreement" means an agreement that creates or provides for a security interest.

(75) "Send", in connection with a record or notification, means:

    (A) to deposit in the mail, deliver for transmission, or transmit by any other usual means of communication, with postage or cost of transmission provided for, addressed to any address reasonable under the circumstances; or

    (B) to cause the record or notification to be received within the time that it would have been received if properly sent under subparagraph (A).

(76) "Software" means a computer program and any supporting information provided in connection with a transaction relating to the program. The term does not include a computer program that is included in the definition of goods.

(77) "State" means a State of the United States, the District of Columbia, Puerto Rico, the United States Virgin Islands, or any territory or insular possession subject to the jurisdiction of the United States.

(78) "Supporting obligation" means a letter-of-credit right or secondary obligation that supports the payment or performance of an account, chattel paper, a document, a general intangible, an instrument, or investment property.

(79) "Tangible chattel paper" means chattel paper evidenced by a record or records consisting of information that is inscribed on a tangible medium.

(80) "Termination statement" means an amendment of a financing statement which:

    (A) identifies, by its file number, the initial financing statement to which it relates; and

    (B) indicates either that it is a termination statement or that the identified financing statement is no longer effective.

(81) "Transmitting utility" means a person primarily engaged in the business of:

    (A)   operating a railroad, subway, street railway, or trolley bus;

    (B)   transmitting communications electrically, electromagnetically, or by light;

    (C)   transmitting goods by pipeline or sewer; or

    (D)   transmitting or producing and transmitting electricity, steam, gas, or water.

(b)   **[Definitions in other articles.]** "Control" as provided in Section 7–106 and the following definitions in other articles apply to this article:

"Applicant". Section 5–102.
"Beneficiary". Section 5–102.
"Broker". Section 8–102.
"Certificated security". Section 8–102.
"Check". Section 3–104.
"Clearing corporation". Section 8–102.
"Contract for sale". Section 2–106.
"Customer". Section 4–104.
"Entitlement holder". Section 8–102.
"Financial asset". Section 8–102.
"Holder in due course". Section 3–302.
"Issuer" (with respect to a letter of credit or letter-of-credit right). Section 5–102.
"Issuer" (with respect to a security). Section 8–201.
"Issuer" (with respect to a document of title). Section 7–102.
"Lease". Section 2A–103.
"Lease agreement". Section 2A–103.
"Lease contract". Section 2A–103.
"Leasehold interest". Section 2A–103.
"Lessee". Section 2A–103.
"Lessee in ordinary course of business". Section 2A–103.
"Lessor". Section 2A–103.
"Lessor's residual interest". Section 2A–103.
"Letter of credit". Section 5–102.
"Merchant". Section 2–104.
"Negotiable instrument". Section 3–104.
"Nominated person". Section 5–102.
"Note". Section 3–104.
"Proceeds of a letter of credit". Section 5–114.
"Prove". Section 3–103.
"Sale". Section 2–106.
"Securities account". Section 8–501.
"Securities intermediary". Section 8–102.
"Security". Section 8–102.
"Security certificate". Section 8–102.
"Security entitlement". Section 8–102.
"Uncertificated security". Section 8–102.

(c)   **[Article 1 definitions and principles.]** Article 1 contains general definitions and principles of construction and interpretation applicable throughout this article.

As amended in 1999, 2000, 2001, 2003, and 2010.

Official Comment

1.   **Source.** All terms that are defined in Article 9 and used in more than one section are consolidated in this section. Note that the definition of "security interest" is found in Section 1–201, not in this Article, and has

been revised. See Appendix I.* Many of the definitions in this section are new; many others derive from those in former Section 9–105. The following Comments also indicate other sections of former Article 9 that defined (or explained) terms.

2. **Parties to Secured Transactions.**

a. **"Debtor"; "Obligor"; "Secondary Obligor."** Determining whether a person was a "debtor" under former Section 9–105(1)(d) required a close examination of the context in which the term was used. To reduce the need for this examination, this Article redefines "debtor" and adds new defined terms, "secondary obligor" and "obligor." In the context of Part 6 (default and enforcement), these definitions distinguish among three classes of persons: (i) those persons who may have a stake in the proper enforcement of a security interest by virtue of their non-lien property interest (typically, an ownership interest) in the collateral, (ii) those persons who may have a stake in the proper enforcement of the security interest because of their obligation to pay the secured debt, and (iii) those persons who have an obligation to pay the secured debt but have no stake in the proper enforcement of the security interest. Persons in the first class are debtors. Persons in the second class are secondary obligors if any portion of the obligation is secondary or if the obligor has a right of recourse against the debtor or another obligor with respect to an obligation secured by collateral. One must consult the law of suretyship to determine whether an obligation is secondary. The Restatement (3d), Suretyship and Guaranty § 1 (1996), contains a useful explanation of the concept. Obligors in the third class are neither debtors nor secondary obligors. With one exception (Section 9–616, as it relates to a consumer obligor), the rights and duties provided by Part 6 affect non-debtor obligors only if they are "secondary obligors."

By including in the definition of "debtor" all persons with a property interest (other than a security interest in or other lien on collateral), the definition includes transferees of collateral, whether or not the secured party knows of the transfer or the transferee's identity. Exculpatory provisions in Part 6 protect the secured party in that circumstance. See Sections 9–605 and 9–628. The definition renders unnecessary former Section 9–112, which governed situations in which collateral was not owned by the debtor. The definition also includes a "consignee," as defined in this section, as well as a seller of accounts, chattel paper, payment intangibles, or promissory notes.

Secured parties and other lienholders are excluded from the definition of "debtor" because the interests of those parties normally derive from and encumber a debtor's interest. However, if in a *separate* secured transaction a secured party grants, *as debtor*, a security interest in its own interest (i.e., its security interest and any obligation that it secures), the secured party is a debtor *in that transaction*. This typically occurs when a secured party with a security interest in specific goods assigns chattel paper.

Consider the following examples:

Example 1: Behnfeldt borrows money and grants a security interest in her Miata to secure the debt. Behnfeldt is a debtor and an obligor.

Example 2: Behnfeldt borrows money and grants a security interest in her Miata to secure the debt. Bruno co-signs a negotiable note as maker. As before, Behnfeldt is the debtor and an obligor. As an accommodation party (see Section 3–419), Bruno is a secondary obligor. Bruno has this status even if the note states that her obligation is a primary obligation and that she waives all suretyship defenses.

Example 3: Behnfeldt borrows money on an unsecured basis. Bruno co-signs the note and grants a security interest in her Honda to secure her obligation. Inasmuch as Behnfeldt does not have a property interest in the Honda, Behnfeldt is not a debtor. Having granted the security interest, Bruno is the debtor. Because Behnfeldt is a principal obligor, she is not a secondary obligor. Whatever the outcome of enforcement of the security interest against the Honda or Bruno's secondary obligation, Bruno will look to Behnfeldt for her losses. The enforcement will not affect Behnfeldt's aggregate obligations.

When the principal obligor (borrower) and the secondary obligor (surety) each has granted a security interest in different collateral, the status of each is determined by the collateral involved.

Example 4: Behnfeldt borrows money and grants a security interest in her Miata to secure the debt. Bruno co-signs the note and grants a security interest in her Honda to secure her obligation. When the secured party enforces the security interest in Behnfeldt's Miata, Behnfeldt is the debtor, and Bruno is a secondary obligor. When the secured party enforces the security interest in the Honda, Bruno is the "debtor." As in Example 3, Behnfeldt is an obligor, but not a secondary obligor.

---

* *Note from West Advisory Panel: Appendix I is omitted from this volume.*

b.   **"Secured Party."** The secured party is the person in whose favor the security interest has been created, as determined by reference to the security agreement. This definition controls, among other things, which person has the duties and potential liability that Part 6 imposes upon a secured party. The definition of "secured party" also includes a "consignor," a person to which accounts, chattel paper, payment intangibles, or promissory notes have been sold, and the holder of an agricultural lien.

The definition of "secured party" clarifies the status of various types of representatives. Consider, for example, a multi-bank facility under which Bank A, Bank B, and Bank C are lenders and Bank A serves as the collateral agent. If the security interest is granted to the banks, then they are the secured parties. If the security interest is granted to Bank A as collateral agent, then Bank A is the secured party.

c.   **Other Parties.** A "consumer obligor" is defined as the obligor in a consumer transaction. Definitions of "new debtor" and "original debtor" are used in the special rules found in Sections 9–326 and 9–508.

3.   **Definitions Relating to Creation of a Security Interest.**

a.   **"Collateral."** As under former Section 9–105, "collateral" is the property subject to a security interest and includes accounts and chattel paper that have been sold. It has been expanded in this Article. The term now explicitly includes proceeds subject to a security interest. It also reflects the broadened scope of the Article. It includes property subject to an agricultural lien as well as payment intangibles and promissory notes that have been sold.

b.   **"Security Agreement."** The definition of "security agreement" is substantially the same as under former Section 9–105—an agreement that creates or provides for a security interest. However, the term frequently was used colloquially in former Article 9 to refer to the document or writing that contained a debtor's security agreement. This Article eliminates that usage, reserving the term for the more precise meaning specified in the definition.

Whether an agreement creates a security interest depends not on whether the parties intend that the law *characterize* the transaction as a security interest but rather on whether the transaction falls within the definition of "security interest" in Section 1–201. Thus, an agreement that the parties characterize as a "lease" of goods may be a "security agreement," notwithstanding the parties' stated intention that the law treat the transaction as a lease and not as a secured transaction. See Section 1–203.

4.   **Goods-Related Definitions.**

a.   **"Goods"; "Consumer Goods"; "Equipment"; "Farm Products"; "Farming Operation"; "Inventory."** The definition of "goods" is substantially the same as the definition in former Section 9–105. This Article also retains the four mutually-exclusive "types" of collateral that consist of goods: "consumer goods," "equipment," "farm products," and "inventory." The revisions are primarily for clarification.

The classes of goods are mutually exclusive. For example, the same property cannot simultaneously be both equipment and inventory. In borderline cases—a physician's car or a farmer's truck that might be either consumer goods or equipment—the principal use to which the property is put is determinative. Goods can fall into different classes at different times. For example, a radio may be inventory in the hands of a dealer and consumer goods in the hands of a consumer. As under former Article 9, goods are "equipment" if they do not fall into another category.

The definition of "consumer goods" follows former Section 9–109. The classification turns on whether the debtor uses or bought the goods for use "primarily for personal, family, or household purposes."

Goods are inventory if they are leased by a lessor or held by a person for sale or lease. The revised definition of "inventory" makes clear that the term includes goods leased by the debtor to others as well as goods held for lease. (The same result should have obtained under the former definition.) Goods to be furnished or furnished under a service contract, raw materials, and work in process also are inventory. Implicit in the definition is the criterion that the sales or leases are or will be in the ordinary course of business. For example, machinery used in manufacturing is equipment, not inventory, even though it is the policy of the debtor to sell machinery when it becomes obsolete or worn. Inventory also includes goods that are consumed in a business (e.g., fuel used in operations). In general, goods used in a business are equipment if they are fixed assets or have, as identifiable units, a relatively long period of use, but are inventory, even though not held for sale or lease, if they are used up or consumed in a short period of time in producing a product or providing a service.

Goods are "farm products" if the debtor is engaged in farming operations with respect to the goods. Animals in a herd of livestock are covered whether the debtor acquires them by purchase or as a result of natural increase. Products of crops or livestock remain farm products as long as they have not been subjected to a manufacturing

719

process. The terms "crops" and "livestock" are not defined. The new definition of "farming operations" is for clarification only.

Crops, livestock, and their products cease to be "farm products" when the debtor ceases to be engaged in farming operations with respect to them. If, for example, they come into the possession of a marketing agency for sale or distribution or of a manufacturer or processor as raw materials, they become inventory. Products of crops or livestock, even though they remain in the possession of a person engaged in farming operations, lose their status as farm products if they are subjected to a manufacturing process. What is and what is not a manufacturing operation is not specified in this Article. At one end of the spectrum, some processes are so closely connected with farming—such as pasteurizing milk or boiling sap to produce maple syrup or sugar—that they would not constitute manufacturing. On the other hand an extensive canning operation would be manufacturing. Once farm products have been subjected to a manufacturing operation, they normally become inventory.

The revised definition of "farm products" clarifies the distinction between crops and standing timber and makes clear that aquatic goods produced in aquacultural operations may be either crops or livestock. Although aquatic goods that are vegetable in nature often would be crops and those that are animal would be livestock, this Article leaves the courts free to classify the goods on a case-by-case basis. See Section 9–324, Comment 11.

The definitions of "goods" and "software" are also mutually exclusive. Computer programs usually constitute "software," and, as such, are not "goods" as this Article uses the terms. However, under the circumstances specified in the definition of "goods," computer programs embedded in goods are part of the "goods" and are not "software."

b. **"Accession"; "Manufactured Home"; "Manufactured-Home Transaction."** Other specialized definitions of goods include "accession" (see the special priority and enforcement rules in Section 9–335), and "manufactured home" (see Section 9–515, permitting a financing statement in a "manufactured-home transaction" to be effective for 30 years). The definition of "manufactured home" borrows from the federal Manufactured Housing Act, 42 U.S.C. §§ 5401 *et seq.*, and is intended to have the same meaning.

c. **"As-Extracted Collateral."** Under this Article, oil, gas, and other minerals that have not been extracted from the ground are treated as real property, to which this Article does not apply. Upon extraction, minerals become personal property (goods) and eligible to be collateral under this Article. See the definition of "goods," which excludes "oil, gas, and other minerals before extraction." To take account of financing practices reflecting the shift from real to personal property, this Article contains special rules for perfecting security interests in minerals which attach upon extraction and in accounts resulting from the sale of minerals at the wellhead or minehead. See, e.g., Sections 9–301(4) (law governing perfection and priority); 9–501 (place of filing), 9–502 (contents of financing statement), 9–519 (indexing of records). The new term, "as-extracted collateral," refers to the minerals and related accounts to which the special rules apply. The term "at the wellhead" encompasses arrangements based on a sale of the produce at the moment that it issues from the ground and is measured, without technical distinctions as to whether title passes at the "Christmas tree" of a well, the far side of a gathering tank, or at some other point. The term "at . . . the minehead" is comparable.

The following examples explain the operation of these provisions.

Example 5: Debtor owns an interest in oil that is to be extracted. To secure Debtor's obligations to Lender, Debtor enters into an authenticated agreement granting Lender an interest in the oil. Although Lender may acquire an interest in the oil under real-property law, Lender does not acquire a security interest under this Article until the oil becomes personal property, i.e., until is extracted and becomes "goods" to which this Article applies. Because Debtor had an interest in the oil before extraction and Lender's security interest attached to the oil as extracted, the oil is "as-extracted collateral."

Example 6: Debtor owns an interest in oil that is to be extracted and contracts to sell the oil to Buyer at the wellhead. In an authenticated agreement, Debtor agrees to sell to Lender the right to payment from Buyer. This right to payment is an account that constitutes "as-extracted collateral." If Lender then resells the account to Financer, Financer acquires a security interest. However, inasmuch as the debtor-seller in that transaction, Lender, had no interest in the oil before extraction, Financer's collateral (the account it owns) is not "as-extracted collateral."

Example 7: Under the facts of Example 6, before extraction, Buyer grants a security interest in the oil to Bank. Although Bank's security interest attaches when the oil is extracted, Bank's security interest is not in "as-extracted collateral," inasmuch as its debtor, Buyer, did not have an interest in the oil before extraction.

5.   **Receivables-related Definitions.**

a.   **"Account"; "Health-Care-Insurance Receivable"; "As-Extracted Collateral."** The definition of "account" has been expanded and reformulated. It is no longer limited to rights to payment relating to goods or services. Many categories of rights to payment that were classified as general intangibles under former Article 9 are accounts under this Article. Thus, if they are sold, a financing statement must be filed to perfect the buyer's interest in them. As used in the definition of "account," a right to payment "arising out of the use of a credit or charge card or information contained on or for use with the card" is the right of a card issuer to payment from its cardholder. A credit-card or charge-card transaction may give rise to other rights to payments; however, those other rights do not "arise out of the use" of the card or information contained on or for use with the card. Among the types of property that are expressly excluded from the definition of account is "a right to payment for money or funds advanced or sold." As defined in Section 1–201, "money" is limited essentially to currency. As used in the exclusion from the definition of "account," however, "funds" is a broader concept (although the term is not defined). For example, when a bank-lender credits a borrower's deposit account for the amount of a loan, the bank's advance of funds is not a transaction giving rise to an account.

The definition of "health-care-insurance receivable" is new. It is a subset of the definition of "account." However, the rules generally applicable to account debtors on accounts do not apply to insurers obligated on health-care-insurance receivables. See Sections 9–404(e), 9–405(d), 9–406(i).

Note that certain accounts also are "as-extracted collateral." See Comment 4.c., Examples 6 and 7.

b.   **"Chattel Paper"; "Electronic Chattel Paper"; "Tangible Chattel Paper."** "Chattel paper" consists of a monetary obligation together with a security interest in or a lease of specific goods if the obligation and security interest or lease are evidenced by "a record or records." The definition has been expanded from that found in former Article 9 to include records that evidence a monetary obligation and a security interest in specific goods and software used in the goods, *a security interest in specific goods and license of software used in the goods, or a lease of specific goods and license of software used in the goods. The expanded definition covers transactions in which the debtor's or lessee's monetary obligation includes amounts owed with respect to software used in the goods. The monetary obligation with respect to the software need not be owed under a license from the secured party or lessor, and the secured party or lessor need not be a party to the license transaction itself. Among the types of monetary obligations that are included in "chattel paper" are amounts that have been advanced by the secured party or lessor to enable the debtor or lessee to acquire or obtain financing for a license of the software used in the goods.*[*] The definition also makes clear that rights to payment arising out of credit-card transactions are not chattel paper.

Charters of vessels are expressly excluded from the definition of chattel paper; they are accounts. The term "charter" as used in this section includes bareboat charters, time charters, successive voyage charters, contracts of affreightment, contracts of carriage, and all other arrangements for the use of vessels. Under former Section 9–105, only if the evidence of an obligation consisted of "a writing or writings" could an obligation qualify as chattel paper. In this Article, traditional, written chattel paper is included in the definition of "tangible chattel paper." "Electronic chattel paper" is chattel paper that is stored in an electronic medium instead of in tangible form.

The concept of an electronic medium should be construed liberally to include electrical, digital, magnetic, optical, electromagnetic, or any other current or similar emerging technologies.

c.   **"Instrument"; "Promissory Note."** The definition of "instrument" includes a negotiable instrument. As under former Section 9–105, it also includes any other right to payment of a monetary obligation that is evidenced by a writing of a type that in ordinary course of business is transferred by delivery (and, if necessary, an indorsement or assignment). Except in the case of chattel paper, the fact that an instrument is secured by a security interest or encumbrance on property does not change the character of the instrument as such or convert the combination of the instrument and collateral into a separate classification of personal property. The definition makes clear that rights to payment arising out of credit-card transactions are not instruments. The definition of "promissory note" is new, necessitated by the inclusion of sales of promissory notes within the scope of Article 9. It explicitly excludes obligations arising out of "orders" to pay (e.g., checks) as opposed to "promises" to pay. See Section 3–104.

d.   **"General Intangible"; "Payment Intangible."** "General intangible" is the residual category of personal property, including things in action, that is not included in the other defined types of collateral. Examples are various categories of intellectual property and the right to payment of a loan of funds that is not evidenced by

---

[*]   Amendment in italics approved by the Permanent Editorial Board for Uniform Commercial Code October 20, 1999.

chattel paper or an instrument. As used in the definition of "general intangible," "things in action" includes rights that arise under a license of intellectual property, including the right to exploit the intellectual property without liability for infringement. The definition has been revised to exclude commercial tort claims, deposit accounts, and letter-of-credit rights. Each of the three is a separate type of collateral. One important consequence of this exclusion is that tortfeasors (commercial tort claims), banks (deposit accounts), and persons obligated on letters of credit (letter-of-credit rights) are not "account debtors" having the rights and obligations set forth in Sections 9–404, 9–405, and 9–406. In particular, tortfeasors, banks, and persons obligated on letters of credit are not obligated to pay an assignee (secured party) upon receipt of the notification described in Section 9–404(a). See Comment 5.h. Another important consequence relates to the adequacy of the description in the security agreement. See Section 9–108.

"Payment intangible" is a subset of the definition of "general intangible." The sale of a payment intangible is subject to this Article. See Section 9–109(a)(3). Virtually any intangible right could give rise to a right to payment of money once one hypothesizes, for example, that the account debtor is in breach of its obligation. The term "payment intangible," however, embraces only those general intangibles "under which the account debtor's *principal* obligation is a monetary obligation." (Emphasis added.) A debtor's right to payment from another person of amounts received by the other person on the debtor's behalf, including the right of a merchant in a credit-card, debit-card, prepaid-card, or other payment-card transaction to payment of amounts received by its bank from the card system in settlement of the transaction, is a "payment intangible." (In contrast, the right of a credit-card issuer to payment arising out of the use of a credit card is an "account.")

In classifying intangible collateral, a court should begin by identifying the particular rights that have been assigned. The account debtor (promisor) under a particular contract may owe several types of monetary obligations as well as other, nonmonetary obligations. If the promisee's right to payment of money is assigned separately, the right is an account or payment intangible, depending on how the account debtor's obligation arose. When all the promisee's rights are assigned together, an account, a payment intangible, and a general intangible all may be involved, depending on the nature of the rights.

A right to the payment of money is frequently buttressed by ancillary rights, such as rights arising from covenants in a purchase agreement, note, or mortgage requiring insurance on the collateral or forbidding removal of the collateral, rights arising from covenants to preserve the creditworthiness of the promisor, and the lessor's rights with respect to leased goods that arise upon the lessee's default (see Section 2A–523). This Article does not treat these ancillary rights separately from the rights to payment to which they relate. For example, attachment and perfection of an assignment of a right to payment of a monetary obligation, whether it be an account or payment intangible, also carries these ancillary rights. Thus, an assignment of the lessor's right to payment under a lease also transfers the lessor's rights with respect to the leased goods under Section 2A–523. If, taken together, the lessor's rights to payment and with respect to the leased goods are evidenced by chattel paper, then, contrary to *In re Commercial Money Center, Inc.*, 350 B.R. 465 (Bankr. App. 9th Cir. 2006), an assignment of the lessor's right to payment constitutes an assignment of the chattel paper. Although an agreement excluding the lessor's rights with respect to the leased goods from an assignment of the lessor's right to payment may be effective between the parties, the agreement does not affect the characterization of the collateral to the prejudice of creditors of, and purchasers from, the assignor.

Every "payment intangible" is also a "general intangible." Likewise, "software" is a "general intangible" for purposes of this Article. See Comment 25. Accordingly, except as otherwise provided, statutory provisions applicable to general intangibles apply to payment intangibles and software.

e.   **"Letter-of-Credit Right."** The term "letter-of-credit right" embraces the rights to payment and performance under a letter of credit (defined in Section 5–102). However, it does not include a beneficiary's right to demand payment or performance. Transfer of those rights to a transferee beneficiary is governed by Article 5. See Sections 9–107, Comment 4, and 9–329, Comments 3 and 4.

f.   **"Supporting Obligation."** This new term covers the most common types of credit enhancements— suretyship obligations (including guarantees) and letter-of-credit rights that support one of the types of collateral specified in the definition. As explained in Comment 2.a., suretyship law determines whether an obligation is "secondary" for purposes of this definition. Section 9–109 generally excludes from this Article transfers of interests in insurance policies. However, the regulation of a secondary obligation as an insurance product does not necessarily mean that it is a "policy of insurance" for purposes of the exclusion in Section 9–109. Thus, this Article may cover a secondary obligation (as a supporting obligation), even if the obligation is issued by a regulated insurance company and the obligation is subject to regulation as an "insurance" product.

This Article contains rules explicitly governing attachment, perfection, and priority of security interests in supporting obligations. See Sections 9–203, 9–308, 9–310, and 9–322. These provisions reflect the principle that a supporting obligation is an incident of the collateral it supports.

Collections of or other distributions under a supporting obligation are "proceeds" of the supported collateral as well as "proceeds" of the supporting obligation itself. See Section 9–102 (defining "proceeds") and Comment 13.b. As such, the collections and distributions are subject to the priority rules applicable to proceeds generally. See Section 9–322. However, under the special rule governing security interests in a letter-of-credit right, a secured party's failure to obtain control (Section 9–107) of a letter-of-credit right supporting collateral may leave its security interest exposed to a priming interest of a party who does take control. See Section 9–329 (security interest in a letter-of-credit right perfected by control has priority over a conflicting security interest).

g. **"Commercial Tort Claim."** This term is new. A tort claim may serve as original collateral under this Article only if it is a "commercial tort claim." See Section 9–109(d). Although security interests in commercial tort claims are within its scope, this Article does not override other applicable law restricting the assignability of a tort claim. See Section 9–401. A security interest in a tort claim also may exist under this Article if the claim is proceeds of other collateral.

h. **"Account Debtor."** An "account debtor" is a person obligated on an account, chattel paper, or general intangible. The account debtor's obligation often is a monetary obligation; however, this is not always the case. For example, if a franchisee uses its rights under a franchise agreement (a general intangible) as collateral, then the franchisor is an "account debtor." As a general matter, Article 3, and not Article 9, governs obligations on negotiable instruments. Accordingly, the definition of "account debtor" excludes obligors on negotiable instruments constituting part of chattel paper. The principal effect of this change from the definition in former Article 9 is that the rules in Sections 9–403, 9–404, 9–405, and 9–406, dealing with the rights of an assignee and duties of an account debtor, do not apply to an assignment of chattel paper in which the obligation to pay is evidenced by a negotiable instrument. (Section 9–406(d), however, does apply to promissory notes, including negotiable promissory notes.) Rather, the assignee's rights are governed by Article 3. Similarly, the duties of an obligor on a nonnegotiable instrument are governed by non-Article 9 law unless the nonnegotiable instrument is a part of chattel paper, in which case the obligor is an account debtor.

i. **Receivables Under Government Entitlement Programs**. This Article does not contain a defined term that encompasses specifically rights to payment or performance under the many and varied government entitlement programs. Depending on the nature of a right under a program, it could be an account, a payment intangible, a general intangible other than a payment intangible, or another type of collateral. The right also might be proceeds of collateral (e.g., crops).

6. **Investment-Property-Related Definitions: "Commodity Account"; "Commodity Contract"; "Commodity Customer"; "Commodity Intermediary"; "Investment Property."** These definitions are substantially the same as the corresponding definitions in former Section 9–115. "Investment property" includes securities, both certificated and uncertificated, securities accounts, security entitlements, commodity accounts, and commodity contracts. The term investment property includes a "securities account" in order to facilitate transactions in which a debtor wishes to create a security interest in all of the investment positions held through a particular account rather than in particular positions carried in the account. Former Section 9–115 was added in conjunction with Revised Article 8 and contained a variety of rules applicable to security interests in investment property. These rules have been relocated to the appropriate sections of Article 9. See, e.g., Sections 9–203 (attachment), 9–314 (perfection by control), 9–328 (priority).

The terms "security," "security entitlement," and related terms are defined in Section 8–102, and the term "securities account" is defined in Section 8–501. The terms "commodity account," "commodity contract," "commodity customer," and "commodity intermediary" are defined in this section. Commodity contracts are not "securities" or "financial assets" under Article 8. See Section 8–103(f). Thus, the relationship between commodity intermediaries and commodity customers is not governed by the indirect-holding-system rules of Part 5 of Article 8. For securities, Article 9 contains rules on security interests, and Article 8 contains rules on the rights of transferees, including secured parties, on such matters as the rights of a transferee if the transfer was itself wrongful and gives rise to an adverse claim. For commodity contracts, Article 9 establishes rules on security interests, but questions of the sort dealt with in Article 8 for securities are left to other law.

The indirect-holding-system rules of Article 8 are sufficiently flexible to be applied to new developments in the securities and financial markets, where that is appropriate. Accordingly, the definition of "commodity contract" is narrowly drafted to ensure that it does not operate as an obstacle to the application of the Article 8 indirect-holding-system rules to new products. The term "commodity contract" covers those contracts that are traded on or subject to the rules of a designated contract market and foreign commodity contracts that are carried on the books of American commodity intermediaries. The effect of this definition is that the category of commodity contracts that are excluded from Article 8 but governed by Article 9 is essentially the same as the category of contracts that fall within the exclusive regulatory jurisdiction of the federal Commodity Futures Trading Commission.

Commodity contracts are different from securities or other financial assets. A person who enters into a commodity futures contract is not buying an asset having a certain value and holding it in anticipation of increase in value. Rather the person is entering into a contract to buy or sell a commodity at set price for delivery at a future time. That contract may become advantageous or disadvantageous as the price of the commodity fluctuates during the term of the contract. The rules of the commodity exchanges require that the contracts be marked to market on a daily basis; that is, the customer pays or receives any increment attributable to that day's price change. Because commodity customers may incur obligations on their contracts, they are required to provide collateral at the outset, known as "original margin," and may be required to provide additional amounts, known as "variation margin," during the term of the contract.

The most likely setting in which a person would want to take a security interest in a commodity contract is where a lender who is advancing funds to finance an inventory of a physical commodity requires the borrower to enter into a commodity contract as a hedge against the risk of decline in the value of the commodity. The lender will want to take a security interest in both the commodity itself and the hedging commodity contract. Typically, such arrangements are structured as security interests in the entire commodity account in which the borrower carries the hedging contracts, rather than in individual contracts.

One important effect of including commodity contracts and commodity accounts in Article 9 is to provide a clearer legal structure for the analysis of the rights of commodity clearing organizations against their participants and futures commission merchants against their customers. The rules and agreements of commodity clearing organizations generally provide that the clearing organization has the right to liquidate any participant's positions in order to satisfy obligations of the participant to the clearing corporation. Similarly, agreements between futures commission merchants and their customers generally provide that the futures commission merchant has the right to liquidate a customer's positions in order to satisfy obligations of the customer to the futures commission merchant.

The main property that a commodity intermediary holds as collateral for the obligations that the commodity customer may incur under its commodity contracts is not other commodity contracts carried by the customer but the other property that the customer has posted as margin. Typically, this property will be securities. The commodity intermediary's security interest in such securities is governed by the rules of this Article on security interests in securities, not the rules on security interests in commodity contracts or commodity accounts.

Although there are significant analytic and regulatory differences between commodities and securities, the development of commodity contracts on financial products in the past few decades has resulted in a system in which the commodity markets and securities markets are closely linked. The rules on security interests in commodity contracts and commodity accounts provide a structure that may be essential in times of stress in the financial markets. Suppose, for example that a firm has a position in a securities market that is hedged by a position in a commodity market, so that payments that the firm is obligated to make with respect to the securities position will be covered by the receipt of funds from the commodity position. Depending upon the settlement cycles of the different markets, it is possible that the firm could find itself in a position where it is obligated to make the payment with respect to the securities position before it receives the matching funds from the commodity position. If cross-margining arrangements have not been developed between the two markets, the firm may need to borrow funds temporarily to make the earlier payment. The rules on security interests in investment property would facilitate the use of positions in one market as collateral for loans needed to cover obligations in the other market.

7. **Consumer-Related Definitions: "Consumer Debtor"; "Consumer Goods"; "Consumer-goods transaction"; "Consumer Obligor"; "Consumer Transaction."** The definition of "consumer goods" (discussed above) is substantially the same as the definition in former Section 9–109. The definitions of "consumer debtor," "consumer obligor," "consumer-goods transaction," and "consumer transaction" have been added in connection with various new (and old) consumer-related provisions and to designate certain provisions that are inapplicable in consumer transactions.

"Consumer-goods transaction" is a subset of "consumer transaction." Under each definition, both the obligation secured and the collateral must have a personal, family, or household purpose. However, "mixed" business and personal transactions also may be characterized as a consumer-goods transaction or consumer transaction. Subparagraph (A) of the definition of consumer-goods transactions and clause (i) of the definition of consumer transaction are primary purposes tests. Under these tests, it is necessary to determine the primary purpose of the obligation or obligations secured. Subparagraph (B) and clause (iii) of these definitions are satisfied if any of the collateral is consumer goods, in the case of a consumer-goods transaction, or "is held or acquired primarily for personal, family, or household purposes," in the case of a consumer transaction. The fact that some of the obligations secured or some of the collateral for the obligation does not satisfy the tests (e.g., some of the collateral is acquired for a business purpose) does not prevent a transaction from being a "consumer transaction" or "consumer-goods transaction."

8. **Filing-Related Definitions: "Continuation Statement"; "File Number"; "Filing Office"; "Filing-office Rule"; "Financing Statement"; "Fixture Filing"; "Manufactured-Home Transaction"; "New Debtor"; "Original Debtor"; "Public-Finance Transaction"; "Termination Statement"; "Transmitting Utility."** These definitions are used exclusively or primarily in the filing-related provisions in Part 5. Most are self-explanatory and are discussed in the Comments to Part 5. A financing statement filed in a manufactured-home transaction or a public-finance transaction may remain effective for 30 years instead of the 5 years applicable to other financing statements. See Section 9–515(b). The definitions relating to medium neutrality also are significant for the filing provisions. See Comment 9.

The definition of "transmitting utility" has been revised to embrace the business of transmitting communications generally to take account of new and future types of communications technology. The term designates a special class of debtors for whom separate filing rules are provided in Part 5, thereby obviating the many local fixture filings that would be necessary under the rules of Section 9–501 for a far-flung public-utility debtor. A transmitting utility will not necessarily be regulated by or operating as such in a jurisdiction where fixtures are located. For example, a utility might own transmission lines in a jurisdiction, although the utility generates no power and has no customers in the jurisdiction.

9. **Definitions Relating to Medium Neutrality.**

a. **"Record."** In many, but not all, instances, the term "record" replaces the term "writing" and "written." A "record" includes information that is in intangible form (e.g., electronically stored) as well as tangible form (e.g., written on paper). Given the rapid development and commercial adoption of modern communication and storage technologies, requirements that documents or communications be "written," "in writing," or otherwise in tangible form do not necessarily reflect or aid commercial practices.

A "record" need not be permanent or indestructible, but the term does not include any oral or other communication that is not stored or preserved by any means. The information must be stored on paper or in some other medium. Information that has not been retained other than through human memory does not qualify as a record. Examples of current technologies commercially used to communicate or store information include, but are not limited to, magnetic media, optical discs, digital voice messaging systems, electronic mail, audio tapes, and photographic media, as well as paper. "Record" is an inclusive term that includes all of these methods of storing or communicating information. Any "writing" is a record. A record may be authenticated. See Comment 9.b. A record may be created without the knowledge or intent of a particular person.

Like the terms "written" or "in writing," the term "record" does not establish the purposes, permitted uses, or legal effect that a record may have under any particular provision of law. Whatever is filed in the Article 9 filing system, including financing statements, continuation statements, and termination statements, whether transmitted in tangible or intangible form, would fall within the definition. However, in some instances, statutes or filing-office rules may require that a paper record be filed. In such cases, even if this Article permits the filing of an electronic record, compliance with those statutes or rules is necessary. Similarly, a filer must comply with a statute or rule that requires a particular type of encoding or formatting for an electronic record.

This Article sometimes uses the terms "for record," "of record," "record or legal title," and "record owner." Some of these are terms traditionally used in real-property law. The definition of "record" in this Article now explicitly excepts these usages from the defined term. Also, this Article refers to a record that is filed or recorded in real-property recording systems to record a mortgage as a "record of a mortgage." This usage recognizes that the defined term "mortgage" means an interest in real property; it does not mean the record that evidences, or is filed or recorded with respect to, the mortgage.

b. **"Authenticate"; "Communicate"; "Send."** The terms "authenticate" and "authenticated" generally replace "sign" and "signed." "Authenticated" replaces and broadens the definition of "signed," in Section 1–201, to encompass authentication of all records, not just writings. (References to authentication of, e.g., an agreement, demand, or notification mean, of course, authentication of a record containing an agreement, demand, or notification.) The terms "communicate" and "send" also contemplate the possibility of communication by nonwritten media. These definitions include the act of transmitting both tangible and intangible records. The definition of "send" replaces, for purposes of this Article, the corresponding term in Section 1–201. The reference to "usual means of communication" in that definition contemplates an inquiry into the appropriateness of the method of transmission used in the particular circumstances involved.

10.   **Scope-Related Definitions.**

a.   **Expanded Scope of Article: "Agricultural Lien"; "Consignment"; "Payment Intangible"; "Promissory Note."** These new definitions reflect the expanded scope of Article 9, as provided in Section 9–109(a).

b.   **Reduced Scope of Exclusions: "Governmental Unit"; "Health-Care-Insurance Receivable"; "Commercial Tort Claims."** These new definitions reflect the reduced scope of the exclusions, provided in Section 9–109(c) and (d), of transfers by governmental debtors and assignments of interests in insurance policies and commercial tort claims.

11.   **Choice-of-Law-Related Definitions: "Certificate of Title"; "Governmental Unit"; "Jurisdiction of Organization"; "Public Organic Record"; "Registered Organization"; "State."** These new definitions reflect the changes in the law governing perfection and priority of security interests and agricultural liens provided in Part 3, Subpart 1.

Statutes often require applicants for a certificate of title to identify all security interests on the application and require the issuing agency to indicate the identified security interests on the certificate. Some of these statutes provide that priority over the rights of a lien creditor (i.e., perfection of a security interest) in goods covered by the certificate occurs upon indication of the security interest on the certificate; that is, they provide for the indication of the security interest on the certificate as a "condition" of perfection. Other statutes contemplate that perfection is achieved upon the occurrence of another act, e.g., delivery of the application to the issuing agency, that "results" in the indication of the security interest on the certificate. A certificate governed by either type of statute can qualify as a "certificate of title" under this Article. The statute providing for the indication of a security interest need not expressly state the connection between the indication and perfection. For example, a certificate issued pursuant to a statute that requires applicants to identify security interests, requires the issuing agency to indicate the identified security interests on the certificate, but is silent concerning the legal consequences of the indication would be a "certificate of title" if, under a judicial interpretation of the statute, perfection of a security interest is a legal consequence of the indication. Likewise, a certificate would be a "certificate of title" if another statute provides, expressly or as interpreted, the requisite connection between the indication and perfection.

The first sentence of the definition of "certificate of title" includes certificates consisting of tangible records, of electronic records, and of combinations of tangible and electronic records.

In many States, a certificate of title covering goods that are encumbered by a security interest is delivered to the secured party by the issuing authority. To eliminate the need for the issuance of a paper certificate under these circumstances, several States have revised their certificate-of-title statutes to permit or require a State agency to maintain an electronic record that evidences ownership of the goods and in which a security interest in the goods may be noted. The second sentence of the definition provides that such a record is a "certificate of title" if it is in fact maintained as an alternative to the issuance of a paper certificate of title, regardless of whether the certificate-of-title statute provides that the record is a certificate of title and even if the statute does not expressly state that the record is maintained instead of issuing a paper certificate.

Not every organization that may provide information about itself in the public records is a "registered organization." For example, a general partnership is not a "registered organization," even if it files a statement of partnership authority under Section 303 of the Uniform Partnership Act (1994) or an assumed name ("dba") certificate. This is because such a partnership is not formed or organized by the filing of a record with, or the issuance of a record by, a State or the United States. In contrast, corporations, limited liability companies, and limited partnerships ordinarily are "registered organizations."

Not every record concerning a registered organization that is filed with, or issued by, a State or the United States is a "public organic record." For example, a certificate of good standing issued with respect to a corporation or a published index of domestic corporations would not be a "public organic record" because its issuance or publication does not form or organize the corporations named.

When collateral is held in a trust, one must look to non-UCC law to determine whether the trust is a "registered organization." Non-UCC law typically distinguishes between statutory trusts and common-law trusts.

A statutory trust is formed by the filing of a record, commonly referred to as a certificate of trust, in a public office pursuant to a statute. See, e.g., Uniform Statutory Trust Entity Act § 201 (2009); Delaware Statutory Trust Act, Del. Code Ann. tit. 12, § 3801 et seq. A statutory trust is a juridical entity, separate from its trustee and beneficial owners, that may sue and be sued, own property, and transact business in its own name. Inasmuch as a statutory trust is a "legal or commercial entity," it qualifies as a "person other than an individual," and therefore as an "organization," under Section 1–201. A statutory trust that is formed by the filing of a record in a public office is a "registered organization," and the filed record is a "public organic record" of the statutory trust, if the filed record is available to the public for inspection. (The requirement that a record be "available to the public for inspection" is satisfied if a copy of the relevant record is available for public inspection.)

Unlike a statutory trust, a common-law trust—whether its purpose is donative or commercial—arises from private action without the filing of a record in a public office. See Uniform Trust Code § 401 (2000); Restatement (Third) of Trusts § 10 (2003). Moreover, under traditional law, a common-law trust is not itself a juridical entity and therefore must sue and be sued, own property, and transact business in the name of the trustee acting in the capacity of trustee. A common-law trust that is a "business trust," i.e., that has a business or commercial purpose, is an "organization" under Section 1–201. However, such a trust would not be a "registered organization" if, as is typically the case, the filing of a public record is not needed to form it.

In some states, however, the trustee of a common-law trust that has a commercial or business purpose is required by statute to file a record in a public office following the trust's formation. See, e.g., Mass. Gen. Laws Ch. 182, § 2; Fla. Stat. Ann. § 609.02. A business trust that is required to file its organic record in a public office is a "registered organization" under the second sentence of the definition if the filed record is available to the public for inspection. Any organic record required to be filed, and filed, with respect to a common-law business trust after the trust is formed is a "public organic record" of the trust. Some statutes require a trust or other organization to file, after formation or organization, a record other than an organic record. See, e.g., N.Y. Gen. Assn's Law § 18 (requiring associations doing business within New York to file a certificate designating the secretary of state as an agent upon whom process may be served). This requirement does not render the organization a "registered organization" under the second sentence of the definition, and the record is not a "public organic record."

12. **Deposit-Account-Related Definitions: "Deposit Account"; "Bank."** The revised definition of "deposit account" incorporates the definition of "bank," which is new. The definition derives from the definitions of "bank" in Sections 4–105(1) and 4A–105(a)(2), which focus on whether the organization is "engaged in the business of banking."

Deposit accounts evidenced by Article 9 "instruments" are excluded from the term "deposit account." In contrast, former Section 9–105 excluded from the former definition "an account evidenced by a certificate of deposit." The revised definition clarifies the proper treatment of nonnegotiable or uncertificated certificates of deposit. Under the definition, an uncertificated certificate of deposit would be a deposit account (assuming there is no writing evidencing the bank's obligation to pay) whereas a nonnegotiable certificate of deposit would be a deposit account only if it is not an "instrument" as defined in this section (a question that turns on whether the nonnegotiable certificate of deposit is "of a type that in ordinary course of business is transferred by delivery with any necessary indorsement or assignment.")

A deposit account evidenced by an instrument is subject to the rules applicable to instruments generally. As a consequence, a security interest in such an instrument cannot be perfected by "control" (see Section 9–104), and the special priority rules applicable to deposit accounts (see Sections 9–327 and 9–340) do not apply.

The term "deposit account" does not include "investment property," such as securities and security entitlements. Thus, the term also does not include shares in a money-market mutual fund, even if the shares are redeemable by check.

13. **Proceeds-Related Definitions: "Cash Proceeds"; "Noncash Proceeds"; "Proceeds."** The revised definition of "proceeds" expands the definition beyond that contained in former Section 9–306 and resolves ambiguities in the former section.

a. **Distributions on Account of Collateral.** The phrase "whatever is collected on, or distributed on account of, collateral," in subparagraph (B), is broad enough to cover cash or stock dividends distributed on account of securities or other investment property that is original collateral. Compare former Section 9–306 ("Any payments or distributions made with respect to investment property collateral are proceeds."). This section rejects the holding of *FDIC v. Hastie*, 2 F.3d 1042 (10th Cir. 1993) (postpetition cash dividends on stock subject to a prepetition pledge are not "proceeds" under Bankruptcy Code Section 552(b)), to the extent the holding relies on the Article 9 definition of "proceeds."

b.   **Distributions on Account of Supporting Obligations.** Under subparagraph (B), collections on and distributions on account of collateral consisting of various credit-support arrangements ("supporting obligations," as defined in Section 9–102) also are proceeds. Consequently, they are afforded treatment identical to proceeds collected from or distributed by the obligor on the underlying (supported) right to payment or other collateral. Proceeds of supporting obligations also are proceeds of the underlying rights to payment or other collateral.

c.   **Proceeds of Proceeds.** The definition of "proceeds" no longer provides that proceeds of proceeds are themselves proceeds. That idea is expressed in the revised definition of "collateral" in Section 9–102. No change in meaning is intended.

d.   **Proceeds Received by Person Who Did Not Create Security Interest.** When collateral is sold subject to a security interest and the buyer then resells the collateral, a question arose under former Article 9 concerning whether the "debtor" had "received" what the buyer received on resale and, therefore, whether those receipts were "proceeds" under former Section 9–306(2). This Article contains no requirement that property be "received" by the debtor for the property to qualify as proceeds. It is necessary only that the property be traceable, directly or indirectly, to the original collateral.

e.   **Cash Proceeds and Noncash Proceeds.** The definition of "cash proceeds" is substantially the same as the corresponding definition in former Section 9–306. The phrase "and the like" covers property that is functionally equivalent to "money, checks, or deposit accounts," such as some money-market accounts that are securities or part of securities entitlements. Proceeds other than cash proceeds are noncash proceeds.

14.   **Consignment-Related Definitions: "Consignee"; "Consignment"; "Consignor."** The definition of "consignment" excludes, in subparagraphs (B) and (C), transactions for which filing would be inappropriate or of insufficient benefit to justify the costs. A consignment excluded from the application of this Article by one of those subparagraphs may still be a true consignment; however, it is governed by non-Article 9 law. The definition also excludes, in subparagraph (D), what have been called "consignments intended for security." These "consignments" are not bailments but secured transactions. Accordingly, all of Article 9 applies to them. See Sections 1–201(b)(35), 9–109(a)(1). The "consignor" is the person who delivers goods to the "consignee" in a consignment.

The definition of "consignment" requires that the goods be delivered "to a merchant for the purpose of sale." If the goods are delivered for another purpose as well, such as milling or processing, the transaction is a consignment nonetheless because a purpose of the delivery is "sale." On the other hand, if a merchant-processor-bailee will not be selling the goods itself but will be delivering to buyers to which the owner-bailor agreed to sell the goods, the transaction would not be a consignment.

15.   **"Accounting."** This definition describes the record and information that a debtor is entitled to request under Section 9–210.

16.   **"Document."** The definition of "document" incorporates both tangible and electronic documents of title. See Section 1–201(b)16 and Comment 16.

18.   **"Fixtures."** This definition is unchanged in substance from the corresponding definition in former Section 9–313. See Section 9–334 (priority of security interests in fixtures and crops).

19.   **"Good Faith."** This Article expands the definition of "good faith" to include "the observance of reasonable commercial standards of fair dealing." The definition in this section applies when the term is used in this Article, and the same concept applies in the context of this Article for purposes of the obligation of good faith imposed by Section 1–203.* See subsection (c).

20.   **"Lien Creditor"** This definition is unchanged in substance from the corresponding definition in former Section 9–301.

21.   **"New Value."** This Article deletes former Section 9–108. Its broad formulation of new value, which embraced the taking of after-acquired collateral for a pre-existing claim, was unnecessary, counterintuitive, and ineffective for its original purpose of sheltering after-acquired collateral from attack as a voidable preference in bankruptcy. The new definition derives from Bankruptcy Code Section 547(a). The term is used with respect to temporary perfection of security interests in instruments, certificated securities, or negotiable documents under Section 9–312(e) and with respect to chattel paper priority in Section 9–330.

_____

*   _Referring to unrevised Article 1 (Appendix A)._

22. **"Person Related To."** Section 9–615 provides a special method for calculating a deficiency or surplus when "the secured party, a person related to the secured party, or a secondary obligor" acquires the collateral at a foreclosure disposition. Separate definitions of the term are provided with respect to an individual secured party and with respect to a secured party that is an organization. The definitions are patterned on the corresponding definition in Section 1.301(32) of the Uniform Consumer Credit Code (1974).

23. **"Proposal."** This definition describes a record that is sufficient to propose to retain collateral in full or partial satisfaction of a secured obligation. See Sections 9–620, 9–621, 9–622.

24. **"Pursuant to Commitment."** This definition is unchanged in substance from the corresponding definition in former Section 9–105. It is used in connection with special priority rules applicable to future advances. See Section 9–323.

25. **"Software."** The definition of "software" is used in connection with the priority rules applicable to purchase-money security interests. See Sections 9–103, 9–324. Software, like a payment intangible, is a type of general intangible for purposes of this Article. See Comment 4.a., above, regarding the distinction between "goods" and "software."

26. **Terminology: "Assignment" and "Transfer."** In numerous provisions, this Article refers to the "assignment" or the "transfer" of property interests. These terms and their derivatives are not defined. This Article generally follows common usage by using the terms "assignment" and "assign" to refer to transfers of rights to payment, claims, and liens and other security interests. It generally uses the term "transfer" to refer to other transfers of interests in property. Except when used in connection with a letter-of-credit transaction (see Section 9–107, Comment 4), no significance should be placed on the use of one term or the other. Depending on the context, each term may refer to the assignment or transfer of an outright ownership interest or to the assignment or transfer of a limited interest, such as a security interest.

As amended in 1999, 2000, 2001, 2003, and 2010.

§ 9–103. Purchase-Money Security Interest; Application of Payments; Burden of Establishing.

(a) **[Definitions.]** In this section:

(1) "purchase-money collateral" means goods or software that secures a purchase-money obligation incurred with respect to that collateral; and

(2) "purchase-money obligation" means an obligation of an obligor incurred as all or part of the price of the collateral or for value given to enable the debtor to acquire rights in or the use of the collateral if the value is in fact so used.

(b) **[Purchase-money security interest in goods.]** A security interest in goods is a purchase-money security interest:

(1) to the extent that the goods are purchase-money collateral with respect to that security interest;

(2) if the security interest is in inventory that is or was purchase-money collateral, also to the extent that the security interest secures a purchase-money obligation incurred with respect to other inventory in which the secured party holds or held a purchase-money security interest; and

(3) also to the extent that the security interest secures a purchase-money obligation incurred with respect to software in which the secured party holds or held a purchase-money security interest.

(c) **[Purchase-money security interest in software.]** A security interest in software is a purchase-money security interest to the extent that the security interest also secures a purchase-money obligation incurred with respect to goods in which the secured party holds or held a purchase-money security interest if:

(1) the debtor acquired its interest in the software in an integrated transaction in which it acquired an interest in the goods; and

(2) the debtor acquired its interest in the software for the principal purpose of using the software in the goods.

(d)   **[Consignor's inventory purchase-money security interest.]** The security interest of a consignor in goods that are the subject of a consignment is a purchase-money security interest in inventory.

(e)   **[Application of payment in non-consumer-goods transaction.]** In a transaction other than a consumer-goods transaction, if the extent to which a security interest is a purchase-money security interest depends on the application of a payment to a particular obligation, the payment must be applied:

(1)   in accordance with any reasonable method of application to which the parties agree;

(2)   in the absence of the parties' agreement to a reasonable method, in accordance with any intention of the obligor manifested at or before the time of payment; or

(3)   in the absence of an agreement to a reasonable method and a timely manifestation of the obligor's intention, in the following order:

(A)   to obligations that are not secured; and

(B)   if more than one obligation is secured, to obligations secured by purchase-money security interests in the order in which those obligations were incurred.

(f)   **[No loss of status of purchase-money security interest in non-consumer-goods transaction.]** In a transaction other than a consumer-goods transaction, a purchase-money security interest does not lose its status as such, even if:

(1)   the purchase-money collateral also secures an obligation that is not a purchase-money obligation;

(2)   collateral that is not purchase-money collateral also secures the purchase-money obligation; or

(3)   the purchase-money obligation has been renewed, refinanced, consolidated, or restructured.

(g)   **[Burden of proof in non-consumer-goods transaction.]** In a transaction other than a consumer-goods transaction, a secured party claiming a purchase-money security interest has the burden of establishing the extent to which the security interest is a purchase-money security interest.

(h)   **[Non-consumer-goods transactions; no inference.]** The limitation of the rules in subsections (e), (f), and (g) to transactions other than consumer-goods transactions is intended to leave to the court the determination of the proper rules in consumer-goods transactions. The court may not infer from that limitation the nature of the proper rule in consumer-goods transactions and may continue to apply established approaches.

Official Comment

1.   **Source.** Former Section 9–107.

2.   **Scope of This Section.** Under Section 9–309(1), a purchase-money security interest in consumer goods is perfected when it attaches. Sections 9–317 and 9–324 provide special priority rules for purchase-money security interests in a variety of contexts. This section explains when a security interest enjoys purchase-money status.

3.   **"Purchase-Money Collateral"; "Purchase-Money Obligation"; "Purchase-Money Security Interest."** Subsection (a) defines "purchase-money collateral" and "purchase-money obligation." These terms are essential to the description of what constitutes a purchase-money security interest under subsection (b). As used in subsection (a)(2), the definition of "purchase-money obligation," the "price" of collateral or the "value given to enable" includes obligations for expenses incurred in connection with acquiring rights in the collateral, sales taxes, duties, finance charges, interest, freight charges, costs of storage in transit, demurrage, administrative charges, expenses of collection and enforcement, attorney's fees, and other similar obligations.

The concept of "purchase-money security interest" requires a close nexus between the acquisition of collateral and the secured obligation. Thus, a security interest does not qualify as a purchase-money security interest if a debtor acquires property on unsecured credit and subsequently creates the security interest to secure the purchase price.

4.   **Cross-Collateralization of Purchase-Money Security Interests in Inventory.** Subsection (b)(2) deals with the problem of cross-collateralized purchase-money security interests in inventory. Consider a simple example:

Example: Seller (S) sells an item of inventory (Item-1) to Debtor (D), retaining a security interest in Item-1 to secure Item-1's price and all other obligations, existing and future, of D to S. S then sells another item of inventory to D (Item-2), again retaining a security interest in Item-2 to secure Item-2's price as well as all other obligations of D to S. D then pays to S Item-1's price. D then sells Item-2 to a buyer in ordinary course of business, who takes Item-2 free of S's security interest.

Under subsection (b)(2), S's security interest in *Item-1* securing *Item-2's unpaid price* would be a purchase-money security interest. This is so because S has a purchase-money security interest in Item-1, Item-1 secures the price of (a "purchase-money obligation incurred with respect to") Item-2 ("other inventory"), and Item-2 itself was subject to a purchase-money security interest. Note that, to the extent Item-1 secures the price of Item-2, S's security interest in Item-1 would not be a purchase-money security interest under subsection (b)(1). The security interest in Item-1 is a purchase-money security interest under subsection (b)(1) only to the extent that Item-1 is "purchase-money collateral," i.e., only to the extent that Item-1 "secures a purchase-money obligation incurred with respect to that collateral" (i.e., Item-1). See subsection (a)(1).

5. **Purchase-Money Security Interests in Goods and Software.** Subsections (b) and (c) limit purchase-money security interests to security interests in goods, including fixtures, and software. Otherwise, no change in meaning from former Section 9–107 is intended. The second sentence of former Section 9–115(5)(f) made the purchase-money priority rule (former Section 9–312(4)) inapplicable to investment property. This section's limitation makes that provision unnecessary.

Subsection (c) describes the limited circumstances under which a security interest in goods may be accompanied by a purchase-money security interest in software. The software must be acquired by the debtor in a transaction integrated with the transaction in which the debtor acquired the goods, and the debtor must acquire the software for the principal purpose of using the software in the goods. "Software" is defined in Section 9–102.

6. **Consignments.** Under former Section 9–114, the priority of the consignor's interest is similar to that of a purchase-money security interest. Subsection (d) achieves this result more directly, by defining the interest of a "consignor," defined in Section 9–102, to be a purchase-money security interest in inventory for purposes of this Article. This drafting convention obviates any need to set forth special priority rules applicable to the interest of a consignor. Rather, the priority of the consignor's interest as against the rights of lien creditors of the consignee, competing secured parties, and purchasers of the goods from the consignee can be determined by reference to the priority rules generally applicable to inventory, such as Sections 9–317, 9–320, 9–322, and 9–324. For other purposes, including the rights and duties of the consignor and consignee as between themselves, the consignor would remain the owner of goods under a bailment arrangement with the consignee. See Section 9–319.

7. **Provisions Applicable Only to Non-Consumer-Goods Transactions.**

a. **"Dual-Status" Rule.** For transactions other than consumer-goods transactions, this Article approves what some cases have called the "dual-status" rule, under which a security interest may be a purchase-money security interest to some extent and a non-purchase-money security interest to some extent. (Concerning consumer-goods transactions, see subsection (h) and Comment 8.) Some courts have found this rule to be explicit or implicit in the words "to the extent," found in former Section 9–107 and continued in subsections (b)(1) and (b)(2). The rule is made explicit in subsection (e). For non-consumer-goods transactions, this Article rejects the "transformation" rule adopted by some cases, under which any cross-collateralization, refinancing, or the like destroys the purchase-money status entirely.

Consider, for example, what happens when a $10,000 loan secured by a purchase-money security interest is refinanced by the original lender, and, as part of the transaction, the debtor borrows an additional $2,000 secured by the collateral. Subsection (f) resolves any doubt that the security interest remains a purchase-money security interest. Under subsection (b), however, it enjoys purchase-money status only to the extent of $10,000.

b. **Allocation of Payments.** Continuing with the example, if the debtor makes a $1,000 payment on the $12,000 obligation, then one must determine the extent to which the security interest remains a purchase-money security interest—$9,000 or $10,000. Subsection (e)(1) expresses the overriding principle, applicable in cases other than consumer-goods transactions, for determining the extent to which a security interest is a purchase-money security interest under these circumstances: freedom of contract, as limited by principle of reasonableness. An unconscionable method of application, for example, is not a reasonable one and so would not be given effect under subsection (e)(1). In the absence of agreement, subsection (e)(2) permits the obligor to determine how payments should be allocated. If the obligor fails to manifest its intention, obligations that are not secured will be paid first. (As used in this Article, the concept of "obligations that are not secured" means obligations for which the debtor has not created a security interest. This concept is different from and should not be confused with the concept of an "unsecured claim" as it appears in Bankruptcy Code Section 506(a).) The obligor may prefer this approach, because unsecured debt is likely to carry a higher interest rate than secured debt. A creditor who would prefer to be secured rather than unsecured also would prefer this approach.

After the unsecured debt is paid, payments are to be applied first toward the obligations secured by purchase-money security interests. In the event that there is more than one such obligation, payments first received are to be applied to obligations first incurred. See subsection (e)(3). Once these obligations are paid, there are no purchase-money security interests and no additional allocation rules are needed.

Subsection (f) buttresses the dual-status rule by making it clear that (in a transaction other than a consumer-goods transaction) cross-collateralization and renewals, refinancings, and restructurings do not cause a purchase-money security interest to lose its status as such. The statutory terms "renewed," "refinanced," and "restructured" are not defined. Whether the terms encompass a particular transaction depends upon whether, under the particular facts, the purchase-money character of the security interest fairly can be said to survive. Each term contemplates that an identifiable portion of the purchase-money obligation could be traced to the new obligation resulting from a renewal, refinancing, or restructuring.

c.   **Burden of Proof.** As is the case when the extent of a security interest is in issue, under subsection (g) the secured party claiming a purchase-money security interest in a transaction other than a consumer-goods transaction has the burden of establishing whether the security interest retains its purchase-money status. This is so whether the determination is to be made following a renewal, refinancing, or restructuring or otherwise.

8.   **Consumer-Goods Transactions; Characterization Under Other Law.** Under subsection (h), the limitation of subsections (e), (f), and (g) to transactions other than consumer-goods transactions leaves to the court the determination of the proper rules in consumer-goods transactions. Subsection (h) also instructs the court not to draw any inference from this limitation as to the proper rules for consumer-goods transactions and leaves the court free to continue to apply established approaches to those transactions.

This section addresses only whether a security interest is a "purchase-money security interest" under this Article, primarily for purposes of perfection and priority. See, e.g., Sections 9–317, 9–324. In particular, its adoption of the dual-status rule, allocation of payments rules, and burden of proof standards for non-consumer-goods transactions is not intended to affect or influence characterizations under other statutes. Whether a security interest is a "purchase-money security interest" under other law is determined by that law. For example, decisions under Bankruptcy Code Section 522(f) have applied both the dual-status and the transformation rules. The Bankruptcy Code does not expressly adopt the state law definition of "purchase-money security interest." Where federal law does not defer to this Article, this Article does not, and could not, determine a question of federal law.

§ 9–104.   Control of Deposit Account.

(a)   **[Requirements for control.]** A secured party has control of a deposit account if:

(1)   the secured party is the bank with which the deposit account is maintained;

(2)   the debtor, secured party, and bank have agreed in an authenticated record that the bank will comply with instructions originated by the secured party directing disposition of the funds in the deposit account without further consent by the debtor; or

(3)   the secured party becomes the bank's customer with respect to the deposit account.

(b)   **[Debtor's right to direct disposition.]** A secured party that has satisfied subsection (a) has control, even if the debtor retains the right to direct the disposition of funds from the deposit account.

Official Comment

1.   **Source.** New; derived from Section 8–106.

2.   **Why "Control" Matters.** This section explains the concept of "control" of a deposit account. "Control" under this section may serve two functions. First, "control . . . pursuant to the debtor's agreement" may substitute for an authenticated security agreement as an element of attachment. See Section 9–203(b)(3)(D). Second, when a deposit account is taken as original collateral, the only method of perfection is obtaining control under this section. See Section 9–312(b)(1).

3.   **Requirements for "Control."** This section derives from Section 8–106 of Revised Article 8, which defines "control" of securities and certain other investment property. Under subsection (a)(1), the bank with which

the deposit account is maintained has control. The effect of this provision is to afford the bank automatic perfection. No other form of public notice is necessary; all actual and potential creditors of the debtor are always on notice that the bank with which the debtor's deposit account is maintained may assert a claim against the deposit account.

> **Example:** D maintains a deposit account with Bank A. To secure a loan from Banks X, Y, and Z, D creates a security interest in the deposit account in favor of Bank A, as agent for Banks X, Y, and Z. Because Bank A is a "secured party" as defined in Section 9–102, the security interest is perfected by control under subsection (a)(1).

Under subsection (a)(2), a secured party may obtain control by obtaining the bank's authenticated agreement that it will comply with the secured party's instructions without further consent by the debtor. The analogous provision in Section 8–106 does not require that the agreement be authenticated. An agreement to comply with the secured party's instructions suffices for "control" of a deposit account under this section even if the bank's agreement is subject to specified conditions, e.g., that the secured party's instructions are accompanied by a certification that the debtor is in default. (Of course, if the condition is the *debtor's* further consent, the statute explicitly provides that the agreement would *not* confer control.) See revised Section 8–106, Comment 7.

Under subsection (a)(3), a secured party may obtain control by becoming the bank's "customer," as defined in Section 4–104. As the customer, the secured party would enjoy the right (but not necessarily the exclusive right) to withdraw funds from, or close, the deposit account. See Sections 4–401(a), 4–403(a).

As is the case with possession under Section 9–313, in determining whether a particular person has control under subsection (a), the principles of agency apply. See Section 1–103 and Restatement (3d), Agency § 8.12, Comment *b*.

Although the arrangements giving rise to control may themselves prevent, or may enable the secured party at its discretion to prevent, the debtor from reaching the funds on deposit, subsection (b) makes clear that the debtor's ability to reach the funds is not inconsistent with "control."

Perfection by control is not available for bank accounts evidenced by an instrument (e.g., certain certificates of deposit), which by definition are "instruments" and not "deposit accounts." See Section 9–102 (defining "deposit account" and "instrument").

As amended in 2010.

§ 9–105.   Control of Electronic Chattel Paper.

(a)   **[General rule: control of electronic chattel paper.]** A secured party has control of electronic chattel paper if a system employed for evidencing the transfer of interests in the chattel paper reliably establishes the secured party as the person to which the chattel paper was assigned.

(b)   **[Specific facts giving control.]** A system satisfies subsection (a) if the record or records comprising the chattel paper are created, stored, and assigned in such a manner that:

(1)   a single authoritative copy of the record or records exists which is unique, identifiable, and, except as otherwise provided in paragraphs (4), (5), and (6), unalterable;

(2)   the authoritative copy identifies the secured party as the assignee of the record or records;

(3)   the authoritative copy is communicated to and maintained by the secured party or its designated custodian;

(4)   copies or amendments that add or change an identified assignee of the authoritative copy can be made only with the consent of the secured party;

(5)   each copy of the authoritative copy and any copy of a copy is readily identifiable as a copy that is not the authoritative copy; and

(6)   any amendment of the authoritative copy is readily identifiable as authorized or unauthorized.

As amended in 2010.

Official Comment

1. **Source.** New.

2. **"Control" of Electronic Chattel Paper.** This Article covers security interests in "electronic chattel paper," a new term defined in Section 9–102. This section governs how "control" of electronic chattel paper may be obtained. Subsection (a), which derives from Section 16 of the Uniform Electronic Transactions Act, sets forth the general test for control. Subsection (b) sets forth a safe harbor test that, if satisfied, establishes control under the general test in subsection (a).

A secured party's control of electronic chattel paper (i) may substitute for an authenticated security agreement for purposes of attachment under Section 9–203, (ii) is a method of perfection under Section 9–314, and (iii) is a condition for obtaining special, non-temporal priority under Section 9–330. Because electronic chattel paper cannot be transferred, assigned, or possessed in the same manner as tangible chattel paper, a special definition of control is necessary. In descriptive terms, this section provides that control of electronic chattel paper is the functional equivalent of possession of "tangible chattel paper" (a term also defined in Section 9–102).

3. **Development of Control Systems.** This Article leaves to the marketplace the development of systems and procedures, through a combination of suitable technologies and business practices, for dealing with control of electronic chattel paper in a commercial context. Systems that evolve for control of electronic chattel paper may or may not involve a third party custodian of the relevant records. As under UETA, a system must be shown to reliably establish that the secured party is the assignee of the chattel paper. Reliability is a high standard and encompasses the general principles of uniqueness, identifiability, and unalterability found in subsection (b) without setting forth specific guidelines as to how these principles must be achieved. However, the standards applied to determine whether a party is in control of electronic chattel paper should not be more stringent than the standards now applied to determine whether a party is in possession of tangible chattel paper. For example, just as a secured party does not lose possession of tangible chattel paper merely by virtue of the possibility that a person acting on its behalf *could* wrongfully redeliver the chattel paper to the debtor, so control of electronic chattel paper would not be defeated by the possibility that the secured party's interest *could* be subverted by the wrongful conduct of a person (such as a custodian) acting on its behalf.

This section and the concept of control of electronic chattel paper are not based on the same concepts as are control of deposit accounts (Section 9–104), security entitlements, a type of investment property (Section 9–106), and letter-of-credit rights (Section 9–107). The rules for control of those types of collateral are based on existing market practices and legal and regulatory regimes for institutions such as banks and securities intermediaries. Analogous practices for electronic chattel paper are developing nonetheless. The flexible approach adopted by this section, moreover, should not impede the development of these practices and, eventually, legal and regulatory regimes, which may become analogous to those for, e.g., investment property.

4. **"Authoritative Copy" of Electronic Chattel Paper.** One requirement for establishing control under subsection (b) is that a particular copy be an "authoritative copy." Although other copies may exist, they must be distinguished from the authoritative copy. This may be achieved, for example, through the methods of authentication that are used or by business practices involving the marking of any additional copies. When tangible chattel paper is converted to electronic chattel paper, in order to establish that a copy of the electronic chattel paper is the authoritative copy it may be necessary to show that the tangible chattel paper no longer exists or has been permanently marked to indicate that it is not the authoritative copy.

As amended in 2010.

§ 9–106.   Control of Investment Property.

(a) **[Control under Section 8–106.]** A person has control of a certificated security, uncertificated security, or security entitlement as provided in Section 8–106.

(b) **[Control of commodity contract.]** A secured party has control of a commodity contract if:

(1) the secured party is the commodity intermediary with which the commodity contract is carried; or

(2) the commodity customer, secured party, and commodity intermediary have agreed that the commodity intermediary will apply any value distributed on account of the commodity contract as directed by the secured party without further consent by the commodity customer.

(c)   **[Effect of control of securities account or commodity account.]** A secured party having control of all security entitlements or commodity contracts carried in a securities account or commodity account has control over the securities account or commodity account.

Official Comment

1.   **Source.** Former Section 9–115(e).

2.   **"Control" Under Article 8.** For an explanation of "control" of securities and certain other investment property, see Section 8–106, Comments 4 and 7.

3.   **"Control" of Commodity Contracts.** This section, as did former Section 9–115(1)(e), contains provisions relating to control of commodity contracts which are analogous to those in Section 8–106 for other types of investment property.

4.   **Securities Accounts and Commodity Accounts.** For drafting convenience, control with respect to a securities account or commodity account is defined in terms of obtaining control over the security entitlements or commodity contracts. Of course, an agreement that provides that (without further consent of the debtor) the securities intermediary or commodity intermediary will honor instructions from the secured party concerning a securities account or commodity account described as such is sufficient. Such an agreement necessarily implies that the intermediary will honor instructions concerning all security entitlements or commodity contracts carried in the account and thus affords the secured party control of all the security entitlements or commodity contracts.

§ 9–107.   Control of Letter-of-Credit Right.

A secured party has control of a letter-of-credit right to the extent of any right to payment or performance by the issuer or any nominated person if the issuer or nominated person has consented to an assignment of proceeds of the letter of credit under Section 5–114(c) or otherwise applicable law or practice.

Official Comment

1.   **Source.** New.

2.   **"Control" of Letter-of-Credit Right.** Whether a secured party has control of a letter-of-credit right may determine the secured party's priority as against competing secured parties. See Section 9–329. This section provides that a secured party acquires control of a letter-of-credit right by receiving an assignment if the secured party obtains the consent of the issuer or any nominated person, such as a confirmer or negotiating bank, under Section 5–114 or other applicable law or practice. Because both issuers and nominated persons may give or be obligated to give value under a letter of credit, this section contemplates that a secured party obtains control of a letter-of-credit right with respect to the issuer or a particular nominated person only to the extent that the issuer or that nominated person consents to the assignment. For example, if a secured party obtains control to the extent of an issuer's obligation but fails to obtain the consent of a nominated person, the secured party does not have control to the extent that the nominated person gives value. In many cases the person or persons who will give value under a letter of credit will be clear from its terms. In other cases, prudence may suggest obtaining consent from more than one person. The details of the consenting issuer's or nominated person's duties to pay or otherwise render performance to the secured party are left to the agreement of the parties.

3.   **"Proceeds of a Letter of Credit."** Section 5–114 follows traditional banking terminology by referring to a letter of credit beneficiary's assignment of its right to receive payment thereunder as an assignment of the "proceeds of a letter of credit." However, as the seller of goods can assign its right to receive payment (an "account") before it has been earned by delivering the goods to the buyer, so the beneficiary of a letter of credit can assign its contingent right to payment before the letter of credit has been honored. See Section 5–114(b). If the assignment creates a security interest, the security interest can be perfected at the time it is created. An assignment of, including the creation of a security interest in, a letter-of-credit right is an assignment of a present interest.

4.   **"Transfer" vs. "Assignment."** Letter-of-credit law and practice distinguish the "transfer" of a letter of credit from an "assignment." Under a transfer, the transferee itself becomes the beneficiary and acquires the right to draw. Whether a new, substitute credit is issued or the issuer advises the transferee of its status as such, the transfer constitutes a novation under which the transferee is the new, substituted beneficiary (but only to the extent of the transfer, in the case of a partial transfer).

Section 5–114(e) provides that the rights of a transferee beneficiary or nominated person are independent of the beneficiary's assignment of the proceeds of a letter of credit and are superior to the assignee's right to the proceeds. For this reason, transfer does not appear in this Article as a means of control or perfection. Section 9–109(c)(4) recognizes the independent and superior rights of a transferee beneficiary under Section 5–114(e); this Article does not apply to the rights of a transferee beneficiary or nominated person to the extent that those rights are independent and superior under Section 5–114.

5. **Supporting Obligation: Automatic Attachment and Perfection.** A letter-of-credit right is a type of "supporting obligation," as defined in Section 9–102. Under Sections 9–203 and 9–308, a security interest in a letter-of-credit right automatically attaches and is automatically perfected if the security interest in the supported obligation is a perfected security interest. However, unless the secured party has control of the letter-of-credit right or itself becomes a transferee beneficiary, it cannot obtain any rights against the issuer or a nominated person under Article 5. Consequently, as a practical matter, the secured party's rights would be limited to its ability to locate and identify proceeds distributed by the issuer or nominated person under the letter of credit.

§ 9–108. Sufficiency of Description.

(a) **[Sufficiency of description.]** Except as otherwise provided in subsections (c), (d), and (e), a description of personal or real property is sufficient, whether or not it is specific, if it reasonably identifies what is described.

(b) **[Examples of reasonable identification.]** Except as otherwise provided in subsection (d), a description of collateral reasonably identifies the collateral if it identifies the collateral by:

(1) specific listing;

(2) category;

(3) except as otherwise provided in subsection (e), a type of collateral defined in [the Uniform Commercial Code];

(4) quantity;

(5) computational or allocational formula or procedure; or

(6) except as otherwise provided in subsection (c), any other method, if the identity of the collateral is objectively determinable.

(c) **[Supergeneric description not sufficient.]** A description of collateral as "all the debtor's assets" or "all the debtor's personal property" or using words of similar import does not reasonably identify the collateral.

(d) **[Investment property.]** Except as otherwise provided in subsection (e), a description of a security entitlement, securities account, or commodity account is sufficient if it describes:

(1) the collateral by those terms or as investment property; or

(2) the underlying financial asset or commodity contract.

(e) **[When description by type insufficient.]** A description only by type of collateral defined in [the Uniform Commercial Code] is an insufficient description of:

(1) a commercial tort claim; or

(2) in a consumer transaction, consumer goods, a security entitlement, a securities account, or a commodity account.

Official Comment

1. **Source.** Former Sections 9–110, 9–115(3).

2. **General Rules.** Subsection (a) retains substantially the same formulation as former Section 9–110. Subsection (b) expands upon subsection (a) by indicating a variety of ways in which a description might reasonably identify collateral. Whereas a provision similar to subsection (b) was applicable only to investment property under former Section 9–115(3), subsection (b) applies to all types of collateral, subject to the limitation in subsection (d). Subsection (b) is subject to subsection (c), which follows prevailing case law and adopts the view that an "all assets" or "all personal property" description for purposes of a *security agreement* is *not* sufficient. Note, however, that

under Section 9–504, a *financing statement* sufficiently indicates the collateral if it "covers all assets or all personal property."

The purpose of requiring a description of collateral in a security agreement under Section 9–203 is evidentiary. The test of sufficiency of a description under this section, as under former Section 9–110, is that the description do the job assigned to it: make possible the identification of the collateral described. This section rejects any requirement that a description is insufficient unless it is exact and detailed (the so-called "serial number" test).

3. **After-Acquired Collateral.** Much litigation has arisen over whether a description in a security agreement is sufficient to include after-acquired collateral if the agreement does not explicitly so provide. This question is one of contract interpretation and is not susceptible to a statutory rule (other than a rule to the effect that it is a question of contract interpretation). Accordingly, this section contains no reference to descriptions of after-acquired collateral.

4. **Investment Property.** Under subsection (d), the use of the wrong Article 8 terminology does not render a description invalid (e.g., a security agreement intended to cover a debtor's "security entitlements" is sufficient if it refers to the debtor's "securities"). Note also that given the broad definition of "securities account" in Section 8–501, a security interest in a securities account also includes all other rights of the debtor against the securities intermediary arising out of the securities account. For example, a security interest in a securities account would include credit balances due to the debtor from the securities intermediary, whether or not they are proceeds of a security entitlement. Moreover, describing collateral as a securities account is a simple way of describing all of the security entitlements carried in the account.

5. **Consumer Investment Property; Commercial Tort Claims.** Subsection (e) requires greater specificity of description in order to prevent debtors from inadvertently encumbering certain property. Subsection (e) requires that a description by defined "type" of collateral alone of a commercial tort claim or, in a consumer transaction, of a security entitlement, securities account, or commodity account, is not sufficient. For example, "all existing and after-acquired investment property" or "all existing and after-acquired security entitlements," without more, would be insufficient in a consumer transaction to describe a security entitlement, securities account, or commodity account. The reference to "*only* by type" in subsection (e) means that a description is sufficient if it satisfies subsection (a) and contains a descriptive component beyond the "type" alone. Moreover, if the collateral consists of a securities account or commodity account, a description of the account is sufficient to cover all existing and future security entitlements or commodity contracts carried in the account. See Section 9–203(h), (i).

Under Section 9–204, an after-acquired collateral clause in a security agreement will not reach future commercial tort claims. It follows that when an effective security agreement covering a commercial tort claim is entered into the claim already will exist. Subsection (e) does not require a description to be specific. For example, a description such as "all tort claims arising out of the explosion of debtor's factory" would suffice, even if the exact amount of the claim, the theory on which it may be based, and the identity of the tortfeasor(s) are not described. (Indeed, those facts may not be known at the time.)

[SUBPART 2. APPLICABILITY OF ARTICLE]

§ 9–109. Scope.

(a) **[General scope of article.]** Except as otherwise provided in subsections (c) and (d), this article applies to:

(1) a transaction, regardless of its form, that creates a security interest in personal property or fixtures by contract;

(2) an agricultural lien;

(3) a sale of accounts, chattel paper, payment intangibles, or promissory notes;

(4) a consignment;

(5) a security interest arising under Section 2–401, 2–505, 2–711(3), or 2A–508(5), as provided in Section 9–110; and

(6) a security interest arising under Section 4–210 or 5–118.

(b) **[Security interest in secured obligation.]** The application of this article to a security interest in a secured obligation is not affected by the fact that the obligation is itself secured by a transaction or interest to which this article does not apply.

(c) **[Extent to which article does not apply.]** This article does not apply to the extent that:

(1) a statute, regulation, or treaty of the United States preempts this article;

(2) another statute of this State expressly governs the creation, perfection, priority, or enforcement of a security interest created by this State or a governmental unit of this State;

(3) a statute of another State, a foreign country, or a governmental unit of another State or a foreign country, other than a statute generally applicable to security interests, expressly governs creation, perfection, priority, or enforcement of a security interest created by the State, country, or governmental unit; or

(4) the rights of a transferee beneficiary or nominated person under a letter of credit are independent and superior under Section 5–114.

(d) **[Inapplicability of article.]** This article does not apply to:

(1) a landlord's lien, other than an agricultural lien;

(2) a lien, other than an agricultural lien, given by statute or other rule of law for services or materials, but Section 9–333 applies with respect to priority of the lien;

(3) an assignment of a claim for wages, salary, or other compensation of an employee;

(4) a sale of accounts, chattel paper, payment intangibles, or promissory notes as part of a sale of the business out of which they arose;

(5) an assignment of accounts, chattel paper, payment intangibles, or promissory notes which is for the purpose of collection only;

(6) an assignment of a right to payment under a contract to an assignee that is also obligated to perform under the contract;

(7) an assignment of a single account, payment intangible, or promissory note to an assignee in full or partial satisfaction of a preexisting indebtedness;

(8) a transfer of an interest in or an assignment of a claim under a policy of insurance, other than an assignment by or to a health-care provider of a health-care-insurance receivable and any subsequent assignment of the right to payment, but Sections 9–315 and 9–322 apply with respect to proceeds and priorities in proceeds;

(9) an assignment of a right represented by a judgment, other than a judgment taken on a right to payment that was collateral;

(10) a right of recoupment or set-off, but:

(A) Section 9–340 applies with respect to the effectiveness of rights of recoupment or set-off against deposit accounts; and

(B) Section 9–404 applies with respect to defenses or claims of an account debtor;

(11) the creation or transfer of an interest in or lien on real property, including a lease or rents thereunder, except to the extent that provision is made for:

(A) liens on real property in Sections 9–203 and 9–308;

(B) fixtures in Section 9–334;

(C) fixture filings in Sections 9–501, 9–502, 9–512, 9–516, and 9–519; and

(D) security agreements covering personal and real property in Section 9–604;

(12) an assignment of a claim arising in tort, other than a commercial tort claim, but Sections 9–315 and 9–322 apply with respect to proceeds and priorities in proceeds; or

(13) an assignment of a deposit account in a consumer transaction, but Sections 9–315 and 9–322 apply with respect to proceeds and priorities in proceeds.

Official Comment

1.   **Source.** Former Sections 9–102, 9–104.

2.   **Basic Scope Provision.** Subsection (a)(1) derives from former Section 9–102(1) and (2). These subsections have been combined and shortened. No change in meaning is intended. Under subsection (a)(1), all consensual security interests in personal property and fixtures are covered by this Article, except for transactions excluded by subsections (c) and (d). As to which transactions give rise to a "security interest," the definition of that term in Section 1–201 must be consulted. When a security interest is created, this Article applies regardless of the form of the transaction or the name that parties have given to it. Likewise, the subjective intention of the parties with respect to the legal characterization of their transaction is irrelevant to whether this Article applies, as it was to the application of former Article 9 under the proper interpretation of former Section 9–102.

3.   **Agricultural Liens.** Subsection (a)(2) is new. It expands the scope of this Article to cover agricultural liens, as defined in Section 9–102.

4.   **Sales of Accounts, Chattel Paper, Payment Intangibles, Promissory Notes, and Other Receivables.** Under subsection (a)(3), as under former Section 9–102, this Article applies to sales of accounts and chattel paper. This approach generally has been successful in avoiding difficult problems of distinguishing between transactions in which a receivable secures an obligation and those in which the receivable has been sold outright. In many commercial financing transactions the distinction is blurred.

Subsection (a)(3) expands the scope of this Article by including the sale of a "payment intangible" (defined in Section 9–102 as "a general intangible under which the account debtor's principal obligation is a monetary obligation") and a "promissory note" (also defined in Section 9–102). To a considerable extent, this Article affords these transactions treatment identical to that given sales of accounts and chattel paper. In some respects, however, sales of payment intangibles and promissory notes are treated differently from sales of other receivables. See, e.g., Sections 9–309 (automatic perfection upon attachment), 9–408 (effect of restrictions on assignment). By virtue of the expanded definition of "account" (defined in Section 9–102), this Article now covers sales of (and other security interests in) "health-care-insurance receivables" (also defined in Section 9–102). Although this Article occasionally distinguishes between outright sales of receivables and sales that secure an obligation, neither this Article nor the definition of "security interest" (Section 1–201(37)*) delineates how a particular transaction is to be classified. That issue is left to the courts.

5.   **Transfer of Ownership in Sales of Receivables.** A "sale" of an account, chattel paper, a promissory note, or a payment intangible includes a sale of a right in the receivable, such as a sale of a participation interest. The term also includes the sale of an enforcement right. For example, a "[p]erson entitled to enforce" a negotiable promissory note (Section 3–301) may sell its ownership rights in the instrument. See Section 3–203, Comment 1 ("Ownership rights in instruments may be determined by principles of the law of property, independent of Article 3, which do not depend upon whether the instrument was transferred under Section 3–203."). Also, the right under Section 3–309 to enforce a lost, destroyed, or stolen negotiable promissory note may be sold to a purchaser who could enforce that right by causing the seller to provide the proof required under that section. This Article rejects decisions reaching a contrary result, e.g., *Dennis Joslin Co. v. Robinson Broadcasting*, 977 F. Supp. 491 (D.D.C. 1997).

Nothing in this section or any other provision of Article 9 prevents the transfer of full and complete ownership of an account, chattel paper, an instrument, or a payment intangible in a transaction of sale. However, as mentioned in Comment 4, neither this Article nor the definition of "security interest" in Section 1–201 provides rules for distinguishing sales transactions from those that create a security interest securing an obligation. This Article applies to both types of transactions. The principal effect of this coverage is to apply this Article's perfection and priority rules to these sales transactions. Use of terminology such as "security interest," "debtor," and "collateral" is merely a drafting convention adopted to reach this end, and its use has no relevance to distinguishing sales from other transactions. See PEB Commentary No. 14.

---

*   *Referring to unrevised Article 1 (Appendix A).*

Following a debtor's outright sale and transfer of ownership of a receivable, the debtor-seller retains no legal or equitable rights in the receivable that has been sold. See Section 9–318(a). This is so whether or not the buyer's security interest is perfected. (A security interest arising from the sale of a promissory note or payment intangible is perfected upon attachment without further action. See Section 9–309.) However, if the buyer's interest in accounts or chattel paper is unperfected, a subsequent lien creditor, perfected secured party, or qualified buyer can reach the sold receivable and achieve priority over (or take free of) the buyer's unperfected security interest under Section 9–317. This is so not because the seller of a receivable retains rights in the property sold; it does not. Nor is this so because the seller of a receivable is a "debtor" and the buyer of a receivable is a "secured party" under this Article (they are). It is so for the simple reason that Sections 9–318(b), 9–317, and 9–322 make it so, as did former Sections 9–301 and 9–312. Because the buyer's security interest is unperfected, for purposes of determining the rights of creditors of and purchasers for value from the debtor-seller, under Section 9–318(b) the debtor-seller is deemed to have the rights and title it sold. Section 9–317 subjects the buyer's unperfected interest in accounts and chattel paper to that of the debtor-seller's lien creditor and other persons who qualify under that section.

6. **Consignments.** Subsection (a)(4) is new. This Article applies to every "consignment." The term, defined in Section 9–102, includes many but not all "true" consignments (i.e., bailments for the purpose of sale). If a transaction is a "sale or return," as defined in revised Section 2–326, it is not a "consignment." In a "sale or return" transaction, the buyer becomes the owner of the goods, and the seller may obtain an enforceable security interest in the goods only by satisfying the requirements of Section 9–203.

Under common law, creditors of a bailee were unable to reach the interest of the bailor (in the case of a consignment, the consignor-owner). Like former Section 2–326 and former Article 9, this Article changes the common-law result; however, it does so in a different manner. For purposes of determining the rights and interests of third-party creditors of, and purchasers of the goods from, the consignee, but not for other purposes, such as remedies of the consignor, the consignee is deemed to acquire under this Article whatever rights and title the consignor had or had power to transfer. See Section 9–319. The interest of a consignor is defined to be a security interest under revised Section 1–201(37),* more specifically, a purchase-money security interest in the consignee's inventory. See Section 9–103(d). Thus, the rules pertaining to lien creditors, buyers, and attachment, perfection, and priority of competing security interests apply to consigned goods. The relationship between the consignor and consignee is left to other law. Consignors also have no duties under Part 6. See Section 9–601(g).

Sometimes parties characterize transactions that secure an obligation (other than the bailee's obligation to returned bailed goods) as "consignments." These transactions are not "consignments" as contemplated by Section 9–109(a)(4). See Section 9–102. This Article applies also to these transactions, by virtue of Section 9–109(a)(1). They create a security interest within the meaning of the first sentence of Section 1–201(37).*

This Article does not apply to bailments for sale that fall outside the definition of "consignment" in Section 9–102 and that do not create a security interest that secures an obligation.

7. **Security Interest in Obligation Secured by Non-Article 9 Transaction.** Subsection (b) is unchanged in substance from former Section 9–102(3). The following example provides an illustration.

Example 1: O borrows $10,000 from M and secures its repayment obligation, evidenced by a promissory note, by granting to M a mortgage on O's land. This Article does not apply to the creation of the real-property mortgage. However, if M sells the promissory note to X or gives a security interest in the note to secure M's own obligation to X, this Article applies to the security interest thereby created in favor of X. The security interest in the promissory note is covered by this Article even though the note is secured by a real-property mortgage. Also, X's security interest in the note gives X an attached security interest in the mortgage lien that secures the note and, if the security interest in the note is perfected, the security interest in the mortgage lien likewise is perfected. See Sections 9–203, 9–308.

It also follows from subsection (b) that an attempt to obtain or perfect a security interest in a secured obligation by complying with non-Article 9 law, as by an assignment of record of a real-property mortgage, would be ineffective. Finally, it is implicit from subsection (b) that one cannot obtain a security interest in a lien, such as a mortgage on real property, that is not also coupled with an equally effective security interest in the secured obligation. This Article rejects cases such as In re *Maryville Savings & Loan Corp.*, 743 F.2d 413 (6th Cir. 1984), clarified on reconsideration, 760 F.2d 119 (1985).

---

* *Referring to unrevised Article 1 (Appendix A).*

8. **Federal Preemption.** Former Section 9–104(a) excluded from Article 9 "a security interest subject to any statute of the United States, to the extent that such statute governs the rights of parties to and third parties affected by transactions in particular types of property." Some (erroneously) read the former section to suggest that Article 9 sometimes deferred to federal law even when federal law did not preempt Article 9. Subsection (c)(1) recognizes explicitly that this Article defers to federal law only when and to the extent that it must—i.e., when federal law preempts it.

9. **Governmental Debtors.** Former Section 9–104(e) excluded transfers by governmental debtors. It has been revised and replaced by the exclusions in new paragraphs (2) and (3) of subsection (c). These paragraphs reflect the view that Article 9 should apply to security interests created by a State, foreign country, or a "governmental unit" (defined in Section 9–102) of either except to the extent that another statute governs the issue in question. Under paragraph (2), this Article defers to all statutes of the forum State. (A forum cannot determine whether it should consult the choice-of-law rules in the forum's UCC unless it first determines that its UCC applies to the transaction before it.) Paragraph (3) defers to statutes of another State or a foreign country only to the extent that those statutes contain rules applicable specifically to security interests created by the governmental unit in question.

> **Example 2:** A New Jersey state commission creates a security interest in favor of a New York bank. The validity of the security interest is litigated in New York. The relevant security agreement provides that it is governed by New York law. To the extent that a New Jersey statute contains rules peculiar to creation of security interests by governmental units generally, to creation of security interests by state commissions, or to creation of security interests by this particular state commission, then that law will govern. On the other hand, to the extent that New Jersey law provides that security interests created by governmental units, state commissions, or this state commission are governed by the law generally applicable to secured transactions (i.e., New Jersey's Article 9), then New York's Article 9 will govern.

> **Example 3:** An airline that is an instrumentality of a foreign country creates a security interest in favor of a New York bank. The analysis used in the previous example would apply here. That is, if the matter is litigated in New York, New York law would govern except to the extent that the foreign country enacted a statute applicable to security interests created by governmental units generally or by the airline specifically.

The fact that New York law applies does not necessarily mean that perfection is accomplished by filing in New York. Rather, it means that the court should apply New York's Article 9, including its choice-of-law provisions. Under New York's Section 9–301, perfection is governed by the law of the jurisdiction in which the debtor is located. Section 9–307 determines the debtor's location for choice-of-law purposes.

If a transaction does not bear an appropriate relation to the forum State, then that State's Article 9 will not apply, regardless of whether the transaction would be excluded by paragraph (3).

> **Example 4:** A Belgian governmental unit grants a security interest in its equipment to a Swiss secured party. The equipment is located in Belgium. A dispute arises and, for some reason, an action is brought in a New Mexico state court. Inasmuch as the transaction bears no "appropriate relation" to New Mexico, New Mexico's UCC, including its Article 9, is inapplicable. See Section 1–105(1).* New Mexico's Section 9–109(c) on excluded transactions should not come into play. Even if the parties agreed that New Mexico law would govern, the parties' agreement would not be effective because the transaction does not bear a "reasonable relation" to New Mexico. See Section 1–105(1).*

Conversely, Article 9 will come into play only if the litigation arises in a UCC jurisdiction or if a foreign choice-of-law rule leads a foreign court to apply the law of a UCC jurisdiction. For example, if issues concerning a security interest granted by a foreign airline to a New York bank are litigated overseas, the court may be bound to apply the law of the debtor's jurisdiction and not New York's Article 9.

10. **Certain Statutory and Common-Law Liens; Interests in Real Property.** With few exceptions (nonconsensual agricultural liens being one), this Article applies only to consensual security interests in personal property. Following former Section 9–104(b) and (j), paragraphs (1) and (11) of subsection (d) exclude landlord's liens and leases and most other interests in or liens on real property. These exclusions generally reiterate the limitations on coverage (i.e., "by contract," "in personal property and fixtures") made explicit in subsection (a)(1). Similarly, most jurisdictions provide special liens to suppliers of many types of services and materials, either by statute or by common law. With the exception of agricultural liens, it is not necessary for this Article to provide general codification of this lien structure, which is determined in large part by local conditions and which is far

---

* *Referring to unrevised Article 1 (Appendix A).*

removed from ordinary commercial financing. As under former Section 9–104(c), subsection (d)(2) excludes these suppliers' liens (other than agricultural liens) from this Article. However, Section 9–333 provides a rule for determining priorities between certain possessory suppliers' liens and security interests covered by this Article.

11. **Wage and Similar Claims.** As under former Section 9–104(d), subsection (d)(3) excludes assignments of claims for wages and the like from this Article. These assignments present important social issues that other law addresses. The Federal Trade Commission has ruled that, with some exceptions, the taking of an assignment of wages or other earnings is an unfair act or practice under the Federal Trade Commission Act. See 16 C.F.R. Part 444. State statutes also may regulate such assignments.

12. **Certain Sales and Assignments of Receivables; Judgments.** In general this Article covers security interests in (including sales of) accounts, chattel paper, payment intangibles, and promissory notes. Paragraphs (4), (5), (6), and (7) of subsection (d) exclude from the Article certain sales and assignments of receivables that, by their nature, do not concern commercial financing transactions. These paragraphs add to the exclusions in former Section 9–104(f) analogous sales and assignments of payment intangibles and promissory notes. For similar reasons, subsection (d)(9) retains the exclusion of assignments of judgments under former Section 9–104(h) (other than judgments taken on a right to payment that itself was collateral under this Article).

13. **Insurance.** Subsection (d)(8) narrows somewhat the broad exclusion of interests in insurance policies under former Section 9–104(g). This Article now covers assignments by or to a health-care provider of "health-care-insurance receivables" (defined in Section 9–102).

14. **Set-Off.** Subsection (d)(10) adds two exceptions to the general exclusion of set-off rights from Article 9 under former Section 9–104(i). The first takes account of new Section 9–340, which regulates the effectiveness of a set-off against a deposit account that stands as collateral. The second recognizes Section 9–404, which affords the obligor on an account, chattel paper, or general intangible the right to raise claims and defenses against an assignee (secured party).

15. **Tort Claims.** Subsection (d)(12) narrows somewhat the broad exclusion of transfers of tort claims under former Section 9–104(k). This Article now applies to assignments of "commercial tort claims" (defined in Section 9–102) as well as to security interests in tort claims that constitute proceeds of other collateral (e.g., a right to payment for negligent destruction of the debtor's inventory). Note that once a claim arising in tort has been settled and reduced to a contractual obligation to pay, the right to payment becomes a payment intangible and ceases to be a claim arising in tort.

This Article contains two special rules governing creation of a security interest in tort claims. First, a description of collateral in a security agreement as "all tort claims" is insufficient to meet the requirement for attachment. See Section 9–108(e). Second, no security interest attaches under an after-acquired property clause to a tort claim. See Section 9–204(b). In addition, this Article does not determine whom the tortfeasor must pay to discharge its obligation. Inasmuch as a tortfeasor is not an "account debtor," the rules governing waiver of defenses and discharge of an obligation by an obligor (Sections 9–403, 9–404, 9–405, and 9–406) are inapplicable to tort-claim collateral.

16. **Deposit Accounts.** Except in consumer transactions, deposit accounts may be taken as original collateral under this Article. Under former Section 9–104(*l*), deposit accounts were excluded as original collateral, leaving security interests in deposit accounts to be governed by the common law. The common law is nonuniform, often difficult to discover and comprehend, and frequently costly to implement. As a consequence, debtors who wished to use deposit accounts as collateral sometimes were precluded from doing so as a practical matter. By excluding deposit accounts from the Article's scope as original collateral in consumer transactions, subsection (d)(13) leaves those transactions to law other than this Article. However, in both consumer and non-consumer transactions, sections 9–315 and 9–322 apply to deposit accounts as proceeds and with respect to priorities in proceeds.

This Article contains several safeguards to protect debtors against inadvertently encumbering deposit accounts and to reduce the likelihood that a secured party will realize a windfall from a debtor's deposit accounts. For example, because "deposit account" is a separate type of collateral, a security agreement covering general intangibles will not adequately describe deposit accounts. Rather, a security agreement must reasonably identify the deposit accounts that are the subject of a security interest, e.g., by using the term "deposit accounts." See Section 9–108. To perfect a security interest in a deposit account as original collateral, a secured party (other than the bank with which the deposit account is maintained) must obtain "control" of the account either by obtaining the bank's authenticated agreement or by becoming the bank's customer with respect to the deposit account. See Sections 9–312(b)(1), 9–104. Either of these steps requires the debtor's consent.

This Article also contains new rules that determine which State's law governs perfection and priority of a security interest in a deposit account (Section 9–304), priority of conflicting security interests in and set-off rights against a deposit account (Sections 9–327, 9–340), the rights of transferees of funds from an encumbered deposit account (Section 9–332), the obligations of the bank (Section 9–341), enforcement of security interests in a deposit account (Section 9–607(c)), and the duty of a secured party to terminate control of a deposit account (Section 9–208(b)).

As amended in 2000 and 2010.

§ 9–110. Security Interests Arising Under Article 2 or 2A.

A security interest arising under Section 2–401, 2–505, 2–711(3), or 2A–508(5) is subject to this article. However, until the debtor obtains possession of the goods:

(1) the security interest is enforceable, even if Section 9–203(b)(3) has not been satisfied;

(2) filing is not required to perfect the security interest;

(3) the rights of the secured party after default by the debtor are governed by Article 2 or 2A; and

(4) the security interest has priority over a conflicting security interest created by the debtor.

Official Comments

1. **Source.** Former Section 9–113.

2. **Background.** Former Section 9–113, from which this section derives, referred generally to security interests "arising solely under the Article on Sales (Article 2) or the Article on Leases (Article 2A)." Views differed as to the precise scope of that section. In contrast, Section 9–110 specifies the security interests to which it applies.

3. **Security Interests Under Articles 2 and 2A.** Section 2–505 explains how a seller of goods may reserve a security interest in them. Section 2–401 indicates that a reservation of title by the seller of goods, despite delivery to the buyer, is limited to reservation of a security interest. As did former Article 9, this Article governs a security interest arising solely under one of those sections; however, until the buyer obtains possession of the goods, the security interest is enforceable even in the absence of a security agreement, filing is not necessary to perfect the security interest, and the seller-secured party's rights on the buyer's default are governed by Article 2.

Sections 2–711(3) and 2A–508(5) create a security interest in favor of a buyer or lessee in possession of goods that were rightfully rejected or as to which acceptance was justifiably revoked. As did former Article 9, this Article governs a security interest arising solely under one of those sections; however, until the seller or lessor obtains possession of the goods, the security interest is enforceable even in the absence of a security agreement, filing is not necessary to perfect the security interest, and the secured party's (buyer's or lessee's) rights on the debtor's (seller's or lessor's) default are governed by Article 2 or 2A, as the case may be.

4. **Priority.** This section adds to former Section 9–113 a priority rule. Until the debtor obtains possession of the goods, a security interest arising under one of the specified sections of Article 2 or 2A has priority over conflicting security interests created by the debtor. Thus, a security interest arising under Section 2–401 or 2–505 has priority over a conflicting security interest in the buyer's after-acquired goods, even if the goods in question are inventory. Arguably, the same result would obtain under Section 9–322, but even if it would not, a purchase-money-like priority is appropriate. Similarly, a security interest under Section 2–711(3) or 2A–508(5) has priority over security interests claimed by the seller's or lessor's secured lender. This result is appropriate, inasmuch as the payments giving rise to the debt secured by the Article 2 or 2A security interest are likely to be included among the lender's proceeds.

Example: Seller owns equipment subject to a security interest created by Seller in favor of Lender. Buyer pays for the equipment, accepts the goods, and then justifiably revokes acceptance. As long as Seller does not recover possession of the equipment, Buyer's security interest under Section 2–711(3) is senior to that of Lender.

In the event that a security interest referred to in this section conflicts with a security interest that is created by a person other than the debtor, Section 9–325 applies. Thus, if Lender's security interest in the example was created not by Seller but by the person from whom Seller acquired the goods, Section 9–325 would govern.

5. **Relationship to Other Rights and Remedies Under Articles 2 and 2A.** This Article does not specifically address the conflict between (i) a security interest created by a buyer or lessee and (ii) the seller's or

lessor's right to withhold delivery under Section 2–702(1), 2–703(a), or 2A–525, the seller's or lessor's right to stop delivery under Section 2–705 or 2A–526, or the seller's right to reclaim under Section 2–507(2) or 2–702(2). These conflicts are governed by the first sentence of Section 2–403(1), under which the buyer's secured party obtains no greater rights in the goods than the buyer had or had power to convey, or Section 2A–307(1), under which creditors of the lessee take subject to the lease contract.

PART 2

EFFECTIVENESS OF SECURITY AGREEMENT; ATTACHMENT OF SECURITY INTEREST; RIGHTS OF PARTIES TO SECURITY AGREEMENT

[SUBPART 1. EFFECTIVENESS AND ATTACHMENT]

§ 9–201.   General Effectiveness of Security Agreement.

(a)   **[General effectiveness.]** Except as otherwise provided in [the Uniform Commercial Code], a security agreement is effective according to its terms between the parties, against purchasers of the collateral, and against creditors.

(b)   **[Applicable consumer laws and other law.]** A transaction subject to this article is subject to any applicable rule of law which establishes a different rule for consumers and [insert reference to (i) any other statute or regulation that regulates the rates, charges, agreements, and practices for loans, credit sales, or other extensions of credit and (ii) any consumer-protection statute or regulation].

(c)   **[Other applicable law controls.]** In case of conflict between this article and a rule of law, statute, or regulation described in subsection (b), the rule of law, statute, or regulation controls. Failure to comply with a statute or regulation described in subsection (b) has only the effect the statute or regulation specifies.

(d)   **[Further deference to other applicable law.]** This article does not:

(1)   validate any rate, charge, agreement, or practice that violates a rule of law, statute, or regulation described in subsection (b); or

(2)   extend the application of the rule of law, statute, or regulation to a transaction not otherwise subject to it.

Official Comment

1.   **Source.** Former Sections 9–201, 9–203(4).

2.   **Effectiveness of Security Agreement.** Subsection (a) provides that a security agreement is generally effective. With certain exceptions, a security agreement is effective between the debtor and secured party and is likewise effective against third parties. Note that "security agreement" is used here (and elsewhere in this Article) as it is defined in Section 9–102: "an agreement that creates or provides for a security interest." It follows that subsection (a) does not provide that every term or provision contained in a record that contains a security agreement or that is so labeled is effective. Properly read, former Section 9–201 was to the same effect. Exceptions to the general rule of subsection (a) arise where there is an overriding provision in this Article or any other Article of the UCC. For example, Section 9–317 subordinates unperfected security interests to lien creditors and certain buyers, and several provisions in Part 3 subordinate some security interests to other security interests and interests of purchasers.

3.   **Law, Statutes, and Regulations Applicable to Certain Transactions.** Subsection (b) makes clear that certain transactions, although subject to this Article, also are subject to other applicable laws relating to consumers or specified in that subsection. Subsection (c) provides that the other law is controlling in the event of a conflict, and that a violation of other law does not *ipso facto* constitute a violation of this Article. Subsection (d) provides that this Article does not validate violations under or extend the application of the other applicable laws.

§ 9–202.   Title to Collateral Immaterial.

Except as otherwise provided with respect to consignments or sales of accounts, chattel paper, payment intangibles, or promissory notes, the provisions of this article with regard to rights and obligations apply whether title to collateral is in the secured party or the debtor.

Official Comment

1.   **Source.** Former Section 9–202.

2.   **Title Immaterial.** The rights and duties of parties to a secured transaction and affected third parties are provided in this Article without reference to the location of "title" to the collateral. For example, the characteristics of a security interest that secures the purchase price of goods are the same whether the secured party appears to have retained title or the debtor appears to have obtained title and then conveyed title or a lien to the secured party.

3.   **When Title Matters.**

a.   **Under This Article.** This section explicitly acknowledges two circumstances in which the effect of certain Article 9 provisions turns on ownership (title). First, in some respects sales of accounts, chattel paper, payment intangibles, and promissory notes receive special treatment. See, e.g., Sections 9–207(a), 9–210(b), 9–615(e). Buyers of receivables under former Article 9 were treated specially, as well. See, e.g., former Section 9–502(2). Second, the remedies of a consignor under a true consignment and, for the most part, the remedies of a buyer of accounts, chattel paper, payment intangibles, or promissory notes are determined by other law and not by Part 6. See Section 9–601(g).

b.   **Under Other Law.** This Article does not determine which line of interpretation (e.g., title theory or lien theory, retained title or conveyed title) should be followed in cases in which the applicability of another rule of law depends upon who has title. If, for example, a revenue law imposes a tax on the "legal" owner of goods or if a corporation law makes a vote of the stockholders prerequisite to a corporation "giving" a security interest but not if it acquires property "subject" to a security interest, this Article does not attempt to define whether the secured party is a "legal" owner or whether the transaction "gives" a security interest for the purpose of such laws. Other rules of law or the agreement of the parties determines the location and source of title for those purposes.

§ 9–203.   Attachment and Enforceability of Security Interest; Proceeds; Supporting Obligations; Formal Requisites.

(a)   **[Attachment.]** A security interest attaches to collateral when it becomes enforceable against the debtor with respect to the collateral, unless an agreement expressly postpones the time of attachment.

(b)   **[Enforceability.]** Except as otherwise provided in subsections (c) through (i), a security interest is enforceable against the debtor and third parties with respect to the collateral only if:

(1)   value has been given;

(2)   the debtor has rights in the collateral or the power to transfer rights in the collateral to a secured party; and

(3)   one of the following conditions is met:

(A)   the debtor has authenticated a security agreement that provides a description of the collateral and, if the security interest covers timber to be cut, a description of the land concerned;

(B)   the collateral is not a certificated security and is in the possession of the secured party under Section 9–313 pursuant to the debtor's security agreement;

(C)   the collateral is a certificated security in registered form and the security certificate has been delivered to the secured party under Section 8–301 pursuant to the debtor's security agreement; or

(D)   the collateral is deposit accounts, electronic chattel paper, investment property, letter-of-credit rights, or electronic documents, and the secured party has control under Section 7–106, 9–104, 9–105, 9–106, or 9–107 pursuant to the debtor's security agreement.

(c)　**[Other UCC provisions.]** Subsection (b) is subject to Section 4–210 on the security interest of a collecting bank, Section 5–118 on the security interest of a letter-of-credit issuer or nominated person, Section 9–110 on a security interest arising under Article 2 or 2A, and Section 9–206 on security interests in investment property.

(d)　**[When person becomes bound by another person's security agreement.]** A person becomes bound as debtor by a security agreement entered into by another person if, by operation of law other than this article or by contract:

(1)　the security agreement becomes effective to create a security interest in the person's property; or

(2)　the person becomes generally obligated for the obligations of the other person, including the obligation secured under the security agreement, and acquires or succeeds to all or substantially all of the assets of the other person.

(e)　**[Effect of new debtor becoming bound.]** If a new debtor becomes bound as debtor by a security agreement entered into by another person:

(1)　the agreement satisfies subsection (b)(3) with respect to existing or after-acquired property of the new debtor to the extent the property is described in the agreement; and

(2)　another agreement is not necessary to make a security interest in the property enforceable.

(f)　**[Proceeds and supporting obligations.]** The attachment of a security interest in collateral gives the secured party the rights to proceeds provided by Section 9–315 and is also attachment of a security interest in a supporting obligation for the collateral.

(g)　**[Lien securing right to payment.]** The attachment of a security interest in a right to payment or performance secured by a security interest or other lien on personal or real property is also attachment of a security interest in the security interest, mortgage, or other lien.

(h)　**[Security entitlement carried in securities account.]** The attachment of a security interest in a securities account is also attachment of a security interest in the security entitlements carried in the securities account.

(i)　**[Commodity contracts carried in commodity account.]** The attachment of a security interest in a commodity account is also attachment of a security interest in the commodity contracts carried in the commodity account.

As amended in 2003.

Official Comment

1.　**Source.** Former Sections 9–203, 9–115(2), (6).

2.　**Creation, Attachment, and Enforceability.** Subsection (a) states the general rule that a security interest attaches to collateral only when it becomes enforceable against the debtor. Subsection (b) specifies the circumstances under which a security interest becomes enforceable. Subsection (b) states three basic prerequisites to the existence of a security interest: value (paragraph (1)), rights or power to transfer rights in collateral (paragraph (2)), and agreement plus satisfaction of an evidentiary requirement (paragraph (3)). When all of these elements exist, a security interest becomes enforceable between the parties and attaches under subsection (a). Subsection (c) identifies certain exceptions to the general rule of subsection (b).

3.　**Security Agreement; Authentication.** Under subsection (b)(3), enforceability requires the debtor's security agreement and compliance with an evidentiary requirement in the nature of a Statute of Frauds. Paragraph (3)(A) represents the most basic of the evidentiary alternatives, under which the debtor must authenticate a security agreement that provides a description of the collateral. Under Section 9–102, a "security agreement" is "an agreement that creates or provides for a security interest." Neither that definition nor the requirement of paragraph (3)(A) rejects the deeply rooted doctrine that a bill of sale, although absolute in form, may be shown in fact to have been given as security. Under this Article, as under prior law, a debtor may show by parol evidence that a transfer purporting to be absolute was in fact for security. Similarly, a self-styled "lease" may serve as a security agreement if the agreement creates a security interest. See Section 1–203 (distinguishing security interest from lease).

4. **Possession, Delivery, or Control Pursuant to Security Agreement.** The other alternatives in subsection (b)(3) dispense with the requirement of an authenticated security agreement and provide alternative evidentiary tests. Under paragraph (3)(B), the secured party's possession substitutes for the debtor's authentication under paragraph (3)(A) if the secured party's possession is "pursuant to the debtor's security agreement." That phrase refers to the debtor's agreement to the secured party's possession for the purpose of creating a security interest. The phrase should not be confused with the phrase "debtor has authenticated a security agreement," used in paragraph (3)(A), which contemplates the debtor's authentication of a record. In the unlikely event that possession is obtained without the debtor's agreement, possession would not suffice as a substitute for an authenticated security agreement. However, once the security interest has become enforceable and has attached, it is not impaired by the fact that the secured party's possession is maintained without the agreement of a subsequent debtor (e.g., a transferee). Possession as contemplated by Section 9–313 is possession for purposes of subsection (b)(3)(B), even though it may not constitute possession "pursuant to the debtor's agreement" and consequently might not serve as a substitute for an authenticated security agreement under subsection (b)(3)(A). Subsection (b)(3)(C) provides that delivery of a certificated security to the secured party under Section 8–301 pursuant to the debtor's security agreement is sufficient as a substitute for an authenticated security agreement. Similarly, under subsection (b)(3)(D), control of investment property, a deposit account, electronic chattel paper, a letter-of-credit right, or electronic documents satisfies the evidentiary test if control is pursuant to the debtor's security agreement.

5. **Collateral Covered by Other Statute or Treaty.** One evidentiary purpose of the formal requisites stated in subsection (b) is to minimize the possibility of future disputes as to the terms of a security agreement (e.g., as to the property that stands as collateral for the obligation secured). One should distinguish the evidentiary functions of the formal requisites of attachment and enforceability (such as the requirement that a security agreement contain a description of the collateral) from the more limited goals of "notice filing" for financing statements under Part 5, explained in Section 9–502, Comment 2. When perfection is achieved by compliance with the requirements of a statute or treaty described in Section 9–311(a), such as a federal recording act or a certificate-of-title statute, the manner of describing the collateral in a registry imposed by the statute or treaty may or may not be adequate for purposes of this section and Section 9–108. However, the description contained in the security agreement, not the description in a public registry or on a certificate of title, controls for purposes of this section.

6. **Debtor's Rights; Debtor's Power to Transfer Rights.** Subsection (b)(2) conditions attachment on the debtor's having "rights in the collateral or the power to transfer rights in the collateral to a secured party." A debtor's limited rights in collateral, short of full ownership, are sufficient for a security interest to attach. However, in accordance with basic personal property conveyancing principles, the baseline rule is that a security interest attaches only to whatever rights a debtor may have, broad or limited as those rights may be.

Certain exceptions to the baseline rule enable a debtor to transfer, and a security interest to attach to, greater rights than the debtor has. See Part 3, Subpart 3 (priority rules). The phrase, "or the power to transfer rights in the collateral to a secured party," accommodates those exceptions. In some cases, a debtor may have power to transfer another person's rights only to a class of transferees that excludes secured parties. See, e.g., Section 2–403(2) (giving certain merchants power to transfer an entruster's rights to a buyer in ordinary course of business). Under those circumstances, the debtor would not have the power to create a security interest in the other person's rights, and the condition in subsection (b)(2) would not be satisfied.

7. **New Debtors.** Subsection (e) makes clear that the enforceability requirements of subsection (b)(3) are met when a new debtor becomes bound under an original debtor's security agreement. If a new debtor becomes bound as debtor by a security agreement entered into by another person, the security agreement satisfies the requirement of subsection (b)(3) as to the existing and after-acquired property of the new debtor to the extent the property is described in the agreement.

Subsection (d) explains when a new debtor becomes bound. Persons who become bound under paragraph (2) are limited to those who both become primarily liable for the original debtor's obligations and succeed to (or acquire) its assets. Thus, the paragraph excludes sureties and other secondary obligors as well as persons who become obligated through veil piercing and other non-successorship doctrines. In many cases, paragraph (2) will exclude successors to the assets and liabilities of a division of a debtor. See also Section 9–508, Comment 3.

8. **Supporting Obligations.** Under subsection (f), a security interest in a "supporting obligation" (defined in Section 9–102) automatically follows from a security interest in the underlying, supported collateral. This result was implicit under former Article 9. Implicit in subsection (f) is the principle that the secured party's interest in a supporting obligation extends to the supporting obligation only to the extent that it supports the collateral in which the secured party has a security interest. Complex issues may arise, however, if a supporting

obligation supports many separate obligations of a particular account debtor and if the supported obligations are separately assigned as security to several secured parties. The problems may be exacerbated if a supporting obligation is limited to an aggregate amount that is less than the aggregate amount of the obligations it supports. This Article does not contain provisions dealing with competing claims to a limited supporting obligation. As under former Article 9, the law of suretyship and the agreements of the parties will control.

9. **Collateral Follows Right to Payment or Performance.** Subsection (g) codifies the common-law rule that a transfer of an obligation secured by a security interest or other lien on personal or real property also transfers the security interest or lien. See Restatement (3d), Property (Mortgages) § 5.4(a) (1997). See also Section 9–308(e) (analogous rule for perfection).

10. **Investment Property.** Subsections (h) and (i) make clear that attachment of a security interest in a securities account or commodity account is also attachment in security entitlements or commodity contracts carried in the accounts.

As amended in 2003 and 2010.

§ 9–204.   After-Acquired Property; Future Advances.

(a) **[After-acquired collateral.]** Except as otherwise provided in subsection (b), a security agreement may create or provide for a security interest in after-acquired collateral.

(b) **[When after-acquired property clause not effective.]** A security interest does not attach under a term constituting an after-acquired property clause to:

(1) consumer goods, other than an accession when given as additional security, unless the debtor acquires rights in them within 10 days after the secured party gives value; or

(2) a commercial tort claim.

(c) **[Future advances and other value.]** A security agreement may provide that collateral secures, or that accounts, chattel paper, payment intangibles, or promissory notes are sold in connection with, future advances or other value, whether or not the advances or value are given pursuant to commitment.

Official Comment

1. **Source.** Former Section 9–204.

2. **After-Acquired Property; Continuing General Lien.** Subsection (a) makes clear that a security interest arising by virtue of an after-acquired property clause is no less valid than a security interest in collateral in which the debtor has rights at the time value is given. A security interest in after-acquired property is not merely an "equitable" interest; no further action by the secured party—such as a supplemental agreement covering the new collateral—is required. This section adopts the principle of a "continuing general lien" or "floating lien." It validates a security interest in the debtor's existing and (upon acquisition) future assets, even though the debtor has liberty to use or dispose of collateral without being required to account for proceeds or substitute new collateral. See Section 9–205. Subsection (a), together with subsection (c), also validates "cross-collateral" clauses under which collateral acquired at any time secures advances whenever made.

3. **After-Acquired Consumer Goods.** Subsection (b)(1) makes ineffective an after-acquired property clause covering consumer goods (defined in Section 9–109), except as accessions (see Section 9–335), acquired more than 10 days after the secured party gives value. Subsection (b)(1) is unchanged in substance from the corresponding provision in former Section 9–204(2).

4. **Commercial Tort Claims.** Subsection (b)(2) provides that an after-acquired property clause in a security agreement does not reach future commercial tort claims. In order for a security interest in a tort claim to attach, the claim must be in existence when the security agreement is authenticated. In addition, the security agreement must describe the tort claim with greater specificity than simply "all tort claims." See Section 9–108(e).

5. **Future Advances; Obligations Secured.** Under subsection (c) collateral may secure future as well as past or present advances if the security agreement so provides. This is in line with the policy of this Article toward security interests in after-acquired property under subsection (a). Indeed, the parties are free to agree that a security interest secures any obligation whatsoever. Determining the obligations secured by collateral is solely a matter of construing the parties' agreement under applicable law. This Article rejects the holdings of cases decided under former Article 9 that applied other tests, such as whether a future advance or other subsequently

incurred obligation was of the same or a similar type or class as earlier advances and obligations secured by the collateral.

6. **Sales of Receivables.** Subsections (a) and (c) expressly validate after-acquired property and future advance clauses not only when the transaction is for security purposes but also when the transaction is the sale of accounts, chattel paper, payment intangibles, or promissory notes. This result was implicit under former Article 9.

7. **Financing Statements.** The effect of after-acquired property and future advance clauses as components of a security agreement should not be confused with the requirements applicable to financing statements under this Article's system of perfection by notice filing. The references to after-acquired property clauses and future advance clauses in this section are limited to security agreements. There is no need to refer to after-acquired property or future advances or other obligations secured in a financing statement. See Section 9–502, Comment 2.

As amended in 2000.

§ 9–205.   Use or Disposition of Collateral Permissible.

(a)   **[When security interest not invalid or fraudulent.]** A security interest is not invalid or fraudulent against creditors solely because:

(1)   the debtor has the right or ability to:

(A)   use, commingle, or dispose of all or part of the collateral, including returned or repossessed goods;

(B)   collect, compromise, enforce, or otherwise deal with collateral;

(C)   accept the return of collateral or make repossessions; or

(D)   use, commingle, or dispose of proceeds; or

(2)   the secured party fails to require the debtor to account for proceeds or replace collateral.

(b)   **[Requirements of possession not relaxed.]** This section does not relax the requirements of possession if attachment, perfection, or enforcement of a security interest depends upon possession of the collateral by the secured party.

Official Comment

1.   **Source.** Former Section 9–205.

2.   **Validity of Unrestricted "Floating Lien."** This Article expressly validates the "floating lien" on shifting collateral. See Sections 9–201, 9–204 and Comment 2. This section provides that a security interest is not invalid or fraudulent by reason of the debtor's liberty to dispose of the collateral without being required to account to the secured party for proceeds or substitute new collateral. As did former Section 9–205, this section repeals the rule of *Benedict v. Ratner*, 268 U.S. 353 (1925), and other cases which held such arrangements void as a matter of law because the debtor was given unfettered dominion or control over collateral. The *Benedict* rule did not effectively discourage or eliminate security transactions in inventory and receivables. Instead, it forced financing arrangements to be self-liquidating. Although this section repeals *Benedict*, the filing and other perfection requirements (see Part 3, Subpart 2, and Part 5) provide for public notice that overcomes any potential misleading effects of a debtor's use and control of collateral. Moreover, nothing in this section prevents the debtor and secured party from agreeing to procedures by which the secured party polices or monitors collateral or to restrictions on the debtor's dominion. However, this Article leaves these matters to agreement based on business considerations, not on legal requirements.

3.   **Possessory Security Interests.** Subsection (b) makes clear that this section does not relax the requirements for perfection by possession under Section 9–313. If a secured party allows the debtor access to and control over collateral its security interest may be or become unperfected.

4.   **Permissible Freedom for Debtor to Enforce Collateral.** Former Section 9–205 referred to a debtor's "liberty. . .to collect or compromise accounts or chattel paper." This section recognizes the broader rights of a debtor to "enforce," as well as to "collect" and "compromise" collateral. This section's reference to collecting,

compromising, and enforcing "collateral" instead of "accounts or chattel paper" contemplates the many other types of collateral that a debtor may wish to "collect, compromise, or enforce": e.g., deposit accounts, documents, general intangibles, instruments, investment property, and letter-of-credit rights.

§ 9–206.   Security Interest Arising in Purchase or Delivery of Financial Asset.

(a)   **[Security interest when person buys through securities intermediary.]** A security interest in favor of a securities intermediary attaches to a person's security entitlement if:

(1)   the person buys a financial asset through the securities intermediary in a transaction in which the person is obligated to pay the purchase price to the securities intermediary at the time of the purchase; and

(2)   the securities intermediary credits the financial asset to the buyer's securities account before the buyer pays the securities intermediary.

(b)   **[Security interest secures obligation to pay for financial asset.]** The security interest described in subsection (a) secures the person's obligation to pay for the financial asset.

(c)   **[Security interest in payment against delivery transaction.]** A security interest in favor of a person that delivers a certificated security or other financial asset represented by a writing attaches to the security or other financial asset if:

(1)   the security or other financial asset:

(A)   in the ordinary course of business is transferred by delivery with any necessary indorsement or assignment; and

(B)   is delivered under an agreement between persons in the business of dealing with such securities or financial assets; and

(2)   the agreement calls for delivery against payment.

(d)   **[Security interest secures obligation to pay for delivery.]** The security interest described in subsection (c) secures the obligation to make payment for the delivery.

Official Comment

1.   **Source.** Former 9–116.

2.   **Codification of "Broker's Lien."** Depending upon a securities intermediary's arrangements with its entitlement holders, the securities intermediary may treat the entitlement holder as entitled to financial assets before the entitlement holder has actually made payment for them. For example, many brokers permit retail customers to pay for financial assets by check. The broker may not receive final payment of the check until several days after the broker has credited the customer's securities account for the financial assets. Thus, the customer will have acquired a security entitlement prior to payment. Subsection (a) provides that, in such circumstances, the securities intermediary has a security interest in the entitlement holder's security entitlement. Under subsection (b) the security interest secures the customer's obligation to pay for the financial asset in question. Subsections (a) and (b) codify and adapt to the indirect holding system the so-called "broker's lien," which has long been recognized. See Restatement, Security § 12.

3.   **Financial Assets Delivered Against Payment.** Subsection (c) creates a security interest in favor of persons who deliver certificated securities or other financial assets in physical form, such as money market instruments, if the agreed payment is not received. In some arrangements for settlement of transactions in physical financial assets, the seller's securities custodian will deliver physical certificates to the buyer's securities custodian and receive a time-stamped delivery receipt. The buyer's securities custodian will examine the certificate to ensure that it is in good order, and that the delivery matches a trade in which the buyer has instructed the seller to deliver to that custodian. If all is in order, the receiving custodian will settle with the delivering custodian through whatever funds settlement system has been agreed upon or is used by custom and usage in that market. The understanding of the trade, however, is that the delivery is conditioned upon payment, so that if payment is not made for any reason, the security will be returned to the deliverer. Subsection (c) clarifies the rights of persons making deliveries in such circumstances. It provides the person making delivery with a security interest in the securities or other financial assets; under subsection (d), the security interest secures the seller's right to receive

payment for the delivery. Section 8–301 specifies when delivery of a certificated security occurs; that section should be applied as well to other financial assets as well for purposes of this section.

4. **Automatic Attachment and Perfection.** Subsections (a) and (c) refer to attachment of a security interest. Attachment under this section has the same incidents (enforceability, right to proceeds, etc.) as attachment under Section 9–203. This section overrides the general attachment rules in Section 9–203. See Section 9–203(c). A securities intermediary's security interest under subsection (a) is perfected by control without further action. See Section 8–106 (control); 9–314 (perfection). Security interests arising under subsection (c) are automatically perfected. See Section 9–309(9).

[SUBPART 2. RIGHTS AND DUTIES]

§ 9–207. Rights and Duties of Secured Party Having Possession or Control of Collateral.

(a) **[Duty of care when secured party in possession.]** Except as otherwise provided in subsection (d), a secured party shall use reasonable care in the custody and preservation of collateral in the secured party's possession. In the case of chattel paper or an instrument, reasonable care includes taking necessary steps to preserve rights against prior parties unless otherwise agreed.

(b) **[Expenses, risks, duties, and rights when secured party in possession.]** Except as otherwise provided in subsection (d), if a secured party has possession of collateral:

(1) reasonable expenses, including the cost of insurance and payment of taxes or other charges, incurred in the custody, preservation, use, or operation of the collateral are chargeable to the debtor and are secured by the collateral;

(2) the risk of accidental loss or damage is on the debtor to the extent of a deficiency in any effective insurance coverage;

(3) the secured party shall keep the collateral identifiable, but fungible collateral may be commingled; and

(4) the secured party may use or operate the collateral:

(A) for the purpose of preserving the collateral or its value;

(B) as permitted by an order of a court having competent jurisdiction; or

(C) except in the case of consumer goods, in the manner and to the extent agreed by the debtor.

(c) **[Duties and rights when secured party in possession or control.]** Except as otherwise provided in subsection (d), a secured party having possession of collateral or control of collateral under Section 7–106, 9–104, 9–105, 9–106, or 9–107:

(1) may hold as additional security any proceeds, except money or funds, received from the collateral;

(2) shall apply money or funds received from the collateral to reduce the secured obligation, unless remitted to the debtor; and

(3) may create a security interest in the collateral.

(d) **[Buyer of certain rights to payment.]** If the secured party is a buyer of accounts, chattel paper, payment intangibles, or promissory notes or a consignor:

(1) subsection (a) does not apply unless the secured party is entitled under an agreement:

(A) to charge back uncollected collateral; or

(B) otherwise to full or limited recourse against the debtor or a secondary obligor based on the nonpayment or other default of an account debtor or other obligor on the collateral; and

(2) subsections (b) and (c) do not apply.

As amended in 2003.

Official Comment

1.   **Source.** Former Section 9–207.

2.   **Duty of Care for Collateral in Secured Party's Possession.** Like former section 9–207, subsection (a) imposes a duty of care, similar to that imposed on a pledgee at common law, on a secured party in possession of collateral. See Restatement, Security §§ 17, 18. In many cases a secured party in possession of collateral may satisfy this duty by notifying the debtor of action that should be taken and allowing the debtor to take the action itself. If the secured party itself takes action, its reasonable expenses may be added to the secured obligation. The revised definitions of "collateral," "debtor," and "secured party" in Section 9–102 make this section applicable to collateral subject to an agricultural lien if the collateral is in the lienholder's possession. Under Section 1–302 the duty to exercise reasonable care may not be disclaimed by agreement, although under that section the parties remain free to determine by agreement standards that are not manifestly unreasonable as to what constitutes reasonable care. Unless otherwise agreed, for a secured party in possession of chattel paper or an instrument, reasonable care includes the preservation of rights against prior parties. The secured party's right to have instruments or documents indorsed or transferred to it or its order is dealt with in the relevant sections of Articles 3, 7, and 8. See Sections 3–203(c), 7–506, 8–304(d).

3.   **Specific Rules When Secured Party in Possession or Control of Collateral.** Subsections (b) and (c) provide rules following common-law precedents which apply unless the parties otherwise agree. The rules in subsection (b) apply to typical issues that may arise while a secured party is in possession of collateral, including expenses, insurance, and taxes, risk of loss or damage, identifiable and fungible collateral, and use or operation of collateral. Subsection (c) contains rules that apply in certain circumstances that may arise when a secured party is in either possession or control of collateral. These circumstances include the secured party's receiving proceeds from the collateral and the secured party's creation of a security interest in the collateral.

4.   **Applicability Following Default.** This section applies when the secured party has possession of collateral either before or after default. See Sections 9–601(b), 9–609. Subsection (b)(4)(C) limits agreements concerning the use or operation of collateral to collateral other than consumer goods. Under Section 9–602(1), a debtor cannot waive or vary that limitation.

5.   **"Repledges" and Right of Redemption.** Subsection (c)(3) eliminates the qualification in former Section 9–207 to the effect that the terms of a "repledge" may not "impair" a debtor's "right to redeem" collateral. The change is primarily for clarification. There is no basis on which to draw from subsection (c)(3) any inference concerning the debtor's right to redeem the collateral. The debtor enjoys that right under Section 9–623; this section need not address it. For example, if the collateral is a negotiable note that the secured party (SP–1) repledges to SP–2, nothing in this section suggests that the debtor (D) does not retain the right to redeem the note upon payment to SP–1 of all obligations secured by the note. But, as explained below, the debtor's unimpaired right to redeem as against the debtor's original secured party nevertheless may not be enforceable as against the new secured party.

In resolving questions that arise from the creation of a security interest by SP–1, one must take care to distinguish D's rights against SP–1 from D's rights against SP–2. Once D discharges the secured obligation, D becomes entitled to the note; SP–1 has no legal basis upon which to withhold it. If, as a practical matter, SP–1 is unable to return the note because SP–2 holds it as collateral for SP–1's unpaid debt, then SP–1 is liable to D under the law of conversion.

Whether SP–2 would be liable to D depends on the relative priority of SP–2's security interest and D's interest. By permitting SP–1 to create a security interest in the collateral (repledge), subsection (c)(3) provides a statutory power for SP–1 to give SP–2 a security interest (subject, of course, to any agreement by SP–1 not to give a security interest). In the vast majority of cases where repledge rights are significant, the security interest of the second secured party, SP–2 in the example, will be senior to the debtor's interest. By virtue of the debtor's consent or applicable legal rules, SP–2 typically would cut off D's rights in investment property or be immune from D's claims. See Sections 9–331, 3–306 (holder in due course), 8–303 (protected purchaser), 8–502 (acquisition of a security entitlement), 8–503(e) (action by entitlement holder). Moreover, the expectations and business practices in some markets, such as the securities markets, are such that D's consent to SP–2's taking free of D's rights inheres in D's creation of SP–1's security interest which gives rise to SP–1's power under this section. In these situations, D would have no right to recover the collateral or recover damages from SP–2. Nevertheless, D would have a damage claim against SP–1 if SP–1 had given a security interest to SP–2 in breach of its agreement with D. Moreover, if SP–2's security interest secures an amount that is less than the amount secured by SP–1's security interest (granted by D), then D's exercise of its right to redeem would provide value sufficient to discharge SP–1's obligations to SP–2.

For the most part this section does not change the law under former Section 9–207, although eliminating the reference to the debtor's right of redemption may alter the secured party's right to repledge in one respect. Former Section 9–207 could have been read to limit the secured party's statutory right to repledge collateral to repledge transactions in which the collateral did not secure a greater obligation than that of the original debtor. Inasmuch as this is a matter normally dealt with by agreement between the debtor and secured party, any change would appear to have little practical effect.

6. **"Repledges" of Investment Property.** The following example will aid the discussion of "repledges" of investment property.

Example. Debtor grants Alpha Bank a security interest in a security entitlement that includes 1000 shares of XYZ Co. stock that Debtor holds through an account with Able & Co. Alpha does not have an account with Able. Alpha uses Beta Bank as its securities custodian. Debtor instructs Able to transfer the shares to Beta, for the account of Alpha, and Able does so. Beta then credits Alpha's account. Alpha has control of the security entitlement for the 1000 shares under Section 8–106(d). (These are the facts of Example 2, Section 8–106, Comment 4.) Although, as between Debtor and Alpha, Debtor may have become the beneficial owner of the new securities entitlement with Beta, Beta has agreed to act on Alpha's entitlement orders because, as between Beta and Alpha, Alpha has become the entitlement holder.

Next, Alpha grants Gamma Bank a security interest in the security entitlement with Beta that includes the 1000 shares of XYZ Co. stock. In order to afford Gamma control of the entitlement, Alpha instructs Beta to transfer the stock to Gamma's custodian, Delta Bank, which credits Gamma's account for 1000 shares. At this point Gamma holds its securities entitlement for its benefit as well as that of its debtor, Alpha. Alpha's derivative rights also are for the benefit of Debtor.

In many, probably most, situations and at any particular point in time, it will be impossible for Debtor or Alpha to "trace" Alpha's "repledge" to any particular securities entitlement or financial asset of Gamma or anyone else. Debtor would retain, of course, a right to redeem the collateral from Alpha upon satisfaction of the secured obligation. However, in the absence of a traceable interest, Debtor would retain only a personal claim against Alpha in the event Alpha failed to restore the security entitlement to Debtor. Moreover, even in the unlikely event that Debtor could trace a property interest, in the context of the financial markets, normally the operation of this section, Debtor's explicit agreement to permit Alpha to create a senior security interest, or legal rules permitting Gamma to cut off Debtor's rights or become immune from Debtor's claims would effectively subordinate Debtor's interest to the holder of a security interest created by Alpha. And, under the shelter principle, all subsequent transferees would obtain interests to which Debtor's interest also would be subordinate.

7. **Buyers of Chattel Paper and Other Receivables; Consignors.** This section has been revised to reflect the fact that a seller of accounts, chattel paper, payment intangibles, or promissory notes retains no interest in the collateral and so is not disadvantaged by the secured party's noncompliance with the requirements of this section. Accordingly, subsection (d) provides that subsection (a) applies only to security interests that secure an obligation and to sales of receivables in which the buyer has recourse against the debtor. (Of course, a buyer of accounts or payment intangibles could not have "possession" of original collateral, but might have possession of proceeds, such as promissory notes or checks.) The meaning of "recourse" in this respect is limited to recourse arising out of the account debtor's failure to pay or other default.

Subsection (d) makes subsections (b) and (c) inapplicable to buyers of accounts, chattel paper, payment intangibles, or promissory notes and consignors. Of course, there is no reason to believe that a buyer of receivables or a consignor could not, for example, create a security interest or otherwise transfer an interest in the collateral, regardless of who has possession of the collateral. However, this section leaves the rights of those owners to law other than Article 9.

As amended in 2000 and 2010.

§ 9–208. Additional Duties of Secured Party Having Control of Collateral.

(a) **[Applicability of section.]** This section applies to cases in which there is no outstanding secured obligation and the secured party is not committed to make advances, incur obligations, or otherwise give value.

(b) **[Duties of secured party after receiving demand from debtor.]** Within 10 days after receiving an authenticated demand by the debtor:

(1)   a secured party having control of a deposit account under Section 9–104(a)(2) shall send to the bank with which the deposit account is maintained an authenticated statement that releases the bank from any further obligation to comply with instructions originated by the secured party;

(2)   a secured party having control of a deposit account under Section 9–104(a)(3) shall:

    (A)   pay the debtor the balance on deposit in the deposit account; or

    (B)   transfer the balance on deposit into a deposit account in the debtor's name;

(3)   a secured party, other than a buyer, having control of electronic chattel paper under Section 9–105 shall:

    (A)   communicate the authoritative copy of the electronic chattel paper to the debtor or its designated custodian;

    (B)   if the debtor designates a custodian that is the designated custodian with which the authoritative copy of the electronic chattel paper is maintained for the secured party, communicate to the custodian an authenticated record releasing the designated custodian from any further obligation to comply with instructions originated by the secured party and instructing the custodian to comply with instructions originated by the debtor; and

    (C)   take appropriate action to enable the debtor or its designated custodian to make copies of or revisions to the authoritative copy which add or change an identified assignee of the authoritative copy without the consent of the secured party;

(4)   a secured party having control of investment property under Section 8–106(d)(2) or 9–106(b) shall send to the securities intermediary or commodity intermediary with which the security entitlement or commodity contract is maintained an authenticated record that releases the securities intermediary or commodity intermediary from any further obligation to comply with entitlement orders or directions originated by the secured party;

(5)   a secured party having control of a letter-of-credit right under Section 9–107 shall send to each person having an unfulfilled obligation to pay or deliver proceeds of the letter of credit to the secured party an authenticated release from any further obligation to pay or deliver proceeds of the letter of credit to the secured party; and

(6)   a secured party having control of an electronic document shall:

    (A)   give control of the electronic document to the debtor or its designated custodian;

    (B)   if the debtor designates a custodian that is the designated custodian with which the authoritative copy of the electronic document is maintained for the secured party, communicate to the custodian an authenticated record releasing the designated custodian from any further obligation to comply with instructions originated by the secured party and instructing the custodian to comply with instructions originated by the debtor; and

    (C)   take appropriate action to enable the debtor or its designated custodian to make copies of or revisions to the authoritative copy which add or change an identified assignee of the authoritative copy without the consent of the secured party.

As amended in 2003.

Official Comment

1.   **Source.** New.

2.   **Scope and Purpose.** This section imposes duties on a secured party who has control of a deposit account, electronic chattel paper, investment property, a letter-of-credit right, or electronic documents of title. The duty to terminate the secured party's control is analogous to the duty to file a termination statement, imposed by Section 9–513. Under subsection (a), it applies only when there is no outstanding secured obligation and the secured party is not committed to give value. The requirements of this section can be varied by agreement under

Section 1–102(3).* For example, a debtor could by contract agree that the secured party may comply with subsection (b) by releasing control more than 10 days after demand. Also, duties under this section should not be read to conflict with the terms of the collateral itself. For example, if the collateral is a time deposit account, subsection (b)(2) should not require a secured party with control to make an early withdrawal of the funds (assuming that were possible) in order to pay them over to the debtor or put them in an account in the debtor's name.

3. **Remedy for Failure to Relinquish Control.** If a secured party fails to comply with the requirements of subsection (b), the debtor has the remedy set forth in Section 9–625(e). This remedy is identical to that applicable to failure to provide or file a termination statement under Section 9–513.

4. **Duty to Relinquish Possession.** Although Section 9–207 addresses directly the duties of a secured party in possession of collateral, that section does not require the secured party to relinquish possession when the secured party ceases to hold a security interest. Under common law, absent agreement to the contrary, the failure to relinquish possession of collateral upon satisfaction of the secured obligation would constitute a conversion. Inasmuch as problems apparently have not surfaced in the absence of statutory duties under former Article 9 and the common-law duty appears to have been sufficient, this Article does not impose a statutory duty to relinquish possession.

As amended in 2000 and 2003.

§ 9–209. Duties of Secured Party if Account Debtor Has Been Notified of Assignment.

(a) **[Applicability of section.]** Except as otherwise provided in subsection (c), this section applies if:

(1) there is no outstanding secured obligation; and

(2) the secured party is not committed to make advances, incur obligations, or otherwise give value.

(b) **[Duties of secured party after receiving demand from debtor.]** Within 10 days after receiving an authenticated demand by the debtor, a secured party shall send to an account debtor that has received notification of an assignment to the secured party as assignee under Section 9–406(a) an authenticated record that releases the account debtor from any further obligation to the secured party.

(c) **[Inapplicability to sales.]** This section does not apply to an assignment constituting the sale of an account, chattel paper, or payment intangible.

Official Comment

1. **Source.** New.

2. **Scope and Purpose.** Like Sections 9–208 and 9–513, which require a secured party to relinquish control of collateral and to file or provide a termination statement for a financing statement, this section requires a secured party to free up collateral when there no longer is any outstanding secured obligation or any commitment to give value in the future. This section addresses the case in which account debtors have been notified to pay a secured party to whom the receivables have been assigned. It requires the secured party (assignee) to inform the account debtors that they no longer are obligated to make payment to the secured party. See subsection (b). It does not apply to account debtors whose obligations on an account, chattel paper, or payment intangible have been sold. See subsection (c).

§ 9–210. Request for Accounting; Request Regarding List of Collateral or Statement of Account.

(a) **[Definitions.]** In this section:

(1) "Request" means a record of a type described in paragraph (2), (3), or (4).

---

* *Referring to unrevised Article 1 (Appendix A).*

(2) "Request for an accounting" means a record authenticated by a debtor requesting that the recipient provide an accounting of the unpaid obligations secured by collateral and reasonably identifying the transaction or relationship that is the subject of the request.

(3) "Request regarding a list of collateral" means a record authenticated by a debtor requesting that the recipient approve or correct a list of what the debtor believes to be the collateral securing an obligation and reasonably identifying the transaction or relationship that is the subject of the request.

(4) "Request regarding a statement of account" means a record authenticated by a debtor requesting that the recipient approve or correct a statement indicating what the debtor believes to be the aggregate amount of unpaid obligations secured by collateral as of a specified date and reasonably identifying the transaction or relationship that is the subject of the request.

(b) **[Duty to respond to requests.]** Subject to subsections (c), (d), (e), and (f), a secured party, other than a buyer of accounts, chattel paper, payment intangibles, or promissory notes or a consignor, shall comply with a request within 14 days after receipt:

(1) in the case of a request for an accounting, by authenticating and sending to the debtor an accounting; and

(2) in the case of a request regarding a list of collateral or a request regarding a statement of account, by authenticating and sending to the debtor an approval or correction.

(c) **[Request regarding list of collateral; statement concerning type of collateral.]** A secured party that claims a security interest in all of a particular type of collateral owned by the debtor may comply with a request regarding a list of collateral by sending to the debtor an authenticated record including a statement to that effect within 14 days after receipt.

(d) **[Request regarding list of collateral; no interest claimed.]** A person that receives a request regarding a list of collateral, claims no interest in the collateral when it receives the request, and claimed an interest in the collateral at an earlier time shall comply with the request within 14 days after receipt by sending to the debtor an authenticated record:

(1) disclaiming any interest in the collateral; and

(2) if known to the recipient, providing the name and mailing address of any assignee of or successor to the recipient's interest in the collateral.

(e) **[Request for accounting or regarding statement of account; no interest in obligation claimed.]** A person that receives a request for an accounting or a request regarding a statement of account, claims no interest in the obligations when it receives the request, and claimed an interest in the obligations at an earlier time shall comply with the request within 14 days after receipt by sending to the debtor an authenticated record:

(1) disclaiming any interest in the obligations; and

(2) if known to the recipient, providing the name and mailing address of any assignee of or successor to the recipient's interest in the obligations.

(f) **[Charges for responses.]** A debtor is entitled without charge to one response to a request under this section during any six-month period. The secured party may require payment of a charge not exceeding $25 for each additional response.

As amended in 1999.

Official Comment

1. **Source.** Former Section 9–208.

2. **Scope and Purpose.** This section provides a procedure whereby a debtor may obtain from a secured party information about the secured obligation and the collateral in which the secured party may claim a security interest. It clarifies and resolves some of the issues that arose under former Section 9–208 and makes information concerning the secured indebtedness readily available to debtors, both before and after default. It applies to

agricultural lien transactions (see the definitions of "debtor," "secured party," and "collateral" in Section 9–102), but generally not to sales of receivables. See subsection (b).

3. **Requests by Debtors Only.** A financing statement filed under Part 5 may disclose only that a secured party may have a security interest in specified types of collateral. In most cases the financing statement will contain no indication of the obligation (if any) secured, whether any security interest actually exists, or the particular property subject to a security interest. Because creditors of and prospective purchasers from a debtor may have legitimate needs for more detailed information, it is necessary to provide a procedure under which the secured party will be required to provide information. On the other hand, the secured party should not be under a duty to disclose any details of the debtor's financial affairs to any casual inquirer or competitor who may inquire. For this reason, this section gives the right to request information to the debtor only. The debtor may submit a request in connection with negotiations with subsequent creditors and purchasers, as well as for the purpose of determining the status of its credit relationship or demonstrating which of its assets are free of a security interest.

4. **Permitted Types of Requests for Information.** Subsection (a) contemplates that a debtor may request three types of information by submitting three types of "requests" to the secured party. First, the debtor may request the secured party to prepare and send an "accounting" (defined in Section 9–102). Second, the debtor may submit to the secured party a list of collateral for the secured party's approval or correction. Third, the debtor may submit to the secured party for its approval or correction a statement of the aggregate amount of unpaid secured obligations. Inasmuch as a secured party may have numerous transactions and relationships with a debtor, each request must identify the relevant transactions or relationships. Subsections (b) and (c) require the secured party to respond to a request within 14 days following receipt of the request.

5. **Recipients Claiming No Interest in the Transaction.** A debtor may be unaware that a creditor with whom it has dealt has assigned its security interest or the secured obligation. Subsections (d) and (e) impose upon recipients of requests under this section the duty to inform the debtor that they claim no interest in the collateral or secured obligation, respectively, and to inform the debtor of the name and mailing address of any known assignee or successor. As under subsections (b) and (c), a response to a request under subsection (d) or (e) is due 14 days following receipt.

6. **Waiver; Remedy for Failure to Comply.** The debtor's rights under this section may not be waived or varied. See Section 9–602(2). Section 9–625 sets forth the remedies for noncompliance with the requirements of this section.

7. **Limitation on Free Responses to Requests.** Under subsection (f), during a six-month period a debtor is entitled to receive from the secured party one free response to a request. The debtor is not entitled to a free response to *each* type of request (i.e., three free responses) during a six-month period.

As amended in 2000.

PART 3

PERFECTION AND PRIORITY

[SUBPART 1. LAW GOVERNING PERFECTION AND PRIORITY]

§ 9–301.   Law Governing Perfection and Priority of Security Interests.

Except as otherwise provided in Sections 9–303 through 9–306, the following rules determine the law governing perfection, the effect of perfection or nonperfection, and the priority of a security interest in collateral:

(1)   Except as otherwise provided in this section, while a debtor is located in a jurisdiction, the local law of that jurisdiction governs perfection, the effect of perfection or nonperfection, and the priority of a security interest in collateral.

(2)   While collateral is located in a jurisdiction, the local law of that jurisdiction governs perfection, the effect of perfection or nonperfection, and the priority of a possessory security interest in that collateral.

(3)   Except as otherwise provided in paragraph (4), while tangible negotiable documents, goods, instruments, money, or tangible chattel paper is located in a jurisdiction, the local law of that jurisdiction governs:

    (A)   perfection of a security interest in the goods by filing a fixture filing;

    (B)   perfection of a security interest in timber to be cut; and

    (C)   the effect of perfection or nonperfection and the priority of a nonpossessory security interest in the collateral.

    (4)   The local law of the jurisdiction in which the wellhead or minehead is located governs perfection, the effect of perfection or nonperfection, and the priority of a security interest in as-extracted collateral.

As amended in 2003.

Official Comment

    1.   **Source.** Former Sections 9–103(1)(a), (b), 9–103(3)(a), (b), 9–103(5), substantially modified.

    2.   **Scope of This Subpart.** Part 3, Subpart 1 (Sections 9–301 through 9–307) contains choice-of-law rules similar to those of former Section 9–103. Former Section 9–103 generally addresses which State's law governs "perfection and the effect of perfection or non-perfection of" security interests. See, e.g., former Section 9–103(1)(b). This Article follows the broader and more precise formulation in former Section 9–103(6)(b), which was revised in connection with the promulgation of Revised Article 8 in 1994: "perfection, the effect of perfection or non-perfection, and the priority of" security interests. Priority, in this context, subsumes all of the rules in Part 3, including "cut off" or "take free" rules such as Sections 9–317(b), (c), and (d), 9–320(a), (b), and (d), and 9–332. This subpart does not address choice of law for other purposes. For example, the law applicable to issues such as attachment, validity, characterization (e.g., true lease or security interest), and enforcement is governed by the rules in Section 1–301; that governing law typically is specified in the same agreement that contains the security agreement. And, another jurisdiction's law may govern other third-party matters addressed in this Article. See Section 9–401, Comment 3.

    3.   **Scope of Referral.** In designating the jurisdiction whose law governs, this Article directs the court to apply only the substantive ("local") law of a particular jurisdiction and not its choice-of-law rules.

    Example 1: Litigation over the priority of a security interest in accounts arises in State X. State X has adopted the official text of this Article, which provides that priority is determined by the local law of the jurisdiction in which the debtor is located. See Section 9–301(1). The debtor is located in State Y. Even if State Y has retained former Article 9 or enacted a nonuniform choice-of-law rule (e.g., one that provides that perfection is governed by the law of State Z), a State X court should look only to the substantive law of State Y and disregard State Y's choice-of-law rule. State Y's substantive law (e.g., its Section 9–501) provides that financing statements should be filed in a filing office in State Y. Note, however, that if the identical perfection issue were to be litigated in State Y, the court would look to State Y's former Section 9–103 or nonuniform 9–301 and conclude that a filing in State Y is ineffective.

    Example 2: In the preceding Example, assume that State X has adopted the official text of this Article, and State Y has adopted a nonuniform Section 9–301(1) under which perfection is governed by the whole law of State X, including its choice-of-law rules. If litigation occurs in State X, the court should look to the substantive law of State Y, which provides that financing statements are to be filed in a filing office in State Y. If litigation occurs in State Y, the court should look to the law of State X, whose choice-of-law rule requires that the court apply the substantive law of State Y. Thus, regardless of the jurisdiction in which the litigation arises, the financing statement should be filed in State Y.

    4.   **Law Governing Perfection: General Rule.** Paragraph (1) contains the general rule: the law governing perfection of security interests in both tangible and intangible collateral, whether perfected by filing or automatically, is the law of the jurisdiction of the debtor's location, as determined under Section 9–307.

    Paragraph (1) substantially simplifies the choice-of-law rules. Former Section 9–103 contained different choice-of-law rules for different types of collateral. Under Section 9–301(1), the law of a single jurisdiction governs perfection with respect to most types of collateral, both tangible and intangible. Paragraph (1) eliminates the need for former Section 9–103(1)(c), which concerned purchase-money security interests in tangible collateral that is intended to move from one jurisdiction to the other. It is likely to reduce the frequency of cases in which the governing law changes after a financing statement is properly filed. (Presumably, debtors change their own location less frequently than they change the location of their collateral.) The approach taken in paragraph (1) also eliminates some difficult priority issues and the need to distinguish between "mobile" and "ordinary" goods, and it reduces the number of filing offices in which secured parties must file or search when collateral is located in several jurisdictions.

758

5. **Law Governing Perfection: Exceptions.** The general rule is subject to several exceptions. It does not apply to goods covered by a certificate of title (see Section 9–303), deposit accounts (see Section 9–304), investment property (see Section 9–305), or letter-of-credit rights (see Section 9–306). Nor does it apply to possessory security interests, i.e., security interests that the secured party has perfected by taking possession of the collateral (see paragraph (2)), security interests perfected by filing a fixture filing (see subparagraph (3)(A)), security interests in timber to be cut (subparagraph (3)(B)), or security interests in as-extracted collateral (see paragraph (4)).

a. **Possessory Security Interests.** Paragraph (2) applies to possessory security interests and provides that perfection is governed by the local law of the jurisdiction in which the collateral is located. This is the rule of former Section 9–103(1)(b), except paragraph (2) eliminates the troublesome "last event" test of former law.

The distinction between nonpossessory and possessory security interests creates the potential for the same jurisdiction to apply two different choice-of-law rules to determine perfection in the same collateral. For example, were a secured party in possession of an instrument or a tangible document to relinquish possession in reliance on temporary perfection, the applicable law immediately would change from that of the location of the collateral to that of the location of the debtor. The applicability of two different choice-of-law rules for perfection is unlikely to lead to any material practical problems. The perfection rules of one Article 9 jurisdiction are likely to be identical to those of another. Moreover, under paragraph (3), the relative priority of competing security interests in tangible collateral is resolved by reference to the law of the jurisdiction in which the collateral is located, regardless of how the security interests are perfected.

b. **Fixture Filings.** Under the general rule in paragraph (1), a security interest in fixtures may be perfected by filing in the office specified by Section 9–501(a) as enacted in the jurisdiction in which the debtor is located. However, application of this rule to perfection of a security interest by filing a fixture filing could yield strange results. For example, perfection of a security interest in fixtures located in Arizona and owned by a Delaware corporation would be governed by the law of Delaware. Although Delaware law would send one to a filing office in Arizona for the place to file a financing statement as a fixture filing, see Section 9–501, Delaware law would not take account of local, nonuniform, real-property filing and recording requirements that Arizona law might impose. For this reason, paragraph (3)(A) contains a special rule for security interests perfected by a fixture filing; the law of the jurisdiction in which the fixtures are located governs perfection, including the formal requisites of a fixture filing. Under paragraph (3)(C), the same law governs priority. Fixtures are "goods" as defined in Section 9–102.

The filing of a financing statement to perfect a security interest in collateral of a transmitting utility constitutes a fixture filing with respect to goods that are or become fixtures. See Section 9–501(b). Accordingly, to perfect a security interest in goods of this kind by a fixture filing, a financing statement must be filed in the office specified by Section 9–501(b) as enacted in the jurisdiction in which the goods are located. If the fixtures collateral is located in more than one State, filing in all of those States will be necessary to perfect a security interest in all the fixtures collateral by a fixture filing. Of course, a security interest in nearly all types of collateral (including fixtures) of a transmitting utility may be perfected by filing in the office specified by Section 9–501(b) as enacted in the jurisdiction in which the transmitting utility is located. However, such a filing will not be effective as a fixture filing except with respect to goods that are located in that jurisdiction.

c. **Timber to Be Cut.** Application of the general rule in paragraph (1) to perfection of a security interest in timber to be cut would yield undesirable results analogous to those described with respect to fixtures. Paragraph (3)(B) adopts a similar solution: perfection is governed by the law of the jurisdiction in which the timber is located. As with fixtures, under paragraph (3)(C), the same law governs priority. Timber to be cut also is "goods" as defined in Section 9–102.

Paragraph (3)(B) applies only to "timber to be cut," not to timber that has been cut. Consequently, once the timber is cut, the general choice-of-law rule in paragraph (1) becomes applicable. To ensure continued perfection, a secured party should file in both the jurisdiction in which the timber to be cut is located and in the state where the debtor is located. The former filing would be with the office in which a real property mortgage would be filed, and the latter would be a central filing. See Section 9–501.

d. **As-Extracted Collateral.** Paragraph (4) adopts the rule of former Section 9–103(5) with respect to certain security interests in minerals and related accounts. Like security interests in fixtures perfected by filing a fixture filing, security interests in minerals that are as-extracted collateral are perfected by filing in the office designated for the filing or recording of a mortgage on the real property. For the same reasons, the law governing perfection and priority is the law of the jurisdiction in which the wellhead or minehead is located.

6.   **Change in Law Governing Perfection.** When the debtor changes its location to another jurisdiction, the jurisdiction whose law governs perfection under paragraph (1) changes, as well. Similarly, the law governing perfection of a possessory security interest in collateral under paragraph (2) changes when the collateral is removed to another jurisdiction. Nevertheless, these changes will not result in an immediate loss of perfection. See Section 9–316(a), (b).

7.   **Law Governing Effect of Perfection and Priority: Goods, Documents, Instruments, Money, Negotiable Documents, and Tangible Chattel Paper.** Under former Section 9–103, the law of a single jurisdiction governed both questions of perfection and those of priority. This Article generally adopts that approach. See paragraph (1). But the approach may create problems if the debtor and collateral are located in different jurisdictions. For example, assume a security interest in equipment located in Pennsylvania is perfected by filing in Illinois, where the debtor is located. If the law of the jurisdiction in which the debtor is located were to govern priority, then the priority of an execution lien on goods located in Pennsylvania would be governed by rules enacted by the Illinois legislature.

To address this problem, paragraph (3)(C) divorces questions of perfection from questions of "the effect of perfection or nonperfection and the priority of a security interest." Under paragraph (3)(C), the rights of competing claimants to tangible collateral are resolved by reference to the law of the jurisdiction in which the collateral is located. A similar bifurcation applied to security interests in investment property under former Section 9–103(6). See Section 9–305.

Paragraph (3)(C) applies the law of the situs to determine priority only with respect to goods (including fixtures), instruments, money, tangible negotiable documents, and tangible chattel paper. Compare former Section 9–103(1), which applied the law of the location of the collateral to documents, instruments, and "ordinary" (as opposed to "mobile") goods. This Article does not distinguish among types of goods. The ordinary/mobile goods distinction appears to address concerns about where to file and search, rather than concerns about priority. There is no reason to preserve this distinction under the bifurcated approach.

Particularly serious confusion may arise when the choice-of-law rules of a given jurisdiction result in each of two competing security interests in the same collateral being governed by a different priority rule. The potential for this confusion existed under former Section 9–103(4) with respect to chattel paper: Perfection by possession was governed by the law of the location of the paper, whereas perfection by filing was governed by the law of the location of the debtor. Consider the mess that would have been created if the language or interpretation of former Section 9–308 were to differ in the two relevant States, or if one of the relevant jurisdictions (e.g., a foreign country) had not adopted Article 9. The potential for confusion could have been exacerbated when a secured party perfected both by taking possession in the State where the collateral is located (State A) and by filing in the State where the debtor is located (State B)—a common practice for some chattel paper financers. By providing that the law of the jurisdiction in which the collateral is located governs priority, paragraph (3) substantially diminishes this problem.

8.   **Non-U.S. Debtors.** This Article applies the same choice-of-law rules to all debtors, foreign and domestic. For example, it adopts the bifurcated approach for determining the law applicable to security interests in goods and other tangible collateral. See Comment 5.a., above. The Article contains a new rule specifying the location of non-U.S. debtors for purposes of this Part. The rule appears in Section 9–307 and is explained in the Comments to that section. Former Section 9–103(3)(c), which contained a special choice-of-law rule governing security interests created by debtors located in a non-U.S. jurisdiction, proved unsatisfactory and was deleted.

As amended in 2003 and 2010.

§ 9–302.   Law Governing Perfection and Priority of Agricultural Liens.

While farm products are located in a jurisdiction, the local law of that jurisdiction governs perfection, the effect of perfection or nonperfection, and the priority of an agricultural lien on the farm products.

Official Comment

1.   **Source.** New.

2.   **Agricultural Liens.** This section provides choice-of-law rules for agricultural liens on farm products. Perfection, the effect of perfection or nonperfection, and priority all are governed by the law of the jurisdiction in which the farm products are located. Other choice-of-law rules, including Section 1–301, determine which jurisdiction's law governs other matters, such as the secured party's rights on default. See Section 9–301, Comment 2. Inasmuch as no agricultural lien on proceeds arises under this Article, this section does not expressly apply to

proceeds of agricultural liens. However, if another statute creates an agricultural lien on proceeds, it may be appropriate for courts to apply the choice-of-law rule in this section to determine priority in the proceeds.

As amended in 2010.

§ 9–303. Law Governing Perfection and Priority of Security Interests in Goods Covered by a Certificate of Title.

(a) **[Applicability of section.]** This section applies to goods covered by a certificate of title, even if there is no other relationship between the jurisdiction under whose certificate of title the goods are covered and the goods or the debtor.

(b) **[When goods covered by certificate of title.]** Goods become covered by a certificate of title when a valid application for the certificate of title and the applicable fee are delivered to the appropriate authority. Goods cease to be covered by a certificate of title at the earlier of the time the certificate of title ceases to be effective under the law of the issuing jurisdiction or the time the goods become covered subsequently by a certificate of title issued by another jurisdiction.

(c) **[Applicable law.]** The local law of the jurisdiction under whose certificate of title the goods are covered governs perfection, the effect of perfection or nonperfection, and the priority of a security interest in goods covered by a certificate of title from the time the goods become covered by the certificate of title until the goods cease to be covered by the certificate of title.

Official Comment

1. **Source.** Former Section 9–103(2)(a), (b), substantially revised.

2. **Scope of This Section.** This section applies to "goods covered by a certificate of title." The new definition of "certificate of title" in Section 9–102 makes clear that this section applies not only to certificate-of-title statutes under which perfection occurs upon notation of the security interest on the certificate but also to those that contemplate notation but provide that perfection is achieved by another method, e.g., delivery of designated documents to an official. Subsection (a), which is new, makes clear that this section applies to certificates of a jurisdiction having no other contacts with the goods or the debtor. This result comports with most of the reported cases on the subject and with contemporary business practices in the trucking industry.

3. **Law Governing Perfection and Priority.** Subsection (c) is the basic choice-of-law rule for goods covered by a certificate of title. Perfection and priority of a security interest are governed by the law of the jurisdiction under whose certificate of title the goods are covered from the time the goods become covered by the certificate of title until the goods cease to be covered by the certificate of title.

Normally, under the law of the relevant jurisdiction, the perfection step would consist of compliance with that jurisdiction's certificate-of-title statute and a resulting notation of the security interest on the certificate of title. See Section 9–311(b). In the typical case of an automobile or over-the-road truck, a person who wishes to take a security interest in the vehicle can ascertain whether it is subject to any security interests by looking at the certificate of title. But certificates of title cover certain types of goods in some States but not in others. A secured party who does not realize this may extend credit and attempt to perfect by filing in the jurisdiction in which the debtor is located. If the goods had been titled in another jurisdiction, the lender would be unperfected.

Subsection (b) explains when goods become covered by a certificate of title and when they cease to be covered. Goods may become covered by a certificate of title, even though no certificate of title has issued. Former Section 9–103(2)(b) provided that the law of the jurisdiction issuing the certificate ceases to apply upon "surrender" of the certificate. This Article eliminates the concept of "surrender." However, if the certificate is surrendered in conjunction with an appropriate application for a certificate to be issued by another jurisdiction, the law of the original jurisdiction ceases to apply because the goods became covered subsequently by a certificate of title from another jurisdiction. Alternatively, the law of the original jurisdiction ceases to apply when the certificate "ceases to be effective" under the law of that jurisdiction. Given the diversity in certificate-of-title statutes, the term "effective" is not defined.

4. **Continued Perfection.** The fact that the law of one State ceases to apply under subsection (b) does not mean that a security interest perfected under that law becomes unperfected automatically. In most cases, the security interest will remain perfected. See Section 9–316(d), (e). Moreover, a perfected security interest may be subject to defeat by certain buyers and secured parties. See Section 9–337.

5.　　**Inventory.** Compliance with a certificate-of-title statute generally is *not* the method of perfecting security interests in inventory. Section 9–311(d) provides that a security interest created in inventory held by a person in the business of selling goods of that kind is subject to the normal filing rules; compliance with a certificate-of-title statute is not necessary or effective to perfect the security interest. Most certificate-of-title statutes are in accord.

The following example explains the subtle relationship between this rule and the choice-of-law rules in Section 9–303 and former Section 9–103(2):

Example: Goods are located in State A and covered by a certificate of title issued under the law of State A. The State A certificate of title is "clean"; it does not reflect a security interest. Owner takes the goods to State B and sells (trades in) the goods to Dealer, who is in the business of selling goods of that kind and is located (within the meaning of Section 9–307) in State B. As is customary, Dealer retains the duly assigned State A certificate of title pending resale of the goods. Dealer's inventory financer, SP, obtains a security interest in the goods under its after-acquired property clause.

Under Section 9–311(d) of both State A and State B, Dealer's inventory financer, SP, must perfect by filing instead of complying with a certificate-of-title statute. If Section 9–303 were read to provide that the law applicable to perfection of SP's security interest is that of State A, because the goods are covered by a State A certificate, then SP would be required to file in State A under State A's Section 9–501. That result would be anomalous, to say the least, since the principle underlying Section 9–311(d) is that the inventory should be treated as ordinary goods.

Section 9–303 (and former Section 9–103(2)) should be read as providing that the law of State B, not State A, applies. A court looking to the forum's Section 9–303(a) would find that Section 9–303 applies only if two conditions are met: (i) the goods are covered by the certificate as explained in Section 9–303(b), i.e., application had been made for a State (here, State A) to issue a certificate of title covering the goods and (ii) the certificate is a "certificate of title" as defined in Section 9–102, i.e., "a statute provides for the security interest in question to be indicated on the certificate as a condition or result of the security interest's obtaining priority over the rights of a lien creditor." Stated otherwise, Section 9–303 applies only when compliance with a certificate-of-title statute, and not filing, is the appropriate method of perfection. Under the law of State A, *for purposes of perfecting SP's security interest in the dealer's inventory*, the proper method of perfection is filing—not compliance with State A's certificate-of-title statute. For that reason, the goods are not covered by a "certificate of title," and the second condition is not met. Thus, Section 9–303 does not apply to the goods. Instead, Section 9–301 applies, and the applicable law is that of State B, where the debtor (dealer) is located.

6.　　**External Constraints on This Section.** The need to coordinate Article 9 with a variety of nonuniform certificate-of-title statutes, the need to provide rules to take account of situations in which multiple certificates of title are outstanding with respect to particular goods, and the need to govern the transition from perfection by filing in one jurisdiction to perfection by notation in another all create pressure for a detailed and complex set of rules. In an effort to minimize complexity, this Article does not attempt to coordinate Article 9 with the entire array of certificate-of-title statutes. In particular, Sections 9–303, 9–311, and 9–316(d) and (e) assume that the certificate-of-title statutes to which they apply do not have relation-back provisions (i.e., provisions under which perfection is deemed to occur at a time earlier than when the perfection steps actually are taken). A Legislative Note to Section 9–311 recommends the elimination of relation-back provisions in certificate-of-title statutes affecting perfection of security interests.

Ideally, at any given time, only one certificate of title is outstanding with respect to particular goods. In fact, however, sometimes more than one jurisdiction issues more than one certificate of title with respect to the same goods. This situation results from defects in certificate-of-title laws and the interstate coordination of those laws, not from deficiencies in this Article. As long as the possibility of multiple certificates of title remains, the potential for innocent parties to suffer losses will continue. At best, this Article can identify clearly which innocent parties will bear the losses in familiar fact patterns.

As amended in 2000.

§ 9–304. Law Governing Perfection and Priority of Security Interests in Deposit Accounts.

(a) **[Law of bank's jurisdiction governs.]** The local law of a bank's jurisdiction governs perfection, the effect of perfection or nonperfection, and the priority of a security interest in a deposit account maintained with that bank.

(b) **[Bank's jurisdiction.]** The following rules determine a bank's jurisdiction for purposes of this part:

(1) If an agreement between the bank and its customer governing the deposit account expressly provides that a particular jurisdiction is the bank's jurisdiction for purposes of this part, this article, or [the Uniform Commercial Code], that jurisdiction is the bank's jurisdiction.

(2) If paragraph (1) does not apply and an agreement between the bank and its customer governing the deposit account expressly provides that the agreement is governed by the law of a particular jurisdiction, that jurisdiction is the bank's jurisdiction.

(3) If neither paragraph (1) nor paragraph (2) applies and an agreement between the bank and its customer governing the deposit account expressly provides that the deposit account is maintained at an office in a particular jurisdiction, that jurisdiction is the bank's jurisdiction.

(4) If none of the preceding paragraphs applies, the bank's jurisdiction is the jurisdiction in which the office identified in an account statement as the office serving the customer's account is located.

(5) If none of the preceding paragraphs applies, the bank's jurisdiction is the jurisdiction in which the chief executive office of the bank is located.

Official Comment

1. **Source.** New; derived from Section 8–110(e) and former Section 9–103(6).

2. **Deposit Accounts.** Under this section, the law of the "bank's jurisdiction" governs perfection and priority of a security interest in deposit accounts. Subsection (b) contains rules for determining the "bank's jurisdiction." The substance of these rules is substantially similar to that of the rules determining the "security intermediary's jurisdiction" under former Section 8–110(e), except that subsection (b)(1) provides more flexibility than the analogous provision in former Section 8–110(e)(1). Subsection (b)(1) permits the parties to choose the law of one jurisdiction to govern perfection and priority of security interests and a different governing law for other purposes. The parties' choice is effective, even if the jurisdiction whose law is chosen bears no relationship to the parties or the transaction. Section 8–110(e)(1) has been conformed to subsection (b)(1) of this section, and Section 9–305(b)(1), concerning a commodity intermediary's jurisdiction, makes a similar departure from former Section 9–103(6)(e)(i).

3. **Change in Law Governing Perfection.** When the bank's jurisdiction changes, the jurisdiction whose law governs perfection under subsection (a) changes, as well. Nevertheless, the change will not result in an immediate loss of perfection. See Section 9–316(f), (g).

§ 9–305. Law Governing Perfection and Priority of Security Interests in Investment Property.

(a) **[Governing law: general rules.]** Except as otherwise provided in subsection (c), the following rules apply:

(1) While a security certificate is located in a jurisdiction, the local law of that jurisdiction governs perfection, the effect of perfection or nonperfection, and the priority of a security interest in the certificated security represented thereby.

(2) The local law of the issuer's jurisdiction as specified in Section 8–110(d) governs perfection, the effect of perfection or nonperfection, and the priority of a security interest in an uncertificated security.

763

(3)   The local law of the securities intermediary's jurisdiction as specified in Section 8–110(e) governs perfection, the effect of perfection or nonperfection, and the priority of a security interest in a security entitlement or securities account.

(4)   The local law of the commodity intermediary's jurisdiction governs perfection, the effect of perfection or nonperfection, and the priority of a security interest in a commodity contract or commodity account.

(b)   **[Commodity intermediary's jurisdiction.]** The following rules determine a commodity intermediary's jurisdiction for purposes of this part:

(1)   If an agreement between the commodity intermediary and commodity customer governing the commodity account expressly provides that a particular jurisdiction is the commodity intermediary's jurisdiction for purposes of this part, this article, or [the Uniform Commercial Code], that jurisdiction is the commodity intermediary's jurisdiction.

(2)   If paragraph (1) does not apply and an agreement between the commodity intermediary and commodity customer governing the commodity account expressly provides that the agreement is governed by the law of a particular jurisdiction, that jurisdiction is the commodity intermediary's jurisdiction.

(3)   If neither paragraph (1) nor paragraph (2) applies and an agreement between the commodity intermediary and commodity customer governing the commodity account expressly provides that the commodity account is maintained at an office in a particular jurisdiction, that jurisdiction is the commodity intermediary's jurisdiction.

(4)   If none of the preceding paragraphs applies, the commodity intermediary's jurisdiction is the jurisdiction in which the office identified in an account statement as the office serving the commodity customer's account is located.

(5)   If none of the preceding paragraphs applies, the commodity intermediary's jurisdiction is the jurisdiction in which the chief executive office of the commodity intermediary is located.

(c)   **[When perfection governed by law of jurisdiction where debtor located.]** The local law of the jurisdiction in which the debtor is located governs:

(1)   perfection of a security interest in investment property by filing;

(2)   automatic perfection of a security interest in investment property created by a broker or securities intermediary; and

(3)   automatic perfection of a security interest in a commodity contract or commodity account created by a commodity intermediary.

Official Comment

1.   **Source.** Former Section 9–103(6).

2.   **Investment Property: General Rules.** This section specifies choice-of-law rules for perfection and priority of security interests in investment property. Subsection (a)(1) covers security interests in certificated securities. Subsection (a)(2) covers security interests in uncertificated securities. Subsection (a)(3) covers security interests in security entitlements and securities accounts. Subsection (a)(4) covers security interests in commodity contracts and commodity accounts. The approach of each of these paragraphs is essentially the same. They identify the jurisdiction's law that governs questions of perfection and priority by using the same principles that Article 8 uses to determine other questions concerning that form of investment property. Thus, for certificated securities, the law of the jurisdiction in which the certificate is located governs. Cf. Section 8–110(c). For uncertificated securities, the law of the issuer's jurisdiction governs. Cf. Section 8–110(a). For security entitlements and securities accounts, the law of the securities intermediary's jurisdiction governs. Cf. Section 8–110(b). For commodity contracts and commodity accounts, the law of the commodity intermediary's jurisdiction governs. Because commodity contracts and commodity accounts are not governed by Article 8, subsection (b) contains rules that specify the commodity intermediary's jurisdiction. These are analogous to the rules in Section 8–110(e) specifying a securities intermediary's jurisdiction. Subsection (b)(1) affords the parties greater flexibility than did

former Section 9–103(6)(3). See also Section 9–304(b) (bank's jurisdiction); Revised Section 8–110(e)(1) (securities intermediary's jurisdiction).

3. **Investment Property: Exceptions.** Subsection (c) establishes an exception to the general rules set out in subsection (a). It provides that perfection of a security interest by filing, automatic perfection of a security interest in investment property created by a debtor who is a broker or securities intermediary (see Section 9–309(10)), and automatic perfection of a security interest in a commodity contract or commodity account of a debtor who is a commodity intermediary (see Section 9–309(11)) are governed by the law of the jurisdiction in which the debtor is located, as determined under Section 9–307.

4. **Examples:** The following examples illustrate the rules in this section:

Example 1: A customer residing in New Jersey maintains a securities account with Able & Co. The agreement between the customer and Able specifies that it is governed by Pennsylvania law but expressly provides that the law of California is Able's jurisdiction for purposes of the Uniform Commercial Code. Through the account the customer holds securities of a Massachusetts corporation, which Able holds through a clearing corporation located in New York. The customer obtains a margin loan from Able. Subsection (a)(3) provides that California law—the law of the securities intermediary's jurisdiction—governs perfection and priority of the security interest, even if California has no other relationship to the parties or the transaction.

Example 2: A customer residing in New Jersey maintains a securities account with Able & Co. The agreement between the customer and Able specifies that it is governed by Pennsylvania law. Through the account the customer holds securities of a Massachusetts corporation, which Able holds through a clearing corporation located in New York. The customer obtains a loan from a lender located in Illinois. The lender takes a security interest and perfects by obtaining an agreement among the debtor, itself, and Able, which satisfies the requirement of Section 8–106(d)(2) to give the lender control. Subsection (a)(3) provides that Pennsylvania law—the law of the securities intermediary's jurisdiction—governs perfection and priority of the security interest, even if Pennsylvania has no other relationship to the parties or the transaction.

Example 3: A customer residing in New Jersey maintains a securities account with Able & Co. The agreement between the customer and Able specifies that it is governed by Pennsylvania law. Through the account, the customer holds securities of a Massachusetts corporation, which Able holds through a clearing corporation located in New York. The customer borrows from SP–1, and SP–1 files a financing statement in New Jersey. Later, the customer obtains a loan from SP–2. SP–2 takes a security interest and perfects by obtaining an agreement among the debtor, itself, and Able, which satisfies the requirement of Section 8–106(d)(2) to give the SP–2 control. Subsection (c) provides that perfection of SP–1's security interest by filing is governed by the location of the debtor, so the filing in New Jersey was appropriate. Subsection (a)(3), however, provides that Pennsylvania law—the law of the securities intermediary's jurisdiction—governs all other questions of perfection and priority. Thus, Pennsylvania law governs perfection of SP–2's security interest, and Pennsylvania law also governs the priority of the security interests of SP–1 and SP–2.

5. **Change in Law Governing Perfection.** When the issuer's jurisdiction, the securities intermediary's jurisdiction, or commodity intermediary's jurisdiction changes, the jurisdiction whose law governs perfection under subsection (a) changes, as well. Similarly, the law governing perfection of a possessory security interest in a certificated security changes when the collateral is removed to another jurisdiction, see subsection (a)(1), and the law governing perfection by filing changes when the debtor changes its location. See subsection (c). Nevertheless, these changes will not result in an immediate loss of perfection. See Section 9–316(f), (g).

As amended in 2010.

§ 9–306. Law Governing Perfection and Priority of Security Interests in Letter-of-Credit Rights.

(a) **[Governing law: issuer's or nominated person's jurisdiction.]** Subject to subsection (c), the local law of the issuer's jurisdiction or a nominated person's jurisdiction governs perfection, the effect of perfection or nonperfection, and the priority of a security interest in a letter-of-credit right if the issuer's jurisdiction or nominated person's jurisdiction is a State.

(b) **[Issuer's or nominated person's jurisdiction.]** For purposes of this part, an issuer's jurisdiction or nominated person's jurisdiction is the jurisdiction whose law governs the liability of the issuer or nominated person with respect to the letter-of-credit right as provided in Section 5–116.

(c)   **[When section not applicable.]** This section does not apply to a security interest that is perfected only under Section 9–308(d).

Official Comment

1.   **Source.** New; derived in part from Section 8–110(e) and former Section 9–103(6).

2.   *Sui Generis* **Treatment.** This section governs the applicable law for perfection and priority of security interests in letter-of-credit rights, other than a security interest perfected only under Section 9–308(d) (i.e., as a supporting obligation). The treatment differs substantially from that provided in Section 9–304 for deposit accounts. The basic rule is that the law of the issuer's or nominated person's (e.g., confirmer's) jurisdiction, derived from the terms of the letter of credit itself, controls perfection and priority, but only if the issuer's or nominated person's jurisdiction is a State, as defined in Section 9–102. If the issuer's or nominated person's jurisdiction is not a State, the baseline rule of Section 9–301 applies—perfection and priority are governed by the law of the debtor's location, determined under Section 9–307. Export transactions typically involve a foreign issuer and a domestic nominated person, such as a confirmer, located in a State. The principal goal of this section is to reduce the likelihood that perfection and priority would be governed by the law of a foreign jurisdiction in a transaction that is essentially domestic from the standpoint of the debtor-beneficiary, its creditors, and a domestic nominated person.

3.   **Issuer's or Nominated Person's Jurisdiction.** Subsection (b) defers to the rules established under Section 5–116 for determination of an issuer's or nominated person's jurisdiction.

Example: An Italian bank issues a letter of credit that is confirmed by a New York bank. The beneficiary is a Connecticut corporation. The letter of credit provides that the issuer's liability is governed by Italian law, and the confirmation provides that the confirmer's liability is governed by the law of New York. Under Sections 9–306(b) and 5–116(a), Italy is the issuer's jurisdiction and New York is the confirmer's (nominated person's) jurisdiction. Because the confirmer's jurisdiction is a State, the law of New York governs perfection and priority of a security interest in the beneficiary's letter-of-credit right against the confirmer. See Section 9–306(a). However, because the issuer's jurisdiction is not a State, the law of that jurisdiction does not govern. See Section 9–306(a). Rather, the choice-of-law rule in Section 9–301(1) applies to perfection and priority of a security interest in the beneficiary's letter-of-credit right against the issuer. Under that section, perfection and priority are governed by the law of the jurisdiction in which the debtor (beneficiary) is located. That jurisdiction is Connecticut. See Section 9–307.

4.   **Scope of this Section.** This section specifies only the law governing perfection, the effect of perfection or nonperfection, and priority of security interests. Section 5–116 specifies the law governing the liability of, and Article 5 (or other applicable law) deals with the rights and duties of, an issuer or nominated person. Perfection, nonperfection, and priority have no effect on those rights and duties.

5.   **Change in Law Governing Perfection.** When the issuer's jurisdiction, or nominated person's jurisdiction changes, the jurisdiction whose law governs perfection under subsection (a) changes, as well. Nevertheless, this change will not result in an immediate loss of perfection. See Section 9–316(f), (g).

§ 9–307.   Location of Debtor.

(a)   **["Place of business."]** In this section, "place of business" means a place where a debtor conducts its affairs.

(b)   **[Debtor's location: general rules.]** Except as otherwise provided in this section, the following rules determine a debtor's location:

(1)   A debtor who is an individual is located at the individual's principal residence.

(2)   A debtor that is an organization and has only one place of business is located at its place of business.

(3)   A debtor that is an organization and has more than one place of business is located at its chief executive office.

(c)   **[Limitation of applicability of subsection (b).]** Subsection (b) applies only if a debtor's residence, place of business, or chief executive office, as applicable, is located in a jurisdiction whose law gene.ally requires information concerning the existence of a nonpossessory security interest to be made generally available in a filing, recording, or registration system as a condition or result of the security interest's obtaining priority over the rights of a lien creditor with respect to the collateral. If subsection (b) does not apply, the debtor is located in the District of Columbia.

(d) **[Continuation of location: cessation of existence, etc.]** A person that ceases to exist, have a residence, or have a place of business continues to be located in the jurisdiction specified by subsections (b) and (c).

(e) **[Location of registered organization organized under State law.]** A registered organization that is organized under the law of a State is located in that State.

(f) **[Location of registered organization organized under federal law; bank branches and agencies.]** Except as otherwise provided in subsection (i), a registered organization that is organized under the law of the United States and a branch or agency of a bank that is not organized under the law of the United States or a State are located:

(1) in the State that the law of the United States designates, if the law designates a State of location;

(2) in the State that the registered organization, branch, or agency designates, if the law of the United States authorizes the registered organization, branch, or agency to designate its State of location, including by designating its main office, home office, or other comparable office; or

(3) in the District of Columbia, if neither paragraph (1) nor paragraph (2) applies.

(g) **[Continuation of location: change in status of registered organization.]** A registered organization continues to be located in the jurisdiction specified by subsection (e) or (f) notwithstanding:

(1) the suspension, revocation, forfeiture, or lapse of the registered organization's status as such in its jurisdiction of organization; or

(2) the dissolution, winding up, or cancellation of the existence of the registered organization.

(h) **[Location of United States.]** The United States is located in the District of Columbia.

(i) **[Location of foreign bank branch or agency if licensed in only one state.]** A branch or agency of a bank that is not organized under the law of the United States or a State is located in the State in which the branch or agency is licensed, if all branches and agencies of the bank are licensed in only one State.

(j) **[Location of foreign air carrier.]** A foreign air carrier under the Federal Aviation Act of 1958, as amended, is located at the designated office of the agent upon which service of process may be made on behalf of the carrier.

(k) **[Section applies only to this part.]** This section applies only for purposes of this part.

As amended in 2010.

Official Comment

1. **Source.** Former Section 9–103(3)(d), substantially revised.

2. **General Rules.** As a general matter, the location of the debtor determines the jurisdiction whose law governs perfection of a security interest. See Sections 9–301(1), 9–305(c). It also governs priority of a security interest in certain types of intangible collateral, such as accounts, electronic chattel paper, and general intangibles. This section determines the location of the debtor for choice-of-law purposes, but not for other purposes. See subsection (k).

Subsection (b) states the general rules: An individual debtor is deemed to be located at the individual's principal residence with respect to both personal and business assets. Any other debtor is deemed to be located at its place of business if it has only one, or at its chief executive office if it has more than one place of business.

As used in this section, a "place of business" means a place where the debtor conducts its affairs. See subsection (a). Thus, every organization, even eleemosynary institutions and other organizations that do not conduct "for profit" business activities, has a "place of business." Under subsection (d), a person who ceases to exist, have a residence, or have a place of business continues to be located in the jurisdiction determined by subsection (b).

The term "chief executive office" is not defined in this Section or elsewhere in the Uniform Commercial Code. "Chief executive office" means the place from which the debtor manages the main part of its business operations or other affairs. This is the place where persons dealing with the debtor would normally look for credit information, and is the appropriate place for filing. With respect to most multi-state debtors, it will be simple to determine which of the debtor's offices is the "chief executive office." Even when a doubt arises, it would be rare that there could be more than two possibilities. A secured party in such a case may protect itself by perfecting under the law of each possible jurisdiction.

Similarly, the term "principal residence" is not defined. If the security interest in question is a purchase-money security interest in consumer goods which is perfected upon attachment, see Section 9–309(1), the choice of law may make no difference. In other cases, when a doubt arises, prudence may dictate perfecting under the law of each jurisdiction that might be the debtor's "principal residence."

Questions sometimes arise about the location of the debtor with respect to collateral held in a common-law trust. A typical common-law trust is not itself a juridical entity capable of owning property and so would not be a "debtor" as defined in Section 9–102. Rather, the debtor with respect to property held in a common-law trust typically is the trustee of the trust acting in the capacity of trustee. (The beneficiary would be a "debtor" with respect to its beneficial interest in the trust, but not with respect to the property held in the trust.) If a common-law trust has multiple trustees located in different jurisdictions, a secured party who perfects by filing would be well advised to file a financing statement in each jurisdiction in which a trustee is located, as determined under Section 9–307. Filing in all relevant jurisdictions would insure perfection and minimize any priority complications that otherwise might arise.

The general rules are subject to several exceptions, each of which is discussed below.

3.   **Non-U.S. Debtors.** Under the general rules of this section, a non-U.S. debtor normally would be located in a foreign jurisdiction and, as a consequence, foreign law would govern perfection. When foreign law affords no public notice of security interests, the general rule yields unacceptable results.

Accordingly, subsection (c) provides that the normal rules for determining the location of a debtor (i.e., the rules in subsection (b)) apply only if they yield a location that is "a jurisdiction whose law generally requires information concerning the existence of a nonpossessory security interest to be made generally available in a filing, recording, or registration system as a condition or result of the security interest's obtaining priority over the rights of a lien creditor with respect to the collateral." The phrase "generally requires" is meant to include legal regimes that generally require notice in a filing or recording system as a condition of perfecting nonpossessory security interests, but which permit perfection by another method (e.g., control, automatic perfection, temporary perfection) in limited circumstances. A jurisdiction that has adopted this Article or an earlier version of this Article is such a jurisdiction. If the rules in subsection (b) yield a jurisdiction whose law does not generally require notice in a filing or registration system and none of the special rules in subsection (e), (f), (i) and (j) applies, the debtor is located in the District of Columbia.

Example 1: Debtor is an English corporation with 7 offices in the United States and its chief executive office in London, England. Debtor creates a security interest in its accounts. Under subsection (b)(3), Debtor would be located in England. However, subsection (c) provides that subsection (b) applies only if English law generally conditions perfection on giving public notice in a filing, recording, or registration system. Otherwise, Debtor is located in the District of Columbia. Under Section 9–301(1), perfection, the effect of perfection, and priority are governed by the law of the jurisdiction of the debtor's location—here, England or the District of Columbia (depending on the content of English law).

Example 2: Debtor is an English corporation with 7 offices in the United States and its chief executive office in London, England. Debtor creates a security interest in equipment located in London. Under subsection (b)(3) Debtor would be located in England. However, subsection (c) provides that subsection (b) applies only if English law generally conditions perfection on giving public notice in a filing, recording, or registration system. Otherwise, Debtor is located in the District of Columbia. Under Section 9–301(1), perfection is governed by the law of the jurisdiction of the debtor's location, whereas, under Section 9–301(3), the law of the jurisdiction in which the collateral is located—here, England—governs priority.

The foregoing discussion assumes that each transaction bears an appropriate relation to the forum State. In the absence of an appropriate relation, the forum State's entire UCC, including the choice-of-law provisions in Article 9 (Sections 9–301 through 9–307), will not apply. See Section 9–109, Comment 9.

4. **Registered Organizations Organized Under Law of a State.** Under subsection (e), a "registered organization" (defined in Section 9–102 so as to ordinarily include corporations, limited partnerships, limited liability companies, and statutory trusts) organized under the law of a "State" (defined in Section 9–102) is located in its State of organization. The term "registered organization" includes a business trust described in the second sentence of the term's definition. See Section 9–102. The trust's public organic record, typically the trust agreement, usually will indicate the jurisdiction under whose law the trust is organized.

Determining the registered organization-debtor's location by reference to the jurisdiction of organization could provide some important side benefits for the filing systems. A jurisdiction could structure its filing system so that it would be impossible to make a mistake in a registered organization-debtor's name on a financing statement. For example, a filer would be informed if a filed record designated an incorrect corporate name for the debtor. Linking filing to the jurisdiction of organization also could reduce pressure on the system imposed by transactions in which registered organizations cease to exist—as a consequence of merger or consolidation, for example. The jurisdiction of organization might prohibit such transactions unless steps were taken to ensure that existing filings were refiled against a successor or terminated by the secured party.

5. **Registered Organizations Organized Under Law of United States; Branches and Agencies of Banks Not Organized Under Law of United States.** Subsection (f) specifies the location of a debtor that is a registered organization organized under the law of the United States. It defers to the law of the United States, to the extent that that law determines, or authorizes the debtor to determine, the debtor's location. Thus, if the law of the United States designates a particular State as the debtor's location, that State is the debtor's location for purposes of this Article's choice-of-law rules. Similarly, if the law of the United States authorizes the registered organization to designate its State of location, the State that the registered organization designates is the State in which it is located for purposes of this Article's choice-of-law rules. In other cases, the debtor is located in the District of Columbia.

In some cases, the law of the United States authorizes the registered organization to designate a main office, home office, or other comparable office. See, e.g., 12 U.S.C. §§ 22 and 1464(a); 12 C.F.R. § 552.3. Designation of such an office constitutes the designation of the State of location for purposes of Section 9–307(f)(2).

Subsection (f) also specifies the location of a branch or agency in the United States of a foreign bank that has one or more branches or agencies in the United States. The law of the United States authorizes a foreign bank (or, on behalf of the bank, a federal agency) to designate a single home state for all of the foreign bank's branches and agencies in the United States. See 12 U.S.C. Section 3103(c) and 12 C.F.R. Section 211.22. As authorized, the designation constitutes the State of location for the branch or agency for purposes of Section 9–307(f), unless all of a foreign bank's branches or agencies that are in the United States are licensed in only one State, in which case the branches and agencies are located in that State. See subsection (i).

In cases not governed by subsection (f) or (i), the location of a foreign bank is determined by subsections (b) and (c).

6. **United States.** To the extent that Article 9 governs (see Sections 1–301, 9–109(c)), the United States is located in the District of Columbia for purposes of this Article's choice-of-law rules. See subsection (h).

7. **Foreign Air Carriers.** Subsection (j) follows former Section 9–103(3)(d). To the extent that it is applicable, the Convention on the International Recognition of Rights in Aircraft (Geneva Convention) supersedes state legislation on this subject, as set forth in Section 9–311(b), but some nations are not parties to that Convention.

As amended in 2010.

[SUBPART 2. PERFECTION]

§ 9–308. When Security Interest or Agricultural Lien Is Perfected; Continuity of Perfection.

(a) **[Perfection of security interest.]** Except as otherwise provided in this section and Section 9–309, a security interest is perfected if it has attached and all of the applicable requirements for perfection in Sections 9–310 through 9–316 have been satisfied. A security interest is perfected when it attaches if the applicable requirements are satisfied before the security interest attaches.

(b) **[Perfection of agricultural lien.]** An agricultural lien is perfected if it has become effective and all of the applicable requirements for perfection in Section 9–310 have been satisfied. An agricultural lien is perfected when it becomes effective if the applicable requirements are satisfied before the agricultural lien becomes effective.

(c) **[Continuous perfection; perfection by different methods.]** A security interest or agricultural lien is perfected continuously if it is originally perfected by one method under this article and is later perfected by another method under this article, without an intermediate period when it was unperfected.

(d) **[Supporting obligation.]** Perfection of a security interest in collateral also perfects a security interest in a supporting obligation for the collateral.

(e) **[Lien securing right to payment.]** Perfection of a security interest in a right to payment or performance also perfects a security interest in a security interest, mortgage, or other lien on personal or real property securing the right.

(f) **[Security entitlement carried in securities account.]** Perfection of a security interest in a securities account also perfects a security interest in the security entitlements carried in the securities account.

(g) **[Commodity contract carried in commodity account.]** Perfection of a security interest in a commodity account also perfects a security interest in the commodity contracts carried in the commodity account.

Legislative Note: Any statute conflicting with subsection (e) must be made expressly subject to that subsection.

Official Comment

1. **Source.** Former Sections 9–303, 9–115(2).

2. **General Rule.** This Article uses the term "attach" to describe the point at which property becomes subject to a security interest. The requisites for attachment are stated in Section 9–203. When it attaches, a security interest may be either perfected or unperfected. "Perfected" means that the security interest has attached and the secured party has taken all the steps required by this Article as specified in Sections 9–310 through 9–316. A perfected security interest may still be or become subordinate to other interests. See, e.g., Sections 9–320, 9–322. However, in general, after perfection the secured party is protected against creditors and transferees of the debtor and, in particular, against any representative of creditors in insolvency proceedings instituted by or against the debtor. See, e.g., Section 9–317.

Subsection (a) explains that the time of perfection is when the security interest has attached and any necessary steps for perfection, such as taking possession or filing, have been taken. The "except" clause refers to the perfection-upon-attachment rules appearing in Section 9–309. It also reflects that other subsections of this section, e.g., subsection (d), contain automatic-perfection rules. If the steps for perfection have been taken in advance, as when the secured party files a financing statement before giving value or before the debtor acquires rights in the collateral, then the security interest is perfected when it attaches.

3. **Agricultural Liens.** Subsection (b) is new. It describes the elements of perfection of an agricultural lien.

4. **Continuous Perfection.** The following example illustrates the operation of subsection (c):

Example 1: Debtor, an importer, creates a security interest in goods that it imports and the documents of title that cover the goods. The secured party, Bank, takes possession of a tangible negotiable bill of lading covering certain imported goods and thereby perfects its security interest in the bill of lading and the goods. See Sections 9–313(a), 9–312(c)(1). Bank releases the bill of lading to the debtor for the purpose of procuring the goods from the carrier and selling them. Under Section 9–312(f), Bank continues to have a perfected security interest in the document and goods for 20 days. Bank files a financing statement covering the collateral before the expiration of the 20-day period. Its security interest now continues perfected for as long as the filing is good.

If the successive stages of Bank's security interest succeed each other without an intervening gap, the security interest is "perfected continuously," and the date of perfection is when the security interest first became perfected (i.e., when Bank received possession of the tangible bill of lading). If, however, there is a gap between stages—for example, if Bank does not file until after the expiration of the 20-day period specified in Section 9–312(f) and leaves the collateral in the debtor's possession—then, the chain being broken, the perfection is no longer continuous. The date of perfection would now be the date of filing (after expiration of the 20-day period). Bank's security interest would be vulnerable to any interests arising during the gap period which under Section 9–317 take priority over an unperfected security interest.

5. **Supporting Obligations.** Subsection (d) is new. It provides for automatic perfection of a security interest in a supporting obligation for collateral if the security interest in the collateral is perfected. This is unlikely to effect any change in the law prior to adoption of this Article.

Example 2: Buyer is obligated to pay Debtor for goods sold. Buyer's president guarantees the obligation. Debtor creates a security interest in the right to payment (account) in favor of Lender. Under Section 9–203(f), the security interest attaches to Debtor's rights under the guarantee (supporting obligation). Under subsection (d), perfection of the security interest in the account constitutes perfection of the security interest in Debtor's rights under the guarantee.

6. **Rights to Payment Secured by Lien.** Subsection (e) is new. It deals with the situation in which a security interest is created in a right to payment that is secured by a security interest, mortgage, or other lien.

Example 3: Owner gives to Mortgagee a mortgage on Blackacre to secure a loan. Owner's obligation to pay is evidenced by a promissory note. In need of working capital, Mortgagee borrows from Financer and creates a security interest in the note in favor of Financer. Section 9–203(g) adopts the traditional view that the mortgage follows the note; i.e., the transferee of the note acquires the mortgage, as well. This subsection adopts a similar principle: perfection of a security interest in the right to payment constitutes perfection of a security interest in the mortgage securing it.

An important consequence of the rules in Section 9–203(g) and subsection (e) is that, by acquiring a perfected security interest in a mortgage (or other secured) note, the secured party acquires a security interest in the mortgage (or other lien) that is senior to the rights of a person who becomes a lien creditor of the mortgagee (Article 9 debtor). See Section 9–317(a)(2). This result helps prevent the separation of the mortgage (or other lien) from the note.

Under this Article, attachment and perfection of a security interest in a secured right to payment do not of themselves affect the obligation to pay. For example, if the obligation is evidenced by a negotiable note, then Article 3 dictates the person whom the maker must pay to discharge the note and any lien securing it. See Section 3–602. If the right to payment is a payment intangible, then Section 9–406 determines whom the account debtor must pay.

Similarly, this Article does not determine who has the power to release a mortgage of record. That issue is determined by real-property law.

7. **Investment Property.** Subsections (f) and (g) follow former Section 9–115(2).

As amended in 2003.

§ 9–309. Security Interest Perfected Upon Attachment.

The following security interests are perfected when they attach:

(1) a purchase-money security interest in consumer goods, except as otherwise provided in Section 9–311(b) with respect to consumer goods that are subject to a statute or treaty described in Section 9–311(a);

(2) an assignment of accounts or payment intangibles which does not by itself or in conjunction with other assignments to the same assignee transfer a significant part of the assignor's outstanding accounts or payment intangibles;

(3) a sale of a payment intangible;

(4) a sale of a promissory note;

(5) a security interest created by the assignment of a health-care-insurance receivable to the provider of the health-care goods or services;

(6) a security interest arising under Section 2–401, 2–505, 2–711(3), or 2A–508(5), until the debtor obtains possession of the collateral;

(7) a security interest of a collecting bank arising under Section 4–210;

(8) a security interest of an issuer or nominated person arising under Section 5–118;

(9) a security interest arising in the delivery of a financial asset under Section 9–206(c);

(10) a security interest in investment property created by a broker or securities intermediary;

(11) a security interest in a commodity contract or a commodity account created by a commodity intermediary;

(12) an assignment for the benefit of all creditors of the transferor and subsequent transfers by the assignee thereunder;

(13) a security interest created by an assignment of a beneficial interest in a decedent's estate; and

(14) a sale by an individual of an account that is a right to payment of winnings in a lottery or other game of chance.

Official Comment

1. **Source.** Derived from former Sections 9–302(1), 9–115(4)(c), (d), 9–116.

2. **Automatic Perfection.** This section contains the perfection-upon-attachment rules previously located in former Sections 9–302(1), 9–115(4)(c), (d), and 9–116. Rather than continue to state the rule by indirection, this section explicitly provides for perfection upon attachment.

3. **Purchase-Money Security Interest in Consumer Goods.** Former Section 9–302(1)(d) has been revised and appears here as paragraph (1). No filing or other step is required to perfect a purchase-money security interest in consumer goods, other than goods, such as automobiles, that are subject to a statute or treaty described in Section 9–311(a). However, filing is required to perfect a non-purchase-money security interest in consumer goods and is necessary to prevent a buyer of consumer goods from taking free of a security interest under Section 9–320(b). A fixture filing is required for priority over conflicting interests in fixtures to the extent provided in Section 9–334.

4. **Rights to Payment.** Paragraph (2) expands upon former Section 9–302(1)(e) by affording automatic perfection to certain assignments of payment intangibles as well as accounts. The purpose of paragraph (2) is to save from *ex post facto* invalidation casual or isolated assignments—assignments which no one would think of filing. Any person who regularly takes assignments of any debtor's accounts or payment intangibles should file. In this connection Section 9–109(d)(4) through (7), which excludes certain transfers of accounts, chattel paper, payment intangibles, and promissory notes from this Article, should be consulted.

Paragraphs (3) and (4), which are new, afford automatic perfection to sales of payment intangibles and promissory notes, respectively. They reflect the practice under former Article 9. Under that Article, filing a financing statement did not affect the rights of a buyer of payment intangibles or promissory notes, inasmuch as the former Article did not cover those sales. To the extent that the exception in paragraph (2) covers outright sales of payment intangibles, which automatically are perfected under paragraph (3), the exception is redundant.

Paragraph (14), which is new, affords automatic perfection to sales by individuals of an "account" (as defined in Section 9–102) consisting of the right to winnings in a lottery or other game of chance. Payments on these accounts typically extend for periods of twenty years or more. It would be unduly burdensome for the secured party, who would have no other reason to maintain contact with the seller, to monitor the the seller's whereabouts for such a length of time. This paragraph was added in 2001. It applies to a sale of an account described in it, even if the sale was entered into before the effective date of the paragraph. However, if the relative priorities of conflicting claims to the account were established before the paragraph took effect, Article 9 as in effect immediately prior to the date the paragraph took effect determines priority.

5. **Health-Care-Insurance Receivables.** Paragraph (5) extends automatic perfection to assignments of health-care-insurance receivables if the assignment is made to the health-care provider that provided the health-care goods or services. The primary effect is that, when an individual assigns a right to payment under an insurance policy to the person who provided health-care goods or services, the provider has no need to file a financing statement against the individual. The normal filing requirements apply to other assignments of health-care-insurance receivables covered by this Article, e.g., assignments from the health-care provider to a financer.

6. **Investment Property.** Paragraph (9) replaces the last clause of former Section 9–116(2), concerning security interests that arise in the delivery of a financial asset.

772

Paragraphs (10) and (11) replace former Section 9–115(4)(c) and (d), concerning secured financing of securities and commodity firms and clearing corporations. The former sections indicated that, with respect to certain security interests created by a securities intermediary or commodity intermediary, "[t]he filing of a financing statement . . . has no effect for purposes of perfection or priority with respect to that security interest." No change in meaning is intended by the deletion of the quoted phrase.

Secured financing arrangements for securities firms are currently implemented in various ways. In some circumstances, lenders may require that the transactions be structured as "hard pledges," where the securities are transferred on the books of a clearing corporation from the debtor's account to the lender's account or to a special pledge account for the lender where they cannot be disposed of without the specific consent of the lender. In other circumstances, lenders are content with so-called "agreement to pledge" or "agreement to deliver" arrangements, where the debtor retains the positions in its own account, but reflects on its books that the positions have been hypothecated and promises that the securities will be transferred to the secured party's account on demand.

The perfection and priority rules of this Article are designed to facilitate current secured financing arrangements for securities firms as well as to provide sufficient flexibility to accommodate new arrangements that develop in the future. Hard pledge arrangements are covered by the concept of control. See Sections 9–314, 9–106, 8–106. Non-control secured financing arrangements for securities firms are covered by the automatic perfection rule of paragraph (10). Before the 1994 revision of Articles 8 and 9, agreement to pledge arrangements could be implemented under a provision that a security interest in securities given for new value under a written security agreement was perfected without filing or possession for a period of 21 days. Although the security interests were temporary in legal theory, the financing arrangements could, in practice, be continued indefinitely by rolling over the loans at least every 21 days. Accordingly, a knowledgeable creditor of a securities firm realizes that the firm's securities may be subject to security interests that are not discoverable from any public records. The automatic-perfection rule of paragraph (10) makes it unnecessary to engage in the purely formal practice of rolling over these arrangements every 21 days.

In some circumstances, a clearing corporation may be the debtor in a secured financing arrangement. For example, a clearing corporation that settles delivery-versus-payment transactions among its participants on a net, same-day basis relies on timely payments from all participants with net obligations due to the system. If a participant that is a net debtor were to default on its payment obligation, the clearing corporation would not receive some of the funds needed to settle with participants that are net creditors to the system. To complete end-of-day settlement after a payment default by a participant, a clearing corporation that settles on a net, same-day basis may need to draw on credit lines and pledge securities of the defaulting participant or other securities pledged by participants in the clearing corporation to secure such drawings. The clearing corporation may be the top-tier securities intermediary for the securities pledged, so that it would not be practical for the lender to obtain control. Even where the clearing corporation holds some types of securities through other intermediaries, however, the clearing corporation is unlikely to be able to complete the arrangements necessary to convey "control" over the securities to be pledged in time to complete settlement in a timely manner. However, the term "securities intermediary" is defined in Section 8–102(a)(14) to include clearing corporations. Thus, the perfection rule of paragraph (10) applies to security interests in investment property granted by clearing corporations.

7.   **Beneficial Interests in Trusts.** Under former Section 9–302(1)(c), filing was not required to perfect a security interest created by an assignment of a beneficial interest in a trust. Because beneficial interests in trusts are now used as collateral with greater frequency in commercial transactions, under this Article filing is required to perfect a security interest in a beneficial interest.

8.   **Assignments for Benefit of Creditors.** No filing or other action is required to perfect an assignment for the benefit of creditors. These assignments are not financing transactions, and the debtor ordinarily will not be engaging in further credit transactions.

§ 9–310.   When Filing Required to Perfect Security Interest or Agricultural Lien; Security Interests and Agricultural Liens to Which Filing Provisions Do Not Apply.

(a)   **[General rule: perfection by filing.]** Except as otherwise provided in subsection (b) and Section 9–312(b), a financing statement must be filed to perfect all security interests and agricultural liens.

(b)   **[Exceptions: filing not necessary.]** The filing of a financing statement is not necessary to perfect a security interest:

(1)   that is perfected under Section 9–308(d), (e), (f), or (g);

(2)   that is perfected under Section 9–309 when it attaches;

(3)   in property subject to a statute, regulation, or treaty described in Section 9–311(a);

(4)   in goods in possession of a bailee which is perfected under Section 9–312(d)(1) or (2);

(5)   in certificated securities, documents, goods, or instruments which is perfected without filing, control, or possession under Section 9–312(e), (f), or (g);

(6)   in collateral in the secured party's possession under Section 9–313;

(7)   in a certificated security which is perfected by delivery of the security certificate to the secured party under Section 9–313;

(8)   in deposit accounts, electronic chattel paper, electronic documents, investment property, or letter-of-credit rights which is perfected by control under Section 9–314;

(9)   in proceeds which is perfected under Section 9–315; or

(10) that is perfected under Section 9–316.

(c)   **[Assignment of perfected security interest.]** If a secured party assigns a perfected security interest or agricultural lien, a filing under this article is not required to continue the perfected status of the security interest against creditors of and transferees from the original debtor.

As amended in 2003.

Official Comment

1.   **Source.** Former Section 9–302(1), (2).

2.   **General Rule.** Subsection (a) establishes a central Article 9 principle: Filing a financing statement is necessary for perfection of security interests and agricultural liens. However, filing is not necessary to perfect a security interest that is perfected by another permissible method, see subsection (b), nor does filing ordinarily perfect a security interest in a deposit account, letter-of-credit right, or money. See Section 9–312(b). Part 5 of the Article deals with the office in which to file, mechanics of filing, and operations of the filing office.

3.   **Exemptions from Filing.** Subsection (b) lists the security interests for which filing is not required as a condition of perfection, because they are perfected automatically upon attachment (subsections (b)(2) and (b)(9)) or upon the occurrence of another event (subsections (b)(1), (b)(5), and (b)(9)), because they are perfected under the law of another jurisdiction (subsection (b)(10)), or because they are perfected by another method, such as by the secured party's taking possession or control (subsections (b)(3), (b)(4), (b)(5), (b)(6), (b)(7), and (b)(8)).

4.   **Assignments of Perfected Security Interests.** Subsection (c) concerns assignment of a perfected security interest or agricultural lien. It provides that no filing is necessary in connection with an assignment by a secured party to an assignee in order to maintain perfection as against creditors of and transferees from the original debtor.

Example 1: Buyer buys goods from Seller, who retains a security interest in them. After Seller perfects the security interest by filing, Seller assigns the perfected security interest to X. The security interest, in X's hands and without further steps on X's part, continues perfected against *Buyer's* transferees and creditors.

Example 2: Dealer creates a security interest in specific equipment in favor of Lender. After Lender perfects the security interest in the equipment by filing, Lender assigns the chattel paper (which includes the perfected security interest in Dealer's equipment) to X. The security interest in the equipment, in X's hands and without further steps on X's part, continues perfected against *Dealer's* transferees and creditors. However, regardless of whether Lender made the assignment to secure Lender's obligation to X or whether the assignment was an outright sale of the chattel paper, the assignment creates a security interest in the chattel paper in favor of X. Accordingly, X must take whatever steps may be required for perfection in order to be protected against *Lender's* transferees and creditors with respect to the chattel paper.

Subsection (c) applies not only to an assignment of a security interest perfected by filing but also to an assignment of a security interest perfected by a method other than by filing, such as by control or by possession. Although subsection (c) addresses explicitly only the absence of an additional filing requirement, the same result normally will follow in the case of an assignment of a security interest perfected by a method other than by filing. For example, as long as possession of collateral is maintained by an assignee or by the assignor or another person on behalf of the assignee, no further perfection steps need be taken on account of the assignment to continue perfection as against creditors and transferees of the original debtor. Of course, additional action may be required for perfection of the assignee's interest as against creditors and transferees of the *assignor*.

Similarly, subsection (c) applies to the assignment of a security interest perfected by compliance with a statute, regulation, or treaty under Section 9–311(b), such as a certificate-of-title statute. Unless the statute expressly provides to the contrary, the security interest will remain perfected against creditors of and transferees from the original debtor, even if the assignee takes no action to cause the certificate of title to reflect the assignment or to cause its name to appear on the certificate of title. See PEB Commentary No. 12, which discusses this issue under former Section 9–302(3). Compliance with the statute is "equivalent to filing" under Section 9–311(b).

§ 9–311. Perfection of Security Interests in Property Subject to Certain Statutes, Regulations, and Treaties.

(a) **[Security interest subject to other law.]** Except as otherwise provided in subsection (d), the filing of a financing statement is not necessary or effective to perfect a security interest in property subject to:

(1) a statute, regulation, or treaty of the United States whose requirements for a security interest's obtaining priority over the rights of a lien creditor with respect to the property preempt Section 9–310(a);

(2) [list any statute covering automobiles, trailers, mobile homes, boats, farm tractors, or the like, which provides for a security interest to be indicated on a certificate of title as a condition or result of perfection, and any non-Uniform Commercial Code central filing statute]; or

(3) a statute of another jurisdiction which provides for a security interest to be indicated on a certificate of title as a condition or result of the security interest's obtaining priority over the rights of a lien creditor with respect to the property.

(b) **[Compliance with other law.]** Compliance with the requirements of a statute, regulation, or treaty described in subsection (a) for obtaining priority over the rights of a lien creditor is equivalent to the filing of a financing statement under this article. Except as otherwise provided in subsection (d) and Sections 9–313 and 9–316(d) and (e) for goods covered by a certificate of title, a security interest in property subject to a statute, regulation, or treaty described in subsection (a) may be perfected only by compliance with those requirements, and a security interest so perfected remains perfected notwithstanding a change in the use or transfer of possession of the collateral.

(c) **[Duration and renewal of perfection.]** Except as otherwise provided in subsection (d) and Section 9–316(d) and (e), duration and renewal of perfection of a security interest perfected by compliance with the requirements prescribed by a statute, regulation, or treaty described in subsection (a) are governed by the statute, regulation, or treaty. In other respects, the security interest is subject to this article.

(d) **[Inapplicability to certain inventory.]** During any period in which collateral subject to a statute specified in subsection (a)(2) is inventory held for sale or lease by a person or leased by that person as lessor and that person is in the business of selling goods of that kind, this section does not apply to a security interest in that collateral created by that person.

Legislative Note: This Article contemplates that perfection of a security interest in goods covered by a certificate of title occurs upon receipt by appropriate State officials of a properly tendered application for a certificate of title on which the security interest is to be indicated, without a relation back to an earlier time. States whose certificate-of-title statutes provide for perfection at a different time or contain a relation-back provision should amend the statutes accordingly.

As amended in 2000 and 2010.

Official Comment

1. **Source.** Former Section 9–302(3), (4).

2. **Federal Statutes, Regulations, and Treaties.** Subsection (a)(1) exempts from the filing provisions of this Article transactions as to which a system of filing—state or federal—has been established under federal law. Subsection (b) makes clear that when such a system exists, perfection of a relevant security interest can be achieved only through compliance with that system (i.e., filing under this Article is not a permissible alternative).

An example of the type of federal statute referred to in subsection (a)(1) is 49 U.S.C. §§ 44107–11, for civil aircraft of the United States. The Assignment of Claims Act of 1940, as amended, provides for notice to contracting and disbursing officers and to sureties on bonds but does not establish a national filing system and therefore is not within the scope of subsection (a)(1). An assignee of a claim against the United States may benefit from compliance with the Assignment of Claims Act. But regardless of whether the assignee complies with that Act, the assignee must file under this Article in order to perfect its security interest against creditors and transferees of its assignor.

Subsection (a)(1) provides explicitly that the filing requirement of this Article defers only to federal statutes, regulations, or treaties whose requirements for a security interest's obtaining priority over the rights of a lien creditor preempt Section 9–310(a). The provision eschews reference to the term "perfection," inasmuch as Section 9–308 specifies the meaning of that term and a preemptive rule may use other terminology.

3. **State Statutes.** Subsections (a)(2) and (3) exempt from the filing requirements of this Article transactions covered by State certificate-of-title statutes covering motor vehicles and the like. The description of certificate-of-title statutes in subsections (a)(2) and (a)(3) tracks the language of the definition of "certificate of title" in Section 9–102. For a discussion of the operation of state certificate-of-title statutes in interstate contexts, see the Comments to Section 9–303.

Some states have enacted central filing statutes with respect to secured transactions in kinds of property that are of special importance in the local economy. Subsection (a)(2) defers to these statutes with respect to filing for that property.

4. **Inventory Covered by Certificate of Title.** Under subsection (d), perfection of a security interest in the inventory of a person in the business of selling goods of that kind is governed by the normal perfection rules, even if the inventory is subject to a certificate-of-title statute. Compliance with a certificate-of-title statute is both unnecessary and ineffective to perfect a security interest in inventory to which this subsection applies. Thus, a secured party who finances an automobile dealer that is in the business of selling and leasing its inventory of automobiles can perfect a security interest in all the automobiles by filing a financing statement but not by compliance with a certificate-of-title statute.

Subsection (d), and thus the filing and other perfection provisions of this Article, does not apply to inventory that is subject to a certificate-of-title statute and is of a kind that the debtor is not in the business of selling. For example, if goods are subject to a certificate-of-title statute and the debtor is in the business of leasing but not of selling, goods of that kind, the other subsections of this section govern perfection of a security interest in the goods. The fact that the debtor eventually sells the goods does not, of itself, mean that the debtor "is in the business of selling goods of that kind."

The filing and other perfection provisions of this Article apply to goods subject to a certificate-of-title statute only "during any period in which collateral is inventory held for sale or lease or leased." If the debtor takes goods of this kind out of inventory and uses them, say, as equipment, a filed financing statement would not remain effective to perfect a security interest.

5. **Compliance with Perfection Requirements of Other Statute.** Subsection (b) makes clear that compliance with the perfection requirements (i.e., the requirements for obtaining priority over a lien creditor), but not other requirements, of a statute, regulation, or treaty described in subsection (a) is sufficient for perfection under this Article. Perfection of a security interest under such a statute, regulation, or treaty has all the consequences of perfection under this Article.

The interplay of this section with certain certificate-of-title statutes may create confusion and uncertainty. For example, statutes under which perfection does not occur until a certificate of title is issued will create a gap between the time that the goods are covered by the certificate under Section 9–303 and the time of perfection. If the gap is long enough, it may result in turning some unobjectionable transactions into avoidable preferences under Bankruptcy Code Section 547. (The preference risk arises if more than 30 days passes between the time a security interest attaches (or the debtor receives possession of the collateral, in the case of a purchase-money security interest) and the time it is perfected.) Accordingly, the Legislative Note to this section instructs the legislature to amend the applicable certificate-of-title statute to provide that perfection occurs upon receipt by the appropriate State official of a properly tendered application for a certificate of title on which the security interest is to be indicated.

Under some certificate-of-title statutes, including the Uniform Motor Vehicle Certificate of Title and Anti-Theft Act, perfection generally occurs upon delivery of specified documents to a state official but may, under certain circumstances, relate back to the time of attachment. This relation-back feature can create great difficulties for the application of the rules in Sections 9–303 and 9–311(b). Accordingly, the Legislative Note also recommends to legislatures that they remove any relation-back provisions from certificate-of-title statutes affecting security interests.

6. **Compliance with Perfection Requirements of Other Statute as Equivalent to Filing.** Under Subsection (b), compliance with the perfection requirements (i.e., the requirements for obtaining priority over a lien creditor) of a statute, regulation, or treaty described in subsection (a) "is equivalent to the filing of a financing statement."

The quoted phrase appeared in former Section 9–302(3). Its meaning was unclear, and many questions arose concerning the extent to which and manner in which Article 9 rules referring to "filing" were applicable to perfection by compliance with a certificate-of-title statute. This Article takes a variety of approaches for applying Article 9's filing rules to compliance with other statutes and treaties. First, as discussed above in Comment 5, it leaves the determination of some rules, such as the rule establishing time of perfection (Section 9–516(a)), to the other statutes themselves. Second, this Article explicitly applies some Article 9 filing rules to perfection under other statutes or treaties. See, e.g., Section 9–505. Third, this Article makes other Article 9 rules applicable to security interests perfected by compliance with another statute through the "equivalent to . . . filing" provision in the first sentence of Section 9–311(b). The third approach is reflected for the most part in occasional Comments explaining how particular rules apply when perfection is accomplished under Section 9–311(b). See, e.g., Section 9–310, Comment 4; Section 9–315, Comment 6; Section 9–317, Comment 8. The absence of a Comment indicating that a particular filing provision applies to perfection pursuant to Section 9–311(b) does not mean the provision is inapplicable.

7. **Perfection by Possession of Goods Covered by Certificate-of-Title Statute.** A secured party who holds a security interest perfected under the law of State A in goods that subsequently are covered by a State B certificate of title may face a predicament. Ordinarily, the secured party will have four months under State B's Section 9–316(c) and (d) in which to (re)perfect as against a purchaser of the goods by having its security interest noted on a State B certificate. This procedure is likely to require the cooperation of the debtor and any competing secured party whose security interest has been noted on the certificate. Comment 4(e) to former Section 9–103 observed that "that cooperation is not likely to be forthcoming from an owner who wrongfully procured the issuance of a new certificate not showing the out-of-state security interest, or from a local secured party finding himself in a priority contest with the out-of-state secured party." According to that Comment, "[t]he only solution for the out-of-state secured party under present certificate of title statutes seems to be to reperfect by possession, i.e., by repossessing the goods." But the "solution" may not have worked: Former Section 9–302(4) provided that a security interest in property subject to a certificate-of-title statute "can be perfected only by compliance therewith."

Sections 9–316(d) and (e), 9–311(c), and 9–313(b) of this Article resolve the conflict by providing that a security interest that remains perfected solely by virtue of Section 9–316(e) can be (re)perfected by the secured party's taking possession of the collateral. These sections contemplate only that taking possession of goods covered by a certificate of title will work as a method of perfection. None of these sections creates a right to take possession. Section 9–609 and the agreement of the parties define the secured party's right to take possession.

As amended in 2000 and 2010.

§ 9–312. Perfection of Security Interests in Chattel Paper, Deposit Accounts, Documents, Goods Covered by Documents, Instruments, Investment Property, Letter-of-Credit Rights, and Money; Perfection by Permissive Filing; Temporary Perfection Without Filing or Transfer of Possession.

(a) **[Perfection by filing permitted.]** A security interest in chattel paper, negotiable documents, instruments, or investment property may be perfected by filing.

(b)　**[Control or possession of certain collateral.]** Except as otherwise provided in Section 9–315(c) and (d) for proceeds:

(1)　a security interest in a deposit account may be perfected only by control under Section 9–314;

(2)　and except as otherwise provided in Section 9–308(d), a security interest in a letter-of-credit right may be perfected only by control under Section 9–314; and

(3)　a security interest in money may be perfected only by the secured party's taking possession under Section 9–313.

(c)　**[Goods covered by negotiable document.]** While goods are in the possession of a bailee that has issued a negotiable document covering the goods:

(1)　a security interest in the goods may be perfected by perfecting a security interest in the document; and

(2)　a security interest perfected in the document has priority over any security interest that becomes perfected in the goods by another method during that time.

(d)　**[Goods covered by nonnegotiable document.]** While goods are in the possession of a bailee that has issued a nonnegotiable document covering the goods, a security interest in the goods may be perfected by:

(1)　issuance of a document in the name of the secured party;

(2)　the bailee's receipt of notification of the secured party's interest; or

(3)　filing as to the goods.

(e)　**[Temporary perfection: new value.]** A security interest in certificated securities, negotiable documents, or instruments is perfected without filing or the taking of possession or control for a period of 20 days from the time it attaches to the extent that it arises for new value given under an authenticated security agreement.

(f)　**[Temporary perfection: goods or documents made available to debtor.]** A perfected security interest in a negotiable document or goods in possession of a bailee, other than one that has issued a negotiable document for the goods, remains perfected for 20 days without filing if the secured party makes available to the debtor the goods or documents representing the goods for the purpose of:

(1)　ultimate sale or exchange; or

(2)　loading, unloading, storing, shipping, transshipping, manufacturing, processing, or otherwise dealing with them in a manner preliminary to their sale or exchange.

(g)　**[Temporary perfection: delivery of security certificate or instrument to debtor.]** A perfected security interest in a certificated security or instrument remains perfected for 20 days without filing if the secured party delivers the security certificate or instrument to the debtor for the purpose of:

(1)　ultimate sale or exchange; or

(2)　presentation, collection, enforcement, renewal, or registration of transfer.

(h)　**[Expiration of temporary perfection.]** After the 20-day period specified in subsection (e), (f), or (g) expires, perfection depends upon compliance with this article.

As amended in 2003.

Official Comment

1.　**Source.** Former Section 9–304, with additions and some changes.

2.　**Instruments.** Under subsection (a), a security interest in instruments may be perfected by filing. This rule represents an important change from former Article 9, under which the secured party's taking possession of an instrument was the only method of achieving long-term perfection. The rule is likely to be particularly useful in transactions involving a large number of notes that a debtor uses as collateral but continues to collect from the makers. A security interest perfected by filing is subject to defeat by certain subsequent purchasers (including

778

secured parties). Under Section 9–330(d), purchasers for value who take possession of an instrument without knowledge that the purchase violates the rights of the secured party generally would achieve priority over a security interest in the instrument perfected by filing. In addition, Section 9–331 provides that filing a financing statement does not constitute notice that would preclude a subsequent purchaser from becoming a holder in due course and taking free of all claims under Section 3–306.

3. **Chattel Paper; Negotiable Documents.** Subsection (a) further provides that filing is available as a method of perfection for security interests in chattel paper and negotiable documents. Tangible chattel paper is sometimes delivered to the assignee, and sometimes left in the hands of the assignor for collection. Subsection (a) allows the assignee to perfect its security interest by filing in the latter case. Alternatively, the assignee may perfect by taking possession. See Section 9–313(a). An assignee of electronic chattel paper may perfect by taking control. See Sections 9–314(a), 9–105. The security interest of an assignee who takes possession or control may qualify for priority over a competing security interest perfected by filing. See Section 9–330.

Negotiable documents may be, and usually are, delivered to the secured party. See Article 1, Section 1–201 (definition of "delivery"). The secured party's taking possession of a tangible document or control of an electronic document will suffice as a perfection step. See Sections 9–313(a), 9–314 and 7–106. However, as is the case with chattel paper, a security interest in a negotiable document may be perfected by filing.

4. **Investment Property.** A security interest in investment property, including certificated securities, uncertificated securities, security entitlements, and securities accounts, may be perfected by filing. However, security interests created by brokers, securities intermediaries, or commodity intermediaries are automatically perfected; filing is of no effect. See Section 9–309(10), (11). A security interest in all kinds of investment property also may be perfected by control, see Sections 9–314, 9–106, and a security interest in a certificated security also may be perfected by the secured party's taking delivery under Section 8–301. See Section 9–313(a). A security interest perfected only by filing is subordinate to a conflicting security interest perfected by control or delivery. See Section 9–328(1), (5). Thus, although filing is a permissible method of perfection, a secured party who perfects by filing takes the risk that the debtor has granted or will grant a security interest in the same collateral to another party who obtains control. Also, perfection by filing would not give the secured party protection against other types of adverse claims, since the Article 8 adverse claim cut-off rules require control. See Section 8–510.

5. **Deposit Accounts.** Under new subsection (b)(1), the only method of perfecting a security interest in a deposit account as original collateral is by control. Filing is ineffective, except as provided in Section 9–315 with respect to proceeds. As explained in Section 9–104, "control" can arise as a result of an agreement among the secured party, debtor, and bank, whereby the bank agrees to comply with instructions of the secured party with respect to disposition of the funds on deposit, even though the debtor retains the right to direct disposition of the funds. Thus, subsection (b)(1) takes an intermediate position between certain non-UCC law, which conditions the effectiveness of a security interest on the secured party's enjoyment of such dominion and control over the deposit account that the debtor is unable to dispose of the funds, and the approach this Article takes to securities accounts, under which a secured party who is unable to reach the collateral without resort to judicial process may perfect by filing. By conditioning perfection on "control," rather than requiring the secured party to enjoy absolute dominion to the exclusion of the debtor, subsection (b)(1) permits perfection in a wide variety of transactions, including those in which the secured party actually relies on the deposit account in extending credit and maintains some meaningful dominion over it, but does not wish to deprive the debtor of access to the funds altogether.

6. **Letter-of-Credit Rights.** Letter-of-credit rights commonly are "supporting obligations," as defined in Section 9–102. Perfection as to the related account, chattel paper, document, general intangible, instrument, or investment property will perfect as to the letter-of-credit rights. See Section 9–308(d). Subsection (b)(2) provides that, in other cases, a security interest in a letter-of-credit right may be perfected only by control. "Control," for these purposes, is explained in Section 9–107.

7. **Goods Covered by Document of Title.** Subsection (c) applies to goods in the possession of a bailee who has issued a negotiable document covering the goods. Subsection (d) applies to goods in the possession of a bailee who has issued a nonnegotiable document of title, including a document of title that is "non-negotiable" under Section 7–104. Section 9–313 governs perfection of a security interest in goods in the possession of a bailee who has not issued a document of title.

Subsection (c) clarifies the perfection and priority rules in former Section 9–304(2). Consistently with the provisions of Article 7, subsection (c) takes the position that, as long as a negotiable document covering goods is outstanding, title to the goods is, so to say, locked up in the document. Accordingly, a security interest in goods covered by a negotiable document may be perfected by perfecting a security interest in the document. The security interest also may be perfected by another method, e.g., by filing. The priority rule in subsection (c) governs only priority between (i) a security interest in goods which is perfected by perfecting in the document and (ii) a security interest in the goods which becomes perfected by another method while the goods are covered by the document.

Example 1: While wheat is in a grain elevator and covered by a negotiable warehouse receipt, Debtor creates a security interest in the wheat in favor of SP–1 and SP–2. SP–1 perfects by filing a financing statement covering "wheat." Thereafter, SP–2 perfects by filing a financing statement describing the warehouse receipt. Subsection (c)(1) provides that SP–2's security interest is perfected. Subsection (c)(2) provides that SP–2's security interest is senior to SP–1's.

Example 2: The facts are as in Example 1, but SP–1's security interest attached and was perfected before the goods were delivered to the grain elevator. Subsection (c)(2) does not apply, because SP–1's security interest did not become perfected during the time that the wheat was in the possession of a bailee. Rather, the first-to-file-or-perfect priority rule applies. See Sections 9–322 and 7–503.

A secured party may become "a holder to whom a negotiable document of title has been duly negotiated" under Section 7–501. If so, the secured party acquires the rights specified by Article 7. Article 9 does not limit those rights, which may include the right to priority over an earlier-perfected security interest. See Section 9–331(a).

Subsection (d) takes a different approach to the problem of goods covered by a nonnegotiable document. Here, title to the goods is not looked on as being locked up in the document, and the secured party may perfect its security interest directly in the goods by filing as to them. The subsection provides two other methods of perfection: issuance of the document in the secured party's name (as consignee of a straight bill of lading or the person to whom delivery would be made under a non-negotiable warehouse receipt) and receipt of notification of the secured party's interest by the bailee. Perfection under subsection (d) occurs when the bailee receives notification of the secured party's interest in the goods, regardless of who sends the notification. Receipt of notification is effective to perfect, regardless of whether the bailee responds. Unlike former Section 9–304(3), from which it derives, subsection (d) does not apply to goods in the possession of a bailee who has not issued a document of title. Section 9–313(c) covers that case and provides that perfection by possession as to goods not covered by a document requires the bailee's acknowledgment.

8. **Temporary Perfection Without Having First Otherwise Perfected.** Subsection (e) follows former Section 9–304(4) in giving perfected status to security interests in certificated securities, instruments, and negotiable documents for a short period (reduced from 21 to 20 days, which is the time period generally applicable in this Article), although there has been no filing and the collateral is in the debtor's possession or control. The 20-day temporary perfection runs from the date of attachment. There is no limitation on the purpose for which the debtor is in possession, but the secured party must have given "new value" (defined in Section 9–102) under an authenticated security agreement.

9. **Maintaining Perfection After Surrendering Possession.** There are a variety of legitimate reasons—many of them are described in subsections (f) and (g)—why certain types of collateral must be released temporarily to a debtor. No useful purpose would be served by cluttering the files with records of such exceedingly short term transactions.

Subsection (f) affords the possibility of 20-day perfection in negotiable documents and goods in the possession of a bailee but not covered by a negotiable document. Subsection (g) provides for 20-day perfection in certificated securities and instruments. These subsections derive from former Section 9–305(5). However, the period of temporary perfection has been reduced from 21 to 20 days, which is the time period generally applicable in this Article, and "enforcement" has been added in subsection (g) as one of the special and limited purposes for which a secured party can release an instrument or certificated security to the debtor and still remain perfected. The period of temporary perfection runs from the date a secured party who already has a perfected security interest turns over the collateral to the debtor. There is no new value requirement, but the turnover must be for one or more of the purposes stated in subsection (f) or (g). The 20-day period may be extended by perfecting as to the collateral by another method before the period expires. However, if the security interest is not perfected by another method until after the 20-day period expires, there will be a gap during which the security interest is unperfected.

Temporary perfection extends only to the negotiable document or goods under subsection (f) and only to the certificated security or instrument under subsection (g). It does not extend to proceeds. If the collateral is sold, the security interest will continue in the proceeds for the period specified in Section 9–315.

Subsections (f) and (g) deal only with perfection. Other sections of this Article govern the priority of a security interest in goods after surrender of possession or control of the document covering them. In the case of a purchase-money security interest in inventory, priority may be conditioned upon giving notification to a prior inventory financer. See Section 9–324.

As amended in 2003.

§ 9–313. When Possession by or Delivery to Secured Party Perfects Security Interest Without Filing.

(a) **[Perfection by possession or delivery.]** Except as otherwise provided in subsection (b), a secured party may perfect a security interest in tangible negotiable documents, goods, instruments, money, or tangible chattel paper by taking possession of the collateral. A secured party may perfect a security interest in certificated securities by taking delivery of the certificated securities under Section 8–301.

(b) **[Goods covered by certificate of title.]** With respect to goods covered by a certificate of title issued by this State, a secured party may perfect a security interest in the goods by taking possession of the goods only in the circumstances described in Section 9–316(d).

(c) **[Collateral in possession of person other than debtor.]** With respect to collateral other than certificated securities and goods covered by a document, a secured party takes possession of collateral in the possession of a person other than the debtor, the secured party, or a lessee of the collateral from the debtor in the ordinary course of the debtor's business, when:

(1) the person in possession authenticates a record acknowledging that it holds possession of the collateral for the secured party's benefit; or

(2) the person takes possession of the collateral after having authenticated a record acknowledging that it will hold possession of collateral for the secured party's benefit.

(d) **[Time of perfection by possession; continuation of perfection.]** If perfection of a security interest depends upon possession of the collateral by a secured party, perfection occurs no earlier than the time the secured party takes possession and continues only while the secured party retains possession.

(e) **[Time of perfection by delivery; continuation of perfection.]** A security interest in a certificated security in registered form is perfected by delivery when delivery of the certificated security occurs under Section 8–301 and remains perfected by delivery until the debtor obtains possession of the security certificate.

(f) **[Acknowledgment not required.]** A person in possession of collateral is not required to acknowledge that it holds possession for a secured party's benefit.

(g) **[Effectiveness of acknowledgment; no duties or confirmation.]** If a person acknowledges that it holds possession for the secured party's benefit:

(1) the acknowledgment is effective under subsection (c) or Section 8–301(a), even if the acknowledgment violates the rights of a debtor; and

(2) unless the person otherwise agrees or law other than this article otherwise provides, the person does not owe any duty to the secured party and is not required to confirm the acknowledgment to another person.

(h) **[Secured party's delivery to person other than debtor.]** A secured party having possession of collateral does not relinquish possession by delivering the collateral to a person other than the debtor or a lessee of the collateral from the debtor in the ordinary course of the debtor's business if the person was instructed before the delivery or is instructed contemporaneously with the delivery:

(1) to hold possession of the collateral for the secured party's benefit; or

(2) to redeliver the collateral to the secured party.

(i) **[Effect of delivery under subsection (h); no duties or confirmation.]** A secured party does not relinquish possession, even if a delivery under subsection (h) violates the rights of a debtor. A person to which collateral is delivered under subsection (h) does not owe any duty to the secured party and is not required to confirm the delivery to another person unless the person otherwise agrees or law other than this article otherwise provides.

As amended in 2003.

Official Comment

1.   **Source.** Former Sections 9–305, 9–115(6).

2.   **Perfection by Possession.** As under the common law of pledge, no filing is required by this Article to perfect a security interest if the secured party takes possession of the collateral. See Section 9–310(b)(6).

This section permits a security interest to be perfected by the taking of possession only when the collateral is goods, instruments, tangible negotiable documents, money, or tangible chattel paper. Accounts, commercial tort claims, deposit accounts, investment property, letter-of-credit rights, letters of credit, and oil, gas, or other minerals before extraction are excluded. (But see Comment 6, below, regarding certificated securities.) A security interest in accounts and payment intangibles—property not ordinarily represented by any writing whose delivery operates to transfer the right to payment—may under this Article be perfected only by filing. This rule would not be affected by the fact that a security agreement or other record described the assignment of such collateral as a "pledge." Section 9–309(2) exempts from filing certain assignments of accounts or payment intangibles which are out of the ordinary course of financing. These exempted assignments are perfected when they attach. Similarly, under Section 9–309(3), sales of payment intangibles are automatically perfected.

3.   **"Possession."** This section does not define "possession." It adopts the general concept as it developed under former Article 9. As under former Article 9, in determining whether a particular person has possession, the principles of agency apply. For example, if the collateral is in possession of an agent of the secured party for the purposes of possessing on behalf of the secured party, and if the agent is not also an agent of the debtor, the secured party has taken actual possession, and subsection (c) does not apply. Sometimes a person holds collateral both as an agent of the secured party and as an agent of the debtor. The fact of dual agency is not of itself inconsistent with the secured party's having taken possession (and thereby having rendered subsection (c) inapplicable). The debtor cannot qualify as an agent for the secured party for purposes of the secured party's taking possession. And, under appropriate circumstances, a court may determine that a person in possession is so closely connected to or controlled by the debtor that the debtor has retained effective possession, even though the person may have agreed to take possession on behalf of the secured party. If so, the person's taking possession would not constitute the secured party's taking possession and would not be sufficient for perfection. See also Section 9–205(b). In a typical escrow arrangement, where the escrowee has possession of collateral as agent for both the secured party and the debtor, the debtor's relationship to the escrowee is not such as to constitute retention of possession by the debtor.

4.   **Goods in Possession of Third Party: Perfection.** Former Section 9–305 permitted perfection of a security interest by notification to a bailee in possession of collateral. This Article distinguishes between goods in the possession of a bailee who has issued a document of title covering the goods and goods in the possession of a third party who has not issued a document. Section 9–312(c) or (d) applies to the former, depending on whether the document is negotiable. Section 9–313(c) applies to the latter. It provides a method of perfection by possession when the collateral is possessed by a third person who is not the secured party's agent.

Notification of a third person does not suffice to perfect under Section 9–313(c). Rather, perfection does not occur unless the third person authenticates an acknowledgment that it holds possession of the collateral for the secured party's benefit. Compare Section 9–312(d), under which receipt of notification of the security party's interest by a bailee holding goods covered by a nonnegotiable document is sufficient to perfect, even if the bailee does not acknowledge receipt of the notification. A third person may acknowledge that it will hold for the secured party's benefit goods to be received in the future. Under these circumstances, perfection by possession occurs when the third person obtains possession of the goods.

Under subsection (c), acknowledgment of notification by a "lessee . . . in . . . ordinary course of . . . business" (defined in Section 2A–103) does not suffice for possession. The section thus rejects the reasoning of *In re Atlantic Systems, Inc.*, 135 B.R. 463 (Bankr. S.D.N.Y. 1992) (holding that notification to debtor-lessor's lessee sufficed to perfect security interest in leased goods). See Steven O. Weise, *Perfection by Possession: The Need for an Objective Test*, 29 Idaho Law Rev. 705 (1992–93) (arguing that lessee's possession in ordinary course of debtor-lessor's business does not provide adequate public notice of possible security interest in leased goods). Inclusion of a per se rule concerning lessees is not meant to preclude a court, under appropriate circumstances, from determining that a third person is so closely connected to or controlled by the debtor that the debtor has retained effective possession. If so, the third person's acknowledgment would not be sufficient for perfection.

In some cases, it may be uncertain whether a person who has possession of collateral is an agent of the secured party or a non-agent bailee. Under those circumstances, prudence might suggest that the secured party obtain the person's acknowledgment to avoid litigation and ensure perfection by possession regardless of how the relationship between the secured party and the person is characterized.

5. **No Relation Back.** Former Section 9–305 provided that a security interest is perfected by possession from the time possession is taken "without a relation back." As the Comment to former Section 9–305 observed, the relation-back theory, under which the taking of possession was deemed to relate back to the date of the original security agreement, has had little vitality since the 1938 revision of the Federal Bankruptcy Act. The theory is inconsistent with former Article 9 and with this Article. See Section 9–313(d). Accordingly, this Article deletes the quoted phrase as unnecessary. Where a pledge transaction is contemplated, perfection dates only from the time possession is taken, although a security interest may attach, unperfected. The only exceptions to this rule are the short, 20-day periods of perfection provided in Section 9–312(e), (f), and (g), during which a debtor may have possession of specified collateral in which there is a perfected security interest.

6. **Certificated Securities.** The second sentence of subsection (a) reflects the traditional rule for perfection of a security interest in certificated securities. Compare Section 9–115(6) (1994 Official Text); Sections 8–321, 8–313(1)(a) (1978 Official Text); Section 9–305 (1972 Official Text). It has been modified to refer to "delivery" under Section 8–301. Corresponding changes appear in Section 9–203(b).

Subsection (e), which is new, applies to a secured party in possession of security certificates or another person who has taken delivery of security certificates and holds them for the secured party's benefit under Section 8–301. See Comment 8.

Under subsection (e), a possessory security interest in a certificated security remains perfected until the debtor obtains possession of the security certificate. This rule is analogous to that of Section 9–314(c), which deals with perfection of security interests in investment property by control. See Section 9–314, Comment 3.

7. **Goods Covered by Certificate of Title.** Subsection (b) is necessary to effect changes to the choice-of-law rules governing goods covered by a certificate of title. These changes are described in the Comments to Section 9–311. Subsection (b), like subsection (a), does not create a right to take possession. Rather, it indicates the circumstances under which the secured party's taking possession of goods covered by a certificate of title is effective to perfect a security interest in the goods: the goods become covered by a certificate of title issued by this State at a time when the security interest is perfected by any method under the law of another jurisdiction.

8. **Goods in Possession of Third Party: No Duty to Acknowledge; Consequences of Acknowledgment.** Subsections (f) and (g) are new and address matters as to which former Article 9 was silent. They derive in part from Section 8–106(g). Subsection (f) provides that a person in possession of collateral is not required to acknowledge that it holds for a secured party. Subsection (g)(1) provides that an acknowledgment is effective even if wrongful as to the debtor. Subsection (g)(2) makes clear that an acknowledgment does not give rise to any duties or responsibilities under this Article. Arrangements involving the possession of goods are hardly standardized. They include bailments for services to be performed on the goods (such as repair or processing), for use (leases), as security (pledges), for carriage, and for storage. This Article leaves to the agreement of the parties and to any other applicable law the imposition of duties and responsibilities upon a person who acknowledges under subsection (c). For example, by acknowledging, a third party does not become obliged to act on the secured party's direction or to remain in possession of the collateral unless it agrees to do so or other law so provides.

9. **Delivery to Third Party by Secured Party.** New subsections (h) and (i) address the practice of mortgage warehouse lenders. These lenders typically send mortgage notes to prospective purchasers under cover of letters advising the prospective purchasers that the lenders hold security interests in the notes. These lenders relied on notification to maintain perfection under former 9–305. Requiring them to obtain authenticated acknowledgments from each prospective purchaser under subsection (c) could be unduly burdensome and disruptive of established practices. Under subsection (h), when a secured party in possession itself delivers the collateral to a third party, instructions to the third party would be sufficient to maintain perfection by possession; an acknowledgment would not be necessary. Under subsection (i), the secured party does not relinquish possession by making a delivery under subsection (h), even if the delivery violates the rights of the debtor. That subsection also makes clear that a person to whom collateral is delivered under subsection (h) does not owe any duty to the secured party and is not required to confirm the delivery to another person unless the person otherwise agrees or law other than this Article provides otherwise.

As amended in 2000 and 2003.

§ 9–314.   Perfection by Control.

(a)   **[Perfection by control.]** A security interest in investment property, deposit accounts, letter-of-credit rights, electronic chattel paper, or electronic documents may be perfected by control of the collateral under Section 7–106, 9–104, 9–105, 9–106, or 9–107.

(b)   **[Specified collateral: time of perfection by control; continuation of perfection.]** A security interest in deposit accounts, electronic chattel paper, letter-of-credit rights, or electronic documents is perfected by control under Section 7–106, 9–104, 9–105, or 9–107 when the secured party obtains control and remains perfected by control only while the secured party retains control.

(c)   **[Investment property: time of perfection by control; continuation of perfection.]** A security interest in investment property is perfected by control under Section 9–106 from the time the secured party obtains control and remains perfected by control until:

(1)   the secured party does not have control; and

(2)   one of the following occurs:

(A)   if the collateral is a certificated security, the debtor has or acquires possession of the security certificate;

(B)   if the collateral is an uncertificated security, the issuer has registered or registers the debtor as the registered owner; or

(C)   if the collateral is a security entitlement, the debtor is or becomes the entitlement holder.

As amended in 2003.

Official Comment

1.   **Source.** Substantially new; derived in part from former Section 9–115(4).

2.   **Control.** This section provides for perfection by control with respect to investment property, deposit accounts, letter-of-credit rights, electronic chattel paper, and electronic documents. For explanations of how a secured party takes control of these types of collateral, see Sections 9–104 through 9–107 and Section 7–106. Subsection (b) explains when a security interest is perfected by control and how long a security interest remains perfected by control. Like Section 9–313(d) and for the same reasons, subsection (b) makes no reference to the doctrine of "relation back." See Section 9–313, Comment 5. As to an electronic document that is reissued in a tangible medium, Section 7–105, a secured party that is perfected by control in the electronic document should file as to the document before relinquishing control in order to maintain continuous perfection in the document. See Section 9–308.

3.   **Investment Property.** Subsection (c) provides a special rule for investment property. Once a secured party has control, its security interest remains perfected by control until the secured party ceases to have control and the debtor receives possession of collateral that is a certificated security, becomes the registered owner of collateral that is an uncertificated security, or becomes the entitlement holder of collateral that is a security entitlement. The result is particularly important in the "repledge" context. See Section 9–207, Comment 5.

In a transaction in which a secured party who has control grants a security interest in investment property or sells outright the investment property, by virtue of the debtor's consent or applicable legal rules, a purchaser from the secured party typically will cut off the debtor's rights in the investment property or be immune from the debtor's claims. See Section 9–207, Comments 5 and 6. If the investment property is a security, the debtor normally would retain no interest in the security following the purchase from the secured party, and a claim of the debtor against the secured party for redemption (Section 9–623) or otherwise with respect to the security would be a purely personal claim. If the investment property transferred by the secured party is a financial asset in which the debtor had a security entitlement credited to a securities account maintained with the secured party as a securities intermediary, the debtor's claim against the secured party could arise as a part of its securities account notwithstanding its personal nature. (This claim would be analogous to a "credit balance" in the securities account, which is a component of the securities account even though it is a personal claim against the intermediary.) In the case in which the debtor may retain an interest in investment property notwithstanding a repledge or sale by the secured party, subsection (c) makes clear that the security interest will remain perfected by control.

As amended in 2003.

§ 9–315. Secured Party's Rights on Disposition of Collateral and in Proceeds.

(a) **[Disposition of collateral: continuation of security interest or agricultural lien; proceeds.]** Except as otherwise provided in this article and in Section 2–403(2):

(1) a security interest or agricultural lien continues in collateral notwithstanding sale, lease, license, exchange, or other disposition thereof unless the secured party authorized the disposition free of the security interest or agricultural lien; and

(2) a security interest attaches to any identifiable proceeds of collateral.

(b) **[When commingled proceeds identifiable.]** Proceeds that are commingled with other property are identifiable proceeds:

(1) if the proceeds are goods, to the extent provided by Section 9–336; and

(2) if the proceeds are not goods, to the extent that the secured party identifies the proceeds by a method of tracing, including application of equitable principles, that is permitted under law other than this article with respect to commingled property of the type involved.

(c) **[Perfection of security interest in proceeds.]** A security interest in proceeds is a perfected security interest if the security interest in the original collateral was perfected.

(d) **[Continuation of perfection.]** A perfected security interest in proceeds becomes unperfected on the 21st day after the security interest attaches to the proceeds unless:

(1) the following conditions are satisfied:

(A) a filed financing statement covers the original collateral;

(B) the proceeds are collateral in which a security interest may be perfected by filing in the office in which the financing statement has been filed; and

(C) the proceeds are not acquired with cash proceeds;

(2) the proceeds are identifiable cash proceeds; or

(3) the security interest in the proceeds is perfected other than under subsection (c) when the security interest attaches to the proceeds or within 20 days thereafter.

(e) **[When perfected security interest in proceeds becomes unperfected.]** If a filed financing statement covers the original collateral, a security interest in proceeds which remains perfected under subsection (d)(1) becomes unperfected at the later of:

(1) when the effectiveness of the filed financing statement lapses under Section 9–515 or is terminated under Section 9–513; or

(2) the 21st day after the security interest attaches to the proceeds.

Official Comment

1. **Source.** Former Section 9–306.

2. **Continuation of Security Interest or Agricultural Lien Following Disposition of Collateral.** Subsection (a)(1), which derives from former Section 9–306(2), contains the general rule that a security interest survives disposition of the collateral. In these cases, the secured party may repossess the collateral from the transferee or, in an appropriate case, maintain an action for conversion. The secured party may claim both any proceeds and the original collateral but, of course, may have only one satisfaction.

In many cases, a purchaser or other transferee of collateral will take free of a security interest, and the secured party's only right will be to proceeds. For example, the general rule does not apply, and a security interest does not continue in collateral, if the secured party authorized the disposition, in the agreement that contains the security agreement or otherwise. Subsection (a)(1) adopts the view of PEB Commentary No. 3 and makes explicit that the authorized disposition to which it refers is an authorized disposition "free of" the security interest or agricultural lien. The secured party's right to proceeds under this section or under the express terms of an agreement does not in itself constitute an authorization of disposition. The change in language from former Section

9–306(2) is not intended to address the frequently litigated situation in which the effectiveness of the secured party's consent to a disposition is conditioned upon the secured party's receipt of the proceeds. In that situation, subsection (a) leaves the determination of authorization to the courts, as under former Article 9.

This Article contains several provisions under which a transferee takes free of a security interest or agricultural lien. For example, Section 9–317 states when transferees take free of unperfected security interests; Sections 9–320 and 9–321 on goods, 9–321 on general intangibles, 9–330 on chattel paper and instruments, and 9–331 on negotiable instruments, negotiable documents, and securities state when purchasers of such collateral take free of a security interest, even though perfected and even though the disposition was not authorized. Section 9–332 enables most transferees (including non-purchasers) of funds from a deposit account and most transferees of money to take free of a perfected security interest in the deposit account or money.

Likewise, the general rule that a security interest survives disposition does not apply if the secured party entrusts goods collateral to a merchant who deals in goods of that kind and the merchant sells the collateral to a buyer in ordinary course of business. Section 2–403(2) gives the merchant the power to transfer all the secured party's rights to the buyer, even if the sale is wrongful as against the secured party. Thus, under subsection (a)(1), an entrusting secured party runs the same risk as any other entruster.

3. **Secured Party's Right to Identifiable Proceeds.** Under subsection (a)(2), which derives from former Section 9–306(2), a security interest attaches to any identifiable "proceeds," as defined in Section 9–102. See also Section 9–203(f). Subsection (b) is new. It indicates when proceeds commingled with other property are identifiable proceeds and permits the use of whatever methods of tracing other law permits with respect to the type of property involved. Among the "equitable principles" whose use other law may permit is the "lowest intermediate balance rule." See Restatement (2d), Trusts § 202.

4. **Automatic Perfection in Proceeds: General Rule.** Under subsection (c), a security interest in proceeds is a perfected security interest if the security interest in the original collateral was perfected. This Article extends the period of automatic perfection in proceeds from 10 days to 20 days. Generally, a security interest in proceeds becomes unperfected on the 21st day after the security interest attaches to the proceeds. See subsection (d). The loss of perfected status under subsection (d) is prospective only. Compare, e.g., Section 9–515(c) (deeming security interest unperfected retroactively).

5. **Automatic Perfection in Proceeds: Proceeds Acquired with Cash Proceeds.** Subsection (d)(1) derives from former Section 9–306(3)(a). It carries forward the basic rule that a security interest in proceeds remains perfected beyond the period of automatic perfection if a filed financing statement covers the original collateral (e.g., inventory) and the proceeds are collateral in which a security interest may be perfected by filing in the office where the financing statement has been filed (e.g., equipment). A different rule applies if the proceeds are acquired with cash proceeds, as is the case if the original collateral (inventory) is sold for cash (cash proceeds) that is used to purchase equipment (proceeds). Under these circumstances, the security interest in the equipment proceeds remains perfected only if the description in the filed financing indicates the type of property constituting the proceeds (e.g., "equipment").

This section reaches the same result but takes a different approach. It recognizes that the treatment of proceeds acquired with cash proceeds under former Section 9–306(3)(a) essentially was superfluous. In the example, had the filing covered "equipment" as well as "inventory," the security interest in the proceeds would have been perfected under the usual rules governing after-acquired equipment (see former Sections 9–302, 9–303); paragraph (3)(a) added only an exception to the general rule. Subsection (d)(1)(C) of this section takes a more direct approach. It makes the general rule of continued perfection inapplicable to proceeds acquired with cash proceeds, leaving perfection of a security interest in those proceeds to the generally applicable perfection rules under subsection (d)(3).

Example 1: Lender perfects a security interest in Debtor's inventory by filing a financing statement covering "inventory." Debtor sells the inventory and deposits the buyer's check into a deposit account. Debtor draws a check on the deposit account and uses it to pay for equipment. Under the "lowest intermediate balance rule," which is a permitted method of tracing in the relevant jurisdiction, see Comment 3, the funds used to pay for the equipment were identifiable proceeds of the inventory. Because the proceeds (equipment) were acquired with cash proceeds (deposit account), subsection (d)(1) does not extend perfection beyond the 20-day automatic period.

Example 2: Lender perfects a security interest in Debtor's inventory by filing a financing statement covering "all debtor's property." As in Example 1, Debtor sells the inventory, deposits the buyer's check into a deposit account, draws a check on the deposit account, and uses the check to pay for equipment. Under the "lowest intermediate balance rule," which is a permitted method of tracing in the relevant jurisdiction, see Comment 3, the funds used to pay for the equipment were identifiable proceeds of the inventory. Because the proceeds (equipment) were acquired with cash proceeds (deposit account), subsection (d)(1) does not extend perfection beyond the 20-day automatic period. However, because the financing statement is sufficient to perfect a security interest in debtor's equipment, under subsection (d)(3) the security interest in the equipment proceeds remains perfected beyond the 20-day period.

6. **Automatic Perfection in Proceeds: Lapse or Termination of Financing Statement During 20-Day Period; Perfection Under Other Statute or Treaty.** Subsection (e) provides that a security interest in proceeds perfected under subsection (d)(1) ceases to be perfected when the financing statement covering the original collateral lapses or is terminated. If the lapse or termination occurs before the 21st day after the security interest attaches, however, the security interest in the proceeds remains perfected until the 21st day. Section 9–311(b) provides that compliance with the perfection requirements of a statute or treaty described in Section 9–311(a) "is equivalent to the filing of a financing statement." It follows that collateral subject to a security interest perfected by such compliance under Section 9–311(b) is covered by a "filed financing statement" within the meaning of Section 9–315(d) and (e).

7. **Automatic Perfection in Proceeds: Continuation of Perfection in Cash Proceeds.** Former Section 9–306(3)(b) provided that if a filed financing statement covered original collateral, a security interest in identifiable cash proceeds of the collateral remained perfected beyond the ten-day period of automatic perfection. Former Section 9–306(3)(c) contained a similar rule with respect to identifiable cash proceeds of investment property. Subsection (d)(2) extends the benefits of former Sections 9–306(3)(b) and (3)(c) to identifiable cash proceeds of all types of original collateral in which a security interest is perfected by any method. Under subsection (d)(2), if the security interest in the original collateral was perfected, a security interest in identifiable cash proceeds will remain perfected indefinitely, regardless of whether the security interest in the original collateral remains perfected. In many cases, however, a purchaser or other transferee of the cash proceeds will take free of the perfected security interest. See, e.g., Sections 9–330(d) (purchaser of check), 9–331 (holder in due course of check), 9–332 (transferee of money or funds from a deposit account).

8. **Insolvency Proceedings; Returned and Repossessed Goods.** This Article deletes former Section 9–306(4), which dealt with proceeds in insolvency proceedings. Except as otherwise provided by the Bankruptcy Code, the debtor's entering into bankruptcy does not affect a secured party's right to proceeds.

This Article also deletes former Section 9–306(5), which dealt with returned and repossessed goods. Section 9–330, Comments 9 to 11 explain and clarify the application of priority rules to returned and repossessed goods as proceeds of chattel paper.

9. **Proceeds of Collateral Subject to Agricultural Lien.** This Article does not determine whether a lien extends to proceeds of farm products encumbered by an agricultural lien. If, however, the proceeds are themselves farm products on which an "agricultural lien" (defined in Section 9–102) arises under other law, then the agricultural-lien provisions of this Article apply to the agricultural lien on the proceeds in the same way in which they would apply had the farm products not been proceeds.

§ 9–316.   Effect of Change in Governing Law.

(a) **[General rule: effect on perfection of change in governing law.]** A security interest perfected pursuant to the law of the jurisdiction designated in Section 9–301(1) or 9–305(c) remains perfected until the earliest of:

(1) the time perfection would have ceased under the law of that jurisdiction;

(2) the expiration of four months after a change of the debtor's location to another jurisdiction; or

(3) the expiration of one year after a transfer of collateral to a person that thereby becomes a debtor and is located in another jurisdiction.

(b) **[Security interest perfected or unperfected under law of new jurisdiction.]** If a security interest described in subsection (a) becomes perfected under the law of the other jurisdiction before the earliest time or event described in that subsection, it remains perfected thereafter. If the security interest does not become perfected under the law of the other jurisdiction before the earliest time or event, it becomes unperfected and is deemed never to have been perfected as against a purchaser of the collateral for value.

(c) **[Possessory security interest in collateral moved to new jurisdiction.]** A possessory security interest in collateral, other than goods covered by a certificate of title and as-extracted collateral consisting of goods, remains continuously perfected if:

(1) the collateral is located in one jurisdiction and subject to a security interest perfected under the law of that jurisdiction;

(2) thereafter the collateral is brought into another jurisdiction; and

(3) upon entry into the other jurisdiction, the security interest is perfected under the law of the other jurisdiction.

(d) **[Goods covered by certificate of title from this state.]** Except as otherwise provided in subsection (e), a security interest in goods covered by a certificate of title which is perfected by any method under the law of another jurisdiction when the goods become covered by a certificate of title from this State remains perfected until the security interest would have become unperfected under the law of the other jurisdiction had the goods not become so covered.

(e) **[When subsection (d) security interest becomes unperfected against purchasers.]** A security interest described in subsection (d) becomes unperfected as against a purchaser of the goods for value and is deemed never to have been perfected as against a purchaser of the goods for value if the applicable requirements for perfection under Section 9–311(b) or 9–313 are not satisfied before the earlier of:

(1) the time the security interest would have become unperfected under the law of the other jurisdiction had the goods not become covered by a certificate of title from this State; or

(2) the expiration of four months after the goods had become so covered.

(f) **[Change in jurisdiction of bank, issuer, nominated person, securities intermediary, or commodity intermediary.]** A security interest in deposit accounts, letter-of-credit rights, or investment property which is perfected under the law of the bank's jurisdiction, the issuer's jurisdiction, a nominated person's jurisdiction, the securities intermediary's jurisdiction, or the commodity intermediary's jurisdiction, as applicable, remains perfected until the earlier of:

(1) the time the security interest would have become unperfected under the law of that jurisdiction; or

(2) the expiration of four months after a change of the applicable jurisdiction to another jurisdiction.

(g) **[Subsection (f) security interest perfected or unperfected under law of new jurisdiction.]** If a security interest described in subsection (f) becomes perfected under the law of the other jurisdiction before the earlier of the time or the end of the period described in that subsection, it remains perfected thereafter. If the security interest does not become perfected under the law of the other jurisdiction before the earlier of that time or the end of that period, it becomes unperfected and is deemed never to have been perfected as against a purchaser of the collateral for value.

(h) **[Effect on filed financing statement of change in governing law.]** The following rules apply to collateral to which a security interest attaches within four months after the debtor changes its location to another jurisdiction:

(1) A financing statement filed before the change pursuant to the law of the jurisdiction designated in Section 9–301(1) or 9–305(c) is effective to perfect a security interest in the collateral if the financing statement would have been effective to perfect a security interest in the collateral had the debtor not changed its location.

(2) If a security interest perfected by a financing statement that is effective under paragraph (1) becomes perfected under the law of the other jurisdiction before the earlier of the time the financing statement would have become ineffective under the law of the jurisdiction designated in Section 9–301(1) or 9–305(c) or the expiration of the four-month period, it remains perfected thereafter. If the security interest does not become perfected under the law of the other

jurisdiction before the earlier time or event, it becomes unperfected and is deemed never to have been perfected as against a purchaser of the collateral for value.

(i) **[Effect of change in governing law on financing statement filed against original debtor.]** If a financing statement naming an original debtor is filed pursuant to the law of the jurisdiction designated in Section 9–301(1) or 9–305(c) and the new debtor is located in another jurisdiction, the following rules apply:

(1) The financing statement is effective to perfect a security interest in collateral acquired by the new debtor before, and within four months after, the new debtor becomes bound under Section 9–203(d), if the financing statement would have been effective to perfect a security interest in the collateral had the collateral been acquired by the original debtor.

(2) A security interest perfected by the financing statement and which becomes perfected under the law of the other jurisdiction before the earlier of the time the financing statement would have become ineffective under the law of the jurisdiction designated in Section 9–301(1) or 9–305(c) or the expiration of the four-month period remains perfected thereafter. A security interest that is perfected by the financing statement but which does not become perfected under the law of the other jurisdiction before the earlier time or event becomes unperfected and is deemed never to have been perfected as against a purchaser of the collateral for value.

As amended in 2010.

Official Comment

1. **Source.** Former Section 9–103(1)(d), (2)(b), (3)(e), as modified.

2. **Continued Perfection.** Subsections (a) through (g) deal with continued perfection of security interests that have been perfected under the law of another jurisdiction. The fact that the law of a particular jurisdiction ceases to govern perfection under Sections 9–301 through 9–307 does not necessarily mean that a security interest perfected under that law automatically becomes unperfected. To the contrary: This section generally provides that a security interest perfected under the law of one jurisdiction remains perfected for a fixed period of time (four months or one year, depending on the circumstances), even though the jurisdiction whose law governs perfection changes. However, cessation of perfection under the law of the original jurisdiction cuts short the fixed period. The four-month and one-year periods are long enough for a secured party to discover in most cases that the law of a different jurisdiction governs perfection and to reperfect (typically by filing) under the law of that jurisdiction. If a secured party properly reperfects a security interest before it becomes unperfected under subsection (a), then the security interest remains perfected continuously thereafter. See subsection (b).

Example 1: Debtor is a general partnership whose chief executive office is in Pennsylvania. Lender perfects a security interest in Debtor's equipment by filing in Pennsylvania on May 15, 2002. On April 1, 2005, without Lender's knowledge, Debtor moves its chief executive office to New Jersey. Lender's security interest remains perfected for four months after the move. See subsection (a)(2).

Example 2: Debtor is a general partnership whose chief executive office is in Pennsylvania. Lender perfects a security interest in Debtor's equipment by filing in Pennsylvania on May 15, 2002. On April 1, 2007, without Lender's knowledge, Debtor moves its chief executive office to New Jersey. Lender's security interest remains perfected only through May 14, 2007, when the effectiveness of the filed financing statement lapses. See subsection (a)(1). Although, under these facts, Lender would have only a short period of time to discover that Debtor had relocated and to reperfect under New Jersey law, Lender could have protected itself by filing a continuation statement in Pennsylvania before Debtor relocated. By doing so, Lender would have prevented lapse and allowed itself the full four months to discover Debtor's new location and refile there or, if Debtor is in default, to perfect by taking possession of the equipment.

Example 3: Under the facts of Example 2, Lender files a financing statement in New Jersey before the effectiveness of the Pennsylvania financing statement lapses. Under subsection (b), Lender's security interest is continuously perfected beyond May 14, 2007, for a period determined by New Jersey's Article 9.

Subsection (a)(3) allows a one-year period in which to reperfect. The longer period is necessary, because, even with the exercise of due diligence, the secured party may be unable to discover that the collateral has been transferred to a person located in another jurisdiction. In any event, the period is cut short if the financing statement becomes ineffective under the law of the jurisdiction in which it is filed.

Example 4: Debtor is a Pennsylvania corporation. On January 1, Lender perfects a security interest in Debtor's equipment by filing in Pennsylvania. Debtor's shareholders decide to "reincorporate" in Delaware. On March 1, they form a Delaware corporation (Newcorp) into which they merge Debtor. The merger effectuates a transfer of the collateral from Debtor to Newcorp, which thereby becomes a debtor and is located in another jurisdiction. Under subsection (a)(3), the security interest remains perfected for one year after the merger. If a financing statement is filed in Delaware against Newcorp within the year following the merger, then the security interest remains perfected thereafter for a period determined by Delaware's Article 9.

Note that although Newcorp is a "new debtor" as defined in Section 9–102, the application of subsection (a)(3) is not limited to transferees who are new debtors. Note also that, under Section 9–507, the financing statement naming Debtor remains effective even though Newcorp has become the debtor.

Subsection (a) addresses security interests that are perfected (i.e., that have attached and as to which any required perfection step has been taken) before the debtor changes its location. Subsection (h) applies to security interests that have not attached before the location changes. See Comment 7.

3.   **Retroactive Unperfection.** Subsection (b) sets forth the consequences of the failure to reperfect before perfection ceases under subsection (a): the security interest becomes unperfected prospectively and, as against purchasers for value, including buyers and secured parties, but not as against donees or lien creditors, retroactively. The rule applies to agricultural liens, as well. See also Section 9–515 (taking the same approach with respect to lapse). Although this approach creates the potential for circular priorities, the alternative—retroactive unperfection against lien creditors—would create substantial and unjustifiable preference risks.

Example 5: Under the facts of Example 4, six months after the merger, Buyer bought from Newcorp some equipment formerly owned by Debtor. At the time of the purchase, Buyer took subject to Lender's perfected security interest, of which Buyer was unaware. See Section 9–315(a)(1). However, subsection (b) provides that if Lender fails to reperfect in Delaware within a year after the merger, its security interest becomes unperfected and is deemed never to have been perfected against Buyer. Having given value and received delivery of the equipment without knowledge of the security interest and before it was perfected, Buyer would take free of the security interest. See Section 9–317(b).

Example 6: Under the facts of Example 4, one month before the merger, Debtor created a security interest in certain equipment in favor of Financer, who perfected by filing in Pennsylvania. At that time, Financer's security interest is subordinate to Lender's. See Section 9–322(a)(1). Financer reperfects by filing in Delaware within a year after the merger, but Lender fails to do so. Under subsection (b), Lender's security interest is deemed never to have been perfected against Financer, a purchaser for value. Consequently, under Section 9–322(a)(2), Financer's security interest is now senior.

Of course, the expiration of the time period specified in subsection (a) does not of itself prevent the secured party from later reperfecting under the law of the new jurisdiction. If the secured party does so, however, there will be a gap in perfection, and the secured party may lose priority as a result. Thus, in Example 6, if Lender perfects by filing in Delaware more than one year under the merger, it will have a new date of filing and perfection for purposes of Section 9–322(a)(1). Financer's security interest, whose perfection dates back to the filing in Pennsylvania under subsection (b), will remain senior.

4.   **Possessory Security Interests.** Subsection (c) deals with continued perfection of possessory security interests. It applies not only to security interests perfected solely by the secured party's having taken possession of the collateral. It also applies to security interests perfected by a method that includes as an element of perfection the secured party's having taken possession, such as perfection by taking delivery of a certificated security in registered form, see Section 9–313(a), and perfection by obtaining control over a certificated security. See Section 9–314(a).

5.   **Goods Covered by Certificate of Title.** Subsections (d) and (e) address continued perfection of a security interest in goods covered by a certificate of title. The following examples explain the operation of those subsections.

Example 7: Debtor's automobile is covered by a certificate of title issued by Illinois. Lender perfects a security interest in the automobile by complying with Illinois' certificate-of-title statute. Thereafter, Debtor applies for a certificate of title in Indiana. Six months thereafter, Creditor acquires a judicial lien on the automobile. Under Section 9–303(b), Illinois law ceases to govern perfection; rather, once Debtor delivers the application and applicable fee to the appropriate Indiana authority, Indiana law governs. Nevertheless, under Indiana's Section 9–316(d), Lender's security interest remains perfected until it would become unperfected under Illinois law had no certificate of title been issued by Indiana. (For example, Illinois' certificate-of-title statute may provide that the surrender of an Illinois certificate of title in connection with the issuance of a certificate of title by another jurisdiction causes a security interest noted thereon to become unperfected.) If Lender's security interest remains perfected, it is senior to Creditor's judicial lien.

Example 8: Under the facts in Example 7, five months after Debtor applies for an Indiana certificate of title, Debtor sells the automobile to Buyer. Under subsection (e)(2), because Lender did not reperfect within the four months after the goods became covered by the Indiana certificate of title, Lender's security interest is deemed never to have been perfected against Buyer. Under Section 9–317(b), Buyer is likely to take free of the security interest. Lender could have protected itself by perfecting its security interest either under Indiana's certificate-of-title statute, see Section 9–311, or, if it had a right to do so under an agreement or Section 9–609, by taking possession of the automobile. See Section 9–313(b).

The results in Examples 7 and 8 do not depend on the fact that the original perfection was achieved by notation on a certificate of title. Subsection (d) applies regardless of the method by which a security interest is perfected under the law of another jurisdiction when the goods became covered by a certificate of title from this State.

Section 9–337 affords protection to a limited class of persons buying or acquiring a security interest in the goods while a security interest is perfected under the law of another jurisdiction but after this State has issued a clean certificate of title.

6. **Deposit Accounts, Letter-of-Credit Rights, and Investment Property.** Subsections (f) and (g) address changes in the jurisdiction of a bank, issuer of an uncertificated security, issuer of or nominated person under a letter of credit, securities intermediary, and commodity intermediary. The provisions are analogous to those of subsections (a) and (b).

7. **Security Interests that Attach after Debtor Changes Location.** In contrast to subsections (a) and (b), which address security interests that are perfected (i.e., that have attached and as to which any required perfection step has been taken) before the debtor changes its location, subsection (h) addresses security interests that attach within four months after the debtor changes its location. Under subsection (h), a filed financing statement that would have been effective to perfect a security interest in the collateral if the debtor had not changed its location is effective to perfect a security interest in collateral acquired within four months after the relocation.

Example 9: Debtor, an individual whose principal residence is in Pennsylvania, grants to Lender a security interest in Debtor's existing and after-acquired inventory. Lender perfects the security interest by filing a proper financing statement in Pennsylvania on January 2, 2014. On March 31, 2014, Debtor's principal residence is relocated to New Jersey. Upon the relocation, New Jersey law governs perfection of a security interest in Debtor's inventory. See Sections 9–301, 9–307. Under New Jersey's Section 9–316(a), Lender's security interest in Debtor's inventory on hand at the time of the relocation remains perfected for four months thereafter. Had Debtor not relocated, the financing statement filed in Pennsylvania would have been effective to perfect Lender's security interest in inventory acquired by Debtor after March 31, 2014. Accordingly, under subsection (h), the financing statement is effective to perfect Lender's security interest in inventory that Debtor acquires within the four months after Debtor's location changed.

In Example 9, Lender's security interest in the inventory acquired within the four months after Debtor's relocation will be perfected when it attaches. It will remain perfected if, before the expiration of the four-month period, the security interest is perfected under the law of New Jersey. Otherwise, the security interest will become unperfected at the end of the four-month period and will be deemed never to have been perfected as against a purchaser for value. See subsection (h)(2).

8. **Collateral Acquired by New Debtor.** Subsection (i) is similar to subsection (h). Whereas subsection (h) addresses security interests that attach within four months after a debtor changes its location, subsection (i) addresses security interests that attach within four months after a new debtor becomes bound as debtor by a security agreement entered into by another person. Subsection (i) also addresses collateral acquired by the new debtor before it becomes bound.

Example 10: Debtor, a Pennsylvania corporation, grants to Lender a security interest in Debtor's existing and after-acquired inventory. Lender perfects the security interest by filing a proper financing statement in Pennsylvania on January 2, 2014. On March 31, 2014, Debtor merges into Survivor, a Delaware corporation. Because Survivor is located in Delaware, Delaware law governs perfection of a security interest in Survivor's inventory. See Sections 9–301, 9–307. Under Delaware's Section 9–316(a), Lender's security interest in the inventory that Survivor acquired from Debtor remains perfected for one year after the transfer. See Comment 2. By virtue of the merger, Survivor becomes bound as debtor by Debtor's security agreement. See Section 9–203(d). As a consequence, Lender's security interest attaches to all of Survivor's inventory under Section 9–203, and Lender's collateral now includes inventory in which Debtor never had an interest. The financing statement filed in Pennsylvania against Debtor is effective under Delaware's Section 9–316(i) to perfect Lender's security interest in inventory that Survivor acquired before, and within the four months after, becoming bound as debtor by Debtor's security agreement. This is because the financing statement filed in Pennsylvania would have been effective to perfect Lender's security interest in this collateral had Debtor, rather than Survivor, acquired it.

If the financing statement is effective, Lender's security interest in the collateral that Survivor acquired before, and within four months after, Survivor became bound as debtor will be perfected upon attachment. It will remain perfected if, before the expiration of the four-month period, the security interest is perfected under Delaware law. Otherwise, the security interest will become unperfected at the end of the four-month period and will be deemed never to have been perfected as against a purchaser for value.

Section 9–325 contains special rules governing the priority of competing security interests in collateral that is transferred, by merger or otherwise, to a new debtor or other person who becomes a debtor with respect to the collateral. Section 9–326 contains special rules governing the priority of competing security interests in collateral acquired by a new debtor other than by transfer from the original debtor.

9. **Agricultural Liens.** This section does not apply to agricultural liens.

Example 11: Supplier holds an agricultural lien on corn. The lien arises under an Iowa statute. Supplier perfects by filing a financing statement in Iowa, where the corn is located. See Section 9–302. Debtor stores the corn in Missouri. Assume the Iowa agricultural lien survives or an agricultural lien arises under Missouri law (matters that this Article does not govern). Once the corn is located in Missouri, Missouri becomes the jurisdiction whose law governs perfection. See Section 9–302. Thus, the agricultural lien will not be perfected unless Supplier files a financing statement in Missouri.

As amended in 2000 and 2010.

[SUBPART 3. PRIORITY]

§ 9–317.   Interests That Take Priority Over or Take Free of Security Interest or Agricultural Lien.

(a)   **[Conflicting security interests and rights of lien creditors.]** A security interest or agricultural lien is subordinate to the rights of:

(1)   a person entitled to priority under Section 9–322; and

(2)   except as otherwise provided in subsection (e), a person that becomes a lien creditor before the earlier of the time:

(A)   the security interest or agricultural lien is perfected; or

(B)   one of the conditions specified in Section 9–203(b)(3) is met and a financing statement covering the collateral is filed.

(b)   **[Buyers that receive delivery.]** Except as otherwise provided in subsection (e), a buyer, other than a secured party, of tangible chattel paper, tangible documents, goods, instruments, or a certificated security takes free of a security interest or agricultural lien if the buyer gives value and receives delivery of the collateral without knowledge of the security interest or agricultural lien and before it is perfected.

(c)   **[Lessees that receive delivery.]** Except as otherwise provided in subsection (e), a lessee of goods takes free of a security interest or agricultural lien if the lessee gives value and receives delivery of the collateral without knowledge of the security interest or agricultural lien and before it is perfected.

(d)   **[Licensees and buyers of certain collateral.]** A licensee of a general intangible or a buyer, other than a secured party, of collateral other than tangible chattel paper, tangible documents, goods, instruments, or a certificated security takes free of a security interest if the licensee or buyer gives value without knowledge of the security interest and before it is perfected.

(e) **[Purchase-money security interest.]** Except as otherwise provided in Sections 9–320 and 9–321, if a person files a financing statement with respect to a purchase-money security interest before or within 20 days after the debtor receives delivery of the collateral, the security interest takes priority over the rights of a buyer, lessee, or lien creditor which arise between the time the security interest attaches and the time of filing.

As amended in 2000, 2003 and 2010.

Official Comment

1. **Source.** Former Sections 9–301, 2A–307(2).

2. **Scope of This Section.** As did former Section 9–301, this section lists the classes of persons who take priority over, or take free of, an unperfected security interest. Section 9–308 explains when a security interest or agricultural lien is "perfected." A security interest that has attached (see Section 9–203) but as to which a required perfection step has not been taken is "unperfected." Certain provisions have been moved from former Section 9–301. The definition of "lien creditor" now appears in Section 9–102, and the rules governing priority in future advances are found in Section 9–323.

3. **Competing Security Interests.** Section 9–322 states general rules for determining priority among conflicting security interests and refers to other sections that state special rules of priority in a variety of situations. The security interests given priority under Section 9–322 and the other sections to which it refers take priority in general even over a perfected security interest. *A fortiori* they take priority over an unperfected security interest.

4. **Filed but Unattached Security Interest vs. Lien Creditor.** Under former Section 9–301(1)(b), a lien creditor's rights had priority over an unperfected security interest. Perfection required attachment (former Section 9–303), and attachment required the giving of value (former Section 9–203). It followed that, if a secured party had filed a financing statement, but the debtor had not entered into a security agreement and value had not yet been given, an intervening lien creditor whose lien arose after filing but before attachment of the security interest acquired rights that are senior to those of the secured party who later gives value. This result comported with the *nemo dat* concept: When the security interest attached, the collateral was already subject to the judicial lien.

On the other hand, this approach treated the first secured advance differently from all other advances, even in circumstances in which a security agreement covering the collateral had been entered into before the judicial lien attached. The special rule for future advances in former Section 9–301(4) (substantially reproduced in Section 9–323(b)) afforded priority to a discretionary advance made by a secured party within 45 days after the lien creditor's rights arose as long as the secured party was "perfected" when the lien creditor's lien arose—i.e., as long as the advance was not the first one and an earlier advance had been made.

Subsection (a)(2) revises former Section 9–301(1)(b) and, in appropriate cases, treats the first advance the same as subsequent advances. More specifically, a judicial lien that arises after the security-agreement condition of Section 9–203(b)(3) is satisfied and a financing statement is filed, but before the security interest attaches and becomes perfected, is subordinate to all advances secured by the security interest, even the first advance, except as otherwise provided in Section 9–323(b). However, if the security interest becomes unperfected (e.g., because the effectiveness of the filed financing statement lapses) before the judicial lien arises, the security interest is subordinate. If a financing statement is filed but a security interest does not attach, then no priority contest arises. The lien creditor has the only enforceable claim to the property.

5. **Security Interest of Consignor or Receivables Buyer vs. Lien Creditor.** Section 1–201(b)(35) defines "security interest" to include the interest of most true consignors of goods and the interest of most buyers of certain receivables (accounts, chattel paper, payment intangibles, and promissory notes). A consignee of goods or a seller of accounts or chattel paper each is deemed to have rights in the collateral which a lien creditor may reach, as long as the competing security interest of the consignor or buyer is unperfected. This is so even though, as between the consignor and the debtor-consignee, the latter has only limited rights, and, as between the buyer and debtor-seller, the latter does not have any rights in the collateral. See Sections 9–318 (seller), 9–319 (consignee). Security interests arising from sales of payment intangibles and promissory notes are automatically

perfected. See Section 9–309. Accordingly, a subsequent judicial lien always would be subordinate to the rights of a buyer of those types of receivables.

6. **Purchasers Other Than Secured Parties.** Subsections (b), (c), and (d) afford priority over an unperfected security interest to certain purchasers (other than secured parties) of collateral. They derive from former Sections 9–301(1)(c), 2A–307(2), and 9–301(d). Former Section 9–301(1)(c) and (1)(d) provided that unperfected security interests are "subordinate" to the rights of certain purchasers. But, as former Comment 9 suggested, the practical effect of subordination in this context is that the purchaser takes free of the security interest. To avoid any possible misinterpretation, subsections (b) and (d) of this section use the phrase "takes free."

Subsection (b) governs goods, as well as intangibles of the type whose transfer is effected by physical delivery of the representative piece of paper (tangible chattel paper, tangible documents, instruments, and security certificates). To obtain priority, a buyer must both give value and receive delivery of the collateral without knowledge of the existing security interest and before perfection. Even if the buyer gave value without knowledge and before perfection, the buyer would take subject to the security interest if perfection occurred before physical delivery of the collateral to the buyer. Subsection (c) contains a similar rule with respect to lessees of goods. Note that a lessee of goods in ordinary course of business takes free of all security interests created by the lessor, even if perfected. See Section 9–321.

Normally, there will be no question when a buyer of tangible chattel paper, tangible documents, instruments, or security certificates "receives delivery" of the property. See Section 1–201 (defining "delivery"). However, sometimes a buyer or lessee of goods, such as complex machinery, takes delivery of the goods in stages and completes assembly at its own location. Under those circumstances, the buyer or lessee "receives delivery" within the meaning of subsections (b) and (c) when, after an inspection of the portion of the goods remaining with the seller or lessor, it would be apparent to a potential lender to the seller or lessor that another person might have an interest in the goods.

The rule of subsection (b) obviously is not appropriate where the collateral consists of intangibles and there is no representative piece of paper whose physical delivery is the only or the customary method of transfer. Therefore, with respect to such intangibles (including accounts, electronic chattel paper, electronic documents, general intangibles, and investment property other than certificated securities), subsection (d) gives priority to any buyer who gives value without knowledge, and before perfection, of the security interest. A licensee of a general intangible takes free of an unperfected security interest in the general intangible under the same circumstances. Note that a licensee of a general intangible in ordinary course of business takes rights under a nonexclusive license free of security interests created by the licensor, even if perfected. See Section 9–321.

Unless Section 9–109 excludes the transaction from this Article, a buyer of accounts, chattel paper, payment intangibles, or promissory notes is a "secured party" (defined in Section 9–102), and subsections (b) and (d) do not determine priority of the security interest created by the sale. Rather, the priority rules generally applicable to competing security interests apply. See Section 9–322.

7. **Agricultural Liens.** Subsections (a), (b), and (c) subordinate unperfected agricultural liens in the same manner in which they subordinate unperfected security interests.

8. **Purchase-Money Security Interests.** Subsection (e) derives from former Section 9–301(2). It provides that, if a purchase-money security interest is perfected by filing no later than 20 days after the debtor receives delivery of the collateral, the security interest takes priority over the rights of buyers, lessees, or lien creditors which arise between the time the security interest attaches and the time of filing. Subsection (e) differs from former Section 9–301(2) in two significant respects. First, subsection (e) protects a purchase-money security interest against all buyers and lessees, not just against transferees in bulk. Second, subsection (e) conditions this protection on filing within 20, as opposed to ten, days after delivery.

Section 9–311(b) provides that compliance with the perfection requirements of a statute or treaty described in Section 9–311(a) "is equivalent to the filing of a financing statement." It follows that a person who perfects a security interest in goods covered by a certificate of title by complying with the perfection requirements of an applicable certificate-of-title statute "files a financing statement" within the meaning of subsection(e).

As amended in 1999, 2000, 2003 and 2010.

§ 9–318.   No Interest Retained in Right to Payment That Is Sold; Rights and Title of Seller of Account or Chattel Paper With Respect to Creditors and Purchasers.

(a)   **[Seller retains no interest.]** A debtor that has sold an account, chattel paper, payment intangible, or promissory note does not retain a legal or equitable interest in the collateral sold.

(b)   **[Deemed rights of debtor if buyer's security interest unperfected.]** For purposes of determining the rights of creditors of, and purchasers for value of an account or chattel paper from, a debtor that has sold an account or chattel paper, while the buyer's security interest is unperfected, the debtor is deemed to have rights and title to the account or chattel paper identical to those the debtor sold.

Official Comment

1.   **Source.** New.

2.   **Sellers of Accounts, Chattel Paper, Payment Intangibles, and Promissory Notes.** Section 1–201(b)(35) defines "security interest" to include the interest of a buyer of accounts, chattel paper, payment intangibles, or promissory notes. See also Section 9–109(a) and Comment 5. Subsection (a) makes explicit what was implicit, but perfectly obvious, under former Article 9: The fact that a sale of an account or chattel paper gives rise to a "security interest" does not imply that the seller retains an interest in the property that has been sold. To the contrary, a seller of an account or chattel paper retains no interest whatsoever in the property to the extent that it has been sold. Subsection (a) also applies to sales of payment intangibles and promissory notes, transactions that were not covered by former Article 9. Neither this Article nor the definition of "security interest" in Section 1–201 provides rules for distinguishing sales transactions from those that create a security interest securing an obligation.

3.   **Buyers of Accounts and Chattel Paper.** Another aspect of sales of accounts and chattel paper also was implicit, and equally obvious, under former Article 9: If the buyer's security interest is unperfected, then for purposes of determining the rights of certain third parties, the seller (debtor) is deemed to have all rights and title that the seller sold. The seller is deemed to have these rights even though, as between the parties, it has sold all its rights to the buyer. Subsection (b) makes this explicit. As a consequence of subsection (b), if the buyer's security interest is unperfected, the seller can transfer, and the creditors of the seller can reach, the account or chattel paper as if it had not been sold.

Example: Debtor sells accounts or chattel paper to Buyer–1 and retains no interest in them. Buyer–1 does not file a financing statement. Debtor then sells the same receivables to Buyer–2. Buyer–2 files a proper financing statement. Having sold the receivables to Buyer–1, Debtor would not have any rights in the collateral so as to permit Buyer–2's security (ownership) interest to attach. Nevertheless, under this section, for purposes of determining the rights of purchasers for value from Debtor, Debtor is deemed to have the rights that Debtor sold. Accordingly, Buyer–2's security interest attaches, is perfected by the filing, and, under Section 9–322, is senior to Buyer–1's interest.

4.   **Effect of Perfection.** If the security interest of a buyer of accounts or chattel paper is perfected the usual result would take effect: transferees from and creditors of the seller could not acquire an interest in the sold accounts or chattel paper. The same result generally would occur if payment intangibles or promissory notes were sold, inasmuch as the buyer's security interest is automatically perfected under Section 9–309. However, in certain circumstances a purchaser who takes possession of a promissory note will achieve priority, under Sections 9–330 or 9–331, over the security interest of an earlier buyer of the promissory note. It necessarily follows that the seller in those circumstances retains the power to transfer the promissory note, as if it had not been sold, to a purchaser who obtains priority under either of those sections. See Section 9–203(b)(3), Comment 6.

As amended in 2010.

§ 9–319.   Rights and Title of Consignee With Respect to Creditors and Purchasers.

(a)   **[Consignee has consignor's rights.]** Except as otherwise provided in subsection (b), for purposes of determining the rights of creditors of, and purchasers for value of goods from, a consignee, while the goods are in the possession of the consignee, the consignee is deemed to have rights and title to the goods identical to those the consignor had or had power to transfer.

(b)   **[Applicability of other law.]** For purposes of determining the rights of a creditor of a consignee, law other than this article determines the rights and title of a consignee while goods are in the consignee's possession if, under this part, a perfected security interest held by the consignor would have priority over the rights of the creditor.

Official Comment

1.   **Source.** New.

2.   **Consignments.** This section takes an approach to consignments similar to that taken by Section 9–318 with respect to buyers of accounts and chattel paper. Revised Section 1–201(b)(35) defines "security interest" to include the interest of a consignor of goods under many true consignments. Section 9–319(a) provides that, for purposes of determining the rights of certain third parties, the consignee is deemed to acquire all rights and title that the consignor had, if the consignor's security interest is unperfected. The consignee acquires these rights even though, as between the parties, it purchases a limited interest in the goods (as would be the case in a true consignment, under which the consignee acquires only the interest of a bailee). As a consequence of this section, creditors of the consignee can acquire judicial liens and security interests in the goods.

Insofar as creditors of the consignee are concerned, this Article to a considerable extent reformulates the former law, which appeared in former Sections 2–326 and 9–114, without changing the results. However, neither Article 2 nor former Article 9 specifically addresses the rights of non-ordinary course buyers from the consignee. Former Section 9–114 contained priority rules applicable to security interests in consigned goods. Under this Article, the priority rules for purchase-money security interests in inventory apply to consignments. See Section 9–103(d). Accordingly, a special section containing priority rules for consignments no longer is needed. Section 9–317 determines whether the rights of a judicial lien creditor are senior to the interest of the consignor, Sections 9–322 and 9–324 govern competing security interests in consigned goods, and Sections 9–317, 9–315, and 9–320 determine whether a buyer takes free of the consignor's interest.

The following example explains the operation of this section:

Example 1: SP–1 delivers goods to Debtor in a transaction constituting a "consignment" as defined in Section 9–102. SP–1 does not file a financing statement. Debtor then grants a security interest in the goods to SP–2. SP–2 files a proper financing statement. Assuming Debtor is a mere bailee, as in a "true" consignment, Debtor would not have any rights in the collateral (beyond those of a bailee) so as to permit SP–2's security interest to attach to any greater rights. Nevertheless, under this section, for purposes of determining the rights of Debtor's creditors, Debtor is deemed to acquire SP–1's rights. Accordingly, SP–2's security interest attaches, is perfected by the filing, and, under Section 9–322, is senior to SP–1's interest.

3.   **Effect of Perfection.** Subsection (b) contains a special rule with respect to consignments that are perfected. If application of this Article would result in the consignor having priority over a competing creditor, then other law determines the rights and title of the consignee.

Example 2: SP–1 delivers goods to Debtor in a transaction constituting a "consignment" as defined in Section 9–102. SP–1 files a proper financing statement. Debtor then grants a security interest in the goods to SP–2. Under Section 9–322, SP–1's security interest is senior to SP–2's. Subsection (b) indicates that, for purposes of determining SP–2's rights, other law determines the rights and title of the consignee. If, for example, a consignee obtains only the special property of a bailee, then SP–2's security interest would attach only to that special property.

Example 3: SP–1 obtains a security interest in all Debtor's existing and after-acquired inventory. SP–1 perfects its security interest with a proper filing. Then SP–2 delivers goods to Debtor in a transaction constituting a "consignment" as defined in Section 9–102. SP–2 files a proper financing statement but does not send notification to SP–1 under Section 9–324(b). Accordingly, SP–2's security interest is junior to SP–1's under Section 9–322(a). Under Section 9–319(a), Debtor is deemed to have the consignor's rights and title, so that SP–1's security interest attaches to SP–2's ownership interest in the goods. Thereafter, Debtor grants a security interest in the goods to SP–3, and SP–3 perfects by filing. Because SP–2's perfected security interest is senior to SP–3's under Section 9–322(a), Section 9–319(b) applies: Other law determines Debtor's rights and title to the goods insofar as SP–3 is concerned, and SP–3's security interest attaches to those rights.

As amended in 2010.

§ 9–320.   Buyer of Goods.

(a)   **[Buyer in ordinary course of business.]** Except as otherwise provided in subsection (e), a buyer in ordinary course of business, other than a person buying farm products from a person engaged in farming operations, takes free of a security interest created by the buyer's seller, even if the security interest is perfected and the buyer knows of its existence.

(b)   **[Buyer of consumer goods.]** Except as otherwise provided in subsection (e), a buyer of goods from a person who used or bought the goods for use primarily for personal, family, or household purposes takes free of a security interest, even if perfected, if the buyer buys:

(1)   without knowledge of the security interest;

(2)   for value;

(3)   primarily for the buyer's personal, family, or household purposes; and

(4)   before the filing of a financing statement covering the goods.

(c)   **[Effectiveness of filing for subsection (b).]** To the extent that it affects the priority of a security interest over a buyer of goods under subsection (b), the period of effectiveness of a filing made in the jurisdiction in which the seller is located is governed by Section 9–316(a) and (b).

(d)   **[Buyer in ordinary course of business at wellhead or minehead.]** A buyer in ordinary course of business buying oil, gas, or other minerals at the wellhead or minehead or after extraction takes free of an interest arising out of an encumbrance.

(e)   **[Possessory security interest not affected.]** Subsections (a) and (b) do not affect a security interest in goods in the possession of the secured party under Section 9–313.

Official Comment

1.   **Source.** Former Section 9–307.

2.   **Scope of This Section.** This section states when buyers of goods take free of a security interest even though perfected. Of course, a buyer who takes free of a perfected security interest takes free of an unperfected one. Section 9–317 should be consulted to determine what purchasers, in addition to the buyers covered in this section, take free of an unperfected security interest. Article 2 states general rules on purchase of goods from a seller with defective or voidable title (Section 2–403).

3.   **Buyers in Ordinary Course.** Subsection (a) derives from former Section 9–307(1). The definition of "buyer in ordinary course of business" in Section 1–201 restricts its application to buyers "from a person, other than a pawnbroker, in the business of selling goods of that kind." Thus subsection (a) applies primarily to inventory collateral. The subsection further excludes from its operation buyers of "farm products" (defined in Section 9–102) from a person engaged in farming operations. The buyer in ordinary course of business is defined as one who buys goods "in good faith, without knowledge that the sale violates the rights of another person and in the ordinary course." Subsection (a) provides that such a buyer takes free of a security interest, even though perfected, and even though the buyer knows the security interest exists. Reading the definition together with the rule of law results in the buyer's taking free if the buyer merely knows that a security interest covers the goods but taking subject if the buyer knows, in addition, that the sale violates a term in an agreement with the secured party.

As did former Section 9–307(1), subsection (a) applies only to security interests created by the seller of the goods to the buyer in ordinary course. However, under certain circumstances a buyer in ordinary course who buys goods that were encumbered with a security interest created by a person other than the seller may take free of the security interest, as Example 2 explains. See also Comment 6, below.

Example 1: Manufacturer, who is in the business of manufacturing appliances, owns manufacturing equipment subject to a perfected security interest in favor of Lender. Manufacturer sells the equipment to Dealer, who is in the business of buying and selling used equipment. Buyer buys the equipment from Dealer. Even if Buyer qualifies as a buyer in the ordinary course of business, Buyer does not take free of Lender's security interest under subsection (a), because Dealer did not create the security interest; Manufacturer did.

Example 2: Manufacturer, who is in the business of manufacturing appliances, owns manufacturing equipment subject to a perfected security interest in favor of Lender. Manufacturer sells the equipment to

Dealer, who is in the business of buying and selling used equipment. Lender learns of the sale but does nothing to assert its security interest. Buyer buys the equipment from Dealer. Inasmuch as Lender's acquiescence constitutes an "entrusting" of the goods to Dealer within the meaning of Section 2–403(3) Buyer takes free of Lender's security interest under Section 2–403(2) if Buyer qualifies as a buyer in ordinary course of business.

4.   **Buyers of Farm Products.** This section does not enable a buyer of farm products to take free of a security interest created by the seller, even if the buyer is a buyer in ordinary course of business. However, a buyer of farm products may take free of a security interest under Section 1324 of the Food Security Act of 1985, 7 U.S.C. § 1631.

5.   **Buyers of Consumer Goods.** Subsection (b), which derives from former Section 9–307(2), deals with buyers of collateral that the debtor-seller holds as "consumer goods" (defined in Section 9–102). Under Section 9–309(1), a purchase-money interest in consumer goods, except goods that are subject to a statute or treaty described in Section 9–311(a) (such as automobiles that are subject to a certificate-of-title statute), is perfected automatically upon attachment. There is no need to file to perfect. Under subsection (b) a buyer of consumer goods takes free of a security interest, even though perfected, if the buyer buys (1) without knowledge of the security interest, (2) for value, (3) primarily for the buyer's own personal, family, or household purposes, and (4) before a financing statement is filed.

As to purchase money-security interests which are perfected without filing under Section 9–309(1): A secured party may file a financing statement, although filing is not required for perfection. If the secured party does file, all buyers take subject to the security interest. If the secured party does not file, a buyer who meets the qualifications stated in the preceding paragraph takes free of the security interest.

As to security interests for which a perfection step is required: This category includes all non-purchase-money security interests, and all security interests, whether or not purchase-money, in goods subject to a statute or treaty described in Section 9–311(a), such as automobiles covered by a certificate-of-title statute. As long as the required perfection step has not been taken and the security interest remains unperfected, not only the buyers described in subsection (b) but also the purchasers described in Section 9–317 will take free of the security interest. After a financing statement has been filed or the perfection requirements of the applicable certificate-of-title statute have been complied with (compliance is the equivalent of filing a financing statement; see Section 9–311(b)), all subsequent buyers, under the rule of subsection (b), are subject to the security interest.

The rights of a buyer under subsection (b) turn on whether a financing statement has been filed against consumer goods. Occasionally, a debtor changes his or her location after a filing is made. Subsection (c), which derives from former Section 9–103(1)(d)(iii), deals with the continued effectiveness of the filing under those circumstances. It adopts the rules of Sections 9–316(a) and (b). These rules are explained in the Comments to that section.

6.   **Authorized Dispositions.** The limitations that subsections (a) and (b) impose on the persons who may take free of a security interest apply of course only to unauthorized sales by the debtor. If the secured party authorized the sale in an express agreement or otherwise, the buyer takes free under Section 9–315(a) without regard to the limitations of this section. (That section also states the right of a secured party to the proceeds of a sale, authorized or unauthorized.) Moreover, the buyer also takes free if the secured party waived or otherwise is precluded from asserting its security interest against the buyer. See Section 1–103.

7.   **Oil, Gas, and Other Minerals.** Under subsection (d), a buyer in ordinary course of business of minerals at the wellhead or minehead or after extraction takes free of a security interest created by the seller. Specifically, it provides that qualified buyers take free not only of Article 9 security interests but also of interests "arising out of an encumbrance." As defined in Section 9–102, the term "encumbrance" means "a right, other than an ownership interest, in real property." Thus, to the extent that a mortgage encumbers minerals not only before but also after extraction, subsection (d) enables a buyer in ordinary course of the minerals to take free of the mortgage. This subsection does not, however, enable these buyers to take free of interests arising out of ownership interests in the real property. This issue is significant only in a minority of states. Several of them have adopted special statutes and nonuniform amendments to Article 9 to provide special protections to mineral owners, whose interests often are highly fractionalized in the case of oil and gas. See Terry I. Cross, *Oil and Gas Product Liens— Statutory Security Interests for Producers and Royalty Owners Under the Statutes of Kansas, New Mexico, Oklahoma, Texas and Wyoming,* 50 Consumer Fin. L. Q. Rep. 418 (1996). Inasmuch as a complete resolution of the issue would require the addition of complex provisions to this Article, and there are good reasons to believe that a uniform solution would not be feasible, this Article leaves its resolution to other legislation.

8.   **Possessory Security Interests.** Subsection (e) is new. It rejects the holding of *Tanbro Fabrics Corp. v. Deering Milliken, Inc.*, 350 N.E.2d 590 (N.Y. 1976) and, together with Section 9–317(b), prevents a buyer of goods collateral from taking free of a security interest if the collateral is in the possession of the secured party. "The secured party" referred in subsection (e) is the holder of the security interest referred to in subsection (a) or (b). Section 9–313 determines whether a secured party is in possession for purposes of this section. Under some circumstances, Section 9–313 provides that a secured party is in possession of collateral even if the collateral is in the physical possession of a third party.

§ 9–321.   Licensee of General Intangible and Lessee of Goods in Ordinary Course of Business.

(a)   **["Licensee in ordinary course of business."]** In this section, "licensee in ordinary course of business" means a person that becomes a licensee of a general intangible in good faith, without knowledge that the license violates the rights of another person in the general intangible, and in the ordinary course from a person in the business of licensing general intangibles of that kind. A person becomes a licensee in the ordinary course if the license to the person comports with the usual or customary practices in the kind of business in which the licensor is engaged or with the licensor's own usual or customary practices.

(b)   **[Rights of licensee in ordinary course of business.]** A licensee in ordinary course of business takes its rights under a nonexclusive license free of a security interest in the general intangible created by the licensor, even if the security interest is perfected and the licensee knows of its existence.

(c)   **[Rights of lessee in ordinary course of business.]** A lessee in ordinary course of business takes its leasehold interest free of a security interest in the goods created by the lessor, even if the security interest is perfected and the lessee knows of its existence.

Official Comment

1.   **Source.** Derived from Sections 2A–103(1)(*o*), 2A–307(3).

2.   **Licensee in Ordinary Course.** Like the analogous rules in Section 9–320(a) with respect to buyers in ordinary course and subsection (c) with respect to lessees in ordinary course, the new rule in subsection (b) reflects the expectations of the parties and the marketplace: a licensee under a nonexclusive license takes subject to a security interest unless the secured party authorizes the license free of the security interest or other, controlling law such as that of this section (protecting ordinary-course licensees) dictates a contrary result. See Sections 9–201, 9–315. The definition of "licensee in ordinary course of business" in subsection (a) is modeled upon that of "buyer in ordinary course of business."

3.   **Lessee in Ordinary Course.** Subsection (c) contains the rule formerly found in Section 2A–307(3). The rule works in the same way as that of Section 9–320(a).

§ 9–322.   Priorities Among Conflicting Security Interests in and Agricultural Liens on Same Collateral.

(a)   **[General priority rules.]** Except as otherwise provided in this section, priority among conflicting security interests and agricultural liens in the same collateral is determined according to the following rules:

(1)   Conflicting perfected security interests and agricultural liens rank according to priority in time of filing or perfection. Priority dates from the earlier of the time a filing covering the collateral is first made or the security interest or agricultural lien is first perfected, if there is no period thereafter when there is neither filing nor perfection.

(2)   A perfected security interest or agricultural lien has priority over a conflicting unperfected security interest or agricultural lien.

(3)   The first security interest or agricultural lien to attach or become effective has priority if conflicting security interests and agricultural liens are unperfected.

(b)   **[Time of perfection: proceeds and supporting obligations.]** For the purposes of subsection (a)(1):

(1)   the time of filing or perfection as to a security interest in collateral is also the time of filing or perfection as to a security interest in proceeds; and

(2)   the time of filing or perfection as to a security interest in collateral supported by a supporting obligation is also the time of filing or perfection as to a security interest in the supporting obligation.

(c)   **[Special priority rules: proceeds and supporting obligations.]** Except as otherwise provided in subsection (f), a security interest in collateral which qualifies for priority over a conflicting security interest under Section 9–327, 9–328, 9–329, 9–330, or 9–331 also has priority over a conflicting security interest in:

(1)   any supporting obligation for the collateral; and

(2)   proceeds of the collateral if:

(A)   the security interest in proceeds is perfected;

(B)   the proceeds are cash proceeds or of the same type as the collateral; and

(C)   in the case of proceeds that are proceeds of proceeds, all intervening proceeds are cash proceeds, proceeds of the same type as the collateral, or an account relating to the collateral.

(d)   **[First-to-file priority rule for certain collateral.]** Subject to subsection (e) and except as otherwise provided in subsection (f), if a security interest in chattel paper, deposit accounts, negotiable documents, instruments, investment property, or letter-of-credit rights is perfected by a method other than filing, conflicting perfected security interests in proceeds of the collateral rank according to priority in time of filing.

(e)   **[Applicability of subsection (d).]** Subsection (d) applies only if the proceeds of the collateral are not cash proceeds, chattel paper, negotiable documents, instruments, investment property, or letter-of-credit rights.

(f)   **[Limitations on subsections (a) through (e).]** Subsections (a) through (e) are subject to:

(1)   subsection (g) and the other provisions of this part;

(2)   Section 4–210 with respect to a security interest of a collecting bank;

(3)   Section 5–118 with respect to a security interest of an issuer or nominated person; and

(4)   Section 9–110 with respect to a security interest arising under Article 2 or 2A.

(g)   **[Priority under agricultural lien statute.]** A perfected agricultural lien on collateral has priority over a conflicting security interest in or agricultural lien on the same collateral if the statute creating the agricultural lien so provides.

Official Comment

1.   **Source.** Former Section 9–312(5), (6).

2.   **Scope of This Section.** In a variety of situations, two or more people may claim a security interest in the same collateral. This section states general rules of priority among conflicting security interests. As subsection (f) provides, the general rules in subsections (a) through (e) are subject to the rule in subsection (g) governing perfected agricultural liens and to the other rules in this Part of this Article. Rules that override this section include those applicable to purchase-money security interests (Section 9–324) and those qualifying for special priority in particular types of collateral. See, e.g., Section 9–327 (deposit accounts); Section 9–328 (investment property); Section 9–329 (letter-of-credit rights); Section 9–330 (chattel paper and instruments); Section 9–334 (fixtures). In addition, the general rules of sections (a) through (e) are subject to priority rules governing security interests arising under Articles 2, 2A, 4, and 5.

3.   **General Rules.** Subsection (a) contains three general rules. Subsection (a)(1) governs the priority of competing perfected security interests. Subsection (a)(2) governs the priority of competing security interests if one is perfected and the other is not. Subsection (a)(3) governs the priority of competing unperfected security interests. The rules may be regarded as adaptations of the idea, deeply rooted at common law, of a race of diligence among creditors. The first two rules are based on precedence in the time as of which the competing secured parties either

filed their financing statements or obtained perfected security interests. Under subsection (a)(1), the first secured party who files or perfects has priority. Under subsection (a)(2), which is new, a perfected security interest has priority over an unperfected one. Under subsection (a)(3), if both security interests are unperfected, the first to attach has priority. Note that Section 9–709(b) may affect the application of subsection (a) to a filing that occurred before the effective date of this Article and which would be ineffective to perfect a security interest under former Article 9 but effective under this Article.

4. **Competing Perfected Security Interests.** When there is more than one perfected security interest, the security interests rank according to priority in time of filing or perfection. "Filing," of course, refers to the filing of an effective financing statement. "Perfection" refers to the acquisition of a perfected security interest, i.e., one that has attached and as to which any required perfection step has been taken. See Sections 9–308 and 9–309.

Example 1: On February 1, A files a financing statement covering a certain item of Debtor's equipment. On March 1, B files a financing statement covering the same equipment. On April 1, B makes a loan to Debtor and obtains a security interest in the equipment. On May 1, A makes a loan to Debtor and obtains a security interest in the same collateral. A has priority even though B's loan was made earlier and was perfected when made. It makes no difference whether A knew of B's security interest when A made its advance.

The problem stated in Example 1 is peculiar to a notice-filing system under which filing may occur before the security interest attaches (see Section 9–502). The justification for determining priority by order of filing lies in the necessity of protecting the filing system—that is, of allowing the first secured party who has filed to make subsequent advances without each time having to check for subsequent filings as a condition of protection. Note, however, that this first-to-file protection is not absolute. For example, Section 9–324 affords priority to certain purchase-money security interests, even if a competing secured party was the first to file or perfect.

Under a notice-filing system, a filed financing statement indicates to third parties that a person may have a security interest in the collateral indicated. With further inquiry, they may discover the complete state of affairs. When a financing statement that is ineffective when filed becomes effective thereafter, the policy underlying the notice-filing system determines the "time of filing" for purposes of subsection (a)(1). For example, the unauthorized filing of an otherwise sufficient initial financing statement becomes authorized, and the financing statement becomes effective, upon the debtor's post-filing authorization or ratification of the filing. See Section 9–509, Comment 3. Because the notice value of the financing statement is independent of the timing of authorization or ratification, the time of the unauthorized filing is the "time of filing" for purposes of subsection (a)(1). The same policy applies to the other priority rules in this part.

Example 2: A and B make non-purchase-money advances secured by the same collateral. The collateral is in Debtor's possession, and neither security interest is perfected when the second advance is made. Whichever secured party first perfects its security interest (by taking possession of the collateral or by filing) takes priority. It makes no difference whether that secured party knows of the other security interest at the time it perfects its own.

The rule of subsection (a)(1), affording priority to the first to file or perfect, applies to security interests that are perfected by any method, including temporarily (Section 9–312) or upon attachment (Section 9–309), even though there may be no notice to creditors or subsequent purchasers and notwithstanding any common-law rule to the contrary. The form of the claim to priority, i.e., filing or perfection, may shift from time to time, and the rank will be based on the first filing or perfection as long as there is no intervening period without filing or perfection. See Section 9–308(c).

Example 3: On October 1, A acquires a temporarily perfected (20-day) security interest, unfiled, in a tangible negotiable document in the debtor's possession under Section 9–312(e). On October 5, B files and thereby perfects a security interest that previously had attached to the same document. On October 10, A files. A has priority, even after the 20-day period expires, regardless of whether A knows of B's security interest when A files. A was the first to perfect and maintained continuous perfection or filing since the start of the 20-day period. However, the perfection of A's security interest extends only "to the extent it arises for new value given." To the extent A's security interest secures advances made by A beyond the 20-day period, its security interest would be subordinate to B's, inasmuch as B was the first to file.

In general, the rule in subsection (a)(1) does not distinguish among various advances made by a secured party. The priority of every advance dates from the earlier of filing or perfection. However, in rare instances, the priority of an advance dates from the time the advance is made. See Example 3 and Section 9–323.

5.   **Priority in After-Acquired Property.** The application of the priority rules to after-acquired property must be considered separately for each item of collateral. Priority does not depend only on time of perfection but may also be based on priority in filing before perfection.

Example 4: On February 1, A makes advances to Debtor under a security agreement covering "all Debtor's machinery, both existing and after-acquired." A promptly files a financing statement. On April 1, B takes a security interest in all Debtor's machinery, existing and after-acquired, to secure an outstanding loan. The following day, B files a financing statement. On May 1, Debtor acquires a new machine. When Debtor acquires rights in the new machine, both A and B acquire security interests in the machine simultaneously. Both security interests are perfected simultaneously. However, A has priority because A filed before B.

When after-acquired collateral is encumbered by more than one security interest, one of the security interests often is a purchase-money security interest that is entitled to special priority under Section 9–324.

6.   **Priority in Proceeds: General Rule.** Subsection (b)(1) follows former Section 9–312(6). It provides that the baseline rules of subsection (a) apply generally to priority conflicts in proceeds except where otherwise provided (e.g., as in subsections (c) through (e)). Under Section 9–203, attachment cannot occur (and therefore, under Section 9–308, perfection cannot occur) as to particular collateral until the collateral itself comes into existence and the debtor has rights in it. Thus, a security interest in proceeds of original collateral does not attach and is not perfected until the proceeds come into existence and the debtor acquires rights in them.

Example 5: On April 1, Debtor authenticates a security agreement granting to A a security interest in all Debtor's existing and after-acquired inventory. The same day, A files a financing statement covering inventory. On May 1, Debtor authenticates a security agreement granting B a security interest in all Debtor's existing and future accounts. On June 1, Debtor sells inventory to a customer on 30-day unsecured credit. When Debtor acquires the account, B's security interest attaches to it and is perfected by B's financing statement. At the very same time, A's security interest attaches to the account as proceeds of the inventory and is automatically perfected. See Section 9–315. Under subsection (b) of this section, for purposes of determining A's priority in the account, the time of filing as to the original collateral (April 1, as to inventory) is also the time of filing as to proceeds (account). Accordingly, A's security interest in the account has priority over B's. Of course, had B filed its financing statement before A filed (e.g., on March 1), then B would have priority in the accounts.

Section 9–324 governs the extent to which a special purchase-money priority in goods or software carries over into the proceeds of the original collateral.

7.   **Priority in Proceeds: Special Rules.** Subsections (c), (d), and (e), which are new, provide additional priority rules for proceeds of collateral in situations where the temporal (first-in-time) rules of subsection (a)(1) are not appropriate. These new provisions distinguish what these Comments refer to as "non-filing collateral" from what they call "filing collateral." As used in these Comments, non-filing collateral is collateral of a type for which perfection may be achieved by a method other than filing (possession or control, mainly) and for which secured parties who so perfect generally do not expect or need to conduct a filing search. More specifically, non-filing collateral is chattel paper, deposit accounts, negotiable documents, instruments, investment property, and letter-of-credit rights. Other collateral—accounts, commercial tort claims, general intangibles, goods, nonnegotiable documents, and payment intangibles—is filing collateral.

8.   **Proceeds of Non-Filing Collateral: Non-Temporal Priority.** Subsection (c)(2) provides a baseline priority rule for proceeds of non-filing collateral which applies if the secured party has taken the steps required for non-temporal priority over a conflicting security interest in non-filing collateral (e.g., control, in the case of deposit accounts, letter-of-credit rights, investment property, and in some cases, electronic negotiable documents, section 9–331). This rule determines priority in proceeds of non-filing collateral whether or not there exists an actual conflicting security interest in the original non-filing collateral. Under subsection (c)(2), the priority in the original collateral continues in proceeds if the security interest in proceeds is perfected and the proceeds are cash proceeds or non-filing proceeds "of the same type" as the original collateral. As used in subsection (c)(2), "type" means a type of collateral defined in the Uniform Commercial Code and should be read broadly. For example, a security is "of the same type" as a security entitlement (i.e., investment property), and a promissory note is "of the same type" as a draft (i.e., an instrument).

Example 6: SP–1 perfects its security interest in investment property by filing. SP–2 perfects subsequently by taking control of a certificated security. Debtor receives cash proceeds of the security (e.g., dividends deposited into Debtor's deposit account). If the first-to-file-or-perfect rule of subsection (a)(1) were applied, SP–1's security interest in the cash proceeds would be senior, although SP–2's security interest continues perfected under Section 9–315 beyond the 20-day period of automatic perfection. This was the result under former Article 9. Under subsection (c), however, SP–2's security interest is senior.

Note that a different result would obtain in Example 6 (i.e., SP–1's security interest would be senior) if SP–1 were to obtain control of the deposit-account proceeds. This is so because subsection (c) is subject to subsection (f), which in turn provides that the priority rules under subsections (a) through (e) are subject to "the other provisions of this part." One of those "other provisions" is Section 9–327, which affords priority to a security interest perfected by control. See Section 9–327(1).

Example 7: SP–1 perfects its security interest in investment property by filing. SP–2 perfects subsequently by taking control of a certificated security. Debtor receives proceeds of the security consisting of a new certificated security issued as a stock dividend on the original collateral. Although the new security is of the same type as the original collateral (i.e., investment property), once the 20-day period of automatic perfection expires (see Section 9–315(d)), SP–2's security interest is unperfected. (SP–2 has not filed or taken delivery or control, and no temporary-perfection rule applies.) Consequently, once the 20-day period expires, subsection (c) does not confer priority, and, under subsection (a)(2), SP–1's security interest in the security is senior. This was the result under former Article 9.

Example 8: SP–1 perfects its security interest in investment property by filing. SP–2 perfects subsequently by taking control of a certificated security and also by filing against investment property. Debtor receives proceeds of the security consisting of a new certificated security issued as a stock dividend of the collateral. Because the new security is of the same type as the original collateral (i.e., investment property) and (unlike Example 7) SP–2's security interest is perfected by filing, SP–2's security interest is senior under subsection (c). If the new security were redeemed by the issuer upon surrender and yet another security were received by Debtor, SP–2's security interest would continue to enjoy priority under subsection (c). The new security would be proceeds of proceeds.

Example 9: SP–1 perfects its security interest in investment property by filing. SP–2 subsequently perfects its security interest in investment property by taking control of a certificated security and also by filing against investment property. Debtor receives proceeds of the security consisting of a dividend check that it deposits to a deposit account. Because the check and the deposit account are cash proceeds, SP–1's and SP–2's security interests in the cash proceeds are perfected under Section 9–315 beyond the 20-day period of automatic perfection. However, SP–2's security interest is senior under subsection (c).

Example 10: SP–1 perfects its security interest in investment property by filing. SP–2 perfects subsequently by taking control of a certificated security and also by filing against investment property. Debtor receives an instrument as proceeds of the security. (Assume that the instrument is not cash proceeds.) Because the instrument is not of the same type as the original collateral (i.e., investment property), SP–2's security interest, although perfected by filing, does not achieve priority under subsection (c). Under the first-to-file-or-perfect rule of subsection (a)(1), SP–1's security interest in the proceeds is senior.

The proceeds of proceeds are themselves proceeds. See Section 9–102 (defining "proceeds" and "collateral"). Sometimes competing security interests arise in proceeds that are several generations removed from the original collateral. As the following example explains, the applicability of subsection (c) may turn on the nature of the intervening proceeds.

Example 11: SP–1 perfects its security interest in Debtor's deposit account by obtaining control. Thereafter, SP–2 files against inventory, (presumably) searches, finds no indication of a conflicting security interest, and advances against Debtor's existing and after-acquired inventory. Debtor uses funds from the deposit account to purchase inventory, which SP–1 can trace as identifiable proceeds of its security interest in Debtor's deposit account, and which SP–2 claims as original collateral. The inventory is sold and the proceeds deposited into *another* deposit account, as to which SP–1 has not obtained control. Subsection (c) does not govern priority in this other deposit account. This deposit account is cash proceeds and is also the same type of collateral as SP–1's original collateral, as required by subsections (c)(2)(A) and (B). However, SP–1's security interest does not satisfy subsection (c)(2)(C) because the inventory proceeds, which intervened between the original deposit account and the deposit account constituting the proceeds at issue, are not cash proceeds, proceeds of the same type as the collateral (original deposit account), or an account relating to the collateral. Stated otherwise, once proceeds other than cash proceeds, proceeds of the same type as the original collateral, or an account relating to the original collateral intervene in the chain of proceeds, priority under subsection (c) is thereafter unavailable. The special priority rule in subsection (d) also is inapplicable to this case. See Comment 9, Example 13, below. Instead, the general first-to-file-or-perfect rule of subsections (a) and (b) apply. Under that rule, SP–1 has priority unless its security interest in the inventory proceeds became unperfected under Section 9–315(d). Had SP–2 filed against inventory before SP–1 obtained control of the original deposit account, then SP–2 would have had priority even if SP–1's security interest in the inventory proceeds remained perfected.

If two security interests in the same original collateral are entitled to priority in an item of proceeds under subsection (c)(2), the security interest having priority in the original collateral has priority in the proceeds.

9. **Proceeds of Non-Filing Collateral: Special Temporal Priority.** Under subsections (d) and (e), if a security interest in non-filing collateral is perfected by a method other than filing (e.g., control or possession), it does not retain its priority over a conflicting security interest in proceeds that are filing collateral. Moreover, it is not entitled to priority in proceeds under the first-to file-or-perfect rule of subsections (a)(1) and (b). Instead, under subsection (d), priority is determined by a new first-to-file rule.

Example 12: SP–1 perfects its security interest in Debtor's deposit account by obtaining control. Thereafter, SP–2 files against equipment, (presumably) searches, finds no indication of a conflicting security interest, and advances against Debtor's equipment. SP–1 then files against Debtor's equipment. Debtor uses funds from the deposit account to purchase equipment, which SP–1 can trace as proceeds of its security interest in Debtor's deposit account. If the first-to-file-or-perfect rule were applied, SP–1's security interest would be senior under subsections (a)(1) and (b), because it was the first to perfect in the original collateral and there was no period during which its security interest was unperfected. Under subsection (d), however, SP–2's security interest would be senior because it filed first. This corresponds with the likely expectations of the parties.

Note that under subsection (e), the first-to-file rule of subsection (d) applies only if the proceeds in question are other than non-filing collateral (i.e., if the proceeds are filing collateral). If the proceeds are non-filing collateral, either the first-to-file-or-perfect rule under subsections (a) and (b) or the non-temporal priority rule in subsection (c) would apply, depending on the facts.

Example 13: SP–1 perfects its security interest in Debtor's deposit account by obtaining control. Thereafter, SP–2 files against inventory, (presumably) searches, finds no indication of a conflicting security interest, and advances against Debtor's existing and after-acquired inventory. Debtor uses funds from the deposit account to purchase inventory, which SP–1 can trace as identifiable proceeds of its security interest in Debtor's deposit account, and which SP–2 claims as original collateral. The inventory is sold and the proceeds deposited into *another* deposit account, as to which SP–1 has not obtained control. As discussed above in Comment 8, Example 11, subsection (c) does not govern priority in this deposit account. Subsection (d) also does not govern, because the proceeds at issue (the deposit account) are cash proceeds. See subsection (e). Rather, the general rules of subsections (a) and (b) govern.

10. **Priority in Supporting Obligations.** Under subsections (b)(2) and (c)(1), a security interest having priority in collateral also has priority in a supporting obligation for that collateral. However, the rules in these subsections are subject to the special rule in Section 9–329 governing the priority of security interests in a letter-of-credit right. See subsection (f). Under Section 9–329, a secured party's failure to obtain control (Section 9–107) of a letter-of-credit right that serves as supporting collateral leaves its security interest exposed to a priming interest of a party who does take control.

11. **Unperfected Security Interests.** Under subsection (a)(3), if conflicting security interests are unperfected, the first to attach has priority. This rule may be of merely theoretical interest, inasmuch as it is hard to imagine a situation where the case would come into litigation without either secured party's having perfected its security interest. If neither security interest had been perfected at the time of the filing of a petition in bankruptcy, ordinarily neither would be good against the trustee in bankruptcy under the Bankruptcy Code.

12. **Agricultural Liens.** Statutes other than this Article may purport to grant priority to an agricultural lien as against a conflicting security interest or agricultural lien. Under subsection (g), if another statute grants priority to an agricultural lien, the agricultural lien has priority only if the same statute creates the agricultural lien and the agricultural lien is perfected. Otherwise, subsection (a) applies the same priority rules to an agricultural lien as to a security interest, regardless of whether the agricultural lien conflicts with another agricultural lien or with a security interest.

Inasmuch as no agricultural lien on proceeds arises under this Article, subsections (b) through (e) do not apply to proceeds of agricultural liens. However, if an agricultural lien has priority under subsection (g) and the statute creating the agricultural lien gives the secured party a lien on proceeds of the collateral subject to the lien, a court should apply the principle of subsection (g) and award priority in the proceeds to the holder of the perfected agricultural lien.

As amended in 2000, 2003 and 2010.

§ 9–323.   Future Advances.

(a)   **[When priority based on time of advance.]** Except as otherwise provided in subsection (c), for purposes of determining the priority of a perfected security interest under Section 9–322(a)(1), perfection of the security interest dates from the time an advance is made to the extent that the security interest secures an advance that:

(1)   is made while the security interest is perfected only:

(A)   under Section 9–309 when it attaches; or

(B)   temporarily under Section 9–312(e), (f), or (g); and

(2)   is not made pursuant to a commitment entered into before or while the security interest is perfected by a method other than under Section 9–309 or 9–312(e), (f), or (g).

(b)   **[Lien creditor.]** Except as otherwise provided in subsection (c), a security interest is subordinate to the rights of a person that becomes a lien creditor to the extent that the security interest secures an advance made more than 45 days after the person becomes a lien creditor unless the advance is made:

(1)   without knowledge of the lien; or

(2)   pursuant to a commitment entered into without knowledge of the lien.

(c)   **[Buyer of receivables.]** Subsections (a) and (b) do not apply to a security interest held by a secured party that is a buyer of accounts, chattel paper, payment intangibles, or promissory notes or a consignor.

(d)   **[Buyer of goods.]** Except as otherwise provided in subsection (e), a buyer of goods other than a buyer in ordinary course of business takes free of a security interest to the extent that it secures advances made after the earlier of:

(1)   the time the secured party acquires knowledge of the buyer's purchase; or

(2)   45 days after the purchase.

(e)   **[Advances made pursuant to commitment: priority of buyer of goods.]** Subsection (d) does not apply if the advance is made pursuant to a commitment entered into without knowledge of the buyer's purchase and before the expiration of the 45-day period.

(f)   **[Lessee of goods.]** Except as otherwise provided in subsection (g), a lessee of goods, other than a lessee in ordinary course of business, takes the leasehold interest free of a security interest to the extent that it secures advances made after the earlier of:

(1)   the time the secured party acquires knowledge of the lease; or

(2)   45 days after the lease contract becomes enforceable.

(g)   **[Advances made pursuant to commitment: priority of lessee of goods.]** Subsection (f) does not apply if the advance is made pursuant to a commitment entered into without knowledge of the lease and before the expiration of the 45-day period.

As amended in 1999.

Official Comment

1.   **Source.** Former Sections 9–312(7), 9–301(4), 9–307(3), 2A–307(4).

2.   **Scope of This Section.** A security agreement may provide that collateral secures future advances. See Section 9–204(c). This section collects all of the special rules dealing with the priority of advances made by a secured party after a third party acquires an interest in the collateral. Subsection (a) applies when the third party is a competing secured party. It replaces and clarifies former Section 9–312(7). Subsection (b) deals with lien

creditors and replaces former Section 9–301(4). Subsections (d) and (e) deal with buyers and replace former Section 9–307(3). Subsections (f) and (g) deal with lessees and replace former Section 2A–307(4).

3.   **Competing Security Interests.** Under a proper reading of the first-to-file-or-perfect rule of Section 9–322(a)(1) (and former Section 9–312(5)), it is abundantly clear that the time when an advance is made plays no role in determining priorities among conflicting security interests except when a financing statement was not filed and the advance is the giving of value as the last step for attachment and perfection. Thus, a secured party takes subject to all advances secured by a competing security interest having priority under Section 9–322(a)(1). This result generally obtains regardless of how the competing security interest is perfected and regardless of whether the advances are made "pursuant to commitment" (Section 9–102). Subsection (a) of this section states the only other instance when the time of an advance figures in the priority scheme in Section 9–322: when the security interest is perfected only automatically under Section 9–309 or temporarily under Section 9–312(e), (f), or (g), and the advance is not made pursuant to a commitment entered into while the security interest was perfected by another method. Thus, an advance has priority from the date it is made only in the rare case in which it is made without commitment and while the security interest is perfected only temporarily under Section 9–312.

The new formulation in subsection (a) clarifies the result when the initial advance is paid and a new ("future") advance is made subsequently. Under former Section 9–312(7), the priority of the new advance turned on whether it was "made while a security interest is perfected." This section resolves any ambiguity by omitting the quoted phrase.

Example 1: On February 1, A makes an advance secured by machinery in the debtor's possession and files a financing statement. On March 1, B makes an advance secured by the same machinery and files a financing statement. On April 1, A makes a further advance, under the original security agreement, against the same machinery. A was the first to file and so, under the first-to-file-or-perfect rule of Section 9–322(a)(1), A's security interest has priority over B's, both as to the February 1 and as to the April 1 advance. It makes no difference whether A knows of B's intervening advance when A makes the second advance. Note that, as long as A was the first to file or perfect, A would have priority with respect to both advances if either A or B had perfected by taking possession of the collateral. Likewise, A would have priority if A's April 1 advance was not made under the original agreement with the debtor, but was under a new agreement.

Example 2: On October 1, A acquires a temporarily perfected (20-day) security interest, unfiled, in a tangible negotiable document in the debtor's possession under Section 9–312(e) or (f). The security interest secures an advance made on that day as well as future advances. On October 5, B files and thereby perfects a security interest that previously had attached to the same document. On October 8, A makes an additional advance. On October 10, A files. Under Section 9–322(a)(1), because A was the first to perfect and maintained continuous perfection or filing since the start of the 20-day period, A has priority, even after the 20-day period expires. See Section 9–322, Comment 4, Example 3. However, under this section, for purposes of Section 9–322(a)(1), to the extent A's security interest secures the October 8 advance, the security interest was perfected on October 8. Inasmuch as B perfected on October 5, B has priority over the October 8 advance.

The rule in subsection (a) is more liberal toward the priority of future advances than the corresponding rules applicable to intervening lien creditors (subsection (b)), buyers (subsections (d) and (e)), and lessees (subsections (f) and (g)).

4.   **Competing Lien Creditors.** Subsection (b) replaces former Section 9–301(4) and addresses the rights of a "lien creditor," as defined in Section 9–102. Under Section 9–317(a)(2), a security interest is senior to the rights of a person who becomes a lien creditor, unless the person becomes a lien creditor before the security interest is perfected and before a financing statement covering the collateral is filed and Section 9–203(b)(3) is satisfied. Subsection (b) of this section provides that a security interest is subordinate to those rights to the extent that the specified circumstances occur. Subsection (b) does not elevate the priority of a security interest that is subordinate to the rights of a lien creditor under Section 9–317(a)(2); it only subordinates.

As under former Section 9–301(4), a secured party's knowledge does not cut short the 45-day period during which future advances can achieve priority over an intervening lien creditor's interest. Rather, because of the impact of the rule in subsection (b) on the question whether the security interest for future advances is "protected" under Section 6323(c)(2) and (d) of the Internal Revenue Code as amended by the Federal Tax Lien Act of 1966, the priority of the security interest for future advances over a lien creditor is made absolute for 45 days regardless of knowledge of the secured party concerning the lien. If, however, the advance is made after the 45 days, the advance will not have priority unless it was made or committed without knowledge of the lien.

5.   **Sales of Receivables; Consignments.** Subsections (a) and (b) do not apply to outright sales of accounts, chattel paper, payment intangibles, or promissory notes, nor do they apply to consignments.

6.   **Competing Buyers and Lessees.** Under subsections (d) and (e), a buyer will not take subject to a security interest to the extent it secures advances made after the secured party has knowledge that the buyer has purchased the collateral or more than 45 days after the purchase unless the advances were made pursuant to a commitment entered into before the expiration of the 45-day period and without knowledge of the purchase. Subsections (f) and (g) provide an analogous rule for lessees. Of course, a buyer in ordinary course who takes free of the security interest under Section 9–320 and a lessee in ordinary course who takes free under Section 9–321 are not subject to any future advances. Subsections (d) and (e) replace former Section 9–307(3), and subsections (f) and (g) replace former Section 2A–307(4). No change in meaning is intended.

As amended in 1999, 2000 and 2003.

§ 9–324.   Priority of Purchase-Money Security Interests.

(a)   **[General rule: purchase-money priority.]** Except as otherwise provided in subsection (g), a perfected purchase-money security interest in goods other than inventory or livestock has priority over a conflicting security interest in the same goods, and, except as otherwise provided in Section 9–327, a perfected security interest in its identifiable proceeds also has priority, if the purchase-money security interest is perfected when the debtor receives possession of the collateral or within 20 days thereafter.

(b)   **[Inventory purchase-money priority.]** Subject to subsection (c) and except as otherwise provided in subsection (g), a perfected purchase-money security interest in inventory has priority over a conflicting security interest in the same inventory, has priority over a conflicting security interest in chattel paper or an instrument constituting proceeds of the inventory and in proceeds of the chattel paper, if so provided in Section 9–330, and, except as otherwise provided in Section 9–327, also has priority in identifiable cash proceeds of the inventory to the extent the identifiable cash proceeds are received on or before the delivery of the inventory to a buyer, if:

(1)   the purchase-money security interest is perfected when the debtor receives possession of the inventory;

(2)   the purchase-money secured party sends an authenticated notification to the holder of the conflicting security interest;

(3)   the holder of the conflicting security interest receives the notification within five years before the debtor receives possession of the inventory; and

(4)   the notification states that the person sending the notification has or expects to acquire a purchase-money security interest in inventory of the debtor and describes the inventory.

(c)   **[Holders of conflicting inventory security interests to be notified.]** Subsections (b)(2) through (4) apply only if the holder of the conflicting security interest had filed a financing statement covering the same types of inventory:

(1)   if the purchase-money security interest is perfected by filing, before the date of the filing; or

(2)   if the purchase-money security interest is temporarily perfected without filing or possession under Section 9–312(f), before the beginning of the 20-day period thereunder.

(d)   **[Livestock purchase-money priority.]** Subject to subsection (e) and except as otherwise provided in subsection (g), a perfected purchase-money security interest in livestock that are farm products has priority over a conflicting security interest in the same livestock, and, except as otherwise provided in Section 9–327, a perfected security interest in their identifiable proceeds and identifiable products in their unmanufactured states also has priority, if:

(1)   the purchase-money security interest is perfected when the debtor receives possession of the livestock;

(2)   the purchase-money secured party sends an authenticated notification to the holder of the conflicting security interest;

(3)   the holder of the conflicting security interest receives the notification within six months before the debtor receives possession of the livestock; and

(4)   the notification states that the person sending the notification has or expects to acquire a purchase-money security interest in livestock of the debtor and describes the livestock.

(e)   **[Holders of conflicting livestock security interests to be notified.]** Subsections (d)(2) through (4) apply only if the holder of the conflicting security interest had filed a financing statement covering the same types of livestock:

(1)   if the purchase-money security interest is perfected by filing, before the date of the filing; or

(2)   if the purchase-money security interest is temporarily perfected without filing or possession under Section 9–312(f), before the beginning of the 20-day period thereunder.

(f)   **[Software purchase-money priority.]** Except as otherwise provided in subsection (g), a perfected purchase-money security interest in software has priority over a conflicting security interest in the same collateral, and, except as otherwise provided in Section 9–327, a perfected security interest in its identifiable proceeds also has priority, to the extent that the purchase-money security interest in the goods in which the software was acquired for use has priority in the goods and proceeds of the goods under this section.

(g)   **[Conflicting purchase-money security interests.]** If more than one security interest qualifies for priority in the same collateral under subsection (a), (b), (d), or (f):

(1)   a security interest securing an obligation incurred as all or part of the price of the collateral has priority over a security interest securing an obligation incurred for value given to enable the debtor to acquire rights in or the use of collateral; and

(2)   in all other cases, Section 9–322(a) applies to the qualifying security interests.

Official Comment

1.   **Source.** Former Section 9–312(3), (4).

2.   **Priority of Purchase-Money Security Interests.** This section contains the priority rules applicable to purchase-money security interests, as defined in Section 9–103. It affords a special, non-temporal priority to those purchase-money security interests that satisfy the statutory conditions. In most cases, priority will be over a security interest asserted under an after-acquired property clause. See Section 9–204 on the extent to which security interests in after-acquired property are validated.

A purchase-money security interest can be created only in goods and software. See Section 9–103. Section 9–324(a), which follows former Section 9–312(4), contains the general rule for purchase-money security interests in goods. It is subject to subsections (b) and (c), which derive from former Section 9–312(3) and apply to purchase-money security interests in inventory, and subsections (d) and (e), which apply to purchase-money security interests in livestock that are farm products. Subsection (f) applies to purchase-money security interests in software. Subsection (g) deals with the relatively unusual case in which a debtor creates two purchase-money security interests in the same collateral and both security interests qualify for special priority under one of the other subsections.

Former Section 9–312(2) contained a rule affording special priority to those who provided secured credit that enabled a debtor to produce crops. This rule proved unworkable and has been eliminated from this Article. Instead, model Section 9–324A contains a revised production-money priority rule. That section is a model, not uniform, provision. The sponsors of the UCC have taken no position as to whether it should be enacted, instead leaving the matter for state legislatures to consider if they are so inclined.

3.   **Purchase-Money Priority in Goods Other Than Inventory and Livestock.** Subsection (a) states a general rule applicable to all types of goods except inventory and farm-products livestock: the purchase-money interest takes priority if it is perfected when the debtor receives possession of the collateral or within 20 days thereafter. (As to the 20-day "grace period," compare Section 9–317(e). Former Sections 9–312(4) and 9–301(2) contained a 10-day grace period.) The perfection requirement means that the purchase-money secured party either has filed a financing statement before that time or has a temporarily perfected security interest in goods covered by documents under Section 9–312(e) and (f) which is continued in a perfected status by filing before the expiration of the 20-day period specified in that section. A purchase-money security interest qualifies for priority under

subsection (a), even if the purchase-money secured party knows that a conflicting security interest has been created and/or that the holder of the conflicting interest has filed a financing statement covering the collateral.

Normally, there will be no question when "the debtor receives possession of the collateral" for purposes of subsection (a). However, sometimes a debtor buys goods and takes possession of them in stages, and then assembly and testing are completed (by the seller or debtor-buyer) at the debtor's location. Under those circumstances, the buyer "takes possession" within the meaning of subsection (a) when, after an inspection of the portion of the goods in the debtor's possession, it would be apparent to a potential lender to the debtor that the debtor has acquired an interest in the goods taken as a whole.

A similar issue concerning the time when "the debtor receives possession" arises when a person acquires possession of goods under a transaction that is not governed by this Article and then later agrees to buy the goods on secured credit. For example, a person may take possession of goods as lessee under a lease contract and then exercise an option to purchase the goods from the lessor on secured credit. Under Section 2A–307(1), creditors of the lessee generally take subject to the lease contract; filing a financing statement against the lessee is unnecessary to protect the lessor's leasehold or residual interest. Once the lease is converted to a security interest, filing a financing statement is necessary to protect the seller's (former lessor's) security interest. Accordingly, the 20-day period in subsection (a) does not commence until the goods become "collateral" (defined in Section 9–102), i.e., until they are subject to a security interest.

4.   **Purchase-Money Security Interests in Inventory.** Subsections (b) and (c) afford a means by which a purchase-money security interest in inventory can achieve priority over an earlier-filed security interest in the same collateral. To achieve priority, the purchase-money security interest must be perfected when the debtor receives possession of the inventory. For a discussion of when "the debtor receives possession," see Comment 3, above. The 20-day grace period of subsection (a) does not apply.

The arrangement between an inventory secured party and its debtor typically requires the secured party to make periodic advances against incoming inventory or periodic releases of old inventory as new inventory is received. A fraudulent debtor may apply to the secured party for advances even though it has already given a purchase-money security interest in the inventory to another secured party. For this reason, subsections (b)(2) through (4) and (c) impose a second condition for the purchase-money security interest's achieving priority: the purchase-money secured party must give notification to the holder of a conflicting security interest who filed against the same item or type of inventory before the purchase-money secured party filed or its security interest became perfected temporarily under Section 9–312(e) or (f). The notification requirement protects the non-purchase-money inventory secured party in such a situation: if the inventory secured party has received notification, it presumably will not make an advance; if it has not received notification (or if the other security interest does not qualify as purchase-money), any advance the inventory secured party may make ordinarily will have priority under Section 9–322. Inasmuch as an arrangement for periodic advances against incoming goods is unusual outside the inventory field, subsection (a) does not contain a notification requirement.

5.   **Notification to Conflicting Inventory Secured Party: Timing.** Under subsection (b)(3), the perfected purchase-money security interest achieves priority over a conflicting security interest only if the holder of the conflicting security interest receives a notification within five years before the debtor receives possession of the purchase-money collateral. If the debtor never receives possession, the five-year period never begins, and the purchase-money security interest has priority, even if notification is not given. However, where the purchase-money inventory financing began by the purchase-money secured party's possession of a negotiable document of title, to retain priority the secured party must give the notification required by subsection (b) at or before the usual time, i.e., when the debtor gets possession of the inventory, even though the security interest remains perfected for 20 days under Section 9–312(e) or (f).

Some people have mistakenly read former Section 9–312(3)(b) to require, as a condition of purchase-money priority in inventory, that the purchase-money secured party give the notification before it files a financing statement. Read correctly, the "before" clauses compare (i) the time when the holder of the conflicting security interest filed a financing statement with (ii) the time when the purchase-money security interest becomes perfected by filing or automatically perfected temporarily. Only if (i) occurs before (ii) must notification be given to the holder of the conflicting security interest. Subsection (c) has been rewritten to clarify this point.

6.   **Notification to Conflicting Inventory Secured Party: Address.** Inasmuch as the address provided as that of the secured party on a filed financing statement is an "address that is reasonable under the circumstances," the holder of a purchase-money security interest may satisfy the requirement to "send" notification to the holder of a conflicting security interest in inventory by sending a notification to that address,

even if the address is or becomes incorrect. See Section 9–102 (definition of "send"). Similarly, because the address is "held out by [the holder of the conflicting security interest] as the place for receipt of such communications [i.e., communications relating to security interests]," the holder is deemed to have "received" a notification delivered to that address. See Section 1–202(e).

7. **Consignments.** Subsections (b) and (c) also determine the priority of a consignor's interest in consigned goods as against a security interest in the goods created by the consignee. Inasmuch as a consignment subject to this Article is defined to be a purchase-money security interest, see Section 9–103(d), no inference concerning the nature of the transaction should be drawn from the fact that a consignor uses the term "security interest" in its notice under subsection (b)(4). Similarly, a notice stating that the consignor has delivered or expects to deliver goods, properly described, "on consignment" meets the requirements of subsection (b)(4), even if it does not contain the term "security interest," and even if the transaction subsequently is determined to be a security interest. Cf. Section 9–505 (use of "consignor" and "consignee" in financing statement).

8. **Priority in Proceeds: General.** When the purchase-money secured party has priority over another secured party, the question arises whether this priority extends to the proceeds of the original collateral. Subsections (a), (d), and (f) give an affirmative answer, but only as to proceeds in which the security interest is perfected (see Section 9–315). Although this qualification did not appear in former Section 9–312(4), it was implicit in that provision.

In the case of inventory collateral under subsection (b), where financing frequently is based on the resulting accounts, chattel paper, or other proceeds, the special priority of the purchase-money secured interest carries over into only certain types of proceeds. As under former Section 9–312(3), the purchase-money priority in inventory under subsection (b) carries over into identifiable cash proceeds (defined in Section 9–102) received on or before the delivery of the inventory to a buyer.

As a general matter, also like former Section 9–312(3), the purchase-money priority in inventory does *not* carry over into proceeds consisting of accounts or chattel paper. Many parties financing inventory are quite content to protect their first-priority security interest in the inventory itself. They realize that when the inventory is sold, someone else will be financing the resulting receivables (accounts or chattel paper), and the priority for inventory will not run forward to the receivables constituting the proceeds. Indeed, the cash supplied by the receivables financer often will be used to pay the inventory financing. In some situations, the party financing the inventory on a purchase-money basis makes contractual arrangements that the proceeds of receivables financing by another be devoted to paying off the inventory security interest.

However, the purchase-money priority in inventory *does* carry over to proceeds consisting of chattel paper and its proceeds (and also to instruments) to the extent provided in Section 9–330. Under Section 9–330(e), the holder of a purchase-money security interest in inventory is deemed to give new value for proceeds consisting of chattel paper. Taken together, Sections 9–324(b) and 9–330(e) enable a purchase-money inventory secured party to obtain priority in chattel paper constituting proceeds of the inventory, even if the secured party does not actually give new value for the chattel paper, provided the purchase-money secured party satisfies the other conditions for achieving priority.

When the proceeds of original collateral (goods or software) consist of a deposit account, Section 9–327 governs priority to the extent it conflicts with the priority rules of this section.

9. **Priority in Accounts Constituting Proceeds of Inventory.** The application of the priority rules in subsection (b) is shown by the following examples:

Example 1: Debtor creates a security interest in its existing and after-acquired inventory in favor of SP–1, who files a financing statement covering inventory. SP–2 subsequently takes a purchase-money security interest in certain inventory and, under subsection (b), achieves priority in this inventory over SP–1. This inventory is then sold, producing accounts. Accounts are not cash proceeds, and so the special purchase-money priority in the inventory does not control the priority in the accounts. Rather, the first-to-file-or-perfect rule of Section 9–322(a)(1) applies. The time of SP–1's filing as to the inventory is also the time of filing as to the accounts under Section 9–322(b). Assuming that each security interest in the accounts proceeds remains perfected under Section 9–315, SP–1 has priority as to the accounts.

Example 2: In Example 1, if SP–2 had filed directly against accounts, the date of that filing as to accounts would be compared with the date of SP–1's filing as to the inventory. The first filed would prevail under Section 9–322(a)(1).

Example 3: If SP–3 had filed against accounts in Example 1 before either SP–1 or SP–2 filed against inventory, SP–3's filing against accounts would have priority over the filings of SP–1 and SP–2. This result obtains even though the filings against inventory are effective to continue the perfected status of SP–1's and SP–2's security interest in the accounts beyond the 20-day period of automatic perfection. See Section 9–315. SP–1's and SP–2's position as to the inventory does not give them a claim to accounts (as proceeds of the inventory) which is senior to someone who has filed earlier against accounts. If, on the other hand, either SP–1's or SP–2's filing against the inventory preceded SP–3's filing against accounts, SP–1 or SP–2 would outrank SP–3 as to the accounts.

10.   **Purchase-Money Security Interests in Livestock.** New subsections (d) and (e) provide a purchase-money priority rule for farm-products livestock. They are patterned on the purchase-money priority rule for inventory found in subsections (b) and (c) and include a requirement that the purchase-money secured party notify earlier-filed parties. Two differences between subsections (b) and (d) are noteworthy. First, unlike the purchase-money inventory lender, the purchase-money livestock lender enjoys priority in *all* proceeds of the collateral. Thus, under subsection (d), the purchase-money secured party takes priority in accounts over an earlier-filed accounts financer. Second, subsection (d) affords priority in certain products of the collateral as well as proceeds.

11.   **Purchase-Money Security Interests in Aquatic Farm Products.** Aquatic goods produced in aquacultural operations (e.g., catfish raised on a catfish farm) are farm products. See Section 9–102 (definition of "farm products"). The definition does not indicate whether aquatic goods are "crops," as to which the model production money security interest priority in Section 9–324A applies, or "livestock," as to which the purchase-money priority in subsection (d) of this section applies. This Article leaves courts free to determine the classification of particular aquatic goods on a case-by-case basis, applying whichever priority rule makes more sense in the overall context of the debtor's business.

12.   **Purchase-Money Security Interests in Software.** Subsection (f) governs the priority of purchase-money security interests in software. Under Section 9–103(c), a purchase-money security interest arises in software only if the debtor acquires its interest in the software for the principal purpose of using the software in goods subject to a purchase-money security interest. Under subsection (f), a purchase-money security interest in software has the same priority as the purchase-money security interest in the goods in which the software was acquired for use. This priority is determined under subsections (b) and (c) (for inventory) or (a) (for other goods).

13.   **Multiple Purchase-Money Security Interests.** New subsection (g) governs priority among multiple purchase-money security interests in the same collateral. It grants priority to purchase-money security interests securing the price of collateral (i.e., created in favor of the seller) over purchase-money security interests that secure enabling loans. Section 7.2(c) of the Restatement (3d) of the Law of Property (Mortgages) (1997) adopts this rule with respect to real property mortgages. As Comment *d* to that section explains:

> the equities favor the vendor. Not only does the vendor part with specific real estate rather than money, but the vendor would never relinquish it at all except on the understanding that the vendor will be able to use it to satisfy the obligation to pay the price. This is the case even though the vendor may know that the mortgagor is going to finance the transaction in part by borrowing from a third party and giving a mortgage to secure that obligation. In the final analysis, the law is more sympathetic to the vendor's hazard of losing real estate previously owned than to the third party lender's risk of being unable to collect from an interest in real estate that never previously belonged to it.

The first-to-file-or-perfect rule of Section 9–322 applies to multiple purchase-money security interests securing enabling loans.

As amended in 2010.

§ 9–325.   Priority of Security Interests in Transferred Collateral.

(a)   **[Subordination of security interest in transferred collateral.]** Except as otherwise provided in subsection (b), a security interest created by a debtor is subordinate to a security interest in the same collateral created by another person if:

(1)   the debtor acquired the collateral subject to the security interest created by the other person;

(2)   the security interest created by the other person was perfected when the debtor acquired the collateral; and

(3)   there is no period thereafter when the security interest is unperfected.

(b)   **[Limitation of subsection (a) subordination.]** Subsection (a) subordinates a security interest only if the security interest:

(1)   otherwise would have priority solely under Section 9–322(a) or 9–324; or

(2)   arose solely under Section 2–711(3) or 2A–508(5).

Official Comment

1.   **Source.** New.

2.   **"Double Debtor Problem."** This section addresses the "double debtor" problem, which arises when a debtor acquires property that is subject to a security interest created by another debtor.

3.   **Taking Subject to Perfected Security Interest.** Consider the following scenario:

Example 1: A owns an item of equipment subject to a perfected security interest in favor of SP–A. A sells the equipment to B, not in the ordinary course of business. B acquires its interest subject to SP–A's security interest. See Sections 9–201, 9–315(a)(1). Under this section, if B creates a security interest in the equipment in favor of SP–B, SP–B's security interest is subordinate to SP–A's security interest, even if SP–B filed against B before SP–A filed against A, and even if SP–B took a purchase-money security interest. Normally, SP–B could have investigated the source of the equipment and discovered SP–A's filing before making an advance against the equipment, whereas SP–A had no reason to search the filings against someone other than its debtor, A.

4.   **Taking Subject to Unperfected Security Interest.** This section applies only if the security interest in the transferred collateral was perfected when the transferee acquired the collateral. See subsection (a)(2). If this condition is not met, then the normal priority rules apply.

Example 2: A owns an item of equipment subject to an unperfected security interest in favor of SP–A. A sells the equipment to B, who gives value and takes delivery of the equipment without knowledge of the security interest. B takes free of the security interest. See Section 9–317(b). If B then creates a security interest in favor of SP–B, no priority issue arises; SP–B has the only security interest in the equipment.

Example 3: The facts are as in Example 2, except that B knows of SP–A's security interest and therefore takes the equipment subject to it. If B creates a security interest in the equipment in favor of SP–B, this section does not determine the relative priority of the security interests. Rather, the normal priority rules govern. If SP–B perfects its security interest, then, under Section 9–322(a)(2), SP–A's unperfected security interest will be junior to SP–B's perfected security interest. The award of priority to SP–B is premised on the belief that SP–A's failure to file could have misled SP–B.

5.   **Taking Subject to Perfected Security Interest that Becomes Unperfected.** This section applies only if the security interest in the transferred collateral did not become unperfected at any time after the transferee acquired the collateral. See subsection (a)(3). If this condition is not met, then the normal priority rules apply.

Example 4: As in Example 1, A owns an item of equipment subject to a perfected security interest in favor of SP–A. A sells the equipment to B, not in the ordinary course of business. B acquires its interest subject to SP–A's security interest. See Sections 9–201, 9–315(a)(1). B creates a security interest in favor of SP–B, and SP–B perfects its security interest. This section provides that SP–A's security interest is senior to SP–B's. However, if SP–A's financing statement lapses while SP–B's security interest is perfected, then the normal priority rules would apply, and SP–B's security interest would become senior to SP–A's security interest. See Sections 9–322(a)(2), 9–515(c).

6.   **Unusual Situations.** The appropriateness of the rule of subsection (a) is most apparent when it works to subordinate security interests having priority under the basic priority rules of Section 9–322(a) or the purchase-money priority rules of Section 9–324. The rule also works properly when applied to the security interest of a buyer under Section 2–711(3) or a lessee under Section 2A–508(5). However, subsection (a) may provide an inappropriate resolution of the "double debtor" problem in some of the wide variety of other contexts in which the problem may arise. Although subsection (b) limits the application of subsection (a) to those cases in which subordination is known to be appropriate, courts should apply the rule in other settings, if necessary to promote the underlying purposes and policies of the Uniform Commercial Code. See Section 1–103(a).

As amended in 2005.

§ 9–326. Priority of Security Interests Created by New Debtor.

(a) **[Subordination of security interest created by new debtor.]** Subject to subsection (b), a security interest that is created by a new debtor in collateral in which the new debtor has or acquires rights and is perfected solely by a filed financing statement that would be ineffective to perfect the security interest but for the application of Section 9–316(i)(1) or 9–508 is subordinate to a security interest in the same collateral which is perfected other than by such a filed financing statement.

(b) **[Priority under other provisions; multiple original debtors.]** The other provisions of this part determine the priority among conflicting security interests in the same collateral perfected by filed financing statements described in subsection (a). However, if the security agreements to which a new debtor became bound as debtor were not entered into by the same original debtor, the conflicting security interests rank according to priority in time of the new debtor's having become bound.

Official Comment

1. **Source.** New.

2. **Subordination of Security Interests Created by New Debtor.** This section addresses the priority contests that may arise when a new debtor becomes bound by the security agreement of an original debtor and each debtor has a secured creditor.

Subsection (a) subordinates the original debtor's secured party's security interest perfected against the new debtor by a filed financing statement that would be ineffective to perfect the security interest but for Section 9–508 or, if the original debtor and new debtor are located in different jurisdictions, Section 9–316(i)(1). The security interest is subordinated to security interests in the same collateral perfected by another method, e.g., by filing against the new debtor. This section does not subordinate a security interest perfected by a new initial financing statement providing the name of the new debtor, even if the initial financing statement is filed to maintain the effectiveness of a financing statement under the circumstances described in Section 9–508(b). Nor does it subordinate a security interest perfected by a financing statement filed against the original debtor which remains effective against collateral transferred by the original debtor to the new debtor. See Section 9–508(c). Concerning priority contests involving transferred collateral, see Sections 9–325 and 9–507.

Example 1: SP–X holds a perfected-by-filing security interest in X Corp's existing and after-acquired inventory, and SP–Z holds a perfected-by-possession security interest in an item of Z Corp's inventory. Both X Corp and Z Corp are located in the same jurisdiction under Section 9–307. Z Corp becomes bound as debtor by X Corp's security agreement (e.g., Z Corp buys X Corp's assets and assumes its security agreement). See Section 9–203(d). But for Section 9–508, SP–X's financing statement would be ineffective to perfect a security interest in the item of inventory in which Z Corp has rights. However, subsection (a) provides that SP–X's perfected security interest is subordinate to SP–Z's, regardless of whether SP–X's financing statement was filed before SP–Z perfected its security interest.

Example 2: SP–X holds a perfected-by-filing security interest in X Corp's existing and after-acquired inventory, and SP–Z holds a perfected-by-filing security interest in Z Corp's existing and after-acquired inventory. Both X Corp and Z Corp are located in the same jurisdiction under Section 9–307. Z Corp becomes bound as debtor by X Corp's security agreement. Immediately thereafter, and before the effectiveness of SP–X's financing statement lapses, Z Corp acquires a new item of inventory. But for Section 9–508, SP–X's financing statement would be ineffective to perfect a security interest in the new item of inventory in which Z Corp has rights. However, because SP–Z's security interest was perfected by a filing whose effectiveness does not depend on Section 9–316(i)(1) or 9–508, subsection (a) subordinates SP–X's perfected security interest to SP–Z's. This would be the case even if SP–Z filed after Z Corp became bound by X Corp's security agreement, and regardless of which financing statement was filed first.

The same result would obtain if X Corp and Z Corp were located in different jurisdictions. SP–X's security interest would be perfected by a financing statement that would be ineffective but for Section 9–316(i)(1), whereas the effectiveness of SP–Z's filing does not depend on Section 9–316(i)(1) or 9–508.

3. **Other Priority Rules.** Subsection (b) addresses the priority among security interests created by the original debtor (X Corp). By invoking the other priority rules of this subpart, as applicable, subsection (b) preserves the relative priority of security interests created by the original debtor.

Example 3: Under the facts of Example 2, SP–Y also holds a perfected-by-filing security interest in X Corp's existing and after-acquired inventory. SP–Y filed after SP–X. Inasmuch as both SP–X's and SP–Y's security interests in inventory acquired by Z Corp after it became bound would be unperfected but for the application of Section 9–508, the normal priority rules determine their relative priorities. Under the "first-to-file-or-perfect" rule of Section 9–322(a)(1), SP–X has priority over SP–Y.

Example 4: Under the facts of Example 3, after Z Corp became bound by X Corp's security agreement, SP–Y promptly filed a new initial financing statement against Z Corp. SP–X's security interest remains perfected only by virtue of its original filing against X Corp which "would be ineffective to perfect the security interest but for the application of Section 9–508." Because SP–Y's security interest is perfected by the filing of a financing statement whose effectiveness does not depend on Section 9–508 or 9–316(i)(1), subsection (a) subordinates SP–X's security interest to SP–Y's. If both SP–X and SP–Y file a new initial financing statement against Z Corp, then the "first-to-file-or-perfect" rule of Section 9–322(a)(1) governs their priority inter se as well as their priority against SP–Z.

The second sentence of subsection (b) effectively limits the applicability of the first sentence to situations in which a new debtor has become bound by more than one security agreement entered into by the *same* original debtor. When the new debtor has become bound by security agreements entered into by *different* original debtors, the second sentence provides that priority is based on priority in time of the new debtor's becoming bound.

Example 5: Under the facts of Example 2, SP–W holds a perfected-by-filing security interest in W Corp's existing and after-acquired inventory. After Z Corp became bound by X Corp's security agreement in favor of SP–X, Z Corp became bound by W Corp's security agreement. Under subsection (b), SP–W's security interest in inventory acquired by Z Corp is subordinate to that of SP–X, because Z Corp became bound under SP–X's security agreement before it became bound under SP–W's security agreement. This is the result regardless of which financing statement (SP–X's or SP–W's) was filed first.

The second sentence of subsection (b) reflects the generally accepted view that priority based on the first-to-file rule is inappropriate for resolving priority disputes when the filings were made against different debtors. Like subsection (a) and the first sentence of subsection (b), however, the second sentence of subsection (b) relates only to priority conflicts among security interests would be unperfected but for the application of Section 9–316(i)(1) or 9–508.

Example 6: Under the facts of Example 5, after Z Corp became bound by W Corp's security agreement, SP–W promptly filed a new initial financing statement against Z Corp. At that time, SP–X's security interest was perfected only pursuant to its original filing against X Corp which "would be ineffective to perfect the security interest but for the application of Section 9–508." Because SP–W's security interest is perfected by the filing of a financing statement whose effectiveness does not depend on Section 9–316(i)(1) or 9–508, subsection (a) subordinates SP–X's security interest to SP–W's. If both SP–X and SP–W file a new initial financing statement against Z Corp, then the "first-to-file-or-perfect" rule of Section 9–322(a)(1) governs their priority inter se as well as their priority against SP–Z.

As amended in 2010.

§ 9–327.   Priority of Security Interests in Deposit Account.

The following rules govern priority among conflicting security interests in the same deposit account:

(1)   A security interest held by a secured party having control of the deposit account under Section 9–104 has priority over a conflicting security interest held by a secured party that does not have control.

(2)   Except as otherwise provided in paragraphs (3) and (4), security interests perfected by control under Section 9–314 rank according to priority in time of obtaining control.

(3)   Except as otherwise provided in paragraph (4), a security interest held by the bank with which the deposit account is maintained has priority over a conflicting security interest held by another secured party.

(4)   A security interest perfected by control under Section 9–104(a)(3) has priority over a security interest held by the bank with which the deposit account is maintained.

Official Comment

1. **Source.** New; derived from former Section 9–115(5).

2. **Scope of This Section.** This section contains the rules governing the priority of conflicting security interests in deposit accounts. It overrides conflicting priority rules. See Sections 9–322(f)(1), 9–324(a), (b), (d), (f). This section does not apply to accounts evidenced by an instrument (e.g., certain certificates of deposit), which by definition are not "deposit accounts."

3. **Control.** Under paragraph (1), security interests perfected by control (Sections 9–314, 9–104) take priority over those perfected otherwise, e.g., as identifiable cash proceeds under Section 9–315. Secured parties for whom the deposit account is an integral part of the credit decision will, at a minimum, insist upon the right to immediate access to the deposit account upon the debtor's default (i.e., control). Those secured parties for whom the deposit account is less essential will not take control, thereby running the risk that the debtor will dispose of funds on deposit (either outright or for collateral purposes) after default but before the account can be frozen by court order or the secured party can obtain control.

Paragraph (2) governs the case (expected to be very rare) in which a bank enters into a Section 9–104(a)(2) control agreement with more than one secured party. It provides that the security interests rank according to time of obtaining control. If the bank is solvent and the control agreements are well drafted, the bank will be liable to each secured party, and the priority rule will have no practical effect.

4. **Priority of Bank.** Under paragraph (3), the security interest of the bank with which the deposit account is maintained normally takes priority over all other conflicting security interests in the deposit account, regardless of whether the deposit account constitutes the competing secured party's original collateral or its proceeds. A rule of this kind enables banks to extend credit to their depositors without the need to examine either the public record or their own records to determine whether another party might have a security interest in the deposit account.

A secured party who takes a security interest in the deposit account as original collateral can protect itself against the results of this rule in one of two ways. It can take control of the deposit account by becoming the bank's customer. Under paragraph (4), this arrangement operates to subordinate the bank's security interest. Alternatively, the secured party can obtain a subordination agreement from the bank. See Section 9–339.

A secured party who claims the deposit account as proceeds of other collateral can reduce the risk of becoming junior by obtaining the debtor's agreement to deposit proceeds into a specific cash-collateral account and obtaining the agreement of that bank to subordinate all its claims to those of the secured party. But if the debtor violates its agreement and deposits funds into a deposit account other than the cash-collateral account, the secured party risks being subordinated.

5. **Priority in Proceeds of, and Funds Transferred from, Deposit Account.** The priority afforded by this section does not extend to proceeds of a deposit account. Rather, Section 9–322(c) through (e) and the provisions referred to in Section 9–322(f) govern priorities in proceeds of a deposit account. Section 9–315(d) addresses continuation of perfection in proceeds of deposit accounts. As to funds transferred from a deposit account that serves as collateral, see Section 9–332.

§ 9–328. Priority of Security Interests in Investment Property.

The following rules govern priority among conflicting security interests in the same investment property:

(1) A security interest held by a secured party having control of investment property under Section 9–106 has priority over a security interest held by a secured party that does not have control of the investment property.

(2) Except as otherwise provided in paragraphs (3) and (4), conflicting security interests held by secured parties each of which has control under Section 9–106 rank according to priority in time of:

(A) if the collateral is a security, obtaining control;

(B) if the collateral is a security entitlement carried in a securities account and:

    (i) if the secured party obtained control under Section 8–106(d)(1), the secured party's becoming the person for which the securities account is maintained;

  (ii) if the secured party obtained control under Section 8–106(d)(2), the securities intermediary's agreement to comply with the secured party's entitlement orders with respect to security entitlements carried or to be carried in the securities account; or

  (iii) if the secured party obtained control through another person under Section 8–106(d)(3), the time on which priority would be based under this paragraph if the other person were the secured party; or

 (C) if the collateral is a commodity contract carried with a commodity intermediary, the satisfaction of the requirement for control specified in Section 9–106(b)(2) with respect to commodity contracts carried or to be carried with the commodity intermediary.

 (3) A security interest held by a securities intermediary in a security entitlement or a securities account maintained with the securities intermediary has priority over a conflicting security interest held by another secured party.

 (4) A security interest held by a commodity intermediary in a commodity contract or a commodity account maintained with the commodity intermediary has priority over a conflicting security interest held by another secured party.

 (5) A security interest in a certificated security in registered form which is perfected by taking delivery under Section 9–313(a) and not by control under Section 9–314 has priority over a conflicting security interest perfected by a method other than control.

 (6) Conflicting security interests created by a broker, securities intermediary, or commodity intermediary which are perfected without control under Section 9–106 rank equally.

 (7) In all other cases, priority among conflicting security interests in investment property is governed by Sections 9–322 and 9–323.

Official Comment

1. **Source.** Former Section 9–115(5).

2. **Scope of This Section.** This section contains the rules governing the priority of conflicting security interests in investment property. Paragraph (1) states the most important general rule—that a secured party who obtains control has priority over a secured party who does not obtain control. Paragraphs (2) through (4) deal with conflicting security interests each of which is perfected by control. Paragraph (5) addresses the priority of a security interest in a certificated security which is perfected by delivery but not control. Paragraph (6) deals with the relatively unusual circumstance in which a broker, securities intermediary, or commodity intermediary has created conflicting security interests none of which is perfected by control. Paragraph (7) provides that the general priority rules of Sections 9–322 and 9–323 apply to cases not covered by the specific rules in this section. The principal application of this residual rule is that the usual first in time of filing rule applies to conflicting security interests that are perfected only by filing. Because the control priority rule of paragraph (1) provides for the ordinary cases in which persons purchase securities on margin credit from their brokers, there is no need for special rules for purchase-money security interests. See also Section 9–103 (limiting purchase-money collateral to goods and software).

3. **General Rule: Priority of Security Interest Perfected by Control.** Under paragraph (1), a secured party who obtains control has priority over a secured party who does not obtain control. The control priority rule does not turn on either temporal sequence or awareness of conflicting security interests. Rather, it is a structural rule, based on the principle that a lender should be able to rely on the collateral without question if the lender has taken the necessary steps to assure itself that it is in a position where it can foreclose on the collateral without further action by the debtor. The control priority rule is necessary because the perfection rules provide considerable flexibility in structuring secured financing arrangements. For example, at the "retail" level, a secured lender to an investor who wants the full measure of protection can obtain control, but the creditor may be willing to accept the greater measure of risk that follows from perfection by filing. Similarly, at the "wholesale" level, a lender to securities firms can leave the collateral with the debtor and obtain a perfected security interest under the automatic perfection rule of Section 9–309(10), but a lender who wants to be entirely sure of its position will want to obtain control. The control priority rule of paragraph (1) is an essential part of this system of flexibility. It is feasible to provide more than one method of perfecting security interests only if the rules ensure that those who take the necessary steps to obtain the full measure of protection do not run the risk of subordination to those

who have not taken such steps. A secured party who is unwilling to run the risk that the debtor has granted or will grant a conflicting control security interest should not make a loan without obtaining control of the collateral.

As applied to the retail level, the control priority rule means that a secured party who obtains control has priority over a conflicting security interest perfected by filing without regard to inquiry into whether the control secured party was aware of the filed security interest. Prior to the 1994 revisions to Articles 8 and 9, Article 9 did not permit perfection of security interests in securities by filing. Accordingly, parties who deal in securities never developed a practice of searching the UCC files before conducting securities transactions. Although filing is now a permissible method of perfection, in order to avoid disruption of existing practices in this business it is necessary to give perfection by filing a different and more limited effect for securities than for some other forms of collateral. The priority rules are not based on the assumption that parties who perfect by the usual method of obtaining control will search the files. Quite the contrary, the control priority rule is intended to ensure that, with respect to investment property, secured parties who do obtain control are entirely unaffected by filings. To state the point another way, perfection by filing is intended to affect only general creditors or other secured creditors who rely on filing. The rule that a security interest perfected by filing can be primed by a control security interest, without regard to awareness, is a consequence of the system of perfection and priority rules for investment property. These rules are designed to take account of the circumstances of the securities markets, where filing is not given the same effect as for some other forms of property. No implication is made about the effect of filing with respect to security interests in other forms of property, nor about other Article 9 rules, e.g., Section 9–330, which govern the circumstances in which security interests in other forms of property perfected by filing can be primed by subsequent perfected security interests.

The following examples illustrate the application of the priority rule in paragraph (1):

Example 1: Debtor borrows from Alpha and grants Alpha a security interest in a variety of collateral, including all of Debtor's investment property. At that time Debtor owns 1000 shares of XYZ Co. stock for which Debtor has a certificate. Alpha perfects by filing. Later, Debtor borrows from Beta and grants Beta a security interest in the 1000 shares of XYZ Co. stock. Debtor delivers the certificate, properly indorsed, to Beta. Alpha and Beta both have perfected security interests in the XYZ Co. stock. Beta has control, see Section 8–106(b)(1), and hence has priority over Alpha.

Example 2: Debtor borrows from Alpha and grants Alpha a security interest in a variety of collateral, including all of Debtor's investment property. At that time Debtor owns 1000 shares of XYZ Co. stock, held through a securities account with Able & Co. Alpha perfects by filing. Later, Debtor borrows from Beta and grants Beta a security interest in the 1000 shares of XYZ Co. stock. Debtor instructs Able to have the 1000 shares transferred through the clearing corporation to Custodian Bank, to be credited to Beta's account with Custodian Bank. Alpha and Beta both have perfected security interests in the XYZ Co. stock. Beta has control, see Section 8–106(d)(1), and hence has priority over Alpha.

Example 3: Debtor borrows from Alpha and grants Alpha a security interest in a variety of collateral, including all of Debtor's investment property. At that time Debtor owns 1000 shares of XYZ Co. stock, which is held through a securities account with Able & Co. Alpha perfects by filing. Later, Debtor borrows from Beta and grants Beta a security interest in the 1000 shares of XYZ Co. stock. Debtor, Able, and Beta enter into an agreement under which Debtor will continue to receive dividends and distributions, and will continue to have the right to direct dispositions, but Beta will also have the right to direct dispositions and receive the proceeds. Alpha and Beta both have perfected security interests in the XYZ Co. stock (more precisely, in the Debtor's security entitlement to the financial asset consisting of the XYZ Co. stock). Beta has control, see Section 8–106(d)(2), and hence has priority over Alpha.

Example 4: Debtor borrows from Alpha and grants Alpha a security interest in a variety of collateral, including all of Debtor's investment property. At that time Debtor owns 1000 shares of XYZ Co. stock, held through a securities account with Able & Co. Alpha perfects by filing. Debtor's agreement with Able & Co. provides that Able has a security interest in all securities carried in the account as security for any obligations of Debtor to Able. Debtor incurs obligations to Able and later defaults on the obligations to Alpha and Able. Able has control by virtue of the rule of Section 8–106(e) that if a customer grants a security interest to its own intermediary, the intermediary has control. Since Alpha does not have control, Able has priority over Alpha under the general control priority rule of paragraph (1).

4. **Conflicting Security Interests Perfected by Control: Priority of Securities Intermediary or Commodity Intermediary.** Paragraphs (2) through (4) govern the priority of conflicting security interests each

of which is perfected by control. The following example explains the application of the rules in paragraphs (3) and (4):

Example 5: Debtor holds securities through a securities account with Able & Co. Debtor's agreement with Able & Co. provides that Able has a security interest in all securities carried in the account as security for any obligations of Debtor to Able. Debtor borrows from Beta and grants Beta a security interest in 1000 shares of XYZ Co. stock carried in the account. Debtor, Able, and Beta enter into an agreement under which Debtor will continue to receive dividends and distributions and will continue to have the right to direct dispositions, but Beta will also have the right to direct dispositions and receive the proceeds. Debtor incurs obligations to Able and later defaults on the obligations to Beta and Able. Both Beta and Able have control, so the general control priority rule of paragraph (1) does not apply. Compare Example 4. Paragraph (3) provides that a security interest held by a securities intermediary in positions of its own customer has priority over a conflicting security interest of an external lender, so Able has priority over Beta. (Paragraph (4) contains a parallel rule for commodity intermediaries.) The agreement among Able, Beta, and Debtor could, of course, determine the relative priority of the security interests of Able and Beta, see Section 9–339, but the fact that the intermediary has agreed to act on the instructions of a secured party such as Beta does not itself imply any agreement by the intermediary to subordinate.

5. **Conflicting Security Interests Perfected by Control: Temporal Priority.** Former Section 9–115 introduced into Article 9 the concept of conflicting security interests that rank equally. Paragraph (2) of this section governs priority in those circumstances in which more than one secured party (other than a broker, securities intermediary, or commodity intermediary) has control. It replaces the equal-priority rule for conflicting security interests in investment property with a temporal rule. For securities, both certificated and uncertificated, under paragraph (2)(A) priority is based on the time that control is obtained. For security entitlements carried in securities accounts, the treatment is more complex. Paragraph (2)(B) bases priority on the timing of the steps taken to achieve control. The following example illustrates the application of paragraph (2).

Example 6: Debtor borrows from Alpha and grants Alpha a security interest in a variety of collateral, including all of Debtor's investment property. At that time Debtor owns a security entitlement that includes 1000 shares of XYZ Co. stock that Debtor holds through a securities account with Able & Co. Debtor, Able, and Alpha enter into an agreement under which Debtor will continue to receive dividends and distributions, and will continue to have the right to direct dispositions, but Alpha will also have the right to direct dispositions and receive the proceeds. Later, Debtor borrows from Beta and grants Beta a security interest in all its investment property, existing and after-acquired. Debtor, Able, and Beta enter into an agreement under which Debtor will continue to receive dividends and distributions, and will continue to have the right to direct dispositions, but Beta will also have the right to direct dispositions and receive the proceeds. Alpha and Beta both have perfected-by-control security interests in the security entitlement to the XYZ Co. stock by virtue of their agreements with Able. See Sections 9–314(a), 9–106(a), 8–106(d)(2). Under paragraph (2)(B)(ii), the priority of each security interest dates from the time of the secured party's agreement with Able. Because Alpha's agreement was first in time, Alpha has priority. This priority applies equally to security entitlements to financial assets credited to the account after the agreement was entered into.

The priority rule is analogous to "first-to-file" priority under Section 9–322 with respect to after-acquired collateral. Paragraphs (2)(B)(i) and (2)(B)(iii) provide similar rules for security entitlements as to which control is obtained by other methods, and paragraph (2)(C) provides a similar rule for commodity contracts carried in a commodity account. Section 8–510 also has been revised to provide a temporal priority conforming to paragraph (2)(B).

6. **Certificated Securities.** A long-standing practice has developed whereby secured parties whose collateral consists of a security evidenced by a security certificate take possession of the security certificate. If the security certificate is in bearer form, the secured party's acquisition of possession constitutes "delivery" under Section 8–301(a)(1), and the delivery constitutes "control" under Section 8–106(a). Comment 5 discusses the priority of security interests perfected by control of investment property.

If the security certificate is in registered form, the secured party will not achieve control over the security unless the security certificate contains an appropriate indorsement or is (re)registered in the secured party's name. See Section 8–106(b). However, the secured party's acquisition of possession constitutes "delivery" of the security certificate under Section 8–301 and serves to perfect the security interest under Section 9–313(a), even if the security certificate has not been appropriately indorsed and has not been (re)registered in the secured party's name. A security interest perfected by this method has priority over a security interest perfected other than by control (e.g., by filing). See paragraph (5).

The priority rule stated in paragraph (5) may seem anomalous, in that it can afford less favorable treatment to purchasers who buy collateral outright that to those who take a security interest in it. For example, a buyer of a security certificate would cut off a security interest perfected by filing only if the buyer achieves the status of a protected purchaser under Section 8–303. The buyer would not be a protected purchaser, for example, if it does not obtain "control" under Section 8–106 (e.g., if it fails to obtain a proper indorsement of the certificate) or if it had notice of an adverse claim under Section 8–105. The apparent anomaly disappears, however, when one understands the priority rule not as one intended to protect careless or guilty parties, but as one that eliminates the need to conduct a search of the public records only insofar as necessary to serve the needs of the securities markets.

7. **Secured Financing of Securities Firms.** Priority questions concerning security interests granted by brokers and securities intermediaries are governed by the general control-beats-non-control priority rule of paragraph (1), as supplemented by the special rules set out in paragraphs (2) (temporal priority—first to control), (3) (special priority for securities intermediary), and (6) (equal priority for non-control). The following examples illustrate the priority rules as applied to this setting. (In all cases it is assumed that the debtor retains sufficient other securities to satisfy all customers' claims. This section deals with the relative rights of secured lenders to a securities firm. Disputes between a secured lender and the firm's own customers are governed by Section 8–511.)

Example 7: Able & Co., a securities dealer, enters into financing arrangements with two lenders, Alpha Bank and Beta Bank. In each case the agreements provide that the lender will have a security interest in the securities identified on lists provided to the lender on a daily basis, that the debtor will deliver the securities to the lender on demand, and that the debtor will not list as collateral any securities which the debtor has pledged to any other lender. Upon Able's insolvency it is discovered that Able has listed the same securities on the collateral lists provided to both Alpha and Beta. Alpha and Beta both have perfected security interests under the automatic-perfection rule of Section 9–309(10). Neither Alpha nor Beta has control. Paragraph (6) provides that the security interests of Alpha and Beta rank equally, because each of them has a non-control security interest granted by a securities firm. They share pro-rata.

Example 8: Able enters into financing arrangements, with Alpha Bank and Beta Bank as in Example 7. At some point, however, Beta decides that it is unwilling to continue to provide financing on a non-control basis. Able directs the clearing corporation where it holds its principal inventory of securities to move specified securities into Beta's account. Upon Able's insolvency it is discovered that a list of collateral provided to Alpha includes securities that had been moved to Beta's account. Both Alpha and Beta have perfected security interests; Alpha under the automatic-perfection rule of Section 9–309(10), and Beta under that rule and also the perfection-by-control rule in Section 9–314(a). Beta has control but Alpha does not. Beta has priority over Alpha under paragraph (1).

Example 9: Able & Co. carries its principal inventory of securities through Clearing Corporation, which offers a "shared control" facility whereby a participant securities firm can enter into an arrangement with a lender under which the securities firm will retain the power to trade and otherwise direct dispositions of securities carried in its account, but Clearing Corporation agrees that, at any time the lender so directs, Clearing Corporation will transfer any securities from the firm's account to the lender's account or otherwise dispose of them as directed by the lender. Able enters into financing arrangements with two lenders, Alpha and Beta, each of which obtains such a control agreement from Clearing Corporation. The agreement with each lender provides that Able will designate specific securities as collateral on lists provided to the lender on a daily or other periodic basis, and that it will not pledge the same securities to different lenders. Upon Able's insolvency, it is discovered that Able has listed the same securities on the collateral lists provided to both Alpha and Beta. Both Alpha and Beta have control over the disputed securities. Paragraph (2) awards priority to whichever secured party first entered into the agreement with Clearing Corporation.

8. **Relation to Other Law.** Section 1–103* provides that "unless displaced by particular provisions of this Act, the principles of law and equity . . . shall supplement its provisions." There may be circumstances in which a secured party's action in acquiring a security interest that has priority under this section constitutes conduct that is wrongful under other law. Though the possibility of such resort to other law may provide an appropriate "escape valve" for cases of egregious conduct, care must be taken to ensure that this does not impair the certainty and predictability of the priority rules. Whether a court may appropriately look to other law to impose liability upon or estop a secured party from asserting its Article 9 priority depends on an assessment of the secured

---

* *Referring to unrevised Article 1 (Appendix A).*

party's conduct under the standards established by such other law as well as a determination of whether the particular application of such other law is displaced by the UCC.

Some circumstances in which other law is clearly displaced by the UCC rules are readily identifiable. Common law "first in time, first in right" principles, or correlative tort liability rules such as common law conversion principles under which a purchaser may incur liability to a person with a prior property interest without regard to awareness of that claim, are necessarily displaced by the priority rules set out in this section since these rules determine the relative ranking of security interests in investment property. So too, Article 8 provides protections against adverse claims to certain purchasers of interests in investment property. In circumstances where a secured party not only has priority under Section 9–328, but also qualifies for protection against adverse claims under Section 8–303, 8–502, or 8–510, resort to other law would be precluded.

In determining whether it is appropriate in a particular case to look to other law, account must also be taken of the policies that underlie the commercial law rules on securities markets and security interests in securities. A principal objective of the 1994 revision of Article 8 and the provisions of Article 9 governing investment property was to ensure that secured financing transactions can be implemented on a simple, timely, and certain basis. One of the circumstances that led to the revision was the concern that uncertainty in the application of the rules on secured transactions involving securities and other financial assets could contribute to systemic risk by impairing the ability of financial institutions to provide liquidity to the markets in times of stress. The control priority rule is designed to provide a clear and certain rule to ensure that lenders who have taken the necessary steps to establish control do not face a risk of subordination to other lenders who have not done so.

The control priority rule does not turn on an inquiry into the state of a secured party's awareness of potential conflicting claims because a rule under which a person's rights depended on that sort of after-the-fact inquiry could introduce an unacceptable measure of uncertainty. If an inquiry into awareness could provide a complete and satisfactory resolution of the problem in all cases, the priority rules of this section would have incorporated that test. The fact that they do not necessarily means that resort to other law based solely on that factor is precluded, though the question whether a control secured party induced or encouraged its financing arrangement with actual knowledge that the debtor would be violating the rights of another secured party may, in some circumstances, appropriately be treated as a factor in determining whether the control party's action is the kind of egregious conduct for which resort to other law is appropriate.

§ 9–329. Priority of Security Interests in Letter-of-Credit Right.

The following rules govern priority among conflicting security interests in the same letter-of-credit right:

(1) A security interest held by a secured party having control of the letter-of-credit right under Section 9–107 has priority to the extent of its control over a conflicting security interest held by a secured party that does not have control.

(2) Security interests perfected by control under Section 9–314 rank according to priority in time of obtaining control.

Official Comment

1. **Source.** New; loosely modeled after former Section 9–115(5).

2. **General Rule.** Paragraph (1) awards priority to a secured party who perfects a security interest directly in letter-of-credit rights (i.e., one that takes an assignment of proceeds and obtains consent of the issuer or any nominated person under Section 5–114(c)) over another conflicting security interest (i.e., one that is perfected automatically in the letter-of-credit rights as supporting obligations under Section 9–308(d)). This is consistent with international letter-of-credit practice and provides finality to payments made to recognized assignees of letter-of-credit proceeds. If an issuer or nominated person recognizes multiple security interests in a letter-of-credit right, resulting in multiple parties having control (Section 9–107), under paragraph (2) the security interests rank according to the time of obtaining control.

3. **Drawing Rights; Transferee Beneficiaries.** Drawing under a letter of credit is personal to the beneficiary and requires the beneficiary to perform the conditions for drawing under the letter of credit. Accordingly, a beneficiary's grant of a security interest in a letter of credit includes the beneficiary's "letter-of-credit right" as defined in Section 9–102 and the right to "proceeds of [the] letter of credit" as defined in Section 5–114(a), but does not include the right to demand payment under the letter of credit.

Section 5–114(e) provides that the "[r]ights of a transferee beneficiary or nominated person are independent of the beneficiary's assignment of the proceeds of a letter of credit and are superior to the assignee's right to the proceeds." To the extent the rights of a transferee beneficiary or nominated person are independent and superior, this Article does not apply. See Section 9–109(c).

Under Article 5, there is in effect a novation upon the transfer with the issuer becoming bound on a new, independent obligation to the transferee. The rights of nominated persons and transferee beneficiaries under a letter of credit include the right to demand payment from the issuer. Under Section 5–114(e), their rights to payment are independent of their obligations to the beneficiary (or original beneficiary) and superior to the rights of assignees of letter-of-credit proceeds (Section 5–114(c)) and others claiming a security interest in the beneficiary's (or original beneficiary's) letter-of-credit rights.

A transfer of drawing rights under a transferable letter of credit establishes independent Article 5 rights in the transferee and does not create or perfect an Article 9 security interest in the transferred drawing rights. The definition of "letter-of-credit right" in Section 9–102 excludes a beneficiary's drawing rights. The exercise of drawing rights by a transferee beneficiary may breach a contractual obligation of the transferee to the original beneficiary concerning when and how much the transferee may draw or how it may use the funds received under the letter of credit. If, for example, drawing rights are transferred to support a sale or loan from the transferee to the original beneficiary, then the transferee would be obligated to the original beneficiary under the sale or loan agreement to account for any drawing and for the use of any funds received. The transferee's obligation would be governed by the applicable law of contracts or restitution.

4. **Secured Party-Transferee Beneficiaries.** As described in Comment 3, drawing rights under letters of credit are transferred in many commercial contexts in which the transferee is not a secured party claiming a security interest in an underlying receivable supported by the letter of credit. Consequently, a transfer of a letter of credit is not a method of "perfection" of a security interest. The transferee's independent right to draw under the letter of credit and to receive and retain the value thereunder (in effect, priority) is not based on Article 9 but on letter-of-credit law and the terms of the letter of credit. Assume, however, that a secured party does hold a security interest in a receivable that is owned by a beneficiary-debtor and supported by a transferable letter of credit. Assume further that the beneficiary-debtor causes the letter of credit to be transferred to the secured party, the secured party draws under the letter of credit, and, upon the issuer's payment to the secured party-transferee, the underlying account debtor's obligation to the original beneficiary-debtor is satisfied. In this situation, the payment to the secured party-transferee is proceeds of the receivable collected by the secured party-transferee. Consequently, the secured party-transferee would have certain duties to the debtor and third parties under Article 9. For example, it would be obliged to collect under the letter of credit in a commercially reasonable manner and to remit any surplus pursuant to Sections 9–607 and 9–608.

This scenario is problematic under letter-of-credit law and practice, inasmuch as a transferee beneficiary collects in its own right arising from its own performance. Accordingly, under Section 5–114, the independent and superior rights of a transferee control over any inconsistent duties under Article 9. A transferee beneficiary may take a transfer of drawing rights to avoid reliance on the original beneficiary's credit and collateral, and it may consider any Article 9 rights superseded by its Article 5 rights. Moreover, it will not always be clear (i) whether a transferee beneficiary has a security interest in the underlying collateral, (ii) whether any security interest is senior to the rights of others, or (iii) whether the transferee beneficiary is aware that it holds a security interest. There will be clear cases in which the role of a transferee beneficiary as such is merely incidental to a conventional secured financing. There also will be cases in which the existence of a security interest may have little to do with the position of a transferee beneficiary as such. In dealing with these cases and less clear cases involving the possible application of Article 9 to a nominated person or a transferee beneficiary, the right to demand payment under a letter of credit should be distinguished from letter-of-credit rights. The courts also should give appropriate consideration to the policies and provisions of Article 5 and letter-of-credit practice as well as Article 9.

§ 9–330. Priority of Purchaser of Chattel Paper or Instrument.

(a) **[Purchaser's priority: security interest claimed merely as proceeds.]** A purchaser of chattel paper has priority over a security interest in the chattel paper which is claimed merely as proceeds of inventory subject to a security interest if:

(1) in good faith and in the ordinary course of the purchaser's business, the purchaser gives new value and takes possession of the chattel paper or obtains control of the chattel paper under Section 9–105; and

821

(2)   the chattel paper does not indicate that it has been assigned to an identified assignee other than the purchaser.

(b)   **[Purchaser's priority: other security interests.]** A purchaser of chattel paper has priority over a security interest in the chattel paper which is claimed other than merely as proceeds of inventory subject to a security interest if the purchaser gives new value and takes possession of the chattel paper or obtains control of the chattel paper under Section 9–105 in good faith, in the ordinary course of the purchaser's business, and without knowledge that the purchase violates the rights of the secured party.

(c)   **[Chattel paper purchaser's priority in proceeds.]** Except as otherwise provided in Section 9–327, a purchaser having priority in chattel paper under subsection (a) or (b) also has priority in proceeds of the chattel paper to the extent that:

(1)   Section 9–322 provides for priority in the proceeds; or

(2)   the proceeds consist of the specific goods covered by the chattel paper or cash proceeds of the specific goods, even if the purchaser's security interest in the proceeds is unperfected.

(d)   **[Instrument purchaser's priority.]** Except as otherwise provided in Section 9–331(a), a purchaser of an instrument has priority over a security interest in the instrument perfected by a method other than possession if the purchaser gives value and takes possession of the instrument in good faith and without knowledge that the purchase violates the rights of the secured party.

(e)   **[Holder of purchase-money security interest gives new value.]** For purposes of subsections (a) and (b), the holder of a purchase-money security interest in inventory gives new value for chattel paper constituting proceeds of the inventory.

(f)   **[Indication of assignment gives knowledge.]** For purposes of subsections (b) and (d), if chattel paper or an instrument indicates that it has been assigned to an identified secured party other than the purchaser, a purchaser of the chattel paper or instrument has knowledge that the purchase violates the rights of the secured party.

Official Comment

1.   **Source.** Former Section 9–308.

2.   **Non-Temporal Priority.** This Article permits a security interest in chattel paper or instruments to be perfected either by filing or by the secured party's taking possession. This section enables secured parties and other purchasers of chattel paper (both electronic and tangible) and instruments to obtain priority over earlier-perfected security interests, thereby promoting the negotiability of these types of receivables.

3.   **Chattel Paper.** Subsections (a) and (b) follow former Section 9–308 in distinguishing between earlier-perfected security interests in chattel paper that is claimed merely as proceeds of inventory subject to a security interest and chattel paper that is claimed other than merely as proceeds. Like former Section 9–308, this section does not elaborate upon the phrase "merely as proceeds." For an elaboration, see PEB Commentary No. 8.

This section makes explicit the "good faith" requirement and retains the requirements of "the ordinary course of the purchaser's business" and the giving of "new value" as conditions for priority. Concerning the last, this Article deletes former Section 9–108 and adds to Section 9–102 a completely different definition of the term "new value." Under subsection (e), the holder of a purchase-money security interest in inventory is deemed to give "new value" for chattel paper constituting the proceeds of the inventory. Accordingly, the purchase-money secured party may qualify for priority in the chattel paper under subsection (a) or (b), whichever is applicable, even if it does not make an additional advance against the chattel paper.

If a possessory security interest in tangible chattel paper or a perfected-by-control security interest in electronic chattel paper does not qualify for priority under this section, it may be subordinate to a perfected-by-filing security interest under Section 9–322(a)(1).

4.   **Possession and Control.** To qualify for priority under subsection (a) or (b), a purchaser must "take[ ] possession of the chattel paper or obtain[ ] control of the chattel paper under Section 9–105." When chattel paper comprises one or more tangible records and one or more electronic records, a purchaser may satisfy the possession-or-control requirement by taking possession of the tangible records under Section 9–313 and having control of the electronic records under Section 9–105. In determining which of several related records constitutes chattel paper

and thus is relevant to possession or control, the form of the records is irrelevant. Rather, the touchstone is whether possession or control of the record would afford the public notice contemplated by the possession and control requirements. For example, because possession or control of an amendment extending the term of a lease would not afford the contemplated public notice, the amendment would not constitute chattel paper regardless of whether the amendment is in tangible form and the lease is in electronic form, the amendment is electronic and the lease is tangible, the amendment and lease are both tangible, or the amendment and lease are both electronic.

Two common practices have raised particular concerns with respect to the possession requirement. First, in some cases the parties create more than one copy or counterpart of chattel paper evidencing a single secured obligation or lease. This practice raises questions as to which counterpart is the "original" and whether it is necessary for a purchaser to take possession of all counterparts in order to "take possession" of the chattel paper. Second, parties sometimes enter into a single "master" agreement. The master agreement contemplates that the parties will enter into separate "schedules" from time to time, each evidencing chattel paper. Must a purchaser of an obligation or lease evidenced by a single schedule also take possession of the master agreement as well as the schedule in order to "take possession" of the chattel paper?

The problem raised by the first practice is easily solved. The parties may in the terms of their agreement and by designation on the chattel paper identify only one counterpart as the original chattel paper for purposes of taking possession of the chattel paper. Concerns about the second practice also are easily solved by careful drafting. Each schedule should provide that it incorporates the terms of the master agreement, not the other way around. This will make it clear that each schedule is a "stand alone" document.

A secured party may wish to convert tangible chattel paper to electronic chattel paper and vice versa. The priority of a security interest in chattel paper under subsection (a) or (b) may be preserved, even if the form of the chattel paper changes. The principle implied in the preceding paragraph, i.e., that not every copy of chattel paper is relevant, applies to "control" as well as to "possession." When there are multiple copies of chattel paper, a secured party may take "possession" or obtain "control" of the chattel paper if it acts with respect to the copy or copies that are reliably identified as the copy or copies that are relevant for purposes of possession or control. This principle applies as well to chattel paper that has been converted from one form to another, even if the relevant copies are not the "original" chattel paper.

5. **Chattel Paper Claimed Merely as Proceeds.** Subsection (a) revises the rule in former Section 9–308(b) to eliminate reference to what the purchaser knows. Instead, a purchaser who meets the possession or control, ordinary course, and new value requirements takes priority over a competing security interest unless the chattel paper itself indicates that it has been assigned to an identified assignee other than the purchaser. Thus subsection (a) recognizes the common practice of placing a "legend" on chattel paper to indicate that it has been assigned. This approach, under which the chattel paper purchaser who gives new value in ordinary course can rely on possession of unlegended, tangible chattel paper without any concern for other facts that it may know, comports with the expectations of both inventory and chattel paper financers.

6. **Chattel Paper Claimed Other Than Merely as Proceeds.** Subsection (b) eliminates the requirement that the purchaser take without knowledge that the "specific paper" is subject to the security interest and substitutes for it the requirement that the purchaser take "without knowledge that the purchase violates the rights of the secured party." This standard derives from the definition of "buyer in ordinary course of business" in Section 1–201(b)(9). The source of the purchaser's knowledge is irrelevant. Note, however, that "knowledge" means "actual knowledge." Section 1–202(b).

In contrast to a junior secured party in accounts, who may be required in some special circumstances to undertake a search under the "good faith" requirement, see Comment 5 to Section 9–331, a purchaser of chattel paper under this section is not required as a matter of good faith to make a search in order to determine the existence of prior security interests. There may be circumstances where the purchaser undertakes a search nevertheless, either on its own volition or because other considerations make it advisable to do so, e.g., where the purchaser also is purchasing accounts. Without more, a purchaser of chattel paper who has seen a financing statement covering the chattel paper or who knows that the chattel paper is encumbered with a security interest, does not have knowledge that its purchase violates the secured party's rights. However, if a purchaser sees a statement in a financing statement to the effect that a purchase of chattel paper from the debtor would violate the rights of the filed secured party, the purchaser would have such knowledge. Likewise, under new subsection (f), if the chattel paper itself indicates that it had been assigned to an identified secured party other than the purchaser, the purchaser would have wrongful knowledge for purposes of subsection (b), thereby preventing the purchaser from qualifying for priority under that subsection, even if the purchaser did not have actual knowledge. In the case of tangible chattel paper, the indication normally would consist of a written legend on the chattel paper. In the case of electronic chattel paper, this Article leaves to developing market and technological practices the manner in which the chattel paper would indicate an assignment.

7.   **Instruments.** Subsection (d) contains a special priority rule for instruments. Under this subsection, a purchaser of an instrument has priority over a security interest perfected by a method other than possession (e.g., by filing, temporarily under Section 9–312(e) or (g), as proceeds under Section 9–315(d), or automatically upon attachment under Section 9–309(4) if the security interest arises out of a sale of the instrument) if the purchaser gives value and takes possession of the instrument in good faith and without knowledge that the purchase violates the rights of the secured party. Generally, to the extent subsection (d) conflicts with Section 3–306, subsection (d) governs. See Section 3–102(b). For example, notice of a conflicting security interest precludes a purchaser from becoming a holder in due course under Section 3–302 and thereby taking free of all claims to the instrument under Section 3–306. However, a purchaser who takes even with knowledge of the security interest qualifies for priority under subsection (d) if it takes without knowledge that the purchase violates the rights of the holder of the security interest. Likewise, a purchaser qualifies for priority under subsection (d) if it takes for "value" as defined in Section 1–201,* even if it does not take for "value" as defined in Section 3–303.

Subsection (d) is subject to Section 9–331(a), which provides that Article 9 does not limit the rights of a holder in due course under Article 3. Thus, in the rare case in which the purchaser of an instrument qualifies for priority under subsection (d), but another person has the rights of a holder in due course of the instrument, the other person takes free of the purchaser's claim. See Section 3–306.

The rule in subsection (d) is similar to the rules in subsections (a) and (b), which govern priority in chattel paper. The observations in Comment 6 concerning the requirement of good faith and the phrase "without knowledge that the purchase violates the rights of the secured party" apply equally to purchasers of instruments. However, unlike a purchaser of chattel paper, to qualify for priority under this section a purchaser of an instrument need only give "value" as defined in Section 1–201;* it need not give "new value." Also, the purchaser need not purchase the instrument in the ordinary course of its business.

Subsection (d) applies to checks as well as notes. For example, to collect and retain checks that are proceeds (collections) of accounts free of a senior secured party's claim to the same checks, a junior secured party must satisfy the good-faith requirement (honesty in fact and the observance of reasonable commercial standards of fair dealing) of this subsection. This is the same good-faith requirement applicable to holders in due course. See Section 9–331, Comment 5.

8.   **Priority in Proceeds of Chattel Paper.** Subsection (c) sets forth the two circumstances under which the priority afforded to a purchaser of chattel paper under subsection (a) or (b) extends also to proceeds of the chattel paper. The first is if the purchaser would have priority under the normal priority rules applicable to proceeds. The second, which the following Comments discuss in greater detail, is if the proceeds consist of the specific goods covered by the chattel paper. Former Article 9 generally was silent as to the priority of a security interest in proceeds when a purchaser qualifies for priority under Section 9–308 (but see former Section 9–306(5)(b), concerning returned and repossessed goods).

9.   **Priority in Returned and Repossessed Goods.** Returned and repossessed goods may constitute proceeds of chattel paper. The following Comments explain the treatment of returned and repossessed goods as proceeds of chattel paper. The analysis is consistent with that of PEB Commentary No. 5, which these Comments replace, and is based upon the following example:

Example: SP–1 has a security interest in all the inventory of a dealer in goods (Dealer); SP–1's security interest is perfected by filing. Dealer sells some of its inventory to a buyer in the ordinary course of business (BIOCOB) pursuant to a conditional sales contract (chattel paper) that does not indicate that it has been assigned to SP–1. SP–2 purchases the chattel paper from Dealer and takes possession of the paper in good faith, in the ordinary course of business, and without knowledge that the purchase violates the rights of SP–1. Subsequently, BIOCOB returns the goods to Dealer because they are defective. Alternatively, Dealer acquires possession of the goods following BIOCOB's default.

10.   **Assignment of Non-Lease Chattel Paper.**

a.   **Loan by SP–2 to Dealer Secured by Chattel Paper (or Functional Equivalent Pursuant to Recourse Arrangement).**

---

*   *Referring to unrevised Article 1 (Appendix A).*

824

(1) **Returned Goods.** If BIOCOB returns the goods to Dealer for repairs, Dealer is merely a bailee and acquires thereby no meaningful rights in the goods to which SP–1's security interest could attach. (Although SP–1's security interest could attach to Dealer's interest as a bailee, that interest is not likely to be of any particular value to SP–1.) Dealer is the owner of the *chattel paper* (i.e., the owner of a right to payment secured by a security interest in the goods); SP–2 has a security interest in the chattel paper, as does SP–1 (as proceeds of the goods under Section 9–315). Under Section 9–330, SP–2's security interest in the chattel paper is senior to that of SP–1. SP–2 enjoys this priority regardless of whether, or when, SP–2 filed a financing statement covering the chattel paper. Because chattel paper and goods represent different types of collateral, Dealer does not have any meaningful interest in *goods* to which either SP–1's or SP–2's security interest could attach in order to secure Dealer's obligations to either creditor. See Section 9–102 (defining "chattel paper" and "goods").

Now assume that BIOCOB returns the goods to Dealer under circumstances whereby Dealer once again becomes the owner of the goods. This would be the case, for example, if the goods were defective and BIOCOB was entitled to reject or revoke acceptance of the goods. See Sections 2–602 (rejection), 2–608 (revocation of acceptance). Unless BIOCOB has waived its defenses as against assignees of the chattel paper, SP–1's and SP–2's rights against BIOCOB would be subject to BIOCOB's claims and defenses. See Sections 9–403, 9–404. SP–1's security interest would attach again because the returned goods would be proceeds of the chattel paper. Dealer's acquisition of the goods easily can be characterized as "proceeds" consisting of an "in kind" collection on or distribution on account of the chattel paper. See Section 9–102 (definition of "proceeds"). Assuming that SP–1's security interest is perfected by filing against the goods and that the filing is made in the same office where a filing would be made against the chattel paper, SP–1's security interest in the goods would remain perfected beyond the 20-day period of automatic perfection. See Section 9–315(d).

Because Dealer's newly reacquired interest in the goods is proceeds of the chattel paper, SP–2's security interest also would attach in the goods as proceeds. If SP–2 had perfected its security interest in the chattel paper by filing (again, assuming that filing against the chattel paper was made in the same office where a filing would be made against the goods), SP–2's security interest in the reacquired goods would be perfected beyond 20 days. See Section 9–315(d). However, if SP–2 had relied only on its possession of the chattel paper for perfection and had not filed against the chattel paper or the goods, SP–2's security interest would be unperfected after the 20-day period. See Section 9–315(d). Nevertheless, SP–2's unperfected security interest in the goods would be senior to SP–1's security interest under Section 9–330(c). The result in this priority contest is not affected by SP–2's acquiescence or non-acquiescence in the return of the goods to Dealer.

(2) **Repossessed Goods.** As explained above, Dealer owns the chattel paper covering the goods, subject to security interests in favor of SP–1 and SP–2. In Article 9 parlance, Dealer has an interest in chattel paper, not goods. If Dealer, SP–1, or SP–2 repossesses the goods upon BIOCOB's default, whether the repossession is rightful or wrongful as among Dealer, SP–1, or SP–2, Dealer's interest will not change. The location of goods and the party who possesses them does not affect the fact that Dealer's interest is in chattel paper, not goods. The goods continue to be owned by BIOCOB. SP–1's security interest in the goods does not attach until such time as Dealer reacquires an interest (other than a bare possessory interest) in the goods. For example, Dealer might buy the goods at a foreclosure sale from SP–2 (whose security interest in the chattel paper is senior to that of SP–1); that disposition would cut off BIOCOB's rights in the goods. Section 9–617.

In many cases the matter would end upon sale of the goods to Dealer at a foreclosure sale and there would be no priority contest between SP–1 and SP–2; Dealer would be unlikely to buy the goods under circumstances whereby SP–2 would retain its security interest. There can be exceptions, however. For example, Dealer may be obliged to purchase the goods from SP–2 and SP–2 may be obliged to convey the goods to Dealer, but Dealer may fail to pay SP–2. Or, one could imagine that SP–2, like SP–1, has a general security interest in the inventory of Dealer. In the latter case, SP–2 should not receive the benefit of any special priority rule, since its interest in no way derives from priority under Section 9–330. In the former case, SP–2's security interest in the goods reacquired by Dealer is senior to SP–1's security interest under Section 9–330.

b. **Dealer's Outright Sale of Chattel Paper to SP–2.** Article 9 also applies to a transaction whereby SP–2 buys the chattel paper in an outright sale transaction without recourse against Dealer. Sections 1–201(37),[*] 9–109(a). Although Dealer does not, in such a transaction, retain any residual ownership interest in the chattel paper, the chattel paper constitutes proceeds of the goods to which SP–1's security interest will attach and continue following the sale of the goods. Section 9–315(a). Even though Dealer has not retained any interest in the chattel paper, as discussed above BIOCOB subsequently may return the goods to Dealer under circumstances whereby

---

[*] *Referring to unrevised Article 1 (Appendix A).*

Dealer reacquires an interest in the goods. The priority contest between SP–1 and SP–2 will be resolved as discussed above; Section 9–330 makes no distinction among purchasers of chattel paper on the basis of whether the purchaser is an outright buyer of chattel paper or one whose security interest secures an obligation of Dealer.

11.   **Assignment of Lease Chattel Paper.** As defined in Section 9–102, "chattel paper" includes not only writings that evidence security interests in specific goods but also those that evidence true leases of goods.

The analysis with respect to lease chattel paper is similar to that set forth above with respect to non-lease chattel paper. It is complicated, however, by the fact that, unlike the case of chattel paper arising out of a sale, Dealer retains a residual interest in the *goods*. See Section 2A–103(1)(q) (defining "lessor's residual interest"); *In re Leasing Consultants, Inc.*, 486 F.2d 367 (2d Cir. 1973) (lessor's residual interest under true lease is an interest in goods and is a separate type of collateral from lessor's interest in the lease). If Dealer leases goods to a "lessee in ordinary course of business" (LIOCOB), then LIOCOB takes its interest under the lease (i.e., its "leasehold interest") free of the security interest of SP–1. See Sections 2A–307(3), 2A–103(1)(m) (defining "leasehold interest"), (1)(*o*) (defining "lessee in ordinary course of business"). SP–1 would, however, retain its security interest in the residual interest. In addition, SP–1 would acquire an interest in the lease chattel paper as proceeds. If Dealer then assigns the lease chattel paper to SP–2, Section 9–330 gives SP–2 priority over SP–1 with respect to the chattel paper, *but not* with respect to the residual interest in the *goods*. Consequently, assignees of lease chattel paper typically take a security interest in and file against the lessor's residual interest in goods, expecting their priority in the goods to be governed by the first-to-file-or-perfect rule of Section 9–322.

If the goods are returned to Dealer, other than upon expiration of the lease term, then the security interests of both SP–1 and SP–2 normally would attach to the goods as proceeds of the chattel paper. (If the goods are returned to Dealer at the expiration of the lease term and the lessee has made all payments due under the lease, however, then Dealer no longer has any rights under the chattel paper. Dealer's interest in the goods consists solely of its residual interest, as to which SP–2 has no claim.) This would be the case, for example, when the lessee rescinds the lease or when the lessor recovers possession in the exercise of its remedies under Article 2A. See, e.g., Section 2A–525. If SP–2 enjoyed priority in the chattel paper under Section 9–330, then SP–2 likewise would enjoy priority in the returned goods as proceeds. This does not mean that SP–2 necessarily is entitled to the entire value of the returned goods. The value of the goods represents the sum of the present value of (i) the value of their use for the term of the lease and (ii) the value of the residual interest. SP–2 has priority in the former, but SP–1 ordinarily would have priority in the latter. Thus, an allocation of a portion of the value of the goods to each component may be necessary. Where, as here, one secured party has a security interest in the lessor's residual interest and another has a priority security interest in the chattel paper, it may be advisable for the conflicting secured parties to establish a method for making such an allocation and otherwise to determine their relative rights in returned goods by agreement.

As amended in 2000 and 2010.

§ 9–331.   Priority of Rights of Purchasers of Instruments, Documents, and Securities Under Other Articles; Priority of Interests in Financial Assets and Security Entitlements Under Article 8.

(a)   **[Rights under Articles 3, 7, and 8 not limited.]** This article does not limit the rights of a holder in due course of a negotiable instrument, a holder to which a negotiable document of title has been duly negotiated, or a protected purchaser of a security. These holders or purchasers take priority over an earlier security interest, even if perfected, to the extent provided in Articles 3, 7, and 8.

(b)   **[Protection under Article 8.]** This article does not limit the rights of or impose liability on a person to the extent that the person is protected against the assertion of a claim under Article 8.

(c)   **[Filing not notice.]** Filing under this article does not constitute notice of a claim or defense to the holders, or purchasers, or persons described in subsections (a) and (b).

Official Comment

1.   **Source.** Former Section 9–309.

2.   **"Priority."** In some provisions, this Article distinguishes between claimants that take collateral free of a security interest (in the sense that the security interest no longer encumbers the collateral) and those that take an interest in the collateral that is senior to a surviving security interest. See, e.g., Section 9–317. Whether a holder or purchaser referred to in this section takes free or is senior to a security interest depends on whether

the purchaser is a buyer of the collateral or takes a security interest in it. The term "priority" is meant to encompass both scenarios, as it does in Section 9–330.

3. **Rights Acquired by Purchasers.** The rights to which this section refers are set forth in Sections 3–305 and 3–306 (holder in due course), 7–502 (holder to whom a negotiable document of title has been duly negotiated), and 8–303 (protected purchaser). The holders and purchasers referred to in this section do not always take priority over a security interest. See, e.g., Section 7–503 (affording paramount rights to certain owners and secured parties as against holder to whom a negotiable document of title has been duly negotiated). Accordingly, this section adds the clause, "to the extent provided in Articles 3, 7, and 8" to former Section 9–309.

4. **Financial Assets and Security Entitlements.** New subsection (b) provides explicit protection for those who deal with financial assets and security entitlements and who are immunized from liability under Article 8. See, e.g., Sections 8–502, 8–503(e), 8–510, 8–511. The new subsection makes explicit in Article 9 what is implicit in former Article 9 and explicit in several provisions of Article 8. It does not change the law.

5. **Collections by Junior Secured Party.** Under this section, a secured party with a junior security interest in receivables (accounts, chattel paper, promissory notes, or payment intangibles) may collect and retain the proceeds of those receivables free of the claim of a senior secured party to the same receivables, if the junior secured party is a holder in due course of the proceeds. In order to qualify as a holder in due course, the junior must satisfy the requirements of Section 3–302, which include taking in "good faith." This means that the junior not only must act "honestly" but also must observe "reasonable commercial standards of fair dealing" under the particular circumstances. See Section 9–102(a). Although "good faith" does not impose a general duty of inquiry, e.g., a search of the records in filing offices, there may be circumstances in which "reasonable commercial standards of fair dealing" would require such a search.

Consider, for example, a junior secured party in the business of financing or buying accounts who fails to undertake a search to determine the existence of prior security interests. Because a search, under the usages of trade of that business, would enable it to know or learn upon reasonable inquiry that collecting the accounts violated the rights of a senior secured party, the junior may fail to meet the good-faith standard. See *Utility Contractors Financial Services, Inc. v. Amsouth Bank, NA*, 985 F.2d 1554 (11th Cir. 1993). Likewise, a junior secured party who collects accounts when it knows or should know under the particular circumstances that doing so would violate the rights of a senior secured party, because the debtor had agreed not to grant a junior security interest in, or sell, the accounts, may not meet the good-faith test. Thus, if a junior secured party conducted or should have conducted a search and a financing statement filed on behalf of the senior secured party states such a restriction, the junior's collection would not meet the good-faith standard. On the other hand, if there was a course of performance between the senior secured party and the debtor which placed no such restrictions on the debtor and allowed the debtor to collect and use the proceeds without any restrictions, the junior secured party may then satisfy the requirements for being a holder in due course. This would be more likely in those circumstances where the junior secured party was providing additional financing to the debtor on an on-going basis by lending against or buying the accounts and had no notice of any restrictions against doing so. Generally, the senior secured party would not be prejudiced because the practical effect of such payment to the junior secured party is little different than if the debtor itself had made the collections and subsequently paid the secured party from the debtor's general funds. Absent collusion, the junior secured party would take the funds free of the senior security interests. See Section 9–332. In contrast, the senior secured party is likely to be prejudiced if the debtor is going out of business and the junior secured party collects the accounts by notifying the account debtors to make payments directly to the junior. Those collections may not be consistent with "reasonable commercial standards of fair dealing."

Whether the junior secured party qualifies as a holder in due course is fact-sensitive and should be decided on a case-by-case basis in the light of those circumstances. Decisions such as *Financial Management Services, Inc. v. Familian*, 905 P.2d 506 (Ariz. App. Div. 1995) (finding holder in due course status) could be determined differently under this application of the good-faith requirement.

The concepts addressed in this Comment are also applicable to junior secured parties as purchasers of instruments under Section 9–330(d). See Section 9–330, Comment 7.

§ 9–332. Transfer of Money; Transfer of Funds From Deposit Account.

(a) **[Transferee of money.]** A transferee of money takes the money free of a security interest unless the transferee acts in collusion with the debtor in violating the rights of the secured party.

(b) [Transferee of funds from deposit account.] A transferee of funds from a deposit account takes the funds free of a security interest in the deposit account unless the transferee acts in collusion with the debtor in violating the rights of the secured party.

Official Comment

1.   **Source.** New.

2.   **Scope of This Section.** This section affords broad protection to transferees who take funds from a deposit account and to those who take money. The term "transferee" is not defined; however, the debtor itself is not a transferee. Thus this section does not cover the case in which a debtor withdraws money (currency) from its deposit account or the case in which a bank debits an encumbered account and credits another account it maintains for the debtor.

A transfer of funds from a deposit account, to which subsection (b) applies, normally will be made by check, by funds transfer, or by debiting the debtor's deposit account and crediting another depositor's account.

Example 1: Debtor maintains a deposit account with Bank A. The deposit account is subject to a perfected security interest in favor of Lender. Debtor draws a check on the account, payable to Payee. Inasmuch as the check is not the proceeds of the deposit account (it is an order to pay funds from the deposit account), Lender's security interest in the deposit account does not give rise to a security interest in the check. Payee deposits the check into its own deposit account, and Bank A pays it. Unless Payee acted in collusion with Debtor in violating Lender's rights, Payee takes the funds (the credits running in favor of Payee) free of Lender's security interest. This is true regardless of whether Payee is a holder in due course of the check and even if Payee gave no value for the check.

Example 2: Debtor maintains a deposit account with Bank A. The deposit account is subject to a perfected security interest in favor of Lender. At Bank B's suggestion, Debtor moves the funds from the account at Bank A to Debtor's deposit account with Bank B. Unless Bank B acted in collusion with Debtor in violating Lender's rights, Bank B takes the funds (the credits running in favor of Bank B) free from Lender's security interest. See subsection (b). However, inasmuch as the deposit account maintained with Bank B constitutes the proceeds of the deposit account at Bank A, Lender's security interest would attach to that account as proceeds. See Section 9-315.

Subsection (b) also would apply if, in the example, Bank A debited Debtor's deposit account in exchange for the issuance of Bank A's cashier's check. Lender's security interest would attach to the cashier's check as proceeds of the deposit account, and the rules applicable to instruments would govern any competing claims to the cashier's check. See, e.g., Sections 3-306, 9-322, 9-330, 9-331.

If Debtor withdraws money (currency) from an encumbered deposit account and transfers the money to a third party, then subsection (a), to the extent not displaced by federal law relating to money, applies. It contains the same rule as subsection (b).

Subsection (b) applies to *transfers of funds from* a deposit account; it does not apply to *transfers of the deposit account* itself or of an interest therein. For example, this section does not apply to the creation of a security interest in a deposit account. Competing claims to the deposit account itself are dealt with by other Article 9 priority rules. See Sections 9-317(a), 9-327, 9-340, 9-341. Similarly, a corporate merger normally would not result in a transfer of funds from a deposit account. Rather, it might result in a transfer of the deposit account itself. If so, the normal rules applicable to transferred collateral would apply; this section would not.

3.   **Policy.** Broad protection for transferees helps to ensure that security interests in deposit accounts do not impair the free flow of funds. It also minimizes the likelihood that a secured party will enjoy a claim to whatever the transferee purchases with the funds. Rules concerning recovery of payments traditionally have placed a high value on finality. The opportunity to upset a completed transaction, or even to place a completed transaction in jeopardy by bringing suit against the transferee of funds, should be severely limited. Although the giving of value usually is a prerequisite for receiving the ability to take free from third-party claims, where payments are concerned the law is even more protective. Thus, Section 3-418(c) provides that, even where the law of restitution otherwise would permit recovery of funds paid by mistake, no recovery may be had from a person "who in good faith changed position in reliance on the payment." Rather than adopt this standard, this section eliminates all reliance requirements whatsoever. Payments made by mistake are relatively rare, but payments of funds from encumbered deposit accounts (e.g., deposit accounts containing collections from accounts receivable) occur with great regularity. In most cases, unlike payment by mistake, no one would object to these payments. In

828

the vast proportion of cases, the transferee probably would be able to show a change of position in reliance on the payment. This section does not put the transferee to the burden of having to make this proof.

4. **"Bad Actors."** To deal with the question of the "bad actor," this section borrows "collusion" language from Article 8. See, e.g., Sections 8–115, 8–503(e). This is the most protective (i.e., least stringent) of the various standards now found in the UCC. Compare, e.g., Section 1–201(b)(9) ("without knowledge that the sale violates the rights of another person"); Section 1–201(b)(20) ("honesty in fact and the observance of reasonable commercial standards of fair dealing"); Section 3–302(a)(2)(v) ("without notice of any claim").

5. **Transferee Who Does Not Take Free.** This section sets forth the circumstances under which certain transferees of money or funds take free of security interests. It does not determine the rights of a transferee who does not take free of a security interest.

Example 3: The facts are as in Example 2, but, in wrongfully moving the funds from the deposit account at Bank A to Debtor's deposit account with Bank B, Debtor acts in collusion with Bank B. Bank B does not take the funds free of Lender's security interest under this section. If Debtor grants a security interest to Bank B, Section 9–327 governs the relative priorities of Lender and Bank B. Under Section 9–327(3), Bank B's security interest in the Bank B deposit account is senior to Lender's security interest in the deposit account as proceeds. However, Bank B's senior security interest does not protect Bank B against any liability to Lender that might arise from Bank B's wrongful conduct.

As amended in 2010.

§ 9–333. Priority of Certain Liens Arising by Operation of Law.

(a) **["Possessory lien."]** In this section, "possessory lien" means an interest, other than a security interest or an agricultural lien:

(1) which secures payment or performance of an obligation for services or materials furnished with respect to goods by a person in the ordinary course of the person's business;

(2) which is created by statute or rule of law in favor of the person; and

(3) whose effectiveness depends on the person's possession of the goods.

(b) **[Priority of possessory lien.]** A possessory lien on goods has priority over a security interest in the goods unless the lien is created by a statute that expressly provides otherwise.

Official Comment

1. **Source.** Former Section 9–310.

2. **"Possessory Liens."** This section governs the relative priority of security interests arising under this Article and "possessory liens," i.e., common-law and statutory liens whose effectiveness depends on the lienor's possession of goods with respect to which the lienor provided services or furnished materials in the ordinary course of its business. As under former Section 9–310, the possessory lien has priority over a security interest unless the possessory lien is created by a statute that expressly provides otherwise. If the statute creating the possessory lien is silent as to its priority relative to a security interest, this section provides a rule of interpretation that the possessory lien takes priority, even if the statute has been construed judicially to make the possessory lien subordinate.

§ 9–334. Priority of Security Interests in Fixtures and Crops.

(a) **[Security interest in fixtures under this article.]** A security interest under this article may be created in goods that are fixtures or may continue in goods that become fixtures. A security interest does not exist under this article in ordinary building materials incorporated into an improvement on land.

(b) **[Security interest in fixtures under real-property law.]** This article does not prevent creation of an encumbrance upon fixtures under real property law.

(c) **[General rule: subordination of security interest in fixtures.]** In cases not governed by subsections (d) through (h), a security interest in fixtures is subordinate to a conflicting interest of an encumbrancer or owner of the related real property other than the debtor.

(d)   **[Fixtures purchase-money priority.]** Except as otherwise provided in subsection (h), a perfected security interest in fixtures has priority over a conflicting interest of an encumbrancer or owner of the real property if the debtor has an interest of record in or is in possession of the real property and:

(1)   the security interest is a purchase-money security interest;

(2)   the interest of the encumbrancer or owner arises before the goods become fixtures; and

(3)   the security interest is perfected by a fixture filing before the goods become fixtures or within 20 days thereafter.

(e)   **[Priority of security interest in fixtures over interests in real property.]** A perfected security interest in fixtures has priority over a conflicting interest of an encumbrancer or owner of the real property if:

(1)   the debtor has an interest of record in the real property or is in possession of the real property and the security interest:

(A)   is perfected by a fixture filing before the interest of the encumbrancer or owner is of record; and

(B)   has priority over any conflicting interest of a predecessor in title of the encumbrancer or owner;

(2)   before the goods become fixtures, the security interest is perfected by any method permitted by this article and the fixtures are readily removable:

(A)   factory or office machines;

(B)   equipment that is not primarily used or leased for use in the operation of the real property; or

(C)   replacements of domestic appliances that are consumer goods;

(3)   the conflicting interest is a lien on the real property obtained by legal or equitable proceedings after the security interest was perfected by any method permitted by this article; or

(4)   the security interest is:

(A)   created in a manufactured home in a manufactured-home transaction; and

(B)   perfected pursuant to a statute described in Section 9–311(a)(2).

(f)   **[Priority based on consent, disclaimer, or right to remove.]** A security interest in fixtures, whether or not perfected, has priority over a conflicting interest of an encumbrancer or owner of the real property if:

(1)   the encumbrancer or owner has, in an authenticated record, consented to the security interest or disclaimed an interest in the goods as fixtures; or

(2)   the debtor has a right to remove the goods as against the encumbrancer or owner.

(g)   **[Continuation of paragraph (f)(2) priority.]** The priority of the security interest under paragraph (f)(2) continues for a reasonable time if the debtor's right to remove the goods as against the encumbrancer or owner terminates.

(h)   **[Priority of construction mortgage.]** A mortgage is a construction mortgage to the extent that it secures an obligation incurred for the construction of an improvement on land, including the acquisition cost of the land, if a recorded record of the mortgage so indicates. Except as otherwise provided in subsections (e) and (f), a security interest in fixtures is subordinate to a construction mortgage if a record of the mortgage is recorded before the goods become fixtures and the goods become fixtures before the completion of the construction. A mortgage has this priority to the same extent as a construction mortgage to the extent that it is given to refinance a construction mortgage.

(i) **[Priority of security interest in crops.]** A perfected security interest in crops growing on real property has priority over a conflicting interest of an encumbrancer or owner of the real property if the debtor has an interest of record in or is in possession of the real property.

(j) **[Subsection (i) prevails.]** Subsection (i) prevails over any inconsistent provisions of the following statutes:

[List here any statutes containing provisions inconsistent with subsection (i).]

Legislative Note: States that amend statutes to remove provisions inconsistent with subsection (i) need not enact subsection (j).

Official Comment

1. **Source.** Former Section 9–313.

2. **Scope of This Section.** This section contains rules governing the priority of security interests in fixtures and crops as against persons who claim an interest in real property. Priority contests with other Article 9 security interests are governed by the other priority rules of this Article. The provisions with respect to fixtures follow those of former Section 9–313. However, they have been rewritten to conform to Section 2A–309 and to prevailing style conventions. Subsections (i) and (j), which apply to crops, are new.

3. **Security Interests in Fixtures.** Certain goods that are the subject of personal-property (chattel) financing become so affixed or otherwise so related to real property that they become part of the real property. These goods are called "fixtures." See Section 9–102 (definition of "fixtures"). Some fixtures retain their personal-property nature: a security interest under this Article may be created in fixtures and may continue in goods that become fixtures. See subsection (a). However, if the goods are ordinary building materials incorporated into an improvement on land, no security interest in them exists. Rather, the priority of claims to the building materials are determined by the law governing claims to real property. (Of course, the fact that no security interest exists in ordinary building materials incorporated into an improvement on land does not prejudice any rights the secured party may have against the debtor or any other person who violated the secured party's rights by wrongfully incorporating the goods into real property.)

Thus, this section recognizes three categories of goods: (1) those that retain their chattel character entirely and are not part of the real property; (2) ordinary building materials that have become an integral part of the real property and cannot retain their chattel character for purposes of finance; and (3) an intermediate class that has become real property for certain purposes, but as to which chattel financing may be preserved.

To achieve priority under certain provisions of this section, a security interest must be perfected by making a "fixture filing" (defined in Section 9–102) in the real-property records. Because the question whether goods have become fixtures often is a difficult one under applicable real-property law, a secured party may make a fixture filing as a precaution. Courts should not infer from a fixture filing that the secured party concedes that the goods are or will become fixtures.

4. **Priority in Fixtures: General.** In considering priority problems under this section, one must first determine whether real-property claimants per se have an interest in the crops or fixtures as part of real property. If not, it is immaterial, so far as concerns real property parties as such, whether a security interest arising under this Article is perfected or unperfected. In no event does a real-property claimant (e.g., owner or mortgagee) acquire an interest in a "pure" chattel just because a security interest therein is unperfected. If on the other hand real-property law gives real-property parties an interest in the goods, a conflict arises and this section states the priorities.

5. **Priority in Fixtures: Residual Rule.** Subsection (c) states the residual priority rule, which applies only if one of the other rules does not: A security interest in fixtures is subordinate to a conflicting interest of an encumbrancer or owner of the related real property other than the debtor.

6. **Priority in Fixtures: First to File or Record.** Subsection (e)(1), which follows former Section 9–313(4)(b), contains the usual priority rule of conveyancing, that is, the first to file or record prevails. In order to achieve priority under this rule, however, the security interest must be perfected by a "fixture filing" (defined in Section 9–102), i.e., a filing for record in the real property records and indexed therein, so that it will be found in a real-property search . . . The condition in subsection (e)(1)(B), that the security interest must have had priority over any conflicting interest of a predecessor in title of the conflicting encumbrancer or owner, appears to limit to the first-in-time principle. However, this apparent limitation is nothing other than an expression of the usual rule

that a person must be entitled to transfer what he has. Thus, if the fixture security interest is subordinate to a mortgage, it is subordinate to an interest of an assignee of the mortgage, even though the assignment is a later recorded instrument. Similarly if the fixture security interest is subordinate to the rights of an owner, it is subordinate to a subsequent grantee of the owner and likewise subordinate to a subsequent mortgagee of the owner.

7.   **Priority in Fixtures: Purchase-Money Security Interests.** Subsection (d), which follows former Section 9–313(4)(a), contains the principal exception to the first-to-file-or-record rule of subsection (e)(1). It affords priority to purchase-money security interests in fixtures as against *prior* recorded real-property interests, provided that the purchase-money security interest is filed as a fixture filing in the real-property records before the goods become fixtures or within 20 days thereafter. This priority corresponds to the purchase-money priority under Section 9–324(a). (Like other 10-day periods in former Article 9, the 10-day period in this section has been changed to 20 days.)

It should be emphasized that this purchase-money priority with the 20-day grace period for filing is limited to rights against real-property interests that arise *before* the goods become fixtures. There is no such priority with the 20-day grace period as against real-property interests that arise subsequently. The fixture security interest can defeat subsequent real-property interests only if it is filed first and prevails under the usual conveyancing rule in subsection (e)(1) or one of the other rules in this section.

8.   **Priority in Fixtures: Readily Removable Goods.** Subsection (e)(2), which derives from Section 2A–309 and former Section 9–313(4)(d), contains another exception to the usual first-to-file-or-perfect rule. It affords priority to the holders of security interests in certain types of readily removable goods—factory and office machines, equipment that is not primarily used or leased for use in the operation of the real property, and (as discussed below) certain replacements of domestic appliances. This rule is made necessary by the confusion in the law as to whether certain machinery, equipment, and appliances become fixtures. It protects a secured party who, perhaps in the mistaken belief that the readily removable goods will not become fixtures, makes a UCC filing (or otherwise perfects under this Article) rather than making a fixture filing.

Frequently, under applicable law, goods of the type described in subsection (e)(2) will not be considered to have become part of the real property. In those cases, the fixture security interest does not conflict with a real-property interest, and resort to this section is unnecessary. However, if the goods have become part of the real property, subsection (e)(2) enables a fixture secured party to take priority over a conflicting real-property interest if the fixture security interest is perfected by a fixture filing or by any other method permitted by this Article. If perfection is by fixture filing, the fixture security interest would have priority over subsequently recorded real-property interests under subsection (e)(1) and, if the fixture security interest is a purchase-money security interest (a likely scenario), it would also have priority over most real property interests under the purchase-money priority of subsection (d). Note, however, that unlike the purchase-money priority rule in subsection (d), the priority rules in subsection (e) override the priority given to a construction mortgage under subsection (h).

The rule in subsection (e)(2) is limited to readily removable replacements of domestic appliances. It does not apply to original installations. Moreover, it is limited to appliances that are "consumer goods" (defined in Section 9–102) in the hands of the debtor. The principal effect of the rule is to make clear that a secured party financing occasional replacements of domestic appliances in noncommercial, owner-occupied contexts need not concern itself with real-property descriptions or records; indeed, for a purchase-money replacement of consumer goods, perfection without any filing will be possible. See Section 9–309(1).

9.   **Priority in Fixtures: Judicial Liens.** Subsection (e)(3), which follows former Section 9–313(4)(d), adopts a first-in-time rule applicable to conflicts between a fixture security interest and a lien on the real property obtained by legal or equitable proceedings. Such a lien is subordinate to an earlier-perfected security interest, regardless of the method by which the security interest was perfected. Judgment creditors generally are not reliance creditors who search real-property records. Accordingly, a perfected fixture security interest takes priority over a subsequent judgment lien or other lien obtained by legal or equitable proceedings, even if no evidence of the security interest appears in the relevant real-property records. Subsection (e)(3) thus protects a perfected fixture security interest from avoidance by a trustee in bankruptcy under Bankruptcy Code Section 544(a), regardless of the method of perfection.

10.   **Priority in Fixtures: Manufactured Homes.** A manufactured home may become a fixture. New subsection (e)(4) contains a special rule granting priority to certain security interests created in a "manufactured home" as part of a "manufactured-home transaction" (both defined in Section 9–102). Under this rule, a security interest in a manufactured home that becomes a fixture has priority over a conflicting interest of an encumbrancer

or owner of the real property if the security interest is perfected under a certificate-of-title statute (see Section 9–311). Subsection (e)(4) is only one of the priority rules applicable to security interests in a manufactured home that becomes a fixture. Thus, a security interest in a manufactured home which does not qualify for priority under this subsection may qualify under another.

11. **Priority in Fixtures: Construction Mortgages.** The purchase-money priority presents a difficult problem in relation to construction mortgages. The latter ordinarily will have been recorded even before the commencement of delivery of materials to the job, and therefore would take priority over fixture security interests were it not for the purchase-money priority. However, having recorded first, the holder of a construction mortgage reasonably expects to have first priority in the improvement built using the mortgagee's advances. Subsection (g) expressly gives priority to the construction mortgage recorded before the filing of the purchase-money security interest in fixtures. A refinancing of a construction mortgage has the same priority as the construction mortgage itself. The phrase "an obligation incurred for the construction of an improvement" covers both optional advances and advances pursuant to commitment. Both types of advances have the same priority under subsection (g).

The priority under this subsection applies only to goods that become fixtures during the construction period leading to the completion of the improvement. The construction priority will not apply to additions to the building made long after completion of the improvement, even if the additions are financed by the real-property mortgagee under an open-end clause of the construction mortgage. In such case, subsections (d), (e), and (f) govern.

Although this subsection affords a construction mortgage priority over a purchase-money security interest that otherwise would have priority under subsection (d), the subsection is subject to the priority rules in subsections (e) and (f). Thus, a construction mortgage may be junior to a fixture security interest perfected by a fixture filing before the construction mortgage was recorded. See subsection (e)(1).

12. **Crops.** Growing crops are "goods" in which a security interest may be created and perfected under this Article. In some jurisdictions, a mortgage of real property may cover crops, as well. In the event that crops are encumbered by both a mortgage and an Article 9 security interest, subsection (i) provides that the security interest has priority. States whose real-property law provides otherwise should either amend that law directly or override it by enacting subsection (j).

§ 9–335.   Accessions.

(a)   **[Creation of security interest in accession.]** A security interest may be created in an accession and continues in collateral that becomes an accession.

(b)   **[Perfection of security interest.]** If a security interest is perfected when the collateral becomes an accession, the security interest remains perfected in the collateral.

(c)   **[Priority of security interest.]** Except as otherwise provided in subsection (d), the other provisions of this part determine the priority of a security interest in an accession.

(d)   **[Compliance with certificate-of-title statute.]** A security interest in an accession is subordinate to a security interest in the whole which is perfected by compliance with the requirements of a certificate-of-title statute under Section 9–311(b).

(e)   **[Removal of accession after default.]** After default, subject to Part 6, a secured party may remove an accession from other goods if the security interest in the accession has priority over the claims of every person having an interest in the whole.

(f)   **[Reimbursement following removal.]** A secured party that removes an accession from other goods under subsection (e) shall promptly reimburse any holder of a security interest or other lien on, or owner of, the whole or of the other goods, other than the debtor, for the cost of repair of any physical injury to the whole or the other goods. The secured party need not reimburse the holder or owner for any diminution in value of the whole or the other goods caused by the absence of the accession removed or by any necessity for replacing it. A person entitled to reimbursement may refuse permission to remove until the secured party gives adequate assurance for the performance of the obligation to reimburse.

Official Comment

1.   **Source.** Former Section 9–314.

2.   **"Accession."** This section applies to an "accession," as defined in Section 9–102, regardless of the cost or difficulty of removing the accession from the other goods, and regardless of whether the original goods have come to form an integral part of the other goods. This section does not apply to goods whose identity has been lost. Goods of that kind are "commingled goods" governed by Section 9–336. Neither this section nor the following one addresses the case of collateral that changes form without the addition of other goods.

3.   **"Accession" vs. "Other Goods."** This section distinguishes among the "accession," the "other goods," and the "whole." The last term refers to the combination of the "accession" and the "other goods." If one person's collateral becomes physically united with another person's collateral, each is an "accession."

> **Example 1:** SP–1 holds a security interest in the debtor's tractors (which are not subject to a certificate-of-title statute), and SP–2 holds a security interest in a particular tractor engine. The engine is installed in a tractor. From the perspective of SP–1, the tractor becomes an "accession" and the engine is the "other goods." From the perspective of SP–2, the engine is the "accession" and the tractor is the "other goods." The completed tractor—tractor cum engine—constitutes the "whole."

4.   **Scope.** This section governs only a few issues concerning accessions. Subsection (a) contains rules governing continuation of a security interest in an accession. Subsection (b) contains a rule governing continued perfection of a security interest in goods that become an accession. Subsection (d) contains a special priority rule governing accessions that become part of a whole covered by a certificate of title. Subsections (e) and (f) govern enforcement of a security interest in an accession.

5.   **Matters Left to Other Provisions of This Article: Attachment and Perfection.** Other provisions of this Article often govern accession-related issues. For example, this section does not address whether a secured party acquires a security interest in the whole if its collateral becomes an accession. Normally this will turn on the description of the collateral in the security agreement.

> **Example 2:** Debtor owns a computer subject to a perfected security interest in favor of SP–1. Debtor acquires memory and installs it in the computer. Whether SP–1's security interest attaches to the memory depends on whether the security agreement covers it.

Similarly, this section does not determine whether perfection against collateral that becomes an accession is effective to perfect a security interest in the whole. Other provisions of this Article, including the requirements for indicating the collateral covered by a financing statement, resolve that question.

6.   **Matters Left to Other Provisions of This Article: Priority.** With one exception, concerning goods covered by a certificate of title (see subsection (d)), the other provisions of this Part, including the rules governing purchase-money security interests, determine the priority of most security interests in an accession, including the relative priority of a security interest in an accession and a security interest in the whole. See subsection (c).

> **Example 3:** Debtor owns an office computer subject to a security interest in favor of SP–1. Debtor acquires memory and grants a perfected security interest in the memory to SP–2. Debtor installs the memory in the computer, at which time (one assumes) SP–1's security interest attaches to the memory. The first-to-file-or-perfect rule of Section 9–322 governs priority in the memory. If, however, SP–2's security interest is a purchase-money security interest, Section 9–324(a) would afford priority in the memory to SP–2, regardless of which security interest was perfected first.

7.   **Goods Covered by Certificate of Title.** This section does govern the priority of a security interest in an accession that is or becomes part of a whole that is subject to a security interest perfected by compliance with a certificate-of-title statute. Subsection (d) provides that a security interest in the whole, perfected by compliance with a certificate-of-title statute, takes priority over a security interest in the accession. It enables a secured party to rely upon a certificate of title without having to check the UCC files to determine whether any components of the collateral may be encumbered. The subsection imposes a corresponding risk upon those who finance goods that may become part of goods covered by a certificate of title. In doing so, it reverses the priority that appeared reasonable to most pre-UCC courts.

> **Example 4:** Debtor owns an automobile subject to a security interest in favor of SP–1. The security interest is perfected by notation on the certificate of title. Debtor buys tires subject to a perfected-by-filing purchase-money security interest in favor of SP–2 and mounts the tires on the automobile's wheels. If the security interest in the automobile attaches to the tires, then SP–1 acquires priority over SP–2. The same result

would obtain if SP–1's security interest attached to the automobile and was perfected after the tires had been mounted on the wheels.

§ 9–336.   Commingled Goods.

(a)   **["Commingled goods."]** In this section, "commingled goods" means goods that are physically united with other goods in such a manner that their identity is lost in a product or mass.

(b)   **[No security interest in commingled goods as such.]** A security interest does not exist in commingled goods as such. However, a security interest may attach to a product or mass that results when goods become commingled goods.

(c)   **[Attachment of security interest to product or mass.]** If collateral becomes commingled goods, a security interest attaches to the product or mass.

(d)   **[Perfection of security interest.]** If a security interest in collateral is perfected before the collateral becomes commingled goods, the security interest that attaches to the product or mass under subsection (c) is perfected.

(e)   **[Priority of security interest.]** Except as otherwise provided in subsection (f), the other provisions of this part determine the priority of a security interest that attaches to the product or mass under subsection (c).

(f)   **[Conflicting security interests in product or mass]** If more than one security interest attaches to the product or mass under subsection (c), the following rules determine priority:

(1)   A security interest that is perfected under subsection (d) has priority over a security interest that is unperfected at the time the collateral becomes commingled goods.

(2)   If more than one security interest is perfected under subsection (d), the security interests rank equally in proportion to the value of the collateral at the time it became commingled goods.

Official Comment

1.   **Source.** Former Section 9–315.

2.   **"Commingled Goods."** Subsection (a) defines "commingled goods." It is meant to include not only goods whose identity is lost through manufacturing or production (e.g., flour that has become part of baked goods) but also goods whose identity is lost by commingling with other goods from which they cannot be distinguished (e.g., ball bearings).

3.   **Consequences of Becoming "Commingled Goods."** By definition, the identity of the original collateral cannot be determined once the original collateral becomes commingled goods. Consequently, the security interest in the specific original collateral alone is lost once the collateral becomes commingled goods, and no security interest in the original collateral can be created thereafter except as a part of the resulting product or mass. See subsection (b).

Once collateral becomes commingled goods, the secured party's security interest is transferred from the original collateral to the product or mass. See subsection (c). If the security interest in the original collateral was perfected, the security interest in the product or mass is a perfected security interest. See subsection (d). This perfection continues until lapse.

4.   **Priority of Perfected Security Interests That Attach Under This Section.** This section governs the priority of competing security interests in a product or mass only when both security interests arise under this section. In that case, if both security interests are perfected by operation of this section (see subsections (c) and (d)), then the security interests rank equally, in proportion to the value of the collateral at the time it became commingled goods. See subsection (f)(2).

Example 1: SP–1 has a perfected security interest in Debtor's eggs, which have a value of $300 and secure a debt of $400, and SP–2 has a perfected security interest in Debtor's flour, which has a value of $500 and secures a debt of $700. Debtor uses the flour and eggs to make cakes, which have a value of $1000. The two security interests rank equally and share in the ratio of 3:5. Applying this ratio to the entire value of the product, SP–1 would be entitled to $375 (i.e., 3/8 x $1000), and SP–2 would be entitled to $625 (i.e., 5/8 x $1000).

Example 2: Assume the facts of Example 1, except that SP–1's collateral, worth $300, secures a debt of $200. Recall that, if the cake is worth $1000, then applying the ratio of 3:5 would entitle SP–1 to $375 and SP–2 to $625. However, SP–1 is not entitled to collect from the product more than it is owed. Accordingly, SP–1's share would be only $200, SP–2 would receive the remaining value, up to the amount it is owed ($700).

Example 3: Assume that the cakes in the previous examples have a value of only $600. Again, the parties share in the ratio of 3:5. If, as in Example 1, SP–1 is owed $400, then SP–1 is entitled to $225 (i.e., 3/8 x $600), and SP–2 is entitled to $375 (i.e., 5/8 x $600). Debtor receives nothing. If, however, as in Example 2, SP–1 is owed only $200, then SP–2 receives $400.

The results in the foregoing examples remain the same, regardless of whether SP–1 or SP–2 (or each) has a purchase-money security interest.

5. **Perfection: Unperfected Security Interests.** The rule explained in the preceding Comment applies only when both security interests in original collateral are perfected when the goods become commingled goods. If a security interest in original collateral is unperfected at the time the collateral becomes commingled goods, subsection (f)(1) applies.

Example 4: SP–1 has a perfected security interest in the debtor's eggs, and SP–2 has an unperfected security interest in the debtor's flour. Debtor uses the flour and eggs to make cakes. Under subsection (c), both security interests attach to the cakes. But since SP–1's security interest was perfected at the time of commingling and SP–2's was not, only SP–1's security interest in the cakes is perfected. See subsection (d). Under subsection (f)(1) and Section 9–322(a)(2), SP–1's perfected security interest has priority over SP–2's unperfected security interest.

If both security interests are unperfected, the rule of Section 9–322(a)(3) would apply.

6. **Multiple Security Interests.** On occasion, a single input may be encumbered by more than one security interest. In those cases, the multiple secured parties should be treated like a single secured party for purposes of determining their collective share under subsection (f)(2). The normal priority rules would determine how that share would be allocated between them. Consider the following example, which is a variation on Example 1 above:

Example 5: SP–1A has a perfected, first-priority security interest in Debtor's eggs. SP–1B has a perfected, second-priority security interest in the same collateral. The eggs have a value of $300. Debtor owes $200 to SP–1A and $200 to SP–1B. SP–2 has a perfected security interest in Debtor's flour, which has a value of $500 and secures a debt of $600. Debtor uses the flour and eggs to make cakes, which have a value of $1000.

For purposes of subsection (f)(2), SP–1A and SP–1B should be treated like a single secured party. The collective security interest would rank equally with that of SP–2. Thus, the secured parties would share in the ratio of 3 (for SP–1A and SP–1B combined) to 5 (for SP–2). Applying this ratio to the entire value of the product, SP–1A and SP–1B in the aggregate would be entitled to $375 (i.e., 3/8 x $1000), and SP–2 would be entitled to $625 (i.e., 5/8 x $1000).

SP–1A and SP–1B would share the $375 in accordance with their priority, as established under other rules. Inasmuch as SP–1A has first priority, it would receive $200, and SP–1B would receive $175.

7. **Priority of Security Interests That Attach Other Than by Operation of This Section.** Under subsection (e), the normal priority rules determine the priority of a security interest that attaches to the product or mass other than by operation of this section. For example, assume that SP–1 has a perfected security interest in Debtor's existing and after-acquired baked goods, and SP–2 has a perfected security interest in Debtor's flour. When the flour is processed into cakes, subsections (c) and (d) provide that SP–2 acquires a perfected security interest in the cakes. If SP–1 filed against the baked goods before SP–2 filed against the flour, then SP–1 will enjoy priority in the cakes. See Section 9–322 (first-to-file-or-perfect). But if SP–2 filed against the flour before SP–1 filed against the baked goods, then SP–2 will enjoy priority in the cakes to the extent of its security interest.

§ 9–337.   Priority of Security Interests in Goods Covered by Certificate of Title.

If, while a security interest in goods is perfected by any method under the law of another jurisdiction, this State issues a certificate of title that does not show that the goods are subject to the security interest or contain a statement that they may be subject to security interests not shown on the certificate:

(1)   a buyer of the goods, other than a person in the business of selling goods of that kind, takes free of the security interest if the buyer gives value and receives delivery of the goods after issuance of the certificate and without knowledge of the security interest; and

(2)   the security interest is subordinate to a conflicting security interest in the goods that attaches, and is perfected under Section 9–311(b), after issuance of the certificate and without the conflicting secured party's knowledge of the security interest.

Official Comment

1.   **Source.** Derived from former Section 9–103(2)(d).

2.   **Protection for Buyers and Secured Parties.** This section affords protection to certain good-faith purchasers for value who are likely to have relied on a "clean" certificate of title, i.e., one that neither shows that the goods are subject to a particular security interest nor contains a statement that they may be subject to security interests not shown on the certificate. Under this section, a buyer can take free of, and the holder of a conflicting security interest can acquire priority over, a security interest that is perfected by any method under the law of another jurisdiction. The fact that the security interest has been reperfected by possession under Section 9–313 does not of itself disqualify the holder of a conflicting security interest from protection under paragraph (2).

§ 9–338.   Priority of Security Interest or Agricultural Lien Perfected by Filed Financing Statement Providing Certain Incorrect Information.

If a security interest or agricultural lien is perfected by a filed financing statement providing information described in Section 9–516(b)(5) which is incorrect at the time the financing statement is filed:

(1)   the security interest or agricultural lien is subordinate to a conflicting perfected security interest in the collateral to the extent that the holder of the conflicting security interest gives value in reasonable reliance upon the incorrect information; and

(2)   a purchaser, other than a secured party, of the collateral takes free of the security interest or agricultural lien to the extent that, in reasonable reliance upon the incorrect information, the purchaser gives value and, in the case of tangible chattel paper, tangible documents, goods, instruments, or a security certificate, receives delivery of the collateral.

As amended in 2003.

Official Comment

1.   **Source.** New.

2.   **Effect of Incorrect Information in Financing Statement.** Section 9–520(a) requires the filing office to reject financing statements that do not contain information concerning the debtor as specified in Section 9–516(b)(5). An error in this information does not render the financing statement ineffective. On rare occasions, a subsequent purchaser of the collateral (i.e., a buyer or secured party) may rely on the misinformation to its detriment. This section subordinates a security interest or agricultural lien perfected by an effective, but flawed, financing statement to the rights of a buyer or holder of a perfected security interest to the extent that, in reasonable reliance on the incorrect information, the purchaser gives value and, in the case of tangible collateral, receives delivery of the collateral. A purchaser who has not made itself aware of the information in the filing office with respect to the debtor cannot act in "reasonable reliance" upon incorrect information.

3.   **Relationship to Section 9–507.** This section applies to financing statements that contain information that is incorrect at the time of filing and imposes a small risk of subordination on the filer. In contrast, Section 9–507 deals with financing statements containing information that is correct at the time of filing but which becomes incorrect later. Except as provided in Section 9–507 with respect to changes in the name that is sufficient as the name of the debtor under Section 9–503(a), an otherwise effective financing statement does not become ineffective if the information contained in it becomes inaccurate.

As amended in 2010.

§ 9–339.   Priority Subject to Subordination.

This article does not preclude subordination by agreement by a person entitled to priority.

Official Comment

1. **Source.** Former Section 9–316.

2. **Subordination by Agreement.** The preceding sections deal elaborately with questions of priority. This section makes it entirely clear that a person entitled to priority may effectively agree to subordinate its claim. Only the person entitled to priority may make such an agreement: a person's rights cannot be adversely affected by an agreement to which the person is not a party.

[SUBPART 4. RIGHTS OF BANK]

§ 9–340. Effectiveness of Right of Recoupment or Set-Off Against Deposit Account.

(a) **[Exercise of recoupment or set-off.]** Except as otherwise provided in subsection (c), a bank with which a deposit account is maintained may exercise any right of recoupment or set-off against a secured party that holds a security interest in the deposit account.

(b) **[Recoupment or set-off not affected by security interest.]** Except as otherwise provided in subsection (c), the application of this article to a security interest in a deposit account does not affect a right of recoupment or set-off of the secured party as to a deposit account maintained with the secured party.

(c) **[When set-off ineffective.]** The exercise by a bank of a set-off against a deposit account is ineffective against a secured party that holds a security interest in the deposit account which is perfected by control under Section 9–104(a)(3), if the set-off is based on a claim against the debtor.

Official Comment

1. **Source.** New; subsection (b) is based on a nonuniform Illinois amendment.

2. **Set-off vs. Security Interest.** This section resolves the conflict between a security interest in a deposit account and the bank's rights of recoupment and set-off.

Subsection (a) states the general rule and provides that the bank may effectively exercise rights of recoupment and set-off against the secured party. Subsection (c) contains an exception: if the secured party has control under Section 9–104(a)(3) (i.e., if it has become the bank's customer), then any set-off exercised by the bank against a debt owed by the debtor (as opposed to a debt owed to the bank by the secured party) is ineffective. The bank may, however, exercise its recoupment rights effectively. This result is consistent with the priority rule in Section 9–327(4), under which the security interest of a bank in a deposit account is subordinate to that of a secured party who has control under Section 9–104(a)(3).

This section deals with rights of set-off and recoupment that a bank may have under other law. It does not create a right of set-off or recoupment, nor is it intended to override any limitations or restrictions that other law imposes on the exercise of those rights.

3. **Preservation of Set-Off Right.** Subsection (b) makes clear that a bank may hold both a right of set-off against, and an Article 9 security interest in, the same deposit account. By holding a security interest in a deposit account, a bank does not impair any right of set-off it would otherwise enjoy. This subsection does not pertain to accounts evidenced by an instrument (e.g., certain certificates of deposit), which are excluded from the definition of "deposit accounts."

§ 9–341. Bank's Rights and Duties With Respect to Deposit Account.

Except as otherwise provided in Section 9–340(c), and unless the bank otherwise agrees in an authenticated record, a bank's rights and duties with respect to a deposit account maintained with the bank are not terminated, suspended, or modified by:

(1) the creation, attachment, or perfection of a security interest in the deposit account;

(2) the bank's knowledge of the security interest; or

(3) the bank's receipt of instructions from the secured party.

Official Comment

1. **Source.** New.

2. **Free Flow of Funds.** This section is designed to prevent security interests in deposit accounts from impeding the free flow of funds through the payment system. Subject to two exceptions, it leaves the bank's rights and duties with respect to the deposit account and the funds on deposit unaffected by the creation or perfection of a security interest or by the bank's knowledge of the security interest. In addition, the section permits the bank to ignore the instructions of the secured party unless it had agreed to honor them or unless other law provides to the contrary. A secured party who wishes to deprive the debtor of access to funds on deposit or to appropriate those funds for itself needs to obtain the agreement of the bank, utilize the judicial process, or comply with procedures set forth in other law. Section 4–303(a), concerning the effect of notice on a bank's right and duty to pay items, is not to the contrary. That section addresses only whether an otherwise effective notice comes too late; it does not determine whether a timely notice is otherwise effective.

3. **Operation of Rule.** The general rule of this section is subject to Section 9–340(c), under which a bank's right of set-off may not be exercised against a deposit account in the secured party's name if the right is based on a claim against the debtor. This result reflects current law in many jurisdictions and does not appear to have unduly disrupted banking practices or the payments system. The more important function of this section, which is not impaired by Section 9–340, is the bank's right to follow the debtor's (customer's) instructions (e.g., by honoring checks, permitting withdrawals, etc.) until such time as the depository institution is served with judicial process or receives instructions with respect to the funds on deposit from a secured party who has control over the deposit account.

4. **Liability of Bank.** This Article does not determine whether a bank that pays out funds from an encumbered deposit is liable to the holder of a security interest. Although the fact that a secured party has control over the deposit account and the manner by which control was achieved may be relevant to the imposition of liability, whatever rule applies generally when a bank pays out funds in which a third party has an interest would determine liability to a secured party. Often, this rule is found in a non-UCC adverse claim statute.

5. **Certificates of Deposit.** This section does not address the obligations of banks that issue instruments evidencing deposits (e.g., certain certificates of deposit).

§ 9–342. Bank's Right to Refuse to Enter Into or Disclose Existence of Control Agreement.

This article does not require a bank to enter into an agreement of the kind described in Section 9–104(a)(2), even if its customer so requests or directs. A bank that has entered into such an agreement is not required to confirm the existence of the agreement to another person unless requested to do so by its customer.

Official Comment

1. **Source.** New; derived from Section 8–106(g).

2. **Protection for Bank.** This section protects banks from the need to enter into agreements against their will and from the need to respond to inquiries from persons other than their customers.

PART 4

RIGHTS OF THIRD PARTIES

§ 9–401. Alienability of Debtor's Rights.

(a) **[Other law governs alienability; exceptions.]** Except as otherwise provided in subsection (b) and Sections 9–406, 9–407, 9–408, and 9–409, whether a debtor's rights in collateral may be voluntarily or involuntarily transferred is governed by law other than this article.

(b) **[Agreement does not prevent transfer.]** An agreement between the debtor and secured party which prohibits a transfer of the debtor's rights in collateral or makes the transfer a default does not prevent the transfer from taking effect.

Official Comment

1.   **Source.** Former Section 9–311.

2.   **Scope of This Part.** This Part deals with several issues affecting third parties (i.e., parties other than the debtor and the secured party). These issues are not addressed in Part 3, Subpart 3, which deals with priorities. This Part primarily addresses the rights and duties of account debtors and other persons obligated on collateral who are not, themselves, parties to a secured transaction.

3.   **Governing Law.** There was some uncertainty under former Article 9 as to which jurisdiction's law (usually, which jurisdiction's version of Article 9) applied to the matters that this Part addresses. Part 3, Subpart 1, does not determine the law governing these matters because they do not relate to perfection, the effect of perfection or nonperfection, or priority. However, it might be inappropriate for a designation of applicable law by a debtor and secured party under Section 1–301 to control the law applicable to an independent transaction or relationship between the debtor and an account debtor.

Consider an example under Section 9–408.

Example 1: State X has adopted this Article; former Article 9 is the law of State Y. A general intangible (e.g., a franchise agreement) between a debtor-franchisee, D, and an account debtor-franchisor, AD, is governed by the law of State Y. D grants to SP a security interest in its rights under the franchise agreement. The franchise agreement contains a term prohibiting D's assignment of its rights under the agreement. D and SP agree that their secured transaction is governed by the law of State X. Under State X's Section 9–408, the restriction on D's assignment is ineffective to prevent the creation, attachment, or perfection of SP's security interest. State Y's former Section 9–318(4), however, does not address restrictions on the creation of security interests in general intangibles other than general intangibles for money due or to become due. Accordingly, it does not address restrictions on the assignment to SP of D's rights under the franchise agreement. The non-Article-9 law of State Y, which does address restrictions, provides that the prohibition on assignment is effective.

This Article does not provide a specific answer to the question of which State's law applies to the restriction on assignment in the example. However, assuming that under non-UCC choice-of-law principles the effectiveness of the restriction would be governed by the law of State Y, which governs the franchise agreement, the fact that State X's Article 9 governs the secured transaction between SP and D would not override the otherwise applicable law governing the agreement. Of course, to the extent that jurisdictions eventually adopt identical versions of this Article and courts interpret it consistently, the inability to identify the applicable law in circumstances such as those in the example may be inconsequential.

4.   **Inalienability Under Other Law.** Subsection (a) addresses the question whether property necessarily is transferable by virtue of its inclusion (i.e., its eligibility as collateral) within the scope of Article 9. It gives a negative answer, subject to the identified exceptions. The substance of subsection (a) was implicit under former Article 9.

5.   **Negative Pledge Covenant.** Subsection (b) is an exception to the general rule in subsection (a). It makes clear that in secured transactions under this Article the debtor has rights in collateral (whether legal title or equitable) which it can transfer and which its creditors can reach. It is best explained with an example.

Example 2: A debtor, D, grants to SP a security interest to secure a debt in excess of the value of the collateral. D agrees with SP that it will not create a subsequent security interest in the collateral and that any security interest purportedly granted in violation of the agreement will be void. Subsequently, in violation of its agreement with SP, D purports to grant a security interest in the same collateral to another secured party.

Subsection (b) validates D's creation of the subsequent (prohibited) security interest, which might even achieve priority over the earlier security interest. See Comment 7. However, unlike some other provisions of this Part, such as Section 9–406, subsection (b) does not provide that the agreement restricting assignment itself is "ineffective." Consequently, the debtor's breach may create a default.

6.   **Rights of Lien Creditors.** Difficult problems may arise with respect to attachment, levy, and other judicial procedures under which a debtor's creditors may reach collateral subject to a security interest. For example, an obligation may be secured by collateral worth many times the amount of the obligation. If a lien creditor has caused all or a portion of the collateral to be seized under judicial process, it may be difficult to

determine the amount of the debtor's "equity" in the collateral that has been seized. The section leaves resolution of this problem to the courts. The doctrine of marshaling may be appropriate.

7. **Sale of Receivables.** If a debtor sells an account, chattel paper, payment intangible, or promissory note outright, as against the buyer the debtor has no remaining rights to transfer. If, however, the buyer fails to perfect its interest, then solely insofar as the rights of certain third parties are concerned, the debtor is deemed to retain its rights and title. See Section 9–318. The debtor has the power to convey these rights to a subsequent purchaser. If the subsequent purchaser (buyer or secured lender) perfects its interest, it will achieve priority over the earlier, unperfected purchaser. See Section 9–322(a)(1).

As amended in 2010.

§ 9–402. Secured Party Not Obligated on Contract of Debtor or in Tort.

The existence of a security interest, agricultural lien, or authority given to a debtor to dispose of or use collateral, without more, does not subject a secured party to liability in contract or tort for the debtor's acts or omissions.

Official Comment

1. **Source.** Former Section 9–317.

2. **Nonliability of Secured Party.** This section, like former Section 9–317, rejects theories on which a secured party might be held liable on a debtor's contracts or in tort merely because a security interest exists or because the debtor is entitled to dispose of or use collateral. This section expands former Section 9–317 to cover agricultural liens.

§ 9–403. Agreement Not to Assert Defenses Against Assignee.

(a) **["Value."]** In this section, "value" has the meaning provided in Section 3–303(a).

(b) **[Agreement not to assert claim or defense.]** Except as otherwise provided in this section, an agreement between an account debtor and an assignor not to assert against an assignee any claim or defense that the account debtor may have against the assignor is enforceable by an assignee that takes an assignment:

(1) for value;

(2) in good faith;

(3) without notice of a claim of a property or possessory right to the property assigned; and

(4) without notice of a defense or claim in recoupment of the type that may be asserted against a person entitled to enforce a negotiable instrument under Section 3–305(a).

(c) **[When subsection (b) not applicable.]** Subsection (b) does not apply to defenses of a type that may be asserted against a holder in due course of a negotiable instrument under Section 3–305(b).

(d) **[Omission of required statement in consumer transaction.]** In a consumer transaction, if a record evidences the account debtor's obligation, law other than this article requires that the record include a statement to the effect that the rights of an assignee are subject to claims or defenses that the account debtor could assert against the original obligee, and the record does not include such a statement:

(1) the record has the same effect as if the record included such a statement; and

(2) the account debtor may assert against an assignee those claims and defenses that would have been available if the record included such a statement.

(e) **[Rule for individual under other law.]** This section is subject to law other than this article which establishes a different rule for an account debtor who is an individual and who incurred the obligation primarily for personal, family, or household purposes.

(f) **[Other law not displaced.]** Except as otherwise provided in subsection (d), this section does not displace law other than this article which gives effect to an agreement by an account debtor not to assert a claim or defense against an assignee.

Official Comment

1.   **Source.** Former Section 9–206.

2.   **Scope and Purpose.** Subsection (b), like former Section 9–206, generally validates an agreement between an account debtor and an assignor that the account debtor will not assert against an assignee claims and defenses that it may have against the assignor. These agreements are typical in installment sale agreements and leases. However, this section expands former Section 9–206 to apply to all account debtors; it is not limited to account debtors that have bought or leased goods. This section applies only to the obligations of an "account debtor," as defined in Section 9–102. Thus, it does not determine the circumstances under which and the extent to which a person who is obligated on a negotiable instrument is disabled from asserting claims and defenses. Rather, Article 3 must be consulted. See, e.g., Sections 3–305, 3–306. Article 3 governs even when the negotiable instrument constitutes part of chattel paper. See Section 9–102 (an obligor on a negotiable instrument constituting part of chattel paper is not an "account debtor").

3.   **Conditions of Validation; Relationship to Article 3.** Subsection (b) validates an account debtor's agreement only if the assignee takes an assignment for value, in good faith, and without notice of conflicting claims to the property assigned or of certain claims or defenses of the account debtor. Like former Section 9–206, this section is designed to put the assignee in a position that is no better and no worse than that of a holder in due course of a negotiable instrument under Article 3. However, former Section 9–206 left open certain issues, e.g., whether the section incorporated the special Article 3 definition of "value" in Section 3–303 or the generally applicable definition in Section 1–201(44).[*] Subsection (a) addresses this question; it provides that "value" has the meaning specified in Section 3–303(a). Similarly, subsection (c) provides that subsection (b) does not validate an agreement with respect to defenses that could be asserted against a holder in due course under Section 3–305(b) (the so-called "real" defenses). In 1990, the definition of "holder in due course" (Section 3–302) and the articulation of the rights of a holder in due course (Sections 3–305 and 3–306) were revised substantially. This section tracks more closely the rules of Sections 3–302, 3–305, and 3–306.

4.   **Relationship to Terms of Assigned Property.** Former Section 9–206(2), concerning warranties accompanying the sale of goods, has been deleted as unnecessary. This Article does not regulate the terms of the account, chattel paper, or general intangible that is assigned, except insofar as the account, chattel paper, or general intangible itself creates a security interest (as often is the case with chattel paper). Thus, Article 2, and not this Article, determines whether a seller of goods makes or effectively disclaims warranties, even if the sale is secured. Similarly, other law, and not this Article, determines the effectiveness of an account debtor's undertaking to pay notwithstanding, and not to assert, any defenses or claims against an assignor—e.g., a "hell-or-high-water" provision in the underlying agreement that is assigned. If other law gives effect to this undertaking, then, under principles of *nemo dat*, the undertaking would be enforceable by the assignee (secured party). If other law prevents the assignor from enforcing the undertaking, this section nevertheless might permit the assignee to do so. The right of the assignee to enforce would depend upon whether, under the particular facts, the account debtor's undertaking fairly could be construed as an agreement that falls within the scope of this section and whether the assignee meets the requirements of this section.

5.   **Relationship to Federal Trade Commission Rule.** Subsection (d) is new. It applies to rights evidenced by a record that is required to contain, but does not contain, the notice set forth in Federal Trade Commission Rule 433, 16 C.F.R. Part 433 (the "Holder-in-Due-Course Regulations"). Under this subsection, an assignee of such a record takes subject to the consumer account debtor's claims and defenses to the same extent as it would have if the writing had contained the required notice. Thus, subsection (d) effectively renders waiver-of-defense clauses ineffective in the transactions with consumers to which it applies.

6.   **Relationship to Other Law.** Like former Section 9–206(1), this section takes no position on the enforceability of waivers of claims and defenses by consumer account debtors, leaving that question to other law. However, the reference to "law other than this article" in subsection (e) encompasses administrative rules and regulations; the reference in former Section 9–206(1) that it replaces ("statute or decision") arguably did not.

   This section does not displace other law that gives effect to a non-consumer account debtor's agreement not to assert defenses against an assignee, even if the agreement would not qualify under subsection (b). See subsection (f). It validates, but does not invalidate, agreements made by a non-consumer account debtor. This section also does not displace other law to the extent that the other law permits an assignee, who takes an assignment with notice of a claim of a property or possessory right, a defense, or a claim in recoupment, to enforce

---

[*]   *Referring to unrevised Article 1 (Appendix A).*

an account debtor's agreement not to assert claims and defenses against the assign*or* (e.g., a "hell-or-high-water" agreement). See Comment 4. It also does not displace an assignee's right to assert that an account debtor is estopped from asserting a claim or defense. Nor does this section displace other law with respect to waivers of potential future claims and defenses that are the subject of an agreement between the account debtor and the assignee. Finally, it does not displace Section 1–107,* concerning waiver of a breach that allegedly already has occurred.

§ 9–404. Rights Acquired by Assignee; Claims and Defenses Against Assignee.

(a) **[Assignee's rights subject to terms, claims, and defenses; exceptions.]** Unless an account debtor has made an enforceable agreement not to assert defenses or claims, and subject to subsections (b) through (e), the rights of an assignee are subject to:

(1) all terms of the agreement between the account debtor and assignor and any defense or claim in recoupment arising from the transaction that gave rise to the contract; and

(2) any other defense or claim of the account debtor against the assignor which accrues before the account debtor receives a notification of the assignment authenticated by the assignor or the assignee.

(b) **[Account debtor's claim reduces amount owed to assignee.]** Subject to subsection (c) and except as otherwise provided in subsection (d), the claim of an account debtor against an assignor may be asserted against an assignee under subsection (a) only to reduce the amount the account debtor owes.

(c) **[Rule for individual under other law.]** This section is subject to law other than this article which establishes a different rule for an account debtor who is an individual and who incurred the obligation primarily for personal, family, or household purposes.

(d) **[Omission of required statement in consumer transaction.]** In a consumer transaction, if a record evidences the account debtor's obligation, law other than this article requires that the record include a statement to the effect that the account debtor's recovery against an assignee with respect to claims and defenses against the assignor may not exceed amounts paid by the account debtor under the record, and the record does not include such a statement, the extent to which a claim of an account debtor against the assignor may be asserted against an assignee is determined as if the record included such a statement.

(e) **[Inapplicability to health-care-insurance receivable.]** This section does not apply to an assignment of a health-care-insurance receivable.

Official Comment

1. **Source.** Former Section 9–318(1).

2. **Purpose; Rights of Assignee in General.** Subsection (a), like former Section 9–318(1), provides that an assignee generally takes an assignment subject to defenses and claims of an account debtor. Under subsection (a)(1), if the account debtor's defenses on an assigned claim arise from the transaction that gave rise to the contract with the assignor, it makes no difference whether the defense or claim accrues before or after the account debtor is notified of the assignment. Under subsection (a)(2), the assignee takes subject to other defenses or claims only if they accrue before the account debtor has been notified of the assignment. Of course, an account debtor may waive its right to assert defenses or claims against an assignee under Section 9–403 or other applicable law. Subsection (a) tracks Section 3–305(a)(3) more closely than its predecessor.

3. **Limitation on Affirmative Claims.** Subsection (b) is new. It limits the claim that the account debtor may assert against an assignee. Borrowing from Section 3–305(a)(3) and cases construing former Section 9–318, subsection (b) generally does not afford the account debtor the right to an affirmative recovery from an assignee.

4. **Consumer Account Debtors; Relationship to Federal Trade Commission Rule.** Subsections (c) and (d) also are new. Subsection (c) makes clear that the rules of this section are subject to other law establishing special rules for consumer account debtors. An "account debtor who is an individual" as used in subsection (c) includes individuals who are jointly or jointly and severally obligated. Subsection (d) applies to rights evidenced by a record that is required to contain, but does not contain, the notice set forth in Federal Trade Commission Rule

---

* *Referring to unrevised Article 1 (Appendix A).*

433, 16 C.F.R. Part 433 (the "Holder-in-Due-Course Regulations"). Under subsection (d), a consumer account debtor has the same right to an affirmative recovery from an assignee of such a record as the consumer would have had against the assignee had the record contained the required notice.

5.   **Scope; Application to "Account Debtor."** This section deals only with the rights and duties of "account debtors"—and for the most part only with account debtors on accounts, chattel paper, and payment intangibles. Subsection (e) provides that the obligation of an insurer with respect to a health-care-insurance receivable is governed by other law. References in this section to an "account debtor" include account debtors on collateral that is proceeds. Neither this section nor any other provision of this Article, including Sections 9–408 and 9–409, provides analogous regulation of the rights and duties of other obligors on collateral, such as the maker of a negotiable instrument (governed by Article 3), the issuer of or nominated person under a letter of credit (governed by Article 5), or the issuer of a security (governed by Article 8). Article 9 leaves those rights and duties untouched; however, Section 9–409 deals with the special case of letters of credit. When chattel paper is composed in part of a negotiable instrument, the obligor on the instrument is not an "account debtor," and Article 3 governs the rights of the assignee of the chattel paper with respect to the issues that this section addresses. See, e.g., Section 3–601 (dealing with discharge of an obligation to pay a negotiable instrument).

§ 9–405.   Modification of Assigned Contract.

(a)   **[Effect of modification on assignee.]** A modification of or substitution for an assigned contract is effective against an assignee if made in good faith. The assignee acquires corresponding rights under the modified or substituted contract. The assignment may provide that the modification or substitution is a breach of contract by the assignor. This subsection is subject to subsections (b) through (d).

(b)   **[Applicability of subsection (a).]** Subsection (a) applies to the extent that:

(1)   the right to payment or a part thereof under an assigned contract has not been fully earned by performance; or

(2)   the right to payment or a part thereof has been fully earned by performance and the account debtor has not received notification of the assignment under Section 9–406(a).

(c)   **[Rule for individual under other law.]** This section is subject to law other than this article which establishes a different rule for an account debtor who is an individual and who incurred the obligation primarily for personal, family, or household purposes.

(d)   **[Inapplicability to health-care-insurance receivable.]** This section does not apply to an assignment of a health-care-insurance receivable.

Official Comment

1.   **Source.** Former Section 9–318(2).

2.   **Modification of Assigned Contract.** The ability of account debtors and assignors to modify assigned contracts can be important, especially in the case of government contracts and complex contractual arrangements (e.g., construction contracts) with respect to which modifications are customary. Subsections (a) and (b) provide that good-faith modifications of assigned contracts are binding against an assignee to the extent that (i) the right to payment has not been fully earned or (ii) the right to payment has been earned and notification of the assignment has not been given to the account debtor. Former Section 9–318(2) did not validate modifications of fully-performed contracts under any circumstances, whether or not notification of the assignment had been given to the account debtor. Subsection (a) protects the interests of assignees by (i) limiting the effectiveness of modifications to those made in good faith, (ii) affording the assignee with corresponding rights under the contract as modified, and (iii) recognizing that the modification may be a breach of the assignor's agreement with the assignee.

3.   **Consumer Account Debtors.** Subsection (c) is new. It makes clear that the rules of this section are subject to other law establishing special rules for consumer account debtors.

4.   **Account Debtors on Health-Care-Insurance Receivables.** Subsection (d) also is new. It provides that this section does not apply to an assignment of a health-care-insurance receivable. The obligation of an insurer with respect to a health-care-insurance receivable is governed by other law.

§ 9–406. Discharge of Account Debtor; Notification of Assignment; Identification and Proof of Assignment; Restrictions on Assignment of Accounts, Chattel Paper, Payment Intangibles, and Promissory Notes Ineffective.

(a) **[Discharge of account debtor; effect of notification.]** Subject to subsections (b) through (i), an account debtor on an account, chattel paper, or a payment intangible may discharge its obligation by paying the assignor until, but not after, the account debtor receives a notification, authenticated by the assignor or the assignee, that the amount due or to become due has been assigned and that payment is to be made to the assignee. After receipt of the notification, the account debtor may discharge its obligation by paying the assignee and may not discharge the obligation by paying the assignor.

(b) **[When notification ineffective.]** Subject to subsection (h), notification is ineffective under subsection (a):

(1) if it does not reasonably identify the rights assigned;

(2) to the extent that an agreement between an account debtor and a seller of a payment intangible limits the account debtor's duty to pay a person other than the seller and the limitation is effective under law other than this article; or

(3) at the option of an account debtor, if the notification notifies the account debtor to make less than the full amount of any installment or other periodic payment to the assignee, even if:

(A) only a portion of the account, chattel paper, or payment intangible has been assigned to that assignee;

(B) a portion has been assigned to another assignee; or

(C) the account debtor knows that the assignment to that assignee is limited.

(c) **[Proof of assignment.]** Subject to subsection (h), if requested by the account debtor, an assignee shall seasonably furnish reasonable proof that the assignment has been made. Unless the assignee complies, the account debtor may discharge its obligation by paying the assignor, even if the account debtor has received a notification under subsection (a).

(d) **[Term restricting assignment generally ineffective.]** Except as otherwise provided in subsection (e) and Sections 2A–303 and 9–407, and subject to subsection (h), a term in an agreement between an account debtor and an assignor or in a promissory note is ineffective to the extent that it:

(1) prohibits, restricts, or requires the consent of the account debtor or person obligated on the promissory note to the assignment or transfer of, or the creation, attachment, perfection, or enforcement of a security interest in, the account, chattel paper, payment intangible, or promissory note; or

(2) provides that the assignment or transfer or the creation, attachment, perfection, or enforcement of the security interest may give rise to a default, breach, right of recoupment, claim, defense, termination, right of termination, or remedy under the account, chattel paper, payment intangible, or promissory note.

(e) **[Inapplicability of subsection (d) to certain sales.]** Subsection (d) does not apply to the sale of a payment intangible or promissory note, other than a sale pursuant to a disposition under Section 9–610 or as acceptance of collateral under Section 9–620.

(f) **[Legal restrictions on assignment generally ineffective.]** Except as otherwise provided in Sections 2A–303 and 9–407 and subject to subsections (h) and (i), a rule of law, statute, or regulation that prohibits, restricts, or requires the consent of a government, governmental body or official, or account debtor to the assignment or transfer of, or creation of a security interest in, an account or chattel paper is ineffective to the extent that the rule of law, statute, or regulation:

(1) prohibits, restricts, or requires the consent of the government, governmental body or official, or account debtor to the assignment or transfer of, or the creation, attachment, perfection, or enforcement of a security interest in the account or chattel paper; or

845

(2) provides that the assignment or transfer or the creation, attachment, perfection, or enforcement of the security interest may give rise to a default, breach, right of recoupment, claim, defense, termination, right of termination, or remedy under the account or chattel paper.

(g) **[Subsection (b)(3) not waivable.]** Subject to subsection (h), an account debtor may not waive or vary its option under subsection (b)(3).

(h) **[Rule for individual under other law.]** This section is subject to law other than this article which establishes a different rule for an account debtor who is an individual and who incurred the obligation primarily for personal, family, or household purposes.

(i) **[Inapplicability to health-care-insurance receivable.]** This section does not apply to an assignment of a health-care-insurance receivable.

(j) **[Section prevails over specified inconsistent law.]** This section prevails over any inconsistent provisions of the following statutes, rules, and regulations:

[List here any statutes, rules, and regulations containing provisions inconsistent with this section.]

Legislative Note: States that amend statutes, rules, and regulations to remove provisions inconsistent with this section need not enact subsection (j)

As amended in 1999, 2000 and 2010.

Official Comment

1. **Source.** Former Section 9–318(3), (4).

2. **Account Debtor's Right to Pay Assignor Until Notification.** Subsection (a) provides the general rule concerning an account debtor's right to pay the assignor until the account debtor receives appropriate notification. The revision makes clear that once the account debtor receives the notification, the account debtor cannot discharge its obligation by paying the assignor. It also makes explicit that payment to the assignor before notification, or payment to the assignee after notification, discharges the obligation. No change in meaning from former Section 9–318 is intended. Nothing in this section conditions the effectiveness of a notification on the identity of the person who gives it. An account debtor that doubts whether the right to payment has been assigned may avail itself of the procedures in subsection (c). See Comment 4.

An effective notification under subsection (a) must be authenticated. This requirement normally could be satisfied by sending notification on the notifying person's letterhead or on a form on which the notifying person's name appears. In each case the printed name would be a symbol adopted by the notifying person for the purpose of identifying the person and adopting the notification. See Section 9–102 (defining "authenticate").

Subsection (a) applies only to account debtors on accounts, chattel paper, and payment intangibles. (Section 9–102 defines the term "account debtor" more broadly, to include those obligated on all general intangibles.) Although subsection (a) is more precise than its predecessor, it probably does not change the rule that applied under former Article 9. Former Section 9–318(3) referred to the account debtor's obligation to "pay," indicating that the subsection was limited to account debtors on accounts, chattel paper, and other payment obligations.

3. **Limitations on Effectiveness of Notification.** Subsection (b) contains some special rules concerning the effectiveness of a notification under subsection (a).

Subsection (b)(1) tracks former Section 9–318(3) by making ineffective a notification that does not reasonably identify the rights assigned. A reasonable identification need not identify the right to payment with specificity, but what is reasonable also is not left to the arbitrary decision of the account debtor. If an account debtor has doubt as to the adequacy of a notification, it may not be safe in disregarding the notification unless it notifies the assignee with reasonable promptness as to the respects in which the account debtor considers the notification defective.

Subsection (b)(2), which is new, applies only to sales of payment intangibles. It makes a notification ineffective to the extent that other law gives effect to an agreement between an account debtor and a seller of a payment intangible that limits the account debtor's duty to pay a person other than the seller. Payment intangibles are substantially less fungible than accounts and chattel paper. In some (e.g., commercial bank loans), account debtors customarily and legitimately expect that they will not be required to pay any person other than the financial institution that has advanced funds.

It has become common in financing transactions to assign interests in a single obligation to more than one assignee. Requiring an account debtor that owes a single obligation to make multiple payments to multiple assignees would be unnecessarily burdensome. Thus, under subsection (b)(3), an account debtor that is notified to pay an assignee less than the full amount of any installment or other periodic payment has the option to treat the notification as ineffective, ignore the notice, and discharge the assigned obligation by paying the assignor. Some account debtors may not realize that the law affords them the right to ignore certain notices of assignment with impunity. By making the notification ineffective at the account debtor's option, subsection (b)(3) permits an account debtor to pay the assignee in accordance with the notice and thereby to satisfy its obligation *pro tanto*. Under subsection (g), the rights and duties created by subsection (b)(3) cannot be waived or varied.

4. **Proof of Assignment.** Subsection (c) links payment with discharge, as in subsection (a). It follows former Section 9–318(3) in referring to the right of the account debtor to pay the assignor if the requested proof of assignment is not seasonably forthcoming. Even if the proof is not forthcoming, the notification of assignment would remain effective, so that, in the absence of reasonable proof of the assignment, the account debtor could discharge the obligation by paying either the assignee or the assignor. Of course, if the assignee did not in fact receive an assignment, the account debtor cannot discharge its obligation by paying a putative assignee who is a stranger. The observations in Comment 3 concerning the reasonableness of an identification of a right to payment also apply here. An account debtor that questions the adequacy of proof submitted by an assignee would be well advised to promptly inform the assignee of the defects.

An account debtor may face another problem if its obligation becomes due while the account debtor is awaiting reasonable proof of the assignment that it has requested from the assignee. This section does not excuse the account debtor from timely compliance with its obligations. Consequently, an account debtor that has received a notification of assignment and who has requested reasonable proof of the assignment may discharge its obligation by paying the assignor at the time (or even earlier if reasonably necessary to avoid risk of default) when a payment is due, even if the account debtor has not yet received a response to its request for proof. On the other hand, after requesting reasonable proof of the assignment, an account debtor may not discharge its obligation by paying the assignor substantially in advance of the time that the payment is due unless the assignee has failed to provide the proof seasonably.

5. **Contractual Restrictions on Assignment.** Former Section 9–318(4) rendered ineffective an agreement between an account debtor and an assignor which prohibited assignment of an account (whether outright or to secure an obligation) or prohibited a security assignment of a general intangible for the payment of money due or to become due. Subsection (d) essentially follows former Section 9–318(4), but expands the rule of free assignability to chattel paper (subject to Sections 2A–303 and 9–407) and promissory notes and explicitly overrides both restrictions and prohibitions of assignment. The policies underlying the ineffectiveness of contractual restrictions under this section build on common-law developments that essentially have eliminated legal restrictions on assignments of rights to payment as security and other assignments of rights to payment such as accounts and chattel paper. Any that might linger for accounts and chattel paper are addressed by new subsection (f). See Comment 6.

Former Section 9–318(4) did not apply to a sale of a payment intangible (as described in the former provision, "a general intangible for money due or to become due") but did apply to an assignment of a payment intangible for security. Subsection (e) continues this approach and also makes subsection (d) inapplicable to sales of promissory notes. Section 9–408 addresses anti-assignment clauses with respect to sales of payment intangibles and promissory notes.

Like former Section 9–318(4), subsection (d) provides that anti-assignment clauses are "ineffective." The quoted term means that the clause is of no effect whatsoever; the clause does not prevent the assignment from taking effect between the parties and the prohibited assignment does not constitute a default under the agreement between the account debtor and assignor. However, subsection (d) does not override terms that do not directly prohibit, restrict, or require consent to an assignment but which might, nonetheless, present a practical impairment of the assignment. Properly read, however, subsection (d) reaches only covenants that prohibit, restrict, or require consents to assignments; it does not override all terms that might "impair" an assignment in fact.

Example: Buyer enters into an agreement with Seller to buy equipment that Seller is to manufacture according to Buyer's specifications. Buyer agrees to make a series of prepayments during the construction process. In return, Seller agrees to set aside the prepaid funds in a special account and to use the funds solely for the manufacture of the designated equipment. Seller also agrees that it will not assign any of its rights under the sale agreement with Buyer. Nevertheless, Seller grants to Secured Party a security interest in its accounts. Seller's anti-assignment agreement is ineffective under subsection (d); its agreement concerning the use of prepaid funds, which is not a restriction or prohibition on assignment, is not. However, if Secured Party notifies Buyer to make all future payments directly to Secured Party, Buyer will be obliged to do so under subsection (a) if it wishes the payments to discharge its obligation. Unless Secured Party releases the funds to Seller so that Seller can comply with its use-of-funds covenant, Seller will be in breach of that covenant.

In the example, there appears to be a plausible business purpose for the use-of-funds covenant. However, a court may conclude that a covenant with no business purpose other than imposing an impediment to an assignment actually is a direct restriction that is rendered ineffective by subsection (d).

6. **Legal Restrictions on Assignment.** Former Section 9–318(4), like subsection (d) of this section, addressed only contractual restrictions on assignment. The former section was grounded on the reality that legal, as opposed to contractual, restrictions on assignments of rights to payment had largely disappeared. New subsection (f) codifies this principle of free assignability for accounts and chattel paper. For the most part the discussion of contractual restrictions in Comment 5 applies as well to legal restrictions rendered ineffective under subsection (f).

7. **Multiple Assignments.** This section, like former Section 9–318, is not a complete codification of the law of assignments of rights to payment. In particular, it is silent concerning many of the ramifications for an account debtor in cases of multiple assignments of the same right. For example, an assignor might assign the same receivable to multiple assignees (which assignments could be either inadvertent or wrongful). Or, the assignor could assign the receivable to assignee–1, which then might re-assign it to assignee–2, and so forth. The rights and duties of an account debtor in the face of multiple assignments and in other circumstances not resolved in the statutory text are left to the common-law rules. See, e.g., Restatement (2d), Contracts §§ 338(3), 339. The failure of former Article 9 to codify these rules does not appear to have caused problems.

8. **Consumer Account Debtors.** Subsection (h) is new. It makes clear that the rules of this section are subject to other law establishing special rules for consumer account debtors.

9. **Account Debtors on Health-Care-Insurance Receivables.** Subsection (i) also is new. The obligation of an insurer with respect to a health-care-insurance receivable is governed by other law. Section 9–408 addresses contractual and legal restrictions on the assignment of a health-care-insurance receivable.

§ 9–407.   Restrictions on Creation or Enforcement of Security Interest in Leasehold Interest or in Lessor's Residual Interest.

(a) **[Term restricting assignment generally ineffective.]** Except as otherwise provided in subsection (b), a term in a lease agreement is ineffective to the extent that it:

(1) prohibits, restricts, or requires the consent of a party to the lease to the assignment or transfer of, or the creation, attachment, perfection, or enforcement of a security interest in an interest of a party under the lease contract or in the lessor's residual interest in the goods; or

(2) provides that the assignment or transfer or the creation, attachment, perfection, or enforcement of the security interest may give rise to a default, breach, right of recoupment, claim, defense, termination, right of termination, or remedy under the lease.

(b) **[Effectiveness of certain terms.]** Except as otherwise provided in Section 2A–303(7), a term described in subsection (a)(2) is effective to the extent that there is:

(1) a transfer by the lessee of the lessee's right of possession or use of the goods in violation of the term; or

(2) a delegation of a material performance of either party to the lease contract in violation of the term.

(c) **[Security interest not material impairment.]** The creation, attachment, perfection, or enforcement of a security interest in the lessor's interest under the lease contract or the lessor's residual interest in the goods is not a transfer that materially impairs the lessee's prospect of obtaining return performance or materially changes the duty of or materially increases the burden or risk imposed on the lessee within the purview of Section 2A–303(4) unless, and then only to the extent that, enforcement actually results in a delegation of material performance of the lessor.

As amended in 1999.

Official Comment

1. **Source.** Section 2A–303.

2. **Restrictions on Assignment Generally Ineffective.** Under subsection (a), as under former Section 2A–303(3), a term in a lease agreement which prohibits or restricts the creation of a security interest generally is ineffective. This reflects the general policy of Section 9–406(d) and former Section 9–318(4). This section has been conformed in several respects to analogous provisions in Sections 9–406, 9–408, and 9–409, including the substitution of "ineffective" for "not enforceable" and the substitution of "assignment or transfer of, or the creation, attachment, perfection, or enforcement of a security interest" for "creation or enforcement of a security interest."

3. **Exceptions for Certain Transfers and Delegations.** Subsection (b) provides exceptions to the general ineffectiveness of restrictions under subsection (a). A term that otherwise is ineffective under subsection (a)(2) is effective to the extent that a lessee transfers its right to possession and use of goods or if either party delegates material performance of the lease contract in violation of the term. However, under subsection (c), as under former Section 2A–303(3), a lessor's creation of a security interest in its interest in a lease contract or its residual interest in the leased goods is not a material impairment under Section 2A–303(4) (former Section 2A–303(5)), absent an actual delegation of the lessor's material performance. The terms of the lease contract determine whether the lessor, in fact, has any remaining obligations to perform. If it does, it is then necessary to determine whether there has been an actual delegation of "material performance." See Section 2A–303, Comments 3 and 4.

As amended in 1999.

§ 9–408. Restrictions on Assignment of Promissory Notes, Health-Care-Insurance Receivables, and Certain General Intangibles Ineffective.

(a) **[Term restricting assignment generally ineffective.]** Except as otherwise provided in subsection (b), a term in a promissory note or in an agreement between an account debtor and a debtor which relates to a health-care-insurance receivable or a general intangible, including a contract, permit, license, or franchise, and which term prohibits, restricts, or requires the consent of the person obligated on the promissory note or the account debtor to, the assignment or transfer of, or creation, attachment, or perfection of a security interest in, the promissory note, health-care-insurance receivable, or general intangible, is ineffective to the extent that the term:

(1) would impair the creation, attachment, or perfection of a security interest; or

(2) provides that the assignment or transfer or the creation, attachment, or perfection of the security interest may give rise to a default, breach, right of recoupment, claim, defense, termination, right of termination, or remedy under the promissory note, health-care-insurance receivable, or general intangible.

(b) **[Applicability of subsection (a) to sales of certain rights to payment.]** Subsection (a) applies to a security interest in a payment intangible or promissory note only if the security interest arises out of a sale of the payment intangible or promissory note, other than a sale pursuant to a disposition under Section 9–610 or as acceptance of collateral under Section 9–620.

(c) **[Legal restrictions on assignment generally ineffective.]** A rule of law, statute, or regulation that prohibits, restricts, or requires the consent of a government, governmental body or official, person obligated on a promissory note, or account debtor to the assignment or transfer of, or creation of a security interest in, a promissory note, health-care-insurance receivable, or general intangible, including a contract, permit, license, or franchise between an account debtor and a debtor, is ineffective to the extent that the rule of law, statute, or regulation:

(1) would impair the creation, attachment, or perfection of a security interest; or

(2) provides that the assignment or transfer or the creation, attachment, or perfection of the security interest may give rise to a default, breach, right of recoupment, claim, defense, termination, right

of termination, or remedy under the promissory note, health-care-insurance receivable, or general intangible.

(d)   **[Limitation on ineffectiveness under subsections (a) and (c).]** To the extent that a term in a promissory note or in an agreement between an account debtor and a debtor which relates to a health-care-insurance receivable or general intangible or a rule of law, statute, or regulation described in subsection (c) would be effective under law other than this article but is ineffective under subsection (a) or (c), the creation, attachment, or perfection of a security interest in the promissory note, health-care-insurance receivable, or general intangible:

(1)   is not enforceable against the person obligated on the promissory note or the account debtor;

(2)   does not impose a duty or obligation on the person obligated on the promissory note or the account debtor;

(3)   does not require the person obligated on the promissory note or the account debtor to recognize the security interest, pay or render performance to the secured party, or accept payment or performance from the secured party;

(4)   does not entitle the secured party to use or assign the debtor's rights under the promissory note, health-care-insurance receivable, or general intangible, including any related information or materials furnished to the debtor in the transaction giving rise to the promissory note, health-care-insurance receivable, or general intangible;

(5)   does not entitle the secured party to use, assign, possess, or have access to any trade secrets or confidential information of the person obligated on the promissory note or the account debtor; and

(6)   does not entitle the secured party to enforce the security interest in the promissory note, health-care-insurance receivable, or general intangible.

(e)   **[Section prevails over specified inconsistent law.]** This section prevails over any inconsistent provisions of the following statutes, rules, and regulations:

[List here any statutes, rules, and regulations containing provisions inconsistent with this section.]

Legislative Note: States that amend statutes, rules, and regulations to remove provisions inconsistent with this section need not enact subsection (e).

As amended in 1999 and 2010.

Official Comment

1.   **Source.** New.

2.   **Free Assignability.** This section makes ineffective any attempt to restrict the assignment of a general intangible, health-care-insurance receivable, or promissory note, whether the restriction appears in the terms of a promissory note or the agreement between an account debtor and a debtor (subsection (a)) or in a rule of law, including a statute or governmental rule or regulation (subsection (c)). This result allows the creation, attachment, and perfection of a security interest in a general intangible, such as an agreement for the nonexclusive license of software, as well as sales of certain receivables, such as a health-care-insurance receivable (which is an "account"), payment intangible, or promissory note, without giving rise to a default or breach by the assignor or from triggering a remedy of the account debtor or person obligated on a promissory note. This enhances the ability of certain debtors to obtain credit. On the other hand, subsection (d) protects the other party—the "account debtor" on a general intangible or the person obligated on a promissory note—from adverse effects arising from the security interest. It leaves the account debtor's or obligated person's rights and obligations unaffected in all material respects if a restriction rendered ineffective by subsection (a) or (c) would be effective under law other than Article 9.

Example 1: A term of an agreement for the nonexclusive license of computer software prohibits the licensee from assigning any of its rights as licensee with respect to the software. The agreement also provides that an attempt to assign rights in violation of the restriction is a default entitling the licensor to terminate the license agreement. The licensee, as debtor, grants to a secured party a security interest in its rights under the license and in the computers in which it is installed. Under this section, the term prohibiting assignment and providing for a default upon an attempted assignment is ineffective to prevent the creation, attachment, or perfection of the security interest or entitle the licensor to terminate the license agreement. However, under subsection (d), the secured party (absent the licensor's agreement) is not entitled to enforce the license or to use, assign, or otherwise enjoy the benefits of the licensed software, and the licensor need not recognize (or pay any attention to) the secured party. Even if the secured party takes possession of the computers on the debtor's default, the debtor would remain free to remove the software from the computer, load it on another computer, and continue to use it, if the license so permits. If the debtor does not remove the software, other law may require the secured party to remove it before disposing of the computer. Disposition of the software with the computer could violate an effective prohibition on enforcement of the security interest. See subsection (d).

3. **Nature of Debtor's Interest.** Neither this section nor any other provision of this Article determines whether a debtor has a property interest. The definition of the term "security interest" provides that it is an "interest in personal property." See Section 1–201(b)(35). Ordinarily, a debtor can create a security interest in collateral only if it has "rights in the collateral." See Section 9–203(b). Other law determines whether a debtor has a property interest ("rights in the collateral") and the nature of that interest. For example, the nonexclusive license addressed in Example 1 may not create any property interest whatsoever in the intellectual property (e.g., copyright) that underlies the license and that effectively enables the licensor to grant the license. The debtor's property interest may be confined solely to its interest in the promises made by the licensor in the license agreement (e.g., a promise not to sue the debtor for its use of the software).

4. **Scope: Sales of Payment Intangibles and Other General Intangibles; Assignments Unaffected by this Section.** Subsections (a) and (c) render ineffective restrictions on assignments only "to the extent" that the assignments restrict the "creation, attachment, or perfection of a security interest," including sales of payment intangibles and promissory notes. This section does not render ineffective a restriction on an assignment that does not create a security interest. For example, if the debtor in Comment 2, Example 1 purported to assign the license to another entity that would use the computer software itself, other law would govern the effectiveness of the anti-assignment provisions.

Subsection (a) applies to a security interest in payment intangibles only if the security interest arises out of sale of the payment intangibles. Contractual restrictions directed to security interests in payment intangibles which secure an obligation are subject to Section 9–406(d). Subsection (a) also deals with sales of promissory notes which also create security interests. See Section 9–109(a). Subsection (c) deals with all security interests in payment intangibles or promissory notes, whether or not arising out of a sale.

Subsection (a) does not render ineffective any term, and subsection (c) does not render ineffective any law, statute or regulation, that restricts outright sales of general intangibles other than payment intangibles. They deal only with restrictions on security interests. The only sales of general intangibles that create security interests are sales of payment intangibles.

5. **Terminology: "Account Debtor"; "Person Obligated on a Promissory Note."** This section uses the term "account debtor" as it is defined in Section 9–102. The term refers to the party, other than the debtor, to a general intangible, including a permit, license, franchise, or the like, and the person obligated on a health-care-insurance receivable, which is a type of account. The definition of "account debtor" does not limit the term to persons who are obligated to *pay* under a general intangible. Rather, the term includes all persons who are obligated on a general intangible, including those who are obligated to render performance in exchange for payment. In some cases, e.g., the creation of a security interest in a franchisee's rights under a franchise agreement, the principal payment obligation may be owed *by* the debtor (franchisee) *to* the account debtor (franchisor). This section also refers to a "person obligated on a promissory note," inasmuch as those persons do not fall within the definition of "account debtor."

Example 2: A licensor and licensee enter into an agreement for the nonexclusive license of computer software. The licensee's interest in the license agreement is a general intangible. If the licensee grants to a secured party a security interest in its rights under the license agreement, the licensee is the debtor and the licensor is the account debtor. On the other hand, if the licensor grants to a secured party a security interest in its right to payment (an account) under the license agreement, the licensor is the debtor and the licensee is the account debtor. (This section applies to the security interest in the general intangible but not to the security interest in the account, which is not a health-care-insurance receivable.)

6. **Effects on Account Debtors and Persons Obligated on Promissory Notes.** Subsections (a) and (c) affect two classes of persons. These subsections affect account debtors on general intangibles and health-care-insurance receivables and persons obligated on promissory notes. Subsection (c) also affects governmental entities

that enact or determine rules of law. *However, subsection (d) ensures that these affected persons are not affected adversely.* That provision removes any burdens or adverse effects on these persons for which any rational basis could exist to restrict the effectiveness of an assignment or to exercise any remedies. For this reason, the effects of subsections (a) and (c) are immaterial insofar as those persons are concerned.

Subsection (a) does not override terms that do not directly prohibit, restrict, or require consent to an assignment but which might, nonetheless, present a practical impairment of the assignment. Properly read, however, this section, like Section 9–406(d), reaches only covenants that prohibit, restrict, or require consents to assignments; it does not override all terms that might "impair" an assignment in fact.

Example 3: A licensor and licensee enter into an agreement for the nonexclusive license of valuable business software. The license agreement includes terms (i) prohibiting the licensee from assigning its rights under the license, (ii) prohibiting the licensee from disclosing to anyone certain information relating to the software and the licensor, and (iii) deeming prohibited assignments and prohibited disclosures to be defaults. The licensee wishes to obtain financing and, in exchange, is willing to grant a security interest in its rights under the license agreement. The secured party, reasonably, refuses to extend credit unless the licensee discloses the information that it is prohibited from disclosing under the license agreement. The secured party cannot determine the value of the proposed collateral in the absence of this information. Under this section, the terms of the license prohibiting the assignment (grant of the security interest) and making the assignment a default are ineffective. However, the nondisclosure covenant is not a term that prohibits the assignment or creation of a security interest in the license. Consequently, the nondisclosure term is enforceable even though the *practical* effect is to restrict the licensee's ability to use its rights under the license agreement as collateral.

The nondisclosure term also would be effective in the factual setting of Comment 2, Example 1. If the secured party's possession of the computers loaded with software would put it in a position to discover confidential information that the debtor was prohibited from disclosing, the licensor should be entitled to enforce its rights against the secured party. Moreover, the licensor could have required the debtor to obtain the secured party's agreement that (i) it would immediately return all copies of software loaded on the computers and that (ii) it would not examine or otherwise acquire any information contained in the software. This section does not prevent an account debtor from protecting by agreement its independent interests that are unrelated to the "creation, attachment, or perfection" of a security interest. In Example 1, moreover, the secured party is not in possession of copies of software by virtue of its security interest or in connection with enforcing its security interest *in the debtor's license of the software.* Its possession is incidental to its possession of the computers, in which it has a security interest. Enforcing against the secured party a restriction relating to the software in no way interferes with its security interest in the computers.

7.   **Effect in Assignor's Bankruptcy.** This section could have a substantial effect if the assignor enters bankruptcy. Roughly speaking, Bankruptcy Code Section 552 invalidates security interests in property acquired after a bankruptcy petition is filed, except to the extent that the postpetition property constitutes proceeds of prepetition collateral.

Example 4: A debtor is the owner of a cable television franchise that, under applicable law, cannot be assigned without the consent of the municipal franchisor. A lender wishes to extend credit to the debtor, provided that the credit is secured by the debtor's "going business" value. To secure the loan, the debtor grants a security interest in all its existing and after-acquired property. The franchise represents the principal value of the business. The municipality refuses to consent to any assignment for collateral purposes. If other law were given effect, the security interest in the franchise would not attach; and if the debtor were to enter bankruptcy and sell the business, the secured party would receive but a fraction of the business's value. Under this section, however, the security interest would attach to the franchise. As a result, the security interest would attach to the proceeds of any sale of the franchise while a bankruptcy is pending. However, this section would protect the interests of the municipality by preventing the secured party from enforcing its security interest to the detriment of the municipality.

8.   **Effect Outside of Bankruptcy.** The principal effects of this section will take place outside of bankruptcy. Compared to the relatively few debtors that enter bankruptcy, there are many more that do not. By making available previously unavailable property as collateral, this section should enable debtors to obtain additional credit. For purposes of determining whether to extend credit, under some circumstances a secured party may ascribe value to the collateral to which its security interest has attached, even if this section precludes the secured party from enforcing the security interest without the agreement of the account debtor or person obligated on the promissory note. This may be the case where the secured party sees a likelihood of obtaining that agreement

in the future. This may also be the case where the secured party anticipates that the collateral will give rise to a type of proceeds as to which this section would not apply.

Example 5: Under the facts of Example 4, the debtor does not enter bankruptcy. Perhaps in exchange for a fee, the municipality agrees that the debtor may transfer the franchise to a buyer. As consideration for the transfer, the debtor receives from the buyer its check for part of the purchase price and its promissory note for the balance. The security interest attaches to the check and promissory note as proceeds. See Section 9–315(a)(2). This section does not apply to the security interest in the check, which is not a promissory note, health-care-insurance receivable, or general intangible. Nor does it apply to the security interest in the promissory note, inasmuch as it was not sold to the secured party.

9. **Contrary Federal Law.** This section does not override federal law to the contrary. However, it does reflect an important policy judgment that should provide a template for future federal law reforms.

As amended in 2010.

§ 9–409. Restrictions on Assignment of Letter-of-Credit Rights Ineffective.

(a) **[Term or law restricting assignment generally ineffective.]** A term in a letter of credit or a rule of law, statute, regulation, custom, or practice applicable to the letter of credit which prohibits, restricts, or requires the consent of an applicant, issuer, or nominated person to a beneficiary's assignment of or creation of a security interest in a letter-of-credit right is ineffective to the extent that the term or rule of law, statute, regulation, custom, or practice:

(1) would impair the creation, attachment, or perfection of a security interest in the letter-of-credit right; or

(2) provides that the assignment or the creation, attachment, or perfection of the security interest may give rise to a default, breach, right of recoupment, claim, defense, termination, right of termination, or remedy under the letter-of-credit right.

(b) **[Limitation on ineffectiveness under subsection (a).]** To the extent that a term in a letter of credit is ineffective under subsection (a) but would be effective under law other than this article or a custom or practice applicable to the letter of credit, to the transfer of a right to draw or otherwise demand performance under the letter of credit, or to the assignment of a right to proceeds of the letter of credit, the creation, attachment, or perfection of a security interest in the letter-of-credit right:

(1) is not enforceable against the applicant, issuer, nominated person, or transferee beneficiary;

(2) imposes no duties or obligations on the applicant, issuer, nominated person, or transferee beneficiary; and

(3) does not require the applicant, issuer, nominated person, or transferee beneficiary to recognize the security interest, pay or render performance to the secured party, or accept payment or other performance from the secured party.

As amended in 1999.

Official Comment

1. **Source.** New.

2. **Purpose and Relevance.** This section, patterned on Section 9–408, limits the effectiveness of attempts to restrict the creation, attachment, or perfection of a security interest in letter-of-credit rights, whether the restriction appears in the letter of credit or a rule of law, custom, or practice applicable to the letter of credit. It protects the creation, attachment, and perfection of a security interest while preventing these events from giving rise to a default or breach by the assignor or from triggering a remedy or defense of the issuer or other person obligated on a letter of credit. Letter-of-credit rights are a type of supporting obligation. See Section 9–102. Under Sections 9–203 and 9–308, a security interest in a supporting obligation attaches and is perfected automatically if the security interest in the supported obligation attaches and is perfected. See Section 9–107, Comment 5. The automatic attachment and perfection under Article 9 would be anomalous or misleading if, under other law (e.g., Article 5), a restriction on transfer or assignment were effective to block attachment and perfection.

3.   **Relationship to Letter-of-Credit Law.** Although restrictions on an assignment of a letter of credit are ineffective to prevent creation, attachment, and perfection of a security interest, subsection (b) protects the issuer and other parties from any adverse effects of the security interest by preserving letter-of-credit law and practice that limits the right of a beneficiary to transfer its right to draw or otherwise demand performance (Section 5–112) and limits the obligation of an issuer or nominated person to recognize a beneficiary's assignment of letter-of-credit proceeds (Section 5–114). Thus, this section's treatment of letter-of-credit rights differs from this Article's treatment of instruments and investment property. Moreover, under Section 9–109(c)(4), this Article does not apply to the extent that the rights of a transferee beneficiary or nominated person are independent and superior under Section 5–114, thereby preserving the "independence principle" of letter-of-credit law.

PART 5

FILING

[SUBPART 1. FILING OFFICE; CONTENTS AND EFFECTIVENESS OF FINANCING STATEMENT]

§ 9–501.   Filing Office.

(a)   **[Filing offices.]** Except as otherwise provided in subsection (b), if the local law of this State governs perfection of a security interest or agricultural lien, the office in which to file a financing statement to perfect the security interest or agricultural lien is:

(1)   the office designated for the filing or recording of a record of a mortgage on the related real property, if:

(A)   the collateral is as-extracted collateral or timber to be cut; or

(B)   the financing statement is filed as a fixture filing and the collateral is goods that are or are to become fixtures; or

(2)   the office of [ ] [or any office duly authorized by [ ]], in all other cases, including a case in which the collateral is goods that are or are to become fixtures and the financing statement is not filed as a fixture filing.

(b)   **[Filing office for transmitting utilities.]** The office in which to file a financing statement to perfect a security interest in collateral, including fixtures, of a transmitting utility is the office of [ ]. The financing statement also constitutes a fixture filing as to the collateral indicated in the financing statement which is or is to become fixtures.

Legislative Note: The State should designate the filing office where the brackets appear. The filing office may be that of a governmental official (e.g., the Secretary of State) or a private party that maintains the State's filing system.

Official Comment

1.   **Source.** Derived from former Section 9–401.

2.   **Where to File.** Subsection (a) indicates where in a given State a financing statement is to be filed. Former Article 9 afforded each State three alternative approaches, depending on the extent to which the State desires central filing (usually with the Secretary of State), local filing (usually with a county office), or both. As Comment 1 to former Section 9–401 observed, "The principal advantage of state-wide filing is ease of access to the credit information which the files exist to provide. Consider for example the national distributor who wishes to have current information about the credit standing of the thousands of persons he sells to on credit. The more completely the files are centralized on a state-wide basis, the easier and cheaper it becomes to procure credit information; the more the files are scattered in local filing units, the more burdensome and costly." Local filing increases the net costs of secured transactions also by increasing uncertainty and the number of required filings. Any benefit that local filing may have had in the 1950's is now insubstantial. Accordingly, this Article dictates central filing for most situations, while retaining local filing for real-estate-related collateral and special filing provisions for transmitting utilities.

3.   **Minerals and Timber.** Under subsection (a)(1), a filing in the office where a record of a mortgage on the related real property would be filed will perfect a security interest in as-extracted collateral. Inasmuch as the security interest does not attach until extraction, the filing continues to be effective after extraction. A different result occurs with respect to timber to be cut, however. Unlike as-extracted collateral, standing timber may be goods before it is cut. See Section 9–102 (defining "goods"). Once cut, however, it is no longer timber *to be* cut, and the filing in the real-property-mortgage office ceases to be effective. The timber then becomes ordinary goods, and filing in the office specified in subsection (a)(2) is necessary for perfection. Note also that after the timber is cut the law of the debtor's location, not the location of the timber, governs perfection under Section 9–301.

4.   **Fixtures.** There are two ways in which a secured party may file a financing statement to perfect a security interest in goods that are or are to become fixtures. It may file in the Article 9 records, as with most other goods. See subsection (a)(2). Or it may file the financing statement as a "fixture filing," defined in Section 9–102, in the office in which a record of a mortgage on the related real property would be filed. See subsection(a)(1)(B).

5.   **Transmitting Utilities.** The usual filing rules do not apply well for a transmitting utility (defined in Section 9–102). Many pre-UCC statutes provided special filing rules for railroads and in some cases for other public utilities, to avoid the requirements for filing with legal descriptions in every county in which such debtors had property. Former Section 9–401(5) recreated and broadened these provisions, and subsection (b) follows this approach. The nature of the debtor will inform persons searching the record as to where to make a search.

A given State's subsection (b) applies only if the local law of that State governs perfection. As to most collateral, perfection by filing is governed by the law of the jurisdiction in which the debtor is located. See Section 9–301(1). However, the law of the jurisdiction in which goods that are or become fixtures are located governs perfection by filing a fixture filing. See Section 9–301(3)(A). As a consequence, filing in the filing office of more than one State may be necessary to perfect a security interest in fixtures collateral of a transmitting utility by filing a fixture filing. See Section 9–301, Comment 5.b.

As amended in 2010.

§ 9–502. Contents of Financing Statement; Record of Mortgage as Financing Statement; Time of Filing Financing Statement.

(a)   **[Sufficiency of financing statement.]** Subject to subsection (b), a financing statement is sufficient only if it:

(1)   provides the name of the debtor;

(2)   provides the name of the secured party or a representative of the secured party; and

(3)   indicates the collateral covered by the financing statement.

(b)   **[Real-property-related financing statements.]** Except as otherwise provided in Section 9–501(b), to be sufficient, a financing statement that covers as-extracted collateral or timber to be cut, or which is filed as a fixture filing and covers goods that are or are to become fixtures, must satisfy subsection (a) and also:

(1)   indicate that it covers this type of collateral;

(2)   indicate that it is to be filed [for record] in the real property records;

(3)   provide a description of the real property to which the collateral is related [sufficient to give constructive notice of a mortgage under the law of this State if the description were contained in a record of the mortgage of the real property]; and

(4)   if the debtor does not have an interest of record in the real property, provide the name of a record owner.

(c)   **[Record of mortgage as financing statement.]** A record of a mortgage is effective, from the date of recording, as a financing statement filed as a fixture filing or as a financing statement covering as-extracted collateral or timber to be cut only if:

(1)   the record indicates the goods or accounts that it covers;

(2) the goods are or are to become fixtures related to the real property described in the record or the collateral is related to the real property described in the record and is as-extracted collateral or timber to be cut;

(3) the record satisfies the requirements for a financing statement in this section, but:

   (A) the record need not indicate that it is to be filed in the real property records; and

   (B) the record sufficiently provides the name of a debtor who is an individual if it provides the individual name of the debtor or the surname and first personal name of the debtor, even if the debtor is an individual to whom Section 9–503(a)(4) applies; and

(4) the record is [duly] recorded.

(d) **[Filing before security agreement or attachment.]** A financing statement may be filed before a security agreement is made or a security interest otherwise attaches.

Legislative Note: Language in brackets is optional. Where the State has any special recording system for real property other than the usual grantor-grantee index (as, for instance, a tract system or a title registration or Torrens system) local adaptations of subsection (b) and Section 9–519(d) and (e) may be necessary. See, e.g., Mass. Gen. Laws Chapter 106, Section 9–410.

A State should enact the 2010 amendments to Section 9–502 only if the State enacts Alternative A of the 2010 amendments to Section 9–503.

As amended in 2010.

Official Comment

1. **Source.** Former Section 9–402(1), (5), (6).

2. **"Notice Filing."** This section adopts the system of "notice filing." What is required to be filed is not, as under pre-UCC chattel mortgage and conditional sales acts, the security agreement itself, but only a simple record providing a limited amount of information (financing statement). The financing statement may be filed before the security interest attaches or thereafter. See subsection (d). See also Section 9–308(a) (contemplating situations in which a financing statement is filed before a security interest attaches).

The notice itself indicates merely that a person may have a security interest in the collateral indicated. Further inquiry from the parties concerned will be necessary to disclose the complete state of affairs. Section 9–210 provides a statutory procedure under which the secured party, at the debtor's request, may be required to make disclosure. However, in many cases, information may be forthcoming without the need to resort to the formalities of that section.

Notice filing has proved to be of great use in financing transactions involving inventory, accounts, and chattel paper, because it obviates the necessity of refiling on each of a series of transactions in a continuing arrangement under which the collateral changes from day to day. However, even in the case of filings that do not necessarily involve a series of transactions (e.g., a loan secured by a single item of equipment), a financing statement is effective to encompass transactions under a security agreement not in existence and not contemplated at the time the notice was filed, if the indication of collateral in the financing statement is sufficient to cover the collateral concerned. Similarly, a financing statement is effective to cover after-acquired property of the type indicated and to perfect with respect to future advances under security agreements, regardless of whether after-acquired property or future advances are mentioned in the financing statement and even if not in the contemplation of the parties at the time the financing statement was authorized to be filed.

3. **Debtor's Signature; Required Authorization.** Subsection (a) sets forth the simple formal requirements for an effective financing statement. These requirements are: (1) the debtor's name; (2) the name of a secured party or representative of the secured party; and (3) an indication of the collateral.

Whereas former Section 9–402(1) required the debtor's signature to appear on a financing statement, this Article contains no signature requirement. The elimination of the signature requirement facilitates paperless filing. (However, as PEB Commentary No. 15 indicates, a paperless financing statement was sufficient under former Article 9.) Elimination of the signature requirement also makes the exceptions provided by former Section 9–402(2) unnecessary.

The fact that this Article does not require that an authenticating symbol be contained in the public record does not mean that all filings are authorized. Rather, Section 9–509(a) entitles a person to file an initial financing statement, an amendment that adds collateral, or an amendment that adds a debtor only if the debtor authorizes the filing, and Section 9–509(d) entitles a person other than the debtor to file a termination statement only if the secured party of record authorizes the filing. Of course, a filing has legal effect only to the extent it is authorized. See Section 9–510.

Law other than this Article, including the law with respect to ratification of past acts, generally determines whether a person has the requisite authority to file a record under this Article. See Sections 1–103 and 9–509, Comment 3. However, under Section 9–509(b), the debtor's authentication of (or becoming bound by) a security agreement *ipso facto* constitutes the debtor's authorization of the filing of a financing statement covering the collateral described in the security agreement. The secured party need not obtain a separate authorization.

Section 9–625 provides a remedy for unauthorized filings. Making an unauthorized filing also may give rise to civil or criminal liability under other law. In addition, this Article contains provisions that assist in the discovery of unauthorized filings and the amelioration of their practical effect. For example, Section 9–518 provides a procedure whereby a person may add to the public record a statement to the effect that a financing statement indexed under the person's name was wrongfully filed, and Section 9–509(d) entitles any person to file a termination statement if the secured party of record fails to comply with its obligation to file or send one to the debtor, the debtor authorizes the filing, and the termination statement so indicates. However, the filing office is neither obligated nor permitted to inquire into issues of authorization. See Section 9–520(a).

4.   **Certain Other Requirements.** Subsection (a) deletes other provisions of former Section 9–402(1) because they seems unwise (real-property description for financing statements covering crops), unnecessary (adequacy of copies of financing statements), or both (copy of security agreement as financing statement). In addition, the filing office must reject a financing statement lacking certain other information formerly required as a condition of perfection (e.g., an address for the debtor or secured party). See Sections 9–516(b), 9–520(a). However, if the filing office accepts the record, it is effective nevertheless. See Section 9–520(c).

5.   **Real-Property-Related Filings.** Subsection (b) contains the requirements for financing statements filed as fixture filings and financing statements covering timber to be cut or minerals and minerals-related accounts constituting as-extracted collateral. A description of the related real property must be sufficient to reasonably identify it. See Section 9–108. This formulation rejects the view that the real property description must be by metes and bounds, or otherwise conforming to traditional real-property practice in conveyancing, but, of course, the incorporation of such a description by reference to the recording data of a deed, mortgage or other instrument containing the description should suffice under the most stringent standards. The proper test is that a description of real property must be sufficient so that the financing statement will fit into the real-property search system and be found by a real-property searcher. Under the optional language in subsection (b)(3), the test of adequacy of the description is whether it would be adequate in a record of a mortgage of the real property. As suggested in the Legislative Note, more detail may be required if there is a tract indexing system or a land registration system.

If the debtor does not have an interest of record in the real property, a real-property-related financing statement must show the name of a record owner, and Section 9–519(d) requires the financing statement to be indexed in the name of that owner. This requirement also enables financing statements covering as-extracted collateral or timber to be cut and financing statements filed as fixture filings to fit into the real-property search system.

6.   **Record of Mortgage Effective as Financing Statement.** Subsection (c) explains when a record of a mortgage is effective as a financing statement filed as a fixture filing or to cover timber to be cut or as-extracted collateral. Use of the term "record of a mortgage" recognizes that in some systems the record actually filed is not the record pursuant to which a mortgage is created. Moreover, "mortgage" is defined in Section 9–102 as an "interest in real property," not as the record that creates or evidences the mortgage or the record that is filed in the public recording systems. A record creating a mortgage may also create a security interest with respect to fixtures (or other goods) in conformity with this Article. A single agreement creating a mortgage on real property and a security interest in chattels is common and useful for certain purposes. Under subsection (c), the recording of the record evidencing a mortgage (if it satisfies the requirements for a financing statement) constitutes the filing of a financing statement as to the fixtures (but not, of course, as to other goods). Section 9–515(g) makes the usual five-year maximum life for financing statements inapplicable to mortgages that operate as fixture filings under Section 9–502(c). Such mortgages are effective for the duration of the real-property recording.

Of course, if a combined mortgage covers chattels that are not fixtures, a regular financing statement filing is necessary with respect to the chattels, and subsection (c) is inapplicable. Likewise, a financing statement filed as a "fixture filing" is not effective to perfect a security interest in personal property other than fixtures.

In some cases it may be difficult to determine whether goods are or will become fixtures. Nothing in this Part prohibits the filing of a "precautionary" fixture filing, which would provide protection in the event goods are determined to be fixtures. The fact of filing should not be a factor in the determining whether goods are fixtures. Cf. Section 9–505(b).

§ 9–503. Name of Debtor and Secured Party.

(a) **[Sufficiency of debtor's name.]** A financing statement sufficiently provides the name of the debtor:

(1) except as otherwise provided in paragraph (3), if the debtor is a registered organization or the collateral is held in a trust that is a registered organization, only if the financing statement provides the name that is stated to be the registered organization's name on the public organic record most recently filed with or issued or enacted by the registered organization's jurisdiction of organization which purports to state, amend, or restate the registered organization's name;

(2) subject to subsection (f), if the collateral is being administered by the personal representative of a decedent, only if the financing statement provides, as the name of the debtor, the name of the decedent and, in a separate part of the financing statement, indicates that the collateral is being administered by a personal representative;

(3) if the collateral is held in a trust that is not a registered organization, only if the financing statement:

    (A) provides, as the name of the debtor:

        (i) if the organic record of the trust specifies a name for the trust, the name specified; or

        (ii) if the organic record of the trust does not specify a name for the trust, the name of the settlor or testator; and

    (B) in a separate part of the financing statement:

        (i) if the name is provided in accordance with subparagraph (A)(i), indicates that the collateral is held in a trust; or

        (ii) if the name is provided in accordance with subparagraph (A)(ii), provides additional information sufficient to distinguish the trust from other trusts having one or more of the same settlors or the same testator and indicates that the collateral is held in a trust, unless the additional information so indicates;

[ALTERNATIVE A]

(4) subject to subsection (g), if the debtor is an individual to whom this State has issued a [driver's license] that has not expired, only if the financing statement provides the name of the individual which is indicated on the [driver's license];

(5) if the debtor is an individual to whom paragraph (4) does not apply, only if the financing statement provides the individual name of the debtor or the surname and first personal name of the debtor; and

(6) in other cases:

    (A) if the debtor has a name, only if the financing statement provides the organizational name of the debtor; and

    (B) if the debtor does not have a name, only if it provides the names of the partners, members, associates, or other persons comprising the debtor, in a manner that each name provided would be sufficient if the person named were the debtor.

(b) **[Additional debtor-related information.]** A financing statement that provides the name of the debtor in accordance with subsection (a) is not rendered ineffective by the absence of:

(1)   a trade name or other name of the debtor; or

(2)   unless required under subsection (a)(6)(B), names of partners, members, associates, or other persons comprising the debtor.

[ALTERNATIVE B]

(4)   if the debtor is an individual, only if the financing statement:

    (A)   provides the individual name of the debtor;

    (B)   provides the surname and first personal name of the debtor; or

    (C)   subject to subsection (g), provides the name of the individual which is indicated on a [driver's license] that this State has issued to the individual and which has not expired; and

(5)   in other cases:

    (A)   if the debtor has a name, only if the financing statement provides the organizational name of the debtor; and

    (B)   if the debtor does not have a name, only if the financing statement provides the names of the partners, members, associates, or other persons comprising the debtor, in a manner that each name provided would be sufficient if the person named were the debtor.

(b) **[Additional debtor-related information.]** A financing statement that provides the name of the debtor in accordance with subsection (a) is not rendered ineffective by the absence of:

(1)   a trade name or other name of the debtor; or

(2)   unless required under subsection (a)(5)(B), names of partners, members, associates, or other persons comprising the debtor.

[END OF ALTERNATIVES]

(c)   **[Debtor's trade name insufficient.]** A financing statement that provides only the debtor's trade name does not sufficiently provide the name of the debtor.

(d)   **[Representative capacity.]** Failure to indicate the representative capacity of a secured party or representative of a secured party does not affect the sufficiency of a financing statement.

(e)   **[Multiple debtors and secured parties.]** A financing statement may provide the name of more than one debtor and the name of more than one secured party.

(f)   **[Name of decedent.]** The name of the decedent indicated on the order appointing the personal representative of the decedent issued by the court having jurisdiction over the collateral is sufficient as the "name of the decedent" under subsection (a)(2).

[ALTERNATIVE A]

(g)   **[Multiple driver's licenses.]** If this State has issued to an individual more than one [driver's license] of a kind described in subsection (a)(4), the one that was issued most recently is the one to which subsection (a)(4) refers.

[ALTERNATIVE B]

(g)   **[Multiple driver's licenses.]** If this State has issued to an individual more than one [driver's license] of a kind described in subsection (a)(4)(C), the one that was issued most recently is the one to which subsection (a)(4)(C) refers.

[END OF ALTERNATIVES]

(h)   **[Definition.]** In this section, the "name of the settlor or testator" means:

(1) if the settlor is a registered organization, the name that is stated to be the settlor's name on the public organic record most recently filed with or issued or enacted by the settlor's jurisdiction of organization which purports to state, amend, or restate the settlor's name; or

(2) in other cases, the name of the settlor or testator indicated in the trust's organic record.

Legislative Note:

1.   This Act contains two alternative sets of amendments relating to the names of individual debtors. A State should enact the same Alternative, A or B, for both subsections (a) and (i) of Section 9–503. A State that enacts Alternative A of the amendments to this section should also enact the amendments to Section 9–502.

2.   Both Alternatives refer, in part, to the name as shown on a debtor's driver's license. The Legislature should be aware that, in some States, certain characters that may be used by the State's department of motor vehicles (or similar agency) in the name on a driver's license may not be accepted by the State's central or local UCC filing offices under current regulations or internal protocols. This may occur because of technological limitations of the filing offices or merely as a result of inconsistent procedures. Similar issues may exist for field sizes as well. In these situations, perfection of a security interest granted by a debtor with such a driver's license may be impossible under Alternative A of the amendments and the utility of Alternative B, under which the name on the driver's license is one of the names that is sufficient, may be reduced. Accordingly, the State may wish to determine if one or more of these issues exist and, if so, to make certain that such issues have been resolved. A successful resolution might be accomplished by statute, agency regulation, or technological change effectuated before or as part of the enactment of this Act.

3.   Regardless of which Alternative is enacted, in States in which a single agency issues driver's licenses and non-driver identification cards as an alternative to a driver's license, such that at any given time an individual may hold either a driver's license or an identification card but not both, the State should replace each use of the term "driver's license" with a phrase meaning "driver's license or identification card" but containing the analogous terms used in the enacting State. In other States, the State should replace the term "driver's license" with the analogous term used in the enacting State.

As amended in 2010.

Official Comment

1.   **Source.** Subsections (a)(4)(A), (b), and (c) derive from former Section 9–402(7); otherwise, new.

2.   **Debtor's Name.** The requirement that a financing statement provide the debtor's name is particularly important. Financing statements are indexed under the name of the debtor, and those who wish to find financing statements search for them under the debtor's name. Subsection (a) explains what the debtor's name is for purposes of a financing statement.

a.   **Registered Organizations.** As a general matter, if the debtor is a "registered organization" (defined in Section 9–102 so as to ordinarily include corporations, limited partnerships, limited liability companies, and statutory trusts), then the debtor's name is the name shown on the "public organic record" of the debtor's "jurisdiction of organization" (both also defined in Section 9–102).

b.   **Collateral Held in a Trust.** When a financing statement covers collateral that is held in a trust that is a registered organization, subsection (a)(1) governs the name of the debtor. If, however, the collateral is held in a trust that is not a registered organization, subsection (a)(3) applies. (As used in this Article, collateral "held in a trust" includes collateral as to which the trust is the debtor as well as collateral as to which the trustee is the debtor.) This subsection adopts a convention that generally results in the name of the trust or the name of the trust's settlor being provided as the name of the debtor on the financing statement, even if, as typically is the case with common-law trusts, the "debtor" (defined in Section 9–102) is a trustee acting with respect to the collateral. This convention provides more accurate information and eases the burden for searchers, who otherwise would have difficulty with respect to debtor trustees that are large financial institutions.

More specifically, if a trust's organic record specifies a name for the trust, subsection (a)(3) requires the financing statement to provide, as the name of the debtor, the name for the trust specified in the organic record. In addition, the financing statement must indicate, in a separate part of the financing statement, that the collateral is held in a trust.

If the organic record of the trust does not specify a name for the trust, the name required for the financing statement is the name of the settlor or, in the case of a testamentary trust, the testator, in each case as determined under subsection (h). In addition, the financing statement must provide sufficient additional information to distinguish the trust from other trusts having one or more of the same settlors or the same testator. In many cases an indication of the date on which the trust was settled will satisfy this requirement. If neither the name nor the additional information indicates that the collateral is held in a trust, the financing statement must indicate that fact, but not as part of the debtor's name.

Neither the indication that the collateral is held in a trust nor the additional information that distinguishes the trust from other trusts having one or more of the same settlors or the same testator is part of the debtor's name. Nevertheless, a financing statement that fails to provide, in a separate part of the financing statement, any required indication or additional information does not sufficiently provide the name of the debtor under Sections 9–502(a) and 9–503(a)(3), does not "substantially satisfy[ ] the requirements" of Part 5 within the meaning of Section 9–506(a), and so is ineffective.

c.   Collateral Administered by a Personal Representative. Subsection (a)(2) deals with collateral that is being administered by an executor, administrator, or other personal representative of a decedent. Even if, as often is the case, the representative is the "debtor" (defined in Section 9–102), the financing statement must provide the name of the decedent as the name of the debtor. Subsection (f) provides a safe harbor, under which the name of the decedent indicated on the order appointing the personal representative issued by the court having jurisdiction over the collateral is sufficient as the name of the decedent. If the order indicates more than one name for the decedent, the first name in the list qualifies under subsection (f); however, other names in the list also may qualify as the "name of the decedent" within the meaning of subsection (a)(2). In addition to providing the name of the decedent, the financing statement must indicate, in a separate part of the financing statement, that the collateral is being administered by a personal representative. Although the indication is not part of the debtor's name, a financing statement that fails to provide the indication does not sufficiently provide the name of the debtor under Sections 9–502(a) and 9–503(a)(2), does not "substantially satisfy[ ] the requirements" of Part 5 within the meaning of Section 9–506(a), and so is ineffective.

d.   Individuals. This Article provides alternative approaches towards the requirement for providing the name of a debtor who is an individual.

Alternative A. Alternative A distinguishes between two groups of individual debtors. For debtors holding an unexpired driver's license issued by the State where the financing statement is filed (ordinarily the State where the debtor maintains the debtor's principal residence), Alternative A requires that a financing statement provide the name indicated on the license. When a debtor does not hold an unexpired driver's license issued by the relevant State, the requirement can be satisfied in either of two ways. A financing statement is sufficient if it provides the "individual name" of the debtor. Alternatively, a financing statement is sufficient if it provides the debtor's surname (i.e., family name) and first personal name (i.e., first name other than the surname).

Alternative B. Alternative B provides three ways in which a financing statement may sufficiently provide the name of an individual who is a debtor. The "individual name" of the debtor is sufficient, as is the debtor's surname and first personal name. If the individual holds an unexpired driver's license issued by the State where the financing statement is filed (ordinarily the State of the debtor's principal residence), the name indicated on the driver's license also is sufficient.

Name indicated on the driver's license. A financing statement does not "provide the name of the individual which is indicated" on the debtor's driver's license unless the name it provides is the same as the name indicated on the license. This is the case even if the name indicated on the debtor's driver's license contains an error.

Example 1: Debtor, an individual whose principal residence is in Illinois, grants a security interest to SP in certain business equipment. SP files a financing statement with the Illinois filing office. The financing statement provides the name appearing on Debtor's Illinois driver's license, "Joseph Allan Jones." Regardless of which Alternative is in effect in Illinois, this filing would be sufficient under Illinois' Section 9–503(a), even if Debtor's correct middle name is Alan, not Allan.

A filing against "Joseph A. Jones" or "Joseph Jones" would not "provide the name of the individual which is indicated" on the debtor's driver's license. However, these filings might be sufficient if Alternative A is in effect in Illinois and Jones has no current (i.e., unexpired) Illinois driver's license, or if Illinois has enacted Alternative B.

Determining the name that should be provided on the financing statement must not be done mechanically. The order in which the components of an individual's name appear on a driver's license differs among the States. Had the debtor in Example 1 obtained a driver's license from a different State, the license might have indicated the name as "Jones Joseph Allan." Regardless of the order on the driver's license, the debtor's surname must be provided in the part of the financing statement designated for the surname.

Alternatives A and B both refer to a license issued by "this State." Perfection of a security interest by filing ordinarily is determined by the law of the jurisdiction in which the debtor is located. See Section 9–301(1). (Exceptions to the general rule are found in Section 9–301(3) and (4), concerning fixture filings, timber to be cut, and as-extracted collateral.) A debtor who is an individual ordinarily is located at the individual's principal residence. See Section 9–307(b). (An exception appears in Section 9–307(c).) Thus, a given State's Section 9–503 ordinarily will apply during any period when the debtor's principal residence is located in that State, even if during that time the debtor holds or acquires a driver's license from another State.

When a debtor's principal residence changes, the location of the debtor under Section 9–307 also changes and perfection by filing ordinarily will be governed by the law of the debtor's new location. As a consequence of the application of that jurisdiction's Section 9–316, a security interest that is perfected by filing under the law of the debtor's former location will remain perfected for four months after the relocation, and thereafter if the secured party perfects under the law of the debtor's new location. Likewise, a financing statement filed in the former location may be effective to perfect a security interest that attaches after the debtor relocates. See Section 9–316(h).

Individual name of the debtor. Article 9 does not determine the "individual name" of a debtor. Nor does it determine which element or elements in a debtor's name constitute the surname. In some cases, determining the "individual name" of a debtor may be difficult, as may determining the debtor's surname. This is because in the case of individuals, unlike registered organizations, there is no public organic record to which reference can be made and from which the name and its components can be definitively determined.

Names can take many forms in the United States. For example, whereas a surname is often colloquially referred to as a "last name," the sequence in which the elements of a name are presented is not determinative. In some cultures, the surname appears first, while in others it may appear in a location that is neither first nor last. In addition, some surnames are composed of multiple elements that, taken together, constitute a single surname. These elements may or may not be separated by a space or connected by a hyphen, "i," or "y." In other instances, some or all of the same elements may not be part of the surname. In some cases, a debtor's entire name might be composed of only a single element, which should be provided in the part of the financing statement designated for the surname.

In disputes as to whether a financing statement sufficiently provides the "individual name" of a debtor, a court should refer to any non-UCC law concerning names. However, case law about names may have developed in contexts that implicate policies different from those of Article 9. A court considering an individual's name for purposes of determining the sufficiency of a financing statement is not necessarily bound by cases that were decided in other contexts and for other purposes.

Individuals are asked to provide their names on official documents such as tax returns and bankruptcy petitions. An individual may provide a particular name on an official document in response to instructions relating to the document rather than because the name is actually the individual's name. Accordingly, a court should not assume that the name an individual provides on an official document necessarily constitutes the "individual name" for purposes of the sufficiency of the debtor's name on a financing statement. Likewise, a court should not assume that the name as presented on an individual's birth certificate is necessarily the individual's current name.

In applying non-UCC law for purposes of determining the sufficiency of a debtor's name on a financing statement, a court should give effect to the instruction in Section 1–103(a)(1) that the UCC "must be liberally construed and applied to promote its underlying purposes and policies," which include simplifying and clarifying the law governing commercial transactions. Thus, determination of a debtor's name in the context of the Article 9 filing system must take into account the needs of both filers and searchers. Filers need a simple and predictable system in which they can have a reasonable degree of confidence that, without undue burden, they can determine a name that will be sufficient so as to permit their financing statements to be effective. Likewise, searchers need a simple and predictable system in which they can have a reasonable degree of confidence that, without undue burden, they will discover all financing statements pertaining to the debtor in question. The court also should take into account the purpose of the UCC to make the law uniform among the various jurisdictions. See Section 1–103(a)(3).

862

Of course, once an individual debtor's name has been determined to be sufficient for purposes of Section 9–503, a financing statement that provides a variation of that name, such as a "nickname" that does not constitute the debtor's name, does not sufficiently provide the name of the debtor under this section. Cf. Section 9–503(c) (a financing statement providing only a debtor's trade name is not sufficient).

If there is any doubt about an individual debtor's name, a secured party may choose to file one or more financing statements that provide a number of possible names for the debtor and a searcher may similarly choose to search under a number of possible names.

Note that, even if the name provided in an initial financing statement is correct, the filing office nevertheless must reject the financing statement if it does not identify an individual debtor's surname (e.g., if it is not clear whether the debtor's surname is Perry or Mason). See Section 9–516(b)(3)(C).

3.   **Secured Party's Name.** New subsection (d) makes clear that when the secured party is a representative, a financing statement is sufficient if it names the secured party, whether or not it indicates any representative capacity. Similarly, a financing statement that names a representative of the secured party is sufficient, even if it does not indicate the representative capacity.

Example 2: Debtor creates a security interest in favor of Bank X, Bank Y, and Bank Z, but not to their representative, the collateral agent (Bank A). The collateral agent is not itself a secured party. See Section 9–102. Under Sections 9–502(a) and 9–503(d), however, a financing statement is effective if it names as secured party Bank A and not the actual secured parties, even if it omits Bank A's representative capacity.

Each person whose name is provided in an initial financing statement as the name of the secured party or representative of the secured party is a secured party of record. See Section 9–511.

4.   **Multiple Names.** Subsection (e) makes explicit what is implicit under former Article 9: a financing statement may provide the name of more than one debtor and secured party. See Section 1–106 (words in the singular include the plural). With respect to records relating to more than one debtor, see Section 9–520(d). With respect to financing statements providing the name of more than one secured party, see Sections 9–509(e) and 9–510(b).

As amended in 2010.

§ 9–504.   Indication of Collateral.

A financing statement sufficiently indicates the collateral that it covers if the financing statement provides:

(1)   a description of the collateral pursuant to Section 9–108; or

(2)   an indication that the financing statement covers all assets or all personal property.

As amended in 1999.

Official Comment

1.   **Source.** Former Section 9–402(1).

2.   **Indication of Collateral.** To comply with Section 9–502(a), a financing statement must "indicate" the collateral it covers. A financing statement sufficiently indicates collateral claimed to be covered by the financing statement if it satisfies the purpose of conditioning perfection on the filing of a financing statement, i.e., if it provides notice that a person may have a security interest in the collateral claimed. See Section 9–502, Comment 2. In particular, an indication of collateral that would have satisfied the requirements of former Section 9–402(1) (i.e., "a statement indicating the types, or describing the items, of collateral") suffices under Section 9–502(a). An indication may satisfy the requirements of Section 9–502(a), even if it would not have satisfied the requirements of former Section 9–402(1).

This section provides two safe harbors. Under paragraph (1), a "description" of the collateral (as the term is explained in Section 9–108) suffices as an indication for purposes of the sufficiency of a financing statement.

Debtors sometimes create a security interest in all, or substantially all, of their assets. To accommodate this practice, paragraph (2) expands the class of sufficient collateral references to embrace "an indication that the financing statement covers all assets or all personal property." If the property in question belongs to the debtor and is personal property, any searcher will know that the property is covered by the financing statement. Of course, regardless of its breadth, a financing statement has no effect with respect to property indicated but to which a security interest has not attached. Note that a broad statement of this kind (e.g., "all debtor's personal property") would not be a sufficient "description" for purposes of a security agreement. See Sections 9–203(b)(3)(A), 9–108. It follows that a somewhat narrower description than "all assets," e.g., "all assets other than automobiles," is sufficient for purposes of this section, even if it does not suffice for purposes of a security agreement.

As amended in 2000.

§ 9–505. Filing and Compliance With Other Statutes and Treaties for Consignments, Leases, Other Bailments, and Other Transactions.

(a) **[Use of terms other than "debtor" and "secured party."]** A consignor, lessor, or other bailor of goods, a licensor, or a buyer of a payment intangible or promissory note may file a financing statement, or may comply with a statute or treaty described in Section 9–311(a), using the terms "consignor", "consignee", "lessor", "lessee", "bailor", "bailee", "licensor", "licensee", "owner", "registered owner", "buyer", "seller", or words of similar import, instead of the terms "secured party" and "debtor".

(b) **[Effect of financing statement under subsection (a).]** This part applies to the filing of a financing statement under subsection (a) and, as appropriate, to compliance that is equivalent to filing a financing statement under Section 9–311(b), but the filing or compliance is not of itself a factor in determining whether the collateral secures an obligation. If it is determined for another reason that the collateral secures an obligation, a security interest held by the consignor, lessor, bailor, licensor, owner, or buyer which attaches to the collateral is perfected by the filing or compliance.

Official Comment

1. **Source.** Former Section 9–408.

2. **Precautionary Filing.** Occasionally, doubts arise concerning whether a transaction creates a relationship to which this Article or its filing provisions apply. For example, questions may arise over whether a "lease" of equipment in fact creates a security interest or whether the "sale" of payment intangibles in fact secures an obligation, thereby requiring action to perfect the security interest. This section, which derives from former Section 9–408, affords the option of filing of a financing statement with appropriate changes of terminology but without affecting the substantive question of classification of the transaction.

3. **Changes from Former Section 9–408.** This section expands the rule of Section 9–408 to embrace more generally other bailments and transactions, as well as sales transactions, primarily sales of payment intangibles and promissory notes. It provides the same benefits for compliance with a statute or treaty described in Section 9–311(a) that former Section 9–408 provided for filing, in connection with the use of terms such as "lessor," "consignor," etc. The references to "owner" and "registered owner" are intended to address, for example, the situation where a putative lessor is the registered owner of an automobile covered by a certificate of title and the transaction is determined to create a security interest. Although this section provides that the security interest is perfected, the relevant certificate-of-title statute may expressly provide to the contrary or may be ambiguous. If so, it may be necessary or advisable to amend the certificate-of-title statute to ensure that perfection of the security interest will be achieved.

As did former Section 1–201, former Article 9 referred to transactions, including leases and consignments, "intended as security." This misleading phrase created the erroneous impression that the parties to a transaction can dictate how the law will classify it (e.g., as a bailment or as a security interest) and thus affect the rights of third parties. This Article deletes the phrase wherever it appears. Subsection (b) expresses the principle more precisely by referring to a security interest that "secures an obligation."

4. **Consignments.** Although a "true" consignment is a bailment, the filing and priority provisions of former Article 9 applied to "true" consignments. See former Sections 2–326(3), 9–114. A consignment "intended as security" created a security interest that was in all respects subject to former Article 9. This Article subsumes most true consignments under the rubric of "security interest." See Sections 9–102 (definition of "consignment"), 9–109(a)(4), 1–201(b)(35) (definition of "security interest"). Nevertheless, it maintains the distinction between a (true) "consignment," as to which only certain aspects of Article 9 apply, and a so-called consignment that actually "secures an obligation," to which Article 9 applies in full. The revisions to this section reflect the change in terminology.

As amended in 2010.

§ 9–506. Effect of Errors or Omissions.

(a) **[Minor errors and omissions.]** A financing statement substantially satisfying the requirements of this part is effective, even if it has minor errors or omissions, unless the errors or omissions make the financing statement seriously misleading.

(b) **[Financing statement seriously misleading.]** Except as otherwise provided in subsection (c), a financing statement that fails sufficiently to provide the name of the debtor in accordance with Section 9–503(a) is seriously misleading.

(c) **[Financing statement not seriously misleading.]** If a search of the records of the filing office under the debtor's correct name, using the filing office's standard search logic, if any, would disclose a financing statement that fails sufficiently to provide the name of the debtor in accordance with Section 9–503(a), the name provided does not make the financing statement seriously misleading.

(d) **["Debtor's correct name."]** For purposes of Section 9–508(b), the "debtor's correct name" in subsection (c) means the correct name of the new debtor.

Official Comment

1. **Source.** Former Section 9–402(8).

2. **Errors and Omissions.** Like former Section 9–402(8), subsection (a) is in line with the policy of this Article to simplify formal requisites and filing requirements. It is designed to discourage the fanatical and impossibly refined reading of statutory requirements in which courts occasionally have indulged themselves. Subsection (a) provides the standard applicable to indications of collateral. Subsections (b) and (c), which are new, concern the effectiveness of financing statements in which the debtor's name is incorrect. Subsection (b) contains the general rule: a financing statement that fails sufficiently to provide the debtor's name in accordance with Section 9–503(a) is seriously misleading as a matter of law. Subsection (c) provides an exception: If the financing statement nevertheless would be discovered in a search under the debtor's correct name, using the filing office's standard search logic, if any, then as a matter of law the incorrect name does not make the financing statement seriously misleading. A financing statement that is seriously misleading under this section is ineffective even if it is disclosed by (i) using a search logic other than that of the filing office to search the official records, or (ii) using the filing office's standard search logic to search a data base other than that of the filing office. For purposes of subsection (c), any name that satisfies Section 9–503(a) at the time of the search is a "correct name."

This section and Section 9–503 balance the interests of filers and searchers. Searchers are not expected to ascertain nicknames, trade names, and the like by which the debtor may be known and then search under each of them. Rather, it is the secured party's responsibility to provide the name of the debtor sufficiently in a filed financing statement. Subsection (c) sets forth the only situation in which a financing statement that fails sufficiently to provide the name of the debtor is not seriously misleading. As stated in subsection (b), if the name of the debtor provided on a financing statement is insufficient and subsection (c) is not satisfied, the financing statement is seriously misleading. Such a financing statement is ineffective even if the debtor is known in some contexts by the name provided on the financing statement and even if searchers know or have reason to know that the name provided on the financing statement refers to the debtor. Any suggestion to the contrary in a judicial opinion is incorrect.

To satisfy the requirements of Section 9–503(a)(2), a financing statement must indicate that the collateral is being administered by a personal representative. To satisfy the requirements of Section 9–503(a)(3), a financing statement must indicate that the collateral is held in a trust and provide additional information that distinguishes the trust from certain other trusts. The indications and additional information are not part of the debtor's name. Nevertheless, a financing statement that fails to provide an indication or the additional information when required does not sufficiently provide the name of the debtor under Sections 9–502(a) and 9–503(a), does not "substantially satisfy[ ] the requirements" of Part 5 within the meaning of this section and so is ineffective.

In addition to requiring the debtor's name and an indication of the collateral, Section 9–502(a) requires a financing statement to provide the name of the secured party or a representative of the secured party. Inasmuch as searches are not conducted under the secured party's name, and no filing is needed to continue the perfected status of security interest after it is assigned, an error in the name of the secured party or its representative will not be seriously misleading. However, in an appropriate case, an error of this kind may give rise to an estoppel in favor of a particular holder of a conflicting claim to the collateral. See Section 1–103.

3.   **New Debtors.** Subsection (d) provides that, in determining the extent to which a financing statement naming an original debtor is effective against a new debtor, the sufficiency of the financing statement should be tested against the name of the new debtor.

As amended in 2010.

§ 9–507.   Effect of Certain Events on Effectiveness of Financing Statement.

(a)   **[Disposition.]** A filed financing statement remains effective with respect to collateral that is sold, exchanged, leased, licensed, or otherwise disposed of and in which a security interest or agricultural lien continues, even if the secured party knows of or consents to the disposition.

(b)   **[Information becoming seriously misleading.]** Except as otherwise provided in subsection (c) and Section 9–508, a financing statement is not rendered ineffective if, after the financing statement is filed, the information provided in the financing statement becomes seriously misleading under Section 9–506.

(c)   **[Change in debtor's name.]** If the name that a filed financing statement provides for a debtor becomes insufficient as the name of the debtor under Section 9–503(a) so that the financing statement becomes seriously misleading under Section 9–506:

(1)   the financing statement is effective to perfect a security interest in collateral acquired by the debtor before, or within four months after, the filed financing statement becomes seriously misleading; and

(2)   the financing statement is not effective to perfect a security interest in collateral acquired by the debtor more than four months after the filed financing statement becomes seriously misleading, unless an amendment to the financing statement which renders the financing statement not seriously misleading is filed within four months after the financing statement became seriously misleading.

As amended in 2010.

Official Comment

1.   **Source.** Former Section 9–402(7).

2.   **Scope of Section.** This section deals with situations in which the information in a proper financing statement becomes inaccurate after the financing statement is filed. Compare Section 9–338, which deals with situations in which a financing statement contains a particular kind of information concerning the debtor (i.e., the information described in Section 9–516(b)(5)) that is incorrect at the time it is filed.

3.   **Post-Filing Disposition of Collateral.** Under subsection (a), a financing statement remains effective even if the collateral is sold or otherwise disposed of. This subsection clarifies the third sentence of former Section 9–402(7) by providing that a financing statement remains effective following the disposition of collateral only when the security interest or agricultural lien continues in that collateral. This result is consistent with the conclusion of PEB Commentary No. 3. Normally, a security interest does continue after disposition of the collateral. See Section 9–315(a). Law other than this Article determines whether an agricultural lien survives disposition of the collateral.

As a consequence of the disposition, the collateral may be owned by a person other than the debtor against whom the financing statement was filed. Under subsection (a), the secured party remains perfected even if it does not correct the public record. For this reason, any person seeking to determine whether a debtor owns collateral free of security interests must inquire as to the debtor's source of title and, if circumstances seem to require it, search in the name of a former owner. Subsection (a) addresses only the sufficiency of the information contained in the financing statement. A disposition of collateral may result in loss of perfection for other reasons. See Section 9–316.

Example: Dee Corp. is an Illinois corporation. It creates a security interest in its equipment in favor of Secured Party. Secured Party files a proper financing statement in Illinois. Dee Corp. sells an item of equipment to Bee Corp., a Pennsylvania corporation, subject to the security interest. The security interest continues, see Section 9–315(a), and remains perfected, see Section 9–507(a), notwithstanding that the financing statement is filed under "D" (for Dee Corp.) and not under "B." However, because Bee Corp. is located in Pennsylvania and not Illinois, see Section 9–307, unless Secured Party perfects under Pennsylvania law within one year after the transfer, its security interest will become unperfected and will be deemed to have been unperfected against purchasers of the collateral. See Section 9–316.

4.   **Other Post-Filing Changes.** Subsection (b) provides that, as a general matter, post-filing changes that render a financing statement seriously misleading have no effect on a financing statement. The financing statement remains effective. It is subject to two exceptions: Section 9–508 and Section 9–507(c). Section 9–508 addresses the effectiveness of a financing statement filed against an original debtor when a new debtor becomes bound by the original debtor's security agreement. It is discussed in the Comments to that section. Section 9–507(c) addresses cases in which a filed financing statement provides a name that, at the time of filing, satisfies the requirements of Section 9–503(a) with respect to the named debtor but, at a later time, no longer does so.

Example 1: Debtor, an individual whose principal residence is in California, grants a security interest to SP in certain business equipment. SP files a financing statement with the California filing office. Alternative A is in effect in California. The financing statement provides the name appearing on Debtor's California driver's license, "James McGinty." Debtor obtains a court order changing his name to "Roger McGuinn" but does not change his driver's license. Even after the court order issues, the name provided for the debtor in the financing statement is sufficient under Section 9–503(a). Accordingly, Section 9–507(c) does not apply.

The same result would follow if Alternative B is in effect in California.

Under Section 9–503(a)(4) (Alternative A), if the debtor holds a current (i.e., unexpired) driver's license issued by the State where the financing statement is filed, the name required for the financing statement is the name indicated on the license that was issued most recently by that State. If the debtor does not have a current driver's license issued by that State, then the debtor's name is determined under subsection (a)(5). It follows that a debtor's name may change, and a financing statement providing the name on the debtor's then-current driver's license may become seriously misleading, if the license expires and the debtor's name under subsection (a)(5) is different. The same consequences may follow if a debtor's driver's license is renewed and the names on the licenses differ.

Example 2: The facts are as in Example 1. Debtor's driver's license expires one year after the entry of the court order changing Debtor's name. Debtor does not renew the license. Upon expiration of the license, the name required for sufficiency by Section 9–503(a) is the individual name of the debtor or the debtor's surname and first personal name. The name "James McGinty" has become insufficient.

Example 3: The facts are as in Example 1. Before the license expires, Debtor renews the license. The name indicated on the new license is "Roger McGuinn." Upon issuance of the new license, "James McGinty" becomes insufficient as the debtor's name under Section 9–503(a).

The same results would follow if Alternative B is in effect in California (assuming that, following the issuance of the court order, "James McGinty" is neither the individual name of the debtor nor the debtor's surname and first personal name).

Even if the name provided as the name of the debtor becomes insufficient under Section 9–503(a), the filed financing statement does not become seriously misleading, and Section 9–507(c) does not apply, if the financing statement can be found by searching under the debtor's "correct" name, using the filing office's standard search logic. See Section 9–506. Any name that satisfies Section 9–503(a) at the time of the search is a "correct name" for these purposes. Thus, assuming that a search of the records of the California filing office under "Roger McGuinn," using the filing office's standard search logic, would not disclose a financing statement naming "James McGinty," the financing statement in Examples 2 and 3 has become seriously misleading and Section 9–507(c) applies.

If a filed financing statement becomes seriously misleading because the name it provides for a debtor becomes insufficient, the financing statement, unless amended to provide a sufficient name for the debtor, is effective only to perfect a security interest in collateral acquired by the debtor before, or within four months after, the change. If an amendment that provides a sufficient name is filed within four months after the change, the financing statement as amended would be effective also with respect to collateral acquired more than four months after the change. If an amendment that provides a sufficient name is filed more than four months after the change, the financing statement as amended would be effective also with respect to collateral acquired more than four months after the change, but only from the time of the filing of the amendment.

As amended in 2010.

§ 9–508. Effectiveness of Financing Statement if New Debtor Becomes Bound by Security Agreement.

(a) **[Financing statement naming original debtor.]** Except as otherwise provided in this section, a filed financing statement naming an original debtor is effective to perfect a security interest in collateral in which a new debtor has or acquires rights to the extent that the financing statement would have been effective had the original debtor acquired rights in the collateral.

(b) **[Financing statement becoming seriously misleading.]** If the difference between the name of the original debtor and that of the new debtor causes a filed financing statement that is effective under subsection (a) to be seriously misleading under Section 9–506:

(1) the financing statement is effective to perfect a security interest in collateral acquired by the new debtor before, and within four months after, the new debtor becomes bound under Section 9–203(d); and

(2) the financing statement is not effective to perfect a security interest in collateral acquired by the new debtor more than four months after the new debtor becomes bound under Section 9–203(d) unless an initial financing statement providing the name of the new debtor is filed before the expiration of that time.

(c) **[When section not applicable.]** This section does not apply to collateral as to which a filed financing statement remains effective against the new debtor under Section 9–507(a).

Official Comment

1. **Source.** New.

2. **The Problem.** Section 9–203(d) and (e) and this section deal with situations where one party (the "new debtor") becomes bound as debtor by a security agreement entered into by another person (the "original debtor"). These situations often arise as a consequence of changes in business structure. For example, the original debtor may be an individual debtor who operates a business as a sole proprietorship and then incorporates it. Or, the original debtor may be a corporation that is merged into another corporation. Under both former Article 9 and this Article, collateral that is transferred in the course of the incorporation or merger normally would remain subject to a perfected security interest. See Sections 9–315(a), 9–507(a). Former Article 9 was less clear with respect to whether an after-acquired property clause in a security agreement signed by the original debtor would be effective to create a security interest in property acquired by the new corporation or the merger survivor and, if so, whether a financing statement filed against the original debtor would be effective to perfect the security interest. This section and Sections 9–203(d) and (e) are a clarification.

3. **How New Debtor Becomes Bound.** Normally, a security interest is unenforceable unless the debtor has authenticated a security agreement describing the collateral. See Section 9–203(b). New Section 9–203(e) creates an exception, under which a security agreement entered into by one person is effective with respect to the property of another. This exception comes into play if a "new debtor" becomes bound as debtor by a security agreement entered into by another person (the "original debtor"). (The quoted terms are defined in Section 9–102.) If a new debtor does become bound, then the security agreement entered into by the original debtor satisfies the security-agreement requirement of Section 9–203(b)(3) as to existing or after-acquired property of the new debtor to the extent the property is described in the security agreement. In that case, no other agreement is necessary to make a security interest enforceable in that property. See Section 9–203(e).

Section 9–203(d) explains when a new debtor becomes bound by an original debtor's security agreement. Under Section 9–203(d)(1), a new debtor becomes bound as debtor if, by contract or operation of other law, the security agreement becomes effective to create a security interest in the new debtor's property. For example, if the applicable corporate law of mergers provides that when A Corp merges into B Corp, B Corp becomes a debtor under A Corp's security agreement, then B Corp would become bound as debtor following such a merger. Similarly, B Corp would become bound as debtor if B Corp contractually assumes A's obligations under the security agreement.

Under certain circumstances, a new debtor becomes bound for purposes of this Article even though it would not be bound under other law. Under Section 9–203(d)(2), a new debtor becomes bound when, by contract or

868

operation of other law, it (i) becomes obligated not only for the secured obligation but also generally for the obligations of the original debtor and (ii) acquires or succeeds to substantially all the assets of the original debtor. For example, some corporate laws provide that, when two corporations merge, the surviving corporation succeeds to the assets of its merger partner and "has all liabilities" of both corporations. In the case where, for example, A Corp merges into B Corp (and A Corp ceases to exist), some people have questioned whether A Corp's grant of a security interest in its existing and after-acquired property becomes a "liability" of B Corp, such that B Corp's existing and after-acquired property becomes subject to a security interest in favor of A Corp's lender. Even if corporate law were to give a negative answer, under Section 9–203(d)(2), B Corp would become bound for purposes of Section 9–203(e) and this section. The "substantially all of the assets" requirement of Section 9–203(d)(2) excludes sureties and other secondary obligors as well as persons who become obligated through veil piercing and other non-successorship doctrines. In most cases, it will exclude successors to the assets and liabilities of a division of a debtor.

4. **When Financing Statement Effective Against New Debtor.** Subsection (a) provides that a filing against the original debtor generally is effective to perfect a security interest in collateral that a new debtor has at the time it becomes bound by the original debtor's security agreement and collateral that it acquires after the new debtor becomes bound. Under subsection (b), however, if the filing against the original debtor is seriously misleading as to the new debtor's name, the filing is effective as to collateral acquired by the new debtor more than four months after the new debtor becomes bound only if a person files during the four-month period an initial financing statement providing the name of the new debtor. Compare Section 9–507(c) (four-month period of effectiveness with respect to collateral acquired by a debtor after the name provided for the debtor becomes insufficient as the name of the debtor). As to the meaning of "initial financing statement" in this context, see Section 9–512, Comment 5.

5. **Transferred Collateral.** This section does not apply to collateral transferred by the original debtor to a new debtor. See subsection (c). Under those circumstances, the filing against the original debtor continues to be effective until it lapses or perfection is lost for another reason. See sections 9–316, 9–507(a).

6. **Priority.** Section 9–326 governs the priority contest between a secured creditor of the original debtor and a secured creditor of the new debtor.

As amended in 2000 and 2010.

§ 9–509. Persons Entitled to File a Record.

(a) **[Person entitled to file record.]** A person may file an initial financing statement, amendment that adds collateral covered by a financing statement, or amendment that adds a debtor to a financing statement only if:

    (1) the debtor authorizes the filing in an authenticated record or pursuant to subsection (b) or (c); or

    (2) the person holds an agricultural lien that has become effective at the time of filing and the financing statement covers only collateral in which the person holds an agricultural lien.

(b) **[Security agreement as authorization.]** By authenticating or becoming bound as debtor by a security agreement, a debtor or new debtor authorizes the filing of an initial financing statement, and an amendment, covering:

    (1) the collateral described in the security agreement; and

    (2) property that becomes collateral under Section 9–315(a)(2), whether or not the security agreement expressly covers proceeds.

(c) **[Acquisition of collateral as authorization.]** By acquiring collateral in which a security interest or agricultural lien continues under Section 9–315(a)(1), a debtor authorizes the filing of an initial financing statement, and an amendment, covering the collateral and property that becomes collateral under Section 9–315(a)(2).

(d) **[Person entitled to file certain amendments.]** A person may file an amendment other than an amendment that adds collateral covered by a financing statement or an amendment that adds a debtor to a financing statement only if:

    (1) the secured party of record authorizes the filing; or

(2) the amendment is a termination statement for a financing statement as to which the secured party of record has failed to file or send a termination statement as required by Section 9–513(a) or (c), the debtor authorizes the filing, and the termination statement indicates that the debtor authorized it to be filed.

(e) **[Multiple secured parties of record.]** If there is more than one secured party of record for a financing statement, each secured party of record may authorize the filing of an amendment under subsection (d).

As amended in 2000.

Official Comment

1. **Source.** New.

2. **Scope and Approach of This Section.** This section collects in one place most of the rules determining whether a record may be filed. Section 9–510 explains the extent to which a filed record is effective. Under these sections, the identity of the person who effects a filing is immaterial. The filing scheme contemplated by this Part does not contemplate that the identity of a "filer" will be a part of the searchable records. This is consistent with, and a necessary aspect of, eliminating signatures or other evidence of authorization from the system. (Note that the 1972 amendments to this Article eliminated the requirement that a financing statement contain the signature of the secured party.) As long as the appropriate person authorizes the filing, or, in the case of a termination statement, the debtor is entitled to the termination, it is insignificant whether the secured party or another person files any given record. The question of authorization is one for the court, not the filing office. However, a filing office may choose to employ authentication procedures in connection with electronic communications, e.g., to verify the identity of a filer who seeks to charge the filing fee.

3. **Unauthorized Filings.** Records filed in the filing office do not require signatures for their effectiveness. Subsection (a)(1) substitutes for the debtor's signature on a financing statement the requirement that the debtor authorize in an authenticated record the filing of an initial financing statement or an amendment that adds collateral. Also, under subsection (a)(1), if an amendment adds a debtor, the debtor who is added must authorize the amendment. A person who files an unauthorized record in violation of subsection (a)(1) is liable under Section 9–625(b) and (e) for actual and statutory damages. Of course, a filed financing statement is ineffective to perfect a security interest if the filing is not authorized. See Section 9–510(a). Law other than this Article, including the law with respect to ratification of past acts, generally determines whether a person has the requisite authority to file a record under this section. See Sections 1–103, 9–502, Comment 3. This Article applies to other issues, such as the priority of a security interest perfected by the filing of a financing statement. See Section 9–322, Comment 4.

4. *Ipso Facto* **Authorization.** Under subsection (b), the authentication of a security agreement *ipso facto* constitutes the debtor's authorization of the filing of a financing statement covering the collateral described in the security agreement. The secured party need not obtain a separate authorization. Similarly, a new debtor's becoming bound by a security agreement *ipso facto* constitutes the new debtor's authorization of the filing of a financing statement covering the collateral described in the security agreement by which the new debtor has become bound. And, under subsection (c), the acquisition of collateral in which a security interest continues after disposition under Section 9–315(a)(1) *ipso facto* constitutes an authorization to file an initial financing statement against the person who acquired the collateral. The authorization to file an initial financing statement also constitutes an authorization to file a record covering actual proceeds of the original collateral, even if the security agreement is silent as to proceeds. See Section 9–322, Comment 4.

Example 1: Debtor authenticates a security agreement creating a security interest in Debtor's inventory in favor of Secured Party. Secured Party files a financing statement covering inventory and accounts. The financing statement is authorized insofar as it covers inventory and unauthorized insofar as it covers accounts. (Note, however, that the financing statement will be effective to perfect a security interest in accounts constituting proceeds of the inventory to the same extent as a financing statement covering only inventory.)

Example 2: Debtor authenticates a security agreement creating a security interest in Debtor's inventory in favor of Secured Party. Secured Party files a financing statement covering inventory. Debtor sells some inventory, deposits the buyer's payment into a deposit account, and withdraws the funds to purchase equipment. As long as the equipment can be traced to the inventory, the security interest continues in the equipment. See Section 9–315(a)(2). However, because the equipment was acquired with cash proceeds, the financing statement becomes ineffective to perfect the security interest in the equipment on the 21st day after the security interest attaches to the equipment unless Secured Party continues perfection beyond the 20-day period by filing a financing statement against the equipment or amending the filed financing statement to cover equipment. See Section 9–315(d). Debtor's authentication of the security agreement authorizes the filing of an initial financing statement or amendment covering the equipment, which is "property that becomes collateral under Section 9–315(a)(2)." See Section 9–509(b)(2).

5. **Agricultural Liens.** Under subsection (a)(2), the holder of an agricultural lien may file a financing statement covering collateral subject to the lien without obtaining the debtor's authorization. Because the lien arises as matter of law, the debtor's consent is not required. A person who files an unauthorized record in violation of this subsection is liable under Section 9–625(e) for a statutory penalty and damages.

6. **Amendments; Termination Statements Authorized by Debtor.** Most amendments may not be filed unless the secured party of record, as determined under Section 9–511, authorizes the filing. See subsection (d)(1). However, under subsection (d)(2), the authorization of the secured party of record is not required for the filing of a termination statement if the secured party of record failed to send or file a termination statement as required by Section 9–513, the debtor authorizes it to be filed, and the termination statement so indicates. An authorization to file a record under subsection (d) is effective even if the authorization is not in an authenticated record. Compare subsection (a)(1). However, both the person filing the record and the person giving the authorization may wish to obtain and retain a record indicating that the filing was authorized.

7. **Multiple Secured Parties of Record.** Subsection (e) deals with multiple secured parties of record. It permits each secured party of record to authorize the filing of amendments. However, Section 9–510(b) protects the rights and powers of one secured party of record from the effects of filings made by another secured party of record. See Section 9–510, Comment 3.

8. **Successor to Secured Party of Record.** A person may succeed to the powers of the secured party of record by operation of other law, e.g., the law of corporate mergers. In that case, the successor has the power to authorize filings within the meaning of this section.

As amended in 2010.

§ 9–510.   Effectiveness of Filed Record.

(a)   **[Filed record effective if authorized.]** A filed record is effective only to the extent that it was filed by a person that may file it under Section 9–509.

(b)   **[Authorization by one secured party of record.]** A record authorized by one secured party of record does not affect the financing statement with respect to another secured party of record.

(c)   **[Continuation statement not timely filed.]** A continuation statement that is not filed within the six-month period prescribed by Section 9–515(d) is ineffective.

Official Comment

1. **Source.** New.

2. **Ineffectiveness of Unauthorized or Overbroad Filings.** Subsection (a) provides that a filed financing statement is effective only to the extent it was filed by a person entitled to file it.

Example 1: Debtor authorizes the filing of a financing statement covering inventory. Under Section 9–509, the secured party may file a financing statement covering only inventory; it may not file a financing statement covering other collateral. The secured party files a financing statement covering inventory and equipment. This section provides that the financing statement is effective only to the extent the secured party may file it. Thus, the financing statement is effective to perfect a security interest in inventory but ineffective to perfect a security interest in equipment.

3. **Multiple Secured Parties of Record.** Section 9–509(e) permits any secured party of record to authorize the filing of most amendments. Subsection (b) of this section prevents a filing authorized by one secured party of record from affecting the rights and powers of another secured party of record without the latter's consent.

Example 2: Debtor creates a security interest in favor of A and B. The filed financing statement names A and B as the secured parties. An amendment deleting some collateral covered by the financing statement is filed pursuant to B's authorization. Although B's security interest in the deleted collateral becomes unperfected, A's security interest remains perfected in all the collateral.

Example 3: Debtor creates a security interest in favor of A and B. The financing statement names A and B as the secured parties. A termination statement is filed pursuant to B's authorization. Although the effectiveness of the financing statement terminates with respect to B's security interest, A's rights are unaffected. That is, the financing statement continues to be effective to perfect A's security interest.

4.   **Continuation Statements.** A continuation statement may be filed only within the six months immediately before lapse. See Section 9–515(d). The filing office is obligated to reject a continuation statement that is filed outside the six-month period. See Sections 9–520(a), 9–516(b)(7). Subsection (c) provides that if the filing office fails to reject a continuation statement that is not filed in a timely manner, the continuation statement is ineffective nevertheless.

§ 9–511.   Secured Party of Record.

(a)   **[Secured party of record.]** A secured party of record with respect to a financing statement is a person whose name is provided as the name of the secured party or a representative of the secured party in an initial financing statement that has been filed. If an initial financing statement is filed under Section 9–514(a), the assignee named in the initial financing statement is the secured party of record with respect to the financing statement.

(b)   **[Amendment naming secured party of record.]** If an amendment of a financing statement which provides the name of a person as a secured party or a representative of a secured party is filed, the person named in the amendment is a secured party of record. If an amendment is filed under Section 9–514(b), the assignee named in the amendment is a secured party of record.

(c)   **[Amendment deleting secured party of record.]** A person remains a secured party of record until the filing of an amendment of the financing statement which deletes the person.

Official Comment

1.   **Source.** New.

2.   **Secured Party of Record.** This new section explains how the secured party of record is to be determined. If SP–1 is named as the secured party in an initial financing statement, it is the secured party of record. Similarly, if an initial financing statement reflects a total assignment from SP–0 to SP–1, then SP–1 is the secured party of record. See subsection (a). If, subsequently, an amendment is filed assigning SP–1's status to SP–2, then SP–2 becomes the secured party of record in place of SP–1. The same result obtains if a subsequent amendment deletes the reference to SP–1 and substitutes therefor a reference to SP–2. If, however, a subsequent amendment adds SP–2 as a secured party but does not purport to remove SP–1 as a secured party, then SP–2 and SP–1 each is a secured party of record. See subsection (b). An amendment purporting to remove the only secured party of record without providing a successor is ineffective. See Section 9–512(e). At any point in time, all effective records that comprise a financing statement must be examined to determine the person or persons that have the status of secured party of record.

3.   **Successor to Secured Party of Record.** Application of other law may result in a person succeeding to the powers of a secured party of record. For example, if the secured party of record (A) merges into another corporation (B) and the other corporation (B) survives, other law may provide that B has all of A's powers. In that case, B is authorized to take all actions under this Part that A would have been authorized to take. Similarly, acts taken by a person who is authorized under generally applicable principles of agency to act on behalf of the secured party of record are effective under this Part.

§ 9–512.   Amendment of Financing Statement.

[ALTERNATIVE A]

(a)   **[Amendment of information in financing statement.]** Subject to Section 9–509, a person may add or delete collateral covered by, continue or terminate the effectiveness of, or, subject to subsection (e), otherwise amend the information provided in, a financing statement by filing an amendment that:

(1) identifies, by its file number, the initial financing statement to which the amendment relates; and

(2) if the amendment relates to an initial financing statement filed [or recorded] in a filing office described in Section 9–501(a)(1), provides the information specified in Section 9–502(b).

[ALTERNATIVE B]

(a) **[Amendment of information in financing statement.]** Subject to Section 9–509, a person may add or delete collateral covered by, continue or terminate the effectiveness of, or, subject to subsection (e), otherwise amend the information provided in, a financing statement by filing an amendment that:

(1) identifies, by its file number, the initial financing statement to which the amendment relates; and

(2) if the amendment relates to an initial financing statement filed [or recorded] in a filing office described in Section 9–501(a)(1), provides the date [and time] that the initial financing statement was filed [or recorded] and the information specified in Section 9–502(b).

[END OF ALTERNATIVES]

(b) **[Period of effectiveness not affected.]** Except as otherwise provided in Section 9–515, the filing of an amendment does not extend the period of effectiveness of the financing statement.

(c) **[Effectiveness of amendment adding collateral.]** A financing statement that is amended by an amendment that adds collateral is effective as to the added collateral only from the date of the filing of the amendment.

(d) **[Effectiveness of amendment adding debtor.]** A financing statement that is amended by an amendment that adds a debtor is effective as to the added debtor only from the date of the filing of the amendment.

(e) **[Certain amendments ineffective.]** An amendment is ineffective to the extent it:

(1) purports to delete all debtors and fails to provide the name of a debtor to be covered by the financing statement; or

(2) purports to delete all secured parties of record and fails to provide the name of a new secured party of record.

Legislative Note: States whose real-estate filing offices require additional information in amendments and cannot search their records by both the name of the debtor and the file number should enact Alternative B to Sections 9–512(a), 9–518(b), 9–518(d), 9–519(f) and 9–522(a).

As amended in 2010.

Official Comment

1. **Source.** Former 9–402(4).

2. **Changes to Financing Statements.** This section addresses changes to financing statements, including addition and deletion of collateral. Although termination statements, assignments, and continuation statements are types of amendment, this Article follows former Article 9 and contains separate sections containing additional provisions applicable to particular types of amendments. See Section 9–513 (termination statements); 9–514 (assignments); 9–515 (continuation statements). One should not infer from this separate treatment that this Article requires a separate amendment to accomplish each change. Rather, a single amendment would be legally sufficient to, e.g., add collateral and continue the effectiveness of the financing statement.

3. **Amendments.** An amendment under this Article may identify only the information contained in a financing statement that is to be changed; alternatively, it may take the form of an amended and restated financing statement. The latter would state, for example, that the financing statement "is amended and restated to read as follows: . . ." References in this Part to an "amended financing statement" are to a financing statement as amended by an amendment using either technique.

This section revises former Section 9–402(4) to permit secured parties of record to make changes in the public record without the need to obtain the debtor's signature. However, the filing of an amendment that adds collateral or adds a debtor must be authorized by the debtor or it will not be effective. See Sections 9–509(a), 9–510(a).

4. **Amendment Adding Debtor.** An amendment that adds a debtor is effective, provided that the added debtor authorizes the filing. See Section 9–509(a). However, filing an amendment adding a debtor to a previously filed financing statement affords no advantage over filing an initial financing statement against that debtor and may be disadvantageous. With respect to the added debtor, for purposes of determining the priority of the security interest, the time of filing is the time of the filing of the amendment, not the time of the filing of the initial financing statement. See subsection (d). However, the effectiveness of the financing statement lapses with respect to added debtor at the time it lapses with respect to the original debtor. See subsection (b).

5. **Amendment Adding Debtor Name.** Many states have enacted statutes governing the "conversion" of one organization organized under the law of that state, e.g., a corporation, into another such organization, e.g., a limited liability company. This Article defers to those statutes to determine whether the resulting organization is the same legal person as the initial, converting organization (albeit with a different name) or whether the resulting organization is a different legal person. When the governing statute does not clearly resolve the question, a secured party whose debtor is the converting organization may wish to proceed as if the statute provides for both results. In these circumstances, an amendment adding to the initial financing statement the name of the resulting organization may be preferable to an amendment substituting that name for the name of the debtor provided on the initial financing statement. In the event the governing statute is construed as providing that the resulting organization is the same legal person as the converting organization, but with a different name, the timely filing of such an amendment would satisfy the requirement of Section 9–507(c)(2). If, however, the governing statute is construed as providing that the resulting organization is a different legal person, the financing statement (which continues to provide the name of the original debtor) would be effective as to collateral acquired by the resulting organization ("new debtor") before, and within four months after, the conversion. See Section 9–508(b)(1). Inasmuch as it is the first financing statement filed against the resulting organization by the secured party, the record adding the name of the resulting organization as a debtor would constitute "an initial financing statement providing the name of the new debtor" under Section 9–508(b)(2). The secured party also may wish to file another financing statement naming the resulting organization as debtor. See Comment 4.

6. **Deletion of All Debtors or Secured Parties of Record.** Subsection (e) assures that there will be a debtor and secured party of record for every financing statement.

Example: A filed financing statement names A and B as secured parties of record and covers inventory and equipment. An amendment deletes equipment and purports to delete A and B as secured parties of record without adding a substitute secured party. The amendment is ineffective to the extent it purports to delete the secured parties of record but effective with respect to the deletion of collateral. As a consequence, the financing statement, as amended, covers only inventory, but A and B remain as secured parties of record.

As amended in 2010.

§ 9–513.   Termination Statement.

(a) **[Consumer goods.]** A secured party shall cause the secured party of record for a financing statement to file a termination statement for the financing statement if the financing statement covers consumer goods and:

(1) there is no obligation secured by the collateral covered by the financing statement and no commitment to make an advance, incur an obligation, or otherwise give value; or

(2) the debtor did not authorize the filing of the initial financing statement.

(b) **[Time for compliance with subsection (a).]** To comply with subsection (a), a secured party shall cause the secured party of record to file the termination statement:

(1) within one month after there is no obligation secured by the collateral covered by the financing statement and no commitment to make an advance, incur an obligation, or otherwise give value; or

(2) if earlier, within 20 days after the secured party receives an authenticated demand from a debtor.

(c) **[Other collateral.]** In cases not governed by subsection (a), within 20 days after a secured party receives an authenticated demand from a debtor, the secured party shall cause the secured party of record for a financing statement to send to the debtor a termination statement for the financing statement or file the termination statement in the filing office if:

(1) except in the case of a financing statement covering accounts or chattel paper that has been sold or goods that are the subject of a consignment, there is no obligation secured by the collateral covered by the financing statement and no commitment to make an advance, incur an obligation, or otherwise give value;

(2) the financing statement covers accounts or chattel paper that has been sold but as to which the account debtor or other person obligated has discharged its obligation;

(3) the financing statement covers goods that were the subject of a consignment to the debtor but are not in the debtor's possession; or

(4) the debtor did not authorize the filing of the initial financing statement.

(d) **[Effect of filing termination statement.]** Except as otherwise provided in Section 9–510, upon the filing of a termination statement with the filing office, the financing statement to which the termination statement relates ceases to be effective. Except as otherwise provided in Section 9–510, for purposes of Sections 9–519(g), 9–522(a), and 9–523(c), the filing with the filing office of a termination statement relating to a financing statement that indicates that the debtor is a transmitting utility also causes the effectiveness of the financing statement to lapse.

As amended in 2000.

Official Comment

1. **Source.** Former Section 9–404.

2. **Duty to File or Send.** This section specifies when a secured party must cause the secured party of record to file or send to the debtor a termination statement for a financing statement. Because most financing statements expire in five years unless a continuation statement is filed (Section 9–515), no compulsion is placed on the secured party to file a termination statement unless demanded by the debtor, except in the case of consumer goods. Because many consumers will not realize the importance to them of clearing the public record, an affirmative duty is put on the secured party in that case. But many purchase-money security interests in consumer goods will not be filed, except for motor vehicles. See Section 9–309(1). Under Section 9–311(b), compliance with a certificate-of-title statute is "equivalent to the filing of a financing statement under this article." Thus, this section applies to a certificate of title unless the section is superseded by a certificate-of-title statute that contains a specific rule addressing a secured party's duty to cause a notation of a security interest to be removed from a certificate of title. In the context of a certificate of title, however, the secured party could comply with this section by causing the removal itself or providing the debtor with documentation sufficient to enable the debtor to effect the removal.

Subsections (a) and (b) apply to a financing statement covering consumer goods. Subsection (c) applies to other financing statements. Subsection (a) and (c) each makes explicit what was implicit under former Article 9: If the debtor did not authorize the filing of a financing statement in the first place, the secured party of record should file or send a termination statement. The liability imposed upon a secured party that fails to comply with subsection (a) or (c) is identical to that imposed for the filing of an unauthorized financing statement or amendment. See Section 9–625(e).

3. **"Bogus" Filings.** A secured party's duty to send a termination statement arises when the secured party "receives" an authenticated demand from the debtor. In the case of an unauthorized financing statement, the person named as debtor in the financing statement may have no relationship with the named secured party and no reason to know the secured party's address. Inasmuch as the address in the financing statement is "held out by [the person named as secured party in the financing statement] as the place for receipt of such communications [i.e., communications relating to security interests]," the putative secured party is deemed to have "received" a notification delivered to that address. See Section 1–202(e). If a termination statement is not forthcoming, the person named as debtor itself may authorize the filing of a termination statement, which will be effective if it indicates that the person authorized it to be filed. See Sections 9–509(d)(2), 9–510(c).

4.   **Buyers of Receivables.** Applied literally, former Section 9–404(1) would have required many buyers of receivables to file a termination statement immediately upon filing a financing statement because "there is no outstanding secured obligation and no commitment to make advances, incur obligations, or otherwise give value." Subsections (c)(1) and (2) remedy this problem. While the security interest of a buyer of accounts or chattel paper (B–1) is perfected, the debtor is not deemed to retain an interest in the sold receivables and thus could transfer no interest in them to another buyer (B–2) or to a lien creditor (LC). However, for purposes of determining the rights of the debtor's creditors and certain purchasers of accounts or chattel paper from the debtor, while B–1's security interest is unperfected, the debtor-seller is deemed to have rights in the sold receivables, and a competing security interest or judicial lien may attach to those rights. See Sections 9–318, 9–109, Comment 5. Suppose that B–1's security interest in certain accounts and chattel paper is perfected by filing, but the effectiveness of the financing statement lapses. Both before and after lapse, B–1 collects some of the receivables. After lapse, LC acquires a lien on the accounts and chattel paper. B–1's unperfected security interest in the accounts and chattel paper is subordinate to LC's rights. See Section 9–317(a)(2). But collections on accounts and chattel paper are not "accounts" or "chattel paper." Even if B–1's security interest in the accounts and chattel paper is or becomes unperfected, neither the debtor nor LC acquires rights to the collections that B–1 collects (and owns) before LC acquires a lien.

5.   **Effect of Filing.** Subsection (d) states the effect of filing a termination statement: the related financing statement ceases to be effective. If one of several secured parties of record files a termination statement, subsection (d) applies only with respect to the rights of the person who authorized the filing of the termination statement. See Section 9–510(b). The financing statement remains effective with respect to the rights of the others. However, even if a financing statement is *terminated* (and thus no longer is effective) with respect to all secured parties of record, the financing statement, including the termination statement, will remain of record until at least one year after it *lapses* with respect to all secured parties of record. See Section 9–519(g).

As amended in 2010.

§ 9–514.   Assignment of Powers of Secured Party of Record.

(a)   **[Assignment reflected on initial financing statement.]** Except as otherwise provided in subsection (c), an initial financing statement may reflect an assignment of all of the secured party's power to authorize an amendment to the financing statement by providing the name and mailing address of the assignee as the name and address of the secured party.

(b)   **[Assignment of filed financing statement.]** Except as otherwise provided in subsection (c), a secured party of record may assign of record all or part of its power to authorize an amendment to a financing statement by filing in the filing office an amendment of the financing statement which:

(1)   identifies, by its file number, the initial financing statement to which it relates;

(2)   provides the name of the assignor; and

(3)   provides the name and mailing address of the assignee.

(c)   **[Assignment of record of mortgage.]** An assignment of record of a security interest in a fixture covered by a record of a mortgage which is effective as a financing statement filed as a fixture filing under Section 9–502(c) may be made only by an assignment of record of the mortgage in the manner provided by law of this State other than [the Uniform Commercial Code].

Official Comment

1.   **Source.** Former Section 9–405.

2.   **Assignments.** This section provides a permissive device whereby a secured party of record may effectuate an assignment of its power to affect a financing statement. It may also be useful for a secured party who has assigned all or part of its security interest or agricultural lien and wishes to have the fact noted of record, so that inquiries concerning the transaction would be addressed to the assignee. See Section 9–502, Comment 2. Upon the filing of an assignment, the assignee becomes the "secured party of record" and may authorize the filing of a continuation statement, termination statement, or other amendment. Note that under Section 9–310(c) no filing of an assignment is required as a condition of continuing the perfected status of the security interest against creditors and transferees of the original debtor. However, if an assignment is not filed, the assignor remains the

secured party of record, with the power (even if not the right) to authorize the filing of effective amendments. See Sections 9–511(c), 9–509(d).

Where a record of a mortgage is effective as a financing statement filed as a fixture filing (Section 9–502(c)), then an assignment of record of the security interest may be made only in the manner in which an assignment of record of the mortgage may be made under local real-property law.

3. **Comparison to Prior Law.** Most of the changes reflected in this section are for clarification or to embrace medium-neutral drafting. As a general matter, this section preserves the opportunity given by former Section 9–405 to assign a security interest of record in one of two different ways. Under subsection (a), a secured party may assign all of its power to affect a financing statement by naming an assignee in the initial financing statement. The secured party of record may accomplish the same result under subsection (b) by making a subsequent filing. Subsection (b) also may be used for an assignment of only some of the secured party of record's power to affect a financing statement, e.g., the power to affect the financing statement as it relates to particular items of collateral or as it relates to an undivided interest in a security interest in all the collateral. An initial financing statement may not be used to change the secured party of record under these circumstances. However, an amendment adding the assignee as a secured party of record may be used.

§ 9–515. Duration and Effectiveness of Financing Statement; Effect of Lapsed Financing Statement.

(a) **[Five-year effectiveness.]** Except as otherwise provided in subsections (b), (e), (f), and (g), a filed financing statement is effective for a period of five years after the date of filing.

(b) **[Public-finance or manufactured-home transaction.]** Except as otherwise provided in subsections (e), (f), and (g), an initial financing statement filed in connection with a public-finance transaction or manufactured-home transaction is effective for a period of 30 years after the date of filing if it indicates that it is filed in connection with a public-finance transaction or manufactured-home transaction.

(c) **[Lapse and continuation of financing statement.]** The effectiveness of a filed financing statement lapses on the expiration of the period of its effectiveness unless before the lapse a continuation statement is filed pursuant to subsection (d). Upon lapse, a financing statement ceases to be effective and any security interest or agricultural lien that was perfected by the financing statement becomes unperfected, unless the security interest is perfected otherwise. If the security interest or agricultural lien becomes unperfected upon lapse, it is deemed never to have been perfected as against a purchaser of the collateral for value.

(d) **[When continuation statement may be filed.]** A continuation statement may be filed only within six months before the expiration of the five-year period specified in subsection (a) or the 30-year period specified in subsection (b), whichever is applicable.

(e) **[Effect of filing continuation statement.]** Except as otherwise provided in Section 9–510, upon timely filing of a continuation statement, the effectiveness of the initial financing statement continues for a period of five years commencing on the day on which the financing statement would have become ineffective in the absence of the filing. Upon the expiration of the five-year period, the financing statement lapses in the same manner as provided in subsection (c), unless, before the lapse, another continuation statement is filed pursuant to subsection (d). Succeeding continuation statements may be filed in the same manner to continue the effectiveness of the initial financing statement.

(f) **[Transmitting utility financing statement.]** If a debtor is a transmitting utility and a filed initial financing statement so indicates, the financing statement is effective until a termination statement is filed.

(g) **[Record of mortgage as financing statement.]** A record of a mortgage that is effective as a financing statement filed as a fixture filing under Section 9–502(c) remains effective as a financing statement filed as a fixture filing until the mortgage is released or satisfied of record or its effectiveness otherwise terminates as to the real property.

As amended in 2010.

Official Comment

1.   **Source.** Former Section 9–403(2), (3), (6).

2.   **Period of Financing Statement's Effectiveness.** Subsection (a) states the general rule: a financing statement is effective for a five-year period unless its effectiveness is continued under this section or terminated under Section 9–513. Subsection (b) provides that if the financing statement relates to a public-finance transaction or a manufactured-home transaction and so indicates, the financing statement is effective for 30 years. These financings typically extend well beyond the standard, five-year period. Under subsection (f), a financing statement filed against a transmitting utility remains effective indefinitely, until a termination statement is filed. Likewise, under subsection (g), a mortgage effective as a fixture filing remains effective until its effectiveness terminates under real-property law.

3.   **Lapse.** When the period of effectiveness under subsection (a) or (b) expires, the effectiveness of the financing statement lapses. The last sentence of subsection (c) addresses the effect of lapse. The deemed retroactive unperfection applies only with respect to purchasers for value; unlike former Section 9–403(2), it does not apply with respect to lien creditors.

Example 1: SP–1 and SP–2 both hold security interests in the same collateral. Both security interests are perfected by filing. SP–1 filed first and has priority under Section 9–322(a)(1). The effectiveness of SP–1's filing lapses. As long as SP–2's security interest remains perfected thereafter, SP–2 is entitled to priority over SP–1's security interest, which is deemed never to have been perfected as against a purchaser for value (SP–2). See Section 9–322(a)(2).

Example 2: SP holds a security interest perfected by filing. On July 1, LC acquires a judicial lien on the collateral. Two weeks later, the effectiveness of the financing statement lapses. Although the security interest becomes unperfected upon lapse, it was perfected when LC acquired its lien. Accordingly, notwithstanding the lapse, the perfected security interest has priority over the rights of LC, who is not a purchaser. See Section 9–317(a)(2).

4.   **Effect of Debtor's Bankruptcy.** Under former Section 9–403(2), lapse was tolled if the debtor entered bankruptcy or another insolvency proceeding. Nevertheless, being unaware that insolvency proceedings had been commenced, filing offices routinely removed records from the files as if lapse had not been tolled. Subsection (c) deletes the former tolling provision and thereby imposes a new burden on the secured party: to be sure that a financing statement does not lapse during the debtor's bankruptcy. The secured party can prevent lapse by filing a continuation statement, even without first obtaining relief from the automatic stay. See Bankruptcy Code Section 362(b)(3). Of course, if the debtor enters bankruptcy before lapse, the provisions of this Article with respect to lapse would be of no effect to the extent that federal bankruptcy law dictates a contrary result (e.g., to the extent that the Bankruptcy Code determines rights as of the date of the filing of the bankruptcy petition).

5.   **Continuation Statements.** Subsection (d) explains when a continuation statement may be filed. A continuation statement filed at a time other than that prescribed by subsection (d) is ineffective, see Section 9–510(c), and the filing office may not accept it. See Sections 9–520(a), 9–516(b). Subsection (e) specifies the effect of a continuation statement and provides for successive continuation statements.

§ 9–516.   What Constitutes Filing; Effectiveness of Filing.

(a)   **[What constitutes filing.]** Except as otherwise provided in subsection (b), communication of a record to a filing office and tender of the filing fee or acceptance of the record by the filing office constitutes filing.

(b)   **[Refusal to accept record; filing does not occur.]** Filing does not occur with respect to a record that a filing office refuses to accept because:

(1)   the record is not communicated by a method or medium of communication authorized by the filing office;

(2)   an amount equal to or greater than the applicable filing fee is not tendered;

(3)   the filing office is unable to index the record because:

(A)   in the case of an initial financing statement, the record does not provide a name for the debtor;

(B) in the case of an amendment or information statement, the record:

    (i) does not identify the initial financing statement as required by Section 9–512 or 9–518, as applicable; or

    (ii) identifies an initial financing statement whose effectiveness has lapsed under Section 9–515;

(C) in the case of an initial financing statement that provides the name of a debtor identified as an individual or an amendment that provides a name of a debtor identified as an individual which was not previously provided in the financing statement to which the record relates, the record does not identify the debtor's surname; or

(D) in the case of a record filed [or recorded] in the filing office described in Section 9–501(a)(1), the record does not provide a sufficient description of the real property to which it relates;

(4) in the case of an initial financing statement or an amendment that adds a secured party of record, the record does not provide a name and mailing address for the secured party of record;

(5) in the case of an initial financing statement or an amendment that provides a name of a debtor which was not previously provided in the financing statement to which the amendment relates, the record does not:

    (A) provide a mailing address for the debtor;

    (B) indicate whether the name provided as the name of the debtor is the name of an individual or an organization;

(6) in the case of an assignment reflected in an initial financing statement under Section 9–514(a) or an amendment filed under Section 9–514(b), the record does not provide a name and mailing address for the assignee; or

(7) in the case of a continuation statement, the record is not filed within the six-month period prescribed by Section 9–515(d).

(c) **[Rules applicable to subsection (b).]** For purposes of subsection (b):

(1) a record does not provide information if the filing office is unable to read or decipher the information; and

(2) a record that does not indicate that it is an amendment or identify an initial financing statement to which it relates, as required by Section 9–512, 9–514, or 9–518, is an initial financing statement.

(d) **[Refusal to accept record; record effective as filed record.]** A record that is communicated to the filing office with tender of the filing fee, but which the filing office refuses to accept for a reason other than one set forth in subsection (b), is effective as a filed record except as against a purchaser of the collateral which gives value in reasonable reliance upon the absence of the record from the files.

As amended in 2010.

Official Comment

1. **Source.** Subsection (a): former Section 9–403(1); the remainder is new.

2. **What Constitutes Filing.** Subsection (a) deals generically with what constitutes filing of a record, including an initial financing statement and amendments of all kinds (e.g., assignments, termination statements, and continuation statements). It follows former Section 9–403(1), under which either acceptance of a record by the filing office or presentation of the record and tender of the filing fee constitutes filing.

3. **Effectiveness of Rejected Record.** Subsection (b) provides an exclusive list of grounds upon which the filing office may reject a record. See Section 9–520(a). Although some of these grounds would also be grounds for rendering a filed record ineffective (e.g., an initial financing statement does not provide a name for the debtor), many others would not be (e.g., an initial financing statement does not provide a mailing address for the debtor or secured party of record). Neither this section nor Section 9–520 requires or authorizes the filing office to determine, or even consider, the accuracy of information provided in a record.

A financing statement or other record that is communicated to the filing office but which the filing office refuses to accept provides no public notice, regardless of the reason for the rejection. However, this section distinguishes between records that the filing office rightfully rejects and those that it wrongfully rejects. A filer is able to prevent a rightful rejection by complying with the requirements of subsection (b). No purpose is served by giving effect to records that justifiably never find their way into the system, and subsection (b) so provides.

Subsection (d) deals with the filing office's unjustified refusal to accept a record. Here, the filer is in no position to prevent the rejection and as a general matter should not be prejudiced by it. Although wrongfully rejected records generally are effective, subsection (d) contains a special rule to protect a third-party purchaser of the collateral (e.g., a buyer or competing secured party) who gives value in reliance upon the apparent absence of the record from the files. As against a person who searches the public record and reasonably relies on what the public record shows, subsection (d) imposes upon the filer the risk that a record failed to make its way into the filing system because of the filing office's wrongful rejection of it. (Compare Section 9–517, under which a mis-indexed financing statement is fully effective.) This risk is likely to be small, particularly when a record is presented electronically, and the filer can guard against this risk by conducting a post-filing search of the records. Moreover, Section 9–520(b) requires the filing office to give prompt notice of its refusal to accept a record for filing.

4. **Method or Medium of Communication.** Rejection pursuant to subsection (b)(1) for failure to communicate a record properly should be understood to mean noncompliance with procedures relating to security, authentication, or other communication-related requirements that the filing office may impose. Subsection (b)(1) does not authorize a filing office to impose additional substantive requirements. See Section 9–520, Comment 2.

5. **Address for Secured Party of Record.** Under subsection (b)(4) and Section 9–520(a), the lack of a mailing address for the secured party of record requires the filing office to reject an initial financing statement. The failure to include an address for the secured party of record no longer renders a financing statement ineffective. See Section 9–502(a). The function of the address is not to identify the secured party of record but rather to provide an address to which others can send required notifications, e.g., of a purchase-money security interest in inventory or of the disposition of collateral. Inasmuch as the address shown on a filed financing statement is an "address that is reasonable under the circumstances," a person required to send a notification to the secured party may satisfy the requirement by sending a notification to that address, even if the address is or becomes incorrect. See Section 9–102 (definition of "send"). Similarly, because the address is "held out by [the secured party] as the place for receipt of such communications [i.e., communications relating to security interests]," the secured party is deemed to have received a notification delivered to that address. See Section 1–202(e).

6. **Uncertainty Concerning Individual Debtor's Surname.** Subsection (b)(3)(C) requires the filing office to reject an initial financing statement or amendment adding an individual debtor if the office cannot index the record because it does not identify the debtor's surname (e.g., it is unclear whether the debtor's surname is Elton or John).

7. **Inability of Filing Office to Read or Decipher Information.** Under subsection (c)(1), if the filing office cannot read or decipher information, the information is not provided by a record for purposes of subsection (b).

8. **Classification of Records.** For purposes of subsection (b), a record that does not indicate it is an amendment or identify an initial financing statement to which it relates is deemed to be an initial financing statement. See subsection (c)(2).

9. **Effectiveness of Rejectable But Unrejected Record.** Section 9–520(a) requires the filing office to refuse to accept an initial financing statement for a reason set forth in subsection (b). However, if the filing office accepts such a financing statement nevertheless, the financing statement generally is effective if it complies with the requirements of Section 9–502(a) and (b). See Section 9–520(c). Similarly, an otherwise effective financing statement generally remains so even though the information in the financing statement becomes incorrect. See Section 9–507(b). (Note that if the information required by subsection (b)(5) is incorrect when the financing statement is filed, Section 9–338 applies.)

As amended in 2010.

§ 9–517.   Effect of Indexing Errors.

The failure of the filing office to index a record correctly does not affect the effectiveness of the filed record.

1.   **Source.** New.

2.   **Effectiveness of Mis-Indexed Records.** This section provides that the filing office's error in mis-indexing a record does not render ineffective an otherwise effective record. As did former Section 9–401, this section imposes the risk of filing-office error on those who search the files rather than on those who file.

§ 9–518.   Claim Concerning Inaccurate or Wrongfully Filed Record.

(a)   **[Statement with respect to record indexed under person's name.]** A person may file in the filing office an information statement with respect to a record indexed there under the person's name if the person believes that the record is inaccurate or was wrongfully filed.

[ALTERNATIVE A]

(b)   **[Contents of statement under subsection (a).]** An information statement under subsection (a) must:

(1)   identify the record to which it relates by the file number assigned to the initial financing statement to which the record relates;

(2)   indicate that it is an information statement; and

(3)   provide the basis for the person's belief that the record is inaccurate and indicate the manner in which the person believes the record should be amended to cure any inaccuracy or provide the basis for the person's belief that the record was wrongfully filed.

[ALTERNATIVE B]

(b)   **[Contents of statement under subsection (a).]** An information statement under subsection (a) must:

(1)   identify the record to which it relates by:

(A)   the file number assigned to the initial financing statement to which the record relates; and

(B)   if the information statement relates to a record filed [or recorded] in a filing office described in Section 9–501(a)(1), the date [and time] that the initial financing statement was filed [or recorded] and the information specified in Section 9–502(b);

(2)   indicate that it is an information statement; and

(3)   provide the basis for the person's belief that the record is inaccurate and indicate the manner in which the person believes the record should be amended to cure any inaccuracy or provide the basis for the person's belief that the record was wrongfully filed.

[END OF ALTERNATIVES]

(c)   **[Statement by secured party of record.]** A person may file in the filing office an information statement with respect to a record filed there if the person is a secured party of record with respect to the financing statement to which the record relates and believes that the person that filed the record was not entitled to do so under Section 9–509(d).

[ALTERNATIVE A]

(d)   **[Contents of statement under subsection (c).]** An information statement under subsection (c) must:

(1)   identify the record to which it relates by the file number assigned to the initial financing statement to which the record relates;

(2)   indicate that it is an information statement; and

(3)   provide the basis for the person's belief that the person that filed the record was not entitled to do so under Section 9–509(d).

[ALTERNATIVE B]

(d)   **[Contents of statement under subsection (c).]** An information statement under subsection (c) must:

(1)   identify the record to which it relates by:

(A)   the file number assigned to the initial financing statement to which the record relates; and

(B)   if the information statement relates to a record filed [or recorded] in a filing office described in Section 9–501(a)(1), the date [and time] that the initial financing statement was filed [or recorded] and the information specified in Section 9–502(b);

(2)   indicate that it is an information statement; and

(3)   provide the basis for the person's belief that the person that filed the record was not entitled to do so under Section 9–509(d).

[END OF ALTERNATIVES]

(e)   **[Record not affected by information statement.]** The filing of an information statement does not affect the effectiveness of an initial financing statement or other filed record.

Legislative Note: States whose real-estate filing offices require additional information in amendments and cannot search their records by both the name of the debtor and the file number should enact Alternative B to Sections 9–512(a), 9–518(b), 9–518(d), 9–519(f) and 9–522(a).

As amended in 2010.

Official Comment

1.   **Source.** New.

2.   **Information Statements.** Former Article 9 did not afford a nonjudicial means for a debtor to indicate that a financing statement or other record was inaccurate or wrongfully filed. Subsection (a) affords the debtor the right to file an information statement. Among other requirements, the information statement must provide the basis for the debtor's belief that the public record should be corrected. See subsection (b). These provisions, which resemble the analogous remedy in the Fair Credit Reporting Act, 15 U.S.C. § 1681i, afford an aggrieved person the opportunity to state its position on the public record. They do not permit an aggrieved person to change the legal effect of the public record. Thus, although a filed information statement becomes part of the "financing statement," as defined in Section 9–102, the filing does not affect the effectiveness of the initial financing statement or any other filed record. See subsection (e).

Sometimes a person files a termination statement or other record relating to a filed financing statement without being entitled to do so. A secured party of record with respect to the financing statement who believes that such a record has been filed may, but need not, file an information statement indicating that the person that filed the record was not entitled to do so. See subsection (c). An information statement has no legal effect. Its sole purpose is to provide some limited public notice that the efficacy of a filed record is disputed. If the person that filed the record was not entitled to do so, the filed record is ineffective, regardless of whether the secured party of record files an information statement. Likewise, if the person that filed the record was entitled to do so, the filed record is effective, even if the secured party of record files an information statement. See Section 9–510(a), 9–518(e). Because an information statement filed under subsection (c) has no legal effect, a secured party of record—even one who is aware of the unauthorized filing of a record—has no duty to file one. Just as searchers bear the burden of determining whether the filing of initial financing statement was authorized, searchers bear the burden of determining whether the filing of every subsequent record was authorized.

Inasmuch as the filing of an information statement has no legal effect, this section does not provide a mechanism by which a secured party can correct an error that it discovers in its own financing statement.

This section does not displace other provisions of this Article that impose liability for making unauthorized filings or failing to file or send a termination statement (see Section 9–625(e)), nor does it displace any available judicial remedies.

3.   **Resort to Other Law.** This Article cannot provide a satisfactory or complete solution to problems caused by misuse of the public records. The problem of "bogus" filings is not limited to the UCC filing system but

extends to the real-property records, as well. A summary judicial procedure for correcting the public record and criminal penalties for those who misuse the filing and recording systems are likely to be more effective and put less strain on the filing system than provisions authorizing or requiring action by filing and recording offices.

As amended in 2010.

[SUBPART 2. DUTIES AND OPERATION OF FILING OFFICE]

§ 9–519. Numbering, Maintaining, and Indexing Records; Communicating Information Provided in Records.

(a) **[Filing office duties.]** For each record filed in a filing office, the filing office shall:

(1) assign a unique number to the filed record;

(2) create a record that bears the number assigned to the filed record and the date and time of filing;

(3) maintain the filed record for public inspection; and

(4) index the filed record in accordance with subsections (c), (d), and (e).

(b) **[File number.]** A file number [assigned after January 1, 2002,] must include a digit that:

(1) is mathematically derived from or related to the other digits of the file number; and

(2) aids the filing office in determining whether a number communicated as the file number includes a single-digit or transpositional error.

(c) **[Indexing: general.]** Except as otherwise provided in subsections (d) and (e), the filing office shall:

(1) index an initial financing statement according to the name of the debtor and index all filed records relating to the initial financing statement in a manner that associates with one another an initial financing statement and all filed records relating to the initial financing statement; and

(2) index a record that provides a name of a debtor which was not previously provided in the financing statement to which the record relates also according to the name that was not previously provided.

(d) **[Indexing: real-property-related financing statement.]** If a financing statement is filed as a fixture filing or covers as-extracted collateral or timber to be cut, [it must be filed for record and] the filing office shall index it:

(1) under the names of the debtor and of each owner of record shown on the financing statement as if they were the mortgagors under a mortgage of the real property described; and

(2) to the extent that the law of this State provides for indexing of records of mortgages under the name of the mortgagee, under the name of the secured party as if the secured party were the mortgagee thereunder, or, if indexing is by description, as if the financing statement were a record of a mortgage of the real property described.

(e) **[Indexing: real-property-related assignment.]** If a financing statement is filed as a fixture filing or covers as-extracted collateral or timber to be cut, the filing office shall index an assignment filed under Section 9–514(a) or an amendment filed under Section 9–514(b):

(1) under the name of the assignor as grantor; and

(2) to the extent that the law of this State provides for indexing a record of the assignment of a mortgage under the name of the assignee, under the name of the assignee.

[ALTERNATIVE A]

(f) **[Retrieval and association capability.]** The filing office shall maintain a capability:

(1) to retrieve a record by the name of the debtor and by the file number assigned to the initial financing statement to which the record relates; and

(2)   to associate and retrieve with one another an initial financing statement and each filed record relating to the initial financing statement.

[ALTERNATIVE B]

(f)   **[Retrieval and association capability.]** The filing office shall maintain a capability:

(1)   to retrieve a record by the name of the debtor and:

(A)   if the filing office is described in Section 9–501(a)(1), by the file number assigned to the initial financing statement to which the record relates and the date [and time] that the record was filed [or recorded]; or

(B)   if the filing office is described in Section 9–501(a)(2), by the file number assigned to the initial financing statement to which the record relates; and

(2)   to associate and retrieve with one another an initial financing statement and each filed record relating to the initial financing statement.

[END OF ALTERNATIVES]

(g)   **[Removal of debtor's name.]** The filing office may not remove a debtor's name from the index until one year after the effectiveness of a financing statement naming the debtor lapses under Section 9–515 with respect to all secured parties of record.

(h)   **[Timeliness of filing office performance.]** The filing office shall perform the acts required by subsections (a) through (e) at the time and in the manner prescribed by filing-office rule, but not later than two business days after the filing office receives the record in question.

[(i)   **[Inapplicability to real-property-related filing office.]** Subsection[s] [(b)] [and] [(h)] do[es] not apply to a filing office described in Section 9–501(a)(1).]

Legislative Notes:

1.   States whose filing offices currently assign file numbers that include a verification number, commonly known as a "check digit," or can implement this requirement before the effective date of this Article should omit the bracketed language in subsection (b).

2.   In States in which writings will not appear in the real property records and indices unless actually recorded the bracketed language in subsection (d) should be used.

3.   States whose real-estate filing offices require additional information in amendments and cannot search their records by both the name of the debtor and the file number should enact Alternative B to Sections 9–512(a), 9–518(b), 9–518(d), 9–519(f) and 9–522(a).

4.   A State that elects not to require real-estate filing offices to comply with either or both of subsections (b) and (h) may adopt an applicable variation of subsection (i) and add "Except as otherwise provided in subsection (i)," to the appropriate subsection or subsections.

As amended in 2010.

Official Comment

1.   **Source.** Former Sections 9–403(4), (7), 9–405(2).

2.   **Filing Office's Duties.** Subsections (a) through (e) set forth the duties of the filing office with respect to filed records. Subsection (h), which is new, imposes a minimum standard of performance for those duties. Prompt indexing is crucial to the effectiveness of any filing system. An accepted but un-indexed record affords no public notice. Subsection (f) requires the filing office to maintain appropriate storage and retrieval facilities, and subsection (g) contains minimum requirements for the retention of records.

3.   **File Number.** Subsection (a)(1) requires the filing office to assign a unique number to each filed record. That number is the "file number" only if the record is an initial financing statement. See Section 9–102.

4. **Time of Filing.** Subsection (a)(2) and Section 9–523 refer to the "date and time" of filing. The statutory text does not contain any instructions to a filing office as to how the time of filing is to be determined. The method of determining or assigning a time of filing is an appropriate matter for filing-office rules to address.

5. **Related Records.** Subsections (c) and (f) are designed to ensure that an initial financing statement and all filed records relating to it are associated with one another, indexed under the name of the debtor, and retrieved together. To comply with subsection (f), a filing office (other than a real-property recording office in a State that enacts subsection (f), Alternative B) must be capable of retrieving records in each of two ways: by the name of the debtor and by the file number of the initial financing statement to which the record relates.

6. **Prohibition on Deleting Names from Index.** This Article contemplates that the filing office will not delete the name of a debtor from the index until at least one year passes after the effectiveness of the financing statement lapses as to all secured parties of record. See subsection (g). This rule applies even if the filing office accepts an amendment purporting to delete or modify the name of a debtor or terminate the effectiveness of the financing statement. If an amendment provides a modified name for a debtor, the amended name should be added to the index, see subsection (c)(2), but the pre-amendment name should remain in the index.

Compared to former Article 9, the rule in subsection (g) increases the amount of information available to those who search the public records. The rule also contemplates that searchers—not the filing office—will determine the significance and effectiveness of filed records.

§ 9–520. Acceptance and Refusal to Accept Record.

(a) **[Mandatory refusal to accept record.]** A filing office shall refuse to accept a record for filing for a reason set forth in Section 9–516(b) and may refuse to accept a record for filing only for a reason set forth in Section 9–516(b).

(b) **[Communication concerning refusal.]** If a filing office refuses to accept a record for filing, it shall communicate to the person that presented the record the fact of and reason for the refusal and the date and time the record would have been filed had the filing office accepted it. The communication must be made at the time and in the manner prescribed by filing-office rule but [, in the case of a filing office described in Section 9–501(a)(2),] in no event more than two business days after the filing office receives the record.

(c) **[When filed financing statement effective.]** A filed financing statement satisfying Section 9–502(a) and (b) is effective, even if the filing office is required to refuse to accept it for filing under subsection (a). However, Section 9–338 applies to a filed financing statement providing information described in Section 9–516(b)(5) which is incorrect at the time the financing statement is filed.

(d) **[Separate application to multiple debtors.]** If a record communicated to a filing office provides information that relates to more than one debtor, this part applies as to each debtor separately.

Legislative Note: A State that elects not to require real-property filing offices to comply with subsection (b) should include the bracketed language.

Official Comment

1. **Source.** New.

2. **Refusal to Accept Record for Filing.** In some States, filing offices considered themselves obligated by former Article 9 to review the form and content of a financing statement and to refuse to accept those that they determine are legally insufficient. Some filing offices imposed requirements for or conditions to filing that do not appear in the statute. Under this section, the filing office is not expected to make legal judgments and is not permitted to impose additional conditions or requirements.

Subsection (a) both prescribes and limits the bases upon which the filing office must and may reject records by reference to the reasons set forth in Section 9–516(b). For the most part, the bases for rejection are limited to those that prevent the filing office from dealing with a record that it receives—because some of the requisite information (e.g., the debtor's name) is missing or cannot be deciphered, because the record is not communicated by a method (e.g., it is MIME-rather than UU-encoded) or medium (e.g., it is written rather than electronic) that the filing office accepts, or because the filer fails to tender an amount equal to or greater than the filing fee.

3. **Consequences of Accepting Rejectable Record.** Section 9–516(b) includes among the reasons for rejecting an initial financing statement the failure to give certain information that is not required as a condition

of effectiveness. In conjunction with Section 9–516(b)(5), this section requires the filing office to refuse to accept a financing statement that is legally sufficient to perfect a security interest under Section 9–502 but does not contain a mailing address for the debtor or disclose whether the debtor is an individual or an organization. The information required by Section 9–516(b)(5) assists searchers in weeding out "false positives," i.e., records that a search reveals but which do not pertain to the debtor in question. It assists filers by helping to ensure that the debtor's name is correct and that the financing statement is filed in the proper jurisdiction.

If the filing office accepts a financing statement that does not give this information at all, the filing is fully effective. Section 9–520(c). The financing statement also generally is effective if the information is given but is incorrect; however, Section 9–338 affords protection to buyers and holders of perfected security interests who gives value in reasonable reliance upon the incorrect information.

4.   **Filing Office's Duties with Respect to Rejected Record.** Subsection (b) requires the filing office to communicate the fact of rejection and the reason therefor within a fixed period of time. Inasmuch as a rightfully rejected record is ineffective and a wrongfully rejected record is not fully effective, prompt communication concerning any rejection is important.

5.   **Partial Effectiveness of Record.** Under subsection (d), the provisions of this Part apply to each debtor separately. Thus, a filing office may reject an initial financing statement or other record as to one named debtor but accept it as to the other.

Example: An initial financing statement is communicated to the filing office. The financing statement names two debtors, John Smith and Jane Smith. It contains all of the information described in Section 9–516(b)(5) with respect to John but lacks some of the information with respect to Jane. The filing office must accept the financing statement with respect to John, reject it with respect to Jane, and notify the filer of the rejection.

As amended in 2010.

§ 9–521.   Uniform Form of Written Financing Statement and Amendment.

(a)   **[Initial financing statement form.]** A filing office that accepts written records may not refuse to accept a written initial financing statement in the following form and format except for a reason set forth in Section 9–516(b):

UCC FINANCING STATEMENT

FOLLOW INSTRUCTIONS

A. NAME & PHONE OF CONTACT AT FILER (optional)

B. E-MAIL CONTACT AT FILER (optional)

C. SEND ACKNOWLEDGMENT TO: (Name and Address)

⌐   ¬

⌊   ⌋

THE ABOVE SPACE IS FOR FILING OFFICE USE ONLY

1. DEBTOR'S NAME: Provide only one Debtor name (1a or 1b) (use exact, full name; do not omit, modify, or abbreviate any part of the Debtor's name); if any part of the Individual Debtor's name will not fit in line 1b, leave all of item 1 blank, check here ☐ and provide the Individual Debtor information in item 10 of the Financing Statement Addendum (Form UCC1Ad)

1a. ORGANIZATION'S NAME			
OR 1b. INDIVIDUAL'S SURNAME	FIRST PERSONAL NAME	ADDITIONAL NAME(S)/INITIAL(S)	SUFFIX
1c. MAILING ADDRESS	CITY	STATE POSTAL CODE	COUNTRY

2. DEBTOR'S NAME: Provide only one Debtor name (2a or 2b) (use exact, full name; do not omit, modify, or abbreviate any part of the Debtor's name); if any part of the Individual Debtor's name will not fit in line 2b, leave all of item 2 blank, check here ☐ and provide the Individual Debtor information in item 10 of the Financing Statement Addendum (Form UCC1Ad)

2a. ORGANIZATION'S NAME			
OR 2b. INDIVIDUAL'S SURNAME	FIRST PERSONAL NAME	ADDITIONAL NAME(S)/INITIAL(S)	SUFFIX
2c. MAILING ADDRESS	CITY	STATE POSTAL CODE	COUNTRY

3. SECURED PARTY'S NAME (or NAME of ASSIGNEE of ASSIGNOR SECURED PARTY) Provide only one Secured Party name (3a or 3b)

3a. ORGANIZATION'S NAME			
OR 3b. INDIVIDUAL'S SURNAME	FIRST PERSONAL NAME	ADDITIONAL NAME(S)/INITIAL(S)	SUFFIX
3c. MAILING ADDRESS	CITY	STATE POSTAL CODE	COUNTRY

4. COLLATERAL: This financing statement covers the following collateral:

5. Check only if applicable and check only one box: Collateral is ☐ held in a Trust (see UCC1Ad, item 17 and Instructions) ☐ being administered by a Decedent's Personal Representative

6a. Check only if applicable and check only one box: 6b. Check only if applicable and check only one box:
☐ Public-Finance Transaction ☐ Manufactured-Home Transaction ☐ A Debtor is a Transmitting Utility   ☐ Agricultural Lien ☐ Non-UCC Filing

7. ALTERNATIVE DESIGNATION (if applicable): ☐ Lessee/Lessor ☐ Consignee/Consignor ☐ Seller/Buyer ☐ Bailee/Bailor ☐ Licensee/Licensor

8. OPTIONAL FILER REFERENCE DATA:

UCC FINANCING STATEMENT (Form UCC1) (Rev. 04/20/11)

UCC FINANCING STATEMENT ADDENDUM
FOLLOW INSTRUCTIONS

9. NAME OF FIRST DEBTOR: Same as line 1a or 1b on Financing Statement; if line 1b was left blank
because Individual Debtor name did not fit, check here ☐

9a. ORGANIZATION'S NAME

OR 9b. INDIVIDUAL'S SURNAME

FIRST PERSONAL NAME

ADDITIONAL NAME(S)/INITIAL(S)   SUFFIX

THE ABOVE SPACE IS FOR FILING OFFICE USE ONLY

10. DEBTOR'S NAME Provide (10a or 10b) only one additional Debtor name or Debtor name that did not fit in line 1b or 2b of the Financing Statement (Form UCC1) (use exact, full name;
do not omit, modify, or abbreviate any part of the Debtor's name) and enter the mailing address in line 10c

10a. ORGANIZATION'S NAME

OR 10b. INDIVIDUAL'S SURNAME

INDIVIDUAL'S FIRST PERSONAL NAME

INDIVIDUAL'S ADDITIONAL NAME(S)/INITIAL(S)   SUFFIX

10c. MAILING ADDRESS	CITY	STATE	POSTAL CODE	COUNTRY

11. ☐ ADDITIONAL SECURED PARTY'S NAME or ☐ ASSIGNOR SECURED PARTY'S NAME: Provide only one name (11a or 11b)

11a. ORGANIZATION'S NAME

OR 11b. INDIVIDUAL'S SURNAME	FIRST PERSONAL NAME	ADDITIONAL NAME(S)/INITIAL(S)	SUFFIX
11c. MAILING ADDRESS	CITY	STATE	POSTAL CODE	COUNTRY

12. ADDITIONAL SPACE FOR ITEM 4 (Collateral)

13. ☐ This FINANCING STATEMENT is to be filed [for record] (or recorded) in the REAL ESTATE RECORDS (if applicable)	14. This FINANCING STATEMENT: ☐ covers timber to be cut ☐ covers as-extracted collateral ☐ is filed as a fixture filing
15. Name and address of a RECORD OWNER of real estate described in item 16 (if Debtor does not have a record interest):	16. Description of real estate:

17. MISCELLANEOUS:

UCC FINANCING STATEMENT ADDENDUM (Form UCC1Ad) (Rev. 04/20/11)

(b)   **[Amendment form.]** A filing office that accepts written records may not refuse to accept a written record in the following form and format except for a reason set forth in Section 9–516(b):

UCC FINANCING STATEMENT AMENDMENT

FOLLOW INSTRUCTIONS

A. NAME & PHONE OF CONTACT AT FILER (optional)

B. E-MAIL CONTACT AT FILER (optional)

C. SEND ACKNOWLEDGMENT TO: (Name and Address)

THE ABOVE SPACE IS FOR FILING OFFICE USE ONLY

1a. INITIAL FINANCING STATEMENT FILE NUMBER

1b. ☐ This FINANCING STATEMENT AMENDMENT is to be filed [for record] (or recorded) in the REAL ESTATE RECORDS
Filer: attach Amendment Addendum (Form UCC3Ad) and provide Debtor's name in item 13

2. ☐ **TERMINATION:** Effectiveness of the Financing Statement identified above is terminated with respect to the security interest(s) of Secured Party authorizing this Termination Statement

3. ☐ **ASSIGNMENT** (full or partial): Provide name of Assignee in item 7a or 7b, and address of Assignee in item 7c and name of Assignor in item 9
For partial assignment, complete items 7 and 9 and also indicate affected collateral in item 8

4. ☐ **CONTINUATION:** Effectiveness of the Financing Statement identified above with respect to the security interest(s) of Secured Party authorizing this Continuation Statement is continued for the additional period provided by applicable law

5. ☐ **PARTY INFORMATION CHANGE:**

Check one of these two boxes   **AND** Check one of these three boxes to:

This Change affects ☐ Debtor or ☐ Secured Party of record   ☐ CHANGE name and/or address: Complete item 6a or 6b; and item 7a or 7b and item 7c   ☐ ADD name: Complete item 7a or 7b, and item 7c   ☐ DELETE name: Give record name to be deleted in item 6a or 6b

6. **CURRENT RECORD INFORMATION:** Complete for Party Information Change - provide only one name (6a or 6b)

6a. ORGANIZATION'S NAME			
OR 6b. INDIVIDUAL'S SURNAME	FIRST PERSONAL NAME	ADDITIONAL NAME(S)/INITIAL(S)	SUFFIX

7. **CHANGED OR ADDED INFORMATION:** Complete for Assignment or Party Information Change - provide only one name (7a or 7b) (use exact, full name; do not omit, modify, or abbreviate any part of the Debtor's name)

7a. ORGANIZATION'S NAME			
OR 7b. INDIVIDUAL'S SURNAME			
INDIVIDUAL'S FIRST PERSONAL NAME			
INDIVIDUAL'S ADDITIONAL NAME(S)/INITIAL(S)			SUFFIX
7c. MAILING ADDRESS	CITY	STATE POSTAL CODE	COUNTRY

8. ☐ **COLLATERAL CHANGE:** Also check one of these four boxes: ☐ ADD collateral ☐ DELETE collateral ☐ RESTATE covered collateral ☐ ASSIGN collateral

Indicate collateral:

9. **NAME OF SECURED PARTY OF RECORD AUTHORIZING THIS AMENDMENT:** Provide only one name (9a or 9b) (name of Assignor, if this is an Assignment)
If this is an Amendment authorized by a DEBTOR, check here ☐ and provide name of authorizing Debtor

9a. ORGANIZATION'S NAME			
OR 9b. INDIVIDUAL'S SURNAME	FIRST PERSONAL NAME	ADDITIONAL NAME(S)/INITIAL(S)	SUFFIX

10. OPTIONAL FILER REFERENCE DATA:

UCC FINANCING STATEMENT AMENDMENT (Form UCC3) (Rev. 04/20/11)

UCC FINANCING STATEMENT AMENDMENT ADDENDUM
FOLLOW INSTRUCTIONS

11. INITIAL FINANCING STATEMENT FILE NUMBER: Same as item 1a on Amendment form

12. NAME OF PARTY AUTHORIZING THIS AMENDMENT: Same as item 9 on Amendment form

12a. ORGANIZATION'S NAME	
OR 12b. INDIVIDUAL'S SURNAME	
FIRST PERSONAL NAME	
ADDITIONAL NAME(S)/INITIAL(S)	SUFFIX

THE ABOVE SPACE IS FOR FILING OFFICE USE ONLY

13. **Name of DEBTOR on related financing statement** (Name of a current Debtor of record required for indexing purposes only in some filing offices - see Instruction item 13). Provide only <u>one</u> Debtor name (13a or 13b) (use exact, full name; do not omit, modify, or abbreviate any part of the Debtor's name); see Instructions if name does not fit

13a. ORGANIZATION'S NAME			
OR 13b. INDIVIDUAL'S SURNAME	FIRST PERSONAL NAME	ADDITIONAL NAME(S)/INITIAL(S)	SUFFIX

14. ADDITIONAL SPACE FOR ITEM 8 (Collateral)

15. This FINANCING STATEMENT AMENDMENT	17. Description of real estate:
☐ covers timber to be cut ☐ covers as-extracted collateral ☐ is filed as a fixture filing	
16. Name and address of a RECORD OWNER of real estate described in item 17 (if Debtor does not have a record interest):	

18. MISCELLANEOUS:

UCC FINANCING STATEMENT AMENDMENT ADDENDUM (Form UCC3Ad) (Rev. 04/20/11)

As amended in 2010.

Official Comment

1.   **Source.** New.

2.   **"Safe Harbor" Written Forms.** Although Section 9–520 limits the bases upon which the filing office can refuse to accept records, this section provides sample written forms that must be accepted in every filing office

in the country, as long as the filing office's rules permit it to accept written communications. By completing one of the forms in this section, a secured party can be certain that the filing office is obligated to accept it.

The forms in this section are based upon national financing statement forms that were in use under former Article 9. Those forms were developed over an extended period and reflect the comments and suggestions of filing officers, secured parties and their counsel, and service companies. The formatting of those forms and of the ones in this section has been designed to reduce error by both filers and filing offices.

A filing office that accepts written communications may not reject, on grounds of form or format, a filing using these forms. Although filers are not required to use the forms, they are encouraged and can be expected to do so, inasmuch as the forms are well designed and avoid the risk of rejection on the basis of form or format. As their use expands, the forms will rapidly become familiar to both filers and filing-office personnel. Filing offices may and should encourage the use of these forms by declaring them to be the "standard" (but not exclusive) forms for each jurisdiction, albeit without in any way suggesting that alternative forms are unacceptable.

The multi-purpose form in subsection (b) covers changes with respect to the debtor, the secured party, the collateral, and the status of the financing statement (termination and continuation). A single form may be used for several different types of amendments at once (e.g., both to change a debtor's name and continue the effectiveness of the financing statement).

§ 9–522.   Maintenance and Destruction of Records.

[ALTERNATIVE A]

(a)   **[Post-lapse maintenance and retrieval of information.]** The filing office shall maintain a record of the information provided in a filed financing statement for at least one year after the effectiveness of the financing statement has lapsed under Section 9–515 with respect to all secured parties of record. The record must be retrievable by using the name of the debtor and by using the file number assigned to the initial financing statement to which the record relates.

[ALTERNATIVE B]

(a)   **[Post-lapse maintenance and retrieval of information.]** The filing office shall maintain a record of the information provided in a filed financing statement for at least one year after the effectiveness of the financing statement has lapsed under Section 9–515 with respect to all secured parties of record. The record must be retrievable by using the name of the debtor and:

(1)   if the record was filed [or recorded] in the filing office described in Section 9–501(a)(1), by using the file number assigned to the initial financing statement to which the record relates and the date [and time] that the record was filed [or recorded]; or

(2)   if the record was filed in the filing office described in Section 9–501(a)(2), by using the file number assigned to the initial financing statement to which the record relates.

[END OF ALTERNATIVES]

(b)   **[Destruction of written records.]** Except to the extent that a statute governing disposition of public records provides otherwise, the filing office immediately may destroy any written record evidencing a financing statement. However, if the filing office destroys a written record, it shall maintain another record of the financing statement which complies with subsection (a).

Legislative Note: States whose real-estate filing offices require additional information in amendments and cannot search their records by both the name of the debtor and the file number should enact Alternative B to Sections 9–512(a), 9–518(b), 9–518(d), 9–519(f) and 9–522(a).

As amended in 2010.

Official Comment

1.   **Source.** Former Section 9–403(3), revised substantially.

2.   **Maintenance of Records.** Section 9–523 requires the filing office to provide information concerning certain lapsed financing statements. Accordingly, subsection (a) requires the filing office to maintain a record of the information in a financing statement for at least one year after lapse. During that time, the filing office may

not delete any information with respect to a filed financing statement; it may only add information. This approach relieves the filing office from any duty to determine whether to substitute or delete information upon receipt of an amendment. It also assures searchers that they will receive all information with respect to financing statements filed against a debtor and thereby be able themselves to determine the state of the public record.

The filing office may maintain this information in any medium. Subsection (b) permits the filing office immediately to destroy written records evidencing a financing statement, provided that the filing office maintains another record of the information contained in the financing statement as required by subsection (a).

§ 9–523.   Information From Filing Office; Sale or License of Records.

(a)   **[Acknowledgment of filing written record.]** If a person that files a written record requests an acknowledgment of the filing, the filing office shall send to the person an image of the record showing the number assigned to the record pursuant to Section 9–519(a)(1) and the date and time of the filing of the record. However, if the person furnishes a copy of the record to the filing office, the filing office may instead:

(1)   note upon the copy the number assigned to the record pursuant to Section 9–519(a)(1) and the date and time of the filing of the record; and

(2)   send the copy to the person.

(b)   **[Acknowledgment of filing other record.]** If a person files a record other than a written record, the filing office shall communicate to the person an acknowledgment that provides:

(1)   the information in the record;

(2)   the number assigned to the record pursuant to Section 9–519(a)(1); and

(3)   the date and time of the filing of the record.

(c)   **[Communication of requested information.]** The filing office shall communicate or otherwise make available in a record the following information to any person that requests it:

(1)   whether there is on file on a date and time specified by the filing office, but not a date earlier than three business days before the filing office receives the request, any financing statement that:

(A)   designates a particular debtor [or, if the request so states, designates a particular debtor at the address specified in the request];

(B)   has not lapsed under Section 9–515 with respect to all secured parties of record; and

(C)   if the request so states, has lapsed under Section 9–515 and a record of which is maintained by the filing office under Section 9–522(a);

(2)   the date and time of filing of each financing statement; and

(3)   the information provided in each financing statement.

(d)   **[Medium for communicating information.]** In complying with its duty under subsection (c), the filing office may communicate information in any medium. However, if requested, the filing office shall communicate information by issuing [its written certificate] [a record that can be admitted into evidence in the courts of this State without extrinsic evidence of its authenticity].

(e)   **[Timeliness of filing office performance.]** The filing office shall perform the acts required by subsections (a) through (d) at the time and in the manner prescribed by filing-office rule, but not later than two business days after the filing office receives the request.

(f)   **[Public availability of records.]** At least weekly, the [insert appropriate official or governmental agency] [filing office] shall offer to sell or license to the public on a nonexclusive basis, in bulk, copies of all records filed in it under this part, in every medium from time to time available to the filing office.

Legislative Notes:

1.   States whose filing office does not offer the additional service of responding to search requests limited to a particular address should omit the bracketed language in subsection (c)(1)(A).

2. A State that elects not to require real-estate filing offices to comply with either or both of subsections (e) and (f) should specify in the appropriate subsection(s) only the filing office described in Section 9–501(a)(2).

Official Comment

1. **Source.** Former Section 9–407; subsections (d) and (e) are new.

2. **Filing Office's Duty to Provide Information.** Former Section 9–407, dealing with obtaining information from the filing office, was bracketed to suggest to legislatures that its enactment was optional. Experience has shown that the method by which interested persons can obtain information concerning the public records should be uniform. Accordingly, the analogous provisions of this Article are not in brackets.

Most of the other changes from former Section 9–407 are for clarification, to embrace medium-neutral drafting, or to impose standards of performance on the filing office.

3. **Acknowledgments of Filing.** Subsections (a) and (b) require the filing office to acknowledge the filing of a record. Under subsection (a), the filing office is required to acknowledge the filing of a written record only upon request of the filer. Subsection (b) requires the filing office to acknowledge the filing of a non-written record even in the absence of a request from the filer.

4. **Response to Search Request.** Subsection (c)(3) requires the filing office to provide "the information contained in each financing statement" to a person who requests it. This requirement can be satisfied by providing copies, images, or reports. The requirement does not in any manner inhibit the filing office from also offering to provide less than all of the information (presumably for a lower fee) to a person who asks for less. Thus, subsection (c) accommodates the practice of providing only the type of record (e.g., initial financing statement, continuation statement), number assigned to the record, date and time of filing, and names and addresses of the debtor and secured party when a requesting person asks for no more (i.e., when the person does not ask for copies of financing statements). In contrast, the filing office's obligation under subsection (b) to provide an acknowledgment containing "the information contained in the record" is not defined by a customer's request. Thus unless the filer stipulates otherwise, to comply with subsection (b) the filing office's acknowledgment must contain all of the information in a record.

Subsection (c) assures that a minimum amount of information about filed records will be available to the public. It does not preclude a filing office from offering additional services.

5. **Lapsed and Terminated Financing Statements.** This section reflects the policy that terminated financing statements will remain part of the filing office's data base. The filing office may remove from the data base only lapsed financing statements, and then only when at least a year has passed after lapse. See Section 9–519(g). Subsection (c)(1)(C) requires a filing office to conduct a search and report as to lapsed financing statements that have not been removed from the data base, when requested.

6. **Search by Debtor's Address.** Subsection (c)(1)(A) contemplates that, by making a single request, a searcher will receive the results of a search of the entire public record maintained by any given filing office. Addition of the bracketed language in subsection (c)(1)(A) would permit a search report limited to financing statements showing a particular address for the debtor, but only if the search request is so limited. With or without the bracketed language, this subsection does not permit the filing office to compel a searcher to limit a request by address.

7. **Medium of Communication; Certificates.** Former Article 9 provided that the filing office respond to a request for information by providing a certificate. The principle of medium-neutrality would suggest that the statute not require a written certificate. Subsection (d) follows this principle by permitting the filing office to respond by communicating "in any medium." By permitting communication "in any medium," subsection (d) is not inconsistent with a system in which persons other than filing office staff conduct searches of the filing office's (computer) records.

Some searchers find it necessary to introduce the results of their search into evidence. Because official written certificates might be introduced into evidence more easily than official communications in another medium, subsection (d) affords States the option of requiring the filing office to issue written certificates upon request. The alternative bracketed language in subsection (d) recognizes that some States may prefer to permit the filing office to respond in another medium, as long as the response can be admitted into evidence in the courts of that State without extrinsic evidence of its authenticity.

8. **Performance Standard.** The utility of the filing system depends on the ability of searchers to get current information quickly. Accordingly, subsection (e) requires that the filing office respond to a request for

information no later than two business days after it receives the request. The information contained in the response must be current as of a date no earlier than three business days before the filing office receives the request. See subsection (c)(1). The failure of the filing office to comply with performance standards, such as subsection (e), has no effect on the private rights of persons affected by the filing of records.

9. **Sales of Records in Bulk.** Subsection (f), which is new, mandates that the appropriate official or the filing office sell or license the filing records to the public in bulk, on a nonexclusive basis, in every medium available to the filing office. The details of implementation are left to filing-office rules.

§ 9-524. Delay by Filing Office.

Delay by the filing office beyond a time limit prescribed by this part is excused if:

(1) the delay is caused by interruption of communication or computer facilities, war, emergency conditions, failure of equipment, or other circumstances beyond control of the filing office; and

(2) the filing office exercises reasonable diligence under the circumstances.

Official Comment

Source. New; derived from Section 4-109.

§ 9-525. Fees.

(a) **[Initial financing statement or other record: general rule.]** Except as otherwise provided in subsection (e), the fee for filing and indexing a record under this part, other than an initial financing statement of the kind described in subsection (b), is [the amount specified in subsection (c), if applicable, plus]:

(1) $[X] if the record is communicated in writing and consists of one or two pages;

(2) $[2X] if the record is communicated in writing and consists of more than two pages; and

(3) $[½X] if the record is communicated by another medium authorized by filing-office rule.

(b) **[Initial financing statement: public-finance and manufactured-housing transactions.]** Except as otherwise provided in subsection (e), the fee for filing and indexing an initial financing statement of the following kind is [the amount specified in subsection (c), if applicable, plus]:

(1) $_____ if the financing statement indicates that it is filed in connection with a public-finance transaction;

(2) $_____ if the financing statement indicates that it is filed in connection with a manufactured-home transaction.

[ALTERNATIVE A]

(c) **[Number of names.]** The number of names required to be indexed does not affect the amount of the fee in subsections (a) and (b).

[ALTERNATIVE B]

(c) **[Number of names.]** Except as otherwise provided in subsection (e), if a record is communicated in writing, the fee for each name more than two required to be indexed is $_____.

[END OF ALTERNATIVES]

(d) **[Response to information request.]** The fee for responding to a request for information from the filing office, including for [issuing a certificate showing] [communicating] whether there is on file any financing statement naming a particular debtor, is:

(1) $_____ if the request is communicated in writing; and

(2) $_____ if the request is communicated by another medium authorized by filing-office rule.

(e) **[Record of mortgage.]** This section does not require a fee with respect to a record of a mortgage which is effective as a financing statement filed as a fixture filing or as a financing statement covering as-extracted collateral or timber to be cut under Section 9–502(c). However, the recording and satisfaction fees that otherwise would be applicable to the record of the mortgage apply.

Legislative Notes:

1.   *To preserve uniformity, a State that places the provisions of this section together with statutes setting fees for other services should do so without modification.*

2.   *A State should enact subsection (c), Alternative A, and omit the bracketed language in subsections (a) and (b) unless its indexing system entails a substantial additional cost when indexing additional names.*

As amended in 2000.

Official Comment

1.   **Source.** Various sections of former Part 4.

2.   **Fees.** This section contains all fee requirements for filing, indexing, and responding to requests for information. Uniformity in the fee structure (but not necessarily in the amount of fees) makes this Article easier for secured parties to use and reduces the likelihood that a filed record will be rejected for failure to pay at least the correct amount of the fee. See Section 9–516(b)(2).

The costs of processing electronic records are less than those with respect to written records. Accordingly, this section mandates a lower fee as an incentive to file electronically and imposes the additional charge (if any) for multiple debtors only with respect to written records. When written records are used, this Article encourages the use of the uniform forms in Section 9–521. The fee for filing these forms should be no greater than the fee for other written records.

To make the relevant information included in a filed record more accessible once the record is found, this section mandates a higher fee for longer written records than for shorter ones. Finally, recognizing that financing statements naming more than one debtor are most often filed against a husband and wife, any additional charge for multiple debtors applies to records filed with respect to more than two debtors, rather than with respect to more than one.

§ 9–526.   Filing-Office Rules.

(a)   **[Adoption of filing-office rules.]** The [insert appropriate governmental official or agency] shall adopt and publish rules to implement this article. The filing-office rules must be[:

(1)]   consistent with this article[; and

(2)   adopted and published in accordance with the [insert any applicable state administrative procedure act]].

(b)   **[Harmonization of rules.]** To keep the filing-office rules and practices of the filing office in harmony with the rules and practices of filing offices in other jurisdictions that enact substantially this part, and to keep the technology used by the filing office compatible with the technology used by filing offices in other jurisdictions that enact substantially this part, the [insert appropriate governmental official or agency], so far as is consistent with the purposes, policies, and provisions of this article, in adopting, amending, and repealing filing-office rules, shall:

(1)   consult with filing offices in other jurisdictions that enact substantially this part; and

(2)   consult the most recent version of the Model Rules promulgated by the International Association of Corporate Administrators or any successor organization; and

(3)   take into consideration the rules and practices of, and the technology used by, filing offices in other jurisdictions that enact substantially this part.

Official Comment

1.   **Source.** New; subsection (b) derives in part from the Uniform Consumer Credit Code (1974).

2.   **Rules Required.** Operating a filing office is a complicated business, requiring many more rules and procedures than this Article can usefully provide. Subsection (a) requires the adoption of rules to carry out the provisions of Article 9. The filing-office rules must be consistent with the provisions of the statute and adopted in

895

accordance with local procedures. The publication requirement informs secured parties about filing-office practices, aids secured parties in evaluating filing-related risks and costs, and promotes regularity of application within the filing office.

3.   **Importance of Uniformity.** In today's national economy, uniformity of the policies and practices of the filing offices will reduce the costs of secured transactions substantially. The International Association of Corporate Administrators (IACA), referred to in subsection (b), is an organization whose membership includes filing officers from every State. These individuals are responsible for the proper functioning of the Article 9 filing system and have worked diligently to develop model filing-office rules, with a view toward efficiency and uniformity.

Although uniformity is an important desideratum, subsection (a) affords considerable flexibility in the adoption of filing-office rules. Each State may adopt a version of subsection (a) that reflects the desired relationship between the statewide filing office described in Section 9–501(a)(2) and the local filing offices described in Section 9–501(a)(1) and that takes into account the practices of its filing offices. Subsection (a) need not designate a single official or agency to adopt rules applicable to all filing offices, and the rules applicable to the statewide filing office need not be identical to those applicable to the local filing office. For example, subsection (a) might provide for the statewide filing office to adopt filing-office rules, and, if not prohibited by other law, the filing office might adopt one set of rules for itself and another for local offices. Or, subsection (a) might designate one official or agency to adopt rules for the statewide filing office and another to adopt rules for local filing offices.

§ 9–527.   Duty to Report.

The [insert appropriate governmental official or agency] shall report [annually on or before _____] to the [Governor and Legislature] on the operation of the filing office. The report must contain a statement of the extent to which:

(1)   the filing-office rules are not in harmony with the rules of filing offices in other jurisdictions that enact substantially this part and the reasons for these variations; and

(2)   the filing-office rules are not in harmony with the most recent version of the Model Rules promulgated by the International Association of Corporate Administrators, or any successor organization, and the reasons for these variations.

Official Comment

1.   **Source.** New; derived in part from the Uniform Consumer Credit Code (1974).

2.   **Duty to Report.** This section is designed to promote compliance with the standards of performance imposed upon the filing office and with the requirement that the filing office's policies, practices, and technology be consistent and compatible with the policies, practices, and technology of other filing offices.

PART 6

DEFAULT

[SUBPART 1. DEFAULT AND ENFORCEMENT OF SECURITY INTEREST]

§ 9–601.   Rights After Default; Judicial Enforcement; Consignor or Buyer of Accounts, Chattel Paper, Payment Intangibles, or Promissory Notes.

(a)   **[Rights of secured party after default.]** After default, a secured party has the rights provided in this part and, except as otherwise provided in Section 9–602, those provided by agreement of the parties. A secured party:

(1)   may reduce a claim to judgment, foreclose, or otherwise enforce the claim, security interest, or agricultural lien by any available judicial procedure; and

(2)   if the collateral is documents, may proceed either as to the documents or as to the goods they cover.

(b) **[Rights and duties of secured party in possession or control.]** A secured party in possession of collateral or control of collateral under Section 7–106, 9–104, 9–105, 9–106, or 9–107 has the rights and duties provided in Section 9–207.

(c) **[Rights cumulative; simultaneous exercise.]** The rights under subsections (a) and (b) are cumulative and may be exercised simultaneously.

(d) **[Rights of debtor and obligor.]** Except as otherwise provided in subsection (g) and Section 9–605, after default, a debtor and an obligor have the rights provided in this part and by agreement of the parties.

(e) **[Lien of levy after judgment.]** If a secured party has reduced its claim to judgment, the lien of any levy that may be made upon the collateral by virtue of an execution based upon the judgment relates back to the earliest of:

(1) the date of perfection of the security interest or agricultural lien in the collateral;

(2) the date of filing a financing statement covering the collateral; or

(3) any date specified in a statute under which the agricultural lien was created.

(f) **[Execution sale.]** A sale pursuant to an execution is a foreclosure of the security interest or agricultural lien by judicial procedure within the meaning of this section. A secured party may purchase at the sale and thereafter hold the collateral free of any other requirements of this article.

(g) **[Consignor or buyer of certain rights to payment.]** Except as otherwise provided in Section 9–607(c), this part imposes no duties upon a secured party that is a consignor or is a buyer of accounts, chattel paper, payment intangibles, or promissory notes.

As amended in 2003.

Official Comment

1. **Source.** Former Section 9–501(1), (2), (5).

2. **Enforcement: In General.** The rights of a secured party to enforce its security interest in collateral after the debtor's default are an important feature of a secured transaction. (Note that the term "rights," as defined in Section 1–201, includes "remedies.") This Part provides those rights as well as certain limitations on their exercise for the protection of the defaulting debtor, other creditors, and other affected persons. However, subsections (a) and (d) make clear that the rights provided in this Part do not exclude other rights provided by agreement.

3. **When Remedies Arise.** Under subsection (a) the secured party's rights arise "[a]fter default." As did former Section 9–501, this Article leaves to the agreement of the parties the circumstances giving rise to a default. This Article does not determine whether a secured party's post-default conduct can constitute a waiver of default in the face of an agreement stating that such conduct shall not constitute a waiver. Rather, it continues to leave to the parties' agreement, as supplemented by law other than this Article, the determination whether a default has occurred or has been waived. See Section 1–103.

4. **Possession of Collateral; Section 9–207.** After a secured party takes possession of collateral following a default, there is no longer any distinction between a security interest that before default was nonpossessory and a security interest that was possessory before default, as under a common-law pledge. This Part generally does not distinguish between the rights of a secured party with a nonpossessory security interest and those of a secured party with a possessory security interest. However, Section 9–207 addresses rights and duties with respect to collateral in a secured party's possession. Under subsection (b) of this section, Section 9–207 applies not only to possession before default but also to possession after default. Subsection (b) also has been conformed to Section 9–207, which, unlike former Section 9–207, applies to secured parties having control of collateral.

5. **Cumulative Remedies.** Former Section 9–501(1) provided that the secured party's remedies were cumulative, but it did not explicitly provide whether the remedies could be exercised simultaneously. Subsection (c) permits the simultaneous exercise of remedies if the secured party acts in good faith. The liability scheme of Subpart 2 affords redress to an aggrieved debtor or obligor. Moreover, permitting the simultaneous exercise of remedies under subsection (c) does not override any non-UCC law, including the law of tort and statutes regulating

collection of debts, under which the simultaneous exercise of remedies in a particular case constitutes abusive behavior or harassment giving rise to liability.

6.　**Judicial Enforcement.** Under subsection (a) a secured party may reduce its claim to judgment or foreclose its interest by any available procedure outside this Article under applicable law. Subsection (e) generally follows former Section 9–501(5). It makes clear that any judicial lien that the secured party may acquire against the collateral effectively is a continuation of the original security interest (if perfected) and not the acquisition of a new interest or a transfer of property on account of a preexisting obligation. Under former Section 9–501(5), the judicial lien was stated to relate back to the date of perfection of the security interest. Subsection (e), however, provides that the lien relates back to the earlier of the date of filing or the date of perfection. This provides a secured party who enforces a security interest by judicial process with the benefit of the "first-to-file-or-perfect" priority rule of Section 9–322(a)(1).

7.　**Agricultural Liens.** Part 6 provides parallel treatment for the enforcement of agricultural liens and security interests. Because agricultural liens are statutory rather than consensual, this Article does draw a few distinctions between these liens and security interests. Under subsection (e), the statute creating an agricultural lien would govern whether and the date to which an execution lien relates back. Section 9–606 explains when a "default" occurs in the agricultural lien context.

8.　**Execution Sales.** Subsection (f) also follows former Section 9–501(5). It makes clear that an execution sale is an appropriate method of foreclosure contemplated by this Part. However, the sale is governed by other law and not by this Article, and the limitations under Section 9–610 on the right of a secured party to purchase collateral do not apply.

9.　**Sales of Receivables; Consignments.** Subsection (g) provides that, except as provided in Section 9–607(c), the duties imposed on secured parties do not apply to buyers of accounts, chattel paper, payment intangibles, or promissory notes. Although denominated "secured parties," these buyers own the entire interest in the property sold and so may enforce their rights without regard to the seller ("debtor") or the seller's creditors. Likewise, a true consignor may enforce its ownership interest under other law without regard to the duties that this Part imposes on secured parties. Note, however, that Section 9–615 governs cases in which a consignee's secured party (other than a consignor) is enforcing a security interest that is senior to the security interest (i.e., ownership interest) of a true consignor.

§ 9–602.　Waiver and Variance of Rights and Duties.

Except as otherwise provided in Section 9–624, to the extent that they give rights to a debtor or obligor and impose duties on a secured party, the debtor or obligor may not waive or vary the rules stated in the following listed sections:

(1)　Section 9–207(b)(4)(C), which deals with use and operation of the collateral by the secured party;

(2)　Section 9–210, which deals with requests for an accounting and requests concerning a list of collateral and statement of account;

(3)　Section 9–607(c), which deals with collection and enforcement of collateral;

(4)　Sections 9–608(a) and 9–615(c) to the extent that they deal with application or payment of noncash proceeds of collection, enforcement, or disposition;

(5)　Sections 9–608(a) and 9–615(d) to the extent that they require accounting for or payment of surplus proceeds of collateral;

(6)　Section 9–609 to the extent that it imposes upon a secured party that takes possession of collateral without judicial process the duty to do so without breach of the peace;

(7)　Sections 9–610(b), 9–611, 9–613, and 9–614, which deal with disposition of collateral;

(8)　Section 9–615(f), which deals with calculation of a deficiency or surplus when a disposition is made to the secured party, a person related to the secured party, or a secondary obligor;

(9)　Section 9–616, which deals with explanation of the calculation of a surplus or deficiency;

(10)　Sections 9–620, 9–621, and 9–622, which deal with acceptance of collateral in satisfaction of obligation;

(11) Section 9–623, which deals with redemption of collateral;

(12) Section 9–624, which deals with permissible waivers; and

(13) Sections 9–625 and 9–626, which deal with the secured party's liability for failure to comply with this article.

Official Comment

1. **Source.** Former Section 9–501(3).

2. **Waiver: In General.** Section 1–102(3)* addresses which provisions of the UCC are mandatory and which may be varied by agreement. With exceptions relating to good faith, diligence, reasonableness, and care, immediate parties, as between themselves, may vary its provisions by agreement. However, in the context of rights and duties after default, our legal system traditionally has looked with suspicion on agreements that limit the debtor's rights and free the secured party of its duties. As stated in former Section 9–501, Comment 4, "no mortgage clause has ever been allowed to clog the equity of redemption." The context of default offers great opportunity for overreaching. The suspicious attitudes of the courts have been grounded in common sense. This section, like former Section 9–501(3), codifies this long-standing and deeply rooted attitude. The specified rights of the debtor and duties of the secured party may not be waived or varied except as stated. Provisions that are not specified in this section are subject to the general rules in Section 1–102(3).*

3. **Nonwaivable Rights and Duties.** This section revises former Section 9–501(3) by restricting the ability to waive or modify additional specified rights and duties: (i) duties under Section 9–207(b)(4)(C), which deals with the use and operation of consumer goods, (ii) the right to a response to a request for an accounting, concerning a list of collateral, or concerning a statement of account (Section 9–210), (iii) the duty to collect collateral in a commercially reasonable manner (Section 9–607), (iv) the implicit duty to refrain from a breach of the peace in taking possession of collateral under Section 9–609, (v) the duty to apply noncash proceeds of collection or disposition in a commercially reasonable manner (Sections 9–608 and 9–615), (vi) the right to a special method of calculating a surplus or deficiency in certain dispositions to a secured party, a person related to secured party, or a secondary obligor (Section 9–615), (vii) the duty to give an explanation of the calculation of a surplus or deficiency (Section 9–616), (viii) the right to limitations on the effectiveness of certain waivers (Section 9–624), and (ix) the right to hold a secured party liable for failure to comply with this Article (Sections 9–625 and 9–626). For clarity and consistency, this Article uses the term "waive or vary" instead of "renounc[e] or modify[ ]," which appeared in former Section 9–504(3).

This section provides generally that the specified rights and duties "may not be waived or varied." However, it does not restrict the ability of parties to agree to settle, compromise, or renounce claims for past conduct that may have constituted a violation or breach of those rights and duties, even if the settlement involves an express "waiver."

Section 9–610(c) limits the circumstances under which a secured party may purchase at its own private disposition. Transactions of this kind are equivalent to "strict foreclosures" and are governed by Sections 9–620, 9–621, and 9–622. The provisions of these sections can be waived only to the extent provided in Section 9–624(b). See Section 9–602.

4. **Waiver by Debtors and Obligors.** The restrictions on waiver contained in this section apply to obligors as well as debtors. This resolves a question under former Article 9 as to whether secondary obligors, assuming that they were "debtors" for purposes of former Part 5, were permitted to waive, under the law of suretyship, rights and duties under that Part.

5. **Certain Post-Default Waivers.** Section 9–624 permits post-default waivers in limited circumstances. These waivers must be made in agreements that are authenticated. Under Section 1–201, an " 'agreement' means the bargain of the parties in fact." In considering waivers under Section 9–624 and analogous agreements in other contexts, courts should carefully scrutinize putative agreements that appear in records that also address many additional or unrelated matters.

As amended in 2010.

---

*   *Referring to unrevised Article 1 (Appendix A).*

§ 9–603. Agreement on Standards Concerning Rights and Duties.

(a) **[Agreed standards.]** The parties may determine by agreement the standards measuring the fulfillment of the rights of a debtor or obligor and the duties of a secured party under a rule stated in Section 9–602 if the standards are not manifestly unreasonable.

(b) **[Agreed standards inapplicable to breach of peace.]** Subsection (a) does not apply to the duty under Section 9–609 to refrain from breaching the peace.

Official Comment

1. **Source.** Former Section 9–501(3).

2. **Limitation on Ability to Set Standards.** Subsection (a), like former Section 9–501(3), permits the parties to set standards for compliance with the rights and duties under this Part if the standards are not "manifestly unreasonable." Under subsection (b), the parties are not permitted to set standards measuring fulfillment of the secured party's duty to take collateral without breaching the peace.

§ 9–604. Procedure if Security Agreement Covers Real Property or Fixtures.

(a) **[Enforcement: personal and real property.]** If a security agreement covers both personal and real property, a secured party may proceed:

(1) under this part as to the personal property without prejudicing any rights with respect to the real property; or

(2) as to both the personal property and the real property in accordance with the rights with respect to the real property, in which case the other provisions of this part do not apply.

(b) **[Enforcement: fixtures.]** Subject to subsection (c), if a security agreement covers goods that are or become fixtures, a secured party may proceed:

(1) under this part; or

(2) in accordance with the rights with respect to real property, in which case the other provisions of this part do not apply.

(c) **[Removal of fixtures.]** Subject to the other provisions of this part, if a secured party holding a security interest in fixtures has priority over all owners and encumbrancers of the real property, the secured party, after default, may remove the collateral from the real property.

(d) **[Injury caused by removal.]** A secured party that removes collateral shall promptly reimburse any encumbrancer or owner of the real property, other than the debtor, for the cost of repair of any physical injury caused by the removal. The secured party need not reimburse the encumbrancer or owner for any diminution in value of the real property caused by the absence of the goods removed or by any necessity of replacing them. A person entitled to reimbursement may refuse permission to remove until the secured party gives adequate assurance for the performance of the obligation to reimburse.

Official Comment

1. **Source.** Former Sections 9–501(4), 9–313(8).

2. **Real-Property-Related Collateral.** The collateral in many transactions consists of both real and personal property. In the interest of simplicity, speed, and economy, subsection (a), like former Section 9–501(4), permits (but does not require) the secured party to proceed as to both real and personal property in accordance with its rights and remedies with respect to the real property. Subsection (a) also makes clear that a secured party who exercises rights under Part 6 with respect to personal property does not prejudice any rights under real-property law.

This Article does not address certain other real-property-related problems. In a number of States, the exercise of remedies by a creditor who is secured by both real property and non-real property collateral is governed by special legal rules. For example, under some anti-deficiency laws, creditors risk loss of rights against personal property collateral if they err in enforcing their rights against the real property. Under a "one-form-of-action" rule (or rule against splitting a cause of action), a creditor who judicially enforces a real property mortgage and does not proceed in the same action to enforce a security interest in personalty may (among other consequences) lose the right to proceed against the personalty. Although statutes of this kind create impediments to enforcement of security interests, this Article does not override these limitations under other law.

3. **Fixtures.** Subsection (b) is new. It makes clear that a security interest in fixtures may be enforced either under real-property law or under any of the applicable provisions of Part 6, including sale or other disposition either before or after removal of the fixtures (see subsection (c)). Subsection (b) also serves to overrule cases holding that a secured party's only remedy after default is the removal of the fixtures from the real property. See, e.g., *Maplewood Bank & Trust v. Sears, Roebuck & Co.*, 625 A.2d 537 (N.J. Super. Ct. App. Div. 1993).

Subsection (c) generally follows former Section 9–313(8). It gives the secured party the right to remove fixtures under certain circumstances. A secured party whose security interest in fixtures has priority over owners and encumbrancers of the real property may remove the collateral from the real property. However, subsection (d) requires the secured party to reimburse any owner (other than the debtor) or encumbrancer for the cost of repairing any physical injury caused by the removal. This right to reimbursement is implemented by the last sentence of subsection (d), which gives the owner or encumbrancer a right to security or indemnity as a condition for giving permission to remove.

§ 9–605. **Unknown Debtor or Secondary Obligor.**

A secured party does not owe a duty based on its status as secured party:

(1) to a person that is a debtor or obligor, unless the secured party knows:

(A) that the person is a debtor or obligor;

(B) the identity of the person; and

(C) how to communicate with the person; or

(2) to a secured party or lienholder that has filed a financing statement against a person, unless the secured party knows:

(A) that the person is a debtor; and

(B) the identity of the person.

Official Comment

1. **Source.** New.

2. **Duties to Unknown Persons.** This section relieves a secured party from duties owed to a debtor or obligor, if the secured party does not know about the debtor or obligor. Similarly, it relieves a secured party from duties owed to a secured party or lienholder who has filed a financing statement against the debtor, if the secured party does not know about the debtor. For example, a secured party may be unaware that the original debtor has sold the collateral subject to the security interest and that the new owner has become the debtor. If so, the secured party owes no duty to the new owner (debtor) or to a secured party who has filed a financing statement against the new owner. This section should be read in conjunction with the exculpatory provisions in Section 9–628. Note that it relieves a secured party not only from duties arising under this Article but also from duties arising under other law by virtue of the secured party's status as such under this Article, unless the other law otherwise provides.

§ 9–606. **Time of Default for Agricultural Lien.**

For purposes of this part, a default occurs in connection with an agricultural lien at the time the secured party becomes entitled to enforce the lien in accordance with the statute under which it was created.

Official Comment

1. **Source.** New.

2. **Time of Default.** Remedies under this Part become available upon the debtor's "default." See Section 9–601. This section explains when "default" occurs in the agricultural-lien context. It requires one to consult the enabling statute to determine when the lienholder is entitled to enforce the lien.

§ 9–607.   Collection and Enforcement by Secured Party.

(a)   **[Collection and enforcement generally.]** If so agreed, and in any event after default, a secured party:

(1)   may notify an account debtor or other person obligated on collateral to make payment or otherwise render performance to or for the benefit of the secured party;

(2)   may take any proceeds to which the secured party is entitled under Section 9–315;

(3)   may enforce the obligations of an account debtor or other person obligated on collateral and exercise the rights of the debtor with respect to the obligation of the account debtor or other person obligated on collateral to make payment or otherwise render performance to the debtor, and with respect to any property that secures the obligations of the account debtor or other person obligated on the collateral;

(4)   if it holds a security interest in a deposit account perfected by control under Section 9–104(a)(1), may apply the balance of the deposit account to the obligation secured by the deposit account; and

(5)   if it holds a security interest in a deposit account perfected by control under Section 9–104(a)(2) or (3), may instruct the bank to pay the balance of the deposit account to or for the benefit of the secured party.

(b)   **[Nonjudicial enforcement of mortgage.]** If necessary to enable a secured party to exercise under subsection (a)(3) the right of a debtor to enforce a mortgage nonjudicially, the secured party may record in the office in which a record of the mortgage is recorded:

(1)   a copy of the security agreement that creates or provides for a security interest in the obligation secured by the mortgage; and

(2)   the secured party's sworn affidavit in recordable form stating that:

(A)   a default has occurred with respect to the obligation secured by the mortgage; and

(B)   the secured party is entitled to enforce the mortgage nonjudicially.

(c)   **[Commercially reasonable collection and enforcement.]** A secured party shall proceed in a commercially reasonable manner if the secured party:

(1)   undertakes to collect from or enforce an obligation of an account debtor or other person obligated on collateral; and

(2)   is entitled to charge back uncollected collateral or otherwise to full or limited recourse against the debtor or a secondary obligor.

(d)   **[Expenses of collection and enforcement.]** A secured party may deduct from the collections made pursuant to subsection (c) reasonable expenses of collection and enforcement, including reasonable attorney's fees and legal expenses incurred by the secured party.

(e)   **[Duties to secured party not affected.]** This section does not determine whether an account debtor, bank, or other person obligated on collateral owes a duty to a secured party.

As amended in 2010.

Official Comment

1.   **Source.** Former Section 9–502; subsections (b), (d), and (e) are new.

2.   **Collections: In General.** Collateral consisting of rights to payment is not only the most liquid asset of a typical debtor's business but also is property that may be collected without any interruption of the debtor's business This situation is far different from that in which collateral is inventory or equipment, whose removal may bring the business to a halt. Furthermore, problems of valuation and identification, present with collateral that is tangible personal property, frequently are not as serious in the case of rights to payment and other intangible collateral. Consequently, this section, like former Section 9–502, recognizes that financing through assignments of intangibles lacks many of the complexities that arise after default in other types of financing. This section allows the assignee to liquidate collateral by collecting whatever may become due on the collateral, whether

902

or not the method of collection contemplated by the security arrangement before default was direct (i.e., payment by the account debtor to the assignee, "notification" financing) or indirect (i.e., payment by the account debtor to the assignor, "nonnotification" financing).

3. **Scope.** The scope of this section is broader than that of former Section 9–502. It applies not only to collections from account debtors and obligors on instruments but also to enforcement more generally against all persons obligated on collateral. It explicitly provides for the secured party's enforcement of the debtor's rights in respect of the account debtor's (and other third parties') obligations and for the secured party's enforcement of supporting obligations with respect to those obligations. (Supporting obligations are components of the collateral under Section 9–203(f).) The rights of a secured party under subsection (a) include the right to enforce claims that the debtor may enjoy against others. For example, the claims might include a breach-of-warranty claim arising out of a defect in equipment that is collateral or a secured party's action for an injunction against infringement of a patent that is collateral. Those claims typically would be proceeds of original collateral under Section 9–315.

4. **Collection and Enforcement Before Default.** Like Part 6 generally, this section deals with the rights and duties of secured parties following default. However, as did former Section 9–502 with respect to collection rights, this section also applies to the collection and enforcement rights of secured parties even if a default has not occurred, as long as the debtor has so agreed. It is not unusual for debtors to agree that secured parties are entitled to collect and enforce rights against account debtors prior to default.

5. **Collections by Junior Secured Party.** A secured party who holds a security interest in a right to payment may exercise the right to collect and enforce under this section, even if the security interest is subordinate to a conflicting security interest in the same right to payment. Whether the junior secured party has priority in the collected proceeds depends on whether the junior secured party qualifies for priority as a purchaser of an instrument (e.g., the account debtor's check) under Section 9–330(d), as a holder in due course of an instrument under Sections 3–305 and 9–331(a), or as a transferee of money under Section 9–332(a). See Sections 9–330, Comment 7; 9–331, Comment 5; and 9–332.

6. **Relationship to Rights and Duties of Persons Obligated on Collateral.** This section permits a secured party to collect and enforce obligations included in collateral in its capacity as a secured party. It is not necessary for a secured party first to become the owner of the collateral pursuant to a disposition or acceptance. However, the secured party's rights, as between it and the debtor, to collect from and enforce collateral against account debtors and others obligated on collateral under subsection (a) are subject to Section 9–341, Part 4, and other applicable law. *Neither this section nor former Section 9–502 should be understood to regulate the duties of an account debtor or other person obligated on collateral.* Subsection (e) makes this explicit. For example, the secured party may be unable to exercise the debtor's rights under an instrument if the debtor is in possession of the instrument, or under a non-transferable letter of credit if the debtor is the beneficiary. Unless a secured party has control over a letter-of-credit right and is entitled to receive payment or performance from the issuer or a nominated person under Article 5, its remedies with respect to the letter-of-credit right may be limited to the recovery of any identifiable proceeds from the debtor. This section establishes only the baseline rights of the secured party *vis-a-vis the debtor*—the secured party is entitled to enforce and collect after default or earlier if so agreed.

7. **Deposit Account Collateral.** Subsections (a)(4) and (5) set forth the self-help remedy for a secured party whose collateral is a deposit account. Subsection (a)(4) addresses the rights of a secured party that is the bank with which the deposit account is maintained. That secured party automatically has control of the deposit account under Section 9–104(a)(1). After default, and otherwise if so agreed, the bank/secured party may apply the funds on deposit to the secured obligation.

If a security interest of a third party is perfected by control (Section 9–104(a)(2) or (a)(3)), then after default, and otherwise if so agreed, the secured party may instruct the bank to pay out the funds in the account. If the third party has control under Section 9–104(a)(3), the depositary institution is obliged to obey the instruction because the secured party is its customer. See Section 4–401. If the third party has control under Section 9–104(a)(2), the control agreement determines the depositary institution's obligation to obey.

If a security interest in a deposit account is unperfected, or is perfected by filing by virtue of the proceeds rules of Section 9–315, the depositary institution ordinarily owes no obligation to obey the secured party's instructions. See Section 9–341. To reach the funds without the debtor's cooperation, the secured party must use an available judicial procedure.

8. **Rights Against Mortgagor of Real Property.** Subsection (b) addresses the situation in which the collateral consists of a mortgage note (or other obligation secured by a mortgage on real property). After the

debtor's (mortgagee's) default, the secured party (assignee) may wish to proceed with a nonjudicial foreclosure of the mortgage securing the note but may be unable to do so because it has not become the assignee of record. The assignee/secured party may not have taken a recordable assignment at the commencement of the transaction (perhaps the mortgage note in question was one of hundreds assigned to the secured party as collateral). Having defaulted, the mortgagee may be unwilling to sign a recordable assignment. This section enables the secured party (assignee) to become the assignee of record by recording in the applicable real-property records the security agreement and an affidavit certifying default. Of course, the secured party's rights derive from those of its debtor. Subsection (b) would not entitle the secured party to proceed with a foreclosure unless the mortgagor also were in default or the debtor (mortgagee) otherwise enjoyed the right to foreclose.

9.   **Commercial Reasonableness.** Subsection (c) provides that the secured party's collection and enforcement rights under subsection (a) must be exercised in a commercially reasonable manner. These rights include the right to settle and compromise claims against the account debtor. The secured party's failure to observe the standard of commercial reasonableness could render it liable to an aggrieved person under Section 9–625, and the secured party's recovery of a deficiency would be subject to Section 9–626. Subsection (c) does not apply if, as is characteristic of most sales of accounts, chattel paper, payment intangibles, and promissory notes, the secured party (buyer) has no right of recourse against the debtor (seller) or a secondary obligor. However, if the secured party does have a right of recourse, the commercial-reasonableness standard applies to collection and enforcement even though the assignment to the secured party was a "true" sale. The obligation to proceed in a commercially reasonable manner arises because the collection process affects the extent of the seller's recourse liability, not because the seller retains an interest in the sold collateral (the seller does not). Concerning classification of a transaction, see Section 9–109, Comment 4.

10.   **Attorney's Fees and Legal Expenses.** The phrase "reasonable attorney's fees and legal expenses," which appears in subsection (d), includes only those fees and expenses incurred in proceeding against account debtors or other third parties. The secured party's right to recover these expenses from the collections arises automatically under this section. The secured party also may incur other attorney's fees and legal expenses in proceeding against the debtor or obligor. Whether the secured party has a right to recover those fees and expenses depends on whether the debtor or obligor has agreed to pay them, as is the case with respect to attorney's fees and legal expenses under Sections 9–608(a)(1)(A) and 9–615(a)(1). The parties also may agree to allocate a portion of the secured party's overhead to collection and enforcement under subsection (d) or Section 9–608(a).

As amended in 2000.

§ 9–608.   Application of Proceeds of Collection or Enforcement; Liability for Deficiency and Right to Surplus.

(a)   **[Application of proceeds, surplus, and deficiency if obligation secured.]** If a security interest or agricultural lien secures payment or performance of an obligation, the following rules apply:

(1)   A secured party shall apply or pay over for application the cash proceeds of collection or enforcement under Section 9–607 in the following order to:

(A)   the reasonable expenses of collection and enforcement and, to the extent provided for by agreement and not prohibited by law, reasonable attorney's fees and legal expenses incurred by the secured party;

(B)   the satisfaction of obligations secured by the security interest or agricultural lien under which the collection or enforcement is made; and

(C)   the satisfaction of obligations secured by any subordinate security interest in or other lien on the collateral subject to the security interest or agricultural lien under which the collection or enforcement is made if the secured party receives an authenticated demand for proceeds before distribution of the proceeds is completed.

(2)   If requested by a secured party, a holder of a subordinate security interest or other lien shall furnish reasonable proof of the interest or lien within a reasonable time. Unless the holder complies, the secured party need not comply with the holder's demand under paragraph (1)(C).

(3)   A secured party need not apply or pay over for application noncash proceeds of collection and enforcement under Section 9–607 unless the failure to do so would be commercially unreasonable.

A secured party that applies or pays over for application noncash proceeds shall do so in a commercially reasonable manner.

(4)   A secured party shall account to and pay a debtor for any surplus, and the obligor is liable for any deficiency.

(b)   **[No surplus or deficiency in sales of certain rights to payment.]** If the underlying transaction is a sale of accounts, chattel paper, payment intangibles, or promissory notes, the debtor is not entitled to any surplus, and the obligor is not liable for any deficiency.

As amended in 2000.

Official Comment

1.   **Source.** Subsection (a) is new; subsection (b) derives from former Section 9–502(2).

2.   **Modifications of Prior Law.** Subsections (a) and (b) modify former Section 9–502(2) by explicitly providing for the application of proceeds recovered by the secured party in substantially the same manner as provided in Section 9–615(a) and (e) for dispositions of collateral.

3.   **Surplus and Deficiency.** Subsections (a)(4) and (b) omit, as unnecessary, the references contained in former Section 9–502(2) to agreements varying the baseline rules on surplus and deficiency. The parties are always free to agree that an obligor will not be liable for a deficiency, even if the collateral secures an obligation, and that an obligor is liable for a deficiency, even if the transaction is a sale of receivables. For parallel provisions, see Section 9–615(d) and (e).

4.   **Noncash Proceeds.** Subsection (a)(3) addresses the situation in which an enforcing secured party receives noncash proceeds.

> **Example:** An enforcing secured party receives a promissory note from an account debtor who is unable to pay an account when it is due. The secured party accepts the note in exchange for extending the date on which the account debtor's obligation is due. The secured party may wish to credit its debtor (the assignor) with the principal amount of the note upon receipt of the note, but probably will prefer to credit the debtor only as and when the note is paid.

Under subsection (a)(3), the secured party is under no duty to apply the note or its value to the outstanding obligation unless its failure to do so would be commercially unreasonable. If the secured party does apply the note to the outstanding obligation, however, it must do so in a commercially reasonable manner. The parties may provide for the method of application of noncash proceeds by agreement, if the method is not manifestly unreasonable. See Section 9–603. This section does not explain when the failure to apply noncash proceeds would be commercially unreasonable; it leaves that determination to case-by-case adjudication. In the example, the secured party appears to have accepted the account debtor's note in order to increase the likelihood of payment and decrease the likelihood that the account debtor would dispute its obligation. Under these circumstances, it may well be commercially reasonable for the secured party to credit its debtor's obligations only as and when cash proceeds are collected from the account debtor, especially given the uncertainty that attends the account debtor's eventual payment. For an example of a secured party's receipt of noncash proceeds in which it may well be commercially unreasonable for the secured party to delay crediting its debtor's obligations with the value of noncash proceeds, see Section 9–615, Comment 3.

When the secured party is not required to "apply or pay over for application noncash proceeds," the proceeds nonetheless remain collateral subject to this Article. If the secured party were to dispose of them, for example, appropriate notification would be required (see Section 9–611), and the disposition would be subject to the standards provided in this Part (see Section 9–610). Moreover, a secured party in possession of the noncash proceeds would have the duties specified in Section 9–207.

5.   **No Effect on Priority of Senior Security Interest.** The application of proceeds required by subsection (a) does not affect the priority of a security interest in collateral which is senior to the interest of the secured party who is collecting or enforcing collateral under Section 9–607. Although subsection (a) imposes a duty to apply proceeds to the enforcing secured party's expenses and to the satisfaction of the secured obligations owed to it and to subordinate secured parties, that duty applies only among the enforcing secured party and those persons. Concerning the priority of a junior secured party who collects and enforces collateral, see Section 9–607, Comment 5.

§ 9–609.   Secured Party's Right to Take Possession After Default.

(a)   **[Possession; rendering equipment unusable; disposition on debtor's premises.]** After default, a secured party:

(1)   may take possession of the collateral; and

(2)   without removal, may render equipment unusable and dispose of collateral on a debtor's premises under Section 9–610.

(b)   **[Judicial and nonjudicial process.]** A secured party may proceed under subsection (a):

(1)   pursuant to judicial process; or

(2)   without judicial process, if it proceeds without breach of the peace.

(c)   **[Assembly of collateral.]** If so agreed, and in any event after default, a secured party may require the debtor to assemble the collateral and make it available to the secured party at a place to be designated by the secured party which is reasonably convenient to both parties.

Official Comment

1.   **Source.** Former Section 9–503.

2.   **Secured Party's Right to Possession.** This section follows former Section 9–503 and earlier uniform legislation. It provides that the secured party is entitled to take possession of collateral after default.

3.   **Judicial Process; Breach of Peace.** Subsection (b) permits a secured party to proceed under this section without judicial process if it does so "without breach of the peace." Although former Section 9–503 placed the same condition on a secured party's right to take possession of collateral, subsection (b) extends the condition to the right provided in subsection (a)(2) as well. Like former Section 9–503, this section does not define or explain the conduct that will constitute a breach of the peace, leaving that matter for continuing development by the courts. In considering whether a secured party has engaged in a breach of the peace, however, courts should hold the secured party responsible for the actions of others taken on the secured party's behalf, including independent contractors engaged by the secured party to take possession of collateral.

This section does not authorize a secured party who repossesses without judicial process to utilize the assistance of a law-enforcement officer. A number of cases have held that a repossessing secured party's use of a law-enforcement officer without benefit of judicial process constituted a failure to comply with former Section 9–503.

4.   **Damages for Breach of Peace.** Concerning damages that may be recovered based on a secured party's breach of the peace in connection with taking possession of collateral, see Section 9–625, Comment 3.

5.   **Multiple Secured Parties.** More than one secured party may be entitled to take possession of collateral under this section. Conflicting rights to possession among secured parties are resolved by the priority rules of this Article. Thus, a senior secured party is entitled to possession as against a junior claimant. Non-UCC law governs whether a junior secured party in possession of collateral is liable to the senior in conversion. Normally, a junior who refuses to relinquish possession of collateral upon the demand of a secured party having a superior possessory right to the collateral would be liable in conversion.

6.   **Secured Party's Right to Disable and Dispose of Equipment on Debtor's Premises.** In the case of some collateral, such as heavy equipment, the physical removal from the debtor's plant and the storage of the collateral pending disposition may be impractical or unduly expensive. This section follows former Section 9–503 by providing that, in lieu of removal, the secured party may render equipment unusable or may dispose of collateral on the debtor's premises. Unlike former Section 9–503, however, this section explicitly conditions these rights on the debtor's default. Of course, this section does not validate unreasonable action by a secured party. Under Section 9–610, all aspects of a disposition must be commercially reasonable.

7.   **Debtor's Agreement to Assemble Collateral.** This section follows former Section 9–503 also by validating a debtor's agreement to assemble collateral and make it available to a secured party at a place that the secured party designates. Similar to the treatment of agreements to permit collection prior to default under Section 9–607 and former 9–502, however, this section validates these agreements whether or not they are conditioned on the debtor's default. For example, a debtor might agree to make available to a secured party, from time to time, any instruments or negotiable documents that the debtor receives on account of collateral. A court should not infer

from this section's validation that a debtor's agreement to assemble and make available collateral would not be enforceable under other applicable law.

8. **Agreed Standards.** Subject to the limitation imposed by Section 9–603(b), this section's provisions concerning agreements to assemble and make available collateral and a secured party's right to disable equipment and dispose of collateral on a debtor's premises are likely topics for agreement on standards as contemplated by Section 9–603.

§ 9–610. Disposition of Collateral After Default.

(a) **[Disposition after default.]** After default, a secured party may sell, lease, license, or otherwise dispose of any or all of the collateral in its present condition or following any commercially reasonable preparation or processing.

(b) **[Commercially reasonable disposition.]** Every aspect of a disposition of collateral, including the method, manner, time, place, and other terms, must be commercially reasonable. If commercially reasonable, a secured party may dispose of collateral by public or private proceedings, by one or more contracts, as a unit or in parcels, and at any time and place and on any terms.

(c) **[Purchase by secured party.]** A secured party may purchase collateral:

(1) at a public disposition; or

(2) at a private disposition only if the collateral is of a kind that is customarily sold on a recognized market or the subject of widely distributed standard price quotations.

(d) **[Warranties on disposition.]** A contract for sale, lease, license, or other disposition includes the warranties relating to title, possession, quiet enjoyment, and the like which by operation of law accompany a voluntary disposition of property of the kind subject to the contract.

(e) **[Disclaimer of warranties.]** A secured party may disclaim or modify warranties under subsection (d):

(1) in a manner that would be effective to disclaim or modify the warranties in a voluntary disposition of property of the kind subject to the contract of disposition; or

(2) by communicating to the purchaser a record evidencing the contract for disposition and including an express disclaimer or modification of the warranties.

(f) **[Record sufficient to disclaim warranties.]** A record is sufficient to disclaim warranties under subsection (e) if it indicates "There is no warranty relating to title, possession, quiet enjoyment, or the like in this disposition" or uses words of similar import.

Official Comment

1. **Source.** Former Section 9–504(1), (3)

2. **Commercially Reasonable Dispositions.** Subsection (a) follows former Section 9–504 by permitting a secured party to dispose of collateral in a commercially reasonable manner following a default. Although subsection (b) permits both public and private dispositions, including public and private dispositions conducted over the Internet, "every aspect of a disposition . . . must be commercially reasonable." This section encourages private dispositions on the assumption that they frequently will result in higher realization on collateral for the benefit of all concerned. Subsection (a) does not restrict dispositions to sales; collateral may be sold, leased, licensed, or otherwise disposed. Section 9–627 provides guidance for determining the circumstances under which a disposition is "commercially reasonable."

3. **Time of Disposition.** This Article does not specify a period within which a secured party must dispose of collateral. This is consistent with this Article's policy to encourage private dispositions through regular commercial channels. It may, for example, be prudent not to dispose of goods when the market has collapsed. Or, it might be more appropriate to sell a large inventory in parcels over a period of time instead of in bulk. Of course, under subsection (b) every aspect of a disposition of collateral must be commercially reasonable. This requirement explicitly includes the "method, manner, time, place and other terms." For example, if a secured party does not proceed under Section 9–620 and holds collateral for a long period of time without disposing of it, and if there is

no good reason for not making a prompt disposition, the secured party may be determined not to have acted in a "commercially reasonable" manner. See also Section 1–203* (general obligation of good faith).

4.   **Pre-Disposition Preparation and Processing.** Former Section 9–504(1) appeared to give the secured party the choice of disposing of collateral either "in its then condition or following any commercially reasonable preparation or processing." Some courts held that the "commercially reasonable" standard of former Section 9–504(3) nevertheless could impose an affirmative duty on the secured party to process or prepare the collateral prior to disposition. Subsection (a) retains the substance of the quoted language. Although courts should not be quick to impose a duty of preparation or processing on the secured party, subsection (a) does not grant the secured party the right to dispose of the collateral "in its then condition" under *all* circumstances. A secured party may not dispose of collateral "in its then condition" when, taking into account the costs and probable benefits of preparation or processing and the fact that the secured party would be advancing the costs at its risk, it would be commercially unreasonable to dispose of the collateral in that condition.

5.   **Disposition by Junior Secured Party.** Disposition rights under subsection (a) are not limited to first-priority security interests. Rather, any secured party as to whom there has been a default enjoys the right to dispose of collateral under this subsection. The exercise of this right by a secured party whose security interest is subordinate to that of another secured party does not of itself constitute a conversion or otherwise give rise to liability in favor of the holder of the senior security interest. Section 9–615 addresses application of the proceeds of a disposition by a junior secured party. Under Section 9–615(a), a junior secured party owes no obligation to apply the proceeds of disposition to the satisfaction of obligations secured by a senior security interest. Section 9–615(g) builds on this general rule by protecting certain juniors from claims of a senior concerning cash proceeds of the disposition. Even if a senior were to have a non-Article 9 claim to proceeds of a junior's disposition, Section 9–615(g) would protect a junior that acts in good faith and without knowledge that its actions violate the rights of a senior party. Because the disposition by a junior would not cut off a senior's security interest or other lien (see Section 9–617), in many (probably most) cases the junior's receipt of the cash proceeds would not violate the rights of the senior.

The holder of a senior security interest is entitled, by virtue of its priority, to take possession of collateral from the junior secured party and conduct its own disposition, provided that the senior enjoys the right to take possession of the collateral from the debtor. See Section 9–609. The holder of a junior security interest normally must notify the senior secured party of an impending disposition. See Section 9–611. Regardless of whether the senior receives a notification from the junior, the junior's disposition does not of itself discharge the senior's security interest. See Section 9–617. Unless the senior secured party has authorized the disposition free and clear of its security interest, the senior's security interest ordinarily will survive the disposition by the junior and continue under Section 9–315(a). If the senior enjoys the right to repossess the collateral from the debtor, the senior likewise may recover the collateral from the transferee.

When a secured party's collateral is encumbered by another security interest or other lien, one of the claimants may seek to invoke the equitable doctrine of marshaling. As explained by the Supreme Court, that doctrine "rests upon the principle that a creditor having two funds to satisfy his debt, may not by his application of them to his demand, defeat another creditor, who may resort to only one of the funds." *Meyer v. United States*, 375 U.S. 233, 236 (1963), quoting *Sowell v. Federal Reserve Bank*, 268 U.S. 449, 456–57 (1925). The purpose of the doctrine is "to prevent the arbitrary action of a senior lienor from destroying the rights of a junior lienor or a creditor having less security." Id. at 237. Because it is an equitable doctrine, marshaling "is applied only when it can be equitably fashioned as to all of the parties" having an interest in the property. Id. This Article leaves courts free to determine whether marshaling is appropriate in any given case. See Section 1–103.

6.   **Security Interests of Equal Rank.** Sometimes two security interests enjoy the same priority. This situation may arise by contract, e.g., pursuant to "equal and ratable" provisions in indentures, or by operation of law. See Section 9–328(6). This Article treats a security interest having equal priority like a senior security interest in many respects. Assume, for example, that SP–X and SP–Y enjoy equal priority, SP–W is senior to them, and SP–Z is junior. If SP–X disposes of the collateral under this section, then (i) SP–W's and SP–Y's security interests survive the disposition but SP–Z's does not, see Section 9–617, and (ii) neither SP–W nor SP–Y is entitled to receive a distribution of proceeds, but SP–Z is. See Section 9–615(a)(3).

When one considers the ability to obtain possession of the collateral, a secured party with equal priority is unlike a senior secured party. As the senior secured party, SP–W should enjoy the right to possession as against SP–X. See Section 9–609, Comment 5. If SP–W takes possession and disposes of the collateral under this section,

---

*   *Referring to unrevised Article 1 (Appendix A).*

908

it is entitled to apply the proceeds to satisfy its secured claim. SP–Y, however, should not have such a right to take possession from SP–X; otherwise, once SP–Y took possession from SP–X, SP–X would have the right to get possession from SP–Y, which would be obligated to redeliver possession to SP–X, and so on. Resolution of this problem is left to the parties and, if necessary, the courts.

7. **Public vs. Private Dispositions.** This Part maintains two distinctions between "public" and other dispositions: (i) the secured party may buy at the former, but normally not at the latter (Section 9–610(c)), and (ii) the debtor is entitled to notification of "the time and place of a public disposition" and notification of "the time after which" a private disposition or other intended disposition is to be made (Section 9–613(1)(E)). It does not retain the distinction under former Section 9–504(4), under which transferees in a noncomplying public disposition could lose protection more easily than transferees in other noncomplying dispositions. Instead, Section 9–617(b) adopts a unitary standard. Although the term is not defined, as used in this Article, a "public disposition" is one at which the price is determined after the public has had a meaningful opportunity for competitive bidding. "Meaningful opportunity" is meant to imply that some form of advertisement or public notice must precede the sale (or other disposition) and that the public must have access to the sale (disposition).

A secured party's purchase of collateral at its own private disposition is equivalent to a "strict foreclosure" and is governed by Sections 9–620, 9–621, and 9–622. The provisions of these sections can be waived only to the extent provided in Section 9–624(b). See Section 9–602.

8. **Investment Property.** Dispositions of investment property may be regulated by the federal securities laws. Although a "public" disposition of securities under this Article may implicate the registration requirements of the Securities Act of 1933, it need not do so. A disposition that qualifies for a "private placement" exemption under the Securities Act of 1933 nevertheless may constitute a "public" disposition within the meaning of this section. Moreover, the "commercially reasonable" requirements of subsection (b) need not prevent a secured party from conducting a foreclosure sale without the issuer's compliance with federal registration requirements.

9. **"Recognized Market."** A "recognized market," as used in subsection (c) and Section 9–611(d), is one in which the items sold are fungible and prices are not subject to individual negotiation. For example, the New York Stock Exchange is a recognized market. A market in which prices are individually negotiated or the items are not fungible is not a recognized market, even if the items are the subject of widely disseminated price guides or are disposed of through dealer auctions.

10. **Relevance of Price.** While not itself sufficient to establish a violation of this Part, a low price suggests that a court should scrutinize carefully all aspects of a disposition to ensure that each aspect was commercially reasonable. Note also that even if the disposition is commercially reasonable, Section 9–615(f) provides a special method for calculating a deficiency or surplus if (i) the transferee in the disposition is the secured party, a person related to the secured party, or a secondary obligor, and (ii) the amount of proceeds of the disposition is significantly below the range of proceeds that a complying disposition to a person other than the secured party, a person related to the secured party, or a secondary obligor would have brought.

11. **Warranties.** Subsection (d) affords the transferee in a disposition under this section the benefit of any title, possession, quiet enjoyment, and similar warranties that would have accompanied the disposition by operation of non-Article 9 law had the disposition been conducted under other circumstances. For example, the Article 2 warranty of title would apply to a sale of goods, the analogous warranties of Article 2A would apply to a lease of goods, and any common-law warranties of title would apply to dispositions of other types of collateral. See, e.g., Restatement (2d), Contracts § 333 (warranties of assignor).

Subsection (e) explicitly provides that these warranties can be disclaimed either under other applicable law or by communicating a record containing an express disclaimer. The record need not be written, but an oral communication would not be sufficient. See Section 9–102 (definition of "record"). Subsection (f) provides a sample of wording that will effectively exclude the warranties in a disposition under this section, whether or not the exclusion would be effective under non-Article 9 law.

The warranties incorporated by subsection (d) are those relating to "title, possession, quiet enjoyment, and the like." Depending on the circumstances, a disposition under this section also may give rise to other statutory or implied warranties, e.g., warranties of quality or fitness for purpose. Law other than this Article determines whether such other warranties apply to a disposition under this section. Other law also determines issues relating to disclaimer of such warranties. For example, a foreclosure sale of a car by a car dealer could give rise to an implied warranty of merchantability (Section 2–314) unless effectively disclaimed or modified (Section 2–316).

This section's approach to these warranties conflicts with the former Comment to Section 2–312. This Article rejects the baseline assumption that commercially reasonable dispositions under this section are out of the ordinary commercial course or peculiar. The Comment to Section 2–312 has been revised accordingly.

As amended in 2010.

§ 9–611.   Notification Before Disposition of Collateral.

(a)   **["Notification date."]** In this section, "notification date" means the earlier of the date on which:

(1)   a secured party sends to the debtor and any secondary obligor an authenticated notification of disposition; or

(2)   the debtor and any secondary obligor waive the right to notification.

(b)   **[Notification of disposition required.]** Except as otherwise provided in subsection (d), a secured party that disposes of collateral under Section 9–610 shall send to the persons specified in subsection (c) a reasonable authenticated notification of disposition.

(c)   **[Persons to be notified.]** To comply with subsection (b), the secured party shall send an authenticated notification of disposition to:

(1)   the debtor;

(2)   any secondary obligor; and

(3)   if the collateral is other than consumer goods:

(A)   any other person from which the secured party has received, before the notification date, an authenticated notification of a claim of an interest in the collateral;

(B)   any other secured party or lienholder that, 10 days before the notification date, held a security interest in or other lien on the collateral perfected by the filing of a financing statement that:

(i)   identified the collateral;

(ii)   was indexed under the debtor's name as of that date; and

(iii)   was filed in the office in which to file a financing statement against the debtor covering the collateral as of that date; and

(C)   any other secured party that, 10 days before the notification date, held a security interest in the collateral perfected by compliance with a statute, regulation, or treaty described in Section 9–311(a).

(d)   **[Subsection (b) inapplicable: perishable collateral; recognized market.]** Subsection (b) does not apply if the collateral is perishable or threatens to decline speedily in value or is of a type customarily sold on a recognized market.

(e)   **[Compliance with subsection (c)(3)(B).]** A secured party complies with the requirement for notification prescribed by subsection (c)(3)(B) if:

(1)   not later than 20 days or earlier than 30 days before the notification date, the secured party requests, in a commercially reasonable manner, information concerning financing statements indexed under the debtor's name in the office indicated in subsection (c)(3)(B); and

(2)   before the notification date, the secured party:

(A)   did not receive a response to the request for information; or

(B)   received a response to the request for information and sent an authenticated notification of disposition to each secured party or other lienholder named in that response whose financing statement covered the collateral.

Official Comment

1.   **Source.** Former Section 9–504(3).

2.   **Reasonable Notification.** This section requires a secured party who wishes to dispose of collateral under Section 9–610 to send "a reasonable authenticated notification of disposition" to specified interested persons, subject to certain exceptions. The notification must be reasonable as to the manner in which it is sent, its timeliness (i.e., a reasonable time before the disposition is to take place), and its content. See Sections 9–612 (timeliness of notification), 9–613 (contents of notification generally), 9–614 (contents of notification in consumer-goods transactions).

3.   **Notification to Debtors and Secondary Obligors.** This section imposes a duty to send notification of a disposition not only to the debtor but also to any secondary obligor. Subsections (b) and (c) resolve an uncertainty under former Article 9 by providing that secondary obligors (sureties) are entitled to receive notification of an intended disposition of collateral, regardless of who created the security interest in the collateral. If the surety created the security interest, it would be the debtor. If it did not, it would be a secondary obligor. (This Article also resolves the question of the secondary obligor's ability to waive, pre-default, the right to notification—waiver generally is not permitted. See Section 9–602.) Section 9–605 relieves a secured party from any duty to send notification to a debtor or secondary obligor unknown to the secured party.

Under subsection (b), the principal obligor (borrower) is not always entitled to notification of disposition.

Example: Behnfeldt borrows on an unsecured basis, and Bruno grants a security interest in her car to secure the debt. Behnfeldt is a primary obligor, not a secondary obligor. As such, she is not entitled to notification of disposition under this section.

4.   **Notification to Other Secured Parties.** Prior to the 1972 amendments to Article 9, former Section 9–504(3) required the enforcing secured party to send reasonable notification of the disposition:

except in the case of consumer goods to any other person who has a security interest in the collateral and who has duly filed a financing statement indexed in the name of the debtor in this State or who is known by the secured party to have a security interest in the collateral.

The 1972 amendments eliminated the duty to give notice to secured parties other than those from whom the foreclosing secured party had received written notice of a claim of an interest in the collateral.

Many of the problems arising from dispositions of collateral encumbered by multiple security interests can be ameliorated or solved by informing all secured parties of an intended disposition and affording them the opportunity to work with one another. To this end, subsection (c)(3)(B) expands the duties of the foreclosing secured party to include the duty to notify (and the corresponding burden of searching the files to discover) certain competing secured parties. The subsection imposes a search burden that in some cases may be greater than the pre-1972 burden on foreclosing secured parties but certainly is more modest than that faced by a new secured lender.

To determine who is entitled to notification, the foreclosing secured party must determine the proper office for filing a financing statement as of a particular date, measured by reference to the "notification date," as defined in subsection (a). This determination requires reference to the choice-of-law provisions of Part 3. The secured party must ascertain whether any financing statements covering the collateral and indexed under the debtor's name, as the name existed as of that date, in fact were filed in that office. The foreclosing secured party generally need not notify secured parties whose effective financing statements have become more difficult to locate because of changes in the location of the debtor, proceeds rules, or changes in the name that is sufficient as the name of the debtor under Section 9–503(a).

Under subsection (c)(3)(C), the secured party also must notify a secured party who has perfected a security interest by complying with a statute or treaty described in Section 9–311(a), such as a certificate-of-title statute.

Subsection (e) provides a "safe harbor" that takes into account the delays that may be attendant to receiving information from the public filing offices. It provides, generally, that the secured party will be deemed to have satisfied its notification duty under subsection (c)(3)(B) if it requests a search from the proper office at least 20 but not more than 30 days before sending notification to the debtor and if it also sends a notification to all secured parties (and other lienholders) reflected on the search report. The secured party's duty under subsection (c)(3)(B) also will be satisfied if the secured party requests but does not receive a search report before the notification is sent to the debtor. Thus, if subsection (e) applies, a secured party who is entitled to notification under subsection (c)(3)(B) has no remedy against a foreclosing secured party who does not send the notification. The foreclosing secured party has complied with the notification requirement. Subsection (e) has no effect on the requirements of the other paragraphs of subsection (c). For example, if the foreclosing secured party received a notification from the holder of a conflicting security interest in accordance with subsection (c)(3)(A) but failed to send to the holder a notification of the disposition, the holder of the conflicting security interest would have the right to recover any loss under Section 9–625(b).

5. **Authentication Requirement.** Subsections (b) and (c) explicitly provide that a notification of disposition must be "authenticated." Some cases read former Section 9–504(3) as validating oral notification.

6. **Second Try.** This Article leaves to judicial resolution, based upon the facts of each case, the question whether the requirement of "reasonable notification" requires a "second try," i.e., whether a secured party who sends notification and learns that the debtor did not receive it must attempt to locate the debtor and send another notification.

7. **Recognized Market; Perishable Collateral.** New subsection (d) makes it clear that there is no obligation to give notification of a disposition in the case of perishable collateral or collateral customarily sold on a recognized market (e.g., marketable securities). Former Section 9–504(3) might be read (incorrectly) to relieve the secured party from its duty to notify a debtor but not from its duty to notify other secured parties in connection with dispositions of such collateral.

8. **Failure to Conduct Notified Disposition.** Nothing in this Article prevents a secured party from electing not to conduct a disposition after sending a notification. Nor does this Article prevent a secured party from electing to send a revised notification if its plans for disposition change. This assumes, however, that the secured party acts in good faith, the revised notification is reasonable, and the revised plan for disposition and any attendant delay are commercially reasonable.

9. **Waiver.** A debtor or secondary obligor may waive the right to notification under this section only by a post-default authenticated agreement. See Section 9–624(a).

10. **Other Law.** Other State or federal law may contain requirements concerning notification of a disposition of property by a secured party. For example, federal law imposes notification requirements with respect to the enforcement of mortgages on federally documented vessels. Principles of statutory interpretation and, in the context of federal law, supremacy and preemption determine whether and to what extent law other than this Article supplements, displaces, or is displaced by this Article. See Sections 1–103, 1–104, 9–109(c)(1).

As amended in 2010.

§ 9–612. Timeliness of Notification Before Disposition of Collateral.

(a) **[Reasonable time is question of fact.]** Except as otherwise provided in subsection (b), whether a notification is sent within a reasonable time is a question of fact.

(b) **[10-day period sufficient in non-consumer transaction.]** In a transaction other than a consumer transaction, a notification of disposition sent after default and 10 days or more before the earliest time of disposition set forth in the notification is sent within a reasonable time before the disposition.

Official Comment

1. **Source.** New.

2. **Reasonable Notification.** Section 9–611(b) requires the secured party to send a "reasonable authenticated notification." Under that section, as under former Section 9–504(3), one aspect of a reasonable notification is its timeliness. This generally means that the notification must be sent at a reasonable time in advance of the date of a public disposition or the date after which a private disposition is to be made. A notification that is sent so near to the disposition date that a notified person could not be expected to act on or take account of the notification would be unreasonable.

3. **Timeliness of Notification: Safe Harbor.** The 10-day notice period in subsection (b) is intended to be a "safe harbor" and not a minimum requirement. To qualify for the "safe harbor" the notification must be sent after default. A notification also must be sent in a commercially reasonable manner. See Section 9–611(b) ("reasonable authenticated notification"). These requirements prevent a secured party from taking advantage of the "safe harbor" by, for example, giving the debtor a notification at the time of the original extension of credit or sending the notice by surface mail to a debtor overseas.

§ 9–613. Contents and Form of Notification Before Disposition of Collateral: General.

Except in a consumer-goods transaction, the following rules apply:

(1) The contents of a notification of disposition are sufficient if the notification:

(A) describes the debtor and the secured party;

(B) describes the collateral that is the subject of the intended disposition;

(C) states the method of intended disposition;

(D) states that the debtor is entitled to an accounting of the unpaid indebtedness and states the charge, if any, for an accounting; and

(E) states the time and place of a public disposition or the time after which any other disposition is to be made.

(2) Whether the contents of a notification that lacks any of the information specified in paragraph (1) are nevertheless sufficient is a question of fact.

(3) The contents of a notification providing substantially the information specified in paragraph (1) are sufficient, even if the notification includes:

(A) information not specified by that paragraph; or

(B) minor errors that are not seriously misleading.

(4) A particular phrasing of the notification is not required.

(5) The following form of notification and the form appearing in Section 9–614(3), when completed, each provides sufficient information:

NOTIFICATION OF DISPOSITION OF COLLATERAL

To: [*Name of debtor, obligor, or other person to which the notification is sent*]

From: [*Name, address, and telephone number of secured party*]

Name of Debtor(s): [*Include only if debtor(s) are not an addressee*]

[*For a public disposition:*]

We will sell [or lease or license, *as applicable*] the [*describe collateral*] [to the highest qualified bidder] in public as follows:

Day and Date: _____

Time: _____

Place: _____

[*For a private disposition:*]

We will sell [or lease or license, *as applicable*] the [*describe collateral*] privately sometime after [*day and date*].

You are entitled to an accounting of the unpaid indebtedness secured by the property that we intend to sell [or lease or license, *as applicable*] [for a charge of $_____]. You may request an accounting by calling us at [*telephone number*]

[End of Form]

As amended in 2000.

Official Comment

1. **Source.** New.

2. **Contents of Notification.** To comply with the "reasonable authenticated notification" requirement of Section 9–611(b), the contents of a notification must be reasonable. Except in a consumer-goods transaction, the contents of a notification that includes the information set forth in paragraph (1) are sufficient as a matter of law, unless the parties agree otherwise. (The reference to "time" of disposition means here, as it did in former Section 9–504(3), not only the hour of the day but also the date.) Although a secured party may choose to include additional information concerning the transaction or the debtor's rights and obligations, no additional information is required unless the parties agree otherwise. A notification that lacks some of the information set forth in paragraph (1) nevertheless may be sufficient if found to be reasonable by the trier of fact, under paragraph (2). A properly completed sample form of notification in paragraph (5) or in Section 9–614(a)(3) is an example of a notification that would contain the information set forth in paragraph (1). Under paragraph (4), however, no particular phrasing of the notification is required.

This section applies to a notification of a public disposition conducted electronically. A notification of an electronic disposition satisfies paragraph (1)(E) if it states the time when the disposition is scheduled to begin and states the electronic location. For example, under the technology current in 2010, the Uniform Resource Locator (URL) or other Internet address where the site of the public disposition can be accessed suffices as an electronic location.

As amended in 2010.

§ 9–614. Contents and Form of Notification Before Disposition of Collateral: Consumer-Goods Transaction.

In a consumer-goods transaction, the following rules apply:

(1) A notification of disposition must provide the following information:

(A) the information specified in Section 9–613(1);

(B) a description of any liability for a deficiency of the person to which the notification is sent;

(C) a telephone number from which the amount that must be paid to the secured party to redeem the collateral under Section 9–623 is available; and

(D) a telephone number or mailing address from which additional information concerning the disposition and the obligation secured is available.

(2) A particular phrasing of the notification is not required.

(3) The following form of notification, when completed, provides sufficient information:

[*Name and address of secured party*]

[*Date*]

NOTICE OF OUR PLAN TO SELL PROPERTY

[*Name and address of any obligor who is also a debtor*]

Subject: [*Identification of Transaction*]

We have your [*describe collateral*], because you broke promises in our agreement.

[*For a public disposition:*]

We will sell [*describe collateral*] at public sale. A sale could include a lease or license. The sale will be held as follows:

Date: _____

Time: _____

Place: _____

You may attend the sale and bring bidders if you want.

[*For a private disposition:*]

We will sell [*describe collateral*] at private sale sometime after [*date*]. A sale could include a lease or license.

The money that we get from the sale (after paying our costs) will reduce the amount you owe. If we get less money than you owe, you [*will or will not, as applicable*] still owe us the difference. If we get more money than you owe, you will get the extra money, unless we must pay it to someone else.

You can get the property back at any time before we sell it by paying us the full amount you owe (not just the past due payments), including our expenses. To learn the exact amount you must pay, call us at [*telephone number*].

If you want us to explain to you in writing how we have figured the amount that you owe us, you may call us at [*telephone number*] [or write us at [*secured party's address*]] and request a written explanation. [We will charge you $ for the explanation if we sent you another written explanation of the amount you owe us within the last six months.]

If you need more information about the sale call us at [*telephone number*] [or write us at [*secured party's address*]].

We are sending this notice to the following other people who have an interest in [*describe collateral*] or who owe money under your agreement:

[*Names of all other debtors and obligors, if any*]

[End of Form]

(4)   A notification in the form of paragraph (3) is sufficient, even if additional information appears at the end of the form.

(5)   A notification in the form of paragraph (3) is sufficient, even if it includes errors in information not required by paragraph (1), unless the error is misleading with respect to rights arising under this article.

(6)   If a notification under this section is not in the form of paragraph (3), law other than this article determines the effect of including information not required by paragraph (1).

Official Comment

1.   **Source.** New.

2.   **Notification in Consumer-Goods Transactions.** Paragraph (1) sets forth the information required for a reasonable notification in a consumer-goods transaction. A notification that lacks any of the information set forth in paragraph (1) is insufficient as a matter of law. Compare Section 9–613(2), under which the trier of fact may find a notification to be sufficient even if it lacks some information listed in paragraph (1) of that section.

3.   **Safe-Harbor Form of Notification; Errors in Information.** Although paragraph (2) provides that a particular phrasing of a notification is not required, paragraph (3) specifies a safe-harbor form that, when properly completed, satisfies paragraph (1). Paragraphs (4), (5), and (6) contain special rules applicable to erroneous and additional information. Under paragraph (4), a notification in the safe-harbor form specified in paragraph (3) is not rendered insufficient if it contains additional information at the end of the form. Paragraph (5) provides that non-misleading errors in information contained in a notification are permitted if the safe-harbor form is used *and if the errors are in information not required by paragraph (1)*. Finally, if a notification is in a form other than the paragraph (3) safe-harbor form, other law determines the effect of including in the notification information other than that required by paragraph (1).

§ 9–615.   Application of Proceeds of Disposition; Liability for Deficiency and Right to Surplus.

(a)   **[Application of proceeds.]** A secured party shall apply or pay over for application the cash proceeds of disposition under Section 9–610 in the following order to:

(1)   the reasonable expenses of retaking, holding, preparing for disposition, processing, and disposing, and, to the extent provided for by agreement and not prohibited by law, reasonable attorney's fees and legal expenses incurred by the secured party;

(2)   the satisfaction of obligations secured by the security interest or agricultural lien under which the disposition is made;

(3)   the satisfaction of obligations secured by any subordinate security interest in or other subordinate lien on the collateral if:

    (A)   the secured party receives from the holder of the subordinate security interest or other lien an authenticated demand for proceeds before distribution of the proceeds is completed; and

    (B)   in a case in which a consignor has an interest in the collateral, the subordinate security interest or other lien is senior to the interest of the consignor; and

(4)   a secured party that is a consignor of the collateral if the secured party receives from the consignor an authenticated demand for proceeds before distribution of the proceeds is completed.

(b)   **[Proof of subordinate interest.]** If requested by a secured party, a holder of a subordinate security interest or other lien shall furnish reasonable proof of the interest or lien within a reasonable time. Unless the holder does so, the secured party need not comply with the holder's demand under subsection (a)(3).

(c)   **[Application of noncash proceeds.]** A secured party need not apply or pay over for application noncash proceeds of disposition under Section 9–610 unless the failure to do so would be commercially unreasonable. A secured party that applies or pays over for application noncash proceeds shall do so in a commercially reasonable manner.

(d)   **[Surplus or deficiency if obligation secured.]** If the security interest under which a disposition is made secures payment or performance of an obligation, after making the payments and applications required by subsection (a) and permitted by subsection (c):

(1)   unless subsection (a)(4) requires the secured party to apply or pay over cash proceeds to a consignor, the secured party shall account to and pay a debtor for any surplus; and

(2)   the obligor is liable for any deficiency.

(e)   **[No surplus or deficiency in sales of certain rights to payment.]** If the underlying transaction is a sale of accounts, chattel paper, payment intangibles, or promissory notes:

(1)   the debtor is not entitled to any surplus; and

(2)   the obligor is not liable for any deficiency.

(f)   **[Calculation of surplus or deficiency in disposition to person related to secured party.]** The surplus or deficiency following a disposition is calculated based on the amount of proceeds that would have been realized in a disposition complying with this part to a transferee other than the secured party, a person related to the secured party, or a secondary obligor if:

(1)   the transferee in the disposition is the secured party, a person related to the secured party, or a secondary obligor; and

(2)   the amount of proceeds of the disposition is significantly below the range of proceeds that a complying disposition to a person other than the secured party, a person related to the secured party, or a secondary obligor would have brought.

(g)   **[Cash proceeds received by junior secured party.]** A secured party that receives cash proceeds of a disposition in good faith and without knowledge that the receipt violates the rights of the holder of a security interest or other lien that is not subordinate to the security interest or agricultural lien under which the disposition is made:

(1)   takes the cash proceeds free of the security interest or other lien;

916

(2)   is not obligated to apply the proceeds of the disposition to the satisfaction of obligations secured by the security interest or other lien; and

(3)   is not obligated to account to or pay the holder of the security interest or other lien for any surplus.

As amended in 2000.

Official Comment

1.   **Source.** Former Section 9–504(1), (2).

2.   **Application of Proceeds.** This section contains the rules governing application of proceeds and the debtor's liability for a deficiency following a disposition of collateral. Subsection (a) sets forth the basic order of application. The proceeds are applied first to the expenses of disposition, second to the obligation secured by the security interest that is being enforced, and third, in the specified circumstances, to interests that are subordinate to that security interest.

Subsections (a) and (d) also address the right of a consignor to receive proceeds of a disposition by a secured party whose interest is senior to that of the consignor. Subsection (a) requires the enforcing secured party to pay excess proceeds first to subordinate secured parties or lienholders whose interests are senior to that of a consignor and, finally, to a consignor. Inasmuch as a consignor is the owner of the collateral, secured parties and lienholders whose interests are junior to the consignor's interest will not be entitled to any proceeds. In like fashion, under subsection (d)(1) the debtor is not entitled to a surplus when the enforcing secured party is required to pay over proceeds to a consignor.

3.   **Noncash Proceeds.** Subsection (c) addresses the application of noncash proceeds of a disposition, such as a note or lease. The explanation in Section 9–608, Comment 4, generally applies to this subsection.

Example: A secured party in the business of selling or financing automobiles takes possession of collateral (an automobile) following its debtor's default. The secured party decides to sell the automobile in a private disposition under Section 9–610 and sends appropriate notification under Section 9–611. After undertaking its normal credit investigation and in accordance with its normal credit policies, the secured party sells the automobile on credit, on terms typical of the credit terms normally extended by the secured party in the ordinary course of its business. The automobile stands as collateral for the remaining balance of the price. The noncash proceeds received by the secured party are chattel paper. The secured party may wish to credit its debtor (the assignor) with the principal amount of the chattel paper or may wish to credit the debtor only as and when the payments are made on the chattel paper by the buyer.

Under subsection (c), the secured party is under no duty to apply the noncash proceeds (here, the chattel paper) or their value to the secured obligation unless its failure to do so would be commercially unreasonable. If a secured party elects to apply the chattel paper to the outstanding obligation, however, it must do so in a commercially reasonable manner. The facts in the example indicate that it would be commercially unreasonable for the secured party to fail to apply the value of the chattel paper to the original debtor's secured obligation. Unlike the example in Comment 4 to Section 9–608, the noncash proceeds received in this example are of the type that the secured party regularly generates in the ordinary course of its financing business in nonforeclosure transactions. The original debtor should not be exposed to delay or uncertainty in this situation. Of course, there will be many situations that fall between the examples presented in the Comment to Section 9–608 and in this Comment. This Article leaves their resolution to the court based on the facts of each case.

One would expect that where noncash proceeds are or may be material, the secured party and debtor would agree to more specific standards in an agreement entered into before or after default. The parties may agree to the method of application of noncash proceeds if the method is not manifestly unreasonable. See Section 9–603.

When the secured party is not required to "apply or pay over for application noncash proceeds," the proceeds nonetheless remain collateral subject to this Article. See Section 9–608, Comment 4.

4.   **Surplus and Deficiency.** Subsection (d) deals with surplus and deficiency. It revises former Section 9–504(2) by imposing an explicit requirement that the secured party "pay" the debtor for any surplus, while retaining the secured party's duty to "account." Inasmuch as the debtor may not be an obligor, subsection (d) provides that the obligor (not the debtor) is liable for the deficiency. The special rule governing surplus and deficiency when receivables have been sold likewise takes into account the distinction between a debtor and an obligor. Subsection (d) also addresses the situation in which a consignor has an interest that is subordinate to the security interest being enforced.

5.   **Collateral Under New Ownership.** When the debtor sells collateral subject to a security interest, the original debtor (creator of the security interest) is no longer a debtor inasmuch as it no longer has a property interest in the collateral; the buyer is the debtor. See Section 9–102. As between the debtor (buyer of the collateral) and the original debtor (seller of the collateral), the debtor (buyer) normally would be entitled to the surplus following a disposition. Subsection (d) therefore requires the secured party to pay the surplus to the debtor (buyer), not to the original debtor (seller) with which it has dealt. But, because this situation typically arises as a result of the debtor's wrongful act, this Article does not expose the secured party to the risk of determining ownership of the collateral. If the secured party does not know about the buyer and accordingly pays the surplus to the original debtor, the exculpatory provisions of this Article exonerate the secured party from liability to the buyer. See Sections 9–605, 9–628(a), (b). If a debtor sells collateral *free* of a security interest, as in a sale to a buyer in ordinary course of business (see Section 9–320(a)), the property is no longer collateral and the buyer is not a debtor.

6.   **Certain "Low-Price" Dispositions.** Subsection (f) provides a special method for calculating a deficiency or surplus when the secured party, a person related to the secured party (defined in Section 9–102), or a secondary obligor acquires the collateral at a foreclosure disposition. It recognizes that when the foreclosing secured party or a related party is the transferee of the collateral, the secured party sometimes lacks the incentive to maximize the proceeds of disposition. As a consequence, the disposition may comply with the procedural requirements of this Article (e.g., it is conducted in a commercially reasonable manner following reasonable notice) but nevertheless fetch a low price.

Subsection (f) adjusts for this lack of incentive. If the proceeds of a disposition of collateral to a secured party, a person related to the secured party, or a secondary obligor are "significantly below the range of proceeds that a complying disposition to a person other than the secured party, a person related to the secured party, or a secondary obligor would have brought," then instead of calculating a deficiency (or surplus) based on the actual net proceeds, the calculation is based upon the amount that would have been received in a commercially reasonable disposition to a person other than the secured party, a person related to the secured party, or a secondary obligor. Subsection (f) thus rejects the view that the secured party's receipt of such a price necessarily constitutes noncompliance with Part 6. However, such a price may suggest the need for greater judicial scrutiny. See Section 9–610, Comment 10.

7.   **"Person Related To."** Section 9–102 defines "person related to." That term is a key element of the system provided in subsection (f) for low-price dispositions. One part of the definition applies when the secured party is an individual, and the other applies when the secured party is an organization. The definition is patterned closely on the corresponding definition in Section 1.301(32) of the Uniform Consumer Credit Code.

§ 9–616.   Explanation of Calculation of Surplus or Deficiency.

(a)   **[Definitions.]** In this section:

(1)   "Explanation" means a writing that:

    (A)   states the amount of the surplus or deficiency;

    (B)   provides an explanation in accordance with subsection (c) of how the secured party calculated the surplus or deficiency;

    (C)   states, if applicable, that future debits, credits, charges, including additional credit service charges or interest, rebates, and expenses may affect the amount of the surplus or deficiency; and

    (D)   provides a telephone number or mailing address from which additional information concerning the transaction is available.

(2)   "Request" means a record:

    (A)   authenticated by a debtor or consumer obligor;

    (B)   requesting that the recipient provide an explanation; and

    (C)   sent after disposition of the collateral under Section 9–610.

(b)   **[Explanation of calculation.]** In a consumer-goods transaction in which the debtor is entitled to a surplus or a consumer obligor is liable for a deficiency under Section 9–615, the secured party shall:

(1)   send an explanation to the debtor or consumer obligor, as applicable, after the disposition and:

   (A)   before or when the secured party accounts to the debtor and pays any surplus or first makes written demand on the consumer obligor after the disposition for payment of the deficiency; and

   (B)   within 14 days after receipt of a request; or

(2)   in the case of a consumer obligor who is liable for a deficiency, within 14 days after receipt of a request, send to the consumer obligor a record waiving the secured party's right to a deficiency.

(c)   **[Required information.]** To comply with subsection (a)(1)(B), a writing must provide the following information in the following order:

(1)   the aggregate amount of obligations secured by the security interest under which the disposition was made, and, if the amount reflects a rebate of unearned interest or credit service charge, an indication of that fact, calculated as of a specified date:

   (A)   if the secured party takes or receives possession of the collateral after default, not more than 35 days before the secured party takes or receives possession; or

   (B)   if the secured party takes or receives possession of the collateral before default or does not take possession of the collateral, not more than 35 days before the disposition;

(2)   the amount of proceeds of the disposition;

(3)   the aggregate amount of the obligations after deducting the amount of proceeds;

(4)   the amount, in the aggregate or by type, and types of expenses, including expenses of retaking, holding, preparing for disposition, processing, and disposing of the collateral, and attorney's fees secured by the collateral which are known to the secured party and relate to the current disposition;

(5)   the amount, in the aggregate or by type, and types of credits, including rebates of interest or credit service charges, to which the obligor is known to be entitled and which are not reflected in the amount in paragraph (1); and

(6)   the amount of the surplus or deficiency.

(d)   **[Substantial compliance.]** A particular phrasing of the explanation is not required. An explanation complying substantially with the requirements of subsection (a) is sufficient, even if it includes minor errors that are not seriously misleading.

(e)   **[Charges for responses.]** A debtor or consumer obligor is entitled without charge to one response to a request under this section during any six-month period in which the secured party did not send to the debtor or consumer obligor an explanation pursuant to subsection (b)(1). The secured party may require payment of a charge not exceeding $25 for each additional response.

Official Comment

1.   **Source.** New.

2.   **Duty to Send Information Concerning Surplus or Deficiency.** This section reflects the view that, in every consumer-goods transaction, the debtor or obligor is entitled to know the amount of a surplus or deficiency and the basis upon which the surplus or deficiency was calculated. Under subsection (b)(1), a secured party is obligated to provide this information (an "explanation," defined in subsection (a)(1)) no later than the time that it accounts for and pays a surplus or the time of its first written attempt to collect the deficiency. The obligor need not make a request for an accounting in order to receive an explanation. A secured party who does not attempt to collect a deficiency in writing or account for and pay a surplus has no obligation to send an explanation under subsection (b)(1) and, consequently, cannot be liable for noncompliance.

A debtor or secondary obligor need not wait until the secured party commences written collection efforts in order to receive an explanation of how a deficiency or surplus was calculated. Subsection (b)(1)(B) obliges the secured party to send an explanation within 14 days after it receives a "request" (defined in subsection (a)(2)).

3.   **Explanation of Calculation of Surplus or Deficiency.** Subsection (c) contains the requirements for how a calculation of a surplus or deficiency must be explained in order to satisfy subsection (a)(1)(B). It gives a secured party some discretion concerning rebates of interest or credit service charges. The secured party may include these rebates in the aggregate amount of obligations secured, under subsection (c)(1), or may include them with other types of rebates and credits under subsection (c)(5). Rebates of interest or credit service charges are the only types of rebates for which this discretion is provided. If the secured party provides an explanation that includes rebates of pre-computed interest, its explanation must so indicate. The expenses and attorney's fees to be described pursuant to subsection (c)(4) are those relating to the most recent disposition, not those that may have been incurred in connection with earlier enforcement efforts and which have been resolved by the parties.

4.   **Liability for Noncompliance.** A secured party who fails to comply with subsection (b)(2) is liable for any loss caused plus $500. See Section 9–625(b), (c), (e)(6). A secured party who fails to send an explanation under subsection (b)(1) is liable for any loss caused plus, if the noncompliance was "part of a pattern, or consistent with a practice of noncompliance," $500. See Section 9–625(b), (c), (e)(5). However, a secured party who fails to comply with this section is not liable for statutory minimum damages under Section 9–625(c)(2). See Section 9–628(d).

As amended in 2010.

§ 9–617.   Rights of Transferee of Collateral.

(a)   **[Effects of disposition.]** A secured party's disposition of collateral after default:

(1)   transfers to a transferee for value all of the debtor's rights in the collateral;

(2)   discharges the security interest under which the disposition is made; and

(3)   discharges any subordinate security interest or other subordinate lien [other than liens created under [cite acts or statutes providing for liens, if any, that are not to be discharged]].

(b)   **[Rights of good-faith transferee.]** A transferee that acts in good faith takes free of the rights and interests described in subsection (a), even if the secured party fails to comply with this article or the requirements of any judicial proceeding.

(c)   **[Rights of other transferee.]** If a transferee does not take free of the rights and interests described in subsection (a), the transferee takes the collateral subject to:

(1)   the debtor's rights in the collateral;

(2)   the security interest or agricultural lien under which the disposition is made; and

(3)   any other security interest or other lien.

Official Comment

1.   **Source.** Former Section 9–504(4).

2.   **Title Taken by Good-Faith Transferee.** Subsection (a) sets forth the rights acquired by persons who qualify under subsection (b)—transferees who act in good faith. Such a person is a "transferee," inasmuch as a buyer at a foreclosure sale does not meet the definition of "purchaser" in Section 1–201 (the transfer is not, vis-a-vis the debtor, "voluntary"). By virtue of the expanded definition of the term "debtor" in Section 9–102, subsection (a) makes clear that the ownership interest of a person who bought the collateral subject to the security interest is terminated by a subsequent disposition under this Part. Such a person is a debtor under this Article. Under former Article 9, the result arguably was the same, but the statute was less clear. Under subsection (a), a disposition normally discharges the security interest being foreclosed and any subordinate security interests and other liens.

A disposition has the effect specified in subsection (a), even if the secured party fails to comply with this Article. An aggrieved person (e.g., the holder of a subordinate security interest to whom a notification required by Section 9–611 was not sent) has a right to recover any loss under Section 9–625(b).

3.   **Unitary Standard in Public and Private Dispositions.** Subsection (b) now contains a unitary standard that applies to transferees in both private and public dispositions—acting in good faith. However, this change from former Section 9–504(4) should not be interpreted to mean that a transferee acts in good faith even though it has knowledge of defects or buys in collusion, standards applicable to public dispositions under the former section. Properly understood, those standards were specific examples of the absence of good faith.

4. **Title Taken by Nonqualifying Transferee.** Subsection (c) specifies the consequences for a transferee who does not qualify for protection under subsections (a) and (b) (i.e., a transferee who does not act in good faith). The transferee takes subject to the rights of the debtor, the enforcing secured party, and other security interests or other liens.

§ 9–618. Rights and Duties of Certain Secondary Obligors.

(a) **[Rights and duties of secondary obligor.]** A secondary obligor acquires the rights and becomes obligated to perform the duties of the secured party after the secondary obligor:

(1) receives an assignment of a secured obligation from the secured party;

(2) receives a transfer of collateral from the secured party and agrees to accept the rights and assume the duties of the secured party; or

(3) is subrogated to the rights of a secured party with respect to collateral.

(b) **[Effect of assignment, transfer, or subrogation.]** An assignment, transfer, or subrogation described in subsection (a):

(1) is not a disposition of collateral under Section 9–610; and

(2) relieves the secured party of further duties under this article.

Official Comment

1. **Source.** Former Section 9–504(5).

2. **Scope of This Section.** Under this section, assignments of secured obligations and other transactions (regardless of form) that function like assignments of secured obligations are not dispositions to which Part 6 applies. Rather, they constitute assignments of rights and (occasionally) delegations of duties. Application of this section may require an investigation into the agreement of the parties, which may not be reflected in the words of the repurchase agreement (e.g., when the agreement requires a recourse party to "purchase the collateral" but contemplates that the purchaser will then conduct an Article 9 foreclosure disposition).

This section, like former Section 9–504(5), does not constitute a general and comprehensive rule for allocating rights and duties upon assignment of a secured obligation. Rather, it applies only in situations involving a secondary obligor described in subsection (a). In other contexts, the agreement of the parties and applicable law other than Article 9 determine whether the assignment imposes upon the assignee any duty to the debtor and whether the assignor retains its duties to the debtor after the assignment.

Subsection (a)(1) applies when there has been an assignment of an obligation that is secured at the time it is assigned. Thus, if a secondary obligor acquires the collateral at a disposition under Section 9–610 and simultaneously or subsequently discharges the unsecured deficiency claim, subsection (a)(1) is not implicated. Similarly, subsection (a)(3) applies only when the secondary obligor is subrogated to the secured party's rights with respect to collateral. Thus, this subsection will not be implicated if a secondary obligor discharges the debtor's unsecured obligation for a post-disposition deficiency. Similarly, if the secured party disposes of some of the collateral and the secondary obligor thereafter discharges the remaining obligation, subsection (a) applies only with respect to rights and duties concerning the remaining collateral, and, under subsection (b), the subrogation is not a disposition *of the remaining collateral*.

As discussed more fully in Comment 3, a secondary obligor may receive a transfer of collateral in a disposition under Section 9–610 in exchange for a payment that is applied against the secured obligation. However, a secondary obligor who pays and receives a transfer of collateral does not necessarily become subrogated to the rights of the secured party as contemplated by subsection (a)(3). Only to the extent the secondary obligor makes a payment in satisfaction of its secondary obligation would it become subrogated. To the extent its payment constitutes the price of the collateral in a Section 9–610 disposition by the secured party, the secondary obligor would not be subrogated. Thus, if the amount paid by the secondary obligor for the collateral in a Section 9–610 disposition is itself insufficient to discharge the secured obligation, but the secondary obligor makes an additional payment that satisfies the remaining balance, the secondary obligor would be subrogated to the secured party's deficiency claim. However, the duties of the secured party *as such* would have come to an end with respect to that collateral. In some situations the capacity in which the payment is made may be unclear. Accordingly, the parties should in their relationship provide clear evidence of the nature and circumstances of the payment by the secondary obligor.

3. **Transfer of Collateral to Secondary Obligor.** It is possible for a secured party to transfer collateral to a secondary obligor in a transaction that is a disposition under Section 9–610 and that establishes a surplus or deficiency under Section 9–615. Indeed, this Article includes a special rule, in Section 9–615(f), for establishing a deficiency in the case of some dispositions to, *inter alia*, secondary obligors. This Article rejects the view, which some may have ascribed to former Section 9–504(5), that a transfer of collateral to a recourse party can *never* constitute a disposition of collateral which discharges a security interest. Inasmuch as a secured party could itself buy collateral at its own public sale, it makes no sense to prohibit a recourse party ever from buying at the sale.

4. **Timing and Scope of Obligations.** Under subsection (a), a recourse party acquires rights and incurs obligations only "after" one of the specified circumstances occurs. This makes clear that when a successor assignee, transferee, or subrogee becomes obligated it does not assume any liability for earlier actions or inactions of the secured party whom it has succeeded unless it agrees to do so. Once the successor becomes obligated, however, it is responsible for complying with the secured party's duties thereafter. For example, if the successor is in possession of collateral, then it has the duties specified in Section 9–207.

Under subsection (b), the same event (assignment, transfer, or subrogation) that gives rise to rights to, and imposes obligations on, a successor relieves its predecessor of any further duties under this Article. For example, if the security interest is enforced after the secured obligation is assigned, the assignee—but not the assignor— has the duty to comply with this Part. Similarly, the assignment does not excuse the assignor from liability for failure to comply with duties that arose before the event or impose liability on the assignee for the assignor's failure to comply.

§ 9–619. Transfer of Record or Legal Title.

(a) **["Transfer statement."]** In this section, "transfer statement" means a record authenticated by a secured party stating:

(1) that the debtor has defaulted in connection with an obligation secured by specified collateral;

(2) that the secured party has exercised its post-default remedies with respect to the collateral;

(3) that, by reason of the exercise, a transferee has acquired the rights of the debtor in the collateral; and

(4) the name and mailing address of the secured party, debtor, and transferee.

(b) **[Effect of transfer statement.]** A transfer statement entitles the transferee to the transfer of record of all rights of the debtor in the collateral specified in the statement in any official filing, recording, registration, or certificate-of-title system covering the collateral. If a transfer statement is presented with the applicable fee and request form to the official or office responsible for maintaining the system, the official or office shall:

(1) accept the transfer statement;

(2) promptly amend its records to reflect the transfer; and

(3) if applicable, issue a new appropriate certificate of title in the name of the transferee.

(c) **[Transfer not a disposition; no relief of secured party's duties.]** A transfer of the record or legal title to collateral to a secured party under subsection (b) or otherwise is not of itself a disposition of collateral under this article and does not of itself relieve the secured party of its duties under this article.

Official Comment

1. **Source.** New.

2. **Transfer of Record or Legal Title.** Potential buyers of collateral that is covered by a certificate of title (e.g., an automobile) or is subject to a registration system (e.g., a copyright) typically require as a condition of their purchase that the certificate or registry reflect their ownership. In many cases, this condition can be met only with the consent of the record owner. If the record owner is the debtor and, as may be the case after the default, the debtor refuses to cooperate, the secured party may have great difficulty disposing of the collateral.

Subsection (b) provides a simple mechanism for obtaining record or legal title, for use primarily when other law does not provide one. Of course, use of this mechanism will not be effective to clear title to the extent that subsection (b) is preempted by federal law. Subsection (b) contemplates a transfer of record or legal title to a third party, following a secured party's exercise of its disposition or acceptance remedies under this Part, as well as a transfer by a debtor to a secured party prior to the secured party's exercise of those remedies. Under subsection (c), a transfer of record or legal title (under subsection (b) or under other law) to a secured party prior to the exercise of those remedies merely puts the secured party in a position to pass legal or record title to a transferee at foreclosure. A secured party who has obtained record or legal title retains its duties with respect to enforcement of its security interest, and the debtor retains its rights as well.

3. **Title-Clearing Systems Under Other Law.** Applicable non-UCC law (e.g., a certificate-of-title statute, federal registry rules, or the like) may provide a means by which the secured party may obtain or transfer record or legal title for the purpose of a disposition of the property under this Article. The mechanism provided by this section is in addition to any title-clearing provision under law other than this Article.

§ 9–620. Acceptance of Collateral in Full or Partial Satisfaction of Obligation; Compulsory Disposition of Collateral.

(a) **[Conditions to acceptance in satisfaction.]** Except as otherwise provided in subsection (g), a secured party may accept collateral in full or partial satisfaction of the obligation it secures only if:

(1) the debtor consents to the acceptance under subsection (c);

(2) the secured party does not receive, within the time set forth in subsection (d), a notification of objection to the proposal authenticated by:

(A) a person to which the secured party was required to send a proposal under Section 9–621; or

(B) any other person, other than the debtor, holding an interest in the collateral subordinate to the security interest that is the subject of the proposal;

(3) if the collateral is consumer goods, the collateral is not in the possession of the debtor when the debtor consents to the acceptance; and

(4) subsection (e) does not require the secured party to dispose of the collateral or the debtor waives the requirement pursuant to Section 9–624.

(b) **[Purported acceptance ineffective.]** A purported or apparent acceptance of collateral under this section is ineffective unless:

(1) the secured party consents to the acceptance in an authenticated record or sends a proposal to the debtor; and

(2) the conditions of subsection (a) are met.

(c) **[Debtor's consent.]** For purposes of this section:

(1) a debtor consents to an acceptance of collateral in partial satisfaction of the obligation it secures only if the debtor agrees to the terms of the acceptance in a record authenticated after default; and

(2) a debtor consents to an acceptance of collateral in full satisfaction of the obligation it secures only if the debtor agrees to the terms of the acceptance in a record authenticated after default or the secured party:

(A) sends to the debtor after default a proposal that is unconditional or subject only to a condition that collateral not in the possession of the secured party be preserved or maintained;

(B) in the proposal, proposes to accept collateral in full satisfaction of the obligation it secures; and

    (C)   does not receive a notification of objection authenticated by the debtor within 20 days after the proposal is sent.

    (d)   **[Effectiveness of notification.]** To be effective under subsection (a)(2), a notification of objection must be received by the secured party:

    (1)   in the case of a person to which the proposal was sent pursuant to Section 9–621, within 20 days after notification was sent to that person; and

    (2)   in other cases:

        (A)   within 20 days after the last notification was sent pursuant to Section 9–621; or

        (B)   if a notification was not sent, before the debtor consents to the acceptance under subsection (c).

    (e)   **[Mandatory disposition of consumer goods.]** A secured party that has taken possession of collateral shall dispose of the collateral pursuant to Section 9–610 within the time specified in subsection (f) if:

    (1)   60 percent of the cash price has been paid in the case of a purchase-money security interest in consumer goods; or

    (2)   60 percent of the principal amount of the obligation secured has been paid in the case of a non-purchase-money security interest in consumer goods.

    (f)   **[Compliance with mandatory disposition requirement.]** To comply with subsection (e), the secured party shall dispose of the collateral:

    (1)   within 90 days after taking possession; or

    (2)   within any longer period to which the debtor and all secondary obligors have agreed in an agreement to that effect entered into and authenticated after default.

    (g)   **[No partial satisfaction in consumer transaction.]** In a consumer transaction, a secured party may not accept collateral in partial satisfaction of the obligation it secures.

Official Comment

1.   **Source.** Former Section 9–505.

2.   **Overview.** This section and the two sections following deal with strict foreclosure, a procedure by which the secured party acquires the debtor's interest in the collateral without the need for a sale or other disposition under Section 9–610. Although these provisions derive from former Section 9–505, they have been entirely reorganized and substantially rewritten. The more straightforward approach taken in this Article eliminates the fiction that the secured party always will present a "proposal" for the retention of collateral and the debtor will have a fixed period to respond. By eliminating the need (but preserving the possibility) for proceeding in that fashion, this section eliminates much of the awkwardness of former Section 9–505. It reflects the belief that strict foreclosures should be encouraged and often will produce better results than a disposition for all concerned.

Subsection (a) sets forth the conditions necessary to an effective acceptance (formerly, retention) of collateral in full or partial satisfaction of the secured obligation. Section 9–621 requires in addition that a secured party who wishes to proceed under this section notify certain other persons who have or claim to have an interest in the collateral. Unlike the failure to meet the conditions in subsection (a), under Section 9–622(b) the failure to comply with the notification requirement of Section 9–621 does not render the acceptance of collateral ineffective. Rather, the acceptance can take effect notwithstanding the secured party's noncompliance. A person to whom the required notice was not sent has the right to recover damages under Section 9–625(b). Section 9–622(a) sets forth the effect of an acceptance of collateral.

3.   **Conditions to Effective Acceptance.** Subsection (a) contains the conditions necessary to the effectiveness of an acceptance of collateral. Subsection (a)(1) requires the debtor's consent. Under subsections (c)(1) and (c)(2), the debtor may consent by agreeing to the acceptance in writing after default. Subsection (c)(2) contains an alternative method by which to satisfy the debtor's-consent condition in subsection (a)(1). It follows the proposal-and-objection model found in former Section 9–505: The debtor consents if the secured party sends a

proposal to the debtor and does not receive an objection within 20 days. Under subsection (c)(1), however, that silence is not deemed to be consent with respect to acceptances in partial satisfaction. Thus, a secured party who wishes to conduct a "partial strict foreclosure" must obtain the debtor's agreement in a record authenticated after default. In all other respects, the conditions necessary to an effective partial strict foreclosure are the same as those governing acceptance of collateral in full satisfaction. (But see subsection (g), prohibiting partial strict foreclosure of a security interest in consumer transactions.)

The time when a debtor consents to a strict foreclosure is significant in several circumstances under this section and the following one. See Sections 9–620(a)(1), (d)(2), 9–621(a)(1), (a)(2), (a)(3). For purposes of determining the time of consent, a debtor's conditional consent constitutes consent.

Subsection (a)(2) contains the second condition to the effectiveness of an acceptance under this section—the absence of a timely objection from a person holding a junior interest in the collateral or from a secondary obligor. Any junior party—secured party or lienholder—is entitled to lodge an objection to a proposal, even if that person was not entitled to notification under Section 9–621. Subsection (d), discussed below, indicates when an objection is timely.

Subsections (a)(3) and (a)(4) contain special rules for transactions in which consumers are involved. See Comment 12.

4.   **Proposals.** Section 9–102 defines the term "proposal." It is necessary to send a "proposal" to the debtor only if the debtor does not agree to an acceptance in an authenticated record as described in subsection (c)(1) or (c)(2). Section 9–621(a) determines whether it is necessary to send a proposal to third parties. A proposal need not take any particular form as long as it sets forth the terms under which the secured party is willing to accept collateral in satisfaction. A proposal to accept collateral should specify the amount (or a means of calculating the amount, such as by including a per diem accrual figure) of the secured obligations to be satisfied, state the conditions (if any) under which the proposal may be revoked, and describe any other applicable conditions. Note, however, that a conditional proposal generally requires the debtor's agreement in order to take effect. See subsection (c).

5.   **Secured Party's Agreement; No "Constructive" Strict Foreclosure.** The conditions of subsection (a) relate to actual or implied consent by the debtor and any secondary obligor or holder of a junior security interest or lien. To ensure that the debtor cannot unilaterally cause an acceptance of collateral, subsection (b) provides that compliance with these conditions is necessary but not sufficient to cause an acceptance of collateral. Rather, under subsection (b), acceptance does not occur unless, in addition, the secured party consents to the acceptance in an authenticated record or sends to the debtor a proposal. For this reason, a mere delay in collection or disposition of collateral does not constitute a "constructive" strict foreclosure. Instead, delay is a factor relating to whether the secured party acted in a commercially reasonable manner for purposes of Section 9–607 or 9–610. A debtor's voluntary surrender of collateral to a secured party and the secured party's acceptance of possession of the collateral does not, of itself, necessarily raise an implication that the secured party intends or is proposing to accept the collateral in satisfaction of the secured obligation under this section.

6.   **When Acceptance Occurs.** This section does not impose any formalities or identify any steps that a secured party must take in order to accept collateral once the conditions of subsections (a) and (b) have been met. Absent facts or circumstances indicating a contrary intention, the fact that the conditions have been met provides a sufficient indication that the secured party has accepted the collateral on the terms to which the secured party has consented or proposed and the debtor has consented or failed to object. Following a proposal, acceptance of the collateral normally is automatic upon the secured party's becoming bound and the time for objection passing. As a matter of good business practice, an enforcing secured party may wish to memorialize its acceptance following a proposal, such as by notifying the debtor that the strict foreclosure is effective or by placing a written record to that effect in its files. The secured party's agreement to accept collateral is self-executing and cannot be breached. The secured party is bound by its agreement to accept collateral and by any proposal to which the debtor consents.

7.   **No Possession Requirement.** This section eliminates the requirement in former Section 9–505 that the secured party be "in possession" of collateral. It clarifies that intangible collateral, which cannot be possessed, may be subject to a strict foreclosure under this section. However, under subsection (a)(3), if the collateral is consumer goods, acceptance does not occur unless the debtor is not in possession.

8.   **When Objection Timely.** Subsection (d) explains when an objection is timely and thus prevents an acceptance of collateral from taking effect. An objection by a person to which notification was sent under Section 9–621 is effective if it is received by the secured party within 20 days from the date the notification was sent to that person. Other objecting parties (i.e., third parties who are not entitled to notification) may object at any time

within 20 days after the last notification is sent under Section 9–621. If no such notification is sent, third parties must object before the debtor agrees to the acceptance in writing or is deemed to have consented by silence. The former may occur any time after default, and the latter requires a 20-day waiting period. See subsection (c).

9.   **Applicability of Other Law.** This section does not purport to regulate all aspects of the transaction by which a secured party may become the owner of collateral previously owned by the debtor. For example, a secured party's acceptance of a motor vehicle in satisfaction of secured obligations may require compliance with the applicable motor vehicle certificate-of-title law. State legislatures should conform those laws so that they mesh well with this section and Section 9–610, and courts should construe those laws and this section harmoniously. A secured party's acceptance of collateral in the possession of the debtor also may implicate statutes dealing with a seller's retention of possession of goods sold.

10.   **Accounts, Chattel Paper, Payment Intangibles, and Promissory Notes.** If the collateral is accounts, chattel paper, payment intangibles, or promissory notes, then a secured party's acceptance of the collateral in satisfaction of secured obligations would constitute a sale to the secured party. That sale normally would give rise to a new security interest (the ownership interest) under Sections 1–201(37)* and 9–109. In the case of accounts and chattel paper, the new security interest would remain perfected by a filing that was effective to perfect the secured party's original security interest. In the case of payment intangibles or promissory notes, the security interest would be perfected when it attaches. See Section 9–309. However, the procedures for acceptance of collateral under this section satisfy all necessary formalities and a new security agreement authenticated by the debtor would not be necessary.

11.   **Role of Good Faith.** Section 1–304 imposes an obligation of good faith on a secured party's enforcement under this Article. This obligation may not be disclaimed by agreement. See Section 1–302. Thus, a proposal and acceptance made under this section in bad faith would not be effective. For example, a secured party's proposal to accept marketable securities worth $1,000 in full satisfaction of indebtedness in the amount of $100, made in the hopes that the debtor might inadvertently fail to object, would be made in bad faith. On the other hand, in the normal case proposals and acceptances should be not second-guessed on the basis of the "value" of the collateral involved. Disputes about valuation or even a clear excess of collateral value over the amount of obligations satisfied do not necessarily demonstrate the absence of good faith.

12.   **Special Rules in Consumer Cases.** Subsection (e) imposes an obligation on the secured party to dispose of consumer goods under certain circumstances. Subsection (f) explains when a disposition that is required under subsection (e) is timely. An effective acceptance of collateral cannot occur if subsection (e) requires a disposition unless the debtor waives this requirement pursuant to Section 9–624(b). Moreover, a secured party who takes possession of collateral and unreasonably delays disposition violates subsection (e), if applicable, and may also violate Section 9–610 or other provisions of this Part. Subsection (e) eliminates as superfluous the express statutory reference to "conversion" found in former Section 9–505. Remedies available under other law, including conversion, remain available under this Article in appropriate cases. See Sections 1–103, 1–305.

Subsection (g) prohibits the secured party in consumer transactions from accepting collateral in partial satisfaction of the obligation it secures. If a secured party attempts an acceptance in partial satisfaction in a consumer transaction, the attempted acceptance is void.

As amended in 2010.

§ 9–621.   Notification of Proposal to Accept Collateral.

(a)   **[Persons to which proposal to be sent.]** A secured party that desires to accept collateral in full or partial satisfaction of the obligation it secures shall send its proposal to:

(1)   any person from which the secured party has received, before the debtor consented to the acceptance, an authenticated notification of a claim of an interest in the collateral;

(2)   any other secured party or lienholder that, 10 days before the debtor consented to the acceptance, held a security interest in or other lien on the collateral perfected by the filing of a financing statement that:

(A)   identified the collateral;

---

*   *Referring to unrevised Article 1 (Appendix A).*

(B) was indexed under the debtor's name as of that date; and

(C) was filed in the office or offices in which to file a financing statement against the debtor covering the collateral as of that date; and

(3) any other secured party that, 10 days before the debtor consented to the acceptance, held a security interest in the collateral perfected by compliance with a statute, regulation, or treaty described in Section 9–311(a).

(b) **[Proposal to be sent to secondary obligor in partial satisfaction.]** A secured party that desires to accept collateral in partial satisfaction of the obligation it secures shall send its proposal to any secondary obligor in addition to the persons described in subsection (a).

Official Comment

1. **Source.** Former Section 9–505.

2. **Notification Requirement.** Subsection (a) specifies three classes of competing claimants to whom the secured party must send notification of its proposal: (i) those who notify the secured party that they claim an interest in the collateral, (ii) holders of certain security interests and liens who have filed against the debtor, and (iii) holders of certain security interests who have perfected by compliance with a statute (including a certificate-of-title statute), regulation, or treaty described in Section 9–311(a). With regard to (ii), see Section 9–611, Comment 4. Subsection (b) also requires notification to any secondary obligor if the proposal is for acceptance in partial satisfaction.

Unlike Section 9–611, this section contains no "safe harbor," which excuses an enforcing secured party from notifying certain secured parties and other lienholders. This is because, unlike Section 9–610, which requires that a disposition of collateral be commercially reasonable, Section 9–620 permits the debtor and secured party to set the amount of credit the debtor will receive for the collateral subject only to the requirement of good faith. An effective acceptance discharges subordinate security interests and other subordinate liens. See Section 9–622. If collateral is subject to several liens securing debts much larger than the value of the collateral, the debtor may be disinclined to refrain from consenting to an acceptance by the holder of the senior security interest, even though, had the debtor objected and the senior disposed of the collateral under Section 9–610, the collateral may have yielded more than enough to satisfy the senior security interest (but not enough to satisfy all the liens). Accordingly, this section imposes upon the enforcing secured party the risk of the filing office's errors and delay. The holder of a security interest who is entitled to notification under this section but to whom the enforcing secured party does not send notification has the right to recover under Section 9–625(b) any loss resulting from the secured party's noncompliance with this section.

As amended in 2010.

§ 9–622. Effect of Acceptance of Collateral.

(a) **[Effect of acceptance.]** A secured party's acceptance of collateral in full or partial satisfaction of the obligation it secures:

(1) discharges the obligation to the extent consented to by the debtor;

(2) transfers to the secured party all of a debtor's rights in the collateral;

(3) discharges the security interest or agricultural lien that is the subject of the debtor's consent and any subordinate security interest or other subordinate lien; and

(4) terminates any other subordinate interest.

(b) **[Discharge of subordinate interest notwithstanding noncompliance.]** A subordinate interest is discharged or terminated under subsection (a), even if the secured party fails to comply with this article.

Official Comment

1. **Source.** New.

2. **Effect of Acceptance.** Subsection (a) specifies the effect of an acceptance of collateral in full or partial satisfaction of the secured obligation. The acceptance to which it refers is an effective acceptance. If a purported

acceptance is ineffective under Section 9–620, e.g., because the secured party receives a timely objection from a person entitled to notification, then neither this subsection nor subsection (b) applies. Paragraph (1) expresses the fundamental consequence of accepting collateral in full or partial satisfaction of the secured obligation—the obligation is discharged to the extent consented to by the debtor. Unless otherwise agreed, the obligor remains liable for any deficiency. Paragraphs (2) through (4) indicate the effects of an acceptance on various property rights and interests. Paragraph (2) follows Section 9–617(a) in providing that the secured party acquires "all of a debtor's rights in the collateral." Under paragraph (3), the effect of strict foreclosure on holders of junior security interests and other liens is the same regardless of whether the collateral is accepted in full or partial satisfaction of the secured obligation: all junior encumbrances are discharged. Paragraph (4) provides for the termination of other subordinate interests.

Subsection (b) makes clear that subordinate interests are discharged under subsection (a) regardless of whether the secured party complies with this Article. Thus, subordinate interests are discharged regardless of whether a proposal was required to be sent or, if required, was sent. However, a secured party's failure to send a proposal or otherwise to comply with this Article may subject the secured party to liability under Section 9–625.

§ 9–623.   Right to Redeem Collateral.

(a) **[Persons that may redeem.]** A debtor, any secondary obligor, or any other secured party or lienholder may redeem collateral.

(b) **[Requirements for redemption.]** To redeem collateral, a person shall tender:

(1) fulfillment of all obligations secured by the collateral; and

(2) the reasonable expenses and attorney's fees described in Section 9–615(a)(1).

(c) **[When redemption may occur.]** A redemption may occur at any time before a secured party:

(1) has collected collateral under Section 9–607;

(2) has disposed of collateral or entered into a contract for its disposition under Section 9–610; or

(3) has accepted collateral in full or partial satisfaction of the obligation it secures under Section 9–622.

Official Comment

1.   **Source.** Former Section 9–506.

2.   **Redemption Right.** Under this section, as under former Section 9–506, the debtor or another secured party may redeem collateral as long as the secured party has not collected (Section 9–607), disposed of or contracted for the disposition of (Section 9–610), or accepted (Section 9–620) the collateral. Although this section generally follows former Section 9–506, it extends the right of redemption to holders of nonconsensual liens. To redeem the collateral a person must tender fulfillment of all obligations secured, plus certain expenses. If the entire balance of a secured obligation has been accelerated, it would be necessary to tender the entire balance. A tender of fulfillment obviously means more than a new promise to perform an existing promise. It requires payment in full of all monetary obligations then due and performance in full of all other obligations then matured. If unmatured secured obligations remain, the security interest continues to secure them (i.e., as if there had been no default).

3.   **Redemption of Remaining Collateral Following Partial Enforcement.** Under Section 9–610 a secured party may make successive dispositions of portions of its collateral. These dispositions would not affect the debtor's, another secured party's, or a lienholder's right to redeem the remaining collateral.

4.   **Effect of "Repledging."** Section 9–207 generally permits a secured party having possession or control of collateral to create a security interest in the collateral. As explained in the Comments to that section, the debtor's right (as opposed to its practical ability) to redeem collateral is not affected by, and does not affect, the priority of a security interest created by the debtor's secured party.

§ 9–624.   Waiver.

(a)   **[Waiver of disposition notification.]** A debtor or secondary obligor may waive the right to notification of disposition of collateral under Section 9–611 only by an agreement to that effect entered into and authenticated after default.

(b)   **[Waiver of mandatory disposition.]** A debtor may waive the right to require disposition of collateral under Section 9–620(e) only by an agreement to that effect entered into and authenticated after default.

(c)   **[Waiver of redemption right.]** Except in a consumer-goods transaction, a debtor or secondary obligor may waive the right to redeem collateral under Section 9–623 only by an agreement to that effect entered into and authenticated after default.

Official Comment

1.   **Source.** Former Sections 9–504(3), 9–505, 9–506.

2.   **Waiver.** This section is a limited exception to Section 9–602, which generally prohibits waiver by debtors and obligors. It makes no provision for waiver of the rule prohibiting a secured party from buying at its own private disposition. Transactions of this kind are equivalent to "strict foreclosures" and are governed by Sections 9–620, 9–621, and 9–622.

[SUBPART 2. NONCOMPLIANCE WITH ARTICLE]

§ 9–625.   Remedies for Secured Party's Failure to Comply With Article.

(a)   **[Judicial orders concerning noncompliance.]** If it is established that a secured party is not proceeding in accordance with this article, a court may order or restrain collection, enforcement, or disposition of collateral on appropriate terms and conditions.

(b)   **[Damages for noncompliance.]** Subject to subsections (c), (d), and (f), a person is liable for damages in the amount of any loss caused by a failure to comply with this article. Loss caused by a failure to comply may include loss resulting from the debtor's inability to obtain, or increased costs of, alternative financing.

(c)   **[Persons entitled to recover damages; statutory damages if collateral is consumer goods.]** Except as otherwise provided in Section 9–628:

(1)   a person that, at the time of the failure, was a debtor, was an obligor, or held a security interest in or other lien on the collateral may recover damages under subsection (b) for its loss; and

(2)   if the collateral is consumer goods, a person that was a debtor or a secondary obligor at the time a secured party failed to comply with this part may recover for that failure in any event an amount not less than the credit service charge plus 10 percent of the principal amount of the obligation or the time-price differential plus 10 percent of the cash price.

(d)   **[Recovery when deficiency eliminated or reduced.]** A debtor whose deficiency is eliminated under Section 9–626 may recover damages for the loss of any surplus. However, a debtor or secondary obligor whose deficiency is eliminated or reduced under Section 9–626 may not otherwise recover under subsection (b) for noncompliance with the provisions of this part relating to collection, enforcement, disposition, or acceptance.

(e)   **[Statutory damages: noncompliance with specified provisions.]** In addition to any damages recoverable under subsection (b), the debtor, consumer obligor, or person named as a debtor in a filed record, as applicable, may recover $500 in each case from a person that:

(1)   fails to comply with Section 9–208;

(2)   fails to comply with Section 9–209;

(3)   files a record that the person is not entitled to file under Section 9–509(a);

(4)   fails to cause the secured party of record to file or send a termination statement as required by Section 9–513(a) or (c);

(5)   fails to comply with Section 9–616(b)(1) and whose failure is part of a pattern, or consistent with a practice, of noncompliance; or

(6)   fails to comply with Section 9–616(b)(2).

(f)   **[Statutory damages: noncompliance with Section 9–210.]** A debtor or consumer obligor may recover damages under subsection (b) and, in addition, $500 in each case from a person that, without reasonable cause, fails to comply with a request under Section 9–210. A recipient of a request under Section 9–210 which never claimed an interest in the collateral or obligations that are the subject of a request under that section has a reasonable excuse for failure to comply with the request within the meaning of this subsection.

(g)   **[Limitation of security interest: noncompliance with Section 9–210.]** If a secured party fails to comply with a request regarding a list of collateral or a statement of account under Section 9–210, the secured party may claim a security interest only as shown in the list or statement included in the request as against a person that is reasonably misled by the failure.

As amended in 2000 and 2010.

Official Comment

1.   **Source.** Former Section 9–507.

2.   **Remedies for Noncompliance; Scope.** Subsections (a) and (b) provide the basic remedies afforded to those aggrieved by a secured party's failure to comply with this Article. Like all provisions that create liability, they are subject to Section 9–628, which should be read in conjunction with Section 9–605. The principal limitations under this Part on a secured party's right to enforce its security interest against collateral are the requirements that it proceed in good faith (Section 1–203)*, in a commercially reasonable manner (Sections 9–607 and 9–610), and, in most cases, with reasonable notification (Sections 9–611 through 9–614). Following former Section 9–507, under subsection (a) an aggrieved person may seek injunctive relief, and under subsection (b) the person may recover damages for losses caused by noncompliance. Unlike former Section 9–507, however, subsections (a) and (b) are not limited to noncompliance with provisions of this Part of Article 9. Rather, they apply to noncompliance with any provision of this Article. The change makes this section applicable to noncompliance with Sections 9–207 (duties of secured party in possession of collateral), 9–208 (duties of secured party having control over deposit account), 9–209 (duties of secured party if account debtor has been notified of an assignment), 9–210 (duty to comply with request for accounting, etc.), 9–509(a) (duty to refrain from filing unauthorized financing statement), and 9–513(a) or (c) (duty to provide termination statement). Subsection (a) also modifies the first sentence of former Section 9–507(1) by adding the references to "collection" and "enforcement." Subsection (c)(2), which gives a minimum damage recovery in consumer-goods transactions, applies only to noncompliance with the provisions of this Part.

3.   **Damages for Noncompliance with This Article.** Subsection (b) sets forth the basic remedy for failure to comply with the requirements of this Article: a damage recovery in the amount of loss caused by the noncompliance. Subsection (c) identifies who may recover under subsection (b). It affords a remedy to any aggrieved person who is a debtor or obligor. However, a principal obligor who is not a debtor may recover damages only for noncompliance with Section 9–616, inasmuch as none of the other rights and duties in this Article run in favor of such a principal obligor. Such a principal obligor could not suffer any loss or damage on account of noncompliance with rights or duties of which it is not a beneficiary. Subsection (c) also affords a remedy to an aggrieved person who holds a competing security interest or other lien, regardless of whether the aggrieved person is entitled to notification under Part 6. The remedy is available even to holders of senior security interests and other liens. The exercise of this remedy is subject to the normal rules of pleading and proof. A person who has delegated the duties of a secured party but who remains obligated to perform them is liable under this subsection. The last sentence of subsection (d) eliminates the possibility of double recovery or other over-compensation arising out of a reduction or elimination of a deficiency under Section 9–626, based on noncompliance with the provisions of this Part relating to collection, enforcement, disposition, or acceptance. Assuming no double recovery, a debtor whose deficiency is eliminated under Section 9–626 may pursue a claim for a surplus. Because Section 9–626 does

_____
*   *Referring to unrevised Article 1 (Appendix A).*

930

not apply to consumer transactions, the statute is silent as to whether a double recovery or other over-compensation is possible in a consumer transaction.

Damages for violation of the requirements of this Article, including Section 9–609, are those reasonably calculated to put an eligible claimant in the position that it would have occupied had no violation occurred. See Section 1–106.* Subsection (b) supports the recovery of actual damages for committing a breach of the peace in violation of Section 9–609, and principles of tort law supplement this subsection. See Section 1–103. However, to the extent that damages in tort compensate the debtor for the same loss dealt with by this Article, the debtor should be entitled to only one recovery.

4. **Minimum Damages in Consumer-Goods Transactions.** Subsection (c)(2) provides a minimum, statutory, damage recovery for a debtor and secondary obligor in a consumer-goods transaction. It is patterned on former Section 9–507(1) and is designed to ensure that every noncompliance with the requirements of Part 6 in a consumer-goods transaction results in liability, regardless of any injury that may have resulted. Subsection (c)(2) leaves the treatment of statutory damages as it was under former Article 9. A secured party is not liable for statutory damages under this subsection more than once with respect to any one secured obligation (see Section 9–628(e)), nor is a secured party liable under this subsection for failure to comply with Section 9–616 (see Section 9–628(d)).

Following former Section 9–507(1), this Article does not include a definition or explanation of the terms "credit service charge," "principal amount," "time-price differential," or "cash price," as used in subsection (c)(2). It leaves their construction and application to the court, taking into account the subsection's purpose of providing a minimum recovery in consumer-goods transactions.

5. **Supplemental Damages.** Subsections (e) and (f) provide damages that supplement the recovery, if any, under subsection (b). Subsection (e) imposes an additional $500 liability upon a person who fails to comply with the provisions specified in that subsection, and subsection (f) imposes like damages on a person who, without reasonable excuse, fails to comply with a request for an accounting or a request regarding a list of collateral or statement of account under Section 9–210. However, under subsection (f), a person has a reasonable excuse for the failure if the person never claimed an interest in the collateral or obligations that were the subject of the request.

6. **Estoppel.** Subsection (g) limits the extent to which a secured party who fails to comply with a request regarding a list of collateral or statement of account may claim a security interest.

§ 9–626. Action in Which Deficiency or Surplus Is in Issue.

(a) **[Applicable rules if amount of deficiency or surplus in issue.]** In an action arising from a transaction, other than a consumer transaction, in which the amount of a deficiency or surplus is in issue, the following rules apply:

(1) A secured party need not prove compliance with the provisions of this part relating to collection, enforcement, disposition, or acceptance unless the debtor or a secondary obligor places the secured party's compliance in issue.

(2) If the secured party's compliance is placed in issue, the secured party has the burden of establishing that the collection, enforcement, disposition, or acceptance was conducted in accordance with this part.

(3) Except as otherwise provided in Section 9–628, if a secured party fails to prove that the collection, enforcement, disposition, or acceptance was conducted in accordance with the provisions of this part relating to collection, enforcement, disposition, or acceptance, the liability of a debtor or a secondary obligor for a deficiency is limited to an amount by which the sum of the secured obligation, expenses, and attorney's fees exceeds the greater of:

(A) the proceeds of the collection, enforcement, disposition, or acceptance; or

(B) the amount of proceeds that would have been realized had the noncomplying secured party proceeded in accordance with the provisions of this part relating to collection, enforcement, disposition, or acceptance.

---

* *Referring to unrevised Article 1 (Appendix A).*

(4) For purposes of paragraph (3)(B), the amount of proceeds that would have been realized is equal to the sum of the secured obligation, expenses, and attorney's fees unless the secured party proves that the amount is less than that sum.

(5) If a deficiency or surplus is calculated under Section 9–615(f), the debtor or obligor has the burden of establishing that the amount of proceeds of the disposition is significantly below the range of prices that a complying disposition to a person other than the secured party, a person related to the secured party, or a secondary obligor would have brought.

(b) **[Non-consumer transactions; no inference.]** The limitation of the rules in subsection (a) to transactions other than consumer transactions is intended to leave to the court the determination of the proper rules in consumer transactions. The court may not infer from that limitation the nature of the proper rule in consumer transactions and may continue to apply established approaches.

Official Comment

1. **Source.** New.

2. **Scope.** The basic damage remedy under Section 9–625(b) is subject to the special rules in this section for transactions other than consumer transactions. This section addresses situations in which the amount of a deficiency or surplus is in issue, i.e., situations in which the secured party has collected, enforced, disposed of, or accepted the collateral. It contains special rules applicable to a determination of the amount of a deficiency or surplus. Because this section affects a person's liability for a deficiency, it is subject to Section 9–628, which should be read in conjunction with Section 9–605. The rules in this section apply only to noncompliance in connection with the "collection, enforcement, disposition, or acceptance" under Part 6. For other types of noncompliance with Part 6, the general liability rule of Section 9–625(b)—recovery of actual damages—applies. Consider, for example, a repossession that does not comply with Section 9–609 for want of a default. The debtor's remedy is under Section 9–625(b). In a proper case, the secured party also may be liable for conversion under non-UCC law. If the secured party thereafter disposed of the collateral, however, it would violate Section 9–610 at that time, and this section would apply.

3. **Rebuttable Presumption Rule.** Subsection (a) establishes the rebuttable presumption rule for transactions other than consumer transactions. Under paragraph (1), the secured party need not prove compliance with the relevant provisions of this Part as part of its prima facie case. If, however, the debtor or a secondary obligor raises the issue (in accordance with the forum's rules of pleading and practice), then the secured party bears the burden of proving that the collection, enforcement, disposition, or acceptance complied. In the event the secured party is unable to meet this burden, then paragraph (3) explains how to calculate the deficiency. Under this rebuttable presumption rule, the debtor or obligor is to be credited with the greater of the actual proceeds of the disposition or the proceeds that would have been realized had the secured party complied with the relevant provisions. If a deficiency remains, then the secured party is entitled to recover it. The references to "the secured obligation, expenses, and attorney's fees" in paragraphs (3) and (4) embrace the application rules in Sections 9–608(a) and 9–615(a).

Unless the secured party proves that compliance with the relevant provisions would have yielded a smaller amount, under paragraph (4) the amount that a complying collection, enforcement, or disposition would have yielded is deemed to be equal to the amount of the secured obligation, together with expenses and attorney's fees. Thus, the secured party may not recover any deficiency unless it meets this burden.

4. **Consumer Transactions.** Although subsection (a) adopts a version of the rebuttable presumption rule for transactions other than consumer transactions, with certain exceptions Part 6 does not specify the effect of a secured party's noncompliance in consumer transactions. (The exceptions are the provisions for the recovery of damages in Section 9–625.) Subsection (b) provides that the limitation of subsection (a) to transactions other than consumer transactions is intended to leave to the court the determination of the proper rules in consumer transactions. It also instructs the court not to draw any inference from the limitation as to the proper rules for consumer transactions and leaves the court free to continue to apply established approaches to those transactions.

Courts construing former Section 9–507 disagreed about the consequences of a secured party's failure to comply with the requirements of former Part 5. Three general approaches emerged. Some courts have held that a noncomplying secured party may not recover a deficiency (the "absolute bar" rule). A few courts held that the debtor can offset against a claim to a deficiency all damages recoverable under former Section 9–507 resulting from the secured party's noncompliance (the "offset" rule). A plurality of courts considering the issue held that the noncomplying secured party is barred from recovering a deficiency unless it overcomes a rebuttable presumption that compliance with former Part 5 would have yielded an amount sufficient to satisfy the secured debt. In addition to the nonuniformity resulting from court decisions, some States enacted special rules governing the availability of deficiencies.

5. **Burden of Proof When Section 9–615(f) Applies.** In a non-consumer transaction, subsection (a)(5) imposes upon a debtor or obligor the burden of proving that the proceeds of a disposition are so low that, under Section 9–615(f), the actual proceeds should not serve as the basis upon which a deficiency or surplus is calculated. Were the burden placed on the secured party, then debtors might be encouraged to challenge the price received in every disposition to the secured party, a person related to the secured party, or a secondary obligor.

6. **Delay in Applying This Section.** There is an inevitable delay between the time a secured party engages in a noncomplying collection, enforcement, disposition, or acceptance and the time of a subsequent judicial determination that the secured party did not comply with Part 6. During the interim, the secured party, believing that the secured obligation is larger than it ultimately is determined to be, may continue to enforce its security interest in collateral. If some or all of the secured indebtedness ultimately is discharged under this section, a reasonable application of this section would impose liability on the secured party for the amount of any excess, unwarranted recoveries but would not make the enforcement efforts wrongful.

§ 9–627. Determination of Whether Conduct Was Commercially Reasonable.

(a) **[Greater amount obtainable under other circumstances; no preclusion of commercial reasonableness.]** The fact that a greater amount could have been obtained by a collection, enforcement, disposition, or acceptance at a different time or in a different method from that selected by the secured party is not of itself sufficient to preclude the secured party from establishing that the collection, enforcement, disposition, or acceptance was made in a commercially reasonable manner.

(b) **[Dispositions that are commercially reasonable.]** A disposition of collateral is made in a commercially reasonable manner if the disposition is made:

(1) in the usual manner on any recognized market;

(2) at the price current in any recognized market at the time of the disposition; or

(3) otherwise in conformity with reasonable commercial practices among dealers in the type of property that was the subject of the disposition.

(c) **[Approval by court or on behalf of creditors.]** A collection, enforcement, disposition, or acceptance is commercially reasonable if it has been approved:

(1) in a judicial proceeding;

(2) by a bona fide creditors' committee;

(3) by a representative of creditors; or

(4) by an assignee for the benefit of creditors.

(d) **[Approval under subsection (c) not necessary; absence of approval has no effect.]** Approval under subsection (c) need not be obtained, and lack of approval does not mean that the collection, enforcement, disposition, or acceptance is not commercially reasonable.

Official Comment

1. **Source.** Former Section 9–507(2).

2. **Relationship of Price to Commercial Reasonableness.** Some observers have found the notion contained in subsection (a) (derived from former Section 9–507(2)) (the fact that a better price could have been obtained does not establish lack of commercial reasonableness) to be inconsistent with that found in Section 9–610(b) (derived from former Section 9–504(3)) (every aspect of the disposition, including its terms, must be commercially reasonable). There is no such inconsistency. While not itself sufficient to establish a violation of this Part, a low price suggests that a court should scrutinize carefully all aspects of a disposition to ensure that each aspect was commercially reasonable.

The law long has grappled with the problem of dispositions of personal and real property which comply with applicable procedural requirements (e.g., advertising, notification to interested persons, etc.) but which yield a price that seems low. This Article addresses that issue in Section 9–615(f). That section applies only when the transferee is the secured party, a person related to the secured party, or a secondary obligor. It contains a special rule for calculating a deficiency or surplus in a complying disposition that yields a price that is "significantly below the range of proceeds that a complying disposition to a person other than the secured party, a person related to the secured party, or a secondary obligor would have brought."

3. **Determination of Commercial Reasonableness; Advance Approval.** It is important to make clear the conduct and procedures that are commercially reasonable and to provide a secured party with the means of obtaining, by court order or negotiation with a creditors' committee or a representative of creditors, advance approval of a proposed method of enforcement as commercially reasonable. This section contains rules that assist in that determination and provides for advance approval in appropriate situations. However, none of the specific methods of disposition specified in subsection (b) is required or exclusive.

4. **"Recognized Market."** As in Sections 9–610(c) and 9–611(d), the concept of a "recognized market" in subsections (b)(1) and (2) is quite limited; it applies only to markets in which there are standardized price quotations for property that is essentially fungible, such as stock exchanges.

§ 9–628.   Nonliability and Limitation on Liability of Secured Party; Liability of Secondary Obligor.

(a) **[Limitation of liability of secured party for noncompliance with article.]** Unless a secured party knows that a person is a debtor or obligor, knows the identity of the person, and knows how to communicate with the person:

(1) the secured party is not liable to the person, or to a secured party or lienholder that has filed a financing statement against the person, for failure to comply with this article; and

(2) the secured party's failure to comply with this article does not affect the liability of the person for a deficiency.

(b) **[Limitation of liability based on status as secured party.]** A secured party is not liable because of its status as secured party:

(1) to a person that is a debtor or obligor, unless the secured party knows:

(A) that the person is a debtor or obligor;

(B) the identity of the person; and

(C) how to communicate with the person; or

(2) to a secured party or lienholder that has filed a financing statement against a person, unless the secured party knows:

(A) that the person is a debtor; and

(B) the identity of the person.

(c) **[Limitation of liability if reasonable belief that transaction not a consumer-goods transaction or consumer transaction.]** A secured party is not liable to any person, and a person's liability for a deficiency is not affected, because of any act or omission arising out of the secured party's reasonable belief that a transaction is not a consumer-goods transaction or a consumer transaction or that goods are not consumer goods, if the secured party's belief is based on its reasonable reliance on:

(1) a debtor's representation concerning the purpose for which collateral was to be used, acquired, or held; or

(2) an obligor's representation concerning the purpose for which a secured obligation was incurred.

(d) **[Limitation of liability for statutory damages.]** A secured party is not liable to any person under Section 9–625(c)(2) for its failure to comply with Section 9–616.

(e) **[Limitation of multiple liability for statutory damages.]** A secured party is not liable under Section 9–625(c)(2) more than once with respect to any one secured obligation.

Official Comment

1. **Source.** New.

2. **Exculpatory Provisions.** Subsections (a), (b), and (c) contain exculpatory provisions that should be read in conjunction with Section 9–605. Without this group of provisions, a secured party could incur liability to unknown persons and under circumstances that would not allow the secured party to protect itself. The broadened definition of the term "debtor" underscores the need for these provisions.

If a secured party reasonably, but mistakenly, believes that a consumer transaction or consumer-goods transaction is a non-consumer transaction or non-consumer-goods transaction, and if the secured party's belief is based on its reasonable reliance on a representation of the type specified in subsection (c)(1) or (c)(2), then this Article should be applied as if the facts reasonably believed and the representation reasonably relied upon were true. For example, if a secured party reasonably believed that a transaction was a non-consumer transaction and its belief was based on reasonable reliance on the debtor's representation that the collateral secured an obligation incurred for business purposes, the secured party is not liable to any person, and the debtor's liability for a deficiency is not affected, because of any act or omission of the secured party which arises out of the reasonable belief. Of course, if the secured party's belief is not reasonable or, even if reasonable, is not based on reasonable reliance on the debtor's representation, this limitation on liability is inapplicable.

3. **Inapplicability of Statutory Damages to Section 9–616.** Subsection (d) excludes noncompliance with Section 9–616 entirely from the scope of statutory damage liability under Section 9–625(c)(2).

4. **Single Liability for Statutory Minimum Damages.** Subsection (e) ensures that a secured party will incur statutory damages only once in connection with any one secured obligation.

As amended in 2000.

[PART 7 TRANSITION RULES OMITTED]

PART 8

TRANSITION PROVISIONS FOR 2010 AMENDMENTS

§ 9–801.   Effective Date.

This [Act] takes effect on July 1, 2013.

Legislative Note: Because these amendments change the proper place in which to file to perfect certain security interests, it is particularly important that States adopt a uniform effective date. Otherwise, the status of a particular security interest as perfected or unperfected would depend on whether the matter was litigated in a State in which the amendments were in effect or a State in which the amendments were not in effect. Any one State's failure to adopt the uniform effective date will significantly increase the cost and uncertainty surrounding the affected transactions.

Official Comment

These transition provisions largely track the provisions of Part 7, which govern the transition to the 1998 revision of this Article. The Comments to the sections of Part 7 generally are relevant to the corresponding sections of Part 8. The 2010 amendments are less far-reaching than the 1998 revision. Although Part 8 does not carry forward those Part 7 provisions that clearly would have no application to the transition to the amendments, as a matter of prudence Part 8 does carry forward all Part 7 provisions that are even arguably relevant to the transition.

The most significant transition problem raised by the 2010 amendments arises from changes to Section 9–503(a), concerning the name of the debtor that must be provided for a financing statement to be sufficient. Sections 9–805 and 9–806 address this problem.

Example: On November 8, 2012, Debtor, an individual whose "individual name" is "Lon Debtor" and whose principal residence is located in State A, creates a security interest in certain manufacturing equipment. On November 15, 2012, SP perfects a security interest in the equipment under Article 9 (as in effect prior to the 2010 amendments) by filing a financing statement against "Lon Debtor" in the State A filing office. On July 1, 2013, the 2010 amendments, including Alternative A to Section 9–503(a), take effect in State A. Debtor's unexpired State A driver's indicates that Debtor's name is "Polonius Debtor." Assuming that a search under

"Polonius Debtor" using the filing office's standard search logic would not disclose the filed financing statement, the financing statement would be insufficient under amended Section 9–503(a)(4) (Alt. A). However, Section 9–805(b) provides that the 2010 amendments do not render the financing statement ineffective. Rather, the financing statement remains effective—even if it has become seriously misleading—until it would have ceased to be effective had the amendments not taken effect. See Section 9–805(b)(1). SP can continue the effectiveness of the financing statement by filing a continuation statement with the State A filing office. To do so, however, SP must amend Debtor's name on the financing statement to provide the name that is sufficient under Section 9–503(a)(4) (Alt. A) at the time the continuation statement is filed. See Section 9–805(c), (e).

The most significant transition problem addressed by the 1998 revision arose from the change in the choice-of-law rules governing where to file a financing statement. The 2010 amendments do not change the choice-of-law rules. Even so, the amendments will change the place to file in a few cases, because certain entities that were not previously classified as "registered organizations" would fall within that category under the amendments.

§ 9–802.   Savings Clause.

(a)   **[Pre-effective-date transactions or liens.]** Except as otherwise provided in this part, this [Act] applies to a transaction or lien within its scope, even if the transaction or lien was entered into or created before this [Act] takes effect.

(b)   **[Pre-effective-date proceedings.]** This [Act] does not affect an action, case, or proceeding commenced before this [Act] takes effect.

§ 9–803.   Security Interest Perfected Before Effective Date.

(a)   **[Continuing perfection: perfection requirements satisfied.]** A security interest that is a perfected security interest immediately before this [Act] takes effect is a perfected security interest under [Article 9 as amended by this [Act]] if, when this [Act] takes effect, the applicable requirements for attachment and perfection under [Article 9 as amended by this [Act]] are satisfied without further action.

(b)   **[Continuing perfection: perfection requirements not satisfied.]** Except as otherwise provided in Section 9–805, if, immediately before this [Act] takes effect, a security interest is a perfected security interest, but the applicable requirements for perfection under [Article 9 as amended by this [Act]] are not satisfied when this [Act] takes effect, the security interest remains perfected thereafter only if the applicable requirements for perfection under [Article 9 as amended by this [Act]] are satisfied within one year after this [Act] takes effect.]

§ 9–804.   Security Interest Unperfected Before Effective Date.

A security interest that is an unperfected security interest immediately before this [Act] takes effect becomes a perfected security interest:

(1)   without further action, when this [Act] takes effect if the applicable requirements for perfection under [Article 9 as amended by this [Act]] are satisfied before or at that time; or

(2)   when the applicable requirements for perfection are satisfied if the requirements are satisfied after that time.

§ 9–805.   Effectiveness of Action Taken Before Effective Date.

(a)   **[Pre-effective-date filing effective.]** The filing of a financing statement before this [Act] takes effect is effective to perfect a security interest to the extent the filing would satisfy the applicable requirements for perfection under [Article 9 as amended by this [Act]].

(b)   **[When pre-effective-date filing becomes ineffective.]** This [Act] does not render ineffective an effective financing statement that, before this [Act] takes effect, is filed and satisfies the applicable requirements for perfection under the law of the jurisdiction governing perfection as provided in [Article 9 as it existed before amendment]. However, except as otherwise provided in subsections (c) and (d) and Section 9–806, the financing statement ceases to be effective:

(1)   if the financing statement is filed in this State, at the time the financing statement would have ceased to be effective had this [Act] not taken effect; or

(2)   if the financing statement is filed in another jurisdiction, at the earlier of:

    (A)   the time the financing statement would have ceased to be effective under the law of that jurisdiction; or

    (B)   June 30, 2018.

(c)   **[Continuation statement.]** The filing of a continuation statement after this [Act] takes effect does not continue the effectiveness of a financing statement filed before this [Act] takes effect. However, upon the timely filing of a continuation statement after this [Act] takes effect and in accordance with the law of the jurisdiction governing perfection as provided in [Article 9 as amended by this [Act]], the effectiveness of a financing statement filed in the same office in that jurisdiction before this [Act] takes effect continues for the period provided by the law of that jurisdiction.

(d)   **[Application of subsection (b)(2)(B) to transmitting utility financing statement.]** Subsection (b)(2)(B) applies to a financing statement that, before this [Act] takes effect, is filed against a transmitting utility and satisfies the applicable requirements for perfection under the law of the jurisdiction governing perfection as provided in [Article 9 as it existed before amendment], only to the extent that [Article 9 as amended by this [Act]] provides that the law of a jurisdiction other than the jurisdiction in which the financing statement is filed governs perfection of a security interest in collateral covered by the financing statement.

(e)   **[Application of Part 5.]** A financing statement that includes a financing statement filed before this [Act] takes effect and a continuation statement filed after this [Act] takes effect is effective only to the extent that it satisfies the requirements of [Part 5 as amended by this [Act]] for an initial financing statement. A financing statement that indicates that the debtor is a decedent's estate indicates that the collateral is being administered by a personal representative within the meaning of Section 9–503(a)(2) as amended by this [Act]. A financing statement that indicates that the debtor is a trust or is a trustee acting with respect to property held in trust indicates that the collateral is held in a trust within the meaning of Section 9–503(a)(3) as amended by this [Act].

§ 9–806.   When Initial Financing Statement Suffices to Continue Effectiveness of Financing Statement.

(a)   **[Initial financing statement in lieu of continuation statement.]** The filing of an initial financing statement in the office specified in Section 9–501 continues the effectiveness of a financing statement filed before this [Act] takes effect if:

(1)   the filing of an initial financing statement in that office would be effective to perfect a security interest under [Article 9 as amended by this [Act]];

(2)   the pre-effective-date financing statement was filed in an office in another State; and

(3)   the initial financing statement satisfies subsection (c).

(b)   **[Period of continued effectiveness.]** The filing of an initial financing statement under subsection (a) continues the effectiveness of the pre-effective-date financing statement:

(1)   if the initial financing statement is filed before this [Act] takes effect, for the period provided in [unamended Section 9–515] with respect to an initial financing statement; and

(2)   if the initial financing statement is filed after this [Act] takes effect, for the period provided in Section 9–515 as amended by this [Act] with respect to an initial financing statement.

(c)   **[Requirements for initial financing statement under subsection (a).]** To be effective for purposes of subsection (a), an initial financing statement must:

(1)   satisfy the requirements of [Part 5 as amended by this [Act]] for an initial financing statement;

(2)   identify the pre-effective-date financing statement by indicating the office in which the financing statement was filed and providing the dates of filing and file numbers, if any, of the financing statement and of the most recent continuation statement filed with respect to the financing statement; and

(3)   indicate that the pre-effective-date financing statement remains effective.

§ 9–807.   Amendment of Pre-effective-Date Financing Statement.

(a)   **["Pre-effective-date financing statement".]** In this section, "pre-effective-date financing statement" means a financing statement filed before this [Act] takes effect.

(b)   **[Applicable law.]** After this [Act] takes effect, a person may add or delete collateral covered by, continue or terminate the effectiveness of, or otherwise amend the information provided in, a pre-effective-date financing statement only in accordance with the law of the jurisdiction governing perfection as provided in [Article 9 as amended by this [Act]]. However, the effectiveness of a pre-effective-date financing statement also may be terminated in accordance with the law of the jurisdiction in which the financing statement is filed.

(c)   **[Method of amending: general rule.]** Except as otherwise provided in subsection (d), if the law of this State governs perfection of a security interest, the information in a pre-effective-date financing statement may be amended after this [Act] takes effect only if:

(1)   the pre-effective-date financing statement and an amendment are filed in the office specified in Section 9–501;

(2)   an amendment is filed in the office specified in Section 9–501 concurrently with, or after the filing in that office of, an initial financing statement that satisfies Section 9–806(c); or

(3)   an initial financing statement that provides the information as amended and satisfies Section 9–806(c) is filed in the office specified in Section 9–501.

(d)   **[Method of amending: continuation.]** If the law of this State governs perfection of a security interest, the effectiveness of a pre-effective-date financing statement may be continued only under Section 9–805(c) and (e) or 9–806.

(e)   **[Method of amending: additional termination rule.]** Whether or not the law of this State governs perfection of a security interest, the effectiveness of a pre-effective-date financing statement filed in this State may be terminated after this [Act] takes effect by filing a termination statement in the office in which the pre-effective-date financing statement is filed, unless an initial financing statement that satisfies Section 9–806(c) has been filed in the office specified by the law of the jurisdiction governing perfection as provided in [Article 9 as amended by this [Act]] as the office in which to file a financing statement.

§ 9–808.   Person Entitled to File Initial Financing Statement or Continuation Statement.

A person may file an initial financing statement or a continuation statement under this part if:

(1)   the secured party of record authorizes the filing; and

(2)   the filing is necessary under this part:

(A)   to continue the effectiveness of a financing statement filed before this [Act] takes effect; or

(B)   to perfect or continue the perfection of a security interest.

§ 9–809.   Priority.

This [Act] determines the priority of conflicting claims to collateral. However, if the relative priorities of the claims were established before this [Act] takes effect, [Article 9 as it existed before amendment] determines priority.

Legislative Note: The term "this [Act]" as used in this part refers to the legislation enacting these amendments to Article 9, not to the legislation that enacted Article 9. States should substitute appropriate references.

APPENDIX A
UNREVISED UCC ARTICLE 1 (2000)

Set forth below are the text of Article 1 and the Official Comments as they existed in 2000, prior to the 2001 revision. The provisions are marked with strikeout/underline to reflect changes to the 2000 version made in 2003 as part of the 2003 Article 7 revision.

ARTICLE 1
GENERAL PROVISIONS

PART 1.   SHORT TITLE, CONSTRUCTION, APPLICATION AND SUBJECT MATTER OF THE ACT

PART 2.   GENERAL DEFINITIONS AND PRINCIPLES OF INTERPRETATION

PART 1

SHORT TITLE, CONSTRUCTION, APPLICATION AND SUBJECT MATTER OF THE ACT

§ 1–101.   Short Title.

This Act shall be known and may be cited as Uniform Commercial Code.

Official Comment

Each Article of the Code (except this Article and Article 10) may also be cited by its own short title. See Sections 2–101, 3–101, 4–101, 5–101, 6–101, 7–101, 8–101 and 9–101.

§ 1–102.   Purposes; Rules of Construction; Variation by Agreement.

(1)   This Act shall be liberally construed and applied to promote its underlying purposes and policies.

(2)   Underlying purposes and policies of this Act are

(a)   to simplify, clarify and modernize the law governing commercial transactions;

(b)   to permit the continued expansion of commercial practices through custom, usage and agreement of the parties;

(c)   to make uniform the law among the various jurisdictions.

(3)   The effect of provisions of this Act may be varied by agreement, except as otherwise provided in this Act and except that the obligations of good faith, diligence, reasonableness and care prescribed by this Act may not be disclaimed by agreement but the parties may by agreement determine the standards by which the performance of such obligations is to be measured if such standards are not manifestly unreasonable.

(4)   The presence in certain provisions of this Act of the words "unless otherwise agreed" or words of similar import does not imply that the effect of other provisions may not be varied by agreement under subsection (3).

(5)   In this Act unless the context otherwise requires

(a)   words in the singular number include the plural, and in the plural include the singular;

(b)   words of the masculine gender include the feminine and the neuter, and when the sense so indicates words of the neuter gender may refer to any gender.

Official Comment

Prior Uniform Statutory Provision: Section 74, Uniform Sales Act; Section 57, Uniform Warehouse Receipts Act; Section 52, Uniform Bills of Lading Act; Section 19, Uniform Stock Transfer Act; Section 18, Uniform Trust Receipts Act.

Changes: Rephrased and new material added.

Purposes of Changes:

1.   Subsections (1) and (2) are intended to make it clear that:

This Act is drawn to provide flexibility so that, since it is intended to be a semi-permanent piece of legislation, it will provide its own machinery for expansion of commercial practices. It is intended to make it possible for the law embodied in this Act to be developed by the courts in the light of unforeseen and new circumstances and practices. However, the proper construction of the Act requires that its interpretation and application be limited to its reason.

Courts have been careful to keep broad acts from being hampered in their effects by later acts of limited scope. Pacific Wool Growers v. Draper & Co., 158 Or. 1, 73 P.2d 1391 (1937), and compare Section 1–104. They have recognized the policies embodied in an act as applicable in reason to subject-matter which was not expressly included in the language of the act, Commercial Nat. Bank of New Orleans v. Canal-Louisiana Bank & Trust Co., 239 U.S. 520, 36 S.Ct. 194, 60 L.Ed. 417 (1916) (bona fide purchase policy of Uniform Warehouse Receipts Act extended to case not covered but of equivalent nature). They have done the same where reason and policy so required, even where the subject-matter had been intentionally excluded from the act in general. Agar v. Orda, 264 N.Y. 248, 190 N.E. 479 (1934) (Uniform Sales Act change in seller's remedies applied to contract for sale of choses in action even though the general coverage of that Act was intentionally limited to goods "other than things in action.") They have implemented a statutory policy with liberal and useful remedies not provided in the statutory text. They have disregarded a statutory limitation of remedy where the reason of the limitation did not apply. Fiterman v. J. N. Johnson & Co., 156 Minn. 201, 194 N.W. 399 (1923) (requirement of return of the goods as a condition to rescission for breach of warranty; also, partial rescission allowed). Nothing in this Act stands in the way of the continuance of such action by the courts.

The Act should be construed in accordance with its underlying purposes and policies. The text of each section should be read in the light of the purpose and policy of the rule or principle in question, as also of the Act as a whole, and the application of the language should be construed narrowly or broadly, as the case may be, in conformity with the purposes and policies involved.

2.   Subsection (3) states affirmatively at the outset that freedom of contract is a principle of the Code: "the effect" of its provisions may be varied by "agreement." The meaning of the statute itself must be found in its text, including its definitions, and in appropriate extrinsic aids; it cannot be varied by agreement. But the Code seeks to avoid the type of interference with evolutionary growth found in Manhattan Co. v. Morgan, 242 N.Y. 38, 150 N.E. 594 (1926). Thus private parties cannot make an instrument negotiable within the meaning of Article 3 except as provided in Section 3–104; nor can they change the meaning of such terms as "bona fide purchaser," "holder in due course," or "due negotiation," as used in this Act. But an agreement can change the legal consequences which would otherwise flow from the provisions of the Act. "Agreement" here includes the effect given to course of dealing, usage of trade and course of performance by Sections 1–201, 1–205 and 2–208; the effect of an agreement on the rights of third parties is left to specific provisions of this Act and to supplementary principles applicable under the next section. The rights of third parties under Section 9–317 when a security interest is unperfected, for example, cannot be destroyed by a clause in the security agreement.

This principle of freedom of contract is subject to specific exceptions found elsewhere in the Act and to the general exception stated here. The specific exceptions vary in explicitness: the statute of frauds found in Section 2–201, for example, does not explicitly preclude oral waiver of the requirement of a writing, but a fair reading denies enforcement to such a waiver as part of the "contract" made unenforceable; Section 9–602, on the other hand, is quite explicit. Under the exception for "the obligations of good faith, diligence, reasonableness and care prescribed by this Act," provisions of the Act prescribing such obligations are not to be disclaimed. However, the section also recognizes the prevailing practice of having agreements set forth standards by which due diligence is measured and explicitly provides that, in the absence of a showing that the standards manifestly are unreasonable, the agreement controls. In this connection, Section 1–205 incorporating into the agreement prior course of dealing and usages of trade is of particular importance.

3.   Subsection (4) is intended to make it clear that, as a matter of drafting, words such as "unless otherwise agreed" have been used to avoid controversy as to whether the subject matter of a particular section does or does not fall within the exceptions to subsection (3), but absence of such words contains no negative implication since under subsection (3) the general and residual rule is that the effect of all provisions of the Act may be varied by agreement.

4.   Subsection (5) is modelled on 1 U.S.C. Section 1 and New York General Construction Law Sections 22 and 35.

§ 1–103.   Supplementary General Principles of Law Applicable.

Unless displaced by the particular provisions of this Act, the principles of law and equity, including the law merchant and the law relative to capacity to contract, principal and agent, estoppel, fraud, misrepresentation, duress, coercion, mistake, bankruptcy, or other validating or invalidating cause shall supplement its provisions.

Official Comment

Prior Uniform Statutory Provision: Sections 2 and 73, Uniform Sales Act; Section 196, Uniform Negotiable Instruments Act; Section 56, Uniform Warehouse Receipts Act; Section 51, Uniform Bills of Lading Act; Section 18, Uniform Stock Transfer Act; Section 17, Uniform Trust Receipts Act.

Changes: Rephrased, the reference to "estoppel" and "validating" being new.

Purposes of Changes:

1.   While this section indicates the continued applicability to commercial contracts of all supplemental bodies of law except insofar as they are explicitly displaced by this Act, the principle has been stated in more detail and the phrasing enlarged to make it clear that the "validating", as well as the "invalidating" causes referred to in the prior uniform statutory provisions, are included here. "Validating" as used here in conjunction with "invalidating" is not intended as a narrow word confined to original validation, but extends to cover any factor which at any time or in any manner renders or helps to render valid any right or transaction.

2.   The general law of capacity is continued by express mention to make clear that section 2 of the old Uniform Sales Act (omitted in this Act as stating no matter not contained in the general law) is also consolidated

in the present section. Hence, where a statute limits the capacity of a non-complying corporation to sue, this is equally applicable to contracts of sale to which such corporation is a party.

3.   The listing given in this section is merely illustrative; no listing could be exhaustive. Nor is the fact that in some sections particular circumstances have led to express reference to other fields of law intended at any time to suggest the negation of the general application of the principles of this section.

§ 1–104.   Construction Against Implicit Repeal.

This Act being a general act intended as a unified coverage of its subject matter, no part of it shall be deemed to be impliedly repealed by subsequent legislation if such construction can reasonably be avoided.

Official Comment

Prior Uniform Statutory Provision: None.

Purposes:

To express the policy that no Act which bears evidence of carefully considered permanent regulative intention should lightly be regarded as impliedly repealed by subsequent legislation. This Act, carefully integrated and intended as a uniform codification of permanent character covering an entire "field" of law, is to be regarded as particularly resistant to implied repeal. See Pacific Wool Growers v. Draper & Co., 158 Or. 1, 73 P.2d 1391 (1937).

§ 1–105.   Territorial Application of the Act; Parties' Power to Choose Applicable Law.

(1)   Except as provided hereafter in this section, when a transaction bears a reasonable relation to this state and also to another state or nation the parties may agree that the law either of this state or of such other state or nation shall govern their rights and duties. Failing such agreement this Act applies to transactions bearing an appropriate relation to this state.

(2)   Where one of the following provisions of this Act specifies the applicable law, that provision governs and a contrary agreement is effective only to the extent permitted by the law (including the conflict of laws rules) so specified:

Rights of creditors against sold goods. Section 2–402.

Applicability of the Article on Leases. Sections 2A–105 and 2A–106.

Applicability of the Article on Bank Deposits and Collections. Section 4–102.

Governing law in the Article on Funds Transfers. Section 4A–507.

Letters of Credit. Section 5–116.

Bulk sales subject to the Article on Bulk Sales. Section 6–103.

> *[If a state adopts the repealer of Article 6—Bulk Transfers (Alternative A), there should not be any item relating to bulk transfers. If, however, a state adopts revised Article 6—Bulk Sales (Alternative B), then the item relating to bulk sales should read as set out ante.]*

Applicability of the Article on Investment Securities. Section 8–110.

Law governing perfection, the effect of perfection or nonperfection, and the priority of security interests and agricultural liens. Sections 9–301 through 9–307.

As amended in 1972, 1987, 1988, 1989, 1994, 1995, and 1999.

Official Comment

Prior Uniform Statutory Provision: None.

Purposes:

1.   Subsection (1) states affirmatively the right of the parties to a multi-state transaction or a transaction involving foreign trade to choose their own law. That right is subject to the firm rules stated in the five sections listed in subsection (2), and is limited to jurisdictions to which the transaction bears a "reasonable relation." In general, the test of "reasonable relation" is similar to that laid down by the Supreme Court in Seeman v.

Philadelphia Warehouse Co., 274 U.S. 403, 47 S.Ct. 626, 71 L.Ed. 1123 (1927). Ordinarily the law chosen must be that of a jurisdiction where a significant enough portion of the making or performance of the contract is to occur or occurs. But an agreement as to choice of law may sometimes take effect as a shorthand expression of the intent of the parties as to matters governed by their agreement, even though the transaction has no significant contact with the jurisdiction chosen.

2. Where there is no agreement as to the governing law, the Act is applicable to any transaction having an "appropriate" relation to any state which enacts it. Of course, the Act applies to any transaction which takes place in its entirety in a state which has enacted the Act. But the mere fact that suit is brought in a state does not make it appropriate to apply the substantive law of that state. Cases where a relation to the enacting state is not "appropriate" include, for example, those where the parties have clearly contracted on the basis of some other law, as where the law of the place of contracting and the law of the place of contemplated performance are the same and are contrary to the law under the Code.

3. Where a transaction has significant contacts with a state which has enacted the Act and also with other jurisdictions, the question what relation is "appropriate" is left to judicial decision. In deciding that question, the court is not strictly bound by precedents established in other contexts. Thus a conflict-of-laws decision refusing to apply a purely local statute or rule of law to a particular multi-state transaction may not be valid precedent for refusal to apply the Code in an analogous situation. Application of the Code in such circumstances may be justified by its comprehensiveness, by the policy of uniformity, and by the fact that it is in large part a reformulation and restatement of the law merchant and of the understanding of a business community which transcends state and even national boundaries. Compare Global Commerce Corp. v. Clark-Babbitt Industries, Inc., 239 F.2d 716, 719 (2d Cir. 1956). In particular, where a transaction is governed in large part by the Code, application of another law to some detail of performance because of an accident of geography may violate the commercial understanding of the parties.

4. The Act does not attempt to prescribe choice-of-law rules for states which do not enact it, but this section does not prevent application of the Act in a court of such a state. Common-law choice of law often rests on policies of giving effect to agreements and of uniformity of result regardless of where suit is brought. To the extent that such policies prevail, the relevant considerations are similar in such a court to those outlined above.

5. Subsection (2) spells out essential limitations on the parties' right to choose the applicable law. Especially in Article 9 parties taking a security interest or asked to extend credit which may be subject to a security interest must have sure ways to find out whether and where to file and where to look for possible existing filings.

6. Sections 9–301 through 9–307 should be consulted as to the rules for perfection of security interests and agricultural liens, the effect of perfection and nonperfection, and priority.

As amended in 1999.

§ 1–106. Remedies to Be Liberally Administered.

(1) The remedies provided by this Act shall be liberally administered to the end that the aggrieved party may be put in as good a position as if the other party had fully performed but neither consequential or special nor penal damages may be had except as specifically provided in this Act or by other rule of law.

(2) Any right or obligation declared by this Act is enforceable by action unless the provision declaring it specifies a different and limited effect.

Official Comment

Prior Uniform Statutory Provision: Subsection (1)—none; Subsection (2)—Section 72, Uniform Sales Act.

Changes: Reworded.

Purposes of Changes and New Matter: Subsection (1) is intended to effect three things:

1. First, to negate the unduly narrow or technical interpretation of some remedial provisions of prior legislation by providing that the remedies in this Act are to be liberally administered to the end stated in the section. Second, to make it clear that compensatory damages are limited to compensation. They do not include consequential or special damages, or penal damages; and the Act elsewhere makes it clear that damages must be minimized. Cf. Sections 1–203, 2–706(1), and 2–712(2). The third purpose of subsection (1) is to reject any doctrine that damages must be calculable with mathematical accuracy. Compensatory damages are often at best

approximate: they have to be proved with whatever definiteness and accuracy the facts permit, but no more. Cf. Section 2–204(3).

    2.   Under subsection (2) any right or obligation described in this Act is enforceable by court action, even though no remedy may be expressly provided, unless a particular provision specifies a different and limited effect. Whether specific performance or other equitable relief is available is determined not by this section but by specific provisions and by supplementary principles. Cf. Sections 1–103, 2–716.

    3.   "Consequential" or "special" damages and "penal" damages are not defined in terms in the Code, but are used in the sense given them by the leading cases on the subject.

Cross References:

    Sections 1–103, 1–203, 2–204(3), 2–701, 2–706(1), 2–712(2) and 2–716.

Definitional Cross References:

    "Action". Section 1–201.
    "Aggrieved party". Section 1–201.
    "Party". Section 1–201.
    "Remedy". Section 1–201.
    "Rights". Section 1–201.

§ 1–107.   Waiver or Renunciation of Claim or Right After Breach.

Any claim or right arising out of an alleged breach can be discharged in whole or in part without consideration by a written waiver or renunciation signed and delivered by the aggrieved party.

Official Comment

Prior Uniform Statutory Provision: Compare Section 1, Uniform Written Obligations Act; Sections 119(3), 120(2) and 122, Uniform Negotiable Instruments Law.

Purposes:

    This section makes consideration unnecessary to the effective renunciation or waiver of rights or claims arising out of an alleged breach of a commercial contract where such renunciation is in writing and signed and delivered by the aggrieved party. Its provisions, however, must be read in conjunction with the section imposing an obligation of good faith. (Section 1–203). There may, of course, also be an oral renunciation or waiver sustained by consideration but subject to Statute of Frauds provisions and to the section of Article 2 on Sales dealing with the modification of signed writings (Section 2–209). As is made express in the latter section this Act fully recognizes the effectiveness of waiver and estoppel.

Cross References:

    Sections 1–203, 2–201 and 2–209. And see Section 2–719.

Definitional Cross References:

    "Aggrieved party". Section 1–201.
    "Rights". Section 1–201.
    "Signed". Section 1–201.
    "Written". Section 1–201.

§ 1–108.   Severability.

If any provision or clause of this Act or application thereof to any person or circumstances is held invalid, such invalidity shall not affect other provisions or applications of the Act which can be given effect without the invalid provision or application, and to this end the provisions of this Act are declared to be severable.

Official Comment

    This is the model severability section recommended by the National Conference of Commissioners on Uniform State Laws for inclusion in all acts of extensive scope.

Definitional Cross Reference:

"Person". Section 1–201.

§1–109.   Section Captions.

Section captions are parts of this Act.

Official Comment

Prior Uniform Statutory Provision: None.

Purposes:

To make explicit in all jurisdictions that section captions are a part of the text of this Act and not mere surplusage.

As amended in 1999.

PART 2

GENERAL DEFINITIONS AND PRINCIPLES OF INTERPRETATION

§1–201.   General Definitions.

Subject to additional definitions contained in the subsequent Articles of this Act which are applicable to specific Articles or Parts thereof, and unless the context otherwise requires, in this Act:

(1)   "Action" in the sense of a judicial proceeding includes recoupment, counterclaim, set-off, suit in equity and any other proceedings in which rights are determined.

(2)   "Aggrieved party" means a party entitled to resort to a remedy.

(3)   "Agreement" means the bargain of the parties in fact as found in their language or by implication from other circumstances including course of dealing or usage of trade or course of performance as provided in this Act (Sections 1–205, 2–208, and 2A–207). Whether an agreement has legal consequences is determined by the provisions of this Act, if applicable; otherwise by the law of contracts (Section 1–103). (Compare "Contract".)

(4)   "Bank" means any person engaged in the business of banking.

(5)   "Bearer" means a person in control of a negotiable electronic document of title or a the person in possession of an instrument, a negotiable tangible document of title, or a certificated security payable to bearer or indorsed in blank.

(6)   "Bill of lading" means a document of title evidencing the receipt of goods for shipment issued by a person engaged in the business of directly or indirectly transporting or forwarding goods. The term does not include a warehouse receipt, and includes an airbill. "Airbill" means a document serving for air transportation as a bill of lading does for marine or rail transportation, and includes an air consignment note or air waybill.

(7)   "Branch" includes a separately incorporated foreign branch of a bank.

(8)   "Burden of establishing" a fact means the burden of persuading the triers of fact that the existence of the fact is more probable than its non-existence.

(9)   "Buyer in ordinary course of business" means a person that buys goods in good faith, without knowledge that the sale violates the rights of another person in the goods, and in the ordinary course from a person, other than a pawnbroker, in the business of selling goods of that kind. A person buys goods in the ordinary course if the sale to the person comports with the usual or customary practices in the kind of business in which the seller is engaged or with the seller's own usual or customary practices. A person that sells oil, gas, or other minerals at the wellhead or minehead is a person in the business of selling goods of that kind. A buyer in ordinary course of business may buy for cash, by exchange of other property, or on

secured or unsecured credit, and may acquire goods or documents of title under a pre-existing contract for sale. Only a buyer that takes possession of the goods or has a right to recover the goods from the seller under Article 2 may be a buyer in ordinary course of business. A person that acquires goods in a transfer in bulk or as security for or in total or partial satisfaction of a money debt is not a buyer in ordinary course of business.

(10) ~~"Conspicuous": A term or clause is conspicuous when it is so written that a reasonable person against whom it is to operate ought to have noticed it. A printed heading in capitals (as: NON-NEGOTIABLE BILL OF LADING) is conspicuous. Language in the body of a form is "conspicuous" if it is in larger or other contrasting type or color. But in a telegram any stated term is "conspicuous". Whether a term or clause is "conspicuous" or not is for decision by the court.~~

(10) "Conspicuous", with reference to a term, means so written, displayed, or presented that a reasonable person against which it is to operate ought to have noticed it. Whether a term is "conspicuous" or not is a decision for the court. Conspicuous terms include the following:

(A) a heading in capitals equal to or greater in size than the surrounding text, or in contrasting type, font, or color to the surrounding text of the same or lesser size; and

(B) language in the body of a record or display in larger type than the surrounding text, or in contrasting type, font, or color to the surrounding text of the same size, or set off from surrounding text of the same size by symbols or other marks that call attention to the language.

(11) "Contract" means the total legal obligation which results from the parties' agreement as affected by this Act and any other applicable rules of law. (Compare "Agreement".)

(12) "Creditor" includes a general creditor, a secured creditor, a lien creditor and any representative of creditors, including an assignee for the benefit of creditors, a trustee in bankruptcy, a receiver in equity and an executor or administrator of an insolvent debtor's or assignor's estate.

(13) "Defendant" includes a person in the position of defendant in a cross-action or counterclaim.

(14) "Delivery" with respect to an electronic document of title means voluntary transfer of control and with respect to instruments, tangible documents of title, chattel paper, or certificated securities means voluntary transfer of possession.

(15) "Document of title" ~~includes bill of lading, dock warrant, dock receipt, warehouse receipt or order for the delivery of goods, and also any other~~ means a record (i) that ~~document which~~ in the regular course of business or financing is treated as adequately evidencing that the person in possession or control of the record ~~it~~ is entitled to receive, control, hold, and dispose of the record ~~document~~ and the goods ~~it~~ the record covers and (ii) that purports to be issued by or addressed to a bailee and to cover goods in the bailee's possession which are either identified or are fungible portions of an identified mass. The term includes a bill of lading, transport document, dock warrant, dock receipt, warehouse receipt, and order for delivery of goods. ~~To be a document of title, a document must purport to be issued by or addressed to a bailee and purport to cover goods in the bailee's possession which are either identified or are fungible portions of an identified mass.~~ An electronic document of title means a document of title evidenced by a record consisting of information stored in an electronic medium. A tangible document of title means a document of title evidenced by a record consisting of information that is inscribed on a tangible medium.

(16) "Fault" means wrongful act, omission or breach.

(17) "Fungible" with respect to goods or securities means goods or securities of which any unit is, by nature or usage of trade, the equivalent of any other like unit. Goods which are not fungible shall be deemed fungible for the purposes of this Act to the extent that under a particular agreement or document unlike units are treated as equivalents.

(18) "Genuine" means free of forgery or counterfeiting.

(19) "Good faith" means honesty in fact in the conduct or transaction concerned.

(20) ~~"Holder," with respect to a negotiable instrument, means the person in possession if the instrument is payable to bearer or, in the case of an instrument payable to an identified person, if the~~

~~identified person is in possession. "Holder" with respect to a document of title means the person in possession if the goods are deliverable to bearer or to the order of the person in possession.~~

"Holder" means:

(A)   the person in possession of a negotiable instrument that is payable either to bearer or to an identified person that is the person in possession;

(B)   the person in possession of a negotiable tangible document of title if the goods are deliverable either to bearer or to the order of the person in possession; or

(C)   the person in control of a negotiable electronic document of title.

(21)   To "honor" is to pay or to accept and pay, or where a credit so engages to purchase or discount a draft complying with the terms of the credit.

(22)   "Insolvency proceedings" includes any assignment for the benefit of creditors or other proceedings intended to liquidate or rehabilitate the estate of the person involved.

(23)   A person is "insolvent" who either has ceased to pay his debts in the ordinary course of business or cannot pay his debts as they become due or is insolvent within the meaning of the federal bankruptcy law.

(24)   "Money" means a medium of exchange authorized or adopted by a domestic or foreign government and includes a monetary unit of account established by an intergovernmental organization or by agreement between two or more nations.

(25)   Subject to subsection (27), a ~~A~~ person has "notice" of a fact if the person ~~when~~

(a)   ~~he~~ has actual knowledge of it; ~~or~~

(b)   ~~he~~ has received a notice or notification of it; or

(c)   from all the facts and circumstances known to ~~him~~ the person at the time in question, ~~he~~ has reason to know that it exists.

A person "knows" or has "knowledge" of a fact when the person ~~he~~ has actual knowledge of it. "Discover" or "learn" or a word or phrase of similar import refers to knowledge rather than to reason to know. The time and circumstances under which a notice or notification may cease to be effective are not determined by this Act.

(26)   A person "notifies" or "gives" a notice or notification to another person by taking such steps as may be reasonably required to inform the other person in ordinary course, whether or not ~~such other~~ the other person actually comes to know of it. Subject to subsection (27), a ~~A~~ person "receives" a notice or notification when

(a)   it comes to ~~his~~ that person's attention; or

(b)   it is duly delivered in a form reasonable under the circumstances at the place of business through which the contract was made or at another location ~~any other place~~ held out by that person ~~him~~ as the place for receipt of such communications.

(27)   Notice, knowledge, or a notice or notification received by an organization is effective for a particular transaction from the time when it is brought to the attention of the individual conducting that transaction, and in any event, from the time when it would have been brought to the individual's ~~his~~ attention if the organization had exercised due diligence. An organization exercises due diligence if it maintains reasonable routines for communicating significant information to the person conducting the transaction and there is reasonable compliance with the routines. Due diligence does not require an individual acting for the organization to communicate information unless such communication is part of the individual's ~~his~~ regular duties or the individual ~~unless he~~ has reason to know of the transaction and that the transaction would be materially affected by the information.

(28) "Organization" includes a corporation, government or governmental subdivision or agency, business trust, estate, trust, partnership or association, two or more persons having a joint or common interest, or any other legal or commercial entity.

(29) "Party", as distinct from "third party", means a person who has engaged in a transaction or made an agreement within this Act.

(30) "Person" includes an individual or an organization (See Section 1–102).

(31) "Presumption" or "presumed" means that the trier of fact must find the existence of the fact presumed unless and until evidence is introduced which would support a finding of its non-existence.

(32) "Purchase" includes taking by sale, discount, negotiation, mortgage, pledge, lien, security interest, issue or re-issue, gift or any other voluntary transaction creating an interest in property.

(33) "Purchaser" means a person who takes by purchase.

(34) "Remedy" means any remedial right to which an aggrieved party is entitled with or without resort to a tribunal.

(35) "Representative" includes an agent, an officer of a corporation or association, and a trustee, executor or administrator of an estate, or any other person empowered to act for another.

(36) "Rights" includes remedies.

(37) "Security interest" means an interest in personal property or fixtures which secures payment or performance of an obligation. The term also includes any interest of a consignor and a buyer of accounts, chattel paper, a payment intangible, or a promissory note in a transaction that is subject to Article 9. The special property interest of a buyer of goods on identification of those goods to a contract for sale under Section 2–401 is not a "security interest", but a buyer may also acquire a "security interest" by complying with Article 9. Except as otherwise provided in Section 2–505, the right of a seller or lessor of goods under Article 2 or 2A to retain or acquire possession of the goods is not a "security interest", but a seller or lessor may also acquire a "security interest" by complying with Article 9. The retention or reservation of title by a seller of goods notwithstanding shipment or delivery to the buyer (Section 2–401) is limited in effect to a reservation of a "security interest".

Whether a transaction creates a lease or security interest is determined by the facts of each case; however, a transaction creates a security interest if the consideration the lessee is to pay the lessor for the right to possession and use of the goods is an obligation for the term of the lease not subject to termination by the lessee, and

(a)   the original term of the lease is equal to or greater than the remaining economic life of the goods,

(b)   the lessee is bound to renew the lease for the remaining economic life of the goods or is bound to become the owner of the goods,

(c)   the lessee has an option to renew the lease for the remaining economic life of the goods for no additional consideration or nominal additional consideration upon compliance with the lease agreement, or

(d)   the lessee has an option to become the owner of the goods for no additional consideration or nominal additional consideration upon compliance with the lease agreement.

A transaction does not create a security interest merely because it provides that

(a)   the present value of the consideration the lessee is obligated to pay the lessor for the right to possession and use of the goods is substantially equal to or is greater than the fair market value of the goods at the time the lease is entered into,

(b)   the lessee assumes risk of loss of the goods, or agrees to pay taxes, insurance, filing, recording, or registration fees, or service or maintenance costs with respect to the goods,

(c)   the lessee has an option to renew the lease or to become the owner of the goods,

(d) the lessee has an option to renew the lease for a fixed rent that is equal to or greater than the reasonably predictable fair market rent for the use of the goods for the term of the renewal at the time the option is to be performed, or

(e) the lessee has an option to become the owner of the goods for a fixed price that is equal to or greater than the reasonably predictable fair market value of the goods at the time the option is to be performed.

For purposes of this subsection (37):

(x) Additional consideration is not nominal if (i) when the option to renew the lease is granted to the lessee the rent is stated to be the fair market rent for the use of the goods for the term of the renewal determined at the time the option is to be performed, or (ii) when the option to become the owner of the goods is granted to the lessee the price is stated to be the fair market value of the goods determined at the time the option is to be performed. Additional consideration is nominal if it is less than the lessee's reasonably predictable cost of performing under the lease agreement if the option is not exercised;

(y) "Reasonably predictable" and "remaining economic life of the goods" are to be determined with reference to the facts and circumstances at the time the transaction is entered into; and

(z) "Present value" means the amount as of a date certain of one or more sums payable in the future, discounted to the date certain. The discount is determined by the interest rate specified by the parties if the rate is not manifestly unreasonable at the time the transaction is entered into; otherwise, the discount is determined by a commercially reasonable rate that takes into account the facts and circumstances of each case at the time the transaction was entered into.

(38) ~~"Send" in connection with any writing or notice means to deposit in the mail or deliver for transmission by any other usual means of communication with postage or cost of transmission provided for and properly addressed and in the case of an instrument to an address specified thereon or otherwise agreed, or if there be none to any address reasonable under the circumstances. The receipt of any writing or notice within the time at which it would have arrived if properly sent has the effect of a proper signing.~~

(38) "Send" in connection with a writing, record, or notice means:

(A) to deposit in the mail or deliver for transmission by any other usual means of communication with postage or cost of transmission provided for and properly addressed and, in the case of an instrument, to an address specified thereon or otherwise agreed, or if there be none to any address reasonable under the circumstances; or

(B) in any other way to cause to be received any record or notice within the time it would have arrived if properly sent.

(39) "Signed" includes any symbol executed or adopted by a party with present intention to authenticate a writing.

(40) "Surety" includes guarantor.

(41) "Telegram" includes a message transmitted by radio, teletype, cable, any mechanical method of transmission, or the like.

(42) "Term" means that portion of an agreement which relates to a particular matter.

(43) "Unauthorized" signature means one made without actual, implied, or apparent authority and includes a forgery.

(44) "Value". Except as otherwise provided with respect to negotiable instruments and bank collections (Sections 3–303, 4–210 and 4–211) a person gives "value" for rights if he acquires them

(a) in return for a binding commitment to extend credit or for the extension of immediately available credit whether or not drawn upon and whether or not a charge-back is provided for in the event of difficulties in collection; or

(b) as security for or in total or partial satisfaction of a pre-existing claim; or

(c)   by accepting delivery pursuant to a pre-existing contract for purchase; or

(d)   generally, in return for any consideration sufficient to support a simple contract.

(45) "Warehouse receipt" means a <u>document of title</u> <s>receipt</s> issued by a person engaged in the business of storing goods for hire.

(46) "Written" or "writing" includes printing, typewriting or any other intentional reduction to tangible form.

As amended in 1962, 1972, 1977, 1987, 1990, 1994 and 1999.

Official Comment

Prior Uniform Statutory Provision, Changes and New Matter:

1.   "Action". See similar definitions in Section 191, Uniform Negotiable Instruments Law; Section 76, Uniform Sales Act; Section 58, Uniform Warehouse Receipts Act; Section 53, Uniform Bills of Lading Act. The definition has been rephrased and enlarged.

2.   "Aggrieved party". New.

3.   "Agreement". New. As used in this Act the word is intended to include full recognition of usage of trade, course of dealing, course of performance and the surrounding circumstances as effective parts thereof, and of any agreement permitted under the provisions of this Act to displace a stated rule of law.

4.   "Bank". See Section 191, Uniform Negotiable Instruments Law.

5.   "Bearer". From Section 191, Uniform Negotiable Instruments Law. The prior definition has been broadened. <u>The term bearer applies to negotiable documents of title and has been broadened to include a person in control of an electronic negotiable document of title. Control of an electronic document of title is defined in Article 7 (Section 7–106).</u>

6.   "Bill of Lading". See similar definitions in Section 1, Uniform Bills of Lading Act. The definition has been enlarged to include freight forwarders' bills and bills issued by contract carriers as well as those issued by common carriers. <s>The definition of airbill is new.</s> <u>A bill of lading is one type of document of title as defined in subsection (15). This definition should be read in conjunction with the definition of carrier in Article 7 (Section 7–102).</u>

7.   "Branch". New.

8.   "Burden of establishing a fact". New.

9.   "Buyer in ordinary course of business". From Section 1, Uniform Trust Receipts Act. The definition has been expanded to make clear the type of person protected. Its major significance lies in Section 2–403 and in the Article on Secured Transactions (Article 9).

The first sentence of paragraph (9) makes clear that a buyer from a pawnbroker cannot be a buyer in ordinary course of business. The second sentence tracks Section 6–102(1)(m). It explains what it means to buy "in the ordinary course." The penultimate sentence prevents a buyer that does not have the right to possession as against the seller from being a buyer in ordinary course of business. Concerning when a buyer obtains possessory rights, see Sections 2–502 and 2–716. However, the penultimate sentence is not intended to affect a buyer's status as a buyer in ordinary course of business in cases (such as a "drop shipment") involving delivery by the seller to a person buying from the buyer or a donee from the buyer. The requirement relates to whether *as against the seller* the buyer or one taking through the buyer has possessory rights.

10.   "Conspicuous". <s>New. This is intended to indicate some of the methods of making a term attention-calling. But the test is whether attention can reasonably be expected to be called to it.</s> <u>This definition states the general standard that to be conspicuous a term ought to be noticed by a reasonable person. Whether a term is conspicuous is an issue for the court. Subparagraphs (A) and (B) set out several methods for making a term conspicuous. Requiring that a term be conspicuous blends a notice function (the term ought to be noticed) and a planning function (giving guidance to the party relying on the term regarding how that result can be achieved). Although these paragraphs indicate some of the methods for making a term attention-calling, the test is whether attention can reasonably be expected to be called to it. The statutory language should not be construed to permit a result that is inconsistent with that test.</u>

11.   "Contract". New. But see Sections 3 and 71, Uniform Sales Act.

12.   "Creditor". New.

13.   "Defendant". From Section 76, Uniform Sales Act. Rephrased.

14.   "Delivery". Section 76, Uniform Sales Act, Section 191, Uniform Negotiable Instruments Law, Section 58, Uniform Warehouse Receipts Act and Section 53, Uniform Bills of Lading Act. The definition has been revised to accommodate electronic documents of title. Control of an electronic document of title is defined in Article 7 (Section 7–106).

15."Document of title". From Section 76, Uniform Sales Act, but rephrased to eliminate certain ambiguities. This definition makes explicit Thus, by making it explicit that the obligation or designation of a third party as "bailee" is essential to a document, this definition and clearly rejects any such result as obtained in Hixson v. Ward, 254 Ill.App. 505 (1929), which treated a conditional sales contract as a document of title. Also the definition is left open so that new types of documents may be included, including documents which gain commercial recognition in the international arena. See UNCITRAL Draft Instrument on the Carriage of Goods by Sea. It is unforeseeable what documents may one day serve the essential purpose now filled by warehouse receipts and bills of lading. Truck transport has already opened up problems which do not fit the patterns of practice resting upon the assumption that a draft can move through banking channels faster than the goods themselves can reach their destination. There lie ahead air transport and such probabilities as teletype transmission of what may some day be regarded commercially as "Documents of Title". The definition is stated in terms of the function of the documents with the intention that any document which gains commercial recognition as accomplishing the desired result shall be included within its scope. Fungible goods are adequately identified within the language of the definition by identification of the mass of which they are a part.

Dock warrants were within the Sales Act definition of document of title apparently for the purpose of recognizing a valid tender by means of such paper. In current commercial practice a dock warrant or receipt is a kind of interim certificate issued by steamship shipping companies upon delivery of the goods at the dock, entitling a designated person to have issued to him at the company's office to be issued a bill of lading. The receipt itself is invariably nonnegotiable in form although it may indicate that a negotiable bill is to be forthcoming. Such a document is not within the general compass of the definition, although trade usage may in some cases entitle such paper to be treated as a document of title. If the dock receipt actually represents a storage obligation undertaken by the shipping company, then it is a warehouse receipt within this Section regardless of the name given to the instrument.

The goods must be "described", but the description may be by marks or labels and may be qualified in such a way as to disclaim personal knowledge of the issuer regarding contents or condition. However, baggage and parcel checks and similar "tokens" of storage which identify stored goods only as those received in exchange for the token are not covered by this Article. The definition is broad enough to include an airway bill.

A document of title may be either tangible or electronic. Tangible documents of title should be construed to mean traditional paper documents. Electronic documents of title are documents that are stored in an electronic medium instead of in tangible form. The concept of an electronic medium should be construed liberally to include electronic, digital, magnetic, optical, electromagnetic, or any other current or similar emerging technologies. As to reissuing a document of title in an alternative medium, see Article 7, Section 7–105. Control for electronic documents of title is defined in Article 7 (Section 7–106).

16.   "Fault". From Section 76, Uniform Sales Act.

17.   "Fungible". See Sections 5, 6 and 76, Uniform Sales Act; Section 58, Uniform Warehouse Receipts Act. Fungibility of goods "by agreement" has been added for clarity and accuracy. As to securities, see Section 8–107 and Comment. *Amendment approved by the Permanent Editorial Board for Uniform Commercial Code November 4, 1995.*

18.   "Genuine". New.

19.   "Good faith". See Section 76(2), Uniform Sales Act; Section 58(2), Uniform Warehouse Receipts Act; Section 53(2), Uniform Bills of Lading Act; Section 22(2), Uniform Stock Transfer Act. "Good faith", whenever it is used in the Code, means at least what is here stated. In certain Articles, by specific provision, additional requirements are made applicable. See, e.g., Secs. 2–103(1)(b), 7–404. To illustrate, in the Article on Sales, Section 2–103, good faith is expressly defined as including in the case of a merchant observance of reasonable commercial

standards of fair dealing in the trade, so that throughout that Article wherever a merchant appears in the case an inquiry into his observance of such standards is necessary to determine his good faith.

20.　"Holder". See similar definitions in Section 191, Uniform Negotiable Instruments Law; Section 58, Uniform Warehouse Receipts Act; Section 53, Uniform Bills of Lading Act.

21.　"Honor". New.

22.　"Insolvency proceedings". New.

23.　"Insolvent". Section 76(3), Uniform Sales Act. The three tests of insolvency—"ceased to pay his debts in the ordinary course of business," "cannot pay his debts as they become due," and "insolvent within the meaning of the federal bankruptcy law"—are expressly set up as alternative tests and must be approached from a commercial standpoint.

24.　"Money". Section 6(5), Uniform Negotiable Instruments Law. The test adopted is that of sanction of government, whether by authorization before issue or adoption afterward, which recognizes the circulating medium as a part of the official currency of that government. The narrow view that money is limited to legal tender is rejected.

25.　"Notice". ~~New. Compare N.I.L. Sec. 56. Under the definition a person has notice when he has received a notification of the fact in question. But by the last sentence the act leaves open the time and circumstances under which notice or notification may cease to be effective. Therefore such cases as Graham v. White-Phillips Co., 296 U.S. 27, 56 S.Ct. 21, 80 L.Ed. 20 (1935), are not overruled.~~

~~26.　"Notifies". New. This is the word used when the essential fact is the proper dispatch of the notice, not its receipt. Compare "Send". When the essential fact is the other party's receipt of the notice, that is stated. The second sentence states when a notification is received.~~

~~27.　New. This makes clear that reason to know, knowledge, or a notification, although "received" for instance by a clerk in Department A of an organization, is effective for a transaction conducted in Department B only from the time when it was or should have been communicated to the individual conducting that transaction.~~

A person has notice of a fact when, inter alia, the person has received a notification of the fact in question. The word "notifies" is used when the essential fact is the proper dispatch of the notice, not its receipt. Compare "send." When the essential fact is the other party's receipt of the notice, that is stated. Subsection (26) states when a notification is received. Subsection (27) makes clear that notice, knowledge, or a notification, although "received," for instance, by a clerk in Department A of an organization, is effective for a transaction conducted in Department B only from the time when it was or should have been communicated to the individual conducting that transaction.

28.　"Organization". This is the definition of every type of entity or association, excluding an individual, acting as such. Definitions of "person" were included in Section 191, Uniform Negotiable Instruments Law; Section 76, Uniform Sales Act; Section 58, Uniform Warehouse Receipts Act; Section 53, Uniform Bills of Lading Act; Section 22, Uniform Stock Transfer Act; Section 1, Uniform Trust Receipts Act. The definition of "organization" given here includes a number of entities or associations not specifically mentioned in prior definition of "person", namely, government, governmental subdivision or agency, business trust, trust and estate.

29.　"Party". New. Mention of a party includes, of course, a person acting through an agent. However, where an agent comes into opposition or contrast to his principal, particular account is taken of that situation.

30.　"Person". See Comment to definition of "Organization". The reference to Section 1–102 is to subsection (5) of that section.

31.　"Presumption". New.

32.　"Purchase". Section 58, Uniform Warehouse Receipts Act; Section 76, Uniform Sales Act; Section 53, Uniform Bills of Lading Act; Section 22, Uniform Stock Transfer Act; Section 1, Uniform Trust Receipts Act. Rephrased. With the addition of taking "by . . . security interest," the revised definition makes explicit what formerly was implicit.

33.　"Purchaser". Section 58, Uniform Warehouse Receipts Act; Section 76, Uniform Sales Act; Section 53, Uniform Bills of Lading Act; Section 22, Uniform Stock Transfer Act; Section 1, Uniform Trust Receipts Act. Rephrased.

34. "Remedy". New. The purpose is to make it clear that both remedy and rights (as defined) include those remedial rights of "self help" which are among the most important bodies of rights under this Act, remedial rights being those to which an aggrieved party can resort on his own motion.

35. "Representative". New.

36. "Rights". New. See Comment to "Remedy".

37. "Security Interest". See Section 1, Uniform Trust Receipts Act. The definition of "security interest" was revised in connection with the promulgation of Article 2A and also to take account of the expanded scope of Article 9 as revised in the 1998 Official Text. It includes the interest of a consignor and the interest of a buyer of accounts, chattel paper, payment intangibles, or promissory notes. See Section 9–109. It also makes clear that, with certain exceptions, *in rem* rights of sellers and lessors under Articles 2 and 2A are not "security interests." Among the rights that are not security interests are the right to withhold delivery under Section 2–702(1), 2–703(a), or 2A–525, the right to stop delivery under Section 2–705 or 2A–526, and the right to reclaim under Section 2–507(2) or 2–702(2).

One of the reasons it was decided to codify the law with respect to leases was to resolve an issue that has created considerable confusion in the courts: what is a lease? The confusion exists, in part, due to the last two sentences of the definition of security interest in the 1978 Official Text of the Act. Section 1–201(37). The confusion is compounded by the rather considerable change in the federal, state and local tax laws and accounting rules as they relate to leases of goods. The answer is important because the definition of lease determines not only the rights and remedies of the parties to the lease but also those of third parties. If a transaction creates a lease and not a security interest, the lessee's interest in the goods is limited to its leasehold estate; the residual interest in the goods belongs to the lessor. This has significant implications to the lessee's creditors. "On common law theory, the lessor, since he has not parted with title, is entitled to full protection against the lessee's creditors and trustee in bankruptcy . . . ." 1 G. Gilmore, *Security Interests in Personal Property* § 3.6, at 76 (1965).

Under pre-Act chattel security law there was generally no requirement that the lessor file the lease, a financing statement, or the like, to enforce the lease agreement against the lessee or any third party; the Article on Secured Transactions (Article 9) did not change the common law in that respect. Coogan, Leasing and the Uniform Commercial Code, in *Equipment Leasing—Leveraged Leasing* 681, 700 n.25, 729 n.80 (2d ed.1980). The Article on Leases (Article 2A) has not changed the law in that respect, except for leases of fixtures. Section 2A–309. An examination of the common law will not provide an adequate answer to the question of what is a lease. The definition of security interest in Section 1–201(37) of the 1978 Official Text of the Act provides that the Article on Secured Transactions (Article 9) governs security interests disguised as leases, *i.e.,* leases intended as security; however, the definition is vague and outmoded.

Lease is defined in Article 2A as a transfer of the right to possession and use of goods for a term, in return for consideration. Section 2A–103(1)(j). The definition continues by stating that the retention or creation of a security interest is not a lease. Thus, the task of sharpening the line between true leases and security interests disguised as leases continues to be a function of this section.

The first paragraph of this definition is a revised version of the first five sentences of the 1978 Official Text of Section 1–201(37). The changes are modest in that they make a style change in the fourth sentence and delete the reference to lease in the fifth sentence. The balance of this definition is new, although it preserves elements of the last two sentences of the prior definition. The focus of the changes was to draw a sharper line between leases and security interests disguised as leases to create greater certainty in commercial transactions.

Prior to this amendment, Section 1–201(37) provided that whether a lease was intended as security (*i.e.,* a security interest disguised as a lease) was to be determined from the facts of each case; however, (a) the inclusion of an option to purchase did not itself make the lease one intended for security, and (b) an agreement that upon compliance with the terms of the lease the lessee would become, or had the option to become, the owner of the property for no additional consideration, or for a nominal consideration, did make the lease one intended for security.

Reference to the intent of the parties to create a lease or security interest has led to unfortunate results. In discovering intent, courts have relied upon factors that were thought to be more consistent with sales or loans than leases. Most of these criteria, however, are as applicable to true leases as to security interests. Examples include the typical net lease provisions, a purported lessor's lack of storage facilities or its character as a financing party rather than a dealer in goods. Accordingly, amended Section 1–201(37) deletes all reference to the parties' intent.

The second paragraph of the new definition is taken from Section 1(2) of the Uniform Conditional Sales Act (act withdrawn 1943), modified to reflect current leasing practice. Thus, reference to the case law prior to this Act will provide a useful source of precedent. Gilmore, *Security Law, Formalism and Article 9,* 47 Neb.L.Rev. 659, 671 (1968). Whether a transaction creates a lease or a security interest continues to be determined by the facts of each case. The second paragraph further provides that a transaction creates a security interest if the lessee has an obligation to continue paying consideration for the term of the lease, if the obligation is not terminable by the lessee (thus correcting early statutory gloss, *e.g., In re Royer's Bakery, Inc.,* 1 U.C.C. Rep.Serv. (Callaghan) 342 (Bankr.E.D.Pa.1963)) and if one of four additional tests is met. The first of these four tests, subparagraph (a), is that the original lease term is equal to or greater than the remaining economic life of the goods. The second of these tests, subparagraph (b), is that the lessee is either bound to renew the lease for the remaining economic life of the goods or to become the owner of the goods. *In re Gehrke Enters.,* 1 Bankr. 647, 651–52 (Bankr.W.D.Wis.1979). The third of these tests, subparagraph (c), is whether the lessee has an option to renew the lease for the remaining economic life or the goods for no additional consideration or for nominal additional consideration, which is defined later in this section. *In re Celeryvale Transp.,* 44 Bankr. 1007, 1014–15 (Bankr.E.D.Tenn.1984). The fourth of these tests, subparagraph (d), is whether the lessee has an option to become the owner of the goods for no additional consideration or for nominal additional consideration. All of these tests focus on economics, not the intent of the parties. *In re Berge,* 32 Bankr. 370, 371–73 (Bankr.W.D.Wis.1983).

The focus on economics is reinforced by the next paragraph, which is new. It states that a transaction does not create a security interest merely because the transaction has certain characteristics listed therein. Subparagraph (a) has no statutory derivative; it states that a full payout lease does not *per se* create a security interest. *Rushton v. Shea,* 419 F.Supp. 1349, 1365 (D.Del.1976). Subparagraph (b) provides the same regarding the provisions of the typical net lease. *Compare All-States Leasing Co. v. Ochs,* 42 Or.App. 319, 600 P.2d 899 (Ct.App.1979) *with In re Tillery,* 571 F.2d 1361 (5th Cir.1978). Subparagraph (c) restates and expands the provisions of former Section 1–201(37) to make clear that the option can be to buy or renew. Subparagraphs (d) and (e) treat fixed price options and provide that fair market value must be determined at the time the transaction is entered into. *Compare Arnold Mach. Co. v. Balls,* 624 P.2d 678 (Utah 1981) *with Aoki v. Shepherd Mach. Co.,* 665 F.2d 941 (9th Cir.1982).

The relationship of the second paragraph of this subsection to the third paragraph of this subsection deserves to be explored. The fixed price purchase option provides a useful example. A fixed price purchase option in a lease does not of itself create a security interest. This is particularly true if the fixed price is equal to or greater than the reasonably predictable fair market value of the goods at the time the option is to be performed. A security interest is created only if the option price is nominal and the conditions stated in the introduction to the second paragraph of this subsection are met. There is a set of purchase options whose fixed price is less than fair market value but greater than nominal that must be determined on the facts of each case to ascertain whether the transaction in which the option is included creates a lease or a security interest.

It was possible to provide for various other permutations and combinations with respect to options to purchase and renew. For example, this section could have stated a rule to govern the facts of *In re Marhoefer Packing Co.,* 674 F.2d 1139 (7th Cir.1982). This was not done because it would unnecessarily complicate the definition. Further development of this rule is left to the courts.

The fourth paragraph provides definitions and rules of construction.

38. "Send". New. Compare "notifies". The definition of send has been modified to allow for electronic dispatch.

39. "Signed". New. The inclusion of authentication in the definition of "signed" is to make clear that as the term is used in this Act a complete signature is not necessary. Authentication may be printed, stamped or written; it may be by initials or by thumbprint. It may be on any part of the document and in appropriate cases may be found in a billhead or letterhead. No catalog of possible authentications can be complete and the court must use common sense and commercial experience in passing upon these matters. The question always is whether the symbol was executed or adopted by the party with present intention to authenticate the writing.

40. "Surety". New.

41. "Telegram". New.

42. "Term". New.

43.   Under the former version of § 1–201(43), it was not clear whether a reference to an "unauthorized signature" in Articles 3 and 4 applied to indorsements. The words "or indorsement" are deleted so that references to "unauthorized signature" in § 3–406 and elsewhere will unambiguously refer to any signature.

44.   "Value". See Sections 25, 26, 27, 191, Uniform Negotiable Instruments Law; Section 76, Uniform Sales Act; Section 53, Uniform Bills of Lading Act; Section 58, Uniform Warehouse Receipts Act; Section 22(1), Uniform Stock Transfer Act; Section 1, Uniform Trust Receipts Act. All the Uniform Acts in the commercial law field (except the Uniform Conditional Sales Act) have carried definitions of "value". All those definitions provided that value was any consideration sufficient to support a simple contract, including the taking of property in satisfaction of or as security for a pre-existing claim. Subsections (a), (b) and (d) in substance continue the definitions of "value" in the earlier acts. Subsection (c) makes explicit that "value" is also given in a third situation: where a buyer by taking delivery under a pre-existing contract converts a contingent into a fixed obligation.

This definition is not applicable to Articles 3 and 4, but the express inclusion of immediately available credit as value follows the separate definitions in those Articles. See Sections 4–208, 4–209, 3–303. A bank or other financing agency which in good faith makes advances against property held as collateral becomes a bona fide purchaser of that property even though provision may be made for charge-back in case of trouble. Checking credit is "immediately available" within the meaning of this section if the bank would be subject to an action for slander of credit in case checks drawn against the credit were dishonored, and when a charge-back is not discretionary with the bank, but may only be made when difficulties in collection arise in connection with the specific transaction involved.

45.   "Warehouse receipt". See Section 76(1), Uniform Sales Act; Section 1, Uniform Warehouse Receipts Act. Receipts issued by a field warehouse are included, provided the warehouseman and the depositor of the goods are different persons. The definition makes clear that the receipt must qualify as a document of title under subsection (15).

46.   "Written" or "writing". This is a broadening of the definition contained in Section 191 of the Uniform Negotiable Instruments Law.

As amended in 1999.

§ 1–202.   Prima Facie Evidence by Third Party Documents.

A document in due form purporting to be a bill of lading, policy or certificate of insurance, official weigher's or inspector's certificate, consular invoice, or any other document authorized or required by the contract to be issued by a third party shall be prima facie evidence of its own authenticity and genuineness and of the facts stated in the document by the third party.

Official Comment

Prior Uniform Statutory Provision: None.

Purposes:

1.   This section is designed to supply judicial recognition for documents which have traditionally been relied upon as trustworthy by commercial men.

2.   This section is concerned only with documents which have been given a preferred status by the parties themselves who have required their procurement in the agreement and for this reason the applicability of the section is limited to actions arising out of the contract which authorized or required the document. The documents listed are intended to be illustrative and not all inclusive.

3.   The provisions of this section go no further than establishing the documents in question as prima facie evidence and leave to the court the ultimate determination of the facts where the accuracy or authenticity of the documents is questioned. In this connection the section calls for a commercially reasonable interpretation.

Definitional Cross References:

"Bill of lading". Section 1–201.
"Contract". Section 1–201.
"Genuine". Section 1–201.

§ 1-203.   Obligation of Good Faith.

Every contract or duty within this Act imposes an obligation of good faith in its performance or enforcement.

Official Comment

Prior Uniform Statutory Provision: None.

Purposes:

This section sets forth a basic principle running throughout this Act. The principle involved is that in commercial transactions good faith is required in the performance and enforcement of all agreements or duties. Particular applications of this general principle appear in specific provisions of the Act such as the option to accelerate at will (Section 1–208), the right to cure a defective delivery of goods (Section 2–508), the duty of a merchant buyer who has rejected goods to effect salvage operations (Section 2–603), substituted performance (Section 2–614), and failure of presupposed conditions (Section 2–615). The concept, however, is broader than any of these illustrations and applies generally, as stated in this section, to the performance or enforcement of every contract or duty within this Act. It is further implemented by Section 1–205 on course of dealing and usage of trade. This section does not support an independent cause of action for failure to perform or enforce in good faith. Rather, this section means that a failure to perform or enforce, in good faith, a specific duty or obligation under the contract, constitutes a breach of that contract or makes unavailable, under the particular circumstances, a remedial right or power. This distinction makes it clear that the doctrine of good faith merely directs a court towards interpreting contracts within the commercial context in which they are created, performed, and enforced, and does not create a separate duty of fairness and reasonableness which can be independently breached. See PEB Commentary No. 10, dated February 10, 1994 [See Appendix G].

It is to be noted that under the Sales Article definition of good faith (Section 2–103), contracts made by a merchant have incorporated in them the explicit standard not only of honesty in fact (Section 1–201), but also of observance by the merchant of reasonable commercial standards of fair dealing in the trade.

Cross References:

Sections 1–201; 1–205; 1–208; 2–103; 2–508; 2–603; 2–614; 2–615.

Definitional Cross References:

"Contract". Section 1–201.
"Good faith". Sections 1–201; 2–103.

§ 1-204.   Time; Reasonable Time; "Seasonably".

(1)   Whenever this Act requires any action to be taken within a reasonable time, any time which is not manifestly unreasonable may be fixed by agreement.

(2)   What is a reasonable time for taking any action depends on the nature, purpose and circumstances of such action.

(3)   An action is taken "seasonably" when it is taken at or within the time agreed or if no time is agreed at or within a reasonable time.

Official Comment

Prior Uniform Statutory Provision: Compare Section 193, Uniform Negotiable Instruments Law.

Purposes:

1.   Subsection (1) recognizes that nothing is stronger evidence of a reasonable time than the fixing of such time by a fair agreement between the parties. However, provision is made for disregarding a clause which whether by inadvertence or overreaching fixes a time so unreasonable that it amounts to eliminating all remedy under the contract. The parties are not required to fix the most reasonable time but may fix any time which is not obviously unfair as judged by the time of contracting.

2.   Under the section, the agreement which fixes the time need not be part of the main agreement, but may occur separately. Notice also that under the definition of "agreement" (Section 1–201) the circumstances of

the transaction, including course of dealing or usages of trade or course of performance may be material. On the question what is a reasonable time these matters will often be important.

Definitional Cross Reference:

"Agreement". Section 1–201.

§ 1–205.   Course of Dealing and Usage of Trade.

(1)   A course of dealing is a sequence of previous conduct between the parties to a particular transaction which is fairly to be regarded as establishing a common basis of understanding for interpreting their expressions and other conduct.

(2)   A usage of trade is any practice or method of dealing having such regularity of observance in a place, vocation or trade as to justify an expectation that it will be observed with respect to the transaction in question. The existence and scope of such a usage are to be proved as facts. If it is established that such a usage is embodied in a written trade code or similar writing the interpretation of the writing is for the court.

(3)   A course of dealing between parties and any usage of trade in the vocation or trade in which they are engaged or of which they are or should be aware give particular meaning to and supplement or qualify terms of an agreement.

(4)   The express terms of an agreement and an applicable course of dealing or usage of trade shall be construed wherever reasonable as consistent with each other; but when such construction is unreasonable express terms control both course of dealing and usage of trade and course of dealing controls usage of trade.

(5)   An applicable usage of trade in the place where any part of performance is to occur shall be used in interpreting the agreement as to that part of the performance.

(6)   Evidence of a relevant usage of trade offered by one party is not admissible unless and until he has given the other party such notice as the court finds sufficient to prevent unfair surprise to the latter.

Official Comment

Prior Uniform Statutory Provision: No such general provision but see Sections 9(1), 15(5), 18(2), and 71, Uniform Sales Act.

Purposes: This section makes it clear that:

1.   This Act rejects both the "lay-dictionary" and the "conveyancer's" reading of a commercial agreement. Instead the meaning of the agreement of the parties is to be determined by the language used by them and by their action, read and interpreted in the light of commercial practices and other surrounding circumstances. The measure and background for interpretation are set by the commercial context, which may explain and supplement even the language of a formal or final writing.

2.   Course of dealing under subsection (1) is restricted, literally, to a sequence of conduct between the parties previous to the agreement. However, the provisions of the Act on course of performance make it clear that a sequence of conduct after or under the agreement may have equivalent meaning. (Section 2–208.)

3.   "Course of dealing" may enter the agreement either by explicit provisions of the agreement or by tacit recognition.

4.   This Act deals with "usage of trade" as a factor in reaching the commercial meaning of the agreement which the parties have made. The language used is to be interpreted as meaning what it may fairly be expected to mean to parties involved in the particular commercial transaction in a given locality or in a given vocation or trade. By adopting in this context the term "usage of trade" this Act expresses its intent to reject those cases which see evidence of "custom" as representing an effort to displace or negate "established rules of law". A distinction is to be drawn between mandatory rules of law such as the Statute of Frauds provisions of Article 2 on Sales whose very office is to control and restrict the actions of the parties, and which cannot be abrogated by agreement, or by a usage of trade, and those rules of law (such as those in Part 3 of Article 2 on Sales) which fill in points which the parties have not considered and in fact agreed upon. The latter rules hold "unless otherwise agreed" but yield to the contrary agreement of the parties. Part of the agreement of the parties to which such rules yield is to be sought for in the usages of trade which furnish the background and give particular meaning to the language used, and

are the framework of common understanding controlling any general rules of law which hold only when there is no such understanding.

5.   A usage of trade under subsection (2) must have the "regularity of observance" specified. The ancient English tests for "custom" are abandoned in this connection. Therefore, it is not required that a usage of trade be "ancient or immemorial", "universal" or the like. Under the requirement of subsection (2) full recognition is thus available for new usages and for usages currently observed by the great majority of decent dealers, even though dissidents ready to cut corners do not agree. There is room also for proper recognition of usage agreed upon by merchants in trade codes.

6.   The policy of this Act controlling explicit unconscionable contracts and clauses (Sections 1–203, 2–302) applies to implicit clauses which rest on usage of trade and carries forward the policy underlying the ancient requirement that a custom or usage must be "reasonable". However, the emphasis is shifted. The very fact of commercial acceptance makes out a prima facie case that the usage is reasonable, and the burden is no longer on the usage to establish itself as being reasonable. But the anciently established policing of usage by the courts is continued to the extent necessary to cope with the situation arising if an unconscionable or dishonest practice should become standard.

7.   Subsection (3), giving the prescribed effect to usages of which the parties "are or should be aware", reinforces the provision of subsection (2) requiring not universality but only the described "regularity of observance" of the practice or method. This subsection also reinforces the point of subsection (2) that such usages may be either general to trade or particular to a special branch of trade.

8.   Although the terms in which this Act defines "agreement" include the elements of course of dealing and usage of trade, the fact that express reference is made in some sections to those elements is not to be construed as carrying a contrary intent or implication elsewhere. Compare Section 1–102(4).

9.   In cases of a well established line of usage varying from the general rules of this Act where the precise amount of the variation has not been worked out into a single standard, the party relying on the usage is entitled, in any event, to the minimum variation demonstrated. The whole is not to be disregarded because no particular line of detail has been established. In case a dominant pattern has been fairly evidenced, the party relying on the usage is entitled under this section to go to the trier of fact on the question of whether such dominant pattern has been incorporated into the agreement.

10.   Subsection (6) is intended to insure that this Act's liberal recognition of the needs of commerce in regard to usage of trade shall not be made into an instrument of abuse.

Cross References:

Point 1: Sections 1–203, 2–104 and 2–202.
Point 2: Section 2–208.
Point 4: Section 2–201 and Part 3 of Article 2.
Point 6: Sections 1–203 and 2–302.
Point 8: Sections 1–102 and 1–201.
Point 9: Section 2–204(3).

Definitional Cross References:

"Agreement". Section 1–201.
"Contract". Section 1–201.
"Party". Section 1–201.
"Term". Section 1–201.

§ 1–206.   Statute of Frauds for Kinds of Personal Property Not Otherwise Covered.

(1)   Except in the cases described in subsection (2) of this section a contract for the sale of personal property is not enforceable by way of action or defense beyond five thousand dollars in amount or value of remedy unless there is some writing which indicates that a contract for sale has been made between the parties at a defined or stated price, reasonably identifies the subject matter, and is signed by the party against whom enforcement is sought or by his authorized agent.

(2)   Subsection (1) of this section does not apply to contracts for the sale of goods (Section 2–201) nor of securities (Section 8–113) nor to security agreements (Section 9–203).

As amended in 1994.

Official Comment

Prior Uniform Statutory Provision: Section 4, Uniform Sales Act (which was based on Section 17 of the Statute of 29 Charles II).

Changes: Completely rewritten by this and other sections.

Purposes: To fill the gap left by the Statute of Frauds provisions for goods (Section 2–201), securities (Section 8–319), and security interests (Section 9–203). As to securities, see Section 8–113. The Uniform Sales Act covered the sale of "choses in action"; the principal gap relates to sale of the "general intangibles" that are not "payment intangibles" (as those terms are defined in Section 9–102) and to transactions excluded from Article 9 by Section 9–109(d). The informality normal to such transactions is recognized by lifting the limit for oral transactions to $5,000. In such transactions there is often no standard of practice by which to judge, and values can rise or drop without warning; troubling abuses are avoided when the dollar limit is exceeded by requiring that the subject-matter be reasonably identified in a signed writing which indicates that a contract for sale has been made at a defined or stated price. *Amendments approved by the Permanent Editorial Board for Uniform Commercial Code November 4, 1995.*

Definitional Cross References:

"Action". Section 1–201.
"Agreement". Section 1–201.
"Contract". Section 1–201.
"Contract for sale". Section 2–106.
"Goods". Section 2–105.
"Party". Section 1–201.
"Sale". Section 2–106.
"Signed". Section 1–201.
"Writing". Section 1–201.

§ 1–207.   Performance or Acceptance Under Reservation of Rights.

(1)   A party who, with explicit reservation of rights performs or promises performance or assents to performance in a manner demanded or offered by the other party does not thereby prejudice the rights reserved. Such words as "without prejudice", "under protest" or the like are sufficient.

(2)   Subsection (1) does not apply to an accord and satisfaction.

As amended in 1990.

Official Comment

1.   This section provides machinery for the continuation of performance along the lines contemplated by the contract despite a pending dispute, by adopting the mercantile device of going ahead with delivery, acceptance, or payment "without prejudice," "under protest," "under reserve," "with reservation of all our rights," and the like. All of these phrases completely reserve all rights within the meaning of this section. The section therefore contemplates that limited as well as general reservations and acceptance by a party may be made "subject to satisfaction of our purchaser," "subject to acceptance by our customers," or the like.

2.   This section does not add any new requirement of language of reservation where not already required by law, but merely provides a specific measure on which a party can rely as that party makes or concurs in any interim adjustment in the course of performance. It does not affect or impair the provisions of this Act such as those under which the buyer's remedies for defect survive acceptance without being expressly claimed if notice of the defects is given within a reasonable time. Nor does it disturb the policy of those cases which restrict the effect of a waiver of a defect to reasonable limits under the circumstances, even though no such reservation is expressed.

The section is not addressed to the creation or loss of remedies in the ordinary course of performance but rather to a method of procedure where one party is claiming as of right something which the other believes to be unwarranted.

3.   Judicial authority was divided on the issue of whether former Section 1–207 (present subsection (1)) applied to an accord and satisfaction. Typically the cases involved attempts to reach an accord and satisfaction by use of a check tendered in full satisfaction of a claim. Subsection (2) of revised Section 1–207 resolves this conflict by stating that Section 1–207 does not apply to an accord and satisfaction. Section 3–311 of revised Article 3 governs if an accord and satisfaction is attempted by tender of a negotiable instrument as stated in that section. If Section 3–311 does not apply, the issue of whether an accord and satisfaction has been effected is determined by the law of contract. Whether or not Section 3–311 applies, Section 1–207 has no application to an accord and satisfaction.

§ 1–208.   Option to Accelerate at Will.

A term providing that one party or his successor in interest may accelerate payment or performance or require collateral or additional collateral "at will" or "when he deems himself insecure" or in words of similar import shall be construed to mean that he shall have power to do so only if he in good faith believes that the prospect of payment or performance is impaired. The burden of establishing lack of good faith is on the party against whom the power has been exercised.

Official Comment

Prior Uniform Statutory Provision: None.

Purposes:

The increased use of acceleration clauses either in the case of sales on credit or in time paper or in security transactions has led to some confusion in the cases as to the effect to be given to a clause which seemingly grants the power of an acceleration at the whim and caprice of one party. This Section is intended to make clear that despite language which can be so construed and which further might be held to make the agreement void as against public policy or to make the contract illusory or too indefinite for enforcement, the clause means that the option is to be exercised only in the good faith belief that the prospect of payment or performance is impaired.

Obviously this section has no application to demand instruments or obligations whose very nature permits call at any time with or without reason. This section applies only to an agreement or to paper which in the first instance is payable at a future date.

Definitional Cross References:

"Burden of establishing". Section 1–201.
"Good faith". Section 1–201.
"Party". Section 1–201.
"Term". Section 1–201.

§ 1–209.   Subordinated Obligations.

An obligation may be issued as subordinated to payment of another obligation of the person obligated, or a creditor may subordinate his right to payment of an obligation by agreement with either the person obligated or another creditor of the person obligated. Such a subordination does not create a security interest as against either the common debtor or a subordinated creditor. This section shall be construed as declaring the law as it existed prior to the enactment of this section and not as modifying it.

Added in 1966.

Note: *This new section is proposed as an optional provision to make it clear that a subordination agreement does not create a security interest unless so intended.*

Official Comment

Source: New York.

Prior Uniform Statutory Provision: None.

Reason for Change: The drafting history of Article 9 makes it clear that there was no intention to cover agreements by which the rights of one unsecured creditor are subordinated to the rights of another unsecured creditor of a common debtor. Nevertheless, since in insolvency proceedings dividends otherwise payable to a subordinated creditor are turned over to the superior creditor, fears have been expressed that a subordination agreement might be treated as a "security agreement" creating a "security interest" in property of the subordinated creditor, and that inappropriate provisions of Article 9 might be applied. This optional section is intended to allay such fears by making an explicit declaration that a subordination agreement does not of itself create a security interest. Nothing in this section prevents the creation of a security interest in such a case when the parties to the agreement so intend.

Purposes:

1.   Billions of dollars of subordinated debt are held by the public and by institutional investors. Commonly, the subordinated debt is subordinated on issue or acquisition and is evidenced by an investment security or by a negotiable or non-negotiable note. Debt is also sometimes subordinated after it arises, either by agreement between the subordinating creditor and the debtor, by agreement between two creditors of the same debtor, or by agreement of all three parties. The subordinated creditor may be a stockholder or other "insider" interested in the common debtor; the subordinated debt may consist of accounts or other rights to payment not evidenced by any instrument. All such cases are included in the terms "subordinated obligation," "subordination," and "subordinated creditor."

2.   Subordination agreements are enforceable between the parties as contracts; and in the bankruptcy of the common debtor dividends otherwise payable to the subordinated creditor are turned over to the superior creditor. This "turn-over" practice has on occasion been explained in terms of "equitable lien," "equitable assignment," or "constructive trust," but whatever the label the practice is essentially an equitable remedy and does not mean that there is a transaction "intended to create a security interest," a "sale of accounts, contract rights or chattel paper," or a "security interest created by contract," within the meaning of Section 9–102. On the other hand, nothing in this section prevents one creditor from assigning his rights to another creditor of the same debtor in such a way as to create a security interest within Article 9, where the parties so intend.

3.   The last sentence of this section is intended to negate any implication that the section changes the law. It is intended to be declaratory of pre-existing law. Both the history and the text of Article 9 make it clear that it was not intended to cover subordination agreements. The provisions of Section 9–203 for authentication by the "debtor" would be entirely unworkable if read to require authentication by public holders of subordinated investment securities. The priorities, filing provisions and remedies on default provided by Article 9 would also be largely inappropriate in many situations. The precautionary language of Section 9–339 preserving subordination of priority by agreement between secured parties points to the conclusion that similar arrangements among unsecured lenders are not covered unless otherwise within the scope of the Article.

4.   The enforcement of subordination agreements is largely left to supplementary principles under Section 1–103. If the subordinated debt is evidenced by ~~an investment security, Section 8–202(1)~~ a certificated security, Section 8–202(a) authorizes enforcement against purchasers on terms stated or referred to on the security certificate. If the fact of subordination is noted on a negotiable instrument, a holder under Sections 3–302 and 3–306 is subject to the term because notice precludes him from taking free of the subordination. Sections 3–302(3)(a), 3–306 and 8–317 severely limit the rights of levying creditors of a subordinated creditor in such cases. *Amendments approved by the Permanent Editorial Board for Uniform Commercial Code November 4, 1995.*

Definitional Cross References:

   "Agreement". Section 1–201.
   "Creditor". Section 1–201.
   "Debtor". Section 9–102(a)(28).
   "Person". Section 1–201.
   "Rights". Section 1–201.
   "Security interest". Section 1–201.

APPENDIX B

UCC ARTICLES 3 & 4 (PRE-1990 VERSION)

Set forth below are the text and Official Comments of Article 3 and the text of Article 4 as they existed prior to revision in 1990.

ARTICLE 3

COMMERCIAL PAPER

APPENDIX B

PART 4.   LIABILITY OF PARTIES

PART 5.   PRESENTMENT, NOTICE OF DISHONOR AND PROTEST

PART 6.   DISCHARGE

PART 1

SHORT TITLE, FORM AND INTERPRETATION

§ 3–101.   Short Title.

This Article shall be known and may be cited as Uniform Commercial Code—Commercial Paper.

Official Comment

This Article represents a complete revision and modernization of the Uniform Negotiable Instruments Law.

The Comments which follow will point out the respects in which this Article changes the Negotiable Instruments Law, which was promulgated by the National Conference of Commissioners on Uniform State Laws in 1896, and was subsequently enacted in every American jurisdiction. Needless to say, in the 50 odd years of the history of that statute, there have been vast changes in commercial practices relating to the handling of negotiable instruments. The need for revision of this important statute was felt for some years before the present project was undertaken.

It should be noted especially that this Article does not apply in any way to the handling of securities. Article 8 deals with that subject. See Sec. 3–103.

§ 3–102.   Definitions and Index of Definitions.

(1)   In this Article unless the context otherwise requires

(a)   "Issue" means the first delivery of an instrument to a holder or a remitter.

(b)   An "order" is a direction to pay and must be more than an authorization or request. It must identify the person to pay with reasonable certainty. It may be addressed to one or more such persons jointly or in the alternative but not in succession.

(c)   A "promise" is an undertaking to pay and must be more than an acknowledgment of an obligation.

(d)   "Secondary party" means a drawer or endorser.

(e)   "Instrument" means a negotiable instrument.

(2)   Other definitions applying to this Article and the sections in which they appear are:

"Acceptance". Section 3–410.
"Accommodation party". Section 3–415.
"Alteration". Section 3–407.
"Certificate of deposit". Section 3–104.
"Certification". Section 3–411.
"Check". Section 3–104.
"Definite time". Section 3–109.
"Dishonor". Section 3–507.

"Draft". Section 3–104.

"Holder in due course". Section 3–302.

"Negotiation". Section 3–202.

"Note". Section 3–104.

"Notice of dishonor". Section 3–508.

"On demand". Section 3–108.

"Presentment". Section 3–504.

"Protest". Section 3–509.

"Restrictive Indorsement". Section 3–205.

"Signature". Section 3–401.

(3)   The following definitions in other Articles apply to this Article:

"Account". Section 4–104.

"Banking Day". Section 4–104.

"Clearing house". Section 4–104.

"Collecting bank". Section 4–105.

"Customer". Section 4–104.

"Depositary Bank". Section 4–105.

"Documentary Draft". Section 4–104.

"Intermediary Bank". Section 4–105.

"Item". Section 4–104.

"Midnight deadline". Section 4–104.

"Payor bank". Section 4–105.

(4)   In addition Article 1 contains general definitions and principles of construction and interpretation applicable throughout this Article.

Official Comment

Prior Uniform Statutory Provision: Sections 1(5), 128 and 191, Uniform Negotiable Instruments Law.

Changes: See below.

Purposes of Changes:

1.   The definition of "issue" in Section 191 of the original act has been clarified in two respects. The Section 191 definition required that the instrument delivered be "complete in form" inconsistently with the provisions of Sections 14 and 15 (relating to incomplete instruments) of the original act. The "complete in form" language has therefore been deleted. Furthermore the Section 191 definition required that the delivery be "to a person who takes as a holder", thus raising difficulties in the case of the remitter (see Comment 3 to Sec. 3–302) who may not be a party to the instrument and thus not a holder. The definition in subsection (1)(a) of this Section thus provides that the delivery may be to a holder or to a remitter.

2.   The definitions of "order" [subsection (b)] and "promise" [subsection (c)] are new, but state principles clearly recognized by the courts. In the case of orders the dividing line between "a direction to pay" and "an authorization or request" may not be self-evident in the occasional unusual, and therefore non-commercial, case. The prefixing of words of courtesy to the direction—as "please pay" or "kindly pay"—should not lead to a holding that the direction has degenerated into a mere request. On the other hand informal language—such as "I wish you would pay"—would not qualify as an order and such an instrument would be non-negotiable. The definition of "promise" is intended to make it clear that a mere I.O.U. is not a negotiable instrument, and to change the result in occasional cases which have held that "Due Currier & Barker seventeen dollars and fourteen cents, value received," and "I borrowed from P. Shemonia the sum of five hundred dollars with four per cent interest; the borrowed money ought to be paid within four months from the above date" were promises sufficient to make the instruments into notes.

3.   The last sentence of subsection (1)(b) ("order") permits the order to be addressed to one or more persons (as drawees) in the alternative, recognizing the practice of corporations issuing dividend checks and of other drawers who for commercial convenience name a number of drawees, usually in different parts of the country. The section on presentment provides that presentment may be made to any one of such drawees. Drawees in succession

are not permitted because the holder should not be required to make more than one presentment, and upon the first dishonor should have his recourse against the drawer and indorsers.

    4.   Comments on the definitions indexed follow the sections in which the definitions are contained.

Cross Reference:

    Point 3: Section 3–504(3)(a).

Definitional Cross References:

    "Bank". Section 1–201.
    "Delivery". Section 1–201.
    "Holder". Section 1–201.
    "Money". Section 1–201.
    "Person". Section 1–201.

§ 3–103.   Limitations on Scope of Article.

    (1)   This Article does not apply to money, documents of title or investment securities.

    (2)   The provisions of this Article are subject to the provisions of the Article on Bank Deposits and Collections (Article 4) and Secured Transactions (Article 9).

Official Comment

Prior Uniform Statutory Provision: None.

Purposes:

    1.   This Article is restricted to commercial paper—that is to say, to drafts, checks, certificates of deposit and notes as defined in Section 3–104(2). Subsection (1) expressly excludes any money, as defined in this Act (Section 1–201), even though the money may be in the form of a bank note which meets all the requirements of Section 3–104(1). Money is of course negotiable at common law or under separate statutes, but no provision of this Article is applicable to it. Subsection (1) also expressly excludes documents of title and investment securities which fall within Articles 7 and 8, respectively. To this extent the section follows decisions which held that interim certificates calling for the delivery of securities were not negotiable instruments under the original statute. Such paper is now covered under Article 8, but is not within any section of this Article. Likewise, bills of lading, warehouse receipts and other documents of title which fall within Article 7 may be negotiable under the provision of that Article, but are not covered by any section of this Article.

    2.   Instruments which fall within the scope of this Article may also be subject to other Articles of the Code. Many items in course of bank collection will of course be negotiable instruments, and the same may be true of collateral pledged as security for a debt. In such cases this Article, which is general, is, in case of conflicting provisions, subject to the Articles which deal specifically with the type of transaction or instrument involved: Article 4 (Bank Deposits and Collections) and Article 9 (Secured Transactions). In the case of a negotiable instrument which is subject to Article 4 because it is in course of collection or to Article 9 because it is used as collateral, the provisions of this Article continue to be applicable except insofar as there may be conflicting provisions in the Bank Collection or Secured Transactions Article.

    An instrument which qualifies as "negotiable" under this Article may also qualify as a "security" under Article 8. It will be noted that the formal requisites of negotiability (Section 3–104) go to matters of form exclusively; the definition of "security" on the other hand (Section 8–102) looks principally to the manner in which an instrument is used ("commonly dealt in upon securities exchanges . . . or commonly recognized . . . as a medium for investment"). If an instrument negotiable in form under Section 3–104 is, because of the manner of its use, a "security" under Section 8–102, Article 8 and not this Article applies. See subsection (1) of this Section and Section 8–102(1)(b).

Cross References:

    Point 1: Articles 7 and 8; Sections 1–201, 3–104(1) and (2), 3–107.
    Point 2: Articles 4 and 9; Sections 3–104 and 8–102.

Definitional Cross References:

"Document of title". Section 1–201.
"Money". Section 1–201.

§ 3–104.   Form of Negotiable Instruments; "Draft"; "Check"; "Certificate of Deposit"; "Note".

(1)   Any writing to be a negotiable instrument within this Article must

(a)   be signed by the maker or drawer; and

(b)   contain an unconditional promise or order to pay a sum certain in money and no other promise, order, obligation or power given by the maker or drawer except as authorized by this Article; and

(c)   be payable on demand or at a definite time; and

(d)   be payable to order or to bearer.

(2)   A writing which complies with the requirements of this section is

(a)   a "draft" ("bill of exchange") if it is an order;

(b)   a "check" if it is a draft drawn on a bank and payable on demand;

(c)   a "certificate of deposit" if it is an acknowledgment by a bank of receipt of money with an engagement to repay it;

(d)   a "note" if it is a promise other than a certificate of deposit.

(3)   As used in other Articles of this Act, and as the context may require, the terms "draft", "check", "certificate of deposit" and "note" may refer to instruments which are not negotiable within this Article as well as to instruments which are so negotiable.

Official Comment

Prior Uniform Statutory Provision: Sections 1, 5, 10, 126, 184 and 185, Uniform Negotiable Instruments Law.

Changes: Parts of original sections combined and reworded; new provisions; original Section 10 omitted.

Purposes of Changes and New Matter: The changes are intended to bring together in one section related provisions and definitions formerly widely separated.

1.   Under subsection (1)(b) any writing, to be a negotiable instrument within this Article, must be payable in money. In a few states there are special statutes, enacted at an early date when currency was less sound and barter was prevalent, which make promises to pay in commodities negotiable. Even under these statutes commodity notes are now little used and have no general circulation. This Article makes no attempt to provide for such paper, as it is a matter of purely local concern. Even if retention of the old statutes is regarded in any state as important, amendment of this section may not be necessary, since "within this Article" in subsection (1) leaves open the possibility that some writings may be made negotiable by other statutes or by judicial decision. The same is true as to any new type of paper which commercial practice may develop in the future.

2.   While a writing cannot be made a negotiable instrument within this Article by contract or by conduct, nothing in this section is intended to mean that in a particular case a court may not arrive at a result similar to that of negotiability by finding that the obligor is estopped by his conduct from asserting a defense against a bona fide purchaser. Such an estoppel rests upon ordinary principles of the law of simple contract; it does not depend upon negotiability, and it does not make the writing negotiable for any other purpose. But a contract to build a house or to employ a workman, or equally a security agreement does not become a negotiable instrument by the mere insertion of a clause agreeing that it shall be one.

3.   The words "no other promise, order, obligation or power" in subsection (1)(b) are an expansion of the first sentence of the original Section 5. Section 3–112 permits an instrument to carry certain limited obligations or powers in addition to the simple promise or order to pay money. Subsection (1) of this Section is intended to say that it cannot carry others.

4.   Any writing which meets the requirements of subsection (1) and is not excluded under Section 3–103 is a negotiable instrument, and all sections of this Article apply to it, even though it may contain additional language beyond that contemplated by this section. Such an instrument is a draft, a check, a certificate of deposit or a note as defined in subsection (2). Traveler's checks in the usual form, for instance, are negotiable instruments under this Article when they have been completed by the identifying signature.

5.   This Article omits the original Section 10, which provided that the instrument need not follow the language of the act if it "clearly indicates an intention to conform" to it. The provision has served no useful purpose, and it has been an encouragement to bad drafting and to liberality in holding questionable paper to be negotiable. The omission is not intended to mean that the instrument must follow the language of this section, or that one term may not be recognized as clearly the equivalent of another, as in the case of "I undertake" instead of "I promise," or "Pay to holder" instead of "Pay to bearer." It does mean that either the language of the section or a clear equivalent must be found, and that in doubtful cases the decision should be against negotiability.

6.   Subsection (3) is intended to make clear the same policy expressed in Section 3–805.

Cross References:

   Sections 3–105 through 3–112, 3–401, 3–402 and 3–403.
   Point 1: Section 3–107.
   Point 3: Section 3–112.
   Point 4: Sections 3–103 and 3–805.
   Point 6: Section 3–805.

Definitional Cross References:

   "Bank". Section 1–201.
   "Bearer". Section 1–201.
   "Definite time". Section 3–109.
   "Money". Section 1–201.
   "On demand". Section 3–108.
   "Order". Section 3–102.
   "Promise". Section 3–102.
   "Signed". Section 1–201.
   "Term". Section 1–201.
   "Writing". Section 1–201.

§ 3–105.   When Promise or Order Unconditional.

(1)   A promise or order otherwise unconditional is not made conditional by the fact that the instrument

   (a)   is subject to implied or constructive conditions; or

   (b)   states its consideration, whether performed or promised, or the transaction which gave rise to the instrument, or that the promise or order is made or the instrument matures in accordance with or "as per" such transaction; or

   (c)   refers to or states that it arises out of a separate agreement or refers to a separate agreement for rights as to prepayment or acceleration; or

   (d)   states that it is drawn under a letter of credit; or

   (e)   states that it is secured, whether by mortgage, reservation of title or otherwise; or

   (f)   indicates a particular account to be debited or any other fund or source from which reimbursement is expected; or

   (g)   is limited to payment out of a particular fund or the proceeds of a particular source, if the instrument is issued by a government or governmental agency or unit; or

   (h)   is limited to payment out of the entire assets of a partnership, unincorporated association, trust or estate by or on behalf of which the instrument is issued.

(2)   A promise or order is not unconditional if the instrument

(a)   states that it is subject to or governed by any other agreement; or

(b)   states that it is to be paid only out of a particular fund or source except as provided in this section.

As amended in 1962.

Official Comment

Prior Uniform Statutory Provision: Section 3, Uniform Negotiable Instruments Law.

Changes: Completely revised.

Purposes of Changes: The section is intended to make it clear that, so far as negotiability is affected, the conditional or unconditional character of the promise or order is to be determined by what is expressed in the instrument itself; and to permit certain specific limitations upon the terms of payment.

1.   Paragraph (a) of subsection (1) rejects the theory of decisions which have held that a recital in an instrument that it is given in return for an executory promise gives rise to an implied condition that the instrument is not to be paid if the promise is not performed, and that this condition destroys negotiability. Nothing in the section is intended to imply that language may not be fairly construed to mean what it says, but implications, whether of law or fact, are not to be considered in determining negotiability.

2.   Paragraph (b) of subsection (1) is an amplification of Section 3(2) of the original act. The final clause is intended to resolve a conflict in the decisions over the effect of such language as "This note is given for payment as per contract for the purchase of goods of even date, maturity being in conformity with the terms of such contract." It adopts the general commercial understanding that such language is intended as a mere recital of the origin of the instrument and a reference to the transaction for information, but is not meant to condition payment according to the terms of any other agreement.

3.   Paragraph (c) of subsection (1) likewise is intended to resolve a conflict, and to reject cases in which a reference to a separate agreement was held to mean that payment of the instrument must be limited in accordance with the terms of the agreement, and hence was conditioned by it. Such a reference normally is inserted for the purpose of making a record or giving information to anyone who may be interested, and in the absence of any express statement to that effect is not intended to limit the terms of payment. Inasmuch as rights as to prepayment or acceleration has to do with a "speed-up" in payment and since notes frequently refer to separate agreements for a statement of these rights, such reference does not destroy negotiability even though it has mild aspects of incorporation by reference. The general reasoning with respect to subparagraph (c) also applies to a draft which on its face states that it is drawn under a letter of credit (subparagraph (d)). Paragraphs (c) and (d) therefore adopt the position that negotiability is not affected. If the reference goes further and provides that payment must be made according to the terms of the agreement, it falls under paragraph (a) of subsection (2) [As amended 1962].

4.   Paragraph (e) of subsection (1) is intended to settle another conflict in the decisions, over the effect of "title security notes" and other instruments which recite the security given. It rejects cases which have held that the mere statement that the instrument is secured, by reservation of title or otherwise, carries the implied condition that payment is to be made only if the security agreement is fully performed. Again such a recital normally is included only for the purpose of making a record or giving information, and is not intended to condition payment in any way. The provision adopts the position of the great majority of the courts.

5.   Paragraph (f) of subsection (1) is a rewording of Section 3(1) of the original act.

6.   Paragraph (g) of subsection (1) is new. It is intended to permit municipal corporations or other governments or governmental agencies to draw checks or to issue other short-term commercial paper in which payment is limited to a particular fund or to the proceeds of particular taxes or other sources of revenue. The provision will permit some municipal warrants to be negotiable if they are in proper form. Normally such warrants lack the words "order" or "bearer," or are marked "Not Negotiable," or are payable only in serial order, which makes them conditional.

7.   Paragraph (h) of subsection (1) is new. It adopts the policy of decisions holding that an instrument issued by an unincorporated association is negotiable although its payment is expressly limited to the assets of the association, excluding the liability of individual members; and recognizing as negotiable an instrument issued by a trust estate without personal liability of the trustee. The policy is extended to a partnership and to any estate.

The provision affects only the negotiability of the instrument, and is not intended to change the law of any state as to the liability of a partner, trustee, executor, administrator, or any other person on such an instrument.

8.   Paragraph (a) of subsection (2) retains the generally accepted rule that where an instrument contains such language as "subject to terms of contract between maker and payee of this date," its payment is conditioned according to the terms of the agreement and the instrument is not negotiable. The distinction is between a mere recital of the existence of the separate agreement or a reference to it for information, which under paragraph (c) of subsection (1) will not affect negotiability, and any language which, fairly construed, requires the holder to look to the other agreement for the terms of payment. The intent of the provision is that an instrument is not negotiable unless the holder can ascertain all of its essential terms from its face. In the specific instance of rights as to prepayment or acceleration, however, there may be a reference to a separate agreement without destroying negotiability [As amended 1962].

9.   Paragraph (b) of subsection (2) restates the last sentence of Section 3 of the original act. As noted above, exceptions are made by paragraphs (g) and (h) of subsection (1) in favor of instruments issued by governments or governmental agencies, or by a partnership, unincorporated association, trust or estate.

Cross Reference:

Section 3–104.

Definitional Cross References:

"Account". Section 4–104.
"Agreement". Section 1–201.
"Instrument". Section 3–102.
"Issue". Section 3–102.
"Order". Section 3–102.
"Promise". Section 3–102.

§ 3–106.   Sum Certain.

(1)   The sum payable is a sum certain even though it is to be paid

(a)   with stated interest or by stated installments; or

(b)   with stated different rates of interest before and after default or a specified date; or

(c)   with a stated discount or addition if paid before or after the date fixed for payment; or

(d)   with exchange or less exchange, whether at a fixed rate or at the current rate; or

(e)   with costs of collection or an attorney's fee or both upon default.

(2)   Nothing in this section shall validate any term which is otherwise illegal.

Official Comment

Prior Uniform Statutory Provision: Sections 2 and 6(5), Uniform Negotiable Instruments Law.

Changes: Reworded.

Purposes of Changes: The new language is intended to clarify doubts arising under the original section as to interest, discounts or additions, exchange, costs and attorney's fees, and acceleration or extension.

1.   The section rejects decisions which have denied negotiability to a note with a term providing for a discount for early payment on the ground that at the time of issue the amount payable was not certain. It is sufficient that at any time of payment the holder is able to determine the amount then payable from the instrument itself with any necessary computation. Thus a demand note bearing interest at six per cent is negotiable. A stated discount or addition for early or late payment does not affect the certainty of the sum so long as the computation can be made, nor do different rates of interest before and after default or a specified date. The computation must be one which can be made from the instrument itself without reference to any outside source, and this section does not make negotiable a note payable with interest "at the current rate."

2.   Paragraph (d) recognizes the occasional practice of making the instrument payable with exchange deducted rather than added.

3.   In paragraph (e) "upon default" is substituted for the language of the original Section 2(5) in order to include any default in payment of interest or installments.

4.   The section contains no specific language relating to the effect of acceleration clauses on the certainty of the sum payable. Section 2(3) of the original act contained a saving clause for provisions accelerating principal on default in payment of an installment or of interest, which led to doubt as to the effect of other accelerating provisions. This Article (Section 3–109, Definite Time) broadly validates acceleration clauses; it is not necessary to state the matter in this section as well. The disappearance of the language referred to in old Section 2(3) means merely that it was regarded as surplusage.

5.   Most states have usury laws prohibiting excessive rates of interest. In some states there are statutes or rules of law invalidating a term providing for increased interest after maturity, or for costs and attorney's fees. Subsection (2) is intended to make it clear that this section is concerned only with the effect of such terms upon negotiability, and is not meant to change the law of any state as to the validity of the term itself.

Cross References:

Section 3–104.
Point 4: Section 3–109.

Definitional Cross Reference:

"Term". Section 1–201.

§ 3–107.   Money.

(1)   An instrument is payable in money if the medium of exchange in which it is payable is money at the time the instrument is made. An instrument payable in "currency" or "current funds" is payable in money.

(2)   A promise or order to pay a sum stated in a foreign currency is for a sum certain in money and, unless a different medium of payment is specified in the instrument, may be satisfied by payment of that number of dollars which the stated foreign currency will purchase at the buying sight rate for that currency on the day on which the instrument is payable or, if payable on demand, on the day of demand. If such an instrument specifies a foreign currency as the medium of payment the instrument is payable in that currency.

Official Comment

Prior Uniform Statutory Provision: Section 6(5), Uniform Negotiable Instruments Law.

Changes: Completely rewritten.

Purposes of Changes and New Matter: To make clear when an instrument is payable in money and to state rules applicable to instruments drawn payable in a foreign currency.

1.   The term "money" is defined in Section 1–201 as "a medium of exchange authorized or adopted by a domestic or foreign government as a part of its currency". That definition rejects the narrow view of some early cases that "money" is limited to legal tender. Legal tender acts do no more than designate a particular kind of money which the obligee will be required to accept in discharge of an obligation. It rejects also the contention sometimes advanced that "money" includes any medium of exchange current and accepted in the particular community whether it be gold dust, beaver pelts, or cigarettes in occupied Germany. Such unusual "currency" is necessarily of uncertain and fluctuating value, and an instrument intended to pass generally in commerce as negotiable may not be made payable therein.

The test adopted is that of the sanction of government, which recognizes the circulating medium as a part of the official currency of that government. In particular the provision adopts the position that an instrument expressing the amount to be paid in sterling, francs, lire or other recognized currency of a foreign government is negotiable even though payable in the United States.

2.   The provision on "currency" or "current funds" accepts the view of the great majority of the decisions, that "currency" or "current funds" means that the instrument is payable in money.

3.   Either the amount to be paid or the medium of payment may be expressed in terms of a particular kind of money. A draft passing between Toronto and Buffalo may, according to the desire and convenience of the parties,

call for payment of 100 United States dollars or of 100 Canadian dollars; and it may require either sum to be paid in either currency. Under this section an instrument in any of these forms is negotiable, whether payable in Toronto or in Buffalo.

4. As stated in the preceding paragraph the intention of the parties in making an instrument payable in a foreign currency may be that the medium of payment shall be either dollars measured by the foreign currency or the foreign currency in which the instrument is drawn. Under subsection (2) the presumption is, unless the instrument otherwise specifies, that the obligation may be satisfied by payment in dollars in an amount determined by the buying sight rate for the foreign currency on the day the instrument becomes payable. Inasmuch as the buying sight rate will fluctuate from day to day, it might be argued that an instrument expressed in a foreign currency but actually payable in dollars is not for a "sum certain". Subsection (2) makes it clear that for the purposes of negotiability under this Article such an instrument, despite exchange fluctuations, is for a sum certain.

Cross References:

> Section 3–104.
> Point 1: Section 1–201.
> Point 4: Section 4–212(6).

Definitional Cross References:

> "Instrument". Section 3–102.
> "Money". Section 1–201.
> "Order". Section 3–102.
> "Promise". Section 3–102.
> "Purchase". Section 1–201.

§ 3–108.   Payable on Demand.

Instruments payable on demand include those payable at sight or on presentation and those in which no time for payment is stated.

Official Comment

Prior Uniform Statutory Provision: Section 7, Uniform Negotiable Instruments Law.

Changes: Reworded, final sentence of original section omitted.

Purposes of Changes: Except for the omission of the final sentence this section restates the substance of original Section 7. The final sentence dealt with the status of a person issuing, accepting or indorsing an instrument after maturity and provided that as to such a person the instrument was payable on demand. That language implied that the ordinary rules relating to demand instruments as to due course, holding, presentment, notice of dishonor and so on were applicable. This Article abandons that concept which served no special purpose except to trap the unwary. Under Section 3–302 (Holder in Due Course) and in view of the deletion from this section of the final sentence of original Section 7 there is no longer the possibility that one taking time paper after maturity may acquire due course rights against a post-maturity indorser. Section 3–501(4), however, provides that the indorser after maturity is not entitled to presentment, notice of dishonor or protest.

Cross References:

> Sections 3–104, 3–302 and 3–501(4).

Definitional Cross Reference:

> "Instrument". Section 3–102.

§ 3–109.   Definite Time.

(1) An instrument is payable at a definite time if by its terms it is payable

(a) on or before a stated date or at a fixed period after a stated date; or

(b) at a fixed period after sight; or

(c)   at a definite time subject to any acceleration; or

(d)   at a definite time subject to extension at the option of the holder, or to extension to a further definite time at the option of the maker or acceptor or automatically upon or after a specified act or event.

(2)   An instrument which by its terms is otherwise payable only upon an act or event uncertain as to time of occurrence is not payable at a definite time even though the act or event has occurred.

Official Comment

Prior Uniform Statutory Provision: Sections 4 and 17(3), Uniform Negotiable Instruments Law.

Changes: Reworded; new provisions; rule of original Section 4(3) reversed.

Purposes of Changes and New Matter: To remove uncertainties arising under the original section, and to eliminate commercially unacceptable instruments.

1.   Subsection (2) reverses the rule of the original Section 4(3) as to instruments payable after events certain to happen but uncertain as to time. Almost the only use of such instruments has been in the anticipation of inheritance or future interests by borrowing on post-obituary notes. These have been much more common in England than in the United States. They are at best questionable paper, not acceptable in general commerce, with no good reason for according them free circulation as negotiable instruments. As in the case of the occasional note payable "one year after the war" or at a similar uncertain date, they are likely to be made under unusual circumstances suggesting good reason for preserving defenses of the maker. They are accordingly eliminated.

2.   With this change "definite time" is substituted for "fixed or determinable future time." The time of payment is definite if it can be determined from the face of the instrument.

3.   An undated instrument payable "thirty days after date" is not payable at a definite time, since the time of payment cannot be determined on its face. It is, however, an incomplete instrument within the provisions of Section 3–115 dealing with such instruments and may be completed by dating it. It is then payable at a definite time.

4.   Paragraph (c) of subsection (1) resolves a conflict in the decisions on the negotiability of instruments containing acceleration clauses as to the meaning and effect of "on or before a fixed or determinable future time" in the original Section 4(2). (Instruments expressly stated to be payable "on or before" a given date are dealt with in subsection (1)(a). So far as certainty of time of payment is concerned a note payable at a definite time but subject to acceleration is no less certain than a note payable on demand, whose negotiability never has been questioned. It is in fact more certain, since it at least states a definite time beyond which the instrument cannot run. Objections to the acceleration clause must be based rather on the possibility of abuse by the holder, which has nothing to do with negotiability and is not limited to negotiable instruments. That problem is now covered by Section 1–208.

Subsection (1)(c) is intended to mean that the certainty of time of payment or the negotiability of the instrument is not affected by any acceleration clause, whether acceleration be at the option of the maker or the holder, or automatic upon the occurrence of some event, and whether it be conditional or unrestricted. If the acceleration term itself is uncertain it may fail on ordinary contract principles, but the instrument then remains negotiable and is payable at the definite time.

The effect of acceleration clauses upon a holder in due course is covered by the new definition of the holder in due course (Section 3–302) and by the section on notice to purchaser (subsection (3) of Section 3–304). If the purchaser is not aware of any acceleration, his delay in making presentment may be excused under the section dealing with excused presentment (subsection (1) of Section 3–511).

5.   Paragraph (d) of subsection (1) is new. It adopts the generally accepted rule that a clause providing for extension at the option of the holder, even without a time limit, does not affect negotiability since the holder is given only a right which he would have without the clause. If the extension is to be at the option of the maker or acceptor or is to be automatic, a definite time limit must be stated or the time of payment remains uncertain and the instrument is not negotiable. Where such a limit is stated, the effect upon certainty of time of payment is the same as if the instrument were made payable at the ultimate date with a term providing for acceleration.

The construction and effect of extension clauses is covered by paragraph (f) of Section 3–118 on ambiguous terms and rules of construction, to which reference should be made.

Cross References:

Section 3–104.
Point 3: Section 3–115.
Point 4: Sections 1–208, 3–118(f), 3–304(3), and 3–511(1).
Point 5: Section 3–118(f).

Definitional Cross References:

"Holder". Section 1–201.
"Instrument". Section 3–102.
"Term". Section 1–201.

§ 3–110.   Payable to Order.

(1)   An instrument is payable to order when by its terms it is payable to the order or assigns of any person therein specified with reasonable certainty, or to him or his order, or when it is conspicuously designated on its face as "exchange" or the like and names a payee. It may be payable to the order of

(a)   the maker or drawer; or

(b)   the drawee; or

(c)   a payee who is not maker, drawer or drawee; or

(d)   two or more payees together or in the alternative; or

(e)   an estate, trust or fund, in which case it is payable to the order of the representative of such estate, trust or fund or his successors; or

(f)   an office, or an officer by his title as such in which case it is payable to the principal but the incumbent of the office or his successors may act as if he or they were the holder; or

(g)   a partnership or unincorporated association, in which case it is payable to the partnership or association and may be indorsed or transferred by any person thereto authorized.

(2)   An instrument not payable to order is not made so payable by such words as "payable upon return of this instrument properly indorsed."

(3)   An instrument made payable both to order and to bearer is payable to order unless the bearer words are handwritten or typewritten.

Official Comment

Prior Uniform Statutory Provision: Section 8, Uniform Negotiable Instruments Law.

Changes: Reworded, new provisions.

Purposes of Changes and New Matter: The changes are intended to remove uncertainties arising under the original section.

1.   Paragraph (d) of subsection (1) replaces the original subsections (4) and (5). It eliminates the word "jointly," which has carried a possible implication of a right of survivorship. Normally an instrument payable to "A and B" is intended to be payable to the two parties as tenants in common, and there is no survivorship in the absence of express language to that effect. The instrument may be payable to "A or B," in which case it is payable to either A or B individually. It may even be made payable to "A and/or B," in which case it is payable either to A or to B singly, or to the two together. The negotiation, enforcement and discharge of the instrument in all such cases are covered by the section on instruments payable to two or more persons (Sec. 3–116).

2.   Paragraph (e) of subsection (1) is intended to change the result of decisions which have held that an instrument payable to the order of the estate of a decedent was payable to bearer, on the ground that the name of the payee did not purport to be that of any person. The intent in such cases is obviously not to make the instrument payable to bearer, but to the order of the representative of the estate. The provision extends the same principle to an instrument payable to the order of "Tilden Trust," or "Community Fund". So long as the payee can be identified, it is not necessary that it be a legal entity; and in each case the instrument is treated as payable to the order of the appropriate representative or his successor.

3.   Under paragraph (f) of subsection (1) an instrument may be made payable to the office itself ("Swedish Consulate") or to the officer by his title as such ("Treasurer of City Club"). In either case it runs to the incumbent of the office and his successors. The effect of instruments in such a form is covered by the section on instruments payable with words of description (Sec. 3–117).

4.   Vestigial theories relating to the lack of "legal entity" of partnerships and various forms of unincorporated associations—such as labor unions and business trusts—make it the part of wisdom to specify that instruments made payable to such groups are order paper payable as designated and not bearer paper (subsection (1)(g)). As in the case of incorporated associations, any person having authority from the partnership or association to whose order the instrument is payable may indorse or otherwise deal with the instrument.

5.   Subsection (2) is intended to change the result of cases holding that "payable upon return of this certificate properly indorsed" indicated an intention to make the instrument payable to any indorsee and so must be construed as the equivalent of "Pay to order." Ordinarily the purpose of such language is only to insure return of the instrument with indorsement in lieu of a receipt, and the word "order" is omitted with the intention that the instrument shall not be negotiable.

6.   Subsection (3) is directed at occasional instruments reading "Pay to the order of John Doe or bearer." Such language usually is found only where the drawer has filled in the name of the payee on a printed form, without intending the ambiguity or noticing the word "bearer." Under such circumstances the name of the specified payee indicates an intent that the order words shall control. If the word "bearer" is handwritten or typewritten, there is sufficient indication of an intent that the instrument shall be payable to bearer. Instruments payable to "order of bearer" are covered not by this section but by the following Section 3–111.

Cross References:

Sections 3–104 and 3–111.
Point 1: Section 3–116.
Points 2, 3 and 4: Section 3–117.

Definitional Cross References:

"Bearer". Section 1–201.
"Conspicuous". Section 1–201.
"Instrument". Section 3–102.
"Negotiation". Section 3–202.
"Person". Section 1–201.
"Term". Section 1–201.

§ 3–111.   Payable to Bearer.

An instrument is payable to bearer when by its terms it is payable to

(a)   bearer or the order of bearer; or

(b)   a specified person or bearer; or

(c)   "cash" or the order of "cash", or any other indication which does not purport to designate a specific payee.

Official Comment

Prior Uniform Statutory Provision: Section 9, Uniform Negotiable Instruments Law.

Changes: Reworded; original subsections (3) and (5) omitted here but covered by Sections on impostors and signature in name of payee (Section 3–405) and on special and blank indorsements (Section 3–204).

Purposes of Changes: The rewording is intended to remove uncertainties.

1.   Language such as "order of bearer" usually results when a printed form is used and the word "bearer" is filled in. Subsection (a) rejects the view that the instrument is payable to order, and adopts the position that "bearer" is the unusual word and should control. Compare Comment 6 to Section 3–110.

2.   Paragraph (c) is reworded to remove any possible implication that "Pay to the order of _____" makes the instrument payable to bearer. It is an incomplete order instrument, and falls under Section 3–115. Likewise

"Pay Treasurer of X Corporation" does not mean pay bearer, even though there may be no such officer. Instruments payable to the order of an estate, trust, fund, partnership, unincorporated association or office are covered by the preceding section. This subsection applies only to such language as "Pay Cash," "Pay to the order of cash," "Pay bills payable," "Pay to the order of one keg of nails," or other words which do not purport to designate any specific payee.

3. Under Section 40 of the original Act an instrument payable to bearer on its face remained bearer paper negotiable by delivery although subsequently specially indorsed. It should be noted that Section 3–204 on special indorsement reverses this rule and allows the special indorsement to control.

Cross References:

Sections 3–104, 3–405 and 3–204.
Point 2: Sections 3–110(1)(a) and (f) and 3–115.
Point 3: Section 3–204.

Definitional Cross References:

"Bearer". Section 1–201.
"Instrument". Section 3–102.
"Person". Section 1–201.
"Term". Section 1–201.

§ 3–112. Terms and Omissions Not Affecting Negotiability.

(1) The negotiability of an instrument is not affected by

(a) the omission of a statement of any consideration or of the place where the instrument is drawn or payable; or

(b) a statement that collateral has been given to secure obligations either on the instrument or otherwise of an obligor on the instrument or that in case of default on those obligations the holder may realize on or dispose of the collateral; or

(c) a promise or power to maintain or protect collateral or to give additional collateral; or

(d) a term authorizing a confession of judgment on the instrument if it is not paid when due; or

(e) a term purporting to waive the benefit of any law intended for the advantage or protection of any obligor; or

(f) a term in a draft providing that the payee by indorsing or cashing it acknowledges full satisfaction of an obligation of the drawer; or

(g) A statement in a draft drawn in a set of parts (Section 3–801) to the effect that the order is effective only if no other part has been honored.

(2) Nothing in this section shall validate any term which is otherwise illegal.

As amended in 1962.

Official Comment

Prior Uniform Statutory Provision: Sections 5 and 6, Uniform Negotiable Instruments Law.

Changes: Reworded; new provisions; Subsection (4) of original Section 5 omitted. Subsection (4) of the original Section 6 is now covered by Section 3–113, and Subsection (5) by Section 3–107.

Purposes of Changes and New Matter: The changes are intended to remove uncertainties arising under the original sections. Subsection (4) of the original Section 5 is omitted because it has been important only in connection with bonds and other investment securities now covered by Article 8 of this Act. An option to require something to be done in lieu of payment of money is uncommon and not desirable in commercial paper.

This section permits the insertion of certain obligations and powers in addition to the simple promise or order to pay money. Under Section 3–104, dealing with form of negotiable instruments, the instrument may not contain any other promise, order, obligation or power.

1.   Paragraph (b) of subsection (1) permits a clause authorizing the sale or disposition of collateral given to secure obligations either on the instrument or otherwise of an obligor on the instrument upon any default in those obligations, including a default in payment of an installment or of interest. It is not limited, as was the original Section 5(1), to default at maturity. The reference to obligations of an obligor on the instrument is intended to recognize so-called cross collateral provisions that appear in collateral note forms used by banks and others throughout the United States and to permit the use of these provisions without destroying negotiability. Paragraph (c) is new. It permits a clause, apparently not within the original section, containing a promise or power to maintain or protect collateral or to give additional collateral, whether on demand or on some other condition. Such terms frequently are accompanied by a provision for acceleration if the collateral is not given, which is now permitted by the section on what constitutes a definite time. Section 1–208 should be consulted as to the construction to be given such clauses under this Act.

2.   As under the original Section 5(2), paragraph (d) is intended to mean that a confession of judgment may be authorized only if the instrument is not paid when due, and that otherwise negotiability is affected. The use of judgment notes is confined to two or three states, and in others the judgment clauses are made illegal or ineffective either by special statutes or by decision. Subsection (2) is intended to say that any such local rule remains unchanged, and that the clause itself may be invalid, although the negotiability of the instrument is not affected.

3.   As in the case of the original Section 5(3), paragraph (e) applies not only to any waiver of the benefits of this Article, such as presentment, notice of dishonor or protest, but also to a waiver of the benefits of any other law such as a homestead exemption. Again subsection (2) is intended to mean that any rule which invalidates the waiver itself is not changed, and that while negotiability is not affected, a waiver of the statute of limitations contained in an instrument may be invalid.

This paragraph is to be read together with subsection (1) of Section 3–104 on form of negotiable instruments. A waiver cannot make the instrument negotiable within this Article where it does not comply with the requirements of that section.

4.   Paragraph (f) is new. The effect of a clause of acknowledgment of satisfaction upon negotiability has been uncertain under the original section.

5.   Paragraph (g) is intended to insure that a condition arising from the statement in question will not adversely affect negotiability.

Cross References:

Sections 3–104 and 3–105.
Point 1: Sections 1–208 and 3–109(1)(c).
Point 3: Section 3–104.

Definitional Cross References:

"Draft". Section 3–104.
"Instrument". Section 3–102.
"On demand". Section 3–108.
"Promise". Section 3–102.
"Term". Section 1–201.

§ 3–113.   Seal.

An instrument otherwise negotiable is within this Article even though it is under a seal.

Official Comment

Prior Uniform Statutory Provision: Section 6(4), Uniform Negotiable Instruments Law.

Changes: Reworded.

Purposes of Changes: The revised wording is intended to change the result of decisions holding that while a seal does not affect the negotiability of an instrument it may affect it in other respects falling within the statute, such as the conclusiveness of consideration. The section is intended to place sealed instruments on the same footing as any other instruments so far as all sections of this Article are concerned. It does not affect any other statutes or rules of law relating to sealed instruments except insofar as, in the case of negotiable instruments, they are inconsistent with this Article. Thus a sealed instrument which is within this Article may still be subject to a longer statute of limitations than negotiable instruments not under seal, or to such local rules of procedure as that it may be enforced by an action of special assumpsit.

Cross Reference:

Section 3–104.

Definitional Cross Reference:

"Instrument". Section 3–102.

§ 3–114. Date, Antedating, Postdating.

(1) The negotiability of an instrument is not affected by the fact that it is undated, antedated or postdated.

(2) Where an instrument is antedated or postdated the time when it is payable is determined by the stated date if the instrument is payable on demand or at a fixed period after date.

(3) Where the instrument or any signature thereon is dated, the date is presumed to be correct.

Official Comment

Prior Uniform Statutory Provision: Sections 6(1), 11, 12 and 17(3), Uniform Negotiable Instruments Law.

Changes: Reworded; new provision; parts of original section 12 omitted.

Purposes of Changes and New Matter: The rewording is intended to remove uncertainties arising under the original sections.

1. The reference to an "illegal or fraudulent purpose" in the original Section 12 is omitted as inaccurate and misleading. Any fraud or illegality connected with the date of an instrument does not affect its negotiability, but is merely a defense under Sections 3–306 and 3–307 to the same extent as any other fraud or illegality. The provision in the same section as to acquisition of title upon delivery is also omitted, as obvious and unnecessary.

2. Subsection (2) is new. An undated instrument payable "thirty days after date" is uncertain as to time of payment, and does not fall within Section 3–109(1)(a) on definite time. It is, however, an incomplete instrument, and the date may be inserted as provided in the section dealing with such instruments (Section 3–115). When the instrument has been dated, this subsection follows decisions under the original Act in providing that the time of payment is to be determined from the stated date, even though the instrument is antedated or postdated. An antedated instrument may thus be due before it is issued. As to the liability of indorsers in such a case, see Section 3–501(4), on indorsement after maturity.

3. Subsection (3) extends the original Section 11 to any signature on an instrument. As to the meaning of "presumed," see Section 1–201.

Cross References:

Point 1: Sections 3–306 and 3–307.
Point 2: Sections 3–109(1)(a), 3–115 and 3–501(4).
Point 3: Section 1–201.

Definitional Cross References:

"Instrument". Section 3–102.
"Issue". Section 3–102.
"On demand". Section 3–108.
"Presumed". Section 1–201.
"Signature". Section 3–401.

§ 3–115.   Incomplete Instruments.

(1)   When a paper whose contents at the time of signing show that it is intended to become an instrument is signed while still incomplete in any necessary respect it cannot be enforced until completed, but when it is completed in accordance with authority given it is effective as completed.

(2)   If the completion is unauthorized the rules as to material alteration apply (Section 3–407), even though the paper was not delivered by the maker or drawer; but the burden of establishing that any completion is unauthorized is on the party so asserting.

Official Comment

Prior Uniform Statutory Provision: Sections 13, 14 and 15, Uniform Negotiable Instruments Law.

Changes: Condensed and reworded; original Section 13 and parts of Section 14 omitted; rule of Section 15 reversed.

Purposes of Changes:

1.   The original sections were lengthy and confusing. Section 13 is eliminated because it has suggested some uncertain distinction between undated instruments and those incomplete in other respects, and has carried the inference that only a holder may fill in the date. An instrument lacking in an essential date is merely one kind of incomplete instrument, to be treated like any other. The third sentence of Section 14, providing that the instrument must be filled up strictly in accordance with the authority given and within a reasonable time, is eliminated as entirely superfluous, since any authority must always be exercised in accordance with its limitations, and expires within a reasonable time unless a time limit is fixed.

2.   The language "signed while still incomplete in any necessary respect" in subsection (1) is substituted for "wanting in any material particular" in the original Section 14, in order to make it entirely clear that a complete writing which lacks an essential element of an instrument and contains no blanks or spaces or anything else to indicate that what is missing is to be supplied, does not fall within the section. "Necessary" means necessary to a complete instrument. It will always include the promise or order, the designation of the payee, and the amount payable. It may include the time of payment where a blank is left for that time to be filled in; but where it is clear that no time is intended to be stated the instrument is complete, and is payable on demand under Section 3–108. It does not include the date of issue, which under Section 3–114(1) is not essential, unless the instrument is made payable at a fixed period after that date.

3.   This section omits the second sentence of the original Section 14, providing that "a signature on a blank paper delivered by the person making the signature in order that the paper may be converted into a negotiable instrument operates as a prima facie authority to fill it up as such for any amount." This had utility only in connection with the ancient practice of signing blank paper to be filled in later as an acceptance, at a time when communications were slow and difficult. The practice has been obsolete for nearly a century. It affords obvious opportunity for fraud, and should not be encouraged by express sanction in the statute. The omission is not intended, however, to mean that any person may not be authorized to write in an instrument over a signature either before or after delivery.

4.   Subsection (2) states the rule generally recognized by the courts, that any unauthorized completion is an alteration of the instrument which stands on the same footing as any other alteration. Reference is therefore made to Section 3–407 where the effect of alteration is stated. Subsection (3) of that section provides that a subsequent holder in due course may in all cases enforce the instrument as completed, and replaces the final sentence of the original Section 14.

5.   The language "even though the paper was not delivered" reverses the rule of the original Section 15, which provides that where an incomplete instrument has not been delivered it will not, if completed, be a valid contract in the hands of any holder as against any person whose signature was placed thereon before delivery. Since under this Article (Sections 3–305 and 3–407) neither non-delivery nor unauthorized completion is a defense against a holder in due course, it has always been illogical that the two together should invalidate the instrument in his hands. A holder in due course sees and takes the same paper, whether it was complete when stolen or completed afterward by the thief, and in each case he relies in good faith on the maker's signature. The loss should fall upon the party whose conduct in signing blank paper has made the fraud possible, rather than upon the innocent purchaser. The result is consistent with the theory of decisions holding the drawer of a check stolen and afterwards filled in to be estopped from setting up the non-delivery against an innocent party.

A similar provision protecting a depositary bank which pays an item in good faith is contained in Section 4–401. The policy of that Section should apply in favor of drawees other than banks.

6.   The language on burden of establishing unauthorized completion is substituted for the "prima facie authority" of the original section 14. It follows the generally accepted rule that the full burden of proof by a preponderance of the evidence is upon the party attacking the completed instrument. "Burden of establishing" is defined in Section 1–201.

Cross References:

Point 2: Sections 3–108 and 3–114(1).
Point 4: Section 3–407.
Point 5: Sections 3–305(2), 3–407(3) and 4–401.
Point 6: Section 1–201.

Definitional Cross References:

"Alteration". Section 3–407.
"Burden of establishing". Section 1–201.
"Delivery". Section 1–201.
"Instrument". Section 3–102.
"Party". Section 1–201.
"Signed". Section 1–201.

§ 3–116.   Instruments Payable to Two or More Persons.

An instrument payable to the order of two or more persons

(a)   if in the alternative is payable to any one of them and may be negotiated, discharged or enforced by any of them who has possession of it;

(b)   if not in the alternative is payable to all of them and may be negotiated, discharged or enforced only by all of them.

Official Comment

Prior Uniform Statutory Provision: Section 41, Uniform Negotiable Instruments Law.

Changes: Revised in wording and substance.

Purposes of Changes: The changes are intended to make clear the distinction between an instrument payable to "A or B" and one payable to "A and B." The first names either A or B as payee, so that either of them who is in possession becomes a holder as that term is defined in Section 1–201 and may negotiate, enforce or discharge the instrument. The second is payable only to A and B together, and as provided in the original section both must indorse in order to negotiate the instrument, although one may of course be authorized to sign for the other. Likewise both must join in any action to enforce the instrument, and the rights of one are not discharged without his consent by the act of the other.

If the instrument is payable to "A and/or B," it is payable in the alternative to A, or to B, or to A and B together, and it may be negotiated, enforced or discharged accordingly.

Cross Reference:

Section 1–201.

Definitional Cross References:

"Instrument". Section 3–102.
"Person". Section 1–201.

§ 3–117.   Instruments Payable With Words of Description.

An instrument made payable to a named person with the addition of words describing him

(a)   as agent or officer of a specified person is payable to his principal but the agent or officer may act as if he were the holder;

(b)   as any other fiduciary for a specified person or purpose is payable to the payee and may be negotiated, discharged or enforced by him;

(c)   in any other manner is payable to the payee unconditionally and the additional words are without effect on subsequent parties.

Official Comment

Prior Uniform Statutory Provision: Section 42, Uniform Negotiable Instruments Law.

Changes: Revised and extended.

Purposes of Changes:

1.   Subsection (a) extends the policy of the original Section 42, which covered only cashiers and fiscal officers of banks and corporations, to any case where a payee is named with words describing him as agent or officer of another named person. The intent is to include all such descriptions as "John Doe, Treasurer of Town of Framingham," "John Doe, President Home Telephone Co.," "John Doe, Secretary of City Club," or "John Doe, agent of Richard Roe." In all such cases it is commercial understanding that the description is not added for mere identification but for the purpose of making the instrument payable to the principal, and that the agent or officer is named as payee only for convenience in enabling him to cash the check.

2.   Subsection (b) covers such descriptions as "John Doe, Trustee of Smithers Trust," "John Doe, Administrator of the Estate of Richard Roe," or "John Doe, Executor under Will of Richard Roe." In such cases the instrument is payable to the individual named, and he may negotiate it, enforce it or discharge it, but he remains subject to any liability for breach of his obligation as a fiduciary. Any subsequent holder of the instrument is put on notice of the fiduciary position, and under the section on notice to purchaser (Section 3–304) is not a holder in due course if he takes with notice that John Doe has negotiated the instrument in payment of or as security for his own debt or in any transaction for his own benefit, or otherwise in breach of duty.

3.   Any other words of description, such as "John Doe, 1121 Main Street," "John Doe, Attorney," or "Jane Doe, unremarried widow," are to be treated as mere identification, and not in any respect as a condition of payment. The same is true of any description of the payee as "Treasurer," "President," "Agent," "Trustee," "Executor," or "Administrator," which does not name the principal or beneficiary. In all such cases the person named may negotiate, enforce or discharge the instrument if he is otherwise identified, even though he does not meet the description. Any subsequent party dealing with the instrument may disregard the description and treat the paper as payable unconditionally to the individual, and is fully protected in the absence of independent notice of other facts sufficient to affect his position.

Cross Reference:

Point 2: Section 3–304(2).

Definitional Cross References:

"Holder". Section 1–201.
"Instrument". Section 3–102.
"Party". Section 1–201.
"Person". Section 1–201.

§ 3–118.   Ambiguous Terms and Rules of Construction.

The following rules apply to every instrument:

(a)   Where there is doubt whether the instrument is a draft or a note the holder may treat it as either. A draft drawn on the drawer is effective as a note.

(b)   Handwritten terms control typewritten and printed terms, and typewritten control printed.

(c)   Words control figures except that if the words are ambiguous figures control.

(d) Unless otherwise specified a provision for interest means interest at the judgment rate at the place of payment from the date of the instrument, or if it is undated from the date of issue.

(e) Unless the instrument otherwise specifies two or more persons who sign as maker, acceptor or drawer or indorser and as a part of the same transaction are jointly and severally liable even though the instrument contains such words as "I promise to pay."

(f) Unless otherwise specified consent to extension authorizes a single extension for not longer than the original period. A consent to extension, expressed in the instrument, is binding on secondary parties and accommodation makers. A holder may not exercise his option to extend an instrument over the objection of a maker or acceptor or other party who in accordance with Section 3-604 tenders full payment when the instrument is due.

Official Comment

Prior Uniform Statutory Provision: Sections 17 and 68, Uniform Negotiable Instruments Law.

Changes: Reworded; new provisions; original subsections (3) and (6) of Section 17 omitted. The original Section 17(3) is covered, so far as the question can arise, by Sections 3-109(1)(a) and 3-114 of this Article. The original Section 17(6) is now covered by Section 3-402.

Purposes of Changes and New Matter:

1. The purpose of this section is to protect holders and to encourage the free circulation of negotiable paper by stating rules of law which will preclude a resort to parol evidence for any purpose except reformation of the instrument. Except as to such reformation, these rules cannot be varied by any proof that any party intended the contrary.

2. Subsection (a): The language of the original Section 17(5) is changed to make it clear that the provision is not limited to ambiguities of phrasing, but extends to any case where the form of the instrument leaves its character as a draft or a note in doubt.

3. Subsection (b): The original Section 17(4) is revised to cover typewriting because of its frequent use in instruments, particularly in promissory notes.

4. Subsection (c): The rewording of the original Section 17(1) is intended to make it clear that figures control only where the words are ambiguous and the figures are not.

5. Subsection (d): The revision of the original Section 17(2) is intended to make it clear that where the instrument provides for payment "with interest" without specifying the rate, the judgment rate of interest of the place of payment is to be taken as intended.

6. Subsection (e): This subsection combines and revises the original Section 17(7) and the last sentence of the original Section 68. The rule applies to any two or more persons who sign in the same capacity, whether as makers, drawers, acceptors or indorsers. It applies only where such parties sign as a part of the same transaction; successive indorsers are, of course, liable severally but not jointly.

7. Subsection (f): This provision is new. It has reference to such clauses as "The makers and indorsers of this note consent that it may be extended without notice to them." Such terms usually are inserted to obtain the consent of the indorsers and any accommodation maker to extension which might otherwise discharge them under Section 3-606 dealing with impairment of recourse or collateral. An extension in accord with these terms binds secondary parties. The holder may not force an extension on a maker or acceptor who makes due tender; the holder is not free to refuse payment and keep interest running on a good note or other instrument by extending it over the objection of a maker or acceptor or other party who in accordance with Section 3-604 tenders full payment when the instrument is due. Where consent to extension has been given, the subsection provides that unless otherwise specified the consent is to be construed as authorizing only one extension for not longer than the original period of the note.

Cross References:

Sections 3-109, 3-114, 3-402 and 3-606.
Point 7: Sections 3-604 and 3-606.

Definitional Cross References:

"Draft". Section 3-104.

"Holder". Section 1–201.

"Instrument". Section 3–102.

"Issue". Section 3–102.

"Note". Section 3–104.

"Person". Section 1–201.

"Promise". Section 3–102.

"Signed". Section 1–201.

"Term". Section 1–201.

§ 3–119.   Other Writings Affecting Instrument.

(1)   As between the obligor and his immediate obligee or any transferee the terms of an instrument may be modified or affected by any other written agreement executed as a part of the same transaction, except that a holder in due course is not affected by any limitation of his rights arising out of the separate written agreement if he had no notice of the limitation when he took the instrument.

(2)   A separate agreement does not affect the negotiability of an instrument.

Official Comment

Prior Uniform Statutory Provision: None.

Purposes: This section is new. It is intended to resolve conflicts as to the effect of a separate writing upon a negotiable instrument.

1.   This Article does not attempt to state general rules as to when an instrument may be varied or affected by parol evidence, except to the extent indicated by the comment to the preceding section. This section is limited to the effect of a separate written agreement executed as a part of the same transaction. The separate writing is most commonly an agreement creating or providing for a security interest such as a mortgage, chattel mortgage, conditional sale or pledge. It may, however, be any type of contract, including an agreement that upon certain conditions the instrument shall be discharged or is not to be paid, or even an agreement that it is a sham and not to be enforced at all. Nothing in this section is intended to validate any such agreement which is fraudulent or void as against public policy, as in the case of a note given to deceive a bank examiner.

2.   Other parties, such as an accommodation indorser, are not affected by the separate writing unless they were also parties to it as a part of the transaction by which they became bound on the instrument.

3.   The section applies to negotiable instruments the ordinary rule that writings executed as a part of the same transaction are to be read together as a single agreement. As between the immediate parties a negotiable instrument is merely a contract, and is no exception to the principle that the courts will look to the entire contract in writing. Accordingly a note may be affected by an acceleration clause, a clause providing for discharge under certain conditions, or any other relevant term in the separate writing. "May be modified or affected" does not mean that the separate agreement must necessarily be given effect. There is still room for construction of the writing as not intended to affect the instrument at all, or as intended to affect it only for a limited purpose such as foreclosure or other realization of collateral. If there is outright contradiction between the two, as where the note is for $1,000 but the accompanying mortgage recites that it is for $2,000, the note may be held to stand on its own feet and not to be affected by the contradiction.

4.   Under this Article a purchaser of the instrument may become a holder in due course although he takes it with knowledge that it was accompanied by a separate agreement, if he has no notice of any defense or claim arising from the terms of the agreement. If any limitation in the separate writing in itself amounts to a defense or claim, as in the case of an agreement that the note is a sham and cannot be enforced, a purchaser with notice of it cannot be a holder in due course. The section also covers limitations which do not in themselves give notice of any present defense or claim, such as conditions providing that under certain conditions the note shall be extended for one year. A purchaser with notice of such limitations may be a holder in due course, but he takes the instrument subject to the limitation. If he is without such notice, he is not affected by such a limiting clause in the separate writing.

5.   Subsection (2) rejects decisions which have carried the rule that contemporaneous writings must be read together to the length of holding that a clause in a mortgage affecting a note destroyed the negotiability of the note. The negotiability of an instrument is always to be determined by what appears on the face of the instrument alone, and if it is negotiable in itself a purchaser without notice of a separate writing is in no way

affected by it. If the instrument itself states that it is subject to or governed by any other agreement, it is not negotiable under this Article; but if it merely refers to a separate agreement or states that it arises out of such an agreement, it is negotiable.

Cross References:

> Point 1: Section 3–119.
> Point 4: Section 3–304(4)(b).
> Point 5: Section 3–105(2)(a) and (1)(c).

Definitional Cross References:

> "Agreement". Section 1–201.
> "Holder in due course". Section 3–302.
> "Instrument". Section 3–102.
> "Notice". Section 1–201.
> "Rights". Section 1–201.
> "Term". Section 1–201.
> "Written" and "writing". Section 1–201.

§ 3–120.   Instruments "Payable Through" Bank.

An instrument which states that it is "payable through" a bank or the like designates that bank as a collecting bank to make presentment but does not of itself authorize the bank to pay the instrument.

Official Comment

Prior Uniform Statutory Provision: None.

Purposes: Insurance, dividend or payroll checks, and occasionally other types of instruments, are sometimes made payable "through" a particular bank. This section states the commercial understanding as to the effect of such language. The bank is not named as drawee, and it is not ordered or even authorized to pay the instrument out of the drawer's account or any other funds of the drawer in its hands. Neither is it required to take the instrument for collection in the absence of special agreement to that effect. It is merely designated as a collecting bank through which presentment is properly made to the drawee.

Definitional Cross References:

> "Bank". Section 1–201.
> "Collecting bank". Section 4–105.
> "Instrument". Section 3–102.
> "Presentment". Section 3–504.

§ 3–121.   Instruments Payable at Bank.

Note: *If this Act is introduced in the Congress of the United States this section should be omitted.*

(States to select either alternative)

ALTERNATIVE A

A note or acceptance which states that it is payable at a bank is the equivalent of a draft drawn on the bank payable when it falls due out of any funds of the maker or acceptor in current account or otherwise available for such payment.

ALTERNATIVE B

A note or acceptance which states that it is payable at a bank is not of itself an order or authorization to the bank to pay it.

Official Comment

Prior Uniform Statutory Provision: Section 87, Uniform Negotiable Instruments Law.

Changes: Alternative sections offered.

Purposes of Changes: The original section 87 has been amended so extensively that no uniformity has been achieved; and in many parts of the country it has been consistently disregarded in practice.

The original section represents the commercial and banking practice of New York and the surrounding states, according to which a note or acceptance made payable at a bank is treated as the equivalent of a draft drawn on the bank. The bank is not only authorized but ordered to make payment out of the account of the maker or acceptor when the instrument falls due, and it is expected to do so without consulting him. In the western and southern states a contrary understanding prevails. The note or acceptance payable at a bank is treated as merely designating a place of payment, as if the instrument were made payable at the office of an attorney. The bank's only function is to notify the maker or acceptor that the instrument has been presented and to ask for his instructions; and in the absence of specific instructions it is not regarded as required or even authorized to pay. Notwithstanding the original section western and southern banks have consistently followed the practice of asking for instructions and treating a direction not to pay as a revocation, equivalent to a direction to stop payment.

Both practices are well established, and the division is along geographical lines. A change in either practice might lead to undesirable consequences for holders, banks or depositors. The instruments involved are chiefly promissory notes, which infrequently cross state lines. There is no great need for uniformity. This section therefore offers alternative provisions, the first of which states the New York commercial understanding, and the second that of the south and west.

Cross Reference:

Section 3–502.

Definitional Cross References:

"Acceptance". Section 3–410.
"Account". Section 4–104.
"Bank". Section 1–201.
"Draft". Section 3–104.
"Instrument". Section 3–102.
"Note". Section 3–104.
"Order". Section 3–102.

§ 3–122.   Accrual of Cause of Action.

(1)   A cause of action against a maker or an acceptor accrues

(a)   in the case of a time instrument on the day after maturity;

(b)   in the case of a demand instrument upon its date or, if no date is stated, on the date of issue.

(2)   A cause of action against the obligor of a demand or time certificate of deposit accrues upon demand, but demand on a time certificate may not be made until on or after the date of maturity.

(3)   A cause of action against a drawer of a draft or an indorser of any instrument accrues upon demand following dishonor of the instrument. Notice of dishonor is a demand.

(4)   Unless an instrument provides otherwise, interest runs at the rate provided by law for a judgment

(a)   in the case of a maker, acceptor or other primary obligor of a demand instrument, from the date of demand;

(b)   in all other cases from the date of accrual of the cause of action.

As amended in 1962.

Official Comment

Prior Uniform Statutory Provision: None.

Purpose:

1.   This section is new. It follows the generally accepted rule that action may be brought on a demand note immediately upon issue, without demand, since presentment is not required to charge the maker under the original Act or under this Article. An exception is made in the case of certificates of deposit for the reason that

banking custom and expectation is that demand will be made before any liability is incurred by the bank, and the additional reason that such certificates are issued with the understanding that they will be held for a considerable length of time, which in many instances exceeds the period of the statute of limitations. As to makers and acceptors of time instruments generally, the cause of action accrues on the day after maturity. As to drawers of drafts (including checks) and all indorsers, the cause of action accrues, in conformity with their underlying contract on the instrument (Sections 3–413 and 3–414), only upon demand made, typically in the form of a notice of dishonor, after the instrument has been presented to and dishonored by the person designated on the instrument to pay it.

2.   Closely related to the accrual of a cause of action is the question of when interest begins to run where the instrument is blank on the point. A term in the instrument providing for interest controls. (See Section 3–118(d) for the construction of a term which provides for interest but does not specify the rate or the time from which it runs.) In the absence of such a term and except in the case of a maker, acceptor or other primary obligor of a demand instrument subsection (4) states the rule that interest at the judgment rate runs from the date the cause of action accrues. In the case of a primary obligor of a demand instrument, interest runs from the date of demand although the cause of action (subsection (1)(a)) accrues on the stated date of the instrument or on issue. There has been a conflict in the decisions as to when "legal" interest begins to run on a demand note. Some courts have taken the view that, since the note is due when issued without demand, it should follow that interest runs from the same date. On the other hand it is clear that there is no default until after demand by the holder and thus no reason for the imposition of the penalty on the maker. Subsection (4), therefore, adopts the position of the majority of the courts that on a demand note interest runs only from demand. This same rule is applied to acceptors and other primary obligors on a demand instrument.

Cross References:

Point 1: Sections 3–501, 3–413 and 3–414.
Point 2: Section 3–118(d).

Definitional Cross References:

"Action". Section 1–201.
"Certificate of deposit". Section 3–102.
"Dishonor". Section 3–507.
"Draft". Section 3–104.
"Instrument". Section 3–102.
"Note". Section 3–104.
"Notice of dishonor". Section 3–508.
"On demand". Section 3–108.

PART 2

TRANSFER AND NEGOTIATION

§ 3–201.   Transfer: Right to Indorsement.

(1)   Transfer of an instrument vests in the transferee such rights as the transferor has therein, except that a transferee who has himself been a party to any fraud or illegality affecting the instrument or who as a prior holder had notice of a defense or claim against it cannot improve his position by taking from a later holder in due course.

(2)   A transfer of a security interest in an instrument vests the foregoing rights in the transferee to the extent of the interest transferred.

(3)   Unless otherwise agreed any transfer for value of an instrument not then payable to bearer gives the transferee the specifically enforceable right to have the unqualified indorsement of the transferor. Negotiation takes effect only when the indorsement is made and until that time there is no presumption that the transferee is the owner.

Official Comment

Prior Uniform Statutory Provision: Sections 27, 49 and 58, Uniform Negotiable Instruments Law.

Changes: Combined and reworded; new provisions.

Purposes of Changes and New Matter: To make it clear that:

1.　　The section applies to any transfer, whether by a holder or not. Any person who transfers an instrument transfers whatever rights he has in it. The transferee acquires those rights even though they do not amount to "title."

2.　　The transfer of rights is not limited to transfers for value. An instrument may be transferred as a gift, and the donee acquires whatever rights the donor had.

3.　　A holder in due course may transfer his rights as such. The "shelter" provision of the last sentence of the original Section 58 is merely one illustration of the rule that anyone may transfer what he has. Its policy is to assure the holder in due course a free market for the paper, and that policy is continued in this section. The provision is not intended and should not be used to permit any holder who has himself been a party to any fraud or illegality affecting the instrument, or who has received notice of any defense or claim against it, to wash the paper clean by passing it into the hands of a holder in due course and then repurchasing it. The operation of the provision is illustrated by the following examples:

(a)　　A induces M by fraud to make an instrument payable to A, A negotiates it to B, who takes as a holder in due course. After the instrument is overdue B gives it to C, who has notice of the fraud. C succeeds to B's rights as a holder in due course, cutting off the defense.

(b)　　A induces M by fraud to make an instrument payable to A, A negotiates it to B, who takes as a holder in due course. A then repurchases the instrument from B. A does not succeed to B's rights as a holder in due course, and remains subject to the defense of fraud.

(c)　　A induces M by fraud to make an instrument payable to A, A negotiates it to B, who takes with notice of the fraud. B negotiates it to C, a holder in due course, and then repurchases the instrument from C. B does not succeed to C's rights as a holder in due course, and remains subject to the defense of fraud.

(d)　　The same facts as (c), except that B had no notice of the fraud when he first acquired the instrument, but learned of it while he was a holder and with such knowledge negotiated to C. B does not succeed to C's rights as a holder in due course, and his position is not improved by the negotiation and repurchase.

4.　　The rights of a transferee with respect to collateral for the instrument are determined by Article 9 (Secured Transactions).

5.　　Subsection (2) restates original Section 27 and is intended to make it clear that a transfer of a limited interest in the instrument passes the rights of the transferor to the extent of the interest given. Thus a transferee for security acquires all such rights subject of course to the provisions of Article 9 (Secured Transactions).

6.　　Subsection (3) applies only to the transfer for value of an instrument payable to order or specially indorsed. It has no application to a gift, or to an instrument payable or indorsed to bearer or indorsed in blank. The transferee acquires, in the absence of any agreement to the contrary, the right to have the indorsement of the transferor. This right is now made enforceable by an action for specific performance. Unless otherwise agreed, it is a right to the general indorsement of the transferor with full liability as indorser, rather than to an indorsement without recourse. The question commonly arises where the purchaser has paid in advance and the indorsement is omitted fraudulently or through oversight; a transferor who is willing to indorse only without recourse or unwilling to indorse at all should make his intentions clear. The agreement for the transferee to take less than an unqualified indorsement need not be an express one, and the understanding may be implied from conduct, from past practice, or from the circumstances of the transaction.

7.　　Subsection (3) follows the second sentence of the original Section 49 in providing that there is no effective negotiation until the indorsement is made. Until that time the purchaser does not become a holder, and if he receives earlier notice of defense against or claim to the instrument he does not qualify as a holder in due course under Section 3–302(1)(c).

8.　　The final clause of subsection (3), which is new, is intended to make it clear that the transferee without indorsement of an order instrument is not a holder and so is not aided by the presumption that he is entitled to recover on the instrument provided in Section 3–307(2). The terms of the obligation do not run to him, and he must account for his possession of the unindorsed paper by proving the transaction through which he acquired it. Proof of a transfer to him by a holder is proof that he has acquired the rights of a holder and that he is entitled to the presumption.

Cross References:

> Sections 3–202 and 3–416.
> Point 5: Article 9.
> Point 7: Section 3–302(1)(c).
> Point 8: Section 3–307(2).

Definitional Cross References:

> "Bearer". Section 1–201.
> "Holder". Section 1–201.
> "Holder in due course". Section 3–302.
> "Instrument". Section 3–102.
> "Negotiation". Section 3–202.
> "Notice". Section 1–201.
> "Party". Section 1–201.
> "Presumption". Section 1–201.
> "Rights". Section 1–201.
> "Security interest". Section 1–201.

§ 3–202.   Negotiation.

(1)   Negotiation is the transfer of an instrument in such form that the transferee becomes a holder. If the instrument is payable to order it is negotiated by delivery with any necessary indorsement; if payable to bearer it is negotiated by delivery.

(2)   An indorsement must be written by or on behalf of the holder and on the instrument or on a paper so firmly affixed thereto as to become a part thereof.

(3)   An indorsement is effective for negotiation only when it conveys the entire instrument or any unpaid residue. If it purports to be of less it operates only as a partial assignment.

(4)   Words of assignment, condition, waiver, guaranty, limitation or disclaimer of liability and the like accompanying an indorsement do not affect its character as an indorsement.

Official Comment

Prior Uniform Statutory Provision: Sections 30, 31 and 32, Uniform Negotiable Instruments Law.

Changes: Combined and reworded; new provisions.

Purposes of Changes and New Matter: To make it clear that:

1.   Negotiation is merely a special form of transfer, the importance of which lies entirely in the fact that it makes the transferee a holder as defined in Section 1–201. Any negotiation carries a transfer of rights as provided in the section on transfer (subsections (1) and (2) of Section 3–201).

2.   Any instrument which has been specially indorsed can be negotiated only with the indorsement of the special indorsee as provided in Section 3–204 on special indorsement. An instrument indorsed in blank may be negotiated by delivery alone, provided that it bears the indorsement of all prior special indorsees.

3.   Subsection (2) follows decisions holding that a purported indorsement on a mortgage or other separate paper pinned or clipped to an instrument is not sufficient for negotiation. The indorsement must be on the instrument itself or on a paper intended for the purpose which is so firmly affixed to the instrument as to become an extension or part of it. Such a paper is called an allonge.

4.   The cause of action on an instrument cannot be split. Any indorsement which purports to convey to any party less than the entire amount of the instrument is not effective for negotiation. This is true of either "Pay A one-half," or "Pay A two-thirds and B one-third," and neither A nor B becomes a holder. On the other hand an indorsement reading merely "Pay A and B" is effective, since it transfers the entire cause of action to A and B as tenants in common.

The partial indorsement does, however, operate as a partial assignment of the cause of action. The provision makes no attempt to state the legal effect of such an assignment, which is left to the local law. In a jurisdiction in which a partial assignee has any rights, either at law or in equity, the partial indorsee has such rights; and in any jurisdiction where a partial assignee has no rights the partial indorsee has none.

5.   Subsection (4) is intended to reject decisions holding that the addition of such words as "I hereby assign all my right, title and interest in the within note" prevents the signature from operating as an indorsement. Such words usually are added by laymen out of an excess of caution and a desire to indicate formally that the instrument is conveyed, rather than with any intent to limit the effect of the signature.

6.   Subsection (4) is also intended to reject decisions which have held that the addition of "I guarantee payment" indicates an intention not to indorse but merely to guarantee. Any signature with such added words is an indorsement, and if it is made by a holder is effective for negotiation; but the liability of the indorser may be affected by the words of guarantee as provided in the section on the contract of a guarantor. (Section 3–416.)

Cross References:

> Section 3–417.
> Point 1: Sections 1–201 and 3–201(1) and (2).
> Point 2: Section 3–204.
> Point 6: Section 3–416.

Definitional Cross References:

> "Bearer". Section 1–201.
> "Delivery". Section 1–201.
> "Holder". Section 1–201.
> "Instrument". Section 3–102.
> "Written". Section 1–201.

§ 3–203.   Wrong or Misspelled Name.

Where an instrument is made payable to a person under a misspelled name or one other than his own he may indorse in that name or his own or both; but signature in both names may be required by a person paying or giving value for the instrument.

Official Comment

Prior Uniform Statutory Provision: Section 43, Uniform Negotiable Instruments Law.

Changes: Reworded.

Purposes of Changes: To make it clear that:

1.   The party whose name is wrongly designated or misspelled may make an indorsement effective for negotiation by signing in his true name only. This is not commercially satisfactory, since any subsequent purchaser may be left in doubt as to the state of the title; but whether it is done intentionally or through oversight, the party transfers his rights and is liable on his indorsement, and there is a negotiation if identity exists.

2.   He may make an effective indorsement in the wrongly designated or misspelled name only. This again is not commercially satisfactory, since his liability as an indorser may require proof of identity.

3.   He may indorse in both names. This is the proper and desirable form of indorsement, and any person called upon to pay an instrument or under contract to purchase it may protect his interest by demanding indorsement in both names, and is not in default if such demand is refused.

Cross Reference:

> Section 3–401(2).

Definitional Cross References:

> "Instrument". Section 3–102.
> "Person". Section 1–201.
> "Signature". Section 3–401.

§ 3–204.   Special Indorsement; Blank Indorsement.

(1)   A special indorsement specifies the person to whom or to whose order it makes the instrument payable. Any instrument specially indorsed becomes payable to the order of the special indorsee and may be further negotiated only by his indorsement.

(2)   An indorsement in blank specifies no particular indorsee and may consist of a mere signature. An instrument payable to order and indorsed in blank becomes payable to bearer and may be negotiated by delivery alone until specially indorsed.

(3)   The holder may convert a blank indorsement into a special indorsement by writing over the signature of the indorser in blank any contract consistent with the character of the indorsement.

Official Comment

Prior Uniform Statutory Provision: Sections 9(5), 33, 34, 35, 36, and 40, Uniform Negotiable Instruments Law.

Changes: Combined and reworded; rule of Section 40 reversed.

Purposes of Changes:

The last sentence of subsection (1) reverses the rule of the original Section 40, under which an instrument drawn payable to bearer and specially indorsed could be further negotiated by delivery alone. The principle here adopted is that the special indorser, as the owner even of a bearer instrument, has the right to direct the payment and to require the indorsement of his indorsee as evidence of the satisfaction of his own obligation. The special indorsee may of course make it payable to bearer again by himself indorsing in blank.

Cross Reference:

Section 3–202.

Definitional Cross References:

"Bearer". Section 1–201.
"Delivery". Section 1–201.
"Instrument". Section 3–102.
"Person". Section 1–201.
"Signature". Section 3–401.

§ 3–205.   Restrictive Indorsements.

An indorsement is restrictive which either

(a)   is conditional; or

(b)   purports to prohibit further transfer of the instrument; or

(c)   includes the words "for collection", "for deposit", "pay any bank", or like terms signifying a purpose of deposit or collection; or

(d)   otherwise states that it is for the benefit or use of the indorser or of another person.

Official Comment

Prior Uniform Statutory Provision: Sections 36 and 39, Uniform Negotiable Instruments Law.

Changes: Combined and reworded; new provisions.

Purposes of Changes and New Matter:

1.   This section is intended to provide a definition of restrictive indorsements which will include the varieties of indorsement described in original Sections 36 and 39. The separate mention of conditional indorsements, those prohibiting transfer, indorsements in the bank deposit or collection process, and other indorsements to a fiduciary, permits separate treatment in subsequent sections where policy so requires.

2.   This is part of a series of changes of the prior uniform statutory provisions effected by Sections 3–102, 3–205, 3–206, 3–304, 3–419, 3–603, and in Article 4, Sections 4–203 and 4–205. The purpose of the changes is generally to require a taker or payor under restrictive indorsement to apply or pay value given consistently with the indorsement, but to provide certain exceptions applying to banks in the collection process (other than depositary banks), and to some other takers and payors.

Cross References:

Sections 3–102, 3–202(2), 3–205, 3–206, 3–304, 3–419, 3–603, 4–203 and 4–205.

Definitional Cross References:

"Instrument". Section 3–102.
"Person". Section 1–201.

§ 3–206.   Effect of Restrictive Indorsement.

(1)   No restrictive indorsement prevents further transfer or negotiation of the instrument.

(2)   An intermediary bank, or a payor bank which is not the depositary bank, is neither given notice nor otherwise affected by a restrictive indorsement of any person except the bank's immediate transferor or the person presenting for payment.

(3)   Except for an intermediary bank, any transferee under an indorsement which is conditional or includes the words "for collection", "for deposit", "pay any bank", or like terms (subparagraphs (a) and (c) of Section 3–205) must pay or apply any value given by him for or on the security of the instrument consistently with the indorsement and to the extent that he does so he becomes a holder for value. In addition such transferee is a holder in due course if he otherwise complies with the requirements of Section 3–302 on what constitutes a holder in due course.

(4)   The first taker under an indorsement for the benefit of the indorser or another person (subparagraph (d) of Section 3–205) must pay or apply any value given by him for or on the security of the instrument consistently with the indorsement and to the extent that he does so he becomes a holder for value. In addition such taker is a holder in due course if he otherwise complies with the requirements of Section 3–302 on what constitutes a holder in due course. A later holder for value is neither given notice nor otherwise affected by such restrictive indorsement unless he has knowledge that a fiduciary or other person has negotiated the instrument in any transaction for his own benefit or otherwise in breach of duty (subsection (2) of Section 3–304).

Official Comment

Prior Uniform Statutory Provision: Sections 36, 37, 39 and 47, Uniform Negotiable Instruments Law.

Changes: Completely revised.

Purposes of Changes:

1.   Subsections (1) and (2) apply to all four classes of restrictive indorsements defined in Section 3–205. Conditional indorsements and indorsements for deposit or collection, defined in paragraphs (a) and (c) of Section 3–205, are also subject to subsection (3); and trust indorsements as defined in paragraph (d) of Section 3–205 are subject to subsection (4). This section negates the implication which has sometimes been found in the original Sections 37 and 47, that under a restrictive indorsement neither the indorsee nor any subsequent taker from him could become a holder in due course. By omitting the original Section 47, this Article also avoids any implication that a discharge is effective against a holder in due course. See Section 3–602.

2.   Under subsection (1) an indorsement reading "Pay A only," or any other indorsement purporting to prohibit further transfer, is without effect for that purpose. Such indorsements have rarely appeared in reported American cases. Ordinarily further negotiation will be contemplated by the indorser, if only for bank collection. The indorsee becomes a holder, and the indorsement does not of itself give notice to subsequent parties of any defense or claim of the indorser. Hence this section gives such an indorsement the same effect as an unrestricted indorsement.

3.   Subsection (2) permits an intermediary bank (Sections 3–102(3) and 4–105) or a payor bank which is not a depositary bank (Sections 3–102(3) and 4–105) to disregard any restrictive indorsement except that of the

bank's immediate transferor. Such banks ordinarily handle instruments, especially checks, in bulk and have no practicable opportunity to consider the effect of restrictive indorsements. Subsection (2) does not affect the rights of the restrictive indorser against parties outside the bank collection process or against the first bank in the collection process; such rights are governed by subsections (3) and (4) and Section 3–603.

4. Conditional indorsements are treated by this section like indorsements for deposit or collection. Under subsection (3) any transferee under such an indorsement except an intermediary bank becomes a holder for value to the extent that he acts consistently with the indorsement in paying or applying any value given by him for or on the security of the instrument. Contrary to the original Section 39, subsection (3) permits a transferee under a conditional indorsement to become a holder in due course free of the conditional indorser's claim.

5. Of the indorsements covered by this section those "for collection", "for deposit" and "pay any bank" are overwhelmingly the most frequent. Indorsements "for collection" or "for deposit" may be either special or blank; indorsements "pay any bank" are governed by Section 4–201(2). Instruments so indorsed are almost invariably destined to be lodged in a bank for collection. Subsection (3) requires any transferee other than an intermediary bank to act consistently with the purpose of collection, and Section 3–603 lays down a similar rule for payors not covered by subsection (2).

6. Subsection (4), applying to trust indorsements other than those for deposit or collection (paragraph (d) of Section 3–205) is similar to subsection (3); but in subsection (4) the duty to act consistently with the indorsement is limited to the first taker under it. If an instrument is indorsed "Pay T in trust for B" or "Pay T for B" or "Pay T for account of B" or "Pay T as agent for B," whether B is the indorser or a third person, T is of course subject to liability for any breach of his obligation as fiduciary. But trustees commonly and legitimately sell trust assets in transactions entirely outside the bank collection process; the trustee therefore has power to negotiate the instrument and make his transferee a holder in due course. Whether transferees from T have notice of a breach of trust such as to deny them the status of holders in due course is governed by the section on notice to purchasers (Section 3–304); the trust indorsement does not of itself give such notice. Payors are immunized either by subsection (2) of this section or by Section 3–603: payment to the trustee or to a purchaser from the trustee is "consistent with the terms" of the trust indorsement under Section 3–603(1)(b).

7. Several sections of Article 3 and Article 4 are explicitly made subject to the rules stated in this section. See Sections 3–306, 3–419, 4–203 and 4–205.

Cross References:

Point 1: Sections 3–205 and 3–602.
Point 2: Section 3–205(b).
Point 3: Sections 3–102(3), 3–419(4), 3–603, 4–105, 4–205(2).
Point 4: Section 3–205(a).
Point 5: Sections 3–205, 3–603 and 4–201.
Point 6: Sections 3–205, 3–304 and 3–603.
Point 7: Sections 3–306, 3–419, 4–203 and 4–205.

Definitional Cross References:

"Bank". Section 1–201.
"Depositary bank". Sections 3–102(3) and 4–105.
"Holder in due course". Section 3–302.
"Intermediary bank". Sections 3–102(3) and 4–105.
"Negotiation". Sections 3–102(2) and 3–202.
"Payor bank". Sections 3–102(3) and 4–105.
"Restrictive indorsement". Section 3–205.
"Transfer". Section 3–201.

§ 3–207. Negotiation Effective Although It May Be Rescinded.

(1) Negotiation is effective to transfer the instrument although the negotiation is

(a) made by an infant, a corporation exceeding its powers, or any other person without capacity; or

(b) obtained by fraud, duress or mistake of any kind; or

(c)   part of an illegal transaction; or

(d)   made in breach of duty.

(2)   Except as against a subsequent holder in due course such negotiation is in an appropriate case subject to rescission, the declaration of a constructive trust or any other remedy permitted by law.

Official Comment

Prior Uniform Statutory Provision: Sections 22, 58 and 59, Uniform Negotiable Instruments Law.

Changes: Completely revised.

Purposes of Changes: To make it clear that:

1.   The original Section 22, which covered only negotiation by an infant or a corporation, is extended by this section to include other negotiations which may be rescinded. The provision applies even though the party's lack of capacity, or the illegality, is of a character which goes to the essence of the transaction and makes it entirely void, and even though the party negotiating has incurred no liability and is entitled to recover the instrument and have his indorsement cancelled.

2.   It is inherent in the character of negotiable paper that any person in possession of an instrument which by its terms runs to him is a holder, and that anyone may deal with him as a holder. The principle finds its most extreme application in the well settled rule that a holder in due course may take the paper even from a thief and be protected against the claim of the rightful owner. Where there is actual negotiation, even in an entirely void transaction, it is no less effective. The policy of this provision, as well as of the last sentence of the original Section 59, is that any person to whom an instrument is negotiated is a holder until the instrument has been recovered from his possession; and that any person who negotiates an instrument thereby parts with all his rights in it until such recovery. The remedy of any such claimant is to recover the paper by replevin or otherwise; to impound it or to enjoin its enforcement, collection or negotiation; to recover its proceeds from the holder; or to intervene in any action brought by the holder against the obligor. As provided in the section on the rights of one not a holder in due course (Section 3–306) his claim is not a defense to the obligor unless he himself defends the action.

3.   Negotiation under this Article always includes delivery. (Section 3–202, and see Section 1–201(14)). Acquisition of possession by a thief can therefore never be negotiation under this section. But delivery by the thief to another person may be.

4.   Nothing in this section is intended to impose any liability on the party negotiating. He may assert any defense available to him under Sections 3–305, 3–306 and 3–307.

5.   A holder in due course takes the instrument free from all claims to it on the part of any person (Section 3–305(1)). Against him there can be no rescission or other remedy, even though the prior negotiation may have been fraudulent or illegal in its essence and entirely void. As against any other party the claimant may have any remedy permitted by law. This section is not intended to specify what that remedy may be, or to prevent any court from imposing conditions or limitations such as prompt action or return of the consideration received. All such questions are left to the law of the particular jurisdiction. Subsection (2) of Section 3–207 gives no right where it would not otherwise exist. The section is intended to mean that any remedies afforded by the local law are cut off only by a holder in due course, and that other parties, such as a bona fide purchaser with notice that the instrument is overdue, take it subject to the claim as provided in paragraph (a) of the section on the rights of one not a holder in due course (Section 3–306).

Cross References:

Point 2: Sections 1–201 and 3–306(d).
Point 3: Sections 1–201 and 3–202.
Point 4: Sections 3–305, 3–306 and 3–307.
Point 5: Sections 3–305(1) and 3–306(a).

Definitional Cross References:

"Holder in due course". Section 3–302.
"Instrument". Section 3–102.
"Negotiation". Section 3–202.
"Person". Section 1–201.

"Remedy". Section 1–201.

§ 3–208.   Reacquisition.

Where an instrument is returned to or reacquired by a prior party he may cancel any indorsement which is not necessary to his title and reissue or further negotiate the instrument, but any intervening party is discharged as against the reacquiring party and subsequent holders not in due course and if his indorsement has been cancelled is discharged as against subsequent holders in due course as well.

Official Comment

Prior Uniform Statutory Provision: Sections 48, 50 and 121, Uniform Negotiable Instruments Law.

Changes: Parts of original sections combined and rephrased.

Purposes of Changes: No change in the substance of the law is intended. "Returned to or reacquired by" is substituted for "negotiated back to" in the original Section 50 in order to make it clear that the section applies to a return by an indorsee who does not himself indorse. "Discharged" is substituted for the original language to make it clear that the discharge of the intervening party is included within the rule of the section on effect of discharge against a holder in due course (Section 3–602) and is not effective against a subsequent holder in due course who takes without notice of it.

The reacquirer may keep the instrument himself or he may further negotiate it. On further negotiation he may or may not cancel intervening indorsements. In any case intervening indorsers are discharged as to the reacquirer, since if he attempted to enforce it against them they would have an action back against him. Where the reacquirer negotiates without cancelling the intervening indorsements, the section provides that such indorsers are discharged except against subsequent holders in due course. The intervening indorser whose indorsement is stricken is, in conformity with Section 3–605, discharged even as against subsequent holders in due course.

Cross References:

Sections 3–602, 3–603(2) and 3–605.

Definitional Cross References:

"Holder in due course". Section 3–302.
"Instrument". Section 3–102.
"Party". Section 1–201.

PART 3

RIGHTS OF A HOLDER

§ 3–301.   Rights of a Holder.

The holder of an instrument whether or not he is the owner may transfer or negotiate it and, except as otherwise provided in Section 3–603 on payment or satisfaction, discharge it or enforce payment in his own name.

Official Comment

Prior Uniform Statutory Provision: Section 51, Uniform Negotiable Instruments Law.

Changes: Reworded. The provision in the original Section 51 as to discharge by payment is now covered by Section 3–603(1).

Purposes of Changes: The section is revised to state in one provision all the rights of a holder, and to make it clear that every holder has such rights. The only limitations are those found in Section 3–603 on payment or satisfaction. That section provides (with stated exceptions) that payment to a holder discharges the liability of the party paying even though made with knowledge of a claim of another person to the instrument, unless the adverse claimant posts indemnity or procures the issuance of appropriate legal process restraining the payment. Thus payment to a holder in an adverse claim situation would not give discharge if the adverse claimant had followed either of the procedures provided for in the "unless" clause of Section 3–603; nor would a discharge result from payment in two other specific situations described in Section 3–603.

Cross References:

Sections 1–201, 3–307 and 3–603(1).

Definitional Cross References:

"Holder". Section 1–201.
"Instrument". Section 3–102.
"Rights". Section 1–201.

§ 3–302.   Holder in Due Course.

(1)   A holder in due course is a holder who takes the instrument

   (a)   for value; and

   (b)   in good faith; and

   (c)   without notice that it is overdue or has been dishonored or of any defense against or claim to it on the part of any person.

(2)   A payee may be a holder in due course.

(3)   A holder does not become a holder in due course of an instrument:

   (a)   by purchase of it at judicial sale or by taking it under legal process; or

   (b)   by acquiring it in taking over an estate; or

   (c)   by purchasing it as part of a bulk transaction not in regular course of business of the transferor.

(4)   A purchaser of a limited interest can be a holder in due course only to the extent of the interest purchased.

Official Comment

Prior Uniform Statutory Provision: Section 52, Uniform Negotiable Instruments Law.

Changes: Reworded; new provisions.

Purposes of Changes and New Matter: The changes are intended to remove uncertainties arising under the original section.

1.   The language "without notice that it is overdue" is substituted for that of the original subsection (2) in order to make it clear that the purchaser of an instrument which is in fact overdue may be a holder in due course if he takes it without notice that it is overdue. Such notice is covered by the section on notice to purchaser (Section 3–304).

2.   Subsection (2) is intended to settle the long continued conflict over the status of the payee as a holder in due course. This conflict has turned very largely upon the word "negotiated" in the original Section 52(4), which is now eliminated. The position here taken is that the payee may become a holder in due course to the same extent and under the same circumstances as any other holder. This is true whether he takes the instrument by purchase from a third person or directly from the obligor. All that is necessary is that the payee meet the requirements of this section. In the following cases, among others, the payee is a holder in due course:

   a.   A remitter, purchasing goods from P, obtains a bank draft payable to P and forwards it to P, who takes it for value, in good faith and without notice as required by this section.

   b.   The remitter buys the bank draft payable to P, but it is forwarded by the bank directly to P, who takes it in good faith and without notice in payment of the remitter's obligation to him.

   c.   A and B sign a note as comakers. A induces B to sign by fraud, and without authority from B delivers the note to P, who takes it for value, in good faith and without notice.

   d.   A defrauds the maker into signing an instrument payable to P. P pays A for it in good faith and without notice, and the maker delivers the instrument directly to P.

e.   D draws a check payable to P and gives it to his agent to be delivered to P in payment of D's debt. The agent delivers it to P, who takes it in good faith and without notice in payment of the agent's debt to P. But as to this case see Section 3–304(2), which may apply.

f.   D draws a check payable to P but blank as to the amount, and gives it to his agent to be delivered to P. The agent fills in the check with an excessive amount, and P takes it for value, in good faith and without notice.

g.   D draws a check blank as to the name of the payee, and gives it to his agent to be filled in with the name of A and delivered to A. The agent fills in the name of P, and P takes the check in good faith, for value and without notice.

3.   Subsection (3) is intended to state existing case law. It covers a few situations in which the purchaser takes the instrument under unusual circumstances which indicate that he is merely a successor in interest to the prior holder and can acquire no better rights. (If such prior holder was himself a holder in due course, the purchaser succeeds to that status under Section 3–201 on Transfer.) The provision applies to a purchaser at an execution sale, a sale in bankruptcy or a sale by a state bank commissioner of the assets of an insolvent bank. It applies equally to an attaching creditor or any other person who acquires the instrument by legal process, even under an antecedent claim; and equally to a representative, such as an executor, administrator, receiver or assignee for the benefit of creditors, who takes over the instrument as part of an estate, even though he is representing antecedent creditors.

Subsection (3)(c) applies to bulk purchases lying outside of the ordinary course of business of the seller. It applies, for example, when a new partnership takes over for value all of the assets of an old one after a new member has entered the firm, or to a reorganized or consolidated corporation taking over in bulk the assets of a predecessor. It has particular application to the purchase by one bank of a substantial part of the paper held by another bank which is threatened with insolvency and seeking to liquidate its assets.

4.   A purchaser of a limited interest—as a pledgee in a security transaction—may become a holder in due course, but he may enforce the instrument over defenses only to the extent of his interest, and defenses good against the pledgor remain available insofar as the pledgor retains an equity in the instrument. This is merely a special application of the general rule (Section 1–201) that a purchaser of a limited interest acquires rights only to the extent of the interest purchased. Section 27 of the original Act contained a similar provision.

Cross References:

Sections 1–201, 3–303, 3–305 and 3–306.
Point 1: Section 3–304(5).
Point 3: Section 3–201.
Point 4: Section 1–201.

Definitional Cross References:

"Good faith". Section 1–201.
"Holder". Section 1–201.
"Instrument". Section 3–102.
"Notice". Section 1–201.
"Notice of dishonor". Section 3–508.
"Person". Section 1–201.
"Purchase". Section 1–201.
"Purchaser". Section 1–201.
"Value". Section 3–303.

§ 3–303.   Taking for Value.

A holder takes the instrument for value

(a)   to the extent that the agreed consideration has been performed or that he acquires a security interest in or a lien on the instrument otherwise than by legal process; or

(b)   when he takes the instrument in payment of or as security for an antecedent claim against any person whether or not the claim is due; or

(c) when he gives a negotiable instrument for it or makes an irrevocable commitment to a third person.

Official Comment

Prior Uniform Statutory Provision: Sections 25, 26, 27 and 54, Uniform Negotiable Instruments Law.

Changes: Combined and reworded; original Section 26 omitted.

Purposes of Changes: The changes are intended to remove uncertainties arising under the original Act.

1.   The original Section 26 which had reference to the liability of accommodation parties is omitted as erroneous and misleading, since a holder who does not himself give value cannot qualify as a holder in due course in his own right merely because value has previously been given for the instrument.

2.   In this Article value is divorced from consideration (Section 3–408). The latter is important only on the question of whether the obligation of a party can be enforced against him; while value is important only on the question of whether the holder who has acquired that obligation qualifies as a particular kind of holder.

3.   Paragraph (a) resolves an apparent conflict between the original Section 54 and the first sentence of the original Section 25, by requiring that the agreed consideration shall actually have been given. An executory promise to give value is not itself value, except as provided in paragraph (c). The underlying reason of policy is that when the purchaser learns of a defense against the instrument or of a defect in the title he is not required to enforce the instrument, but is free to rescind the transaction for breach of the transferor's warranty (Section 3–417). There is thus not the same necessity for giving him the status of a holder in due course, cutting off claims and defenses, as where he has actually paid value. A common illustration is the bank credit not drawn upon, which can be and is revoked when a claim or defense appears.

4.   Paragraph (a) limits the language of the original Section 27, eliminating the attaching creditor or any other person who acquires a lien by legal process. Any such lienor has been uniformly held not to be a holder in due course.

5.   Paragraph (b) restates the last sentence of the original Section 25. It adopts the generally accepted rule that the holder takes for value when he takes the instrument as security for an antecedent debt, even though there is no extension of time or other concession, and whether or not the debt is due. The provision extends the same rule to any claim against any person; there is no requirement that the claim arise out of contract. In particular the provision is intended to apply to an instrument given in payment of or as security for the debt of a third person, even though no concession is made in return.

6.   Paragraph (c) is new, but states generally recognized exceptions to the rule that an executory promise is not value. A negotiable instrument is value because it carries the possibility of negotiation to a holder in due course, after which the party who gives it cannot refuse to pay. The same reasoning applies to any irrevocable commitment to a third person, such as a letter of credit issued when an instrument is taken.

Cross References:

Sections 3–302 and 3–415.
Point 1: Section 3–415.
Point 2: Section 3–408.
Point 3: Section 3–417.

Definitional Cross References:

"Holder". Section 1–201.
"Instrument". Section 3–102.
"Person". Section 1–201.
"Security interest". Section 1–201.

§ 3–304.   Notice to Purchaser.

(1)   The purchaser has notice of a claim or defense if

(a) the instrument is so incomplete, bears such visible evidence of forgery or alteration, or is otherwise so irregular as to call into question its validity, terms or ownership or to create an ambiguity as to the party to pay; or

(b) the purchaser has notice that the obligation of any party is voidable in whole or in part, or that all parties have been discharged.

(2) The purchaser has notice of a claim against the instrument when he has knowledge that a fiduciary has negotiated the instrument in payment of or as security for his own debt or in any transaction for his own benefit or otherwise in breach of duty.

(3) The purchaser has notice that an instrument is overdue if he has reason to know

(a) that any part of the principal amount is overdue or that there is an uncured default in payment of another instrument of the same series; or

(b) that acceleration of the instrument has been made; or

(c) that he is taking a demand instrument after demand has been made or more than a reasonable length of time after its issue. A reasonable time for a check drawn and payable within the states and territories of the United States and the District of Columbia is presumed to be thirty days.

(4) Knowledge of the following facts does not of itself give the purchaser notice of a defense or claim

(a) that the instrument is antedated or postdated;

(b) that it was issued or negotiated in return for an executory promise or accompanied by a separate agreement, unless the purchaser has notice that a defense or claim has arisen from the terms thereof;

(c) that any party has signed for accommodation;

(d) that an incomplete instrument has been completed, unless the purchaser has notice of any improper completion;

(e) that any person negotiating the instrument is or was a fiduciary;

(f) that there has been default in payment of interest on the instrument or in payment of any other instrument, except one of the same series.

(5) The filing or recording of a document does not of itself constitute notice within the provisions of this Article to a person who would otherwise be a holder in due course.

(6) To be effective notice must be received at such time and in such manner as to give a reasonable opportunity to act on it.

Official Comment

Prior Uniform Statutory Provision: Sections 45, 52, 53, 55 and 56, Uniform Negotiable Instruments Law.

Changes: Combined and reworded; new provisions.

Purposes of Changes and New Matter: The original sections are expanded, with the addition of specific provisions intended to remove uncertainties in the existing law.

1. "Notice" is defined in Section 1–201.

2. Paragraph (a) of subsection (1) replaces the provision in the original Section 52(1) requiring that the instrument be "complete and regular on its face." An instrument may be blank as to some unnecessary particular, may contain minor erasures, or even have an obvious change in the date, as where "January 2, 1948" is changed to "January 2, 1949", without even exciting suspicion. Irregularity is properly a question of notice to the purchaser of something wrong, and is so treated here.

3. "Voidable" obligation in paragraph (b) of subsection (1) is intended to limit the provision to notice of defense which will permit any party to avoid his original obligation on the instrument, as distinguished from a set-off or counterclaim.

4.   Notice that one party has been discharged is not notice to the purchaser of an infirmity in the obligation of other parties who remain liable on the instrument. A purchaser with notice that an indorser is discharged takes subject to that discharge as provided in the section on effect of discharge against a holder in due course (Section 3–602) but is not prevented from taking the obligation of the maker in due course. If he has notice that all parties are discharged he cannot be a holder in due course.

5.   Subsection (2) follows the policy of Section 6 of the Uniform Fiduciaries Act, and specifies the same elements as notice of improper conduct of a fiduciary. Under paragraph (e) of subsection (4) mere notice of the existence of the fiduciary relation is not enough in itself to prevent the holder from taking in due course, and he is free to take the instrument on the assumption that the fiduciary is acting properly. The purchaser may pay cash into the hands of the fiduciary without notice of any breach of the obligation. Section 3–206 should be consulted for the effect of a restrictive indorsement.

6.   Subsection (3) removes an uncertainty in the original Act by providing that reason to know of an overdue installment or other part of the principal amount is notice that the instrument is overdue and thus prevents the purchaser from taking in due course. On the other hand subsection (4)(f) makes notice that interest is overdue insufficient, on the basis of banking and commercial practice, the decisions under the original Act, and the frequency with which interest payments are in fact delayed. Notice of default in payment of any other instrument, except an uncured default in another instrument of the same series, is likewise insufficient.

7.   Subsection (3) departs from the original Section 52(2) by providing that the purchaser may take accelerated paper, or a demand instrument on which demand has in fact been made, as a holder in due course if he takes without notice of the acceleration or demand. With this change the original Section 45 is eliminated, as the presumption that any negotiation has taken place before the instrument was in fact overdue is of importance only in aid of a holder in due course. Under this section it is not conclusive that the instrument was in fact overdue when it was negotiated, if the holder takes without notice of that fact.

The "reasonable time after issue" is retained from the original Section 53, but paragraph (c) adds a presumption, as that term is defined in this Act (Section 1–201), that a domestic check is stale after thirty days.

8.   Paragraph (a) of subsection (4) rejects decisions holding that an instrument known to be antedated or postdated is not "regular." Such knowledge does not prevent a holder from taking in due course.

9.   Paragraph (b) of subsection (4) is to be read together with the provisions of this Article as to when a promise or order is unconditional and as to other writings affecting the instrument (Sections 3–105 and 3–119). Mere notice of the existence of an executory promise or a separate agreement does not prevent the holder from taking in due course, and such notice may even appear in the instrument itself. If the purchaser has notice of any default in the promise or agreement which gives rise to a defense or claim against the instrument, he is on notice to the same extent as in the case of any other information as to the existence of a defense or claim.

10.   Paragraph (d) of subsection (4) follows the policy of the original Section 14, under which any person in possession of an instrument has prima facie authority to fill blanks. It is intended to mean that the holder may take in due course even though a blank is filled in his presence, if he is without notice that the filling is improper. Section 3–407 on alteration should be consulted as to the rights of subsequent holders following such an alteration.

11.   Subsection (5) is new. It removes an uncertainty arising under the original Act as to the effect of "constructive notice" through public filing or recording.

12.   Subsection (6) is new. It means that notice must be received with a sufficient margin of time to afford a reasonable opportunity to act on it, and that a notice received by the president of a bank one minute before the bank's teller cashes a check is not effective to prevent the bank from becoming a holder in due course. See in this connection the provision on notice to an organization, Sec. 1–201(27).

Cross References:

Sections 3–201 and 3–302.
Point 1: Section 1–201.
Point 4: Section 3–602.
Point 5: Section 3–206.
Point 7: Section 1–201.
Point 9: Sections 3–105(1)(b) and (c) and 3–119.
Point 10: Section 3–407.

Point 12: Section 1–201.

Definitional Cross References:

"Accommodation party". Section 3–415.

"Agreement". Section 1–201.

"Alteration". Section 3–407.

"Bank". Section 1–201.

"Check". Section 3–104.

"Holder in due course". Section 3–302.

"Instrument". Section 3–102.

"Issue". Section 3–102.

"Negotiation". Section 3–202.

"Notice". Section 1–201.

"Party". Section 1–201.

"Person". Section 1–201.

"Presumed". Section 1–201.

"Promise". Section 3–102.

"Purchaser". Section 1–201.

"Reasonable time". Section 1–204.

"Signed". Section 1–201.

"Term". Section 1–201.

§ 3–305.   Rights of a Holder in Due Course.

To the extent that a holder is a holder in due course he takes the instrument free from

(1)   all claims to it on the part of any person; and

(2)   all defenses of any party to the instrument with whom the holder has not dealt except

(a)   infancy, to the extent that it is a defense to a simple contract; and

(b)   such other incapacity, or duress, or illegality of the transaction, as renders the obligation of the party a nullity; and

(c)   such misrepresentation as has induced the party to sign the instrument with neither knowledge nor reasonable opportunity to obtain knowledge of its character or its essential terms; and

(d)   discharge in insolvency proceedings; and

(e)   any other discharge of which the holder has notice when he takes the instrument.

Official Comment

Prior Uniform Statutory Provision: Sections 15, 16 and 57, Uniform Negotiable Instruments Law.

Changes: Combined and reworded; new provisions; rule of original Section 15 reversed.

Purposes of Changes and New Matter:

1.   The section applies to any person who is himself a holder in due course, and equally to any transferee who acquires the rights of one (Section 3–201). "Takes" is substituted for "holds" in the original Section 57 because a holder in due course may still be subject to any claims or defenses which arise against him after he has taken the instrument.

2.   The language "all claims to it on the part of any person" is substituted for "any defect of title of prior parties" in the original Section 57 in order to make it clear that the holder in due course takes the instrument free not only from any claim of legal title but also from all liens, equities or claims of any other kind. This includes any claim for rescission of a prior negotiation, in accordance with the provisions of the section on reacquisition (Section 3–208).

3.   "All defenses" includes nondelivery, conditional delivery or delivery for a special purpose. Under this Article such nondelivery or qualified delivery is a defense (Sections 3–306 and 3–307) and the defendant has the full burden of establishing it. Accordingly the "conclusive presumption" of the third sentence of the original Section 16 is abrogated in favor of a rule of law cutting off the defense.

The effect of this section, together with the sections dealing with incomplete instruments (Section 3–115) and alteration (Section 3–407) is to cut off the defense of nondelivery of an incomplete instrument against a holder in due course, and to change the rule of the original Section 15.

4.   Paragraph (a) of subsection (2) is new. It follows the decisions under the original Act in providing that the defense of infancy may be asserted against a holder in due course, even though its effect is to render the instrument voidable but not void. The policy is one of protection of the infant against those who take advantage of him, even at the expense of occasional loss to an innocent purchaser. No attempt is made to state when infancy is available as a defense or the conditions under which it may be asserted. In some jurisdictions it is held that an infant cannot rescind the transaction or set up the defense unless he restores the holder to his former position, which in the case of a holder in due course is normally impossible. In other states an infant who has misrepresented his age may be estopped to assert his infancy. Such questions are left to the local law, as an integral part of the policy of each state as to the protection of infants.

5.   Paragraph (b) of subsection (2) is new. It covers mental incompetence, guardianship, ultra vires acts or lack of corporate capacity to do business, any remaining incapacity of married women, or any other incapacity apart from infancy. Such incapacity is largely statutory. Its existence and effect is left to the law of each state. If under the local law the effect is to render the obligation of the instrument entirely null and void, the defense may be asserted against a holder in due course. If the effect is merely to render the obligation voidable at the election of the obligor, the defense is cut off.

6.   Duress is a matter of degree. An instrument signed at the point of a gun is void, even in the hands of a holder in due course. One signed under threat to prosecute the son of the maker for theft may be merely voidable, so that the defense is cut off. Illegality is most frequently a matter of gambling or usury, but may arise in many other forms under a great variety of statutes. The statutes differ greatly in their provisions and the interpretations given them. They are primarily a matter of local concern and local policy. All such matters are therefore left to the local law. If under that law the effect of the duress or the illegality is to make the obligation entirely null and void, the defense may be asserted against a holder in due course. Otherwise it is cut off.

7.   Paragraph (c) of subsection (2) is new. It follows the great majority of the decisions under the original Act in recognizing the defense of "real" or "essential" fraud, sometimes called fraud in the essence or fraud in the factum, as effective against a holder in due course. The common illustration is that of the maker who is tricked into signing a note in the belief that it is merely a receipt or some other document. The theory of the defense is that his signature on the instrument is ineffective because he did not intend to sign such an instrument at all. Under this provision the defense extends to an instrument signed with knowledge that it is a negotiable instrument, but without knowledge of its essential terms.

The test of the defense here stated is that of excusable ignorance of the contents of the writing signed. The party must not only have been in ignorance, but must also have had no reasonable opportunity to obtain knowledge. In determining what is a reasonable opportunity all relevant factors are to be taken into account, including the age and sex of the party, his intelligence, education and business experience; his ability to read or to understand English, the representations made to him and his reason to rely on them or to have confidence in the person making them; the presence or absence of any third person who might read or explain the instrument to him, or any other possibility of obtaining independent information; and the apparent necessity, or lack of it, for acting without delay.

Unless the misrepresentation meets this test, the defense is cut off by a holder in due course.

8.   Paragraph (d) is also new. It is inserted to make it clear that any discharge in bankruptcy or other insolvency proceedings, as defined in this Article, is not cut off when the instrument is purchased by a holder in due course.

9.   Paragraph (e) of subsection (2) is also new. Under the notice to purchaser section of this Article (Section 3–304), notice of any discharge which leaves other parties liable on the instrument does not prevent the purchaser from becoming a holder in due course. The obvious case is that of the cancellation of an indorsement, which leaves the maker and prior indorsers liable. As to such parties the purchaser may be a holder in due course, but he takes

the instrument subject to the discharge of which he has notice. If he is without such notice, the discharge is not effective against him (Section 3–602).

Cross References:

> Point 1: Section 3–201(1).
> Point 2: Section 3–208.
> Point 3: Sections 3–115(2), 3–306(c), 3–307(2) and 3–407(3).
> Point 9: Sections 3–304(1)(b) and 3–602.

Definitional Cross References:

> "Contract". Section 1–201.
> "Holder in due course". Section 3–302.
> "Insolvency proceedings". Section 1–201.
> "Instrument". Section 3–102.
> "Notice". Section 1–201.
> "Party". Section 1–201.
> "Person". Section 1–201.
> "Term". Section 1–201.

§ 3–306.   Rights of One Not Holder in Due Course.

Unless he has the rights of a holder in due course any person takes the instrument subject to

(a)   all valid claims to it on the part of any person; and

(b)   all defenses of any party which would be available in an action on a simple contract; and

(c)   the defenses of want or failure of consideration, non-performance of any condition precedent, non-delivery, or delivery for a special purpose (Section 3–408); and

(d)   the defense that he or a person through whom he holds the instrument acquired it by theft, or that payment or satisfaction to such holder would be inconsistent with the terms of a restrictive indorsement. The claim of any third person to the instrument is not otherwise available as a defense to any party liable thereon unless the third person himself defends the action for such party.

Official Comment

Prior Uniform Statutory Provision: Sections 16, 28, 58 and 59, Uniform Negotiable Instruments Law.

Changes: Combined, condensed and reworded.

Purposes of Changes: The changes are intended to remove the following uncertainties arising under the original sections:

1.   Any transferee who acquires the rights of a holder in due course under the transfer section of this Article (Section 3–201) is included within the provisions of the preceding Section 305. This section covers any person who neither qualifies in his own right as a holder in due course nor has acquired the rights of one by transfer. In particular the section applies to a bona fide purchaser with notice that the instrument is overdue.

2.   "All valid claims to it on the part of any person" includes not only claims of legal title, but all liens, equities, or other claims of right against the instrument or its proceeds. It includes claims to rescind a prior negotiation and to recover the instrument or its proceeds.

3.   Paragraph (b) restates the first sentence of the original Section 58.

4.   Paragraph (c) condenses the original Sections 16 and 28. Want or failure of consideration is specifically mentioned, as in the original Section 28, in order to make it clear that either is a defense which the defendant has the burden of establishing under the following section of this Article. The language as to an "ascertained or liquidated amount or otherwise" in the original Section 28 is omitted because it is believed to be superfluous. The third sentence of Section 16 is now covered by the preceding section. The fourth sentence is omitted in favor of the rule stated in the following section, which places the full burden of establishing the defense of non-delivery,

conditional delivery or delivery for a special purpose upon the defendant, and makes any presumption unnecessary.

5.   Paragraph (d) is substituted for the last sentence of the original Section 59, as a more detailed and explicit statement of the same policy, which is also found in the original Section 22. The contract of the obligor is to pay the holder of the instrument, and the claims of other persons against the holder are generally not his concern. He is not required to set up such a claim as a defense, since he usually will have no satisfactory evidence of his own on the issue; and the provision that he may not do so is intended as much for his protection as for that of the holder. The claimant who has lost possession of an instrument so payable or indorsed that another may become a holder has lost his rights on the instrument, which by its terms no longer runs to him. The provision includes all claims for rescission of a negotiation, whether based in incapacity, fraud, duress, mistake, illegality, breach of trust or duty or any other reason. It includes claims based on conditional delivery or delivery for a special purpose. It includes claims of legal title, lien, constructive trust or other equity against the instrument or its proceeds. The exception made in the case of theft is based on the policy which refuses to aid a proved thief to recover, and refuses to aid him indirectly by permitting his transferee to recover unless the transferee is a holder in due course. The exception concerning restrictive indorsements is intended to achieve consistency with Section 3–603 and related sections.

Nothing in this section is intended to prevent the claimant from intervening in the holder's action against the obligor or defending the action for the latter, and asserting his claim in the course of such intervention or defense. Nothing here stated is intended to prevent any interpleader, deposit in court or other available procedure under which the defendant may bring the claimant into court or be discharged without himself litigating the claim as a defense. Compare Section 3–803 on vouching in other parties alleged to be liable.

Cross References:

Section 3–302.
Point 1: Sections 3–201(1) and 3–305.
Point 2: Section 3–207.
Point 3: Section 3–307(2).
Point 4: Sections 3–305 and 3–307(2).
Point 5: Section 3–803.

Definitional Cross References:

"Action". Section 1–201.
"Contract". Section 1–201.
"Delivery". Section 1–201.
"Holder in due course". Section 3–302.
"Instrument". Section 3–102.
"Party". Section 1–201.
"Person". Section 1–201.
"Rights". Section 1–201.

§ 3–307.   Burden of Establishing Signatures, Defenses and Due Course.

(1)   Unless specifically denied in the pleadings each signature on an instrument is admitted. When the effectiveness of a signature is put in issue

(a)   the burden of establishing it is on the party claiming under the signature; but

(b)   the signature is presumed to be genuine or authorized except where the action is to enforce the obligation of a purported signer who has died or become incompetent before proof is required.

(2)   When signatures are admitted or established, production of the instrument entitles a holder to recover on it unless the defendant establishes a defense.

(3)   After it is shown that a defense exists a person claiming the rights of a holder in due course has the burden of establishing that he or some person under whom he claims is in all respects a holder in due course.

Official Comment

Prior Uniform Statutory Provision: Section 59, Uniform Negotiable Instruments Law.

Changes: Reworded; new provisions.

Purposes of Changes and New Matter:

1. Subsection (1) is new, although similar provisions are found in a number of states. The purpose of the requirement of a specific denial in the pleadings is to give the plaintiff notice that he must meet a claim of forgery or lack of authority as to the particular signature, and to afford him an opportunity to investigate and obtain evidence. Where local rules of pleading permit, the denial may be on information and belief, or it may be a denial of knowledge or information sufficient to form a belief. It need not be under oath unless the local statutes or rules require verification. In the absence of such specific denial the signature stands admitted, and is not in issue. Nothing in this section is intended, however, to prevent amendment of the pleading in a proper case.

The question of the burden of establishing the signature arises only when it has been put in issue by specific denial. "Burden of establishing" is defined in the definitions section of this Act (Section 1–201). The burden is on the party claiming under the signature, but he is aided by the presumption that it is genuine or authorized [as] stated in paragraph (b). "Presumption" is also defined in this Act (Section 1–201). It means that until some evidence is introduced which would support a finding that the signature is forged or unauthorized the plaintiff is not required to prove that it is authentic. The presumption rests upon the fact that in ordinary experience forged or unauthorized signatures are very uncommon, and normally any evidence is within the control of the defendant or more accessible to him. He is therefore required to make some sufficient showing of the grounds for his denial before the plaintiff is put to his proof. His evidence need not be sufficient to require a directed verdict in his favor, but it must be enough to support his denial by permitting a finding in his favor. Until he introduces such evidence the presumption requires a finding for the plaintiff. Once such evidence is introduced the burden of establishing the signature by a preponderance of the total evidence is on the plaintiff.

Under paragraph (b) this presumption does not arise where the action is to enforce the obligation of a purported signer who has died or become incompetent before the evidence is required, and so is disabled from obtaining or introducing it. "Action" of course includes a claim asserted against the estate of a deceased or an incompetent.

2. Subsection (2) is substituted for the first clause of the original Section 59. Once signatures are proved or admitted, a holder makes out his case by mere production of the instrument, and is entitled to recover in the absence of any further evidence. The defendant has the burden of establishing any and all defenses, not only in the first instance but by a preponderance of the total evidence. The provision applies only to a holder, as defined in this Act (Section 1–201). Any other person in possession of an instrument must prove his right to it and account for the absence of any necessary indorsement. If he establishes a transfer which gives him the rights of a holder (Section 3–201), this provision becomes applicable, and he is then entitled to recover unless the defendant establishes a defense.

3. Subsection (3) rephrases the last clause of the first sentence of the original Section 59. Until it is shown that a defense exists the issue as to whether the holder is a holder in due course does not arise. In the absence of a defense any holder is entitled to recover and there is no occasion to say that he is deemed prima facie to be a holder in due course. When it is shown that a defense exists the plaintiff may, if he so elects, seek to cut off the defense by establishing that he is himself a holder in due course, or that he has acquired the rights of a prior holder in due course (Section 3–201). On this issue he has the full burden of proof by a preponderance of the total evidence. "In all respects" means that he must sustain this burden by affirmative proof that the instrument was taken for value, that it was taken in good faith, and that it was taken without notice (Section 3–302).

Nothing in this section is intended to say that the plaintiff must necessarily prove that he is a holder in due course. He may elect to introduce no further evidence, in which case a verdict may be directed for the plaintiff or the defendant, or the issue of the defense may be left to the jury, according to the weight and sufficiency of the defendant's evidence. He may elect to rebut the defense itself by proof to the contrary, in which case again a verdict may be directed for either party or the issue may be for the jury. This subsection means only that if the plaintiff claims the rights of a holder in due course against the defense he has the burden of proof upon that issue.

Cross References:

Sections 3–305, 3–306, 3–401, 3–403 and 3–404.
Point 1: Section 1–201.

Point 2: Sections 1–201 and 3–201(1).

Point 3: Sections 3–201(1) and 3–302.

Definitional Cross References:

"Action". Section 1–201.

"Burden of establishing". Section 1–201.

"Defendant". Section 1–201.

"Genuine". Section 1–201.

"Holder". Section 1–201.

"Holder in due course". Section 3–302.

"Instrument". Section 3–102.

"Party". Section 1–201.

"Person". Section 1–201.

"Presumed". Section 1–201.

"Rights". Section 1–201.

"Signature". Section 3–401.

PART 4

LIABILITY OF PARTIES

§ 3–401.   Signature.

(1)   No person is liable on an instrument unless his signature appears thereon.

(2)   A signature is made by use of any name, including any trade or assumed name, upon an instrument, or by any word or mark used in lieu of a written signature.

Official Comment

Prior Uniform Statutory Provision: Section 18, Uniform Negotiable Instruments Law.

Changes: Reworded.

Purposes of Changes: To make it clear that:

1.   No one is liable on an instrument unless and until he has signed it. The chief application of the rule has been in cases holding that a principal whose name does not appear on an instrument signed by his agent is not liable on the instrument even though the payee knew when it was issued that it was intended to be the obligation of one who did not sign. The exceptions made as to collateral and virtual acceptances by the original Sections 134 and 135 are now abrogated by the definition of an acceptance and the rules governing its operation. An allonge is part of the instrument to which it is affixed. Section 3–202(2).

Nothing in this section is intended to prevent any liability arising apart from the instrument itself. The party who does not sign may still be liable on the original obligation for which the instrument was given, or for breach of any agreement to sign, or in tort for misrepresentation, or even on an oral guaranty of payment where the statute of frauds is satisfied. He may of course be liable under any separate writing. The provision is not intended to prevent an estoppel to deny that the party has signed, as where the instrument is purchased in good faith reliance upon his assurance that a forged signature is genuine.

2.   A signature may be handwritten, typed, printed or made in any other manner. It need not be subscribed, and may appear in the body of the instrument, as in the case of "I, John Doe, promise to pay—" without any other signature. It may be made by mark, or even by thumbprint. It may be made in any name, including any trade name or assumed name, however false and fictitious, which is adopted for the purpose. Parol evidence is admissible to identify the signer, and when he is identified the signature is effective.

This section is not intended to affect any local statute or rule of law requiring a signature by mark to be witnessed, or any signature to be otherwise authenticated, or requiring any form of proof. It is to be read together with the provision under which a person paying or giving value for the instrument may require indorsement in both the right name and the wrong one; and with the provision that the absence of an indorsement in the right name may make an instrument so irregular as to call its ownership into question and put a purchaser upon notice which will prevent his taking as a holder in due course.

Cross References:

Sections 3–202(2), 3–402 through 3–406.
Point 1: Section 3–410.
Point 2: Section 3–203.

Definitional Cross References:

"Person". Section 1–201.
"Instrument". Section 3–102.
"Signed". Section 1–201.
"Written". Section 1–201.

§ 3–402. Signature in Ambiguous Capacity.

Unless the instrument clearly indicates that a signature is made in some other capacity it is an indorsement.

Official Comment

Prior Uniform Statutory Provision: Sections 17(6) and 63, Uniform Negotiable Instruments Law.

Changes: Combined and reworded.

Purposes of Changes: The revised language is intended to say that any ambiguity as to the capacity in which a signature is made must be resolved by a rule of law that it is an indorsement. Parol evidence is not admissible to show any other capacity, except for the purpose of reformation of the instrument as it may be permitted under the rules of the particular jurisdiction. The question is to be determined from the face of the instrument alone, and unless the instrument itself makes it clear that he has signed in some other capacity the signer must be treated as an indorser.

The indication that the signature is made in another capacity must be clear without reference to anything but the instrument. It may be found in the language used. Thus if John Doe signs after "I, John Doe, promise to pay," he is clearly a maker; and "John Doe, witness" is not liable at all. The capacity may be found in any clearly evidenced purpose of the signature, as where a drawee signing in an unusual place on the paper has no visible reason to sign at all unless he is an acceptor. It may be found in usage or custom. Thus by long established practice judicially noticed or otherwise established a signature in the lower right hand corner of an instrument indicates an intent to sign as the maker of a note or the drawer of a draft. Any similar clear indication of an intent to sign in some other capacity may be enough to remove the signature from the application of this section.

Cross Reference:

Section 3–401.

Definitional Cross References:

"Instrument". Section 3–102.
"Signature". Section 3–401.

§ 3–403. Signature by Authorized Representative.

(1) A signature may be made by an agent or other representative, and his authority to make it may be established as in other cases of representation. No particular form of appointment is necessary to establish such authority.

(2) An authorized representative who signs his own name to an instrument

(a) is personally obligated if the instrument neither names the person represented nor shows that the representative signed in a representative capacity;

(b) except as otherwise established between the immediate parties, is personally obligated if the instrument names the person represented but does not show that the representative signed in a representative capacity, or if the instrument does not name the person represented but does show that the representative signed in a representative capacity.

(3)   Except as otherwise established the name of an organization preceded or followed by the name and office of an authorized individual is a signature made in a representative capacity.

Official Comment

Prior Uniform Statutory Provision: Sections 19, 20 and 21, Uniform Negotiable Instruments Law.

Changes: Combined and reworded; original Section 21 omitted.

Purposes of Changes:

1.   The definition of "representative" in this Act (Section 1–201) includes an officer of a corporation or association, a trustee, an executor or administrator of an estate, or any person empowered to act for another. It is not intended to mean that a trust or an estate is necessarily a legal entity with the capacity to issue negotiable instruments, but merely that if it can issue them they may be signed by the representative.

The power to sign for another may be an express authority, or it may be implied in law or in fact, or it may rest merely upon apparent authority. It may be established as in other cases of representation, and when relevant parol evidence is admissible to prove or to deny it.

2.   Subsection (2) applies only to the signature of a representative whose authority to sign for another is established. If he is not authorized his signature has the effect of an unauthorized signature (Section 3–404). Even though he is authorized the principal is not liable on the instrument, under the provisions (Section 3–401) relating to signatures, unless the instrument names him and clearly shows that the signature is made on his behalf.

3.   Assuming that Peter Pringle is a principal and Arthur Adams is his agent, an instrument might, for example, bear the following signatures affixed by the agent—

    (a)   "Peter Pringle", or

    (b)   "Arthur Adams", or

    (c)   "Peter Pringle by Arthur Adams, Agent", or

    (d)   "Arthur Adams, Agent", or

    (e)   "Peter Pringle Arthur Adams".

A signature in form (a) does not bind Adams if authorized (Sections 3–401 and 3–404).

A signature as in (b) personally obligates the agent and parol evidence is inadmissible under subsection (2)(a) to disestablish his obligation.

The unambiguous way to make the representation clear is to sign as in (c). Any other definite indication is sufficient, as where the instrument reads "Peter Pringle promises to pay" and it is signed "Arthur Adams, Agent." Adams is not bound if he is authorized (Section 3–404).

Subsection 2(b) adopts the New York (minority) rule of Megowan v. Peterson, 173 N.Y. 1 (1902), in such a case as (d); and adopts the majority rule in such a case as (e). In both cases the section admits parol evidence in litigation between the immediate parties to prove signature by the agent in his representative capacity. [Paragraph 3 was amended in 1966].

4.   The original Section 21, covering signatures by "procuration," is omitted. It was based on English practice under which the words "per procuration" added to any signature are understood to mean that the signer is acting under a power of attorney which the holder is free to examine. The holder is thus put on notice of the limited authority, and there can be no apparent authority extending beyond the power of attorney. This meaning of "per procuration" is almost unknown in the United States, and the words are understood by the ordinary banker or attorney to be merely the equivalent of "by." The omission is not intended to suggest that a signature "by procuration" can no longer have the effect which it had under the original Section 21, in any case where a party chooses to use the expression.

Cross References:

     Point 1: Section 1–201.

     Point 2: Sections 3–401(1), 3–404 and 3–405.

Definitional Cross References:

"Instrument". Section 3–102.
"Person". Section 1–201.
"Representative". Section 1–201.
"Signature". Section 3–401.

§ 3–404.   Unauthorized Signatures.

(1)   Any unauthorized signature is wholly inoperative as that of the person whose name is signed unless he ratifies it or is precluded from denying it; but it operates as the signature of the unauthorized signer in favor of any person who in good faith pays the instrument or takes it for value.

(2)   Any unauthorized signature may be ratified for all purposes of this Article. Such ratification does not of itself affect any rights of the person ratifying against the actual signer.

Official Comment

Prior Uniform Statutory Provision: Section 23, Uniform Negotiable Instruments Law.

Changes: Reworded; new provisions.

Purpose of Changes and New Matter: The changes are intended to remove uncertainties arising under the original section:

1.   "Unauthorized signature" is a defined term (Section 1–201). It includes both a forgery and a signature made by an agent exceeding his actual or apparent authority.

2.   The final clause of subsection (1) is new. It states the generally accepted rule that the unauthorized signature, while it is wholly inoperative as that of the person whose name is signed, is effective to impose liability upon the actual signer or to transfer any rights that he may have in the instrument. His liability is not in damages for breach of a warranty of his authority, but is full liability on the instrument in the capacity in which he has signed. It is, however, limited to parties who take or pay the instrument in good faith; and one who knows that the signature is unauthorized cannot recover from the signer on the instrument.

3.   Subsection (2) is new. It settles the conflict which has existed in the decisions as to whether a forgery may be ratified. A forged signature may at least be adopted; and the word "ratified" is used in order to make it clear that the adoption is retroactive, and that it may be found from conduct as well as from express statements. Thus it may be found from the retention of benefits received in the transaction with knowledge of the unauthorized signature; and although the forger is not an agent, the ratification is governed by the same rules and principles as if he were.

This provision makes ratification effective only for the purposes of this Article. The unauthorized signature becomes valid so far as its effect as a signature is concerned. The ratification relieves the actual signer from liability on the signature. It does not of itself relieve him from liability to the person whose name is signed. It does not in any way affect the criminal law. No policy of the criminal law requires that the person whose name is forged shall not assume liability to others on the instrument; but he cannot affect the rights of the state. While the ratification may be taken into account with other relevant facts in determining punishment, it does not relieve the signer of criminal liability.

4.   The words "or is precluded from denying it" are retained in subsection (1) to recognize the possibility of an estoppel against the person whose name is signed, as where he expressly or tacitly represents to an innocent purchaser that the signature is genuine; and to recognize the negligence which precludes a denial of the signature.

Cross References:

Sections 3–307, 3–401, 3–403 and 3–405.
Point 1: Section 1–201.
Point 4: Section 3–406.

Definitional Cross References:

"Good faith". Section 1–201.
"Instrument". Section 3–102.
"Person". Section 1–201.

"Rights". Section 1–201.
"Signature". Section 3–401.
"Signed". Section 1–201.
"Unauthorized signature". Section 1–201.
"Value". Section 3–303.

§ 3–405.　Impostors; Signature in Name of Payee.

(1)　An indorsement by any person in the name of a named payee is effective if

(a)　an impostor by use of the mails or otherwise has induced the maker or drawer to issue the instrument to him or his confederate in the name of the payee; or

(b)　a person signing as or on behalf of a maker or drawer intends the payee to have no interest in the instrument; or

(c)　an agent or employee of the maker or drawer has supplied him with the name of the payee intending the latter to have no such interest.

(2)　Nothing in this section shall affect the criminal or civil liability of the person so indorsing.

Official Comment

Prior Uniform Statutory Provision: Section 9(3), Uniform Negotiable Instruments Law.

Changes: Reworded; new provisions.

Purposes of Changes and New Matter:

1.　This section enlarges the original subsection to include additional situations which it has not been held to cover. The words "fictitious or nonexisting person" have been eliminated as misleading, since the existence or nonexistence of the named payee is not decisive and is important only as it may bear on the intent that he shall have no interest in the instrument. The instrument is not made payable to bearer and indorsements are still necessary to negotiation. The section however recognizes as effective indorsement of the types of paper covered no matter by whom made. This solution is thought preferable to making such instruments bearer paper; on the face of things they are payable to order and a subsequent taker should require what purports to be a regular chain of indorsements. On the other hand it is thought to be unduly restrictive to require that the actual indorsement be made by the impostor or other fraudulent actor. In most cases the person whose fraud procured the instrument to be issued will himself indorse; when some other third person indorses it will most probably be a case of theft or a second independent fraud superimposed upon the original fraud. In neither case does there seem to be sufficient reason to reverse the rule of the section. To recapitulate: the instrument does not become bearer paper, a purportedly regular chain in indorsements is required, but any person—first thief, second impostor or third murderer—can effectively indorse in the name of the payee.

2.　Subsection (1)(a) is new. It rejects decisions which distinguish between face-to-face imposture and imposture by mail and hold that where the parties deal by mail the dominant intent of the drawer is to deal with the name rather than with the person so that the resulting instrument may be negotiated only by indorsement of the payee whose name has been taken in vain. The result of the distinction has been under some prior law, to throw the loss in the mail imposture forward to a subsequent holder or to the drawee. Since the maker or drawer believes the two to be one and the same, the two intentions cannot be separated, and the "dominant intent" is a fiction. The position here taken is that the loss, regardless of the type of fraud which the particular impostor has committed, should fall upon the maker or drawer.

"Impostor" refers to impersonation, and does not extend to a false representation that the party is the authorized agent of the payee. The maker or drawer who takes the precaution of making the instrument payable to the principal is entitled to have his indorsement.

3.　Subsection (1)(b) restates the substance of the original subsection 9(3). The test stated is not whether the named payee is "fictitious," but whether the signer intends that he shall have no interest in the instrument. The following situations illustrate the application of the subsection.

a.　The drawer of a check, for his own reasons, makes it payable to P knowing that P does not exist.

b.   The drawer makes the check payable in the name of P. A person named P exists, but the drawer does not know it.

c.   The drawer makes the check payable to P, an existing person whom he knows, intending to receive the money himself and that P shall have no interest in the check.

d.   The treasurer of a corporation draws its check payable to P, who to the knowledge of the treasurer does not exist.

e.   The treasurer of a corporation draws its check payable to P. P exists but the treasurer has fraudulently added his name to the payroll intending that he shall not receive the check.

f.   The president and the treasurer of a corporation both sign its check payable to P. P does not exist. The treasurer knows it but the president does not.

g.   The same facts as f, except that P exists and the treasurer knows it, but intends that P shall have no interest in the check.

In all the cases stated an indorsement by any person in the name of P is effective.

4.   Paragraph (c) is new. It extends the rule of the original Subsection 9(3) to include the padded payroll cases, where the drawer's agent or employee prepares the check for signature or otherwise furnishes the signing officer with the name of the payee. The principle followed is that the loss should fall upon the employer as a risk of his business enterprise rather than upon the subsequent holder or drawee. The reasons are that the employer is normally in a better position to prevent such forgeries by reasonable care in the selection or supervision of his employees, or, if he is not, is at least in a better position to cover the loss by fidelity insurance; and that the cost of such insurance is properly an expense of his business rather than of the business of the holder or drawee.

The provision applies only to the agent or employee of the drawer, and only to the agent or employee who supplies him with the name of the payee. The following situations illustrate its application.

a.   An employee of a corporation prepares a padded payroll for its treasurer, which includes the name of P. P does not exist, and the employee knows it, but the treasurer does not. The treasurer draws the corporation's check payable to P.

b.   The same facts as a, except that P exists and the employee knows it but intends him to have no interest in the check. In both cases an indorsement by any person in the name of P is effective and the loss falls on the corporation.

5.   The section is not intended to affect criminal liability for forgery or any other crime, or civil liability to the drawer or to any other person. It is to be read together with the section under which an unauthorized signer is personally liable on the signature to any person who takes the instrument in good faith (3–404(1)).

Cross References:

Sections 3–401, 3–403, 3–404 and 3–406.
Point 5: Section 3–404(1).

Definitional Cross References:

"Instrument". Section 3–102.
"Issue". Section 3–102.
"Person". Section 1–201.
"Signature". Section 3–401.

§ 3–406.   Negligence Contributing to Alteration or Unauthorized Signature.

Any person who by his negligence substantially contributes to a material alteration of the instrument or to the making of an unauthorized signature is precluded from asserting the alteration or lack of authority against a holder in due course or against a drawee or other payor who pays the instrument in good faith and in accordance with the reasonable commercial standards of the drawee's or payor's business.

Official Comment

Prior Uniform Statutory Provision: None.

Purposes:

1. This section is new. It adopts the doctrine of Young v. Grote, 4 Bing. 253 (1827), which held that a drawer who so negligently draws an instrument as to facilitate its material alteration is liable to a drawee who pays the altered instrument in good faith. It should be noted that the rule as stated in the section requires that the negligence "substantially" contribute to the alteration.

2. The section extends the above principle to the protection of a holder in due course and of payors who may not technically be drawees. It rejects decisions which have held that the maker of a note owes no duty of care to the holder because at the time the instrument is drawn there is no contract between them. By drawing the instrument and "setting it afloat upon a sea of strangers" the maker or drawer voluntarily enters into a relation with later holders which justifies his responsibility. In this respect an instrument so negligently drawn as to facilitate alteration does not differ in principle from an instrument containing blanks which may be filled.

The holder in due course under the rules governing alteration (Section 3–407) may enforce the altered instrument according to its original tenor. Where negligence of the obligor has substantially contributed to the alteration, this section gives the holder the alternative right to enforce the instrument as altered.

3. No attempt is made to define negligence which will contribute to an alteration. The question is left to the court or the jury upon the circumstances of the particular cases. Negligence usually has been found where spaces are left in the body of the instrument in which words or figures may be inserted. No unusual precautions are required, and the section is not intended to change decisions holding that the drawer of a bill is under no duty to use sensitized paper, indelible ink or a protectograph; or that it is not negligence to leave spaces between the lines or at the end of the instrument in which a provision for interest or the like can be written.

4. The section applies only where the negligence contributes to the alteration. It must afford an opportunity of which advantage is in fact taken. The section approves decisions which have refused to hold the drawer responsible where he has left spaces in a check but the payee erased all the writing with chemicals and wrote in an entirely new check.

5. This section does not make the negligent party liable in tort for damages resulting from the alteration. Instead it estops him from asserting it against the holder in due course or drawee. The reason is that in the usual case the extent of the loss, which involves the possibility of ultimate recovery from the wrongdoer, cannot be determined at the time of litigation, and the decision would have to be made on the unsatisfactory basis of burden of proof. The holder or drawee is protected by an estoppel, and the task of pursuing the wrongdoer is left to the negligent party. Any amount in fact recovered from the wrongdoer must be held for the benefit of the negligent party under ordinary principles of equity.

6. The section protects parties who act not only in good faith, (Section 1–201) but also in observance of the reasonable standards of their business. Thus any bank which takes or pays an altered check which ordinary banking standards would require it to refuse cannot take advantage of the estoppel.

7. The section applies the same rule to negligence which contributes to a forgery or other unauthorized signature, as defined in this Act (Section 1–201). The most obvious case is that of the drawer who makes use of a signature stamp or other automatic signing device and is negligent in looking after it. The section extends, however, to cases where the party has notice that forgeries of his signature have occurred and is negligent in failing to prevent further forgeries by the same person. It extends to negligence which contributes to a forgery of the signature of another, as in the case where a check is negligently mailed to the wrong person having the same name as the payee. As in the case of alteration, no attempt is made to specify what is negligence, and the question is one for the court or the jury on the facts of the particular case.

Cross References:

Sections 3–401 and 3–404.
Point 2: Section 3–407(3).
Point 6: Section 1–201.
Point 7: Section 1–201.

Definitional Cross References:

"Alteration". Section 3–407.

"Good faith". Section 1–201.

"Holder in due course". Section 3–302.

"Instrument". Section 3–102.

"Person". Section 1–201.

"Unauthorized signature". Section 1–201.

§3–407. Alteration.

(1) Any alteration of an instrument is material which changes the contract of any party thereto in any respect, including any such change in

(a) the number or relations of the parties; or

(b) an incomplete instrument, by completing it otherwise than as authorized; or

(c) the writing as signed, by adding to it or by removing any part of it.

(2) As against any person other than a subsequent holder in due course.

(a) alteration by the holder which is both fraudulent and material discharges any party whose contract is thereby changed unless that party assents or is precluded from asserting the defense;

(b) no other alteration discharges any party and the instrument may be enforced according to its original tenor, or as to incomplete instruments according to the authority given.

(3) A subsequent holder in due course may in all cases enforce the instrument according to its original tenor, and when an incomplete instrument has been completed, he may enforce it as completed.

Official Comment

Prior Uniform Statutory Provision: Sections 14, 15, 124 and 125, Uniform Negotiable Instruments Law.

Changes: Combined and reworded; new provisions; rule of original Section 15 reversed.

Purposes of Changes and New Matter: The changes are intended to remove uncertainties arising under the original sections, and to modify the rules as to discharge:

1. Subsection (1) substitutes a general definition for the list of illustrations in the original Section 125. Any alteration is material only as it may change the contract of a party to the instrument; and the addition or deletion of words which do not in any way affect the contract of any previous signer is not material. But any change in the contract of a party, however slight, is a material alteration; and the addition of one cent to the amount payable, or an advance of one day in the date of payment, will operate as a discharge if it is fraudulent.

Specific mention is made of a change in the number or relations of the parties in order to make it clear that any such change is material only if it changes the contract of one who has signed. The addition of a co-maker or a surety does not change in most jurisdictions the contract of one who has already signed as maker and should not be held material as to him. The addition of the name of an alternative payee is material, since it changes his obligation. Paragraph (c) makes special mention of a change in the writing signed in order to cover occasional cases of addition of sticker clauses, scissoring or perforating instruments where the separation is not authorized.

2. Paragraph (b) of subsection (1) is to be read together with Section 3–115 on incomplete instruments. Where an instrument contains blanks or is otherwise incomplete, it may be completed in accordance with the authority given and is then valid and effective as completed. If the completion is unauthorized and has the effect of changing the contract of any previous signer, this provision follows the generally accepted rule in treating it as a material alteration which may operate as a discharge.

3. Subsection (2) modifies the very rigorous rule of the original Section 124. The changes made are as follows:

a. A material alteration does not discharge any party unless it is made by the holder. Spoliation by any meddling stranger does not affect the rights of the holder. It is of course intended that the acts of the holder's authorized agent or employee, or of his confederates, are to be attributed to him.

b.   A material alteration does not discharge any party unless it is made for a fraudulent purpose. There is no discharge where a blank is filled in the honest belief that it is as authorized; or where a change is made with a benevolent motive such as a desire to give the obligor the benefit of a lower interest rate. Changes favorable to the obligor are unlikely to be made with any fraudulent intent; but if such an intent is found the alteration may operate as a discharge.

c.   The discharge is a personal defense of the party whose contract is changed by the alteration, and anyone whose contract is not affected cannot assert it. The contract of any party is necessarily affected, however, by the discharge of any party against whom he has a right of recourse on the instrument. Assent to the alteration given before or after it is made will prevent the party from asserting the discharge. "Or is precluded from asserting the defense" is added in paragraph (a) to recognize the possibility of an estoppel or other ground barring the defense which does not rest on assent.

d.   If the alteration is not material or if it is not made for a fraudulent purpose there is no discharge, and the instrument may be enforced according to its original tenor. Where blanks are filled or an incomplete instrument is otherwise completed there is no original tenor, but the instrument may be enforced according to the authority in fact given.

4.   Subsection (3) combines the final sentences of the original Sections 14 and 124, and provides that a subsequent holder in due course takes free of the discharge in all cases. The provision is merely one form of the general rule governing the effect of discharge against a holder in due course (Section 3–602). The holder in due course may enforce the instrument according to its original tenor. In this connection reference should be made to the section giving the holder in due course the right, where the maker's or drawer's negligence has substantially contributed to the alteration, to enforce the instrument in its altered form (Section 3–406). Reference should also be made to Section 4–401 covering a bank's right to charge its customer's account in the case of altered instruments.

Where blanks are filled or an incomplete instrument is otherwise completed, this subsection follows the original Section 14 in placing the loss upon the party who left the instrument incomplete and permitting the holder to enforce it in its completed form. As indicated in the comment to Section 3–115 on incomplete instruments, this result is intended even though the instrument was stolen from the maker or drawer and completed after the theft; and the effect of this subsection, together with the section on incomplete instruments is to reverse the rule of the original Section 15.

There is no inconsistency between subsection (3) and paragraph (b) of subsection (2). The holder in due course may elect to enforce the instrument either as provided in that paragraph or as provided in subsection (3).

It should be noted that a purchaser who takes the instrument with notice of any material alteration, including the unauthorized completion of an incomplete instrument, takes with notice of a claim or defense and cannot be a holder in due course (Section 3–304).

Cross References:

Sections 3–305, 3–306 and 3–307.
Point 2: Section 3–115.
Point 4: Sections 3–115, 3–304(2), 3–602 and 4–401.

Definitional Cross References:

"Contract". Section 1–201.
"Holder". Section 1–201.
"Holder in due course". Section 3–302.
"Instrument". Section 3–102.
"Party". Section 1–201.
"Person". Section 1–201.
"Signed". Section 1–201.
"Writing". Section 1–201.

§ 3–408.   Consideration.

Want or failure of consideration is a defense as against any person not having the rights of a holder in due course (Section 3–305), except that no consideration is necessary for an instrument or obligation thereon given in payment of or as security for an antecedent obligation of any kind. Nothing in this section shall be taken to displace any statute outside this Act under which a promise is enforceable notwithstanding lack or failure of consideration. Partial failure of consideration is a defense pro tanto whether or not the failure is in an ascertained or liquidated amount.

Official Comment

Prior Uniform Statutory Provision: Sections 24, 25 and 28, Uniform Negotiable Instruments Law.

Changes: Combined and reworded.

Purposes of Changes:

1. "Consideration" is distinguished from "value" throughout this Article. "Consideration" refers to what the obligor has received for his obligation, and is important only on the question of whether his obligation can be enforced against him.

2. The "except" clause is intended to remove the difficulties which have arisen where a note or a draft, or an indorsement of either, is given as payment or as security for a debt already owed by the party giving it, or by a third person. The provision is intended to change the result of decisions holding that where no extension of time or other concession is given by the creditor the new obligation fails for lack of legal consideration. It is intended also to mean that an instrument given for more or less than the amount of a liquidated obligation does not fail by reason of the common law rule that an obligation for a lesser liquidated amount cannot be consideration for the surrender of a greater.

3. With respect to the necessity or sufficiency of consideration other obligations on an instrument are subject to the ordinary rules of contract law relating to contracts not under seal. Promissory estoppel or any other equivalent or substitute for consideration is to be recognized as in other contract cases. The provision of the original Section 28 as to absence or failure of consideration is now covered by the section dealing with the rights of one not a holder in due course; and the "presumption" of consideration in the original Section 24 is replaced by the provision relating to the burden of establishing defenses.

Cross References:

Point 1: Section 3–303.
Point 3: Sections 3–306(c) and 3–307(2).

Definitional Cross References:

"Holder in due course". Section 3–302.
"Instrument". Section 3–102.
"Person". Section 1–201.
"Rights". Section 1–201.

§ 3–409. Draft Not an Assignment.

(1) A check or other draft does not of itself operate as an assignment of any funds in the hands of the drawee available for its payment, and the drawee is not liable on the instrument until he accepts it.

(2) Nothing in this section shall affect any liability in contract, tort or otherwise arising from any letter of credit or other obligation or representation which is not an acceptance.

Official Comment

Prior Uniform Statutory Provision: Sections 127 and 189, Uniform Negotiable Instruments Law.

Changes: Combined and reworded; new provisions.

Purposes of Changes and New Matter:

The two original sections are combined, brought forward to appear in connection with acceptance, and reworded to remove uncertainties.

1. As under the original sections, a check or other draft does not of itself operate as an assignment in law or equity. The assignment may, however, appear from other facts, and particularly from other agreements, express or implied; and when the intent to assign is clear the check may be the means by which the assignment is effected.

2.　The language of the original Section 189, that the drawee is not liable "to the holder", is changed as inaccurate and not intended. The drawee is not liable on the instrument until he accepts; but he remains subject to any other liability to the holder. In this connection reference should be made to Section 4–302 on the payor bank's liability for late return. Such a bank if it does not either make prompt settlement or return on an item received by it will become liable to a holder of the item.

3.　Subsection (2) is new. It is intended to make it clear that this section does not in any way affect any liability which may arise apart from the instrument itself. The drawee who fails to accept may be liable to the drawer or to the holder for breach of the terms of a letter of credit or any other agreement by which he is obligated to accept. He may be liable in tort or upon any other basis because of his representation that he has accepted, or that he intends to accept. The section leaves unaffected any liability of any kind apart from the instrument.

Cross References:

Sections 3–410, 3–411, 3–412 and 3–415.
Point 2: Section 4–302.

Definitional Cross References:

"Acceptance". Section 3–410.
"Check". Section 3–104.
"Contract". Section 1–201.
"Draft". Section 3–104.
"Instrument". Section 3–102.
"Letter of credit". Section 5–104.

§ 3–410.　Definition and Operation of Acceptance.

(1)　Acceptance is the drawee's signed engagement to honor the draft as presented. It must be written on the draft, and may consist of his signature alone. It becomes operative when completed by delivery or notification.

(2)　A draft may be accepted although it has not been signed by the drawer or is otherwise incomplete or is overdue or has been dishonored.

(3)　Where the draft is payable at a fixed period after sight and the acceptor fails to date his acceptance the holder may complete it by supplying a date in good faith.

Official Comment

Prior Uniform Statutory Provision: Sections 132, 133, 134, 135, 136, 137, 138, 161–170, and 191, Uniform Negotiable Instruments Law.

Changes: Combined, reworded; original Sections 134, 135, 137 and 161–170 eliminated.

Purposes of Changes:

1.　The original Sections 161–170 providing for acceptance for honor are omitted from this Article. This ancient practice developed at a time when communications were slow, and particularly in overseas transactions there might be a delay of several months before the drawer could be notified of dishonor by nonacceptance and take steps to protect his credit. The need for intervention by a third party has passed with the development of the cable transfer, the letter of credit, and numerous other devices by which a substitute arrangement is promptly made. The practice has been obsolete for many years, and the sections are therefore eliminated.

2.　Under Section 3–417 a person obtaining acceptance gives a warranty against alteration of the instrument before acceptance.

3.　Subsection (1) adopts the rule of Section 17 of the English Bills of Exchange Act that the acceptance must be written on the draft. It eliminates the original Sections 134 and 135, providing for "virtual" acceptance by a written promise to accept drafts to be drawn, and "collateral" acceptance by a separate writing. Both have been anomalous exceptions to the policy that no person is liable on an instrument unless his signature appears on it. Both are derived from a line of early American cases decided at a time when difficulties of communication, particularly overseas, might leave the holder in doubt for a long period whether the draft was accepted. Such conditions have long since ceased to exist, and the "virtual" or "collateral" acceptance is now almost entirely obsolete. Good commercial and banking practice does not sanction acceptance by any separate writing because of the dangers and uncertainties arising when it becomes separated from the draft. The instrument is now forwarded to the drawee for his acceptance upon it, or reliance is placed upon the obligation of the separate writing itself, as in the case of a letter of credit.

Nothing in this section is intended to eliminate any liability of the drawee in contract, tort or otherwise arising from the separate writing or any other obligation or representation, as provided in Section 3–409.

Subsection (1) likewise eliminates the original section 137, providing for acceptance by delay or refusal to return the instrument but the drawee may be liable for a conversion of the instrument under Section 3–419.

4. Subsection (1) states the generally recognized rule that the mere signature of the drawee on the instrument is a sufficient acceptance. Customarily the signature is written vertically across the face of the instrument; but since the drawee has no reason to sign for any other purpose his signature in any other place, even on the back of the instrument, is sufficient. It need not be accompanied by such words as "Accepted," "Certified," or "Good." It must not, however, bear any words indicating an intent to refuse to honor the bill; and nothing in this provision is intended to change such decisions as Norton v. Knapp, 64 Iowa 112, 19 N.W. 867 (1884), holding that the drawee's signature accompanied by the words "Kiss my foot" is not an acceptance.

5. The final sentence of subsection (1) expressly states the generally recognized rule, implied in the definition of acceptance in the original Section 191, that an acceptance written on the draft takes effect when the drawee notifies the holder or gives notice according to his instructions. Acceptance is thus an exception to the usual rule that no obligation on an instrument is effective until delivery.

6. Subsection (3) changes the last sentence of the original Section 138. The purpose of the provision is to provide a definite date of payment where none appears on the instrument. An undated acceptance of a draft payable "thirty days after sight" is incomplete; and unless the acceptor himself writes in a different date the holder is authorized to complete the acceptance according to the terms of the draft by supplying a date of presentment. Any date which the holder chooses to write in is effective providing his choice of date is made in good faith. Any different agreement not written on the draft is not effective, and parol evidence is not admissible to show it.

Cross References:

Sections 3–411, 3–412 and 3–418.
Point 2: Section 3–417.
Point 3: Sections 3–401(1), 3–409(2) and 3–419.
Point 6: Section 3–412.

Definitional Cross References:

"Delivery". Section 1–201.
"Dishonor". Section 3–507.
"Draft". Section 3–104.
"Good faith". Section 1–201.
"Holder". Section 1–201.
"Honor". Section 1–201.
"Notification". Section 1–201.
"Presentment". Section 3–504.
"Signature". Section 3–401.
"Signed". Section 1–201.
"Written". Section 1–201.

§3–411. Certification of a Check.

(1) Certification of a check is acceptance. Where a holder procures certification the drawer and all prior indorsers are discharged.

(2) Unless otherwise agreed a bank has no obligation to certify a check.

(3) A bank may certify a check before returning it for lack of proper indorsement. If it does so the drawer is discharged.

Official Comment

Prior Uniform Statutory Provision: Sections 187 and 188, Uniform Negotiable Instruments Law.

Changes: Combined and reworded; new provisions.

Purposes of Changes and New Matter:

1.   The second sentence of subsection (1) continues the rule of original Section 188 that, while certification procured by a holder discharges the drawer and other prior parties, certification procured by the drawer leaves him liable. Under this provision any certification procured by a holder discharges the drawer and prior indorsers. Any indorsement made after a certification so procured remains effective; and where it is intended that any indorser shall remain liable notwithstanding certification, he may indorse with the words "after certification" to make his liability clear.

2.   Subsection (2) is new. It states the generally recognized rule that in the absence of agreement a bank is under no obligation to certify a check, because it is a demand instrument calling for payment rather than acceptance. The bank may be liable for breach of any agreement with the drawer, the holder, or any other person by which it undertakes to certify. Its liability is not on the instrument, since the drawee is not so liable until acceptance (Section 3–409(1)). Any liability is for breach of the separate agreement.

3.   Subsection (3) is new. It recognizes the banking practice of certifying a check which is returned for proper indorsement in order to protect the drawer against a longer contingent liability. It is consistent with the provision of Section 3–410(2) permitting certification although the check has not been signed or is otherwise incomplete.

Cross References:

Sections 3–412, 3–413, 3–417 and 3–418.
Point 2: Section 3–409(1).
Point 3: Section 3–410(2).

Definitional Cross References:

"Acceptance". Section 3–410.
"Bank". Section 1–201.
"Check". Section 3–104.
"Holder". Section 1–201.

§ 3–412.   Acceptance Varying Draft.

(1)   Where the drawee's proffered acceptance in any manner varies the draft as presented the holder may refuse the acceptance and treat the draft as dishonored in which case the drawee is entitled to have his acceptance cancelled.

(2)   The terms of the draft are not varied by an acceptance to pay at any particular bank or place in the United States, unless the acceptance states that the draft is to be paid only at such bank or place.

(3)   Where the holder assents to an acceptance varying the terms of the draft each drawer and indorser who does not affirmatively assent is discharged.

As amended in 1962.

Official Comment

Prior Uniform Statutory Provision: Sections 139, 140, 141 and 142, Uniform Negotiable Instruments Law.

Changes: Combined and reworded; law changed as to qualified acceptances.

Purposes of Changes:

1.   The section applies to conditional acceptances, acceptances for part of the amount, acceptances to pay at a different time from that required by the draft, or to the acceptance of less than all of the drawees, all of which are covered by the original Section 141. It applies to any other engagement changing the essential terms of the draft.

2.   Where the drawee offers such a varied engagement the holder has an election. He may reject the offer, insist on acceptance of the draft as presented, and treat the refusal to give it as a dishonor. In that event the drawee is not bound by his engagement, and is entitled to have it cancelled. After any necessary notice of dishonor and protest the holder may have his recourse against the drawer and indorsers.

If the holder elects to accept the offer, this section does not invalidate the drawee's varied engagement. It remains his effective obligation, which the holder may enforce against him. By his assent, however, the holder discharges any drawer or indorser who does not also assent. The rule of the original Section 142 is changed to require that the assent of the drawer or indorser be affirmatively expressed. Mere failure to object within a reasonable time is not assent which will prevent the discharge.

3.   The rule of original Section 140 that an acceptance to pay at a particular place is an unqualified acceptance is modified by the provision of subsection (2) that the terms of the draft are not varied by an acceptance to pay at any particular bank or place in the United States unless the acceptance states that the draft is to be paid only at such bank or place. Section 3–504(4) provides that a draft accepted payable at a bank in the United States must be presented at the bank designated [As amended 1962].

Cross References:

Sections 3–410 and 3–413.
Point 3: Section 3–504(4).

Definitional Cross References:

"Acceptance". Section 3–410.
"Bank". Section 1–201.
"Dishonor". Section 3–507.
"Draft". Section 3–104.
"Holder". Section 1–201.
"Term". Section 1–201.
"Written". Section 1–201.

§ 3–413.   Contract of Maker, Drawer and Acceptor.

(1)   The maker or acceptor engages that he will pay the instrument according to its tenor at the time of his engagement or as completed pursuant to Section 3–115 on incomplete instruments.

(2)   The drawer engages that upon dishonor of the draft and any necessary notice of dishonor or protest he will pay the amount of the draft to the holder or to any indorser who takes it up. The drawer may disclaim this liability by drawing without recourse.

(3)   By making, drawing or accepting the party admits as against all subsequent parties including the drawee the existence of the payee and his then capacity to indorse.

Official Comment

Prior Uniform Statutory Provision: Sections 60, 61 and 62, Uniform Negotiable Instruments Law.

Changes: Combined and reworded.

Purposes of Changes:

The original sections are combined for convenience and condensed to avoid duplication of language. This section should be read in connection with the sections on incomplete instruments (3–115), negligence contributing to alteration or unauthorized signature (3–406), alteration (3–407), acceptances varying a draft (3–412) and finality of payment or acceptance (3–418). Thus a maker who signs an incomplete note engages under this section to pay it according to its tenor at the time he signs it, but by virtue of Sections 3–115 and 3–407 the note may thereafter be completed and enforced against him. In the same way, if the maker's negligence substantially contributes to alteration of the instrument, he will become liable on his note as altered under Section 3–406. When a holder assents to an acceptance varying a draft (Section 3–412) he can of course hold the acceptor only according to the form of acceptance to which the holder agreed. Section 3–418 applies the rule of Price v. Neal both to acceptance and payment; thus an acceptor may not, after acceptance, assert that the drawer's signature is unauthorized.

Subsection (1) applies to all drafts (including checks) the rule that the acceptance relates to the instrument as it was at the time of its acceptance and not (in case of alteration before acceptance) to its original tenor. The cases on this point under the original act (all of which involved checks) have been in conflict. It should be noted that under Section 3–417 a person who obtains acceptance warrants to the acceptor that the instrument has not been materially altered.

Except as indicated in the foregoing comment the section makes no change in substance from the provision of the original act.

Cross References:

Sections 3–115, 3–406, 3–407, 3–412, 3–417 and 3–418.

Definitional Cross References:

"Contract". Section 1–201.
"Dishonor". Section 3–507.
"Draft". Section 3–104.
"Holder". Section 1–201.
"Instrument". Section 3–102.
"Notice of dishonor". Section 3–508.
"Party". Section 1–201.
"Protest". Section 3–509.

§ 3–414.   Contract of Indorser; Order of Liability.

(1)   Unless the indorsement otherwise specifies (as by such words as "without recourse") every indorser engages that upon dishonor and any necessary notice of dishonor and protest he will pay the instrument according to its tenor at the time of his indorsement to the holder or to any subsequent indorser who takes it up, even though the indorser who takes it up was not obligated to do so.

(2)   Unless they otherwise agree indorsers are liable to one another in the order in which they indorse, which is presumed to be the order in which their signatures appear on the instrument.

Official Comment

Prior Uniform Statutory Provision: Sections 38, 44, 66, 67 and 68, Uniform Negotiable Instruments Law.

Changes: Combined and reworded.

Purposes of Changes:

1.   Subsection (1) states the contract of indorsement—that if the instrument is dishonored and any protest or notice of dishonor which may be necessary under Section 3–501 is given, the indorser will pay the instrument. The indorser's engagement runs to any holder (whether or not for value) and to any indorser subsequent to him who has taken the instrument up. An indorser may disclaim his liability on the contract of indorsement, but only if the indorsement itself so specifies. Since the disclaimer varies the written contract of indorsement, the disclaimer itself must be written on the instrument and cannot be proved by parol. The customary manner of disclaiming the indorser's liability under this section is to indorse "without recourse". Apart from such a disclaimer all indorsers incur this liability, without regard to whether or not the indorser transferred the instrument for value or received consideration for his indorsement.

Original Section 44, permitting a representative to indorse in such terms as to exclude personal liability, is omitted as unnecessary and included in the broader right to disclaim any liability. No change in the law is intended by this omission.

2.   In addition to his liability on the contract of indorsement, an indorser, if a transferor, gives the warranties stated in Section 3–417.

3.   As in the case of acceptor's liability (Section 3–413), this section conditions the indorser's liability on the tenor of the instrument at the time of his indorsement. Thus if a person indorses an altered instrument he assumes liability as indorser on the instrument as altered.

4.   Subsection (2) is intended to clarify existing law under original Section 68.

The section states two presumptions: One is that the indorsers are liable to one another in the order in which they have in fact indorsed. The other is that they have in fact indorsed in the order in which their names appear. Parol evidence is admissible to show that they have indorsed in another order, or that they have otherwise agreed as to their liability to one another.

The last sentence of the original Section 68 is now covered by Section 3–118(e) (Ambiguous Terms and Rules of Construction).

Cross References:

Point 1: Section 3–501.
Point 2: Section 3–417.
Point 3: Section 3–413.
Point 4: Section 3–118(e).

Definitional Cross References:

"Contract". Section 1–201.
"Dishonor". Section 3–507.
"Holder". Section 1–201.
"Instrument". Section 3–102.
"Notice of dishonor". Section 3–508.
"Presumed". Section 1–201.
"Protest". Section 3–509.
"Signature". Section 3–401.

§ 3–415.   Contract of Accommodation Party.

(1)   An accommodation party is one who signs the instrument in any capacity for the purpose of lending his name to another party to it.

(2)   When the instrument has been taken for value before it is due the accommodation party is liable in the capacity in which he has signed even though the taker knows of the accommodation.

(3)   As against a holder in due course and without notice of the accommodation oral proof of the accommodation is not admissible to give the accommodation party the benefit of discharges dependent on his character as such. In other cases the accommodation character may be shown by oral proof.

(4)   An indorsement which shows that it is not in the chain of title is notice of its accommodation character.

(5)   An accommodation party is not liable to the party accommodated, and if he pays the instrument has a right of recourse on the instrument against such party.

Official Comment

Prior Uniform Statutory Provision: Sections 28, 29 and 64, Uniform Negotiable Instruments Law.

Changes: Combined and reworded; new provisions.

Purposes of Changes and New Matter: To make it clear that:

1.   Subsection (1) recognizes that an accommodation party is always a surety (which includes a guarantor), and it is his only distinguishing feature. He differs from other sureties only in that his liability is on the instrument and he is a surety for another party to it. His obligation is therefore determined by the capacity in which he signs. An accommodation maker or acceptor is bound on the instrument without any resort to his principal, while an accommodation indorser may be liable only after presentment, notice of dishonor and protest. The subsection recognizes the defenses of a surety in accordance with the provisions subjecting one not a holder in due course to all simple contract defenses, as well as his rights against his principal after payment. Under subsection (3) except as against a holder in due course without notice of the accommodation, parol evidence is admissible to prove that the party has signed for accommodation. In any case, however, under subsection (4) an indorsement which is not in the chain of title (the irregular or anomalous indorsement) is notice to all subsequent takers of the instrument of the accommodation character of the indorsement.

1023

2.   Subsection (1) eliminates the language of the old Section 29 requiring that the accommodation party sign the instrument "without receiving value therefor." The essential characteristic is that the accommodation party is a surety, and not that he has signed gratuitously. He may be a paid surety, or receive other compensation from the party accommodated. He may even receive it from the payee, as where A and B buy goods and it is understood that A is to pay for all of them and that B is to sign a note only as a surety for A.

3.   The obligation of the accommodation party is supported by any consideration for which the instrument is taken before it is due. Subsection (2) is intended to change occasional decisions holding that there is no sufficient consideration where an accommodation party signs a note after it is in the hands of a holder who has given value. The party is liable to the holder in such a case even though there is no extension of time or other concession. This is consistent with the provision as to antecedent obligations as consideration (Section 3–408). The limitation to "before it is due" is one of suretyship law, by which the obligation of the surety is terminated at the time limit unless in the meantime the obligation of the principal has become effective.

4.   As a surety the accommodation party is not liable to the party accommodated; but he is otherwise liable on the instrument in the capacity in which he has signed. This general statement of the rule makes unnecessary the detailed provisions of the original Section 64, which is therefore eliminated, without any change in substance.

5.   Subsection (5) is intended to change the result of such decisions as Quimby v. Varnum, 190 Mass. 211, 76 N.E. 671 (1906), which held that an accommodation indorser who paid the instrument could not maintain an action on it against the accommodated party since he had no "former rights" to which he was remitted. Under ordinary principles of suretyship the accommodation party who pays is subrogated to the rights of the holder paid, and should have his recourse on the instrument.

Cross References:

Sections 3–305, 3–408, 3–603, 3–604 and 3–606.
Point 1: Section 3–306(b).
Point 3: Section 3–408.

Definitional Cross References:

"Holder in due course". Section 3–302.
"Instrument". Section 3–102.
"Notice". Section 1–201.
"Party". Section 1–201.
"Presentment". Section 3–504.
"Signed". Section 1–201.
"Writing". Section 1–201.

§ 3–416.   Contract of Guarantor.

(1)   "Payment guaranteed" or equivalent words added to a signature mean that the signer engages that if the instrument is not paid when due he will pay it according to its tenor without resort by the holder to any other party.

(2)   "Collection guaranteed" or equivalent words added to a signature mean that the signer engages that if the instrument is not paid when due he will pay it according to its tenor, but only after the holder has reduced his claim against the maker or acceptor to judgment and execution has been returned unsatisfied, or after the maker or acceptor has become insolvent or it is otherwise apparent that it is useless to proceed against him.

(3)   Words of guaranty which do not otherwise specify guarantee payment.

(4)   No words of guaranty added to the signature of a sole maker or acceptor affect his liability on the instrument. Such words added to the signature of one of two or more makers or acceptors create a presumption that the signature is for the accommodation of the others.

(5)   When words of guaranty are used presentment, notice of dishonor and protest are not necessary to charge the user.

(6)   Any guaranty written on the instrument is enforceable notwithstanding any statute of frauds.

Official Comment

Prior Uniform Statutory Provision: None.

Purposes: The section is new. It states the commercial understanding as to the meaning and effect of words of guaranty added to a signature.

An indorser who guarantees payment waives not only presentment, notice of dishonor and protest, but also all demand upon the maker or drawee. Words of guaranty do not affect the character of the indorsement as an indorsement (Section 3–202(4)); but the liability of the indorser becomes indistinguishable from that of a co-maker. A guaranty of collection likewise waives formal presentment, notice of dishonor and protest, but requires that the holder first proceed against the maker or acceptor by suit and execution, or show that such proceeding would be useless.

Subsection (6) is concerned chiefly with the type of statute of frauds which provides that no promise to answer for the debt, default or miscarriage of another is enforceable unless it is evidenced by a writing which states the consideration for the promise. It is unusual to state any consideration when a guaranty is added to a signature on a negotiable instrument, which in itself sufficiently shows the nature of the transaction; and such statutes have commonly been held not to apply to such guaranties.

Cross References:

Sections 3–202(4) and 3–415.

Definitional Cross References:

"Holder". Section 1–201.
"Insolvent". Section 1–201.
"Instrument". Section 3–102.
"Notice of dishonor". Section 3–508.
"Party". Section 1–201.
"Presumption". Section 1–201.
"Protest". Section 3–509.
"Signature". Section 3–401.
"Written". Section 1–201.

§ 3–417.   Warranties on Presentment and Transfer.

(1)   Any person who obtains payment or acceptance and any prior transferor warrants to a person who in good faith pays or accepts that

    (a)   he has a good title to the instrument or is authorized to obtain payment or acceptance on behalf of one who has a good title; and

    (b)   he has no knowledge that the signature of the maker or drawer is unauthorized, except that this warranty is not given by a holder in due course acting in good faith

        (i)   to a maker with respect to the maker's own signature; or

        (ii)   to a drawer with respect to the drawer's own signature, whether or not the drawer is also the drawee; or

        (iii)   to an acceptor of a draft if the holder in due course took the draft after the acceptance or obtained the acceptance without knowledge that the drawer's signature was unauthorized; and

    (c)   the instrument has not been materially altered, except that this warranty is not given by a holder in due course acting in good faith

        (i)   to the maker of a note; or

        (ii)   to the drawer of a draft whether or not the drawer is also the drawee; or

    (iii) to the acceptor of a draft with respect to an alteration made prior to the acceptance if the holder in due course took the draft after the acceptance, even though the acceptance provided "payable as originally drawn" or equivalent terms; or

    (iv) to the acceptor of a draft with respect to an alteration made after the acceptance.

(2)   Any person who transfers an instrument and receives consideration warrants to his transferee and if the transfer is by indorsement to any subsequent holder who takes the instrument in good faith that

    (a)   he has a good title to the instrument or is authorized to obtain payment or acceptance on behalf of one who has a good title and the transfer is otherwise rightful; and

    (b)   all signatures are genuine or authorized; and

    (c)   the instrument has not been materially altered; and

    (d)   no defense of any party is good against him; and

    (e)   he has no knowledge of any insolvency proceeding instituted with respect to the maker or acceptor or the drawer of an unaccepted instrument.

(3)   By transferring "without recourse" the transferor limits the obligation stated in subsection (2)(d) to a warranty that he has no knowledge of such a defense.

(4)   A selling agent or broker who does not disclose the fact that he is acting only as such gives the warranties provided in this section, but if he makes such disclosure warrants only his good faith and authority.

Official Comment

Prior Uniform Statutory Provision: Sections 65 and 69, Uniform Negotiable Instruments Law.

Changes: Combined and reworded; new provisions added.

Purposes of Changes and New Matter:

1.   The obligations imposed by this section are stated in terms of warranty. Warranty terms, which are not limited to sale transactions, are used with the intention of bringing in all the usual rules of law applicable to warranties, and in particular the necessity of reliance in good faith and the availability of all remedies for breach of warranty, such as rescission of the transaction or an action for damages. Like other warranties, those stated in this section may be disclaimed by agreement between the immediate parties. In the case of an indorser, disclaimer of his liability as a transferor, to be effective, must appear in the form of the indorsement, and no parol proof of "agreement otherwise" is admissible. For corresponding warranties in the case of items in the bank collection process, Section 4–207 should be consulted.

2.   Subsection (1) is new. It is intended to state the undertaking to a party who accepts or pays of one who obtains payment or acceptance or of any prior transferor. It is closely connected with the following section on the finality of acceptance or payment (Section 3–418), and should be read together with it.

3.   Subsection (1)(a) retains the generally accepted rule that the party who accepts or pays does not "admit" the genuineness of indorsements, and may recover from the person presenting the instrument when they turn out to be forged. The justification for the distinction between forgery of the signature of the drawer and forgery of an indorsement is that the drawee is in a position to verify the drawer's signature by comparison with one in his hands, but has ordinarily no opportunity to verify an indorsement.

4.   Subsection (1)(b) recognizes and deals with competing equities of parties accepting or paying instruments bearing unauthorized maker's or drawer's signatures and those obtaining acceptances or receiving payment. The warranties prescribed and exceptions thereto follow closely principles established at common law, particularly, those under Price v. Neal, 3 Burr. 1354 (1762).

The basic warranty that the person obtaining payment or acceptance and any prior transferor warrants that he has no knowledge that the signature of the maker or drawer is unauthorized stems from the general principle that one who presents an instrument knowing that the signature of the maker or drawer is forged or unauthorized commits an obvious fraud upon the party to whom presentment is made. However, few cases present this simple fact situation. If the signature of a maker or drawer has been forged, the parties include the dishonest forger himself and usually one or more innocent holders taking from him. Frequently, the state of knowledge of a holder is difficult to determine and sometimes a holder takes such a forged instrument in perfect good faith but subsequently learns of the forgery. Since in different fact situations holders have equities of varying strength, it is necessary to have some exceptions to the basic warranty.

The exceptions apply only in favor of a holder in due course and, within the provisions of Section 3–201, to all subsequent transferees from a holder in due course. Since a condition of the status of a holder in due course under Section 3–302(1)(a) is that the holder takes the instrument without notice of any defense against it, this condition presupposes that at the time of taking such a holder had no knowledge of the unauthorized signature. Consequently, the warranty of subsection (1)(b) is pertinent in the case of a holder in due course only in the relatively few cases where he acquires knowledge of the forgery after the taking but before the presentment. In this situation the holder in due course must continue to act in good faith to be exempted from the basic warranty.

The first exemption from the warranty by such a holder, made by subparagraph (i), is that the warranty does not run to a maker of a note with respect to the maker's own signature. This codifies the rule of Price v. Neal, and related cases. Since a maker of a note is presumed to know his own signature, if he fails to detect a forgery of his own signature and pays the note, under the Price v. Neal principle he should not be permitted to recover such payment from a holder in due course acting in good faith. Similarly, under subparagraph (ii) a drawer of a draft is presumed to know his own signature and if he fails to detect a forgery of his signature and pays a draft he may not recover that payment from a holder in due course acting in good faith. This rule applies if the drawer pays the instrument as drawer and also if he pays the instrument as drawee in a case where he is both drawer and drawee.

Under the principle of Price v. Neal a drawee of a draft is presumed to know the signature of his customer, the drawer. However, under subsection (1)(b) and subparagraph (iii) of this subsection this presumption is not strong enough to deprive such a drawee (either in accepting or paying an instrument) of the warranty of no knowledge of the unauthorized drawer's signature, unless the holder in due course took the instrument and became such a holder after the drawee's acceptance; or obtained the acceptance without knowledge that the drawer's signature was unauthorized. In the former case, the holder taking after and thereby presumably in reliance on the acceptance should be protected as against the drawee who accepted without detecting the unauthorized signature. In the latter case the holder, having no knowledge of the unauthorized signature at the time of the drawee's acceptance, would not be charged with this warranty and would be entitled to enforce such acceptance under Section 3–418, even if thereafter he acquired knowledge of the unauthorized signature prior to enforcement of the acceptance. Such right of the holder to enforce the acceptance would be valueless if immediately upon enforcing it and obtaining payment the holder became obligated to return the payment by reason of breach of the warranty of no knowledge at the time of payment.

5. Subsection (1)(c) retains the common law rule, followed by several decisions under the original Act, which has permitted a party paying a materially altered instrument in good faith to recover, and a party who accepts such an instrument to avoid such acceptance. As in the case of subsection (1)(b) this warranty is not imposed against a holder in due course acting in good faith in favor of a maker of a note or a drawer of a draft on the ground that such maker or drawer should know the form and amount of the note or draft which he has signed. The exception made by subparagraph (iii) in the case of a holder in due course of a draft accepted after the alteration follows the decisions in National City Bank of Chicago v. National Bank of Republic of Chicago, 300 Ill. 103, 132 N.E. 832, 22 A.L.R. 1153 (1921), and Wells Fargo Bank & Union Trust Company v. Bank of Italy, 214 Cal. 156, 4 P.2d 781 (1931), and is based on the principle that an acceptance is an undertaking relied upon in good faith by an innocent party. The attempt to avoid this result by certifying checks "payable as originally drawn" leaves the subsequent purchaser in uncertainty as to the amount for which the instrument is certified, and so defeats the entire purpose of certification, which is to obtain the definite obligation of the bank to honor a definite instrument. Subparagraph (iii) accordingly provides that such language is not sufficient to impose on the holder in due course the warranty of no material alteration where the holder took the draft after the acceptance and presumably in reliance on it.

Subparagraph (iv) of subsection (1)(c) exempts a holder in due course from the warranty of no material alteration to the acceptor of a draft with respect to an alteration made after the acceptance. A drawee accepting a draft has an opportunity of ascertaining the form and particularly the amount of the draft accepted. If, thereafter, the draft is materially altered and is thereupon presented for payment to the acceptor, the acceptor has the necessary information in its records to verify the form and particularly the amount of the draft. If in spite of this available information it pays the draft, there is as much reason to leave the responsibility for such payment upon the acceptor (as against a holder in due course acting in good faith) as there is in the case of a maker or drawer paying a materially altered note or draft.

6.　Under Section 3–201 parties taking from or holding under a holder in due course, within the limits of that section, will have the same rights under Section 3–417(1) as a holder in due course. Of course such parties claiming under a holder in due course must act in good faith and be free from fraud, illegality and notice as provided in Section 3–201.

7.　The liabilities imposed by subsection (2) in favor of the immediate transferee apply to all persons who transfer an instrument for consideration whether or not the transfer is accompanied by indorsement. Any consideration sufficient to support a simple contract will support those warranties.

8.　Subsection (2) changes the original Section 65 to extend the warranties of any *indorser* beyond the immediate transferee in all cases. Where there is an indorsement the warranty runs with the instrument and the remote holder may sue the indorser-warrantor directly and thus avoid a multiplicity of suits which might be interrupted by the insolvency of an intermediate transferor. The language of subsections (2)(b) and (2)(c) is substituted for "genuine and what it purports to be" in the original Section 65(1). The language of subsection (2)(a) is substituted for that of Section 65(2) in order to cover the case of the agent who transfers for another.

9.　Subsection (2)(d) resolves a conflict in the decisions as to whether the transferor warrants that there are no defenses to the instrument good against him. The position taken is that the buyer does not undertake to buy an instrument incapable of enforcement, and that in the absence of contrary understanding the warranty is implied. Even where the buyer takes as a holder in due course who will cut off the defense, he still does not undertake to buy a lawsuit with the necessity of proving his status. Subsection (3) however provides that an indorsement "without recourse" limits the (2)(d) warranty to one that the indorser has no knowledge of such defenses. With this exception the liabilities of a "without recourse" indorser under this section are the same as those of any other transferor. Under Section 3–414 "without recourse" in an indorsement is effective to disclaim the general contract of the indorser stated in that section.

10.　Subsection (2)(e) is substituted for Section 65(4). The transferor does not warrant against difficulties of collection, apart from defenses, or against impairment of the credit of the obligor or even his insolvency in the commercial sense. The buyer is expected to determine such questions for himself before he takes the obligation. If insolvency proceedings as defined in this Act (Section 1–201) have been instituted against the party who is expected to pay and the transferor knows it, the concealment of that fact amounts to a fraud upon the buyer, and the warranty against knowledge of such proceedings is provided accordingly.

11.　Subsection (4) is substituted for Section 69 of the original Act. It applies only to a selling agent, as distinguished from an agent for collection. It follows the rule generally accepted that an agent who makes the disclosure warrants his good faith and authority and may not by contract assume a lesser warranty.

Cross References:

Sections 3–404, 3–405, 3–406, 3–414 and 4–207.
Point 1: Section 4–207.
Point 2: Section 3–418.
Point 4: Sections 3–201, 3–302 and 3–418.
Point 9: Section 3–414.
Point 10: Section 1–201.

Definitional Cross References:

"Acceptance". Section 3–410.
"Alteration". Section 3–407.
"Bank". Section 1–201.
"Draft". Section 3–104.
"Genuine". Section 1–201.
"Good faith". Section 1–201.
"Holder in due course". Section 3–302.
"Instrument". Section 3–102.
"Note". Section 3–104.
"Party". Section 1–201.
"Person". Section 1–201.
"Signature". Section 3–401.

"Term". Section 1–201.

§ 3–418.   Finality of Payment or Acceptance.

Except for recovery of bank payments as provided in the Article on Bank Deposits and Collections (Article 4) and except for liability for breach of warranty on presentment under the preceding section, payment or acceptance of any instrument is final in favor of a holder in due course, or a person who has in good faith changed his position in reliance on the payment.

Official Comment

Prior Uniform Statutory Provision: Section 62, Uniform Negotiable Instruments Law.

Changes: Completely restated.

Purposes of Changes:

The rewording is intended to remove a number of uncertainties arising under the original section.

1.   The section follows the rule of Price v. Neal, 3 Burr. 1354 (1762), under which a drawee who accepts or pays an instrument on which the signature of the drawer is forged is bound on his acceptance and cannot recover back his payment. Although the original Act is silent as to payment, the common law rule has been applied to it by all but a very few jurisdictions. The traditional justification for the result is that the drawee is in a superior position to detect a forgery because he has the maker's signature and is expected to know and compare it; a less fictional rationalization is that it is highly desirable to end the transaction on an instrument when it is paid rather than reopen and upset a series of commercial transactions at a later date when the forgery is discovered.

The rule as stated in the section is not limited to drawees, but applies equally to the maker of a note or to any other party who pays an instrument.

2.   The section follows the decisions under the original Act applying the rule of Price v. Neal to the payment of overdrafts, or any other payment made in error as to the state of the drawer's account. The same argument for finality applies, with the additional reason that the drawee is responsible for knowing the state of the account before he accepts or pays.

3.   The section follows decisions under the original Act, in making payment or acceptance final only in favor of a holder in due course, or a transferee who has the rights of a holder in due course under the shelter principle. If no value has been given for the instrument the holder loses nothing by the recovery of the payment or the avoidance of the acceptance, and is not entitled to profit at the expense of the drawee; and if he has given only an executory promise or credit he is not compelled to perform it after the forgery or other reason for recovery is discovered. If he has taken the instrument in bad faith or with notice he has no equities as against the drawee.

4.   The section rejects decisions under the original Act permitting recovery on the basis of mere negligence of the holder in taking the instrument. If such negligence amounts to a lack of good faith as defined in this Act (Section 1–201) or to notice under the rules (Section 3–304) relating to notice to a purchaser of an instrument, the holder is not a holder in due course and is not protected; but otherwise the holder's negligence does not affect the finality of the payment or acceptance.

5.   This section is to be read together with the preceding section, which states the warranties given by the person obtaining acceptance or payment. It is also limited by the bank collection provision (Section 4–301) permitting a payor bank to recover a payment improperly paid if it returns the item or sends notice of dishonor within the limited time provided in that section. But notice that the latter right is sharply limited in time, and terminates in any case when the bank has made final payment, as defined in Section 4–213.

Cross References:

Sections 3–302, 3–303 and 3–417.
Point 2: Section 3–201(1).
Point 4: Sections 1–201, 3–302 and 3–304.
Point 5: Sections 3–417, 4–213 and 4–301.

Definitional Cross References:

"Acceptance". Section 3–410.
"Account". Section 4–104.

"Bank". Section 1–201.
"Holder in due course". Section 3–302.
"Instrument". Section 3–102.
"Presentment". Section 3–504.

§ 3–419. Conversion of Instrument; Innocent Representative.

(1)   An instrument is converted when

(a)   a drawee to whom it is delivered for acceptance refuses to return it on demand; or

(b)   any person to whom it is delivered for payment refuses on demand either to pay or to return it; or

(c)   it is paid on a forged indorsement.

(2)   In an action against a drawee under subsection (1) the measure of the drawee's liability is the face amount of the instrument. In any other action under subsection (1) the measure of liability is presumed to be the face amount of the instrument.

(3)   Subject to the provisions of this Act concerning restrictive indorsements a representative, including a depositary or collecting bank, who has in good faith and in accordance with the reasonable commercial standards applicable to the business of such representative dealt with an instrument or its proceeds on behalf of one who was not the true owner is not liable in conversion or otherwise to the true owner beyond the amount of any proceeds remaining in his hands.

(4)   An intermediary bank or payor bank which is not a depositary bank is not liable in conversion solely by reason of the fact that proceeds of an item indorsed restrictively (Sections 3–205 and 3–206) are not paid or applied consistently with the restrictive indorsement of an indorser other than its immediate transferor.

Official Comment

Prior Uniform Statutory Provision: Section 137, Uniform Negotiable Instruments Law.

Changes: Rule changed; new provisions.

Purposes of Changes and New Matter: To remove difficulties arising under the original section, and to cover additional situations:

1.   The provision of the original Section 137 that refusal to return a bill presented for acceptance is deemed to be acceptance has led to difficulties. If the bill is accepted it is not dishonored, and the holder is left without recourse against the drawer and indorsers when he has most need for immediate recourse. The drawee does not in fact accept and does everything he can to display an intention not to accept; and the "acceptance" is useless to the holder for any purpose other than an action against the drawee, since he has nothing that he can negotiate. The original rule has therefore been changed (see Section 3–410).

2.   A negotiable instrument is the property of the holder. It is a mercantile specialty which embodies rights against other parties, and a thing of value. This section adopts the generally recognized rule that a refusal to return it on demand is a conversion. The provision is not limited to drafts presented for acceptance, but extends to any instrument presented for payment, including a note presented to the maker. The action is not on the instrument, but in tort for its conversion.

The detention of an instrument voluntarily delivered is not wrongful unless and until there is demand for its return. Demand for a return at a particular time may, however, be made at the time of delivery; or it may be implied under the circumstances or understood as a matter of custom. If the holder is to call for the instrument and fails to do so, he is to be regarded as extending the time. "Refuses" is meant to cover any intentional failure to return the instrument, including its intentional destruction. It does not cover a negligent loss or destruction, or any other unintentional failure to return. In such a case the party may be liable in tort for any damage sustained as a result of his negligence, but he is not liable as a converter under this section.

3.   Subsection (1)(c) is new. It adopts the prevailing view of decisions holding that payment on a forged indorsement is not an acceptance, but that even though made in good faith it is an exercise of dominion and control over the instrument inconsistent with the rights of the owner, and results in liability for conversion.

4.   Subsection (2) is new. It adopts the rule generally applied to the conversion of negotiable instruments, that the obligation of any party on the instrument is presumed, in the sense that the term is defined in this Act (Section 1–201), to be worth its face value. Evidence is admissible to show that for any reason such as insolvency or the existence of a defense the obligation is in fact worth less, or even that it is without value. In the case of the drawee, however, the presumption is replaced by a rule of absolute liability.

5.   Subsection (3), which is new, is intended to adopt the rule of decisions which has held that a representative, such as a broker or depositary bank, who deals with a negotiable instrument for his principal in good faith is not liable to the true owner for conversion of the instrument or otherwise, except that he may be compelled to turn over to the true owner the instrument itself or any proceeds of the instrument remaining in his hands. The provisions of subsection (3) are, however, subject to the provisions of this Act concerning restrictive indorsements (Sections 3–205, 3–206 and related sections).

6.   The provisions of this section are not intended to eliminate any liability on warranties of presentment and transfer (Section 3–417). Thus a collecting bank might be liable to a drawee bank which had been subject to liability under this section, even though the collecting bank might not be liable directly to the owner of the instrument.

Cross References:

Sections 3–409, 3–410, 3–411 and 3–603.
Point 4: Section 1–201.
Point 5: Sections 1–201, 3–205 and 3–206.
Point 6: Section 3–417.

Definitional Cross References:

"Acceptance". Section 3–410.
"Action". Section 1–201.
"Bank". Section 1–201.
"Collecting bank". Sections 3–102 and 4–105.
"Depositary bank". Sections 3–102 and 4–105.
"Good faith". Section 1–201.
"Instrument". Section 3–102.
"Intermediary bank". Sections 3–102 and 4–105.
"On demand". Section 3–108.
"Person". Section 1–201.
"Presumed". Section 1–201.
"Representative". Section 1–201.

PART 5

PRESENTMENT, NOTICE OF DISHONOR AND PROTEST

§ 3–501.   When Presentment, Notice of Dishonor, and Protest Necessary or Permissible.

(1)   Unless excused (Section 3–511) presentment is necessary to charge secondary parties as follows:

(a)   presentment for acceptance is necessary to charge the drawer and indorsers of a draft where the draft so provides, or is payable elsewhere than at the residence or place of business of the drawee, or its date of payment depends upon such presentment. The holder may at his option present for acceptance any other draft payable at a stated date;

(b)   presentment for payment is necessary to charge any indorser;

(c)   in the case of any drawer, the acceptor of a draft payable at a bank or the maker of a note payable at a bank, presentment for payment is necessary, but failure to make presentment discharges such drawer, acceptor or maker only as stated in Section 3–502(1)(b).

(2)   Unless excused (Section 3–511)

(a)   notice of any dishonor is necessary to charge any indorser;

(b)   in the case of any drawer, the acceptor of a draft payable at a bank or the maker of a note payable at a bank, notice of any dishonor is necessary, but failure to give such notice discharges such drawer, acceptor or maker only as stated in Section 3–502(1)(b).

(3)   Unless excused (Section 3–511) protest of any dishonor is necessary to charge the drawer and indorsers of any draft which on its face appears to be drawn or payable outside of the states, territories, dependencies and possessions of the United States, the District of Columbia and the Commonwealth of Puerto Rico. The holder may at his option make protest of any dishonor of any other instrument and in the case of a foreign draft may on insolvency of the acceptor before maturity make protest for better security.

(4)   Notwithstanding any provision of this section, neither presentment nor notice of dishonor nor protest is necessary to charge an indorser who has indorsed an instrument after maturity.

As amended in 1966.

Official Comment

Prior Uniform Statutory Provision: Sections 70, 89, 118, 129, 143, 144, 150, 151, 152, 157, 158 and 186, Uniform Negotiable Instruments Law.

Changes: Combined and simplified.

Purposes of Changes:

1.   Part 5 simplifies the requirements of the original Act as to presentment for acceptance or payment, notice of dishonor and protest. This section assembles in one place all provisions as to when any such proceeding is necessary. It eliminates some of the requirements and simplifies others. The effect of unexcused delay in any such proceeding as a discharge is covered by the next section, and the sections following prescribe the details of the proceedings.

2.   The words "Necessary to charge" are retained from the original Act. They mean that the necessary proceeding is a condition precedent to any right of action against the drawer or indorser. He is not liable and cannot be sued without the proceedings however long delayed. Under some circumstances delay is excused. If it is not excused it may operate as a discharge under the next section. Under some circumstances the proceeding may be entirely excused and the drawer or indorser is then liable as if the proceeding had been duly taken. Section 3–511 states the circumstances under which delay may be excused or the proceeding entirely excused.

3.   Subsection (1)(a) retains the substance of the original Sections 143, 144 and 150. The last sentence of the subsection states the rule of the decisions both at common law and under the original Act, that the holder may at his option present any time draft for acceptance, and is not required to wait until the due date to know whether the drawee will accept it; but that if he does make presentment and acceptance is refused he must give notice of dishonor. There is no similar right to present for acceptance a draft payable on demand, since a demand draft entitles the holder to immediate payment but not to acceptance.

4.   Subsections (1)(b) and (1)(c) on presentment for payment follow Section 70 of the original Act with one important change. Under the original Act and under this section ((1)(b)) presentment for payment is necessary (unless excused) to charge any drawer. Under the original Act drawers of drafts other than checks were wholly discharged by a failure to make due presentment but drawers of checks (Section 70 in conjunction with Section 186) were discharged only "to the extent of the loss caused by the delay"—that is to say, when insolvency of the drawee bank occurred after the time when presentment was due. The check rule of the original Act (somewhat modified—see Section 3–502(1)(b) and Comment thereto) is by subsection (1)(c) extended to all drawers, and also to the acceptors and makers of domiciled—"payable at a bank"—drafts and notes. Thus drawers of drafts other than checks are not, as they were under Section 70, wholly discharged by failure to make due presentment but, like drawers of checks, are discharged only as they may have suffered loss as provided in Section 3–502(1)(b). As to domiciled paper original Section 70 provided that ability and willingness to pay at the place named at maturity were "equivalent to a tender of payment"—that is to say would stop the running of interest, but had no other effect. Accordingly cases have held that makers and acceptors of domiciled paper were not discharged to any extent by the holder's failure to make presentment even when the obligor had funds available in the paying bank on the date for presentment and the bank subsequently failed. Subsection (1)(c) applies the check rule to such makers and acceptors; the "tender" language of Section 70 is eliminated; and the result in the cases referred to in the

preceding sentence is reversed. Under this section as under the original act presentment for payment is not necessary to charge primary parties (makers and acceptors of undomiciled paper).

5. Under subsection (2) the rules as to necessity of notice of dishonor run parallel with the rules as to necessity of presentment stated in subsection (1).

6. Under the original Sections 129 and 152 protest is required in the case of every "foreign draft", defined as a draft which on its face is not both drawn and payable "within this state." The result has been that upon dishonor in New York a check which appears on its face to be drawn in Jersey City must be protested in order to sue the drawer or any indorser. This has led to great inconvenience and expense of protest fees. The only function of protest is that of proof of dishonor, and it adds nothing to notice of dishonor as such.

Subsection (3) eliminates the requirement of protest except upon dishonor of a draft which on its face appears to be either drawn or payable outside of the states, territories, dependencies and possessions of the United States, the District of Columbia and the Commonwealth of Puerto Rico. The requirement is left as to such international drafts because it is generally required by foreign law, which this Article cannot affect. The formalities of protest are covered by Section 3–509 on protest, and substitutes for protest as proof of dishonor are provided for in Section 3–510 on evidence of dishonor and of notice. [This paragraph was amended in 1966].

This provision retains from the original Section 118 the rule permitting the holder at his option to make protest of any dishonor of any other instrument. Even where not required protest may have definite convenience where process does not run to another state and the taking of depositions is a slow and expensive matter. Even where the instrument is drawn and payable entirely within a state there may be convenience in saving the trip of a witness from Buffalo to New York to testify to dishonor, where the substitute evidence of dishonor and notice of dishonor cannot be relied on. Either required or optional protest is presumptive evidence of dishonor. (Section 3–510.)

7. The permissible "protest for better security" of original Section 158 is retained in the case of a foreign draft, as the practice is common in certain foreign countries.

8. Under the final sentence of Section 7 of the original Act an instrument indorsed when overdue became payable on demand as to the indorser. That language has been deleted from this Article—see Section 3–108 and Comment. It meant, among other things and in view of the provisions of the original Act as to demand paper, that such an indorser was discharged unless the instrument was presented for payment within a reasonable time after his indorsement. Presentment of overdue paper for the purpose of charging an indorser is unusual and not an expected commercial practice; the rule has been little more than a trap for those not familiar with the Act. Subsection (4), reversing the original Act, provides that as to indorsers after maturity neither presentment nor notice of dishonor nor protest is necessary; like primary parties therefore they will remain liable on the instrument for the period of the applicable statute of limitations.

Cross References:

> Point 1: Sections 3–502 through 3–508.
> Point 2: Sections 3–413, 3–414 and 3–511.
> Point 3: Sections 3–413, 3–414 and 3–511.
> Point 4: Section 3–502.
> Point 6: Sections 3–413, 3–414, 3–509, 3–510 and 3–511.
> Point 8: Section 3–108.

Definitional Cross References:

> "Acceptance". Section 3–410.
> "Bank". Section 1–201.
> "Certificate of deposit". Section 3–104.
> "Dishonor". Section 3–507.
> "Draft". Section 3–104.
> "Holder". Section 1–201.
> "Instrument". Section 3–102.
> "Note". Section 3–104.
> "Notice of dishonor". Section 3–508.
> "Party". Section 1–201.

"Presentment". Section 3–504.
"Protest". Section 3–509.
"Secondary party". Section 3–102.
"Signature". Section 3–401.

§ 3–502.   Unexcused Delay; Discharge.

(1)   Where without excuse any necessary presentment or notice of dishonor is delayed beyond the time when it is due

(a)   any indorser is discharged; and

(b)   any drawer or the acceptor of a draft payable at a bank or the maker of a note payable at a bank who because the drawee or payor bank becomes insolvent during the delay is deprived of funds maintained with the drawee or payor bank to cover the instrument may discharge his liability by written assignment to the holder of his rights against the drawee or payor bank in respect of such funds, but such drawer, acceptor or maker is not otherwise discharged.

(2)   Where without excuse a necessary protest is delayed beyond the time when it is due any drawer or indorser is discharged.

Official Comment

Prior Uniform Statutory Provision: Sections 7, 70, 89, 144, 150, 152 and 186, Uniform Negotiable Instruments Law.

Changes: Combined and simplified.

This section is the complement of the preceding section. It covers in one section widely scattered provisions of the original Act:

1.   The circumstances under which presentment or notice of dishonor or protest or delay therein are excused are stated in Section 3–511. When not excused delay operates as a discharge as provided in this section.

2.   Subsection (1)(b) applies to any drawer, as well as to the makers and acceptors of drafts and notes payable at a bank, the rule of the original Section 186 providing for discharge only where the drawer of a check has sustained loss through the delay. This section expressly limits the rule to loss sustained through insolvency of the drawee or payor which was the only type of loss to which the Section 186 rule has ever been applied in the cases arising under it.

The purpose of the rule is to avoid hardship upon the holder through complete discharge, and unjust enrichment of the drawer or other party who normally has received goods or other consideration for the issue of the instrument. He is "deprived of funds" in any case where bank failure or other insolvency of the drawee or payor has prevented him from receiving the benefit of funds which would have paid the instrument if it had been duly presented.

The original language discharging the drawer "to the extent of the loss caused by the delay" has not worked out satisfactorily in the decided cases, since the amount of the loss caused by the failure of a bank is almost never ascertainable at the time of suit and may not be ascertained until some years later. The decisions have turned upon burden of proof, and the drawer has seldom succeeded in proving his discharge. Subsection (1)(b) therefore substitutes a right to discharge liability by written assignment to the holder of rights against the drawee or payor as to the funds which cover the particular instrument. The assignment is intended to give the holder an effective right to claim against the drawee or payor.

3.   Subsection (2) retains the rule of the original Section 152, that any unexcused delay of a required protest is a complete discharge of all drawers and indorsers.

Cross References:

Point 1: Section 3–511(1).
Point 2: Section 3–501.
Point 3: Section 3–509.

Definitional Cross References:

"Bank". Section 1–201.
"Draft". Section 3–104.
"Holder". Section 1–201.
"Insolvent". Section 1–201.
"Instrument". Section 3–102.
"Note". Section 3–104.
"Notice of dishonor". Section 3–508.
"Payor bank". Section 4–105.
"Presentment". Section 3–504.
"Protest". Section 3–509.
"Rights". Section 1–201.
"Signature". Section 3–401.
"Written". Section 1–201.

§ 3–503.   Time of Presentment.

(1)   Unless a different time is expressed in the instrument the time for any presentment is determined as follows:

(a)   where an instrument is payable at or a fixed period after a stated date any presentment for acceptance must be made on or before the date it is payable;

(b)   where an instrument is payable after sight it must either be presented for acceptance or negotiated within a reasonable time after date or issue whichever is later;

(c)   where an instrument shows the date on which it is payable presentment for payment is due on that date;

(d)   where an instrument is accelerated presentment for payment is due within a reasonable time after the acceleration;

(e)   with respect to the liability of any secondary party presentment for acceptance or payment of any other instrument is due within a reasonable time after such party becomes liable thereon.

(2)   A reasonable time for presentment is determined by the nature of the instrument, any usage of banking or trade and the facts of the particular case. In the case of an uncertified check which is drawn and payable within the United States and which is not a draft drawn by a bank the following are presumed to be reasonable periods within which to present for payment or to initiate bank collection:

(a)   with respect to the liability of the drawer, thirty days after date or issue whichever is later; and

(b)   with respect to the liability of an indorser, seven days after his indorsement.

(3)   Where any presentment is due on a day which is not a full business day for either the person making presentment or the party to pay or accept, presentment is due on the next following day which is a full business day for both parties.

(4)   Presentment to be sufficient must be made at a reasonable hour, and if at a bank during its banking day.

Official Comment

Prior Uniform Statutory Provision: Sections 71, 72, 75, 85, 86, 144, 145, 146, 186 and 193, Uniform Negotiable Instruments Law.

Changes: Combined and simplified; new provisions.

Purposes of Changes and New Matter:

1.   This section states in one place all of the rules applicable to the time of presentment. Excused delay is covered by Section 3–511 on waiver and excuse, and the effect of unexcused delay by Section 3–502 on discharge.

The original Section 86, as to the determination of the time of payment by calculation from the day the time is to run, is omitted as superfluous. It states a rule universally applied to all time calculations in the law of contracts, and has no special application to negotiable instruments. No change in the law is intended.

2. Subsection (1) contains new provisions stating the commercial understanding as to the presentment of instruments payable after sight, and of accelerated paper.

3. Subsection (2) retains the substance of the original Section 193 as to the determination of a reasonable time. It provides specific time limits which are presumed, as that term is defined in this Act (Section 1–201), to be reasonable for uncertified checks drawn and payable within the continental limits of the United States. The court-made time limit of one day after the receipt of the instrument found in decisions under the original Act has proved to be too short a time for some holders, such as the department store or other large business clearing many checks through its books shortly after the first of the month, as well as the farmer or other individual at a distance from a bank.

The time limit provided differs as to drawer and indorser. The drawer, who has himself issued the check and normally expects to have it paid and charged to his account is reasonably required to stand behind it for a longer period, especially in view of the protection now provided by Federal Deposit Insurance. The thirty days specified coincides with the time after which a purchaser has notice that a check has become stale (Section 3–304(3)(c)). The indorser, who has normally merely received the check and passed it on, and does not expect to have to pay it, is entitled to know more promptly whether it is to be dishonored, in order that he may have recourse against the person with whom he has dealt.

4. Subsection (3) replaces the original Sections 85 and 146. It is intended to make allowance for the increasing practice of closing banks or businesses on Saturday or other days of the week. It is not intended to mean that any drawee or obligor can avoid dishonor of instruments by extended closing.

5. Subsection (4) eliminates the provision of the original Section 75 permitting presentment "at any hour before the bank is closed" if the drawer has no funds in the bank. The change is made to avoid inconvenience to the bank.

"Banking day" is defined in Section 4–104.

Cross References:

Point 1: Sections 3–501, 3–502, 3–505, 3–506 and 3–511.
Point 3: Sections 1–201 and 3–304(3)(c).
Point 5: Section 4–104.

Definitional Cross References:

"Acceptance". Section 3–410.
"Bank". Section 1–201.
"Banking day". Section 4–104.
"Check". Section 3–104.
"Draft". Section 3–104.
"Instrument". Section 3–102.
"Issue". Section 3–102.
"Party". Section 1–201.
"Person". Section 1–201.
"Presentment". Section 3–504.
"Presumed". Section 1–201.
"Reasonable time". Section 1–204.
"Secondary party". Section 3–102.
"Usage of trade". Section 1–205.

§ 3–504. How Presentment Made.

(1) Presentment is a demand for acceptance or payment made upon the maker, acceptor, drawee or other payor by or on behalf of the holder.

(2) Presentment may be made

(a) by mail, in which event the time of presentment is determined by the time of receipt of the mail; or

(b) through a clearing house; or

(c) at the place of acceptance or payment specified in the instrument or if there be none at the place of business or residence of the party to accept or pay. If neither the party to accept or pay nor anyone authorized to act for him is present or accessible at such place presentment is excused.

(3) It may be made

(a) to any one of two or more makers, acceptors, drawees or other payors; or

(b) to any person who has authority to make or refuse the acceptance or payment.

(4) A draft accepted or a note made payable at a bank in the United States must be presented at such bank.

(5) In the cases described in Section 4–210 presentment may be made in the manner and with the result stated in that section.

As amended in 1962.

<h2 style="text-align:center">Official Comment</h2>

Prior Uniform Statutory Provision: Sections 72, 73, 77, 78 and 145, Uniform Negotiable Instruments Law.

Changes: Combined and simplified.

Purposes of Changes:

1. This section is intended to simplify the rules as to how presentment is made and to make it clear that any demand upon the party to pay is a presentment no matter where or how. Former technical requirements of exhibition of the instrument and the like are not required unless insisted upon by the party to pay (Section 3–505).

2. Paragraph (a) of subsection (2) authorizes presentment by mail directly to the obligor. The presentment is sufficient and the instrument is dishonored by non-acceptance or nonpayment even though the party making presentment may be liable for improper collection methods. "Through a clearing-house" means that presentment is not made when the demand reaches the clearing-house, but when it reaches the obligor. Section 4–210 should also be consulted for the methods of presenting which may properly be employed by a collecting bank. Subsection (5) of this section makes it clear that presentment made under Section 4–210 is proper presentment.

3. Paragraph (a) of subsection (3) eliminates the requirement of the original Sections 78 and 145(1) that presentment be made to each of two or more makers, acceptors or drawees unless they are partners or one has authority to act for the others. The holder is entitled to expect that any one of the named parties will pay or accept, and should not be required to go to the trouble and expense of making separate presentment to a number of them.

4. Section 3–412 provides that an acceptance made payable at a bank in the United States does not vary the draft. Subsection (4) of this section makes it clear that a draft so accepted must be presented at the bank so designated. The same rule is applied to notes made payable at a bank. The rule of the subsection is in conformity with the provisions of Section 3–501 on presentment and Section 3–502 on the effect of failure to make presentment with reference to domiciled paper [This paragraph was amended in 1962].

Cross References:

Point 1: Sections 3–501, 3–502, 3–505 and 3–511.
Point 2: Section 4–210.
Point 5: Sections 3–412, 3–501 and 3–502.

Definitional Cross References:

"Acceptance". Section 3–410.
"Bank". Section 1–201.
"Clearing house". Section 4–104.

"Draft". Section 3–104.
"Holder". Section 1–201.
"Instrument". Section 3–102.
"Note". Section 3–104.
"Party". Section 1–201.
"Person". Section 1–201.

§ 3–505.　　Rights of Party to Whom Presentment Is Made.

(1)　The party to whom presentment is made may without dishonor require

(a)　exhibition of the instrument; and

(b)　reasonable identification of the person making presentment and evidence of his authority to make it if made for another; and

(c)　that the instrument be produced for acceptance or payment at a place specified in it, or if there be none at any place reasonable in the circumstances; and

(d)　a signed receipt on the instrument for any partial or full payment and its surrender upon full payment.

(2)　Failure to comply with any such requirement invalidates the presentment but the person presenting has a reasonable time in which to comply and the time for acceptance or payment runs from the time of compliance.

Official Comment

Prior Uniform Statutory Provision: Section 74, Uniform Negotiable Instruments Law.

Changes: Expanded and modified.

Purposes of Changes: To supplement the provisions as to how presentment is made, by permitting the party to whom it is made to insist on additional requirements:

1.　In the first instance a mere demand for acceptance or payment is sufficient presentment, and if the payment is unqualifiedly refused nothing more is required. The party to whom presentment is made may, however, require exhibition of the instrument, its production at the proper place, identification of the party making presentment, and a signed receipt on the instrument, or its surrender on full payment. Failure to comply with any such requirement invalidates the presentment and means that the instrument is not dishonored. The time for presentment is, however, extended to give the person presenting a reasonable opportunity to comply with the requirements.

2.　"Reasonable identification" means identification reasonable under all the circumstances. If the party on whom demand is made knows the person making presentment, no requirement of identification is reasonable, while if the circumstances are suspicious a great deal may be required. The requirement applies whether the instrument presented is payable to order or to bearer.

Cross References:

Point 1: Sections 3–504 and 3–506.

Definitional Cross References:

"Acceptance". Section 3–410.
"Dishonor". Section 3–507.
"Instrument". Section 3–102.
"Party". Section 1–201.
"Person". Section 1–201.
"Presentment". Section 3–504.
"Reasonable time". Section 1–204.
"Signed". Section 1–201.

§ 3-506. Time Allowed for Acceptance or Payment.

(1) Acceptance may be deferred without dishonor until the close of the next business day following presentment. The holder may also in a good faith effort to obtain acceptance and without either dishonor of the instrument or discharge of secondary parties allow postponement of acceptance for an additional business day.

(2) Except as a longer time is allowed in the case of documentary drafts drawn under a letter of credit, and unless an earlier time is agreed to by the party to pay, payment of an instrument may be deferred without dishonor pending reasonable examination to determine whether it is properly payable, but payment must be made in any event before the close of business on the day of presentment.

Official Comment

Prior Uniform Statutory Provision: Section 136, Uniform Negotiable Instruments Law.

Changes: Expanded.

Purposes of Changes: The original section covered only the time allowed to the drawee on presentment for acceptance. This section also covers the time allowed on presentment for payment.

Section 5-112 (Time Allowed for Honor) states the time, longer than here provided, during which a bank to which drafts are presented under a letter of credit may defer payment or acceptance without dishonor of the drafts. As to drafts drawn under a letter of credit Section 5-112 of course controls.

Section 4-301 on deferred posting should be consulted for the right of a payor bank to recover tentative settlements made by it on the day an item is received. That right does not survive final payment (Section 4-213).

Cross References:

Sections 4-301 and 5-112.

Definitional Cross References:

"Acceptance". Section 3-410.
"Dishonor". Section 3-507.
"Documentary draft". Sections 3-102 and 4-104.
"Instrument". Section 3-102.
"Letter of credit". Section 5-103.
"Party". Section 1-201.
"Presentment". Section 3-504.

§ 3-507. Dishonor; Holder's Right of Recourse; Term Allowing Re-presentment.

(1) An instrument is dishonored when

(a) a necessary or optional presentment is duly made and due acceptance or payment is refused or cannot be obtained within the prescribed time or in case of bank collections the instrument is seasonably returned by the midnight deadline (Section 4-301); or

(b) presentment is excused and the instrument is not duly accepted or paid.

(2) Subject to any necessary notice of dishonor and protest, the holder has upon dishonor an immediate right of recourse against the drawers and indorsers.

(3) Return of an instrument for lack of proper indorsement is not dishonor.

(4) A term in a draft or an indorsement thereof allowing a stated time for re-presentment in the event of any dishonor of the draft by nonacceptance if a time draft or by nonpayment if a sight draft gives the holder as against any secondary party bound by the term an option to waive the dishonor without affecting the liability of the secondary party and he may present again up to the end of the stated time.

Official Comment

Prior Uniform Statutory Provision: Sections 83 and 149, Uniform Negotiable Instruments Law.

Changes: Reworded.

Purposes of Changes:

1.   The language of the section is changed in accordance with the provisions of the preceding section as to the time allowed for acceptance or payment.

2.   Subsection (3) is new. It states general banking and commercial understanding. The time within which a payor bank must return items, and the methods of returning, are stated in Section 4–301. Under Section 3–411(3) a bank may certify an item so returned.

Cross References:

Point 1: Sections 3–503, 3–504, 3–505, 3–508 and 4–301.
Point 2: Sections 3–411(3), 4–301.

Definitional Cross References:

"Acceptance". Section 3–410.
"Bank". Section 1–201.
"Draft". Section 3–104.
"Holder". Section 1–201.
"Instrument". Section 3–102.
"Midnight deadline". Section 4–104.
"Notice of dishonor". Section 3–508.
"Presentment". Section 3–504.
"Protest". Section 3–509.
"Right". Section 1–201.
"Seasonably". Section 1–204.
"Secondary party". Section 3–102.
"Term". Section 1–201.

§ 3–508.   Notice of Dishonor.

(1)   Notice of dishonor may be given to any person who may be liable on the instrument by or on behalf of the holder or any party who has himself received notice, or any other party who can be compelled to pay the instrument. In addition an agent or bank in whose hands the instrument is dishonored may give notice to his principal or customer or to another agent or bank from which the instrument was received.

(2)   Any necessary notice must be given by a bank before its midnight deadline and by any other person before midnight of the third business day after dishonor or receipt of notice of dishonor.

(3)   Notice may be given in any reasonable manner. It may be oral or written and in any terms which identify the instrument and state that it has been dishonored. A misdescription which does not mislead the party notified does not vitiate the notice. Sending the instrument bearing a stamp, ticket or writing stating that acceptance or payment has been refused or sending a notice of debit with respect to the instrument is sufficient.

(4)   Written notice is given when sent although it is not received.

(5)   Notice to one partner is notice to each although the firm has been dissolved.

(6)   When any party is in insolvency proceedings instituted after the issue of the instrument notice may be given either to the party or to the representative of his estate.

(7)   When any party is dead or incompetent notice may be sent to his last known address or given to his personal representative.

(8)   Notice operates for the benefit of all parties who have rights on the instrument against the party notified.

Official Comment

Prior Uniform Statutory Provision: Sections 90 through 108, Uniform Negotiable Instruments Law.

Changes: Combined and simplified.

Purposes of Changes: To simplify notice of dishonor and eliminate many of the detailed requirements of the original Act:

1. Notice is normally given by the holder or by an indorser who has himself received notice. Subsection (1) is intended to encourage and facilitate notice of dishonor by permitting any party who may be compelled to pay the instrument to notify any party who may be liable on it. Thus an indorser may notify another indorser who is not liable to the one who gives notice, even when the latter has not received notice from any other party to the instrument.

2. Except as to collecting banks, as to whom Section 4–212 controls, the time within which necessary notice must be given is extended to three days after dishonor or receipt of notice from another party. In the case of individuals the one-day time limit of the original Act has proved too short in many cases. It is extended to give the party a margin of time within which to ascertain what is required of him and get out an ordinary business letter. This time leeway eliminates the elaborate provisions as to the time of mailing in the original Sections 103 and 104.

3. Subsection (3) retains the substance of the original Sections 95 and 96. The provision approves the bank practice of returning the instrument bearing a stamp, ticket or other writing, or a notice of debit of the account, as sufficient notice. Subsection (4) retains the substance of the original Section 105.

4. Subsection (7) permits notice to be sent to the last known address of a party who is dead or incompetent rather than to his personal representative. The provision is intended to save time, as the name of the personal representative often cannot easily be ascertained, and mail addressed to the original party will reach the representative.

Cross References:

Sections 3–501, 3–507 and 3–511.
Point 2: Section 4–212.

Definitional Cross References:

"Acceptance". Section 3–410.
"Bank". Section 1–201.
"Customer". Section 4–104.
"Dishonor". Section 3–507.
"Holder". Section 1–201.
"Insolvency proceedings". Section 1–201.
"Instrument". Section 3–102.
"Issue". Section 3–102.
"Midnight deadline". Section 4–104.
"Notifies". Section 1–201.
"Party". Section 1–201.
"Person". Section 1–201.
"Representative". Section 1–201.
"Rights". Section 1–201.
"Send". Section 1–201.
"Written" and "writing". Section 1–201.

§ 3–509. Protest; Noting for Protest.

(1) A protest is a certificate of dishonor made under the hand and seal of a United States consul or vice consul or a notary public or other person authorized to certify dishonor by the law of the place where dishonor occurs. It may be made upon information satisfactory to such person.

(2) The protest must identify the instrument and certify either that due presentment has been made or the reason why it is excused and that the instrument has been dishonored by non-acceptance or nonpayment.

(3)   The protest may also certify that notice of dishonor has been given to all parties or to specified parties.

(4)   Subject to subsection (5) any necessary protest is due by the time that notice of dishonor is due.

(5)   If, before protest is due, an instrument has been noted for protest by the officer to make protest, the protest may be made at any time thereafter as of the date of the noting.

Official Comment

Prior Uniform Statutory Provision: Sections 153, 154, 155, 156, 158 and 160, Uniform Negotiable Instruments Law.

Changes: Combined and simplified.

Purposes of Changes:

1.   Protest is not necessary except on drafts drawn or payable outside of the United States. Section 3–501(3) which also permits the holder at his option to make protest on dishonor of any other instrument. This section is intended to simplify either necessary or optional protest when it is made.

2.   "Protest" has been used to mean the act of making protest, and sometimes loosely to refer to the entire process of presentment, notice of dishonor and protest. In this Article it is given its original, technical meaning, that of the official certificate of dishonor.

3.   Subsection (1) adds to the notary public the United States consul or vice consul, and any other person authorized to certify dishonor by the law of the place where dishonor occurs. It eliminates the requirement of the original Section 156 that protest must be made at the place of dishonor. It eliminates also the provision of the original Section 154 permitting protest by "any respectable resident of the place where the bill is dishonored, in the presence of two or more credible witnesses." This has at least left uncertainty as to the identity and credibility of the persons certifying, and has almost never been used. Any necessary delay in finding the proper officer to make protest is excused under Section 3–511.

4.   "Information satisfactory to such person" does away with the requirement occasionally stated, that the person making protest must certify as of his own knowledge. The requirement has been more honored in the breach than in the observance, and in practice protest has been made upon hearsay which the officer regards as reliable, upon the admission of the person who has dishonored, or at most upon re-presentment, which is only indirect proof of the original dishonor. There is seldom any possible motive for false protest, and the basis on which it is made is never questioned. Subsection (1) leaves to the certifying officer the responsibility for determining whether he has satisfactory information. The provision is not intended to affect any personal liability of the officer for making a false certificate.

5.   The protest need not be in any particular form, so long as it certifies the matters stated in Subsection (2). It need not be annexed to the instrument, and may be forwarded separately; but annexation may identify the instrument. If the instrument is lost, destroyed, or wrongfully withheld, protest is still sufficient if it identifies the instrument; but the owner must prove his rights as in any action under this Article on a lost, destroyed or stolen instrument (Section 3–804).

6.   Subsection (3) recognizes the practice of including in the protest a certification that notice of dishonor has been given to all parties or to specified parties. The next section makes such a certification presumptive evidence that the notice has been given.

7.   Protest is normally forwarded with notice of dishonor. Subsection (4) extends the time for making a necessary protest to coincide with the time for giving notice of dishonor. Any delay due to circumstances beyond the holder's control is excused under Section 3–511 on waiver or excuse. Any protest which is not necessary but merely optional with the holder may be made at any time before it is used as evidence.

8.   Subsection (5) retains from the original Section 155 the provision permitting the officer to note the protest and extend it formally later.

Cross References:

Point 1: Sections 3–501(3) and 3–511.
Point 3: Section 3–511(1).
Point 5: Section 3–804.

Point 6: Section 3–510(a).

Point 7: Sections 3–508(2) and 3–511(1).

Definitional Cross References:

"Dishonor". Section 3–507.

"Instrument". Section 3–102.

"Notice of dishonor". Section 3–508.

"Party". Section 1–201.

"Person". Section 1–201.

"Presentment". Section 3–504.

§ 3–510. Evidence of Dishonor and Notice of Dishonor.

The following are admissible as evidence and create a presumption of dishonor and of any notice of dishonor therein shown:

(a) a document regular in form as provided in the preceding section which purports to be a protest;

(b) the purported stamp or writing of the drawee, payor bank or presenting bank on the instrument or accompanying it stating that acceptance or payment has been refused for reasons consistent with dishonor;

(c) any book or record of the drawee, payor bank, or any collecting bank kept in the usual course of business which shows dishonor, even though there is no evidence of who made the entry.

Official Comment

Prior Uniform Statutory Provision: None.

Purposes: This section is new. It states the effect of protest as evidence, and provides two substitutes for protest as proof of dishonor:

1. Paragraph (a) states the generally accepted rule that a protest is not only admissible as evidence, but creates a presumption, as that term is defined in this Act (Section 1–201), of the dishonor which it certifies. The rule is extended to include the giving of any notice of dishonor certified by the protest. The provision also relieves the holder of the necessity of proving that a document regular in form which purports to be a protest is authentic, or that the person making it was qualified. Nothing in the provision is intended to prevent the obligor from overthrowing the presumption by evidence that there was in fact no dishonor, that notice was not given, or that the protest is not authentic or not made by a proper officer.

2. Paragraph (b) recognizes as the full equivalent of protest the stamp, ticket or other writing of the drawee, payor or presenting bank. The drawee's statement that payment is refused on account of insufficient funds always has been commercially acceptable as full proof of dishonor. It should be satisfactory evidence in any court. It is therefore made admissible, and creates a presumption of dishonor. The provision applies only where the stamp or writing states reasons for refusal which are consistent with dishonor. Thus the following reasons for refusal are not evidence of dishonor, but of justifiable refusal to pay or accept:

Indorsement missing
Signature missing
Signature illegible
Forgery
Payee altered
Date altered
Post dated
Not on us

On the other hand the following reasons are satisfactory evidence of dishonor, consistent with due presentment, and are within this provision:

Not sufficient funds
Account garnisheed
No account

1043

Payment stopped

3.   Paragraph (c) recognizes as the full equivalent of protest any books or records of the drawee, payor bank or any collecting bank kept in its usual course of business, even though there is no evidence of who made the entries. The provision, as well as that of paragraph (b), rests upon the inherent improbability that bank records, or those of the drawee, will show any dishonor which has not in fact occurred, or that the holder will attempt to proceed on the basis of dishonor if he could in fact have obtained payment.

Cross References:

> Sections 3–501 and 3–508.
> Point 1: Section 1–201.

Definitional Cross References:

> "Acceptance". Section 3–410.
> "Collecting bank". Section 4–105.
> "Dishonor". Section 3–507.
> "Instrument". Section 3–102.
> "Notice of dishonor". Section 3–508.
> "Payor bank". Section 4–105.
> "Presumption". Section 1–201.
> "Protest." Section 3–509.
> "Writing". Section 1–201.

§ 3–511.   Waived or Excused Presentment, Protest or Notice of Dishonor or Delay Therein.

(1)   Delay in presentment, protest or notice of dishonor is excused when the party is without notice that it is due or when the delay is caused by circumstances beyond his control and he exercises reasonable diligence after the cause of the delay ceases to operate.

(2)   Presentment or notice or protest as the case may be is entirely excused when

(a)   the party to be charged has waived it expressly or by implication either before or after it is due; or

(b)   such party has himself dishonored the instrument or has countermanded payment or otherwise has no reason to expect or right to require that the instrument be accepted or paid; or

(c)   by reasonable diligence the presentment or protest cannot be made or the notice given.

(3)   Presentment is also entirely excused when

(a)   the maker, acceptor or drawee of any instrument except a documentary draft is dead or in insolvency proceedings instituted after the issue of the instrument; or

(b)   acceptance or payment is refused but not for want of proper presentment.

(4)   Where a draft has been dishonored by nonacceptance a later presentment for payment and any notice of dishonor and protest for nonpayment are excused unless in the meantime the instrument has been accepted.

(5)   A waiver of protest is also a waiver of presentment and of notice of dishonor even though protest is not required.

(6)   Where a waiver of presentment or notice or protest is embodied in the instrument itself it is binding upon all parties; but where it is written above the signature of an indorser it binds him only.

Official Comment

Prior Uniform Statutory Provision: Sections 79, 80, 81, 82, 109, 111, 112, 113, 114, 115, 116, 130, 147, 148, 150, 151, 159, Uniform Negotiable Instruments Law.

Changes: Combined and simplified.

Purposes of Changes: This section combines widely scattered sections of the original act, and is intended to simplify the rules as to when presentment, notice or protest is excused:

1. The single term "excused" is substituted for "excused," "dispensed with," "not necessary," "not required," as used variously in the original act. No change in meaning is intended.

2. Subsection (1) combines provisions found in the original Sections 81, 113, 147 and 159. Delay in making presentment either for payment or for acceptance, in giving notice of dishonor or in making protest is excused when the party has acted with reasonable diligence and the delay is not his fault. This is true where an instrument has been accelerated without his knowledge, or demand has been made by a prior holder immediately before his purchase. It is true under any other circumstances where the delay is beyond his control. The words "not imputable to his default, misconduct or negligence" found in the original Sections 81, 113 and 159 are omitted as superfluous, but no change in substance is intended.

3. Any waived presentment, notice or protest is excused, as under the original Sections 82, 109, 110 and 111. The waiver may be express or implied, oral or written, and before or after the proceeding waived is due. It may be, and often is, a term of the instrument when it is issued. Subsection (5) retains as standard commercial usage the meaning attached by the original Section 111 to "protest waived."

4. Paragraph (b) of subsection (2) combines the substance of provisions found in the original Sections 79, 80, 114, 115 and 130. A party who has no right to require or reason to expect that the instrument will be honored is not entitled to presentment, notice or protest. This is of course true where he has himself dishonored the instrument or has countermanded payment. It is equally true, for example, where he is an accommodated party and has himself broken the accommodation agreement.

5. Paragraph (c) of subsection (2) combines provisions found in the original Sections 82(1), 112 and 159. The excuse is established only by proof that reasonable diligence has been exercised without success, or that reasonable diligence would in any case have been unsuccessful.

6. Paragraph (a) of subsection (3) is new. It excuses presentment in situations where immediate payment or acceptance is impossible or so unlikely that the holder cannot reasonably be expected to make presentment. He is permitted instead to have his immediate recourse upon the drawer or indorser, and let the latter file any necessary claim in probate or insolvency proceedings. The exception for the documentary draft is to preserve any profit on the resale of goods for the creditors of the drawee if his representative can find the funds to pay.

7. Paragraph (b) of subsection (3) extends the original Section 148(3) to include any case where payment or acceptance is definitely refused and the refusal is not on the ground that there has been no proper presentment. The purpose of presentment is to determine whether or not the maker, acceptor or drawee will pay or accept; and when that question is clearly determined the holder is not required to go through a useless ceremony. The provision applies to a definite refusal stating no reasons.

8. Subsection (4) retains the rule of the original Sections 116 and 151.

9. Subsection (6) retains the rule of original Section 110.

Cross References:

Sections 3–501, 3–502, 3–503, 3–507 and 3–509.

Definitional Cross References:

"Acceptance". Section 3–410.
"Dishonor". Section 3–507.
"Documentary draft". Section 4–104.
"Draft". Section 3–104.
"Insolvency proceedings". Section 1–201.
"Instrument". Section 3–102.
"Issue". Section 3–102.
"Notice of dishonor". Section 3–508.
"Party". Section 1–201.
"Presentment". Section 3–504.
"Protest". Section 3–509.
"Right". Section 1–201.

PART 6

DISCHARGE

§ 3–601.   Discharge of Parties.

(1)   The extent of the discharge of any party from liability on an instrument is governed by the sections on

    (a)   payment or satisfaction (Section 3–603); or

    (b)   tender of payment (Section 3–604); or

    (c)   cancellation or renunciation (Section 3–605); or

    (d)   impairment of right of recourse or of collateral (Section 3–606); or

    (e)   reacquisition of the instrument by a prior party (Section 3–208); or

    (f)   fraudulent and material alteration (Section 3–407); or

    (g)   certification of a check (Section 3–411); or

    (h)   acceptance varying a draft (Section 3–412); or

    (i)   unexcused delay in presentment or notice of dishonor or protest (Section 3–502).

(2)   Any party is also discharged from his liability on an instrument to another party by any other act or agreement with such party which would discharge his simple contract for the payment of money.

(3)   The liability of all parties is discharged when any party who has himself no right of action or recourse on the instrument

    (a)   reacquires the instrument in his own right; or

    (b)   is discharged under any provision of this Article, except as otherwise provided with respect to discharge for impairment of recourse or of collateral (Section 3–606).

Official Comment

Prior Uniform Statutory Provision: Sections 119, 120 and 121, Uniform Negotiable Instruments Law.

Changes: Portions of original sections combined and reworded; new provisions.

Purposes of Changes:

1.   Subsection (1) contains an index referring to all of the sections of this Article which provide for the discharge of any party. The list is exclusive so far as the provisions of this Article are concerned, but it is not intended to prevent or affect any discharge arising apart from this statute, as for example a discharge in bankruptcy or a statutory provision for discharge if the instrument is negotiated in a gaming transaction.

2.   A negotiable instrument is in itself merely a piece of paper bearing a writing, and strictly speaking is incapable of being discharged. The parties are rather discharged from liability on their contracts on the instrument. The language of the original Section 119 as to discharge of the instrument itself has left uncertainties as to the effect of the discharge upon the rights of a subsequent holder in due course. It is therefore eliminated, and this section now distinguishes instead between the discharge of a single party and the discharge of all parties.

So far as the discharge of any one party is concerned a negotiable instrument differs from any other contract only in the special rules arising out of its character to which paragraphs (a) to (i) of subsection (1) are an index, and in the effect of the discharge against a subsequent holder in due course (Section 3–602). Subsection (2) therefore retains from the original Section 119(4) the provision for discharge by "any other act which will discharge a simple contract for the payment of money," and specifically recognizes the possibility of a discharge by agreement.

The discharge of any party is a defense available to that party as provided in sections on rights of those who are and are not holders in due course (Sections 3–305 and 3–306). He has the burden of establishing the defense (Section 3–307).

3.   Subsection (3) substitutes for the "discharge of the instrument" the discharge of all parties from liability on their contracts on the instrument. It covers a part of the substance of the original Section 119(1), (2) and (5), the original Section 120(1) and (3), and the original Section 121(1) and (2). It states a general principle in lieu of the original detailed provisions. The principle is that all parties to an instrument are discharged when no party is left with rights against any other party on the paper.

When any party reacquires the instrument in his own right his own liability is discharged; and any intervening party to whom he was liable is also discharged as provided in Section 3–208 on reacquisition. When he is left with no right of action against an intervening party and no right of recourse against any prior party, all parties are obviously discharged. The instrument itself is not necessarily extinct, since it may be reissued or renegotiated with a new and further liability; and if it subsequently reaches the hands of a holder in due course without notice of the discharge he may still enforce it as provided in Section 3–602 on effect of discharge against a holder in due course.

Under Section 3–606 on impairment of recourse or collateral, the discharge of any party discharges those who have a right of recourse against him, except in the case of a release with reservation of rights or a failure to give notice of dishonor. A discharge of one who has himself no right of action or recourse on the instrument may thus discharge all parties. Again the instrument itself is not necessarily extinct, and if it is negotiated to a subsequent holder in due course without notice of the discharge he may enforce it as provided in Section 3–602 on effect of discharge against a holder in due course.

4.   The language "any party who has himself no right of action or recourse on the instrument" is substituted for "principal debtor," which is not defined by the original Act and has been misleading. This Article also omits the original Section 192, defining the "person primarily liable." Under Section 3–415 on accommodation parties an accommodation maker or acceptor, although he is primarily liable on the instrument in the sense that he is obligated to pay it without recourse upon another, has himself a right of recourse against the accommodated payee; and his reacquisition or discharge leaves the accommodated party liable to him. The accommodated payee, although he is not primarily liable to others, has no right of action or recourse against the accommodation maker, and his reacquisition or discharge may discharge all parties.

Cross References:

Sections 3–406, 3–411, 3–412, 3–509, 3–603, 3–604 and 3–605.
Point 2: Sections 3–305, 3–306, 3–307 and 3–602.
Point 3: Sections 3–208, 3–602 and 3–606.
Point 4: Section 3–415.

Definitional Cross References:

"Action". Section 1–201.
"Agreement". Section 1–201.
"Alteration". Section 3–407.
"Certification". Section 3–411.
"Check". Section 3–104.
"Contract". Section 1–201.
"Draft". Section 3–104.
"Instrument". Section 3–102.
"Money". Section 1–201.
"Notice of dishonor". Section 3–508.
"Party". Section 1–201.
"Presentment". Section 3–504.
"Rights". Section 1–201.

§ 3–602.   Effect of Discharge Against Holder in Due Course.

No discharge of any party provided by this Article is effective against a subsequent holder in due course unless he has notice thereof when he takes the instrument.

Official Comment

Prior Uniform Statutory Provision: None.

Purposes:

The section is intended to remove an uncertainty as to which the original Act is silent. It rests on the principle that any discharge of a party provided under any section of this Article is a personal defense of the party, which is cut off when a subsequent holder in due course takes the instrument without notice of the defense. Thus where an instrument is paid without surrender such a subsequent purchase cuts off the defense. This section applies only to discharges arising under the provisions of this Article, and it has no application to any discharge arising apart from it, such as a discharge in bankruptcy.

Under Section 3–304(1)(b) on notice to purchaser it is possible for a holder to take the instrument in due course even though he has notice that one or more parties have been discharged, so long as any party remains undischarged. Thus he may take with notice that an indorser of a note has been released, and still be a holder in due course as to the liability of the maker. In that event, the holder in due course is subject to the defense of the discharge of which he had notice when he took the instrument.

Cross References:

Sections 3–302, 3–304, 3–305 and 3–601.

Definitional Cross References:

"Holder in due course". Section 3–302.
"Instrument". Section 3–102.
"Notice". Section 1–201.
"Party". Section 1–201.

§ 3–603.   Payment or Satisfaction.

(1)   The liability of any party is discharged to the extent of his payment or satisfaction to the holder even though it is made with knowledge of a claim of another person to the instrument unless prior to such payment or satisfaction the person making the claim either supplies indemnity deemed adequate by the party seeking the discharge or enjoins payment or satisfaction by order of a court of competent jurisdiction in an action in which the adverse claimant and the holder are parties. This subsection does not, however, result in the discharge of the liability

    (a)   of a party who in bad faith pays or satisfies a holder who acquired the instrument by theft or who (unless having the rights of a holder in due course) holds through one who so acquired it; or

    (b)   of a party (other than an intermediary bank or a payor bank which is not a depositary bank) who pays or satisfies the holder of an instrument which has been restrictively indorsed in a manner not consistent with the terms of such restrictive indorsement.

(2)   Payment or satisfaction may be made with the consent of the holder by any person including a stranger to the instrument. Surrender of the instrument to such a person gives him the rights of a transferee (Section 3–201).

Official Comment

Prior Uniform Statutory Provision: Sections 51, 88, 119, 121 and 171–177, Uniform Negotiable Instruments Law.

Changes: Parts of original sections combined and reworded; law changed.

Purposes of Changes: This section changes the law as follows:

1.   It eliminates the "payment in due course" found in the original Sections 51, 88 and 119. "Payment in due course" discharged all parties where it was made by one who has no right of recourse on the instrument; but this is true of any other discharge of such a party, and is now covered by Section 3–601(3) on discharge of parties. Such payment was effective as a discharge against a subsequent purchaser; but since it is made at or after maturity of the instrument a purchaser with notice of that fact cannot be a holder in due course, and one who

takes without notice of the payment and the maturity should be protected against failure to take up the instrument. The matter is now covered by Section 3–602.

2.   The original Sections 171–177 provide for payment of a draft "for honor" after protest. The practice originated at a time when communications were slow and difficult, and in overseas transactions there might be a delay of several months before the drawer could act upon any dishonor. It provided a method by which a third party might intervene to protect the credit of the drawer and at the same time preserve his own rights. Cable, telegraph and telephone have made the practice obsolete for nearly a century, and it is today almost entirely unknown. It has been replaced by the cable transfer, the letter of credit and numerous other devices by which a substitute arrangement is promptly made. "Payment for honor" is therefore eliminated; and subsection (2) now provides that any person may pay with the consent of the holder.

3.   Payment to the holder discharges the party who makes it from his own liability on the instrument, and a part payment discharges him pro tanto. The same is true of any other satisfaction. Subsection (1) changes the law by eliminating the requirement of the original Section 88 that the payment be made in good faith and without notice that the title of the holder is defective. It adopts as a general principle the position that a payor is not required to obey an order to stop payment received from an indorser. However, this general principle is qualified by the provisions of subsection (1)(a) and (b) respecting persons who acquire an instrument by theft, or through a restrictive indorsement (Section 3–205). These provisions are thus consistent with Section 3–306 covering the rights of one not a holder in due course.

When the party to pay is notified of an adverse claim to the instrument he has normally no means of knowing whether the assertion is true. The "unless" clause of subsection (1) follows statutes which have been passed in many states on adverse claims to bank deposits. The paying party may pay despite notification of the adverse claim unless the adverse claimant supplies indemnity deemed adequate by the paying party or procures the issuance of process restraining payment in an action in which the adverse claimant and the holder of the instrument are both parties. If the paying party chooses to refuse payment and stand suit, even though not indemnified or enjoined, he is free to do so, although, under Section 3–306(d) on the rights of one not a holder in due course, except where theft or taking through a restrictive indorsement is alleged the payor must rely on the third party claimant to litigate the issue and may not himself defend on such a ground. His contract is to pay the holder of the instrument, and he performs it by making such payment. Except in cases of theft or restrictive indorsement there is no good reason to put him to inconvenience because of a dispute between two other parties unless he is indemnified or served with appropriate process.

4.   With the elimination of "payment for honor", subsection (2) provides that with the consent of the holder payment may be made by anyone, including a stranger. The subsection omits the provision of the original Section 121 by which the payor is "remitted to his former rights". It rejects such decisions as Quimby v. Varnum, 190 Mass. 211, 76 N.E. 671 (1906), holding that an irregular indorser who makes payment cannot recover on the instrument. The same result is reached under Section 3–415(5) on accommodation parties. Upon payment and surrender of the paper the payor succeeds to the rights of the holder, subject to the limitation found in Section 3–201 on transfer that one who has himself been a party to any fraud or illegality affecting the instrument or who as a prior holder had notice of a defense or claim against it cannot improve his position by taking from a later holder in due course.

5.   Payment discharges the liability of the person making it. It discharges the liability of other parties only as

a.   The discharge of the payor discharges others who have a right of recourse against him under Section 3–606; or

b.   Reacquisition of the instrument discharges intervening parties under Section 3–208 on reacquisition; or

c.   The discharge of one who has himself no right of recourse on the instrument discharges all parties under Section 3–601 on discharge of parties.

Cross References:

Sections 3–604 and 3–606.
Point 1: Section 3–601(3).
Point 3: Sections 3–205 and 3–306(d).
Point 4: Sections 3–201 and 3–415(5).

Point 5: Sections 3–606, 3–208, 3–601.

Definitional Cross References:

"Action". Section 1–201.

"Holder". Section 1–201.

"Instrument". Section 3–102.

"Order". Section 3–102.

"Party". Section 1–201.

"Person". Section 1–201.

"Rights". Section 1–201.

§ 3–604.   Tender of Payment.

(1) Any party making tender of full payment to a holder when or after it is due is discharged to the extent of all subsequent liability for interest, costs and attorney's fees.

(2) The holder's refusal of such tender wholly discharges any party who has a right of recourse against the party making the tender.

(3) Where the maker or acceptor of an instrument payable otherwise than on demand is able and ready to pay at every place of payment specified in the instrument when it is due, it is equivalent to tender.

Official Comment

Prior Uniform Statutory Provision: Sections 70 and 120, Uniform Negotiable Instruments Law.

Changes: Parts of original sections combined and reworded; new provisions.

Purposes of Changes and New Matter:

1. Subsection (1) is new. It states the generally accepted rule as to the effect of tender.

2. Subsection (2) rewords the original subsection 120(4). The party discharged is one who has a right of recourse against the party making tender, whether the latter be a prior party or a subsequent one who has been accommodated.

3. Subsection (3) rewords the final clause of the first sentence of the original Section 70. Where the instrument is payable at any one of two or more specified places, the maker or acceptor must be able and ready to pay at each of them. The language in original Section 70 was taken to mean that makers and acceptors of notes and drafts payable at a bank were not discharged by failure of a holder to make due presentment of such paper at the designated bank. This Article reverses that rule. See Sections 3–501 on necessity of presentment, 3–504 on how presentment is made, and 3–502 on effect of delay in presentment.

Cross References:

Section 3–601.

Point 3: Sections 3–501, 3–502 and 3–504.

Definitional Cross References:

"Holder". Section 1–201.

"Instrument". Section 3–102.

"On demand". Section 3–108.

"Party". Section 1–201.

"Right". Section 1–201.

§ 3–605.   Cancellation and Renunciation.

(1) The holder of an instrument may even without consideration discharge any party

(a) in any manner apparent on the face of the instrument or the indorsement, as by intentionally cancelling the instrument or the party's signature by destruction or mutilation, or by striking out the party's signature; or

(b)   by renouncing his rights by a writing signed and delivered or by surrender of the instrument to the party to be discharged.

(2)   Neither cancellation nor renunciation without surrender of the instrument affects the title thereto.

Official Comment

Prior Uniform Statutory Provision: Sections 48, 119(3), 120(2), 122 and 123, Uniform Negotiable Instruments Law.

Changes: Combined and reworded.

Purposes of Changes:

1.   The original Act does not state how cancellation is to be effected, except as to striking indorsements under the original Section 48. It must be done in such a manner as to be apparent on the face of the instrument, and the methods stated, which are supported by the decisions, are exclusive.

2.   Subsection (1)(b) restates the original Section 122. The provision as to "discharge of the instrument" is now covered by discharge, Section 3–601(3); that as to subsequent holders in due course by Section 3–602 on effect of discharge against a holder in due course.

3.   Subsection (2) is new. It is intended to make it clear that the striking of an indorsement, or any other cancellation or renunciation, does not affect the title.

Cross References:

Point 2: Sections 3–601 and 3–602.

Definitional Cross References:

"Holder". Section 1–201.
"Instrument". Section 3–102.
"Party". Section 1–201.
"Rights". Section 1–201.
"Signature". Section 3–401.
"Signed". Section 1–201.
"Writing". Section 1–201.

§ 3–606.   Impairment of Recourse or of Collateral.

(1)   The holder discharges any party to the instrument to the extent that without such party's consent the holder

(a)   without express reservation of rights releases or agrees not to sue any person against whom the party has to the knowledge of the holder a right of recourse or agrees to suspend the right to enforce against such person the instrument or collateral or otherwise discharges such person, except that failure or delay in effecting any required presentment, protest or notice of dishonor with respect to any such person does not discharge any party as to whom presentment, protest or notice of dishonor is effective or unnecessary; or

(b)   unjustifiably impairs any collateral for the instrument given by or on behalf of the party or any person against whom he has a right of recourse.

(2)   By express reservation of rights against a party with a right of recourse the holder preserves

(a)   all his rights against such party as of the time when the instrument was originally due; and

(b)   the right of the party to pay the instrument as of that time; and

(c)   all rights of such party to recourse against others.

Official Comment

Prior Uniform Statutory Provision: Section 120, Uniform Negotiable Instruments Law.

Changes: Reworded; new provisions.

Purposes of Changes and New Matter: To make it clear that:

1.   The words "any party to the instrument" remove an uncertainty arising under the original section. The suretyship defenses here provided are not limited to parties who are "secondarily liable," but are available to any party who is in the position of a surety, having a right of recourse either on the instrument or dehors it, including an accommodation maker or acceptor known to the holder to be so.

2.   Consent may be given in advance, and is commonly incorporated in the instrument; or it may be given afterward. It requires no consideration, and operates as a waiver of the consenting party's right to claim his own discharge.

3.   The words "to the knowledge of the holder" exclude the latent surety, as for example the accommodation maker where there is nothing on the instrument to show that he has signed for accommodation and the holder is ignorant of that fact. In such a case the holder is entitled to proceed according to what is shown by the face of the paper or what he otherwise knows, and does not discharge the surety when he acts in ignorance of the relation.

4.   This section retains the right of the holder to release one party, or to postpone his time of payment, while expressly reserving rights against others. Subsection (2), which is new, states the generally accepted rule as to the effect of such an express reservation of rights. [Comment 4 was amended in 1966].

5.   Paragraph (b) of subsection (1) is new. The suretyship defense stated has been generally recognized as available to indorsers or accommodation parties. As to when a holder's actions in dealing with collateral may be "unjustifiable", the section on rights and duties with respect to collateral in the possession of a secured party (Section 9–207) should be consulted.

Cross Reference:

Point 5: Section 9–207.

Definitional Cross References:

"Agreement". Section 1–201.
"Holder". Section 1–201.
"Instrument". Section 3–102.
"Notice of dishonor". Section 3–508.
"Party". Section 1–201.
"Person". Section 1–201.
"Rights". Section 1–201.

PART 7

ADVICE OF INTERNATIONAL SIGHT DRAFT

§ 3–701.   Letter of Advice of International Sight Draft.

(1)   A "letter of advice" is a drawer's communication to the drawee that a described draft has been drawn.

(2)   Unless otherwise agreed when a bank receives from another bank a letter of advice of an international sight draft the drawee bank may immediately debit the drawer's account and stop the running of interest pro tanto. Such a debit and any resulting credit to any account covering outstanding drafts leaves in the drawer full power to stop payment or otherwise dispose of the amount and creates no trust or interest in favor of the holder.

(3)   Unless otherwise agreed and except where a draft is drawn under a credit issued by the drawee, the drawee of an international sight draft owes the drawer no duty to pay an unadvised draft but if it does so and the draft is genuine, may appropriately debit the drawer's account.

Official Comment

Prior Uniform Statutory Provision: None.

Purposes: To recognize and clarify, in law, certain established practices of international banking.

1.   Checks drawn by one international bank on the account it carries (in a currency foreign to itself) in another international bank are still handled under practices which reflect older conditions, but which have a real, continuing reason in the typical, European rule that a bank paying a check in good faith and in ordinary course can charge its depositor's account notwithstanding forgery of a necessary indorsement. To decrease the risk that forgery will prove successful, the practice is to send a letter of advice that a draft has been drawn and will be forthcoming. Subsection 3 recognizes that a drawer who sends no such letter forfeits any rights for improper dishonor, while still permitting the drawee to protect his delinquent drawer's credit.

2.   Subsection (2) clears up for American courts, the meaning of another international practice: that of charging the drawer's account on receipt of the letter of advice. This practice involves no conception of trust or the like and the rule of Section 3–409(1) (Draft not an assignment) still applies. The debit has to do with the payment of interest only. The section recognizes the fact.

Cross Reference:

Point 2: Section 3–409(1).

Definitional Cross References:

"Account". Section 4–104.
"Bank". Section 1–201.
"Credit". Section 5–103.
"Draft". Section 3–104.
"Genuine". Section 1–201.
"Holder". Section 1–201.

PART 8

MISCELLANEOUS

§ 3–801.   Drafts in a Set.

(1)   Where a draft is drawn in a set of parts, each of which is numbered and expressed to be an order only if no other part has been honored, the whole of the parts constitutes one draft but a taker of any part may become a holder in due course of the draft.

(2)   Any person who negotiates, indorses or accepts a single part of a draft drawn in a set thereby becomes liable to any holder in due course of that part as if it were the whole set, but as between different holders in due course to whom different parts have been negotiated the holder whose title first accrues has all rights to the draft and its proceeds.

(3)   As against the drawee the first presented part of a draft drawn in a set is the part entitled to payment, or if a time draft to acceptance and payment. Acceptance of any subsequently presented part renders the drawee liable thereon under subsection (2). With respect both to a holder and to the drawer payment of a subsequently presented part of a draft payable at sight has the same effect as payment of a check notwithstanding an effective stop order (Section 4–407).

(4)   Except as otherwise provided in this section, where any part of a draft in a set is discharged by payment or otherwise the whole draft is discharged.

Official Comment

Prior Uniform Statutory Provision: Sections 178–183, Uniform Negotiable Instruments Law.

Changes: Combined and reworded.

Purposes of Changes:

The revised language makes no important change in substance, and is intended only as a clarification and supplementation of the original sections:

1.   Drafts in a set customarily contain such language as "Pay _____ this first of exchange (second unpaid)," with equivalent language in the second part. Today a part also commonly bears conspicuous indication of its number. At least the first factor is necessary to notify the holder of his rights, and is therefore necessary in order to make this section apply. Subsection (1) so provides, thus stating in the statute a matter left previously to a commercial practice long uniform but expensive to establish in court.

2.   The final sentence of subsection (3) is new. Payment of the part of the draft subsequently presented is improper and the drawee may not charge it to the account of the drawer, but some one has probably been unjustly enriched on the total transaction, at the expense of the drawee. So the drawee is like a bank which has paid a check over an effective stop payment order, and is subrogated as provided in that situation. Section 4–407.

3.   A statement in a draft drawn in a set of parts to the effect that the order is effective only if no other part has been honored does not render the draft nonnegotiable as conditional. See Section 3–112(1)(g).

Cross References:

> Point 2: Section 4–407.
>
> Point 3: Section 3–112.

Definitional Cross References:

> "Acceptance". Section 3–410.
>
> "Check". Section 3–104.
>
> "Draft". Section 3–104.
>
> "Holder". Section 1–201.
>
> "Holder in due course". Section 3–302.
>
> "Honor". Section 1–201.
>
> "Person". Section 1–201.
>
> "Rights". Section 1–201.

§ 3–802.   Effect of Instrument on Obligation for Which It Is Given.

(1)   Unless otherwise agreed where an instrument is taken for an underlying obligation

(a)   the obligation is pro tanto discharged if a bank is drawer, maker or acceptor of the instrument and there is no recourse on the instrument against the underlying obligor; and

(b)   in any other case the obligation is suspended pro tanto until the instrument is due or if it is payable on demand until its presentment. If the instrument is dishonored action may be maintained on either the instrument or the obligation; discharge of the underlying obligor on the instrument also discharges him on the obligation.

(2)   The taking in good faith of a check which is not post-dated does not of itself so extend the time on the original obligation as to discharge a surety.

Official Comment

Prior Uniform Statutory Provision: None.

Purposes:

1.   The section is new. It is intended to settle conflicts as to the effect of an instrument as payment of the obligation for which it is given.

2.   Where a holder procures certification of a check the drawer is discharged under Section 3–411 on check certification. Thereafter the original obligation is regarded as paid, and the holder must look to the certifying bank. The circumstances may indicate a similar intent in other transactions, and the question may be one of fact for the jury. Subsection (1)(a) states a rule discharging the obligation pro tanto when the instrument taken carries the obligation of a bank as drawer, maker or acceptor and there is no recourse on the instrument against the underlying obligor.

3.   It is commonly said that a check or other negotiable instrument is "conditional payment." By this it is normally meant that taking the instrument is a surrender of the right to sue on the obligation until the instrument is due, but if the instrument is not paid on due presentment the right to sue on the obligation is "revived."

Subsection (1)(b) states this result in terms of suspension of the obligation, which is intended to include suspension of the running of the statute of limitations. On dishonor of the instrument the holder is given his option to sue either on the instrument or on the underlying obligation. If, however, the original obligor has been discharged on the instrument (see Section 3–601) he is also discharged on the original obligation.

4. Subsection (2) is intended to remove any implication that a check given in payment of an obligation discharges a surety. The check is taken as a means of immediate payment; the thirty day period for presentment specified in Section 3–503 does not affect the surety's liability.

Cross References:

> Point 2: Sections 1–201, 3–411 and 3–601.
> Point 4: Section 3–503.

Definitional Cross References:

> "Action". Section 1–201.
> "Bank". Section 1–201.
> "Check". Section 3–104.
> "Dishonor". Section 3–507.
> "Good faith". Section 1–201.
> "Instrument". Section 3–102.
> "On demand". Section 3–108.
> "Presentment". Section 3–504.

§ 3–803. Notice to Third Party.

Where a defendant is sued for breach of an obligation for which a third person is answerable over under this Article he may give the third person written notice of the litigation, and the person notified may then give similar notice to any other person who is answerable over to him under this Article. If the notice states that the person notified may come in and defend and that if the person notified does not do so he will in any action against him by the person giving the notice be bound by any determination of fact common to the two litigations, then unless after seasonable receipt of the notice the person notified does come in and defend he is so bound.

Official Comment

Prior Uniform Statutory Provisions: None.

Purposes:

The section is new. It is intended to supplement, not to displace existing procedures for interpleader or joinder of parties.

The section conforms to the analogous provision in Section 2–607. It extends to such liabilities as those arising from forged indorsements even though not "on the instrument," and is intended to make it clear that the notification is not effective until received. In Hartford Accident & Indemnity Co. v. First Nat. Bank & Trust Co., 281 N.Y. 162, 22 N.E.2d 324, 123 A.L.R. 1149 (1939), the common-law doctrine of "vouching in" was held inapplicable where the party notified had no direct liability to the party giving the notice. In that case the drawer of a check, sued by the payee whose indorsement had been forged, gave notice to a collecting bank. In a second action the drawee was held liable to the drawer; but in an action by the drawee for judgment over against the collecting bank the determinations of fact in the first action were held not conclusive. This section does not disturb this result; the section is limited to cases where the person notified is "answerable over" to the person giving the notice.

Cross Reference:

> Section 2–607.

Definitional Cross References:

> "Action". Section 1–201.
> "Defendant". Section 1–201.

"Instrument". Section 3–102.
"Notifies". Section 1–201.
"Person". Section 1–201.
"Right". Section 1–201.
"Seasonably". Section 1–204.
"Written". Section 1–201.

§ 3–804.   Lost, Destroyed or Stolen Instruments.

The owner of an instrument which is lost, whether by destruction, theft or otherwise, may maintain an action in his own name and recover from any party liable thereon upon due proof of his ownership, the facts which prevent his production of the instrument and its terms. The court may require security indemnifying the defendant against loss by reason of further claims on the instrument.

Official Comment

Prior Uniform Statutory Provision: None.

Purposes:

This section is new. It is intended to provide a method of recovery on instruments which are lost, destroyed or stolen. The plaintiff who claims to be the owner of such an instrument is not a holder as that term is defined in this Act, since he is not in possession of the paper, and he does not have the holder's prima facie right to recover under the section on the burden of establishing signatures. He must prove his case. He must establish the terms of the instrument and his ownership, and must account for its absence.

If the claimant testifies falsely, or if the instrument subsequently turns up in the hands of a holder in due course, the obligor may be subjected to double liability. The court is therefore authorized to require security indemnifying the obligor against loss by reason of such possibilities. There may be cases in which so much time has elapsed, or there is so little possible doubt as to the destruction of the instrument and its ownership that there is no good reason to require the security. The requirement is therefore not an absolute one, and the matter is left to the discretion of the court.

Cross References:

Sections 1–201 and 3–307.

Definitional Cross References:

"Action". Section 1–201.
"Defendant". Section 1–201.
"Instrument". Section 3–102.
"Party". Section 1–201.
"Term". Section 1–201.

§ 3–805.   Instruments Not Payable to Order or to Bearer.

This Article applies to any instrument whose terms do not preclude transfer and which is otherwise negotiable within this Article but which is not payable to order or to bearer, except that there can be no holder in due course of such an instrument.

Official Comment

Prior Uniform Statutory Provision: None.

Purposes:

This section covers the "non-negotiable instrument." As it has been used by most courts, this term has been a technical one of art. It does not refer to a writing, such as a note containing an express condition, which is not negotiable and is entirely outside of the scope of this Article and to be treated as a simple contract. It refers to a particular type of instrument which meets all requirements as to form of a negotiable instrument except that it is not payable to order or to bearer. The typical example is the check reading merely "Pay John Doe."

Such a check is not a negotiable instrument under this Article. At the same time it is still a check, a mercantile specialty which differs in many respects from a simple contract. Commercial and banking practice treats it as a check, and a long line of decisions before and after the original Act have made it clear that it is subject to the law merchant as distinguished from ordinary contract law. Although the Negotiable Instruments Law has been held by its terms not to apply to such "non-negotiable instruments" it has been recognized as a codification and restatement of the law merchant, and has in fact been applied to them by analogy.

Thus the holder of the check reading "Pay A" establishes his case by production of the instrument and proof of signatures; and the burden of proving want of consideration or any other defense is upon the obligor. Such a check passes by indorsement and delivery without words of assignment, and the indorser undertakes greater liabilities than those of an assignor. This section resolves a conflict in the decisions as to the extent of that undertaking by providing in effect that the indorser of such an instrument is not distinguished from any indorser of a negotiable instrument. The indorser is entitled to presentment, notice of dishonor and protest, and the procedure and liabilities in bank collection are the same. The rules as to alteration, the filling of blanks, accommodation parties, the liability of signing agents, discharge, and the like are those applied to negotiable instruments.

In short, the "non-negotiable instrument" is treated as a negotiable instrument, so far as its form permits. Since it lacks words of negotiability there can be no holder in due course of such an instrument, and any provision of any section of this Article peculiar to a holder in due course cannot apply to it. With this exception, such instruments are covered by all sections of this Article.

Cross Reference:

Section 3–104.

Definitional Cross References:

"Bearer". Section 1–201.
"Holder in due course". Section 3–302.
"Instrument". Section 3–102.
"Term". Section 1–201.

ARTICLE 4

BANK DEPOSITS AND COLLECTIONS

(Official Comments omitted)

PART 1
GENERAL PROVISIONS AND DEFINITIONS

§ 4–101.   Short Title.

This Article shall be known and may be cited as Uniform Commercial Code—Bank Deposits and Collections.

§ 4–102.   Applicability.

(1)   To the extent that items within this Article are also within the scope of Articles 3 and 8, they are subject to the provisions of those Articles. In the event of conflict the provisions of this Article govern those of Article 3 but the provisions of Article 8 govern those of this Article.

(2)   The liability of a bank for action or non-action with respect to any item handled by it for purposes of presentment, payment or collection is governed by the law of the place where the bank is located. In the case of action or non-action by or at a branch or separate office of a bank, its liability is governed by the law of the place where the branch or separate office is located.

§ 4–103.   Variation by Agreement; Measure of Damages; Certain Action Constituting Ordinary Care.

(1)   The effect of the provisions of this Article may be varied by agreement except that no agreement can disclaim a bank's responsibility for its own lack of good faith or failure to exercise ordinary care or can limit the measure of damages for such lack or failure; but the parties may by agreement determine the standards by which such responsibility is to be measured if such standards are not manifestly unreasonable.

(2)   Federal Reserve regulations and operating letters, clearing house rules, and the like, have the effect of agreements under subsection (1), whether or not specifically assented to by all parties interested in items handled.

(3)   Action or non-action approved by this Article or pursuant to Federal Reserve regulations or operating letters constitutes the exercise of ordinary care and, in the absence of special instructions, action or non-action consistent with clearing house rules and the like or with a general banking usage not disapproved by this Article, prima facie constitutes the exercise of ordinary care.

(4)   The specification or approval of certain procedures by this Article does not constitute disapproval of other procedures which may be reasonable under the circumstances.

(5)   The measure of damages for failure to exercise ordinary care in handling an item is the amount of the item reduced by an amount which could not have been realized by the use of ordinary care, and where there is bad faith it includes other damages, if any, suffered by the party as a proximate consequence.

§ 4–104.   Definitions and Index of Definitions.

(1)   In this Article unless the context otherwise requires

(a) "Account" means any account with a bank and includes a checking, time, interest or savings account;

(b) "Afternoon" means the period of a day between noon and midnight;

(c) "Banking day" means that part of any day on which a bank is open to the public for carrying on substantially all of its banking functions;

(d) "Clearing house" means any association of banks or other payors regularly clearing items;

(e) "Customer" means any person having an account with a bank or for whom a bank has agreed to collect items and includes a bank carrying an account with another bank;

(f) "Documentary draft" means any negotiable or non-negotiable draft with accompanying documents, securities or other papers to be delivered against honor of the draft;

(g) "Item" means any instrument for the payment of money even though it is not negotiable but does not include money;

(h) "Midnight deadline" with respect to a bank is midnight on its next banking day following the banking day on which it receives the relevant item or notice or from which the time for taking action commences to run, whichever is later;

(i) "Properly payable" includes the availability of funds for payment at the time of decision to pay or dishonor;

(j) "Settle" means to pay in cash, by clearing house settlement, in a charge or credit or by remittance, or otherwise as instructed. A settlement may be either provisional or final;

(k) "Suspends payments" with respect to a bank means that it has been closed by order of the supervisory authorities, that a public officer has been appointed to take it over or that it ceases or refuses to make payments in the ordinary course of business.

(2) Other definitions applying to this Article and the sections in which they appear are:

"Collecting bank"	Section 4–105.
"Depositary bank"	Section 4–105.
"Intermediary bank"	Section 4–105.
"Payor bank"	Section 4–105.
"Presenting bank"	Section 4–105.
"Remitting bank"	Section 4–105.

(3) The following definitions in other Articles apply to this Article:

"Acceptance"	Section 3–410.
"Certificate of deposit"	Section 3–104.
"Certification"	Section 3–411.
"Check"	Section 3–104.
"Draft"	Section 3–104.
"Holder in due course"	Section 3–302.
"Notice of dishonor"	Section 3–508.
"Presentment"	Section 3–504.
"Protest"	Section 3–509.
"Secondary party"	Section 3–102.

(4) In addition Article 1 contains general definitions and principles of construction and interpretation applicable throughout this Article.

§ 4–105. "Depositary Bank"; "Intermediary Bank"; "Collecting Bank"; "Payor Bank"; "Presenting Bank"; "Remitting Bank".

In this Article unless the context otherwise requires:

(a)   "Depositary bank" means the first bank to which an item is transferred for collection even though it is also the payor bank;

(b)   "Payor bank" means a bank by which an item is payable as drawn or accepted;

(c)   "Intermediary bank" means any bank to which an item is transferred in course of collection except the depositary or payor bank;

(d)   "Collecting bank" means any bank handling the item for collection except the payor bank;

(e)   "Presenting bank" means any bank presenting an item except a payor bank;

(f)   "Remitting bank" means any payor or intermediary bank remitting for an item.

§ 4–106.   Separate Office of a Bank.

A branch or separate office of a bank [maintaining its own deposit ledgers] is a separate bank for the purpose of computing the time within which and determining the place at or to which action may be taken or notices or orders shall be given under this Article and under Article 3.

As amended in 1962.

Note: *The brackets are to make it optional with the several states whether to require a branch to maintain its own deposit ledgers in order to be considered to be a separate bank for certain purposes under Article 4. In some states "maintaining its own deposit ledgers" is a satisfactory test. In others branch banking practices are such that this test would not be suitable.*

§ 4–107.   Time of Receipt of Items.

(1)   For the purpose of allowing time to process items, prove balances and make the necessary entries on its books to determine its position for the day, a bank may fix an afternoon hour of 2 P.M. or later as a cut-off hour for the handling of money and items and the making of entries on its books.

(2)   Any item or deposit of money received on any day after a cut-off hour so fixed or after the close of the banking day may be treated as being received at the opening of the next banking day.

§ 4–108.   Delays.

(1)   Unless otherwise instructed, a collecting bank in a good faith effort to secure payment may, in the case of specific items and with or without the approval of any person involved, waive, modify or extend time limits imposed or permitted by this Act for a period not in excess of an additional banking day without discharge of secondary parties and without liability to its transferor or any prior party.

(2)   Delay by a collecting bank or payor bank beyond time limits prescribed or permitted by this Act or by instructions is excused if caused by interruption of communication facilities, suspension of payments by another bank, war, emergency conditions or other circumstances beyond the control of the bank provided it exercises such diligence as the circumstances require.

§ 4–109.   Process of Posting.

The "process of posting" means the usual procedure followed by a payor bank in determining to pay an item and in recording the payment including one or more of the following or other steps as determined by the bank:

(a)   verification of any signature;

(b)   ascertaining that sufficient funds are available;

(c)   affixing a "paid" or other stamp;

(d)   entering a charge or entry to a customer's account;

(e)   correcting or reversing an entry or erroneous action with respect to the item.

Added in 1962.

PART 2

COLLECTION OF ITEMS: DEPOSITARY AND COLLECTING BANKS

§ 4–201. **Presumption and Duration of Agency Status of Collecting Banks and Provisional Status of Credits; Applicability of Article; Item Indorsed "Pay Any Bank".**

(1) Unless a contrary intent clearly appears and prior to the time that a settlement given by a collecting bank for an item is or becomes final (subsection (3) of Section 4–211 and Sections 4–212 and 4–213) the bank is an agent or sub-agent of the owner of the item and any settlement given for the item is provisional. This provision applies regardless of the form of indorsement or lack of indorsement and even though credit given for the item is subject to immediate withdrawal as of right or is in fact withdrawn; but the continuance of ownership of an item by its owner and any rights of the owner to proceeds of the item are subject to rights of a collecting bank such as those resulting from outstanding advances on the item and valid rights of setoff. When an item is handled by banks for purposes of presentment, payment and collection, the relevant provisions of this Article apply even though action of parties clearly establishes that a particular bank has purchased the item and is the owner of it.

(2) After an item has been indorsed with the words "pay any bank" or the like, only a bank may acquire the rights of a holder

   (a) until the item has been returned to the customer initiating collection; or

   (b) until the item has been specially indorsed by a bank to a person who is not a bank.

§ 4–202. **Responsibility for Collection; When Action Seasonable.**

(1) A collecting bank must use ordinary care in

   (a) presenting an item or sending it for presentment; and

   (b) sending notice of dishonor or non-payment or returning an item other than a documentary draft to the bank's transferor [or directly to the depositary bank under subsection (2) of Section 4–212] (*see note to Section 4–212*) after learning that the item has not been paid or accepted, as the case may be; and

   (c) settling for an item when the bank receives final settlement; and

   (d) making or providing for any necessary protest; and

   (e) notifying its transferor of any loss or delay in transit within a reasonable time after discovery thereof.

(2) A collecting bank taking proper action before its midnight deadline following receipt of an item, notice or payment acts seasonably; taking proper action within a reasonably longer time may be seasonable but the bank has the burden of so establishing.

(3) Subject to subsection (1)(a), a bank is not liable for the insolvency, neglect, misconduct, mistake or default of another bank or person or for loss or destruction of an item in transit or in the possession of others.

§ 4–203. **Effect of Instructions.**

Subject to the provisions of Article 3 concerning conversion of instruments (Section 3–419) and the provisions of both Article 3 and this Article concerning restrictive indorsements only a collecting bank's transferor can give instructions which affect the bank or constitute notice to it and a collecting bank is not liable to prior parties for any action taken pursuant to such instructions or in accordance with any agreement with its transferor.

§ 4–204.   Methods of Sending and Presenting; Sending Direct to Payor Bank.

(1)   A collecting bank must send items by reasonably prompt method taking into consideration any relevant instructions, the nature of the item, the number of such items on hand, and the cost of collection involved and the method generally used by it or others to present such items.

(2)   A collecting bank may send

(a)   any item direct to the payor bank;

(b)   any item to any non-bank payor if authorized by its transferor; and

(c)   any item other than documentary drafts to any non-bank payor, if authorized by Federal Reserve regulation or operating letter, clearing house rule or the like.

(3)   Presentment may be made by a presenting bank at a place where the payor bank has requested that presentment be made.

As amended in 1962.

§ 4–205.   Supplying Missing Indorsement; No Notice from Prior Indorsement.

(1)   A depositary bank which has taken an item for collection may supply any indorsement of the customer which is necessary to title unless the item contains the words "payee's indorsement required" or the like. In the absence of such a requirement a statement placed on the item by the depositary bank to the effect that the item was deposited by a customer or credited to his account is effective as the customer's indorsement.

(2)   An intermediary bank, or payor bank which is not a depositary bank, is neither given notice nor otherwise affected by a restrictive indorsement of any person except the bank's immediate transferor.

§ 4–206.   Transfer Between Banks.

Any agreed method which identifies the transferor bank is sufficient for the item's further transfer to another bank.

§ 4–207.   Warranties of Customer and Collecting Bank on Transfer or Presentment of Items; Time for Claims.

(1)   Each customer or collecting bank who obtains payment or acceptance of an item and each prior customer and collecting bank warrants to the payor bank or other payor who in good faith pays or accepts the item that

(a)   he has a good title to the item or is authorized to obtain payment or acceptance on behalf of one who has a good title; and

(b)   he has no knowledge that the signature of the maker or drawer is unauthorized, except that this warranty is not given by any customer or collecting bank that is a holder in due course and acts in good faith

(i)   to a maker with respect to the maker's own signature; or

(ii)   to a drawer with respect to the drawer's own signature, whether or not the drawer is also the drawee; or

(iii)   to an acceptor of an item if the holder in due course took the item after the acceptance or obtained the acceptance without knowledge that the drawer's signature was unauthorized; and

    (c)   the item has not been materially altered, except that this warranty is not given by any customer or collecting bank that is a holder in due course and acts in good faith

        (i)   to the maker of a note; or

        (ii)   to the drawer of a draft whether or not the drawer is also the drawee; or

        (iii)   to the acceptor of an item with respect to an alteration made prior to the acceptance if the holder in due course took the item after the acceptance, even though the acceptance provided "payable as originally drawn" or equivalent terms; or

        (iv)   to the acceptor of an item with respect to an alteration made after the acceptance.

    (2)   Each customer and collecting bank who transfers an item and receives a settlement or other consideration for it warrants to his transferee and to any subsequent collecting bank who takes the item in good faith that

    (a)   he has a good title to the item or is authorized to obtain payment or acceptance on behalf of one who has a good title and the transfer is otherwise rightful; and

    (b)   all signatures are genuine or authorized; and

    (c)   the item has not been materially altered; and

    (d)   no defense of any party is good against him; and

    (e)   he has no knowledge of any insolvency proceeding instituted with respect to the maker or acceptor or the drawer of an unaccepted item.

In addition each customer and collecting bank so transferring an item and receiving a settlement or other consideration engages that upon dishonor and any necessary notice of dishonor and protest he will take up the item.

    (3)   The warranties and the engagement to honor set forth in the two preceding subsections arise notwithstanding the absence of indorsement or words of guaranty or warranty in the transfer or presentment and a collecting bank remains liable for their breach despite remittance to its transferor. Damages for breach of such warranties or engagement to honor shall not exceed the consideration received by the customer or collecting bank responsible plus finance charges and expenses related to the item, if any.

    (4)   Unless a claim for breach of warranty under this section is made within a reasonable time after the person claiming learns of the breach, the person liable is discharged to the extent of any loss caused by the delay in making claim.

§ 4–208.   Security Interest of Collecting Bank in Items, Accompanying Documents and Proceeds.

    (1)   A bank has a security interest in an item and any accompanying documents or the proceeds of either

    (a)   in case of an item deposited in an account to the extent to which credit given for the item has been withdrawn or applied;

    (b)   in case of an item for which it has given credit available for withdrawal as of right, to the extent of the credit given whether or not the credit is drawn upon and whether or not there is a right of charge-back; or

    (c)   if it makes an advance on or against the item.

    (2)   When credit which has been given for several items received at one time or pursuant to a single agreement is withdrawn or applied in part the security interest remains upon all the items, any accompanying documents or the proceeds of either. For the purpose of this section, credits first given are first withdrawn.

    (3)   Receipt by a collecting bank of a final settlement for an item is a realization on its security interest in the item, accompanying documents and proceeds. To the extent and so long as the bank does not receive

final settlement for the item or give up possession of the item or accompanying documents for purposes other than collection, the security interest continues and is subject to the provisions of Article 9 except that

(a)   no security agreement is necessary to make the security interest enforceable (subsection (1)(a) of Section 9–203); and

(b)   no filing is required to perfect the security interest; and

(c)   the security interest has priority over conflicting perfected security interests in the item, accompanying documents or proceeds.

§ 4–209.   When Bank Gives Value for Purposes of Holder in Due Course.

For purposes of determining its status as a holder in due course, the bank has given value to the extent that it has a security interest in an item provided that the bank otherwise complies with the requirements of Section 3–302 on what constitutes a holder in due course.

§ 4–210.   Presentment by Notice of Item Not Payable by, Through or at a Bank; Liability of Secondary Parties.

(1)   Unless otherwise instructed, a collecting bank may present an item not payable by, through or at a bank by sending to the party to accept or pay a written notice that the bank holds the item for acceptance or payment. The notice must be sent in time to be received on or before the day when presentment is due and the bank must meet any requirement of the party to accept or pay under Section 3–505 by the close of the bank's next banking day after it knows of the requirement.

(2)   Where presentment is made by notice and neither honor nor request for compliance with a requirement under Section 3–505 is received by the close of business on the day after maturity or in the case of demand items by the close of business on the third banking day after notice was sent, the presenting bank may treat the item as dishonored and charge any secondary party by sending him notice of the facts.

§ 4–211.   Media of Remittance; Provisional and Final Settlement in Remittance Cases.

(1)   A collecting bank may take in settlement of an item

(a)   a check of the remitting bank or of another bank on any bank except the remitting bank; or

(b)   a cashier's check or similar primary obligation of a remitting bank which is a member of or clears through a member of the same clearing house or group as the collecting bank; or

(c)   appropriate authority to charge an account of the remitting bank or of another bank with the collecting bank; or

(d)   if the item is drawn upon or payable by a person other than a bank, a cashier's check, certified check or other bank check or obligation.

(2)   If before its midnight deadline the collecting bank properly dishonors a remittance check or authorization to charge on itself or presents or forwards for collection a remittance instrument of or on another bank which is of a kind approved by subsection (1) or has not been authorized by it, the collecting bank is not liable to prior parties in the event of the dishonor of such check, instrument or authorization.

(3)   A settlement for an item by means of a remittance instrument or authorization to charge is or becomes a final settlement as to both the person making and the person receiving the settlement

(a)   if the remittance instrument or authorization to charge is of a kind approved by subsection (1) or has not been authorized by the person receiving the settlement and in either case the person receiving the settlement acts seasonably before its midnight deadline in presenting, forwarding for collection or paying the instrument or authorization,—at the time the remittance instrument or authorization is finally paid by the payor by which it is payable;

(b)   if the person receiving the settlement has authorized remittance by a non-bank check or obligation or by a cashier's check or similar primary obligation of or a check upon the payor or other remitting bank which is not of a kind approved by subsection (1)(b),—at the time of the receipt of such remittance check or obligation; or

(c) if in a case not covered by sub-paragraphs (a) or (b) the person receiving the settlement fails to seasonably present, forward for collection, pay or return a remittance instrument or authorization to it to charge before its midnight deadline,—at such midnight deadline.

§ 4–212. Right of Charge-Back or Refund.

(1) If a collecting bank has made provisional settlement with its customer for an item and itself fails by reason of dishonor, suspension of payments by a bank or otherwise to receive a settlement for the item which is or becomes final, the bank may revoke the settlement given by it, charge back the amount of any credit given for the item to its customer's account or obtain refund from its customer whether or not it is able to return the items if by its midnight deadline or within a longer reasonable time after it learns the facts it returns the item or sends notification of the facts. These rights to revoke, charge-back and obtain refund terminate if and when a settlement for the item received by the bank is or becomes final (subsection (3) of Section 4–211 and subsections (2) and (3) of Section 4–213).

[(2) Within the time and manner prescribed by this section and Section 4–301, an intermediary or payor bank, as the case may be, may return an unpaid item directly to the depositary bank and may send for collection a draft on the depositary bank and obtain reimbursement. In such case, if the depositary bank has received provisional settlement for the item, it must reimburse the bank drawing the draft and any provisional credits for the item between banks shall become and remain final.]

Note: *Direct returns is recognized as an innovation that is not yet established bank practice, and therefore, Paragraph 2 has been bracketed. Some lawyers have doubts whether it should be included in legislation or left to development by agreement.*

(3) A depositary bank which is also the payor may charge-back the amount of an item to its customer's account or obtain refund in accordance with the section governing return of an item received by a payor bank for credit on its books. (Section 4–301).

(4) The right to charge-back is not affected by

(a) prior use of the credit given for the item; or

(b) failure by any bank to exercise ordinary care with respect to the item but any bank so failing remains liable.

(5) A failure to charge-back or claim refund does not affect other rights of the bank against the customer or any other party.

(6) If credit is given in dollars as the equivalent of the value of an item payable in a foreign currency the dollar amount of any charge-back or refund shall be calculated on the basis of the buying sight rate for the foreign currency prevailing on the day when the person entitled to the charge-back or refund learns that it will not receive payment in ordinary course.

§ 4–213. Final Payment of Item by Payor Bank; When Provisional Debits and Credits Become Final; When Certain Credits Become Available for Withdrawal.

(1) An item is finally paid by a payor bank when the bank has done any of the following, whichever happens first:

(a) paid the item in cash; or

(b) settled for the item without reserving a right to revoke the settlement and without having such right under statute, clearing house rule or agreement; or

(c) completed the process of posting the item to the indicated account of the drawer, maker or other person to be charged therewith; or

(d)   made a provisional settlement for the item and failed to revoke the settlement in the time and manner permitted by statute, clearing house rule or agreement.

Upon a final payment under subparagraphs (b), (c) or (d) the payor bank shall be accountable for the amount of the item.

(2)   If provisional settlement for an item between the presenting and payor banks is made through a clearing house or by debits or credits in an account between them, then to the extent that provisional debits or credits for the item are entered in accounts between the presenting and payor banks or between the presenting and successive prior collecting banks seriatim, they become final upon final payment of the item by the payor bank.

(3)   If a collecting bank receives a settlement for an item which is or becomes final (subsection (3) of Section 4–211, subsection (2) of Section 4–213) the bank is accountable to its customer for the amount of the item and any provisional credit given for the item in an account with its customer becomes final.

(4)   Subject to any right of the bank to apply the credit to an obligation of the customer, credit given by a bank for an item in an account with its customer becomes available for withdrawal as of right

(a)   in any case where the bank has received a provisional settlement for the item,—when such settlement becomes final and the bank has had a reasonable time to learn that the settlement is final;

(b)   in any case where the bank is both a depositary bank and a payor bank and the item is finally paid,—at the opening of the bank's second banking day following receipt of the item.

(5)   A deposit of money in a bank is final when made but, subject to any right of the bank to apply the deposit to an obligation of the customer, the deposit becomes available for withdrawal as of right at the opening of the bank's next banking day following receipt of the deposit.

§ 4–214.   Insolvency and Preference.

(1)   Any item in or coming into the possession of a payor or collecting bank which suspends payment and which item is not finally paid shall be returned by the receiver, trustee or agent in charge of the closed bank to the presenting bank or the closed bank's customer.

(2)   If a payor bank finally pays an item and suspends payments without making a settlement for the item with its customer or the presenting bank which settlement is or becomes final, the owner of the item has a preferred claim against the payor bank.

(3)   If a payor bank gives or a collecting bank gives or receives a provisional settlement for an item and thereafter suspends payments, the suspension does not prevent or interfere with the settlement becoming final if such finality occurs automatically upon the lapse of certain time or the happening of certain events (subsection (3) of Section 4–211, subsections (1)(d), (2) and (3) of Section 4–213).

(4)   If a collecting bank receives from subsequent parties settlement for an item which settlement is or becomes final and suspends payments without making a settlement for the item with its customer which is or becomes final, the owner of the item has a preferred claim against such collecting bank.

PART 3

COLLECTION OF ITEMS: PAYOR BANKS

§ 4–301.   Deferred Posting; Recovery of Payment by Return of Items; Time of Dishonor.

(1)   Where an authorized settlement for a demand item (other than a documentary draft) received by a payor bank otherwise than for immediate payment over the counter has been made before midnight of the banking day of receipt the payor bank may revoke the settlement and recover any payment if before it has made final payment (subsection (1) of Section 4–213) and before its midnight deadline it

(a)   returns the item; or

(b)   sends written notice of dishonor or nonpayment if the item is held for protest or is otherwise unavailable for return.

(2)   If a demand item is received by a payor bank for credit on its books it may return such item or send notice of dishonor and may revoke any credit given or recover the amount thereof withdrawn by its customer, if it acts within the time limit and in the manner specified in the preceding subsection.

(3)   Unless previous notice of dishonor has been sent an item is dishonored at the time when for purposes of dishonor it is returned or notice sent in accordance with this section.

(4)   An item is returned:

(a)   as to an item received through a clearing house, when it is delivered to the presenting or last collecting bank or to the clearing house or is sent or delivered in accordance with its rules; or

(b)   in all other cases, when it is sent or delivered to the bank's customer or transferor or pursuant to his instructions.

§ 4–302.   Payor Bank's Responsibility for Late Return of Item.

In the absence of a valid defense such as breach of a presentment warranty (subsection (1) of Section 4–207), settlement effected or the like, if an item is presented on and received by a payor bank the bank is accountable for the amount of

(a)   a demand item other than a documentary draft whether properly payable or not if the bank, in any case where it is not also the depositary bank, retains the item beyond midnight of the banking day of receipt without settling for it or, regardless of whether it is also the depositary bank, does not pay or return the item or send notice of dishonor until after its midnight deadline; or

(b)   any other properly payable item unless within the time allowed for acceptance or payment of that item the bank either accepts or pays the item or returns it and accompanying documents.

§ 4–303.   When Items Subject to Notice, Stop-Order, Legal Process or Setoff; Order in Which Items May Be Charged or Certified.

(1)   Any knowledge, notice or stop-order received by, legal process served upon or setoff exercised by a payor bank, whether or not effective under other rules of law to terminate, suspend or modify the bank's right or duty to pay an item or to charge its customer's account for the item, comes too late to so terminate, suspend or modify such right or duty if the knowledge, notice, stop-order or legal process is received or served and a reasonable time for the bank to act thereon expires or the setoff is exercised after the bank has done any of the following:

(a)   accepted or certified the item;

(b)   paid the item in cash;

(c)   settled for the item without reserving a right to revoke the settlement and without having such right under statute, clearing house rule or agreement;

(d)   completed the process of posting the item to the indicated account of the drawer, maker or other person to be charged therewith or otherwise has evidenced by examination of such indicated account and by action its decision to pay the item; or

(e)   become accountable for the amount of the item under subsection (1)(d) of Section 4–213 and Section 4–302 dealing with the payor bank's responsibility for late return of items.

(2)   Subject to the provisions of subsection (1) items may be accepted, paid, certified or charged to the indicated account of its customer in any order convenient to the bank.

PART 4

RELATIONSHIP BETWEEN PAYOR BANK AND ITS CUSTOMER

§ 4–401. When Bank May Charge Customer's Account.

(1) As against its customer, a bank may charge against his account any item which is otherwise properly payable from that account even though the charge creates an overdraft.

(2) A bank which in good faith makes payment to a holder may charge the indicated account of its customer according to

(a) the original tenor of his altered item; or

(b) the tenor of his completed item, even though the bank knows the item has been completed unless the bank has notice that the completion was improper.

§ 4–402. Bank's Liability to Customer for Wrongful Dishonor.

A payor bank is liable to its customer for damages proximately caused by the wrongful dishonor of an item. When the dishonor occurs through mistake liability is limited to actual damages proved. If so proximately caused and proved damages may include damages for an arrest or prosecution of the customer or other consequential damages. Whether any consequential damages are proximately caused by the wrongful dishonor is a question of fact to be determined in each case.

§ 4–403. Customer's Right to Stop Payment; Burden of Proof of Loss.

(1) A customer may by order to his bank stop payment of any item payable for his account but the order must be received at such time and in such manner as to afford the bank a reasonable opportunity to act on it prior to any action by the bank with respect to the item described in Section 4–303.

(2) An oral order is binding upon the bank only for fourteen calendar days unless confirmed in writing within that period. A written order is effective for only six months unless renewed in writing.

(3) The burden of establishing the fact and amount of loss resulting from the payment of an item contrary to a binding stop payment order is on the customer.

§ 4–404. Bank Not Obligated to Pay Check More Than Six Months Old.

A bank is under no obligation to a customer having a checking account to pay a check, other than a certified check, which is presented more than six months after its date, but it may charge its customer's account for a payment made thereafter in good faith.

§ 4–405. Death or Incompetence of Customer.

(1) A payor or collecting bank's authority to accept, pay or collect an item or to account for proceeds of its collection if otherwise effective is not rendered ineffective by incompetence of a customer of either bank existing at the time the item is issued or its collection is undertaken if the bank does not know of an adjudication of incompetence. Neither death nor incompetence of a customer revokes such authority to accept, pay, collect or account until the bank knows of the fact of death or of an adjudication of incompetence and has reasonable opportunity to act on it.

(2) Even with knowledge a bank may for 10 days after the date of death pay or certify checks drawn on or prior to that date unless ordered to stop payment by a person claiming an interest in the account.

§4–406. Customer's Duty to Discover and Report Unauthorized Signature or Alteration.

(1) When a bank sends to its customer a statement of account accompanied by items paid in good faith in support of the debit entries or holds the statement and items pursuant to a request or instructions of its customer or otherwise in a reasonable manner makes the statement and items available to the customer, the customer must exercise reasonable care and promptness to examine the statement and items to discover his unauthorized signature or any alteration on an item and must notify the bank promptly after discovery thereof.

(2) If the bank establishes that the customer failed with respect to an item to comply with the duties imposed on the customer by subsection (1) the customer is precluded from asserting against the bank

    (a) his unauthorized signature or any alteration on the item if the bank also establishes that it suffered a loss by reason of such failure; and

    (b) an unauthorized signature or alteration by the same wrongdoer on any other item paid in good faith by the bank after the first item and statement was available to the customer for a reasonable period not exceeding fourteen calendar days and before the bank receives notification from the customer of any such unauthorized signature or alteration.

(3) The preclusion under subsection (2) does not apply if the customer establishes lack of ordinary care on the part of the bank in paying the item(s).

(4) Without regard to care or lack of care of either the customer or the bank a customer who does not within one year from the time the statement and items are made available to the customer (subsection (1)) discover and report his unauthorized signature or any alteration on the face or back of the item or does not within 3 years from that time discover and report any unauthorized indorsement is precluded from asserting against the bank such unauthorized signature or indorsement or such alteration.

(5) If under this section a payor bank has a valid defense against a claim of a customer upon or resulting from payment of an item and waives or fails upon request to assert the defense the bank may not assert against any collecting bank or other prior party presenting or transferring the item a claim based upon the unauthorized signature or alteration giving rise to the customer's claim.

§4–407. Payor Bank's Right to Subrogation on Improper Payment.

If a payor bank has paid an item over the stop payment order of the drawer or maker or otherwise under circumstances giving a basis for objection by the drawer or maker, to prevent unjust enrichment and only to the extent necessary to prevent loss to the bank by reason of its payment of the item, the payor bank shall be subrogated to the rights

    (a) of any holder in due course on the item against the drawer or maker; and

    (b) of the payee or any other holder of the item against the drawer or maker either on the item or under the transaction out of which the item arose; and

    (c) of the drawer or maker against the payee or any other holder of the item with respect to the transaction out of which the item arose.

PART 5

COLLECTION OF DOCUMENTARY DRAFTS

§4–501. Handling of Documentary Drafts; Duty to Send for Presentment and to Notify Customer of Dishonor.

A bank which takes a documentary draft for collection must present or send the draft and accompanying documents for presentment and upon learning that the draft has not been paid or accepted in due course must seasonably notify its customer of such fact even though it may have discounted or bought the draft or extended credit available for withdrawal as of right.

§ 4–502.   Presentment of "On Arrival" Drafts.

When a draft or the relevant instructions require presentment "on arrival", "when goods arrive" or the like, the collecting bank need not present until in its judgment a reasonable time for arrival of the goods has expired. Refusal to pay or accept because the goods have not arrived is not dishonor; the bank must notify its transferor of such refusal but need not present the draft again until it is instructed to do so or learns of the arrival of the goods.

§ 4–503.   Responsibility of Presenting Bank for Documents and Goods; Report of Reasons for Dishonor; Referee in Case of Need.

Unless otherwise instructed and except as provided in Article 5 a bank presenting a documentary draft

(a)   must deliver the documents to the drawee on acceptance of the draft if it is payable more than three days after presentment; otherwise, only on payment; and

(b)   upon dishonor, either in the case of presentment for acceptance or presentment for payment, may seek and follow instructions from any referee in case of need designated in the draft or if the presenting bank does not choose to utilize his services it must use diligence and good faith to ascertain the reason for dishonor, must notify its transferor of the dishonor and of the results of its effort to ascertain the reasons therefor and must request instructions.

But the presenting bank is under no obligation with respect to goods represented by the documents except to follow any reasonable instructions seasonably received; it has a right to reimbursement for any expense incurred in following instructions and to prepayment of or indemnity for such expenses.

§ 4–504.   Privilege of Presenting Bank to Deal With Goods; Security Interest for Expenses.

(1)   A presenting bank which, following the dishonor of a documentary draft, has seasonably requested instructions but does not receive them within a reasonable time may store, sell, or otherwise deal with the goods in any reasonable manner.

(2)   For its reasonable expenses incurred by action under subsection (1) the presenting bank has a lien upon the goods or their proceeds, which may be foreclosed in the same manner as an unpaid seller's lien.

APPENDIX C

2002 AMENDMENTS TO UCC ARTICLES 3 AND 4

In strikeout/underline format

DRAFTING COMMITTEE TO AMEND UNIFORM COMMERCIAL CODE ARTICLES 3 AND 4

Edwin E. Smith, Boston, Massachusetts, *Chair*
Michael M. Greenfield, St. Louis, Missouri, *The American Law Institute Representative*
Michael Houghton, Wilmington, Delaware, *Enactment Plan Coordinator*
H. Kathleen Patchel, Indianapolis, Indiana
Donald J. Rapson, Deal, New Jersey, *The American Law Institute Representative*
Carlyle C. Ring, Jr., Washington, DC
Paul M. Shupack, New York, New York, *The American Law Institute Representative*
Ronald Mann, Ann Arbor, Michigan, *Reporter*

EX OFFICIO

K. King Burnett, Salisbury, Maryland, *President*
Joseph P. Mazurek, Helena, Montana, *Division Chair*

AMERICAN BAR ASSOCIATION ADVISORS

Stephanie Heller, Brooklyn, New York, *ABA Advisor*
Michael A. Ferry, St. Louis, Missouri, *ABA Business Law Section Advisor*
Richard L. Field, Cliffside Park, New Jersey, *ABA Science and Technology Section Advisor*

EXECUTIVE DIRECTOR

William H. Henning, Columbia, Missouri, *Executive Director*
Fred H. Miller, Norman, Oklahoma, *Executive Director Emeritus*
William J. Pierce, Ann Arbor, Michigan, *Executive Director Emeritus*

PREFATORY NOTE

This project involves a small number of amendments to Articles 3 and 4 with respect to which there is a general consensus that the need for reform is plain and the opportunity for justifiable controversy small. The specific amendments cover the following topics.

1. <u>Transferring Lost Instruments.</u>—At least one case has held that the receiver of a failed bank cannot enforce an instrument transferred to it in the portfolio of a failed bank if the instrument was lost before the transfer. The result in that case poses a serious problem for the FDIC. An amendment to UCC § 3–309 calls for a contrary result, making it clear that the party seeking to enforce a lost instrument need not have been in possession of the instrument at the time that it was lost.

2. <u>Payment and Discharge.</u>—Amendments to UCC §§ 3–602 conform that provision to the rules for payment that appear in the *Restatement of Mortgages* and in the *Restatement of Contracts.*

3. <u>Telephonically Generated Checks.</u>—Several States have adopted non-uniform amendments dealing with the responsibility for unauthorized telephone-generated checks. The amendments include warranties that generally place the responsibility for such checks on depositary banks rather than payor banks. The warranties are limited to items that are drawn on a consumer account and do not bear a manual signature.

4. <u>Suretyship.</u>—Amendments to UCC §§ 3–419 and 3–605 generally conform those provisions to the rules in the *Restatement of Suretyship and Guaranty.*

5.   Electronic Communications.—Amendments to various provisions of Articles 3 and 4 implement the policy of the Uniform Electronic Transactions Act to remove unnecessary obstacles to electronic communications.

6.   Consumer Notes.—A provision analogous to UCC § 9–404(d) indicates that a note for which the Federal Trade Commission requires a notice to be included will be treated is if the notice had been included.

7.   United Nations Convention on International Bills of Exchange and International Promissory Notes.—The draft includes several comments indicating similarities and differences between Article 3 and the United Nations Convention, designed to facilitate implementation of the Convention if the United States ratifies that convention in the coming years.

_____

AMENDMENTS TO ARTICLE 3
NEGOTIABLE INSTRUMENTS

§ 3–102.   Subject Matter.

Official Comment
* * *

5.   In 1989 the United Nations Commission on International Trade Law completed a Convention on International Bills of Exchange and International Promissory Notes. If the United States becomes a party to this Convention, the Convention will preempt state law with respect to international bills and notes governed by the Convention. Thus, an international bill of exchange or promissory note that meets the definition of instrument in Section 3–104 will not be governed by Article 3 if it is governed by the Convention. That Convention applies only to bills and notes that indicate on their face that they involve cross-border transactions. It does not apply at all to checks. Convention Articles 1(3), 2(1), 2(2). Moreover, because it applies only if the bill or note specifically calls for application of the Convention, Convention Article 1, there is little chance that the Convention will apply accidentally to a transaction that the parties intended to be governed by this Article. *Amendments approved by the Permanent Editorial Board for Uniform Commercial Code November 2, 2002.*

§ 3–103.   Definitions.

(a)   In this Article:

(1)   "Acceptor" means a drawee who has accepted a draft.

(2)   "Consumer account" means an account established by an individual primarily for personal, family, or household purposes.

(3)   "Consumer transaction" means a transaction in which an individual incurs an obligation primarily for personal, family, or household purposes.

(4)   "Drawee" means a person ordered in a draft to make payment.

(3) (5)   "Drawer" means a person who signs or is identified in a draft as a person ordering payment.

(4) (6)   ["Good faith" means honesty in fact and the observance of reasonable commercial standards of fair dealing.]

(5) (7)   "Maker" means a person who signs or is identified in a note as a person undertaking to pay.

(6) (8)   "Order" means a written instruction to pay money signed by the person giving the instruction. The instruction may be addressed to any person, including the person giving the instruction, or to one or more persons jointly or in the alternative but not in succession. An authorization to pay is not an order unless the person authorized to pay is also instructed to pay.

~~(7)~~ (9) "Ordinary care" in the case of a person engaged in business means observance of reasonable commercial standards, prevailing in the area in which the person is located, with respect to the business in which the person is engaged. In the case of a bank that takes an instrument for processing for collection or payment by automated means, reasonable commercial standards do not require the bank to examine the instrument if the failure to examine does not violate the bank's prescribed procedures and the bank's procedures do not vary unreasonably from general banking usage not disapproved by this Article or Article 4.

~~(8)~~ (10) "Party" means a party to an instrument.

(11) "Principal obligor," with respect to an instrument, means the accommodated party or any other party to the instrument against whom a secondary obligor has recourse under this article.

~~(9)~~ (12) "Promise" means a written undertaking to pay money signed by the person undertaking to pay. An acknowledgment of an obligation by the obligor is not a promise unless the obligor also undertakes to pay the obligation.

~~(10)~~ (13) "Prove" with respect to a fact means to meet the burden of establishing the fact (Section 1–201(8)).

(14) ["Record" means information that is inscribed on a tangible medium or that is stored in an electronic or other medium and is retrievable in perceivable form.]

~~(11)~~ (15) "Remitter" means a person who purchases an instrument from its issuer if the instrument is payable to an identified person other than the purchaser.

(16) "Remotely-created consumer item" means an item drawn on a consumer account, which is not created by the payor bank and does not bear a handwritten signature purporting to be the signature of the drawer.

(17) "Secondary obligor," with respect to an instrument, means (a) an indorser or an accommodation party, (b) a drawer having the obligation described in Section 3–414(d), or (c) any other party to the instrument that has recourse against another party to the instrument pursuant to Section 3–116(b).

(b)   Other definitions applying to this Article and the sections in which they appear are:

"Acceptance" Section 3–409
"Accommodated party" Section 3–419
"Accommodation party" Section 3–419
"Account" Section 4–104
"Alteration" Section 3–407
"Anomalous indorsement" Section 3–205
"Blank indorsement" Section 3–205
"Cashier's check" Section 3–104
"Certificate of deposit" Section 3–104
"Certified check" Section 3–409
"Check" Section 3–104
"Consideration" Section 3–303
"Draft" Section 3–104
"Holder in due course" Section 3–302
"Incomplete instrument" Section 3–115
"Indorsement" Section 3–204
"Indorser" Section 3–204
"Instrument" Section 3–104
"Issue" Section 3–105
"Issuer" Section 3–105
"Negotiable instrument" Section 3–104
"Negotiation" Section 3–201
"Note" Section 3–104

"Payable at a definite time" Section 3–108
"Payable on demand" Section 3–108
"Payable to bearer" Section 3–109
"Payable to order" Section 3–109
"Payment" Section 3–602
"Person entitled to enforce" Section 3–301
"Presentment" Section 3–501
"Reacquisition" Section 3–207
"Special indorsement" Section 3–205
"Teller's check" Section 3–104
"Transfer of instrument" Section 3–203
"Traveler's check" Section 3–104
"Value" Section 3–303
(c)   The following definitions in other Articles apply to this Article:
~~"Bank" Section 4–105~~
"Banking day" Section 4–104
"Clearing house" Section 4–104
"Collecting bank" Section 4–105
"Depositary bank" Section 4–105
"Documentary draft" Section 4–104
"Intermediary bank" Section 4–105
"Item" Section 4–104
"Payor bank" Section 4–105
"Suspends payments" Section 4–104

(d)   In addition, Article 1 contains general definitions and principles of construction and interpretation applicable throughout this Article.

Legislative Note. A jurisdiction that enacts this statute that has not yet enacted the revised version of UCC Article 1 should add to Section 3–103 the definition of "good faith" that appears in the official version of Section 1–201(b)(20) and the definition of "record" that appears in the official version of Section 1–201(b)(31). Sections 3–103(a)(6) and (14) are reserved for that purpose. A jurisdiction that already has adopted or simultaneously adopts the revised Article 1 should not add those definitions, but should leave those numbers "reserved." If jurisdictions follow the numbering suggested here, the subsections will have the same numbering in all jurisdictions that have adopted these amendments (whether they have or have not adopted the revised version of UCC Article 1).

Official Comment

* * *

4.   ~~Subsection (a)(4) introduces a definition of good faith to apply to Articles 3 and 4. Former Articles 3 and 4 used the definition in Section 1–201(19).~~ This Article now uses the broadened definition of good faith in revised Article 1. The definition requires not only honesty in fact but also "observance of reasonable commercial standards of fair dealing." Although fair dealing is a broad term that must be defined in context, it is clear that it is concerned with the fairness of conduct rather than the care with which an act is performed. Failure to exercise ordinary care in conducting a transaction is an entirely different concept than failure to deal fairly in conducting the transaction. Both fair dealing and ordinary care, which is defined in Section 3–103(a)(9), are to be judged in the light of reasonable commercial standards, but those standards in each case are directed to different aspects of commercial conduct.

5.   Subsection (a)(9) is a definition of ordinary care which is applicable not only to Article 3 but to Article 4 as well. See Section 4–104(c). The general rule is stated in the first sentence of subsection (a)(9) and it applies both to banks and to persons engaged in businesses other than banking. Ordinary care means observance of reasonable commercial standards of the relevant businesses prevailing in the area in which the person is located. The second sentence of subsection (a)(9) is a particular rule limited to the duty of a bank to examine an instrument taken by a bank for processing for collection or payment by automated means. This particular rule applies primarily to Section 4–406 and it is discussed in Comment 4 to that section. Nothing in Section 3–103(a)(9) is

intended to prevent a customer from proving that the procedures followed by a bank are unreasonable, arbitrary, or unfair.

6. ~~In subsection (c) reference is made to a new definition of "bank" in amended Article 4.~~ The definition of consumer account includes a joint account established by more than one individual. See Section 1–106(1).

§ 3–104. Negotiable Instrument.

Official Comment

* * *

5. There are some differences between the requirements of Article 3 and the requirements included in Article 3 of the Convention on International Bills of Exchange and International Promissory Notes. Most obviously, the Convention does not include the limitation on extraneous undertakings set forth in Section 3–104(a)(3), and does not permit documents payable to bearer that would be permissible under Section 3–104(a)(1) and Section 3–109. See Convention Article 3. In most respects, however, the requirements of Section 3–104 and Article 3 of the Convention are quite similar.*

§ 3–106. Unconditional Promise or Order.

(a) Except as provided in this section, for the purposes of Section 3–104(a), a promise or order is unconditional unless it states (i) an express condition to payment, (ii) that the promise or order is subject to or governed by another ~~writing,~~ record, or (iii) that rights or obligations with respect to the promise or order are stated in another ~~writing.~~ record. A reference to another ~~writing~~ record does not of itself make the promise or order conditional.

(b) A promise or order is not made conditional (i) by a reference to another ~~writing~~ record for a statement of rights with respect to collateral, prepayment, or acceleration, or (ii) because payment is limited to resort to a particular fund or source.

* * *

§ 3–116. Joint and Several Liability; Contribution.

* * *

~~(c) Discharge of one party having joint and several liability by a person entitled to enforce the instrument does not affect the right under subsection (b) of a party having the same joint and several liability to receive contribution from the party discharged.~~

Official Comment

1. Subsection (a) replaces subsection (e) of former Section 3–118. Subsection (b) states contribution rights of parties with joint and several liability by referring to applicable law. But subsection (b) is subject to Section ~~3–419(e)~~ 3–419(f). If one of the parties with joint and several liability is an accommodation party and the other is the accommodated party, Section ~~3–419(e)~~ 3–419(f) applies. ~~Subsection (c) deals with discharge. The discharge of a jointly and severally liable obligor does not affect the right of other obligors to seek contribution from the discharged obligor.~~ Because one of the joint and several obligors may have recourse against the other joint and several obligor under subsection (b), each party that is jointly and severally liable under subsection (a) is a secondary obligor in part and a principal obligor in part, as those terms are defined in Section 3–103(a). Accordingly, Section 3–605 determines the effect of a release, an extension of time, or a modification of the obligation of one of the joint and several obligors, as well as the effect of an impairment of collateral provided by one of those obligors.

* * *

---

* Amendment approved by the Permanent Editorial Board for Uniform Commercial Code November 2, 2002.

§ 3–118.   Statute of Limitations.

Official Comment

* * *

7.   One of the most significant differences between this Article and the Convention on International Bills of Exchange and International Promissory Notes is that the statute of limitation under the Convention generally is only four years, rather than the six years provided by this section. See Convention Article 84.*

§ 3–119.   Notice of Right to Defend Action.

In an action for breach of an obligation for which a third person is answerable over pursuant to this article or article 4, the defendant may give the third person ~~written~~ notice of the litigation in a record, and the person notified may then give similar notice to any other person who is answerable over. if the notice states (i) that the person notified may come in and defend and (ii) that failure to do so will bind the person notified in an action later brought by the person giving the notice as to any determination of fact common to the two litigations, the person notified is so bound unless after seasonable receipt of the notice the person notified does come in and defend.

§ 3–203.   Transfer of Instrument; Rights Acquired by Transfer.

Official Comment

* * *

6.   The rules for transferring instruments set out in this section are similar to the rules in Article 13 of the Convention on International Bills of Exchange and International Promissory Notes.*

§ 3–205.   Special Indorsement; Blank Indorsement; Anomalous Indorsement.

Official Comment

* * *

4.   Articles 14 and 16 of the Convention on International Bills of Exchange and International Promissory Notes includes similar rules for blank and special indorsements.*

§ 3–301.   Person Entitled to Enforce Instrument.

Official Comment

This section replaces former Section 3–301 that stated the rights of a holder. The rights stated in former Section 3–301 to transfer, negotiate, enforce, or discharge an instrument are stated in other sections of Article 3. In revised Article 3, Section 3–301 defines "person entitled to enforce" an instrument. The definition recognizes that enforcement is not limited to holders. The quoted phrase includes a person enforcing a lost or stolen instrument. Section 3–309. It also includes a person in possession of an instrument who is not a holder. A nonholder in possession of an instrument includes a person that acquired rights of a holder by subrogation or under Section 3–203(a). ~~It also includes any other person who under applicable law is a successor to the holder or otherwise acquires the holder's rights.~~ It also includes both a remitter that has received an instrument from the issuer but has not yet transferred or negotiated the instrument to another person and also any other person who under applicable law is a successor to the holder or otherwise acquires the holder's rights.*

---

*   Amendments approved by the Permanent Editorial Board for Uniform Commercial Code November 2, 2002.

§ 3–302.   Holder in Due Course.

Official Comment

* * *

8.   The status of holder in due course resembles the status of protected holder under Article 29 of the Convention on International Bills of Exchange and International Promissory Notes. The requirements for being a protected holder under Article 29 generally track those of Section 3–302.*

§ 3–303.   Value and Consideration.

Official Comment

* * *

6.   The term "promise" in paragraph (a)(1) is used in the phrase "promise of performance" and for that reason does not have the specialized meaning given that term in Section 3–103(a)(12). See Section 1–201 ("Changes from Former Law"). No inference should be drawn from the decision to use the phrase "promise of performance," although the phrase does include the word "promise," which has the specialized definition set forth in Section 3–103. Indeed, that is true even though "undertaking" is used instead of "promise" in Section 3–104(a)(3). See Section 3–104 comment 1 (explaining the use of the term "undertaking" in Section 3–104 to avoid use of the defined term "promise").*

§ 3–305.   Defenses and Claims in Recoupment; Claims in Consumer Transactions.

(a)   Except as ~~stated in subsection (b),~~ otherwise provided in this section, the right to enforce the obligation of a party to pay an instrument is subject to the following:

* * *

(e)   In a consumer transaction, if law other than this article requires that an instrument include a statement to the effect that the rights of a holder or transferee are subject to a claim or defense that the issuer could assert against the original payee, and the instrument does not include such a statement:

(1)   the instrument has the same effect as if the instrument included such a statement;

(2)   the issuer may assert against the holder or transferee all claims and defenses that would have been available if the instrument included such a statement; and

(3)   the extent to which claims may be asserted against the holder or transferee is determined as if the instrument included such a statement.

(f)   This section is subject to law other than this article that establishes a different rule for consumer transactions.

Legislative Note: If a consumer protection law in this state addresses the same issue as subsection (g), it should be examined for consistency with subsection (g) and, if inconsistent, should be amended.

Official Comment

* * *

5.   Subsection (d) applies to instruments signed for accommodation (Section 3–419) and this subsection equates the obligation of the accommodation party to that of the accommodated party. The accommodation party can assert whatever defense or claim the accommodated party had against the person enforcing the instrument. The only exceptions are discharge in bankruptcy, infancy and lack of capacity. The same rule does not apply to an indorsement by a holder of the instrument in negotiating the instrument. The indorser, as transferor, makes a warranty to the indorsee, as transferee, that no defense or claim in recoupment is good against the indorser. Section 3–416(a)(4). Thus, if the indorsee sues the indorser because of dishonor of the instrument, the indorser may not assert the defense or claim in recoupment of the maker or drawer against the indorsee.

Section 3–305(d) must be read in conjunction with Section 3–605, which provides rules (usually referred to as suretyship defenses) for determining when the obligation of an accommodation party is discharged, in whole or in part, because of some act or omission of a person entitled to enforce the instrument. To the extent a rule stated in Section 3–605 is inconsistent with Section 3–305(d), the Section 3–605 rule governs. For example, ~~under Section 3–605(b), discharge under Section 3–604 of the accommodated party does not discharge the accommodation party~~ <u>Section 3–605(a) provides rules for determining when and to what extent a discharge of the accommodated party under Section 3–604 will discharge the accommodation party</u>. As explained in Comment ~~3~~<u>2</u> to Section 3–605, discharge of the accommodated party is normally part of a settlement under which the holder of a note accepts partial payment from an accommodated party who is financially unable to pay the entire amount of the note. If the holder then brings an action against the accommodation party to recover the remaining unpaid amount of the note, the accommodation party cannot use Section 3–305(d) to nullify Section 3–605(~~b~~<u>a</u>) by asserting the discharge of the accommodated party as a defense. On the other hand, suppose the accommodated party is a buyer of goods who issued the note to the seller who took the note for the buyer's obligation to pay for the goods. Suppose the buyer has a claim for breach of warranty with respect to the goods against the seller and the warranty claim may be asserted against the holder of the note. The warranty claim is a claim in recoupment. If the holder and the accommodated party reach a settlement under which the holder accepts payment less than the amount of the note in full satisfaction of the note and the warranty claim, the accommodation party could defend an action on the note by the holder by asserting the accord and satisfaction under Section 3–305(d). There is no conflict with Section 3–605(~~b~~<u>a</u>) because that provision is not intended to apply to settlement of disputed claims. ~~Another example of the use of Section 3–305(d) in cases in which Section 3–605 applies is stated in Comment 4 to Section 3–605. See PEB Commentary No. 11, dated February 10, 1994 [Appendix V, infra].~~

    <u>6.   Subsection (e) is added to clarify the treatment of an instrument that omits the notice currently required by the Federal Trade Commission Rule related to certain consumer credit sales and consumer purchase money loans (16 C.F.R. Part 433). This subsection adopts the view that the instrument should be treated as if the language required by the FTC Rule were present. It is based on the language describing that rule in Section 3–106(d) and the analogous provision in Section 9–404(d).</u>

    <u>7.   Subsection (f) is modeled on Sections 9–403(e) and 9–404(c). It ensures that Section 3–305 is interpreted to accommodate relevant consumer-protection laws. The absence of such a provision from other sections in Article 3 should not justify any inference about the meaning of those sections.</u>

    <u>8.   Articles 28 and 30 of the Convention on International Bills of Exchange and International Promissory Notes includes a similar dichotomy, with a narrower group of defenses available against a protected holder under Articles 28(1) and 30 than are available under Article 28(2) against a holder that is not a protected holder.</u>

§ 3–306.   Claims to an Instrument.

Official Comment

    This section expands on the reference to "claims to" the instrument mentioned in former Sections 3–305 and 3–306. Claims covered by the section include not only claims to ownership but also any other claim of a property or possessory right. It includes the claim to a lien or the claim of a person in rightful possession of an instrument who was wrongfully deprived of possession. Also included is a claim based on Section 3–202(b) for rescission of a negotiation of the instrument by the claimant. Claims to an instrument under Section 3–306 are different from claims in recoupment referred to in Section 3–305(a)(3). <u>The rule of this section is similar to the rule of Article 30(2) of the Convention on International Bills of Exchange and International Promissory Notes.</u>[*]

§ 3–309.   Enforcement of Lost, Destroyed, or Stolen Instrument.

(a)   A person not in possession of an instrument is entitled to enforce the instrument if:

    (1)   the person seeking to enforce the instrument:

        ~~(i)   the person was in possession of the instrument and~~ <u>(A) was</u> entitled to enforce ~~it~~ <u>the instrument</u> when loss of possession occurred; <u>or</u>

        <u>(B)   has directly or indirectly acquired ownership of the instrument from a person who was entitled to enforce the instrument when loss of possession occurred;</u>

        ~~(ii)~~ <u>(2)</u>   the loss of possession was not the result of a transfer by the person or a lawful <u>seizure;</u> ~~and~~

---

  [*]   Amendment approved by the Permanent Editorial Board for Uniform Commercial Code November 2, 2002.

~~seizure, and (iii)~~ (3) the person cannot reasonably obtain possession of the instrument because the instrument was destroyed, its whereabouts cannot be determined, or it is in the wrongful possession of an unknown person or a person that cannot be found or is not amenable to service of process.

(b) A person seeking enforcement of an instrument under subsection (a) must prove the terms of the instrument and the person's right to enforce the instrument. If that proof is made, Section 3–308 applies to the case as if the person seeking enforcement had produced the instrument. The court may not enter judgment in favor of the person seeking enforcement unless it finds that the person required to pay the instrument is adequately protected against loss that might occur by reason of a claim by another person to enforce the instrument. Adequate protection may be provided by any reasonable means.

Official Comment

1. Section 3–309 is a modification of former Section 3–804. The rights stated are those of "a person entitled to enforce the instrument" at the time of loss rather than those of an "owner" as in former Section 3–804. Under subsection (b), judgment to enforce the instrument cannot be given unless the court finds that the defendant will be adequately protected against a claim to the instrument by a holder that may appear at some later time. The court is given discretion in determining how adequate protection is to be assured. Former Section 3–804 allowed the court to "require security indemnifying the defendant against loss." Under Section 3–309 adequate protection is a flexible concept. For example, there is substantial risk that a holder in due course may make a demand for payment if the instrument was payable to bearer when it was lost or stolen. On the other hand if the instrument was payable to the person who lost the instrument and that person did not indorse the instrument, no other person could be a holder of the instrument. In some cases there is risk of loss only if there is doubt about whether the facts alleged by the person who lost the instrument are true. Thus, the type of adequate protection that is reasonable in the circumstances may depend on the degree of certainty about the facts in the case.

2. Subsection (a) is intended to reject the result in Dennis Joslin Co. v. Robinson Broadcasting Corp., 977 F. Supp. 491 (D.D.C. 1997). A transferee of a lost instrument need prove only that its transferor was entitled to enforce, not that the transferee was in possession at the time the instrument was lost. The protections of subsection (a) should also be available when instruments are lost during transit, because whatever the precise status of ownership at the point of loss, either the sender or the receiver ordinarily would have been entitled to enforce the instrument during the course of transit. The amendments to subsection (a) are not intended to alter in any way the rules that apply to the preservation of checks in connection with truncation or any other expedited method of check collection or processing.

3. A security interest may attach to the right of a person not in possession of an instrument to enforce the instrument. Although the secured party may not be the owner of the instrument, the secured party may nevertheless be entitled to exercise its debtor's right to enforce the instrument by resorting to its collection rights under the circumstances described in Section 9–607. This section does not address whether the person required to pay the instrument owes any duty to a secured party that is not itself the owner of the instrument.

§ 3–310. Effect of Instrument on Obligation for Which Taken.

Official Comment

* * *

3. Subsection (b) concerns cases in which an uncertified check or a note is taken for an obligation. The typical case is that in which a buyer pays for goods or services by giving the seller the buyer's personal check, or in which the buyer signs a note for the purchase price. Subsection (b) also applies to the uncommon cases in which a check or note of a third person is given in payment of the obligation. Subsection (b) preserves the rule under former Section 3–802(1)(b) that the buyer's obligation to pay the price is suspended, but subsection (b) spells out the effect more precisely. If the check or note is dishonored, the seller may sue on either the dishonored instrument or the contract of sale if the seller has possession of the instrument and is the person entitled to enforce it. If the right to enforce the instrument is held by somebody other than the seller, the seller can't enforce the right to payment of the price under the sales contract because that right is represented by the instrument which is enforceable by somebody else. Thus, if the seller sold the note or the check to a holder and has not reacquired it after dishonor, the only right that survives is the right to enforce the instrument. What that means is that even

though the suspension of the obligation may end upon dishonor under paragraph (b)(1), the obligation is not revived in the circumstances described in paragraph (b)(4).*

* * *

§ 3–312.   Lost, Destroyed, or Stolen Cashier's Check, Teller's Check, or Certified Check.

(a)   In this section:

(1)   "Check" means a cashier's check, teller's check, or certified check.

(2)   "Claimant" means a person who claims the right to receive the amount of a cashier's check, teller's check, or certified check that was lost, destroyed, or stolen.

(3)   "Declaration of loss" means a ~~written~~ statement, made in a record under penalty of perjury, to the effect that (i) the declarer lost possession of a check, (ii) the declarer is the drawer or payee of the check, in the case of a certified check, or the remitter or payee of the check, in the case of a cashier's check or teller's check, (iii) the loss of possession was not the result of a transfer by the declarer or a lawful seizure, and (iv) the declarer cannot reasonably obtain possession of the check because the check was destroyed, its whereabouts cannot be determined, or it is in the wrongful possession of an unknown person or a person that cannot be found or is not amenable to service of process.

* * *

§ 3–412.   Obligation of Issuer of Note or Cashier's Check.

Official Comment

* * *

4.   The rule of this section is similar to the rule of Article 39 of the Convention on International Bills of Exchange and International Promissory Notes.*

§ 3–413.   Obligation of Acceptor.

Official Comment

* * *

Subsection (a) is consistent with former Section 3–413(1). Subsection (b) has primary importance with respect to certified checks. It protects the holder in due course of a certified check that was altered after certification and before negotiation to the holder in due course. A bank can avoid liability for the altered amount by stating on the check the amount the bank agrees to pay. The subsection applies to other accepted drafts as well. The rule of this section is similar to the rule of Articles 41 of the Convention on International Bills of Exchange and International Promissory Notes. Articles 42 and 43 of the Convention include more detailed rules that in many respects do not have parallels in this Article.*

§ 3–414.   Obligation of Drawer.

Official Comment

* * *

7.   The obligation of the drawer under this section is similar to the obligation of the drawer under Article 38 of the Convention on International Bills of Exchange and International Promissory Notes.**

---

*   Amendment approved by the Permanent Editorial Board for Uniform Commercial Code November 2, 2002.

**   Amendments approved by the Permanent Editorial Board for Uniform Commercial Code November 2, 2002.

§ **3–415.** **Obligation of Indorser.**

Official Comment

* * *

6. The rule of this section is similar to the rule of Article 44 of the Convention on International Bills of Exchange and International Promissory Notes.*

§ **3–416.** **Transfer Warranties.**

(a) A person who transfers an instrument for consideration warrants to the transferee and, if the transfer is by indorsement, to any subsequent transferee that:

(1) the warrantor is a person entitled to enforce the instrument;

(2) all signatures on the instrument are authentic and authorized;

(3) the instrument has not been altered;

(4) the instrument is not subject to a defense or claim in recoupment of any party which can be asserted against the warrantor; ~~and~~

(5) the warrantor has no knowledge of any insolvency proceeding commenced with respect to the maker or acceptor or, in the case of an unaccepted draft, the ~~drawer.~~ drawer; and

(6) with respect to a remotely-created consumer item, that the person on whose account the item is drawn authorized the issuance of the item in the amount for which the item is drawn.

* * *

Official Comment

* * *

8. Subsection (a)(6) is based on a number of nonuniform amendments designed to address concerns about certain kinds of check fraud. The provision implements a limited rejection of Price v. Neal, 97 Eng. Rep. 871 (K.B. 1762), so that in certain circumstances (those involving remotely-created consumer items) the payor bank can use a warranty claim to absolve itself of responsibility for honoring an unauthorized item. The provision rests on the premise that monitoring by depositary banks can control this type of fraud more effectively than any practices readily available to payor banks. The provision expressly includes both the case in which the consumer does not authorize the item at all and also the case in which the consumer authorizes the item but in an amount different from the amount in which the item is drawn. Similar provisions appear in Sections 3–417, 4–207, and 4–208.

The provision supplements applicable federal law, which requires telemarketers who submit instruments for payment to obtain the customer's "express verifiable authorization," which may be either in writing or tape recorded and must be made available upon request to the customer's bank. Federal Trade Commission's Telemarketing Sales Rule, 16 C.F.R. § 310.3(a)(3), implementing the Telemarketing and Consumer Fraud and Abuse Prevention Act, 15 U.S.C. §§ 6101–6108. Some states also have consumer-protection laws governing authorization of instruments in telemarketing transactions. See, e.g., 9 Vt. Stat. Ann. § 2464.

9. Article 45 of the Convention on International Bills of Exchange and International Promissory Notes includes warranties that are similar (except for the warranty in subsection (a)(6)).

§ **3–417.** **Presentment Warranties.**

(a) If an unaccepted draft is presented to the drawee for payment or acceptance and the drawee pays or accepts the draft, (i) the person obtaining payment or acceptance, at the time of presentment, and (ii) a previous transferor of the draft, at the time of transfer, warrant to the drawee making payment or accepting the draft in good faith that:

(1) the warrantor is, or was, at the time the warrantor transferred the draft, a person entitled to enforce the draft or authorized to obtain payment or acceptance of the draft on behalf of a person entitled to enforce the draft;

(2)   the draft has not been altered; ~~and~~

(3)   the warrantor has no knowledge that the signature of the drawer of the draft is ~~unauthorized.~~ unauthorized; and

(4)   with respect to any remotely-created consumer item, that the person on whose account the item is drawn authorized the issuance of the item in the amount for which the item is drawn.

* * *

Official Comment

* * *

9.   For discussion of subsection (a)(4), see Comment 8 to Section 3–416.

§ 3–419.   Instruments Signed for Accommodation.

* * *

(e)   If the signature of a party to an instrument is accompanied by words indicating that the party guarantees payment or the signer signs the instrument as an accommodation party in some other manner that does not unambiguously indicate an intention to guarantee collection rather than payment, the signer is obliged to pay the amount due on the instrument to a person entitled to enforce the instrument in the same circumstances as the accommodated party would be obliged, without prior resort to the accommodated party by the person entitled to enforce the instrument.

(f)   An accommodation party who pays the instrument is entitled to reimbursement from the accommodated party and is entitled to enforce the instrument against the accommodated party. In proper circumstances, an accommodation party may obtain relief that requires the accommodated party to perform its obligations on the instrument. An accommodated party ~~who~~ that pays the instrument has no right of recourse against, and is not entitled to contribution from, an accommodation party.

Official Comment

* * *

3.   As stated in Comment 1, whether a person is an accommodation party is a question of fact. But it is almost always the case that a co-maker who signs with words of guaranty after the signature is an accommodation party. The same is true of an anomalous indorser. In either case a person taking the instrument is put on notice of the accommodation status of the co-maker or indorser. This is relevant to Section 3–605(~~h~~e). But, under subsection (c), signing with words of guaranty or as an anomalous indorser also creates a presumption that the signer is an accommodation party. A party challenging accommodation party status would have to rebut this presumption by producing evidence that the signer was in fact a direct beneficiary of the value given for the instrument.

* * *

§ 3–502.   Dishonor.

Official Comment

* * *

4.   ~~Subsection (b) applies to unaccepted drafts other than documentary drafts. Subsection (b)(1) applies to checks. Except for checks presented for immediate payment over the counter, which are covered by subsection (b)(2), dishonor occurs according to rules stated in Article 4. When a check is presented for payment through the check-collection system, the drawee bank normally makes settlement for the amount of the check to the presenting bank. Under Section 4–301 the drawee bank may recover this settlement if it returns the check within its midnight deadline (Section 4–104). In that case the check is not paid and dishonor occurs under Section 3–502(b)(1). If the drawee bank does not return the check or give notice of dishonor or nonpayment within the midnight deadline, the settlement becomes final payment of the check. Section 4–215. Thus, no dishonor occurs regardless of whether the check is retained or is returned after the midnight deadline. In some cases the drawee bank might not settle for the check when it is received. Under Section 4–302 if the drawee bank is not also the depositary bank and~~

retains the check without settling for it beyond midnight of the day it is presented for payment, the bank becomes "accountable" for the amount of the check, i.e. it is obliged to pay the amount of the check. If the drawee bank is also the depositary bank, the bank is accountable for the amount of the check if the bank does not pay the check or return it or send notice of dishonor within the midnight deadline. In all cases in which the drawee bank becomes accountable, the check has not been paid and, under Section 3-502(b)(1), the check is dishonored. The fact that the bank is obliged to pay the check does not mean that the check has been paid. When a check is presented for payment, the person presenting the check is entitled to payment not just the obligation of the drawee to pay. Until that payment is made, the check is dishonored. To say that the drawee bank is obliged to pay the check necessarily means that the check has not been paid. If the check is eventually paid, the drawee bank no longer is accountable.

4. Subsection (b) applies to unaccepted drafts other than documentary drafts. Subsection (b)(1) applies to checks. Except for checks presented for immediate payment over the counter, which are covered by subsection (b)(2), dishonor occurs according to rules stated in Article 4. Those rules contemplate four separate situations that warrant discussion. The first two situations arise in the normal course of affairs, in which the drawee bank makes settlement for the amount of the check to the presenting bank. In the first situation, the drawee bank under Section 4-301 recovers this settlement if it returns the check by its midnight deadline (Section 4-104). In that case the check is not paid and dishonor occurs under Section 3-502(b)(1). The second situation arises if the drawee bank has made such a settlement and does not return the check or give notice of dishonor or nonpayment within the midnight deadline. In that case, the settlement becomes final payment of the check under Section 4-215. Because the drawee bank already has paid such an item, it cannot be "accountable" for the item under the terms of Section 4-302(a)(1). Thus, no dishonor occurs regardless of whether the drawee bank retains the check indefinitely or for some reason returns the check after its midnight deadline.

The third and fourth situations arise less commonly, in cases in which the drawee bank does not settle for the check when it is received. Under Section 4-302 if the drawee bank is not also the depositary bank and retains the check without settling for it beyond midnight of the day it is presented for payment, the bank at that point becomes "accountable" for the amount of the check, i.e., it is obliged to pay the amount of the check. If the drawee bank is also the depositary bank, the bank becomes accountable for the amount of the check if the bank does not pay the check or return it or send notice of dishonor by its midnight deadline. Hence, if the drawee bank is also the depositary bank and does not either settle for the check when it is received (a settlement that would ripen into final payment if the drawee bank failed to take action to recover the settlement by its midnight deadline) or return the check or an appropriate notice by its midnight deadline, the drawee bank will become accountable for the amount of the check under Section 4-302. Thus, in all cases in which the drawee bank becomes accountable under Section 4-302, the check has not been paid (either by a settlement that became unrecoverable or otherwise) and thus, under Section 3-502(b)(1), the check is dishonored.

The fact that a bank that is accountable for the amount of the check under Section 4-302 is obliged to pay the check does not mean that the check has been paid. Indeed, because each of the paragraphs of Section 4-302(b) is limited by its terms to situations in which a bank has not paid the item, a drawee bank will be accountable under Section 4-302 only in situations in which it has not previously paid the check. Section 3-502(b)(1) reflects the view that a person presenting a check is entitled to payment, not just the ability to hold the drawee accountable under Section 4-302. If that payment is not made in a timely manner, the check is dishonored.

Regulation CC Section 229.36(d) provides that settlement between banks for the forward collection of checks is final. The relationship of that section to Articles 3 and 4 is discussed in the Commentary to that section.*

* * *

§ 3-602.   Payment.

(a)   Subject to subsection ~~(b)~~, (e), an instrument is paid to the extent payment is made ~~(i)~~ by or on behalf of a party obliged to pay the instrument, and ~~(ii)~~ to a person entitled to enforce the instrument.

(b)   Subject to subsection (e), a note is paid to the extent payment is made by or on behalf of a party obliged to pay the note to a person that formerly was entitled to enforce the note only if at the time of the payment the party obliged to pay has not received adequate notification that the note has been transferred and that payment is to be made to the transferee. A notification is adequate only if it is signed by the transferor or the transferee; reasonably identifies the transferred note; and provides an address at which payments subsequently are to be made. Upon request, a transferee shall seasonably furnish reasonable

---

*   Amendment approved by the Permanent Editorial Board for Uniform Commercial Code November 2, 2002.

proof that the note has been transferred. Unless the transferee complies with the request, a payment to the person that formerly was entitled to enforce the note is effective for purposes of subsection (c) even if the party obliged to pay the note has received a notification under this paragraph.

(c)   Subject to subsection (e), to the extent of ~~the payment,~~ a payment under subsections (a) and (b), the obligation of the party obliged to pay the instrument is discharged even though payment is made with knowledge of a claim to the instrument under Section 3–306 by another person.

(d)   Subject to subsection (e), a transferee, or any party that has acquired rights in the instrument directly or indirectly from a transferee, including any such party that has rights as a holder in due course, is deemed to have notice of any payment that is made under subsection (b) after the date that the note is transferred to the transferee but before the party obliged to pay the note receives adequate notification of the transfer.

~~(b)~~ (e)   The obligation of a party to pay the instrument is not discharged under ~~subsection (a)~~ subsections (a) through (d) if:

(1)   a claim to the instrument under Section 3–306 is enforceable against the party receiving payment and (i) payment is made with knowledge by the payor that payment is prohibited by injunction or similar process of a court of competent jurisdiction, or (ii) in the case of an instrument other than a cashier's check, teller's check, or certified check, the party making payment accepted, from the person having a claim to the instrument, indemnity against loss resulting from refusal to pay the person entitled to enforce the instrument; or

(2)   the person making payment knows that the instrument is a stolen instrument and pays a person it knows is in wrongful possession of the instrument.

(f)   As used in this section, "signed," with respect to a record that is not a writing, includes the attachment to or logical association with the record of an electronic symbol, sound, or process with the present intent to adopt or accept the record.

Official Comment

1.   This section replaces former Section 3–603(1). The phrase "claim to the instrument" in subsection (a) means, by reference to Section 3–306, a claim of ownership or possession and not a claim in recoupment. Subsection ~~(b)~~(e)(1)(ii) is added to conform to Section 3–411. Section 3–411 is intended to discourage an obligated bank from refusing payment of a cashier's check, certified check or dishonored teller's check at the request of a claimant to the check who provided the bank with indemnity against loss. See Comment 1 to Section 3–411. An obligated bank that refuses payment under those circumstances not only remains liable on the check but may also be liable to the holder of the check for consequential damages. Section 3–602~~(b)~~(e)(1)(ii) and Section 3–411, read together, change the rule of former Section 3–603(1) with respect to the obligation of the obligated bank on the check. Payment to the holder of a cashier's check, teller's check, or certified check discharges the obligation of the obligated bank on the check to both the holder and the claimant even though indemnity has been given by the person asserting the claim. If the obligated bank pays the check in violation of an agreement with the claimant in connection with the indemnity agreement, any liability that the bank may have for violation of the agreement is not governed by Article 3, but is left to other law. This section continues the rule that the obligor is not discharged on the instrument if payment is made in violation of an injunction against payment. See Section 3–411(c)(iv).

2.   Subsection (a) covers payments made in a traditional manner, to the person entitled to enforce the instrument. Subsection (b), which provides an alternative method of payment, deals with the situation in which a person entitled to enforce the instrument transfers the instrument without giving notice to parties obligated to pay the instrument. If that happens and one of those parties subsequently makes a payment to the transferor, the payment is effective even though it is not made to the person entitled to enforce the instrument. Unlike the earlier version of Section 3–602, this rule is consistent with Section 9–406(a), Restatement of Mortgages § 5.5, and Restatement of Contracts § 338(1).

3.   In determining the party to whom a payment is made for purposes of this section, courts should look to traditional rules of agency. Thus, if the original payee of a note transfers ownership of the note to a third party but continues to service the obligation, the law of agency might treat payments made to the original payee as payments made to the third party.

§ 3–604.   Discharge by Cancellation or Renunciation.

(a)   A person entitled to enforce an instrument, with or without consideration, may discharge the obligation of a party to pay the instrument (i) by an intentional voluntary act, such as surrender of the instrument to the party, destruction, mutilation, or cancellation of the instrument, cancellation or striking out of the party's signature, or the addition of words to the instrument indicating discharge, or (ii) by agreeing not to sue or otherwise renouncing rights against the party by a signed ~~writing.~~ record.

(b)   Cancellation or striking out of an indorsement pursuant to subsection (a) does not affect the status and rights of a party derived from the indorsement.

(c)   In this section, "signed," with respect to a record that is not a writing, includes the attachment to or logical association with the record of an electronic symbol, sound, or process with the present intent to adopt or accept the record.

§ 3–605.   Discharge of Secondary Obligors. ~~Discharge of Indorsers and Accommodation Parties.~~

(a)   If a person entitled to enforce an instrument releases the obligation of a principal obligor in whole or in part, and another party to the instrument is a secondary obligor with respect to the obligation of that principal obligor, the following rules apply:

(1)   Any obligations of the principal obligor to the secondary obligor with respect to any previous payment by the secondary obligor are not affected. Unless the terms of the release preserve the secondary obligor's recourse, the principal obligor is discharged, to the extent of the release, from any other duties to the secondary obligor under this article.

(2)   Unless the terms of the release provide that the person entitled to enforce the instrument retains the right to enforce the instrument against the secondary obligor, the secondary obligor is discharged to the same extent as the principal obligor from any unperformed portion of its obligation on the instrument. If the instrument is a check and the obligation of the secondary obligor is based on an indorsement of the check, the secondary obligor is discharged without regard to the language or circumstances of the discharge or other release.

(3)   If the secondary obligor is not discharged under paragraph (2), the secondary obligor is discharged to the extent of the value of the consideration for the release, and to the extent that the release would otherwise cause the secondary obligor a loss.

(b)   If a person entitled to enforce an instrument grants a principal obligor an extension of the time at which one or more payments are due on the instrument and another party to the instrument is a secondary obligor with respect to the obligation of that principal obligor, the following rules apply:

(1)   Any obligations of the principal obligor to the secondary obligor with respect to any previous payment by the secondary obligor are not affected. Unless the terms of the extension preserve the secondary obligor's recourse, the extension correspondingly extends the time for performance of any other duties owed to the secondary obligor by the principal obligor under this article.

(2)   The secondary obligor is discharged to the extent that the extension would otherwise cause the secondary obligor a loss.

(3)   To the extent that the secondary obligor is not discharged under paragraph (2), the secondary obligor may perform its obligations to a person entitled to enforce the instrument as if the time for payment had not been extended or, unless the terms of the extension provide that the person entitled to enforce the instrument retains the right to enforce the instrument against the secondary obligor as if the time for payment had not been extended, treat the time for performance of its obligations as having been extended correspondingly.

(c)   If a person entitled to enforce an instrument agrees, with or without consideration, to a modification of the obligation of a principal obligor other than a complete or partial release or an extension of the due date and another party to the instrument is a secondary obligor with respect to the obligation of that principal obligor, the following rules apply:

(1)　Any obligations of the principal obligor to the secondary obligor with respect to any previous payment by the secondary obligor are not affected. The modification correspondingly modifies any other duties owed to the secondary obligor by the principal obligor under this article.

(2)　The secondary obligor is discharged from any unperformed portion of its obligation to the extent that the modification would otherwise cause the secondary obligor a loss.

(3)　To the extent that the secondary obligor is not discharged under paragraph (2), the secondary obligor may satisfy its obligation on the instrument as if the modification had not occurred, or treat its obligation on the instrument as having been modified correspondingly.

(d)　If the obligation of a principal obligor is secured by an interest in collateral, another party to the instrument is a secondary obligor with respect to that obligation, and a person entitled to enforce the instrument impairs the value of the interest in collateral, the obligation of the secondary obligor is discharged to the extent of the impairment. The value of an interest in collateral is impaired to the extent the value of the interest is reduced to an amount less than the amount of the recourse of the secondary obligor, or the reduction in value of the interest causes an increase in the amount by which the amount of the recourse exceeds the value of the interest. For purposes of this subsection, impairing the value of an interest in collateral includes failure to obtain or maintain perfection or recordation of the interest in collateral, release of collateral without substitution of collateral of equal value or equivalent reduction of the underlying obligation, failure to perform a duty to preserve the value of collateral owed, under Article 9 or other law, to a debtor or other person secondarily liable, and failure to comply with applicable law in disposing of or otherwise enforcing the interest in collateral.

(e)　A secondary obligor is not discharged under subsections (a)(3), (b), (c), or (d) unless the person entitled to enforce the instrument knows that the person is a secondary obligor or has notice under Section 3–419(c) that the instrument was signed for accommodation.

(f)　A secondary obligor is not discharged under this section if the secondary obligor consents to the event or conduct that is the basis of the discharge, or the instrument or a separate agreement of the party provides for waiver of discharge under this section specifically or by general language indicating that parties waive defenses based on suretyship or impairment of collateral. Unless the circumstances indicate otherwise, consent by the principal obligor to an act that would lead to a discharge under this section constitutes consent to that act by the secondary obligor if the secondary obligor controls the principal obligor or deals with the person entitled to enforce the instrument on behalf of the principal obligor.

(g)　A release or extension preserves a secondary obligor's recourse if the terms of the release or extension provide that:

(1)　the person entitled to enforce the instrument retains the right to enforce the instrument against the secondary obligor; and

(2)　the recourse of the secondary obligor continues as if the release or extension had not been granted.

(h)　Except as otherwise provided in subsection (i), a secondary obligor asserting discharge under this section has the burden of persuasion both with respect to the occurrence of the acts alleged to harm the secondary obligor and loss or prejudice caused by those acts.

(i)　If the secondary obligor demonstrates prejudice caused by an impairment of its recourse, and the circumstances of the case indicate that the amount of loss is not reasonably susceptible of calculation or requires proof of facts that are not ascertainable, it is presumed that the act impairing recourse caused a loss or impairment equal to the liability of the secondary obligor on the instrument. In that event, the burden of persuasion as to any lesser amount of the loss is on the person entitled to enforce the instrument.

(a)　In this section, the term "indorser" includes a drawer having the obligation described in Section 3–414(d).

(b)　Discharge, under Section 3–604, of the obligation of a party to pay an instrument does not discharge the obligation of an indorser or accommodation party having a right of recourse against the discharged party.

(c) If a person entitled to enforce an instrument agrees, with or without consideration, to an extension of the due date of the obligation of a party to pay the instrument, the extension discharges an indorser or accommodation party having a right of recourse against the party whose obligation is extended to the extent the indorser or accommodation party proves that the extension caused loss to the indorser or accommodation party with respect to the right of recourse.

(d) If a person entitled to enforce an instrument agrees, with or without consideration, to a material modification of the obligation of a party other than an extension of the due date, the modification discharges the obligation of an indorser or accommodation party having a right of recourse against the person whose obligation is modified to the extent the modification causes loss to the indorser or accommodation party with respect to the right of recourse. The loss suffered by the indorser or accommodation party as a result of the modification is equal to the amount of the right of recourse unless the person enforcing the instrument proves that no loss was caused by the modification or that the loss caused by the modification was an amount less than the amount of the right of recourse.

(e) If the obligation of a party to pay an instrument is secured by an interest in collateral and a person entitled to enforce the instrument impairs the value of the interest in collateral, the obligation of an indorser or accommodation party having a right of recourse against the obligor is discharged to the extent of the impairment. The value of an interest in collateral is impaired to the extent (i) the value of the interest is reduced to an amount less than the amount of the right of recourse of the party asserting discharge, or (ii) the reduction in value of the interest causes an increase in the amount by which the amount of the right of recourse exceeds the value of the interest. The burden of proving impairment is on the party asserting discharge.

(f) If the obligation of a party is secured by an interest in collateral not provided by an accommodation party and a person entitled to enforce the instrument impairs the value of the interest in collateral, the obligation of any party who is jointly and severally liable with respect to the secured obligation is discharged to the extent the impairment causes the party asserting discharge to pay more than that party would have been obliged to pay, taking into account rights of contribution, if impairment had not occurred. If the party asserting discharge is an accommodation party not entitled to discharge under subsection (e), the party is deemed to have a right to contribution based on joint and several liability rather than a right to reimbursement. The burden of proving impairment is on the party asserting discharge.

(g) Under subsection (e) or (f), impairing value of an interest in collateral includes (i) failure to obtain or maintain perfection or recordation of the interest in collateral, (ii) release of collateral without substitution of collateral of equal value, (iii) failure to perform a duty to preserve the value of collateral owed, under Article 9 or other law, to a debtor or surety or other person secondarily liable, or (iv) failure to comply with applicable law in disposing of collateral.

(h) An accommodation party is not discharged under subsection (c), (d), or (e) unless the person entitled to enforce the instrument knows of the accommodation or has notice under Section 3–419(c) that the instrument was signed for accommodation.

(i) A party is not discharged under this section if (i) the party asserting discharge consents to the event or conduct that is the basis of the discharge, or (ii) the instrument or a separate agreement of the party provides for waiver of discharge under this section either specifically or by general language indicating that parties waive defenses based on suretyship or impairment of collateral.

Official Comment

1. Section 3–605, which replaces former Section 3–606, can be illustrated by an example. Bank lends $10,000 to Borrower who signs a note under which Borrower is obliged to pay $10,000 to Bank on a due date stated in the note. Bank insists, however, that Accommodation Party also become liable to pay the note. Accommodation Party can incur this liability by signing the note as a co-maker or by indorsing the note. In either case the note is signed for accommodation and Borrower is the accommodated party. Rights and obligations of Accommodation Party in this case are stated in Section 3–419. Suppose that after the note is signed, Bank agrees to a modification of the rights and obligations between Bank and Borrower. For example, Bank agrees that Borrower may pay the note at some date after the due date, or that Borrower may discharge Borrower's $10,000 obligation to pay the note by paying Bank $3,000, or that Bank releases collateral given by Borrower to secure the note. Under the law of suretyship Borrower is usually referred to as the principal debtor and Accommodation Party is referred to as

the surety. Under that law, the surety can be discharged under certain circumstances if changes of this kind are made by Bank, the creditor, without the consent of Accommodation Party, the surety. Rights of the surety to discharge in such cases are commonly referred to as suretyship defenses. Section 3–605 is concerned with this kind of problem in the context of a negotiable instrument to which the principal debtor and the surety are parties. But Section 3–605 has a wider scope. It also applies to indorsers who are not accommodation parties. Unless an indorser signs without recourse, the indorser's liability under Section 3–415(a) is that of a guarantor of payment. If Bank in our hypothetical case indorsed the note and transferred it to Second Bank, Bank has rights given to an indorser under Section 3–605 if it is Second Bank that modifies rights and obligations of Borrower. Both accommodation parties and indorsers will be referred to in these Comments as sureties. The scope of Section 3–605 is also widened by subsection (e) which deals with rights of a non-accommodation party co-maker when collateral is impaired.

2.   The importance of suretyship defenses is greatly diminished by the fact that they can be waived. The waiver is usually made by a provision in the note or other writing that represents the obligation of the principal debtor. It is standard practice to include a waiver of suretyship defenses in notes given to financial institutions or other commercial creditors. Section 3–605(i) allows waiver. Thus, Section 3–605 applies to the occasional case in which the creditor did not include a waiver clause in the instrument or in which the creditor did not obtain the permission of the surety to take the action that triggers the suretyship defense.

3.   Subsection (b) addresses the effect of discharge under Section 3–604 of the principal debtor. In the hypothetical case stated in Comment 1, release of Borrower by Bank does not release Accommodation Party. As a practical matter, Bank will not gratuitously release Borrower. Discharge of Borrower normally would be part of a settlement with Borrower if Borrower is insolvent or in financial difficulty. If Borrower is unable to pay all creditors, it may be prudent for Bank to take partial payment, but Borrower will normally insist on a release of the obligation. If Bank takes $3,000 and releases Borrower from the $10,000 debt, Accommodation Party is not injured. To the extent of the payment Accommodation Party's obligation to Bank is reduced. The release of Borrower by Bank does not affect the right of Accommodation Party to obtain reimbursement from Borrower or to enforce the note against Borrower if Accommodation Party pays Bank. Section 3–419(e). Subsection (b) is designed to allow a creditor to settle with the principal debtor without risk of losing rights against sureties. Settlement is in the interest of sureties as well as the creditor. Subsection (b), however, is not intended to apply to a settlement of a disputed claim which discharges the obligation.

Subsection (b) changes the law stated in former Section 3–606 but the change relates largely to formalities rather than substance. Under former Section 3–606, Bank in the hypothetical case stated in Comment 1 could settle with and release Borrower without releasing Accommodation Party, but to accomplish that result Bank had to either obtain the consent of Accommodation Party or make an express reservation of rights against Accommodation Party at the time it released Borrower. The reservation of rights was made in the agreement between Bank and Borrower by which the release of Borrower was made. There was no requirement in former Section 3–606 that any notice be given to Accommodation Party. Section 3–605 eliminates the necessity that Bank formally reserve rights against Accommodation Party in order to retain rights of recourse against Accommodation Party. See PEB Commentary No. 11, dated February 10, 1994 [Appendix V, infra].

4.   Subsection (c) relates to extensions of the due date of the instrument. In most cases an extension of time to pay a note is a benefit to both the principal debtor and sureties having recourse against the principal debtor. In relatively few cases the extension may cause loss if deterioration of the financial condition of the principal debtor reduces the amount that the surety will be able to recover on its right of recourse when default occurs. Former Section 3–606(1)(a) did not take into account the presence or absence of loss to the surety. For example, suppose the instrument is an installment note and the principal debtor is temporarily short of funds to pay a monthly installment. The payee agrees to extend the due date of the installment for a month or two to allow the debtor to pay when funds are available. Under former Section 3–606 surety was discharged if consent was not given unless the payee expressly reserved rights against the surety. It did not matter that the extension of time was a trivial change in the guaranteed obligation and that there was no evidence that the surety suffered any loss because of the extension. Wilmington Trust Co. v. Gesullo, 29 U.C.C.Rep. 144 (Del.Super.Ct.1980). Under subsection (c) an extension of time results in discharge only to the extent the surety proves that the extension caused loss. For example, if the extension is for a long period the surety might be able to prove that during the period of extension the principal debtor became insolvent, thus reducing the value of the right of recourse of the surety. By putting the burden on the surety to prove loss, subsection (c) more accurately reflects what the parties would have done by agreement, and it facilitates workouts.

Under other provisions of Article 3, what is the effect of an extension agreement between the holder of a note and the maker who is an accommodated party? The question is illustrated by the following case:

Case #1. A borrows money from Lender and issues a note payable on April 1, 1992. B signs the note for accommodation at the request of Lender. B signed the note either as co-maker or as an anomalous indorser. In either case Lender subsequently makes an agreement with A extending the due date of A's obligation to pay the note to July 1, 1992. In either case B did not agree to the extension.

What is the effect of the extension agreement on B? Could Lender enforce the note against B if the note is not paid on April 1, 1992? A's obligation to Lender to pay the note on April 1, 1992 may be modified by the agreement of Lender. If B is an anomalous indorser Lender cannot enforce the note against B unless the note has been dishonored. Section 3–415(a). Under Section 3–502(a)(3) dishonor occurs if it is not paid on the day it becomes payable. Since the agreement between A and Lender extended the due date of A's obligation to July 1, 1992 there is no dishonor because A was not obligated to pay Lender on April 1, 1992. If B is a co-maker the analysis is somewhat different. Lender has no power to amend the terms of the note without the consent of both A and B. By an agreement with A, Lender can extend the due date of A's obligation to Lender to pay the note but B's obligation is to pay the note according to the terms of the note at the time of issue. Section 3–412. However, B's obligation to pay the note is subject to a defense because B is an accommodation party. B is not obliged to pay Lender if A is not obliged to pay Lender. Under Section 3–305(d), B as an accommodation party can assert against Lender any defense of A. A has a defense based on the extension agreement. Thus, the result is that Lender could not enforce the note against B until July 1, 1992. This result is consistent with the right of B if B is an anomalous indorser.

As a practical matter an extension of the due date will normally occur when the accommodated party is unable to pay on the due date. The interest of the accommodation party normally is to defer payment to the holder rather than to pay right away and rely on an action against the accommodated party that may have little or no value. But in unusual cases the accommodation party may prefer to pay the holder on the original due date. In such cases, the accommodation party may do so. This is because the extension agreement between the accommodated party and the holder cannot bind the accommodation party to a change in its obligation without the accommodation party's consent. The effect on the recourse of the accommodation party against the accommodation party of performance by the accommodation party on the original due date is not addressed in § 3–419 and is left to the general law of suretyship.

Even though an accommodation party has the option of paying the instrument on the original due date, the accommodation party is not precluded from asserting its rights to discharge under Section 3–605(c) if it does not exercise that option. The critical issue is whether the extension caused the accommodation party a loss by increasing the difference between its cost of performing its obligation on the instrument and the amount recoverable from the accommodated party pursuant to Section 3–419(e). The decision by the accommodation party not to exercise its option to pay on the original due date may, under the circumstances, be a factor to be considered in the determination of that issue. See PEB Commentary No. 11, supra.

5.   Former Section 3–606 applied to extensions of the due date of a note but not to other modifications of the obligation of the principal debtor. There was no apparent reason why former Section 3–606 did not follow general suretyship law in covering both. Under Section 3–605(d) a material modification of the obligation of the principal debtor, other than an extension of the due date, will result in discharge of the surety to the extent the modification caused loss to the surety with respect to the right of recourse. The loss caused by the modification is deemed to be the entire amount of the right of recourse unless the person seeking enforcement of the instrument proves that no loss occurred or that the loss was less than the full amount of the right of recourse. In the absence of that proof, the surety is completely discharged. The rationale for having different rules with respect to loss for extensions of the due date and other modifications is that extensions are likely to be beneficial to the surety and they are often made. Other modifications are less common and they may very well be detrimental to the surety. Modification of the obligation of the principal debtor without permission of the surety is unreasonable unless the modification is benign. Subsection (d) puts the burden on the person seeking enforcement of the instrument to prove the extent to which loss was not caused by the modification.

The following is an illustration of the kind of case to which Section 3–605(d) would apply:

Case #2. Corporation borrows money from Lender and issues a note payable to Lender. X signs the note as an accommodation party for Corporation. The loan agreement under which the note was issued states various events of default which allow Lender to accelerate the due date of the note. Among the events of default are breach of covenants not to incur debt beyond specified limits and not to engage in any line of business substantially different from that currently carried on by Corporation. Without consent of X, Lender agrees to modify the covenants to allow Corporation to enter into a new line of business that X considers to be risky, and to incur debt beyond the limits specified in the loan agreement to finance the new venture. This modification releases X unless Lender proves that the modification did not cause loss to X or that the loss caused by the modification was less than X's right of recourse.

Sometimes there is both an extension of the due date and some other modification. In that case both subsections (c) and (d) apply. The following is an example:

Case #3. Corporation was indebted to Lender on a note payable on April 1, 1992 and X signed the note as an accommodation party for Corporation. The interest rate on the note was 12 percent. Lender and Corporation agreed to a six-month extension of the due date of the note to October 1, 1992 and an increase in the interest rate to 14 percent after April 1, 1992. Corporation defaulted on October 1, 1992. Corporation paid no interest during the six-month extension period. Corporation is insolvent and has no assets from which unsecured creditors can be paid. Lender demanded payment from X.

Assume X is an anomalous indorser. First consider Section 3–605(c) alone. If there had been no change in the interest rate, the fact that Lender gave an extension of six months to Corporation would not result in discharge unless X could prove loss with respect to the right of recourse because of the extension. If the financial condition of Corporation on April 1, 1992 would not have allowed any recovery on the right of recourse, X can't show any loss as a result of the extension with respect to the amount due on the note on April 1, 1992. Since the note accrued interest during the six-month extension, is there a loss equal to the accrued interest? Since the interest rate was not raised, only Section 3–605(c) would apply and X probably could not prove any loss. The obligation of X includes interest on the note until the note is paid. To the extent payment was delayed X had the use of the money that X otherwise would have had to pay to Lender. X could have prevented the running of interest by paying the debt. Since X did not do so, X suffered no loss as the result of the extension.

If the interest rate was raised, Section 3–605(d) also must be considered. If X is an anomalous indorser, X's liability is to pay the note according to its terms at the time of indorsement. Section 3–415(a). Thus, X's obligation to pay interest is measured by the terms of the note (12%) rather than by the increased amount of 14 percent. The same analysis applies if X had been a co-maker. Under Section 3–412 the liability of the issuer of a note is to pay the note according to its terms at the time it was issued. Either obligation could be changed by contract and that occurred with respect to Corporation when it agreed to the increase in the interest rate, but X did not join in that agreement and is not bound by it. Thus, the most that X can be required to pay is the amount due on the note plus interest at the rate of 12 percent.

Does the modification discharge X under Section 3–605(d)? Any modification that increases the monetary obligation of X is material. An increase of the interest rate from 12 percent to 14 percent is certainly a material modification. There is a presumption that X is discharged because Section 3–605(d) creates a presumption that the modification caused a loss to X equal to the amount of the right of recourse. Thus, Lender has the burden of proving absence of loss or a loss less than the amount of the right of recourse. Since Corporation paid no interest during the six-month period, the issue is like the issue presented under Section 3–605(c) which we have just discussed. The increase in the interest rate could not have affected the right of recourse because no interest was paid by Corporation. X is in the same position as X would have been in if there had been an extension without an increase in the interest rate.

The analysis with respect to Section 3–605(c) and (d) would have been different if we change the assumptions. Suppose Corporation was not insolvent on April 1, 1992, that Corporation paid interest at the higher rate during the six-month period, and that Corporation was insolvent at the end of the six-month period. In this case it is possible that the extension and the additional burden placed on Corporation by the increased interest rate may have been detrimental to X.

There are difficulties in properly allocating burden of proof when the agreement between Lender and Corporation involves both an extension under Section 3–605(c) and a modification under Section 3–605(d). The agreement may have caused loss to X but it may be difficult to identify the extent to which the loss was caused by the extension or the other modification. If neither Lender nor X introduces evidence on the issue, the result is full discharge because Section 3–605(d) applies. Thus, Lender has the burden of overcoming the presumption in Section 3–605(d). In doing so, Lender should be entitled to a presumption that the extension of time by itself caused no loss. Section 3–605(c) is based on such a presumption and X should be required to introduce evidence on the effect of the extension on the right of recourse. Lender would have to introduce evidence on the effect of the increased interest rate. Thus both sides will have to introduce evidence. On the basis of this evidence the court will have to make a determination of the overall effect of the agreement on X's right of recourse. See PEB Commentary No. 11, supra.

6. Subsection (e) deals with discharge of sureties by impairment of collateral. It generally conforms to former Section 3–606(1)(b). Subsection (g) states common examples of what is meant by impairment. By using the term "includes," it allows a court to find impairment in other cases as well. There is extensive case law on impairment of collateral. The surety is discharged to the extent the surety proves that impairment was caused by a person entitled to enforce the instrument. For example, suppose the payee of a secured note fails to perfect the security interest. The collateral is owned by the principal debtor who subsequently files in bankruptcy. As a result of the failure to perfect, the security interest is not enforceable in bankruptcy. If the payee obtains payment from the surety, the surety is subrogated to the payee's security interest in the collateral. In this case the value of the security interest is impaired completely because the security interest is unenforceable. If the value of the collateral is as much or more than the amount of the note there is a complete discharge.

In some states a real property grantee who assumes the obligation of the grantor as maker of a note secured by the real property becomes by operation of law a principal debtor and the grantor becomes a surety. The meager case authority was split on whether former Section 3–606 applied to release the grantor if the holder released or extended the obligation of the grantee. Revised Article 3 takes no position on the effect of the release of the grantee in this case. Section 3–605(b) does not apply because the holder has not discharged the obligation of a "party," a term defined in Section 3–103(a)(8) as "party to an instrument." The assuming grantee is not a party to the instrument. The resolution of this question is governed by general principles of law, including the law of suretyship. See PEB Commentary No. 11, supra.

7. Subsection (f) is illustrated by the following case. X and Y sign a note for $1,000 as co-makers. Neither is an accommodation party. X grants a security interest in X's property to secure the note. The collateral is worth more than $1,000. Payee fails to perfect the security interest in X's property before X files in bankruptcy. As a result the security interest is not enforceable in bankruptcy. Had Payee perfected the security interest, Y could have paid the note and gained rights to X's collateral by subrogation. If the security interest had been perfected, Y could have realized on the collateral to the extent of $500 to satisfy its right of contribution against X. Payee's failure to perfect deprived Y of the benefit of the collateral. Subsection (f) discharges Y to the extent of its loss. If there are no assets in the bankruptcy for unsecured claims, the loss is $500, the amount of Y's contribution claim against X which now has a zero value. If some amount is payable on unsecured claims, the loss is reduced by the amount receivable by Y. The same result follows if Y is an accommodation party but Payee has no knowledge of the accommodation or notice under Section 3–419(c). In that event Y is not discharged under subsection (e), but subsection (f) applies because X and Y are jointly and severally liable on the note. Under subsection (f), Y is treated as a co-maker with a right of contribution rather than an accommodation party with a right of reimbursement. Y is discharged to the extent of $500. If Y is the principal debtor and X is the accommodation party subsection (f) doesn't apply. Y, as principal debtor, is not injured by the impairment of collateral because Y would have been obliged to reimburse X for the entire $1,000 even if Payee had obtained payment from sale of the collateral.

8. Subsection (i) is a continuation of former law which allowed suretyship defenses to be waived. As the subsection provides, a party is not discharged under this section if the instrument or a separate agreement of the party waives discharge either specifically or by general language indicating that defenses based on suretyship and impairment of collateral are waived. No particular language or form of agreement is required, and the standards for enforcing such a term are the same as the standards for enforcing any other term in an instrument or agreement.

Subsection (i), however, applies only to a "discharge under this section." The right of an accommodation party to be discharged under Section 3–605(e) because of an impairment of collateral can be waived. But with respect to a note secured by personal property collateral, Article 9 also applies. If an accommodation party is a "debtor" under Section 9–105(1)(d), the accommodation party has rights under Article 9. Under Section 9–501(3)(b) rights of an Article 9 debtor under Section 9–504(3) and Section 9–505(1), which deal with disposition of collateral, cannot be waived except as provided in Article 9. These Article 9 rights are independent of rights under Section 3–605. Since Section 3–605(i) is specifically limited to discharge under Section 3–605, a waiver of rights with respect to Section 3–605 has no effect on rights under Article 9. With respect to Article 9 rights, Section 9–501(3)(b) controls. See PEB Commentary No. 11, supra.

1. This section contains rules that are applicable when a secondary obligor (as defined in Section 3–103(a)(17)) is a party to an instrument. These rules essentially parallel modern interpretations of the law of suretyship and guaranty that apply when a secondary obligor is not a party to an instrument. See generally *Restatement of the Law, Third, Suretyship and Guaranty* (1996). Of course, the rules in this section do not resolve

all possible issues concerning the rights and duties of the parties. In the event that a situation is presented that is not resolved by this section (or the other related sections of this Article), the resolution may be provided by the general law of suretyship because, pursuant to Section 1–103, that law is applicable unless displaced by provisions of this Act.

2.   Like the law of suretyship and guaranty, Section 3–605 provides secondary obligors with defenses that are not available to other parties to instruments. The general operation of Section 3–605, and its relationship to the law of suretyship and guaranty, can be illustrated by an example. Bank agrees to lend $10,000 to Borrower, but only if Backer also is liable for repayment of the loan. The parties could consummate that transaction in three different ways. First, if Borrower and Backer incurred those obligations with contracts not governed by this Article (such as a note that is not an instrument for purposes of this Article), the general law of suretyship and guaranty would be applicable. Under modern nomenclature, Bank is the "obligee," Borrower is the "principal obligor," and Backer is the "secondary obligor." See *Restatement of Suretyship and Guaranty* § 1. Then assume that Bank and Borrower agree to a modification of their rights and obligations after the note is signed. For example, they might agree that Borrower may repay the loan at some date after the due date, or that Borrower may discharge its repayment obligation by paying Bank $3,000 rather than $10,000. Alternatively, suppose that Bank releases collateral that Borrower has given to secure the loan. Under the law of suretyship and guaranty, the secondary obligor may be discharged under certain circumstances if these modifications of the obligations between Bank (the obligee) and Borrower (the principal obligor) are made without the consent of Backer (the secondary obligor). The rights that the secondary obligor has to a discharge of its liability in such cases commonly are referred to as suretyship defenses. The extent of the discharge depends upon the particular circumstances. See *Restatement of Suretyship and Guaranty* §§ 37, 39–44.

A second possibility is that the parties might decide to evidence the loan by a negotiable instrument. In that scenario, Borrower signs a note under which Borrower is obliged to pay $10,000 to the order of Bank on a due date stated in the note. Backer becomes liable for the repayment obligation by signing the note as a co-maker or indorser. In either case the note is signed for accommodation, Backer is an accommodation party, and Borrower is the accommodated party. See Section 3–419 (describing the obligations of accommodation parties). For purposes of Section 3–605, Backer is also a "secondary obligor" and Borrower is a "principal obligor," as those terms are defined in Section 3–103. Because Backer is a party to the instrument, its rights to a discharge based on any modification of obligations between Bank and Borrower are governed by Section 3–605 rather than by the general law of suretyship and guaranty. Within Section 3–605, subsection (a) describes the consequences of a release of Borrower, subsection (b) describes the consequences of an extension of time, and subsection (c) describes the consequences of other modifications.

The third possibility is that Borrower would use an instrument governed by this Article to evidence its repayment obligation, but Backer's obligation would be created in some way other than by becoming party to that instrument. In that case, Backer's rights are determined by suretyship and guaranty law rather than by this Article. See Comment 3 to Section 3–419.

A person also can acquire secondary liability without having been a secondary obligor at the time that the principal obligation was created. For example, a transferee of real or personal property that assumes the obligation of the transferor as maker of a note secured by the property becomes by operation of law a principal obligor, with the transferor becoming a secondary obligor. *Restatement of Suretyship and Guaranty* § 2(e); *Restatement of Mortgages* § 5.1. Article 3 does not determine the effect of the release of the transferee in that case because the assuming transferee is not a "party" to the instrument as defined in Section 3–103(a)(10). Section 3–605(a) does not apply then because the holder has not discharged the obligation of a "principal obligor," a term defined in Section 3–103(a)(11). Thus, the resolution of that question is governed by the law of suretyship. See *Restatement of Suretyship and Guaranty* § 39.

3.   Section 3–605 is not, however, limited to the conventional situation of the accommodation party discussed in Comment 2. It also applies in four other situations. First, it applies to indorsers of notes who are not accommodation parties. Unless an indorser signs without recourse, the indorser's liability under Section 3–415(a) is functionally similar to that of a guarantor of payment. For example, if Bank in the second hypothetical discussed in Comment 2 indorsed the note and transferred it to Second Bank, Bank is liable to Second Bank in the event of dishonor of the note by Borrower. Section 3–415(a). Because of that secondary liability as indorser, Bank qualifies as a "secondary obligor" under Section 3–103(a)(17) and has the same rights under Section 3–605 as an accommodation party.

Second, a similar analysis applies to the drawer of a draft that is accepted by a party that is not a bank. Under Section 3–414(d), that drawer has liability on the same terms as an indorser under Section 3–415(a). Thus, the drawer in that case is a "secondary obligor" under Section 3–103(a)(17) and has rights under Section 3–605 to that extent.

Third, a similar principle justifies application of Section 3–605 to persons who indorse a check. Assume that Drawer draws a check to the order of Payee. Payee then indorses the check and transfers it to Transferee. If Transferee presents the check and it is dishonored, Transferee may recover from Drawer under Section 3–414 or Payee under Section 3–415. Because of that secondary liability as an indorser, Payee is a secondary obligor under Section 3–103(a)(17). Drawer is a "principal obligor" under Section 3–103(a)(11). As noted in Comment 4, below, however, Section 3–605(a)(3) will discharge indorsers of checks in some cases in which other secondary obligors will not be discharged by this section.

Fourth, this section also deals with the rights of co-makers of instruments, even when those co-makers do not qualify as accommodation parties. The co-makers' rights of contribution under Section 3–116 make each co-maker a secondary obligor to the extent of that right of contribution.

4.   Subsection (a) is based on *Restatement of Suretyship and Guaranty* § 39. It addresses the effects of a release of the principal obligor by the person entitled to enforce the instrument. Paragraph (a)(1) governs the effect of that release on the principal obligor's duties to the secondary obligor; paragraphs (a)(2) and (a)(3) govern the effect of that release on the secondary obligor's duties to the person entitled to enforce the instrument.

With respect to the duties of the principal obligor, the release of course cannot affect obligations of the principal obligor with respect to payments that the secondary obligor already has made. But with respect to future payments by the secondary obligor, paragraph (a)(1) (based on *Restatement of Suretyship and Guaranty* § 39(a)) provides that the principal obligor is discharged, to the extent of the release, from any other duties to the secondary obligor. That rule is appropriate because otherwise the discharge granted to the principal obligor would be illusory: it would have obtained a release from a person entitled to enforce that instrument, but it would be directly liable for the same sum to the secondary obligor if the secondary obligor later complied with its secondary obligation to pay the instrument. This discharge does not occur, though, if the terms of the release effect a "preservation of recourse" as described in subsection (g). See Comment 10, below.

The discharge under paragraph (a)(1) of the principal obligor's duties to the secondary obligor is broad, applying to all duties under this article. This includes not only the principal obligor's liability as a party to an instrument (as a maker, drawer or indorser under Sections 3–412 through 3–415) but also obligations under Sections 3–116 and 3–419.

Paragraph (a)(2) is based closely on *Restatement of Suretyship and Guaranty* § 39(b). It articulates a default rule that the release of a principal obligor also discharges the secondary obligor, to the extent of the release granted to the principal obligor, from any unperformed portion of its obligation on the instrument. The discharge of the secondary obligor under paragraph (a)(2) is phrased more narrowly than the discharge of the principal obligor is phrased under paragraph (a)(1) because, unlike principal obligors, the only obligations of secondary obligors in Article 3 are "on the instrument" as makers or indorsers.

The parties can opt out of that rule by including a contrary statement in the terms of the release. The provision does not contemplate that any "magic words" are necessary. Thus, discharge of the secondary obligor under paragraph (a)(2) is avoided not only if the terms of the release track the statutory language (e.g., the person entitled to enforce the instrument "retains the right to enforce the instrument" against the secondary obligor), or if the terms of the release effect a preservation of recourse under subsection (g), but also if the terms of the release include a simple statement that the parties intend to "release the principal obligor but not the secondary obligor" or that the person entitled to enforce the instrument "reserves its rights" against the secondary obligor. At the same time, because paragraph (a)(2) refers to the "terms of the release," extrinsic circumstances cannot be used to establish that the parties intended the secondary obligor to remain obligated. If a release of the principal obligor includes such a provision, the secondary obligor is, nonetheless, discharged to the extent of the consideration that is paid for the release; that consideration is treated as a payment in partial satisfaction of the instrument.

Notwithstanding language in the release that prevents discharge of the secondary obligor under paragraph (a)(2), paragraph (a)(3) discharges the secondary obligor from its obligation to a person entitled to enforce the instrument to the extent that the release otherwise would cause the secondary obligor a loss. The rationale for that provision is that a release of the principal obligor changes the economic risk for which the secondary obligor contracted. This risk may be increased in two ways. First, by releasing the principal obligor, the person entitled to enforce the instrument has eliminated the likelihood of future payments by the principal obligor that would lessen the obligation of the secondary obligor. Second, unless the release effects a preservation of the secondary obligor's recourse, the release eliminates the secondary obligor's claims against the principal obligor with respect to any future payment by the secondary obligor. The discharge provided by this paragraph prevents that increased risk from causing the secondary obligor a loss. Moreover, permitting releases to be negotiated between the principal obligor and the person entitled to enforce the instrument without regard to the consequences to the secondary obligor would create an undue risk of opportunistic behavior by the obligee and principal obligor. That concern is lessened, and the discharge is not provided by paragraph (a)(3), if the secondary obligor has consented to the release or is deemed to have consented to it under subsection (f) (which presumes consent by a secondary obligor to actions taken by a principal obligor if the secondary obligor controls the principal obligor or deals with the person entitled to enforce the instrument on behalf of the principal obligor). See Comment 9, below.

Subsection (a) (and Restatement Section 39(b), the concepts of which it follows quite closely) is designed to facilitate negotiated workouts between a creditor and a principal obligor, so long as they are not at the expense of a secondary obligor who has not consented to the arrangement (either specifically or by waiving its rights to discharge under this section). Thus, for example, the provision facilitates an arrangement in which the principal obligor pays some portion of a guaranteed obligation, the person entitled to enforce the instrument grants a release to the principal obligor in exchange for that payment, and the person entitled to enforce the instrument pursues the secondary obligor for the remainder of the obligation. Under paragraph (a)(2), the person entitled to enforce the instrument may pursue the secondary obligor despite the release of the principal obligor so long as the terms of the release provide for this result. Under paragraph (a)(3), though, the secondary obligor will be protected against any loss it might suffer by reason of that release (if the secondary obligor has not waived discharge under subsection (f)). It should be noted that the obligee may be able to minimize the risk of such loss (and, thus, of the secondary obligor's discharge) by giving the secondary obligor prompt notice of the release even though such notice is not required.

The foregoing principles are illustrated by the following cases:

Case 1. D borrows $1000 from C. The repayment obligation is evidenced by a note issued by D, payable to the order of C. S is an accommodation indorser of the note. As the due date of the note approaches, it becomes obvious that D cannot pay the full amount of the note and may soon be facing bankruptcy. C, in order to collect as much as possible from D and lessen the need to seek recovery from S, agrees to release D from its obligation under the note in exchange for $100 in cash. The agreement to release D is silent as to the effect of the release on S. Pursuant to Section 3–605(a)(2), the release of D discharges S from its obligations to C on the note.

Case 2. Same facts as Case 1, except that the terms of the release provide that C retains its rights to enforce the instrument against S. D is discharged from its obligations to S pursuant to Section 3–605(a)(1), but S is not discharged from its obligations to C pursuant to Section 3–605(a)(2). However, if S could have recovered from D any sum it paid to C (had D not been discharged from its obligation to S), S has been harmed by the release and is discharged pursuant to Section 3–605(a)(3) to the extent of that harm.

Case 3. Same facts as Case 1, except that the terms of the release provide that C retains its rights to enforce the instrument against S and that S retains its recourse against D. Under subsection (g), the release effects a preservation of recourse. Thus, S is not discharged from its obligations to C pursuant to Section 3–605(a)(2) and D is not discharged from its obligations to S pursuant to Section 3–605(a)(1). Because S's claims against D are preserved, S will not suffer the kind of loss described in Case 2. If no other loss is suffered by S as a result of the release, S is not discharged pursuant to this section.

Case 4. Same facts as Case 3, except that D had made arrangements to work at a second job in order to earn the money to fulfill its obligations on the note. When C released D, however, D canceled the plans for the second job. While S still retains its recourse against D, S may be discharged from its obligation under the instrument to the extent that D's decision to forgo the second job causes S a loss because forgoing the job renders D unable to fulfill its obligations to S under Section 3–419.

Subsection (a) reflects a change from former Section 3–605(b), which provided categorically that the release of a principal obligor by the person entitled to enforce the instrument did not discharge a secondary obligor's obligation on the instrument and assumed that the release also did not discharge the principal obligor's obligations to the secondary obligor under Section 3–419. The rule under subsection (a) is much closer to the policy of the *Restatement of Suretyship and Guaranty* than was former Section 3–605(b). The change, however, is likely to affect only a narrow category of cases. First, as discussed above, Section 3–605 applies only to transactions in which the payment obligation is represented by a negotiable instrument, and, within that set of transactions, only to those transactions in which the secondary obligation is incurred by indorsement or cosigning, not to transactions that involve a separate document of guaranty. See Comment 2, above. Second, as provided in subsection (f), secondary obligors cannot obtain a discharge under subsection (a) in any transaction in which they have consented to the challenged conduct. Thus, subsection (a) will not apply to any transaction that includes a provision waiving suretyship defenses (a provision that is almost universally included in commercial loan documentation) or to any transaction in which the creditor obtains the consent of the secondary obligor at the time of the release.

The principal way in which subsection (a) goes beyond the policy of *Restatement* § 39 is with respect to the liability of indorsers of checks. Specifically, the last sentence of paragraph (a)(2) provides that a release of a principal obligor grants a complete discharge to the indorser of a check, without requiring the indorser to prove harm. In that particular context, it seems likely that continuing responsibility for the indorser often would be so inconsistent with the expectations of the parties as to create a windfall for the creditor and an unfair surprise for the indorser. Thus, the statute implements a simple rule that grants a complete discharge. The creditor, of course, can avoid that rule by contracting with the secondary obligor for a different result at the time that the creditor grants the release to the principal obligor.

5.　　Subsection (b) is based on *Restatement of Suretyship and Guaranty* § 40 and relates to extensions of the due date of the instrument. An extension of time to pay a note is often beneficial to the secondary obligor because the additional time may enable the principal obligor to obtain the funds to pay the instrument. In some cases, however, the extension may cause loss to the secondary obligor, particularly if deterioration of the financial condition of the principal obligor reduces the amount that the secondary obligor is able to recover on its right of recourse when default occurs. For example, suppose that the instrument is an installment note and the principal debtor is temporarily short of funds to pay a monthly installment. The payee agrees to extend the due date of the installment for a month or two to allow the debtor to pay when funds are available. Paragraph (b)(2) provides that an extension of time results in a discharge of the secondary obligor, but only to the extent that the secondary obligor proves that the extension caused loss. See subsection (h) (discussing the burden of proof under Section 3–605). Thus, if the extension is for a long period, the secondary obligor might be able to prove that during the period of extension the principal obligor became insolvent, reducing the value of the right of recourse of the secondary obligor. In such a case, paragraph (b)(2) discharges the secondary obligor to the extent of that harm. Although not required to notify the secondary obligor of the extension, the payee can minimize the risk of loss by the secondary obligor by giving the secondary obligor prompt notice of the extension; prompt notice can enhance the likelihood that the secondary obligor's right of recourse can remain valuable, and thus can limit the likelihood that the secondary obligor will suffer a loss because of the extension. See *Restatement of Suretyship and Guaranty* Section 38 comment b.

If the secondary obligor is not discharged under paragraph (b)(2) (either because it would not suffer a loss by reason of the extension or because it has waived its right to discharge pursuant to subsection (f)), it is important to understand the effect of the extension on the rights and obligations of the secondary obligor. Consider the following cases:

Case 5. A borrows money from Lender and issues a note payable to the order of Lender that is due on April 1, 2002. B signs the note for accommodation at the request of Lender. B signed the note either as co-maker or as an anomalous indorser. In either case Lender subsequently makes an agreement with A extending the due date of A's obligation to pay the note to July 1, 2002. In either case B did not agree to the extension, and the extension did not address Lender's rights against B. Under paragraph (b)(1), A's obligations to B under this article are also extended to July 1, 2002. Under paragraph (b)(3), if B is not discharged, B may treat its obligations to Lender as also extended, or may pay the instrument on the original due date.

Case 6. Same facts as Case 5, except that the extension agreement includes a statement that the Lender retains its right to enforce the note against B on its original terms. Under paragraph (b)(3), B is liable on the original due date, but under paragraph (b)(1), A's obligations to B under Section 3–419 are not due until July 1, 2002.

Case 7. Same facts as Case 5, except that the extension agreement includes a statement that the Lender retains its right to enforce the note against B on its original terms and B retains its recourse against A as though no extension had been granted. Under paragraph (b)(3), B is liable on the original due date. Under paragraph (b)(1), A's obligations to B under Section 3–419 are not extended.

Under section 3–605(b), the results in Case 5 and Case 7 are identical to the results that follow from the law of suretyship and guaranty. See *Restatement of Suretyship and Guaranty* § 40. The situation in Case 6 is not specifically addressed in the Restatement, but the resolution in this Section is consistent with the concepts of suretyship and guaranty law as reflected in the Restatement. If the secondary obligor is called upon to pay on the due date, it may be difficult to quantify the extent to which the extension has impaired the right of recourse of the secondary obligor at that time. Still, the secondary obligor does have a right to make a claim against the obligee at that time. As a practical matter a suit making such a claim should establish the facts relevant to the extent of the impairment. *See Restatement of Suretyship and Guaranty* § 37(4).

As a practical matter, an extension of the due date will normally occur only when the principal obligor is unable to pay on the due date. The interest of the secondary obligor normally is to acquiesce in the willingness of the person entitled to enforce the instrument to wait for payment from the principal obligor rather than to pay right away and rely on an action against the principal obligor that may have little or no value. But in unusual cases the secondary obligor may prefer to pay the holder on the original due date so as to avoid continuing accrual of interest. In such cases, the secondary obligor may do so. See paragraph (b)(3). If the terms of the extension provide that the person entitled to enforce the instrument retains its right to enforce the instrument against the secondary obligor on the original due date, though, those terms are effective and the secondary obligor may not delay payment until the extended due date. Unless the extension agreement effects a preservation of recourse, however, the secondary obligor may not proceed against the principal obligor under Section 3–419 until the extended due date. See paragraph (b)(1). To the extent that delay causes loss to the secondary obligor it is discharged under paragraph (b)(2).

Even in those cases in which a secondary obligor does not have a duty to pay the instrument on the original due date, it always has the right to pay the instrument on that date, and perhaps minimize its loss by doing so. The secondary obligor is not precluded, however, from asserting its rights to discharge under Section 3–605(b)(2) if it does not exercise that option. The critical issue is whether the extension caused the secondary obligor a loss by increasing the difference between its cost of performing its obligation on the instrument and the amount recoverable from the principal obligor under this Article. The decision by the secondary obligor not to exercise its option to pay on the original due date may, under the circumstances, be a factor to be considered in the determination of that issue, especially if the secondary obligor has been given prompt notice of the extension (as discussed above).

6.   Subsection (c) is based on *Restatement of Suretyship and Guaranty* § 41. It is a residual provision, which applies to modifications of the obligation of the principal obligor that are not covered by subsections (a) and (b). Under subsection (c)(1), a modification of the obligation of the principal obligor on the instrument (other than a release covered by subsection (a) or an extension of the due date covered by subsection (b)), will correspondingly modify the duties of the principal obligor to the secondary obligor. Under subsection (c)(2), such a modification also will result in discharge of the secondary obligor to the extent the modification causes loss to the secondary obligor. To the extent that the secondary obligor is not discharged and the obligation changes the amount of money payable on the instrument, or the timing of such payment, subsection (c)(3) provides the secondary obligor with a choice: it may satisfy its obligation on the instrument as if the modification had not occurred, or it may treat its obligation to pay the instrument as having been modified in a manner corresponding to the modification of the principal obligor's obligation.

The following cases illustrate the application of subsection (c):

Case 8. Corporation borrows money from Lender and issues a note payable to Lender. X signs the note as an accommodation party for Corporation. The note refers to a loan agreement under which the note was issued, which states various events of default that allow Lender to accelerate the due date of the note. Among the events of default are breach of covenants not to incur debt beyond specified limits and not to engage in any line of business substantially different from that currently carried on by Corporation. Without consent of X, Lender agrees to modify the covenants to allow Corporation to enter into a new line of business that X considers to be risky, and to incur debt beyond the limits specified in the loan agreement to finance the new venture. This modification discharges X to the extent that the modification otherwise would cause X a loss.

Case 9. Corporation borrows money from Lender and issues a note payable to Lender in the amount of $100,000. X signs the note as an accommodation party for Corporation. The note calls for 60 equal monthly payments of interest and principal. Before the first payment is made, Corporation and Lender agree to modify the note by changing the repayment schedule to require four annual payments of interest only, followed by a fifth payment of interest and the entire $100,000 principal balance. To the extent that the modification does not discharge X, X has the option of fulfilling its obligation on the note in accordance with the original terms or the modified terms.

7.   Subsection (d) is based on *Restatement of Suretyship and Guaranty* § 42 and deals with the discharge of secondary obligors by impairment of collateral. The last sentence of subsection (d) states four common examples of what is meant by impairment. Because it uses the term "includes," the provision allows a court to find

impairment in other cases as well. There is extensive case law on impairment of collateral. The secondary obligor is discharged to the extent that the secondary obligor proves that impairment was caused by a person entitled to enforce the instrument. For example, assume that the payee of a secured note fails to perfect the security interest. The collateral is owned by the principal obligor who subsequently files in bankruptcy. As a result of the failure to perfect, the security interest is not enforceable in bankruptcy. If the payee were to obtain payment from the secondary obligor, the secondary obligor would be subrogated to the payee's security interest in the collateral under Section 3–419 and general principles of suretyship law. See *Restatement of Suretyship and Guaranty § 28(1)(c).* In this situation, though, the value of the security interest is impaired completely because the security interest is unenforceable. Thus, the secondary obligor is discharged from its obligation on the note to the extent of that impairment. If the value of the collateral impaired is as much or more than the amount of the note, and if there will be no recovery on the note as an unsecured claim, there is a complete discharge. Subsection (d) applies whether the collateral is personalty or realty, whenever the obligation in question is in the form of a negotiable instrument.

8.   Subsection (e) is based on the former Section 3–605(h). The requirement of knowledge in the first clause is consistent with Section 9–628. The requirement of notice in the second clause is consistent with Section 3–419(c).

9.   The importance of the suretyship defenses provided in Section 3–605 is greatly diminished by the fact that the right to discharge can be waived as provided in subsection (f). The waiver can be effectuated by a provision in the instrument or in a separate agreement. It is standard practice to include such a waiver of suretyship defenses in notes prepared by financial institutions or other commercial creditors. Thus, Section 3–605 will result in the discharge of an accommodation party on a note only in the occasional case in which the note does not include such a waiver clause and the person entitled to enforce the note nevertheless takes actions that would give rise to a discharge under this section without obtaining the consent of the secondary obligor.

Because subsection (f) by its terms applies only to a discharge "under this section," subsection (f) does not operate to waive a defense created by other law (such as the law governing enforcement of security interests under Article 9) that cannot be waived under that law. See, e.g., Section 9–602.

The last sentence of subsection (f) creates an inference of consent on the part of the secondary obligor whenever the secondary obligor controls the principal obligor or deals with the creditor on behalf of the principal obligor. That sentence is based on *Restatement of Suretyship and Guaranty § 48(2).*

10.   Subsection (g) explains the criteria for determining whether the terms of a release or extension preserve the secondary obligor's recourse, a concept of importance in the application of subsections (a) and (b). First, the terms of the release or extension must provide that the person entitled to enforce the instrument retains the right to enforce the instrument against the secondary obligor. Second, the terms of the release or extension must provide that the recourse of the secondary obligor against the principal obligor continues as though the release or extension had not been granted. Those requirements are drawn from *Restatement of Suretyship and Guaranty § 38.*

11.   Subsections (h) and (i) articulate rules for the burden of persuasion under Section 3–605. Those rules are based on *Restatement of Suretyship and Guaranty § 49.*

———————

AMENDMENTS TO ARTICLE 4

BANK DEPOSITS AND COLLECTIONS

§ 4–103.   **Variation by Agreement; Measure of Damages; Action Constituting Ordinary Care.**

Official Comment
* * *

4.   Under this Article banks come under the general obligations of the use of good faith and the exercise of ordinary care. "Good faith" is defined in ~~Section 3–103(a)(4)~~ Section 1–201(b)(20). The term "ordinary care" is defined in Section 3–103(a)(9). These definitions are made to apply to Article 4 by Section 4–104(c). Section 4–202 states respects in which collecting banks must use ordinary care. Subsection (c) of Section 4–103 provides that

action or non-action approved by the Article or pursuant to Federal Reserve regulations or operating circulars constitutes the exercise of ordinary care. Federal Reserve regulations and operating circulars constitute an affirmative standard of ordinary care equally with the provisions of Article 4 itself.

* * *

§ 4–104.　　Definitions and Index of Definitions.

* * *

(b)　Other definitions applying to this Article and the sections in which they appear are:

"Agreement for electronic presentment" Section 4–110.

~~"Bank" Section 4–105.~~

"Collecting bank" Section 4–105.

"Depositary bank" Section 4–105.

"Intermediary bank" Section 4–105.

"Payor bank" Section 4–105.

"Presenting bank" Section 4–105.

"Presentment notice" Section 4–110.

(c)　The following definitions in other Articles apply to this Article:

"Acceptance" Section 3–409.

"Alteration" Section 3–407.

"Cashier's check" Section 3–104.

"Certificate of deposit" Section 3–104.

"Certified check" Section 3–409.

"Check" Section 3–104.

"Good faith" Section 3–103.

"Holder in due course" Section 3–302.

"Instrument" Section 3–104.

"Notice of dishonor" Section 3–503.

"Order" Section 3–103.

"Ordinary care" Section 3–103.

"Person entitled to enforce" Section 3–301.

"Presentment" Section 3–501.

"Promise" Section 3–103.

"Prove" Section 3–103.

"Record" Section 3–103.

"Remotely-Created Consumer item" Section 3–103.

"Teller's check" Section 3–104.

"Unauthorized signature" Section 3–403.

(d)　In addition, Article 1 contains general definitions and principles of construction and interpretation applicable throughout this Article.

§ 4–105.　　Definitions of Types of Banks "Bank"; "Depositary Bank"; "Payor Bank"; "Intermediary Bank"; "Collecting Bank"; "Presenting Bank".

In this Article:

(1)　["Bank" means a person engaged in the business of banking, including a savings bank, savings and loan association, credit union, or trust company;]

(2)　"Depositary bank" means the first bank to take an item even though it is also the payor bank, unless the item is presented for immediate payment over the counter;

(3)   "Payor bank" means a bank that is the drawee of a draft;

(4)   "Intermediary bank" means a bank to which an item is transferred in course of collection except the depositary or payor bank;

(5)   "Collecting bank" means a bank handling an item for collection except the payor bank;

(6)   "Presenting bank" means a bank presenting an item except a payor bank.

Legislative Note: A jurisdiction that enacts this statute that has not yet enacted the revised version of UCC Article 1 should leave the definition of "Bank" in Section 4–105(1). Section 4–105(1) is reserved for that purpose. A jurisdiction that has adopted or simultaneously adopts the revised Article 1 should delete the definition of "Bank" from Section 4–105(1), but should leave those numbers "reserved." If jurisdictions follow the numbering suggested here, the subsections will have the same numbering in all jurisdictions that have adopted these amendments (whether they have or have not adopted the revised version of UCC Article 1). In either case, they should change the title of the section, as indicated in these revisions, so that all jurisdictions will have the same title for the section.

§ 4–207.   Transfer Warranties.

(a)   A customer or collecting bank that transfers an item and receives a settlement or other consideration warrants to the transferee and to any subsequent collecting bank that:

(1)   the warrantor is a person entitled to enforce the item;

(2)   all signatures on the item are authentic and authorized;

(3)   the item has not been altered;

(4)   the item is not subject to a defense or claim in recoupment (Section 3–305(a)) of any party that can be asserted against the warrantor; ~~and~~

(5)   the warrantor has no knowledge of any insolvency proceeding commenced with respect to the maker or acceptor or, in the case of an unaccepted draft, the ~~drawer.~~ drawer; and

(6)   with respect to any remotely-created consumer item, that the person on whose account the item is drawn authorized the issuance of the item in the amount for which the item is drawn.

* * *

Official Comment

1.   Except for subsection (b), this section conforms to Section 3–416 and extends its coverage to items. The substance of this section is discussed in the Comment to Section 3–416. Subsection (b) provides that customers or collecting banks that transfer items, whether by indorsement or not, undertake to pay the item if the item is dishonored. This obligation cannot be disclaimed by a "without recourse" indorsement or otherwise. With respect to checks, Regulation CC Section 229.34 states the warranties made by paying and returning banks.

2.   For an explanation of subsection (a)(6), see comment 8 to Section 3–416.

§ 4–208.   Presentment Warranties.

(a)   If an unaccepted draft is presented to the drawee for payment or acceptance and the drawee pays or accepts the draft, (i) the person obtaining payment or acceptance, at the time of presentment, and (ii) a previous transferor of the draft, at the time of transfer, warrant to the drawee that pays or accepts the draft in good faith that:

(1)   the warrantor is, or was, at the time the warrantor transferred the draft, a person entitled to enforce the draft or authorized to obtain payment or acceptance of the draft on behalf of a person entitled to enforce the draft;

(2)   the draft has not been altered; and

(3)   the warrantor has no knowledge that the signature of the purported drawer of the draft is ~~unauthorized.~~ unauthorized; and

1101

(4)   with respect to any remotely-created consumer item, that the person on whose account the item is drawn authorized the issuance of the item in the amount for which the item is drawn.

* * *

Official Comment

1.   This section conforms to Section 3–417 and extends its coverage to items. The substance of this section is discussed in the Comment to Section 3–417. "Draft" is defined in Section 4–104 as including an item that is an order to pay so as to make clear that the term "draft" in Article 4 may include items that are not instruments within Section 3–104.

2.   For an explanation of subsection (a)(4), see comment 8 to Section 3–416.

§ 4–212.   Presentment by Notice of Item Not Payable by, Through, or at Bank; Liability of Drawer or Indorser.

(a)   Unless otherwise instructed, a collecting bank may present an item not payable by, through, or at a bank by sending to the party to accept or pay a ~~written~~ record providing notice that the bank holds the item for acceptance or payment. The notice must be sent in time to be received on or before the day when presentment is due and the bank must meet any requirement of the party to accept or pay under Section 3–501 by the close of the bank's next banking day after it knows of the requirement.

* * *

§ 4–301.   Posting; Recovery of Payment by Return of Items; Time of Dishonor; Return of Items by Payor Bank.

(a)   If a payor bank settles for a demand item other than a documentary draft presented otherwise than for immediate payment over the counter before midnight of the banking day of receipt, the payor bank may revoke the settlement and recover the settlement if, before it has made final payment and before its midnight deadline, it

(1)   ~~returns the item;~~ (1) returns the item;

(2)   returns an image of the item, if the party to which the return is made has entered into an agreement to accept an image as a return of the item and the image is returned in accordance with that agreement; or

(2)   ~~sends written~~ (3) sends a record providing notice of dishonor or nonpayment if the item is unavailable for return.

* * *

Official Comment

* * *

8.   Paragraph (a)(2) is designed to facilitate electronic check-processing by authorizing the payor bank to return an image of the item instead of the actual item. It applies only when the payor bank and the party to which the return has been made have agreed that the payor bank can make such a return and when the return complies with the agreement. The purpose of the paragraph is to prevent third parties (such as the depositor of the check) from contending that the payor bank missed its midnight deadline because it failed to return the actual item in a timely manner. If the payor bank missed its midnight deadline, payment would have become final under Section 4–215 and the depositary bank would have lost its right of chargeback under Section 4–214. Of course, the depositary bank might enter into an agreement with its depositor to resolve that problem, but it is not clear that agreements by banks with their customers can resolve all such issues. In any event, paragraph (a)(2) should eliminate the need for such agreements. The provision rests on the premise that it is inappropriate to penalize a payor bank simply because it returns the actual item a few business days after the midnight deadline of the payor bank sent notice before that deadline to a collecting bank that had agreed to accept such notices.

Nothing in paragraph (a)(2) authorizes the payor bank to destroy the check.

§ 4–302. Payor's Bank Responsibility for Late Return of Item.

Official Comment

* * *

2. If the settlement given by the payor bank does not become final, there has been no payment under Section 4–215(b), and the payor bank giving the failed settlement is accountable under subsection (a)(1) of Section 4–302. For instance, the payor bank makes provisional settlement by sending a teller's check that is dishonored. In such a case settlement is not final under Section 4–213(c) and no payment occurs under Section 4–215(b). Payor bank is accountable on the item. The general principle is that unless settlement provides the presenting bank with usable funds, settlement has failed and the payor bank is accountable for the amount of the item. <u>On the other hand, if the payor bank makes a settlement for the item that becomes final under Section 4–215, the item has been paid and thus the payor bank is not accountable for the item under this Section.</u>*

* * *

§ 4–403. Customer's Right to Stop Payment; Burden of Proof of Loss.

* * *

(b) A stop-payment order is effective for six months, but it lapses after 14 calendar days if the original order was oral and was not confirmed in ~~writing~~ <u>a record</u> within that period. A stop-payment order may be renewed for additional six-month periods by a ~~writing~~ <u>record</u> given to the bank within a period during which the stop-payment order is effective.

* * *

§ 4–406. Customer's Duty to Discover and Report Unauthorized Signature or Alteration.

Official Comment

* * *

4. Subsection (e) replaces former subsection (3) and poses a modified comparative negligence test for determining liability. See the discussion on this point in the Comments to Sections 3–404, 3–405, and 3–406. The term "good faith" is defined in ~~Section 3–103(a)(4)~~ <u>Section 1–201(b)(20)</u> as including "observance of reasonable commercial standards of fair dealing." The connotation of this standard is fairness and not absence of negligence.

* * *

---

* Amendment approved by the Permanent Editorial Board for Uniform Commercial Code November 2, 2002.

APPENDIX D
UNREVISED UCC ARTICLE 7 (2002)

ARTICLE 7

WAREHOUSE RECEIPTS, BILLS OF LADING AND OTHER DOCUMENTS OF TITLE

PART 1. GENERAL

PART 2. WAREHOUSE RECEIPTS: SPECIAL PROVISIONS

PART 3. BILLS OF LADING: SPECIAL PROVISIONS

PART 4. WAREHOUSE RECEIPTS AND BILLS OF LADING: GENERAL OBLIGATIONS

PART 5. WAREHOUSE RECEIPTS AND BILLS OF LADING: NEGOTIATION AND TRANSFER

PART 6. WAREHOUSE RECEIPTS AND BILLS OF LADING: MISCELLANEOUS PROVISIONS

PART 1
GENERAL

§ 7–101. Short Title.

This Article shall be known and may be cited as Uniform Commercial Code—Documents of Title.

Official Comment

This Article is a consolidation and revision of the Uniform Warehouse Receipts Act and the Uniform Bills of Lading Act, and embraces also the provisions of the Uniform Sales Act relating to negotiation of documents of title.

The only substantial omissions of material covered in the previous uniform acts are the criminal provisions found in the Warehouse Receipts and Bills of Lading acts. These criminal provisions are inappropriate to a Commercial Code, and for the most part duplicate portions of the ordinary criminal law relating to frauds.

The Article does not attempt to define the tort liability of bailees, except to hold certain classes of bailees to a minimum standard of reasonable care. For important classes of bailees, liabilities in case of loss, damage or destruction, as well as other legal questions associated with particular documents of title, are governed by federal statutes, international treaties, and in some cases regulatory state laws, which supersede the provisions of this Article in case of inconsistency. See Section 7–103.

§ 7–102. Definitions and Index of Definitions.

(1) In this Article, unless the context otherwise requires:

(a) "Bailee" means the person who by a warehouse receipt, bill of lading or other document of title acknowledges possession of goods and contracts to deliver them.

(b) "Consignee" means the person named in a bill to whom or to whose order the bill promises delivery.

(c) "Consignor" means the person named in a bill as the person from whom the goods have been received for shipment.

(d) "Delivery order" means a written order to deliver goods directed to a warehouseman, carrier or other person who in the ordinary course of business issues warehouse receipts or bills of lading.

(e) "Document" means document of title as defined in the general definitions in Article 1 (Section 1–201).

(f) "Goods" means all things which are treated as movable for the purposes of a contract of storage or transportation.

(g) "Issuer" means a bailee who issues a document except that in relation to an unaccepted delivery order it means the person who orders the possessor of goods to deliver. Issuer includes any person for whom an agent or employee purports to act in issuing a document if the agent or employee has real or apparent authority to issue documents, notwithstanding that the issuer received no goods or that the goods were misdescribed or that in any other respect the agent or employee violated his instructions.

(h) "Warehouseman" is a person engaged in the business of storing goods for hire.

(2) Other definitions applying to this Article or to specified Parts thereof, and the sections in which they appear are:

"Duly negotiate". Section 7–501.

"Person entitled under the document". Section 7–403(4).

(3) Definitions in other Articles applying to this Article and the sections in which they appear are:

"Contract for sale". Section 2–106.

"Overseas". Section 2–323.

"Receipt" of goods. Section 2–103.

(4) In addition Article 1 contains general definitions and principles of construction and interpretation applicable throughout this Article.

Official Comment

Prior Uniform Statutory Provision: Section 76, Uniform Sales Act; Section 58, Uniform Warehouse Receipts Act; Sections 1 and 53, Uniform Bills of Lading Act.

Changes: Applicable definitions from the uniform acts have been consolidated and revised; definition of delivery order is new.

Purposes of Changes and New Matter:

1. "Bailee" was not defined in the old uniform acts. It is used in this Article as a blanket term to designate carriers, warehousemen and others who normally issue documents of title on the basis of goods which they have received. The definition does not, however, require actual possession of the goods. If a bailee acknowledges possession when he does not have it he is bound by sections of this Article which declare the "bailee's" obligations. (See definition of "Issuer" in this section and Sections 7–203 and 7–301 on liability in case of non-receipt.)

2. The definition of warehouse receipt contained in the general definitions section of this Act (Section 1–201) eliminates the requirement of the Uniform Warehouse Receipts Act that the issuing warehouseman be "lawfully engaged" in business. The warehouseman's compliance with applicable state regulations such as the filing of a bond has no bearing on the substantive issues dealt with in this Article. Certainly the issuer's violations of law should not diminish his responsibility on documents he has put in commercial circulation. The Uniform Warehouse Receipts Act requirement that the warehouseman be engaged "for profit" has also been eliminated in view of the existence of state operated and co-operative warehouses. But it is still essential that the business be storing goods "for hire" (Section 1–201 and this section). A person does not become a warehouseman by storing his own goods.

3. Delivery orders, which were included without qualification in the Uniform Sales Act definition of document of title, must be treated differently in this consolidation of provisions from the three uniform acts. When a delivery order has been accepted by the bailee it is for practical purposes indistinguishable from a warehouse

receipt. Prior to such acceptance there is no basis for imposing obligations on the bailee other than the ordinary obligation of contract which the bailee may have assumed to the depositor of the goods.

Cross References:

Point 1: Sections 7–203 and 7–301.

Point 2: Sections 1–201 and 7–203.

See general comment to document of title in Section 1–201.

Definitional Cross References:

"Bill of lading". Section 1–201.

"Contract". Section 1–201.

"Contract for sale". Section 2–106.

"Delivery". Section 1–201.

"Document of title". Section 1–201.

"Person". Section 1–201.

"Purchase". Section 1–201.

"Receipt of goods". Section 2–103.

"Right". Section 1–201.

"Warehouse receipt". Section 1–201.

"Written". Section 1–201.

§ 7–103. Relation of Article to Treaty, Statute, Tariff, Classification or Regulation.

To the extent that any treaty or statute of the United States, regulatory statute of this State or tariff, classification or regulation filed or issued pursuant thereto is applicable, the provisions of this Article are subject thereto.

Official Comment

Prior Uniform Statutory Provision: None.

Purposes:

1.   To make clear what would of course be true without the Section, that applicable Federal law is paramount.

2.   To make clear also that *regulatory* state statutes (such as those fixing or authorizing a commission to fix rates and prescribe services, authorizing different charges for goods of different values, and limiting liability for loss to the declared value on which the charge was based) are not affected by the Article and are controlling on the matters which they cover. Notice that the reference is not only to such statutes, but to tariffs, classifications and regulations filed or issued pursuant to them.

Cross References:

Sections 7–201, 7–202, 7–204, 7–206, 7–309, 7–401, and 7–403.

Definitional Cross Reference:

"Bill of lading". Section 1–201.

§ 7–104. Negotiable and Non-negotiable Warehouse Receipt, Bill of Lading or Other Document of Title.

(1)   A warehouse receipt, bill of lading or other document of title is negotiable

(a)   if by its terms the goods are to be delivered to bearer or to the order of a named person; or

(b)   where recognized in overseas trade, if it runs to a named person or assigns.

(2)   Any other document is non-negotiable. A bill of lading in which it is stated that the goods are consigned to a named person is not made negotiable by a provision that the goods are to be delivered only against a written order signed by the same or another named person.

Official Comment

Prior Uniform Statutory Provision: Sections 27 and 76, Uniform Sales Act; Sections 2, 3, 4, and 5, Uniform Warehouse Receipts Act; Sections 2, 3, 4, 5 and 53, Uniform Bills of Lading Act.

Changes: Consolidated and rewritten.

Purposes of Changes:

This Article deals with a class of commercial paper representing commodities in storage or transportation. This "commodity paper" is to be distinguished from what might be called "money paper" dealt with in the Article of this Act on Commercial Paper (Article 3) and "investment paper" dealt with in the Article of this Act on Investment Securities (Article 8). The class of "commodity paper" is designated "document of title" following the terminology of the Uniform Sales Act Section 76. Section 1–201. The distinctions between negotiable and nonnegotiable documents in this section makes the most important subclassification employed in the Article, in that the holder of negotiable documents may acquire more rights than his transferor had (See Section 7–502).

A document of title is negotiable only if it satisfies this section. "Deliverable on proper indorsement and surrender of this receipt" will not render a document negotiable. Bailees often include such provisions as a means of insuring return of non-negotiable receipts for record purposes. Such language may be regarded as insistence by the bailee upon a particular kind of receipt in connection with delivery of the goods. Subsections (1)(a) and (2) make it clear that a document is not negotiable which provides for delivery to order or bearer only if written instructions to that effect are given by a named person.

Cross Reference:

Section 7–502.

Definitional Cross References:

"Bearer". Section 1–201.
"Bill of lading". Section 1–201.
"Delivery". Section 1–201.
"Document of title". Section 1–201.
"Overseas". Section 2–323.
"Person". Section 1–201.
"Warehouse receipt". Section 1–201.

§ 7–105.　Construction Against Negative Implication.

The omission from either Part 2 or Part 3 of this Article of a provision corresponding to a provision made in the other Part does not imply that a corresponding rule of law is not applicable.

Official Comment

Prior Uniform Statutory Provision: None.

Purposes:

To avoid any impairment, for example, of any common-law right of indemnity a warehouseman may have corresponding to Section 7–301(5), or of any contractual security interest a carrier might have corresponding to Section 7–209(2).

Cross References:

Parts 2 and 3 of Article 7.

PART 2

WAREHOUSE RECEIPTS: SPECIAL PROVISIONS

§ 7–201.　Who May Issue a Warehouse Receipt; Storage Under Government Bond.

(1)　A warehouse receipt may be issued by any warehouseman.

(2)   Where goods including distilled spirits and agricultural commodities are stored under a statute requiring a bond against withdrawal or a license for the issuance of receipts in the nature of warehouse receipts, a receipt issued for the goods has like effect as a warehouse receipt even though issued by a person who is the owner of the goods and is not a warehouseman.

Official Comment

Prior Uniform Statutory Provision: Section 1, Uniform Warehouse Receipts Act.

Changes: Provision added to cover storage under government bond or under licensing statute.

Purposes:

It is not intended by reenactment of subsection (1) to repeal any provisions of special licensing or other statutes regulating who may become a warehouseman. See Section 10–103. Subsection (2) covers receipts issued by the owner for whiskey or other goods stored in bonded warehouses under such statutes as 26 U.S.C. Chapter 26. Limitations on the transfer of the receipts and criminal sanctions for violation of such limitations are not impaired. Section 7–103. Compare Section 7–401(d) on the liability of the issuer in such cases.

Cross References:

Sections 7–103, 7–401, 10–103.

Definitional Cross References:

"Warehouse receipt". Section 1–201.
"Warehouseman". Section 7–102.

§ 7–202.   Form of Warehouse Receipt; Essential Terms; Optional Terms.

(1)   A warehouse receipt need not be in any particular form.

(2)   Unless a warehouse receipt embodies within its written or printed terms each of the following, the warehouseman is liable for damages caused by the omission to a person injured thereby:

(a)   the location of the warehouse where the goods are stored;

(b)   the date of issue of the receipt;

(c)   the consecutive number of the receipt;

(d)   a statement whether the goods received will be delivered to the bearer, to a specified person, or to a specified person or his order;

(e)   the rate of storage and handling charges, except that where goods are stored under a field warehousing arrangement a statement of that fact is sufficient on a non-negotiable receipt;

(f)   a description of the goods or of the packages containing them;

(g)   the signature of the warehouseman, which may be made by his authorized agent;

(h)   if the receipt is issued for goods of which the warehouseman is owner, either solely or jointly or in common with others, the fact of such ownership; and

(i)   a statement of the amount of advances made and of liabilities incurred for which the warehouseman claims a lien or security interest (Section 7–209). If the precise amount of such advances made or of such liabilities incurred is, at the time of the issue of the receipt, unknown to the warehouseman or to his agent who issues it, a statement of the fact that advances have been made or liabilities incurred and the purpose thereof is sufficient.

(3)   A warehouseman may insert in his receipt any other terms which are not contrary to the provisions of this Act and do not impair his obligation of delivery (Section 7–403) or his duty of care (Section 7–204). Any contrary provisions shall be ineffective.

Official Comment

Prior Uniform Statutory Provision: Section 2, Uniform Warehouse Receipts Act.

Changes: Exemption for field warehouse receipts added in subsection (2)(e).

Purposes:

To make clear that the formal requirements of the Uniform Warehouse Receipts Act are continued but not to displace particular legislation requiring other or different specifications of form, see Sections 7–103 and 10–103. This section does not require that a receipt be issued but states formal requirements for those which are issued.

Cross References:

Sections 7–103 and 10–103.

Definitional Cross References:

"Bearer". Section 1–201.
"Delivery". Section 1–201.
"Goods". Section 7–102.
"Person". Section 1–201.
"Security interest". Section 1–201.
"Term". Section 1–201.
"Warehouse receipt". Section 1–201.
"Warehouseman". Section 7–102.
"Written". Section 1–201.

§ 7–203. Liability for Non-receipt or Misdescription.

A party to or purchaser for value in good faith of a document of title other than a bill of lading relying in either case upon the description therein of the goods may recover from the issuer damages caused by the non-receipt or misdescription of the goods, except to the extent that the document conspicuously indicates that the issuer does not know whether any part or all of the goods in fact were received or conform to the description, as where the description is in terms of marks or labels or kind, quantity or condition, or the receipt or description is qualified by "contents, condition and quality unknown", "said to contain" or the like, if such indication be true, or the party or purchaser otherwise has notice.

Official Comment

Prior Uniform Statutory Provision: Section 20, Uniform Warehouse Receipts Act.

Changes: New section confined to problem of non-receipt and misdescription.

Purposes of Changes and New Matter:

This section is a simplified restatement of existing law as to the method by which a bailee may avoid responsibility for the accuracy of descriptions which are made by or in reliance upon information furnished by the depositor. The issuer is liable on documents issued by an agent, contrary to instructions of his principal, without receiving goods. No disclaimer of the latter liability is permitted.

Cross References:

Sections 7–301 and 7–203.

Definitional Cross References:

"Conspicuous". Section 1–201.
"Document". Section 7–102.
"Document of title". Section 1–201.
"Goods". Section 7–102.
"Issuer". Section 7–102.
"Notice". Section 1–201.
"Party". Section 1–201.
"Purchaser". Section 1–201.
"Receipt of goods". Section 2–103.

"Value". Section 1–201.

§ 7–204. Duty of Care; Contractual Limitation of Warehouseman's Liability.

(1)   A warehouseman is liable for damages for loss of or injury to the goods caused by his failure to exercise such care in regard to them as a reasonably careful man would exercise under like circumstances but unless otherwise agreed he is not liable for damages which could not have been avoided by the exercise of such care.

(2)   Damages may be limited by a term in the warehouse receipt or storage agreement limiting the amount of liability in case of loss or damage, and setting forth a specific liability per article or item, or value per unit of weight, beyond which the warehouseman shall not be liable; provided, however, that such liability may on written request of the bailor at the time of signing such storage agreement or within a reasonable time after receipt of the warehouse receipt be increased on part or all of the goods thereunder, in which event increased rates may be charged based on such increased valuation, but that no such increase shall be permitted contrary to a lawful limitation of liability contained in the warehouseman's tariff, if any. No such limitation is effective with respect to the warehouseman's liability for conversion to his own use.

(3)   Reasonable provisions as to the time and manner of presenting claims and instituting actions based on the bailment may be included in the warehouse receipt or tariff.

(4)   This section does not impair or repeal . . .

Note: *Insert in subsection (4) a reference to any statute which imposes a higher responsibility upon the warehouseman or invalidates contractual limitations which would be permissible under this Article.*

Official Comment

Prior Uniform Statutory Provision: Sections 3 and 21, Uniform Warehouse Receipts Act.

Changes: Consolidated and rewritten; material on limitation of remedy is new.

Purposes of Changes:

The old uniform acts provided that receipts could not contain terms impairing the obligation of reasonable care. Whether this is violated by a stipulation that in case of loss the bailee's liability is limited to stated amounts has been much controverted. The section is intended to eliminate that controversy by setting forth the conditions under which liability is so limited. However, as subsection (4) makes clear, the states as well as the federal government may supplement this section with more rigid standards of responsibility for some or all bailees.

Cross References:

Sections 7–103 and 10–103.

Definitional Cross References:

"Action". Section 1–201.
"Agreed". Section 1–201.
"Goods". Section 7–102.
"Reasonable time". Section 1–204.
"Sign". Section 1–201.
"Term". Section 1–201.
"Value". Section 1–201.
"Warehouse receipt". Section 1–201.
"Warehouseman". Section 7–102.
"Written". Section 1–201.

§ 7–205. Title Under Warehouse Receipt Defeated in Certain Cases.

A buyer in the ordinary course of business of fungible goods sold and delivered by a warehouseman who is also in the business of buying and selling such goods takes free of any claim under a warehouse receipt even though it has been duly negotiated.

Official Comment

Prior Uniform Statutory Provision: None.

Purposes:

The typical case covered by this section is that of the warehouseman-dealer in grain, and the substantive question at issue is whether in case the warehouseman becomes insolvent the receipt holders shall be able to trace and recover grain shipped to farmers and other purchasers from the elevator. This was possible under the old acts, although courts were eager to find estoppels to prevent it. The practical difficulty of tracing fungible grain means that the preservation of this theoretical right adds little to the commercial acceptability of negotiable grain receipts, which really circulate on the credit of the warehouseman. Moreover, on default of the warehouseman, the receipt holders at least share in what grain remains, whereas retaking the grain from a good faith cash purchaser reduces him completely to the status of general creditor in a situation where there was very little he could do to guard against the loss. Compare 15 U.S.C. Section 714p, enacted in 1955.

Cross References:

Sections 2–403 and 9–320.

Definitional Cross References:

"Buyer in ordinary course of business". Section 1–201.
"Delivery". Section 1–201.
"Duly negotiate". Section 7–501.
"Fungible" goods. Section 1–201.
"Goods". Section 7–102.
"Value". Section 1–201.
"Warehouse receipt". Section 1–201.
"Warehouseman". Section 7–102.

§ 7–206.   Termination of Storage at Warehouseman's Option.

(1)   A warehouseman may on notifying the person on whose account the goods are held and any other person known to claim an interest in the goods require payment of any charges and removal of the goods from the warehouse at the termination of the period of storage fixed by the document, or, if no period is fixed, within a stated period not less than thirty days after the notification. If the goods are not removed before the date specified in the notification, the warehouseman may sell them in accordance with the provisions of the section on enforcement of a warehouseman's lien (Section 7–210).

(2)   If a warehouseman in good faith believes that the goods are about to deteriorate or decline in value to less than the amount of his lien within the time prescribed in subsection (1) for notification, advertisement and sale, the warehouseman may specify in the notification any reasonable shorter time for removal of the goods and in case the goods are not removed, may sell them at public sale held not less than one week after a single advertisement or posting.

(3)   If as a result of a quality or condition of the goods of which the warehouseman had no notice at the time of deposit the goods are a hazard to other property or to the warehouse or to persons, the warehouseman may sell the goods at public or private sale without advertisement on reasonable notification to all persons known to claim an interest in the goods. If the warehouseman after a reasonable effort is unable to sell the goods he may dispose of them in any lawful manner and shall incur no liability by reason of such disposition.

(4)   The warehouseman must deliver the goods to any person entitled to them under this Article upon due demand made at any time prior to sale or other disposition under this section.

(5)   The warehouseman may satisfy his lien from the proceeds of any sale or disposition under this section but must hold the balance for delivery on the demand of any person to whom he would have been bound to deliver the goods.

Official Comment

Prior Uniform Statutory Provision: Section 34, Uniform Warehouse Receipts Act.

Changes: Rewritten and expanded to define the warehouseman's right to terminate the storage not only where the goods are perishable or hazardous as in Uniform Warehouse Receipts Act, Section 34, but also for any other reason including decline in value of the goods imperilling the warehouseman's security for charges.

Purposes of Changes:

1.   Most warehousing is for an indefinite term, the bailor being entitled to delivery on reasonable demand. It is necessary to define the warehouseman's power to terminate the bailment, since it would be commercially intolerable to allow warehousemen to order removal of the goods on short notice. The thirty day period provided where the document does not carry its own period of termination corresponds to commercial practice of computing rates on a monthly basis. The right to terminate under subsection (1) includes a right to require payment of "any charges", but does not depend on the existence of unpaid charges.

2.   In permitting expeditious disposition of perishable and hazardous goods Uniform Warehouse Receipts Act, Section 34, made no distinction between cases where the warehouseman knowingly undertook to store such goods and cases where the goods were discovered to be of that character subsequent to storage. The former situation presents no such emergency as justifies the summary power of removal and sale. Subsections (2) and (3) distinguish between the two situations.

3.   Protection of his lien is the only interest which the warehouseman has to justify summary sale of perishable goods which are not hazardous. This same interest must be recognized when the stored goods, although not perishable, decline in market value to a point which threatens the warehouseman's security.

4.   The right to order removal of stored goods is subject to provisions of the public warehousing laws of some states forbidding warehousemen from discriminating among customers. Nor does the section relieve the warehouseman of any obligation under the states laws to secure the approval of a public official before disposing of deteriorating goods. Such *regulatory* statutes and the regulations under them remain in force and operative. Sections 7–103, 10–103.

Cross References:

Sections 7–103, 7–403, 10–103.

Definitional Cross References:

"Delivery". Section 1–201.
"Document". Section 7–102.
"Good faith". Section 1–201.
"Goods". Section 7–102.
"Notice". Section 1–201.
"Notification". Section 1–201.
"Person". Section 1–201.
"Reasonable time". Section 1–204.
"Value". Section 1–201.
"Warehouseman". Section 7–102.

§ 7–207.   Goods Must Be Kept Separate; Fungible Goods.

(1)   Unless the warehouse receipt otherwise provides, a warehouseman must keep separate the goods covered by each receipt so as to permit at all times identification and delivery of those goods except that different lots of fungible goods may be commingled.

(2)   Fungible goods so commingled are owned in common by the persons entitled thereto and the warehouseman is severally liable to each owner for that owner's share. Where because of overissue a mass of fungible goods is insufficient to meet all the receipts which the warehouseman has issued against it, the persons entitled include all holders to whom overissued receipts have been duly negotiated.

Official Comment

Prior Uniform Statutory Provision: Sections 22, 23 and 24, Uniform Warehouse Receipts Act.

Changes: Consolidated and revised; holders of overissued receipts permitted to share in mass of fungible goods.

Purposes of Changes:

No change of substance is made other than the explicit statement that holders to whom overissued receipts have been duly negotiated shall share in a mass of fungible goods. Where individual ownership interests are merged into claims on a common fund, as is necessarily the case with fungible goods, there is no policy reason for discriminating between successive purchasers of similar claims.

Definitional Cross References:

"Delivery". Section 1–201.
"Duly negotiate". Section 7–501.
"Fungible" goods. Section 1–201.
"Goods". Section 7–102.
"Holder". Section 1–201.
"Person". Section 1–201.
"Warehouse receipt". Section 1–201.
"Warehouseman". Section 7–102.

§ 7–208.   Altered Warehouse Receipts.

Where a blank in a negotiable warehouse receipt has been filled in without authority, a purchaser for value and without notice of the want of authority may treat the insertion as authorized. Any other unauthorized alteration leaves any receipt enforceable against the issuer according to its original tenor.

Official Comment

Prior Uniform Statutory Provision: Section 13, Uniform Warehouse Receipts Act.

Changes: Generally revised and simplified; explicit treatment of the situation where a blank in an executed document is filled without authority.

Purposes of Changes:

1.   The execution of warehouse receipts in blank is a dangerous practice. As between the issuer and an innocent purchaser the risks should clearly fall on the former.

2.   An unauthorized alteration whether made with or without fraudulent intent does not relieve the issuer of his liability on the warehouse receipt as originally executed. The unauthorized alteration itself is of course ineffective against the warehouseman.

Definitional Cross References:

"Issuer". Section 7–102.
"Notice". Section 1–201.
"Purchaser". Section 1–201.
"Value". Section 1–201.
"Warehouse receipt". Section 1–201.

§ 7–209.   Lien of Warehouseman.

(1)   A warehouseman has a lien against the bailor on the goods covered by a warehouse receipt or on the proceeds thereof in his possession for charges for storage or transportation (including demurrage and terminal charges), insurance, labor, or charges present or future in relation to the goods, and for expenses necessary for preservation of the goods or reasonably incurred in their sale pursuant to law. If the person on whose account the goods are held is liable for like charges or expenses in relation to other goods whenever deposited and it is stated in the receipt that a lien is claimed for charges and expenses in relation to other goods, the warehouseman also has a lien against him for such charges and expenses whether or not the other goods have been delivered by the warehouseman. But against a person to whom a negotiable warehouse receipt is duly negotiated a warehouseman's lien is limited to charges in an amount or at a rate specified on the receipt or if no charges are so specified then to a reasonable charge for storage of the goods covered by the receipt subsequent to the date of the receipt.

(2) The warehouseman may also reserve a security interest against the bailor for a maximum amount specified on the receipt for charges other than those specified in subsection (1), such as for money advanced and interest. Such a security interest is governed by the Article on Secured Transactions (Article 9).

(3)(a) A warehouseman's lien for charges and expenses under subsection (1) or a security interest under subsection (2) is also effective against any person who so entrusted the bailor with possession of the goods that a pledge of them by him to a good faith purchaser for value would have been valid but is not effective against a person as to whom the document confers no right in the goods covered by it under Section 7–503.

(b) A warehouseman's lien on household goods for charges and expenses in relation to the goods under subsection (1) is also effective against all persons if the depositor was the legal possessor of the goods at the time of deposit. "Household goods" means furniture, furnishings and personal effects used by the depositor in a dwelling.

(4) A warehouseman loses his lien on any goods which he voluntarily delivers or which he unjustifiably refuses to deliver.

As amended in 1966.

Official Comment

Prior Uniform Statutory Provision: Sections 27 through 32, Uniform Warehouse Receipts Act.

Changes: Rewritten.

Purposes of Changes:

1. Subsection (1) defines the warehouseman's statutory lien. A specific lien attaches automatically, without express notation on the receipt, to goods stored under a non-negotiable receipt. That lien is limited to the usual charges arising out of a storage transaction; by notation on the receipt it can be made a general lien extending to like charges in relation to other goods. The same rules apply where the receipt is negotiable, except that as against a holder by due negotiation the lien is limited to the amount or rate specified on the receipt, or, if none is specified, to a reasonable charge for storage of the specific goods after the date of the receipt.

2. Subsection (2) provides for a security interest based upon agreement. Such a security interest arises out of relations between the parties other than bailment for storage or transportation, as where the bailee assumes the role of financer or performs a manufacturing operation, extending credit in reliance upon the goods covered by the receipt. Such a security interest is not a statutory lien. Compare Sections 9–109 and 9–333. It is governed in all respects by Article 9, except that subsection (2) requires that the receipt specify a maximum amount and limits the security interest to the amount specified.

3. Subsections (1) and (2) validate the lien and security interest "against the bailor." As against third parties, subsection (3)(a) continues the rule under the prior uniform statutory provision that to validate the lien the owner must have entrusted the goods to the depositor, and that the circumstances must be such that a pledge by the depositor to a good faith purchaser for value would have been valid. Thus the owner's interest will not be subjected to a lien or security interest arising out of a deposit of his goods by a thief. The warehouseman may be protected because of the actual, implied or apparent authority of the depositor, because of a Factor's Act, or because of other circumstances which would protect a bona fide pledgee, unless those circumstances are denied effect under Section 7–503. Where the third party is the holder of a security interest, the rights of the warehouseman depend on the priority given to a hypothetical bona fide pledgee by Article 9, particularly Section 9–322. Thus the special priority granted to statutory liens by Section 9–333 does not apply to liens under subsection (1) of this section, since subsection (3) "expressly provides otherwise" within the meaning of Section 9–333. As to household goods, however, subsection (3)(b) makes the warehouseman's lien "for charges and expenses in relation to the goods" effective against all persons if the depositor was the legal possessor. The purpose of the exception is to permit the warehouseman to accept household goods for storage in sole reliance on the value of the goods themselves, especially in situations of family emergency. [This paragraph was amended in 1966].

4. It is unnecessary to state here, as in Uniform Warehouse Receipts Act 31, that a bailee with a valid lien need not deliver until the lien is satisfied. Section 7–403 provides that a person demanding delivery under a document must be prepared to satisfy the bailee's lien.

5.   Where goods have been stored under a non-negotiable warehouse receipt and are sold by the person to whom the receipt has been issued, frequently the goods are not withdrawn by the new owner. The obligations of the seller of the goods in this situation are set forth in Section 2–503(4) on tender of delivery and include procurement of an acknowledgment by the bailee of the buyer's right to possession of the goods. If a new receipt is requested, such an acknowledgment can be withheld until storage charges have been paid or provided for. The statutory lien for charges on the goods sold, granted by the first sentence of subsection (1), continues valid unless the bailee gives it up. But once a new receipt is issued to the buyer, the buyer becomes "the person on whose account the goods are held" under the second sentence of subsection (1); unless he undertakes liability for charges in relation to other goods stored by the seller, there is no general lien against the buyer for such charges. Of course, the bailee may preserve the general lien in such a case either by an arrangement by which the buyer "is liable for" such charges, or by reserving a security interest under subsection (2).

Cross References:

Point 2: Sections 9–109 and 9–333.

Point 3: Sections 7–503, 9–333 and 9–322.

Point 4: Section 7–403.

Point 5: Section 2–503.

Definitional Cross References:

"Deliver". Section 1–201.

"Document". Section 7–102.

"Goods". Section 7–102.

"Money". Section 1–201.

"Person". Section 1–201.

"Purchaser". Section 1–201.

"Right". Section 1–201.

"Security interest". Section 1–201.

"Value". Section 1–201.

"Warehouse receipt". Section 1–201.

"Warehouseman". Section 7–102.

§ 7–210.   Enforcement of Warehouseman's Lien.

(1)   Except as provided in subsection (2), a warehouseman's lien may be enforced by public or private sale of the goods in block or in parcels, at any time or place and on any terms which are commercially reasonable, after notifying all persons known to claim an interest in the goods. Such notification must include a statement of the amount due, the nature of the proposed sale and the time and place of any public sale. The fact that a better price could have been obtained by a sale at a different time or in a different method from that selected by the warehouseman is not of itself sufficient to establish that the sale was not made in a commercially reasonable manner. If the warehouseman either sells the goods in the usual manner in any recognized market therefor, or if he sells at the price current in such market at the time of his sale, or if he has otherwise sold in conformity with commercially reasonable practices among dealers in the type of goods sold, he has sold in a commercially reasonable manner. A sale of more goods than apparently necessary to be offered to insure satisfaction of the obligation is not commercially reasonable except in cases covered by the preceding sentence.

(2)   A warehouseman's lien on goods other than goods stored by a merchant in the course of his business may be enforced only as follows:

(a)   All persons known to claim an interest in the goods must be notified.

(b)   The notification must be delivered in person or sent by registered or certified letter to the last known address of any person to be notified.

(c)   The notification must include an itemized statement of the claim, a description of the goods subject to the lien, a demand for payment within a specified time not less than ten days after receipt of the notification, and a conspicuous statement that unless the claim is paid within that time the goods will be advertised for sale and sold by auction at a specified time and place.

(d)   The sale must conform to the terms of the notification.

(e)   The sale must be held at the nearest suitable place to that where the goods are held or stored.

(f)   After the expiration of the time given in the notification, an advertisement of the sale must be published once a week for two weeks consecutively in a newspaper of general circulation where the sale is to be held. The advertisement must include a description of the goods, the name of the person on whose account they are being held, and the time and place of the sale. The sale must take place at least fifteen days after the first publication. If there is no newspaper of general circulation where the sale is to be held, the advertisement must be posted at least ten days before the sale in not less than six conspicuous places in the neighborhood of the proposed sale.

(3)   Before any sale pursuant to this section any person claiming a right in the goods may pay the amount necessary to satisfy the lien and the reasonable expenses incurred under this section. In that event the goods must not be sold, but must be retained by the warehouseman subject to the terms of the receipt and this Article.

(4)   The warehouseman may buy at any public sale pursuant to this section.

(5)   A purchaser in good faith of goods sold to enforce a warehouseman's lien takes the goods free of any rights of persons against whom the lien was valid, despite noncompliance by the warehouseman with the requirements of this section.

(6)   The warehouseman may satisfy his lien from the proceeds of any sale pursuant to this section but must hold the balance, if any, for delivery on demand to any person to whom he would have been bound to deliver the goods.

(7)   The rights provided by this section shall be in addition to all other rights allowed by law to a creditor against his debtor.

(8)   Where a lien is on goods stored by a merchant in the course of his business the lien may be enforced in accordance with either subsection (1) or (2).

(9)   The warehouseman is liable for damages caused by failure to comply with the requirements for sale under this section and in case of willful violation is liable for conversion.

As amended in 1962.

Official Comment

Prior Uniform Statutory Provision: Section 33, Uniform Warehouse Receipts Act.

Changes: Rewritten; simplified foreclosure proceeding provided for all liens other than warehousemen's lien in non-commercial storage.

Purposes of Changes:

1.   Subsection (1) makes "commercial reasonableness" the standard for foreclosure proceedings in all cases except non-commercial storage with a warehouseman. The latter category embraces principally storage of household goods by private owners; and for such cases the detailed provisions as to notification, publication and public sale, found in Section 33 of the Uniform Warehouse Receipts Act are retained in subsection (2). The swifter, more flexible procedure of subsection (1) is appropriate to commercial storage. Compare seller's power of resale on breach by buyer under the provisions of the Article on Sales (Section 2–706).

2.   The provisions of subsections (4) and (5) permitting the bailee to bid at public sales and confirming the title of purchasers at foreclosure sales are designed to secure more bidding and better prices.

Cross Reference:

Section 7–403.

Definitional Cross References:

"Bill of lading". Section 1–201.

"Conspicuous". Section 1–201.

"Creditor". Section 1–201.

"Delivery". Section 1–201.
"Document". Section 7–102.
"Good faith". Section 1–201.
"Goods". Section 7–102.
"Notification". Section 1–201.
"Notifies". Section 1–201.
"Person". Section 1–201.
"Purchaser". Section 1–201.
"Rights". Section 1–201.
"Term". Section 1–201.
"Warehouseman". Section 7–102.

PART 3

BILLS OF LADING: SPECIAL PROVISIONS

§ 7–301. Liability for Non-receipt or Misdescription; "Said to Contain"; "Shipper's Load and Count"; Improper Handling.

(1) A consignee of a non-negotiable bill who has given value in good faith or a holder to whom a negotiable bill has been duly negotiated relying in either case upon the description therein of the goods, or upon the date therein shown, may recover from the issuer damages caused by the misdating of the bill or the non-receipt or misdescription of the goods, except to the extent that the document indicates that the issuer does not know whether any part or all of the goods in fact were received or conform to the description, as where the description is in terms of marks or labels or kind, quantity, or condition or the receipt or description is qualified by "contents or condition of contents of packages unknown", "said to contain", "shipper's weight, load and count" or the like, if such indication be true.

(2) When goods are loaded by an issuer who is a common carrier, the issuer must count the packages of goods if package freight and ascertain the kind and quantity if bulk freight. In such cases "shipper's weight, load and count" or other words indicating that the description was made by the shipper are ineffective except as to freight concealed by packages.

(3) When bulk freight is loaded by a shipper who makes available to the issuer adequate facilities for weighing such freight, an issuer who is a common carrier must ascertain the kind and quantity within a reasonable time after receiving the written request of the shipper to do so. In such cases "shipper's weight" or other words of like purport are ineffective.

(4) The issuer may by inserting in the bill the words "shipper's weight, load and count" or other words of like purport indicate that the goods were loaded by the shipper; and if such statement be true the issuer shall not be liable for damages caused by the improper loading. But their omission does not imply liability for such damages.

(5) The shipper shall be deemed to have guaranteed to the issuer the accuracy at the time of shipment of the description, marks, labels, number, kind, quantity, condition and weight, as furnished by him; and the shipper shall indemnify the issuer against damage caused by inaccuracies in such particulars. The right of the issuer to such indemnity shall in no way limit his responsibility and liability under the contract of carriage to any person other than the shipper.

Official Comment

Prior Uniform Statutory Provision: Section 23, Uniform Bills of Lading Act.

Changes: Rewritten in part.

Purposes of Changes:

1. The provision as to misdating in subsection (1) conforms to the policy of the amendment to the Federal Bills of Lading Act by 44 Stat. 1450 (1927), as amended 49 U.S.C. Section 102, after the holding in Browne v. Union Pac. R. Co., 113 Kan. 726, 216 P. 299 (1923), affirmed on other grounds 267 U.S. 255, 45 S.Ct. 315, 69 L.Ed.

601 (1925). Subsections (2) and (3) conform to the policy of the Federal Bills of Lading Act, 49 U.S.C. Sections 100, 101, and the laws of several states. See, e.g., N.Y.Pers.Prop.Law Section 209; Report of N.Y. Law Revision Commission, N.Y.Leg.Doc. (1941) No. 65(F).

2.   The language of the old Uniform Act suggested that a carrier is ordinarily liable for damage caused by improper loading, but may relieve himself of liability by disclosing on the bill that shipper actually loaded. A more accurate statement of the law is that the carrier is not liable for losses caused by act or default of the shipper, which would include improper loading. There is some question whether under present law a carrier is liable even to a good faith purchaser of a negotiable bill for such losses, if the shipper's faulty loading in fact caused the loss. It is this doubtful liability which subsection (4) permits the carrier to bar by disclosure of shipper's loading. There is no implication that decisions such as Modern Tool Corp. v. Pennsylvania R. Co., 100 F.Supp. 595 (D.N.J.1951), are disapproved.

3.   This section is a simplified restatement of existing law as to the method by which a bailee may avoid responsibility for the accuracy of descriptions which are made by or in reliance upon information furnished by the depositor or shipper. The issuer is liable on documents issued by an agent, contrary to instructions of his principal, without receiving goods. No disclaimer of this liability is permitted since it is not a matter either of the care of the goods or their description.

4.   The shipper's erroneous report to the carrier concerning the goods may cause damage to the carrier. Subsection (5) therefore provides appropriate indemnity.

Cross References:

Sections 7–203 and 7–309.

Definitional Cross References:

"Bill of lading". Section 1–201.
"Consignee". Section 7–102.
"Document". Section 7–102.
"Duly negotiate". Section 7–501.
"Good faith". Section 1–201.
"Goods". Section 7–102.
"Holder". Section 1–201.
"Issuer". Section 7–102.
"Notice". Section 1–201.
"Party". Section 1–201.
"Purchaser". Section 1–201.
"Receipt of goods". Section 2–103.
"Value". Section 1–201.

§ 7–302.   Through Bills of Lading and Similar Documents.

(1)   The issuer of a through bill of lading or other document embodying an undertaking to be performed in part by persons acting as its agents or by connecting carriers is liable to anyone entitled to recover on the document for any breach by such other persons or by a connecting carrier of its obligation under the document but to the extent that the bill covers an undertaking to be performed overseas or in territory not contiguous to the continental United States or an undertaking including matters other than transportation this liability may be varied by agreement of the parties.

(2)   Where goods covered by a through bill of lading or other document embodying an undertaking to be performed in part by persons other than the issuer are received by any such person, he is subject with respect to his own performance while the goods are in his possession to the obligation of the issuer. His obligation is discharged by delivery of the goods to another such person pursuant to the document, and does not include liability for breach by any other such persons or by the issuer.

(3)   The issuer of such through bill of lading or other document shall be entitled to recover from the connecting carrier or such other person in possession of the goods when the breach of the obligation under the document occurred, the amount it may be required to pay to anyone entitled to recover on the document therefor, as may be evidenced by any receipt, judgment, or transcript thereof, and the amount of any expense

reasonably incurred by it in defending any action brought by anyone entitled to recover on the document therefor.

Official Comment

Prior Uniform Statutory Provision: None.

Purposes:

1.   The purpose of this section is to subject the initial carrier under a through bill to suit for breach of the contract of carriage by any connecting carrier and to make it clear that any such connecting carrier holds the goods on terms which are defined by the document of title even though such connecting carrier did not issue the document. Since the connecting carrier does hold on the terms of the document, it must honor a proper demand for delivery or a diversion order just as the original bailee would have to. Similarly it has the benefits of the excuses for nondelivery and limitations of liability provided for the original bailee. Unlike the original bailee-issuer, the connecting carrier's responsibility is limited to the period while the goods are in its possession. The section is patterned generally after the Interstate Commerce Act, but does not impose any obligation to issue through bills.

2.   The reference to documents other than through bills looks to the possibility that multi-purpose documents may come into use, e.g., combination warehouse receipts and bills of lading.

3.   Where the obligations or standards applicable to different parties bound by a document of title are different, the initial carrier's responsibility for portions of the journey not on its own lines will be determined by the standards appropriate to the connecting carrier. Thus a land carrier issuing a through bill of lading involving water carriage at a later stage will have the benefit of the water carrier's immunity from liability for negligence of its servants in navigating the vessel, where the law provides such an immunity for water carriers and the loss occurred while the goods were in the water carrier's possession.

4.   Under Subsection (1) the issuer of a through bill of lading may become liable for the fault of another person. Subsection (3) gives it appropriate rights of recourse.

Definitional Cross References:

"Agreement". Section 1–201.
"Bailee". Section 7–102.
"Bill of lading". Section 1–201.
"Delivery". Section 1–201.
"Document". Section 7–102.
"Goods". Section 7–102.
"Issuer". Section 7–102.
"Overseas". Section 2–323.
"Party". Section 1–201.
"Person". Section 1–201.

§ 7–303.   Diversion; Reconsignment; Change of Instructions.

(1)   Unless the bill of lading otherwise provides, the carrier may deliver the goods to a person or destination other than that stated in the bill or may otherwise dispose of the goods on instructions from

(a)   the holder of a negotiable bill; or

(b)   the consignor on a non-negotiable bill notwithstanding contrary instructions from the consignee; or

(c)   the consignee on a non-negotiable bill in the absence of contrary instructions from the consignor, if the goods have arrived at the billed destination or if the consignee is in possession of the bill; or

(d)   the consignee on a non-negotiable bill if he is entitled as against the consignor to dispose of them.

(2)   Unless such instructions are noted on a negotiable bill of lading, a person to whom the bill is duly negotiated can hold the bailee according to the original terms.

Official Comment

Prior Uniform Statutory Provision: None.

Purposes:

1.   The old Acts contained no reference to diversion, a very common commercial practice which defeats delivery to the consignee originally named in a bill of lading. The carrier was protected under the heading of "justified delivery" if the substituted consignee who received delivery was "a person lawfully entitled to possession of the goods." Cf. subsection (1)(d). This in turn depended on whether the person ordering the diversion was the owner of the goods or empowered to dispose of them, which again might depend upon whether under sales law title had passed from the consignor-seller to the consignee-buyer. The carrier is plainly not in a position to decide such questions when directed by the person with whom it has contracted for transportation to change the destination of the goods in transit. Carriers may as a business matter be willing to accept instructions from consignees in which case, as under the old uniform acts, the carrier will be liable for misdelivery if the consignee was not the owner or otherwise empowered to dispose of the goods. The section imposes no duty on carriers to undertake diversion; it is of course subject to the provisions of filed tariffs. Section 7–103.

2.   It should be noted that the section provides only an immunity for carriers against liability for "misdelivery." It does not, for example, defeat the title to the goods which the consignee-buyer may have acquired from the consignor-seller upon delivery of the goods to the carrier under a non-negotiable bill of lading. Thus if the carrier, upon instructions from the consignor, returns the goods to him, the consignee may recover the goods from the consignor or his insolvent estate. However, under certain circumstances, the consignee's title may be defeated by diversion of the goods in transit to a different consignee.

Cross References:

Point 2: Sections 7–403 and 7–504(3).

Definitional Cross References:

"Bailee". Section 7–102.
"Bill of lading". Section 1–201.
"Consignee". Section 7–102.
"Consignor". Section 7–102.
"Delivery". Section 1–201.
"Goods". Section 7–102.
"Holder". Section 1–201.
"Notice". Section 1–201.
"Person". Section 1–201.
"Purchaser". Section 1–201.
"Term". Section 1–201.

§ 7–304.   Bills of Lading in a Set.

(1)   Except where customary in overseas transportation, a bill of lading must not be issued in a set of parts. The issuer is liable for damages caused by violation of this subsection.

(2)   Where a bill of lading is lawfully drawn in a set of parts, each of which is numbered and expressed to be valid only if the goods have not been delivered against any other part, the whole of the parts constitute one bill.

(3)   Where a bill of lading is lawfully issued in a set of parts and different parts are negotiated to different persons, the title of the holder to whom the first due negotiation is made prevails as to both the document and the goods even though any later holder may have received the goods from the carrier in good faith and discharged the carrier's obligation by surrender of his part.

(4)   Any person who negotiates or transfers a single part of a bill of lading drawn in a set is liable to holders of that part as if it were the whole set.

(5)   The bailee is obliged to deliver in accordance with Part 4 of this Article against the first presented part of a bill of lading lawfully drawn in a set. Such delivery discharges the bailee's obligation on the whole bill.

Official Comment

Prior Uniform Statutory Provision: Section 6, Uniform Bills of Lading Act.

Changes: This section adds to existing legislation, which merely prohibits bills in a set in ordinary domestic trade, a statement of the legal effect of a lawfully issued set.

Purposes of Changes:

The statement of the legal effect of a lawfully issued set is in accord with existing commercial law relating to maritime and other overseas bills. This law has been codified in the Hague and Warsaw Conventions and in the Carriage of Goods by Sea Act, the provisions of which would ordinarily govern in situations where bills in a set are recognized by this Article.

Cross Reference:

Section 10–103.

Definitional Cross References:

"Bailee". Section 7–102.
"Bill of lading". Section 7–102.
"Delivery". Section 1–201.
"Document". Section 7–102.
"Duly negotiate". Section 7–501.
"Good faith". Section 1–201.
"Goods". Section 7–102.
"Holder". Section 1–201.
"Issuer". Section 7–102.
"Overseas". Section 2–323.
"Person". Section 1–201.
"Receipt of goods". Section 2–103.

§ 7–305.   Destination Bills.

(1)   Instead of issuing a bill of lading to the consignor at the place of shipment a carrier may at the request of the consignor procure the bill to be issued at destination or at any other place designated in the request.

(2)   Upon request of anyone entitled as against the carrier to control the goods while in transit and on surrender of any outstanding bill of lading or other receipt covering such goods, the issuer may procure a substitute bill to be issued at any place designated in the request.

Official Comment

Prior Uniform Statutory Provision: None.

Purposes:

This proposal is designed to facilitate the use of order bills in connection with fast shipments. Use of order bills on high speed shipments is impeded by the fact that the goods may arrive at destination before the documents, so that no one is ready to take delivery from the carrier. This is especially inconvenient for carriers by truck and air, who do not have terminal facilities where shipments can be held to await consignee's appearance. Order bills would be useful to take advantage of bank collection. This may be preferable to C.O.D. shipment in which the carrier, e.g. a truck driver, is the collecting and remitting agent. Financing of shipments under this plan would be handled as follows: seller at San Francisco delivers the goods to an airline with instructions to issue a bill in New York to a named bank. Seller receives a receipt embodying this undertaking to issue a destination bill. Airline wires its New York freight agent to issue the bill as instructed by the seller. Seller wires the New York bank a draft on buyer. New York bank indorses the bill to buyer when he honors the draft. Normally seller would act through his own bank in San Francisco, which would extend him credit in reliance on the airline's contract to deliver a bill to the order of its New York correspondent. This section is entirely permissive; it imposes no duty to issue such bills. Whether a connecting carrier will act as issuing agent is left to agreement between carriers.

Definitional Cross References:

"Bill of lading". Section 1–201.

"Consignor". Section 7–102.

"Goods". Section 7–102.

"Issuer". Section 7–102.

"Receipt of goods". Section 2–103.

§ 7–306. Altered Bills of Lading.

An unauthorized alteration or filling in of a blank in a bill of lading leaves the bill enforceable according to its original tenor.

Official Comment

Prior Uniform Statutory Provision: Section 16, Uniform Bills of Lading Act.

Changes: Generally revised and simplified; explicit treatment of the situation where a blank in an executed document is filled without authority.

Purposes of Changes:

An unauthorized alteration whether made with or without fraudulent intent does not relieve the issuer of his liability on the document as originally executed. Uniform Warehouse Receipts Act 13 excused the issuer from any liability to a fraudulent alterer, other than the liability to deliver the goods according to the terms of the original document. It is difficult to conceive what liability the draftsman intended to excuse. Uniform Bills of Lading Act 16 contains no such excuse provision, and is followed in this respect in the present section. Uniform Bills of Lading Act 16 characterizes an unauthorized alteration as "void" but apparently nothing more was intended than that the alteration did not change the obligation of the issuer. This is sufficiently covered by the terms of this Section. Moreover cases are conceivable in which an alteration would not be "void"; for example, an alteration made by common consent of a transferor and transferee of a document might evidence an enforceable contract between them. The same rule is made applicable to the filling in of blanks, a matter on which the prior Acts were silent.

Definitional Cross References:

"Bill of lading". Section 1–201.

"Issuer". Section 7–102.

§ 7–307. Lien of Carrier.

(1) A carrier has a lien on the goods covered by a bill of lading for charges subsequent to the date of its receipt of the goods for storage or transportation (including demurrage and terminal charges) and for expenses necessary for preservation of the goods incident to their transportation or reasonably incurred in their sale pursuant to law. But against a purchaser for value of a negotiable bill of lading a carrier's lien is limited to charges stated in the bill or the applicable tariffs, or if no charges are stated then to a reasonable charge.

(2) A lien for charges and expenses under subsection (1) on goods which the carrier was required by law to receive for transportation is effective against the consignor or any person entitled to the goods unless the carrier had notice that the consignor lacked authority to subject the goods to such charges and expenses. Any other lien under subsection (1) is effective against the consignor and any person who permitted the bailor to have control or possession of the goods unless the carrier had notice that the bailor lacked such authority.

(3) A carrier loses his lien on any goods which he voluntarily delivers or which he unjustifiably refuses to deliver.

Official Comment

Prior Uniform Statutory Provision: Sections 27 through 32, Uniform Warehouse Receipts Act.

Changes: Rewritten; lien extended to carrier. Lien of common carrier validated unless carrier had notice that consignor lacked authority to subject the goods to charges and expenses. Where the carrier is not required by law to receive the goods for transportation, lien validated against anyone who permitted the bailor to have possession even if he had no real or apparent authority.

Purposes of Changes:

The section is intended to give carriers a specific statutory lien for charges and expenses similar to that given to warehousemen by the first sentence of Section 7–209. But since carriers do not commonly claim a lien for charges in relation to other goods or lend money on the security of goods in their hands, provisions for a general lien or a security interest similar to those in Section 7–209(1) and (2) are omitted. See Comment to Section 7–105. Since the lien given by this section is specific, and the storage or transportation often preserves or increases the value of the goods, subsection (2) validates the lien against anyone who permitted the bailor to have possession of the goods. Where the carrier is required to receive the goods for transportation, the owner's interest may be subjected to charges and expenses arising out of deposit of his goods by a thief. Cf. Section 9–333. The crucial mental element is the carrier's knowledge or reason to know of the bailor's lack of authority.

Cross References:

Sections 7–209, 9–109 and 9–333.

Definitional Cross References:

"Bill of lading". Section 1–201.
"Consignor". Section 7–102.
"Delivery". Section 1–201.
"Goods". Section 7–102.
"Person". Section 1–201.
"Purchaser". Section 1–201.
"Value". Section 1–201.

§ 7–308. Enforcement of Carrier's Lien.

(1) A carrier's lien may be enforced by public or private sale of the goods, in block or in parcels, at any time or place and on any terms which are commercially reasonable, after notifying all persons known to claim an interest in the goods. Such notification must include a statement of the amount due, the nature of the proposed sale and the time and place of any public sale. The fact that a better price could have been obtained by a sale at a different time or in a different method from that selected by the carrier is not of itself sufficient to establish that the sale was not made in a commercially reasonable manner. If the carrier either sells the goods in the usual manner in any recognized market therefor or if he sells at the price current in such market at the time of his sale or if he has otherwise sold in conformity with commercially reasonable practices among dealers in the type of goods sold he has sold in a commercially reasonable manner. A sale of more goods than apparently necessary to be offered to ensure satisfaction of the obligation is not commercially reasonable except in cases covered by the preceding sentence.

(2) Before any sale pursuant to this section any person claiming a right in the goods may pay the amount necessary to satisfy the lien and the reasonable expenses incurred under this section. In that event the goods must not be sold, but must be retained by the carrier subject to the terms of the bill and this Article.

(3) The carrier may buy at any public sale pursuant to this section.

(4) A purchaser in good faith of goods sold to enforce a carrier's lien takes the goods free of any rights of persons against whom the lien was valid, despite noncompliance by the carrier with the requirements of this section.

(5)   The carrier may satisfy his lien from the proceeds of any sale pursuant to this section but must hold the balance, if any, for delivery on demand to any person to whom he would have been bound to deliver the goods.

(6)   The rights provided by this section shall be in addition to all other rights allowed by law to a creditor against his debtor.

(7)   A carrier's lien may be enforced in accordance with either subsection (1) or the procedure set forth in subsection (2) of Section 7–210.

(8)   The carrier is liable for damages caused by failure to comply with the requirements for sale under this section and in case of willful violation is liable for conversion.

Official Comment

Prior Uniform Statutory Provision: Section 33, Uniform Warehouse Receipts Act.

Changes: Rewritten; provisions extended to carriers' liens; simplified foreclosure proceeding provided.

Purposes of Changes:

This section is intended to give the carrier an enforcement procedure of his lien coextensive with that given the warehousemen in cases other than those covering noncommercial storage by him. See Comment to Section 7–210.

Cross Reference:

Section 7–210.

Definitional Cross References:

"Bill of lading". Section 1–201.
"Creditor". Section 1–201.
"Delivery". Section 1–201.
"Good faith". Section 1–201.
"Goods". Section 7–102.
"Notification". Section 1–201.
"Notifies". Section 1–201.
"Person". Section 1–201.
"Purchaser". Section 1–201.
"Rights". Section 1–201.
"Term". Section 1–201.

§ 7–309.   Duty of Care; Contractual Limitation of Carrier's Liability.

(1)   A carrier who issues a bill of lading whether negotiable or non-negotiable must exercise the degree of care in relation to the goods which a reasonably careful man would exercise under like circumstances. This subsection does not repeal or change any law or rule of law which imposes liability upon a common carrier for damages not caused by its negligence.

(2)   Damages may be limited by a provision that the carrier's liability shall not exceed a value stated in the document if the carrier's rates are dependent upon value and the consignor by the carrier's tariff is afforded an opportunity to declare a higher value or a value as lawfully provided in the tariff, or where no tariff is filed he is otherwise advised of such opportunity; but no such limitation is effective with respect to the carrier's liability for conversion to its own use.

(3)   Reasonable provisions as to the time and manner of presenting claims and instituting actions based on the shipment may be included in a bill of lading or tariff.

Official Comment

Prior Uniform Statutory Provision: Section 3, Uniform Bills of Lading Act.

Changes: Consolidated and rewritten.

Purposes of Changes:

The old uniform act provided that bills of lading could not contain terms impairing the obligation of reasonable care. Whether this is violated by a stipulation that in case of loss the bailee's liability is limited to stated amounts has been much controverted. For interstate rail transportation the matter is settled by the Carmack Amendment to the Interstate Commerce Act (See 49 U.S.C.A. § 20(11)). The present section is a generalized version of the Interstate Commerce Act provisions. The obligation of due care is radically qualified, in the case of maritime bills and international airbills, by federal legislation and treaty. All this special legislation would remain in effect even if Congress enacts this Code, including the present Article. See Section 7–103.

Subsection (1) does not impair any rule of law imposing the liability of an insurer on a common carrier in intrastate commerce. Subsection (2), however, applies to such liability as well as to liability based on negligence. The entire section is subject under Section 7–103 to applicable provisions in filed tariffs, such as the common disclaimer of responsibility for undeclared articles of extraordinary value, hidden from view. Tariffs which lawfully provide a maximum unit value beyond which goods are not taken fall within the same principle, and are expressly covered by the words "value as lawfully provided in the tariff."

Cross Reference:

Section 7–103.

Definitional Cross References:

"Action". Section 1–201.
"Bill of lading". Section 1–201.
"Consignor". Section 7–102.
"Document". Section 7–102.
"Goods". Section 7–102.
"Value". Section 1–201.

PART 4

WAREHOUSE RECEIPTS AND BILLS OF LADING: GENERAL OBLIGATIONS

§ 7–401.　Irregularities in Issue of Receipt or Bill or Conduct of Issuer.

The obligations imposed by this Article on an issuer apply to a document of title regardless of the fact that

(a)　the document may not comply with the requirements of this Article or of any other law or regulation regarding its issue, form or content; or

(b)　the issuer may have violated laws regulating the conduct of his business; or

(c)　the goods covered by the document were owned by the bailee at the time the document was issued; or

(d)　the person issuing the document does not come within the definition of warehouseman if it purports to be a warehouse receipt.

Official Comment

Prior Uniform Statutory Provision: Section 20, Uniform Warehouse Receipts Act; Section 23, Uniform Bills of Lading Act.

Changes: Most of the material is new; the uniform act sections cited deal only with non-receipt and misdescription.

Purposes of Changes and New Matter:

The bailee's liability on his document despite non-receipt or misdescription of the goods is affirmed in Sections 7–203 and 7–301. The purpose of this section is to make it clear that regardless of irregularities a document which falls within the definition of document of title imposes on the issuer the obligations stated in this

Article. For example, a bailee will not be permitted to avoid his obligation to deliver the goods (Section 7–403) or his obligation of due care with respect to them (Sections 7–204 and 7–309) by taking the position that no valid "document" was issued because he failed to file a statutory bond or did not pay stamp taxes or did not disclose the place of storage in the document. Sanctions against violations of statutory or administrative duties with respect to documents should be limited to revocation of license or other measures prescribed by the regulation imposing the duty. As to the continuing vitality of regulations, in addition to those found in this Article, of documents of title, see Sections 7–103 and 10–103.

Cross References:

Sections 7–103, 7–203, 7–204, 7–301, 7–309 and 10–103.

Definitional Cross References:

"Bailee". Section 7–102.
"Document". Section 7–102.
"Document of title". Section 1–201.
"Goods". Section 7–102.
"Issuer". Section 7–102.
"Person". Section 1–201.
"Warehouse receipt". Section 1–201.
"Warehouseman". Section 7–102.

§ 7–402.   Duplicate Receipt or Bill; Overissue.

Neither a duplicate nor any other document of title purporting to cover goods already represented by an outstanding document of the same issuer confers any right in the goods, except as provided in the case of bills in a set, overissue of documents for fungible goods and substitutes for lost, stolen or destroyed documents. But the issuer is liable for damages caused by his overissue or failure to identify a duplicate document as such by conspicuous notation on its face.

Official Comment

Prior Uniform Statutory Provision: Section 6, Uniform Warehouse Receipts Act; Section 7, Uniform Bills of Lading Act.

Changes: Consolidated and rewritten.

Purposes of Changes:

1.   This section treats a duplicate which is not properly identified as such like any other overissue of documents: a purchaser of such a document acquires no title but only a cause of action for damages against the person who made his deception possible, except in the cases noted in the section. But parts of a bill lawfully issued in a set of parts are not "overissue" (Section 7–304). Of course, if the issuer has clearly indicated that a document is a duplicate so that no one can be deceived by it, and in fact the duplicate is a correct copy of the original, the warehouseman is not liable for preparing and delivering such a duplicate copy.

2.   The section applies to nonnegotiable documents to the extent of providing an action for damages for one who acquires an unmarked duplicate from a transferor who knew the facts and would therefore himself have had no cause of action against the issuer of the duplicate. Ordinarily the transferee of a nonnegotiable document acquires only the rights of his transferor.

3.   Overissue is defined so as to exclude the common situation where two valid documents of different issuers are outstanding for the same goods at the same time. Thus freight forwarders commonly issue bills of lading to their customers for small shipments to be combined into carload shipments for which the railroad will issue a bill of lading to the forwarder. So also a warehouse receipt may be outstanding against goods, and the holder of the receipt may issue delivery orders against the same goods. In these cases dealings with the subsequently issued documents may be effective to transfer title; e.g. negotiation of a delivery order will effectively transfer title in the ordinary case where no dishonesty has occurred and the goods are available to satisfy the orders. Section 7–503 provides for cases of conflict between documents of different issuers.

Cross References:

Point 1: Sections 7–207, 7–304, and 7–601.

Point 3: Section 7–503.

Definitional Cross References:

"Bill of lading". Section 1–201.

"Conspicuous". Section 1–201.

"Document". Section 7–102.

"Document of title". Section 1–201.

"Fungible" goods. Section 1–201.

"Goods". Section 7–102.

"Issuer". Section 7–102.

"Right". Section 1–201.

§ 7–403.   Obligation of Warehouseman or Carrier to Deliver; Excuse.

(1)   The bailee must deliver the goods to a person entitled under the document who complies with subsections (2) and (3), unless and to the extent that the bailee establishes any of the following:

(a)   delivery of the goods to a person whose receipt was rightful as against the claimant;

(b)   damage to or delay, loss or destruction of the goods for which the bailee is not liable [, but the burden of establishing negligence in such cases is on the person entitled under the document];

Note: *The brackets in (1)(b) indicate that State enactments may differ on this point without serious damage to the principle of uniformity.*

(c)   previous sale or other disposition of the goods in lawful enforcement of a lien or on warehouseman's lawful termination of storage;

(d)   the exercise by a seller of his right to stop delivery pursuant to the provisions of the Article on Sales (Section 2–705);

(e)   a diversion, reconsignment or other disposition pursuant to the provisions of this Article (Section 7–303) or tariff regulating such right;

(f)   release, satisfaction or any other fact affording a personal defense against the claimant;

(g)   any other lawful excuse.

(2)   A person claiming goods covered by a document of title must satisfy the bailee's lien where the bailee so requests or where the bailee is prohibited by law from delivering the goods until the charges are paid.

(3)   Unless the person claiming is one against whom the document confers no right under Sec. 7–503(1), he must surrender for cancellation or notation of partial deliveries any outstanding negotiable document covering the goods, and the bailee must cancel the document or conspicuously note the partial delivery thereon or be liable to any person to whom the document is duly negotiated.

(4)   "Person entitled under the document" means holder in the case of a negotiable document, or the person to whom delivery is to be made by the terms of or pursuant to written instructions under a non-negotiable document.

Official Comment

Prior Uniform Statutory Provision: Sections 8 through 12, 16 and 19, Uniform Warehouse Receipts Act; Sections 11 through 15, 19 and 22, Uniform Bills of Lading Act.

Changes: Consolidated and rewritten.

Purposes of Changes:

1.   The general and primary purpose of this revision is to simplify the statement of the bailee's obligation on the document. The interrelations of the separate sections of the old uniform acts dealing with "obligation to deliver," "justification in delivering," and "liability for misdelivery" are obscure. The present section is constructed on the basis of stating what previous deliveries or other circumstances operate to excuse the bailee's normal

obligation on the document. Accordingly, "justified" deliveries under the old uniform acts now find their place as "excuse" under subsection (1). Unjustified deliveries, i.e., "misdeliveries" under the old acts, are simply omitted from the list of excuses, thus permitting the normal obligation on the document to be asserted.

    2.   The principal case covered by subsection (1)(a) is delivery to a person whose title is paramount to the rights represented by the document. For example, if a thief deposits stolen goods in a warehouse and takes a negotiable receipt, the warehouseman is not liable on the receipt if he has surrendered the goods to the true owner, even though the receipt is held by a good faith purchaser. See Section 7–503(1). However, if the owner entrusted the goods to a person with power of disposition, and that person deposited the goods and took a negotiable document, the owner's receipt would not be rightful as against a holder to whom the negotiable document was duly negotiated, and delivery to the owner would not give the bailee a defense against such a holder. See Sections 7–502(1)(b), 7–503(1)(a).

    3.   Subsection (1)(b) amounts to a cross reference to all the tort law that determines the varying responsibilities and standards of care applicable to commercial bailees. A restatement of this tort law would be beyond the scope of this Act. Much of the applicable law as to responsibility of bailees for the preservation of the goods and limitation of liability in case of loss has been codified for particular classes of bailees in interstate and foreign commerce by federal legislation and treaty and for intrastate carriers and other bailees by the regulatory state laws preserved by Section 7–103. In the absence of governing legislation the common law will prevail subject to the minimum standard of reasonable care prescribed by Sections 7–204 and 7–309 of this Article. The optional language in subsection (1)(b) states the rule laid down for interstate carriers in many federal cases. State decisions are in conflict as to both carriers and warehousemen. Particular states may prefer to adopt the federal rule.

    4.   Subsection (2) eliminates the implication of the old uniform acts that a request for delivery must be accompanied by a formal tender of the amount of the charges due. Rather, the bailee must request payment of the amount of his lien when asked to deliver, and only in case this request is refused is he justified in declining to deliver because of nonpayment of charges. Where delivery without payment is forbidden by law, the request is treated as implicit. Such a prohibition reflects a policy of uniformity to prevent discrimination by failure to request payment in particular cases.

    5.   Subsection (3) states the obvious duty of a bailee to take up a negotiable document or note partial deliveries conspicuously thereon, and the result of failure in that duty. It is subject to only one exception, that stated in subsection 1(a) of this section and in Section 7–503(1). It is limited to cases of delivery to a claimant; it has no application, for example, where goods held under a negotiable document are lawfully sold to enforce the bailee's lien.

Cross References:

    Point 2: Sections 7–502 and 7–503.

    Point 3: Sections 7–103, 7–204, 7–309 and 10–103.

    Point 5: Section 7–503(1).

Definitional Cross References:

    "Bailee". Section 7–102.

    "Conspicuous". Section 1–201.

    "Delivery". Section 1–201.

    "Document". Section 7–102.

    "Document of title". Section 1–201.

    "Duly negotiate". Section 7–501.

    "Goods". Section 7–102.

    "Person". Section 1–201.

    "Receipt of goods". Section 2–103.

    "Right". Section 1–201.

    "Terms". Section 1–201.

    "Warehouseman". Section 7–102.

    "Written". Section 1–201.

§ 7–404.   No Liability for Good Faith Delivery Pursuant to Receipt or Bill.

A bailee who in good faith including observance of reasonable commercial standards has received goods and delivered or otherwise disposed of them according to the terms of the document of title or pursuant to this Article is not liable therefor. This rule applies even though the person from whom he received the goods had no authority to procure the document or to dispose of the goods and even though the person to whom he delivered the goods had no authority to receive them.

Official Comment

Prior Uniform Statutory Provision: Section 10, Uniform Warehouse Receipts Act; Section 13, Uniform Bills of Lading Act.

Changes: Consolidated and rewritten.

Purposes of Changes:

The generalized test of good faith and observance of reasonable commercial standards is substituted for the attempts to particularize what constitutes good faith in the cited sections of the old uniform acts. The section states explicitly what is perhaps an implication from the old acts that the common law rule of "innocent conversion" by unauthorized "intermeddling" with another's property is inapplicable to the operations of commercial carriers and warehousemen, who in good faith and with reasonable observance of commercial standards perform obligations which they have assumed and which generally they are under a legal compulsion to assume. The section applies to delivery to a fraudulent holder of a valid document as well as to delivery to the holder of an invalid document.

Definitional Cross References:

"Bailee". Section 7–102.
"Delivery". Section 1–201.
"Document of title". Section 1–201.
"Good faith". Section 1–201.
"Goods". Section 7–102.
"Person". Section 1–201.
"Receipt of goods". Section 2–103.
"Term". Section 1–201.

PART 5

WAREHOUSE RECEIPTS AND BILLS OF LADING: NEGOTIATION AND TRANSFER

§ 7–501.   Form of Negotiation and Requirements of "Due Negotiation".

(1)   A negotiable document of title running to the order of a named person is negotiated by his indorsement and delivery. After his indorsement in blank or to bearer any person can negotiate it by delivery alone.

(2)(a)   A negotiable document of title is also negotiated by delivery alone when by its original terms it runs to bearer.

(b)   When a document running to the order of a named person is delivered to him the effect is the same as if the document had been negotiated.

(3)   Negotiation of a negotiable document of title after it has been indorsed to a specified person requires indorsement by the special indorsee as well as delivery.

(4)   A negotiable document of title is "duly negotiated" when it is negotiated in the manner stated in this section to a holder who purchases it in good faith without notice of any defense against or claim to it on the part of any person and for value, unless it is established that the negotiation is not in the regular course of business or financing or involves receiving the document in settlement or payment of a money obligation.

(5)   Indorsement of a non-negotiable document neither makes it negotiable nor adds to the transferee's rights.

(6)   The naming in a negotiable bill of a person to be notified of the arrival of the goods does not limit the negotiability of the bill nor constitute notice to a purchaser thereof of any interest of such person in the goods.

Official Comment

Prior Uniform Statutory Provision: Sections 28, 29, 31, 32 and 38, Uniform Sales Act; Sections 37, 38, 39, 40 and 47, Uniform Warehouse Receipts Act; Sections 9, 28, 29, 30, 31 and 38, Uniform Bills of Lading Act.

Changes: Consolidated and rewritten.

Purposes of Changes:

1.   In general this section is intended to clarify the language of the old acts and to restate the effect of the better decisions thereunder. An important new concept is added, however, in the requirement of "regular course of business or financing" to effect the "due negotiation" which will transfer greater rights than those held by the person negotiating. The foundation of the mercantile doctrine of good faith purchase for value has always been, as shown by the case situations, the furtherance and protection of the regular course of trade. The reason for allowing a person, in bad faith or in error, to convey away rights which are not his own has from the beginning been to make possible the speedy handling of that great run of commercial transactions which are patently usual and normal.

There are two aspects to the usual and normal course of mercantile dealings, namely, the person making the transfer and the nature of the transaction itself. The first question which arises is: Is the transferor a person with whom it is reasonable to deal as having full powers? In regard to documents of title the only holder whose possession appears, commercially, to be in order is almost invariably a person in the trade. No commercial purpose is served by allowing a tramp or a professor to "duly negotiate" an order bill of lading for hides or cotton not his own, and since such a transfer is obviously not in the regular course of business, it is excluded from the scope of the protection of subsection (4).

The second question posed by the "regular course" qualification is: Is the transaction one which is normally proper to pass full rights without inquiry, even though the transferor himself may not have such rights to pass, and even though he may be acting in breach of duty? In raising this question the "regular course" criterion has the further advantage of limiting, the effective wrongful disposition to transactions whose protection will really further trade. Obviously, the snapping up of goods for quick resale at a price suspiciously below the market deserves no protection as a matter of policy: it is also clearly outside the range of regular course.

Any notice from the face of the document sufficient to put a merchant on inquiry as to the "regular course" quality of the transaction will frustrate a "due negotiation". Thus irregularity of the document on its face or unexplained staleness of a bill of lading may appropriately be recognized as negating a negotiation in "regular" course.

A pre-existing claim constitutes value, and "due negotiation" does not require "new value." A usual and ordinary transaction in which documents are received as security for credit previously extended may be in "regular" course, even though there is a demand for additional collateral because the creditor "deems himself insecure." But the matter has moved out of the regular course of financing if the debtor is thought to be insolvent, the credit previously extended is in effect cancelled, and the creditor snatches a plank in the shipwreck under the guise of a demand for additional collateral. Where a money debt is "paid" in commodity paper, any question of "regular" course disappears, as the case is explicitly excepted from "due negotiation".

2.   Negotiation under this section may be made by any holder no matter how he acquired possession of the document. The present section follows in this respect the Uniform Bills of Lading Act and amendments of the original Uniform Sales Act and Uniform Warehouse Receipts Act proposed by the Commissioners on Uniform State Laws in 1922.

3.   Subsection (2)(b) makes explicit a matter upon which the intent of the old acts was clear but the language somewhat obscure: a negotiation results from a delivery to a banker or buyer to whose order the document has been taken by the person making the bailment. There is no presumption of irregularity in such a negotiation; it may very well be in "regular course."

1132

4.   This Article does not contain any provision creating a presumption of due negotiation to, and full rights in, a holder of a document of title akin to that created by Sections 16, 24 and 59 of the Negotiable Instruments Law. But the reason of the provisions of this Act (Section 1–202) on the prima facie authenticity and accuracy of third party documents, joins with the reason of the present section to work such a presumption in favor of any person who has power to make a due negotiation. It would not make sense for this Act to authorize a purchaser to indulge the presumption of regularity if the courts were not also called upon to do so.

Cross References:

Point 1: Sections 7–502 and 7–503.

Point 2: Section 7–502.

Definitional Cross References:

"Bearer". Section 1–201.

"Delivery". Section 1–201.

"Document". Section 7–102.

"Document of title". Section 1–201.

"Good faith". Section 1–201.

"Holder". Section 1–201.

"Notice". Section 1–201.

"Person". Section 1–201.

"Purchase". Section 1–201.

"Rights". Section 1–201.

"Term". Section 1–201.

"Value". Section 1–201.

§ 7–502.   Rights Acquired by Due Negotiation.

(1)   Subject to the following section and to the provisions of Section 7–205 on fungible goods, a holder to whom a negotiable document of title has been duly negotiated acquires thereby:

(a)   title to the document;

(b)   title to the goods;

(c)   all rights accruing under the law of agency or estoppel, including rights to goods delivered to the bailee after the document was issued; and

(d)   the direct obligation of the issuer to hold or deliver the goods according to the terms of the document free of any defense or claim by him except those arising under the terms of the document or under this Article. In the case of a delivery order the bailee's obligation accrues only upon acceptance and the obligation acquired by the holder is that the issuer and any indorser will procure the acceptance of the bailee.

(2)   Subject to the following section, title and rights so acquired are not defeated by any stoppage of the goods represented by the document or by surrender of such goods by the bailee, and are not impaired even though the negotiation or any prior negotiation constituted a breach of duty or even though any person has been deprived of possession of the document by misrepresentation, fraud, accident, mistake, duress, loss, theft or conversion, or even though a previous sale or other transfer of the goods or document has been made to a third person.

Official Comment

Prior Uniform Statutory Provision: Sections 20(4), 25, 33, 38 and 62, Uniform Sales Act; Sections 41, 47, 48 and 49, Uniform Warehouse Receipts Act; Sections 32, 38, 39, 40 and 42, Uniform Bills of Lading Act.

Changes: Rewritten.

Purposes of Changes:

1.   The several necessary qualifications of the broad principle that the holder of a document acquired in a due negotiation is the owner of the document and the goods have been brought together in the next section.

2.   Subsection (1)(c) covers the case of "feeding" of a duly negotiated document by subsequent delivery to the bailee of such goods as the document falsely purported to cover; the bailee in such case is estopped as against the holder of the document.

3.   The explicit statement in subsection (1)(d) of the bailee's direct obligation to the holder precludes the defense, sometimes successfully asserted under the old acts, that the document in question was "spent" after the carrier had delivered the goods to a previous holder. But the holder is subject to such defenses as non-negligent destruction even though not apparent on the face of the document, and the bailee's obligation is of course subject to lawful provisions in filed classifications and tariffs. See Sections 7–103, 7–403. The sentence on delivery orders applies only to delivery orders in negotiable form which have been duly negotiated. On delivery orders, see also Section 7–503(2) and Comment.

4.   Subsection (2) condenses and continues the law of a number of sections of the prior acts which gave full effect to the issuance or due negotiation of a negotiable document. The subsection adds nothing to the effect of the rules stated in subsection (1), but it has been included since such explicit references were relied upon under the prior acts to preserve the rights of a purchaser by due negotiation unimpaired. The listing is not exhaustive. Only those matters have been repeated in this subsection which were explicitly reserved in the prior acts except in the case of stoppage in transit. Here, the language has been broadened to include "any stoppage" lest an inference be drawn that a stoppage of the goods before or after transit might cut off or otherwise impair the purchaser's rights.

Cross References:

Sections 7–103, 7–205, 7–403 and 7–503.

Definitional Cross References:

"Bailee". Section 7–102.
"Delivery". Section 1–201.
"Delivery order". Section 7–102.
"Document". Section 7–102.
"Document of title". Section 1–201.
"Duly negotiate". Section 7–501.
"Fungible". Section 1–201.
"Goods". Section 7–102.
"Holder". Section 1–201.
"Issuer". Section 7–102.
"Person". Section 1–201.
"Rights". Section 1–201.
"Term". Section 1–201.
"Warehouse receipt". Section 1–201.

§ 7–503.   Document of Title to Goods Defeated in Certain Cases.

(1)   A document of title confers no right in goods against a person who before issuance of the document had a legal interest or a perfected security interest in them and who neither

(a)   delivered or entrusted them or any document of title covering them to the bailor or his nominee with actual or apparent authority to ship, store or sell or with power to obtain delivery under this Article (Section 7–403) or with power of disposition under this Act (Sections 2–403 and 9–320) or other statute or rule of law; nor

(b)   acquiesced in the procurement by the bailor or his nominee of any document of title.

(2)   Title to goods based upon an unaccepted delivery order is subject to the rights of anyone to whom a negotiable warehouse receipt or bill of lading covering the goods has been duly negotiated. Such a title may be defeated under the next section to the same extent as the rights of the issuer or a transferee from the issuer.

(3)   Title to goods based upon a bill of lading issued to a freight forwarder is subject to the rights of anyone to whom a bill issued by the freight forwarder is duly negotiated; but delivery by the carrier in

accordance with Part 4 of this Article pursuant to its own bill of lading discharges the carrier's obligation to deliver.

As amended in 1999.

Official Comment

Prior Uniform Statutory Provision: Section 33, Uniform Sales Act; Section 41, Uniform Warehouse Receipts Act; Section 32, Uniform Bills of Lading Act.

Changes: Subsection (1) narrows, as compared to the cited sections, the occasions for defeating the document holder's title.

Purposes of Changes:

1. In general it may be said that the title of a purchaser by due negotiation prevails over almost any interest in the goods which existed prior to the procurement of the document of title if the possession of the goods by the person obtaining the document derived from any action by the prior claimant which introduced the goods into the stream of commerce or carried them along that stream. A thief of the goods cannot indeed by shipping or storing them to his own order acquire power to transfer them to a good faith purchaser. Nor can a tenant or mortgagor defeat any rights of a landlord or mortgagee which have been perfected under the local law merely by wrongfully shipping or storing a portion of the crop or other goods. However, "acquiescence" by the landlord or tenant does not require active consent under subsection (1)(b) and knowledge of the likelihood of storage or shipment with no objection or effort to control it is sufficient to defeat his rights as against one who takes by "due" negotiation of a negotiable document.

On the other hand, where goods are delivered to a factor for sale, even though the factor has made no advances and is limited in his duty to sell for cash, the goods are "entrusted" to him "with actual . . . authority . . . to sell" under subsection (1)(a), and if he procures a negotiable document of title he can transfer the owner's interest to a purchaser by due negotiation. Further, where the factor is in the business of selling, goods entrusted to him simply for safekeeping or storage may be entrusted under circumstances which give him "apparent authority to ship, store or sell" under subsection (1)(a), or power of disposition under Section 2–403, 7–205 or 9–320, or under a statute such as the earlier Factors Acts, or under a rule of law giving effect to apparent ownership. See Section 1–103.

Persons having an interest in goods also frequently deliver or entrust them to agents or servants other than factors for the purpose of shipping or warehousing or under circumstances reasonably contemplating such action. Rounding out the case law development under the prior Acts, this Act is clear that such persons assume full risk that the agent to whom the goods are so delivered may ship or store in breach of duty, take a document to his own order and then proceed to misappropriate it. This Act makes no distinction between possession or mere custody in such situations and finds no exception in the case of larceny by a bailee or the like. The safeguard in such situations lies in the requirement that a due negotiation can occur only "in the regular course of business or financing" and that the purchase be in good faith and without notice. See Section 7–501. Documents of title have no market among the commercially inexperienced and the commercially experienced do not take them without inquiry from persons known to be truck drivers or petty clerks even though such persons purport to be operating in their own names.

Again, where the seller allows a buyer to receive goods under a contract for sale, though as a "conditional delivery" or under "cash sale" terms and on explicit agreement for immediate payment, the buyer thereby acquires power to defeat the seller's interest by transfer of the goods to certain good faith purchasers. See Section 2–403. Both in policy and under the language of subsection (1)(a) that same power must be extended to accomplish the same result if the buyer procures a negotiable document of title to the goods and duly negotiates it.

2. Under subsection (1) a delivery order issued by a person having no right in or power over the goods is ineffective unless the owner acts as provided in subsection (1)(a) or (b). Thus the rights of a transferee of a non-negotiable warehouse receipt can be defeated by a delivery order subsequently issued by the transferor only if the transferee "delivers or entrusts" to the "person procuring" the delivery order or "acquiesces" in his procurement. Similarly, a second delivery order issued by the same issuer for the same goods will ordinarily be subject to the first, both under this section and under Section 7–402. After a delivery order is validly issued but before it is accepted, it may nevertheless be defeated under subsection (2) in much the same way that the rights of a transferee may be defeated under Section 7–504. For example, a buyer in ordinary course from the issuer may defeat the rights of the holder of a prior delivery order if the bailee receives notification of the buyer's rights before notification of the holder's rights. Section 7–504(2)(b). But an accepted delivery order has the same effect as a document issued by the bailee.

3. Under subsection (3) a bill of lading issued to a freight forwarder is subordinated to the freight forwarder's certificate, since the bill on its face gives notice of the fact that a freight forwarder is in the picture and has in all probability issued a certificate. But the carrier is protected in following the terms of its own bill of lading.

Cross References:

Point 1: Sections 2–403, 7–205, 7–501, 9–320, and 9–331.
Point 2: Sections 7–402 and 7–504.
Point 3: Sections 7–402, 7–403 and 7–404.

Definitional Cross References:

"Bill of lading". Section 1–201.
"Contract for sale". Section 2–106.
"Delivery". Section 1–201.
"Delivery order". Section 7–102.
"Document". Section 7–102.
"Document of title". Section 1–201.
"Duly negotiate". Section 7–501.
"Goods". Section 7–102.
"Person". Section 1–201.
"Right". Section 1–201.
"Warehouse receipt". Section 1–201.

§ 7–504. Rights Acquired in the Absence of Due Negotiation; Effect of Diversion; Seller's Stoppage of Delivery.

(1) A transferee of a document, whether negotiable or non-negotiable, to whom the document has been delivered but not duly negotiated, acquires the title and rights which his transferor had or had actual authority to convey.

(2) In the case of a non-negotiable document, until but not after the bailee receives notification of the transfer, the rights of the transferee may be defeated

(a) by those creditors of the transferor who could treat the sale as void under Section 2–402; or

(b) by a buyer from the transferor in ordinary course of business if the bailee has delivered the goods to the buyer or received notification of his rights; or

(c) as against the bailee by good faith dealings of the bailee with the transferor.

(3) A diversion or other change of shipping instructions by the consignor in a non-negotiable bill of lading which causes the bailee not to deliver to the consignee defeats the consignee's title to the goods if they have been delivered to a buyer in ordinary course of business and in any event defeats the consignee's rights against the bailee.

(4) Delivery pursuant to a non-negotiable document may be stopped by a seller under Section 2–705, and subject to the requirement of due notification there provided. A bailee honoring the seller's instructions is entitled to be indemnified by the seller against any resulting loss or expense.

Official Comment

Prior Uniform Statutory Provision: Section 34, Uniform Sales Act; Sections 41(b) and 42, Uniform Warehouse Receipts Act; Sections 32(b) and 33, Uniform Bills of Lading Act.

Changes: Generally rewritten; Subsection (3) is new.

Purposes of Changes and New Matter:

1. Under the general principles controlling negotiable documents, it is clear that in the absence of due negotiation a transferor cannot convey greater rights than he himself has, even when the negotiation is formally perfect. This section recognizes the transferor's power to transfer rights which he himself has or has "actual

authority to convey." Thus, where a negotiable document of title is being transferred the operation of the principle of estoppel is not recognized, as contrasted with situations involving the transfer of the goods themselves. (Compare Section 2–403 on good faith purchase of goods.)

A necessary part of the price for the protection of regular dealings with negotiable documents of title is an insistence that no dealing which is in any way irregular shall be recognized as a good faith purchase of the document or of any rights pertaining to it. So, where the transfer of a negotiable document fails as a negotiation because a requisite indorsement is forged or otherwise missing, the purchaser in good faith and for value may be in the anomalous position of having less rights, in part, than if he had purchased the goods themselves. True, his rights are not subject to defeat by attachment of the goods or surrender of them to his transferor [Contrast subsection (2)]; but on the other hand, he cannot acquire enforceable rights to control or receive the goods over the bailee's objection merely by giving notice to the bailee. Similarly, a consignee who makes payment to his consignor against a straight bill of lading can thereby acquire the position of a good faith purchaser of goods under provisions of the Article of this Act on Sales (Section 2–403), whereas the same payment made in good faith against an unindorsed order bill would not have such effect. The appropriate remedy of a purchaser in such a situation is to regularize his status by compelling indorsement of the document (see Section 7–506).

2.   As in the case of transfer—as opposed to "due negotiation"—of negotiable documents, subsection (1) empowers the transferor of a nonnegotiable document to transfer only such rights as he himself has or has "actual authority" to convey. In contrast to situations involving the goods themselves the operation of estoppel or agency principles is not here recognized to enable the transferor to convey greater rights than he actually has. Subsection (2) makes it clear, however, that the transferee of a nonnegotiable document may acquire rights greater in some respects than those of his transferor by giving notice of the transfer to the bailee.

3.   Subsection (3) is in part a reiteration of the carrier's immunity from liability if it honors instructions of the consignor to divert, but there is added a provision protecting the title of the substituted consignee if the latter is a buyer in ordinary course of business. A typical situation would be where a manufacturer, having shipped a lot of standardized goods to A on nonnegotiable bill of lading, diverts the goods to customer B who pays for them. Under orthodox passage-of-title-by-appropriation doctrine A might reclaim the goods from B. However, no consideration of commercial policy supports this involvement of an innocent third party in the default of the manufacturer on his contract to A; and the common commercial practice of diverting goods in transit suggests a trade understanding in accordance with this subsection.

4.   Subsection (4) gives the carrier an express right to indemnity where he honors a seller's request to stop delivery.

5.   Section 1–201(27) gives the bailee protection, if due diligence is exercised, similar to that found in the third paragraph of Section 33, Uniform Bills of Lading Act, where the bailee's organization has not had time to act on a notification.

Cross References:

Point 1: Sections 2–403 and 7–506.
Point 2: Section 2–403.
Point 3: Sections 7–303 and 7–403(1)(e).
Point 4: Sections 2–705 and 7–403(1)(d).

Definitional Cross References:

"Bailee". Section 7–102.
"Bill of lading". Section 1–201.
"Buyer in ordinary course of business". Section 1–201.
"Consignee". Section 7–102.
"Consignor". Section 7–102.
"Creditor". Section 1–201.
"Delivery". Section 1–201.
"Document". Section 7–102.
"Duly negotiate". Section 7–501.
"Good faith". Section 1–201.
"Goods". Section 7–102.
"Honor". Section 1–201.

"Notification". Section 1–201.
"Purchaser". Section 1–201.
"Rights". Section 1–201.

§ 7–505.   Indorser Not a Guarantor for Other Parties.

The indorsement of a document of title issued by a bailee does not make the indorser liable for any default by the bailee or by previous indorsers.

Official Comment

Prior Uniform Statutory Provision: Section 37, Uniform Sales Act; Section 45, Uniform Warehouse Receipts Act; Section 36, Uniform Bills of Lading Act.

Changes: No substantial change.

Purposes of Changes:

The indorsement of a document of title is generally understood to be directed towards perfecting the transferee's rights rather than towards assuming additional obligations. The language of the present section, however, does not preclude the one case in which an indorsement given for value guarantees future action, namely, that in which the bailee has not yet become liable upon the document at the time of the indorsement. Under such circumstances the indorser, of course, engages that appropriate honor of the document by the bailee will occur. See Section 7–502(1)(d) as to negotiable delivery orders. However, even in such a case, once the bailee attorns to the transferee, the indorser's obligation has been fulfilled and the policy of this section excludes any continuing obligation on the part of the indorser for the bailee's ultimate actual performance.

Cross Reference:

Section 7–502.

Definitional Cross References:

"Bailee". Section 7–102.
"Document of title". Section 1–201.
"Party". Section 1–201.

§ 7–506.   Delivery Without Indorsement: Right to Compel Indorsement.

The transferee of a negotiable document of title has a specifically enforceable right to have his transferor supply any necessary indorsement but the transfer becomes a negotiation only as of the time the indorsement is supplied.

Official Comment

Prior Uniform Statutory Provision: Section 35, Uniform Sales Act; Section 43, Uniform Warehouse Receipts Act; Section 34, Uniform Bills of Lading Act.

Changes: Consolidated and rewritten; former requirement that transfer be "for value" eliminated.

Purposes of Changes:

1.   From a commercial point of view the intention to transfer a negotiable document of title which requires an indorsement for its transfer, is incompatible with an intention to withhold such indorsement and so defeat the effective use of the document. This position is sustained by the absence of any reported case applying the prior provisions in almost forty years of decisions. Further, the preceding section and the Comment thereto make it clear that an indorsement generally imposes no responsibility on the indorser.

2.   Although this section provides that delivery of a document of title without the necessary indorsement is effective as a transfer, the transferee, of course, has not regularized his position until such indorsement is supplied. Until this is done he cannot claim rights under due negotiation within the requirements of this Article (subsection (4) of Section 7–501) on "due negotiation". Similarly, despite the transfer to him of his transferor's title, he cannot demand the goods from the bailee until the negotiation has been completed and the document is in proper form for surrender. See Section 7–403(3).

Cross References:

> Point 1: Section 7–505.
> Point 2: Sections 7–501(4) and 7–403(2).

Definitional Cross References:

> "Document of title". Section 1–201.
> "Rights". Section 1–201.

§ 7–507.   Warranties on Negotiation or Transfer of Receipt or Bill.

Where a person negotiates or transfers a document of title for value otherwise than as a mere intermediary under the next following section, then unless otherwise agreed he warrants to his immediate purchaser only in addition to any warranty made in selling the goods

   (a)   that the document is genuine; and

   (b)   that he has no knowledge of any fact which would impair its validity or worth; and

   (c)   that his negotiation or transfer is rightful and fully effective with respect to the title to the document and the goods it represents.

Official Comment

Prior Uniform Statutory Provision: Section 36, Uniform Sales Act; Section 44, Uniform Warehouse Receipts Act; Section 35, Uniform Bills of Lading Act.

Changes: Consolidated and rewritten without change in policy.

Purposes of Changes:

   1.   This section omits provisions of the prior acts on warranties as to the goods as unnecessary and incomplete. It is unnecessary because such warranties derive from the contract of sale and not from the transfer of the documents. The fact that transfer of control occurs by way of a document of title does not limit or displace the ordinary obligations of a seller. The former provision, moreover, was incomplete because it did not expressly include all of the warranties which might rest upon a seller under such circumstances. This Act handles the problem by means of the precautionary reference to "any warranty made in selling the goods." If the transfer of documents attends or follows the making of a contract for the sale of goods, the general obligations on warranties as to the goods (Sections 2–312 through 2–318) are brought to bear as well as the special warranties under this section.

   2.   The limited warranties of a delivering or collecting intermediary are stated in Section 7–508.

Cross References:

> Point 1: Sections 2–312 through 2–318.
> Point 2: Section 7–508.

Definitional Cross References:

> "Document". Section 7–102.
> "Document of title". Section 1–201.
> "Genuine". Section 1–201.
> "Goods". Section 7–102.
> "Person". Section 1–201.
> "Purchaser". Section 1–201.
> "Value". Section 1–201.

§ 7–508.   Warranties of Collecting Bank as to Documents.

A collecting bank or other intermediary known to be entrusted with documents on behalf of another or with collection of a draft or other claim against delivery of documents warrants by such delivery of the documents only its own good faith and authority. This rule applies even though the intermediary has purchased or made advances against the claim or draft to be collected.

Official Comment

Prior Uniform Statutory Provision: None.

Purposes:

1.   To state the limited warranties given with respect to the documents accompanying a documentary draft.

2.   In warranting its authority a bank only warrants its authority from its transferor. See Section 4–203. It does not warrant the genuineness or effectiveness of the document. Compare Section 7–507.

3.   Other duties and rights of banks handling documentary drafts for collection are stated in Article 4, Part 5.

Cross References:

Sections 4–203 and 7–507, 4–501 through 4–504.

Definitional Cross References:

"Collecting bank". Section 4–105.
"Delivery". Section 1–201.
"Document". Section 7–102.
"Draft". Section 5–103.
"Good faith". Section 1–201.

§ 7–509.   Receipt or Bill: When Adequate Compliance With Commercial Contract.

The question whether a document is adequate to fulfill the obligations of a contract for sale or the conditions of a credit is governed by the Articles on Sales (Article 2) and on Letters of Credit (Article 5).

Official Comment

Prior Uniform Statutory Provision: None.

Purposes:

To cross-refer to the Articles of this Act which deal with the substantive issues of the type of document of title required under the contract entered into by the parties.

Cross References:

Articles 2 and 5.
"Document". Section 7–102.

Definitional Cross References:

"Contract for sale". Section 2–106.

PART 6

WAREHOUSE RECEIPTS AND BILLS OF LADING: MISCELLANEOUS PROVISIONS

§ 7–601.   Lost and Missing Documents.

(1)   If a document has been lost, stolen or destroyed, a court may order delivery of the goods or issuance of a substitute document and the bailee may without liability to any person comply with such order. If the document was negotiable the claimant must post security approved by the court to indemnify any person who may suffer loss as a result of non-surrender of the document. If the document was not negotiable, such security may be required at the discretion of the court. The court may also in its discretion order payment of the bailee's reasonable costs and counsel fees.

(2)   A bailee who without court order delivers goods to a person claiming under a missing negotiable document is liable to any person injured thereby, and if the delivery is not in good faith becomes liable for conversion. Delivery in good faith is not conversion if made in accordance with a filed classification or tariff or, where no classification or tariff is filed, if the claimant posts security with the bailee in an amount at least double the value of the goods at the time of posting to indemnify any person injured by the delivery who files a notice of claim within one year after the delivery.

Official Comment

Prior Uniform Statutory Provision: Section 14, Uniform Warehouse Receipts Act; Section 17, Uniform Bills of Lading Act.

Changes: General Revision. Principal innovations include: affirmation of bailee's privilege to deliver to claimant without resort to judicial proceedings if the bailee acts in good faith and is willing to take the full risk of loss in case the lost document turns up in the hands of an innocent purchaser; explicit authorization to the court to order bailee to issue a substitute document rather than make physical delivery of the goods; inclusion of "stolen" as well as lost documents; extension of section to non-negotiable documents.

Purposes of Changes: The purposes of the changes insofar as they are not self-evident are as follows:

1.   As to bailee's privilege to deliver without court order, doubt had arisen as to the propriety of such action under Section 54 of the Uniform Warehouse Receipts Act, which made it a crime to deliver goods covered by negotiable receipts without taking up the receipts "except in the cases provided for in Section 14" (the lost receipts section). This has been interpreted by one court as exempting from criminal liability only if the judicial procedure of Section 14 was followed. Dahl v. Winter-Truesdell-Diercks Co., 61 N.D. 84, 237 N.W. 202 (1931). Although the criminal provisions are not being re-enacted in this Act (and the Uniform Bills of Lading Act never did include such a criminal provision), it seems advisable to clarify the legality of the well established commercial practice of bailees to make delivery where they are satisfied that the claimant is the person entitled under a lost document. Since the bailee remains liable on the document in such cases, he will usually insist that the claimant provide an indemnity bond.

2.   The old acts provide only for compulsory delivery of goods; this Section provides also for compulsory issuance of a substitute document. If continuance of the bailment is desirable there is no reason to require the goods to be withdrawn and redeposited in order to secure a negotiable document. The present acts would probably be so interpreted. Section 20 of the Federal Warehouse Act and some state laws expressly require issuance of a new receipt on proof of loss and posting of bond.

3.   Claimants on non-negotiable instruments are permitted to avail themselves of this procedure because straight bills of lading sometimes contain provisions that the goods shall not be delivered except upon production of the bill. If the carrier should choose to insist upon production of the bill, the consignee should have some means of compelling delivery on satisfactory proof of entitlement.

Ordinarily no security would be necessary to indemnify a bailee in delivering to the person named in a non-negotiable document. But disputes as to negotiability may arise, in which case if there is a reasonable doubt on the point the bailee should be protected against the possibility that the missing document would, in the hands of an innocent purchaser for value, be held negotiable.

4.   It seems unnecessary to state, as do the present acts, that the court shall act "on satisfactory proof of such loss or destruction." The right of action created by the section is conditioned on a document being lost, stolen or destroyed. Plaintiff must of course bring himself within the section. There is nothing in the language of the old acts to suggest that they intended to impose anything but the normal burden of proof on the plaintiff in such proceedings.

5.   Subsection (2) makes it clear that after delivery without court order the bailee remains liable for actual damages. Liability for conversion is provided where the delivery is dishonest, but excluded where a filed classification or tariff is followed in good faith, or where the described bond is posted in good faith and no classification or tariff is filed. Liability for conversion in other cases is left to judicial decision.

Definitional Cross References:

"Bailee". Section 7–102.
"Bill of lading". Section 1–201.
"Delivery". Section 1–201.

"Document". Section 7–102.
"Good faith". Section 1–201.
"Goods". Section 7–102.
"Person". Section 1–201.
"Warehouse receipt". Section 1–201.
"Warehouseman". Section 7–102.

§ 7–602.   Attachment of Goods Covered by a Negotiable Document.

Except where the document was originally issued upon delivery of the goods by a person who had no power to dispose of them, no lien attaches by virtue of any judicial process to goods in the possession of a bailee for which a negotiable document of title is outstanding unless the document be first surrendered to the bailee or its negotiation enjoined, and the bailee shall not be compelled to deliver the goods pursuant to process until the document is surrendered to him or impounded by the court. One who purchases the document for value without notice of the process or injunction takes free of the lien imposed by judicial process.

Official Comment

Prior Uniform Statutory Provisions: Section 25, Uniform Warehouse Receipts Act; Section 24, Uniform Bills of Lading Act.

Changes: Consolidated and rewritten.

Purposes of Changes:

1.   The purpose of the section is to protect the bailee from conflicting claims of the document holder and the judgment creditors of the person who deposited the goods. The rights of the former prevail unless, in effect, the judgment creditors immobilize the negotiable document. However, if the document was issued upon deposit of the goods by a person who had no power to dispose of the goods so that the document is ineffective to pass title, judgment liens are valid to the extent of the debtor's interest in the goods.

2.   The last sentence covers the possibility that the holder of a document who has been enjoined from negotiating it will violate the injunction by negotiating to an innocent purchaser for value. In such case the lien will be defeated.

Cross Reference:

Point 1: Section 7–503.

Definitional Cross References:

"Bailee". Section 7–102.
"Delivery". Section 1–201.
"Document". Section 7–102.
"Goods". Section 7–102.
"Notice". Section 1–201.
"Person". Section 1–201.
"Purchase". Section 1–201.
"Value". Section 1–201.

§ 7–603.   Conflicting Claims; Interpleader.

If more than one person claims title or possession of the goods, the bailee is excused from delivery until he has had a reasonable time to ascertain the validity of the adverse claims or to bring an action to compel all claimants to interplead and may compel such interpleader, either in defending an action for non-delivery of the goods, or by original action, whichever is appropriate.

Official Comment

Prior Uniform Statutory Provision: Sections 16 and 17, Uniform Warehouse Receipts Act; Sections 20 and 21, Uniform Bills of Lading Act.

Changes: Consolidation without substantial change.

Purposes of Changes:

The section enables a bailee faced with conflicting claims to the goods to compel the claimants to litigate their claims with each other rather than with him.

Definitional Cross References:

"Action". Section 1–201.
"Bailee". Section 7–102.
"Delivery". Section 1–201.
"Goods". Section 7–102.
"Person". Section 1–201.
"Reasonable time". Section 1–204.

APPENDIX E

PEB COMMENTARIES AND REPORTS ON THE UNIFORM COMMERCIAL CODE

Current Permanent Editorial Board (PEB) for the UCC

Chair

Richard L. Revesz

Members

Boris Auerbach

E. Carolan Berkley

Carl S. Bjerre

Amelia H. Boss

Patricia Brumfield Fry

Teresa W. Harmon

Stephanie Heller

Lisa I. Karsai

Lance Liebman

Carlyle C. Ring, Jr.

Edwin E. Smith

Steven O. Weise

ABA Advisors

Carter H. Klein

Norman M. Powell

Division E Chair Member

John T. McGarvey

Ex Officio

Richard T. Cassidy

Roberta Cooper Ramo

Emeritus Members

William H. Henning

Frederick H. Miller

James J. White

Director of Research

Neil B. Cohen

CONTENTS

APPENDIX E

PEB RESOLUTION ON PURPOSES, STANDARDS AND PROCEDURES FOR PEB COMMENTARY TO THE UCC

1.   The Permanent Editorial Board (PEB), in accordance with the standards and procedures set out in this resolution of March 14, 1987, and the authority given in the agreement between the American Law Institute and the National Conference of Commissioners on Uniform State Laws dated July 31, 1986, will issue supplemental commentary on the Uniform Commercial Code (UCC) from time to time.

a.   The supplemental commentary of the PEB generally will be known as *PEB Commentary,* to distinguish it from the Official Comments to the UCC, and will be preserved separately from the Official Comments.

b.   The underlying purposes and policies of the *PEB Commentary* are those specified in UCC § 1–102(2). A *PEB Commentary* should come within one or more of the following specific purposes, which should be made apparent at the inception of the Commentary: (1) to resolve an ambiguity in the UCC by restating more clearly what the PEB considers to be the legal rule; (2) to state a preferred resolution of an issue on which judicial opinion or scholarly writing diverges; (3) to elaborate on the application of the UCC where the statute and/or the Official Comment leaves doubt as to inclusion or exclusion of, or application to, particular circumstances or transactions; (4) consistent with UCC § 1–102(2)(b), to apply the principles of the UCC to new or changed circumstances; (5) to clarify or elaborate upon the operation of the UCC as it relates to other statutes (such as the Bankruptcy Code and various federal and state consumer protection statutes) and general principles of law and equity pursuant to UCC § 1–103; or (6) to otherwise improve the operation of the UCC.

c.   The format of the *PEB Commentary* normally will consist of an identification of the issue, a discussion concerning the possible resolutions of the issue to be addressed, and a statement of the view of the PEB as to how the issue should be resolved. On a carefully selected basis supplemental commentary may be issued as an identified supplement to the Official Comments, in which case it generally should take the form of a brief exposition modeled substantially on the form and style of the Official Comments.

d.   Topics for *PEB Commentary* will be selected periodically by the PEB from suggestions, accompanied by supporting reasons, made by PEB members and by other persons. *PEB Commentary* may be issued whether or not a perceived issue has been litigated or is in litigation, and whether or not the position taken by the PEB accords with the weight of authority on the issue. The number of topics and topics that are chosen at any given time will be determined by the PEB weighing criteria appropriate under the circumstances, which may include the practical importance of the issue, the absence of other means of resolution, the time and effort to be involved in the preparation of the *PEB Commentary,* the extent to which the *PEB Commentary* is likely to be successful in addressing an issue, whether it is known to the PEB that the topic of the *PEB Commentary* is in specific litigation and, if so, the probable impact upon that litigation, and the availability of resources. However, normally no *PEB Commentary* should be begun with respect to a UCC Article that is undergoing amendment or initial promulgation except upon consultation with and concurrence of the study or drafting committee for such amendment or initial promulgation. Moreover, except in extraordinary cases and in the case of *PEB Commentary* identified as specific supplements to Official Comments, an Official Comment, as opposed to the text of the UCC, should not be the specific subject of *PEB Commentary.*

e. For a variety of reasons, topics initially identified by the PEB for *PEB Commentary* and advisors' drafts of *PEB Commentary* (discussed in paragraph 2 below) may not result in the final approval of *PEB Commentary.* Such reasons might include the failure of a consensus to emerge on the substance of an issue or a conclusion that the issue would better be treated by a change in the UCC Official Text. No inference should be drawn from, and no weight should be accorded to, any withdrawal of an advisor's draft or any failure to proceed with a *PEB Commentary* on any particular topic.

2. The process by which *PEB Commentary* is prepared and issued by the PEB should be flexible, but usually should include:

a. periodic publication of the topics under consideration by the PEB with a request for comment by interested persons by a stated date as to whether any listed topic should be deleted or a related topic added and as to the appropriate resolution of the issues presented by the topics under consideration;

b. selection of one or more appropriate advisers, who are not members of the PEB, to review any comments submitted by interested persons and other relevant materials and to prepare a tentative adviser's draft of the proposed *PEB Commentary;*

c. publication of the adviser's draft of the *PEB Commentary,* after supervisory review of the PEB, soliciting comments by interested persons by a stated date on the substance and style of the work;

d. approval by the PEB of the substance and style of the *PEB Commentary* as finally submitted by the adviser(s) and comments submitted by interested persons or, when warranted, the withdrawal of the proposal with the reasons for withdrawal stated; and

e. periodic publication of such *PEB Commentary* as is approved by the PEB on a regular schedule.

Approval by the PEB of *PEB Commentary* shall be by three quarters of the members of the PEB voting on the *Commentary.* The manner of publication of *PEB Commentary* by the PEB will be in accordance with procedures formulated under a resolution related to that subject generally.

PEB COMMENTARY NO. 1
SECTION 2–507(2)
(March 10, 1990)

ISSUE

A cash seller has the right to be paid upon delivery of goods and, if not paid, to reclaim the goods. This right is codified by § 2–507(2). Payment may be made by a check, but such payment is conditional and defeated by dishonor of the check giving rise to the seller's right of reclamation. Comment 3 to § 2–507(2) states:

"Subsection (2) deals with the effect of a conditional delivery by the seller and in such a situation makes the buyer's 'right as against the seller' conditional upon payment. These words are used as words of limitation to conform with the policy set forth in the bona fide purchase sections of this Article. Should the seller after making such a conditional delivery fail to follow up his rights, the condition is waived.

APPENDIX E

The provision of this Article for a ten day limit within which the seller may reclaim goods delivered on credit to an insolvent buyer is also applicable here." (emphasis supplied)

If the payment is tendered by check, the seller payee will only learn that the check has been or will be dishonored *after* the goods are delivered. The seller will gain this information either by learning from the bank where the check was deposited that it had been dishonored by the payor bank; or, sometimes by inquiring directly of the payor bank and being told that there is no such account or there is an account but with insufficient funds to cover the check. Oftentimes, the seller may not learn of the dishonor or anticipated dishonor until more than ten days after delivery of the goods.[1] Does the reference in the Comment to the requirement of § 2–702(2) requiring a credit seller to demand reclamation of the goods "within ten days after the receipt" mean that the cash seller also loses the right of reclamation where demand is made more than ten days after delivery of the goods, even though the seller did not learn of the dishonor before then?

DISCUSSION

The cash seller's right of reclamation was a common law remedy in the nature of a lien. "The ground upon which an unpaid seller is allowed a lien and kindred remedies is the inherent injustice of depriving him of goods with which he has not finally parted where it is evident that he has not been paid or will not be paid the price for them when it is due." Williston, *Sales*, 99 (1948).

The "cash sale" is expressly mentioned in the voidable title provision of § 2–403(1)(c) (along with payment by check (§ 2–403(1)(b))), but the right of reclamation is not specifically mentioned. Instead, it is implicit in § 2–507(2) and § 2–511(3). As noted by the First Circuit in Szabo v. Vinton Motors, 630 F.2d 1, 3, 29 UCC Rep.Serv. (Callaghan) 737 (1st Cir.1980):

> "Although the right of such a cash seller to reclaim goods sold in a 'bad check' transaction is not specifically set forth in the Code provisions, [footnote omitted] such a reclamation right is inherent in 2–507(2) and 2–511(3) of the Code, Mass. Gen. Laws ch. 106, §§ 2–507(2), 2–511(3). In re Mort Co., 208 F.Supp. 309, 310 [1 UCC Rep. 166] (ED Pa.1962); In re Helms Veneer Corp., 287 F.Supp. 840, 845–46 [5 UCC Rep. 977, 983–4] (WD Va.1968). See generally Mann & Phillips, The Cash Seller Under the Uniform Commercial Code, 20 B.C.L.Rev. 370, 375–84 (1979). Section 2–507(2) makes a buyer's 'right as against the seller to retain or dispose of [the goods] . . . conditional upon his making the payment due.' Section 2–511(3), in turn, provides that 'payment by check is conditional and is defeated as between the parties by dishonor of the check on due presentment.' Taking these two Code provisions together, the clear implication is that a buyer cannot retain and, conversely, a seller has the right to reclaim goods sold in a cash transaction if the buyer's check is dishonored.

"The existence of the cash seller's right to reclaim is further supported, and limited, by Comment 3 to section 2–507:

> "[quotation omitted]

"The reference in the last sentence of Comment 3 is to the limitation contained in § 2–702(2) requiring a credit seller to reclaim goods within ten days of receipt. See note 1 supra. Based on this reference, courts have invariably held that a cash seller must make a demand for the return of the goods within ten days after the goods are received by the buyer. E.g., In re Samuels & Co., 526 F.2d 1238, 1245 (5th Cir.) (en banc), cert. denied 429 U.S. 834 (1976); In re Helms Veneer Corp., supra, at 846 * * * [footnote omitted]."

See also Dugan, *Cash Sellers Under Articles 2 and 9 of the UCC,* 8 UCC L.J. 330, 345–349 (1976).

Szabo, which represents the majority view by reason of the Comment, went on to hold that the seller's right of reclamation is lost if demand is made more than ten days after delivery of the goods:

---

[1] This problem should become less significant under Federal Reserve Board Regulation CC, 12 CFR Part 229, issued pursuant to the Expedited Funds Availability Act, 12 USC Section 4001 et seq. Under Section 229.30, the payor bank has a duty to effect an "expeditious return" of the check and if the check is for $2,500 or more, Section 229.33 requires that it provide notice of non-payment that is received by the depositary bank by 4:00 P.M. on the second business day following the banking day on which the check was presented; and that the depositary bank send notice to its customer by midnight of the banking day following its receipt of the notice or within a reasonable longer time.

PEB COMMENTARY NO. 1

"Appellee urges us to disregard the limitation contained in Comment 3 on the ground that it directly contradicts the language of the Code. Although official Code Comments do not have the force of law, they are helpful in explaining the Code provisions and their purpose is to promote uniformity in construction. Mass.Gen. Laws ch. 106, Comment to Title; Thompson v. United States, 408 F.2d 1075, 1084 n. 15 (8th Cir.1969). See generally Skilton, Some Comments on the Comments to the Uniform Commercial Code, 1966 Wisc.L.Rev. 597. It has been stated that the Official Comments 'are powerful dicta.' In re Yale Express System, Inc., 370 F.2d 433, 437 (2d Cir.1966). Nevertheless, it is the Code provisions and not the Comments which control. We do not, however, accept appellee's argument that there is a direct conflict between the cash sale provisions of the Code and Comment 3 to § 2–507. As noted above, Comment 3 supports a reclamation right which is only implicit in §§ 2–507(2) and 2–511(3), and limits that right by reference to another Code provision, § 2–702(2), dealing with credit sales. Comment 3 does not contradict, but merely complements and explains the Code. We decline to disregard it." (630 F.2d at 3–4).

The Eighth Circuit, however, rejected *Szabo* in Burk v. Emmick, 637 F.2d 1172, 29 UCC Rep.Serv. (Callaghan) 1489 (8th Cir.1980):

"We reject this reasoning. In our view, it would tend to coerce the cash seller who reasonably expects the buyer to tender payment at delivery to go through the cautious motions of a credit seller dealing with an economically unstable buyer. This we are not prepared to do. . . ." (637 F.2d at 1175 n. 6).

"Our holding is quite limited. We determine that as between the seller and the buyer, where a cash seller reclaims goods sold to a breaching buyer, the only limitation imposed upon the seller's right is a reasonableness requirement. . . ." (637 F.2d at 1176).

There is nothing in the language of § 2–507(2) supporting the imposition of the "ten day limit" mentioned in Comment 3. At common law, there was no specific time limitation. Rather, an attempt to reclaim after excessive delay would be defeated by doctrines such as waiver, estoppel, or ratification of the buyer's property interest. See, e.g., Frech v. Lewis, 218 Pa. 141, 67 A. 45 (1907). Under § 1–103, common law principles supplement Code provisions, unless "displaced by the particular provisions." Proper implementation of this doctrine compels the conclusion that the codification of the "cash sale" concept implicit in § 2–507(2), without any mention of a time limit, means that common law rules governing enforcement are still applicable. Indeed, the third sentence of Comment 3 is consistent with this interpretation in referring to waiver where a seller fails "to follow up his rights." The cases which, even though they rely on Comment 3, impose a ten day limit, must be considered to have reached an improper result. There is no need to impose a specific time limitation for enforcement of a cash seller's right of reclamation. The common law rules defeating the right where there is delay resulting in prejudice to the buyer adequately cover instances where only the seller and buyer are involved: If the rights of third parties are implicated § 2–403(1)(b) and (c) protect good faith purchasers.

CONCLUSION

There is no justification for barring the cash seller's right or remedy of reclamation before discovery of non-payment. There is no specific time limit for a cash seller to exercise the right of reclamation. The right may be exercised as long as there has not been an excessive delay causing inequitable prejudice to the buyer. Common law rules and precedents governing such circumstances are applicable.

The last sentence of Official Comment 3 to § 2–507 is deleted as inappropriate and replaced by the following:

. . . This subsection (2) codifies the cash seller's right of reclamation which is in the nature of a lien. There is no specific time limit for a cash seller to exercise the right of reclamation. However, the right will be defeated by delay causing prejudice to the buyer, waiver, estoppel, or ratification of the buyer's right to retain possession. Common law rules and precedents governing such principles are applicable (Section 1–103). If third parties are involved, Section 2–403(1) protects good faith purchasers. See PEB Commentary No. 1, dated March 10, 1990.

PEB COMMENTARY NO. 2
SECTION 9–301(4)*
(March 10, 1990)

ISSUE

Section 9–301(4) provides: "A person who becomes a lien creditor while a security interest is perfected takes subject to the security interest only to the extent that it secures advances made before he becomes a lien creditor or within 45 days thereafter or made without knowledge of the lien or pursuant to a commitment entered into without knowledge of the lien." Does the phrase "only to the extent that it secures advances" limit the priority of the security interest to advances, as distinguished from, e.g., accruing interest, collection expenses, and similar ancillary rights (all herein called "non-advances")?

DISCUSSION

An example to illustrate the issue is the question whether non-advances, e.g., interest on advances accruing either before or after the lien arises, or expenses of foreclosure of the security interest arising after the lien arises, are excluded from the priority of pre-lien advances under the security interest by the language quoted above.

If § 9–301(4) were read in an exclusionary fashion as suggested in the issue above, it would put on the priority of a security interest a limitation which does not have any pre-Code precedents in chattel security law or similar real estate mortgage law. Even if the language were to be read as excluding only interest and expenses incurred after the creditor's lien arose, the limitation is believed to be without precedent except for some situations in which accruing interest and expenses were considered to be "inchoate" as that concept developed in federal law concerned with rights of the United States against secured parties under the Federal Preference Act, R.S. 3166, now 31 USC 3713, and under the Federal Tax Lien Act, 26 USC 6321–6323.

Section 9–301(4) was one of three sections (the others being §§ 9–307(3) and 9–312(7)) adopted by the 1972 amendments to Article 9 to solve the much debated question of the priority of future advances against intermediate security interests or buyers of the collateral or creditors having non-consensual liens on the collateral. See the 1972 General Comments of the Review Committee for Article 9, paragraphs E–39 to –45 (republished in West's Uniform Commercial Code, 1987 Official Text with Comments, pp. 910–912), which neither by their heading nor by their text offered any suggestion that the priority considered related to anything other than the future advances themselves, as distinguished from non-advances. To the same effect, the "Reasons for 1972 Change" to §§ 9–301(4) (Rights of Lien Creditors), 9–307(3) (Rights of Buyers) and 9–312(7) (Rights of Intervening Secured Parties) do not contain any suggestion that the sections undertake to affect the priorities of non-advances. The three sections are *in pari materia,* although they use somewhat different combinations of the same elements to reach varying results in three situations.

Sections 9–301(4) and 9–307(3) provide nearly identical rules as to the priority of subsequent advances against lien creditors and buyers respectively. Section 9–307(3) reads: "A buyer . . . takes free of a security interest to the extent that it secures future advances made after the secured party acquires knowledge of the purchase, or more than 45 days after the purchase, whichever first occurs, unless made pursuant to a commitment entered into without knowledge of the purchase and before the expiration of the 45 day period." The only substantive difference between this and § 9–301(4), quoted at the beginning of the Commentary, is that in § 9–307(3) the effect of knowledge of the intervening rights is to shorten the specified 45-day period during which advances may be made with the same priority as the original advance, while in § 9–301(4) absence of knowledge is a factor which can extend beyond the 45 days the right to make post-lien advances with the same priority as the original advance.

The language in § 9–307(3) sets forth the rule for future advances without suggesting that it is exclusive and excludes any priority for nonadvances, while § 9–301(4) is so phrased with the word "only" that on its face it excludes any right to non-advances. It is believed that this phraseology in § 9–301(4) was just an accident of draftmanship as the draftsmen concentrated on the problem discussed in the last

---

* *Note from West Advisory Panel: Referring to unrevised Article 9. See revised § 9–323.*

paragraph of the "Reasons for 1972 Change" for § 9–301(4), namely, the effect of the rule chosen on priority of the security interest as against the Federal Tax Lien under the Federal Tax Lien Act of 1966.

CONCLUSION

Section 9–301(4) should not be read as excluding or limiting interest on advances or expenses made in their collection and enforcement, or other non-advances ancillary to advances having priority against the lien creditor.

This issue was presented in Dick Warner Cargo Handling Corp. v. Aetna Business Credit, Inc., 746 F.2d 126, 39 UCC Rep.Serv. (Callaghan) 762 (2d Cir.1984), and the Court held in accordance with this conclusion.

The Official Comment to § 9–301 is amended by adding the following:

8.   The word "only" in subsection (4) is limited in its effect to the lien creditor's subjection to the specified advances. It does not limit the lien creditor's subjection to whatever other rights the secured party may have by contract or law, e.g., the right to interest before or after the attachment of the judgment lien to the collateral or the right to foreclosure expenses or other collection expenses. See PEB Commentary No. 2, dated March 10, 1990.

PEB COMMENTARY NO. 3
SECTIONS 9–306(2) AND 9–402(7)*
(March 10, 1990)

ISSUE

Is there a conflict between UCC § 9–306(2), which terminates a security interest upon any disposition of the collateral that has been authorized by the secured party, and the last sentence of UCC § 9–402(7), which continues the effectiveness of a financing statement with respect to collateral that has been transferred even though the secured party knows of and consents to the transfer?

The issue can be described by the following hypothetical: Debtor ("D") has granted to Secured Party ("SP") a security interest in collateral consisting of equipment. The security interest is perfected by the filing of a financing statement naming D as the debtor. D disposes of the collateral to Transferee ("T") who assumes D's obligations under the security agreement. SP is aware of and consents to the disposition but only on the conditions that D remain liable on the secured indebtedness and that T make all payments and perform all obligations under the security agreement in a timely manner.

DISCUSSION

1.   Section 9–306(2)

Section 9–306(2) (1972 Official Text) provides:

"Except where this Article otherwise provides, a security interest continues in collateral notwithstanding sale, exchange or other disposition thereof unless the disposition was authorized by the secured party in the security agreement or otherwise, and also continues in any identifiable proceeds including collections received by the debtor."

Section 9–306(2) treats only the issue of whether a security interest continues in collateral following disposition of the collateral. Assuming the security interest continues in the collateral after disposition, this Section does not deal with the issue of whether the secured party must take further action to continue the perfected status of its security interest in the collateral. Section 9–306(2) states the general rule that a security interest in collateral is not terminated upon a disposition of the collateral and can be enforced against the collateral in the hands of the transferee. See Official Comment No. 3 to UCC § 9–306(2).

Section 9–306(2), however, sets forth an exception to this rule if the secured party has authorized the disposition of the collateral in the security agreement or otherwise. The intent underlying this exception is to permit a disposition of the collateral free and clear of the security interest when the secured party has

---

*   Note from West Advisory Panel: Referring to unrevised Article 9. See revised § 9–315 and § 9–507.

authorized the disposition free and clear of its security interest in the security agreement or otherwise. In the case of such an authorized disposition, the general rule of survivability of the security interest set forth in § 9–306(2) will not apply and the security interest will terminate upon the disposition. However, this exception to the rule of survivability only applies if the secured party has authorized the disposition, by agreement or otherwise, *free and clear of the security interest*. The exception will not apply if the secured party did not authorize the disposition of the collateral or if the secured party authorized the disposition subject to its security interest. This authorization issue presents a factual question. The questions of what facts will constitute an effective express or implied authorization for purposes of this Section and what standard of proof is applicable to this determination are not addressed in the Code but are instead left to other law.

If the disposition of the collateral has been authorized by the secured party free and clear of the security interest, the security interest will terminate upon the disposition and there will be no need to determine whether the secured party must take further action to continue the perfected status of the security interest in the collateral following its disposition. On the other hand, if the security interest in the collateral survives the disposition, the secured party must then determine whether further action is necessary to continue the perfected status of its security interest following the disposition. This is a perfection issue which is not governed by § 9–306(2). This perfection issue is governed by § 9–402(7).

2.   Section 9–402(7)

The last sentence of § 9–402(7) provides that "a filed financing statement remains effective with respect to collateral transferred by the debtor even though the secured party knows of or consents to the transfer."

This sentence, which was added in the 1972 Official Text, was intended to resolve an ambiguity in the 1962 Code as to whether a secured party is required to file an amended or new financing statement when the collateral is transferred. Substantial policy arguments can be made on both sides of this issue. Those favoring a refiling obligation when collateral is transferred argue that, absent refiling in the name of the transferee, secured creditors searching in the name of the transferee could be misled since they would not discover a financing statement filed in the name of the transferor. Allowing a filing against the transferor to be effective against creditors of the transferee would thus promote hidden liens in violation of the public notice purposes of Article 9. Those who argue against a refiling obligation as to collateral transferred by the debtor point to the enormous policing responsibility that a refiling duty would impose on secured creditors of the transferor, most of whom have no continuing contact with the transferor after the secured transaction other than to receive installment payments on the secured indebtedness. A refiling obligation linked to the secured creditor's "notice" or "knowledge" of the transfer would create difficult problems of proof and would foster litigation with all of its resultant costs and uncertainties. Secured creditors of the transferee can protect themselves against filings in the name of prior owners of the collateral by tracing ownership of the collateral and searching in the names of prior owners. This tracing obligation, it is argued, is not an unreasonable burden to place on creditors of the transferee since they would have this responsibility anyway in order to insure that their debtor (the transferee) has rights in the collateral sufficient to grant a security interest.

Balancing these competing policy concerns, the National Conference of Commissioners on Uniform State Laws and the American Law Institute, in adopting § 9–402(7), opted in favor of the no refiling rule as to collateral transferred by the debtor. Thus, the last sentence of § 9–402(7) makes it clear that the secured party has no refiling obligation even if the secured party knows that the collateral has been transferred or even authorized or consented to the transfer. Official Comment 8 to § 9–402(7) explains the purpose of the last sentence in § 9–402(7):

"Subsection (7) also deals with a different problem, namely whether a new filing is necessary where the collateral has been transferred from one debtor to another. This question has been much debated both in pre-Code law and under the Code. This Article now answers the questions in the negative. Thus, any person searching the condition of the ownership of a debtor must make inquiry as to the debtor's source of title, and must search in the name of a former owner if circumstances seem to require it."

3.   Harmonizing Sections 9–306(2) and 9–402(7)

Read together, §§ 9–306(2) and 9–402(7) lead to the following results when collateral is disposed of:

If the secured party does not authorize the disposition or if the secured party authorizes the disposition subject to the security interest, the security interest will continue in the collateral following the disposition (§ 9–306(2)) and no new financing statement or amendment to the existing financing statement will be required in order to continue the perfected status of the security interest in the collateral following the disposition (§ 9–402(7)).

If the secured party, in the security agreement or otherwise, authorizes the disposition free and clear of the security interest, the security interest will terminate the disposition (§ 9–306(2)) and there will be no need to be concerned with perfection issues under § 9–402(7).

Returning to the hypothetical, this analysis yields the following results: D's disposition of the collateral to T will not terminate SP's security interest under § 9–306(2) since SP did not authorize the disposition free and clear of its security interest. The disposition of the collateral was authorized by SP but subject to T's recognition of SP's security interest in the collateral. Thus, under § 9–306(2), SP's security interest continues in the collateral following the disposition. Under § 9–402(7), SP's filed financing statement remains effective following the disposition of the collateral by D to T even though SP was aware of and consented to the disposition. Therefore, SP need not file a new financing statement in the names of D or T or take any other action to continue the perfected status of its security interest in the collateral. This Commentary does not imply that the secured creditor need not take filing action if required by other Sections of the Code (e.g., Sections 9–103(1), 9–103(3) or 9–401(3)) based upon a change in location of the collateral or a change in the debtor's location following the transfer of the collateral by the debtor.

CONCLUSION

There is no conflict between § 9–306(2) and the last sentence of § 9–402(7). Section 9–306(2) deals with the effect of a disposition of the collateral upon a security interest in the collateral and sets forth a general rule of survivability which applies unless the secured party authorizes the disposition free and clear of the security interest. The last sentence of § 9–402(7) only has operative effect if the security interest survives the disposition under § 9–306(2). In this instance, the last sentence of § 9–402(7) continues the perfected status of the security interest in the transferred collateral even though the secured party may have authorized or consented to the disposition. Cases reaching this conclusion as to the interplay between UCC §§ 9–306(2) and 9–402(7) include In re Southern Properties, Inc., 44 B.R. 838, 40 UCC Rep.Serv. (Callaghan) 1089 (Bkcy.E.D.Va.1989); Loeb v. Franchise Distributors, Inc. (In re Franchise Systems, Inc.), 46 B.R. 158, 40 UCC Rep.Serv. (Callaghan) 689 (Bkcy.N.D.Ga.1985); and Matto's Inc. v. Olde Colonie Place (In re Matto's Inc.), 30 UCC Rep.Serv. (Callaghan) 1750 (Bkcy.E.D.Mich.1981).

The second paragraph of Official Comment 3 to UCC § 9–306 is supplemented as follows:

In many cases a purchaser or other transferee of collateral will take free of a security interest: in such cases the secured party's only right will be to proceeds. A transferee will acquire the collateral free and clear of a preexisting security interest only if the disposition of the collateral by the debtor was authorized by the secured party free and clear of the secured party's security interest. If the disposition was not authorized by the secured party, or was authorized by the secured party subject to the secured party's security interest, the transferee will not acquire the collateral free and clear of the security interest. The authorization may be contained in the security agreement or otherwise given. The right to proceeds, either under the rules of this section or under specific mention thereof in a security agreement or financing statement does not in itself constitute an authorization of sale. PEB Commentary No. 3, dated March 10, 1990, analyzes the interplay between this Section and Section 9–402(7).

Official Comment 8 to UCC § 9–402 is amended to add the following paragraph at the end of the Comment:

PEB Commentary No. 3, dated March 10, 1990, explains the interplay between this Section and Section 9–306(2). As explained in this Commentary, this Section is consistent with Section 9–306(2) since Section 9–306(2) deals with the continuation or termination of a security interest in collateral

APPENDIX E

following a disposition of the collateral. The last sentence of Section 9–402(7), on the other hand, deals with the continued effectiveness of a filed financing statement to perfect any security interest that continues in the collateral following its disposition.

PEB COMMENTARY NO. 4
SECTION 8–207(1)*
(March 10, 1990)

ISSUE

Section 8–207(1) provides that

> (1)   Prior to due presentment for registration of transfer of a certificated security in registered form, the issuer or indenture trustee may treat the registered owner as the person exclusively entitled to vote, to receive notifications, and otherwise to exercise all the rights and powers of an owner.

This section has been part of the UCC since its inception, the only change made by the 1977 amendments being the addition of the word "certificated."

Under what circumstances will a distribution of money or other property to the registered owner of a certificated security provide the issuer with a defense against a claim to that distribution asserted by a pledgee who was a bona fide purchaser and in possession of that security at the time of such distribution?

DISCUSSION

1.   The Statutory Scheme

As between the parties, the rights of the owner of a registered certificated security are transferred to a purchaser when the security is delivered to the purchaser. § 8–313(1)(a). The issuer is required to register that transfer when the security is presented to it with an appropriate request. § 8–401(1). Thus, between the time of delivery and presentment, the registered owner and the person ultimately entitled to the rights of ownership will be different parties. The objective of § 8–207(1) is to protect the issuer by express authorization to treat the original registered owner of a security, during this "gap" period, as the person entitled to the rights of ownership, including the right to receive distributions with respect thereto. Such protection is clearly necessary, since, in the vast majority of cases, the issuer would have no knowledge that a transfer had been made or know the identity of the purchaser. Inherent in this scheme is that a distribution to the registered owner will relieve the issuer from any liability to the purchaser for the same distribution. Without that protection, no issuer could safely make any distribution without requiring the surrender, or exhibition, of the security by the distributee—a patently impractical requirement.

In the context of outright sales of securities, the rule of § 8–207(1) does not constitute a serious problem. In such transactions, the period of incongruity between registered and actual ownership will be of limited duration, since the purchaser will normally present the security for registration of transfer as promptly as possible. The nature, amount, and record date of any imminent distributions can usually be ascertained and can be reflected in the price or otherwise adjusted between the parties.

In the context of pledges of securities, however, the pledgee, in most cases, takes delivery of the security, duly endorsed for transfer, but does not present it to the issuer for registration of transfer. Possession of the security by the pledgee effectively prevents the pledgor from transferring it to another purchaser and places the pledgee in the position where registration of transfer can be obtained in the event of the pledgor's default. When the loan is repaid, as most loans are, the securities, still registered in the pledgor's name, are returned to the pledgor. This procedure avoids two unnecessary registrations of transfer—pledgor to pledgee and, then, pledgee back to pledgor.

Furthermore, while the loan is outstanding, the pledgor, who remains the registered owner, continues to receive reports, proxy materials, and periodic dividend or interest payments, directly from the issuer and without inconvenience to the pledgee. This is precisely the result normally intended by the parties to the pledge transaction. See § 9–207(2)(c). Hence, even in the pledge context, the rule of § 8–207(1),

---

*   *Note from West Advisory Panel: Referring to unrevised Article 8. See revised § 8–207(a).*

notwithstanding the existence of dual interests in the security, generally produces results that are both efficient and fair.

2.   The Problem

Section 8–207(1) does not define or limit the phrase "all the rights and powers of an owner." If that phrase is construed, as it logically might be, to include the right to receive *all* distributions, the issuer may, with impunity, distribute, to the registered owner, not only regular cash dividends and interest payments, but also extraordinary cash dividends, negotiable securities in connection with stock dividends, stock splits and spin-offs and, indeed, cash in complete liquidation of stock or partial or complete redemption of debt or redeemable equity securities.

Thus, the pledgee that fails to present its collateral for registration of transfer subjects itself to the continuing risk that the issuer will distribute cash and/or negotiable securities to the pledgor, which, if not turned over to the pledgee as the pledge agreement would normally require, will have the effect of substantially reducing or eliminating the value of the collateral in its possession. For example, the distribution of stock to the pledgor, in connection with a two-for-one split, would leave the pledgee with collateral worth only half its pre-split value, and the distribution of cash to the pledgor, as a final liquidating dividend, would render the pledgee's collateral worthless.

The pledgee, of course, is not without power to avoid these dire consequences. It could, routinely, present its collateral for registration of transfer in every pledge transaction, but only with the attendant extra expense, which would ultimately be borne by all borrowers. Alternatively, it can evaluate the risk in any particular transaction, taking into account such factors as the financial strength and integrity of the pledgor, the identity of the issuers and the likelihood that any contemplated extraordinary distributions will receive advance public notice, the extent to which the pledged securities are diversified, and the magnitude of any collateral "cushion." The fact remains, however, that part of the price paid for the protection afforded the issuer by § 8–207(1) is the risk borne by the pledgee who does not register the transfer.

3.   The Cases

It is encouraging to note that only two reported cases have raised the question of the scope of issuer protection for distributions made to registered owners pursuant to § 8–207(1). Because of the aberrational fact situations involved, neither case directly addressed the issue as stated.

In New England Merchants Bank of Boston v. Old Colony Trust Co., 385 Mass. 24, 429 N.E.2d 1143, 32 UCC Rep.Serv. (Callaghan) 1592 (Mass.1982), affirming 11 Mass.App. 539, 417 N.E.2d 471, 30 UCC Rep.Serv. (Callaghan) 1661 (Mass.App.1981), the issuer, in paying a liquidating dividend, did not rely on § 8–207(1), which permits, but does not require, an issuer to recognize the registered owner, without further proof, as the person entitled to receive distributions. Rather, with an abundance of prudence, it required surrender of the stock certificates as a condition of payment. The certificates that were surrendered had been issued to the registered owner, five years earlier, to replace the original certificates which the owner had asserted were lost. Pursuant to § 8–405(2), the issuer had obtained a lost securities indemnity bond.

The claimant was the administrator of an intestate estate who had found the original certificates among the decedent's papers. Apparently, they had been delivered to the decedent, endorsed in blank, almost thirty years before, and no attempt had been made to have the transfer registered on the books of the issuer. Upon surrender of the certificates to the issuer, the claimant demanded payment of the liquidating dividend.

In denying the claim, the court stated: (1) that payment to the registered owner, pursuant to § 8–207(1) constitutes a defense against the possessor of the certificates; (2) that § 8–207(1) makes no distinction between ordinary and liquidating dividends; and (3) that the plaintiff had not established that he was a bona fide purchaser, implying that the result might have been different if he had so established. The question of bona fide purchase is relevant to the case, but only under the provisions of § 8–405(3), which deals with the rights of the holder of a security that has been reported lost and has previously been replaced.

In Bank of Honolulu v. Hawaii Corp., 829 F.2d 813, 4 UCC Rep.Serv.2d (Callaghan) 837 (9th Cir.1987), reversing 59 B.R. 410, 42 UCC Rep.Serv. (Callaghan) 1736 (Bkcy.D.Haw.1986), the claimant, a pledgee bank that had received stock certificates as collateral for a loan to the issuer's president, was unquestionably a bona fide purchaser. Subsequently, the issuer entered a Chapter X bankruptcy proceeding. The issuer's Trustee brought suit against the pledgor which was ultimately settled. As part of the settlement, the pledgor released the Trustee from "all claims . . . or interests." When it later developed that there would be a distribution to stockholders, the bank filed a Proof of Stock Interest, based on the pledged stock.

The Trustee refused to honor the bank's Proof on the ground that § 8–207(1) permitted the issuer to treat the pledgor, who remained the registered owner, as the person who could "exercise all the rights and powers of an owner." In his view, these included the right to dispose of the stock, free of the pledgee's interest, in what was, essentially, a privately negotiated transaction. The trial court agreed.

The Ninth Circuit reversed, ordering entry of judgment for the bank. In so holding, however, the court stated: (1) that payment, even pursuant to § 8–207(1), does not constitute "a defense . . . going to the validity of the security," which, in the court's view, is required under § 8–105(2)(c); (2) "that § 8–207 is meant to apply [only] in what might be called the normal case . . . the payment of dividends in the normal course of business"; and (3) that "negotiability is negated when the transferor retains rights which . . . will frustrate the exercise of rights by the transferee."

While the results in both these cases are probably correct under their own peculiar facts, the gratuitous statements of the respective courts, supporting their holdings, are in conflict with each other and tend to confuse, rather than clarify, the proper construction of the intent, scope, and limitations of § 8–207(1).

CONCLUSION

In light of this confusion, and in an effort to promote a reasonable and uniform construction of § 8–207(1), the Board offers the following guidelines:

(1) *A distribution to the registered owner of a security is protected under § 8–207(1) only if it is distributable to the owners of all securities of the same issue.* This rule would prevent an issuer from acquiring a security, free of claims, in a negotiated transaction with the registered owner without requiring surrender of the security. In such a transaction, which is, in effect, a purchase rather than a distribution by the issuer, requiring delivery of the security imposes no burden on the issuer that is not borne by any purchaser. It supports the result in the Hawaii case.

(2) *If the terms of a security require its surrender as a condition of payment or exchange, a distribution to the registered owner in payment or exchange is not protected under § 8–207(1) unless the security is surrendered.* The requirement of surrender is commonly included in the terms of debt securities, redeemable equity securities, and convertible securities. Since the outstanding security is rendered worthless by the redemption or exchange, it is clearly in the interest of all concerned to get it out of circulation. Even if surrender is not required by the terms of the security, issuers may, and, as a matter of prudence, frequently do, as did the issuer in the *New England Merchants* case, require surrender as a condition of payment of a liquidating dividend.

(3) *Distributions to all the registered owners of a security, the terms of which do not require the surrender thereof, are protected under § 8–207(1), regardless of the regularity, amount, or nature of such distributions.* This rule rejects the suggestion that only regular dividend and interest payments can be safely distributed to the registered owners. The issuer's lack of knowledge of unregistered transfers, which requires protection for regular payments to the registered owners, also demands similar protection for the distributions in stock dividends, stock splits, spin-offs, and other extraordinary distributions, even though they may substantially impair the value of the outstanding securities.

(4) *A distribution to the registered owner that is protected under § 8–207(1) constitutes a defense against a claim to such distribution by a person in possession of the security, even if such person is a bona fide purchaser.* The entire purpose of § 8–207(1) would be vitiated if a distribution protected by it could *not* be successfully asserted against a claim by a person in possession of the security, who, in most cases, will be a bona fide purchaser. This result can be justified by charging the transferee who elects not to register a transfer with knowledge of § 8–207(1) and notice that any distributions protected under that section will be made directly to the registered owner.

The Board believes that these guidelines strike a proper balance between the right of an issuer to rely solely on its registration records in making distributions and the ability of a pledgee to rely on its possession of a security to protect it against diminutions of value that cannot be reasonably anticipated.

The Official Comment to § 8–207 is supplemented by the addition of the following paragraph, immediately following the first paragraph of Official Comment 1:

> The issuer may, under this section, make distributions of money or securities to the registered owners of certificated securities without requiring further proof of ownership, provided that such distributions are distributable to the owners of all securities of the same issue and the terms of the security do not require its surrender as a condition of payment or exchange. Any such distribution shall constitute a defense against a claim for the same distribution by a person, even if that person is in possession of the security and is a bona fide purchaser of the security. See PEB Commentary No. 4, dated March 10, 1990.

PEB COMMENTARY NO. 5
SECTION 9–306(5)*
(March 10, 1990)

ISSUE

Section 9–306(5)(b) gives a purchaser of a conditional sales contract or other chattel paper ("chattel paper financer") a security interest in the goods covered by the chattel paper against the seller of the goods (and of the chattel paper) if the chattel paper financer is "unpaid" and the goods are "returned to or are repossessed by the seller or the secured party." If the chattel paper financer had obtained priority in the chattel paper pursuant to § 9–308 over a secured party with a security interest in the seller's goods ("inventory financer"), does § 9–306(5)(b) enable the chattel paper financer to retain that priority without having to further perfect "for protection" under § 9–306(5)(d) against the inventory financer?

DISCUSSION

The issue will usually arise in the context of the following fact situation: (I) Secured Party #1 ("inventory financer") has a perfected security interest in all the inventory of a dealer in goods ("Dealer"); (II) Dealer sells some of its inventory to a buyer in the ordinary course of business ("BIOCOB") pursuant to a conditional sales contract ("chattel paper"); and (III) Secured Party #2 ("chattel paper financer") purchases the chattel paper from Dealer and takes possession of the paper in the ordinary course of its business.

Secured Party #1's security interest in the sold goods terminates under § 9–307(1) when they are sold to BIOCOB. However, Secured Party #1's security interest continues in the chattel paper as proceeds. If the goods are thereafter returned to Dealer, § 9–306(5)(a) provides that "if the goods were collateral at the time of sale for an indebtedness of the seller which is still unpaid," Secured Party #1's security interest in the goods "attaches again to the goods and continues as a perfected security interest." In effect, the returned goods are proceeds of the chattel paper.

Section 9–306(5)(b) also gives Secured Party #2 a security interest in the same returned goods against Dealer and states that this security interest is "prior to a security interest under [§ 9–306(5)(a)] to the extent that the [chattel paper financer] was entitled to priority under Section 9–308." This interplay between § 9–306(5)(a) and (b) arises in the following two circumstances.

First, when BIOCOB's obligation is terminated because the goods are returned to Dealer pursuant to an agreement with Dealer or because BIOCOB had a right to rescind the sale, e.g., revoke acceptance under § 2–608. See Official Comment 4 to § 9–306(5). In that circumstance, the goods once again become part of Dealer's inventory and are subject to Secured Party #1's security interest. However, because Secured Party #2 has not been paid pursuant to the chattel paper, § 9–306(5)(b) gives Secured Party #2, as an "unpaid

---

*   *Note from West Advisory Panel: Referring to unrevised Article 9. See revised § 9–330.*

transferee" of the chattel paper, a security interest in the goods against Dealer to secure the amount remaining unpaid under the chattel paper at the time BIOCOB's obligation was terminated.[1]

Second, when the goods are repossessed because BIOCOB has defaulted under the chattel paper and are returned to Dealer whereat Secured Party #2 then sells the goods pursuant to § 9–504. In that circumstance, if the goods are purchased at the foreclosure sale either (a) by Dealer or (b) by Secured Party #2 who then conveys the goods to Dealer pursuant to an agreement by Dealer to repurchase the goods, § 9–306(5) is applicable if Dealer does not then pay Secured Party #2 the purchase price.[2] In both of these instances, the goods once again become part of Dealer's inventory and are subject to Secured Party #1's security interest. However, because Dealer has not paid Secured Party #2 the purchase price for the goods, § 9–306(5)(b) gives Secured Party #2, as an unpaid transferee, a security interest in the goods against Dealer to secure Dealer's obligation to pay the purchase price, i.e. the successful bid price at the foreclosure sale[3] or the amount due under the repurchase agreement,[4] as the case may be.

This security interest of Secured Party #2 in the goods against Dealer is separate and distinct from the security interest evidenced by the chattel paper itself in which BIOCOB is the debtor. It attaches to the goods when returned to Dealer, whether voluntarily or through revocation of acceptance or repossession, and upon Dealer acquiring "rights in the collateral" by reason of the (i) revocation of acceptance or (ii) agreement with BIOCOB or (iii) purchase of the goods at the foreclosure sale or (iv) repurchase agreement. § 9–203(1)(c). In essence, Secured Party #2 has a security interest against Dealer in the returned goods as the proceeds of the secured transaction represented by the purchase of the chattel paper from the Dealer. In both instances, Secured Party #2 is the secured party and Dealer is the debtor. ". . . When the underlying goods are returned or repossessed, the chattel paper interest automatically shifts to the goods. . . ." 2 Gilmore, *Security Interests in Personal Property,* § 27.5.

Under § 9–306(5)(b), Secured Party #2's security interest in the returned goods against Dealer is

". . . prior to a security interest under paragraph (a) [i.e. that of Secured Party #1] to the extent that the transferee of the chattel paper [Secured Party #2] was entitled to priority under Section 9–308."

In the above circumstances, Secured Party #2 had priority in the chattel paper at the time it purchased the chattel paper for new value from Dealer over Secured Party #1's claim to the chattel paper as proceeds of the inventory. § 9–308(b). Accordingly, § 9–306(5)(b) gives Secured Party #2 priority over Secured Party #1 in the returned goods. This result is consistent with the policy of encouraging the purchase of chattel paper reflected by § 9–308. Furthermore, it is not unfair to Secured Party #1 because Secured Party #1 is entitled

---

[1] Dealer's sale of the chattel paper is usually accompanied by a warranty that the chattel paper is genuine, valid and enforceable according to its term. Inasmuch as BIOCOB's obligation has been terminated, Secured Party has lost the benefit of the bargain it made in purchasing the chattel paper from Dealer, i.e., the right to receive all payments required thereunder. Dealer, who has reacquired the goods, either by agreement or because BIOCOB had the right to revoke acceptance, is, therefore, liable to Secured Party #2 for those remaining payments.

[2] Frequently, there will be an agreement that Dealer need not pay the purchase price until it is able to re-sell the goods.

[3] When the sale or disposition to enforce the security interest in the goods is made, the proceeds are applied to BIOCOB's indebtedness under the chattel paper and BIOCOB is entitled to any surplus and liable for any deficiency. § 9–504(1) and (2). The amount due from Dealer on the sale is usually the same as the amount due under the chattel paper, but might be a different amount. Secured Party #2's security interest against Dealer terminates upon payment of that amount to Secured Party #2, but if that amount is less than that due under the chattel paper, BIOCOB remains liable to Secured Party #2 for that deficiency.

[4] Instead of an agreement for Dealer to repurchase the goods, there could be an agreement to repurchase the chattel paper. That repurchase is not a sale or disposition under § 9–504(5). Upon that repurchase, Dealer becomes the secured party. If Dealer then sells the goods under § 9–504 and buys them at the sale, the same analysis applies. That is, the goods are once again part of Dealer's inventory and subject to Secured Party #1's security interest; but, if Dealer has not paid the repurchase price to Secured Party #2, § 9–306(5)(b) likewise gives Secured Party #2, as an unpaid transferee, a security interest in the goods against Dealer to secure Dealer's obligation to pay that repurchase price.

to receive the money paid to Dealer by Secured Party #2 upon purchase of the chattel paper as proceeds of its security interest in the goods sold to BIOCOB.[5]

The interpretative problem is presented by § 9–306(5)(d):

"A security interest of an unpaid transferee [Secured Party #2] asserted under paragraph (b) . . . must be perfected for protection against creditors of the transferor [Dealer] and purchasers of the returned or repossessed goods."

Does this negate § 9–306(5)(b) and mean that Secured Party #2 does not have priority over Secured Party #1 in the returned goods under § 9–306(5)(b) unless Secured Party #2's security interest in the goods is perfected against Dealer? Stated differently, is Secured Party #1 a "creditor" of Dealer or a "purchaser" of the returned or repossessed goods within the purview of § 9–306(5)(d)?[6] Furthermore, assuming Secured Party #1 is such a "creditor" or "purchaser," does the requirement that Secured Party #2's security interest be "perfected for protection" against Secured Party #1 mean that Secured Party #2 must acquire priority under § 9–312? If Secured Party #1's position was prior in time under § 9–312(5)(a), must Secured Party #2 somehow follow a procedure sufficient to give it a purchase money super-priority over Secured Party #1? This priority issue will be significant in the event Secured Party #1 and Secured Party #2 both claim the goods or the proceeds of any sale or disposition thereof by Dealer.

J.I. Case v. Borg-Warner, 669 S.W.2d 543, 37 UCC Rep.Serv. (Callaghan) 1025 (Ky.App.1984), and Northwest Accept. Corp. v. Lynnwood Equipment, Inc., 1 UCC Rep.Serv.2d (Callaghan) 980, motion for reconsideration denied, 1 UCC Rep.Serv.2d (Callaghan) 171 (D.W.D.Wash.1986), both held that the chattel paper financer had priority without having to take further action to perfect with respect to the inventory financer. The courts held that in the context of § 9–306(5) the definitions of "creditor" and "purchaser" in § 1–201 are not applicable to Secured Party #1. Since Secured Party #1 is neither a "creditor" nor "purchaser" as used in § 9–306(5)(d), Secured Party #2 has priority under § 9–306(5)(b). These decisions are consistent with the intent of §§ 9–306(5)(b) and 9–308. See 2 Gilmore, Security Interests in Personal Property, § 27.5; Smith, Annual Survey: Secured Transactions, 40 The Business Lawyer 1487, 1505–1508 (1985). Cf. the opposite treatment of a transferee of accounts under § 9–306(5)(c). To conclude otherwise (i.e. that Secured Party #1 is a "creditor" or "purchaser") would nullify the intent of § 9–306(5)(b). Crocker Nat. Bank v. Clark, 724 F.2d 696, 37 UCC Rep.Serv. (Callaghan) 673 (8th Cir.1984), holding that the inventory financer was a "creditor" is not consistent with this analysis.

The drafting history to § 9–306(5) demonstrates that the inventory financer (Secured Party #1) is neither a "creditor" nor a "purchaser" within the purview of § 9–306(5)(d). In the 1952 Official Draft of the UCC, § 9–306(5) read as follows:

"(5) If collateral which has been sold is returned to the debtor, the following rules determine the priorities:

(a) As between the debtor and a secured party to whom the indebtedness originally secured by the collateral has not been paid, the original security interest continues;

(b) As between the debtor and an unpaid transferee of the chattel paper arising from the sale, the transferee shall have a security interest in the property returned, but such security interest must be perfected for protection against third parties;

(c) The security interest of an unpaid transferee under (b) shall have priority over a security interest claimed under (a)."

This section was redrafted to its present form pursuant to the 1956 Recommendations of the Editorial Board. The revision covered repossessions in addition to returns and added present subsection (c) which affords

---

[5] If Secured Party #2 had purchased accounts instead of chattel paper, § 9–306(5)(c) subordinates Secured Party #2 to Secured Party #1's rights in the returned goods. This Commentary does not undertake to explore this different treatment for purchasers of accounts—or the reasons for this difference.

[6] A secured creditor is included within both the definitions of "creditor" in § 1–201(12) and "purchaser" in § 1–201(32), (33), "unless the context otherwise requires."

subordinate priority status to the purchaser of an account. The rule of former subsection (c) which affords first priority to the chattel paper purchaser was carried over to present subsection (b).

Present § 9–306(5)(d) states the rule that both the chattel paper purchaser and the account purchaser must be "perfected for protection against creditors of the transferor and purchasers of the returned or repossessed goods." The 1952 Draft, which had dealt only with the priority of the chattel paper purchaser, had set forth the same rule in then § 9–306(5)(b):

"As between the debtor and an unpaid transferee of the chattel paper arising from the sale, the transferee shall have a security interest in the property returned, but such security interest must be perfected for protection against *third parties*." (emphasis supplied)

It is evident from that 1952 Draft that "third parties" as used in subsection (b) did not include "a security interest claimed under (a)," because that interest was expressly covered in subsection (c). Rather, "third parties" could have referred only to "creditors of the transferor and purchasers of the returned or repossessed goods," namely, the parties more particularly identified in the reformulation of the same rule now set forth in § 9–306(5)(d). That is, "third parties" meant "creditors of the transferor" and "purchasers of the returned or repossessed goods" *other than* the inventory financer.

Accordingly, the meaning and intent of "perfected for protection" in § 9–306(5)(d) is that by reason of the goods being in the possession of Dealer, Secured Party #2 must give constructive notice of its security interest in those goods by filing a financing statement against Dealer in order to be perfected against those creditors and purchasers of Dealer (other than Secured Party #1) as to whom an unperfected security interest would otherwise be subordinate under § 9–301. Secured Party #2 should file a signed financing statement covering those returned goods either at the time it first purchases the chattel paper or prior to returning the repossessed goods to Dealer. Note, however, that filing the financing statement does not affect Secured Party #2's rights against Secured Party #1 under § 9–306(5) and will not protect Secured Party #2 against the risk that the goods may be sold by Dealer to buyers in the ordinary course of business who will take free of that security interest. § 2–403(2); § 9–307(1); see the fifth paragraph of Official Comment 4 to § 9–306.

If Secured Party #2 fails to perfect against Dealer, it will retain its priority against Secured Party #1 but may become subordinate to others under § 9–301. This may result in a circular priority, the resolution of which is beyond the scope of this Commentary. See 2 Gilmore, *Security Interests in Personal Property*, § 27.5.

CONCLUSION

"Creditors" and "purchasers" as used in § 9–306(5)(d) do not include the original secured inventory financer of the seller of goods under subsection (a). Accordingly, a purchaser of chattel paper generated by a sale of the goods by that seller, attaining priority over the inventory financer under § 9–308, retains that priority in the event the goods covered by that chattel paper are returned to the seller, without having to further perfect against that inventory financer.

The Official Comment to § 9–306 is amended by adding the following:

5. "Creditors" and "purchasers" as used in paragraph (5)(d) do not include the original secured inventory financer of the seller of goods under subsection (a). If a purchaser of chattel paper generated by a sale of the goods attains priority over the seller's inventory financer under Section 9–308, the purchaser retains that priority in the event the goods covered by the chattel paper are returned to the seller, without having to further perfect against the inventory financer. This priority issue will usually arise in the context of the original inventory financer and the chattel paper purchaser both claiming the goods or the proceeds of any sale or disposition thereof by the seller. See PEB Commentary No. 5, dated March 10, 1990.

PEB COMMENTARY NO. 6

PEB COMMENTARY NO. 6
SECTION 9–301(1)*
(March 10, 1990)

ISSUE

Section 9–301(1) provides (with an exception that is not relevant here) that a security interest is subordinate to members of various specified classes (herein called "the protected classes") who acquired their interests while the security interest was unperfected, subject to conditions set forth for each specified class.

When a security interest is subordinated under this rule in favor of a member of a protected class, does the security interest continue subordinated under the "shelter principle" to an assignee of that protected person, although the assignee does not fit the specific requirements for a member of the protected class because he acquired his interest after the security interest was perfected? In other words, does the protected status of an assignor "shelter" the position of an assignee who by himself would not meet the standards for protection?

DISCUSSION

A right of ownership of personal property ordinarily consists in part of the right to transfer it to others in the same form and with the same attributes, e.g., freedom from competing ownership interests or defenses or security interests that are not valid against the transferring owner. This right is known as the "shelter principle."

Section 2–403(1) states the shelter principle: "A purchaser of goods acquires all title which his transferor had. . . ." As Official Comment 1 states: "The *basic principle of our law is generally continued and expanded* under subsection (1)." [emphasis added]. Since the principle existed before the Code, it is not dependent on its codification in § 2–403(1). Examples of its use appear in four Articles of the Code:

(a) Sections 3–201(1) and Official Comment 3, 3–305 and Official Comment, and 3–306 and Official Comment 1 illustrate the concept. These provisions set forth the ability of a holder in due course of a negotiable instrument to transfer the instrument free of the defenses and claims which the transferor's status as holder in due course has cut off. It is clear that the transferor's status as holder in due course and the value of his ownership of the instrument would be impaired if he could not transfer the instrument and confer the same status upon his transferee without the transferee qualifying on his own as a holder in due course (when the transfer was a gift or because the instrument had matured or because the transferee had knowledge of a defect). To protect the holder in due course fully, the law must protect the holder's transferee.

(b) Similar shelter provisions are found in connection with equivalent negotiability rules in §§ 8–301(1) and 8–302(4) and Official Comment 5 to the latter.

(c) Similar shelter provisions are found in connection with equivalent negotiability rules in §§ 7–504(1) and 7–502(1).

(d) A similar shelter provision in respect to property rights other than those resting on negotiability is found in Article 9, § 9–313(4)(b). Under specified circumstances this provision gives the holder of a security interest in a fixture priority over the interest of an owner or an incumbrancer of the realty; but this rule is expressly subject to the condition that a real estate interest is not subordinated to the fixture security interest if the real estate interest's predecessor in title was not subject to defeat by the fixture security interest, thus applying the shelter principle. For variation of the shelter principle, see also § 9–313(6), which shelters refinancings of a superior interest from a subordinate interest which would otherwise have priority over the later refinancing.

The case of Aircraft Trading and Services, Inc. v. Braniff, Inc., 819 F.2d 1227, 3 UCC Rep.Serv.2d (Callaghan) 1297 (2d Cir.1987), first called attention to the absence of express shelter provisions in § 9–301(1). Simplifying the facts, A sold an aircraft engine to B and took back a purchase-money mortgage (security interest), which for a time A failed to record as required by federal law. B sold the engine to C, who

---

* *Note from West Advisory Panel: Referring to unrevised Article 9. See revised § 9–317.*

APPENDIX E

searched the record and ascertained that there was no recorded mortgage. Thus A's mortgage was subordinate to C's interest, under § 9–301(1)(c), which provides that an unperfected security interest is subordinate to a buyer like C to the extent that he gives value and receives delivery of the collateral without knowledge of the security interest and before it is perfected. Thereafter the mortgage was recorded, thus perfecting the security interest, and still later C sold the engine to D. (D had actual knowledge of the recording, but the Court's opinion did not rest on that fact.)

The Court of Appeals held that since D did not acquire his interest while the security interest was unperfected, D's interest was subject to the security interest. The Court identified the shelter principle with § 2–403(1), then rejected its application in reliance on § 2–402(3), which reads: "Nothing in this Article should be deemed to impair the rights of creditors of the seller (a) under the provisions of the Article on Secured Transactions (Article 9). . . ." This Commentary does not adhere to that interpretation. Application of the shelter principle of § 2–403(1) in favor of a buyer from one who has obtained senior status under § 9–301(1) does not "impair the rights of creditors." The rights of the unperfected secured creditor have *already* been impaired by the operation of § 9–301(1). The shelter principle should be applied to protect D. Otherwise the value of C's status, as one taking free of the security interest, is unjustifiably impaired if he cannot confer that status upon his transferee. Section 2–402(3)(a) does not compel a different result. Article 2 does not apply the shelter principle, although the principle is stated in § 2–403(1) as an introduction to rules stating when the purchaser can receive *more* than the transferor had.

Once a protected party achieves such senior rights, § 9–301(1) should not be construed to interfere with those rights and the shelter principle should be deemed applicable. The Code is a "complex and interrelated statutory scheme." Bank of Honolulu v. Hawaii Corp., 829 F.2d 813, 815, 4 UCC Rep.Serv.2d (Callaghan) 837, 841 (9th Cir.1987). The Code should be interpreted to produce equivalent results in situations comparable to the four cited above. This broad approach is supported by § 1–102 and its Official Comment 1.

CONCLUSION

Underlying principles of fairness require a broad reading and a broad application of the shelter concept, even when not expressly stated. The importance of shelter is too great in the Code's scheme to support a narrow reading of the Code. Section 9–301(1) should be interpreted and applied in this circumstance to incorporate the shelter principle so that a member of a protected class who prevails thereunder can transfer what he has, even though the security interest which was unperfected when the transferor acquired his rights has since been perfected. The shelter principle also should operate even though the transferee from the protected party has knowledge of the earlier subordinated security interest. The Official Comment to § 9–301 is amended by adding the following:

9.   There is no conflict between the principle of § 9–301(1) and the "shelter principle," which is applied at several points in the statute, but is most explicitly stated in § 2–403(1): "A purchaser of goods acquires all title which his transferor had. . . ."

Although § 9–301(1) fails to state the shelter principle expressly, that principle is applicable where a person who had met the conditions for prevailing over an unperfected security interest transfers his right to another person after the security interest is perfected. See PEB Commentary No. 6, dated March 10, 1990.

The rules for subordination of unperfected security interests have a purpose—in common with similar rules in all filing and recording systems—to impose sanctions for not adhering to filing or recording requirements. Such rules are necessary to make the system effective and enforce the policy against secret liens. The shelter principle recognizes that when a person in a protected class transfers his right after the security interest has been perfected, the right will be diminished in value unless the sanction is continued. The sanction imposed by § 9–301(1) is that members of protected classes take free of an unperfected security interest. That sanction should be continued to protect transferees from those members in order to fulfill the purpose of the section.

PEB COMMENTARY NO. 7
THE RELATIVE PRIORITIES OF SECURITY INTERESTS IN THE CASH PROCEEDS OF ACCOUNTS, CHATTEL PAPER, AND GENERAL INTANGIBLES*
(March 10, 1990)

ISSUE

Secured party A and secured party B each has a perfected security interest in the same account, chattel paper, or general intangible, with A having priority over B. If the account debtor makes payment to secured party B, directly or through the debtor, may A recover the payment from B?

DISCUSSION

The issue under discussion arises when two secured parties have a perfected security interest in an account, chattel paper, or general intangible and the secured party that does not have priority (B) receives a payment from the account debtor. The debtor, having received the payment from the account debtor, may remit it to B, or B may receive payment directly from the account debtor. See § 9–502(2) (secured parties' right to notify account debtor to make payment to the secured party); § 9–318(3) (account debtor may discharge obligation by paying assignee after receiving notification that right to receive payment has been assigned and that payment is to be made to assignee). Under these circumstances, may A, the secured party having priority in the account, chattel paper, or general intangible, recover the payment from B?

A. Payment by Check

Article 9 determines the relative priorities of security interests in accounts, chattel paper, and general intangibles. See § 9–312(5) (general rule); § 9–308 (special rule with respect to chattel paper). The Article also determines the relative priorities of security interests in payments made by the account debtor, which payments are the proceeds of the original collateral. See § 9–312(6); § 9–306(1).

When the account debtor pays B by check, or when the debtor indorses and delivers to B a check drawn by the account debtor to the order of the debtor, B will be a holder of the check. If B takes the check under the circumstances described in § 3–302(1), B will be a holder in due course. See § 3–302(1) and (2). A's filed financing statement does not constitute notice to B of A's claim to the check and does not preclude B from being a holder in due course. See § 3–305(1). Specifically, B takes priority over A's earlier, perfected security interest in the check and is entitled to keep the funds received when the check is paid. See § 9–309; Dallas Bank & Trust Co. v. Frigiking, Inc., 692 S.W.2d 163, 41 UCC Rep.Serv. (Callaghan) 1334 (Tex.Ct.App.1985); Thorp Commercial Corp. v. Northgate Industries, Inc., 490 F.Supp. 197, 203–04, 29 UCC Rep.Serv. (Callaghan) 297, 306–307 (D.Minn.1980) (alternate holding), rev'd on other grounds, 654 F.2d 1245, 31 UCC Rep.Serv. (Callaghan) 801 (8th Cir.1981). Contra Bank of the West v. Commercial Credit Financial Services, Inc., 655 F.Supp. 807, 819–20, 3 UCC Rep.Serv.2d (Callaghan) 240, 258–259 (N.D.Cal.1987), rev'd on other grounds, 852 F.2d 1162, 6 UCC Rep.Serv.2d (Callaghan) 602 (9th Cir.1988).

Even if B is not a holder in due course, § 9–308 may give priority to B's security interest in the check. But if B takes the check under circumstances that preclude B from being a holder in due course (e.g., if a notation on the check gives B reason to know that the check constitutes A's proceeds) and from taking priority under § 9–308, then B would take the check subject to A's security interest. See § 3–306(a).

B. Payment in Cash

The Code does not specifically address the right of B to retain a cash payment from the account debtor. Accordingly, resort must be had to the principles of law and equity. See § 1–103. Under those principles, when a person assigns the same claim to two persons and the assignee without priority (B) receives payment from the obligor, the assignee receiving payment owes a duty of restitution to the assignee having priority (A). But if B gave value for the assignment (as B must have, see § 9–203(1)(b)) and obtained the payment in good faith and without knowledge or reason to know of the prior assignment, then B may retain the

---

* *Note from West Advisory Panel: Referring to unrevised Article 9. See revised § 9–608.*

payment. See Restatement, Second, Contracts § 342(b), Comment *e* & Illustration 3; see also Restatement of Restitution § 126, Comment *f* & Illustration 8. Cf. § 9–306 Comment 2(c) (recipients of cash proceeds paid from the debtor's checking account in the operation of the debtor's business take free of a security interest in the proceeds). In determining whether B had reason to know of A's security interest, courts should apply § 9–309 by analogy. Otherwise, cash would be rendered less negotiable than a check.

CONCLUSION

Whether B will be entitled to keep a cash payment from an account debtor or will be under a duty of restitution to A depends on whether B received the payment in good faith and without knowledge or reason to know of A's security interest. Whether B will be entitled to keep a payment made by a check drawn by the account debtor depends on whether B is a holder in due course of the check or is entitled to priority under § 9–308. A's filed financing statement should not constitute notice to B of A's security interest in either case.

The Official Comment to § 9–309 is amended by adding the following:

3.   The operation of this section can be seen when two secured parties have a perfected security interest in an account, chattel paper, or general intangible and the secured party that does not have priority receives a payment by check directly or indirectly from the account debtor. If the recipient takes the check under circumstances that give the recipient the rights of a holder in due course (Section 3–302), then the recipient's security interest in the check will take priority over the competing security interest and the recipient will be entitled to keep the payment. See Commentary No. 7, dated March 10, 1990.

The Official Comment to § 9–312 is amended by adding the following:

9.   Under some circumstances, a secured party, who does not have priority in an account, chattel paper, or general intangible may be entitled to keep a cash payment received directly or indirectly from the account debtor. See PEB Commentary No. 7, dated March 10, 1990.

PEB COMMENTARY NO. 8
(December 10, 1991 as amended to apply to
Revised Article 9)*
SECTION 9–330

ISSUE

Section 9–330(a) provides a special priority rule for purchasers of chattel paper who give new value and take possession, or obtain control, of the chattel paper in the ordinary course of their business. Subsection (a) provides that such purchasers take priority over a security interest in the chattel paper "which is claimed merely as proceeds of inventory subject to a security interest . . ."

This Commentary addresses an issue that may arise under § 9–330(a): When is a security interest in chattel paper "claimed merely as proceeds of inventory subject to a security interest" so that the subsequent chattel paper financer who meets the other requirements of § 9–330(a) takes free of it?

---

*   PEB Commentary No. 8 was originally issued in 1991, and covered two issues that arose under former UCC Section 9–308. Revised UCC Section 9–330 continues the basic provisions of former Section 9–308 with minor changes. One of the questions addressed in the original Commentary—whether a financer of chattel paper that takes possession of it has a duty to make inquiry or search to determine whether there is an existing security interest in that chattel paper—is answered in the negative by Comment 6 to Revised UCC Section 9–330. The other question dealt with in the original Commentary—when does a secured party have an interest in chattel paper "merely as proceeds"—is not resolved in Revised UCC Section 9–330 or addressed in the Comments to that section. Accordingly, that discussion has been continued in this amended Commentary, modified to conform to the differences between former UCC Section 9–308 and Revised UCC Section 9–330. Unless otherwise indicated, references in this amended Commentary to sections of Article 9 are references to Revised Article 9.

1164

PEB COMMENTARY NO. 8

INTRODUCTORY DISCUSSION

Most chattel paper is generated by dealers in automobiles, trucks, machinery, and other durable goods of substantial value. Such dealers frequently sell their chattel paper or use it as collateral for loans. Buyers of chattel paper usually take possession of the paper and collect from the debtors thereon themselves. Also, some lenders on chattel paper will take possession and handle collections. (Financers with a security interest in chattel paper covering smaller appliances, television sets, etc., frequently do not take possession of the paper.)

Under the ordinary priority rules of the Code (first to file or perfect has priority) the buyer of, or lender on, chattel paper would have to make a filing search before the transaction to determine whether a prior party has filed a financing statement covering chattel paper or inventory of which the chattel paper might be proceeds. (If a security interest in inventory is perfected by filing, there is also an automatically perfected proceeds security interest in chattel paper which is generated when inventory subject to the security interest is sold.) A filing search requirement before each transaction would entail substantial delays and significant expense even if the search revealed no prior filed financing statement. In the many cases in which there is a prior filed financing statement covering chattel paper or inventory, or both, the application of the general § 9–322 priority rules would always give the first filer priority. Such a system would make it difficult for any buyer or lender other than the first filed secured party to purchase or lend on the security of chattel paper and would make it particularly difficult for a dealer to deal as to chattel paper with anyone other than the inventory financer. Prior filings would have to be limited to specific chattel paper or subordination agreements or releases would have to be secured from prior filed inventory or chattel paper financers each time items of chattel paper are transferred to a different financer.

When Article 9 was being drafted in the 1950s, some financers of chattel paper left it with the dealer who had generated it and others took possession of the paper. The drafters of the Code did not want to disrupt those practices. Therefore, the problem presented to the drafters was how to structure priority rules so that both forms of financing could continue efficiently and safely. The Code drafters might have encouraged the practice of purchasing and taking possession of chattel paper by treating chattel paper like instruments and providing that a security interest in chattel paper could be perfected only by taking possession. That rule, however, would have denied perfected status to security interests in chattel paper left with the debtor and would have disrupted that widely used form of financing. Requiring possession for perfection of chattel paper would also have meant that an inventory financer's proceeds interest in chattel paper would be lost after 20 days unless the financer took possession of the paper. On the other hand, as already noted, applying the ordinary Code priority rules to chattel paper would have imposed substantial impediments to the widespread business of buying and taking possession of chattel paper. The drafters, therefore, struck a compromise between the interests of non-possessory financers of chattel paper and inventory financers with a non-possessory proceeds interest in the paper on the one hand, and, on the other hand, competing chattel paper financers who take possession of the paper. Section 9–330 continues that compromise and extends it to protect financers who gain control of electronic chattel paper. (See § 9–105 regarding control of electronic chattel paper.)

Under that compromise a secured party can have a non-possessory security interest in chattel paper perfected through filing (including a proceeds interest therein) which will be good against subsequent non-possessory security interests and judgment creditors including the trustee in bankruptcy, but, under § 9–330, that security interest will frequently be junior to a chattel paper purchaser who gives new value and takes possession, or obtains control, of the paper in the ordinary course of its business. (See also § 9–322(c) regarding proceeds.)

The above discussion has reviewed the basic reason for the adoption of the rules set out in § 9–330. The discussion now turns to the specific issue arising under § 9–330 which this Commentary addresses.

ISSUE

When is a security interest in chattel paper claimed "merely as proceeds of inventory subject to a security interest" so that a chattel paper financer that gives new value and takes possession, or obtains control, of the paper in the ordinary course of its business has priority unless the chattel paper indicates that it has been assigned to an identified assignee other than the financer?

APPENDIX E

DISCUSSION

Preliminarily, it should be noted that this issue may be of limited importance since, even if the security interest is more than a mere proceeds interest, the chattel paper financer under § 9–330 will take free of the interest unless it has knowledge that the purchase violates the rights of the secured party. The following discussion should be read with this caveat in mind.

A brief description of two common types of inventory secured financing will help put the discussion of the meaning of a "mere proceeds interest" in its business context.

(a)　The first type, which will be called "type A," is inventory financing of automobiles and large items of equipment in which the financing is primarily item by item (each item of inventory secures a precise amount loaned against that item even though there may be a cross-security provision), with a requirement that the associated inventory debt be paid off when the item is sold, or after a maximum period (usually 90 days subject to renewal), whichever first occurs.

(b)　The second ("type B") is a general floating loan secured by inventory *and* receivables (sometimes called an "availability loan") under which the debtor is entitled to borrow from the secured party such amounts as the debtor may desire, subject to a maximum availability determined by a formula, e.g., 50% of cost of saleable inventory plus 80% of the amount of receivables not in default more than 30 days. This type of financing is usually used in situations involving smaller items of inventory as to which it would be too burdensome to account on an individual basis and in which the receivables are accounts rather than chattel paper so that § 9–330 issues do not arise. However, such financing arrangements may sometimes involve larger, more expensive items of inventory which are frequently sold on credit generating chattel paper.

For the reasons stated below, the Board believes that a type A inventory financer will frequently have only a "mere proceeds interest" in chattel paper which is generated when items of inventory subject to its security interest are sold. On the other hand, as noted below, the Board believes that a type B financer has more than a mere proceeds interest in any chattel paper generated on sale of the inventory.

The type A inventory financer having a proceeds claim to the chattel paper must do something more than rest on that proceeds claim in order to prevail against the person described in § 9–330(a)(1), namely, a purchaser who "in good faith and in the ordinary course of the purchaser's business . . . gives new value and takes possession of the chattel paper or obtains control of the chattel paper under Section 9–105." Such an inventory financer takes the chattel paper out of the "mere proceeds" category only by giving value against it in some new transaction. Such a lender gives new value, as it commonly will, by purchasing the chattel paper (or, in some types of transactions, making a specific loan against it). Whether the type A inventory financer will be willing to give value against the chattel paper instead of merely resting on its proceeds claim until payment will depend on the quality of the paper. That quality depends upon such factors as the credit worthiness of the buyer who is the principal obligor on the chattel paper, the amount of the buyer's down payment and hence the amount of the chattel paper debt as compared to the value of the collateral (the former inventory), and the terms under which the dealer (the former inventory debtor) is willing to assume full or limited recourse to support the buyer's obligation under the chattel paper. Not infrequently the financer and the dealer will negotiate a package purchase of several items of chattel paper in which the total price is determined by the quality of the paper, the extent of the recourse, and so on. When the financer buys, or lends against, chattel paper in the way just outlined, there is a "new transaction" by which the financer has acquired an interest in the specific chattel paper which is more than a "mere proceeds interest."

If, however, the type A inventory financer does not by some new transaction give value against specific chattel paper, the fact that the inventory debt is unpaid and that the security agreement specifically claims the chattel paper proceeds as additional collateral does not give the financer more than a mere proceeds interest. Further, while no doubt much inventory financing is carried out with nominal profit to the financer in anticipation that it will be given the opportunity to acquire the chattel paper, in the Board's opinion this anticipation of receiving the chattel paper does not take the case out of the "mere proceeds" phrase of the statute.

As pointed out above, the Board believes that the type B financer at all times has more than a mere proceeds interest in the chattel paper on hand whether or not at any specific time there is sufficient inventory on hand to secure the amount of the loan outstanding at that time. The structure of the deal is such that the chattel paper is part of the primary collateral for the debt. That interest extends to any chattel paper subsequently generated by a sale of inventory whether or not at any particular time the existing inventory is adequate security for the debt actually outstanding.

A number of reported cases under former Article 9 involved priority conflicts between inventory financers and purchasers of chattel paper who took possession, gave new value, and acted in the ordinary course of their business. In those cases, the courts applied the "mere proceeds" rules of former § 9–308, and the chattel paper financer always won.[1] The courts have not always carefully reported the facts, but it is clear that in at least one of the cases, the security agreement did specifically claim an interest in chattel paper and the court did not treat that fact as significant.[2] In most of the cases, the court did not carefully consider whether the chattel paper financer had knowledge of the prior interest in the chattel paper, but in several cases the court either assumed that the chattel paper financer had knowledge or the findings of fact show that the chattel paper financer did have knowledge.[3] The results in all those cases are consistent with the position taken in this Commentary.

CONCLUSION

If a financer loans or extends credit for the cost of specific items of inventory and expects to be paid upon the sale of the items, the financer's security interest in chattel paper generated when the items are sold is a mere proceeds interest unless the financer in a new transaction gives value against the specific paper. On the other hand, a lender who agrees to lend up to a specified percentage of the cost of inventory and of receivables has more than a mere proceeds interest in chattel paper which is a part of the receivables covered by the security agreement. In inventory financing transactions which do not fall within the above two categories, whether the financer has more than a mere proceeds interest in chattel paper generated when inventory subject to its secured interest is sold must be determined from an examination of all the facts of the case.

PEB COMMENTARY NO. 9
SECTION 9–306(1)*
(June 25, 1992)

ISSUE

Section 9–306(1) provides: " 'Proceeds' includes whatever is received upon the sale, exchange, collection or other disposition of collateral or proceeds." Where a debtor has granted to a secured party a security interest in goods and the debtor later leases those goods as lessor, do the lease rentals constitute proceeds of the secured party's collateral?

DISCUSSION

Where a debtor has granted to a secured party a security interest in goods that the debtor later leases as lessor, the lease rentals would constitute proceeds of the secured party's collateral for the reason that the debtor's conveyance of a leasehold interest in the goods constitutes a disposition of the goods for purposes of § 9–306(1).

---

[1]   See e.g. *Aetna Finance Corp. v. Massey-Ferguson, Inc.,* 626 F. Supp. 482, 42 UCC Rep. Serv. (Callaghan) 1501 (S.D. Ind. 1985); *Northwest Acceptance Corp. v. Lynnwood Equipment, Inc.,* 1 UCC Rep.Serv.2d (Callaghan) 980, 1710 (W.D. Wash. 1986); *Rex Financial Corp. v. Great Western Bank & Trust,* 23 Ariz. App. 286, 532 P.2d 558, 16 UCC Rep.Serv. (Callaghan) 1155 (Ariz. App. 1975); *Commercial Credit Corp. v. National Credit Corp.,* 251 Ark. 541, 473 S.W.2d 876, 10 UCC Rep.Serv. (Callaghan) 232 (Ark. 1971); *American State Bank v. Avco Financial Services of the United States, Inc.,* 71 Cal. App. 3d 774, 139 Cal.Rptr. 658, 22 UCC Rep.Serv. (Callaghan) 235 (Cal. App. 1977); *Home Savings Ass'n v. General Electric Credit Corp.,* 101 Nev. 595, 708 P.2d 280, 42 UCC Rep.Serv. (Callaghan) 1489 (Nev. 1985); *Chrysler Credit Corp. v. Sharp,* 56 Misc.2d 261, 288 N.Y.S.2d 525, 5 UCC Rep.Serv. (Callaghan) 226 (N.Y. Sup. Ct. 1968); *Bank of Beulah v. Chase,* 231 N.W.2d 738, 17 UCC Rep.Serv. (Callaghan) 259 (N.D. 1975); *Associates Discount Corp. v. Old Freeport Bank,* 421 Pa. 609, 220 A.2d 621, 3 UCC Rep.Serv. (Callaghan) 481 (Pa. 1966); *Borg-Warner Acceptance Corp. v. C.I.T. Corp.,* 679 S.W.2d 140, 39 UCC Rep.Serv. (Callaghan) 1864 (Tex. Ct. App. 1984).

[2]   *Home Savings Ass'n, supra* note 1.

[3]   *American State Bank, Rex Financial Corp.,* both *supra* note 1.

*   *Note from West Advisory Panel: Referring to unrevised Article 9. See revised § 9–102 (definition of "proceeds").*

This would certainly be the case where the lease creates a security interest under § 1–201(37). In that instance the lease is nothing more than a disguised sale of the goods, and the secured party would be entitled to a security interest in any chattel paper or payments on that chattel paper, all as proceeds resulting from that sales transaction. The following examples illustrate this conclusion:

Example 1. Debtor grants to Secured Party a security interest in Debtor's drill press. Debtor sells the drill press to Buyer who pays for the drill press by issuing to Debtor Buyer's five-year promissory note secured by a security interest in the drill press. The promissory note and security interest together constitute chattel paper under § 9–105(1)(b), and, since the chattel paper was received by Debtor upon the sale of the drill press, the chattel paper constitutes proceeds of Secured Party's collateral. When payments are made by Buyer on the promissory note, those payments, arising upon the "collection" of "proceeds," also constitute proceeds of Secured Party's collateral.

Example 2. Debtor grants to Secured Party a security interest in Debtor's drill press. Debtor leases the drill press to Lessee for a fixed term of five years not subject to termination by Lessee. The drill press is predicted to have exhausted its useful life at the end of that five-year term, and Lessee will then be entitled to purchase the drill press for the cash sum of $10. The lease constitutes chattel paper under § 9–105(1)(b). Since the chattel paper was received by Debtor upon the granting to Lessee of a leasehold interest for the entire useful life of the drill press and Lessee can become the owner of the drill press at the end of the nonterminable lease term by paying a nominal consideration, the transaction will be viewed as creating a security interest under § 1–201(37) and will be treated for Article 9 purposes as a disguised sale. Just as the chattel paper arising upon the sale of the drill press in Example 1 constituted proceeds of Secured Party's collateral, so does the chattel paper arising upon the granting of a security lease constitute proceeds of Secured Party's collateral in this example; the two transactions have precisely the same economic effect although labeled by the parties as a "sale" in Example 1 and a "lease" in this example. Similarly, when rental payments are made by Lessee on the security lease, those payments, arising upon the "collection" of "proceeds," also constitute proceeds of Secured Party's collateral.

In both Example 1 and Example 2 it is irrelevant to the payments to Debtor being treated as proceeds whether the sale or lease was authorized by Secured Party or whether the drill press constituted equipment or inventory in the hands of Debtor. This is because under § 9–306(2) Secured Party's security interest will continue "in any identifiable proceeds including collections received by the debtor" even when the disposition of the collateral was authorized by the Secured Party or where the collateral subject to the disposition was transferred to a buyer in the ordinary course as contemplated by § 9–307(1).

Lease rentals would also constitute proceeds of a secured party's collateral consisting of goods where the subsequent lease of those goods creates a "true" lease governed by Article 2A. Consider the following example:

Example 3. Debtor grants to Secured Party a security interest in Debtor's drill press which then has a predicted useful life of five years. Debtor leases the drill press to Lessee for a fixed term, not subject to termination by Lessee, of two years with no purchase option. The lease would appear to be a "true" lease governed by Article 2A. See §§ 1–201(37), 2A–102, and 2A–103(1)(j). Once again, the lease constitutes chattel paper under § 9–105(1)(b). The chattel paper was received by Debtor upon the granting of a leasehold interest in the drill press for a non-terminable period of two years out of a predicted useful life of the drill press of five years. Debtor has remaining to it a residual interest in the drill press, i.e., a right to the drill press arising only at the end of the two-year lease term. See § 2A–103(1)(q) (defining "lessor's residual interest"). But an interest in the drill press constituting a right by Lessee to use the drill press for a two-year period out of the drill press's predicted five-year useful life was conveyed by Debtor to Lessee. The granting of the leasehold interest constitutes a disposition of a portion of Debtor's interest in the drill press, and the chattel paper arising upon that disposition constitutes proceeds of Secured Party's collateral. When rental payments are made by Lessee on the true lease, those payments, arising upon the "collection" of "proceeds," also constitute proceeds of Secured Party's collateral.

The foregoing analysis in Example 3, by concluding that the granting of a true leasehold interest in goods constitutes a "disposition" of the goods for purposes of § 9–306(1), is consistent with the common law rule that the granting of a real estate leasehold interest constitutes a disposition of a portion of the lessor's ownership interest in the leased estate. See, e.g., *Hueschen v. Stalie,* 98 N.M. 696, 652 P.2d 246 (1982) (real estate lease is a conveyance of an estate for a limited term with conditions); Powell, *Law of Real Property,* § 221 (1990). It is also consistent with Article 9 cases which treat the totality of a debtor's interest in goods as comprising the debtor's leasehold interest as lessor plus the debtor's residual interest in the leased goods as owner, with the necessity of a secured party's security interest in the leasehold being perfected in one manner (e.g., possession or filing as to the chattel paper) and its security interest in the lessor's residual interest being perfected in another manner (e.g., filing as to the goods). See, e.g., *In re Leasing Consultants, Inc.,* 486 F.2d 367, 13 UCC Rep.Serv. (Callaghan) 189 (2d Cir.1973). Furthermore, this analysis is consistent with Article 2A's definition of a lease being a "transfer" of a right to possession and use of the leased goods even without being a "sale" of the goods. See §§ 2–106(1) and 2A–103(1)(j). Cf. *Feldman v. Philadelphia Nat. Bank,* 408 F.Supp. 24, 37–38, 18 UCC Rep.Serv. (Callaghan) 776, 786–788 (E.D.Pa.1976) (while the court referred to chattel paper as "proceeds" of a security interest in underlying goods, the reference may be viewed as dicta since the secured party had in any event taken possession of the chattel paper). Cases such as *General Electric Credit Corp. v. Cleary Brothers Construction Co., Inc. (In re Cleary Brothers Construction Co., Inc.),* 9 B.R. 40, 30 UCC Rep.Serv. (Callaghan) 1444 (Bkrtcy.S.D.Fla.1980), and *In re A.E.I. Corp.,* 11 B.R. 97, 31 UCC Rep.Serv. (Callaghan) 1467 (Bkrtcy.E.D.Pa.1981), to the extent that they hold that a subsequent lease of goods or payments thereon cannot constitute proceeds of a secured party's pre-existing collateral consisting of the goods, are not consistent with this analysis.

Lease rentals would constitute proceeds of a secured party's collateral consisting of goods even where the subsequent lease of the goods is for a term which is of a short duration in relation to the useful life of the goods. Where the goods have a limited useful life, any transfer of the use and possession of the goods in return for a consideration constitutes a disposition, however small, of the debtor's interest in the goods. If that consideration consists of chattel paper, that chattel paper and the payments thereon constitute proceeds of the secured party's collateral. For a case reaching an analogous conclusion in the context of a real estate mortgage, see *Old Stone Bank v. Tycon I Building Limited Partnership,* 946 F.2d 271 (4th Cir.1991) (forfeited earnest money deposit under a sales contract for mortgaged real estate constituted "proceeds" to which undersecured mortgagee is entitled under its mortgage since the deposit resulted from a disposition of valuable "lock up" rights to the collateral while the sales contract was in effect).

The foregoing analysis is intended to clarify the treatment of rental payments as proceeds of a secured party's collateral consisting of goods subsequently leased. It is not intended to address transactions where the goods become subject to the secured party's security interest at a time when the goods are already under lease by the debtor as lessor. See § 2A–307; *In re Leasing Consultants, Inc.,* 486 F.2d 367, 13 UCC Rep.Serv. (Callaghan) 189 (2d Cir.1973). Nor is it intended to address transactions where the goods, although subject to a secured party's pre-existing security interest, are not subsequently leased by the debtor as lessor. For example, the foregoing analysis is not intended to suggest that income generated from the debtor's own use and possession of goods should constitute proceeds of a secured party's pre-existing collateral consisting of the goods. Similarly, it is not intended to address other transactions where no disposition of the goods by security lease, determined by reference to § 1–201(37), or true lease, governed by Article 2A, has taken place. Cf. *In re S & J Holding Corp.,* 42 B.R. 249, 39 UCC Rep.Serv. (Callaghan) 668 (Bkrtcy.S.D.Fla.1984) (payments for playing video games on game machines).

Moreover, the foregoing analysis is not intended to suggest that, as a matter of federal bankruptcy law, a secured party is necessarily entitled to "adequate protection" compensation for the debtor's use of rental payments made under a post-petition lease by the debtor as lessor of goods in which a secured party held a perfected and unavoidable pre-petition security interest. Factors such as the term of the lease in relation to the useful life of the leased goods and the provision by the debtor of post-petition services associated with the post-petition lease of the goods may well affect the secured party's entitlement to such "adequate protection" compensation, without, however, affecting the status of the lease or the rental payments thereon as proceeds of the secured party's pre-existing collateral as a matter of state law. See 11 U.S.C. §§ 361, 363(e), and 552(b); cf. *General Electric Credit Corp. v. Cleary Brothers Construction Co., Inc. (In re Cleary Brothers Construction Co., Inc.),* 9 B.R. 40, 30 UCC Rep.Serv. (Callaghan) 1444 (Bkrtcy.S.D.Fla.1980) (instead of holding that the secured party could not claim, as proceeds of its pre-petition security interest in a crane, the rentals under a post-petition lease of the crane for a 10-day period, the court could have reached the same result by concluding that, although the rentals were proceeds of the secured party's collateral, the secured party was adequately protected).

CONCLUSION

Where a debtor has granted to a secured party a security interest in goods and the debtor later leases those goods as lessor, the lease rentals will constitute proceeds of the secured party's collateral consisting of the goods.

The Official Comment to § 9–306 is amended by adding the following:

6. Where a debtor has granted to a secured party a security interest in goods and the debtor later leases those goods as lessor, the lease rentals constitute proceeds of the secured party's collateral consisting of the goods. See PEB Commentary No. 9, dated June 25, 1992.

PEB COMMENTARY NO. 10
SECTION 1–203*
(February 10, 1994)

ISSUE

Section 1–203 provides that "Every contract or duty within this Act imposes an obligation of good faith in its performance or enforcement." [1] While this concept applies generally to every contract, it finds particular expression throughout the Code. For example, out of over 400 Code provisions, more than 50 sections make specific reference to "good faith." [2]

The meaning of "good faith" varies with the context. Sometimes the context is as a standard of performance or enforcement; other times the context is that of good faith purchase. [3] This Commentary deals only with good faith performance or enforcement of a right or duty under a contract that is within the Code.

In the context in which the obligation of good faith functions as the standard of contract performance or enforcement, can the failure to meet this standard support a cause of action where no other basis for a cause of action exists? This Commentary examines this question in order to promote a uniform understanding of what it means to say that a general obligation of good faith is imposed on every contracting party. In so doing, several principles are discussed.

DISCUSSION

1. *Good Faith, Commercial Expectations, and the Concept of Agreement*

Section 1–201(19) defines good faith as "honesty in fact in the conduct or transaction concerned." [4] Commentators have said that this general requirement of good faith sets a "subjective" standard, [5] while the

---

* *Note from West Advisory Panel: Referring to unrevised Article 1 (Appendix A). See revised § 1–304.*

[1] This does not mean that the obligation of good faith as defined in the Code will necessarily apply to all aspects of the same transaction. As written, the scope of § 1–203 is co-extensive with the Code's coverage. For example, if a loan agreement that provides for an Article 9 security interest also contains financial covenants which are not governed by the Code, § 1–203 would apply to the former and the general law of contracts would apply to the latter. See, e.g., Restatement, Second, Contracts § 205 (1981).

[2] Farnsworth, *Good Faith Performance and Commercial Reasonableness Under the Uniform Commercial Code,* 30 U.Chi.L.Rev. 666, 667 (1963).

[3] See, e.g., UCC §§ 2–403 (good faith purchaser); 3–302 (holder in due course); 9–307 (buyer in the ordinary course of business). On the distinction between the doctrines of good faith performance and good faith purchase, see generally id.

[4] This sparse definition found in Article 1 is expanded elsewhere in the Code for purposes of particular Articles. See, e.g., §§ 2–103(1)(b); 2A–103(2); 3–103(a)(4); 4–104(c); 4A–105(a)(6). This expanded definition "is concerned with the fairness of conduct rather than the care with which an act is performed." UCC § 3–103, Comment 4.

[5] See Aronstein, *Good Faith Performance of Security Agreements: The Liability of Corporate Managers,* 120 U.Pa.L.Rev. 1, 31 (1971) ("Good faith [as] defined in § 1–201(19) . . . [has] been historically construed as applying only to the actor's subjective state of mind."); Braucher, *The Legislative History of the Uniform Commercial Code,* 58 Colum.L.Rev. 798, 812 (1958) (describing the test of good faith in § 1–201(19) as a "subjective" test, sometimes known as the rule of "the pure heart and empty head"); Lawrence, *The Prematurely Reported Demise of the Perfect Tender Rule,* 35

particularized definitions elsewhere also create an additional "objective" standard of the observance of reasonable commercial standards of fair dealing. This Commentary applies with equal force to both standards of good faith.

The principal author of the Code, Karl Llewellyn, recognized that parties develop expectations over time against the background of commercial practices and that if commercial law fails to account for those practices, it will cut against the parties' actual expectations. In an unpublished commentary on the Proposed Final Draft of the Uniform Revised Sales Act, Llewellyn had this to say about good faith:

> No inconsistency of language and background exists merely because the words used mean something different to an outsider than they do to the merchants who used that language in the light of the commercial background against which they contracted. This is the necessary result of applying commercial standards and principles of good faith to the agreement. . . . Moreover, where the commercial background normally gives to a term in question some breadth of meaning so that it describes a range of acceptable tolerances rather than a sharp-edged single line of action, any attempted narrowing of this meaning by one party is so unusual as not likely to be expected or perceived by the other. Therefore, attention must be called to a desire to contract at material variance from the accepted commercial pattern of contract or use of language. Thus, this Act rejects any "surprise" variation from the fair and normal meaning of the agreement.[6]

Explaining the doctrine of good faith in such terms is thus a recognition that, as expressed in the Code, it serves as a directive to protect the reasonable expectations of the contracting parties. The general imperative that the reasonable expectations of the parties are the measure of the good faith of each suggests that good faith is a concept with conceptual content related to that of agreement.

The Code definition of "Agreement" reads:

> "Agreement" means the bargain of the parties in fact as found in their language or by implication from other circumstances including course of dealing or usage of trade or course of performance as provided in this Act (Sections 1–205 and 2–208).[7]

The agreement of the parties consists of more than their language alone. In elaborating on this theme, Comment 3 to § 1–201 emphasizes that "the word [agreement] is intended to include full recognition of usage of trade, course of dealing, *course of performance* and the surrounding circumstances as effective parts thereof. . . ." (emphasis added).[8]

U.Kan.L.Rev. 557, 571 (1987) ("Good faith is a subjective term meaning 'honesty in fact in the contract or transaction concerned.' ").

[6] The Karl Llewellyn Papers, The University of Chicago Law Library, File J.X.2.K. 1, 9, *reprinted in* D. Patterson, *Good Faith and Lender Liability* 217 (1990).

[7] UCC § 1–201(3). Furthermore, Comment 1 to § 1–205 ("Course of Dealing and Usage of Trade") reinforces this definition by stating:

> This Act rejects both the "lay-dictionary" and the "conveyancer's" reading of a commercial agreement. Instead the meaning of the agreement of the parties is to be determined by the language used by them and by their action, read and interpreted in the light of commercial practices and other surrounding circumstances. The measure and background for interpretation are set by the commercial context, which may explain and supplement even the language of a formal or final writing.

[8] This Commentary recognizes the fact that course of performance is defined in Articles 2 and 2A and was originally not a part of the general definition of "Agreement" in Article 1. The concept is included here as an element of the agreement of the parties because there exists no plausible justification for excluding it. This view is strongly supported by Comments 1 and 2 to § 2–208. Comment 2, in particular, emphasizes that "a course of performance is always relevant to determine the meaning of the agreement." See also Westinghouse Credit Corp. v. Shelton, 645 F.2d 869, 31 UCC Rep.Serv. (Callaghan) 410 (10th Cir.1981) (course of performance may also be used for discerning the meaning of "Agreement" in Article 9).

The Restatement, Second, of Contracts does not reflect the Code's isolation of course of performance in Articles 2 and 2A. The Restatement provides that all four elements—express terms, course of dealing, course of performance, and usage of trade—are all elements of the meaning of "contract." See Restatement, Second, Contracts § 203. In fact, § 202(4) states that "any course of performance accepted or acquiesced in without objection is given great weight in the interpretation of the agreement."

"Course of dealing" is defined as follows:

A course of dealing is a sequence of previous conduct between the parties to a particular transaction which is fairly to be regarded as establishing a common basis of understanding for interpreting their expressions and other conduct.[9]

"Usage of trade" is defined as follows:

A usage of trade is any practice or method of dealing having such regularity of observance in a place, vocation or trade as to justify an expectation that it will be observed with respect to the transaction in question. The existence and scope of such a usage are to be proved as facts. If it is established that such a usage is embodied in a written trade code or similar writing the interpretation of the writing is for the court.[10]

"Course of performance" is defined as follows:

Where the contract for sale involves repeated occasions for performance by either party with knowledge of the nature of the performance and opportunity for objection to it by the other, any course of performance accepted or acquiesced in without objection shall be relevant to determine the meaning of the agreement.[11]

In addition to two definitional sections, § 1–205 contains two additional methodological sections which direct how express terms, course of dealing, and usage of trade are to be synthesized:

(3)   A course of dealing between parties and any usage of trade in the vocation or trade in which they are engaged or of which they are or should be aware give particular meaning to and supplement or qualify terms of an agreement.

(4)   The express terms of an agreement and an applicable course of dealing or usage of trade shall be construed wherever reasonable as consistent with each other; but when such construction is unreasonable express terms control both course of dealing and usage of trade and course of dealing controls usage of trade.[12]

At this juncture it is important to recognize that one acts in good faith relative to the agreement of the parties. To decide the question whether a party has acted in good faith, a court must first ascertain the substance of the parties' agreement.

The performance and enforcement of agreements in a manner consistent with the reasonable expectations of the parties is in keeping with the broadest understanding of contract doctrine.[13] The Code

---

[9]   UCC § 1–205(1).

[10]   UCC § 1–205(2).

[11]   UCC § 2–208(1). This definition is duplicated in § 2A–207(1).

[12]   UCC § 1–205(3)–(4). The connection between § 1–205 and good faith is made explicit in the Comment to § 1–203, wherein it is stated that the obligation of good faith "is further implemented by Section 1–205 on course of dealing and usage of trade."

The interpretational priorities set forth in § 1–205 are, with the added inclusion of course of performance, duplicated in § 2–208(2). That section states as follows:

The express terms of the agreement and any such course of performance, as well as any course of dealing and usage of trade, shall be construed whenever reasonable as consistent with each other; but when such construction is unreasonable, express terms shall control course of performance and course of performance shall control both course of dealing and usage of trade (Section 1–205).

See also UCC § 2A–207(2).

[13]   See 3 A. Corbin, *Corbin on Contracts* § 570 (West Supp.1993).

If the purpose of contract law is to enforce the reasonable expectations of parties induced by promises, then at some point it becomes necessary for courts to look to the substance rather than to the form of the agreement, and to hold that substance controls over form. What courts are doing here, whether calling the process "implication" of promises, or interpreting the requirements of "good faith," as the current fashion may be, is but a recognition that the parties occasionally have understandings or expectations that were so fundamental that they did not need to negotiate about those expectations. When the court "implies a promise" or holds that "good faith" requires a party not to violate those expectations, it is recognizing that sometimes silence says more than words, and it is understanding its duty to the spirit of the bargain is higher than its duty to the technicalities of the language.

is consistent with this tradition of thought. However, the Code's concept of agreement broadens the sources for determining the meaning of the parties' agreement. The concept of agreement is not limited to the terms of the parties' writing: it includes a variety of elements, all of which must be synthesized.

Under § 1–205(4), the initial interpretive effort is to read all the terms as consistent with one another. Only when this is impossible does the interpreter then move to a lexical ordering of the terms, with express terms at the head of the list. Cases which make no attempt to reconcile the various terms before according priority to express terms in the construction of the parties' agreement must be considered to have proceeded improperly.[14] The better application of § 1–205(4), and the issues of interpretation which are central to it, is illustrated in cases like *Nanakuli Paving & Rock Co. v. Shell Oil Co.,* 664 F.2d 772, 32 UCC Rep.Serv. (Callaghan) 1025 (9th Cir.1981) (upholding a finding that the written price term in an asphalt supply contract was qualified by a trade practice requiring suppliers to delay price increases for jobs on which buyers have already bid). Accordingly, in order to answer the question, "Has a party performed or enforced a contractual right or duty in good faith?", the content of the parties' agreement must first be determined.[15]

2. *UCC § 1–203 Does Not Create an Independent Cause of Action*

The inherent flaw in the view that § 1–203 supports an independent cause of action is the belief that the obligation of good faith has an existence which is conceptually separate from the underlying agreement. As the above discussion demonstrates, however, this is an incorrect view of the duty. "A party cannot simply 'act in good faith.' One acts in good faith relative to the agreement of the parties. Thus the real question is 'What is the Agreement of the parties?' "[16] Put differently, good faith merely directs attention to the parties' reasonable expectations; it is not an independent source from which rights and duties evolve.[17] The language of § 1–203 itself makes this quite clear by providing that the obligation to perform or enforce in good faith extends only to the rights and duties resulting from the parties' contract. The term "contract" is, in turn, defined as "the total legal obligation which results from the parties' *agreement.* . . ."[18] Consequently, resort to principles of law or equity outside the Code are not appropriate to create rights, duties, and liabilities inconsistent with those stated in the Code.[19] For example, a breach of a contract or duty within the Code arising from a failure to act in good faith does not give rise to a claim for punitive damages unless specifically permitted.[20]

Id. Reiter & Swan, Contracts and the Protection of Reasonable Expectations, in *Studies in Contract Law* 1, 11 (B. Reiter & J. Swan eds. 1980) ("[T]hroughout the law of contract, a striving to protect reasonable expectations is visible. . . .").

[14] See, e.g., Southern Concrete Servs. v. Mableton Contractors, Inc., 407 F.Supp. 581, 19 UCC Rep.Serv. (Callaghan) 79 (N.D.Ga.1975), *aff'd mem.,* 569 F.2d 1154 (5th Cir.1978); Division of Triple T Serv. v. Mobil Oil Corp., 304 N.Y.S.2d 191, 6 UCC Rep.Serv. (Callaghan) 1011 (Sup.Ct.1969).

[15] For a non-Code decision which is consistent with this approach, see Southwest Savings and Loan Association v. Sunamp Systems, Inc., 838 P.2d 1314 (Ariz.App.1992) (holding that inquiry does not stop with recognition that lender had general authority in written loan agreement to take the particular action, but inquiry extends to whether lender exercised that authority "for a reason beyond the risks" assumed by borrower in loan agreement, or beyond borrower's "justified expectations," in the context of how a reasonable lender might act).

[16] Patterson, *supra,* at 143. Good faith is sometimes the basis of an implied term to fill a gap or deal with an omitted case, e.g., the duty of cooperation frequently imposed on a party whose cooperation is essential and not unreasonably burdensome; or, the duty to give notice within a reasonable time of some important fact of which the other party would otherwise be unaware. See § 2–309(3) and Comment 8; 2 Farnsworth on Contracts §§ 7.17, 7.17a (1990). A breach of such duties gives rise to a cause of action for breach of the contract of which the implied term becomes a part. Although such a cause of action arguably has the same practical content as a cause of action based upon a purported breach of § 1–203, there is an important methodological difference in that this Commentary requires, in the case of contracts within the Code, that the focus be upon the Agreement of the parties and their reasonable expectations.

[17] Cases reaching this conclusion include Management Assistance, Inc. v. Computer Dimensions, Inc., 546 F.Supp. 666 (N.D.Ga.1982), *aff'd* 747 F.2d 708 (11th Cir.1984), and Chandler v. Hunter, 340 So.2d 818, 21 UCC Rep.Serv. (Callaghan) 484 (Ala.Civ.App.1976). A contrary conclusion was reached in Reid v. Key Bank of Southern Maine, Inc., 821 F.2d 9, 3 UCC Rep.Serv.2d (Callaghan) 1665 (1st Cir.1987).

[18] UCC § 1–201(11) (emphasis supplied).

[19] See UCC § 1–103.

[20] See UCC § 1–106(1).

APPENDIX E

CONCLUSION

Section 1–203 does not support a cause of action where no other basis for a cause of action exists.

The concept of Agreement permeates the entirety of the Code. For example, § 9–105(1)(*l*) incorporates the Article 1 concept of Agreement directly into Article 9. The "agreement of the parties" cannot be read off the face of a document, but must be discerned against the background of actual commercial practice. Not only does the Code recognize "the reasonable practices and standards of the commercial community . . . [as] an appropriate source of legal obligation,"[21] but it also rejects the "premise that the language used [by the parties] has the meaning attributable to [it] by rules of construction existing in the law rather than the meaning which arises out of the commercial context in which it was used."[22] The correct perspective on the meaning of good faith performance and enforcement is the Agreement of the parties. The critical question is, "Has 'X' acted in good faith with respect to the performance or enforcement of some right or duty under the terms of the Agreement?" It is therefore wrong to conclude that as long as the agreement allows a party to do something, it is under all terms and conditions permissible. Such a conclusion overlooks completely the distinction between merely performing or enforcing a right or duty under an agreement on the one hand and, on the other hand, doing so in a way that recognizes that the agreement should be interpreted in a manner consistent with the reasonable expectations of the parties in the light of the commercial conditions existing in the context under scrutiny. The latter is the correct approach. Examples are: (1) Is it reasonable for a buyer in a particular locale or trade to expect that an express quantity term in a contract is "not really" a quantity term, but a mere projection to be adjusted according to market forces?;[23] (2) Does a party to a sales contract that permits discretionary termination have the right to expect that the decision whether to terminate will be made on the basis of sound business criteria?

The Official Comment to § 1–203 is amended by adding the following language at the end of the first paragraph:

This section does not support an independent cause of action for failure to perform or enforce in good faith. Rather, this section means that a failure to perform or enforce, in good faith, a specific duty or obligation under the contract, constitutes a breach of that contract or makes unavailable, under the particular circumstances, a remedial right or power. This distinction makes it clear that the doctrine of good faith merely directs a court towards interpreting contracts within the commercial context in which they are created, performed, and enforced, and does not create a separate duty of fairness and reasonableness which can be independently breached. See PEB Commentary No. 10, dated February 10, 1994.

PEB COMMENTARY NO. 11
(February 10, 1994, as amended to apply to Revised Article 9)*
SURETYSHIP ISSUES UNDER SECTIONS 3–116, 3–305, 3–415, 3–419, AND 3–605

INTRODUCTION

The promulgation of revised Article 3 of the Uniform Commercial Code has given rise to a number of questions concerning the provisions in that Article governing the rights and duties of accommodation

---

[21] Kastely, *Stock Equipment for the Bargain in Fact: Trade Usage, "Express Terms," and Consistency Under Section 1–205 of the Uniform Commercial Code*, 64 N.C.L.Rev. 777, 780 (1986).

[22] UCC § 2–202, Comment 1.

[23] See Columbia Nitrogen Corp. v. Royster Co., 451 F.2d 3, 9 UCC Rep.Serv. (Callaghan) 977 (4th Cir.1971).

* PEB Commentary No. 11, which addresses suretyship issues that arise under Article 3 of the Uniform Commercial Code, was originally issued in 1994. Issue 11 in the original Commentary dealt with the power of an accommodation party on an instrument that is secured by a security interest governed by Uniform Commercial Code Article 9 to waive the rights of that party that were provided for in Part 5 of former Article 9. Since the issuance of the original Commentary, former Article 9 has been replaced with Revised Article 9 and the Restatement of Suretyship and Guaranty, which was in the process of being drafted in 1994, has been promulgated by the American Law Institute. This

parties. This heightened level of interest results from many factors. In particular, the provisions in revised Article 3 concerning accommodation parties differ significantly from those in former Article 3 in ways that are complex and not always obvious. Application of these rules often raises issues that were not pertinent under prior law. In addition, the promulgation in 1995 of the Restatement of Suretyship and Guaranty by The American Law Institute has generated greater interest in the rights and duties of sureties, including, of course, accommodation parties.

As a result of this heightened interest, the suretyship rules in Article 3 have been the subject of a great deal of scrutiny, which has resulted in a recognition that the treatment of some suretyship issues in revised Article 3 should be clarified. It is the purpose of this Commentary to answer several questions that have arisen concerning the rights and duties of accommodation parties. This Commentary concludes with a series of revisions and additions to the Comments to various sections in Article 3 that govern suretyship issues.

ISSUE 1

If another person agrees to be liable for the obligation of the maker of a note, are the rights and duties of that person determined by the provisions of Article 3 governing accommodation parties, by the general law of suretyship, or both?

DISCUSSION

A person who agrees to be liable for the debt of another is clearly a surety. See Restatement of Suretyship and Guaranty § 1. If the person effectuates the agreement by becoming a party (i.e., a co-maker or indorser) to the same instrument that creates the obligation, the surety is also an accommodation party. In such a case, the rules in §§ 3–116, 3–305, 3–415, 3–419, and 3–605 concerning accommodation parties are applicable. Of course, these sections will not resolve all possible issues concerning the rights and duties of the surety. In the event that a situation is presented that is not resolved by those sections, the resolution may be provided by the general law of suretyship because, pursuant to § 1–103, that law is applicable unless displaced by provisions of this Act. If the surety does not effectuate the obligation by becoming a party to the note, the surety is not an accommodation party. In that case, the surety's rights and duties are determined by the general law of suretyship.

In unusual cases, two parties to an instrument may have a surety relationship that is not governed by Article 3 because the requirements of § 3–419(a) are not fulfilled. For example, assume that the payee of an instrument would like to sell it, but the potential buyer will agree to buy the instrument only if, in the event that the instrument is dishonored, the buyer has recourse not only against the issuer and the payee but also against someone more creditworthy. Accordingly, the payee produces a creditworthy person who agrees to stand behind the payee's obligations with respect to the instrument. The transfer to the buyer is then made after both the payee and the creditworthy person indorse the instrument. The creditworthy person is a party to the instrument as an indorser and is an accommodation party for the issuer who is the accommodated party. The creditworthy person is also a surety with respect to the obligation of both the issuer and the payee as indorser. The creditworthy person, however, is not an accommodation party for the payee and the payee is not an accommodated party under § 3–419(a) inasmuch as the instrument was not issued for value given for the benefit of the payee. Therefore, the general law of suretyship, and not the provisions in Article 3 concerning accommodation parties, provides the rules that govern the suretyship relationship between the creditworthy person and the payee.[1]

ISSUE 2

What are the differences between the rights of an accommodation party with respect to the accommodated party under revised Article 3 and former Article 3?

---

amended Commentary updates the discussion of Issue 11 to reflect Revised Article 9 and the promulgation of the Restatement of Suretyship and Guaranty.

[1] The revisions to Comment 3 to § 3–419 and Comment 6 to § 3–605 reflect this discussion. See Appendix, par. 3 and par. 10.

APPENDIX E

DISCUSSION

Under the general law of suretyship, as between the principal obligor and the secondary obligor, it is the principal obligor who ought to bear the cost of performance. Restatement of Suretyship and Guaranty § 1. Suretyship law provides three mechanisms to effectuate that cost allocation. First, if the principal obligor is charged with notice of the secondary obligation, the principal obligor owes the secondary obligor a duty of performance; this duty of performance can be enforced by the secondary obligor through the mechanism commonly known as exoneration. Restatement of Suretyship and Guaranty § 21. Second, a secondary obligor who performs may be subrogated to the rights of the obligee against the principal obligor (regardless of whether the principal obligor was charged with notice of the secondary obligation). Restatement of Suretyship and Guaranty § 27. Third, if the principal obligor is charged with notice of the secondary obligation, the principal obligor must reimburse a secondary obligor who performs the obligation. Restatement of Suretyship and Guaranty § 22. If the principal obligor is not charged with notice of the secondary obligation, a secondary obligor who performs is nonetheless entitled to restitution from the principal obligor. Restatement of Suretyship and Guaranty § 26.

An accommodation party is always a surety. Former Article 3 explicitly provided in § 3–415(5) that an accommodation party who paid the instrument was entitled to enforce the instrument against the accommodated party. This right essentially codified the surety's right of subrogation. Other rights of the accommodation party against the accommodated party were left to the general law of suretyship through § 1–103. In § 3–419(e), revised Article 3 also in effect sets forth subrogation rights of accommodation parties by providing that such parties are "entitled to enforce the instrument against the accommodated party." That section also codifies the accommodation party's right to be reimbursed by the accommodated party. Unlike the general law of suretyship, however, that right is not limited to situations in which the accommodated party was charged with notice of the accommodation party's obligation. Thus, it need not be determined whether the accommodated party is charged with notice of the accommodation party's obligation, and the right of restitution that is present in the general law of suretyship is superfluous. Revised Article 3, like former Article 3, leaves the accommodated party's duty of performance and the accommodation party's concomitant right of exoneration to the general law of suretyship through § 1–103.[2]

ISSUE 3

Is an accommodation party entitled to reimbursement if the accommodated party had a defense to its obligation that could have been raised by the accommodation party against the person entitled to enforce the instrument?

DISCUSSION

The juxtaposition of the accommodated party's duty to reimburse the accommodation party (§ 3–419(e)) with the accommodated party's right to raise defenses (§ 3–305(b)) raises important policy issues. If a duty to reimburse exists even when the accommodated party had a defense, that duty could be said to obviate the value of the defense. On the other hand, if no duty to reimburse exists in such circumstances, the cost of performance will be borne ultimately by the accommodation party rather than the accommodated party.

There are a number of different contexts in which the situation may arise. Generally speaking, the accommodation party may raise as a defense to its obligation the defenses of the accommodated party to *its* obligation. See § 3–305(d). There are three exceptions. The accommodated party's defenses of discharge in insolvency proceedings, infancy, and lack of legal capacity are not available to the accommodation party. If the accommodation party pays the instrument when the accommodated party had one of these defenses, the accommodated party has no duty to reimburse the accommodation party. The accommodation party has, in a sense, assumed the risk that such defenses will exist.

Occasionally, an accommodation party will pay an instrument even though the accommodated party has a defense that is available to the accommodation party. In such cases, the existence of the duty to reimburse may depend on whether the accommodation party was aware of the defense at the time it paid the instrument. If the accommodation party was unaware of the defense, there is a duty to reimburse. Thus, there is an incentive for the accommodated party to make the accommodation party aware of any defenses

---

[2]   The revision to Comment 5 to § 3–419 reflects this discussion. See Appendix, par. 5.

it may have. If the accommodation party pays the instrument while aware of a defense of the accommodated party, however, reimbursement would ordinarily not be justified but might be justified in some circumstances. Resolution of this issue is left to the general law of suretyship through § 1–103.[3]

ISSUE 4

Section 3–415(a) provides that an indorser's obligation to pay the instrument upon dishonor is owed, *inter alia*, to a subsequent indorser who pays the instrument. What if both the prior indorser and subsequent indorser are anomalous indorsers?

DISCUSSION

In the general law of suretyship, when there are two secondary obligors for the same underlying obligation, the relationship between those two secondary obligors may be that of co-suretyship or sub-suretyship. In a co-suretyship situation, the two secondary obligors are jointly and severally liable and, as between themselves, have a right of contribution against each other. In a sub-suretyship situation, on the other hand, the second secondary obligor is, in a sense, a surety for the obligation of the first secondary obligor. Thus, as between the two secondary obligors, the first obligor occupies the position of a principal obligor while the later one occupies the position of a secondary obligor. It is often difficult to determine whether the two secondary obligors are co-sureties or sub-sureties, especially in the context of negotiable instruments when the obligations of those parties may be created by a signature alone, unaccompanied by words of explanation.

Article 3 treats successive anomalous indorsers as having joint and several liability on the instrument. See § 3–116(a). If one of the anomalous indorsers pays the instrument, that indorser has a right to receive contribution from the other indorser. See § 3–116(b). Accordingly, the general rule of § 3–415(a), that a subsequent indorser who pays the instrument may recover the full amount of the instrument from a prior indorser, does not apply in such cases. Section 3–116(b) does not recognize a distinction between a co-surety and a sub-surety, but in providing for a right to contribution, § 3–116(b) has the effect of treating anomalous indorsers as though they were co-sureties. Section 3–116(b), however, is subject to "agreement of the affected parties." If the subsequent indorser can prove an agreement with the prior indorser giving the subsequent indorser rights as a sub-surety, that agreement changes the rule of § 3–116(b). If the subsequent indorser pays the instrument and has rights under the agreement as a sub-surety, the subsequent indorser has a right of recourse against the prior indorser for the amount of the payment rather than only a right to contribution; if the prior indorser pays the instrument, there is no right of recourse against the subsequent indorser.[4]

ISSUE 5

What effect do words of guaranty have on the obligation of an indorser to a person entitled to enforce an instrument?

DISCUSSION

Under former § 3–416, the obligation of an indorser who added the words "payment guaranteed" or "collection guaranteed" to the indorsement was different than that of an indorser who did not add those words. The addition of the words "payment guaranteed" (or their equivalent) meant that if the instrument was not paid when due the indorser would pay it without resort to any other party. Thus, an indorser who guaranteed payment could be said to have waived presentment, notice of dishonor, and protest, as well as all demand upon the maker or drawee. In contrast, the addition of the words "collection guaranteed" (or their equivalent) meant that the indorser was required to pay only after the holder reduced its claim against the maker or acceptor to judgment or it was shown that such a proceeding would be useless.

Section 3–419(d) preserves the concept of a guaranty of collection, but no provision is made for a guaranty of payment. Moreover, the preferred treatment given to a guarantor of collection is only applicable when the words accompanying the indorsement indicate "unambiguously that the party is guaranteeing collection rather than payment of the obligation of another party to the instrument." Thus, an indorser who

---

[3] The addition of Comments 6 and 7 to § 3–419 reflect this discussion. See Appendix, par. 6.

[4] The addition of Comment 5 to § 3–415 reflects this discussion. See Appendix, par. 2.

adds the words "payment guaranteed," or the like, to the indorsement has the same liability as an indorser who added no special words to the indorsement. Such an indorser may be entitled, *inter alia*, to notice of dishonor pursuant to § 3–503.[5]

ISSUE 6

May a person entitled to enforce an instrument avoid discharge of an accommodation party pursuant to § 3–605 by "reserving rights" against that party in conjunction with a release, extension, or other modification of the duty of the accommodated party?

DISCUSSION

Under former UCC § 3–606(1)(a), a release, extension, or other modification of the accommodated party's duty accompanied by an express "reservation of rights" against the accommodation party would not discharge that party. This provision paralleled the general law of suretyship in many jurisdictions.

Article 3 rejects the reservation of rights doctrine. The effects of a release, extension, or other modification of the accommodated party's duty cannot be changed by the incantation of a "reservation of rights." Pursuant to § 3–605(b), a release of the accommodated party does not discharge the accommodation party, so there is no need for the person entitled to enforce the instrument to take any action, such as a reservation of rights, to preserve recourse against the accommodation party. Pursuant to § 3–605(c)–(d), an extension or modification of the accommodated party's duty discharges the accommodation party to the extent that the extension or modification would otherwise cause the accommodation party a loss. This discharge cannot be avoided by a "reservation of rights" by the person entitled to enforce the instrument.[6]

ISSUE 7

If a person entitled to enforce an instrument agrees to extend the due date of the accommodated party's performance and, pursuant to § 3–605(c), the extension does not discharge the accommodation party, what is the effect of the extension on the obligation of the accommodation party? In particular, is the due date for the accommodation party's performance extended correspondingly? May the accommodation party perform on the original due date?

DISCUSSION

The person entitled to enforce the instrument will not be able to enforce the instrument against the accommodation party until the extended due date. If the accommodation party is an indorser, this is because an indorser is not liable until dishonor of the instrument, which, under these circumstances, cannot occur until it is unpaid on the extended due date. If the accommodation party is a co-maker, this is because, under § 3–305(d), until the extended due date the accommodation party will be able to assert the accommodated party's defense that, pursuant to the extension agreement, performance is not yet due.

The accommodation party may, however, perform on the original due date. The accommodation party is bound in accordance with the terms of its original engagement. The agreement between the accommodated party and the person entitled to enforce the instrument cannot bind the accommodation party to a change in its obligation without the accommodation party's consent. The effect on the recourse of the accommodation party against the accommodated party of performance by the accommodation party on the original due date is not addressed in § 3–419 and is left to the general law of suretyship.

Even though the accommodation party has the option of paying the instrument on the original due date, the accommodation party is not precluded from asserting its rights to discharge under § 3–605(c) if it does not exercise that option. The critical issue is whether the extension caused the accommodation party a loss by increasing the difference between the accommodation party's cost of performing its obligation on the instrument and the amount recoverable from the accommodated party pursuant to § 3–419(e). The decision by the accommodation party not to exercise its option to pay on the original due date may, under the circumstances, be a factor to be considered in the determination of that issue.[7]

---

[5] The revision to Comment 4 to § 3–419 reflects this discussion. See Appendix, par. 4.

[6] The revision to Comment 3 to § 3–605 reflects this discussion. See Appendix, par. 7.

[7] The revision to Comment 4 to § 3–605 reflects this discussion. See Appendix, par. 8.

PEB COMMENTARY NO. 11

ISSUE 8

What if the person entitled to enforce the instrument agrees, in one transaction, to both an extension of time for the accommodated party's performance and another modification of the accommodation party's obligation? What if there is a dispute as to whether, as a result of these changes, the accommodation party has suffered a loss?

DISCUSSION

This question highlights the difficulties in properly allocating the burden of persuasion when the agreement between the person entitled to enforce the instrument and the accommodated party involves both an extension governed by § 3–605(c) and a modification governed by § 3–605(d). The accommodation party has the burden of demonstrating loss from an extension, but the person entitled to enforce the instrument has the burden of overcoming a presumption of loss from other modifications.

If neither party introduces evidence as to loss causation, the result is full discharge of the accommodation party because § 3–605(d) applies. If the person entitled to enforce the instrument seeks to overcome the presumption of loss from the modification, it is entitled to a presumption that the extension alone caused no loss. Thus, the accommodation party will have to introduce evidence as to the effect of the extension, while the person entitled to enforce the instrument will have to introduce evidence as to the effect of the modification. On the basis of this evidence, the court will make an overall determination of the effect of the changes on the accommodation party's right of recourse against the accommodated party.[8]

ISSUE 9

How can § 3–305(d), which provides that the accommodation party can raise defenses of the accommodated party, be reconciled with § 3–605(b), which provides that a release of the accommodated party does not discharge the accommodation party?

DISCUSSION

While § 3–305(d) provides that an accommodation party can raise most defenses of the accommodated party, that section must be read in conjunction with § 3–605, which governs the effect on the obligation of the accommodation party of an act or omission of the person entitled to enforce the instrument. Section 3–605(b) provides that a release of the accommodated party does not discharge the accommodation party. Thus, while examined in isolation, § 3–305(d) might seem to allow the accommodation party to raise, as a defense to *its* obligation, a release of the accommodated party granted by the person entitled to enforce the instrument, the applicability of that section to such a release must be considered in light of § 3–605(b). If the release of the accommodated party is part of a settlement pursuant to which the person entitled to enforce the instrument accepts partial payment from an accommodated party who is financially unable to pay the entire amount of the note, the transaction falls within the scope of § 3–605(b) and the accommodation party cannot escape liability by asserting § 3–305(d) essentially to nullify § 3–605(b). If, on the other hand, the release of the accommodated party is part of an accord and satisfaction settling a dispute as to the obligation of the accommodated party, the accommodation party may utilize § 3–305(d) to assert that release as a defense to its obligation because § 3–605(b) is not intended to apply to settlement of disputed claims.[9]

ISSUE 10

What sort of language is sufficient to waive discharge under § 3–605?

DISCUSSION

Section 3–605(i) provides that a party is not discharged under that section if the instrument or a separate agreement of the party waives such discharge "either specifically or by general language indicating that parties waive defenses based on suretyship or impairment of collateral." Thus, no particular language or form of agreement is required, and the standards for enforcing such a term are the same as the standards for enforcing any other term in an instrument or agreement. There is no requirement of particularity in

---

8   The revision to Comment 5 to § 3–605 reflects this discussion. See Appendix, par. 9.

9   The revision to Comment 5 to § 3–305 reflects this discussion. See Appendix, par. 1.

referring to the four grounds for discharge established by § 3–605 so long as the language used indicates that suretyship defenses are waived. By allowing the use of general language, the rule recognizes that the use of lengthy provisions containing detailed waivers or even separate identification of each ground for discharge does not necessarily promote greater understanding of an instrument's terms. Yet, the requirement that the language indicate that defenses are being waived assures that a diligent indorser or accommodation party will, at the least, not be unjustly surprised when it is asserted that the terms of the instrument or agreement delete protections that would otherwise be available. In adopting this course, § 3–605 is consistent with the general law of suretyship. See Restatement of Suretyship and Guaranty § 48.[10]

ISSUE 11

As a result of § 3–605(i), may an accommodation party waive whatever protections it may have pursuant to Part 6 of Article 9?

DISCUSSION

Section 3–605(e) provides that impairment of an interest in collateral for the obligation of the accommodated party may discharge the accommodation party. Section 3–605(g) defines impairment of an interest in collateral as including, *inter alia,* failure to comply with applicable law in disposing of collateral. In the case of personal property or fixtures, applicable law includes, of course, Article 9. Thus, failure to comply with the rules in Part 6 of Article 9 concerning disposition of collateral for the accommodated party's obligation constitutes impairment of an interest in collateral. In addition, the accommodation party will qualify as an "obligor" and a "secondary obligor" with respect to that collateral. See § 9–102(a)(59), (71). Obligors and, to a much greater extent, secondary obligors, are provided with substantial protections in Part 6 of Article 9. Section 9–602 provides that, with few exceptions, obligors may not waive these protections. Section 3–605(i), on the other hand, provides that an accommodation party may waive discharge under this section (including discharge for impairment of an interest in collateral pursuant to § 3–605(e)). This does not mean that the accommodation party may waive *all* protections it may have concerning disposition of collateral; rather, it provides for the waiver of protections created by § 3–605. To the extent that Article 9 also provides the accommodation party similar protections, waiver of those protections is governed by Article 9 as interpreted in each jurisdiction.[11]

APPENDIX

1. Comment 5 to § 3–305 is amended by adding an unnumbered paragraph as follows:

Section 3–305(d) must be read in conjunction with Section 3–605, which provides rules (usually referred to as suretyship defenses) for determining when the obligation of an accommodation party is discharged, in whole or in part, because of some act or omission of a person entitled to enforce the instrument. To the extent a rule stated in Section 3–605 is inconsistent with Section 3–305(d), the Section 3–605 rule governs. For example, under Section 3–605(b), discharge under Section 3–604 of the accommodated party does not discharge the accommodation party. As explained in Comment 3 to Section 3–605, discharge of the accommodated party is normally part of a settlement under which the holder of a note accepts partial payment from an accommodated party who is financially unable to pay the entire amount of the note. If the holder then brings an action against the accommodation party to recover the remaining unpaid amount of the note, the accommodation party cannot use Section 3–305(d) to nullify Section 3–605(b) by asserting the discharge of the accommodated party as a defense. On the other hand, suppose the accommodated party is a buyer of goods who issued the note to the seller who took the note for the buyer's obligation to pay for the goods. Suppose the buyer has a claim for breach of warranty with respect to the goods against the seller and the warranty claim may be asserted against the holder of the note. The warranty claim is a claim in recoupment. If the holder and the accommodated party reach a settlement under which the holder accepts payment less than the amount of the note in full satisfaction of the note and the warranty claim, the accommodation party could defend an action on the note by the holder by asserting the accord and satisfaction under Section 3–305(d). There is no conflict with Section 3–605(b) because that provision is not intended to apply to settlement of disputed claims. Other examples of the use of Section 3–305(d) in cases in which Section

---

[10]   The revision to Comment 8 to § 3–605 reflects this discussion. See Appendix, par. 11.

[11]   The revision to Comment 8 to § 3–605 reflects this discussion. See Appendix, par. 11.

PEB COMMENTARY NO. 11

3–605 applies are stated in Comment 4 to Section 3–605. See PEB Commentary No. 11, dated February 10, 1994.

2.   A new Comment 5 to § 3–415 is added as follows:

5.   As stated in subsection (a), the obligation of an indorser to pay the amount due on the instrument is generally owed not only to a person entitled to enforce the instrument but also to a subsequent indorser who paid the instrument. But if the prior indorser and the subsequent indorser are both anomalous indorsers, this rule does not apply. In that case, Section 3–116 applies. Under Section 3–116(a), the anomalous indorsers are jointly and severally liable and if either pays the instrument the indorser who pays has a right of contribution against the other. Section 3–116(b). The right to contribution in Section 3–116(b) is subject to "agreement of the affected parties." Suppose the subsequent indorser can prove an agreement with the prior indorser under which the prior indorser agreed to treat the subsequent indorser as a guarantor of the obligation of the prior indorser. Rights of the two indorsers between themselves would be governed by the agreement. Under suretyship law, the subsequent indorser under such an agreement is referred to as a sub-surety. Under the agreement, if the subsequent indorser pays the instrument there is a right to reimbursement from the prior indorser; if the prior indorser pays the instrument, there is no right of recourse against the subsequent indorser. See PEB Commentary No. 11, dated February 10, 1994.

3.   Comment 3 to § 3–419 is amended by adding an unnumbered paragraph as follows:

An accommodation party is always a surety. A surety who is not a party to the instrument, however, is not an accommodation party. For example, if M issues a note payable to the order of P, and S signs a separate contract in which S agrees to pay P the amount of the instrument if it is dishonored, S is a surety but is not an accommodation party. In such a case, S's rights and duties are determined under the general law of suretyship. In unusual cases two parties to an instrument may have a surety relationship that is not governed by Article 3 because the requirements of Section 3–419(a) are not met. In those cases the general law of suretyship applies to the relationship. See PEB Commentary No. 11, dated February 10, 1994.

4.   Comment 4 to § 3–419 is amended by adding the following two sentences:

Words added to an anomalous indorsement indicating that payment of the instrument is guaranteed by the indorser do not change the liability of the indorser as stated in Section 3–415. This is a change from former Section 3–416(5). See PEB Commentary No. 11, supra.

5.   Comment 5 to § 3–419 is amended by deleting the struck-out words and adding the underlined words as follows:

5.   Subsection (e) ~~restates subsection (5) of present Section 3–415~~ _like former Section 3–415(5), provides that an accommodation party that pays the instrument is entitled to enforce the instrument against the accommodated party._ Since the accommodation party that pays the instrument is entitled to enforce the instrument against the accommodated party, the accommodation party also obtains rights to any security interest or other collateral that secures payment of the instrument. _Subsection (e) also provides that an accommodation party that pays the instrument is entitled to reimbursement from the accommodated party._ See PEB Commentary No. 11, supra.

6.   A new Comment 6 and a new Comment 7 to § 3–419 are added as follows:

6.   In occasional cases, the accommodation party might pay the instrument even though the accommodated party had a defense to its obligation that was available to the accommodation party under Section 3–305(d). In such cases, the accommodation party's right to reimbursement may conflict with the accommodated party's right to raise its defense. For example, suppose the accommodation party pays the instrument without being aware of the defense. In that case the accommodation party should be entitled to reimbursement. Suppose the accommodation party paid the instrument with knowledge of the defense. In that case, to the extent of the defense, reimbursement ordinarily would not be justified, but under some circumstances reimbursement may be justified depending upon the facts of the case. The resolution of this conflict is left to the general law of suretyship. Section 1–103. See PEB Commentary No. 11, supra.

7.   Section 3–419, along with Section 3–116(a) and (b), Section 3–305(d) and Section 3–605, provides rules governing the rights of accommodation parties. In addition, except to the extent that it is displaced by provisions of this Article, the general law of suretyship also applies to the rights of accommodation parties. Section 1–103. See PEB Commentary No. 11, supra.

7.   Comment 3 to § 3–605 is amended by dividing it into two paragraphs, deleting the struck-out words, and adding the underlined words as follows:

3.   Subsection (b) addresses the effect of discharge under Section 3–604 of the principal debtor. In the hypothetical case stated in Comment 1, release of Borrower by Bank does not release Accommodation Party. As a practical matter, Bank will not gratuitously release Borrower. Discharge of Borrower normally would be part of a settlement with Borrower if Borrower is insolvent or in financial difficulty. If Borrower is unable to pay all creditors, it may be prudent for Bank to take partial payment, but Borrower will normally insist on a release of the obligation. If Bank takes $3,000 and releases Borrower from the $10,000 debt, Accommodation Party is not injured. To the extent of the payment Accommodation Party's obligation to Bank is reduced. The release of Borrower by Bank does not affect the right of Accommodation Party to obtain reimbursement from Borrower or to enforce the note against Borrower if Accommodation Party pays Bank. Section 3–419(e). Subsection (b) is designed to allow a creditor to settle with the principal debtor without risk of losing rights against sureties. Settlement is in the interest of sureties as well as the creditor. Subsection (b), however, is not intended to apply to a settlement of a disputed claim which discharges the obligation.

Subsection (b) changes the law stated in former Section 3–606 but the change relates largely to formalities rather than substance. Under former Section 3–606, Bank in the hypothetical case stated in Comment 1 could settle with and release Borrower without releasing Accommodation Party, but to accomplish that result Bank had to either obtain the consent of Accommodation Party or make an express reservation of rights against Accommodation Party at the time it released Borrower. The reservation of rights was made in the agreement between Bank and Borrower by which the release of Borrower was made. There was no requirement in former Section 3–606 that any notice be given to Accommodation Party. The reservation of rights doctrine is abolished in Section 3–605 with respect to rights on instruments eliminates the necessity that Bank formally reserve rights against Accommodation Party in order to retain rights of recourse against Accommodation Party. See PEB Commentary No. 11, dated February 10, 1994.

8.   Comment 4 to § 3–605 is amended by adding six unnumbered paragraphs as follows:

Under other provisions of Article 3, what is the effect of an extension agreement between the holder of a note and the maker who is an accommodated party? The question is illustrated by the following case:

Case #1. A borrows money from Lender and issues a note payable on April 1, 1992. B signs the note for accommodation at the request of Lender. B signed the note either as co-maker or as an anomalous indorser. In either case Lender subsequently makes an agreement with A extending the due date of A's obligation to pay the note to July 1, 1992. In either case B did not agree to the extension.

What is the effect of the extension agreement on B? Could Lender enforce the note against B if the note is not paid on April 1, 1992? A's obligation to Lender to pay the note on April 1, 1992 may be modified by the agreement of Lender. If B is an anomalous indorser Lender cannot enforce the note against B unless the note has been dishonored. Section 3–415(a). Under Section 3–502(a)(3) dishonor occurs if it is not paid on the day it becomes payable. Since the agreement between A and Lender extended the due date of A's obligation to July 1, 1992 there is no dishonor because A was not obligated to pay Lender on April 1, 1992. If B is a co-maker the analysis is somewhat different. Lender has no power to amend the terms of the note without the consent of both A and B. By an agreement with A, Lender can extend the due date of A's obligation to Lender to pay the note but B's obligation is to pay the note according to the terms of the note at the time of issue. Section 3–412. However, B's obligation to pay the note is subject to a defense because B is an accommodation party. B is not obliged to pay Lender if A is not obliged to pay Lender. Under Section 3–305(d), B as an accommodation party can assert against Lender any defense of A. A has a defense based on the extension agreement. Thus, the result is that Lender could not enforce the note against B until July 1, 1992. This result is consistent with the right of B if B is an anomalous indorser.

As a practical matter an extension of the due date will normally occur when the accommodated party is unable to pay on the due date. The interest of the accommodation party normally is to defer payment to the holder rather than to pay right away and rely on an action against the accommodated party that may have little or no value. But in unusual cases the accommodation party may prefer to pay the holder on the original due date. In such cases, the accommodation party may do so. This is because the extension agreement between the accommodated party and the holder cannot bind the accommodation party to a change in its obligation without the accommodation party's consent. The effect on the recourse of the accommodation party against the accommodated party of performance by the accommodation party on the original due date is not addressed in § 3–419 and is left to the general law of suretyship.

Even though X has the option of paying the instrument on the original due date, X is not precluded from asserting its rights to discharge under Section 3–605(c) if it does not exercise that option. The critical issue is whether the extension caused X a loss by increasing the difference between X's cost of performing its obligation on the instrument and the amount recoverable from Corporation pursuant to Section 3–419(e). The decision by X not to exercise its option to pay on the original due date may, under the circumstances, be a factor to be considered in the determination of that issue. See PEB Commentary No. 11, supra.

9. Comment 5 to § 3–605 is amended by adding seven unnumbered paragraphs as follows:

The following is an illustration of the kind of case to which Section 3–605(d) would apply:

Case #2. Corporation borrows money from Lender and issues a note payable to Lender. X signs the note as an accommodation party for Corporation. The loan agreement under which the note was issued states various events of default which allow Lender to accelerate the due date of the note. Among the events of default are breach of covenants not to incur debt beyond specified limits and not to engage in any line of business substantially different from that currently carried on by Corporation. Without consent of X, Lender agrees to modify the covenants to allow Corporation to enter into a new line of business that X considers to be risky, and to incur debt beyond the limits specified in the loan agreement to finance the new venture. This modification releases X unless Lender proves that the modification did not cause loss to X or that the loss caused by the modification was less than X's right of recourse.

Sometimes there is both an extension of the due date and some other modification. In that case both subsections (c) and (d) apply. The following is an example:

Case #3. Corporation was indebted to Lender on a note payable on April 1, 1992 and X signed the note as an accommodation party for Corporation. The interest rate on the note was 12 percent. Lender and Corporation agreed to a six-month extension of the due date of the note to October 1, 1992 and an increase in the interest rate to 14 percent after April 1, 1992. Corporation defaulted on October 1, 1992. Corporation paid no interest during the six-month extension period. Corporation is insolvent and has no assets from which unsecured creditors can be paid. Lender demanded payment from X.

Assume X is an anomalous indorser. First consider Section 3–605(c) alone. If there had been no change in the interest rate, the fact that Lender gave an extension of six months to Corporation would not result in discharge unless X could prove loss with respect to the right of recourse because of the extension. If the financial condition of Corporation on April 1, 1992 would not have allowed any recovery on the right of recourse, X can't show any loss as a result of the extension with respect to the amount due on the note on April 1, 1992. Since the note accrued interest during the six-month extension, is there a loss equal to the accrued interest? Since the interest rate was not raised, only Section 3–605(c) would apply and X probably could not prove any loss. The obligation of X includes interest on the note until the note is paid. To the extent payment was delayed X had the use of the money that X otherwise would have had to pay to Lender. X could have prevented the running of interest by paying the debt. Since X did not do so, X suffered no loss as the result of the extension.

If the interest rate was raised, Section 3–605(d) also must be considered. If X is an anomalous indorser, X's liability is to pay the note according to its terms at the time of indorsement. Section 3–415(a). Thus, X's obligation to pay interest is measured by the terms of the note (12%) rather than by the increased amount of 14 percent. The same analysis applies if X had been a co-maker. Under Section 3–412 the liability of the issuer of a note is to pay the note according to its terms at the time it was issued. Either obligation could be changed by contract and that occurred with respect to Corporation when it agreed to the increase in the interest rate, but X did not join in that agreement and is not bound by it. Thus, the most that X can be required to pay is the amount due on the note plus interest at the rate of 12 percent.

Does the modification discharge X under Section 3–605(d)? Any modification that increases the monetary obligation of X is material. An increase of the interest rate from 12 percent to 14 percent is certainly a material modification. There is a presumption that X is discharged because Section 3–605(d) creates a presumption that the modification caused a loss to X equal to the amount of the right of recourse. Thus, Lender has the burden of proving absence of loss or a loss less than the amount of the right of recourse. Since Corporation paid no interest during the six-month period, the issue is like the issue presented under Section 3–605(c) which we have just discussed. The increase in the interest rate could not have affected the right of recourse because no interest was paid by Corporation. X is in the same position as X would have been in if there had been an extension without an increase in the interest rate.

The analysis with respect to Section 3–605(c) and (d) would have been different if we change the assumptions. Suppose Corporation was not insolvent on April 1, 1992, that Corporation paid interest at the higher rate during the six-month period, and that Corporation was insolvent at the end of the six-month period. In this case it is possible that the extension and the additional burden placed on Corporation by the increased interest rate may have been detrimental to X.

There are difficulties in properly allocating burden of proof when the agreement between Lender and Corporation involves both an extension under Section 3–605(c) and a modification under Section 3–605(d). The agreement may have caused loss to X but it may be difficult to identify the extent to which the loss was caused by the extension or the other modification. If neither Lender nor X introduces evidence on the issue, the result is full discharge because Section 3–605(d) applies. Thus, Lender has the burden of overcoming the presumption in Section 3–605(d). In doing so, Lender should be entitled to a presumption that the extension of time by itself caused no loss. Section 3–605(c) is based on such a presumption and X should be required to introduce evidence on the effect of the extension on the right of recourse. Lender would have to introduce evidence on the effect of the increased interest rate. Thus both sides will have to introduce evidence. On the basis of this evidence the court will have to make a determination of the overall effect of the agreement on X's right of recourse. See PEB Commentary No. 11, supra.

10.   The second paragraph of Comment 6 to § 3–605 is amended to read as follows:

In some states a real property grantee who assumes the obligation of the grantor as maker of a note secured by the real property becomes by operation of law a principal debtor and the grantor becomes a surety. The meager case authority was split on whether former Section 3–606 applied to release the grantor if the holder released or extended the obligation of the grantee. Revised Article 3 takes no position on the effect of the release of the grantee in this case. Section 3–605(b) does not apply because the holder has not discharged the obligation of a "party," a term defined in Section 3–103(a)(8) as "party to an instrument." The assuming grantee is not a party to the instrument. The resolution of this question is governed by general principles of law, including the law of suretyship. See PEB Commentary No. 11, supra.

11.   Comment 8 to § 3–605 is amended by adding the underlined words as follows:

8.   Subsection (i) is a continuation of former law which allowed suretyship defenses to be waived. <u>As the subsection provides, a party is not discharged under this section if the instrument or a separate agreement of the party waives discharge either specifically or by general language indicating that defenses based on suretyship and impairment of collateral are waived.</u> No particular language or

form of agreement is required, and the standards for enforcing such a term are the same as the standards for enforcing any other term in an instrument or agreement.

Subsection (i), however, applies only to a "discharge under this section." The right of an accommodation party to be discharged under Section 3–605(e) because of an impairment of collateral can be waived. But with respect to a note secured by personal property collateral, Article 9 also applies. If an accommodation party is a "debtor" under Section 9–105(1)(d) 9–102(a)(28), an "obligor" under Section 9–102(a)(59), or a "secondary obligor" under Section 9–102(a)(71), the accommodation party has rights under Article 9. Under Section 9–501(3)(b) 9–602, many rights of an Article 9 debtor or obligor under Part 6 of Article 9 under Section 9–504(3) and Section 9–505(1), which deal with disposition of collateral, cannot be waived except as provided in Article 9. These Article 9 rights are independent of rights under Section 3–605. Since Section 3–605(i) is specifically limited to discharge under Section 3–605, a waiver of rights with respect to Section 3–605 has no effect on rights under Article 9. With respect to Article 9 rights, Section 9–501(3)(b) 9–602 controls. See PEB Commentary No. 11, supra.

PEB COMMENTARY NO. 12
SECTION 9–302*
(February 10, 1994)

ISSUE

Section 9–302(3) provides that the filing requirements of Article 9 are not applicable to the perfection of a security interest in goods covered by a certificate of title statute. In that circumstance, perfection of a relevant security interest can be had only through compliance with the certificate of title statute. If the secured party perfects its security interest pursuant to such a statute and then assigns the security interest, must the assignee take some further action to reflect that it has become the secured party in order to continue such perfection, for example, having the certificate of title endorsed or reissued to name itself as the secured party or lienholder? Or is § 9–302(2), which provides that if a secured party assigns a perfected security interest, "no filing under this Article is required in order to continue the perfected status of the security interest against creditors of and transferees from the original debtor," applicable in this instance so that the assignee need not take any further action?

DISCUSSION

Section 9–302(1) states the general rule that in order to perfect a security interest under Article 9, a financing statement must be filed, except for certain specified transactions. See Comment 1. Section 9–302(3) provides for an additional exception: "The filing of a financing statement *otherwise required by this Article* is not necessary or effective to *perfect* a security interest in property" (emphasis supplied) that is subject to a filing system set up outside the UCC, including specifically, the certificate of title statute "of this state" (subsection (b)) or "a certificate of title statute of another jurisdiction under the law of which indication of a security interest on the certificate is required as a condition of perfection (subsection (2) of Section 9–103)" (subsection (c)).[1]

Inasmuch as every jurisdiction that has enacted Article 9 has also enacted a certificate of title (or ownership) statute, the effect of these provisions is that perfection of Article 9 security interests in property covered by certificate of title laws must always be accomplished by compliance with those laws. In essence, § 9–302(3) substitutes compliance with the requirements of the applicable certificate of title statute for filing a financing statement under Article 9 as the means for perfecting a security interest in the affected property.

---

* *Note from West Advisory Panel: Referring to unrevised Article 9. See revised § 9–310.*

[1] Although some certificate of title statutes condition perfection on a physical notation being placed on the certificate and are clearly covered by § 9–302(3)(c) and the conflict provisions of § 9–103(2), others, while contemplating notation, provide that perfection is achieved by delivery of designated documents to a state official and could, therefore, arguably fall outside of the provisions of § 9–302(3)(c) and § 9–103(2). The Alabama Supreme Court in *Lightfoot v. Harris Trust & Savings Bank,* 357 So.2d 654, 23 UCC Rep.Serv. (Callaghan) 750 (Ala.1978), dismissed the argument and held that Article 9 applies to goods covered by a certificate of title issued under either kind of statute. This Commentary supports the position taken in *Lightfoot.*

(A major exception to this rule is that the filing provisions of Article 9 remain applicable where the collateral is inventory held for sale by a person who is in the business of selling goods of that kind, for example, an automobile dealer. Section 9–302(3)(b).)

Section 9–302(2) states a corollary rule to § 9–302(1)'s general rule on perfection, which is that the perfected security interest can be assigned by the secured party to another person without the need for a further filing under Article 9 and that the security interest of the assignee continues to be perfected, without further action, against the creditors of and transferees from the original debtor. The security interest created in favor of the secured party is transferred by the assignment to the assignee;[2] it is the same security interest and not a new security interest. Accordingly, neither a new financing statement nor a statement of assignment is required to continue the perfection of the assignee's security interest in the property. Section 9–405 permits, but does not require, the assignee to file a statement of assignment against the original debtor. By not filing, the assignee may encounter certain risks with adverse business and legal consequences, and therefore, the assignee may opt to file a statement of assignment even though not required to do so. Some risks an assignee may encounter if the statement of assignment is not filed are: the assignor might fraudulently or inadvertently release or terminate the security interest; the assignor might assign the security interest to an innocent third party who might then file a statement of assignment and become the secured party of record; or the assignor might go out of business or disappear and make it difficult or impossible for the assignee to be able to respond to inquiries from third parties concerning the status of the security interest. The decision whether to file or not file a statement of assignment is essentially a business decision for the assignee to make, taking into account these various risk factors, as well as the cost, administrative convenience, and the like.

Inasmuch as the purpose of § 9–302(3) and (4) is to substitute compliance with the perfection requirements of the applicable certificate of title statute for filing under Article 9, § 9–302(4) makes it clear that it is only with regard to such perfection requirements that Article 9 is displaced by the certificate of title statute: "in all other respects the security interest is subject to" Article 9. Therefore, in order to determine whether § 9–302(2) is applicable to security interests perfected under § 9–302(3) and (4), it is first necessary to ascertain whether the certificate of title statute applicable to the particular transaction contains provisions concerning an assignment of a security interest and, if so, whether such provisions relate to perfection.

Even though all jurisdictions have enacted certificate of title statutes, there is a wide variation among those statutes. The Uniform Motor Vehicle Certificate of Title and Anti-Theft Act (the "Uniform Act") has been enacted in 11 jurisdictions. 11 Uniform Laws Annotated 250 (1993 Supp.). In a jurisdiction that has enacted the Uniform Act, it is clear from the provisions thereof concerning the assignment of a security interest that such provisions do not affect the perfected status of the assigned security interest. Section 22(b) of the Uniform Act expressly provides that the "assignee may, *but need not to perfect the assignment,* have the certificate of title endorsed or issued with the assignee named as lienholder, upon delivering to the Department [of Motor Vehicles] the certificate and an assignment by the lienholder named in the certificate in the form the Department prescribes." (Emphasis supplied.)

In other jurisdictions, however, the certificate of title statute contains provisions concerning the assignment of a security interest, but the statute is not clear whether such provisions relate to perfection. In that circumstance, the guiding principle is that "[t]he certificate of title statutes, when applied as lien perfection statutes, should be construed in harmony with the general U.C.C. scheme for perfection of security interests." *In re Littlejohn,* 519 F.2d 356, 358, 17 UCC Rep.Serv. (Callaghan) 254, 257 (10th

---

2   The assignment of that security interest, whether a grant of a security interest in the underlying security agreement (chattel paper) between the assignor-secured party and the original debtor, or a sale of that chattel paper (§ 9–102(1)(b)), is a separate and distinct secured transaction and involves different considerations. The validity and perfection of the assignee's security interest against *the creditors of and transferees from the assignor-secured party* is governed entirely by Article 9 and a jurisdiction's certificate of title statute has no applicability. Perfection would be accomplished by the assignee either taking possession of the chattel paper (§ 9–305) or by filing a financing statement against the assignor-secured party (§ 9–304(1)). Comment 7 to § 9–302 makes it clear that the rules set forth in § 9–302(1) and (2) do not apply to the perfection of the assignee's interest in the security agreement when viewed in relation to the creditors of and transferees from the assignor-secured party. Section 9–302(2) only obviates the need to take further steps in order to continue perfection of the security interest in the underlying vehicle against *the creditors of and transferees from the original debtor.*

Cir.1975). Accord, *General Motors Acceptance Corp. v. Rupp,* 951 F.2d 283, 16 UCC Rep.Serv.2d (Callaghan) 510 (10th Cir.1991); *In re Circus Time, Inc.,* 641 F.2d 39, 30 UCC Rep.Serv. (Callaghan) 1475 (1st Cir.1981). In so construing the statutes, the courts have recognized that the primary purposes of the certificate of title statutes are to facilitate the identification of motor vehicles or boats, the ascertainment of their owners, and the prevention of theft or fraud in their transfer; to provide the state with a convenient and accessible record of title for tax purposes; and to lend stability to the business climate surrounding the sale of motor vehicles and like goods. As observed by the court in *In re Circus Time, Inc.:*

> Absolute compliance with the requirements of the Certificate of Title Acts is not necessary to perfect a security interest in a vehicle. Courts have properly interpreted such acts in light of the perfection provisions of the Uniform Commercial Code, which recognize as effective to perfect a security interest any filing that 'substantially compl[ies] with the requirements of [the Code] . . . even though it contains minor errors which are not seriously misleading.' U.C.C. § 9–402(8); [other citations omitted]. . . .

641 F.2d at 42, 30 UCC Rep.Serv. at 1479. To the extent that § 9–302(2) and the certificate of title statutes can be construed as consistent with each other, the Code's underlying purpose and policy of making "uniform the law among the various jurisdictions" (§ 1–102(2)(c)) will, of course, be better served. See *In re Hollis,* 301 F.Supp. 1, 3 (D.Conn.1969) ("[I]t is the duty of a court construing the [Certificate of Title] Act to create a uniform national interpretation.").

The corollary of the foregoing principle is that a strict and literal construction of a certificate of title statute should be avoided if it produces a result that unnecessarily conflicts with the Uniform Commercial Code. Additionally, courts have refused to apply a highly refined and technical interpretation to a certificate of title statute to defeat the perfection of a security interest. See *In re Williams,* 608 F.2d 1015 (5th Cir.1979) and *Janney v. Bell,* 111 F.2d 103 (4th Cir.1940). By way of analogy, the overwhelming majority of courts have upheld the rights of a buyer in ordinary course of business under § 2–403 even though the buyer did not obtain certificate of title. See, e.g., *Dugdale of Nebraska, Inc. v. First State Bank,* 420 N.W.2d 273, 277, 6 UCC Rep.Serv.2d (Callaghan) 111, 116–17 (Neb.1988) and Comment 7 to § 2A–304, approving this line of cases; see also *Associates Discount Corp. v. Rattan Chevrolet, Inc.,* 462 S.W.2d 546, 8 UCC Rep.Serv. (Callaghan) 117 (Tex.1970) and *Sterling Acceptance Co. v. Grimes,* 168 A.2d 600, 1 UCC Rep.Serv. (Callaghan) 487 (Pa.Super.1961), applying the same rationale to § 9–307. This same rationale should be applied to the question of whether an assignee must do something under a certificate of title statute to continue the perfected status of an assigned security interest when the statute contains provisions on assignments but does not specifically mandate any action by the assignee for perfection, or makes no or only isolated references to assignments, or is ambiguous as to what action an assignee must take and makes no mention of the consequence of the assignee's failure to take action with respect to the issue of perfection.

A number of other jurisdictions have incorporated parts of § 22 of the Uniform Act into their certificate of title statutes, but most of these states did not include the phrase "but need not to perfect the assignment" in their versions of § 22. See, e.g., Code of Alabama § 32–8–63. Even without the quoted phrase, it would be consistent with § 9–302(2) to view these statutes as permitting but not requiring the assignment to be noted on the certificate of title. This would also be consistent with § 9–405, which provides a permissive device for noting assignments in the public records. Those certificate of title statutes that do not specifically require, as a condition of perfection, that an assignee have the certificate of title endorsed or reissued to name itself as lienholder, but instead contain phrases like: "the title officer *shall* file each assignment received," or "*upon* receiving a certificate," or other words of similar import, may be construed consistently with § 9–302(2) as being merely permissive on this issue and as not requiring further action in order to continue perfection.

Section 9–302(2) can also be construed consistently with the certificate of title statutes in those jurisdictions where the latter is either silent as to assignments, e.g., Arizona Revised Statutes Annotated § 28–325 (Liens and encumbrances), or where there is an isolated reference to an assignee but no mention of perfection. For example, New Jersey Statutes Annotated § 39:10–9 states that "the name and the business or residence address of the secured party or his assignee shall be noted on the certificate of ownership," but makes no reference to the assignee having to note its name on the certificate in place of a secured party whose name is already noted or taking any other action such as filing a notice or document with the Division of Motor Vehicles. In those circumstances, § 9–302(3) and (4) do not have the effect of substituting the requirements of the certificate of title statute relating to perfection for "filing under this Article," inasmuch

APPENDIX E

as the certificate of title statute does not state, within the purview of those UCC provisions, any requirement that the assignment of the security interest be noted on the certificate of title. As a result, § 9–302(2) remains applicable.

Some jurisdictions have certificate of title statutes that are ambiguous about what an assignee must do or whether the assignee must act in a particular way, but do not, within the meaning of § 9–302(2), relate such required action by the assignee to the continued perfection of the security interest. Pennsylvania is an example of a jurisdiction having such a statute. Section 1134(b) of Pennsylvania Consolidated Statutes Annotated, 75 Pa.C.S.A. § 1134(b), is an assignment section in the certificate of title statute which provides that the "assignee shall deliver to the department the certificate of title and an assignment by the lienholder. . . ." The certificate of title statute does not specify either a time period within which such action is to be performed or the consequences of the assignee's failure to act with respect to perfection. Id. The only consequence specified in the statute for the assignee's failure to act is contained in § 1134(a) which says, "any person without notice of the assignment is protected in dealing with the lienholder as the holder of the security interest and the lienholder remains liable for any obligations as lienholder until the assignee is named as lienholder on the certificate." 75 Pa.C.S.A. § 1134(a). That language is identical to that in § 22(a) of the Uniform Act. Section 9–302(2) and these statutes may be construed consistently with each other as not requiring the security interest to become unperfected because of the assignee's failure to have its name noted on the certificate of title. In view of the express provision in § 22(b) obviating the need for the assignee to take any action "to perfect the assignment" (see pages 3–4), the language in § 22(a), viewed in that context, does not appear to relate to perfection. The language merely restates the other potential risks and adverse business and legal consequences discussed above that might result from the failure of the assignee to have its name noted on the certificate. (See page 3.)

In summary, § 9–302(2) and certificate of title statutes that do not specifically address perfection in connection with the assignment of a security interest can be construed consistently. As a result, in accordance with the mandate of § 9–302(4) that "in all other respects the security interest is subject to" Article 9, § 9–302(2) remains applicable. In order to interpret and apply § 9–302(2) in a manner that is harmonious with the various certificate of title statutes and to simplify, clarify, and modernize the law applicable to the assignment of security interests, "no filing under this Article" as used in § 9–302(2) should be liberally and broadly construed to include "no notation of a security interest on a certificate of title" when not expressly required as a condition for perfection by the applicable certificate of title statute. See § 1–102. This interpretation is consistent with the basic function of certificate of title statutes in that the continued notation of the security interest on the certificate gives notice to creditors of and transferees from the original debtor of the existence of the security interest in the property covered by the certificate of title.

CONCLUSION

If a security interest has been perfected under the applicable certificate of title statute and is thereafter assigned, and that statute does not expressly require the assignee to take some further action with respect to the certificate of title to reflect that it has become the secured party in order to continue such perfection, § 9–302(2) is applicable and the assignee is not required to place its name on the certificate of title "in order to continue the perfected status of the security interest against creditors of and transferees from the original debtor." If the assignee, nevertheless, wishes to have the assignment noted on the certificate of title, its right to do so and the procedure therefor are governed by the applicable certificate of title statute.

The Official Comment to § 9–302 is amended by adding the following:

10. If a security interest has been perfected under the applicable certificate of title statute and is thereafter assigned, and that statute does not expressly require the assignee to take some further action with respect to the certificate of title to reflect that it has become the secured party in order to continue such perfection, § 9–302(2) is applicable and the assignee is not required to note its name on the certificate of title "in order to continue the perfected status of the security interest against creditors of and transferees from the original debtor." See PEB Commentary No. 12, dated February 10, 1994.

PEB COMMENTARY NO. 13
THE PLACE OF ARTICLE 4A IN A WORLD OF
ELECTRONIC FUNDS TRANSFERS
(February 16, 1994)

ISSUE

Article 4A of the UCC deals primarily with electronic funds transfers made through the banking system.[1] Adopted by the ALI and the National Conference of Commissioners on Uniform State Laws in 1989, Article 4A has had a substantial measure of success. At this time it is law in all but a few states, has been incorporated into Regulation J of the Federal Reserve System[2] and, through their incorporation of New York State law, has been written into the Rules of CHIPS[3] and NACHA.[4]

For a transfer of funds to be governed by Article 4A, an instruction must be given to a bank ("Bank I" in this scenario) either to make payment to the person who is the ultimate recipient of the funds or to instruct some other bank ("Bank II") to make the payment.[5] If the instruction is that Bank I make payment to the ultimate recipient, the bank is dealing with its own depositor or someone who has a direct customer relationship with the bank. That relationship, while occasionally dealt with by Article 4A, is largely outside the coverage of the statute.[6]

Article 4A concentrates principally upon the relationship of one bank with another bank. Assuming that the instruction given to Bank I is that Bank I instruct Bank II to make the payment,[7] Bank II can as easily be located abroad as in the United States. For this reason, it is desirable that Article 4A find compatibility with such international law as exists in this area.

The major international legal document dealing with the subject of electronic funds transfers is the Model Law on International Credit Transfers ("Model Law") adopted in 1992 by the United Nations Commission on International Trade Law ("UNCITRAL"). It covers basically the same type of transaction as does Article 4A, although it requires the funds transferred to have an international component.[8]

No foreign State has, to date, adopted the Model Law as its own local law. Nevertheless, in examining international payments, this Commentary assumes that the United States is subject to Article 4A and that the remainder of the world, because of the lack of development in the law otherwise, has adopted the Model Law now offered to it by the United Nations.[9]

---

[1] While Article 4A was clearly drafted with electronic funds transfers in mind and while its present effect will be upon such transfers, it is not limited to electronic transfers and applies by its terms to all transfers among banks outside the checking system. This concept is elaborated upon in Comment 6 to § 4A–104.

[2] 12 C.F.R. Part 210, Appendix B (1993).

[3] New York Clearing House Interbank Payments Systems, CHIPS Rule 3.

[4] National Automatic Clearing House Association, ACH Rule 1.7.

[5] We need not deal with who gives the instruction to Bank I. It might be a company or an individual originating a funds transfer; it might be another bank which is moving along an instruction that had been given to it.

[6] Provisions of Article 4A that do deal with the relationship of beneficiary's bank and beneficiary are §§ 4A–404 and 4A–405.

[7] Bank II can, having received the instruction from Bank I, in turn instruct another bank to make the payment. In this way, a series of banks can be involved in one transfer of funds from the party originating the transfer (called the "Originator") to the party ultimately receiving it (called the "Beneficiary").

[8] Model Law, Article 1(1) requires that "any sending bank and its receiving bank (be) in different States." Henceforth, references to Article numbers will refer to the Model Law; references to sections beginning with "4A" will refer to the UCC.

[9] Full uniformity would of course occur if the United States adopted the Model Law. It is unlikely in the extreme that this will occur. See the Conclusion to this Commentary.

APPENDIX E

DISCUSSION

We will hypothesize two funds transfers. One is sent by a New York bank to San Francisco ("NY–SF") and the other to London ("NY–L").[10]

We may correctly assume that a New York bank will have both business reason and technical capacity to send funds with equal ease to both San Francisco and London. Administratively, it will normally make little if any difference to the bank whether the transfer goes east or west. For the two transfers to be subject to different legal regimes can, however, create problems. For example, if New York imposes a different level of responsibility upon the bank for completion of the funds transfer depending upon where it goes, the bank's fee structure might vary between the two. Similarly, if there are different requirements, depending upon the location of the receiving bank, of persons who must receive notices or duties as to correcting a transfer made in error, different expectations will be created for the bank's systems. The banking system was clear in its reactions to Article 4A and the Model Law through its drafting that it would find it both difficult and expensive to administer electronic funds transfers subject to conflicting legal systems.

In its final form, the Model Law is close to Article 4A both in its overall structure and in its details, but is not the same.

A.   Conflicts of Laws

The conflicts of law provisions of Article 4A and the Model Law tell us what law will apply to these transfers. In this respect, the two statutes are essentially harmonious: § 4A–507(a)(1) and an optional Article Y[11] in the Model Law both prescribe that, for most issues, the law of the receiving bank will govern.[12] Thus, Article 4A will generally govern for NY–SF, and the Model Law for NY–L.[13]

B.   Working of the Two Laws

Some examples will illustrate differences between Article 4A and the Model Law:

1.   Consumer Transactions

Both Article 4A and the Model Law were written without a focus on consumer-related transactions and, therefore, without the particular protections that typically accompany laws written for the benefit of consumers. In Article 4A, this is evidenced by an exclusion through § 4A–108 of transactions covered by the federal Electronic Fund Transfer Act of 1978 ("EFTA"), which is tailored for the consumer funds transfer. In the Model Law, a footnote to Article 1 provides that the Law "does not deal with issues related to the protection of consumers."[14]

---

[10]   We need not deal with funds transfers made to New York from different sending banks. The UCC and the Model Law generally base their choice of law provisions on the law of the receiving bank. Thus, all funds transfers received in New York would be dealt with by New York law and there would be no problem of inconsistencies. See the discussion, *infra,* under A. Conflicts of Laws.

[11]   UNCITRAL was unable to agree whether a conflicts of law article belonged in the Model Law and, consequently, created an optional provision.

[12]   Details of both Article 4A and the Model Law introduce complexities. For example, both permit the parties to select the applicable law. In an Article 4A transaction, the relationship between a beneficiary (that is, the party who will ultimately receive the money being transferred) and its bank are governed pursuant to § 4A–507(a)(2) by the law of the jurisdiction where the bank is located. Article 4A also contains rules that will govern when the funds transfer is made through a funds-transfer system (see text *infra,* at Notes 22–24), and that system has its own choice of law rules. This Commentary does not deal with such variations.

[13]   One cannot exhaust the potential conflicts problems that arise even within this simple structure. For example, when the originator of the funds transfer instructs its New York bank to send funds to San Francisco or to London, the relationship of originator and bank is governed by the law of the receiving bank—New York. A funds transfer may also pass through several jurisdictions and raise additional issues. For the NY–SF and the NY–L transfers, however, the rule is that the law of California and of England will, respectively, apply.

[14]   The Model Law does not present the sharp distinction between consumer and business transactions represented by the positioning of Article 4A and EFTA. The quoted language reflects the philosophy behind the Model Law—that its design is really for large, commercially oriented funds transfers—and justifies the positions taken on various issues. The Model Law on its face governs both consumer and commercial funds transfers and it was left to individual states to decide how their consumers would be treated.

This surface harmony leads, however, to problems. For example, the EFTA does not deal with the number of issues treated by Article 4A. It does not, for example, define the time when the originator of a consumer funds transfer has made payment to the beneficiary, a question answered by both Article 4A and the Model Law. If the NY–L and the NY–SF funds transfers were consumer in nature and this question arose, it would be answered for NY–L and not for NY–SF (since the latter would be governed by the EFTA).[15]

2. Variation by Agreement

Both Article 4A[16] and the Model Law[17] generally permit the parties to vary their statutory obligations by agreement except as may be specifically prohibited. Areas of specific prohibition vary, however, between the two laws.

For example, the obligation of a receiving bank that is also the beneficiary's bank to pay the amount of an order that it has accepted to the beneficiary may not be varied by agreement under § 4A–404(c). It may be varied under Article 10 of the Model Law. If our New York bank were to enter into agreements with its receiving banks defining circumstances under which an accepted order should not thereupon be paid to the beneficiary, the agreements would be effective for the NY–L transfer and not for the NY–SF transfer.[18]

3. Use of a Funds-Transfer System

Most electronic funds transfers are executed through funds-transfer systems.[19] Section 4A–206(a) provides that a funds-transfer system is the agent of the sender. Errors made by a funds-transfer system are, therefore, the errors of the bank that sent the funds through the system. (For this purpose, however, the FedWire system is excluded, and the Federal Reserve bank operating FedWire is deemed to be just another bank.) The Model Law is silent on this subject.

Thus, if, in a NY–SF transfer, the New York bank gives a payment order of $100,000 to the CHIPS system and CHIPS mistakenly transmits $1,000,000, the error is that of the New York bank, which is considered to have sent $1,000,000.[20] In a NY–L transfer, one cannot be certain. It appears, however, that the error is that of CHIPS.[21]

Under Article 4A,[22] funds-transfer system rules are given legal effect and may bind even parties who are not members of the system. Under the Model Law, the effect of a systems rule upon nonparties is not

---

[15] Presumably a court would look to analogies in other laws to see how the question should be answered in the NY–SF context. Presumably, the closest law for this purpose would be Article 4A and the court would use the Article 4A solution.

A limited number of consumer transactions—those handled through the FedWire system and a few others such as unplanned telephone transfers—are excluded from the EFTA by Federal Reserve Regulation E and returned to coverage under Article 4A. See 12 C.F.R. § 205.3(b) (1992).

[16] Section 4A–501(a).

[17] Article 4.

[18] One might imagine a New York bank agreeing with certain of its correspondents that they would not pay money to certain named beneficiaries without checking first with New York. That such an agreement would be effective for foreign banks but not for American banks was not the subject of detailed discussion, but one might imagine that foreign spokesmen could have wanted to support greater freedom for their banking system than the United States believes should be tolerated.

[19] A "funds-transfer system" is defined under § 4A–105(a)(5) as a "wire transfer network, automated clearing house, or other communication system of a clearing house or other association of banks through which a payment order by a bank may be transmitted to the bank to which the order is addressed." Well-known domestic funds-transfer systems include the FedWire system of the Federal Reserve Banks, the CHIPS system of the New York Clearing House Association, and the systems of the National Automated Clearing House Association. Foreign systems include the Society of Worldwide Interbank Financial Telecommunication ("SWIFT"), the United Kingdom Clearing House Automated Payments System ("CHAPS"), and the Japanese BOJ-NET system.

[20] See Comment 2 to § 4A–206.

[21] This sort of event and its consequences are typically covered in the rules of a funds-transfer system. As discussed above, both Article 4A, § 4A–501, and the Model Law, Article 4, authorize agreements varying their provisions. Rules of a funds-transfer system would probably be considered agreements under the Model Law and are agreements specifically under § 4A–501.

[22] Section 4A–501(b).

prescribed and, therefore, will be determined according to the law of contracts.[23] Generally, under American contract law, those who are not parties to a contract are not bound by its terms. If a funds-transfer system with its own rules is part of the two described funds transfers, the law applicable to the NY–L and the NY–SF transfers can be different.

4. Authentication Procedures

For the protection of the banking system and bank customers, both Article 4A and the Model Law establish procedures for the authentication of messages. The two systems work in similar manners.[24] Both protect a receiving bank if it properly authenticates a message, even if the message was sent without the sender's proper authority.[25] Both also relieve the sender of responsibility if it can prove that the message was sent by someone outside the sender's influence.[26] The Model Law[27] reimposes responsibility on the sender if the receiver can prove that the sender was responsible. Article 4A does not contain the reimposition responsibility, although this is implicit since the receiving bank will attempt to disclaim its liability by proving that the sender was responsible.

The effect of agreements varying the terms of the law again varies between Article 4A and the Model Law. Article 4A holds that (subject to certain limited and restricted exceptions) the parties may not vary its statutory authentication rights and liabilities by agreement.[28] The Model Law has no such prescription and the parties may alter their legal authentication relationships by agreement.[29] Thus, if the New York bank in our hypothetical agrees with its customers for a result other than as provided by the statutes, it will be effective for the NY–L transfer, but not for the NY–SF transfer.

5. Acceptance and Rejection

Under both Article 4A and the Model Law, a receiving bank is given the essentially unrestricted power to accept or reject an order sent to it. An order may be rejected by a notice sent to the sender.[30]

a. Receiving Banks Other Than the Beneficiary's Bank

If a bank (other than the beneficiary's bank) does not send a rejection notice, the legal consequences vary between the two laws; on the other hand, they resolve themselves, as the following discussion illustrates, without undue tension between them.

Under Article 4A, an order may be accepted by a bank other than the beneficiary's bank only by that bank executing a new order in favor of the next bank in line.[31] Failure to give a notice of rejection does not cause the bank to incur a penalty; neither does it result in acceptance. If the bank does not move, or "execute," the order, it is not deemed to have accepted the order, and the order is automatically canceled by operation of law in five days.[32] If the receiving bank has received actual funds covering the order, it must return the funds and pay interest to the sending bank until cancellation.[33]

Under the Model Law, a receiving bank that executes a new order is deemed to have accepted the order sent to it as under Article 4A.[34] An order that is neither executed nor rejected is deemed—unlike the Article

---

[23] *Report of UNCITRAL,* U.N. Doc. A/46/17 (1991), par. 98.

[24] The relevant sections are §§ 4A–201, 4A–202, and 4A–203 for Article 4A, and Article 5 for the Model Law.

[25] Section 4A–202(b); Article 5(2).

[26] Section 4A–203(a)(2); Article 5(4).

[27] Article 5(4).

[28] Section 4A–202(f).

[29] Article 5(3) does provide that for the parties to agree that a sending bank will be bound by an authenticated message, the authentication must be reasonable. Section 4A–202(b) has a similar requirement.

[30] Section 4A–210(a) and Model Law Articles 7 and 9.

[31] Section 4A–209(a).

[32] Section 4A–211(d).

[33] Section 4A–210(b) and §§ 4A–402(c) and 4A–402(d).

[34] Article 7(2)(c).

4A approach—to be accepted if funds covering the order have been paid to the receiving bank.[35] The receiving bank then is obligated to issue a new order in accordance with the responsibilities put by the Model Law upon the acceptor of an order. Similar to Article 4A, the payment order ceases to have effect after five days.[36] If the transfer is not completed, however, the bank must return any payment received by it plus interest to the date of payment[37] and does not suffer any further liability for its failure to execute the accepted order.

In the instant situation, still assuming that the San Francisco and the London banks are receiving banks that are not the beneficiary's bank, if an order is neither accepted nor rejected and if funds have been advanced to that bank (that is, if the order is "covered"), there would not be any duty upon the San Francisco bank to accept (that is, to execute the order in favor of the next bank in line) and the funds paid would bear interest for five days; for the NY–L transfer, the payment order would be accepted by the London bank, there would be a duty—albeit for a brief time—to move the funds, the acceptance would cease after five days, and the payment (the "cover") would bear interest until returned. The financial differences do not appear consequential since the receiving bank has the use of the funds until they are returned. Under the general structure of both laws not to impose more than interest penalties for failure to reject, the receiving bank in London would not incur other penalties for failing to honor its responsibility to move the funds.

b. The Beneficiary's Bank as a Receiving Bank

The ability of the beneficiary's bank to accept or reject payment orders is handled with essential comparability under the two laws. Under Article 4A, there are three events that trigger such a bank's acceptance, including rules based upon the relationship between the bank and the beneficiary, "cover" of the order to the bank, and the passage of time.[38] The Model Law contains eight events signifying acceptance by the beneficiary's bank.[39] One does not anticipate significant variations in practice between the two laws.

6. Time for Execution

Although their approaches to the question of when a receiving bank must take action upon an accepted payment order differ in the two laws, they have an essential similarity. For example, both Article 4A[40] and the Model Law[41] basically require that an order be executed on the day it is received. The Model Law, however, permits the order to be sent on the next day. In the event that occurs, however, the receiver must "execute for value as of" the prior day (that is, must give the next bank in line interest for the day that execution was delayed).

7. Cancellation

Both statutes provide the mechanism for a payment order to be canceled. Under Article 4A, if there is a security procedure between sender and receiver guarding the authenticity of the original order, "the" (that is, the same) procedure must be followed for cancellations.[42] If the original order was not subject to a security procedure, the cancellation order need not be authenticated. Under the Model Law, it is necessary that every cancellation be subject to some security procedure, not necessarily the same one originally used and even if no security procedure was originally used.[43] If the cancellation order is not authenticated, it is ineffective.

In addition, under the Model Law, it appears that every cancellation order must be authenticated. Under Article 4A, the cancellation must be authenticated only if there was an authentication procedure applicable to the original order.

---

[35] While there is also a five-day cancellation provision, it is applicable only if the order is neither accepted nor rejected and we are dealing here with a deemed acceptance. Article 7(2), 7(3), and 7(4).

[36] Article 7(4).

[37] Article 14(1). This differs from Article 4A, which requires interest only for the five days.

[38] Section 4A–209(b).

[39] Article 9(1).

[40] Section 4A–301(b).

[41] Article 11(1).

[42] Section 4A–211(a).

[43] Article 12(4).

The Article 4A approach is applicable in the NY–SF transfer; the Model Law governs the NY–L transfer.

8.   The "Money-Back Guarantee"

As part of their underlying philosophy that the originator's funds will be transferred by the banking system, both Article 4A and the Model Law contain a so-called "money-back guarantee." This provides that, if the total transfer of money is not completed, the originator (who, under the model we have been following, either gave an order to the New York bank or was someone who gave an order at an earlier stage in the total funds transfer that was transmitted by another bank to the New York bank) will obtain a refund plus accumulated interest and certain other charges.[44] The provisions of the two laws are consistent in major respects. Neither permits variation by agreement. The Model Law, however, relieves receiving banks from the guarantee if they can demonstrate that they accepted the transfer despite what had been perceived as "a significant risk."[45]

9.   Underpayments and the Recovery of Overpayments

Both laws contain essentially comparable provisions requiring sending banks who sent orders in amounts less than the amounts sent to them to send the differences and to permit banks who sent excessive payments to recover the excess.[46]

10.   Consequential Damages

In general, the measure of damages provided by both laws for violations of their standards is the payment of interest for moneys held for the times beyond which the law allows. Occasionally, additional charges incident to the transfer will be included.[47]

Probably the single most controversial issue underlying the drafting of Article 4A was whether banks should have liability for consequential damages resulting from their negligence or failure to comply with the requirements of the statute. The banks argued that, given the traditionally low fees that they charged to transfer funds electronically, they could not at the same time subject themselves to the risk of immense and unquantifiable consequential damage recoveries. Business users of electronic funds-transfer systems asserted that consequential damages were an appropriate result of the banks' transfer responsibilities. Consequential damages were ultimately eliminated from Article 4A.[48]

Consequential damages may, however, be imposed against a bank under the Model Law. In view of the intense opposition of some national banking systems and their representatives in the United Nations to this concept, however, they were reduced in scope to where they will be imposed only where a bank has acted "(a) with the specific intent to cause loss, or (b) recklessly and with actual knowledge that loss would be likely to result."[49]

Thus, the NY–L transfer by a New York bank involves greater risk than does the NY–SF transfer.

11.   Request for Assistance

Article 13 of the Model Law "requests" a bank that receives a payment order to assist the originator and each prior bank and to seek the assistance of the next receiving bank "in completing the banking

---

[44]   Section 4A–402 and Model Law Article 14.

[45]   A "prudent" originator's bank may agree with the originator that the money-back guarantee will not apply to a funds transfer if the bank accepted the transfer despite what it perceived as a "significant risk" that the transfer might not be completed. The example frequently given for this situation is where the transfer is to pass through areas involved in armed conflict.

[46]   Section 4A–303(a) and § 4A–303(b), and Model Law Articles 15 and 16.

[47]   See §§ 4A–303(b) and 4A–305(b).

[48]   This result was ultimately agreed to by the major business interests in exchange for the consent by the banks to the "money-back guarantee" discussed in paragraph 8 above. Consequential damages were, however, authorized in favor of an ultimate beneficiary of a funds transfer against its bank that refuses to pay it after being notified of the particular circumstances giving rise to such damages. Section 4A–404(a). Consequential damages may also be provided for by express written agreement with a receiving bank. Section 4A–305(c).

[49]   Article 18. The terms used within the quotation marks have established meanings under United States tort law with the exception of "actual knowledge that loss would be likely to result."

procedures of the credit transfer." Article 4A has no equivalent. In the NY–L transfer, the New York bank is subject to the request; in the NY–SF transfer, it is not. There is no penalty for failing to abide by the request.[50]

The absence of penalty may suggest that a bank need have no concern about the requirement. On the other hand, the presence of a law does impose an obligation to comply. In addition, assuming that there are bank regulators enforcing compliance, the regulators in London could bring an action against the New York bank for specific performance of its obligation to assist under Article 13; United States regulators could not.

CONCLUSION

The Model Law was drafted for world-wide enactment. It is, however, unlikely in the extreme that it will be enacted in the United States in the foreseeable future.[51] It was generally accepted by the foreign states in UNCITRAL that there would be no movement to repeal Article 4A in the United States and adopt the Model Law in its stead. The two laws basically live together in harmony, but to the extent there are differences they must be recognized and, to the extent possible, avoided or adjusted by agreement.

The PREFATORY NOTE to Article 4A is amended by adding the following paragraph at the end of the PREFATORY NOTE:

International transfers.

The major international legal document dealing with the subject of electronic funds transfers is the Model Law on International Credit Transfers adopted in 1992 by the United Nations Commission on International Trade Law. It covers basically the same type of transaction as does Article 4A, although it requires the funds transferred to have an international component. The Model Law and Article 4A basically live together in harmony, but to the extent there are differences they must be recognized and, to the extent possible, avoided or adjusted by agreement. See PEB Commentary No. 13, dated February 16, 1994.

PEB COMMENTARY NO. 14
SECTION 9–102(1)(b)*
(June 10, 1994)

ISSUE

Does the application of Article 9 to the sale of accounts and chattel paper prevent the transfer of ownership of accounts or chattel paper?

DISCUSSION

Section 9–102(1)(b) provides, subject to certain exceptions,[1] that Article 9 applies "to any sale of accounts or chattel paper."[2] Comment 2 to § 9–102 explains that "a sale of [accounts or chattel paper is] covered by subsection (1)(b) whether intended for security or not. . . . The buyer then is treated as a secured party, and his interest as a security interest."[3] This Commentary examines whether that application means

---

[50] Banks normally engage in this type of assistance even without statutory direction.

[51] For further material on the subject of this Commentary, see Bhala, Rakesh K., *Paying for the Deal*, 42 Kan.L.Rev. No. 3 (1993), in which Professor Bhala uses micro-economic and banking concepts to evaluate the utility of both Article 4A and the UNCITRAL Model Law.

[*] *Note from West Advisory Panel: Referring to unrevised Article 9. See revised § 9–318.*

[1] See § 9–104(f).

[2] For ease of reference, this Commentary refers to accounts and chattel paper collectively as "receivables."

[3] This drafting technique is implemented by conforming definitions. Section 1–201(37), for example, states that the term "security interest" includes "any interest of a buyer of accounts or chattel paper which is subject to Article 9." Section 9–105(1)(m) provides that the term "secured party" includes "a person to whom accounts or chattel paper have been sold." Section 9–105(1)(d) provides that the term "debtor" includes "the seller of accounts or chattel paper." Section 9–105(1)(c) provides that the term "collateral" includes "accounts and chattel paper which have been sold." That such inclusion was simply a drafting technique was long ago freely acknowledged by Homer Kripke in paragraph 2 of his Practice Commentary to § 9–502 of the New York UCC, Cons.Laws N.Y.Annot.Book 62½, Part 3 (McKinney 1964): "Subsection (2) of [§ 9–502] recognizes throughout the fact that this article [9] includes within its

APPENDIX E

that ownership of receivables may not be transferred or that a buyer's interest in receivables is limited to one of security.

It is a fundamental principle of law that an owner of property may transfer ownership to another person.[4] Were a statute intended to take away that right, it would do so explicitly and such a significant curtailment of rights would be supported by substantial reason. No such reason is expressed or implied in the Code or the Official Comments. Indeed, the sale of receivables long antedates adoption of the Code, and it cannot be supposed that either the drafters of the Code or the legislatures that enacted it intended to work so drastic a change in existing law without clearly saying so. Moreover, a close reading of the text of Article 9 and its Comments, particularly in the context of the pre-Code history, compels the conclusion that Article 9 does not prevent the transfer of ownership.

Article 9 contemplates that sales of receivables may exist, and that the consequences of a sale differ from those of a transfer for security. For example, § 9–502(2) recognizes a distinction in the consequences under Article 9 between sales of receivables and transactions secured by receivables. It provides that, "[i]f the security agreement secures an indebtedness, the secured party must account to the debtor for any surplus. . . . But, if the underlying transaction was a sale of accounts or chattel paper, the debtor [as seller of the receivables] is entitled to any surplus [from collections of the sold receivables] . . . *only if* the security agreement so provides." (Emphasis added.) Section 9–504(2) has virtually identical language. Furthermore, Comment 4 to § 9–502, after acknowledging that "there may be a true sale of accounts or chattel paper," clarifies that "[t]he determination whether a particular assignment constitutes a sale or a transfer for security is left to the courts."[5]

Why, then, was Article 9 made "applicable" to the sale of receivables? The introductory Comment and Comment 2 to § 9–102 explain that Article 9 applies to both sales and security transfers of receivables to avoid the need to distinguish between such transfers for Article 9 purposes:

[C]ertain sales of accounts and chattel paper are brought within this Article [9] to avoid difficult problems of distinguishing between transactions intended for security and those not so intended.

* * *

2. * * *

Commercial financing on the basis of accounts and chattel paper is often so conducted that the distinction between a security transfer and a sale is blurred, and a sale of such property is therefore covered by subsection (1)(b) whether intended for security or not. . . .

The reason for subjecting both sales and secured transactions to Article 9 was to inform third parties of existing interests in a debtor's receivables and to provide protection for all types of assignments of receivables:

There was an obvious reason for the inclusion of sales: it was necessary to *protect* [transferees] not only [in] straight accounts receivable financing but also [in] arrangements of the factoring type. [Emphasis added.] Article 9 merely follows the pre-Code accounts receivable statutes [covering sales of accounts and chattel paper as well as security transfers].[6]

---

coverage not only true security transactions in which accounts are collateral, but also sales of accounts . . . which are included by artificial definitions."

[4] See, e.g., Comment 1 to § 2–403.

[5] This Commentary likewise does not discuss what factors a court should look to in determining whether a particular transfer of receivables constitutes a sale or a secured loan. It addresses only whether Article 9 negates sale treatment even though a court viewing those factors would, but for Article 9, determine that the transfer was a sale. For a discussion of factors that courts have found relevant in determining whether a given transfer of receivables constitutes a sale or a secured loan, see Steven L. Schwarcz, *Structured Finance, A Guide to The Principles of Asset Securitization,* at 28–35 (2d ed. 1993).

[6] 1 Gilmore, *Security Interests in Personal Property* § 8.7, at 275; § 10.5, at 308 (Little Brown & Co. 1965). Indeed, § 1–201(37) of the 1952 Official Draft of the UCC referred to a "financing buyer" of receivables and § 9–102(1)(b) referred to a "financing sale" of receivables. The word "financing" was deleted from both sections in Supplement No. 1 to the 1952 Official Draft, January 1955, pursuant to the 1954 Recommendations of the Editorial Board, for the reason that the phrases "financing buyer" and "financing sale" were perceived as "undefined concepts" and it was thought better to include

This is not to say, however, that Article 9 has no impact upon a buyer's ownership rights regarding the purchased receivables. For example, a failure to perfect as required by Article 9 may leave the transferee's ownership of the receivables subject to the claims of third parties, such as the seller's lien creditors or trustee in bankruptcy.[7] This perfection requirement, however, does not by its terms or by implication affect the transfer of ownership as between the seller and buyer.[8]

At least two Circuit Court opinions interpret the Code consistently with this Commentary. In *Major's Furniture Mart v. Castle Credit Corp.,*[9] the Third Circuit considered whether a transfer of a company's receivables should be construed as a sale or a secured loan. By considering that question, the court started from the premise that a transaction that Article 9 calls a security interest could nonetheless be a sale. If the transaction was a sale, the transferee would be entitled to surplus collections of the receivables. If the transaction was only for security, then the transferor would be entitled to the surplus collections. The court followed Comment 4 to § 9–502 and looked to non-UCC law to determine whether the transaction was a sale.

In *In re Contractors Equipment Supply Co.,*[10] the Ninth Circuit affirmed a lower court decision by looking to non-UCC law to determine that the transfer of receivables in question was a loan. The court stated that had there been a sale, the transferor would *not* be entitled to any surplus because "[a] sale entails the passage of title."[11]

In *Octagon Gas Systems, Inc. v. Rimmer,*[12] however, the Tenth Circuit, after stating that a purchased royalty interest in a natural gas system was an account, erroneously stated that "[t]he impact of applying Article 9 to [the buyer's] account is that Article 9's treatment of accounts sold as collateral would place [the buyer's] account within the property of [the seller's] bankruptcy estate."[13] The court reached this determination despite the transfer of the royalty interest purporting to be an outright sale of all the seller's interest. To the extent the court relied on Article 9 in reaching its determination, this Commentary adopts a contrary position.

CONCLUSION

Article 9's application to sales of receivables does not prevent the transfer of ownership. Official Comment 2 to § 9–102 therefore is amended by adding the following paragraph:

> Neither Section 9–102 nor any other provision of Article 9 is intended to prevent the transfer of ownership of accounts or chattel paper. The determination of whether a particular transfer of accounts

---

all sales of receivables, subject to the exclusion provisions of § 9–104. The exclusion in § 9–104(f) was correspondingly broadened to exclude from Article 9 certain types of sales of receivables that, "by their nature, have nothing to do with commercial financing transactions." See Comment 6 to § 9–104.

[7] Section 9–301(1). Just as Article 9's perfection requirement may impact upon the rights of a buyer of receivables without negating that a sale has occurred, so too does the requirement of § 9–502(2) that a buyer of receivables with a right of recourse against the seller "must proceed in a commercially reasonable manner. . . ." Section 9–502(2) does not, however, articulate an ownership principle but rather is an abbreviated codification of the rule that would be applicable in any event under common law and § 1–103, whether the recourse right is characterized as one of suretyship or contract. Assuming perfection, the sold receivables are beyond the reach of the seller's creditors or purported transferees from the seller not earlier filed or perfected. The buyer does not have to account in any way to the seller or its creditors, and the seller has no right of redemption or other legal or equitable interests in the receivables. These absolute ownership rights can exist in the buyer even if the purchase of the receivables is "with recourse." See Comment 4 to § 9–502.

[8] Provisions of Article 9 that deal with matters other than perfection and priority likewise are not intended to give a seller any legal or equitable interests in receivables that have been sold. For example, the debtor's right under § 9–506 to redeem collateral prior to consummation of foreclosure by a secured party applies only where the transfer of the collateral was intended for security because it is only there that the debtor has retained rights that must be foreclosed.

[9] 602 F.2d 538, 26 UCC Rep.Serv. (Callaghan) 1319 (3d Cir.1979).

[10] 861 F.2d 241, 7 UCC Rep.Serv.2d (Callaghan) 583 (9th Cir.1988).

[11] 861 F.2d at 245, 7 UCC Rep.Serv.2d at 587 (referring to § 9–502). Also see 861 F.2d at 245 n. 8, 7 UCC Rep.Serv.2d at 587–88 n. 8: "If the present case involved a true [sale], under basic contract law principles, the notification would have taken the account receivable out of the estate."

[12] 995 F.2d 948, 20 UCC Rep.Serv.2d (Callaghan) 1330 (10th Cir.1993), cert. denied, [510] U.S. [993], 114 S.Ct. 554, 126 L.Ed.2d 455 (1993).

[13] 995 F.2d at 955, 20 UCC Rep.Serv.2d at 1338.

or chattel paper constitutes a sale or a transfer for security purposes (such as in connection with a loan) is not governed by Article 9. Article 9 applies both to sales of accounts or chattel paper and loans secured by accounts or chattel paper primarily to incorporate Article 9's perfection rules. The use of terminology such as "security interest" to include the interest of a buyer of accounts or chattel paper, "secured party" to include a buyer of accounts or chattel paper, "debtor" to include a seller of accounts or chattel paper, and "collateral" to include accounts or chattel paper that have been sold is intended solely as a drafting technique to achieve this end and is not relevant to the sale or secured transaction determination. See PEB Commentary No. 14, dated June 10, 1994.

PEB COMMENTARY NO. 15
ELECTRONIC FILING UNDER ARTICLE 9*
(July 16, 1996)

ISSUE

Do data transmitted electronically to a filing office, which provide all the information required under the applicable provision of Article 9, constitute a financing statement or other filing under Article 9?

DISCUSSION

Under § 9–402(1), a financing statement is sufficient if it gives the names of the debtor and secured party, is signed by the debtor, and gives the specified other information. Similar signing and writing requirements appear for amendments, continuation and termination statements, assignments, and other filings. Under § 1–201(39), "signed" includes any symbol executed or adopted by a party with present intention to authenticate a writing. A "writing" includes any intentional reduction to tangible form. Section 1–201(46). Obviously a paper signed by the debtor meeting the other requirements of § 9–402(1) qualifies as a financing statement.

The UCC mandates that it is to "be liberally construed and applied to . . . modernize the law governing commercial transactions [and] to permit the continued expansion of commercial practices." Section 1–102. This provision mandates that the provisions of the UCC be interpreted and applied in a manner that is consistent with and furthers the utilization of advances in technology and resultant changes in commercial practices. See, e.g., Goss v. Trinity Sav. & Loan Ass'n, 813 P.2d 492, 13 UCC Rep. Serv. 2d (Callaghan) 1138 (Okla. 1991) (intent of UCC is to aid in expansion of commercial practices; court, when faced with widespread commercial practice, should acknowledge it). Two of the stated purposes of the PEB Commentaries are "to apply the principles of the UCC to new or changed circumstances" and "to otherwise improve the operation of the UCC." Applying the statutory mandate, this Commentary concludes that data transmitted electronically to a filing office which provide all the information required under the applicable provision of Article 9 constitute a financing statement or other filing under Article 9. No statutory change is required to accommodate electronic filing.

This Commentary addresses only the issue of electronic filing under Article 9. Conclusions concerning the meaning of "signed" and "writing" in that context are not intended to suggest a meaning for those terms in other contexts, where relevant policies and factual considerations may differ. This Commentary also does not mandate that any state offer electronic filing or require any filing party to utilize that technique merely because it is offered. Prudent business practices to guard against fraud and forgery should be observed in the electronic environment just as they should be in the paper environment.

With respect to electronic filing under Article 9, Iowa has been accepting electronically transmitted financing statements and other filings since 1992, and Kansas initiated an electronic filing system in 1995. Texas, the state with the largest annual volume of filings in the nation, has recently implemented an electronic filing system. The American National Standards Institute has already created a standard (ANSI standard X12 154) for the electronic transmission to filing offices of financing statements and subsequent Article 9 filings. The Texas program is based on this standard.

---

*   *Note from West Advisory Panel: Referring to unrevised Article 9.*

PEB COMMENTARY NO. 15

Nothing in Article 9 mandates a particular mode of transmission of a filing to the filing office. Section 9–403 is written in media neutral language, providing that either "[p]resentation for filing . . . or acceptance of the statement by the filing officer constitutes filing. . . ." Indeed, although Part 4 of Article 9 does not utilize the term "send" with respect to filing a financing statement, it is instructive that the drafters defined that term as follows: "in connection with any writing . . . [send] means to deposit in the mail or deliver for transmission by any other usual means of communication. . . . The receipt of any writing . . . within the time at which it would have arrived if properly sent has the effect of a proper sending." Section 1–201(38). This definition further illustrates the Code's policy of flexibility, a desire to enable commercial practices to utilize future technological development, and a methodology of looking to practical results. Moreover, nothing in Article 9 appears to limit the filing officer's use of any particular technology for the receipt, storage, or retrieval of filings, whether such use occurs pursuant to published rules or regulations or simply as a matter of administrative procedure, suggesting that filing officers have the authority to adopt procedures and methodologies deemed by them to be reasonably suited to carrying out their legislatively mandated tasks. Finally, nothing in Article 9 mandates that a financing statement or other filing be on paper or any other particular medium. Article 9 prescribes the sufficiency of a financing statement filing not in terms of its form but in terms of its content, i.e., the presence or absence of the required data.

Signing is not limited to the cursive writing of the letters of the party's name by means of a pen grasped in the hand.[1] The focus of the definition is not on the technique but rather on the intent to authenticate. Official Comment 39 to § 1–201 states: "The inclusion of authentication in the definition of 'signed' is to make clear that as the term is used in this Act a complete signature is not necessary. Authentication may be printed, stamped or written; it may be by initials or by thumbprint. It may be on any part of the document and in appropriate cases may be found in a billhead or letterhead. No catalog of possible authentications can be complete and the court must use common sense and commercial experience in passing upon these matters. The question always is whether the symbol was executed or adopted by the party with present intention to authenticate the writing."

The statute and the Official Comment support the conclusions that (i) any symbol, including a typed or printed expression of the person's name, can constitute a signature; (ii) the person need not be the party who places it, physically or otherwise, on the financing statement; and (iii) the adoption of the symbol by the signer need not occur at the instant of such placement but can occur theretofore or thereafter.[2] In an electronically transmitted financing statement or other filing, the signature requirement is satisfied by the signer's adoption of a symbol that is transmitted electronically to the filing office. The symbol may be the signer's name, an asterisk, or any other symbol, provided that it is adopted by the signer. The symbol may be keyed or otherwise placed on the electronic "form" in the signature "box" (a field agreed upon by the sender and the filing office as the field for authentication data, such as that approved for such use under the ANSI standard). For validity as a "signature," there is no statutory requirement that the authentication data or symbol be transmitted to or received by the filing office in any particular medium or form.[3] The

---

[1] With respect to sufficiency of a typed or printed (i.e., non-manually written) name as a signature, see, e.g., In re Save-On-Carpets of Arizona, Inc., 545 F.2d 1239, 20 UCC Rep. Serv. (Callaghan) 1081 (9th Cir. 1976) (secured party's intent to authenticate manifested by typed corporate name and its credit manager's name typed in appropriate spaces and submission for filing). Cases such as In re Kane, 1 UCC Rep. Serv. (Callaghan) 582, 587 (E.D. Pa. 1962) (required "an actual signature manually produced by a writing instrument in the hand of the signer in direct contact with the document being executed"), and In re Carlstrom, 3 UCC Rep. Serv. (Callaghan) 766, 772, 773 (D. Me. 1966) (stating that to incorporate § 1–201(39) into § 9–402 "does considerable violence to the language and context of § 9–402," and that § 1–201(39) "must be held to be inconsistent with the context of § 9–402 and hence inapplicable") are disapproved. Other cases where a filing without a manual signature was held insufficient are consistent with the analysis set forth in this Commentary because they are grounded not on the proposition that a manual signature is absolutely required but on the absence of evidence that the debtor had adopted some other symbol or otherwise intended to authenticate.

[2] For example, in Barber & Ross Co. v. Lifetime Doors, Inc., 810 F.2d 1276, 3 UCC Rep. Serv. 2d (Callaghan) 41 (4th Cir. 1987), cert. denied, 484 U.S. 823 (1987), the seller's pre-printed sales literature, given to the buyer prior to the making of an oral requirements agreement, was sufficient to satisfy the statute of frauds requirement of a signed writing by virtue of the printed trademark on the literature. See also John Deere Co. v. First Interstate Bank of Arizona, N.A., 709 P.2d 890, 42 UCC Rep. Serv. (Callaghan) 1110 (Ariz. App. 1985) (corporate debtor's name signed by principal in his representative capacity sufficient as debtor's signature although debtor did not come into existence until six days later).

[3] In Barber-Greene Co. v. National City Bank of Minneapolis, 816 F.2d 1267, 3 UCC Rep. Serv. 2d (Callaghan) 1234 (8th Cir. 1987), the court held that the adoption need not be in writing. In that case, a financing statement was signed by the debtor's typewritten name followed by a cursive writing of the debtor's name that had been manually

ultimate fact of legal significance, the signer's intent to authenticate, can be established by any evidence lawfully admissible in court. A common mode of establishing such intent to authenticate will likely be the presentation of language to that effect in a security agreement or other writing signed by the debtor. A prudent secured party, of course, will obtain and preserve evidence of the debtor's adoption of a particular data or symbol with the intent to authenticate.

"Writing" *includes* any intentional reduction to tangible form. Even when the electronically transmitted filing data are not in tangible form before or during transmission, they are reducible to such form by the filing officer. Data in fact reduced to such form constitute "writings." Data transmitted electronically to the filing office may be reduced to tangible form in a variety of ways; common forms include microfilm, microfiche, magnetic tape, CD-ROM, other disks, other tapes, optical storage devices, and paper. All of these (and no attempt is here made to be exhaustive) are tangible and are writings.

Courts have repeatedly demonstrated their ability and willingness, in many contexts, in and outside of the Uniform Commercial Code, to accommodate technological developments and resultant changes in business practices. For example, telegrams have long been accepted by the courts as "writings" sufficient to satisfy the statute of frauds.[4] See, e.g., Howley v. Whipple, 48 N.H. 487 (1869) ("it makes no difference whether [the agent] writes the offer or the acceptance in the presence of his principal and by his express direction, with a steel pen an inch long attached to an ordinary penholder, or whether his pen be a copper wire a thousand miles long"). More recently, the statute of frauds was held to have been satisfied by a telegram transmitted pursuant to telephonic instructions to the telegraph operator. Hillstrom v. Gosnay, 188 Mont. 388, 614 P.2d 466 (1980). To the same effect in the case of a "signed writing" sent by teletype, see Joseph Denunzio Fruit Co. v. Crane, 79 F. Supp. 117 (S.D. Cal. 1948), mot. for new trial granted, 89 F. Supp. 962 (S.D. Cal. 1950), rev'd, 188 F.2d 569 (9th Cir. 1951), cert. denied, 342 U.S. 820 (1951), and cert. denied, 344 U.S. 829 (1952), and by mailgram, see Hessenthaler v. Farzin, 388 Pa. Super. 37, 564 A.2d 990 (1989) (mailgram is a "signed writing" within real estate statute of frauds; dictum in a footnote alludes favorably to e-mail, telexes, and faxes), and McMillan, Ltd. v. Warrior Drilling & Engineering Co., Inc., 512 So.2d 14, 4 UCC Rep. Serv. 2d (Callaghan) 1546 (Ala. 1986). In Apex Oil Co. v. Vanguard Oil & Service Co., Inc., 760 F.2d 417, 40 UCC Rep. Serv. (Callaghan) 1221 (2d Cir. 1985), a telex was held to constitute a "writing" satisfying the requirement of § 2–201(2) of a writing confirming the existence of a contract.

A telecopy or "fax" is a commonly used device for the electronic transmission of data. A fax may send data directly from one computer to another without the data having been on paper at the outset or being "printed out" on paper by the recipient; or the data might be on paper at one end and not the other; or the data might be on paper at both ends, giving the appearance of a reproduction.[5] Accepting telecopies as writings within the meaning of § 2–201, see International Products & Technologies, Inc. v. Iomega Corp.,

---

performed by the secured party's manager. The jury was instructed that the debtor had signed the financing statement by adoption if the debtor "intended [it] to be valid and expressed that intent by word or deed. . . ." 816 F.2d at 1269, 3 UCC Rep. Serv. 2d at 1237. The jury found that the debtor had knowingly authorized the secured party to sign on its behalf and had, before the filing, adopted the signature with present intent to authenticate. Id. The appellate court reviewed the statutory definition of "signed" and the related Official Comment, and looked to the policy supportive of continued expansion of commercial practices. 816 F.2d at 1270–71, 3 UCC Rep. Serv. 2d at 1239. It rejected the argument that adoption required a writing, relying both on the "common sense and commercial practice" language in the Official Comment and on Benedict v. Lebowitz, 346 F.2d 120, 2 UCC Rep. Serv. (Callaghan) 747 (2d Cir. 1965) ("creditor had not [manually] signed the financing statement but court held that the act of typing in the name [in body of the statement, not in the signature block at the bottom] coupled with [the] subsequent act of filing the statement indicated creditor's intent to authenticate"). 816 F.2d at 1271, 3 UCC Rep. Serv. 2d at 1240. Rejecting the assertion that a requirement of adoption in writing was intended by the draftsmen in order to eliminate issues of authentication or fraud, the court stated: "But it is undisputed in this case that the debtor was aware of the financing statement, the debtor had read the statement, and by its word and deed had accepted the statement as authentic. From time to time, [debtor] requested and received from [secured party] releases of its security interest. A written adoption in this case was unnecessary." Id.

[4]   Article 9 does not state that a financing statement must be in writing. It is only the signature requirement, an authentication requirement, that speaks in terms of a "writing." The Article 9 requirement of a financing statement serves a notice function which can be fulfilled electronically; the requirement is not based on possibilities of fraud. Statute of frauds cases are mentioned simply as illustrations of courts being able to deal with new technology in relation to a pre-existing statutory framework.

[5]   Electronically transmitted data ordinarily do not purport to be copies of the data in a prior medium. Thus, cases and statutory language concerning "copies" are not relevant to the issue dealt with in this Commentary.

PEB COMMENTARY NO. 16

1989 U.S. Dist. LEXIS 13589, 10 UCC Rep. Serv. 2d (Callaghan) 694 (E.D. Pa. 1989), aff'd without op., 908 F.2d 962 (3d Cir. 1990); Bazak Int'l Corp. v. Mast Industries, Inc., 73 N.Y.2d 113, 538 N.Y.S.2d 503, 535 N.E.2d 633, 7 UCC Rep. Serv. 2d (Callaghan) 1380 (1989). Approximately a dozen states presently accept financing statements transmitted to the filing office by fax.

CONCLUSION

Data transmitted electronically to a filing office, which provide all the information required under the applicable provision of Article 9, constitute a financing statement or other filing under Article 9 and no statutory change is required to accommodate electronic filing under Article 9. Official Comment 1 to § 9–402 is amended by the addition of the following language at the end: Nothing in Article 9 mandates a particular mode of transmission to the filing office of the data required to be supplied for a financing statement or other filing, mandates that a filing be on paper or any particular medium, or limits the filing officer's use of any particular technology for the receipt, storage, or retrieval of filings. Accordingly, data transmitted electronically to the filing office and reduced to tangible form constitute a financing statement or other filing under Article 9 if they provide all the information required under the applicable provision of Article 9. See PEB Commentary No. 15, dated July 16, 1996.

PEB COMMENTARY NO. 16
SECTIONS 4A–502(d) AND 4A–503
(July 1, 2009)

INTRODUCTION

A funds transfer is a series of payment orders starting with an originator's order to the originator's bank to cause a sum certain amount of money to be paid to a beneficiary. The series of payment orders culminates with a beneficiary bank crediting the account of a beneficiary for that sum certain. U.C.C. § 4A–104(a) (definition of funds transfer). The series of payment orders is a mechanism used to make a transfer of value through the debiting and crediting of bank accounts from the originator to the beneficiary. The funds transfer often involves one or more intermediary banks that receive a payment order from the originator's bank or another bank. The receiving intermediary bank then issues its own payment order to another intermediary bank or the beneficiary's bank. Several cases have raised the issue of whether a creditor of the beneficiary may serve creditor process on an intermediary bank and thus capture the value transfer while it is in process.

Article 4A provides that the creditor of the beneficiary may not serve creditor process on any bank other than the beneficiary's bank. U.C.C. § 4A–502(d). Official Comment 4 to § 4A–502 further explains the concept, and does so in relation to a creditor of either the beneficiary or the originator:

> A creditor of the originator can levy on the account of the originator in the originator's bank before the funds transfer is initiated . . . [but] cannot reach any other funds *because no property of the originator is being transferred*. A creditor of the beneficiary cannot levy on property of the originator and until the funds transfer is completed by acceptance by the beneficiary's bank of a payment order for the benefit of the beneficiary, *the beneficiary has no property interest in the funds transfer which the beneficiary's creditor can reach* (emphasis supplied).

Official Comment to § 4A–503 further explains both § 4A–502(d) and § 4A–503 are designed to prevent interruption of a funds transfer after it has been set in motion and that, in particular, intermediary banks are protected.

A funds transfer is a series of payment orders that create contractual obligations only as to the sender and receiver of each payment order. Those contractual obligations are not the property of either the originator or the beneficiary. In a simple funds transfer, the originator instructs its bank, the originator's bank, to debit the originator's account and order the beneficiary's bank to credit the beneficiary. Those instructions are payment orders. U.C.C. § 4A–103 (definition of payment order, "beneficiary," and "beneficiary's bank"); § 4A–104 (definition of "funds transfer," "originator," and "originator's bank"). See also Regulation J, 12 C.F.R. § 210.26 (governing payment orders issued to or by a federal reserve bank). The originator is the sender of the payment order and the originator's bank is the receiving bank. U.C.C. § 4A–

103 (definitions of "sender" and "receiving bank"). If the originator's bank accepts the originator's payment order, the originator owes an obligation to the originator's bank to pay the amount of the payment order. U.C.C. § 4A–402(b). The originator's bank owes an obligation to the originator to execute the accepted payment order according to the instructions of the originator. U.C.C. § 4A–302.

In execution of the originator's payment order, the originator's bank may send its own payment order to the beneficiary's bank, but more commonly it will send its payment order to an intermediary bank. U.C.C. § 4A–104 (definition of "intermediary bank"). The originator's bank is the sender of its payment order and the intermediary bank is the receiving bank of that second payment order. Upon acceptance of that second payment order, the intermediary bank owes an obligation to the originator's bank, not the originator, to execute its own payment order that replicates *the originator's bank's payment order* (emphasis supplied). U.C.C. § 4A–302 (obligation in execution owed by receiving bank to its sender). The originator's bank, not the originator, owes payment of the originator bank's payment order to the intermediary bank. U.C.C. § 4A–402(b) (sender owes obligation to pay the amount of an accepted payment order to its receiving bank). In the event the originator is not able to pay the amount of its payment order to the originator's bank, but the originator's bank's payment order has been accepted by the intermediary bank, the originator's bank still owes a payment obligation to the intermediary bank. The intermediary bank has no right of recovery against the originator, but only has a right of recovery against the originator's bank (its sender) for payment of the payment order.

Further, the intermediary bank will then issue its own payment order to the beneficiary's bank for the beneficiary's bank to credit the account of the beneficiary when the beneficiary's bank accepts that payment order. Accordingly, the intermediary bank owes an obligation to pay for that order to the beneficiary bank, not the beneficiary. U.C.C. § 4A–402(b). Upon the beneficiary bank's acceptance of the payment order, it is the beneficiary's bank that owes an obligation to pay the beneficiary, usually by crediting an account of the beneficiary. U.C.C. § 4A–404. See also Regulation J §§ 210.28, 210.29, 210.30, 210.31, and 210.32.

In summation, under the Article 4A structure, the issuance and acceptance of payment orders create rights and obligations only as between the sender of the payment order and its receiving bank (e.g., between originator and originator's bank as to the originator's payment order), between the originator's bank and an intermediary bank as to the originator's bank's payment order, between the intermediary bank and the beneficiary bank as to the intermediary bank's payment order, and finally as between the beneficiary bank that has accepted a payment order and the beneficiary. Accepted and executed payment orders thus create contractual obligations that result in a series of credits and debits to bank accounts. They do not involve a transfer of property of the originator to the beneficiary. A receiving bank owes its contractual obligation to its sender to execute the payment order and the sender owes its contractual obligation to pay the amount of the payment order to its receiving bank. The intermediary bank has no contractual obligation to the originator or to the beneficiary, and neither the originator nor the beneficiary has any contractual obligation to or rights flowing from the intermediary bank. Thus, credits in an intermediary bank are credits in favor of the originator's bank, *and are not property of either the originator or the beneficiary* (emphasis supplied).

DISCUSSION

In a series of cases applying Admiralty Rule B regarding attachment, the federal courts in New York have held that the intermediary bank in a funds transfer is holding "property" of the originator or beneficiary and have thus allowed creditor process on an intermediary bank in an effort to collect a debt owed by either the originator or the beneficiary (as the case may be).[1] See, e.g., Winter Storm Shipping, Ltd. v. TPI, 310 F.3d 263 (2d Cir. 2002), cert. denied, 539 U.S. 927 (2003); Aqua Stoli Shipping Ltd. v. Gardner Smith Pty Ltd., 460 F.3d 434 (2d Cir. 2006); Con-sub Delaware LLC v. Schahin Engenharia Limitada and Standard Chartered Bank, 534 F.3d 104 (2d Cir. 2008); Navalmar (U.K.) Ltd. v. Welspun Gujarat Stahl Rohren, Ltd., 485 F. Supp. 2d 399 (S.D.N.Y. 2007); Compania Sudamericana de Vapores S.A. v. Sinochem Tianjin Co., 2007 WL 1002265 (S.D.N.Y. 2007); but see Seamar Shipping Corp. v. Kremikovtzi Trade Ltd., 461 F. Supp. 2d 222 (S.D.N.Y. 2006).

---

[1]   Federal Rules of Civil Procedure, Supplemental Rules for Certain Admiralty and Maritime Claims, Admiralty Rule B(1)(a) permits attachment of "the defendant's tangible or intangible personal property" in the hands of named garnishees and thus allows garnishment of such property held by a bank.

These decisions stem from the opinion of the court in *Winter Storm* that the value held by the intermediary bank is property of the originator. Under Article 4A, which is also adopted federal law in Regulation J for funds transfers through a federal reserve bank, the originator does not have any claim against the intermediary bank for return of the value in the event the funds transfer is not completed. Rather, the only party with a claim against the intermediary bank is the sender to that bank, which is typically the originator's bank. In an uncompleted funds transfer, it is the originator's bank that must refund the value to the originator. U.C.C. § 4A–402(d). The intermediary bank owes its refund obligation to its sender, the originator's bank, not to the originator. The originator's bank must refund to the originator even if it cannot recover from the intermediary bank.[2] The beneficiary likewise has no claim to any payment from the intermediary bank. The beneficiary's only claim to the funds is against its bank, the beneficiary bank, and then only when the beneficiary bank has accepted the payment order. U.C.C. § 4A–404. The intermediary bank thus holds no property of either the originator or the beneficiary. Since Admiralty Rule B does not define what is "property" of a party, normally courts look to other law on that issue.

Other law is sufficient to define the parties' rights in a funds transfer. Article 4A is uniform law, enacted in every state in the United States, and Regulation J, which adopts in large part Article 4A's provisions, is uniform in applying to all funds transfers through the federal reserve system. Both define uniformly the rights of parties in a funds transfer. The *Consub* court reasoned that leaving the functional usefulness of Rule B attachments to the vagaries of the laws of 50 states would create a measure of anarchy, but did not take into account that Article 4A is uniform law in all U.S. jurisdictions and is adopted federal law.[3] Neither did the court explain how Rule B provides any basis for determining whether anyone had any property rights in the value held at the intermediary bank.[4]

Further, looking for a federal precedent concerning the "susceptibility of funds involved in an EFT to attachment under Admiralty Rule B," *Winter Storm* turned to *United States v. Dac-carett*, 6 F.3d 37 (2d Cir. 1993), a forfeiture case involving the drug trafficking and money laundering activities of a Colombian drug cartel, 310 F.3d at 276–77 ("The case is instructive in the admiralty field because the attachments of funds in *Daccarett* were accomplished pursuant to the Admiralty Rules, incorporated by reference into the forfeiture statute.") Reasoning from *Daccarett's* holding that " 'an EFT while it takes the form of a bank credit at an intermediary bank is clearly a seizable *res* under the forfeiture statutes,' " id. at 276 (quoting *Daccarett*, 6 F.3d at 55), *Winter Storm* concluded that the "inclusive language of [Rule B] and the EFT analysis in *Daccarett* combine to fashion a rule in this Circuit that EFT funds in the hands of an intermediary bank may be attached pursuant to [Rule B]." 310 F.3d at 276. *Consub* endorsed *Winter Storm's* reliance on *Daccarett*, with minimal independent analysis. See 543 F.3d at 110–11. It should be noted that Rule B remains unchanged for all relevant intents and purposes since *Winter Storm* was decided in 2002 even though, effective December 1, 2006, the rules embodying the practice of maritime attachment in civil

---

2   A simple example illustrates how these courts conflated privity-based contract claims between two parties to create property rights in a third party. Assume A owes B an obligation, B owes C an obligation, and C owes D an obligation. Under garnishment law, D cannot garnish A to satisfy the obligation C owes D. A holds no property of C (A owes B). Now substitute the Article 4A terms to this simple example. A is the intermediary bank who has received payment of a payment order issued by B, the originator's bank, and C is the originator. D is the garnishing creditor. The court in *Winter Storm* and its progeny have in essence allowed D (the originator's creditor) to garnish A (the intermediary bank) to collect on the debt C (the originator) owes to D.

3   The courts following *Winter Storm* have not followed the applicable law directly on point regarding property rights, but have also not followed applicable precedent predating Article 4A. The court in Reibor International Limited v. Cargo Carriers (Kacz-Co.) Ltd., 759 F.2d 262 (2d Cir. 1985), considered whether the CHIPS credit involved was property subject to attachment under the Admiralty Rules. The court said that federal law generally governs questions as to the validity of Rule B attachments, but the Admiralty Rules themselves offered little guidance and so the court agreed with the district court that state law more directly in point should be turned to. This is entirely consistent with respect to other contexts where federal law relies on state law to determine whether property is involved, such as in bankruptcy. See, e.g., Butner v. United States, 440 U.S. 48 (1979). Also the Court in *Grain Traders, Inc. v. Citibank, N.A.*, 160 F.2d 97 (2d Cir. 1998), recognized the applicability of U.C.C. Article 4A when it held that law prevents an originator of a funds transfer from suing an intermediary bank. Id. at 102. *Grain Traders* remains good law in the Second Circuit and its logic applies to suits by beneficiaries as well.

4   The *Consub* court believed that the *Winter Storm* rule was not shown to be unworkable. Note that U.C.C. Article 4A is substantially premised on the ability to net obligations because of the large sums involved. U.C.C. § 4A–403. If a particular creditor can seize funds and frustrate that plan, the resultant systemic risk may provide the demonstration that the *Winter Storm* approach and its progeny are unworkable.

APPENDIX E

forfeiture actions and other in rem proceedings have been re-named the Supplemental Rules for Admiralty or Maritime Claims and Asset Forfeiture Actions (the "Supplemental Rules"). The revised Supplemental Rules added, inter alia, the reference to "Asset Forfeiture Actions," and Rule G, governing forfeiture actions in rem arising from a federal statute, "to bring together the central procedures that govern civil forfeiture actions." Supplemental Rule G, Advisory Committee's Note. The point is that *Daccarett* never decided whether either an originator or a beneficiary of the funds transfer had a *property interest* in the amount involved in a funds transfer received by an intermediary bank. It did not need to do so because in a forfeiture case funds can be seized even if they do not constitute property of the defendant. The *Daccarett* court, as appropriate in a forfeiture case, identified the amount of the funds as traceable to an illicit activity and therefore subject to attachment under 21 U.S.C. § 881(a). This is a critical difference.

Moreover, as a remedy quasi in rem, the validity of a Rule B attachment depends entirely on the determination that the res at issue is property of the judgment debtor at the moment it is attached. See J. Lauritzen A/S v. Dashwood Shipping, Ltd., 65 F.3d 139, 141 (9th Cir. 1995) (Rule B attachment characterized as quasi in rem jurisdiction because jurisdiction is derived solely from the attachment of the property of the defendant). Forfeiture, on the other hand, is a remedy in rem, based as it is on the legal fiction that " 'property used in violation of law [is] itself the wrongdoer that must be held to account for the harms it [has] caused.' " United States v. 92 Buena Vista Avenue, 507 U.S. 111, 125 (1993). This is a critical distinction between actions proceeding under Supplemental Rule C—now Rule G—and those brought under Rule B; it is not a "distinction without a difference," as *Winter Storm* found. 310 F.3d at 278.

Accordingly, unless there is superseding federal law, such as a drug forfeiture law or a regulation of the Treasury Department's Office of Foreign Assets Control ("OFAC"), Article 4A must be honored. Rule B is not such a superseding law.

Even absent that scenario, the Winter Storm approach is proving to be practically un-workable. The result of the *Winter Storm* approach has been a staggering number of maritime writs that New York banks are required to process on a daily basis. For example, from October 1, 2008 to January 31, 2009, maritime plaintiffs filed 962 lawsuits seeking to attach more than $1.35 billion. These lawsuits constituted 33 percent of all lawsuits filed in the Southern District of New York during that period, and the resulting maritime writs only add to the burden of 800 to 900 prior writs already served daily on the District's banks. The numbers have tapered off only slightly during the past months; from February 1, 2009 to April 30, 2009, maritime plaintiffs filed 498 lawsuits seeking to attach a total of $720 million. The explosion of maritime writs served on the banks has been logistically overwhelming.

Of even more significance, however, this explosion of writs creates an additional threat to the U.S. dollar as the world's primary reserve currency and New York's standing as a center of international banking and finance. Confronted with this situation, companies around the world may well consider restructuring their transactions to provide for payments in euros, sterling, yen, or some other currency to avoid using U.S. dollars cleared through intermediary banks in the United States, or clear transactions through one of the proliferating off-shore dollar clearing networks. Because the only contact with the United States in most of these transactions is the use of an intermediary bank in the United States to clear U.S. dollars, the U.S. litigation apparatus can be avoided entirely by the relatively simple expedient of using a different currency. As a result, *Winter Storm* and its progeny have had a far greater, and damaging, potential impact on U.S. and foreign banks located in New York than might have been anticipated.

An additional significant problem for banks is that the only practical way in which they can accommodate post-*Winter Storm* attachments is by frequent amendments to their software filters used to identify transactions involving entities and other persons whose financial transactions are blocked under OFAC regulations. OFAC administers U.S. economic sanctions pro-grams arising under the Trading with the Enemy Act, 50 U.S.C. app. § 5, the International Emergency Economic Powers Act, 50 U.S.C. §§ 1701–1706, and other statutes. OFAC regularly issues bulletins that add or delete entities or persons from its lists, and banks must update their screening software to reflect these changes. This year, OFAC has updated its lists 19 times through May 6, 2009 (83 business days). By contrast, new maritime attachment orders were filed nearly every business day. The process of constantly amending the software filters to deal with this flood of maritime attachments has greatly increased the burden on the banks, requiring them to take down their OFAC filters almost every day, vastly increasing the chance that the OFAC database will be corrupted by the manipulation, and substantially increasing the number of "hits," including numerous false positives that these filters now generate, creating real risks of inefficiency and error.

In addition, permitting a beneficiary's creditor to attach a funds-transfer credit, ordinarily held only momentarily in New York, would exacerbate the considerable due-process concerns inherent in restraining a funds transfer. The defendants in maritime cases invariably are foreign corporations with few or no contacts with the United States. In many of the cases the defendant does not appear to have significant contacts, if any, with New York. Indeed, for a maritime defendant's property to be prima facie subject to a Rule B attachment, the plaintiff is required to attest, pursuant to Rule B(1)(b), that the defendant could not be found within the District. See STX Panocean (UK) Co., Ltd. v. Glory Wealth Shipping Pte Ltd., 560 F.3d 127, 130–31 (2d Cir. 2009). Moreover, the funds transfers at issue are often meant to effect payment from a third party's non-U.S. account to the defendant's non-U.S. account, or vice versa. The New York garnishee banks in most cases are involved as intermediary banks only because the payment was denominated in U.S. dollars.

CONCLUSION

In uniform law under Article 4A and under Regulation J, neither the originator nor the beneficiary of a funds transfer has any property claim to the value held by an intermediary bank in a funds transfer. Thus, neither a creditor of an originator nor the creditor of a beneficiary may successfully issue creditor process[5] to an intermediary bank as the intermediary bank is not holding property of either the originator or the beneficiary. To the extent that the cases cited earlier indicate to the contrary, that reasoning is disapproved and should not be followed.

PEB COMMENTARY NO. 17
LIMITED LIABILITY PARTNERSHIPS UNDER THE
CHOICE OF LAW RULES OF ARTICLE 9
(June 29, 2012)

BACKGROUND

The location of an organization,[1] as "location" is determined under U.C.C. § 9–307, plays an important role in determining the local law that governs perfection, the effect of perfection or nonperfection, and the priority of a security interest. See U.C.C. § 9–301(1). As a general matter, a "registered organization" is located, as determined under U.C.C. § 9–307(e), in the State under whose laws the organization is organized while an organization that is not a registered organization is considered under U.C.C. § 9–307(b)(2) to be located in the State in which the organization has its place of business.[2]

The 2010 amendments to Article 9 clarified and expanded the definition of "registered organization" by providing in relevant part that the term "means an organization formed or organized solely under the law of a single State . . . by the filing of a public organic record with . . . the State. . . ." See U.C.C. § 9–102(a)(71)(2010).

The 2010 amendments also added a new definition of "public organic record." The term in relevant part means "a record that is available to the public for inspection and is . . . a record consisting of the record initially filed with . . . a State . . . to form or organize an organization and any record filed with . . . the State . . . which amends or restates the initial record." See U.C.C. § 9–102(a)(68)(2010).

---

[5] "Creditor process" means levy, attachment, garnishment, notice of lien, sequestration, or similar process issued by or on behalf of a creditor or other claimant with respect to an account. As to account, see authorized account defined in U.C.C. § 4A–105(a)(1).

[1] The term "organization" is defined in U.C.C. § 1–201(b)(25) as a "person" other than an individual. The term "person" is defined in U.C.C. § 1–201(b)(27) to include not only an individual but also a corporation, partnership or other legal or commercial entity.

[2] If an organization that is not a registered organization has more than one place of business, it is considered under U.C.C. § 9–307(b)(3) to be located where its chief executive office is located.

APPENDIX E

ISSUE

Under the 2010 amendments to Article 9, should a limited liability partnership organized under the law of a State be considered a registered organization or an organization that is not a registered organization?

ANALYSIS

A full survey of the limited liability partnership law of each State is beyond the scope of this Commentary. This Commentary focuses upon the Uniform Partnership Act promulgated by the Uniform Law Commission in 1997 (the "1997 UPA") as a typical example of a State's limited liability partnership law.[3]

Under the 1997 UPA a general partnership is formed from the association of the partners and not from any public filing with the State. *See* 1997 UPA § 202. Under Section 1001 of the 1997 UPA a general partnership may become a limited liability partnership by obtaining a vote of its partners to become a limited liability partnership and by filing with the State a statement of qualification. The already existing partnership becomes a limited liability partnership on the date of the filing of the statement or on such later date as is designated in the statement. *See* 1997 UPA § 1001(e). Once the statement of qualification becomes effective, Section 306(c) of the 1997 UPA establishes a liability shield that protects the partnership's partners from vicarious personal liability for all partnership obligations incurred while the partnership is a limited liability partnership. The partnership's status as a limited liability partnership remains in effect until the statement is canceled or revoked. *See* 1997 UPA §§ 105(d), 1001(e), and 1003.

Under the 1997 UPA a limited liability partnership is not a new entity; rather, the original partnership, formed by the association of the partners, continues as a partnership, albeit with the liability shield for its partners. Section 201(b) of the 1997 UPA states categorically: "A limited liability partnership continues to be the same entity that existed before the filing of a statement of qualification under Section 1001." An official comment elaborates:

> [T]he filing of a statement of qualification does not create a "new" partnership. The filing partnership continues to be the same partnership entity that existed before the filing. Similarly, the amendment or cancellation of a statement of qualification under Section 105(d) or the revocation of a statement of qualification under Section 1003(c) does not terminate the partnership and create a "new" partnership. See Section 1003(d). Accordingly, a partnership remains the same entity regardless of a filing, cancellation, or revocation of a statement of qualification.

It follows that the statement of qualification filed with the State and by which a partnership becomes a limited liability partnership under the 1997 UPA is not a "public organic record" under the 2010 amendments to Article 9. The statement of qualification is not a record filed with the State to "form or organize" the partnership. It is the association of the partners that forms the partnership, not any record publicly filed with the State. Both conceptually and legally, a partnership is formed wholly apart from the filing of a statement of qualification with the State.

Because a limited liability partnership is not formed or organized by the filing of a public organic record, it cannot be a "registered organization" under the 2010 amendments to Article 9.[4]

The forgoing analysis does not suggest that a change of law for the characterization of a limited liability partnership, as discussed in this Commentary, was effected by the 2010 amendments to Article 9. Even before giving effect to the 2010 amendments, a limited liability partnership would not be considered a "registered organization." That is because the public filing of a statement of qualification would not be a record that "the State . . . must maintain . . . showing the organization to have been organized." *See* U.C.C.

---

[3] The reasoning and conclusions of this Commentary would also apply to legislation similar to the 1997 UPA that has the material attributes of the 1997 UPA discussed in this Commentary, including those provisions (discussed later in the text) that state that a limited liability partnership is a continuation of the pre-existing general partnership.

[4] A limited liability partnership should be distinguished from a limited partnership. This Commentary does not address a limited partnership. A limited partnership is ordinarily considered to be a registered organization. *See* U.C.C. § 9–102 cmt. 11.

§ 9–102(a)(70)(2009). The statement of qualification maintained by the State would show only that the partners have the benefit of the liability shield, not that the partnership itself has been organized.

CONCLUSION

The 2010 amendments to Article 9 did not change the law on whether a limited liability partnership should be characterized as a registered organization under Article 9. Whether before or after giving effect to the 2010 amendments to Article 9, a limited liability partnership organized under the law of a State that has adopted the 1997 UPA, or similar legislation having the material attributes of the 1997 UPA discussed in this Commentary, is an organization that is not a "registered organization" as defined by U.C.C. § 9–102(a).

Official Comment 11 to U.C.C. § 9–102 is amended by adding at the end of the penultimate sentence of the second paragraph of the Official Comment (the fifth paragraph after giving effect to the changes to the Official Comment made in connection with the 2010 amendments to Article 9):

> Likewise, a limited liability partnership, which is a form of general partnership under the Uniform Partnership Act (1997), is not a "registered organization" even if it has filed a record that is a statement of qualification under Section 1001 of the Uniform Partnership Act (1997). The filing of the record does not form or organize the partnership. The filing only provides the partners in the general partnership with a limited liability shield and evidences that the general partnership has limited liability partnership status. See PEB Commentary No. 17. As discussed in PEB Commentary No. 17 the same conclusion would apply to a limited liability partnership formed under the law of state that has not adopted the Uniform Partnership Act (1997) but has adopted for limited liability partnerships similar legislation having the material attributes of that Act. Also as discussed in PEB Commentary No. 17, the same conclusion would apply whether before or after giving effect to the 2010 amendments to this Article.

PEB COMMENTARY NO. 18
HIGHLAND CAPITAL COMMENTARY (JULY 2014)

ISSUE

Does an obligation of an issuer which satisfies the requirements of subparagraphs (ii) and (iii) of U.C.C. § 8–102(a)(15), and is represented by a certificate that is not in bearer form and that specifies a person entitled to the obligation, qualify as a "security" if (a) the certificate lacks any statement about registration of transfer, and (b) no books are maintained by the issuer for registration of transfers?

BACKGROUND

The 2010 Amendments to Article 9 of the Uniform Commercial Code, approved and promulgated by the American Law Institute and the Uniform Law Commission, contain an Appendix adding a new paragraph to Comment 13 to U.C.C. § 8–102. That comment addresses the definition of "registered form" in U.C.C. § 8–102(a)(13), which is an important element of the definition of "security" in U.C.C. § 8–102(a)(15). This issue is quite important, and the amendment to the Comment affects matters beyond those governed by Article 9. Accordingly, the Permanent Editorial Board for the Uniform Commercial Code has determined that the promulgation of this Commentary will be useful in explaining, in somewhat greater depth than possible in the amended Comment, the importance of the issue and the circumstances that gave rise to its addition to the Uniform Commercial Code.

Depending on their nature, rights to the payment of money may fit into a number of different categories of personal property defined in the Uniform Commercial Code. For example, a right to payment may be evidenced by a "note" (which is a type of "negotiable instrument") governed by Article 3 of the Uniform Commercial Code; it may be a "security" governed by Article 8 of the Uniform Commercial Code; or it may be one of several different types of personal property identified in Article 9 of the Uniform Commercial Code. Within Article 9, the right to payment may be an "account," "chattel paper," a "payment intangible," or a "promissory note" (which is a type of "instrument"); if the right to payment is a "security" (as defined in, and governed by, Article 8) it is also "investment property" under Article 9. Each of these types of property that encompass a right to the payment of money is governed by a different set of rules in the Uniform Commercial

Code. Accordingly, a misapplication of the rules governing one property type to a right that is actually a different property type will yield an erroneous answer; thus, the definitions of each of the property types are quite important.

The opinion of the New York Court of Appeals in Highland Capital Management LP v. Schneider, 866 N.E.2d 1020, 834 N.Y.S.2d 692 (2007), raised important questions about application of the definition of "security" to certain rights to the payment of money. Because of the importance of accurately categorizing payment rights in order to determine correctly the legal rules governing those property rights under the Uniform Commercial Code, the opinion is worthy of attention. More particularly, in *Highland Capital* the court interpreted U.C.C. § 8–102(a)(15)—the definition of "security"—as including an obligation "the transfer of which may be registered upon books maintained for that purpose by or on behalf of the issuer" even if such books do not exist and are not maintained, so long as the issuer would, as a practical necessity, eventually have to maintain books upon which such transfers were recorded. Because the reasoning in this opinion could be determinative of whether an obligation is a "security" in a large number of factual contexts and because the definition of "security" has broad effects throughout the Uniform Commercial Code, both the Permanent Editorial Board and the Joint Review Committee that prepared the 2010 Amendments to Article 9 concluded that the matter should be addressed explicitly in the Official Comments to the Uniform Commercial Code.

I.   Importance of the Issue

Among the effects of concluding that a monetary obligation constitutes a "security" rather than another type of personal property such as a "note" or "negotiable instrument" governed by Article 3, or an "account," "chattel paper," "instrument," "promissory note," or "payment intangible" governed by Article 9 are the following:[1]

(i)   The statute of frauds in former Article 1 of the Uniform Commercial Code does not apply if the obligation is a security.[2]

(ii)   The protections available to good-faith purchasers of securities for value are different than those available to similar purchasers of negotiable instruments. In the case of securities, such a purchaser may qualify for protection against certain defenses under U.C.C. § 8–202 and may qualify as a "protected purchaser" under U.C.C. § 8–303 and thereby take the security free of any adverse claim. In the case of negotiable instruments, such a good-faith purchaser may qualify as a "holder in due course" and take free of certain defenses and claims in recoupment under U.C.C. § 3–305 and take free of claims to the instrument under U.C.C. § 3–306. The criteria for qualifying for these protections, and the details of the protections, differ as between Article 8 and Article 3, however.[3]

(iii)   The non-temporal priority rules in U.C.C. § 9–330(d) that apply to instruments are inapplicable.

(iv)   The issuer would have the duties described in Article 8 rather than those described in Article 3 (if the obligation would otherwise qualify as a negotiable instrument) or contract law.

(v)   The obligations of an indorser would be those set out in Article 8 rather than in Article 3 (in the case of a negotiable instrument) or the common law. For example, under Article 3 an indorser is responsible if the maker of a note does not pay the note; this is not the case under Article 8.[4]

(vi)   Certain automatic perfection rules and priority rules that govern "investment property" under Article 9 would apply.[5]

---

[1]   See also Official Comment 2 to U.C.C. § 3–102 for further discussion of this point.

[2]   U.C.C. § 1–206 (1962).

[3]   Compare U.C.C. § 8–202 (2012) (issuer's limited defenses against purchaser of security), and *id.* § 8–303 ("protected purchaser" of a security takes free of any adverse claim) with *id.* § 3–302 (defining "holder in due course" of a negotiable instrument), *id.* § 3–305(b) (issuer's limited defenses against a holder in due course), and *id.* § 3–306 (holder in due course of a negotiable instrument takes free of any adverse claim).

[4]   Compare U.C.C. § 8–304(f) (2012) with *id.* § 3–415.

[5]   U.C.C. § 9–309(10) (2012) (automatic perfection); *id.* § 9–328 (priority of competing security interests).

(vii) The provisions of U.C.C. §§ 9–406 and 9–408 that limit the effect of restrictions on assignment would be inapplicable.

II.   The *Highland Capital* Case

In *Highland Capital*, the plaintiff alleged that the defendant had entered into an oral agreement to sell some promissory notes and had breached that agreement. The defendant both denied the existence of the agreement and asserted the statute of frauds in former U.C.C. § 1–206(1) as an additional defense. In response, the plaintiff asserted that the promissory notes constituted securities and, therefore, § 1–206 was inapplicable. (Former U.C.C. § 1–206(2) provides that the statute of frauds in subsection (1) "does not apply to contracts for the sale of . . . securities. . . .")

The facts of *Highland Capital* are complex, but they revolve around promissory notes with an aggregate face value of $69 million issued by Norton McNaughton, Inc. ("McNaughton") to various members of the Schneider family (the "Schneiders") in conjunction with the acquisition of some women's apparel companies. As described by the New York Court of Appeals:

> The eight notes with an aggregate face value of $69 million . . . , running 12 pages apiece, were each payable to one or another of the four Schneiders. The notes required McNaughton to make quarterly principal and monthly interest payments to the named payee. McNaughton was designated the maker of the notes, each of which bore the following restrictive legend: "THIS NOTE HAS NOT BEEN REGISTERED UNDER THE SECURITIES ACT OF 1933, AS AMENDED. IT MAY NOT BE TRANSFERRED IN THE ABSENCE OF AN EFFECTIVE REGISTRATION STATEMENT UNDER SUCH ACT OR AN OPINION OF COUNSEL TO THE MAKER THAT SUCH REGISTRATION IS NOT REQUIRED." Each note was marked "SUBORDINATED PROMISSORY NOTE" on its face because these notes were subordinate to McNaughton's existing bank and bond debt amounting to roughly $350 million. Upon McNaughton's default, the payee had the right to declare the entire amount under the note due and owing, and to elect either to receive payment in stock or to accelerate payment. The notes stated that they were "governed by and construed in accordance with" New York law.

> The securities industry professionals who subsequently dealt with the notes considered them to be high-risk debt akin to junk bonds. Consequently, it was anticipated that any potential purchaser would expect a high yield or internal rate of return. Concomitantly, the notes carried a substantial, variable interest rate (initially, 9.34% on the December notes).

McNaughton did not maintain books on which the transfer of any of the promissory notes could be registered.

According to Highland Capital, at a time when it appeared that McNaughton would be unable to pay the full amount of the notes when due, the Schneiders retained RBC Dominion Securities to market the notes on their behalf and subsequently orally agreed to sell the promissory notes to RBC at almost 50% below their face value; RBC, in turn, entered into a contract to sell the promissory notes to Highland Capital. Then, according to Highland Capital, when McNaughton was acquired by a larger company and became able to pay the full amount of the promissory notes, the Schneiders reneged on their oral agreement.

Highland Capital brought suit against the Schneiders for breach of contract in a Texas state court, but the case was removed to federal court on diversity grounds and eventually transferred to the United States District Court for the Southern District of New York. In its ruling on a motion by the Schneiders to dismiss the suit on the basis of the U.C.C. § 1–206 statute of frauds, the court noted that if the promissory notes that were the subject of the *Highland Capital* dispute constituted "securities," the § 1–206 statute of frauds would be inapplicable and the oral agreement, if proven, would be enforceable.[6] If, on the other hand, the promissory notes did not constitute securities, the court noted that the § 1–206 statute of frauds would apply and the contract would be enforceable only to the extent of $5000.[7] The court held that the promissory notes

---

[6]   See U.C.C. § 8–113. U.C.C. § 1–206 (1962) was deleted from the official text by the 2001 revision of Article 1, but it was in force in New York at the time of the events and decision in *Highland Capital*.

[7]   The court did not consider the possibility that the sale of the promissory notes was governed by revised U.C.C. Article 9 and, thus, by its statute of frauds in U.C.C. § 9–203(b). While the events in the case occurred before the effective date of revised Article 9 on July 1, 2001, litigation was not commenced until after that date. See U.C.C. §§ 9–701, 9–702(c).

did not constitute securities and granted the motion to dismiss.[8] The decision was appealed to the United States Court of Appeals for the Second Circuit, which certified the matter to the New York Court of Appeals, asking whether "the eight promissory notes issued by [McNaughton] to the Schneiders fall within the definition of a security as contemplated by § 8–102(a)(15) of the New York Uniform Commercial Code."

III. Analysis of the Issue Addressed in *Highland Capital*

Uniform Commercial Code § 8–102(a)(15) defines "security" as follows:

an obligation of an issuer or a share, participation, or other interest in an issuer or in property or an enterprise of an issuer:

(i) which is represented by a security certificate in bearer or registered form, or the transfer of which may be registered upon books maintained for that purpose by or on behalf of the issuer;

(ii) which is one of a class or series or by its terms is divisible into a class or series of shares, participations, interests, or obligations; and

(iii) which:

(A) is, or is of a type, dealt in or traded on securities exchanges or securities markets; or

(B) is a medium for investment and by its terms expressly provides that it is a security governed by this Article.

Thus, in order to qualify as securities, the promissory notes in *Highland Capital* must fulfill the requirements of subparagraph (i) (transferability and registrability), subparagraph (ii) (divisibility), and clause (A) of subparagraph (iii) (investment-function test) of § 8–102(a)(15).[9]

In applying these criteria, we are guided by § 1–103(a) of the Uniform Commercial Code. That section provides that the Code "must be liberally construed and applied to promote its underlying purposes and policies." This fundamental principle is further articulated in the Prefatory Note to Revised Article 8:

In analyzing these classification questions, courts should take care to avoid mechanical jurisprudence based solely upon exegesis of the wording of definitions in Article 8. The result of classification questions is that different sets of rules come into play. In order to decide the classification question it is necessary to understand fully the commercial setting and consider which set of rules best fits the transaction. Rather than letting the choice of rules turn on interpretation of the words of the definitions, the interpretation of the words of the definitions should turn on the suitability of the application of the substantive rules.[10]

The *Highland Capital* court devoted most of its analysis to the transferability/registrability test of subparagraph (i) of U.C.C. § 8–102(a)(15). It was common ground that the notes were not in bearer form. Thus, the court was required to determine whether the promissory notes were represented by security certificates in "registered form."[11] (The court seems to have assumed that the divisibility and investment-

---

[8] Because the U.C.C. § 1–206 statute of frauds allows enforcement up to $5000, the motion to dismiss was granted on the ground that the amount in controversy no longer met the jurisdictional standard for a diversity case.

[9] The promissory notes need not satisfy the investment-function test of clause (A) of subparagraph (iii) if they satisfy clause (B) of that subparagraph. However, these notes evidently did not satisfy clause (B) because they evidently did not provide expressly that they were securities subject to Article 8. Accordingly, the effects of such an "opt in" were not considered by the court, nor are they considered in this Commentary.

[10] Section III.C.14. Similarly, in the context of the indirect-holding-system rules of Article 8, Comment 1 to § 8–501 warns that "the question whether a given arrangement is a securities account should be decided not by dictionary analysis of the words of the definition taken out of context, but by considering whether it promotes the objectives of Article 8 to include the arrangement within the term securities account." The interpretation of the term "security" in Article 8 must be approached with these principles in mind.

[11] Formally, an item may satisfy subparagraph (i) of § 8–102(a)(15) without being in bearer or registered form if "the transfer of [the item] may be registered upon books maintained for that purpose by or on behalf of the issuer." That language was added in 1977 with reference to uncertificated securities, which are excluded from the definition of "registered form." The current text of Article 8 does not expressly limit the application of that language in subparagraph (i) to uncertificated securities. However, the same language is an element of the definition of "registered form." Hence an

function tests were satisfied. The opinion does not treat these issues in any detail, and, accordingly, this Commentary does not address them.[12])

U.C.C. § 8–102(a)(13) provides as follows:

"Registered form," as applied to a certificated security, means a form in which:

(i)   the security certificate specifies a person entitled to the security; and

(ii)   a transfer of the security may be registered upon books maintained for that purpose by or on behalf of the issuer, or the security certificate so states.

The notes in *Highland Capital* satisfied subparagraph (i) of this definition, because each specified the person entitled to be paid. The notes evidently did not satisfy the second clause of subparagraph (ii) ("or the security certificate so states"), because they apparently said nothing about registration of transfer. Accordingly, the issue in *Highland Capital* reduced to the single question of whether the notes satisfied the first clause of subparagraph (ii). That question can be restated as follows: given that McNaughton did not maintain books on which the transfer of the promissory notes may be registered but, presumably McNaughton *might have* maintained such books, was it the case that "a transfer of the [promissory notes] may be registered upon books maintained for that purpose by or on behalf of [McNaughton]"?

The court answered that question in the affirmative:

McNaughton ultimately would have been constrained to [register the transfer of the notes to a third-party at the Schneiders' request]. McNaughton did not restrict transfer of the notes other than by the legend . . . And the restrictive legend itself suggests that the parties contemplated the possibility of future transfer. As . . . a practical matter, McNaughton would have to have recorded any transfer of the notes in order to protect itself and the senior debt holders. For example, in the event of default, the payee of the notes could have elected conversion of the principal to common stock, thus diluting other shareholders' value; and because the notes called for hefty payments of principal and interest, McNaughton had to have a way to keep track of the proper payees.

The Permanent Editorial Board believes that records kept by an obligor as to the identity of the owners of its obligations are not sufficient to satisfy the definition of "registered form" unless, among other things, those records are maintained for the purpose of registering transfer. Registration of transfer of a certificated security as referred to in U.C.C. § 8–102(a)(13)(ii) entails the issuer marking its books to reflect the change in record ownership, and also entails the issuance of a new certificate in the name of the transferee and, if less than the whole amount of the security is transferred, issuance of a new certificate for the difference in the name of the transferor. Neither McNaughton nor the Schneiders seem to have contemplated that McNaughton would be obligated to take such actions. Moreover, the notes involved in *Highland Capital* were not subject to any agreement or arrangement by which McNaughton was entitled to treat as owner of a note the person identified as such in its records, as contemplated by U.C.C. § 8–207. Hence any records that McNaughton might have maintained as to the identity of the owners of the notes would not have been maintained for the purpose of registering transfer.

The *Highland Capital* opinion stated that "the proper inquiry is whether the notes *could have been* registered on transfer books maintained by McNaughton, not whether they were registered on transfer books at the time of the litigation." The dissenting opinion took this to be the court's argument:

[The majority] emphasizes the words "may be" [in the definition of "registered form,"] which the majority seemingly takes to mean that the notes are registrable if any books could possibly exist in which transfers of the notes could be registered. Read so broadly, the words "may be" deprive the registrability requirement of any meaning—it is always theoretically possible there could be books on which transfers of anything could be registered. The words "may be registered upon books maintained for that purpose" are much more plausibly read to mean that "books maintained for that purpose" must

---

item that is not in bearer form must satisfy that language in order to qualify under subparagraph (i) in any case. For simplicity, this Commentary refers to the language as it appears in the definition of "registered form."

12   For analysis of these issues, see, e.g., Howard Darmstadter, U.C.C. Survey Article 8—Investment Securities, 62 Bus. Lawyer 1623 (2007).

exist, on which transfers may (or may not) be registered. In other words, the requirement is met whether transfers are actually registered on the books or not, but not if there are no books "maintained for that purpose" on which registration could occur.

The Permanent Editorial Board agrees with the dissenting opinion in *Highland Capital*. If an issuer of obligations not in bearer form does not maintain books on which transfer of those obligations may be registered, those obligations do not satisfy the registrability criterion and those obligations are not "securities." A contrary reading deprives the distinction between debt obligations that are negotiable notes or Article 9 promissory notes and debt obligations that are securities of both the substantive content intended by the drafters and of the predictability and certainty needed for commercial transactions. This is because, under the *Highland Capital* majority, all such obligations in the form of negotiable notes or promissory notes might nonetheless be characterized as securities. Inasmuch as many important legal rights with respect to debt obligations (of which the existence or nonexistence of an applicable statute of frauds—the primary issue of the *Highland Capital* case—is only one) depend on the characterization of such obligations, a reading of the statute that creates uncertainty as to that characterization creates not only uncertainty as to the resolution of disputes in litigation but also transactional uncertainty that adds risk and cost to transactions.

IV. Conclusion

The definitions of "registered form" and "security" in U.C.C. §§ 8–102(a)(13) and 8–102(a)(15) should be interpreted so that an obligation of an issuer that is represented by a certificate, that satisfies subparagraphs (ii) and (iii) of § 8–102(a)(13), that is not in bearer form, and that specifies a person entitled to the security, is not a "security" unless (a) the certificate states that a transfer of the obligation may be registered upon books maintained by or on behalf of the issuer for the purpose of registering transfer, or (b) any records that the issuer maintains (or that it would eventually have to maintain pursuant to the undertaking referred to in the preceding clause (a)) do not merely record transfers of such obligations but are instead maintained for the purpose of registering transfer of such obligations.

As noted above, the 2010 Amendments to Article 9 of the Uniform Commercial Code, approved and promulgated by the American Law Institute and the Uniform Law Commission, contain an Appendix adding a new paragraph to Comment 13 to U.C.C. § 8–102 to preclude that incorrect interpretation of the definition of "registered form." The new Comment states:

> Contrary to the holding in Highland Capital Management LP v. Schneider, 8 N.Y.3d 406 (2007), the registrability requirement in the definition of "registered form," and its parallel in the definition of "security," are satisfied only if books are maintained by or on behalf of the issuer for the purpose of registration of transfer, including the determination of rights under § 8–207(a) (or if, in the case of a certificated security, the security certificate so states). It is not sufficient that the issuer records ownership, or records transfers thereof, for other purposes. Nor is it sufficient that the issuer, while not in fact maintaining books for the purpose of registration of transfer, could do so, for such is always the case.

This amendment to Comment 13 to U.C.C. § 8–102 is not limited to matters governed by the provisions of the Uniform Commercial Code that are amended by the 2010 Amendments. Accordingly, the amended Comment reflects the view of the Permanent Editorial Board for the Uniform Commercial Code of the law prior to the effective date of the 2010 Amendments as well as the law after the effective date of those amendments.

REPORT

PERMANENT EDITORIAL BOARD
FOR THE UNIFORM COMMERCIAL CODE

REPORT

EFFECT OF NON-UNIFORM SCOPE PROVISIONS IN
REVISED ARTICLE 9 OF THE
UNIFORM COMMERCIAL CODE
(December 1, 2004)

I. Introduction

Revised Article 9 has now been enacted in all 50 states and in the District of Columbia. As has been the case with other Articles of the Uniform Commercial Code, the various state enactments contain a number of deviations from the Official Text of Revised Article 9.

While some deviations from the Official Text reflect accommodation of uniquely local issues, others represent substantive policy choices by the enacting legislatures to differ from the national model provided by the Official Text of Revised Article 9. While non-uniformities in the latter category are inconsistent with the ideal of a truly *Uniform* Commercial Code, they are, of course, inevitable in a democratic system that entrusts enactment to 51 different legislatures. Moreover, it must be recognized that the Uniform Commercial Code has never been enacted in a truly uniform way. There have been local variations ever since the widespread enactment of the Code, including variations in Article 9. The substantive non-uniformities in the enactment of Revised Article 9 are well-catalogued in two articles by Penelope L. Christophorou, Kenneth C. Kettering, Lynn A. Soukup, and Steven O. Weise: *Under the Surface of Revised Article 9: Selected Variations in State Enactments from the Official Text of Revised Article 9*,[1] and *Analysis of State Variations*.[2]

Such non-uniformities have the potential to be problematic in our national economy, where transactions frequently cross state lines and where more than one jurisdiction can be the forum in which litigation establishing the rights of parties can be instituted. Nonetheless, most of the deviations from the Official Text of Revised Article 9 will not cause serious transactional difficulties so long as the parties involved educate themselves as to the applicable law.

There is one group of non-uniformities, though, that has the potential to cause transactional difficulty and legal uncertainty, because these non-uniformities can create difficult conflict of laws issues. This group of non-uniform enactments relates to the scope provisions of Revised Article 9.

II. Uncertainties Arising from Non-uniformities as to Scope

Uniform Commercial Code Section 9–109(a)[3] provides that, "[e]xcept as otherwise provided in subsections (c) and (d)," Revised Article 9 applies, *inter alia*, to all transactions, regardless of their form, that create a security interest in personal property or fixtures by contract and to sales of accounts, chattel paper, payment intangibles, or promissory notes. Section 9–109(c) excludes application of Revised Article 9 in certain situations *to the extent that* the transactions are governed by other law referred to in that subsection.[4] Section 9–109(d) excludes application of Revised Article 9 altogether to the transactions and

---

[1] 34 Uniform Commercial Code Law Journal 331 (2002).

[2] 34 Uniform Commercial Code Law Journal 358 (2002) (hereinafter referred to as "State Variations").

[3] Unless otherwise noted, all references to Article 9 are to the Official Text of Revised Article 9.

[4] Section 9–109(c) provides:

This article does not apply to the extent that:

(1) a statute, regulation, or treaty of the United States preempts this article;

(2) another statute of this State expressly governs the creation, perfection, priority, or enforcement of a security interest created by this State or a governmental unit of this State;

APPENDIX E

interests listed in that subsection.[5] While there are non-uniformities in enactment with respect to subsection (c), variations with respect to subsection (d) raise more difficult issues. In most cases, these non-uniform enactments add further exclusions to the 13 listed exclusions in the Official Text of the subsection. Thus, Article 9 as enacted in a state with such a non-uniform enactment does not govern some transactions that are governed by Article 9 in states that have followed the Official Text. In a few states, however, the non-uniform variations delete an exclusion that appears in subsection (d) of the Official Text, with the result that transactions not governed by Article 9 in states that have followed the Official Text are governed by Article 9 of such states.

A. Non-uniform Exclusions

For purposes of this Report, attention is drawn particularly to the most common types of non-uniform enactments of Section 9–109(d)—those that exclude from the scope of Article 9 transactions that are otherwise within the scope of the Official Text of the Article: (i) 18 states exclude from Article 9 transfers by the government of any state,[6] (ii) 18 states exclude from Article 9 transfers of interests in workers

---

(3) statute of another State, a foreign country, or a governmental unit of another State or a foreign country, other than a statute generally applicable to security interests, expressly governs creation, perfection, priority, or enforcement of a security interest created by the State, country, or governmental unit; or

(4) the rights of a transferee beneficiary or nominated person under a letter of credit are independent and superior under Section 5–114.

[5] Section 9–109(d) provides:

This article does not apply to:

(1) a landlord's lien, other than an agricultural lien;

(2) a lien, other than an agricultural lien, given by statute or other rule of law for services or materials, but Section 9–333 applies with respect to priority of the lien;

(3) an assignment of a claim for wages, salary, or other compensation of an employee;

(4) a sale of accounts, chattel paper, payment intangibles, or promissory notes as part of a sale of the business out of which they arose;

(5) an assignment of accounts, chattel paper, payment intangibles, or promissory notes which is for the purpose of collection only;

(6) an assignment of a right to payment under a contract to an assignee that is also obligated to perform under the contract;

(7) an assignment of a single account, payment intangible, or promissory note to an assignee in full or partial satisfaction of a preexisting indebtedness;

(8) a transfer of an interest in or an assignment of a claim under a policy of insurance, other than an assignment by or to a health-care provider of a health-care-insurance receivable and any subsequent assignment of the right to payment, but Sections 9–315 and 9–322 apply with respect to proceeds and priorities in proceeds;

(9) an assignment of a right represented by a judgment, other than a judgment taken on a right to payment that was collateral;

(10)   a right of recoupment or set-off, but:

(A) Section 9–340 applies with respect to the effectiveness of rights of recoupment or set-off against deposit accounts; and

(B) Section 9–404 applies with respect to defenses or claims of an account debtor;

(11)   the creation or transfer of an interest in or lien on real property, including a lease or rents thereunder, except to the extent that provision is made for:

(A) liens on real property in Sections 9–203 and 9–308;

(B) fixtures in Section 9–334;

(C) fixture filings in Sections 9–501, 9–502, 9–512, 9–516, and 9–519; and

(D) security agreements covering personal and real property in Section 9–604;

(12)   an assignment of a claim arising in tort, other than a commercial tort claim, but Sections 9–315 and 9–322 apply with respect to proceeds and priorities in proceeds; or

(13)   an assignment of a deposit account in a consumer transaction, but Sections 9–315 and 9–322 apply with respect to proceeds and priorities in proceeds.

[6] See *State Variations* at 361–82. Thirteen other states exclude transfers only by "this state." By their limited nature, these exclusions are likely to cause fewer choice of law problems. See *id.*

compensation and similar programs,[7] and (iii)13 states exclude from Article 9 transfers of interests in special needs trusts.[8] The relatively large number of states with these non-uniform exclusions makes it likely that conflict of laws issues will arise with some frequency.

If a transaction that is the subject of a non-uniform exclusion from Article 9 does not have a relationship to any state other than the state that has excluded that transaction from Article 9, and litigation takes place in a forum in that state, Revised Article 9 would not be applicable to the transaction. However, such a purely local transaction (accompanied by local litigation) may not be the norm. In many cases, the parties (or some other aspect of the transaction) may relate to a state that has not excluded the transaction from Article 9, or the litigation may take place in a state that has not excluded the transaction from Article 9. Accordingly, conflict of laws issues must be addressed.

1. Litigation in non-excluding forum

What happens if litigation concerning a security interest excluded from the scope of Article 9 as enacted in State X is instituted in the courts of State Y, which has not excluded the transaction from the scope of Article 9? In such a case, the conflict of laws rules of State Y determine which state's law applies. The Uniform Commercial Code of State Y contains two sets of rules that determine the state whose law will govern secured transactions issues in the litigation. With respect to issues of perfection and priority, UCC Sections 9–301 through 9–307 of State Y provide the rules that determine which state's law governs.[9] With respect to issues of enforceability, attachment, and other rights and duties between debtor and secured party, though, the applicable law is determined by the conflict of laws rules in UCC Article 1 of State Y. Article 1's conflict of laws rules appear in Section 1–301 of Revised Article 1 and Section 1–105 of former Article 1. As the following analysis demonstrates, it is possible for a court in State Y to conclude, by application of that forum's conflict of laws rules, that the law of State Y (or another state that has not excluded the transaction from the scope of Article 9) is applicable, even if the transaction has significant contacts with State X.

a. Enforceability, attachment, and other rights between the parties

If litigation concerning a transaction that is excluded from the scope of Article 9 in State X takes place in the courts of State Y, which has not excluded the transaction from its Article 9, the law that governs enforceability, attachment, and other rights between the parties will be determined by application of Revised Section 1–301 or former Section 1–105, as enacted in the forum state. If application of Revised Section 1–301 or former Section 1–105 directs the State Y court to apply the law of State X, the court will apply that law—which, as a result of the exclusion in State X, will not be Article 9, but, rather, whatever other law of State X governs in light of the fact that the transaction has been excluded from State X's Article 9.[10] It is possible, of course, for Revised Section 1–301 or former Section 1–105 to direct the State Y court to apply the law of State Y (or another state that has not excluded the transaction from Article 9) even though the transaction has some connection to State X. In this regard, it should be noted that both Revised Section 1–301 and former Section 1–105 provide the parties to a transaction with some autonomy as to selection of the governing law.[11]

b. Perfection and priority

If, under the law of the state determined to be applicable pursuant to State Y's enactment of Revised Section 1–301 or former Section 1–105 (whether the applicable law is the non-Article 9 law of State X or Article 9 of State Y), the security interest in question is enforceable and attached, issues of perfection of that

---

[7] See *id.*

[8] See *id.*

[9] More precisely, these sections govern issues of perfection, the effect of perfection or nonperfection, and the priority of a security interest in collateral.

[10] It is important in this regard to recall that excluding a transaction from the scope of Article 9 is not the same thing as prohibiting that transaction. Exclusion from Article 9 merely means that other law governs the transaction. Only if other law prohibits the transaction is the transaction prohibited. As a practical matter, though, parties may be unwilling to enter into a transaction if the other law that would govern it is uncertain or antiquated.

[11] Section 1–301 provides somewhat greater party autonomy in non-consumer transactions but is also explicitly limited by considerations of public policy. See Revised UCC Section 1–301(f).

APPENDIX E

security interest and the priority of that security interest are likely to arise. If the litigation concerning these issues takes place in the courts of State Y, those courts must apply the conflict of laws rules in UCC Sections 9–301 through 9–307 to determine which state's law governs issues of perfection and priority. Once again, depending on the situation, the State Y court might be directed by these sections to apply the non-Article 9 law of State X for either or both of these issues, or it might be directed to apply the law of State Y (or another state that has not excluded application of Article 9 to the transaction at hand);[12] in the latter case, the rules in Article 9 of State Y or such other state would apply even though the transaction has some connection with State X.

2. Litigation in excluding forum

It is also possible for litigation concerning a security interest excluded from the scope of Article 9 in State X to be instituted in the courts of State X, even if the transaction has significant contacts with State Y, which has not excluded the transaction from its enactment of Article 9. In such a case, the conflict of laws rules of State X determine which state's law applies. If all aspects of the transaction relate to no state other than State X, the analysis is likely trivial, resulting in application of the law of State X to all aspects of the transaction; but, as noted above, such a purely local transaction may not be the norm. In cases in which the law of a state other than State X might conceivably apply, the analysis is made much more difficult by the fact that the conflict of laws rules that will determine the applicable law may not be the conflict of laws rules found in the Uniform Commercial Code.

a. Enforceability, attachment, and other rights between the parties

If litigation concerning a transaction that is excluded from the scope of Article 9 in State X takes place in a court of State X, it is not clear which conflict of laws rules the court must apply in order to determine the state whose law governs enforceability, attachment, and other rights between the parties. If no other aspect of the transaction is within the scope of Article 9 of State X or within the scope of another Article of the Uniform Commercial Code of State X, it is likely that the conflict of laws rules in UCC Article 1 do not apply. This result is stated explicitly in Revised UCC Section 1–301(b), and is implicit in former Section 1–105. Thus, the general conflict of laws principles of State X determine whether the non-Article 9 law of State X applies to these issues or, rather, whether the Article 9 of State Y (or another state that has not excluded the transaction from Article 9) applies. Because conflict of laws rules outside the UCC are not uniform in the various states, it may be difficult to predict which state's law would be applied by the courts of a state that has excluded a transaction from Article 9. *It is the view of the Permanent Editorial Board that a court in a state that has excluded from the scope of its Article 9 a transaction that would otherwise be within the scope of that Article should give serious consideration to applying to such a transaction the conflict of laws rules in that state's enactment of Article 1, even though those rules may not, strictly speaking, be binding on the court, on the theory that those rules represent a general statement of legislative policy as to conflict of laws issues in secured transactions.*

b. Perfection and priority

If litigation concerning a transaction that is excluded from the scope of Article 9 in State X takes place in a court of State X, and, under the law applied by that court (whether that law is the non-Article 9 law of State X or Article 9 of State Y), the security interest granted by the debtor to the secured party is enforceable and attached, issues of perfection of that security interest and the priority of that security interest are likely to arise. In such a case, it is also not clear which conflict of laws rules the court must apply in order to determine the state whose law governs issues of perfection and priority. In this situation, UCC Sections 9–301 through 9–307 of State X are not, strictly speaking, applicable to determine which state's law governs issues of perfection and priority. This is because Sections 9–301 through 9–307 are part of Article 9, and, as a result of State X's non-uniform scope provision, Article 9 of State X (including Sections 9–301 through 9–307) does not apply to the transaction. As a result, a State X court will be required to determine (without the explicit legislative guidance in the Uniform Commercial Code) the nature of State X's conflict of laws rule for issues relating to perfection and priority of security interests that are outside the scope of State X's Article 9. A search for such conflict of laws rules might be quite difficult, and the search could conceivably

---

[12] The conflict of laws rules in Sections 9–301 through 9–307, unlike those in Revised Section 1–301 and former Section 1–105, do not generally defer to choices made by the parties.

lead to a rule directing the court to apply the law of a state other than the state whose law that would be applicable by virtue of UCC Sections 9–301 through 9–307. Such a result would be unfortunate, because it would necessitate parties to secured transactions that are excluded from the scope of Article 9 in *any* state to consider the possibility that litigation concerning the security interest might take place in such a state, and that the courts of that state might look to the law of a different state for perfection (and, thus, the location of any required filing) than would a state that has enacted the Official Text of Article 9. Requiring parties to perform such complex conflict of laws analyses not based on application of the conflict of laws rules of the Uniform Commercial Code, and to make protective filings in various states in order to be sure of perfection regardless of where litigation takes place, is wasteful. *Accordingly, it is the view of the Permanent Editorial Board that a court in a state that has excluded from the scope of its Article 9 a transaction that would otherwise be within the scope of that Article should give serious consideration to applying to such a transaction the conflict of laws rules in that state's enactment of Sections 9–301 through 9–307, even though those rules may not, strictly speaking, be binding on the court, on the theory that those rules represent a general statement of legislative policy as to conflict of laws issues in secured transactions.*

B. Non-uniform Inclusions

For purposes of this Report, attention is drawn to non-uniform enactments of UCC Section 9–109(d) which delete the exclusion in Section 9–109(d)(13) for "an assignment of a deposit account in a consumer transaction."[13] This exclusion is deleted in the enactment of Revised Article 9 in four states—Idaho, Illinois, Mississippi, and North Dakota. As in the case of non-uniform exclusions from the scope of Article 9, this leads to the possibility of differing determinations of applicable law depending on whether a dispute is litigated in a state that has enacted the Official Text of Article 9 or a state that has enacted this non-uniform inclusion with respect to Article 9.

The basic conflict of laws analysis for this non-uniform inclusion is the same as described in Part A of this Report. If an issue concerning a security interest in a deposit account in a consumer transaction is litigated in a state that has enacted the Official Text of Revised Article 9 and, thus, in which assignments of deposit accounts in consumer transactions are outside the scope of Article 9, neither the conflict of laws rules in Revised Section 1–301 or former Section 1–105 (governing attachment, enforceability, and other bilateral issues) nor the conflict of laws rules in Sections 9–301 through 9–307 (governing perfection and priority) are applicable. This can lead to uncertainty as to the applicability of Article 9 if the transaction also touches upon one of the states that has enacted the non-uniform inclusion of deposit accounts in consumer transactions. *As is the case with respect to non-uniform exclusions from the scope of Article 9, discussed in Part A, it is the view of the Permanent Editorial Board that a court in a state that has followed the Official Text of Revised Article 9 and, accordingly, has enacted the exclusion of assignments of deposit accounts in consumer transactions from the scope of Article 9, should consider its legislature's enactment of the conflict of laws rules in that state's enactment of Article 1 and Sections 9–301 through 9–307 as general statements of legislative policy as to conflict of laws issues in secured transactions and apply the principles of those sections to conflict of laws issues relating to assignments of such deposit accounts even though, strictly speaking, they may not be binding on the court.*

If, on the other hand, an issue concerning a security interest in a deposit account in a consumer transaction is litigated in a state that has enacted the non-uniform inclusion of these transactions in the scope of Article 9, the conflict of laws rules in Revised Section 1–301 and former Section 1–105 (governing attachment, enforceability, and other bilateral issues) and the conflict of laws rules in Sections 9–301 through 9–307 (governing perfection and priority) are applicable.

III. Conclusion

The non-uniform enactments of the scope provisions of Revised Article 9 leads to the possibility of non-uniform determinations of which state's law governs legal issues arising from a secured transaction. As a result, different rules could be applied to a secured transaction depending on the location of the court in which litigation takes place. This situation would impose significant costs and uncertainty on transactions that are the subject of non-uniform scope provisions. This difficulty can be avoided if courts in states with

---

[13] Section 9–109(d)(13) provides, however, that "sections 9–315 and 9–322 apply with respect to proceeds and priorities in proceeds."

non-uniform scope provisions nonetheless consider their legislatures' enactments of Revised Section 1–301 or former Section 1–105 and Sections 9–301 through 9–307 as general statements of legislative policy as to conflict of laws issues in secured transactions and apply the principles of those sections even though, strictly speaking, they may not be binding on the court. If this practice is followed, all U.S. courts should make the same determination of which state's law governs issues arising under a secured transaction that is within the scope of Article 9 in some, but not all, states.

REPORT OF THE PERMANENT EDITORIAL BOARD FOR THE UNIFORM COMMERCIAL CODE

APPLICATION OF THE UNIFORM COMMERCIAL CODE TO SELECTED ISSUES RELATING TO MORTGAGE NOTES
(November 14, 2011)

Preface

In 1961, the American Law Institute and the Uniform Law Commission, the organizations that jointly sponsor the Uniform Commercial Code, established the Permanent Editorial Board for the Uniform Commercial Code (PEB). One of the charges of the PEB is to issue commentaries "and other articulations as appropriate to reflect the correct interpretation of the [Uniform Commercial] Code and issuing the same in a manner and at times best calculated to advance the uniformity and orderly development of commercial law." Such commentaries and other articulations are issued directly by the PEB rather than by action of the American Law Institute and the Uniform Law Commission.

This Report of the Permanent Editorial Board is such an articulation, addressing the application of the Uniform Commercial Code to issues of legal, economic, and social importance arising from the issuance and transfer of mortgage notes. A draft of this Report was made available to the public for comment on March 29, 2011, and the comments that were received have been taken into account in preparing the final Report.

Introduction

Recent economic developments have brought to the forefront complex legal issues about the enforcement and collection of mortgage debt. Many of these issues are governed by local real property law and local rules of foreclosure procedure, but others are addressed in a uniform way throughout the United States by provisions of the Uniform Commercial Code (UCC).[1] Although the UCC provisions are settled law, it has become apparent that not all courts and attorneys are familiar with them. In addition, the complexity of some of the rules has proved daunting.

The Permanent Editorial Board for the Uniform Commercial Code[2] has prepared this Report in order to further the understanding of this statutory background by identifying and explaining several key rules in the UCC that govern the transfer and enforcement of notes secured by a mortgage[3] on real property. The

---

[1] The UCC is a uniform law sponsored by the American Law Institute and the Uniform Law Commission. It has been enacted in every state (as well as the District of Columbia, Puerto Rico, and the United States Virgin Islands) in whole or significant part. This Report is based on the current Official Text of the UCC. Some states have enacted some non-uniform provisions that are generally not relevant to the issues discussed in this Report. Of course, the enacted text of the UCC in the state whose law is applicable governs. See note 6, *infra*, regarding the various different versions of Article 3 of the UCC in effect in the states.

[2] In 1961, the American Law Institute and the Uniform Law Commission, the organizations that jointly sponsor the UCC, established the Permanent Editorial Board for the Uniform Commercial Code (PEB). One of the charges of the PEB is to issue commentaries "and other articulations as appropriate to reflect the correct interpretation of the [Uniform Commercial] Code and issuing the same in a manner and at times best calculated to advance the uniformity and orderly development of commercial law."

[3] This Report, like Article 9 of the UCC, uses the term "mortgage" to include a consensual interest in real property to secure an obligation whether created by mortgage, trust deed, or the like. See UCC § 9–102(a)(55) and Official Comment 17 thereto and former UCC § 9–105(1)(j). This Report uses the term "mortgage note" to refer to a note secured by a mortgage, whether or not the note is a negotiable instrument under UCC Article 3.

REPORT OF THE PERMANENT EDITORIAL BOARD

UCC, of course, does not resolve all issues in this field. Most particularly, as to both substance and procedure, the enforcement of real estate mortgages by foreclosure is primarily the province of a state's real property law (although determinations made pursuant to the UCC are typically relevant under that law). Accordingly, this Report should be understood as providing guidance only as to the issues the Report addresses.[4]

Background

Issues relating to the transfer, ownership, and enforcement of mortgage notes are primarily governed by two Articles of the UCC:

- In cases in which the mortgage note is a negotiable instrument,[5] Article 3 of the UCC[6] provides rules governing the obligations of parties on the note[7] and the enforcement of those obligations.

- In cases involving either negotiable or non-negotiable notes, Article 9 of the UCC[8] contains important rules governing how ownership of those notes may be transferred, the effect of the transfer of ownership of the notes on the ownership of the mortgages securing those notes, and the right of the transferee, under certain circumstances, to record its interest in the mortgage in the applicable real estate recording office.

This Report explains the application of the rules in both of those UCC Articles to provide guidance in:

- Identifying the person who is entitled to enforce the payment obligation of the maker[9] of a mortgage note, and to whom the maker owes that obligation; and

- Determining who owns the rights represented by the note and mortgage.

Together, the provisions in Articles 3 and 9 of the UCC (along with general principles that appear in Article 1 and that apply to all transactions governed by the UCC) provide legal rules that apply to these questions.[10]

---

[4] Of course, the application of the UCC rules to particular factual circumstances depends on the nature of those circumstances. Facts raising legal issues other than those addressed in this Report can result in different rights and obligations than would be the case in the absence of those facts. Accordingly, this Report should not be read as a statement of the total legal implications of any factual scenario. Rather, the Report sets out the UCC rules that are common to the transactions discussed so as to provide a common basis for understanding the application of those rules. The impact of non-UCC law that applies to other aspects of such transactions is beyond the scope of this Report.

[5] The requirements that must be satisfied in order for a note to be a negotiable instrument are set out in UCC § 3–104.

[6] Except for New York, every state (as well as the District of Columbia, Puerto Rico, and the United States Virgin Islands) has enacted either the 1990 Official Text of Article 3 or the newer 2002 Official Text (the latter having been adopted in ten states as of the date of this Report). Unless indicated to the contrary all discussions of provisions in Article 3 apply equally to both versions. Much of the analysis of UCC Article 3 in this Report also applies under the older version of Article 3 in effect in New York, although many section numbers differ. The Report does not address those aspects of New York's Article 3 that are different from the 1990 or 2002 texts.

[7] In this Report, such notes are sometimes referred to as "negotiable notes."

[8] Unlike Article 3 (which has not been enacted in its modern form in New York), the current version of Article 9 has been enacted in all 50 states, the District of Columbia, and the United States Virgin Islands. Some states have enacted non-uniform provisions that are generally not relevant to the issues discussed in this Report (but see note 31 with respect to one relevant non-uniformity). A limited set of amendments to Article 9 was approved by the American Law Institute and the Uniform Law Commission in 2010. Except as noted in this Report, those amendments (which provide for a uniform effective date of July 1, 2013) are not germane to the matters addressed in this Report.

[9] A note can have more than one obligor. In some cases, this is because there is more than one maker (in which case they are jointly and severally liable; see UCC § 3–116(a)). In other cases, there may be an indorser. The obligation of an indorser is different from that of a maker in that the indorser's obligation is triggered by dishonor of the note (see UCC § 3–415) and, unless waived, indorsers have additional procedural protections (such as notice of dishonor; see UCC § 3–503)). These differences do not affect the issues addressed in this Report. For simplicity, this Report uses the term "maker" to refer to both makers and indorsers.

[10] Subject to limitations on the ability to affect the rights of third parties, the effect of these provisions may be varied by agreement. UCC § 1–302. Variation by agreement is not permitted when the variation would disclaim obligations of good faith, diligence, reasonableness, or care prescribed by the UCC or when the UCC otherwise so indicates (see, *e.g.*, UCC § 9–602). But the meaning of the statute itself cannot be varied by agreement. Thus, for example, private parties cannot make a note negotiable unless it complies with UCC § 3–104. See Official Comment 1 to UCC § 1–302. Similarly,

Moreover, these rules displace any inconsistent common law rules that might have otherwise previously governed the same questions.[11]

This Report does not, however, address all of the rules in the UCC relating to enforcement, transfer, and ownership of mortgage notes. Rather, it reviews the rules relating to four specific questions:

- Who is the person entitled to enforce a mortgage note and, correspondingly, to whom is the obligation to pay the note owed?

- How can the owner of a mortgage note effectively transfer ownership of that note to another person or effectively use that note as collateral for an obligation?

- What is the effect of transfer of an interest in a mortgage note on the mortgage securing it?

- May a person to whom an interest in a mortgage note has been transferred, but who has not taken a recordable assignment of the mortgage, take steps to become the assignee of record in the real estate recording system of the mortgage securing the note?[12]

Question One—To Whom is the Obligation to Pay a Mortgage Note Owed?

If the mortgage note is a negotiable instrument,[13] Article 3 of the UCC provides a largely complete set of rules governing the obligations of parties on the note, including how to determine who may enforce those obligations and, thus, to whom those obligations are owed. The following discussion analyzes the application of these rules to that determination in the context of mortgage notes that are negotiable instruments.[14]

In the context of mortgage notes that have been sold or used as collateral to secure an obligation, the central concept for making that determination is identification of the "person entitled to enforce" the note.[15] Several issues are resolved by that determination. Most particularly:

(i) the maker's obligation on the note is to pay the amount of the note to *the person entitled to enforce the note*,[16]

---

parties may not avoid the application of UCC Article 9 to a transaction that falls within its scope. See *id.* and Official Comment 2 to UCC § 9–109.

[11] UCC § 1–103(b). As noted in Official Comment 2 to UCC § 1–103:

The Uniform Commercial Code was drafted against the backdrop of existing bodies of law, including the common law and equity, and relies on those bodies of law to supplement its provisions in many important ways. At the same time, the Uniform Commercial Code is the primary source of commercial law rules in areas that it governs, and its rules represent choices made by its drafters and the enacting legislatures about the appropriate policies to be furthered in the transactions it covers. Therefore, while principles of common law and equity may *supplement* provisions of the Uniform Commercial Code, they may not be used to *supplant* its provisions, or the purposes and policies those provisions reflect, unless a specific provision of the Uniform Commercial Code provides otherwise. In the absence of such a provision, the Uniform Commercial Code preempts principles of common law and equity that are inconsistent with either its provisions or its purposes and policies.

[12] The Report does not discuss the application of common law principles, such as the law of agency, that supplement the provisions of the UCC other than to note some situations in which the text or comments of the UCC identify such principles as being relevant. See UCC § 1–103(b).

[13] See UCC § 3–104 for the requirements that must be fulfilled in order for a payment obligation to qualify as a negotiable instrument. It should not be assumed that all mortgage notes are negotiable instruments. The issue of the negotiability of a particular mortgage note, which requires application of the standards in UCC § 3–104 to the words of the particular note, is beyond the scope of this Report.

[14] Law other than Article 3, including contract law, governs this determination for non-negotiable mortgage notes. That law is beyond the scope of this Report.

[15] The concept of "person entitled to enforce" a note is not synonymous with "owner" of the note. See Official Comment 1 to UCC § 3–203. A person need not be the owner of a note to be the person entitled to enforce it, and not all owners will qualify as persons entitled to enforce. Rules that address transfer of ownership of a note are addressed in the discussion of Question 2 below.

[16] UCC § 3–412. (If the note has been dishonored, and an indorser has paid the note to the person entitled to enforce it, the maker's obligation runs to the indorser.)

(ii) the maker's payment to *the person entitled to enforce the note* results in discharge of the maker's obligation,[17] and

(iii) the maker's failure to pay, when due, the amount of the note to *the person entitled to enforce the note* constitutes dishonor of the note.[18]

Thus, a person seeking to enforce rights based on the failure of the maker to pay a mortgage note must identify the person entitled to enforce the note and establish that that person has not been paid. This portion of this Report sets out the criteria for qualifying as a "person entitled to enforce" a mortgage note. The discussion of Question Two addresses how ownership of a mortgage note may be effectively transferred from an owner to another person.

UCC Section 3–301 provides only three ways in which a person may qualify as the person entitled to enforce a note, two of which require the person to be in possession of the note (which may include possession by a third party that possesses it for the person):[19]

- The first way that a person may qualify as the person entitled to enforce a note is to be its "holder." This familiar concept, set out in detail in UCC Section 1–201(b)(21)(A), requires that the person be in possession of the note and either (i) the note is payable to that person or (ii) the note is payable to bearer. Determining to whom a note is payable requires examination not only of the face of the note but also of any indorsements. This is because the party to whom a note is payable may be changed by indorsement[20] so that, for example, a note payable to the order of a named payee that is indorsed in blank by that payee becomes payable to bearer.[21]

- The second way that a person may be the person entitled to enforce a note is to be a "nonholder in possession of the [note] who has the rights of a holder."

  o How can a person who is not the holder of a note have the rights of a holder? This can occur by operation of law outside the UCC, such as the law of subrogation or estate administration, by which one person is the successor to or acquires another person's rights.[22] It can also occur if the delivery of the note to that person constitutes a "transfer" (as that term is defined in UCC Section 3–203, see below) because transfer of a note "vests in the transferee any right of the transferor to enforce the instrument."[23] Thus, if a holder (who, as seen above, is a person entitled to enforce a note) transfers the note to another person, that other person

---

[17] UCC § 3–602. The law of agency is applicable in determining whether a payment has been made to a person entitled to enforce. See *id.*, Official Comment 3. Note that, in states that have enacted the 2002 Official Text of UCC Article 3, UCC § 3–602(b) provides that a maker is also discharged by paying a person formerly entitled to enforce the note if the maker has not received adequate notification that the note has been transferred and that payment is to be made to the transferee. This amendment aligns the protection afforded to makers of notes that have been assigned with comparable protection afforded to obligors on other payment rights that have been assigned. See, *e.g.*, UCC § 9–406(a); Restatement (Second), Contracts § 338(1).

[18] See UCC § 3–502. See also UCC § 3–602.

[19] See UCC § 1–103(b) (unless displaced by particular provisions of the UCC, the law of, *inter alia*, principal and agent supplements the provisions of the UCC). See also UCC § 3–420, Comment 1 ("Delivery to an agent [of a payee] is delivery to the payee."). Note that "delivery" of a negotiable instrument is defined in UCC § 1–201(b)(15) as voluntary transfer of possession. This Report does not address the determination of whether a particular person is an agent of another person under the law of agency and the agency law implications of such a determination.

[20] "Indorsement," as defined in UCC § 3–204(a), requires the signature of the indorser. The law of agency determines whether a signature made by a person purporting to act as a representative binds the represented person. UCC § 3–402(a); see note 12, supra. An indorsement may appear either on the instrument or on a separate piece of paper (usually referred to as an *allonge*) affixed to the instrument. See UCC § 3–204(a) and Comment 1, par. 4.

[21] UCC Section 3–205 contains the rules concerning the effect of various types of indorsement on the party to whom a note is payable. Either a "special indorsement" (see UCC § 3–205(a)) or a "blank indorsement" (see UCC § 3–205(b)) can change the identity of the person to whom the note is payable. A special indorsement is an indorsement that identifies the person to whom it makes the note payable, while a blank indorsement is an indorsement that does not identify such a person and results in the instrument becoming payable to bearer. When an instrument is indorsed in blank (and, thus, is payable to bearer), it may be negotiated by transfer of possession alone until specially indorsed. UCC § 3–205(b).

[22] See Official Comment to UCC § 3–301.

[23] UCC § 3–203(b).

(the transferee) obtains from the holder the right to enforce the note even if the transferee does not become the holder (as in the example below). Similarly, a subsequent transfer will result in the subsequent transferee being a person entitled to enforce the note.

o Under what circumstances does delivery of a note qualify as a transfer? As stated in UCC Section 3–203(a), a note is transferred "when it is delivered by a person other than its issuer for the purpose of giving to the person receiving delivery the right to enforce the instrument." For example, assume that the payee of a note sells it to an assignee, intending to transfer all of the payee's rights to the note, but delivers the note to the assignee without indorsing it. The assignee will not qualify as a holder (because the note is still payable to the payee) but, because the transaction between the payee and the assignee qualifies as a transfer, the assignee now has all of the payee's rights to enforce the note and thereby qualifies as the person entitled to enforce it. Thus, the failure to obtain the indorsement of the payee does not prevent a person in possession of the note from being the person entitled to enforce it, but demonstrating that status is more difficult. This is because the person in possession of the note must also demonstrate the purpose of the delivery of the note to it in order to qualify as the person entitled to enforce.[24]

- There is a third method of qualifying as a person entitled to enforce a note that, unlike the previous two methods, does not require possession of the note. This method is quite limited—it applies only in cases in which "the person cannot reasonably obtain possession of the instrument because the instrument was destroyed, its whereabouts cannot be determined, or it is in the wrongful possession of an unknown person or a person that cannot be found or is not amenable to service of process."[25] In such a case, a person qualifies as a person entitled to enforce the note if the person demonstrates not only that one of those circumstances is present but also demonstrates that the person was formerly in possession of the note and entitled to enforce it when the loss of possession occurred and that the loss of possession was not as a result of transfer (as defined above) or lawful seizure. If the person proves those facts, as well as the terms of the note, the person is a person entitled to enforce the note and may seek to enforce it even though it is not in possession of the note,[26] but the court may not enter judgment in favor of the person unless the court finds that the maker is adequately protected against loss that might occur if the note subsequently reappears.[27]

Illustrations:

1. Maker issued a negotiable mortgage note payable to the order of Payee. Payee is in possession of the note, which has not been indorsed. Payee is the holder of the note and, therefore, is the person entitled to enforce it. UCC §§ 1–201(b)(21)(A), 3–301(i).

2. Maker issued a negotiable mortgage note payable to the order of Payee. Payee indorsed the note in blank and gave possession of it to Transferee. Transferee is the holder of the note and, therefore, is the person entitled to enforce it. UCC §§ 1–201(b)(21)(A), 3–301(i).

3. Maker issued a negotiable mortgage note payable to the order of Payee. Payee sold the note to Transferee and gave possession of it to Transferee for the purpose of giving Transferee the right

---

[24] If the note was transferred for value and the transferee does not qualify as a holder because of the lack of indorsement by the transferor, "the transferee has a specifically enforceable right to the unqualified indorsement of the transferor." See UCC § 3–203(c).

[25] UCC § 3–309(a)(iii) (1990 text), 3–309(a)(3) (2002 text). The 2002 text goes on to provide that a transferee from the person who lost possession of a note may also qualify as a person entitled to enforce it. See UCC § 3–309(a)(1)(B) (2002). This point was thought to be implicit in the 1990 text, but was rejected in some cases in which the issue was raised. The reasoning of those cases was rejected in Official Comment 5 to UCC § 9–109 and the point was made explicit in the 2002 text of Article 3.

[26] To prevail the person must establish not only that the person is a person entitled to enforce the note but also the other elements of the maker's obligation to pay such a person. See generally UCC §§ 3–309(b), 3–412. Moreover, as is the case with respect to the enforcement of all rights under the UCC, the person enforcing the note must act in good faith in enforcing the note. UCC § 1–304.

[27] See *id*. UCC § 3–309(b) goes on to state that "Adequate protection may be provided by any reasonable means."

to enforce the note. Payee did not, however, indorse the note. Transferee is not the holder of the note because, while Transferee is in possession of the note, it is payable neither to bearer nor to Transferee. UCC § 1–201(b)(21)(A). Nonetheless, Transferee is a person entitled to enforce the note. This is because the note was transferred to Transferee and the transfer vested in Transferee Payee's right to enforce the note. UCC § 3–203(a)–(b). As a result, Transferee is a nonholder in possession of the note with the rights of a holder and, accordingly, a person entitled to enforce the note. UCC § 3–301(ii).

4. Same facts as Illustrations 2 and 3, except that (i) under the law of agency, Agent is the agent of Transferee for purposes of possessing the note and (ii) it is Agent, rather than Transferee, to whom actual physical possession of the note is given by Payee. In the facts of Illustration 2, Transferee is a holder of the note and a person entitled to enforce it. In the context of Illustration 3, Transferee is a person entitled to enforce the note. Whether Agent may enforce the note or mortgage on behalf of Transferee depends in part on the law of agency and, in the case of the mortgage, real property law.

5. Same facts as Illustration 2, except that after obtaining possession of the note, Transferee lost the note and its whereabouts cannot be determined. Transferee is a person entitled to enforce the note even though Transferee does not have possession of it. UCC § 3–309(a). If Transferee brings an action on the note against Maker, Transferee must establish the terms of the note and the elements of Maker's obligation on it. The court may not enter judgment in favor of Transferee, however, unless the court finds that Maker is adequately protected against loss that might occur by reason of a claim of another person (such as the finder of the note) to enforce the note. UCC § 3–309(b).

Question Two—What Steps Must be Taken for the Owner of a Mortgage Note to Transfer Ownership of the Note to Another Person or Use the Note as Collateral for an Obligation?

In the discussion of Question One, this Report addresses identification of the person who is entitled to enforce a note. That discussion does not address who "owns" the note. While, in many cases, the person entitled to enforce a note is also its owner, this need not be the case. The rules that determine whether a person is a person entitled to enforce a note do not require that person to be the owner of the note,[28] and a change in ownership of a note does not necessarily bring about a concomitant change in the identity of the person entitled to enforce the note. This is because the rules that determine who is entitled to enforce a note and the rules that determine whether the note, or an interest in it, have been effectively transferred serve different functions:

- The rules that determine who is entitled to enforce a note are concerned primarily with the maker of the note, providing the maker with a relatively simple way of determining to whom his or her obligation is owed and, thus, whom to pay in order to be discharged.

- The rules concerning transfer of ownership and other interests in a note, on the other hand, primarily relate to who, among competing claimants, is entitled to the economic value of the note.

In a typical transaction, when a note is issued to a payee, the note is initially owned by that payee. If that payee seeks either to use the note as collateral or sell the note outright, Article 9 of the UCC governs that transaction and determines whether the creditor or buyer has obtained a property right in the note. As is generally known, Article 9 governs transactions in which property is used as collateral for an obligation.[29] In addition, however, Article 9 governs the sale of most payment rights, including the sale of both negotiable and non-negotiable notes.[30] With very few exceptions, the same Article 9 rules that apply to transactions in

---

28 See UCC § 3–301, which provides, in relevant part, that "A person may be a person entitled to enforce the instrument even though the person is not the owner of the instrument. . . ."

29 UCC § 9–109(a)(1).

30 With certain limited exceptions not germane to this Report, Article 9 governs the sale of accounts, chattel paper, payment intangibles, and promissory notes. UCC § 9–109(a)(3). The term "promissory note" includes not only notes that fulfill the requirements of a negotiable instrument under UCC § 3–104 but also notes that do not fulfill those requirements but nonetheless are of a "type that in ordinary business is transferred by delivery with any necessary

which a payment right is collateral for an obligation also apply to transactions in which a payment right is sold. Rather than contain two parallel sets of rules—one for transactions in which payment rights are collateral and the other for sales of payment rights—Article 9 uses nomenclature conventions to apply one set of rules to both types of transactions. This is accomplished primarily by defining the term "security interest" to include not only an interest in property that secures an obligation but also the right of a buyer of a payment right in a transaction governed by Article 9.[31] Similarly, definitional conventions denominate the seller of such a payment right as the "debtor," the buyer as the "secured party," and the sold payment right as the "collateral."[32] As a result, for purposes of Article 9, the buyer of a promissory note is a "secured party" that has acquired a "security interest" in the note from the "debtor," and the rules that apply to security interests that secure an obligation generally also apply to transactions in which a promissory note is sold.

Section 9–203(b) of the Uniform Commercial Code provides that three criteria must be fulfilled in order for the owner of a mortgage note effectively to create a "security interest" (either an interest in the note securing an obligation or the outright sale of the note to a buyer) in it.

- The first two criteria are straightforward—"value" must be given[33] and the debtor/seller must have rights in the note or the power to transfer rights in the note to a third party.[34]

- The third criterion may be fulfilled in either one of two ways. Either the debtor/seller must "authenticate"[35] a "security agreement"[36] that describes the note[37] or the secured party must take possession[38] of the note pursuant to the debtor's security agreement.[39]

---

indorsement or assignment." See UCC §§ 9–102(a)(65) (definition of "promissory note") and 9–102(a)(47) (definition of "instrument" as the term is used in Article 9).

[31] See UCC § 1–201(b)(35) [UCC § 1–201(37) in states that have not yet enacted the 2001 revised text of UCC Article 1]. (For reasons that are not apparent, when South Carolina enacted the 1998 revised text of UCC Article 9, which included an amendment to UCC § 1–201 to expand the definition of "security interest" to include the right of a buyer of a promissory note, it did not enact the amendment to § 1–201. This Report does not address the effect of that omission.) The limitation to transactions governed by Article 9 refers to the exclusion, in cases not germane to this Report, of certain assignments of payment rights from the reach of Article 9.

[32] UCC §§ 9–102(a)(28)(B); 9–102(a)(72)(D); 9–102(a)(12)(B).

[33] UCC § 9–203(b)(1). UCC § 1–204 provides that giving "value" for rights includes not only acquiring them for consideration but also acquiring them in return for a binding commitment to extend credit, as security for or in complete or partial satisfaction of a preexisting claim, or by accepting delivery of them under a preexisting contract for their purchase.

[34] UCC § 9–203(b)(2). Limited rights that are short of full ownership are sufficient for this purpose. See Official Comment 6 to UCC § 9–203.

[35] This term is defined to include signing and its electronic equivalent. See UCC § 9–102(a)(7).

[36] A "security agreement" is an agreement that creates or provides for a security interest (including the rights of a buyer arising upon the outright sale of a payment right). See UCC § 9–102(a)(73).

[37] Article 9's criteria for descriptions of property in a security agreement are quite flexible. Generally speaking, any description suffices, whether or not specific, if it reasonably identifies the property. See UCC § 9–108(a)–(b). A "supergeneric" description consisting solely of words such as "all of the debtor's assets" or "all of the debtor's personal property" is not sufficient, however. UCC § 9–108(c). A narrower description, limiting the property to a particular category or type, such as "all notes," is sufficient. For example, a description that refers to "all of the debtor's notes" is sufficient.

[38] See UCC § 9–313. As noted in Official Comment 3 to UCC § 9–313, "in determining whether a particular person has possession, the principles of agency apply." In addition, UCC § 9–313 also contains two special rules under which possession by a non-agent may constitute possession by the secured party. First, if a person who is not an agent is in possession of the collateral and the person authenticates a record acknowledging that the person holds the collateral for the secured party's benefit, possession by that person constitutes possession by the secured party. UCC § 9–313(c). Second, a secured party that has possession of collateral does not relinquish possession by delivering the collateral to another person (other than the debtor or a lessee of the collateral from the debtor in the ordinary course of the debtor's business) if the delivery is accompanied by instructions to that person to hold possession of the collateral for the benefit of the secured party or redeliver it to the secured party. UCC § 9–313(h). See also Official Comment 9 to UCC § 9–313 ("New subsections (h) and (i) address the practice of mortgage warehouse lenders.") Possession as contemplated by UCC § 9–313 is also possession for purposes of UCC § 9–203. See UCC § 9–203, Comment 4.

[39] UCC §§ 9–203(b)(3)(A)–(B).

- o Thus, if the secured party (including a buyer) takes possession of the mortgage note pursuant to the security agreement of the debtor (including a seller), this criterion is satisfied even if that agreement is oral or otherwise not evidenced by an authenticated record.

- o Alternatively, if the debtor authenticates a security agreement describing the note, this criterion is satisfied even if the secured party does *not* take possession of the note. (Note that in this situation, in which the seller of a note may retain possession of it, the owner of a note may be a different person than the person entitled to enforce the note.)[40]

Satisfaction of these three criteria of Section 9–203(b) results in the secured party (including a buyer of the note) obtaining a property right (whether outright ownership or a security interest to secure an obligation) in the note from the debtor (including a seller of the note).[41]

Illustrations:

6. Maker issued a mortgage note payable to the order of Payee.[42] Payee borrowed money from Funder and, to secure Payee's repayment obligation, Payee and Funder agreed that Funder would have a security interest in the note. Simultaneously with the funding of the loan, Payee gave possession of the note to Funder. Funder has an attached and enforceable security interest in the note. UCC § 9–203(b). This is the case even if Payee's agreement is oral or otherwise not evidenced by an authenticated record. Payee is no longer a person entitled to enforce the note (because Payee is no longer in possession of it and it has not been lost, stolen, or destroyed). UCC § 3–301. Funder is a person entitled to enforce the note if either (i) Payee indorsed the note by blank indorsement or by a special indorsement identifying Funder as the person to whom the indorsement makes the note payable (because, in such cases, Funder would be the holder of the note), or (ii) the delivery of the note from Payee to Funder constitutes a transfer of the note under UCC § 3–203 (because, in such case, Funder would be a nonholder in possession of the note with the rights of a holder). See also UCC §§ 1–201(b)(21)(A), 3–205(a)–(b), and 3–301(i)–(ii).

7. Maker issued a mortgage note payable to the order of Payee. Payee borrowed money from Funder and, in a signed writing that reasonably identified the note (whether specifically or as part of a category or a type of property defined in the UCC), granted Funder a security interest in the note to secure Payee's repayment obligation. Payee, however, retained possession of the note. Funder has an attached and enforceable security interest in the note. UCC § 9–203(b). If the note is negotiable, Payee remains the holder and the person entitled to enforce the note because Payee is in possession of it and it is payable to the order of Payee. UCC §§ 1–201(b)(21)(A), 3–301(i).

---

[40] As noted in the discussion of Question One, payment by the maker of a negotiable note to the person entitled to enforce it discharges the maker's obligations on the note. UCC § 3–602. This is the case even if the person entitled to enforce the note is not its owner. As between the person entitled to enforce the note and the owner of the note, the right to the money paid by the maker is determined by the UCC and other applicable law, such as the law of contract and the law of restitution, as well as agency law. See, e.g., UCC §§ 3–306 and 9–315(a)(2). As noted in comment 3 to UCC § 3–602, "if the original payee of the note transfers ownership of the note to a third party but continues to service the obligation, the law of agency might treat payments made to the original payee as payments made to the third party."

[41] For cases in which another person claims an interest in the note (whether as a result of another voluntary transfer by the debtor or otherwise), reference to Article 9's rules governing perfection and priority of security interests may be required in order to rank order those claims (and, in some cases, determine whether a party has taken the note free of competing claims to the note). In the case of notes that are negotiable instruments, the Article 3 concept of "holder in due course" (see UCC § 3–302) should be considered as well, because a holder in due course takes its rights in an instrument free of competing property claims to it (as well as free of most defenses to obligations on it). See UCC §§ 3–305 and 3–306. With respect to determining whether the owner of a note has effectively transferred a property interest to a transferee, however, the perfection and priority rules are largely irrelevant. (The application of the perfection and priority rules can result in the rights of the transferee either being subordinate to the rights of a competing claimant or being extinguished by the rights of the competing claimant. See, e.g., UCC §§ 9–317(b), 9–322(a), 9–330(d), and 9–331(a).)

[42] For this Illustration, as well as Illustrations 7–11, the analysis under UCC Article 9 is the same whether the mortgage note is negotiable or non-negotiable. This is because, in either case, the mortgage note will qualify as a "promissory note" and, therefore, an "instrument" under UCC Article 9. See UCC §§ 9–102(a)(47), (65).

8.   Maker issued a mortgage note payable to the order of Payee. Payee sold the note to Funder, giving possession of the note to Funder in exchange for the purchase price. The sale of the note is governed by Article 9 and the rights of Funder as buyer constitute a "security interest." UCC §§ 9–109(a)(3), 1–201(b)(35). The security interest is attached and is enforceable. UCC § 9–203(b). This is the case even if the sales agreement was oral or otherwise not evidenced by an authenticated record. If the note is negotiable, Funder is also a person entitled to enforce the note, whether or not Payee indorsed it, because either (i) Funder is a holder of the note (if Payee indorsed it by blank indorsement or by a special indorsement identifying Funder as the person to whom the indorsement makes the note payable) or (ii) Funder is a nonholder in possession of the note (if there is no such indorsement) who has obtained the rights of Payee by transfer of the note pursuant to UCC § 3–203. See also UCC §§ 1–201(b)(21)(A), 3–205(a)–(b), and 3–301(i)–(ii).

9.   Maker issued a mortgage note payable to the order of Payee. Pursuant to a signed writing that reasonably identified the note (whether specifically or as part of a category or a type of property defined in the UCC), Payee sold the note to Funder. Payee, however, retained possession of the note. The sale of the note is governed by Article 9 and the rights of Funder as buyer constitute a "security interest." UCC § 1–201(b)(35). The security interest is attached and is enforceable. UCC § 9–203(b). If the note is negotiable, Payee remains the holder and the person entitled to enforce the note (even though, as between Payee and Funder, Funder owns the note) because Payee is in possession of it and it is payable to the order of Payee. UCC §§ 1–201(b)(21)(A), 3–301(i).

Question Three—What is the Effect of Transfer of an Interest in a Mortgage Note on the Mortgage Securing It?

What if a note secured by a mortgage is sold (or the note is used as collateral to secure an obligation), but the parties do not take any additional actions to assign the mortgage that secures payment of the note, such as execution of a recordable assignment of the mortgage? UCC Section 9–203(g) explicitly provides that, in such cases, the assignment of the interest of the seller or other grantor of a security interest in the note automatically transfers a corresponding interest in the mortgage to the assignee: "The attachment of a security interest in a right to payment or performance secured by a security interest or other lien on personal or real property is also attachment of a security interest in the security interest, mortgage, or other lien." (As noted previously, a "security interest" in a note includes the right of a buyer of the note.)

While this question has provoked some uncertainty and has given rise to some judicial analysis that disregards the impact of Article 9,[43] the UCC is unambiguous: the sale of a mortgage note (or other grant of a security interest in the note) not accompanied by a separate conveyance of the mortgage securing the note does not result in the mortgage being severed from the note.[44]

It is important to note in this regard, however, that UCC Section 9–203(g) addresses only whether, as between the seller of a mortgage note (or a debtor who uses it as collateral) and the buyer or other secured

---

[43] *See, e.g.,* the discussion of this issue in *U.S. Bank v. Ibanez,* 458 Mass. 637 at 652–53, 941 N.E.2d 40 at 53–54 (2011). In that discussion, the court cited Massachusetts common law precedents pre-dating the enactment of the current text of Article 9 to the effect that a mortgage does not follow a note in the absence of a separate assignment of the mortgage, but did not address the effect of Massachusetts's subsequent enactment of UCC § 9–203(g) on those precedents. Under the rule in UCC § 9–203(g), if the holder of the note in question demonstrated that it had an attached security interest (including the interest of a buyer) in the note, the holder of the note in question would also have a security interest in the mortgage securing the note even in the absence of a separate assignment of the mortgage. (This Report does not address whether, under the facts of the *Ibanez* case, the holder of the note had an attached security interest in the note and, thus, qualified for the application of UCC § 9–203(g). Moreover, even if the holder had an attached security interest in the note and, thus, had a security interest in the mortgage, this would not, of itself, mean that the holder could enforce the mortgage without a recordable assignment of the mortgage to the holder. Whatever steps are required in order to enforce a mortgage in the absence of a recordable assignment are the province of real property law. The matter is addressed, in part, in the discussion of Question 4 below.)

[44] Official Comment 9 to UCC § 9–203 confirms this point: "Subsection (g) codifies the common-law rule that a transfer of an obligation secured by a security interest or other lien on personal or real property also transfers the security interest or lien." Pursuant to UCC § 1–302(a), the parties to the transaction may agree that an interest in the mortgage securing the note does not accompany the note, but such an agreement is unlikely. See, *e.g.,* Restatement (3d), Property (Mortgages) § 5.4, comment *a* ("It is conceivable that on rare occasions a mortgagee will wish to disassociate the obligation and the mortgage, but that result should follow only upon evidence that the parties to the transfer so agreed.").

party, the interest of the seller (or debtor) in the mortgage has been correspondingly transferred to the secured party. UCC Section 9–308(e) goes on to state that, if the secured party's security interest in the note is perfected, the secured party's security interest in the mortgage securing the note is also perfected,[45] with result that the right of the secured party is senior to the rights of a person who then or later becomes a lien creditor of the seller of (or other grantor of a security interest in) the note. Neither of these rules, however, determines the ranking of rights in the underlying real property itself, or the effect of recordation or non-recordation in the real property recording system on enforcement of the mortgage.[46]

Illustration:

10. Same facts as Illustration 9. The signed writing was silent with respect to the mortgage securing the note and the parties made no other agreement with respect to the mortgage. The attachment of Funder's interest in the rights of Payee in the note also constitutes attachment of an interest in the rights of Payee in the mortgage. UCC § 9–203(g).

Question Four—What Actions May a Person to Whom an Interest in a Mortgage Note Has Been Transferred, but Who Has not Taken a Recordable Assignment of the Mortgage, Take in Order to Become the Assignee of Record of the Mortgage Securing the Note?

In some states, a party without a recorded interest in a mortgage may not enforce the mortgage non-judicially. In such states, even though the buyer of a mortgage note (or a creditor to whom a security interest in the note has been granted to secure an obligation) automatically obtains corresponding rights in the mortgage,[47] this may be insufficient as a matter of applicable real estate law to enable that buyer or secured creditor to enforce the mortgage upon default of the maker if the buyer or secured creditor does not have a recordable assignment. The buyer or other secured party may attempt to obtain such a recordable assignment from the seller or debtor at the time it seeks to enforce the mortgage, but such an attempt may be unsuccessful.[48]

Article 9 of the UCC provides such a buyer or secured creditor a mechanism by which it can record its interest in the realty records in order to conduct a non-judicial foreclosure. UCC Section 9–607(b) provides that "if necessary to enable a secured party [including the buyer of a mortgage note] to exercise . . . the right of [its transferor]to enforce a mortgage nonjudicially," the secured party may record in the office in which the mortgage is recorded (i) a copy of the security agreement transferring an interest in the note to the secured party and (ii) the secured party's sworn affidavit in recordable form stating that default has occurred[49] and that the secured party is entitled to enforce the mortgage non-judicially.[50]

Illustration:

11. Same facts as Illustration 10. Maker has defaulted on the note and mortgage and Funder would like to enforce the mortgage non-judicially. In the relevant state, however, only a party with a recorded interest in a mortgage may enforce it non-judicially. Funder may record in the relevant mortgage recording office a copy of the signed writing pursuant to which the note was sold to

---

[45] See Official Comment 6 to UCC § 9–308, which also observes that "this result helps prevent the separation of the mortgage (or other lien) from the note." Note also that, as explained in Official Comment 7 to UCC § 9–109, "It also follows from [UCC § 9–109(b)] that an attempt to obtain or perfect a security interest in a secured obligation by complying with non-Article 9 law, as by an assignment of record of a real-property mortgage, would be ineffective."

[46] Similarly, Official Comment 6 to UCC § 9–308 states that "this Article does not determine who has the power to release a mortgage of record. That issue is determined by real-property law."

[47] See discussion of Question Three, *supra*.

[48] In some cases, the seller or debtor may no longer be in business. In other cases, it may simply be unresponsive to requests for execution of documents with respect to a transaction in which it no longer has an economic interest. Moreover, in cases in which mortgage note was collateral for an obligation owed to the secured party, the defaulting debtor may simply be unwilling to assist its secured party. See Official Comment 8 to UCC § 9–607.

[49] The 2010 amendments to Article 9 (see fn. 8, *supra*) add language to this provision to clarify that "default," in this context, means default with respect to the note or other obligation secured by the mortgage.

[50] UCC § 9–607(b) does not address other conditions that must be satisfied for judicial or non-judicial enforcement of a mortgage.

Funder and a sworn affidavit stating that Maker has defaulted and that Funder is entitled to enforce the mortgage non-judicially. UCC § 9–607(b).

Summary

The Uniform Commercial Code provides four sets of rules that determine matters that are important in the context of enforcement of mortgage notes and the mortgages that secure them:

- First, in the case of a mortgage note that is a negotiable instrument, Article 3 of the UCC determines the identity of the person who is entitled to enforce the note and to whom the maker owes its payment obligation; payment to the person entitled to enforce the note discharges the maker's obligation, but failure to pay that party when the note is due constitutes dishonor.

- Second, for both negotiable and non-negotiable mortgage notes, Article 9 of the UCC determines whether a transferee of the note from its owner has obtained an attached property right in the note.

- Third, Article 9 of the UCC provides that a transferee of a mortgage note whose property right in the note has attached also automatically has an attached property right in the mortgage that secures the note.

- Finally, Article 9 of the UCC provides a mechanism by which the owner of a note and the mortgage securing it may, upon default of the maker of the note, record its interest in the mortgage in the realty records in order to conduct a non-judicial foreclosure.

As noted previously, these UCC rules do not resolve all issues in this field. The enforcement of real estate mortgages by foreclosure is primarily the province of a state's real property law, but legal determinations made pursuant to the four sets of UCC rules described in this Report will, in many cases, be central to administration of that law. In such cases, proper application of real property law requires proper application of the UCC rules discussed in this Report.

UNIFORM VOIDABLE TRANSACTIONS ACT*

---

§ 1.   Definitions.

As used in this [Act]:

(1) "Affiliate" means:

(i) a person that directly or indirectly owns, controls, or holds with power to vote, 20 percent or more of the outstanding voting securities of the debtor, other than a person that holds the securities:

(A) as a fiduciary or agent without sole discretionary power to vote the securities; or

(B) solely to secure a debt, if the person has not in fact exercised the power to vote;

(ii) a corporation 20 percent or more of whose outstanding voting securities are directly or indirectly owned, controlled, or held with power to vote, by the debtor or a person that directly or indirectly owns, controls, or holds, with power to vote, 20 percent or more of the outstanding voting securities of the debtor, other than a person that holds the securities:

(A) as a fiduciary or agent without sole discretionary power to vote the securities; or

(B) solely to secure a debt, if the person has not in fact exercised the power to vote;

(iii) a person whose business is operated by the debtor under a lease or other agreement, or a person substantially all of whose assets are controlled by the debtor; or

(iv) a person that operates the debtor's business under a lease or other agreement or controls substantially all of the debtor's assets.

(2) "Asset" means property of a debtor, but the term does not include:

(i) property to the extent it is encumbered by a valid lien;

      (ii)   property to the extent it is generally exempt under nonbankruptcy law; or

      (iii)   an interest in property held in tenancy by the entireties to the extent it is not subject to process by a creditor holding a claim against only one tenant.

    (3)   "Claim", except as used in "claim for relief", means a right to payment, whether or not the right is reduced to judgment, liquidated, unliquidated, fixed, contingent, matured, unmatured, disputed, undisputed, legal, equitable, secured, or unsecured.

    (4)   "Creditor" means a person that has a claim.

    (5)   "Debt" means liability on a claim.

    (6)   "Debtor" means a person that is liable on a claim.

    (7)   "Electronic" means relating to technology having electrical, digital, magnetic, wireless, optical, electromagnetic, or similar capabilities.

    (8)   "Insider" includes:

      (i)   if the debtor is an individual:

        (A)   a relative of the debtor or of a general partner of the debtor;

        (B)   a partnership in which the debtor is a general partner;

        (C)   a general partner in a partnership described in clause (B); or

        (D)   a corporation of which the debtor is a director, officer, or person in control;

      (ii)   if the debtor is a corporation:

        (A)   a director of the debtor;

        (B)   an officer of the debtor;

        (C)   a person in control of the debtor;

        (D)   a partnership in which the debtor is a general partner;

        (E)   a general partner in a partnership described in clause (D); or

        (F)   a relative of a general partner, director, officer, or person in control of the debtor;

      (iii)   if the debtor is a partnership:

        (A)   a general partner in the debtor;

        (B)   a relative of a general partner in, a general partner of, or a person in control of the debtor;

        (C)   another partnership in which the debtor is a general partner;

        (D)   a general partner in a partnership described in clause (C); or

        (E)   a person in control of the debtor;

      (iv)   an affiliate, or an insider of an affiliate as if the affiliate were the debtor; and

      (v)   a managing agent of the debtor.

    (9)   "Lien" means a charge against or an interest in property to secure payment of a debt or performance of an obligation, and includes a security interest created by agreement, a judicial lien obtained by legal or equitable process or proceedings, a common-law lien, or a statutory lien.

    (10)   "Organization" means a person other than an individual.

    (11)   "Person" means an individual, estate, partnership, association, trust, business or nonprofit entity, public corporation, government or governmental subdivision, agency, or instrumentality, or other legal or commercial entity.

    (12)   "Property" means anything that may be the subject of ownership.

(13) "Record" means information that is inscribed on a tangible medium or that is stored in an electronic or other medium and is retrievable in perceivable form.

(14) "Relative" means an individual related by consanguinity within the third degree as determined by the common law, a spouse, or an individual related to a spouse within the third degree as so determined, and includes an individual in an adoptive relationship within the third degree.

(15) "Sign" means, with present intent to authenticate or adopt a record:

    (i)   to execute or adopt a tangible symbol; or

    (ii) to attach to or logically associate with the record an electronic symbol, sound, or process.

(16) "Transfer" means every mode, direct or indirect, absolute or conditional, voluntary or involuntary, of disposing of or parting with an asset or an interest in an asset, and includes payment of money, release, lease, license, and creation of a lien or other encumbrance.

(17) "Valid lien" means a lien that is effective against the holder of a judicial lien subsequently obtained by legal or equitable process or proceedings.

§ 2.   Insolvency.

(a)   A debtor is insolvent if, at a fair valuation, the sum of the debtor's debts is greater than the sum of the debtor's assets.

(b)   A debtor that is generally not paying the debtor's debts as they become due other than as a result of a bona fide dispute is presumed to be insolvent. The presumption imposes on the party against which the presumption is directed the burden of proving that the nonexistence of insolvency is more probable than its existence.

(c)   Assets under this section do not include property that has been transferred, concealed, or removed with intent to hinder, delay, or defraud creditors or that has been transferred in a manner making the transfer voidable under this [Act].

(d)   Debts under this section do not include an obligation to the extent it is secured by a valid lien on property of the debtor not included as an asset.

§ 3.   Value.

(a)   Value is given for a transfer or an obligation if, in exchange for the transfer or obligation, property is transferred or an antecedent debt is secured or satisfied, but value does not include an unperformed promise made otherwise than in the ordinary course of the promisor's business to furnish support to the debtor or another person.

(b)   For the purposes of Section 4(a)(2) and Section 5, a person gives a reasonably equivalent value if the person acquires an interest of the debtor in an asset pursuant to a regularly conducted, noncollusive foreclosure sale or execution of a power of sale for the acquisition or disposition of the interest of the debtor upon default under a mortgage, deed of trust, or security agreement.

(c)   A transfer is made for present value if the exchange between the debtor and the transferee is intended by them to be contemporaneous and is in fact substantially contemporaneous.

§ 4.   Transfer or Obligation Voidable as to Present or Future Creditor.

(a)   A transfer made or obligation incurred by a debtor is voidable as to a creditor, whether the creditor's claim arose before or after the transfer was made or the obligation was incurred, if the debtor made the transfer or incurred the obligation:

    (1) with actual intent to hinder, delay, or defraud any creditor of the debtor; or

    (2) without receiving a reasonably equivalent value in exchange for the transfer or obligation, and the debtor:

        (i)   was engaged or was about to engage in a business or a transaction for which the remaining assets of the debtor were unreasonably small in relation to the business or transaction; or

        (ii)   intended to incur, or believed or reasonably should have believed that the debtor would incur, debts beyond the debtor's ability to pay as they became due.

    (b)   In determining actual intent under subsection (a)(1), consideration may be given, among other factors, to whether:

        (1)   the transfer or obligation was to an insider;

        (2)   the debtor retained possession or control of the property transferred after the transfer;

        (3)   the transfer or obligation was disclosed or concealed;

        (4)   before the transfer was made or obligation was incurred, the debtor had been sued or threatened with suit;

        (5)   the transfer was of substantially all the debtor's assets;

        (6)   the debtor absconded;

        (7)   the debtor removed or concealed assets;

        (8)   the value of the consideration received by the debtor was reasonably equivalent to the value of the asset transferred or the amount of the obligation incurred;

        (9)   the debtor was insolvent or became insolvent shortly after the transfer was made or the obligation was incurred;

        (10) the transfer occurred shortly before or shortly after a substantial debt was incurred; and

        (11) the debtor transferred the essential assets of the business to a lienor who transferred the assets to an insider of the debtor.

    (c)   A creditor making a claim for relief under subsection (a) has the burden of proving the elements of the claim for relief by a preponderance of the evidence.

§ 5.   Transfer or Obligation Voidable as to Present Creditor.

    (a)   A transfer made or obligation incurred by a debtor is voidable as to a creditor whose claim arose before the transfer was made or the obligation was incurred if the debtor made the transfer or incurred the obligation without receiving a reasonably equivalent value in exchange for the transfer or obligation and the debtor was insolvent at that time or the debtor became insolvent as a result of the transfer or obligation.

    (b)   A transfer made by a debtor is voidable as to a creditor whose claim arose before the transfer was made if the transfer was made to an insider for an antecedent debt, the debtor was insolvent at that time, and the insider had reasonable cause to believe that the debtor was insolvent.

    (c)   Subject to Section 2(b), a creditor making a claim for relief under subsection (a) or (b) has the burden of proving the elements of the claim for relief by a preponderance of the evidence.

§ 6.   When Transfer Is Made or Obligation Is Incurred.

For the purposes of this [Act]:

        (1)   a transfer is made:

        (i)   with respect to an asset that is real property other than a fixture, but including the interest of a seller or purchaser under a contract for the sale of the asset, when the transfer is so far perfected that a good-faith purchaser of the asset from the debtor against which applicable law permits the transfer to be perfected cannot acquire an interest in the asset that is superior to the interest of the transferee; and

(ii)   with respect to an asset that is not real property or that is a fixture, when the transfer is so far perfected that a creditor on a simple contract cannot acquire a judicial lien otherwise than under this [Act] that is superior to the interest of the transferee;

(2)   if applicable law permits the transfer to be perfected as provided in paragraph (1) and the transfer is not so perfected before the commencement of an action for relief under this [Act], the transfer is deemed made immediately before the commencement of the action;

(3)   if applicable law does not permit the transfer to be perfected as provided in paragraph (1), the transfer is made when it becomes effective between the debtor and the transferee;

(4)   a transfer is not made until the debtor has acquired rights in the asset transferred; and

(5)   an obligation is incurred:

(i)   if oral, when it becomes effective between the parties; or

(ii)   if evidenced by a record, when the record signed by the obligor is delivered to or for the benefit of the obligee.

§ 7.   Remedies of Creditor.

(a)   In an action for relief against a transfer or obligation under this [Act], a creditor, subject to the limitations in Section 8, may obtain:

(1)   avoidance of the transfer or obligation to the extent necessary to satisfy the creditor's claim;

(2)   an attachment or other provisional remedy against the asset transferred or other property of the transferee if available under applicable law; and

(3)   subject to applicable principles of equity and in accordance with applicable rules of civil procedure:

(i)   an injunction against further disposition by the debtor or a transferee, or both, of the asset transferred or of other property;

(ii)   appointment of a receiver to take charge of the asset transferred or of other property of the transferee; or

(iii)   any other relief the circumstances may require.

(b)   If a creditor has obtained a judgment on a claim against the debtor, the creditor, if the court so orders, may levy execution on the asset transferred or its proceeds.

§ 8.   Defenses, Liability, and Protection of Transferee or Obligee.

(a)   A transfer or obligation is not voidable under Section 4(a)(1) against a person that took in good faith and for a reasonably equivalent value given the debtor or against any subsequent transferee or obligee.

(b)   To the extent a transfer is avoidable in an action by a creditor under Section 7(a)(1), the following rules apply:

(1)   Except as otherwise provided in this section, the creditor may recover judgment for the value of the asset transferred, as adjusted under subsection (c), or the amount necessary to satisfy the creditor's claim, whichever is less. The judgment may be entered against:

(i)   the first transferee of the asset or the person for whose benefit the transfer was made; or

(ii)   an immediate or mediate transferee of the first transferee, other than:

(a)   a good-faith transferee that took for value; or

(b)   an immediate or mediate good-faith transferee of a person described in clause (A).

(2)   Recovery pursuant to Section 7(a)(1) or (b) of or from the asset transferred or its proceeds, by levy or otherwise, is available only against a person described in paragraph 1(i) or (ii).

(c)   If the judgment under subsection (b) is based upon the value of the asset transferred, the judgment must be for an amount equal to the value of the asset at the time of the transfer, subject to adjustment as the equities may require.

(d)   Notwithstanding voidability of a transfer or an obligation under this [Act], a good-faith transferee or obligee is entitled, to the extent of the value given the debtor for the transfer or obligation, to:

(1)   a lien on or a right to retain an interest in the asset transferred;

(2)   enforcement of an obligation incurred; or

(3)   a reduction in the amount of the liability on the judgment.

(e)   A transfer is not voidable under Section 4(a)(2) or Section 5 if the transfer results from:

(1)   termination of a lease upon default by the debtor when the termination is pursuant to the lease and applicable law; or

(2)   enforcement of a security interest in compliance with Article 9 of the Uniform Commercial Code, other than acceptance of collateral in full or partial satisfaction of the obligation it secures.

(f)   A transfer is not voidable under Section 5(b):

(1)   to the extent the insider gave new value to or for the benefit of the debtor after the transfer was made, except to the extent the new value was secured by a valid lien;

(2)   if made in the ordinary course of business or financial affairs of the debtor and the insider; or

(3)   if made pursuant to a good-faith effort to rehabilitate the debtor and the transfer secured present value given for that purpose as well as an antecedent debt of the debtor.

(g)   The following rules determine the burden of proving matters referred to in this section:

(1)   A party that seeks to invoke subsection (a), (d), (e), or (f) has the burden of proving the applicability of that subsection.

(2)   Except as otherwise provided in paragraphs (3) and (4), the creditor has the burden of proving each applicable element of subsection (b) or (c).

(3)   The transferee has the burden of proving the applicability to the transferee of subsection (b)(1)(ii)(A) or (B).

(4)   A party that seeks adjustment under subsection (c) has the burden of proving the adjustment.

(h)   The standard of proof required to establish matters referred to in this section is preponderance of the evidence.

§ 9.   Extinguishment of Claim for Relief.

A claim for relief with respect to a transfer or obligation under this [Act] is extinguished unless action is brought:

(a)   under Section 4(a)(1), not later than four years after the transfer was made or the obligation was incurred or, if later, not later than one year after the transfer or obligation was or could reasonably have been discovered by the claimant;

(b)   under Section 4(a)(2) or 5(a), not later than four years after the transfer was made or the obligation was incurred; or

(c)   under Section 5(b), not later than one year after the transfer was made.

§ 10.   Governing Law.

(a)   In this section, the following rules determine a debtor's location:

(1)   A debtor who is an individual is located at the individual's principal residence.

(2)   A debtor that is an organization and has only one place of business is located at its place of business.

(3)   A debtor that is an organization and has more than one place of business is located at its chief executive office.

(b)   A claim for relief in the nature of a claim for relief under this [Act] is governed by the local law of the jurisdiction in which the debtor is located when the transfer is made or the obligation is incurred.

§ 11.   Application to Series Organization.

(a)   In this section:

(1)   "Protected series" means an arrangement, however denominated, created by a series organization that, pursuant to the law under which the series organization is organized, has the characteristics set forth in paragraph (2).

(2)   "Series organization" means an organization that, pursuant to the law under which it is organized, has the following characteristics:

(i)   The organic record of the organization provides for creation by the organization of one or more protected series, however denominated, with respect to specified property of the organization, and for records to be maintained for each protected series that identify the property of or associated with the protected series.

(ii)   Debt incurred or existing with respect to the activities of, or property of or associated with, a particular protected series is enforceable against the property of or associated with the protected series only, and not against the property of or associated with the organization or other protected series of the organization.

(iii)   Debt incurred or existing with respect to the activities or property of the organization is enforceable against the property of the organization only, and not against the property of or associated with a protected series of the organization.

(b)   A series organization and each protected series of the organization is a separate person for purposes of this [Act], even if for other purposes a protected series is not a person separate from the organization or other protected series of the organization.

Legislative Note: This section should be enacted even if the enacting jurisdiction does not itself have legislation enabling the creation of protected series. For example, in such an enacting jurisdiction this section will apply if a protected series of a series organization organized under the law of a different jurisdiction makes a transfer to another protected series of that organization and, under applicable choice of law rules, the voidability of the transfer is governed by the law of the enacting jurisdiction.

§ 12.   Supplementary Provisions.

Unless displaced by the provisions of this [Act], the principles of law and equity, including the law merchant and the law relating to principal and agent, estoppel, laches, fraud, misrepresentation, duress, coercion, mistake, insolvency, or other validating or invalidating cause, supplement its provisions.

§ 13.   Uniformity of Application and Construction.

This [Act] shall be applied and construed to effectuate its general purpose to make uniform the law with respect to the subject of this [Act] among states enacting it.

§ 14.   Relation to Electronic Signatures in Global and National Commerce Act.

This [Act] modifies, limits, or supersedes the Electronic Signatures in Global and National Commerce Act, 15 U.S.C. Section 7001 et seq., but does not modify, limit, or supersede Section 101(c) of that act, 15 U.S.C. Section 7001(c), or authorize electronic delivery of any of the notices described in Section 103(b) of that act, 15 U.S.C. Section 7003(b).

§ 15. Short Title.

This [Act], which was formerly cited as the Uniform Fraudulent Transfer Act, may be cited as the Uniform Voidable Transactions Act.

§ 16. Repeals; Conforming Amendments.

(a) . . .

(b) . . .

(c) . . .

UNIFORM ELECTRONIC TRANSACTIONS ACT (1999)[*]

PREFATORY NOTE

With the advent of electronic means of communication and information transfer, business models and methods for doing business have evolved to take advantage of the speed, efficiencies, and cost benefits of electronic technologies. These developments have occurred in the face of existing legal barriers to the legal efficacy of records and documents which exist solely in electronic media. Whether the legal requirement that information or an agreement or contract must be contained or set forth in a pen and paper writing derives from a statute of frauds affecting the enforceability of an agreement, or from a record retention statute that calls for keeping the paper record of a transaction, such legal requirements raise real barriers to the effective use of electronic media.

One striking example of electronic barriers involves so called check retention statutes in every State. A study conducted by the Federal Reserve Bank of Boston identified more than 2500 different state laws which require the retention of canceled checks by the issuers of those checks. These requirements not only impose burdens on the issuers, but also effectively restrain the ability of banks handling the checks to automate the process. Although check truncation is validated under the Uniform Commercial Code, if the bank's customer must store the canceled paper check, the bank will not be able to deal with the item through electronic transmission of the information. By establishing the equivalence of an electronic record of the information, the Uniform Electronic Transactions Act (UETA) removes these barriers without affecting the underlying legal rules and requirements.

It is important to understand that the purpose of the UETA is to remove barriers to electronic commerce by validating and effectuating electronic records and signatures. It is NOT a general contracting statute—the substantive rules of contracts remain unaffected by UETA. Nor is it a digital signature statute.

---

[*]   Reproduced by permission of the Uniform Law Commission.

UNIFORM ELECTRONIC TRANSACTIONS ACT

To the extent that a State has a Digital Signature Law, the UETA is designed to support and compliment that statute.

A.   Scope of the Act and Procedural Approach. The scope of this Act provides coverage which sets forth a clear framework for covered transactions, and also avoids unwarranted surprises for unsophisticated parties dealing in this relatively new media. The clarity and certainty of the scope of the Act have been obtained while still providing a solid legal framework that allows for the continued development of innovative technology to facilitate electronic transactions.

With regard to the general scope of the Act, the Act's coverage is inherently limited by the definition of "transaction." The Act does not apply to *all* writings and signatures, but only to electronic records and signatures relating to a transaction, defined as those interactions between people relating to business, commercial and governmental affairs. In general, there are few writing or signature requirements imposed by law on many of the "standard" transactions that had been considered for exclusion. A good example relates to trusts, where the general rule on creation of a trust imposes no formal writing requirement. Further, the writing requirements in other contexts derived from governmental filing issues. For example, real estate transactions were considered potentially troublesome because of the need to file a deed or other instrument for protection against third parties. Since the efficacy of a real estate purchase contract, or even a deed, between the parties is not affected by any sort of filing, the question was raised why these transactions should not be validated by this Act if done via an electronic medium. No sound reason was found. Filing requirements fall within Sections 17–19 on governmental records. An exclusion of all real estate transactions would be particularly unwarranted in the event that a State chose to convert to an electronic recording system, as many have for Article 9 financing statement filings under the Uniform Commercial Code.

The exclusion of specific Articles of the Uniform Commercial Code reflects the recognition that, particularly in the case of Articles 5, 8 and revised Article 9, electronic transactions were addressed in the specific contexts of those revision processes. In the context of Articles 2 and 2A the UETA provides the vehicle for assuring that such transactions may be accomplished and effected via an electronic medium. At such time as Articles 2 and 2A are revised the extent of coverage in those Articles/Acts may make application of this Act as a gap-filling law desirable. Similar considerations apply to the recently promulgated Uniform Computer Information Transactions Act ("UCITA").

The need for certainty as to the scope and applicability of this Act is critical, and makes any sort of a broad, general exception based on notions of inconsistency with existing writing and signature requirements unwise at best. The uncertainty inherent in leaving the applicability of the Act to judicial construction of this Act with other laws is unacceptable if electronic transactions are to be facilitated.

Finally, recognition that the paradigm for the Act involves two willing parties conducting a transaction electronically, makes it necessary to expressly provide that some form of acquiescence or intent on the part of a person to conduct transactions electronically is necessary before the Act can be invoked. Accordingly, Section 5 specifically provides that the Act only applies between parties that have agreed to conduct transactions electronically. In this context, the construction of the term agreement must be broad in order to assure that the Act applies whenever the circumstances show the parties intention to transact electronically, regardless of whether the intent rises to the level of a formal agreement.

B.   Procedural Approach. Another fundamental premise of the Act is that it be minimalist and procedural. The general efficacy of existing law in an electronic context, so long as biases and barriers to the medium are removed, validates this approach. The Act defers to existing substantive law. Specific areas of deference to other law in this Act include: (1) the meaning and effect of "sign" under existing law, (2) the method and manner of displaying, transmitting and formatting information in Section 8, (3) rules of attribution in Section 9, and (4) the law of mistake in Section 10.

The Act's treatment of records and signatures demonstrates best the minimalist approach that has been adopted. Whether a record is attributed to a person is left to law outside this Act. Whether an electronic signature has any effect is left to the surrounding circumstances and other law. These provisions are salutary directives to assure that records and signatures will be treated in the same manner, under currently existing law, as written records and manual signatures.

The deference of the Act to other substantive law does not negate the necessity of setting forth rules and standards for using electronic media. The Act expressly validates electronic records, signatures and contracts. It provides for the use of electronic records and information for retention purposes, providing certainty in an area with great potential in cost savings and efficiency. The Act makes clear that the actions of machines ("electronic agents") programmed and used by people will bind the user of the machine, regardless of whether human review of a particular transaction has occurred. It specifies the standards for sending and receipt of electronic records, and it allows for innovation in financial services through the implementation of transferable records. In these ways the Act permits electronic transactions to be accomplished with certainty under existing substantive rules of law.

§ 1.   Short Title.

This [Act] may be cited as the Uniform Electronic Transactions Act.

§ 2.   Definitions.

In this [Act]:

(1)   "Agreement" means the bargain of the parties in fact, as found in their language or inferred from other circumstances and from rules, regulations, and procedures given the effect of agreements under laws otherwise applicable to a particular transaction.

(2)   "Automated transaction" means a transaction conducted or performed, in whole or in part, by electronic means or electronic records, in which the acts or records of one or both parties are not reviewed by an individual in the ordinary course in forming a contract, performing under an existing contract, or fulfilling an obligation required by the transaction.

(3)   "Computer program" means a set of statements or instructions to be used directly or indirectly in an information processing system in order to bring about a certain result.

(4)   "Contract" means the total legal obligation resulting from the parties' agreement as affected by this [Act] and other applicable law.

(5)   "Electronic" means relating to technology having electrical, digital, magnetic, wireless, optical, electromagnetic, or similar capabilities.

(6)   "Electronic agent" means a computer program or an electronic or other automated means used independently to initiate an action or respond to electronic records or performances in whole or in part, without review or action by an individual.

(7)   "Electronic record" means a record created, generated, sent, communicated, received, or stored by electronic means.

(8)   "Electronic signature" means an electronic sound, symbol, or process attached to or logically associated with a record and executed or adopted by a person with the intent to sign the record.

(9)   "Governmental agency" means an executive, legislative, or judicial agency, department, board, commission, authority, institution, or instrumentality of the federal government or of a State or of a county, municipality, or other political subdivision of a State.

(10) "Information" means data, text, images, sounds, codes, computer programs, software, databases, or the like.

(11) "Information processing system" means an electronic system for creating, generating, sending, receiving, storing, displaying, or processing information.

(12) "Person" means an individual, corporation, business trust, estate, trust, partnership, limited liability company, association, joint venture, governmental agency, public corporation, or any other legal or commercial entity.

(13) "Record" means information that is inscribed on a tangible medium or that is stored in an electronic or other medium and is retrievable in perceivable form.

(14) "Security procedure" means a procedure employed for the purpose of verifying that an electronic signature, record, or performance is that of a specific person or for detecting changes or errors in the information in an electronic record. The term includes a procedure that requires the use of algorithms or other codes, identifying words or numbers, encryption, or callback or other acknowledgment procedures.

(15) "State" means a State of the United States, the District of Columbia, Puerto Rico, the United States Virgin Islands, or any territory or insular possession subject to the jurisdiction of the United States. The term includes an Indian tribe or band, or Alaskan native village, which is recognized by federal law or formally acknowledged by a State.

(16) "Transaction" means an action or set of actions occurring between two or more persons relating to the conduct of business, commercial, or governmental affairs.

Sources: UNCITRAL Model Law on Electronic Commerce; Uniform Commercial Code; Uniform Computer Information Transactions Act; Restatement 2d Contracts.

Comment

1. **"Agreement."** Whether the parties have reached an agreement is determined by their express language and all surrounding circumstances. The Restatement 2d Contracts § 3 provides that, "An agreement is a manifestation of mutual assent on the part of two or more persons." See also Restatement 2d Contracts, Section 2, Comment b. The Uniform Commercial Code specifically includes in the circumstances from which an agreement may be inferred "course of performance, course of dealing and usage of trade . . ." as defined in the UCC. Although the definition of agreement in this Act does not make specific reference to usage of trade and other party conduct, this definition is not intended to affect the construction of the parties' agreement under the substantive law applicable to a particular transaction. Where that law takes account of usage and conduct in informing the terms of the parties' agreement, the usage or conduct would be relevant as "other circumstances" included in the definition under this Act.

Where the law applicable to a given transaction provides that system rules and the like constitute part of the agreement of the parties, such rules will have the same effect in determining the parties agreement under this Act. For example, UCC Article 4 (Section 4–103(b)) provides that Federal Reserve regulations and operating circulars and clearinghouse rules have the effect of agreements. Such agreements by law properly would be included in the definition of agreement in this Act.

The parties' agreement is relevant in determining whether the provisions of this Act have been varied by agreement. In addition, the parties' agreement may establish the parameters of the parties' use of electronic records and signatures, security procedures and similar aspects of the transaction. See Model Trading Partner Agreement, 45 Business Lawyer Supp. Issue (June 1990). See Section 5(b) and Comments thereto.

2. **"Automated Transaction."** An automated transaction is a transaction performed or conducted by electronic means in which machines are used without human intervention to form contracts and perform obligations under existing contracts. Such broad coverage is necessary because of the diversity of transactions to which this Act may apply.

As with electronic agents, this definition addresses the circumstance where electronic records may result in action or performance by a party although no human review of the electronic records is anticipated. Section 14 provides specific rules to assure that where one or both parties do not review the electronic records, the resulting agreement will be effective.

The critical element in this definition is the lack of a human actor on one or both sides of a transaction. For example, if one orders books from Bookseller.com through Bookseller's website, the transaction would be an automated transaction because Bookseller took and confirmed the order via its machine. Similarly, if Automaker and supplier do business through Electronic Data Interchange, Automaker's computer, upon receiving information within certain pre-programmed parameters, will send an electronic order to supplier's computer. If Supplier's computer confirms the order and processes the shipment because the order falls within pre-programmed parameters in Supplier's computer, this would be a fully automated transaction. If, instead, the Supplier relies on a human employee to review, accept, and process the Buyer's order, then only the Automaker's side of the transaction would be automated. In either case, the entire transaction falls within this definition.

3.   "**Computer program.**" This definition refers to the functional and operating aspects of an electronic, digital system. It relates to operating instructions used in an electronic system such as an electronic agent. (See definition of "Electronic Agent.")

4.   "**Electronic.**" The basic nature of most current technologies and the need for a recognized, single term warrants the use of "electronic" as the defined term. The definition is intended to assure that the Act will be applied broadly as new technologies develop. The term must be construed broadly in light of developing technologies in order to fulfill the purpose of this Act to validate commercial transactions regardless of the medium used by the parties. Current legal requirements for "writings" can be satisfied by almost any tangible media, whether paper, other fibers, or even stone. The purpose and applicability of this Act covers intangible media which are technologically capable of storing, transmitting and reproducing information in human perceivable form, but which lack the tangible aspect of paper, papyrus or stone.

While not all technologies listed are technically "electronic" in nature (e.g., optical fiber technology), the term "electronic" is the most descriptive term available to describe the majority of current technologies. For example, the development of biological and chemical processes for communication and storage of data, while not specifically mentioned in the definition, are included within the technical definition because such processes operate on electromagnetic impulses. However, whether a particular technology may be characterized as technically "electronic," i.e., operates on electromagnetic impulses, should not be determinative of whether records and signatures created, used and stored by means of a particular technology are covered by this Act. This Act is intended to apply to all records and signatures created, used and stored by any medium which permits the information to be retrieved in perceivable form.

5.   "**Electronic agent.**" This definition establishes that an electronic agent is a machine. As the term "electronic agent" has come to be recognized, it is limited to a tool function. The effect on the party using the agent is addressed in the operative provisions of the Act (e.g., Section 14)

An electronic agent, such as a computer program or other automated means employed by a person, is a tool of that person. As a general rule, the employer of a tool is responsible for the results obtained by the use of that tool since the tool has no independent volition of its own. However, an electronic agent, by definition, is capable within the parameters of its programming, of initiating, responding or interacting with other parties or their electronic agents once it has been activated by a party, without further attention of that party.

While this Act proceeds on the paradigm that an electronic agent is capable of performing only within the technical strictures of its preset programming, it is conceivable that, within the useful life of this Act, electronic agents may be created with the ability to act autonomously, and not just automatically. That is, through developments in artificial intelligence, a computer may be able to "learn through experience, modify the instructions in their own programs, and even devise new instructions." Allen and Widdison, "Can Computers Make Contracts?" *9 Harv. J.L. & Tech 25* (Winter, 1996). If such developments occur, courts may construe the definition of electronic agent accordingly, in order to recognize such new capabilities.

The examples involving Bookseller.com and Automaker in the Comment to the definition of Automated Transaction are equally applicable here. Bookseller acts through an electronic agent in processing an order for books. Automaker and the supplier each act through electronic agents in facilitating and effectuating the just-in-time inventory process through EDI.

6.   "**Electronic record.**" An electronic record is a subset of the broader defined term "record." It is any record created, used or stored in a medium other than paper (see definition of electronic). The defined term is also used in this Act as a limiting definition in those provisions in which it is used.

Information processing systems, computer equipment and programs, electronic data interchange, electronic mail, voice mail, facsimile, telex, telecopying, scanning, and similar technologies all qualify as electronic under this Act. Accordingly information stored on a computer hard drive or floppy disc, facsimiles, voice mail messages, messages on a telephone answering machine, audio and video tape recordings, among other records, all would be electronic records under this Act.

7.   "**Electronic signature.**" The idea of a signature is broad and not specifically defined. Whether any particular record is "signed" is a question of fact. Proof of that fact must be made under other applicable law. This Act simply assures that the signature may be accomplished through electronic means. No specific technology need be used in order to create a valid signature. One's voice on an answering machine may suffice if the requisite intention is present. Similarly, including one's name as part of an electronic mail communication also may suffice, as may the firm name on a facsimile. It also may be shown that the requisite intent was not present and

accordingly the symbol, sound or process did not amount to a signature. One may use a digital signature with the requisite intention, or one may use the private key solely as an access device with no intention to sign, or otherwise accomplish a legally binding act. In any case the critical element is the intention to execute or adopt the sound or symbol or process for the purpose of signing the related record.

The definition requires that the signer execute or adopt the sound, symbol, or process with the intent to sign the record. The act of applying a sound, symbol or process to an electronic record could have differing meanings and effects. The consequence of the act and the effect of the act as a signature are determined under other applicable law. However, the essential attribute of a signature involves applying a sound, symbol or process with an intent to do a legally significant act. It is that intention that is understood in the law as a part of the word "sign", without the need for a definition.

This Act establishes, to the greatest extent possible, the equivalency of electronic signatures and manual signatures. Therefore the term "signature" has been used to connote and convey that equivalency. The purpose is to overcome unwarranted biases against electronic methods of signing and authenticating records. The term "authentication," used in other laws, often has a narrower meaning and purpose than an electronic signature as used in this Act. However, an authentication under any of those other laws constitutes an electronic signature under this Act.

The precise effect of an electronic signature will be determined based on the surrounding circumstances under Section 9(b).

This definition includes as an electronic signature the standard webpage click through process. For example, when a person orders goods or services through a vendor's website, the person will be required to provide information as part of a process which will result in receipt of the goods or services. When the customer ultimately gets to the last step and clicks "I agree," the person has adopted the process and has done so with the intent to associate the person with the record of that process. The actual effect of the electronic signature will be determined from all the surrounding circumstances, however, the person adopted a process which the circumstances indicate s/he intended to have the effect of getting the goods/services and being bound to pay for them. The adoption of the process carried the intent to do a legally significant act, the hallmark of a signature.

Another important aspect of this definition lies in the necessity that the electronic signature be linked or logically associated with the record. In the paper world, it is assumed that the symbol adopted by a party is attached to or located somewhere in the same paper that is intended to be authenticated, e.g., an allonge firmly attached to a promissory note, or the classic signature at the end of a long contract. These tangible manifestations do not exist in the electronic environment, and accordingly, this definition expressly provides that the symbol must in some way be linked to, or connected with, the electronic record being signed. This linkage is consistent with the regulations promulgated by the Food and Drug Administration. 21 CFR Part 11 (March 20, 1997).

A digital signature using public key encryption technology would qualify as an electronic signature, as would the mere inclusion of one's name as a part of an e-mail message—so long as in each case the signer executed or adopted the symbol with the intent to sign.

8. **"Governmental agency."** This definition is important in the context of optional Sections 17–19.

9. **"Information processing system."** This definition is consistent with the UNCITRAL Model Law on Electronic Commerce. The term includes computers and other information systems. It is principally used in Section 15 in connection with the sending and receiving of information. In that context, the key aspect is that the information enter a system from which a person can access it.

10. **"Record."** This is a standard definition designed to embrace all means of communicating or storing information except human memory. It includes any method for storing or communicating information, including "writings." A record need not be indestructible or permanent, but the term does not include oral or other communications which are not stored or preserved by some means. Information that has not been retained other than through human memory does not qualify as a record. As in the case of the terms "writing" or "written," the term "record" does not establish the purposes, permitted uses or legal effect which a record may have under any particular provision of substantive law. ABA Report on Use of the Term "Record," October 1, 1996.

11. **"Security procedure."** A security procedure may be applied to verify an electronic signature, verify the identity of the sender, or assure the informational integrity of an electronic record. The definition does not identify any particular technology. This permits the use of procedures which the parties select or which are established by law. It permits the greatest flexibility among the parties and allows for future technological development.

The definition in this Act is broad and is used to illustrate one way of establishing attribution or content integrity of an electronic record or signature. The use of a security procedure is not accorded operative legal effect, through the use of presumptions or otherwise, by this Act. In this Act, the use of security procedures is simply one method for proving the source or content of an electronic record or signature.

A security procedure may be technologically very sophisticated, such as an asymmetric cryptographic system. At the other extreme the security procedure may be as simple as a telephone call to confirm the identity of the sender through another channel of communication. It may include the use of a mother's maiden name or a personal identification number (PIN). Each of these examples is a method for confirming the identity of a person or accuracy of a message.

12. **"Transaction."** The definition has been limited to actions between people taken in the context of business, commercial or governmental activities. The term includes all interactions between people for business, commercial, including specifically consumer, or governmental purposes. However, the term does not include unilateral or non-transactional actions. As such it provides a structural limitation on the scope of the Act as stated in the next section.

It is essential that the term commerce and business be understood and construed broadly to include commercial and business transactions involving individuals who may qualify as "consumers" under other applicable law. If Alice and Bob agree to the sale of Alice's car to Bob for $2000 using an internet auction site, that transaction is fully covered by this Act. Even if Alice and Bob each qualify as typical "consumers" under other applicable law, their interaction is a transaction in commerce. Accordingly their actions would be related to commercial affairs, and fully qualify as a transaction governed by this Act.

Other transaction types include:

1. A single purchase by an individual from a retail merchant, which may be accomplished by an order from a printed catalog sent by facsimile, or by exchange of electronic mail.

2. Recurring orders on a weekly or monthly basis between large companies which have entered into a master trading partner agreement to govern the methods and manner of their transaction parameters.

3. A purchase by an individual from an online internet retail vendor. Such an arrangement may develop into an ongoing series of individual purchases, with security procedures and the like, as a part of doing ongoing business.

4. The closing of a business purchase transaction via facsimile transmission of documents or even electronic mail. In such a transaction, all parties may participate through electronic conferencing technologies. At the appointed time all electronic records are executed electronically and transmitted to the other party. In such a case, the electronic records and electronic signatures are validated under this Act, obviating the need for "in person" closings.

A transaction must include interaction between two or more persons. Consequently, to the extent that the execution of a will, trust, or a health care power of attorney or similar health care designation does not involve another person and is a unilateral act, it would not be covered by this Act because not occurring as a part of a transaction as defined in this Act. However, this Act *does* apply to all electronic records and signatures *related* to a transaction, and so does cover, for example, internal auditing and accounting records related to a transaction.

§ 3. Scope

(a) Except as otherwise provided in subsection (b), this [Act] applies to electronic records and electronic signatures relating to a transaction.

(b) This [Act] does not apply to a transaction to the extent it is governed by:

(1) a law governing the creation and execution of wills, codicils, or testamentary trusts;

(2) [The Uniform Commercial Code other than Sections 1–107 and 1–206, Article 2, and Article 2A];

(3) [the Uniform Computer Information Transactions Act]; and

(4) [other laws, if any, identified by State].

(c)   This [Act] applies to an electronic record or electronic signature otherwise excluded from the application of this [Act] under subsection (b) to the extent it is governed by a law other than those specified in subsection (b).

(d)   A transaction subject to this [Act] is also subject to other applicable substantive law.

See Legislative Note below, following Comment.

Comment

1.   The scope of this Act is inherently limited by the fact that it only applies to transactions related to business, commercial (including consumer) and governmental matters. Consequently, transactions with no relation to business, commercial or governmental transactions would not be subject to this Act. Unilaterally generated electronic records and signatures which are not part of a transaction also are not covered by this Act. See Section 2, Comment 12.

2.   This Act affects the medium in which information, records and signatures may be presented and retained under current legal requirements. While this Act covers all electronic records and signatures which are used in a business, commercial (including consumer) or governmental transaction, the operative provisions of the Act relate to requirements for writings and signatures under other laws. Accordingly, the exclusions in subsection (b) focus on those legal rules imposing certain writing and signature requirements which will *not* be affected by this Act.

3.   The exclusions listed in subsection (b) provide clarity and certainty regarding the laws which are and are not affected by this Act. This section provides that transactions subject to specific laws are unaffected by this Act and leaves the balance subject to this Act.

4.   Paragraph (1) excludes wills, codicils and testamentary trusts. This exclusion is largely salutary given the unilateral context in which such records are generally created and the unlikely use of such records in a transaction as defined in this Act (i.e., actions taken by two or more persons in the context of business, commercial or governmental affairs). Paragraph (2) excludes all of the Uniform Commercial Code other than UCC Sections 1–107 and 1–206, and Articles 2 and 2A. This Act does not apply to the excluded UCC articles, whether in "current" or "revised" form. The Act does apply to UCC Articles 2 and 2A and to UCC Sections 1–107 and 1–206.

5.   Articles 3, 4 and 4A of the UCC impact payment systems and have specifically been removed from the coverage of this Act. The check collection and electronic fund transfer systems governed by Articles 3, 4 and 4A involve systems and relationships involving numerous parties beyond the parties to the underlying contract. The impact of validating electronic media in such systems involves considerations beyond the scope of this Act. Articles 5, 8 and 9 have been excluded because the revision process relating to those Articles included significant consideration of electronic practices. Paragraph 4 provides for exclusion from this Act of the Uniform Computer Information Transactions Act (UCITA) because the drafting process of that Act also included significant consideration of electronic contracting provisions.

6.   The very limited application of this Act to Transferable Records in Section 16 does not affect payment systems, and the section is designed to apply to a transaction only through express agreement of the parties. The exclusion of Articles 3 and 4 will not affect the Act's coverage of Transferable Records. Section 16 is designed to allow for the development of systems which will provide "control" as defined in Section 16. Such control is necessary as a substitute for the idea of possession which undergirds negotiable instrument law. The technology has yet to be developed which will allow for the possession of a unique electronic token embodying the rights associated with a negotiable promissory note. Section 16's concept of control is intended as a substitute for possession.

The provisions in Section 16 operate as free standing rules, establishing the rights of parties using Transferable Records *under this Act*. The references in Section 16 to UCC Sections 3–302, 7–501, and 9–308 (R9–330(d)) are designed to incorporate the substance of those provisions into this Act for the limited purposes noted in Section 16(c). Accordingly, an electronic record which is also a Transferable Record, would not be used for purposes of a transaction governed by Articles 3, 4, or 9, but would be an electronic record used for purposes of a transaction governed by Section 16. However, it is important to remember that those UCC Articles will still apply to the transferable record in their own right. Accordingly any other substantive requirements, e.g., method and manner of perfection under Article 9, must be complied with under those other laws. See Comments to Section 16.

7.   This Act does apply, *in toto*, to transactions under unrevised Articles 2 and 2A. There is every reason to validate electronic contracting in these situations. Sale and lease transactions do not implicate broad systems beyond the parties to the underlying transaction, such as are present in check collection and electronic funds

transfers. Further sales and leases generally do not have as far reaching effect on the rights of third parties beyond the contracting parties, such as exists in the secured transactions system. Finally, it is in the area of sales, licenses and leases that electronic commerce is occurring to its greatest extent today. To exclude these transactions would largely gut the purpose of this Act.

In the event that Articles 2 and 2A are revised and adopted in the future, UETA will only apply to the extent provided in those Acts.

8. An electronic record/signature may be used for purposes of more than one legal requirement, or may be covered by more than one law. Consequently, it is important to make clear, despite any apparent redundancy, in subsection (c) that an electronic record used for purposes of a law which is **not** affected by this Act under subsection (b) may nonetheless be used and validated for purposes of other laws not excluded by subsection (b). For example, this Act does not apply to an electronic record of a check when used for purposes of a transaction governed by Article 4 of the Uniform Commercial Code, i.e., the Act does not validate so-called electronic checks. However, for purposes of check retention statutes, the same electronic record of the check is covered by this Act, so that retention of an electronic image/record of a check will satisfy such retention statutes, so long as the requirements of Section 12 are fulfilled.

In another context, subsection (c) would operate to allow this Act to apply to what would appear to be an excluded transaction under subsection (b). For example, Article 9 of the Uniform Commercial Code applies generally to any transaction that creates a security interest in personal property. However, Article 9 excludes landlord's liens. Accordingly, although this Act excludes from its application transactions subject to Article 9, this Act would apply to the creation of a landlord lien if the law otherwise applicable to landlord's liens did not provide otherwise, because the landlord's lien transaction is excluded from Article 9.

9. Additional exclusions under subparagraph (b)(4) should be limited to laws which govern electronic records and signatures which may be used in transactions as defined in Section 2(16). Records used unilaterally, or which do not relate to business, commercial (including consumer), or governmental affairs are not governed by this Act in any event, and exclusion of laws relating to such records may create unintended inferences about whether other records and signatures are covered by this Act.

It is also important that additional exclusions, if any, be incorporated under subsection (b)(4). As noted in Comment 8 above, an electronic record used in a transaction excluded under subsection (b), e.g., a check used to pay one's taxes, will nonetheless be validated for purposes of other, non-excluded laws under subsection (c), e.g., the check when used as proof of payment. It is critical that additional exclusions, if any, be incorporated into subsection (b) so that the salutary effect of subsection (c) apply to validate those records in other, non-excluded transactions. While a legislature may determine that a particular notice, such as a utility shutoff notice, be provided to a person in writing on paper, it is difficult to see why the utility should not be entitled to use electronic media for storage and evidentiary purposes.

Legislative Note Regarding Possible Additional Exclusions under Section 3(b)(4).

The following discussion is derived from the Report dated September 21, 1998 of The Task Force on State Law Exclusions (the "Task Force") presented to the Drafting Committee. After consideration of the Report, the Drafting Committee determined that exclusions other than those specified in the Act were not warranted. In addition, other inherent limitations on the applicability of the Act (the definition of transaction, the requirement that the parties acquiesce in the use of an electronic format) also militate against additional exclusions. Nonetheless, the Drafting Committee recognized that some legislatures may wish to exclude additional transactions from the Act, and determined that guidance in some major areas would be helpful to those legislatures considering additional areas for exclusion.

Because of the overwhelming number of references in state law to writings and signatures, the following list of possible transactions is not exhaustive. However, they do represent those areas most commonly raised during the course of the drafting process as areas that might be inappropriate for an electronic medium. It is important to keep in mind however, that the Drafting Committee determined that exclusion of these additional areas was not warranted.

1. **Trusts** (other than testamentary trusts). Trusts can be used for both business and personal purposes. By virtue of the definition of transaction, trusts used outside the area of business and commerce would not be governed by this Act. With respect to business or commercial trusts, the laws governing their formation contain few or no requirements for paper or signatures. Indeed, in most jurisdictions trusts of any kind may be created orally. Consequently, the Drafting Committee believed that the Act should apply to any transaction where the law

leaves to the parties the decision of whether to use a writing. Thus, in the absence of legal requirements for writings, there is no sound reason to exclude laws governing trusts from the application of this Act.

2.   **Powers of Attorney.** A power of attorney is simply a formalized type of agency agreement. In general, no formal requirements for paper or execution were found to be applicable to the validity of powers of attorney.

Special health powers of attorney have been established by statute in some States. These powers may have special requirements under state law regarding execution, acknowledgment and possibly notarization. In the normal case such powers will not arise in a transactional context and so would not be covered by this Act. However, even if such a record were to arise in a transactional context, this Act operates simply to remove the barrier to the use of an electronic medium, and preserves other requirements of applicable substantive law, avoiding any necessity to exclude such laws from the operation of this Act. Especially in light of the provisions of Sections 8 and 11, the substantive requirements under such laws will be preserved and may be satisfied in an electronic format.

3.   **Real Estate Transactions.** It is important to distinguish between the efficacy of paper documents involving real estate between the parties, as opposed to their effect on third parties. As between the parties it is unnecessary to maintain existing barriers to electronic contracting. There are no unique characteristics to contracts relating to real property as opposed to other business and commercial (including consumer) contracts. Consequently, the decision whether to use an electronic medium for their agreements should be a matter for the parties to determine. Of course, to be effective against third parties state law generally requires filing with a governmental office. Pending adoption of electronic filing systems by States, the need for a piece of paper to file to perfect rights against third parties, will be a consideration for the parties. In the event notarization and acknowledgment are required under other laws, Section 11 provides a means for such actions to be accomplished electronically.

With respect to the requirements of government filing, those are left to the individual States in the decision of whether to adopt and implement electronic filing systems. (See optional Sections 17–19.) However, government recording systems currently require paper deeds including notarized, manual signatures. Although California and Illinois are experimenting with electronic filing systems, until such systems become widespread, the parties likely will choose to use, at the least, a paper deed for filing purposes. Nothing in this Act precludes the parties from selecting the medium best suited to the needs of the particular transaction. Parties may wish to consummate the transaction using electronic media in order to avoid expensive travel. Yet the actual deed may be in paper form to assure compliance with existing recording systems and requirements. The critical point is that nothing in this Act prevents the parties from selecting paper or electronic media for all or part of their transaction.

4.   **Consumer Protection Statutes.** Consumer protection provisions in state law often require that information be disclosed or provided to a consumer in writing. Because this Act does apply to such transactions, the question of whether such laws should be specifically excluded was considered. Exclusion of consumer transactions would eliminate a huge group of commercial transactions which benefit consumers by enabling the efficiency of the electronic medium. Commerce over the internet is driven by consumer demands and concerns and must be included.

At the same time, it is important to recognize the protective effects of many consumer statutes. Consumer statutes often require that information be provided in writing, or may require that the consumer separately sign or initial a particular provision to evidence that the consumer's attention was brought to the provision. Subsection (1) requires electronic records to be retainable by a person whenever the law requires information to be delivered in writing. The section imposes a significant burden on the sender of information. The sender must assure that the information system of the recipient is compatible with, and capable of retaining the information sent by, the sender's system. Furthermore, nothing in this Act permits the avoidance of legal requirements of separate signatures or initialing. The Act simply permits the signature or initialing to be done electronically.

Other consumer protection statutes require (expressly or implicitly) that certain information be presented in a certain manner or format. Laws requiring information to be presented in particular fonts, formats or in similar fashion, as well as laws requiring conspicuous displays of information are preserved. Section 8(b)(3) specifically preserves the applicability of such requirements in an electronic environment. In the case of legal requirements that information be presented or appear conspicuous, the determination of what is conspicuous will be left to other law. Section 8 was included to specifically preserve the protective functions of such disclosure statutes, while at the same time allowing the use of electronic media if the substantive requirements of the other laws could be satisfied in the electronic medium.

Formatting and separate signing requirements serve a critical purpose in much consumer protection legislation, to assure that information is not slipped past the unsuspecting consumer. Not only does this Act not disturb those requirements, it preserves those requirements. In addition, other bodies of substantive law continue to operate to allow the courts to police any such bad conduct or overreaching, e.g., unconscionability, fraud, duress, mistake and the like. These bodies of law remain applicable regardless of the medium in which a record appears.

The requirement that both parties agree to conduct a transaction electronically also prevents the imposition of an electronic medium on unwilling parties See Section 5(b). In addition, where the law requires inclusion of specific terms or language, those requirements are preserved broadly by Section 5(e).

Requirements that information be sent to, or received by, someone have been preserved in Section 15. As in the paper world, obligations to send do not impose any duties on the sender to assure receipt, other than reasonable methods of dispatch. In those cases where receipt is required legally, Sections 5, 8, and 15 impose the burden on the sender to assure delivery to the recipient if satisfaction of the legal requirement is to be fulfilled.

The preservation of existing safeguards, together with the ability to opt out of the electronic medium entirely, demonstrate the lack of any need generally to exclude consumer protection laws from the operation of this Act. Legislatures may wish to focus any review on those statutes which provide for post-contract formation and post-breach notices to be in paper. However, any such consideration must also balance the needed protections against the potential burdens which may be imposed. Consumers and others will not be well served by restrictions which preclude the employment of electronic technologies sought and desired by consumers.

§ 4. Prospective Application.

This [Act] applies to any electronic record or electronic signature created, generated, sent, communicated, received, or stored on or after the effective date of this [Act].

Comment

This section makes clear that the Act only applies to validate electronic records and signatures which arise subsequent to the effective date of the Act. Whether electronic records and electronic signatures arising before the effective date of this Act are valid is left to other law.

§ 5. Use of Electronic Records and Electronic Signatures; Variation by Agreement.

(a) This [Act] does not require a record or signature to be created, generated, sent, communicated, received, stored, or otherwise processed or used by electronic means or in electronic form.

(b) This [Act] applies only to transactions between parties each of which has agreed to conduct transactions by electronic means. Whether the parties agree to conduct a transaction by electronic means is determined from the context and surrounding circumstances, including the parties' conduct.

(c) A party that agrees to conduct a transaction by electronic means may refuse to conduct other transactions by electronic means. The right granted by this subsection may not be waived by agreement.

(d) Except as otherwise provided in this [Act], the effect of any of its provisions may be varied by agreement. The presence in certain provisions of this [Act] of the words "unless otherwise agreed", or words of similar import, does not imply that the effect of other provisions may not be varied by agreement.

(e) Whether an electronic record or electronic signature has legal consequences is determined by this [Act] and other applicable law.

Comment

This section limits the applicability of this Act to transactions which parties have agreed to conduct electronically. Broad interpretation of the term agreement is necessary to assure that this Act has the widest possible application consistent with its purpose of removing barriers to electronic commerce.

1.   This section makes clear that this Act is intended to facilitate the use of electronic means, but does not require the use of electronic records and signatures. This fundamental principle is set forth in subsection (a) and elaborated by subsections (b) and (c), which require an intention to conduct transactions electronically and preserve the right of a party to refuse to use electronics in any subsequent transaction.

2.   The paradigm of this Act is two willing parties doing transactions electronically. It is therefore appropriate that the Act is voluntary and preserves the greatest possible party autonomy to refuse electronic

transactions. The requirement that party agreement be found from all the surrounding circumstances is a limitation on the scope of this Act.

    3.   If this Act is to serve to facilitate electronic transactions, it must be applicable under circumstances not rising to a full fledged contract to use electronics. While absolute certainty can be accomplished by obtaining an explicit contract before relying on electronic transactions, such an explicit contract should not be necessary before one may feel safe in conducting transactions electronically. Indeed, such a requirement would itself be an unreasonable barrier to electronic commerce, at odds with the fundamental purpose of this Act. Accordingly, the requisite agreement, express or implied, must be determined from all available circumstances and evidence.

    4.   Subsection (b) provides that the Act applies to transactions in which the parties have agreed to conduct the transaction electronically. In this context it is essential that the parties' actions and words be broadly construed in determining whether the requisite agreement exists. Accordingly, the Act expressly provides that the party's agreement is to be found from all circumstances, including the parties' conduct. The critical element is the intent of a party to conduct a transaction electronically. Once that intent is established, this Act applies. See Restatement 2d Contracts, Sections 2, 3, and 19.

Examples of circumstances from which it may be found that parties have reached an agreement to conduct transactions electronically include the following:

    A.   Automaker and supplier enter into a Trading Partner Agreement setting forth the terms, conditions and methods for the conduct of business between them electronically.

    B.   Joe gives out his business card with his business e-mail address. It may be reasonable, under the circumstances, for a recipient of the card to infer that Joe has agreed to communicate electronically for business purposes. However, in the absence of additional facts, it would not necessarily be reasonable to infer Joe's agreement to communicate electronically for purposes outside the scope of the business indicated by use of the business card.

    C.   Sally may have several e-mail addresses—home, main office, office of a non-profit organization on whose board Sally sits. In each case, it may be reasonable to infer that Sally is willing to communicate electronically with respect to business related to the business/purpose associated with the respective e-mail addresses. However, depending on the circumstances, it may not be reasonable to communicate with Sally for purposes other than those related to the purpose for which she maintained a particular e-mail account.

    D.   Among the circumstances to be considered in finding an agreement would be the time when the assent occurred relative to the timing of the use of electronic communications. If one orders books from an on-line vendor, such as Bookseller.com, the intention to conduct that transaction and to receive any correspondence related to the transaction electronically can be inferred from the conduct. Accordingly, as to information related to that transaction it is reasonable for Bookseller to deal with the individual electronically.

The examples noted above are intended to focus the inquiry on the party's agreement to conduct a transaction electronically. Similarly, if two people are at a meeting and one tells the other to send an e-mail to confirm a transaction—the requisite agreement under subsection (b) would exist. In each case, the use of a business card, statement at a meeting, or other evidence of willingness to conduct a transaction electronically must be viewed in light of all the surrounding circumstances with a view toward broad validation of electronic transactions.

    5.   Just as circumstances may indicate the existence of agreement, express or implied from surrounding circumstances, circumstances may also demonstrate the absence of true agreement. For example:

    A.   If Automaker, Inc. were to issue a recall of automobiles via its Internet website, it would not be able to rely on this Act to validate that notice in the case of a person who never logged on to the website, or indeed, had no ability to do so, notwithstanding a clause in a paper purchase contract by which the buyer agreed to receive such notices in such a manner.

    B.   Buyer executes a standard form contract in which an agreement to receive all notices electronically in set forth on page 3 in the midst of other fine print. Buyer has never communicated with Seller electronically, and has not provided any other information in the contract to suggest a willingness to deal electronically. Not only is it unlikely that any but the most formalistic of agreements may be found, but nothing in this Act prevents courts from policing such form contracts under common law doctrines relating to contract formation, unconscionability and the like.

6.   Subsection (c) has been added to make clear the ability of a party to refuse to conduct a transaction electronically, even if the person has conducted transactions electronically in the past. The effectiveness of a party's refusal to conduct a transaction electronically will be determined under other applicable law in light of all surrounding circumstances. Such circumstances must include an assessment of the transaction involved.

A party's right to decline to act electronically under a specific contract, on the ground that each action under that contract amounts to a separate "transaction," must be considered in light of the purpose of the contract and the action to be taken electronically. For example, under a contract for the purchase of goods, the giving and receipt of notices electronically, as provided in the contract, should not be viewed as discreet transactions. Rather such notices amount to separate actions which are part of the "transaction" of purchase evidenced by the contract. Allowing one party to require a change of medium in the middle of the transaction evidenced by that contract is not the purpose of this subsection. Rather this subsection is intended to preserve the party's right to conduct the next purchase in a non-electronic medium.

7.   Subsection (e) is an essential provision in the overall scheme of this Act. While this Act validates and effectuates electronic records and electronic signatures, the legal effect of such records and signatures is left to existing substantive law outside this Act except in very narrow circumstances. See, e.g., Section 16. Even when this Act operates to validate records and signatures in an electronic medium, it expressly preserves the substantive rules of other law applicable to such records. See, e.g., Section 11.

For example, beyond validation of records, signatures and contracts based on the medium used, Section 7 (a) and (b) should not be interpreted as establishing the legal effectiveness of any given record, signature or contract. Where a rule of law requires that the record contain minimum substantive content, the legal effect of such a record will depend on whether the record meets the substantive requirements of other applicable law.

Section 8 expressly preserves a number of legal requirements in currently existing law relating to the presentation of information in writing. Although this Act now would allow such information to be presented in an electronic record, Section 8 provides that the other substantive requirements of law must be satisfied in the electronic medium as well.

§ 6.   Construction and Application.

This [Act] must be construed and applied:

(1)   to facilitate electronic transactions consistent with other applicable law;

(2)   to be consistent with reasonable practices concerning electronic transactions and with the continued expansion of those practices; and

(3)   to effectuate its general purpose to make uniform the law with respect to the subject of this [Act] among States enacting it.

Comment

1.   The purposes and policies of this Act are

(a)   to facilitate and promote commerce and governmental transactions by validating and authorizing the use of electronic records and electronic signatures;

(b)   to eliminate barriers to electronic commerce and governmental transactions resulting from uncertainties relating to writing and signature requirements;

(c)   to simplify, clarify and modernize the law governing commerce and governmental transactions through the use of electronic means;

(d)   to permit the continued expansion of commercial and governmental electronic practices through custom, usage and agreement of the parties;

(e)   to promote uniformity of the law among the States (and worldwide) relating to the use of electronic and similar technological means of effecting and performing commercial and governmental transactions;

(f)   to promote public confidence in the validity, integrity and reliability of electronic commerce and governmental transactions; and

(g)   to promote the development of the legal and business infrastructure necessary to implement electronic commerce and governmental transactions.

2.   This Act has been drafted to permit flexible application consistent with its purpose to validate electronic transactions. The provisions of this Act validating and effectuating the employ of electronic media allow the courts to apply them to new and unforeseen technologies and practices. As time progresses, it is anticipated that what is new and unforeseen today will be commonplace tomorrow. Accordingly, this legislation is intended to set a framework for the validation of media which may be developed in the future and which demonstrate the same qualities as the electronic media contemplated and validated under this Act.

§ 7.   Legal Recognition of Electronic Records, Electronic Signatures, and Electronic Contracts.

(a)   A record or signature may not be denied legal effect or enforceability solely because it is in electronic form.

(b)   A contract may not be denied legal effect or enforceability solely because an electronic record was used in its formation.

(c)   If a law requires a record to be in writing, an electronic record satisfies the law.

(d)   If a law requires a signature, an electronic signature satisfies the law.

Source: UNCITRAL Model Law on Electronic Commerce, Articles 5, 6, and 7.

Comment

1.   This section sets forth the fundamental premise of this Act: namely, that the medium in which a record, signature, or contract is created, presented or retained does not affect it's legal significance. Subsections (a) and (b) are designed to eliminate the single element of medium as a reason to deny effect or enforceability to a record, signature, or contract. The fact that the information is set forth in an electronic, as opposed to paper, record is irrelevant.

2.   Under Restatement 2d Contracts Section 8, a contract may have legal effect and yet be unenforceable. Indeed, one circumstance where a record or contract may have effect but be unenforceable is in the context of the Statute of Frauds. Though a contract may be unenforceable, the records may have collateral effects, as in the case of a buyer that insures goods purchased under a contract unenforceable under the Statute of Frauds. The insurance company may not deny a claim on the ground that the buyer is not the owner, though the buyer may have no direct remedy against seller for failure to deliver. See Restatement 2d Contracts, Section 8, Illustration 4.

While this section would validate an electronic record for purposes of a statute of frauds, if an agreement to conduct the transaction electronically cannot reasonably be found (See Section 5(b)) then a necessary predicate to the applicability of this Act would be absent and this Act would not validate the electronic record. Whether the electronic record might be valid under other law is not addressed by this Act.

3.   Subsections (c) and (d) provide the positive assertion that electronic records and signatures satisfy legal requirements for writings and signatures. The provisions are limited to requirements in laws that a record be in writing or be signed. This section does not address requirements imposed by other law in addition to requirements for writings and signatures See, e.g., Section 8.

Subsections (c) and (d) are particularized applications of subsection (a). The purpose is to validate and effectuate electronic records and signatures as the equivalent of writings, subject to all of the rules applicable to the efficacy of a writing, except as such other rules are modified by the more specific provisions of this Act.

Illustration 1: A sends the following e-mail to B: "I hereby offer to buy widgets from you, delivery next Tuesday. /s/ A." B responds with the following e-mail: "I accept your offer to buy widgets for delivery next Tuesday. /s/ B." The e-mails may not be denied effect solely because they are electronic. In addition, the e-mails do qualify as records under the Statute of Frauds. However, because there is no quantity stated in either record, the parties' agreement would be unenforceable under existing UCC Section 2–201(1).

Illustration 2: A sends the following e-mail to B: "I hereby offer to buy 100 widgets for $1000, delivery next Tuesday. /s/ A." B responds with the following e-mail: "I accept your offer to purchase 100 widgets for $1000, delivery next Tuesday. /s/ B." In this case the analysis is the same as in Illustration 1 except that here the records otherwise satisfy the requirements of UCC Section 2–201(1). The transaction may not be denied legal effect solely because there is not a pen and ink "writing" or "signature".

4.   Section 8 addresses additional requirements imposed by other law which may affect the legal effect or enforceability of an electronic record in a particular case. For example, in Section 8(a) the legal requirement addressed is *the provision of information* in writing. The section then sets forth the standards to be applied in determining whether the provision of information by an electronic record is the equivalent of the provision of information in writing. The requirements in Section 8 are in addition to the bare validation that occurs under this section.

5.   Under the substantive law applicable to a particular transaction within this Act, the legal effect of an electronic record may be separate from the issue of whether the record contains a signature. For example, where notice must be given as part of a contractual obligation, the effectiveness of the notice will turn on whether the party provided the notice regardless of whether the notice was signed (See Section 15). An electronic record attributed to a party under Section 9 and complying with the requirements of Section 15 would suffice in that case, notwithstanding that it may not contain an electronic signature.

§ 8.   Provision of Information in Writing; Presentation of Records.

(a)   If parties have agreed to conduct a transaction by electronic means and a law requires a person to provide, send, or deliver information in writing to another person, the requirement is satisfied if the information is provided, sent, or delivered, as the case may be, in an electronic record capable of retention by the recipient at the time of receipt. An electronic record is not capable of retention by the recipient if the sender or its information processing system inhibits the ability of the recipient to print or store the electronic record.

(b)   If a law other than this [Act] requires a record (i) to be posted or displayed in a certain manner, (ii) to be sent, communicated, or transmitted by a specified method, or (iii) to contain information that is formatted in a certain manner, the following rules apply:

(1)   The record must be posted or displayed in the manner specified in the other law.

(2)   Except as otherwise provided in subsection (d)(2), the record must be sent, communicated, or transmitted by the method specified in the other law.

(3)   The record must contain the information formatted in the manner specified in the other law.

(c)   If a sender inhibits the ability of a recipient to store or print an electronic record, the electronic record is not enforceable against the recipient.

(d)   The requirements of this section may not be varied by agreement, but:

(1)   to the extent a law other than this [Act] requires information to be provided, sent, or delivered in writing but permits that requirement to be varied by agreement, the requirement under subsection (a) that the information be in the form of an electronic record capable of retention may also be varied by agreement; and

(2)   a requirement under a law other than this [Act] to send, communicate, or transmit a record by [first-class mail, postage prepaid] [regular United States mail], may be varied by agreement to the extent permitted by the other law.

Source: Canadian-Uniform Electronic Commerce Act

Comment

1.   This section is a savings provision, designed to assure, consistent with the fundamental purpose of this Act, that otherwise applicable substantive law will not be overridden by this Act. The section makes clear that while the pen and ink provisions of such other law may be satisfied electronically, nothing in this Act vitiates the other requirements of such laws. The section addresses a number of issues related to disclosures and notice provisions in other laws.

2.   This section is independent of the prior section. Section 7 refers to legal requirements for a writing. This section refers to legal requirements for the provision of information in writing or relating to the method or manner of presentation or delivery of information. The section addresses more specific legal requirements of other laws, provides standards for satisfying the more particular legal requirements, and defers to other law for satisfaction of requirements under those laws.

3.   Under subsection (a), to meet a requirement of other law that information be provided in writing, the recipient of an electronic record of the information must be able to get to the electronic record and read it, and must have the ability to get back to the information in some way at a later date. Accordingly, the section requires that the electronic record be capable of retention for later review.

The section specifically provides that any inhibition on retention imposed by the sender or the sender's system will preclude satisfaction of this section. Use of technological means now existing or later developed which prevents the recipient from retaining a copy the information would result in a determination that information has not been provided under subsection (a). The policies underlying laws requiring the provision of information in writing warrant the imposition of an additional burden on the sender to make the information available in a manner which will permit subsequent reference. A difficulty does exist for senders of information because of the disparate systems of their recipients and the capabilities of those systems. However, in order to satisfy the *legal requirement* of other law to make information available, the sender must assure that the recipient receives and can retain the information. However, it is left for the courts to determine whether the sender has complied with this subsection if evidence demonstrates that it is something peculiar the recipient's system which precludes subsequent reference to the information.

4.   Subsection (b) is a savings provision for laws which provide for the means of delivering or displaying information and which are not affected by the Act. For example, if a law requires delivery of notice by first class US mail, that means of delivery would not be affected by this Act. The information to be delivered may be provided on a disc, i.e., in electronic form, but the particular means of delivery must still be via the US postal service. Display, delivery and formatting requirements will continue to be applicable to electronic records and signatures. If those legal requirements can be satisfied in an electronic medium, e.g., the information can be presented in the equivalent of 20 point bold type as required by other law, this Act will validate the use of the medium, leaving to the other applicable law the question of whether the particular electronic record meets the other legal requirements. If a law requires that particular records be delivered together, or attached to other records, this Act does not preclude the delivery of the records together in an electronic communication, so long as the records are connected or associated with each other in a way determined to satisfy the other law.

5.   Subsection (c) provides incentives for senders of information to use systems which will not inhibit the other party from retaining the information. However, there are circumstances where a party providing certain information may wish to inhibit retention in order to protect intellectual property rights or prevent the other party from retaining confidential information about the sender. In such cases inhibition is understandable, but if the sender wishes to enforce the record in which the information is contained, the sender may not inhibit its retention by the recipient. Unlike subsection (a), subsection (c) applies in all transactions and simply provides for unenforceability against the recipient. Subsection (a) applies only where another law imposes the writing requirement, and subsection (a) imposes a broader responsibility on the sender to assure retention capability by the recipient.

6.   The protective purposes of this section justify the non-waivability provided by subsection (d). However, since the requirements for sending and formatting and the like are imposed by other law, to the extent other law permits waiver of such protections, there is no justification for imposing a more severe burden in an electronic environment.

§ 9.   Attribution and Effect of Electronic Record and Electronic Signature.

(a)   An electronic record or electronic signature is attributable to a person if it was the act of the person. The act of the person may be shown in any manner, including a showing of the efficacy of any security procedure applied to determine the person to which the electronic record or electronic signature was attributable.

(b)   The effect of an electronic record or electronic signature attributed to a person under subsection (a) is determined from the context and surrounding circumstances at the time of its creation, execution, or adoption, including the parties' agreement, if any, and otherwise as provided by law.

Comment

1.   Under subsection (a), so long as the electronic record or electronic signature resulted from a person's action it will be attributed to that person—the legal effect of that attribution is addressed in subsection (b). This section does not alter existing rules of law regarding attribution. The section assures that such rules will be applied in the electronic environment. A person's actions include actions taken by human agents of the person, as well as

actions taken by an electronic agent, i.e., the tool, of the person. Although the rule may appear to state the obvious, it assures that the record or signature is not ascribed to a machine, as opposed to the person operating or programing the machine.

In each of the following cases, both the electronic record and electronic signature would be attributable to a person under subsection (a):

A.   The person types his/her name as part of an e-mail purchase order;

B.   The person's employee, pursuant to authority, types the person's name as part of an e-mail purchase order;

C.   The person's computer, programmed to order goods upon receipt of inventory information within particular parameters, issues a purchase order which includes the person's name, or other identifying information, as part of the order.

In each of the above cases, law other than this Act would ascribe both the signature and the action to the person if done in a paper medium. Subsection (a) expressly provides that the same result will occur when an electronic medium is used.

2.   Nothing in this section affects the use of a signature as a device for attributing a record to a person. Indeed, a signature is often the primary method for attributing a record to a person. In the foregoing examples, once the electronic signature is attributed to the person, the electronic record would also be attributed to the person, unless the person established fraud, forgery, or other invalidating cause. However, a signature is not the only method for attribution.

3.   The use of facsimile transmissions provides a number of examples of attribution using information other than a signature. A facsimile may be attributed to a person because of the information printed across the top of the page that indicates the machine from which it was sent. Similarly, the transmission may contain a letterhead which identifies the sender. Some cases have held that the letterhead actually constituted a signature because it was a symbol adopted by the sender with intent to authenticate the facsimile. However, the signature determination resulted from the necessary finding of intention in that case. Other cases have found facsimile letterheads NOT to be signatures because the requisite intention was not present. The critical point is that with or without a signature, information within the electronic record may well suffice to provide the facts resulting in attribution of an electronic record to a particular party.

In the context of attribution of records, normally the content of the record will provide the necessary information for a finding of attribution. It is also possible that an established course of dealing between parties may result in a finding of attribution Just as with a paper record, evidence of forgery or counterfeiting may be introduced to rebut the evidence of attribution.

4.   Certain information may be present in an electronic environment that does not appear to attribute but which clearly links a person to a particular record. Numerical codes, personal identification numbers, public and private key combinations all serve to establish the party to whom an electronic record should be attributed. Of course security procedures will be another piece of evidence available to establish attribution.

The inclusion of a specific reference to security procedures as a means of proving attribution is salutary because of the unique importance of security procedures in the electronic environment. In certain processes, a technical and technological security procedure may be the best way to convince a trier of fact that a particular electronic record or signature was that of a particular person. In certain circumstances, the use of a security procedure to establish that the record and related signature came from the person's business might be necessary to overcome a claim that a hacker intervened. The reference to security procedures is not intended to suggest that other forms of proof of attribution should be accorded less persuasive effect. It is also important to recall that the particular strength of a given procedure does not affect the procedure's status as a security procedure, but only affects the weight to be accorded the evidence of the security procedure as tending to establish attribution.

5.   This section does apply in determining the effect of a "click-through" transaction. A "click-through" transaction involves a process which, if executed with an intent to "sign," will be an electronic signature. See definition of Electronic Signature. In the context of an anonymous "click-through," issues of proof will be paramount. This section will be relevant to establish that the resulting electronic record is attributable to a particular person upon the requisite proof, including security procedures which may track the source of the click-through.

6.　　Once it is established that a record or signature is attributable to a particular party, the effect of a record or signature must be determined in light of the context and surrounding circumstances, including the parties' agreement, if any. Also informing the effect of any attribution will be other legal requirements considered in light of the context. Subsection (b) addresses the effect of the record or signature once attributed to a person.

§ 10.　　Effect of Change or Error.

If a change or error in an electronic record occurs in a transmission between parties to a transaction, the following rules apply:

(1)　If the parties have agreed to use a security procedure to detect changes or errors and one party has conformed to the procedure, but the other party has not, and the nonconforming party would have detected the change or error had that party also conformed, the conforming party may avoid the effect of the changed or erroneous electronic record.

(2)　In an automated transaction involving an individual, the individual may avoid the effect of an electronic record that resulted from an error made by the individual in dealing with the electronic agent of another person if the electronic agent did not provide an opportunity for the prevention or correction of the error and, at the time the individual learns of the error, the individual:

(A)　promptly notifies the other person of the error and that the individual did not intend to be bound by the electronic record received by the other person;

(B)　takes reasonable steps, including steps that conform to the other person's reasonable instructions, to return to the other person or, if instructed by the other person, to destroy the consideration received, if any, as a result of the erroneous electronic record; and

(C)　has not used or received any benefit or value from the consideration, if any, received from the other person.

(3)　If neither paragraph (1) nor paragraph (2) applies, the change or error has the effect provided by other law, including the law of mistake, and the parties' contract, if any.

(4)　Paragraphs (2) and (3) may not be varied by agreement.

Source: Restatement 2d Contracts, Sections 152–155.

Comment

1.　　This section is limited to changes and errors occurring in transmissions between parties—whether person-person (paragraph 1) or in an automated transaction involving an individual and a machine (paragraphs 1 and 2). The section focuses on the effect of changes and errors occurring when records are exchanged between parties. In cases where changes and errors occur in contexts other than transmission, the law of mistake is expressly made applicable to resolve the conflict.

The section covers both changes and errors. For example, if Buyer sends a message to Seller ordering 100 widgets, but Buyer's information processing system changes the order to 1000 widgets, a "change" has occurred between what Buyer transmitted and what Seller received. If on the other hand, Buyer typed in 1000 intending to order only 100, but sent the message before noting the mistake, an error would have occurred which would also be covered by this section.

2.　　Paragraph (1) deals with any transmission where the parties have agreed to use a security procedure to detect changes and errors. It operates against the non-conforming party, i.e., the party in the best position to have avoided the change or error, regardless of whether that person is the sender or recipient. The source of the error/change is not indicated, and so both human and machine errors/changes would be covered. With respect to errors or changes that would not be detected by the security procedure even if applied, the parties are left to the general law of mistake to resolve the dispute.

3.　　Paragraph (1) applies only in the situation where a security procedure would detect the error/change but one party fails to use the procedure and does not detect the error/change. In such a case, consistent with the law of mistake generally, the record is made avoidable at the instance of the party who took all available steps to avoid the mistake. See Restatement 2d Contracts Sections 152–154.

Making the erroneous record avoidable by the conforming party is consistent with Sections 153 and 154 of the Restatement 2d Contracts because the non-conforming party was in the best position to avoid the problem, and would bear the risk of mistake. Such a case would constitute mistake by one party. The mistaken party (the conforming party) would be entitled to avoid any resulting contract under Section 153 because s/he does not have the risk of mistake and the non-conforming party had reason to know of the mistake.

4.   As with paragraph (1), paragraph (2), when applicable, allows the mistaken party to avoid the effect of the erroneous electronic record. However, the subsection is limited to human error on the part of an individual when dealing with the electronic agent of the other party. In a transaction between individuals there is a greater ability to correct the error before parties have acted on it. However, when an individual makes an error while dealing with the electronic agent of the other party, it may not be possible to correct the error before the other party has shipped or taken other action in reliance on the erroneous record.

Paragraph (2) applies only to errors made by individuals. If the error results from the electronic agent, it would constitute a system error. In such a case the effect of that error would be resolved under paragraph (1) if applicable, otherwise under paragraph (3) and the general law of mistake.

5.   The party acting through the electronic agent/machine is given incentives by this section to build in safeguards which enable the individual to prevent the sending of an erroneous record, or correct the error once sent. For example, the electronic agent may be programmed to provide a "confirmation screen" to the individual setting forth all the information the individual initially approved. This would provide the individual with the ability to prevent the erroneous record from ever being sent. Similarly, the electronic agent might receive the record sent by the individual and then send back a confirmation which the individual must again accept before the transaction is completed. This would allow for correction of an erroneous record. In either case, the electronic agent would "provide an opportunity for prevention or correction of the error," *and the subsection would not apply*. Rather, the affect of any error is governed by other law.

6.   Paragraph (2) also places additional requirements on the mistaken individual before the paragraph may be invoked to avoid an erroneous electronic record. The individual must take prompt action to advise the other party of the error and the fact that the individual did not intend the electronic record. Whether the action is prompt must be determined from all the circumstances including the individual's ability to contact the other party. The individual should advise the other party both of the error and of the lack of intention to be bound (i.e., avoidance) by the electronic record received. Since this provision allows avoidance by the mistaken party, that party should also be required to expressly note that it is seeking to avoid the electronic record, i.e., lacked the intention to be bound.

Second, restitution is normally required in order to undo a mistaken transaction. Accordingly, the individual must also return or destroy any consideration received, adhering to instructions from the other party in any case. This is to assure that the other party retains control over the consideration sent in error.

Finally, and most importantly in regard to transactions involving intermediaries which may be harmed because transactions cannot be unwound, the individual cannot have received any benefit from the transaction. This section prevents a party from unwinding a transaction after the delivery of value and consideration which cannot be returned or destroyed. For example, if the consideration received is information, it may not be possible to avoid the benefit conferred. While the information itself could be returned, mere access to the information, or the ability to redistribute the information would constitute a benefit precluding the mistaken party from unwinding the transaction. It may also occur that the mistaken party receives consideration which changes in value between the time of receipt and the first opportunity to return. In such a case restitution cannot be made adequately, and the transaction would not be avoidable. In each of the foregoing cases, under subparagraph (2)(c), the individual would have received the benefit of the consideration and would NOT be able to avoid the erroneous electronic record under this section.

7.   In all cases not covered by paragraphs (1) or (2), where error or change to a record occur, the parties' contract, or other law, specifically including the law of mistake, applies to resolve any dispute. In the event that the parties' contract and other law would achieve different results, the construction of the parties' contract is left to the other law. If the error occurs in the context of record retention, Section 12 will apply. In that case the standard is one of accuracy and retrievability of the information.

8.   Paragraph (4) makes the error correction provision in paragraph (2) and the application of the law of mistake in paragraph (3) non-variable. Paragraph (2) provides incentives for parties using electronic agents to establish safeguards for individuals dealing with them. It also avoids unjustified windfalls to the individual by erecting stringent requirements before the individual may exercise the right of avoidance under the paragraph.

Therefore, there is no reason to permit parties to avoid the paragraph by agreement. Rather, parties should satisfy the paragraph's requirements.

§ 11.   Notarization and Acknowledgment.

If a law requires a signature or record to be notarized, acknowledged, verified, or made under oath, the requirement is satisfied if the electronic signature of the person authorized to perform those acts, together with all other information required to be included by other applicable law, is attached to or logically associated with the signature or record.

Comment

This section permits a notary public and other authorized officers to act electronically, effectively removing the stamp/seal requirements. However, the section does not eliminate any of the other requirements of notarial laws, and consistent with the entire thrust of this Act, simply allows the signing and information to be accomplished in an electronic medium.

For example, Buyer wishes to send a notarized Real Estate Purchase Agreement to Seller via e-mail. The notary must appear in the room with the Buyer, satisfy him/herself as to the identity of the Buyer, and swear to that identification. All that activity must be reflected as part of the electronic Purchase Agreement and the notary's electronic signature must appear as a part of the electronic real estate purchase contract.

As another example, Buyer seeks to send Seller an affidavit averring defects in the products received. A court clerk, authorized under state law to administer oaths, is present with Buyer in a room. The Clerk administers the oath and includes the statement of the oath, together with any other requisite information, in the electronic record to be sent to the Seller. Upon administering the oath and witnessing the application of Buyer's electronic signature to the electronic record, the Clerk also applies his electronic signature to the electronic record. So long as all substantive requirements of other applicable law have been fulfilled and are reflected in the electronic record, the sworn electronic record of Buyer is as effective as if it had been transcribed on paper.

§ 12.   Retention of Electronic Records; Originals.

(a) If a law requires that a record be retained, the requirement is satisfied by retaining an electronic record of the information in the record which:

(1) accurately reflects the information set forth in the record after it was first generated in its final form as an electronic record or otherwise; and

(2) remains accessible for later reference.

(b) A requirement to retain a record in accordance with subsection (a) does not apply to any information the sole purpose of which is to enable the record to be sent, communicated, or received.

(c) A person may satisfy subsection (a) by using the services of another person if the requirements of that subsection are satisfied.

(d) If a law requires a record to be presented or retained in its original form, or provides consequences if the record is not presented or retained in its original form, that law is satisfied by an electronic record retained in accordance with subsection (a).

(e) If a law requires retention of a check, that requirement is satisfied by retention of an electronic record of the information on the front and back of the check in accordance with subsection (a).

(f) A record retained as an electronic record in accordance with subsection (a) satisfies a law requiring a person to retain a record for evidentiary, audit, or like purposes, unless a law enacted after the effective date of this [Act] specifically prohibits the use of an electronic record for the specified purpose.

(g) This section does not preclude a governmental agency of this State from specifying additional requirements for the retention of a record subject to the agency's jurisdiction.

Source: UNCITRAL Model Law On Electronic Commerce Articles 8 and 10.

Comment

1.   This section deals with the serviceability of electronic records as retained records and originals. So long as there exists reliable assurance that the electronic record accurately reproduces the information, this section continues the theme of establishing the functional equivalence of electronic and paper-based records. This is consistent with Fed.R.Evid. 1001(3) and Unif.R.Evid. 1001(3) (1974). This section assures that information stored electronically will remain effective for all audit, evidentiary, archival and similar purposes.

2.   In an electronic medium, the concept of an original document is problematic. For example, as one drafts a document on a computer the "original" is either on a disc or the hard drive to which the document has been initially saved. If one periodically saves the draft, the fact is that at times a document may be first saved to disc then to hard drive, and at others vice versa. In such a case the "original" may change from the information on the disc to the information on the hard drive. Indeed, it may be argued that the "original" exists solely in RAM and, in a sense, the original is destroyed when a "copy" is saved to a disc or to the hard drive. In any event, in the context of record retention, the concern focuses on the integrity of the information, and not with its "originality."

3.   Subsection (a) requires accuracy and the ability to access at a later time. The requirement of accuracy is derived from the Uniform and Federal Rules of Evidence. The requirement of continuing accessibility addresses the issue of technology obsolescence and the need to update and migrate information to developing systems. It is not unlikely that within the span of 5–10 years (a period during which retention of much information is required) a corporation may evolve through one or more generations of technology. More to the point, this technology may be incompatible with each other necessitating the reconversion of information from one system to the other.

For example, certain operating systems from the early 1980's, e.g., memory typewriters, became obsolete with the development of personal computers. The information originally stored on the memory typewriter would need to be converted to the personal computer system in a way meeting the standards for accuracy contemplated by this section. It is also possible that the medium on which the information is stored is less stable. For example, information stored on floppy discs is generally less stable, and subject to a greater threat of disintegration, that information stored on a computer hard drive. In either case, the continuing accessibility issue must be satisfied to validate information stored by electronic means under this section.

This section permits parties to convert original written records to electronic records for retention so long as the requirements of subsection (a) are satisfied. Accordingly, in the absence of specific requirements to retain written records, written records may be destroyed once saved as electronic records satisfying the requirements of this section.

The subsection refers to the information contained in an electronic record, rather than relying on the term electronic record, as a matter of clarity that the critical aspect in retention is the information itself. What information must be retained is determined by the purpose for which the information is needed. If the addressing and pathway information regarding an e-mail is relevant, then that information should also be retained. However if it is the substance of the e-mail that is relevant, only that information need be retained. Of course, wise record retention would include all such information since what information will be relevant at a later time will not be known.

4.   Subsections (b) and (c) simply make clear that certain ancillary information or the use of third parties, does not affect the serviceability of records and information retained electronically. Again, the relevance of particular information will not be known until that information is required at a subsequent time.

5.   Subsection (d) continues the theme of the Act as validating electronic records as originals where the law requires retention of an original. The validation of electronic records and electronic information as originals is consistent with the Uniform Rules of Evidence. See Uniform Rules of Evidence 1001(3), 1002, 1003 and 1004.

6.   Subsection (e) specifically addresses particular concerns regarding check retention statutes in many jurisdictions. A Report compiled by the Federal Reserve Bank of Boston identifies hundreds of state laws which require the retention or production of original canceled checks. Such requirements preclude state banks and their customers from realizing the benefits and efficiencies related to truncation processes otherwise validated under current law. The benefits to banks and their customers from electronic check retention are effectuated by this provision.

7.   Subsections (f) and (g) generally address other record retention statutes. As with check retention, all businesses and individuals may realize significant savings from electronic record retention. So long as the standards in Section 12 are satisfied, this section permits all parties to obtain those benefits. As always the

government may require records in any medium, however, these subsections require a governmental agency to specifically identify the types of records and requirements that will be imposed.

§ 13.   Admissibility in Evidence.

In a proceeding, evidence of a record or signature may not be excluded solely because it is in electronic form.

Source: UNCITRAL Model Law on Electronic Commerce Article 9.

Comment

Like Section 7, this section prevents the nonrecognition of electronic records and signatures solely on the ground of the media in which information is presented.

Nothing in this section relieves a party from establishing the necessary foundation for the admission of an electronic record. See Uniform Rules of Evidence 1001(3), 1002,1003 and 1004.

§ 14.   Automated Transaction.

In an automated transaction, the following rules apply:

(1)   A contract may be formed by the interaction of electronic agents of the parties, even if no individual was aware of or reviewed the electronic agents' actions or the resulting terms and agreements.

(2)   A contract may be formed by the interaction of an electronic agent and an individual, acting on the individual's own behalf or for another person, including by an interaction in which the individual performs actions that the individual is free to refuse to perform and which the individual knows or has reason to know will cause the electronic agent to complete the transaction or performance.

(3)   The terms of the contract are determined by the substantive law applicable to it.

Source: UNCITRAL Model Law on Electronic Commerce Article 11.

Comment

1.   This section confirms that contracts can be formed by machines functioning as electronic agents for parties to a transaction. It negates any claim that lack of human intent, at the time of contract formation, prevents contract formation. When machines are involved, the requisite intention flows from the programing and use of the machine. As in other cases, these are salutary provisions consistent with the fundamental purpose of the Act to remove barriers to electronic transactions while leaving the substantive law, e.g., law of mistake, law of contract formation, unaffected to the greatest extent possible.

2.   The process in paragraph (2) validates an anonymous click-through transaction. It is possible that an anonymous click-through process may simply result in no recognizable legal relationship, e.g., A goes to a person's website and acquires access without in any way identifying herself, or otherwise indicating agreement or assent to any limitation or obligation, and the owner's site grants A access. In such a case no legal relationship has been created.

On the other hand it may be possible that A's actions indicate agreement to a particular term. For example, A goes to a website and is confronted by an initial screen which advises her that the information at this site is proprietary, that A may use the information for her own personal purposes, but that, by clicking below, A agrees that any other use without the site owner's permission is prohibited. If A clicks "agree" and downloads the information and then uses the information for other, prohibited purposes, should not A be bound by the click? It seems the answer properly should be, and would be, yes.

If the owner can show that the only way A could have obtained the information was from his website, and that the process to access the subject information required that A must have clicked the "I agree" button after having the ability to see the conditions on use, A has performed actions which A was free to refuse, which A knew would cause the site to grant her access, i.e., "complete the transaction." The terms of the resulting contract will be determined under general contract principles, but will include the limitation on A's use of the information, as a condition precedent to granting her access to the information.

3.   In the transaction set forth in Comment 2, the record of the transaction also will include an electronic signature. By clicking "I agree" A adopted a process with the intent to "sign," i.e., bind herself to a legal obligation, the resulting record of the transaction. If a "signed writing" were required under otherwise applicable law, this transaction would be enforceable. If a "signed writing" were not required, it may be sufficient to establish that the electronic record is attributable to A under Section 9. Attribution may be shown in any manner reasonable including showing that, of necessity, A could only have gotten the information through the process at the website.

§ 15.   Time and Place of Sending and Receipt.

(a)   Unless otherwise agreed between the sender and the recipient, an electronic record is sent when it:

(1)   is addressed properly or otherwise directed properly to an information processing system that the recipient has designated or uses for the purpose of receiving electronic records or information of the type sent and from which the recipient is able to retrieve the electronic record;

(2)   is in a form capable of being processed by that system; and

(3)   enters an information processing system outside the control of the sender or of a person that sent the electronic record on behalf of the sender or enters a region of the information processing system designated or used by the recipient which is under the control of the recipient.

(b)   Unless otherwise agreed between a sender and the recipient, an electronic record is received when:

(1)   it enters an information processing system that the recipient has designated or uses for the purpose of receiving electronic records or information of the type sent and from which the recipient is able to retrieve the electronic record; and

(2)   it is in a form capable of being processed by that system.

(c)   Subsection (b) applies even if the place the information processing system is located is different from the place the electronic record is deemed to be received under subsection (d).

(d)   Unless otherwise expressly provided in the electronic record or agreed between the sender and the recipient, an electronic record is deemed to be sent from the sender's place of business and to be received at the recipient's place of business. For purposes of this subsection, the following rules apply:

(1)   If the sender or recipient has more than one place of business, the place of business of that person is the place having the closest relationship to the underlying transaction.

(2)   If the sender or the recipient does not have a place of business, the place of business is the sender's or recipient's residence, as the case may be.

(e)   An electronic record is received under subsection (b) even if no individual is aware of its receipt.

(f)   Receipt of an electronic acknowledgment from an information processing system described in subsection (b) establishes that a record was received but, by itself, does not establish that the content sent corresponds to the content received.

(g)   If a person is aware that an electronic record purportedly sent under subsection (a), or purportedly received under subsection (b), was not actually sent or received, the legal effect of the sending or receipt is determined by other applicable law. Except to the extent permitted by the other law, the requirements of this subsection may not be varied by agreement.

Source: UNCITRAL Model Law on Electronic Commerce Article 15.

Comment

1.   This section provides default rules regarding when and from where an electronic record is sent and when and where an electronic record is received. This section does not address the efficacy of the record that is sent or received. That is, whether a record is unintelligible or unusable by a recipient is a separate issue from whether that record was sent or received. The effectiveness of an illegible record, whether it binds any party, are questions left to other law.

2.   Subsection (a) furnishes rules for determining when an electronic record is sent. The effect of the sending and its import are determined by other law once it is determined that a sending has occurred.

In order to have a proper sending, the subsection requires that information be properly addressed or otherwise directed to the recipient. In order to send within the meaning of this section, there must be specific information which will direct the record to the intended recipient. Although mass electronic sending is not precluded, a general broadcast message, sent to systems rather than individuals, would not suffice as a sending.

The record will be considered sent once it leaves the control of the sender, or comes under the control of the recipient. Records sent through e-mail or the internet will pass through many different server systems. Accordingly, the critical element when more than one system is involved is the loss of control by the sender.

However, the structure of many message delivery systems is such that electronic records may actually never leave the control of the sender. For example, within a university or corporate setting, e-mail sent within the system to another faculty member is technically not out of the sender's control since it never leaves the organization's server. Accordingly, to qualify as a sending, the e-mail must arrive at a point where the recipient has control. This section does not address the effect of an electronic record that is thereafter "pulled back," e.g., removed from a mailbox. The analog in the paper world would be removing a letter from a person's mailbox. As in the case of providing information electronically under Section 8, the recipient's ability to receive a message should be judged from the perspective of whether the sender has done any action which would preclude retrieval. This is especially the case in regard to sending, since the sender must direct the record to a system designated or used by the recipient.

3.   Subsection (b) provides simply that when a record enters the system which the recipient has designated or uses and to which it has access, in a form capable of being processed by that system, it is received. Keying receipt to a system accessible by the recipient removes the potential for a recipient leaving messages with a server or other service in order to avoid receipt. However, the section does not resolve the issue of how the sender proves the time of receipt.

To assure that the recipient retains control of the place of receipt, subsection (b) requires that the system be specified or used by the recipient, and that the system be used or designated for the type of record being sent. Many people have multiple e-mail addresses for different purposes. Subsection (b) assures that recipients can designate the e-mail address or system to be used in a particular transaction. For example, the recipient retains the ability to designate a home e-mail for personal matters, work e-mail for official business, or a separate organizational e-mail solely for the business purposes of that organization. If A sends B a notice at his home which relates to business, it may not be deemed received if B designated his business address as the sole address for business purposes. Whether actual knowledge upon seeing it at home would qualify as receipt is determined under the otherwise applicable substantive law.

4.   Subsections (c) and (d) provide default rules for determining where a record will be considered to have been sent or received. The focus is on the place of business of the recipient and not the physical location of the information processing system, which may bear absolutely no relation to the transaction between the parties. It is not uncommon for users of electronic commerce to communicate from one State to another without knowing the location of information systems through which communication is operated. In addition, the location of certain communication systems may change without either of the parties being aware of the change. Accordingly, where the place of sending or receipt is an issue under other applicable law, e.g., conflict of laws issues, tax issues, the relevant location should be the location of the sender or recipient and not the location of the information processing system.

Subsection (d) assures individual flexibility in designating the place from which a record will be considered sent or at which a record will be considered received. Under subsection (d) a person may designate the place of sending or receipt unilaterally in an electronic record. This ability, as with the ability to designate by agreement, may be limited by otherwise applicable law to places having a reasonable relationship to the transaction.

5.   Subsection (e) makes clear that receipt is not dependent on a person having notice that the record is in the person's system. Receipt occurs when the record reaches the designated system whether or not the recipient ever retrieves the record. The paper analog is the recipient who never reads a mail notice.

6.   Subsection (f) provides legal certainty regarding the effect of an electronic acknowledgment. It only addresses the fact of receipt, not the quality of the content, nor whether the electronic record was read or "opened."

7.   Subsection (g) limits the parties' ability to vary the method for sending and receipt provided in subsections (a) and (b), when there is a legal requirement for the sending or receipt. As in other circumstances

where legal requirements derive from other substantive law, to the extent that the other law permits variation by agreement, this Act does not impose any additional requirements, and provisions of this Act may be varied to the extent provided in the other law.

§ 16. Transferable Records.

(a) In this section, "transferable record" means an electronic record that:

(1) would be a note under [Article 3 of the Uniform Commercial Code] or a document under [Article 7 of the Uniform Commercial Code] if the electronic record were in writing; and

(2) the issuer of the electronic record expressly has agreed is a transferable record.

(b) A person has control of a transferable record if a system employed for evidencing the transfer of interests in the transferable record reliably establishes that person as the person to which the transferable record was issued or transferred.

(c) A system satisfies subsection (b), and a person is deemed to have control of a transferable record, if the transferable record is created, stored, and assigned in such a manner that:

(1) a single authoritative copy of the transferable record exists which is unique, identifiable, and, except as otherwise provided in paragraphs (4), (5), and (6), unalterable;

(2) the authoritative copy identifies the person asserting control as:

(A) the person to which the transferable record was issued; or

(B) if the authoritative copy indicates that the transferable record has been transferred, the person to which the transferable record was most recently transferred;

(3) the authoritative copy is communicated to and maintained by the person asserting control or its designated custodian;

(4) copies or revisions that add or change an identified assignee of the authoritative copy can be made only with the consent of the person asserting control;

(5) each copy of the authoritative copy and any copy of a copy is readily identifiable as a copy that is not the authoritative copy; and

(6) any revision of the authoritative copy is readily identifiable as authorized or unauthorized.

(d) Except as otherwise agreed, a person having control of a transferable record is the holder, as defined in [Section 1–201(20) of the Uniform Commercial Code], of the transferable record and has the same rights and defenses as a holder of an equivalent record or writing under [the Uniform Commercial Code], including, if the applicable statutory requirements under [Section 3–302(a), 7–501, or 9–308 of the Uniform Commercial Code] are satisfied, the rights and defenses of a holder in due course, a holder to which a negotiable document of title has been duly negotiated, or a purchaser, respectively. Delivery, possession, and indorsement are not required to obtain or exercise any of the rights under this subsection.

(e) Except as otherwise agreed, an obligor under a transferable record has the same rights and defenses as an equivalent obligor under equivalent records or writings under [the Uniform Commercial Code].

(f) If requested by a person against which enforcement is sought, the person seeking to enforce the transferable record shall provide reasonable proof that the person is in control of the transferable record. Proof may include access to the authoritative copy of the transferable record and related business records sufficient to review the terms of the transferable record and to establish the identity of the person having control of the transferable record.

Source: Revised Article 9, Section 9–105.

Comment

1. Paper negotiable instruments and documents are unique in the fact that a tangible token—a piece of paper—actually embodies intangible rights and obligations. The extreme difficulty of creating a unique electronic

token which embodies the singular attributes of a paper negotiable document or instrument dictates that the rules relating to negotiable documents and instruments not be simply amended to allow the use of an electronic record for the requisite paper writing. However, the desirability of establishing rules by which business parties might be able to acquire some of the benefits of negotiability in an electronic environment is recognized by the inclusion of this section on Transferable Records.

This section provides legal support for the creation, transferability and enforceability of electronic note and document equivalents, as against the issuer/obligor. The certainty created by the section provides the requisite incentive for industry to develop the systems and processes, which involve significant expenditures of time and resources, to enable the use of such electronic documents.

The importance of facilitating the development of systems which will permit electronic equivalents is a function of cost, efficiency and safety for the records. The storage cost and space needed for the billions of paper notes and documents is phenomenal. Further, natural disasters can wreak havoc on the ability to meet legal requirements for retaining, retrieving and delivering paper instruments. The development of electronic systems meeting the rigorous standards of this section will permit retention of copies which reflect the same integrity as the original. As a result storage, transmission and other costs will be reduced, while security and the ability to satisfy legal requirements governing such paper records will be enhanced.

Section 16 provides for the creation of an electronic record which may be controlled by the holder, who in turn may obtain the benefits of holder in due course and good faith purchaser status. If the benefits and efficiencies of electronic media are to be realized in this industry it is essential to establish a means by which transactions involving paper promissory notes may be accomplished completely electronically. Particularly as other aspects of such transactions are accomplished electronically, the drag on the transaction of requiring a paper note becomes evident. In addition to alleviating the logistical problems of generating, storing and retrieving paper, the mailing and transmission costs associated with such transactions will also be reduced.

2.   The definition of transferable record is limited in two significant ways. First, only the equivalent of paper promissory notes and paper documents of title can be created as transferable records. Notes and Documents of Title do not impact the broad systems that relate to the broader payments mechanisms related, for example, to checks. Impacting the check collection system by allowing for "electronic checks" has ramifications well beyond the ability of this Act to address. Accordingly, this Act excludes from its scope transactions governed by UCC Articles 3 and 4. The limitation to promissory note equivalents in Section 16 is quite important in that regard because of the ability to deal with many enforcement issues by contract without affecting such systemic concerns.

Second, not only is Section 16 limited to electronic records which would qualify as negotiable promissory notes or documents if they were in writing, but the issuer of the electronic record must expressly agree that the electronic record is to be considered a transferable record. The definition of transferable record as "an electronic record that . . . the issuer of the electronic record expressly has agreed is a transferable record" indicates that the electronic record itself will likely set forth the issuer's agreement, though it may be argued that a contemporaneous electronic or written record might set forth the issuer's agreement. However, conversion of a paper note issued as such would not be possible because the issuer would not be the issuer, in such a case, of an electronic record. The purpose of such a restriction is to assure that transferable records can only be created at the time of issuance by the obligor. The possibility that a paper note might be converted to an electronic record and then intentionally destroyed, and the effect of such action, was not intended to be covered by Section 16.

The requirement that the obligor expressly agree in the electronic record to its treatment as a transferable record does not otherwise affect the characterization of a transferable record (i.e., does not affect what would be a paper note) because it is a statutory condition. Further, it does not obligate the issuer to undertake to do any other act than the payment of the obligation evidenced by the transferable record. Therefore, it does not make the transferable record "conditional" within the meaning of Section 3–104(a)(3) of the Uniform Commercial Code.

3.   Under Section 16 acquisition of "control" over an electronic record serves as a substitute for "possession" in the paper analog. More precisely, "control" under Section 16 serves as the substitute for delivery, indorsement and possession of a negotiable promissory note or negotiable document of title. Section 16(b) allows control to be found so long as "a system employed for evidencing the transfer of interests in the transferable record reliably establishes [the person claiming control] as the person to which the transferable record was issued or transferred." The key point is that a system, whether involving third party registry or technological safeguards, must be shown to reliably establish the identity of *the* person entitled to payment. Section 16(c) then sets forth a safe harbor list of very strict requirements for such a system. The specific provisions listed in Section 16(c) are derived from Section 105 of Revised Article 9 of the Uniform Commercial Code. Generally, the transferable record must be unique,

identifiable, and except as specifically permitted, unalterable. That "authoritative copy" must (i) identify the person claiming control as the person to whom the record was issued or most recently transferred, (ii) be maintained by the person claiming control or its designee, and (iii) be unalterable except with the permission of the person claiming control. In addition any copy of the authoritative copy must be readily identifiable as a copy and all revisions must be readily identifiable as authorized or unauthorized.

The control requirements may be satisfied through the use of a trusted third party registry system. Such systems are currently in place with regard to the transfer of securities entitlements under Article 8 of the Uniform Commercial Code, and in the transfer of cotton warehouse receipts under the program sponsored by the United States Department of Agriculture. This Act would recognize the use of such a system so long as the standards of subsection (c) were satisfied. In addition, a technological system which met such exacting standards would also be permitted under Section 16.

For example, a borrower signs an electronic record which would be a promissory note or document if it were paper. The borrower specifically agrees in the electronic record that it will qualify as a transferable record under this section. The lender implements a newly developed technological system which dates, encrypts, and stores all the electronic information in the transferable record in a manner which lender can demonstrate reliably establishes lender as the person to which the transferable record was issued. In the alternative, the lender may contract with a third party to act as a registry for all such transferable records, retaining records establishing the party to whom the record was issued and all subsequent transfers of the record. An example of this latter method for assuring control is the system established for the issuance and transfer of electronic cotton warehouse receipts under 7 C.F.R. section 735 et seq.

Of greatest importance in the system used is the ability to securely and demonstrably be able to transfer the record to others in a manner which assures that only one "holder" exists. The need for such certainty and security resulted in the very stringent standards for a system outlined in subsection (c). A system relying on a third party registry is likely the most effective way to satisfy the requirements of subsection (c) that the transferable record remain unique, identifiable and unalterable, while also providing the means to assure that the transferee is clearly noted and identified.

It must be remembered that Section 16 was drafted in order to provide sufficient legal certainty regarding the rights of those in control of such electronic records, that legal incentives would exist to warrant the development of systems which would establish the requisite control. During the drafting of Section 16, representatives from the Federal Reserve carefully scrutinized the impact of any electronicization of any aspect of the national payment system. Section 16 represents a compromise position which, as noted, serves as a bridge pending more detailed study and consideration of what legal changes, if any, are necessary or appropriate in the context of the payment systems impacted. Accordingly, Section 16 provides limited scope for the attainment of important rights derived from the concept of negotiability, in order to permit the development of systems which will satisfy its strict requirements for control.

4.   It is important to note what the section does not provide. Issues related to enforceability against intermediate transferees and transferors (i.e., indorser liability under a paper note), warranty liability that would attach in a paper note, and issues of the effect of taking a transferable record on the underlying obligation, are NOT addressed by this section. Such matters must be addressed, if at all, by contract between and among the parties in the chain of transmission and transfer of the transferable record. In the event that such matters are not addressed by the contract, the issues would need to be resolved under otherwise applicable law. Other law may include general contract principles of assignment and assumption, or may include rules from Article 3 of the Uniform Commercial Code applied by analogy.

For example, Issuer agrees to pay a debt by means of a transferable record issued to A. Unless there is agreement between issuer and A that the transferable record "suspends" the underlying obligation (see Section 3–310 of the Uniform Commercial Code), A would not be prevented from enforcing the underlying obligation without the transferable record. Similarly, if A transfers the transferable record to B by means granting B control, B may obtain holder in due course rights against the obligor/issuer, but B's recourse against A would not be clear unless A agreed to remain liable under the transferable record. Although the rules of Article 3 may be applied by analogy in an appropriate context, in the absence of an express agreement in the transferable record or included by applicable system rules, the liability of the transferor would not be clear.

5.   Current business models exist which rely for their efficacy on the benefits of negotiability. A principal example, and one which informed much of the development of Section 16, involves the mortgage backed securities industry. Aggregators of commercial paper acquire mortgage secured promissory notes following a chain of

transfers beginning with the origination of the mortgage loan by a mortgage broker. In the course of the transfers of this paper, buyers of the notes and lenders/secured parties for these buyers will intervene. For the ultimate purchaser of the paper, the ability to rely on holder in due course and good faith purchaser status creates the legal security necessary to issue its own investment securities which are backed by the obligations evidenced by the notes purchased. Only through their HIDC status can these purchasers be assured that third party claims will be barred. Only through their HIDC status can the end purchaser avoid the incredible burden of requiring and assuring that each person in the chain of transfer has waived any and all defenses to performance which may be created during the chain of transfer.

6.   This section is a stand-alone provision. Although references are made to specific provisions in Article 3, Article 7, and Article 9 of the Uniform Commercial Code, these provisions are incorporated into this Act and made the applicable rules for purposes of this Act. The rights of parties to transferable records are established under subsections (d) and (e). Subsection (d) provides rules for determining the rights of a party in control of a transferable record. The subsection makes clear that the rights are determined under this section, and not under other law, by incorporating the rules on the manner of acquisition into this statute. The last sentence of subsection (d) is intended to assure that requirements related to notions of possession, which are inherently inconsistent with the idea of an electronic record, are not incorporated into this statute.

If a person establishes control, Section 16(d) provides that that person is the "holder" of the transferable record which is equivalent to a holder of an analogous paper negotiable instrument. More importantly, if the person acquired control in a manner which would make it a holder in due course of an equivalent paper record, the person acquires the rights of a HIDC. The person in control would therefore be able to enforce the transferable record against the obligor regardless of intervening claims and defenses. However, by pulling these rights into Section 16, this Act does NOT validate the wholesale electrification of promissory notes under Article 3 of the Uniform Commercial Code.

Further, it is important to understand that a transferable record under Section 16, while having no counterpart under Article 3 of the Uniform Commercial Code, would be an "account," "general intangible," or "payment intangible" under Article 9 of the Uniform Commercial Code. Accordingly, two separate bodies of law would apply to that asset of the obligee. A taker of the transferable record under Section 16 may acquire purchaser rights under Article 9 of the Uniform Commercial Code, however, those rights may be defeated by a trustee in bankruptcy of a prior person in control unless perfection under Article 9 of the Uniform Commercial Code by filing is achieved. If the person in control also takes control in a manner granting it holder in due course status, of course that person would take free of any claim by a bankruptcy trustee or lien creditor.

7.   Subsection (e) accords to the obligor of the transferable record rights equal to those of an obligor under an equivalent paper record. Accordingly, unless a waiver of defense clause is obtained in the electronic record, or the transferee obtains HDC rights under subsection (d), the obligor has all the rights and defenses available to it under a contract assignment. Additionally, the obligor has the right to have the payment noted or otherwise included as part of the electronic record.

8.   Subsection (f) grants the obligor the right to have the transferable record and other information made available for purposes of assuring the correct person to pay. This will allow the obligor to protect its interest and obtain the defense of discharge by payment or performance. This is particularly important because a person receiving subsequent control under the appropriate circumstances may well qualify as a holder in course who can enforce payment of the transferable record.

9.   Section 16 is a singular exception to the thrust of this Act to simply validate electronic media used in commercial transactions. Section 16 actually provides a means for expanding electronic commerce. It provides certainty to lenders and investors regarding the enforceability of a new class of financial services. It is hoped that the legal protections afforded by Section 16 will engender the development of technological and business models which will permit realization of the significant cost savings and efficiencies available through electronic transacting in the financial services industry. Although only a bridge to more detailed consideration of the broad issues related to negotiability in an electronic context, Section 16 provides the impetus for that broader consideration while allowing continuation of developing technological and business models.

§ 17. Creation and Retention of Electronic Records and Conversion of Written Records by Governmental Agencies.

[Each governmental agency] [The [designated state officer]] of this State shall determine whether, and the extent to which, [it] [a governmental agency] will create and retain electronic records and convert written records to electronic records.]

Comment

See Comments following Section 19.

§ 18. Acceptance and Distribution of Electronic Records by Governmental Agencies.

(a) Except as otherwise provided in Section 12(f), [each governmental agency] [the [designated state officer]] of this State shall determine whether, and the extent to which, [it] [a governmental agency] will send and accept electronic records and electronic signatures to and from other persons and otherwise create, generate, communicate, store, process, use, and rely upon electronic records and electronic signatures.

(b) To the extent that a governmental agency uses electronic records and electronic signatures under subsection (a), the [governmental agency] [designated state officer], giving due consideration to security, may specify:

(1) the manner and format in which the electronic records must be created, generated, sent, communicated, received, and stored and the systems established for those purposes;

(2) if electronic records must be signed by electronic means, the type of electronic signature required, the manner and format in which the electronic signature must be affixed to the electronic record, and the identity of, or criteria that must be met by, any third party used by a person filing a document to facilitate the process;

(3) control processes and procedures as appropriate to ensure adequate preservation, disposition, integrity, security, confidentiality, and auditability of electronic records; and

(4) any other required attributes for electronic records which are specified for corresponding nonelectronic records or reasonably necessary under the circumstances.

(c) Except as otherwise provided in Section 12(f), this [Act] does not require a governmental agency of this State to use or permit the use of electronic records or electronic signatures.]

Source: Illinois Act Section 25–101; Florida Electronic Signature Act, Chapter 96–324, Section 7 (1996).

Comment

See Comments following Section 19.

§ 19. Interoperability.

The [governmental agency] [designated officer] of this State which adopts standards pursuant to Section 18 may encourage and promote consistency and interoperability with similar requirements adopted by other governmental agencies of this and other States and the federal government and nongovernmental persons interacting with governmental agencies of this State. If appropriate, those standards may specify differing levels of standards from which governmental agencies of this State may choose in implementing the most appropriate standard for a particular application.]

Source: Illinois Act Section 25–115.

See Legislative Note below, following Comment.

Comment

1. Sections 17–19 have been bracketed as optional provisions to be considered for adoption by each State. Among the barriers to electronic commerce are barriers which exist in the use of electronic media by state governmental agencies—whether among themselves or in external dealing with the private sector. In those circumstances where the government acts as a commercial party, e.g., in areas of procurement, the general

validation provisions of this Act will apply. That is to say, the government must agree to conduct transactions electronically with vendors and customers of government services.

However, there are other circumstances when government ought to establish the ability to proceed in transactions electronically. Whether in regard to records and communications within and between governmental agencies, or with respect to information and filings which must be made with governmental agencies, these sections allow a State to establish the ground work for such electronicization.

2. The provisions in Sections 17–19 are broad and very general. In many States they will be unnecessary because enacted legislation designed to facilitate governmental use of electronic records and communications is in place. However, in many States broad validating rules are needed and desired. Accordingly, this Act provides these sections as a baseline.

Of paramount importance in all States however, is the need for States to assure that whatever systems and rules are adopted, the systems established are compatible with the systems of other governmental agencies and with common systems in the private sector. A very real risk exists that implementation of systems by myriad governmental agencies and offices may create barriers because of a failure to consider compatibility, than would be the case otherwise.

3. The provisions in Section 17–19 are broad and general to provide the greatest flexibility and adaptation to the specific needs of the individual States. The differences and variations in the organization and structure of governmental agencies mandates this approach. However, it is imperative that each State always keep in mind the need to prevent the erection of barriers through appropriate coordination of systems and rules within the parameters set by the State.

4. Section 17 authorizes state agencies to use electronic records and electronic signatures generally for intra-governmental purposes, and to convert written records and manual signatures to electronic records and electronic signatures. By its terms the section gives enacting legislatures the option to leave the decision to use electronic records or convert written records and signatures to the governmental agency or assign that duty to a designated state officer. It also authorizes the destruction of written records after conversion to electronic form.

5. Section 18 broadly authorizes state agencies to send and receive electronic records and signatures in dealing with non-governmental persons. Again, the provision is permissive and not obligatory (see subsection (c)). However, it does provide specifically that with respect to electronic records used for evidentiary purposes, Section 12 will apply unless a particular agency expressly opts out.

6. Section 19 is the most important section of the three. It requires governmental agencies or state officers to take account of consistency in applications and interoperability to the extent practicable when promulgating standards. This section is critical in addressing the concern that inconsistent applications may promote barriers greater than currently exist. Without such direction the myriad systems that could develop independently would be new barriers to electronic commerce, not a removal of barriers. The key to interoperability is flexibility and adaptability. The requirement of a single system may be as big a barrier as the proliferation of many disparate systems.

Legislative Note Regarding Adoption of Sections 17–19

1. Sections 17–19 are optional sections for consideration by individual legislatures for adoption, and have been bracketed to make this clear. The inclusion or exclusion of Sections 17–19 will not have a detrimental impact on the uniformity of adoption of this Act, so long as Sections 1–16 are adopted uniformly as presented. In some States Sections 17–19 will be unnecessary because legislation is already in place to authorize and implement government use of electronic media. However, the general authorization provided by Sections 17–19 may be critical in some States which desire to move forward in this area.

2. In the event that a state legislature chooses to adopt Sections 17–19, a number of issues must be addressed:

A. Is the general authorization to adopt electronic media, provided by Sections 17–19 sufficient for the needs of the particular jurisdiction, or is more detailed and specific authorization necessary? This determination may be affected by the decision regarding the appropriate entity or person to oversee implementation of the use of electronic media (See next paragraph). Sections 17–19 are broad and general in the authorization granted. Certainly greater specificity can be added subsequent to adoption of these sections. The question for the legislature is whether greater direction and specificity is needed at this time. If so, the legislature should not enact Sections 17–19 at this time.

B.   Assuming a legislature decides to enact Sections 17–19, what entity or person should oversee implementation of the government's use of electronic media? As noted in each of Sections 17–19, again by brackets, a choice must be made regarding the entity to make critical decisions regarding the systems and rules which will govern the use of electronic media by the State. Each State will need to consider its particular structure and administration in making this determination. However, legislatures are strongly encouraged to make compatibility and interoperability considerations paramount in making this determination.

C.   Finally, a decision will have to be made regarding the process by which coordination of electronic systems will occur between the various branches of state government and among the various levels of government within the State. Again this will require consideration of the unique situation in each State.

3.   If a State chooses not to enact Sections 17–19, UETA Sections 1–16 will still apply to governmental entities when acting as a "person" engaging in "transactions" within its scope. The definition of transaction includes "governmental affairs." Of course, like any other party, the circumstances surrounding a transaction must indicate that the governmental actor has agreed to act electronically (See Section 5(b)), but otherwise all the provisions of Sections 1–16 will apply to validate the use of electronic records and signatures in transactions involving governmental entities.

If a State does choose to enact Sections 17–19, Sections 1–16 will continue to apply as above. In addition, Sections 17–19 will provide authorization for intra-governmental uses of electronic media. Finally, Sections 17–19 provide a broader authorization for the State to develop systems and procedures for the use of electronic media in its relations with non-governmental entities and persons.

§ 20.   Severability Clause.

If any provision of this [Act] or its application to any person or circumstance is held invalid, the invalidity does not affect other provisions or applications of this [Act] which can be given effect without the invalid provision or application, and to this end the provisions of this [Act] are severable.

§ 21.   Effective Date.

This [Act] takes effect [ ].

ELECTRONIC SIGNATURES IN GLOBAL AND NATIONAL COMMERCE ACT (ESIGN)

---

15 U.S.C.A. §§ 7001–7031

Current through March 30, 2016; P.L. 114–141

For updates, see http://uscode.house.gov

SUBCHAPTER I—ELECTRONIC RECORDS AND SIGNATURES IN COMMERCE

§ 7001.   General Rule of Validity [§ 101]

(a) In general

Notwithstanding any statute, regulation, or other rule of law (other than this subchapter and subchapter II of this chapter), with respect to any transaction in or affecting interstate or foreign commerce—

(1)   a signature, contract, or other record relating to such transaction may not be denied legal effect, validity, or enforceability solely because it is in electronic form; and

(2)   a contract relating to such transaction may not be denied legal effect, validity, or enforceability solely because an electronic signature or electronic record was used in its formation.

(b) Preservation of rights and obligations

This subchapter does not—

(1)   limit, alter, or otherwise affect any requirement imposed by a statute, regulation, or rule of law relating to the rights and obligations of persons under such statute, regulation, or rule of law other than a requirement that contracts or other records be written, signed, or in nonelectronic form; or

(2)   require any person to agree to use or accept electronic records or electronic signatures, other than a governmental agency with respect to a record other than a contract to which it is a party.

(c) Consumer disclosures

(1) Consent to electronic records

Notwithstanding subsection (a), if a statute, regulation, or other rule of law requires that information relating to a transaction or transactions in or affecting interstate or foreign commerce be provided or made available to a consumer in writing, the use of an electronic record to provide or make available (whichever is required) such information satisfies the requirement that such information be in writing if—

(A)   the consumer has affirmatively consented to such use and has not withdrawn such consent;

(B)   the consumer, prior to consenting, is provided with a clear and conspicuous statement—

(i)   informing the consumer of (I) any right or option of the consumer to have the record provided or made available on paper or in nonelectronic form, and (II) the right of the consumer to withdraw the consent to have the record provided or made available in an electronic form and of any conditions, consequences (which may include termination of the parties' relationship), or fees in the event of such withdrawal;

(ii)   informing the consumer of whether the consent applies (I) only to the particular transaction which gave rise to the obligation to provide the record, or (II) to identified categories of records that may be provided or made available during the course of the parties' relationship;

(iii)   describing the procedures the consumer must use to withdraw consent as provided in clause (i) and to update information needed to contact the consumer electronically; and

(iv)   informing the consumer (I) how, after the consent, the consumer may, upon request, obtain a paper copy of an electronic record, and (II) whether any fee will be charged for such copy;

(C)   the consumer—

(i)   prior to consenting, is provided with a statement of the hardware and software requirements for access to and retention of the electronic records; and

(ii)   consents electronically, or confirms his or her consent electronically, in a manner that reasonably demonstrates that the consumer can access information in the electronic form that will be used to provide the information that is the subject of the consent; and

(D)   after the consent of a consumer in accordance with subparagraph (A), if a change in the hardware or software requirements needed to access or retain electronic records creates a material risk that the consumer will not be able to access or retain a subsequent electronic record that was the subject of the consent, the person providing the electronic record—

(i)   provides the consumer with a statement of (I) the revised hardware and software requirements for access to and retention of the electronic records, and (II) the right to withdraw consent without the imposition of any fees for such withdrawal and without the imposition of any condition or consequence that was not disclosed under subparagraph (B)(i); and

(ii)   again complies with subparagraph (C).

(2) Other rights

(A) Preservation of consumer protections

Nothing in this subchapter affects the content or timing of any disclosure or other record required to be provided or made available to any consumer under any statute, regulation, or other rule of law.

(B) Verification or acknowledgment

If a law that was enacted prior to this chapter expressly requires a record to be provided or made available by a specified method that requires verification or acknowledgment of receipt, the record may be provided or made available electronically only if the method used provides verification or acknowledgment of receipt (whichever is required).

(3)   Effect of failure to obtain electronic consent or confirmation of consent

The legal effectiveness, validity, or enforceability of any contract executed by a consumer shall not be denied solely because of the failure to obtain electronic consent or confirmation of consent by that consumer in accordance with paragraph (1)(C)(ii).

(4)   Prospective effect

Withdrawal of consent by a consumer shall not affect the legal effectiveness, validity, or enforceability of electronic records provided or made available to that consumer in accordance with paragraph (1) prior to implementation of the consumer's withdrawal of consent. A consumer's withdrawal of consent shall be effective within a reasonable period of time after receipt of the withdrawal by the provider of the record. Failure to comply with paragraph (1)(D) may, at the election of the consumer, be treated as a withdrawal of consent for purposes of this paragraph.

(5)   Prior consent

This subsection does not apply to any records that are provided or made available to a consumer who has consented prior to the effective date of this subchapter to receive such records in electronic form as permitted by any statute, regulation, or other rule of law.

(6)   Oral communications

An oral communication or a recording of an oral communication shall not qualify as an electronic record for purposes of this subsection except as otherwise provided under applicable law.

(d)   Retention of contracts and records

(1)   Accuracy and accessibility

If a statute, regulation, or other rule of law requires that a contract or other record relating to a transaction in or affecting interstate or foreign commerce be retained, that requirement is met by retaining an electronic record of the information in the contract or other record that—

(A)   accurately reflects the information set forth in the contract or other record; and

(B)   remains accessible to all persons who are entitled to access by statute, regulation, or rule of law, for the period required by such statute, regulation, or rule of law, in a form that is capable of being accurately reproduced for later reference, whether by transmission, printing, or otherwise.

(2)   Exception

A requirement to retain a contract or other record in accordance with paragraph (1) does not apply to any information whose sole purpose is to enable the contract or other record to be sent, communicated, or received.

(3)   Originals

If a statute, regulation, or other rule of law requires a contract or other record relating to a transaction in or affecting interstate or foreign commerce to be provided, available, or retained in its original form, or provides consequences if the contract or other record is not provided, available, or retained in its original form, that statute, regulation, or rule of law is satisfied by an electronic record that complies with paragraph (1).

(4)   Checks

If a statute, regulation, or other rule of law requires the retention of a check, that requirement is satisfied by retention of an electronic record of the information on the front and back of the check in accordance with paragraph (1).

(e)   Accuracy and ability to retain contracts and other records

Notwithstanding subsection (a), if a statute, regulation, or other rule of law requires that a contract or other record relating to a transaction in or affecting interstate or foreign commerce be in writing, the legal effect, validity, or enforceability of an electronic record of such contract or other record may be denied if such electronic record is not in a form that is capable of being retained and accurately reproduced for later reference by all parties or persons who are entitled to retain the contract or other record.

(f) Proximity

Nothing in this subchapter affects the proximity required by any statute, regulation, or other rule of law with respect to any warning, notice, disclosure, or other record required to be posted, displayed, or publicly affixed.

(g) Notarization and acknowledgment

If a statute, regulation, or other rule of law requires a signature or record relating to a transaction in or affecting interstate or foreign commerce to be notarized, acknowledged, verified, or made under oath, that requirement is satisfied if the electronic signature of the person authorized to perform those acts, together with all other information required to be included by other applicable statute, regulation, or rule of law, is attached to or logically associated with the signature or record.

(h) Electronic agents

A contract or other record relating to a transaction in or affecting interstate or foreign commerce may not be denied legal effect, validity, or enforceability solely because its formation, creation, or delivery involved the action of one or more electronic agents so long as the action of any such electronic agent is legally attributable to the person to be bound.

(i) Insurance

It is the specific intent of the Congress that this subchapter and subchapter II of this chapter apply to the business of insurance.

(j) Insurance agents and brokers

An insurance agent or broker acting under the direction of a party that enters into a contract by means of an electronic record or electronic signature may not be held liable for any deficiency in the electronic procedures agreed to by the parties under that contract if—

(1)   the agent or broker has not engaged in negligent, reckless, or intentional tortious conduct;

(2)   the agent or broker was not involved in the development or establishment of such electronic procedures; and

(3)   the agent or broker did not deviate from such procedures.

§ 7002.   Exemption to Preemption [§ 102]

(a) In general

A State statute, regulation, or other rule of law may modify, limit, or supersede the provisions of section 7001 of this title with respect to State law only if such statute, regulation, or rule of law—

(1)   constitutes an enactment or adoption of the Uniform Electronic Transactions Act as approved and recommended for enactment in all the States by the National Conference of Commissioners on Uniform State Laws in 1999, except that any exception to the scope of such Act enacted by a State under section 3(b)(4) of such Act shall be preempted to the extent such exception is inconsistent with this subchapter or subchapter II of this chapter, or would not be permitted under paragraph (2)(A)(ii) of this subsection; or

(2)(A)   specifies the alternative procedures or requirements for the use or acceptance (or both) of electronic records or electronic signatures to establish the legal effect, validity, or enforceability of contracts or other records, if—

(i)   such alternative procedures or requirements are consistent with this subchapter and subchapter II of this chapter; and

    (ii)   such alternative procedures or requirements do not require, or accord greater legal status or effect to, the implementation or application of a specific technology or technical specification for performing the functions of creating, storing, generating, receiving, communicating, or authenticating electronic records or electronic signatures; and

    (B)   if enacted or adopted after June 30, 2000, makes specific reference to this chapter.

(b) Exceptions for actions by States as market participants

Subsection (a)(2)(A)(ii) of this section shall not apply to the statutes, regulations, or other rules of law governing procurement by any State, or any agency or instrumentality thereof.

(c) Prevention of circumvention

Subsection (a) of this section does not permit a State to circumvent this subchapter or subchapter II of this chapter through the imposition of nonelectronic delivery methods under section 8(b)(2) of the Uniform Electronic Transactions Act.

§ 7003.   Specific Exceptions [§ 103]

(a) Excepted requirements

The provisions of section 7001 of this title shall not apply to a contract or other record to the extent it is governed by—

    (1)   a statute, regulation, or other rule of law governing the creation and execution of wills, codicils, or testamentary trusts;

    (2)   a State statute, regulation, or other rule of law governing adoption, divorce, or other matters of family law; or

    (3)   the Uniform Commercial Code, as in effect in any State, other than sections 1–107 and 1–206 and Articles 2 and 2A.

(b) Additional exceptions

The provisions of section 7001 of this title shall not apply to—

    (1)   court orders or notices, or official court documents (including briefs, pleadings, and other writings) required to be executed in connection with court proceedings;

    (2)   any notice of—

        (A)   the cancellation or termination of utility services (including water, heat, and power);

        (B)   default, acceleration, repossession, foreclosure, or eviction, or the right to cure, under a credit agreement secured by, or a rental agreement for, a primary residence of an individual;

        (C)   the cancellation or termination of health insurance or benefits or life insurance benefits (excluding annuities); or

        (D)   recall of a product, or material failure of a product, that risks endangering health or safety; or

    (3)   any document required to accompany any transportation or handling of hazardous materials, pesticides, or other toxic or dangerous materials.

(c) Review of exceptions

(1) Evaluation required

The Secretary of Commerce, acting through the Assistant Secretary for Communications and Information, shall review the operation of the exceptions in subsections (a) and (b) of this section to evaluate, over a period of 3 years, whether such exceptions continue to be necessary for the protection of consumers. Within 3 years after June 30, 2000, the Assistant Secretary shall submit a report to the Congress on the results of such evaluation.

(2) Determinations

If a Federal regulatory agency, with respect to matter within its jurisdiction, determines after notice and an opportunity for public comment, and publishes a finding, that one or more such exceptions are no longer necessary for the protection of consumers and eliminating such exceptions will not increase the material risk of harm to consumers, such agency may extend the application of section 7001 of this title to the exceptions identified in such finding.

§ 7004. Applicability to Federal and State Governments [§ 104]

(a) Filing and access requirements

Subject to subsection (c)(2) of this section, nothing in this subchapter limits or supersedes any requirement by a Federal regulatory agency, self-regulatory organization, or State regulatory agency that records be filed with such agency or organization in accordance with specified standards or formats.

(b) Preservation of existing rulemaking authority

(1) Use of authority to interpret

Subject to paragraph (2) and subsection (c) of this section, a Federal regulatory agency or State regulatory agency that is responsible for rulemaking under any other statute may interpret section 7001 of this title with respect to such statute through—

(A) the issuance of regulations pursuant to a statute; or

(B) to the extent such agency is authorized by statute to issue orders or guidance, the issuance of orders or guidance of general applicability that are publicly available and published (in the Federal Register in the case of an order or guidance issued by a Federal regulatory agency).

This paragraph does not grant any Federal regulatory agency or State regulatory agency authority to issue regulations, orders, or guidance pursuant to any statute that does not authorize such issuance.

(2) Limitations on interpretation authority

Notwithstanding paragraph (1), a Federal regulatory agency shall not adopt any regulation, order, or guidance described in paragraph (1), and a State regulatory agency is preempted by section 7001 of this title from adopting any regulation, order, or guidance described in paragraph (1), unless—

(A) such regulation, order, or guidance is consistent with section 7001 of this title;

(B) such regulation, order, or guidance does not add to the requirements of such section; and

(C) such agency finds, in connection with the issuance of such regulation, order, or guidance, that—

(i) there is a substantial justification for the regulation, order, or guidance;

(ii) the methods selected to carry out that purpose—

(I) are substantially equivalent to the requirements imposed on records that are not electronic records; and

(II) will not impose unreasonable costs on the acceptance and use of electronic records; and

(iii) the methods selected to carry out that purpose do not require, or accord greater legal status or effect to, the implementation or application of a specific technology or technical specification for performing the functions of creating, storing, generating, receiving, communicating, or authenticating electronic records or electronic signatures.

(3) Performance standards

(A) Accuracy, record integrity, accessibility

Notwithstanding paragraph (2)(C)(iii), a Federal regulatory agency or State regulatory agency may interpret section 7001(d) of this title to specify performance standards to assure accuracy, record integrity, and accessibility of records that are required to be retained. Such performance standards may be specified in a manner that imposes a requirement in violation of paragraph (2)(C)(iii) if the requirement (i) serves an important governmental objective; and (ii) is substantially related to the achievement of that objective. Nothing in this paragraph shall be construed to grant any Federal regulatory agency or State regulatory agency authority to require use of a particular type of software or hardware in order to comply with section 7001(d) of this title.

(B) Paper or printed form

Notwithstanding subsection (c)(1) of this section, a Federal regulatory agency or State regulatory agency may interpret section 7001(d) of this title to require retention of a record in a tangible printed or paper form if—

(i) there is a compelling governmental interest relating to law enforcement or national security for imposing such requirement; and

(ii) imposing such requirement is essential to attaining such interest.

(4) Exceptions for actions by Government as market participant

Paragraph (2)(C)(iii) shall not apply to the statutes, regulations, or other rules of law governing procurement by the Federal or any State government, or any agency or instrumentality thereof.

(c) Additional limitations

(1) Reimposing paper prohibited

Nothing in subsection (b) of this section (other than paragraph (3)(B) thereof) shall be construed to grant any Federal regulatory agency or State regulatory agency authority to impose or reimpose any requirement that a record be in a tangible printed or paper form.

(2) Continuing obligation under Government Paperwork Elimination Act

Nothing in subsection (a) or (b) of this section relieves any Federal regulatory agency of its obligations under the Government Paperwork Elimination Act (title XVII of Public Law 105–277).

(d) Authority to exempt from consent provision

(1) In general

A Federal regulatory agency may, with respect to matter within its jurisdiction, by regulation or order issued after notice and an opportunity for public comment, exempt without condition a specified category or type of record from the requirements relating to consent in section 7001(c) of this title if such exemption is necessary to eliminate a substantial burden on electronic commerce and will not increase the material risk of harm to consumers.

(2) Prospectuses

Within 30 days after June 30, 2000, the Securities and Exchange Commission shall issue a regulation or order pursuant to paragraph (1) exempting from section 7001(c) of this title any records that are required to be provided in order to allow advertising, sales literature, or other information concerning a security issued by an investment company that is registered under the Investment Company Act of 1940 [15 U.S.C.A. § 80a–1 et seq.], or concerning the issuer thereof, to be excluded from the definition of a prospectus under section 77b(a)(10)(A) of this title.

(e) Electronic letters of agency

The Federal Communications Commission shall not hold any contract for telecommunications service or letter of agency for a preferred carrier change, that otherwise complies with the Commission's rules, to be legally ineffective, invalid, or unenforceable solely because an electronic record or electronic signature was used in its formation or authorization.

§ 7005.   Studies [§ 105]

(a) Delivery

Within 12 months after June 30, 2000, the Secretary of Commerce shall conduct an inquiry regarding the effectiveness of the delivery of electronic records to consumers using electronic mail as compared with delivery of written records via the United States Postal Service and private express mail services. The Secretary shall submit a report to the Congress regarding the results of such inquiry by the conclusion of such 12-month period.

(b) Study of electronic consent

Within 12 months after June 30, 2000, the Secretary of Commerce and the Federal Trade Commission shall submit a report to the Congress evaluating any benefits provided to consumers by the procedure required by section 7001(c)(1)(C)(ii) of this title; any burdens imposed on electronic commerce by that provision; whether the benefits outweigh the burdens; whether the absence of the procedure required by section 7001(c)(1)(C)(ii) of this title would increase the incidence of fraud directed against consumers; and suggesting any revisions to the provision deemed appropriate by the Secretary and the Commission. In conducting this evaluation, the Secretary and the Commission shall solicit comment from the general public, consumer representatives, and electronic commerce businesses.

§ 7006.   Definitions [§ 106]

For purposes of this subchapter:

(1) Consumer

The term "consumer" means an individual who obtains, through a transaction, products or services which are used primarily for personal, family, or household purposes, and also means the legal representative of such an individual.

(2) Electronic

The term "electronic" means relating to technology having electrical, digital, magnetic, wireless, optical, electromagnetic, or similar capabilities.

(3) Electronic agent

The term "electronic agent" means a computer program or an electronic or other automated means used independently to initiate an action or respond to electronic records or performances in whole or in part without review or action by an individual at the time of the action or response.

(4) Electronic record

The term "electronic record" means a contract or other record created, generated, sent, communicated, received, or stored by electronic means.

(5) Electronic signature

The term "electronic signature" means an electronic sound, symbol, or process, attached to or logically associated with a contract or other record and executed or adopted by a person with the intent to sign the record.

(6) Federal regulatory agency

The term "Federal regulatory agency" means an agency, as that term is defined in section 552(f) of Title 5.

(7) Information

The term "information" means data, text, images, sounds, codes, computer programs, software, databases, or the like.

(8) Person

The term "person" means an individual, corporation, business trust, estate, trust, partnership, limited liability company, association, joint venture, governmental agency, public corporation, or any other legal or commercial entity.

(9) Record

The term "record" means information that is inscribed on a tangible medium or that is stored in an electronic or other medium and is retrievable in perceivable form.

(10) Requirement

The term "requirement" includes a prohibition.

(11) Self-regulatory organization

The term "self-regulatory organization" means an organization or entity that is not a Federal regulatory agency or a State, but that is under the supervision of a Federal regulatory agency and is authorized under Federal law to adopt and administer rules applicable to its members that are enforced by such organization or entity, by a Federal regulatory agency, or by another self-regulatory organization.

(12) State

The term "State" includes the District of Columbia and the territories and possessions of the United States.

(13) Transaction

The term "transaction" means an action or set of actions relating to the conduct of business, consumer, or commercial affairs between two or more persons, including any of the following types of conduct—

(A) the sale, lease, exchange, licensing, or other disposition of (i) personal property, including goods and intangibles, (ii) services, and (iii) any combination thereof; and

(B) the sale, lease, exchange, or other disposition of any interest in real property, or any combination thereof.

SUBCHAPTER II—TRANSFERABLE RECORDS

§ 7021.   Transferable Records [§ 201]

(a) Definitions

For purposes of this section:

(1) Transferable record

The term "transferable record" means an electronic record that—

(A) would be a note under Article 3 of the Uniform Commercial Code if the electronic record were in writing;

(B) the issuer of the electronic record expressly has agreed is a transferable record; and

(C) relates to a loan secured by real property.

A transferable record may be executed using an electronic signature.

(2) Other definitions

The terms "electronic record", "electronic signature", and "person" have the same meanings provided in section 7006 of this title.

(b) Control

A person has control of a transferable record if a system employed for evidencing the transfer of interests in the transferable record reliably establishes that person as the person to which the transferable record was issued or transferred.

(c) Conditions

A system satisfies subsection (b) of this section, and a person is deemed to have control of a transferable record, if the transferable record is created, stored, and assigned in such a manner that—

(1) a single authoritative copy of the transferable record exists which is unique, identifiable, and, except as otherwise provided in paragraphs (4), (5), and (6), unalterable;

(2) the authoritative copy identifies the person asserting control as—

(A) the person to which the transferable record was issued; or

(B) if the authoritative copy indicates that the transferable record has been transferred, the person to which the transferable record was most recently transferred;

(3) the authoritative copy is communicated to and maintained by the person asserting control or its designated custodian;

(4) copies or revisions that add or change an identified assignee of the authoritative copy can be made only with the consent of the person asserting control;

(5) each copy of the authoritative copy and any copy of a copy is readily identifiable as a copy that is not the authoritative copy; and

(6) any revision of the authoritative copy is readily identifiable as authorized or unauthorized.

(d) Status as holder

Except as otherwise agreed, a person having control of a transferable record is the holder, as defined in section 1–201(20) of the Uniform Commercial Code, of the transferable record and has the same rights and defenses as a holder of an equivalent record or writing under the Uniform Commercial Code, including, if the applicable statutory requirements under section 3–302(a), 9–308, or revised section 9–330 of the Uniform Commercial Code are satisfied, the rights and defenses of a holder in due course or a purchaser, respectively. Delivery, possession, and endorsement are not required to obtain or exercise any of the rights under this subsection.

(e) Obligor rights

Except as otherwise agreed, an obligor under a transferable record has the same rights and defenses as an equivalent obligor under equivalent records or writings under the Uniform Commercial Code.

(f) Proof of control

If requested by a person against which enforcement is sought, the person seeking to enforce the transferable record shall provide reasonable proof that the person is in control of the transferable record. Proof may include access to the authoritative copy of the transferable record and related business records sufficient to review the terms of the transferable record and to establish the identity of the person having control of the transferable record.

(g) UCC references

For purposes of this subsection, all references to the Uniform Commercial Code are to the Uniform Commercial Code as in effect in the jurisdiction the law of which governs the transferable record.

SUBCHAPTER III—PROMOTION OF INTERNATIONAL ELECTRONIC COMMERCE

§ 7031. Principles Governing the Use of Electronic Signatures in International Transactions [§ 301]

(a) Promotion of electronic signatures

(1) Required actions

The Secretary of Commerce shall promote the acceptance and use, on an international basis, of electronic signatures in accordance with the principles specified in paragraph (2) and in a manner consistent with section 7001 of this title. The Secretary of Commerce shall take all actions necessary in a manner consistent with such principles to eliminate or reduce, to the maximum extent possible, the impediments to commerce in electronic signatures, for the purpose of facilitating the development of interstate and foreign commerce.

(2) Principles

The principles specified in this paragraph are the following:

(A) Remove paper-based obstacles to electronic transactions by adopting relevant principles from the Model Law on Electronic Commerce adopted in 1996 by the United Nations Commission on International Trade Law.

(B) Permit parties to a transaction to determine the appropriate authentication technologies and implementation models for their transactions, with assurance that those technologies and implementation models will be recognized and enforced.

(C) Permit parties to a transaction to have the opportunity to prove in court or other proceedings that their authentication approaches and their transactions are valid.

(D) Take a nondiscriminatory approach to electronic signatures and authentication methods from other jurisdictions.

(b) Consultation

In conducting the activities required by this section, the Secretary shall consult with users and providers of electronic signature products and services and other interested persons.

(c) Definitions

As used in this section, the terms "electronic record" and "electronic signature" have the same meanings provided in section 7006 of this title.

(Pub.L. 106–229, Title I, § 101, June 30, 2000, 114 Stat. 464.)

MAGNUSON-MOSS WARRANTY—FEDERAL TRADE COMMISSION IMPROVEMENT ACT (1975)

15 U.S.C.A. §§ 2301–2312

Current through March 30, 2016; P.L. 114–141

For updates, see http://uscode.house.gov

TITLE I. CONSUMER PRODUCT WARRANTIES

§ 101. Definitions [15 U.S.C.A. § 2301]

For the purposes of this chapter:

(1) The term "consumer product" means any tangible personal property which is distributed in commerce and which is normally used for personal, family, or household purposes (including any such property intended to be attached to or installed in any real property without regard to whether it is so attached or installed).

(2) The term "Commission" means the Federal Trade Commission.

(3) The term "consumer" means a buyer (other than for purposes of resale) of any consumer product, any person to whom such product is transferred during the duration of an implied or written warranty (or service contract) applicable to the product, and any other person who is entitled by the terms of such warranty (or service contract) or under applicable State law to enforce against the warrantor (or service contractor) the obligations of the warranty (or service contract).

(4) The term "supplier" means any person engaged in the business of making a consumer product directly or indirectly available to consumers.

(5) The term "warrantor" means any supplier or other person who gives or offers to give a written warranty or who is or may be obligated under an implied warranty.

(6) The term "written warranty" means—

(A) any written affirmation of fact or written promise made in connection with the sale of a consumer product by a supplier to a buyer which relates to the nature of the material or workmanship and affirms or promises that such material or workmanship is defect free or will meet a specified level of performance over a specified period of time, or

(B) any undertaking in writing in connection with the sale by a supplier of a consumer product to refund, repair, replace, or take other remedial action with respect to such product in the event that such product fails to meet the specifications set forth in the undertaking,

which written affirmation, promise, or undertaking becomes part of the basis of the bargain between a supplier and a buyer for purposes other than resale of such product.

(7) The term "implied warranty" means an implied warranty arising under State law (as modified by sections 2308 and 2304(a) of this title) in connection with the sale by a supplier of a consumer product.

(8) The term "service contract" means a contract in writing to perform, over a fixed period of time or for a specified duration, services relating to the maintenance or repair (or both) of a consumer product.

(9) The term "reasonable and necessary maintenance" consists of those operations (A) which the consumer reasonably can be expected to perform or have performed and (B) which are necessary to keep any consumer product performing its intended function and operating at a reasonable level of performance.

(10) The term "remedy" means whichever of the following actions the warrantor elects:

(A) repair,

(B) replacement, or

(C) refund;

except that the warrantor may not elect refund unless (i) the warrantor is unable to provide replacement and repair is not commercially practicable or cannot be timely made, or (ii) the consumer is willing to accept such refund.

(11) The term "replacement" means furnishing a new consumer product which is identical or reasonably equivalent to the warranted consumer product.

(12) The term "refund" means refunding the actual purchase price (less reasonable depreciation based on actual use where permitted by rules of the Commission).

(13) The term "distributed in commerce" means sold in commerce, introduced or delivered for introduction into commerce, or held for sale or distribution after introduction into commerce.

(14) The term "commerce" means trade, traffic, commerce, or transportation—

(A) between a place in a State and any place outside thereof, or

(B) which affects trade, traffic, commerce, or transportation described in subparagraph (A).

(15) The term "State" means a State, the District of Columbia, the Commonwealth of Puerto Rico, the Virgin Islands, Guam, the Canal Zone, or American Samoa. The term "State law" includes a law of the United States applicable only to the District of Columbia or only to a territory or possession of the United States; and the term "Federal law" excludes any State law.

§ 102. Rules governing contents of warranties [15 U.S.C.A. § 2302]

(a) Full and conspicuous disclosure of terms and conditions; additional requirements for contents

In order to improve the adequacy of information available to consumers, prevent deception, and improve competition in the marketing of consumer products, any warrantor warranting a consumer product to a consumer by means of a written warranty shall, to the extent required by rules of the Commission, fully and conspicuously disclose in simple and readily understood language the terms and conditions of such warranty. Such rules may require inclusion in the written warranty of any of the following items among others:

(1)   The clear identification of the names and addresses of the warrantors.

(2)   The identity of the party or parties to whom the warranty is extended.

(3)   The products or parts covered.

(4)   A statement of what the warrantor will do in the event of a defect, malfunction, or failure to conform with such written warranty—at whose expense—and for what period of time.

(5)   A statement of what the consumer must do and expenses he must bear.

(6)   Exceptions and exclusions from the terms of the warranty.

(7)   The step-by-step procedure which the consumer should take in order to obtain performance of any obligation under the warranty, including the identification of any person or class of persons authorized to perform the obligations set forth in the warranty.

(8)   Information respecting the availability of any informal dispute settlement procedure offered by the warrantor and a recital, where the warranty so provides, that the purchaser may be required to resort to such procedure before pursuing any legal remedies in the courts.

(9)   A brief, general description of the legal remedies available to the consumer.

(10)   The time at which the warrantor will perform any obligations under the warranty.

(11)   The period of time within which, after notice of a defect, malfunction, or failure to conform with the warranty, the warrantor will perform any obligations under the warranty.

(12)   The characteristics or properties of the products, or parts thereof, that are not covered by the warranty.

(13)   The elements of the warranty in words or phrases which would not mislead a reasonable, average consumer as to the nature or scope of the warranty.

(b)   Availability of terms to consumer; manner and form for presentation and display of information; duration; extension of period for written warranty or service contract

(1)(A)   The Commission shall prescribe rules requiring that the terms of any written warranty on a consumer product be made available to the consumer (or prospective consumer) prior to the sale of the product to him.

(B)   The Commission may prescribe rules for determining the manner and form in which information with respect to any written warranty of a consumer product shall be clearly and conspicuously presented or displayed so as not to mislead the reasonable, average consumer, when such information is contained in advertising, labeling, point-of-sale material, or other representations in writing.

(2)   Nothing in this chapter (other than paragraph (3) of this subsection) shall be deemed to authorize the Commission to prescribe the duration of written warranties given or to require that a consumer product or any of its components be warranted.

(3)   The Commission may prescribe rules for extending the period of time a written warranty or service contract is in effect to correspond with any period of time in excess of a reasonable period (not less than 10 days) during which the consumer is deprived of the use of such consumer product by reason of failure of the product to conform with the written warranty or by reason of the failure of the warrantor (or service contractor) to carry out such warranty (or service contract) within the period specified in the warranty (or service contract).

(4)(A)   Except as provided in subparagraph (B), the rules prescribed under this subsection shall allow for the satisfaction of all requirements concerning the availability of terms of a written warranty on a consumer product under this subsection by—

(i)   making available such terms in an accessible digital format on the Internet website of the manufacturer of the consumer product in a clear and conspicuous manner; and

(ii)   providing to the consumer (or prospective consumer) information with respect to how to obtain and review such terms by indicating on the product or product packaging or in the product manual—

(I)   the Internet website of the manufacturer where such terms can be obtained and reviewed; and

(II)   the phone number of the manufacturer, the postal mailing address of the manufacturer, or another reasonable non-Internet based means of contacting the manufacturer to obtain and review such terms.

(B)   With respect to any requirement that the terms of any written warranty for a consumer product be made available to the consumer (or prospective consumer) prior to sale of the product, in a case in which a consumer product is offered for sale in a retail location, by catalog, or through door-to-door sales, subparagraph (A) shall only apply if the seller makes available, through electronic or other means, at the location of the sale to the consumer purchasing the consumer product the terms of the warranty for the consumer product before the purchase.

(c)   Prohibition on conditions for written or implied warranty; waiver by Commission

No warrantor of a consumer product may condition his written or implied warranty of such product on the consumer's using, in connection with such product, any article or service (other than article or service provided without charge under the terms of the warranty) which is identified by brand, trade, or corporate name; except that the prohibition of this subsection may be waived by the Commission if—

(1)   the warrantor satisfies the Commission that the warranted product will function properly only if the article or service so identified is used in connection with the warranted product, and

(2)   the Commission finds that such a waiver is in the public interest.

The Commission shall identify in the Federal Register, and permit public comment on, all applications for waiver of the prohibition of this subsection, and shall publish in the Federal Register its disposition of any such application, including the reasons therefor.

(d)   Incorporation by reference of detailed substantive warranty provisions

The Commission may by rule devise detailed substantive warranty provisions which warrantors may incorporate by reference in their warranties.

(e)   Applicability to consumer products costing more than $5

The provisions of this section apply only to warranties which pertain to consumer products actually costing the consumer more than $5.

§ 103.   Designation of written warranties [15 U.S.C.A. § 2303]

(a)   Full (statement of duration) or limited warranty

Any warrantor warranting a consumer product by means of a written warranty shall clearly and conspicuously designate such warranty in the following manner, unless exempted from doing so by the Commission pursuant to subsection (c) of this section:

(1)   If the written warranty meets the Federal minimum standards for warranty set forth in section 2304 of this title, then it shall be conspicuously designated a "full (statement of duration) warranty".

(2)   If the written warranty does not meet the Federal minimum standards for warranty set forth in section 2304 of this title, then it shall be conspicuously designated a "limited warranty".

(b) Applicability of requirements, standards, etc., to representations or statements of customer satisfaction

This section and sections 2302 and 2304 of this title shall not apply to statements or representations which are similar to expressions of general policy concerning customer satisfaction and which are not subject to any specific limitations.

(c) Exemptions by Commission

In addition to exercising the authority pertaining to disclosure granted in section 2302 of this title, the Commission may by rule determine when a written warranty does not have to be designated either "full (statement of duration)" or "limited" in accordance with this section.

(d) Applicability to consumer products costing more than $10 and not designated as full warranties

The provisions of subsections (a) and (c) of this section apply only to warranties which pertain to consumer products actually costing the consumer more than $10 and which are not designated "full (statement of duration) warranties".

§ 104. Federal minimum standards for warranties [15 U.S.C.A. § 2304]

(a) Remedies under written warranty; duration of implied warranty; exclusion or limitation on consequential damages for breach of written or implied warranty; election of refund or replacement

In order for a warrantor warranting a consumer product by means of a written warranty to meet the Federal minimum standards for warranty—

(1) such warrantor must as a minimum remedy such consumer product within a reasonable time and without charge, in the case of a defect, malfunction, or failure to conform with such written warranty;

(2) notwithstanding section 2308(b) of this title, such warrantor may not impose any limitation on the duration of any implied warranty on the product;

(3) such warrantor may not exclude or limit consequential damages for breach of any written or implied warranty on such product, unless such exclusion or limitation conspicuously appears on the face of the warranty; and

(4) if the product (or a component part thereof) contains a defect or malfunction after a reasonable number of attempts by the warrantor to remedy defects or malfunctions in such product, such warrantor must permit the consumer to elect either a refund for, or replacement without charge of, such product or part (as the case may be). The Commission may by rule specify for purposes of this paragraph, what constitutes a reasonable number of attempts to remedy particular kinds of defects or malfunctions under different circumstances. If the warrantor replaces a component part of a consumer product, such replacement shall include installing the part in the product without charge.

(b) Duties and conditions imposed on consumer by warrantor

(1) In fulfilling the duties under subsection (a) of this section respecting a written warranty, the warrantor shall not impose any duty other than notification upon any consumer as a condition of securing remedy of any consumer product which malfunctions, is defective, or does not conform to the written warranty, unless the warrantor has demonstrated in a rulemaking proceeding, or can demonstrate in an administrative or judicial enforcement proceeding (including private enforcement), or in an informal dispute settlement proceeding, that such a duty is reasonable.

(2) Notwithstanding paragraph (1), a warrantor may require, as a condition to replacement of, or refund for, any consumer product under subsection (a) of this section, that such consumer product shall be made available to the warrantor free and clear of liens and other encumbrances, except as otherwise provided by rule or order of the Commission in cases in which such a requirement would not be practicable.

(3)　The Commission may, by rule define in detail the duties set forth in subsection (a) of this section and the applicability of such duties to warrantors of different categories of consumer products with "full (statement of duration)" warranties.

(4)　The duties under subsection (a) of this section extend from the warrantor to each person who is a consumer with respect to the consumer product.

(c)　Waiver of standards

The performance of the duties under subsection (a) of this section shall not be required of the warrantor if he can show that the defect, malfunction, or failure of any warranted consumer product to conform with a written warranty, was caused by damage (not resulting from defect or malfunction) while in the possession of the consumer, or unreasonable use (including failure to provide reasonable and necessary maintenance).

(d)　Remedy without charge

For purposes of this section and of section 2302(c) of this title, the term "without charge" means that the warrantor may not assess the consumer for any costs the warrantor or his representatives incur in connection with the required remedy of a warranted consumer product. An obligation under subsection (a)(1)(A) of this section to remedy without charge does not necessarily require the warrantor to compensate the consumer for incidental expenses; however, if any incidental expenses are incurred because the remedy is not made within a reasonable time or because the warrantor imposed an unreasonable duty upon the consumer as a condition of securing remedy, then the consumer shall be entitled to recover reasonable incidental expenses which are so incurred in any action against the warrantor.

(e)　Incorporation of standards to products designated with full warranty for purposes of judicial actions

If a supplier designates a warranty applicable to a consumer product as a "full (statement of duration)" warranty, then the warranty on such product shall, for purposes of any action under section 2310(d) of this title or under any State law, be deemed to incorporate at least the minimum requirements of this section and rules prescribed under this section.

§ 105.　Full and limited warranting of a consumer product [15 U.S.C.A. § 2305]

Nothing in this chapter shall prohibit the selling of a consumer product which has both full and limited warranties if such warranties are clearly and conspicuously differentiated.

§ 106.　Service contracts; rules for full, clear and conspicuous disclosure of terms and conditions; addition to or in lieu of written warranty [15 U.S.C.A. § 2306]

(a)　The Commission may prescribe by rule the manner and form in which the terms and conditions of service contracts shall be fully, clearly, and conspicuously disclosed.

(b)　Nothing in this chapter shall be construed to prevent a supplier or warrantor from entering into a service contract with the consumer in addition to or in lieu of a written warranty if such contract fully, clearly, and conspicuously discloses its terms and conditions in simple and readily understood language.

§ 107.　Designation of representatives by warrantor to perform duties under written or implied warranty [15 U.S.C.A. § 2307]

Nothing in this chapter shall be construed to prevent any warrantor from designating representatives to perform duties under the written or implied warranty: *Provided*, That such warrantor shall make reasonable arrangements for compensation of such designated representatives, but no such designation shall relieve the warrantor of his direct responsibilities to the consumer or make the representative a cowarrantor.

§ 108. Implied warranties

(a) Restrictions on disclaimers or modifications [15 U.S.C.A. § 2308]

No supplier may disclaim or modify (except as provided in subsection (b) of this section) any implied warranty to a consumer with respect to such consumer product if (1) such supplier makes any written warranty to the consumer with respect to such consumer product, or (2) at the time of sale, or within 90 days thereafter, such supplier enters into a service contract with the consumer which applies to such consumer product.

(b) Limitation on duration

For purposes of this chapter (other than section 2304(a)(2) of this title), implied warranties may be limited in duration to the duration of a written warranty of reasonable duration, if such limitation is conscionable and is set forth in clear and unmistakable language and prominently displayed on the face of the warranty.

(c) Effectiveness of disclaimers, modifications, or limitations

A disclaimer, modification, or limitation made in violation of this section shall be ineffective for purposes of this chapter and State law.

§ 109. Procedures applicable to promulgation of rules by Commission [15 U.S.C.A. § 2309]

(a) Oral presentation

Any rule prescribed under this chapter shall be prescribed in accordance with section 553 of Title 5; except that the Commission shall give interested persons an opportunity for oral presentations of data, views, and arguments, in addition to written submissions. A transcript shall be kept of any oral presentation. Any such rule shall be subject to judicial review under section 57a(e) of this title in the same manner as rules prescribed under section 57a(a)(1)(B) of this title, except that section 57a(e)(3)(B) of this title shall not apply.

(b) Warranties and warranty practices involved in sale of used motor vehicles

The Commission shall initiate within one year after January 4, 1975, a rulemaking proceeding dealing with warranties and warranty practices in connection with the sale of used motor vehicles; and, to the extent necessary to supplement the protections offered the consumer by this chapter, shall prescribe rules dealing with such warranties and practices. In prescribing rules under this subsection, the Commission may exercise any authority it may have under this chapter, or other law, and in addition it may require disclosure that a used motor vehicle is sold without any warranty and specify the form and content of such disclosure.

§ 110. Remedies in consumer disputes [15 U.S.C.A. § 2310]

(a) Informal dispute settlement procedures; establishment; rules setting forth minimum requirements; effect of compliance by warrantor; review of informal procedures or implementation by Commission; application to existing informal procedures

(1) Congress hereby declares it to be its policy to encourage warrantors to establish procedures whereby consumer disputes are fairly and expeditiously settled through informal dispute settlement mechanisms.

(2) The Commission shall prescribe rules setting forth minimum requirements for any informal dispute settlement procedure which is incorporated into the terms of a written warranty to which any provision of this chapter applies. Such rules shall provide for participation in such procedure by independent or governmental entities.

(3) One or more warrantors may establish an informal dispute settlement procedure which meets the requirements of the Commission's rules under paragraph (2). If—

(A) a warrantor establishes such a procedure,

(B)   such procedure, and its implementation, meets the requirements of such rules, and

(C)   he incorporates in a written warranty a requirement that the consumer resort to such procedure before pursuing any legal remedy under this section respecting such warranty,

then (i) the consumer may not commence a civil action (other than a class action) under subsection (d) of this section unless he initially resorts to such procedure; and (ii) a class of consumers may not proceed in a class action under subsection (d) of this section except to the extent the court determines necessary to establish the representative capacity of the named plaintiffs, unless the named plaintiffs (upon notifying the defendant that they are named plaintiffs in a class action with respect to a warranty obligation) initially resort to such procedure. In the case of such a class action which is brought in a district court of the United States, the representative capacity of the named plaintiffs shall be established in the application of rule 23 of the Federal Rules of Civil Procedure. In any civil action arising out of a warranty obligation and relating to a matter considered in such a procedure, any decision in such procedure shall be admissible in evidence.

(4)   The Commission on its own initiative may, or upon written complaint filed by any interested person shall, review the bona fide operation of any dispute settlement procedure resort to which is stated in a written warranty to be a prerequisite to pursuing a legal remedy under this section. If the Commission finds that such procedure or its implementation fails to comply with the requirements of the rules under paragraph (2), the Commission may take appropriate remedial action under any authority it may have under this chapter or any other provision of law.

(5)   Until rules under paragraph (2) take effect, this subsection shall not affect the validity of any informal dispute settlement procedure respecting consumer warranties, but in any action under subsection (d) of this section, the court may invalidate any such procedure if it finds that such procedure is unfair.

(b)   Prohibited acts

It shall be a violation of section 45(a)(1) of this title for any person to fail to comply with any requirement imposed on such person by this chapter (or a rule thereunder) or to violate any prohibition contained in this chapter (or a rule thereunder).

(c)   Injunction proceedings by Attorney General or Commission for deceptive warranty, noncompliance with requirements, or violating prohibitions; procedures; definitions

(1)   The district courts of the United States shall have jurisdiction of any action brought by the Attorney General (in his capacity as such), or by the Commission by any of its attorneys designated by it for such purpose, to restrain (A) any warrantor from making a deceptive warranty with respect to a consumer product, or (B) any person from failing to comply with any requirement imposed on such person by or pursuant to this chapter or from violating any prohibition contained in this chapter. Upon proper showing that, weighing the equities and considering the Commission's or Attorney General's likelihood of ultimate success, such action would be in the public interest and after notice to the defendant, a temporary restraining order or preliminary injunction may be granted without bond. In the case of an action brought by the Commission, if a complaint under section 45 of this title is not filed within such period (not exceeding 10 days) as may be specified by the court after the issuance of the temporary restraining order or preliminary injunction, the order or injunction shall be dissolved by the court and be of no further force and effect. Any suit shall be brought in the district in which such person resides or transacts business. Whenever it appears to the court that the ends of justice require that other persons should be parties in the action, the court may cause them to be summoned whether or not they reside in the district in which the court is held, and to that end process may be served in any district.

(2)   For the purposes of this subsection, the term "deceptive warranty" means (A) a written warranty which (i) contains an affirmation, promise, description, or representation which is either false or fraudulent, or which, in light of all of the circumstances, would mislead a reasonable individual exercising due care; or (ii) fails to contain information which is necessary in light of all of the circumstances, to make the warranty not misleading to a reasonable individual exercising due care; or (B) a written warranty created by the use of such terms as "guaranty" or "warranty", if the terms and conditions of such warranty so limit its scope and application as to deceive a reasonable individual.

(d) Civil action by consumer for damages, etc.; jurisdiction; recovery of costs and expenses; cognizable claims

(1)   Subject to subsections (a)(3) and (e) of this section, a consumer who is damaged by the failure of a supplier, warrantor, or service contractor to comply with any obligation under this chapter, or under a written warranty, implied warranty, or service contract, may bring suit for damages and other legal and equitable relief—

(A)   in any court of competent jurisdiction in any State or the District of Columbia; or

(B)   in an appropriate district court of the United States, subject to paragraph (3) of this subsection.

(2)   If a consumer finally prevails in any action brought under paragraph (1) of this subsection, he may be allowed by the court to recover as part of the judgment a sum equal to the aggregate amount of cost and expenses (including attorneys' fees based on actual time expended) determined by the court to have been reasonably incurred by the plaintiff for or in connection with the commencement and prosecution of such action, unless the court in its discretion shall determine that such an award of attorneys' fees would be inappropriate.

(3)   No claim shall be cognizable in a suit brought under paragraph (1)(B) of this subsection—

(A)   if the amount in controversy of any individual claim is less than the sum or value of $25;

(B)   if the amount in controversy is less than the sum or value of $50,000 (exclusive of interests and costs) computed on the basis of all claims to be determined in this suit; or

(C)   if the action is brought as a class action, and the number of named plaintiffs is less than one hundred.

(e) Class actions; conditions; procedures applicable

No action (other than a class action or an action respecting a warranty to which subsection (a)(3) of this section applies) may be brought under subsection (d) of this section for failure to comply with any obligation under any written or implied warranty or service contract, and a class of consumers may not proceed in a class action under such subsection with respect to such a failure except to the extent the court determines necessary to establish the representative capacity of the named plaintiffs, unless the person obligated under the warranty or service contract is afforded a reasonable opportunity to cure such failure to comply. In the case of such a class action (other than a class action respecting a warranty to which subsection (a)(3) of this section applies) brought under subsection (d) of this section for breach of any written or implied warranty or service contract, such reasonable opportunity will be afforded by the named plaintiffs and they shall at that time notify the defendant that they are acting on behalf of the class. In the case of such a class action which is brought in a district court of the United States, the representative capacity of the named plaintiffs shall be established in the application of rule 23 of the Federal Rules of Civil Procedure.

(f) Warrantors subject to enforcement of remedies

For purposes of this section, only the warrantor actually making a written affirmation of fact, promise, or undertaking shall be deemed to have created a written warranty, and any rights arising thereunder may be enforced under this section only against such warrantor and no other person.

§ 111.   Applicability to other laws [15 U.S.C.A. § 2311]

(a) Federal Trade Commission Act and Federal Seed Act

(1)   Nothing contained in this chapter shall be construed to repeal, invalidate, or supersede the Federal Trade Commission Act [15 U.S.C.A. § 41 et seq.] or any statute defined therein as an Antitrust Act.

(2)   Nothing in this chapter shall be construed to repeal, invalidate, or supersede the Federal Seed Act [7 U.S.C.A. § 1551 et seq.] and nothing in this chapter shall apply to seed for planting.

(b) Rights, remedies, and liabilities

(1)   Nothing in this chapter shall invalidate or restrict any right or remedy of any consumer under State law or any other Federal law.

(2)   Nothing in this chapter (other than sections 2308 and 2304(a)(2) and (4) of this title) shall (A) affect the liability of, or impose liability on, any person for personal injury, or (B) supersede any provision of State law regarding consequential damages for injury to the person or other injury.

(c) State warranty laws

(1)   Except as provided in subsection (b) of this section and in paragraph (2) of this subsection, a State requirement—

    (A)   which relates to labeling or disclosure with respect to written warranties or performance thereunder;

    (B)   which is within the scope of an applicable requirement of sections 2302, 2303, and 2304 of this title (and rules implementing such sections), and

    (C)   which is not identical to a requirement of section 2302, 2303, or 2304 of this title (or a rule thereunder),

shall not be applicable to written warranties complying with such sections (or rules thereunder).

(2)   If, upon application of an appropriate State agency, the Commission determines (pursuant to rules issued in accordance with section 2309 of this title) that any requirement of such State covering any transaction to which this chapter applies (A) affords protection to consumers greater than the requirements of this chapter and (B) does not unduly burden interstate commerce, then such State requirement shall be applicable (notwithstanding the provisions of paragraph (1) of this subsection) to the extent specified in such determination for so long as the State administers and enforces effectively any such greater requirement.

(d) Other Federal warranty laws

This chapter (other than section 2302(c) of this title) shall be inapplicable to any written warranty the making or content of which is otherwise governed by Federal law. If only a portion of a written warranty is so governed by Federal law, the remaining portion shall be subject to this chapter.

§ 112.   Effective dates [15 U.S.C.A. § 2312]

(a) Effective date of chapter

Except as provided in subsection (b) of this section, this chapter shall take effect 6 months after January 4, 1975, but shall not apply to consumer products manufactured prior to such date.

(b) Effective date of section 2302(a)

Section 2302(a) of this title shall take effect 6 months after the final publication of rules respecting such section; except that the Commission, for good cause shown, may postpone the applicability of such sections until one year after such final publication in order to permit any designated classes of suppliers to bring their written warranties into compliance with rules promulgated pursuant to this chapter.

(c) Promulgation of rules

The Commission shall promulgate rules for initial implementation of this chapter as soon as possible after January 4, 1975, but in no event later than one year after such date.

Pub.L. 93–637, Title I, § 101, Jan. 4, 1975, 88 Stat. 2183.)

MAGNUSON-MOSS WARRANTY ACT REGULATIONS

16 C.F.R. Parts 700–703

Current through March 31, 2016; 80 F.R. 18737

For updates, see www.gpo.gov/fdsys

PART 700. INTERPRETATIONS OF
MAGNUSON-MOSS WARRANTY ACT

§ 700.1   Products covered.

(a)   The Act applies to written warranties on tangible personal property which is normally used for personal, family, or household purposes. This definition includes property which is intended to be attached to or installed in any real property without regard to whether it is so attached or installed. This means that a product is a "consumer product" if the use of that type of product is not uncommon. The percentage of sales or the use to which a product is put by any individual buyer is not determinative. For example, products such as automobiles and typewriters which are used for both personal and commercial purposes come within the definition of consumer product. Where it is unclear whether a particular product is covered under the definition of consumer product, any ambiguity will be resolved in favor of coverage.

(b)   Agricultural products such as farm machinery, structures and implements used in the business or occupation of farming are not covered by the Act where their personal, family, or household use is uncommon. However, those agricultural products normally used for personal or household gardening (for example, to produce goods for personal consumption, and not for resale) are consumer products under the Act.

(c)   The definition of "Consumer product" limits the applicability of the Act to personal property, "including any such property intended to be attached to or installed in any real property without regard to whether it is so attached or installed." This provision brings under the Act separate items of equipment attached to real property, such as air conditioners, furnaces, and water heaters.

(d)   The coverage of separate items of equipment attached to real property includes, but is not limited to, appliances and other thermal, mechanical, and electrical equipment. (It does not extend to the wiring, plumbing, ducts, and other items which are integral component parts of the structure.) State law would classify many such products as fixtures to, and therefore a part of, realty. The statutory definition is designed to bring such products under the Act regardless of whether they may be considered fixtures under state law.

(e)   The coverage of building materials which are not separate items of equipment is based on the nature of the purchase transaction. An analysis of the transaction will determine whether the goods are real or personal property. The numerous products which go into the construction of a consumer dwelling are all consumer products when sold "over the counter," as by hardware and building supply retailers. This is also true where a consumer contracts for the purchase of such materials in connection with the improvement, repair, or modification of a home (for example, paneling, dropped ceilings, siding, roofing, storm windows, remodeling). However, where such products are at the time of sale integrated into the structure of a dwelling they are not consumer products as they cannot be practically distinguished from realty. Thus, for example, the beams, wallboard, wiring, plumbing, windows, roofing, and other structural components of a dwelling are not consumer products when they are sold as part of real estate covered by a written warranty.

(f)   In the case where a consumer contracts with a builder to construct a home, a substantial addition to a home, or other realty (such as a garage or an in-ground swimming pool) the building materials to be used are not consumer products. Although the materials are separately identifiable at the time the contract is made, it is the intention of the parties to contract for the construction of realty which will integrate the component materials. Of course, as noted above, any separate items of equipment to be attached to such realty are consumer products under the Act.

(g)   Certain provisions of the Act apply only to products actually costing the consumer more than a specified amount. Section 103, 15 U.S.C. 2303, applies to consumer products actually costing the consumer more than $10, excluding tax. The $10 minimum will be interpreted to include multiple-packaged items which may individually sell for less than $10, but which have been packaged in a manner that does not permit breaking the package to purchase an item or items at a price less than $10. Thus, a written warranty on a dozen items packaged and priced for sale at $12 must be designated, even though identical items may be offered in smaller quantities at under $10. This interpretation applies in the same manner to the minimum dollar limits in section 102, 15 U.S.C. 2302, and rules promulgated under that section.

(h)   Warranties on replacement parts and components used to repair consumer products are covered; warranties on services are not covered. Therefore, warranties which apply solely to a repairer's workmanship in performing repairs are not subject to the Act. Where a written agreement warrants both the parts provided to effect a repair and the workmanship in making that repair, the warranty must comply with the Act and the rules thereunder.

(i)   The Act covers written warranties on consumer products "distributed in commerce" as that term is defined in section 101(13), 15 U.S.C. 2301(13). Thus, by its terms the Act arguably applies to products exported to foreign jurisdictions. However, the public interest would not be served by the use of Commission resources to enforce the Act with respect to such products. Moreover, the legislative intent to apply the requirements of the Act to such products is not sufficiently clear to justify such an extraordinary result. The Commission does not contemplate the enforcement of the Act with respect to consumer products exported to foreign jurisdictions. Products exported for sale at military post exchanges remain subject to the same enforcement standards as products sold within the United States, its territories and possessions.

§ 700.2   Date of manufacture.

Section 112 of the Act, 15 U.S.C. 2312, provides that the Act shall apply only to those consumer products manufactured after July 4, 1975. When a consumer purchases repair of a consumer product the date of manufacture of any replacement parts used is the measuring date for determining coverage under the Act. The date of manufacture of the consumer product being repaired is in this instance not relevant. Where a consumer purchases or obtains on an exchange basis a rebuilt consumer product, the date that the rebuilding process is completed determines the Act's applicability.

§ 700.3   Written warranty.

(a)   The Act imposes specific duties and liabilities on suppliers who offer written warranties on consumer products. Certain representations, such as energy efficiency ratings for electrical appliances, care labeling of wearing apparel, and other product information disclosures may be express warranties under the Uniform Commercial Code. However, these disclosures alone are not written warranties under this Act. Section 101(6), 15 U.S.C. 2301(6), provides that a written affirmation of fact or a written promise of a specified level of performance must relate to a specified period of time in order to be considered a "written warranty."[1] A product information disclosure without a specified time period to which the disclosure relates is therefore not a written warranty. In addition, section 111(d), 15 U.S.C. 2311(d), exempts from the Act (except section 102(c), 15 U.S.C. 2302(c)) any written warranty the making or content of which is required by federal law. The Commission encourages the disclosure of product information which is not deceptive and which may benefit consumers, and will not construe the Act to impede information disclosure in product advertising or labeling.

(b)   Certain terms, or conditions, of sale of a consumer product may not be "written warranties" as that term is defined in section 101(6), 15 U.S.C. 2301(6), and should not be offered or described in a manner that may deceive consumers as to their enforceability under the Act. For example, a seller of consumer products may give consumers an unconditional right to revoke acceptance of goods within a certain number of days after delivery without regard to defects or failure to meet a specified level of performance. Or a seller may permit consumers to return products for any reason for credit toward purchase of another item. Such terms of sale taken alone are not written warranties under the Act. Therefore, suppliers should avoid any characterization of such terms of sale as warranties. The use of such terms as "free trial period" and "trade-in credit policy" in this regard would be appropriate. Furthermore, such terms of sale should be stated separately from any written warranty. Of course, the offering and performance of such terms of sale remain subject to section 5 of the Federal Trade Commission Act, 15 U.S.C. 45.

---

[1]   A "written warranty" is also created by a written affirmation of fact or a written promise that the product is defect free, or by a written undertaking of remedial action within the meaning of section 101(6)(B), 15 U.S.C. 2301(6)(B).

(c)   The Magnuson-Moss Warranty Act generally applies to written warranties covering consumer products. Many consumer products are covered by warranties which are neither intended for, nor enforceable by, consumers. A common example is a warranty given by a component supplier to a manufacturer of consumer products. (The manufacturer may, in turn, warrant these components to consumers.) The component supplier's warranty is generally given solely to the product manufacturer, and is neither intended to be conveyed to the consumer nor brought to the consumer's attention in connection with the sale. Such warranties are not subject to the Act, since a written warranty under section 101(6) of the Act, 15 U.S.C. 2301(6), must become "part of the basis of the bargain between a supplier and a buyer for purposes other than resale." However, the Act applies to a component supplier's warranty in writing which is given to the consumer. An example is a supplier's written warranty to the consumer covering a refrigerator that is sold installed in a boat or recreational vehicle. The supplier of the refrigerator relies on the boat or vehicle assembler to convey the written agreement to the consumer. In this case, the supplier's written warranty is to a consumer, and is covered by the Act.

§ 700.4   Parties "actually making" a written warranty.

Section 110(f) of the Act, 15 U.S.C. 2310(f), provides that only the supplier "actually making" a written warranty is liable for purposes of FTC and private enforcement of the Act. A supplier who does no more than distribute or sell a consumer product covered by a written warranty offered by another person or business and which identifies that person or business as the warrantor is not liable for failure of the written warranty to comply with the Act or rules thereunder. However, other actions and written and oral representations of such a supplier in connection with the offer or sale of a warranted product may obligate that supplier under the Act. If under state law the supplier is deemed to have "adopted" the written affirmation of fact, promise, or undertaking, the supplier is also obligated under the Act. Suppliers are advised to consult state law to determine those actions and representations which may make them co-warrantors, and therefore obligated under the warranty of the other person or business.

§ 700.5   Expressions of general policy.

(a)   Under section 103(b), 15 U.S.C. 2303(b), statements or representations of general policy concerning customer satisfaction which are not subject to any specific limitation need not be designated as full or limited warranties, and are exempt from the requirements of sections 102, 103, and 104 of the Act, 15 U.S.C. 2302–2304, and rules thereunder. However, such statements remain subject to the enforcement provisions of section 110 of the Act, 15 U.S.C. 2310, and to section 5 of the Federal Trade Commission Act, 15 U.S.C. 45.

(b)   The section 103(b), 15 U.S.C. 2303(b), exemption applies only to general policies, not to those which are limited to specific consumer products manufactured or sold by the supplier offering such a policy. In addition, to qualify for an exemption under section 103(b), 15 U.S.C. 2303(b), such policies may not be subject to any specific limitations. For example, policies which have an express limitation of duration or a limitation of the amount to be refunded are not exempted. This does not preclude the imposition of reasonable limitations based on the circumstances in each instance a consumer seeks to invoke such an agreement. For instance, a warrantor may refuse to honor such an expression of policy where a consumer has used a product for 10 years without previously expressing any dissatisfaction with the product. Such a refusal would not be a specific limitation under this provision.

§ 700.6   Designation of warranties.

(a)   Section 103 of the Act, 15 U.S.C. 2303, provides that written warranties on consumer products manufactured after July 4, 1975, and actually costing the consumer more than $10, excluding tax, must be designated either "Full (statement of duration) Warranty" or "Limited Warranty". Warrantors may include a statement of duration in a limited warranty designation. The designation or designations should appear clearly and conspicuously as a caption, or prominent title, clearly separated from the text of the warranty. The full (statement of duration) warranty and limited warranty are the exclusive designations permitted under the Act, unless a specific exception is created by rule.

(b)   Based on section 104(b)(4), 15 U.S.C. 2304(b)(4), the duties under subsection (a) of section 104, 15 U.S.C. 2304, extend from the warrantor to each person who is a consumer with respect to the consumer product. Section 101(3), 15 U.S.C. 2301(3), defines a consumer as a buyer (other than for purposes of resale) of any consumer product, any person to whom such product is transferred during the duration of an implied or written warranty (or service contract) applicable to the product. Therefore, a full warranty may not expressly restrict the warranty rights of a transferee during its stated duration. However, where the duration of a full warranty is defined solely in terms of first purchaser ownership there can be no violation of section 104(b)(4), 15 U.S.C. 2304(b)(4), since the duration of the warranty expires, by definition, at the time of transfer. No rights of a subsequent transferee are cut off as there is no transfer of ownership "during the duration of (any) warranty." Thus, these provisions do not preclude the offering of a full warranty with its duration determined exclusively by the period during which the first purchaser owns the product, or uses it in conjunction with another product. For example, an automotive battery or muffler warranty may be designated as "full warranty for as long as you own your car." Because this type of warranty leads the consumer to believe that proof of purchase is not needed so long as he or she owns the product a duty to furnish documentary proof may not be reasonably imposed on the consumer under this type of warranty. The burden is on the warrantor to prove that a particular claimant under this type of warranty is not the original purchaser or owner of the product. Warrantors or their designated agents may, however, ask consumers to state or affirm that they are the first purchaser of the product.

§ 700.7   Use of warranty registration cards.

(a)   Under section 104(b)(1) of the Act, 15 U.S.C. 2304(b)(1), a warrantor offering a full warranty may not impose on consumers any duty other than notification of a defect as a condition of securing remedy of the defect or malfunction, unless such additional duty can be demonstrated by the warrantor to be reasonable. Warrantors have in the past stipulated the return of a "warranty registration" or similar card. By "warranty registration card" the Commission means a card which must be returned by the consumer shortly after purchase of the product and which is stipulated or implied in the warranty to be a condition precedent to warranty coverage and performance.

(b)   A requirement that the consumer return a warranty registration card or a similar notice as a condition of performance under a full warranty is an unreasonable duty. Thus, a provision such as, "This warranty is void unless the warranty registration card is returned to the warrantor" is not permissible in a full warranty, nor is it permissible to imply such a condition in a full warranty.

(c)   This does not prohibit the use of such registration cards where a warrantor suggests use of the card as one possible means of proof of the date the product was purchased. For example, it is permissible to provide in a full warranty that a consumer may fill out and return a card to place on file proof of the date the product was purchased. Any such suggestion to the consumer must include notice that failure to return the card will not affect rights under the warranty, so long as the consumer can show in a reasonable manner the date the product was purchased. Nor does this interpretation prohibit a seller from obtaining from purchasers at the time of sale information requested by the warrantor.

§ 700.8   Warrantor's decision as final.

A warrantor shall not indicate in any written warranty or service contract either directly or indirectly that the decision of the warrantor, service contractor, or any designated third party is final or binding in any dispute concerning the warranty or service contract. Nor shall a warrantor or service contractor state that it alone shall determine what is a defect under the agreement. Such statements are deceptive since section 110(d) of the Act, 15 U.S.C. 2310(d), gives state and federal courts jurisdiction over suits for breach of warranty and service contract.

§ 700.9   Duty to install under a full warranty.

Under section 104(a)(1) of the Act, 15 U.S.C. 2304(a)(1), the remedy under a full warranty must be provided to the consumer without charge. If the warranted product has utility only when installed, a full warranty must provide such installation without charge regardless of whether or not the consumer originally paid for installation by the warrantor or his agent. However, this does not preclude the warrantor from imposing on the consumer a duty to remove, return, or reinstall where such duty can be demonstrated by the warrantor to meet the standard of reasonableness under section 104(b)(1), 15 U.S.C. 2304(b)(1).

§ 700.10   Section 102(c).

(a)   Section 102(c), 15 U.S.C. 2302(c), prohibits tying arrangements that condition coverage under a written warranty on the consumer's use of an article or service identified by brand, trade, or corporate name unless that article or service is provided without charge to the consumer.

(b)   Under a limited warranty that provides only for replacement of defective parts and no portion of labor charges, section 102(c), 15 U.S.C. 2302(c), prohibits a condition that the consumer use only service (labor) identified by the warrantor to install the replacement parts. A warrantor or his designated representative may not provide parts under the warranty in a manner which impedes or precludes the choice by the consumer of the person or business to perform necessary labor to install such parts.

(c)   No warrantor may condition the continued validity of a warranty on the use of only authorized repair service and/or authorized replacement parts for non-warranty service and maintenance (other than an article of service provided without charge under the warranty or unless the warrantor has obtained a waiver pursuant to section 102(c) of the Act, 15 U.S.C. 2302(c)). For example, provisions such as, "This warranty is void if service is performed by anyone other than an authorized 'ABC' dealer and all replacement parts must be genuine 'ABC' parts," and the like, are prohibited where the service or parts are not covered by the warranty. These provisions violate the Act in two ways. First, they violate the section 102(c), 15 U.S.C. 2302(c), ban against tying arrangements. Second, such provisions are deceptive under section 110 of the Act, 15 U.S.C. 2310, because a warrantor cannot, as a matter of law, avoid liability under a written warranty where a defect is unrelated to the use by a consumer of "unauthorized" articles or service. In addition, warranty language that implies to a consumer acting reasonably in the circumstances that warranty coverage requires the consumer's purchase of an article or service identified by brand, trade or corporate name is similarly deceptive. For example, a provision in the warranty such as, "use only an authorized 'ABC' dealer" or "use only 'ABC' replacement parts," is prohibited where the service or parts are not provided free of charge pursuant to the warranty. This does not preclude a warrantor from expressly excluding liability for defects or damage caused by such "unauthorized" articles or service; nor does it preclude the warrantor from denying liability where the warrantor can demonstrate that the defect or damage was so caused.

§ 700.11   Written warranty, service contract, and insurance distinguished for purposes of compliance under the Act.

(a)   The Act recognizes two types of agreements which may provide similar coverage of consumer products, the written warranty, and the service contract. In addition, other agreements may meet the statutory definitions of either "written warranty" or "service contract," but are sold and regulated under state law as contracts of insurance. One example is the automobile breakdown insurance policies sold in many jurisdictions and regulated by the state as a form of casualty insurance. The McCarran-Ferguson Act, 15 U.S.C. 1011 et seq., provides that most federal laws (including the Magnuson-Moss Warranty Act) shall not be construed to invalidate, impair, or supersede any law enacted by any State for the purpose of regulating the business of insurance. While three specific laws are subject to a separate proviso, the Magnuson-Moss Warranty Act is not one of them. Thus, to the extent the Magnuson-Moss Warranty Act's service contract provisions apply to the business of insurance, they are effective so long as they do not invalidate, impair, or supersede a State law enacted for the purpose of regulating the business of insurance.

(b)   "Written warranty" and "service contract" are defined in sections 101(6) and 101(8) of the Act, 15 U.S.C. 2301(6) and 15 U.S.C. 2301(8), respectively. A written warranty must be "part of the basis of the bargain." This means that it must be conveyed at the time of sale of the consumer product and the consumer must not give any consideration beyond the purchase price of the consumer product in order to benefit from the agreement. It is not a requirement of the Act that an agreement obligate a supplier of the consumer product to a written warranty, but merely that it be part of the basis of the bargain between a supplier and a consumer. This contemplates written warranties by third-party non-suppliers.

(c)   A service contract under the Act must meet the definitions of section 101(8), 15 U.S.C. 2301(8). An agreement which would meet the definition of written warranty in section 101(6)(A) or (B), 15 U.S.C. 2301(6)(A) or (B), but for its failure to satisfy the basis of the bargain test is a service contract. For example, an agreement which calls for some consideration in addition to the purchase price of the consumer product, or which is entered into at some date after the purchase of the consumer product to which it applies, is a service contract. An agreement which relates only to the performance of maintenance and/or inspection services and which is not an undertaking, promise, or affirmation with respect to a specified level of performance, or that the product is free of defects in materials or workmanship, is a service contract. An agreement to perform periodic cleaning and inspection of a product over a specified period of time, even when offered at the time of sale and without charge to the consumer, is an example of such a service contract.

§ 700.12   Effective date of 16 CFR, Parts 701 and 702.

The Statement of Basis and Purpose of the final rules promulgated on December 31, 1975, provides that parts 701 and 702 of this chapter will become effective one year after the date of promulgation, December 31, 1976. The Commission intends this to mean that these rules apply only to written warranties on products manufactured after December 31, 1976.

PART 701. DISCLOSURE OF WRITTEN CONSUMER PRODUCT WARRANTY TERMS AND CONDITIONS

§ 701.1   Definitions.

(a)   The Act means the Magnuson-Moss Warranty Federal Trade Commission Improvement Act, 15 U.S.C. 2301, et seq.

(b)   Consumer product means any tangible personal property which is distributed in commerce and which is normally used for personal, family, or household purposes (including any such property intended to be attached to or installed in any real property without regard to whether it is so attached or installed). Products which are purchased solely for commercial or industrial use are excluded solely for purposes of this Part.

(c)   Written warranty means:

(1)   Any written affirmation of fact or written promise made in connection with the sale of a consumer product by a supplier to a buyer which relates to the nature of the material or workmanship and affirms or promises that such material or workmanship is defect free or will meet a specified level of performance over a specified period of time, or

(2)   Any undertaking in writing in connection with the sale by a supplier of a consumer product to refund, repair, replace, or take other remedial action with respect to such product in the event that such product fails to meet the specifications set forth in the undertaking, which written affirmation, promise or undertaking becomes part of the basis of the bargain between a supplier and a buyer for purposes other than resale of such product.

(d)   Implied warranty means an implied warranty arising under State law (as modified by sections 104(a) and 108 of the Act, 15 U.S.C. 2304(a) and 2308), in connection with the sale by a supplier of a consumer product.

(e)   Remedy means whichever of the following actions the warrantor elects:

(1)   Repair,

(2)   Replacement, or

(3)   Refund; except that the warrantor may not elect refund unless:

(i)   The warrantor is unable to provide replacement and repair is not commercially practicable or cannot be timely made, or

(ii) The consumer is willing to accept such refund.

(f)   Supplier means any person engaged in the business of making a consumer product directly or indirectly available to consumers.

(g)   Warrantor means any supplier or other person who gives or offers to give a written warranty.

(h)   Consumer means a buyer (other than for purposes of resale or use in the ordinary course of the buyer's business) of any consumer product, any person to whom such product is transferred during the duration of an implied or written warranty applicable to the product, and any other such person who is entitled by the terms of such warranty or under applicable State law to enforce against the warrantor the obligations of the warranty.

(i)   On the face of the warranty means:

(1)   Where the warranty is a single sheet with printing on both sides of the sheet or where the warranty is comprised of more than one sheet, the page on which the warranty text begins;

(2)   Where the warranty is included as part of a larger document, such as a use and care manual, the page in such document on which the warranty text begins.

§ 701.2   Scope.

The regulations in this part establish requirements for warrantors for disclosing the terms and conditions of written warranties on consumer products actually costing the consumer more than $15.00.

§ 701.3   Written warranty terms.

(a)   Any warrantor warranting to a consumer by means of a written warranty a consumer product actually costing the consumer more than $15.00 shall clearly and conspicuously disclose in a single document in simple and readily understood language, the following items of information:

(1)   The identity of the party or parties to whom the written warranty is extended, if the enforceability of the written warranty is limited to the original consumer purchaser or is otherwise limited to persons other than every consumer owner during the term of the warranty;

(2)   A clear description and identification of products, or parts, or characteristics, or components or properties covered by and where necessary for clarification, excluded from the warranty;

(3)   A statement of what the warrantor will do in the event of a defect, malfunction or failure to conform with the written warranty, including the items or services the warrantor will pay for or provide, and, where necessary for clarification, those which the warrantor will not pay for or provide;

(4)   The point in time or event on which the warranty term commences, if different from the purchase date, and the time period or other measurement of warranty duration;

(5)   A step-by-step explanation of the procedure which the consumer should follow in order to obtain performance of any warranty obligation, including the persons or class of persons authorized to perform warranty obligations. This includes the name(s) of the warrantor(s), together with: The mailing address(es) of the warrantor(s), and/or the name or title and the address of any employee or department of the warrantor responsible for the performance of warranty obligations, and/or a telephone number which consumers may use without charge to obtain information on warranty performance;

(6)   Information respecting the availability of any informal dispute settlement mechanism elected by the warrantor in compliance with part 703 of this subchapter;

(7)   Any limitations on the duration of implied warranties, disclosed on the face of the warranty as provided in section 108 of the Act, 15 U.S.C. 2308, accompanied by the following statement:

Some States do not allow limitations on how long an implied warranty lasts, so the above limitation may not apply to you.

(8)   Any exclusions of or limitations on relief such as incidental or consequential damages, accompanied by the following statement, which may be combined with the statement required in paragraph (a)(7) of this section:

> Some States do not allow the exclusion or limitation of incidental or consequential damages, so the above limitation or exclusion may not apply to you.

(9)   A statement in the following language:

> This warranty gives you specific legal rights, and you may also have other rights which vary from State to State.

(b)   Paragraphs (a)(1) through (9) of this section shall not be applicable with respect to statements of general policy on emblems, seals or insignias issued by third parties promising replacement or refund if a consumer product is defective, which statements contain no representation or assurance of the quality or performance characteristics of the product; *Provided* That: (1) The disclosures required by paragraphs (a)(1) through (9) of this section are published by such third parties in each issue of a publication with a general circulation, and (2) such disclosures are provided free of charge to any consumer upon written request.

§ 701.4   Owner registration cards.

When a warrantor employs any card such as an owner's registration card, a warranty registration card, or the like, and the return of such card is a condition precedent to warranty coverage and performance, the warrantor shall disclose this fact in the warranty. If the return of such card reasonably appears to be a condition precedent to warranty coverage and performance, but is not such a condition, that fact shall be disclosed in the warranty.

PART 702.   PRE-SALE AVAILABILITY OF WRITTEN WARRANTY TERMS

§ 702.1   Definitions.

(a)   The Act means the Magnuson-Moss Warranty Federal Trade Commission Improvement Act, 15 U.S.C. 2301, et seq.

(b)   Consumer product means any tangible personal property which is distributed in commerce and which is normally used for personal, family, or household purposes (including any such property intended to be attached to or installed in any real property without regard to whether it is so attached or installed). Products which are purchased solely for commercial or industrial use are excluded solely for purposes of this Part.

(c)   Written warranty means—

(1)   Any written affirmation of fact or written promise made in connection with the sale of a consumer product by a supplier to a buyer which relates to the nature of the material or workmanship and affirms or promises that such material or workmanship is defect free or will meet a specified level of performance over a specified period of time, or

(2)   Any undertaking in writing in connection with the sale by a supplier of a consumer product to refund, repair, replace or take other remedial action with respect to such product in the event that such product fails to meet the specifications set forth in the undertaking, which written affirmation, promise, or undertaking becomes part of the basis of the bargain between a supplier and a buyer for purposes other than resale of such product.

(d)   Warrantor means any supplier or other person who gives or offers to give a written warranty.

(e)   Seller means any person who sells or offers for sale for purposes other than resale or use in the ordinary course of the buyer's business any consumer product.

(f)   Supplier means any person engaged in the business of making a consumer product directly or indirectly available to consumers.

§ 702.2   Scope.

The regulations in this part establish requirements for sellers and warrantors for making the terms of any written warranty on a consumer product available to the consumer prior to sale.

§ 702.3   Pre-sale availability of written warranty terms.

The following requirements apply to consumer products actually costing the consumer more than $15.00:

(a) **Duties of seller.** Except as provided in paragraphs (c) through (d) of this section, the seller of a consumer product with a written warranty shall make a text of the warranty readily available for examination by the prospective buyer by:

(1) Displaying it in close proximity to the warranted product, or

(2) Furnishing it upon request prior to sale and placing signs reasonably calculated to elicit the prospective buyer's attention in prominent locations in the store or department advising such prospective buyers of the availability of warranties upon request.

(b) **Duties of the warrantor.**

(1) A warrantor who gives a written warranty warranting to a consumer a consumer product actually costing the consumer more than $15.00 shall:

(i) Provide sellers with warranty materials necessary for such sellers to comply with the requirements set forth in paragraph (a) of this section, by the use of one or more by the following means:

(A) Providing a copy of the written warranty with every warranted consumer product; and/or

(B) Providing a tag, sign, sticker, label, decal or other attachment to the product, which contains the full text of the written warranty; and/or

(C) Printing on or otherwise attaching the text of the written warranty to the package, carton, or other container if that package, carton or other container is normally used for display purposes. If the warrantor elects this option a copy of the written warranty must also accompany the warranted product; and/or

(D) Providing a notice, sign, or poster disclosing the text of a consumer product warranty. If the warrantor elects this option, a copy of the written warranty must also accompany each warranted product.

(ii) Provide catalog, mail order, and door-to-door sellers with copies of written warranties necessary for such sellers to comply with the requirements set forth in paragraphs (c) and (d) of this section.

(2) Paragraph (a)(1) of this section shall not be applicable with respect to statements of general policy on emblems, seals or insignias issued by third parties promising replacement or refund if a consumer product is defective, which statements contain no representation or assurance of the quality or performance characteristics of the product; provided that

(i) The disclosures required by § 701.3(a)(1) through (9) of this part are published by such third parties in each issue of a publication with a general circulation, and

(ii) Such disclosures are provided free of charge to any consumer upon written request.

(c) **Catalog and mail order sales.**

(1) For purposes of this paragraph:

(i) Catalog or mail order sales means any offer for sale, or any solicitation for an order for a consumer product with a written warranty, which includes instructions for ordering the product which do not require a personal visit to the seller's establishment.

(ii)   Close conjunction means on the page containing the description of the warranted product, or on the page facing that page.

(2)   Any seller who offers for sale to consumers consumer products with written warranties by means of a catalog or mail order solicitation shall:

(i)   Clearly and conspicuously disclose in such catalog or solicitation in close conjunction to the description of warranted product, or in an information section of the catalog or solicitation clearly referenced, including a page number, in close conjunction to the description of the warranted product, either:

(A)   The full text of the written warranty; or

(B)   That the written warranty can be obtained free upon specific written request, and the address where such warranty can be obtained. If this option is elected, such seller shall promptly provide a copy of any written warranty requested by the consumer.

(d)   **Door-to-door sales.**

(1)   For purposes of this paragraph:

(i)   Door-to-door sale means a sale of consumer products in which the seller or his representative personally solicits the sale, including those in response to or following an invitation by a buyer, and the buyer's agreement to offer to purchase is made at a place other than the place of business of the seller.

(ii)   Prospective buyer means an individual solicited by a door-to-door seller to buy a consumer product who indicates sufficient interest in that consumer product or maintains sufficient contact with the seller for the seller reasonably to conclude that the person solicited is considering purchasing the product.

(2)   Any seller who offers for sale to consumers consumer products with written warranties by means of door-to-door sales shall, prior to the consummation of the sale, disclose the fact that the sales representative has copies of the warranties for the warranted products being offered for sale, which may be inspected by the prospective buyer at any time during the sales presentation. Such disclosure shall be made orally and shall be included in any written materials shown to prospective buyers.

PART 703. INFORMAL DISPUTE
SETTLEMENT PROCEDURES

§ 703.1   Definitions.

(a)   The Act means the Magnuson-Moss Warranty—Federal Trade Commission Improvement Act, 15 U.S.C. 2301, et seq.

(b)   Consumer product means any tangible personal property which is distributed in commerce and which is normally used for personal, family, or household purposes (including any such property intended to be attached to or installed in any real property without regard to whether it is so attached or installed).

(c)   Written warranty means:

(1)   Any written affirmation of fact or written promise made in connection with the sale of a consumer product by a supplier to a buyer which relates to the nature of the material or workmanship and affirms or promises that such material or workmanship is defect free or will meet a specified level of performance over a specified period of time, or

(2)   Any undertaking in writing in connection with the sale by a supplier of a consumer product to refund, repair, replace, or take other remedial action with respect to such product in the event that such product fails to meet the specifications set forth in the undertaking, which written affirmation, promise or undertaking becomes part of the basis of the bargain between a supplier and a buyer for purposes other than resale of such product.

(d)   Warrantor means any person who gives or offers to give a written warranty which incorporates an informal dispute settlement mechanism.

(e)   Mechanism means an informal dispute settlement procedure which is incorporated into the terms of a written warranty to which any provision of Title I of the Act applies, as provided in section 110 of the Act, 15 U.S.C. 2310.

(f)   Members means the person or persons within a Mechanism actually deciding disputes.

(g)   Consumer means a buyer (other than for purposes of resale) of any consumer product, any person to whom such product is transferred during the duration of a written warranty applicable to the product, and any other person who is entitled by the terms of such warranty or under applicable state law to enforce against the warrantor the obligations of the warranty.

(h)   On the face of the warranty means:

(1)   If the warranty is a single sheet with printing on both sides of the sheet, or if the warranty is comprised of more than one sheet, the page on which the warranty text begins;

(2)   If the warranty is included as part of a longer document, such as a use and care manual, the page in such document on which the warranty text begins.

§ 703.2   Duties of warrantor.

(a)   The warrantor shall not incorporate into the terms of a written warranty a Mechanism that fails to comply with the requirements contained in §§ 703.3 through 703.8 of this part. This paragraph (a) shall not prohibit a warrantor from incorporating into the terms of a written warranty the step-by-step procedure which the consumer should take in order to obtain performance of any obligation under the warranty as described in section 102(a)(7) of the Act, 15 U.S.C. 2302(a)(7), and required by part 701 of this subchapter.

(b)   The warrantor shall disclose clearly and conspicuously at least the following information on the face of the written warranty:

(1)   A statement of the availability of the informal dispute settlement mechanism;

(2)   The name and address of the Mechanism, or the name and a telephone number of the Mechanism which consumers may use without charge;

(3)   A statement of any requirement that the consumer resort to the Mechanism before exercising rights or seeking remedies created by Title I of the Act; together with the disclosure that if a consumer chooses to seek redress by pursuing rights and remedies not created by Title I of the Act, resort to the Mechanism would not be required by any provision of the Act; and

(4)   A statement, if applicable, indicating where further information on the Mechanism can be found in materials accompanying the product, as provided in § 703.2(c) of this section.

(c)   The warrantor shall include in the written warranty or in a separate section of materials accompanying the product, the following information:

(1)   Either (i) a form addressed to the Mechanism containing spaces requesting the information which the Mechanism may require for prompt resolution of warranty disputes; or (ii) a telephone number of the Mechanism which consumers may use without charge;

(2)   The name and address of the Mechanism;

(3)   A brief description of Mechanism procedures;

(4)   The time limits adhered to by the Mechanism; and

(5)   The types of information which the Mechanism may require for prompt resolution of warranty disputes.

(d)   The warrantor shall take steps reasonably calculated to make consumers aware of the Mechanism's existence at the time consumers experience warranty disputes. Nothing contained in paragraphs (b), (c), or (d) of this section shall limit the warrantor's option to encourage consumers to seek redress directly from the warrantor as long as the warrantor does not expressly require consumers to seek redress directly from the warrantor. The warrantor shall proceed fairly and expeditiously to attempt to resolve all disputes submitted directly to the warrantor.

(e)   Whenever a dispute is submitted directly to the warrantor, the warrantor shall, within a reasonable time, decide whether, and to what extent, it will satisfy the consumer, and inform the consumer of its decision. In its notification to the consumer of its decision, the warrantor shall include the information required in § 703.2(b) and (c) of this section.

(f)   The warrantor shall:

(1)   Respond fully and promptly to reasonable requests by the Mechanism for information relating to disputes;

(2)   Upon notification of any decision of the Mechanism that would require action on the part of the warrantor, immediately notify the Mechanism whether, and to what extent, warrantor will abide by the decision; and

(3)   Perform any obligations it has agreed to.

(g)   The warrantor shall act in good faith in determining whether, and to what extent, it will abide by a Mechanism decision.

(h)   The warrantor shall comply with any reasonable requirements imposed by the Mechanism to fairly and expeditiously resolve warranty disputes.

MINIMUM REQUIREMENTS OF THE MECHANISM

§ 703.3   Mechanism organization.

(a)   The Mechanism shall be funded and competently staffed at a level sufficient to ensure fair and expeditious resolution of all disputes, and shall not charge consumers any fee for use of the Mechanism.

(b)   The warrantor and the sponsor of the Mechanism (if other than the warrantor) shall take all steps necessary to ensure that the Mechanism, and its members and staff, are sufficiently insulated from the warrantor and the sponsor, so that the decisions of the members and the performance of the staff are not influenced by either the warrantor or the sponsor. Necessary steps shall include, at a minimum, committing funds in advance, basing personnel decisions solely on merit, and not assigning conflicting warrantor or sponsor duties to Mechanism staff persons.

(c)   The Mechanism shall impose any other reasonable requirements necessary to ensure that the members and staff act fairly and expeditiously in each dispute.

§ 703.4   Qualification of members.

(a)   No member deciding a dispute shall be:

(1)   A party to the dispute, or an employee or agent of a party other than for purposes of deciding disputes; or

(2)   A person who is or may become a party in any legal action, including but not limited to class actions, relating to the product or complaint in dispute, or an employee or agent of such person other than for purposes of deciding disputes. For purposes of this paragraph (a) a person shall not be considered a "party" solely because he or she acquires or owns an interest in a party solely for investment, and the acquisition or ownership of an interest which is offered to the general public shall be prima facie evidence of its acquisition or ownership solely for investment.

(b)   When one or two members are deciding a dispute, all shall be persons having no direct involvement in the manufacture, distribution, sale or service of any product. When three or more members are deciding a dispute, at least two-thirds shall be persons having no direct involvement in the manufacture, distribution, sale or service of any product. "Direct involvement" shall not include acquiring or owning an interest solely for investment, and the acquisition or ownership of an interest which is offered to the general public shall be prima facie evidence of its acquisition or ownership solely for investment. Nothing contained in this section shall prevent the members from consulting with any persons knowledgeable in the technical, commercial or other areas relating to the product which is the subject of the dispute.

(c)   Members shall be persons interested in the fair and expeditious settlement of consumer disputes.

§ 703.5   Operation of the Mechanism.

(a)   The Mechanism shall establish written operating procedures which shall include at least those items specified in paragraphs (b) through (j) of this section. Copies of the written procedures shall be made available to any person upon request.

(b)   Upon notification of a dispute, the Mechanism shall immediately inform both the warrantor and the consumer of receipt of the dispute.

(c)   The Mechanism shall investigate, gather and organize all information necessary for a fair and expeditious decision in each dispute. When any evidence gathered by or submitted to the Mechanism raises issues relating to the number of repair attempts, the length of repair periods, the possibility of unreasonable use of the product, or any other issues relevant in light of Title I of the Act (or rules thereunder), including issues relating to consequential damages, or any other remedy under the Act (or rules thereunder), the Mechanism shall investigate these issues. When information which will or may be used in the decision, submitted by one party, or a consultant under § 703.4(b) of this part, or any other source tends to contradict facts submitted by the other party, the Mechanism shall clearly, accurately, and completely disclose to both parties the contradictory information (and its source) and shall provide both parties an opportunity to explain or rebut the information and to submit additional materials. The Mechanism shall not require any information not reasonably necessary to decide the dispute.

(d)   If the dispute has not been settled, the Mechanism shall, as expeditiously as possible but at least within 40 days of notification of the dispute, except as provided in paragraph (e) of this section:

(1)   Render a fair decision based on the information gathered as described in paragraph (c) of this section, and on any information submitted at an oral presentation which conforms to the requirements of paragraph (f) of this section (A decision shall include any remedies appropriate under the circumstances, including repair, replacement, refund, reimbursement for expenses, compensation for damages, and any other remedies available under the written warranty or the Act (or rules thereunder); and a decision shall state a specified reasonable time for performance);

(2)   Disclose to the warrantor its decision and the reasons therefor;

(3)   If the decision would require action on the part of the warrantor, determine whether, and to what extent, warrantor will abide by its decision; and

(4)   Disclose to the consumer its decision, the reasons therefor, warrantor's intended actions (if the decision would require action on the part of the warrantor), and the information described in paragraph (g) of this section. For purposes of paragraph (d) of this section a dispute shall be deemed settled when the Mechanism has ascertained from the consumer that:

(i)   The dispute has been settled to the consumer's satisfaction; and

(ii)   The settlement contains a specified reasonable time for performance.

(e)   The Mechanism may delay the performance of its duties under paragraph (d) of this section beyond the 40 day time limit:

(1)   Where the period of delay is due solely to failure of a consumer to provide promptly his or her name and address, brand name and model number of the product involved, and a statement as to the nature of the defect or other complaint; or

(2)   For a 7 day period in those cases where the consumer has made no attempt to seek redress directly from the warrantor.

(f)   The Mechanism may allow an oral presentation by a party to a dispute (or a party's representative) only if:

(1)   Both warrantor and consumer expressly agree to the presentation;

(2)   Prior to agreement the Mechanism fully discloses to the consumer the following information:

(i)   That the presentation by either party will take place only if both parties so agree, but that if they agree, and one party fails to appear at the agreed upon time and place, the presentation by the other party may still be allowed;

(ii)   That the members will decide the dispute whether or not an oral presentation is made;

(iii)   The proposed date, time and place for the presentation; and

(iv)   A brief description of what will occur at the presentation including, if applicable, parties' rights to bring witnesses and/or counsel; and

(3)   Each party has the right to be present during the other party's oral presentation. Nothing contained in this paragraph (b) of this section shall preclude the Mechanism from allowing an oral presentation by one party, if the other party fails to appear at the agreed upon time and place, as long as all of the requirements of this paragraph have been satisfied.

(g)   The Mechanism shall inform the consumer, at the time of disclosure required in paragraph (d) of this section that:

(1)   If he or she is dissatisfied with its decision or warrantor's intended actions, or eventual performance, legal remedies, including use of small claims court, may be pursued;

(2)   The Mechanism's decision is admissible in evidence as provided in section 110(a)(3) of the Act, 15 U.S.C. 2310(a)(3); and

(3)   The consumer may obtain, at reasonable cost, copies of all Mechanism records relating to the consumer's dispute.

(h)   If the warrantor has agreed to perform any obligations, either as part of a settlement agreed to after notification to the Mechanism of the dispute or as a result of a decision under paragraph (d) of this section, the Mechanism shall ascertain from the consumer within 10 working days of the date for performance whether performance has occurred.

(i)   A requirement that a consumer resort to the Mechanism prior to commencement of an action under section 110(d) of the Act, 15 U.S.C. 2310(d), shall be satisfied 40 days after notification to the Mechanism of the dispute or when the Mechanism completes all of its duties under paragraph (d) of this section, whichever occurs sooner. Except that, if the Mechanism delays performance of its paragraph (d) of this section duties as allowed by paragraph (e) of this section, the requirement that the consumer initially resort to the Mechanism shall not be satisfied until the period of delay allowed by paragraph (e) of this section has ended.

(j)   Decisions of the Mechanism shall not be legally binding on any person. However, the warrantor shall act in good faith, as provided in § 703.2(g) of this part. In any civil action arising out of a warranty obligation and relating to a matter considered by the Mechanism, any decision of the Mechanism shall be admissible in evidence, as provided in section 110(a)(3) of the Act, 15 U.S.C. 2310(a)(3).

§ 703.6   Recordkeeping.

(a)   The Mechanism shall maintain records on each dispute referred to it which shall include:

(1)   Name, address and telephone number of the consumer;

(2)   Name, address, telephone number and contact person of the warrantor;

(3)   Brand name and model number of the product involved;

(4)   The date of receipt of the dispute and the date of disclosure to the consumer of the decision;

(5)   All letters or other written documents submitted by either party;

(6)   All other evidence collected by the Mechanism relating to the dispute, including summaries of relevant and material portions of telephone calls and meetings between the Mechanism and any other person (including consultants described in § 703.4(b) of this part);

(7)   A summary of any relevant and material information presented by either party at an oral presentation;

(8)   The decision of the members including information as to date, time and place of meeting, and the identity of members voting; or information on any other resolution;

(9)   A copy of the disclosure to the parties of the decision;

(10)   A statement of the warrantor's intended action(s);

(11)   Copies of follow-up letters (or summaries of relevant and material portions of follow-up telephone calls) to the consumer, and responses thereto; and

(12)   Any other documents and communications (or summaries of relevant and material portions of oral communications) relating to the dispute.

(b)   The Mechanism shall maintain an index of each warrantor's disputes grouped under brand name and sub-grouped under product model.

(c)   The Mechanism shall maintain an index for each warrantor as will show:

(1)   All disputes in which the warrantor has promised some performance (either by settlement or in response to a Mechanism decision) and has failed to comply; and

(2)   All disputes in which the warrantor has refused to abide by a Mechanism decision.

(d)   The Mechanism shall maintain an index as will show all disputes delayed beyond 40 days.

(e)   The Mechanism shall compile semi-annually and maintain statistics which show the number and percent of disputes in each of the following categories:

(1)   Resolved by staff of the Mechanism and warrantor has complied;

(2)   Resolved by staff of the Mechanism, time for compliance has occurred, and warrantor has not complied;

(3)   Resolved by staff of the Mechanism and time for compliance has not yet occurred;

(4)   Decided by members and warrantor has complied;

(5)   Decided by members, time for compliance has occurred, and warrantor has not complied;

(6)   Decided by members and time for compliance has not yet occurred;

(7)   Decided by members adverse to the consumer;

(8)   No jurisdiction;

(9)   Decision delayed beyond 40 days under § 703.5(e)(1) of this part;

(10)   Decision delayed beyond 40 days under § 703.5(e)(2) of this part;

(11)   Decision delayed beyond 40 days for any other reason; and

(12)   Pending decision.

(f)   The Mechanism shall retain all records specified in paragraphs (a) through (e) of this section for at least 4 years after final disposition of the dispute.

§ 703.7   Audits.

(a)   The Mechanism shall have an audit conducted at least annually, to determine whether the Mechanism and its implementation are in compliance with this part. All records of the Mechanism required to be kept under § 703.6 of this part shall be available for audit.

(b)   Each audit provided for in paragraph (a) of this section shall include at a minimum the following:

(1)   Evaluation of warrantors' efforts to make consumers aware of the Mechanism's existence as required in § 703.2(d) of this part;

(2)   Review of the indexes maintained pursuant to § 703.6(b), (c), and (d) of this part; and

(3)   Analysis of a random sample of disputes handled by the Mechanism to determine the following:

(i)   Adequacy of the Mechanism's complaint and other forms, investigation, mediation and follow-up efforts, and other aspects of complaint handling; and

(ii)   Accuracy of the Mechanism's statistical compilations under § 703.6(e) of this part. (For purposes of this subparagraph "analysis" shall include oral or written contact with the consumers involved in each of the disputes in the random sample.)

(c)   A report of each audit under this section shall be submitted to the Federal Trade Commission, and shall be made available to any person at reasonable cost. The Mechanism may direct its auditor to delete names of parties to disputes, and identity of products involved, from the audit report.

(d)   Auditors shall be selected by the Mechanism. No auditor may be involved with the Mechanism as a warrantor, sponsor or member, or employee or agent thereof, other than for purposes of the audit.

§ 703.8   Openness of records and proceedings.

(a)   The statistical summaries specified in § 703.6(e) of this part shall be available to any person for inspection and copying.

(b)   Except as provided under paragraphs (a) and (e) of this section, and paragraph (c) of § 703.7 of this part, all records of the Mechanism may be kept confidential, or made available only on such terms and conditions, or in such form, as the Mechanism shall permit.

(c)   The policy of the Mechanism with respect to records made available at the Mechanism's option shall be set out in the procedures under § 703.5(a) of this part; the policy shall be applied uniformly to all requests for access to or copies of such records.

(d)   Meetings of the members to hear and decide disputes shall be open to observers on reasonable and nondiscriminatory terms. The identity of the parties and products involved in disputes need not be disclosed at meetings.

(e)   Upon request the Mechanism shall provide to either party to a dispute:

(1)   Access to all records relating to the dispute; and

(2)   Copies of any records relating to the dispute, at reasonable cost.

(f)   The Mechanism shall make available to any person upon request, information relating to the qualifications of Mechanism staff and members.

FOOD SECURITY ACT OF 1985

7 U.S.C.A. § 1631

Current through March 30, 2016; P.L. 114–141

For updates, see http://uscode.house.gov

§ 1631.   Protection for purchasers of farm products

(a) Congressional findings

Congress finds that—

(1)   certain State laws permit a secured lender to enforce liens against a purchaser of farm products even if the purchaser does not know that the sale of the products violates the lender's security interest in the products, lacks any practical method for discovering the existence of the security interest, and has no reasonable means to ensure that the seller uses the sales proceeds to repay the lender;

(2)   these laws subject the purchaser of farm products to double payment for the products, once at the time of purchase, and again when the seller fails to repay the lender;

(3)   the exposure of purchasers of farm products to double payment inhibits free competition in the market for farm products; and

(4)   this exposure constitutes a burden on and an obstruction to interstate commerce in farm products.

(b) Declaration of purpose

The purpose of this section is to remove such burden on and obstruction to interstate commerce in farm products.

(c) Definitions

For the purposes of this section—

(1)   The term "buyer in the ordinary course of business" means a person who, in the ordinary course of business, buys farm products from a person engaged in farming operations who is in the business of selling farm products.

(2)   The term "central filing system" means a system for filing effective financing statements or notice of such financing statements on a statewide basis and which has been certified by the Secretary of the United States Department of Agriculture; the Secretary shall certify such system if the system complies with the requirements of this section; specifically under such system—

(A)   effective financing statements or notice of such financing statements are filed with the office of the Secretary of State of a State;

(B)   the Secretary of State records the date and hour of the filing of such statements;

(C)   the Secretary of State compiles all such statements into a master list—

(i)   organized according to farm products;

(ii)   arranged within each such product—

(I)   in alphabetical order according to the last name of the individual debtors, or, in the case of debtors doing business other than as individuals, the first word in the name of such debtors; and

(II) in numerical order according to the social security number, or other approved unique identifier, of the individual debtors or, in the case of debtors doing business other than as individuals, the Internal Revenue Service taxpayer identification number, or other approved unique identifier, of such debtors, except that the numerical list containing social security or taxpayer identification numbers may be encrypted for security purposes if the Secretary of State provides a method by which an effective search of the encrypted numbers may be conducted to determine whether the farm product at issue is subject to 1 or more liens; and

(III) geographically by county or parish; and

(IV) by crop year;

(iii) containing the information referred to in paragraph (4)(D);

(D) the Secretary of State maintains a list of all buyers of farm products, commission merchants, and selling agents who register with the Secretary of State, on a form indicating—

(i) the name and address of each buyer, commission merchant and selling agent;

(ii) the interest of each buyer, commission merchant, and selling agent in receiving the lists described in subparagraph (E); and

(iii) the farm products in which each buyer, commission merchant, and selling agent has an interest;

(E) the Secretary of State distributes regularly as prescribed by the State to each buyer, commission merchant, and selling agent on the list described in subparagraph (D) a copy in written or printed form of those portions of the master list described in subparagraph (C) that cover the farm products in which such buyer, commission merchant, or selling agent has registered an interest except that—

(i) the distribution of the portion of the master list may be in electronic, written, or printed form; and

(ii) if social security or taxpayer identification numbers on the master list are encrypted, the Secretary of State may distribute the master list only—

(I) by compact disc or other electronic media that contains—

(aa) the recorded list of debtor names; and

(bb) an encryption program that enables the buyer, commission merchant, and selling agent to enter a social security number for matching against the recorded list of encrypted social security or taxpayer identification numbers; and

(II) on the written request of the buyer, commission merchant, or selling agent, by paper copy of the list to the requestor;

(F) the Secretary of State furnishes to those who are not registered pursuant to (2)(D) of this section[1] oral confirmation within 24 hours of any effective financing statement on request followed by written confirmation to any buyer of farm products buying from a debtor, or commission merchant or selling agent selling for a seller covered by such statement.

(3) The term "commission merchant" means any person engaged in the business of receiving any farm product for sale, on commission, or for or on behalf of another person.

(4) The term "effective financing statement" means a statement that—

(A) is an original or reproduced copy of the statement, or, in the case of a State which (under the applicable State law provisions of the Uniform Commercial Code) allows the electronic

---

[1]   So in original. Probably should be "pursuant to subparagraph (D)". [*Note from West Advisory Panel: the revisor's note refers to (c)(2)(D).*]

filing of financing statements without the signature of the debtor, is an electronically reproduced copy of the statement;

(B) other than in the case of an electronically reproduced copy of the statement, is signed, authorized, or otherwise authenticated by the debtor, and filed with the Secretary of State of a State by the secured party;

(C) contains,

    (i) the name and address of the secured party;

    (ii) the name and address of the person indebted to the secured party;

    (iii) the social security number, or other approved unique identifier, of the debtor or, in the case of a debtor doing business other than as an individual, the Internal Revenue Service taxpayer identification number, or other approved unique identifier, of such debtor; and

    (iv) a description of the farm products subject to the security interest created by the debtor, including the amount of such products where applicable, and the name of each county or parish in which the farm products are produced or located;

(D) must be amended in writing, within 3 months, similarly signed, authorized, or otherwise authenticated by the debtor and filed, to reflect material changes;

(E) remains effective for a period of 5 years from the date of filing, subject to extensions for additional periods of 5 years each by refiling or filing a continuation statement within 6 months before the expiration of the initial 5 year period;

(F) lapses on either the expiration of the effective period of the statement or the filing of a notice signed, authorized, or otherwise authenticated by the secured party that the statement has lapsed, whichever occurs first;

(G) is accompanied by the requisite filing fee set by the Secretary of State; and

(H) substantially complies with the requirements of this subparagraph even though it contains minor errors that are not seriously misleading.

(5)[2] The term "farm product" means an agricultural commodity such as wheat, corn, soybeans, or a species of livestock such as cattle, hogs, sheep, horses, or poultry used or produced in farming operations, or a product of such crop or livestock in its unmanufactured state (such as ginned cotton, wool-clip, maple syrup, milk, and eggs), that is in the possession of a person engaged in farming operations.

(6) The term "knows" or "knowledge" means actual knowledge.

(7) The term "security interest" means an interest in farm products that secures payment or performance of an obligation.

(8) The term "selling agent" means any person, other than a commission merchant, who is engaged in the business of negotiating the sale and purchase of any farm product on behalf of a person engaged in farming operations.

(9) The term "State" means each of the 50 States, the District of Columbia, the Commonwealth of Puerto Rico, Guam, the Virgin Islands of the United States, American Samoa, the Commonwealth of the Northern Mariana Islands, or the Trust Territory of the Pacific Islands.

(10) The term "person" means any individual, partnership, corporation, trust, or any other business entity.

(11) The term "Secretary of State" means the Secretary of State or the designee of the State.

---

  2 So in original. Another par. (5) follows par. (11).

(5)[3] The term "approved unique identifier" means a number, combination of numbers and letters, or other identifier selected by the Secretary of State using a selection system or method approved by the Secretary of Agriculture.

(d) Purchases free of security interest

Except as provided in subsection (e) of this section and notwithstanding any other provision of Federal, State, or local law, a buyer who in the ordinary course of business buys a farm product from a seller engaged in farming operations shall take free of a security interest created by the seller, even though the security interest is perfected; and the buyer knows of the existence of such interest.

(e) Purchases subject to security interest

A buyer of farm products takes subject to a security interest created by the seller if—

(1)(A) within 1 year before the sale of the farm products, the buyer has received from the secured party or the seller written notice of the security interest organized according to farm products that—

(i) is an original or reproduced copy thereof;

(ii) contains,

(I) the name and address of the secured party;

(II) the name and address of the person indebted to the secured party;

(III) the social security number, or other approved unique identifier, of the debtor or, in the case of a debtor doing business other than as an individual, the Internal Revenue Service taxpayer identification number, or other approved unique identifier, of such debtor; and

(IV) a description of the farm products subject to the security interest created by the debtor, including the amount of such products where applicable, crop year, and the name of each county or parish in which the farm products are produced or located;

(iii) must be amended in writing, within 3 months, similarly signed, authorized, or otherwise authenticated and transmitted, to reflect material changes;

(iv) will lapse on either the expiration period of the statement or the transmission of a notice signed, authorized, or otherwise authenticated by the secured party that the statement has lapsed, whichever occurs first; and

(v) contains any payment obligations imposed on the buyer by the secured party as conditions for waiver or release of the security interest; and

(B) the buyer has failed to perform the payment obligations, or

(2) in the case of a farm product produced in a State that has established a central filing system—

(A) the buyer has failed to register with the Secretary of State of such State prior to the purchase of farm products; and

(B) the secured party has filed an effective financing statement or notice that covers the farm products being sold; or

(3) in the case of a farm product produced in a State that has established a central filing system, the buyer—

(A) receives from the Secretary of State of such State written notice as provided in subsection (c)(2)(E) or (c)(2)(F) that specifies both the seller and the farm product being sold by such seller as being subject to an effective financing statement or notice; and

---

[3]   So in original. Another par. (5) follows par. (4).

(B) does not secure a waiver or release of the security interest specified in such effective financing statement or notice from the secured party by performing any payment obligation or otherwise.

(f) Law governing "receipt"

What constitutes receipt, as used in this section, shall be determined by the law of the State in which the buyer resides.

(g) Commission merchants or selling agents: sales free of or subject to security interest; law governing "receipt"

(1) Except as provided in paragraph (2) and notwithstanding any other provision of Federal, State, or local law, a commission merchant or selling agent who sells, in the ordinary course of business, a farm product for others, shall not be subject to a security interest created by the seller in such farm product even though the security interest is perfected and even though the commission merchant or selling agent knows of the existence of such interest.

(2) A commission merchant or selling agent who sells a farm product for others shall be subject to a security interest created by the seller in such farm product if—

(A) within 1 year before the sale of such farm product the commission merchant or selling agent has received from the secured party or the seller written notice of the security interest; organized according to farm products, that—

(i) is an original or reproduced copy thereof;

(ii) contains,

(I) the name and address of the secured party;

(II) the name and address of the person indebted to the secured party;

(III) the social security number, or other approved unique identifier, of the debtor or, in the case of a debtor doing business other than as an individual, the Internal Revenue Service taxpayer identification number, or other approved unique identifier, of such debtor; and

(IV) a description of the farm products subject to the security interest created by the debtor, including the amount of such products, where applicable, crop year, and the name of each county or parish in which the farm products are produced or located;

(iii) must be amended in writing, within 3 months, similarly signed, authorized, or otherwise authenticated and transmitted, to reflect material changes;

(iv) will lapse on either the expiration period of the statement or the transmission of a notice signed, authorized, or otherwise authenticated by the secured party that the statement has lapsed, whichever occurs first; and

(v) contains any payment obligations imposed on the commission merchant or selling agent by the secured party as conditions for waiver or release of the security interest; and

(B) the commission merchant or selling agent has failed to perform the payment obligations;

(C) in the case of a farm product produced in a State that has established a central filing system—

(i) the commission merchant or selling agent has failed to register with the Secretary of State of such State prior to the purchase of farm products; and

(ii) the secured party has filed an effective financing statement or notice that covers the farm products being sold; or

(D) in the case of a farm product produced in a State that has established a central filing system, the commission merchant or selling agent—

(i) receives from the Secretary of State of such State written notice as provided in subsection (c)(2)(E) or (c)(2)(F) of this section that specifies both the seller and the farm products being sold by such seller as being subject to an effective financing statement or notice; and

(ii) does not secure a waiver or release of the security interest specified in such effective financing statement or notice from the secured party by performing any payment obligation or otherwise.

(3) What constitutes receipt, as used in this section, shall be determined by the law of the State in which the buyer resides.

(h) Security agreements; identity lists; notice of identity or accounting for proceeds; violations

(1) A security agreement in which a person engaged in farming operations creates a security interest in a farm product may require the person to furnish to the secured party a list of the buyers, commission merchants, and selling agents to or through whom the person engaged in farming operations may sell such farm product.

(2) If a security agreement contains a provision described in paragraph (1) and such person engaged in farming operations sells the farm product collateral to a buyer or through a commission merchant or selling agent not included on such list, the person engaged in farming operations shall be subject to paragraph (3) unless the person—

(A) has notified the secured party in writing of the identity of the buyer, commission merchant, or selling agent at least 7 days prior to such sale; or

(B) has accounted to the secured party for the proceeds of such sale not later than 10 days after such sale.

(3) A person violating paragraph (2) shall be fined $5,000 or 15 per centum of the value or benefit received for such farm product described in the security agreement, whichever is greater.

(i) Regulations

The Secretary of Agriculture shall prescribe regulations not later than 90 days after December 23, 1985, to aid States in the implementation and management of a central filing system.

(j) Effective date

This section shall become effective 12 months after December 23, 1985.

(Pub.L. 99–198, Title XIII, § 1324, Dec. 23, 1985, 99 Stat. 1535; Pub.L. 104–127, Title VI, § 662, Apr. 4, 1996, 110 Stat. 1107; Pub.L. 107–171, Title X, § 10604, May 13, 2002, 116 Stat. 512; Pub.L. 108–447, Div. A, Title VII, § 776, Dec, 8, 2004, 118 Stat. 2849; Pub.L. 110–234, Title XIV, § 14215, May 22, 2008, 122 Stat. 1466; Pub.L. 110–246, § 4(a), Title XIV, § 14215, June 18, 2008, 122 Stat. 1664, 2228.)

CHECK CLEARING
FOR THE 21ST CENTURY ACT
(CHECK 21 ACT)

---

12 U.S.C.A. §§ 5001–5018

Current through March 30, 2016; P.L. 114–141

For updates, see http://uscode.house.gov

---

§ 5001.   Findings; purposes

(a)   Findings

The Congress finds as follows:

(1)   In the Expedited Funds Availability Act, enacted on August 10, 1987 [12 U.S.C.A. § 4001 et seq.], the Congress directed the Board of Governors of the Federal Reserve System to consider establishing regulations requiring Federal reserve banks and depository institutions to provide for check truncation, in order to improve the check processing system.

(2)   In that same Act, the Congress—

(A)   provided the Board of Governors of the Federal Reserve System with full authority to regulate all aspects of the payment system, including the receipt, payment, collection, and clearing of checks, and related functions of the payment system pertaining to checks; and

(B)   directed that the exercise of such authority by the Board superseded any State law, including the Uniform Commercial Code, as in effect in any State.

(3)   Check truncation is no less desirable in 2003 for both financial service customers and the financial services industry, to reduce costs, improve efficiency in check collections, and expedite funds

1315

availability for customers than it was over 15 years ago when Congress first directed the Board to consider establishing such a process.

(b) Purposes

The purposes of this chapter are as follows:

(1) To facilitate check truncation by authorizing substitute checks.

(2) To foster innovation in the check collection system without mandating receipt of checks in electronic form.

(3) To improve the overall efficiency of the Nation's payments system.

§ 5002.   Definitions

For purposes of this chapter, the following definitions shall apply:

(1) Account

The term "account" means a deposit account at a bank.

(2) Bank

The term "bank" means any person that is located in a State and engaged in the business of banking and includes—

(A) any depository institution (as defined in section 461 (b)(1)(A) of this title);

(B) any Federal reserve bank;

(C) any Federal home loan bank; or

(D) to the extent it acts as a payor—

(i) the Treasury of the United States;

(ii) the United States Postal Service;

(iii) a State government; or

(iv) a unit of general local government (as defined in section 4001(24) of this title).

(3) Banking terms

(A) Collecting bank

The term "collecting bank" means any bank handling a check for collection except the paying bank.

(B) Depositary bank

The term "depositary bank" means—

(i) the first bank to which a check is transferred, even if such bank is also the paying bank or the payee; or

(ii) a bank to which a check is transferred for deposit in an account at such bank, even if the check is physically received and indorsed first by another bank.

(C) Paying bank

The term "paying bank" means—

(i) the bank by which a check is payable, unless the check is payable at or through another bank and is sent to the other bank for payment or collection; or

(ii) the bank at or through which a check is payable and to which the check is sent for payment or collection.

(D) Returning bank

(i) In general

The term "returning bank" means a bank (other than the paying or depositary bank) handling a returned check or notice in lieu of return.

(ii) Treatment as collecting bank

No provision of this chapter shall be construed as affecting the treatment of a returning bank as a collecting bank for purposes of section 4–202(b) of the Uniform Commercial Code.

(4) Board

The term "Board" means the Board of Governors of the Federal Reserve System.

(5) Business day

The term "business day" has the same meaning as in section 4001(3) of this title.

(6) Check

The term "check"—

(A) means a draft, payable on demand and drawn on or payable through or at an office of a bank, whether or not negotiable, that is handled for forward collection or return, including a substitute check and a travelers check; and

(B) does not include a noncash item or an item payable in a medium other than United States dollars.

(7) Consumer

The term "consumer" means an individual who—

(A) with respect to a check handled for forward collection, draws the check on a consumer account; or

(B) with respect to a check handled for return, deposits the check into, or cashes the check against, a consumer account.

(8) Consumer account

The term "consumer account" has the same meaning as in section 4001(10) of this title.

(9) Customer

The term "customer" means a person having an account with a bank.

(10) Forward collection

The term "forward collection" means the transfer by a bank of a check to a collecting bank for settlement or the paying bank for payment.

(11) Indemnifying bank

The term "indemnifying bank" means a bank that is providing an indemnity under section 5005 of this title with respect to a substitute check.

(12) MICR line

The terms "MICR line" and "magnetic ink character recognition line" mean the numbers, which may include the bank routing number, account number, check number, check amount, and other information, that are printed near the bottom of a check in magnetic ink in accordance with generally applicable industry standards.

(13) Noncash item

The term "noncash item" has the same meaning as in section 4001(14) of this title.

(14) Person

The term "person" means a natural person, corporation, unincorporated company, partnership, government unit or instrumentality, trust, or any other entity or organization.

(15) Reconverting bank

The term "reconverting bank" means—

(A)　the bank that creates a substitute check; or

(B)　if a substitute check is created by a person other than a bank, the first bank that transfers or presents such substitute check.

(16) Substitute check

The term "substitute check" means a paper reproduction of the original check that—

(A)　contains an image of the front and back of the original check;

(B)　bears a MICR line containing all the information appearing on the MICR line of the original check, except as provided under generally applicable industry standards for substitute checks to facilitate the processing of substitute checks;

(C)　conforms, in paper stock, dimension, and otherwise, with generally applicable industry standards for substitute checks; and

(D)　is suitable for automated processing in the same manner as the original check.

(17) State

The term "State" has the same meaning as in 1813(a) of this title.

(18) Truncate

The term "truncate" means to remove an original paper check from the check collection or return process and send to a recipient, in lieu of such original paper check, a substitute check or, by agreement, information relating to the original check (including data taken from the MICR line of the original check or an electronic image of the original check), whether with or without subsequent delivery of the original paper check.

(19) Uniform Commercial Code

The term "Uniform Commercial Code" means the Uniform Commercial Code in effect in a State.

(20) Other terms

Unless the context requires otherwise, the terms not defined in this section shall have the same meanings as in the Uniform Commercial Code.

§ 5003.　　　　General provisions governing substitute checks

(a)　No agreement required

A person may deposit, present, or send for collection or return a substitute check without an agreement with the recipient, so long as a bank has made the warranties in section 5004 of this title with respect to such substitute check.

(b)　Legal equivalence

A substitute check shall be the legal equivalent of the original check for all purposes, including any provision of any Federal or State law, and for all persons if the substitute check—

(1)　accurately represents all of the information on the front and back of the original check as of the time the original check was truncated; and

(2)　bears the legend: "This is a legal copy of your check. You can use it the same way you would use the original check."

(c) Endorsements

A bank shall ensure that the substitute check for which the bank is the reconverting bank bears all endorsements applied by parties that previously handled the check (whether in electronic form or in the form of the original paper check or a substitute check) for forward collection or return.

(d) Identification of reconverting bank

A bank shall identify itself as a reconverting bank on any substitute check for which the bank is a reconverting bank so as to preserve any previous reconverting bank identifications in conformance with generally applicable industry standards.

(e) Applicable law

A substitute check that is the legal equivalent of the original check under subsection (b) of this section shall be subject to any provision, including any provision relating to the protection of customers, of part 229 of title 12 of the Code of Federal Regulations, the Uniform Commercial Code, and any other applicable Federal or State law as if such substitute check were the original check, to the extent such provision of law is not inconsistent with this chapter.

§ 5004.   Substitute check warranties

A bank that transfers, presents, or returns a substitute check and receives consideration for the check warrants, as a matter of law, to the transferee, any subsequent collecting or returning bank, the depositary bank, the drawee, the drawer, the payee, the depositor, and any endorser (regardless of whether the warrantee receives the substitute check or another paper or electronic form of the substitute check or original check) that—

> (1)   the substitute check meets all the requirements for legal equivalence under section 5003(b) of this title; and

> (2)   no depositary bank, drawee, drawer, or endorser will receive presentment or return of the substitute check, the original check, or a copy or other paper or electronic version of the substitute check or original check such that the bank, drawee, drawer, or endorser will be asked to make a payment based on a check that the bank, drawee, drawer, or endorser has already paid.

§ 5005.   Indemnity

(a) Indemnity

A reconverting bank and each bank that subsequently transfers, presents, or returns a substitute check in any electronic or paper form, and receives consideration for such transfer, presentment, or return shall indemnify the transferee, any subsequent collecting or returning bank, the depositary bank, the drawee, the drawer, the payee, the depositor, and any endorser, up to the amount described in subsections (b) and (c) of this section, as applicable, to the extent of any loss incurred by any recipient of a substitute check if that loss occurred due to the receipt of a substitute check instead of the original check.

(b) Indemnity amount

(1) Amount in event of breach of warranty

The amount of the indemnity under subsection (a) of this section shall be the amount of any loss (including costs and reasonable attorney's fees and other expenses of representation) proximately caused by a breach of a warranty provided under section 5004 of this title.

(2) Amount in absence of breach of warranty

In the absence of a breach of a warranty provided under section 5004 of this title, the amount of the indemnity under subsection (a) of this section shall be the sum of—

> (A)   the amount of any loss, up to the amount of the substitute check; and

(B) interest and expenses (including costs and reasonable attorney's fees and other expenses of representation).

(c) Comparative negligence

(1) In general

If a loss described in subsection (a) of this section results in whole or in part from the negligence or failure to act in good faith on the part of an indemnified party, then that party's indemnification under this section shall be reduced in proportion to the amount of negligence or bad faith attributable to that party.

(2) Rule of construction

Nothing in this subsection reduces the rights of a consumer or any other person under the Uniform Commercial Code or other applicable provision of Federal or State law.

(d) Effect of producing original check or copy

(1) In general

If the indemnifying bank produces the original check or a copy of the original check (including an image or a substitute check) that accurately represents all of the information on the front and back of the original check (as of the time the original check was truncated) or is otherwise sufficient to determine whether or not a claim is valid, the indemnifying bank shall—

(A) be liable under this section only for losses covered by the indemnity that are incurred up to the time that the original check or copy is provided to the indemnified party; and

(B) have a right to the return of any funds it has paid under the indemnity in excess of those losses.

(2) Coordination of indemnity with implied warranty

The production of the original check, a substitute check, or a copy under paragraph (1) by an indemnifying bank shall not absolve the bank from any liability on a warranty established under this chapter or any other provision of law.

(e) Subrogation of rights

(1) In general

Each indemnifying bank shall be subrogated to the rights of any indemnified party to the extent of the indemnity.

(2) Recovery under warranty

A bank that indemnifies a party under this section may attempt to recover from another party based on a warranty or other claim.

(3) Duty of indemnified party

Each indemnified party shall have a duty to comply with all reasonable requests for assistance from an indemnifying bank in connection with any claim the indemnifying bank brings against a warrantor or other party related to a check that forms the basis for the indemnification.

§ 5006.   Expedited recredit for consumers

(a) Recredit claims

(1) In general

A consumer may make a claim for expedited recredit from the bank that holds the account of the consumer with respect to a substitute check, if the consumer asserts in good faith that—

(A) the bank charged the consumer's account for a substitute check that was provided to the consumer;

(B) either—

    (i) the check was not properly charged to the consumer's account; or

    (ii) the consumer has a warranty claim with respect to such substitute check;

(C) the consumer suffered a resulting loss; and

(D) the production of the original check or a better copy of the original check is necessary to determine the validity of any claim described in subparagraph (B).

(2) 40-day period

Any claim under paragraph (1) with respect to a consumer account may be submitted by a consumer before the end of the 40-day period beginning on the later of—

(A) the date on which the financial institution mails or delivers, by a means agreed to by the consumer, the periodic statement of account for such account which contains information concerning the transaction giving rise to the claim; or

(B) the date on which the substitute check is made available to the consumer.

(3) Extension under extenuating circumstances

If the ability of the consumer to submit the claim within the 40-day period under paragraph (2) is delayed due to extenuating circumstances, including extended travel or the illness of the consumer, the 40-day period shall be extended by a reasonable amount of time.

(b) Procedures for claims

(1) In general

To make a claim for an expedited recredit under subsection (a) of this section with respect to a substitute check, the consumer shall provide to the bank that holds the account of such consumer—

(A) a description of the claim, including an explanation of—

    (i) why the substitute check was not properly charged to the consumer's account; or

    (ii) the warranty claim with respect to such check;

(B) a statement that the consumer suffered a loss and an estimate of the amount of the loss;

(C) the reason why production of the original check or a better copy of the original check is necessary to determine the validity of the charge to the consumer's account or the warranty claim; and

(D) sufficient information to identify the substitute check and to investigate the claim.

(2) Claim in writing

(A) In general

The bank holding the consumer account that is the subject of a claim by the consumer under subsection (a) of this section may, in the discretion of the bank, require the consumer to submit the information required under paragraph (1) in writing.

(B) Means of submission

A bank that requires a submission of information under subparagraph (A) may permit the consumer to make the submission electronically, if the consumer has agreed to communicate with the bank in that manner.

(c) Recredit to consumer

(1) Conditions for recredit

The bank shall recredit a consumer account in accordance with paragraph (2) for the amount of a substitute check that was charged against the consumer account if—

(A) a consumer submits a claim to the bank with respect to that substitute check that meets the requirement of subsection (b) of this section; and

(B) the bank has not—

(i) provided to the consumer—

(I) the original check; or

(II) a copy of the original check (including an image or a substitute check) that accurately represents all of the information on the front and back of the original check, as of the time at which the original check was truncated; and

(ii) demonstrated to the consumer that the substitute check was properly charged to the consumer account.

(2) Timing of recredit

(A) In general

The bank shall recredit the consumer's account for the amount described in paragraph (1) no later than the end of the business day following the business day on which the bank determines the consumer's claim is valid.

(B) Recredit pending investigation

If the bank has not yet determined that the consumer's claim is valid before the end of the 10th business day after the business day on which the consumer submitted the claim, the bank shall recredit the consumer's account for—

(i) the lesser of the amount of the substitute check that was charged against the consumer account, or $2,500, together with interest if the account is an interest-bearing account, no later than the end of such 10th business day; and

(ii) the remaining amount of the substitute check that was charged against the consumer account, if any, together with interest if the account is an interest-bearing account, not later than the 45th calendar day following the business day on which the consumer submits the claim.

(d) Availability of recredit

(1) Next business day availability

Except as provided in paragraph (2), a bank that provides a recredit to a consumer account under subsection (c) of this section shall make the recredited funds available for withdrawal by the consumer by the start of the next business day after the business day on which the bank recredits the consumer's account under subsection (c) of this section.

(2) Safeguard exceptions

A bank may delay availability to a consumer of a recredit provided under subsection (c)(2)(B)(i) of this section until the start of either the business day following the business day on which the bank determines that the consumer's claim is valid or the 45th calendar day following the business day on which the consumer submits a claim for such recredit in accordance with subsection (b) of this section, whichever is earlier, in any of the following circumstances:

(A) New accounts

The claim is made during the 30-day period beginning on the business day the consumer account was established.

(B) Repeated overdrafts

Without regard to the charge that is the subject of the claim for which the recredit was made—

(i) on 6 or more business days during the 6-month period ending on the date on which the consumer submits the claim, the balance in the consumer account was negative or would have become negative if checks or other charges to the account had been paid; or

(ii) on 2 or more business days during such 6-month period, the balance in the consumer account was negative or would have become negative in the amount of $5,000 or more if checks or other charges to the account had been paid.

(C) Prevention of fraud losses

The bank has reasonable cause to believe that the claim is fraudulent, based on facts (other than the fact that the check in question or the consumer is of a particular class) that would cause a well-grounded belief in the mind of a reasonable person that the claim is fraudulent.

(3) Overdraft fees

No bank that, in accordance with paragraph (2), delays the availability of a recredit under subsection (c) of this section to any consumer account may impose any overdraft fees with respect to drafts drawn by the consumer on such recredited amount before the end of the 5-day period beginning on the date notice of the delay in the availability of such amount is sent by the bank to the consumer.

(e) Reversal of recredit

A bank may reverse a recredit to a consumer account if the bank—

(1) determines that a substitute check for which the bank recredited a consumer account under subsection (c) of this section was in fact properly charged to the consumer account; and

(2) notifies the consumer in accordance with subsection (f)(3) of this section.

(f) Notice to consumer

(1) Notice if consumer claim not valid

If a bank determines that a substitute check subject to the consumer's claim was in fact properly charged to the consumer's account, the bank shall send to the consumer, no later than the business day following the business day on which the bank makes a determination—

(A) the original check or a copy of the original check (including an image or a substitute check) that—

(i) accurately represents all of the information on the front and back of the original check (as of the time the original check was truncated); or

(ii) is otherwise sufficient to determine whether or not the consumer's claim is valid; and

(B) an explanation of the basis for the determination by the bank that the substitute check was properly charged, including a statement that the consumer may request copies of any information or documents on which the bank relied in making the determination.

(2) Notice of recredit

If a bank recredits a consumer account under subsection (c) of this section, the bank shall send to the consumer, no later than the business day following the business day on which the bank makes the recredit, a notice of—

(A)   the amount of the recredit; and

(B)   the date the recredited funds will be available for withdrawal.

(3)   Notice of reversal of recredit

In addition to the notice required under paragraph (1), if a bank reverses a recredited amount under subsection (e) of this section, the bank shall send to the consumer, no later than the business day following the business day on which the bank reverses the recredit, a notice of—

(A)   the amount of the reversal; and

(B)   the date the recredit was reversed.

(4)   Mode of delivery

A notice described in this subsection shall be delivered by United States mail or by any other means through which the consumer has agreed to receive account information.

(g)   Other claims not affected

Providing a recredit in accordance with this section shall not absolve the bank from liability for a claim made under any other law, such as a claim for wrongful dishonor under the Uniform Commercial Code, or from liability for additional damages under section 5005 or 5009 of this title.

(h)   Clarification concerning consumer possession

A consumer who was provided a substitute check may make a claim for an expedited recredit under this section with regard to a transaction involving the substitute check whether or not the consumer is in possession of the substitute check.

(i)   Scope of application

This section shall only apply to customers who are consumers.

§ 5007.   Expedited recredit procedures for banks

(a)   Recredit claims

(1)   In general

A bank may make a claim against an indemnifying bank for expedited recredit for which that bank is indemnified if—

(A)   the claimant bank (or a bank that the claimant bank has indemnified) has received a claim for expedited recredit from a consumer under section 5006 of this title with respect to a substitute check or would have been subject to such a claim had the consumer's account been charged;

(B)   the claimant bank has suffered a resulting loss or is obligated to recredit a consumer account under section 5006 of this title with respect to such substitute check; and

(C)   production of the original check, another substitute check, or a better copy of the original check is necessary to determine the validity of the charge to the customer account or any warranty claim connected with such substitute check.

(2)   120-day period

Any claim under paragraph (1) may be submitted by the claimant bank to an indemnifying bank before the end of the 120-day period beginning on the date of the transaction that gave rise to the claim.

(b) Procedures for claims

(1) In general

To make a claim under subsection (a) of this section for an expedited recredit relating to a substitute check, the claimant bank shall send to the indemnifying bank—

(A) a description of—

(i) the claim, including an explanation of why the substitute check cannot be properly charged to the consumer account; or

(ii) the warranty claim;

(B) a statement that the claimant bank has suffered a loss or is obligated to recredit the consumer's account under section 5006 of this title, together with an estimate of the amount of the loss or recredit;

(C) the reason why production of the original check, another substitute check, or a better copy of the original check is necessary to determine the validity of the charge to the consumer account or the warranty claim; and

(D) information sufficient for the indemnifying bank to identify the substitute check and to investigate the claim.

(2) Requirements relating to copies of substitute checks

If the information submitted by a claimant bank pursuant to paragraph (1) in connection with a claim for an expedited recredit includes a copy of any substitute check for which any such claim is made, the claimant bank shall take reasonable steps to ensure that any such copy cannot be—

(A) mistaken for the legal equivalent of the check under section 5003(b) of this title; or

(B) sent or handled by any bank, including the indemnifying bank, as a forward collection or returned check.

(3) Claim in writing

(A) In general

An indemnifying bank may, in the discretion of the bank, require the claimant bank to submit the information required by paragraph (1) in writing, including a copy of the written or electronically submitted claim, if any, that the consumer provided in accordance with section 5006(b) of this title.

(B) Means of submission

An indemnifying bank that requires a submission of information under subparagraph (A) may permit the claimant bank to make the submission electronically, if the claimant bank has agreed to communicate with the indemnifying bank in that manner.

(c) Recredit by indemnifying bank

(1) Prompt action required

No later than 10 business days after the business day on which an indemnifying bank receives a claim under subsection (a) of this section from a claimant bank with respect to a substitute check, the indemnifying bank shall—

(A) provide, to the claimant bank, the original check (with respect to such substitute check) or a copy of the original check (including an image or a substitute check) that—

(i) accurately represents all of the information on the front and back of the original check (as of the time the original check was truncated); or

(ii) is otherwise sufficient to determine the bank's claim is not valid; and

(B) recredit the claimant bank for the amount of the claim up to the amount of the substitute check, plus interest if applicable; or

(C) provide information to the claimant bank as to why the indemnifying bank is not obligated to comply with subparagraph (A) or (B).

(2) Recredit does not abrogate other liabilities

Providing a recredit under this subsection to a claimant bank with respect to a substitute check shall not absolve the indemnifying bank from liability for claims brought under any other law or from additional damages under section 5005 or 5009 of this title with respect to such check.

(3) Refund to indemnifying bank

If a claimant bank reverses, in accordance with section 5006(e) of this title, a recredit previously made to a consumer account under section 5006(c) of this title, or otherwise receives a credit or recredit with regard to such substitute check, the claimant bank shall promptly refund to any indemnifying bank any amount previously advanced by the indemnifying bank in connection with such substitute check.

(d) Production of original check or a sufficient copy governed by section 5005(d) of this title

If the indemnifying bank provides the claimant bank with the original check or a copy of the original check (including an image or a substitute check) under subsection (c)(1)(A) of this section, section 5005(d) of this title shall govern any right of the indemnifying bank to any repayment of any funds the indemnifying bank has recredited to the claimant bank pursuant to subsection (c) of this section.

§ 5008.   Delays in an emergency

A delay by a bank beyond the time limits prescribed or permitted by this chapter shall be excused if the delay is caused by interruption of communication or computer facilities, suspension of payments by another bank, war, emergency conditions, failure of equipment, or other circumstances beyond the control of a bank and if the bank uses such diligence as the circumstances require.

§ 5009.   Measure of damages

(a) Liability

(1) In general

Except as provided in section 5005 of this title, any person who, in connection with a substitute check, breaches any warranty under this chapter or fails to comply with any requirement imposed by, or regulation prescribed pursuant to, this chapter with respect to any other person shall be liable to such person in an amount equal to the sum of—

(A) the lesser of—

(i) the amount of the loss suffered by the other person as a result of the breach or failure; or

(ii) the amount of the substitute check; and

(B) interest and expenses (including costs and reasonable attorney's fees and other expenses of representation) related to the substitute check.

(2) Offset of recredits

The amount of damages any person receives under paragraph (1), if any, shall be reduced by the amount, if any, that the claimant receives and retains as a recredit under section 5006 or 5007 of this title.

(b) Comparative negligence

(1) In general

If a person incurs damages that resulted in whole or in part from the negligence or failure of that person to act in good faith, then the amount of any liability due to that person under subsection (a) of this section shall be reduced in proportion to the amount of negligence or bad faith attributable to that person.

(2) Rule of construction

Nothing in this subsection reduces the rights of a consumer or any other person under the Uniform Commercial Code or other applicable provision of Federal or State law.

§ 5010. Statute of limitations and notice of claim

(a) Actions under this chapter

(1) In general

An action to enforce a claim under this chapter may be brought in any United States district court, or in any other court of competent jurisdiction, before the end of the 1-year period beginning on the date the cause of action accrues.

(2) Accrual

A cause of action accrues as of the date the injured party first learns, or by which such person reasonably should have learned, of the facts and circumstances giving rise to the cause of action.

(b) Discharge of claims

Except as provided in subsection (c) of this section, unless a person gives notice of a claim to the indemnifying or warranting bank within 30 days after the person has reason to know of the claim and the identity of the indemnifying or warranting bank, the indemnifying or warranting bank is discharged from liability in an action to enforce a claim under this chapter to the extent of any loss caused by the delay in giving notice of the claim.

(c) Notice of claim by consumer

A timely claim by a consumer under section 5006 of this title for expedited recredit constitutes timely notice of a claim by the consumer for purposes of subsection (b) of this section.

§ 5011. Consumer awareness

(a) In general

Each bank shall provide, in accordance with subsection (b) of this section, a brief notice about substitute checks that describes—

(1) how a substitute check is the legal equivalent of an original check for all purposes, including any provision of any Federal or State law, and for all persons, if the substitute check—

(A) accurately represents all of the information on the front and back of the original check as of the time at which the original check was truncated; and

(B) bears the legend: "This is a legal copy of your check. You can use it in the same way you would use the original check."; and

(2) the consumer recredit rights established under section 5006 of this title when a consumer believes in good faith that a substitute check was not properly charged to the account of the consumer.

(b) Distribution

(1) Existing customers

With respect to consumers who are customers of a bank on the effective date of this chapter and who receive original checks or substitute checks, a bank shall provide the notice described in subsection (a) of this section to each such consumer no later than the first regularly scheduled communication with the consumer after the effective date of this chapter.

(2) New account holders

A bank shall provide the notice described in subsection (a) of this section to each consumer who will receive original checks or substitute checks, other than existing customers referred to in paragraph (1), at the time at which the customer relationship is initiated.

(3) Mode of delivery

A bank may send the notices required by this subsection by United States mail or by any other means through which the consumer has agreed to receive account information.

(4) Consumers who request copies of checks

Notice shall be provided to each consumer of the bank that requests a copy of a check and receives a substitute check, at the time of the request.

(c) Model language

(1) In general

Before the end of the 9-month period beginning on October 28, 2003, the Board shall publish model forms and clauses that a bank may use to describe each of the elements required by subsection (a) of this section.

(2) Safe harbor

(A) In general

A bank shall be treated as being in compliance with the requirements of subsection (a) of this section if the bank's substitute check notice uses a model form or clause published by the Board and such model form or clause accurately describes the bank's policies and practices.

(B) Deletion or rearrangement

A bank may delete any information in the model form or clause that is not required by this chapter or rearrange the format.

(3) Use of model language not required

This section shall not be construed as requiring any bank to use a model form or clause that the Board prepares under this subsection.

§ 5012.   Effect on other law

This chapter shall supersede any provision of Federal or State law, including the Uniform Commercial Code, that is inconsistent with this chapter, but only to the extent of the inconsistency.

§ 5013.   Variation by agreement

(a) Section 5007 of this title.

Any provision of section 5007 of this title may be varied by agreement of the banks involved.

(b) No other provisions may be varied

Except as provided in subsection (a) of this section, no provision of this chapter may be varied by agreement of any person or persons.

§ 5014.   Regulations

The Board may prescribe such regulations as the Board determines to be necessary to implement, prevent circumvention or evasion of, or facilitate compliance with the provisions of this chapter.

§ 5015.   Study and report on funds availability

(a) Study

In order to evaluate the implementation and the impact of this chapter, the Board shall conduct a study of—

(1)   the percentage of total checks cleared in which the paper check is not returned to the paying bank;

(2)   the extent to which banks make funds available to consumers for local and nonlocal checks prior to the expiration of maximum hold periods;

(3)   the length of time within which depositary banks learn of the nonpayment of local and nonlocal checks;

(4)   the increase or decrease in check-related losses over the study period; and

(5)   the appropriateness of the time periods and amount limits applicable under sections 4002 and 4003 of this title, as in effect on October 28, 2003.

(b) Report to Congress

Before the end of the 30-month period beginning on the effective date of this chapter, the Board shall submit a report to the Congress containing the results of the study conducted under this section, together with recommendations for legislative action.

§ 5016.   Statistical reporting of costs and revenues for transporting checks between reserve banks

In the annual report prepared by the Board for the first full calendar year after October 28, 2003 and in each of the 9 subsequent annual reports by the Board, the Board shall include the amount of operating costs attributable to, and an estimate of the Federal Reserve banks' imputed revenues derived from, the transportation of commercial checks between Federal Reserve bank check processing centers.

§ 5017.   Evaluation and report by the comptroller general

(a) Study

During the 5-year period beginning on October 28, 2003, the Comptroller General of the United States shall evaluate the implementation and administration of this chapter, including—

(1)   an estimate of the gains in economic efficiency made possible from check truncation;

(2)   an evaluation of the benefits accruing to consumers and financial institutions from reduced transportation costs, longer hours for accepting deposits for credit within 1 business day, the impact of fraud losses, and an estimate of consumers' share of the total benefits derived from this chapter; and

(3)   an assessment of consumer acceptance of the check truncation process resulting from this chapter, as well as any new costs incurred by consumers who had their original checks returned with their regular monthly statements prior to October 28, 2003.

(b) Report to Congress

Before the end of the 5-year period referred to in subsection (a) of this section, the Comptroller General shall submit a report to the Congress containing the findings and conclusions of the Comptroller General in connection with the evaluation conducted pursuant to subsection (a) of this section, together with such recommendations for legislative and administrative action as the Comptroller General may determine to be appropriate.

§ 5018.   Depositary services efficiency and cost reduction

(a)   Findings

The Congress finds as follows:

(1)   The Secretary of the Treasury has long compensated financial institutions for various critical depositary and financial agency services provided for or on behalf of the United States by—

     (A)   placing large balances, commonly referred to as "compensating balances", on deposit at such institutions; and

     (B)   using imputed interest on such funds to offset charges for the various depositary and financial agency services provided to or on behalf of the Government.

(2)   As a result of sharp declines in interest rates over the last few years to record low levels, or the public debt outstanding reaching the statutory debt limit, the Department of the Treasury often has had to dramatically increase or decrease the size of the compensating balances on deposit at these financial institutions.

(3)   The fluctuation of the compensating balances, and the necessary pledging of collateral by financial institutions to secure the value of compensating balances placed with those institutions, have created unintended financial uncertainty for the Secretary of the Treasury and for the management by financial institutions of their cash and securities.

(4)   It is imperative that the process for providing financial services to the Government be transparent, and provide the information necessary for the Congress to effectively exercise its appropriation and oversight responsibilities.

(5)   The use of direct payment for services rendered would strengthen cash and debt management responsibilities of the Secretary of the Treasury because the Secretary would no longer need to dramatically increase or decrease the level of such balances when interest rates fluctuate sharply or when the public debt outstanding reaches the statutory debt limit.

(6)   An alternative to the use of compensating balances, such as direct payments to financial institutions, would ensure that payments to financial institutions for the services they provide would be made in a more predictable manner and could result in cost savings.

(7)   Limiting the use of compensating balances could result in a more direct and cost-efficient method of obtaining those services currently provided under compensating balance arrangements.

(8)   A transition from the use of compensating balances to another compensation method must be carefully managed to prevent higher-than-necessary transitional costs and enable participating financial institutions to modify their planned investment of cash and securities.

(b)   Authorization of appropriations for services rendered by depositaries and financial agencies of the United States

There are authorized to be appropriated for fiscal years beginning after fiscal year 2003 to the Secretary of the Treasury such sums as may be necessary for reimbursing financial institutions in their capacity as depositaries and financial agents of the United States for all services required or directed by the Secretary of the Treasury, or a designee of the Secretary, to be performed by such financial institutions on behalf of the Secretary of the Treasury or another Federal agency, including services rendered before fiscal year 2004.

(c)   Orderly transition

(1)   In general

As appropriations authorized in subsection (b) of this section become available, the Secretary of the Treasury shall promptly begin the process of phasing in the use of the appropriations to pay financial institutions serving as depositaries and financial agents of the United States, and transitioning from the use of compensating balances to fund these services.

(2) Post-transition use limited to extraordinary circumstances

(A) In general

Following the transition to the use of the appropriations authorized in subsection (b) of this section, the Secretary of the Treasury may use the compensating balances to pay financial institutions serving as depositaries and financial agents of the United States only in extraordinary situations where the Secretary determines that they are needed to ensure the fiscal operations of the Government continue to function in an efficient and effective manner.

(B) Report

Any use of compensating balances pursuant to subparagraph (A) shall promptly be reported by the Secretary of the Treasury to the Committee on Financial Services of the House of Representatives and the Committee on Banking, Housing, and Urban Affairs of the Senate.

(3) Requirements for orderly transition

In transitioning to the use of the appropriations authorized in subsection (b) of this section, the Secretary of the Treasury shall take such steps as may be appropriate to—

(A) prevent abrupt financial disruption to the functions of the Department of the Treasury or to the participating financial institutions; and

(B) maintain adequate accounting and management controls to ensure that payments to financial institutions for their banking services provided to the Government as depositaries and financial agents are accurate and that the arrangements last no longer than is necessary.

(4) Reports required

(A) Annual report

(i) In general

For each fiscal year, the Secretary of the Treasury shall submit a report to the Congress on the use of compensating balances and on the use of appropriations authorized in subsection (b) of this section during that fiscal year.

(ii) Inclusion in budget

The report required under clause (i) may be submitted as part of the budget submitted by the President under section 1105 of Title 31 for the following fiscal year and if so, the report shall be submitted concurrently to the Committee on Financial Services of the House of Representatives and the Committee on Banking, Housing, and Urban Affairs of the Senate.

(B) Final report following transition

(i) In general

Following completion of the transition from the use of compensating balances to the use of the appropriations authorized in subsection (b) of this section to pay financial institutions for their services as depositaries and financial agents of the United States, the Secretary of the Treasury shall submit a report on the transition to the Committee on Financial Services of the House of Representatives and the Committee on Banking, Housing, and Urban Affairs of the Senate.

(ii) Contents of report

The report submitted under clause (i) shall include a detailed analysis of—

(I) the cost of transition;

(II) the direct costs of the services being paid from the appropriations authorized in subsection (b) of this section; and

        (III) the benefits realized from the use of direct payment for such services, rather than the use of compensating balance arrangements.

(d)   Omitted

(e)   Effective date

Notwithstanding section 20, this section shall take effect on October 28, 2003.

    (Pub.L. 108–100, § 4, Oct. 28, 2003, 117 Stat. 1180.)

EXPEDITED FUNDS AVAILABILITY ACT

12 U.S.C.A. §§ 4001–4010

Current through March 13, 2016; P.L. 114–133

For updates, see http://uscode.house.gov

---

§ 4001.   Definitions

For purposes of this chapter—

(1)   Account

The term "account" means a demand deposit account or other similar transaction account at a depository institution.

(2)   Board

The term "Board" means the Board of Governors of the Federal Reserve System.

(3)   Business day

The term "business day" means any day other than a Saturday, Sunday, or legal holiday.

(4)   Cash

The term "cash" means United States coins and currency, including Federal Reserve notes.

(5)   Cashier's check

The term "cashier's check" means any check which—

    (A)   is drawn on a depository institution;

    (B)   is signed by an officer or employee of such depository institution; and

    (C)   is a direct obligation of such depository institution.

(6)   Certified check

The term "certified check" means any check with respect to which a depository institution certifies that—

    (A)   the signature on the check is genuine; and

    (B)   such depository institution has set aside funds which—

        (i)   are equal to the amount of the check; and

1333

    (ii)　will be used only to pay such check.

(7)　Check

The term "check" means any negotiable demand draft drawn on or payable through an office of a depository institution located in the United States. Such term does not include noncash items.

(8)　Check clearinghouse association

The term "check clearinghouse association" means any arrangement by which participant depository institutions exchange deposited checks on a local basis, including an entire metropolitan area, without using the check processing facilities of the Federal Reserve System.

(9)　Check processing region

The term "check processing region" means the geographical area served by a Federal Reserve bank check processing center or such larger area as the Board may prescribe by regulations.

(10)　Consumer account

The term "consumer account" means any account used primarily for personal, family, or household purposes.

(11)　Depository check

The term "depository check" means any cashier's check, certified check, teller's check, and any other functionally equivalent instrument as determined by the Board.

(12)　Depository institution

The term "depository institution" has the meaning given such term in clauses (i) through (vi) of section 461(b)(1)(A) of this title. Such term also includes an office, branch, or agency of a foreign bank located in the United States.

(13)　Local originating depository institution

The term "local originating depository institution" means any originating depository institution which is located in the same check processing region as the receiving depository institution.

(14)　Noncash item

The term "noncash item" means—

    (A)　a check or other demand item to which a passbook, certificate, or other document is attached;

    (B)　a check or other demand item which is accompanied by special instructions, such as a request for special advise of payment or dishonor; or

    (C)　any similar item which is otherwise classified as a noncash item in regulations of the Board.

(15)　Nonlocal originating depository institution

The term "nonlocal originating depository institution" means any originating depository institution which is not a local depository institution.

(16)　Proprietary ATM

The term "proprietary ATM" means an automated teller machine which is—

    (A)　located—

        (i)　at or adjacent to a branch of the receiving depository institution; or

        (ii)　in close proximity, as defined by the Board, to a branch of the receiving depository institution; or

    (B)　owned by, operated exclusively for, or operated by the receiving depository institution.

(17) Originating depository institution

The term "originating depository institution" means the branch of a depository institution on which a check is drawn.

(18) Nonproprietary ATM

The term "nonproprietary ATM" means an automated teller machine which is not a proprietary ATM.

(19) Participant

The term "participant" means a depository institution which—

(A) is located in the same geographic area as that served by a check clearinghouse association; and

(B) exchanges checks through the check clearinghouse association, either directly or through an intermediary.

(20) Receiving depository institution

The term "receiving depository institution" means the branch of a depository institution or the proprietary ATM in which a check is first deposited.

(21) State

The term "State" means any State, the District of Columbia, the Commonwealth of Puerto Rico, or the Virgin Islands.

(22) Teller's check

The term "teller's check" means any check issued by a depository institution and drawn on another depository institution.

(23) United States

The term "United States" means the several States, the District of Columbia, the Commonwealth of Puerto Rico, and the Virgin Islands.

(24) Unit of general local government

The term "unit of general local government" means any city, county, town, township, parish, village, or other general purpose political subdivision of a State.

(25) Wire transfer

The term "wire transfer" has such meaning as the Board shall prescribe by regulations.

(Pub.L. 100–86, Title VI, § 602, Aug. 10, 1987, 101 Stat. 635.)

§ 4002. Expedited funds availability schedules

(a) Next business day availability for certain deposits

(1) Cash deposits; wire transfers

Except as provided in subsection (e) of this section and in section 4003 of this title, in any case in which—

(A) any cash is deposited in an account at a receiving depository institution staffed by individuals employed by such institution, or

(B) funds are received by a depository institution by wire transfer for deposit in an account at such institution,

such cash or funds shall be available for withdrawal not later than the business day after the business day on which such cash is deposited or such funds are received for deposit.

(2) Government checks; certain other checks

Funds deposited in an account at a depository institution by check shall be available for withdrawal not later than the business day after the business day on which such funds are deposited in the case of—

(A) a check which—

(i) is drawn on the Treasury of the United States; and

(ii) is endorsed only by the person to whom it was issued;

(B) a check which—

(i) is drawn by a State;

(ii) is deposited in a receiving depository institution which is located in such State and is staffed by individuals employed by such institution;

(iii) is deposited with a special deposit slip which indicates it is a check drawn by a State; and

(iv) is endorsed only by the person to whom it was issued;

(C) a check which—

(i) is drawn by a unit of general local government;

(ii) is deposited in a receiving depository institution which is located in the same State as such unit of general local government and is staffed by individuals employed by such institution;

(iii) is deposited with a special deposit slip which indicates it is a check drawn by a unit of general local government; and

(iv) is endorsed only by the person to whom it was issued;

(D) the first $200 deposited by check or checks on any one business day;

(E) a check deposited in a branch of a depository institution and drawn on the same or another branch of the same depository institution if both such branches are located in the same State or the same check processing region;

(F) a cashier's check, certified check, teller's check, or depository check which—

(i) is deposited in a receiving depository institution which is staffed by individuals employed by such institution;

(ii) is deposited with a special deposit slip which indicates it is a cashier's check, certified check, teller's check, or depository check, as the case may be; and

(iii) is endorsed only by the person to whom it was issued.

(b) Permanent schedule

(1) Availability of funds deposited by local checks

Subject to paragraph (3) of this subsection, subsections (a)(2), (d), and (e) of this section, and section 4003 of this title, not more than 1 business day shall intervene between the business day on which funds are deposited in an account at a depository institution by a check drawn on a local originating depository institution and the business day on which the funds involved are available for withdrawal.

(2) Availability of funds deposited by nonlocal checks

Subject to paragraph (3) of this subsection, subsections (a)(2), (d), and (e) of this section, and section 4003 of this title, not more than 4 business days shall intervene between the business day on which funds are deposited in an account at a depository institution by a check drawn on a nonlocal originating depository institution and the business day on which such funds are available for withdrawal.

(3) Time period adjustments for cash withdrawal of certain checks

(A) In general

Except as provided in subparagraph (B), funds deposited in an account in a depository institution by check (other than a check described in subsection (a)(2) of this section) shall be available for cash withdrawal not later than the business day after the business day on which such funds otherwise are available under paragraph (1) or (2).

(B) 5 p.m. cash availability

Not more than $400 (or the maximum amount allowable in the case of a withdrawal from an automated teller machine but not more than $400) of funds deposited by one or more checks to which this paragraph applies shall be available for cash withdrawal not later than 5 o'clock post meridian of the business day on which such funds are available under paragraph (1) or (2). If funds deposited by checks described in both paragraph (1) and paragraph (2) become available for cash withdrawal under this paragraph on the same business day, the limitation contained in this subparagraph shall apply to the aggregate amount of such funds.

(C) $200 availability

Any amount available for withdrawal under this paragraph shall be in addition to the amount available under subsection (a)(2)(D) of this section.

(4) Applicability

This subsection shall apply with respect to funds deposited by check in an account at a depository institution on or after September 1, 1990, except that the Board may, by regulation, make this subsection or any part of this subsection applicable earlier than September 1, 1990.

(c) Temporary schedule

(1) Availability of local checks

(A) In general

Subject to subparagraph (B) of this paragraph, subsections (a)(2), (d), and (e) of this section, and section 4003 of this title, not more than 2 business days shall intervene between the business day on which funds are deposited in an account at a depository institution by a check drawn on a local originating depository institution and the business day on which such funds are available for withdrawal.

(B) Time period adjustment for cash withdrawal of certain checks

(i) In general

Except as provided in clause (ii), funds deposited in an account in a depository institution by check drawn on a local depository institution that is not a participant in the same check clearinghouse association as the receiving depository institution (other than a check described in subsection (a)(2) of this section) shall be available for cash withdrawal not later than the business day after the business day on which such funds otherwise are available under subparagraph (A).

(ii) 5 p.m. cash availability

Not more than $400 (or the maximum amount allowable in the case of a withdrawal from an automated teller machine but not more than $400) of funds deposited by one or more checks to which this subparagraph applies shall be available for cash withdrawal not later than 5 o'clock post meridian of the business day on which such funds are available under subparagraph (A).

(iii) $100 availability

Any amount available for withdrawal under this subparagraph shall be in addition to the amount available under subsection (a)(2)(D) of this section.

(2) Availability of nonlocal checks

Subject to subsections (a)(2), (d), and (e) of this section and section 4003 of this title, not more than 6 business days shall intervene between the business day on which funds are deposited in an account at a depository institution by a check drawn on a nonlocal originating depository institution and the business day on which such funds are available for withdrawal.

(3) Applicability

This subsection shall apply with respect to funds deposited by check in an account at a depository institution after August 31, 1988, and before September 1, 1990, except as may be otherwise provided under subsection (b)(4) of this section.

(d) Time period adjustments

(1) Reduction generally

Notwithstanding any other provision of law, the Board, jointly with the Director of the Bureau of Consumer Financial Protection, shall, by regulation, reduce the time periods established under subsections (b), (c), and (e) of this section to as short a time as possible and equal to the period of time achievable under the improved check clearing system for a receiving depository institution to reasonably expect to learn of the nonpayment of most items for each category of checks.

(2) Extension for certain deposits in noncontiguous States or territories

Notwithstanding any other provision of law, any time period established under subsection (b), (c), or (e) of this section shall be extended by 1 business day in the case of any deposit which is both—

(A)   deposited in an account at a depository institution which is located in Alaska, Hawaii, Puerto Rico, or the Virgin Islands; and

(B)   deposited by a check drawn on an originating depository institution which is not located in the same State, commonwealth, or territory as the receiving depository institution.

(e) Deposits at ATM

(1) Nonproprietary ATM

(A) In general

Not more than 4 business days shall intervene between the business day a deposit described in subparagraph (B) is made at a nonproprietary automated teller machine (for deposit in an account at a depository institution) and the business day on which funds from such deposit are available for withdrawal.

(B) Deposits described in this paragraph[1]

A deposit is described in this subparagraph if it is—

(i)   a cash deposit;

(ii)   a deposit made by a check described in subsection (a)(2) of this section;

(iii)   a deposit made by a check drawn on a local originating depository institution (other than a check described in subsection (a)(2) of this section); or

(iv)   a deposit made by a check drawn on a nonlocal originating depository institution (other than a check described in subsection (a)(2) of this section).

---

[1]   So in original. Probably should be "subparagraph".

(2) Proprietary ATM—temporary and permanent schedules

The provisions of subsections (a), (b), and (c) of this section shall apply with respect to any funds deposited at a proprietary automated teller machine for deposit in an account at a depository institution.

(3) Study and report on ATM's

The Board shall, either directly or through the Consumer Advisory Council, establish and maintain a dialogue with depository institutions and their suppliers on the computer software and hardware available for use by automated teller machines, and shall, not later than September 1 of each of the first 3 calendar years beginning after August 10, 1987, report to the Congress regarding such software and hardware and regarding the potential for improving the processing of automated teller machine deposits.

(f) Check return; notice of nonpayment

No provision of this section shall be construed as requiring that, with respect to all checks deposited in a receiving depository institution—

(1) such checks be physically returned to such depository institution; or

(2) any notice of nonpayment of any such check be given to such depository institution within the times set forth in subsection (a), (b), (c), or (e) of this section or in the regulations issued under any such subsection.

(Pub.L. 100–86, Title VI, § 603, Aug. 10, 1987, 101 Stat. 637; Pub.L. 101–625, Title X, § 1001, Nov. 28, 1990, 104 Stat. 4424; Pub.L. 102–242, Title II, § 227(a), (b)(1), Dec. 19, 1991, 105 Stat. 2307, 2308; Pub.L. 111–203, Title X, § 1086, July 21, 2010, 124 Stat. 2085, 2086.)

§ 4003. Safeguard exceptions

(a) New accounts

Notwithstanding section 4002 of this title, in the case of any account established at a depository institution by a new depositor, the following provisions shall apply with respect to any deposit in such account during the 30-day period (or such shorter period as the Board, jointly with the Director of the Bureau of Consumer Financial Protection, may establish) beginning on the date such account is established—

(1) Next business day availability of cash and certain items

Except as provided in paragraph (3), in the case of—

(A) any cash deposited in such account;

(B) any funds received by such depository institution by wire transfer for deposit in such account;

(C) any funds deposited in such account by cashier's check, certified check, teller's check, depository check, or traveler's check; and

(D) any funds deposited by a government check which is described in subparagraph (A), (B), or (C) of section 4002(a)(2) of this title,

such cash or funds shall be available for withdrawal on the business day after the business day on which such cash or funds are deposited or, in the case of a wire transfer, on the business day after the business day on which such funds are received for deposit.

(2) Availability of other items

In the case of any funds deposited in such account by a check (other than a check described in subparagraph (C) or (D) of paragraph (1)), the availability for withdrawal of such funds shall not be subject to the provisions of section 4002(b), 4002(c), or paragraphs[1] (1) of section 4002(e) of this title.

---

[1] So in original. Probably should be "paragraph".

(3)   Limitation relating to certain checks in excess of $5,000

In the case of funds deposited in such account during such period by checks described in subparagraph (C) or (D) of paragraph (1) the aggregate amount of which exceeds $5,000—

(A)   paragraph (1) shall apply only with respect to the first $5,000 of such aggregate amount; and

(B)   not more than 8 business days shall intervene between the business day on which any such funds are deposited and the business day on which such excess amount shall be available for withdrawal.

(b)   Large or redeposited checks; repeated overdrafts

The Board, jointly with the Director of the Bureau of Consumer Financial Protection, may, by regulation, establish reasonable exceptions to any time limitation established under subsection (a)(2), (b), (c), or (e) of section 4002 of this title for—

(1)   the amount of deposits by one or more checks that exceeds the amount of $5,000 in any one day;

(2)   checks that have been returned unpaid and redeposited; and

(3)   deposit accounts which have been overdrawn repeatedly.

(c)   Reasonable cause exception

(1)   In general

In accordance with regulations which the Board, jointly with the Director of the Bureau of Consumer Financial Protection, shall prescribe, subsections (a)(2), (b), (c), and (e) of section 4002 of this title shall not apply with respect to any check deposited in an account at a depository institution if the receiving depository institution has reasonable cause to believe that the check is uncollectible from the originating depository institution. For purposes of the preceding sentence, reasonable cause to believe requires the existence of facts which would cause a well-grounded belief in the mind of a reasonable person. Such reasons shall be included in the notice required under subsection (f) of this section.

(2)   Basis for determination

No determination under this subsection may be based on any class of checks or persons.

(3)   Overdraft fees

If the receiving depository institution determines that a check deposited in an account is a check described in paragraph (1), the receiving depository institution shall not assess any fee for any subsequent overdraft with respect to such account, if—

(A)   the depositor was not provided with the written notice required under subsection (f) of this section (with respect to such determination) at the time the deposit was made;

(B)   the overdraft would not have occurred but for the fact that the funds so deposited are not available; and

(C)   the amount of the check is collected from the originating depository institution.

(4)   Compliance

Each agency referred to in section 4009(a) of this title shall monitor compliance with the requirements of this subsection in each regular examination of a depository institution and shall describe in each report to the Congress the extent to which this subsection is being complied with. For the purpose of this paragraph, each depository institution shall retain a record of each notice provided under subsection (f) of this section as a result of the application of this subsection.

(d) Emergency conditions

Subject to such regulations as the Board, jointly with the Director of the Bureau of Consumer Financial Protection, may prescribe, subsections (a)(2), (b), (c), and (e) of section 4002 of this title shall not apply to funds deposited by check in any receiving depository institution in the case of—

(1) any interruption of communication facilities;

(2) suspension of payments by another depository institution;

(3) any war; or

(4) any emergency condition beyond the control of the receiving depository institution,

if the receiving depository institution exercises such diligence as the circumstances require.

(e) Prevention of fraud losses

(1) In general

The Board, jointly with the Director of the Bureau of Consumer Financial Protection, may, by regulation or order, suspend the applicability of this chapter, or any portion thereof, to any classification of checks if the Board, jointly with the Director of the Bureau of Consumer Financial Protection, determines that—

(A) depository institutions are experiencing an unacceptable level of losses due to check-related fraud, and

(B) suspension of this chapter, or such portion of this chapter, with regard to the classification of checks involved in such fraud is necessary to diminish the volume of such fraud.

(2) Sunset provision

No regulation prescribed or order issued under paragraph (1) shall remain in effect for more than 45 days (excluding Saturdays, Sundays, legal holidays, or any day either House of Congress is not in session).

(3) Report to Congress

(A) Notice of each suspension

Within 10 days of prescribing any regulation or issuing any order under paragraph (1), the Board, jointly with the Director of the Bureau of Consumer Financial Protection, shall transmit a report of such action to the Committee on Banking, Finance and Urban Affairs of the House of Representatives and the Committee on Banking, Housing, and Urban Affairs of the Senate.

(B) Contents of report

Each report under subparagraph (A) shall contain—

(i) the specific reason for prescribing the regulation or issuing the order;

(ii) evidence considered by the Board in making the determination under paragraph (1) with respect to such regulation or order; and

(iii) specific examples of the check-related fraud giving rise to such regulation or order.

(f) Notice of exception; availability within reasonable time

(1) In general

If any exception contained in this section (other than subsection (a) of this section) applies with respect to funds deposited in an account at a depository institution—

(A) the depository institution shall provide notice in the manner provided in paragraph (2) of—

(i) the time period within which the funds shall be made available for withdrawal; and

      (ii)   the reason the exception was invoked; and

    (B)   except where other time periods are specifically provided in this chapter, the availability of the funds deposited shall be governed by the policy of the receiving depository institution, but shall not exceed a reasonable period of time as determined by the Board, jointly with the Director of the Bureau of Consumer Financial Protection.

(2)   Time for notice

The notice required under paragraph (1)(A) with respect to a deposit to which an exception contained in this section applies shall be made by the time provided in the following subparagraphs:

    (A)   In the case of a deposit made in person by the depositor at the receiving depository institution, the depository institution shall immediately provide such notice in writing to the depositor.

    (B)   In the case of any other deposit (other than a deposit described in subparagraph (C)), the receiving depository institution shall mail the notice to the depositor not later than the close of the next business day following the business day on which the deposit is received.

    (C)   In the case of a deposit to which subsection (d) or (e) of this section applies, notice shall be provided by the depository institution in accordance with regulations of the Board, jointly with the Director of the Bureau of Consumer Financial Protection.

    (D)   In the case of a deposit to which subsection (b)(1) or (b)(2) of this section applies, the depository institution may, for nonconsumer accounts and other classes of accounts, as defined by the Board, that generally have a large number of such deposits, provide notice at or before the time it first determines that the subsection applies.

    (E)   In the case of a deposit to which subsection (b)(3) of this section applies, the depository institution may, subject to regulations of the Board, provide notice at the beginning of each time period it determines that the subsection applies. In addition to the requirements contained in paragraph (1)(A), the notice shall specify the time period for which the exception will apply.

(3)   Subsequent determinations

If the facts upon which the determination of the applicability of an exception contained in subsection (b) or (c) of this section to any deposit only become known to the receiving depository institution after the time notice is required under paragraph (2) with respect to such deposit, the depository institution shall mail such notice to the depositor as soon as practicable, but not later than the first business day following the day such facts become known to the depository institution.

(Pub.L. 100–86, Title VI, § 604, Aug. 10, 1987, 101 Stat. 637; Pub.L. 102–242, Title II, § 225, 227(b)(2), Dec. 19, 1991, 105 Stat. 2307, 2308; Pub.L. 111–203, Title X, § 1086(b), July 21, 2010, 124 Stat. 2085.)

§ 4004.   Disclosure of funds availability policies

(a)   Notice for new accounts

Before an account is opened at a depository institution, the depository institution shall provide written notice to the potential customer of the specific policy of such depository institution with respect to when a customer may withdraw funds deposited into the customer's account.

(b)   Preprinted deposit slips

All preprinted deposit slips that a depository institution furnishes to its customers shall contain a summary notice, as prescribed by the Board, jointly with the Director of the Bureau of Consumer Financial Protection, in regulations, that deposited items may not be available for immediate withdrawal.

(c) Mailing of notice

(1) First mailing after enactment

In the first regularly scheduled mailing to customers occurring after September 1, 1988, but not more than 60 days after September 1, 1988, each depository institution shall send a written notice containing the specific policy of such depository institution with respect to when a customer may withdraw funds deposited into such customer's account, unless the depository institution has provided a disclosure which meets the requirements of this section before September 1, 1988.

(2) Subsequent changes

A depository institution shall send a written notice to customers at least 30 days before implementing any change to the depository institution's policy with respect to when customers may withdraw funds deposited into consumer accounts, except that any change which expedites the availability of such funds shall be disclosed not later than 30 days after implementation.

(3) Upon request

Upon the request of any person, a depository institution shall provide or send such person a written notice containing the specific policy of such depository institution with respect to when a customer may withdraw funds deposited into a customer's account.

(d) Posting of notice

(1) Specific notice at manned teller stations

Each depository institution shall post, in a conspicuous place in each location where deposits are accepted by individuals employed by such depository institution, a specific notice which describes the time periods applicable to the availability of funds deposited in a consumer account.

(2) General notice at automated teller machines

In the case of any automated teller machine at which any funds are received for deposit in an account at any depository institution, the Board, jointly with the Director of the Bureau of Consumer Financial Protection, shall prescribe, by regulations, that the owner or operator of such automated teller machine shall post or provide a general notice that funds deposited in such machine may not be immediately available for withdrawal.

(e) Notice of interest payment policy

If a depository institution described in section 4005(b) of this title begins the accrual of interest or dividends at a later date than the date described in section 4005(a) of this title with respect to all funds, including cash, deposited in an interest-bearing account at such depository institution, any notice required to be provided under subsections (a) and (c) of this section shall contain a written description of the time at which such depository institution begins to accrue interest or dividends on such funds.

(f) Model disclosure forms

(1) Prepared by Board and Bureau

The Board, jointly with the Director of the Bureau of Consumer Financial Protection, shall publish model disclosure forms and clauses for common transactions to facilitate compliance with the disclosure requirements of this section and to aid customers by utilizing readily understandable language.

(2) Use of forms to achieve compliance

A depository institution shall be deemed to be in compliance with the requirements of this section if such institution—

    (A) uses any appropriate model form or clause as published by the Board, jointly with the Director of the Bureau of Consumer Financial Protection,,[1] or

    (B) uses any such model form or clause and changes such form or clause by—

        (i)   deleting any information which is not required by this chapter; or

        (ii) rearranging the format.

(3) Voluntary use

Nothing in this chapter requires the use of any such model form or clause prescribed by the Board, jointly with the Director of the Bureau of Consumer Financial Protection, under this subsection.

(4) Notice and comment

Model disclosure forms and clauses shall be adopted by the Board, jointly with the Director of the Bureau of Consumer Financial Protection, only after notice duly given in the Federal Register and an opportunity for public comment in accordance with section 553 of Title 5.

(Pub.L. 100–86, Title VI, § 605, Aug. 10, 1987, 101 Stat. 644; Pub.L. 111–203, Title X, § 1086(c), July 21, 2010, 124 Stat. 2086.)

§ 4005.   Payment of interest

(a) In general

Except as provided in subsection (b) or (c) of this section and notwithstanding any other provision of law, interest shall accrue on funds deposited in an interest-bearing account at a depository institution beginning not later than the business day on which the depository institution receives provisional credit for such funds.

(b) Special rule for credit unions

Subsection (a) of this section shall not apply to an account at a depository institution described in section 461(b)(1)(A)(iv) of this title if the depository institution—

    (1) begins the accrual of interest or dividends at a later date than the date described in subsection (a) of this section with respect to all funds, including cash, deposited in such account; and

    (2) provides notice of the interest payment policy in the manner required under section 4004(e) of this title.

(c) Exception for checks returned unpaid

No provision of this chapter shall be construed as requiring the payment of interest or dividends on funds deposited by a check which is returned unpaid.

(Pub.L. 100–86, Title VI, § 606, Aug. 10, 1987, 101 Stat. 646.)

§ 4006.   Miscellaneous provisions

(a) After-hours deposits

For purposes of this chapter, any deposit which is made on a Saturday, Sunday, legal holiday, or after the close of business on any business day shall be deemed to have been made on the next business day.

(b) Availability at start of business day

Except as provided in subsections (b)(3) and (c)(1)(B) of section 4002 of this title, if any provision of this chapter requires that funds be available for withdrawal on any business day, such funds shall be available for withdrawal at the start of such business day.

---

[1] So in original.

(c) Effect on policies of depository institutions

No provision of this chapter shall be construed as—

(1) prohibiting a depository institution from making funds available for withdrawal in a shorter period of time than the period of time required by this chapter; or

(2) affecting a depository institution's right—

(A) to accept or reject a check for deposit;

(B) to revoke any provisional settlement made by the depository institution with respect to a check accepted by such institution for deposit;

(C) to charge back the depositor's account for the amount of such check; or

(D) to claim a refund of such provisional credit.

(d) Prohibition on freezing certain funds in an account

In any case in which a check is deposited in an account at a depository institution and the funds represented by such check are not yet available for withdrawal pursuant to this chapter, the depository institution may not freeze any other funds in such account (which are otherwise available for withdrawal pursuant to this chapter) solely because the funds so deposited are not yet available for withdrawal.

(e) Employee training on and compliance with requirements of this chapter

Each depository institution shall—

(1) take such actions as may be necessary fully to inform each employee (who performs duties subject to the requirements of this chapter) of the requirements of this chapter; and

(2) establish and maintain procedures reasonably designed to assure and monitor employee compliance with such requirements.

(f) Adjustments to dollar amounts for inflation

The dollar amounts under this title shall be adjusted every 5 years after December 31, 2011, by the annual percentage increase in the Consumer Price Index for Urban Wage Earners and Clerical Workers, as published by the Bureau of Labor Statistics, rounded to the nearest multiple of $25.

(Pub.L. 100–86, Title VI, § 607, Aug. 10, 1987, 101 Stat. 646; Pub.L. 111–203, Title X, § 1086(f), July 21, 2010, 124 Stat. 2086.)

§ 4007. Effect on State law

(a) In general

Any law or regulation of any State in effect on September 1, 1989, which requires that funds deposited or received for deposit in an account at a depository institution chartered by such State be made available for withdrawal in a shorter period of time than the period of time provided in this chapter or in regulations prescribed by the Board under this chapter (as in effect on September 1, 1989) shall—

(1) supersede the provisions of this chapter and any regulations by the Board to the extent such provisions relate to the time by which funds deposited or received for deposit in an account shall be available for withdrawal; and

(2) apply to all federally insured depository institutions located within such State.

(b) Override of certain State laws

Except as provided in subsection (a) of this section, this chapter and regulations prescribed under this chapter shall supersede any provision of the law of any State, including the Uniform Commercial Code as in effect in such State, which is inconsistent with this chapter or such regulations.

(Pub.L. 100–86, Title VI, § 608, Aug. 10, 1987, 101 Stat. 647.)

§ 4008.   Regulations and reports by Board

(a) In general

After notice and opportunity to submit comment in accordance with section 553(c) of Title 5, the Board, jointly with the Director of the Bureau of Consumer Financial Protection, shall prescribe regulations—

(1)   to carry out the provisions of this chapter;

(2)   to prevent the circumvention or evasion of such provisions; and

(3)   to facilitate compliance with such provisions.

(b) Regulations relating to improvement of check processing system

In order to improve the check processing system, the Board shall consider (among other proposals) requiring, by regulation, that—

(1)   depository institutions be charged based upon notification that a check or similar instrument will be presented for payment;

(2)   the Federal Reserve banks and depository institutions provide for check truncation;

(3)   depository institutions be provided incentives to return items promptly to the depository institution of first deposit;

(4)   the Federal Reserve banks and depository institutions take such actions as are necessary to automate the process of returning unpaid checks;

(5)   each depository institution and Federal Reserve bank—

(A)   place its endorsement, and other notations specified in regulations of the Board, on checks in the positions specified in such regulations; and

(B)   take such actions as are necessary to—

(i)   automate the process of reading endorsements; and

(ii)   eliminate unnecessary endorsements;

(6)   within one business day after an originating depository institution is presented a check (for more than such minimum amount as the Board may prescribe)—

(A)   such originating depository institution determines whether it will pay such check; and

(B)   if such originating depository institution determines that it will not pay such check, such originating depository institution directly notify the receiving depository institution of such determination;

(7)   regardless of where a check is cleared initially, all returned checks be eligible to be returned through the Federal Reserve System;

(8)   Federal Reserve banks and depository institutions participate in the development and implementation of an electronic clearinghouse process to the extent the Board determines, pursuant to the study under subsection (f) of this section, that such a process is feasible; and

(9)   originating depository institutions be permitted to return unpaid checks directly to, and obtain reimbursement for such checks directly from, the receiving depository institution.

(c) Regulatory responsibility of Board for payment system

(1) Responsibility for payment system

In order to carry out the provisions of this chapter, the Board of Governors of the Federal Reserve System shall have the responsibility to regulate—

(A)   any aspect of the payment system, including the receipt, payment, collection, or clearing of checks; and

(B) any related function of the payment system with respect to checks.

(2) Regulations

The Board shall prescribe such regulations as it may determine to be appropriate to carry out its responsibility under paragraph (1).

(d) Reports

(1) Implementation progress reports

(A) Required reports

The Board shall transmit a report to both Houses of the Congress not later than 18, 30, and 48 months after August 10, 1987.

(B) Contents of report

Each such report shall describe—

(i) the actions taken and progress made by the Board to implement the schedules established in section 4002 of this title, and

(ii) the impact of this chapter on consumers and depository institutions.

(2) Evaluation of temporary schedule report

(A) Report required

The Board shall transmit a report to both Houses of the Congress not later than 2 years after August 10, 1987, regarding the effects the temporary schedule established under section 4002(c) of this title have had on depository institutions and the public.

(B) Contents of report

Such report shall also assess the potential impact the implementation of the schedule established in section 4002(b) of this title will have on depository institutions and the public, including an estimate of the risks to and losses of depository institutions and the benefits to consumers. Such report shall also contain such recommendations for legislative or administrative action as the Board may determine to be necessary.

(3) Comptroller General evaluation report

Not later than 6 months after September 1, 1988, the Comptroller General of the United States shall transmit a report to the Congress evaluating the implementation and administration of this chapter.

(e) Consultations

In prescribing regulations under subsections (a) and (b), the Board and the Director of the Bureau of Consumer Financial Protection, in the case of subsection (a), and the Board, in the case of subsection (b), shall consult with the Comptroller of the Currency, the Board of Directors of the Federal Deposit Insurance Corporation, and the National Credit Union Administration Board.

(f) Electronic clearinghouse study

(1) Study required

The Board shall study the feasibility of modernizing and accelerating the check payment system through the development of an electronic clearinghouse process utilizing existing telecommunications technology to avoid the necessity of actual presentment of the paper instrument to a payor institution before such institution is charged for the item.

(2) Consultation; factors to be studied

In connection with the study required under paragraph (1), the Board shall—

(A) consult with appropriate experts in telecommunications technology; and

1347

(B) consider all practical and legal impediments to the development of an electronic clearinghouse process.

(3) Report required

The Board shall report its conclusions to the Congress within 9 months of August 10, 1987.

(Pub.L. 100–86, Title VI, § 609, Aug. 10, 1987, 101 Stat. 647; Pub.L. 111–203, Title X, 108 6(d), July 21, 2010, 124 Stat. 2086.)

§ 4009.   Administrative enforcement

(a) Administrative enforcement

Compliance with the requirements imposed under this chapter, including regulations prescribed by and orders issued by the Board of Governors of the Federal Reserve System under this chapter, shall be enforced under—

(1) section 8 of the Federal Deposit Insurance Act [12 U.S.C.A. § 1818] in the case of—

(A) national banks, and Federal branches and Federal agencies of foreign banks, by the Office of the Comptroller of the Currency;

(B) member banks of the Federal Reserve System (other than national banks), and offices, branches, and agencies of foreign banks located in the United States (other than Federal branches, Federal agencies, and insured State branches of foreign banks), by the Board of Governors of the Federal Reserve System; and

(C) banks insured by the Federal Deposit Insurance Corporation (other than members of the Federal Reserve System) and insured State branches of foreign banks, by the Board of Directors of the Federal Deposit Insurance Corporation;

(2) section 8 of the Federal Deposit Insurance Act [12 U.S.C.A. § 1818], by the Director of the Office of Thrift Supervision in the case of savings associations the deposits of which are insured by the Federal Deposit Insurance Corporation; and

(3) the Federal Credit Union Act [12 U.S.C.A. § 1751 et seq.], by the National Credit Union Administration Board with respect to any Federal credit union or insured credit union.

The terms used in paragraph (1) that are not defined in this chapter or otherwise defined in section 3(s) of the Federal Deposit Insurance Act (12 U.S.C. 1813(s)) shall have the meaning given to them in section 1(b) of the International Banking Act of 1978 (12 U.S.C. 3101).

(b) Additional powers

(1) Violation of this chapter treated as violation of other Acts

For purposes of the exercise by any agency referred to in subsection (a) of this section of its powers under any Act referred to in that subsection, a violation of any requirement imposed under this chapter shall be deemed to be a violation of a requirement imposed under that Act.

(2) Enforcement authority under other Acts

In addition to its powers under any provision of law specifically referred to in subsection (a) of this section, each of the agencies referred to in such subsection may exercise, for purposes of enforcing compliance with any requirement imposed under this chapter, any other authority conferred on it by law.

(c) Enforcement by Board

(1) In general

Except to the extent that enforcement of the requirements imposed under this chapter is specifically committed to some other Government agency under subsection (a) of this section, the Board of Governors of the Federal Reserve System shall enforce such requirements.

(2) Additional remedy

If the Board determines that—

(A)   any depository institution which is not a depository institution described in subsection (a) of this section, or

(B)   any other person subject to the authority of the Board under this chapter, including any person subject to the authority of the Board under section 4004(d)(2) or 4008(c) of this title,

has failed to comply with any requirement imposed by this chapter or by the Board under this chapter, the Board may issue an order prohibiting any depository institution, any Federal Reserve bank, or any other person subject to the authority of the Board from engaging in any activity or transaction which directly or indirectly involves such noncomplying depository institution or person (including any activity or transaction involving the receipt, payment, collection, and clearing of checks and any related function of the payment system with respect to checks).

(d) Procedural rules

The authority of the Board to prescribe regulations under this chapter does not impair the authority of any other agency designated in this section to make rules regarding its own procedures in enforcing compliance with requirements imposed under this chapter.

(Pub.L. 100–86, Title VI, § 610, Aug. 10, 1987, 101 Stat. 649; Pub.L. 101–73, Title VII, § 744(d), Aug. 9, 1989, 103 Stat. 438; Pub.L. 102–242, Title II, § 212(h), Dec. 19, 1991, 105 Stat. 2303.)

§ 4010.   Civil liability

(a) Civil liability

Except as otherwise provided in this section, any depository institution which fails to comply with any requirement imposed under this chapter or any regulation prescribed under this chapter with respect to any person other than another depository institution is liable to such person in an amount equal to the sum of—

(1)   any actual damage sustained by such person as a result of the failure;

(2)(A)   in the case of an individual action, such additional amount as the court may allow, except that the liability under this subparagraph shall not be less than $100 nor greater than $1,000; or

(B)   in the case of a class action, such amount as the court may allow, except that—

(i)   as to each member of the class, no minimum recovery shall be applicable; and

(ii)   the total recovery under this subparagraph in any class action or series of class actions arising out of the same failure to comply by the same depository institution shall not be more than the lesser of $500,000 or 1 percent of the net worth of the depository institution involved; and

(3)   in the case of any successful action to enforce the foregoing liability, the costs of the action, together with a reasonable attorney's fee as determined by the court.

(b) Class action awards

In determining the amount of any award in any class action, the court shall consider, among other relevant factors—

(1)   the amount of any actual damages awarded;

(2)   the frequency and persistence of failures of compliance;

(3)   the resources of the depository institution;

(4)   the number of persons adversely affected; and

(5)   the extent to which the failure of compliance was intentional.

(c)   Bona fide errors

(1)   General rule

A depository institution may not be held liable in any action brought under this section for a violation of this chapter if the depository institution demonstrates by a preponderance of the evidence that the violation was not intentional and resulted from a bona fide error, notwithstanding the maintenance of procedures reasonably adapted to avoid any such error.

(2)   Examples

Examples of a bona fide error include clerical, calculation, computer malfunction and programming, and printing errors, except that an error of legal judgment with respect to a depository institution's obligation under this chapter is not a bona fide error.

(d)   Jurisdiction

Any action under this section may be brought in any United States district court, or in any other court of competent jurisdiction, within one year after the date of the occurrence of the violation involved.

(e)   Reliance on Board rulings

No provision of this section imposing any liability shall apply to any act done or omitted in good faith in conformity with any rule, regulation, or interpretation thereof by the Board of Governors of the Federal Reserve System, notwithstanding the fact that after such act or omission has occurred, such rule, regulation, or interpretation is amended, rescinded, or determined by judicial or other authority to be invalid for any reason.

(f)   Authority to establish rules regarding losses and liability among depository institutions

The Board is authorized to impose on or allocate among depository institutions the risks of loss and liability in connection with any aspect of the payment system, including the receipt, payment, collection, or clearing of checks, and any related function of the payment system with respect to checks. Liability under this subsection shall not exceed the amount of the check giving proximate consequence of any act or omission rise to the loss or liability, and, where there is bad faith, other damages, if any, suffered as a giving rise to the loss or liability.

(Pub.L. 100–86, Title VI, § 611, Aug. 10, 1987, 101 Stat. 650.)

CONSUMER CREDIT PROTECTION ACT (CCPA)

15 U.S.C.A. §§ 1601–1693r

Current through Mar. 13, 2016; P.L. 114–133

For updates, see http://uscode.house.gov

SUBCHAPTER I—CONSUMER CREDIT COST DISCLOSURE

PART A—GENERAL PROVISIONS

PART B—CREDIT TRANSACTIONS

CONSUMER CREDIT PROTECTION ACT (CCPA)

CONSUMER CREDIT PROTECTION ACT (CCPA)

CONSUMER CREDIT PROTECTION ACT (CCPA)

SUBCHAPTER I—CONSUMER CREDIT COST DISCLOSURE

PART A—GENERAL PROVISIONS

§ 1601.   Congressional findings and declaration of purpose [CCPA § 102]

(a)   Informed use of credit

The Congress finds that economic stabilization would be enhanced and the competition among the various financial institutions and other firms engaged in the extension of consumer credit would be strengthened by the informed use of credit. The informed use of credit results from an awareness of the cost thereof by consumers. It is the purpose of this subchapter to assure a meaningful disclosure of credit terms so that the consumer will be able to compare more readily the various credit terms available to him and avoid the uninformed use of credit, and to protect the consumer against inaccurate and unfair credit billing and credit card practices.

(b)   Terms of personal property leases

The Congress also finds that there has been a recent trend toward leasing automobiles and other durable goods for consumer use as an alternative to installment credit sales and that these leases have been offered without adequate cost disclosures. It is the purpose of this subchapter to assure a meaningful disclosure of the terms of leases of personal property for personal, family, or household purposes so as to enable the lessee to compare more readily the various lease terms available to him, limit balloon payments in consumer leasing, enable comparison of lease terms with credit terms where appropriate, and to assure meaningful and accurate disclosures of lease terms in advertisements.

(Pub.L. 90–321, Title I, § 102, May 29, 1968, 82 Stat. 146; Pub.L. 93–495, Title III, § 302, Oct. 28, 1974, 88 Stat. 1511; Pub.L. 94–240, § 2, Mar. 23, 1976, 90 Stat. 257.)

§ 1602.   Definitions and rules of construction [CCPA § 103]

(a)   The definitions and rules of construction set forth in this section are applicable for the purposes of this subchapter.

(b)   The term "Bureau" means the Bureau of Consumer Financial Protection.[*]

(c)   The term "Board" refers to the Board of Governors of the Federal Reserve System.

(d)   The term "organization" means a corporation, government or governmental subdivision or agency, trust, estate, partnership, cooperative, or association.

(e)   The term "person" means a natural person or an organization.

(f)   The term "credit" means the right granted by a creditor to a debtor to defer payment of debt or to incur debt and defer its payment.

(g)   The term "creditor" refers only to a person who both (1) regularly extends, whether in connection with loans, sales of property or services, or otherwise, consumer credit which is payable by agreement in more than four installments or for which the payment of a finance charge is or may be required, and (2) is the person to whom the debt arising from the consumer credit transaction is initially payable on the face of

---

[*]   *Note from West Advisory Panel: This definition was inserted as part of Pub.L. 111–203 (Dodd-Frank), changing the numbering of all subsequent definitions. Dodd-Frank appears to contain many clerical errors. Cross-references to definitions may not reflect the Dodd-Frank changes.*

the evidence of indebtedness or, if there is no such evidence of indebtedness, by agreement. Notwithstanding the preceding sentence, in the case of an open-end credit plan involving a credit card, the card issuer and any person who honors the credit card and offers a discount which is a finance charge are creditors. For the purpose of the requirements imposed under part D of this subchapter and sections 1637(a)(5), 1637(a)(6), 1637(a)(7), 1637(b)(1), 1637(b)(2), 1637(b)(3), 1637(b)(8), and 1637(b)(10) of this title, the term "creditor" shall also include card issuers whether or not the amount due is payable by agreement in more than four installments or the payment of a finance charge is or may be required, and the Board shall, by regulation, apply these requirements to such card issuers, to the extent appropriate, even though the requirements are by their terms applicable only to creditors offering open-end credit plans. Any person who originates 2 or more mortgages referred to in subsection (aa) of this section in any 12-month period or any person who originates 1 or more such mortgages through a mortgage broker shall be considered to be a creditor for purposes of this subchapter. The term "creditor" includes a private educational lender (as that term is defined in section 1650 of this title) for purposes of this subchapter.

(h)   The term "credit sale" refers to any sale in which the seller is a creditor. The term includes any contract in the form of a bailment or lease if the bailee or lessee contracts to pay as compensation for use a sum substantially equivalent to or in excess of the aggregate value of the property and services involved and it is agreed that the bailee or lessee will become, or for no other or a nominal consideration has the option to become, the owner of the property upon full compliance with his obligations under the contract.

(i)   The adjective "consumer", used with reference to a credit transaction, characterizes the transaction as one in which the party to whom credit is offered or extended is a natural person, and the money, property, or services which are the subject of the transaction are primarily for personal, family, or household purposes.

(j)   terms "open end credit plan" and "open end consumer credit plan" mean a plan under which the creditor reasonably contemplates repeated transactions, which prescribes the terms of such transactions, and which provides for a finance charge which may be computed from time to time on the outstanding unpaid balance. A credit plan or open end consumer credit plan which is an open end credit plan or open end consumer credit plan within the meaning of the preceding sentence is an open end credit plan even if credit information is verified from time to time.

(k)   The term "adequate notice," as used in section 1643 of this title, means a printed notice to a cardholder which sets forth the pertinent facts clearly and conspicuously so that a person against whom it is to operate could reasonably be expected to have noticed it and understood its meaning. Such notice may be given to a cardholder by printing the notice on any credit card, or on each periodic statement of account, issued to the cardholder, or by any other means reasonably assuring the receipt thereof by the cardholder.

(l)   The term "credit card" means any card, plate, coupon book or other credit device existing for the purpose of obtaining money, property, labor, or services on credit.

(m)   The term "accepted credit card" means any credit card which the cardholder has requested and received or has signed or has used, or authorized another to use, for the purpose of obtaining money, property, labor, or services on credit.

(n)   The term "cardholder" means any person to whom a credit card is issued or any person who has agreed with the card issuer to pay obligations arising from the issuance of a credit card to another person.

(o)   The term "card issuer" means any person who issues a credit card, or the agent of such person with respect to such card.

(p)   The term "unauthorized use," as used in section 1643 of this title, means a use of a credit card by a person other than the cardholder who does not have actual, implied, or apparent authority for such use and from which the cardholder receives no benefit.

(q)   The term "discount" as used in section 1666f of this title means a reduction made from the regular price. The term "discount" as used in section 1666f of this title shall not mean a surcharge.

(r)   The term "surcharge" as used in this section and section 1666f of this title means any means of increasing the regular price to a cardholder which is not imposed upon customers paying by cash, check, or similar means.

(s) The term "State" refers to any State, the Commonwealth of Puerto Rico, the District of Columbia, and any territory or possession of the United States.

(t) The term "agricultural purposes" includes the production, harvest, exhibition, marketing, transportation, processing, or manufacture of agricultural products by a natural person who cultivates, plants, propagates, or nurtures those agricultural products, including but not limited to the acquisition of farmland, real property with a farm residence, and personal property and services used primarily in farming.

(u) The term "agricultural products" includes agricultural, horticultural, viticultural, and dairy products, livestock, wildlife, poultry, bees, forest products, fish and shellfish, and any products thereof, including processed and manufactured products, and any and all products raised or produced on farms and any processed or manufactured products thereof.

(v) The term "material disclosures" means the disclosure, as required by this subchapter, of the annual percentage rate, the method of determining the finance charge and the balance upon which a finance charge will be imposed, the amount of the finance charge, the amount to be financed, the total of payments, the number and amount of payments, the due dates or periods of payments scheduled to repay the indebtedness, and the disclosures required by section 1639(a) of this title.

(w) The term "dwelling" means a residential structure or mobile home which contains one to four family housing units, or individual units of condominiums or cooperatives.

(x) The term "residential mortgage transaction" means a transaction in which a mortgage, deed of trust, purchase money security interest arising under an installment sales contract, or equivalent consensual security interest is created or retained against the consumer's dwelling to finance the acquisition or initial construction of such dwelling.

(y) As used in this section and section 1666f of this title, the term "regular price" means the tag or posted price charged for the property or service if a single price is tagged or posted, or the price charged for the property or service when payment is made by use of an open-end credit plan or a credit card if either (1) no price is tagged or posted, or (2) two prices are tagged or posted, one of which is charged when payment is made by use of an open-end credit plan or a credit card and the other when payment is made by use of cash, check, or similar means. For purposes of this definition, payment by check, draft, or other negotiable instrument which may result in the debiting of an open-end credit plan or a credit cardholder's open-end account shall not be considered payment made by use of the plan or the account.

(z) Any reference to any requirement imposed under this subchapter or any provision thereof includes reference to the regulations of the Bureau under this subchapter or the provision thereof in question.

(aa) The disclosure of an amount or percentage which is greater than the amount or percentage required to be disclosed under this subchapter does not in itself constitute a violation of this subchapter.

(bb) High-cost mortgage

(1) Definition

(A) In general

The term "high-cost mortgage", and a mortgage referred to in this subsection, means a consumer credit transaction that is secured by the consumer's principal dwelling, other than a reverse mortgage transaction, if—

(i) in the case of a credit transaction secured—

(I) by a first mortgage on the consumer's principal dwelling, the annual percentage rate at consummation of the transaction will exceed by more than 6.5 percentage points (8.5 percentage points, if the dwelling is personal property and the transaction is for less than $50,000) the average prime offer rate, as defined in section 1639c(b)(2)(B) of this title, for a comparable transaction; or

(II) by a subordinate or junior mortgage on the consumer's principal dwelling, the annual percentage rate at consummation of the transaction will exceed by more than 8.5

percentage points the average prime offer rate, as defined in section 1639c(b)(2)(B) of this title, for a comparable transaction;

(ii) the total points and fees payable in connection with the transaction, other than bona fide third party charges not retained by the mortgage originator, creditor, or an affiliate of the creditor or mortgage originator, exceed—

     (I) in the case of a transaction for $20,000 or more, 5 percent of the total transaction amount; or

     (II) in the case of a transaction for less than $20,000, the lesser of 8 percent of the total transaction amount or $1,000 (or such other dollar amount as the Board shall prescribe by regulation); or

(iii) the credit transaction documents permit the creditor to charge or collect prepayment fees or penalties more than 36 months after the transaction closing or such fees or penalties exceed, in the aggregate, more than 2 percent of the amount prepaid.

(B) Introductory rates taken into account

For purposes of subparagraph (A)(i), the annual percentage rate of interest shall be determined based on the following interest rate:

(i) In the case of a fixed-rate transaction in which the annual percentage rate will not vary during the term of the loan, the interest rate in effect on the date of consummation of the transaction.

(ii) In the case of a transaction in which the rate of interest varies solely in accordance with an index, the interest rate determined by adding the index rate in effect on the date of consummation of the transaction to the maximum margin permitted at any time during the loan agreement.

(iii) In the case of any other transaction in which the rate may vary at any time during the term of the loan for any reason, the interest charged on the transaction at the maximum rate that may be charged during the term of the loan.

(C) Mortgage insurance

For the purposes of computing the total points and fees under paragraph (4), the total points and fees shall exclude—

(i) any premium provided by an agency of the Federal Government or an agency of a State;

(ii) any amount that is not in excess of the amount payable under policies in effect at the time of origination under section 203(c)(2)(A) of the National Housing Act (12 U.S.C. 1709(c)(2)(A)), provided that the premium, charge, or fee is required to be refundable on a pro-rated basis and the refund is automatically issued upon notification of the satisfaction of the underlying mortgage loan; and

(iii) any premium paid by the consumer after closing.

(2)(A) After the 2-year period beginning on the effective date of the regulations promulgated under section 155 of the Riegle Community Development and Regulatory Improvement Act of 1994, and no more frequently than biennially after the first increase or decrease under this subparagraph, the Board may by regulation increase or decrease the number of percentage points specified in paragraph (1)(A), if the Board determines that the increase or decrease is—

(i) consistent with the consumer protections against abusive lending provided by the amendments made by subtitle B of title I of the Riegle Community Development and Regulatory Improvement Act of 1994; and

(ii) warranted by the need for credit.

(B) An increase or decrease under subparagraph (A)—

(i) may not result in the number of percentage points referred to in paragraph (1)(A)(i)(I) being less than 6 percentage points or greater than 10 percentage points; and

(ii) may not result in the number of percentage points referred to in paragraph (1)(A)(i)(II) being less than 8 percentage points or greater than 12 percentage points.

(C) In determining whether to increase or decrease the number of percentage points referred to in subparagraph (A), the Board shall consult with representatives of consumers, including low-income consumers, and lenders.

(3) The amount specified in paragraph (1)(B)(ii) shall be adjusted annually on January 1 by the annual percentage change in the Consumer Price Index, as reported on June 1 of the year preceding such adjustment.

(4) For purposes of paragraph (1)(B), points and fees shall include—

(A) all items included in the finance charge, except interest or the time-price differential;

(B) all compensation paid directly or indirectly by a consumer or creditor to a mortgage originator from any source, including a mortgage originator that is also the creditor in a table-funded transaction;

(C) each of the charges listed in section 1605(e) of this title (except an escrow for future payment of taxes), unless—

(i) the charge is reasonable;

(ii) the creditor receives no direct or indirect compensation; and

(iii) the charge is paid to a third party unaffiliated with the creditor; and

(D) premiums or other charges payable at or before closing for any credit life, credit disability, credit unemployment, or credit property insurance, or any other accident, loss-of-income, life or health insurance, or any payments directly or indirectly for any debt cancellation or suspension agreement or contract, except that insurance premiums or debt cancellation or suspension fees calculated and paid in full a monthly basis shall not be considered financed by the creditor;

(E) the maximum prepayment fees and penalties which may be charged or collected under the terms of the credit transaction;

(F) all prepayment fees or penalties that are incurred by the consumer if the loan refinances a previous loan made or currently held by the same creditor or an affiliate of the creditor; and

(G) such other charges as the Bureau determines to be appropriate.

(5) Calculation of points and fees for open-end consumer credit plans

In the case of open-end consumer credit plans, points and fees shall be calculated, for purposes of this section and section 1639 of this title, by adding the total points and fees known at or before closing, including the maximum prepayment penalties which may be charged or collected under the terms of the credit transaction, plus the minimum additional fees the consumer would be required to pay to draw down an amount equal to the total credit line.

(6) This subsection shall not be construed to limit the rate of interest or the finance charge that a person may charge a consumer for any extension of credit.

(cc)[1] The term "reverse mortgage transaction" means a nonrecourse transaction in which a mortgage, deed of trust, or equivalent consensual security interest is created against the consumer's principal dwelling—

(1) securing one or more advances; and

(2) with respect to which the payment of any principal, interest, and shared appreciation or equity is due and payable (other than in the case of default) only after—

---

[1] So in original. There are two subsections designated (cc).

    (A) the transfer of the dwelling;

    (B) the consumer ceases to occupy the dwelling as a principal dwelling; or

    (C) the death of the consumer.

(cc)[1] **Definitions relating to mortgage origination and residential mortgage loans**

(1) Commission

Unless otherwise specified, the term "Commission" means the Federal Trade Commission.

(2) Mortgage originator

The term "mortgage originator"—

    (A) means any person who, for direct or indirect compensation or gain, or in the expectation of direct or indirect compensation or gain—

        (i) takes a residential mortgage loan application;

        (ii) assists a consumer in obtaining or applying to obtain a residential mortgage loan; or

        (iii) offers or negotiates terms of a residential mortgage loan;

    (B) includes any person who represents to the public, through advertising or other means of communicating or providing information (including the use of business cards, stationery, brochures, signs, rate lists, or other promotional items), that such person can or will provide any of the services or perform any of the activities described in subparagraph (A);

    (C) does not include any person who is (i) not otherwise described in subparagraph (A) or (B) and who performs purely administrative or clerical tasks on behalf of a person who is described in any such subparagraph, or (ii) an employee of a retailer of manufactured homes who is not described in clause (i) or (iii) of subparagraph (A) and who does not advise a consumer on loan terms (including rates, fees, and other costs);

    (D) does not include a person or entity that only performs real estate brokerage activities and is licensed or registered in accordance with applicable State law, unless such person or entity is compensated by a lender, a mortgage broker, or other mortgage originator or by any agent of such lender, mortgage broker, or other mortgage originator;

    (E) does not include, with respect to a residential mortgage loan, a person, estate, or trust that provides mortgage financing for the sale of 3 properties in any 12-month period to purchasers of such properties, each of which is owned by such person, estate, or trust and serves as security for the loan, provided that such loan—

        (i) is not made by a person, estate, or trust that has constructed, or acted as a contractor for the construction of, a residence on the property in the ordinary course of business of such person, estate, or trust;

        (ii) is fully amortizing;

        (iii) is with respect to a sale for which the seller determines in good faith and documents that the buyer has a reasonable ability to repay the loan;

        (iv) has a fixed rate or an adjustable rate that is adjustable after 5 or more years, subject to reasonable annual and lifetime limitations on interest rate increases; and

        (v) meets any other criteria the Board may prescribe;

    (F) does not include the creditor (except the creditor in a table-funded transaction) under paragraph (1), (2), or (4) of section 1639b(c) of this title; and

    (G) does not include a servicer or servicer employees, agents and contractors, including but not limited to those who offer or negotiate terms of a residential mortgage loan for purposes of renegotiating, modifying, replacing and subordinating principal of existing mortgages where borrowers

---

[1] So in original. There are two subsections designated (cc).

are behind in their payments, in default or have a reasonable likelihood of being in default or falling behind.

(3) Nationwide Mortgage Licensing System and Registry

The term "Nationwide Mortgage Licensing System and Registry" has the same meaning as in the Secure and Fair Enforcement for Mortgage Licensing Act of 2008.

(4) Other definitions relating to mortgage originator

For purposes of this subsection, a person "assists a consumer in obtaining or applying to obtain a residential mortgage loan" by, among other things, advising on residential mortgage loan terms (including rates, fees, and other costs), preparing residential mortgage loan packages, or collecting information on behalf of the consumer with regard to a residential mortgage loan.

(5) Residential mortgage loan

The term "residential mortgage loan" means any consumer credit transaction that is secured by a mortgage, deed of trust, or other equivalent consensual security interest on a dwelling or on residential real property that includes a dwelling, other than a consumer credit transaction under an open end credit plan or, for purposes of sections 1639b and 1639c of this title and section 1638(a)(16), (17), (18), and (19) of this title, and sections 1638(f) and 1640(k) of this title, and any regulations promulgated thereunder, an extension of credit relating to a plan described in section 101(53D) of Title 11.

(6) Secretary

The term "Secretary", when used in connection with any transaction or person involved with a residential mortgage loan, means the Secretary of Housing and Urban Development.

(7) Servicer

The term "servicer" has the same meaning as in section 2605(i)(2) of Title 12.

(dd) Bona fide discount points and prepayment penalties

For the purposes of determining the amount of points and fees for purposes of subsection (aa), either the amounts described in paragraph (1) or (2) of the following paragraphs, but not both, shall be excluded:

(1) Up to and including 2 bona fide discount points payable by the consumer in connection with the mortgage, but only if the interest rate from which the mortgage's interest rate will be discounted does not exceed by more than 1 percentage point—

> **(A)** the average prime offer rate, as defined in section 1639c of this title; or

> **(B)** if secured by a personal property loan, the average rate on a loan in connection with which insurance is provided under title I of the National Housing Act (12 U.S.C. 1702 et seq.).

(2) Unless 2 bona fide discount points have been excluded under paragraph (1), up to and including 1 bona fide discount point payable by the consumer in connection with the mortgage, but only if the interest rate from which the mortgage's interest rate will be discounted does not exceed by more than 2 percentage points—

> **(A)** the average prime offer rate, as defined in section 1639c of this title; or

> **(B)** if secured by a personal property loan, the average rate on a loan in connection with which insurance is provided under title I of the National Housing Act (12 U.S.C. 1702 et seq.).

(3) For purposes of paragraph (1), the term "bona fide discount points" means loan discount points which are knowingly paid by the consumer for the purpose of reducing, and which in fact result in a bona fide reduction of, the interest rate or time-price differential applicable to the mortgage.

(4) Paragraphs (1) and (2) shall not apply to discount points used to purchase an interest rate reduction unless the amount of the interest rate reduction purchased is reasonably consistent with established industry norms and practices for secondary mortgage market transactions.

(Pub.L. 90–321, Title I, § 103, May 29, 1968, 82 Stat. 147; Pub.L. 91–508, Title V, § 501, Oct. 26, 1970, 84 Stat. 1126; Pub.L. 93–495, Title III, § 303, Oct. 28, 1974, 88 Stat. 1511; Pub.L. 94–222, § 3(a), Feb. 27,

1976, 90 Stat. 197; Pub.L. 96–221, Title VI, §§ 602, 603(a), (b), 604, 612(a)(2), (b), Mar. 31, 1980, 94 Stat. 168, 169, 175, 176; Pub.L. 97–25, Title I, § 102, July 27, 1981, 95 Stat. 144; Pub.L. 97–320, Title VII, § 702(a), Oct. 15, 1982, 96 Stat. 1538; Pub.L. 103–325, Title I, §§ 152(a) to (c), 154(a), Sept. 23, 1994, 108 Stat. 2190, 2191, 2196; Pub.L. 110–315, Title X, § 1011(b), Aug. 14, 2008, 122 Stat. 3481; Pub.L. 111–24, Title I, § 108, May 22, 2009, 123 Stat. 1743; Pub.L. 111–203, Title X, §§ 1100A(2), 1100H, Title XIV, §§ 1400(c), 1401, 1431, 1432, 1433, July 21, 2010, 124 Stat. 2107, 2113, 2136, 2137, 2157, 2158, 2159.)

§ 1603.   Exempted transactions [CCPA § 104]

This subchapter does not apply to the following:

(1)   Credit transactions involving extensions of credit primarily for business, commercial, or agricultural purposes, or to government or governmental agencies or instrumentalities, or to organizations.

(2)   Transactions in securities or commodities accounts by a broker-dealer registered with the Securities and Exchange Commission.

(3)   Credit transactions, other than those in which a security interest is or will be acquired in real property, or in personal property used or expected to be used as the principal dwelling of the consumer and other than private education loans (as that term is defined in section 1650(a) of this title), in which the total amount financed exceeds $50,000.

(4)   Transactions under public utility tariffs, if the Bureau determines that a State regulatory body regulates the charges for the public utility services involved, the charges for delayed payment, and any discount allowed for early payment.

(5)   Transactions for which the Bureau, by rule, determines that coverage under this subchapter is not necessary to carry out the purposes of this subchapter.

(6)   Repealed. Pub.L. 96–221, Title VI, § 603(c) (3), Mar. 31, 1980, 94 Stat. 169

(7)   Loans made, insured, or guaranteed pursuant to a program authorized by Title IV of the Higher Education Act of 1965 (20 U.S.C. 1070 et seq.).

(Pub.L. 90–321, Title I, § 104, May 29, 1968, 82 Stat. 147; Pub.L. 93–495, Title IV, § 402, Oct. 28, 1974, 88 Stat. 1517; Pub.L. 96–221, Title VI, § 603(c), Mar. 31, 1980, 94 Stat. 169; Pub.L. 97–320, Title VII, § 701(a), Oct. 15, 1982, 96 Stat. 1538; Pub.L. 104–208, Div. A, Title II, § 2102(a), Sept. 30, 1996, 110 Stat. 3009–398; Pub.L. 110–315, Title X, § 1022, Aug. 14, 2008, 122 Stat. 3488; Pub.L. 111–203, Title X, §§ 1100A(2), 1100E(a)(1), 124 Stat. 2107, 2111.)

§ 1604.   Disclosure guidelines [CCPA § 105]

(a)   Promulgation, contents, etc., of regulations

The Bureau shall prescribe regulations to carry out the purposes of this subchapter. Except with respect to the provisions of section 1639 of this title that apply to a mortgage referred to in section 1602(aa)* of this title, such regulations may contain such additional requirements, classifications, differentiations, or other provisions, and may provide for such adjustments and exceptions for all or any class of transactions, as in the judgment of the Bureau are necessary or proper to effectuate the purposes of this subchapter, to prevent circumvention or evasion thereof, or to facilitate compliance therewith.

(b)   Model disclosure forms and clauses; publication, criteria, compliance, etc.

The Bureau shall publish a single, integrated disclosure for mortgage loan transactions (including real estate settlement cost statements) which includes the disclosure requirements of this subchapter in conjunction with the disclosure requirements of the Real Estate Settlement Procedures Act of 1974 that, taken together, may apply to a transaction that is subject to both or either provisions of law. The purpose of such model disclosure shall be to facilitate compliance with the disclosure requirements of this subchapter and the Real Estate Settlement Procedures Act of 1974, and to aid the borrower or lessee in understanding

---

*   *Note from West Advisory Panel: Pub. L. 111–203 (Dodd-Frank) appears to contain clerical errors. We believe this reference should be to § 1602(bb).*

the transaction by utilizing readily understandable language to simplify the technical nature of the disclosures. In devising such forms, the Bureau shall consider the use by creditors or lessors of data processing or similar automated equipment. Nothing in this subchapter may be construed to require a creditor or lessor to use any such model form or clause prescribed by the Bureau under this section. A creditor or lessor shall be deemed to be in compliance with the disclosure provisions of this subchapter with respect to other than numerical disclosures if the creditor or lessor (1) uses any appropriate model form or clause as published by the Bureau, or (2) uses any such model form or clause and changes it by (A) deleting any information which is not required by this subchapter, or (B) rearranging the format, if in making such deletion or rearranging the format, the creditor or lessor does not affect the substance, clarity, or meaningful sequence of the disclosure.

(c) Procedures applicable for adoption of model forms and clauses

Model disclosure forms and clauses shall be adopted by the Bureau after notice duly given in the Federal Register and an opportunity for public comment in accordance with section 553 of Title 5.

(d) Effective dates of regulations containing new disclosure requirements

Any regulation of the Bureau, or any amendment or interpretation thereof, requiring any disclosure which differs from the disclosures previously required by this part, part D, or part E of this subchapter or by any regulation of the Bureau promulgated thereunder shall have an effective date of that October 1 which follows by at least six months the date of promulgation, except that the Bureau may at its discretion take interim action by regulation, amendment, or interpretation to lengthen the period of time permitted for creditors or lessors to adjust their forms to accommodate new requirements or shorten the length of time for creditors or lessors to make such adjustments when it makes a specific finding that such action is necessary to comply with the findings of a court or to prevent unfair or deceptive disclosure practices. Notwithstanding the previous sentence, any creditor or lessor may comply with any such newly promulgated disclosure requirements prior to the effective date of the requirements.

(e)[1] [Omitted.]

(f) Exemption authority

(1) In general

The Bureau may exempt, by regulation, from all or part of this subchapter all or any class of transactions, other than transactions involving any mortgage described in section 1602(aa)[*] of this title, for which, in the determination of the Bureau, coverage under all or part of this subchapter does not provide a meaningful benefit to consumers in the form of useful information or protection.

(2) Factors for consideration

In determining which classes of transactions to exempt in whole or in part under paragraph (1), the Bureau shall consider the following factors and publish its rationale at the time a proposed exemption is published for comment:

(A) The amount of the loan and whether the disclosures, right of rescission, and other provisions provide a benefit to the consumers who are parties to such transactions, as determined by the Bureau.

(B) The extent to which the requirements of this subchapter complicate, hinder, or make more expensive the credit process for the class of transactions.

(C) The status of the borrower, including—

(i) any related financial arrangements of the borrower, as determined by the Bureau;

(ii) the financial sophistication of the borrower relative to the type of transaction; and

---

[1] So in original. No subsec. (e) has been enacted.
 * *Note from West Advisory Panel: Pub. L. 111–203 (Dodd-Frank) appears to contain clerical errors. We believe this reference should be to § 1602(bb).*

        (iii) the importance to the borrower of the credit, related supporting property, and coverage under this subchapter, as determined by the Bureau;

    (D) whether the loan is secured by the principal residence of the consumer; and

    (E) whether the goal of consumer protection would be undermined by such an exemption.

(g) Waiver for certain borrowers

(1) In general

The Bureau, by regulation, may exempt from the requirements of this subchapter certain credit transactions if—

    (A) the transaction involves a consumer—

        (i) with an annual earned income of more than $200,000; or

        (ii) having net assets in excess of $1,000,000 at the time of the transaction; and

    (B) a waiver that is handwritten, signed, and dated by the consumer is first obtained from the consumer.

(2) Adjustments by the Bureau

The Bureau, at its discretion, may adjust the annual earned income and net asset requirements of paragraph (1) for inflation.

(h) Deference

Notwithstanding any power granted to any Federal agency under this subchapter, the deference that a court affords to the Bureau with respect to a determination made by the Bureau relating to the meaning or interpretation of any provision of this subchapter, other than section 1639e or 1639h of this title, shall be applied as if the Bureau were the only agency authorized to apply, enforce, interpret, or administer the provisions of this subchapter.

(i) Authority of the Board to prescribe rules

Notwithstanding subsection (a), the Board shall have authority to prescribe rules under this subchapter with respect to a person described in section 5519(a) of Title 12. Regulations prescribed under this subsection may contain such classifications, differentiations, or other provisions, as in the judgment of the Board are necessary or proper to effectuate the purposes of this subchapter, to prevent circumvention or evasion thereof, or to facilitate compliance therewith.

    (Pub.L. 90–321, Title I, § 105, May 29, 1968, 82 Stat. 148; Pub.L. 96–221, Title VI, § 605, Mar. 31, 1980, 94 Stat. 170; Pub.L. 103–325, Title I, § 152(e)(2)(A), Sept. 23, 1994, 108 Stat. 2194; Pub.L. 104–208, Div. A, Title II, §§ 2102(b), 2104, Sept. 30, 1996, 110 Stat. 3009–399, 3009–401; Pub.L. 111–203, Title X, §§ 1100A(2), 1100A(3), 1100A(5), 1100A(6), Title XIV, §§ 1400(c), 1472(c), July 21, 2010, 124 Stat. 2107, 2108, 2136, 2190.)

§ 1605.   Determination of finance charge [CCPA § 106]

(a) "Finance charge" defined

Except as otherwise provided in this section, the amount of the finance charge in connection with any consumer credit transaction shall be determined as the sum of all charges, payable directly or indirectly by the person to whom the credit is extended, and imposed directly or indirectly by the creditor as an incident to the extension of credit. The finance charge does not include charges of a type payable in a comparable cash transaction. The finance charge shall not include fees and amounts imposed by third party closing agents (including settlement agents, attorneys, and escrow and title companies) if the creditor does not require the imposition of the charges or the services provided and does not retain the charges. Examples of charges which are included in the finance charge include any of the following types of charges which are applicable:

    (1) Interest, time price differential, and any amount payable under a point, discount, or other system of additional charges.

    (2) Service or carrying charge.

(3) Loan fee, finder's fee, or similar charge.

(4) Fee for an investigation or credit report.

(5) Premium or other charge for any guarantee or insurance protecting the creditor against the obligor's default or other credit loss.

(6) Borrower-paid mortgage broker fees, including fees paid directly to the broker or the lender (for delivery to the broker) whether such fees are paid in cash or financed.

(b) Life, accident, or health insurance premiums included in finance charge

Charges or premiums for credit life, accident, or health insurance written in connection with any consumer credit transaction shall be included in the finance charges unless

(1) the coverage of the debtor by the insurance is not a factor in the approval by the creditor of the extension of credit, and this fact is clearly disclosed in writing to the person applying for or obtaining the extension of credit; and

(2) in order to obtain the insurance in connection with the extension of credit, the person to whom the credit is extended must give specific affirmative written indication of his desire to do so after written disclosure to him of the cost thereof.

(c) Property damage and liability insurance premiums included in finance charge

Charges or premiums for insurance, written in connection with any consumer credit transaction, against loss of or damage to property or against liability arising out of the ownership or use of property, shall be included in the finance charge unless a clear and specific statement in writing is furnished by the creditor to the person to whom the credit is extended, setting forth the cost of the insurance if obtained from or through the creditor, and stating that the person to whom the credit is extended may choose the person through which the insurance is to be obtained.

(d) Items exempted from computation of finance charge in all credit transactions

If any of the following items is itemized and disclosed in accordance with the regulations of the Bureau in connection with any transaction, then the creditor need not include that item in the computation of the finance charge with respect to that transaction:

(1) Fees and charges prescribed by law which actually are or will be paid to public officials for determining the existence of or for perfecting or releasing or satisfying any security related to the credit transaction.

(2) The premium payable for any insurance in lieu of perfecting any security interest otherwise required by the creditor in connection with the transaction, if the premium does not exceed the fees and charges described in paragraph (1) which would otherwise be payable.

(3) Any tax levied on security instruments or on documents evidencing indebtedness if the payment of such taxes is a precondition for recording the instrument securing the evidence of indebtedness.

(e) Items exempted from computation of finance charge in extensions of credit secured by an interest in real property

The following items, when charged in connection with any extension of credit secured by an interest in real property, shall not be included in the computation of the finance charge with respect to that transaction:

(1) Fees or premiums for title examination, title insurance, or similar purposes.

(2) Fees for preparation of loan-related documents.

(3) Escrows for future payments of taxes and insurance.

(4) Fees for notarizing deeds and other documents.

(5) Appraisal fees, including fees related to any pest infestation or flood hazard inspections conducted prior to closing.

(6) Credit reports.

(f)   **Tolerances for accuracy**

In connection with credit transactions not under an open end credit plan that are secured by real property or a dwelling, the disclosure of the finance charge and other disclosures affected by any finance charge—

    (1)   shall be treated as being accurate for purposes of this subchapter if the amount disclosed as the finance charge—

        (A)   does not vary from the actual finance charge by more than $100; or

        (B)   is greater than the amount required to be disclosed under this subchapter; and

    (2)   shall be treated as being accurate for purposes of section 1635 of this title if—

        (A)   except as provided in subparagraph (B), the amount disclosed as the finance charge does not vary from the actual finance charge by more than an amount equal to one-half of one percent of the total amount of credit extended; or

        (B)   in the case of a transaction, other than a mortgage referred to in section 1602(aa) of this title, which—

            (i)   is a refinancing of the principal balance then due and any accrued and unpaid finance charges of a residential mortgage transaction as defined in section 1602(w) of this title, or is any subsequent refinancing of such a transaction; and

            (ii)   does not provide any new consolidation or new advance;

if the amount disclosed as the finance charge does not vary from the actual finance charge by more than an amount equal to one percent of the total amount of credit extended.

(Pub.L. 90–321, Title I, § 106, May 29, 1968, 82 Stat. 148; Pub.L. 96–221, Title VI, § 606, Mar. 31, 1980, 94 Stat. 170; Pub.L. 104–29, §§ 2(a), (b)(1), (c) to (e), 3(a), Sept. 30, 1995, 109 Stat. 271, 272; Pub.L. 111–203, Title X, § 1100A(2), July 21, 2010, 124 Stat. 2107.)

§ 1606.   Determination of annual percentage rate [CCPA § 107]

(a)   **"Annual percentage rate" defined**

The annual percentage rate applicable to any extension of consumer credit shall be determined, in accordance with the regulations of the Bureau,

    (1)   in the case of any extension of credit other than under an open end credit plan, as

        (A)   that nominal annual percentage rate which will yield a sum equal to the amount of the finance charge when it is applied to the unpaid balances of the amount financed, calculated according to the actuarial method of allocating payments made on a debt between the amount financed and the amount of the finance charge, pursuant to which a payment is applied first to the accumulated finance charge and the balance is applied to the unpaid amount financed; or

        (B)   the rate determined by any method prescribed by the Bureau as a method which materially simplifies computation while retaining reasonable accuracy as compared with the rate determined under subparagraph (A).

    (2)   in the case of any extension of credit under an open end credit plan, as the quotient (expressed as a percentage) of the total finance charge for the period to which it relates divided by the amount upon which the finance charge for that period is based, multiplied by the number of such periods in a year.

(b)   **Computation of rate of finance charges for balances within a specified range**

Where a creditor imposes the same finance charge for balances within a specified range, the annual percentage rate shall be computed on the median balance within the range, except that if the Bureau determines that a rate so computed would not be meaningful, or would be materially misleading, the annual percentage rate shall be computed on such other basis as the Bureau may by regulation require.

(c) Allowable tolerances for purposes of compliance with disclosure requirements

The disclosure of an annual percentage rate is accurate for the purpose of this subchapter if the rate disclosed is within a tolerance not greater than one-eighth of 1 per centum more or less than the actual rate or rounded to the nearest one-fourth of 1 per centum. The Bureau may allow a greater tolerance to simplify compliance where irregular payments are involved.

(d) Use of rate tables or charts having allowable variance from determined rates

The Bureau may authorize the use of rate tables or charts which may provide for the disclosure of annual percentage rates which vary from the rate determined in accordance with subsection (a)(1)(A) of this section by not more than such tolerances as the Bureau may allow. The Bureau may not allow a tolerance greater than 8 per centum of that rate except to simplify compliance where irregular payments are involved.

(e) Authorization of tolerances in determining annual percentage rates

In the case of creditors determining the annual percentage rate in a manner other than as described in subsection (d) of this section, the Bureau may authorize other reasonable tolerances.

(Pub.L. 90–321, Title I, § 107, May 29, 1968, 82 Stat. 149; Pub.L. 96–221, Title VI, § 607, Mar. 31, 1980, 94 Stat. 170; Pub.L. 111–203, Title X, § 1100A(2), July 21, 2010, 124 Stat. 2107.)

§ 1607. Administrative enforcement [CCPA § 108]

(a) Enforcing agencies

Subject to subtitle B of the Consumer Financial Protection Act of 2010 [12 U.S.C.A. §§ 5511–5519] compliance with the requirements imposed under this subchapter shall be enforced under—

(1) section 1818 of Title 12, by the appropriate Federal banking agency, as defined in section 1813(q) of Title 12, with respect to—

(A) national banks, Federal savings associations, and Federal branches and Federal agencies of foreign banks;

(B) member banks of the Federal Reserve System (other than national banks), branches and agencies of foreign banks (other than Federal branches, Federal agencies, and insured State branches of foreign banks), commercial lending companies owned or controlled by foreign banks, and organizations operating under section 25 or 25A of the Federal Reserve Act; and

(C) banks and State savings associations insured by the Federal Deposit Insurance Corporation (other than members of the Federal Reserve System), and insured State branches of foreign banks;

(2) the Federal Credit Union Act, by the Director of the National Credit Union Administration, with respect to any Federal credit union;

(3) part A of subtitle VII of Title 49, by the Secretary of Transportation, with respect to any air carrier or foreign air carrier subject to that part;

(4) the Packers and Stockyards Act, 1921 (except as provided in section 406 of that Act), by the Secretary of Agriculture, with respect to any activities subject to that Act;

(5) the Farm Credit Act of 1971, by the Farm Credit Administration with respect to any Federal land bank, Federal land bank association, Federal intermediate credit bank, or production credit association; and

(6) subtitle E of the Consumer Financial Protection Act of 2010 [12 U.S.C.A. §§ 5561–5567], by the Bureau, with respect to any person subject to this subchapter.

(7) sections 78u–2 and 78u–3 of this title, in the case of a broker or dealer, other than a depository institution, by the Securities and Exchange Commission.

(b) Violations of this subchapter deemed violations of pre-existing statutory requirements; additional agency powers

For the purpose of the exercise by any agency referred to in subsection (a) of this section of its powers under any Act referred to in that subsection, a violation of any requirement imposed under this subchapter shall be deemed to be a violation of a requirement imposed under that Act. In addition to its powers under any provision of law specifically referred to in subsection (a) of this section, each of the agencies referred to in that subsection may exercise, for the purpose of enforcing compliance with any requirement imposed under this subchapter, any other authority conferred on it by law.

(c) Overall enforcement authority of the Federal Trade Commission

Except to the extent that enforcement of the requirements imposed under this subchapter is specifically committed to some other Government agency under any of paragraphs (1) through (5) of subsection (a), and subject to subtitle B of the Consumer Financial Protection Act of 2010 [12 U.S.C.A. §§ 5511–5519], the Federal Trade Commission shall be authorized to enforce such requirements. For the purpose of the exercise by the Federal Trade Commission of its functions and powers under the Federal Trade Commission Act [15 U.S.C.A. § 41 et seq.], a violation of any requirement imposed under this subchapter shall be deemed a violation of a requirement imposed under that Act. All of the functions and powers of the Federal Trade Commission under the Federal Trade Commission Act are available to the Federal Trade Commission to enforce compliance by any person with the requirements under this subchapter, irrespective of whether that person is engaged in commerce or meets any other jurisdictional tests under the Federal Trade Commission Act.

(d) Rules and regulations

The authority of the Bureau to issue regulations under this subchapter does not impair the authority of any other agency designated in this section to make rules respecting its own procedures in enforcing compliance with requirements imposed under this subchapter.

(e) Adjustment of finance charges; procedures applicable, coverage, criteria, etc.

(1) In carrying out its enforcement activities under this section, each agency referred to in subsection (a) or (c) of this section, in cases where an annual percentage rate or finance charge was inaccurately disclosed, shall notify the creditor of such disclosure error and is authorized in accordance with the provisions of this subsection to require the creditor to make an adjustment to the account of the person to whom credit was extended, to assure that such person will not be required to pay a finance charge in excess of the finance charge actually disclosed or the dollar equivalent of the annual percentage rate actually disclosed, whichever is lower. For the purposes of this subsection, except where such disclosure error resulted from a willful violation which was intended to mislead the person to whom credit was extended, in determining whether a disclosure error has occurred and in calculating any adjustment, (A) each agency shall apply (i) with respect to the annual percentage rate, a tolerance of one-quarter of 1 percent more or less than the actual rate, determined without regard to section 1606(c) of this title, and (ii) with respect to the finance charge, a corresponding numerical tolerance as generated by the tolerance provided under this subsection for the annual percentage rate; except that (B) with respect to transactions consummated after two years following March 31, 1980, each agency shall apply (i) for transactions that have a scheduled amortization of ten years or less, with respect to the annual percentage rate, a tolerance not to exceed one-quarter of 1 percent more or less than the actual rate, determined without regard to section 1606(c) of this title, but in no event a tolerance of less than the tolerances allowed under section 1606(c) of this title, (ii) for transactions that have a scheduled amortization of more than ten years, with respect to the annual percentage rate, only such tolerances as are allowed under section 1606(c) of this title, and (iii) for all transactions, with respect to the finance charge, a corresponding numerical tolerance as generated by the tolerances provided under this subsection for the annual percentage rate.

(2) Each agency shall require such an adjustment when it determines that such disclosure error resulted from (A) a clear and consistent pattern or practice of violations, (B) gross negligence, or (C) a willful violation which was intended to mislead the person to whom the credit was extended. Notwithstanding the preceding sentence, except where such disclosure error resulted from a willful violation which was intended to mislead the person to whom credit was extended, an agency need not require such an adjustment if it determines that such disclosure error—

(A) resulted from an error involving the disclosure of a fee or charge that would otherwise be excludable in computing the finance charge, including but not limited to violations involving the disclosures described in sections 1605(b), (c) and (d) of this title, in which event the agency may require such remedial action as it determines to be equitable, except that for transactions consummated after two years after March 31, 1980, such an adjustment shall be ordered for violations of section 1605(b) of this title;

(B) involved a disclosed amount which was 10 per centum or less of the amount that should have been disclosed and (i) in cases where the error involved a disclosed finance charge, the annual percentage rate was disclosed correctly, and (ii) in cases where the error involved a disclosed annual percentage rate, the finance charge was disclosed correctly; in which event the agency may require such adjustment as it determines to be equitable;

(C) involved a total failure to disclose either the annual percentage rate or the finance charge, in which event the agency may require such adjustment as it determines to be equitable; or

(D) resulted from any other unique circumstance involving clearly technical and nonsubstantive disclosure violations that do not adversely affect information provided to the consumer and that have not misled or otherwise deceived the consumer.

In the case of other such disclosure errors, each agency may require such an adjustment.

(3) Notwithstanding paragraph (2), no adjustment shall be ordered—

(A) if it would have a significantly adverse impact upon the safety or soundness of the creditor, but in any such case, the agency may—

    (i) require a partial adjustment in an amount which does not have such an impact; or

    (ii) require the full adjustment, but permit the creditor to make the required adjustment in partial payments over an extended period of time which the agency considers to be reasonable, if (in the case of an agency referred to in paragraph (1), (2), or (3) of subsection (a) of this section), the agency determines that a partial adjustment or making partial payments over an extended period is necessary to avoid causing the creditor to become undercapitalized pursuant to section 38 of the Federal Deposit Insurance Act [12 U.S.C.A. § 1831*o*];

(B) the[1] amount of the adjustment would be less than $1, except that if more than one year has elapsed since the date of the violation, the agency may require that such amount be paid into the Treasury of the United States, or

(C) except where such disclosure error resulted from a willful violation which was intended to mislead the person to whom credit was extended, in the case of an open-end credit plan, more than two years after the violation, or in the case of any other extension of credit, as follows:

    (i) with respect to creditors that are subject to examination by the agencies referred to in paragraphs (1) through (3) of subsection (a) of this section, except in connection with violations arising from practices identified in the current examination and only in connection with transactions that are consummated after the date of the immediately preceding examination, except that where practices giving rise to violations identified in earlier examinations have not been corrected, adjustments for those violations shall be required in connection with transactions consummated after the date of examination in which such practices were first identified;

    (ii) with respect to creditors that are not subject to examination by such agencies, except in connection with transactions that are consummated after May 10, 1978; and

    (iii) in no event after the later of (I) the expiration of the life of the credit extension, or (II) two years after the agreement to extend credit was consummated.

(4)(A) Notwithstanding any other provision of this section, an adjustment under this subsection may be required by an agency referred to in subsection (a) or (c) of this section only by an order issued in accordance with cease and desist procedures provided by the provision of law referred to in such subsections.

---

[1] So in original. Probably should be preceded by "if".

(B) In case of an agency which is not authorized to conduct cease and desist proceedings, such an order may be issued after an agency hearing on the record conducted at least thirty but not more than sixty days after notice of the alleged violation is served on the creditor. Such a hearing shall be deemed to be a hearing which is subject to the provisions of section 8(h) of the Federal Deposit Insurance Act [12 U.S.C.A. § 1818(h)] and shall be subject to judicial review as provided therein.

(5) Except as otherwise specifically provided in this subsection and notwithstanding any provision of law referred to in subsection (a) or (c) of this section, no agency referred to in subsection (a) or (c) of this section may require a creditor to make dollar adjustments for errors in any requirements under this subchapter, except with regard to the requirements of section 1666d of this title.

(6) A creditor shall not be subject to an order to make an adjustment, if within sixty days after discovering a disclosure error, whether pursuant to a final written examination report or through the creditor's own procedures, the creditor notifies the person concerned of the error and adjusts the account so as to assure that such person will not be required to pay a finance charge in excess of the finance charge actually disclosed or the dollar equivalent of the annual percentage rate actually disclosed, whichever is lower.

(7) Notwithstanding the second sentence of subsection (e)(1), subsection (e)(3)(C)(i), and subsection (e)(3)(C)(ii) of this section, each agency referred to in subsection (a) or (c) of this section shall require an adjustment for an annual percentage rate disclosure error that exceeds a tolerance of one quarter of one percent less than the actual rate, determined without regard to section 1606(c) of this title, with respect to any transaction consummated between January 1, 1977, and March 31, 1980.

(Pub.L. 90–321, Title I, § 108, May 29, 1968, 82 Stat. 150; Pub.L. 91–206, §§ 1, 3, Mar. 10, 1970, 84 Stat. 49; Pub.L. 93–495, Title IV, § 403, Oct. 28, 1974, 88 Stat. 1517; Pub.L. 95–630, Title V, § 501, Nov. 10, 1978, 92 Stat. 3680; Pub.L. 96–221, Title VI, § 608(a), (c), Mar. 21, 1980, 94 Stat. 171, 173; Pub.L. 98–443, § 9(n), Oct. 4, 1984, 98 Stat. 1708; Pub.L. 101–73, Title VII, § 744(k), Aug. 9, 1989, 103 Stat. 439; Pub.L. 102–242, Title II, § 212(b), Dec. 19, 1991, 105 Stat. 2299; Pub.L. 102–550, Title XVI, § 1604(a)(5), Oct. 28, 1992, 106 Stat. 4082; Pub.L. 104–208, Div. A, Title II, § 2106, Sept. 30, 1996, 110 Stat. 3009–402; Pub.L. 111–203, Title X, §§ 1100A(2), 1100A(8), Title XIV, §§ 1400(c), 1414(b), July 21, 2010, 124 Stat. 2107, 2108, 2109, 2136, 2152.)

§ 1608. Views of other agencies [CCPA § 109]

In the exercise of its functions under this subchapter, the Bureau may obtain upon requests the views of any other Federal agency which, in the judgment of the Bureau, exercises regulatory or supervisory functions with respect to any class of creditors subject to this subchapter.

(Pub.L. 90–321, Title I, § 109, May 29, 1968, 82 Stat. 150; Pub.L. 111–203, Title X, § 1100A(2), July 21, 2010, 124 Stat. 2107.)

§ 1609. Repealed. Pub.L. 94–239, § 3(b)(1), Mar. 23, 1976, 90 Stat. 253

§ 1610. Effect on other laws [CCPA § 111]

(a) Inconsistent provisions; procedures applicable for determination

(1) Except as provided in subsection (e) of this section, this part and parts B and C of this subchapter do not annul, alter, or affect the laws of any State relating to the disclosure of information in connection with credit transactions, except to the extent that those laws are inconsistent with the provisions of this subchapter and then only to the extent of the inconsistency. Upon its own motion or upon the request of any creditor, State or other interested party which is submitted in accordance with procedures prescribed in regulations of the Bureau, the Bureau shall determine whether any such inconsistency exists. If the Bureau determines that a State-required disclosure is inconsistent, creditors located in that State may not make disclosures using the inconsistent term or form, and shall incur no liability under the law of that State for failure to use such term or form, notwithstanding that such determination is subsequently amended, rescinded, or determined by judicial or other authority to be invalid for any reason.

(2) Upon its own motion or upon the request of any creditor, State, or other interested party which is submitted in accordance with procedures prescribed in regulations of the Bureau, the Bureau shall determine whether any disclosure required under the law of any State is substantially the same in meaning as a disclosure required under this subchapter. If the Bureau determines that a State-required disclosure is substantially the same in meaning as a disclosure required by this subchapter, then creditors located in that State may make such disclosure in compliance with such State law in lieu of the disclosure required by this subchapter, except that the annual percentage rate and finance charge shall be disclosed as required by section 1632 of this title, and such State-required disclosure may not be made in lieu of the disclosures applicable to certain mortgages under section 1639 of this title.

(b) State credit charge statutes

Except as provided in section 1639 of this title, this subchapter does not otherwise annul, alter or affect in any manner the meaning, scope or applicability of the laws of any State, including, but not limited to, laws relating to the types, amounts or rates of charges, or any element or elements of charges, permissible under such laws in connection with the extension or use of credit, nor does this subchapter extend the applicability of those laws to any class of persons or transactions to which they would not otherwise apply. The provisions of section 1639 of this title do not annul, alter, or affect the applicability of the laws of any State or exempt any person subject to the provisions of section 1639 of this title from complying with the laws of any State, with respect to the requirements for mortgages referred to in section 1602(aa) of this title, except to the extent that those State laws are inconsistent with any provisions of section 1639 of this title, and then only to the extent of the inconsistency.

(c) Disclosure as evidence

In any action or proceeding in any court involving a consumer credit sale, the disclosure of the annual percentage rate as required under this subchapter in connection with that sale may not be received as evidence that the sale was a loan or any type of transaction other than a credit sale.

(d) Contract or other obligations under State or Federal law

Except as specified in sections 1635, 1640, and 1666e of this title, this subchapter and the regulations issued thereunder do not affect the validity or enforceability of any contract or obligation under State or Federal law.

(e) Certain credit and charge card application and solicitation disclosure provisions

The provisions of subsection (c) of section 1632 of this title and subsections (c), (d), (e), and (f) of section 1637 of this title shall supersede any provision of the law of any State relating to the disclosure of information in any credit or charge card application or solicitation which is subject to the requirements of section 1637(c) of this title or any renewal notice which is subject to the requirements of section 1637(d) of this title, except that any State may employ or establish State laws for the purpose of enforcing the requirements of such sections.

(Pub.L. 90–321, Title I, § 111, May 29, 1968, 82 Stat. 151; Pub.L. 93–495, Title III, § 307(b), Oct. 28, 1974, 88 Stat. 1516; Pub.L. 96–221, Title VI, § 609, Mar. 31, 1980, 94 Stat. 173; Pub.L. 100–583, § 4, Nov. 3, 1988, 102 Stat. 2967; Pub.L. 103–325, Title I, § 152(e)(2)(B), (C), Sept. 23, 1994, 108 Stat. 2194; Pub.L. 111–203, Title X, § 1100A(2), July 21, 2010, 124 Stat. 2107.)

§ 1611. Criminal liability for willful and knowing violation [CCPA § 112]

Whoever willfully and knowingly

(1) gives false or inaccurate information or fails to provide information which he is required to disclose under the provisions of this subchapter or any regulation issued thereunder,

(2) uses any chart or table authorized by the Bureau under section 1606 of this title in such a manner as to consistently understate the annual percentage rate determined under section 1606(a)(1)(A) of this title, or

(3) otherwise fails to comply with any requirement imposed under this subchapter,

shall be fined not more than $5,000 or imprisoned not more than one year, or both.

(Pub.L. 90–321, Title I, § 112, May 29, 1968, 82 Stat. 151; Pub.L. 111–203, Title X, § 1100A(2), July 21, 2010, 124 Stat. 2107.)

§ 1612.   Effect on government agencies [CCPA § 113]

(a) Consultation requirements respecting compliance of credit instruments issued to participating creditor

Any department or agency of the United States which administers a credit program in which it extends, insures, or guarantees consumer credit and in which it provides instruments to a creditor which contain any disclosures required by this subchapter shall, prior to the issuance or continued use of such instruments, consult with the Bureau to assure that such instruments comply with this subchapter.

(b) Inapplicability of Federal civil or criminal penalties to Federal, state, and local agencies

No civil or criminal penalty provided under this subchapter for any violation thereof may be imposed upon the United States or any department or agency thereof, or upon any State or political subdivision thereof, or any agency of any State or political subdivision.

(c) Inapplicability of Federal civil or criminal penalties to participating creditor where violating instrument issued by United States

A creditor participating in a credit program administered, insured, or guaranteed by any department or agency of the United States shall not be held liable for a civil or criminal penalty under this subchapter in any case in which the violation results from the use of an instrument required by any such department or agency.

(d) Applicability of State penalties to violations by participating creditor

A creditor participating in a credit program administered, insured, or guaranteed by any department or agency of the United States shall not be held liable for a civil or criminal penalty under the laws of any State (other than laws determined under section 1610 of this title to be inconsistent with this subchapter) for any technical or procedural failure, such as a failure to use a specific form, to make information available at a specific place on an instrument, or to use a specific typeface, as required by State law, which is caused by the use of an instrument required to be used by such department or agency.

(Pub.L. 90–321, Title I, § 113, May 29, 1968, 82 Stat. 151; Pub.L. 96–221, Title VI, § 622(a), Mar. 31, 1980, 94 Stat. 184; Pub.L. 111–203, Title X, § 1100A(2), July 21, 2010, 124 Stat. 2107.)

§ 1613.   Annual reports to Congress by Bureau [CCPA § 114]

Each year the Bureau shall make a report to the Congress concerning the administration of its functions under this subchapter, including such recommendations as the Bureau deems necessary or appropriate. In addition, each report of the Bureau shall include its assessment of the extent to which compliance with the requirements imposed under this subchapter is being achieved.

(Pub.L. 90–321, Title I, § 114, May 29, 1968, 82 Stat. 151; Pub.L. 96–221, Title VI, § 610(a), Mar. 31, 1980, 94 Stat. 174; Pub.L. 97–375, Title II, § 209(b), Dec. 21, 1982, 96 Stat. 1825; Pub.L. 111–203, Title X, § 1100A(2), July 21, 2010, 124 Stat. 2107.)

§ 1614.   Repealed. Pub.L. 96–221, Title VI, 616(b), Mar. 31, 1980, 94 Stat. 182

§ 1615.   Prohibition on use of "Rule of 78's" in connection with mortgage refinancings and other consumer loans [CCPA § 116]

(a) Prompt refund of unearned interest required

(1) In general

If a consumer prepays in full the financed amount under any consumer credit transaction, the creditor shall promptly refund any unearned portion of the interest charge to the consumer.

(2) Exception for refund of de minimus amount

No refund shall be required under paragraph (1) with respect to the prepayment of any consumer credit transaction if the total amount of the refund would be less than $1.

(3) Applicability to refinanced transactions and acceleration by the creditor

This subsection shall apply with respect to any prepayment of a consumer credit transaction described in paragraph (1) without regard to the manner or the reason for the prepayment, including—

(A) any prepayment made in connection with the refinancing, consolidation, or restructuring of the transaction; and

(B) any prepayment made as a result of the acceleration of the obligation to repay the amount due with respect to the transaction.

(b) Use of "Rule of 78's" prohibited

For the purpose of calculating any refund of interest required under subsection (a) of this section for any precomputed consumer credit transaction of a term exceeding 61 months which is consummated after September 30, 1993, the creditor shall compute the refund based on a method which is at least as favorable to the consumer as the actuarial method.

(c) Statement of prepayment amount

(1) In general

Before the end of the 5-day period beginning on the date an oral or written request is received by a creditor from a consumer for the disclosure of the amount due on any precomputed consumer credit account, the creditor or assignee shall provide the consumer with a statement of—

(A) the amount necessary to prepay the account in full; and

(B) if the amount disclosed pursuant to subparagraph (A) includes an amount which is required to be refunded under this section with respect to such prepayment, the amount of such refund.

(2) Written statement required if request is in writing

If the customer's request is in writing, the statement under paragraph (1) shall be in writing.

(3) 1 free annual statement

A consumer shall be entitled to obtain 1 statement under paragraph (1) each year without charge.

(4) Additional statements subject to reasonable fees

Any creditor may impose a reasonable fee to cover the cost of providing any statement under paragraph (1) to any consumer in addition to the 1 free annual statement required under paragraph (3) if the amount of the charge for such additional statement is disclosed to the consumer before furnishing such statement.

(d) Definitions

For the purpose of this section—

(1) Actuarial method

The term "actuarial method" means the method of allocating payments made on a debt between the amount financed and the finance charge pursuant to which a payment is applied first to the accumulated finance charge and any remainder is subtracted from, or any deficiency is added to, the unpaid balance of the amount financed.

(2) Consumer, credit

The terms "consumer" and "creditor" have the meanings given to such terms in section 1602 of this title.

(3) Creditor

The term "creditor"—

(A) has the meaning given to such term in section 1602 of this title; and

(B) includes any assignee of any creditor with respect to credit extended in connection with any consumer credit transaction and any subsequent assignee with respect to such credit.

(Pub.L. 102–550, Title IX, § 933, Oct. 28, 1992, 106 Stat. 3891.)

§ 1616.   Board review of consumer credit plans and regulations

(a)   Required review

Not later than 2 years after the effective date of this Act and every 2 years thereafter, except as provided in subsection (c)(2), the Board shall conduct a review, within the limits of its existing resources available for reporting purposes, of the consumer credit card market, including—

(1)   the terms of credit card agreements and the practices of credit card issuers;

(2)   the effectiveness of disclosure of terms, fees, and other expenses of credit card plans;

(3)   the adequacy of protections against unfair or deceptive acts or practices relating to credit card plans; and

(4)   whether or not, and to what extent, the implementation of this Act and the amendments made by this Act has affected—

(A)   cost and availability of credit, particularly with respect to non-prime borrowers;

(B)   the safety and soundness of credit card issuers;

(C)   the use of risk-based pricing; or

(D)   credit card product innovation.

(b)   Solicitation of public comment

In connection with conducting the review required by subsection (a), the Board shall solicit comment from consumers, credit card issuers, and other interested parties, such as through hearings or written comments.

(c)   Regulations

(1)   Notice

Following the review required by subsection (a), the Board shall publish a notice in the Federal Register that—

(A)   summarizes the review, the comments received from the public solicitation, and other evidence gathered by the Board, such as through consumer testing or other research; and

(B)   either—

(i)   proposes new or revised regulations or interpretations to update or revise disclosures and protections for consumer credit cards, as appropriate; or

(ii)   states the reason for the determination of the Board that new or revised regulations are not necessary.

(2)   Revision of review period following material revision of regulations

In the event that the Board materially revises regulations on consumer credit card plans, a review need not be conducted until 2 years after the effective date of the revised regulations, which thereafter shall be treated as the new date for the biennial review required by subsection (a).

(d)   Board report to the Congress

The Board shall report to Congress not less frequently than every 2 years, except as provided in subsection (c)(2), on the status of its most recent review, its efforts to address any issues identified from the review, and any recommendations for legislation.

(e) Additional reporting

The Federal banking agencies (as that term is defined in section 1813 of Title 12) and the Federal Trade Commission shall provide annually to the Board, and the Board shall include in its annual report to Congress under section 10 of the Federal Reserve Act, information about the supervisory and enforcement activities of the agencies with respect to compliance by credit card issuers with applicable Federal consumer protection statutes and regulations, including—

(1) this Act, the amendments made by this Act, and regulations prescribed under this Act and such amendments; and

(2) section 5 of the Federal Trade Commission Act, and regulations prescribed under the Federal Trade Commission Act, including part 227 of title 12 of the Code of Federal Regulations, as prescribed by the Board (referred to as "Regulation AA").

(Pub.L. 111–24, Title V, § 502, May 22, 2009, 123 Stat. 1755.)

PART B—CREDIT TRANSACTIONS

§ 1631. Disclosure requirements [CCPA § 121]

(a) Duty of creditor or lessor respecting one or more than one obligor

Subject to subsection (b) of this section, a creditor or lessor shall disclose to the person who is obligated on a consumer lease or a consumer credit transaction the information required under this subchapter. In a transaction involving more than one obligor, a creditor or lessor, except in a transaction under section 1635 of this title, need not disclose to more than one of such obligors if the obligor given disclosure is a primary obligor.

(b) Creditor or lessor required to make disclosure

If a transaction involves one creditor as defined in section 1602(f) of this title, or one lessor as defined in section 1667(3) of this title, such creditor or lessor shall make the disclosures. If a transaction involves more than one creditor or lessor, only one creditor or lessor shall be required to make the disclosures. The Bureau shall by regulation specify which creditor or lessor shall make the disclosures.

(c) Estimates as satisfying statutory requirements; basis of disclosure for per diem interest

The Bureau may provide by regulation that any portion of the information required to be disclosed by this subchapter may be given in the form of estimates where the provider of such information is not in a position to know exact information. In the case of any consumer credit transaction a portion of the interest on which is determined on a per diem basis and is to be collected upon the consummation of such transaction, any disclosure with respect to such portion of interest shall be deemed to be accurate for purposes of this subchapter if the disclosure is based on information actually known to the creditor at the time that the disclosure documents are being prepared for the consummation of the transaction.

(d) Tolerances for numerical disclosures

The Bureau shall determine whether tolerances for numerical disclosures other than the annual percentage rate are necessary to facilitate compliance with this subchapter, and if it determines that such tolerances are necessary to facilitate compliance, it shall by regulation permit disclosures within such tolerances. The Bureau shall exercise its authority to permit tolerances for numerical disclosures other than the annual percentage rate so that such tolerances are narrow enough to prevent such tolerances from resulting in misleading disclosures or disclosures that circumvent the purposes of this subchapter.

(Pub.L. 90–321, Title I, § 121, May 29, 1968, 82 Stat. 152; Pub.L. 93–495, Title III, § 307(c), (d), Title IV, § 409, Oct. 28, 1974, 88 Stat. 1516, 1519; Pub.L. 94–205, § 11, Jan. 2, 1976, 89 Stat. 1159; Pub.L. 96–221, Title VI, § 611, Mar. 31, 1980, 94 Stat. 174; Pub.L. 104–29, § 3(b), Sept. 30, 1995, 109 Stat. 273; Pub.L. 111–203, Title X, § 1100A(2), July 21, 2010, 124 Stat. 2107.)

§ 1632.   Form of disclosure; additional information [CCPA § 122]

(a) Information clearly and conspicuously disclosed; "annual percentage rate" and "finance charge"; order of disclosures and use of different terminology

Information required by this subchapter shall be disclosed clearly and conspicuously, in accordance with regulations of the Bureau. The terms "annual percentage rate" and "finance charge" shall be disclosed more conspicuously than other terms, data, or information provided in connection with a transaction, except information relating to the identity of the creditor. Except as provided in subsection (c) of this section, regulations of the Bureau need not require that disclosures pursuant to this subchapter be made in the order set forth in this subchapter and, except as otherwise provided, may permit the use of terminology different from that employed in this subchapter if it conveys substantially the same meaning.

(b) Optional information by creditor or lessor

Any creditor or lessor may supply additional information or explanation with any disclosures required under parts D and E of this subchapter and, except as provided in sections 1637a(b)(3) and 1638(b)(1) of this title, under this part.

(c) Tabular format required for certain disclosures under section 1637(c)

(1) In general

The information described in paragraphs (1)(A), (3)(B)(i)(I), (4)(A), and (4)(C)(i)(I) of section 1637(c) of this title shall be—

(A) disclosed in the form and manner which the Bureau shall prescribe by regulations; and

(B) placed in a conspicuous and prominent location on or with any written application, solicitation, or other document or paper with respect to which such disclosure is required.

(2) Tabular format

(A) Form of table to be prescribed

In the regulations prescribed under paragraph (1)(A) of this subsection, the Bureau shall require that the disclosure of such information shall, to the extent the Bureau determines to be practicable and appropriate, be in the form of a table which—

(i) contains clear and concise headings for each item of such information; and

(ii) provides a clear and concise form for stating each item of information required to be disclosed under each such heading.

(B) Bureau discretion in prescribing order and wording of table

In prescribing the form of the table under subparagraph (A), the Bureau may—

(i) list the items required to be included in the table in a different order than the order in which such items are set forth in paragraph (1)(A) or (4)(A) of section 1637(c) of this title; and

(ii) subject to subparagraph (C), employ terminology which is different than the terminology which is employed in section 1637(c) of this title if such terminology conveys substantially the same meaning.

(C) Grace period

Either the heading or the statement under the heading which relates to the time period referred to in section 1637(c)(1)(A)(iii) of this title shall contain the term "grace period".

(d) Additional electronic disclosures

(1) Posting agreements

Each creditor shall establish and maintain an Internet site on which the creditor shall post the written agreement between the creditor and the consumer for each credit card account under an open-end consumer credit plan.

(2) Creditor to provide contracts to the Bureau

Each creditor shall provide to the Bureau, in electronic format, the consumer credit card agreements that it publishes on its Internet site.

(3) Record repository

The Bureau shall establish and maintain on its publicly available Internet site a central repository of the consumer credit card agreements received from creditors pursuant to this subsection, and such agreements shall be easily accessible and retrievable by the public.

(4) Exception

This subsection shall not apply to individually negotiated changes to contractual terms, such as individually modified workouts or renegotiations of amounts owed by a consumer under an open end consumer credit plan.

(5) Regulations

The Bureau, in consultation with the other Federal banking agencies (as that term is defined in section 603) and the Bureau,[1] may promulgate regulations to implement this subsection, including specifying the format for posting the agreements on the Internet sites of creditors and establishing exceptions to paragraphs (1) and (2), in any case in which the administrative burden outweighs the benefit of increased transparency, such as where a credit card plan has a de minimis number of consumer account holders.

(Pub.L. 90–321, Title I, § 122, May 29, 1968, 82 Stat. 152; Pub.L. 93–495, Title III, § 307(e), (f), Oct. 28, 1974, 88 Stat. 1516, 1517; Pub.L. 96–221, Title VI, § 611, Mar. 31, 1980, 94 Stat. 175; Pub.L. 100–583, § 2(b), Nov. 3, 1988, 102 Stat. 2966; Pub.L. 100–709, § 2(d), Nov. 23, 1988, 102 Stat. 4731; Pub.L. 111–24, Title II, § 204(a), May 22, 2009, 123 Stat. 1746; Pub.L. 111–203, Title X, § 1100A(2), (3), July 21, 2010, 124 Stat. 2107.)

§ 1633. Exemption for State-regulated transactions [CCPA § 123]

The Bureau shall by regulation exempt from the requirements of this part any class of credit transactions within any State if it determines that under the law of that State that class of transactions is subject to requirements substantially similar to those imposed under this part, and that there is adequate provision for enforcement.

(Pub.L. 90–321, Title I, § 123, May 29, 1968, 82 Stat. 152; Pub.L. 111–203, Title X, § 1100A(2), July 21, 2010, 124 Stat. 2107.)

§ 1634. Effect of subsequent occurrence [CCPA § 124]

If information disclosed in accordance with this part is subsequently rendered inaccurate as the result of any act, occurrence, or agreement subsequent to the delivery of the required disclosures, the inaccuracy resulting therefrom does not constitute a violation of this part.

(Pub.L. 90–321, Title I, § 124, May 29, 1968, 82 Stat. 152.)

§ 1635. Right of rescission as to certain transactions [CCPA § 125]

(a) Disclosure of obligor's right to rescind

Except as otherwise provided in this section, in the case of any consumer credit transaction (including opening or increasing the credit limit for an open end credit plan) in which a security interest, including any such interest arising by operation of law, is or will be retained or acquired in any property which is used as the principal dwelling of the person to whom credit is extended, the obligor shall have the right to rescind the transaction until midnight of the third business day following the consummation of the transaction or the delivery of the information and rescission forms required under this section together with a statement containing the material disclosures required under this subchapter, whichever is later, by notifying the

---

[1] So in original.

creditor, in accordance with regulations of the Bureau, of his intention to do so. The creditor shall clearly and conspicuously disclose, in accordance with regulations of the Bureau, to any obligor in a transaction subject to this section the rights of the obligor under this section. The creditor shall also provide, in accordance with regulations of the Bureau, appropriate forms for the obligor to exercise his right to rescind any transaction subject to this section.

(b) Return of money or property following rescission

When an obligor exercises his right to rescind under subsection (a) of this section, he is not liable for any finance or other charge, and any security interest given by the obligor, including any such interest arising by operation of law, becomes void upon such a rescission. Within 20 days after receipt of a notice of rescission, the creditor shall return to the obligor any money or property given as earnest money, downpayment, or otherwise, and shall take any action necessary or appropriate to reflect the termination of any security interest created under the transaction. If the creditor has delivered any property to the obligor, the obligor may retain possession of it. Upon the performance of the creditor's obligations under this section, the obligor shall tender the property to the creditor, except that if return of the property in kind would be impracticable or inequitable, the obligor shall tender its reasonable value. Tender shall be made at the location of the property or at the residence of the obligor, at the option of the obligor. If the creditor does not take possession of the property within 20 days after tender by the obligor, ownership of the property vests in the obligor without obligation on his part to pay for it. The procedures prescribed by this subsection shall apply except when otherwise ordered by a court.

(c) Rebuttable presumption of delivery of required disclosures

Notwithstanding any rule of evidence, written acknowledgment of receipt of any disclosures required under this subchapter by a person to whom information, forms, and a statement is required to be given pursuant to this section does no more than create a rebuttable presumption of delivery thereof.

(d) Modification and waiver of rights

The Bureau may, if it finds that such action is necessary in order to permit homeowners to meet bona fide personal financial emergencies, prescribe regulations authorizing the modification or waiver of any rights created under this section to the extent and under the circumstances set forth in those regulations.

(e) Exempted transactions; reapplication of provisions

This section does not apply to—

(1) a residential mortgage transaction as defined in section 1602(w) of this title;

(2) a transaction which constitutes a refinancing or consolidation (with no new advances) of the principal balance then due and any accrued and unpaid finance charges of an existing extension of credit by the same creditor secured by an interest in the same property;

(3) a transaction in which an agency of a State is the creditor; or

(4) advances under a preexisting open end credit plan if a security interest has already been retained or acquired and such advances are in accordance with a previously established credit limit for such plan.

(f) Time limit for exercise of right

An obligor's right of rescission shall expire three years after the date of consummation of the transaction or upon the sale of the property, whichever occurs first, notwithstanding the fact that the information and forms required under this section or any other disclosures required under this part have not been delivered to the obligor, except that if (1) any agency empowered to enforce the provisions of this subchapter institutes a proceeding to enforce the provisions of this section within three years after the date of consummation of the transaction, (2) such agency finds a violation of this section, and (3) the obligor's right to rescind is based in whole or in part on any matter involved in such proceeding, then the obligor's right of rescission shall expire three years after the date of consummation of the transaction or upon the earlier sale of the property, or upon the expiration of one year following the conclusion of the proceeding, or any judicial review or period for judicial review thereof, whichever is later.

(g) Additional relief

In any action in which it is determined that a creditor has violated this section, in addition to rescission the court may award relief under section 1640 of this title for violations of this subchapter not relating to the right to rescind.

(h) Limitation on rescission

An obligor shall have no rescission rights arising solely from the form of written notice used by the creditor to inform the obligor of the rights of the obligor under this section, if the creditor provided the obligor the appropriate form of written notice published and adopted by the Bureau, or a comparable written notice of the rights of the obligor, that was properly completed by the creditor, and otherwise complied with all other requirements of this section regarding notice.

(i) Rescission rights in foreclosure

(1) In general

Notwithstanding section 1649 of this title, and subject to the time period provided in subsection (f) of this section, in addition to any other right of rescission available under this section for a transaction, after the initiation of any judicial or nonjudicial foreclosure process on the primary dwelling of an obligor securing an extension of credit, the obligor shall have a right to rescind the transaction equivalent to other rescission rights provided by this section, if—

(A) a mortgage broker fee is not included in the finance charge in accordance with the laws and regulations in effect at the time the consumer credit transaction was consummated; or

(B) the form of notice of rescission for the transaction is not the appropriate form of written notice published and adopted by the Bureau or a comparable written notice, and otherwise complied with all the requirements of this section regarding notice.

(2) Tolerance for disclosures

Notwithstanding section 1605(f) of this title, and subject to the time period provided in subsection (f) of this section, for the purposes of exercising any rescission rights after the initiation of any judicial or nonjudicial foreclosure process on the principal dwelling of the obligor securing an extension of credit, the disclosure of the finance charge and other disclosures affected by any finance charge shall be treated as being accurate for purposes of this section if the amount disclosed as the finance charge does not vary from the actual finance charge by more than $35 or is greater than the amount required to be disclosed under this subchapter.

(3) Right of recoupment under State law

Nothing in this subsection affects a consumer's right of rescission in recoupment under State law.

(4) Applicability

This subsection shall apply to all consumer credit transactions in existence or consummated on or after September 30, 1995.

(Pub.L. 90–321, Title I, § 125, May 29, 1968, 82 Stat. 153; Pub.L. 93–495, Title IV, §§ 404, 405, 412, Oct. 28, 1974, 88 Stat. 1517, 1519; Pub.L. 96–221, Title VI, § 612(a)(1), (3) to (6), Mar. 31, 1980, 94 Stat. 175, 176; Pub.L. 98–479, Title II, § 205, Oct. 17, 1984, 98 Stat. 2234; Pub.L. 104–29, §§ 5, 8, Sept. 30, 1995, 109 Stat. 274, 275; Pub.L. 111–203, Title X, § 1100A(2), July 21, 2010, 124 Stat. 2107.)

§ 1636. Repealed. Pub.L. 96–221, Title VI, § 614(e)(1), Mar. 31, 1980, 94 Stat. 180

§ 1637. Open end consumer credit plans [CCPA § 127]

(a) Required disclosures by creditor

Before opening any account under an open end consumer credit plan, the creditor shall disclose to the person to whom credit is to be extended each of the following items, to the extent applicable:

(1) The conditions under which a finance charge may be imposed, including the time period (if any) within which any credit extended may be repaid without incurring a finance charge, except that the creditor may, at his election and without disclosure, impose no such finance charge if payment is received after the termination of such time period. If no such time period is provided, the creditor shall disclose such fact.

(2) The method of determining the balance upon which a finance charge will be imposed.

(3) The method of determining the amount of the finance charge, including any minimum or fixed amount imposed as a finance charge.

(4) Where one or more periodic rates may be used to compute the finance charge, each such rate, the range of balances to which it is applicable, and the corresponding nominal annual percentage rate determined by multiplying the periodic rate by the number of periods in a year.

(5) Identification of other charges which may be imposed as part of the plan, and their method of computation, in accordance with regulations of the Bureau.

(6) In cases where the credit is or will be secured, a statement that a security interest has been or will be taken in (A) the property purchased as part of the credit transaction, or (B) property not purchased as part of the credit transaction identified by item or type.

(7) A statement, in a form prescribed by regulations of the Bureau of the protection provided by sections 1666 and 1666i of this title to an obligor and the creditor's responsibilities under sections 1666a and 1666i of this title. With respect to one billing cycle per calendar year, at intervals of not less than six months or more than eighteen months, the creditor shall transmit such statement to each obligor to whom the creditor is required to transmit a statement pursuant to subsection (b) of this section for such billing cycle.

(8) In the case of any account under an open end consumer credit plan which provides for any extension of credit which is secured by the consumer's principal dwelling, any information which—

(A) is required to be disclosed under section 1637a(a) of this title; and

(B) the Bureau determines is not described in any other paragraph of this subsection.

(b) Statement required with each billing cycle

The creditor of any account under an open end consumer credit plan shall transmit to the obligor, for each billing cycle at the end of which there is an outstanding balance in that account or with respect to which a finance charge is imposed, a statement setting forth each of the following items to the extent applicable:

(1) The outstanding balance in the account at the beginning of the statement period.

(2) The amount and date of each extension of credit during the period, and a brief identification, on or accompanying the statement of each extension of credit in a form prescribed by the Bureau sufficient to enable the obligor either to identify the transaction or to relate it to copies of sales vouchers or similar instruments previously furnished, except that a creditor's failure to disclose such information in accordance with this paragraph shall not be deemed a failure to comply with this part or this subchapter if (A) the creditor maintains procedures reasonably adapted to procure and provide such information, and (B) the creditor responds to and treats any inquiry for clarification or documentation as a billing error and an erroneously billed amount under section 1666 of this title. In lieu of complying with the requirements of the previous sentence, in the case of any transaction in which the creditor and seller are the same person, as defined by the Bureau, and such person's open end credit plan has fewer than 15,000 accounts, the creditor may elect to provide only the amount and date of each extension of credit during the period and the seller's name and location where the transaction took place if (A) a brief identification of the transaction has been previously furnished, and (B) the creditor responds to and treats any inquiry for clarification or documentation as a billing error and an erroneously billed amount under section 1666 of this title.

(3) The total amount credited to the account during the period.

(4) The amount of any finance charge added to the account during the period, itemized to show the amounts, if any, due to the application of percentage rates and the amount, if any, imposed as a minimum or fixed charge.

(5) Where one or more periodic rates may be used to compute the finance charge, each such rate, the range of balances to which it is applicable, and, unless the annual percentage rate (determined under section 1606(a)(2) of this title) is required to be disclosed pursuant to paragraph (6), the corresponding nominal annual percentage rate determined by multiplying the periodic rate by the number of periods in a year.

(6) Where the total finance charge exceeds 50 cents for a monthly or longer billing cycle, or the pro rata part of 50 cents for a billing cycle shorter than monthly, the total finance charge expressed as an annual percentage rate (determined under section 1606(a)(2) of this title), except that if the finance charge is the sum of two or more products of a rate times a portion of the balance, the creditor may, in lieu of disclosing a single rate for the total charge, disclose each such rate expressed as an annual percentage rate, and the part of the balance to which it is applicable.

(7) The balance on which the finance charge was computed and a statement of how the balance was determined. If the balance is determined without first deducting all credits during the period, that fact and the amount of such payments shall also be disclosed.

(8) The outstanding balance in the account at the end of the period.

(9) The date by which or the period (if any) within which, payment must be made to avoid additional finance charges, except that the creditor may, at his election and without disclosure, impose no such additional finance charge if payment is received after such date or the termination of such period.

(10) The address to be used by the creditor for the purpose of receiving billing inquiries from the obligor.

(11)(A) A written statement in the following form: "Minimum Payment Warning: Making only the minimum payment will increase the amount of interest you pay and the time it takes to repay your balance.", or such similar statement as is established by the Bureau pursuant to consumer testing.

(B) Repayment information that would apply to the outstanding balance of the consumer under the credit plan, including—

    (i) the number of months (rounded to the nearest month) that it would take to pay the entire amount of that balance, if the consumer pays only the required minimum monthly payments and if no further advances are made;

    (ii) the total cost to the consumer, including interest and principal payments, of paying that balance in full, if the consumer pays only the required minimum monthly payments and if no further advances are made;

    (iii) the monthly payment amount that would be required for the consumer to eliminate the outstanding balance in 36 months, if no further advances are made, and the total cost to the consumer, including interest and principal payments, of paying that balance in full if the consumer pays the balance over 36 months; and

    (iv) a toll-free telephone number at which the consumer may receive information about accessing credit counseling and debt management services.

(C)(i) Subject to clause (ii), in making the disclosures under subparagraph (B), the creditor shall apply the interest rate or rates in effect on the date on which the disclosure is made until the date on which the balance would be paid in full.

    (ii) If the interest rate in effect on the date on which the disclosure is made is a temporary rate that will change under a contractual provision applying an index or formula for subsequent interest rate adjustment, the creditor shall apply the interest rate in effect on the date on which the disclosure is made for as long as that interest rate will apply under that contractual provision, and then apply an interest rate based on the index or formula in effect on the applicable billing date.

(D) All of the information described in subparagraph (B) shall—

(i) be disclosed in the form and manner which the Bureau shall prescribe, by regulation, and in a manner that avoids duplication; and

(ii) be placed in a conspicuous and prominent location on the billing statement.

(E) In the regulations prescribed under subparagraph (D), the Bureau shall require that the disclosure of such information shall be in the form of a table that—

(i) contains clear and concise headings for each item of such information; and

(ii) provides a clear and concise form stating each item of information required to be disclosed under each such heading.

(F) In prescribing the form of the table under subparagraph (E), the board shall require that—

(i) all of the information in the table, and not just a reference to the table, be placed on the billing statement, as required by this paragraph; and

(ii) the items required to be included in the table shall be listed in the order in which such items are set forth in subparagraph (B).

(G) In prescribing the form of the table under subparagraph (D), the Bureau shall employ terminology which is different than the terminology which is employed in subparagraph (B), if such terminology is more easily understood and conveys substantially the same meaning.

(12) Requirements relating to late payment deadlines and penalties

(A) Late payment deadline required to be disclosed

In the case of a credit card account under an open end consumer credit plan under which a late fee or charge may be imposed due to the failure of the obligor to make payment on or before the due date for such payment, the periodic statement required under subsection (b) with respect to the account shall include, in a conspicuous location on the billing statement, the date on which the payment is due or, if different, the date on which a late payment fee will be charged, together with the amount of the fee or charge to be imposed if payment is made after that date.

(B) Disclosure of increase in interest rates for late payments

If 1 or more late payments under an open end consumer credit plan may result in an increase in the annual percentage rate applicable to the account, the statement required under subsection (b) with respect to the account shall include conspicuous notice of such fact, together with the applicable penalty annual percentage rate, in close proximity to the disclosure required under subparagraph (A) of the date on which payment is due under the terms of the account.

(C) Payments at local branches

If the creditor, in the case of a credit card account referred to in subparagraph (A), is a financial institution which maintains branches or offices at which payments on any such account are accepted from the obligor in person, the date on which the obligor makes a payment on the account at such branch or office shall be considered to be the date on which the payment is made for purposes of determining whether a late fee or charge may be imposed due to the failure of the obligor to make payment on or before the due date for such payment.

(c) Disclosure in credit and charge card applications and solicitations

(1) Direct mail applications and solicitations

(A) Information in tabular format

Any application to open a credit card account for any person under an open end consumer credit plan, or a solicitation to open such an account without requiring an application, that is mailed to consumers shall disclose the following information, subject to subsection (e) of this section and section 1632(c) of this title:

(i) Annual percentage rates

(I) Each annual percentage rate applicable to extensions of credit under such credit plan.

(II) Where an extension of credit is subject to a variable rate, the fact that the rate is variable, the annual percentage rate in effect at the time of the mailing, and how the rate is determined.

(III) Where more than one rate applies, the range of balances to which each rate applies.

(ii) Annual and other fees

(I) Any annual fee, other periodic fee, or membership fee imposed for the issuance or availability of a credit card, including any account maintenance fee or other charge imposed based on activity or inactivity for the account during the billing cycle.

(II) Any minimum finance charge imposed for each period during which any extension of credit which is subject to a finance charge is outstanding.

(III) Any transaction charge imposed in connection with use of the card to purchase goods or services.

(iii) Grace period

(I) The date by which or the period within which any credit extended under such credit plan for purchases of goods or services must be repaid to avoid incurring a finance charge, and, if no such period is offered, such fact shall be clearly stated.

(II) If the length of such "grace period" varies, the card issuer may disclose the range of days in the grace period, the minimum number of days in the grace period, or the average number of days in the grace period, if the disclosure is identified as such.

(iv) Balance calculation method

(I) The name of the balance calculation method used in determining the balance on which the finance charge is computed if the method used has been defined by the Bureau, or a detailed explanation of the balance calculation method used if the method has not been so defined.

(II) In prescribing regulations to carry out this clause, the Bureau shall define and name not more than the 5 balance calculation methods determined by the Bureau to be the most commonly used methods.

(B) Other information

In addition to the information required to be disclosed under subparagraph (A), each application or solicitation to which such subparagraph applies shall disclose clearly and conspicuously the following information, subject to subsections (e) and (f) of this section:

(i) Cash advance fee

Any fee imposed for an extension of credit in the form of cash.

(ii) Late fee

Any fee imposed for a late payment.

(iii) Over-the-limit fee

Any fee imposed in connection with an extension of credit in excess of the amount of credit authorized to be extended with respect to such account.

(2) Telephone solicitations

(A) In general

In any telephone solicitation to open a credit card account for any person under an open end consumer credit plan, the person making the solicitation shall orally disclose the information described in paragraph (1)(A).

(B) Exception

Subparagraph (A) shall not apply to any telephone solicitation if—

    (i) the credit card issuer—

        (I) does not impose any fee described in paragraph (1)(A)(ii)(I); or

        (II) does not impose any fee in connection with telephone solicitations unless the consumer signifies acceptance by using the card;

    (ii) the card issuer discloses clearly and conspicuously in writing the information described in paragraph (1) within 30 days after the consumer requests the card, but in no event later than the date of delivery of the card; and

    (iii) the card issuer discloses clearly and conspicuously that the consumer is not obligated to accept the card or account and the consumer will not be obligated to pay any of the fees or charges disclosed unless the consumer elects to accept the card or account by using the card.

(3) Applications and solicitations by other means

(A) In general

Any application to open a credit card account for any person under an open end consumer credit plan, and any solicitation to open such an account without requiring an application, that is made available to the public or contained in catalogs, magazines, or other publications shall meet the disclosure requirements of subparagraph (B), (C), or (D).

(B) Specific information

An application or solicitation described in subparagraph (A) meets the requirement of this subparagraph if such application or solicitation contains—

    (i) the information—

        (I) described in paragraph (1)(A) in the form required under section 1632(c) of this title, subject to subsection (e) of this section, and

        (II) described in paragraph (1)(B) in a clear and conspicuous form, subject to subsections (e) and (f) of this section;

    (ii) a statement, in a conspicuous and prominent location on the application or solicitation, that—

        (I) the information is accurate as of the date the application or solicitation was printed;

        (II) the information contained in the application or solicitation is subject to change after such date; and

        (III) the applicant should contact the creditor for information on any change in the information contained in the application or solicitation since it was printed;

    (iii) a clear and conspicuous disclosure of the date the application or solicitation was printed; and

    (iv) a disclosure, in a conspicuous and prominent location on the application or solicitation, of a toll free telephone number or a mailing address at which the applicant may contact the creditor to obtain any change in the information provided in the application or solicitation since it was printed.

(C) General information without any specific term

An application or solicitation described in subparagraph (A) meets the requirement of this subparagraph if such application or solicitation—

(i) contains a statement, in a conspicuous and prominent location on the application or solicitation, that—

(I) there are costs associated with the use of credit cards; and

(II) the applicant may contact the creditor to request disclosure of specific information of such costs by calling a toll free telephone number or by writing to an address, specified in the application;

(ii) contains a disclosure, in a conspicuous and prominent location on the application or solicitation, of a toll free telephone number and a mailing address at which the applicant may contact the creditor to obtain such information; and

(iii) does not contain any of the items described in paragraph (1).

(D) Applications or solicitations containing subsection (a) disclosures

An application or solicitation meets the requirement of this subparagraph if it contains, or is accompanied by—

(i) the disclosures required by paragraphs (1) through (6) of subsection (a) of this section;

(ii) the disclosures required by subparagraphs (A) and (B) of paragraph (1) of this subsection included clearly and conspiciously[1] (except that the provisions of section 1632(c) of this title shall not apply); and

(iii) a toll free telephone number or a mailing address at which the applicant may contact the creditor to obtain any change in the information provided.

(E) Prompt response to information requests

Upon receipt of a request for any of the information referred to in subparagraph (B), (C), or (D), the card issuer or the agent of such issuer shall promptly disclose all of the information described in paragraph (1).

(4) Charge card applications and solicitations

(A) In general

Any application or solicitation to open a charge card account shall disclose clearly and conspicuously the following information in the form required by section 1632(c) of this title, subject to subsection (e) of this section:

(i) Any annual fee, other periodic fee, or membership fee imposed for the issuance or availability of the charge card, including any account maintenance fee or other charge imposed based on activity or inactivity for the account during the billing cycle.

(ii) Any transaction charge imposed in connection with use of the card to purchase goods or services.

(iii) A statement that charges incurred by use of the charge card are due and payable upon receipt of a periodic statement rendered for such charge card account.

---

[1] So in original. Probably should be "conspicuously".

(B) Other information

In addition to the information required to be disclosed under subparagraph (A), each written application or solicitation to which such subparagraph applies shall disclose clearly and conspicuously the following information, subject to subsections (e) and (f) of this section:

(i) Cash advance fee

Any fee imposed for an extension of credit in the form of cash.

(ii) Late fee

Any fee imposed for a late payment.

(iii) Over-the-limit fee

Any fee imposed in connection with an extension of credit in excess of the amount of credit authorized to be extended with respect to such account.

(C) Applications and solicitations by other means

Any application to open a charge card account, and any solicitation to open such an account without requiring an application, that is made available to the public or contained in catalogs, magazines, or other publications shall contain—

(i) the information—

(I) described in subparagraph (A) in the form required under section 1632(c) of this title, subject to subsection (e) of this section, and

(II) described in subparagraph (B) in a clear and conspicuous form, subject to subsections (e) and (f) of this section;

(ii) a statement, in a conspicuous and prominent location on the application or solicitation, that—

(I) the information is accurate as of the date the application or solicitation was printed;

(II) the information contained in the application or solicitation is subject to change after such date; and

(III) the applicant should contact the creditor for information on any change in the information contained in the application or solicitation since it was printed;

(iii) a clear and conspicuous disclosure of the date the application or solicitation was printed; and

(iv) a disclosure, in a conspicuous and prominent location on the application or solicitation, of a toll free telephone number or a mailing address at which the applicant may contact the creditor to obtain any change in the information provided in the application or solicitation since it was printed.

(D) Issuers of charge cards which provide access to open end consumer credit plans

If a charge card permits the card holder to receive an extension of credit under an open end consumer credit plan, which is not maintained by the charge card issuer, the charge card issuer may provide the information described in subparagraphs (A) and (B) in the form required by such subparagraphs in lieu of the information required to be provided under paragraph (1), (2), or (3) with respect to any credit extended under such plan, if the charge card issuer discloses clearly and conspicuously to the consumer in the application or solicitation that—

(i) the charge card issuer will make an independent decision as to whether to issue the card;

(ii) the charge card may arrive before the decision is made with respect to an extension of credit under an open end consumer credit plan; and

(iii) approval by the charge card issuer does not constitute approval by the issuer of the extension of credit.

The information required to be disclosed under paragraph (1) shall be provided to the charge card holder by the creditor which maintains such open end consumer credit plan before the first extension of credit under such plan.

(E) Charge card defined

For the purposes of this subsection, the term "charge card" means a card, plate, or other single credit device that may be used from time to time to obtain credit which is not subject to a finance charge.

(5) Regulatory authority of the Bureau

The Bureau may, by regulation, require the disclosure of information in addition to that otherwise required by this subsection or subsection (d) of this section, and modify any disclosure of information required by this subsection or subsection (d) of this section, in any application to open a credit card account for any person under an open end consumer credit plan or any application to open a charge card account for any person, or a solicitation to open any such account without requiring an application, if the Bureau determines that such action is necessary to carry out the purposes of, or prevent evasions of, any paragraph of this subsection.

(6) Additional notice concerning "introductory rates"—

(A) In general

Except as provided in subparagraph (B), an application or solicitation to open a credit card account and all promotional materials accompanying such application or solicitation for which a disclosure is required under paragraph (1), and that offers a temporary annual percentage rate of interest, shall—

(i) use the term "introductory" in immediate proximity to each listing of the temporary annual percentage rate applicable to such account, which term shall appear clearly and conspicuously;

(ii) if the annual percentage rate of interest that will apply after the end of the temporary rate period will be a fixed rate, state in a clear and conspicuous manner in a prominent location closely proximate to the first listing of the temporary annual percentage rate (other than a listing of the temporary annual percentage rate in the tabular format described in section 1632(c) of this title), the time period in which the introductory period will end and the annual percentage rate that will apply after the end of the introductory period; and

(iii) if the annual percentage rate that will apply after the end of the temporary rate period will vary in accordance with an index, state in a clear and conspicuous manner in a prominent location closely proximate to the first listing of the temporary annual percentage rate (other than a listing in the tabular format prescribed by section 1632(c) of this title), the time period in which the introductory period will end and the rate that will apply after that, based on an annual percentage rate that was in effect within 60 days before the date of mailing the application or solicitation.

(B) Exception

Clauses (ii) and (iii) of subparagraph (A) do not apply with respect to any listing of a temporary annual percentage rate on an envelope or other enclosure in which an application or solicitation to open a credit card account is mailed.

(C) Conditions for introductory rates

An application or solicitation to open a credit card account for which a disclosure is required under paragraph (1), and that offers a temporary annual percentage rate of interest shall, if that rate of interest is revocable under any circumstance or upon any event, clearly and conspicuously disclose, in a prominent manner on or with such application or solicitation—

    (i)   a general description of the circumstances that may result in the revocation of the temporary annual percentage rate; and

    (ii)   if the annual percentage rate that will apply upon the revocation of the temporary annual percentage rate—

        (I)   will be a fixed rate, the annual percentage rate that will apply upon the revocation of the temporary annual percentage rate; or

        (II)   will vary in accordance with an index, the rate that will apply after the temporary rate, based on an annual percentage rate that was in effect within 60 days before the date of mailing the application or solicitation.

(D)   **Definitions**

In this paragraph—

    (i)   the terms "temporary annual percentage rate of interest" and "temporary annual percentage rate" mean any rate of interest applicable to a credit card account for an introductory period of less than 1 year, if that rate is less than an annual percentage rate that was in effect within 60 days before the date of mailing the application or solicitation; and

    (ii)   the term "introductory period" means the maximum time period for which the temporary annual percentage rate may be applicable.

(E)   **Relation to other disclosure requirements**

Nothing in this paragraph may be construed to supersede subsection (a) of section 1632 of this title, or any disclosure required by paragraph (1) or any other provision of this subsection.

(7)   **Internet-based solicitations**

(A)   **In general**

In any solicitation to open a credit card account for any person under an open end consumer credit plan using the Internet or other interactive computer service, the person making the solicitation shall clearly and conspicuously disclose—

    (i)   the information described in subparagraphs (A) and (B) of paragraph (1); and

    (ii)   the information described in paragraph (6).

(B)   **Form of disclosure**

The disclosures required by subparagraph (A) shall be—

    (i)   readily accessible to consumers in close proximity to the solicitation to open a credit card account; and

    (ii)   updated regularly to reflect the current policies, terms, and fee amounts applicable to the credit card account.

(C)   **Definitions**

For purposes of this paragraph—

    (i)   the term "Internet" means the international computer network of both Federal and non-Federal interoperable packet switched data networks; and

    (ii)   the term "interactive computer service" means any information service, system, or access software provider that provides or enables computer access by multiple users to a computer server, including specifically a service or system that provides access to the Internet and such systems operated or services offered by libraries or educational institutions.

(8) Applications from underage consumers

(A) Prohibition on issuance

No credit card may be issued to, or open end consumer credit plan established by or on behalf of, a consumer who has not attained the age of 21, unless the consumer has submitted a written application to the card issuer that meets the requirements of subparagraph (B).

(B) Application requirements

An application to open a credit card account by a consumer who has not attained the age of 21 as of the date of submission of the application shall require—

(i) the signature of a cosigner, including the parent, legal guardian, spouse, or any other individual who has attained the age of 21 having a means to repay debts incurred by the consumer in connection with the account, indicating joint liability for debts incurred by the consumer in connection with the account before the consumer has attained the age of 21; or

(ii) submission by the consumer of financial information, including through an application, indicating an independent means of repaying any obligation arising from the proposed extension of credit in connection with the account.

(C) Safe harbor

The Bureau shall promulgate regulations providing standards that, if met, would satisfy the requirements of subparagraph (B)(ii).

(d) Disclosure prior to renewal

(1) In general

A card issuer that has changed or amended any term of the account since the last renewal that has not been previously disclosed or that imposes any fee described in subsection (c)(1)(A)(ii)(I) or (c)(4)(A)(i) of this section shall transmit to a consumer at least 30 days prior to the scheduled renewal date of the consumer's credit or charge card account a clear and conspicuous disclosure of—

(A) the date by which, the month by which, or the billing period at the close of which, the account will expire if not renewed;

(B) the information described in subsection (c)(1)(A) or (c)(4)(A) of this section that would apply if the account were renewed, subject to subsection (e) of this section; and

(C) the method by which the consumer may terminate continued credit availability under the account.

(2) Short-term renewals

The Bureau may by regulation provide for fewer disclosures than are required by paragraph (1) in the case of an account which is renewable for a period of less than 6 months.

(e) Other rules for disclosures under subsections (c) and (d)

(1) Fees determined on the basis of a percentage

If the amount of any fee required to be disclosed under subsection (c) or (d) of this section is determined on the basis of a percentage of another amount, the percentage used in making such determination and the identification of the amount against which such percentage is applied shall be disclosed in lieu of the amount of such fee.

(2) Disclosure only of fees actually imposed

If a credit or charge card issuer does not impose any fee required to be disclosed under any provision of subsection (c) or (d) of this section, such provision shall not apply with respect to such issuer.

(f) Disclosure of range of certain fees which vary by State allowed

If the amount of any fee required to be disclosed by a credit or charge card issuer under paragraph (1)(B), (3)(B)(i)(II), (4)(B), or (4)(C)(i)(II) of subsection (c) of this section varies from State to State, the card issuer may disclose the range of such fees for purposes of subsection (c) of this section in lieu of the amount for each applicable State, if such disclosure includes a statement that the amount of such fee varies from State to State.

(g) Insurance in connection with certain open end credit card plans

(1) Change in insurance carrier

Whenever a card issuer that offers any guarantee or insurance for repayment of all or part of the outstanding balance of an open end credit card plan proposes to change the person providing that guarantee or insurance, the card issuer shall send each insured consumer written notice of the proposed change not less than 30 days prior to the change, including notice of any increase in the rate or substantial decrease in coverage or service which will result from such change. Such notice may be included on or with the monthly statement provided to the consumer prior to the month in which the proposed change would take effect.

(2) Notice of new insurance coverage

In any case in which a proposed change described in paragraph (1) occurs, the insured consumer shall be given the name and address of the new guarantor or insurer and a copy of the policy or group certificate containing the basic terms and conditions, including the premium rate to be charged.

(3) Right to discontinue guarantee or insurance

The notices required under paragraphs (1) and (2) shall each include a statement that the consumer has the option to discontinue the insurance or guarantee.

(4) No preemption of State law

No provision of this subsection shall be construed as superseding any provision of State law which is applicable to the regulation of insurance.

(5) Bureau definition of substantial decrease in coverage or service

The Bureau shall define, in regulations, what constitutes a "substantial decrease in coverage or service" for purposes of paragraph (1).

(h) Prohibition on certain actions for failure to incur finance charges

A creditor of an account under an open end consumer credit plan may not terminate an account prior to its expiration date solely because the consumer has not incurred finance charges on the account. Nothing in this subsection shall prohibit a creditor from terminating an account for inactivity in 3 or more consecutive months.

(i) Advance notice of rate increase and other changes required

(1) Advance notice of increase in interest rate required

In the case of any credit card account under an open end consumer credit plan, a creditor shall provide a written notice of an increase in an annual percentage rate (except in the case of an increase described in paragraph (1), (2), or (3) of section 1666i–1(b) of this title) not later than 45 days prior to the effective date of the increase.

(2) Advance notice of other significant changes required

In the case of any credit card account under an open end consumer credit plan, a creditor shall provide a written notice of any significant change, as determined by rule of the Bureau, in the terms (including an increase in any fee or finance charge, other than as provided in paragraph (1)) of the cardholder agreement between the creditor and the obligor, not later than 45 days prior to the effective date of the change.

(3) Notice of right to cancel

Each notice required by paragraph (1) or (2) shall be made in a clear and conspicuous manner, and shall contain a brief statement of the right of the obligor to cancel the account pursuant to rules established by the Bureau before the effective date of the subject rate increase or other change.

(4) Rule of construction

Closure or cancellation of an account by the obligor shall not constitute a default under an existing cardholder agreement, and shall not trigger an obligation to immediately repay the obligation in full or through a method that is less beneficial to the obligor than one of the methods described in section 1666i–1(c)(2) of this title, or the imposition of any other penalty or fee.

(j) Prohibition on penalties for on-time payments

(1) Prohibition on double-cycle billing and penalties for on-time payments

Except as provided in paragraph (2), a creditor may not impose any finance charge on a credit card account under an open end consumer credit plan as a result of the loss of any time period provided by the creditor within which the obligor may repay any portion of the credit extended without incurring a finance charge, with respect to—

    (A) any balances for days in billing cycles that precede the most recent billing cycle; or

    (B) any balances or portions thereof in the current billing cycle that were repaid within such time period.

(2) Exceptions

Paragraph (1) does not apply to—

    (A) any adjustment to a finance charge as a result of the resolution of a dispute; or

    (B) any adjustment to a finance charge as a result of the return of a payment for insufficient funds.

(k) Opt-in required for over-the-limit transactions if fees are imposed

(1) In general

In the case of any credit card account under an open end consumer credit plan under which an over-the-limit fee may be imposed by the creditor for any extension of credit in excess of the amount of credit authorized to be extended under such account, no such fee shall be charged, unless the consumer has expressly elected to permit the creditor, with respect to such account, to complete transactions involving the extension of credit under such account in excess of the amount of credit authorized.

(2) Disclosure by creditor

No election by a consumer under paragraph (1) shall take effect unless the consumer, before making such election, received a notice from the creditor of any over-the-limit fee in the form and manner, and at the time, determined by the Bureau. If the consumer makes the election referred to in paragraph (1), the creditor shall provide notice to the consumer of the right to revoke the election, in the form prescribed by the Bureau, in any periodic statement that includes notice of the imposition of an over-the-limit fee during the period covered by the statement.

(3) Form of election

A consumer may make or revoke the election referred to in paragraph (1) orally, electronically, or in writing, pursuant to regulations prescribed by the Bureau. The Bureau shall prescribe regulations to ensure that the same options are available for both making and revoking such election.

(4) Time of election

A consumer may make the election referred to in paragraph (1) at any time, and such election shall be effective until the election is revoked in the manner prescribed under paragraph (3).

(5) Regulations

The Bureau shall prescribe regulations—

    (A) governing disclosures under this subsection; and

    (B) that prevent unfair or deceptive acts or practices in connection with the manipulation of credit limits designed to increase over-the-limit fees or other penalty fees.

(6) Rule of construction

Nothing in this subsection shall be construed to prohibit a creditor from completing an over-the-limit transaction, provided that a consumer who has not made a valid election under paragraph (1) is not charged an over-the-limit fee for such transaction.

(7) Restriction on fees charged for an over-the-limit transaction

With respect to a credit card account under an open end consumer credit plan, an over-the-limit fee may be imposed only once during a billing cycle if the credit limit on the account is exceeded, and an over-the-limit fee, with respect to such excess credit, may be imposed only once in each of the 2 subsequent billing cycles, unless the consumer has obtained an additional extension of credit in excess of such credit limit during any such subsequent cycle or the consumer reduces the outstanding balance below the credit limit as of the end of such billing cycle.

(*l*) Limit on fees related to method of payment

With respect to a credit card account under an open end consumer credit plan, the creditor may not impose a separate fee to allow the obligor to repay an extension of credit or finance charge, whether such repayment is made by mail, electronic transfer, telephone authorization, or other means, unless such payment involves an expedited service by a service representative of the creditor.

(m) Use of term "fixed rate"

With respect to the terms of any credit card account under an open end consumer credit plan, the term "fixed", when appearing in conjunction with a reference to the annual percentage rate or interest rate applicable with respect to such account, may only be used to refer to an annual percentage rate or interest rate that will not change or vary for any reason over the period specified clearly and conspicuously in the terms of the account.

(n) Standards applicable to initial issuance of subprime or "fee harvester" cards

(1) In general

If the terms of a credit card account under an open end consumer credit plan require the payment of any fees (other than any late fee, over-the-limit fee, or fee for a payment returned for insufficient funds) by the consumer in the first year during which the account is opened in an aggregate amount in excess of 25 percent of the total amount of credit authorized under the account when the account is opened, no payment of any fees (other than any late fee, over-the-limit fee, or fee for a payment returned for insufficient funds) may be made from the credit made available under the terms of the account.

(2) Rule of construction

No provision of this subsection may be construed as authorizing any imposition or payment of advance fees otherwise prohibited by any provision of law.

(o) Due dates for credit card accounts

(1) In general

The payment due date for a credit card account under an open end consumer credit plan shall be the same day each month.

(2) Weekend or holiday due dates

If the payment due date for a credit card account under an open end consumer credit plan is a day on which the creditor does not receive or accept payments by mail (including weekends and holidays), the creditor may not treat a payment received on the next business day as late for any purpose.

(p) Parental approval required to increase credit lines for accounts for which parent is jointly liable

No increase may be made in the amount of credit authorized to be extended under a credit card account for which a parent, legal guardian, or spouse of the consumer, or any other individual has assumed joint liability for debts incurred by the consumer in connection with the account before the consumer attains the age of 21, unless that parent, guardian, or spouse approves in writing, and assumes joint liability for, such increase.

(q) Omitted

(r) College card agreements

(1) Definitions

For purposes of this subsection, the following definitions shall apply:

(A) College affinity card

The term "college affinity card" means a credit card issued by a credit card issuer under an open end consumer credit plan in conjunction with an agreement between the issuer and an institution of higher education, or an alumni organization or foundation affiliated with or related to such institution, under which such cards are issued to college students who have an affinity with such institution, organization and—

(i) the creditor has agreed to donate a portion of the proceeds of the credit card to the institution, organization, or foundation (including a lump sum or 1-time payment of money for access);

(ii) the creditor has agreed to offer discounted terms to the consumer; or

(iii) the credit card bears the name, emblem, mascot, or logo of such institution, organization, or foundation, or other words, pictures, or symbols readily identified with such institution, organization, or foundation.

(B) College student credit card account

The term "college student credit card account" means a credit card account under an open end consumer credit plan established or maintained for or on behalf of any college student.

(C) College student

The term "college student" means an individual who is a full-time or a part-time student attending an institution of higher education.

(D) Institution of higher education

The term "institution of higher education" has the same meaning as in section[2] 1001 and 1002 of Title 20.

(2) Reports by creditors

(A) In general

Each creditor shall submit an annual report to the Bureau containing the terms and conditions of all business, marketing, and promotional agreements and college affinity card agreements with an institution of higher education, or an alumni organization or foundation affiliated with or related to such institution, with respect to any college student credit card issued to a college student at such institution.

---

[2] So in original. Probably should be "sections".

(B) Details of report

The information required to be reported under subparagraph (A) includes—

    (i) any memorandum of understanding between or among a creditor, an institution of higher education, an alumni association, or foundation that directly or indirectly relates to any aspect of any agreement referred to in such subparagraph or controls or directs any obligations or distribution of benefits between or among any such entities;

    (ii) the amount of any payments from the creditor to the institution, organization, or foundation during the period covered by the report, and the precise terms of any agreement under which such amounts are determined; and

    (iii) the number of credit card accounts covered by any such agreement that were opened during the period covered by the report, and the total number of credit card accounts covered by the agreement that were outstanding at the end of such period.

(C) Aggregation by institution

The information required to be reported under subparagraph (A) shall be aggregated with respect to each institution of higher education or alumni organization or foundation affiliated with or related to such institution.

(D) Initial report

The initial report required under subparagraph (A) shall be submitted to the Bureau before the end of the 9-month period beginning on May 22, 2009.

(3) Reports by Bureau

The Bureau shall submit to the Congress, and make available to the public, an annual report that lists the information concerning credit card agreements submitted to the Bureau under paragraph (2) by each institution of higher education, alumni organization, or foundation.

    (Pub.L. 90–321, Title I, § 127, May 29, 1968, 82 Stat. 153; Pub.L. 93–495, Title III, §§ 304, 305, Title IV, §§ 411, 415, Oct. 28, 1974, 88 Stat. 1511, 1519, 1521; Pub.L. 96–221, Title VI, § 613(a) to (e), Mar. 31, 1980, 94 Stat. 176, 177; Pub.L. 100–583, §§ 2(a), 6, Nov. 3, 1988, 102 Stat. 2960, 2968; Pub.L. 100–709, § 2(b), Nov. 23, 1988, 102 Stat. 4729; Pub.L. 109–8, Title XIII, §§ 1301(a), 1303(a), 1304(a), 1305(a), 1306(a), Apr. 20, 2005, 119 Stat. 204, 209, 211, 212; Pub.L. 111–24, Title I, § 101(a)(1), 102(a), 103, 105, 106(a) Title II, 201(a), 202, 203, Title III, 301, 303, 305(a), May 22, 2009, 123 Stat. 1738, 1741, 1742, 1743, 1745, 1746, 1747, 1748, 1749; Pub.L. 111–203, Title X, § 1100A(2), July 21, 2010, 124 Stat. 2107.)

§ 1637a. Disclosure requirements for open end consumer credit plans secured by consumer's principal dwelling [CCPA § 127A]

(a) Application disclosures

In the case of any open end consumer credit plan which provides for any extension of credit which is secured by the consumer's principal dwelling, the creditor shall make the following disclosures in accordance with subsection (b) of this section:

(1) Fixed annual percentage rate

Each annual percentage rate imposed in connection with extensions of credit under the plan and a statement that such rate does not include costs other than interest.

(2) Variable percentage rate

In the case of a plan which provides for variable rates of interest on credit extended under the plan—

    (A) a description of the manner in which such rate will be computed and a statement that such rate does not include costs other than interest;

    (B) a description of the manner in which any changes in the annual percentage rate will be made, including—

    (i) any negative amortization and interest rate carryover;

    (ii) the timing of any such changes;

    (iii) any index or margin to which such changes in the rate are related; and

    (iv) a source of information about any such index;

  (C) if an initial annual percentage rate is offered which is not based on an index—

    (i) a statement of such rate and the period of time such initial rate will be in effect; and

    (ii) a statement that such rate does not include costs other than interest;

  (D) a statement that the consumer should ask about the current index value and interest rate;

  (E) a statement of the maximum amount by which the annual percentage rate may change in any 1-year period or a statement that no such limit exists;

  (F) a statement of the maximum annual percentage rate that may be imposed at any time under the plan;

  (G) subject to subsection (b)(3) of this section, a table, based on a $10,000 extension of credit, showing how the annual percentage rate and the minimum periodic payment amount under each repayment option of the plan would have been affected during the preceding 15-year period by changes in any index used to compute such rate;

  (H) a statement of—

    (i) the maximum annual percentage rate which may be imposed under each repayment option of the plan;

    (ii) the minimum amount of any periodic payment which may be required, based on a $10,000 outstanding balance, under each such option when such maximum annual percentage rate is in effect; and

    (iii) the earliest date by which such maximum annual interest rate may be imposed; and

  (I) a statement that interest rate information will be provided on or with each periodic statement.

(3) Other fees imposed by the creditor

An itemization of any fees imposed by the creditor in connection with the availability or use of credit under such plan, including annual fees, application fees, transaction fees, and closing costs (including costs commonly described as "points"), and the time when such fees are payable.

(4) Estimates of fees which may be imposed by third parties

  (A) Aggregate amount

An estimate, based on the creditor's experience with such plans and stated as a single amount or as a reasonable range, of the aggregate amount of additional fees that may be imposed by third parties (such as governmental authorities, appraisers, and attorneys) in connection with opening an account under the plan.

  (B) Statement of availability

A statement that the consumer may ask the creditor for a good faith estimate by the creditor of the fees that may be imposed by third parties.

(5) Statement of risk of loss of dwelling

A statement that—

  (A) any extension of credit under the plan is secured by the consumer's dwelling; and

(B) in the event of any default, the consumer risks the loss of the dwelling.

(6) Conditions to which disclosed terms are subject

(A) Period during which such terms are available

A clear and conspicuous statement—

(i) of the time by which an application must be submitted to obtain the terms disclosed; or

(ii) if applicable, that the terms are subject to change.

(B) Right of refusal if certain terms change

A statement that—

(i) the consumer may elect not to enter into an agreement to open an account under the plan if any term changes (other than a change contemplated by a variable feature of the plan) before any such agreement is final; and

(ii) if the consumer makes an election described in clause (i), the consumer is entitled to a refund of all fees paid in connection with the application.

(C) Retention of information

A statement that the consumer should make or otherwise retain a copy of information disclosed under this subparagraph.

(7) Rights of creditor with respect to extensions of credit

A statement that—

(A) under certain conditions, the creditor may terminate any account under the plan and require immediate repayment of any outstanding balance, prohibit any additional extension of credit to the account, or reduce the credit limit applicable to the account; and

(B) the consumer may receive, upon request, more specific information about the conditions under which the creditor may take any action described in subparagraph (A).

(8) Repayment options and minimum periodic payments

The repayment options under the plan, including—

(A) if applicable, any differences in repayment options with regard to—

(i) any period during which additional extensions of credit may be obtained; and

(ii) any period during which repayment is required to be made and no additional extensions of credit may be obtained;

(B) the length of any repayment period, including any differences in the length of any repayment period with regard to the periods described in clauses (i) and (ii) of subparagraph (A); and

(C) an explanation of how the amount of any minimum monthly or periodic payment will be determined under each such option, including any differences in the determination of any such amount with regard to the periods described in clauses (i) and (ii) of subparagraph (A).

(9) Example of minimum payments and maximum repayment period

An example, based on a $10,000 outstanding balance and the interest rate (other than a rate not based on the index under the plan) which is, or was recently, in effect under such plan, showing the minimum monthly or periodic payment, and the time it would take to repay the entire $10,000 if the consumer paid only the minimum periodic payments and obtained no additional extensions of credit.

(10) Statement concerning balloon payments

If, under any repayment option of the plan, the payment of not more than the minimum periodic payments required under such option over the length of the repayment period—

(A) would not repay any of the principal balance; or

(B) would repay less than the outstanding balance by the end of such period,

as the case may be, a statement of such fact, including an explicit statement that at the end of such repayment period a balloon payment (as defined in section 1665b(f) of this title) would result which would be required to be paid in full at that time.

(11) Negative amortization

If applicable, a statement that—

(A) any limitation in the plan on the amount of any increase in the minimum payments may result in negative amortization;

(B) negative amortization increases the outstanding principal balance of the account; and

(C) negative amortization reduces the consumer's equity in the consumer's dwelling.

(12) Limitations and minimum amount requirements on extensions of credit

(A) Number and dollar amount limitations

Any limitation contained in the plan on the number of extensions of credit and the amount of credit which may be obtained during any month or other defined time period.

(B) Minimum balance and other transaction amount requirements

Any requirement which establishes a minimum amount for—

(i) the initial extension of credit to an account under the plan;

(ii) any subsequent extension of credit to an account under the plan; or

(iii) any outstanding balance of an account under the plan.

(13) Statement regarding tax deductibility

A statement that—

(A) the consumer should consult a tax advisor regarding the deductibility of interest and charges under the plan; and

(B) in any case in which the extension of credit exceeds the fair market value (as defined under Title 26) of the dwelling, the interest on the portion of the credit extension that is greater than the fair market value of the dwelling is not tax deductible for Federal income tax purposes.

(14) Disclosure requirements established by Bureau

Any other term which the Bureau requires, in regulations, to be disclosed.

(b) Time and form of disclosures

(1) Time of disclosure

(A) In general

The disclosures required under subsection (a) of this section with respect to any open end consumer credit plan which provides for any extension of credit which is secured by the consumer's principal dwelling and the pamphlet required under subsection (e) of this section shall be provided to any consumer at the time the creditor distributes an application to establish an account under such plan to such consumer.

(B) Telephone, publications, and third party applications

In the case of telephone applications, applications contained in magazines or other publications, or applications provided by a third party, the disclosures required under subsection (a) of this section and the pamphlet required under subsection (e) of this section shall be provided by the creditor before the end of the 3-day period beginning on the date the creditor receives a completed application from a consumer.

(2) Form

(A) In general

Except as provided in paragraph (1)(B), the disclosures required under subsection (a) of this section shall be provided on or with any application to establish an account under an open end consumer credit plan which provides for any extension of credit which is secured by the consumer's principal dwelling.

(B) Segregation of required disclosures from other information

The disclosures required under subsection (a) of this section shall be conspicuously segregated from all other terms, data, or additional information provided in connection with the application, either by grouping the disclosures separately on the application form or by providing the disclosures on a separate form, in accordance with regulations of the Bureau.

(C) Precedence of certain information

The disclosures required by paragraphs (5), (6), and (7) of subsection (a) of this section shall precede all of the other required disclosures.

(D) Special provision relating to variable interest rate information

Whether or not the disclosures required under subsection (a) of this section are provided on the application form, the variable rate information described in subsection (a)(2) of this section may be provided separately from the other information required to be disclosed.

(3) Requirement for historical table

In preparing the table required under subsection (a)(2)(G) of this section, the creditor shall consistently select one rate of interest for each year and the manner of selecting the rate from year to year shall be consistent with the plan.

(c) Third party applications

In the case of an application to open an account under any open end consumer credit plan described in subsection (a) of this section which is provided to a consumer by any person other than the creditor—

(1) such person shall provide such consumer with—

(A) the disclosures required under subsection (a) of this section with respect to such plan, in accordance with subsection (b) of this section; and

(B) the pamphlet required under subsection (e) of this section; or

(2) if such person cannot provide specific terms about the plan because specific information about the plan terms is not available, no nonrefundable fee may be imposed in connection with such application before the end of the 3-day period beginning on the date the consumer receives the disclosures required under subsection (a) of this section with respect to the application.

(d) "Principal dwelling" defined

For purposes of this section and sections 1647 and 1665b of this title, the term "principal dwelling" includes any second or vacation home of the consumer.

(e) Pamphlet

In addition to the disclosures required under subsection (a) of this section with respect to an application to open an account under any open end consumer credit plan described in such subsection, the creditor or other person providing such disclosures to the consumer shall provide—

(1) a pamphlet published by the Bureau pursuant to section 4 of the Home Equity Consumer Protection Act of 1988; or

(2) any pamphlet which provides substantially similar information to the information described in such section, as determined by the Bureau.

(Pub.L. 90–321, Title I, § 127A, as added Pub.L. 100–709, § 2(a), Nov. 23, 1988, 102 Stat. 4725, and amended Pub.L. 109–8, Title XIII, § 1302(a)(1), Apr. 20, 2005, 119 Stat. 208; Pub.L. 111–203, Title X, § 1100A(2), July 21, 2010, 124 Stat. 2107.)

§ 1638. Transactions other than under an open end credit plan [CCPA § 128]

(a) Required disclosures by creditor

For each consumer credit transaction other than under an open end credit plan, the creditor shall disclose each of the following items, to the extent applicable:

(1) The identity of the creditor required to make disclosure.

(2)(A) The "amount financed", using that term, which shall be the amount of credit of which the consumer has actual use. This amount shall be computed as follows, but the computations need not be disclosed and shall not be disclosed with the disclosures conspicuously segregated in accordance with subsection (b)(1) of this section:

(i) take the principal amount of the loan or the cash price less downpayment and trade-in;

(ii) add any charges which are not part of the finance charge or of the principal amount of the loan and which are financed by the consumer, including the cost of any items excluded from the finance charge pursuant to section 1605 of this title; and

(iii) subtract any charges which are part of the finance charge but which will be paid by the consumer before or at the time of the consummation of the transaction, or have been withheld from the proceeds of the credit.

(B) In conjunction with the disclosure of the amount financed, a creditor shall provide a statement of the consumer's right to obtain, upon a written request, a written itemization of the amount financed. The statement shall include spaces for a "yes" and "no" indication to be initialed by the consumer to indicate whether the consumer wants a written itemization of the amount financed. Upon receiving an affirmative indication, the creditor shall provide, at the time other disclosures are required to be furnished, a written itemization of the amount financed. For the purposes of this subparagraph, "itemization of the amount financed" means a disclosure of the following items, to the extent applicable:

(i) the amount that is or will be paid directly to the consumer;

(ii) the amount that is or will be credited to the consumer's account to discharge obligations owed to the creditor;

(iii) each amount that is or will be paid to third persons by the creditor on the consumer's behalf, together with an identification of or reference to the third person; and

(iv) the total amount of any charges described in the preceding subparagraph (A)(iii).

(3) The "finance charge", not itemized, using that term.

(4) The finance charge expressed as an "annual percentage rate", using that term. This shall not be required if the amount financed does not exceed $75 and the finance charge does not exceed $5, or if the amount financed exceeds $75 and the finance charge does not exceed $7.50.

(5) The sum of the amount financed and the finance charge, which shall be termed the "total of payments".

(6) The number, amount, and due dates or period of payments scheduled to repay the total of payments.

(7) In a sale of property or services in which the seller is the creditor required to disclose pursuant to section 1631(b) of this title, the "total sale price", using that term, which shall be the total of the cash price of the property or services, additional charges, and the finance charge.

(8) Descriptive explanations of the terms "amount financed", "finance charge", "annual percentage rate", "total of payments", and "total sale price" as specified by the Bureau. The descriptive explanation of "total sale price" shall include reference to the amount of the downpayment.

(9) Where the credit is secured, a statement that a security interest has been taken in (A) the property which is purchased as part of the credit transaction, or (B) property not purchased as part of the credit transaction identified by item or type.

(10) Any dollar charge or percentage amount which may be imposed by a creditor solely on account of a late payment, other than a deferral or extension charge.

(11) A statement indicating whether or not the consumer is entitled to a rebate of any finance charge upon refinancing or prepayment in full pursuant to acceleration or otherwise, if the obligation involves a precomputed finance charge. A statement indicating whether or not a penalty will be imposed in those same circumstances if the obligation involves a finance charge computed from time to time by application of a rate to the unpaid principal balance.

(12) A statement that the consumer should refer to the appropriate contract document for any information such document provides about nonpayment, default, the right to accelerate the maturity of the debt, and prepayment rebates and penalties.

(13) In any residential mortgage transaction, a statement indicating whether a subsequent purchaser or assignee of the consumer may assume the debt obligation on its original terms and conditions.

(14) In the case of any variable interest rate residential mortgage transaction, in disclosures provided at application as prescribed by the Bureau for a variable rate transaction secured by the consumer's principal dwelling, at the option of the creditor, a statement that the periodic payments may increase or decrease substantially, and the maximum interest rate and payment for a $10,000 loan originated at a recent interest rate, as determined by the Bureau, assuming the maximum periodic increases in rates and payments under the program, or a historical example illustrating the effects of interest rate changes implemented according to the loan program.

(15) In the case of a consumer credit transaction that is secured by the principal dwelling of the consumer, in which the extension of credit may exceed the fair market value of the dwelling, a clear and conspicuous statement that—

    (A) the interest on the portion of the credit extension that is greater than the fair market value of the dwelling is not tax deductible for Federal income tax purposes; and

    (B) the consumer should consult a tax adviser for further information regarding the deductibility of interest and charges.

(16) In the case of a variable rate residential mortgage loan for which an escrow or impound account will be established for the payment of all applicable taxes, insurance, and assessments—

    (A) the amount of initial monthly payment due under the loan for the payment of principal and interest, and the amount of such initial monthly payment including the monthly payment deposited in the account for the payment of all applicable taxes, insurance, and assessments; and

    (B) the amount of the fully indexed monthly payment due under the loan for the payment of principal and interest, and the amount of such fully indexed monthly payment including the monthly payment deposited in the account for the payment of all applicable taxes, insurance, and assessments.

(17) In the case of a residential mortgage loan, the aggregate amount of settlement charges for all settlement services provided in connection with the loan, the amount of charges that are included in the loan and the amount of such charges the borrower must pay at closing, the approximate amount of the wholesale rate of funds in connection with the loan, and the aggregate amount of other fees or required payments in connection with the loan.

(18) In the case of a residential mortgage loan, the aggregate amount of fees paid to the mortgage originator in connection with the loan, the amount of such fees paid directly by the consumer, and any additional amount received by the originator from the creditor.

(19) In the case of a residential mortgage loan, the total amount of interest that the consumer will pay over the life of the loan as a percentage of the principal of the loan. Such amount shall be computed assuming the consumer makes each monthly payment in full and on-time, and does not make any over-payments.

(b) Form and timing of disclosures; residential mortgage transaction requirements

(1) Except as otherwise provided in this part, the disclosures required under subsection (a) of this section shall be made before the credit is extended. Except for the disclosures required by subsection (a)(1) of this section, all disclosures required under subsection (a) of this section and any disclosure provided for in subsection (b), (c), or (d) of section 1605 of this title shall be conspicuously segregated from all other terms, data, or information provided in connection with a transaction, including any computations or itemization.

(2)(A) Except as provided in subparagraph (G), in the case of any extension of credit that is secured by the dwelling of a consumer, which is also subject to the Real Estate Settlement Procedures Act [12 U.S.C. 2601 et seq.], good faith estimates of the disclosures required under subsection (a) of this section shall be made in accordance with regulations of the Bureau under section 1631(c) of this title and shall be delivered or placed in the mail not later than three business days after the creditor receives the consumer's written application, which shall be at least 7 business days before consummation of the transaction.

(B) In the case of an extension of credit that is secured by the dwelling of a consumer, the disclosures provided under subparagraph (A),[1] shall be in addition to the other disclosures required by subsection (a), and shall—

(i) state in conspicuous type size and format, the following: "You are not required to complete this agreement merely because you have received these disclosures or signed a loan application."; and

(ii) be provided in the form of final disclosures at the time of consummation of the transaction, in the form and manner prescribed by this section.

(C) In the case of an extension of credit that is secured by the dwelling of a consumer, under which the annual rate of interest is variable, or with respect to which the regular payments may otherwise be variable, in addition to the other disclosures required by subsection (a), the disclosures provided under this subsection shall do the following:

(i) Label the payment schedule as follows: "Payment Schedule: Payments Will Vary Based on Interest Rate Changes".

(ii) State in conspicuous type size and format examples of adjustments to the regular required payment on the extension of credit based on the change in the interest rates specified by the contract for such extension of credit. Among the examples required to be provided under this clause is an example that reflects the maximum payment amount of the regular required payments on the extension of credit, based on the maximum interest rate allowed under the contract, in accordance with the rules of the Bureau. Prior to issuing any rules pursuant to this clause, the Bureau shall conduct consumer testing to determine the appropriate format for providing the disclosures required under this subparagraph to consumers so that such disclosures can be easily understood, including the fact that the initial regular payments are for a specific time period that will end on a certain date, that payments will adjust afterwards potentially to a higher amount, and that there is no guarantee that the borrower will be able to refinance to a lower amount.

(D) In any case in which the disclosure statement under subparagraph (A) contains an annual percentage rate of interest that is no longer accurate, as determined under section 1606(c)

---

[1] So in original. The comma probably should not appear.

of this title, the creditor shall furnish an additional, corrected statement to the borrower, not later than 3 business days before the date of consummation of the transaction.

    (E) The consumer shall receive the disclosures required under this paragraph before paying any fee to the creditor or other person in connection with the consumer's application for an extension of credit that is secured by the dwelling of a consumer. If the disclosures are mailed to the consumer, the consumer is considered to have received them 3 business days after they are mailed. A creditor or other person may impose a fee for obtaining the consumer's credit report before the consumer has received the disclosures under this paragraph, provided the fee is bona fide and reasonable in amount.

(F) Waiver of timeliness of disclosures

    To expedite consummation of a transaction, if the consumer determines that the extension of credit is needed to meet a bona fide personal financial emergency, the consumer may waive or modify the timing requirements for disclosures under subparagraph (A), provided that—

    (i) the term "bona fide personal emergency" may be further defined in regulations issued by the Bureau;

    (ii) the consumer provides to the creditor a dated, written statement describing the emergency and specifically waiving or modifying those timing requirements, which statement shall bear the signature of all consumers entitled to receive the disclosures required by this paragraph; and

    (iii) the creditor provides to the consumers at or before the time of such waiver or modification, the final disclosures required by paragraph (1).

    (G)(i) In the case of an extension of credit relating to a plan described in section 101(53D) of Title 11—

    (I) the requirements of subparagraphs (A) through (E) shall not apply; and

    (II) a good faith estimate of the disclosures required under subsection (a) shall be made in accordance with regulations of the Bureau under section 1631(c) of this title before such credit is extended, or shall be delivered or placed in the mail not later than 3 business days after the date on which the creditor receives the written application of the consumer for such credit, whichever is earlier.

    (ii) If a disclosure statement furnished within 3 business days of the written application (as provided under clause (i)(II)) contains an annual percentage rate which is subsequently rendered inaccurate, within the meaning of section 1606(c) of this title, the creditor shall furnish another disclosure statement at the time of settlement or consummation of the transaction.

    (3) In the case of a credit transaction described in paragraph (15) of subsection (a) of this section, disclosures required by that paragraph shall be made to the consumer at the time of application for such extension of credit.

(4) Repayment analysis required to include escrow payments

(A) In general

    In the case of any consumer credit transaction secured by a first mortgage or lien on the principal dwelling of the consumer, other than a consumer credit transaction under an open end credit plan or a reverse mortgage, for which an impound, trust, or other type of account has been or will be established in connection with the transaction for the payment of property taxes, hazard and flood (if any) insurance premiums, or other periodic payments or premiums with respect to the property, the information required to be provided under subsection (a) with respect to the number, amount, and due dates or period of payments scheduled to repay the total of payments shall take into account the amount of any monthly payment to such account for each such repayment in accordance with section 10(a)(2) of the Real Estate Settlement Procedures Act of 1974.

(B) Assessment value

The amount taken into account under subparagraph (A) for the payment of property taxes, hazard and flood (if any) insurance premiums, or other periodic payments or premiums with respect to the property shall reflect the taxable assessed value of the real property securing the transaction after the consummation of the transaction, including the value of any improvements on the property or to be constructed on the property (whether or not such construction will be financed from the proceeds of the transaction), if known, and the replacement costs of the property for hazard insurance, in the initial year after the transaction.

(c) Timing of disclosures on unsolicited mailed or telephone purchase orders or loan requests

(1) If a creditor receives a purchase order by mail or telephone without personal solicitation, and the cash price and the total sale price and the terms of financing, including the annual percentage rate, are set forth in the creditor's catalog or other printed material distributed to the public, then the disclosures required under subsection (a) of this section may be made at any time not later than the date the first payment is due.

(2) If a creditor receives a request for a loan by mail or telephone without personal solicitation and the terms of financing, including the annual percentage rate for representative amounts of credit, are set forth in the creditor's printed material distributed to the public, or in the contract of loan or other printed material delivered to the obligor, then the disclosures required under subsection (a) of this section may be made at any time not later than the date the first payment is due.

(d) Timing of disclosure in cases of an addition of a deferred payment price to an existing outstanding balance

If a consumer credit sale is one of a series of consumer credit sales transactions made pursuant to an agreement providing for the addition of the deferred payment price of that sale to an existing outstanding balance, and the person to whom the credit is extended has approved in writing both the annual percentage rate or rates and the method of computing the finance charge or charges, and the creditor retains no security interest in any property as to which he has received payments aggregating the amount of the sales price including any finance charges attributable thereto, then the disclosure required under subsection (a) of this section for the particular sale may be made at any time not later than the date the first payment for that sale is due. For the purposes of this subsection, in the case of items purchased on different dates, the first purchased shall be deemed first paid for, and in the case of items purchased on the same date, the lowest price shall be deemed first paid for.

(e) Terms and disclosure with respect to private education loans

(1) Disclosures required in private education loan applications and solicitations

In any application for a private education loan, or a solicitation for a private education loan without requiring an application, the private educational lender shall disclose to the borrower, clearly and conspicuously—

(A) the potential range of rates of interest applicable to the private education loan;

(B) whether the rate of interest applicable to the private education loan is fixed or variable;

(C) limitations on interest rate adjustments, both in terms of frequency and amount, or the lack thereof, if applicable;

(D) requirements for a co-borrower, including any changes in the applicable interest rates without a co-borrower;

(E) potential finance charges, late fees, penalties, and adjustments to principal, based on defaults or late payments of the borrower;

(F) fees or range of fees applicable to the private education loan;

(G) the term of the private education loan;

(H) whether interest will accrue while the student to whom the private education loan relates is enrolled at a covered educational institution;

(I)   payment deferral options;

(J)   general eligibility criteria for the private education loan;

(K)   an example of the total cost of the private education loan over the life of the loan—

(i)   which shall be calculated using the principal amount and the maximum rate of interest actually offered by the private educational lender; and

(ii)   calculated both with and without capitalization of interest, if an option exists for postponing interest payments;

(L)   that a covered educational institution may have school-specific education loan benefits and terms not detailed on the disclosure form;

(M)   that the borrower may qualify for Federal student financial assistance through a program under title IV of the Higher Education Act of 1965 (20 U.S.C. 1070 et seq.), in lieu of, or in addition to, a loan from a non-Federal source;

(N)   the interest rates available with respect to such Federal student financial assistance through a program under title IV of the Higher Education Act of 1965 (20 U.S.C. 1070 et seq.);

(O)   that, as provided in paragraph (6)—

(i)   the borrower shall have the right to accept the terms of the loan and consummate the transaction at any time within 30 calendar days (or such longer period as the private educational lender may provide) following the date on which the application for the private education loan is approved and the borrower receives the disclosure documents required under this subsection for the loan; and

(ii)   except for changes based on adjustments to the index used for a loan, the rates and terms of the loan may not be changed by the private educational lender during the period described in clause (i);

(P)   that, before a private education loan may be consummated, the borrower must obtain from the relevant institution of higher education the form required under paragraph (3), and complete, sign, and return such form to the private educational lender;

(Q)   that the consumer may obtain additional information concerning such Federal student financial assistance from their institution of higher education, or at the website of the Department of Education; and

(R)   such other information as the Bureau shall prescribe, by rule, as necessary or appropriate for consumers to make informed borrowing decisions.

(2) Disclosures at the time of private education loan approval

Contemporaneously with the approval of a private education loan application, and before the loan transaction is consummated, the private educational lender shall disclose to the borrower, clearly and conspicuously—

(A)   the applicable rate of interest in effect on the date of approval;

(B)   whether the rate of interest applicable to the private education loan is fixed or variable;

(C)   limitations on interest rate adjustments, both in terms of frequency and amount, or the lack thereof, if applicable;

(D)   the initial approved principal amount;

(E)   applicable finance charges, late fees, penalties, and adjustments to principal, based on borrower defaults or late payments, including limitations on the discharge of a private education loan in bankruptcy;

(F)   fees or range of fees applicable to the private education loan;

(G)   the maximum term under the private education loan program;

(H) an estimate of the total amount for repayment, at both the interest rate in effect on the date of approval and at the maximum possible rate of interest offered by the private educational lender and applicable to the borrower, to the extent that such maximum rate may be determined, or if not, a good faith estimate thereof;

(I) any principal and interest payments required while the student for whom the private education loan is intended is enrolled at a covered educational institution and unpaid interest that will accrue during such enrollment;

(J) payment deferral options applicable to the borrower;

(K) whether monthly payments are graduated;

(L) that, as provided in paragraph (6)—

(i) the borrower shall have the right to accept the terms of the loan and consummate the transaction at any time within 30 calendar days (or such longer period as the private educational lender may provide) following the date on which the application for the private education loan is approved and the borrower receives the disclosure documents required under this subsection for the loan; and

(ii) except for changes based on adjustments to the index used for a loan, the rates and terms of the loan may not be changed by the private educational lender during the period described in clause (i);

(M) that the borrower—

(i) may qualify for Federal financial assistance through a program under title IV of the Higher Education Act of 1965 (20 U.S.C. 1070 et seq.), in lieu of, or in addition to, a loan from a non-Federal source; and

(ii) may obtain additional information concerning such assistance from their institution of higher education or the website of the Department of Education;

(N) the interest rates available with respect to such Federal financial assistance through a program under title IV of the Higher Education Act of 1965 (20 U.S.C. 1070 et seq.);

(O) the maximum monthly payment, calculated using the maximum rate of interest actually offered by the private educational lender and applicable to the borrower, to the extent that such maximum rate may be determined, or if not, a good faith estimate thereof; and

(P) such other information as the Bureau shall prescribe, by rule, as necessary or appropriate for consumers to make informed borrowing decisions.

(3) Self-certification of information

(A) In general

Before a private educational lender may consummate a private education loan with respect to a student attending an institution of higher education, the lender shall obtain from the applicant for the private education loan the form developed by the Secretary of Education under section 155 of the Higher Education Act of 1965, signed by the applicant, in written or electronic form.

(B) Rule of construction

No other provision of this subsection shall be construed to require a private educational lender to perform any additional duty under this paragraph, other than collecting the form required under subparagraph (A).

(4) Disclosures at the time of private education loan consummation

Contemporaneously with the consummation of a private education loan, a private educational lender shall make to the borrower each of the disclosures described in—

(A) paragraph (2)(A) (adjusted, as necessary, for the rate of interest in effect on the date of consummation, based on the index used for the loan);

(B)　subparagraphs (B) through (K) and (M) through (P) of paragraph (2); and

(C)　paragraph (7).

(5)　Format of disclosures

(A)　Model form

Not later than 2 years after August 14, 2008, the Bureau shall, based on consumer testing, and in consultation with the Secretary of Education, develop and issue model forms that may be used, at the option of the private educational lender, for the provision of disclosures required under this subsection.

(B)　Format

Model forms developed under this paragraph shall—

(i)　be comprehensible to borrowers, with a clear format and design;

(ii)　provide for clear and conspicuous disclosures;

(iii)　enable borrowers easily to identify material terms of the loan and to compare such terms among private education loans; and

(iv)　be succinct, and use an easily readable type font.

(C)　Safe harbor

Any private educational lender that elects to provide a model form developed under this subsection that accurately reflects the practices of the private educational lender shall be deemed to be in compliance with the disclosures required under this subsection.

(6)　Effective period of approved rate of interest and loan terms

(A)　In general

With respect to a private education loan, the borrower shall have the right to accept the terms of the loan and consummate the transaction at any time within 30 calendar days (or such longer period as the private educational lender may provide) following the date on which the application for the private education loan is approved and the borrower receives the disclosure documents required under this subsection for the loan, and the rates and terms of the loan may not be changed by the private educational lender during that period.

(B)　Prohibition on changes

Except for changes based on adjustments to the index used for a loan, the rates and terms of the loan may not be changed by the private educational lender prior to the earlier of—

(i)　the date of acceptance of the terms of the loan and consummation of the transaction by the borrower, as described in subparagraph (A); or

(ii)　the expiration of the period described in subparagraph (A).

(7)　Right to cancel

With respect to a private education loan, the borrower may cancel the loan, without penalty to the borrower, at any time within 3 business days of the date on which the loan is consummated, and the private educational lender shall disclose such right to the borrower in accordance with paragraph (4).

(8)　Prohibition on disbursement

No funds may be disbursed with respect to a private education loan until the expiration of the 3-day period described in paragraph (7).

(9)　Bureau regulations

In issuing regulations under this subsection, the Bureau shall prevent, to the extent possible, duplicative disclosure requirements for private educational lenders that are otherwise required to make disclosures under this subchapter, except that in any case in which the disclosure requirements of this subsection differ or conflict with the disclosure requirements of any other provision of this subchapter, the requirements of this subsection shall be controlling.

(10) Definitions

For purposes of this subsection, the terms "covered educational institution", "private educational lender", and "private education loan" have the same meanings as in section 1650 of Title 15.

(11) Duties of lenders participating in preferred lender arrangements

Each private educational lender that has a preferred lender arrangement with a covered educational institution shall annually, by a date determined by the Bureau, in consultation with the Secretary of Education, provide to the covered educational institution such information as the Bureau determines to include in the model form developed under paragraph (5) for each type of private education loan that the lender plans to offer to students attending the covered educational institution, or to the families of such students, for the next award year (as that term is defined in section 481 of the Higher Education Act of 1965).

(f) Periodic statements for residential mortgage loans

(1) In general

The creditor, assignee, or servicer with respect to any residential mortgage loan shall transmit to the obligor, for each billing cycle, a statement setting forth each of the following items, to the extent applicable, in a conspicuous and prominent manner:

(A) The amount of the principal obligation under the mortgage.

(B) The current interest rate in effect for the loan.

(C) The date on which the interest rate may next reset or adjust.

(D) The amount of any prepayment fee to be charged, if any.

(E) A description of any late payment fees.

(F) A telephone number and electronic mail address that may be used by the obligor to obtain information regarding the mortgage.

(G) The names, addresses, telephone numbers, and Internet addresses of counseling agencies or programs reasonably available to the consumer that have been certified or approved and made publicly available by the Secretary of Housing and Urban Development or a State housing finance authority (as defined in section 1441a–1 of Title 12).

(H) Such other information as the Board may prescribe in regulations.

(2) Development and use of standard form

The Board[2] shall develop and prescribe a standard form for the disclosure required under this subsection, taking into account that the statements required may be transmitted in writing or electronically.

(3) Exception

Paragraph (1) shall not apply to any fixed rate residential mortgage loan where the creditor, assignee, or servicer provides the obligor with a coupon book that provides the obligor with substantially the same information as required in paragraph (1).

(Pub.L. 90–321, Title I, § 128, May 29, 1968, 82 Stat. 155; Pub.L. 96–221, Title VI, § 614(a) to (c), Mar. 31, 1980, 94 Stat. 178, 179; Pub.L. 104–208, Div. A, Title II, § 2105, Sept. 30, 1996, 110 Stat. 3009–402; Pub.L. 109–8, Title XIII, § 1302(b)(1), Apr. 20, 2005, 119 Stat. 209; Pub.L. 110–289, Div. B, Title V, § 2502(a), July 30, 2008, 122 Stat. 2855; Pub.L. 110–315, Title X, § 1021(a), Aug. 14, 2008, 122 Stat. 3483; Pub.L. 110–343, Div. A, Title I, § 130(a), Oct. 3, 2008, 122 Stat. 3797; Pub.L. 111–203, Title X, § 1100A(2), Title XIV, §§ 1400(c), 1419, 1420, 1465, July 21, 2010, 124 Stat. 2107, 2136, 2154, 2155, 2185.)

---

2   So in original. Probably should be "Bureau".

§ 1638a.　　Reset of hybrid adjustable rate mortgages [CCPA 128A]

(a)　Hybrid adjustable rate mortgages defined

For purposes of this section, the term "hybrid adjustable rate mortgage" means a consumer credit transaction secured by the consumer's principal residence with a fixed interest rate for an introductory period that adjusts or resets to a variable interest rate after such period.

(b)　Notice of reset and alternatives

During the 1-month period that ends 6 months before the date on which the interest rate in effect during the introductory period of a hybrid adjustable rate mortgage adjusts or resets to a variable interest rate or, in the case of such an adjustment or resetting that occurs within the first 6 months after consummation of such loan, at consummation, the creditor or servicer of such loan shall provide a written notice, separate and distinct from all other correspondence to the consumer, that includes the following:

(1)　Any index or formula used in making adjustments to or resetting the interest rate and a source of information about the index or formula.

(2)　An explanation of how the new interest rate and payment would be determined, including an explanation of how the index was adjusted, such as by the addition of a margin.

(3)　A good faith estimate, based on accepted industry standards, of the creditor or servicer of the amount of the monthly payment that will apply after the date of the adjustment or reset, and the assumptions on which this estimate is based.

(4)　A list of alternatives consumers may pursue before the date of adjustment or reset, and descriptions of the actions consumers must take to pursue these alternatives, including—

(A)　refinancing;

(B)　renegotiation of loan terms;

(C)　payment forbearances; and

(D)　pre-foreclosure sales.

(5)　The names, addresses, telephone numbers, and Internet addresses of counseling agencies or programs reasonably available to the consumer that have been certified or approved and made publicly available by the Secretary of Housing and Urban Development or a State housing finance authority (as defined in section 1441a–1 of Title 12).

(6)　The address, telephone number, and Internet address for the State housing finance authority (as so defined) for the State in which the consumer resides.

(c)　Savings clause

The Board may require the notice in paragraph (b) or other notice consistent with this chapter for adjustable rate mortgage loans that are not hybrid adjustable rate mortgage loans.

(Pub.L. 90–321, Title I, § 128A, as added Pub.L. 111–203, Title XIV, § 1418(a), July 21, 2010, 124 Stat. 2153.)

§ 1639.　　Requirements for certain mortgages [CCPA § 129]

(a)　Disclosures

(1)　Specific disclosures

In addition to other disclosures required under this subchapter, for each mortgage referred to in section 1602(aa) of this title, the creditor shall provide the following disclosures in conspicuous type size:

(A)　"You are not required to complete this agreement merely because you have received these disclosures or have signed a loan application.".

(B) "If you obtain this loan, the lender will have a mortgage on your home. You could lose your home, and any money you have put into it, if you do not meet your obligations under the loan.".

(2) Annual percentage rate

In addition to the disclosures required under paragraph (1), the creditor shall disclose—

(A) in the case of a credit transaction with a fixed rate of interest, the annual percentage rate and the amount of the regular monthly payment; or

(B) in the case of any other credit transaction, the annual percentage rate of the loan, the amount of the regular monthly payment, a statement that the interest rate and monthly payment may increase, and the amount of the maximum monthly payment, based on the maximum interest rate allowed pursuant to section 3806 of Title 12.

(b) Time of disclosures

(1) In general

The disclosures required by this section shall be given not less than 3 business days prior to consummation of the transaction.

(2) New disclosures required

(A) In general

After providing the disclosures required by this section, a creditor may not change the terms of the extension of credit if such changes make the disclosures inaccurate, unless new disclosures are provided that meet the requirements of this section.

(B) Telephone disclosure

A creditor may provide new disclosures pursuant to subparagraph (A) by telephone, if—

(i) the change is initiated by the consumer; and

(ii) at the consummation of the transaction under which the credit is extended—

(I) the creditor provides to the consumer the new disclosures, in writing; and

(II) the creditor and consumer certify in writing that the new disclosures were provided by telephone, by not later than 3 days prior to the date of consummation of the transaction.

(3) Modifications

The Bureau may, if it finds that such action is necessary to permit homeowners to meet bona fide personal financial emergencies, prescribe regulations authorizing the modification or waiver of rights created under this subsection, to the extent and under the circumstances set forth in those regulations.

(c) No prepayment penalty

(1) In general

(A) Limitation on terms

A mortgage referred to in section 1602(aa) of this title may not contain terms under which a consumer must pay a prepayment penalty for paying all or part of the principal before the date on which the principal is due.

(B) Construction

For purposes of this subsection, any method of computing a refund of unearned scheduled interest is a prepayment penalty if it is less favorable to the consumer than the actuarial method (as that term is defined in section 1615(d) of this title).

(2) Repealed. Pub.L. 111–203, Title XIV, § 1432(a), July 21, 2010, 124 Stat. 2160

(d) Limitations after default

A mortgage referred to in section 1602(aa) of this title may not provide for an interest rate applicable after default that is higher than the interest rate that applies before default. If the date of maturity of a mortgage referred to in subsection[1] 1602(aa) of this title is accelerated due to default and the consumer is entitled to a rebate of interest, that rebate shall be computed by any method that is not less favorable than the actuarial method (as that term is defined in section 1615(d) of this title).

(e) No balloon payments

No high-cost mortgage may contain a scheduled payment that is more than twice as large as the average of earlier scheduled payments. This subsection shall not apply when the payment schedule is adjusted to the seasonal or irregular income of the consumer.

(f) No negative amortization

A mortgage referred to in section 1602(aa) of this title may not include terms under which the outstanding principal balance will increase at any time over the course of the loan because the regular periodic payments do not cover the full amount of interest due.

(g) No prepaid payments

A mortgage referred to in section 1602(aa) of this title may not include terms under which more than 2 periodic payments required under the loan are consolidated and paid in advance from the loan proceeds provided to the consumer.

(h) Prohibition on extending credit without regard to payment ability of consumer

A creditor shall not engage in a pattern or practice of extending credit to consumers under mortgages referred to in section 1602(aa) of this title based on the consumers' collateral without regard to the consumers' repayment ability, including the consumers' current and expected income, current obligations, and employment.

(i) Requirements for payments under home improvement contracts

A creditor shall not make a payment to a contractor under a home improvement contract from amounts extended as credit under a mortgage referred to in section 1602(aa) of this title, other than—

    (1) in the form of an instrument that is payable to the consumer or jointly to the consumer and the contractor; or

    (2) at the election of the consumer, by a third party escrow agent in accordance with terms established in a written agreement signed by the consumer, the creditor, and the contractor before the date of payment.

(j) Recommended default

No creditor shall recommend or encourage default on an existing loan or other debt prior to and in connection with the closing or planned closing of a high-cost mortgage that refinances all or any portion of such existing loan or debt.

(k) Late fees

    (1) In general

No creditor may impose a late payment charge or fee in connection with a high-cost mortgage—

      (A) in an amount in excess of 4 percent of the amount of the payment past due;

      (B) unless the loan documents specifically authorize the charge or fee;

      (C) before the end of the 15-day period beginning on the date the payment is due, or in the case of a loan on which interest on each installment is paid in advance, before the end of the 30-day period beginning on the date the payment is due; or

---

[1] So in original. Probably should be "section".

(D) more than once with respect to a single late payment.

(2) Coordination with subsequent late fees

If a payment is otherwise a full payment for the applicable period and is paid on its due date or within an applicable grace period, and the only delinquency or insufficiency of payment is attributable to any late fee or delinquency charge assessed on any earlier payment, no late fee or delinquency charge may be imposed on such payment.

(3) Failure to make installment payment

If, in the case of a loan agreement the terms of which provide that any payment shall first be applied to any past due principal balance, the consumer fails to make an installment payment and the consumer subsequently resumes making installment payments but has not paid all past due installments, the creditor may impose a separate late payment charge or fee for any principal due (without deduction due to late fees or related fees) until the default is cured.

(*l*) Acceleration of debt

No high-cost mortgage may contain a provision which permits the creditor to accelerate the indebtedness, except when repayment of the loan has been accelerated by default in payment, or pursuant to a due-on-sale provision, or pursuant to a material violation of some other provision of the loan document unrelated to payment schedule.

(m) Restriction on financing points and fees

No creditor may directly or indirectly finance, in connection with any high-cost mortgage, any of the following.

(1) Any prepayment fee or penalty payable by the consumer in a refinancing transaction if the creditor or an affiliate of the creditor is the noteholder of the note being refinanced.

(2) Any points or fees.

(n) Consequence of failure to comply

Any mortgage that contains a provision prohibited by this section shall be deemed a failure to deliver the material disclosures required under this subchapter, for the purpose of section 1635 of this title.

(o) "Affiliate" defined

For purposes of this section, the term "affiliate" has the same meaning as in section 1841(k) of Title 12.

(p) Discretionary regulatory authority of Bureau

(1) Exemptions

The Bureau may, by regulation or order, exempt specific mortgage products or categories of mortgages from any or all of the prohibitions specified in subsections (c) through (i) of this section, if the Bureau finds that the exemption—

(A) is in the interest of the borrowing public; and

(B) will apply only to products that maintain and strengthen home ownership and equity protection.

(2) Prohibitions

The Bureau, by regulation or order, shall prohibit acts or practices in connection with—

(A) mortgage loans that the Bureau finds to be unfair, deceptive, or designed to evade the provisions of this section; and

(B) refinancing of mortgage loans that the Bureau finds to be associated with abusive lending practices, or that are otherwise not in the interest of the borrower.

(q) Civil penalties in Federal Trade Commission enforcement actions

For purposes of enforcement by the Federal Trade Commission, any violation of a regulation issued by the Bureau pursuant to subsection (*l*)(2) of this section shall be treated as a violation of a rule promulgated under section 57a of this title regarding unfair or deceptive acts or practices.

(r) Prohibitions on evasions, structuring of transactions, and reciprocal arrangements

A creditor may not take any action in connection with a high-cost mortgage—

    (1) to structure a loan transaction as an open-end credit plan or another form of loan for the purpose and with the intent of evading the provisions of this subchapter; or

    (2) to divide any loan transaction into separate parts for the purpose and with the intent of evading provisions of this subchapter.

(s) Modification and deferral fees prohibited

A creditor, successor in interest, assignee, or any agent of any of the above, may not charge a consumer any fee to modify, renew, extend, or amend a high-cost mortgage, or to defer any payment due under the terms of such mortgage.

(t) Payoff statement

    (1) Fees

        (A) In general

Except as provided in subparagraph (B), no creditor or servicer may charge a fee for informing or transmitting to any person the balance due to pay off the outstanding balance on a high-cost mortgage.

        (B) Transaction fee

When payoff information referred to in subparagraph (A) is provided by facsimile transmission or by a courier service, a creditor or servicer may charge a processing fee to cover the cost of such transmission or service in an amount not to exceed an amount that is comparable to fees imposed for similar services provided in connection with consumer credit transactions that are secured by the consumer's principal dwelling and are not high-cost mortgages.

        (C) Fee disclosure

Prior to charging a transaction fee as provided in subparagraph (B), a creditor or servicer shall disclose that payoff balances are available for free pursuant to subparagraph (A).

        (D) Multiple requests

If a creditor or servicer has provided payoff information referred to in subparagraph (A) without charge, other than the transaction fee allowed by subparagraph (B), on 4 occasions during a calendar year, the creditor or servicer may thereafter charge a reasonable fee for providing such information during the remainder of the calendar year.

    (2) Prompt delivery

Payoff balances shall be provided within 5 business days after receiving a request by a consumer or a person authorized by the consumer to obtain such information.

(u) Pre-loan counseling

    (1) In general

A creditor may not extend credit to a consumer under a high-cost mortgage without first receiving certification from a counselor that is approved by the Secretary of Housing and Urban Development, or at the discretion of the Secretary, a State housing finance authority, that the consumer has received counseling on the advisability of the mortgage. Such counselor shall not be employed by the creditor or an affiliate of the creditor or be affiliated with the creditor.

(2) Disclosures required prior to counseling

No counselor may certify that a consumer has received counseling on the advisability of the high-cost mortgage unless the counselor can verify that the consumer has received each statement required (in connection with such loan) by this section or the Real Estate Settlement Procedures Act of 1974 with respect to the transaction.

(3) Regulations

The Board may prescribe such regulations as the Board determines to be appropriate to carry out the requirements of paragraph (1).

(v) Corrections and unintentional violations

A creditor or assignee in a high-cost mortgage who, when acting in good faith, fails to comply with any requirement under this section will not be deemed to have violated such requirement if the creditor or assignee establishes that either—

(1) within 30 days of the loan closing and prior to the institution of any action, the consumer is notified of or discovers the violation, appropriate restitution is made, and whatever adjustments are necessary are made to the loan to either, at the choice of the consumer—

(A) make the loan satisfy the requirements of this part; or

(B) in the case of a high-cost mortgage, change the terms of the loan in a manner beneficial to the consumer so that the loan will no longer be a high-cost mortgage; or

(2) within 60 days of the creditor's discovery or receipt of notification of an unintentional violation or bona fide error and prior to the institution of any action, the consumer is notified of the compliance failure, appropriate restitution is made, and whatever adjustments are necessary are made to the loan to either, at the choice of the consumer—

(A) make the loan satisfy the requirements of this part; or

(B) in the case of a high-cost mortgage, change the terms of the loan in a manner beneficial so that the loan will no longer be a high-cost mortgage.

(Pub.L. 90–321, Title I, § 129, as added Pub.L. 103–325, Title I, § 152(d), Sept. 23, 1994, 108 Stat. 2191, and amended Pub.L. 111–8, Div. D, Title VI, § 626(c), Mar. 11, 2009, 123 Stat. 679; Pub.L. 111–203, Title X, §§ 1100A(2), 1100A(9), 1100H, Title XIV, §§ 1400(c), 1433, July 21, 2010, 124 Stat. 2107, 2109, 2160.)

§ 1639a. Duty of servicers of residential mortgages [CCPA § 129A]

(a) In general

Notwithstanding any other provision of law, whenever a servicer of residential mortgages agrees to enter into a qualified loss mitigation plan with respect to 1 or more residential mortgages originated before May 20, 2009, including mortgages held in a securitization or other investment vehicle—

(1) to the extent that the servicer owes a duty to investors or other parties to maximize the net present value of such mortgages, the duty shall be construed to apply to all such investors and parties, and not to any individual party or group of parties; and

(2) the servicer shall be deemed to have satisfied the duty set forth in paragraph (1) if, before December 31, 2012, the servicer implements a qualified loss mitigation plan that meets the following criteria:

(A) Default on the payment of such mortgage has occurred, is imminent, or is reasonably foreseeable, as such terms are defined by guidelines issued by the Secretary of the Treasury or his designee under the Emergency Economic Stabilization Act of 2008.

(B) The mortgagor occupies the property securing the mortgage as his or her principal residence.

(C) The servicer reasonably determined, consistent with the guidelines issued by the Secretary of the Treasury or his designee, that the application of such qualified loss mitigation plan to a mortgage or class of mortgages will likely provide an anticipated recovery on the outstanding principal mortgage debt that will exceed the anticipated recovery through foreclosures.

(b) No liability

A servicer that is deemed to be acting in the best interests of all investors or other parties under this section shall not be liable to any party who is owed a duty under subsection (a)(1), and shall not be subject to any injunction, stay, or other equitable relief to such party, based solely upon the implementation by the servicer of a qualified loss mitigation plan.

(c) Standard industry practice

The qualified loss mitigation plan guidelines issued by the Secretary of the Treasury under the Emergency Economic Stabilization Act of 2008 shall constitute standard industry practice for purposes of all Federal and State laws.

(d) Scope of safe harbor

Any person, including a trustee, issuer, and loan originator, shall not be liable for monetary damages or be subject to an injunction, stay, or other equitable relief, based solely upon the cooperation of such person with a servicer when such cooperation is necessary for the servicer to implement a qualified loss mitigation plan that meets the requirements of subsection (a).

(e) Reporting

Each servicer that engages in qualified loss mitigation plans under this section shall regularly report to the Secretary of the Treasury the extent, scope, and results of the servicer's modification activities. The Secretary of the Treasury shall prescribe regulations or guidance specifying the form, content, and timing of such reports.

(f) Definitions

As used in this section—

(1) the term "qualified loss mitigation plan" means—

(A) a residential loan modification, workout, or other loss mitigation plan, including to the extent that the Secretary of the Treasury determines appropriate, a loan sale, real property disposition, trial modification, pre-foreclosure sale, and deed in lieu of foreclosure, that is described or authorized in guidelines issued by the Secretary of the Treasury or his designee under the Emergency Economic Stabilization Act of 2008; and

(B) a refinancing of a mortgage under the Hope for Homeowners program;

(2) the term "servicer" means the person responsible for the servicing for others of residential mortgage loans (including of a pool of residential mortgage loans); and

(3) the term "securitization vehicle" means a trust, special purpose entity, or other legal structure that is used to facilitate the issuing of securities, participation certificates, or similar instruments backed by or referring to a pool of assets that includes residential mortgages (or instruments that are related to residential mortgages such as credit-linked notes).

(g) Rule of construction

No provision of subsection (b) or (d) shall be construed as affecting the liability of any servicer or person as described in subsection (d) for actual fraud in the origination or servicing of a loan or in the implementation of a qualified loss mitigation plan, or for the violation of a State or Federal law, including laws regulating the origination of mortgage loans, commonly referred to as predatory lending laws.

(Pub.L. 90–321, Title I, § 129, formerly § 129A, as added Pub.L. 110–289, Div. A, Title IV, § 1403, July 30, 2008, 122 Stat. 2809; renumbered § 129, Pub.L. 111–22, Div. A, Title II, § 201(b), May 20, 2009, 123 Stat. 1638; renumbered § 129A, Pub.L. 111–203, Title XIV, §§ 1400(c), 1402(a)(1), July 21, 2010, 124 Stat. 2136, 2138.)

§ 1639b. Residential mortgage loan origination [CCPA 129B]

(a) Finding and purpose

(1) Finding

The Congress finds that economic stabilization would be enhanced by the protection, limitation, and regulation of the terms of residential mortgage credit and the practices related to such credit, while ensuring that responsible, affordable mortgage credit remains available to consumers.

(2) Purpose

It is the purpose of this section and section 1639c of this title to assure that consumers are offered and receive residential mortgage loans on terms that reasonably reflect their ability to repay the loans and that are understandable and not unfair, deceptive or abusive.

(b) Duty of care

(1) Standard

Subject to regulations prescribed under this subsection, each mortgage originator shall, in addition to the duties imposed by otherwise applicable provisions of State or Federal law—

(A) be qualified and, when required, registered and licensed as a mortgage originator in accordance with applicable State or Federal law, including the Secure and Fair Enforcement for Mortgage Licensing Act of 2008; and

(B) include on all loan documents any unique identifier of the mortgage originator provided by the Nationwide Mortgage Licensing System and Registry.

(2) Compliance procedures required

The Bureau shall prescribe regulations requiring depository institutions to establish and maintain procedures reasonably designed to assure and monitor the compliance of such depository institutions, the subsidiaries of such institutions, and the employees of such institutions or subsidiaries with the requirements of this section and the registration procedures established under section 1507 of the Secure and Fair Enforcement for Mortgage Licensing Act of 2008.

(c) Prohibition on steering incentives

(1) In general

For any residential mortgage loan, no mortgage originator shall receive from any person and no person shall pay to a mortgage originator, directly or indirectly, compensation that varies based on the terms of the loan (other than the amount of the principal).

(2) Restructuring of financing origination fee

(A) In general

For any mortgage loan, a mortgage originator may not receive from any person other than the consumer and no person, other than the consumer, who knows or has reason to know that a consumer has directly compensated or will directly compensate a mortgage originator may pay a mortgage originator any origination fee or charge except bona fide third party charges not retained by the creditor, mortgage originator, or an affiliate of the creditor or mortgage originator.

(B) Exception

Notwithstanding subparagraph (A), a mortgage originator may receive from a person other than the consumer an origination fee or charge, and a person other than the consumer may pay a mortgage originator an origination fee or charge, if—

(i) the mortgage originator does not receive any compensation directly from the consumer; and

(ii) the consumer does not make an upfront payment of discount points, origination points, or fees, however denominated (other than bona fide third party charges not retained

by the mortgage originator, creditor, or an affiliate of the creditor or originator), except that the Bureau may, by rule, waive or provide exemptions to this clause if the Bureau determines that such waiver or exemption is in the interest of consumers and in the public interest.

(3) Regulations

The Bureau shall prescribe regulations to prohibit—

    (A) mortgage originators from steering any consumer to a residential mortgage loan that—

        (i) the consumer lacks a reasonable ability to repay (in accordance with regulations prescribed under section 1639c(a) of this title); or

        (ii) has predatory characteristics or effects (such as equity stripping, excessive fees, or abusive terms);

    (B) mortgage originators from steering any consumer from a residential mortgage loan for which the consumer is qualified that is a qualified mortgage (as defined in section 1639c(b)(2) of this title) to a residential mortgage loan that is not a qualified mortgage;

    (C) abusive or unfair lending practices that promote disparities among consumers of equal credit worthiness but of different race, ethnicity, gender, or age; and

    (D) mortgage originators from—

        (i) mischaracterizing the credit history of a consumer or the residential mortgage loans available to a consumer;

        (ii) mischaracterizing or suborning the mischaracterization of the appraised value of the property securing the extension of credit; or

        (iii) if unable to suggest, offer, or recommend to a consumer a loan that is not more expensive than a loan for which the consumer qualifies, discouraging a consumer from seeking a residential mortgage loan secured by a consumer's principal dwelling from another mortgage originator.

(4) Rules of construction

No provision of this subsection shall be construed as—

    (A) permitting any yield spread premium or other similar compensation that would, for any residential mortgage loan, permit the total amount of direct and indirect compensation from all sources permitted to a mortgage originator to vary based on the terms of the loan (other than the amount of the principal);

    (B) limiting or affecting the amount of compensation received by a creditor upon the sale of a consummated loan to a subsequent purchaser;

    (C) restricting a consumer's ability to finance, at the option of the consumer, including through principal or rate, any origination fees or costs permitted under this subsection, or the mortgage originator's right to receive such fees or costs (including compensation) from any person, subject to paragraph (2)(B), so long as such fees or costs do not vary based on the terms of the loan (other than the amount of the principal) or the consumer's decision about whether to finance such fees or costs; or

    (D) prohibiting incentive payments to a mortgage originator based on the number of residential mortgage loans originated within a specified period of time.

(d) Liability for violations

(1) In general

For purposes of providing a cause of action for any failure by a mortgage originator, other than a creditor, to comply with any requirement imposed under this section and any regulation prescribed under this section, section 1640 of this title shall be applied with respect to any such failure by substituting "mortgage originator" for "creditor" each place such term appears in each such subsection.[1]

(2) Maximum

The maximum amount of any liability of a mortgage originator under paragraph (1) to a consumer for any violation of this section shall not exceed the greater of actual damages or an amount equal to 3 times the total amount of direct and indirect compensation or gain accruing to the mortgage originator in connection with the residential mortgage loan involved in the violation, plus the costs to the consumer of the action, including a reasonable attorney's fee.

(e) Discretionary regulatory authority

(1) In general

The Bureau shall, by regulations, prohibit or condition terms, acts or practices relating to residential mortgage loans that the Bureau finds to be abusive, unfair, deceptive, predatory, necessary or proper to ensure that responsible, affordable mortgage credit remains available to consumers in a manner consistent with the purposes of this section and section 1639c of this title, necessary or proper to effectuate the purposes of this section and section 1639c of this title, to prevent circumvention or evasion thereof, or to facilitate compliance with such sections, or are not in the interest of the borrower.

(2) Application

The regulations prescribed under paragraph (1) shall be applicable to all residential mortgage loans and shall be applied in the same manner as regulations prescribed under section 1604 of this title.

(f) Section 1639b of this title and any regulations promulgated thereunder do not apply to an extension of credit relating to a plan described in section 101(53D) of Title 11.

(Pub.L. 90–321, Title I, § 129B, as added and amended Pub.L. 111–203, Title X, § 1100A(2), Title XIV, §§ 1402(a)(2), 1403, 1404, 1405(a), July 21, 2010, 124 Stat. 2107, 2139, 2141.)

§ 1639c.   Minimum standards for residential mortgage loans [CCPA 129C]

(a) Ability to repay

(1) In general

In accordance with regulations prescribed by the Bureau, no creditor may make a residential mortgage loan unless the creditor makes a reasonable and good faith determination based on verified and documented information that, at the time the loan is consummated, the consumer has a reasonable ability to repay the loan, according to its terms, and all applicable taxes, insurance (including mortgage guarantee insurance), and assessments.

(2) Multiple loans

If the creditor knows, or has reason to know, that 1 or more residential mortgage loans secured by the same dwelling will be made to the same consumer, the creditor shall make a reasonable and good faith determination, based on verified and documented information, that the consumer has a reasonable ability to repay the combined payments of all loans on the same dwelling according to the terms of those loans and all applicable taxes, insurance (including mortgage guarantee insurance), and assessments.

(3) Basis for determination

A determination under this subsection of a consumer's ability to repay a residential mortgage loan shall include consideration of the consumer's credit history, current income, expected income the consumer is reasonably assured of receiving, current obligations, debt-to-income ratio or the residual income the consumer will have after paying non-mortgage debt and mortgage-related obligations, employment status, and other financial resources other than the consumer's equity in the dwelling or real property that secures repayment of the loan. A creditor shall determine the ability of the consumer to repay using a payment schedule that fully amortizes the loan over the term of the loan.

---

[1]   So in original. Probably should be "in such section."

(4) Income verification

A creditor making a residential mortgage loan shall verify amounts of income or assets that such creditor relies on to determine repayment ability, including expected income or assets, by reviewing the consumer's Internal Revenue Service Form W-2, tax returns, payroll receipts, financial institution records, or other third-party documents that provide reasonably reliable evidence of the consumer's income or assets. In order to safeguard against fraudulent reporting, any consideration of a consumer's income history in making a determination under this subsection shall include the verification of such income by the use of—

    (A) Internal Revenue Service transcripts of tax returns; or

    (B) a method that quickly and effectively verifies income documentation by a third party subject to rules prescribed by the Bureau.

(5) Exemption

With respect to loans made, guaranteed, or insured by Federal departments or agencies identified in subsection (b)(3)(B)(ii), such departments or agencies may exempt refinancings under a streamlined refinancing from this income verification requirement as long as the following conditions are met:

    (A) The consumer is not 30 days or more past due on the prior existing residential mortgage loan.

    (B) The refinancing does not increase the principal balance outstanding on the prior existing residential mortgage loan, except to the extent of fees and charges allowed by the department or agency making, guaranteeing, or insuring the refinancing.

    (C) Total points and fees (as defined in section 1602(aa)(4) of this title, other than bona fide third party charges not retained by the mortgage originator, creditor, or an affiliate of the creditor or mortgage originator) payable in connection with the refinancing do not exceed 3 percent of the total new loan amount.

    (D) The interest rate on the refinanced loan is lower than the interest rate of the original loan, unless the borrower is refinancing from an adjustable rate to a fixed-rate loan, under guidelines that the department or agency shall establish for loans they make, guarantee, or issue.

    (E) The refinancing is subject to a payment schedule that will fully amortize the refinancing in accordance with the regulations prescribed by the department or agency making, guaranteeing, or insuring the refinancing.

    (F) The terms of the refinancing do not result in a balloon payment, as defined in subsection (b)(2)(A)(ii).

    (G) Both the residential mortgage loan being refinanced and the refinancing satisfy all requirements of the department or agency making, guaranteeing, or insuring the refinancing.

(6) Nonstandard loans

    (A) Variable rate loans that defer repayment of any principal or interest

    For purposes of determining, under this subsection, a consumer's ability to repay a variable rate residential mortgage loan that allows or requires the consumer to defer the repayment of any principal or interest, the creditor shall use a fully amortizing repayment schedule.

    (B) Interest-only loans

    For purposes of determining, under this subsection, a consumer's ability to repay a residential mortgage loan that permits or requires the payment of interest only, the creditor shall use the payment amount required to amortize the loan by its final maturity.

    (C) Calculation for negative amortization

    In making any determination under this subsection, a creditor shall also take into consideration any balance increase that may accrue from any negative amortization provision.

(D) Calculation process

For purposes of making any determination under this subsection, a creditor shall calculate the monthly payment amount for principal and interest on any residential mortgage loan by assuming—

    (i) the loan proceeds are fully disbursed on the date of the consummation of the loan;

    (ii) the loan is to be repaid in substantially equal monthly amortizing payments for principal and interest over the entire term of the loan with no balloon payment, unless the loan contract requires more rapid repayment (including balloon payment), in which case the calculation shall be made (I) in accordance with regulations prescribed by the Bureau, with respect to any loan which has an annual percentage rate that does not exceed the average prime offer rate for a comparable transaction, as of the date the interest rate is set, by 1.5 or more percentage points for a first lien residential mortgage loan; and by 3.5 or more percentage points for a subordinate lien residential mortgage loan; or (II) using the contract's repayment schedule, with respect to a loan which has an annual percentage rate, as of the date the interest rate is set, that is at least 1.5 percentage points above the average prime offer rate for a first lien residential mortgage loan; and 3.5 percentage points above the average prime offer rate for a subordinate lien residential mortgage loan; and

    (iii) the interest rate over the entire term of the loan is a fixed rate equal to the fully indexed rate at the time of the loan closing, without considering the introductory rate.

(E) Refinance of hybrid loans with current lender

In considering any application for refinancing an existing hybrid loan by the creditor into a standard loan to be made by the same creditor in any case in which there would be a reduction in monthly payment and the mortgagor has not been delinquent on any payment on the existing hybrid loan, the creditor may—

    (i) consider the mortgagor's good standing on the existing mortgage;

    (ii) consider if the extension of new credit would prevent a likely default should the original mortgage reset and give such concerns a higher priority as an acceptable underwriting practice; and

    (iii) offer rate discounts and other favorable terms to such mortgagor that would be available to new customers with high credit ratings based on such underwriting practice.

(7) Fully-indexed rate defined

For purposes of this subsection, the term "fully indexed rate" means the index rate prevailing on a residential mortgage loan at the time the loan is made plus the margin that will apply after the expiration of any introductory interest rates.

(8) Reverse mortgages and bridge loans

This subsection shall not apply with respect to any reverse mortgage or temporary or bridge loan with a term of 12 months or less, including to any loan to purchase a new dwelling where the consumer plans to sell a different dwelling within 12 months.

(9) Seasonal income

If documented income, including income from a small business, is a repayment source for a residential mortgage loan, a creditor may consider the seasonality and irregularity of such income in the underwriting of and scheduling of payments for such credit.

(b) Presumption of ability to repay

(1) In general

Any creditor with respect to any residential mortgage loan, and any assignee of such loan subject to liability under this subchapter, may presume that the loan has met the requirements of subsection (a), if the loan is a qualified mortgage.

(2) Definitions

For purposes of this subsection, the following definitions shall apply:

(A) Qualified mortgage

The term "qualified mortgage" means any residential mortgage loan—

  (i) for which the regular periodic payments for the loan may not—

    (I) result in an increase of the principal balance; or

    (II) except as provided in subparagraph (E), allow the consumer to defer repayment of principal;

  (ii) except as provided in subparagraph (E), the terms of which do not result in a balloon payment, where a "balloon payment" is a scheduled payment that is more than twice as large as the average of earlier scheduled payments;

  (iii) for which the income and financial resources relied upon to qualify the obligors on the loan are verified and documented;

  (iv) in the case of a fixed rate loan, for which the underwriting process is based on a payment schedule that fully amortizes the loan over the loan term and takes into account all applicable taxes, insurance, and assessments;

  (v) in the case of an adjustable rate loan, for which the underwriting is based on the maximum rate permitted under the loan during the first 5 years, and a payment schedule that fully amortizes the loan over the loan term and takes into account all applicable taxes, insurance, and assessments;

  (vi) that complies with any guidelines or regulations established by the Bureau relating to ratios of total monthly debt to monthly income or alternative measures of ability to pay regular expenses after payment of total monthly debt, taking into account the income levels of the borrower and such other factors as the Bureau may determine relevant and consistent with the purposes described in paragraph (3)(B)(i);

  (vii) for which the total points and fees (as defined in subparagraph (C)) payable in connection with the loan do not exceed 3 percent of the total loan amount;

  (viii)   for which the term of the loan does not exceed 30 years, except as such term may be extended under paragraph (3), such as in high-cost areas; and

  (ix) in the case of a reverse mortgage (except for the purposes of subsection (a) of this section, to the extent that such mortgages are exempt altogether from those requirements), a reverse mortgage which meets the standards for a qualified mortgage, as set by the Bureau in rules that are consistent with the purposes of this subsection.

(B) Average prime offer rate

The term "average prime offer rate" means the average prime offer rate for a comparable transaction as of the date on which the interest rate for the transaction is set, as published by the Bureau..[1]

(C) Points and fees

(i)   In general

For purposes of subparagraph (A), the term "points and fees" means points and fees as defined by section 1602(aa)(4) of this title (other than bona fide third party charges not retained by the mortgage originator, creditor, or an affiliate of the creditor or mortgage originator).

---

[1]   So in original. Second period probably should not appear.

(ii) Computation

For purposes of computing the total points and fees under this subparagraph, the total points and fees shall exclude either of the amounts described in the following subclauses, but not both:

(I) Up to and including 2 bona fide discount points payable by the consumer in connection with the mortgage, but only if the interest rate from which the mortgage's interest rate will be discounted does not exceed by more than 1 percentage point the average prime offer rate.

(II) Unless 2 bona fide discount points have been excluded under subclause (I), up to and including 1 bona fide discount point payable by the consumer in connection with the mortgage, but only if the interest rate from which the mortgage's interest rate will be discounted does not exceed by more than 2 percentage points the average prime offer rate.

(iii) Bona fide discount points defined

For purposes of clause (ii), the term "bona fide discount points" means loan discount points which are knowingly paid by the consumer for the purpose of reducing, and which in fact result in a bona fide reduction of, the interest rate or time-price differential applicable to the mortgage.

(iv) Interest rate reduction

Subclauses (I) and (II) of clause (ii) shall not apply to discount points used to purchase an interest rate reduction unless the amount of the interest rate reduction purchased is reasonably consistent with established industry norms and practices for secondary mortgage market transactions.

(D) Smaller loans

The Bureau shall prescribe rules adjusting the criteria under subparagraph (A)(vii) in order to permit lenders that extend smaller loans to meet the requirements of the presumption of compliance under paragraph (1). In prescribing such rules, the Bureau shall consider the potential impact of such rules on rural areas and other areas where home values are lower.

(E) Balloon loans

The Bureau may, by regulation, provide that the term "qualified mortgage" includes a balloon loan—

(i) that meets all of the criteria for a qualified mortgage under subparagraph (A) (except clauses (i)(II), (ii), (iv), and (v) of such subparagraph);

(ii) for which the creditor makes a determination that the consumer is able to make all scheduled payments, except the balloon payment, out of income or assets other than the collateral;

(iii) for which the underwriting is based on a payment schedule that fully amortizes the loan over a period of not more than 30 years and takes into account all applicable taxes, insurance, and assessments; and

(iv) that is extended by a creditor that—

(I) operates in rural or underserved areas;

(II) together with all affiliates, has total annual residential mortgage loan originations that do not exceed a limit set by the Bureau;

(III) retains the balloon loans in portfolio; and

(IV) meets any asset size threshold and any other criteria as the Bureau may establish, consistent with the purposes of this subtitle.

(3) Regulations

(A) In general

The Bureau shall prescribe regulations to carry out the purposes of this subsection.

(B) Revision of safe harbor criteria

(i) In general

The Bureau may prescribe regulations that revise, add to, or subtract from the criteria that define a qualified mortgage upon a finding that such regulations are necessary or proper to ensure that responsible, affordable mortgage credit remains available to consumers in a manner consistent with the purposes of this section, necessary and appropriate to effectuate the purposes of this section and section 1639b of this title, to prevent circumvention or evasion thereof, or to facilitate compliance with such sections.

(ii) Loan definition

The following agencies shall, in consultation with the Bureau, prescribe rules defining the types of loans they insure, guarantee, or administer, as the case may be, that are qualified mortgages for purposes of paragraph (2)(A), and such rules may revise, add to, or subtract from the criteria used to define a qualified mortgage under paragraph (2)(A), upon a finding that such rules are consistent with the purposes of this section and section 1639b of this title, to prevent circumvention or evasion thereof, or to facilitate compliance with such sections:

> **(I)** The Department of Housing and Urban Development, with regard to mortgages insured under the National Housing Act (12 U.S.C. 1707 et seq.).

> **(II)** The Department of Veterans Affairs, with regard to a loan made or guaranteed by the Secretary of Veterans Affairs.

> **(III)** The Department of Agriculture, with regard[2] loans guaranteed by the Secretary of Agriculture pursuant to 42 U.S.C. 1472(h).

> **(IV)** The Rural Housing Service, with regard to loans insured by the Rural Housing Service.

(c) Prohibition on certain prepayment penalties

(1) Prohibited on certain loans

(A) In general

A residential mortgage loan that is not a "qualified mortgage", as defined under subsection (b)(2), may not contain terms under which a consumer must pay a prepayment penalty for paying all or part of the principal after the loan is consummated.

(B) Exclusions

For purposes of this subsection, a "qualified mortgage" may not include a residential mortgage loan that—

> **(i)** has an adjustable rate; or

> **(ii)** has an annual percentage rate that exceeds the average prime offer rate for a comparable transaction, as of the date the interest rate is set—

> > **(I)** by 1.5 or more percentage points, in the case of a first lien residential mortgage loan having a original principal obligation amount that is equal to or less than the amount of the maximum limitation on the original principal obligation of mortgage in effect for a residence of the applicable size, as of the date of such interest rate set, pursuant to the 6th sentence of section 1454(a)(2) of Title 12;

> > **(II)** by 2.5 or more percentage points, in the case of a first lien residential mortgage loan having a original principal obligation amount that is more than the amount of the maximum limitation on the original principal obligation of mortgage in effect for a residence of the applicable size, as of the date of such interest rate set, pursuant to the 6th sentence of section 1454(a)(2) of Title 12; and

---

2   So in original. Probably should be followed by "to."

(III) by 3.5 or more percentage points, in the case of a subordinate lien residential mortgage loan.

(2) Publication of average prime offer rate and APR thresholds

The Bureau—

(A) shall publish, and update at least weekly, average prime offer rates;

(B) may publish multiple rates based on varying types of mortgage transactions; and

(C) shall adjust the thresholds established under subclause (I), (II), and (III) of paragraph (1)(B)(ii) as necessary to reflect significant changes in market conditions and to effectuate the purposes of the Mortgage Reform and Anti-Predatory Lending Act.

(3) Phased-out penalties on qualified mortgages

A qualified mortgage (as defined in subsection (b)(2)) may not contain terms under which a consumer must pay a prepayment penalty for paying all or part of the principal after the loan is consummated in excess of the following limitations:

(A) During the 1-year period beginning on the date the loan is consummated, the prepayment penalty shall not exceed an amount equal to 3 percent of the outstanding balance on the loan.

(B) During the 1-year period beginning after the period described in subparagraph (A), the prepayment penalty shall not exceed an amount equal to 2 percent of the outstanding balance on the loan.

(C) During the 1-year period beginning after the 1-year period described in subparagraph (B), the prepayment penalty shall not exceed an amount equal to 1 percent of the outstanding balance on the loan.

(D) After the end of the 3-year period beginning on the date the loan is consummated, no prepayment penalty may be imposed on a qualified mortgage.

(4) Option for no prepayment penalty required

A creditor may not offer a consumer a residential mortgage loan product that has a prepayment penalty for paying all or part of the principal after the loan is consummated as a term of the loan without offering the consumer a residential mortgage loan product that does not have a prepayment penalty as a term of the loan.

(d) Single premium credit insurance prohibited

No creditor may finance, directly or indirectly, in connection with any residential mortgage loan or with any extension of credit under an open end consumer credit plan secured by the principal dwelling of the consumer, any credit life, credit disability, credit unemployment, or credit property insurance, or any other accident, loss-of-income, life, or health insurance, or any payments directly or indirectly for any debt cancellation or suspension agreement or contract, except that—

(1) insurance premiums or debt cancellation or suspension fees calculated and paid in full on a monthly basis shall not be considered financed by the creditor; and

(2) this subsection shall not apply to credit unemployment insurance for which the unemployment insurance premiums are reasonable, the creditor receives no direct or indirect compensation in connection with the unemployment insurance premiums, and the unemployment insurance premiums are paid pursuant to another insurance contract and not paid to an affiliate of the creditor.

(e) Arbitration

(1) In general

No residential mortgage loan and no extension of credit under an open end consumer credit plan secured by the principal dwelling of the consumer may include terms which require arbitration or any other nonjudicial procedure as the method for resolving any controversy or settling any claims arising out of the transaction.

(2) Post-controversy agreements

Subject to paragraph (3), paragraph (1) shall not be construed as limiting the right of the consumer and the creditor or any assignee to agree to arbitration or any other nonjudicial procedure as the method for resolving any controversy at any time after a dispute or claim under the transaction arises.

(3) No waiver of statutory cause of action

No provision of any residential mortgage loan or of any extension of credit under an open end consumer credit plan secured by the principal dwelling of the consumer, and no other agreement between the consumer and the creditor relating to the residential mortgage loan or extension of credit referred to in paragraph (1), shall be applied or interpreted so as to bar a consumer from bringing an action in an appropriate district court of the United States, or any other court of competent jurisdiction, pursuant to section 1640 of this title or any other provision of law, for damages or other relief in connection with any alleged violation of this section, any other provision of this subchapter, or any other Federal law.

(f) Mortgages with negative amortization

No creditor may extend credit to a borrower in connection with a consumer credit transaction under an open or closed end consumer credit plan secured by a dwelling or residential real property that includes a dwelling, other than a reverse mortgage, that provides or permits a payment plan that may, at any time over the term of the extension of credit, result in negative amortization unless, before such transaction is consummated—

 (1) the creditor provides the consumer with a statement that—

  (A) the pending transaction will or may, as the case may be, result in negative amortization;

  (B) describes negative amortization in such manner as the Bureau shall prescribe;

  (C) negative amortization increases the outstanding principal balance of the account; and

  (D) negative amortization reduces the consumer's equity in the dwelling or real property; and

 (2) in the case of a first-time borrower with respect to a residential mortgage loan that is not a qualified mortgage, the first-time borrower provides the creditor with sufficient documentation to demonstrate that the consumer received homeownership counseling from organizations or counselors certified by the Secretary of Housing and Urban Development as competent to provide such counseling.

(g) Protection against loss of anti-deficiency protection

(1) Definition

For purposes of this subsection, the term "anti-deficiency law" means the law of any State which provides that, in the event of foreclosure on the residential property of a consumer securing a mortgage, the consumer is not liable, in accordance with the terms and limitations of such State law, for any deficiency between the sale price obtained on such property through foreclosure and the outstanding balance of the mortgage.

(2) Notice at time of consummation

In the case of any residential mortgage loan that is, or upon consummation will be, subject to protection under an anti-deficiency law, the creditor or mortgage originator shall provide a written notice to the consumer describing the protection provided by the anti-deficiency law and the significance for the consumer of the loss of such protection before such loan is consummated.

(3) Notice before refinancing that would cause loss of protection

In the case of any residential mortgage loan that is subject to protection under an anti-deficiency law, if a creditor or mortgage originator provides an application to a consumer, or receives an application from a consumer, for any type of refinancing for such loan that would cause the loan to lose the protection of such anti-deficiency law, the creditor or mortgage originator shall provide a written notice to the consumer describing the protection provided by the anti-deficiency law and the significance for the consumer of the loss of such protection before any agreement for any such refinancing is consummated.

(h) Policy regarding acceptance of partial payment

In the case of any residential mortgage loan, a creditor shall disclose prior to settlement or, in the case of a person becoming a creditor with respect to an existing residential mortgage loan, at the time such person becomes a creditor—

(1) the creditor's policy regarding the acceptance of partial payments; and

(2) if partial payments are accepted, how such payments will be applied to such mortgage and if such payments will be placed in escrow.

(i) Timeshare plans

This section and any regulations promulgated under this section do not apply to an extension of credit relating to a plan described in section 101(53D) of Title 11.

(Pub.L. 90–321, Title I, § 129C; Pub.L. 111–203, Title X, § 1100A(2), Title XIV, §§ 1411(a)(2), 1412, 1414(a), (c), (d), July 21, 2010, 124 Stat. 2107, 2142, 2145, 2149, 2152; Pub.L. 114–94, Div. G, Title LXXXIX, § 89003, Dec. 4, 2015, 129 Stat. 1801.)

§ 1639d. Escrow or impound accounts relating to certain consumer credit transactions [CCPA 129D]

(a) In general

Except as provided in subsection (b), (c), (d), or (e), a creditor, in connection with the consummation of a consumer credit transaction secured by a first lien on the principal dwelling of the consumer, other than a consumer credit transaction under an open end credit plan or a reverse mortgage, shall establish, before the consummation of such transaction, an escrow or impound account for the payment of taxes and hazard insurance, and, if applicable, flood insurance, mortgage insurance, ground rents, and any other required periodic payments or premiums with respect to the property or the loan terms, as provided in, and in accordance with, this section.

(b) When required

No impound, trust, or other type of account for the payment of property taxes, insurance premiums, or other purposes relating to the property may be required as a condition of a real property sale contract or a loan secured by a first deed of trust or mortgage on the principal dwelling of the consumer, other than a consumer credit transaction under an open end credit plan or a reverse mortgage, except when—

(1) any such impound, trust, or other type of escrow or impound account for such purposes is required by Federal or State law;

(2) a loan is made, guaranteed, or insured by a State or Federal governmental lending or insuring agency;

(3) the transaction is secured by a first mortgage or lien on the consumer's principal dwelling having an original principal obligation amount that—

(A) does not exceed the amount of the maximum limitation on the original principal obligation of mortgage in effect for a residence of the applicable size, as of the date such interest rate set, pursuant to the sixth sentence of section 1454(a)(2) of Title 12, and the annual percentage rate will exceed the average prime offer rate as defined in section 1639c of this title by 1.5 or more percentage points; or

(B) exceeds the amount of the maximum limitation on the original principal obligation of mortgage in effect for a residence of the applicable size, as of the date such interest rate set, pursuant to the sixth sentence of section 1454(a)(2) of Title 12, and the annual percentage rate will exceed the average prime offer rate as defined in section 1639c of this title by 2.5 or more percentage points; or

    (4)   so required pursuant to regulation.

(c) **Exemptions**

The Bureau may, by regulation, exempt from the requirements of subsection (a) a creditor that—

    (1)   operates in rural or underserved areas;

    (2)   together with all affiliates, has total annual mortgage loan originations that do not exceed a limit set by the Bureau;

    (3)   retains its mortgage loan originations in portfolio; and

    (4)   meets any asset size threshold and any other criteria the Bureau may establish, consistent with the purposes of this subtitle.

(d) **Duration of mandatory escrow or impound account**

An escrow or impound account established pursuant to subsection (b) shall remain in existence for a minimum period of 5 years, beginning with the date of the consummation of the loan, unless and until—

    (1)   such borrower has sufficient equity in the dwelling securing the consumer credit transaction so as to no longer be required to maintain private mortgage insurance;

    (2)   such borrower is delinquent;

    (3)   such borrower otherwise has not complied with the legal obligation, as established by rule; or

    (4)   the underlying mortgage establishing the account is terminated.

(e) **Limited exemptions for loans secured by shares in a cooperative or in which an association must maintain a master insurance policy**

Escrow accounts need not be established for loans secured by shares in a cooperative. Insurance premiums need not be included in escrow accounts for loans secured by dwellings or units, where the borrower must join an association as a condition of ownership, and that association has an obligation to the dwelling or unit owners to maintain a master policy insuring the dwellings or units.

(f) **Clarification on escrow accounts for loans not meeting statutory test**

For mortgages not covered by the requirements of subsection (b), no provision of this section shall be construed as precluding the establishment of an impound, trust, or other type of account for the payment of property taxes, insurance premiums, or other purposes relating to the property—

    (1)   on terms mutually agreeable to the parties to the loan;

    (2)   at the discretion of the lender or servicer, as provided by the contract between the lender or servicer and the borrower; or

    (3)   pursuant to the requirements for the escrowing of flood insurance payments for regulated lending institutions in section 102(d) of the Flood Disaster Protection Act of 1973.

(g) **Administration of mandatory escrow or impound accounts**

    (1) **In general**

Except as may otherwise be provided for in this subchapter or in regulations prescribed by the Bureau, escrow or impound accounts established pursuant to subsection (b) shall be established in a federally insured depository institution or credit union.

    (2) **Administration**

Except as provided in this section or regulations prescribed under this section, an escrow or impound account subject to this section shall be administered in accordance with—

    (A) the Real Estate Settlement Procedures Act of 1974 and regulations prescribed under such Act;

    (B) the Flood Disaster Protection Act of 1973 and regulations prescribed under such Act; and

    (C) the law of the State, if applicable, where the real property securing the consumer credit transaction is located.

(3) Applicability of payment of interest

If prescribed by applicable State or Federal law, each creditor shall pay interest to the consumer on the amount held in any impound, trust, or escrow account that is subject to this section in the manner as prescribed by that applicable State or Federal law.

(4) Penalty coordination with RESPA

Any action or omission on the part of any person which constitutes a violation of the Real Estate Settlement Procedures Act of 1974 or any regulation prescribed under such Act for which the person has paid any fine, civil money penalty, or other damages shall not give rise to any additional fine, civil money penalty, or other damages under this section, unless the action or omission also constitutes a direct violation of this section.

(h) Disclosures relating to mandatory escrow or impound account

In the case of any impound, trust, or escrow account that is required under subsection (b), the creditor shall disclose by written notice to the consumer at least 3 business days before the consummation of the consumer credit transaction giving rise to such account or in accordance with timeframes established in prescribed regulations the following information:

    (1) The fact that an escrow or impound account will be established at consummation of the transaction.

    (2) The amount required at closing to initially fund the escrow or impound account.

    (3) The amount, in the initial year after the consummation of the transaction, of the estimated taxes and hazard insurance, including flood insurance, if applicable, and any other required periodic payments or premiums that reflects, as appropriate, either the taxable assessed value of the real property securing the transaction, including the value of any improvements on the property or to be constructed on the property (whether or not such construction will be financed from the proceeds of the transaction) or the replacement costs of the property.

    (4) The estimated monthly amount payable to be escrowed for taxes, hazard insurance (including flood insurance, if applicable) and any other required periodic payments or premiums.

    (5) The fact that, if the consumer chooses to terminate the account in the future, the consumer will become responsible for the payment of all taxes, hazard insurance, and flood insurance, if applicable, as well as any other required periodic payments or premiums on the property unless a new escrow or impound account is established.

    (6) Such other information as the Bureau determines necessary for the protection of the consumer.

(i) Definitions

For purposes of this section, the following definitions shall apply:

(1) Flood insurance

The term "flood insurance" means flood insurance coverage provided under the national flood insurance program pursuant to the National Flood Insurance Act of 1968.

(2) Hazard insurance

The term "hazard insurance" shall have the same meaning as provided for "hazard insurance", "casualty insurance", "homeowner's insurance", or other similar term under the law of the State where the real property securing the consumer credit transaction is located.

(j) Disclosure notice required for consumers who waive escrow services

> **(1) In general**
>
> If—
>
> > **(A)** an impound, trust, or other type of account for the payment of property taxes, insurance premiums, or other purposes relating to real property securing a consumer credit transaction is not established in connection with the transaction; or
> >
> > **(B)** a consumer chooses, and provides written notice to the creditor or servicer of such choice, at any time after such an account is established in connection with any such transaction and in accordance with any statute, regulation, or contractual agreement, to close such account, the creditor or servicer shall provide a timely and clearly written disclosure to the consumer that advises the consumer of the responsibilities of the consumer and implications for the consumer in the absence of any such account.
>
> **(2) Disclosure requirements**
>
> Any disclosure provided to a consumer under paragraph (1) shall include the following:
>
> > **(A)** Information concerning any applicable fees or costs associated with either the non-establishment of any such account at the time of the transaction, or any subsequent closure of any such account.
> >
> > **(B)** A clear and prominent statement that the consumer is responsible for personally and directly paying the non-escrowed items, in addition to paying the mortgage loan payment, in the absence of any such account, and the fact that the costs for taxes, insurance, and related fees can be substantial.
> >
> > **(C)** A clear explanation of the consequences of any failure to pay non-escrowed items, including the possible requirement for the forced placement of insurance by the creditor or servicer and the potentially higher cost (including any potential commission payments to the servicer) or reduced coverage for the consumer in the event of any such creditor-placed insurance.
> >
> > **(D)** Such other information as the Bureau determines necessary for the protection of the consumer.

(Pub.L. 90–321, Title I, § 129D; Pub.L. 111–203, Title X, § 1100A(2), Title XIV, §§ 1461(a), 1462, July 21, 2010, 124 Stat. 2107, 2178, 2181; Pub.L. 114–94, Div. G, Title LXXXIX, § 89003(1), Dec. 4, 2015, 129 Stat. 1801.)

§ 1639e.   Appraisal independence requirements [CCPA 129E]

(a) In general

It shall be unlawful, in extending credit or in providing any services for a consumer credit transaction secured by the principal dwelling of the consumer, to engage in any act or practice that violates appraisal independence as described in or pursuant to regulations prescribed under this section.

(b) Appraisal independence

For purposes of subsection (a), acts or practices that violate appraisal independence shall include—

> **(1)** any appraisal of a property offered as security for repayment of the consumer credit transaction that is conducted in connection with such transaction in which a person with an interest in the underlying transaction compensates, coerces, extorts, colludes, instructs, induces, bribes, or intimidates a person, appraisal management company, firm, or other entity conducting or involved in an appraisal, or attempts, to compensate, coerce, extort, collude, instruct, induce, bribe, or intimidate such a person, for the purpose of causing the appraised value assigned, under the appraisal, to the property to be based on any factor other than the independent judgment of the appraiser;
>
> **(2)** mischaracterizing, or suborning any mischaracterization of, the appraised value of the property securing the extension of the credit;

(3) seeking to influence an appraiser or otherwise to encourage a targeted value in order to facilitate the making or pricing of the transaction; and

(4) withholding or threatening to withhold timely payment for an appraisal report or for appraisal services rendered when the appraisal report or services are provided for in accordance with the contract between the parties.

(c) Exceptions

The requirements of subsection (b) shall not be construed as prohibiting a mortgage lender, mortgage broker, mortgage banker, real estate broker, appraisal management company, employee of an appraisal management company, consumer, or any other person with an interest in a real estate transaction from asking an appraiser to undertake 1 or more of the following:

(1) Consider additional, appropriate property information, including the consideration of additional comparable properties to make or support an appraisal.

(2) Provide further detail, substantiation, or explanation for the appraiser's value conclusion.

(3) Correct errors in the appraisal report.

(d) Prohibitions on conflicts of interest

No certified or licensed appraiser conducting, and no appraisal management company procuring or facilitating, an appraisal in connection with a consumer credit transaction secured by the principal dwelling of a consumer may have a direct or indirect interest, financial or otherwise, in the property or transaction involving the appraisal.

(e) Mandatory reporting

Any mortgage lender, mortgage broker, mortgage banker, real estate broker, appraisal management company, employee of an appraisal management company, or any other person involved in a real estate transaction involving an appraisal in connection with a consumer credit transaction secured by the principal dwelling of a consumer who has a reasonable basis to believe an appraiser is failing to comply with the Uniform Standards of Professional Appraisal Practice, is violating applicable laws, or is otherwise engaging in unethical or unprofessional conduct, shall refer the matter to the applicable State appraiser certifying and licensing agency.

(f) No extension of credit

In connection with a consumer credit transaction secured by a consumer's principal dwelling, a creditor who knows, at or before loan consummation, of a violation of the appraisal independence standards established in subsections[1] (b) or (d) shall not extend credit based on such appraisal unless the creditor documents that the creditor has acted with reasonable diligence to determine that the appraisal does not materially misstate or misrepresent the value of such dwelling.

(g) Rules and interpretive guidelines

(1) In general

Except as provided under paragraph (2), the Board, the Comptroller of the Currency, the Federal Deposit Insurance Corporation, the National Credit Union Administration Board, the Federal Housing Finance Agency, and the Bureau may jointly issue rules, interpretive guidelines, and general statements of policy with respect to acts or practices that violate appraisal independence in the provision of mortgage lending services for a consumer credit transaction secured by the principal dwelling of the consumer and mortgage brokerage services for such a transaction, within the meaning of subsections (a), (b), (c), (d), (e), (f), (h), and (i).

(2) Interim final regulations

The Board shall, for purposes of this section, prescribe interim final regulations no later than 90 days after July 21, 2010, defining with specificity acts or practices that violate appraisal independence in the provision of mortgage lending services for a consumer credit transaction secured by the principal

---

[1]   So in original. Probably should be "subsection".

dwelling of the consumer or mortgage brokerage services for such a transaction and defining any terms in this section or such regulations. Rules prescribed by the Board under this paragraph shall be deemed to be rules prescribed by the agencies jointly under paragraph (1).

(h) Appraisal report portability

Consistent with the requirements of this section, the Board, the Comptroller of the Currency, the Federal Deposit Insurance Corporation, the National Credit Union Administration Board, the Federal Housing Finance Agency, and the Bureau may jointly issue regulations that address the issue of appraisal report portability, including regulations that ensure the portability of the appraisal report between lenders for a consumer credit transaction secured by a 1–4 unit single family residence that is the principal dwelling of the consumer, or mortgage brokerage services for such a transaction.

(i) Customary and reasonable fee

    (1) In general

Lenders and their agents shall compensate fee appraisers at a rate that is customary and reasonable for appraisal services performed in the market area of the property being appraised. Evidence for such fees may be established by objective third-party information, such as government agency fee schedules, academic studies, and independent private sector surveys. Fee studies shall exclude assignments ordered by known appraisal management companies.

    (2) Fee appraiser definition

For purposes of this section, the term "fee appraiser" means a person who is not an employee of the mortgage loan originator or appraisal management company engaging the appraiser and is—

        (A) a State licensed or certified appraiser who receives a fee for performing an appraisal and certifies that the appraisal has been prepared in accordance with the Uniform Standards of Professional Appraisal Practice; or

        (B) a company not subject to the requirements of section 3353 of Title 12 that utilizes the services of State licensed or certified appraisers and receives a fee for performing appraisals in accordance with the Uniform Standards of Professional Appraisal Practice.

    (3) Exception for complex assignments

In the case of an appraisal involving a complex assignment, the customary and reasonable fee may reflect the increased time, difficulty, and scope of the work required for such an appraisal and include an amount over and above the customary and reasonable fee for non-complex assignments.

(j) Sunset

Effective on the date the interim final regulations are promulgated pursuant to subsection (g), the Home Valuation Code of Conduct announced by the Federal Housing Finance Agency on December 23, 2008, shall have no force or effect.

(k) Penalties

    (1) First violation

In addition to the enforcement provisions referred to in section 1640 of this title, each person who violates this section shall forfeit and pay a civil penalty of not more than $10,000 for each day any such violation continues.

    (2) Subsequent violations

In the case of any person on whom a civil penalty has been imposed under paragraph (1), paragraph (1) shall be applied by substituting "$20,000" for "$10,000" with respect to all subsequent violations.

    (3) Assessment

The agency referred to in subsection (a) or (c) of section 1607 of this title with respect to any person described in paragraph (1) shall assess any penalty under this subsection to which such person is subject.

(Pub.L. 90–321, Title I, § 129E, as added Pub.L. 111–203, Title XIV, § 1472, July 21, 2010, Stat. 2187.)

§ 1639f. Requirements for prompt crediting of home loan payments [CCPA 129F]

(a) In general

In connection with a consumer credit transaction secured by a consumer's principal dwelling, no servicer shall fail to credit a payment to the consumer's loan account as of the date of receipt, except when a delay in crediting does not result in any charge to the consumer or in the reporting of negative information to a consumer reporting agency, except as required in subsection (b).

(b) Exception

If a servicer specifies in writing requirements for the consumer to follow in making payments, but accepts a payment that does not conform to the requirements, the servicer shall credit the payment as of 5 days after receipt.

(Pub.L. 90–321, Title I, § 129F, as added Pub.L. 111–203, Title XIV, § 1464(a), July 21, 2010, 124 Stat. 2184.)

§ 1639g. Requests for payoff amounts of home loan [CCPA § 129G]

A creditor or servicer of a home loan shall send an accurate payoff balance within a reasonable time, but in no case more than 7 business days, after the receipt of a written request for such balance from or on behalf of the borrower.

(Pub.L. 90–321, Title I, § 129G, as added Pub.L. 111–203, Title XIV, § 1464(b), July 21, 2010, 124 Stat. 2184.)

§ 1639h. Property appraisal requirements [CCPA § 129H]

(a) In general

A creditor may not extend credit in the form of a higher-risk mortgage to any consumer without first obtaining a written appraisal of the property to be mortgaged prepared in accordance with the requirements of this section.

(b) Appraisal requirements

(1) Physical property visit

Subject to the rules prescribed under paragraph (4), an appraisal of property to be secured by a higher-risk mortgage does not meet the requirement of this section unless it is performed by a certified or licensed appraiser who conducts a physical property visit of the interior of the mortgaged property.

(2) Second appraisal under certain circumstances

(A) In general

If the purpose of a higher-risk mortgage is to finance the purchase or acquisition of the mortgaged property from a person within 180 days of the purchase or acquisition of such property by that person at a price that was lower than the current sale price of the property, the creditor shall obtain a second appraisal from a different certified or licensed appraiser. The second appraisal shall include an analysis of the difference in sale prices, changes in market conditions, and any improvements made to the property between the date of the previous sale and the current sale.

(B) No cost to applicant

The cost of any second appraisal required under subparagraph (A) may not be charged to the applicant.

(3) Certified or licensed appraiser defined

For purposes of this section, the term "certified or licensed appraiser" means a person who—

> (A) is, at a minimum, certified or licensed by the State in which the property to be appraised is located; and

> (B) performs each appraisal in conformity with the Uniform Standards of Professional Appraisal Practice and title XI of the Financial Institutions Reform, Recovery, and Enforcement Act of 1989, and the regulations prescribed under such title, as in effect on the date of the appraisal.

(4) Regulations

(A) In general

The Board, the Comptroller of the Currency, the Federal Deposit Insurance Corporation, the National Credit Union Administration Board, the Federal Housing Finance Agency, and the Bureau shall jointly prescribe regulations to implement this section.

(B) Exemption

The agencies listed in subparagraph (A) may jointly exempt, by rule, a class of loans from the requirements of this subsection or subsection (a) if the agencies determine that the exemption is in the public interest and promotes the safety and soundness of creditors.

(c) Free copy of appraisal

A creditor shall provide 1 copy of each appraisal conducted in accordance with this section in connection with a higher-risk mortgage to the applicant without charge, and at least 3 days prior to the transaction closing date.

(d) Consumer notification

At the time of the initial mortgage application, the applicant shall be provided with a statement by the creditor that any appraisal prepared for the mortgage is for the sole use of the creditor, and that the applicant may choose to have a separate appraisal conducted at the expense of the applicant.

(e) Violations

In addition to any other liability to any person under this subchapter, a creditor found to have willfully failed to obtain an appraisal as required in this section shall be liable to the applicant or borrower for the sum of $2,000.

(f) Higher-risk mortgage defined

For purposes of this section, the term "higher-risk mortgage" means a residential mortgage loan, other than a reverse mortgage loan that is a qualified mortgage, as defined in section 1639c of this title, secured by a principal dwelling—

> (1) that is not a qualified mortgage, as defined in section 1639c of this title; and

> (2) with an annual percentage rate that exceeds the average prime offer rate for a comparable transaction, as defined in section 1639c of this title, as of the date the interest rate is set—

> > (A) by 1.5 or more percentage points, in the case of a first lien residential mortgage loan having an original principal obligation amount that does not exceed the amount of the maximum limitation on the original principal obligation of mortgage in effect for a residence of the applicable size, as of the date of such interest rate set, pursuant to the sixth sentence of section 1454(a)(2) of Title 12;

> > (B) by 2.5 or more percentage points, in the case of a first lien residential mortgage loan having an original principal obligation amount that exceeds the amount of the maximum limitation on the original principal obligation of mortgage in effect for a residence of the applicable size, as of the date of such interest rate set, pursuant to the sixth sentence of section 1454(a)(2) of Title 12; and

> > (C) by 3.5 or more percentage points for a subordinate lien residential mortgage loan.

(Pub.L. 90–321, Title I, § 129H, as added Pub.L. 111–203, Title XIV, § 1471, July 21, 2010, Stat. 2185.)

§ 1640. Civil liability [CCPA § 130]

(a) Individual or class action for damages; amount of award; factors determining amount of award

Except as otherwise provided in this section, any creditor who fails to comply with any requirement imposed under this part, including any requirement under section 1635 of this title, subsection (f) or (g) of section 1641 of this title, or part D or E of this subchapter with respect to any person is liable to such person in an amount equal to the sum of—

(1) any actual damage sustained by such person as a result of the failure;

(2)(A) (i) in the case of an individual action twice the amount of any finance charge in connection with the transaction, (ii) in the case of an individual action relating to a consumer lease under part E of this subchapter, 25 per centum of the total amount of monthly payments under the lease, except that the liability under this subparagraph shall not be less than $200 nor greater than $2,000, (iii) in the case of an individual action relating to an open end consumer credit plan that is not secured by real property or a dwelling, twice the amount of any finance charge in connection with the transaction, with a minimum of $500 and a maximum of $5,000, or such higher amount as may be appropriate in the case of an established pattern or practice of such failures;[1] or (iv) in the case of an individual action relating to a credit transaction not under an open end credit plan that is secured by real property or a dwelling, not less than $400 or greater than $4,000; or

(B) in the case of a class action, such amount as the court may allow, except that as to each member of the class no minimum recovery shall be applicable, and the total recovery under this subparagraph in any class action or series of class actions arising out of the same failure to comply by the same creditor shall not be more than the lesser of $1,000,000 or 1 per centum of the net worth of the creditor;

(3) in the case of any successful action to enforce the foregoing liability or in any action in which a person is determined to have a right of rescission under section 1635 or 1638(e)(7) of this title, the costs of the action, together with a reasonable attorney's fee as determined by the court; and

(4) in the case of a failure to comply with any requirement under section 1639, paragraph (1) or (2) of section 1639b(c) of this title, or section 1639c(a) of this title, an amount equal to the sum of all finance charges and fees paid by the consumer, unless the creditor demonstrates that the failure to comply is not material.

In determining the amount of award in any class action, the court shall consider, among other relevant factors, the amount of any actual damages awarded, the frequency and persistence of failures of compliance by the creditor, the resources of the creditor, the number of persons adversely affected, and the extent to which the creditor's failure of compliance was intentional. In connection with the disclosures referred to in subsections (a) and (b) of section 1637 of this title, a creditor shall have a liability determined under paragraph (2) only for failing to comply with the requirements of section 1635, 1637(a)[2] of this title, or any of paragraphs (4) through (13) of section 1637(b) of this title, or for failing to comply with disclosure requirements under State law for any term or item that the Bureau has determined to be substantially the same in meaning under section 1610(a)(2) of this title as any of the terms or items referred to in section 1637(a) of this title, or any of paragraphs (4) through (13) of section 1637(b) of this title. In connection with the disclosures referred to in subsection (c) or (d) of section 1637 of this title, a card issuer shall have a liability under this section only to a cardholder who pays a fee described in section 1637(c)(1)(A)(ii)(I) or section 1637(c)(4)(A)(i) of this title or who uses the credit card or charge card. In connection with the disclosures referred to in section 1638 of this title, a creditor shall have a liability determined under paragraph (2) only for failing to comply with the requirements of section 1635 of this title, of paragraph (2) (insofar as it requires a disclosure of the "amount financed"), (3), (4), (5), (6), or (9) of section 1638(a) of this title, or section 1638(b)(2)(C)(ii) of this title, of subparagraphs (A), (B), (D), (F), or (J) of section 1638(e)(2) of this title (for purposes of paragraph (2) or (4) of section 1638(e) of this title), or paragraph (4)(C), (6), (7), or (8) of section 1638(e) of this title, or for failing to comply with disclosure requirements under State law for

---

[1]   So in original. The semicolon probably should be a comma.
[2]   So in original. Probably should be preceded by "section".

any term which the Bureau has determined to be substantially the same in meaning under section 1610(a)(2) of this title as any of the terms referred to in any of those paragraphs of section 1638(a) of this title or section 1638(b)(2)(C)(ii) of this title. With respect to any failure to make disclosures required under this part or part D or E of this subchapter, liability shall be imposed only upon the creditor required to make disclosure, except as provided in section 1641 of this title.

(b) Correction of errors

A creditor or assignee has no liability under this section or section 1607 of this title or section 1611 of this title for any failure to comply with any requirement imposed under this part or part E of this subchapter, if within sixty days after discovering an error, whether pursuant to a final written examination report or notice issued under section 1607(e)(1) of this title or through the creditor's or assignee's own procedures, and prior to the institution of an action under this section or the receipt of written notice of the error from the obligor, the creditor or assignee notifies the person concerned of the error and makes whatever adjustments in the appropriate account are necessary to assure that the person will not be required to pay an amount in excess of the charge actually disclosed, or the dollar equivalent of the annual percentage rate actually disclosed, whichever is lower.

(c) Unintentional violations; bona fide errors

A creditor or assignee may not be held liable in any action brought under this section or section 1635 of this title for a violation of this subchapter if the creditor or assignee shows by a preponderance of evidence that the violation was not intentional and resulted from a bona fide error notwithstanding the maintenance of procedures reasonably adapted to avoid any such error. Examples of a bona fide error include, but are not limited to, clerical, calculation, computer malfunction and programing, and printing errors, except that an error of legal judgment with respect to a person's obligations under this subchapter is not a bona fide error.

(d) Liability in transaction or lease involving multiple obligors

When there are multiple obligors in a consumer credit transaction or consumer lease, there shall be no more than one recovery of damages under subsection (a)(2) of this section for a violation of this subchapter.

(e) Jurisdiction of courts; limitations on actions; State attorney general enforcement

Except as provided in the subsequent sentence, any action under this section may be brought in any United States district court, or in any other court of competent jurisdiction, within one year from the date of the occurrence of the violation or, in the case of a violation involving a private education loan (as that term is defined in section 1650(a) of this title), 1 year from the date on which the first regular payment of principal is due under the loan. Any action under this section with respect to any violation of section 1639, 1639b, or 1639c of this title may be brought in any United States district court, or in any other court of competent jurisdiction, before the end of the 3-year period beginning on the date of the occurrence of the violation. This subsection does not bar a person from asserting a violation of this subchapter in an action to collect the debt which was brought more than one year from the date of the occurrence of the violation as a matter of defense by recoupment or set-off in such action, except as otherwise provided by State law. An action to enforce a violation of section 1639, 1639b, 1639c, 1639d, 1639e, 1639f, 1639g, or 1639h of this title may also be brought by the appropriate State attorney general in any appropriate United States district court, or any other court of competent jurisdiction, not later than 3 years after the date on which the violation occurs. The State attorney general shall provide prior written notice of any such civil action to the Federal agency responsible for enforcement under section 1607 of this title and shall provide the agency with a copy of the complaint. If prior notice is not feasible, the State attorney general shall provide notice to such agency immediately upon instituting the action. The Federal agency may—

    (1)   intervene in the action;

    (2)   upon intervening—

        (A)   remove the action to the appropriate United States district court, if it was not originally brought there; and

        (B)   be heard on all matters arising in the action; and

    (3)   file a petition for appeal.

(f) Good faith compliance with rule, regulation, or interpretation of Board or with interpretation or approval of duly authorized official or employee of Federal Reserve System

No provision of this section, section 1607(b) of this title, section 1607(c) of this title, section 1607(e) of this title, or section 1611 of this title imposing any liability shall apply to any act done or omitted in good faith in conformity with any rule, regulation, or interpretation thereof by the Bureau or in conformity with any interpretation or approval by an official or employee of the Federal Reserve System duly authorized by the Bureau to issue such interpretations or approvals under such procedures as the Bureau may prescribe therefor, notwithstanding that after such act or omission has occurred, such rule, regulation, interpretation, or approval is amended, rescinded, or determined by judicial or other authority to be invalid for any reason.

(g) Recovery for multiple failures to disclose

The multiple failure to disclose to any person any information required under this part or part D or E of this subchapter to be disclosed in connection with a single account under an open end consumer credit plan, other single consumer credit sale, consumer loan, consumer lease, or other extension of consumer credit, shall entitle the person to a single recovery under this section but continued failure to disclose after a recovery has been granted shall give rise to rights to additional recoveries. This subsection does not bar any remedy permitted by section 1635 of this title.

(h) Offset from amount owed to creditor or assignee; rights of defaulting consumer

A person may not take any action to offset any amount for which a creditor or assignee is potentially liable to such person under subsection (a)(2) of this section against any amount owed by such person, unless the amount of the creditor's or assignee's liability under this subchapter has been determined by judgment of a court of competent jurisdiction in an action of which such person was a party. This subsection does not bar a consumer then in default on the obligation from asserting a violation of this subchapter as an original action, or as a defense or counterclaim to an action to collect amounts owed by the consumer brought by a person liable under this subchapter.

(i) Class action moratorium

(1) In general

During the period beginning on May 18, 1995, and ending on October 1, 1995, no court may enter any order certifying any class in any action under this subchapter—

(A) which is brought in connection with any credit transaction not under an open end credit plan which is secured by a first lien on real property or a dwelling and constitutes a refinancing or consolidation of an existing extension of credit; and

(B) which is based on the alleged failure of a creditor—

(i) to include a charge actually incurred (in connection with the transaction) in the finance charge disclosed pursuant to section 1638 of this title;

(ii) to properly make any other disclosure required under section 1638 of this title as a result of the failure described in clause (i); or

(iii) to provide proper notice of rescission rights under section 1635(a) of this title due to the selection by the creditor of the incorrect form from among the model forms prescribed by the Bureau or from among forms based on such model forms.

(2) Exceptions for certain alleged violations

Paragraph (1) shall not apply with respect to any action—

(A) described in clause (i) or (ii) of paragraph (1)(B), if the amount disclosed as the finance charge results in an annual percentage rate that exceeds the tolerance provided in section 1606(c) of this title; or

(B) described in paragraph (1)(B)(iii), if—

(i) no notice relating to rescission rights under section 1635(a) of this title was provided in any form; or

            (ii) proper notice was not provided for any reason other than the reason described in such paragraph.

(j)   Private educational lender

A private educational lender (as that term is defined in section 1650(a) of this title) has no liability under this section for failure to comply with section 1638(e)(3) of this title).[3]

(k)   Defense to foreclosure

(1)   In general

Notwithstanding any other provision of law, when a creditor, assignee, or other holder of a residential mortgage loan or anyone acting on behalf of such creditor, assignee, or holder, initiates a judicial or nonjudicial foreclosure of the residential mortgage loan, or any other action to collect the debt in connection with such loan, a consumer may assert a violation by a creditor of paragraph (1) or (2) of section 1639b(c) of this title, or of section 1639c(a) of this title, as a matter of defense by recoupment or set off without regard for the time limit on a private action for damages under subsection (e).

(2)   Amount of recoupment or setoff

(A)   In general

The amount of recoupment or set-off under paragraph (1) shall equal the amount to which the consumer would be entitled under subsection (a) for damages for a valid claim brought in an original action against the creditor, plus the costs to the consumer of the action, including a reasonable attorney's fee.

(B)   Special rule

Where such judgment is rendered after the expiration of the applicable time limit on a private action for damages under subsection (e), the amount of recoupment or set-off under paragraph (1) derived from damages under subsection (a)(4) shall not exceed the amount to which the consumer would have been entitled under subsection (a)(4) for damages computed up to the day preceding the expiration of the applicable time limit.

(l)   Exemption from liability and rescission in case of borrower fraud or deception

In addition to any other remedy available by law or contract, no creditor or assignee shall be liable to an obligor under this section, if such obligor, or co-obligor has been convicted of obtaining by actual fraud such residential mortgage loan.

(Pub.L. 90–321, Title I, § 130, May 29, 1968, 82 Stat. 157; Pub.L. 93–495, Title IV, §§ 406, 407, 408(a) to (d), Oct. 28, 1974, 88 Stat. 1518; Pub.L. 94–222, § 3(b), Feb. 27, 1976, 90 Stat. 197; Pub.L. 94–240, § 4, Mar. 23, 1976, 90 Stat. 260; Pub.L. 96–221, Title VI, § 615, Mar. 31, 1980, 94 Stat. 180; Pub.L. 100–583, § 3, Nov. 3, 1988, 102 Stat. 2966; Pub.L. 103–325, Title I, § 153(a), (b), Sept. 23, 1994, 108 Stat. 2195; Pub.L. 104–12, § 2, May 18, 1995, 109 Stat. 161; Pub.L. 104–29, § 6, Sept. 30, 1995, 109 Stat. 274; Pub.L. 110–289, Div. B, Title V, § 2502(b), July 30, 2008, 122 Stat. 2857; Pub.L. 110–315, Title X, § 1012(a), Aug. 14, 2008, 122 Stat. 3483; Pub.L. 111–22, Div. A, Title IV, § 404(b), May 20, 2009, 123 Stat. 1658; Pub.L. 111–24, Title I, § 107, Title II, § 201(b), May 22, 2009, 123 Stat. 1743, 1745; Pub.L. 111–203, Title X, § 1100A(2), Title XIV, §§ 1400(c), 1413, 1416, 1417, 1422, July 21, 2010, 124 Stat. 2107, 2148, 2153, 2157.)

§ 1641.   Liability of assignees [CCPA § 131]

(a)   Prerequisites

Except as otherwise specifically provided in this subchapter, any civil action for a violation of this subchapter or proceeding under section 1607 of this title which may be brought against a creditor may be maintained against any assignee of such creditor only if the violation for which such action or proceeding is brought is apparent on the face of the disclosure statement, except where the assignment was involuntary. For the purpose of this section, a violation apparent on the face of the disclosure statement includes, but is not limited to (1) a disclosure which can be determined to be incomplete or inaccurate from the face of the

---

    [3]   So in original. The closing parenthesis probably should not appear.

disclosure statement or other documents assigned, or (2) a disclosure which does not use the terms required to be used by this subchapter.

(b) Proof of compliance with statutory provisions

Except as provided in section 1635(c) of this title, in any action or proceeding by or against any subsequent assignee of the original creditor without knowledge to the contrary by the assignee when he acquires the obligation, written acknowledgement of receipt by a person to whom a statement is required to be given pursuant to this subchapter shall be conclusive proof of the delivery thereof and, except as provided in subsection (a) of this section, of compliance with this part. This section does not affect the rights of the obligor in any action against the original creditor.

(c) Right of rescission by consumer unaffected

Any consumer who has the right to rescind a transaction under section 1635 of this title may rescind the transaction as against any assignee of the obligation.

(d) Rights upon assignment of certain mortgages

(1) In general

Any person who purchases or is otherwise assigned a mortgage referred to in section 1602(aa)* of this title shall be subject to all claims and defenses with respect to that mortgage that the consumer could assert against the creditor of the mortgage, unless the purchaser or assignee demonstrates, by a preponderance of the evidence, that a reasonable person exercising ordinary due diligence, could not determine, based on the documentation required by this subchapter, the itemization of the amount financed, and other disclosure of disbursements that the mortgage was a mortgage referred to in section 1602(aa)* of this title. The preceding sentence does not affect rights of a consumer under subsection (a), (b), or (c) of this section or any other provision of this subchapter.

(2) Limitation on damages

Notwithstanding any other provision of law, relief provided as a result of any action made permissible by paragraph (1) may not exceed—

(A) with respect to actions based upon a violation of this subchapter, the amount specified in section 1640 of this title; and

(B) with respect to all other causes of action, the sum of—

(i) the amount of all remaining indebtedness; and

(ii) the total amount paid by the consumer in connection with the transaction.

(3) Offset

The amount of damages that may be awarded under paragraph (2)(B) shall be reduced by the amount of any damages awarded under paragraph (2)(A).

(4) Notice

Any person who sells or otherwise assigns a mortgage referred to in section 1602(aa)* of this title shall include a prominent notice of the potential liability under this subsection as determined by the Bureau.

(e) Liability of assignee for consumer credit transactions secured by real property

(1) In general

Except as otherwise specifically provided in this subchapter, any civil action against a creditor for a violation of this subchapter, and any proceeding under section 1607 of this title against a creditor, with respect to a consumer credit transaction secured by real property may be maintained against any assignee of such creditor only if—

---

* *Note from West Advisory Panel: Pub. L. 111–203 (Dodd-Frank) appears to contain clerical errors. We believe this reference should be to § 1602(bb).*

    (A) the violation for which such action or proceeding is brought is apparent on the face of the disclosure statement provided in connection with such transaction pursuant to this subchapter; and

    (B) the assignment to the assignee was voluntary.

(2) Violation apparent on the face of the disclosure described

    For the purpose of this section, a violation is apparent on the face of the disclosure statement if—

    (A) the disclosure can be determined to be incomplete or inaccurate by a comparison among the disclosure statement, any itemization of the amount financed, the note, or any other disclosure of disbursement; or

    (B) the disclosure statement does not use the terms or format required to be used by this subchapter.

(f) Treatment of servicer

(1) In general

    A servicer of a consumer obligation arising from a consumer credit transaction shall not be treated as an assignee of such obligation for purposes of this section unless the servicer is or was the owner of the obligation.

(2) Servicer not treated as owner on basis of assignment for administrative convenience

    A servicer of a consumer obligation arising from a consumer credit transaction shall not be treated as the owner of the obligation for purposes of this section on the basis of an assignment of the obligation from the creditor or another assignee to the servicer solely for the administrative convenience of the servicer in servicing the obligation. Upon written request by the obligor, the servicer shall provide the obligor, to the best knowledge of the servicer, with the name, address, and telephone number of the owner of the obligation or the master servicer of the obligation.

(3) "Servicer" defined

    For purposes of this subsection, the term "servicer" has the same meaning as in section 2605(i)(2) of Title 12.

(4) Applicability

    This subsection shall apply to all consumer credit transactions in existence or consummated on or after September 30, 1995.

(g) Notice of new creditor

(1) In general

    In addition to other disclosures required by this subchapter, not later than 30 days after the date on which a mortgage loan is sold or otherwise transferred or assigned to a third party, the creditor that is the new owner or assignee of the debt shall notify the borrower in writing of such transfer, including—

    (A) the identity, address, telephone number of the new creditor;

    (B) the date of transfer;

    (C) how to reach an agent or party having authority to act on behalf of the new creditor;

    (D) the location of the place where transfer of ownership of the debt is recorded; and

    (E) any other relevant information regarding the new creditor.

(2) Definition

    As used in this subsection, the term "mortgage loan" means any consumer credit transaction that is secured by the principal dwelling of a consumer.

(Pub.L. 90–321, Title I, § 131, May 29, 1968, 82 Stat. 157; Pub.L. 96–221, Title VI, § 616(a), Mar. 31, 1980, 94 Stat. 182; Pub.L. 103–325, Title I, § 153(c), Sept. 23, 1994, 108 Stat. 2195; Pub.L. 104–29, § 7, Sept. 30, 1995, 109 Stat. 274; Pub.L. 111–22, Title IV, § 404(a), May 20, 2009, 123 Stat. 1658; Pub.L. 111–203, Title X, § 1100A(2), July 21, 2010, 124 Stat. 2107.)

§ 1642. Issuance of credit cards [CCPA § 132]

No credit card shall be issued except in response to a request or application therefor. This prohibition does not apply to the issuance of a credit card in renewal of, or in substitution for, an accepted credit card.

(Pub.L. 90–321, Title I, § 132, as added Pub.L. 91–508, Title V, § 502(a), Oct. 26, 1970, 84 Stat. 1126.)

§ 1643. Liability of holder of credit card [CCPA § 133]

(a) Limits on liability

(1) A cardholder shall be liable for the unauthorized use of a credit card only if—

(A) the card is an accepted credit card;

(B) the liability is not in excess of $50;

(C) the card issuer gives adequate notice to the cardholder of the potential liability;

(D) the card issuer has provided the cardholder with a description of a means by which the card issuer may be notified of loss or theft of the card, which description may be provided on the face or reverse side of the statement required by section 1637(b) of this title or on a separate notice accompanying such statement;

(E) the unauthorized use occurs before the card issuer has been notified that an unauthorized use of the credit card has occurred or may occur as the result of loss, theft, or otherwise; and

(F) the card issuer has provided a method whereby the user of such card can be identified as the person authorized to use it.

(2) For purposes of this section, a card issuer has been notified when such steps as may be reasonably required in the ordinary course of business to provide the card issuer with the pertinent information have been taken, whether or not any particular officer, employee, or agent of the card issuer does in fact receive such information.

(b) Burden of proof

In any action by a card issuer to enforce liability for the use of a credit card, the burden of proof is upon the card issuer to show that the use was authorized or, if the use was unauthorized, then the burden of proof is upon the card issuer to show that the conditions of liability for the unauthorized use of a credit card, as set forth in subsection (a) of this section, have been met.

(c) Liability imposed by other laws or by agreement with issuer

Nothing in this section imposes liability upon a cardholder for the unauthorized use of a credit card in excess of his liability for such use under other applicable law or under any agreement with the card issuer.

(d) Exclusiveness of liability

Except as provided in this section, a cardholder incurs no liability from the unauthorized use of a credit card.

(Pub.L. 90–321, Title I, § 133, as added Pub.L. 91–508, Title V, § 502(a), Oct. 26, 1970, 84 Stat. 1126, and amended Pub.L. 96–221, Title VI, § 617, Mar. 31, 1980, 94 Stat. 182.)

§ 1644.   Fraudulent use of credit cards; penalties [CCPA § 134]

(a)   Use, attempt or conspiracy to use card in transaction affecting interstate or foreign commerce

Whoever knowingly in a transaction affecting interstate or foreign commerce, uses or attempts or conspires to use any counterfeit, fictitious, altered, forged, lost, stolen, or fraudulently obtained credit card to obtain money, goods, services, or anything else of value which within any one-year period has a value aggregating $1,000 or more; or

(b)   Transporting, attempting or conspiring to transport card in interstate commerce

Whoever, with unlawful or fraudulent intent, transports or attempts or conspires to transport in interstate or foreign commerce a counterfeit, fictitious, altered, forged, lost, stolen, or fraudulently obtained credit card knowing the same to be counterfeit, fictitious, altered, forged, lost, stolen, or fraudulently obtained; or

(c)   Use of interstate commerce to sell or transport card

Whoever, with unlawful or fraudulent intent, uses any instrumentality of interstate or foreign commerce to sell or transport a counterfeit, fictitious, altered, forged, lost, stolen, or fraudulently obtained credit card knowing the same to be counterfeit, fictitious, altered, forged, lost, stolen, or fraudulently obtained; or

(d)   Receipt, concealment, etc., of goods obtained by use of card

Whoever knowingly receives, conceals, uses, or transports money, goods, services, or anything else of value (except tickets for interstate or foreign transportation) which (1) within any one-year period has a value aggregating $1,000 or more, (2) has moved in or is part of, or which constitutes interstate or foreign commerce, and (3) has been obtained with a counterfeit, fictitious, altered, forged, lost, stolen, or fraudulently obtained credit card; or

(e)   Receipt, concealment, etc., of tickets for interstate or foreign transportation obtained by use of card

Whoever knowingly receives, conceals, uses, sells, or transports in interstate or foreign commerce one or more tickets for interstate or foreign transportation, which (1) within any one-year period have a value aggregating $500 or more, and (2) have been purchased or obtained with one or more counterfeit, fictitious, altered, forged, lost, stolen, or fraudulently obtained credit cards; or

(f)   Furnishing of money, etc., through use of card

Whoever in a transaction affecting interstate or foreign commerce furnishes money, property, services, or anything else of value, which within any one-year period has a value aggregating $1,000 or more, through the use of any counterfeit, fictitious, altered, forged, lost, stolen, or fraudulently obtained credit card knowing the same to be counterfeit, fictitious, altered, forged, lost, stolen, or fraudulently obtained—

shall be fined not more than $10,000 or imprisoned not more than ten years, or both.

> (Pub.L. 90–321, Title I, § 134, as added Pub.L. 91–508, Title V, § 502(a), Oct. 26, 1970, 84 Stat. 1127, and amended Pub.L. 93–495, Title IV, § 414, Oct. 28, 1974, 88 Stat. 1520.)

§ 1645.   Business credit cards; limits on liability of employees [CCPA § 135]

The exemption provided by section 1603(1) of this title does not apply to the provisions of sections 1642, 1643, and 1644 of this title, except that a card issuer and a business or other organization which provides credit cards issued by the same card issuer to ten or more of its employees may by contract agree as to liability of the business or other organization with respect to unauthorized use of such credit cards without regard to the provisions of section 1643 of this title, but in no case may such business or other organization or card issuer impose liability upon any employee with respect to unauthorized use of such a credit card except in accordance with and subject to the limitations of section 1643 of this title.

> (Pub.L. 90–321, Title I, § 135, as added Pub.L. 93–495, Title IV, § 410(a), Oct. 28, 1974, 88 Stat. 1519.)

§ 1646. Dissemination of annual percentage rates; implementation, etc. [CCPA § 136]

(a) Annual percentage rates

The Bureau shall collect, publish, and disseminate to the public, on a demonstration basis in a number of standard metropolitan statistical areas to be determined by the Bureau, the annual percentage rates charged for representative types of nonsale credit by creditors in such areas. For the purpose of this section, the Bureau is authorized to require creditors in such areas to furnish information necessary for the Bureau to collect, publish, and disseminate such information.

(b) Credit card price and availability information

(1) Collection required

The Bureau shall collect, on a semiannual basis, credit card price and availability information, including the information required to be disclosed under section 1637(c) of this title, from a broad sample of financial institutions which offer credit card services.

(2) Sample requirements

The broad sample of financial institutions required under paragraph (1) shall include—

(A) the 25 largest issuers of credit cards; and

(B) not less than 125 additional financial institutions selected by the Board in a manner that ensures—

(i) an equitable geographical distribution within the sample; and

(ii) the representation of a wide spectrum of institutions within the sample.

(3) Report of information from sample

Each financial institution in the broad sample established pursuant to paragraph (2) shall report the information to the Bureau in accordance with such regulations or orders as the Bureau may prescribe.

(4) Public availability of collected information; report to Congress

The Bureau shall—

(A) make the information collected pursuant to this subsection available to the public upon request; and

(B) report such information semiannually to Congress.

(c) Implementation

The Bureau is authorized to enter into contracts or other arrangements with appropriate persons, organizations, or State agencies to carry out its functions under subsections (a) and (b) of this section and to furnish financial assistance in support thereof.

(Pub.L. 90–321, Title I, § 136, as added Pub.L. 96–221, Title VI, § 618(a), Mar. 31, 1980, 94 Stat. 183, and amended Pub.L. 100–583, § 5, Nov. 3, 1988, 102 Stat. 2967; Pub.L. 111–203, Title X, § 1100A(2), July 21, 2010, 124 Stat. 2107.)

§ 1647. Home equity plans [CCPA § 137]

(a) Index requirement

In the case of extensions of credit under an open end consumer credit plan which are subject to a variable rate and are secured by a consumer's principal dwelling, the index or other rate of interest to which changes in the annual percentage rate are related shall be based on an index or rate of interest which is publicly available and is not under the control of the creditor.

(b) Grounds for acceleration of outstanding balance

A creditor may not unilaterally terminate any account under an open end consumer credit plan under which extensions of credit are secured by a consumer's principal dwelling and require the immediate repayment of any outstanding balance at such time, except in the case of—

(1) fraud or material misrepresentation on the part of the consumer in connection with the account;

(2) failure by the consumer to meet the repayment terms of the agreement for any outstanding balance; or

(3) any other action or failure to act by the consumer which adversely affects the creditor's security for the account or any right of the creditor in such security.

This subsection does not apply to reverse mortgage transactions.

(c) Change in terms

(1) In general

No open end consumer credit plan under which extensions of credit are secured by a consumer's principal dwelling may contain a provision which permits a creditor to change unilaterally any term required to be disclosed under section 1637a(a) of this title or any other term, except a change in insignificant terms such as the address of the creditor for billing purposes.

(2) Certain changes not precluded

Notwithstanding the provisions of subsection[1] (1), a creditor may make any of the following changes:

(A) Change the index and margin applicable to extensions of credit under such plan if the index used by the creditor is no longer available and the substitute index and margin would result in a substantially similar interest rate.

(B) Prohibit additional extensions of credit or reduce the credit limit applicable to an account under the plan during any period in which the value of the consumer's principal dwelling which secures any outstanding balance is significantly less than the original appraisal value of the dwelling.

(C) Prohibit additional extensions of credit or reduce the credit limit applicable to the account during any period in which the creditor has reason to believe that the consumer will be unable to comply with the repayment requirements of the account due to a material change in the consumer's financial circumstances.

(D) Prohibit additional extensions of credit or reduce the credit limit applicable to the account during any period in which the consumer is in default with respect to any material obligation of the consumer under the agreement.

(E) Prohibit additional extensions of credit or reduce the credit limit applicable to the account during any period in which—

(i) the creditor is precluded by government action from imposing the annual percentage rate provided for in the account agreement; or

(ii) any government action is in effect which adversely affects the priority of the creditor's security interest in the account to the extent that the value of the creditor's secured interest in the property is less than 120 percent of the amount of the credit limit applicable to the account.

(F) Any change that will benefit the consumer.

---

[1] So in original. Probably should be "paragraph".

(3) Material obligations

Upon the request of the consumer and at the time an agreement is entered into by a consumer to open an account under an open end consumer credit plan under which extensions of credit are secured by the consumer's principal dwelling, the consumer shall be given a list of the categories of contract obligations which are deemed by the creditor to be material obligations of the consumer under the agreement for purposes of paragraph (2)(D).

(4) Consumer benefit

(A) In general

For purposes of paragraph (2)(F), a change shall be deemed to benefit the consumer if the change is unequivocally beneficial to the borrower and the change is beneficial through the entire term of the agreement.

(B) Bureau categorization

The Bureau may, by regulation, determine categories of changes that benefit the consumer.

(d) Terms changed after application

If any term or condition described in section 1637a(a) of this title which is disclosed to a consumer in connection with an application to open an account under an open end consumer credit plan described in such section (other than a variable feature of the plan) changes before the account is opened, and if, as a result of such change, the consumer elects not to enter into the plan agreement, the creditor shall refund all fees paid by the consumer in connection with such application.

(e) Additional requirements relating to refunds and imposition of nonrefundable fees

(1) In general

No nonrefundable fee may be imposed by a creditor or any other person in connection with any application by a consumer to establish an account under any open end consumer credit plan which provides for extensions of credit which are secured by a consumer's principal dwelling before the end of the 3-day period beginning on the date such consumer receives the disclosure required under section 1637a(a) of this title and the pamphlet required under section 1637a(e) of this title with respect to such application.

(2) Constructive receipt

For purposes of determining when a nonrefundable fee may be imposed in accordance with this subsection if the disclosures and pamphlet referred to in paragraph (1) are mailed to the consumer, the date of the receipt of the disclosures by such consumer shall be deemed to be 3 business days after the date of mailing by the creditor.

(Pub.L. 100–709, § 3, Nov. 23, 1988, 102 Stat. 4731; Pub.L. 103–325, Title I, § 154(c), Sept. 23, 1994, 108 Stat. 2197; Pub.L. 111–203, Title X, § 1100A(2), July 21, 2010, 124 Stat. 2107.)

§ 1648. Reverse mortgages [CCPA § 138]

(a) In general

In addition to the disclosures required under this subchapter, for each reverse mortgage, the creditor shall, not less than 3 days prior to consummation of the transaction, disclose to the consumer in conspicuous type a good faith estimate of the projected total cost of the mortgage to the consumer expressed as a table of annual interest rates. Each annual interest rate shall be based on a projected total future credit extension balance under a projected appreciation rate for the dwelling and a term for the mortgage. The disclosure shall include—

(1) statements of the annual interest rates for not less than 3 projected appreciation rates and not less than 3 credit transaction periods, as determined by the Bureau, including—

(A) a short-term reverse mortgage;

(B) a term equaling the actuarial life expectancy of the consumer; and

    (C) such longer term as the Bureau deems appropriate; and

    (2) a statement that the consumer is not obligated to complete the reverse mortgage transaction merely because the consumer has received the disclosure required under this section or has signed an application for the reverse mortgage.

(b) Projected total cost

In determining the projected total cost of the mortgage to be disclosed to the consumer under subsection (a) of this section, the creditor shall take into account—

    (1) any shared appreciation or equity that the lender will, by contract, be entitled to receive;

    (2) all costs and charges to the consumer, including the costs of any associated annuity that the consumer elects or is required to purchase as part of the reverse mortgage transaction;

    (3) all payments to and for the benefit of the consumer, including, in the case in which an associated annuity is purchased (whether or not required by the lender as a condition of making the reverse mortgage), the annuity payments received by the consumer and financed from the proceeds of the loan, instead of the proceeds used to finance the annuity; and

    (4) any limitation on the liability of the consumer under reverse mortgage transactions (such as nonrecourse limits and equity conservation agreements).

    (Pub.L. 90–321, Title I, § 138, as added Pub.L. 103–325, Title I, § 154(b), Sept. 23, 1994, 108 Stat. 2196; Pub.L. 111–203, Title X, § 1100A(2), July 21, 2010, 124 Stat. 2107.)

§ 1649.   Certain limitations on liability [CCPA § 139]

(a) Limitations on liability

For any closed end consumer credit transaction that is secured by real property or a dwelling, that is subject to this subchapter, and that is consummated before September 30, 1995, a creditor or any assignee of a creditor shall have no civil, administrative, or criminal liability under this subchapter for, and a consumer shall have no extended rescission rights under section 1635(f) of this title with respect to—

    (1) the creditor's treatment, for disclosure purposes, of—

        (A) taxes described in section 1605(d)(3) of this title;

        (B) fees described in section 1605(e)(2) and (5) of this title;

        (C) fees and amounts referred to in the 3rd sentence of section 1605(a) of this title; or

        (D) borrower-paid mortgage broker fees referred to in section 1605(a)(6) of this title;

    (2) the form of written notice used by the creditor to inform the obligor of the rights of the obligor under section 1635 of this title if the creditor provided the obligor with a properly dated form of written notice published and adopted by the Bureau or a comparable written notice, and otherwise complied with all the requirements of this section regarding notice; or

    (3) any disclosure relating to the finance charge imposed with respect to the transaction if the amount or percentage actually disclosed—

        (A) may be treated as accurate for purposes of this subchapter if the amount disclosed as the finance charge does not vary from the actual finance charge by more than $200;

        (B) may, under section 1605(f)(2) of this title, be treated as accurate for purposes of section 1635 of this title; or

        (C) is greater than the amount or percentage required to be disclosed under this subchapter.

(b) Exceptions

Subsection (a) of this section shall not apply to—

(1) any individual action or counterclaim brought under this subchapter which was filed before June 1, 1995;

(2) any class action brought under this subchapter for which a final order certifying a class was entered before January 1, 1995;

(3) the named individual plaintiffs in any class action brought under this subchapter which was filed before June 1, 1995; or

(4) any consumer credit transaction with respect to which a timely notice of rescission was sent to the creditor before June 1, 1995.

(Pub.L. 90–321, Title I, § 139, as added Pub.L. 104–29, § 4(a), Sept. 30, 1995, 109 Stat. 273, and amended Pub.L. 104–208, Div. A, Title II, § 2107(a), Sept. 30, 1996, 110 Stat. 3009–402; Pub.L. 111–203, Title X, § 1100A(2), July 21, 2010, 124 Stat. 2107.)

§ 1650. Preventing unfair and deceptive private educational lending practices and eliminating conflicts of interest [CCPA § 140]

(a) Definitions

As used in this section—

(1) the term "covered educational institution"—

(A) means any educational institution that offers a postsecondary educational degree, certificate, or program of study (including any institution of higher education); and

(B) includes an agent, officer, or employee of the educational institution;

(2) the term "gift"—

(A)(i) means any gratuity, favor, discount, entertainment, hospitality, loan, or other item having more than a de minimis monetary value, including services, transportation, lodging, or meals, whether provided in kind, by purchase of a ticket, payment in advance, or reimbursement after the expense has been incurred; and

(ii) includes an item described in clause (i) provided to a family member of an officer, employee, or agent of a covered educational institution, or to any other individual based on that individual's relationship with the officer, employee, or agent, if—

(I) the item is provided with the knowledge and acquiescence of the officer, employee, or agent; and

(II) the officer, employee, or agent has reason to believe the item was provided because of the official position of the officer, employee, or agent; and

(B) does not include—

(i) standard informational material related to a loan, default aversion, default prevention, or financial literacy;

(ii) food, refreshments, training, or informational material furnished to an officer, employee, or agent of a covered educational institution, as an integral part of a training session or through participation in an advisory council that is designed to improve the service of the private educational lender to the covered educational institution, if such training or participation contributes to the professional development of the officer, employee, or agent of the covered educational institution;

(iii) favorable terms, conditions, and borrower benefits on a private education loan provided to a student employed by the covered educational institution, if such terms, conditions, or benefits are not provided because of the student's employment with the covered educational institution;

    (iv) the provision of financial literacy counseling or services, including counseling or services provided in coordination with a covered educational institution, to the extent that such counseling or services are not undertaken to secure—

        (I) applications for private education loans or private education loan volume;

        (II) applications or loan volume for any loan made, insured, or guaranteed under title IV of the Higher Education Act of 1965 (20 U.S.C. 1070 et seq.); or

        (III) the purchase of a product or service of a specific private educational lender;

    (v) philanthropic contributions to a covered educational institution from a private educational lender that are unrelated to private education loans and are not made in exchange for any advantage related to private education loans; or

    (vi) State education grants, scholarships, or financial aid funds administered by or on behalf of a State;

(3) the term "institution of higher education" has the same meaning as in section 102 of the Higher Education Act of 1965 (20 U.S.C. 1002);

(4) the term "postsecondary educational expenses" means any of the expenses that are included as part of the cost of attendance of a student, as defined under section 472 of the Higher Education Act of 1965 (20 U.S.C. 1087*ll*);

(5) the term "preferred lender arrangement" has the same meaning as in section 151 of the Higher Education Act of 1965 [20 U.S.C.A. § 1019];

(6) the term "private educational lender" means—

    (A) a financial institution, as defined in section 1813 of Title 12 that solicits, makes, or extends private education loans;

    (B) a Federal credit union, as defined in section 1752 of Title 12 that solicits, makes, or extends private education loans; and

    (C) any other person engaged in the business of soliciting, making, or extending private education loans;

(7) the term "private education loan"—

    (A) means a loan provided by a private educational lender that—

        (i) is not made, insured, or guaranteed under of[1] title IV of the Higher Education Act of 1965 (20 U.S.C. 1070 et seq.); and

        (ii) is issued expressly for postsecondary educational expenses to a borrower, regardless of whether the loan is provided through the educational institution that the subject student attends or directly to the borrower from the private educational lender; and

    (B) does not include an extension of credit under an open end consumer credit plan, a reverse mortgage transaction, a residential mortgage transaction, or any other loan that is secured by real property or a dwelling; and

(8) the term "revenue sharing" means an arrangement between a covered educational institution and a private educational lender under which—

    (A) a private educational lender provides or issues private education loans with respect to students attending the covered educational institution;

    (B) the covered educational institution recommends to students or others the private educational lender or the private education loans of the private educational lender; and

    (C) the private educational lender pays a fee or provides other material benefits, including profit sharing, to the covered educational institution in connection with the private education

---

    [1]   So in original. The word "of" probably should not appear.

loans provided to students attending the covered educational institution or a borrower acting on behalf of a student.

(b) Prohibition on certain gifts and arrangements

A private educational lender may not, directly or indirectly—

(1) offer or provide any gift to a covered educational institution in exchange for any advantage or consideration provided to such private educational lender related to its private education loan activities; or

(2) engage in revenue sharing with a covered educational institution.

(c) Prohibition on co-branding

A private educational lender may not use the name, emblem, mascot, or logo of the covered educational institution, or other words, pictures, or symbols readily identified with the covered educational institution, in the marketing of private education loans in any way that implies that the covered educational institution endorses the private education loans offered by the private educational lender.

(d) Advisory board compensation

Any person who is employed in the financial aid office of a covered educational institution, or who otherwise has responsibilities with respect to private education loans or other financial aid of the institution, and who serves on an advisory board, commission, or group established by a private educational lender or group of such lenders shall be prohibited from receiving anything of value from the private educational lender or group of lenders. Nothing in this subsection prohibits the reimbursement of reasonable expenses incurred by an employee of a covered educational institution as part of their service on an advisory board, commission, or group described in this subsection.

(e) Prohibition on prepayment or repayment fees or penalty

It shall be unlawful for any private educational lender to impose a fee or penalty on a borrower for early repayment or prepayment of any private education loan.

(f) Credit card protections for college students

(1) Disclosure required

An institution of higher education shall publicly disclose any contract or other agreement made with a card issuer or creditor for the purpose of marketing a credit card.

(2) Inducements prohibited

No card issuer or creditor may offer to a student at an institution of higher education any tangible item to induce such student to apply for or participate in an open end consumer credit plan offered by such card issuer or creditor, if such offer is made—

(A) on the campus of an institution of higher education;

(B) near the campus of an institution of higher education, as determined by rule of the Bureau; or

(C) at an event sponsored by or related to an institution of higher education.

(3) Sense of the Congress

It is the sense of the Congress that each institution of higher education should consider adopting the following policies relating to credit cards:

(A) That any card issuer that markets a credit card on the campus of such institution notify the institution of the location at which such marketing will take place.

(B) That the number of locations on the campus of such institution at which the marketing of credit cards takes place be limited.

(C) That credit card and debt education and counseling sessions be offered as a regular part of any orientation program for new students of such institution.

(Pub.L. 90–321, Title I, § 140, as added Pub.L. 110–315, Title X, § 1011(a), Aug. 14, 2008, 122 Stat. 3479, and amended Pub.L. 111–24, Title III, § 304, May 22, 2009, 123 Stat. 1749; Pub.L. 111–203, Title X, § 1100A(2), July 21, 2010, 124 Stat. 2107.)

§ 1651.   Procedure for timely settlement of estates of decedent obligors [CCPA § 140A]

The Bureau,[1] in consultation with the Bureau[1] and each other agency referred to in section 1607(a) of this title, shall prescribe regulations to require any creditor, with respect to any credit card account under an open end consumer credit plan, to establish procedures to ensure that any administrator of an estate of any deceased obligor with respect to such account can resolve outstanding credit balances in a timely manner.

(Pub.L. 90–321, Title I, § 140A, as added Pub.L. 111–24, Title V, § 504(a), May 22, 2009, 123 Stat. 1756; Pub.L. 111–203, Title X, § 1100A(2), (3), July 21, 2010, 124 Stat. 2107.)

PART C—CREDIT ADVERTISING AND LIMITS ON CREDIT CARD FEES

§ 1661.   Catalogs and multiple-page advertisements [CCPA § 141]

For the purposes of this part, a catalog or other multiple-page advertisement shall be considered a single advertisement if it clearly and conspicuously displays a credit terms table on which the information required to be stated under this part is clearly set forth.

(Pub.L. 90–321, Title I, § 141, May 29, 1968, 82 Stat. 158.)

§ 1662.   Advertising of downpayments and installments [CCPA § 142]

No advertisement to aid, promote, or assist directly or indirectly any extension of consumer credit may state

    (1) that a specific periodic consumer credit amount or installment amount can be arranged, unless the creditor usually and customarily arranges credit payments or installments for that period and in that amount.

    (2) that a specified downpayment is required in connection with any extension of consumer credit, unless the creditor usually and customarily arranges downpayments in that amount.

(Pub.L. 90–321, Title I, § 142, May 29, 1968, 82 Stat. 158.)

§ 1663.   Advertising of open end credit plans [CCPA § 143]

No advertisement to aid, promote, or assist directly or indirectly the extension of consumer credit under an open end credit plan may set forth any of the specific terms of that plan unless it also clearly and conspicuously sets forth all of the following items:

    (1) Any minimum or fixed amount which could be imposed.

    (2) In any case in which periodic rates may be used to compute the finance charge, the periodic rates expressed as annual percentage rates.

    (3) Any other term that the Bureau may by regulation require to be disclosed.

(Pub.L. 90–321, Title I, § 143, May 29, 1968, 82 Stat. 158; Pub.L. 96–221, Title VI, §§ 613(f), 619(a), Mar. 31, 1980, 94 Stat. 177, 183; Pub.L. 111–203, Title X, § 1100A(2), July 21, 2010, 124 Stat. 2107.)

---

[1]   So in original.

§ 1664.   Advertising of credit other than open end plans [CCPA § 144]

(a)   Exclusion of open end credit plans

Except as provided in subsection (b) of this section, this section applies to any advertisement to aid, promote, or assist directly or indirectly any consumer credit sale, loan, or other extension of credit subject to the provisions of this subchapter, other than an open end credit plan.

(b)   Advertisements of residential real estate

The provisions of this section do not apply to advertisements of residential real estate except to the extent that the Bureau may by regulation require.

(c)   Rate of finance charge expressed as annual percentage rate

If any advertisement to which this section applies states the rate of a finance charge, the advertisement shall state the rate of that charge expressed as an annual percentage rate.

(d)   Requisite disclosures in advertisement

If any advertisement to which this section applies states the amount of the downpayment, if any, the amount of any installment payment, the dollar amount of any finance charge, or the number of installments or the period of repayment, then the advertisement shall state all of the following items:

> **(1)**   The downpayment, if any.
>
> **(2)**   The terms of repayment.
>
> **(3)**   The rate of the finance charge expressed as an annual percentage rate.

(e)   Credit transaction secured by principal dwelling of consumer

Each advertisement to which this section applies that relates to a consumer credit transaction that is secured by the principal dwelling of a consumer in which the extension of credit may exceed the fair market value of the dwelling, and which advertisement is disseminated in paper form to the public or through the internet, as opposed to by radio or television, shall clearly and conspicuously State that—

> **(1)**   the interest on the portion of the credit extension that is greater than the fair market value of the dwelling is not tax deductible for Federal income tax purposes; and
>
> **(2)**   the consumer should consult a tax adviser for further information regarding the deductibility of interest and charges.

(Pub.L. 90–321, Title I, § 144, May 29, 1968, 82 Stat. 158; Pub.L. 96–221, Title VI, § 619(b), Mar. 31, 1980, 94 Stat. 183; Pub.L. 109–8, Title XIII, § 1302(b)(2), Apr. 20, 2005, 119 Stat. 209; Pub.L. 111–203, Title X, § 1100A(2), July 21, 2010, 124 Stat. 2107.)

§ 1665.   Nonliability of advertising media [CCPA § 145]

There is no liability under this part on the part of any owner or personnel, as such, of any medium in which an advertisement appears or through which it is disseminated.

(Pub.L. 90–321, Title I, § 145, May 29, 1968, 82 Stat. 159.)

§ 1665a.   Use of annual percentage rate in oral disclosures; exceptions [CCPA § 146]

In responding orally to any inquiry about the cost of credit, a creditor, regardless of the method used to compute finance charges, shall state rates only in terms of the annual percentage rate, except that in the case of an open end credit plan, the periodic rate also may be stated and, in the case of an other than open end credit plan where a major component of the finance charge consists of interest computed at a simple annual rate, the simple annual rate also may be stated. The Bureau may, by regulation, modify the requirements of this section or provide an exception from this section for a transaction or class of transactions for which the creditor cannot determine in advance the applicable annual percentage rate.

(Pub.L. 90–321, Title I, § 146, as added Pub.L. 93–495, Title IV, § 401(a), Oct. 28, 1974, 88 Stat. 1517, and amended Pub.L. 96–221, Title VI, § 623(a), Mar. 31, 1980, 94 Stat. 185; Pub.L. 111–203, Title X, § 1100A(2), July 21, 2010, 124 Stat. 2107.)

§ 1665b.   Advertising of open end consumer credit plans secured by consumer's principal dwelling [CCPA § 147]

(a)   In general

If any advertisement to aid, promote, or assist, directly or indirectly, the extension of consumer credit through an open end consumer credit plan under which extensions of credit are secured by the consumer's principal dwelling states, affirmatively or negatively, any of the specific terms of the plan, including any periodic payment amount required under such plan, such advertisement shall also clearly and conspicuously set forth the following information, in such form and manner as the Bureau may require:

(1)   Loan fees and opening cost estimates

Any loan fee the amount of which is determined as a percentage of the credit limit applicable to an account under the plan and an estimate of the aggregate amount of other fees for opening the account, based on the creditor's experience with the plan and stated as a single amount or as a reasonable range.

(2)   Periodic rates

In any case in which periodic rates may be used to compute the finance charge, the periodic rates expressed as an annual percentage rate.

(3)   Highest annual percentage rate

The highest annual percentage rate which may be imposed under the plan.

(4)   Other information

Any other information the Bureau may by regulation require.

(b)   Tax deductibility

(1)   In general

If any advertisement described in subsection (a) of this section contains a statement that any interest expense incurred with respect to the plan is or may be tax deductible, the advertisement shall not be misleading with respect to such deductibility.

(2)   Credit in excess of fair market value

Each advertisement described in subsection (a) of this section that relates to an extension of credit that may exceed the fair market value of the dwelling, and which advertisement is disseminated in paper form to the public or through the Internet, as opposed to by radio or television, shall include a clear and conspicuous statement that—

     (A) the interest on the portion of the credit extension that is greater than the fair market value of the dwelling is not tax deductible for Federal income tax purposes; and

     (B) the consumer should consult a tax adviser for further information regarding the deductibility of interest and charges.

(c)   Certain terms prohibited

No advertisement described in subsection (a) of this section with respect to any home equity account may refer to such loan as "free money" or use other terms determined by the Bureau by regulation to be misleading.

(d) Discounted initial rate

(1) In general

If any advertisement described in subsection (a) of this section includes an initial annual percentage rate that is not determined by the index or formula used to make later interest rate adjustments, the advertisement shall also state with equal prominence the current annual percentage rate that would have been applied using the index or formula if such initial rate had not been offered.

(2) Quoted rate must be reasonably current

The annual percentage rate required to be disclosed under the paragraph (1) rate must be current as of a reasonable time given the media involved.

(3) Period during which initial rate is in effect

Any advertisement to which paragraph (1) applies shall also state the period of time during which the initial annual percentage rate referred to in such paragraph will be in effect.

(e) Balloon payment

If any advertisement described in subsection (a) of this section contains a statement regarding the minimum monthly payment under the plan, the advertisement shall also disclose, if applicable, the fact that the plan includes a balloon payment.

(f) "Balloon payment" defined

For purposes of this section and section 1637a of this title, the term "balloon payment" means, with respect to any open end consumer credit plan under which extensions of credit are secured by the consumer's principal dwelling, any repayment option under which—

(1) the account holder is required to repay the entire amount of any outstanding balance as of a specified date or at the end of a specified period of time, as determined in accordance with the terms of the agreement pursuant to which such credit is extended; and

(2) the aggregate amount of the minimum periodic payments required would not fully amortize such outstanding balance by such date or at the end of such period.

(Pub.L. 90–321, Title I, § 147, as added Pub.L. 100–709, § 2(c), Nov. 23, 1988, 102 Stat. 4730; Pub.L. 109–8, Title XIII, § 1302(a)(2), Apr. 20, 2005, 119 Stat. 208; Pub.L. 111–203, Title X, § 1100A(2), July 21, 2010, 124 Stat. 2107.)

§ 1665c. Interest rate reduction on open end consumer credit plans [CCPA § 148]

(a) In general

If a creditor increases the annual percentage rate applicable to a credit card account under an open end consumer credit plan, based on factors including the credit risk of the obligor, market conditions, or other factors, the creditor shall consider changes in such factors in subsequently determining whether to reduce the annual percentage rate for such obligor.

(b) Requirements

With respect to any credit card account under an open end consumer credit plan, the creditor shall—

(1) maintain reasonable methodologies for assessing the factors described in subsection (a);

(2) not less frequently than once every 6 months, review accounts as to which the annual percentage rate has been increased since January 1, 2009, to assess whether such factors have changed (including whether any risk has declined);

(3) reduce the annual percentage rate previously increased when a reduction is indicated by the review; and

(4) in the event of an increase in the annual percentage rate, provide in the written notice required under section 1637(i) of this title a statement of the reasons for the increase.

(c)   Rule of construction

This section shall not be construed to require a reduction in any specific amount.

(d)   Rulemaking

The Bureau[1] shall issue final rules not later than 9 months May 22, 2009 to implement the requirements of and evaluate compliance with this section, and subsections (a), (b), and (c) shall become effective 15 months after May 22, 2009.

(Pub.L. 90–321, Title I, § 148, as added Pub.L. 111–24, Title I, § 101(c), May 22, 2009, 123 Stat. 1737; Pub.L. 111–203, Title X, § 1100A(2), July 21, 2010, 124 Stat. 2107.)

§ 1665d.   Reasonable penalty fees on open end consumer credit plans [CCPA § 149]

(a)   In general

The amount of any penalty fee or charge that a card issuer may impose with respect to a credit card account under an open end consumer credit plan in connection with any omission with respect to, or violation of, the cardholder agreement, including any late payment fee, over-the-limit fee, or any other penalty fee or charge, shall be reasonable and proportional to such omission or violation.

(b)   Rulemaking required

The Bureau, in consultation with the Comptroller of the Currency, the Board of Directors of the Federal Deposit Insurance Corporation, the Director of the Office of Thrift Supervision, and the National Credit Union Administration Board, shall issue final rules not later than 9 months after May 22, 2009, to establish standards for assessing whether the amount of any penalty fee or charge described under subsection (a) is reasonable and proportional to the omission or violation to which the fee or charge relates. Subsection (a) shall become effective 15 months after May 22, 2009.

(c)   Considerations

In issuing rules required by this section, the Bureau shall consider—

    (1)   the cost incurred by the creditor from such omission or violation;

    (2)   the deterrence of such omission or violation by the cardholder;

    (3)   the conduct of the cardholder; and

    (4)   such other factors as the Bureau may deem necessary or appropriate.

(d)   Differentiation permitted

In issuing rules required by this subsection, the Bureau may establish different standards for different types of fees and charges, as appropriate.

(e)   Safe harbor rule authorized

The Bureau, in consultation with the Comptroller of the Currency, the Board of Directors of the Federal Deposit Insurance Corporation, the Director of the Office of Thrift Supervision, and the National Credit Union Administration Board may issue rules to provide an amount for any penalty fee or charge described under subsection (a) that is presumed to be reasonable and proportional to the omission or violation to which the fee or charge relates.

(Pub.L. 90–321, Title I, § 149, as added Pub.L. 111–24, Title I, § 102(b)(1), May 22, 2009, 123 Stat. 1740; Pub.L. 111–203, Title X, § 1100A(2), July 21, 2010, 124 Stat. 2107.)

§ 1665e.   Consideration of ability to repay [CCPA § 150]

A card issuer may not open any credit card account for any consumer under an open end consumer credit plan, or increase any credit limit applicable to such account, unless the card issuer considers the ability of the consumer to make the required payments under the terms of such account.

---

[1]   So in original. Probably should be "Board".

(Pub.L. 90–321, Title I, § 150, as added Pub.L. 111–24, Title I, § 109(a), May 22, 2009, 123 Stat. 1743.)

PART D—CREDIT BILLING

§ 1666.   Correction of billing errors [CCPA § 161]

(a)   Written notice by obligor to creditor; time for and contents of notice; procedure upon receipt of notice by creditor

If a creditor, within sixty days after having transmitted to an obligor a statement of the obligor's account in connection with an extension of consumer credit, receives at the address disclosed under section 1637(b)(10) of this title a written notice (other than notice on a payment stub or other payment medium supplied by the creditor if the creditor so stipulates with the disclosure required under section 1637(a)(7) of this title) from the obligor in which the obligor—

    (1)   sets forth or otherwise enables the creditor to identify the name and account number (if any) of the obligor,

    (2)   indicates the obligor's belief that the statement contains a billing error and the amount of such billing error, and

    (3)   sets forth the reasons for the obligor's belief (to the extent applicable) that the statement contains a billing error,

the creditor shall, unless the obligor has, after giving such written notice and before the expiration of the time limits herein specified, agreed that the statement was correct—

    (A)   not later than thirty days after the receipt of the notice, send a written acknowledgment thereof to the obligor, unless the action required in subparagraph (B) is taken within such thirty-day period, and

    (B)   not later than two complete billing cycles of the creditor (in no event later than ninety days) after the receipt of the notice and prior to taking any action to collect the amount, or any part thereof, indicated by the obligor under paragraph (2) either—

       (i)   make appropriate corrections in the account of the obligor, including the crediting of any finance charges on amounts erroneously billed, and transmit to the obligor a notification of such corrections and the creditor's explanation of any change in the amount indicated by the obligor under paragraph (2) and, if any such change is made and the obligor so requests, copies of documentary evidence of the obligor's indebtedness; or

       (ii)   send a written explanation or clarification to the obligor, after having conducted an investigation, setting forth to the extent applicable the reasons why the creditor believes the account of the obligor was correctly shown in the statement and, upon request of the obligor, provide copies of documentary evidence of the obligor's indebtedness. In the case of a billing error where the obligor alleges that the creditor's billing statement reflects goods not delivered to the obligor or his designee in accordance with the agreement made at the time of the transaction, a creditor may not construe such amount to be correctly shown unless he determines that such goods were actually delivered, mailed, or otherwise sent to the obligor and provides the obligor with a statement of such determination.

After complying with the provisions of this subsection with respect to an alleged billing error, a creditor has no further responsibility under this section if the obligor continues to make substantially the same allegation with respect to such error.

(b)   Billing error

For the purpose of this section, a "billing error" consists of any of the following:

    (1)   A reflection on a statement of an extension of credit which was not made to the obligor or, if made, was not in the amount reflected on such statement.

    (2)   A reflection on a statement of an extension of credit for which the obligor requests additional clarification including documentary evidence thereof.

(3)   A reflection on a statement of goods or services not accepted by the obligor or his designee or not delivered to the obligor or his designee in accordance with the agreement made at the time of a transaction.

(4)   The creditor's failure to reflect properly on a statement a payment made by the obligor or a credit issued to the obligor.

(5)   A computation error or similar error of an accounting nature of the creditor on a statement.

(6)   Failure to transmit the statement required under section 1637(b) of this title to the last address of the obligor which has been disclosed to the creditor, unless that address was furnished less than twenty days before the end of the billing cycle for which the statement is required.

(7)   Any other error described in regulations of the Bureau.

(c)   Action by creditor to collect amount or any part thereof regarded by obligor to be a billing error

For the purposes of this section, "action to collect the amount, or any part thereof, indicated by an obligor under paragraph (2)" does not include the sending of statements of account, which may include finance charges on amounts in dispute, to the obligor following written notice from the obligor as specified under subsection (a) of this section, if—

(1)   the obligor's account is not restricted or closed because of the failure of the obligor to pay the amount indicated under paragraph (2) of subsection (a) of this section, and

(2)   the creditor indicates the payment of such amount is not required pending the creditor's compliance with this section.

Nothing in this section shall be construed to prohibit any action by a creditor to collect any amount which has not been indicated by the obligor to contain a billing error.

(d)   Restricting or closing by creditor of account regarded by obligor to contain a billing error

Pursuant to regulations of the Bureau, a creditor operating an open end consumer credit plan may not, prior to the sending of the written explanation or clarification required under paragraph (B)(ii), restrict or close an account with respect to which the obligor has indicated pursuant to subsection (a) of this section that he believes such account to contain a billing error solely because of the obligor's failure to pay the amount indicated to be in error. Nothing in this subsection shall be deemed to prohibit a creditor from applying against the credit limit on the obligor's account the amount indicated to be in error.

(e)   Effect of noncompliance with requirements by creditor

Any creditor who fails to comply with the requirements of this section or section 1666a of this title forfeits any right to collect from the obligor the amount indicated by the obligor under paragraph (2) of subsection (a) of this section, and any finance charges thereon, except that the amount required to be forfeited under this subsection may not exceed $50.

(Pub.L. 90–321, Title I, § 161, as added Pub.L. 93–495, Title III, § 306, Oct. 28, 1974, 88 Stat. 1512, and amended Pub.L. 96–221, Title VI, §§ 613(g), 620, Mar. 31, 1980, 94 Stat. 177, 184; Pub.L. 111–203, Title X, §§ 1087, 1100A(2), July 21, 2010, 124 Stat. 2086, 2107.)

§ 1666a.   Regulation of credit reports [CCPA § 162]

(a)   Reports by creditor on obligor's failure to pay amount regarded as billing error

After receiving a notice from an obligor as provided in section 1666(a) of this title, a creditor or his agent may not directly or indirectly threaten to report to any person adversely on the obligor's credit rating or credit standing because of the obligor's failure to pay the amount indicated by the obligor under section 1666(a)(2) of this title, and such amount may not be reported as delinquent to any third party until the creditor has met the requirements of section 1666 of this title and has allowed the obligor the same number of days (not less than ten) thereafter to make payment as is provided under the credit agreement with the obligor for the payment of undisputed amounts.

(b) Reports by creditor on delinquent amounts in dispute; notification of obligor of parties notified of delinquency

If a creditor receives a further written notice from an obligor that an amount is still in dispute within the time allowed for payment under subsection (a) of this section, a creditor may not report to any third party that the amount of the obligor is delinquent because the obligor has failed to pay an amount which he has indicated under section 1666(a)(2) of this title, unless the creditor also reports that the amount is in dispute and, at the same time, notifies the obligor of the name and address of each party to whom the creditor is reporting information concerning the delinquency.

(c) Reports by creditor of subsequent resolution of delinquent amounts

A creditor shall report any subsequent resolution of any delinquencies reported pursuant to subsection (b) of this section to the parties to whom such delinquencies were initially reported.

(Pub.L. 90–321, Title I, § 162, as added Pub.L. 93–495, Title III, § 306, Oct. 28, 1974, 88 Stat. 1513.)

§ 1666b. Timing of payments [CCPA § 163]

(a) Time to make payments

A creditor may not treat a payment on a credit card account under an open end consumer credit plan as late for any purpose, unless the creditor has adopted reasonable procedures designed to ensure that each periodic statement including the information required by section 1637(b) of this title is mailed or delivered to the consumer not later than 21 days before the payment due date.

(b) Grace period

If an open end consumer credit plan provides a time period within which an obligor may repay any portion of the credit extended without incurring an additional finance charge, such additional finance charge may not be imposed with respect to such portion of the credit extended for the billing cycle of which such period is a part, unless a statement which includes the amount upon which the finance charge for the period is based was mailed or delivered to the consumer not later than 21 days before the date specified in the statement by which payment must be made in order to avoid imposition of that finance charge.

(Pub.L. 90–321, Title I, § 163, as added Pub.L. 93–495, Title III, § 306, Oct. 28, 1974, 88 Stat. 1514, and amended Pub.L. 111–24, Title I, § 106(b)(1), May 22, 2009, 123 Stat. 1735; Pub.L. 111–93, § 2, Nov. 6, 2009, 123 Stat. 2998.)

§ 1666c. Prompt and fair crediting of payments [CCPA § 164]

(a) In general

Payments received from an obligor under an open end consumer credit plan by the creditor shall be posted promptly to the obligor's account as specified in regulations of the Bureau. Such regulations shall prevent a finance charge from being imposed on any obligor if the creditor has received the obligor's payment in readily identifiable form, by 5:00 p.m. on the date on which such payment is due, in the amount, manner, and location indicated by the creditor to avoid the imposition thereof.

(b) Application of payments

(1) In general

Upon receipt of a payment from a cardholder, the card issuer shall apply amounts in excess of the minimum payment amount first to the card balance bearing the highest rate of interest, and then to each successive balance bearing the next highest rate of interest, until the payment is exhausted.

(2) Clarification relating to certain deferred interest arrangements

A creditor shall allocate the entire amount paid by the consumer in excess of the minimum payment amount to a balance on which interest is deferred during the last 2 billing cycles immediately preceding the expiration of the period during which interest is deferred.

(c) Changes by card issuer

If a card issuer makes a material change in the mailing address, office, or procedures for handling cardholder payments, and such change causes a material delay in the crediting of a cardholder payment made during the 60-day period following the date on which such change took effect, the card issuer may not impose any late fee or finance charge for a late payment on the credit card account to which such payment was credited.

(Pub.L. 90–321, Title I, § 164, as added Pub.L. 93–495, Title III, § 306, Oct. 28, 1974, 88 Stat. 1514, and amended Pub.L. 111–24, Title I, § 104, May 22, 2009, 123 Stat. 1741; Pub.L. 111–203, Title X, § 1100A(2), July 21, 2010, 124 Stat. 2107.)

§ 1666d.   Treatment of credit balances [CCPA § 165]

Whenever a credit balance in excess of $1 is created in connection with a consumer credit transaction through (1) transmittal of funds to a creditor in excess of the total balance due on an account, (2) rebates of unearned finance charges or insurance premiums, or (3) amounts otherwise owed to or held for the benefit of an obligor, the creditor shall—

(A) credit the amount of the credit balance to the consumer's account;

(B) refund any part of the amount of the remaining credit balance, upon request of the consumer; and

(C) make a good faith effort to refund to the consumer by cash, check, or money order any part of the amount of the credit balance remaining in the account for more than six months, except that no further action is required in any case in which the consumer's current location is not known by the creditor and cannot be traced through the consumer's last known address or telephone number.

(Pub.L. 90–321, Title I, § 165, as added Pub.L. 93–495, Title III, § 306, Oct. 28, 1974, 88 Stat. 1514, and amended Pub.L. 96–221, Title VI, § 621(a), Mar. 31, 1980, 94 Stat. 184.)

§ 1666e.   Notification of credit card issuer by seller of return of goods, etc., by obligor; credit for account of obligor [CCPA § 166]

With respect to any sales transaction where a credit card has been used to obtain credit, where the seller is a person other than the card issuer, and where the seller accepts or allows a return of the goods or forgiveness of a debit for services which were the subject of such sale, the seller shall promptly transmit to the credit card issuer, a credit statement with respect thereto and the credit card issuer shall credit the account of the obligor for the amount of the transaction.

(Pub.L. 90–321, Title I, § 166, as added Pub.L. 93–495, Title III, § 306, Oct. 28, 1974, 88 Stat. 1514.)

§ 1666f.   Inducements to cardholders by sellers of cash discounts for payments by cash, check or similar means; finance charge for sales transactions involving cash discounts [CCPA § 167]

(a) Cash discounts

With respect to credit card which may be used for extensions of credit in sales transactions in which the seller is a person other than the card issuer, the card issuer may not, by contract, or otherwise, prohibit any such seller from offering a discount to a cardholder to induce the cardholder to pay by cash, check, or similar means rather than use a credit card.

(b) Finance charge

With respect to any sales transaction, any discount from the regular price offered by the seller for the purpose of inducing payment by cash, checks, or other means not involving the use of an open-end credit plan or a credit card shall not constitute a finance charge as determined under section 1605 of this title if such discount is offered to all prospective buyers and its availability is disclosed clearly and conspicuously.

(Pub.L. 90–321, Title I, § 167, as added Pub.L. 93–495, Title III, § 306, Oct. 28, 1974, 88 Stat. 1515, and amended Pub.L. 94–222, § 3(c)(1), Feb. 27, 1976, 90 Stat. 197; Pub.L. 97–25, Title I, § 101, July 27, 1981, 95 Stat. 144.)

§ 1666g.   Tie-in services prohibited for issuance of credit card [CCPA § 168]

Notwithstanding any agreement to the contrary, a card issuer may not require a seller, as a condition to participating in a credit card plan, to open an account with or procure any other service from the card issuer or its subsidiary or agent.

(Pub.L. 90–321, Title I, § 168, as added Pub.L. 93–495, Title III, § 306, Oct. 28, 1974, 88 Stat. 1515.)

§ 1666h.   Offset of cardholder's indebtedness by issuer of credit card with funds deposited with issuer by cardholder; remedies of creditors under State law not affected [CCPA § 169]

(a) Offset against consumer's funds

A card issuer may not take any action to offset a cardholder's indebtedness arising in connection with a consumer credit transaction under the relevant credit card plan against funds of the cardholder held on deposit with the card issuer unless—

    (1) such action was previously authorized in writing by the cardholder in accordance with a credit plan whereby the cardholder agrees periodically to pay debts incurred in his open end credit account by permitting the card issuer periodically to deduct all or a portion of such debt from the cardholder's deposit account, and

    (2) such action with respect to any outstanding disputed amount not be taken by the card issuer upon request of the cardholder.

In the case of any credit card account in existence on the effective date of this section, the previous written authorization referred to in clause (1) shall not be required until the date (after such effective date) when such account is renewed, but in no case later than one year after such effective date. Such written authorization shall be deemed to exist if the card issuer has previously notified the cardholder that the use of his credit card account will subject any funds which the card issuer holds in deposit accounts of such cardholder to offset against any amounts due and payable on his credit card account which have not been paid in accordance with the terms of the agreement between the card issuer and the cardholder.

(b) Attachments and levies

This section does not alter or affect the right under State law of a card issuer to attach or otherwise levy upon funds of a cardholder held on deposit with the card issuer if that remedy is constitutionally available to creditors generally.

(Pub.L. 90–321, Title I, § 169, as added Pub.L. 93–495, Title III, § 306, Oct. 28, 1974, 88 Stat. 1515.)

§ 1666i.   Assertion by cardholder against card issuer of claims and defenses arising out of credit card transaction; prerequisites; limitation on amount of claims or defenses [CCPA § 170]

(a) Claims and defenses assertible

Subject to the limitation contained in subsection (b) of this section, a card issuer who has issued a credit card to a cardholder pursuant to an open end consumer credit plan shall be subject to all claims (other than tort claims) and defenses arising out of any transaction in which the credit card is used as a method of payment or extension of credit if (1) the obligor has made a good faith attempt to obtain satisfactory resolution of a disagreement or problem relative to the transaction from the person honoring the credit card; (2) the amount of the initial transaction exceeds $50; and (3) the place where the initial transaction occurred was in the same State as the mailing address previously provided by the cardholder or was within 100 miles from such address, except that the limitations set forth in clauses (2) and (3) with respect to an obligor's right to assert claims and defenses against a card issuer shall not be applicable to any transaction in which the person honoring the credit card (A) is the same person as the card issuer, (B) is controlled by the card issuer, (C) is under direct or indirect common control with the card issuer, (D) is a franchised dealer in the card issuer's products or services, or (E) has obtained the order for such transaction through a mail solicitation made by or participated in by the card issuer in which the cardholder is solicited to enter into such transaction by using the credit card issued by the card issuer.

(b) Amount of claims and defenses assertible

The amount of claims or defenses asserted by the cardholder may not exceed the amount of credit outstanding with respect to such transaction at the time the cardholder first notifies the card issuer or the person honoring the credit card of such claim or defense. For the purpose of determining the amount of credit outstanding in the preceding sentence, payments and credits to the cardholder's account are deemed to have been applied, in the order indicated, to the payment of: (1) late charges in the order of their entry to the account; (2) finance charges in order of their entry to the account; and (3) debits to the account other than those set forth above, in the order in which each debit entry to the account was made.

(Pub.L. 90–321, Title I, § 170, as added Pub.L. 93–495, Title III, § 306, Oct. 28, 1974, 88 Stat. 1515.)

§ 1666i–1. Limits on interest rate, fee, and finance charge increases applicable to outstanding balances [CCPA § 171]

(a) In general

In the case of any credit card account under an open end consumer credit plan, no creditor may increase any annual percentage rate, fee, or finance charge applicable to any outstanding balance, except as permitted under subsection (b).

(b) Exceptions

The prohibition under subsection (a) shall not apply to—

(1) an increase in an annual percentage rate upon the expiration of a specified period of time, provided that—

(A) prior to commencement of that period, the creditor disclosed to the consumer, in a clear and conspicuous manner, the length of the period and the annual percentage rate that would apply after expiration of the period;

(B) the increased annual percentage rate does not exceed the rate disclosed pursuant to subparagraph (A); and

(C) the increased annual percentage rate is not applied to transactions that occurred prior to commencement of the period;

(2) an increase in a variable annual percentage rate in accordance with a credit card agreement that provides for changes in the rate according to operation of an index that is not under the control of the creditor and is available to the general public;

(3) an increase due to the completion of a workout or temporary hardship arrangement by the obligor or the failure of the obligor to comply with the terms of a workout or temporary hardship arrangement, provided that—

(A) the annual percentage rate, fee, or finance charge applicable to a category of transactions following any such increase does not exceed the rate, fee, or finance charge that applied to that category of transactions prior to commencement of the arrangement; and

(B) the creditor has provided the obligor, prior to the commencement of such arrangement, with clear and conspicuous disclosure of the terms of the arrangement (including any increases due to such completion or failure); or

(4) an increase due solely to the fact that a minimum payment by the obligor has not been received by the creditor within 60 days after the due date for such payment, provided that the creditor shall—

(A) include, together with the notice of such increase required under section 1637(i) of this title, a clear and conspicuous written statement of the reason for the increase and that the increase will terminate not later than 6 months after the date on which it is imposed, if the creditor receives the required minimum payments on time from the obligor during that period; and

(B) terminate such increase not later than 6 months after the date on which it is imposed, if the creditor receives the required minimum payments on time during that period.

(c) Repayment of outstanding balance

(1) In general

The creditor shall not change the terms governing the repayment of any outstanding balance, except that the creditor may provide the obligor with one of the methods described in paragraph (2) of repaying any outstanding balance, or a method that is no less beneficial to the obligor than one of those methods.

(2) Methods

The methods described in this paragraph are—

(A) an amortization period of not less than 5 years, beginning on the effective date of the increase set forth in the notice required under section 1637(i) of this title; or

(B) a required minimum periodic payment that includes a percentage of the outstanding balance that is equal to not more than twice the percentage required before the effective date of the increase set forth in the notice required under section 1637(i) of this title.

(d) Outstanding balance defined

For purposes of this section, the term "outstanding balance" means the amount owed on a credit card account under an open end consumer credit plan as of the end of the 14th day after the date on which the creditor provides notice of an increase in the annual percentage rate, fee, or finance charge in accordance with section 1637(i) of this title.

(Pub.L. 90–321, Title I, § 171, as added Pub.L. 111–24, Title I, § 101(b)(2), May 22, 2009, 123 Stat. 1736.)

§ 1666i–2. Additional limits on interest rate increases [CCPA § 172]

(a) Limitation on increases within first year

Except in the case of an increase described in paragraph (1), (2), (3), or (4) of section 1666i–1(b) of this title, no increase in any annual percentage rate, fee, or finance charge on any credit card account under an open end consumer credit plan shall be effective before the end of the 1-year period beginning on the date on which the account is opened.

(b) Promotional rate minimum term

No increase in any annual percentage rate applicable to a credit card account under an open end consumer credit plan that is a promotional rate (as that term is defined by the Bureau) shall be effective before the end of the 6-month period beginning on the date on which the promotional rate takes effect, subject to such reasonable exceptions as the Bureau may establish, by rule.

(Pub.L. 90–321, Title I, § 172, as added Pub.L. 111–24, Title I, § 101(d), May 22, 2009, 123 Stat. 1738; Pub.L. 111–203, Title X, § 1100A(2), July 21, 2010, 124 Stat. 2107.)

§ 1666j. Applicability of State laws [CCPA § 173]

(a) Consistency of provisions

This part does not annul, alter, or affect, or exempt any person subject to the provisions of this part from complying with, the laws of any State with respect to credit billing practices, except to the extent that those laws are inconsistent with any provision of this part, and then only to the extent of the inconsistency. The Bureau is authorized to determine whether such inconsistencies exist. The Bureau may not determine that any State law is inconsistent with any provision of this part if the Bureau determines that such law gives greater protection to the consumer.

(b) Exemptions by Bureau from credit billing requirements

The Bureau shall by regulation exempt from the requirements of this part any class of credit transactions within any State if it determines that under the law of that State that class of transactions is subject to requirements substantially similar to those imposed under this part or that such law gives greater protection to the consumer, and that there is adequate provision for enforcement.

(c) Finance charge or other charge for credit for sales transactions involving cash discounts

Notwithstanding any other provisions of this subchapter, any discount offered under section 1666f(b) of this title shall not be considered a finance charge or other charge for credit under the usury laws of any State or under the laws of any State relating to disclosure of information in connection with credit transactions, or relating to the types, amounts or rates of charges, or to any element or elements of charges permissible under such laws in connection with the extension or use of credit.

> (Pub.L. 90–321, Title I, § 173, formerly § 171, as added Pub.L. 93–495, Title III, § 306, Oct. 28, 1974, 88 Stat. 1516, and amended Pub.L. 94–222, § 3(d), Feb. 27, 1976, 90 Stat. 198; renumbered § 173, P.L. 111–22, Title I, § 101(b)(1), May 20, 2009, 123 Stat. 1638; Pub.L. 111–203, Title X, §§ 1087, 1100A(2), July 21, 2010, 124 Stat. 2086, 2107.)

PART E—CONSUMER LEASES

§ 1667.   Definitions [CCPA § 181]

For purposes of this part—

    (1) The term "consumer lease" means a contract in the form of a lease or bailment for the use of personal property by a natural person for a period of time exceeding four months, and for a total contractual obligation not exceeding $50,000, primarily for personal, family, or household purposes, whether or not the lessee has the option to purchase or otherwise become the owner of the property at the expiration of the lease, except that such term shall not include any credit sale as defined in section 1602(g)* of this title. Such term does not include a lease for agricultural, business, or commercial purposes, or to a government or governmental agency or instrumentality, or to an organization.

    (2) The term "lessee" means a natural person who leases or is offered a consumer lease.

    (3) The term "lessor" means a person who is regularly engaged in leasing, offering to lease, or arranging to lease under a consumer lease.

    (4) The term "personal property" means any property which is not real property under the laws of the State where situated at the time offered or otherwise made available for lease.

    (5) The terms "security" and "security interest" mean any interest in property which secures payment or performance of an obligation.

> (Pub.L. 90–321, Title I, § 181, as added Pub.L. 94–240, § 3, Mar. 23, 1976, 90 Stat. 257; Pub.L. 111–203, Title X, § 1100E(a)(2), July 21, 2010, 124 Stat. 2111.)

§ 1667a.   Consumer lease disclosures [CCPA § 182]

Each lessor shall give a lessee prior to the consummation of the lease a dated written statement on which the lessor and lessee are identified setting out accurately and in a clear and conspicuous manner the following information with respect to that lease, as applicable:

    (1) A brief description or identification of the leased property;

    (2) The amount of any payment by the lessee required at the inception of the lease;

    (3) The amount paid or payable by the lessee for official fees, registration, certificate of title, or license fees or taxes;

---

* *Note from West Advisory Panel: This section was redesignated section 1602(h) of this title by Pub.L. 111–203, Title X, § 1100A(1)(A), July 21, 2010, 124 Stat. 2107.*

(4) The amount of other charges payable by the lessee not included in the periodic payments, a description of the charges and that the lessee shall be liable for the differential, if any, between the anticipated fair market value of the leased property and its appraised actual value at the termination of the lease, if the lessee has such liability;

(5) A statement of the amount or method of determining the amount of any liabilities the lease imposes upon the lessee at the end of the term and whether or not the lessee has the option to purchase the leased property and at what price and time;

(6) A statement identifying all express warranties and guarantees made by the manufacturer or lessor with respect to the leased property, and identifying the party responsible for maintaining or servicing the leased property together with a description of the responsibility;

(7) A brief description of insurance provided or paid for by the lessor or required of the lessee, including the types and amounts of the coverages and costs;

(8) A description of any security interest held or to be retained by the lessor in connection with the lease and a clear identification of the property to which the security interest relates;

(9) The number, amount, and due dates or periods of payments under the lease and the total amount of such periodic payments;

(10) Where the lease provides that the lessee shall be liable for the anticipated fair market value of the property on expiration of the lease, the fair market value of the property at the inception of the lease, the aggregate cost of the lease on expiration, and the differential between them; and

(11) A statement of the conditions under which the lessee or lessor may terminate the lease prior to the end of the term and the amount or method of determining any penalty or other charge for delinquency, default, late payments, or early termination.

The disclosures required under this section may be made in the lease contract to be signed by the lessee. The Bureau may provide by regulation that any portion of the information required to be disclosed under this section may be given in the form of estimates where the lessor is not in a position to know exact information.

(Pub.L. 90–321, Title I, § 182, as added Pub.L. 94–240, § 3, Mar. 23, 1976, 90 Stat. 258; Pub.L. 111–203, Title X, §§ 1100A(2), 1100A(10)(B), July 21, 2010, 124 Stat. 2107, 2109.)

§ 1667b. Lessee's liability on expiration or termination of lease [CCPA § 183]

(a) Estimated residual value of property as basis; presumptions; action by lessor for excess liability; mutually agreeable final adjustment

Where the lessee's liability on expiration of a consumer lease is based on the estimated residual value of the property such estimated residual value shall be a reasonable approximation of the anticipated actual fair market value of the property on lease expiration. There shall be a rebuttable presumption that the estimated residual value is unreasonable to the extent that the estimated residual value exceeds the actual residual value by more than three times the average payment allocable to a monthly period under the lease. In addition, where the lessee has such liability on expiration of a consumer lease there shall be a rebuttable presumption that the lessor's estimated residual value is not in good faith to the extent that the estimated residual value exceeds the actual residual value by more than three times the average payment allocable to a monthly period under the lease and such lessor shall not collect from the lessee the amount of such excess liability on expiration of a consumer lease unless the lessor brings a successful action with respect to such excess liability. In all actions, the lessor shall pay the lessee's reasonable attorney's fees. The presumptions stated in this section shall not apply to the extent the excess of estimated over actual residual value is due to physical damage to the property beyond reasonable wear and use, or to excessive use, and the lease may set standards for such wear and use if such standards are not unreasonable. Nothing in this subsection shall preclude the right of a willing lessee to make any mutually agreeable final adjustment with respect to such excess residual liability, provided such an agreement is reached after termination of the lease.

(b) Penalties and charges for delinquency, default, or early termination

Penalties or other charges for delinquency, default, or early termination may be specified in the lease but only at an amount which is reasonable in the light of the anticipated or actual harm caused by the delinquency, default, or early termination, the difficulties of proof of loss, and the inconvenience or nonfeasibility of otherwise obtaining an adequate remedy.

(c) Independent professional appraisal of residual value of property at termination of lease; finality

If a lease has a residual value provision at the termination of the lease, the lessee may obtain at his expense, a professional appraisal of the leased property by an independent third party agreed to by both parties. Such appraisal shall be final and binding on the parties.

(Pub.L. 90–321, Title I, § 183, as added Pub.L. 94–240, § 3, Mar. 23, 1976, 90 Stat. 259.)

§ 1667c.   Consumer lease advertising; liability of advertising media [CCPA § 184]

(a) In general

If an advertisement for a consumer lease includes a statement of the amount of any payment or a statement that any or no initial payment is required, the advertisement shall clearly and conspicuously state, as applicable—

    (1) the transaction advertised is a lease;

    (2) the total amount of any initial payments required on or before consummation of the lease or delivery of the property, whichever is later;

    (3) that a security deposit is required;

    (4) the number, amount, and timing of scheduled payments; and

    (5) with respect to a lease in which the liability of the consumer at the end of the lease term is based on the anticipated residual value of the property, that an extra charge may be imposed at the end of the lease term.

(b) Advertising medium not liable

No owner or employee of any entity that serves as a medium in which an advertisement appears or through which an advertisement is disseminated, shall be liable under this section.

(c) Radio advertisements

    (1) In general

        An advertisement by radio broadcast to aid, promote, or assist, directly or indirectly, any consumer lease shall be deemed to be in compliance with the requirements of subsection (a) of this section if such advertisement clearly and conspicuously—

        (A) states the information required by paragraphs (1) and (2) of subsection (a) of this section;

        (B) states the number, amounts, due dates or periods of scheduled payments, and the total of such payments under the lease;

        (C) includes—

            (i) a referral to—

                (I) a toll-free telephone number established in accordance with paragraph (2) that may be used by consumers to obtain the information required under subsection (a) of this section; or

                (II) a written advertisement that—

                    (aa) appears in a publication in general circulation in the community served by the radio station on which such advertisement is broadcast during the period beginning 3 days before any such broadcast and ending 10 days after such broadcast; and

(bb) includes the information required to be disclosed under subsection (a) of this section; and

(ii) the name and dates of any publication referred to in clause (i)(II); and

(D) includes any other information which the Bureau determines necessary to carry out this part.

(2) Establishment of toll-free number

(A) In general

In the case of a radio broadcast advertisement described in paragraph (1) that includes a referral to a toll-free telephone number, the lessor who offers the consumer lease shall—

(i) establish such a toll-free telephone number not later than the date on which the advertisement including the referral is broadcast;

(ii) maintain such telephone number for a period of not less than 10 days, beginning on the date of any such broadcast; and

(iii) provide the information required under subsection (a) of this section with respect to the lease to any person who calls such number.

(B) Form of information

The information required to be provided under subparagraph (A)(iii) shall be provided verbally or, if requested by the consumer, in written form.

(3) No effect on other law

Nothing in this subsection shall affect the requirements of Federal law as such requirements apply to advertisement by any medium other than radio broadcast.

(Pub.L. 90–321, Title I, § 184, as added Pub.L. 94–240, § 3, Mar. 23, 1976, 90 Stat. 259, and amended Pub.L. 103–325, Title III, § 336(a), Sept. 23, 1994, 108 Stat. 2234; Pub.L. 104–208, Div. A, Title II, § 2605(c), Sept. 30, 1996, 110 Stat. 3009–473; Pub.L. 111–203, Title X, §§ 1100A(2), 1100A(10)(A), July 21, 2010, 124 Stat. 2107, 2109.)

§ 1667d. Civil liability of lessors [CCPA § 185]

(a) Grounds for maintenance of action

Any lessor who fails to comply with any requirement imposed under section 1667a or 1667b of this title with respect to any person is liable to such person as provided in section 1640 of this title.

(b) Additional grounds for maintenance of action; "creditor" defined

Any lessor who fails to comply with any requirement imposed under section 1667c of this title with respect to any person who suffers actual damage from the violation is liable to such person as provided in section 1640 of this title. For the purposes of this section, the term "creditor" as used in sections 1640 and 1641 of this title shall include a lessor as defined in this part.

(c) Jurisdiction of courts; time limitation

Notwithstanding section 1640(e) of this title, any action under this section may be brought in any United States district court or in any other court of competent jurisdiction. Such actions alleging a failure to disclose or otherwise comply with the requirements of this part shall be brought within one year of the termination of the lease agreement.

(Pub.L. 90–321, Title I, § 185, as added Pub.L. 94–240, § 3, Mar. 23, 1976, 90 Stat. 260, and amended Pub.L. 96–221, Title VI, § 624, Mar. 31, 1980, 94 Stat. 185.)

§ **1667e.   Applicability of State laws; exemptions by Board from leasing requirements [CCPA § 186]**

(a)   This part does not annul, alter, or affect, or exempt any person subject to the provisions of this part from complying with, the laws of any State with respect to consumer leases, except to the extent that those laws are inconsistent with any provision of this part, and then only to the extent of the inconsistency. The Bureau is authorized to determine whether such inconsistencies exist. The Bureau may not determine that any State law is inconsistent with any provision of this part if the Bureau determines that such law gives greater protection and benefit to the consumer.

(b)   The Bureau shall by regulation exempt from the requirements of this part any class of lease transactions within any State if it determines that under the law of that State that class of transactions is subject to requirements substantially similar to those imposed under this part or that such law gives greater protection and benefit to the consumer, and that there is adequate provision for enforcement.

(Pub.L. 90–321, Title I, § 186, as added Pub.L. 94–240, § 3, Mar. 23, 1976, 90 Stat. 260; Pub.L. 111–203, Title X, §§ 1100A(2), 1100A(10), July 21, 2010, 124 Stat. 2107, 2109.)

§ **1667f.   Regulations [CCPA § 187]**

(a) Regulations authorized

(1) In general

The Bureau shall prescribe regulations to update and clarify the requirements and definitions applicable to lease disclosures and contracts, and any other issues specifically related to consumer leasing, to the extent that the Bureau determines such action to be necessary—

(A)   to carry out this part;

(B)   to prevent any circumvention of this part; or

(C)   to facilitate compliance with the requirements of the[1] part.

(2) Classifications, adjustments

Any regulations prescribed under paragraph (1) may contain classifications and differentiations, and may provide for adjustments and exceptions for any class of transactions, as the Bureau considers appropriate.

(b) Model disclosure

(1) Publication

The Bureau shall establish and publish model disclosure forms to facilitate compliance with the disclosure requirements of this part and to aid the consumer in understanding the transaction to which the subject disclosure form relates.

(2) Use of automated equipment

In establishing model forms under this subsection, the Bureau shall consider the use by lessors of data processing or similar automated equipment.

(3) Use optional

A lessor may utilize a model disclosure form established by the Bureau under this subsection for purposes of compliance with this part, at the discretion of the lessor.

(4) Effect of use

Any lessor who properly uses the material aspects of any model disclosure form established by the Bureau under this subsection shall be deemed to be in compliance with the disclosure requirements to which the form relates.

---

[1]   So in original. Probably should be "this".

(Pub.L. 90–321, Title I, § 187, as added Pub.L. 104–208, Div. A, Title II, § 2605(b)(1), Sept. 30, 1996, 110 Stat. 3009–471; Pub.L. 111–203, Title X, §§ 1100A(2), 1100A(10), July 21, 2010, 124 Stat. 2107, 2109.)

SUBCHAPTER II—RESTRICTIONS ON GARNISHMENT

§ 1671.   Congressional findings and declaration of purpose [CCPA § 301]

(a) Disadvantages of garnishment

The Congress finds:

   (1)   The unrestricted garnishment of compensation due for personal services encourages the making of predatory extensions of credit. Such extensions of credit divert money into excessive credit payments and thereby hinder the production and flow of goods in interstate commerce.

   (2)   The application of garnishment as a creditors' remedy frequently results in loss of employment by the debtor, and the resulting disruption of employment, production, and consumption constitutes a substantial burden on interstate commerce.

   (3)   The great disparities among the laws of the several States relating to garnishment have, in effect, destroyed the uniformity of the bankruptcy laws and frustrated the purposes thereof in many areas of the country.

(b) Necessity for regulation

On the basis of the findings stated in subsection (a) of this section, the Congress determines that the provisions of this subchapter are necessary and proper for the purpose of carrying into execution the powers of the Congress to regulate commerce and to establish uniform bankruptcy laws.

   (Pub.L. 90–321, Title III, § 301, May 29, 1968, 82 Stat. 163.)

§ 1672.   Definitions [CCPA § 302]

For the purposes of this subchapter:

   (a)   The term "earnings" means compensation paid or payable for personal services, whether denominated as wages, salary, commission, bonus, or otherwise, and includes periodic payments pursuant to a pension or retirement program.

   (b)   The term "disposable earnings" means that part of the earnings of any individual remaining after the deduction from those earnings of any amounts required by law to be withheld.

   (c)   The term "garnishment" means any legal or equitable procedure through which the earnings of any individual are required to be withheld for payment of any debt.

   (Pub.L. 90–321, Title III, § 302, May 29, 1968, 82 Stat. 163.)

§ 1673.   Restriction on garnishment [CCPA § 303]

(a) Maximum allowable garnishment

Except as provided in subsection (b) of this section and in section 1675 of this title, the maximum part of the aggregate disposable earnings of an individual for any workweek which is subjected to garnishment may not exceed

   (1)   25 per centum of his disposable earnings for that week, or

   (2)   the amount by which his disposable earnings for that week exceed thirty times the Federal minimum hourly wage prescribed by section 206(a)(1) of Title 29 in effect at the time the earnings are payable,

whichever is less. In the case of earnings for any pay period other than a week, the Secretary of Labor shall by regulation prescribe a multiple of the Federal minimum hourly wage equivalent in effect to that set forth in paragraph (2).

(b) Exceptions

    (1) The restrictions of subsection (a) of this section do not apply in the case of

        (A) any order for the support of any person issued by a court of competent jurisdiction or in accordance with an administrative procedure, which is established by State law, which affords substantial due process, and which is subject to judicial review.

        (B) any order of any court of the United States having jurisdiction over cases under chapter 13 of Title 11.

        (C) any debt due for any State or Federal tax.

    (2) The maximum part of the aggregate disposable earnings of an individual for any workweek which is subject to garnishment to enforce any order for the support of any person shall not exceed—

        (A) where such individual is supporting his spouse or dependent child (other than a spouse or child with respect to whose support such order is used), 50 per centum of such individual's disposable earnings for that week; and

        (B) where such individual is not supporting such a spouse or dependent child described in clause (A), 60 per centum of such individual's disposable earnings for that week;

except that, with respect to the disposable earnings of any individual for any workweek, the 50 per centum specified in clause (A) shall be deemed to be 55 per centum and the 60 per centum specified in clause (B) shall be deemed to be 65 per centum, if and to the extent that such earnings are subject to garnishment to enforce a support order with respect to a period which is prior to the twelve-week period which ends with the beginning of such workweek.

(c) Execution or enforcement of garnishment order or process prohibited

    No court of the United States or any State, and no State (or officer or agency thereof), may make, execute, or enforce any order or process in violation of this section.

    (Pub.L. 90–321, Title III, § 303, May 29, 1968, 82 Stat. 163; Pub.L. 95–30, Title V, § 501(e)(1) to (3), May 23, 1977, 91 Stat. 161, 162; Pub.L. 95–598, Title III, § 312(a), Nov. 6, 1978, 92 Stat. 2676.)

§ 1674.   Restriction on discharge from employment by reason of garnishment [CCPA § 304]

(a) Termination of employment

    No employer may discharge any employee by reason of the fact that his earnings have been subjected to garnishment for any one indebtedness.

(b) Penalties

    Whoever willfully violates subsection (a) of this section shall be fined not more than $1,000, or imprisoned not more than one year, or both.

    (Pub.L. 90–321, Title III, § 304, May 29, 1968, 82 Stat. 163.)

§ 1675.   Exemption for State-regulated garnishments [CCPA § 305]

    The Secretary of Labor may by regulation exempt from the provisions of section 1673(a) and (b)(2) of this title garnishments issued under the laws of any State if he determines that the laws of that State provide restrictions on garnishment which are substantially similar to those provided in section 1673(a) and (b)(2) of this title.

    (Pub.L. 90–321, Title III, § 305, May 29, 1968, 82 Stat. 164; Pub.L. 95–30, Title V, § 501(e)(4), May 23, 1977, 91 Stat. 162.)

§ 1676.   Enforcement by Secretary of Labor [CCPA § 306]

    The Secretary of Labor, acting through the Wage and Hour Division of the Department of Labor, shall enforce the provisions of this subchapter.

(Pub.L. 90–321, Title III, § 306, May 29, 1968, 82 Stat. 164.)

§ 1677.   Effect on State laws [CCPA § 307]

This subchapter does not annul, alter, or affect, or exempt any person from complying with, the laws of any State

(1)   prohibiting garnishments or providing for more limited garnishment than are allowed under this subchapter, or

(2)   prohibiting the discharge of any employee by reason of the fact that his earnings have been subjected to garnishment for more than one indebtedness.

(Pub.L. 90–321, Title III, § 307, May 29, 1968, 82 Stat. 164.)

SUBCHAPTER II–A—CREDIT REPAIR ORGANIZATIONS

§ 1679.   Findings and purposes [CCPA § 402]

(a)   Findings

The Congress makes the following findings:

(1)   Consumers have a vital interest in establishing and maintaining their credit worthiness[1] and credit standing in order to obtain and use credit. As a result, consumers who have experienced credit problems may seek assistance from credit repair organizations which offer to improve the credit standing of such consumers.

(2)   Certain advertising and business practices of some companies engaged in the business of credit repair services have worked a financial hardship upon consumers, particularly those of limited economic means and who are inexperienced in credit matters.

(b)   Purposes

The purposes of this subchapter are—

(1)   to ensure that prospective buyers of the services of credit repair organizations are provided with the information necessary to make an informed decision regarding the purchase of such services; and

(2)   to protect the public from unfair or deceptive advertising and business practices by credit repair organizations.

(Pub.L. 90–321, Title IV, § 402, as added Pub.L. 104–208, Div. A, Title II, § 2451, Sept. 30, 1996, 110 Stat. 3009–462.)

§ 1679a.   Definitions [CCPA § 403]

For purposes of this subchapter, the following definitions apply:

(1)   Consumer

The term "consumer" means an individual.

(2)   Consumer credit transaction

The term "consumer credit transaction" means any transaction in which credit is offered or extended to an individual for personal, family, or household purposes.

(3)   Credit repair organization

The term "credit repair organization"—

---

[1]   So in original. Probably should be "creditworthiness".

(A)   means any person who uses any instrumentality of interstate commerce or the mails to sell, provide, or perform (or represent that such person can or will sell, provide, or perform) any service, in return for the payment of money or other valuable consideration, for the express or implied purpose of—

(i)   improving any consumer's credit record, credit history, or credit rating; or

(ii)   providing advice or assistance to any consumer with regard to any activity or service described in clause (i); and

(B)   does not include—

(i)   any nonprofit organization which is exempt from taxation under section 501(c)(3) of Title 26;

(ii)   any creditor (as defined in section 1602 of this title), with respect to any consumer, to the extent the creditor is assisting the consumer to restructure any debt owed by the consumer to the creditor; or

(iii)   any depository institution (as that term is defined in section 1813 of Title 12) or any Federal or State credit union (as those terms are defined in section 1752 of Title 12), or any affiliate or subsidiary of such a depository institution or credit union.

(4)   Credit

The term "credit" has the meaning given to such term in section 1602(e) of this title.

(Pub.L. 90–321, Title IV, § 403, as added Pub.L. 104–208, Div. A, Title II, § 2451, Sept. 30, 1996, 110 Stat. 3009–455.)

§ 1679b.   Prohibited practices [CCPA § 404]

(a)   In general

No person may—

(1)   make any statement, or counsel or advise any consumer to make any statement, which is untrue or misleading (or which, upon the exercise of reasonable care, should be known by the credit repair organization, officer, employee, agent, or other person to be untrue or misleading) with respect to any consumer's credit worthiness,[1] credit standing, or credit capacity to—

(A)   any consumer reporting agency (as defined in section 1681a(f) of this title); or

(B)   any person—

(i)   who has extended credit to the consumer; or

(ii)   to whom the consumer has applied or is applying for an extension of credit;

(2)   make any statement, or counsel or advise any consumer to make any statement, the intended effect of which is to alter the consumer's identification to prevent the display of the consumer's credit record, history, or rating for the purpose of concealing adverse information that is accurate and not obsolete to—

(A)   any consumer reporting agency;

(B)   any person—

(i)   who has extended credit to the consumer; or

(ii)   to whom the consumer has applied or is applying for an extension of credit;

(3)   make or use any untrue or misleading representation of the services of the credit repair organization; or

---

[1]   So in original. Probably should be "creditworthiness".

(4) engage, directly or indirectly, in any act, practice, or course of business that constitutes or results in the commission of, or an attempt to commit, a fraud or deception on any person in connection with the offer or sale of the services of the credit repair organization.

(b) Payment in advance

No credit repair organization may charge or receive any money or other valuable consideration for the performance of any service which the credit repair organization has agreed to perform for any consumer before such service is fully performed.

(Pub.L. 90–321, Title IV, § 404, as added Pub.L. 104–208, Div. A, Title II, § 2451, Sept. 30, 1996, 110 Stat. 3009–456.)

§ 1679c. Disclosures [CCPA § 405]

(a) Disclosure required

Any credit repair organization shall provide any consumer with the following written statement before any contract or agreement between the consumer and the credit repair organization is executed:

"Consumer Credit File Rights Under State and Federal Law

"You have a right to dispute inaccurate information in your credit report by contacting the credit bureau directly. However, neither you nor any 'credit repair' company or credit repair organization has the right to have accurate, current, and verifiable information removed from your credit report. The credit bureau must remove accurate, negative information from your report only if it is over 7 years old. Bankruptcy information can be reported for 10 years.

"You have a right to obtain a copy of your credit report from a credit bureau. You may be charged a reasonable fee. There is no fee, however, if you have been turned down for credit, employment, insurance, or a rental dwelling because of information in your credit report within the preceding 60 days. The credit bureau must provide someone to help you interpret the information in your credit file. You are entitled to receive a free copy of your credit report if you are unemployed and intend to apply for employment in the next 60 days, if you are a recipient of public welfare assistance, or if you have reason to believe that there is inaccurate information in your credit report due to fraud.

"You have a right to sue a credit repair organization that violates the Credit Repair Organization Act. This law prohibits deceptive practices by credit repair organizations.

"You have the right to cancel your contract with any credit repair organization for any reason within 3 business days from the date you signed it.

"Credit bureaus are required to follow reasonable procedures to ensure that the information they report is accurate. However, mistakes may occur.

"You may, on your own, notify a credit bureau in writing that you dispute the accuracy of information in your credit file. The credit bureau must then reinvestigate and modify or remove inaccurate or incomplete information. The credit bureau may not charge any fee for this service. Any pertinent information and copies of all documents you have concerning an error should be given to the credit bureau.

"If the credit bureau's reinvestigation does not resolve the dispute to your satisfaction, you may send a brief statement to the credit bureau, to be kept in your file, explaining why you think the record is inaccurate. The credit bureau must include a summary of your statement about disputed information with any report it issues about you.

"The Federal Trade Commission regulates credit bureaus and credit repair organizations. For more information contact:

"The Public Reference Branch

"Federal Trade Commission

"Washington, D.C. 20580".

(b) Separate statement requirement

The written statement required under this section shall be provided as a document which is separate from any written contract or other agreement between the credit repair organization and the consumer or any other written material provided to the consumer.

(c) Retention of compliance records

(1) In general

The credit repair organization shall maintain a copy of the statement signed by the consumer acknowledging receipt of the statement.

(2) Maintenance for 2 years

The copy of any consumer's statement shall be maintained in the organization's files for 2 years after the date on which the statement is signed by the consumer.

(Pub.L. 90–321, Title IV, § 405, as added Pub.L. 104–208, Div. A, Title II, § 2451, Sept. 30, 1996, 110 Stat. 3009–457.)

§ 1679d.   Credit repair organizations contracts [CCPA § 406]

(a) Written contracts required

No services may be provided by any credit repair organization for any consumer—

(1) unless a written and dated contract (for the purchase of such services) which meets the requirements of subsection (b) of this section has been signed by the consumer; or

(2) before the end of the 3-business-day period beginning on the date the contract is signed.

(b) Terms and conditions of contract

No contract referred to in subsection (a) of this section meets the requirements of this subsection unless such contract includes (in writing)—

(1) the terms and conditions of payment, including the total amount of all payments to be made by the consumer to the credit repair organization or to any other person;

(2) a full and detailed description of the services to be performed by the credit repair organization for the consumer, including—

(A) all guarantees of performance; and

(B) an estimate of—

(i) the date by which the performance of the services (to be performed by the credit repair organization or any other person) will be complete; or

(ii) the length of the period necessary to perform such services;

(3) the credit repair organization's name and principal business address; and

(4) a conspicuous statement in bold face type, in immediate proximity to the space reserved for the consumer's signature on the contract, which reads as follows: "You may cancel this contract without penalty or obligation at any time before midnight of the 3rd business day after the date on which you signed the contract. See the attached notice of cancellation form for an explanation of this right.".

(Pub.L. 90–321, Title IV, § 406, as added Pub.L. 104–208, Div. A, Title II, § 2451, Sept. 30, 1996, 110 Stat. 3009–458.)

§ 1679e.   Right to cancel contract [CCPA § 407]

(a) In general

Any consumer may cancel any contract with any credit repair organization without penalty or obligation by notifying the credit repair organization of the consumer's intention to do so at any time before midnight of the 3rd business day which begins after the date on which the contract or agreement between the consumer and the credit repair organization is executed or would, but for this subsection, become enforceable against the parties.

(b) Cancellation form and other information

Each contract shall be accompanied by a form, in duplicate, which has the heading "Notice of Cancellation" and contains in bold face type the following statement:

"You may cancel this contract, without any penalty or obligation, at any time before midnight of the 3rd day which begins after the date the contract is signed by you.

"To cancel this contract, mail or deliver a signed, dated copy of this cancellation notice, or any other written notice to [name of credit repair organization] at [address of credit repair organization] before midnight on [date]

"I hereby cancel this transaction,

[date]

[purchaser's signature].".

(c) Consumer copy of contract required

Any consumer who enters into any contract with any credit repair organization shall be given, by the organization—

(1) a copy of the completed contract and the disclosure statement required under section 1679c of this title; and

(2) a copy of any other document the credit repair organization requires the consumer to sign,

at the time the contract or the other document is signed.

(Pub.L. 90–321, Title IV, § 407, as added Pub.L. 104–208, Div. A, Title II, § 2451, Sept. 30, 1996, 110 Stat. 3009–459.)

§ 1679f.   Noncompliance with this subchapter [CCPA § 408]

(a) Consumer waivers invalid

Any waiver by any consumer of any protection provided by or any right of the consumer under this subchapter—

(1) shall be treated as void; and

(2) may not be enforced by any Federal or State court or any other person.

(b) Attempt to obtain waiver

Any attempt by any person to obtain a waiver from any consumer of any protection provided by or any right of the consumer under this subchapter shall be treated as a violation of this subchapter.

(c) Contracts not in compliance

Any contract for services which does not comply with the applicable provisions of this subchapter—

(1) shall be treated as void; and

(2) may not be enforced by any Federal or State court or any other person.

(Pub.L. 90–321, Title IV, § 408, as added Pub.L. 104–208, Div. A, Title II, § 2451, Sept. 30, 1996, 110 Stat. 3009–459.)

§ 1679g.   Civil liability [CCPA § 409]

(a)   Liability established

Any person who fails to comply with any provision of this subchapter with respect to any other person shall be liable to such person in an amount equal to the sum of the amounts determined under each of the following paragraphs:

(1)   Actual damages

The greater of—

(A)   the amount of any actual damage sustained by such person as a result of such failure; or

(B)   any amount paid by the person to the credit repair organization.

(2)   Punitive damages

(A)   Individual actions

In the case of any action by an individual, such additional amount as the court may allow.

(B)   Class actions

In the case of a class action, the sum of—

(i)   the aggregate of the amount which the court may allow for each named plaintiff; and

(ii)   the aggregate of the amount which the court may allow for each other class member, without regard to any minimum individual recovery.

(3)   Attorneys' fees

In the case of any successful action to enforce any liability under paragraph (1) or (2), the costs of the action, together with reasonable attorneys' fees.

(b)   Factors to be considered in awarding punitive damages

In determining the amount of any liability of any credit repair organization under subsection (a)(2) of this section, the court shall consider, among other relevant factors—

(1)   the frequency and persistence of noncompliance by the credit repair organization;

(2)   the nature of the noncompliance;

(3)   the extent to which such noncompliance was intentional; and

(4)   in the case of any class action, the number of consumers adversely affected.

(Pub.L. 90–321, Title IV, § 409, as added Pub.L. 104–208, Div. A, Title II, § 2451, Sept. 30, 1996, 110 Stat. 3009–459.)

§ 1679h.   Administrative enforcement [CCPA § 410]

(a)   In general

Compliance with the requirements imposed under this subchapter with respect to credit repair organizations shall be enforced under the Federal Trade Commission Act [15 U.S.C.A. § 41 et seq.] by the Federal Trade Commission.

(b)   Violations of this subchapter treated as violations of Federal Trade Commission Act

(1)   In general

For the purpose of the exercise by the Federal Trade Commission of the Commission's functions and powers under the Federal Trade Commission Act [15 U.S.C.A. § 41 et seq.], any violation of any requirement or prohibition imposed under this subchapter with respect to credit repair organizations shall constitute an unfair or deceptive act or practice in commerce in violation of section 5(a) of the Federal Trade Commission Act [15 U.S.C.A. § 45(a)].

(2) Enforcement authority under other law

All functions and powers of the Federal Trade Commission under the Federal Trade Commission Act [15 U.S.C.A. § 41 et seq.] shall be available to the Commission to enforce compliance with this subchapter by any person subject to enforcement by the Federal Trade Commission pursuant to this subsection, including the power to enforce the provisions of this subchapter in the same manner as if the violation had been a violation of any Federal Trade Commission trade regulation rule, without regard to whether the credit repair organization—

    (A) is engaged in commerce; or

    (B) meets any other jurisdictional tests in the Federal Trade Commission Act [15 U.S.C.A. § 41 et seq.].

(c) State action for violations

(1) Authority of States

In addition to such other remedies as are provided under State law, whenever the chief law enforcement officer of a State, or an official or agency designated by a State, has reason to believe that any person has violated or is violating this subchapter, the State—

    (A) may bring an action to enjoin such violation;

    (B) may bring an action on behalf of its residents to recover damages for which the person is liable to such residents under section 1679g of this title as a result of the violation; and

    (C) in the case of any successful action under subparagraph (A) or (B), shall be awarded the costs of the action and reasonable attorney fees as determined by the court.

(2) Rights of Commission

    (A) Notice to Commission

The State shall serve prior written notice of any civil action under paragraph (1) upon the Federal Trade Commission and provide the Commission with a copy of its complaint, except in any case where such prior notice is not feasible, in which case the State shall serve such notice immediately upon instituting such action.

    (B) Intervention

The Commission shall have the right—

    (i) to intervene in any action referred to in subparagraph (A);

    (ii) upon so intervening, to be heard on all matters arising in the action; and

    (iii) to file petitions for appeal.

(3) Investigatory powers

For purposes of bringing any action under this subsection, nothing in this subsection shall prevent the chief law enforcement officer, or an official or agency designated by a State, from exercising the powers conferred on the chief law enforcement officer or such official by the laws of such State to conduct investigations or to administer oaths or affirmations or to compel the attendance of witnesses or the production of documentary and other evidence.

(4) Limitation

Whenever the Federal Trade Commission has instituted a civil action for violation of this subchapter, no State may, during the pendency of such action, bring an action under this section against any defendant named in the complaint of the Commission for any violation of this subchapter that is alleged in that complaint.

(Pub.L. 90–321, Title IV, § 410, as added Pub.L. 104–208, Div. A, Title II, § 2451, Sept. 30, 1996, 110 Stat. 3009–459.)

§ 1679i.   Statute of limitations [CCPA § 411]

Any action to enforce any liability under this subchapter may be brought before the later of—

   (1)   the end of the 5-year period beginning on the date of the occurrence of the violation involved; or

   (2)   in any case in which any credit repair organization has materially and willfully misrepresented any information which—

      (A)   the credit repair organization is required, by any provision of this subchapter, to disclose to any consumer; and

      (B)   is material to the establishment of the credit repair organization's liability to the consumer under this subchapter,

the end of the 5-year period beginning on the date of the discovery by the consumer of the misrepresentation.

(Pub.L. 90–321, Title IV, § 411, as added Pub.L. 104–208, Div. A, Title II, § 2451, Sept. 30, 1996, 110 Stat. 3009–459.)

§ 1679j.   Relation to State law [CCPA § 412]

This subchapter shall not annul, alter, affect, or exempt any person subject to the provisions of this subchapter from complying with any law of any State except to the extent that such law is inconsistent with any provision of this subchapter, and then only to the extent of the inconsistency.

(Pub.L. 90–321, Title IV, § 412, as added Pub.L. 104–208, Div. A, Title II, § 2451, Sept. 30, 1996, 110 Stat. 3009–459.)

SUBCHAPTER III—CREDIT REPORTING AGENCIES

§ 1681.   Congressional findings and statement of purpose [CCPA § 602]

(a)   Accuracy and fairness of credit reporting

The Congress makes the following findings:

   (1)   The banking system is dependent upon fair and accurate credit reporting. Inaccurate credit reports directly impair the efficiency of the banking system, and unfair credit reporting methods undermine the public confidence which is essential to the continued functioning of the banking system.

   (2)   An elaborate mechanism has been developed for investigating and evaluating the credit worthiness,[1] credit standing, credit capacity, character, and general reputation of consumers.

   (3)   Consumer reporting agencies have assumed a vital role in assembling and evaluating consumer credit and other information on consumers.

   (4)   There is a need to insure that consumer reporting agencies exercise their grave responsibilities with fairness, impartiality, and a respect for the consumer's right to privacy.

(b)   Reasonable procedures

It is the purpose of this subchapter to require that consumer reporting agencies adopt reasonable procedures for meeting the needs of commerce for consumer credit, personnel, insurance, and other information in a manner which is fair and equitable to the consumer, with regard to the confidentiality, accuracy, relevancy, and proper utilization of such information in accordance with the requirements of this subchapter.

(Pub.L. 90–321, Title VI, § 602, as added Pub.L. 91–508, Title VI, § 601, Oct. 26, 1970, 84 Stat. 1128.)

---

[1]   So in original. Probably should be "creditworthiness".

§ 1681a.   **Definitions; rules of construction [CCPA § 603]**

(a)   Definitions and rules of construction set forth in this section are applicable for the purposes of this subchapter.

(b)   The term "person" means any individual, partnership, corporation, trust, estate, cooperative, association, government or governmental subdivision or agency, or other entity.

(c)   The term "consumer" means an individual.

(d)   Consumer report.

(1)   In general.

The term "consumer report" means any written, oral, or other communication of any information by a consumer reporting agency bearing on a consumer's credit worthiness[1], credit standing, credit capacity, character, general reputation, personal characteristics, or mode of living which is used or expected to be used or collected in whole or in part for the purpose of serving as a factor in establishing the consumer's eligibility for—

(A)   credit or insurance to be used primarily for personal, family, or household purposes;

(B)   employment purposes; or

(C)   any other purpose authorized under section 1681b of this title.

(2)   Exclusions.

Except as provided in paragraph (3), the term "consumer report" does not include—

(A)   subject to section 1681s–3 of this title, any—

(i)   report containing information solely as to transactions or experiences between the consumer and the person making the report;

(ii)   communication of that information among persons related by common ownership or affiliated by corporate control; or

(iii)   communication of other information among persons related by common ownership or affiliated by corporate control, if it is clearly and conspicuously disclosed to the consumer that the information may be communicated among such persons and the consumer is given the opportunity, before the time that the information is initially communicated, to direct that such information not be communicated among such persons;

(B)   any authorization or approval of a specific extension of credit directly or indirectly by the issuer of a credit card or similar device;

(C)   any report in which a person who has been requested by a third party to make a specific extension of credit directly or indirectly to a consumer conveys his or her decision with respect to such request, if the third party advises the consumer of the name and address of the person to whom the request was made, and such person makes the disclosures to the consumer required under section 1681m of this title; or

(D)   a communication described in subsection (*o*) or (x) of this section.

(3)   Restriction on sharing of medical information

Except for information or any communication of information disclosed as provided in section 1681b(g)(3) of this title, the exclusions in paragraph (2) shall not apply with respect to information disclosed to any person related by common ownership or affiliated by corporate control, if the information is—

(A)   medical information;

(B)   an individualized list or description based on the payment transactions of the consumer for medical products or services; or

    (C) an aggregate list of identified consumers based on payment transactions for medical products or services.

    (e) The term "investigative consumer report" means a consumer report or portion thereof in which information on a consumer's character, general reputation, personal characteristics, or mode of living is obtained through personal interviews with neighbors, friends, or associates of the consumer reported on or with others with whom he is acquainted or who may have knowledge concerning any such items of information. However, such information shall not include specific factual information on a consumer's credit record obtained directly from a creditor of the consumer or from a consumer reporting agency when such information was obtained directly from a creditor of the consumer or from the consumer.

    (f) The term "consumer reporting agency" means any person which, for monetary fees, dues, or on a cooperative nonprofit basis, regularly engages in whole or in part in the practice of assembling or evaluating consumer credit information or other information on consumers for the purpose of furnishing consumer reports to third parties, and which uses any means or facility of interstate commerce for the purpose of preparing or furnishing consumer reports.

    (g) The term "file", when used in connection with information on any consumer, means all of the information on that consumer recorded and retained by a consumer reporting agency regardless of how the information is stored.

    (h) The term "employment purposes" when used in connection with a consumer report means a report used for the purpose of evaluating a consumer for employment, promotion, reassignment or retention as an employee.

(i)   **Medical information**

The term "medical information"—

    (1) means information or data, whether oral or recorded, in any form or medium, created by or derived from a health care provider or the consumer, that relates to—

        (A) the past, present, or future physical, mental, or behavioral health or condition of an individual;

        (B) the provision of health care to an individual; or

        (C) the payment for the provision of health care to an individual.[1]

    (2) does not include the age or gender of a consumer, demographic information about the consumer, including a consumer's residence address or e-mail address, or any other information about a consumer that does not relate to the physical, mental, or behavioral health or condition of a consumer, including the existence or value of any insurance policy.

(j)   **Definitions relating to child support obligations**

(1)   **Overdue support**

The term "overdue support" has the meaning given to such term in section 666(e) of Title 42.

(2)   **State or local child support enforcement agency**

The term "State or local child support enforcement agency" means a State or local agency which administers a State or local program for establishing and enforcing child support obligations.

(k)   **Adverse action.**

(1)   **Actions included.**

The term "adverse action"—

    (A) has the same meaning as in section 1691(d)(6) of this title; and

    (B) means—

---

[1] So in original. The period probably should be "; and".

(i) a denial or cancellation of, an increase in any charge for, or a reduction or other adverse or unfavorable change in the terms of coverage or amount of, any insurance, existing or applied for, in connection with the underwriting of insurance;

(ii) a denial of employment or any other decision for employment purposes that adversely affects any current or prospective employee;

(iii) a denial or cancellation of, an increase in any charge for, or any other adverse or unfavorable change in the terms of, any license or benefit described in section 1681b(a)(3)(D) of this title; and

(iv) an action taken or determination that is—

(I) made in connection with an application that was made by, or a transaction that was initiated by, any consumer, or in connection with a review of an account under section 1681b(a)(3)(F)(ii) of this title; and

(II) adverse to the interests of the consumer.

(2) Applicable findings, decisions, commentary, and orders.

For purposes of any determination of whether an action is an adverse action under paragraph (1)(A), all appropriate final findings, decisions, commentary, and orders issued under section 1691(d)(6) of this title by the Bureau or any court shall apply.

(*l*) Firm offer of credit or insurance.

The term "firm offer of credit or insurance" means any offer of credit or insurance to a consumer that will be honored if the consumer is determined, based on information in a consumer report on the consumer, to meet the specific criteria used to select the consumer for the offer, except that the offer may be further conditioned on one or more of the following:

(1) The consumer being determined, based on information in the consumer's application for the credit or insurance, to meet specific criteria bearing on credit worthiness or insurability, as applicable, that are established—

(A) before selection of the consumer for the offer; and

(B) for the purpose of determining whether to extend credit or insurance pursuant to the offer.

(2) Verification

(A) that the consumer continues to meet the specific criteria used to select the consumer for the offer, by using information in a consumer report on the consumer, information in the consumer's application for the credit or insurance, or other information bearing on the credit worthiness or insurability of the consumer; or

(B) of the information in the consumer's application for the credit or insurance, to determine that the consumer meets the specific criteria bearing on credit worthiness[1] or insurability.

(3) The consumer furnishing any collateral that is a requirement for the extension of the credit or insurance that was—

(A) established before selection of the consumer for the offer of credit or insurance; and

(B) disclosed to the consumer in the offer of credit or insurance.

(m) credit or insurance transaction that is not initiated by the consumer.

The term "credit or insurance transaction that is not initiated by the consumer" does not include the use of a consumer report by a person with which the consumer has an account or insurance policy, for purposes of—

---

[1] So in original. Probably should be "creditworthiness".

    (1)   reviewing the account or insurance policy; or

    (2)   collecting the account.

(n)   State.

The term "State" means any State, the Commonwealth of Puerto Rico, the District of Columbia, and any territory or possession of the United States.

(o)   Excluded communications.

A communication is described in this subsection if it is a communication—

    (1)   that, but for subsection (d)(2)(D) of this section, would be an investigative consumer report;

    (2)   that is made to a prospective employer for the purpose of—

        (A)   procuring an employee for the employer; or

        (B)   procuring an opportunity for a natural person to work for the employer;

    (3)   that is made by a person who regularly performs such procurement;

    (4)   that is not used by any person for any purpose other than a purpose described in subparagraph (A) or (B) of paragraph (2); and

    (5)   with respect to which—

        (A)   the consumer who is the subject of the communication—

            (i)   consents orally or in writing to the nature and scope of the communication, before the collection of any information for the purpose of making the communication;

            (ii)   consents orally or in writing to the making of the communication to a prospective employer, before the making of the communication; and

            (iii)   in the case of consent under clause (i) or (ii) given orally, is provided written confirmation of that consent by the person making the communication, not later than 3 business days after the receipt of the consent by that person;

        (B)   the person who makes the communication does not, for the purpose of making the communication, make any inquiry that if made by a prospective employer of the consumer who is the subject of the communication would violate any applicable Federal or State equal employment opportunity law or regulation; and

        (C)   the person who makes the communication—

            (i)   discloses in writing to the consumer who is the subject of the communication, not later than 5 business days after receiving any request from the consumer for such disclosure, the nature and substance of all information in the consumer's file at the time of the request, except that the sources of any information that is acquired solely for use in making the communication and is actually used for no other purpose, need not be disclosed other than under appropriate discovery procedures in any court of competent jurisdiction in which an action is brought; and

            (ii)   notifies the consumer who is the subject of the communication, in writing, of the consumer's right to request the information described in clause (i).

(p)   Consumer reporting agency that compiles and maintains files on consumers on a nationwide basis.

The term "consumer reporting agency that compiles and maintains files on consumers on a nationwide basis" means a consumer reporting agency that regularly engages in the practice of assembling or evaluating, and maintaining, for the purpose of furnishing consumer reports to third parties bearing on a consumer's credit worthiness, credit standing, or credit capacity, each of the following regarding consumers residing nationwide:

    (1)   Public record information.

(2)   credit account information from persons who furnish that information regularly and in the ordinary course of business.

(q)   Definitions relating to fraud alerts

(1)   Active duty military consumer

The term "active duty military consumer" means a consumer in military service who—

(A)   is on active duty (as defined in section 101(d)(1) of Title 10) or is a reservist performing duty under a call or order to active duty under a provision of law referred to in section 101(a)(13) of Title 10; and

(B)   is assigned to service away from the usual duty station of the consumer.

(2)   Fraud alert; active duty alert

The terms "fraud alert" and "active duty alert" mean a statement in the file of a consumer that—

(A)   notifies all prospective users of a consumer report relating to the consumer that the consumer may be a victim of fraud, including identity theft, or is an active duty military consumer, as applicable; and

(B)   is presented in a manner that facilitates a clear and conspicuous view of the statement described in subparagraph (A) by any person requesting such consumer report.

(3)   Identity theft

The term "identity theft" means a fraud committed using the identifying information of another person, subject to such further definition as the Bureau may prescribe, by regulation.

(4)   Identity theft report

The term "identity theft report" has the meaning given that term by rule of the Bureau, and means, at a minimum, a report—

(A)   that alleges an identity theft;

(B)   that is a copy of an official, valid report filed by a consumer with an appropriate Federal, State, or local law enforcement agency, including the United States Postal Inspection Service, or such other government agency deemed appropriate by the Bureau; and

(C)   the filing of which subjects the person filing the report to criminal penalties relating to the filing of false information if, in fact, the information in the report is false.

(5)   New credit plan

The term "new credit plan" means a new account under an open end credit plan (as defined in section 1602(i) of this title) or a new credit transaction not under an open end credit plan.

(r)   credit and debit related terms

(1)   Card issuer

The term "card issuer" means—

(A)   a credit card issuer, in the case of a credit card; and

(B)   a debit card issuer, in the case of a debit card.

(2)   credit card

The term "credit card" has the same meaning as in section 1602 of this title.

(3)   Debit card

The term "debit card" means any card issued by a financial institution to a consumer for use in initiating an electronic fund transfer from the account of the consumer at such financial institution, for the purpose of transferring money between accounts or obtaining money, property, labor, or services.

(4) Account and electronic fund transfer

The terms "account" and "electronic fund transfer" have the same meanings as in section 1693a of this title.

(5) credit and creditor

The terms "credit" and "creditor" have the same meanings as in section 1691a of this title.

(s) Federal banking agency

The term "Federal banking agency" has the same meaning as in section 1813 of Title 12.

(t) Financial institution

The term "financial institution" means a State or National bank, a State or Federal savings and loan association, a mutual savings bank, a State or Federal credit union, or any other person that, directly or indirectly, holds a transaction account (as defined in section 461(b) of Title 12) belonging to a consumer.

(u) Reseller

The term "reseller" means a consumer reporting agency that—

(1) assembles and merges information contained in the database of another consumer reporting agency or multiple consumer reporting agencies concerning any consumer for purposes of furnishing such information to any third party, to the extent of such activities; and

(2) does not maintain a database of the assembled or merged information from which new consumer reports are produced.

(v) Commission

The term "Commission" means the Bureau.[2]

(w) The term "Bureau" means the Bureau of Consumer Financial Protection.

(x) Nationwide specialty consumer reporting agency

The term "nationwide specialty consumer reporting agency" means a consumer reporting agency that compiles and maintains files on consumers on a nationwide basis relating to—

(1) medical records or payments;

(2) residential or tenant history;

(3) check writing history;

(4) employment history; or

(5) insurance claims.

(y) Exclusion of certain communications for employee investigations

(1) Communications described in this subsection

A communication is described in this subsection if—

(A) but for subsection (d)(2)(D) of this section, the communication would be a consumer report;

(B) the communication is made to an employer in connection with an investigation of—

(i) suspected misconduct relating to employment; or

(ii) compliance with Federal, State, or local laws and regulations, the rules of a self-regulatory organization, or any preexisting written policies of the employer;

(C) the communication is not made for the purpose of investigating a consumer's credit worthiness, credit standing, or credit capacity; and

---

[2] So in original.

(D) the communication is not provided to any person except—

(i) to the employer or an agent of the employer;

(ii) to any Federal or State officer, agency, or department, or any officer, agency, or department of a unit of general local government;

(iii) to any self-regulatory organization with regulatory authority over the activities of the employer or employee;

(iv) as otherwise required by law; or

(v) pursuant to section 1681f of this title.

(2) Subsequent disclosure

After taking any adverse action based in whole or in part on a communication described in paragraph (1), the employer shall disclose to the consumer a summary containing the nature and substance of the communication upon which the adverse action is based, except that the sources of information acquired solely for use in preparing what would be but for subsection (d)(2)(D) of this section an investigative consumer report need not be disclosed.

(3) Self-regulatory organization defined

For purposes of this subsection, the term "self-regulatory organization" includes any self-regulatory organization (as defined in section 78c(a)(26) of this title), any entity established under title I of the Sarbanes-Oxley Act of 2002, any board of trade designated by the Commodity Futures Trading Commission, and any futures association registered with such Commission.

(Pub.L. 90–321, Title VI, § 603, as added Pub.L. 91–508, Title VI, § 601, Oct. 26, 1970, 84 Stat. 1128, and amended Pub.L. 102–537, § 2(b), Oct. 27, 1992, 106 Stat. 3531; Pub.L. 104–208, Div. A, Title II, § 2402(a) to (g), Sept. 30, 1996, 110 Stat. 3009–428; Pub.L. 105–347, § 6(1) to (3), Nov. 2, 1998, 112 Stat. 3211; Pub.L. 108–159, Title I, § 111, Title II, § 214(c)(1), Title IV, § 411(b), (c), Title VI, § 611, Dec. 4, 2003, 117 Stat. 1954, 1983, 2001, 2010; Pub.L. 111–203, Title X, § 1088(a)(1), (2)(A), (C), (3), July 21, 2010, 124 Stat. 2086, 2087.)

§ 1681b. Permissible purposes of consumer reports [CCPA § 604]

(a) In general

Subject to subsection (c) of this section, any consumer reporting agency may furnish a consumer report under the following circumstances and no other:

(1) In response to the order of a court having jurisdiction to issue such an order, or a subpoena issued in connection with proceedings before a Federal grand jury.

(2) In accordance with the written instructions of the consumer to whom it relates.

(3) To a person which it has reason to believe—

(A) intends to use the information in connection with a credit transaction involving the consumer on whom the information is to be furnished and involving the extension of credit to, or review or collection of an account of, the consumer; or

(B) intends to use the information for employment purposes; or

(C) intends to use the information in connection with the underwriting of insurance involving the consumer; or

(D) intends to use the information in connection with a determination of the consumer's eligibility for a license or other benefit granted by a governmental instrumentality required by law to consider an applicant's financial responsibility or status; or

(E) intends to use the information, as a potential investor or servicer, or current insurer, in connection with a valuation of, or an assessment of the credit or prepayment risks associated with, an existing credit obligation; or

(F) otherwise has a legitimate business need for the information—

(i)   in connection with a business transaction that is initiated by the consumer; or

(ii)   to review an account to determine whether the consumer continues to meet the terms of the account.

(G)   executive departments and agencies in connection with the issuance of government-sponsored individually-billed travel charge cards.

(4)   In response to a request by the head of a State or local child support enforcement agency (or a State or local government official authorized by the head of such an agency), if the person making the request certifies to the consumer reporting agency that—

(A)   the consumer report is needed for the purpose of establishing an individual's capacity to make child support payments, determining the appropriate level of such payments, or enforcing a child support order, award, agreement, or judgment;

(B)   the parentage of the consumer for the child to which the obligation relates has been established or acknowledged by the consumer in accordance with State laws under which the obligation arises (if required by those laws); and

(C)   the consumer report will be kept confidential, will be used solely for a purpose described in subparagraph (A), and will not be used in connection with any other civil, administrative, or criminal proceeding, or for any other purpose.

(5)   To an agency administering a State plan under section 654 of Title 42 for use to set an initial or modified child support award.

(6)   To the Federal Deposit Insurance Corporation or the National Credit Union Administration as part of its preparation for its appointment or as part of its exercise of powers, as conservator, receiver, or liquidating agent for an insured depository institution or insured credit union under the Federal Deposit Insurance Act or the Federal Credit Union Act, or other applicable Federal or State law, or in connection with the resolution or liquidation of a failed or failing insured depository institution or insured credit union, as applicable.

(b)   Conditions for furnishing and using consumer reports for employment purposes

(1)   Certification from user

A consumer reporting agency may furnish a consumer report for employment purposes only if—

(A)   the person who obtains such report from the agency certifies to the agency that—

(i)   the person has complied with paragraph (2) with respect to the consumer report, and the person will comply with paragraph (3) with respect to the consumer report if paragraph (3) becomes applicable; and

(ii)   information from the consumer report will not be used in violation of any applicable Federal or State equal employment opportunity law or regulation; and

(B)   the consumer reporting agency provides with the report, or has previously provided, a summary of the consumer's rights under this subchapter, as prescribed by the Bureau under section 1681g(c)(3) of this title.

(2)   Disclosure to consumer

(A)   In general

Except as provided in subparagraph (B), a person may not procure a consumer report, or cause a consumer report to be procured, for employment purposes with respect to any consumer, unless—

(i)   a clear and conspicuous disclosure has been made in writing to the consumer at any time before the report is procured or caused to be procured, in a document that consists solely of the disclosure, that a consumer report may be obtained for employment purposes; and

(ii) the consumer has authorized in writing (which authorization may be made on the document referred to in clause (i)) the procurement of the report by that person.

(B) Application by mail, telephone, computer, or other similar means

If a consumer described in subparagraph (C) applies for employment by mail, telephone, computer, or other similar means, at any time before a consumer report is procured or caused to be procured in connection with that application—

(i) the person who procures the consumer report on the consumer for employment purposes shall provide to the consumer, by oral, written, or electronic means, notice that a consumer report may be obtained for employment purposes, and a summary of the consumer's rights under section 1681m(a)(3) of this title; and

(ii) the consumer shall have consented, orally, in writing, or electronically to the procurement of the report by that person.

(C) Scope

Subparagraph (B) shall apply to a person procuring a consumer report on a consumer in connection with the consumer's application for employment only if—

(i) the consumer is applying for a position over which the Secretary of Transportation has the power to establish qualifications and maximum hours of service pursuant to the provisions of section 31502 of Title 49, or a position subject to safety regulation by a State transportation agency; and

(ii) as of the time at which the person procures the report or causes the report to be procured the only interaction between the consumer and the person in connection with that employment application has been by mail, telephone, computer, or other similar means.

(3) Conditions on use for adverse actions

(A) In general

Except as provided in subparagraph (B), in using a consumer report for employment purposes, before taking any adverse action based in whole or in part on the report, the person intending to take such adverse action shall provide to the consumer to whom the report relates—

(i) a copy of the report; and

(ii) a description in writing of the rights of the consumer under this subchapter, as prescribed by the Bureau under section 1681g(c)(3) of this title.

(B) Application by mail, telephone, computer, or other similar means

(i) If a consumer described in subparagraph (C) applies for employment by mail, telephone, computer, or other similar means, and if a person who has procured a consumer report on the consumer for employment purposes takes adverse action on the employment application based in whole or in part on the report, then the person must provide to the consumer to whom the report relates, in lieu of the notices required under subparagraph (A) of this section and under section 1681m(a) of this title, within 3 business days of taking such action, an oral, written or electronic notification—

(I) that adverse action has been taken based in whole or in part on a consumer report received from a consumer reporting agency;

(II) of the name, address and telephone number of the consumer reporting agency that furnished the consumer report (including a toll-free telephone number established by the agency if the agency compiles and maintains files on consumers on a nationwide basis);

(III) that the consumer reporting agency did not make the decision to take the adverse action and is unable to provide to the consumer the specific reasons why the adverse action was taken; and

1483

(IV) that the consumer may, upon providing proper identification, request a free copy of a report and may dispute with the consumer reporting agency the accuracy or completeness of any information in a report.

(ii) If, under clause (B)(i)(IV), the consumer requests a copy of a consumer report from the person who procured the report, then, within 3 business days of receiving the consumer's request, together with proper identification, the person must send or provide to the consumer a copy of a report and a copy of the consumer's rights as prescribed by the Bureau under section 1681g(c)(3) of this title.

(C) Scope

Subparagraph (B) shall apply to a person procuring a consumer report on a consumer in connection with the consumer's application for employment only if—

(i) the consumer is applying for a position over which the Secretary of Transportation has the power to establish qualifications and maximum hours of service pursuant to the provisions of section 31502 of Title 49, or a position subject to safety regulation by a State transportation agency; and

(ii) as of the time at which the person procures the report or causes the report to be procured the only interaction between the consumer and the person in connection with that employment application has been by mail, telephone, computer, or other similar means.

(4) Exception for national security investigations

(A) In general

In the case of an agency or department of the United States Government which seeks to obtain and use a consumer report for employment purposes, paragraph (3) shall not apply to any adverse action by such agency or department which is based in part on such consumer report, if the head of such agency or department makes a written finding that—

(i) the consumer report is relevant to a national security investigation of such agency or department;

(ii) the investigation is within the jurisdiction of such agency or department;

(iii) there is reason to believe that compliance with paragraph (3) will—

(I) endanger the life or physical safety of any person;

(II) result in flight from prosecution;

(III) result in the destruction of, or tampering with, evidence relevant to the investigation;

(IV) result in the intimidation of a potential witness relevant to the investigation;

(V) result in the compromise of classified information; or

(VI) otherwise seriously jeopardize or unduly delay the investigation or another official proceeding.

(B) Notification of consumer upon conclusion of investigation

Upon the conclusion of a national security investigation described in subparagraph (A), or upon the determination that the exception under subparagraph (A) is no longer required for the reasons set forth in such subparagraph, the official exercising the authority in such subparagraph shall provide to the consumer who is the subject of the consumer report with regard to which such finding was made—

(i) a copy of such consumer report with any classified information redacted as necessary;

(ii) notice of any adverse action which is based, in part, on the consumer report; and

(iii) the identification with reasonable specificity of the nature of the investigation for which the consumer report was sought.

(C) Delegation by head of agency or department

For purposes of subparagraphs (A) and (B), the head of any agency or department of the United States Government may delegate his or her authorities under this paragraph to an official of such agency or department who has personnel security responsibilities and is a member of the Senior Executive Service or equivalent civilian or military rank.

(D) Definitions

For purposes of this paragraph, the following definitions shall apply:

(i) Classified information.—The term "classified information" means information that is protected from unauthorized disclosure under Executive Order No. 12958 or successor orders.

(ii) National security investigation.—The term "national security investigation" means any official inquiry by an agency or department of the United States Government to determine the eligibility of a consumer to receive access or continued access to classified information or to determine whether classified information has been lost or compromised.

(c) Furnishing reports in connection with credit or insurance transactions that are not initiated by the consumer

(1) In general

A consumer reporting agency may furnish a consumer report relating to any consumer pursuant to subparagraph (A) or (C) of subsection (a)(3) of this section in connection with any credit or insurance transaction that is not initiated by the consumer only if—

(A) the consumer authorizes the agency to provide such report to such person; or

(B)(i) the transaction consists of a firm offer of credit or insurance;

(ii) the consumer reporting agency has complied with subsection (e) of this section;

(iii) there is not in effect an election by the consumer, made in accordance with subsection (e) of this section, to have the consumer's name and address excluded from lists of names provided by the agency pursuant to this paragraph; and

(iv) the consumer report does not contain a date of birth that shows that the consumer has not attained the age of 21, or, if the date of birth on the consumer report shows that the consumer has not attained the age of 21, such consumer consents to the consumer reporting agency to such furnishing.

(2) Limits on information received under paragraph (1)(B)

A person may receive pursuant to paragraph (1)(B) only—

(A) the name and address of a consumer;

(B) an identifier that is not unique to the consumer and that is used by the person solely for the purpose of verifying the identity of the consumer; and

(C) other information pertaining to a consumer that does not identify the relationship or experience of the consumer with respect to a particular creditor or other entity.

(3) Information regarding inquiries

Except as provided in section 1681g(a)(5) of this title, a consumer reporting agency shall not furnish to any person a record of inquiries in connection with a credit or insurance transaction that is not initiated by a consumer.

(d) Reserved

(e) Election of consumer to be excluded from lists

(1) In general

A consumer may elect to have the consumer's name and address excluded from any list provided by a consumer reporting agency under subsection (c)(1)(B) of this section in connection with a credit or insurance transaction that is not initiated by the consumer, by notifying the agency in accordance with paragraph (2) that the consumer does not consent to any use of a consumer report relating to the consumer in connection with any credit or insurance transaction that is not initiated by the consumer.

(2) Manner of notification

A consumer shall notify a consumer reporting agency under paragraph (1)—

(A) through the notification system maintained by the agency under paragraph (5); or

(B) by submitting to the agency a signed notice of election form issued by the agency for purposes of this subparagraph.

(3) Response of agency after notification through system

Upon receipt of notification of the election of a consumer under paragraph (1) through the notification system maintained by the agency under paragraph (5), a consumer reporting agency shall—

(A) inform the consumer that the election is effective only for the 5-year period following the election if the consumer does not submit to the agency a signed notice of election form issued by the agency for purposes of paragraph (2)(B); and

(B) provide to the consumer a notice of election form, if requested by the consumer, not later than 5 business days after receipt of the notification of the election through the system established under paragraph (5), in the case of a request made at the time the consumer provides notification through the system.

(4) Effectiveness of election

An election of a consumer under paragraph (1)—

(A) shall be effective with respect to a consumer reporting agency beginning 5 business days after the date on which the consumer notifies the agency in accordance with paragraph (2);

(B) shall be effective with respect to a consumer reporting agency—

(i) subject to subparagraph (C), during the 5-year period beginning 5 business days after the date on which the consumer notifies the agency of the election, in the case of an election for which a consumer notifies the agency only in accordance with paragraph (2)(A); or

(ii) until the consumer notifies the agency under subparagraph (C), in the case of an election for which a consumer notifies the agency in accordance with paragraph (2)(B);

(C) shall not be effective after the date on which the consumer notifies the agency, through the notification system established by the agency under paragraph (5), that the election is no longer effective; and

(D) shall be effective with respect to each affiliate of the agency.

(5) Notification system

(A) In general

Each consumer reporting agency that, under subsection (c)(1)(B) of this section, furnishes a consumer report in connection with a credit or insurance transaction that is not initiated by a consumer, shall—

(i)   establish and maintain a notification system, including a toll-free telephone number, which permits any consumer whose consumer report is maintained by the agency to notify the agency, with appropriate identification, of the consumer's election to have the consumer's name and address excluded from any such list of names and addresses provided by the agency for such a transaction; and

(ii)   publish by not later than 365 days after September 30, 1996, and not less than annually thereafter, in a publication of general circulation in the area served by the agency—

(I)   a notification that information in consumer files maintained by the agency may be used in connection with such transactions; and

(II)   the address and toll-free telephone number for consumers to use to notify the agency of the consumer's election under clause (i).

(B)   Establishment and maintenance as compliance

Establishment and maintenance of a notification system (including a toll-free telephone number) and publication by a consumer reporting agency on the agency's own behalf and on behalf of any of its affiliates in accordance with this paragraph is deemed to be compliance with this paragraph by each of those affiliates.

(6)   Notification system by agencies that operate nationwide

Each consumer reporting agency that compiles and maintains files on consumers on a nationwide basis shall establish and maintain a notification system for purposes of paragraph (5) jointly with other such consumer reporting agencies.

(f)   Certain use or obtaining of information prohibited

A person shall not use or obtain a consumer report for any purpose unless—

(1) the consumer report is obtained for a purpose for which the consumer report is authorized to be furnished under this section; and

(2) the purpose is certified in accordance with section 1681e of this title by a prospective user of the report through a general or specific certification.

(g)   Protection of medical information

(1)   Limitation on consumer reporting agencies

A consumer reporting agency shall not furnish for employment purposes, or in connection with a credit or insurance transaction, a consumer report that contains medical information (other than medical contact information treated in the manner required under section 605(a)(6) of this title) about a consumer, unless—

(A) if furnished in connection with an insurance transaction, the consumer affirmatively consents to the furnishing of the report;

(B) if furnished for employment purposes or in connection with a credit transaction—

(i)   the information to be furnished is relevant to process or effect the employment or credit transaction; and

(ii)   the consumer provides specific written consent for the furnishing of the report that describes in clear and conspicuous language the use for which the information will be furnished; or

(C) the information to be furnished pertains solely to transactions, accounts, or balances relating to debts arising from the receipt of medical services, products, or devises, where such information, other than account status or amounts, is restricted or reported using codes that do not identify, or do not provide information sufficient to infer, the specific provider or the nature of such services, products, or devices, as provided in section 1681c(a)(6) of this title.

(2) Limitation on creditors

Except as permitted pursuant to paragraph (3)(C) or regulations prescribed under paragraph (5)(A), a creditor shall not obtain or use medical information (other than medical information treated in the manner required under section 605(a)(6) of this title) pertaining to a consumer in connection with any determination of the consumer's eligibility, or continued eligibility, for credit.

(3) Actions authorized by Federal law, insurance activities and regulatory determinations

Section 1681a(d)(3) of this title shall not be construed so as to treat information or any communication of information as a consumer report if the information or communication is disclosed—

(A) in connection with the business of insurance or annuities, including the activities described in section 18B of the model Privacy of Consumer Financial and Health Information Regulation issued by the National Association of Insurance Commissioners (as in effect on January 1, 2003);

(B) for any purpose permitted without authorization under the Standards for Individually Identifiable Health Information promulgated by the Department of Health and Human Services pursuant to the Health Insurance Portability and Accountability Act of 1996, or referred to under section 1179 of such Act, or described in section 6802(e) of this title; or

(C) as otherwise determined to be necessary and appropriate, by regulation or order, by the Bureau or the applicable state insurance authority (with respect to any persons engaged in providing insurance or annuities).

(4) Limitation on redisclosure of medical information

Any person that receives medical information pursuant to paragraph (1) or (3) shall not disclose such information to any other person, except as necessary to carry out the purpose for which the information was initially disclosed, or as otherwise permitted by statute, regulation, or order.

(5) Regulations and effective date for paragraph (2)

(A)[1] Regulations required

The Bureau may, after notice and opportunity for comment, prescribe regulations that permit transactions under paragraph (2) that are determined to be necessary and appropriate to protect legitimate operational, transactional, risk, consumer, and other needs (and which shall include permitting actions necessary for administrative verification purposes), consistent with the intent of paragraph (2) to restrict the use of medical information for inappropriate purposes.

(6) Coordination with other laws

No provision of this subsection shall be construed as altering, affecting, or superseding the applicability of any other provision of Federal law relating to medical confidentiality.

(Pub.L. 90–321, Title VI, § 604, as added Pub.L. 91–508, Title VI, § 601, Oct. 26, 1970, 84 Stat. 1129, and amended Pub.L. 101–73, Title IX, § 964(c), Aug. 9, 1989, 103 Stat. 506; Pub.L. 104–193, Title III, § 352, Aug. 22, 1996, 110 Stat. 2240; Pub.L. 104–208, Div. A, Title II, §§ 2403, 2404(a), (b), 2405, Sept. 30, 1996, 110 Stat. 3009–430, 3009–433, 3009–434; Pub.L. 105–107, Title III, § 311(a), Nov. 20, 1997, 111 Stat. 2255; Pub.L. 105–347, §§ 2, 3, 6(4), Nov. 2, 1998, 112 Stat. 3208, 3210, 3211; Pub.L. 107–306, Title VIII, § 811(b)(8)(A), Nov. 27, 2002, 116 Stat. 2426; Pub.L. 108–159, Title II, § 213(c), Title IV, § 411(a), (f), Title VIII, § 811(b), Dec. 4, 2003, 117 Stat. 1979, 1999, 2003, 2011; Pub.L. 108–177, Title III, § 361(j), Dec. 13, 2003, 117 Stat. 2625; Pub.L. 109–351, Title VII, § 719, Oct. 13, 2006, 120 Stat. 1998; Pub.L. 110–161, Div. D, Title VII, § 743, Dec. 26, 2007, 121 Stat. 2032; Pub.L. 111–24, Title III, § 302, May 22, 2009, 123 Stat. 1748; Pub.L. 111–203, Title X, § 1088(a)(2)(A), (4), July 21, 2010, 124 Stat. 2087; Pub.L. 114–94, Div. G, Title LXXX § 80001, Dec. 4, 2015, 192 Stat. 1792.)

---

[1] So in original. No subpart (B) has been enacted.

§ 1681c. Requirements relating to information contained in consumer reports [CCPA § 605]

(a) Information excluded from consumer reports

Except as authorized under subsection (b) of this section, no consumer reporting agency may make any consumer report containing any of the following items of information:

(1) Cases under Title 11 or under the Bankruptcy Act that, from the date of entry of the order for relief or the date of adjudication, as the case may be, antedate the report by more than 10 years.

(2) Civil suits, civil judgments, and records of arrest that, from date of entry, antedate the report by more than seven years or until the governing statute of limitations has expired, whichever is the longer period.

(3) Paid tax liens which, from date of payment, antedate the report by more than seven years.

(4) Accounts placed for collection or charged to profit and loss which antedate the report by more than seven years.

(5) Any other adverse item of information, other than records of convictions of crimes which antedates the report by more than seven years.

(6) The name, address, and telephone number of any medical information furnisher that has notified the agency of its status, unless—

(A) such name, address, and telephone number are restricted or reported using codes that do not identify, or provide information sufficient to infer, the specific provider or the nature of such services, products, or devices to a person other than the consumer; or

(B) the report is being provided to an insurance company for a purpose relating to engaging in the business of insurance other than property and casualty insurance.

(b) Exempted cases

The provisions of paragraphs (1) through (5) of subsection (a) of this section are not applicable in the case of any consumer credit report to be used in connection with—

(1) a credit transaction involving, or which may reasonably be expected to involve, a principal amount of $150,000 or more;

(2) the underwriting of life insurance involving, or which may reasonably be expected to involve, a face amount of $150,000 or more; or

(3) the employment of any individual at an annual salary which equals, or which may reasonably be expected to equal $75,000, or more.

(c) Running of reporting period

(1) **In general.**—The 7-year period referred to in paragraphs (4) and (6) of subsection (a) of this section shall begin, with respect to any delinquent account that is placed for collection (internally or by referral to a third party, whichever is earlier), charged to profit and loss, or subjected to any similar action, upon the expiration of the 180-day period beginning on the date of the commencement of the delinquency which immediately preceded the collection activity, charge to profit and loss, or similar action.

(2) **Effective date.**—Paragraph (1) shall apply only to items of information added to the file of a consumer on or after the date that is 455 days after September 30, 1996.

(d) Information required to be disclosed

(1) Title 11 information

Any consumer reporting agency that furnishes a consumer report that contains information regarding any case involving the consumer that arises under Title 11 shall include in the report an identification of the chapter of such Title 11 under which such case arises if provided by the source of the information. If any case arising or filed under Title 11 is withdrawn by the consumer before a final judgment, the consumer reporting agency shall include in the report that such case or filing was withdrawn upon receipt of documentation certifying such withdrawal.

(2) Key factor in credit score information

Any consumer reporting agency that furnishes a consumer report that contains any credit score or any other risk score or predictor on any consumer shall include in the report a clear and conspicuous statement that a key factor (as defined in section 1681g(f)(2)(B) of this title) that adversely affected such score or predictor was the number of enquiries, if such a predictor was in fact a key factor that adversely affected such score. This paragraph shall not apply to a check services company, acting as such, which issues authorizations for the purpose of approving or processing negotiable instruments, electronic fund transfers, or similar methods of payments, but only to the extent that such company is engaged in such activities.

(e) Indication of closure of account by consumer

If a consumer reporting agency is notified pursuant to section 1681s–2(a)(4) of this title that a credit account of a consumer was voluntarily closed by the consumer, the agency shall indicate that fact in any consumer report that includes information related to the account.

(f) Indication of dispute by consumer

If a consumer reporting agency is notified pursuant to section 1681s–2(a)(3) of this title that information regarding a consumer who[1] was furnished to the agency is disputed by the consumer, the agency shall indicate that fact in each consumer report that includes the disputed information.

(g) Truncation of credit card and debit card numbers

(1) In general

Except as otherwise provided in this subsection, no person that accepts credit cards or debit cards for the transaction of business shall print more than the last 5 digits of the card number or the expiration date upon any receipt provided to the cardholder at the point of the sale or transaction.

(2) Limitation

This subsection shall apply only to receipts that are electronically printed, and shall not apply to transactions in which the sole means of recording a credit card or debit card account number is by handwriting or by an imprint or copy of the card.

(3) Effective date

This subsection shall become effective—

(A) 3 years after December 4, 2003, with respect to any cash register or other machine or device that electronically prints receipts for credit card or debit card transactions that is in use before January 1, 2005; and

(B) 1 year after December 4, 2003, with respect to any cash register or other machine or device that electronically prints receipts for credit card or debit card transactions that is first put into use on or after January 1, 2005.

(h) Notice of discrepancy in address

(1) In general

If a person has requested a consumer report relating to a consumer from a consumer reporting agency described in section 1681a(p) of this title, the request includes an address for the consumer that substantially differs from the addresses in the file of the consumer, and the agency provides a consumer report in response to the request, the consumer reporting agency shall notify the requester of the existence of the discrepancy.

---

[1]   So in original. Probably should be "which".

(2) Regulations

(A) Regulations required

The Bureau shall,,[2] in consultation with the Federal banking agencies, the National Credit Union Administration, and the Federal Trade Commission,,[2] prescribe regulations providing guidance regarding reasonable policies and procedures that a user of a consumer report should employ when such user has received a notice of discrepancy under paragraph (1).

(B) Policies and procedures to be included

The regulations prescribed under subparagraph (A) shall describe reasonable policies and procedures for use by a user of a consumer report—

(i) to form a reasonable belief that the user knows the identity of the person to whom the consumer report pertains; and

(ii) if the user establishes a continuing relationship with the consumer, and the user regularly and in the ordinary course of business furnishes information to the consumer reporting agency from which the notice of discrepancy pertaining to the consumer was obtained, to reconcile the address of the consumer with the consumer reporting agency by furnishing such address to such consumer reporting agency as part of information regularly furnished by the user for the period in which the relationship is established.

(Pub.L. 90–321, Title VI, § 605, as added Pub.L. 91–508, Title VI, § 601, Oct. 26, 1970, 84 Stat. 1129, and amended Pub.L. 95–598, Title III, § 312(b), Nov. 6, 1978, 92 Stat. 2676; Pub.L. 104–208, Div. A, Title II, §§ 2406(a) to (e), Sept. 30, 1996, 110 Stat. 3009–434, 3009–435; Pub.L. 105–347, § 5, Nov. 2, 1998, 112 Stat. 3211; Pub.L. 108–159, Title II, §§ 113, 212(d), Title III, § 315, Title IV, § 412(b), (c), Title VIII, § 811(c)(1), (2)(A), Dec. 4, 2003, 117 Stat. 1959, 1977, 1996, 2002, 2011; Pub.L. 111–203, Title X, § 1088(a)(2)(D), (5), July 21, 2010, 124 Stat. 2087.)

§ 1681c–1. Identity theft prevention; fraud alerts and active duty alerts [CCPA § 605A]

(a) One-call fraud alerts

(1) Initial alerts

Upon the direct request of a consumer, or an individual acting on behalf of or as a personal representative of a consumer, who asserts in good faith a suspicion that the consumer has been or is about to become a victim of fraud or related crime, including identity theft, a consumer reporting agency described in section 1681a(p) of this title that maintains a file on the consumer and has received appropriate proof of the identity of the requester shall—

(A) include a fraud alert in the file of that consumer, and also provide that alert along with any credit score generated in using that file, for a period of not less than 90 days, beginning on the date of such request, unless the consumer or such representative requests that such fraud alert be removed before the end of such period, and the agency has received appropriate proof of the identity of the requester for such purpose; and

(B) refer the information regarding the fraud alert under this paragraph to each of the other consumer reporting agencies described in section 1681a(p) of this title, in accordance with procedures developed under section 1681s(f) of this title.

(2) Access to free reports

In any case in which a consumer reporting agency includes a fraud alert in the file of a consumer pursuant to this subsection, the consumer reporting agency shall—

(A) disclose to the consumer that the consumer may request a free copy of the file of the consumer pursuant to section 1681j(d) of this title; and

---

[2] So in original.

(B) provide to the consumer all disclosures required to be made under section 1681a of this title, without charge to the consumer, not later than 3 business days after any request described in subparagraph (A).

(b) Extended alerts

(1) In general

Upon the direct request of a consumer, or an individual acting on behalf of or as a personal representative of a consumer, who submits an identity theft report to a consumer reporting agency described in section 1681a(p) of this title that maintains a file on the consumer, if the agency has received appropriate proof of the identity of the requester, the agency shall—

(A) include a fraud alert in the file of that consumer, and also provide that alert along with any credit score generated in using that file, during the 7-year period beginning on the date of such request, unless the consumer or such representative requests that such fraud alert be removed before the end of such period and the agency has received appropriate proof of the identity of the requester for such purpose;

(B) during the 5-year period beginning on the date of such request, exclude the consumer from any list of consumers prepared by the consumer reporting agency and provided to any third party to offer credit or insurance to the consumer as part of a transaction that was not initiated by the consumer, unless the consumer or such representative requests that such exclusion be rescinded before the end of such period; and

(C) refer the information regarding the extended fraud alert under this paragraph to each of the other consumer reporting agencies described in section 1681a(p) of this title, in accordance with procedures developed under section 1681s(f) of this title.

(2) Access to free reports

In any case in which a consumer reporting agency includes a fraud alert in the file of a consumer pursuant to this subsection, the consumer reporting agency shall—

(A) disclose to the consumer that the consumer may request 2 free copies of the file of the consumer pursuant to section 1681j(d) of this title during the 12-month period beginning on the date on which the fraud alert was included in the file; and

(B) provide to the consumer all disclosures required to be made under section 1681g of this title, without charge to the consumer, not later than 3 business days after any request described in subparagraph (A).

(c) Active duty alerts

Upon the direct request of an active duty military consumer, or an individual acting on behalf of or as a personal representative of an active duty military consumer, a consumer reporting agency described in section 1681a(p) of this title that maintains a file on the active duty military consumer and has received appropriate proof of the identity of the requester shall—

(1) include an active duty alert in the file of that active duty military consumer, and also provide that alert along with any credit score generated in using that file, during a period of not less than 12 months, or such longer period as the Bureau shall determine, by regulation, beginning on the date of the request, unless the active duty military consumer or such representative requests that such fraud alert be removed before the end of such period, and the agency has received appropriate proof of the identity of the requester for such purpose;

(2) during the 2-year period beginning on the date of such request, exclude the active duty military consumer from any list of consumers prepared by the consumer reporting agency and provided to any third party to offer credit or insurance to the consumer as part of a transaction that was not initiated by the consumer, unless the consumer requests that such exclusion be rescinded before the end of such period; and

(3) refer the information regarding the active duty alert to each of the other consumer reporting agencies described in section 1681a(p) of this title, in accordance with procedures developed under section 1681s(f) of this title.

(d) Procedures

Each consumer reporting agency described in section 1681a(p) of this title shall establish policies and procedures to comply with this section, including procedures that inform consumers of the availability of initial, extended, and active duty alerts and procedures that allow consumers and active duty military consumers to request initial, extended, or active duty alerts (as applicable) in a simple and easy manner, including by telephone.

(e) Referrals of alerts

Each consumer reporting agency described in section 1681a(p) of this title that receives a referral of a fraud alert or active duty alert from another consumer reporting agency pursuant to this section shall, as though the agency received the request from the consumer directly, follow the procedures required under—

(1) paragraphs (1)(A) and (2) of subsection (a) of this section, in the case of a referral under subsection (a)(1)(B) of this section;

(2) paragraphs (1)(A), (1)(B), and (2) of subsection (b) of this section, in the case of a referral under subsection (b)(1)(C) of this section; and

(3) paragraphs (1) and (2) of subsection (c) of this section, in the case of a referral under subsection (c)(3) of this section.

(f) Duty of reseller to reconvey alert

A reseller shall include in its report any fraud alert or active duty alert placed in the file of a consumer pursuant to this section by another consumer reporting agency.

(g) Duty of other consumer reporting agencies to provide contact information

If a consumer contacts any consumer reporting agency that is not described in section 1681a(p) of this title to communicate a suspicion that the consumer has been or is about to become a victim of fraud or related crime, including identity theft, the agency shall provide information to the consumer on how to contact the Bureau and the consumer reporting agencies described in section 1681a(p) of this title to obtain more detailed information and request alerts under this section.

(h) Limitations on use of information for credit extensions

(1) Requirements for initial and active duty alerts

(A) Notification

Each initial fraud alert and active duty alert under this section shall include information that notifies all prospective users of a consumer report on the consumer to which the alert relates that the consumer does not authorize the establishment of any new credit plan or extension of credit, other than under an open-end credit plan (as defined in section 1602(i) of this title), in the name of the consumer, or issuance of an additional card on an existing credit account requested by a consumer, or any increase in credit limit on an existing credit account requested by a consumer, except in accordance with subparagraph (B).

(B) Limitation on users

(i) In general

No prospective user of a consumer report that includes an initial fraud alert or an active duty alert in accordance with this section may establish a new credit plan or extension of credit, other than under an open-end credit plan (as defined in section 1602(i) of this title), in the name of the consumer, or issue an additional card on an existing credit account requested by a consumer, or grant any increase in credit limit on an existing credit account requested by a consumer, unless the user utilizes reasonable policies and procedures to form a reasonable belief that the user knows the identity of the person making the request.

(ii) Verification

If a consumer requesting the alert has specified a telephone number to be used for identity verification purposes, before authorizing any new credit plan or extension described in clause (i) in the name of such consumer, a user of such consumer report shall contact the consumer using that telephone number or take reasonable steps to verify the consumer's identity and confirm that the application for a new credit plan is not the result of identity theft.

(2) Requirements for extended alerts

(A) Notification

Each extended alert under this section shall include information that provides all prospective users of a consumer report relating to a consumer with—

(i) notification that the consumer does not authorize the establishment of any new credit plan or extension of credit described in clause (i), other than under an open-end credit plan (as defined in section 1602(i) of this title), in the name of the consumer, or issuance of an additional card on an existing credit account requested by a consumer, or any increase in credit limit on an existing credit account requested by a consumer, except in accordance with subparagraph (B); and

(ii) a telephone number or other reasonable contact method designated by the consumer.

(B) Limitation on users

No prospective user of a consumer report or of a credit score generated using the information in the file of a consumer that includes an extended fraud alert in accordance with this section may establish a new credit plan or extension of credit, other than under an open-end credit plan (as defined in section 1602(i) of this title), in the name of the consumer, or issue an additional card on an existing credit account requested by a consumer, or any increase in credit limit on an existing credit account requested by a consumer, unless the user contacts the consumer in person or using the contact method described in subparagraph (A)(ii) to confirm that the application for a new credit plan or increase in credit limit, or request for an additional card is not the result of identity theft.

(Pub.L. 90–321, Title VI, § 605A, as added Pub.L. 108–159, Title I, § 112(a), Dec. 4, 2003, 117 Stat. 1955; Pub.L. 111–203, Title X, § 1088(a)(2)(C), July 21, 2010, 124 Stat. 2087.)

§ 1681c–2.   Block of information resulting from identity theft [CCPA § 605B]

(a) Block

Except as otherwise provided in this section, a consumer reporting agency shall block the reporting of any information in the file of a consumer that the consumer identifies as information that resulted from an alleged identity theft, not later than 4 business days after the date of receipt by such agency of—

(1) appropriate proof of the identity of the consumer;

(2) a copy of an identity theft report;

(3) the identification of such information by the consumer; and

(4) a statement by the consumer that the information is not information relating to any transaction by the consumer.

(b) Notification

A consumer reporting agency shall promptly notify the furnisher of information identified by the consumer under subsection (a) of this section—

(1) that the information may be a result of identity theft;

(2) that an identity theft report has been filed;

(3) that a block has been requested under this section; and

(4) of the effective dates of the block.

(c) Authority to decline or rescind

(1) In general

A consumer reporting agency may decline to block, or may rescind any block, of information relating to a consumer under this section, if the consumer reporting agency reasonably determines that—

(A) the information was blocked in error or a block was requested by the consumer in error;

(B) the information was blocked, or a block was requested by the consumer, on the basis of a material misrepresentation of fact by the consumer relevant to the request to block; or

(C) the consumer obtained possession of goods, services, or money as a result of the blocked transaction or transactions.

(2) Notification to consumer

If a block of information is declined or rescinded under this subsection, the affected consumer shall be notified promptly, in the same manner as consumers are notified of the reinsertion of information under section 1681i(a)(5)(B) of this title.

(3) Significance of block

For purposes of this subsection, if a consumer reporting agency rescinds a block, the presence of information in the file of a consumer prior to the blocking of such information is not evidence of whether the consumer knew or should have known that the consumer obtained possession of any goods, services, or money as a result of the block.

(d) Exception for resellers

(1) No reseller file

This section shall not apply to a consumer reporting agency, if the consumer reporting agency—

(A) is a reseller;

(B) is not, at the time of the request of the consumer under subsection (a) of this section, otherwise furnishing or reselling a consumer report concerning the information identified by the consumer; and

(C) informs the consumer, by any means, that the consumer may report the identity theft to the Bureau to obtain consumer information regarding identity theft.

(2) Reseller with file

The sole obligation of the consumer reporting agency under this section, with regard to any request of a consumer under this section, shall be to block the consumer report maintained by the consumer reporting agency from any subsequent use, if—

(A) the consumer, in accordance with the provisions of subsection (a) of this section, identifies, to a consumer reporting agency, information in the file of the consumer that resulted from identity theft; and

(B) the consumer reporting agency is a reseller of the identified information.

(3) Notice

In carrying out its obligation under paragraph (2), the reseller shall promptly provide a notice to the consumer of the decision to block the file. Such notice shall contain the name, address, and telephone number of each consumer reporting agency from which the consumer information was obtained for resale.

(e) Exception for verification companies

The provisions of this section do not apply to a check services company, acting as such, which issues authorizations for the purpose of approving or processing negotiable instruments, electronic fund transfers, or similar methods of payments, except that, beginning 4 business days after receipt of information described in paragraphs (1) through (3) of subsection (a) of this section, a check services company shall not report to a national consumer reporting agency described in section 1681a(p) of this title, any information identified in the subject identity theft report as resulting from identity theft.

(f) Access to blocked information by law enforcement agencies

No provision of this section shall be construed as requiring a consumer reporting agency to prevent a Federal, State, or local law enforcement agency from accessing blocked information in a consumer file to which the agency could otherwise obtain access under this title.

(Pub.L. 90–321, Title VI, § 605B, as added Pub.L. 108–159, Title I, § 152(a), Dec. 4, 2003, 117 Stat. 1964; Pub.L. 111–203, Title X, § 1088(a)(2)(C), July 21, 2010, 124 Stat. 2087.)

§ 1681d.   Disclosure of investigative consumer reports [CCPA § 606]

(a) Disclosure of fact of preparation

A person may not procure or cause to be prepared an investigative consumer report on any consumer unless—

    (1) it is clearly and accurately disclosed to the consumer that an investigative consumer report including information as to his character, general reputation, personal characteristics, and mode of living, whichever are applicable, may be made, and such disclosure (A) is made in a writing mailed, or otherwise delivered, to the consumer, not later than three days after the date on which the report was first requested, and (B) includes a statement informing the consumer of his right to request the additional disclosures provided for under subsection (b) of this section and the written summary of the rights of the consumer prepared pursuant to section 1681g(c) of this title; and

    (2) the person certifies or has certified to the consumer reporting agency that—

        (A) the person has made the disclosures to the consumer required by paragraph (1); and

        (B) the person will comply with subsection (b) of this section.

(b) Disclosure on request of nature and scope of investigation

Any person who procures or causes to be prepared an investigative consumer report on any consumer shall, upon written request made by the consumer within a reasonable period of time after the receipt by him of the disclosure required by subsection (a)(1) of this section, make a complete and accurate disclosure of the nature and scope of the investigation requested. This disclosure shall be made in a writing mailed, or otherwise delivered, to the consumer not later than five days after the date on which the request for such disclosure was received from the consumer or such report was first requested, whichever is the later.

(c) Limitation on liability upon showing of reasonable procedures for compliance with provisions

No person may be held liable for any violation of subsection (a) or (b) of this section if he shows by a preponderance of the evidence that at the time of the violation he maintained reasonable procedures to assure compliance with subsection (a) or (b) of this section.

(d) Prohibitions

    (1) **Certification.**—A consumer reporting agency shall not prepare or furnish an investigative consumer report unless the agency has received a certification under subsection (a)(2) of this section from the person who requested the report.

    (2) **Inquiries.**—A consumer reporting agency shall not make an inquiry for the purpose of preparing an investigative consumer report on a consumer for employment purposes if the making of the inquiry by an employer or prospective employer of the consumer would violate any applicable Federal or State equal employment opportunity law or regulation.

(3) **Certain public record information.**—Except as otherwise provided in section 1681k of this title, a consumer reporting agency shall not furnish an investigative consumer report that includes information that is a matter of public record and that relates to an arrest, indictment, conviction, civil judicial action, tax lien, or outstanding judgment, unless the agency has verified the accuracy of the information during the 30-day period ending on the date on which the report is furnished.

(4) **Certain adverse information.**—A consumer reporting agency shall not prepare or furnish an investigative consumer report on a consumer that contains information that is adverse to the interest of the consumer and that is obtained through a personal interview with a neighbor, friend, or associate of the consumer or with another person with whom the consumer is acquainted or who has knowledge of such item of information, unless—

(A) the agency has followed reasonable procedures to obtain confirmation of the information, from an additional source that has independent and direct knowledge of the information; or

(B) the person interviewed is the best possible source of the information.

(Pub.L. 90–321, Title VI, § 606, as added Pub.L. 91–508, Title VI, § 601, Oct. 26, 1970, 84 Stat. 1130; amended Pub.L. 104–208, Div. A, Title II, §§ 2408(d)(2), 2414(1) to (3), Sept. 30, 1996, 110 Stat. 3009–438, 3009–449.)

§ 1681e. Compliance procedures [CCPA § 607]

(a) Identity and purposes of credit users

Every consumer reporting agency shall maintain reasonable procedures designed to avoid violations of section 1681c of this title and to limit the furnishing of consumer reports to the purposes listed under section 1681b of this title. These procedures shall require that prospective users of the information identify themselves, certify the purposes for which the information is sought, and certify that the information will be used for no other purpose. Every consumer reporting agency shall make a reasonable effort to verify the identity of a new prospective user and the uses certified by such prospective user prior to furnishing such user a consumer report. No consumer reporting agency may furnish a consumer report to any person if it has reasonable grounds for believing that the consumer report will not be used for a purpose listed in section 1681b of this title.

(b) Accuracy of report

Whenever a consumer reporting agency prepares a consumer report it shall follow reasonable procedures to assure maximum possible accuracy of the information concerning the individual about whom the report relates.

(c) Disclosure of consumer reports by users allowed

A consumer reporting agency may not prohibit a user of a consumer report furnished by the agency on a consumer from disclosing the contents of the report to the consumer, if adverse action against the consumer has been taken by the user based in whole or in part on the report.

(d) Notice to users and furnishers of information

(1) **Notice requirement.**—A consumer reporting agency shall provide to any person—

(A) who regularly and in the ordinary course of business furnishes information to the agency with respect to any consumer; or

(B) to whom a consumer report is provided by the agency;

a notice of such person's responsibilities under this subchapter.

(2) **Content of notice.**—The Bureau shall prescribe the content of notices under paragraph (1), and a consumer reporting agency shall be in compliance with this subsection if it provides a notice under paragraph (1) that is substantially similar to the Bureau prescription under this paragraph.

(e) Procurement of consumer report for resale

(1) **Disclosure.**—A person may not procure a consumer report for purposes of reselling the report (or any information in the report) unless the person discloses to the consumer reporting agency that originally furnishes the report—

(A) the identity of the end-user of the report (or information); and

(B) each permissible purpose under section 1681b of this title for which the report is furnished to the end-user of the report (or information).

(2) **Responsibilities of procurers for resale.**—A person who procures a consumer report for purposes of reselling the report (or any information in the report) shall—

(A) establish and comply with reasonable procedures designed to ensure that the report (or information) is resold by the person only for a purpose for which the report may be furnished under section 1681b of this title, including by requiring that each person to which the report (or information) is resold and that resells or provides the report (or information) to any other person—

(i) identifies each end user of the resold report (or information);

(ii) certifies each purpose for which the report (or information) will be used; and

(iii) certifies that the report (or information) will be used for no other purpose; and

(B) before reselling the report, make reasonable efforts to verify the identifications and certifications made under subparagraph (A).

(3) **Resale of consumer report to a federal agency or department.**—Notwithstanding paragraph (1) or (2), a person who procures a consumer report for purposes of reselling the report (or any information in the report) shall not disclose the identity of the end-user of the report under paragraph (1) or (2) if—

(A) the end user is an agency or department of the United States Government which procures the report from the person for purposes of determining the eligibility of the consumer concerned to receive access or continued access to classified information (as defined in section 1681b(b)(4)(E)(i) of this title); and

(B) the agency or department certifies in writing to the person reselling the report that nondisclosure is necessary to protect classified information or the safety of persons employed by or contracting with, or undergoing investigation for work or contracting with the agency or department.

(Pub.L. 90–321, Title VI, § 607, as added Pub.L. 91–508, Title VI, § 601, Oct. 26, 1970, 84 Stat. 1130; amended Pub.L. 104–208, Div. A, Title II, § 2407, Sept. 30, 1996, 110 Stat. 3009–435; Pub.L. 105–107, Title III, § 311(b), Nov. 20, 1997, 111 Stat. 2256; Pub.L. 111–203, Title X, § 1088(a)(2)(A), July 21, 2010, 124 Stat. 2087.)

§ 1681f.   Disclosures to governmental agencies [CCPA § 608]

Notwithstanding the provisions of section 1681b of this title, a consumer reporting agency may furnish identifying information respecting any consumer, limited to his name, address, former addresses, places of employment, or former places of employment, to a governmental agency.

(Pub.L. 90–321, Title VI, § 608, as added Pub.L. 91–508, Title VI, § 601, Oct. 26, 1970, 84 Stat. 1131.)

§ 1681g.   Disclosures to consumers [CCPA § 609]

(a) Information on file; sources; report recipients

Every consumer reporting agency shall, upon request, and subject to section 1681h(a)(1) of this title, clearly and accurately disclose to the consumer:

(1) All information in the consumer's file at the time of the request, except that—

(A) if the consumer to whom the file relates requests that the first 5 digits of the social security number (or similar identification number) of the consumer not be included in the disclosure and the consumer reporting agency has received appropriate proof of the identity of the requester, the consumer reporting agency shall so truncate such number in such disclosure; and

(B) nothing in this paragraph shall be construed to require a consumer reporting agency to disclose to a consumer any information concerning credit scores or any other risk scores or predictors relating to the consumer.

(2) The sources of the information; except that the sources of information acquired solely for use in preparing an investigative consumer report and actually used for no other purpose need not be disclosed: *Provided*, That in the event an action is brought under this subchapter, such sources shall be available to the plaintiff under appropriate discovery procedures in the court in which the action is brought.

(3)(A) Identification of each person (including each end-user identified under section 1681e(e)(1) of this title) that procured a consumer report—

(i) for employment purposes, during the 2-year period preceding the date on which the request is made; or

(ii) for any other purpose, during the 1-year period preceding the date on which the request is made.

(B) An identification of a person under subparagraph (A) shall include—

(i) the name of the person or, if applicable, the trade name (written in full) under which such person conducts business; and

(ii) upon request of the consumer, the address and telephone number of the person.

(C) Subparagraph (A) does not apply if—

(i) the end user is an agency or department of the United States Government that procures the report from the person for purposes of determining the eligibility of the consumer to whom the report relates to receive access or continued access to classified information (as defined in section 1681b(b)(4)(E)(i) of this title); and

(ii) the head of the agency or department makes a written finding as prescribed under section 1681b(b)(4)(A) of this title.

(4) The dates, original payees, and amounts of any checks upon which is based any adverse characterization of the consumer, included in the file at the time of the disclosure.

(5) A record of all inquiries received by the agency during the 1-year period preceding the request that identified the consumer in connection with a credit or insurance transaction that was not initiated by the consumer.

(6) If the consumer requests the credit file and not the credit score, a statement that the consumer may request and obtain a credit score.

(b) Exempt information

The requirements of subsection (a) of this section respecting the disclosure of sources of information and the recipients of consumer reports do not apply to information received or consumer reports furnished prior to the effective date of this subchapter except to the extent that the matter involved is contained in the files of the consumer reporting agency on that date.

(c) Summary of rights to obtain and dispute information in consumer reports and to obtain credit scores

(1) Commission[1] summary of rights required

(A) In general

---

[1]   So in original.

The Commission[1] shall prepare a model summary of the rights of consumers under this subchapter.

(B) Content of summary

The summary of rights prepared under subparagraph (A) shall include a description of—

(i) the right of a consumer to obtain a copy of a consumer report under subsection (a) of this section from each consumer reporting agency;

(ii) the frequency and circumstances under which a consumer is entitled to receive a consumer report without charge under section 1681j of this title;

(iii) the right of a consumer to dispute information in the file of the consumer under section 1681i of this title;

(iv) the right of a consumer to obtain a credit score from a consumer reporting agency, and a description of how to obtain a credit score;

(v) the method by which a consumer can contact, and obtain a consumer report from, a consumer reporting agency without charge, as provided in the regulations of the Bureau prescribed under section 211(c) of the Fair and Accurate Credit Transactions Act of 2003; and

(vi) the method by which a consumer can contact, and obtain a consumer report from, a consumer reporting agency described in section 1681a(w) of this title, as provided in the regulations of the Bureau prescribed under section 1681j(a)(1)(C) of this title.

(C) Availability of summary of rights

The Commission[1] shall—

(i) actively publicize the availability of the summary of rights prepared under this paragraph;

(ii) conspicuously post on its Internet website the availability of such summary of rights; and

(iii) promptly make such summary of rights available to consumers, on request.

(2) Summary of rights required to be included with agency disclosures

A consumer reporting agency shall provide to a consumer, with each written disclosure by the agency to the consumer under this section—

(A) the summary of rights prepared by the Bureau under paragraph (1);

(B) in the case of a consumer reporting agency described in section 1681a(p) of this title, a toll-free telephone number established by the agency, at which personnel are accessible to consumers during normal business hours;

(C) a list of all Federal agencies responsible for enforcing any provision of this subchapter, and the address and any appropriate phone number of each such agency, in a form that will assist the consumer in selecting the appropriate agency;

(D) a statement that the consumer may have additional rights under State law, and that the consumer may wish to contact a State or local consumer protection agency or a State attorney general (or the equivalent thereof) to learn of those rights; and

(E) a statement that a consumer reporting agency is not required to remove accurate derogatory information from the file of a consumer, unless the information is outdated under section 1681c of this title or cannot be verified.

---

[1] So in original.

(d) Summary of rights of identity theft victims

(1) In general

The Commission,[1] in consultation with the Federal banking agencies and the National Credit Union Administration, shall prepare a model summary of the rights of consumers under this subchapter with respect to the procedures for remedying the effects of fraud or identity theft involving credit, an electronic fund transfer, or an account or transaction at or with a financial institution or other creditor.

(2) Summary of rights and contact information

Beginning 60 days after the date on which the model summary of rights is prescribed in final form by the Bureau pursuant to paragraph (1), if any consumer contacts a consumer reporting agency and expresses a belief that the consumer is a victim of fraud or identity theft involving credit, an electronic fund transfer, or an account or transaction at or with a financial institution or other creditor, the consumer reporting agency shall, in addition to any other action that the agency may take, provide the consumer with a summary of rights that contains all of the information required by the Bureau under paragraph (1), and information on how to contact the Bureau to obtain more detailed information.

(e) Information available to victims

(1) In general

For the purpose of documenting fraudulent transactions resulting from identity theft, not later than 30 days after the date of receipt of a request from a victim in accordance with paragraph (3), and subject to verification of the identity of the victim and the claim of identity theft in accordance with paragraph (2), a business entity that has provided credit to, provided for consideration products, goods, or services to, accepted payment from, or otherwise entered into a commercial transaction for consideration with, a person who has allegedly made unauthorized use of the means of identification of the victim, shall provide a copy of application and business transaction records in the control of the business entity, whether maintained by the business entity or by another person on behalf of the business entity, evidencing any transaction alleged to be a result of identity theft to—

(A) the victim;

(B) any Federal, State, or local government law enforcement agency or officer specified by the victim in such a request; or

(C) any law enforcement agency investigating the identity theft and authorized by the victim to take receipt of records provided under this subsection.

(2) Verification of identity and claim

Before a business entity provides any information under paragraph (1), unless the business entity, at its discretion, otherwise has a high degree of confidence that it knows the identity of the victim making a request under paragraph (1), the victim shall provide to the business entity—

(A) as proof of positive identification of the victim, at the election of the business entity—

(i) the presentation of a government-issued identification card;

(ii) personally identifying information of the same type as was provided to the business entity by the unauthorized person; or

(iii) personally identifying information that the business entity typically requests from new applicants or for new transactions, at the time of the victim's request for information, including any documentation described in clauses (i) and (ii); and

(B) as proof of a claim of identity theft, at the election of the business entity—

(i) a copy of a police report evidencing the claim of the victim of identity theft; and

---

[1] So in original.

    (ii) a properly completed—

        (I) copy of a standardized affidavit of identity theft developed and made available by the Bureau; or

        (II) an[2] affidavit of fact that is acceptable to the business entity for that purpose.

(3) Procedures

The request of a victim under paragraph (1) shall—

    (A) be in writing;

    (B) be mailed to an address specified by the business entity, if any; and

    (C) if asked by the business entity, include relevant information about any transaction alleged to be a result of identity theft to facilitate compliance with this section including—

        (i) if known by the victim (or if readily obtainable by the victim), the date of the application or transaction; and

        (ii) if known by the victim (or if readily obtainable by the victim), any other identifying information such as an account or transaction number.

(4) No charge to victim

Information required to be provided under paragraph (1) shall be so provided without charge.

(5) Authority to decline to provide information

A business entity may decline to provide information under paragraph (1) if, in the exercise of good faith, the business entity determines that—

    (A) this subsection does not require disclosure of the information;

    (B) after reviewing the information provided pursuant to paragraph (2), the business entity does not have a high degree of confidence in knowing the true identity of the individual requesting the information;

    (C) the request for the information is based on a misrepresentation of fact by the individual requesting the information relevant to the request for information; or

    (D) the information requested is Internet navigational data or similar information about a person's visit to a website or online service.

(6) Limitation on liability

Except as provided in section 1681s of this title, sections 1681n and 1681o of this title do not apply to any violation of this subsection.

(7) Limitation on civil liability

No business entity may be held civilly liable under any provision of Federal, State, or other law for disclosure, made in good faith pursuant to this subsection.

(8) No new recordkeeping obligation

Nothing in this subsection creates an obligation on the part of a business entity to obtain, retain, or maintain information or records that are not otherwise required to be obtained, retained, or maintained in the ordinary course of its business or under other applicable law.

(9) Rule of construction

    (A) In general

---

[2] So in original. The word "an" probably should not appear.

No provision of subtitle A of title V of Public Law 106–102, prohibiting the disclosure of financial information by a business entity to third parties shall be used to deny disclosure of information to the victim under this subsection.

(B) Limitation

Except as provided in subparagraph (A), nothing in this subsection permits a business entity to disclose information, including information to law enforcement under subparagraphs (B) and (C) of paragraph (1), that the business entity is otherwise prohibited from disclosing under any other applicable provision of Federal or State law.

(10) Affirmative defense

In any civil action brought to enforce this subsection, it is an affirmative defense (which the defendant must establish by a preponderance of the evidence) for a business entity to file an affidavit or answer stating that—

(A) the business entity has made a reasonably diligent search of its available business records; and

(B) the records requested under this subsection do not exist or are not reasonably available.

(11) Definition of victim

For purposes of this subsection, the term "victim" means a consumer whose means of identification or financial information has been used or transferred (or has been alleged to have been used or transferred) without the authority of that consumer, with the intent to commit, or to aid or abet, an identity theft or a similar crime.

(12) Effective date

This subsection shall become effective 180 days after December 4, 2003.

(13) Effectiveness study

Not later than 18 months after December 4, 2003, the Comptroller General of the United States shall submit a report to Congress assessing the effectiveness of this provision.

(f) Disclosure of credit scores

(1) In general

Upon the request of a consumer for a credit score, a consumer reporting agency shall supply to the consumer a statement indicating that the information and credit scoring model may be different than the credit score that may be used by the lender, and a notice which shall include—

(A) the current credit score of the consumer or the most recent credit score of the consumer that was previously calculated by the credit reporting agency for a purpose related to the extension of credit;

(B) the range of possible credit scores under the model used;

(C) all of the key factors that adversely affected the credit score of the consumer in the model used, the total number of which shall not exceed 4, subject to paragraph (9);

(D) the date on which the credit score was created; and

(E) the name of the person or entity that provided the credit score or credit file upon which the credit score was created.

(2) Definitions

For purposes of this subsection, the following definitions shall apply:

(A) credit score

The term "credit score"—

    (i) means a numerical value or a categorization derived from a statistical tool or modeling system used by a person who makes or arranges a loan to predict the likelihood of certain credit behaviors, including default (and the numerical value or the categorization derived from such analysis may also be referred to as a "risk predictor" or "risk score"); and

    (ii) does not include—

        (I) any mortgage score or rating of an automated underwriting system that considers one or more factors in addition to credit information, including the loan to value ratio, the amount of down payment, or the financial assets of a consumer; or

        (II) any other elements of the underwriting process or underwriting decision.

(B) Key factors

    The term "key factors" means all relevant elements or reasons adversely affecting the credit score for the particular individual, listed in the order of their importance based on their effect on the credit score.

(3) Timeframe and manner of disclosure

    The information required by this subsection shall be provided in the same timeframe and manner as the information described in subsection (a) of this section.

(4) Applicability to certain uses

    This subsection shall not be construed so as to compel a consumer reporting agency to develop or disclose a score if the agency does not—

    (A) distribute scores that are used in connection with residential real property loans; or

    (B) develop scores that assist credit providers in understanding the general credit behavior of a consumer and predicting the future credit behavior of the consumer.

(5) Applicability to credit scores developed by another person

    (A) In general

    This subsection shall not be construed to require a consumer reporting agency that distributes credit scores developed by another person or entity to provide a further explanation of them, or to process a dispute arising pursuant to section 1681i of this title, except that the consumer reporting agency shall provide the consumer with the name and address and website for contacting the person or entity who developed the score or developed the methodology of the score.

    (B) Exception

    This paragraph shall not apply to a consumer reporting agency that develops or modifies scores that are developed by another person or entity.

(6) Maintenance of credit scores not required

    This subsection shall not be construed to require a consumer reporting agency to maintain credit scores in its files.

(7) Compliance in certain cases

    In complying with this subsection, a consumer reporting agency shall—

    (A) supply the consumer with a credit score that is derived from a credit scoring model that is widely distributed to users by that consumer reporting agency in connection with residential real property loans or with a credit score that assists the consumer in understanding the credit scoring assessment of the credit behavior of the consumer and predictions about the future credit behavior of the consumer; and

    (B) a statement indicating that the information and credit scoring model may be different than that used by the lender.

(8) Fair and reasonable fee

A consumer reporting agency may charge a fair and reasonable fee, as determined by the Bureau, for providing the information required under this subsection.

(9) Use of enquiries as a key factor

If a key factor that adversely affects the credit score of a consumer consists of the number of enquiries made with respect to a consumer report, that factor shall be included in the disclosure pursuant to paragraph (1)(C) without regard to the numerical limitation in such paragraph.

(g) Disclosure of credit scores by certain mortgage lenders

(1) In general

Any person who makes or arranges loans and who uses a consumer credit score, as defined in subsection (f) of this section, in connection with an application initiated or sought by a consumer for a closed end loan or the establishment of an open end loan for a consumer purpose that is secured by 1 to 4 units of residential real property (hereafter in this subsection referred to as the "lender") shall provide the following to the consumer as soon as reasonably practicable:

(A) Information required under subsection (f)—

(i) In general

A copy of the information identified in subsection (f) of this section that was obtained from a consumer reporting agency or was developed and used by the user of the information.

(ii) Notice under subparagraph (D)

In addition to the information provided to it by a third party that provided the credit score or scores, a lender is only required to provide the notice contained in subparagraph (D).

(B) Disclosures in case of automated underwriting system

(i) In general

If a person that is subject to this subsection uses an automated underwriting system to underwrite a loan, that person may satisfy the obligation to provide a credit score by disclosing a credit score and associated key factors supplied by a consumer reporting agency.

(ii) Numerical credit score

However, if a numerical credit score is generated by an automated underwriting system used by an enterprise, and that score is disclosed to the person, the score shall be disclosed to the consumer consistent with subparagraph (C).

(iii) Enterprise defined

For purposes of this subparagraph, the term "enterprise" has the same meaning as in paragraph (6) of section 4502 of Title 12.

(C) Disclosures of credit scores not obtained from a consumer reporting agency

A person that is subject to the provisions of this subsection and that uses a credit score, other than a credit score provided by a consumer reporting agency, may satisfy the obligation to provide a credit score by disclosing a credit score and associated key factors supplied by a consumer reporting agency.

(D) Notice to home loan applicants

A copy of the following notice, which shall include the name, address, and telephone number of each consumer reporting agency providing a credit score that was used:

NOTICE TO THE HOME LOAN APPLICANT

In connection with your application for a home loan, the lender must disclose to you the score that a consumer reporting agency distributed to users and the lender used in connection with your home loan, and the key factors affecting your credit scores.

The credit score is a computer generated summary calculated at the time of the request and based on information that a consumer reporting agency or lender has on file. The scores are based on data about your credit history and payment patterns. credit scores are important because they are used to assist the lender in determining whether you will obtain a loan. They may also be used to determine what interest rate you may be offered on the mortgage. credit scores can change over time, depending on your conduct, how your credit history and payment patterns change, and how credit scoring technologies change.

Because the score is based on information in your credit history, it is very important that you review the credit-related information that is being furnished to make sure it is accurate. Credit records may vary from one company to another.

If you have questions about your credit score or the credit information that is furnished to you, contact the consumer reporting agency at the address and telephone number provided with this notice, or contact the lender, if the lender developed or generated the credit score. The consumer reporting agency plays no part in the decision to take any action on the loan application and is unable to provide you with specific reasons for the decision on a loan application.

If you have questions concerning the terms of the loan, contact the lender.

(E) Actions not required under this subsection

This subsection shall not require any person to—

    (i) explain the information provided pursuant to subsection (f) of this section;

    (ii) disclose any information other·than a credit score or key factors, as defined in subsection (f) of this section;

    (iii) disclose any credit score or related information obtained by the user after a loan has closed;

    (iv) provide more than 1 disclosure per loan transaction; or

    (v) provide the disclosure required by this subsection when another person has made the disclosure to the consumer for that loan transaction.

(F) No obligation for content

    (i) In general

The obligation of any person pursuant to this subsection shall be limited solely to providing a copy of the information that was received from the consumer reporting agency.

    (ii) Limit on liability

No person has liability under this subsection for the content of that information or for the omission of any information within the report provided by the consumer reporting agency.

(G) Person defined as excluding enterprise

As used in this subsection, the term "person" does not include an enterprise (as defined in paragraph (6) of section 4502 of Title 12).

(2) Prohibition on disclosure clauses null and void

    (A) In general

Any provision in a contract that prohibits the disclosure of a credit score by a person who makes or arranges loans or a consumer reporting agency is void.

(B) No liability for disclosure under this subsection

A lender shall not have liability under any contractual provision for disclosure of a credit score pursuant to this subsection.

(Pub.L. 90–321, Title VI, § 609, as added Pub.L. 91–508, Title VI, § 601, Oct. 26, 1970, 84 Stat. 1131, and amended Pub.L. 103–325, Title III, § 339, Sept. 23, 1994, 108 Stat. 2237; Pub.L. 104–208, Div. A, Title II, § 2408(a) to (d)(1), (e)(5)(A), Sept. 30, 1996, 110 Stat. 3009–436, 3009–437, 3009–439; Pub.L. 105–347, § 4(a), Nov. 2, 1998, 112 Stat. 3210; Pub.L. 108–159, Title I, §§ 115, 151(a)(1), Title II, §§ 211(c), 212(a) to (c), Title VIII, § 811(d), Dec. 4, 2003, 117 Stat. 1961, 1970, 1973 to 1975, 2011; Pub.L. 111–203, Title X, § 1088(a)(2)(C), July 21, 2010, 124 Stat. 2087.)

§ 1681h. Conditions and form of disclosure to consumers [CCPA § 610]

(a) In general

(1) Proper identification.—A consumer reporting agency shall require, as a condition of making the disclosures required under section 1681g of this title, that the consumer furnish proper identification.

(2) Disclosure in writing.—Except as provided in subsection (b) of this section, the disclosures required to be made under section 1681(g) of this title shall be provided under that section in writing.

(b) Other forms of disclosure

(1) In general.—If authorized by a consumer, a consumer reporting agency may make the disclosures required under[1] 1681g of this title—

(A) other than in writing; and

(B) in such form as may be—

(i) specified by the consumer in accordance with paragraph (2); and

(ii) available from the agency.

(2) Form.—A consumer may specify pursuant to paragraph (1) that disclosures under section 1681g of this title shall be made—

(A) in person, upon the appearance of the consumer at the place of business of the consumer reporting agency where disclosures are regularly provided, during normal business hours, and on reasonable notice;

(B) by telephone, if the consumer has made a written request for disclosure by telephone;

(C) by electronic means, if available from the agency; or

(D) by any other reasonable means that is available from the agency.

(c) Trained personnel

Any consumer reporting agency shall provide trained personnel to explain to the consumer any information furnished to him pursuant to section 1681g of this title.

(d) Persons accompanying consumer

The consumer shall be permitted to be accompanied by one other person of his choosing, who shall furnish reasonable identification. A consumer reporting agency may require the consumer to furnish a written statement granting permission to the consumer reporting agency to discuss the consumer's file in such person's presence.

(e) Limitation of liability

Except as provided in sections 1681n and 1681o of this title, no consumer may bring any action or proceeding in the nature of defamation, invasion of privacy, or negligence with respect to the reporting of information against any consumer reporting agency, any user of information, or any person who furnishes

---

[1] So in original. Probably should be followed by "section".

information to a consumer reporting agency, based on information disclosed pursuant to section 1681g, 1681h, or 1681m of this title, or based on information disclosed by a user of a consumer report to or for a consumer against whom the user has taken adverse action, based in whole or in part on the report[2] except as to false information furnished with malice or willful intent to injure such consumer.

(Pub.L. 90–321, Title VI, § 610, as added Pub.L. 91–508, Title VI, § 601, Oct. 26, 1970, 84 Stat. 1131, and amended Pub.L. 104–208, Div. A, Title II, § 2408(e)(1), (e)(4), (e)(5)(B), Sept. 30, 1996, 110 Stat. 3009–438, 3009–439.)

§ 1681i.   Procedure in case of disputed accuracy [CCPA § 611]

(a) **Reinvestigations of disputed information**

(1) **Reinvestigation required.—**

(A) **In general.**—Subject to subsection (f) of this section, if the completeness or accuracy of any item of information contained in a consumer's file at a consumer reporting agency is disputed by the consumer and the consumer notifies the agency directly, or indirectly through a reseller, of such dispute, the agency shall, free of charge, conduct a reasonable reinvestigation to determine whether the disputed information is inaccurate and record the current status of the disputed information, or delete the item from the file in accordance with paragraph (5), before the end of the 30-day period beginning on the date on which the agency receives the notice of the dispute from the consumer or reseller.

(B) **Extension of period to reinvestigate.**—Except as provided in subparagraph (C), the 30-day period described in subparagraph (A) may be extended for not more than 15 additional days if the consumer reporting agency receives information from the consumer during that 30-day period that is relevant to the reinvestigation.

(C) **Limitations on extension of period to reinvestigate.**—Subparagraph (B) shall not apply to any reinvestigation in which, during the 30-day period described in subparagraph (A), the information that is the subject of the reinvestigation is found to be inaccurate or incomplete or the consumer reporting agency determines that the information cannot be verified.

(2) **Prompt notice of dispute to furnisher of information.—**

(A) **In general.**—Before the expiration of the 5-business-day period beginning on the date on which a consumer reporting agency receives notice of a dispute from any consumer or a reseller in accordance with paragraph (1), the agency shall provide notification of the dispute to any person who provided any item of information in dispute, at the address and in the manner established with the person. The notice shall include all relevant information regarding the dispute that the agency has received from the consumer or reseller.

(B) **Provision of other information.**—The consumer reporting agency shall promptly provide to the person who provided the information in dispute all relevant information regarding the dispute that is received by the agency from the consumer or the reseller after the period referred to in subparagraph (A) and before the end of the period referred to in paragraph (1)(A).

(3) **Determination that dispute is frivolous or irrelevant.—**

(A) **In general.**—Notwithstanding paragraph (1), a consumer reporting agency may terminate a reinvestigation of information disputed by a consumer under that paragraph if the agency reasonably determines that the dispute by the consumer is frivolous or irrelevant, including by reason of a failure by a consumer to provide sufficient information to investigate the disputed information.

(B) **Notice of determination.**—Upon making any determination in accordance with subparagraph (A) that a dispute is frivolous or irrelevant, a consumer reporting agency shall notify the consumer of such determination not later than 5 business days after making such determination, by mail or, if authorized by the consumer for that purpose, by any other means available to the agency.

---

[2] So in original. Probably should be followed by a comma.

(C) Contents of notice.—A notice under subparagraph (B) shall include—

(i) the reasons for the determination under subparagraph (A); and

(ii) identification of any information required to investigate the disputed information, which may consist of a standardized form describing the general nature of such information.

(4) Consideration of consumer information.—In conducting any reinvestigation under paragraph (1) with respect to disputed information in the file of any consumer, the consumer reporting agency shall review and consider all relevant information submitted by the consumer in the period described in paragraph (1)(A) with respect to such disputed information.

(5) Treatment of inaccurate or unverifiable information.—

(A) In general.—If, after any reinvestigation under paragraph (1) of any information disputed by a consumer, an item of the information is found to be inaccurate or incomplete or cannot be verified, the consumer reporting agency shall—

(i) promptly delete that item of information from the file of the consumer, or modify that item of information, as appropriate, based on the results of the reinvestigation; and

(ii) promptly notify the furnisher of that information that the information has been modified or deleted from the file of the consumer.

(B) Requirements relating to reinsertion of previously deleted material.—

(i) **Certification of accuracy of information.**—If any information is deleted from a consumer's file pursuant to subparagraph (A), the information may not be reinserted in the file by the consumer reporting agency unless the person who furnishes the information certifies that the information is complete and accurate.

(ii) **Notice to consumer.**—If any information that has been deleted from a consumer's file pursuant to subparagraph (A) is reinserted in the file, the consumer reporting agency shall notify the consumer of the reinsertion in writing not later than 5 business days after the reinsertion or, if authorized by the consumer for that purpose, by any other means available to the agency.

(iii) **Additional information.**—As part of, or in addition to, the notice under clause (ii), a consumer reporting agency shall provide to a consumer in writing not later than 5 business days after the date of the reinsertion—

(I) a statement that the disputed information has been reinserted;

(II) the business name and address of any furnisher of information contacted and the telephone number of such furnisher, if reasonably available, or of any furnisher of information that contacted the consumer reporting agency, in connection with the reinsertion of such information; and

(III) a notice that the consumer has the right to add a statement to the consumer's file disputing the accuracy or completeness of the disputed information.

(C) Procedures to prevent reappearance.—A consumer reporting agency shall maintain reasonable procedures designed to prevent the reappearance in a consumer's file, and in consumer reports on the consumer, of information that is deleted pursuant to this paragraph (other than information that is reinserted in accordance with subparagraph (B)(i)).

(D) Automated reinvestigation system.—Any consumer reporting agency that compiles and maintains files on consumers on a nationwide basis shall implement an automated system through which furnishers of information to that consumer reporting agency may report the results of a reinvestigation that finds incomplete or inaccurate information in a consumer's file to other such consumer reporting agencies.

(6) Notice of results of reinvestigation.—

(A) In general.—A consumer reporting agency shall provide written notice to a consumer of the results of a reinvestigation under this subsection not later than 5 business days after the completion of the reinvestigation, by mail or, if authorized by the consumer for that purpose, by other means available to the agency.

(B) Contents.—As part of, or in addition to, the notice under subparagraph (A), a consumer reporting agency shall provide to a consumer in writing before the expiration of the 5-day period referred to in subparagraph (A)—

(i) a statement that the reinvestigation is completed;

(ii) a consumer report that is based upon the consumer's file as that file is revised as a result of the reinvestigation;

(iii) a notice that, if requested by the consumer, a description of the procedure used to determine the accuracy and completeness of the information shall be provided to the consumer by the agency, including the business name and address of any furnisher of information contacted in connection with such information and the telephone number of such furnisher, if reasonably available;

(iv) a notice that the consumer has the right to add a statement to the consumer's file disputing the accuracy or completeness of the information; and

(v) a notice that the consumer has the right to request under subsection (d) of this section that the consumer reporting agency furnish notifications under that subsection.

(7) Description of reinvestigation procedure.—A consumer reporting agency shall provide to a consumer a description referred to in paragraph (6)(B)(iii) by not later than 15 days after receiving a request from the consumer for that description.

(8) Expedited dispute resolution.—If a dispute regarding an item of information in a consumer's file at a consumer reporting agency is resolved in accordance with paragraph (5)(A) by the deletion of the disputed information by not later than 3 business days after the date on which the agency receives notice of the dispute from the consumer in accordance with paragraph (1)(A), then the agency shall not be required to comply with paragraphs (2), (6), and (7) with respect to that dispute if the agency—

(A) provides prompt notice of the deletion to the consumer by telephone;

(B) includes in that notice, or in a written notice that accompanies a confirmation and consumer report provided in accordance with subparagraph (C), a statement of the consumer's right to request under subsection (d) of this section that the agency furnish notifications under that subsection; and

(C) provides written confirmation of the deletion and a copy of a consumer report on the consumer that is based on the consumer's file after the deletion, not later than 5 business days after making the deletion.

(b) Statement of dispute

If the reinvestigation does not resolve the dispute, the consumer may file a brief statement setting forth the nature of the dispute. The consumer reporting agency may limit such statements to not more than one hundred words if it provides the consumer with assistance in writing a clear summary of the dispute.

(c) Notification of consumer dispute in subsequent consumer reports

Whenever a statement of a dispute is filed, unless there is reasonable grounds to believe that it is frivolous or irrelevant, the consumer reporting agency shall, in any subsequent consumer report containing the information in question, clearly note that it is disputed by the consumer and provide either the consumer's statement or a clear and accurate codification or summary thereof.

(d) Notification of deletion of disputed information

Following any deletion of information which is found to be inaccurate or whose accuracy can no longer be verified or any notation as to disputed information, the consumer reporting agency shall, at the request of the consumer, furnish notification that the item has been deleted or the statement, codification or summary pursuant to subsection (b) or (c) of this section to any person specifically designated by the consumer who has within two years prior thereto received a consumer report for employment purposes, or within six months prior thereto received a consumer report for any other purpose, which contained the deleted or disputed information.

(e) Treatment of complaints and report to Congress

(1) In general

The Commission[1] shall—

    (A) compile all complaints that it receives that a file of a consumer that is maintained by a consumer reporting agency described in section 1681a(p) of this title contains incomplete or inaccurate information, with respect to which, the consumer appears to have disputed the completeness or accuracy with the consumer reporting agency or otherwise utilized the procedures provided by subsection (a) of this section; and

    (B) transmit each such complaint to each consumer reporting agency involved.

(2) Exclusion

Complaints received or obtained by the Bureau pursuant to its investigative authority under the Consumer Financial Protection Act of 2010 shall not be subject to paragraph (1).

(3) Agency responsibilities

Each consumer reporting agency described in section 1681a(p) of this title that receives a complaint transmitted by the Bureau pursuant to paragraph (1) shall—

    (A) review each such complaint to determine whether all legal obligations imposed on the consumer reporting agency under this subchapter (including any obligation imposed by an applicable court or administrative order) have been met with respect to the subject matter of the complaint;

    (B) provide reports on a regular basis to the Bureau regarding the determinations of and actions taken by the consumer reporting agency, if any, in connection with its review of such complaints; and

    (C) maintain, for a reasonable time period, records regarding the disposition of each such complaint that is sufficient to demonstrate compliance with this subsection.

(4) Rulemaking authority

The Commission[1] may prescribe regulations, as appropriate to implement this subsection.

(5) Annual report

The Commission[1] shall submit to the Committee on Banking, Housing, and Urban Affairs of the Senate and the Committee on Financial Services of the House of Representatives an annual report regarding information gathered by the Bureau under this subsection.

(f) Reinvestigation requirement applicable to resellers

(1) Exemption from general reinvestigation requirement

Except as provided in paragraph (2), a reseller shall be exempt from the requirements of this section.

(2) Action required upon receiving notice of a dispute

If a reseller receives a notice from a consumer of a dispute concerning the completeness or accuracy of any item of information contained in a consumer report on such consumer produced by the reseller, the reseller shall, within 5 business days of receiving the notice, and free of charge—

---

[1] So in original. Probably should be "Bureau".

(A) determine whether the item of information is incomplete or inaccurate as a result of an act or omission of the reseller; and

(B) if—

(i) the reseller determines that the item of information is incomplete or inaccurate as a result of an act or omission of the reseller, not later than 20 days after receiving the notice, correct the information in the consumer report or delete it; or

(ii) if the reseller determines that the item of information is not incomplete or inaccurate as a result of an act or omission of the reseller, convey the notice of the dispute, together with all relevant information provided by the consumer, to each consumer reporting agency that provided the reseller with the information that is the subject of the dispute, using an address or a notification mechanism specified by the consumer reporting agency for such notices.

(3) Responsibility of consumer reporting agency to notify consumer through reseller

Upon the completion of a reinvestigation under this section of a dispute concerning the completeness or accuracy of any information in the file of a consumer by a consumer reporting agency that received notice of the dispute from a reseller under paragraph (2)—

(A) the notice by the consumer reporting agency under paragraph (6), (7), or (8) of subsection (a) of this section shall be provided to the reseller in lieu of the consumer; and

(B) the reseller shall immediately reconvey such notice to the consumer, including any notice of a deletion by telephone in the manner required under paragraph (8)(A).

(4) Reseller reinvestigations

No provision of this subsection shall be construed as prohibiting a reseller from conducting a reinvestigation of a consumer dispute directly.

(Pub.L. 90–321, Title VI, § 611, as added Pub.L. 91–508, Title VI, § 601, Oct. 26, 1970, 84 Stat. 1132, and amended Pub.L. 104–208, Div. A, Title II, § 2409(a), (b), Sept. 30, 1996, 110 Stat. 3009–439, 3009–442; Pub.L. 105–347, § 6(5), Nov. 2, 1998, 112 Stat. 3211; Pub.L. 108–159, Title III, §§ 313(a), 314(a), 316, 317, Dec. 4, 2003, 117 Stat. 1994, 1995, 1996, 1998; Pub.L. 111–203, Title X, § 1088(a)(2)(C), (6), July 21, 2010, 124 Stat. 2087.)

§ 1681j. Charges for certain disclosures [CCPA § 612]

(a) Free annual disclosure

(1) Nationwide consumer reporting agencies

(A) In general

All consumer reporting agencies described in subsections (p) and (w) of section 1681a of this title shall make all disclosures pursuant to section 1681g of this title once during any 12-month period upon request of the consumer and without charge to the consumer.

(B) Centralized source

Subparagraph (A) shall apply with respect to a consumer reporting agency described in section 1681a(p) of this title only if the request from the consumer is made using the centralized source established for such purpose in accordance with section 211(c) of the Fair and Accurate Credit Transactions Act of 2003.

(C) Nationwide specialty consumer reporting agency

(i) In general

The Commission[1] shall prescribe regulations applicable to each consumer reporting agency described in section 1681a of this title to require the establishment of a streamlined process for

---

[1] So in original.

consumers to request consumer reports under subparagraph (A), which shall include, at a minimum, the establishment by each such agency of a toll-free telephone number for such requests.

(ii) Considerations

In prescribing regulations under clause (i), the Bureau shall consider—

(I) the significant demands that may be placed on consumer reporting agencies in providing such consumer reports;

(II) appropriate means to ensure that consumer reporting agencies can satisfactorily meet those demands, including the efficacy of a system of staggering the availability to consumers of such consumer reports; and

(III) the ease by which consumers should be able to contact consumer reporting agencies with respect to access to such consumer reports.

(iii) Date of issuance

The Commission[1] shall issue the regulations required by this subparagraph in final form not later than 6 months after December 4, 2003.

(iv) Consideration of ability to comply

The regulations of the Bureau under this subparagraph shall establish an effective date by which each nationwide specialty consumer reporting agency (as defined in section 1681a of this title) shall be required to comply with subsection (a) of this section, which effective date—

(I) shall be established after consideration of the ability of each nationwide specialty consumer reporting agency to comply with subsection (a) of this section; and

(II) shall be not later than 6 months after the date on which such regulations are issued in final form (or such additional period not to exceed 3 months, as the Bureau determines appropriate).

(2) Timing

A consumer reporting agency shall provide a consumer report under paragraph (1) not later than 15 days after the date on which the request is received under paragraph (1).

(3) Reinvestigations

Notwithstanding the time periods specified in section 1681i(a)(1) of this title, a reinvestigation under that section by a consumer reporting agency upon a request of a consumer that is made after receiving a consumer report under this subsection shall be completed not later than 45 days after the date on which the request is received.

(4) Exception for first 12 months of operation

This subsection shall not apply to a consumer reporting agency that has not been furnishing consumer reports to third parties on a continuing basis during the 12-month period preceding a request under paragraph (1), with respect to consumers residing nationwide.

(b) Free disclosure after adverse notice to consumer

Each consumer reporting agency that maintains a file on a consumer shall make all disclosures pursuant to section 1681g of this title without charge to the consumer if, not later than 60 days after receipt by such consumer of a notification pursuant to section 1681m of this title, or of a notification from a debt collection agency affiliated with that consumer reporting agency stating that the consumer's credit rating may be or has been adversely affected, the consumer makes a request under section 1681g of this title.

(c) Free disclosure under certain other circumstances

Upon the request of the consumer, a consumer reporting agency shall make all disclosures pursuant to section 1681g of this title once during any 12-month period without charge to that consumer if the consumer certifies in writing that the consumer—

(1)   is unemployed and intends to apply for employment in the 60-day period beginning on the date on which the certification is made;

(2)   is a recipient of public welfare assistance; or

(3)   has reason to believe that the file on the consumer at the agency contains inaccurate information due to fraud.

(d)   Free disclosures in connection with fraud alerts

Upon the request of a consumer, a consumer reporting agency described in section 1681a(p) of this title shall make all disclosures pursuant to section 1681g of this title without charge to the consumer, as provided in subsections (a)(2) and (b)(2) of section 1681c–1 of this title, as applicable.

(e)   Other charges prohibited

A consumer reporting agency shall not impose any charge on a consumer for providing any notification required by this subchapter or making any disclosure required by this subchapter, except as authorized by subsection (f) of this section.

(f)   Reasonable charges allowed for certain disclosures

(1)   **In general.**—In the case of a request from a consumer other than a request that is covered by any of subsections (a) through (d) of this section, a consumer reporting agency may impose a reasonable charge on a consumer—

(A)   for making a disclosure to the consumer pursuant to section 1681g of this title, which charge—

(i)   shall not exceed $8; and

(ii)   shall be indicated to the consumer before making the disclosure; and

(B)   for furnishing, pursuant to section 1681i(d) of this title, following a reinvestigation under section 1681i(a) of this title, a statement, codification, or summary to a person designated by the consumer under that section after the 30-day period beginning on the date of notification of the consumer under paragraph (6) or (8) of section 1681i(a) of this title with respect to the reinvestigation, which charge—

(i)   shall not exceed the charge that the agency would impose on each designated recipient for a consumer report; and

(ii)   shall be indicated to the consumer before furnishing such information.

(2)   **Modification of amount.**—The Bureau shall increase the amount referred to in paragraph (1)(A)(i) on January 1 of each year, based proportionally on changes in the Consumer Price Index, with fractional changes rounded to the nearest fifty cents.

(g)   Prevention of deceptive marketing of credit reports

(1)   In general

Subject to rulemaking pursuant to section 205(b) of the Credit CARD Act of 2009, any advertisement for a free credit report in any medium shall prominently disclose in such advertisement that free credit reports are available under Federal law at: 'AnnualCreditReport.com' (or such other source as may be authorized under Federal law).

(2)   Television and radio advertisement

In the case of an advertisement broadcast by television, the disclosures required under paragraph (1) shall be included in the audio and visual part of such advertisement. In the case of an advertisement broadcast by television[1] or radio, the disclosure required under paragraph (1) shall consist only of the following: "This is not the free credit report provided for by Federal law".

---

[1]   So in original. Probably should be "television".

(Pub.L. 90–321, Title VI, § 612, as added Pub.L. 91–508, Title VI, § 601, Oct. 26, 1970, 84 Stat. 1132, and amended Pub.L. 104–208, Div. A, Title II, § 2410, Sept. 30, 1996, 110 Stat. 3009–442; Pub.L. 108–159, Title II, § 211(a), Dec. 4, 2003, 117 Stat. 1968; Pub.L. 111–24, Title II, § 205(a), May 22, 2009, 123 Stat. 1747; Pub.L. 111–203, Title X, § 1088(a)(2)(A), (C), July 21, 2010, 124 Stat. 2087.)

§ 1681k. Public record information for employment purposes [CCPA § 613]

(a) In general

A consumer reporting agency which furnishes a consumer report for employment purposes and which for that purpose compiles and reports items of information on consumers which are matters of public record and are likely to have an adverse effect upon a consumer's ability to obtain employment shall—

(1) at the time such public record information is reported to the user of such consumer report, notify the consumer of the fact that public record information is being reported by the consumer reporting agency, together with the name and address of the person to whom such information is being reported; or

(2) maintain strict procedures designed to insure that whenever public record information which is likely to have an adverse effect on a consumer's ability to obtain employment is reported it is complete and up to date. For purposes of this paragraph, items of public record relating to arrests, indictments, convictions, suits, tax liens, and outstanding judgments shall be considered up to date if the current public record status of the item at the time of the report is reported.

(b) Exemption for National security investigations

Subsection (a) of this section does not apply in the case of an agency or department of the United States Government that seeks to obtain and use a consumer report for employment purposes, if the head of the agency or department makes a written finding as prescribed under section 1681b(b)(4)(A) of this title.

(Pub.L. 90–321, Title VI, § 613, as added Pub.L. 91–508, Title VI, § 601, Oct. 26, 1970, 84 Stat. 1133, and amended Pub.L. 105–347, § 4(b), Nov. 2, 1998, 112 Stat. 3210.)

§ 1681*l*. Restrictions on investigative consumer reports [CCPA § 614]

Whenever a consumer reporting agency prepares an investigative consumer report, no adverse information in the consumer report (other than information which is a matter of public record) may be included in a subsequent consumer report unless such adverse information has been verified in the process of making such subsequent consumer report, or the adverse information was received within the three-month period preceding the date the subsequent report is furnished.

(Pub.L. 90–321, Title VI, § 614, as added Pub.L. 91–508, Title VI, § 601, Oct. 26, 1970, 84 Stat. 1133.)

§ 1681m. Requirements on users of consumer reports [CCPA § 615]

(a) Duties of users taking adverse actions on basis of information contained in consumer reports

If any person takes any adverse action with respect to any consumer that is based in whole or in part on any information contained in a consumer report, the person shall—

(1) provide oral, written, or electronic notice of the adverse action to the consumer;

(2) provide to the consumer written or electronic disclosure—

(A) of a numerical credit score as defined in section 1681g(f)(2)(A) of this title used by such person in taking any adverse action based in whole or in part on any information in a consumer report; and

(B) of the information set forth in subparagraphs (B) through (E) of section 1681g(f)(1) of this title;

(3) provide to the consumer orally, in writing, or electronically—

(A) the name, address, and telephone number of the consumer reporting agency (including a toll-free telephone number established by the agency if the agency compiles and maintains files on consumers on a nationwide basis) that furnished the report to the person; and

(B) a statement that the consumer reporting agency did not make the decision to take the adverse action and is unable to provide the consumer the specific reasons why the adverse action was taken; and

(4) provide to the consumer an oral, written, or electronic notice of the consumer's right—

(A) to obtain, under section 1681j of this title, a free copy of a consumer report on the consumer from the consumer reporting agency referred to in paragraph (3), which notice shall include an indication of the 60-day period under that section for obtaining such a copy; and

(B) to dispute, under section 1681i of this title, with a consumer reporting agency the accuracy or completeness of any information in a consumer report furnished by the agency.

(b) Adverse action based on information obtained from third parties other than consumer reporting agencies

(1) **In general.**—Whenever credit for personal, family, or household purposes involving a consumer is denied or the charge for such credit is increased either wholly or partly because of information obtained from a person other than a consumer reporting agency bearing upon the consumer's credit worthiness[1], credit standing, credit capacity, character, general reputation, personal characteristics, or mode of living, the user of such information shall, within a reasonable period of time, upon the consumer's written request for the reasons for such adverse action received within sixty days after learning of such adverse action, disclose the nature of the information to the consumer. The user of such information shall clearly and accurately disclose to the consumer his right to make such written request at the time such adverse action is communicated to the consumer.

(2) **Duties of person taking certain actions based on information provided by affiliate.**—

(A) **Duties, generally.**—If a person takes an action described in subparagraph (B) with respect to a consumer, based in whole or in part on information described in subparagraph (C), the person shall—

(i) notify the consumer of the action, including a statement that the consumer may obtain the information in accordance with clause (ii); and

(ii) upon a written request from the consumer received within 60 days after transmittal of the notice required by clause (i), disclose to the consumer the nature of the information upon which the action is based by not later than 30 days after receipt of the request.

(B) **Action described.**—An action referred to in subparagraph (A) is an adverse action described in section 1681a(k)(1)(A) of this title, taken in connection with a transaction initiated by the consumer, or any adverse action described in clause (i) or (ii) of section 1681a(k)(1)(B) of this title.

(C) **Information described.**—Information referred to in subparagraph (A)—

(i) except as provided in clause (ii), is information that—

(I) is furnished to the person taking the action by a person related by common ownership or affiliated by common corporate control to the person taking the action; and

(II) bears on the credit worthiness[1], credit standing, credit capacity, character, general reputation, personal characteristics, or mode of living of the consumer; and

(ii) does not include—

(I) information solely as to transactions or experiences between the consumer and the person furnishing the information; or

(II) information in a consumer report.

---

[1] So in original. Probably should be "creditworthiness".

(c) Reasonable procedures to assure compliance

No person shall be held liable for any violation of this section if he shows by a preponderance of the evidence that at the time of the alleged violation he maintained reasonable procedures to assure compliance with the provisions of this section.

(d) Duties of users making written credit or insurance solicitations on the basis of information contained in consumer files

(1) **In general.**—Any person who uses a consumer report on any consumer in connection with any credit or insurance transaction that is not initiated by the consumer, that is provided to that person under section 1681b(c)(1)(B) of this title, shall provide with each written solicitation made to the consumer regarding the transaction a clear and conspicuous statement that—

(A) information contained in the consumer's consumer report was used in connection with the transaction;

(B) the consumer received the offer of credit or insurance because the consumer satisfied the criteria for credit worthiness[1] or insurability under which the consumer was selected for the offer;

(C) if applicable, the credit or insurance may not be extended if, after the consumer responds to the offer, the consumer does not meet the criteria used to select the consumer for the offer or any applicable criteria bearing on credit worthiness[1] or insurability or does not furnish any required collateral;

(D) the consumer has a right to prohibit information contained in the consumer's file with any consumer reporting agency from being used in connection with any credit or insurance transaction that is not initiated by the consumer; and

(E) the consumer may exercise the right referred to in subparagraph (D) by notifying a notification system established under section 1681b(e) of this title.

(2) **Disclosure of address and telephone number; format**

A statement under paragraph (1) shall—

(A) include the address and toll-free telephone number of the appropriate notification system established under section 1681b(e) of this title; and

(B) be presented in such format and in such type size and manner as to be simple and easy to understand, as established by the Bureau, by rule, in consultation with the Federal Trade Commission, the Federal banking agencies, and the National Credit Union Administration.

(3) **Maintaining criteria on file.**—A person who makes an offer of credit or insurance to a consumer under a credit or insurance transaction described in paragraph (1) shall maintain on file the criteria used to select the consumer to receive the offer, all criteria bearing on credit worthiness[1] or insurability, as applicable, that are the basis for determining whether or not to extend credit or insurance pursuant to the offer, and any requirement for the furnishing of collateral as a condition of the extension of credit or insurance, until the expiration of the 3-year period beginning on the date on which the offer is made to the consumer.

(4) **Authority of Federal agencies regarding unfair or deceptive acts or practices not affected.**—This section is not intended to affect the authority of any Federal or State agency to enforce a prohibition against unfair or deceptive acts or practices, including the making of false or misleading statements in connection with a credit or insurance transaction that is not initiated by the consumer.

(e) Red flag guidelines and regulations required

(1) **Guidelines**

The Federal banking agencies, the National Credit Union Administration, the Federal Trade Commission, the Commodity Futures Trading Commission, and the Securities and Exchange

---

[1] So in original. Probably should be "creditworthiness".

Commission shall jointly, with respect to the entities that are subject to their respective enforcement authority under section 1681s of this title—

(A) establish and maintain guidelines for use by each financial institution and each creditor regarding identity theft with respect to account holders at, or customers of, such entities, and update such guidelines as often as necessary;

(B) prescribe regulations requiring each financial institution and each creditor to establish reasonable policies and procedures for implementing the guidelines established pursuant to subparagraph (A), to identify possible risks to account holders or customers or to the safety and soundness of the institution or customers; and

(C) prescribe regulations applicable to card issuers to ensure that, if a card issuer receives notification of a change of address for an existing account, and within a short period of time (during at least the first 30 days after such notification is received) receives a request for an additional or replacement card for the same account, the card issuer may not issue the additional or replacement card, unless the card issuer, in accordance with reasonable policies and procedures—

(i) notifies the cardholder of the request at the former address of the cardholder and provides to the cardholder a means of promptly reporting incorrect address changes;

(ii) notifies the cardholder of the request by such other means of communication as the cardholder and the card issuer previously agreed to; or

(iii) uses other means of assessing the validity of the change of address, in accordance with reasonable policies and procedures established by the card issuer in accordance with the regulations prescribed under subparagraph (B).

(2) Criteria

(A) In general

In developing the guidelines required by paragraph (1)(A), the agencies described in paragraph (1) shall identify patterns, practices, and specific forms of activity that indicate the possible existence of identity theft.

(B) Inactive accounts

In developing the guidelines required by paragraph (1)(A), the agencies described in paragraph (1) shall consider including reasonable guidelines providing that when a transaction occurs with respect to a credit or deposit account that has been inactive for more than 2 years, the creditor or financial institution shall follow reasonable policies and procedures that provide for notice to be given to a consumer in a manner reasonably designed to reduce the likelihood of identity theft with respect to such account.

(3) Consistency with verification requirements

Guidelines established pursuant to paragraph (1) shall not be inconsistent with the policies and procedures required under section 5318(*l*) of Title 31.

(4) Definitions

As used in this subsection, the term "creditor"—

(A) means a creditor, as defined in section 1691a of this title, that regularly and in the ordinary course of business—

(i) obtains or uses consumer reports, directly or indirectly, in connection with a credit transaction;

(ii) furnishes information to consumer reporting agencies, as described in section 1681s–2 of this title, in connection with a credit transaction; or

(iii) advances funds to or on behalf of a person, based on an obligation of the person to repay the funds or repayable from specific property pledged by or on behalf of the person;

(B) does not include a creditor described in subparagraph (A)(iii) that advances funds on behalf of a person for expenses incidental to a service provided by the creditor to that person; and

(C) includes any other type of creditor, as defined in that section 1691a of this title, as the agency described in paragraph (1) having authority over that creditor may determine appropriate by rule promulgated by that agency, based on a determination that such creditor offers or maintains accounts that are subject to a reasonably foreseeable risk of identity theft.

(f) Prohibition on sale or transfer of debt caused by identity theft

(1) In general

No person shall sell, transfer for consideration, or place for collection a debt that such person has been notified under section 1681c–2 of this title has resulted from identity theft.

(2) Applicability

The prohibitions of this subsection shall apply to all persons collecting a debt described in paragraph (1) after the date of a notification under paragraph (1).

(3) Rule of construction

Nothing in this subsection shall be construed to prohibit—

(A) the repurchase of a debt in any case in which the assignee of the debt requires such repurchase because the debt has resulted from identity theft;

(B) the securitization of a debt or the pledging of a portfolio of debt as collateral in connection with a borrowing; or

(C) the transfer of debt as a result of a merger, acquisition, purchase and assumption transaction, or transfer of substantially all of the assets of an entity.

(g) Debt collector communications concerning identity theft

If a person acting as a debt collector (as that term is defined in subchapter V of this chapter) on behalf of a third party that is a creditor or other user of a consumer report is notified that any information relating to a debt that the person is attempting to collect may be fraudulent or may be the result of identity theft, that person shall—

(1) notify the third party that the information may be fraudulent or may be the result of identity theft; and

(2) upon request of the consumer to whom the debt purportedly relates, provide to the consumer all information to which the consumer would otherwise be entitled if the consumer were not a victim of identity theft, but wished to dispute the debt under provisions of law applicable to that person.

(h) Duties of users in certain credit transactions

(1) In general

Subject to rules prescribed as provided in paragraph (6), if any person uses a consumer report in connection with an application for, or a grant, extension, or other provision of, credit on material terms that are materially less favorable than the most favorable terms available to a substantial proportion of consumers from or through that person, based in whole or in part on a consumer report, the person shall provide an oral, written, or electronic notice to the consumer in the form and manner required by regulations prescribed in accordance with this subsection.

(2) Timing

The notice required under paragraph (1) may be provided at the time of an application for, or a grant, extension, or other provision of, credit or the time of communication of an approval of an application for, or grant, extension, or other provision of, credit, except as provided in the regulations prescribed under paragraph (6).

(3) Exceptions

No notice shall be required from a person under this subsection if—

(A) the consumer applied for specific material terms and was granted those terms, unless those terms were initially specified by the person after the transaction was initiated by the consumer and after the person obtained a consumer report; or

(B) the person has provided or will provide a notice to the consumer under subsection (a) of this section in connection with the transaction.

(4) Other notice not sufficient

A person that is required to provide a notice under subsection (a) of this section cannot meet that requirement by providing a notice under this subsection.

(5) Content and delivery of notice

A notice under this subsection shall, at a minimum—

(A) include a statement informing the consumer that the terms offered to the consumer are set based on information from a consumer report;

(B) identify the consumer reporting agency furnishing the report;

(C) include a statement informing the consumer that the consumer may obtain a copy of a consumer report from that consumer reporting agency without charge;

(D) include the contact information specified by that consumer reporting agency for obtaining such consumer reports (including a toll-free telephone number established by the agency in the case of a consumer reporting agency described in section 1681a(p) of this title); and

(E) include a statement informing the consumer of—

(i) a numerical credit score as defined in section 1681g(f)(2)(A) of this title, used by such person in making the credit decision described in paragraph (1) based in whole or in part on any information in a consumer report; and

(ii) the information set forth in subparagraphs (B) through (E) of section 1681g(f)(1) of this title.

(6) Rulemaking

(A) Rules required

The Bureau shall prescribe rules to carry out this subsection.

(B) Content

Rules required by subparagraph (A) shall address, but are not limited to—

(i) the form, content, time, and manner of delivery of any notice under this subsection;

(ii) clarification of the meaning of terms used in this subsection, including what credit terms are material, and when credit terms are materially less favorable;

(iii) exceptions to the notice requirement under this subsection for classes of persons or transactions regarding which the agencies determine that notice would not significantly benefit consumers;

(iv) a model notice that may be used to comply with this subsection; and

(v) the timing of the notice required under paragraph (1), including the circumstances under which the notice must be provided after the terms offered to the consumer were set based on information from a consumer report.

(7) Compliance

A person shall not be liable for failure to perform the duties required by this section if, at the time of the failure, the person maintained reasonable policies and procedures to comply with this section.

(8) Enforcement

(A) No civil actions

Sections 1681n and 1681o of this title shall not apply to any failure by any person to comply with this section.

(B) Administrative enforcement

This section shall be enforced exclusively under section 1681s of this title by the Federal agencies and officials identified in that section.

(Pub.L. 90–321, Title VI, § 615, as added Pub.L. 91–508, Title VI, § 601, Oct. 26, 1970, 84 Stat. 1133, and amended Pub.L. 104–208, Div. A, Title II, § 2411(a), (b), (d), (e), Sept. 30, 1996, 110 Stat. 3009–443, 3009–444, 3009–445; Pub.L. 108–159, Title I, §§ 114, 154(b), 155, Title II, § 213(a), Title III, § 311(a), Title VIII, § 811(h), Dec. 4, 2003, 117 Stat. 1960, 1967, 1978, 1988, 2012; Pub.L. 111–319, § 2(a), Dec. 18, 2010, 124 Stat. 3457; Pub.L. 111–203, Title X, § 1088(a)(2)(C), (7) to (9), 1100F, July 21, 2010, 124 Stat. 2087, 2088, 2112.)

§ 1681n. Civil liability for willful noncompliance [CCPA § 616]

(a) In general

Any person who willfully fails to comply with any requirement imposed under this subchapter with respect to any consumer is liable to that consumer in an amount equal to the sum of—

(1)(A) any actual damages sustained by the consumer as a result of the failure or damages of not less than $100 and not more than $1,000; or

(B) in the case of liability of a natural person for obtaining a consumer report under false pretenses or knowingly without a permissible purpose, actual damages sustained by the consumer as a result of the failure or $1,000, whichever is greater;

(2) such amount of punitive damages as the court may allow; and

(3) in the case of any successful action to enforce any liability under this section, the costs of the action together with reasonable attorney's fees as determined by the court.

(b) Civil liability for knowing noncompliance

Any person who obtains a consumer report from a consumer reporting agency under false pretenses or knowingly without a permissible purpose shall be liable to the consumer reporting agency for actual damages sustained by the consumer reporting agency or $1,000, whichever is greater.

(c) Attorney's fees

Upon a finding by the court that an unsuccessful pleading, motion, or other paper filed in connection with an action under this section was filed in bad faith or for purposes of harassment, the court shall award to the prevailing party attorney's fees reasonable in relation to the work expended in responding to the pleading, motion, or other paper.

(d) Clarification of willful noncompliance

For the purposes of this section, any person who printed an expiration date on any receipt provided to a consumer cardholder at a point of sale or transaction between December 4, 2004, and June 3, 2008, but otherwise complied with the requirements of section 1681c(g) of this title for such receipt shall not be in willful noncompliance with section 1681c(g) of this title by reason of printing such expiration date on the receipt.

(Pub.L. 90–321, Title VI, § 616, as added Pub.L. 91–508, Title VI, § 601, Oct. 26, 1970, 84 Stat. 1134, and amended Pub.L. 104–208, Div. A, Title II, § 2412(a) to (c), (e)(1), Sept. 30, 1996, 110 Stat. 3009–446; Pub.L. 110–241, § 3(a), June 3, 2008, 122 Stat. 1566.)

§ 1681o.   Civil liability for negligent noncompliance [CCPA § 617]

(a) In general

Any person who is negligent in failing to comply with any requirement imposed under this subchapter with respect to any consumer is liable to that consumer in an amount equal to the sum of—

(1) any actual damages sustained by the consumer as a result of the failure; and

(2) in the case of any successful action to enforce any liability under this section, the costs of the action together with reasonable attorney's fees as determined by the court.

(b) Attorney's fees

On a finding by the court that an unsuccessful pleading, motion, or other paper filed in connection with an action under this section was filed in bad faith or for purposes of harassment, the court shall award to the prevailing party attorney's fees reasonable in relation to the work expended in responding to the pleading, motion, or other paper.

(Pub.L. 90–321, Title VI, § 617, as added Pub.L. 91–508, Title VI, § 601, Oct. 26, 1970, 84 Stat. 1134, and amended Pub.L. 104–208, Div. A, Title II, § 2412(d), (e)(2), Sept. 30, 1996, 110 Stat. 3009–446; Pub.L. 108–159, Title VIII, § 811(e), Dec. 4, 2003, 117 Stat. 2012.)

§ 1681p.   Jurisdiction of courts; limitation of actions [CCPA § 618]

An action to enforce any liability created under this subchapter may be brought in any appropriate United States district court, without regard to the amount in controversy, or in any other court of competent jurisdiction, not later than the earlier of—

(1) 2 years after the date of discovery by the plaintiff of the violation that is the basis for such liability; or

(2) 5 years after the date on which the violation that is the basis for such liability occurs.

(Pub.L. 90–321, Title VI, § 618, as added Pub.L. 91–508, Title VI, § 601, Oct. 26, 1970, 84 Stat. 1134, and amended Pub.L. 108–159, Title I, § 156, Dec. 4, 2003, 117 Stat. 1968.)

§ 1681q.   Obtaining information under false pretenses [CCPA § 619]

Any person who knowingly and willfully obtains information on a consumer from a consumer reporting agency under false pretenses shall be fined under Title 18, imprisoned for not more than 2 years, or both.

(Pub.L. 90–321, Title VI, § 619, as added Pub.L. 91–508, Title VI, § 601, Oct. 26, 1970, 84 Stat. 1134, and amended Pub.L. 104–208, Div. A, Title II, § 2415(a), Sept. 30, 1996, 110 Stat. 3009–450.)

§ 1681r.   Unauthorized disclosures by officers or employees [CCPA § 620]

Any officer or employee of a consumer reporting agency who knowingly and willfully provides information concerning an individual from the agency's files to a person not authorized to receive that information shall be fined under Title 18, imprisoned for not more than 2 years, or both.

(Pub.L. 90–321, Title VI, § 620, as added Pub.L. 91–508, Title VI, § 601, Oct. 26, 1970, 84 Stat. 1134, and amended Pub.L. 104–208, Div. A, Title II, § 2415(b), Sept. 30, 1996, 110 Stat. 3009–450.)

§ 1681s.   Administrative enforcement [CCPA § 621]

(a) Enforcement by Federal Trade Commission

(1) In general

The Federal Trade Commission shall be authorized to enforce compliance with the requirements imposed by this subchapter under the Federal Trade Commission Act (15 U.S.C. § 41 et seq.), with respect to consumer reporting agencies and all other persons subject thereto, except to the extent that enforcement of the requirements imposed under this subchapter is specifically committed to some other Government agency under any of subparagraphs (A) through (G) of subsection (b)(1), and subject to subtitle B of the

Consumer Financial Protection Act of 2010, subsection (b).[1] For the purpose of the exercise by the Federal Trade Commission of its functions and powers under the Federal Trade Commission Act, a violation of any requirement or prohibition imposed under this subchapter shall constitute an unfair or deceptive act or practice in commerce, in violation of section 5(a) of the Federal Trade Commission Act (15 U.S.C. § 45(a)), and shall be subject to enforcement by the Federal Trade Commission under section 5(b) of that Act with respect to any consumer reporting agency or person that is subject to enforcement by the Federal Trade Commission pursuant to this subsection, irrespective of whether that person is engaged in commerce or meets any other jurisdictional tests under the Federal Trade Commission Act. The Federal Trade Commission shall have such procedural, investigative, and enforcement powers, including the power to issue procedural rules in enforcing compliance with the requirements imposed under this subchapter and to require the filing of reports, the production of documents, and the appearance of witnesses, as though the applicable terms and conditions of the Federal Trade Commission Act were part of this subchapter. Any person violating any of the provisions of this subchapter shall be subject to the penalties and entitled to the privileges and immunities provided in the Federal Trade Commission Act as though the applicable terms and provisions of such Act are part of this subchapter.

(2) Penalties

(A) Knowing violations

Except as otherwise provided by subtitle B of the Consumer Financial Protection Act of 2010, in the event of a knowing violation, which constitutes a pattern or practice of violations of this subchapter, the Federal Trade Commission may commence a civil action to recover a civil penalty in a district court of the United States against any person that violates this subchapter. In such action, such person shall be liable for a civil penalty of not more than $2,500 per violation.

(B) Determining penalty amount

In determining the amount of a civil penalty under subparagraph (A), the court shall take into account the degree of culpability, any history of such prior conduct, ability to pay, effect on ability to continue to do business, and such other matters as justice may require.

(C) Limitation

Notwithstanding paragraph (2), a court may not impose any civil penalty on a person for a violation of section 1681s–2(a)(1) of this title, unless the person has been enjoined from committing the violation, or ordered not to commit the violation, in an action or proceeding brought by or on behalf of the Federal Trade Commission, and has violated the injunction or order, and the court may not impose any civil penalty for any violation occurring before the date of the violation of the injunction or order.

(b) Enforcement by other agencies

(1) In general

Subject to subtitle B of the Consumer Financial Protection Act of 2010, compliance with the requirements imposed under this subchapter with respect to consumer reporting agencies, persons who use consumer reports from such agencies, persons who furnish information to such agencies, and users of information that are subject to section 1681m(d) of this title shall be enforced under—

(A) section 1818 of Title 12, by the appropriate Federal banking agency, as defined in section 1813(q) of Title 12, with respect to—

(i) any national bank or State savings association, and any Federal branch or Federal agency of a foreign bank;

(ii) any member bank of the Federal Reserve System (other than a national bank), a branch or agency of a foreign bank (other than a Federal branch, Federal agency, or insured State branch of a foreign bank), a commercial lending company owned or controlled by a foreign bank, and any organization operating under section 25 or 25A of the Federal Reserve Act; and

---

[1] So in original.

(iii) any bank or Federal savings association insured by the Federal Deposit Insurance Corporation (other than a member of the Federal Reserve System) and any insured State branch of a foreign bank;

(B)   the Federal Credit Union Act (12 U.S.C. § 1751 et seq.), by the Administrator of the National Credit Union Administration with respect to any Federal credit union;

(C)   subtitle IV of Title 49, by the Secretary of Transportation, with respect to all carriers subject to the jurisdiction of the Surface Transportation Board;

(D)   part A of subtitle VII of Title 49, by the Secretary of Transportation, with respect to any air carrier or foreign air carrier subject to that Act;

(E)   the Packers and Stockyards Act, 1921 (7 U.S.C. § 181 et seq.) (except as provided in section 406 of that Act), by the Secretary of Agriculture, with respect to any activities subject to that Act;

(F)   the Commodity Exchange Act, with respect to a person subject to the jurisdiction of the Commodity Futures Trading Commission;

(G)   the Federal securities laws, and any other laws that are subject to the jurisdiction of the Securities and Exchange Commission, with respect to a person that is subject to the jurisdiction of the Securities and Exchange Commission; and

(H)   subtitle E of the Consumer Financial Protection Act of 2010, by the Bureau, with respect to any person subject to this subchapter.

(2)   Incorporated definitions

The terms used in paragraph (1) that are not defined in this subchapter or otherwise defined in section 1813(s) of Title 12 have the same meanings as in section 3101(b) of Title 12.

(c)   State action for violations

(1)   Authority of States.—In addition to such other remedies as are provided under State law, if the chief law enforcement officer of a State, or an official or agency designated by a State, has reason to believe that any person has violated or is violating this subchapter, the State—

(A)   may bring an action to enjoin such violation in any appropriate United States district court or in any other court of competent jurisdiction;

(B)   subject to paragraph (5), may bring an action on behalf of the residents of the State to recover—

(i)   damages for which the person is liable to such residents under sections 1681n and 1681o of this title as a result of the violation;

(ii)   in the case of a violation described in any of paragraphs (1) through (3) of section 1681s–2(c) of this title, damages for which the person would, but for section 1681s–2(c) of this title, be liable to such residents as a result of the violation; or

(iii)   damages of not more than $1,000 for each willful or negligent violation; and

(C)   in the case of any successful action under subparagraph (A) or (B), shall be awarded the costs of the action and reasonable attorney fees as determined by the court.

(2)   Rights of Federal regulators.—The State shall serve prior written notice of any action under paragraph (1) upon the Bureau and the Federal Trade Commission or the appropriate Federal regulator determined under subsection (b) of this section and provide the Bureau and the Federal Trade Commission or appropriate Federal regulator with a copy of its complaint, except in any case in which such prior notice is not feasible, in which case the State shall serve such notice immediately upon instituting such action. The Bureau and the Federal Trade Commission or appropriate Federal regulator shall have the right—

(A)   to intervene in the action;

(B)   upon so intervening, to be heard on all matters arising therein;

(C)   to remove the action to the appropriate United States district court; and

(D) to file petitions for appeal.

(3) Investigatory powers.—For purposes of bringing any action under this subsection, nothing in this subsection shall prevent the chief law enforcement officer, or an official or agency designated by a State, from exercising the powers conferred on the chief law enforcement officer or such official by the laws of such State to conduct investigations or to administer oaths or affirmations or to compel the attendance of witnesses or the production of documentary and other evidence.

(4) Limitation on State action while Federal action pending.—If the Bureau and the Federal Trade Commission or the appropriate Federal regulator has instituted a civil action or an administrative action under section 8 of the Federal Deposit Insurance Act [12 U.S.C.A. § 1818] for a violation of this subchapter, no State may, during the pendency of such action, bring an action under this section against any defendant named in the complaint of the Bureau and the Federal Trade Commission or the appropriate Federal regulator for any violation of this subchapter that is alleged in that complaint.

(5) Limitations on State actions for certain violations

(A) Violation of injunction required.—A State may not bring an action against a person under paragraph (1)(B) for a violation described in any of paragraphs (1) through (3) of section 1681s–2(c) of this title, unless—

(i) the person has been enjoined from committing the violation, in an action brought by the State under paragraph (1)(A); and

(ii) the person has violated the injunction.

(B) Limitation on damages recoverable.—In an action against a person under paragraph (1)(B) for a violation described in any of paragraphs (1) through (3) of section 1681s–2(c) of this title, a State may not recover any damages incurred before the date of the violation of an injunction on which the action is based.

(d) Enforcement under other authority

For the purpose of the exercise by any agency referred to in subsection (b) of this section of its powers under any Act referred to in that subsection, a violation of any requirement imposed under this subchapter shall be deemed to be a violation of a requirement imposed under that Act. In addition to its powers under any provision of law specifically referred to in subsection (b) of this section, each of the agencies referred to in that subsection may exercise, for the purpose of enforcing compliance with any requirement imposed under this subchapter any other authority conferred on it by law.

(e) Regulatory authority

(1) In general

The Bureau shall prescribe such regulations as are necessary to carry out the purposes of this subchapter, except with respect to sections 1681m(e) and 1681w of this title. The Bureau may prescribe regulations as may be necessary or appropriate to administer and carry out the purposes and objectives of this subchapter, and to prevent evasions thereof or to facilitate compliance therewith. Except as provided in section 5519(a) of Title 12, the regulations prescribed by the Bureau under this subchapter shall apply to any person that is subject to this subchapter, notwithstanding the enforcement authorities granted to other agencies under this section.

(2) Deference

Notwithstanding any power granted to any Federal agency under this subchapter, the deference that a court affords to a Federal agency with respect to a determination made by such agency relating to the meaning or interpretation of any provision of this subchapter that is subject to the jurisdiction of such agency shall be applied as if that agency were the only agency authorized to apply, enforce, interpret, or administer the provisions of this subchapter[2] The regulations prescribed by the Bureau under this subchapter shall apply to any person that is subject to this subchapter, notwithstanding the enforcement authorities granted to other agencies under this section.

---

2   So in original. Probably should be followed by a period.

(f) Coordination of consumer complaint investigations

(1) In general

Each consumer reporting agency described in section 1681a(p) of this title shall develop and maintain procedures for the referral to each other such agency of any consumer complaint received by the agency alleging identity theft, or requesting a fraud alert under section 1681c–1 of this title or a block under section 1681c–2 of this title.

(2) Model form and procedure for reporting identity theft

The Commission,[3] in consultation with the Federal Trade Commission, the Federal banking agencies, and the National Credit Union Administration, shall develop a model form and model procedures to be used by consumers who are victims of identity theft for contacting and informing creditors and consumer reporting agencies of the fraud.

(3) Annual summary reports

Each consumer reporting agency described in section 1681a(p) of this title shall submit an annual summary report to the Bureau on consumer complaints received by the agency on identity theft or fraud alerts.

(g) Bureau regulation of coding of trade names

If the Bureau determines that a person described in paragraph (9) of section 1681s–c(a) of this title has not met the requirements of such paragraph, the Bureau shall take action to ensure the person's compliance with such paragraph, which may include issuing model guidance or prescribing reasonable policies and procedures, as necessary to ensure that such person complies with such paragraph.

(Pub.L. 90–321, Title VI, § 621, as added Pub.L. 91–508, Title VI, § 601, Oct. 26, 1970, 84 Stat. 1134, and amended Pub.L. 98–443, § 9(n), Oct. 4, 1984, 98 Stat. 1708; Pub.L. 101–73, Title VII, § 744(*l*), Aug. 9, 1989, 103 Stat. 439; Pub.L. 102–242, Title II, § 212(c), Dec. 19, 1991, 105 Stat. 2300; Pub.L. 102–550, Title XVI, § 1604(a)(6), Oct. 28, 1992, 106 Stat. 4082; Pub.L. 104–88, Title III, § 314, Dec. 29, 1995, 109 Stat. 948; Pub.L. 104–208, Div. A, Title II, §§ 2416 to 2418, Sept. 30, 1996, 110 Stat. 3009–450 to 3009–452; Pub.L. 105–347, § 6(6), Nov. 2, 1998, 112 Stat. 3211; Pub.L. 106–102, Title V, § 506(a), (b), Nov. 12, 1999, 113 Stat. 1441, 1442; Pub.L. 108–159, Title I, § 153, Title III, § 312(e)(2), Title IV, § 411(e), Title VIII, § 811(f), Dec. 4, 2003, 117 Stat. 1966, 1993, 2003, 2012; Pub.L. 111–203, Title X, § 1088(a)(2)(A) to (C), July 21, 2010, 124 Stat. 2087.)

§ 1681s–1.   Information on overdue child support obligations [CCPA § 622]

Notwithstanding any other provision of this subchapter, a consumer reporting agency shall include in any consumer report furnished by the agency in accordance with section 1681b of this title, any information on the failure of the consumer to pay overdue support which—

(1) is provided—

(A) to the consumer reporting agency by a State or local child support enforcement agency; or

(B) to the consumer reporting agency and verified by any local, State, or Federal Government agency; and

(2) antedates the report by 7 years or less.

(Pub.L. 90–321, Title VI, § 622, as added Pub.L. 102–537, § 2(a), Oct. 27, 1992, 106 Stat. 3531.)

§ 1681s–2.   Responsibilities of furnishers of information to consumer reporting agencies [CCPA § 623]

(a) Duty of furnishers of information to provide accurate information

(1) Prohibition

---

[3] So in original. Probably should be "The Bureau".

(A) Reporting information with actual knowledge of errors

A person shall not furnish any information relating to a consumer to any consumer reporting agency if the person knows or has reasonable cause to believe that the information is inaccurate.

(B) Reporting information after notice and confirmation of errors

A person shall not furnish information relating to a consumer to any consumer reporting agency if—

(i) the person has been notified by the consumer, at the address specified by the person for such notices, that specific information is inaccurate; and

(ii) the information is, in fact, inaccurate.

(C) No address requirement

A person who clearly and conspicuously specifies to the consumer an address for notices referred to in subparagraph (B) shall not be subject to subparagraph (A); however, nothing in subparagraph (B) shall require a person to specify such an address.

(D) Definition

For purposes of subparagraph (A), the term "reasonable cause to believe that the information is inaccurate" means having specific knowledge, other than solely allegations by the consumer, that would cause a reasonable person to have substantial doubts about the accuracy of the information.

(2) Duty to correct and update information

A person who—

(A) regularly and in the ordinary course of business furnishes information to one or more consumer reporting agencies about the person's transactions or experiences with any consumer; and

(B) has furnished to a consumer reporting agency information that the person determines is not complete or accurate,

shall promptly notify the consumer reporting agency of that determination and provide to the agency any corrections to that information, or any additional information, that is necessary to make the information provided by the person to the agency complete and accurate, and shall not thereafter furnish to the agency any of the information that remains not complete or accurate.

(3) Duty to provide notice of dispute

If the completeness or accuracy of any information furnished by any person to any consumer reporting agency is disputed to such person by a consumer, the person may not furnish the information to any consumer reporting agency without notice that such information is disputed by the consumer.

(4) Duty to provide notice of closed accounts

A person who regularly and in the ordinary course of business furnishes information to a consumer reporting agency regarding a consumer who has a credit account with that person shall notify the agency of the voluntary closure of the account by the consumer, in information regularly furnished for the period in which the account is closed.

(5) Duty to provide notice of delinquency of accounts

(A) In general

A person who furnishes information to a consumer reporting agency regarding a delinquent account being placed for collection, charged to profit or loss, or subjected to any similar action shall, not later than 90 days after furnishing the information, notify the agency of the date of delinquency on the account, which shall be the month and year of the commencement of the delinquency on the account that immediately preceded the action.

(B) Rule of construction

For purposes of this paragraph only, and provided that the consumer does not dispute the information, a person that furnishes information on a delinquent account that is placed for collection, charged for profit or loss, or subjected to any similar action, complies with this paragraph, if—

(i) the person reports the same date of delinquency as that provided by the creditor to which the account was owed at the time at which the commencement of the delinquency occurred, if the creditor previously reported that date of delinquency to a consumer reporting agency;

(ii) the creditor did not previously report the date of delinquency to a consumer reporting agency, and the person establishes and follows reasonable procedures to obtain the date of delinquency from the creditor or another reliable source and reports that date to a consumer reporting agency as the date of delinquency; or

(iii) the creditor did not previously report the date of delinquency to a consumer reporting agency and the date of delinquency cannot be reasonably obtained as provided in clause (ii), the person establishes and follows reasonable procedures to ensure the date reported as the date of delinquency precedes the date on which the account is placed for collection, charged to profit or loss, or subjected to any similar action, and reports such date to the credit reporting agency.

(6) Duties of furnishers upon notice of identity theft-related information

(A) Reasonable procedures

A person that furnishes information to any consumer reporting agency shall have in place reasonable procedures to respond to any notification that it receives from a consumer reporting agency under section 1681c–2 of this title relating to information resulting from identity theft, to prevent that person from refurnishing such blocked information.

(B) Information alleged to result from identity theft

If a consumer submits an identity theft report to a person who furnishes information to a consumer reporting agency at the address specified by that person for receiving such reports stating that information maintained by such person that purports to relate to the consumer resulted from identity theft, the person may not furnish such information that purports to relate to the consumer to any consumer reporting agency, unless the person subsequently knows or is informed by the consumer that the information is correct.

(7) Negative information

(A) Notice to consumer required

(i) In general

If any financial institution that extends credit and regularly and in the ordinary course of business furnishes information to a consumer reporting agency described in section 1681a(p) of this title furnishes negative information to such an agency regarding credit extended to a customer, the financial institution shall provide a notice of such furnishing of negative information, in writing, to the customer.

(ii) Notice effective for subsequent submissions

After providing such notice, the financial institution may submit additional negative information to a consumer reporting agency described in section 1681a(p) of this title with respect to the same transaction, extension of credit, account, or customer without providing additional notice to the customer.

(B) Time of notice

(i) In general

The notice required under subparagraph (A) shall be provided to the customer prior to, or no later than 30 days after, furnishing the negative information to a consumer reporting agency described in section 1681a(p) of this title.

(ii) Coordination with new account disclosures

If the notice is provided to the customer prior to furnishing the negative information to a consumer reporting agency, the notice may not be included in the initial disclosures provided under section 1637(a) of this title.

(C) Coordination with other disclosures

The notice required under subparagraph (A)—

(i) may be included on or with any notice of default, any billing statement, or any other materials provided to the customer; and

(ii) must be clear and conspicuous.

(D) Model disclosure

(i) Duty of bureau

The Bureau shall prescribe a brief model disclosure that a financial institution may use to comply with subparagraph (A), which shall not exceed 30 words.

(ii) Use of model not required

No provision of this paragraph may be construed to require a financial institution to use any such model form prescribed by the Bureau.

(iii) Compliance using model

A financial institution shall be deemed to be in compliance with subparagraph (A) if the financial institution uses any model form prescribed by the Bureau under this subparagraph, or the financial institution uses any such model form and rearranges its format.

(E) Use of notice without submitting negative information

No provision of this paragraph shall be construed as requiring a financial institution that has provided a customer with a notice described in subparagraph (A) to furnish negative information about the customer to a consumer reporting agency.

(F) Safe harbor

A financial institution shall not be liable for failure to perform the duties required by this paragraph if, at the time of the failure, the financial institution maintained reasonable policies and procedures to comply with this paragraph or the financial institution reasonably believed that the institution is prohibited, by law, from contacting the consumer.

(G) Definitions

For purposes of this paragraph, the following definitions shall apply:

(i) Negative information

The term "negative information" means information concerning a customer's delinquencies, late payments, insolvency, or any form of default.

(ii) Customer; financial institution

The terms "customer" and "financial institution" have the same meanings as in section 6809 of this title.

(8)   **Ability of consumer to dispute information directly with furnisher**

(A) In general

The Bureau, in consultation with the Federal Trade Commission, the Federal banking agencies, and the National Credit Union Administration, shall prescribe regulations that shall identify the circumstances under which a furnisher shall be required to reinvestigate a dispute concerning the accuracy of information contained in a consumer report on the consumer, based on a direct request of a consumer.

(B) Considerations

In prescribing regulations under subparagraph (A), the agencies shall weigh—

(i)   the benefits to consumers with the costs on furnishers and the credit reporting system;

(ii)   the impact on the overall accuracy and integrity of consumer reports of any such requirements;

(iii)   whether direct contact by the consumer with the furnisher would likely result in the most expeditious resolution of any such dispute; and

(iv)   the potential impact on the credit reporting process if credit repair organizations, as defined in section 1679a(3) of this title, including entities that would be a credit repair organization, but for section 1679a(3)(B)(i) of this title, are able to circumvent the prohibition in subparagraph (G).

(C) Applicability

Subparagraphs (D) through (G) shall apply in any circumstance identified under the regulations promulgated under subparagraph (A).

(D) Submitting a notice of dispute

A consumer who seeks to dispute the accuracy of information shall provide a dispute notice directly to such person at the address specified by the person for such notices that—

(i)   identifies the specific information that is being disputed;

(ii)   explains the basis for the dispute; and

(iii)   includes all supporting documentation required by the furnisher to substantiate the basis of the dispute.

(E) Duty of person after receiving notice of dispute

After receiving a notice of dispute from a consumer pursuant to subparagraph (D), the person that provided the information in dispute to a consumer reporting agency shall—

(i)   conduct an investigation with respect to the disputed information;

(ii)   review all relevant information provided by the consumer with the notice;

(iii)   complete such person's investigation of the dispute and report the results of the investigation to the consumer before the expiration of the period under section 1681i(a)(1) of this title within which a consumer reporting agency would be required to complete its action if the consumer had elected to dispute the information under that section; and

(iv)   if the investigation finds that the information reported was inaccurate, promptly notify each consumer reporting agency to which the person furnished the inaccurate information of that determination and provide to the agency any correction to that information that is necessary to make the information provided by the person accurate.

(F) Frivolous or irrelevant dispute

(i) In general

This paragraph shall not apply if the person receiving a notice of a dispute from a consumer reasonably determines that the dispute is frivolous or irrelevant, including—

(I) by reason of the failure of a consumer to provide sufficient information to investigate the disputed information; or

(II) the submission by a consumer of a dispute that is substantially the same as a dispute previously submitted by or for the consumer, either directly to the person or through a consumer reporting agency under subsection (b) of this section, with respect to which the person has already performed the person's duties under this paragraph or subsection (b), as applicable.

(ii) Notice of determination

Upon making any determination under clause (i) that a dispute is frivolous or irrelevant, the person shall notify the consumer of such determination not later than 5 business days after making such determination, by mail or, if authorized by the consumer for that purpose, by any other means available to the person.

(iii) Contents of notice

A notice under clause (ii) shall include—

(I) the reasons for the determination under clause (i); and

(II) identification of any information required to investigate the disputed information, which may consist of a standardized form describing the general nature of such information.

(G) Exclusion of credit repair organizations

This paragraph shall not apply if the notice of the dispute is submitted by, is prepared on behalf of the consumer by, or is submitted on a form supplied to the consumer by, a credit repair organization, as defined in section 1679a(3) of this title, or an entity that would be a credit repair organization, but for section 1679a(3)(B)(i) of this title.

(9) Duty to provide notice of status as medical information furnisher

A person whose primary business is providing medical services, products, or devices, or the person's agent or assignee, who furnishes information to a consumer reporting agency on a consumer shall be considered a medical information furnisher for purposes of this subchapter, and shall notify the agency of such status.

(b) Duties of furnishers of information upon notice of dispute

(1) In general

After receiving notice pursuant to section 1681i(a)(2) of this title of a dispute with regard to the completeness or accuracy of any information provided by a person to a consumer reporting agency, the person shall—

(A) conduct an investigation with respect to the disputed information;

(B) review all relevant information provided by the consumer reporting agency pursuant to section 1681i(a)(2) of this title;

(C) report the results of the investigation to the consumer reporting agency;

(D) if the investigation finds that the information is incomplete or inaccurate, report those results to all other consumer reporting agencies to which the person furnished the information and that compile and maintain files on consumers on a nationwide basis; and

(E) if an item of information disputed by a consumer is found to be inaccurate or incomplete or cannot be verified after any reinvestigation under paragraph (1), for purposes of reporting to a consumer reporting agency only, as appropriate, based on the results of the reinvestigation promptly—

    (i)   modify that item of information;

    (ii)   delete that item of information; or

    (iii)   permanently block the reporting of that item of information.

(2) Deadline

A person shall complete all investigations, reviews, and reports required under paragraph (1) regarding information provided by the person to a consumer reporting agency, before the expiration of the period under section 1681i(a)(1) of this title within which the consumer reporting agency is required to complete actions required by that section regarding that information.

(c) Limitation on liability

Except as provided in section 1681s(c)(1)(B) of this title, sections 1681n and 1681o of this title do not apply to any violation of—

    (1)   subsection (a) of this section, including any regulations issued thereunder;

    (2)   subsection (e) of this section, except that nothing in this paragraph shall limit, expand, or otherwise affect liability under section 1681n or 1681o of this title, as applicable, for violations of subsection (b) of this section; or

    (3)   subsection (e) of section 1681m of this title.

(d) Limitation on enforcement

The provisions of law described in paragraphs (1) through (3) of subsection (c) of this section (other than with respect to the exception described in paragraph (2) of subsection (c) of this section) shall be enforced exclusively as provided under section 1681s of this title by the Federal agencies and officials and the State officials identified in section 1681s of this title.

(e) Accuracy guidelines and regulations required

(1) Guidelines

The Bureau shall, with respect to persons or entities that are subject to the enforcement authority of the Bureau under section 1681s of this title—

    (A)   establish and maintain guidelines for use by each person that furnishes information to a consumer reporting agency regarding the accuracy and integrity of the information relating to consumers that such entities furnish to consumer reporting agencies, and update such guidelines as often as necessary; and

    (B)   prescribe regulations requiring each person that furnishes information to a consumer reporting agency to establish reasonable policies and procedures for implementing the guidelines established pursuant to subparagraph (A).

(2) Criteria

In developing the guidelines required by paragraph (1)(A), the Bureau shall—

    (A)   identify patterns, practices, and specific forms of activity that can compromise the accuracy and integrity of information furnished to consumer reporting agencies;

    (B)   review the methods (including technological means) used to furnish information relating to consumers to consumer reporting agencies;

    (C)   determine whether persons that furnish information to consumer reporting agencies maintain and enforce policies to ensure the accuracy and integrity of information furnished to consumer reporting agencies; and

(D) examine the policies and processes that persons that furnish information to consumer reporting agencies employ to conduct reinvestigations and correct inaccurate information relating to consumers that has been furnished to consumer reporting agencies.

(Pub.L. 90–321, Title VI, § 623, as added Pub.L. 104–208, Div. A, Title II, § 2413(a)(2), Sept. 30, 1996, 110 Stat. 3009–447, and amended Pub.L. 108–159, Title I, § 154(a), Title II, § 217(a), Title III, §§ 312(a) to (e)(1), 314(b), Title IV, § 412(a), (f), Dec. 4, 2003, 117 Stat. 1966, 1986, 1989 to 1993, 1995, 2002, 2003; Pub.L. 111–203, Title X, § 1088(a)(2)(D), (11), July 21, 2010, 124 Stat. 2087, 2090.)

§ 1681s–3.   Affiliate sharing [CCPA § 624]

(a) Special rule for solicitation for purposes of marketing

(1) Notice

Any person that receives from another person related to it by common ownership or affiliated by corporate control a communication of information that would be a consumer report, but for clauses (i), (ii), and (iii) of section 1681a(d)(2)(A) of this title, may not use the information to make a solicitation for marketing purposes to a consumer about its products or services, unless—

(A) it is clearly and conspicuously disclosed to the consumer that the information may be communicated among such persons for purposes of making such solicitations to the consumer; and

(B) the consumer is provided an opportunity and a simple method to prohibit the making of such solicitations to the consumer by such person.

(2) Consumer choice

(A) In general

The notice required under paragraph (1) shall allow the consumer the opportunity to prohibit all solicitations referred to in such paragraph, and may allow the consumer to choose from different options when electing to prohibit the sending of such solicitations, including options regarding the types of entities and information covered, and which methods of delivering solicitations the consumer elects to prohibit.

(B) Format

Notwithstanding subparagraph (A), the notice required under paragraph (1) shall be clear, conspicuous, and concise, and any method provided under paragraph (1)(B) shall be simple. The regulations prescribed to implement this section shall provide specific guidance regarding how to comply with such standards.

(3) Duration

(A) In general

The election of a consumer pursuant to paragraph (1)(B) to prohibit the making of solicitations shall be effective for at least 5 years, beginning on the date on which the person receives the election of the consumer, unless the consumer requests that such election be revoked.

(B) Notice upon expiration of effective period

At such time as the election of a consumer pursuant to paragraph (1)(B) is no longer effective, a person may not use information that the person receives in the manner described in paragraph (1) to make any solicitation for marketing purposes to the consumer, unless the consumer receives a notice and an opportunity, using a simple method, to extend the opt-out for another period of at least 5 years, pursuant to the procedures described in paragraph (1).

(4) Scope

This section shall not apply to a person—

(A) using information to make a solicitation for marketing purposes to a consumer with whom the person has a pre-existing business relationship;

(B) using information to facilitate communications to an individual for whose benefit the person provides employee benefit or other services pursuant to a contract with an employer related to and arising out of the current employment relationship or status of the individual as a participant or beneficiary of an employee benefit plan;

(C) using information to perform services on behalf of another person related by common ownership or affiliated by corporate control, except that this subparagraph shall not be construed as permitting a person to send solicitations on behalf of another person, if such other person would not be permitted to send the solicitation on its own behalf as a result of the election of the consumer to prohibit solicitations under paragraph (1)(B);

(D) using information in response to a communication initiated by the consumer;

(E) using information in response to solicitations authorized or requested by the consumer; or

(F) if compliance with this section by that person would prevent compliance by that person with any provision of State insurance laws pertaining to unfair discrimination in any State in which the person is lawfully doing business.

(5) No retroactivity

This subsection shall not prohibit the use of information to send a solicitation to a consumer if such information was received prior to the date on which persons are required to comply with regulations implementing this subsection.

(b) Notice for other purposes permissible

A notice or other disclosure under this section may be coordinated and consolidated with any other notice required to be issued under any other provision of law by a person that is subject to this section, and a notice or other disclosure that is equivalent to the notice required by subsection (a) of this section, and that is provided by a person described in subsection (a) of this section to a consumer together with disclosures required by any other provision of law, shall satisfy the requirements of subsection (a) of this section.

(c) User requirements

Requirements with respect to the use by a person of information received from another person related to it by common ownership or affiliated by corporate control, such as the requirements of this section, constitute requirements with respect to the exchange of information among persons affiliated by common ownership or common corporate control, within the meaning of section 1681t(b)(2) of this title.

(d) Definitions

For purposes of this section, the following definitions shall apply:

(1) Pre-existing business relationship

The term "pre-existing business relationship" means a relationship between a person, or a person's licensed agent, and a consumer, based on—

(A) a financial contract between a person and a consumer which is in force;

(B) the purchase, rental, or lease by the consumer of that person's goods or services, or a financial transaction (including holding an active account or a policy in force or having another continuing relationship) between the consumer and that person during the 18-month period immediately preceding the date on which the consumer is sent a solicitation covered by this section;

(C) an inquiry or application by the consumer regarding a product or service offered by that person, during the 3-month period immediately preceding the date on which the consumer is sent a solicitation covered by this section; or

(D) any other pre-existing customer relationship defined in the regulations implementing this section.

(2) Solicitation

The term "solicitation" means the marketing of a product or service initiated by a person to a particular consumer that is based on an exchange of information described in subsection (a) of this section, and is intended to encourage the consumer to purchase such product or service, but does not include communications that are directed at the general public or determined not to be a solicitation by the regulations prescribed under this section.

(Pub.L. 90–321, Title VI, § 624, as added Pub.L. 108–159, Title II, § 214(a)(2), Dec. 4, 2003, 117 Stat. 1980.)

§ 1681t.   Relation to State laws [CCPA § 625]

(a) In general

Except as provided in subsections (b) and (c) of this section, this subchapter does not annul, alter, affect, or exempt any person subject to the provisions of this subchapter from complying with the laws of any State with respect to the collection, distribution, or use of any information on consumers, or for the prevention or mitigation of identity theft, except to the extent that those laws are inconsistent with any provision of this subchapter, and then only to the extent of the inconsistency.

(b) General exceptions

No requirement or prohibition may be imposed under the laws of any State—

(1) with respect to any subject matter regulated under—

(A) subsection (c) or (e) of section 1681b of this title, relating to the prescreening of consumer reports;

(B) section 1681i of this title, relating to the time by which a consumer reporting agency must take any action, including the provision of notification to a consumer or other person, in any procedure related to the disputed accuracy of information in a consumer's file, except that this subparagraph shall not apply to any State law in effect on September 30, 1996;

(C) subsections (a) and (b) of section 1681m of this title, relating to the duties of a person who takes any adverse action with respect to a consumer;

(D) section 1681m(d) of this title, relating to the duties of persons who use a consumer report of a consumer in connection with any credit or insurance transaction that is not initiated by the consumer and that consists of a firm offer of credit or insurance;

(E) section 1681c of this title, relating to information contained in consumer reports, except that this subparagraph shall not apply to any State law in effect on September 30, 1996;

(F) section 1681s–2 of this title, relating to the responsibilities of persons who furnish information to consumer reporting agencies, except that this paragraph shall not apply—

(i) with respect to section 54A(a) of chapter 93 of the Massachusetts Annotated Laws (as in effect on September 30, 1996); or

(ii) with respect to section 1785.25(a) of the California Civil Code (as in effect on September 30, 1996);

(G) section 1681g(e) of this title, relating to information available to victims under section 1681g(e) of this title;

(H) section 1681s–3 of this title, relating to the exchange and use of information to make a solicitation for marketing purposes; or

(I) section 1681m(h) of this title, relating to the duties of users of consumer reports to provide notice with respect to terms in certain credit transactions;

(2) with respect to the exchange of information among persons affiliated by common ownership or common corporate control, except that this paragraph shall not apply with respect to subsection (a) or (c)(1) of section 2480e of title 9, Vermont Statutes Annotated (as in effect on September 30, 1996);

    (3) with respect to the disclosures required to be made under subsection (c), (d), (e), or (g) of section 1681g of this title, or subsection (f) of section 1681g of this title relating to the disclosure of credit scores for credit granting purposes, except that this paragraph—

        (A) shall not apply with respect to sections 1785.10, 1785.16, and 1785.20.2 of the California Civil Code (as in effect on December 4, 2003) and section 1785.15 through section 1785.15.2 of such Code (as in effect on such date);

        (B) shall not apply with respect to sections 5–3–106(2) and 212–14.3–104.3 of the Colorado Revised Statutes (as in effect on December 4, 2003); and

        (C) shall not be construed as limiting, annulling, affecting, or superseding any provision of the laws of any State regulating the use in an insurance activity, or regulating disclosures concerning such use, of a credit-based insurance score of a consumer by any person engaged in the business of insurance;

    (4) with respect to the frequency of any disclosure under section 1681j(a) of this title, except that this paragraph shall not apply—

        (A) with respect to section 12–14.3–105(1)(d) of the Colorado Revised Statutes (as in effect on December 4, 2003);

        (B) with respect to section 10–1–393(29)(C) of the Georgia Code (as in effect on December 4, 2003);

        (C) with respect to section 1316.2 of title 10 of the Maine Revised Statutes (as in effect on December 4, 2003);

        (D) with respect to sections 14–1209(a)(1) and 14–1209(b)(1)(i) of the Commercial Law Article of the Code of Maryland (as in effect on December 4, 2003);

        (E) with respect to section 59(d) and section 59(e) of chapter 93 of the General Laws of Massachusetts (as in effect December 4, 2003);

        (F) with respect to section 56:11–37.10(a)(1) of the New Jersey Revised Statutes (as in effect on December 4, 2003); or

        (G) with respect to section 2480c(a)(1) of title 9 of the Vermont Statutes Annotated (as in effect on December 4, 2003); or

    (5) with respect to the conduct required by the specific provisions of—

        (A) section 1681c(g) of this title;

        (B) section 1681c–1 of this title;

        (C) section 1681c–2 of this title;

        (D) section 1681g(a)(1)(A) of this title;

        (E) section 1681j(a) of this title;

        (F) subsections (e), (f), and (g) of section 1681m of this title;

        (G) section 1681s(f) of this title;

        (H) section 1681s–2(a)(6) of this title; or

        (I) section 1681w of this title.

(c)   **"Firm offer of credit or insurance" defined**

    Notwithstanding any definition of the term "firm offer of credit or insurance" (or any equivalent term) under the laws of any State, the definition of that term contained in section 1681a(*l*) of this title shall be construed to apply in the enforcement and interpretation of the laws of any State governing consumer reports.

(d) Limitations

Subsections (b) and (c) of this section do not affect any settlement, agreement, or consent judgment between any State Attorney General and any consumer reporting agency in effect on September 30, 1996.

(Pub.L. 90–321, Title VI, § 625, formerly § 622, as added Pub.L. 91–508, Title VI, § 601, Oct. 26, 1970, 84 Stat. 1136, and renumbered § 623, Pub.L. 102–537, § 2(a), Oct. 27, 1992, 106 Stat. 3531; renumbered § 624 and amended Pub.L. 104–208, Div. A, Title II, §§ 2413(a)(1), 2419, Sept. 30, 1996, 110 Stat. 3009–447, 3009–452; renumbered § 625 and amended Pub.L. 108–159, Title I, § 151(a)(2), Title II, §§ 212(e), 214(a)(1), (c)(2), Title III, § 311(b), Title VII, § 711, Dec. 4, 2003, 117 Stat. 1964, 1977, 1980, 1983, 1989, 2011.)

§ 1681u. Disclosures to FBI for counterintelligence purposes [CCPA § 626]

(a) Identity of financial institutions

Notwithstanding section 1681b of this title or any other provision of this subchapter, a consumer reporting agency shall furnish to the Federal Bureau of Investigation the names and addresses of all financial institutions (as that term is defined in section 3401 of Title 12) at which a consumer maintains or has maintained an account, to the extent that information that includes a term that specifically identifies a consumer or account to be used as the basis for the production of that information is in the files of the agency, when presented with a written request for that information, signed by the Director of the Federal Bureau of Investigation, or the Director's designee in a position not lower than Deputy Assistant Director at Bureau headquarters or a Special Agent in Charge of a Bureau field office designated by the Director, which certifies compliance with this section. The Director or the Director's designee may make such a certification only if the Director or the Director's designee has determined in writing, that such information is sought for the conduct of an authorized investigation to protect against international terrorism or clandestine intelligence activities, provided that such an investigation of a United States person is not conducted solely upon the basis of activities protected by the first amendment to the Constitution of the United States.

(b) Identifying information

Notwithstanding the provisions of section 1681b of this title or any other provision of this subchapter, a consumer reporting agency shall furnish identifying information respecting a consumer, limited to name, address, former addresses, places of employment, or former places of employment, to the Federal Bureau of Investigation when presented with a written request that includes a term that specifically identifies a consumer or account to be used as the basis for the production of that information, signed by the Director or the Director's designee in a position not lower than Deputy Assistant Director at Bureau headquarters or a Special Agent in Charge of a Bureau field office designated by the Director, which certifies compliance with this subsection. The Director or the Director's designee may make such a certification only if the Director or the Director's designee has determined in writing that such information is sought for the conduct of an authorized investigation to protect against international terrorism or clandestine intelligence activities, provided that such an investigation of a United States person is not conducted solely upon the basis of activities protected by the first amendment to the Constitution of the United States.

(c) Court order for disclosure of consumer reports

Notwithstanding section 1681b of this title or any other provision of this subchapter, if requested in writing by the Director of the Federal Bureau of Investigation, or a designee of the Director in a position not lower than Deputy Assistant Director at Bureau headquarters or a Special Agent in Charge in a Bureau field office designated by the Director, a court may issue an order ex parte, which shall include a term that specifically identifies a consumer or account to be used as the basis for the production of the information directing a consumer reporting agency to furnish a consumer report to the Federal Bureau of Investigation, upon a showing in camera that the consumer report is sought for the conduct of an authorized investigation to protect against international terrorism or clandestine intelligence activities, provided that such an investigation of a United States person is not conducted solely upon the basis of activities protected by the first amendment to the Constitution of the United States.

The terms of an order issued under this subsection shall not disclose that the order is issued for purposes of a counterintelligence investigation.

(d) Prohibition of certain disclosure

    (1) Prohibition

        (A) In general.

        If a certification is issued under subparagraph (B) and notice of the right to judicial review under subsection (e) is provided, no consumer reporting agency that receives a request under subsection (a) or (b) or an order under subsection (c), or officer, employee, or agent thereof, shall disclose or specify in any consumer report, that the Federal Bureau of Investigation has sought or obtained access to information or records under subsection (a), (b), or (c).

        (B) Certification.

        The requirements of subparagraph (A) shall apply if the Director of the Federal Bureau of Investigation, or a designee of the Director whose rank shall be no lower than Deputy Assistant Director at Bureau headquarters or a Special Agent in Charge of a Bureau field office, certifies that the absence of a prohibition of disclosure under this subsection may result in—

            (i) a danger to the national security of the United States;

            (ii) interference with a criminal, counterterrorism, or counterintelligence investigation;

            (iii) interference with diplomatic relations; or

            (iv) danger to the life or physical safety of any person.

    (2) Exception

        (A) In general.

        A consumer reporting agency that receives a request under subsection (a) or (b) or an order under subsection (c), or officer, employee, or agent thereof, may disclose information otherwise subject to any applicable nondisclosure requirement to—

            (i) those persons to whom disclosure is necessary in order to comply with the request;

            (ii) an attorney in order to obtain legal advice or assistance regarding the request; or

            (iii) other persons as permitted by the Director of the Federal Bureau of Investigation or the designee of the Director.

        (B) Application.

        A person to whom disclosure is made under subparagraph (A) shall be subject to the nondisclosure requirements applicable to a person to whom a request under subsection (a) or (b) or an order under subsection (c) is issued in the same manner as the person to whom the request is issued.

        (C) Notice.

        Any recipient that discloses to a person described in subparagraph (A) information otherwise subject to a nondisclosure requirement shall inform the person of the applicable nondisclosure requirement.

        (D) Identification of disclosure recipients.

        At the request of the Director of the Federal Bureau of Investigation or the designee of the Director, any person making or intending to make a disclosure under clause (i) or (iii) of subparagraph (A) shall identify to the Director or such designee the person to whom such disclosure will be made or to whom such disclosure was made prior to the request.

(e) Judicial review

(1) In general.

A request under subsection (a) or (b) or an order under subsection (c) or a non-disclosure requirement imposed in connection with such request under subsection (d) shall be subject to judicial review under section 3511 of title 18, United States Code.

(2) Notice.

A request under subsection (a) or (b) or an order under subsection (c) shall include notice of the availability of judicial review described in paragraph (1).

(f) Payment of fees

The Federal Bureau of Investigation shall, subject to the availability of appropriations, pay to the consumer reporting agency assembling or providing report or information in accordance with procedures established under this section a fee for reimbursement for such costs as are reasonably necessary and which have been directly incurred in searching, reproducing, or transporting books, papers, records, or other data required or requested to be produced under this section.

(g) Limit on dissemination

The Federal Bureau of Investigation may not disseminate information obtained pursuant to this section outside of the Federal Bureau of Investigation, except to other Federal agencies as may be necessary for the approval or conduct of a foreign counterintelligence investigation, or, where the information concerns a person subject to the Uniform Code of Military Justice, to appropriate investigative authorities within the military department concerned as may be necessary for the conduct of a joint foreign counterintelligence investigation.

(h) Rules of construction

Nothing in this section shall be construed to prohibit information from being furnished by the Federal Bureau of Investigation pursuant to a subpoena or court order, in connection with a judicial or administrative proceeding to enforce the provisions of this subchapter. Nothing in this section shall be construed to authorize or permit the withholding of information from the Congress.

(i) Reports to Congress

(1) On a semiannual basis, the Attorney General shall fully inform the Permanent Select Committee on Intelligence and the Committee on Banking, Finance and Urban Affairs of the House of Representatives, and the Select Committee on Intelligence and the Committee on Banking, Housing, and Urban Affairs of the Senate concerning all requests made pursuant to subsections (a), (b), and (c) of this section.

(2) In the case of the semiannual reports required to be submitted under paragraph (1) to the Permanent Select Committee on Intelligence of the House of Representatives and the Select Committee on Intelligence of the Senate, the submittal dates for such reports shall be as provided in section 415b of Title 50.

(j) Damages

Any agency or department of the United States obtaining or disclosing any consumer reports, records, or information contained therein in violation of this section is liable to the consumer to whom such consumer reports, records, or information relate in an amount equal to the sum of—

(1) $100, without regard to the volume of consumer reports, records, or information involved;

(2) any actual damages sustained by the consumer as a result of the disclosure;

(3) if the violation is found to have been willful or intentional, such punitive damages as a court may allow; and

(4) in the case of any successful action to enforce liability under this subsection, the costs of the action, together with reasonable attorney fees, as determined by the court.

(k) Disciplinary actions for violations

If a court determines that any agency or department of the United States has violated any provision of this section and the court finds that the circumstances surrounding the violation raise questions of whether or not an officer or employee of the agency or department acted willfully or intentionally with respect to the violation, the agency or department shall promptly initiate a proceeding to determine whether or not disciplinary action is warranted against the officer or employee who was responsible for the violation.

(*l*) Good-faith exception

Notwithstanding any other provision of this subchapter, any consumer reporting agency or agent or employee thereof making disclosure of consumer reports or identifying information pursuant to this subsection in good-faith reliance upon a certification of the Federal Bureau of Investigation pursuant to provisions of this section shall not be liable to any person for such disclosure under this subchapter, the constitution of any State, or any law or regulation of any State or any political subdivision of any State.

(m) Limitation of remedies

Notwithstanding any other provision of this subchapter, the remedies and sanctions set forth in this section shall be the only judicial remedies and sanctions for violation of this section.

(n) Injunctive relief

In addition to any other remedy contained in this section, injunctive relief shall be available to require compliance with the procedures of this section. In the event of any successful action under this subsection, costs together with reasonable attorney fees, as determined by the court, may be recovered.

(Pub.L. 90–321, Title VI, § 625, formerly § 624, as added Pub.L. 104–93, Title VI, § 601(a), Jan. 6, 1996, 109 Stat. 974; renumbered § 625 and amended Pub.L. 107–56, Title III, § 358(g)(1)(A), Title V, § 505(c), Oct. 26, 2001, 115 Stat. 327, 366; Pub.L. 107–306, Title VIII, § 811(b)(8)(B), Nov. 27, 2002, 116 Stat. 2426; renumbered § 626, Pub.L. 108–159, Title II, § 214(a)(1), Dec. 4, 2003, 117 Stat. 1980; Pub.L. 109–177, Title I, § 116(b), Mar. 9, 2006, 120 Stat. 214; Pub.L. 109–178, § 4(c)(1), Mar. 9, 2006, 120 Stat. 280; Pub.L. 114–23, Title V, §§ 501(c), 502(c), 503(c), June 2, 2015, 129 Stat. 282, 285, 290.)

§ 1681v. Disclosures to governmental agencies for counterterrorism purposes [CCPA § 627]

(a) Disclosure

Notwithstanding section 1681b of this title or any other provision of this subchapter, a consumer reporting agency shall furnish a consumer report of a consumer and all other information in a consumer's file to a government agency authorized to conduct investigations of, or intelligence or counterintelligence activities or analysis related to, international terrorism when presented with a written certification by such government agency that such information is necessary for the agency's conduct or such investigation, activity or analysis and that includes a term that specifically identifies a consumer or account to be used as the basis for the production of such information.

(b) Form of certification

The certification described in subsection (a) of this section shall be signed by a supervisory official designated by the head of a Federal agency or an officer of a Federal agency whose appointment to office is required to be made by the President, by and with the advice and consent of the Senate.

(c) Prohibition of certain disclosure

(1) Prohibition

(A) In general.

If a certification is issued under subparagraph (B) and notice of the right to judicial review under subsection (d) is provided, no consumer reporting agency that receives a request under subsection (a), or officer, employee, or agent thereof, shall disclose or specify in any consumer report, that a government agency described in subsection (a) has sought or obtained access to information or records under subsection (a).

(B) Certification.

The requirements of subparagraph (A) shall apply if the head of the government agency described in subsection (a), or a designee, certifies that the absence of a prohibition of disclosure under this subsection may result in—

　(i) a danger to the national security of the United States;

　(ii) interference with a criminal, counterterrorism, or counterintelligence investigation;

　(iii) interference with diplomatic relations; or

　(iv) danger to the life or physical safety of any person.

(2) Exception

(A) In general.

A consumer reporting agency that receives a request under subsection (a), or officer, employee, or agent thereof, may disclose information otherwise subject to any applicable nondisclosure requirement to—

　(i) those persons to whom disclosure is necessary in order to comply with the request;

　(ii) an attorney in order to obtain legal advice or assistance regarding the request; or

　(iii) other persons as permitted by the head of the government agency described in subsection (a) or a designee.

(B) Application.

A person to whom disclosure is made under subparagraph (A) shall be subject to the nondisclosure requirements applicable to a person to whom a request under subsection (a) is issued in the same manner as the person to whom the request is issued.

(C) Notice.

Any recipient that discloses to a person described in subparagraph (A) information otherwise subject to a nondisclosure requirement shall inform the person of the applicable nondisclosure requirement.

(D) Identification of disclosure recipients.

At the request of the head of the government agency described in subsection (a) or a designee, any person making or intending to make a disclosure under clause (i) or (iii) of subparagraph (A) shall identify to the head or such designee the person to whom such disclosure will be made or to whom such disclosure was made prior to the request.

(d) Judicial review

(1) In general.

A request under subsection (a) or a non-disclosure requirement imposed in connection with such request under subsection (c) shall be subject to judicial review under section 3511 of title 18, United States Code.

(2) Notice.

A request under subsection (a) shall include notice of the availability of judicial review described in paragraph (1).

(e) Rule of construction

Nothing in section 1681u of this title shall be construed to limit the authority of the Director of the Federal Bureau of Investigation under this section.

(f) Safe harbor

Notwithstanding any other provision of this subchapter, any consumer reporting agency or agent or employee thereof making disclosure of consumer reports or other information pursuant to this section in good-faith reliance upon a certification of a government agency pursuant to the provisions of this section shall not be liable to any person for such disclosure under this subchapter, the constitution of any State, or any law or regulation of any State or any political subdivision of any State.

(g) Reports to Congress

(1) On a semi-annual basis, the Attorney General shall fully inform the Committee on the Judiciary, the Committee on Financial Services, and the Permanent Select Committee on Intelligence of the House of Representatives and the Committee on the Judiciary, the Committee on Banking, Housing, and Urban Affairs, and the Select Committee on Intelligence of the Senate concerning all requests made pursuant to subsection (a) of this section.

(2) In the case of the semiannual reports required to be submitted under paragraph (1) to the Permanent Select Committee on Intelligence of the House of Representatives and the Select Committee on Intelligence of the Senate, the submittal dates for such reports shall be as provided in section 415b of Title 50.

(Pub.L. 90–321, Title VI, § 627, formerly § 626, as added Pub.L. 107–56, Title III, § 358(g)(1)(B), Oct. 26, 2001, 115 Stat. 327; renumbered § 627 and amended Pub.L. 108–159, Title II, § 214(a)(1), (c)(3), Dec. 4, 2003, 117 Stat. 1980, 1983; Pub.L. 108–458, Title VI, § 6203(*l*), Dec. 17, 2004, 118 Stat. 3747; Pub.L. 109–177, Title I, §§ 116(c), 118(b), Mar. 9, 2006, 120 Stat. 214, 217; Pub.L. 109–178, § 4(c)(2), Mar. 9, 2006, 120 Stat. 280; Pub.L. 114–23, Title V, §§ 501(d), 502(d), 503(d), June 2, 2015, 129 Stat. 282, 286, 290.)

§ 1681w. Disposal of records [CCPA § 628]

(a) Regulations

(1) In general

The Federal Trade Commission, the Securities and Exchange Commission, the Commodity Futures Trading Commission, the Federal banking agencies, and the National Credit Union Administration, with respect to the entities that are subject to their respective enforcement authority under section 1681s of this title, and in coordination as described in paragraph (2), shall issue final regulations requiring any person that maintains or otherwise possesses consumer information, or any compilation of consumer information, derived from consumer reports for a business purpose to properly dispose of any such information or compilation.

(2) Coordination

Each agency required to prescribe regulations under paragraph (1) shall—

(A) consult and coordinate with each other such agency so that, to the extent possible, the regulations prescribed by each such agency are consistent and comparable with the regulations by each such other agency; and

(B) ensure that such regulations are consistent with the requirements and regulations issued pursuant to Public Law 106–102 and other provisions of Federal law.

(3) Exemption authority

In issuing regulations under this section, the agencies identified in paragraph (1) may exempt any person or class of persons from application of those regulations, as such agency deems appropriate to carry out the purpose of this section.

(b) Rule of construction

Nothing in this section shall be construed—

(1) to require a person to maintain or destroy any record pertaining to a consumer that is not imposed under other law; or

(2) to alter or affect any requirement imposed under any other provision of law to maintain or destroy such a record.

(Pub.L. 90–321, Title VI, § 628, as added Pub.L. 108–159, Title II, § 216(a), Dec. 4, 2003, 117 Stat. 1985; Pub.L. 111–203, Title X, § 1088(a)(12), (13), July 21, 2010, 124 Stat. 2091, 2092.)

§ 1681x. Corporate and technological circumvention prohibited [CCPA § 629]

The Commission shall prescribe regulations, to become effective not later than 90 days after December 4, 2003, to prevent a consumer reporting agency from circumventing or evading treatment as a consumer reporting agency described in section 1681a(p) of this title for purposes of this subchapter, including—

(1) by means of a corporate reorganization or restructuring, including a merger, acquisition, dissolution, divestiture, or asset sale of a consumer reporting agency; or

(2) by maintaining or merging public record and credit account information in a manner that is substantially equivalent to that described in paragraphs (1) and (2) of section 1681a(p) of this title, in the manner described in section 1681a(p) of this title.

(Pub.L. 90–321, Title VI, § 629, as added Pub.L. 108–159, Title II, § 211(b), Dec. 4, 2003, 117 Stat. 1970.)

SUBCHAPTER IV—EQUAL CREDIT OPPORTUNITY

§ 1691. Scope of prohibition [CCPA § 701]

(a) Activities constituting discrimination

It shall be unlawful for any creditor to discriminate against any applicant, with respect to any aspect of a credit transaction—

(1) on the basis of race, color, religion, national origin, sex or marital status, or age (provided the applicant has the capacity to contract);

(2) because all or part of the applicant's income derives from any public assistance program; or

(3) because the applicant has in good faith exercised any right under this chapter.

(b) Activities not constituting discrimination

It shall not constitute discrimination for purposes of this subchapter for a creditor—

(1) to make an inquiry of marital status if such inquiry is for the purpose of ascertaining the creditor's rights and remedies applicable to the particular extension of credit and not to discriminate in a determination of credit-worthiness;[1]

(2) to make an inquiry of the applicant's age or of whether the applicant's income derives from any public assistance program if such inquiry is for the purpose of determining the amount and probable continuance of income levels, credit history, or other pertinent element of credit-worthiness as provided in regulations of the Bureau;

(3) to use any empirically derived credit system which considers age if such system is demonstrably and statistically sound in accordance with regulations of the Bureau, except that in the operation of such system the age of an elderly applicant may not be assigned a negative factor or value;

(4) to make an inquiry or to consider the age of an elderly applicant when the age of such applicant is to be used by the creditor in the extension of credit in favor of such applicant;

(5) to make an inquiry under section 1691c–2 of this title, in accordance with the requirements of that section.

---

[1] So in original. Probably should not be hyphenated.

(c) Additional activities not constituting discrimination

It is not a violation of this section for a creditor to refuse to extend credit offered pursuant to—

(1) any credit assistance program expressly authorized by law for an economically disadvantaged class of persons;

(2) any credit assistance program administered by a nonprofit organization for its members or an economically disadvantaged class of persons; or

(3) any special purpose credit program offered by a profit-making organization to meet special social needs which meets standards prescribed in regulations by the Bureau;

if such refusal is required by or made pursuant to such program.

(d) Reason for adverse action; procedure applicable; "adverse action" defined

(1) Within thirty days (or such longer reasonable time as specified in regulations of the Bureau for any class of credit transaction) after receipt of a completed application for credit, a creditor shall notify the applicant of its action on the application.

(2) Each applicant against whom adverse action is taken shall be entitled to a statement of reasons for such action from the creditor. A creditor satisfies this obligation by—

(A) providing statements of reasons in writing as a matter of course to applicants against whom adverse action is taken; or

(B) giving written notification of adverse action which discloses (i) the applicant's right to a statement of reasons within thirty days after receipt by the creditor of a request made within sixty days after such notification, and (ii) the identity of the person or office from which such statement may be obtained. Such statement may be given orally if the written notification advises the applicant of his right to have the statement of reasons confirmed in writing on written request.

(3) A statement of reasons meets the requirements of this section only if it contains the specific reasons for the adverse action taken.

(4) Where a creditor has been requested by a third party to make a specific extension of credit directly or indirectly to an applicant, the notification and statement of reasons required by this subsection may be made directly by such creditor, or indirectly through the third party, provided in either case that the identity of the creditor is disclosed.

(5) The requirements of paragraph (2), (3), or (4) may be satisfied by verbal statements or notifications in the case of any creditor who did not act on more than one hundred and fifty applications during the calendar year preceding the calendar year in which the adverse action is taken, as determined under regulations of the Board.

(6) For purposes of this subsection, the term "adverse action" means a denial or revocation of credit, a change in the terms of an existing credit arrangement, or a refusal to grant credit in substantially the amount or on substantially the terms requested. Such term does not include a refusal to extend additional credit under an existing credit arrangement where the applicant is delinquent or otherwise in default, or where such additional credit would exceed a previously established credit limit.

(e) Copies furnished to applicants

(1) In general

Each creditor shall furnish to an applicant a copy of any and all written appraisals and valuations developed in connection with the applicant's application for a loan that is secured or would have been secured by a first lien on a dwelling promptly upon completion, but in no case later than 3 days prior to the closing of the loan, whether the creditor grants or denies the applicant's request for credit or the application is incomplete or withdrawn.

(2) Waiver

The applicant may waive the 3 day requirement provided for in paragraph (1), except where otherwise required in law.

(3) Reimbursement

The applicant may be required to pay a reasonable fee to reimburse the creditor for the cost of the appraisal, except where otherwise required in law.

(4) Free copy

Notwithstanding paragraph (3), the creditor shall provide a copy of each written appraisal or valuation at no additional cost to the applicant.

(5) Notification to applicants

At the time of application, the creditor shall notify an applicant in writing of the right to receive a copy of each written appraisal and valuation under this subsection.

(6) Valuation defined

For purposes of this subsection, the term "valuation" shall include any estimate of the value of a dwelling developed in connection with a creditor's decision to provide credit, including those values developed pursuant to a policy of a government sponsored enterprise or by an automated valuation model, a broker price opinion, or other methodology or mechanism.

> (Pub.L. 90–321, Title VII, § 701, as added Pub.L. 93–495, Title V, § 503, Oct. 28, 1974, 88 Stat. 1521, and amended Pub.L. 94–239, § 2, Mar. 23, 1976, 90 Stat. 251; Pub.L. 102–242, Title II, § 223(d), Dec. 19, 1991, 105 Stat. 2306; Pub.L. 111–203, Title X, §§ 1071(b), 1085(1), Title XIV, §§ 1400(c), 1474, July 21, 2010, 124 Stat. 2059, 2083, 2136, 2199.)

§ 1691a.   Definitions; rules of construction [CCPA § 702]

(a) The definitions and rules of construction set forth in this section are applicable for the purposes of this subchapter.

(b) The term "applicant" means any person who applies to a creditor directly for an extension, renewal, or continuation of credit, or applies to a creditor indirectly by use of an existing credit plan for an amount exceeding a previously established credit limit.

(c) The term "Bureau" means the Bureau of Consumer Financial Protection.

(d) The term "credit" means the right granted by a creditor to a debtor to defer payment of debt or to incur debts and defer its payment or to purchase property or services and defer payment therefor.

(e) The term "creditor" means any person who regularly extends, renews, or continues credit; any person who regularly arranges for the extension, renewal, or continuation of credit; or any assignee of an original creditor who participates in the decision to extend, renew, or continue credit.

(f) The term "person" means a natural person, a corporation, government or governmental subdivision or agency, trust, estate, partnership, cooperative, or association.

(g) Any reference to any requirement imposed under this subchapter or any provision thereof includes reference to the regulations of the Bureau under this subchapter or the provision thereof in question.

> (Pub.L. 90–321, Title VII, § 702, as added Pub.L. 93–495, Title V, § 503, Oct. 28, 1974, 88 Stat. 1522; Pub.L. 111–203, Title X, § 1085(1), (2), July 21, 2010, 124 Stat. 2083.)

§ 1691b.   Promulgation of regulations by the Bureau [CCPA § 703]

(a) The Bureau shall prescribe regulations to carry out the purposes of this subchapter. These regulations may contain but are not limited to such classifications, differentiation, or other provision, and may provide for such adjustments and exceptions for any class of transactions, as in the judgment of the Bureau are necessary or proper to effectuate the purposes of this subchapter, to prevent circumvention or evasion thereof, or to facilitate or substantiate compliance therewith.

(b) Such regulations may exempt from the provisions of this subchapter any class of transactions that are not primarily for personal, family, or household purposes, or business or commercial loans made available by a financial institution, except that a particular type within a class of such transactions may be exempted if the Bureau determines, after making an express finding that the application of this subchapter or of any provision of this subchapter of such transaction would not contribute substantially to effecting the purposes of this subchapter.

(c)   An exemption granted pursuant to subsection (b) shall be for no longer than five years and shall be extended only if the Bureau makes a subsequent determination, in the manner described by such paragraph[1], that such exemption remains appropriate.

(d)   Pursuant to Bureau regulations, entities making business or commercial loans shall maintain such records or other data relating to such loans as may be necessary to evidence compliance with this subsection[2] or enforce any action pursuant to the authority of this chapter. In no event shall such records or data be maintained for a period of less than one year. The Bureau shall promulgate regulations to implement this paragraph[3] in the manner prescribed by chapter 5 of Title 5.

(e)   The Bureau shall provide in regulations that an applicant for a business or commercial loan shall be provided a written notice of such applicant's right to receive a written statement of the reasons for the denial of such loan.

(f)   Board authority

Notwithstanding subsection (a), the Board shall prescribe regulations to carry out the purposes of this subchapter with respect to a person described in section 5519(a) of Title 12. These regulations may contain but are not limited to such classifications, differentiation, or other provision, and may provide for such adjustments and exceptions for any class of transactions, as in the judgment of the Board are necessary or proper to effectuate the purposes of this subchapter, to prevent circumvention or evasion thereof, or to facilitate or substantiate compliance therewith.

(g)   Deference

Notwithstanding any power granted to any Federal agency under this subchapter, the deference that a court affords to a Federal agency with respect to a determination made by such agency relating to the meaning or interpretation of any provision of this subchapter that is subject to the jurisdiction of such agency shall be applied as if that agency were the only agency authorized to apply, enforce, interpret, or administer the provisions of this subchapter[4]

(Pub.L. 90–321, Title VII, § 703, as added Pub.L. 93–495, Title V, § 503, Oct. 28, 1974, 88 Stat. 1522, and amended Pub.L. 94–239, § 3(a), Mar. 23, 1976, 90 Stat. 252; Pub.L. 100–533, Title III, § 301, Oct. 25, 1988, 102 Stat. 2692; Pub.L. 111–203, Title X, § 1085(1), (3), July 21, 2010, 124 Stat. 2083.)

§ 1691c.   Administrative enforcement [CCPA § 704]

(a)   Enforcing agencies

Subject to subtitle B of the Consumer Protection Financial Protection Act of 2010[1] with[2] the requirements imposed under this subchapter shall be enforced under:

(1)   section 1818 of Title 12, by the appropriate Federal banking agency, as defined in section 1813(q) of Title 12, with respect to—

(A)   national banks, Federal savings associations, and Federal branches and Federal agencies of foreign banks;

(B)   member banks of the Federal Reserve System (other than national banks), branches and agencies of foreign banks (other than Federal branches, Federal agencies, and insured State

---

[1]   So in original. Probably should be "subsection,".
[2]   So in original.
[3]   So in original. Probably should be "subsection".
[4]   So in original. Probably should be followed by a period.
[1]   So in original. Probably should be "Consumer Financial Protection Act of 2010".
[2]   So in original. Probably should be ", compliance with".

branches of foreign banks), commercial lending companies owned or controlled by foreign banks, and organizations operating under section 25 or 25A of the Federal Reserve Act; and

(C) banks and State savings associations insured by the Federal Deposit Insurance Corporation (other than members of the Federal Reserve System), and insured State branches of foreign banks;

(2) The Federal Credit Union Act [12 U.S.C.A. § 1751 et seq.], by the Administrator of the National Credit Union Administration with respect to any Federal Credit Union.

(3) Subtitle IV of Title 49, by the Secretary of Transportation, with respect to all carriers subject to the jurisdiction of the Surface Transportation Board.

(4) Part A of subtitle VII of title 49, by the Secretary of Transportation with respect to any air carrier or foreign air carrier subject to that part.

(5) The Packers and Stockyards Act, 1921 [7 U.S.C.A. § 181 et seq.] (except as provided in section 406 of that Act [7 U.S.C.A. §§ 226, 227]), by the Secretary of Agriculture with respect to any activities subject to that Act.

(6) The Farm Credit Act of 1971 [12 U.S.C.A. § 2001 et seq.], by the Farm Credit Administration with respect to any Federal land bank, Federal land bank association, Federal intermediate credit bank, and production credit association;

(7) The Securities Exchange Act of 1934 [15 U.S.C.A. § 78a et seq.], by the Securities and Exchange Commission with respect to brokers and dealers; and

(8) The Small Business Investment Act of 1958 [15 U.S.C.A. § 661 et seq.], by the Small Business Administration, with respect to small business investment companies;

(9) Subtitle E of the Consumer Financial Protection Act of 2010, by the Bureau, with respect to any person subject to this subchapter.

The terms used in paragraph (1) that are not defined in this subchapter or otherwise defined in section 3(s) of the Federal Deposit Insurance Act (12 U.S.C. 1813(s)) shall have the meaning given to them in section 1(b) of the International Banking Act of 1978 (12 U.S.C. 3101).

(b) Violations of subchapter deemed violations of preexisting statutory requirements; additional agency powers

For the purpose of the exercise by any agency referred to in subsection (a) of this section of its powers under any Act referred to in that subsection, a violation of any requirement imposed under this subchapter shall be deemed to be a violation of a requirement imposed under that Act. In addition to its powers under any provision of law specifically referred to in subsection (a) of this section, each of the agencies referred to in that subsection may exercise for the purpose of enforcing compliance with any requirement imposed under this subchapter, any other authority conferred on it by law. The exercise of the authorities of any of the agencies referred to in subsection (a) of this section for the purpose of enforcing compliance with any requirement imposed under this subchapter shall in no way preclude the exercise of such authorities for the purpose of enforcing compliance with any other provision of law not relating to the prohibition of discrimination on the basis of sex or marital status with respect to any aspect of a credit transaction.

(c) Overall enforcement authority of Federal Trade Commission

Except to the extent that enforcement of the requirements imposed under this subchapter is specifically committed to some other Government agency under any of paragraphs (1) through (8) of subsection (a), and subject to subtitle B of the Consumer Financial Protection Act of 2010, the Federal Trade Commission shall be authorized to enforce such requirements. For the purpose of the exercise by the Federal Trade Commission of its functions and powers under the Federal Trade Commission Act (15 U.S.C. 41 et seq.), a violation of any requirement imposed under this subchapter shall be deemed a violation of a requirement imposed under that Act. All of the functions and powers of the Federal Trade Commission under the Federal Trade Commission Act are available to the Federal Trade Commission to enforce compliance by any person with the requirements imposed under this subchapter, irrespective of whether that person is engaged in commerce or meets any other jurisdictional tests under the Federal Trade

Commission Act, including the power to enforce any rule prescribed by the Bureau under this subchapter in the same manner as if the violation had been a violation of a Federal Trade Commission trade regulation rule.

(d) Rules and regulations by enforcing agencies

The authority of the Bureau to issue regulations under this subchapter does not impair the authority of any other agency designated in this section to make rules respecting its own procedures in enforcing compliance with requirements imposed under this subchapter.

(Pub.L. 90–321, Title VII, § 704, as added Pub.L. 93–495, Title V, § 503, Oct. 28, 1974, 88 Stat. 1522, and amended Pub.L. 94–239, § 4, Mar. 23, 1976, 90 Stat. 253; Pub.L. 95–473, § 3(b), Oct. 17, 1978, 92 Stat. 1466; Pub.L. 98–443, § 9(n), Oct. 4, 1984, 98 Stat. 1708; Pub.L. 101–73, Title VII, § 744(m), Aug. 9, 1989, 103 Stat. 439; Pub.L. 102–242, Title II, § 212(d), Dec. 19, 1991, 105 Stat. 2300; Pub.L. 102–550, Title XVI, § 1604(a)(7), Oct. 28, 1992, 106 Stat. 4082; Pub.L. 104–88, Title III, § 315, Dec. 29, 1995, 109 Stat. 948; Pub.L. 111–203, Title X, § 1085(4), July 21, 2010, 124 Stat. 2084.)

§ 1691c–1.　　　Incentives for self-testing and self-correction [CCPA § 704A]

(a) Privileged information

(1) Conditions for privilege

A report or result of a self-test (as that term is defined by regulations of the Bureau) shall be considered to be privileged under paragraph (2) if a creditor—

(A) conducts, or authorizes an independent third party to conduct, a self-test of any aspect of a credit transaction by a creditor, in order to determine the level or effectiveness of compliance with this subchapter by the creditor; and

(B) has identified any possible violation of this subchapter by the creditor and has taken, or is taking, appropriate corrective action to address any such possible violation.

(2) Privileged self-test

If a creditor meets the conditions specified in subparagraphs (A) and (B) of paragraph (1) with respect to a self-test described in that paragraph, any report or results of that self-test—

(A) shall be privileged; and

(B) may not be obtained or used by any applicant, department, or agency in any—

(i) proceeding or civil action in which one or more violations of this subchapter are alleged; or

(ii) examination or investigation relating to compliance with this subchapter.

(b) Results of self-testing

(1) In general

No provision of this section may be construed to prevent an applicant, department, or agency from obtaining or using a report or results of any self-test in any proceeding or civil action in which a violation of this subchapter is alleged, or in any examination or investigation of compliance with this subchapter if—

(A) the creditor or any person with lawful access to the report or results—

(i) voluntarily releases or discloses all, or any part of, the report or results to the applicant, department, or agency, or to the general public; or

(ii) refers to or describes the report or results as a defense to charges of violations of this subchapter against the creditor to whom the self-test relates; or

(B) the report or results are sought in conjunction with an adjudication or admission of a violation of this subchapter for the sole purpose of determining an appropriate penalty or remedy.

(2) Disclosure for determination of penalty or remedy

Any report or results of a self-test that are disclosed for the purpose specified in paragraph (1)(B)—

(A) shall be used only for the particular proceeding in which the adjudication or admission referred to in paragraph (1)(B) is made; and

(B) may not be used in any other action or proceeding.

(c) Adjudication

An applicant, department, or agency that challenges a privilege asserted under this section may seek a determination of the existence and application of that privilege in—

(1) a court of competent jurisdiction; or

(2) an administrative law proceeding with appropriate jurisdiction.

(Pub.L. 90–321, Title VII, § 704A, as added Pub.L. 104–208, Div. A, Title II, § 2302(a)(1), Sept. 30, 1996, 110 Stat. 3009–420; Pub.L. 111–203, Title X, § 1085(1), July 21, 2010, 124 Stat. 2083.)

§ 1691c–2. Small business loan data collection

(a) Purpose

The purpose of this section is to facilitate enforcement of fair lending laws and enable communities, governmental entities, and creditors to identify business and community development needs and opportunities of women-owned, minority-owned, and small businesses.

(b) Information gathering

Subject to the requirements of this section, in the case of any application to a financial institution for credit for women-owned, minority-owned, or small business, the financial institution shall—

(1) inquire whether the business is a women-owned, minority-owned, or small business, without regard to whether such application is received in person, by mail, by telephone, by electronic mail or other form of electronic transmission, or by any other means, and whether or not such application is in response to a solicitation by the financial institution; and

(2) maintain a record of the responses to such inquiry, separate from the application and accompanying information.

(c) Right to refuse

Any applicant for credit may refuse to provide any information requested pursuant to subsection (b) in connection with any application for credit.

(d) No access by underwriters

(1) Limitation

Where feasible, no loan underwriter or other officer or employee of a financial institution, or any affiliate of a financial institution, involved in making any determination concerning an application for credit shall have access to any information provided by the applicant pursuant to a request under subsection (b) in connection with such application.

(2) Limited access

If a financial institution determines that a loan underwriter or other officer or employee of a financial institution, or any affiliate of a financial institution, involved in making any determination concerning an application for credit should have access to any information provided by the applicant pursuant to a request under subsection (b), the financial institution shall provide notice to the applicant of the access of the underwriter to such information, along with notice that the financial institution may not discriminate on the basis of such information.

(e) Form and manner of information

(1) In general

Each financial institution shall compile and maintain, in accordance with regulations of the Bureau, a record of the information provided by any loan applicant pursuant to a request under subsection (b).

(2) Itemization

Information compiled and maintained under paragraph (1) shall be itemized in order to clearly and conspicuously disclose—

(A) the number of the application and the date on which the application was received;

(B) the type and purpose of the loan or other credit being applied for;

(C) the amount of the credit or credit limit applied for, and the amount of the credit transaction or the credit limit approved for such applicant;

(D) the type of action taken with respect to such application, and the date of such action;

(E) the census tract in which is located the principal place of business of the women-owned, minority-owned, or small business loan applicant;

(F) the gross annual revenue of the business in the last fiscal year of the women-owned, minority-owned, or small business loan applicant preceding the date of the application;

(G) the race, sex, and ethnicity of the principal owners of the business; and

(H) any additional data that the Bureau determines would aid in fulfilling the purposes of this section.

(3) No personally identifiable information

In compiling and maintaining any record of information under this section, a financial institution may not include in such record the name, specific address (other than the census tract required under paragraph (1)(E))[1], telephone number, electronic mail address, or any other personally identifiable information concerning any individual who is, or is connected with, the women-owned, minority-owned, or small business loan applicant.

(4) Discretion to delete or modify publicly available data

The Bureau may, at its discretion, delete or modify data collected under this section which is or will be available to the public, if the Bureau determines that the deletion or modification of the data would advance a privacy interest.

(f) Availability of information

(1) Submission to Bureau

The data required to be compiled and maintained under this section by any financial institution shall be submitted annually to the Bureau.

(2) Availability of information

Information compiled and maintained under this section shall be—

(A) retained for not less than 3 years after the date of preparation;

(B) made available to any member of the public, upon request, in the form required under regulations prescribed by the Bureau;

(C) annually made available to the public generally by the Bureau, in such form and in such manner as is determined by the Bureau, by regulation.

(3) Compilation of aggregate data

---

[1]   So in original. Probably should be "(2)(E)),".

The Bureau may, at its discretion—

    (A) compile and aggregate data collected under this section for its own use; and

    (B) make public such compilations of aggregate data.

(g) Bureau action

    (1) In general

The Bureau shall prescribe such rules and issue such guidance as may be necessary to carry out, enforce, and compile data pursuant to this section.

    (2) Exceptions

The Bureau, by rule or order, may adopt exceptions to any requirement of this section and may, conditionally or unconditionally, exempt any financial institution or class of financial institutions from the requirements of this section, as the Bureau deems necessary or appropriate to carry out the purposes of this section.

    (3) Guidance

The Bureau shall issue guidance designed to facilitate compliance with the requirements of this section, including assisting financial institutions in working with applicants to determine whether the applicants are women-owned, minority-owned, or small businesses for purposes of this section.

(h) Definitions

For purposes of this section, the following definitions shall apply:

    (1) Financial institution

The term "financial institution" means any partnership, company, corporation, association (incorporated or unincorporated), trust, estate, cooperative organization, or other entity that engages in any financial activity.

    (2) Small business

The term "small business" has the same meaning as the term "small business concern" in section 632 of this title.

    (3) Small business loan

The term "small business loan" means a loan made to a small business.

    (4) Minority

The term "minority" has the same meaning as in section 1204(c)(3) of the Financial Institutions Reform, Recovery, and Enforcement Act of 1989.

    (5) Minority-owned business

The term "minority-owned business" means a business—

    (A) more than 50 percent of the ownership or control of which is held by 1 or more minority individuals; and

    (B) more than 50 percent of the net profit or loss of which accrues to 1 or more minority individuals.

    (6) Women-owned business

The term "women-owned business" means a business—

    (A) more than 50 percent of the ownership or control of which is held by 1 or more women; and

    (B) more than 50 percent of the net profit or loss of which accrues to 1 or more women.

(Pub.L. 90–321, Title VII, § 704A, as added Pub.L. 111–203, Title X, § 1071(a), July 21, 2010, 124 Stat. 2056.)

§ 1691d.   Applicability of other laws [CCPA § 705]

(a)   Requests for signature of husband and wife for creation of valid lien, etc.

A request for the signature of both parties to a marriage for the purpose of creating a valid lien, passing clear title, waiving inchoate rights to property, or assigning earnings, shall not constitute discrimination under this subchapter: *Provided, however*, That this provision shall not be construed to permit a creditor to take sex or marital status into account in connection with the evaluation of creditworthiness of any applicant.

(b)   State property laws affecting creditworthiness

Consideration or application of State property laws directly or indirectly affecting creditworthiness shall not constitute discrimination for purposes of this subchapter.

(c)   State laws prohibiting separate extension of consumer credit to husband and wife

Any provision of State law which prohibits the separate extension of consumer credit to each party to a marriage shall not apply in any case where each party to a marriage voluntarily applies for separate credit from the same creditor: *Provided*, That in any case where such a State law is so preempted, each party to the marriage shall be solely responsible for the debt so contracted.

(d)   Combining credit accounts of husband and wife with same creditor to determine permissible finance charges or loan ceilings under Federal or State laws

When each party to a marriage separately and voluntarily applies for and obtains separate credit accounts with the same creditor, those accounts shall not be aggregated or otherwise combined for purposes of determining permissible finance charges or permissible loan ceilings under the laws of any State or of the United States.

(e)   Election of remedies under subchapter or State law; nature of relief determining applicability

Where the same act or omission constitutes a violation of this subchapter and of applicable State law, a person aggrieved by such conduct may bring a legal action to recover monetary damages either under this subchapter or under such State law, but not both. This election of remedies shall not apply to court actions in which the relief sought does not include monetary damages or to administrative actions.

(f)   Compliance with inconsistent State laws; determination of inconsistency

This subchapter does not annul, alter, or affect, or exempt any person subject to the provisions of this subchapter from complying with, the laws of any State with respect to credit discrimination, except to the extent that those laws are inconsistent with any provision of this subchapter, and then only to the extent of the inconsistency. The Bureau is authorized to determine whether such inconsistencies exist. The Bureau may not determine that any State law is inconsistent with any provision of this subchapter if the Bureau determines that such law gives greater protection to the applicant.

(g)   Exemption by regulation of credit transactions covered by State law; failure to comply with State law

The Bureau shall by regulation exempt from the requirements of sections 1691 and 1691a of this title any class of credit transactions within any State if it determines that under the law of that State that class of transactions is subject to requirements substantially similar to those imposed under this subchapter or that such law gives greater protection to the applicant, and that there is adequate provision for enforcement. Failure to comply with any requirement of such State law in any transaction so exempted shall constitute a violation of this subchapter for the purposes of section 1691e of this title.

(Pub.L. 90–321, Title VII, § 705, as added Pub.L. 93–495, Title V, § 503, Oct. 28, 1974, 88 Stat. 1523, and amended Pub.L. 94–239, § 5, Mar. 23, 1976, 90 Stat. 253; Pub.L. 111–203, Title X, § 1085(1), July 21, 2010, 124 Stat. 2083.)

§ 1691e.   Civil liability [CCPA § 706]

(a)   Individual or class action for actual damages

Any creditor who fails to comply with any requirement imposed under this subchapter shall be liable to the aggrieved applicant for any actual damages sustained by such applicant acting either in an individual capacity or as a member of a class.

(b)   Recovery of punitive damages in individual and class action for actual damages; exemptions; maximum amount of punitive damages in individual actions; limitation on total recovery in class actions; factors determining amount of award

Any creditor, other than a government or governmental subdivision or agency, who fails to comply with any requirement imposed under this subchapter shall be liable to the aggrieved applicant for punitive damages in an amount not greater than $10,000, in addition to any actual damages provided in subsection (a) of this section, except that in the case of a class action the total recovery under this subsection shall not exceed the lesser of $500,000 or 1 per centum of the net worth of the creditor. In determining the amount of such damages in any action, the court shall consider, among other relevant factors, the amount of any actual damages awarded, the frequency and persistence of failures of compliance by the creditor, the resources of the creditor, the number of persons adversely affected, and the extent to which the creditor's failure of compliance was intentional.

(c)   Action for equitable and declaratory relief

Upon application by an aggrieved applicant, the appropriate United States district court or any other court of competent jurisdiction may grant such equitable and declaratory relief as is necessary to enforce the requirements imposed under this subchapter.

(d)   Recovery of costs and attorney fees

In the case of any successful action under subsection (a), (b), or (c) of this section, the costs of the action, together with a reasonable attorney's fee as determined by the court, shall be added to any damages awarded by the court under such subsection.

(e)   Good faith compliance with rule, regulation, or interpretation of Bureau or interpretation or approval by an official or employee of Bureau of Consumer Financial Protection duly authorized by Bureau

No provision of this subchapter imposing liability shall apply to any act done or omitted in good faith in conformity with any official rule, regulation, or interpretation thereof by the Bureau or in conformity with any interpretation or approval by an official or employee of the Bureau of Consumer Financial Protection duly authorized by the Bureau to issue such interpretations or approvals under such procedures as the Bureau may prescribe therefor, notwithstanding that after such act or omission has occurred, such rule, regulation, interpretation, or approval is amended, rescinded, or determined by judicial or other authority to be invalid for any reason.

(f)   Jurisdiction of courts; time for maintenance of action; exceptions

Any action under this section may be brought in the appropriate United States district court without regard to the amount in controversy, or in any other court of competent jurisdiction. No such action shall be brought later than 5 years after the date of the occurrence of the violation, except that—

(1)   whenever any agency having responsibility for administrative enforcement under section 1691c of this title commences an enforcement proceeding within 5 years after the date of the occurrence of the violation,

(2)   whenever the Attorney General commences a civil action under this section within 5 years after the date of the occurrence of the violation,

then any applicant who has been a victim of the discrimination which is the subject of such proceeding or civil action may bring an action under this section not later than one year after the commencement of that proceeding or action.

(g) Request by responsible enforcement agency to Attorney General for civil action

The agencies having responsibility for administrative enforcement under section 1691c of this title, if unable to obtain compliance with section 1691 of this title, are authorized to refer the matter to the Attorney General with a recommendation that an appropriate civil action be instituted. Each agency referred to in paragraphs (1), (2), and (9) of section 1691c(a) of this title shall refer the matter to the Attorney General whenever the agency has reason to believe that 1 or more creditors has engaged in a pattern or practice of discouraging or denying applications for credit in violation of section 1691(a) of this title. Each such agency may refer the matter to the Attorney General whenever the agency has reason to believe that 1 or more creditors has violated section 1691(a) of this title.

(h) Authority for Attorney General to bring civil action; jurisdiction

When a matter is referred to the Attorney General pursuant to subsection (g) of this section, or whenever he has reason to believe that one or more creditors are engaged in a pattern or practice in violation of this subchapter, the Attorney General may bring a civil action in any appropriate United States district court for such relief as may be appropriate, including actual and punitive damages and injunctive relief.

(i) Recovery under both subchapter and fair housing enforcement provisions prohibited for violation based on same transaction

No person aggrieved by a violation of this subchapter and by a violation of section 3605 of Title 42 shall recover under this subchapter and section 3612 of Title 42, if such violation is based on the same transaction.

(j) Discovery of creditor's granting standards

Nothing in this subchapter shall be construed to prohibit the discovery of a creditor's credit granting standards under appropriate discovery procedures in the court or agency in which an action or proceeding is brought.

(k) Notice to HUD of violations

Whenever an agency referred to in paragraph (1), (2), or (3) of section 1691c(a) of this title—

    (1) has reason to believe, as a result of receiving a consumer complaint, conducting a consumer compliance examination, or otherwise, that a violation of this subchapter has occurred;

    (2) has reason to believe that the alleged violation would be a violation of the Fair Housing Act [42 U.S.C.A. § 3601 et seq.]; and

    (3) does not refer the matter to the Attorney General pursuant to subsection (g) of this section,

the agency shall notify the Secretary of Housing and Urban Development of the violation, and shall notify the applicant that the Secretary of Housing and Urban Development has been notified of the alleged violation and that remedies for the violation may be available under the Fair Housing Act.

    (Pub.L. 90–321, Title VII, § 706, as added Pub.L. 93–495, Title V, § 503, Oct. 28, 1974, 88 Stat. 1524, and amended Pub.L. 94–239, § 6, Mar. 23, 1976, 90 Stat. 253; Pub.L. 102–242, Title II, § 223(a) to (c), Dec. 19, 1991, 105 Stat. 2306; Pub.L. 111–203, Title X, §§ 1085(1), (5) to (7), July 21, 2010, 124 Stat. 2083, 2085.)

§ 1691f.   Annual reports to Congress; contents [CCPA § 707]

Each year, the Bureau and the Attorney General shall, respectively, make reports to the Congress concerning the administration of their functions under this subchapter, including such recommendations as the Bureau and the Attorney General, respectively, deem necessary or appropriate. In addition, each report of the Bureau shall include its assessment of the extent to which compliance with the requirements of this subchapter is being achieved, and a summary of the enforcement actions taken by each of the agencies assigned administrative enforcement responsibilities under section 1691c of this title.

    (Pub.L. 90–321, Title VII, § 707, as added Pub.L. 94–239, § 7, Mar. 23, 1976, 90 Stat. 255, and amended Pub.L. 96–221, Title VI, § 610(c), Mar. 31, 1980, 94 Stat. 174; Pub.L. 111–203, Title X, § 1085(1), July 21, 2010, 124 Stat. 2083.)

SUBCHAPTER V—DEBT COLLECTION PRACTICES

§ 1692.   Congressional findings and declaration of purpose [CCPA § 802]

(a) Abusive practices

There is abundant evidence of the use of abusive, deceptive, and unfair debt collection practices by many debt collectors. Abusive debt collection practices contribute to the number of personal bankruptcies, to marital instability, to the loss of jobs, and to invasions of individual privacy.

(b) Inadequacy of laws

Existing laws and procedures for redressing these injuries are inadequate to protect consumers.

(c) Available non-abusive collection methods

Means other than misrepresentation or other abusive debt collection practices are available for the effective collection of debts.

(d) Interstate commerce

Abusive debt collection practices are carried on to a substantial extent in interstate commerce and through means and instrumentalities of such commerce. Even where abusive debt collection practices are purely intrastate in character, they nevertheless directly affect interstate commerce.

(e) Purposes

It is the purpose of this subchapter to eliminate abusive debt collection practices by debt collectors, to insure that those debt collectors who refrain from using abusive debt collection practices are not competitively disadvantaged, and to promote consistent State action to protect consumers against debt collection abuses.

(Pub.L. 90–321, Title VIII, § 802, as added Pub.L. 95–109, Sept. 20, 1977, 91 Stat. 874.)

§ 1692a.   Definitions [CCPA § 803]

As used in this subchapter—

(1) The term "Bureau" means the Bureau of Consumer Financial Protection.

(2) The term "communication" means the conveying of information regarding a debt directly or indirectly to any person through any medium.

(3) The term "consumer" means any natural person obligated or allegedly obligated to pay any debt.

(4) The term "creditor" means any person who offers or extends credit creating a debt or to whom a debt is owed, but such term does not include any person to the extent that he receives an assignment or transfer of a debt in default solely for the purpose of facilitating collection of such debt for another.

(5) The term "debt" means any obligation or alleged obligation of a consumer to pay money arising out of a transaction in which the money, property, insurance, or services which are the subject of the transaction are primarily for personal, family, or household purposes, whether or not such obligation has been reduced to judgment.

(6) The term "debt collector" means any person who uses any instrumentality of interstate commerce or the mails in any business the principal purpose of which is the collection of any debts, or who regularly collects or attempts to collect, directly or indirectly, debts owed or due or asserted to be owed or due another. Notwithstanding the exclusion provided by clause (F) of the last sentence of this paragraph, the term includes any creditor who, in the process of collecting his own debts, uses any name other than his own which would indicate that a third person is collecting or attempting to collect such debts. For the purpose of section 1692f(6) of this title, such term also includes any person who uses any instrumentality of interstate commerce or the mails in any business the principal purpose of which is the enforcement of security interests. The term does not include—

(A)   any officer or employee of a creditor while, in the name of the creditor, collecting debts for such creditor;

(B)   any person while acting as a debt collector for another person, both of whom are related by common ownership or affiliated by corporate control, if the person acting as a debt collector does so only for persons to whom it is so related or affiliated and if the principal business of such person is not the collection of debts;

(C)   any officer or employee of the United States or any State to the extent that collecting or attempting to collect any debt is in the performance of his official duties;

(D)   any person while serving or attempting to serve legal process on any other person in connection with the judicial enforcement of any debt;

(E)   any nonprofit organization which, at the request of consumers, performs bona fide consumer credit counseling and assists consumers in the liquidation of their debts by receiving payments from such consumers and distributing such amounts to creditors; and

(F)   any person collecting or attempting to collect any debt owed or due or asserted to be owed or due another to the extent such activity (i) is incidental to a bona fide fiduciary obligation or a bona fide escrow arrangement; (ii) concerns a debt which was originated by such person; (iii) concerns a debt which was not in default at the time it was obtained by such person; or (iv) concerns a debt obtained by such person as a secured party in a commercial credit transaction involving the creditor.

(7)   The term "location information" means a consumer's place of abode and his telephone number at such place, or his place of employment.

(8)   The term "State" means any State, territory, or possession of the United States, the District of Columbia, the Commonwealth of Puerto Rico, or any political subdivision of any of the foregoing.

(Pub.L. 90–321, Title VIII, § 803, as added Pub.L. 95–109, Sept. 20, 1977, 91 Stat. 875, and amended Pub.L. 99–361, July 9, 1986, 100 Stat. 768; Pub.L. 111–203, Title X, § 1089(2), July 21, 2010, 124 Stat. 2092.)

§ 1692b.   Acquisition of location information [CCPA § 804]

Any debt collector communicating with any person other than the consumer for the purpose of acquiring location information about the consumer shall—

(1)   identify himself, state that he is confirming or correcting location information concerning the consumer, and, only if expressly requested, identify his employer;

(2)   not state that such consumer owes any debt;

(3)   not communicate with any such person more than once unless requested to do so by such person or unless the debt collector reasonably believes that the earlier response of such person is erroneous or incomplete and that such person now has correct or complete location information;

(4)   not communicate by post card;

(5)   not use any language or symbol on any envelope or in the contents of any communication effected by the mails or telegram that indicates that the debt collector is in the debt collection business or that the communication relates to the collection of a debt; and

(6)   after the debt collector knows the consumer is represented by an attorney with regard to the subject debt and has knowledge of, or can readily ascertain, such attorney's name and address, not communicate with any person other than that attorney, unless the attorney fails to respond within a reasonable period of time to communication from the debt collector.

(Pub.L. 90–321, Title VIII, § 804, as added Pub.L. 95–109, Sept. 20, 1977, 91 Stat. 876.)

§ 1692c. Communication in connection with debt collection [CCPA § 805]

(a) Communication with the consumer generally

Without the prior consent of the consumer given directly to the debt collector or the express permission of a court of competent jurisdiction, a debt collector may not communicate with a consumer in connection with the collection of any debt—

(1) at any unusual time or place or a time or place known or which should be known to be inconvenient to the consumer. In the absence of knowledge of circumstances to the contrary, a debt collector shall assume that the convenient time for communicating with a consumer is after 8 o'clock antemeridian and before 9 o'clock postmeridian, local time at the consumer's location;

(2) if the debt collector knows the consumer is represented by an attorney with respect to such debt and has knowledge of, or can readily ascertain, such attorney's name and address, unless the attorney fails to respond within a reasonable period of time to a communication from the debt collector or unless the attorney consents to direct communication with the consumer; or

(3) at the consumer's place of employment if the debt collector knows or has reason to know that the consumer's employer prohibits the consumer from receiving such communication.

(b) Communication with third parties

Except as provided in section 1692b of this title, without the prior consent of the consumer given directly to the debt collector, or the express permission of a court of competent jurisdiction, or as reasonably necessary to effectuate a postjudgment judicial remedy, a debt collector may not communicate, in connection with the collection of any debt, with any person other than the consumer, his attorney, a consumer reporting agency if otherwise permitted by law, the creditor, the attorney of the creditor, or the attorney of the debt collector.

(c) Ceasing communication

If a consumer notifies a debt collector in writing that the consumer refuses to pay a debt or that the consumer wishes the debt collector to cease further communication with the consumer, the debt collector shall not communicate further with the consumer with respect to such debt, except—

(1) to advise the consumer that the debt collector's further efforts are being terminated;

(2) to notify the consumer that the debt collector or creditor may invoke specified remedies which are ordinarily invoked by such debt collector or creditor; or

(3) where applicable, to notify the consumer that the debt collector or creditor intends to invoke a specified remedy.

If such notice from the consumer is made by mail, notification shall be complete upon receipt.

(d) "Consumer" defined

For the purpose of this section, the term "consumer" includes the consumer's spouse, parent (if the consumer is a minor), guardian, executor, or administrator.

(Pub.L. 90–321, Title VIII, § 805, as added Pub.L. 95–109, Sept. 20, 1977, 91 Stat. 876.)

§ 1692d. Harassment or abuse [CCPA § 806]

A debt collector may not engage in any conduct the natural consequence of which is to harass, oppress, or abuse any person in connection with the collection of a debt. Without limiting the general application of the foregoing, the following conduct is a violation of this section:

(1) The use or threat of use of violence or other criminal means to harm the physical person, reputation, or property of any person.

(2) The use of obscene or profane language or language the natural consequence of which is to abuse the hearer or reader.

(3)   The publication of a list of consumers who allegedly refuse to pay debts, except to a consumer reporting agency or to persons meeting the requirements of section 1681a(f) or 1681b(3) of this title.

(4)   The advertisement for sale of any debt to coerce payment of the debt.

(5)   Causing a telephone to ring or engaging any person in telephone conversation repeatedly or continuously with intent to annoy, abuse, or harass any person at the called number.

(6)   Except as provided in section 1692b of this title, the placement of telephone calls without meaningful disclosure of the caller's identity.

(Pub.L. 90–321, Title VIII, § 806, as added Pub.L. 95–109, Sept. 20, 1977, 91 Stat. 877.)

§ 1692e.   False or misleading representations [CCPA § 807]

A debt collector may not use any false, deceptive, or misleading representation or means in connection with the collection of any debt. Without limiting the general application of the foregoing, the following conduct is a violation of this section:

(1)   The false representation or implication that the debt collector is vouched for, bonded by, or affiliated with the United States or any State, including the use of any badge, uniform, or facsimile thereof.

(2)   The false representation of—

(A)   the character, amount, or legal status of any debt; or

(B)   any services rendered or compensation which may be lawfully received by any debt collector for the collection of a debt.

(3)   The false representation or implication that any individual is an attorney or that any communication is from an attorney.

(4)   The representation or implication that nonpayment of any debt will result in the arrest or imprisonment of any person or the seizure, garnishment, attachment, or sale of any property or wages of any person unless such action is lawful and the debt collector or creditor intends to take such action.

(5)   The threat to take any action that cannot legally be taken or that is not intended to be taken.

(6)   The false representation or implication that a sale, referral, or other transfer of any interest in a debt shall cause the consumer to—

(A)   lose any claim or defense to payment of the debt; or

(B)   become subject to any practice prohibited by this subchapter.

(7)   The false representation or implication that the consumer committed any crime or other conduct in order to disgrace the consumer.

(8)   Communicating or threatening to communicate to any person credit information which is known or which should be known to be false, including the failure to communicate that a disputed debt is disputed.

(9)   The use or distribution of any written communication which simulates or is falsely represented to be a document authorized, issued, or approved by any court, official, or agency of the United States or any State, or which creates a false impression as to its source, authorization, or approval.

(10)   The use of any false representation or deceptive means to collect or attempt to collect any debt or to obtain information concerning a consumer.

(11)   The failure to disclose in the initial written communication with the consumer and, in addition, if the initial communication with the consumer is oral, in that initial oral communication, that the debt collector is attempting to collect a debt and that any information obtained will be used for that purpose, and the failure to disclose in subsequent communications that the communication is

from a debt collector, except that this paragraph shall not apply to a formal pleading made in connection with a legal action.

(12) The false representation or implication that accounts have been turned over to innocent purchasers for value.

(13) The false representation or implication that documents are legal process.

(14) The use of any business, company, or organization name other than the true name of the debt collector's business, company, or organization.

(15) The false representation or implication that documents are not legal process forms or do not require action by the consumer.

(16) The false representation or implication that a debt collector operates or is employed by a consumer reporting agency as defined by section 1681a(f) of this title.

(Pub.L. 90–321, Title VIII, § 807, as added Pub.L. 95–109, Sept. 20, 1977, 91 Stat. 877, and amended Pub.L. 104–208, Title II, § 2305(a), Sept. 30, 1996, 110 Stat. 3009–425.)

§ 1692f. Unfair practices [CCPA § 808]

A debt collector may not use unfair or unconscionable means to collect or attempt to collect any debt. Without limiting the general application of the foregoing, the following conduct is a violation of this section:

(1) The collection of any amount (including any interest, fee, charge, or expense incidental to the principal obligation) unless such amount is expressly authorized by the agreement creating the debt or permitted by law.

(2) The acceptance by a debt collector from any person of a check or other payment instrument postdated by more than five days unless such person is notified in writing of the debt collector's intent to deposit such check or instrument not more than ten nor less than three business days prior to such deposit.

(3) The solicitation by a debt collector of any postdated check or other postdated payment instrument for the purpose of threatening or instituting criminal prosecution.

(4) Depositing or threatening to deposit any postdated check or other postdated payment instrument prior to the date on such check or instrument.

(5) Causing charges to be made to any person for communications by concealment of the true purpose of the communication. Such charges include, but are not limited to, collect telephone calls and telegram fees.

(6) Taking or threatening to take any nonjudicial action to effect dispossession or disablement of property if—

    (A) there is no present right to possession of the property claimed as collateral through an enforceable security interest;

    (B) there is no present intention to take possession of the property; or

    (C) the property is exempt by law from such dispossession or disablement.

(7) Communicating with a consumer regarding a debt by post card.

(8) Using any language or symbol, other than the debt collector's address, on any envelope when communicating with a consumer by use of the mails or by telegram, except that a debt collector may use his business name if such name does not indicate that he is in the debt collection business.

(Pub.L. 90–321, Title VIII, § 808, as added Pub.L. 95–109, Sept. 20, 1977, 91 Stat. 879.)

§ 1692g.   Validation of debts [CCPA § 809]

(a) Notice of debt; contents

Within five days after the initial communication with a consumer in connection with the collection of any debt, a debt collector shall, unless the following information is contained in the initial communication or the consumer has paid the debt, send the consumer a written notice containing—

    (1)   the amount of the debt;

    (2)   the name of the creditor to whom the debt is owed;

    (3)   a statement that unless the consumer, within thirty days after receipt of the notice, disputes the validity of the debt, or any portion thereof, the debt will be assumed to be valid by the debt collector;

    (4)   a statement that if the consumer notifies the debt collector in writing within the thirty-day period that the debt, or any portion thereof, is disputed, the debt collector will obtain verification of the debt or a copy of a judgment against the consumer and a copy of such verification or judgment will be mailed to the consumer by the debt collector; and

    (5)   a statement that, upon the consumer's written request within the thirty-day period, the debt collector will provide the consumer with the name and address of the original creditor, if different from the current creditor.

(b) Disputed debts

If the consumer notifies the debt collector in writing within the thirty-day period described in subsection (a) of this section that the debt, or any portion thereof, is disputed, or that the consumer requests the name and address of the original creditor, the debt collector shall cease collection of the debt, or any disputed portion thereof, until the debt collector obtains verification of the debt or a copy of a judgment, or the name and address of the original creditor, and a copy of such verification or judgment, or name and address of the original creditor, is mailed to the consumer by the debt collector. Collection activities and communications that do not otherwise violate this subchapter may continue during the 30-day period referred to in subsection (a) of this section unless the consumer has notified the debt collector in writing that the debt, or any portion of the debt, is disputed or that the consumer requests the name and address of the original creditor. Any collection activities and communication during the 30-day period may not overshadow or be inconsistent with the disclosure of the consumer's right to dispute the debt or request the name and address of the original creditor.

(c) Admission of liability

The failure of a consumer to dispute the validity of a debt under this section may not be construed by any court as an admission of liability by the consumer.

(d) Legal pleadings

A communication in the form of a formal pleading in a civil action shall not be treated as an initial communication for purposes of subsection (a) of this section.

(e) Notice provisions

The sending or delivery of any form or notice which does not relate to the collection of a debt and is expressly required by the Internal Revenue Code of 1986, chapter 94 of this title [15 U.S.C.A. § 6801 et seq.], or any provision of Federal or State law relating to notice of data security breach or privacy, or any regulation prescribed under any such provision of law, shall not be treated as an initial communication in connection with debt collection for purposes of this section.

    (Pub.L. 90–321, Title VIII, § 809, as added Pub.L. 95–109, Sept. 20, 1977, 91 Stat. 879, and amended Pub.L. 109–351, Title VIII, § 802, Oct. 13, 2006, 120 Stat. 2006.)

§ 1692h.   Multiple debts [CCPA § 810]

If any consumer owes multiple debts and makes any single payment to any debt collector with respect to such debts, such debt collector may not apply such payment to any debt which is disputed by the consumer and, where applicable, shall apply such payment in accordance with the consumer's directions.

(Pub.L. 90–321, Title VIII, § 810, as added Pub.L. 95–109, Sept. 20, 1977, 91 Stat. 880.)

§ 1692i. Legal actions by debt collectors [CCPA § 811]

(a) Venue

Any debt collector who brings any legal action on a debt against any consumer shall—

(1) in the case of an action to enforce an interest in real property securing the consumer's obligation, bring such action only in a judicial district or similar legal entity in which such real property is located; or

(2) in the case of an action not described in paragraph (1), bring such action only in the judicial district or similar legal entity—

(A) in which such consumer signed the contract sued upon; or

(B) in which such consumer resides at the commencement of the action.

(b) Authorization of actions

Nothing in this subchapter shall be construed to authorize the bringing of legal actions by debt collectors.

(Pub.L. 90–321, Title VIII, § 811, as added Pub.L. 95–109, Sept. 20, 1977, 91 Stat. 880.)

§ 1692j. Furnishing certain deceptive forms [CCPA § 812]

(a) It is unlawful to design, compile, and furnish any form knowing that such form would be used to create the false belief in a consumer that a person other than the creditor of such consumer is participating in the collection of or in an attempt to collect a debt such consumer allegedly owes such creditor, when in fact such person is not so participating.

(b) Any person who violates this section shall be liable to the same extent and in the same manner as a debt collector is liable under section 1692k of this title for failure to comply with a provision of this subchapter.

(Pub.L. 90–321, Title VIII, § 812, as added Pub.L. 95–109, Sept. 20, 1977, 91 Stat. 880.)

§ 1692k. Civil liability [CCPA § 813]

(a) Amount of damages

Except as otherwise provided by this section, any debt collector who fails to comply with any provision of this subchapter with respect to any person is liable to such person in an amount equal to the sum of—

(1) any actual damage sustained by such person as a result of such failure;

(2)(A) in the case of any action by an individual, such additional damages as the court may allow, but not exceeding $1,000; or

(B) in the case of a class action, (i) such amount for each named plaintiff as could be recovered under subparagraph (A), and (ii) such amount as the court may allow for all other class members, without regard to a minimum individual recovery, not to exceed the lesser of $500,000 or 1 per centum of the net worth of the debt collector; and

(3) in the case of any successful action to enforce the foregoing liability, the costs of the action, together with a reasonable attorney's fee as determined by the court. On a finding by the court that an action under this section was brought in bad faith and for the purpose of harassment, the court may award to the defendant attorney's fees reasonable in relation to the work expended and costs.

(b) Factors considered by court

In determining the amount of liability in any action under subsection (a) of this section, the court shall consider, among other relevant factors—

    (1) in any individual action under subsection (a)(2)(A) of this section, the frequency and persistence of noncompliance by the debt collector, the nature of such noncompliance, and the extent to which such noncompliance was intentional; or

    (2) in any class action under subsection (a)(2)(B) of this section, the frequency and persistence of noncompliance by the debt collector, the nature of such noncompliance, the resources of the debt collector, the number of persons adversely affected, and the extent to which the debt collector's noncompliance was intentional.

(c)   Intent

    A debt collector may not be held liable in any action brought under this subchapter if the debt collector shows by a preponderance of evidence that the violation was not intentional and resulted from a bona fide error notwithstanding the maintenance of procedures reasonably adapted to avoid any such error.

(d)   Jurisdiction

    An action to enforce any liability created by this subchapter may be brought in any appropriate United States district court without regard to the amount in controversy, or in any other court of competent jurisdiction, within one year from the date on which the violation occurs.

(e)   Advisory opinions of Bureau

    No provision of this section imposing any liability shall apply to any act done or omitted in good faith in conformity with any advisory opinion of the Bureau, notwithstanding that after such act or omission has occurred, such opinion is amended, rescinded, or determined by judicial or other authority to be invalid for any reason.

    (Pub.L. 90–321, Title VIII, § 813, as added Pub.L. 95–109, Sept. 20, 1977, 91 Stat. 881; Pub.L. 111–203, Title X, § 1089(1), July 21, 2010, 124 Stat. 2092.)

§ 1692*l*.   Administrative enforcement [CCPA § 814]

(a)   Federal Trade Commission

    The Federal Trade Commission shall be authorized to enforce compliance with this subchapter, except to the extent that enforcement of the requirements imposed under this subchapter is specifically committed to another Government agency under any of paragraphs (1) through (5) of subsection (b), subject to subtitle B of the Consumer Financial Protection Act of 2010. For purpose of the exercise by the Federal Trade Commission of its functions and powers under the Federal Trade Commission Act (15 U.S.C. 41 et seq.), a violation of this subchapter shall be deemed an unfair or deceptive act or practice in violation of that Act. All of the functions and powers of the Federal Trade Commission under the Federal Trade Commission Act are available to the Federal Trade Commission to enforce compliance by any person with this subchapter, irrespective of whether that person is engaged in commerce or meets any other jurisdictional tests under the Federal Trade Commission Act, including the power to enforce the provisions of this subchapter, in the same manner as if the violation had been a violation of a Federal Trade Commission trade regulation rule.

(b)   Applicable provisions of law

    Subject to subtitle B of the Consumer Financial Protection Act of 2010, compliance with any requirements imposed under this subchapter shall be enforced under—

    (1) section 1818 of Title 12, by the appropriate Federal banking agency, as defined in section 1813(q) of Title 12, with respect to—

        (A) national banks, Federal savings associations, and Federal branches and Federal agencies of foreign banks;

        (B) member banks of the Federal Reserve System (other than national banks), branches and agencies of foreign banks (other than Federal branches, Federal agencies, and insured State branches of foreign banks), commercial lending companies owned or controlled by foreign banks, and organizations operating under section 25 or 25A of the Federal Reserve Act; and

(C) banks and State savings associations insured by the Federal Deposit Insurance Corporation (other than members of the Federal Reserve System), and insured State branches of foreign banks;

(2) the Federal Credit Union Act [12 U.S.C.A. § 1751 et seq.], by the National Credit Union Administration Board with respect to any Federal Credit union;

(3) subtitle IV of Title 49, by the Secretary of Transportation, with respect to all carriers subject to the jurisdiction of the Surface Transportation Board;

(4) part A of subtitle VII of Title 49, by the Secretary of Transportation with respect to any air carrier or any foreign air carrier subject to that part;

(5) the Packers and Stockyards Act, 1921 [7 U.S.C.A. § 181 et seq.] (except as provided in section 406 of that Act [7 U.S.C.A. §§ 226, 227]), by the Secretary of Agriculture with respect to any activities subject to that Act; and

(6) subtitle E of the Consumer Financial Protection Act of 2010, by the Bureau, with respect to any person subject to this subchapter,

The terms used in paragraph (1) that are not defined in this subchapter or otherwise defined in section 3(s) of the Federal Deposit Insurance Act (12 U.S.C. 1813(s)) shall have the meaning given to them in section 1(b) of the International Banking Act of 1978 (12 U.S.C. 3101).

(c) Agency powers

For the purpose of the exercise by any agency referred to in subsection (b) of this section of its powers under any Act referred to in that subsection, a violation of any requirement imposed under this subchapter shall be deemed to be a violation of a requirement imposed under that Act. In addition to its powers under any provision of law specifically referred to in subsection (b) of this section, each of the agencies referred to in that subsection may exercise, for the purpose of enforcing compliance with any requirement imposed under this subchapter any other authority conferred on it by law, except as provided in subsection (d) of this section.

(d) Rules and regulations

Except as provided in section 5519(a) of Title 12, the Bureau may prescribe rules with respect to the collection of debt collectors, as defined in this subchapter.

(Pub.L. 90–321, Title VIII, § 814, as added Pub.L. 95–109, Sept. 20, 1977, 91 Stat. 881, and amended Pub.L. 95–473, § 3(b), Oct. 17, 1978, 92 Stat. 1466; Pub.L. 95–630, Title V, § 501, Nov. 10, 1978, 92 Stat. 3680; Pub.L. 98–443, § 9(n), Oct. 4, 1984, 98 Stat. 1708; Pub.L. 101–73, Title VII, § 744(n), Aug. 9, 1989, 103 Stat. 440; Pub.L. 102–242, Title II, § 212(e), Dec. 19, 1991, 105 Stat. 2301; Pub.L. 102–550, Title XVI, § 1604(a)(8), Oct. 28, 1992, 106 Stat. 4082; Pub.L. 104–88, Title III, § 316, Dec. 29, 1995, 109 Stat. 949; Pub.L. 111–203, Title X, §§ 1089(3), (4), July 21, 2010, 124 Stat. 2092.)

§ 1692m. Reports to Congress by the Bureau; views of other Federal agencies [CCPA § 815]

(a) Not later than one year after the effective date of this subchapter and at one-year intervals thereafter, the Bureau shall make reports to the Congress concerning the administration of its functions under this subchapter, including such recommendations as the Bureau deems necessary or appropriate. In addition, each report of the Bureau shall include its assessment of the extent to which compliance with this subchapter is being achieved and a summary of the enforcement actions taken by the Bureau under section 1692*l* of this title.

(b) In the exercise of its functions under this subchapter, the Bureau may obtain upon request the views of any other Federal agency which exercises enforcement functions under section 1692*l* of this title.

(Pub.L. 90–321, Title VIII, § 815, as added Pub.L. 95–109, Sept. 20, 1977, 91 Stat. 882, and amended Pub.L. 111–203, Title X, § 1089(1), July 21, 2010, 124 Stat. 2092.)

§ 1692n.   Relation to State laws [CCPA § 816]

This subchapter does not annul, alter, or affect, or exempt any person subject to the provisions of this subchapter from complying with the laws of any State with respect to debt collection practices, except to the extent that those laws are inconsistent with any provision of this subchapter, and then only to the extent of the inconsistency. For purposes of this section, a State law is not inconsistent with this subchapter if the protection such law affords any consumer is greater than the protection provided by this subchapter.

(Pub.L. 90–321, Title VIII, § 816, as added Pub.L. 95–109, Sept. 20, 1977, 91 Stat. 883.)

§ 1692o.   Exemption for State regulation [CCPA § 817]

The Bureau shall by regulation exempt from the requirements of this subchapter any class of debt collection practices within any State if the Bureau determines that under the law of that State that class of debt collection practices is subject to requirements substantially similar to those imposed by this subchapter, and that there is adequate provision for enforcement.

(Pub.L. 90–321, Title VIII, § 817, as added Pub.L. 95–109, Sept. 20, 1977, 91 Stat. 883, and amended Pub.L. 111–203, Title X, § 1089(1), July 21, 2010, 124 Stat. 2092.)

§ 1692p.   Exception for certain bad check enforcement programs operated by private entities [CCPA § 818]

(a) **In general**

(1) **Treatment of certain private entities**

Subject to paragraph (2), a private entity shall be excluded from the definition of a debt collector, pursuant to the exception provided in section 1692a(6) of this title, with respect to the operation by the entity of a program described in paragraph (2)(A) under a contract described in paragraph (2)(B).

(2) **Conditions of applicability**

Paragraph (1) shall apply if—

(A) a State or district attorney establishes, within the jurisdiction of such State or district attorney and with respect to alleged bad check violations that do not involve a check described in subsection (b) of this section, a pretrial diversion program for alleged bad check offenders who agree to participate voluntarily in such program to avoid criminal prosecution;

(B) a private entity, that is subject to an administrative support services contract with a State or district attorney and operates under the direction, supervision, and control of such State or district attorney, operates the pretrial diversion program described in subparagraph (A); and

(C) in the course of performing duties delegated to it by a State or district attorney under the contract, the private entity referred to in subparagraph (B)—

(i) complies with the penal laws of the State;

(ii) conforms with the terms of the contract and directives of the State or district attorney;

(iii) does not exercise independent prosecutorial discretion;

(iv) contacts any alleged offender referred to in subparagraph (A) for purposes of participating in a program referred to in such paragraph—

(I) only as a result of any determination by the State or district attorney that probable cause of a bad check violation under State penal law exists, and that contact with the alleged offender for purposes of participation in the program is appropriate; and

(II) the alleged offender has failed to pay the bad check after demand for payment, pursuant to State law, is made for payment of the check amount;

(v) includes as part of an initial written communication with an alleged offender a clear and conspicuous statement that—

(I) the alleged offender may dispute the validity of any alleged bad check violation;

(II) where the alleged offender knows, or has reasonable cause to believe, that the alleged bad check violation is the result of theft or forgery of the check, identity theft, or other fraud that is not the result of the conduct of the alleged offender, the alleged offender may file a crime report with the appropriate law enforcement agency; and

(III) if the alleged offender notifies the private entity or the district attorney in writing, not later than 30 days after being contacted for the first time pursuant to clause (iv), that there is a dispute pursuant to this subsection, before further restitution efforts are pursued, the district attorney or an employee of the district attorney authorized to make such a determination makes a determination that there is probable cause to believe that a crime has been committed; and

(vi) charges only fees in connection with services under the contract that have been authorized by the contract with the State or district attorney.

(b) Certain checks excluded

A check is described in this subsection if the check involves, or is subsequently found to involve—

(1) a postdated check presented in connection with a payday loan, or other similar transaction, where the payee of the check knew that the issuer had insufficient funds at the time the check was made, drawn, or delivered;

(2) a stop payment order where the issuer acted in good faith and with reasonable cause in stopping payment on the check;

(3) a check dishonored because of an adjustment to the issuer's account by the financial institution holding such account without providing notice to the person at the time the check was made, drawn, or delivered;

(4) a check for partial payment of a debt where the payee had previously accepted partial payment for such debt;

(5) a check issued by a person who was not competent, or was not of legal age, to enter into a legal contractual obligation at the time the check was made, drawn, or delivered; or

(6) a check issued to pay an obligation arising from a transaction that was illegal in the jurisdiction of the State or district attorney at the time the check was made, drawn, or delivered.

(c) Definitions

For purposes of this section, the following definitions shall apply:

(1) State or district attorney

The term "State or district attorney" means the chief elected or appointed prosecuting attorney in a district, county (as defined in section 2 of title 1, United States Code), municipality, or comparable jurisdiction, including State attorneys general who act as chief elected or appointed prosecuting attorneys in a district, county (as so defined), municipality or comparable jurisdiction, who may be referred to by a variety of titles such as district attorneys, prosecuting attorneys, commonwealth's attorneys, solicitors, county attorneys, and state's attorneys, and who are responsible for the prosecution of State crimes and violations of jurisdiction-specific local ordinances.

(2) Check

The term "check" has the same meaning as in section 5002(6) of Title 12.

(3)   Bad check violation

The term "bad check violation" means a violation of the applicable State criminal law relating to the writing of dishonored checks.

(Pub.L. 90–321, Title VIII, § 818, as added Pub.L. 109–351, Title VIII, § 801(a)(2), Oct. 13, 2006, 120 Stat. 2004.)

SUBCHAPTER VI—ELECTRONIC FUND TRANSFERS

§ 1693.   Congressional findings and declaration of purpose [CCPA § 902]

(a)   Rights and liabilities undefined

The Congress finds that the use of electronic systems to transfer funds provides the potential for substantial benefits to consumers. However, due to the unique characteristics of such systems, the application of existing consumer protection legislation is unclear, leaving the rights and liabilities of consumers, financial institutions, and intermediaries in electronic fund transfers undefined.

(b)   Purposes

It is the purpose of this subchapter to provide a basic framework establishing the rights, liabilities, and responsibilities of participants in electronic fund and remittance transfer systems. The primary objective of this subchapter, however, is the provision of individual consumer rights.

(Pub.L. 90–321, Title IX, § 902, as added Pub.L. 95–630, Title XX, § 2001, Nov. 10, 1978, 92 Stat. 3728, and amended Pub.L. 111–203, Title X, § 1073(a)(1), July 21, 2010, 124 Stat. 2060.)

§ 1693a.   Definitions [CCPA § 903]

As used in this subchapter—

(1)   the term "accepted card or other means of access" means a card, code, or other means of access to a consumer's account for the purpose of initiating electronic fund transfers when the person to whom such card or other means of access was issued has requested and received or has signed or has used, or authorized another to use, such card or other means of access for the purpose of transferring money between accounts or obtaining money, property, labor, or services;

(2)   the term "account" means a demand deposit, savings deposit, or other asset account (other than an occasional or incidental credit balance in an open end credit plan as defined in section 1602(i) of this title), as described in regulations of the Bureau, established primarily for personal, family, or household purposes, but such term does not include an account held by a financial institution pursuant to a bona fide trust agreement;

(4)[1]   the term "Board" means the Board of Governors of the Federal Reserve System;

(4)[1]   the term "Bureau" means the Bureau of Consumer Financial Protection;

(5)   the term "business day" means any day on which the offices of the consumer's financial institution involved in an electronic fund transfer are open to the public for carrying on substantially all of its business functions;

(6)   the term "consumer" means a natural person;

(7)   the term "electronic fund transfer" means any transfer of funds, other than a transaction originated by check, draft, or similar paper instrument, which is initiated through an electronic terminal, telephonic instrument, or computer or magnetic tape so as to order, instruct, or authorize a financial institution to debit or credit an account. Such term includes, but is not limited to, point-of-sale transfers, automated teller machine transactions, direct deposits or withdrawals of funds, and transfers initiated by telephone. Such term does not include—

---

[1]   So in original. There are two paragraphs designated "(4)" and no paragraph "(3)".

(A) any check guarantee or authorization service which does not directly result in a debit or credit to a consumer's account:[2]

(B) any transfer of funds, other than those processed by automated clearinghouse, made by a financial institution on behalf of a consumer by means of a service that transfers funds held at either Federal Reserve banks or other depository institutions and which is not designed primarily to transfer funds on behalf of a consumer;

(C) any transaction the primary purpose of which is the purchase or sale of securities or commodities through a broker-dealer registered with or regulated by the Securities and Exchange Commission;

(D) any automatic transfer from a savings account to a demand deposit account pursuant to an agreement between a consumer and a financial institution for the purpose of covering an overdraft or maintaining an agreed upon minimum balance in the consumer's demand deposit account; or

(E) any transfer of funds which is initiated by a telephone conversation between a consumer and an officer or employee of a financial institution which is not pursuant to a prearranged plan and under which periodic or recurring transfers are not contemplated;

as determined under regulations of the Bureau;

(8) the term "electronic terminal" means an electronic device, other than a telephone operated by a consumer, through which a consumer may initiate an electronic fund transfer. Such term includes, but is not limited to, point-of-sale terminals, automated teller machines, and cash dispensing machines;

(9) the term "financial institution" means a State or National bank, a State or Federal savings and loan association, a mutual savings bank, a State or Federal credit union, or any other person who, directly or indirectly, holds an account belonging to a consumer;

(10) the term "preauthorized electronic fund transfer" means an electronic fund transfer authorized in advance to recur at substantially regular intervals;

(11) the term "State" means any State, territory, or possession of the United States, the District of Columbia, the Commonwealth of Puerto Rico, or any political subdivision of any of the foregoing; and

(12) the term "unauthorized electronic fund transfer" means an electronic fund transfer from a consumer's account initiated by a person other than the consumer without actual authority to initiate such transfer and from which the consumer receives no benefit, but the term does not include any electronic fund transfer (A) initiated by a person other than the consumer who was furnished with the card, code, or other means of access to such consumer's account by such consumer, unless the consumer has notified the financial institution involved that transfers by such other person are no longer authorized, (B) initiated with fraudulent intent by the consumer or any person acting in concert with the consumer, or (C) which constitutes an error committed by a financial institution.

(Pub.L. 90–321, Title IX, § 903, as added Pub.L. 95–630, Title XX, § 2001, Nov. 10, 1978, 92 Stat. 3728, and amended Pub.L. 111–203, Title X, §§ 1084(1), (2), July 21, 2010, 124 Stat. 2081.)

§ 1693b. Regulations [CCPA § 904]

(a) Prescription by the Bureau and the Board

(1) In General

Except as provided in paragraph (2), the Bureau shall prescribe rules to carry out the purposes of this title.

---

[2] So in original. The colon probably should be a semi colon.

(2) Authority of the Board

The Board shall have sole authority to prescribe rules—

   (A) to carry out the purposes of this title with respect to a person described section 5519(a) of Title 12; and

   (B) to carry out the purposes of section 1693o–2 of this title.

In prescribing such regulations, the Board shall:

   (1) consult with the other agencies referred to in section 1693o of this title and take into account, and allow for, the continuing evolution of electronic banking services and the technology utilized in such services,

   (2) prepare an analysis of economic impact which considers the costs and benefits to financial institutions, consumers, and other users of electronic fund transfers, including the extent to which additional documentation, reports, records, or other paper work would be required, and the effects upon competition in the provision of electronic banking services among large and small financial institutions and the availability of such services to different classes of consumers, particularly low income consumers,

   (3) to the extent practicable, the Board shall demonstrate that the consumer protections of the proposed regulations outweigh the compliance costs imposed upon consumers and financial institutions, and

   (4) any proposed regulations and accompanying analyses shall be sent promptly to Congress by the Board.

(b) Issuance of model clauses

The Bureau shall issue model clauses for optional use by financial institutions to facilitate compliance with the disclosure requirements of section 1693c of this title and to aid consumers in understanding the rights and responsibilities of participants in electronic fund transfers by utilizing readily understandable language. Such model clauses shall be adopted after notice duly given in the Federal Register and opportunity for public comment in accordance with section 553 of Title 5. With respect to the disclosures required by section 1693c(a)(3) and (4) of this title, the Bureau shall take account of variations in the services and charges under different electronic fund transfer systems and, as appropriate, shall issue alternative model clauses for disclosure of these differing account terms.

(c) Criteria; modification of requirements

Regulations prescribed hereunder may contain such classifications, differentiations, or other provisions, and may provide for such adjustments and exceptions for any class of electronic fund transfers or remittance transfers, as in the judgment of the Bureau are necessary or proper to effectuate the purposes of this subchapter, to prevent circumvention or evasion thereof, or to facilitate compliance therewith. The Bureau shall by regulation modify the requirements imposed by this subchapter on small financial institutions if the Bureau determines that such modifications are necessary to alleviate any undue compliance burden on small financial institutions and such modifications are consistent with the purpose and objective of this subchapter.

(d) Applicability to service providers other than certain financial institutions

(1) In general

If electronic fund transfer services are made available to consumers by a person other than a financial institution holding a consumer's account, the Bureau shall by regulation assure that the disclosures, protections, responsibilities, and remedies created by this subchapter are made applicable to such persons and services.

(2) State and local government electronic benefit transfer systems

(A) "Electronic benefit transfer system" defined

In this paragraph, the term "electronic benefit transfer system"—

(i) means a system under which a government agency distributes needs-tested benefits by establishing accounts that may be accessed by recipients electronically, such as through automated teller machines or point-of-sale terminals; and

(ii) does not include employment-related payments, including salaries and pension, retirement, or unemployment benefits established by a Federal, State, or local government agency.

(B) Exemption generally

The disclosures, protections, responsibilities, and remedies established under this subchapter, and any regulation prescribed or order issued by the Bureau in accordance with this subchapter, shall not apply to any electronic benefit transfer system established under State or local law or administered by a State or local government.

(C) Exception for direct deposit into recipient's account

Subparagraph (B) shall not apply with respect to any electronic funds transfer under an electronic benefit transfer system for a deposit directly into a consumer account held by the recipient of the benefit.

(D) Rule of construction

No provision of this paragraph—

(i) affects or alters the protections otherwise applicable with respect to benefits established by any other provision[1] Federal, State, or local law; or

(ii) otherwise supersedes the application of any State or local law.

(3) Fee disclosures at automated teller machines

(A) In general

The regulations prescribed under paragraph (1) shall require any automated teller machine operator who imposes a fee on any consumer for providing host transfer services to such consumer to provide notice in accordance with subparagraph (B) to the consumer (at the time the service is provided) of—

(i) the fact that a fee is imposed by such operator for providing the service; and

(ii) the amount of any such fee.

(B) Notice requirement

The notice required under clauses (i) and (ii) of subparagraph (A) with respect to any fee described in such subparagraph shall appear on the screen of the automated teller machine, or on a paper notice issued from such machine, after the transaction is initiated and before the consumer is irrevocably committed to completing the transaction.

(C) Prohibition on fees not properly disclosed and explicitly assumed by consumer

No fee may be imposed by any automated teller machine operator in connection with any electronic fund transfer initiated by a consumer for which a notice is required under subparagraph (A), unless—

(i) the consumer receives such notice in accordance with subparagraph (B); and

(ii) the consumer elects to continue in the manner necessary to effect the transaction after receiving such notice.

(D) Definitions

For purposes of this paragraph, the following definitions shall apply:

---

[1] So in original. Probably should be followed by "of".

(i)   Automated teller machine operator

The term "automated teller machine operator" means any person who—

     (I)   operates an automated teller machine at which consumers initiate electronic fund transfers; and

     (II)   is not the financial institution that holds the account of such consumer from which the transfer is made.

(ii)   Electronic fund transfer

The term "electronic fund transfer" includes a transaction that involves a balance inquiry initiated by a consumer in the same manner as an electronic fund transfer, whether or not the consumer initiates a transfer of funds in the course of the transaction.

(iii)   Host transfer services

The term "host transfer services" means any electronic fund transfer made by an automated teller machine operator in connection with a transaction initiated by a consumer at an automated teller machine operated by such operator.

(e)   Deference

No provision of this subchapter may be construed as altering, limiting, or otherwise affecting the deference that a court affords to—

     (1)   the Bureau in making determinations regarding the meaning or interpretation of any provision of this subchapter for which the Bureau has authority to prescribe regulations; or

     (2)   the Board in making determinations regarding the meaning or interpretation of section 1693*o*–2 of this title.

     (Pub.L. 90–321, Title IX, § 904, as added Pub.L. 95–630, Title XX, § 2001, Nov. 10, 1978, 92 Stat. 3730, and amended Pub.L. 104–193, Title VIII, § 891, Title IX, § 907, Aug. 22, 1996, 110 Stat. 2346, 2350; Pub.L. 106–102, Title VII, § 702, Nov. 12, 1999, 113 Stat. 1463; Pub.L. 111–203, Title X, §§ 1073(a)(2), 1084(1), (3), July 21, 2010, 124 Stat. 2060, 2081; Pub.L. 112–216, § 1, Dec. 20, 2012, 126 Stat. 1590.)

§ 1693c.   Terms and conditions of transfers [CCPA § 905]

(a)   Disclosures; time; form; contents

The terms and conditions of electronic fund transfers involving a consumer's account shall be disclosed at the time the consumer contracts for an electronic fund transfer service, in accordance with regulations of the Bureau. Such disclosures shall be in readily understandable language and shall include, to the extent applicable—

     (1)   the consumer's liability for unauthorized electronic fund transfers and, at the financial institution's option, notice of the advisability of prompt reporting of any loss, theft, or unauthorized use of a card, code, or other means of access;

     (2)   the telephone number and address of the person or office to be notified in the event the consumer believes than[1] an unauthorized electronic fund transfer has been or may be effected;

     (3)   the type and nature of electronic fund transfers which the consumer may initiate, including any limitations on the frequency or dollar amount of such transfers, except that the details of such limitations need not be disclosed if their confidentiality is necessary to maintain the security of an electronic fund transfer system, as determined by the Bureau;

     (4)   any charges for electronic fund transfers or for the right to make such transfers;

     (5)   the consumer's right to stop payment of a preauthorized electronic fund transfer and the procedure to initiate such a stop payment order;

---

[1]   So in original. Probably should be "that".

(6) the consumer's right to receive documentation of electronic fund transfers under section 1693d of this title;

(7) a summary, in a form prescribed by regulations of the Bureau, of the error resolution provisions of section 1693f of this title and the consumer's rights thereunder. The financial institution shall thereafter transmit such summary at least once per calendar year;

(8) the financial institution's liability to the consumer under section 1693h of this title;

(9) under what circumstances the financial institution will in the ordinary course of business disclose information concerning the consumer's account to third persons; and

(10) a notice to the consumer that a fee may be imposed by—

(A) an automated teller machine operator (as defined in section 1693b(d)(3)(D)(i) of this title) if the consumer initiates a transfer from an automated teller machine that is not operated by the person issuing the card or other means of access; and

(B) any national, regional, or local network utilized to effect the transaction.

(b) Notification of changes to consumer

A financial institution shall notify a consumer in writing at least twenty-one days prior to the effective date of any change in any term or condition of the consumer's account required to be disclosed under subsection (a) of this section if such change would result in greater cost or liability for such consumer or decreased access to the consumer's account. A financial institution may, however, implement a change in the terms or conditions of an account without prior notice when such change is immediately necessary to maintain or restore the security of an electronic fund transfer system or a consumer's account. Subject to subsection (a)(3) of this section, the Bureau shall require subsequent notification if such a change is made permanent.

(c) Time for disclosures respecting accounts accessible prior to effective date of this subchapter

For any account of a consumer made accessible to electronic fund transfers prior to the effective date of this subchapter, the information required to be disclosed to the consumer under subsection (a) of this section shall be disclosed not later than the earlier of—

(1) the first periodic statement required by section 1693d(c) of this title after the effective date of this subchapter; or

(2) thirty days after the effective date of this subchapter.

(Pub.L. 90–321, Title IX, § 905, as added Pub.L. 95–630, Title XX, § 2001, Nov. 10, 1978, 92 Stat. 3730, and amended Pub.L. 106–102, Title VII, § 703, Nov. 12, 1999, 113 Stat. 1464; Pub.L. 111–203, Title X, § 1084(1), July 21, 2010, 124 Stat. 2081.)

§ 1693d. Documentation of transfers [CCPA § 906]

(a) Availability of written documentation to consumer; contents

For each electronic fund transfer initiated by a consumer from an electronic terminal, the financial institution holding such consumer's account shall, directly or indirectly, at the time the transfer is initiated, make available to the consumer written documentation of such transfer. The documentation shall clearly set forth to the extent applicable—

(1) the amount involved and date the transfer is initiated;

(2) the type of transfer;

(3) the identity of the consumer's account with the financial institution from which or to which funds are transferred;

(4) the identity of any third party to whom or from whom funds are transferred; and

(5) the location or identification of the electronic terminal involved.

(b) Notice of credit to consumer

For a consumer's account which is scheduled to be credited by a preauthorized electronic fund transfer from the same payor at least once in each successive sixty-day period, except where the payor provides positive notice of the transfer to the consumer, the financial institution shall elect to provide promptly either positive notice to the consumer when the credit is made as scheduled, or negative notice to the consumer when the credit is not made as scheduled, in accordance with regulations of the Bureau. The means of notice elected shall be disclosed to the consumer in accordance with section 1693c of this title.

(c) Periodic statement; contents

A financial institution shall provide each consumer with a periodic statement for each account of such consumer that may be accessed by means of an electronic fund transfer. Except as provided in subsections (d) and (e) of this section, such statement shall be provided at least monthly for each monthly or shorter cycle in which an electronic fund transfer affecting the account has occurred, or every three months, whichever is more frequent. The statement, which may include information regarding transactions other than electronic fund transfers, shall clearly set forth—

    (1) with regard to each electronic fund transfer during the period, the information described in subsection (a) of this section, which may be provided on an accompanying document;

    (2) the amount of any fee or charge assessed by the financial institution during the period for electronic fund transfers or for account maintenance;

    (3) the balances in the consumer's account at the beginning of the period and at the close of the period; and

    (4) the address and telephone number to be used by the financial institution for the purpose of receiving any statement inquiry or notice of account error from the consumer. Such address and telephone number shall be preceded by the caption "Direct Inquiries To:" or other similar language indicating that the address and number are to be used for such inquiries or notices.

(d) Consumer passbook accounts

In the case of a consumer's passbook account which may not be accessed by electronic fund transfers other than preauthorized electronic fund transfers crediting the account, a financial institution may, in lieu of complying with the requirements of subsection (c) of this section, upon presentation of the passbook provide the consumer in writing with the amount and date of each such transfer involving the account since the passbook was last presented.

(e) Accounts other than passbook accounts

In the case of a consumer's account, other than a passbook account, which may not be accessed by electronic fund transfers other than preauthorized electronic fund transfers crediting the account, the financial institution may provide a periodic statement on a quarterly basis which otherwise complies with the requirements of subsection (c) of this section.

(f) Documentation as evidence

In any action involving a consumer, any documentation required by this section to be given to the consumer which indicates that an electronic fund transfer was made to another person shall be admissible as evidence of such transfer and shall constitute prima facie proof that such transfer was made.

    (Pub.L. 90–321, Title IX, § 906, as added Pub.L. 95–630, Title XX, § 2001, Nov. 10, 1978, 92 Stat. 3731; Pub.L. 111–203, Title X, § 1084(1), July 21, 2010, 124 Stat. 2081.)

§ 1693e.   Preauthorized transfers [CCPA § 907]

    (a) A preauthorized electronic fund transfer from a consumer's account may be authorized by the consumer only in writing, and a copy of such authorization shall be provided to the consumer when made. A consumer may stop payment of a preauthorized electronic fund transfer by notifying the financial institution orally or in writing at any time up to three business days preceding the scheduled date of such transfer. The financial institution may require written confirmation to be provided to it within fourteen days of an oral notification if, when the oral notification is made, the consumer is advised of such requirement and the address to which such confirmation should be sent.

(b) In the case of preauthorized transfers from a consumer's account to the same person which may vary in amount, the financial institution or designated payee shall, prior to each transfer, provide reasonable advance notice to the consumer, in accordance with regulations of the Bureau.

(Pub.L. 90–321, Title IX, § 907, as added Pub.L. 95–630, Title XX, § 2001, Nov. 10, 1978, 92 Stat. 3733; Pub.L. 111–203, Title X, § 1084(1), July 21, 2010, 124 Stat. 2081.)

§ 1693f.   Error resolution [CCPA § 908]

(a)   Notification to financial institution of error

If a financial institution, within sixty days after having transmitted to a consumer documentation pursuant to section 1693d(a), (c), or (d) of this title or notification pursuant to section 1693d(b) of this title, receives oral or written notice in which the consumer—

(1) sets forth or otherwise enables the financial institution to identify the name and account number of the consumer;

(2) indicates the consumer's belief that the documentation, or, in the case of notification pursuant to section 1693d(b) of this title, the consumer's account, contains an error and the amount of such error; and

(3) sets forth the reasons for the consumer's belief (where applicable) that an error has occurred,

the financial institution shall investigate the alleged error, determine whether an error has occurred, and report or mail the results of such investigation and determination to the consumer within ten business days. The financial institution may require written confirmation to be provided to it within ten business days of an oral notification of error if, when the oral notification is made, the consumer is advised of such requirement and the address to which such confirmation should be sent. A financial institution which requires written confirmation in accordance with the previous sentence need not provisionally recredit a consumer's account in accordance with subsection (c) of this section, nor shall the financial institution be liable under subsection (e) of this section if the written confirmation is not received within the ten-day period referred to in the previous sentence.

(b)   Correction of error; interest

If the financial institution determines that an error did occur, it shall promptly, but in no event more than one business day after such determination, correct the error, subject to section 1693g of this title, including the crediting of interest where applicable.

(c)   Provisional recredit of consumer's account

If a financial institution receives notice of an error in the manner and within the time period specified in subsection (a) of this section, it may, in lieu of the requirements of subsections (a) and (b) of this section, within ten business days after receiving such notice provisionally recredit the consumer's account for the amount alleged to be in error, subject to section 1693g of this title, including interest where applicable, pending the conclusion of its investigation and its determination of whether an error has occurred. Such investigation shall be concluded not later than forty-five days after receipt of notice of the error. During the pendency of the investigation, the consumer shall have full use of the funds provisionally recredited.

(d)   Absence of error; finding; explanation

If the financial institution determines after its investigation pursuant to subsection (a) or (c) of this section that an error did not occur, it shall deliver or mail to the consumer an explanation of its findings within 3 business days after the conclusion of its investigation, and upon request of the consumer promptly deliver or mail to the consumer reproductions of all documents which the financial institution relied on to conclude that such error did not occur. The financial institution shall include notice of the right to request reproductions with the explanation of its findings.

(e)   Treble damages

If in any action under section 1693m of this title, the court finds that—

    (1)   the financial institution did not provisionally recredit a consumer's account within the ten-day period specified in subsection (c) of this section, and the financial institution (A) did not make a good faith investigation of the alleged error, or (B) did not have a reasonable basis for believing that the consumer's account was not in error; or

    (2)   the financial institution knowingly and willfully concluded that the consumer's account was not in error when such conclusion could not reasonably have been drawn from the evidence available to the financial institution at the time of its investigation,

then the consumer shall be entitled to treble damages determined under section 1693m(a)(1) of this title.

(f)   Acts constituting error

For the purpose of this section, an error consists of—

    (1)   an unauthorized electronic fund transfer;

    (2)   an incorrect electronic fund transfer from or to the consumer's account;

    (3)   the omission from a periodic statement of an electronic fund transfer affecting the consumer's account which should have been included;

    (4)   a computational error by the financial institution;

    (5)   the consumer's receipt of an incorrect amount of money from an electronic terminal;

    (6)   a consumer's request for additional information or clarification concerning an electronic fund transfer or any documentation required by this subchapter; or

    (7)   any other error described in regulations of the Bureau.

    (Pub.L. 90–321, Title IX, § 908, as added Pub.L. 95–630, Title XX, § 2001, Nov. 10, 1978, 92 Stat. 3733; Pub.L. 111–203, Title X, § 1084(1), July 21, 2010, 124 Stat. 2081.)

§ 1693g.   Consumer liability [CCPA § 909]

(a)   Unauthorized electronic fund transfers; limit

A consumer shall be liable for any unauthorized electronic fund transfer involving the account of such consumer only if the card or other means of access utilized for such transfer was an accepted card or other meanas[1] of access and if the issuer of such card, code, or other means of access has provided a means whereby the user of such card, code, or other means of access can be identified as the person authorized to use it, such as by signature, photograph, or fingerprint or by electronic or mechanical confirmation. In no event, however, shall a consumer's liability for an unauthorized transfer exceed the lesser of—

    (1) $50; or

    (2)   the amount of money or value of property or services obtained in such unauthorized electronic fund transfer prior to the time the financial institution is notified of, or otherwise becomes aware of, circumstances which lead to the reasonable belief that an unauthorized electronic fund transfer involving the consumer's account has been or may be effected. Notice under this paragraph is sufficient when such steps have been taken as may be reasonably required in the ordinary course of business to provide the financial institution with the pertinent information, whether or not any particular officer, employee, or agent of the financial institution does in fact receive such information.

Notwithstanding the foregoing, reimbursement need not be made to the consumer for losses the financial institution establishes would not have occurred but for the failure of the consumer to report within sixty days of transmittal of the statement (or in extenuating circumstances such as extended travel or hospitalization, within a reasonable time under the circumstances) any unauthorized electronic fund transfer or account error which appears on the periodic statement provided to the consumer under section

---

[1]   So in original. Probably should be "means".

1693d of this title. In addition, reimbursement need not be made to the consumer for losses which the financial institution establishes would not have occurred but for the failure of the consumer to report any loss or theft of a card or other means of access within two business days after the consumer learns of the loss or theft (or in extenuating circumstances such as extended travel or hospitalization, within a longer period which is reasonable under the circumstances), but the consumer's liability under this subsection in any such case may not exceed a total of $500, or the amount of unauthorized electronic fund transfers which occur following the close of two business days (or such longer period) after the consumer learns of the loss or theft but prior to notice to the financial institution under this subsection, whichever is less.

(b) Burden of proof

In any action which involves a consumer's liability for an unauthorized electronic fund transfer, the burden of proof is upon the financial institution to show that the electronic fund transfer was authorized or, if the electronic fund transfer was unauthorized, then the burden of proof is upon the financial institution to establish that the conditions of liability set forth in subsection (a) of this section have been met, and, if the transfer was initiated after the effective date of section 1693c of this title, that the disclosures required to be made to the consumer under section 1693c(a)(1) and (2) of this title were in fact made in accordance with such section.

(c) Determination of limitation on liability

In the event of a transaction which involves both an unauthorized electronic fund transfer and an extension of credit as defined in section 1602(e) of this title pursuant to an agreement between the consumer and the financial institution to extend such credit to the consumer in the event the consumer's account is overdrawn, the limitation on the consumer's liability for such transaction shall be determined solely in accordance with this section.

(d) Restriction on liability

Nothing in this section imposes liability upon a consumer for an unauthorized electronic fund transfer in excess of his liability for such a transfer under other applicable law or under any agreement with the consumer's financial institution.

(e) Scope of liability

Except as provided in this section, a consumer incurs no liability from an unauthorized electronic fund transfer.

(Pub.L. 90–321, Title IX, § 909, as added Pub.L. 95–630, Title XX, § 2001, Nov. 10, 1978, 92 Stat. 3734.)

§ 1693h. Liability of financial institutions [CCPA § 910]

(a) Action or failure to act proximately causing damages

Subject to subsections (b) and (c) of this section, a financial institution shall be liable to a consumer for all damages proximately caused by—

    (1) the financial institution's failure to make an electronic fund transfer, in accordance with the terms and conditions of an account, in the correct amount or in a timely manner when properly instructed to do so by the consumer, except where—

        (A) the consumer's account has insufficient funds;

        (B) the funds are subject to legal process or other encumbrance restricting such transfer;

        (C) such transfer would exceed an established credit limit;

        (D) an electronic terminal has insufficient cash to complete the transaction; or

        (E) as otherwise provided in regulations of the Bureau;

    (2) the financial institution's failure to make an electronic fund transfer due to insufficient funds when the financal[1] institution failed to credit, in accordance with the terms and conditions of an

---

[1] So in original. Probably should be "financial".

account, a deposit of funds to the consumer's account which would have provided sufficient funds to make the transfer, and

(3) the financial institution's failure to stop payment of a preauthorized transfer from a consumer's account when instructed to do so in accordance with the terms and conditions of the account.

(b) Acts of God and technical malfunctions

A financial institution shall not be liable under subsection (a)(1) or (2) of this section if the financial institution shows by a preponderance of the evidence that its action or failure to act resulted from—

(1) an act of God or other circumstance beyond its control, that it exercised reasonable care to prevent such an occurrence, and that it exercised such diligence as the circumstances required; or

(2) a technical malfunction which was known to the consumer at the time he attempted to initiate an electronic fund transfer or, in the case of a preauthorized transfer, at the time such transfer should have occurred.

(c) Intent

In the case of a failure described in subsection (a) of this section which was not intentional and which resulted from a bona fide error, notwithstanding the maintenance of procedures reasonably adapted to avoid any such error, the financial institution shall be liable for actual damages proved.

(d) Exception for damaged notices

If the notice required to be posted pursuant to section 1693b(d)(3)(B)(i) of this title by an automated teller machine operator has been posted by such operator in compliance with such section and the notice is subsequently removed, damaged, or altered by any person other than the operator of the automated teller machine, the operator shall have no liability under this section for failure to comply with section 1693b(d)(3)(B)(i) of this title.

> (Pub.L. 90–321, Title IX, § 910, as added Pub.L. 95–630, Title XX, § 2001, Nov. 10, 1978, 92 Stat. 3735, and amended Pub.L. 106–102, Title VII, § 705, Nov. 12, 1999, 113 Stat. 1465; Pub.L. 111–203, Title X, § 1084(1), July 21, 2010, 124 Stat. 2081.)

§ 1693i.   Issuance of cards or other means of access [CCPA § 911]

(a) Prohibition; proper issuance

No person may issue to a consumer any card, code, or other means of access to such consumer's account for the purpose of initiating an electronic fund transfer other than—

(1) in response to a request or application therefor; or

(2) as a renewal of, or in substitution for, an accepted card, code, or other means of access, whether issued by the initial issuer or a successor.

(b) Exceptions

Notwithstanding the provisions of subsection (a) of this section, a person may distribute to a consumer on an unsolicited basis a card, code, or other means of access for use in initiating an electronic fund transfer from such consumer's account, if—

(1) such card, code, or other means of access is not validated;

(2) such distribution is accompanied by a complete disclosure, in accordance with section 1693c of this title, of the consumer's rights and liabilities which will apply if such card, code, or other means of access is validated;

(3) such distribution is accompanied by a clear explanation, in accordance with regulations of the Bureau, that such card, code, or other means of access is not validated and how the consumer may dispose of such code, card, or other means of access if validation is not desired; and

(4) such card, code, or other means of access is validated only in response to a request or application from the consumer, upon verification of the consumer's identity.

(c) Validation

For the purpose of subsection (b) of this section, a card, code, or other means of access is validated when it may be used to initiate an electronic fund transfer.

(Pub.L. 90–321, Title IX, § 911, as added Pub.L. 95–630, Title XX, § 2001, Nov. 10, 1978, 92 Stat. 3736; Pub.L. 111–203, Title X, § 1084(1), July 21, 2010, 124 Stat. 2081.)

§ 1693j. Suspension of obligations [CCPA § 912]

If a system malfunction prevents the effectuation of an electronic fund transfer initiated by a consumer to another person, and such other person has agreed to accept payment by such means, the consumer's obligation to the other person shall be suspended until the malfunction is corrected and the electronic fund transfer may be completed, unless such other person has subsequently, by written request, demanded payment by means other than an electronic fund transfer.

(Pub.L. 90–321, Title IX, § 912, as added Pub.L. 95–630, Title XX, § 2001, Nov. 10, 1978, 92 Stat. 3737.)

§ 1693k. Compulsory use of electronic fund transfers [CCPA § 913]

No person may—

(1) condition the extension of credit to a consumer on such consumer's repayment by means of preauthorized electronic fund transfers; or

(2) require a consumer to establish an account for receipt of electronic fund transfers with a particular financial institution as a condition of employment or receipt of a government benefit.

(Pub.L. 90–321, Title IX, § 913, as added Pub.L. 95–630, Title XX, § 2001, Nov. 10, 1978, 92 Stat. 3737.)

§ 1693*l*. Waiver of rights [CCPA § 914]

No writing or other agreement between a consumer and any other person may contain any provision which constitutes a waiver of any right conferred or cause of action created by this subchapter. Nothing in this section prohibits, however, any writing or other agreement which grants to a consumer a more extensive right or remedy or greater protection than contained in this subchapter or a waiver given in settlement of a dispute or action.

(Pub.L. 90–321, Title IX, § 914, as added Pub.L. 95–630, Title XX, § 2001, Nov. 10, 1978, 92 Stat. 3737.)

§ 1693*l*–1. General-use prepaid cards, gift certificates, and store gift cards [CCPA § 915]

(a) Definitions

In this section, the following definitions shall apply:

(1) Dormancy fee; inactivity charge or fee

The terms "dormancy fee" and "inactivity charge or fee" mean a fee, charge, or penalty for non-use or inactivity of a gift certificate, store gift card, or general-use prepaid card.

(2) General use prepaid card, gift certificate, and store gift card

(A) General use[1] prepaid card

The term "general-use prepaid card" means a card or other payment code or device issued by any person that is—

(i) redeemable at multiple, unaffiliated merchants or service providers, or automated teller machines;

---

[1]   So in original. Probably should be "General-use".

    (ii) issued in a requested amount, whether or not that amount may, at the option of the issuer, be increased in value or reloaded if requested by the holder;

    (iii) purchased or loaded on a prepaid basis; and

    (iv) honored, upon presentation, by merchants for goods or services, or at automated teller machines.

(B) Gift certificate

The term "gift certificate" means an electronic promise that is—

    (i) redeemable at a single merchant or an affiliated group of merchants that share the same name, mark, or logo;

    (ii) issued in a specified amount that may not be increased or reloaded;

    (iii) purchased on a prepaid basis in exchange for payment; and

    (iv) honored upon presentation by such single merchant or affiliated group of merchants for goods or services.

(C) Store gift card

The term "store gift card" means an electronic promise, plastic card, or other payment code or device that is—

    (i) redeemable at a single merchant or an affiliated group of merchants that share the same name, mark, or logo;

    (ii) issued in a specified amount, whether or not that amount may be increased in value or reloaded at the request of the holder;

    (iii) purchased on a prepaid basis in exchange for payment; and

    (iv) honored upon presentation by such single merchant or affiliated group of merchants for goods or services.

(D) Exclusions

The terms "general-use prepaid card", "gift certificate", and "store gift card" do not include an electronic promise, plastic card, or payment code or device that is—

    (i) used solely for telephone services;

    (ii) reloadable and not marketed or labeled as a gift card or gift certificate;

    (iii) a loyalty, award, or promotional gift card, as defined by the Bureau;

    (iv) not marketed to the general public;

    (v) issued in paper form only (including for tickets and events); or

    (vi) redeemable solely for admission to events or venues at a particular location or group of affiliated locations, which may also include services or goods obtainable—

        (I) at the event or venue after admission; or

        (II) in conjunction with admission to such events or venues, at specific locations affiliated with and in geographic proximity to the event or venue.

(3) Service fee

(A) In general

The term "service fee" means a periodic fee, charge, or penalty for holding or use of a gift certificate, store gift card, or general-use prepaid card.

(B) Exclusion

With respect to a general-use prepaid card, the term "service fee" does not include a one-time initial issuance fee.

(b) Prohibition on imposition of fees or charges

(1) In general

Except as provided under paragraphs (2) through (4), it shall be unlawful for any person to impose a dormancy fee, an inactivity charge or fee, or a service fee with respect to a gift certificate, store gift card, or general-use prepaid card.

(2) Exceptions

A dormancy fee, inactivity charge or fee, or service fee may be charged with respect to a gift certificate, store gift card, or general-use prepaid card, if—

    (A) there has been no activity with respect to the certificate or card in the 12-month period ending on the date on which the charge or fee is imposed;

    (B) the disclosure requirements of paragraph (3) have been met;

    (C) not more than one fee may be charged in any given month; and

    (D) any additional requirements that the Bureau may establish through rulemaking under subsection (d) have been met.

(3) Disclosure requirements

The disclosure requirements of this paragraph are met if—

    (A) the gift certificate, store gift card, or general-use prepaid card clearly and conspicuously states—

        (i) that a dormancy fee, inactivity charge or fee, or service fee may be charged;

        (ii) the amount of such fee or charge;

        (iii) how often such fee or charge may be assessed; and

        (iv) that such fee or charge may be assessed for inactivity; and

    (B) the issuer or vendor of such certificate or card informs the purchaser of such charge or fee before such certificate or card is purchased, regardless of whether the certificate or card is purchased in person, over the Internet, or by telephone.

(4) Exclusion

The prohibition under paragraph (1) shall not apply to any gift certificate—

    (A) that is distributed pursuant to an award, loyalty, or promotional program, as defined by the Bureau; and

    (B) with respect to which, there is no money or other value exchanged.

(c) Prohibition on sale of gift cards with expiration dates

(1) In general

Except as provided under paragraph (2), it shall be unlawful for any person to sell or issue a gift certificate, store gift card, or general-use prepaid card that is subject to an expiration date.

(2) Exceptions

A gift certificate, store gift card, or general-use prepaid card may contain an expiration date if—

    (A) the expiration date is not earlier than 5 years after the date on which the gift certificate was issued, or the date on which card funds were last loaded to a store gift card or general-use prepaid card; and

(B) the terms of expiration are clearly and conspicuously stated.

(d) Additional rulemaking

(1) In general

The Bureau shall—

(A) prescribe regulations to carry out this section, in addition to any other rules or regulations required by this subchapter, including such additional requirements as appropriate relating to the amount of dormancy fees, inactivity charges or fees, or service fees that may be assessed and the amount of remaining value of a gift certificate, store gift card, or general-use prepaid card below which such charges or fees may be assessed; and

(B) shall[2] determine the extent to which the individual definitions and provisions of this subchapter or Regulation E should apply to general-use prepaid cards, gift certificates, and store gift cards.

(2) Consultation

In prescribing regulations under this subsection, the Bureau shall consult with the Federal Trade Commission.

(3) Timing; effective date

The regulations required by this subsection shall be issued in final form not later than 9 months after May 22, 2009.

(Pub.L. 90–321, Title IX, § 915, as added Pub.L. 111–24, Title IV, § 401(2), May 22, 2009, 123 Stat. 1751; Pub.L. 111–203, Title X, § 1084(1), July 21, 2010, 124 Stat. 2081.)

§ 1693m.   Civil liability [CCPA § 916]

(a) Individual or class action for damages; amount of award

Except as otherwise provided by this section and section 1693h of this title, any person who fails to comply with any provision of this subchapter with respect to any consumer, except for an error resolved in accordance with section 1693f of this title, is liable to such consumer in an amount equal to the sum of—

(1) any actual damage sustained by such consumer as a result of such failure;

(2)(A) in the case of an individual action, an amount not less than $100 nor greater than $1,000; or

(B) in the case of a class action, such amount as the court may allow, except that (i) as to each member of the class no minimum recovery shall be applicable, and (ii) the total recovery under this subparagraph in any class action or series of class actions arising out of the same failure to comply by the same person shall not be more than the lesser of $500,000 or 1 per centum of the net worth of the defendant; and

(3) in the case of any successful action to enforce the foregoing liability, the costs of the action, together with a reasonable attorney's fee as determined by the court.

(b) Factors determining amount of award

In determining the amount of liability in any action under subsection (a) of this section, the court shall consider, among other relevant factors—

(1) in any individual action under subsection (a)(2)(A) of this section, the frequency and persistence of noncompliance, the nature of such noncompliance, and the extent to which the noncompliance was intentional; or

---

[2] So in original. The word "shall" probably should not appear.

(2) in any class action under subsection (a)(2)(B) of this section, the frequency and persistence of noncompliance, the nature of such noncompliance, the resources of the defendant, the number of persons adversely affected, and the extent to which the noncompliance was intentional.

(c) Unintentional violations; bona fide error

Except as provided in section 1693h of this title, a person may not be held liable in any action brought under this section for a violation of this subchapter if the person shows by a preponderance of evidence that the violation was not intentional and resulted from a bona fide error notwithstanding the maintenance of procedures reasonably adapted to avoid any such error.

(d) Good faith compliance with rule, regulation, or interpretation

No provision of this section or section 1693n of this title imposing any liability shall apply to—

(1) any act done or omitted in good faith in conformity with any rule, regulation, or interpretation thereof by the Bureau or the Board or in conformity with any interpretation or approval by an official or employee of the Bureau of Consumer Financial Protection or the Federal Reserve System duly authorized by the Bureau or the Board to issue such interpretations or approvals under such procedures as the Bureau or the Board may prescribe therefor; or

(2) any failure to make disclosure in proper form if a financial institution utilized an appropriate model clause issued by the Bureau or the Board,

notwithstanding that after such act, omission, or failure has occurred, such rule, regulation, approval, or model clause is amended, rescinded, or determined by judicial or other authority to be invalid for any reason.

(e) Notification to consumer prior to action; adjustment of consumer's account

A person has no liability under this section for any failure to comply with any requirement under this subchapter if, prior to the institution of an action under this section, the person notifies the consumer concerned of the failure, complies with the requirements of this subchapter, and makes an appropriate adjustment to the consumer's account and pays actual damages or, where applicable, damages in accordance with section 1693h of this title.

(f) Action in bad faith or for harassment; attorney's fees

On a finding by the court that an unsuccessful action under this section was brought in bad faith or for purposes of harassment, the court shall award to the defendant attorney's fees reasonable in relation to the work expended and costs.

(g) Jurisdiction of courts; time for maintenance of action

Without regard to the amount in controversy, any action under this section may be brought in any United States district court, or in any other court of competent jurisdiction, within one year from the date of the occurrence of the violation.

(Pub.L. 90–321, Title IX, § 916, formerly § 915, as added Pub.L. 95–630, Title XX, § 2001, Nov. 10, 1978, 92 Stat. 3737; renumbered § 916, Pub.L. 111–24, Title IV, § 401(1), May 22, 2009, 123 Stat. 1751; Pub.L. 111–203, Title X, §§ 1084(1), (4), July 21, 2010, 124 Stat. 2081, 2082.)

§ 1693n.   Criminal liability [CCPA § 917]

(a) Violations respecting giving of false or inaccurate information, failure to provide information, and failure to comply with provisions of this subchapter

Whoever knowingly and willfully—

(1) gives false or inaccurate information or fails to provide information which he is required to disclose by this subchapter or any regulation issued thereunder; or

(2) otherwise fails to comply with any provision of this subchapter;

shall be fined not more than $5,000 or imprisoned not more than one year, or both.

(b) Violations affecting interstate or foreign commerce

Whoever—

(1) knowingly, in a transaction affecting interstate or foreign commerce, uses or attempts or conspires to use any counterfeit, fictitious, altered, forged, lost, stolen, or fraudulently obtained debit instrument to obtain money, goods, services, or anything else of value which within any one-year period has a value aggregating $1,000 or more; or

(2) with unlawful or fraudulent intent, transports or attempts or conspires to transport in interstate or foreign commerce a counterfeit, fictitious, altered, forged, lost, stolen, or fraudulently obtained debit instrument knowing the same to be counterfeit, fictitious, altered, forged, lost, stolen, or fraudulently obtained; or

(3) with unlawful or fraudulent intent, uses any instrumentality of interstate or foreign commerce to sell or transport a counterfeit, fictitious, altered, forged, lost, stolen, or fraudulently obtained debit instrument knowing the same to be counterfeit, fictitious, altered, forged, lost, stolen, or fraudulently obtained; or

(4) knowingly receives, conceals, uses, or transports money, goods, services, or anything else of value (except tickets for interstate or foreign transportation) which (A) within any one-year period has a value aggregating $1,000 or more, (B) has moved in or is part of, or which constitutes interstate or foreign commerce, and (C) has been obtained with a counterfeit, fictitious, altered, forged, lost, stolen, or fraudulently obtained debit instrument; or

(5) knowingly receives, conceals, uses, sells, or transports in interstate or foreign commerce one or more tickets for interstate or foreign transportation, which (A) within any one-year period have a value aggregating $500 or more, and (B) have been purchased or obtained with one or more counterfeit, fictitious, altered, forged, lost, stolen, or fraudulently obtained debit instrument; or

(6) in a transaction affecting interstate or foreign commerce, furnishes money, property, services, or anything else of value, which within any one-year period has a value aggregating $1,000 or more, through the use of any counterfeit, fictitious, altered, forged, lost, stolen, or fraudulently obtained debit instrument knowing the same to be counterfeit, fictitious, altered, forged, lost, stolen, or fraudulently obtained—

shall be fined not more than $10,000 or imprisoned not more than ten years, or both.

(c) "Debit instrument" defined

As used in this section, the term "debit instrument" means a card, code, or other device, other than a check, draft, or similar paper instrument, by the use of which a person may initiate an electronic fund transfer.

(Pub.L. 90–321, Title IX, § 917, formerly § 916, as added Pub.L. 95–630, Title XX, § 2001, Nov. 10, 1978, 92 Stat. 3738; renumbered § 917, Pub.L. 111–24, Title IV, § 401(1), May 22, 2009, 123 Stat. 1751.)

§ 1693*o*.   Administrative enforcement [CCPA § 918]

(a) Enforcing agencies

Subject to subtitle B of the Consumer Protection Act of 2010 [12 U.S.C. §§ 5511–5519] compliance with the requirements imposed under this subchapter shall be enforced under—

(1) section 1818 of Title 12, by the appropriate Federal banking agency, as defined in section 1813(q) of Title 12, with respect to—

(A) national banks, Federal savings associations, and Federal branches and Federal agencies of foreign banks;

(B) member banks of the Federal Reserve System (other than national banks), branches and agencies of foreign banks (other than Federal branches, Federal agencies, and insured State branches of foreign banks), commercial lending companies owned or controlled by foreign banks, and organizations operating under section 25 or 25A of the Federal Reserve Act; and

(C) banks and State savings associations insured by the Federal Deposit Insurance Corporation (other than members of the Federal Reserve System), and insured State branches of foreign banks;

(2) the Federal Credit Union Act [12 U.S.C.A. § 1751 et seq.], by the Administrator of the National Credit Union Administration with respect to any Federal credit union;

(3) part A of subtitle VII of title 49, by the Secretary of Transportation, with respect to any air carrier or foreign air carrier subject to that part;

(4) the Securities Exchange Act of 1934 [15 U.S.C.A. § 78a et seq.], by the Securities and Exchange Commission, with respect to any broker or dealer subject to that Act and[1]

(5) subtitle E of the Consumer Financial Protection Act of 2010, by the Bureau, with respect to any person subject to this subchapter, except that the Bureau shall not have authority to enforce the requirements of section 1693o–2 of this title or any regulations prescribed by the Board under section 1693o–2 of this title.

The terms used in paragraph (1) that are not defined in this subchapter or otherwise defined in section 3(s) of the Federal Deposit Insurance Act (12 U.S.C. 1813(s)) shall have the meaning given to them in section 1(b) of the International Banking Act of 1978 (12 U.S.C. 3101).

(b) Violations of subchapter deemed violations of pre-existing statutory requirements; additional powers

For the purpose of the exercise by any agency referred to in any of paragraphs (1) through (4) subsection (a) of this section of its powers under any Act referred to in that subsection, a violation of any requirement imposed under this subchapter shall be deemed to be a violation of a requirement imposed under that Act. In addition to its powers under any provision of law specifically referred to in any of paragraphs (1) through (4) subsection (a) of this section, each of the agencies referred to in that subsection may exercise, for the purpose of enforcing compliance with any requirement imposed under this subchapter, any other authority conferred on it by law.

(c) Overall enforcement authority of the Federal Trade Commission

Except to the extent that enforcement of the requirements imposed under this subchapter is specifically committed to some other Government agency under any of paragraphs (1) through (4) of subsection (a), and subject to subtitle B of the Consumer Financial Protection Act of 2010, the Federal Trade Commission shall be authorized to enforce such requirements. For the purpose of the exercise by the Federal Trade Commission of its functions and powers under the Federal Trade Commission Act, a violation of any requirement imposed under this subchapter shall be deemed a violation of a requirement imposed under that Act. All of the functions and powers of the Federal Trade Commission under the Federal Trade Commission Act are available to the Federal Trade Commission to enforce compliance by any person subject to the jurisdiction of the Federal Trade Commission with the requirements imposed under this subchapter, irrespective of whether that person is engaged in commerce or meets any other jurisdictional tests under the Federal Trade Commission Act.

(Pub.L. 90–321, Title IX, § 918, formerly § 917, as added Pub.L. 95–630, Title XX, § 2001, Nov. 10, 1978, 92 Stat. 3739, and amended Pub.L. 101–73, Title VII, § 744(o), Aug. 9, 1989, 103 Stat. 440; Pub.L. 102–242, Title II, § 212(f), Dec. 19, 1991, 105 Stat. 2301; Pub.L. 104–287, § 6(h), Oct. 11, 1996, 110 Stat. 3399; renumbered § 918, Pub.L. 111–24, Title IV, § 401(1), May 22, 2009, 123 Stat. 1751; Pub.L. 111–203, Title X, § 1084(5), July 21, 2010, 124 Stat. 2082.)

§ 1693o–1. Remittance transfers [CCPA § 919]

(a) Disclosures required for remittance transfers

(1) In general

---

[1] So in original. Probably should be "; and".

Each remittance transfer provider shall make disclosures as required under this section and in accordance with rules prescribed by the Bureau. Disclosures required under this section shall be in addition to any other disclosures applicable under this subchapter.

(2)   Disclosures

Subject to rules prescribed by the Bureau, a remittance transfer provider shall provide, in writing and in a form that the sender may keep, to each sender requesting a remittance transfer, as applicable to the transaction—

(A)   at the time at which the sender requests a remittance transfer to be initiated, and prior to the sender making any payment in connection with the remittance transfer, a disclosure describing—

(i)   the amount of currency that will be received by the designated recipient, using the values of the currency into which the funds will be exchanged;

(ii)   the amount of transfer and any other fees charged by the remittance transfer provider for the remittance transfer; and

(iii) any exchange rate to be used by the remittance transfer provider for the remittance transfer, to the nearest 1/100th of a point; and

(B)   at the time at which the sender makes payment in connection with the remittance transfer—

(i)   a receipt showing—

(I)   the information described in subparagraph (A);

(II)   the promised date of delivery to the designated recipient; and

(III) the name and either the telephone number or the address of the designated recipient, if either the telephone number or the address of the designated recipient is provided by the sender; and

(ii)   a statement containing—

(I)   information about the rights of the sender under this section regarding the resolution of errors; and

(II)   appropriate contact information for—

(aa) the remittance transfer provider; and

(bb) the State agency that regulates the remittance transfer provider and the Bureau, including the toll-free telephone number established under section 5493 of Title 12.

(3)   Requirements relating to disclosures

With respect to each disclosure required to be provided under paragraph (2) a remittance transfer provider shall—

(A)   provide an initial notice and receipt, as required by subparagraphs (A) and (B) of paragraph (2), and an error resolution statement, as required by subsection (d), that clearly and conspicuously describe the information required to be disclosed therein; and

(B)   with respect to any transaction that a sender conducts electronically, comply with the Electronic Signatures in Global and National Commerce Act (15 U.S.C. § 7001 et seq.).

(4)   Exception for disclosures of amount received

(A)   In general

Subject to the rules prescribed by the Bureau, and except as provided under subparagraph (B), the disclosures required regarding the amount of currency that will be received by the designated recipient shall be deemed to be accurate, so long as the disclosures provide a reasonably accurate estimate of the foreign currency to be received. This paragraph shall apply only to a remittance transfer provider who is an insured depository institution, (as defined in section 1813 of Title 12), or an insured credit union, as defined in section 1752 of Title 12, and if—

(i) a remittance transfer is conducted through a demand deposit, savings deposit, or other asset account that the sender holds with such remittance transfer provider; and

(ii) at the time at which the sender requests the transaction, the remittance transfer provider is unable to know, for reasons beyond its control, the amount of currency that will be made available to the designated recipient.

(B) Deadline

The application of subparagraph (A) shall terminate 5 years after July 21, 2010, unless the Bureau determines that termination of such provision would negatively affect the ability of remittance transfer providers described in subparagraph (A) to send remittances to locations in foreign countries, in which case, the Bureau may, by rule, extend the application of subparagraph (A) to not longer than 10 years after July 21, 2010.

(5) Exemption authority

The Bureau may, by rule, permit a remittance transfer provider to satisfy the requirements of—

(A) paragraph (2)(A) orally, if the transaction is conducted entirely by telephone;

(B) paragraph (2)(B), in the case of a transaction conducted entirely by telephone, by mailing the disclosures required under such subparagraph to the sender, not later than 1 business day after the date on which the transaction is conducted, or by including such documents in the next periodic statement, if the telephone transaction is conducted through a demand deposit, savings deposit, or other asset account that the sender holds with the remittance transfer provider;

(C) subparagraphs (A) and (B) of paragraph (2) together in one written disclosure, but only to the extent that the information provided in accordance with paragraph (3)(A) is accurate at the time at which payment is made in connection with the subject remittance transfer; and

(D) paragraph (2)(A), without compliance with section 101(c) of the Electronic Signatures in Global Commerce Act, if a sender initiates the transaction electronically and the information is displayed electronically in a manner that the sender can keep.

(6) Storefront and Internet notices

(A) In general

(i) Prominent posting

Subject to subparagraph (B), the Bureau may prescribe rules to require a remittance transfer provider to prominently post, and timely update, a notice describing a model remittance transfer for one or more amounts, as the Bureau may determine, which notice shall show the amount of currency that will be received by the designated recipient, using the values of the currency into which the funds will be exchanged.

(ii) Onsite displays

The Bureau may require the notice prescribed under this subparagraph to be displayed in every physical storefront location owned or controlled by the remittance transfer provider.

(iii) Internet notices

Subject to paragraph (3), the Bureau shall prescribe rules to require a remittance transfer provider that provides remittance transfers via the Internet to provide a notice, comparable to a storefront notice described in this subparagraph, located on the home page or landing page (with respect to such remittance transfer services) owned or controlled by the remittance transfer provider.

(iv) Rulemaking authority

In prescribing rules under this subparagraph, the Bureau may impose standards or requirements regarding the provision of the storefront and Internet notices required under this subparagraph and the provision of the disclosures required under paragraphs (2) and (3).

(B) Study and analysis

Prior to proposing rules under subparagraph (A), the Bureau shall undertake appropriate studies and analyses, which shall be consistent with section 1693b(a)(2) of this title, and may include an advanced notice of proposed rulemaking, to determine whether a storefront notice or Internet notice facilitates the ability of a consumer—

(i) to compare prices for remittance transfers; and

(ii) to understand the types and amounts of any fees or costs imposed on remittance transfers.

(b) Foreign language disclosures

The disclosures required under this section shall be made in English and in each of the foreign languages principally used by the remittance transfer provider, or any of its agents, to advertise, solicit, or market, either orally or in writing, at that office.

(c) Regulations regarding transfers to certain nations

If the Bureau determines that a recipient nation does not legally allow, or the method by which transactions are made in the recipient country do not allow, a remittance transfer provider to know the amount of currency that will be received by the designated recipient, the Bureau may prescribe rules (not later than 18 months after July 21, 2010) addressing the issue, which rules shall include standards for a remittance transfer provider to provide—

(1) a receipt that is consistent with subsections (a) and (b); and

(2) a reasonably accurate estimate of the foreign currency to be received, based on the rate provided to the sender by the remittance transfer provider at the time at which the transaction was initiated by the sender.

(d) Remittance transfer errors

(1) Error resolution

(A) In general

If a remittance transfer provider receives oral or written notice from the sender within 180 days of the promised date of delivery that an error occurred with respect to a remittance transfer, including the amount of currency designated in subsection (a)(3)(A) that was to be sent to the designated recipient of the remittance transfer, using the values of the currency into which the funds should have been exchanged, but was not made available to the designated recipient in the foreign country, the remittance transfer provider shall resolve the error pursuant to this subsection and investigate the reason for the error.

(B) Remedies

Not later than 90 days after the date of receipt of a notice from the sender pursuant to subparagraph (A), the remittance transfer provider shall, as applicable to the error and as designated by the sender—

(i) refund to the sender the total amount of funds tendered by the sender in connection with the remittance transfer which was not properly transmitted;

(ii) make available to the designated recipient, without additional cost to the designated recipient or to the sender, the amount appropriate to resolve the error;

(iii) provide such other remedy, as determined appropriate by rule of the Bureau for the protection of senders; or

(iv) provide written notice to the sender that there was no error with an explanation responding to the specific complaint of the sender.

(2) Rules

The Bureau shall establish, by rule issued not later than 18 months after July 21, 2010, clear and appropriate standards for remittance transfer providers with respect to error resolution relating to remittance transfers, to protect senders from such errors. Standards prescribed under this paragraph shall include appropriate standards regarding record keeping, as required, including documentation—

(A) of the complaint of the sender;

(B) that the sender provides the remittance transfer provider with respect to the alleged error; and

(C) of the findings of the remittance transfer provider regarding the investigation of the alleged error that the sender brought to their attention.

(3) Cancellation and refund policy rules

Not later than 18 months after July 21, 2010, the Bureau shall issue final rules regarding appropriate remittance transfer cancellation and refund policies for consumers.

(e) Applicability of this subchapter

(1) In general

A remittance transfer that is not an electronic fund transfer, as defined in section 1693a of this title, shall not be subject to any of the provisions of sections 1693c through 1693k of this title. A remittance transfer that is an electronic fund transfer, as defined in section 1693a of this title, shall be subject to all provisions of this subchapter, except for section 1693f of this title, that are otherwise applicable to electronic fund transfers under this subchapter.

(2) Rule of construction

Nothing in this section shall be construed—

(A) to affect the application to any transaction, to any remittance provider, or to any other person of any of the provisions of subchapter II of chapter 53 of Title 31, section 1829b of Title 12, or chapter 2 of title I of Public Law 91–508 (12 U.S.C. §§ 1951–1959), or any regulations promulgated thereunder; or

(B) to cause any fund transfer that would not otherwise be treated as such under paragraph (1) to be treated as an electronic fund transfer, or as otherwise subject to this subchapter, for the purposes of any of the provisions referred to in subparagraph (A) or any regulations promulgated thereunder.

(f) Acts of agents

(1) In general

A remittance transfer provider shall be liable for any violation of this section by any agent, authorized delegate, or person affiliated with such provider, when such agent, authorized delegate, or affiliate acts for that remittance transfer provider.

(2) Obligations of remittance transfer providers

The Bureau shall prescribe rules to implement appropriate standards or conditions of, liability of a remittance transfer provider, including a provider who acts through an agent or authorized delegate. An agency charged with enforcing the requirements of this section, or rules prescribed by the Bureau under this section, may consider, in any action or other proceeding against a remittance transfer provider, the extent to which the provider had established and maintained policies or procedures for compliance, including policies, procedures, or other appropriate oversight measures designed to assure compliance by an agent or authorized delegate acting for such provider.

(g) Definitions

As used in this section—

(1) the term "designated recipient" means any person located in a foreign country and identified by the sender as the authorized recipient of a remittance transfer to be made by a remittance transfer provider, except that a designated recipient shall not be deemed to be a consumer for purposes of this chapter;

(2) the term "remittance transfer"—

(A) means the electronic (as defined in section 106(2) of the Electronic Signatures in Global and National Commerce Act (15 U.S.C. § 7006(2))) transfer of funds requested by a sender located in any State to a designated recipient that is initiated by a remittance transfer provider, whether or not the sender holds an account with the remittance transfer provider or whether or not the remittance transfer is also an electronic fund transfer, as defined in section 1693a of this title; and

(B) does not include a transfer described in subparagraph (A) in an amount that is equal to or lesser than the amount of a small-value transaction determined, by rule, to be excluded from the requirements under section 1693d(a) of this title;

(3) the term "remittance transfer provider" means any person or financial institution that provides remittance transfers for a consumer in the normal course of its business, whether or not the consumer holds an account with such person or financial institution; and

(4) the term "sender" means a consumer who requests a remittance provider to send a remittance transfer for the consumer to a designated recipient.

(Pub.L. 90–321, Title IX, § 919, as added and amended Pub.L. 111–203, Title X, §§ 1073(a)(4), 1084(1), July 21, 2010, 124 Stat. 2060, 2081.)

§ 1693o–2.   Reasonable fees and rules for payment card transactions [CCPA § 920]

(a) Reasonable interchange transaction fees for electronic debit transactions

(1) Regulatory authority over interchange transaction fees

The Board may prescribe regulations, pursuant to section 553 of Title 5, regarding any interchange transaction fee that an issuer may receive or charge with respect to an electronic debit transaction, to implement this subsection (including related definitions), and to prevent circumvention or evasion of this subsection.

(2) Reasonable interchange transaction fees

The amount of any interchange transaction fee that an issuer may receive or charge with respect to an electronic debit transaction shall be reasonable and proportional to the cost incurred by the issuer with respect to the transaction.

(3) Rulemaking required

(A) In general

The Board shall prescribe regulations in final form not later than 9 months after July 21, 2010, to establish standards for assessing whether the amount of any interchange transaction fee described in paragraph (2) is reasonable and proportional to the cost incurred by the issuer with respect to the transaction.

(B) Information collection

The Board may require any issuer (or agent of an issuer) or payment card network to provide the Board with such information as may be necessary to carry out the provisions of this subsection and the Board, in issuing rules under subparagraph (A) and on at least a bi-annual basis thereafter, shall disclose such aggregate or summary information concerning the costs incurred, and interchange transaction fees charged or received, by issuers or payment card networks in connection with the authorization, clearance or settlement of electronic debit transactions as the Board considers appropriate and in the public interest.

(4) Considerations; consultation

In prescribing regulations under paragraph (3)(A), the Board shall—

(A) consider the functional similarity between—

(i) electronic debit transactions; and

(ii) checking transactions that are required within the Federal Reserve bank system to clear at par;

(B) distinguish between—

(i) the incremental cost incurred by an issuer for the role of the issuer in the authorization, clearance, or settlement of a particular electronic debit transaction, which cost shall be considered under paragraph (2); and

(ii) other costs incurred by an issuer which are not specific to a particular electronic debit transaction, which costs shall not be considered under paragraph (2); and

(C) consult, as appropriate, with the Comptroller of the Currency, the Board of Directors of the Federal Deposit Insurance Corporation, the Director of the Office of Thrift Supervision, the National Credit Union Administration Board, the Administrator of the Small Business Administration, and the Director of the Bureau of Consumer Financial Protection.

(5) Adjustments to interchange transaction fees for fraud prevention costs

(A) Adjustments

The Board may allow for an adjustment to the fee amount received or charged by an issuer under paragraph (2), if—

(i) such adjustment is reasonably necessary to make allowance for costs incurred by the issuer in preventing fraud in relation to electronic debit transactions involving that issuer; and

(ii) the issuer complies with the fraud-related standards established by the Board under subparagraph (B), which standards shall—

(I) be designed to ensure that any fraud-related adjustment of the issuer is limited to the amount described in clause (i) and takes into account any fraud-related reimbursements (including amounts from charge-backs) received from consumers, merchants, or payment card networks in relation to electronic debit transactions involving the issuer; and

(II) require issuers to take effective steps to reduce the occurrence of, and costs from, fraud in relation to electronic debit transactions, including through the development and implementation of cost-effective fraud prevention technology.

(B) Rulemaking required

(i) In general

The Board shall prescribe regulations in final form not later than 9 months after July 21, 2010, to establish standards for making adjustments under this paragraph.

(ii) Factors for consideration

In issuing the standards and prescribing regulations under this paragraph, the Board shall consider—

(I) the nature, type, and occurrence of fraud in electronic debit transactions;

(II) the extent to which the occurrence of fraud depends on whether authorization in an electronic debit transaction is based on signature, PIN, or other means;

(III) the available and economical means by which fraud on electronic debit transactions may be reduced;

(IV) the fraud prevention and data security costs expended by each party involved in electronic debit transactions (including consumers, persons who accept debit cards as a form of payment, financial institutions, retailers and payment card networks);

(V) the costs of fraudulent transactions absorbed by each party involved in such transactions (including consumers, persons who accept debit cards as a form of payment, financial institutions, retailers and payment card networks);

(VI) the extent to which interchange transaction fees have in the past reduced or increased incentives for parties involved in electronic debit transactions to reduce fraud on such transactions; and

(VII) such other factors as the Board considers appropriate.

(6) Exemption for small issuers

(A) In general

This subsection shall not apply to any issuer that, together with its affiliates, has assets of less than $10,000,000,000, and the Board shall exempt such issuers from regulations prescribed under paragraph (3)(A).

(B) Definition

For purposes of this paragraph, the term "issuer" shall be limited to the person holding the asset account that is debited through an electronic debit transaction.

(7) Exemption for government-administered payment programs and reloadable prepaid cards

(A) In general

This subsection shall not apply to an interchange transaction fee charged or received with respect to an electronic debit transaction in which a person uses—

(i) a debit card or general-use prepaid card that has been provided to a person pursuant to a Federal, State or local government-administered payment program, in which the person may only use the debit card or general-use prepaid card to transfer or debit funds, monetary value, or other assets that have been provided pursuant to such program; or

(ii) a plastic card, payment code, or device that is—

(I) linked to funds, monetary value, or assets which are purchased or loaded on a prepaid basis;

(II) not issued or approved for use to access or debit any account held by or for the benefit of the card holder (other than a subaccount or other method of recording or tracking funds purchased or loaded on the card on a prepaid basis);

(III) redeemable at multiple, unaffiliated merchants or service providers, or automated teller machines;

(IV) used to transfer or debit funds, monetary value, or other assets; and

(V) reloadable and not marketed or labeled as a gift card or gift certificate.

(B) Exception

Notwithstanding subparagraph (A), after the end of the 1-year period beginning on the effective date provided in paragraph (9), this subsection shall apply to an interchange transaction fee charged or received with respect to an electronic debit transaction described in subparagraph (A)(i) in which a person uses a general-use prepaid card, or an electronic debit transaction described in subparagraph (A)(ii), if any of the following fees may be charged to a person with respect to the card:

(i) A fee for an overdraft, including a shortage of funds or a transaction processed for an amount exceeding the account balance.

(ii) A fee imposed by the issuer for the first withdrawal per month from an automated teller machine that is part of the issuer's designated automated teller machine network.

(C) Definition

For purposes of subparagraph (B), the term "designated automated teller machine network" means either—

(i) all automated teller machines identified in the name of the issuer; or

(ii) any network of automated teller machines identified by the issuer that provides reasonable and convenient access to the issuer's customers.

(D) Reporting

Beginning 12 months after July 21, 2010, the Board shall annually provide a report to the Congress regarding—

(i) the prevalence of the use of general-use prepaid cards in Federal, State or local government-administered payment programs; and

(ii) the interchange transaction fees and cardholder fees charged with respect to the use of such general-use prepaid cards.

(8) Regulatory authority over network fees

(A) In general

The Board may prescribe regulations, pursuant to section 553 of Title 5, regarding any network fee.

(B) Limitation

The authority under subparagraph (A) to prescribe regulations shall be limited to regulations to ensure that—

(i) a network fee is not used to directly or indirectly compensate an issuer with respect to an electronic debit transaction; and

(ii) a network fee is not used to circumvent or evade the restrictions of this subsection and regulations prescribed under such subsection.

(C) Rulemaking required

The Board shall prescribe regulations in final form before the end of the 9-month period beginning on July 21, 2010, to carry out the authorities provided under subparagraph (A).

(9) Effective date

This subsection shall take effect at the end of the 12-month period beginning on July 21, 2010.

(b) Limitation on payment card network restrictions

(1) Prohibitions against exclusivity arrangements

(A) No exclusive network

The Board shall, before the end of the 1-year period beginning on July 21, 2010, prescribe regulations providing that an issuer or payment card network shall not directly or through any agent, processor, or licensed member of a payment card network, by contract, requirement, condition, penalty, or otherwise, restrict the number of payment card networks on which an electronic debit transaction may be processed to—

    (i)   1 such network; or

    (ii)   2 or more such networks which are owned, controlled, or otherwise operated by—

        (I)   affiliated persons; or

        (II)   networks affiliated with such issuer.

(B) No routing restrictions

The Board shall, before the end of the 1-year period beginning on July 21, 2010, prescribe regulations providing that an issuer or payment card network shall not, directly or through any agent, processor, or licensed member of the network, by contract, requirement, condition, penalty, or otherwise, inhibit the ability of any person who accepts debit cards for payments to direct the routing of electronic debit transactions for processing over any payment card network that may process such transactions.

(2) Limitation on restrictions on offering discounts for use of a form of payment

(A) In general

A payment card network shall not, directly or through any agent, processor, or licensed member of the network, by contract, requirement, condition, penalty, or otherwise, inhibit the ability of any person to provide a discount or in-kind incentive for payment by the use of cash, checks, debit cards, or credit cards to the extent that—

    (i)   in the case of a discount or in-kind incentive for payment by the use of debit cards, the discount or in-kind incentive does not differentiate on the basis of the issuer or the payment card network;

    (ii)   in the case of a discount or in-kind incentive for payment by the use of credit cards, the discount or in-kind incentive does not differentiate on the basis of the issuer or the payment card network; and

    (iii)   to the extent required by Federal law and applicable State law, such discount or in-kind incentive is offered to all prospective buyers and disclosed clearly and conspicuously.

(B) Lawful discounts

For purposes of this paragraph, the network may not penalize any person for the providing of a discount that is in compliance with Federal law and applicable State law.

(3) Limitation on restrictions on setting transaction minimums or maximums

(A) In general

A payment card network shall not, directly or through any agent, processor, or licensed member of the network, by contract, requirement, condition, penalty, or otherwise, inhibit the ability—

    (i)   of any person to set a minimum dollar value for the acceptance by that person of credit cards, to the extent that—

        (I)   such minimum dollar value does not differentiate between issuers or between payment card networks; and

        (II)   such minimum dollar value does not exceed $10.00; or

    (ii)   of any Federal agency or institution of higher education to set a maximum dollar value for the acceptance by that Federal agency or institution of higher education of credit cards, to the extent that such maximum dollar value does not differentiate between issuers or between payment card networks.

(B) Increase in minimum dollar amount

The Board may, by regulation prescribed pursuant to section 553 of Title 5, increase the amount of the dollar value listed in subparagraph (A)(i)(II).

(4) Rule of construction

No provision of this subsection shall be construed to authorize any person—

(A) to discriminate between debit cards within a payment card network on the basis of the issuer that issued the debit card; or

(B) to discriminate between credit cards within a payment card network on the basis of the issuer that issued the credit card.

(c) Definitions

For purposes of this section, the following definitions shall apply:

(1) Affiliate

The term "affiliate" means any company that controls, is controlled by, or is under common control with another company.

(2) Debit card

The term "debit card"—

(A) means any card, or other payment code or device, issued or approved for use through a payment card network to debit an asset account (regardless of the purpose for which the account is established), whether authorization is based on signature, PIN, or other means;

(B) includes a general-use prepaid card, as that term is defined in section 1693l–1(a)(2)(A) of this title; and

(C) does not include paper checks.

(3) Credit card

The term "credit card" has the same meaning as in section 1602 of this title.

(4) Discount

The term "discount"—

(A) means a reduction made from the price that customers are informed is the regular price; and

(B) does not include any means of increasing the price that customers are informed is the regular price.

(5) Electronic debit transaction

The term "electronic debit transaction" means a transaction in which a person uses a debit card.

(6) Federal agency

The term "Federal agency" means—

(A) an agency (as defined in section 101 of Title 31); and

(B) a Government corporation (as defined in section 103 of Title 5).

(7) Institution of higher education

The term "institution of higher education" has the same meaning as in 1001[1] and 1002 of Title 20.

(8) Interchange transaction fee

---

[1] So in original. Probably should be preceded by "sections".

The term "interchange transaction fee" means any fee established, charged or received by a payment card network for the purpose of compensating an issuer for its involvement in an electronic debit transaction.

(9) Issuer

The term "issuer" means any person who issues a debit card, or credit card, or the agent of such person with respect to such card.

(10) Network fee

The term "network fee" means any fee charged and received by a payment card network with respect to an electronic debit transaction, other than an interchange transaction fee.

(11) Payment card network

The term "payment card network" means an entity that directly, or through licensed members, processors, or agents, provides the proprietary services, infrastructure, and software that route information and data to conduct debit card or credit card transaction authorization, clearance, and settlement, and that a person uses in order to accept as a form of payment a brand of debit card, credit card or other device that may be used to carry out debit or credit transactions.

(d) Enforcement

(1) In general

Compliance with the requirements imposed under this section shall be enforced under section 1693o of this title.

(2) Exception

Sections 1693m and 1693n of this title shall not apply with respect to this section or the requirements imposed pursuant to this section.

(Pub.L. 90–321, Title IX, § 920, as added Pub.L. 111–203, Title X, § 1075(a)(2), July 21, 2010, 124 Stat. 2068.)

§ 1693p.   Reports to Congress [CCPA § 921]

(a) Not later than twelve months after the effective date of this subchapter and at one-year intervals thereafter, the Bureau shall make reports to the Congress concerning the administration of its functions under this subchapter, including such recommendations as the Bureau deems necessary and appropriate. In addition, each report of the Bureau shall include its assessment of the extent to which compliance with this subchapter is being achieved, and a summary of the enforcement actions taken under section 1693o of this title. In such report, the Bureau shall particularly address the effects of this subchapter on the costs and benefits to financial institutions and consumers, on competition, on the introduction of new technology, on the operations of financial institutions, and on the adequacy of consumer protection.

(b) In the exercise of its functions under this subchapter, the Bureau may obtain upon request the views of any other Federal agency which, in the judgment of the Bureau, exercises regulatory or supervisory functions with respect to any class of persons subject to this subchapter.

(Pub.L. 90–321, Title IX, § 921, formerly § 918, as added Pub.L. 95–630, Title XX, § 2001, Nov. 10, 1978, 92 Stat. 3740, and amended Pub.L. 97–375, Title II, § 209(a), Dec. 21, 1982, 96 Stat. 1825; renumbered § 919, Pub.L. 111–24, Title IV, § 401(1), May 22, 2009, 123 Stat. 1751; renumbered §§ 920, 921 and amended Pub.L. 111–203, Title X, §§ 1073(a)(3), 1075(a)(1), 1084(1), July 21, 2010, 124 Stat. 2060, 2068, 2081.)

§ 1693q.   Relation to State laws [CCPA § 922]

This subchapter does not annul, alter, or affect the laws of any State relating to electronic fund transfers, dormancy fees, inactivity charges or fees, service fees, or expiration dates of gift certificates, store gift cards, or general-use prepaid cards, except to the extent that those laws are inconsistent with the provisions of this subchapter, and then only to the extent of the inconsistency. A State law is not inconsistent with this subchapter if the protection such law affords any consumer is greater than the protection afforded by this subchapter. The Bureau shall, upon its own motion or upon the request of any financial institution,

State, or other interested party, submitted in accordance with procedures prescribed in regulations of the Bureau, determine whether a State requirement is inconsistent or affords greater protection. If the Bureau determines that a State requirement is inconsistent, financial institutions shall incur no liability under the law of that State for a good faith failure to comply with that law, notwithstanding that such determination is subsequently amended, rescinded, or determined by judicial or other authority to be invalid for any reason. This subchapter does not extend the applicability of any such law to any class of persons or transactions to which it would not otherwise apply.

> (Pub.L. 90–321, Title IX, § 922, formerly § 919, as added Pub.L. 95–630, Title XX, § 2001, Nov. 10, 1978, 92 Stat. 3741, and renumbered § 920 and amended Pub.L. 111–24, Title IV, §§ 401(1), 402, May 22, 2009, 123 Stat. 1751, 1754; renumbered §§ 921, 922 and amended Pub.L. 111–203, Title X, §§ 1073(a)(3), 1075(a)(1), 1084(1), July 21, 2010, 124 Stat. 2060, 2068, 2081.)

§ 1693r. Exemption for State regulation [CCPA § 922]*

The Bureau shall by regulation exempt from the requirements of this subchapter any class of electronic fund transfers within any State if the Bureau determines that under the law of that State that class of electronic fund transfers is subject to requirements substantially similar to those imposed by this subchapter, and that there is adequate provision for enforcement.

> (Pub.L. 90–321, Title IX, § 922, formerly § 920, as added Pub.L. 95–630, Title XX, § 2001, Nov. 10, 1978, 92 Stat. 3741; renumbered § 921, Pub.L. 111–24, Title IV, § 401(1), May 22, 2009, 123 Stat. 1638, renumbered § 922 and amended Pub.L. 111–203, Title X, §§ 1073(a)(3), 1084(1), July 21, 2010, 124 Stat. 2060, 2081.)

---

* *Note from West Advisory Panel: So in original. Probably should have been redesignated § 923.*

TRUTH IN LENDING
(REGULATION Z)

12 C.F.R. Part 1026

Current through March 13, 2016; 81 F.R. 12795

For updates, see www.ecfr.gov

Note from West Advisory Board

This regulation is the Consumer Financial Protection Bureau's recodification of the Federal Reserve Board's Regulation Z (12 C.F.R. Part 226), as mandated by the Dodd-Frank Wall Street Reform and Consumer Protection Act of 2010. The Federal Reserve Board's regulation still has some applicability, primarily to auto dealers. The text of that regulation can be found at www.ecfr.gov.

SUBPART D.   MISCELLANEOUS

SUBPART E.   SPECIAL RULES FOR CERTAIN HOME MORTGAGE TRANSACTIONS

SUBPART F.   SPECIAL RULES FOR PRIVATE EDUCATION LOANS

SUBPART G.   SPECIAL RULES APPLICABLE TO CREDIT CARD ACCOUNTS AND OPEN-END CREDIT OFFERED TO COLLEGE STUDENTS

SUBPART A. GENERAL

§ 1026.1   Authority, purpose, coverage, organization, enforcement, and liability.

(a)   **Authority.** This part, known as Regulation Z, is issued by the Bureau of Consumer Financial Protection to implement the Federal Truth in Lending Act, which is contained in title I of the Consumer

Credit Protection Act, as amended (15 U.S.C. 1601 et seq.). This part also implements Title XII, section 1204 of the Competitive Equality Banking Act of 1987 (Pub.L. 100–86, 101 Stat. 552). Furthermore, this part implements certain provisions of the Real Estate Settlement Procedures Act of 1974, as amended (12 U.S.C. 2601 et seq.). In addition, this part implements certain provisions of the Financial Institutions Reform, Recovery, and Enforcement Act, as amended (12 U.S.C. 3331 et seq.). The Bureau's information-collection requirements contained in this part have been approved by the Office of Management and Budget under the provisions of 44 U.S.C. 3501 et seq. and have been assigned OMB No. 3170–0015 (Truth in Lending).

(b) Purpose. The purpose of this part is to promote the informed use of consumer credit by requiring disclosures about its terms and cost, to ensure that consumers are provided with greater and more timely information on the nature and costs of the residential real estate settlement process, and to effect certain changes in the settlement process for residential real estate that will result in more effective advance disclosure to home buyers and sellers of settlement costs. The regulation also includes substantive protections. It gives consumers the right to cancel certain credit transactions that involve a lien on a consumer's principal dwelling, regulates certain credit card practices, and provides a means for fair and timely resolution of credit billing disputes. The regulation does not generally govern charges for consumer credit, except that several provisions in subpart G set forth special rules addressing certain charges applicable to credit card accounts under an open-end (not home-secured) consumer credit plan. The regulation requires a maximum interest rate to be stated in variable-rate contracts secured by the consumer's dwelling. It also imposes limitations on home-equity plans that are subject to the requirements of § 1026.40 and mortgages that are subject to the requirements of § 1026.32. The regulation prohibits certain acts or practices in connection with credit secured by a dwelling in § 1026.36, and credit secured by a consumer's principal dwelling in § 1026.35. The regulation also regulates certain practices of creditors who extend private education loans as defined in § 1026.46(b)(5). In addition, it imposes certain limitations on increases in costs for mortgage transactions subject to § 1026.19(e) and (f).

(c) Coverage.

(1) In general, this part applies to each individual or business that offers or extends credit, other than a person excluded from coverage of this part by section 1029 of the Consumer Financial Protection Act of 2010, Title X of the Dodd-Frank Wall Street Reform and Consumer Protection Act, Public Law 111–203, 124 Stat. 1376, when four conditions are met:

(i) The credit is offered or extended to consumers;

(ii) The offering or extension of credit is done regularly;

(iii) The credit is subject to a finance charge or is payable by a written agreement in more than four installments; and

(iv) The credit is primarily for personal, family, or household purposes.

(2) If a credit card is involved, however, certain provisions apply even if the credit is not subject to a finance charge, or is not payable by a written agreement in more than four installments, or if the credit card is to be used for business purposes.

(3) In addition, certain requirements of § 1026.40 apply to persons who are not creditors but who provide applications for home-equity plans to consumers.

(4) Furthermore, certain requirements of § 1026.57 apply to institutions of higher education.

(5) Except in transactions subject to § 1026.19(e) and (f), no person is required to provide the disclosures required by sections 128(a)(16) through (19), 128(b)(4), 129C(f)(1), 129C(g)(2) and (3), 129D(h), or 129D(j)(1)(A) of the Truth in Lending Act, section 4(c) of the Real Estate Settlement Procedures Act, or the disclosure required prior to settlement by section 129C(h) of the Truth in Lending Act. Except in transactions subject to § 1026.20(e), no person is required to provide the disclosure required by section 129D(j)(1)(B) of the Truth in Lending Act. Except in transactions subject to § 1026.39(d)(5), no person becoming a creditor with respect to an existing residential mortgage loan is required to provide the disclosure required by section 129C(h) of the Truth in Lending Act.

(d) Organization. The regulation is divided into subparts and appendices as follows:

(1)   Subpart A contains general information. It sets forth:

    (i)   The authority, purpose, coverage, and organization of the regulation;

    (ii)   The definitions of basic terms;

    (iii)   The transactions that are exempt from coverage; and

    (iv)   The method of determining the finance charge.

(2)   Subpart B contains the rules for open-end credit. It requires that account-opening disclosures and periodic statements be provided, as well as additional disclosures for credit and charge card applications and solicitations and for home-equity plans subject to the requirements of § 1026.60 and § 1026.40, respectively. It also describes special rules that apply to credit card transactions, treatment of payments and credit balances, procedures for resolving credit billing errors, annual percentage rate calculations, rescission requirements, and advertising.

(3)   Subpart C relates to closed-end credit. It contains rules on disclosures, treatment of credit balances, annual percentage rate calculations, rescission requirements, and advertising.

(4)   Subpart D contains rules on oral disclosures, disclosures in languages other than English, record retention, effect on state laws, state exemptions, and rate limitations.

(5)   Subpart E contains special rules for mortgage transactions. Section 1026.32 requires certain disclosures and provides limitations for closed-end credit transactions and open-end credit plans that have rates or fees above specified amounts or certain prepayment penalties. Section 1026.33 requires special disclosures, including the total annual loan cost rate, for reverse mortgage transactions. Section 1026.34 prohibits specific acts and practices in connection with high-cost mortgages, as defined in § 1026.32(a). Section 1026.35 prohibits specific acts and practices in connection with closed-end higher-priced mortgage loans, as defined in § 1026.35(a). Section 1026.36 prohibits specific acts and practices in connection with an extension of credit secured by a dwelling. Sections 1026.37 and 1026.38 set forth special disclosure requirements for certain closed-end transactions secured by real property, as required by § 1026.19(e) and (f).

(6)   Subpart F relates to private education loans. It contains rules on disclosures, limitations on changes in terms after approval, the right to cancel the loan, and limitations on co-branding in the marketing of private education loans.

(7)   Subpart G relates to credit card accounts under an open-end (not home-secured) consumer credit plan (except for § 1026.57(c), which applies to all open-end credit plans). Section 1026.51 contains rules on evaluation of a consumer's ability to make the required payments under the terms of an account. Section 1026.52 limits the fees that a consumer can be required to pay with respect to an open-end (not home-secured) consumer credit plan during the first year after account opening. Section 1026.53 contains rules on allocation of payments in excess of the minimum payment. Section 1026.54 sets forth certain limitations on the imposition of finance charges as the result of a loss of a grace period. Section 1026.55 contains limitations on increases in annual percentage rates, fees, and charges for credit card accounts. Section 1026.56 prohibits the assessment of fees or charges for over-the-limit transactions unless the consumer affirmatively consents to the creditor's payment of over-the-limit transactions. Section 1026.57 sets forth rules for reporting and marketing of college student open-end credit. Section 1026.58 sets forth requirements for the Internet posting of credit card accounts under an open-end (not home-secured) consumer credit plan.

(8)   Several appendices contain information such as the procedures for determinations about state laws, state exemptions and issuance of official interpretations, special rules for certain kinds of credit plans, and the rules for computing annual percentage rates in closed-end credit transactions and total-annual-loan-cost rates for reverse mortgage transactions.

(e)   **Enforcement and liability.** Section 108 of the Truth in Lending Act contains the administrative enforcement provisions for that Act. Sections 112, 113, 130, 131, and 134 contain provisions relating to liability for failure to comply with the requirements of the Truth in Lending Act and the regulation. Section 1204(c) of title XII of the Competitive Equality Banking Act of 1987, Public Law 100–86, 101 Stat. 552, incorporates by reference administrative enforcement and civil liability provisions of sections 108 and 130 of the Truth in Lending Act. Section 19 of the Real Estate Settlement Procedures Act contains the administrative enforcement provisions for that Act.

§ 1026.2   Definitions and rules of construction.

(a) **Definitions.** For purposes of this part, the following definitions apply:

(1) *Act* means the Truth in Lending Act (15 U.S.C. 1601 et seq.).

(2) *Advertisement* means a commercial message in any medium that promotes, directly or indirectly, a credit transaction.

(3)(i) *Application* means the submission of a consumer's financial information for the purposes of obtaining an extension of credit.

(ii) For transactions subject to § 1026.19(e), (f), or (g) of this part, an application consists of the submission of the consumer's name, the consumer's income, the consumer's social security number to obtain a credit report, the property address, an estimate of the value of the property, and the mortgage loan amount sought.

(4) *Billing cycle or cycle* means the interval between the days or dates of regular periodic statements. These intervals shall be equal and no longer than a quarter of a year. An interval will be considered equal if the number of days in the cycle does not vary more than four days from the regular day or date of the periodic statement.

(5) *Bureau* means the Bureau of Consumer Financial Protection.

(6) *Business day* means a day on which the creditor's offices are open to the public for carrying on substantially all of its business functions. However, for purposes of rescission under §§ 1026.15 and 1026.23, and for purposes of §§ 1026.19(a)(1)(ii), 1026.19(a)(2), 1026.19(e)(1)(iii)(B), 1026.19(e)(1)(iv), 1026.19(e)(2)(i)(A), 1026.19(e)(4)(ii), 1026.19(f)(1)(ii), 1026.19(f)(1)(iii), 1026.20(e)(5), 1026.31, and 1026.46(d)(4), the term means all calendar days except Sundays and the legal public holidays specified in 5 U.S.C. 6103(a), such as New Year's Day, the Birthday of Martin Luther King, Jr., Washington's Birthday, Memorial Day, Independence Day, Labor Day, Columbus Day, Veterans Day, Thanksgiving Day, and Christmas Day.

(7) *Card issuer* means a person that issues a credit card or that person's agent with respect to the card.

(8) *Cardholder* means a natural person to whom a credit card is issued for consumer credit purposes, or a natural person who has agreed with the card issuer to pay consumer credit obligations arising from the issuance of a credit card to another natural person. For purposes of § 1026.12(a) and (b), the term includes any person to whom a credit card is issued for any purpose, including business, commercial or agricultural use, or a person who has agreed with the card issuer to pay obligations arising from the issuance of such a credit card to another person.

(9) *Cash price* means the price at which a creditor, in the ordinary course of business, offers to sell for cash property or service that is the subject of the transaction. At the creditor's option, the term may include the price of accessories, services related to the sale, service contracts and taxes and fees for license, title, and registration. The term does not include any finance charge.

(10) *Closed-end credit* means consumer credit other than "open-end credit" as defined in this section.

(11) *Consumer* means a cardholder or natural person to whom consumer credit is offered or extended. However, for purposes of rescission under §§ 1026.15 and 1026.23, the term also includes a natural person in whose principal dwelling a security interest is or will be retained or acquired, if that person's ownership interest in the dwelling is or will be subject to the security interest.

(12) *Consumer credit* means credit offered or extended to a consumer primarily for personal, family, or household purposes.

(13) Consummation means the time that a consumer becomes contractually obligated on a credit transaction.

(14) Credit means the right to defer payment of debt or to incur debt and defer its payment.

(15)(i) Credit card means any card, plate, or other single credit device that may be used from time to time to obtain credit.

(ii) Credit card account under an open-end (not home-secured) consumer credit plan means any open-end credit account that is accessed by a credit card, except:

(A) A home-equity plan subject to the requirements of § 1026.40 that is accessed by a credit card; or

(B) An overdraft line of credit that is accessed by a debit card or an account number.

(iii) Charge card means a credit card on an account for which no periodic rate is used to compute a finance charge.

(16) Credit sale means a sale in which the seller is a creditor. The term includes a bailment or lease (unless terminable without penalty at any time by the consumer) under which the consumer:

(i) Agrees to pay as compensation for use a sum substantially equivalent to, or in excess of, the total value of the property and service involved; and

(ii) Will become (or has the option to become), for no additional consideration or for nominal consideration, the owner of the property upon compliance with the agreement.

(17) Creditor means:

(i) A person who regularly extends consumer credit that is subject to a finance charge or is payable by written agreement in more than four installments (not including a down payment), and to whom the obligation is initially payable, either on the face of the note or contract, or by agreement when there is no note or contract.

(ii) For purposes of §§ 1026.4(c)(8) (Discounts), 1026.9(d) (Finance charge imposed at time of transaction), and 1026.12(e) (Prompt notification of returns and crediting of refunds), a person that honors a credit card.

(iii) For purposes of subpart B, any card issuer that extends either open-end credit or credit that is not subject to a finance charge and is not payable by written agreement in more than four installments.

(iv) For purposes of subpart B (except for the credit and charge card disclosures contained in §§ 1026.60 and 1026.9(e) and (f), the finance charge disclosures contained in § 1026.6(a)(1) and (b)(3)(i) and § 1026.7(a)(4) through (7) and (b)(4) through (6) and the right of rescission set forth in § 1026.15) and subpart C, any card issuer that extends closed-end credit that is subject to a finance charge or is payable by written agreement in more than four installments.

(v) A person regularly extends consumer credit only if it extended credit (other than credit subject to the requirements of § 1026.32) more than 25 times (or more than 5 times for transactions secured by a dwelling) in the preceding calendar year. If a person did not meet these numerical standards in the preceding calendar year, the numerical standards shall be applied to the current calendar year. A person regularly extends consumer credit if, in any 12-month period, the person originates more than one credit extension that is subject to the requirements of § 1026.32 or one or more such credit extensions through a mortgage broker.

(18) Downpayment means an amount, including the value of property used as a trade-in, paid to a seller to reduce the cash price of goods or services purchased in a credit sale transaction. A deferred portion of a downpayment may be treated as part of the downpayment if it is payable not later than the due date of the second otherwise regularly scheduled payment and is not subject to a finance charge.

(19) Dwelling means a residential structure that contains one to four units, whether or not that structure is attached to real property. The term includes an individual condominium unit, cooperative unit, mobile home, and trailer, if it is used as a residence.

(20) Open-end credit means consumer credit extended by a creditor under a plan in which:

(i) The creditor reasonably contemplates repeated transactions;

(ii) The creditor may impose a finance charge from time to time on an outstanding unpaid balance; and

(iii) The amount of credit that may be extended to the consumer during the term of the plan (up to any limit set by the creditor) is generally made available to the extent that any outstanding balance is repaid.

(21) Periodic rate means a rate of finance charge that is or may be imposed by a creditor on a balance for a day, week, month, or other subdivision of a year.

(22) Person means a natural person or an organization, including a corporation, partnership, proprietorship, association, cooperative, estate, trust, or government unit.

(23) Prepaid finance charge means any finance charge paid separately in cash or by check before or at consummation of a transaction, or withheld from the proceeds of the credit at any time.

(24) Residential mortgage transaction means a transaction in which a mortgage, deed of trust, purchase money security interest arising under an installment sales contract, or equivalent consensual security interest is created or retained in the consumer's principal dwelling to finance the acquisition or initial construction of that dwelling.

(25) Security interest means an interest in property that secures performance of a consumer credit obligation and that is recognized by state or Federal law. It does not include incidental interests such as interests in proceeds, accessions, additions, fixtures, insurance proceeds (whether or not the creditor is a loss payee or beneficiary), premium rebates, or interests in after-acquired property. For purposes of disclosures under §§ 1026.6, 1026.18, 1026.19(e) and (f), and 1026.38(*l*)(6). the term does not include an interest that arises solely by operation of law. However, for purposes of the right of rescission under §§ 1026.15 and 1026.23, the term does include interests that arise solely by operation of law.

(26) State means any state, the District of Columbia, the Commonwealth of Puerto Rico, and any territory or possession of the United States.

(b) **Rules of construction.** For purposes of this part, the following rules of construction apply:

(1) Where appropriate, the singular form of a word includes the plural form and plural includes singular.

(2) Where the words obligation and transaction are used in the regulation, they refer to a consumer credit obligation or transaction, depending upon the context. Where the word credit is used in the regulation, it means consumer credit unless the context clearly indicates otherwise.

(3) Unless defined in this part, the words used have the meanings given to them by state law or contract.

(4) Where the word amount is used in this part to describe disclosure requirements, it refers to a numerical amount.

§ 1026.3   Exempt transactions.

The following transactions are not subject to this part or, if the exemption is limited to specified provisions of this part, are not subject to those provisions:

(a) **Business, commercial, agricultural, or organizational credit.**

(1) An extension of credit primarily for a business, commercial or agricultural purpose.

(2) An extension of credit to other than a natural person, including credit to government agencies or instrumentalities.

(b) Credit over applicable threshold amount.[*]

(1) Exemption.

(i) Requirements. An extension of credit in which the amount of credit extended exceeds the applicable threshold amount or in which there is an express written commitment to extend credit in excess of the applicable threshold amount, unless the extension of credit is:

(A) Secured by any real property, or by personal property used or expected to be used as the principal dwelling of the consumer; or

(B) A private education loan as defined in § 1026.46(b)(5).

(ii) Annual adjustments. The threshold amount in paragraph (b)(1)(i) of this section is adjusted annually to reflect increases in the Consumer Price Index for Urban Wage Earners and Clerical Workers, as applicable. See the official commentary to this paragraph (b) for the threshold amount applicable to a specific extension of credit or express written commitment to extend credit.

(2) Transition rule for open-end accounts exempt prior to July 21, 2011. An open-end account that is exempt on July 20, 2011 based on an express written commitment to extend credit in excess of $25,000 remains exempt until December 31, 2011 unless:

(i) The creditor takes a security interest in any real property, or in personal property used or expected to be used as the principal dwelling of the consumer; or

(ii) The creditor reduces the express written commitment to extend credit to $25,000 or less.

(c) Public utility credit. An extension of credit that involves public utility services provided through pipe, wire, other connected facilities, or radio or similar transmission (including extensions of such facilities), if the charges for service, delayed payment, or any discounts for prompt payment are filed with or regulated by any government unit. The financing of durable goods or home improvements by a public utility is not exempt.

(d) Securities or commodities accounts. Transactions in securities or commodities accounts in which credit is extended by a broker-dealer registered with the Securities and Exchange Commission or the Commodity Futures Trading Commission.

(e) Home fuel budget plans. An installment agreement for the purchase of home fuels in which no finance charge is imposed.

(f) Student loan programs. Loans made, insured, or guaranteed pursuant to a program authorized by Title IV of the Higher Education Act of 1965 (20 U.S.C. 1070 et seq.).

(g) Employer-sponsored retirement plans. An extension of credit to a participant in an employer-sponsored retirement plan qualified under section 401(a) of the Internal Revenue Code, a tax-sheltered annuity under section 403(b) of the Internal Revenue Code, or an eligible governmental deferred compensation plan under section 457(b) of the Internal Revenue Code (26 U.S.C. 401(a); 26 U.S.C. 403(b); 26 U.S.C. 457(b)), provided that the extension of credit is comprised of fully vested funds from such participant's account and is made in compliance with the Internal Revenue Code (26 U.S.C. 1 et seq.).

(h) Partial exemption for certain mortgage loans. The special disclosure requirements in § 1026.19(e), (f), and (g) do not apply to a transaction that satisfies all of the following criteria:

(1) The transaction is secured by a subordinate lien;

(2) The transaction is for the purpose of:

---

[*] *Note from West Advisory Panel: From Jan. 1 through Dec. 31, 2016 the threshold amount is $54,600. See Supplement I (Part I) to Part 1026—Official Interpretations, Section 1026.3—Exempt Transactions.*

(i) Downpayment, closing costs, or other similar home buyer assistance, such as principal or interest subsidies;

(ii) Property rehabilitation assistance;

(iii) Energy efficiency assistance; or

(iv) Foreclosure avoidance or prevention;

(3) The credit contract does not require the payment of interest;

(4) The credit contract provides that repayment of the amount of credit extended is:

(i) Forgiven either incrementally or in whole, at a date certain, and subject only to specified ownership and occupancy conditions, such as a requirement that the consumer maintain the property as the consumer's principal dwelling for five years;

(ii) Deferred for a minimum of 20 years after consummation of the transaction;

(iii) Deferred until sale of the property securing the transaction; or

(iv) Deferred until the property securing the transaction is no longer the principal dwelling of the consumer;

(5) The total of costs payable by the consumer in connection with the transaction at consummation is less than one percent of the amount of credit extended and includes no charges other than:

(i) Fees for recordation of security instruments, deeds, and similar documents;

(ii) A bona fide and reasonable application fee; and

(iii) A bona fide and reasonable fee for housing counseling services; and

(6) The creditor complies with all other applicable requirements of this part in connection with the transaction, including without limitation the disclosures required by § 1026.18.

§ 1026.4   Finance charge.

(a) Definition. The finance charge is the cost of consumer credit as a dollar amount. It includes any charge payable directly or indirectly by the consumer and imposed directly or indirectly by the creditor as an incident to or a condition of the extension of credit. It does not include any charge of a type payable in a comparable cash transaction.

(1) **Charges by third parties.** The finance charge includes fees and amounts charged by someone other than the creditor, unless otherwise excluded under this section, if the creditor:

(2) **Special rule;** closing agent charges. Fees charged by a third party that conducts the loan closing (such as a settlement agent, attorney, or escrow or title company) are finance charges only if the creditor:

(i) Requires the particular services for which the consumer is charged;

(ii) Requires the imposition of the charge; or

(iii) Retains a portion of the third-party charge, to the extent of the portion retained.

(3) **Special rule;** mortgage broker fees. Fees charged by a mortgage broker (including fees paid by the consumer directly to the broker or to the creditor for delivery to the broker) are finance charges even if the creditor does not require the consumer to use a mortgage broker and even if the creditor does not retain any portion of the charge.

(b) Examples of finance charges. The finance charge includes the following types of charges, except for charges specifically excluded by paragraphs (c) through (e) of this section:

(1) Interest, time price differential, and any amount payable under an add-on or discount system of additional charges.

(2) Service, transaction, activity, and carrying charges, including any charge imposed on a checking or other transaction account to the extent that the charge exceeds the charge for a similar account without a credit feature.

(3) Points, loan fees, assumption fees, finder's fees, and similar charges.

(4) Appraisal, investigation, and credit report fees.

(5) Premiums or other charges for any guarantee or insurance protecting the creditor against the consumer's default or other credit loss.

(6) Charges imposed on a creditor by another person for purchasing or accepting a consumer's obligation, if the consumer is required to pay the charges in cash, as an addition to the obligation, or as a deduction from the proceeds of the obligation.

(7) Premiums or other charges for credit life, accident, health, or loss-of-income insurance, written in connection with a credit transaction.

(8) Premiums or other charges for insurance against loss of or damage to property, or against liability arising out of the ownership or use of property, written in connection with a credit transaction.

(9) Discounts for the purpose of inducing payment by a means other than the use of credit.

(10) Charges or premiums paid for debt cancellation or debt suspension coverage written in connection with a credit transaction, whether or not the coverage is insurance under applicable law.

(c) **Charges excluded from the finance charge.** The following charges are not finance charges:

(1) Application fees charged to all applicants for credit, whether or not credit is actually extended.

(2) Charges for actual unanticipated late payment, for exceeding a credit limit, or for delinquency, default, or a similar occurrence.

(3) Charges imposed by a financial institution for paying items that overdraw an account, unless the payment of such items and the imposition of the charge were previously agreed upon in writing.

(4) Fees charged for participation in a credit plan, whether assessed on an annual or other periodic basis.

(5) Seller's points.

(6) Interest forfeited as a result of an interest reduction required by law on a time deposit used as security for an extension of credit.

(7) Real-estate related fees. The following fees in a transaction secured by real property or in a residential mortgage transaction, if the fees are bona fide and reasonable in amount:

(i) Fees for title examination, abstract of title, title insurance, property survey, and similar purposes.

(ii) Fees for preparing loan-related documents, such as deeds, mortgages, and reconveyance or settlement documents.

(iii) Notary and credit-report fees.

(iv) Property appraisal fees or fees for inspections to assess the value or condition of the property if the service is performed prior to closing, including fees related to pest-infestation or flood-hazard determinations.

(v) Amounts required to be paid into escrow or trustee accounts if the amounts would not otherwise be included in the finance charge.

(8) Discounts offered to induce payment for a purchase by cash, check, or other means, as provided in section 167(b) of the Act.

(d)   **Insurance and debt cancellation and debt suspension coverage.**

(1)   **Voluntary credit insurance premiums.** Premiums for credit life, accident, health, or loss-of-income insurance may be excluded from the finance charge if the following conditions are met:

    (i)   The insurance coverage is not required by the creditor, and this fact is disclosed in writing.

    (ii)   The premium for the initial term of insurance coverage is disclosed in writing. If the term of insurance is less than the term of the transaction, the term of insurance also shall be disclosed. The premium may be disclosed on a unit-cost basis only in open-end credit transactions, closed-end credit transactions by mail or telephone under § 1026.17(g), and certain closed-end credit transactions involving an insurance plan that limits the total amount of indebtedness subject to coverage.

    (iii) The consumer signs or initials an affirmative written request for the insurance after receiving the disclosures specified in this paragraph, except as provided in paragraph (d)(4) of this section. Any consumer in the transaction may sign or initial the request.

(2)   **Property insurance premiums.** Premiums for insurance against loss of or damage to property, or against liability arising out of the ownership or use of property, including single interest insurance if the insurer waives all right of subrogation against the consumer, may be excluded from the finance charge if the following conditions are met:

    (i)   The insurance coverage may be obtained from a person of the consumer's choice, and this fact is disclosed. (A creditor may reserve the right to refuse to accept, for reasonable cause, an insurer offered by the consumer.)

    (ii)   If the coverage is obtained from or through the creditor, the premium for the initial term of insurance coverage shall be disclosed. If the term of insurance is less than the term of the transaction, the term of insurance shall also be disclosed. The premium may be disclosed on a unit-cost basis only in open-end credit transactions, closed-end credit transactions by mail or telephone under § 1026.17(g), and certain closed-end credit transactions involving an insurance plan that limits the total amount of indebtedness subject to coverage.

(3)   **Voluntary debt cancellation or debt suspension fees.** Charges or premiums paid for debt cancellation coverage for amounts exceeding the value of the collateral securing the obligation or for debt cancellation or debt suspension coverage in the event of the loss of life, health, or income or in case of accident may be excluded from the finance charge, whether or not the coverage is insurance, if the following conditions are met:

    (i)   The debt cancellation or debt suspension agreement or coverage is not required by the creditor, and this fact is disclosed in writing;

    (ii)   The fee or premium for the initial term of coverage is disclosed in writing. If the term of coverage is less than the term of the credit transaction, the term of coverage also shall be disclosed. The fee or premium may be disclosed on a unit-cost basis only in open-end credit transactions, closed-end credit transactions by mail or telephone under § 1026.17(g), and certain closed-end credit transactions involving a debt cancellation agreement that limits the total amount of indebtedness subject to coverage;

    (iii) The following are disclosed, as applicable, for debt suspension coverage: That the obligation to pay loan principal and interest is only suspended, and that interest will continue to accrue during the period of suspension.

    (iv) The consumer signs or initials an affirmative written request for coverage after receiving the disclosures specified in this paragraph, except as provided in paragraph (d)(4) of this section. Any consumer in the transaction may sign or initial the request.

(4)   **Telephone purchases.** If a consumer purchases credit insurance or debt cancellation or debt suspension coverage for an open-end (not home-secured) plan by telephone, the creditor must make the disclosures under paragraphs (d)(1)(i) and (ii) or (d)(3)(i) through (iii) of this section, as applicable, orally. In such a case, the creditor shall:

(i)   Maintain evidence that the consumer, after being provided the disclosures orally, affirmatively elected to purchase the insurance or coverage; and

(ii)   Mail the disclosures under paragraphs (d)(1)(i) and (ii) or (d)(3)(i) through (iii) of this section, as applicable, within three business days after the telephone purchase.

(e)   **Certain security interest charges.** If itemized and disclosed, the following charges may be excluded from the finance charge:

(1)   Taxes and fees prescribed by law that actually are or will be paid to public officials for determining the existence of or for perfecting, releasing, or satisfying a security interest.

(2)   The premium for insurance in lieu of perfecting a security interest to the extent that the premium does not exceed the fees described in paragraph (e)(1) of this section that otherwise would be payable.

(3)   **Taxes on security instruments.** Any tax levied on security instruments or on documents evidencing indebtedness if the payment of such taxes is a requirement for recording the instrument securing the evidence of indebtedness.

(f)   **Prohibited offsets.** Interest, dividends, or other income received or to be received by the consumer on deposits or investments shall not be deducted in computing the finance charge.

SUBPART B. OPEN-END CREDIT

§ 1026.5   General disclosure requirements.

(a)   **Form of disclosures.**

(1)   **General.**

(i)   The creditor shall make the disclosures required by this subpart clearly and conspicuously.

(ii)   The creditor shall make the disclosures required by this subpart in writing, in a form that the consumer may keep, except that:

(A)   The following disclosures need not be written: Disclosures under § 1026.6(b)(3) of charges that are imposed as part of an open-end (not home-secured) plan that are not required to be disclosed under § 1026.6(b)(2) and related disclosures of charges under § 1026.9(c)(2)(iii)(B); disclosures under § 1026.9(c)(2)(vi); disclosures under § 1026.9(d) when a finance charge is imposed at the time of the transaction; and disclosures under § 1026.56(b)(1)(i).

(B)   The following disclosures need not be in a retainable form: Disclosures that need not be written under paragraph (a)(1)(ii)(A) of this section; disclosures for credit and charge card applications and solicitations under § 1026.60; home-equity disclosures under § 1026.40(d); the alternative summary billing-rights statement under § 1026.9(a)(2); the credit and charge card renewal disclosures required under § 1026.9(e); and the payment requirements under § 1026.10(b), except as provided in § 1026.7(b)(13).

(iii)   The disclosures required by this subpart may be provided to the consumer in electronic form, subject to compliance with the consumer consent and other applicable provisions of the Electronic Signatures in Global and National Commerce Act (E-Sign Act) (15 U.S.C. 7001 et seq.). The disclosures required by §§ 1026.60, 1026.40, and 1026.16 may be provided to the consumer in electronic form without regard to the consumer consent or other provisions of the E-Sign Act in the circumstances set forth in those sections.

(2) Terminology.

(i) Terminology used in providing the disclosures required by this subpart shall be consistent.

(ii) For home-equity plans subject to § 1026.40, the terms finance charge and annual percentage rate, when required to be disclosed with a corresponding amount or percentage rate, shall be more conspicuous than any other required disclosure. The terms need not be more conspicuous when used for periodic statement disclosures under § 1026.7(a)(4) and for advertisements under § 1026.16.

(iii) If disclosures are required to be presented in a tabular format pursuant to paragraph (a)(3) of this section, the term penalty APR shall be used, as applicable. The term penalty APR need not be used in reference to the annual percentage rate that applies with the loss of a promotional rate, assuming the annual percentage rate that applies is not greater than the annual percentage rate that would have applied at the end of the promotional period; or if the annual percentage rate that applies with the loss of a promotional rate is a variable rate, the annual percentage rate is calculated using the same index and margin as would have been used to calculate the annual percentage rate that would have applied at the end of the promotional period. If credit insurance or debt cancellation or debt suspension coverage is required as part of the plan, the term required shall be used and the program shall be identified by its name. If an annual percentage rate is required to be presented in a tabular format pursuant to paragraph (a)(3)(i) or (a)(3)(iii) of this section, the term fixed, or a similar term, may not be used to describe such rate unless the creditor also specifies a time period that the rate will be fixed and the rate will not increase during that period, or if no such time period is provided, the rate will not increase while the plan is open.

(3) Specific formats.

(i) Certain disclosures for credit and charge card applications and solicitations must be provided in a tabular format in accordance with the requirements of § 1026.60(a)(2).

(ii) Certain disclosures for home-equity plans must precede other disclosures and must be given in accordance with the requirements of § 1026.40(a).

(iii) Certain account-opening disclosures must be provided in a tabular format in accordance with the requirements of § 1026.6(b)(1).

(iv) Certain disclosures provided on periodic statements must be grouped together in accordance with the requirements of § 1026.7(b)(6) and (b)(13).

(v) Certain disclosures provided on periodic statements must be given in accordance with the requirements of § 1026.7(b)(12).

(vi) Certain disclosures accompanying checks that access a credit card account must be provided in a tabular format in accordance with the requirements of § 1026.9(b)(3).

(vii) Certain disclosures provided in a change-in-terms notice must be provided in a tabular format in accordance with the requirements of § 1026.9(c)(2)(iv)(D).

(viii) Certain disclosures provided when a rate is increased due to delinquency, default or as a penalty must be provided in a tabular format in accordance with the requirements of § 1026.9(g)(3)(ii).

(b) Time of disclosures.

(1) Account-opening disclosures.

(i) General rule. The creditor shall furnish account-opening disclosures required by § 1026.6 before the first transaction is made under the plan.

(ii) Charges imposed as part of an open-end (not home-secured) plan. Charges that are imposed as part of an open-end (not home-secured) plan and are not required to be disclosed under § 1026.6(b)(2) may be disclosed after account opening but before the consumer agrees to pay or becomes obligated to pay for the charge, provided they are disclosed at a time and in a manner that a consumer would be likely to notice them. This provision does not apply to charges imposed as part of a home-equity plan subject to the requirements of § 1026.40.

(iii) **Telephone purchases.** Disclosures required by § 1026.6 may be provided as soon as reasonably practicable after the first transaction if:

(A) The first transaction occurs when a consumer contacts a merchant by telephone to purchase goods and at the same time the consumer accepts an offer to finance the purchase by establishing an open-end plan with the merchant or third-party creditor;

(B) The merchant or third-party creditor permits consumers to return any goods financed under the plan and provides consumers with a sufficient time to reject the plan and return the goods free of cost after the merchant or third-party creditor has provided the written disclosures required by § 1026.6; and

(C) The consumer's right to reject the plan and return the goods is disclosed to the consumer as a part of the offer to finance the purchase.

(iv) **Membership fees.**

(A) **General.** In general, a creditor may not collect any fee before account-opening disclosures are provided. A creditor may collect, or obtain the consumer's agreement to pay, membership fees, including application fees excludable from the finance charge under § 1026.4(c)(1), before providing account-opening disclosures if, after receiving the disclosures, the consumer may reject the plan and have no obligation to pay these fees (including application fees) or any other fee or charge. A membership fee for purposes of this paragraph has the same meaning as a fee for the issuance or availability of credit described in § 1026.60(b)(2). If the consumer rejects the plan, the creditor must promptly refund the membership fee if it has been paid, or take other action necessary to ensure the consumer is not obligated to pay that fee or any other fee or charge.

(B) **Home-equity plans.** Creditors offering home-equity plans subject to the requirements of § 1026.40 are not subject to the requirements of paragraph (b)(1)(iv)(A) of this section.

(v) **Application fees.** A creditor may collect an application fee excludable from the finance charge under § 1026.4(c)(1) before providing account-opening disclosures. However, if a consumer rejects the plan after receiving account-opening disclosures, the consumer must have no obligation to pay such an application fee, or if the fee was paid, it must be refunded. See § 1026.5(b)(1)(iv)(A).

(2) **Periodic statements.**

(i) **Statement required.** The creditor shall mail or deliver a periodic statement as required by § 1026.7 for each billing cycle at the end of which an account has a debit or credit balance of more than $1 or on which a finance charge has been imposed. A periodic statement need not be sent for an account if the creditor deems it uncollectible, if delinquency collection proceedings have been instituted, if the creditor has charged off the account in accordance with loan-loss provisions and will not charge any additional fees or interest on the account, or if furnishing the statement would violate Federal law.

(ii) **Timing requirements.**

(A) **Credit card accounts under an open-end (not home-secured) consumer credit plan.** For credit card accounts under an open-end (not home-secured) consumer credit plan, a card issuer must adopt reasonable procedures designed to ensure that:

(1) Periodic statements are mailed or delivered at least 21 days prior to the payment due date disclosed on the statement pursuant to § 1026.7(b)(11)(i)(A); and

(2) The card issuer does not treat as late for any purpose a required minimum periodic payment received by the card issuer within 21 days after mailing or delivery of the periodic statement disclosing the due date for that payment.

(B) Open-end consumer credit plans. For accounts under an open-end consumer credit plan, a creditor must adopt reasonable procedures designed to ensure that:

(1) If a grace period applies to the account:

(i) Periodic statements are mailed or delivered at least 21 days prior to the date on which the grace period expires; and

(ii) The creditor does not impose finance charges as a result of the loss of the grace period if a payment that satisfies the terms of the grace period is received by the creditor within 21 days after mailing or delivery of the periodic statement.

(2) Regardless of whether a grace period applies to the account:

(i) Periodic statements are mailed or delivered at least 14 days prior to the date on which the required minimum periodic payment must be received in order to avoid being treated as late for any purpose; and

(ii) The creditor does not treat as late for any purpose a required minimum periodic payment received by the creditor within 14 days after mailing or delivery of the periodic statement.

(3) For purposes of paragraph (b)(2)(ii)(B) of this section, "grace period" means a period within which any credit extended may be repaid without incurring a finance charge due to a periodic interest rate.

(3) Credit and charge card application and solicitation disclosures. The card issuer shall furnish the disclosures for credit and charge card applications and solicitations in accordance with the timing requirements of § 1026.60.

(4) Home-equity plans. Disclosures for home-equity plans shall be made in accordance with the timing requirements of § 1026.40(b).

(c) Basis of disclosures and use of estimates. Disclosures shall reflect the terms of the legal obligation between the parties. If any information necessary for accurate disclosure is unknown to the creditor, it shall make the disclosure based on the best information reasonably available and shall state clearly that the disclosure is an estimate.

(d) Multiple creditors; multiple consumers. If the credit plan involves more than one creditor, only one set of disclosures shall be given, and the creditors shall agree among themselves which creditor must comply with the requirements that this part imposes on any or all of them. If there is more than one consumer, the disclosures may be made to any consumer who is primarily liable on the account. If the right of rescission under § 1026.15 is applicable, however, the disclosures required by §§ 1026.6 and 1026.15(b) shall be made to each consumer having the right to rescind.

(e) Effect of subsequent events. If a disclosure becomes inaccurate because of an event that occurs after the creditor mails or delivers the disclosures, the resulting inaccuracy is not a violation of this part, although new disclosures may be required under § 1026.9(c).

§ 1026.6 Account-opening disclosures.

(a) Rules affecting home-equity plans. The requirements of this paragraph (a) apply only to home-equity plans subject to the requirements of § 1026.40. A creditor shall disclose the items in this section, to the extent applicable:

(1) Finance charge. The circumstances under which a finance charge will be imposed and an explanation of how it will be determined, as follows:

(i) A statement of when finance charges begin to accrue, including an explanation of whether or not any time period exists within which any credit extended may be repaid without incurring a finance charge. If such a time period is provided, a creditor may, at its option and without disclosure, impose no finance charge when payment is received after the time period's expiration.

(ii) A disclosure of each periodic rate that may be used to compute the finance charge, the range of balances to which it is applicable, and the corresponding annual percentage rate. If a creditor offers a variable-rate plan, the creditor shall also disclose: The circumstances under which the rate(s) may increase; any limitations on the increase; and the effect(s) of an increase. When different periodic rates apply to different types of transactions, the types of transactions to which the periodic rates shall apply shall also be disclosed. A creditor is not required to adjust the range of balances disclosure to reflect the balance below which only a minimum charge applies.

(iii) An explanation of the method used to determine the balance on which the finance charge may be computed.

(iv) An explanation of how the amount of any finance charge will be determined, including a description of how any finance charge other than the periodic rate will be determined.

(2) **Other charges.** The amount of any charge other than a finance charge that may be imposed as part of the plan, or an explanation of how the charge will be determined.

(3) **Home-equity plan information.** The following disclosures described in § 1026.40(d), as applicable:

(i) A statement of the conditions under which the creditor may take certain action, as described in § 1026.40(d)(4)(i), such as terminating the plan or changing the terms.

(ii) The payment information described in § 1026.40(d)(5)(i) and (ii) for both the draw period and any repayment period.

(iii) A statement that negative amortization may occur as described in § 1026.40(d)(9).

(iv) A statement of any transaction requirements as described in § 1026.40(d)(10).

(v) A statement regarding the tax implications as described in § 1026.40(d)(11).

(vi) A statement that the annual percentage rate imposed under the plan does not include costs other than interest as described in § 1026.40(d)(6) and (d)(12)(ii).

(vii) The variable-rate disclosures described in § 1026.40(d)(12)(viii), (d)(12)(x), (d)(12)(xi), and (d)(12)(xii), as well as the disclosure described in § 1026.40(d)(5)(iii), unless the disclosures provided with the application were in a form the consumer could keep and included a representative payment example for the category of payment option chosen by the consumer.

(4) **Security interests.** The fact that the creditor has or will acquire a security interest in the property purchased under the plan, or in other property identified by item or type.

(5) **Statement of billing rights.** A statement that outlines the consumer's rights and the creditor's responsibilities under §§ 1026.12(c) and 1026.13 and that is substantially similar to the statement found in Model Form G–3 or, at the creditor's option, G–3(A), in Appendix G to this part.

(b) **Rules affecting open-end (not home-secured) plans.** The requirements of paragraph (b) of this section apply to plans other than home-equity plans subject to the requirements of § 1026.40.

(1) **Form of disclosures; tabular format for open-end (not home-secured) plans.** Creditors must provide the account-opening disclosures specified in paragraph (b)(2)(i) through (b)(2)(v) (except for (b)(2)(i)(D)(2)) and (b)(2)(vii) through (b)(2)(xiv) of this section in the form of a table with the headings, content, and format substantially similar to any of the applicable tables in G–17 in Appendix G.

(i) **Highlighting.** In the table, any annual percentage rate required to be disclosed pursuant to paragraph (b)(2)(i) of this section; any introductory rate permitted to be disclosed pursuant to paragraph (b)(2)(i)(B) or required to be disclosed under paragraph (b)(2)(i)(F) of this section, any rate that will apply after a premium initial rate expires permitted to be disclosed pursuant to paragraph (b)(2)(i)(C) or required to be disclosed pursuant to paragraph (b)(2)(i)(F), and any fee or percentage amounts or maximum limits on fee amounts disclosed pursuant to paragraphs (b)(2)(ii), (b)(2)(iv), (b)(2)(vii) through (b)(2)(xii) of this section must be disclosed in bold text. However, bold text shall not be used for: The amount of any periodic fee disclosed pursuant to paragraph (b)(2) of this section that is not an annualized amount; and other annual percentage rates or fee amounts disclosed in the table.

(ii) **Location.** Only the information required or permitted by paragraphs (b)(2)(i) through (v) (except for (b)(2)(i)(D)(2)) and (b)(2)(vii) through (xiv) of this section shall be in the table. Disclosures required by paragraphs (b)(2)(i)(D)(2), (b)(2)(i)(D)(3), (b)(2)(vi), and (b)(2)(xv) of this section shall be placed directly below the table. Disclosures required by paragraphs (b)(3) through (5) of this section that are not otherwise required to be in the table and other information may be presented with the account agreement or account-opening disclosure statement, provided such information appears outside the required table.

(iii) **Fees that vary by state.** Creditors that impose fees referred to in paragraphs (b)(2)(vii) through (b)(2)(xi) of this section that vary by state and that provide the disclosures required by paragraph (b) of this section in person at the time the open-end (not home-secured) plan is established in connection with financing the purchase of goods or services may, at the creditor's option, disclose in the account-opening table the specific fee applicable to the consumer's account, or the range of the fees, if the disclosure includes a statement that the amount of the fee varies by state and refers the consumer to the account agreement or other disclosure provided with the account-opening table where the amount of the fee applicable to the consumer's account is disclosed. A creditor may not list fees for multiple states in the account-opening summary table.

(iv) **Fees based on a percentage**. If the amount of any fee required to be disclosed under this section is determined on the basis of a percentage of another amount, the percentage used and the identification of the amount against which the percentage is applied may be disclosed instead of the amount of the fee.

(2) **Required disclosures for account-opening table for open-end (not home-secured) plans.** A creditor shall disclose the items in this section, to the extent applicable:

(i) **Annual percentage rate.** Each periodic rate that may be used to compute the finance charge on an outstanding balance for purchases, a cash advance, or a balance transfer, expressed as an annual percentage rate (as determined by § 1026.14(b)). When more than one rate applies for a category of transactions, the range of balances to which each rate is applicable shall also be disclosed. The annual percentage rate for purchases disclosed pursuant to this paragraph shall be in at least 16-point type, except for the following: A penalty rate that may apply upon the occurrence of one or more specific events.

(A) **Variable-rate information.** If a rate disclosed under paragraph (b)(2)(i) of this section is a variable rate, the creditor shall also disclose the fact that the rate may vary and how the rate is determined. In describing how the applicable rate will be determined, the creditor must identify the type of index or formula that is used in setting the rate. The value of the index and the amount of the margin that are used to calculate the variable rate shall not be disclosed in the table. A disclosure of any applicable limitations on rate increases or decreases shall not be included in the table.

(B) **Discounted initial rates.** If the initial rate is an introductory rate, as that term is defined in § 1026.16(g)(2)(ii), the creditor must disclose the rate that would otherwise apply to the account pursuant to paragraph (b)(2)(i) of this section. Where the rate is not tied to an index or formula, the creditor must disclose the rate that will apply after the introductory rate expires. In a variable-rate account, the creditor must disclose a rate based on the applicable index or formula in accordance with the accuracy requirements of paragraph (b)(4)(ii)(G) of this section. Except as provided in paragraph (b)(2)(i)(F) of this section, the creditor is not required to, but may disclose in the table the introductory rate along with the rate that would otherwise apply to the account if the creditor also discloses the time period during which the introductory rate will remain in effect, and uses the term "introductory" or "intro" in immediate proximity to the introductory rate.

(C) Premium initial rate. If the initial rate is temporary and is higher than the rate that will apply after the temporary rate expires, the creditor must disclose the premium initial rate pursuant to paragraph (b)(2)(i) of this section. Consistent with paragraph (b)(2)(i) of this section, the premium initial rate for purchases must be in at least 16-point type. Except as provided in paragraph (b)(2)(i)(F) of this section, the creditor is not required to, but may disclose in the table the rate that will apply after the premium initial rate expires if the creditor also discloses the time period during which the premium initial rate will remain in effect. If the creditor also discloses in the table the rate that will apply after the premium initial rate for purchases expires, that rate also must be in at least 16-point type.

(D) Penalty rates.

(1) In general. Except as provided in paragraph (b)(2)(i)(D)(2) and (b)(2)(i)(D)(3) of this section, if a rate may increase as a penalty for one or more events specified in the account agreement, such as a late payment or an extension of credit that exceeds the credit limit, the creditor must disclose pursuant to paragraph (b)(2)(i) of this section the increased rate that may apply, a brief description of the event or events that may result in the increased rate, and a brief description of how long the increased rate will remain in effect. If more than one penalty rate may apply, the creditor at its option may disclose the highest rate that could apply, instead of disclosing the specific rates or the range of rates that could apply.

(2) Introductory rates. If the creditor discloses in the table an introductory rate, as that term is defined in § 1026.16(g)(2)(ii), creditors must briefly disclose directly beneath the table the circumstances under which the introductory rate may be revoked, and the rate that will apply after the introductory rate is revoked.

(3) Employee preferential rates. If a creditor discloses in the table a preferential annual percentage rate for which only employees of the creditor, employees of a third party, or other individuals with similar affiliations with the creditor or third party, such as executive officers, directors, or principal shareholders are eligible, the creditor must briefly disclose directly beneath the table the circumstances under which such preferential rate may be revoked, and the rate that will apply after such preferential rate is revoked.

(E) Point of sale where APRs vary by state or based on creditworthiness. Creditors imposing annual percentage rates that vary by state or based on the consumer's creditworthiness and providing the disclosures required by paragraph (b) of this section in person at the time the open-end (not home-secured) plan is established in connection with financing the purchase of goods or services may, at the creditor's option, disclose pursuant to paragraph (b)(2)(i) of this section in the account-opening table:

(1) The specific annual percentage rate applicable to the consumer's account; or

(2) The range of the annual percentage rates, if the disclosure includes a statement that the annual percentage rate varies by state or will be determined based on the consumer's creditworthiness and refers the consumer to the account agreement or other disclosure provided with the account-opening table where the annual percentage rate applicable to the consumer's account is disclosed. A creditor may not list annual percentage rates for multiple states in the account-opening table.

(F) Credit card accounts under an open-end (not home-secured) consumer credit plan. Notwithstanding paragraphs (b)(2)(i)(B) and (b)(2)(i)(C) of this section, for credit card accounts under an open-end (not home-secured) plan, issuers must disclose in the table:

(1) Any introductory rate as that term is defined in § 1026.16(g)(2)(ii) that would apply to the account, consistent with the requirements of paragraph (b)(2)(i)(B) of this section, and

(2) Any rate that would apply upon the expiration of a premium initial rate, consistent with the requirements of paragraph (b)(2)(i)(C) of this section.

(ii) Fees for issuance or availability.

(A) Any annual or other periodic fee that may be imposed for the issuance or availability of an open-end plan, including any fee based on account activity or inactivity; how frequently it will be imposed; and the annualized amount of the fee.

(B) Any non-periodic fee that relates to opening the plan. A creditor must disclose that the fee is a one-time fee.

(iii) Fixed finance charge; minimum interest charge. Any fixed finance charge and a brief description of the charge. Any minimum interest charge if it exceeds $1.00 that could be imposed during a billing cycle, and a brief description of the charge. The $1.00 threshold amount shall be adjusted periodically by the Bureau to reflect changes in the Consumer Price Index. The Bureau shall calculate each year a price level adjusted minimum interest charge using the Consumer Price Index in effect on the June 1 of that year. When the cumulative change in the adjusted minimum value derived from applying the annual Consumer Price level to the current minimum interest charge threshold has risen by a whole dollar, the minimum interest charge will be increased by $1.00. The creditor may, at its option, disclose in the table minimum interest charges below this threshold.

(iv) Transaction charges. Any transaction charge imposed by the creditor for use of the open-end plan for purchases.

(v) Grace period. The date by which or the period within which any credit extended may be repaid without incurring a finance charge due to a periodic interest rate and any conditions on the availability of the grace period. If no grace period is provided, that fact must be disclosed. If the length of the grace period varies, the creditor may disclose the range of days, the minimum number of days, or the average number of the days in the grace period, if the disclosure is identified as a range, minimum, or average. In disclosing in the tabular format a grace period that applies to all features on the account, the phrase "How to Avoid Paying Interest" shall be used as the heading for the row describing the grace period. If a grace period is not offered on all features of the account, in disclosing this fact in the tabular format, the phrase "Paying Interest" shall be used as the heading for the row describing this fact.

(vi) Balance computation method. The name of the balance computation method listed in § 1026.60(g) that is used to determine the balance on which the finance charge is computed for each feature, or an explanation of the method used if it is not listed, along with a statement that an explanation of the method(s) required by paragraph (b)(4)(i)(D) of this section is provided with the account-opening disclosures. In determining which balance computation method to disclose, the creditor shall assume that credit extended will not be repaid within any grace period, if any.

(vii) Cash advance fee. Any fee imposed for an extension of credit in the form of cash or its equivalent.

(viii) Late payment fee. Any fee imposed for a late payment.

(ix) Over-the-limit fee. Any fee imposed for exceeding a credit limit.

(x) Balance transfer fee. Any fee imposed to transfer an outstanding balance.

(xi) Returned-payment fee. Any fee imposed by the creditor for a returned payment.

(xii) Required insurance, debt cancellation or debt suspension coverage.

   (A) A fee for insurance described in § 1026.4(b)(7) or debt cancellation or suspension coverage described in § 1026.4(b)(10), if the insurance, or debt cancellation or suspension coverage is required as part of the plan; and

   (B) A cross reference to any additional information provided about the insurance or coverage, as applicable.

   (xiii) Available credit. If a creditor requires fees for the issuance or availability of credit described in paragraph (b)(2)(ii) of this section, or requires a security deposit for such credit, and the total amount of those required fees and/or security deposit that will be imposed and charged to the account when the account is opened is 15 percent or more of the minimum credit limit for the plan, a creditor must disclose the available credit remaining after these fees or security deposit are debited to the account. The determination whether the 15 percent threshold is met must be based on the minimum credit limit for the plan. However, the disclosure provided under this paragraph must be based on the actual initial credit limit provided on the account. In determining whether the 15 percent threshold test is met, the creditor must only consider fees for issuance or availability of credit, or a security deposit, that are required. If fees for issuance or availability are optional, these fees should not be considered in determining whether the disclosure must be given. Nonetheless, if the 15 percent threshold test is met, the creditor in providing the disclosure must disclose the amount of available credit calculated by excluding those optional fees, and the available credit including those optional fees. The creditor shall also disclose that the consumer has the right to reject the plan and not be obligated to pay those fees or any other fee or charges until the consumer has used the account or made a payment on the account after receiving a periodic statement. This paragraph does not apply with respect to fees or security deposits that are not debited to the account.

   (xiv) Web site reference. For issuers of credit cards that are not charge cards, a reference to the Web site established by the Bureau and a statement that consumers may obtain on the Web site information about shopping for and using credit cards. Until January 1, 2013, issuers may substitute for this reference a reference to the Web site established by the Board of Governors of the Federal Reserve System.

   (xv) Billing error rights reference. A statement that information about consumers' right to dispute transactions is included in the account-opening disclosures.

   (3) Disclosure of charges imposed as part of open-end (not home-secured) plans. A creditor shall disclose, to the extent applicable:

   (i) For charges imposed as part of an open-end (not home-secured) plan, the circumstances under which the charge may be imposed, including the amount of the charge or an explanation of how the charge is determined. For finance charges, a statement of when the charge begins to accrue and an explanation of whether or not any time period exists within which any credit that has been extended may be repaid without incurring the charge. If such a time period is provided, a creditor may, at its option and without disclosure, elect not to impose a finance charge when payment is received after the time period expires.

   (ii) Charges imposed as part of the plan are:

   (A) Finance charges identified under § 1026.4(a) and § 1026.4(b).

   (B) Charges resulting from the consumer's failure to use the plan as agreed, except amounts payable for collection activity after default, attorney's fees whether or not automatically imposed, and post-judgment interest rates permitted by law.

   (C) Taxes imposed on the credit transaction by a state or other governmental body, such as documentary stamp taxes on cash advances.

(D) Charges for which the payment, or nonpayment, affect the consumer's access to the plan, the duration of the plan, the amount of credit extended, the period for which credit is extended, or the timing or method of billing or payment.

(E) Charges imposed for terminating a plan.

(F) Charges for voluntary credit insurance, debt cancellation or debt suspension.

(iii) Charges that are not imposed as part of the plan include:

(A) Charges imposed on a cardholder by an institution other than the card issuer for the use of the other institution's ATM in a shared or interchange system.

(B) A charge for a package of services that includes an open-end credit feature, if the fee is required whether or not the open-end credit feature is included and the non-credit services are not merely incidental to the credit feature.

(C) Charges under § 1026.4(e) disclosed as specified.

(4) **Disclosure of rates for open-end (not home-secured) plans.** A creditor shall disclose, to the extent applicable:

(i) For each periodic rate that may be used to calculate interest:

(A) Rates. The rate, expressed as a periodic rate and a corresponding annual percentage rate.

(B) Range of balances. The range of balances to which the rate is applicable; however, a creditor is not required to adjust the range of balances disclosure to reflect the balance below which only a minimum charge applies.

(C) Type of transaction. The type of transaction to which the rate applies, if different rates apply to different types of transactions.

(D) Balance computation method. An explanation of the method used to determine the balance to which the rate is applied.

(ii) **Variable-rate accounts.** For interest rate changes that are tied to increases in an index or formula (variable-rate accounts) specifically set forth in the account agreement:

(A) The fact that the annual percentage rate may increase.

(B) How the rate is determined, including the margin.

(C) The circumstances under which the rate may increase.

(D) The frequency with which the rate may increase.

(E) Any limitation on the amount the rate may change.

(F) The effect(s) of an increase.

(G) Except as specified in paragraph (b)(4)(ii)(H) of this section, a rate is accurate if it is a rate as of a specified date and this rate was in effect within the last 30 days before the disclosures are provided.

(H) Creditors imposing annual percentage rates that vary according to an index that is not under the creditor's control that provide the disclosures required by paragraph (b) of this section in person at the time the open-end (not home-secured) plan is established in connection with financing the purchase of goods or services may disclose in the table a rate, or range of rates to the extent permitted by § 1026.6(b)(2)(i)(E), that was in effect within the last 90 days before the disclosures are provided, along with a reference directing the consumer to the account agreement or other disclosure provided with the account-opening table where an annual percentage rate applicable to the consumer's account in effect within the last 30 days before the disclosures are provided is disclosed.

(iii) Rate changes not due to index or formula. For interest rate changes that are specifically set forth in the account agreement and not tied to increases in an index or formula:

(A) The initial rate (expressed as a periodic rate and a corresponding annual percentage rate) required under paragraph (b)(4)(i)(A) of this section.

(B) How long the initial rate will remain in effect and the specific events that cause the initial rate to change.

(C) The rate (expressed as a periodic rate and a corresponding annual percentage rate) that will apply when the initial rate is no longer in effect and any limitation on the time period the new rate will remain in effect.

(D) The balances to which the new rate will apply.

(E) The balances to which the current rate at the time of the change will apply.

(5) Additional disclosures for open-end (not home-secured) plans. A creditor shall disclose, to the extent applicable:

(i) Voluntary credit insurance, debt cancellation or debt suspension. The disclosures in §§ 1026.4(d)(1)(i) and (d)(1)(ii) and (d)(3)(i) through (d)(3)(iii) if the creditor offers optional credit insurance or debt cancellation or debt suspension coverage that is identified in § 1026.4(b)(7) or (b)(10).

(ii) Security interests. The fact that the creditor has or will acquire a security interest in the property purchased under the plan, or in other property identified by item or type.

(iii) Statement of billing rights. A statement that outlines the consumer's rights and the creditor's responsibilities under §§ 1026.12(c) and 1026.13 and that is substantially similar to the statement found in Model Form G–3(A) in Appendix G to this part.

§ 1026.7 Periodic statement.

The creditor shall furnish the consumer with a periodic statement that discloses the following items, to the extent applicable:

(a) Rules affecting home-equity plans. The requirements of paragraph (a) of this section apply only to home-equity plans subject to the requirements of § 1026.40. Alternatively, a creditor subject to this paragraph may, at its option, comply with any of the requirements of paragraph (b) of this section; however, any creditor that chooses not to provide a disclosure under paragraph (a)(7) of this section must comply with paragraph (b)(6) of this section.

(1) Previous balance. The account balance outstanding at the beginning of the billing cycle.

(2) Identification of transactions. An identification of each credit transaction in accordance with § 1026.8.

(3) Credits. Any credit to the account during the billing cycle, including the amount and the date of crediting. The date need not be provided if a delay in accounting does not result in any finance or other charge.

(4) Periodic rates.

(i) Except as provided in paragraph (a)(4)(ii) of this section, each periodic rate that may be used to compute the finance charge, the range of balances to which it is applicable, and the corresponding annual percentage rate. If no finance charge is imposed when the outstanding balance is less than a certain amount, the creditor is not required to disclose that fact, or the balance below which no finance charge will be imposed. If different periodic rates apply to different types of transactions, the types of transactions to which the periodic rates apply shall also be disclosed. For variable-rate plans, the fact that the periodic rate(s) may vary.

(ii) Exception. An annual percentage rate that differs from the rate that would otherwise apply and is offered only for a promotional period need not be disclosed except in periods in which the offered rate is actually applied.

(5) Balance on which finance charge computed. The amount of the balance to which a periodic rate was applied and an explanation of how that balance was determined. When a balance is determined without first deducting all credits and payments made during the billing cycle, the fact and the amount of the credits and payments shall be disclosed.

(6) Amount of finance charge and other charges. Creditors may comply with paragraphs (a)(6) of this section, or with paragraph (b)(6) of this section, at their option.

(i) Finance charges. The amount of any finance charge debited or added to the account during the billing cycle, using the term finance charge. The components of the finance charge shall be individually itemized and identified to show the amount(s) due to the application of any periodic rates and the amounts(s) of any other type of finance charge. If there is more than one periodic rate, the amount of the finance charge attributable to each rate need not be separately itemized and identified.

(ii) Other charges. The amounts, itemized and identified by type, of any charges other than finance charges debited to the account during the billing cycle.

(7) Annual percentage rate. At a creditor's option, when a finance charge is imposed during the billing cycle, the annual percentage rate(s) determined under § 1026.14(c) using the term annual percentage rate.

(8) Grace period. The date by which or the time period within which the new balance or any portion of the new balance must be paid to avoid additional finance charges. If such a time period is provided, a creditor may, at its option and without disclosure, impose no finance charge if payment is received after the time period's expiration.

(9) Address for notice of billing errors. The address to be used for notice of billing errors. Alternatively, the address may be provided on the billing rights statement permitted by § 1026.9(a)(2).

(10) Closing date of billing cycle; new balance. The closing date of the billing cycle and the account balance outstanding on that date.

(b) Rules affecting open-end (not home-secured) plans. The requirements of paragraph (b) of this section apply only to plans other than home-equity plans subject to the requirements of § 1026.40.

(1) Previous balance. The account balance outstanding at the beginning of the billing cycle.

(2) Identification of transactions. An identification of each credit transaction in accordance with § 1026.8.

(3) Credits. Any credit to the account during the billing cycle, including the amount and the date of crediting. The date need not be provided if a delay in crediting does not result in any finance or other charge.

(4) Periodic rates.

(i) Except as provided in paragraph (b)(4)(ii) of this section, each periodic rate that may be used to compute the interest charge expressed as an annual percentage rate and using the term Annual Percentage Rate, along with the range of balances to which it is applicable. If no interest charge is imposed when the outstanding balance is less than a certain amount, the creditor is not required to disclose that fact, or the balance below which no interest charge will be imposed. The types of transactions to which the periodic rates apply shall also be disclosed. For variable-rate plans, the fact that the annual percentage rate may vary.

(ii) Exception. A promotional rate, as that term is defined in § 1026.16(g)(2)(i), is required to be disclosed only in periods in which the offered rate is actually applied.

(5)   Balance on which finance charge computed. The amount of the balance to which a periodic rate was applied and an explanation of how that balance was determined, using the term Balance Subject to Interest Rate. When a balance is determined without first deducting all credits and payments made during the billing cycle, the fact and the amount of the credits and payments shall be disclosed. As an alternative to providing an explanation of how the balance was determined, a creditor that uses a balance computation method identified in § 1026.60(g) may, at the creditor's option, identify the name of the balance computation method and provide a toll-free telephone number where consumers may obtain from the creditor more information about the balance computation method and how resulting interest charges were determined. If the method used is not identified in § 1026.60(g), the creditor shall provide a brief explanation of the method used.

(6)   Charges imposed.

(i)   The amounts of any charges imposed as part of a plan as stated in § 1026.6(b)(3), grouped together, in proximity to transactions identified under paragraph (b)(2) of this section, substantially similar to Sample G–18(A) in Appendix G to this part.

(ii)   Interest. Finance charges attributable to periodic interest rates, using the term Interest Charge, must be grouped together under the heading Interest Charged, itemized and totaled by type of transaction, and a total of finance charges attributable to periodic interest rates, using the term Total Interest, must be disclosed for the statement period and calendar year to date, using a format substantially similar to Sample G–18(A) in Appendix G to this part.

(iii)   Fees. Charges imposed as part of the plan other than charges attributable to periodic interest rates must be grouped together under the heading Fees, identified consistent with the feature or type, and itemized, and a total of charges, using the term Fees, must be disclosed for the statement period and calendar year to date, using a format substantially similar to Sample G–18(A) in Appendix G to this part.

(7)   Change-in-terms and increased penalty rate summary for open-end (not home-secured) plans. Creditors that provide a change-in-terms notice required by § 1026.9(c), or a rate increase notice required by § 1026.9(g), on or with the periodic statement, must disclose the information in § 1026.9(c)(2)(iv)(A) and (c)(2)(iv)(B) (if applicable) or § 1026.9(g)(3)(i) on the periodic statement in accordance with the format requirements in § 1026.9(c)(2)(iv)(D), and § 1026.9(g)(3)(ii). See Forms G–18(F) and G–18(G) in Appendix G to this part.

(8)   Grace period. The date by which or the time period within which the new balance or any portion of the new balance must be paid to avoid additional finance charges. If such a time period is provided, a creditor may, at its option and without disclosure, impose no finance charge if payment is received after the time period's expiration.

(9)   Address for notice of billing errors. The address to be used for notice of billing errors. Alternatively, the address may be provided on the billing rights statement permitted by § 1026.9(a)(2).

(10) Closing date of billing cycle; new balance. The closing date of the billing cycle and the account balance outstanding on that date. The new balance must be disclosed in accordance with the format requirements of paragraph (b)(13) of this section.

(11) Due date; late payment costs.

(i)   Except as provided in paragraph (b)(11)(ii) of this section and in accordance with the format requirements in paragraph (b)(13) of this section, for a credit card account under an open-end (not home-secured) consumer credit plan, a card issuer must provide on each periodic statement:

(A)   The due date for a payment. The due date disclosed pursuant to this paragraph shall be the same day of the month for each billing cycle.

(B)   The amount of any late payment fee and any increased periodic rate(s) (expressed as an annual percentage rate(s)) that may be imposed on the account as a result of a late payment. If a range of late payment fees may be assessed, the card issuer may state the range of fees, or the highest fee and an indication that the fee imposed could be lower. If the rate may be increased for more than one feature or balance, the card issuer may state the range of rates or the highest rate that could apply and at the issuer's option an indication that the rate imposed could be lower.

(ii) **Exception.** The requirements of paragraph (b)(11)(i) of this section do not apply to the following:

(A) Periodic statements provided solely for charge card accounts; and

(B) Periodic statements provided for a charged-off account where payment of the entire account balance is due immediately.

(12) **Repayment disclosures.**

(i) **In general.** Except as provided in paragraphs (b)(12)(ii) and (b)(12)(v) of this section, for a credit card account under an open-end (not home-secured) consumer credit plan, a card issuer must provide the following disclosures on each periodic statement:

(A) The following statement with a bold heading: "Minimum Payment Warning: If you make only the minimum payment each period, you will pay more in interest and it will take you longer to pay off your balance;"

(B) The minimum payment repayment estimate, as described in Appendix M1 to this part. If the minimum payment repayment estimate is less than 2 years, the card issuer must disclose the estimate in months. Otherwise, the estimate must be disclosed in years and rounded to the nearest whole year;

(C) The minimum payment total cost estimate, as described in Appendix M1 to this part. The minimum payment total cost estimate must be rounded either to the nearest whole dollar or to the nearest cent, at the card issuer's option;

(D) A statement that the minimum payment repayment estimate and the minimum payment total cost estimate are based on the current outstanding balance shown on the periodic statement. A statement that the minimum payment repayment estimate and the minimum payment total cost estimate are based on the assumption that only minimum payments are made and no other amounts are added to the balance;

(E) A toll-free telephone number where the consumer may obtain from the card issuer information about credit counseling services consistent with paragraph (b)(12)(iv) of this section; and

(F)(1) Except as provided in paragraph (b)(12)(i)(F)(2) of this section, the following disclosures:

(i) The estimated monthly payment for repayment in 36 months, as described in Appendix M1 to this part. The estimated monthly payment for repayment in 36 months must be rounded either to the nearest whole dollar or to the nearest cent, at the card issuer's option;

(ii) A statement that the card issuer estimates that the consumer will repay the outstanding balance shown on the periodic statement in 3 years if the consumer pays the estimated monthly payment each month for 3 years;

(iii) The total cost estimate for repayment in 36 months, as described in Appendix M1 to this part. The total cost estimate for repayment in 36 months must be rounded either to the nearest whole dollar or to the nearest cent, at the card issuer's option; and

(iv) The savings estimate for repayment in 36 months, as described in Appendix M1 to this part. The savings estimate for repayment in 36 months must be rounded either to the nearest whole dollar or to the nearest cent, at the card issuer's option.

(2) The requirements of paragraph (b)(12)(i)(F)(1) of this section do not apply to a periodic statement in any of the following circumstances:

(i) The minimum payment repayment estimate that is disclosed on the periodic statement pursuant to paragraph (b)(12)(i)(B) of this section after rounding is three years or less;

(ii) The estimated monthly payment for repayment in 36 months, as described in Appendix M1 to this part, after rounding as set forth in paragraph (b)(12)(i)(F)(1)(i) of this section that is calculated for a particular billing cycle is less than the minimum payment required for the plan for that billing cycle; and

(iii) A billing cycle where an account has both a balance in a revolving feature where the required minimum payments for this feature will not amortize that balance in a fixed amount of time specified in the account agreement and a balance in a fixed repayment feature where the required minimum payment for this fixed repayment feature will amortize that balance in a fixed amount of time specified in the account agreement which is less than 36 months.

(ii) Negative or no amortization. If negative or no amortization occurs when calculating the minimum payment repayment estimate as described in Appendix M1 of this part, a card issuer must provide the following disclosures on the periodic statement instead of the disclosures set forth in paragraph (b)(12)(i) of this section:

(A) The following statement: "Minimum Payment Warning: Even if you make no more charges using this card, if you make only the minimum payment each month we estimate you will never pay off the balance shown on this statement because your payment will be less than the interest charged each month";

(B) The following statement: "If you make more than the minimum payment each period, you will pay less in interest and pay off your balance sooner";

(C) The estimated monthly payment for repayment in 36 months, as described in Appendix M1 to this part. The estimated monthly payment for repayment in 36 months must be rounded either to the nearest whole dollar or to the nearest cent, at the issuer's option;

(D) A statement that the card issuer estimates that the consumer will repay the outstanding balance shown on the periodic statement in 3 years if the consumer pays the estimated monthly payment each month for 3 years; and

(E) A toll-free telephone number where the consumer may obtain from the card issuer information about credit counseling services consistent with paragraph (b)(12)(iv) of this section.

(iii) Format requirements. A card issuer must provide the disclosures required by paragraph (b)(12)(i) or (b)(12)(ii) of this section in accordance with the format requirements of paragraph (b)(13) of this section, and in a format substantially similar to Samples G–18(C)(1), G–18(C)(2) and G–18(C)(3) in Appendix G to this part, as applicable.

(iv) Provision of information about credit counseling services.

(A) Required information. To the extent available from the United States Trustee or a bankruptcy administrator, a card issuer must provide through the toll-free telephone number disclosed pursuant to paragraphs (b)(12)(i) or (b)(12)(ii) of this section the name, street address, telephone number, and Web site address for at least three organizations that have been approved by the United States Trustee or a bankruptcy administrator pursuant to 11 U.S.C. 111(a)(1) to provide credit counseling services in, at the card issuer's option, either the state in which the billing address for the account is located or the state specified by the consumer.

(B) Updating required information. At least annually, a card issuer must update the information provided pursuant to paragraph (b)(12)(iv)(A) of this section for consistency with the information available from the United States Trustee or a bankruptcy administrator.

(v) Exemptions. Paragraph (b)(12) of this section does not apply to:

(A) Charge card accounts that require payment of outstanding balances in full at the end of each billing cycle;

(B) A billing cycle immediately following two consecutive billing cycles in which the consumer paid the entire balance in full, had a zero outstanding balance or had a credit balance; and

(C) A billing cycle where paying the minimum payment due for that billing cycle will pay the entire outstanding balance on the account for that billing cycle.

(13) Format requirements. The due date required by paragraph (b)(11) of this section shall be disclosed on the front of the first page of the periodic statement. The amount of the late payment fee and the annual percentage rate(s) required by paragraph (b)(11) of this section shall be stated in close proximity to the due date. The ending balance required by paragraph (b)(10) of this section and the disclosures required by paragraph (b)(12) of this section shall be disclosed closely proximate to the minimum payment due. The due date, late payment fee and annual percentage rate, ending balance, minimum payment due, and disclosures required by paragraph (b)(12) of this section shall be grouped together. Sample G–18(D) in Appendix G to this part sets forth an example of how these terms may be grouped.

(14) Deferred interest or similar transactions. For accounts with an outstanding balance subject to a deferred interest or similar program, the date by which that outstanding balance must be paid in full in order to avoid the obligation to pay finance charges on such balance must be disclosed on the front of any page of each periodic statement issued during the deferred interest period beginning with the first periodic statement issued during the deferred interest period that reflects the deferred interest or similar transaction. The disclosure provided pursuant to this paragraph must be substantially similar to Sample G–18(H) in Appendix G to this part.

§ 1026.8   Identifying transactions on periodic statements.

The creditor shall identify credit transactions on or with the first periodic statement that reflects the transaction by furnishing the following information, as applicable:

(a) Sale credit.

(1) Except as provided in paragraph (a)(2) of this section, for each credit transaction involving the sale of property or services, the creditor must disclose the amount and date of the transaction, and either:

(i) A brief identification of the property or services purchased, for creditors and sellers that are the same or related; or

(ii) The seller's name; and the city and state or foreign country where the transaction took place. The creditor may omit the address or provide any suitable designation that helps the consumer to identify the transaction when the transaction took place at a location that is not fixed; took place in the consumer's home; or was a mail, Internet, or telephone order.

(2) Creditors need not comply with paragraph (a)(1) of this section if an actual copy of the receipt or other credit document is provided with the first periodic statement reflecting the transaction, and the amount of the transaction and either the date of the transaction to the consumer's account or the date of debiting the transaction are disclosed on the copy or on the periodic statement.

(b) Nonsale credit. For each credit transaction not involving the sale of property or services, the creditor must disclose a brief identification of the transaction; the amount of the transaction; and at least one of the following dates: The date of the transaction, the date the transaction was debited to the consumer's account, or, if the consumer signed the credit document, the date appearing on the document. If an actual copy of the receipt or other credit document is provided and that copy shows the amount and at least one of the specified dates, the brief identification may be omitted.

(c) Alternative creditor procedures; consumer inquiries for clarification or documentation. The following procedures apply to creditors that treat an inquiry for clarification or documentation as a notice of a billing error, including correcting the account in accordance with § 1026.13(e):

(1) Failure to disclose the information required by paragraphs (a) and (b) of this section is not a failure to comply with the regulation, provided that the creditor also maintains procedures reasonably designed to obtain and provide the information. This applies to transactions that take place outside a state, as defined in § 1026.2(a)(26), whether or not the creditor maintains procedures reasonably adapted to obtain the required information.

(2) As an alternative to the brief identification for sale or nonsale credit, the creditor may disclose a number or symbol that also appears on the receipt or other credit document given to the consumer, if the number or symbol reasonably identifies that transaction with that creditor.

§ 1026.9   Subsequent disclosure requirements.

(a) Furnishing statement of billing rights.

(1) **Annual statement.** The creditor shall mail or deliver the billing rights statement required by § 1026.6(a)(5) and (b)(5)(iii) at least once per calendar year, at intervals of not less than 6 months nor more than 18 months, either to all consumers or to each consumer entitled to receive a periodic statement under § 1026.5(b)(2) for any one billing cycle.

(2) **Alternative summary statement.** As an alternative to paragraph (a)(1) of this section, the creditor may mail or deliver, on or with each periodic statement, a statement substantially similar to Model Form G–4 or Model Form G–4(A) in Appendix G to this part, as applicable. Creditors offering home-equity plans subject to the requirements of § 1026.40 may use either Model Form, at their option.

(b) Disclosures for supplemental credit access devices and additional features.

(1) If a creditor, within 30 days after mailing or delivering the account-opening disclosures under § 1026.6(a)(1) or (b)(3)(ii)(A), as applicable, adds a credit feature to the consumer's account or mails or delivers to the consumer a credit access device, including but not limited to checks that access a credit card account, for which the finance charge terms are the same as those previously disclosed, no additional disclosures are necessary. Except as provided in paragraph (b)(3) of this section, after 30 days, if the creditor adds a credit feature or furnishes a credit access device (other than as a renewal, resupply, or the original issuance of a credit card) on the same finance charge terms, the creditor shall disclose, before the consumer uses the feature or device for the first time, that it is for use in obtaining credit under the terms previously disclosed.

(2) Except as provided in paragraph (b)(3) of this section, whenever a credit feature is added or a credit access device is mailed or delivered to the consumer, and the finance charge terms for the feature or device differ from disclosures previously given, the disclosures required by § 1026.6(a)(1) or (b)(3)(ii)(A), as applicable, that are applicable to the added feature or device shall be given before the consumer uses the feature or device for the first time.

(3) **Checks that access a credit card account.**

(i) **Disclosures.** For open-end plans not subject to the requirements of § 1026.40, if checks that can be used to access a credit card account are provided more than 30 days after account-opening disclosures under § 1026.6(b) are mailed or delivered, or are provided within 30 days of the account-opening disclosures and the finance charge terms for the checks differ from the finance charge terms previously disclosed, the creditor shall disclose on the front of the page containing the checks the following terms in the form of a table with the headings, content, and form substantially similar to Sample G–19 in Appendix G to this part:

(A) If a promotional rate, as that term is defined in § 1026.16(g)(2)(i) applies to the checks:

(1) The promotional rate and the time period during which the promotional rate will remain in effect;

(2) The type of rate that will apply (such as whether the purchase or cash advance rate applies) after the promotional rate expires, and the annual percentage rate that will apply after the promotional rate expires. For a variable-rate account, a creditor must disclose an annual percentage rate based on the applicable index or formula in accordance with the accuracy requirements set forth in paragraph (b)(3)(ii) of this section; and

(3) The date, if any, by which the consumer must use the checks in order to qualify for the promotional rate. If the creditor will honor checks used after such date but will apply an annual percentage rate other than the promotional rate, the creditor must disclose this fact and the type of annual percentage rate that will apply if the consumer uses the checks after such date.

(B) If no promotional rate applies to the checks:

(1) The type of rate that will apply to the checks and the applicable annual percentage rate. For a variable-rate account, a creditor must disclose an annual percentage rate based on the applicable index or formula in accordance with the accuracy requirements set forth in paragraph (b)(3)(ii) of this section.

(2) [Reserved]

(C) Any transaction fees applicable to the checks disclosed under § 1026.6(b)(2)(iv); and

(D) Whether or not a grace period is given within which any credit extended by use of the checks may be repaid without incurring a finance charge due to a periodic interest rate. When disclosing whether there is a grace period, the phrase "How to Avoid Paying Interest on Check Transactions" shall be used as the row heading when a grace period applies to credit extended by the use of the checks. When disclosing the fact that no grace period exists for credit extended by use of the checks, the phrase "Paying Interest" shall be used as the row heading.

(ii) Accuracy. The disclosures in paragraph (b)(3)(i) of this section must be accurate as of the time the disclosures are mailed or delivered. A variable annual percentage rate is accurate if it was in effect within 60 days of when the disclosures are mailed or delivered.

(iii) Variable rates. If any annual percentage rate required to be disclosed pursuant to paragraph (b)(3)(i) of this section is a variable rate, the card issuer shall also disclose the fact that the rate may vary and how the rate is determined. In describing how the applicable rate will be determined, the card issuer must identify the type of index or formula that is used in setting the rate. The value of the index and the amount of the margin that are used to calculate the variable rate shall not be disclosed in the table. A disclosure of any applicable limitations on rate increases shall not be included in the table.

(c) **Change in terms.**

(1) **Rules affecting home-equity plans.**

(i) Written notice required. For home-equity plans subject to the requirements of § 1026.40, whenever any term required to be disclosed under § 1026.6(a) is changed or the required minimum periodic payment is increased, the creditor shall mail or deliver written notice of the change to each consumer who may be affected. The notice shall be mailed or delivered at least 15 days prior to the effective date of the change. The 15-day timing requirement does not apply if the change has been agreed to by the consumer; the notice shall be given, however, before the effective date of the change.

(ii) Notice not required. For home-equity plans subject to the requirements of § 1026.40, a creditor is not required to provide notice under this section when the change involves a reduction of any component of a finance or other charge or when the change results from an agreement involving a court proceeding.

(iii) Notice to restrict credit. For home-equity plans subject to the requirements of § 1026.40, if the creditor prohibits additional extensions of credit or reduces the credit limit pursuant to § 1026.40(f)(3)(i) or (f)(3)(vi), the creditor shall mail or deliver written notice of the action to each consumer who will be affected. The notice must be provided not later than three business days after the action is taken and shall contain specific reasons for the action. If the creditor requires the consumer to request reinstatement of credit privileges, the notice also shall state that fact.

(2) Rules affecting open-end (not home-secured) plans.

(i) Changes where written advance notice is required.

(A) General. For plans other than home-equity plans subject to the requirements of § 1026.40, except as provided in paragraphs (c)(2)(i)(B), (c)(2)(iii) and (c)(2)(v) of this section, when a significant change in account terms as described in paragraph (c)(2)(ii) of this section is made, a creditor must provide a written notice of the change at least 45 days prior to the effective date of the change to each consumer who may be affected. The 45-day timing requirement does not apply if the consumer has agreed to a particular change as described in paragraph (c)(2)(i)(B) of this section; for such changes, notice must be given in accordance with the timing requirements of paragraph (c)(2)(i)(B) of this section. Increases in the rate applicable to a consumer's account due to delinquency, default or as a penalty described in paragraph (g) of this section that are not due to a change in the contractual terms of the consumer's account must be disclosed pursuant to paragraph (g) of this section instead of paragraph (c)(2) of this section.

(B) Changes agreed to by the consumer. A notice of change in terms is required, but it may be mailed or delivered as late as the effective date of the change if the consumer agrees to the particular change. This paragraph (c)(2)(i)(B) applies only when a consumer substitutes collateral or when the creditor can advance additional credit only if a change relatively unique to that consumer is made, such as the consumer's providing additional security or paying an increased minimum payment amount. The following are not considered agreements between the consumer and the creditor for purposes of this paragraph (c)(2)(i)(B): The consumer's general acceptance of the creditor's contract reservation of the right to change terms; the consumer's use of the account (which might imply acceptance of its terms under state law); the consumer's acceptance of a unilateral term change that is not particular to that consumer, but rather is of general applicability to consumers with that type of account; and the consumer's request to reopen a closed account or to upgrade an existing account to another account offered by the creditor with different credit or other features.

(ii) Significant changes in account terms. For purposes of this section, a "significant change in account terms" means a change to a term required to be disclosed under § 1026.6(b)(1) and (b)(2), an increase in the required minimum periodic payment, a change to a term required to be disclosed under § 1026.6(b)(4), or the acquisition of a security interest.

(iii) Charges not covered by § 1026.6(b)(1) and (b)(2). Except as provided in paragraph (c)(2)(vi) of this section, if a creditor increases any component of a charge, or introduces a new charge, required to be disclosed under § 1026.6(b)(3) that is not a significant change in account terms as described in paragraph (c)(2)(ii) of this section, a creditor must either, at its option:

(A) Comply with the requirements of paragraph (c)(2)(i) of this section; or

(B) Provide notice of the amount of the charge before the consumer agrees to or becomes obligated to pay the charge, at a time and in a manner that a consumer would be likely to notice the disclosure of the charge. The notice may be provided orally or in writing.

(iv) Disclosure requirements.

(A) Significant changes in account terms. If a creditor makes a significant change in account terms as described in paragraph (c)(2)(ii) of this section, the notice provided pursuant to paragraph (c)(2)(i) of this section must provide the following information:

(1) A summary of the changes made to terms required by § 1026.6(b)(1) and (b)(2) or § 1026.6(b)(4), a description of any increase in the required minimum periodic payment, and a description of any security interest being acquired by the creditor;

(2) A statement that changes are being made to the account;

(3) For accounts other than credit card accounts under an open-end (not home-secured) consumer credit plan subject to § 1026.9(c)(2)(iv)(B), a statement indicating the consumer has the right to opt out of these changes, if applicable, and a reference to additional information describing the opt-out right provided in the notice, if applicable;

(4) The date the changes will become effective;

(5) If applicable, a statement that the consumer may find additional information about the summarized changes, and other changes to the account, in the notice;

(6) If the creditor is changing a rate on the account, other than a penalty rate, a statement that if a penalty rate currently applies to the consumer's account, the new rate described in the notice will not apply to the consumer's account until the consumer's account balances are no longer subject to the penalty rate;

(7) If the change in terms being disclosed is an increase in an annual percentage rate, the balances to which the increased rate will be applied. If applicable, a statement identifying the balances to which the current rate will continue to apply as of the effective date of the change in terms; and

(8) If the change in terms being disclosed is an increase in an annual percentage rate for a credit card account under an open-end (not home-secured) consumer credit plan, a statement of no more than four principal reasons for the rate increase, listed in their order of importance.

(B) Right to reject for credit card accounts under an open-end (not home-secured) credit plan. In addition to the disclosures in paragraph (c)(2)(iv)(A) of this section, if a card issuer makes a significant change in account terms on a credit card account under an open-end (not home-secured) consumer credit plan, the creditor must generally provide the following information on the notice provided pursuant to paragraph (c)(2)(i) of this section. This information is not required to be provided in the case of an increase in the required minimum periodic payment, an increase in a fee as a result of a reevaluation of a determination made under § 1026.52(b)(1)(i) or an adjustment to the safe harbors in § 1026.52(b)(1)(ii) to reflect changes in the Consumer Price Index, a change in an annual percentage rate applicable to a consumer's account, an increase in a fee previously reduced consistent with 50 U.S.C. app. 527 or a similar Federal or state statute or regulation if the amount of the increased fee does not exceed the amount of that fee prior to the reduction, or when the change results from the creditor not receiving the consumer's required minimum periodic payment within 60 days after the due date for that payment:

(1) A statement that the consumer has the right to reject the change or changes prior to the effective date of the changes, unless the consumer fails to make a required minimum periodic payment within 60 days after the due date for that payment;

(2) Instructions for rejecting the change or changes, and a toll-free telephone number that the consumer may use to notify the creditor of the rejection; and

(3) If applicable, a statement that if the consumer rejects the change or changes, the consumer's ability to use the account for further advances will be terminated or suspended.

(C) Changes resulting from failure to make minimum periodic payment within 60 days from due date for credit card accounts under an open-end (not home-secured) consumer credit plan. For a credit card account under an open-end (not home-secured) consumer credit plan:

(1) If the significant change required to be disclosed pursuant to paragraph (c)(2)(i) of this section is an increase in an annual percentage rate or a fee or charge required to be disclosed under § 1026.6(b)(2)(ii), (b)(2)(iii), or (b)(2)(xii) based on the consumer's failure to make a minimum periodic payment within 60 days from the due date for that payment, the notice provided pursuant to paragraph (c)(2)(i) of this section must state that the increase will cease to apply to transactions that occurred prior to or within 14 days of provision of the notice, if the creditor receives six consecutive required minimum periodic payments on or before the payment due date, beginning with the first payment due following the effective date of the increase.

(2) If the significant change required to be disclosed pursuant to paragraph (c)(2)(i) of this section is an increase in a fee or charge required to be disclosed under § 1026.6(b)(2)(ii), (b)(2)(iii), or (b)(2)(xii) based on the consumer's failure to make a minimum periodic payment within 60 days from the due date for that payment, the notice provided pursuant to paragraph (c)(2)(i) of this section must also state the reason for the increase.

(D) Format requirements.

(1) **Tabular format.** The summary of changes described in paragraph (c)(2)(iv)(A)(1) of this section must be in a tabular format (except for a summary of any increase in the required minimum periodic payment, a summary of a term required to be disclosed under § 1026.6(b)(4) that is not required to be disclosed under § 1026.6(b)(1) and (b)(2), or a description of any security interest being acquired by the creditor), with headings and format substantially similar to any of the account-opening tables found in G–17 in Appendix G to this part. The table must disclose the changed term and information relevant to the change, if that relevant information is required by § 1026.6(b)(1) and (b)(2). The new terms shall be described in the same level of detail as required when disclosing the terms under § 1026.6(b)(2).

(2) **Notice included with periodic statement.** If a notice required by paragraph (c)(2)(i) of this section is included on or with a periodic statement, the information described in paragraph (c)(2)(iv)(A)(1) of this section must be disclosed on the front of any page of the statement. The summary of changes described in paragraph (c)(2)(iv)(A)(1) of this section must immediately follow the information described in paragraph (c)(2)(iv)(A)(2) through (c)(2)(iv)(A)(7) and, if applicable, paragraphs (c)(2)(iv)(A)(8), (c)(2)(iv)(B), and (c)(2)(iv)(C) of this section, and be substantially similar to the format shown in Sample G–20 or G–21 in Appendix G to this part.

(3) **Notice provided separately from periodic statement.** If a notice required by paragraph (c)(2)(i) of this section is not included on or with a periodic statement, the information described in paragraph (c)(2)(iv)(A)(1) of this section must, at the creditor's option, be disclosed on the front of the first page of the notice or segregated on a separate page from other information given with the notice. The summary of changes required to be in a table pursuant to paragraph (c)(2)(iv)(A)(1) of this section may be on more than one page, and may use both the front and reverse sides, so long as the table begins on the front of the first page of the notice and there is a reference on the first page indicating that the table continues on the following page. The summary of changes described in paragraph (c)(2)(iv)(A)(1) of this section must immediately follow the information described in paragraph (c)(2)(iv)(A)(2) through (c)(2)(iv)(A)(7) and, if applicable, paragraphs (c)(2)(iv)(A)(8), (c)(2)(iv)(B), and (c)(2)(iv)(C), of this section, substantially similar to the format shown in Sample G–20 or G–21 in Appendix G to this part.

(v) Notice not required. For open-end plans (other than home equity plans subject to the requirements of § 1026.40) a creditor is not required to provide notice under this section:

(A) When the change involves charges for documentary evidence; a reduction of any component of a finance or other charge; suspension of future credit privileges (except as provided in paragraph (c)(2)(vi) of this section) or termination of an account or plan; when the change results from an agreement involving a court proceeding; when the change is an extension of the grace period; or if the change is applicable only to checks that access a credit card account and the changed terms are disclosed on or with the checks in accordance with paragraph (b)(3) of this section;

(B) When the change is an increase in an annual percentage rate or fee upon the expiration of a specified period of time, provided that:

(1) Prior to commencement of that period, the creditor disclosed in writing to the consumer, in a clear and conspicuous manner, the length of the period and the annual percentage rate or fee that would apply after expiration of the period;

(2) The disclosure of the length of the period and the annual percentage rate or fee that would apply after expiration of the period are set forth in close proximity and in equal prominence to the first listing of the disclosure of the rate or fee that applies during the specified period of time; and

(3) The annual percentage rate or fee that applies after that period does not exceed the rate or fee disclosed pursuant to paragraph (c)(2)(v)(B)(1) of this paragraph or, if the rate disclosed pursuant to paragraph (c)(2)(v)(B)(1) of this section was a variable rate, the rate following any such increase is a variable rate determined by the same formula (index and margin) that was used to calculate the variable rate disclosed pursuant to paragraph (c)(2)(v)(B)(1);

(C) When the change is an increase in a variable annual percentage rate in accordance with a credit card or other account agreement that provides for changes in the rate according to operation of an index that is not under the control of the creditor and is available to the general public; or

(D) When the change is an increase in an annual percentage rate, a fee or charge required to be disclosed under § 1026.6(b)(2)(ii), (b)(2)(iii), (b)(2)(viii), (b)(2)(ix), or (b)(2)(xii), or the required minimum periodic payment due to the completion of a workout or temporary hardship arrangement by the consumer or the consumer's failure to comply with the terms of such an arrangement, provided that:

(1) The annual percentage rate or fee or charge applicable to a category of transactions or the required minimum periodic payment following any such increase does not exceed the rate or fee or charge or required minimum periodic payment that applied to that category of transactions prior to commencement of the arrangement or, if the rate that applied to a category of transactions prior to the commencement of the workout or temporary hardship arrangement was a variable rate, the rate following any such increase is a variable rate determined by the same formula (index and margin) that applied to the category of transactions prior to commencement of the workout or temporary hardship arrangement; and

(2) The creditor has provided the consumer, prior to the commencement of such arrangement, with a clear and conspicuous disclosure of the terms of the arrangement (including any increases due to such completion or failure). This disclosure must generally be provided in writing. However, a creditor may provide the disclosure of the terms of the arrangement orally by telephone, provided that the creditor mails or delivers a written disclosure of the terms of the arrangement to the consumer as soon as reasonably practicable after the oral disclosure is provided.

(vi) Reduction of the credit limit. For open-end plans that are not subject to the requirements of § 1026.40, if a creditor decreases the credit limit on an account, advance notice of the decrease must be provided before an over-the-limit fee or a penalty rate can be imposed solely as a result of the consumer exceeding the newly decreased credit limit. Notice shall be provided in writing or orally at least 45 days prior to imposing the over-the-limit fee or penalty rate and shall state that the credit limit on the account has been or will be decreased.

(d) Finance charge imposed at time of transaction.

(1)   Any person, other than the card issuer, who imposes a finance charge at the time of honoring a consumer's credit card, shall disclose the amount of that finance charge prior to its imposition.

(2)   The card issuer, other than the person honoring the consumer's credit card, shall have no responsibility for the disclosure required by paragraph (d)(1) of this section, and shall not consider any such charge for the purposes of §§ 1026.60, 1026.6 and 1026.7.

(e)   Disclosures upon renewal of credit or charge card.

(1)   **Notice prior to renewal.** A card issuer that imposes any annual or other periodic fee to renew a credit or charge card account of the type subject to § 1026.60, including any fee based on account activity or inactivity or any card issuer that has changed or amended any term of a cardholder's account required to be disclosed under § 1026.6(b)(1) and (b)(2) that has not previously been disclosed to the consumer, shall mail or deliver written notice of the renewal to the cardholder. If the card issuer imposes any annual or other periodic fee for renewal, the notice shall be provided at least 30 days or one billing cycle, whichever is less, before the mailing or the delivery of the periodic statement on which any renewal fee is initially charged to the account. If the card issuer has changed or amended any term required to be disclosed under § 1026.6(b)(1) and (b)(2) and such changed or amended term has not previously been disclosed to the consumer, the notice shall be provided at least 30 days prior to the scheduled renewal date of the consumer's credit or charge card. The notice shall contain the following information:

(i)   The disclosures contained in § 1026.60(b)(1) through (b)(7) that would apply if the account were renewed; and

(ii)   How and when the cardholder may terminate credit availability under the account to avoid paying the renewal fee, if applicable.

(2)   **Notification on periodic statements.** The disclosures required by this paragraph may be made on or with a periodic statement. If any of the disclosures are provided on the back of a periodic statement, the card issuer shall include a reference to those disclosures on the front of the statement.

(f)   Change in credit card account insurance provider.

(1)   **Notice prior to change.** If a credit card issuer plans to change the provider of insurance for repayment of all or part of the outstanding balance of an open-end credit card account of the type subject to § 1026.60, the card issuer shall mail or deliver to the cardholder written notice of the change not less than 30 days before the change in provider occurs. The notice shall also include the following items, to the extent applicable:

(i)   Any increase in the rate that will result from the change;

(ii)   Any substantial decrease in coverage that will result from the change; and

(iii)   A statement that the cardholder may discontinue the insurance.

(2)   **Notice when change in provider occurs.** If a change described in paragraph (f)(1) of this section occurs, the card issuer shall provide the cardholder with a written notice no later than 30 days after the change, including the following items, to the extent applicable:

(i)   The name and address of the new insurance provider;

(ii)   A copy of the new policy or group certificate containing the basic terms of the insurance, including the rate to be charged; and

(iii) A statement that the cardholder may discontinue the insurance.

(3) **Substantial decrease in coverage.** For purposes of this paragraph, a substantial decrease in coverage is a decrease in a significant term of coverage that might reasonably be expected to affect the cardholder's decision to continue the insurance. Significant terms of coverage include, for example, the following:

(i) Type of coverage provided;

(ii) Age at which coverage terminates or becomes more restrictive;

(iii) Maximum insurable loan balance, maximum periodic benefit payment, maximum number of payments, or other term affecting the dollar amount of coverage or benefits provided;

(iv) Eligibility requirements and number and identity of persons covered;

(v) Definition of a key term of coverage such as disability;

(vi) Exclusions from or limitations on coverage; and

(vii) Waiting periods and whether coverage is retroactive.

(4) **Combined notification.** The notices required by paragraph (f)(1) and (2) of this section may be combined provided the timing requirement of paragraph (f)(1) of this section is met. The notices may be provided on or with a periodic statement.

(g) **Increase in rates due to delinquency or default or as a penalty.**

(1) **Increases subject to this section.** For plans other than home-equity plans subject to the requirements of § 1026.40, except as provided in paragraph (g)(4) of this section, a creditor must provide a written notice to each consumer who may be affected when:

(i) A rate is increased due to the consumer's delinquency or default; or

(ii) A rate is increased as a penalty for one or more events specified in the account agreement, such as making a late payment or obtaining an extension of credit that exceeds the credit limit.

(2) **Timing of written notice.** Whenever any notice is required to be given pursuant to paragraph (g)(1) of this section, the creditor shall provide written notice of the increase in rates at least 45 days prior to the effective date of the increase. The notice must be provided after the occurrence of the events described in paragraphs (g)(1)(i) and (g)(1)(ii) of this section that trigger the imposition of the rate increase.

(3)(i) **Disclosure requirements for rate increases.**

(A) **General.** If a creditor is increasing the rate due to delinquency or default or as a penalty, the creditor must provide the following information on the notice sent pursuant to paragraph (g)(1) of this section:

(1) A statement that the delinquency or default rate or penalty rate, as applicable, has been triggered;

(2) The date on which the delinquency or default rate or penalty rate will apply;

(3) The circumstances under which the delinquency or default rate or penalty rate, as applicable, will cease to apply to the consumer's account, or that the delinquency or default rate or penalty rate will remain in effect for a potentially indefinite time period;

(4) A statement indicating to which balances the delinquency or default rate or penalty rate will be applied;

(5) If applicable, a description of any balances to which the current rate will continue to apply as of the effective date of the rate increase, unless a consumer fails to make a minimum periodic payment within 60 days from the due date for that payment; and

(6)   For a credit card account under an open-end (not home-secured) consumer credit plan, a statement of no more than four principal reasons for the rate increase, listed in their order of importance.

(B) Rate increases resulting from failure to make minimum periodic payment within 60 days from due date. For a credit card account under an open-end (not home-secured) consumer credit plan, if the rate increase required to be disclosed pursuant to paragraph (g)(1) of this section is an increase pursuant to § 1026.55(b)(4) based on the consumer's failure to make a minimum periodic payment within 60 days from the due date for that payment, the notice provided pursuant to paragraph (g)(1) of this section must also state that the increase will cease to apply to transactions that occurred prior to or within 14 days of provision of the notice, if the creditor receives six consecutive required minimum periodic payments on or before the payment due date, beginning with the first payment due following the effective date of the increase.

(ii)   Format requirements.

(A)   If a notice required by paragraph (g)(1) of this section is included on or with a periodic statement, the information described in paragraph (g)(3)(i) of this section must be in the form of a table and provided on the front of any page of the periodic statement, above the notice described in paragraph (c)(2)(iv) of this section if that notice is provided on the same statement.

(B)   If a notice required by paragraph (g)(1) of this section is not included on or with a periodic statement, the information described in paragraph (g)(3)(i) of this section must be disclosed on the front of the first page of the notice. Only information related to the increase in the rate to a penalty rate may be included with the notice, except that this notice may be combined with a notice described in paragraph (c)(2)(iv) or (g)(4) of this section.

(4)   Exception for decrease in credit limit. A creditor is not required to provide a notice pursuant to paragraph (g)(1) of this section prior to increasing the rate for obtaining an extension of credit that exceeds the credit limit, provided that:

(i)   The creditor provides at least 45 days in advance of imposing the penalty rate a notice, in writing, that includes:

(A)   A statement that the credit limit on the account has been or will be decreased.

(B)   A statement indicating the date on which the penalty rate will apply, if the outstanding balance exceeds the credit limit as of that date;

(C)   A statement that the penalty rate will not be imposed on the date specified in paragraph (g)(4)(i)(B) of this section, if the outstanding balance does not exceed the credit limit as of that date;

(D)   The circumstances under which the penalty rate, if applied, will cease to apply to the account, or that the penalty rate, if applied, will remain in effect for a potentially indefinite time period;

(E)   A statement indicating to which balances the penalty rate may be applied; and

(F)   If applicable, a description of any balances to which the current rate will continue to apply as of the effective date of the rate increase, unless the consumer fails to make a minimum periodic payment within 60 days from the due date for that payment; and

(ii)   The creditor does not increase the rate applicable to the consumer's account to the penalty rate if the outstanding balance does not exceed the credit limit on the date set forth in the notice and described in paragraph (g)(4)(i)(B) of this section.

(iii)(A) If a notice provided pursuant to paragraph (g)(4)(i) of this section is included on or with a periodic statement, the information described in paragraph (g)(4)(i) of this section must be in the form of a table and provided on the front of any page of the periodic statement; or

(B) If a notice required by paragraph (g)(4)(i) of this section is not included on or with a periodic statement, the information described in paragraph (g)(4)(i) of this section must be disclosed on the front of the first page of the notice. Only information related to the reduction in credit limit may be included with the notice, except that this notice may be combined with a notice described in paragraph (c)(2)(iv) or (g)(1) of this section.

(h) Consumer rejection of certain significant changes in terms.

(1) Right to reject. If paragraph (c)(2)(iv)(B) of this section requires disclosure of the consumer's right to reject a significant change to an account term, the consumer may reject that change by notifying the creditor of the rejection before the effective date of the change.

(2) Effect of rejection. If a creditor is notified of a rejection of a significant change to an account term as provided in paragraph (h)(1) of this section, the creditor must not:

(i) Apply the change to the account;

(ii) Impose a fee or charge or treat the account as in default solely as a result of the rejection; or

(iii) Require repayment of the balance on the account using a method that is less beneficial to the consumer than one of the methods listed in § 1026.55(c)(2).

(3) Exception. Section 1026.9(h) does not apply when the creditor has not received the consumer's required minimum periodic payment within 60 days after the due date for that payment.

§ 1026.10 Payments.

(a) General rule. A creditor shall credit a payment to the consumer's account as of the date of receipt, except when a delay in crediting does not result in a finance or other charge or except as provided in paragraph (b) of this section.

(b) Specific requirements for payments.

(1) General rule. A creditor may specify reasonable requirements for payments that enable most consumers to make conforming payments.

(2) Examples of reasonable requirements for payments. Reasonable requirements for making payment may include:

(i) Requiring that payments be accompanied by the account number or payment stub;

(ii) Setting reasonable cut-off times for payments to be received by mail, by electronic means, by telephone, and in person (except as provided in paragraph (b)(3) of this section), provided that such cut-off times shall be no earlier than 5 p.m. on the payment due date at the location specified by the creditor for the receipt of such payments;

(iii) Specifying that only checks or money orders should be sent by mail;

(iv) Specifying that payment is to be made in U.S. dollars; or

(v) Specifying one particular address for receiving payments, such as a post office box.

(3) In-person payments on credit card accounts.

(i) General. Notwithstanding § 1026.10(b), payments on a credit card account under an open-end (not home-secured) consumer credit plan made in person at a branch or office of a card issuer that is a financial institution prior to the close of business of that branch or office shall be considered received on the date on which the consumer makes the payment. A card issuer that is a financial institution shall not impose a cut-off time earlier than the close of business for any such payments made in person at any branch or office of the card issuer at which such payments are accepted. Notwithstanding § 1026.10(b)(2)(ii), a card issuer may impose a cut-off time earlier than 5 p.m. for such payments, if the close of business of the branch or office is earlier than 5 p.m.

(ii) **Financial institution.** For purposes of paragraph (b)(3) of this section, "financial institution" shall mean a bank, savings association, or credit union.

(4) **Nonconforming payments.**

(i) **In general.** Except as provided in paragraph (b)(4)(ii) of this section, if a creditor specifies, on or with the periodic statement, requirements for the consumer to follow in making payments as permitted under this § 1026.10, but accepts a payment that does not conform to the requirements, the creditor shall credit the payment within five days of receipt.

(ii) **Payment methods promoted by creditor.** If a creditor promotes a method for making payments, such payments shall be considered conforming payments in accordance with this paragraph (b) and shall be credited to the consumer's account as of the date of receipt, except when a delay in crediting does not result in a finance or other charge.

(c) **Adjustment of account.** If a creditor fails to credit a payment, as required by paragraphs (a) or (b) of this section, in time to avoid the imposition of finance or other charges, the creditor shall adjust the consumer's account so that the charges imposed are credited to the consumer's account during the next billing cycle.

(d) **Crediting of payments when creditor does not receive or accept payments on due date.**

(1) **General.** Except as provided in paragraph (d)(2) of this section, if a creditor does not receive or accept payments by mail on the due date for payments, the creditor may generally not treat a payment received the next business day as late for any purpose. For purposes of this paragraph (d), the "next business day" means the next day on which the creditor accepts or receives payments by mail.

(2) **Payments accepted or received other than by mail.** If a creditor accepts or receives payments made on the due date by a method other than mail, such as electronic or telephone payments, the creditor is not required to treat a payment made by that method on the next business day as timely, even if it does not accept mailed payments on the due date.

(e) **Limitations on fees related to method of payment.** For credit card accounts under an open-end (not home-secured) consumer credit plan, a creditor may not impose a separate fee to allow consumers to make a payment by any method, such as mail, electronic, or telephone payments, unless such payment method involves an expedited service by a customer service representative of the creditor. For purposes of paragraph (e) of this section, the term "creditor" includes a third party that collects, receives, or processes payments on behalf of a creditor.

(f) **Changes by card issuer.** If a card issuer makes a material change in the address for receiving payments or procedures for handling payments, and such change causes a material delay in the crediting of a payment to the consumer's account during the 60-day period following the date on which such change took effect, the card issuer may not impose any late fee or finance charge for a late payment on the credit card account during the 60-day period following the date on which the change took effect.

§ 1026.11   Treatment of credit balances; account termination.

(a) **Credit balances.** When a credit balance in excess of $1 is created on a credit account (through transmittal of funds to a creditor in excess of the total balance due on an account, through rebates of unearned finance charges or insurance premiums, or through amounts otherwise owed to or held for the benefit of the consumer), the creditor shall:

(1) Credit the amount of the credit balance to the consumer's account;

(2) Refund any part of the remaining credit balance within seven business days from receipt of a written request from the consumer;

(3) Make a good faith effort to refund to the consumer by cash, check, or money order, or credit to a deposit account of the consumer, any part of the credit balance remaining in the account for more than six months. No further action is required if the consumer's current location is not known to the creditor and cannot be traced through the consumer's last known address or telephone number.

(b) Account termination.

(1) A creditor shall not terminate an account prior to its expiration date solely because the consumer does not incur a finance charge.

(2) Nothing in paragraph (b)(1) of this section prohibits a creditor from terminating an account that is inactive for three or more consecutive months. An account is inactive for purposes of this paragraph if no credit has been extended (such as by purchase, cash advance or balance transfer) and if the account has no outstanding balance.

(c) Timely settlement of estate debts.

(1) General rule.

(i) Reasonable policies and procedures required. For credit card accounts under an open-end (not home-secured) consumer credit plan, card issuers must adopt reasonable written policies and procedures designed to ensure that an administrator of an estate of a deceased accountholder can determine the amount of and pay any balance on the account in a timely manner.

(ii) Application to joint accounts. Paragraph (c) of this section does not apply to the account of a deceased consumer if a joint accountholder remains on the account.

(2) Timely statement of balance.

(i) Requirement. Upon request by the administrator of an estate, a card issuer must provide the administrator with the amount of the balance on a deceased consumer's account in a timely manner.

(ii) Safe harbor. For purposes of paragraph (c)(2)(i) of this section, providing the amount of the balance on the account within 30 days of receiving the request is deemed to be timely.

(3) Limitations after receipt of request from administrator.

(i) Limitation on fees and increases in annual percentage rates. After receiving a request from the administrator of an estate for the amount of the balance on a deceased consumer's account, a card issuer must not impose any fees on the account (such as a late fee, annual fee, or over-the-limit fee) or increase any annual percentage rate, except as provided by § 1026.55(b)(2).

(ii) Limitation on trailing or residual interest. A card issuer must waive or rebate any additional finance charge due to a periodic interest rate if payment in full of the balance disclosed pursuant to paragraph (c)(2) of this section is received within 30 days after disclosure.

§ 1026.12   Special credit card provisions.

(a) Issuance of credit cards. Regardless of the purpose for which a credit card is to be used, including business, commercial, or agricultural use, no credit card shall be issued to any person except:

(1) In response to an oral or written request or application for the card; or

(2) As a renewal of, or substitute for, an accepted credit card.

(b) Liability of cardholder for unauthorized use.

(1)(i) Definition of unauthorized use. For purposes of this section, the term "unauthorized use" means the use of a credit card by a person, other than the cardholder, who does not have actual, implied, or apparent authority for such use, and from which the cardholder receives no benefit.

(ii) **Limitation on amount.** The liability of a cardholder for unauthorized use of a credit card shall not exceed the lesser of $50 or the amount of money, property, labor, or services obtained by the unauthorized use before notification to the card issuer under paragraph (b)(3) of this section.

(2) **Conditions of liability.** A cardholder shall be liable for unauthorized use of a credit card only if:

(i)   The credit card is an accepted credit card;

(ii)   The card issuer has provided adequate notice of the cardholder's maximum potential liability and of means by which the card issuer may be notified of loss or theft of the card. The notice shall state that the cardholder's liability shall not exceed $50 (or any lesser amount) and that the cardholder may give oral or written notification, and shall describe a means of notification (for example, a telephone number, an address, or both); and

(iii) The card issuer has provided a means to identify the cardholder on the account or the authorized user of the card.

(3) **Notification to card issuer.** Notification to a card issuer is given when steps have been taken as may be reasonably required in the ordinary course of business to provide the card issuer with the pertinent information about the loss, theft, or possible unauthorized use of a credit card, regardless of whether any particular officer, employee, or agent of the card issuer does, in fact, receive the information. Notification may be given, at the option of the person giving it, in person, by telephone, or in writing. Notification in writing is considered given at the time of receipt or, whether or not received, at the expiration of the time ordinarily required for transmission, whichever is earlier.

(4) **Effect of other applicable law or agreement.** If state law or an agreement between a cardholder and the card issuer imposes lesser liability than that provided in this paragraph, the lesser liability shall govern.

(5) **Business use of credit cards.** If 10 or more credit cards are issued by one card issuer for use by the employees of an organization, this section does not prohibit the card issuer and the organization from agreeing to liability for unauthorized use without regard to this section. However, liability for unauthorized use may be imposed on an employee of the organization, by either the card issuer or the organization, only in accordance with this section.

(c) **Right of cardholder to assert claims or defenses against card issuer.**

(1) **General rule.** When a person who honors a credit card fails to resolve satisfactorily a dispute as to property or services purchased with the credit card in a consumer credit transaction, the cardholder may assert against the card issuer all claims (other than tort claims) and defenses arising out of the transaction and relating to the failure to resolve the dispute. The cardholder may withhold payment up to the amount of credit outstanding for the property or services that gave rise to the dispute and any finance or other charges imposed on that amount.

(2) **Adverse credit reports prohibited.** If, in accordance with paragraph (c)(1) of this section, the cardholder withholds payment of the amount of credit outstanding for the disputed transaction, the card issuer shall not report that amount as delinquent until the dispute is settled or judgment is rendered.

(3) **Limitations.**

(i)   **General.** The rights stated in paragraphs (c)(1) and (c)(2) of this section apply only if:

(A)   The cardholder has made a good faith attempt to resolve the dispute with the person honoring the credit card; and

(B)   The amount of credit extended to obtain the property or services that result in the assertion of the claim or defense by the cardholder exceeds $50, and the disputed transaction occurred in the same state as the cardholder's current designated address or, if not within the same state, within 100 miles from that address.

(ii) **Exclusion.** The limitations stated in paragraph (c)(3)(i)(B) of this section shall not apply when the person honoring the credit card:

(A) Is the same person as the card issuer;

(B) Is controlled by the card issuer directly or indirectly;

(C) Is under the direct or indirect control of a third person that also directly or indirectly controls the card issuer;

(D) Controls the card issuer directly or indirectly;

(E) Is a franchised dealer in the card issuer's products or services; or

(F) Has obtained the order for the disputed transaction through a mail solicitation made or participated in by the card issuer.

(d) **Offsets by card issuer prohibited.**

(1) A card issuer may not take any action, either before or after termination of credit card privileges, to offset a cardholder's indebtedness arising from a consumer credit transaction under the relevant credit card plan against funds of the cardholder held on deposit with the card issuer.

(2) This paragraph does not alter or affect the right of a card issuer acting under state or Federal law to do any of the following with regard to funds of a cardholder held on deposit with the card issuer if the same procedure is constitutionally available to creditors generally: Obtain or enforce a consensual security interest in the funds; attach or otherwise levy upon the funds; or obtain or enforce a court order relating to the funds.

(3) This paragraph does not prohibit a plan, if authorized in writing by the cardholder, under which the card issuer may periodically deduct all or part of the cardholder's credit card debt from a deposit account held with the card issuer (subject to the limitations in § 1026.13(d)(1)).

(e) **Prompt notification of returns and crediting of refunds.**

(1) When a creditor other than the card issuer accepts the return of property or forgives a debt for services that is to be reflected as a credit to the consumer's credit card account, that creditor shall, within 7 business days from accepting the return or forgiving the debt, transmit a credit statement to the card issuer through the card issuer's normal channels for credit statements.

(2) The card issuer shall, within 3 business days from receipt of a credit statement, credit the consumer's account with the amount of the refund.

(3) If a creditor other than a card issuer routinely gives cash refunds to consumers paying in cash, the creditor shall also give credit or cash refunds to consumers using credit cards, unless it discloses at the time the transaction is consummated that credit or cash refunds for returns are not given. This section does not require refunds for returns nor does it prohibit refunds in kind.

(f) **Discounts; tie-in arrangements.** No card issuer may, by contract or otherwise:

(1) Prohibit any person who honors a credit card from offering a discount to a consumer to induce the consumer to pay by cash, check, or similar means rather than by use of a credit card or its underlying account for the purchase of property or services; or

(2) Require any person who honors the card issuer's credit card to open or maintain any account or obtain any other service not essential to the operation of the credit card plan from the card issuer or any other person, as a condition of participation in a credit card plan. If maintenance of an account for clearing purposes is determined to be essential to the operation of the credit card plan, it may be required only if no service charges or minimum balance requirements are imposed.

(g) **Relation to Electronic Fund Transfer Act and Regulation E.** For guidance on whether Regulation Z (12 CFR part 1026) or Regulation E (12 CFR part 1005) applies in instances involving both credit and electronic fund transfer aspects, refer to Regulation E, 12 CFR 1005.12(a) regarding issuance and liability for unauthorized use. On matters other than issuance and liability, this section applies to the credit aspects of combined credit/electronic fund transfer transactions, as applicable.

§ 1026.13   Billing error resolution.

(a)   **Definition of billing error.** For purposes of this section, the term billing error means:

(1)   A reflection on or with a periodic statement of an extension of credit that is not made to the consumer or to a person who has actual, implied, or apparent authority to use the consumer's credit card or open-end credit plan.

(2)   A reflection on or with a periodic statement of an extension of credit that is not identified in accordance with the requirements of §§ 1026.7(a)(2) or (b)(2), as applicable, and 1026.8.

(3)   A reflection on or with a periodic statement of an extension of credit for property or services not accepted by the consumer or the consumer's designee, or not delivered to the consumer or the consumer's designee as agreed.

(4)   A reflection on a periodic statement of the creditor's failure to credit properly a payment or other credit issued to the consumer's account.

(5)   A reflection on a periodic statement of a computational or similar error of an accounting nature that is made by the creditor.

(6)   A reflection on a periodic statement of an extension of credit for which the consumer requests additional clarification, including documentary evidence.

(7)   The creditor's failure to mail or deliver a periodic statement to the consumer's last known address if that address was received by the creditor, in writing, at least 20 days before the end of the billing cycle for which the statement was required.

(b)   **Billing error notice.** A billing error notice is a written notice from a consumer that:

(1)   Is received by a creditor at the address disclosed under § 1026.7(a)(9) or (b)(9), as applicable, no later than 60 days after the creditor transmitted the first periodic statement that reflects the alleged billing error;

(2)   Enables the creditor to identify the consumer's name and account number; and

(3)   To the extent possible, indicates the consumer's belief and the reasons for the belief that a billing error exists, and the type, date, and amount of the error.

(c)   **Time for resolution; general procedures.**

(1)   The creditor shall mail or deliver written acknowledgment to the consumer within 30 days of receiving a billing error notice, unless the creditor has complied with the appropriate resolution procedures of paragraphs (e) and (f) of this section, as applicable, within the 30-day period; and

(2)   The creditor shall comply with the appropriate resolution procedures of paragraphs (e) and (f) of this section, as applicable, within 2 complete billing cycles (but in no event later than 90 days) after receiving a billing error notice.

(d)   **Rules pending resolution.** Until a billing error is resolved under paragraph (e) or (f) of this section, the following rules apply:

(1)   **Consumer's right to withhold disputed amount; collection action prohibited.** The consumer need not pay (and the creditor may not try to collect) any portion of any required payment that the consumer believes is related to the disputed amount (including related finance or other charges). If the cardholder has enrolled in an automatic payment plan offered by the card issuer and has agreed to pay the credit card indebtedness by periodic deductions from the cardholder's deposit account, the card issuer shall not deduct any part of the disputed amount or related finance or other charges if a billing error notice is received any time up to 3 business days before the scheduled payment date.

(2) Adverse credit reports prohibited. The creditor or its agent shall not (directly or indirectly) make or threaten to make an adverse report to any person about the consumer's credit standing, or report that an amount or account is delinquent, because the consumer failed to pay the disputed amount or related finance or other charges.

(3) Acceleration of debt and restriction of account prohibited. A creditor shall not accelerate any part of the consumer's indebtedness or restrict or close a consumer's account solely because the consumer has exercised in good faith rights provided by this section. A creditor may be subject to the forfeiture penalty under 15 U.S.C. 1666(e) for failure to comply with any of the requirements of this section.

(4) Permitted creditor actions. A creditor is not prohibited from taking action to collect any undisputed portion of the item or bill; from deducting any disputed amount and related finance or other charges from the consumer's credit limit on the account; or from reflecting a disputed amount and related finance or other charges on a periodic statement, provided that the creditor indicates on or with the periodic statement that payment of any disputed amount and related finance or other charges is not required pending the creditor's compliance with this section.

(e) Procedures if billing error occurred as asserted. If a creditor determines that a billing error occurred as asserted, it shall within the time limits in paragraph (c)(2) of this section:

(1) Correct the billing error and credit the consumer's account with any disputed amount and related finance or other charges, as applicable; and

(2) Mail or deliver a correction notice to the consumer.

(f) Procedures if different billing error or no billing error occurred. If, after conducting a reasonable investigation, a creditor determines that no billing error occurred or that a different billing error occurred from that asserted, the creditor shall within the time limits in paragraph (c)(2) of this section:

(1) Mail or deliver to the consumer an explanation that sets forth the reasons for the creditor's belief that the billing error alleged by the consumer is incorrect in whole or in part;

(2) Furnish copies of documentary evidence of the consumer's indebtedness, if the consumer so requests; and

(3) If a different billing error occurred, correct the billing error and credit the consumer's account with any disputed amount and related finance or other charges, as applicable.

(g) Creditor's rights and duties after resolution. If a creditor, after complying with all of the requirements of this section, determines that a consumer owes all or part of the disputed amount and related finance or other charges, the creditor:

(1) Shall promptly notify the consumer in writing of the time when payment is due and the portion of the disputed amount and related finance or other charges that the consumer still owes;

(2) Shall allow any time period disclosed under § 1026.6(a)(1) or (b)(2)(v), as applicable, and § 1026.7(a)(8) or (b)(8), as applicable, during which the consumer can pay the amount due under paragraph (g)(1) of this section without incurring additional finance or other charges;

(3) May report an account or amount as delinquent because the amount due under paragraph (g)(1) of this section remains unpaid after the creditor has allowed any time period disclosed under § 1026.6(a)(1) or (b)(2)(v), as applicable, and § 1026.7(a)(8) or (b)(8), as applicable or 10 days (whichever is longer) during which the consumer can pay the amount; but

(4) May not report that an amount or account is delinquent because the amount due under paragraph (g)(1) of the section remains unpaid, if the creditor receives (within the time allowed for payment in paragraph (g)(3) of this section) further written notice from the consumer that any portion of the billing error is still in dispute, unless the creditor also:

(i) Promptly reports that the amount or account is in dispute;

(ii)   Mails or delivers to the consumer (at the same time the report is made) a written notice of the name and address of each person to whom the creditor makes a report; and

(iii)   Promptly reports any subsequent resolution of the reported delinquency to all persons to whom the creditor has made a report.

(h)   **Reassertion of billing error.** A creditor that has fully complied with the requirements of this section has no further responsibilities under this section (other than as provided in paragraph (g)(4) of this section) if a consumer reasserts substantially the same billing error.

(i)   **Relation to Electronic Fund Transfer Act and Regulation E.** If an extension of credit is incident to an electronic fund transfer, under an agreement between a consumer and a financial institution to extend credit when the consumer's account is overdrawn or to maintain a specified minimum balance in the consumer's account, the creditor shall comply with the requirements of Regulation E, 12 CFR 1005.11 governing error resolution rather than those of paragraphs (a), (b), (c), (e), (f), and (h) of this section.

§ 1026.14   Determination of annual percentage rate.

(a)   **General rule.** The annual percentage rate is a measure of the cost of credit, expressed as a yearly rate. An annual percentage rate shall be considered accurate if it is not more than 1/8th of 1 percentage point above or below the annual percentage rate determined in accordance with this section. An error in disclosure of the annual percentage rate or finance charge shall not, in itself, be considered a violation of this part if:

(1)   The error resulted from a corresponding error in a calculation tool used in good faith by the creditor; and

(2)   Upon discovery of the error, the creditor promptly discontinues use of that calculation tool for disclosure purposes, and notifies the Bureau in writing of the error in the calculation tool.

(b)   **Annual percentage rate—in general.** Where one or more periodic rates may be used to compute the finance charge, the annual percentage rate(s) to be disclosed for purposes of §§ 1026.60, 1026.40, 1026.6, 1026.7(a)(4) or (b)(4), 1026.9, 1026.15, 1026.16, 1026.26, 1026.55, and 1026.56 shall be computed by multiplying each periodic rate by the number of periods in a year.

(c)   **Optional effective annual percentage rate for periodic statements for creditors offering open-end credit plans secured by a consumer's dwelling.** A creditor offering an open-end plan subject to the requirements of § 1026.40 need not disclose an effective annual percentage rate. Such a creditor may, at its option, disclose an effective annual percentage rate(s) pursuant to § 1026.7(a)(7) and compute the effective annual percentage rate as follows:

(1)   **Solely periodic rates imposed.** If the finance charge is determined solely by applying one or more periodic rates, at the creditor's option, either:

(i)   By multiplying each periodic rate by the number of periods in a year; or

(ii)   By dividing the total finance charge for the billing cycle by the sum of the balances to which the periodic rates were applied and multiplying the quotient (expressed as a percentage) by the number of billing cycles in a year.

(2)   **Minimum or fixed charge, but not transaction charge, imposed.** If the finance charge imposed during the billing cycle is or includes a minimum, fixed, or other charge not due to the application of a periodic rate, other than a charge with respect to any specific transaction during the billing cycle, by dividing the total finance charge for the billing cycle by the amount of the balance(s) to which it is applicable and multiplying the quotient (expressed as a percentage) by the number of billing cycles in a year. If there is no balance to which the finance charge is applicable, an annual percentage rate cannot be determined under this section. Where the finance charge imposed during the billing cycle is or includes a loan fee, points, or similar charge that relates to opening, renewing, or continuing an account, the amount of such charge shall not be included in the calculation of the annual percentage rate.

(3) Transaction charge imposed. If the finance charge imposed during the billing cycle is or includes a charge relating to a specific transaction during the billing cycle (even if the total finance charge also includes any other minimum, fixed, or other charge not due to the application of a periodic rate), by dividing the total finance charge imposed during the billing cycle by the total of all balances and other amounts on which a finance charge was imposed during the billing cycle without duplication, and multiplying the quotient (expressed as a percentage) by the number of billing cycles in a year, except that the annual percentage rate shall not be less than the largest rate determined by multiplying each periodic rate imposed during the billing cycle by the number of periods in a year. Where the finance charge imposed during the billing cycle is or includes a loan fee, points, or similar charge that relates to the opening, renewing, or continuing an account, the amount of such charge shall not be included in the calculation of the annual percentage rate. See Appendix F to this part regarding determination of the denominator of the fraction under this paragraph.

(4) If the finance charge imposed during the billing cycle is or includes a minimum, fixed, or other charge not due to the application of a periodic rate and the total finance charge imposed during the billing cycle does not exceed 50 cents for a monthly or longer billing cycle, or the pro rata part of 50 cents for a billing cycle shorter than monthly, at the creditor's option, by multiplying each applicable periodic rate by the number of periods in a year, notwithstanding the provisions of paragraphs (c)(2) and (c)(3) of this section.

(d) Calculations where daily periodic rate applied. If the provisions of paragraph (c)(1)(ii) or (c)(2) of this section apply and all or a portion of the finance charge is determined by the application of one or more daily periodic rates, the annual percentage rate may be determined either:

(1) By dividing the total finance charge by the average of the daily balances and multiplying the quotient by the number of billing cycles in a year; or

(2) By dividing the total finance charge by the sum of the daily balances and multiplying the quotient by 365.

§ 1026.15 Right of rescission.

(a) Consumer's right to rescind.

(1)(i) Except as provided in paragraph (a)(1)(ii) of this section, in a credit plan in which a security interest is or will be retained or acquired in a consumer's principal dwelling, each consumer whose ownership interest is or will be subject to the security interest shall have the right to rescind: each credit extension made under the plan; the plan when the plan is opened; a security interest when added or increased to secure an existing plan; and the increase when a credit limit on the plan is increased.

(ii) As provided in section 125(e) of the Act, the consumer does not have the right to rescind each credit extension made under the plan if such extension is made in accordance with a previously established credit limit for the plan.

(2) To exercise the right to rescind, the consumer shall notify the creditor of the rescission by mail, telegram, or other means of written communication. Notice is considered given when mailed, or when filed for telegraphic transmission, or, if sent by other means, when delivered to the creditor's designated place of business.

(3) The consumer may exercise the right to rescind until midnight of the third business day following the occurrence described in paragraph (a)(1) of this section that gave rise to the right of rescission, delivery of the notice required by paragraph (b) of this section, or delivery of all material disclosures, whichever occurs last. If the required notice and material disclosures are not delivered, the right to rescind shall expire 3 years after the occurrence giving rise to the right of rescission, or upon transfer of all of the consumer's interest in the property, or upon sale of the property, whichever occurs first. In the case of certain administrative proceedings, the rescission period shall be extended in accordance with section 125(f) of the Act. The term material disclosures means the information that must be provided to satisfy the requirements in § 1026.6 with regard to the method of determining the finance charge and the balance upon which a finance charge will be imposed, the annual percentage rate, the amount or method of determining the amount of any membership or participation fee that may be imposed as part of the plan, and the payment information described in § 1026.40(d)(5)(i) and (ii) that is required under § 1026.6(e)(2).

(4)   When more than one consumer has the right to rescind, the exercise of the right by one consumer shall be effective as to all consumers.

(b)   **Notice of right to rescind.** In any transaction or occurrence subject to rescission, a creditor shall deliver two copies of the notice of the right to rescind to each consumer entitled to rescind (one copy to each if the notice is delivered in electronic form in accordance with the consumer consent and other applicable provisions of the E-Sign Act). The notice shall identify the transaction or occurrence and clearly and conspicuously disclose the following:

(1)   The retention or acquisition of a security interest in the consumer's principal dwelling.

(2)   The consumer's right to rescind, as described in paragraph (a)(1) of this section.

(3)   How to exercise the right to rescind, with a form for that purpose, designating the address of the creditor's place of business.

(4)   The effects of rescission, as described in paragraph (d) of this section.

(5)   The date the rescission period expires.

(c)   **Delay of creditor's performance.** Unless a consumer waives the right to rescind under paragraph (e) of this section, no money shall be disbursed other than in escrow, no services shall be performed, and no materials delivered until after the rescission period has expired and the creditor is reasonably satisfied that the consumer has not rescinded. A creditor does not violate this section if a third party with no knowledge of the event activating the rescission right does not delay in providing materials or services, as long as the debt incurred for those materials or services is not secured by the property subject to rescission.

(d)   **Effects of rescission.**

(1)   When a consumer rescinds a transaction, the security interest giving rise to the right of rescission becomes void, and the consumer shall not be liable for any amount, including any finance charge.

(2)   Within 20 calendar days after receipt of a notice of rescission, the creditor shall return any money or property that has been given to anyone in connection with the transaction and shall take any action necessary to reflect the termination of the security interest.

(3)   If the creditor has delivered any money or property, the consumer may retain possession until the creditor has met its obligation under paragraph (d)(2) of this section. When the creditor has complied with that paragraph, the consumer shall tender the money or property to the creditor or, where the latter would be impracticable or inequitable, tender its reasonable value. At the consumer's option, tender of property may be made at the location of the property or at the consumer's residence. Tender of money must be made at the creditor's designated place of business. If the creditor does not take possession of the money or property within 20 calendar days after the consumer's tender, the consumer may keep it without further obligation.

(4)   The procedures outlined in paragraphs (d)(2) and (3) of this section may be modified by court order.

(e)   **Consumer's waiver of right to rescind.** The consumer may modify or waive the right to rescind if the consumer determines that the extension of credit is needed to meet a bona fide personal financial emergency. To modify or waive the right, the consumer shall give the creditor a dated written statement that describes the emergency, specifically modifies or waives the right to rescind, and bears the signature of all the consumers entitled to rescind. Printed forms for this purpose are prohibited.

(f)   **Exempt transactions.** The right to rescind does not apply to the following:

(1)   A residential mortgage transaction.

(2) A credit plan in which a state agency is a creditor.

§ 1026.16   Advertising.

(a) Actually available terms. If an advertisement for credit states specific credit terms, it shall state only those terms that actually are or will be arranged or offered by the creditor.

(b) Advertisement of terms that require additional disclosures.

(1) Any term required to be disclosed under § 1026.6(b)(3) set forth affirmatively or negatively in an advertisement for an open-end (not home-secured) credit plan triggers additional disclosures under this section. Any term required to be disclosed under § 1026.6(a)(1) or (a)(2) set forth affirmatively or negatively in an advertisement for a home-equity plan subject to the requirements of § 1026.40 triggers additional disclosures under this section. If any of the terms that trigger additional disclosures under this paragraph is set forth in an advertisement, the advertisement shall also clearly and conspicuously set forth the following:

(i) Any minimum, fixed, transaction, activity or similar charge that is a finance charge under § 1026.4 that could be imposed.

(ii) Any periodic rate that may be applied expressed as an annual percentage rate as determined under § 1026.14(b). If the plan provides for a variable periodic rate, that fact shall be disclosed.

(iii) Any membership or participation fee that could be imposed.

(2) If an advertisement for credit to finance the purchase of goods or services specified in the advertisement states a periodic payment amount, the advertisement shall also state the total of payments and the time period to repay the obligation, assuming that the consumer pays only the periodic payment amount advertised. The disclosure of the total of payments and the time period to repay the obligation must be equally prominent to the statement of the periodic payment amount.

(c) Catalogs or other multiple-page advertisements; electronic advertisements.

(1) If a catalog or other multiple-page advertisement, or an electronic advertisement (such as an advertisement appearing on an Internet Web site), gives information in a table or schedule in sufficient detail to permit determination of the disclosures required by paragraph (b) of this section, it shall be considered a single advertisement if:

(i) The table or schedule is clearly and conspicuously set forth; and

(ii) Any statement of terms set forth in § 1026.6 appearing anywhere else in the catalog or advertisement clearly refers to the page or location where the table or schedule begins.

(2) A catalog or other multiple-page advertisement or an electronic advertisement (such as an advertisement appearing on an Internet Web site) complies with this paragraph if the table or schedule of terms includes all appropriate disclosures for a representative scale of amounts up to the level of the more commonly sold higher-priced property or services offered.

(d) Additional requirements for home-equity plans.

(1) Advertisement of terms that require additional disclosures. If any of the terms required to be disclosed under § 1026.6(a)(1) or (a)(2) or the payment terms of the plan are set forth, affirmatively or negatively, in an advertisement for a home-equity plan subject to the requirements of § 1026.40, the advertisement also shall clearly and conspicuously set forth the following:

(i) Any loan fee that is a percentage of the credit limit under the plan and an estimate of any other fees imposed for opening the plan, stated as a single dollar amount or a reasonable range.

(ii) Any periodic rate used to compute the finance charge, expressed as an annual percentage rate as determined under § 1026.14(b).

(iii) The maximum annual percentage rate that may be imposed in a variable-rate plan.

(2)   Discounted and premium rates. If an advertisement states an initial annual percentage rate that is not based on the index and margin used to make later rate adjustments in a variable-rate plan, the advertisement also shall state with equal prominence and in close proximity to the initial rate:

   (i)   The period of time such initial rate will be in effect; and

   (ii)   A reasonably current annual percentage rate that would have been in effect using the index and margin.

(3)   Balloon payment. If an advertisement contains a statement of any minimum periodic payment and a balloon payment may result if only the minimum periodic payments are made, even if such a payment is uncertain or unlikely, the advertisement also shall state with equal prominence and in close proximity to the minimum periodic payment statement that a balloon payment may result, if applicable. A balloon payment results if paying the minimum periodic payments does not fully amortize the outstanding balance by a specified date or time, and the consumer is required to repay the entire outstanding balance at such time. If a balloon payment will occur when the consumer makes only the minimum payments required under the plan, an advertisement for such a program which contains any statement of any minimum periodic payment shall also state with equal prominence and in close proximity to the minimum periodic payment statement:

   (i)   That a balloon payment will result; and

   (ii)   The amount and timing of the balloon payment that will result if the consumer makes only the minimum payments for the maximum period of time that the consumer is permitted to make such payments.

(4)   Tax implications. An advertisement that states that any interest expense incurred under the home-equity plan is or may be tax deductible may not be misleading in this regard. If an advertisement distributed in paper form or through the Internet (rather than by radio or television) is for a home-equity plan secured by the consumer's principal dwelling, and the advertisement states that the advertised extension of credit may exceed the fair market value of the dwelling, the advertisement shall clearly and conspicuously state that:

   (i)   The interest on the portion of the credit extension that is greater than the fair market value of the dwelling is not tax deductible for Federal income tax purposes; and

   (ii)   The consumer should consult a tax adviser for further information regarding the deductibility of interest and charges.

(5)   Misleading terms. An advertisement may not refer to a home-equity plan as "free money" or contain a similarly misleading term.

(6)   Promotional rates and payments.

   (i)   **Definitions.** The following definitions apply for purposes of paragraph (d)(6) of this section:

      (A)   **Promotional rate.** The term "promotional rate" means, in a variable-rate plan, any annual percentage rate that is not based on the index and margin that will be used to make rate adjustments under the plan, if that rate is less than a reasonably current annual percentage rate that would be in effect under the index and margin that will be used to make rate adjustments under the plan.

      (B)   **Promotional payment.** The term "promotional payment" means:

         (1)   For a variable-rate plan, any minimum payment applicable for a promotional period that:

            (i)   Is not derived by applying the index and margin to the outstanding balance when such index and margin will be used to determine other minimum payments under the plan; and

1644

(ii) Is less than other minimum payments under the plan derived by applying a reasonably current index and margin that will be used to determine the amount of such payments, given an assumed balance.

(2) For a plan other than a variable-rate plan, any minimum payment applicable for a promotional period if that payment is less than other payments required under the plan given an assumed balance.

(C) **Promotional period.** A "promotional period" means a period of time, less than the full term of the loan, that the promotional rate or promotional payment may be applicable.

(ii) **Stating the promotional period and post-promotional rate or payments.** If any annual percentage rate that may be applied to a plan is a promotional rate, or if any payment applicable to a plan is a promotional payment, the following must be disclosed in any advertisement, other than television or radio advertisements, in a clear and conspicuous manner with equal prominence and in close proximity to each listing of the promotional rate or payment:

(A) The period of time during which the promotional rate or promotional payment will apply;

(B) In the case of a promotional rate, any annual percentage rate that will apply under the plan. If such rate is variable, the annual percentage rate must be disclosed in accordance with the accuracy standards in §§ 1026.40 or 1026.16(b)(1)(ii) as applicable; and

(C) In the case of a promotional payment, the amounts and time periods of any payments that will apply under the plan. In variable-rate transactions, payments that will be determined based on application of an index and margin shall be disclosed based on a reasonably current index and margin.

(iii) **Envelope excluded.** The requirements in paragraph (d)(6)(ii) of this section do not apply to an envelope in which an application or solicitation is mailed, or to a banner advertisement or pop-up advertisement linked to an application or solicitation provided electronically.

(e) **Alternative disclosures—television or radio advertisements.** An advertisement made through television or radio stating any of the terms requiring additional disclosures under paragraphs (b)(1) or (d)(1) of this section may alternatively comply with paragraphs (b)(1) or (d)(1) of this section by stating the information required by paragraphs (b)(1)(ii) or (d)(1)(ii) of this section, as applicable, and listing a toll-free telephone number, or any telephone number that allows a consumer to reverse the phone charges when calling for information, along with a reference that such number may be used by consumers to obtain the additional cost information.

(f) **Misleading terms.** An advertisement may not refer to an annual percentage rate as "fixed," or use a similar term, unless the advertisement also specifies a time period that the rate will be fixed and the rate will not increase during that period, or if no such time period is provided, the rate will not increase while the plan is open.

(g) **Promotional rates and fees.**

(1) **Scope.** The requirements of this paragraph apply to any advertisement of an open-end (not home-secured) plan, including promotional materials accompanying applications or solicitations subject to § 1026.60(c) or accompanying applications or solicitations subject to § 1026.60(e).

(2) **Definitions.**

(i) Promotional rate means any annual percentage rate applicable to one or more balances or transactions on an open-end (not home-secured) plan for a specified period of time that is lower than the annual percentage rate that will be in effect at the end of that period on such balances or transactions.

(ii) Introductory rate means a promotional rate offered in connection with the opening of an account.

(iii) Promotional period means the maximum time period for which a promotional rate or promotional fee may be applicable.

(iv) Promotional fee means a fee required to be disclosed under § 1026.6(b)(1) and (2) applicable to an open-end (not home-secured) plan, or to one or more balances or transactions on an open-end (not home-secured) plan, for a specified period of time that is lower than the fee that will be in effect at the end of that period for such plan or types of balances or transactions.

(v) Introductory fee means a promotional fee offered in connection with the opening of an account.

(3)   Stating the term "introductory". If any annual percentage rate or fee that may be applied to the account is an introductory rate or introductory fee, the term introductory or intro must be in immediate proximity to each listing of the introductory rate or introductory fee in a written or electronic advertisement.

(4)   Stating the promotional period and post-promotional rate or fee. If any annual percentage rate that may be applied to the account is a promotional rate under paragraph (g)(2)(i) of this section or any fee that may be applied to the account is a promotional fee under paragraph (g)(2)(iv) of this section, the information in paragraphs (g)(4)(i) and, as applicable, (g)(4)(ii) or (iii) of this section must be stated in a clear and conspicuous manner in the advertisement. If the rate or fee is stated in a written or electronic advertisement, the information in paragraphs (g)(4)(i) and, as applicable, (g)(4)(ii) or (iii) of this section must also be stated in a prominent location closely proximate to the first listing of the promotional rate or promotional fee.

(i)   When the promotional rate or promotional fee will end;

(ii)   The annual percentage rate that will apply after the end of the promotional period. If such rate is variable, the annual percentage rate must comply with the accuracy standards in §§ 1026.60(c)(2), 1026.60(d)(3), 1026.60(e)(4), or 1026.16(b)(1)(ii), as applicable. If such rate cannot be determined at the time disclosures are given because the rate depends at least in part on a later determination of the consumer's creditworthiness, the advertisement must disclose the specific rates or the range of rates that might apply; and

(iii)   The fee that will apply after the end of the promotional period.

(5)   Envelope excluded. The requirements in paragraph (g)(4) of this section do not apply to an envelope or other enclosure in which an application or solicitation is mailed, or to a banner advertisement or pop-up advertisement, linked to an application or solicitation provided electronically.

(h)   Deferred interest or similar offers.

(1)   Scope. The requirements of this paragraph apply to any advertisement of an open-end credit plan not subject to § 1026.40, including promotional materials accompanying applications or solicitations subject to § 1026.60(c) or accompanying applications or solicitations subject to § 1026.60(e).

(2)   Definitions. "Deferred interest" means finance charges, accrued on balances or transactions, that a consumer is not obligated to pay or that will be waived or refunded to a consumer if those balances or transactions are paid in full by a specified date. The maximum period from the date the consumer becomes obligated for the balance or transaction until the specified date by which the consumer must pay the balance or transaction in full in order to avoid finance charges, or receive a waiver or refund of finance charges, is the "deferred interest period." "Deferred interest" does not include any finance charges the consumer avoids paying in connection with any recurring grace period.

(3)   Stating the deferred interest period. If a deferred interest offer is advertised, the deferred interest period must be stated in a clear and conspicuous manner in the advertisement. If the phrase "no interest" or similar term regarding the possible avoidance of interest obligations under the deferred interest program is stated, the term "if paid in full" must also be stated in a clear and conspicuous manner preceding the disclosure of the deferred interest period in the advertisement. If the deferred interest offer is included in a written or electronic advertisement, the deferred interest period and, if applicable, the term "if paid in full" must also be stated in immediate proximity to each statement of "no interest," "no payments," "deferred interest," "same as cash," or similar term regarding interest or payments during the deferred interest period.

(4) **Stating the terms of the deferred interest or similar offer.** If any deferred interest offer is advertised, the information in paragraphs (h)(4)(i) and (h)(4)(ii) of this section must be stated in the advertisement, in language similar to Sample G–24 in Appendix G to this part. If the deferred interest offer is included in a written or electronic advertisement, the information in paragraphs (h)(4)(i) and (h)(4)(ii) of this section must also be stated in a prominent location closely proximate to the first statement of "no interest," "no payments," "deferred interest," "same as cash," or similar term regarding interest or payments during the deferred interest period.

(i) A statement that interest will be charged from the date the consumer becomes obligated for the balance or transaction subject to the deferred interest offer if the balance or transaction is not paid in full within the deferred interest period; and

(ii) A statement, if applicable, that interest will be charged from the date the consumer incurs the balance or transaction subject to the deferred interest offer if the account is in default before the end of the deferred interest period.

(5) **Envelope excluded.** The requirements in paragraph (h)(4) of this section do not apply to an envelope or other enclosure in which an application or solicitation is mailed, or to a banner advertisement or pop-up advertisement linked to an application or solicitation provided electronically.

SUBPART C. CLOSED-END CREDIT

§ 1026.17 General disclosure requirements.

(a) **Form of disclosures.** Except for the disclosures required by § 1026.19(e), (f), and (g):

(1) The creditor shall make the disclosures required by this subpart clearly and conspicuously in writing, in a form that the consumer may keep. The disclosures required by this subpart may be provided to the consumer in electronic form, subject to compliance with the consumer consent and other applicable provisions of the Electronic Signatures in Global and National Commerce Act (E-Sign Act) (15 U.S.C. 7001 et seq.). The disclosures required by §§ 1026.17(g), 1026.19(b), and 1026.24 may be provided to the consumer in electronic form without regard to the consumer consent or other provisions of the E-Sign Act in the circumstances set forth in those sections. The disclosures shall be grouped together, shall be segregated from everything else, and shall not contain any information not directly related to the disclosures required under § 1026.18, § 1026.20(c) and (d), or § 1026.47. The disclosures required by § 1026.20(d) shall be provided as a separate document from all other written materials. The disclosures may include an acknowledgment of receipt, the date of the transaction, and the consumer's name, address, and account number. The following disclosures may be made together with or separately from other required disclosures: The creditor's identity under § 1026.18(a), the variable rate example under § 1026.18(f)(1)(iv), insurance or debt cancellation under § 1026.18(n), and certain security interest charges under § 1026.18(o). The itemization of the amount financed under § 1026.18(c)(1) must be separate from the other disclosures under § 1026.18, except for private education loan disclosures made in compliance with § 1026.47.

(2) Except for private education loan disclosures made in compliance with § 1026.47, the terms "finance charge" and "annual percentage rate," when required to be disclosed under § 1026.18(d) and (e) together with a corresponding amount or percentage rate, shall be more conspicuous than any other disclosure, except the creditor's identity under § 1026.18(a). For private education loan disclosures made in compliance with § 1026.47, the term "annual percentage rate," and the corresponding percentage rate must be less conspicuous than the term "finance charge" and corresponding amount under § 1026.18(d), the interest rate under §§ 1026.47(b)(1)(i) and (c)(1), and the notice of the right to cancel under § 1026.47(c)(4).

(b) Time of disclosures. The creditor shall make disclosures before consummation of the transaction. In certain residential mortgage transactions, special timing requirements are set forth in § 1026.19(a). In certain variable-rate transactions, special timing requirements for variable-rate disclosures are set forth in § 1026.19(b) and § 1026.20(c) and (d). For private education loan disclosures made in compliance with § 1026.47, special timing requirements are set forth in § 1026.46(d). In certain transactions involving mail or telephone orders or a series of sales, the timing of disclosures may be delayed in accordance with paragraphs (g) and (h) of this section. This paragraph (b) does not apply to the disclosures required by §§ 1026.19(e), (f), and (g) and 1026.20(e).

(c) Basis of disclosures and use of estimates.

(1) The disclosures shall reflect the terms of the legal obligation between the parties.

(2)(i) If any information necessary for an accurate disclosure is unknown to the creditor, the creditor shall make the disclosure based on the best information reasonably available at the time the disclosure is provided to the consumer, and shall state clearly that the disclosure is an estimate.

(ii) For a transaction in which a portion of the interest is determined on a per-diem basis and collected at consummation, any disclosure affected by the per-diem interest shall be considered accurate if the disclosure is based on the information known to the creditor at the time that the disclosure documents are prepared for consummation of the transaction.

(3) The creditor may disregard the effects of the following in making calculations and disclosures.

(i) That payments must be collected in whole cents.

(ii) That dates of scheduled payments and advances may be changed because the scheduled date is not a business day.

(iii) That months have different numbers of days.

(iv) The occurrence of leap year.

(4) In making calculations and disclosures, the creditor may disregard any irregularity in the first period that falls within the limits described below and any payment schedule irregularity that results from the irregular first period:

(i) For transactions in which the term is less than 1 year, a first period not more than 6 days shorter or 13 days longer than a regular period;

(ii) For transactions in which the term is at least 1 year and less than 10 years, a first period not more than 11 days shorter or 21 days longer than a regular period; and

(iii) For transactions in which the term is at least 10 years, a first period shorter than or not more than 32 days longer than a regular period.

(5) If an obligation is payable on demand, the creditor shall make the disclosures based on an assumed maturity of 1 year. If an alternate maturity date is stated in the legal obligation between the parties, the disclosures shall be based on that date.

(6)(i) A series of advances under an agreement to extend credit up to a certain amount may be considered as one transaction.

(ii) When a multiple-advance loan to finance the construction of a dwelling may be permanently financed by the same creditor, the construction phase and the permanent phase may be treated as either one transaction or more than one transaction.

(d) Multiple creditors; multiple consumers. If a transaction involves more than one creditor, only one set of disclosures shall be given and the creditors shall agree among themselves which creditor must comply with the requirements that this part imposes on any or all of them. If there is more than one consumer, the disclosures may be made to any consumer who is primarily liable on the obligation. If the transaction is rescindable under § 1026.23, however, the disclosures shall be made to each consumer who has the right to rescind.

(e)   Effect of subsequent events. If a disclosure becomes inaccurate because of an event that occurs after the creditor delivers the required disclosures, the inaccuracy is not a violation of this part, although new disclosures may be required under paragraph (f) of this section, § 1026.19, § 1026.20, or § 1026.48(c)(4).

(f)   Early disclosures. Except for private education loan disclosures made in compliance with § 1026.47, if disclosures required by this subpart are given before the date of consummation of a transaction and a subsequent event makes them inaccurate, the creditor shall disclose before consummation (subject to the provisions of § 1026.19(a)(2), (e), and (f):

(1)   Any changed term unless the term was based on an estimate in accordance with § 1026.17(c)(2) and was labeled an estimate;

(2)   All changed terms, if the annual percentage rate at the time of consummation varies from the annual percentage rate disclosed earlier by more than $1/8$ of 1 percentage point in a regular transaction, or more than $1/4$ of 1 percentage point in an irregular transaction, as defined in § 1026.22(a).

(g)   Mail or telephone orders—delay in disclosures. Except for private education loan disclosures made in compliance with § 1026.47 and mortgage disclosures made in compliance with § 1026.19(a) or (e), (f), and (g), if a creditor receives a purchase order or a request for an extension of credit by mail, telephone, or facsimile machine without face-to-face or direct telephone solicitation, the creditor may delay the disclosures until the due date of the first payment, if the following information for representative amounts or ranges of credit is made available in written form or in electronic form to the consumer or to the public before the actual purchase order or request:

(1)   The cash price or the principal loan amount.

(2)   The total sale price.

(3)   The finance charge.

(4)   The annual percentage rate, and if the rate may increase after consummation, the following disclosures:

(i)   The circumstances under which the rate may increase.

(ii)   Any limitations on the increase.

(iii) The effect of an increase.

(5)   The terms of repayment.

(h)   Series of sales—delay in disclosures. Except for mortgage disclosures made in compliance with § 1026.19(a) or (e), (f), and (g), if a credit sale is one of a series made under an agreement providing that subsequent sales may be added to an outstanding balance, the creditor may delay the required disclosures until the due date of the first payment for the current sale, if the following two conditions are met:

(1)   The consumer has approved in writing the annual percentage rate or rates, the range of balances to which they apply, and the method of treating any unearned finance charge on an existing balance.

(2)   The creditor retains no security interest in any property after the creditor has received payments equal to the cash price and any finance charge attributable to the sale of that property. For purposes of this provision, in the case of items purchased on different dates, the first purchased is deemed the first item paid for; in the case of items purchased on the same date, the lowest priced is deemed the first item paid for.

(i)   Interim student credit extensions. For transactions involving an interim credit extension under a student credit program for which an application is received prior to the mandatory compliance date of §§ 1026.46, 47, and 48, the creditor need not make the following disclosures: the finance charge under § 1026.18(d), the payment schedule under § 1026.18(g), the total of payments under § 1026.18(h), or the total sale price under § 1026.18(j) at the time the credit is actually extended. The creditor must make complete disclosures at the time the creditor and consumer agree upon the repayment schedule for the total obligation. At that time, a new set of disclosures must be made of all applicable items under § 1026.18.

§ 1026.18   Content of disclosures.

For each transaction other than a mortgage transaction subject to § 1026.19(e) and (f), the creditor shall disclose the following information as applicable:

(a)   Creditor. The identity of the creditor making the disclosures.

(b)   Amount financed. The amount financed, using that term, and a brief description such as the amount of credit provided to you or on your behalf. The amount financed is calculated by:

(1)   Determining the principal loan amount or the cash price (subtracting any downpayment);

(2)   Adding any other amounts that are financed by the creditor and are not part of the finance charge; and

(3)   Subtracting any prepaid finance charge.

(c)   Itemization of amount financed.

(1)   Except as provided in paragraphs (c)(2) and (c)(3) of this section, a separate written itemization of the amount financed, including:

(i)   The amount of any proceeds distributed directly to the consumer.

(ii)   The amount credited to the consumer's account with the creditor.

(iii)   Any amounts paid to other persons by the creditor on the consumer's behalf. The creditor shall identify those persons. The following payees may be described using generic or other general terms and need not be further identified: public officials or government agencies, credit reporting agencies, appraisers, and insurance companies.

(iv)   The prepaid finance charge.

(2)   The creditor need not comply with paragraph (c)(1) of this section if the creditor provides a statement that the consumer has the right to receive a written itemization of the amount financed, together with a space for the consumer to indicate whether it is desired, and the consumer does not request it.

(3)   Good faith estimates of settlement costs provided for transactions subject to the Real Estate Settlement Procedures Act (12 U.S.C. 2601 et seq.) may be substituted for the disclosures required by paragraph (c)(1) of this section.

(d)   Finance charge. The finance charge, using that term, and a brief description such as "the dollar amount the credit will cost you."

(1)   Mortgage loans. In a transaction secured by real property or a dwelling, the disclosed finance charge and other disclosures affected by the disclosed finance charge (including the amount financed and the annual percentage rate) shall be treated as accurate if the amount disclosed as the finance charge:

(i)   Is understated by no more than $100; or

(ii)   Is greater than the amount required to be disclosed.

(2)   Other credit. In any other transaction, the amount disclosed as the finance charge shall be treated as accurate if, in a transaction involving an amount financed of $1,000 or less, it is not more than $5 above or below the amount required to be disclosed; or, in a transaction involving an amount financed of more than $1,000, it is not more than $10 above or below the amount required to be disclosed.

(e)   Annual percentage rate. The annual percentage rate, using that term, and a brief description such as "the cost of your credit as a yearly rate." For any transaction involving a finance charge of $5 or less on an amount financed of $75 or less, or a finance charge of $7.50 or less on an amount financed of more than $75, the creditor need not disclose the annual percentage rate.

(f) Variable rate.

(1) Except as provided in paragraph (f)(3) of this section, if the annual percentage rate may increase after consummation in a transaction not secured by the consumer's principal dwelling or in a transaction secured by the consumer's principal dwelling with a term of one year or less, the following disclosures:

    (i) The circumstances under which the rate may increase.

    (ii) Any limitations on the increase.

    (iii) The effect of an increase.

    (iv) An example of the payment terms that would result from an increase.

(2) If the annual percentage rate may increase after consummation in a transaction secured by the consumer's principal dwelling with a term greater than one year, the following disclosures:

    (i) The fact that the transaction contains a variable-rate feature.

    (ii) A statement that variable-rate disclosures have been provided earlier.

(3) Information provided in accordance with §§ 1026.18(f)(2) and 1026.19(b) may be substituted for the disclosures required by paragraph (f)(1) of this section.

(g) Payment schedule. Other than for a transaction that is subject to paragraph (s) of this section, the number, amounts, and timing of payments scheduled to repay the obligation.

(1) In a demand obligation with no alternate maturity date, the creditor may comply with this paragraph by disclosing the due dates or payment periods of any scheduled interest payments for the first year.

(2) In a transaction in which a series of payments varies because a finance charge is applied to the unpaid principal balance, the creditor may comply with this paragraph by disclosing the following information:

    (i) The dollar amounts of the largest and smallest payments in the series.

    (ii) A reference to the variations in the other payments in the series.

(h) Total of payments. The total of payments, using that term, and a descriptive explanation such as "the amount you will have paid when you have made all scheduled payments." In any transaction involving a single payment, the creditor need not disclose the total of payments.

(i) Demand feature. If the obligation has a demand feature, that fact shall be disclosed. When the disclosures are based on an assumed maturity of 1 year as provided in § 1026.17(c)(5), that fact shall also be disclosed.

(j) Total sale price. In a credit sale, the total sale price, using that term, and a descriptive explanation (including the amount of any downpayment) such as "the total price of your purchase on credit, including your downpayment of $__." The total sale price is the sum of the cash price, the items described in paragraph (b)(2), and the finance charge disclosed under paragraph (d) of this section.

(k) Prepayment.

(1) When an obligation includes a finance charge computed from time to time by application of a rate to the unpaid principal balance, a statement indicating whether or not a charge may be imposed for paying all or part of a loan's principal balance before the date on which the principal is due.

(2) When an obligation includes a finance charge other than the finance charge described in paragraph (k)(1) of this section, a statement indicating whether or not the consumer is entitled to a rebate of any finance charge if the obligation is prepaid in full or in part.

(*l*)   **Late payment.** Any dollar or percentage charge that may be imposed before maturity due to a late payment, other than a deferral or extension charge.

(m)   **Security interest.** The fact that the creditor has or will acquire a security interest in the property purchased as part of the transaction, or in other property identified by item or type.

(n)   **Insurance and debt cancellation.** The items required by § 1026.4(d) in order to exclude certain insurance premiums and debt cancellation fees from the finance charge.

(o)   **Certain security interest charges.** The disclosures required by § 1026.4(e) in order to exclude from the finance charge certain fees prescribed by law or certain premiums for insurance in lieu of perfecting a security interest.

(p)   **Contract reference.** A statement that the consumer should refer to the appropriate contract document for information about nonpayment, default, the right to accelerate the maturity of the obligation, and prepayment rebates and penalties. At the creditor's option, the statement may also include a reference to the contract for further information about security interests and, in a residential mortgage transaction, about the creditor's policy regarding assumption of the obligation.

(q)   **Assumption policy.** In a residential mortgage transaction, a statement whether or not a subsequent purchaser of the dwelling from the consumer may be permitted to assume the remaining obligation on its original terms.

(r)   **Required deposit.** If the creditor requires the consumer to maintain a deposit as a condition of the specific transaction, a statement that the annual percentage rate does not reflect the effect of the required deposit. A required deposit need not include, for example:

   (1)   An escrow account for items such as taxes, insurance or repairs;

   (2)   A deposit that earns not less than 5 percent per year; or

   (3)   Payments under a Morris Plan.

(s)   **Interest rate and payment summary for mortgage transactions.** For a closed-end transaction secured by real property or a dwelling, other than a transaction that is subject to § 1026.19(e) and (f), the creditor shall disclose the following information about the interest rate and payments:

   (1)   **Form of disclosures.** The information in paragraphs (s)(2)–(4) of this section shall be in the form of a table, with no more than five columns, with headings and format substantially similar to Model Clause H–4(E), H–4(F), H–4(G), or H–4(H) in Appendix H to this part. The table shall contain only the information required in paragraphs (s)(2)–(4) of this section, shall be placed in a prominent location, and shall be in a minimum 10-point font.

   (2)   **Interest rates.**

      (i)   **Amortizing loans.**

         (A)   For a fixed-rate mortgage, the interest rate at consummation.

         (B)   For an adjustable-rate or step-rate mortgage:

            (1)   The interest rate at consummation and the period of time until the first interest rate adjustment may occur, labeled as the "introductory rate and monthly payment";

            (2)   The maximum interest rate that may apply during the first five years after the date on which the first regular periodic payment will be due and the earliest date on which that rate may apply, labeled as "maximum during first five years"; and

            (3)   The maximum interest rate that may apply during the life of the loan and the earliest date on which that rate may apply, labeled as "maximum ever."

         (C)   If the loan provides for payment increases as described in paragraph (s)(3)(i)(B) of this section, the interest rate in effect at the time the first such payment increase is scheduled to occur and the date on which the increase will occur, labeled as "first adjustment" if the loan is an adjustable-rate mortgage or, otherwise, labeled as "first increase."

(ii) Negative amortization loans. For a negative amortization loan:

(A) The interest rate at consummation and, if it will adjust after consummation, the length of time until it will adjust, and the label "introductory" or "intro";

(B) The maximum interest rate that could apply when the consumer must begin making fully amortizing payments under the terms of the legal obligation;

(C) If the minimum required payment will increase before the consumer must begin making fully amortizing payments, the maximum interest rate that could apply at the time of the first payment increase and the date the increase is scheduled to occur; and

(D) If a second increase in the minimum required payment may occur before the consumer must begin making fully amortizing payments, the maximum interest rate that could apply at the time of the second payment increase and the date the increase is scheduled to occur.

(iii) Introductory rate disclosure for amortizing adjustable-rate mortgages. For an amortizing adjustable-rate mortgage, if the interest rate at consummation is less than the fully-indexed rate, placed in a box directly beneath the table required by paragraph (s)(1) of this section, in a format substantially similar to Model Clause H–4(I) in Appendix H to this part:

(A) The interest rate that applies at consummation and the period of time for which it applies;

(B) A statement that, even if market rates do not change, the interest rate will increase at the first adjustment and a designation of the place in sequence of the month or year, as applicable, of such rate adjustment; and

(C) The fully-indexed rate.

(3) Payments for amortizing loans.

(i) Principal and interest payments. If all periodic payments will be applied to accrued interest and principal, for each interest rate disclosed under paragraph (s)(2)(i) of this section:

(A) The corresponding periodic principal and interest payment, labeled as "principal and interest;"

(B) If the periodic payment may increase without regard to an interest rate adjustment, the payment that corresponds to the first such increase and the earliest date on which the increase could occur;

(C) If an escrow account will be established, an estimate of the amount of taxes and insurance, including any mortgage insurance or any functional equivalent, payable with each periodic payment; and

(D) The sum of the amounts disclosed under paragraphs (s)(3)(i)(A) and (C) of this section or (s)(3)(i)(B) and (C) of this section, as applicable, labeled as "total estimated monthly payment."

(ii) Interest-only payments. If the loan is an interest-only loan, for each interest rate disclosed under paragraph (s)(2)(i) of this section, the corresponding periodic payment and:

(A) If the payment will be applied to only accrued interest, the amount applied to interest, labeled as "interest payment," and a statement that none of the payment is being applied to principal;

(B) If the payment will be applied to accrued interest and principal, an itemization of the amount of the first such payment applied to accrued interest and to principal, labeled as "interest payment" and "principal payment," respectively;

(C) The escrow information described in paragraph (s)(3)(i)(C) of this section; and

(D) The sum of all amounts required to be disclosed under paragraphs (s)(3)(ii)(A) and (C) of this section or (s)(3)(ii)(B) and (C) of this section, as applicable, labeled as "total estimated monthly payment."

(4) Payments for negative amortization loans. For negative amortization loans:

(i)(A) The minimum periodic payment required until the first payment increase or interest rate increase, corresponding to the interest rate disclosed under paragraph (s)(2)(ii)(A) of this section;

(B) The minimum periodic payment that would be due at the first payment increase and the second, if any, corresponding to the interest rates described in paragraphs (s)(2)(ii)(C) and (D) of this section; and

(C) A statement that the minimum payment pays only some interest, does not repay any principal, and will cause the loan amount to increase;

(ii) The fully amortizing periodic payment amount at the earliest time when such a payment must be made, corresponding to the interest rate disclosed under paragraph (s)(2)(ii)(B) of this section; and

(iii) If applicable, in addition to the payments in paragraphs (s)(4)(i) and (ii) of this section, for each interest rate disclosed under paragraph (s)(2)(ii) of this section, the amount of the fully amortizing periodic payment, labeled as the "full payment option," and a statement that these payments pay all principal and all accrued interest.

(5) Balloon payments.

(i) Except as provided in paragraph (s)(5)(ii) of this section, if the transaction will require a balloon payment, defined as a payment that is more than two times a regular periodic payment, the balloon payment shall be disclosed separately from other periodic payments disclosed in the table under this paragraph (s), outside the table and in a manner substantially similar to Model Clause H–4(J) in Appendix H to this part.

(ii) If the balloon payment is scheduled to occur at the same time as another payment required to be disclosed in the table pursuant to paragraph (s)(3) or (s)(4) of this section, then the balloon payment must be disclosed in the table.

(6) Special disclosures for loans with negative amortization. For a negative amortization loan, the following information, in close proximity to the table required in paragraph (s)(1) of this section, with headings, content, and format substantially similar to Model Clause H–4(G) in Appendix H to this part:

(i) The maximum interest rate, the shortest period of time in which such interest rate could be reached, the amount of estimated taxes and insurance included in each payment disclosed, and a statement that the loan offers payment options, two of which are shown.

(ii) The dollar amount of the increase in the loan's principal balance if the consumer makes only the minimum required payments for the maximum possible time and the earliest date on which the consumer must begin making fully amortizing payments, assuming that the maximum interest rate is reached at the earliest possible time.

(7) Definitions. For purposes of this § 1026.18(s):

(i) The term "adjustable-rate mortgage" means a transaction secured by real property or a dwelling for which the annual percentage rate may increase after consummation.

(ii) The term "step-rate mortgage" means a transaction secured by real property or a dwelling for which the interest rate will change after consummation, and the rates that will apply and the periods for which they will apply are known at consummation.

(iii) The term "fixed-rate mortgage" means a transaction secured by real property or a dwelling that is not an adjustable-rate mortgage or a step-rate mortgage.

(iv) The term "interest-only" means that, under the terms of the legal obligation, one or more of the periodic payments may be applied solely to accrued interest and not to loan principal; an "interest-only loan" is a loan that permits interest-only payments.

(v) The term "amortizing loan" means a loan in which payment of the periodic payments does not result in an increase in the principal balance under the terms of the legal obligation; the term "negative amortization" means payment of periodic payments that will result in an increase in the principal balance under the terms of the legal obligation; the term "negative amortization loan" means a loan, other than a reverse mortgage subject to §1026.33, that provides for a minimum periodic payment that covers only a portion of the accrued interest, resulting in negative amortization.

(vi) The term "fully-indexed rate" means the interest rate calculated using the index value and margin at the time of consummation.

(t)   "No-guarantee-to-refinance" statement.

(1)   Disclosure. For a closed-end transaction secured by real property or a dwelling, other than a transaction that is subject to §1026.19(e) and (f), the creditor shall disclose a statement that there is no guarantee the consumer can refinance the transaction to lower the interest rate or periodic payments.

(2)   Format. The statement required by paragraph (t)(1) of this section must be in a form substantially similar to Model Clause H–4(K) in Appendix H to this part.

§1026.19   Certain mortgage and variable-rate transactions.

(a)   Mortgage transactions subject to RESPA.

(1)(i)   Time of disclosures. In a reverse mortgage transaction subject to both §1026.33 and the Real Estate Settlement Procedures Act (12 U.S.C. 2601 et seq.) that is secured by the consumer's dwelling, the creditor shall provide the consumer with good faith estimates of the disclosures required by §1026.18 and shall deliver or place them in the mail not later than the third business day after the creditor receives the consumer's written application.

(ii)   Imposition of fees. Except as provided in paragraph (a)(1)(iii) of this section, neither a creditor nor any other person may impose a fee on a consumer in connection with the consumer's application for a reverse mortgage transaction subject to paragraph (a)(1)(i) of this section before the consumer has received the disclosures required by paragraph (a)(1)(i) of this section. If the disclosures are mailed to the consumer, the consumer is considered to have received them three business days after they are mailed.

(iii)   Exception to fee restriction. A creditor or other person may impose a fee for obtaining the consumer's credit history before the consumer has received the disclosures required by paragraph (a)(1)(i) of this section, provided the fee is bona fide and reasonable in amount.

(2)   Waiting periods for early disclosures and corrected disclosures.

(i)   The creditor shall deliver or place in the mail the good faith estimates required by paragraph (a)(1)(i) of this section not later than the seventh business day before consummation of the transaction.

(ii)   If the annual percentage rate disclosed under paragraph (a)(1)(i) of this section becomes inaccurate, as defined in §1026.22, the creditor shall provide corrected disclosures with all changed terms. The consumer must receive the corrected disclosures no later than three business days before consummation. If the corrected disclosures are mailed to the consumer or delivered to the consumer by means other than delivery in person, the consumer is deemed to have received the corrected disclosures three business days after they are mailed or delivered.

(3) Consumer's waiver of waiting period before consummation. If the consumer determines that the extension of credit is needed to meet a bona fide personal financial emergency, the consumer may modify or waive the seven-business-day waiting period or the three-business-day waiting period required by paragraph (a)(2) of this section, after receiving the disclosures required by § 1026.18. To modify or waive a waiting period, the consumer shall give the creditor a dated written statement that describes the emergency, specifically modifies or waives the waiting period, and bears the signature of all the consumers who are primarily liable on the legal obligation. Printed forms for this purpose are prohibited.

(4) Notice. Disclosures made pursuant to paragraph (a)(1) or paragraph (a)(2) of this section shall contain the following statement: "You are not required to complete this agreement merely because you have received these disclosures or signed a loan application." The disclosure required by this paragraph shall be grouped together with the disclosures required by paragraphs (a)(1) or (a)(2) of this section.

(5) Timeshare plans. In a mortgage transaction subject to the Real Estate Settlement Procedures Act (12 U.S.C. 2601 et seq.) that is secured by a consumer's interest in a timeshare plan described in 11 U.S.C. 101(53(D)):

(i) The requirements of paragraphs (a)(1) through (a)(4) of this section do not apply;

(ii) The creditor shall make good faith estimates of the disclosures required by § 1026.18 before consummation, or shall deliver or place them in the mail not later than three business days after the creditor receives the consumer's written application, whichever is earlier; and

(iii) If the annual percentage rate at the time of consummation varies from the annual percentage rate disclosed under paragraph (a)(5)(ii) of this section by more than $^1/_8$ of 1 percentage point in a regular transaction or more than ¼ of 1 percentage point in an irregular transaction, as defined in § 1026.22, the creditor shall disclose all the changed terms no later than consummation or settlement.

(b) Certain variable-rate transactions. Except as provided in paragraph (d) of this section, if the annual percentage rate may increase after consummation in a transaction secured by the consumer's principal dwelling with a term greater than one year, the following disclosures must be provided at the time an application form is provided or before the consumer pays a non-refundable fee, whichever is earlier (except that the disclosures may be delivered or placed in the mail not later than three business days following receipt of a consumer's application when the application reaches the creditor by telephone, or through an intermediary agent or broker):

(1) The booklet titled Consumer Handbook on Adjustable Rate Mortgages, or a suitable substitute.

(2) A loan program disclosure for each variable-rate program in which the consumer expresses an interest. The following disclosures, as applicable, shall be provided:

(i) The fact that the interest rate, payment, or term of the loan can change.

(ii) The index or formula used in making adjustments, and a source of information about the index or formula.

(iii) An explanation of how the interest rate and payment will be determined, including an explanation of how the index is adjusted, such as by the addition of a margin.

(iv) A statement that the consumer should ask about the current margin value and current interest rate.

(v) The fact that the interest rate will be discounted, and a statement that the consumer should ask about the amount of the interest rate discount.

(vi) The frequency of interest rate and payment changes.

(vii) Any rules relating to changes in the index, interest rate, payment amount, and outstanding loan balance including, for example, an explanation of interest rate or payment limitations, negative amortization, and interest rate carryover.

(viii) At the option of the creditor, either of the following:

(A) A historical example, based on a $10,000 loan amount, illustrating how payments and the loan balance would have been affected by interest rate changes implemented according to the terms of the loan program disclosure. The example shall reflect the most recent 15 years of index values. The example shall reflect all significant loan program terms, such as negative amortization, interest rate carryover, interest rate discounts, and interest rate and payment limitations, that would have been affected by the index movement during the period.

(B) The maximum interest rate and payment for a $10,000 loan originated at the initial interest rate (index value plus margin, adjusted by the amount of any discount or premium) in effect as of an identified month and year for the loan program disclosure assuming the maximum periodic increases in rates and payments under the program; and the initial interest rate and payment for that loan and a statement that the periodic payment may increase or decrease substantially depending on changes in the rate.

(ix) An explanation of how the consumer may calculate the payments for the loan amount to be borrowed based on either:

(A) The most recent payment shown in the historical example in paragraph (b)(2)(viii)(A) of this section; or

(B) The initial interest rate used to calculate the maximum interest rate and payment in paragraph (b)(2)(viii)(B) of this section.

(x) The fact that the loan program contains a demand feature.

(xi) The type of information that will be provided in notices of adjustments and the timing of such notices.

(xii) A statement that disclosure forms are available for the creditor's other variable-rate loan programs.

(c) **Electronic disclosures.** For an application that is accessed by the consumer in electronic form, the disclosures required by paragraph (b) of this section may be provided to the consumer in electronic form on or with the application.

(d) Information provided in accordance with variable-rate regulations of other Federal agencies may be substituted for the disclosures required by paragraph (b) of this section.

(e) **Mortgage loans secured by real property—early disclosures.**

(1) **Provision of disclosures.**

(i) **Creditor.** In a closed-end consumer credit transaction secured by real property, other than a reverse mortgage subject to § 1026.33, the creditor shall provide the consumer with good faith estimates of the disclosures in § 1026.37.

(ii) **Mortgage broker.**

(A) If a mortgage broker receives a consumer's application, either the creditor or the mortgage broker shall provide a consumer with the disclosures required under paragraph (e)(1)(i) of this section in accordance with paragraph (e)(1)(iii) of this section. If the mortgage broker provides the required disclosures, the mortgage broker shall comply with all relevant requirements of this paragraph (e). The creditor shall ensure that such disclosures are provided in accordance with all requirements of this paragraph (e). Disclosures provided by a mortgage broker in accordance with the requirements of this paragraph (e) satisfy the creditor's obligation under this paragraph (e).

(B) If a mortgage broker provides any disclosure under § 1026.19(e), the mortgage broker shall also comply with the requirements of § 1026.25(c).

(iii) Timing.

(A) The creditor shall deliver or place in the mail the disclosures required under paragraph (e)(1)(i) of this section not later than the third business day after the creditor receives the consumer's application, as defined in § 1026.2(a)(3).

(B) Except as set forth in paragraph (e)(1)(iii)(C) of this section, the creditor shall deliver or place in the mail the disclosures required under paragraph (e)(1)(i) of this section not later than the seventh business day before consummation of the transaction.

(C) For a transaction secured by a consumer's interest in a timeshare plan described in 11 U.S.C. 101(53D), paragraph (e)(1)(iii)(B) of this section does not apply.

(iv) Receipt of early disclosures. If any disclosures required under paragraph (e)(1)(i) of this section are not provided to the consumer in person, the consumer is considered to have received the disclosures three business days after they are delivered or placed in the mail.

(v) Consumer's waiver of waiting period before consummation. If the consumer determines that the extension of credit is needed to meet a bona fide personal financial emergency, the consumer may modify or waive the seven-business-day waiting period for early disclosures required under paragraph (e)(1)(iii)(B) of this section, after receiving the disclosures required under paragraph (e)(1)(i) of this section. To modify or waive the waiting period, the consumer shall give the creditor a dated written statement that describes the emergency, specifically modifies or waives the waiting period, and bears the signature of all the consumers who are primarily liable on the legal obligation. Printed forms for this purpose are prohibited.

(vi) Shopping for settlement service providers.

(A) Shopping permitted. A creditor permits a consumer to shop for a settlement service if the creditor permits the consumer to select the provider of that service, subject to reasonable requirements.

(B) Disclosure of services. The creditor shall identify the settlement services for which the consumer is permitted to shop in the disclosures required under paragraph (e)(1)(i) of this section.

(C) Written list of providers. If the consumer is permitted to shop for a settlement service, the creditor shall provide the consumer with a written list identifying available providers of that settlement service and stating that the consumer may choose a different provider for that service. The creditor must identify at least one available provider for each settlement service for which the consumer is permitted to shop. The creditor shall provide this written list of settlement service providers separately from the disclosures required by paragraph (e)(1)(i) of this section but in accordance with the timing requirements in paragraph (e)(1)(iii) of this section.

(2) Predisclosure activity.

(i) Imposition of fees on consumer.

(A) Fee restriction. Except as provided in paragraph (e)(2)(i)(B) of this section, neither a creditor nor any other person may impose a fee on a consumer in connection with the consumer's application for a mortgage transaction subject to paragraph (e)(1)(i) of this section before the consumer has received the disclosures required under paragraph (e)(1)(i) of this section and indicated to the creditor an intent to proceed with the transaction described by those disclosures. A consumer may indicate an intent to proceed with a transaction in any manner the consumer chooses, unless a particular manner of communication is required by the creditor. The creditor must document this communication to satisfy the requirements of § 1026.25.

(B) Exception to fee restriction. A creditor or other person may impose a bona fide and reasonable fee for obtaining the consumer's credit report before the consumer has received the disclosures required under paragraph (e)(1)(i) of this section.

(ii) Written information provided to consumer. If a creditor or other person provides a consumer with a written estimate of terms or costs specific to that consumer before the consumer receives the disclosures required under paragraph (e)(1)(i) of this section, the creditor or such person shall clearly and conspicuously state at the top of the front of the first page of the estimate in a font size that is no smaller than 12-point font: "Your actual rate, payment, and costs could be higher. Get an official Loan Estimate before choosing a loan." The written estimate of terms or costs may not be made with headings, content, and format substantially similar to form H–24 or H–25 of appendix H to this part.

(iii) Verification of information. The creditor or other person shall not require a consumer to submit documents verifying information related to the consumer's application before providing the disclosures required by paragraph (e)(1)(i) of this section.

(3) Good faith determination for estimates of closing costs.

(i) General rule. An estimated closing cost disclosed pursuant to paragraph (e) of this section is in good faith if the charge paid by or imposed on the consumer does not exceed the amount originally disclosed under paragraph (e)(1)(i) of this section, except as otherwise provided in paragraphs (e)(3)(ii) through (iv) of this section.

(ii) Limited increases permitted for certain charges. An estimate of a charge for a third-party service or a recording fee is in good faith if:

(A) The aggregate amount of charges for third-party services and recording fees paid by or imposed on the consumer does not exceed the aggregate amount of such charges disclosed under paragraph (e)(1)(i) of this section by more than 10 percent;

(B) The charge for the third-party service is not paid to the creditor or an affiliate of the creditor; and

(C) The creditor permits the consumer to shop for the third-party service, consistent with paragraph (e)(1)(vi) of this section.

(iii) Variations permitted for certain charges. An estimate of the following charges is in good faith if it is consistent with the best information reasonably available to the creditor at the time it is disclosed, regardless of whether the amount paid by the consumer exceeds the amount disclosed under paragraph (e)(1)(i) of this section:

(A) Prepaid interest;

(B) Property insurance premiums;

(C) Amounts placed into an escrow, impound, reserve, or similar account;

(D) Charges paid to third-party service providers selected by the consumer consistent with paragraph (e)(1)(vi)(A) of this section that are not on the list provided pursuant to paragraph (e)(1)(vi)(C) of this section; and

(E) Charges paid for third-party services not required by the creditor. These charges may be paid to affiliates of the creditor.

(iv) Revised estimates. For the purpose of determining good faith under paragraph (e)(3)(i) and (ii) of this section, a creditor may use a revised estimate of a charge instead of the estimate of the charge originally disclosed under paragraph (e)(1)(i) of this section if the revision is due to any of the following reasons:

(A) Changed circumstance affecting settlement charges. Changed circumstances cause the estimated charges to increase or, in the case of estimated charges identified in paragraph (e)(3)(ii) of this section, cause the aggregate amount of such charges to increase by more than 10 percent. For purposes of this paragraph, "changed circumstance" means:

(1)   An extraordinary event beyond the control of any interested party or other unexpected event specific to the consumer or transaction;

(2)   Information specific to the consumer or transaction that the creditor relied upon when providing the disclosures required under paragraph (e)(1)(i) of this section and that was inaccurate or changed after the disclosures were provided; or

(3)   New information specific to the consumer or transaction that the creditor did not rely on when providing the original disclosures required under paragraph (e)(1)(i) of this section.

(B)   **Changed circumstance affecting eligibility.** The consumer is ineligible for an estimated charge previously disclosed because a changed circumstance, as defined under paragraph (e)(3)(iv)(A) of this section, affected the consumer's creditworthiness or the value of the security for the loan.

(C)   **Revisions requested by the consumer.** The consumer requests revisions to the credit terms or the settlement that cause an estimated charge to increase.

(D)   **Interest rate dependent charges.** The points or lender credits change because the interest rate was not locked when the disclosures required under paragraph (e)(1)(i) of this section were provided. No later than three business days after the date the interest rate is locked, the creditor shall provide a revised version of the disclosures required under paragraph (e)(1)(i) of this section to the consumer with the revised interest rate, the points disclosed pursuant to § 1026.37(f)(1), lender credits, and any other interest rate dependent charges and terms.

(E)   **Expiration.** The consumer indicates an intent to proceed with the transaction more than ten business days after the disclosures required under paragraph (e)(1)(i) of this section are provided pursuant to paragraph (e)(1)(iii) of this section.

(F)   **Delayed settlement date on a construction loan.** In transactions involving new construction, where the creditor reasonably expects that settlement will occur more than 60 days after the disclosures required under paragraph (e)(1)(i) of this section are provided pursuant to paragraph (e)(1)(iii) of this section, the creditor may provide revised disclosures to the consumer if the original disclosures required under paragraph (e)(1)(i) of this section state clearly and conspicuously that at any time prior to 60 days before consummation, the creditor may issue revised disclosures. If no such statement is provided, the creditor may not issue revised disclosures, except as otherwise provided in paragraph (f) of this section.

(4)   **Provision and receipt of revised disclosures.**

(i)   **General rule.** Subject to the requirements of paragraph (e)(4)(ii) of this section, if a creditor uses a revised estimate pursuant to paragraph (e)(3)(iv) of this section for the purpose of determining good faith under paragraphs (e)(3)(i) and (ii) of this revised version of the disclosures required under paragraph (e)(1)(i) of this section reflecting the revised estimate within three business days of receiving information sufficient to establish that one of the reasons for revision provided under paragraphs (e)(3)(iv)(A) through (C), (E) and (F) of this section applies.

(ii)   **Relationship to disclosures required under § 1026.19(f)(1)(i).** The creditor shall not provide a revised version of the disclosures required under paragraph (e)(1)(i) of this section on or after the date on which the creditor provides the disclosures required under paragraph (f)(1)(i) of this section. The consumer must receive a revised version of the disclosures required under paragraph (e)(1)(i) of this section not later than four business days prior to consummation. If the revised version of the disclosures required under paragraph (e)(1)(i) of this section is not provided to the consumer in person, the consumer is considered to have received such version three business days after the creditor delivers or places such version in the mail.

(f)   **Mortgage loans secured by real property—final disclosures.**

     (1)   **Provision of disclosures.**

        (i)   **Scope.** In a closed-end consumer credit transaction secured by real property, other than a reverse mortgage subject to § 1026.33, the creditor shall provide the consumer with the disclosures in § 1026.38 reflecting the actual terms of the transaction.

        (ii)   **Timing.**

           (A)   **In general.** Except as provided in paragraphs (f)(1)(ii)(B), (f)(2)(i), (f)(2)(iii), (f)(2)(iv), and (f)(2)(v) of this section, the creditor shall ensure that the consumer receives the disclosures required under paragraph (f)(1)(i) of this section no later than three business days before consummation.

           (B)   **Timeshares.** For transactions secured by a consumer's interest in a timeshare plan described in 11 U.S.C. 101(53D), the creditor shall ensure that the consumer receives the disclosures required under paragraph (f)(1)(i) of this section no later than consummation.

        (iii) Receipt of disclosures. If any disclosures required under paragraph (f)(1)(i) of this section are not provided to the consumer in person, the consumer is considered to have received the disclosures three business days after they are delivered or placed in the mail.

        (iv) Consumer's waiver of waiting period before consummation. If the consumer determines that the extension of credit is needed to meet a bona fide personal financial emergency, the consumer may modify or waive the three-business-day waiting period under paragraph (f)(1)(ii)(A) or (f)(2)(ii) of this section, after receiving the disclosures required under paragraph (f)(1)(i) of this section. To modify or waive the waiting period, the consumer shall give the creditor a dated written statement that describes the emergency, specifically modifies or waives the waiting period, and bears the signature of all consumers who are primarily liable on the legal obligation. Printed forms for this purpose are prohibited.

        (v) Settlement agent. A settlement agent may provide a consumer with the disclosures required under paragraph (f)(1)(i) of this section, provided the settlement agent complies with all relevant requirements of this paragraph (f). The creditor shall ensure that such disclosures are provided in accordance with all requirements of this paragraph (f). Disclosures provided by a settlement agent in accordance with the requirements of this paragraph (f) satisfy the creditor's obligation under this paragraph (f).

     (2)   **Subsequent changes.**

        (i)   **Changes before consummation not requiring a new waiting period.** Except as provided in paragraph (f)(2)(ii), if the disclosures provided under paragraph (f)(1)(i) of this section become inaccurate before consummation, the creditor shall provide corrected disclosures reflecting any changed terms to the consumer so that the consumer receives the corrected disclosures at or before consummation. Notwithstanding the requirement to provide corrected disclosures at or before consummation, the creditor shall permit the consumer to inspect the disclosures provided under this paragraph, completed to set forth those items that are known to the creditor at the time of inspection, during the business day immediately preceding consummation, but the creditor may omit from inspection items related only to the seller's transaction.

        (ii)   **Changes before consummation requiring a new waiting period.** If one of the following disclosures provided under paragraph (f)(1)(i) of this section becomes inaccurate in the following manner before consummation, the creditor shall ensure that the consumer receives corrected disclosures containing all changed terms in accordance with the requirements of paragraph (f)(1)(ii)(A) of this section:

           (A)   The annual percentage rate disclosed under § 1026.38(o)(4) becomes inaccurate, as defined in § 1026.22.

(B) The loan product is changed, causing the information disclosed under § 1026.38(a)(5)(iii) to become inaccurate.

(C) A prepayment penalty is added, causing the statement regarding a prepayment penalty required under § 1026.38(b) to become inaccurate.

(iii) Changes due to events occurring after consummation. If during the 30-day period following consummation, an event in connection with the settlement of the transaction occurs that causes the disclosures required under paragraph (f)(1)(i) of this section to become inaccurate, and such inaccuracy results in a change to an amount actually paid by the consumer from that amount disclosed under paragraph (f)(1)(i) of this section, the creditor shall deliver or place in the mail corrected disclosures not later than 30 days after receiving information sufficient to establish that such event has occurred.

(iv) Changes due to clerical errors. A creditor does not violate paragraph (f)(1)(i) of this section if the disclosures provided under paragraph (f)(1)(i) contain non-numeric clerical errors, provided the creditor delivers or places in the mail corrected disclosures no later than 60 days after consummation.

(v) Refunds related to the good faith analysis. If amounts paid by the consumer exceed the amounts specified under paragraph (e)(3)(i) or (ii) of this section, the creditor complies with paragraph (e)(1)(i) of this section if the creditor refunds the excess to the consumer no later than 60 days after consummation, and the creditor complies with paragraph (f)(1)(i) of this section if the creditor delivers or places in the mail corrected disclosures that reflect such refund no later than 60 days after consummation.

(3) Charges disclosed.

(i) Actual charge. The amount imposed upon the consumer for any settlement service shall not exceed the amount actually received by the settlement service provider for that service, except as otherwise provided in paragraph (f)(3)(ii) of this section.

(ii) Average charge. A creditor or settlement service provider may charge a consumer or seller the average charge for a settlement service if the following conditions are satisfied:

(A) The average charge is no more than the average amount paid for that service by or on behalf of all consumers and sellers for a class of transactions;

(B) The creditor or settlement service provider defines the class of transactions based on an appropriate period of time, geographic area, and type of loan;

(C) The creditor or settlement service provider uses the same average charge for every transaction within the defined class; and

(D) The creditor or settlement service provider does not use an average charge:

(1) For any type of insurance;

(2) For any charge based on the loan amount or property value; or by law.

(4) Transactions involving a seller.

(i) Provision to seller. In a closed-end consumer credit transaction secured by real property that involves a seller, other than a reverse mortgage subject to § 1026.33, the settlement agent shall provide the seller with the disclosures in § 1026.38 that relate to the seller's transaction reflecting the actual terms of the seller's transaction.

(ii) Timing. The settlement agent shall provide the disclosures required under paragraph (f)(4)(i) of this section no later than the day of consummation. If during the 30-day period following consummation, an event in connection with the settlement of the transaction occurs that causes disclosures required under paragraph (f)(4)(i) of this section to become inaccurate, and such inaccuracy results in a change to the amount actually paid by the seller from that amount disclosed under paragraph (f)(4)(i) of this section, the settlement agent shall deliver or place in the mail corrected disclosures not later than 30 days after receiving information sufficient to establish that such event has occurred.

(iii) Charges disclosed. The amount imposed on the seller for any settlement service shall not exceed the amount actually received by the service provider for that service, except as otherwise provided in paragraph (f)(3)(ii) of this section.

(iv) Creditor's copy. When the consumer's and seller's disclosures under this paragraph (f) are provided on separate documents, as permitted under § 1026.38(t)(5), the settlement agent shall provide to the creditor (if the creditor is not the settlement agent) a copy of the disclosures provided to the seller under paragraph (f)(4)(i) of this section.

(5) No fee. No fee may be imposed on any person, as a part of settlement costs or otherwise, by a creditor or by a servicer (as that term is defined under 12 U.S.C. 2605(i)(2)) for the preparation or delivery of the disclosures required under paragraph (f)(1)(i) of this section.

(g) Special information booklet at time of application.

(1) Creditor to provide special information booklet. Except as provided in paragraphs (g)(1)(ii) and (iii) of this section, the creditor shall provide a copy of the special information booklet (required pursuant to section 5 of the Real Estate Settlement Procedures Act (12 U.S.C. 2604) to help consumers applying for federally related mortgage loans understand the nature and cost of real estate settlement services) to a consumer who applies for a consumer credit transaction secured by real property.

(i) The creditor shall deliver or place in the mail the special information booklet not later than three business days after the consumer's application is received. However, if the creditor denies the consumer's application before the end of the three-business-day period, the creditor need not provide the booklet. If a consumer uses a mortgage broker, the mortgage broker shall provide the special information booklet and the creditor need not do so.

(ii) In the case of a home equity line of credit subject to § 1026.40, a creditor or mortgage broker that provides the consumer with a copy of the brochure entitled "When Your Home is On the Line: What You Should Know About Home Equity Lines of Credit," or any successor brochure issued by the Bureau, is deemed to be in compliance with this section.

(iii) The creditor or mortgage broker need not provide the booklet to the consumer for a consumer credit transaction secured by real property, the purpose of which is not the purchase of a one-to-four family residential property, including, but not limited to, the following:

(A) Refinancing transactions;

(B) Closed-end loans secured by a subordinate lien; and

(C) Reverse mortgages.

(2) Permissible changes. Creditors may not make changes to, deletions from, or additions to the special information booklet other than the changes specified in paragraphs (g)(2)(i) through (iv) of this section.

(i) In the "Complaints" section of the booklet, "the Bureau of Consumer Financial Protection" may be substituted for "HUD's Office of RESPA" and "the RESPA office."

(ii) In the "Avoiding Foreclosure" section of the booklet, it is permissible to inform homeowners that they may find information on and assistance in avoiding foreclosures at http://www.consumerfinance.gov. The reference to the HUD Web site, http://www.hud.gov/foreclosure/, in the "Avoiding Foreclosure" section of the booklet shall not be deleted.

(iii) In the "No Discrimination" section of the appendix to the booklet, "the Bureau of Consumer Financial Protection" may be substituted for the reference to the "Board of Governors of the Federal Reserve System." In the Contact Information section of the appendix to the booklet, the following contact information for the Bureau may be added: "Bureau of Consumer Financial Protection, 1700 G Street NW., Washington, DC 20552; www.consumerfinance.gov/learnmore."

The contact information for HUD's Office of RESPA and Interstate Land Sales may be removed from the "Contact Information" section of the appendix to the booklet.

(iv) The cover of the booklet may be in any form and may contain any drawings, pictures or artwork, provided that the title appearing on the cover shall not be changed. Names, addresses, and telephone numbers of the creditor or others and similar information may appear on the cover, but no discussion of the matters covered in the booklet shall appear on the cover. References to HUD on the cover of the booklet may be changed to references to the Bureau.

§ 1026.20 Disclosure requirements regarding post-consummation events.

(a) **Refinancings.** A refinancing occurs when an existing obligation that was subject to this subpart is satisfied and replaced by a new obligation undertaken by the same consumer. A refinancing is a new transaction requiring new disclosures to the consumer. The new finance charge shall include any unearned portion of the old finance charge that is not credited to the existing obligation. The following shall not be treated as a refinancing:

(1) A renewal of a single payment obligation with no change in the original terms.

(2) A reduction in the annual percentage rate with a corresponding change in the payment schedule.

(3) An agreement involving a court proceeding.

(4) A change in the payment schedule or a change in collateral requirements as a result of the consumer's default or delinquency, unless the rate is increased, or the new amount financed exceeds the unpaid balance plus earned finance charge and premiums for continuation of insurance of the types described in § 1026.4(d).

(5) The renewal of optional insurance purchased by the consumer and added to an existing transaction, if disclosures relating to the initial purchase were provided as required by this subpart.

(b) **Assumptions.** An assumption occurs when a creditor expressly agrees in writing with a subsequent consumer to accept that consumer as a primary obligor on an existing residential mortgage transaction. Before the assumption occurs, the creditor shall make new disclosures to the subsequent consumer, based on the remaining obligation. If the finance charge originally imposed on the existing obligation was an add-on or discount finance charge, the creditor need only disclose:

(1) The unpaid balance of the obligation assumed.

(2) The total charges imposed by the creditor in connection with the assumption.

(3) The information required to be disclosed under § 1026.18(k), (*l*), (m), and (n).

(4) The annual percentage rate originally imposed on the obligation.

(5) The payment schedule under § 1026.18(g) and the total of payments under § 1026.18(h) based on the remaining obligation.

(c) **Rate adjustments with a corresponding change in payment.** The creditor, assignee, or servicer of an adjustable-rate mortgage shall provide consumers with disclosures, as described in this paragraph (c), in connection with the adjustment of interest rates pursuant to the loan contract that results in a corresponding adjustment to the payment. To the extent that other provisions of this subpart C govern the disclosures required by this paragraph (c), those provisions apply to assignees and servicers as well as to creditors. The disclosures required by this paragraph (c) also shall be provided for an interest rate adjustment resulting from the conversion of an adjustable-rate mortgage to a fixed-rate transaction, if that interest rate adjustment results in a corresponding payment change.

(1) **Coverage.**

(i) **In general.** For purposes of this paragraph (c), an adjustable-rate mortgage or "ARM" is a closed-end consumer credit transaction secured by the consumer's principal dwelling in which the annual percentage rate may increase after consummation.

    (ii) Exemptions. The requirements of this paragraph (c) do not apply to:

        (A) ARMs with terms of one year or less;

        (B) The first interest rate adjustment to an ARM if the first payment at the adjusted level is due within 210 days after consummation and the new interest rate disclosed at consummation pursuant to § 1026.20(d) was not an estimate; or

        (C) The creditor, assignee or servicer of an adjustable-rate mortgage when the servicer on the loan is subject to the Fair Debt Collections Practices Act (FDCPA) (15 U.S.C. 1692 et seq.) with regard to the loan and the consumer has sent a notification pursuant to FDCPA section 805(c) (15 U.S.C. 1692c(c)).

    (2) Timing and content. Except as otherwise provided in paragraph (c)(2) of this section, the disclosures required by this paragraph (c) shall be provided to consumers at least 60, but no more than 120, days before the first payment at the adjusted level is due. The disclosures shall be provided to consumers at least 25, but no more than 120, days before the first payment at the adjusted level is due for ARMs with uniformly scheduled interest rate adjustments occurring every 60 days or more frequently and for ARMs originated prior to January 10, 2015 in which the loan contract requires the adjusted interest rate and payment to be calculated based on the index figure available as of a date that is less than 45 days prior to the adjustment date. The disclosures shall be provided to consumers as soon as practicable, but not less than 25 days before the first payment at the adjusted level is due, for the first adjustment to an ARM if it occurs within 60 days of consummation and the new interest rate disclosed at consummation pursuant to § 1026.20(d) was an estimate. The disclosures required by this paragraph (c) shall include:

    (i) A statement providing:

        (A) An explanation that under the terms of the consumer's adjustable-rate mortgage, the specific time period in which the current interest rate has been in effect is ending and the interest rate and mortgage payment will change;

        (B) The effective date of the interest rate adjustment and when additional future interest rate adjustments are scheduled to occur; and

        (C) Any other changes to loan terms, features, or options taking effect on the same date as the interest rate adjustment, such as the expiration of interest-only or payment-option features.

    (ii) A table containing the following information:

        (A) The current and new interest rates;

        (B) The current and new payments and the date the first new payment is due; and

        (C) For interest-only or negatively-amortizing payments, the amount of the current and new payment allocated to principal, interest, and taxes and insurance in escrow, as applicable. The current payment allocation disclosed shall be the payment allocation for the last payment prior to the date of the disclosure. The new payment allocation disclosed shall be the expected payment allocation for the first payment for which the new interest rate will apply.

    (iii) An explanation of how the interest rate is determined, including:

        (A) The specific index or formula used in making interest rate adjustments and a source of information about the index or formula; and

        (B) The type and amount of any adjustment to the index, including any margin and an explanation that the margin is the addition of a certain number of percentage points to the index, and any application of previously foregone interest rate increases from past interest rate adjustments.

(iv) Any limits on the interest rate or payment increases at each interest rate adjustment and over the life of the loan, as applicable, including the extent to which such limits result in the creditor, assignee, or servicer foregoing any increase in the interest rate and the earliest date that such foregone interest rate increases may apply to future interest rate adjustments, subject to those limits.

(v) An explanation of how the new payment is determined, including:

(A) The index or formula used;

(B) Any adjustment to the index or formula, such as the addition of a margin or the application of any previously foregone interest rate increases from past interest rate adjustments;

(C) The loan balance expected on the date of the interest rate adjustment; and

(D) The length of the remaining loan term expected on the date of the interest rate adjustment and any change in the term of the loan caused by the adjustment.

(vi) If applicable, a statement that the new payment will not be allocated to pay loan principal and will not reduce the loan balance. If the new payment will result in negative amortization, a statement that the new payment will not be allocated to pay loan principal and will pay only part of the loan interest, thereby adding to the balance of the loan. If the new payment will result in negative amortization as a result of the interest rate adjustment, the statement shall set forth the payment required to amortize fully the remaining balance at the new interest rate over the remainder of the loan term.

(vii) The circumstances under which any prepayment penalty, as defined in § 1026.32(b)(6)(i), may be imposed, such as when paying the loan in full or selling or refinancing the principal dwelling; the time period during which such a penalty may be imposed; and a statement that the consumer may contact the servicer for additional information, including the maximum amount of the penalty.

(3) Format.

(i) The disclosures required by this paragraph (c) shall be provided in the form of a table and in the same order as, and with headings and format substantially similar to, forms H–4(D)(1) and (2) in appendix H to this part; and

(ii) The disclosures required by paragraph (c)(2)(ii) of this section shall be in the form of a table located within the table described in paragraph (c)(3)(i) of this section. These disclosures shall appear in the same order as, and with headings and format substantially similar to, the table inside the larger table in forms H–4(D)(1) and (2) in appendix H to this part.

(d) Initial rate adjustment. The creditor, assignee, or servicer of an adjustable-rate mortgage shall provide consumers with disclosures, as described in this paragraph (d), in connection with the initial interest rate adjustment pursuant to the loan contract. To the extent that other provisions of this subpart C govern the disclosures required by this paragraph (d), those provisions apply to assignees and servicers as well as to creditors. The disclosures required by this paragraph (d) shall be provided as a separate document from other documents provided by the creditor, assignee, or servicer. The disclosures shall be provided to consumers at least 210, but no more than 240, days before the first payment at the adjusted level is due. If the first payment at the adjusted level is due within the first 210 days after consummation, the disclosures shall be provided at consummation.

(1) Coverage.

(i)   In general. For purposes of this paragraph (d), an adjustable-rate mortgage or "ARM" is a closed-end consumer credit transaction secured by the consumer's principal dwelling in which the annual percentage rate may increase after consummation.

(ii)   Exemptions. The requirements of this paragraph (d) do not apply to ARMs with terms of one year or less.

(2) Content. If the new interest rate (or the new payment calculated from the new interest rate) is not known as of the date of the disclosure, an estimate shall be disclosed and labeled as such. This estimate shall be based on the calculation of the index reported in the source of information described in paragraph (d)(2)(iv)(A) of this section within fifteen business days prior to the date of the disclosure. The disclosures required by this paragraph (d) shall include:

(i) The date of the disclosure.

(ii) A statement providing:

(A) An explanation that under the terms of the consumer's adjustable-rate mortgage, the specific time period in which the current interest rate has been in effect is ending and that any change in the interest rate may result in a change in the mortgage payment;

(B) The effective date of the interest rate adjustment and when additional future interest rate adjustments are scheduled to occur; and

(C) Any other changes to loan terms, features, or options taking effect on the same date as the interest rate adjustment, such as the expiration of interest-only or payment-option features.

(iii) A table containing the following information:

(A) The current and new interest rates;

(B) The current and new payments and the date the first new payment is due; and

(C) For interest-only or negatively-amortizing payments, the amount of the current and new payment allocated to principal, interest, and taxes and insurance in escrow, as applicable. The current payment allocation disclosed shall be the payment allocation for the last payment prior to the date of the disclosure. The new payment allocation disclosed shall be the expected payment allocation for the first payment for which the new interest rate will apply.

(iv) An explanation of how the interest rate is determined, including:

(A) The specific index or formula used in making interest rate adjustments and a source of information about the index or formula; and

(B) The type and amount of any adjustment to the index, including any margin and an explanation that the margin is the addition of a certain number of percentage points to the index.

(v) Any limits on the interest rate or payment increases at each interest rate adjustment and over the life of the loan, as applicable, including the extent to which such limits result in the creditor, assignee, or servicer foregoing any increase in the interest rate and the earliest date that such foregone interest rate increases may apply to future interest rate adjustments, subject to those limits.

(vi) An explanation of how the new payment is determined, including:

(A) The index or formula used;

(B) Any adjustment to the index or formula, such as the addition of a margin;

(C) The loan balance expected on the date of the interest rate adjustment;

(D) The length of the remaining loan term expected on the date of the interest rate adjustment and any change in the term of the loan caused by the adjustment; and

(E) If the new interest rate or new payment provided is an estimate, a statement that another disclosure containing the actual new interest rate and new payment will be provided to the consumer between two and four months before the first payment at the adjusted level is due for interest rate adjustments that result in a corresponding payment change.

(vii) If applicable, a statement that the new payment will not be allocated to pay loan principal and will not reduce the loan balance. If the new payment will result in negative amortization, a statement that the new payment will not be allocated to pay loan principal and will pay only part of the loan interest, thereby adding to the balance of the loan. If the new payment will result in negative amortization as a result of the interest rate adjustment, the statement shall set forth the payment required to amortize fully the remaining balance at the new interest rate over the remainder of the loan term.

(viii) The circumstances under which any prepayment penalty, as defined in § 1026.32(b)(6)(i), may be imposed, such as when paying the loan in full or selling or refinancing the principal dwelling; the time period during which such a penalty may be imposed; and a statement that the consumer may contact the servicer for additional information, including the maximum amount of the penalty.

(ix) The telephone number of the creditor, assignee, or servicer for consumers to call if they anticipate not being able to make their new payments.

(x) The following alternatives to paying at the new rate that consumers may be able to pursue and a brief explanation of each alternative, expressed in simple and clear terms:

(A) Refinancing the loan with the current or another creditor or assignee;

(B) Selling the property and using the proceeds to pay the loan in full;

(C) Modifying the terms of the loan with the creditor, assignee, or servicer; and

(D) Arranging payment forbearance with the creditor, assignee, or servicer.

(xi) The Web site to access either the Bureau list or the HUD list of homeownership counselors and counseling organizations, the HUD toll-free telephone number to access the HUD list of homeownership counselors and counseling organizations, and the Bureau Web site to access contact information for State housing finance authorities (as defined in § 1301 of the Financial Institutions Reform, Recovery, and Enforcement Act of 1989).

(3)   Format.

(i) Except for the disclosures required by paragraph (d)(2)(i) of this section, the disclosures required by this paragraph (d) shall be provided in the form of a table and in the same order as, and with headings and format substantially similar to, forms H–4(D)(3) and (4) in appendix H to this part;

(ii) The disclosures required by paragraph (d)(2)(i) of this section shall appear outside of and above the table required in paragraph (d)(3)(i) of this section; and

(iii) The disclosures required by paragraph (d)(2)(iii) of this section shall be in the form of a table located within the table described in paragraph (d)(3)(i) of this section. These disclosures shall appear in the same order as, and with headings and format substantially similar to, the table inside the larger table in forms H–4(D)(3) and (4) in appendix H to this part.

(e)   Escrow account cancellation notice for certain mortgage transactions—

(1)   Scope. In a closed-end consumer credit transaction secured by a first lien on real property or a dwelling, other than a reverse mortgage subject to § 1026.33, for which an escrow account was established in connection with the transaction and will be cancelled, the creditor or servicer shall disclose the information specified in paragraph (e)(2) of this section in accordance with the form requirements in paragraph (e)(4) of this section, and the timing requirements in paragraph (e)(5) of this section. For purposes of this paragraph (e), the term "escrow account" has the same meaning as under 12 CFR 1024.17(b), and the term "servicer" has the same meaning as under 12 CFR 1024.2(b).

(2)   Content requirements. If an escrow account was established in connection with a transaction subject to this paragraph (e) and the escrow account will be cancelled, the creditor or servicer shall clearly and conspicuously disclose, under the heading "Escrow Closing Notice," the following information:

(i)   A statement informing the consumer of the date on which the consumer will no longer have an escrow account; a statement that an escrow account may also be called an impound or trust account; a statement of the reason why the escrow account will be closed; a statement that without an escrow account, the consumer must pay all property costs, such as taxes and homeowner's insurance, directly, possibly in one or two large payments a year; and a table, titled "Cost to you," that contains an itemization of the amount of any fee the creditor or servicer imposes on the consumer in connection with the closure of the consumer's escrow account, labeled "Escrow Closing Fee," and a statement that the fee is for closing the escrow account.

(ii)   Under the reference "In the future":

(A)   A statement of the consequences if the consumer fails to pay property costs, including the actions that a State or local government may take if property taxes are not paid and the actions the creditor or servicer may take if the consumer does not pay some or all property costs, such as adding amounts to the loan balance, adding an escrow account to the loan, or purchasing a property insurance policy on the consumer's behalf that may be more expensive and provide fewer benefits than a policy that the consumer could obtain directly;

(B)   A statement with a telephone number that the consumer can use to request additional information about the cancellation of the escrow account;

(C)   A statement of whether the creditor or servicer offers the option of keeping the escrow account open and, as applicable, a telephone number the consumer can use to request that the account be kept open; and

(D)   A statement of whether there is a cut-off date by which the consumer can request that the account be kept open.

(3)   **Optional information.** The creditor or servicer may, at its option, include its name or logo, the consumer's name, phone number, mailing address and property address, the issue date of the notice, the loan number, or the consumer's account number on the notice required by this paragraph (e). Except for the name and logo of the creditor or servicer, the information described in this paragraph may be placed between the heading required by paragraph (e)(2) of this section and the disclosures required by paragraphs (e)(2)(i) and (ii) of this section. The name and logo may be placed above the heading required by paragraph (e)(2) of this section.

(4)   **Form of disclosures.** The disclosures required by paragraph (e)(2) of this section shall be provided in a minimum 10-point font, grouped together on the front side of a one-page document, separate from all other materials, with the headings, content, order, and format substantially similar to model form H–29 in appendix H to this part. The disclosure of the heading required by paragraph (e)(2) of this section shall be more conspicuous than, and shall precede, the other disclosures required by paragraph (e)(2) of this section.

(5)   **Timing—**

(i)   Cancellation upon consumer's request. If the creditor or servicer cancels the escrow account at the consumer's request, the creditor or servicer shall ensure that the consumer receives the disclosures required by paragraph (e)(2) of this section no later than three business days before the closure of the consumer's escrow account.

(ii)   Cancellations other than upon the consumer's request. If the creditor or servicer cancels the escrow account and the cancellation is not at the consumer's request, the creditor or servicer shall ensure that the consumer receives the disclosures required by paragraph (e)(2) of this section no later than 30 business days before the closure of the consumer's escrow account.

(iii)   Receipt of disclosure. If the disclosures required by paragraph (e)(2) of this section are not provided to the consumer in person, the consumer is considered to have received the disclosures three business days after they are delivered or placed in the mail.

§ 1026.21 Treatment of credit balances.

When a credit balance in excess of $1 is created in connection with a transaction (through transmittal of funds to a creditor in excess of the total balance due on an account, through rebates of unearned finance charges or insurance premiums, or through amounts otherwise owed to or held for the benefit of a consumer), the creditor shall:

(a) Credit the amount of the credit balance to the consumer's account;

(b) Refund any part of the remaining credit balance, upon the written request of the consumer; and

(c) Make a good faith effort to refund to the consumer by cash, check, or money order, or credit to a deposit account of the consumer, any part of the credit balance remaining in the account for more than 6 months, except that no further action is required if the consumer's current location is not known to the creditor and cannot be traced through the consumer's last known address or telephone number.

§ 1026.22 Determination of annual percentage rate.

(a) Accuracy of annual percentage rate.

(1) The annual percentage rate is a measure of the cost of credit, expressed as a yearly rate, that relates the amount and timing of value received by the consumer to the amount and timing of payments made. The annual percentage rate shall be determined in accordance with either the actuarial method or the United States Rule method. Explanations, equations and instructions for determining the annual percentage rate in accordance with the actuarial method are set forth in Appendix J to this part. An error in disclosure of the annual percentage rate or finance charge shall not, in itself, be considered a violation of this part if:

(i) The error resulted from a corresponding error in a calculation tool used in good faith by the creditor; and

(ii) Upon discovery of the error, the creditor promptly discontinues use of that calculation tool for disclosure purposes and notifies the Bureau in writing of the error in the calculation tool.

(2) As a general rule, the annual percentage rate shall be considered accurate if it is not more than 1/8 of 1 percentage point above or below the annual percentage rate determined in accordance with paragraph (a)(1) of this section.

(3) In an irregular transaction, the annual percentage rate shall be considered accurate if it is not more than ¼ of 1 percentage point above or below the annual percentage rate determined in accordance with paragraph (a)(1) of this section. For purposes of this paragraph (a)(3), an irregular transaction is one that includes one or more of the following features: multiple advances, irregular payment periods, or irregular payment amounts (other than an irregular first period or an irregular first or final payment).

(4) Mortgage loans. If the annual percentage rate disclosed in a transaction secured by real property or a dwelling varies from the actual rate determined in accordance with paragraph (a)(1) of this section, in addition to the tolerances applicable under paragraphs (a)(2) and (3) of this section, the disclosed annual percentage rate shall also be considered accurate if:

(i) The rate results from the disclosed finance charge; and

(ii)(A) The disclosed finance charge would be considered accurate under § 1026.18(d)(1) or § 1026.38(o)(2), as applicable; or

(B) For purposes of rescission, if the disclosed finance charge would be considered accurate under § 1026.23(g) or (h), whichever applies.

(5) Additional tolerance for mortgage loans. In a transaction secured by real property or a dwelling, in addition to the tolerances applicable under paragraphs (a)(2) and (3) of this section, if the disclosed finance charge is calculated incorrectly but is considered accurate under § 1026.18(d)(1) or

§ 1026.38(*o*)(2), as applicable, or § 1026.23(g) or (h), the disclosed annual percentage rate shall be considered accurate:

 (i) If the disclosed finance charge is understated, and the disclosed annual percentage rate is also understated but it is closer to the actual annual percentage rate than the rate that would be considered accurate under paragraph (a)(4) of this section;

 (ii) If the disclosed finance charge is overstated, and the disclosed annual percentage rate is also overstated but it is closer to the actual annual percentage rate than the rate that would be considered accurate under paragraph (a)(4) of this section.

(b) **Computation tools.**

 (1) The Regulation Z Annual Percentage Rate Tables produced by the Bureau may be used to determine the annual percentage rate, and any rate determined from those tables in accordance with the accompanying instructions complies with the requirements of this section. Volume I of the tables applies to single advance transactions involving up to 480 monthly payments or 104 weekly payments. It may be used for regular transactions and for transactions with any of the following irregularities: an irregular first period, an irregular first payment, and an irregular final payment. Volume II of the tables applies to transactions involving multiple advances and any type of payment or period irregularity.

 (2) Creditors may use any other computation tool in determining the annual percentage rate if the rate so determined equals the rate determined in accordance with Appendix J to this part, within the degree of accuracy set forth in paragraph (a) of this section.

(c) **Single add-on rate transactions.** If a single add-on rate is applied to all transactions with maturities up to 60 months and if all payments are equal in amount and period, a single annual percentage rate may be disclosed for all those transactions, so long as it is the highest annual percentage rate for any such transaction.

(d) **Certain transactions involving ranges of balances.** For purposes of disclosing the annual percentage rate referred to in § 1026.17(g)(4) (Mail or telephone orders—delay in disclosures) and (h) (Series of sales—delay in disclosures), if the same finance charge is imposed on all balances within a specified range of balances, the annual percentage rate computed for the median balance may be disclosed for all the balances. However, if the annual percentage rate computed for the median balance understates the annual percentage rate computed for the lowest balance by more than 8 percent of the latter rate, the annual percentage rate shall be computed on whatever lower balance will produce an annual percentage rate that does not result in an understatement of more than 8 percent of the rate determined on the lowest balance.

§ 1026.23 Right of rescission.

(a) **Consumer's right to rescind.**

 (1) In a credit transaction in which a security interest is or will be retained or acquired in a consumer's principal dwelling, each consumer whose ownership interest is or will be subject to the security interest shall have the right to rescind the transaction, except for transactions described in paragraph (f) of this section. For purposes of this section, the addition to an existing obligation of a security interest in a consumer's principal dwelling is a transaction. The right of rescission applies only to the addition of the security interest and not the existing obligation. The creditor shall deliver the notice required by paragraph (b) of this section but need not deliver new material disclosures. Delivery of the required notice shall begin the rescission period.

 (2) To exercise the right to rescind, the consumer shall notify the creditor of the rescission by mail, telegram or other means of written communication. Notice is considered given when mailed, when filed for telegraphic transmission or, if sent by other means, when delivered to the creditor's designated place of business.

 (3)(i) The consumer may exercise the right to rescind until midnight of the third business day following consummation, delivery of the notice required by paragraph (b) of this section, or delivery of all material disclosures, whichever occurs last. If the required notice or material disclosures are not delivered, the right to rescind shall expire 3 years after consummation, upon transfer of all of the consumer's interest in the property, or upon sale of the property, whichever occurs first. In the case of certain administrative proceedings, the rescission period shall be extended in accordance with section 125(f) of the Act.

(ii) For purposes of this paragraph (a)(3), the term "material disclosures" means the required disclosures of the annual percentage rate, the finance charge, the amount financed, the total of payments, the payment schedule, and the disclosures and limitations referred to in §§ 1026.32(c) and (d) and 1026.43(g).

(4) When more than one consumer in a transaction has the right to rescind, the exercise of the right by one consumer shall be effective as to all consumers.

(b)(1) **Notice of right to rescind.** In a transaction subject to rescission, a creditor shall deliver two copies of the notice of the right to rescind to each consumer entitled to rescind (one copy to each if the notice is delivered in electronic form in accordance with the consumer consent and other applicable provisions of the E-Sign Act). The notice shall be on a separate document that identifies the transaction and shall clearly and conspicuously disclose the following:

(i) The retention or acquisition of a security interest in the consumer's principal dwelling.

(ii) The consumer's right to rescind the transaction.

(iii) How to exercise the right to rescind, with a form for that purpose, designating the address of the creditor's place of business.

(iv) The effects of rescission, as described in paragraph (d) of this section.

(v) The date the rescission period expires.

(2) **Proper form of notice.** To satisfy the disclosure requirements of paragraph (b)(1) of this section, the creditor shall provide the appropriate model form in Appendix H of this part or a substantially similar notice.

(c) **Delay of creditor's performance.** Unless a consumer waives the right of rescission under paragraph (e) of this section, no money shall be disbursed other than in escrow, no services shall be performed and no materials delivered until the rescission period has expired and the creditor is reasonably satisfied that the consumer has not rescinded.

(d) **Effects of rescission.**

(1) When a consumer rescinds a transaction, the security interest giving rise to the right of rescission becomes void and the consumer shall not be liable for any amount, including any finance charge.

(2) Within 20 calendar days after receipt of a notice of rescission, the creditor shall return any money or property that has been given to anyone in connection with the transaction and shall take any action necessary to reflect the termination of the security interest.

(3) If the creditor has delivered any money or property, the consumer may retain possession until the creditor has met its obligation under paragraph (d)(2) of this section. When the creditor has complied with that paragraph, the consumer shall tender the money or property to the creditor or, where the latter would be impracticable or inequitable, tender its reasonable value. At the consumer's option, tender of property may be made at the location of the property or at the consumer's residence. Tender of money must be made at the creditor's designated place of business. If the creditor does not take possession of the money or property within 20 calendar days after the consumer's tender, the consumer may keep it without further obligation.

(4) The procedures outlined in paragraphs (d)(2) and (3) of this section may be modified by court order.

(e) **Consumer's waiver of right to rescind.** The consumer may modify or waive the right to rescind if the consumer determines that the extension of credit is needed to meet a bona fide personal financial emergency. To modify or waive the right, the consumer shall give the creditor a dated written statement that describes the emergency, specifically modifies or waives the right to rescind, and bears the signature of all the consumers entitled to rescind. Printed forms for this purpose are prohibited.

(f) **Exempt transactions.** The right to rescind does not apply to the following:

(1) A residential mortgage transaction.

(2) A refinancing or consolidation by the same creditor of an extension of credit already secured by the consumer's principal dwelling. The right of rescission shall apply, however, to the extent the new amount financed exceeds the unpaid principal balance, any earned unpaid finance charge on the existing debt, and amounts attributed solely to the costs of the refinancing or consolidation.

(3) A transaction in which a state agency is a creditor.

(4) An advance, other than an initial advance, in a series of advances or in a series of single-payment obligations that is treated as a single transaction under § 1026.17(c)(6), if the notice required by paragraph (b) of this section and all material disclosures have been given to the consumer.

(5) A renewal of optional insurance premiums that is not considered a refinancing under § 1026.20(a)(5).

(g) **Tolerances for accuracy.**

(1) **One-half of 1 percent tolerance.** Except as provided in paragraphs (g)(2) and (h)(2) of this section, the finance charge and other disclosures affected by the finance charge (such as the amount financed and the annual percentage rate) shall be considered accurate for purposes of this section if the disclosed finance charge:

(i) Is understated by no more than ½ of 1 percent of the face amount of the note or $100, whichever is greater; or

(ii) Is greater than the amount required to be disclosed.

(2) **One percent tolerance.** In a refinancing of a residential mortgage transaction with a new creditor (other than a transaction covered by § 1026.32), if there is no new advance and no consolidation of existing loans, the finance charge and other disclosures affected by the finance charge (such as the amount financed and the annual percentage rate) shall be considered accurate for purposes of this section if the disclosed finance charge:

(i) Is understated by no more than 1 percent of the face amount of the note or $100, whichever is greater; or

(ii) Is greater than the amount required to be disclosed.

(h) **Special rules for foreclosures.**

(1) **Right to rescind.** After the initiation of foreclosure on the consumer's principal dwelling that secures the credit obligation, the consumer shall have the right to rescind the transaction if:

(i) A mortgage broker fee that should have been included in the finance charge was not included; or

(ii) The creditor did not provide the properly completed appropriate model form in Appendix H of this part, or a substantially similar notice of rescission.

(2) **Tolerance for disclosures.** After the initiation of foreclosure on the consumer's principal dwelling that secures the credit obligation, the finance charge and other disclosures affected by the finance charge (such as the amount financed and the annual percentage rate) shall be considered accurate for purposes of this section if the disclosed finance charge:

(i) Is understated by no more than $35; or

(ii) Is greater than the amount required to be disclosed.

§ 1026.24   Advertising.

(a) Actually available terms. If an advertisement for credit states specific credit terms, it shall state only those terms that actually are or will be arranged or offered by the creditor.

(b) Clear and conspicuous standard. Disclosures required by this section shall be made clearly and conspicuously.

(c) Advertisement of rate of finance charge. If an advertisement states a rate of finance charge, it shall state the rate as an "annual percentage rate," using that term. If the annual percentage rate may be increased after consummation, the advertisement shall state that fact. If an advertisement is for credit not secured by a dwelling, the advertisement shall not state any other rate, except that a simple annual rate or periodic rate that is applied to an unpaid balance may be stated in conjunction with, but not more conspicuously than, the annual percentage rate. If an advertisement is for credit secured by a dwelling, the advertisement shall not state any other rate, except that a simple annual rate that is applied to an unpaid balance may be stated in conjunction with, but not more conspicuously than, the annual percentage rate.

(d) Advertisement of terms that require additional disclosures.

(1) Triggering terms. If any of the following terms is set forth in an advertisement, the advertisement shall meet the requirements of paragraph (d)(2) of this section:

(i) The amount or percentage of any downpayment.

(ii) The number of payments or period of repayment.

(iii) The amount of any payment.

(iv) The amount of any finance charge.

(2) Additional terms. An advertisement stating any of the terms in paragraph (d)(1) of this section shall state the following terms, as applicable (an example of one or more typical extensions of credit with a statement of all the terms applicable to each may be used):

(i) The amount or percentage of the downpayment.

(ii) The terms of repayment, which reflect the repayment obligations over the full term of the loan, including any balloon payment.

(iii) The "annual percentage rate," using that term, and, if the rate may be increased after consummation, that fact.

(e) Catalogs or other multiple-page advertisements; electronic advertisements.

(1) If a catalog or other multiple-page advertisement, or an electronic advertisement (such as an advertisement appearing on an Internet Web site), gives information in a table or schedule in sufficient detail to permit determination of the disclosures required by paragraph (d)(2) of this section, it shall be considered a single advertisement if:

(i) The table or schedule is clearly and conspicuously set forth; and

(ii) Any statement of the credit terms in paragraph (d)(1) of this section appearing anywhere else in the catalog or advertisement clearly refers to the page or location where the table or schedule begins.

(2) A catalog or other multiple-page advertisement or an electronic advertisement (such as an advertisement appearing on an Internet Web site) complies with paragraph (d)(2) of this section if the table or schedule of terms includes all appropriate disclosures for a representative scale of amounts up to the level of the more commonly sold higher-priced property or services offered.

(f) Disclosure of rates and payments in advertisements for credit secured by a dwelling.

(1) Scope. The requirements of this paragraph apply to any advertisement for credit secured by a dwelling, other than television or radio advertisements, including promotional materials accompanying applications.

(2) Disclosure of rates.

(i) In general. If an advertisement for credit secured by a dwelling states a simple annual rate of interest and more than one simple annual rate of interest will apply over the term of the advertised loan, the advertisement shall disclose in a clear and conspicuous manner:

(A) Each simple annual rate of interest that will apply. In variable-rate transactions, a rate determined by adding an index and margin shall be disclosed based on a reasonably current index and margin;

(B) The period of time during which each simple annual rate of interest will apply; and

(C) The annual percentage rate for the loan. If such rate is variable, the annual percentage rate shall comply with the accuracy standards in §§ 1026.17(c) and 1026.22.

(ii) Clear and conspicuous requirement. For purposes of paragraph (f)(2)(i) of this section, clearly and conspicuously disclosed means that the required information in paragraphs (f)(2)(i)(A) through (C) shall be disclosed with equal prominence and in close proximity to any advertised rate that triggered the required disclosures. The required information in paragraph (f)(2)(i)(C) may be disclosed with greater prominence than the other information.

(3) Disclosure of payments.

(i) In general. In addition to the requirements of paragraph (c) of this section, if an advertisement for credit secured by a dwelling states the amount of any payment, the advertisement shall disclose in a clear and conspicuous manner:

(A) The amount of each payment that will apply over the term of the loan, including any balloon payment. In variable-rate transactions, payments that will be determined based on the application of the sum of an index and margin shall be disclosed based on a reasonably current index and margin;

(B) The period of time during which each payment will apply; and

(C) In an advertisement for credit secured by a first lien on a dwelling, the fact that the payments do not include amounts for taxes and insurance premiums, if applicable, and that the actual payment obligation will be greater.

(ii) Clear and conspicuous requirement. For purposes of paragraph (f)(3)(i) of this section, a clear and conspicuous disclosure means that the required information in paragraphs (f)(3)(i)(A) and (B) shall be disclosed with equal prominence and in close proximity to any advertised payment that triggered the required disclosures, and that the required information in paragraph (f)(3)(i)(C) shall be disclosed with prominence and in close proximity to the advertised payments.

(4) Envelope excluded. The requirements in paragraphs (f)(2) and (f)(3) of this section do not apply to an envelope in which an application or solicitation is mailed, or to a banner advertisement or pop-up advertisement linked to an application or solicitation provided electronically.

(g) Alternative disclosures—television or radio advertisements. An advertisement made through television or radio stating any of the terms requiring additional disclosures under paragraph (d)(2) of this section may comply with paragraph (d)(2) of this section either by:

(1) Stating clearly and conspicuously each of the additional disclosures required under paragraph (d)(2) of this section; or

(2) Stating clearly and conspicuously the information required by paragraph (d)(2)(iii) of this section and listing a toll-free telephone number, or any telephone number that allows a consumer to reverse the phone charges when calling for information, along with a reference that such number may be used by consumers to obtain additional cost information.

(h) Tax implications. If an advertisement distributed in paper form or through the Internet (rather than by radio or television) is for a loan secured by the consumer's principal dwelling, and the advertisement states that the advertised extension of credit may exceed the fair market value of the dwelling, the advertisement shall clearly and conspicuously state that:

    (1) The interest on the portion of the credit extension that is greater than the fair market value of the dwelling is not tax deductible for Federal income tax purposes; and

    (2) The consumer should consult a tax adviser for further information regarding the deductibility of interest and charges.

(i) Prohibited acts or practices in advertisements for credit secured by a dwelling. The following acts or practices are prohibited in advertisements for credit secured by a dwelling:

    (1) *Misleading advertising of "fixed" rates and payments.* Using the word "fixed" to refer to rates, payments, or the credit transaction in an advertisement for variable-rate transactions or other transactions where the payment will increase, unless:

        (i) In the case of an advertisement solely for one or more variable-rate transactions,

            (A) The phrase "Adjustable-Rate Mortgage," "Variable-Rate Mortgage," or "ARM" appears in the advertisement before the first use of the word "fixed" and is at least as conspicuous as any use of the word "fixed" in the advertisement; and

            (B) Each use of the word "fixed" to refer to a rate or payment is accompanied by an equally prominent and closely proximate statement of the time period for which the rate or payment is fixed, and the fact that the rate may vary or the payment may increase after that period;

        (ii) In the case of an advertisement solely for non-variable-rate transactions where the payment will increase (e.g., a stepped-rate mortgage transaction with an initial lower payment), each use of the word "fixed" to refer to the payment is accompanied by an equally prominent and closely proximate statement of the time period for which the payment is fixed, and the fact that the payment will increase after that period; or

        (iii) In the case of an advertisement for both variable-rate transactions and non-variable-rate transactions,

            (A) The phrase "Adjustable-Rate Mortgage," "Variable-Rate Mortgage," or "ARM" appears in the advertisement with equal prominence as any use of the term "fixed," "Fixed-Rate Mortgage," or similar terms; and

            (B) Each use of the word "fixed" to refer to a rate, payment, or the credit transaction either refers solely to the transactions for which rates are fixed and complies with paragraph (i)(1)(ii) of this section, if applicable, or, if it refers to the variable-rate transactions, is accompanied by an equally prominent and closely proximate statement of the time period for which the rate or payment is fixed, and the fact that the rate may vary or the payment may increase after that period.

    (2) *Misleading comparisons in advertisements.* Making any comparison in an advertisement between actual or hypothetical credit payments or rates and any payment or simple annual rate that will be available under the advertised product for a period less than the full term of the loan, unless:

        (i) In general. The advertisement includes a clear and conspicuous comparison to the information required to be disclosed under § 1026.24(f)(2) and (3); and

        (ii) Application to variable-rate transactions. If the advertisement is for a variable-rate transaction, and the advertised payment or simple annual rate is based on the index and margin that will be used to make subsequent rate or payment adjustments over the term of the loan, the advertisement includes an equally prominent statement in close proximity to the payment or rate that the payment or rate is subject to adjustment and the time period when the first adjustment will occur.

(3) Misrepresentations about government endorsement. Making any statement in an advertisement that the product offered is a "government loan program", "government-supported loan", or is otherwise endorsed or sponsored by any Federal, state, or local government entity, unless the advertisement is for an FHA loan, VA loan, or similar loan program that is, in fact, endorsed or sponsored by a Federal, state, or local government entity.

(4) Misleading use of the current lender's name. Using the name of the consumer's current lender in an advertisement that is not sent by or on behalf of the consumer's current lender, unless the advertisement:

    (i) Discloses with equal prominence the name of the person or creditor making the advertisement; and

    (ii) Includes a clear and conspicuous statement that the person making the advertisement is not associated with, or acting on behalf of, the consumer's current lender.

(5) Misleading claims of debt elimination. Making any misleading claim in an advertisement that the mortgage product offered will eliminate debt or result in a waiver or forgiveness of a consumer's existing loan terms with, or obligations to, another creditor.

(6) Misleading use of the term "counselor". Using the term "counselor" in an advertisement to refer to a for-profit mortgage broker or mortgage creditor, its employees, or persons working for the broker or creditor that are involved in offering, originating or selling mortgages.

(7) Misleading foreign-language advertisements. Providing information about some trigger terms or required disclosures, such as an initial rate or payment, only in a foreign language in an advertisement, but providing information about other trigger terms or required disclosures, such as information about the fully-indexed rate or fully amortizing payment, only in English in the same advertisement.

SUBPART D. MISCELLANEOUS

§ 1026.25   Record retention.

(a) General rule. A creditor shall retain evidence of compliance with this part (other than advertising requirements under §§ 1026.16 and 1026.24, and other than the requirements under § 1026.19(e) and (f)) for two years after the date disclosures are required to be made or action is required to be taken. The administrative agencies responsible for enforcing the regulation may require creditors under their jurisdictions to retain records for a longer period if necessary to carry out their enforcement responsibilities under section 108 of the Act.

(b) Inspection of records. A creditor shall permit the agency responsible for enforcing this part with respect to that creditor to inspect its relevant records for compliance.

(c) Records related to certain requirements for mortgage loans.

    (1) Records related to requirements for loans secured by real property—

        (i) General rule. Except as provided under paragraph (c)(1)(ii) of this section, a creditor shall retain evidence of compliance with the requirements of § 1026.19(e) and (f) for three years after the later of the date of consumption, the date disclosures are required to be made, or the date the action is required to be taken.

        (ii) Closing disclosures. (A) A creditor shall retain each completed disclosure required under § 1026.19(f)(1)(i) or (f)(4)(i), and all documents related to such disclosures, for five years after consumption, notwithstanding paragraph (c)(1)(ii)(B) of this section.

            (B) If a creditor sells, transfers, or otherwise disposes of its interest in a mortgage loan subject to § 1026.19(f) and does not service the mortgage loan, the creditor shall provide a copy of the disclosures required under § 1026.19(f)(1)(i) or (f)(4)(i) to the owner or servicer of the mortgage as a part of the transfer of the loan file. Such owner or servicer shall retain such disclosures for the remainder of the five-year period described under paragraph (c)(1)(ii)(A) of this section.

(C) The Bureau shall have the right to require provision of copies of records related to the disclosures required under § 1026.19(f)(1)(i) and (f)(4)(i).

(2) Records related to requirements for loan originator compensation. Notwithstanding paragraph (a) of this section, for transactions subject to § 1026.36:

(i) A creditor shall maintain records sufficient to evidence all compensation it pays to a loan originator, as defined in § 1026.36(a)(1), and the compensation agreement that governs those payments for three years after the date of payment.

(ii) A loan originator organization, as defined in § 1026.36(a)(1)(iii), shall maintain records sufficient to evidence all compensation it receives from a creditor, a consumer, or another person; all compensation it pays to any individual loan originator, as defined in § 1026.36(a)(1)(ii); and the compensation agreement that governs each such receipt or payment, for three years after the date of each such receipt or payment.

(3) Records related to minimum standards for transactions secured by a dwelling. Notwithstanding paragraph (a) of this section, a creditor shall retain evidence of compliance with § 1026.43 of this regulation for three years after consummation of a transaction covered by that section.

§ 1026.26   Use of annual percentage rate in oral disclosures.

(a)   Open-end credit. In an oral response to a consumer's inquiry about the cost of open-end credit, only the annual percentage rate or rates shall be stated, except that the periodic rate or rates also may be stated. If the annual percentage rate cannot be determined in advance because there are finance charges other than a periodic rate, the corresponding annual percentage rate shall be stated, and other cost information may be given.

(b)   Closed-end credit. In an oral response to a consumer's inquiry about the cost of closed-end credit, only the annual percentage rate shall be stated, except that a simple annual rate or periodic rate also may be stated if it is applied to an unpaid balance. If the annual percentage rate cannot be determined in advance, the annual percentage rate for a sample transaction shall be stated, and other cost information for the consumer's specific transaction may be given.

§ 1026.27   Language of disclosures.

Disclosures required by this part may be made in a language other than English, provided that the disclosures are made available in English upon the consumer's request. This requirement for providing English disclosures on request does not apply to advertisements subject to §§ 1026.16 and 1026.24.

§ 1026.28   Effect on state laws.

(a)   Inconsistent disclosure requirements.

(1) Except as provided in paragraph (d) of this section, State law requirements that are inconsistent with the requirements contained in chapter 1 (General Provisions), chapter 2 (Credit Transactions), or chapter 3 (Credit Advertising) of the Act and the implementing provisions of this part are preempted to the extent of the inconsistency. A State law is inconsistent if it requires a creditor to make disclosures or take actions that contradict the requirements of the Federal law. A State law is contradictory if it requires the use of the same term to represent a different amount or a different meaning than the Federal law, or if it requires the use of a term different from that required in the Federal law to describe the same item. A creditor, State, or other interested party may request the Bureau to determine whether a State law requirement is inconsistent. After the Bureau determines that a state law is inconsistent, a creditor may not make disclosures using the inconsistent term or form. A determination as to whether a State law is inconsistent with the requirements of sections 4 and 5 of RESPA (other than the RESPA section 5(c) requirements regarding provision of a list of certified homeownership counselors) and §§ 1026.19(e) and (f), 1026.37, and 1026.38 shall be made in accordance with this section and not 12 CFR 1024.13.

(2)(i) State law requirements are inconsistent with the requirements contained in sections 161 (Correction of billing errors) or 162 (Regulation of credit reports) of the Act and the implementing provisions of this part and are preempted if they provide rights, responsibilities, or procedures for consumers or creditors that are different from those required by the Federal law. However, a state law that allows a consumer to inquire about an open-end credit account and imposes on the creditor an obligation to respond to such inquiry after the time allowed in the Federal law for the consumer to submit written notice of a billing error shall not be preempted in any situation where the time period for making written notice under this part has expired. If a creditor gives written notice of a consumer's rights under such state law, the notice shall state that reliance on the longer time period available under state law may result in the loss of important rights that could be preserved by acting more promptly under Federal law; it shall also explain that the state law provisions apply only after expiration of the time period for submitting a proper written notice of a billing error under the Federal law. If the state disclosures are made on the same side of a page as the required Federal disclosures, the state disclosures shall appear under a demarcation line below the Federal disclosures, and the Federal disclosures shall be identified by a heading indicating that they are made in compliance with Federal law.

(ii) State law requirements are inconsistent with the requirements contained in chapter 4 (Credit billing) of the Act (other than section 161 or 162) and the implementing provisions of this part and are preempted if the creditor cannot comply with state law without violating Federal law.

(iii) A state may request the Bureau to determine whether its law is inconsistent with chapter 4 of the Act and its implementing provisions.

(b) **Equivalent disclosure requirements.** If the Bureau determines that a disclosure required by state law (other than a requirement relating to the finance charge, annual percentage rate, or the disclosures required under § 1026.32) is substantially the same in meaning as a disclosure required under the Act or this part, creditors in that state may make the state disclosure in lieu of the Federal disclosure. A creditor, state, or other interested party may request the Bureau to determine whether a state disclosure is substantially the same in meaning as a Federal disclosure.

(c) **Request for determination.** The procedures under which a request for a determination may be made under this section are set forth in Appendix A.

(d) **Special rule for credit and charge cards.** State law requirements relating to the disclosure of credit information in any credit or charge card application or solicitation that is subject to the requirements of section 127(c) of chapter 2 of the Act (§ 1026.60 of the regulation) or in any renewal notice for a credit or charge card that is subject to the requirements of section 127(d) of chapter 2 of the Act (§ 1026.9(e) of the regulation) are preempted. State laws relating to the enforcement of section 127(c) and (d) of the Act are not preempted.

§ 1026.29 State exemptions.

(a) **General rule.** Any state may apply to the Bureau to exempt a class of transactions within the state from the requirements of chapter 2 (Credit transactions) or chapter 4 (Credit billing) of the Act and the corresponding provisions of this part. The Bureau shall grant an exemption if it determines that:

(1) The state law is substantially similar to the Federal law or, in the case of chapter 4, affords the consumer greater protection than the Federal law; and

(2) There is adequate provision for enforcement.

(b) Civil liability.

(1) No exemptions granted under this section shall extend to the civil liability provisions of sections 130 and 131 of the Act.

(2) If an exemption has been granted, the disclosures required by the applicable state law (except any additional requirements not imposed by Federal law) shall constitute the disclosures required by the Act.

(c) Applications. The procedures under which a state may apply for an exemption under this section are set forth in Appendix B to this part.

§ 1026.30   Limitation on rates.

A creditor shall include in any consumer credit contract secured by a dwelling and subject to the Act and this part the maximum interest rate that may be imposed during the term of the obligation when:

(a) In the case of closed-end credit, the annual percentage rate may increase after consummation, or

(b) In the case of open-end credit, the annual percentage rate may increase during the plan.

SUBPART E. SPECIAL RULES FOR CERTAIN HOME MORTGAGE TRANSACTIONS

§ 1026.31   General rules.

(a) Relation to other subparts in this part. The requirements and limitations of this subpart are in addition to and not in lieu of those contained in other subparts of this part.

(b) Form of disclosures. The creditor shall make the disclosures required by this subpart clearly and conspicuously in writing, in a form that the consumer may keep. The disclosures required by this subpart may be provided to the consumer in electronic form, subject to compliance with the consumer consent and other applicable provisions of the Electronic Signatures in Global and National Commerce Act (E-Sign Act) (15 U.S.C. 7001 et seq.).

(c) Timing of disclosure.

(1) Disclosures for high-cost mortgages. The creditor shall furnish the disclosures required by § 1026.32 at least three business days prior to consummation or account opening of a high-cost mortgage as defined in § 1026.32(a).

(i) Change in terms. After complying with this paragraph (c)(1) and prior to consummation or account opening, if the creditor changes any term that makes the disclosures inaccurate, new disclosures shall be provided in accordance with the requirements of this subpart.

(ii) Telephone disclosures. A creditor may provide new disclosures required by paragraph (c)(1)(i) of this section by telephone if the consumer initiates the change and if, prior to or at consummation or account opening:

(A) The creditor provides new written disclosures; and

(B) The consumer and creditor sign a statement that the new disclosures were provided by telephone at least three days prior to consummation or account opening, as applicable.

(iii) Consumer's waiver of waiting period before consummation or account opening. The consumer may, after receiving the disclosures required by this paragraph (c)(1), modify or waive the three-day waiting period between delivery of those disclosures and consummation or account opening if the consumer determines that the extension of credit is needed to meet a bona fide personal financial emergency. To modify or waive the right, the consumer shall give the creditor a dated written statement that describes the emergency, specifically modifies or waives the waiting period, and bears the signature of all the consumers entitled to the waiting period. Printed forms for this purpose are prohibited, except when creditors are permitted to use printed forms pursuant to § 1026.23(e)(2).

(2) Disclosures for reverse mortgages. The creditor shall furnish the disclosures required by § 1026.33 at least three business days prior to:

(i) Consummation of a closed-end credit transaction; or

(ii) The first transaction under an open-end credit plan.

(d) Basis of disclosures and use of estimates.

(1) Legal Obligation. Disclosures shall reflect the terms of the legal obligation between the parties.

(2) Estimates. If any information necessary for an accurate disclosure is unknown to the creditor, the creditor shall make the disclosure based on the best information reasonably available at the time the disclosure is provided, and shall state clearly that the disclosure is an estimate.

(3) Per-diem interest. For a transaction in which a portion of the interest is determined on a per-diem basis and collected at consummation, any disclosure affected by the per-diem interest shall be considered accurate if the disclosure is based on the information known to the creditor at the time that the disclosure documents are prepared.

(e) Multiple creditors; multiple consumers. If a transaction involves more than one creditor, only one set of disclosures shall be given and the creditors shall agree among themselves which creditor must comply with the requirements that this part imposes on any or all of them. If there is more than one consumer, the disclosures may be made to any consumer who is primarily liable on the obligation. If the transaction is rescindable under § 1026.15 or § 1026.23, however, the disclosures shall be made to each consumer who has the right to rescind.

(f) Effect of subsequent events. If a disclosure becomes inaccurate because of an event that occurs after the creditor delivers the required disclosures, the inaccuracy is not a violation of Regulation Z (12 CFR part 1026), although new disclosures may be required for mortgages covered by § 1026.32 under paragraph (c) of this section, § 1026.9(c), § 1026.19, or § 1026.20.

(g) Accuracy of annual percentage rate. For purposes of § 1026.32, the annual percentage rate shall be considered accurate, and may be used in determining whether a transaction is covered by § 1026.32, if it is accurate according to the requirements and within the tolerances under § 1026.22 for closed-end credit transactions or 1026.6(a) for open-end credit plans. The finance charge tolerances for rescission under § 1026.23(g) or (h) shall not apply for this purpose.

(h) Corrections and unintentional violations. A creditor or assignee in a high-cost mortgage, as defined in § 1026.32(a), who, when acting in good faith, failed to comply with any requirement under section 129 of the Act will not be deemed to have violated such requirement if the creditor or assignee satisfies either of the following sets of conditions:

(1)(i) Within 30 days of consummation or account opening and prior to the institution of any action, the consumer is notified of or discovers the violation;

(ii) Appropriate restitution is made within a reasonable time; and

(iii) Within a reasonable time, whatever adjustments are necessary are made to the loan or credit plan to either, at the choice of the consumer:

(A) Make the loan or credit plan satisfy the requirements of 15 U.S.C. 1631–1651; or

(B) Change the terms of the loan or credit plan in a manner beneficial to the consumer so that the loan or credit plan will no longer be a high-cost mortgage.

(2)(i) Within 60 days of the creditor's discovery or receipt of notification of an unintentional violation or bona fide error and prior to the institution of any action, the consumer is notified of the compliance failure;

    (ii) Appropriate restitution is made within a reasonable time; and

    (iii) Within a reasonable time, whatever adjustments are necessary are made to the loan or credit plan to either, at the choice of the consumer:

        (A) Make the loan or credit plan satisfy the requirements of 15 U.S.C. 1631–1651; or

        (B) Change the terms of the loan or credit plan in a manner beneficial to the consumer so that the loan or credit plan will no longer be a high-cost mortgage.

§ 1026.32   Requirements for high-cost home mortgages.

    (a) Coverage. (1) The requirements of this section apply to a high-cost mortgage, which is any consumer credit transaction that is secured by the consumer's principal dwelling, other than as provided in paragraph (a)(2) of this section, and in which:

    (i) The annual percentage rate applicable to the transaction, as determined in accordance with paragraph (a)(3) of this section, will exceed the average prime offer rate, as defined in § 1026.35(a)(2), for a comparable transaction by more than:

        (A) 6.5 percentage points for a first-lien transaction, other than as described in paragraph (a)(1)(i)(B) of this section;

        (B) 8.5 percentage points for a first-lien transaction if the dwelling is personal property and the loan amount is less than $50,000; or

        (C) 8.5 percentage points for a subordinate-lien transaction; or

    (ii) The transaction's total points and fees, as defined in paragraphs (b)(1) and (2) of this section, will exceed:

        (A) 5 percent of the total loan amount for a transaction with a loan amount of $20,000 or more; the $20,000 figure shall be adjusted annually on January 1 by the annual percentage change in the Consumer Price Index that was reported on the preceding June 1; or

        (B) The lesser of 8 percent of the total loan amount or $1,000 for a transaction with a loan amount of less than $20,000; the $1,000 and $20,000 figures shall be adjusted annually on January 1 by the annual percentage change in the Consumer Price Index that was reported on the preceding June 1; or

    (iii) Under the terms of the loan contract or open-end credit agreement, the creditor can charge a prepayment penalty, as defined in paragraph (b)(6) of this section, more than 36 months after consummation or account opening, or prepayment penalties that can exceed, in total, more than 2 percent of the amount prepaid.

    (2) Exemptions. This section does not apply to the following:

    (i) A reverse mortgage transaction subject to § 1026.33;

    (ii) A transaction to finance the initial construction of a dwelling;

    (iii) A transaction originated by a Housing Finance Agency, where the Housing Finance Agency is the creditor for the transaction; or

    (iv) A transaction originated pursuant to the United States Department of Agriculture's Rural Development Section 502 Direct Loan Program.

    (3) Determination of annual percentage rate. For purposes of paragraph (a)(1)(i) of this section, a creditor shall determine the annual percentage rate for a closed-or open-end credit transaction based on the following:

    (i) For a transaction in which the annual percentage rate will not vary during the term of the loan or credit plan, the interest rate in effect as of the date the interest rate for the transaction is set;

(ii) For a transaction in which the interest rate may vary during the term of the loan or credit plan in accordance with an index, the interest rate that results from adding the maximum margin permitted at any time during the term of the loan or credit plan to the value of the index rate in effect as of the date the interest rate for the transaction is set, or the introductory interest rate, whichever is greater; and

(iii) For a transaction in which the interest rate may or will vary during the term of the loan or credit plan, other than a transaction described in paragraph (a)(3)(ii) of this section, the maximum interest rate that may be imposed during the term of the loan or credit plan.

(b) **Definitions.** For purposes of this subpart, the following definitions apply:

(1) **In connection with a closed-end credit transaction**, points and fees means the following fees or charges that are known at or before consummation:

(i) All items included in the finance charge under § 1026.4(a) and (b), except that the following items are excluded:

(A) Interest or the time-price differential;

(B) Any premium or other charge imposed in connection with any Federal or State agency program for any guaranty or insurance that protects the creditor against the consumer's default or other credit loss;

(C) For any guaranty or insurance that protects the creditor against the consumer's default or other credit loss and that is not in connection with any Federal or State agency program:

(1) If the premium or other charge is payable after consummation, the entire amount of such premium or other charge; or

(2) If the premium or other charge is payable at or before consummation, the portion of any such premium or other charge that is not in excess of the amount payable under policies in effect at the time of origination under section 203(c)(2)(A) of the National Housing Act (12 U.S.C. 1709(c)(2)(A)), provided that the premium or charge is required to be refundable on a pro rata basis and the refund is automatically issued upon notification of the satisfaction of the underlying mortgage loan;

(D) Any bona fide third-party charge not retained by the creditor, loan originator, or an affiliate of either, unless the charge is required to be included in points and fees under paragraph (b)(1)(i)(C), (iii), or (iv) of this section;

(E) Up to two bona fide discount points paid by the consumer in connection with the transaction, if the interest rate without any discount does not exceed:

(1) The average prime offer rate, as defined in § 1026.35(a)(2), by more than one percentage point; or

(2) For purposes of paragraph (a)(1)(ii) of this section, for transactions that are secured by personal property, the average rate for a loan insured under Title I of the National Housing Act (12 U.S.C. 1702 et seq.) by more than one percentage point; and

(F) If no discount points have been excluded under paragraph (b)(1)(i)(E) of this section, then up to one bona fide discount point paid by the consumer in connection with the transaction, if the interest rate without any discount does not exceed:

(1) The average prime offer rate, as defined in § 1026.35(a)(2), by more than two percentage points; or

(2) For purposes of paragraph (a)(1)(ii) of this section, for transactions that are secured by personal property, the average rate for a loan insured under Title I of the National Housing Act (12 U.S.C. 1702 et seq.) by more than two percentage points;

(ii) All compensation paid directly or indirectly by a consumer or creditor to a loan originator, as defined in § 1026.36(a)(1), that can be attributed to that transaction at the time the interest rate is set unless:

(A) That compensation is paid by a consumer to a mortgage broker, as defined in § 1026.36(a)(2), and already has been included in points and fees under paragraph (b)(1)(i) of this section;

(B) That compensation is paid by a mortgage broker, as defined in § 1026.36(a)(2), to a loan originator that is an employee of the mortgage broker;

(C) That compensation is paid by a creditor to a loan originator that is an employee of the creditor; or

(D) That compensation is paid by a retailer of manufactured homes to its employee.

(iii) All items listed in § 1026.4(c)(7) (other than amounts held for future payment of taxes), unless:

(A) The charge is reasonable;

(B) The creditor receives no direct or indirect compensation in connection with the charge; and

(C) The charge is not paid to an affiliate of the creditor;

(iv) Premiums or other charges payable at or before consummation for any credit life, credit disability, credit unemployment, or credit property insurance, or any other life, accident, health, or loss-of-income insurance for which the creditor is a beneficiary, or any payments directly or indirectly for any debt cancellation or suspension agreement or contract;

(v) The maximum prepayment penalty, as defined in paragraph (b)(6)(i) of this section, that may be charged or collected under the terms of the mortgage loan; and

(vi) The total prepayment penalty, as defined in paragraph (b)(6)(i) or (ii) of this section, as applicable, incurred by the consumer if the consumer refinances the existing mortgage loan, or terminates an existing open-end credit plan in connection with obtaining a new mortgage loan, with the current holder of the existing loan or plan, a servicer acting on behalf of the current holder, or an affiliate of either.

(2) **In connection with an open-end credit plan**, points and fees means the following fees or charges that are known at or before account opening:

(i) All items included in the finance charge under § 1026.4(a) and (b), except that the following items are excluded:

(A) Interest or the time-price differential;

(B) Any premium or other charge imposed in connection with any Federal or State agency program for any guaranty or insurance that protects the creditor against the consumer's default or other credit loss;

(C) For any guaranty or insurance that protects the creditor against the consumer's default or other credit loss and that is not in connection with any Federal or State agency program:

(1) If the premium or other charge is payable after account opening, the entire amount of such premium or other charge; or

(2) If the premium or other charge is payable at or before account opening, the portion of any such premium or other charge that is not in excess of the amount payable under policies in effect at the time of account opening under section 203(c)(2)(A) of the National Housing Act (12 U.S.C. 1709(c)(2)(A)), provided that the premium or charge

is required to be refundable on a pro rata basis and the refund is automatically issued upon notification of the satisfaction of the underlying mortgage transaction;

(D) Any bona fide third-party charge not retained by the creditor, loan originator, or an affiliate of either, unless the charge is required to be included in points and fees under paragraphs (b)(2)(i)(C), (b)(2)(iii) or (b)(2)(iv) of this section;

(E) Up to two bona fide discount points payable by the consumer in connection with the transaction, provided that the conditions specified in paragraph (b)(1)(i)(E) of this section are met; and

(F) Up to one bona fide discount point payable by the consumer in connection with the transaction, provided that no discount points have been excluded under paragraph (b)(2)(i)(E) of this section and the conditions specified in paragraph (b)(1)(i)(F) of this section are met;

(ii) All compensation paid directly or indirectly by a consumer or creditor to a loan originator, as defined in § 1026.36(a)(1), that can be attributed to that transaction at the time the interest rate is set unless:

(A) That compensation is paid by a consumer to a mortgage broker, as defined in § 1026.36(a)(2), and already has been included in points and fees under paragraph (b)(2)(i) of this section;

(B) That compensation is paid by a mortgage broker, as defined in § 1026.36(a)(2), to a loan originator that is an employee of the mortgage broker;

(C) That compensation is paid by a creditor to a loan originator that is an employee of the creditor; or

(D) That compensation is paid by a retailer of manufactured homes to its employee.

(iii) All items listed in § 1026.4(c)(7) (other than amounts held for future payment of taxes) unless:

(A) The charge is reasonable;

(B) The creditor receives no direct or indirect compensation in connection with the charge; and

(C) The charge is not paid to an affiliate of the creditor;

(iv) Premiums or other charges payable at or before account opening for any credit life, credit disability, credit unemployment, or credit property insurance, or any other life, accident, health, or loss-of-income insurance for which the creditor is a beneficiary, or any payments directly or indirectly for any debt cancellation or suspension agreement or contract;

(v) The maximum prepayment penalty, as defined in paragraph (b)(6)(ii) of this section, that may be charged or collected under the terms of the open-end credit plan;

(vi) The total prepayment penalty, as defined in paragraph (b)(6)(i) or (ii) of this section, as applicable, incurred by the consumer if the consumer refinances an existing closed-end credit transaction with an open-end credit plan, or terminates an existing open-end credit plan in connection with obtaining a new open-end credit plan, with the current holder of the existing transaction or plan, a servicer acting on behalf of the current holder, or an affiliate of either;

(vii) Any fees charged for participation in an open-end credit plan, payable at or before account opening, as described in § 1026.4(c)(4); and

(viii) Any transaction fee, including any minimum fee or per-transaction fee, that will be charged for a draw on the credit line, where the creditor must assume that the consumer will make at least one draw during the term of the plan.

(3) Bona fide discount point—

(i) Closed-end credit. The term bona fide discount point means an amount equal to 1 percent of the loan amount paid by the consumer that reduces the interest rate or time-price differential applicable to the transaction based on a calculation that is consistent with established industry practices for determining the amount of reduction in the interest rate or time-price differential appropriate for the amount of discount points paid by the consumer.

(ii) Open-end credit. The term bona fide discount point means an amount equal to 1 percent of the credit limit for the plan when the account is opened, paid by the consumer, and that reduces the interest rate or time-price differential applicable to the transaction based on a calculation that is consistent with established industry practices for determining the amount of reduction in the interest rate or time-price differential appropriate for the amount of discount points paid by the consumer. See comment 32(b)(3)(i)–1 for additional guidance in determining whether a discount point is bona fide.

(4) Total loan amount—

(i) Closed-end credit. The total loan amount for a closed-end credit transaction is calculated by taking the amount financed, as determined according to § 1026.18(b), and deducting any cost listed in § 1026.32(b)(1)(iii), (iv), or (vi) that is both included as points and fees under § 1026.32(b)(1) and financed by the creditor.

(ii) Open-end credit. The total loan amount for an open-end credit plan is the credit limit for the plan when the account is opened.

(5) Affiliate means any company that controls, is controlled by, or is under common control with another company, as set forth in the Bank Holding Company Act of 1956 (12 U.S.C. 1841 et seq.).

(6) Prepayment penalty—

(i) Closed-end credit transactions. For a closed-end credit transaction, prepayment penalty means a charge imposed for paying all or part of the transaction's principal before the date on which the principal is due, other than a waived, bona fide third-party charge that the creditor imposes if the consumer prepays all of the transaction's principal sooner than 36 months after consummation, provided, however, that interest charged consistent with the monthly interest accrual amortization method is not a prepayment penalty for extensions of credit insured by the Federal Housing Administration that are consummated before January 21, 2015.

(ii) Open-end credit. For an open-end credit plan, prepayment penalty means a charge imposed by the creditor if the consumer terminates the open-end credit plan prior to the end of its term, other than a waived, bona fide third-party charge that the creditor imposes if the consumer terminates the open-end credit plan sooner than 36 months after account opening.

(c) Disclosures. In addition to other disclosures required by this part, in a mortgage subject to this section, the creditor shall disclose the following in conspicuous type size:

(1) Notices. The following statement: "You are not required to complete this agreement merely because you have received these disclosures or have signed a loan application. If you obtain this loan, the lender will have a mortgage on your home. You could lose your home, and any money you have put into it, if you do not meet your obligations under the loan."

(2) Annual percentage rate. The annual percentage rate.

(3) Regular payment; minimum periodic payment example; balloon payment.

(i) For a closed-end credit transaction, the amount of the regular monthly (or other periodic) payment and the amount of any balloon payment provided in the credit contract, if permitted under paragraph (d)(1) of this section. The regular payment disclosed under this paragraph shall be treated as accurate if it is based on an amount borrowed that is deemed accurate and is disclosed under paragraph (c)(5) of this section.

(ii) For an open-end credit plan:

(A) An example showing the first minimum periodic payment for the draw period, the first minimum periodic payment for any repayment period, and the balance outstanding at the beginning of any repayment period. The example must be based on the following assumptions:

(1) The consumer borrows the full credit line, as disclosed in paragraph (c)(5) of this section, at account opening and does not obtain any additional extensions of credit;

(2) The consumer makes only minimum periodic payments during the draw period and any repayment period; and

(3) The annual percentage rate used to calculate the example payments remains the same during the draw period and any repayment period. The creditor must provide the minimum periodic payment example based on the annual percentage rate for the plan, as described in paragraph (c)(2) of this section, except that if an introductory annual percentage rate applies, the creditor must use the rate that will apply to the plan after the introductory rate expires.

(B) If the credit contract provides for a balloon payment under the plan as permitted under paragraph (d)(1) of this section, a disclosure of that fact and an example showing the amount of the balloon payment based on the assumptions described in paragraph (c)(3)(ii)(A) of this section.

(C) A statement that the example payments show the first minimum periodic payments at the current annual percentage rate if the consumer borrows the maximum credit available when the account is opened and does not obtain any additional extensions of credit, or a substantially similar statement.

(D) A statement that the example payments are not the consumer's actual payments and that the actual minimum periodic payments will depend on the amount the consumer borrows, the interest rate applicable to that period, and whether the consumer pays more than the required minimum periodic payment, or a substantially similar statement.

(4) Variable-rate. For variable-rate transactions, a statement that the interest rate and monthly payment may increase, and the amount of the single maximum monthly payment, based on the maximum interest rate required to be included in the contract by § 1026.30.

(5) Amount borrowed; credit limit.

(i) For a closed-end credit transaction, the total amount the consumer will borrow, as reflected by the face amount of the note. Where the amount borrowed includes financed charges that are not prohibited under § 1026.34(a)(10), that fact shall be stated, grouped together with the disclosure of the amount borrowed. The disclosure of the amount borrowed shall be treated as accurate if it is not more than $100 above or below the amount required to be disclosed.

(ii) For an open-end credit plan, the credit limit for the plan when the account is opened.

(d) Limitations. A high-cost mortgage shall not include the following terms:

(1)(i) Balloon payment. Except as provided by paragraphs (d)(1)(ii) and (iii) of this section, a payment schedule with a payment that is more than two times a regular periodic payment.

(ii) Exceptions. The limitations in paragraph (d)(1)(i) of this section do not apply to:

(A) A mortgage transaction with a payment schedule that is adjusted to the seasonal or irregular income of the consumer;

(B) A loan with maturity of 12 months or less, if the purpose of the loan is a "bridge" loan connected with the acquisition or construction of a dwelling intended to become the consumer's principal dwelling; or

(C) A loan that meets the criteria set forth in §§ 1026.43(f)(1)(i) through (vi) and 1026.43(f)(2), or the conditions set forth in § 1026.43(e)(6).

(iii) Open-end credit plans. If the terms of an open-end credit plan provide for a repayment period during which no further draws may be taken, the limitations in paragraph (d)(1)(i) of this section do not apply to any adjustment in the regular periodic payment that results solely from the credit plan's transition from the draw period to the repayment period. If the terms of an open-end credit plan do not provide for any repayment period, the limitations in paragraph (d)(1)(i) of this section apply to all periods of the credit plan.

(2) Negative amortization. A payment schedule with regular periodic payments that cause the principal balance to increase.

(3) Advance payments. A payment schedule that consolidates more than two periodic payments and pays them in advance from the proceeds.

(4) Increased interest rate. An increase in the interest rate after default.

(5) Rebates. A refund calculated by a method less favorable than the actuarial method (as defined by section 933(d) of the Housing and Community Development Act of 1992, 15 U.S.C. 1615(d)), for rebates of interest arising from a loan acceleration due to default.

(6) Prepayment penalties. A prepayment penalty, as defined in paragraph (b)(6) of this section.

(7) [Reserved.]

(8) Acceleration of debt. A demand feature that permits the creditor to accelerate the indebtedness by terminating the high-cost mortgage in advance of the original maturity date and to demand repayment of the entire outstanding balance, except in the following circumstances:

(i) There is fraud or material misrepresentation by the consumer in connection with the loan or open-end credit agreement;

(ii) The consumer fails to meet the repayment terms of the agreement for any outstanding balance that results in a default in payment under the loan; or

(iii) There is any action or inaction by the consumer that adversely affects the creditor's security for the loan, or any right of the creditor in such security.

§ 1026.33   Requirements for reverse mortgages.

(a) Definition. For purposes of this subpart, reverse mortgage transaction means a nonrecourse consumer credit obligation in which:

(1) A mortgage, deed of trust, or equivalent consensual security interest securing one or more advances is created in the consumer's principal dwelling; and

(2) Any principal, interest, or shared appreciation or equity is due and payable (other than in the case of default) only after:

(i) The consumer dies;

(ii) The dwelling is transferred; or

(iii) The consumer ceases to occupy the dwelling as a principal dwelling.

(b) Content of disclosures. In addition to other disclosures required by this part, in a reverse mortgage transaction the creditor shall provide the following disclosures in a form substantially similar to the model form found in paragraph (d) of Appendix K of this part:

(1) Notice. A statement that the consumer is not obligated to complete the reverse mortgage transaction merely because the consumer has received the disclosures required by this section or has signed an application for a reverse mortgage loan.

(2) Total annual loan cost rates. A good-faith projection of the total cost of the credit, determined in accordance with paragraph (c) of this section and expressed as a table of "total annual loan cost rates," using that term, in accordance with Appendix K of this part.

(3) Itemization of pertinent information. An itemization of loan terms, charges, the age of the youngest borrower and the appraised property value.

(4) Explanation of table. An explanation of the table of total annual loan cost rates as provided in the model form found in paragraph (d) of Appendix K of this part.

(c) Projected total cost of credit. The projected total cost of credit shall reflect the following factors, as applicable:

(1) Costs to consumer. All costs and charges to the consumer, including the costs of any annuity the consumer purchases as part of the reverse mortgage transaction.

(2) Payments to consumer. All advances to and for the benefit of the consumer, including annuity payments that the consumer will receive from an annuity that the consumer purchases as part of the reverse mortgage transaction.

(3) Additional creditor compensation. Any shared appreciation or equity in the dwelling that the creditor is entitled by contract to receive.

(4) Limitations on consumer liability. Any limitation on the consumer's liability (such as nonrecourse limits and equity conservation agreements).

(5) Assumed annual appreciation rates. Each of the following assumed annual appreciation rates for the dwelling:

    (i) 0 percent.

    (ii) 4 percent.

    (iii) 8 percent.

(6) Assumed loan period.

    (i) Each of the following assumed loan periods, as provided in Appendix L of this part:

        (A) Two years.

        (B) The actuarial life expectancy of the consumer to become obligated on the reverse mortgage transaction (as of that consumer's most recent birthday). In the case of multiple consumers, the period shall be the actuarial life expectancy of the youngest consumer (as of that consumer's most recent birthday).

        (C) The actuarial life expectancy specified by paragraph (c)(6)(i)(B) of this section, multiplied by a factor of 1.4 and rounded to the nearest full year.

    (ii) At the creditor's option, the actuarial life expectancy specified by paragraph (c)(6)(i)(B) of this section, multiplied by a factor of .5 and rounded to the nearest full year.

§1026.34 Prohibited acts or practices in connection with high-cost mortgages.

(a) Prohibited acts or practices for high-cost mortgages.

(1) Home improvement contracts. A creditor shall not pay a contractor under a home improvement contract from the proceeds of a high-cost mortgage, other than:

    (i) By an instrument payable to the consumer or jointly to the consumer and the contractor; or

    (ii) At the election of the consumer, through a third-party escrow agent in accordance with terms established in a written agreement signed by the consumer, the creditor, and the contractor prior to the disbursement.

(2)   Notice to assignee. A creditor may not sell or otherwise assign a high-cost mortgage without furnishing the following statement to the purchaser or assignee: "Notice: This is a mortgage subject to special rules under the Federal Truth in Lending Act. Purchasers or assignees of this mortgage could be liable for all claims and defenses with respect to the mortgage that the consumer could assert against the creditor."

(3)   Refinancings within one-year period. Within one year of having extended a high-cost mortgage, a creditor shall not refinance any high-cost mortgage to the same consumer into another high-cost mortgage, unless the refinancing is in the consumer's interest. An assignee holding or servicing a high-cost mortgage shall not, for the remainder of the one-year period following the date of origination of the credit, refinance any high-cost mortgage to the same consumer into another high-cost mortgage, unless the refinancing is in the consumer's interest. A creditor (or assignee) is prohibited from engaging in acts or practices to evade this provision, including a pattern or practice of arranging for the refinancing of its own loans by affiliated or unaffiliated creditors.

(4)   Repayment ability for high-cost mortgages. In connection with an open-end, high-cost mortgage, a creditor shall not open a plan for a consumer where credit is or will be extended without regard to the consumer's repayment ability as of account opening, including the consumer's current and reasonably expected income, employment, assets other than the collateral, and current obligations including any mortgage-related obligations that are required by another credit obligation undertaken prior to or at account opening, and are secured by the same dwelling that secures the high-cost mortgage transaction. The requirements set forth in § 1026.34(a)(4)(i) through (iv) apply to open-end high-cost mortgages, but do not apply to closed-end high-cost mortgages. In connection with a closed-end, high-cost mortgage, a creditor must comply with the repayment ability requirements set forth in § 1026.43. Temporary or "bridge" loans with terms of twelve months or less, such as a loan to purchase a new dwelling where the consumer plans to sell a current dwelling within twelve months, are exempt from this repayment ability requirement.

(i)   Mortgage-related obligations. For purposes of this paragraph (a)(4), mortgage-related obligations are expected property taxes, premiums for mortgage-related insurance required by the creditor as set forth in § 1026.35(b), and similar expenses.

(ii)   Basis for determination of repayment ability. Under this paragraph (a)(4) a creditor must determine the consumer's repayment ability in connection with an open-end, high cost mortgage as follows:

(A)   A creditor must verify amounts of income or assets that it relies on to determine repayment ability, including expected income or assets, by the consumer's Internal Revenue Service Form W-2, tax returns, payroll receipts, financial institution records, or other third-party documents that provide reasonably reliable evidence of the consumer's income or assets.

(B)   A creditor must verify the consumer's current obligations, including any mortgage-related obligations that are required by another credit obligation undertaken prior to or at account opening, and are secured by the same dwelling that secures the high-cost mortgage transaction.

(iii) Presumption of compliance. For an open-end, high cost mortgage, a creditor is presumed to have complied with this paragraph (a)(4) with respect to a transaction if the creditor:

(A)   Determines the consumer's repayment ability as provided in paragraph (a)(4)(ii);

(B)   Determines the consumer's repayment ability taking into account current obligations and mortgage-related obligations as defined in paragraph (a)(4)(i) of this section, and using the largest required minimum periodic payment based on the following assumptions:

(1) The consumer borrows the full credit line at account opening with no additional extensions of credit;

(2) The consumer makes only required minimum periodic payments during the draw period and any repayment period;

(3) If the annual percentage rate may increase during the plan, the maximum annual percentage rate that is included in the contract, as required by § 1026.30, applies to the plan at account opening and will apply during the draw period and any repayment period.

(C) Assesses the consumer's repayment ability taking into account at least one of the following: The ratio of total current obligations, including any mortgage-related obligations that are required by another credit obligation undertaken prior to or at account opening, and are secured by the same dwelling that secures the high-cost mortgage transaction, to income, or the income the consumer will have after paying current obligations.

(iv) Exclusions from presumption of compliance. Notwithstanding the previous paragraph, no presumption of compliance is available for an open-end, high-cost mortgage transaction for which the regular periodic payments when aggregated do not fully amortize the outstanding principal balance except as otherwise provided by § 1026.32(d)(1)(ii).

(5) Pre-loan counseling.

(i) Certification of counseling required. A creditor shall not extend a high-cost mortgage to a consumer unless the creditor receives written certification that the consumer has obtained counseling on the advisability of the mortgage from a counselor that is approved to provide such counseling by the Secretary of the U.S. Department of Housing and Urban Development or, if permitted by the Secretary, by a State housing finance authority.

(ii) Timing of counseling. The counseling required under this paragraph (a)(5) must occur after:

(A) The consumer receives either the disclosure required by section 5(c) of the Real Estate Settlement Procedures Act of 1974 (12 U.S.C. 2604(c)) or the disclosures required by § 1026.40; or

(B) The consumer receives the disclosures required by § 1026.32(c), for transactions in which neither of the disclosures listed in paragraph (a)(5)(ii)(A) of this section are provided.

(iii) Affiliation prohibited. The counseling required under this paragraph (a)(5) shall not be provided by a counselor who is employed by or affiliated with the creditor.

(iv) Content of certification. The certification of counseling required under paragraph (a)(5)(i) must include:

(A) The name(s) of the consumer(s) who obtained counseling;

(B) The date(s) of counseling;

(C) The name and address of the counselor;

(D) A statement that the consumer(s) received counseling on the advisability of the high-cost mortgage based on the terms provided in either the disclosure required by section 5(c) of the Real Estate Settlement Procedures Act of 1974 (12 U.S.C. 2604(c)) or the disclosures required by § 1026.40.

(E) For transactions for which neither of the disclosures listed in paragraph (a)(5)(ii)(A) of this section are provided, a statement that the consumer(s) received counseling on the advisability of the high-cost mortgage based on the terms provided in the disclosures required by § 1026.32(c); and

(F) A statement that the counselor has verified that the consumer(s) received the disclosures required by either § 1026.32(c) or the Real Estate Settlement Procedures Act of 1974 (12 U.S.C. 2601 et seq.) with respect to the transaction.

(v) **Counseling fees**. A creditor may pay the fees of a counselor or counseling organization for providing counseling required under this paragraph (a)(5) but may not condition the payment of such fees on the consummation or account-opening of a mortgage transaction. If the consumer withdraws the application that would result in the extension of a high-cost mortgage, a creditor may not condition the payment of such fees on the receipt of certification from the counselor required by paragraph (a)(5)(i) of this section. A creditor may, however, confirm that a counselor has provided counseling to the consumer pursuant to this paragraph (a)(5) prior to paying the fee of a counselor or counseling organization.

(vi) **Steering prohibited**. A creditor that extends a high-cost mortgage shall not steer or otherwise direct a consumer to choose a particular counselor or counseling organization for the counseling required under this paragraph (a)(5).

(6) **Recommended default**. A creditor or mortgage broker, as defined in section 1026.36(a)(2), may not recommend or encourage default on an existing loan or other debt prior to and in connection with the consummation or account opening of a high-cost mortgage that refinances all or any portion of such existing loan or debt.

(7) **Modification and deferral fees**. A creditor, successor-in-interest, assignee, or any agent of such parties may not charge a consumer any fee to modify, renew, extend or amend a high-cost mortgage, or to defer any payment due under the terms of such mortgage.

(8) **Late fees.**

(i) **General.** Any late payment charge imposed in connection with a high-cost mortgage must be specifically permitted by the terms of the loan contract or open-end credit agreement and may not exceed 4 percent of the amount of the payment past due. No such charge may be imposed more than once for a single late payment.

(ii) **Timing.** A late payment charge may be imposed in connection with a high-cost mortgage only if the payment is not received by the end of the 15-day period beginning on the date the payment is due or, in the case of a high-cost mortgage on which interest on each installment is paid in advance, the end of the 30-day period beginning on the date the payment is due.

(iii) **Multiple late charges assessed on payment subsequently paid**. A late payment charge may not be imposed in connection with a high-cost mortgage payment if any delinquency is attributable only to a late payment charge imposed on an earlier payment, and the payment otherwise is a full payment for the applicable period and is paid by the due date or within any applicable grace period.

(iv) **Failure to make required payment**. The terms of a high-cost mortgage agreement may provide that any payment shall first be applied to any past due balance. If the consumer fails to make a timely payment by the due date and subsequently resumes making payments but has not paid all past due payments, the creditor may impose a separate late payment charge for any payment(s) outstanding (without deduction due to late fees or related fees) until the default is cured.

(9) **Payoff statements.**

(i) **Fee prohibition.** In general, a creditor or servicer (as defined in 12 CFR 1024.2(b)) may not charge a fee for providing to a consumer, or a person authorized by the consumer to obtain such information, a statement of the amount due to pay off the outstanding balance of a high-cost mortgage.

(ii) **Processing fee.** A creditor or servicer may charge a processing fee to cover the cost of providing a payoff statement, as described in paragraph (a)(9)(i) of this section, by fax or courier, provided that such fee may not exceed an amount that is comparable to fees imposed for similar services provided in connection with consumer credit transactions that are secured by the consumer's principal dwelling and are not high-cost mortgages. A creditor or servicer shall make a payoff statement available to a consumer, or a person authorized by the consumer to obtain such information, by a method other than by fax or courier and without charge pursuant to paragraph (a)(9)(i) of this section.

(iii) **Processing fee disclosure.** Prior to charging a processing fee for provision of a payoff statement by fax or courier, as permitted pursuant to paragraph (a)(9)(ii) of this section, a creditor or servicer shall disclose to a consumer or a person authorized by the consumer to obtain the consumer's payoff statement that payoff statements, as described in paragraph (a)(9)(i) of this section, are available by a method other than by fax or courier without charge.

(iv) **Fees permitted after multiple requests.** A creditor or servicer that has provided a payoff statement, as described in paragraph (a)(9)(i) of this section, to a consumer, or a person authorized by the consumer to obtain such information, without charge, other than the processing fee permitted under paragraph (a)(9)(ii) of this section, four times during a calendar year, may thereafter charge a reasonable fee for providing such statements during the remainder of the calendar year. Fees for payoff statements provided to a consumer, or a person authorized by the consumer to obtain such information, in a subsequent calendar year are subject to the requirements of this section.

(v) **Timing of delivery of payoff statements**. A payoff statement, as described in paragraph (a)(9)(i) of this section, for a high-cost mortgage shall be provided by a creditor or servicer within five business days after receiving a request for such statement by a consumer or a person authorized by the consumer to obtain such statement.

(10) **Financing of points and fees.** A creditor that extends credit under a high-cost mortgage may not finance charges that are required to be included in the calculation of points and fees, as that term is defined in § 1026.32(b)(1) and (2). Credit insurance premiums or debt cancellation or suspension fees that are required to be included in points and fees under § 1026.32(b)(1)(iv) or (2)(iv) shall not be considered financed by the creditor when they are calculated and paid in full on a monthly basis.

(b) **Prohibited acts or practices for dwelling-secured loans; structuring loans to evade high-cost mortgage requirements.** A creditor shall not structure any transaction that is otherwise a high-cost mortgage in a form, for the purpose, and with the intent to evade the requirements of a high-cost mortgage subject to this subpart, including by dividing any loan transaction into separate parts.

§ 1026.35   Requirements for higher-priced mortgage loans.

(a) **Definitions**. For purposes of this section:

(1) "Higher-priced mortgage loan" means a closed-end consumer credit transaction secured by the consumer's principal dwelling with an annual percentage rate that exceeds the average prime offer rate for a comparable transaction as of the date the interest rate is set:

(i) By 1.5 or more percentage points, for a loan secured by a first lien with a principal obligation at consumption that does not exceed the limit in effect as of the date the transaction's interest rate is set for the maximum principal obligation eligible for purchase by Freddie Mac;

(ii) By 2.5 or more percentage points, for a loan secured by a first lien with a principal obligation at consumption that exceeds the limit in effect as of the date the transaction's interest rate is set for the maximum principal obligation eligible for purchase by Freddie Mac; or

(iii) By 3.5 or more percentage points, for a loan secured by a subordinate lien.

(2) "Average prime offer rate" means an annual percentage rate that is derived from average interest rates, points, and other loan pricing terms currently offered to consumers by a representative sample of creditors for mortgage transactions that have low-risk pricing characteristics. The Bureau publishes average prime offer rates for a broad range of types of transactions in a table updated at least weekly as well as the methodology the Bureau uses to derive these rates.

(b) Escrow accounts—

(1) Requirement to escrow for property taxes and insurance. Except as provided in paragraph (b)(2) of this section, a creditor may not extend a higher-priced mortgage loan secured by a first lien on a consumer's principal dwelling unless an escrow account is established before consummation for payment of property taxes and premiums for mortgage-related insurance required by the creditor, such as insurance against loss of or damage to property, or against liability arising out of the ownership or use of the property, or insurance protecting the creditor against the consumer's default or other credit loss. For purposes of this paragraph (b), the term "escrow account" has the same meaning as under Regulation X (12 C.F.R. 1024.17(b)), as amended.

(2) Exemptions. Notwithstanding paragraph (b)(1) of this section:

(i) An escrow account need not be established for:

(A) A transaction secured by shares in a cooperative;

(B) A transaction to finance the initial construction of a dwelling;

(C) A temporary or "bridge" loan with a loan term of twelve months or less, such as a loan to purchase a new dwelling where the consumer plans to *4754 sell a current dwelling within twelve months; or

(D) A reverse mortgage transaction subject to § 1026.33.

(ii) Insurance premiums described in paragraph (b)(1) of this section need not be included in escrow accounts for loans secured by dwellings in condominiums, planned unit developments, or other common interest communities in which dwelling ownership requires participation in a governing association, where the governing association has an obligation to the dwelling owners to maintain a master policy insuring all dwellings.

(iii) Except as provided in paragraph (b)(2)(v) of this section, an escrow account need not be established for a transaction if, at the time of consummation:

(A) During the preceding calendar year, or, if the application for the transaction was received before April 1 of the current calendar year, during either of the two preceding calendar years, the creditor extended more than 50 percent of its total covered transactions, as defined by § 1026.43(b)(1), secured by first liens on properties that are located in areas that are either "rural" or "underserved," as set forth in paragraph (b)(2)(iv) of this section;

(B) During the preceding calendar year, or, if the application for the transaction was received before April 1 of the current calendar year, during either of the two preceding calendar years, the creditor and its affiliates together extended no more than 2,000 covered transactions, as defined by § 1026.43(b)(1), secured by first liens, that were sold, assigned, or otherwise transferred to another person, or that were subject at the time of consummation to a commitment to be acquired by another person;

(C) As of the preceding December 31st, or, if the application for the transaction was received before April 1 of the current calendar year, as of either of the two preceding December 31sts, the creditor and its affiliates that regularly extended covered transactions, as defined by § 1026.43(b)(1), secured by first liens, together, had total assets of less than $2,000,000,000; this asset threshold shall adjust automatically each year, based on the year-to-year change in the average of the Consumer Price Index for Urban Wage Earners and Clerical Workers, not seasonally adjusted, for each 12-month period ending in November, with rounding to the nearest million dollars (see comment 35(b)(2)(iii)–1.iii for the applicable threshold); and

(D) Neither the creditor nor its affiliate maintains an escrow account of the type described in paragraph (b)(1) of this section for any extension of consumer credit secured by real property or a dwelling that the creditor or its affiliate currently services, other than:

(1) Escrow accounts established for first-lien higher-priced mortgage loans for which applications were received on or after April 1, 2010, and before January 1, 2016; or

(2) Escrow accounts established after consummation as an accommodation to distressed consumers to assist such consumers in avoiding default or foreclosure.

(iv) For purposes of paragraph (b)(2)(iii)(A) of this section:

(A) An area is "rural" during a calendar year if it is:

(1) A county that is neither in a metropolitan statistical area nor in a micropolitan statistical area that is adjacent to a metropolitan statistical area, as those terms are defined by the U.S. Office of Management and Budget and as they are applied under currently applicable Urban Influence Codes (UICs), established by the United States Department of Agriculture's Economic Research Service (USDA-ERS); or

(2) A census block that is not in an urban area, as defined by the U.S. Census Bureau using the latest decennial census of the United States.

(B) An area is "underserved" during a calendar year if, according to Home Mortgage Disclosure Act (HMDA) data for the preceding calendar year, it is a county in which no more than two creditors extended covered transactions, as defined in § 1026.43(b)(1), secured by first liens on properties in the county five or more times.

(C) A property shall be deemed to be in an area that is rural or underserved in a particular calendar year if the property is:

(1) Located in a county that appears on the lists published by the Bureau of counties that are rural or underserved, as defined by § 1026.35(b)(2)(iv)(A)(1) or § 1026.35(b)(2)(iv)(B), for that calendar year,

(2) Designated as rural or underserved for that calendar year by any automated tool that the Bureau provides on its public Web site, or

(3) Not designated as located in an urban area, as defined by the most recent delineation of urban areas announced by the Census Bureau, by any automated address search tool that the U.S. Census Bureau provides on its public Web site for that purpose and that specifically indicates the urban or rural designations of properties.

(v) Notwithstanding paragraph (b)(2)(iii) of this section, an escrow account must be established pursuant to paragraph (b)(1) of this section for any first-lien higher-priced mortgage loan that, at consummation, is subject to a commitment to be acquired by a person that does not satisfy the conditions in paragraph (b)(2)(iii) of this section, unless otherwise exempted by this paragraph (b)(2).

(3) **Cancellation—**

(i) **General.** Except as provided in paragraph (b)(3)(ii) of this section, a creditor or servicer may cancel an escrow account required in paragraph (b)(1) of this section only upon the earlier of:

(A) Termination of the underlying debt obligation; or

(B) Receipt no earlier than five years after consummation of a consumer's request to cancel the escrow account.

(ii) **Delayed cancellation.** Notwithstanding paragraph (b)(3)(i) of this section, a creditor or servicer shall not cancel an escrow account pursuant to a consumer's request described in paragraph (b)(3)(i)(B) of this section unless the following conditions are satisfied:

(A) The unpaid principal balance is less than 80 percent of the original value of the property securing the underlying debt obligation; and

(B) The consumer currently is not delinquent or in default on the underlying debt obligation.

(c) **Appraisals—**

(1) **Definitions.** For purposes of this section:

(i) Certified or licensed appraiser means a person who is certified or licensed by the State agency in the State in which the property that secures the transaction is located, and who performs the appraisal in conformity with the Uniform Standards of Professional Appraisal Practice and the requirements applicable to appraisers in title XI of the Financial Institutions Reform, Recovery, and Enforcement Act of 1989, as amended (12 U.S.C. 3331 et seq.), and any implementing regulations in effect at the time the appraiser signs the appraiser's certification.

(ii) Credit risk means the financial risk that a consumer will default on a loan.

(iii) Manufactured home has the same meaning as in 24 CFR 3280.2.

(iv) Manufacturer's invoice means a document issued by a manufacturer and provided with a manufactured home to a retail dealer that separately details the wholesale (base) prices at the factory for specific models or series of manufactured homes and itemized options (large appliances, built-in items and equipment), plus actual itemized charges for freight from the factory to the dealer's lot or the homesite (including any rental of wheels and axles) and for any sales taxes to be paid by the dealer. The invoice may recite such prices and charges on an itemized basis or by stating an aggregate price or charge, as appropriate, for each category.

(v) National Registry means the database of information about State certified and licensed appraisers maintained by the Appraisal Subcommittee of the Federal Financial Institutions Examination Council.

(vi) New manufactured home means a manufactured home that has not been previously occupied.

(vii) State agency means a "State appraiser certifying and licensing agency" recognized in accordance with section 1118(b) of the Financial Institutions Reform, Recovery, and Enforcement Act of 1989 (12 U.S.C. 3347(b)) and any implementing regulations.

(2) **Exemptions.** Unless otherwise specified, the requirements in paragraph (c)(3) through (6) of this section do not apply to the following types of transactions:

(i) A loan that satisfies the criteria of a qualified mortgage as defined pursuant to 15 U.S.C. 1639c;

(ii) An extension of credit for which the amount of credit extended is equal to or less than the applicable threshold amount, which is adjusted every year to reflect increases in the Consumer Price Index for Urban Wage Earners and Clerical Workers, as applicable, and published in the official staff commentary to this paragraph (c)(2)(ii);

(iii) A transaction secured by a mobile home, boat, or trailer.

(iv) A transaction to finance the initial construction of a dwelling.

(v) A loan with a maturity of 12 months or less, if the purpose of the loan is a "bridge" loan connected with the acquisition of a dwelling intended to become the consumer's principal dwelling.

(vi) A reverse-mortgage transaction subject to 12 CFR 1026.33(a).

(vii) An extension of credit that is a refinancing secured by a first lien, with refinancing defined as in § 1026.20(a) (except that the creditor need not be the original creditor or a holder or servicer of the original obligation), provided that the refinancing meets the following criteria:

(A) Either—

(1) The credit risk of the refinancing is retained by the person that held the credit risk of the existing obligation and there is no commitment, at consummation, to transfer the credit risk to another person; or

(2) The refinancing is insured or guaranteed by the same Federal government agency that insured or guaranteed the existing obligation;

(B) The regular periodic payments under the refinance loan do not—

(1) Cause the principal balance to increase;

(2) Allow the consumer to defer repayment of principal; or

(3) Result in a balloon payment, as defined in § 1026.18(s)(5)(i); and

(C) The proceeds from the refinancing are used solely to satisfy the existing obligation and amounts attributed solely to the costs of the refinancing; and

(viii) A transaction secured by:

(A) A new manufactured home and land, but the exemption shall only apply to the requirement in paragraph (c)(3)(i) of this section that the appraiser conduct a physical visit of the interior of the new manufactured home; or

(B) A manufactured home and not land, for which the creditor obtains one of the following and provides a copy to the consumer no later than three business days prior to consummation of the transaction—

(1) For a new manufactured home, the manufacturer's invoice for the manufactured home securing the transaction, provided that the date of manufacture is no earlier than 18 months prior to the creditor's receipt of the consumer's application for credit;

(2) A cost estimate of the value of the manufactured home securing the transaction obtained from an independent cost service provider; or

(3) A valuation, as defined in § 1026.42(b)(3), of the manufactured home performed by a person who has no direct or indirect interest, financial or otherwise, in the property or transaction for which the valuation is performed and has training in valuing manufactured homes.

(3) Appraisals required—

(i) In general. Except as provided in paragraph (c)(2) of this section, a creditor shall not extend a higher-priced mortgage loan to a consumer without obtaining, prior to consummation, a written appraisal of the property to be mortgaged. The appraisal must be performed by a certified or licensed appraiser who conducts a physical visit of the interior of the property that will secure the transaction.

(ii) Safe harbor. A creditor obtains a written appraisal that meets the requirements for an appraisal required under paragraph (c)(3)(i) of this section if the creditor:

(A) Orders that the appraiser perform the appraisal in conformity with the Uniform Standards of Professional Appraisal Practice and title XI of the Financial Institutions Reform, Recovery, and Enforcement Act of 1989, as amended (12 U.S.C. 3331 et seq.), and any implementing regulations in effect at the time the appraiser signs the appraiser's certification;

(B) Verifies through the National Registry that the appraiser who signed the appraiser's certification was a certified or licensed appraiser in the State in which the appraised property is located as of the date the appraiser signed the appraiser's certification;

(C) Confirms that the elements set forth in appendix N to this part are addressed in the written appraisal; and

(D) Has no actual knowledge contrary to the facts or certifications contained in the written appraisal.

(4) Additional appraisal for certain higher-priced mortgage loans—

(i)   In general. Except as provided in paragraphs (c)(2) and (c)(4)(vii) of this section, a creditor shall not extend a higher-priced mortgage loan to a consumer to finance the acquisition of the consumer's principal dwelling without obtaining, prior to consummation, two written appraisals, if:

(A) The seller acquired the property 90 or fewer days prior to the date of the consumer's agreement to acquire the property and the price in the consumer's agreement to acquire the property exceeds the seller's acquisition price by more than 10 percent; or

(B) The seller acquired the property 91 to 180 days prior to the date of the consumer's agreement to acquire the property and the price in the consumer's agreement to acquire the property exceeds the seller's acquisition price by more than 20 percent.

(ii)   Different certified or licensed appraisers. The two appraisals required under paragraph (c)(4)(i) of this section may not be performed by the same certified or licensed appraiser.

(iii) Relationship to general appraisal requirements. If two appraisals must be obtained under paragraph (c)(4)(i) of this section, each appraisal shall meet the requirements of paragraph (c)(3)(i) of this section.

(iv)   Required analysis in the additional appraisal. One of the two required appraisals must include an analysis of:

(A) The difference between the price at which the seller acquired the property and the price that the consumer is obligated to pay to acquire the property, as specified in the consumer's agreement to acquire the property from the seller;

(B) Changes in market conditions between the date the seller acquired the property and the date of the consumer's agreement to acquire the property; and

(C) Any improvements made to the property between the date the seller acquired the property and the date of the consumer's agreement to acquire the property.

(v)   No charge for the additional appraisal. If the creditor must obtain two appraisals under paragraph (c)(4)(i) of this section, the creditor may charge the consumer for only one of the appraisals.

(vi)   Creditor's determination of prior sale date and price—

(A)   Reasonable diligence. A creditor must obtain two written appraisals under paragraph (c)(4)(i) of this section unless the creditor can demonstrate by exercising reasonable diligence that the requirement to obtain two appraisals does not apply. A creditor acts with reasonable diligence if the creditor bases its determination on information contained in written source documents, such as the documents listed in Appendix O to this part.

(B)   Inability to determine prior sale date or price—modified requirements for additional appraisal. If, after exercising reasonable diligence, a creditor cannot determine whether the conditions in paragraphs (c)(4)(i)(A) and (c)(4)(i)(B) are present and therefore must obtain two written appraisals in accordance with paragraphs (c)(4)(i) through (v) of this section, one of the two appraisals shall include an analysis of the factors in paragraph (c)(4)(iv) of this section only to the extent that the information necessary for the appraiser to perform the analysis can be determined.

(vii) Exemptions from the additional appraisal requirement. The additional appraisal required under paragraph (c)(4)(i) of this section shall not apply to extensions of credit that finance a consumer's acquisition of property:

    (A) From a local, State or Federal government agency;

    (B) From a person who acquired title to the property through foreclosure, deed-in-lieu of foreclosure, or other similar judicial or non-judicial procedure as a result of the person's exercise of rights as the holder of a defaulted mortgage loan;

    (C) From a non-profit entity as part of a local, State, or Federal government program under which the non-profit entity is permitted to acquire title to single-family properties for resale from a seller who acquired title to the property through the process of foreclosure, deed-in-lieu of foreclosure, or other similar judicial or non-judicial procedure;

    (D) From a person who acquired title to the property by inheritance or pursuant to a court order of dissolution of marriage, civil union, or domestic partnership, or of partition of joint or marital assets to which the seller was a party;

    (E) From an employer or relocation agency in connection with the relocation of an employee;

    (F) From a servicemember, as defined in 50 U.S.C. App. 511(1), who received a deployment or permanent change of station order after the servicemember purchased the property;

    (G) Located in an area designated by the President as a federal disaster area, if and for as long as the Federal financial institutions regulatory agencies, as defined in 12 U.S.C. 3350(6), waive the requirements in title XI of the Financial Institutions Reform, Recovery, and Enforcement Act of 1989, as amended (12 U.S.C. 3331 et seq.), and any implementing regulations in that area; or

    (H) Located in a rural county, as defined in 12 CFR 1026.35(b)(2)(iv)(A).

(5) Required disclosure—

    (i) In general. Except as provided in paragraph (c)(2) of this section, a creditor shall disclose the following statement, in writing, to a consumer who applies for a higher-priced mortgage loan: "We may order an appraisal to determine the property's value and charge you for this appraisal. We will give you a copy of any appraisal, even if your loan does not close. You can pay for an additional appraisal for your own use at your own cost." Compliance with the disclosure requirement in Regulation B, 12 CFR 1002.14(a)(2), satisfies the requirements of this paragraph.

    (ii) Timing of disclosure. The disclosure required by paragraph (c)(5)(i) of this section shall be delivered or placed in the mail no later than the third business day after the creditor receives the consumer's application for a higher-priced mortgage loan subject to paragraph (c) of this section. In the case of a loan that is not a higher-priced mortgage loan subject to paragraph (c) of this section at the time of application, but becomes a higher-priced mortgage loan subject to paragraph (c) of this section after application, the disclosure shall be delivered or placed in the mail not later than the third business day after the creditor determines that the loan is a higher-priced mortgage loan subject to paragraph (c) of this section.

(6) Copy of appraisals—

    (i) In general. Except as provided in paragraph (c)(2) of this section, a creditor shall provide to the consumer a copy of any written appraisal performed in connection with a higher-priced mortgage loan pursuant to paragraphs (c)(3) and (c)(4) of this section.

    (ii) Timing. A creditor shall provide to the consumer a copy of each written appraisal pursuant to paragraph (c)(6)(i) of this section:

    (A) No later than three business days prior to consummation of the loan; or

(B) In the case of a loan that is not consummated, no later than 30 days after the creditor determines that the loan will not be consummated.

(iii) Form of copy. Any copy of a written appraisal required by paragraph (c)(6)(i) of this section may be provided to the applicant in electronic form, subject to compliance with the consumer consent and other applicable provisions of the Electronic Signatures in Global and National Commerce Act (E-Sign Act) (15 U.S.C. 7001 et seq.).

(iv) No charge for copy of appraisal. A creditor shall not charge the consumer for a copy of a written appraisal required to be provided to the consumer pursuant to paragraph (c)(6)(i) of this section.

(7)   Relation to other rules. The rules in this paragraph (c) were adopted jointly by the Federal Reserve Board (Board), the Office of the Comptroller of the Currency (OCC), the Federal Deposit Insurance Corporation, the National Credit Union Administration, the Federal Housing Finance Agency, and the Bureau. These rules are substantively identical to the Board's and the OCC's higher-priced mortgage loan appraisal rules published separately in 12 CFR 226.43 (for the Board) and in 12 CFR part 34, subpart G and 12 CFR part 164, subpart B (for the OCC).

(d)   Evasion; open-end credit. In connection with credit secured by a consumer's principal dwelling that does not meet the definition of open-end credit in § 1026.2(a)(20), a creditor shall not structure a home-secured loan as an open-end plan to evade the requirements of this section.

§ 1026.36   Prohibited acts or practices and certain requirements for credit secured by a dwelling.

(a)   Definitions.

(1)   Loan originator.

(i)   For purposes of this section, the term "loan originator" means a person who, in expectation of direct or indirect compensation or other monetary gain or for direct or indirect compensation or other monetary gain, performs any of the following activities: takes an application, offers, arranges, assists a consumer in obtaining or applying to obtain, negotiates, or otherwise obtains or makes an extension of consumer credit for another person; or through advertising or other means of communication represents to the public that such person can or will perform any of these activities. The term "loan originator" includes an employee, agent, or contractor of the creditor or loan originator organization if the employee, agent, or contractor meets this definition. The term "loan originator" includes a creditor that engages in loan origination activities if the creditor does not finance the transaction at consummation out of the creditor's own resources, including by drawing on a bona fide warehouse line of credit or out of deposits held by the creditor. All creditors that engage in any of the foregoing loan origination activities are loan originators for purposes of paragraphs (f) and (g) of this section. The term does not include:

(A)   A person who does not take a consumer credit application or offer or negotiate credit terms available from a creditor to that consumer selected based on the consumer's financial characteristics, but who performs purely administrative or clerical tasks on behalf of a person who does engage in such activities.

(B)   An employee of a manufactured home retailer who does not take a consumer credit application, offer or negotiate credit terms, or advise a consumer on credit terms.

(C)   A person that performs only real estate brokerage activities and is licensed or registered in accordance with applicable State law, unless such person is compensated by a creditor or loan originator or by any agent of such creditor or loan originator for a particular consumer credit transaction subject to this section.

(D)   A seller financer that meets the criteria in paragraph (a)(4) or (a)(5) of this section, as applicable.

  (E) A servicer or servicer's employees, agents, and contractors who offer or negotiate terms for purposes of renegotiating, modifying, replacing, or subordinating principal of existing mortgages where consumers are behind in their payments, in default, or have a reasonable likelihood of defaulting or falling behind. This exception does not apply, however, to a servicer or servicer's employees, agents, and contractors who offer or negotiate a transaction that constitutes a refinancing under § 1026.20(a) or obligates a different consumer on the existing debt.

  (ii) An "**individual loan originator**" is a natural person who meets the definition of "loan originator" in paragraph (a)(1)(i) of this section.

  (iii) A "**loan originator organization**" is any loan originator, as defined in paragraph (a)(1)(i) of this section, that is not an individual loan originator.

 (2) **Mortgage broker.** For purposes of this section, a mortgage broker with respect to a particular transaction is any loan originator that is not an employee of the creditor.

 (3) **Compensation.** The term "compensation" includes salaries, commissions, and any financial or similar incentive.

 (4) **Seller financers; three properties**. A person (as defined in § 1026.2(a)(22)) that meets all of the following criteria is not a loan originator under paragraph (a)(1) of this section:

  (i) The person provides seller financing for the sale of three or fewer properties in any 12-month period to purchasers of such properties, each of which is owned by the person and serves as security for the financing.

  (ii) The person has not constructed, or acted as a contractor for the construction of, a residence on the property in the ordinary course of business of the person.

  (iii) The person provides seller financing that meets the following requirements:

   (A) The financing is fully amortizing.

   (B) The financing is one that the person determines in good faith the consumer has a reasonable ability to repay.

   (C) The financing has a fixed rate or an adjustable rate that is adjustable after five or more years, subject to reasonable annual and lifetime limitations on interest rate increases. If the financing agreement has an adjustable rate, the rate is determined by the addition of a margin to an index rate and is subject to reasonable rate adjustment limitations. The index the adjustable rate is based on is a widely available index such as indices for U.S. Treasury securities or LIBOR.

 (5) **Seller financers; one property.** A natural person, estate, or trust that meets all of the following criteria is not a loan originator under paragraph (a)(1) of this section:

  (i) The natural person, estate, or trust provides seller financing for the sale of only one property in any 12-month period to purchasers of such property, which is owned by the natural person, estate, or trust and serves as security for the financing.

  (ii) The natural person, estate, or trust has not constructed, or acted as a contractor for the construction of, a residence on the property in the ordinary course of business of the person.

  (iii) The natural person, estate, or trust provides seller financing that meets the following requirements:

   (A) The financing has a repayment schedule that does not result in negative amortization.

   (B) The financing has a fixed rate or an adjustable rate that is adjustable after five or more years, subject to reasonable annual and lifetime limitations on interest rate increases. If the financing agreement has an adjustable rate, the rate is determined by the addition of a margin to an index rate and is subject to reasonable rate adjustment limitations. The index the adjustable rate is based on is a widely available index such as indices for U.S. Treasury securities or LIBOR.

(6) Credit terms. For purposes of this section, the term "credit terms" includes rates, fees, and other costs. Credit terms are selected based on the consumer's financial characteristics when those terms are selected based on any factors that may influence a credit decision, such as debts, income, assets, or credit history.

(b) Scope. Paragraphs (c)(1) and (2) of this section apply to closed-end consumer credit transactions secured by a consumer's principal dwelling. Paragraph (c)(3) of this section applies to a consumer credit transaction secured by a dwelling. Paragraphs (d) through (i) of this section apply to closed-end consumer credit transactions secured by a dwelling. This section does not apply to a home equity line of credit subject to § 1026.40, except that paragraphs (h) and (i) of this section apply to such credit when secured by the consumer's principal dwelling and paragraph (c)(3) applies to such credit when secured by a dwelling. Paragraphs (d) through (i) of this section do not apply to a loan that is secured by a consumer's interest in a timeshare plan described in 11 U.S.C. 101(53D).

(c) Servicing practices. For purposes of this paragraph (c), the terms "servicer" and "servicing" have the same meanings as provided in 12 CFR 1024.2(b).

(1) Payment processing. In connection with a consumer credit transaction secured by a consumer's principal dwelling:

(i) Periodic payments. No servicer shall fail to credit a periodic payment to the consumer's loan account as of the date of receipt, except when a delay in crediting does not result in any charge to the consumer or in the reporting of negative information to a consumer reporting agency, or except as provided in paragraph (c)(1)(iii) of this section. A periodic payment, as used in this paragraph (c), is an amount sufficient to cover principal, interest, and escrow (if applicable) for a given billing cycle. A payment qualifies as a periodic payment even if it does not include amounts required to cover late fees, other fees, or non-escrow payments a servicer has advanced on a consumer's behalf.

(ii) Partial payments. Any servicer that retains a partial payment, meaning any payment less than a periodic payment, in a suspense or unapplied funds account shall:

(A) Disclose to the consumer the total amount of funds held in such suspense or unapplied funds account on the periodic statement as required by § 1026.41(d)(3), if a periodic statement is required; and

(B) On accumulation of sufficient funds to cover a periodic payment in any suspense or unapplied funds account, treat such funds as a periodic payment received in accordance with paragraph (c)(1)(i) of this section.

(iii) Non-conforming payments. If a servicer specifies in writing requirements for the consumer to follow in making payments, but accepts a payment that does not conform to the requirements, the servicer shall credit the payment as of five days after receipt.

(2) No pyramiding of late fees. In connection with a consumer credit transaction secured by a consumer's principal dwelling, a servicer shall not impose any late fee or delinquency charge for a payment if:

(i) Such a fee or charge is attributable solely to failure of the consumer to pay a late fee or delinquency charge on an earlier payment; and

(ii) The payment is otherwise a periodic payment received on the due date, or within any applicable courtesy period.

(3) Payoff statements. In connection with a consumer credit transaction secured by a consumer's dwelling, a creditor, assignee or servicer, as applicable, must provide an accurate statement of the total outstanding balance that would be required to pay the consumer's obligation in full as of a specified date. The statement shall be sent within a reasonable time, but in no case more than seven business days, after receiving a written request from the consumer or any person acting on behalf of the consumer. When a creditor, assignee, or servicer, as applicable, is not able to provide the statement within seven business days of such a request because a loan is in bankruptcy or foreclosure, because the loan is a reverse mortgage or shared appreciation mortgage, or because of natural disasters or other similar circumstances, the payoff statement must be provided within a reasonable time. A creditor or assignee that does not currently own the mortgage loan or the mortgage servicing rights is not subject to the requirement in this paragraph (c)(3) to provide a payoff statement.

(d)   Prohibited payments to loan originators.

    (1)   Payments based on a term of a transaction.

        (i)   Except as provided in paragraph (d)(1)(iii) or (iv) of this section, in connection with a consumer credit transaction secured by a dwelling, no loan originator shall receive and no person shall pay to a loan originator, directly or indirectly, compensation in an amount that is based on a term of a transaction, the terms of multiple transactions by an individual loan originator, or the terms of multiple transactions by multiple individual loan originators. If a loan originator's compensation is based in whole or in part on a factor that is a proxy for a term of a transaction, the loan originator's compensation is based on a term of a transaction. A factor that is not itself a term of a transaction is a proxy for a term of the transaction if the factor consistently varies with that term over a significant number of transactions, and the loan originator has the ability, directly or indirectly, to add, drop, or change the factor in originating the transaction.

        (ii)   For purposes of this paragraph (d)(1) only, a "term of a transaction" is any right or obligation of the parties to a credit transaction. The amount of credit extended is not a term of a transaction or a proxy for a term of a transaction, provided that compensation received by or paid to a loan originator, directly or indirectly, is based on a fixed percentage of the amount of credit extended; however, such compensation may be subject to a minimum or maximum dollar amount.

        (iii)   An individual loan originator may receive, and a person may pay to an individual loan originator, compensation in the form of a contribution to a defined contribution plan that is a designated tax-advantaged plan or a benefit under a defined benefit plan that is a designated tax-advantaged plan. In the case of a contribution to a defined contribution plan, the contribution shall not be directly or indirectly based on the terms of that individual loan originator's transactions. As used in this paragraph (d)(1)(iii), "designated tax-advantaged plan" means any plan that meets the requirements of Internal Revenue Code section 401(a), 26 U.S.C. 401(a); employee annuity plan described in Internal Revenue Code section 403(a), 26 U.S.C. 403(a); simple retirement account, as defined in Internal Revenue Code section 408(p), 26 U.S.C. 408(p); simplified employee pension described in Internal Revenue Code section 408(k), 26 U.S.C. 408(k); annuity contract described in Internal Revenue Code section 403(b), 26 U.S.C. 403(b); or eligible deferred compensation plan, as defined in Internal Revenue Code section 457(b), 26 U.S.C. 457(b).

        (iv)   An individual loan originator may receive, and a person may pay to an individual loan originator, compensation under a non-deferred profits-based compensation plan (i.e., any arrangement for the payment of non-deferred compensation that is determined with reference to the profits of the person from mortgage-related business), provided that:

            (A)   The compensation paid to an individual loan originator pursuant to this paragraph (d)(1)(iv) is not directly or indirectly based on the terms of that individual loan originator's transactions that are subject to this paragraph (d); and

            (B)   At least one of the following conditions is satisfied:

                (1)   The compensation paid to an individual loan originator pursuant to this paragraph (d)(1)(iv) does not, in the aggregate, exceed 10 percent of the individual loan originator's total compensation corresponding to the time period for which the compensation under the non-deferred profits-based compensation plan is paid; or

                (2)   The individual loan originator was a loan originator for ten or fewer transactions subject to this paragraph (d) consummated during the 12-month period preceding the date of the compensation determination.

(2) Payments by persons other than consumer.

(i) Dual compensation.

(A) Except as provided in paragraph (d)(2)(i)(C) of this section, if any loan originator receives compensation directly from a consumer in a consumer credit transaction secured by a dwelling:

(1) No loan originator shall receive compensation, directly or indirectly, from any person other than the consumer in connection with the transaction; and

(2) No person who knows or has reason to know of the consumer-paid compensation to the loan originator (other than the consumer) shall pay any compensation to a loan originator, directly or indirectly, in connection with the transaction.

(B) Compensation received directly from a consumer includes payments to a loan originator made pursuant to an agreement between the consumer and a person other than the creditor or its affiliates, under which such other person agrees to provide funds toward the consumer's costs of the transaction (including loan originator compensation).

(C) If a loan originator organization receives compensation directly from a consumer in connection with a transaction, the loan originator organization may pay compensation to an individual loan originator, and the individual loan originator may receive compensation from the loan originator organization, subject to paragraph (d)(1) of this section.

(ii) Exemption. A payment to a loan originator that is otherwise prohibited by section 129B(c)(2)(A) of the Truth in Lending Act is nevertheless permitted pursuant to section 129B(c)(2)(B) of the Act, regardless of whether the consumer makes any upfront payment of discount points, origination points, or fees, as described in section 129B(c)(2)(B)(ii) of the Act, as long as the loan originator does not receive any compensation directly from the consumer as described in section 129B(c)(2)(B)(i) of the Act.

(3) Affiliates. For purposes of this paragraph (d), affiliates shall be treated as a single "person."

(e) Prohibition on steering.

(1) General. In connection with a consumer credit transaction secured by a dwelling, a loan originator shall not direct or "steer" a consumer to consummate a transaction based on the fact that the originator will receive greater compensation from the creditor in that transaction than in other transactions the originator offered or could have offered to the consumer, unless the consummated transaction is in the consumer's interest.

(2) Permissible transactions. A transaction does not violate paragraph (e)(1) of this section if the consumer is presented with loan options that meet the conditions in paragraph (e)(3) of this section for each type of transaction in which the consumer expressed an interest. For purposes of paragraph (e) of this section, the term "type of transaction" refers to whether:

(i) A loan has an annual percentage rate that cannot increase after consummation;

(ii) A loan has an annual percentage rate that may increase after consummation; or

(iii) A loan is a reverse mortgage.

(3) Loan options presented. A transaction satisfies paragraph (e)(2) of this section only if the loan originator presents the loan options required by that paragraph and all of the following conditions are met:

(i) The loan originator must obtain loan options from a significant number of the creditors with which the originator regularly does business and, for each type of transaction in which the consumer expressed an interest, must present the consumer with loan options that include:

(A) The loan with the lowest interest rate;

(B) The loan with the lowest interest rate without negative amortization, a prepayment penalty, interest-only payments, a balloon payment in the first 7 years of the life of the loan, a demand feature, shared equity, or shared appreciation; or, in the case of a reverse mortgage, a loan without a prepayment penalty, or shared equity or shared appreciation; and

(C) The loan with the lowest total dollar amount of discount points, origination points or origination fees (or, if two or more loans have the same total dollar amount of discount points, origination points or origination fees, the loan with the lowest interest rate that has the lowest total dollar amount of discount points, origination points or origination fees).

(ii) The loan originator must have a good faith belief that the options presented to the consumer pursuant to paragraph (e)(3)(i) of this section are loans for which the consumer likely qualifies.

(iii) For each type of transaction, if the originator presents to the consumer more than three loans, the originator must highlight the loans that satisfy the criteria specified in paragraph (e)(3)(i) of this section.

(4) Number of loan options presented. The loan originator can present fewer than three loans and satisfy paragraphs (e)(2) and (e)(3)(i) of this section if the loan(s) presented to the consumer satisfy the criteria of the options in paragraph (e)(3)(i) of this section and the provisions of paragraph (e)(3) of this section are otherwise met.

(f) Loan originator qualification requirements. A loan originator for a consumer credit transaction secured by a dwelling must, when required by applicable State or Federal law, be registered and licensed in accordance with those laws, including the Secure and Fair Enforcement for Mortgage Licensing Act of 2008 (SAFE Act, 12 U.S.C. 5102 et seq.), its implementing regulations (12 CFR part 1007 or part 1008), and State SAFE Act implementing law. To comply with this paragraph (f), a loan originator organization that is not a government agency or State housing finance agency must:

(1) Comply with all applicable State law requirements for legal existence and foreign qualification;

(2) Ensure that each individual loan originator who works for the loan originator organization is licensed or registered to the extent the individual is required to be licensed or registered under the SAFE Act, its implementing regulations, and State SAFE Act implementing law before the individual acts as a loan originator in a consumer credit transaction secured by a dwelling; and

(3) For each of its individual loan originator employees who is not required to be licensed and is not licensed as a loan originator pursuant to § 1008.103 of this chapter or State SAFE Act implementing law:

(i) Obtain for any individual whom the loan originator organization hired on or after January 1, 2014 (or whom the loan originator organization hired before this date but for whom there were no applicable statutory or regulatory background standards in effect at the time of hire or before January 1, 2014, used to screen the individual) and for any individual regardless of when hired who, based on reliable information known to the loan originator organization, likely does not meet the standards under § 1026.36(f)(3)(ii), before the individual acts as a loan originator in a consumer credit transaction secured by a dwelling:

(A) A criminal background check through the Nationwide Mortgage Licensing System and Registry (NMLSR) or, in the case of an individual loan originator who is not a registered loan originator under the NMLSR, a criminal background check from a law enforcement agency or commercial service;

(B) A credit report from a consumer reporting agency described in section 603(p) of the Fair Credit Reporting Act (15 U.S.C. 1681a(p)) secured, where applicable, in compliance with the requirements of section 604(b) of the Fair Credit Reporting Act, 15 U.S.C. 1681b(b); and

(C) Information from the NMLSR about any administrative, civil, or criminal findings by any government jurisdiction or, in the case of an individual loan originator who is not a registered loan originator under the NMLSR, such information from the individual loan originator;

(ii) Determine on the basis of the information obtained pursuant to paragraph (f)(3)(i) of this section and any other information reasonably available to the loan originator organization, for any individual whom the loan originator organization hired on or after January 1, 2014 (or whom the loan originator organization hired before this date but for whom there were no applicable statutory or regulatory background standards in effect at the time of hire or before January 1, 2014, used to screen the individual) and for any individual regardless of when hired who, based on reliable information known to the loan originator organization, likely does not meet the standards under this paragraph (f)(3)(ii), before the individual acts as a loan originator in a consumer credit transaction secured by a dwelling, that the individual loan originator:

(A)(1) Has not been convicted of, or pleaded guilty or nolo contendere to, a felony in a domestic or military court during the preceding seven-year period or, in the case of a felony involving an act of fraud, dishonesty, a breach of trust, or money laundering, at any time;

(2) For purposes of this paragraph (f)(3)(ii)(A):

(i) A crime is a felony only if at the time of conviction it was classified as a felony under the law of the jurisdiction under which the individual was convicted;

(ii) Expunged convictions and pardoned convictions do not render an individual unqualified; and

(iii) A conviction or plea of guilty or nolo contendere does not render an individual unqualified under this § 1026.36(f) if the loan originator organization has obtained consent to employ the individual from the Federal Deposit Insurance Corporation (or the Board of Governors of the Federal Reserve System, as applicable) pursuant to section 19 of the Federal Deposit Insurance Act (FDIA), 12 U.S.C. 1829, the National Credit Union Administration pursuant to section 205 of the Federal Credit Union Act (FCUA), 12 U.S.C. 1785(d), or the Farm Credit Administration pursuant to section 5.65(d) of the Farm Credit Act of 1971 (FCA), 12 U.S.C. 227a–14(d), notwithstanding the bars posed with respect to that conviction or plea by the FDIA, FCUA, and FCA, as applicable; and

(B) Has demonstrated financial responsibility, character, and general fitness such as to warrant a determination that the individual loan originator will operate honestly, fairly, and efficiently; and

(iii) Provide periodic training covering Federal and State law requirements that apply to the individual loan originator's loan origination activities.

(g)   Name and NMLSR ID on loan documents. (1) For a consumer credit transaction secured by a dwelling, a loan originator organization must include on the loan documents described in paragraph (g)(2) of this section, whenever each such loan document is provided to a consumer or presented to a consumer for signature, as applicable:

(i)   Its name and NMLSR ID, if the NMLSR has provided it an NMLSR ID; and

(ii)   The name of the individual loan originator (as the name appears in the NMLSR) with primary responsibility for the origination and, if the NMLSR has provided such person an NMLSR ID, that NMLSR ID.

(2)   The loan documents that must include the names and NMLSR IDs pursuant to paragraph (g)(1) of this section are:

(i)   The credit application;

(ii) The disclosures required by § 1026.19(e) and (f);

(iii) The note or loan contract; and

(iv) The security instrument.

(3) For purposes of this section, NMLSR ID means a number assigned by the Nationwide Mortgage Licensing System and Registry to facilitate electronic tracking and uniform identification of loan originators and public access to the employment history of, and the publicly adjudicated disciplinary and enforcement actions against, loan originators.

(h) Prohibition on mandatory arbitration clauses and waivers of certain consumer rights.

(1) Arbitration. A contract or other agreement for a consumer credit transaction secured by a dwelling (including a home equity line of credit secured by the consumer's principal dwelling) may not include terms that require arbitration or any other non-judicial procedure to resolve any controversy or settle any claims arising out of the transaction. This prohibition does not limit a consumer and creditor or any assignee from agreeing, after a dispute or claim under the transaction arises, to settle or use arbitration or other non-judicial procedure to resolve that dispute or claim.

(2) No waivers of Federal statutory causes of action. A contract or other agreement relating to a consumer credit transaction secured by a dwelling (including a home equity line of credit secured by the consumer's principal dwelling) may not be applied or interpreted to bar a consumer from bringing a claim in court pursuant to any provision of law for damages or other relief in connection with any alleged violation of any Federal law. This prohibition does not limit a consumer and creditor or any assignee from agreeing, after a dispute or claim under the transaction arises, to settle or use arbitration or other non-judicial procedure to resolve that dispute or claim.

(i) Prohibition on financing credit insurance.

(1) A creditor may not finance, directly or indirectly, any premiums or fees for credit insurance in connection with a consumer credit transaction secured by a dwelling (including a home equity line of credit secured by the consumer's principal dwelling). This prohibition does not apply to credit insurance for which premiums or fees are calculated and paid in full on a monthly basis.

(2) For purposes of this paragraph (i):

(i) "Credit insurance":

(A) Means credit life, credit disability, credit unemployment, or credit property insurance, or any other accident, loss-of-income, life, or health insurance, or any payments directly or indirectly for any debt cancellation or suspension agreement or contract, but

(B) Excludes credit unemployment insurance for which the unemployment insurance premiums are reasonable, the creditor receives no direct or indirect compensation in connection with the unemployment insurance premiums, and the unemployment insurance premiums are paid pursuant to a separate insurance contract and are not paid to an affiliate of the creditor;

(ii) A creditor finances premiums or fees for credit insurance if it provides a consumer the right to defer payment of a credit insurance premium or fee owed by the consumer beyond the monthly period in which the premium or fee is due; and

(iii) Credit insurance premiums or fees are calculated on a monthly basis if they are determined mathematically by multiplying a rate by the actual monthly outstanding balance.

(j) Policies and procedures to ensure and monitor compliance.

(1) A depository institution must establish and maintain written policies and procedures reasonably designed to ensure and monitor the compliance of the depository institution, its employees, its subsidiaries, and its subsidiaries' employees with the requirements of paragraphs (d), (e), (f), and (g) of this section. These written policies and procedures must be appropriate to the nature, size, complexity, and scope of the mortgage lending activities of the depository institution and its subsidiaries.

(2) For purposes of this paragraph (j), "depository institution" has the meaning in section 1503(3) of the SAFE Act, 12 U.S.C. 5102(3). For purposes of this paragraph (j), "subsidiary" has the meaning in section 3 of the Federal Deposit Insurance Act, 12 U.S.C. 1813.

(k) Negative amortization counseling. (1) Counseling required. A creditor shall not extend credit to a first-time borrower in connection with a closed-end transaction secured by a dwelling, other than a reverse mortgage transaction subject to § 1026.33 or a transaction secured by a consumer's interest in a timeshare plan described in 11 U.S.C. 101(53D), that may result in negative amortization, unless the creditor receives documentation that the consumer has obtained homeownership counseling from a counseling organization or counselor certified or approved by the U.S. Department of Housing and Urban Development to provide such counseling.

(2) Definitions. For the purposes of this paragraph (k), the following definitions apply:

(i) A "first-time borrower" means a consumer who has not previously received a closed-end credit transaction or open-end credit plan secured by a dwelling.

(ii) "Negative amortization" means a payment schedule with regular periodic payments that cause the principal balance to increase.

(3) Steering prohibited. A creditor that extends credit to a first-time borrower in connection with a closed-end transaction secured by a dwelling, other than a reverse mortgage transaction subject to § 1026.33 or a transaction secured by a consumer's interest in a timeshare plan described in 11 U.S.C. 101(53D), that may result in negative amortization shall not steer or otherwise direct a consumer to choose a particular counselor or counseling organization for the counseling required under this paragraph (k).

§ 1026.37 Content of disclosures for certain mortgage transactions (Loan Estimate).

For each transaction subject to § 1026.19(e), the creditor shall disclose the information in this section:

(a) General information—

(1) Form title. The title of the form, "Loan Estimate," using that term.

(2) Form purpose. The statement, "Save this Loan Estimate to compare with your Closing Disclosure."

(3) Creditor. The name and address of the creditor making the disclosures.

(4) Date issued. The date the disclosures are mailed or delivered to the consumer by the creditor, labeled "Date Issued."

(5) Applicants. The name and mailing address of the consumer(s) applying for the credit, labeled "Applicants."

(6) Property. The address including the zip code of the property that secures or will secure the transaction, or if the address is unavailable, the location of such property including a zip code, labeled "Property."

(7) Sale price. (i) For transactions that involve a seller, the contract sale price of the property identified in paragraph (a)(6) of this section, labeled "Sale Price."

(ii) For transactions that do not involve a seller, the estimated value of the property identified in paragraph (a)(6), labeled "Prop. Value."

(8) Loan term. The term to maturity of the credit transaction, stated in years or months, or both, as applicable, labeled "Loan Term."

(9) Purpose. The consumer's intended use for the credit, labeled "Purpose," using one of the following terms:

(i) **Purchase.** If the credit is to finance the acquisition of the property identified in paragraph (a)(6) of this section, the creditor shall disclose that the loan is for a "Purchase."

(ii) **Refinance.** If the credit is not for the purpose described in paragraph (a)(9)(i) of this section, and if the credit will be used to refinance an existing obligation, as defined in § 1026.20(a) (but without regard to whether the creditor is the original creditor or a holder or servicer of the original obligation), that is secured by the property identified in paragraph (a)(6) of this section, the creditor shall disclose that the loan is for a "Refinance."

(iii) **Construction.** If the credit is not for one of the purposes described in paragraphs (a)(9)(i) or (ii) of this section and the credit will be used to finance the initial construction of a dwelling on the property identified in paragraph (a)(6) of this section, the creditor shall disclose that the loan is for "Construction."

(iv) **Home equity loan.** If the credit is not for one of the purposes described in paragraphs (a)(9)(i) through (iii) of this section, the creditor shall disclose that the loan is a "Home Equity Loan."

(10) **Product.** A description of the loan product, labeled "Product."

(i) The description of the loan product shall include one of the following terms:

(A) **Adjustable rate.** If the interest rate may increase after consumption, but the rates that will apply or the periods for which they will apply are not known at consumption, the creditor shall disclose the loan product as an "Adjustable Rate."

(B) **Step rate.** If the interest rate will change after consumption, and the rates that will apply and the periods for which they will apply are known at consumption, the creditor shall disclose the loan product as a "Step Rate."

(C) **Fixed rate.** If the loan product is not an Adjustable Rate or a Step Rate, as described in paragraphs (a)(10)(i)(A) and (B) of this section, respectively, the creditor shall disclose the loan product as a "Fixed Rate."

(ii) The description of the loan product shall include the features that may change the periodic payment using the following terms, subject to paragraph (a)(10)(iii) of this section, as applicable:

(A) **Negative amortization.** If the principal balance may increase due to the addition of accrued interest to the principal balance, the creditor shall disclose that the loan product has a "Negative Amortization" feature.

(B) **Interest only.** If one or more regular periodic payments may be applied only to interest accrued and not to the loan principal, the creditor shall disclose that the loan product has an "Interest Only" feature.

(C) **Step payment.** If scheduled variations in regular periodic payment amounts occur that are not caused by changes to the interest rate during the loan term, the creditor shall disclose that the loan product has a "Step Payment" feature.

(D) **Balloon payment.** If the terms of the legal obligation include a "balloon payment," as that term is defined in paragraph (b)(5) of this section, the creditor shall disclose that the loan has a "Balloon Payment" feature.

(E) **Seasonal payment.** If the terms of the legal obligation expressly provide that regular periodic payments are not scheduled between specified unit-periods on a regular basis, the creditor shall disclose that the loan product has a "Seasonal Payment" feature.

(iii) The disclosure of a loan feature under paragraph (a)(10)(ii) of this section shall precede the disclosure of the loan product under paragraph (a)(10)(i) of this section. If a transaction has more than one of the loan features described in paragraph (a)(10)(ii) of this section, the creditor shall disclose only the first applicable feature in the order the features are listed in paragraph (a)(10)(ii) of this section.

(iv) The disclosures required by paragraphs (a)(10)(i)(A) and (B), and (a)(10)(ii)(A) through (D) of this section must each be preceded by the duration of any introductory rate or payment period, and the first adjustment period, as applicable.

(11) Loan type. The type of loan, labeled "Loan Type," offered to the consumer using one of the following terms, as applicable:

(i)   Conventional. If the loan is not guaranteed or insured by a Federal or State government agency, the creditor shall disclose that the loan is a "Conventional."

(ii)   FHA. If the loan is insured by the Federal Housing Administration, the creditor shall disclose that the loan is an "FHA."

(iii)   VA. If the loan is guaranteed by the U.S. Department of Veterans Affairs, the creditor shall disclose that the loan is a "VA."

(iv)   Other. For federally-insured or guaranteed loans other than those described in paragraphs (a)(11)(ii) and (iii) of this section, and for loans insured or guaranteed by a State agency, the creditor shall disclose the loan type as "Other," and provide a brief description of the loan type.

(12) Loan identification number (Loan ID #). A number that may be used by the creditor, consumer, and other parties to identify the transaction, labeled "Loan ID #."

(13) Rate lock. A statement of whether the interest rate disclosed pursuant to paragraph (b)(2) of this section is locked for a specific period of time, labeled "Rate Lock."

(i)   For transactions in which the interest rate is locked for a specific period of time, the creditor must provide the date and time (including the applicable time zone) when that period ends.

(ii)   The "Rate Lock" statement required by this paragraph (a)(13) shall be accompanied by a statement that the interest rate, any points, and any lender credits may change unless the interest rate has been locked, and the date and time (including the applicable time zone) at which estimated closing costs expire.

(b)   Loan terms. A separate table under the heading "Loan Terms" that contains the following information and satisfies the following requirements:

(1)   Loan amount. The amount of credit to be extended under the terms of the legal obligation, labeled "Loan Amount."

(2)   Interest rate. The interest rate that will be applicable to the transaction at consummation, labeled "Interest Rate." For an adjustable rate transaction, if the interest rate at consummation is not known, the rate disclosed shall be the fully-indexed rate, which, for purposes of this paragraph, means the interest rate calculated using the index value and margin at the time of consummation.

(3)   Principal and interest payment. The initial periodic payment amount that will be due under the terms of the legal obligation, labeled "Principal & Interest," immediately preceded by the applicable unit-period, and a statement referring to the payment amount that includes any mortgage insurance and escrow payments that is required to be disclosed pursuant to paragraph (c) of this section. If the interest rate at consummation is not known, the amount disclosed shall be calculated using the fully-indexed rate disclosed under paragraph (b)(2) of this section.

(4)   Prepayment penalty. A statement of whether the transaction includes a prepayment penalty, labeled "Prepayment Penalty." For purposes of this paragraph (b)(4), "prepayment penalty" means a charge imposed for paying all or part of a transaction's principal before the date on which the principal is due, other than a waived, bona fide third-party charge that the creditor imposes if the consumer prepays all of the transaction's principal sooner than 36 months after consummation.

(5)   Balloon payment. A statement of whether the transaction includes a balloon payment, labeled "Balloon Payment." For purposes of this paragraph (b)(5), "balloon payment" means a payment that is more than two times a regular periodic payment. "Balloon payment" includes the payment or payments under a transaction that requires only one or two payments during the loan term.

(6) **Adjustments after consummation.** For each amount required to be disclosed by paragraphs (b)(1) through (3) of this section, a statement of whether the amount may increase after consummation as an affirmative or negative answer to the question, and under such question disclosed as a subheading, "Can this amount increase after closing?" and, in the case of an affirmative answer, the following additional information, as applicable:

(i) **Adjustment in loan amount.** The maximum principal balance for the transaction and the due date of the last payment that may cause the principal balance to increase. The disclosure further shall indicate whether the maximum principal balance is potential or is scheduled to occur under the terms of the legal obligation.

(ii) **Adjustment in interest rate.** The frequency of interest rate adjustments, the date when the interest rate may first adjust, the maximum interest rate, and the first date when the interest rate can reach the maximum interest rate, followed by a reference to the disclosure required by paragraph (j) of this section. If the loan term, as defined under paragraph (a)(8) of this section, may increase based on an interest rate adjustment, the disclosure required by this paragraph (b)(6)(ii) shall also state that fact and the maximum possible loan term determined in accordance with paragraph (a)(8) of this section.

(iii) **Increase in periodic payment.** The scheduled frequency of adjustments to the periodic principal and interest payment, the due date of the first adjusted principal and interest payment, the maximum possible periodic principal and interest payment, and the date when the periodic principal and interest payment may first equal the maximum principal and interest payment. If any adjustments to the principal and interest payment are not the result of a change to the interest rate, a reference to the disclosure required by paragraph (i) of this section. If there is a period during which only interest is required to be paid, the disclosure required by this paragraph (b)(6)(iii) shall also state that fact and the due date of the last periodic payment of such period.

(7) **Details about prepayment penalty and balloon payment.** The information required to be disclosed by paragraphs (b)(4) and (5) of this section shall be disclosed as an affirmative or negative answer to the question, and under such question disclosed as a subheading, "Does the loan have these features?" If an affirmative answer for a prepayment penalty or balloon payment is required to be disclosed, the following information shall be included, as applicable:

(i) The maximum amount of the prepayment penalty that may be imposed and the date when the period during which the penalty may be imposed terminates; and

(ii) The maximum amount of the balloon payment and the due date of such payment.

(8) **Timing. (i)** The dates required to be disclosed by paragraph (b)(6)(ii) of this section shall be disclosed as the year in which the event occurs, counting from the date that interest for the first scheduled periodic payment begins to accrue after consummation.

(ii) The dates required to be disclosed by paragraphs (b)(6)(i), (b)(6)(iii) and (b)(7)(ii) of this section shall be disclosed as the year in which the event occurs, counting from the due date of the initial periodic payment.

(iii) The date required to be disclosed by paragraph (b)(7)(i) of this section shall be disclosed as the year in which the event occurs, counting from the date of consummation.

(c) **Projected payments.** In a separate table under the heading "Projected Payments," an itemization of each separate periodic payment or range of payments, together with an estimate of taxes, insurance, and assessments and the payments to be made with escrow account funds.

(1) **Periodic payment or range of payments.**

(i) The initial periodic payment or range of payments is a separate periodic payment or range of payments and, except as otherwise provided in paragraph (c)(1)(ii) and (iii) of this section, the following events require the disclosure of additional separate periodic payments or ranges of payments:

(A) The periodic principal and interest payment or range of such payments may change;

(B) A scheduled balloon payment, as defined in paragraph (b)(5) of this section;

(C) The creditor must automatically terminate mortgage insurance or any functional equivalent under applicable law; and

(D) The anniversary of the due date of the initial periodic payment or range of payments that immediately follows the occurrence of multiple events described in paragraph (c)(1)(i)(A) of this section during a single year.

(ii) The table required by this paragraph (c) shall not disclose more than four separate periodic payments or ranges of payments. For all events requiring disclosure of additional separate periodic payments or ranges of payments described in paragraph (c)(1)(i)(A) through (D) of this section occurring after the third separate periodic payment or range of payments disclosed, the separate periodic payments or ranges of payments shall be disclosed as a single range of payments, subject to the following exceptions:

(A) A balloon payment that is scheduled as a final payment under the terms of the legal obligation shall always be disclosed as a separate periodic payment or range of payments, in which case all events requiring disclosure of additional separate periodic payments or ranges of payments described in paragraph (c)(1)(i)(A) through (D) of this section occurring after the second separate periodic payment or range of payments disclosed, other than the balloon payment that is scheduled as a final payment, shall be disclosed as a single range of payments.

(B) The automatic termination of mortgage insurance or any functional equivalent under applicable law shall require disclosure of an additional separate periodic payment or range of payments only if the total number of separate periodic payments or ranges of payments otherwise disclosed pursuant to this paragraph (c)(1) does not exceed three.

(iii) When a range of payments is required to be disclosed under this paragraph (c)(1), the creditor must disclose the minimum and maximum amount for both the principal and interest payment under paragraph (c)(2)(i) of this section and the total periodic payment under paragraph (c)(2)(iv) of this section. A range of payments is required to be disclosed under this paragraph (c)(1) when:

(A) Multiple events described in paragraph (c)(1)(i) of this section are combined in a single range of payments pursuant to paragraph (c)(1)(ii) of this section;

(B) Multiple events described in paragraph (c)(1)(i)(A) of this section occur during a single year or an event described in paragraph (c)(1)(i)(A) of this section occurs during the same year as the initial periodic payment or range of payments, in which case the creditor discloses the range of payments that would apply during the year in which the events occur; or

(C) The periodic principal and interest payment may adjust based on index rates at the time an interest rate adjustment may occur.

(2) **Itemization.** Each separate periodic payment or range of payments disclosed on the table required by this paragraph (c) shall be itemized as follows:

(i) The amount payable for principal and interest, labeled "Principal & Interest," including the term "only interest" if the payment or range of payments includes any interest only payment:

(A) In the case of a loan that has an adjustable interest rate, the maximum principal and interest payment amounts are determined by assuming that the interest rate in effect throughout the loan term is the maximum possible interest rate, and the minimum amounts are determined by assuming that the interest rate in effect throughout the loan term is the minimum possible interest rate;

(B) In the case of a loan that has an adjustable interest rate and also contains a negative amortization feature, the maximum principal and interest payment amounts after the end of the period of the loan's term during which the loan's principal balance may increase due to the addition of accrued interest are determined by assuming the maximum principal amount permitted under the terms of the legal obligation at the end of such period, and the minimum amounts are determined pursuant to paragraph (c)(2)(i)(A) of this section;

(ii) The maximum amount payable for mortgage insurance premiums corresponding to the principal and interest payment disclosed pursuant to paragraph (c)(2)(i) of this section, labeled "Mortgage Insurance";

(iii) The amount payable into an escrow account to pay some or all of the charges described in paragraph (c)(4)(ii), as applicable, labeled "Escrow," together with a statement that the amount disclosed can increase over time; and

(iv) The total periodic payment, calculated as the sum of the amounts disclosed pursuant to paragraphs (c)(2)(i) through (iii) of this section, labeled "Total Monthly Payment."

(3) Subheadings. (i) The labels required pursuant to paragraph (c)(2) of this section must be listed under the subheading "Payment Calculation."

(ii) Except as provided in paragraph (c)(3)(iii) of this section, each separate periodic payment or range of payments to be disclosed under this paragraph (c) must be disclosed under a subheading that states the years of the loan during which that payment or range of payments will apply. The subheadings must be stated in a sequence of whole years from the due date of the initial periodic payment.

(iii) A balloon payment that is scheduled as a final payment under the terms of the legal obligation must be disclosed under the subheading "Final Payment."

(4) Taxes, insurance, and assessments. Under the information required by paragraphs (c)(1) through (3) of this section:

(i) The label "Taxes, Insurance & Assessments";

(ii) The sum of the charges identified in § 1026.43(b)(8), other than amounts identified in § 1026.4(b)(5), expressed as a monthly amount, even if no escrow account for the payment of some or any of such charges will be established;

(iii) A statement that the amount disclosed pursuant to paragraph (c)(4)(ii) of this section can increase over time;

(iv) A statement of whether the amount disclosed pursuant to paragraph (c)(4)(ii) of this section includes payments for property taxes, amounts identified in § 1026.4(b)(8), and other amounts described in paragraph (c)(4)(ii) of this section, along with a description of any such other amounts, and an indication of whether such amounts will be paid by the creditor using escrow account funds;

(v) A statement that the consumer must pay separately any amounts described in paragraph (c)(4)(ii) of this section that are not paid by the creditor using escrow account funds; and

(vi) A reference to the information disclosed pursuant to paragraph (g)(3) of this section.

(5) Calculation of taxes and insurance. For purposes of paragraphs (c)(2)(iii) and (c)(4)(ii) of this section, estimated property taxes and homeowner's insurance shall reflect:

(i) The taxable assessed value of the real property securing the transaction after consumption, including the value of any improvements on the property or to be constructed on the property, if known, whether or not such construction will be financed from the proceeds of the transaction, for property taxes; and

(ii) The replacement costs of the property during the initial year after the transaction, for amounts identified in § 1026.4(b)(8).

(d) **Costs at closing.**

(1) **Costs at closing table.** In a separate table, under the heading "Costs at Closing":

(i) Labeled "Closing Costs," the dollar amount disclosed pursuant to paragraph (g)(6) of this section, together with:

(A) A statement that the amount disclosed pursuant to paragraph (d)(1)(i) of this section includes the amounts disclosed pursuant to paragraphs (f)(4), (g)(5), and (g)(6)(ii);

(B) The dollar amount disclosed pursuant to paragraph (f)(4) of this section, labeled "Loan Costs";

(C) The dollar amount disclosed pursuant to paragraph (g)(5) of this section, labeled "Other Costs";

(D) The dollar amount disclosed pursuant to paragraph (g)(6)(ii) of this section, labeled "Lender Credits"; and

(E) A statement referring the consumer to the tables disclosed pursuant to paragraphs (f) and (g) of this section for details.

(ii) Labeled "Cash to Close," the dollar amount calculated in accordance with paragraph (h)(1)(viii) of this section, together with:

(A) A statement that the amount includes the amount disclosed pursuant to paragraph (d)(1)(i) of this section, and

(B) A statement referring the consumer to the location of the table required pursuant to paragraph (h) of this section for details.

(2) **Optional alternative table for transactions without a seller.** For transactions that do not involve a seller, instead of the amount and statements described in paragraph (d)(1)(ii) of this section, the creditor may alternatively disclose, using the label "Cash to Close":

(i) The amount calculated in accordance with (h)(2)(iv) of this section;

(ii) A statement of whether the disclosed estimated amount is due from or to the consumer; and

(iii) A statement referring the consumer to the alternative table disclosed pursuant to paragraph (h)(2) of this section for details.

(e) **Web site reference.** A statement that the consumer may obtain general information and tools at the Web site of the Bureau, and the link or uniform resource locator address to the Web site: www. consumerfinance.gov/mortgage-estimate.

(f) **Closing cost details; loan costs.** Under the master heading "Closing Cost Details," in a table under the heading "Loan Costs," all loan costs associated with the transaction. The table shall contain the items and amounts listed under four subheadings, described in paragraphs (f)(1) through (4) of this section.

(1) **Origination charges.** Under the subheading "Origination Charges," an itemization of each amount, and a subtotal of all such amounts, that the consumer will pay to each creditor and loan originator for originating and extending the credit.

(i) The points paid to the creditor to reduce the interest rate shall be itemized separately, as both a percentage of the amount of credit extended and a dollar amount, and using the label "__% of Loan Amount (Points)." If points to reduce the interest rate are not paid, the disclosure required by this paragraph (f)(1)(i) must be blank.

(ii) The number of items disclosed under this paragraph (f)(1), including the points disclosed under paragraph (f)(1)(i) of this section, shall not exceed 13.

(2) Services you cannot shop for. Under the subheading "Services You Cannot Shop For," an itemization of each amount, and a subtotal of all such amounts, the consumer will pay for settlement services for which the consumer cannot shop in accordance with § 1026.19(e)(1)(vi)(A) and that are provided by persons other than the creditor or mortgage broker.

(i) For any item that is a component of title insurance or is for conducting the closing, the introductory description "Title __" shall appear at the beginning of the label for that item.

(ii) The number of items disclosed under this paragraph (f)(2) shall not exceed 13.

(3) Services you can shop for. Under the subheading "Services You Can Shop For," an itemization of each amount and a subtotal of all such amounts the consumer will pay for settlement services for which the consumer can shop in accordance with § 1026.19(e)(1)(vi)(A) and that are provided by persons other than the creditor or mortgage broker.

(i) For any item that is a component of title insurance or is for conducting the closing, the introductory description "Title __" shall appear at the beginning of the label for that item.

(ii) The number of items disclosed under this paragraph (f)(3) shall not exceed 14.

(4) Total loan costs. Under the subheading "Total Loan Costs," the sum of the subtotals disclosed under paragraphs (f)(1) through (3) of this section.

(5) Item descriptions and ordering. The items listed as loan costs pursuant to this paragraph (f) shall be labeled using terminology that describes each item, subject to the requirements of paragraphs (f)(1)(i), (f)(2)(i), and (f)(3)(i) of this section.

(i) The item prescribed in paragraph (f)(1)(i) of this section for points shall be the first item listed in the disclosure pursuant to paragraph (f)(1) of this section.

(ii) All other items must be listed in alphabetical order by their labels under the applicable subheading.

(6) Use of addenda. (i) An addendum to a form of disclosures prescribed by this section may not be used for items described in paragraph (f)(1) or (2) of this section. If the creditor is not able to itemize every service and every corresponding charge required to be disclosed in the number of lines provided by paragraph (f)(1)(ii) or (f)(2)(ii) of this section, the remaining charges shall be disclosed as an aggregate amount in the last line permitted under paragraph (f)(1)(ii) or (f)(2)(ii), as applicable, labeled "Additional Charges."

(ii) An addendum to a form of disclosures prescribed by this section may be used for items described in paragraph (f)(3) of this section. If the creditor is not able to itemize all of the charges required to be disclosed in the number of lines provided by paragraph (f)(3)(ii), the remaining charges shall be disclosed as follows:

(A) Label the last line permitted under paragraph (f)(3)(ii) with an appropriate reference to an addendum and list the remaining items on the addendum in accordance with the requirements in paragraphs (f)(3) and (5) of this section; or

(B) Disclose the remaining charges as an aggregate amount in the last line permitted under paragraph (f)(3)(ii), labeled "Additional Charges."

(g) Closing cost details; other costs. Under the master heading "Closing Cost Details," in a table under the heading "Other Costs," all costs associated with the transaction that are in addition to the costs disclosed under paragraph (f) of this section. The table shall contain the items and amounts listed under six subheadings, described in paragraphs (g)(1) through (6) of this section.

(1) Taxes and other government fees. Under the subheading "Taxes and Other Government Fees," the amounts to be paid to State and local governments for taxes and other government fees, and the subtotal of all such amounts, as follows:

(i) On the first line, the sum of all recording fees and other government fees and taxes, except for transfer taxes paid by the consumer and disclosed pursuant to paragraph (g)(1)(ii) of this section, labeled "Recording Fees and Other Taxes."

(ii) On the second line, the sum of all transfer taxes paid by the consumer, labeled "Transfer Taxes."

(iii) If an amount required to be disclosed by this paragraph (g)(1) is not charged to the consumer, the amount disclosed on the applicable line required by this paragraph (g)(1) must be blank.

(2) Prepaids. Under the subheading "Prepaids," an itemization of the amounts to be paid by the consumer in advance of the first scheduled payment, and the subtotal of all such amounts, as follows:

(i) On the first line, the number of months for which homeowner's insurance premiums are to be paid by the consumer at consummation and the total dollar amount to be paid by the consumer at consummation for such premiums, labeled "Homeowner's Insurance Premium (__ months)."

(ii) On the second line, the number of months for which mortgage insurance premiums are to be paid by the consumer at consummation and the total dollar amount to be paid by the consumer at consummation for such premiums, labeled "Mortgage Insurance Premium (__ months)."

(iii) On the third line, the amount of prepaid interest to be paid per day, the number of days for which prepaid interest will be collected, the interest rate, and the total dollar amount to be paid by the consumer at consummation for such interest, labeled "Prepaid Interest (___ per day for __ days @__ %)."

(iv) On the fourth line, the number of months for which property taxes are to be paid by the consumer at consummation and the total dollar amount to be paid by the consumer at consummation for such taxes, labeled "Property Taxes (__ months)."

(v) If an amount is not charged to the consumer for any item for which this paragraph (g)(2) prescribes a label, each of the amounts required to be disclosed on that line must be blank.

(vi) A maximum of three additional items may be disclosed under this paragraph (g)(2), and each additional item must be identified and include the applicable time period covered by the amount to be paid by the consumer at consummation and the total amount to be paid.

(3) Initial escrow payment at closing. Under the subheading "Initial Escrow Payment at Closing," an itemization of the amounts that the consumer will be expected to place into a reserve or escrow account at consummation to be applied to recurring periodic charges, and the subtotal of all such amounts, as follows:

(i) On the first line, the amount escrowed per month, the number of months covered by an escrowed amount collected at consummation, and the total amount to be paid into the escrow account by the consumer at consummation for homeowner's insurance premiums, labeled "Homeowner's Insurance __ per month for __ mo."

(ii) On the second line, the amount escrowed per month, the number of months covered by an escrowed amount collected at consummation, and the total amount to be paid into the escrow account by the consumer at consummation for mortgage insurance premiums, labeled "Mortgage Insurance __ per month for __ mo."

(iii) On the third line, the amount escrowed per month, the number of months covered by an escrowed amount collected at consummation, and the total amount to be paid into the escrow account by the consumer at consummation for property taxes, labeled "Property Taxes __ per month for __ mo."

(iv) If an amount is not charged to the consumer for any item for which this paragraph (g)(3) prescribes a label, each of the amounts required to be disclosed on that line must be blank.

(v) A maximum of five items may be disclosed pursuant to this paragraph (g)(3) in addition to the items described in paragraph (g)(3)(i) through (iii) of this section, and each such additional item must be identified with a descriptive label and include the applicable amount per month, the number of months collected at consummation, and the total amount to be paid.

(4) Other. Under the subheading "Other," an itemization of any other amounts in connection with the transaction that the consumer is likely to pay or has contracted with a person other than the creditor or loan originator to pay at closing and of which the creditor is aware at the time of issuing the Loan Estimate, a descriptive label of each such amount, and the subtotal of all such amounts.

(i) For any item that is a component of title insurance, the introductory description "Title __" shall appear at the beginning of the label for that item.

(ii) The parenthetical description "(optional)" shall appear at the end of the label for items disclosing any premiums paid for separate insurance, warranty, guarantee, or event-coverage products.

(iii) The number of items disclosed under this paragraph (g)(4) shall not exceed five.

(5) Total other costs. Under the subheading "Total Other Costs," the sum of the subtotals disclosed pursuant to paragraphs (g)(1) through (4) of this section.

(6) Total closing costs. Under the subheading "Total Closing Costs," the component amounts and their sum, as follows:

(i) The sum of the amounts disclosed as loan costs and other costs under paragraphs (f)(4) and (g)(5) of this section, labeled "D + I"; and

(ii) The amount of any lender credits, disclosed as a negative number with the label "Lender Credits" provided that, if no such amount is disclosed, the amount must be blank.

(7) Item descriptions and ordering. The items listed as other costs pursuant to this paragraph (g) shall be labeled using terminology that describes each item.

(i) The items prescribed in paragraphs (g)(1)(i) and (ii), (g)(2)(i) through (iv), and (g)(3)(i) through (iii) of this section must be listed in the order prescribed as the initial items under the applicable subheading, with any additional items to follow.

(ii) All additional items must be listed in alphabetical order under the applicable subheading.

(8) Use of addenda. An addendum to a form of disclosures prescribed by this section may not be used for items required to be disclosed by this paragraph (g). If the creditor is not able to itemize all of the charges described in this paragraph (g) in the number of lines provided by paragraphs (g)(2)(vi), (3)(v), or (4)(iii) of this section, the remaining charges shall be disclosed as an aggregate amount in the last line permitted under paragraphs (g)(2)(vi), (g)(3)(v), or (g)(4)(iii), as applicable, using the label "Additional Charges."

(h) Calculating cash to close—

(1) For all transactions. Under the master heading "Closing Cost Details," under the heading "Calculating Cash to Close," the total amount of cash or other funds that must be provided by the consumer at consummation, with an itemization of that amount into the following component amounts:

(i) Total closing costs. The amount disclosed under paragraph (g)(6) of this section, disclosed as a positive number, labeled "Total Closing Costs";

(ii) Closing costs to be financed. The amount of any closing costs to be paid out of loan proceeds, disclosed as a negative number, labeled "Closing Costs Financed (Paid from your Loan Amount)";

(iii) Downpayment and other funds from borrower. Labeled "Down Payment/Funds from Borrower":

(A) In a purchase transaction as defined in paragraph (a)(9)(i) of this section, the amount of the difference between the purchase price of the property and the principal amount of the loan, disclosed as a positive number; or

(B) In all transactions other than purchase transactions as defined in paragraph (a)(9)(i) of this section, the estimated funds from the consumer as determined in accordance with paragraph (h)(1)(v) of this section;

(iv) Deposit.

(A) In a purchase transaction as defined in paragraph (a)(9)(i) of this section, the amount that is paid to the seller or held in trust or escrow by an attorney or other party under the terms of the agreement for the sale of the property, disclosed as a negative number, labeled "Deposit";

(B) In all transactions other than purchase transactions as defined in paragraph (a)(9)(i) of this section, the amount of $0, labeled "Deposit";

(v) Funds for borrower. The amount of funds for the consumer, labeled "Funds for Borrower." The amount of funds from the consumer disclosed under paragraph (h)(1)(iii)(B) of this section, and of funds for the consumer disclosed under this paragraph (h)(1)(v) of this section, are determined by subtracting the principal amount of the credit extended (excluding any amount disclosed pursuant to paragraph (h)(1)(ii) of this section) from the total amount of all existing debt being satisfied in the transaction (except to the extent the satisfaction of such existing debt is disclosed under paragraph (g) of this section);

(A) If the calculation under this paragraph (h)(1)(v) yields an amount that is a positive number, such amount is disclosed under paragraph (h)(1)(iii)(B) of this section, and $0 is disclosed under this paragraph (h)(1)(v);

(B) If the calculation under this paragraph (h)(1)(v) yields an amount that is a negative number, such amount is disclosed under this paragraph (h)(1)(v) as a negative number, and $0 is disclosed under paragraph (h)(1)(iii)(B) of this section;

(C) If the calculation under this paragraph (h)(1)(v) of this section yields $0, then $0 is disclosed under paragraphs (h)(1)(iii)(B) and paragraph (h)(1)(v) of this section;

(vi) Seller credits. The total amount that the seller will pay for total loan costs as determined by paragraph (f)(4) of this section and total other costs as determined by paragraph (g)(5) of this section, to the extent known, disclosed as a negative number, labeled "Seller Credits";

(vii) Adjustments and other credits. The amount of all loan costs determined pursuant to paragraph (f) and other costs determined pursuant to paragraph (g) that are paid by persons other than the loan originator, creditor, consumer, or seller, together with any other amounts that are required to be paid by the consumer at closing pursuant to a purchase and sale contract, disclosed as a negative number, labeled "Adjustments and Other Credits"; and

(viii) Estimated Cash to Close. The sum of the amounts disclosed under paragraphs (h)(1)(i) through (vii) of this section labeled "Cash to Close."

(2) Optional alternative calculating cash to close table for transactions without a seller. For transactions that do not involve a seller, instead of the table described in paragraph (h)(1) above, the creditor may alternatively provide, in a separate table, under the master heading "Closing Cost Details," under the heading "Calculating Cash to Close," the total amount of cash or other funds that must be provided by the consumer at consummation with an itemization of that amount into the following component amounts:

(i) Loan amount. The amount disclosed under paragraph (b)(1) of this section, labeled "Loan Amount";

(ii) Total closing costs. The amount disclosed under paragraph (g)(6) of this section, disclosed as a negative number, labeled "Total Closing Costs";

(iii) Payoffs and payments. The total amount of payoffs and payments to be made to third parties not otherwise disclosed pursuant to paragraphs (f) and (g) of this section, disclosed as a negative number, labeled "Total Payoffs and Payments";

(iv) Cash to or from consumer. The amount of cash or other funds due from or to the consumer and a statement of whether the disclosed estimated amount is due from or to the consumer, calculated by the sum of the amounts disclosed under paragraphs (h)(2)(i) through (iii) of this section, labeled "Cash to Close"; and

(v) Closing costs financed. The sum of the amounts disclosed under paragraphs (h)(2)(i) and (iii) of this section, but only to the extent that the sum is greater than zero and less than or equal to the sum disclosed under paragraph (g)(6) of this section, labeled "Closing Costs Financed (Paid from your Loan Amount)."

(i) Adjustable payment table. If the periodic principal and interest payment may change after consummation but not based on an adjustment to the interest rate, or if the transaction is a seasonal payment product as described in paragraph (a)(10)(ii)(E) of this section, a separate table under the master heading "Closing Cost Details" required by paragraph (f) of this section and under the heading "Adjustable Payment (AP) Table" that contains the following information and satisfies the following requirements:

(1) Interest only payments. Whether the transaction is an interest only product pursuant to paragraph (a)(10)(ii)(B) of this section as an affirmative or negative answer to the question "Interest Only Payments?" and, if an affirmative answer is disclosed, the period during which interest only periodic payments are scheduled.

(2) Optional payments. Whether the terms of the legal obligation expressly provide that the consumer may elect to pay a specified periodic principal and interest payment in an amount other than the scheduled amount of the payment, as an affirmative or negative answer to the question "Optional Payments?" and, if an affirmative answer is disclosed, the period during which the consumer may elect to make such payments.

(3) Step payments. Whether the transaction is a step payment product pursuant to paragraph (a)(10)(ii)(C) of this section as an affirmative or negative answer to the question "Step Payments?" and, if an affirmative answer is disclosed, the period during which the regular periodic payments are scheduled to increase.

(4) Seasonal payments. Whether the transaction is a seasonal payment product pursuant to paragraph (a)(10)(ii)(E) of this section as an affirmative or negative answer to the question "Seasonal Payments?" and, if an affirmative answer is disclosed, the period during which periodic payments are not scheduled.

(5) Principal and interest payments. Under the subheading "Principal and Interest Payments," which subheading is immediately preceded by the applicable unit-period, the following information:

(i) The number of the payment of the first periodic principal and interest payment that may change under the terms of the legal obligation disclosed under this paragraph (i), counting from the first periodic payment due after consummation, and the amount or range of the periodic principal and interest payment for such payment, labeled "First Change/Amount";

(ii) The frequency of subsequent changes to the periodic principal and interest payment, labeled "Subsequent Changes"; and

(iii) The maximum periodic principal and interest payment that may occur during the term of the transaction, and the first periodic principal and interest payment that can reach such maximum, counting from the first periodic payment due after consummation, labeled "Maximum Payment."

(j) Adjustable interest rate table. If the interest rate may increase after consummation, a separate table under the master heading "Closing Cost Details" required by paragraph (f) of this section and under the heading "Adjustable Interest Rate (AIR) Table" that contains the following information and satisfies the following requirements:

(1) Index and margin. If the interest rate may adjust and the product type is not a "Step Rate" under paragraph (a)(10)(i)(B) of this section, the index upon which the adjustments to the interest rate are based and the margin that is added to the index to determine the interest rate, if any, labeled "Index + Margin."

(2) Increases in interest rate. If the product type is a "Step Rate" and not also an "Adjustable Rate" under paragraph (a)(10)(i)(A) of this section, the maximum amount of any adjustments to the interest rate that are scheduled and pre-determined, labeled "Interest Rate Adjustments."

(3) Initial interest rate. The interest rate at consummation of the loan transaction, labeled "Initial Interest Rate."

(4) Minimum and maximum interest rate. The minimum and maximum interest rates for the loan, after any introductory period expires, labeled "Minimum/Maximum Interest Rate."

(5) Frequency of adjustments. The following information, under the subheading "Change Frequency":

(i) The month when the interest rate after consummation may first change, calculated from the date interest for the first scheduled periodic payment begins to accrue, labeled "First Change"; and

(ii) The frequency of interest rate adjustments after the initial adjustment to the interest rate, labeled, "Subsequent Changes."

(6) Limits on interest rate changes. The following information, under the subheading "Limits on Interest Rate Changes":

(i) The maximum possible change for the first adjustment of the interest rate after consummation, labeled "First Change"; and

(ii) The maximum possible change for subsequent adjustments of the interest rate after consummation, labeled "Subsequent Changes."

(k) Contact information. Under the master heading, "Additional Information About This Loan," the following information:

(1) The name and Nationwide Mortgage Licensing System and Registry identification number (NMLSR ID)(labeled "NMLS ID/License ID") for the creditor (labeled "Lender") and the mortgage broker (labeled "Mortgage Broker"), if any. In the event the creditor or the mortgage broker has not been assigned an NMLSR ID, the license number or other unique identifier issued by the applicable jurisdiction or regulating body with which the creditor or mortgage broker is licensed and/or registered shall be disclosed, with the abbreviation for the State of the applicable jurisdiction or regulatory body stated before the word "License" in the label, if any;

(2) The name and NMLSR ID of the individual loan officer (labeled "Loan Officer" and "NMLS ID/License ID," respectively) of the creditor and the mortgage broker, if any, who is the primary contact for the consumer. In the event the individual loan officer has not been assigned an NMLSR ID, the license number or other unique identifier issued by the applicable jurisdiction or regulating body with which the loan officer is licensed and/or registered shall be disclosed with the abbreviation for the State of the applicable jurisdiction or regulatory body stated before the word "License" in the label, if any; and

(3) The email address and telephone number of the loan officer (labeled "Email" and "Phone," respectively).

(*l*)   **Comparisons.** Under the master heading, "Additional Information About This Loan" required by paragraph (k) of this section, in a separate table under the heading "Comparisons" along with the statement "Use these measures to compare this loan with other loans":

(1)   **In five years.** Using the label "In 5 Years":

(i)   The total principal, interest, mortgage insurance, and loan costs scheduled to be paid through the end of the 60th month after the due date of the first periodic payment, expressed as a dollar amount, along with the statement "Total you will have paid in principal, interest, mortgage insurance, and loan costs"; and

(ii)   The principal scheduled to be paid through the end of the 60th month after the due date of the first periodic payment, expressed as a dollar amount, along with the statement "Principal you will have paid off."

(2)   **Annual percentage rate.** The "Annual Percentage Rate," using that term and the abbreviation "APR" and expressed as a percentage, and the following statement: "Your costs over the loan term expressed as a rate. This is not your interest rate."

(3)   **Total interest percentage.** The total amount of interest that the consumer will pay over the life of the loan, expressed as a percentage of the amount of credit extended, using the term "Total Interest Percentage," the abbreviation "TIP," and the statement "The total amount of interest that you will pay over the loan term as a percentage of your loan amount."

(m)   **Other considerations**. Under the master heading "Additional Information About This Loan" required by paragraph (k) of this section and under the heading "Other Considerations":

(1)   **Appraisal.** For transactions subject to 15 U.S.C. 1639h or 1691(e), as implemented in this part or Regulation B, 12 CFR part 1002, respectively, a statement, labeled "Appraisal," that:

(i)   The creditor may order an appraisal to determine the value of the property identified in paragraph (a)(6) of this section and may charge the consumer for that appraisal;

(ii)   The creditor will promptly provide the consumer a copy of any appraisal, even if the transaction is not consummated; and

(iii)   The consumer may choose to pay for an additional appraisal of the property for the consumer's use.

(2)   **Assumption.** A statement of whether a subsequent purchaser of the property may be permitted to assume the remaining loan obligation on its original terms, labeled "Assumption."

(3)   **Homeowner's insurance.** At the option of the creditor, a statement that homeowner's insurance is required on the property and that the consumer may choose the insurance provider, labeled "Homeowner's Insurance."

(4)   **Late payment.** A statement detailing any charge that may be imposed for a late payment, stated as a dollar amount or percentage charge of the late payment amount, and the number of days that a payment must be late to trigger the late payment fee, labeled "Late Payment."

(5)   **Refinance.** The following statement, labeled "Refinance": "Refinancing this loan will depend on your future financial situation, the property value, and market conditions. You may not be able to refinance this loan."

(6)   **Servicing.** A statement of whether the creditor intends to service the loan or transfer the loan to another servicer, labeled "Servicing."

(7)   **Liability after foreclosure.** If the purpose of the credit transaction is to refinance an extension of credit as described in paragraph (a)(9)(ii) of this section, a brief statement that certain State law protections against liability for any deficiency after foreclosure may be lost, the potential consequences of the loss of such protections, and a statement that the consumer should consult an attorney for additional information, labeled "Liability after Foreclosure."

(8) **Construction loans.** In transactions involving new construction, where the creditor reasonably expects that settlement will occur more than 60 days after the provision of the loan estimate, at the creditor's option, a clear and conspicuous statement that the creditor may issue a revised disclosure any time prior to 60 days before consummation, pursuant to § 1026.19(e)(3)(iv)(F).

(n) Signature statement.

(1) At the creditor's option, under the master heading required by paragraph (k) of this section and under the heading "Confirm Receipt," a line for the signatures of the consumers in the transaction. If the creditor includes a line for the consumer's signature, the creditor must disclose the following above the signature line: "By signing, you are only confirming that you have received this form. You do not have to accept this loan because you have signed or received this form."

(2) If the creditor does not include a line for the consumer's signature, the creditor must disclose the following statement under the heading "Other Considerations" required by paragraph (m) of this section, labeled "Loan Acceptance": "You do not have to accept this loan because you have received this form or signed a loan application."

(o) Form of disclosures—

(1) **General requirements. (i)** The creditor shall make the disclosures required by this section clearly and conspicuously in writing, in a form that the consumer may keep. The disclosures also shall be grouped together and segregated from everything else.

(ii) Except as provided in paragraph (o)(5) of this section, the disclosures shall contain only the information required by paragraphs (a) through (n) of this section and shall be made in the same order, and positioned relative to the master headings, headings, subheadings, labels, and similar designations in the same manner, as shown in form H–24, set forth in appendix H to this part.

(2) **Headings and labels.** If a master heading, heading, subheading, label, or similar designation contains the word "estimated" or a capital letter designation in form H–24, set forth in appendix H to this part, that heading, label, or similar designation shall contain the word "estimated" and the applicable capital letter designation.

(3) **Form.** Except as provided in paragraph (o)(5) of this section:

(i) For a transaction subject to § 1026.19(e) that is a federally related mortgage loan, as defined in Regulation X, 12 CFR 1024.2, the disclosures must be made using form H–24, set forth in appendix H to this part.

(ii) For any other transaction subject to this section, the disclosures must be made with headings, content, and format substantially similar to form H–24, set forth in appendix H to this part.

(iii) The disclosures required by this section may be provided to the consumer in electronic form, subject to compliance with the consumer consent and other applicable provisions of the Electronic Signatures in Global and National Commerce Act (15 U.S.C. 7001 et seq.).

(4) **Rounding—**

(i) **Nearest dollar.**

(A) The dollar amounts required to be disclosed by paragraphs (b)(6) and (7), (c)(1)(iii), (c)(2)(ii) and (iii), (c)(4)(ii), (f), (g), (h), (i), and (l) of this section shall be rounded to the nearest whole dollar, except that the per diem amount required to be disclosed by paragraph (g)(2)(iii) of this section and the monthly amounts required to be disclosed by paragraphs (g)(3)(i) through (iii) and (g)(3)(v) of this section shall not be rounded.

(B) The dollar amount required to be disclosed by paragraph (b)(1) of this section shall not be rounded, and if the amount is a whole number then the amount disclosed shall be truncated at the decimal point.

(C) The dollar amounts required to be disclosed by paragraph (c)(2)(iv) of this section shall be rounded to the nearest whole dollar, if any of the component amounts are required by paragraph (o)(4)(i)(A) of this section to be rounded to the nearest whole dollar.

(ii) **Percentages.** The percentage amounts required to be disclosed under paragraphs (b)(2) and (6), (f)(1)(i), (g)(2)(iii), (j), and (l)(3) of this section shall not be rounded and shall be disclosed up to two or three decimal places. The percentage amount required to be disclosed under paragraph (l)(2) of this section shall be disclosed up to three decimal places. If the amount is a whole number then the amount disclosed shall be truncated at the decimal point.

(5) Exceptions—

(i) **Unit-period.** Wherever the form or this section uses "monthly" to describe the frequency of any payments or uses "month" to describe the applicable unit-period, the creditor shall substitute the appropriate term to reflect the fact that the transaction's terms provide for other than monthly periodic payments, such as bi-weekly or quarterly payments.

(ii) **Translation.** The form may be translated into languages other than English, and creditors may modify form H–24 of appendix H to this part to the extent that translation prevents the headings, labels, designations, and required disclosure items under this section from fitting in the space provided on form H–24.

(iii) **Logo or slogan.** The creditor providing the form may use a logo for, and include a slogan with, the information required by paragraph (a)(3) of this section in any font size or type, provided that such logo or slogan does not cause the information required by paragraph (a)(3) of this section to exceed the space provided for that information, as illustrated in form H–24 of appendix H to this part. If the creditor does not use a logo for the information required by paragraph (a)(3) of this section, the information shall be disclosed in a similar format as form H–24.

(iv) **Business card.** The creditor may physically attach a business card over the information required to be disclosed by paragraph (a)(3) of this section.

(v) **Administrative information.** The creditor may insert at the bottom of each page under the disclosures required by this section as illustrated by form H–24 of appendix H to this part, any administrative information, text, or codes that assist in identification of the form or the information disclosed on the form, provided that the space provided on form H–24 of appendix H to this part for any of the information required by this section is not altered.

§ 1026.38 Content of disclosures for certain mortgage transactions (Closing Disclosure).

For each transaction subject to § 1026.19(f), the creditor shall disclose the information in this section:

(a) General information—

(1) Form title. The title of the form, "Closing Disclosure," using that term.

(2) Form purpose. The following statement: "This form is a statement of final loan terms and closing costs. Compare this document with your Loan Estimate."

(3) Closing information. Under the heading "Closing Information":

(i) **Date issued.** The date the disclosures required by this section are delivered to the consumer, labeled "Date Issued."

(ii) **Closing date.** The date of consummation, labeled "Closing Date."

(iii) **Disbursement date.** The date the amounts disclosed pursuant to paragraphs (j)(3)(iii) and (k)(3)(iii) of this section are expected to be paid in a purchase transaction under § 1026.37(a)(9)(i) to the consumer and seller, respectively, as applicable, or the date the amounts disclosed pursuant to paragraphs (j)(2)(iii) or (t)(5)(vii)(B) of this section are expected to be paid to the consumer or a third party in a transaction that is not a purchase transaction under § 1026.37(a)(9)(i), labeled "Disbursement Date."

(iv) **Settlement agent.** The name of the settlement agent conducting the closing, labeled "Settlement Agent."

(v) **File number.** The number assigned to the transaction by the settlement agent for identification purposes, labeled "File #."

(vi) **Property.** The address or location of the property required to be disclosed under § 1026.37(a)(6), labeled "Property."

(vii) **Sale price. (A)** In credit transactions where there is a seller, the contract sale price of the property identified in paragraph (a)(3)(vi) of this section, labeled "Sale Price."

(**B**)   In credit transactions where there is no seller, the appraised value of the property identified in paragraph (a)(3)(vi) of this section, labeled "Appraised Prop. Value."

(4) **Transaction information.** Under the heading "Transaction Information":

(i) **Borrower.** The consumer's name and mailing address, labeled "Borrower."

(ii) **Seller.** Where applicable, the seller's name and mailing address, labeled "Seller."

(iii) **Lender.** The name of the creditor making the disclosure, labeled "Lender."

(5) **Loan information.** Under the heading "Loan Information":

(i) **Loan term.** The information required to be disclosed under § 1026.37(a)(8), labeled "Loan Term."

(ii) **Purpose.** The information required to be disclosed under § 1026.37(a)(9), labeled "Purpose."

(iii) **Product.** The information required to be disclosed under § 1026.37(a)(10), labeled "Product."

(iv) **Loan type.** The information required to be disclosed under § 1026.37(a)(11), labeled "Loan Type."

(v) **Loan identification number.** The information required to be disclosed under § 1026.37(a)(12), labeled "Loan ID #."

(vi) **Mortgage insurance case number.** The case number for any mortgage insurance policy, if required by the creditor, labeled "MIC #."

(b) **Loan terms.** A separate table under the heading "Loan Terms" that includes the information required by § 1026.37(b).

(c) **Projected payments.** A separate table, under the heading "Projected Payments," that includes and satisfies the following information and requirements:

(1) **Projected payments or range of payments.** The information required to be disclosed pursuant to § 1026.37(c)(1) through (4), other than § 1026.37(c)(4)(vi). In disclosing estimated escrow payments as described in § 1026.37(c)(2)(iii) and (c)(4)(ii), the amount disclosed on the Closing Disclosure:

(i)   For transactions subject to RESPA, is determined under the escrow account analysis described in Regulation X, 12 CFR 1024.17;

(ii)   For transactions not subject to RESPA, may be determined under the escrow account analysis described in Regulation X, 12 CFR 1024.17 or in the manner set forth in § 1026.37(c)(5).

(2) **Estimated taxes, insurance, and assessments.** A reference to the disclosure required by paragraph (l)(7) of this section.

(d)   **Costs at closing—**

(1)   **Costs at closing table.** In a separate table, under the heading "Costs at Closing":

   (i) Labeled "Closing Costs," the sum of the dollar amounts disclosed pursuant to paragraphs (f)(4), (g)(5), and (h)(3) of this section, together with:

      (A) A statement that the amount disclosed pursuant to paragraph (d)(1)(i) of this section includes the amounts disclosed pursuant to paragraphs (f)(4), (g)(5), and (h)(3) of this section;

      (B) The dollar amount disclosed pursuant to paragraph (f)(4) of this section, labeled "Loan Costs";

      (C) The dollar amount disclosed pursuant to paragraph (g)(5) of this section, labeled "Other Costs";

      (D) The dollar amount disclosed pursuant to paragraph (h)(3) of this section, labeled "Lender Credits"; and

      (E) A statement referring the consumer to the tables disclosed pursuant to paragraphs (f) and (g) of this section for details.

   (ii) Labeled "Cash to Close," the sum of the dollar amounts calculated in accordance with paragraph (i)(9)(ii) of this section, together with:

      (A) A statement that the amount disclosed pursuant to paragraph (d)(1)(ii) of this section includes the amount disclosed pursuant to paragraph (d)(1)(i) of this section; and

      (B) A statement referring the consumer to the table required pursuant to paragraph (i) of this section for details.

   (2) **Alternative table for transactions without a seller.** For transactions that do not involve a seller and where the creditor disclosed the optional alternative table pursuant to § 1026.37(d)(2), the creditor shall disclose, with the label "Cash to Close," instead of the sum of the dollar amounts described in paragraph (d)(1)(ii) of this section:

   (i) The amount calculated in accordance with paragraph (e)(5)(ii) of this section;

   (ii) A statement of whether the disclosed amount is due from or to the consumer; and

   (iii) A statement referring the consumer to the table required pursuant to paragraph (e) of this section for details.

   (e) **Alternative calculating cash to close table for transactions without a seller.** For transactions that do not involve a seller and where the creditor disclosed the optional alternative table pursuant to § 1026.37(h)(2), the creditor shall disclose, instead of the table described in paragraph (i) of this section, in a separate table, under the heading "Calculating Cash to Close," together with the statement "Use this table to see what has changed from your Loan Estimate":

   (1) **Loan amount.** Labeled "Loan Amount:"

   (i) Under the subheading "Loan Estimate," the loan amount disclosed on the Loan Estimate under § 1026.37(b)(1);

   (ii) Under the subheading "Final," the loan amount disclosed under paragraph (b) of this section;

   (iii) Disclosed more prominently than the other disclosures under paragraph (e)(1)(i) and (ii) of this section, under the subheading "Did this change?":

      (A) If the amount disclosed under paragraph (e)(1)(ii) of this section is different than the amount disclosed under paragraph (e)(1)(i) of this section (unless the difference is due to rounding), a statement of that fact along with a statement of whether this amount increased or decreased; or

      (B) If the amount disclosed under paragraph (e)(1)(i) of this section is equal to the amount disclosed under paragraph (e)(1)(ii) of this section a statement of that fact.

(2)   **Total closing costs.** Labeled "Total Closing Costs":

(i)   Under the subheading "Loan Estimate," the amount disclosed on the Loan Estimate under § 1026.37(h)(2)(ii);

(ii)   Under the subheading "Final," the amount disclosed under paragraph (h)(1) of this section, disclosed as a negative number; and

(iii) Disclosed more prominently than the other disclosures under this paragraph (e)(2)(i) and (ii) of this section, under the subheading "Did this change?":

> **(A)**   If the amount disclosed under paragraph (e)(2)(ii) of this section is different than the amount disclosed under paragraph (e)(2)(i) of this section (unless the difference is due to rounding):

> > **(1)**   A statement of that fact;

> > **(2)**   If the difference in the amounts disclosed under paragraphs (e)(2)(i) and (e)(2)(ii) is attributable to differences in itemized charges that are included in either or both subtotals, a statement that the consumer should see the total loan costs and total other costs subtotals disclosed under paragraphs (f)(4) and (g)(5) of this section (together with references to such disclosures), as applicable; and

> > **(3)**   If the increase exceeds the limitations on increases in closing costs under § 1026.19(e)(3), a statement that such increase exceeds the legal limits by the dollar amount of the excess and if any refund is provided pursuant to § 1026.19(f)(2)(v), a statement directing the consumer to the disclosure required under paragraph (h)(3) of this section. Such dollar amount shall equal the sum total of all excesses of the limitations on increases in closing costs under § 1026.19(e)(3), taking into account the different methods of calculating excesses of the limitations on increases in closing costs under § 1026.19(e)(3)(i) and (ii).

> **(B)**   If the amount disclosed under paragraph (e)(2)(i) of this section is equal to the amount disclosed under paragraph (e)(2)(ii) of this section, a statement of that fact.

(3)   **Closing costs paid before closing.** Labeled "Closing Costs Paid Before Closing:"

(i)   Under the subheading "Loan Estimate," the amount of $0;

(ii)   Under the subheading "Final," any amount designated as borrower-paid before closing under paragraph (h)(2) of this section, disclosed as a positive number; and

(iii) Disclosed more prominently than the other disclosures under this paragraph (e)(3)(i) and (ii) of this section, under the subheading "Did this change?":

> **(A)**   If the amount disclosed under paragraph (e)(3)(ii) of this section is different than the amount disclosed under paragraph (e)(3)(i) of this section (unless the difference is due to rounding), a statement of that fact, along with a statement that the consumer paid such amounts prior to consummation of the transaction; or

> **(B)**   If the amount disclosed under paragraph (e)(3)(ii) of this section is equal to the amount disclosed under paragraph (e)(3)(i) of this section, a statement of that fact.

(4)   **Payoffs and payments.** Labeled "Total Payoffs and Payments,"

(i)   Under the subheading "Loan Estimate," the total payoffs and payments disclosed on the Loan Estimate under § 1026.37(h)(2)(iii);

(ii)   Under the subheading "Final," the total amount of payoffs and payments made to third parties disclosed pursuant to paragraph (t)(5)(vii)(B) of this section, to the extent known, disclosed as a negative number;

(iii) Disclosed more prominently than the other disclosures under this paragraph (e)(4)(i) and (ii), under the subheading "Did this change?":

(A)   If the amount disclosed under paragraph (e)(4)(ii) of this section is different than the amount disclosed under paragraph (e)(4)(i) of this section (unless the difference is due to rounding), a statement of that fact along with a reference to the table disclosed under paragraph (t)(5)(vii)(B) of this section; or

(B)   If the amount disclosed under paragraph (e)(4)(ii) of this section is equal to the amount disclosed under paragraph (e)(4)(i) of this section, a statement of that fact.

(5)   **Cash to or from consumer.** Labeled "Cash to Close:"

(i)   Under the subheading "Loan Estimate," the estimated cash to close on the Loan Estimate together with the statement of whether the estimated amount is due from or to the consumer as disclosed under § 1026.37(h)(2)(iv);

(ii)   Under the subheading "Final," the amount due from or to the consumer, calculated by the sum of the amounts disclosed under paragraphs (e)(1)(ii), (e)(2)(ii), (e)(3)(ii), and (e)(4)(ii) of this section, disclosed as a positive number, together with a statement of whether the disclosed amount is due from or to the consumer.

(6)   **Closing costs financed.** Labeled "Closing Costs Financed (Paid from your Loan Amount)," the sum of the amounts disclosed under paragraphs (e)(1)(ii) and (e)(4)(ii) of this section, but only to the extent that the sum is greater than zero and less than or equal to the sum disclosed under paragraph (h)(1) of this section minus the sum disclosed under paragraph (h)(2) of this section designated borrower-paid before closing.

(f)   **Closing cost details; loan costs.** Under the master heading "Closing Cost Details" with columns stating whether the charge was borrower-paid at or before closing, seller-paid at or before closing, or paid by others, all loan costs associated with the transaction, listed in a table under the heading "Loan Costs." The table shall contain the items and amounts listed under four subheadings, described in paragraphs (f)(1) through (5) of this section.

(1)   **Origination charges.** Under the subheading "Origination Charges," and in the applicable columns as described in paragraph (f) of this section, an itemization of each amount paid for charges described in § 1026.37(f)(1), the amount of compensation paid by the creditor to a third-party loan originator along with the name of the loan originator ultimately receiving the payment, and the total of all such itemized amounts that are designated borrower-paid at or before closing.

(2)   **Services borrower did not shop for.** Under the subheading "Services Borrower Did Not Shop For" and in the applicable columns as described in paragraph (f) of this section, an itemization of the services and corresponding costs for each of the settlement services required by the creditor for which the consumer did not shop in accordance with § 1026.19(e)(1)(vi)(A) and that are provided by persons other than the creditor or mortgage broker, the name of the person ultimately receiving the payment for each such amount, and the total of all such itemized amounts that are designated borrower-paid at or before closing. Items that were disclosed pursuant to § 1026.37(f)(3) must be disclosed under this paragraph (f)(2) if the consumer was provided a written list of settlement service providers under § 1026.19(e)(1)(vi)(C) and the consumer selected a settlement service provider contained on that written list.

(3)   **Services borrower did shop for.** Under the subheading "Services Borrower Did Shop For" and in the applicable column as described in paragraph (f) of this section, an itemization of the services and corresponding costs for each of the settlement services required by the creditor for which the consumer shopped in accordance with § 1026.19(e)(1)(vi)(A) and that are provided by persons other than the creditor or mortgage broker, the name of the person ultimately receiving the payment for each such amount, and the total of all such itemized costs that are designated borrower-paid at or before closing. Items that were disclosed pursuant to § 1026.37(f)(3) must be disclosed under this paragraph (f)(3) if the consumer was provided a written list of settlement service providers under § 1026.19(e)(1)(vi)(C) and the consumer did not select a settlement service provider contained on that written list.

(4) Total loan costs. Under the subheading "Total Loan Costs (Borrower-Paid)," the sum of the amounts disclosed as borrower-paid pursuant to paragraph (f)(5) of this section.

(5) Subtotal of loan costs. The sum of loan costs, calculated by totaling the amounts described in paragraphs (f)(1) through (3) of this section for costs designated borrower-paid at or before closing, labeled "Loan Costs Subtotals."

(g) Closing cost details; other costs. Under the master heading "Closing Cost Details" disclosed pursuant to paragraph (f) of this section, with columns stating whether the charge was borrower-paid at or before closing, seller-paid at or before closing, or paid by others, all costs in connection with the transaction, other than those disclosed under paragraph (f) of this section, listed in a table with a heading disclosed as "Other Costs." The table shall contain the items and amounts listed under five subheadings, described in paragraphs (g)(1) through (6) of this section.

(1) Taxes and other government fees. Under the subheading "Taxes and Other Government Fees," and in the applicable column as described in paragraph (g) of this section, an itemization of each amount that is expected to be paid to State and local governments for taxes and government fees and the total of all such itemized amounts that are designated borrower-paid at or before closing, as follows:

(i) Recording fees and the amounts paid in the applicable columns; and

(ii) An itemization of transfer taxes, with the name of the government entity assessing the transfer tax.

(2) Prepaids. Under the subheading "Prepaids" and in the applicable column as described in paragraph (g) of this section, an itemization of each amount for charges described in § 1026.37(g)(2), the name of the person ultimately receiving the payment or government entity assessing the property tax, provided that the person ultimately receiving the payment need not be disclosed for the disclosure required by § 1026.37(g)(2)(iii) when disclosed pursuant to this paragraph, and the total of all such itemized amounts that are designated borrower-paid at or before closing.

(3) Initial escrow payment at closing. Under the subheading "Initial escrow payment at closing" and in the applicable column as described in paragraph (g) of this section, an itemization of each amount for charges described in § 1026.37(g)(3), the applicable aggregate adjustment pursuant to 12 CFR 1024.17(d)(2) along with the label "aggregate adjustment," and the total of all such itemized amounts that are designated borrower-paid at or before closing.

(4) Other. Under the subheading "Other" and in the applicable column as described in paragraph (g) of this section, an itemization of each amount for charges in connection with the transaction that are in addition to the charges disclosed under paragraphs (f) and (g)(1) through (3) for services that are required or obtained in the real estate closing by the consumer, the seller, or other party, the name of the person ultimately receiving the payment, and the total of all such itemized amounts that are designated borrower-paid at or before closing.

(i) For any cost that is a component of title insurance services, the introductory description "Title __" shall appear at the beginning of the label for that actual cost.

(ii) The parenthetical description "(optional)" shall appear at the end of the label for costs designated borrower-paid at or before closing for any premiums paid for separate insurance, warranty, guarantee, or event-coverage products.

(5) Total other costs. Under the subheading "Total Other Costs (Borrower-Paid)," the sum of the amounts disclosed as borrower-paid pursuant to paragraph (g)(6) of this section.

(6) Subtotal of costs. The sum of other costs, calculated by totaling the costs disclosed in paragraphs (g)(1) through (4) of this section designated borrower-paid at or before closing, labeled "Other Costs Subtotals."

(h) Closing cost totals.

(1)   The sum of the costs disclosed as borrower-paid pursuant to paragraph (h)(2) of this section and the amount disclosed in paragraph (h)(3) of this section, under the subheading "Total Closing Costs (Borrower-Paid)."

(2)   The sum of the amounts disclosed in paragraphs (f)(5) and (g)(6) of this section, designated borrower-paid at or before closing, and the sum of the costs designated seller-paid at or before closing or paid by others disclosed pursuant to paragraphs (f) and (g) of this section, labeled "Closing Costs Subtotals."

(3)   The amount described in § 1026.37(g)(6)(ii) as a negative number, labeled "Lender Credits" and designated borrower-paid at closing, and if a refund is provided pursuant to § 1026.19(f)(2)(v), a statement that this amount includes a credit for an amount that exceeds the limitations on increases in closing costs under § 1026.19(e)(3), and the amount of such credit under § 1026.19(f)(2)(v).

(4)   The services and costs disclosed pursuant to paragraphs (f) and (g) of this section on the Closing Disclosure shall be labeled using terminology that describes the item disclosed, in a manner that is consistent with the descriptions or prescribed labels, as applicable, used for such items on the Loan Estimate pursuant to § 1026.37. The creditor must also list the items on the Closing Disclosure in the same sequential order as on the Loan Estimate pursuant to § 1026.37.

(i)   Calculating cash to close. In a separate table, under the heading "Calculating Cash to Close," together with the statement "Use this table to see what has changed from your Loan Estimate":

(1)   Total closing costs.

(i)   Under the subheading "Loan Estimate," the "Total Closing Costs" disclosed on the Loan Estimate under § 1026.37(h)(1)(i), labeled using that term.

(ii)   Under the subheading "Final," the amount disclosed under paragraph (h)(1) of this section.

(iii)   Under the subheading "Did this change?," disclosed more prominently than the other disclosures under this paragraph (i)(1):

(A)   If the amount disclosed under paragraph (i)(1)(ii) of this section is different than the amount disclosed under paragraph (i)(1)(i) of this section (unless the difference is due to rounding):

(1)   A statement of that fact;

(2)   If the difference in the "Total Closing Costs" is attributable to differences in itemized charges that are included in either or both subtotals, a statement that the consumer should see the total loan costs and total other costs subtotals disclosed under paragraphs (f)(4) and (g)(5) of this section (together with references to such disclosures), as applicable; and

(3)   If the increase exceeds the limitations on increases in closing costs under § 1026.19(e)(3), a statement that such increase exceeds the legal limits by the dollar amount of the excess, and if any refund is provided pursuant to § 1026.19(f)(2)(v), a statement directing the consumer to the disclosure required under paragraph (h)(3) of this section. Such dollar amount shall equal the sum total of all excesses of the limitations on increases in closing costs under § 1026.19(e)(3), taking into account the different methods of calculating excesses of the limitations on increases in closing costs under § 1026.19(e)(3)(i) and (ii).

(B)   If the amount disclosed under paragraph (i)(1)(ii) of this section is equal to the amount disclosed under paragraph (i)(1)(i) of this section, a statement of that fact.

(2) Closing costs paid before closing.

(i) Under the subheading "Loan Estimate," the dollar amount "$0," labeled "Closing Costs Paid Before Closing."

(ii) Under the subheading "Final," the amount of "Total Closing Costs" disclosed under paragraph (h)(2) of this section and designated as borrower-paid before closing, stated as a negative number.

(iii) Under the subheading "Did this change?," disclosed more prominently than the other disclosures under this paragraph (i)(2):

(A) If the amount disclosed under paragraph (i)(2)(ii) of this section is different than the amount disclosed under paragraph (i)(2)(i) of this section (unless the difference is due to rounding), a statement of that fact, along with a statement that the consumer paid such amounts prior to consummation of the transaction; or

(B) If the amount disclosed under paragraph (i)(2)(ii) of this section is equal to the amount disclosed under paragraph (i)(2)(i) of this section, a statement of that fact.

(3) Closing costs financed.

(i) Under the subheading "Loan Estimate," the amount disclosed under § 1026.37(h)(1)(ii), labeled "Closing Costs Financed (Paid from your Loan Amount)."

(ii) Under the subheading "Final," the actual amount of the closing costs that are to be paid out of loan proceeds, if any, stated as a negative number.

(iii) Under the subheading "Did this change?," disclosed more prominently than the other disclosures under this paragraph (i)(3):

(A) If the amount disclosed under paragraph (i)(3)(ii) of this section is different than the amount disclosed under paragraph (i)(3)(i) of this section (unless the difference is due to rounding), a statement of that fact, along with a statement that the consumer included the closing costs in the loan amount, which increased the loan amount; or

(B) If the amount disclosed under paragraph (i)(3)(ii) of this section is equal to the amount disclosed under paragraph (i)(3)(i) of this section, a statement of that fact.

(4) Down payment/funds from borrower.

(i) Under the subheading "Loan Estimate," the amount disclosed under § 1026.37(h)(1)(iii), labeled "Down Payment/Funds from Borrower."

(ii) Under the subheading "Final":

(A) In a transaction that is a purchase as defined in § 1026.37(a)(9)(i), the amount of the difference between the purchase price of the property and the principal amount of the credit extended, stated as a positive number, labeled "Down Payment/Funds from Borrower"; or

(B) In a transaction other than the type described in paragraph (i)(4)(ii)(A) of this section, the "Funds from Borrower" as determined in accordance with paragraph (i)(6)(iv) of this section, labeled "Down Payment/Funds from Borrower."

(iii) Under the subheading "Did this change?," disclosed more prominently than the other disclosures under this paragraph (i)(4):

(A) If the amount disclosed under paragraph (i)(4)(ii) of this section is different than the amount disclosed under paragraph (i)(4)(i) of this section (unless the difference is due to rounding), a statement of that fact, along with a statement that the consumer increased or decreased this payment and that the consumer should see the details disclosed under paragraph (j)(1) or (j)(2) of this section, as applicable; or

(B) If the amount disclosed under paragraph (i)(4)(ii) of this section is equal to the amount disclosed under paragraph (i)(4)(i) of this section, a statement of that fact.

(5) Deposit.

(i) Under the subheading "Loan Estimate," the amount disclosed under §1026.37(h)(1)(iv), labeled "Deposit."

(ii) Under the subheading "Final," the amount disclosed under paragraph (j)(2)(ii) of this section, stated as a negative number.

(iii) Under the subheading "Did this change?," disclosed more prominently than the other disclosures under this paragraph (i)(5):

(A) If the amount disclosed under paragraph (i)(5)(ii) of this section is different than the amount disclosed under paragraph (i)(5)(i) of this section (unless the difference is due to rounding), a statement of that fact, along with a statement that the consumer increased or decreased this payment, as applicable, and that the consumer should see the details disclosed under paragraph (j)(2)(ii) of this section; or

(B) If the amount disclosed under paragraph (i)(5)(ii) of this section is equal to the amount disclosed under paragraph (i)(5)(i) of this section, a statement of that fact.

(6) Funds for borrower.

(i) Under the subheading "Loan Estimate," the amount disclosed under §1026.37(h)(1)(v), labeled "Funds for Borrower."

(ii) Under the subheading "Final," the "Funds for Borrower," labeled using that term, as determined in accordance with paragraph (i)(6)(iv) of this section.

(iii) Under the subheading "Did this change?," disclosed more prominently than the other disclosures under this paragraph (i)(6):

(A) If the amount disclosed under paragraph (i)(6)(ii) of this section is different than the amount disclosed under paragraph (i)(6)(i) of this section (unless the difference is due to rounding), a statement of that fact, along with a statement that the consumer's available funds from the loan amount have increased or decreased, as applicable; or

(B) If the amount disclosed under paragraph (i)(6)(ii) of this section is equal to the amount disclosed under paragraph (i)(6)(i) of this section, a statement of that fact.

(iv) The "Funds from Borrower" to be disclosed under paragraph (i)(4)(ii)(B) of this section and "Funds for Borrower" to be disclosed under paragraph (i)(6)(ii) of this section are determined by subtracting the principal amount of the credit extended (excluding any amount disclosed pursuant to paragraph (i)(3)(ii) of this section) from the total amount of all existing debt being satisfied in the real estate closing and disclosed under paragraph (j)(1)(v) of this section (except to the extent the satisfaction of such existing debt is disclosed under paragraph (g) of this section).

(A) If the calculation under this paragraph (i)(6)(iv) yields an amount that is a positive number, such amount shall be disclosed under paragraph (i)(4)(ii)(B) of this section, and $0 shall be disclosed under paragraph (i)(6)(ii) of this section.

(B) If the calculation under this paragraph (i)(6)(iv) yields an amount that is a negative number, such amount shall be disclosed under paragraph (i)(6)(ii) of this section, stated as a negative number, and $0 shall be disclosed under paragraph (i)(4)(ii)(B) of this section.

(C) If the calculation under this paragraph (i)(6)(iv) yields $0, $0 shall be disclosed under paragraph (i)(4)(ii)(B) of this section and under paragraph (i)(6)(ii) of this section.

(7) Seller credits.

(i) Under the subheading "Loan Estimate," the amount disclosed under § 1026.37(h)(1)(vi), labeled "Seller Credits."

(ii) Under the subheading "Final," the amount disclosed under paragraph (j)(2)(v) of this section, stated as a negative number.

(iii) Under the subheading "Did this change?," disclosed more prominently than the other disclosures under this paragraph (i)(7):

(A) If the amount disclosed under paragraph (i)(7)(ii) of this section is different than the amount disclosed under paragraph (i)(7)(i) of this section (unless the difference is due to rounding), a statement of that fact, along with a statement that the consumer should see the details disclosed under paragraph (j)(2)(v) of this section; or

(B) If the amount disclosed under paragraph (i)(7)(ii) of this section is equal to the amount disclosed under paragraph (i)(7)(i) of this section, a statement of that fact.

(8) Adjustments and other credits.

(i) Under the subheading "Loan Estimate," the amount disclosed on the Loan Estimate under § 1026.37(h)(1)(vii) rounded to the nearest whole dollar, labeled "Adjustments and Other Credits."

(ii) Under the subheading "Final," the amount equal to the total of the amounts disclosed under paragraphs (j)(1)(iii) and (v) through (x) of this section reduced by the total of the amounts disclosed under paragraphs (j)(2)(vi) through (xi) of this section.

(iii) Under the subheading "Did this change?," disclosed more prominently than the other disclosures under this paragraph (i)(8):

(A) If the amount disclosed under paragraph (i)(8)(ii) of this section is different than the amount disclosed under paragraph (i)(8)(i) of this section (unless the difference is due to rounding), a statement of that fact, along with a statement that the consumer should see the details disclosed under paragraphs (j)(1)(iii) and (v) through (x) and (j)(2)(vi) through (xi) of this section; or

(B) If the amount disclosed under paragraph (i)(8)(ii) of this section is equal to the amount disclosed under paragraph (i)(8)(i) of this section, a statement of that fact.

(9) Cash to close.

(i) Under the subheading "Loan Estimate," the amount disclosed on the Loan Estimate under § 1026.37(h)(1)(viii), labeled "Cash to Close" and disclosed more prominently than the other disclosures under this paragraph (i).

(ii) Under the subheading "Final," the sum of the amounts disclosed under paragraphs (i)(1) through (i)(8) of this section under the subheading "Final," and disclosed more prominently than the other disclosures under this paragraph (i).

(j) Summary of borrower's transaction. Under the heading "Summaries of Transactions," with a statement to "Use this table to see a summary of your transaction," two separate tables are disclosed. The first table shall include, under the subheading "Borrower's Transaction," the following information and shall satisfy the following requirements:

(1) Itemization of amounts due from borrower.

(i) The total amount due from the consumer at closing, calculated as the sum of items required to be disclosed by paragraph (j)(1)(ii) through (x) of this section, excluding items paid from funds other than closing funds as described in paragraph (j)(4)(i) of this section, labeled "Due from Borrower at Closing";

(ii) The amount of the contract sales price of the property being sold in a purchase real estate transaction, excluding the price of any tangible personal property if the consumer and seller have agreed to a separate price for such items, labeled "Sale Price of Property";

(iii) The amount of the sales price of any tangible personal property excluded from the contract sales price pursuant to paragraph (j)(1)(ii) of this section, labeled "Sale Price of Any Personal Property Included in Sale";

(iv) The total amount of closing costs disclosed that are designated borrower-paid at closing, as the sum of the amounts calculated pursuant to paragraphs (h)(2) and (3) of this section, labeled "Closing Costs Paid at Closing";

(v) A description and the amount of any additional items that the seller has paid prior to the real estate closing, but reimbursed by the consumer at the real estate closing, and a description and the amount of any other items owed by the consumer at the real estate closing not otherwise disclosed pursuant to paragraph (f), (g), or (j) of this section;

(vi) The description "Adjustments for Items Paid by Seller in Advance";

(vii) The prorated amount of any prepaid taxes due from the consumer to reimburse the seller at the real estate closing, and the time period corresponding to that amount, labeled "City/Town Taxes";

(viii) The prorated amount of any prepaid taxes due from the consumer to reimburse the seller at the real estate closing, and the time period corresponding to that amount, labeled "County Taxes";

(ix) The prorated amount of any prepaid assessments due from the consumer to reimburse the seller at the real estate closing, and the time period corresponding to that amount, labeled "Assessments"; and

(x) A description and the amount of any additional items paid by the seller prior to the real estate closing that are due from the consumer at the real estate closing.

(2) Itemization of amounts already paid by or on behalf of borrower.

(i) The sum of the amounts disclosed in this paragraphs (j)(2)(ii) through (xi) of this section, excluding items paid from funds other than closing funds as described in paragraph (j)(4)(i) of this section, labeled "Paid Already by or on Behalf of Borrower at Closing";

(ii) Any amount that is paid to the seller or held in trust or escrow by an attorney or other party under the terms of the agreement for the sale of the property, labeled "Deposit";

(iii) The amount of the consumer's new loan amount or first user loan as disclosed pursuant to paragraph (b) of this section, labeled "Loan Amount";

(iv) The amount of any existing loans that the consumer is assuming, or any loans subject to which the consumer is taking title to the property, labeled "Existing Loan(s) Assumed or Taken Subject to";

(v) The total amount of money that the seller will provide at the real estate closing as a lump sum not otherwise itemized to pay for loan costs as determined by paragraph (f) of this section and other costs as determined by paragraph (g) of this section and any other obligations of the seller to be paid directly to the consumer, labeled "Seller Credit";

(vi) The description "Other Credits," together with a description and amount of other items paid by or on behalf of the consumer and not otherwise disclosed pursuant to paragraphs (f), (g), (h), and (j)(2) of this section;

(vii) The description "Adjustments for Items Unpaid by Seller";

(viii) The prorated amount of any unpaid taxes due from the seller to reimburse the consumer at the real estate closing, and the time period corresponding to that amount, labeled "City/Town Taxes";

(ix) The prorated amount of any unpaid taxes due from the seller to reimburse the consumer at the real estate closing, and the time period corresponding to that amount, labeled "County Taxes";

(x) The prorated amount of any unpaid assessments due from the seller to reimburse the consumer at the real estate closing, and the time period corresponding to that amount, labeled "Assessments"; and

(xi) A description and the amount of any additional items which have not yet been paid and which the consumer is expected to pay after the real estate closing, but which are attributable in part to a period of time prior to the real estate closing.

(3) Calculation of borrower's transaction. Under the label "Calculation":

(i) The amount disclosed pursuant to paragraph (j)(1)(i) of this section, labeled "Total Due from Borrower at Closing";

(ii) The amount disclosed pursuant to paragraph (j)(2)(i) of this section, if any, disclosed as a negative number, labeled "Total Paid Already by or on Behalf of Borrower at Closing"; and

(iii) A statement that the disclosed amount is due from or to the consumer, and the amount due from or to the consumer at the real estate closing, calculated by the sum of the amounts disclosed under paragraphs (j)(3)(i) and (ii) of this section, labeled "Cash to Close."

(4) Items paid outside of closing funds.

(i) Costs that are not paid from closing funds but that would otherwise be disclosed in the table required pursuant to paragraph (j) of this section, should be marked with the phrase "Paid Outside of Closing" or the abbreviation "P.O.C." and include the name of the party making the payment.

(ii) For purposes of this paragraph (j), "closing funds" means funds collected and disbursed at real estate closing.

(k) Summary of seller's transaction. Under the heading "Summaries of Transactions" required by paragraph (j) of this section, a separate table under the subheading "Seller's Transaction," that includes the following information and satisfies the following requirements:

(1) Itemization of amounts due to seller.

(i) The total amount due to the seller at the real estate closing, calculated as the sum of items required to be disclosed pursuant to paragraphs (k)(1)(ii) through (ix) of this section, excluding items paid from funds other than closing funds as described in paragraph (k)(4)(i) of this section, labeled "Due to Seller at Closing";

(ii) The amount of the contract sales price of the property being sold, excluding the price of any tangible personal property if the consumer and seller have agreed to a separate price for such items, labeled "Sale Price of Property";

(iii) The amount of the sales price of any tangible personal property excluded from the contract sales price pursuant to paragraph (k)(1)(ii) of this section, labeled "Sale Price of Any Personal Property Included in Sale";

(iv) A description and the amount of other items paid to the seller by the consumer pursuant to the contract of sale or other agreement, such as charges that were not disclosed pursuant to § 1026.37 on the Loan Estimate or items paid by the seller prior to the real estate closing but reimbursed by the consumer at the real estate closing;

(v) The description "Adjustments for Items Paid by Seller in Advance";

(vi) The prorated amount of any prepaid taxes due from the consumer to reimburse the seller at the real estate closing, and the time period corresponding to that amount, labeled "City/Town Taxes";

(vii) The prorated amount of any prepaid taxes due from the consumer to reimburse the seller at the real estate closing, and the time period corresponding to that amount, labeled "County Taxes";

(viii) The prorated amount of any prepaid assessments due from the consumer to reimburse the seller at the real estate closing, and the time period corresponding to that amount, labeled "Assessments"; and

(ix) A description and the amount of additional items paid by the seller prior to the real estate closing that are reimbursed by the consumer at the real estate closing.

(2) Itemization of amounts due from seller.

(i) The total amount due from the seller at the real estate closing, calculated as the sum of items required to be disclosed pursuant to paragraphs (k)(2)(ii) through (xiii) of this section, excluding items paid from funds other than closing funds as described in paragraph (k)(4)(i) of this section, labeled "Due from Seller at Closing";

(ii) The amount of any excess deposit disbursed to the seller prior to the real estate closing, labeled "Excess Deposit";

(iii) The amount of closing costs designated seller-paid at closing disclosed pursuant to paragraph (h)(2) of this section, labeled "Closing Costs Paid at Closing";

(v) The amount of any loan secured by a first lien on the property that will be paid off as part of the real estate closing, labeled "Payoff of First Mortgage Loan";

(vi) The amount of any loan secured by a second lien on the property that will be paid off as part of the real estate closing, labeled "Payoff of Second Mortgage Loan";

(vii) The total amount of money that the seller will provide at the real estate closing as a lump sum not otherwise itemized to pay for loan costs as determined by paragraph (f) of this section and other costs as determined by paragraph (g) of this section and any other obligations of the seller to be paid directly to the consumer, labeled "Seller Credit";

(viii) A description and amount of any and all other obligations required to be paid by the seller at the real estate closing, including any lien-related payoffs, fees, or obligations;

(ix) The description "Adjustments for Items Unpaid by Seller";

(x) The prorated amount of any unpaid taxes due from the seller to reimburse the consumer at the real estate closing, and the time period corresponding to that amount, labeled "City/Town Taxes";

(xi) The prorated amount of any unpaid taxes due from the seller to the consumer at the real estate closing, and the time period corresponding to that amount, labeled "County Taxes";

(xii) The prorated amount of any unpaid assessments due from the seller to reimburse the consumer at the real estate closing, and the time period corresponding to that amount, labeled "Assessments"; and

(xiii) A description and the amount of any additional items which have not yet been paid and which the consumer is expected to pay after the real estate closing, but which are attributable in part to a period of time prior to the real estate closing.

(3) Calculation of seller's transaction. Under the label "Calculation":

(i) The amount described in paragraph (k)(1)(i) of this section, labeled "Total Due to Seller at Closing";

(ii) The amount described in paragraph (k)(2)(i) of this section, disclosed as a negative number, labeled "Total Due from Seller at Closing"; and

(iii) A statement that the disclosed amount is due from or to the seller, and the amount due from or to the seller at closing, calculated by the sum of the amounts disclosed pursuant to paragraphs (k)(3)(i) and (ii) of this section, labeled "Cash."

(4) Items paid outside of closing funds.

(i) Charges that are not paid from closing funds but that would otherwise be disclosed in the table described in paragraph (k) of this section, should be marked with the phrase "Paid Outside of Closing" or the acronym "P.O.C." and include a statement of the party making the payment.

(ii) For purposes of this paragraph (k), "closing funds" are defined as funds collected and disbursed at real estate closing.

(*l*) **Loan disclosures.** Under the master heading "Additional Information About This Loan" and under the heading "Loan Disclosures":

(1) Assumption. Under the subheading "Assumption," the information required by § 1026.37(m)(2).

(2) Demand feature. Under the subheading "Demand Feature," a statement of whether the legal obligation permits the creditor to demand early repayment of the loan and, if the statement is affirmative, a reference to the note or other loan contract for details.

(3) Late payment. Under the subheading "Late Payment," the information required by § 1026.37(m)(4).

(4) Negative amortization. Under the subheading "Negative Amortization (Increase in Loan Amount)," a statement of whether the regular periodic payments may cause the principal balance to increase.

(i) If the regular periodic payments do not cover all of the interest due, the creditor must provide a statement that the principal balance will increase, such balance will likely become larger than the original loan amount, and increases in such balance lower the consumer's equity in the property.

(ii) If the consumer may make regular periodic payments that do not cover all of the interest due, the creditor must provide a statement that, if the consumer chooses a monthly payment option that does not cover all of the interest due, the principal balance may become larger than the original loan amount and the increases in the principal balance lower the consumer's equity in the property.

(5) Partial payment policy. Under the subheading "Partial Payments":

(i) If periodic payments that are less than the full amount due are accepted, a statement that the creditor, using the term "lender," may accept partial payments and apply such payments to the consumer's loan;

(ii) If periodic payments that are less than the full amount due are accepted but not applied to a consumer's loan until the consumer pays the remainder of the full amount due, a statement that the creditor, using the term "lender," may hold partial payments in a separate account until the consumer pays the remainder of the payment and then apply the full periodic payment to the consumer's loan;

(iii) If periodic payments that are less than the full amount due are not accepted, a statement that the creditor, using the term "lender," does not accept any partial payments; and

(iv) A statement that, if the loan is sold, the new creditor, using the term "lender," may have a different policy.

(6) Security interest. Under the subheading "Security Interest," a statement that the consumer is granting a security interest in the property securing the transaction, the property address including a zip code, and a statement that the consumer may lose the property if the consumer does not make the required payments or satisfy other requirements under the legal obligation.

(7) **Escrow account.** Under the subheading "Escrow Account":

(i) Under the reference "For now," a statement that an escrow account may also be called an impound or trust account, a statement of whether the creditor has established or will establish, at or before consumption, an escrow account in connection with the transaction for the costs that will be paid using escrow account funds described in paragraph (l)(7)(i)(A)(1) of this section:

(A) A statement that the creditor may be liable for penalties and interest if it fails to make a payment for any cost for which the escrow account is established, a statement that the consumer would have to pay such costs directly in the absence of the escrow account, and a table, titled "Escrow" that contains, if an escrow account is or will be established, an itemization of the following:

(1) The total amount the consumer will be required to pay into an escrow account over the first year after consumption for payment of the charges described in § 1026.37(c)(4)(ii), labeled "Escrowed Property Costs over Year 1," together with a descriptive name of each such charge, calculated as the amount disclosed under paragraph (l)(7)(i)(A)(4) of this section multiplied by the number of periodic payments scheduled to be made to the escrow account during the first year after consumption;

(2) The estimated amount the consumer is likely to pay during the first year after consumption for charges described in § 1026.37(c)(4)(ii) that are known to the creditor and that will not be paid using escrow account funds, labeled "Non-Escrowed Property Costs over Year 1," together with a descriptive name of each such charge and a statement that the consumer may have to pay other costs that are not listed;

(3) The total amount disclosed pursuant to paragraph (g)(3) of this section, a statement that the payment is a cushion for the escrow account, labeled "Initial Escrow Payment," and a reference to the information disclosed pursuant to paragraph (g)(3) of this section;

(4) The amount the consumer will be required to pay into the escrow account with each periodic payment during the first year after consumption for payment of the charges described in § 1026.37(c)(4)(ii), labeled "Monthly Escrow Payment."

(5) A creditor complies with the requirements of paragraphs (l)(7)(i)(A)(1) and (l)(7)(i)(A)(4) of this section if the creditor bases the numerical disclosures required by those paragraphs on amounts derived from the escrow account analysis required under Regulation X, 12 CFR 1024.17.

(B) A statement of whether the consumer will not have an escrow account, the reason why an escrow account will not be established, a statement that the consumer must pay all property costs, such as taxes and homeowner's insurance, directly, a statement that the consumer may contact the creditor to inquire about the availability of an escrow account, and a table, titled "No Escrow," that contains, if an escrow account will not be established, an itemization of the following:

(1) The estimated total amount the consumer will pay directly for charges described in § 1026.37(c)(4)(ii) during the first year after consumption that are known to the creditor and a statement that, without an escrow account, the consumer must pay the identified costs, possibly in one or two large payments, labeled "Property Costs over Year 1"; and

(2) The amount of any fee the creditor imposes on the consumer for not establishing an escrow account in connection with the transaction, labeled "Escrow Waiver Fee."

(ii) Under the reference "In the future":

(A) A statement that the consumer's property costs may change and that, as a result, the consumer's escrow payment may change;

(B) A statement that the consumer may be able to cancel any escrow account that has been established, but that the consumer is responsible for directly paying all property costs in the absence of an escrow account; and

(C) A description of the consequences if the consumer fails to pay property costs, including the actions that a State or local government may take if property taxes are not paid and the actions the creditor may take if the consumer does not pay some or all property costs, such as adding amounts to the loan balance, adding an escrow account to the loan, or purchasing a property insurance policy on the consumer's behalf that may be more expensive and provide fewer benefits than what the consumer could obtain directly.

(m) **Adjustable payment table.** Under the master heading "Additional Information About This Loan" required by paragraph (l) of this section, and under the heading "Adjustable Payment (AP) Table," the table required to be disclosed by § 1026.37(i).

(n) **Adjustable interest rate table.** Under the master heading "Additional Information About This Loan" required by paragraph (l) of this section, and under the heading "Adjustable Interest Rate (AIR) Table," the table required to be disclosed by § 1026.37(j).

(o) **Loan calculations**. In a separate table under the heading "Loan Calculations":

(1) **Total of payments.** The "Total of Payments," using that term and expressed as a dollar amount, and a statement that the disclosure is the total the consumer will have paid after making all payments of principal, interest, mortgage insurance, and loan costs, as scheduled.

(2) **Finance charge. The** "Finance Charge," using that term and expressed as a dollar amount, and the following statement: "The dollar amount the loan will cost you." The disclosed finance charge and other disclosures affected by the disclosed financed charge (including the amount financed and the annual percentage rate) shall be treated as accurate if the amount disclosed as the finance charge:

(i) Is understated by no more than $100; or

(ii) Is greater than the amount required to be disclosed.

(3) **Amount financed.** The "Amount Financed," using that term and expressed as a dollar amount, and the following statement: "The loan amount available after paying your upfront finance charge."

(4) **Annual percentage rate.** The "Annual Percentage Rate," using that term and the abbreviation "APR" and expressed as a percentage, and the following statement: "Your costs over the loan term expressed as a rate. This is not your interest rate."

(5) **Total interest percentage.** The "Total Interest Percentage," using that term and the abbreviation "TIP" and expressed as a percentage, and the following statement: "The total amount of interest that you will pay over the loan term as a percentage of your loan amount."

(p) **Other disclosures.** Under the heading "Other Disclosures":

(1) **Appraisal.** For transactions subject to 15 U.S.C. 1639h or 1691(e), as implemented in this part or Regulation B, 12 CFR part 1002, respectively, under the subheading "Appraisal," that:

(i) If there was an appraisal of the property in connection with the loan, the creditor is required to provide the consumer with a copy at no additional cost to the consumer at least three days prior to consummation; and

(ii) If the consumer has not yet received a copy of the appraisal, the consumer should contact the creditor using the information disclosed pursuant to paragraph (r) of this section.

(2)   Contract details. A statement that the consumer should refer to the appropriate loan document and security instrument for information about nonpayment, what constitutes a default under the legal obligation, circumstances under which the creditor may accelerate the maturity of the obligation, and prepayment rebates and penalties, under the subheading "Contract Details."

(3)   Liability after foreclosure. A brief statement of whether, and the conditions under which, the consumer may remain responsible for any deficiency after foreclosure under applicable State law, a brief statement that certain protections may be lost if the consumer refinances or incurs additional debt on the property, and a statement that the consumer should consult an attorney for additional information, under the subheading "Liability after Foreclosure."

(4)   Refinance. Under the subheading "Refinance," the statement required by § 1026.37(m)(5).

(5)   Tax deductions. Under the subheading "Tax Deductions," a statement that, if the extension of credit exceeds the fair market value of the property, the interest on the portion of the credit extension that is greater than the fair market value of the property is not tax deductible for Federal income tax purposes and a statement that the consumer should consult a tax adviser for further information.

(q)   Questions notice. In a separate notice labeled "Questions?":

(1)   A statement directing the consumer to use the contact information disclosed under paragraph (r) of this section if the consumer has any questions about the disclosures required pursuant to § 1026.19(f);

(2)   A reference to the Bureau's Web site to obtain more information or to submit a complaint; and the link or uniform resource locator address to the Web site: www.consumerfinance.gov/mortgage-closing; and

(3)   A prominent question mark.

(r)   Contact information. In a separate table, under the heading "Contact Information," the following information for each creditor (under the subheading "Lender"), mortgage broker (under the subheading "Mortgage Broker"), consumer's real estate broker (under the subheading "Real Estate Broker (B)"), seller's real estate broker (under the subheading "Real Estate Broker (S)"), and settlement agent (under the subheading "Settlement Agent") participating in the transaction:

(1)   Name of the person, labeled "Name";

(2)   Address, using that label;

(3)   Nationwide Mortgage Licensing System & Registry (NMLSR ID) identification number, labeled "NMLS ID," or, if none, license number or other unique identifier issued by the applicable jurisdiction or regulating body with which the person is licensed and/or registered, labeled "License ID," with the abbreviation for the State of the applicable jurisdiction or regulatory body stated before the word "License" in the label, for the persons identified in paragraph (r)(1) of this section;

(4)   Name of the natural person who is the primary contact for the consumer with the person identified in paragraph (r)(1) of this section, labeled "Contact";

(5)   NMLSR ID, labeled "Contact NMLS ID," or, if none, license number or other unique identifier issued by the applicable jurisdiction or regulating body with which the person is licensed and/or registered, labeled "Contact License ID," with the abbreviation for the State of the applicable jurisdiction or regulatory body stated before the word "License" in the label, for the natural person identified in paragraph (r)(4) of this section,

(6)   Email address for the person identified in paragraph (r)(4) of this section, labeled "Email"; and

(7)   Telephone number for the person identified in paragraph (r)(4) of this section, labeled "Phone."

(s) Signature statement.

(1) At the creditor's option, under the heading "Confirm Receipt," a line for the signatures of the consumers in the transaction. If the creditor provides a line for the consumer's signature, the creditor must disclose above the signature line the statement required to be disclosed under § 1026.37(n)(1).

(2) If the creditor does not provide a line for the consumer's signature, the statement required to be disclosed under § 1026.37(n)(2) under the heading "Other Disclosures" required by paragraph (p) of this section.

(t) Form of disclosures—

(1) General requirements.

(i) The creditor shall make the disclosures required by this section clearly and conspicuously in writing, in a form that the consumer may keep. The disclosures also shall be grouped together and segregated from everything else.

(ii) Except as provided in paragraph (t)(5), the disclosures shall contain only the information required by paragraphs (a) through (s) of this section and shall be made in the same order, and positioned relative to the master headings, headings, subheadings, labels, and similar designations in the same manner, as shown in form H–25, set forth in appendix H to this part.

(2) Headings and labels. If a master heading, heading, subheading, label, or similar designation contains the word "estimated" or a capital letter designation in form H–25, set forth in appendix H to this part, that heading, label, or similar designation shall contain the word "estimated" and the applicable capital letter designation.

(3) Form. Except as provided in paragraph (t)(5) of this section:

(i) For a transaction subject to § 1026.19(f) that is a federally related mortgage loan, as defined in Regulation X, 12 CFR 1024.2, the disclosures must be made using form H–25, set forth in appendix H to this part.

(ii) For any other transaction subject to this section, the disclosures must be made with headings, content, and format substantially similar to form H–25, set forth in appendix H to this part.

(iii) The disclosures required by this section may be provided to the consumer in electronic form, subject to compliance with the consumer consent and other applicable provisions of the Electronic Signatures in Global and National Commerce Act (15 U.S.C. 7001 et seq.).

(4) Rounding—

(i) Nearest dollar. The following dollar amounts are required to be rounded to the nearest whole dollar:

(A) The dollar amounts required to be disclosed by paragraph (b) of this section that are required to be rounded by § 1026.37(o)(4)(i)(A) when disclosed under § 1026.37(b)(6) and (7);

(B) The dollar amounts required to be disclosed by paragraph (c) of this section that are required to be rounded by § 1026.37(o)(4)(i)(A) when disclosed under § 1026.37(c)(1)(iii);

(C) The dollar amounts required to be disclosed by paragraphs (e) and (i) of this section under the subheading "Loan Estimate";

(D) The dollar amounts required to be disclosed by paragraph (m) of this section; and

(E) The dollar amounts required to be disclosed by paragraph (c) of this section that are required to be rounded by § 1026.37(o)(4)(i)(C) when disclosed under § 1026.37(c)(2)(iv).

(ii) Percentages. The percentage amounts required to be disclosed under paragraphs (b), (f)(1), (n), and (o)(5) of this section shall not be rounded and shall be disclosed up to two or three decimal places. The percentage amount required to be disclosed under paragraph (o)(4) of this section shall not be rounded and shall be disclosed up to three decimal places. If the amount is a whole number then the amount disclosed shall be truncated at the decimal point.

(iii) **Loan amount.** The dollar amount required to be disclosed by paragraph (b) of this section as required by § 1026.37(b)(1) shall be disclosed as an unrounded number, except that if the amount is a whole number then the amount disclosed shall be truncated at the decimal point.

(5) **Exceptions—**

(i) **Unit-period.** Wherever the form or this section uses "monthly" to describe the frequency of any payments or uses "month" to describe the applicable unit-period, the creditor shall substitute the appropriate term to reflect the fact that the transaction's terms provide for other than monthly periodic payments, such as bi-weekly or quarterly payments.

(ii) **Lender credits.** The amount required to be disclosed by paragraph (d)(1)(i)(D) of this section may be omitted from the form if the amount is zero.

(iii) **Administrative information.** The creditor may insert at the bottom of each page under the disclosures required by this section as illustrated by form H–25 of appendix H to this part, any administrative information, text, or codes that assist in identification of the form or the information disclosed on the form, provided that the space provided on form H–25 for any of the information required by this section is not altered.

(iv) **Closing cost details—**

(A) Additional line numbers. Line numbers provided on form H–25 of appendix H to this part for the disclosure of the information required by paragraphs (f)(1) through (3) and (g)(1) through (4) of this section that are not used may be deleted and the deleted line numbers added to the space provided for any other of those paragraphs as necessary to accommodate the disclosure of additional items.

(B) **Two pages.** To the extent that adding or deleting line numbers provided on form H–25 of appendix H to this part, as permitted by paragraph (t)(5)(iv)(A) of this section, does not accommodate an itemization of all information required to be disclosed by paragraphs (f) through (h) on one page, the information required to be disclosed by paragraphs (f) through (h) of this section may be disclosed on two pages, provided that the information required by paragraph (f) is disclosed on a page separate from the information required by paragraph (g). The information required by paragraph (g), if disclosed on a page separate from paragraph (f), shall be disclosed on the same page as the information required by paragraph (h).

(v) **Separation of consumer and seller information.** The creditor or settlement agent preparing the form may use form H–25 of appendix H to this part for the disclosure provided to both the consumer and the seller, with the following modifications to separate the information of the consumer and seller, as necessary:

(A) The information required to be disclosed by paragraphs (j) and (k) of this section may be disclosed on separate pages to the consumer and the seller, respectively, with the information required by the other paragraph left blank. The information disclosed to the consumer pursuant to paragraph (j) of this section must be disclosed on the same page as the information required by paragraph (i) of this section.

(B) The information required to be disclosed by paragraphs (f) and (g) of this section with respect to costs paid by the consumer may be left blank on the disclosure provided to the seller.

(C) The information required by paragraphs (a)(2), (a)(4)(iii), (a)(5), (b) through (d), (i), (l) through (p), (r) with respect to the creditor and mortgage broker, and (s)(2) of this section may be left blank on the disclosure provided to the seller.

(vi) **Modified version of the form for a seller or third-party.** The information required by paragraphs (a)(2), (a)(4)(iii), (a)(5), (b) through (d), (f), and (g) with respect to costs paid by the consumer, (i), (j), (l) through (p), (q)(1), and (r) with respect to the creditor and mortgage broker, and (s) of this section may be deleted from the form provided to the seller or a third-party, as illustrated by form H–25(I) of appendix H to this part.

(vii) **Transaction without a seller.** The following modifications to form H–25 of appendix H to this part may be made for a transaction that does not involve a seller and for which the alternative tables are disclosed pursuant to paragraphs (d)(2) and (e) of this section, as illustrated by form H–25(J) of appendix H to this part:

(A) The information required by paragraph (a)(4)(ii), and paragraphs (f), (g), and (h) of this section with respect to costs paid by the seller, may be deleted.

(B) A table under the master heading "Closing Cost Details" required by paragraph (f) of this section may be added with the heading "Payoffs and Payments" that itemizes the amounts of payments made at closing to other parties from the credit extended to the consumer or funds provided by the consumer in connection with the transaction, including designees of the consumer; the payees and a description of the purpose of such disbursements under the subheading "To"; and the total amount of such payments labeled "Total Payoffs and Payments."

(C) The tables required to be disclosed by paragraphs (j) and (k) of this section may be deleted.

(viii) **Translation.** The form may be translated into languages other than English, and creditors may modify form H–25 of appendix H to this part to the extent that translation prevents the headings, labels, designations, and required disclosure items under this section from fitting in the space provided on form H–25.

(ix) **Customary recitals and information.** An additional page may be attached to the form for the purpose of including customary recitals and information used locally in real estate settlements.

§ 1026.39   Mortgage transfer disclosures.

(a) **Scope.** The disclosure requirements of this section apply to any covered person except as otherwise provided in this section. For purposes of this section:

(1) A "covered person" means any person, as defined in § 1026.2(a)(22), that becomes the owner of an existing mortgage loan by acquiring legal title to the debt obligation, whether through a purchase, assignment or other transfer, and who acquires more than one mortgage loan in any twelve-month period. For purposes of this section, a servicer of a mortgage loan shall not be treated as the owner of the obligation if the servicer holds title to the loan, or title is assigned to the servicer, solely for the administrative convenience of the servicer in servicing the obligation.

(2) A "mortgage loan" means:

(i) An open-end consumer credit transaction that is secured by the principal dwelling of a consumer; and

(ii) A closed-end consumer credit transaction secured by a dwelling or real property.

(b) **Disclosure required.** Except as provided in paragraph (c) of this section, each covered person is subject to the requirements of this section and shall mail or deliver the disclosures required by this section to the consumer on or before the 30th calendar day following the date of transfer.

(1) **Form of disclosures.** The disclosures required by this section shall be provided clearly and conspicuously in writing, in a form that the consumer may keep. The disclosures required by this section may be provided to the consumer in electronic form, subject to compliance with the consumer consent and other applicable provisions of the Electronic Signatures in Global and National Commerce Act (E-Sign Act) (15 U.S.C. 7001 et seq.).

(2)   The date of transfer. For purposes of this section, the date of transfer to the covered person may, at the covered person's option, be either the date of acquisition recognized in the books and records of the acquiring party, or the date of transfer recognized in the books and records of the transferring party.

(3)   Multiple consumers. If more than one consumer is liable on the obligation, a covered person may mail or deliver the disclosures to any consumer who is primarily liable.

(4)   Multiple transfers. If a mortgage loan is acquired by a covered person and subsequently sold, assigned, or otherwise transferred to another covered person, a single disclosure may be provided on behalf of both covered persons if the disclosure satisfies the timing and content requirements applicable to each covered person.

(5)   Multiple covered persons. If an acquisition involves multiple covered persons who jointly acquire the loan, a single disclosure must be provided on behalf of all covered persons.

(c)   Exceptions. Notwithstanding paragraph (b) of this section, a covered person is not subject to the requirements of this section with respect to a particular mortgage loan if:

(1)   The covered person sells, or otherwise transfers or assigns legal title to the mortgage loan on or before the 30th calendar day following the date that the covered person acquired the mortgage loan which shall be the date of transfer recognized for purposes of paragraph (b)(2) of this section;

(2)   The mortgage loan is transferred to the covered person in connection with a repurchase agreement that obligates the transferor to repurchase the loan. However, if the transferor does not repurchase the loan, the covered person must provide the disclosures required by this section within 30 days after the date that the transaction is recognized as an acquisition on its books and records; or

(3)   The covered person acquires only a partial interest in the loan and the party authorized to receive the consumer's notice of the right to rescind and resolve issues concerning the consumer's payments on the loan does not change as a result of the transfer of the partial interest.

(d)   Content of required disclosures. The disclosures required by this section shall identify the mortgage loan that was sold, assigned or otherwise transferred, and state the following, except that the information required by paragraph (d)(5) of this section shall be stated only for a mortgage loan that is a closed-end consumer credit transaction secured by a dwelling or real property other than a reverse mortgage transaction subject to § 1026.33 of this part:

(1)   The name, address, and telephone number of the covered person.

(i)   If a single disclosure is provided on behalf of more than one covered person, the information required by this paragraph shall be provided for each of them unless paragraph (d)(1)(ii) of this section applies.

(ii)   If a single disclosure is provided on behalf of more than one covered person and one of them has been authorized in accordance with paragraph (d)(3) of this section to receive the consumer's notice of the right to rescind and resolve issues concerning the consumer's payments on the loan, the information required by paragraph (d)(1) of this section may be provided only for that covered person.

(2)   The date of transfer.

(3)   The name, address and telephone number of an agent or party authorized to receive notice of the right to rescind and resolve issues concerning the consumer's payments on the loan. However, no information is required to be provided under this paragraph if the consumer can use the information provided under paragraph (d)(1) of this section for these purposes.

(4)   Where transfer of ownership of the debt to the covered person is or may be recorded in public records, or, alternatively, that the transfer of ownership has not been recorded in public records at the time the disclosure is provided.

(5)   Partial payment policy. Under the subheading "Partial Payment":

(i)   If periodic payments that are less than the full amount due are accepted, a statement that the covered person, using the term "lender," may accept partial payments and apply such payments to the consumer's loan;

(ii)   If periodic payments that are less than the full amount due are accepted but not applied to a consumer's loan until the consumer pays the remainder of the full amount due, a statement that the covered person, using the term "lender," may hold partial payments in a separate account until the consumer pays the remainder of the payment and then apply the full periodic payment to the consumer's loan;

(iii)   If periodic payments that are less than the full amount due are not accepted, a statement that the covered person, using the term "lender," does not accept any partial payments; and

(iv)   A statement that, if the loan is sold, the new covered person, using the term "lender," may have a different policy.

(e)   Optional disclosures. In addition to the information required to be disclosed under paragraph (d) of this section, a covered person may, at its option, provide any other information regarding the transaction.

§ 1026.40   Requirements for home equity plans.

The requirements of this section apply to open-end credit plans secured by the consumer's dwelling. For purposes of this section, an annual percentage rate is the annual percentage rate corresponding to the periodic rate as determined under § 1026.14(b).

(a)   Form of disclosures.

(1)   General. The disclosures required by paragraph (d) of this section shall be made clearly and conspicuously and shall be grouped together and segregated from all unrelated information. The disclosures may be provided on the application form or on a separate form. The disclosure described in paragraph (d)(4)(iii), the itemization of third-party fees described in paragraph (d)(8), and the variable-rate information described in paragraph (d)(12) of this section may be provided separately from the other required disclosures.

(2)   Precedence of certain disclosures. The disclosures described in paragraph (d)(1) through (4)(ii) of this section shall precede the other required disclosures.

(3)   For an application that is accessed by the consumer in electronic form, the disclosures required under this section may be provided to the consumer in electronic form on or with the application.

(b)   Time of disclosures. The disclosures and brochure required by paragraphs (d) and (e) of this section shall be provided at the time an application is provided to the consumer. The disclosures and the brochure may be delivered or placed in the mail not later than three business days following receipt of a consumer's application in the case of applications contained in magazines or other publications, or when the application is received by telephone or through an intermediary agent or broker.

(c)   Duties of third parties. Persons other than the creditor who provide applications to consumers for home equity plans must provide the brochure required under paragraph (e) of this section at the time an application is provided. If such persons have the disclosures required under paragraph (d) of this section for a creditor's home equity plan, they also shall provide the disclosures at such time. The disclosures and the brochure may be delivered or placed in the mail not later than three business days following receipt of a consumer's application in the case of applications contained in magazines or other publications, or when the application is received by telephone or through an intermediary agent or broker.

(d)   Content of disclosures. The creditor shall provide the following disclosures, as applicable:

(1) Retention of information. A statement that the consumer should make or otherwise retain a copy of the disclosures.

(2) Conditions for disclosed terms.

(i) A statement of the time by which the consumer must submit an application to obtain specific terms disclosed and an identification of any disclosed term that is subject to change prior to opening the plan.

(ii) A statement that, if a disclosed term changes (other than a change due to fluctuations in the index in a variable-rate plan) prior to opening the plan and the consumer therefore elects not to open the plan, the consumer may receive a refund of all fees paid in connection with the application.

(3) Security interest and risk to home. A statement that the creditor will acquire a security interest in the consumer's dwelling and that loss of the dwelling may occur in the event of default.

(4) Possible actions by creditor.

(i) A statement that, under certain conditions, the creditor may terminate the plan and require payment of the outstanding balance in full in a single payment and impose fees upon termination; prohibit additional extensions of credit or reduce the credit limit; and, as specified in the initial agreement, implement certain changes in the plan.

(ii) A statement that the consumer may receive, upon request, information about the conditions under which such actions may occur.

(iii) In lieu of the disclosure required under paragraph (d)(4)(ii) of this section, a statement of such conditions.

(5) Payment terms. The payment terms of the plan. If different payment terms may apply to the draw and any repayment period, or if different payment terms may apply within either period, the disclosures shall reflect the different payment terms. The payment terms of the plan include:

(i) The length of the draw period and any repayment period.

(ii) An explanation of how the minimum periodic payment will be determined and the timing of the payments. If paying only the minimum periodic payments may not repay any of the principal or may repay less than the outstanding balance, a statement of this fact, as well as a statement that a balloon payment may result. A balloon payment results if paying the minimum periodic payments does not fully amortize the outstanding balance by a specified date or time, and the consumer must repay the entire outstanding balance at such time.

(iii) An example, based on a $10,000 outstanding balance and a recent annual percentage rate, showing the minimum periodic payment, any balloon payment, and the time it would take to repay the $10,000 outstanding balance if the consumer made only those payments and obtained no additional extensions of credit. For fixed-rate plans, a recent annual percentage rate is a rate that has been in effect under the plan within the twelve months preceding the date the disclosures are provided to the consumer. For variable-rate plans, a recent annual percentage rate is the most recent rate provided in the historical example described in paragraph (d)(12)(xi) of this section or a rate that has been in effect under the plan since the date of the most recent rate in the table.

(6) Annual percentage rate. For fixed-rate plans, a recent annual percentage rate imposed under the plan and a statement that the rate does not include costs other than interest. A recent annual percentage rate is a rate that has been in effect under the plan within the twelve months preceding the date the disclosures are provided to the consumer.

(7) Fees imposed by creditor. An itemization of any fees imposed by the creditor to open, use, or maintain the plan, stated as a dollar amount or percentage, and when such fees are payable.

(8) Fees imposed by third parties to open a plan. A good faith estimate, stated as a single dollar amount or range, of any fees that may be imposed by persons other than the creditor to open the plan, as well as a statement that the consumer may receive, upon request, a good faith itemization of such fees. In lieu of the statement, the itemization of such fees may be provided.

(9) Negative amortization. A statement that negative amortization may occur and that negative amortization increases the principal balance and reduces the consumer's equity in the dwelling.

(10) Transaction requirements. Any limitations on the number of extensions of credit and the amount of credit that may be obtained during any time period, as well as any minimum outstanding balance and minimum draw requirements, stated as dollar amounts or percentages.

(11) Tax implications. A statement that the consumer should consult a tax advisor regarding the deductibility of interest and charges under the plan.

(12) Disclosures for variable-rate plans. For a plan in which the annual percentage rate is variable, the following disclosures, as applicable:

(i) The fact that the annual percentage rate, payment, or term may change due to the variable-rate feature.

(ii) A statement that the annual percentage rate does not include costs other than interest.

(iii) The index used in making rate adjustments and a source of information about the index.

(iv) An explanation of how the annual percentage rate will be determined, including an explanation of how the index is adjusted, such as by the addition of a margin.

(v) A statement that the consumer should ask about the current index value, margin, discount or premium, and annual percentage rate.

(vi) A statement that the initial annual percentage rate is not based on the index and margin used to make later rate adjustments, and the period of time such initial rate will be in effect.

(vii) The frequency of changes in the annual percentage rate.

(viii) Any rules relating to changes in the index value and the annual percentage rate and resulting changes in the payment amount, including, for example, an explanation of payment limitations and rate carryover.

(ix) A statement of any annual or more frequent periodic limitations on changes in the annual percentage rate (or a statement that no annual limitation exists), as well as a statement of the maximum annual percentage rate that may be imposed under each payment option.

(x) The minimum periodic payment required when the maximum annual percentage rate for each payment option is in effect for a $10,000 outstanding balance, and a statement of the earliest date or time the maximum rate may be imposed.

(xi) An historical example, based on a $10,000 extension of credit, illustrating how annual percentage rates and payments would have been affected by index value changes implemented according to the terms of the plan. The historical example shall be based on the most recent 15 years of index values (selected for the same time period each year) and shall reflect all significant plan terms, such as negative amortization, rate carryover, rate discounts, and rate and payment limitations, that would have been affected by the index movement during the period.

(xii) A statement that rate information will be provided on or with each periodic statement.

(e) Brochure. The home equity brochure entitled "What You Should Know About Home Equity Lines of Credit" or a suitable substitute shall be provided.

(f) Limitations on home equity plans. No creditor may, by contract or otherwise:

(1) Change the annual percentage rate unless:

(i) Such change is based on an index that is not under the creditor's control; and

(ii) Such index is available to the general public.

(2) Terminate a plan and demand repayment of the entire outstanding balance in advance of the original term (except for reverse mortgage transactions that are subject to paragraph (f)(4) of this section) unless:

(i) There is fraud or material misrepresentation by the consumer in connection with the plan;

(ii) The consumer fails to meet the repayment terms of the agreement for any outstanding balance;

(iii) Any action or inaction by the consumer adversely affects the creditor's security for the plan, or any right of the creditor in such security; or

(iv) Federal law dealing with credit extended by a depository institution to its executive officers specifically requires that as a condition of the plan the credit shall become due and payable on demand, provided that the creditor includes such a provision in the initial agreement.

(3) Change any term, except that a creditor may:

(i) Provide in the initial agreement that it may prohibit additional extensions of credit or reduce the credit limit during any period in which the maximum annual percentage rate is reached. A creditor also may provide in the initial agreement that specified changes will occur if a specified event takes place (for example, that the annual percentage rate will increase a specified amount if the consumer leaves the creditor's employment).

(ii) Change the index and margin used under the plan if the original index is no longer available, the new index has an historical movement substantially similar to that of the original index, and the new index and margin would have resulted in an annual percentage rate substantially similar to the rate in effect at the time the original index became unavailable.

(iii) Make a specified change if the consumer specifically agrees to it in writing at that time.

(iv) Make a change that will unequivocally benefit the consumer throughout the remainder of the plan.

(v) Make an insignificant change to terms.

(vi) Prohibit additional extensions of credit or reduce the credit limit applicable to an agreement during any period in which:

(A) The value of the dwelling that secures the plan declines significantly below the dwelling's appraised value for purposes of the plan;

(B) The creditor reasonably believes that the consumer will be unable to fulfill the repayment obligations under the plan because of a material change in the consumer's financial circumstances;

(C) The consumer is in default of any material obligation under the agreement;

(D) The creditor is precluded by government action from imposing the annual percentage rate provided for in the agreement;

(E) The priority of the creditor's security interest is adversely affected by government action to the extent that the value of the security interest is less than 120 percent of the credit line; or

(F) The creditor is notified by its regulatory agency that continued advances constitute an unsafe and unsound practice.

(4) For reverse mortgage transactions that are subject to § 1026.33, terminate a plan and demand repayment of the entire outstanding balance in advance of the original term except:

(i) In the case of default;

(ii) If the consumer transfers title to the property securing the note;

(iii) If the consumer ceases using the property securing the note as the primary dwelling; or

(iv) Upon the consumer's death.

(g)　Refund of fees. A creditor shall refund all fees paid by the consumer to anyone in connection with an application if any term required to be disclosed under paragraph (d) of this section changes (other than a change due to fluctuations in the index in a variable-rate plan) before the plan is opened and, as a result, the consumer elects not to open the plan.

(h)　Imposition of nonrefundable fees. Neither a creditor nor any other person may impose a nonrefundable fee in connection with an application until three business days after the consumer receives the disclosures and brochure required under this section. If the disclosures and brochure are mailed to the consumer, the consumer is considered to have received them three business days after they are mailed.

§ 1026.41　Periodic statements for residential mortgage loans.

(a)　In general.

(1)　Scope. This section applies to a closed-end consumer credit transaction secured by a dwelling, unless an exemption in paragraph (e) of this section applies. A closed-end consumer credit transaction secured by a dwelling is referred to as a mortgage loan for purposes of this section.

(2)　Periodic statements. A servicer of a transaction subject to this section shall provide the consumer, for each billing cycle, a periodic statement meeting the requirements of paragraphs (b), (c), and (d) of this section. If a mortgage loan has a billing cycle shorter than a period of 31 days (for example, a bi-weekly billing cycle), a periodic statement covering an entire month may be used. For the purposes of this section, servicer includes the creditor, assignee, or servicer, as applicable. A creditor or assignee that does not currently own the mortgage loan or the mortgage servicing rights is not subject to the requirement in this section to provide a periodic statement.

(b)　Timing of the periodic statement. The periodic statement must be delivered or placed in the mail within a reasonably prompt time after the payment due date or the end of any courtesy period provided for the previous billing cycle.

(c)　Form of the periodic statement. The servicer must make the disclosures required by this section clearly and conspicuously in writing, or electronically if the consumer agrees, and in a form that the consumer may keep. Sample forms for periodic statements are provided in appendix H–30. Proper use of these forms complies with the requirements of this paragraph (c) and the layout requirements in paragraph (d) of this section.

(d)　Content and layout of the periodic statement. The periodic statement required by this section shall include:

(1)　Amount due. Grouped together in close proximity to each other and located at the top of the first page of the statement:

(i) The payment due date;

(ii) The amount of any late payment fee, and the date on which that fee will be imposed if payment has not been received; and

(iii) The amount due, shown more prominently than other disclosures on the page and, if the transaction has multiple payment options, the amount due under each of the payment options.

(2)　Explanation of amount due. The following items, grouped together in close proximity to each other and located on the first page of the statement:

(i) The monthly payment amount, including a breakdown showing how much, if any, will be applied to principal, interest, and escrow and, if a mortgage loan has multiple payment options, a breakdown of each of the payment options along with information on whether the principal balance will increase, decrease, or stay the same for each option listed;

    (ii) The total sum of any fees or charges imposed since the last statement; and

    (iii) Any payment amount past due.

    (3) **Past Payment Breakdown.** The following items, grouped together in close proximity to each other and located on the first page of the statement:

    (i) The total of all payments received since the last statement, including a breakdown showing the amount, if any, that was applied to principal, interest, escrow, fees and charges, and the amount, if any, sent to any suspense or unapplied funds account; and

    (ii) The total of all payments received since the beginning of the current calendar year, including a breakdown of that total showing the amount, if any, that was applied to principal, interest, escrow, fees and charges, and the amount, if any, currently held in any suspense or unapplied funds account.

    (4) **Transaction activity.** A list of all the transaction activity that occurred since the last statement. For purposes of this paragraph (d)(4), transaction activity means any activity that causes a credit or debit to the amount currently due. This list must include the date of the transaction, a brief description of the transaction, and the amount of the transaction for each activity on the list.

    (5) **Partial payment information.** If a statement reflects a partial payment that was placed in a suspense or unapplied funds account, information explaining what must be done for the funds to be applied. The information must be on the front page of the statement or, alternatively, may be included on a separate page enclosed with the periodic statement or in a separate letter.

    (6) **Contact information.** A toll-free telephone number and, if applicable, an electronic mailing address that may be used by the consumer to obtain information about the consumer's account, located on the front page of the statement.

    (7) **Account information.** The following information:

    (i) The amount of the outstanding principal balance;

    (ii) The current interest rate in effect for the mortgage loan;

    (iii) The date after which the interest rate may next change;

    (iv) The existence of any prepayment penalty, as defined in § 1026.32(b)(6)(i), that may be charged;

    (v) The Web site to access either the Bureau list or the HUD list of homeownership counselors and counseling organizations and the HUD toll-free telephone number to access contact information for homeownership counselors or counseling organizations; and

    (8) **Delinquency information.** If the consumer is more than 45 days delinquent, the following items, grouped together in close proximity to each other and located on the first page of the statement or, alternatively, on a separate page enclosed with the periodic statement or in a separate letter:

    (i) The date on which the consumer became delinquent;

    (ii) A notification of possible risks, such as foreclosure, and expenses, that may be incurred if the delinquency is not cured;

    (iii) An account history showing, for the previous six months or the period since the last time the account was current, whichever is shorter, the amount remaining past due from each billing cycle or, if any such payment was fully paid, the date on which it was credited as fully paid;

    (iv) A notice indicating any loss mitigation program to which the consumer has agreed, if applicable;

(v) A notice of whether the servicer has made the first notice or filing required by applicable law for any judicial or non-judicial foreclosure process, if applicable;

(vi) The total payment amount needed to bring the account current; and

(vii) A reference to the homeownership counselor information disclosed pursuant to paragraph (d)(7)(v) of this section.

(e) Exemptions.

(1) Reverse mortgages. Reverse mortgage transactions, as defined by § 1026.33(a), are exempt from the requirements of this section.

(2) Timeshare plans. Transactions secured by consumers' interests in timeshare plans, as defined by 11 U.S.C. 101(53D), are exempt from the requirements of this section.

(3) Coupon books. The requirements of paragraph (a) of this section do not apply to fixed-rate loans if the servicer:

(i) Provides the consumer with a coupon book that includes on each coupon the information listed in paragraph (d)(1) of this section;

(ii) Provides the consumer with a coupon book that includes anywhere in the coupon book:

(A) The account information listed in paragraph (d)(7) of this section;

(B) The contact information for the servicer, listed in paragraph (d)(6) of this section; and

(C) Information on how the consumer can obtain the information listed in paragraph (e)(3)(iii) of this section;

(iii) Makes available upon request to the consumer by telephone, in writing, in person, or electronically, if the consumer consents, the information listed in paragraph (d)(2) through (5) of this section; and

(iv) Provides the consumer the information listed in paragraph (d)(8) of this section in writing, for any billing cycle during which the consumer is more than 45 days delinquent.

(4) Small servicers.

(i) Exemption. A creditor, assignee, or servicer is exempt from the requirements of this section for mortgage loans serviced by a small servicer.

(ii) Small servicer defined. A small servicer is a servicer that:

(A) Services, together with any affiliates, 5,000 or fewer mortgage loans, for all of which the servicer (or an affiliate) is the creditor or assignee;

(B) Is a Housing Finance Agency, as defined in 24 CFR 266.5; or

(C) Is a nonprofit entity that services 5,000 or fewer mortgage loans, including any mortgage loans serviced on behalf of associated nonprofit entities, for all of which the servicer or an associated nonprofit entity is the creditor. For purposes of this paragraph (e)(4)(ii)(C), the following definitions apply:

(1) The term "nonprofit entity" means an entity having a tax exemption ruling or determination letter from the Internal Revenue Service under section 501(c)(3) of the Internal Revenue Code of 1986 (26 U.S.C. 501(c)(3); 26 CFR 1.501(c)(3)–(1), and;

(2) The term "associated nonprofit entities" means nonprofit entities that by agreement operate using a common name, trademark, or servicemark to further and support a common charitable mission or purpose.

(iii) Small servicer determination. In determining whether a servicer satisfies paragraph (e)(4)(ii)(A) of this section, the servicer is evaluated based on the mortgage loans serviced by the servicer and any affiliates as of January 1 and for the remainder of the calendar year. In determining whether a servicer satisfies paragraph (e)(4)(ii)(C) of this section, the servicer is evaluated based on the mortgage loans serviced by the servicer as of January 1 and for the remainder of the calendar year. A servicer that ceases to qualify as a small servicer will have six months from the time it ceases to qualify or until the next January 1, whichever is later, to comply with any requirements from which the servicer is no longer exempt as a small servicer. The following mortgage loans are not considered in determining whether a servicer qualifies as a small servicer:

>   **(A)** Mortgage loans voluntarily serviced by the servicer for a creditor or assignee that is not an affiliate of the servicer and for which the servicer does not receive any compensation or fees.

>   **(B)** Reverse mortgage transactions.

>   **(C)** Mortgage loans secured by consumers' interests in timeshare plans.

>   **(5) Consumers in bankruptcy.** A servicer is exempt from the requirements of this section for a mortgage loan while the consumer is a debtor in bankruptcy under Title 11 of the United States Code.

§ 1026.42 Valuation independence.

(a) Scope. This section applies to any consumer credit transaction secured by the consumer's principal dwelling.

(b) Definitions. For purposes of this section:

(1) "Covered person" means a creditor with respect to a covered transaction or a person that provides "settlement services," as defined in 12 U.S.C. 2602(3) and implementing regulations, in connection with a covered transaction.

(2) "Covered transaction" means an extension of consumer credit that is or will be secured by the consumer's principal dwelling, as defined in § 1026.2(a)(19).

(3) "Valuation" means an estimate of the value of the consumer's principal dwelling in written or electronic form, other than one produced solely by an automated model or system.

(4) "Valuation management functions" means:

>   **(i)** Recruiting, selecting, or retaining a person to prepare a valuation;

>   **(ii)** Contracting with or employing a person to prepare a valuation;

>   **(iii)** Managing or overseeing the process of preparing a valuation, including by providing administrative services such as receiving orders for and receiving a valuation, submitting a completed valuation to creditors and underwriters, collecting fees from creditors and underwriters for services provided in connection with a valuation, and compensating a person that prepares valuations; or

>   **(iv)** Reviewing or verifying the work of a person that prepares valuations.

(c) Valuation of consumer's principal dwelling.

(1) Coercion. In connection with a covered transaction, no covered person shall or shall attempt to directly or indirectly cause the value assigned to the consumer's principal dwelling to be based on any factor other than the independent judgment of a person that prepares valuations, through coercion, extortion, inducement, bribery, or intimidation of, compensation or instruction to, or collusion with a person that prepares valuations or performs valuation management functions.

>   **(i)** Examples of actions that violate paragraph (c)(1) include:

>   **(A)** Seeking to influence a person that prepares a valuation to report a minimum or maximum value for the consumer's principal dwelling;

(B) Withholding or threatening to withhold timely payment to a person that prepares a valuation or performs valuation management functions because the person does not value the consumer's principal dwelling at or above a certain amount;

(C) Implying to a person that prepares valuations that current or future retention of the person depends on the amount at which the person estimates the value of the consumer's principal dwelling;

(D) Excluding a person that prepares a valuation from consideration for future engagement because the person reports a value for the consumer's principal dwelling that does not meet or exceed a predetermined threshold; and

(E) Conditioning the compensation paid to a person that prepares a valuation on consummation of the covered transaction.

(2) Mischaracterization of value.

(i) Misrepresentation. In connection with a covered transaction, no person that prepares valuations shall materially misrepresent the value of the consumer's principal dwelling in a valuation. A misrepresentation is material for purposes of this paragraph (c)(2)(i) if it is likely to significantly affect the value assigned to the consumer's principal dwelling. A bona fide error shall not be a misrepresentation.

(ii) Falsification or alteration. In connection with a covered transaction, no covered person shall falsify and no covered person other than a person that prepares valuations shall materially alter a valuation. An alteration is material for purposes of this paragraph (c)(2)(ii) if it is likely to significantly affect the value assigned to the consumer's principal dwelling.

(iii) Inducement of mischaracterization. In connection with a covered transaction, no covered person shall induce a person to violate paragraph (c)(2)(i) or (ii) of this section.

(3) Permitted actions. Examples of actions that do not violate paragraph (c)(1) or (c)(2) include:

(i) Asking a person that prepares a valuation to consider additional, appropriate property information, including information about comparable properties, to make or support a valuation;

(ii) Requesting that a person that prepares a valuation provide further detail, substantiation, or explanation for the person's conclusion about the value of the consumer's principal dwelling;

(iii) Asking a person that prepares a valuation to correct errors in the valuation;

(iv) Obtaining multiple valuations for the consumer's principal dwelling to select the most reliable valuation;

(v) Withholding compensation due to breach of contract or substandard performance of services; and

(vi) Taking action permitted or required by applicable Federal or state statute, regulation, or agency guidance.

(d) Prohibition on conflicts of interest.

(1)(i) In general. No person preparing a valuation or performing valuation management functions for a covered transaction may have a direct or indirect interest, financial or otherwise, in the property or transaction for which the valuation is or will be performed.

(ii) Employees and affiliates of creditors; providers of multiple settlement services. In any covered transaction, no person violates paragraph (d)(1)(i) of this section based solely on the fact that the person:

(A) Is an employee or affiliate of the creditor; or

(B) Provides a settlement service in addition to preparing valuations or performing valuation management functions, or based solely on the fact that the person's affiliate performs another settlement service.

(2) **Employees and affiliates of creditors with assets of more than $250 million for both of the past two calendar years.** For any covered transaction in which the creditor had assets of more than $250 million as of December 31st for both of the past two calendar years, a person subject to paragraph (d)(1)(i) of this section who is employed by or affiliated with the creditor does not have a conflict of interest in violation of paragraph (d)(1)(i) of this section based on the person's employment or affiliate relationship with the creditor if:

(i) The compensation of the person preparing a valuation or performing valuation management functions is not based on the value arrived at in any valuation;

(ii) The person preparing a valuation or performing valuation management functions reports to a person who is not part of the creditor's loan production function, as defined in paragraph (d)(5)(i) of this section, and whose compensation is not based on the closing of the transaction to which the valuation relates; and

(iii) No employee, officer or director in the creditor's loan production function, as defined in paragraph (d)(5)(i) of this section, is directly or indirectly involved in selecting, retaining, recommending or influencing the selection of the person to prepare a valuation or perform valuation management functions, or to be included in or excluded from a list of approved persons who prepare valuations or perform valuation management functions.

(3) **Employees and affiliates of creditors with assets of $250 million or less for either of the past two calendar years.** For any covered transaction in which the creditor had assets of $250 million or less as of December 31st for either of the past two calendar years, a person subject to paragraph (d)(1)(i) of this section who is employed by or affiliated with the creditor does not have a conflict of interest in violation of paragraph (d)(1)(i) of this section based on the person's employment or affiliate relationship with the creditor if:

(i) The compensation of the person preparing a valuation or performing valuation management functions is not based on the value arrived at in any valuation; and

(ii) The creditor requires that any employee, officer or director of the creditor who orders, performs, or reviews a valuation for a covered transaction abstain from participating in any decision to approve, not approve, or set the terms of that transaction.

(4) **Providers of multiple settlement services.** For any covered transaction, a person who prepares a valuation or performs valuation management functions in addition to performing another settlement service for the transaction, or whose affiliate performs another settlement service for the transaction, does not have a conflict of interest in violation of paragraph (d)(1)(i) of this section as a result of the person or the person's affiliate performing another settlement service for the transaction if:

(i) The creditor had assets of more than $250 million as of December 31st for both of the past two calendar years and the conditions in paragraph (d)(2)(i)–(iii) are met; or

(ii) The creditor had assets of $250 million or less as of December 31st for either of the past two calendar years and the conditions in paragraph (d)(3)(i)–(ii) are met.

(5) **Definitions.** For purposes of this paragraph (d), the following definitions apply:

(i) **Loan production function.** The term "loan production function" means an employee, officer, director, department, division, or other unit of a creditor with responsibility for generating covered transactions, approving covered transactions, or both.

(ii) **Settlement service.** The term "settlement service" has the same meaning as in the Real Estate Settlement Procedures Act, 12 U.S.C. 2601 et seq.

(iii) **Affiliate.** The term "affiliate" has the same meaning as in Regulation Y of the Board of Governors of the Federal Reserve System, 12 CFR 225.2(a).

(e) **When extension of credit prohibited.** In connection with a covered transaction, a creditor that knows, at or before consummation, of a violation of paragraph (c) or (d) of this section in connection with a valuation shall not extend credit based on the valuation, unless the creditor documents that it has acted with reasonable diligence to determine that the valuation does not materially misstate or misrepresent the value of the consumer's principal dwelling. For purposes of this paragraph (e), a valuation materially misstates or misrepresents the value of the consumer's principal dwelling if the valuation contains a misstatement or misrepresentation that affects the credit decision or the terms on which credit is extended.

(f) **Customary and reasonable compensation.**

(1) **Requirement to provide customary and reasonable compensation to fee appraisers.** In any covered transaction, the creditor and its agents shall compensate a fee appraiser for performing appraisal services at a rate that is customary and reasonable for comparable appraisal services performed in the geographic market of the property being appraised. For purposes of paragraph (f) of this section, "agents" of the creditor do not include any fee appraiser as defined in paragraph (f)(4)(i) of this section.

(2) **Presumption of compliance.** A creditor and its agents shall be presumed to comply with paragraph (f)(1) of this section if:

(i) The creditor or its agents compensate the fee appraiser in an amount that is reasonably related to recent rates paid for comparable appraisal services performed in the geographic market of the property being appraised. In determining this amount, a creditor or its agents shall review the factors below and make any adjustments to recent rates paid in the relevant geographic market necessary to ensure that the amount of compensation is reasonable:

(A) The type of property,

(B) The scope of work,

(C) The time in which the appraisal services are required to be performed,

(D) Fee appraiser qualifications,

(E) Fee appraiser experience and professional record, and

(F) Fee appraiser work quality; and

(ii) The creditor and its agents do not engage in any anticompetitive acts in violation of state or Federal law that affect the compensation paid to fee appraisers, including:

(A) Entering into any contracts or engaging in any conspiracies to restrain trade through methods such as price fixing or market allocation, as prohibited under section 1 of the Sherman Antitrust Act, 15 U.S.C. 1, or any other relevant antitrust laws; or

(B) Engaging in any acts of monopolization such as restricting any person from entering the relevant geographic market or causing any person to leave the relevant geographic market, as prohibited under section 2 of the Sherman Antitrust Act, 15 U.S.C. 2, or any other relevant antitrust laws.

(3) **Alternative presumption of compliance.** A creditor and its agents shall be presumed to comply with paragraph (f)(1) of this section if the creditor or its agents determine the amount of compensation paid to the fee appraiser by relying on information about rates that:

(i) Is based on objective third-party information, including fee schedules, studies, and surveys prepared by independent third parties such as government agencies, academic institutions, and private research firms;

(ii) Is based on recent rates paid to a representative sample of providers of appraisal services in the geographic market of the property being appraised or the fee schedules of those providers; and

(iii) In the case of information based on fee schedules, studies, and surveys, such fee schedules, studies, or surveys, or the information derived therefrom, excludes compensation paid to fee appraisers for appraisals ordered by appraisal management companies, as defined in paragraph (f)(4)(iii) of this section.

(4) **Definitions.** For purposes of this paragraph (f), the following definitions apply:

(i) **Fee appraiser.** The term "fee appraiser" means:

(A) A natural person who is a state-licensed or state-certified appraiser and receives a fee for performing an appraisal, but who is not an employee of the person engaging the appraiser; or

(B) An organization that, in the ordinary course of business, employs state-licensed or state-certified appraisers to perform appraisals, receives a fee for performing appraisals, and is not subject to the requirements of section 1124 of the Financial Institutions Reform, Recovery, and Enforcement Act of 1989 (12 U.S.C. 3353).

(ii) **Appraisal services.** The term "appraisal services" means the services required to perform an appraisal, including defining the scope of work, inspecting the property, reviewing necessary and appropriate public and private data sources (for example, multiple listing services, tax assessment records and public land records), developing and rendering an opinion of value, and preparing and submitting the appraisal report.

(iii) **Appraisal management company.** The term "appraisal management company" means any person authorized to perform one or more of the following actions on behalf of the creditor:

(A) Recruit, select, and retain fee appraisers;

(B) Contract with fee appraisers to perform appraisal services;

(C) Manage the process of having an appraisal performed, including providing administrative services such as receiving appraisal orders and appraisal reports, submitting completed appraisal reports to creditors and underwriters, collecting fees from creditors and underwriters for services provided, and compensating fee appraisers for services performed; or

(D) Review and verify the work of fee appraisers.

(g) **Mandatory reporting.**

(1) **Reporting required.** Any covered person that reasonably believes an appraiser has not complied with the Uniform Standards of Professional Appraisal Practice or ethical or professional requirements for appraisers under applicable state or Federal statutes or regulations shall refer the matter to the appropriate state agency if the failure to comply is material. For purposes of this paragraph (g)(1), a failure to comply is material if it is likely to significantly affect the value assigned to the consumer's principal dwelling.

(2) **Timing of reporting.** A covered person shall notify the appropriate state agency within a reasonable period of time after the person determines that there is a reasonable basis to believe that a failure to comply required to be reported under paragraph (g)(1) of this section has occurred.

(3) **Definition.** For purposes of this paragraph (g), "state agency" means "state appraiser certifying and licensing agency" under 12 U.S.C. 3350(1) and any implementing regulations. The appropriate state agency to which a covered person must refer a matter under paragraph (g)(1) of this section is the agency for the state in which the consumer's principal dwelling is located.

(h) The Bureau issued a joint rule to implement the appraisal management company minimum requirements in the Financial Institutions Reform, Recovery, and Enforcement Act, as amended by section 1473 of the Dodd-Frank Wall Street Reform and Consumer Protection Act. See 12 CFR part 34.

§ 1026.43   Minimum standards for transactions secured by a dwelling.

(a)   **Scope.** This section applies to any consumer credit transaction that is secured by a dwelling, as defined in § 1026.2(a)(19), including any real property attached to a dwelling, other than:

(1)   A home equity line of credit subject to § 1026.40;

(2)   A mortgage transaction secured by a consumer's interest in a timeshare plan, as defined in 11 U.S.C. 101(53(D); or

(3)   For purposes of paragraphs (c) through (f) of this section:

(i)   A reverse mortgage subject to § 1026.33;

(ii)   A temporary or "bridge" loan with a term of 12 months or less, such as a loan to finance the purchase of a new dwelling where the consumer plans to sell a current dwelling within 12 months or a loan to finance the initial construction of a dwelling;

(iii)   A construction phase of 12 months or less of a construction-to-permanent loan;

(iv)   An extension of credit made pursuant to a program administered by a Housing Finance Agency, as defined under 24 CFR 266.5;

(v)   An extension of credit made by:

(A)   A creditor designated as a Community Development Financial Institution, as defined under 12 CFR 1805.104(h);

(B)   A creditor designated as a Downpayment Assistance through Secondary Financing Provider, pursuant to 24 CFR 200.194(a), operating in accordance with regulations prescribed by the U.S. Department of Housing and Urban Development applicable to such persons;

(C)   A creditor designated as a Community Housing Development Organization provided that the creditor has entered into a commitment with a participating jurisdiction and is undertaking a project under the HOME program, pursuant to the provisions of 24 CFR 92.300(a), and as the terms community housing development organization, commitment, participating jurisdiction, and project are defined under 24 CFR 92.2; or

(D)   A creditor with a tax exemption ruling or determination letter from the Internal Revenue Service under section 501(c)(3) of the Internal Revenue Code of 1986 (26 U.S.C. 501(c)(3); 26 CFR 1.501(c)(3)–1), provided that:

(1)   During the calendar year preceding receipt of the consumer's application, the creditor extended credit secured by a dwelling no more than 200 times, except as provided in paragraph (a)(3)(vii) of this section;

(2)   During the calendar year preceding receipt of the consumer's application, the creditor extended credit secured by a dwelling only to consumers with income that did not exceed the low-and moderate-income household limit as established pursuant to section 102 of the Housing and Community Development Act of 1974 (42 U.S.C. 5302(a)(20)) and amended from time to time by the U.S. Department of Housing and Urban Development, pursuant to 24 CFR 570.3;

(3)   The extension of credit is to a consumer with income that does not exceed the household limit specified in paragraph (a)(3)(v)(D)(2) of this section; and

(4)   The creditor determines, in accordance with written procedures, that the consumer has a reasonable ability to repay the extension of credit.

(vi)   An extension of credit made pursuant to a program authorized by sections 101 and 109 of the Emergency Economic Stabilization Act of 2008 (12 U.S.C. 5211; 5219);[1]

---

[1]   So in original. Probably should be ".".

(vii) Consumer credit transactions that meet the following criteria are not considered in determining whether a creditor exceeds the credit extension limitation in paragraph (a)(3)(v)(D)(1) of this section:

(A) The transaction is secured by a subordinate lien;

(B) The transaction is for the purpose of:

(1) Downpayment, closing costs, or other similar home buyer assistance, such as principal or interest subsidies;

(2) Property rehabilitation assistance;

(3) Energy efficiency assistance; or

(4) Foreclosure avoidance or prevention;

(C) The credit contract does not require payment of interest;

(D) The credit contract provides that repayment of the amount of the credit extended is:

(1) Forgiven either incrementally or in whole, at a date certain, and subject only to specified ownership and occupancy conditions, such as a requirement that the consumer maintain the property as the consumer's principal dwelling for five years;

(2) Deferred for a minimum of 20 years after consummation of the transaction;

(3) Deferred until sale of the property securing the transaction; or

(4) Deferred until the property securing the transaction is no longer the principal dwelling of the consumer;

(E) The total of costs payable by the consumer in connection with the transaction at consummation is less than 1 percent of the amount of credit extended and includes no charges other than:

(1) Fees for recordation of security instruments, deeds, and similar documents;

(2) A bona fide and reasonable application fee; and

(3) A bona fide and reasonable fee for housing counseling services; and

(F) The creditor complies with all other applicable requirements of this part in connection with the transaction.

(b) Definitions. For purposes of this section:

(1) Covered transaction means a consumer credit transaction that is secured by a dwelling, as defined in § 1026.2(a)(19), including any real property attached to a dwelling, other than a transaction exempt from coverage under paragraph (a) of this section.

(2) Fully amortizing payment means a periodic payment of principal and interest that will fully repay the loan amount over the loan term.

(3) Fully indexed rate means the interest rate calculated using the index or formula that will apply after recast, as determined at the time of consummation, and the maximum margin that can apply at any time during the loan term.

(4) Higher-priced covered transaction means a covered transaction with an annual percentage rate that exceeds the average prime offer rate for a comparable transaction as of the date the interest rate is set by 1.5 or more percentage points for a first-lien covered transaction, other than a qualified mortgage under paragraph (e)(5), (e)(6), or (f) of this section; by 3.5 or more percentage points for a first-lien covered transaction that is a qualified mortgage under paragraph (e)(5), (e)(6), or (f) of this section; or by 3.5 or more percentage points for a subordinate-lien covered transaction.

(5) Loan amount means the principal amount the consumer will borrow as reflected in the promissory note or loan contract.

(6) Loan term means the period of time to repay the obligation in full.

(7) Maximum loan amount means the loan amount plus any increase in principal balance that results from negative amortization, as defined in § 1026.18(s)(7)(v), based on the terms of the legal obligation assuming:

   (i) The consumer makes only the minimum periodic payments for the maximum possible time, until the consumer must begin making fully amortizing payments; and

   (ii) The maximum interest rate is reached at the earliest possible time.

(8) Mortgage-related obligations mean property taxes; premiums and similar charges identified in § 1026.4(b)(5), (7), (8), and (10) that are required by the creditor; fees and special assessments imposed by a condominium, cooperative, or homeowners association; ground rent; and leasehold payments.

(9) Points and fees has the same meaning as in § 1026.32(b)(1).

(10) Prepayment penalty has the same meaning as in § 1026.32(b)(6).

(11) Recast means:

   (i) For an adjustable-rate mortgage, as defined in § 1026.18(s)(7)(i), the expiration of the period during which payments based on the introductory fixed interest rate are permitted under the terms of the legal obligation;

   (ii) For an interest-only loan, as defined in § 1026.18(s)(7)(iv), the expiration of the period during which interest-only payments are permitted under the terms of the legal obligation; and

   (iii) For a negative amortization loan, as defined in § 1026.18(s)(7)(v), the expiration of the period during which negatively amortizing payments are permitted under the terms of the legal obligation.

(12) Simultaneous loan means another covered transaction or home equity line of credit subject to § 1026.40 that will be secured by the same dwelling and made to the same consumer at or before consummation of the covered transaction or, if to be made after consummation, will cover closing costs of the first covered transaction.

(13) Third-party record means:

   (i) A document or other record prepared or reviewed by an appropriate person other than the consumer, the creditor, or the mortgage broker, as defined in § 1026.36(a)(2), or an agent of the creditor or mortgage broker;

   (ii) A copy of a tax return filed with the Internal Revenue Service or a State taxing authority;

   (iii) A record the creditor maintains for an account of the consumer held by the creditor; or

   (iv) If the consumer is an employee of the creditor or the mortgage broker, a document or other record maintained by the creditor or mortgage broker regarding the consumer's employment status or employment income.

(c) Repayment ability—

   (1) General requirement. A creditor shall not make a loan that is a covered transaction unless the creditor makes a reasonable and good faith determination at or before consummation that the consumer will have a reasonable ability to repay the loan according to its terms.

   (2) Basis for determination. Except as provided otherwise in paragraphs (d), (e), and (f) of this section, in making the repayment ability determination required under paragraph (c)(1) of this section, a creditor must consider the following:

(i) The consumer's current or reasonably expected income or assets, other than the value of the dwelling, including any real property attached to the dwelling, that secures the loan;

(ii) If the creditor relies on income from the consumer's employment in determining repayment ability, the consumer's current employment status;

(iii) The consumer's monthly payment on the covered transaction, calculated in accordance with paragraph (c)(5) of this section;

(iv) The consumer's monthly payment on any simultaneous loan that the creditor knows or has reason to know will be made, calculated in accordance with paragraph (c)(6) of this section;

(v) The consumer's monthly payment for mortgage-related obligations;

(vi) The consumer's current debt obligations, alimony, and child support;

(vii) The consumer's monthly debt-to-income ratio or residual income in accordance with paragraph (c)(7) of this section; and

(viii) The consumer's credit history.

(3) Verification using third-party records. A creditor must verify the information that the creditor relies on in determining a consumer's repayment ability under § 1026.43(c)(2) using reasonably reliable third-party records, except that:

(i) For purposes of paragraph (c)(2)(i) of this section, a creditor must verify a consumer's income or assets that the creditor relies on in accordance with § 1026.43(c)(4);

(ii) For purposes of paragraph (c)(2)(ii) of this section, a creditor may verify a consumer's employment status orally if the creditor prepares a record of the information obtained orally; and

(iii) For purposes of paragraph (c)(2)(vi) of this section, if a creditor relies on a consumer's credit report to verify a consumer's current debt obligations and a consumer's application states a current debt obligation not shown in the consumer's credit report, the creditor need not independently verify such an obligation.

(4) Verification of income or assets. A creditor must verify the amounts of income or assets that the creditor relies on under § 1026.43(c)(2)(i) to determine a consumer's ability to repay a covered transaction using third-party records that provide reasonably reliable evidence of the consumer's income or assets. A creditor may verify the consumer's income using a tax-return transcript issued by the Internal Revenue Service (IRS). Examples of other records the creditor may use to verify the consumer's income or assets include:

(i) Copies of tax returns the consumer filed with the IRS or a State taxing authority;

(ii) IRS Form W-2s or similar IRS forms used for reporting wages or tax withholding;

(iii) Payroll statements, including military Leave and Earnings Statements;

(iv) Financial institution records;

(v) Records from the consumer's employer or a third party that obtained information from the employer;

(vi) Records from a Federal, State, or local government agency stating the consumer's income from benefits or entitlements;

(vii) Receipts from the consumer's use of check cashing services; and

(viii) Receipts from the consumer's use of a funds transfer service.

(5) Payment calculation—

(i) General rule. Except as provided in paragraph (c)(5)(ii) of this section, a creditor must make the consideration required under paragraph (c)(2)(iii) of this section using:

(A) The fully indexed rate or any introductory interest rate, whichever is greater; and

(B) Monthly, fully amortizing payments that are substantially equal.

(ii) *Special rules for loans with a balloon payment, interest-only loans, and negative amortization loans.* A creditor must make the consideration required under paragraph (c)(2)(iii) of this section for:

(A) A loan with a balloon payment, as defined in § 1026.18(s)(5)(i), using:

(1) The maximum payment scheduled during the first five years after the date on which the first regular periodic payment will be due for a loan that is not a higher-priced covered transaction; or

(2) The maximum payment in the payment schedule, including any balloon payment, for a higher-priced covered transaction;

(B) An interest-only loan, as defined in § 1026.18(s)(7)(iv), using:

(1) The fully indexed rate or any introductory interest rate, whichever is greater; and

(2) Substantially equal, monthly payments of principal and interest that will repay the loan amount over the term of the loan remaining as of the date the loan is recast.

(C) A negative amortization loan, as defined in § 1026.18(s)(7)(v), using:

(1) The fully indexed rate or any introductory interest rate, whichever is greater; and

(2) Substantially equal, monthly payments of principal and interest that will repay the maximum loan amount over the term of the loan remaining as of the date the loan is recast.

(6) *Payment calculation for simultaneous loans.* For purposes of making the evaluation required under paragraph (c)(2)(iv) of this section, a creditor must consider, taking into account any mortgage-related obligations, a consumer's payment on a simultaneous loan that is:

(i) A covered transaction, by following paragraph (c)(5) of this section; or

(ii) A home equity line of credit subject to § 1026.40, by using the periodic payment required under the terms of the plan and the amount of credit to be drawn at or before consummation of the covered transaction.

(7) *Monthly debt-to-income ratio or residual income—*

(i) *Definitions.* For purposes of this paragraph (c)(7), the following definitions apply:

(A) *Total monthly debt obligations.* The term total monthly debt obligations means the sum of: the payment on the covered transaction, as required to be calculated by paragraphs (c)(2)(iii) and (c)(5) of this section; simultaneous loans, as required by paragraphs (c)(2)(iv) and (c)(6) of this section; mortgage-related obligations, as required by paragraph (c)(2)(v) of this section; and current debt obligations, alimony, and child support, as required by paragraph (c)(2)(vi) of this section.

(B) *Total monthly income.* The term total monthly income means the sum of the consumer's current or reasonably expected income, including any income from assets, as required by paragraphs (c)(2)(i) and (c)(4) of this section.

(ii) *Calculations—*

(A) *Monthly debt-to-income ratio.* If a creditor considers the consumer's monthly debt-to-income ratio under paragraph (c)(2)(vii) of this section, the creditor must consider the ratio of the consumer's total monthly debt obligations to the consumer's total monthly income.

(B) Monthly residual income. If a creditor considers the consumer's monthly residual income under paragraph (c)(2)(vii) of this section, the creditor must consider the consumer's remaining income after subtracting the consumer's total monthly debt obligations from the consumer's total monthly income.

(d) Refinancing of non-standard mortgages—

(1) **Definitions.** For purposes of this paragraph (d), the following definitions apply:

(i) **Non-standard mortgage.** The term non-standard mortgage means a covered transaction that is:

(A) An adjustable-rate mortgage, as defined in § 1026.18(s)(7)(i), with an introductory fixed interest rate for a period of one year or longer;

(B) An interest-only loan, as defined in § 1026.18(s)(7)(iv); or

(C) A negative amortization loan, as defined in § 1026.18(s)(7)(v).

(ii) **Standard mortgage.** The term standard mortgage means a covered transaction:

(A) That provides for regular periodic payments that do not:

(1) Cause the principal balance to increase;

(2) Allow the consumer to defer repayment of principal; or

(3) Result in a balloon payment, as defined in § 1026.18(s)(5)(i);

(B) For which the total points and fees payable in connection with the transaction do not exceed the amounts specified in paragraph (e)(3) of this section;

(C) For which the term does not exceed 40 years;

(D) For which the interest rate is fixed for at least the first five years after consummation; and

(E) For which the proceeds from the loan are used solely for the following purposes:

(1) To pay off the outstanding principal balance on the non-standard mortgage; and

(2) To pay closing or settlement charges required to be disclosed under the Real Estate Settlement Procedures Act, 12 U.S.C. 2601 et seq.

(iii) **Refinancing.** The term refinancing has the same meaning as in § 1026.20(a).

(2) **Scope.** The provisions of this paragraph (d) apply to the refinancing of a non-standard mortgage into a standard mortgage when the following conditions are met:

(i) The creditor for the standard mortgage is the current holder of the existing non-standard mortgage or the servicer acting on behalf of the current holder;

(ii) The monthly payment for the standard mortgage is materially lower than the monthly payment for the non-standard mortgage, as calculated under paragraph (d)(5) of this section.

(iii) The creditor receives the consumer's written application for the standard mortgage no later than two months after the non-standard mortgage has recast.

(iv) The consumer has made no more than one payment more than 30 days late on the non-standard mortgage during the 12 months immediately preceding the creditor's receipt of the consumer's written application for the standard mortgage.

(v) The consumer has made no payments more than 30 days late during the six months immediately preceding the creditor's receipt of the consumer's written application for the standard mortgage; and

(vi) If the non-standard mortgage was consummated on or after January 10, 2014, the non-standard mortgage was made in accordance with paragraph (c) or (e) of this section, as applicable.

(3) Exemption from repayment ability requirements. A creditor is not required to comply with the requirements of paragraph (c) of this section if:

(i) The conditions in paragraph (d)(2) of this section are met; and

(ii) The creditor has considered whether the standard mortgage likely will prevent a default by the consumer on the non-standard mortgage once the loan is recast.

(4) Offer of rate discounts and other favorable terms. A creditor making a covered transaction under this paragraph (d) may offer to the consumer rate discounts and terms that are the same as, or better than, the rate discounts and terms that the creditor offers to new consumers, consistent with the creditor's documented underwriting practices and to the extent not prohibited by applicable State or Federal law.

(5) Payment calculations. For purposes of determining whether the consumer's monthly payment for a standard mortgage will be materially lower than the monthly payment for the non-standard mortgage, the following provisions shall be used:

(i) Non-standard mortgage. For purposes of the comparison conducted pursuant to paragraph (d)(2)(ii) of this section, the creditor must calculate the monthly payment for a non-standard mortgage based on substantially equal, monthly, fully amortizing payments of principal and interest using:

(A) The fully indexed rate as of a reasonable period of time before or after the date on which the creditor receives the consumer's written application for the standard mortgage;

(B) The term of the loan remaining as of the date on which the recast occurs, assuming all scheduled payments have been made up to the recast date and the payment due on the recast date is made and credited as of that date; and

(C) A remaining loan amount that is:

(1) For an adjustable-rate mortgage under paragraph (d)(1)(i)(A) of this section, the outstanding principal balance as of the date of the recast, assuming all scheduled payments have been made up to the recast date and the payment due on the recast date is made and credited as of that date;

(2) For an interest-only loan under paragraph (d)(1)(i)(B) of this section, the outstanding principal balance as of the date of the recast, assuming all scheduled payments have been made up to the recast date and the payment due on the recast date is made and credited as of that date; or

(3) For a negative amortization loan under paragraph (d)(1)(i)(C) of this section, the maximum loan amount, determined after adjusting for the outstanding principal balance.

(ii) Standard mortgage. For purposes of the comparison conducted pursuant to paragraph (d)(2)(ii) of this section, the monthly payment for a standard mortgage must be based on substantially equal, monthly, fully amortizing payments based on the maximum interest rate that may apply during the first five years after consummation.

(e) Qualified mortgages—

(1) Safe harbor and presumption of compliance—

(i) Safe harbor for loans that are not higher-priced covered transactions. A creditor or assignee of a qualified mortgage, as defined in paragraphs (e)(2), (e)(4), (e)(5), (e)(6), or (f) of this section, that is not a higher-priced covered transaction, as defined in paragraph (b)(4) of this section, complies with the repayment ability requirements of paragraph (c) of this section.

(ii) Presumption of compliance for higher-priced covered transactions.

(A) A creditor or assignee of a qualified mortgage, as defined in paragraph (e)(2), (e)(4), (e)(5), (e)(6), or (f) of this section, that is a higher-priced covered transaction, as defined in paragraph (b)(4) of this section, is presumed to comply with the repayment ability requirements of paragraph (c) of this section.

(B) To rebut the presumption of compliance described in paragraph (e)(1)(ii)(A) of this section, it must be proven that, despite meeting the prerequisites of paragraph (e)(2), (e)(4), (e)(5), (e)(6), or (f) of this section, the creditor did not make a reasonable and good faith determination of the consumer's repayment ability at the time of consummation, by showing that the consumer's income, debt obligations, alimony, child support, and the consumer's monthly payment (including mortgage-related obligations) on the covered transaction and on any simultaneous loans of which the creditor was aware at consummation would leave the consumer with insufficient residual income or assets other than the value of the dwelling (including any real property attached to the dwelling) that secures the loan with which to meet living expenses, including any recurring and material non-debt obligations of which the creditor was aware at the time of consummation.

(2) Qualified mortgage defined—general. Except as provided in paragraph (e)(4), (e)(5), (e)(6), or (f) of this section, a qualified mortgage is a covered transaction:

(i) That provides for regular periodic payments that are substantially equal, except for the effect that any interest rate change after consummation has on the payment in the case of an adjustable-rate or step-rate mortgage, that do not:

(A) Result in an increase of the principal balance;

(B) Allow the consumer to defer repayment of principal, except as provided in paragraph (f) of this section; or

(C) Result in a balloon payment, as defined in § 1026.18(s)(5)(i), except as provided in paragraph (f) of this section;

(ii) For which the loan term does not exceed 30 years;

(iii) For which the total points and fees payable in connection with the loan do not exceed the amounts specified in paragraph (e)(3) of this section;

(iv) For which the creditor underwrites the loan, taking into account the monthly payment for mortgage-related obligations, using:

(A) The maximum interest rate that may apply during the first five years after the date on which the first regular periodic payment will be due; and

(B) Periodic payments of principal and interest that will repay either:

(1) The outstanding principal balance over the remaining term of the loan as of the date the interest rate adjusts to the maximum interest rate set forth in paragraph (e)(2)(iv)(A) of this section, assuming the consumer will have made all required payments as due prior to that date; or

(2) The loan amount over the loan term;

(v) For which the creditor considers and verifies at or before consummation the following:

(A) The consumer's current or reasonably expected income or assets other than the value of the dwelling (including any real property attached to the dwelling) that secures the loan, in accordance with appendix Q and paragraphs (c)(2)(i) and (c)(4) of this section; and

(B) The consumer's current debt obligations, alimony, and child support in accordance with appendix Q and paragraphs (c)(2)(vi) and (c)(3) of this section; and

(vi) For which the ratio of the consumer's total monthly debt to total monthly income at the time of consummation does not exceed 43 percent. For purposes of this paragraph (e)(2)(vi), the ratio of the consumer's total monthly debt to total monthly income is determined:

(A) Except as provided in paragraph (e)(2)(vi)(B) of this section, in accordance with the standards in appendix Q;

(B) Using the consumer's monthly payment on:

(1) The covered transaction, including the monthly payment for mortgage-related obligations, in accordance with paragraph (e)(2)(iv) of this section; and

(2) Any simultaneous loan that the creditor knows or has reason to know will be made, in accordance with paragraphs (c)(2)(iv) and (c)(6) of this section.

(3) **Limits on points and fees for qualified mortgages.**

(i) Except as provided in paragraph (e)(3)(iii) of this section, a covered transaction is not a qualified mortgage unless the transaction's total points and fees, as defined in § 1026.32(b)(1), do not exceed:

(A) For a loan amount greater than or equal to $100,000 (indexed for inflation): 3 percent of the total loan amount;

(B) For a loan amount greater than or equal to $60,000 (indexed for inflation) but less than $100,000 (indexed for inflation): $3,000 (indexed for inflation);

(C) For a loan amount greater than or equal to $20,000 (indexed for inflation) but less than $60,000 (indexed for inflation): 5 percent of the total loan amount;

(D) For a loan amount greater than or equal to $12,500 (indexed for inflation) but less than $20,000 (indexed for inflation): $1,000 (indexed for inflation);

(E) For a loan amount less than $12,500 (indexed for inflation): 8 percent of the total loan amount.

(ii) The dollar amounts, including the loan amounts, in paragraph (e)(3)(i) of this section shall be adjusted annually on January 1 by the annual percentage change in the Consumer Price Index for All Urban Consumers (CPI-U) that was reported on the preceding June 1. See the official commentary to this paragraph (e)(3)(ii) for the current dollar amounts.

(iii) For covered transactions consummated on or before January 10, 2021, if the creditor or assignee determines after consummation that the transaction's total points and fees exceed the applicable limit under paragraph (e)(3)(i) of this section, the loan is not precluded from being a qualified mortgage, provided:

(A) The loan otherwise meets the requirements of paragraphs (e)(2), (e)(4), (e)(5), (e)(6), or (f) of this section, as applicable;

(B) The creditor or assignee pays to the consumer the amount described in paragraph (e)(3)(iv) of this section within 210 days after consummation and prior to the occurrence of any of the following events:

(1) The institution of any action by the consumer in connection with the loan;

(2) The receipt by the creditor, assignee, or servicer of written notice from the consumer that the transaction's total points and fees exceed the applicable limit under paragraph (e)(3)(i) of this section; or

(3) The consumer becoming 60 days past due on the legal obligation; and

(C) The creditor or assignee, as applicable, maintains and follows policies and procedures for post-consumation review of points and fees and for making payments to consumers in accordance with paragraphs (e)(3)(iii)(B) and (e)(3)(iv) of this section.

(iv) For purposes of paragraph (e)(3)(iii) of this section, the creditor or assignee must pay to the consumer an amount that is not less than the sum of the following:

(A) The dollar amount by which the transaction's total points and fees exceeds the applicable limit under paragraph (e)(3)(i) of this section; and

(B) Interest on the dollar amount described in paragraph (e)(3)(iv)(A) of this section, calculated using the contract interest rate applicable during the period from consummation until the payment described in this paragraph (e)(3)(iv) is made to the consumer.

(4) Qualified mortgage defined—special rules—

(i) General. Notwithstanding paragraph (e)(2) of this section, a qualified mortgage is a covered transaction that satisfies:

(A) The requirements of paragraphs (e)(2)(i) through (iii) of this section; and

(B) One or more of the criteria in paragraph (e)(4)(ii) of this section.

(ii) Eligible loans. A qualified mortgage under this paragraph (e)(4) must be one of the following at consummation:

(A) A loan that is eligible, except with regard to matters wholly unrelated to ability to repay:

(1) To be purchased or guaranteed by the Federal National Mortgage Association or the Federal Home Loan Mortgage Corporation operating under the conservatorship or receivership of the Federal Housing Finance Agency pursuant to section 1367(a) of the Federal Housing Enterprises Financial Safety and Soundness Act of 1992 (12 U.S.C. 4617(a)); or

(2) To be purchased or guaranteed by any limited-life regulatory entity succeeding the charter of either the Federal National Mortgage Association or the Federal Home Loan Mortgage Corporation pursuant to section 1367(i) of the Federal Housing Enterprises Financial Safety and Soundness Act of 1992 (12 U.S.C. 4617(i));

(B) A loan that is eligible to be insured, except with regard to matters wholly unrelated to ability to repay, by the U.S. Department of Housing and Urban Development under the National Housing Act (12 U.S.C. 1707 et seq.);

(C) A loan that is eligible to be guaranteed, except with regard to matters wholly unrelated to ability to repay, by the U.S. Department of Veterans Affairs;

(D) A loan that is eligible to be guaranteed, except with regard to matters wholly unrelated to ability to repay, by the U.S. Department of Agriculture pursuant to 42 U.S.C. 1472(h); or

(E) A loan that is eligible to be insured, except with regard to matters wholly unrelated to ability to repay, by the Rural Housing Service.

(iii) Sunset of special rules. (A) Each respective special rule described in paragraph (e)(4)(ii)(B), (C), (D), or (E) of this section shall expire on the effective date of a rule issued by each respective agency pursuant to its authority under TILA section 129C(b)(3)(ii) to define a qualified mortgage.

(B) Unless otherwise expired under paragraph (e)(4)(iii)(A) of this section, the special rules in this paragraph (e)(4) are available only for covered transactions consummated on or before January 10, 2021.

(5) Qualified mortgage defined—small creditor portfolio loans.

(i) Notwithstanding paragraph (e)(2) of this section, a qualified mortgage is a covered transaction:

(A) That satisfies the requirements of paragraph (e)(2) of this section other than the requirements of paragraph (e)(2)(vi) and without regard to the standards in appendix Q to this part;

(B) For which the creditor considers at or before consummation the consumer's monthly debt-to-income ratio or residual income and verifies the debt obligations and income used to determine that ratio in accordance with paragraph (c)(7) of this section, except that the calculation of the payment on the covered transaction for purposes of determining the consumer's total monthly debt obligations in paragraph (c)(7)(i)(A) shall be determined in accordance with paragraph (e)(2)(iv) of this section instead of paragraph (c)(5) of this section;

(C) That is not subject, at consummation, to a commitment to be acquired by another person, other than a person that satisfies the requirements of paragraph (e)(5)(i)(D) of this section; and

(D) For which the creditor satisfies the requirements stated in § 1026.35(b)(2)(iii)(B) and (C).

(ii) A qualified mortgage extended pursuant to paragraph (e)(5)(i) of this section immediately loses its status as a qualified mortgage under paragraph (e)(5)(i) if legal title to the qualified mortgage is sold, assigned, or otherwise transferred to another person except when:

(A) The qualified mortgage is sold, assigned, or otherwise transferred to another person three years or more after consummation of the qualified mortgage;

(B) The qualified mortgage is sold, assigned, or otherwise transferred to a creditor that satisfies the requirements of paragraph (e)(5)(i)(D) of this section;

(C) The qualified mortgage is sold, assigned, or otherwise transferred to another person pursuant to a capital restoration plan or other action under 12 U.S.C. 1831o, actions or instructions of any person acting as conservator, receiver, or bankruptcy trustee, an order of a State or Federal government agency with jurisdiction to examine the creditor pursuant to State or Federal law, or an agreement between the creditor and such an agency; or

(D) The qualified mortgage is sold, assigned, or otherwise transferred pursuant to a merger of the creditor with another person or acquisition of the creditor by another person or of another person by the creditor.

(6) **Qualified mortgage defined—temporary balloon-payment qualified mortgage rules.**

(i) Notwithstanding paragraph (e)(2) of this section, a qualified mortgage is a covered transaction:

(A) That satisfies the requirements of paragraph (f) of this section other than the requirements of paragraph (f)(1)(vi); and

(B) For which the creditor satisfies the requirements stated in § 1026.35(b)(2)(iii)(B) and (C).

(ii) The provisions of this paragraph (e)(6) apply only to covered transactions for which the application was received before April 1, 2016.

(f) **Balloon-payment qualified mortgages made by certain creditors—**

(1) **Exemption.** Notwithstanding paragraph (e)(2) of this section, a qualified mortgage may provide for a balloon payment, provided:

(i) The loan satisfies the requirements for a qualified mortgage in paragraphs (e)(2)(i)(A), (e)(2)(ii), (e)(2)(iii), and (e)(2)(v) of this section, but without regard to the standards in appendix Q;

(ii) The creditor determines at or before consummation that the consumer can make all of the scheduled payments under the terms of the legal obligation, as described in paragraph (f)(1)(iv) of this section, together with the consumer's monthly payments for all mortgage-related obligations and excluding the balloon payment, from the consumer's current or reasonably expected income or assets other than the dwelling that secures the loan;

(iii) The creditor considers at or before consummation the consumer's monthly debt-to-income ratio or residual income and verifies the debt obligations and income used to determine that ratio in accordance with paragraph (c)(7) of this section, except that the calculation of the payment on the covered transaction for purposes of determining the consumer's total monthly debt obligations in (c)(7)(i)(A) shall be determined in accordance with paragraph (f)(iv)(A) of this section, together with the consumer's monthly payments for all mortgage-related obligations and excluding the balloon payment;

(iv) The legal obligation provides for:

(A) Scheduled payments that are substantially equal, calculated using an amortization period that does not exceed 30 years;

(B) An interest rate that does not increase over the term of the loan; and

(C) A loan term of five years or longer.

(v) The loan is not subject, at consummation, to a commitment to be acquired by another person, other than a person that satisfies the requirements of paragraph (f)(1)(vi) of this section; and

(vi) The creditor satisfies the requirements stated in § 1026.35(b)(2)(iii)(A), (B), and (C).

(2) **Post-consummation transfer of balloon-payment qualified mortgage.** A balloon-payment qualified mortgage, extended pursuant to paragraph (f)(1), immediately loses its status as a qualified mortgage under paragraph (f)(1) if legal title to the balloon-payment qualified mortgage is sold, assigned, or otherwise transferred to another person except when:

(i) The balloon-payment qualified mortgage is sold, assigned, or otherwise transferred to another person three years or more after consummation of the balloon-payment qualified mortgage;

(ii) The balloon-payment qualified mortgage is sold, assigned, or otherwise transferred to a creditor that satisfies the requirements of paragraph (f)(1)(vi) of this section;

(iii) The balloon-payment qualified mortgage is sold, assigned, or otherwise transferred to another person pursuant to a capital restoration plan or other action under 12 U.S.C. 1831o, actions or instructions of any person acting as conservator, receiver or bankruptcy trustee, an order of a State or Federal governmental agency with jurisdiction to examine the creditor pursuant to State or Federal law, or an agreement between the creditor and such an agency; or

(iv) The balloon-payment qualified mortgage is sold, assigned, or otherwise transferred pursuant to a merger of the creditor with another person or acquisition of the creditor by another person or of another person by the creditor.

(g) **Prepayment penalties—**

(1) **When permitted.** A covered transaction must not include a prepayment penalty unless:

(i) The prepayment penalty is otherwise permitted by law; and

(ii) The transaction:

(A) Has an annual percentage rate that cannot increase after consummation;

(B) Is a qualified mortgage under paragraph (e)(2), (e)(4), (e)(5), (e)(6), or (f) of this section; and

(C) Is not a higher-priced mortgage loan, as defined in § 1026.35(a).

(2)   Limits on prepayment penalties. A prepayment penalty:

(i)   Must not apply after the three-year period following consummation; and

(ii)   Must not exceed the following percentages of the amount of the outstanding loan balance prepaid:

(A)   2 percent, if incurred during the first two years following consummation; and

(B)   1 percent, if incurred during the third year following consummation.

(3)   Alternative offer required. A creditor must not offer a consumer a covered transaction with a prepayment penalty unless the creditor also offers the consumer an alternative covered transaction without a prepayment penalty and the alternative covered transaction:

(i)   Has an annual percentage rate that cannot increase after consummation and has the same type of interest rate as the covered transaction with a prepayment penalty; for purposes of this paragraph (g), the term "type of interest rate" refers to whether a transaction:

(A)   Is a fixed-rate mortgage, as defined in § 1026.18(s)(7)(iii); or

(B)   Is a step-rate mortgage, as defined in § 1026.18(s)(7)(ii);

(ii)   Has the same loan term as the loan term for the covered transaction with a prepayment penalty;

(iii)   Satisfies the periodic payment conditions under paragraph (e)(2)(i) of this section;

(iv)   Satisfies the points and fees conditions under paragraph (e)(2)(iii) of this section, based on the information known to the creditor at the time the transaction is offered; and

(v)   Is a transaction for which the creditor has a good faith belief that the consumer likely qualifies, based on the information known to the creditor at the time the creditor offers the covered transaction without a prepayment penalty.

(4)   Offer through a mortgage broker. If the creditor offers a covered transaction with a prepayment penalty to the consumer through a mortgage broker, as defined in § 1026.36(a)(2), the creditor must:

(i)   Present the mortgage broker an alternative covered transaction without a prepayment penalty that satisfies the requirements of paragraph (g)(3) of this section; and

(ii)   Establish by agreement that the mortgage broker must present the consumer an alternative covered transaction without a prepayment penalty that satisfies the requirements of paragraph (g)(3) of this section, offered by:

(A)   The creditor; or

(B)   Another creditor, if the transaction offered by the other creditor has a lower interest rate or a lower total dollar amount of discount points and origination points or fees.

(5)   Creditor that is a loan originator. If the creditor is a loan originator, as defined in § 1026.36(a)(1), and the creditor presents the consumer a covered transaction offered by a person to which the creditor would assign the covered transaction after consummation, the creditor must present the consumer an alternative covered transaction without a prepayment penalty that satisfies the requirements of paragraph (g)(3) of this section, offered by:

(i)   The assignee; or

(ii)   Another person, if the transaction offered by the other person has a lower interest rate or a lower total dollar amount of origination discount points and points or fees.

(6)   Applicability. This paragraph (g) applies only if a covered transaction is consummated with a prepayment penalty and is not violated if:

(i)   A covered transaction is consummated without a prepayment penalty; or

(ii)   The creditor and consumer do not consummate a covered transaction.

(h)   Evasion; open-end credit. In connection with credit secured by a consumer's dwelling that does not meet the definition of open-end credit in § 1026.2(a)(20), a creditor shall not structure the loan as an open-end plan to evade the requirements of this section.

§§ 1026.44 to 1026.45   [Reserved]

SUBPART F. SPECIAL RULES FOR PRIVATE EDUCATION LOANS

§ 1026.46   Special disclosure requirements for private education loans.

(a)   Coverage. The requirements of this subpart apply to private education loans as defined in § 1026.46(b)(5). A creditor may, at its option, comply with the requirements of this subpart for an extension of credit subject to §§ 1026.17 and 1026.18 that is extended to a consumer for expenses incurred after graduation from a law, medical, dental, veterinary, or other graduate school and related to relocation, study for a bar or other examination, participation in an internship or residency program, or similar purposes.

(1)   **Relation to other subparts in this part.** Except as otherwise specifically provided, the requirements and limitations of this subpart are in addition to and not in lieu of those contained in other subparts of this Part.

(2)   [Reserved]

(b)   Definitions. For purposes of this subpart, the following definitions apply:

(1)   Covered educational institution means:

(i)   An educational institution that meets the definition of an institution of higher education, as defined in paragraph (b)(2) of this section, without regard to the institution's accreditation status; and

(ii)   Includes an agent, officer, or employee of the institution of higher education. An agent means an institution-affiliated organization as defined by section 151 of the Higher Education Act of 1965 (20 U.S.C. 1019) or an officer or employee of an institution-affiliated organization.

(2)   Institution of higher education has the same meaning as in sections 101 and 102 of the Higher Education Act of 1965 (20 U.S.C. 1001–1002) and the implementing regulations published by the U.S. Department of Education.

(3)   Postsecondary educational expenses means any of the expenses that are listed as part of the cost of attendance, as defined under section 472 of the Higher Education Act of 1965 (20 U.S.C. 1087ll), of a student at a covered educational institution. These expenses include tuition and fees, books, supplies, miscellaneous personal expenses, room and board, and an allowance for any loan fee, origination fee, or insurance premium charged to a student or parent for a loan incurred to cover the cost of the student's attendance.

(4)   Preferred lender arrangement has the same meaning as in section 151 of the Higher Education Act of 1965 (20 U.S.C. 1019).

(5)   Private education loan means an extension of credit that:

(i)   Is not made, insured, or guaranteed under Title IV of the Higher Education Act of 1965 (20 U.S.C. 1070 et seq.);

(ii)   Is extended to a consumer expressly, in whole or in part, for postsecondary educational expenses, regardless of whether the loan is provided by the educational institution that the student attends;

(iii) Does not include open-end credit or any loan that is secured by real property or a dwelling; and

(iv) Does not include an extension of credit in which the covered educational institution is the creditor if:

(A) The term of the extension of credit is 90 days or less; or

(B) an interest rate will not be applied to the credit balance and the term of the extension of credit is one year or less, even if the credit is payable in more than four installments.

(c)   Form of disclosures.

(1)   Clear and conspicuous. The disclosures required by this subpart shall be made clearly and conspicuously.

(2)   Transaction disclosures.

(i)   The disclosures required under §§ 1026.47(b) and (c) shall be made in writing, in a form that the consumer may keep. The disclosures shall be grouped together, shall be segregated from everything else, and shall not contain any information not directly related to the disclosures required under §§ 1026.47(b) and (c), which include the disclosures required under § 1026.18.

(ii)   The disclosures may include an acknowledgement of receipt, the date of the transaction, and the consumer's name, address, and account number. The following disclosures may be made together with or separately from other required disclosures: the creditor's identity under § 1026.18(a), insurance or debt cancellation under § 1026.18(n), and certain security interest charges under § 1026.18(o).

(iii)   The term "finance charge" and corresponding amount, when required to be disclosed under § 1026.18(d), and the interest rate required to be disclosed under §§ 1026.47(b)(1)(i) and (c)(1), shall be more conspicuous than any other disclosure, except the creditor's identity under § 1026.18(a).

(3)   Electronic disclosures. The disclosures required under §§ 1026.47(b) and (c) may be provided to the consumer in electronic form, subject to compliance with the consumer consent and other applicable provisions of the Electronic Signatures in Global and National Commerce Act (E-Sign Act) (15 U.S.C. 7001 et seq.). The disclosures required by § 1026.47(a) may be provided to the consumer in electronic form on or with an application or solicitation that is accessed by the consumer in electronic form without regard to the consumer consent or other provisions of the E-Sign Act. The form required to be received under § 1026.48(e) may be accepted by the creditor in electronic form as provided for in that section.

(d)   Timing of disclosures.

(1)   Application or solicitation disclosures.

(i)   The disclosures required by § 1026.47(a) shall be provided on or with any application or solicitation. For purposes of this subpart, the term solicitation means an offer of credit that does not require the consumer to complete an application. A "firm offer of credit" as defined in section 603(*l*) of the Fair Credit Reporting Act (15 U.S.C. 1681a(*l*)) is a solicitation for purposes of this section.

(ii)   The creditor may, at its option, disclose orally the information in § 1026.47(a) in a telephone application or solicitation. Alternatively, if the creditor does not disclose orally the information in § 1026.47(a), the creditor must provide the disclosures or place them in the mail no later than three business days after the consumer has applied for the credit, except that, if the creditor either denies the consumer's application or provides or places in the mail the disclosures in § 1026.47(b) no later than three business days after the consumer requests the credit, the creditor need not also provide the § 1026.47(a) disclosures.

(iii)   Notwithstanding paragraph (d)(1)(i) of this section, for a loan that the consumer may use for multiple purposes including, but not limited to, postsecondary educational expenses, the creditor need not provide the disclosures required by § 1026.47(a).

(2) Approval disclosures. The creditor shall provide the disclosures required by § 1026.47(b) before consummation on or with any notice of approval provided to the consumer. If the creditor mails notice of approval, the disclosures must be mailed with the notice. If the creditor communicates notice of approval by telephone, the creditor must mail the disclosures within three business days of providing the notice of approval. If the creditor communicates notice of approval electronically, the creditor may provide the disclosures in electronic form in accordance with § 1026.46(d)(3); otherwise the creditor must mail the disclosures within three business days of communicating the notice of approval. If the creditor communicates approval in person, the creditor must provide the disclosures to the consumer at that time.

(3) Final disclosures. The disclosures required by § 1026.47(c) shall be provided after the consumer accepts the loan in accordance with § 1026.48(c)(1).

(4) Receipt of mailed disclosures. If the disclosures under paragraphs (d)(1), (d)(2) or (d)(3) of this section are mailed to the consumer, the consumer is considered to have received them three business days after they are mailed.

(e) Basis of disclosures and use of estimates.

(1) Legal obligation. Disclosures shall reflect the terms of the legal obligation between the parties.

(2) Estimates. If any information necessary for an accurate disclosure is unknown to the creditor, the creditor shall make the disclosure based on the best information reasonably available at the time the disclosure is provided, and shall state clearly that the disclosure is an estimate.

(f) Multiple creditors; multiple consumers. If a transaction involves more than one creditor, only one set of disclosures shall be given and the creditors shall agree among themselves which creditor will comply with the requirements that this part imposes on any or all of them. If there is more than one consumer, the disclosures may be made to any consumer who is primarily liable on the obligation.

(g) Effect of subsequent events.

(1) Approval disclosures. If a disclosure under § 1026.47(b) becomes inaccurate because of an event that occurs after the creditor delivers the required disclosures, the inaccuracy is not a violation of Regulation Z (12 CFR part 1026), although new disclosures may be required under § 1026.48(c).

(2) Final disclosures. If a disclosure under § 1026.47(c) becomes inaccurate because of an event that occurs after the creditor delivers the required disclosures, the inaccuracy is not a violation of Regulation Z (12 CFR part 1026).

§ 1026.47 Content of disclosures.

(a) Application or solicitation disclosures. A creditor shall provide the disclosures required under paragraph (a) of this section on or with a solicitation or an application for a private education loan.

(1) Interest Rates.

(i) The interest rate or range of interest rates applicable to the loan and actually offered by the creditor at the time of application or solicitation. If the rate will depend, in part, on a later determination of the consumer's creditworthiness or other factors, a statement that the rate for which the consumer may qualify will depend on the consumer's creditworthiness and other factors, if applicable.

(ii) Whether the interest rates applicable to the loan are fixed or variable.

(iii) If the interest rate may increase after consummation of the transaction, any limitations on the interest rate adjustments, or lack thereof; a statement that the consumer's actual rate could be higher or lower than the rates disclosed under paragraph (a)(1)(i) of this section, if applicable; and, if the limitation is determined by applicable law, that fact.

(iv) Whether the applicable interest rates typically will be higher if the loan is not co-signed or guaranteed.

(2) Fees and default or late payment costs.

(i) An itemization of the fees or range of fees required to obtain the private education loan.

(ii) Any fees, changes to the interest rate, and adjustments to principal based on the consumer's defaults or late payments.

(3) Repayment terms.

(i) The term of the loan, which is the period during which regularly scheduled payments of principal and interest will be due.

(ii) A description of any payment deferral options, or, if the consumer does not have the option to defer payments, that fact.

(iii) For each payment deferral option applicable while the student is enrolled at a covered educational institution:

(A) Whether interest will accrue during the deferral period; and

(B) If interest accrues, whether payment of interest may be deferred and added to the principal balance.

(iv) A statement that if the consumer files for bankruptcy, the consumer may still be required to pay back the loan.

(4) Cost estimates. An example of the total cost of the loan calculated as the total of payments over the term of the loan:

(i) Using the highest rate of interest disclosed under paragraph (a)(1) of this section and including all finance charges applicable to loans at that rate;

(ii) Using an amount financed of $10,000, or $5000 if the creditor only offers loans of this type for less than $10,000; and

(iii) Calculated for each payment option.

(5) Eligibility. Any age or school enrollment eligibility requirements relating to the consumer or cosigner.

(6) Alternatives to private education loans.

(i) A statement that the consumer may qualify for Federal student financial assistance through a program under Title IV of the Higher Education Act of 1965 (20 U.S.C. 1070 et seq.).

(ii) The interest rates available under each program under Title IV of the Higher Education Act of 1965 (20 U.S.C. 1070 et seq.) and whether the rates are fixed or variable.

(iii) A statement that the consumer may obtain additional information concerning Federal student financial assistance from the institution of higher education that the student attends, or at the Web site of the U.S. Department of Education, including an appropriate Web site address.

(iv) A statement that a covered educational institution may have school-specific education loan benefits and terms not detailed on the disclosure form.

(7) Rights of the consumer. A statement that if the loan is approved, the terms of the loan will be available and will not change for 30 days except as a result of adjustments to the interest rate and other changes permitted by law.

(8) Self-certification information. A statement that, before the loan may be consummated, the consumer must complete the self-certification form and that the form may be obtained from the institution of higher education that the student attends.

(b) Approval disclosures. On or with any notice of approval provided to the consumer, the creditor shall disclose the information required under § 1026.18 and the following information:

(1) Interest rate.

(i) The interest rate applicable to the loan.

(ii) Whether the interest rate is fixed or variable.

(iii) If the interest rate may increase after consummation of the transaction, any limitations on the rate adjustments, or lack thereof.

(2) Fees and default or late payment costs.

(i) An itemization of the fees or range of fees required to obtain the private education loan.

(ii) Any fees, changes to the interest rate, and adjustments to principal based on the consumer's defaults or late payments.

(3) Repayment terms.

(i) The principal amount of the loan for which the consumer has been approved.

(ii) The term of the loan, which is the period during which regularly scheduled payments of principal and interest will be due.

(iii) A description of the payment deferral option chosen by the consumer, if applicable, and any other payment deferral options that the consumer may elect at a later time.

(iv) Any payments required while the student is enrolled at a covered educational institution, based on the deferral option chosen by the consumer.

(v) The amount of any unpaid interest that will accrue while the student is enrolled at a covered educational institution, based on the deferral option chosen by the consumer.

(vi) A statement that if the consumer files for bankruptcy, the consumer may still be required to pay back the loan.

(vii) An estimate of the total amount of payments calculated based on:

(A) The interest rate applicable to the loan. Compliance with § 1026.18(h) constitutes compliance with this requirement.

(B) The maximum possible rate of interest for the loan or, if a maximum rate cannot be determined, a rate of 25%.

(C) If a maximum rate cannot be determined, the estimate of the total amount for repayment must include a statement that there is no maximum rate and that the total amount for repayment disclosed under paragraph (b)(3)(vii)(B) of this section is an estimate and will be higher if the applicable interest rate increases.

(viii) The maximum monthly payment based on the maximum rate of interest for the loan or, if a maximum rate cannot be determined, a rate of 25%. If a maximum cannot be determined, a statement that there is no maximum rate and that the monthly payment amount disclosed is an estimate and will be higher if the applicable interest rate increases.

(4) Alternatives to private education loans.

(i) A statement that the consumer may qualify for Federal student financial assistance through a program under Title IV of the Higher Education Act of 1965 (20 U.S.C. 1070 et seq.).

(ii) The interest rates available under each program under Title IV of the Higher Education Act of 1965 (20 U.S.C. 1070 et seq.), and whether the rates are fixed or variable.

(iii) A statement that the consumer may obtain additional information concerning Federal student financial assistance from the institution of higher education that the student attends, or at the Web site of the U.S. Department of Education, including an appropriate Web site address.

(5) Rights of the consumer.

(i) A statement that the consumer may accept the terms of the loan until the acceptance period under § 1026.48(c)(1) has expired. The statement must include the specific date on which the acceptance period expires, based on the date upon which the consumer receives the disclosures required under this subsection for the loan. The disclosure must also specify the method or methods by which the consumer may communicate acceptance.

(ii) A statement that, except for changes to the interest rate and other changes permitted by law, the rates and terms of the loan may not be changed by the creditor during the period described in paragraph (b)(5)(i) of this section.

(c) Final disclosures. After the consumer has accepted the loan in accordance with § 1026.48(c)(1), the creditor shall disclose to the consumer the information required by § 1026.18 and the following information:

(1) Interest rate. Information required to be disclosed under § 1026.47(b)(1).

(2) Fees and default or late payment costs. Information required to be disclosed under § 1026.47(b)(2).

(3) Repayment terms. Information required to be disclosed under § 1026.47(b)(3).

(4) Cancellation right. A statement that:

(i) The consumer has the right to cancel the loan, without penalty, at any time before the cancellation period under § 1026.48(d) expires, and

(ii) Loan proceeds will not be disbursed until after the cancellation period under § 1026.48(d) expires. The statement must include the specific date on which the cancellation period expires and state that the consumer may cancel by that date. The statement must also specify the method or methods by which the consumer may cancel. If the creditor permits cancellation by mail, the statement must specify that the consumer's mailed request will be deemed timely if placed in the mail not later than the cancellation date specified on the disclosure. The disclosures required by this paragraph (c)(4) must be made more conspicuous than any other disclosure required under this section, except for the finance charge, the interest rate, and the creditor's identity, which must be disclosed in accordance with the requirements of § 1026.46(c)(2)(iii).

§ 1026.48   Limitations on private education loans.

(a) Co-branding prohibited.

(1) Except as provided in paragraph (b) of this section, a creditor, other than the covered educational institution itself, shall not use the name, emblem, mascot, or logo of a covered educational institution, or other words, pictures, or symbols identified with a covered educational institution, in the marketing of private education loans in a way that implies that the covered education institution endorses the creditor's loans.

(2) A creditor's marketing of private education loans does not imply that the covered education institution endorses the creditor's loans if the marketing includes a clear and conspicuous disclosure that is equally prominent and closely proximate to the reference to the covered educational institution that the covered educational institution does not endorse the creditor's loans and that the creditor is not affiliated with the covered educational institution.

(b) Endorsed lender arrangements. If a creditor and a covered educational institution have entered into an arrangement where the covered educational institution agrees to endorse the creditor's private education loans, and such arrangement is not prohibited by other applicable law or regulation, paragraph (a)(1) of this section does not apply if the private education loan marketing includes a clear and conspicuous disclosure that is equally prominent and closely proximate to the reference to the covered educational institution that the creditor's loans are not offered or made by the covered educational institution, but are made by the creditor.

(c) Consumer's right to accept.

(1) The consumer has the right to accept the terms of a private education loan at any time within 30 calendar days following the date on which the consumer receives the disclosures required under § 1026.47(b).

(2) Except for changes permitted under paragraphs (c)(3) and (c)(4), the rate and terms of the private education loan that are required to be disclosed under §§ 1026.47(b) and (c) may not be changed by the creditor prior to the earlier of:

(i) The date of disbursement of the loan; or

(ii) The expiration of the 30 calendar day period described in paragraph (c)(1) of this section if the consumer has not accepted the loan within that time.

(3) Exceptions not requiring re-disclosure.

(i) Notwithstanding paragraph (c)(2) of this section, nothing in this section prevents the creditor from:

(A) Withdrawing an offer before consummation of the transaction if the extension of credit would be prohibited by law or if the creditor has reason to believe that the consumer has committed fraud in connection with the loan application;

(B) Changing the interest rate based on adjustments to the index used for a loan;

(C) Changing the interest rate and terms if the change will unequivocally benefit the consumer; or

(D) Reducing the loan amount based upon a certification or other information received from the covered educational institution, or from the consumer, indicating that the student's cost of attendance has decreased or the consumer's other financial aid has increased. A creditor may make corresponding changes to the rate and other terms only to the extent that the consumer would have received the terms if the consumer had applied for the reduced loan amount.

(ii) If the creditor changes the rate or terms of the loan under this paragraph (c)(3), the creditor need not provide the disclosures required under § 1026.47(b) for the new loan terms, nor need the creditor provide an additional 30-day period to the consumer to accept the new terms of the loan under paragraph (c)(1) of this section.

(4) Exceptions requiring re-disclosure.

(i) Notwithstanding paragraphs (c)(2) or (c)(3) of this section, nothing in this section prevents the creditor, at its option, from changing the rate or terms of the loan to accommodate a specific request by the consumer. For example, if the consumer requests a different repayment option, the creditor may, but need not, offer to provide the requested repayment option and make any other changes to the rate and terms.

(ii) If the creditor changes the rate or terms of the loan under this paragraph (c)(4), the creditor shall provide the disclosures required under § 1026.47(b) and shall provide the consumer the 30-day period to accept the loan under paragraph (c)(1) of this section. The creditor shall not make further changes to the rates and terms of the loan, except as specified in paragraphs (c)(3) and (4) of this section. Except as permitted under § 1026.48(c)(3), unless the consumer accepts the loan offered by the creditor in response to the consumer's request, the creditor may not withdraw or change the rates or terms of the loan for which the consumer was approved prior to the consumer's request for a change in loan terms.

(d) Consumer's right to cancel. The consumer may cancel a private education loan, without penalty, until midnight of the third business day following the date on which the consumer receives the disclosures required by § 1026.47(c). No funds may be disbursed for a private education loan until the three-business day period has expired.

(e)   Self-certification form. For a private education loan intended to be used for the postsecondary educational expenses of a student while the student is attending an institution of higher education, the creditor shall obtain from the consumer or the institution of higher education the form developed by the Secretary of Education under section 155 of the Higher Education Act of 1965, signed by the consumer, in written or electronic form, before consummating the private education loan.

(f)   Provision of information by preferred lenders. A creditor that has a preferred lender arrangement with a covered educational institution shall provide to the covered educational institution the information required under §§ 1026.47(a)(1) through (5), for each type of private education loan that the lender plans to offer to consumers for students attending the covered educational institution for the period beginning July 1 of the current year and ending June 30 of the following year. The creditor shall provide the information annually by the later of the 1st day of April, or within 30 days after entering into, or learning the creditor is a party to, a preferred lender arrangement.

SUBPART G. SPECIAL RULES APPLICABLE TO CREDIT CARD ACCOUNTS AND OPEN-END CREDIT OFFERED TO COLLEGE STUDENTS

§ 1026.51   Ability to Pay.

(a)   General rule.

(1)(i)   Consideration of ability to pay. A card issuer must not open a credit card account for a consumer under an open-end (not home-secured) consumer credit plan, or increase any credit limit applicable to such account, unless the card issuer considers the consumer's ability to make the required minimum periodic payments under the terms of the account based on the consumer's income or assets and the consumer's current obligations.

(ii)   Reasonable policies and procedures. Card issuers must establish and maintain reasonable written policies and procedures to consider the consumer's ability to make the required minimum payments under the terms of the account based on a consumer's income or assets and a consumer's current obligations. Reasonable policies and procedure include treating any income and assets to which the consumer has a reasonable expectation of access as the consumer's income or assets, or limiting consideration of the consumer's income or assets to the consumer's independent income and assets. Reasonable policies and procedures also include consideration of at least one of the following: The ratio of debt obligations to income; the ratio of debt obligations to assets; or the income the consumer will have after paying debt obligations. It would be unreasonable for a card issuer to not review any information about a consumer's income or assets and current obligations, or to issue a credit card to a consumer who does not have any income or assets.

(2)   Minimum periodic payments.

(i)   Reasonable method. For purposes of paragraph (a)(1) of this section, a card issuer must use a reasonable method for estimating the minimum periodic payments the consumer would be required to pay under the terms of the account.

(ii)   Safe harbor. A card issuer complies with paragraph (a)(2)(i) of this section if it estimates required minimum periodic payments using the following method:

(A)   The card issuer assumes utilization, from the first day of the billing cycle, of the full credit line that the issuer is considering offering to the consumer; and

(B)   The card issuer uses a minimum payment formula employed by the issuer for the product the issuer is considering offering to the consumer or, in the case of an existing account, the minimum payment formula that currently applies to that account, provided that:

(1)   If the applicable minimum payment formula includes interest charges, the card issuer estimates those charges using an interest rate that the issuer is considering offering to the consumer for purchases or, in the case of an existing account, the interest rate that currently applies to purchases; and

(2) If the applicable minimum payment formula includes mandatory fees, the card issuer must assume that such fees have been charged to the account.

(b) Rules affecting young consumers.

(1) Applications from young consumers. A card issuer may not open a credit card account under an open-end (not home-secured) consumer credit plan for a consumer less than 21 years old, unless the consumer has submitted a written application and the cardissuer has:

(i) Financial information indicating the consumer has an independent ability to make the required minimum periodic payments on the proposed extension of credit in connection with the account; or

(ii)(A) A signed agreement of a cosigner, guarantor, or joint applicant who is at least 21 years old to be either secondarily liable for any debt on the account incurred by the consumer before the consumer has attained the age of 21 or jointly liable with the consumer for any debt on the account; and

(B) Financial information indicating such cosigner, guarantor, or joint applicant has the ability to make the required minimum periodic payments on such debts, consistent with paragraph (a) of this section.

(2) Credit line increases for young consumers.

(i) If a credit card account has been opened pursuant to paragraph (b)(1)(i) of this section, no increase in the credit limit may be made on such account before the consumer attains the age of 21 unless:

(A) At the time of the contemplated increase, the consumer has an independent ability to make the required minimum periodic payments on the increased limit consistent with paragraph (b)(1)(i) of this section; or

(B) A cosigner, guarantor, or joint applicant who is at least 21 years old agrees in writing to assume liability for any debt incurred on the account, consistent with paragraph (b)(1)(ii) of this section.

(ii) If a credit card account has been opened pursuant to paragraph (b)(1)(ii) of this section, no increase in the credit limit may be made on such account before the consumer attains the age of 21 unless the cosigner, guarantor, or joint accountholder who assumed liability at account opening agrees in writing to assume liability on the increase.

§ 1026.52   Limitations on fees.

(a) Limitations during first year after account opening.

(1) General rule. Except as provided in paragraph (a)(2) of this section, the total amount of fees a consumer is required to pay with respect to a credit card account under an open-end (not home-secured) consumer credit plan during the first year after account opening must not exceed 25 percent of the credit limit in effect when the account is opened. For purposes of this paragraph, an account is considered open no earlier than the date on which the account may first be used by the consumer to engage in transactions.

(2) Fees not subject to limitations. Paragraph (a) of this section does not apply to:

(i) Late payment fees, over-the-limit fees, and returned-payment fees; or

(ii) Fees that the consumer is not required to pay with respect to the account.

(3) Rule of construction. Paragraph (a) of this section does not authorize the imposition or payment of fees or charges otherwise prohibited by law.

(b) Limitations on penalty fees. A card issuer must not impose a fee for violating the terms or other requirements of a credit card account under an open-end (not home-secured) consumer credit plan unless the dollar amount of the fee is consistent with paragraphs (b)(1) and (b)(2) of this section.

(1) **General rule.** Except as provided in paragraph (b)(2) of this section, a card issuer may impose a fee for violating the terms or other requirements of a credit card account under an open-end (not home-secured) consumer credit plan if the dollar amount of the fee is consistent with either paragraph (b)(1)(i) or (b)(1)(ii) of this section.

(i) **Fees based on costs.** A card issuer may impose a fee for violating the terms or other requirements of an account if the card issuer has determined that the dollar amount of the fee represents a reasonable proportion of the total costs incurred by the card issuer as a result of that type of violation. A card issuer must reevaluate this determination at least once every twelve months. If as a result of the reevaluation the card issuer determines that a lower fee represents a reasonable proportion of the total costs incurred by the card issuer as a result of that type of violation, the card issuer must begin imposing the lower fee within 45 days after completing the reevaluation. If as a result of the reevaluation the card issuer determines that a higher fee represents a reasonable proportion of the total costs incurred by the card issuer as a result of that type of violation, the card issuer may begin imposing the higher fee after complying with the notice requirements in § 1026.9.

(ii) **Safe harbors.** A card issuer may impose a fee for violating the terms or other requirements of an account if the dollar amount of the fee does not exceed, as applicable:

(A) $27.00;

(B) $37.00 if the card issuer previously imposed a fee pursuant to paragraph (b)(1)(ii)(A) of this section for a violation of the same type that occurred during the same billing cycle or one of the next six billing cycles; or

(C) Three percent of the delinquent balance on a charge card account that requires payment of outstanding balances in full at the end of each billing cycle if the card issuer has not received the required payment for two or more consecutive billing cycles.

(D) The amounts in paragraphs (b)(1)(ii)(A) and (b)(1)(ii)(B) of this section will be adjusted annually by the Bureau to reflect changes in the Consumer Price Index.

(2) **Prohibited fees.**

(i) **Fees that exceed dollar amount associated with violation.**

(A) **Generally.** A card issuer must not impose a fee for violating the terms or other requirements of a credit card account under an open-end (not home-secured) consumer credit plan that exceeds the dollar amount associated with the violation.

(B) **No dollar amount associated with violation.** A card issuer must not impose a fee for violating the terms or other requirements of a credit card account under an open-end (not home-secured) consumer credit plan when there is no dollar amount associated with the violation. For purposes of paragraph (b)(2)(i) of this section, there is no dollar amount associated with the following violations:

(1) Transactions that the card issuer declines to authorize;

(2) Account inactivity; and

(3) The closure or termination of an account.

(ii) **Multiple fees based on a single event or transaction.** A card issuer must not impose more than one fee for violating the terms or other requirements of a credit card account under an open-end (not home-secured) consumer credit plan based on a single event or transaction. A card issuer may, at its option, comply with this prohibition by imposing no more than one fee for violating the terms or other requirements of an account during a billing cycle.

§ 1026.53   Allocation of payments.

(a) **General rule.** Except as provided in paragraph (b) of this section, when a consumer makes a payment in excess of the required minimum periodic payment for a credit card account under an open-end (not home-secured) consumer credit plan, the card issuer must allocate the excess amount first to the balance with the highest annual percentage rate and any remaining portion to the other balances in descending order based on the applicable annual percentage rate.

(b) **Special rules.**

(1) **Accounts with balances subject to deferred interest or similar program.** When a balance on a credit card account under an open-end (not home-secured) consumer credit plan is subject to a deferred interest or similar program that provides that a consumer will not be obligated to pay interest that accrues on the balance if the balance is paid in full prior to the expiration of a specified period of time:

(i) **Last two billing cycles.** The card issuer must allocate any amount paid by the consumer in excess of the required minimum periodic payment consistent with paragraph (a) of this section, except that, during the two billing cycles immediately preceding expiration of the specified period, the excess amount must be allocated first to the balance subject to the deferred interest or similar program and any remaining portion allocated to any other balances consistent with paragraph (a) of this section; or

(ii) **Consumer request.** The card issuer may at its option allocate any amount paid by the consumer in excess of the required minimum periodic payment among the balances on the account in the manner requested by the consumer.

(2) **Accounts with secured balances.** When a balance on a credit card account under an open-end (not home-secured) consumer credit plan is secured, the card issuer may at its option allocate any amount paid by the consumer in excess of the required minimum periodic payment to that balance if requested by the consumer.

§ 1026.54   Limitations on the imposition of finance charges.

(a) **Limitations on imposing finance charges as a result of the loss of a grace period.**

(1) **General rule.** Except as provided in paragraph (b) of this section, a card issuer must not impose finance charges as a result of the loss of a grace period on a credit card account under an open-end (not home-secured) consumer credit plan if those finance charges are based on:

(i) Balances for days in billing cycles that precede the most recent billing cycle; or

(ii) Any portion of a balance subject to a grace period that was repaid prior to the expiration of the grace period.

(2) **Definition of grace period.** For purposes of paragraph (a)(1) of this section, "grace period" has the same meaning as in § 1026.5(b)(2)(ii)(B)(3).

(b) **Exceptions.** Paragraph (a) of this section does not apply to:

(1) Adjustments to finance charges as a result of the resolution of a dispute under § 1026.12 or § 1026.13; or

(2) Adjustments to finance charges as a result of the return of a payment.

§ 1026.55   Limitations on increasing annual percentage rates, fees, and charges.

(a) **General rule.** Except as provided in paragraph (b) of this section, a card issuer must not increase an annual percentage rate or a fee or charge required to be disclosed under § 1026.6(b)(2)(ii), (b)(2)(iii), or (b)(2)(xii) on a credit card account under an open-end (not home-secured) consumer credit plan.

(b) **Exceptions.** A card issuer may increase an annual percentage rate or a fee or charge required to be disclosed under § 1026.6(b)(2)(ii), (b)(2)(iii), or (b)(2)(xii) pursuant to an exception set forth in this paragraph even if that increase would not be permitted under a different exception.

(1) **Temporary rate, fee, or charge exception.** A card issuer may increase an annual percentage rate or a fee or charge required to be disclosed under § 1026.6(b)(2)(ii), (b)(2)(iii), or (b)(2)(xii) upon the expiration of a specified period of six months or longer, provided that:

(i) Prior to the commencement of that period, the card issuer disclosed in writing to the consumer, in a clear and conspicuous manner, the length of the period and the annual percentage rate, fee, or charge that would apply after expiration of the period; and

(ii) Upon expiration of the specified period:

(A) The card issuer must not apply an annual percentage rate, fee, or charge to transactions that occurred prior to the period that exceeds the annual percentage rate, fee, or charge that applied to those transactions prior to the period;

(B) If the disclosures required by paragraph (b)(1)(i) of this section are provided pursuant to § 1026.9(c), the card issuer must not apply an annual percentage rate, fee, or charge to transactions that occurred within 14 days after provision of the notice that exceeds the annual percentage rate, fee, or charge that applied to that category of transactions prior to provision of the notice; and

(C) The card issuer must not apply an annual percentage rate, fee, or charge to transactions that occurred during the period that exceeds the increased annual percentage rate, fee, or charge disclosed pursuant to paragraph (b)(1)(i) of this section.

(2) **Variable rate exception.** A card issuer may increase an annual percentage rate when:

(i) The annual percentage rate varies according to an index that is not under the card issuer's control and is available to the general public; and

(ii) The increase in the annual percentage rate is due to an increase in the index.

(3) **Advance notice exception.** A card issuer may increase an annual percentage rate or a fee or charge required to be disclosed under § 1026.6(b)(2)(ii), (b)(2)(iii), or (b)(2)(xii) after complying with the applicable notice requirements in § 1026.9(b), (c), or (g), provided that:

(i) If a card issuer discloses an increased annual percentage rate, fee, or charge pursuant to § 1026.9(b), the card issuer must not apply that rate, fee, or charge to transactions that occurred prior to provision of the notice;

(ii) If a card issuer discloses an increased annual percentage rate, fee, or charge pursuant to § 1026.9(c) or (g), the card issuer must not apply that rate, fee, or charge to transactions that occurred prior to or within 14 days after provision of the notice; and

(iii) This exception does not permit a card issuer to increase an annual percentage rate or a fee or charge required to be disclosed under § 1026.6(b)(2)(ii), (iii), or (xii) during the first year after the account is opened, while the account is closed, or while the card issuer does not permit the consumer to use the account for new transactions. For purposes of this paragraph, an account is considered open no earlier than the date on which the account may first be used by the consumer to engage in transactions.

(4) **Delinquency exception.** A card issuer may increase an annual percentage rate or a fee or charge required to be disclosed under § 1026.6(b)(2)(ii), (b)(2)(iii), or (b)(2)(xii) due to the card issuer not receiving the consumer's required minimum periodic payment within 60 days after the due date for that payment, provided that:

(i) The card issuer must disclose in a clear and conspicuous manner in the notice of the increase pursuant to § 1026.9(c) or (g):

(A) A statement of the reason for the increase; and

(B) That the increased annual percentage rate, fee, or charge will cease to apply if the card issuer receives six consecutive required minimum periodic payments on or before the payment due date beginning with the first payment due following the effective date of the increase; and

(ii) If the card issuer receives six consecutive required minimum periodic payments on or before the payment due date beginning with the first payment due following the effective date of the increase, the card issuer must reduce any annual percentage rate, fee, or charge increased pursuant to this exception to the annual percentage rate, fee, or charge that applied prior to the increase with respect to transactions that occurred prior to or within 14 days after provision of the § 1026.9(c) or (g) notice.

(5) Workout and temporary hardship arrangement exception. A card issuer may increase an annual percentage rate or a fee or charge required to be disclosed under § 1026.6(b)(2)(ii), (b)(2)(iii), or (b)(2)(xii) due to the consumer's completion of a workout or temporary hardship arrangement or the consumer's failure to comply with the terms of such an arrangement, provided that:

(i) Prior to commencement of the arrangement (except as provided in § 1026.9(c)(2)(v)(D)), the card issuer has provided the consumer with a clear and conspicuous written disclosure of the terms of the arrangement (including any increases due to the completion or failure of the arrangement); and

(ii) Upon the completion or failure of the arrangement, the card issuer must not apply to any transactions that occurred prior to commencement of the arrangement an annual percentage rate, fee, or charge that exceeds the annual percentage rate, fee, or charge that applied to those transactions prior to commencement of the arrangement.

(6) Servicemembers Civil Relief Act exception. If an annual percentage rate or a fee or charge required to be disclosed under § 1026.6(b)(2)(ii), (iii), or (xii) has been decreased pursuant to 50 U.S.C. app. 527 or a similar Federal or state statute or regulation, a card issuer may increase that annual percentage rate, fee, or charge once 50 U.S.C. app. 527 or the similar statute or regulation no longer applies, provided that the card issuer must not apply to any transactions that occurred prior to the decrease an annual percentage rate, fee, or charge that exceeds the annual percentage rate, fee, or charge that applied to those transactions prior to the decrease.

(c) Treatment of protected balances.

(1) Definition of protected balance. For purposes of this paragraph, "protected balance" means the amount owed for a category of transactions to which an increased annual percentage rate or an increased fee or charge required to be disclosed under § 1026.6(b)(2)(ii), (b)(2)(iii), or (b)(2)(xii) cannot be applied after the annual percentage rate, fee, or charge for that category of transactions has been increased pursuant to paragraph (b)(3) of this section.

(2) Repayment of protected balance. The card issuer must not require repayment of the protected balance using a method that is less beneficial to the consumer than one of the following methods:

(i) The method of repayment for the account before the effective date of the increase;

(ii) An amortization period of not less than five years, beginning no earlier than the effective date of the increase; or

(iii) A required minimum periodic payment that includes a percentage of the balance that is equal to no more than twice the percentage required before the effective date of the increase.

(d) Continuing application. This section continues to apply to a balance on a credit card account under an open-end (not home-secured) consumer credit plan after:

(1) The account is closed or acquired by another creditor; or

(2) The balance is transferred from a credit card account under an open-end (not home-secured) consumer credit plan issued by a creditor to another credit account issued by the same creditor or its affiliate or subsidiary (unless the account to which the balance is transferred is subject to § 1026.40).

(e) Promotional waivers or rebates of interest, fees, and other charges. If a card issuer promotes the waiver or rebate of finance charges due to a periodic interest rate or fees or charges required to be disclosed under § 1026.6(b)(2)(ii), (iii), or (xii) and applies the waiver or rebate to a credit card account under an open-end (not home-secured) consumer credit plan, any cessation of the waiver or rebate on that account constitutes an increase in an annual percentage rate, fee, or charge for purposes of this section.

§ 1026.56   Requirements for over-the-limit transactions.

(a) Definition. For purposes of this section, the term "over-the-limit transaction" means any extension of credit by a card issuer to complete a transaction that causes a consumer's credit card account balance to exceed the credit limit.

(b) Opt-in requirement.

(1) General. A card issuer shall not assess a fee or charge on a consumer's credit card account under an open-end (not home-secured) consumer credit plan for an over-the-limit transaction unless the card issuer:

(i) Provides the consumer with an oral, written or electronic notice, segregated from all other information, describing the consumer's right to affirmatively consent, or opt in, to the card issuer's payment of an over-the-limit transaction;

(ii) Provides a reasonable opportunity for the consumer to affirmatively consent, or opt in, to the card issuer's payment of over-the-limit transactions;

(iii) Obtains the consumer's affirmative consent, or opt-in, to the card issuer's payment of such transactions;

(iv) Provides the consumer with confirmation of the consumer's consent in writing, or if the consumer agrees, electronically; and

(v) Provides the consumer notice in writing of the right to revoke that consent following the assessment of an over-the-limit fee or charge.

(2) Completion of over-the-limit transactions without consumer consent. Notwithstanding the absence of a consumer's affirmative consent under paragraph (b)(1)(iii) of this section, a card issuer may pay any over-the-limit transaction on a consumer's account provided that the card issuer does not impose any fee or charge on the account for paying that over-the-limit transaction.

(c) Method of election. A card issuer may permit a consumer to consent to the card issuer's payment of any over-the-limit transaction in writing, orally, or electronically, at the card issuer's option. The card issuer must also permit the consumer to revoke his or her consent using the same methods available to the consumer for providing consent.

(d) Timing and placement of notices.

(1) Initial notice.

(i) General. The notice required by paragraph (b)(1)(i) of this section shall be provided prior to the assessment of any over-the-limit fee or charge on a consumer's account.

(ii) Oral or electronic consent. If a consumer consents to the card issuer's payment of any over-the-limit transaction by oral or electronic means, the card issuer must provide the notice required by paragraph (b)(1)(i) of this section immediately prior to obtaining that consent.

(2) Confirmation of opt-in. The notice required by paragraph (b)(1)(iv) of this section may be provided no later than the first periodic statement sent after the consumer has consented to the card issuer's payment of over-the-limit transactions.

(3) **Notice of right of revocation.** The notice required by paragraph (b)(1)(v) of this section shall be provided on the front of any page of each periodic statement that reflects the assessment of an over-the-limit fee or charge on a consumer's account.

(e) **Content.**

(1) **Initial notice.** The notice required by paragraph (b)(1)(i) of this section shall include all applicable items in this paragraph (e)(1) and may not contain any information not specified in or otherwise permitted by this paragraph.

(i) **Fees.** The dollar amount of any fees or charges assessed by the card issuer on a consumer's account for an over-the-limit transaction;

(ii) **APRs.** Any increased periodic rate(s) (expressed as an annual percentage rate(s)) that may be imposed on the account as a result of an over-the-limit transaction; and

(iii) Disclosure of opt-in right. An explanation of the consumer's right to affirmatively consent to the card issuer's payment of over-the-limit transactions, including the method(s) by which the consumer may consent.

(2) **Subsequent notice.** The notice required by paragraph (b)(1)(v) of this section shall describe the consumer's right to revoke any consent provided under paragraph (b)(1)(iii) of this section, including the method(s) by which the consumer may revoke.

(3) **Safe harbor.** Use of Model Forms G–25(A) or G–25(B) of Appendix G to this part, or substantially similar notices, constitutes compliance with the notice content requirements of paragraph (e) of this section.

(f) **Joint relationships.** If two or more consumers are jointly liable on a credit card account under an open-end (not home-secured) consumer credit plan, the card issuer shall treat the affirmative consent of any of the joint consumers as affirmative consent for that account. Similarly, the card issuer shall treat a revocation of consent by any of the joint consumers as revocation of consent for that account.

(g) **Continuing right to opt in or revoke opt-in.** A consumer may affirmatively consent to the card issuer's payment of over-the-limit transactions at any time in the manner described in the notice required by paragraph (b)(1)(i) of this section. Similarly, the consumer may revoke the consent at any time in the manner described in the notice required by paragraph (b)(1)(v) of this section.

(h) **Duration of opt-in.** A consumer's affirmative consent to the card issuer's payment of over-the-limit transactions is effective until revoked by the consumer, or until the card issuer decides for any reason to cease paying over-the-limit transactions for the consumer.

(i) **Time to comply with revocation request.** A card issuer must comply with a consumer's revocation request as soon as reasonably practicable after the card issuer receives it.

(j) **Prohibited practices.** Notwithstanding a consumer's affirmative consent to a card issuer's payment of over-the-limit transactions, a card issuer is prohibited from engaging in the following practices:

(1) **Fees or charges imposed per cycle.**

(i) **General rule.** A card issuer may not impose more than one over-the-limit fee or charge on a consumer's credit card account per billing cycle, and, in any event, only if the credit limit was exceeded during the billing cycle. In addition, except as provided in paragraph (j)(1)(ii) of this section, a card issuer may not impose an over-the-limit fee or charge on the consumer's credit card account for more than three billing cycles for the same over-the-limit transaction where the consumer has not reduced the account balance below the credit limit by the payment due date for either of the last two billing cycles.

(ii) **Exception.** The prohibition in paragraph (j)(1)(i) of this section on imposing an over-the-limit fee or charge in more than three billing cycles for the same over-the-limit transaction(s) does not apply if another over-the-limit transaction occurs during either of the last two billing cycles.

(2) **Failure to promptly replenish.** A card issuer may not impose an over-the-limit fee or charge solely because of the card issuer's failure to promptly replenish the consumer's available credit following the crediting of the consumer's payment under § 1026.10.

(3) **Conditioning.** A card issuer may not condition the amount of a consumer's credit limit on the consumer affirmatively consenting to the card issuer's payment of over-the-limit transactions if the card issuer assesses a fee or charge for such service.

(4) **Over-the-limit fees attributed to fees or interest.** A card issuer may not impose an over-the-limit fee or charge for a billing cycle if a consumer exceeds a credit limit solely because of fees or interest charged by the card issuer to the consumer's account during that billing cycle. For purposes of this paragraph (j)(4), the relevant fees or interest charges are charges imposed as part of the plan under § 1026.6(b)(3).

§ 1026.57   Reporting and marketing rules for college student open-end credit.

(a) **Definitions.**

(1) **College student credit card.** The term "college student credit card" as used in this section means a credit card issued under a credit card account under an open-end (not home-secured) consumer credit plan to any college student.

(2) **College student.** The term "college student" as used in this section means a consumer who is a full-time or part-time student of an institution of higher education.

(3) **Institution of higher education.** The term "institution of higher education" as used in this section has the same meaning as in sections 101 and 102 of the Higher Education Act of 1965 (20 U.S.C. 1001 and 1002).

(4) **Affiliated organization.** The term "affiliated organization" as used in this section means an alumni organization or foundation affiliated with or related to an institution of higher education.

(5) **College credit card agreement.** The term "college credit card agreement" as used in this section means any business, marketing or promotional agreement between a card issuer and an institution of higher education or an affiliated organization in connection with which college student credit cards are issued to college students currently enrolled at that institution.

(b) **Public disclosure of agreements.** An institution of higher education shall publicly disclose any contract or other agreement made with a card issuer or creditor for the purpose of marketing a credit card.

(c) **Prohibited inducements.** No card issuer or creditor may offer a college student any tangible item to induce such student to apply for or open an open-end consumer credit plan offered by such card issuer or creditor, if such offer is made:

(1) On the campus of an institution of higher education;

(2) Near the campus of an institution of higher education; or

(3) At an event sponsored by or related to an institution of higher education.

(d) **Annual report to the Bureau.**

(1) **Requirement to report.** Any card issuer that was a party to one or more college credit card agreements in effect at any time during a calendar year must submit to the Bureau an annual report regarding those agreements in the form and manner prescribed by the Bureau.

(2) **Contents of report.** The annual report to the Bureau must include the following:

(i) Identifying information about the card issuer and the agreements submitted, including the issuer's name, address, and identifying number (such as an RSSD ID number or tax identification number);

(ii) A copy of any college credit card agreement to which the card issuer was a party that was in effect at any time during the period covered by the report;

    (iii) A copy of any memorandum of understanding in effect at any time during the period covered by the report between the card issuer and an institution of higher education or affiliated organization that directly or indirectly relates to the college credit card agreement or that controls or directs any obligations or distribution of benefits between any such entities;

    (iv) The total dollar amount of any payments pursuant to a college credit card agreement from the card issuer to an institution of higher education or affiliated organization during the period covered by the report, and the method or formula used to determine such amounts;

    (v) The total number of credit card accounts opened pursuant to any college credit card agreement during the period covered by the report; and

    (vi) The total number of credit card accounts opened pursuant to any such agreement that were open at the end of the period covered by the report.

    (3) Timing of reports. Except for the initial report described in this paragraph (d)(3), a card issuer must submit its annual report for each calendar year to the Bureau by the first business day on or after March 31 of the following calendar year.

§ 1026.58   Internet posting of credit card agreements.

    (a) Applicability. The requirements of this section apply to any card issuer that issues credit cards under a credit card account under an open-end (not home-secured) consumer credit plan.

    (b) Definitions.

    (1) Agreement. For purposes of this section, "agreement" or "credit card agreement" means the written document or documents evidencing the terms of the legal obligation, or the prospective legal obligation, between a card issuer and a consumer for a credit card account under an open-end (not home-secured) consumer credit plan. "Agreement" or "credit card agreement" also includes the pricing information, as defined in § 1026.58(b)(7).

    (2) Amends. For purposes of this section, an issuer "amends" an agreement if it makes a substantive change (an "amendment") to the agreement. A change is substantive if it alters the rights or obligations of the card issuer or the consumer under the agreement. Any change in the pricing information, as defined in § 1026.58(b)(7), is deemed to be substantive.

    (3) Business day. For purposes of this section, "business day" means a day on which the creditor's offices are open to the public for carrying on substantially all of its business functions.

    (4) Card issuer. For purposes of this section, "card issuer" or "issuer" means the entity to which a consumer is legally obligated, or would be legally obligated, under the terms of a credit card agreement.

    (5) Offers. For purposes of this section, an issuer "offers" or "offers to the public" an agreement if the issuer is soliciting or accepting applications for accounts that would be subject to that agreement.

    (6) Open account. For purposes of this section, an account is an "open account" or "open credit card account" if it is a credit card account under an open-end (not home-secured) consumer credit plan and either:

    (i) The cardholder can obtain extensions of credit on the account; or

    (ii) There is an outstanding balance on the account that has not been charged off. An account that has been suspended temporarily (for example, due to a report by the cardholder of unauthorized use of the card) is considered an "open account" or "open credit card account."

    (7) Pricing information. For purposes of this section, "pricing information" means the information listed in § 1026.6(b)(2)(i) through (b)(2)(xii). Pricing information does not include temporary or promotional rates and terms or rates and terms that apply only to protected balances.

    (8) Private label credit card account and private label credit card plan. For purposes of this section:

(i) "private label credit card account" means a credit card account under an open-end (not home-secured) consumer credit plan with a credit card that can be used to make purchases only at a single merchant or an affiliated group of merchants; and

(ii) "private label credit card plan" means all of the private label credit card accounts issued by a particular issuer with credit cards usable at the same single merchant or affiliated group of merchants.

(c) Submission of agreements to Bureau.

(1) Quarterly submissions. A card issuer must make quarterly submissions to the Bureau, in the form and manner specified by the Bureau. Quarterly submissions must be sent to the Bureau no later than the first business day on or after January 31, April 30, July 31, and October 31 of each year. Each submission must contain:

(i) Identifying information about the card issuer and the agreements submitted, including the issuer's name, address, and identifying number (such as an RSSD ID number or tax identification number);

(ii) The credit card agreements that the card issuer offered to the public as of the last business day of the preceding calendar quarter that the card issuer has not previously submitted to the Bureau;

(iii) Any credit card agreement previously submitted to the Bureau that was amended during the preceding calendar quarter and that the card issuer offered to the public as of the last business day of the preceding calendar quarter, as described in § 1026.58(c)(3); and

(iv) Notification regarding any credit card agreement previously submitted to the Bureau that the issuer is withdrawing, as described in § 1026.58(c)(4), (c)(5), (c)(6), and (c)(7).

(2) [Reserved]

(3) Amended agreements. If a credit card agreement has been submitted to the Bureau, the agreement has not been amended and the card issuer continues to offer the agreement to the public, no additional submission regarding that agreement is required. If a credit card agreement that previously has been submitted to the Bureau is amended and the card issuer offered the amended agreement to the public as of the last business day of the calendar quarter in which the change became effective, the card issuer must submit the entire amended agreement to the Bureau, in the form and manner specified by the Bureau, by the first quarterly submission deadline after the last day of the calendar quarter in which the change became effective.

(4) Withdrawal of agreements. If a card issuer no longer offers to the public a credit card agreement that previously has been submitted to the Bureau, the card issuer must notify the Bureau, in the form and manner specified by the Bureau, by the first quarterly submission deadline after the last day of the calendar quarter in which the issuer ceased to offer the agreement.

(5) De minimis exception.

(i) A card issuer is not required to submit any credit card agreements to the Bureau if the card issuer had fewer than 10,000 open credit card accounts as of the last business day of the calendar quarter.

(ii) If an issuer that previously qualified for the de minimis exception ceases to qualify, the card issuer must begin making quarterly submissions to the Bureau no later than the first quarterly submission deadline after the date as of which the issuer ceased to qualify.

(iii) If a card issuer that did not previously qualify for the de minimis exception qualifies for the de minimis exception, the card issuer must continue to make quarterly submissions to the Bureau until the issuer notifies the Bureau that the card issuer is withdrawing all agreements it previously submitted to the Bureau.

(6) Private label credit card exception.

(i) A card issuer is not required to submit to the Bureau a credit card agreement if, as of the last business day of the calendar quarter, the agreement:

(A) Is offered for accounts under one or more private label credit card plans each of which has fewer than 10,000 open accounts; and

(B) Is not offered to the public other than for accounts under such a plan.

(ii) If an agreement that previously qualified for the private label credit card exception ceases to qualify, the card issuer must submit the agreement to the Bureau no later than the first quarterly submission deadline after the date as of which the agreement ceased to qualify.

(iii) If an agreement that did not previously qualify for the private label credit card exception qualifies for the exception, the card issuer must continue to make quarterly submissions to the Bureau with respect to that agreement until the issuer notifies the Bureau that the agreement is being withdrawn.

(7) Product testing exception.

(i) A card issuer is not required to submit to the Bureau a credit card agreement if, as of the last business day of the calendar quarter, the agreement:

(A) Is offered as part of a product test offered to only a limited group of consumers for a limited period of time;

(B) Is used for fewer than 10,000 open accounts; and

(C) Is not offered to the public other than in connection with such a product test.

(ii) If an agreement that previously qualified for the product testing exception ceases to qualify, the card issuer must submit the agreement to the Bureau no later than the first quarterly submission deadline after the date as of which the agreement ceased to qualify.

(iii) If an agreement that did not previously qualify for the product testing exception qualifies for the exception, the card issuer must continue to make quarterly submissions to the Bureau with respect to that agreement until the issuer notifies the Bureau that the agreement is being withdrawn.

(8) Form and content of agreements submitted to the Bureau.

(i) Form and content generally.

(A) Each agreement must contain the provisions of the agreement and the pricing information in effect as of the last business day of the preceding calendar quarter.

(B) Agreements must not include any personally identifiable information relating to any cardholder, such as name, address, telephone number, or account number.

(C) The following are not deemed to be part of the agreement for purposes of § 1026.58, and therefore are not required to be included in submissions to the Bureau:

(1) Disclosures required by state or Federal law, such as affiliate marketing notices, privacy policies, billing rights notices, or disclosures under the E-Sign Act;

(2) Solicitation materials;

(3) Periodic statements;

(4) Ancillary agreements between the issuer and the consumer, such as debt cancellation contracts or debt suspension agreements;

(5) Offers for credit insurance or other optional products and other similar advertisements; and

(6) Documents that may be sent to the consumer along with the credit card or credit card agreement such as a cover letter, a validation sticker on the card, or other information about card security.

(D) Agreements must be presented in a clear and legible font.

(ii) Pricing information.

(A) Pricing information must be set forth in a single addendum to the agreement. The addendum must contain all of the pricing information, as defined by § 1026.58(b)(7). The addendum may, but is not required to, contain any other information listed in § 1026.6(b), provided that information is complete and accurate as of the applicable date under § 1026.58. The addendum may not contain any other information.

(B) Pricing information that may vary from one cardholder to another depending on the cardholder's creditworthiness or state of residence or other factors must be disclosed either by setting forth all the possible variations (such as purchase APRs of 13 percent, 15 percent, 17 percent, and 19 percent) or by providing a range of possible variations (such as purchase APRs ranging from 13 percent to 19 percent).

(C) If a rate included in the pricing information is a variable rate, the issuer must identify the index or formula used in setting the rate and the margin. Rates that may vary from one cardholder to another must be disclosed by providing the index and the possible margins (such as the prime rate plus 5 percent, 8 percent, 10 percent, or 12 percent) or range of margins (such as the prime rate plus from 5 to 12 percent). The value of the rate and the value of the index are not required to be disclosed.

(iii) Optional variable terms addendum. Provisions of the agreement other than the pricing information that may vary from one cardholder to another depending on the cardholder's creditworthiness or state of residence or other factors may be set forth in a single addendum to the agreement separate from the pricing information addendum.

(iv) Integrated agreement. Issuers may not provide provisions of the agreement or pricing information in the form of change-in-terms notices or riders (other than the pricing information addendum and the optional variable terms addendum). Changes in provisions or pricing information must be integrated into the text of the agreement, the pricing information addendum or the optional variable terms addendum, as appropriate.

(d) Posting of agreements offered to the public.

(1) Except as provided below, a card issuer must post and maintain on its publicly available Web site the credit card agreements that the issuer is required to submit to the Bureau under § 1026.58(c). With respect to an agreement offered solely for accounts under one or more private label credit card plans, an issuer may fulfill this requirement by posting and maintaining the agreement in accordance with the requirements of this section on the publicly available Web site of at least one of the merchants at which credit cards issued under each private label credit card plan with 10,000 or more open accounts may be used.

(2) Except as provided in § 1026.58(d), agreements posted pursuant to § 1026.58(d) must conform to the form and content requirements for agreements submitted to the Bureau specified in § 1026.58(c)(8).

(3) Agreements posted pursuant to § 1026.58(d) may be posted in any electronic format that is readily usable by the general public. Agreements must be placed in a location that is prominent and readily accessible by the public and must be accessible without submission of personally identifiable information.

(4) The card issuer must update the agreements posted on its Web site pursuant to § 1026.58(d) at least as frequently as the quarterly schedule required for submission of agreements to the Bureau under § 1026.58(c). If the issuer chooses to update the agreements on its Web site more frequently, the agreements posted on the issuer's Web site may contain the provisions of the agreement and the pricing information in effect as of a date other than the last business day of the preceding calendar quarter.

(e) Agreements for all open accounts.

(1) Availability of individual cardholder's agreement. With respect to any open credit card account, a card issuer must either:

(i) Post and maintain the cardholder's agreement on its Web site; or

(ii) Promptly provide a copy of the cardholder's agreement to the cardholder upon the cardholder's request. If the card issuer makes an agreement available upon request, the issuer must provide the cardholder with the ability to request a copy of the agreement both by using the issuer's Web site (such as by clicking on a clearly identified box to make the request) and by calling a readily available telephone line the number for which is displayed on the issuer's Web site and clearly identified as to purpose. The card issuer must send to the cardholder or otherwise make available to the cardholder a copy of the cardholder's agreement in electronic or paper form no later than 30 days after the issuer receives the cardholder's request.

(2) Special rule for issuers without interactive Web sites. An issuer that does not maintain a Web site from which cardholders can access specific information about their individual accounts, instead of complying with § 1026.58(e)(1), may make agreements available upon request by providing the cardholder with the ability to request a copy of the agreement by calling a readily available telephone line, the number for which is displayed on the issuer's Web site and clearly identified as to purpose or included on each periodic statement sent to the cardholder and clearly identified as to purpose. The issuer must send to the cardholder or otherwise make available to the cardholder a copy of the cardholder's agreement in electronic or paper form no later than 30 days after the issuer receives the cardholder's request.

(3) Form and content of agreements.

(i) Except as provided in § 1026.58(e), agreements posted on the card issuer's Web site pursuant to § 1026.58(e)(1)(i) or made available upon the cardholder's request pursuant to § 1026.58(e)(1)(ii) or (e)(2) must conform to the form and content requirements for agreements submitted to the Bureau specified in § 1026.58(c)(8).

(ii) If the card issuer posts an agreement on its Web site or otherwise provides an agreement to a cardholder electronically under § 1026.58(e), the agreement may be posted or provided in any electronic format that is readily usable by the general public and must be placed in a location that is prominent and readily accessible to the cardholder.

(iii) Agreements posted or otherwise provided pursuant to § 1026.58(e) may contain personally identifiable information relating to the cardholder, such as name, address, telephone number, or account number, provided that the issuer takes appropriate measures to make the agreement accessible only to the cardholder or other authorized persons.

(iv) Agreements posted or otherwise provided pursuant to § 1026.58(e) must set forth the specific provisions and pricing information applicable to the particular cardholder. Provisions and pricing information must be complete and accurate as of a date no more than 60 days prior to:

(A) The date on which the agreement is posted on the card issuer's Web site under § 1026.58(e)(1)(i); or

(B) The date the cardholder's request is received under § 1026.58(e)(1)(ii) or (e)(2).

(v) Agreements provided upon cardholder request pursuant to § 1026.58(e)(1)(ii) or (e)(2) may be provided by the issuer in either electronic or paper form, regardless of the form of the cardholder's request.

(f) E-Sign Act requirements. Card issuers may provide credit card agreements in electronic form under § 1026.58(d) and (e) without regard to the consumer notice and consent requirements of section 101(c) of the Electronic Signatures in Global and National Commerce Act (E-Sign Act) (15 U.S.C. 7001 et seq.).

(g) Temporary suspension of agreement submission requirement.

(1) Quarterly submissions. The quarterly submission requirement in paragraph (c) of this section is suspended for the submissions that would otherwise be due to the Bureau by the first business day on or after April 30, 2015; July 31, 2015; October 31, 2015; and January 31, 2016.

(2) Posting of agreements offered to the public. Nothing in paragraph (g)(1) of this section shall affect the agreement posting requirements in paragraph (d) of this section.

§ 1026.59   Reevaluation of rate increases.

(a) General rule.

(1) Evaluation of increased rate. If a card issuer increases an annual percentage rate that applies to a credit card account under an open-end (not home-secured) consumer credit plan, based on the credit risk of the consumer, market conditions, or other factors, or increased such a rate on or after January 1, 2009, and 45 days' advance notice of the rate increase is required pursuant to § 1026.9(c)(2) or (g), the card issuer must:

(i) Evaluate the factors described in paragraph (d) of this section; and

(ii) Based on its review of such factors, reduce the annual percentage rate applicable to the consumer's account, as appropriate.

(2) Rate reductions.

(i) Timing. If a card issuer is required to reduce the rate applicable to an account pursuant to paragraph (a)(1) of this section, the card issuer must reduce the rate not later than 45 days after completion of the evaluation described in paragraph (a)(1).

(ii) Applicability of rate reduction. Any reduction in an annual percentage rate required pursuant to paragraph (a)(1) of this section shall apply to:

(A) Any outstanding balances to which the increased rate described in paragraph (a)(1) of this section has been applied; and

(B) New transactions that occur after the effective date of the rate reduction that would otherwise have been subject to the increased rate.

(b) Policies and procedures. A card issuer must have reasonable written policies and procedures in place to conduct the review described in paragraph (a) of this section.

(c) Timing. A card issuer that is subject to paragraph (a) of this section must conduct the review described in paragraph (a)(1) of this section not less frequently than once every six months after the rate increase.

(d) Factors.

(1) In general. Except as provided in paragraph (d)(2) of this section, a card issuer must review either:

(i) The factors on which the increase in an annual percentage rate was originally based; or

(ii) The factors that the card issuer currently considers when determining the annual percentage rates applicable to similar new credit card accounts under an open-end (not home-secured) consumer credit plan.

(2) Rate increases imposed between January 1, 2009 and February 21, 2010. For rate increases imposed between January 1, 2009 and February 21, 2010, an issuer must consider the factors described in paragraph (d)(1)(ii) when conducting the first two reviews required under paragraph (a) of this section, unless the rate increase subject to paragraph (a) of this section was based solely upon factors specific to the consumer, such as a decline in the consumer's credit risk, the consumer's delinquency or default, or a violation of the terms of the account.

(e) Rate increases due to delinquency. If an issuer increases a rate applicable to a consumer's account pursuant to § 1026.55(b)(4) based on the card issuer not receiving the consumer's required minimum periodic payment within 60 days after the due date, the issuer is not required to perform the review described in paragraph (a) of this section prior to the sixth payment due date after the effective date of the increase. However, if the annual percentage rate applicable to the consumer's account is not reduced pursuant to § 1026.55(b)(4)(ii), the card issuer must perform the review described in paragraph (a) of this section. The first such review must occur no later than six months after the sixth payment due following the effective date of the rate increase.

(f) Termination of obligation to review factors. The obligation to review factors described in paragraph (a) and (d) of this section ceases to apply:

(1) If the issuer reduces the annual percentage rate applicable to a credit card account under an open-end (not home-secured) consumer credit plan to the rate applicable immediately prior to the increase, or, if the rate applicable immediately prior to the increase was a variable rate, to a variable rate determined by the same formula (index and margin) that was used to calculate the rate applicable immediately prior to the increase; or

(2) If the issuer reduces the annual percentage rate to a rate that is lower than the rate described in paragraph (f)(1) of this section.

(g) Acquired accounts.

(1) General. Except as provided in paragraph (g)(2) of this section, this section applies to credit card accounts that have been acquired by the card issuer from another card issuer. A card issuer that complies with this section by reviewing the factors described in paragraph (d)(1)(i) must review the factors considered by the card issuer from which it acquired the accounts in connection with the rate increase.

(2) Review of acquired portfolio. If, not later than six months after the acquisition of such accounts, a card issuer reviews all of the credit card accounts it acquires in accordance with the factors that it currently considers in determining the rates applicable to its similar new credit card accounts:

(i) Except as provided in paragraph (g)(2)(iii), the card issuer is required to conduct reviews described in paragraph (a) of this section only for rate increases that are imposed as a result of its review under this paragraph. See §§ 1026.9 and 1026.55 for additional requirements regarding rate increases on acquired accounts.

(ii) Except as provided in paragraph (g)(2)(iii) of this section, the card issuer is not required to conduct reviews in accordance with paragraph (a) of this section for any rate increases made prior to the card issuer's acquisition of such accounts.

(iii) If as a result of the card issuer's review, an account is subject to, or continues to be subject to, an increased rate as a penalty, or due to the consumer's delinquency or default, the requirements of paragraph (a) of this section apply.

(h) Exceptions.

(1) Servicemembers Civil Relief Act exception. The requirements of this section do not apply to increases in an annual percentage rate that was previously decreased pursuant to 50 U.S.C. app. 527, provided that such a rate increase is made in accordance with § 1026.55(b)(6).

(2) Charged off accounts. The requirements of this section do not apply to accounts that the card issuer has charged off in accordance with loan-loss provisions.

§ 1026.60 Credit and charge card applications and solicitations.

(a) General rules. The card issuer shall provide the disclosures required under this section on or with a solicitation or an application to open a credit or charge card account.

(1) Definition of solicitation. For purposes of this section, the term solicitation means an offer by the card issuer to open a credit or charge card account that does not require the consumer to complete an application. A "firm offer of credit" as defined in section 603(*l*) of the Fair Credit Reporting Act (15 U.S.C. 1681a(*l*)) for a credit or charge card is a solicitation for purposes of this section.

(2) Form of disclosures; tabular format.

(i) The disclosures in paragraphs (b)(1) through (5) (except for (b)(1)(iv)(B)) and (b)(7) through (15) of this section made pursuant to paragraph (c), (d)(2), (e)(1) or (f) of this section generally shall be in the form of a table with headings, content, and format substantially similar to any of the applicable tables found in G–10 in Appendix G to this part.

(ii) The table described in paragraph (a)(2)(i) of this section shall contain only the information required or permitted by this section. Other information may be presented on or with an application or solicitation, provided such information appears outside the required table.

(iii) Disclosures required by paragraphs (b)(1)(iv)(B), (b)(1)(iv)(C) and (b)(6) of this section must be placed directly beneath the table.

(iv) When a tabular format is required, any annual percentage rate required to be disclosed pursuant to paragraph (b)(1) of this section, any introductory rate required to be disclosed pursuant to paragraph (b)(1)(ii) of this section, any rate that will apply after a premium initial rate expires required to be disclosed under paragraph (b)(1)(iii) of this section, and any fee or percentage amounts or maximum limits on fee amounts disclosed pursuant to paragraphs (b)(2), (b)(4), (b)(8) through (b)(13) of this section must be disclosed in bold text. However, bold text shall not be used for: The amount of any periodic fee disclosed pursuant to paragraph (b)(2) of this section that is not an annualized amount; and other annual percentage rates or fee amounts disclosed in the table.

(v) For an application or a solicitation that is accessed by the consumer in electronic form, the disclosures required under this section may be provided to the consumer in electronic form on or with the application or solicitation.

(vi)(A) Except as provided in paragraph (a)(2)(vi)(B) of this section, the table described in paragraph (a)(2)(i) of this section must be provided in a prominent location on or with an application or a solicitation.

(B) If the table described in paragraph (a)(2)(i) of this section is provided electronically, it must be provided in close proximity to the application or solicitation.

(3) Fees based on a percentage. If the amount of any fee required to be disclosed under this section is determined on the basis of a percentage of another amount, the percentage used and the identification of the amount against which the percentage is applied may be disclosed instead of the amount of the fee.

(4) Fees that vary by state. Card issuers that impose fees referred to in paragraphs (b)(8) through (12) of this section that vary by state may, at the issuer's option, disclose in the table required by paragraph (a)(2)(i) of this section: The specific fee applicable to the consumer's account; or the range of the fees, if the disclosure includes a statement that the amount of the fee varies by state and refers the consumer to a disclosure provided with the table where the amount of the fee applicable to the consumer's account is disclosed. A card issuer may not list fees for multiple states in the table.

(5) Exceptions. This section does not apply to:

(i) Home-equity plans accessible by a credit or charge card that are subject to the requirements of § 1026.40;

(ii) Overdraft lines of credit tied to asset accounts accessed by check-guarantee cards or by debit cards;

(iii) Lines of credit accessed by check-guarantee cards or by debit cards that can be used only at automated teller machines;

(iv) Lines of credit accessed solely by account numbers;

    (v) Additions of a credit or charge card to an existing open-end plan;

    (vi) General purpose applications unless the application, or material accompanying it, indicates that it can be used to open a credit or charge card account; or

    (vii) Consumer-initiated requests for applications.

  (b) **Required disclosures.** The card issuer shall disclose the items in this paragraph on or with an application or a solicitation in accordance with the requirements of paragraphs (c), (d), (e)(1) or (f) of this section. A credit card issuer shall disclose all applicable items in this paragraph except for paragraph (b)(7) of this section. A charge card issuer shall disclose the applicable items in paragraphs (b)(2), (4), (7) through (12), and (15) of this section.

    (1) **Annual percentage rate.** Each periodic rate that may be used to compute the finance charge on an outstanding balance for purchases, a cash advance, or a balance transfer, expressed as an annual percentage rate (as determined by § 1026.14(b)). When more than one rate applies for a category of transactions, the range of balances to which each rate is applicable shall also be disclosed. The annual percentage rate for purchases disclosed pursuant to this paragraph shall be in at least 16-point type, except for the following: Oral disclosures of the annual percentage rate for purchases; or a penalty rate that may apply upon the occurrence of one or more specific events.

      (i) **Variable rate information.** If a rate disclosed under paragraph (b)(1) of this section is a variable rate, the card issuer shall also disclose the fact that the rate may vary and how the rate is determined. In describing how the applicable rate will be determined, the card issuer must identify the type of index or formula that is used in setting the rate. The value of the index and the amount of the margin that are used to calculate the variable rate shall not be disclosed in the table. A disclosure of any applicable limitations on rate increases shall not be included in the table.

      (ii) **Discounted initial rate.** If the initial rate is an introductory rate, as that term is defined in § 1026.16(g)(2)(ii), the card issuer must disclose in the table the introductory rate, the time period during which the introductory rate will remain in effect, and must use the term "introductory" or "intro" in immediate proximity to the introductory rate. The card issuer also must disclose the rate that would otherwise apply to the account pursuant to paragraph (b)(1) of this section. Where the rate is not tied to an index or formula, the card issuer must disclose the rate that will apply after the introductory rate expires. In a variable-rate account, the card issuer must disclose a rate based on the applicable index or formula in accordance with the accuracy requirements set forth in paragraphs (c)(2), (d)(3), or (e)(4) of this section, as applicable.

      (iii) **Premium initial rate.** If the initial rate is temporary and is higher than the rate that will apply after the temporary rate expires, the card issuer must disclose the premium initial rate pursuant to paragraph (b)(1) of this section and the time period during which the premium initial rate will remain in effect. Consistent with paragraph (b)(1) of this section, the premium initial rate for purchases must be in at least 16-point type. The issuer must also disclose in the table the rate that will apply after the premium initial rate expires, in at least 16-point type.

      (iv) **Penalty rates.**

        (A) **In general.** Except as provided in paragraph (b)(1)(iv)(B) and (C) of this section, if a rate may increase as a penalty for one or more events specified in the account agreement, such as a late payment or an extension of credit that exceeds the credit limit, the card issuer must disclose pursuant to this paragraph (b)(1) the increased rate that may apply, a brief description of the event or events that may result in the increased rate, and a brief description of how long the increased rate will remain in effect.

        (B) **Introductory rates.** If the issuer discloses an introductory rate, as that term is defined in § 1026.16(g)(2)(ii), in the table or in any written or electronic promotional materials accompanying applications or solicitations subject to paragraph (c) or (e) of this section, the issuer must briefly disclose directly beneath the table the circumstances, if any, under which the introductory rate may be revoked, and the type of rate that will apply after the introductory rate is revoked.

(C) **Employee preferential rates.** If a card issuer discloses in the table a preferential annual percentage rate for which only employees of the card issuer, employees of a third party, or other individuals with similar affiliations with the card issuer or third party, such as executive officers, directors, or principal shareholders are eligible, the card issuer must briefly disclose directly beneath the table the circumstances under which such preferential rate may be revoked, and the rate that will apply after such preferential rate is revoked.

(v) **Rates that depend on consumer's creditworthiness.** If a rate cannot be determined at the time disclosures are given because the rate depends, at least in part, on a later determination of the consumer's creditworthiness, the card issuer must disclose the specific rates or the range of rates that could apply and a statement that the rate for which the consumer may qualify at account opening will depend on the consumer's creditworthiness, and other factors if applicable. If the rate that depends, at least in part, on a later determination of the consumer's creditworthiness is a penalty rate, as described in paragraph (b)(1)(iv) of this section, the card issuer at its option may disclose the highest rate that could apply, instead of disclosing the specific rates or the range of rates that could apply.

(vi) **APRs that vary by state.** Issuers imposing annual percentage rates that vary by state may, at the issuer's option, disclose in the table: the specific annual percentage rate applicable to the consumer's account; or the range of the annual percentage rates, if the disclosure includes a statement that the annual percentage rate varies by state and refers the consumer to a disclosure provided with the table where the annual percentage rate applicable to the consumer's account is disclosed. A card issuer may not list annual percentage rates for multiple states in the table.

(2) **Fees for issuance or availability.**

(i) Any annual or other periodic fee that may be imposed for the issuance or availability of a credit or charge card, including any fee based on account activity or inactivity; how frequently it will be imposed; and the annualized amount of the fee.

(ii) Any non-periodic fee that relates to opening an account. A card issuer must disclose that the fee is a one-time fee.

(3) **Fixed finance charge; minimum interest charge.** Any fixed finance charge and a brief description of the charge. Any minimum interest charge if it exceeds $1.00 that could be imposed during a billing cycle, and a brief description of the charge. The $1.00 threshold amount shall be adjusted periodically by the Bureau to reflect changes in the Consumer Price Index. The Bureau shall calculate each year a price level adjusted minimum interest charge using the Consumer Price Index in effect on June 1 of that year. When the cumulative change in the adjusted minimum value derived from applying the annual Consumer Price level to the current minimum interest charge threshold has risen by a whole dollar, the minimum interest charge will be increased by $1.00. The issuer may, at its option, disclose in the table minimum interest charges below this threshold.

(4) **Transaction charges.** Any transaction charge imposed by the card issuer for the use of the card for purchases.

(5) **Grace period.** The date by which or the period within which any credit extended for purchases may be repaid without incurring a finance charge due to a periodic interest rate and any conditions on the availability of the grace period. If no grace period is provided, that fact must be disclosed. If the length of the grace period varies, the card issuer may disclose the range of days, the minimum number of days, or the average number of days in the grace period, if the disclosure is identified as a range, minimum, or average. In disclosing in the tabular format a grace period that applies to all types of purchases, the phrase "How to Avoid Paying Interest on Purchases" shall be used as the heading for the row describing the grace period. If a grace period is not offered on all types of

purchases, in disclosing this fact in the tabular format, the phrase "Paying Interest" shall be used as the heading for the row describing this fact.

(6)   Balance computation method. The name of the balance computation method listed in paragraph (g) of this section that is used to determine the balance for purchases on which the finance charge is computed, or an explanation of the method used if it is not listed. In determining which balance computation method to disclose, the card issuer shall assume that credit extended for purchases will not be repaid within the grace period, if any.

(7)   Statement on charge card payments. A statement that charges incurred by use of the charge card are due when the periodic statement is received.

(8)   Cash advance fee. Any fee imposed for an extension of credit in the form of cash or its equivalent.

(9)   Late payment fee. Any fee imposed for a late payment.

(10)   Over-the-limit fee. Any fee imposed for exceeding a credit limit.

(11)   Balance transfer fee. Any fee imposed to transfer an outstanding balance.

(12)   Returned-payment fee. Any fee imposed by the card issuer for a returned payment.

(13)   Required insurance, debt cancellation or debt suspension coverage.

(i)   A fee for insurance described in § 1026.4(b)(7) or debt cancellation or suspension coverage described in § 1026.4(b)(10), if the insurance or debt cancellation or suspension coverage is required as part of the plan; and

(ii)   A cross reference to any additional information provided about the insurance or coverage accompanying the application or solicitation, as applicable.

(14) Available credit. If a card issuer requires fees for the issuance or availability of credit described in paragraph (b)(2) of this section, or requires a security deposit for such credit, and the total amount of those required fees and/or security deposit that will be imposed and charged to the account when the account is opened is 15 percent or more of the minimum credit limit for the card, a card issuer must disclose the available credit remaining after these fees or security deposit are debited to the account, assuming that the consumer receives the minimum credit limit. In determining whether the 15 percent threshold test is met, the issuer must only consider fees for issuance or availability of credit, or a security deposit, that are required. If fees for issuance or availability are optional, these fees should not be considered in determining whether the disclosure must be given. Nonetheless, if the 15 percent threshold test is met, the issuer in providing the disclosure must disclose the amount of available credit calculated by excluding those optional fees, and the available credit including those optional fees. This paragraph does not apply with respect to fees or security deposits that are not debited to the account.

(15) Web site reference. A reference to the Web site established by the Bureau and a statement that consumers may obtain on the Web site information about shopping for and using credit cards. Until January 1, 2013, issuers may substitute for this reference a reference to the Web site established by the Board of Governors of the Federal Reserve System.

(c)   Direct mail and electronic applications and solicitations.

(1)   General. The card issuer shall disclose the applicable items in paragraph (b) of this section on or with an application or solicitation that is mailed to consumers or provided to consumers in electronic form.

(2)   Accuracy.

(i)   Disclosures in direct mail applications and solicitations must be accurate as of the time the disclosures are mailed. An accurate variable annual percentage rate is one in effect within 60 days before mailing.

(ii)   Disclosures provided in electronic form must be accurate as of the time they are sent, in the case of disclosures sent to a consumer's email address, or as of the time they are viewed by the public, in the case of disclosures made available at a location such as a card issuer's Web site. An accurate variable annual percentage rate provided in electronic form is one in effect within 30 days before it is sent to a consumer's email address, or viewed by the public, as applicable.

(d) Telephone applications and solicitations.

(1) Oral disclosure. The card issuer shall disclose orally the information in paragraphs (b)(1) through (7) and (b)(14) of this section, to the extent applicable, in a telephone application or solicitation initiated by the card issuer.

(2) Alternative disclosure. The oral disclosure under paragraph (d)(1) of this section need not be given if the card issuer either:

(i)(A)   Does not impose a fee described in paragraph (b)(2) of this section; or

(B)   Imposes such a fee but provides the consumer with a right to reject the plan consistent with § 1026.5(b)(1)(iv); and

(ii)   The card issuer discloses in writing within 30 days after the consumer requests the card (but in no event later than the delivery of the card) the following:

(A)   The applicable information in paragraph (b) of this section; and

(B)   As applicable, the fact that the consumer has the right to reject the plan and not be obligated to pay fees described in paragraph (b)(2) or any other fees or charges until the consumer has used the account or made a payment on the account after receiving a billing statement.

(3) Accuracy.

(i)   The oral disclosures under paragraph (d)(1) of this section must be accurate as of the time they are given.

(ii)   The alternative disclosures under paragraph (d)(2) of this section generally must be accurate as of the time they are mailed or delivered. A variable annual percentage rate is one that is accurate if it was:

(A)   In effect at the time the disclosures are mailed or delivered; or

(B)   In effect as of a specified date (which rate is then updated from time to time, but no less frequently than each calendar month).

(e) Applications and solicitations made available to general public. The card issuer shall provide disclosures, to the extent applicable, on or with an application or solicitation that is made available to the general public, including one contained in a catalog, magazine, or other generally available publication. The disclosures shall be provided in accordance with paragraph (e)(1) or (e)(2) of this section.

(1) Disclosure of required credit information. The card issuer may disclose in a prominent location on the application or solicitation the following:

(i)   The applicable information in paragraph (b) of this section;

(ii)   The date the required information was printed, including a statement that the required information was accurate as of that date and is subject to change after that date; and

(iii) A statement that the consumer should contact the card issuer for any change in the required information since it was printed, and a toll-free telephone number or a mailing address for that purpose.

(2) No disclosure of credit information. If none of the items in paragraph (b) of this section is provided on or with the application or solicitation, the card issuer may state in a prominent location on the application or solicitation the following:

(i)   There are costs associated with the use of the card; and

(ii) The consumer may contact the card issuer to request specific information about the costs, along with a toll-free telephone number and a mailing address for that purpose.

(3) **Prompt response to requests for information.** Upon receiving a request for any of the information referred to in this paragraph, the card issuer shall promptly and fully disclose the information requested.

(4) **Accuracy.** The disclosures given pursuant to paragraph (e)(1) of this section must be accurate as of the date of printing. A variable annual percentage rate is accurate if it was in effect within 30 days before printing.

(f) **In-person applications and solicitations.** A card issuer shall disclose the information in paragraph (b) of this section, to the extent applicable, on or with an application or solicitation that is initiated by the card issuer and given to the consumer in person. A card issuer complies with the requirements of this paragraph if the issuer provides disclosures in accordance with paragraph (c)(1) or (e)(1) of this section.

(g) **Balance computation methods defined.** The following methods may be described by name. Methods that differ due to variations such as the allocation of payments, whether the finance charge begins to accrue on the transaction date or the date of posting the transaction, the existence or length of a grace period, and whether the balance is adjusted by charges such as late payment fees, annual fees and unpaid finance charges do not constitute separate balance computation methods.

(1)(i) **Average daily balance (including new purchases).** This balance is figured by adding the outstanding balance (including new purchases and deducting payments and credits) for each day in the billing cycle, and then dividing by the number of days in the billing cycle.

(ii) **Average daily balance (excluding new purchases).** This balance is figured by adding the outstanding balance (excluding new purchases and deducting payments and credits) for each day in the billing cycle, and then dividing by the number of days in the billing cycle.

(2) **Adjusted balance.** This balance is figured by deducting payments and credits made during the billing cycle from the outstanding balance at the beginning of the billing cycle.

(3) **Previous balance.** This balance is the outstanding balance at the beginning of the billing cycle.

(4) **Daily balance.** For each day in the billing cycle, this balance is figured by taking the beginning balance each day, adding any new purchases, and subtracting any payment and credits.

CONSUMER LEASING
(REGULATION M)

12 C.F.R. Part 1013
Current through March 31, 2016; 80 F.R. 18737

For updates, see www.gpo.gov/fdsys

Note from West Advisory Board

This regulation is the Consumer Financial Protection Bureau's recodification of the Federal Reserve Board's Regulation M (12 C.F.R. Part 213), as mandated by the Dodd-Frank Wall Street Reform and Consumer Protection Act of 2010. The Federal Reserve Board's regulation still has the same applicability, primarily to auto dealers. The text of that regulation can be found at www.gpo.gov/fdsys.

§ 1013.1   Authority, scope, purpose, and enforcement.

(a) **Authority.** The regulation in this part, known as Regulation M, is issued by the Bureau of Consumer Financial Protection to implement the consumer leasing provisions of the Truth in Lending Act, which is Title I of the Consumer Credit Protection Act, as amended (15 U.S.C. 1601 et seq.). Information collection requirements contained in this part have been approved by the Office of Management and Budget under the provisions of 44 U.S.C. 3501 et seq. and have been assigned OMB control number 3170–0006.

(b) **Scope and purpose.** This part applies to all persons that are lessors of personal property under consumer leases as those terms are defined in § 1013.2(e)(1) and (h), except persons excluded from coverage of this part by section 1029 of the Consumer Financial Protection Act of 2010, Title X of the Dodd-Frank Wall Street Reform and Consumer Protection Act (Dodd-Frank Act), Public Law 111–203, 124 Stat. 1376. The purpose of this part is:

(1) To ensure that lessees of personal property receive meaningful disclosures that enable them to compare lease terms with other leases and, where appropriate, with credit transactions;

(2) To limit the amount of balloon payments in consumer lease transactions; and

(3) To provide for the accurate disclosure of lease terms in advertising.

(c) **Enforcement and liability.** Section 108 of the Act contains the administrative enforcement provisions. Sections 112, 130, 131, and 185 of the act contain the liability provisions for failing to comply with the requirements of the Act and this part.

§ 1013.2   Definitions.

For the purposes of this part the following definitions apply:

(a) Act means the Truth in Lending Act (15 U.S.C. 1601 et seq.) and the Consumer Leasing Act is chapter 5 of the Truth in Lending Act.

(b) Advertisement means a commercial message in any medium that directly or indirectly promotes a consumer lease transaction.

(c) Bureau refers to the Bureau of Consumer Financial Protection.

(d) Closed-end lease means a consumer lease other than an open-end lease as defined in this section.

(e)(1) Consumer lease means a contract in the form of a bailment or lease for the use of personal property by a natural person primarily for personal, family, or household purposes, for a period exceeding four months and for a total contractual obligation not exceeding the applicable threshold amount, whether or not the lessee has the option to purchase or otherwise become the owner of the property at the expiration of the lease. The threshold amount is adjusted annually to reflect increases in the Consumer Price Index for Urban Wage Earners and Clerical Workers, as applicable. See the official commentary to this paragraph (e) for the threshold amount applicable to a specific consumer lease.* Unless the context indicates otherwise, in this part "lease" means "consumer lease."

    (2) The term does not include a lease that meets the definition of a credit sale in Regulation Z (12 CFR 226.2(a)). It also does not include a lease for agricultural, business, or commercial purposes or a lease made to an organization.

    (3) This part does not apply to a lease transaction of personal property which is incident to the lease of real property and which provides that:

        (i) The lessee has no liability for the value of the personal property at the end of the lease term except for abnormal wear and tear; and

        (ii) The lessee has no option to purchase the leased property.

(f) Gross capitalized cost means the amount agreed upon by the lessor and the lessee as the value of the leased property and any items that are capitalized or amortized during the lease term, including but not limited to taxes, insurance, service agreements, and any outstanding prior credit or lease balance. Capitalized cost reduction means the total amount of any rebate, cash payment, net trade-in allowance, and noncash credit that reduces the gross capitalized cost. The adjusted capitalized cost equals the gross capitalized cost less the capitalized cost reduction, and is the amount used by the lessor in calculating the base periodic payment.

(g) Lessee means a natural person who enters into or is offered a consumer lease.

(h) Lessor means a person who regularly leases, offers to lease, or arranges for the lease of personal property under a consumer lease. A person who has leased, offered, or arranged to lease personal property more than five times in the preceding calendar year or more than five times in the current calendar year is subject to the act and this part.

(i) Open-end lease means a consumer lease in which the lessee's liability at the end of the lease term is based on the difference between the residual value of the leased property and its realized value.

(j) Organization means a corporation, trust, estate, partnership, cooperative, association, or government entity or instrumentality.

(k) Person means a natural person or an organization.

(l) Personal property means any property that is not real property under the law of the state where the property is located at the time it is offered or made available for lease.

(m) Realized value means:

    (1) The price received by the lessor for the leased property at disposition;

---

   * *Note from West Advisory Panel: From Jan. 1 through Dec. 31, 2016, the threshold amount is $54,600. See 80 Fed. Reg. 73945 (Nov. 27, 2015).*

(2) The highest offer for disposition of the leased property; or

(3) The fair market value of the leased property at the end of the lease term.

(n) Residual value means the value of the leased property at the end of the lease term, as estimated or assigned at consummation by the lessor, used in calculating the base periodic payment.

(o) Security interest and security mean any interest in property that secures the payment or performance of an obligation.

(p) State means any state, the District of Columbia, the Commonwealth of Puerto Rico, and any territory or possession of the United States.

§ 1013.3 General disclosure requirements.

(a) **General requirements.** A lessor shall make the disclosures required by § 1013.4, as applicable. The disclosures shall be made clearly and conspicuously in writing in a form the consumer may keep, in accordance with this section. The disclosures required by this part may be provided to the lessee in electronic form, subject to compliance with the consumer consent and other applicable provisions of the Electronic Signatures in Global and National Commerce Act (E-Sign Act) (15 U.S.C. § 7001 et seq.). For an advertisement accessed by the consumer in electronic form, the disclosures required by § 1013.7 may be provided to the consumer in electronic form in the advertisement, without regard to the consumer consent or other provisions of the E-Sign Act.

(1) **Form of disclosures.** The disclosures required by § 1013.4 shall be given to the lessee together in a dated statement that identifies the lessor and the lessee; the disclosures may be made either in a separate statement that identifies the consumer lease transaction or in the contract or other document evidencing the lease. Alternatively, the disclosures required to be segregated from other information under paragraph (a)(2) of this section may be provided in a separate dated statement that identifies the lease, and the other required disclosures may be provided in the lease contract or other document evidencing the lease. In a lease of multiple items, the property description required by § 1013.4(a) may be given in a separate statement that is incorporated by reference in the disclosure statement required by this paragraph.

(2) **Segregation of certain disclosures.** The following disclosures shall be segregated from other information and shall contain only directly related information: §§ 1013.4(b) through (f), (g)(2), (h)(3), (i)(1), (j), and (m)(1). The headings, content, and format for the disclosures referred to in this paragraph (a)(2) shall be provided in a manner substantially similar to the applicable model form in appendix A of this part.

(3) **Timing of disclosures.** A lessor shall provide the disclosures to the lessee prior to the consummation of a consumer lease.

(4) **Language of disclosures.** The disclosures required by § 1013.4 may be made in a language other than English provided that they are made available in English upon the lessee's request.

(5) **[Reserved]**

(b) **Additional information; nonsegregated disclosures.** Additional information may be provided with any disclosure not listed in paragraph (a)(2) of this section, but it shall not be stated, used, or placed so as to mislead or confuse the lessee or contradict, obscure, or detract attention from any disclosure required by this part.

(c) **Multiple lessors or lessees.** When a transaction involves more than one lessor, the disclosures required by this part may be made by one lessor on behalf of all the lessors. When a lease involves more than one lessee, the lessor may provide the disclosures to any lessee who is primarily liable on the lease.

(d) **Use of estimates.** If an amount or other item needed to comply with a required disclosure is unknown or unavailable after reasonable efforts have been made to ascertain the information, the lessor may use a reasonable estimate that is based on the best information available to the lessor, is clearly identified as an estimate, and is not used to circumvent or evade any disclosures required by this part.

(e) Effect of subsequent occurrence. If a required disclosure becomes inaccurate because of an event occurring after consummation, the inaccuracy is not a violation of this part.

(f) Minor variations. A lessor may disregard the effects of the following in making disclosures:

(1) That payments must be collected in whole cents;

(2) That dates of scheduled payments may be different because a scheduled date is not a business day;

(3) That months have different numbers of days; and

(4) That February 29 occurs in a leap year.

§ 1013.4 Content of disclosures.

For any consumer lease subject to this part, the lessor shall disclose the following information, as applicable:

(a) Description of property. A brief description of the leased property sufficient to identify the property to the lessee and lessor.

(b) Amount due at lease signing or delivery. The total amount to be paid prior to or at consummation or by delivery, if delivery occurs after consummation, using the term "amount due at lease signing or delivery." The lessor shall itemize each component by type and amount, including any refundable security deposit, advance monthly or other periodic payment, and capitalized cost reduction; and in motor-vehicle leases, shall itemize how the amount due will be paid, by type and amount, including any net trade-in allowance, rebates, noncash credits, and cash payments in a format substantially similar to the model forms in Appendix A of this part.

(c) Payment schedule and total amount of periodic payments. The number, amount, and due dates or periods of payments scheduled under the lease, and the total amount of the periodic payments.

(d) Other charges. The total amount of other charges payable to the lessor, itemized by type and amount, that are not included in the periodic payments. Such charges include the amount of any liability the lease imposes upon the lessee at the end of the lease term; the potential difference between the residual and realized values referred to in paragraph (k) of this section is excluded.

(e) Total of payments. The total of payments, with a description such as "the amount you will have paid by the end of the lease." This amount is the sum of the amount due at lease signing (less any refundable amounts), the total amount of periodic payments (less any portion of the periodic payment paid at lease signing), and other charges under paragraphs (b), (c), and (d) of this section. In an open-end lease, a description such as "you will owe an additional amount if the actual value of the vehicle is less than the residual value" shall accompany the disclosure.

(f) Payment calculation. In a motor-vehicle lease, a mathematical progression of how the scheduled periodic payment is derived, in a format substantially similar to the applicable model form in Appendix A of this part, which shall contain the following:

(1) **Gross capitalized cost.** The gross capitalized cost, including a disclosure of the agreed upon value of the vehicle, a description such as "the agreed upon value of the vehicle [state the amount] and any items you pay for over the lease term (such as service contracts, insurance, and any outstanding prior credit or lease balance)," and a statement of the lessee's option to receive a separate written itemization of the gross capitalized cost. If requested by the lessee, the itemization shall be provided before consummation.

(2) **Capitalized cost reduction.** The capitalized cost reduction, with a description such as "the amount of any net trade-in allowance, rebate, noncash credit, or cash you pay that reduces the gross capitalized cost."

(3) **Adjusted capitalized cost.** The adjusted capitalized cost, with a description such as "the amount used in calculating your base [periodic] payment."

REGULATION M §1013.4

(4)   Residual value. The residual value, with a description such as "the value of the vehicle at the end of the lease used in calculating your base [periodic] payment."

(5)   Depreciation and any amortized amounts. The depreciation and any amortized amounts, which is the difference between the adjusted capitalized cost and the residual value, with a description such as "the amount charged for the vehicle's decline in value through normal use and for any other items paid over the lease term."

(6)   Rent charge. The rent charge, with a description such as "the amount charged in addition to the depreciation and any amortized amounts." This amount is the difference between the total of the base periodic payments over the lease term minus the depreciation and any amortized amounts.

(7)   Total of base periodic payments. The total of base periodic payments with a description such as "depreciation and any amortized amounts plus the rent charge."

(8)   Lease payments. The lease payments with a description such as "the number of payments in your lease."

(9)   Base periodic payment. The total of the base periodic payments divided by the number of payment periods in the lease.

(10) Itemization of other charges. An itemization of any other charges that are part of the periodic payment.

(11) Total periodic payment. The sum of the base periodic payment and any other charges that are part of the periodic payment.

(g)   Early termination—

(1)   Conditions and disclosure of charges. A statement of the conditions under which the lessee or lessor may terminate the lease prior to the end of the lease term; and the amount or a description of the method for determining the amount of any penalty or other charge for early termination, which must be reasonable.

(2)   Early termination notice. In a motor-vehicle lease, a notice substantially similar to the following: "Early Termination. You may have to pay a substantial charge if you end this lease early. The charge may be up to several thousand dollars. The actual charge will depend on when the lease is terminated. The earlier you end the lease, the greater this charge is likely to be."

(h)   Maintenance responsibilities. The following provisions are required:

(1)   Statement of responsibilities. A statement specifying whether the lessor or the lessee is responsible for maintaining or servicing the leased property, together with a brief description of the responsibility;

(2)   Wear and use standard. A statement of the lessor's standards for wear and use (if any), which must be reasonable; and

(3)   Notice of wear and use standard. In a motor vehicle lease, a notice regarding wear and use substantially similar to the following: "Excessive Wear and Use. You may be charged for excessive wear based on our standards for normal use." The notice shall also specify the amount or method for determining any charge for excess mileage.

(i)   Purchase option. A statement of whether or not the lessee has the option to purchase the leased property, and:

(1)   End of lease term. If at the end of the lease term, the purchase price; and

(2)   During lease term. If prior to the end of the lease term, the purchase price or the method for determining the price and when the lessee may exercise this option.

(j)   Statement referencing nonsegregated disclosures. A statement that the lessee should refer to the lease documents for additional information on early termination, purchase options and maintenance responsibilities, warranties, late and default charges, insurance, and any security interests, if applicable.

(k) Liability between residual and realized values. A statement of the lessee's liability, if any, at early termination or at the end of the lease term for the difference between the residual value of the leased property and its realized value.

(*l*) Right of appraisal. If the lessee's liability at early termination or at the end of the lease term is based on the realized value of the leased property, a statement that the lessee may obtain, at the lessee's expense, a professional appraisal by an independent third party (agreed to by the lessee and the lessor) of the value that could be realized at sale of the leased property. The appraisal shall be final and binding on the parties.

(m) Liability at end of lease term based on residual value. If the lessee is liable at the end of the lease term for the difference between the residual value of the leased property and its realized value:

(1) Rent and other charges. The rent and other charges, paid by the lessee and required by the lessor as an incident to the lease transaction, with a description such as "the total amount of rent and other charges imposed in connection with your lease [state the amount]."

(2) Excess liability. A statement about a rebuttable presumption that, at the end of the lease term, the residual value of the leased property is unreasonable and not in good faith to the extent that the residual value exceeds the realized value by more than three times the base monthly payment (or more than three times the average payment allocable to a monthly period, if the lease calls for periodic payments other than monthly); and that the lessor cannot collect the excess amount unless the lessor brings a successful court action and pays the lessee's reasonable attorney's fees, or unless the excess of the residual value over the realized value is due to unreasonable or excessive wear or use of the leased property (in which case the rebuttable presumption does not apply).

(3) Mutually agreeable final adjustment. A statement that the lessee and lessor are permitted, after termination of the lease, to make any mutually agreeable final adjustment regarding excess liability.

(n) Fees and taxes. The total dollar amount for all official and license fees, registration, title, or taxes required to be paid in connection with the lease.

(o) Insurance. A brief identification of insurance in connection with the lease including:

(1) Through the lessor. If the insurance is provided by or paid through the lessor, the types and amounts of coverage and the cost to the lessee; or

(2) Through a third party. If the lessee must obtain the insurance, the types and amounts of coverage required of the lessee.

(p) Warranties or guarantees. A statement identifying all express warranties and guarantees from the manufacturer or lessor with respect to the leased property that apply to the lessee.

(q) Penalties and other charges for delinquency. The amount or the method of determining the amount of any penalty or other charge for delinquency, default, or late payments, which must be reasonable.

(r) Security interest. A description of any security interest, other than a security deposit disclosed under paragraph (b) of this section, held or to be retained by the lessor; and a clear identification of the property to which the security interest relates.

(s) Limitations on rate information. If a lessor provides a percentage rate in an advertisement or in documents evidencing the lease transaction, a notice stating that "this percentage may not measure the overall cost of financing this lease" shall accompany the rate disclosure. The lessor shall not use the term "annual percentage rate," "annual lease rate," or any equivalent term.

(t) Non-motor vehicle open-end leases. Non-motor vehicle open-end leases remain subject to section 182(10) of the Act regarding end of term liability.

§ 1013.5 Renegotiations, extensions, and assumptions.

(a) Renegotiation. A renegotiation occurs when a consumer lease subject to this part is satisfied and replaced by a new lease undertaken by the same consumer. A renegotiation requires new disclosures, except as provided in paragraph (d) of this section.

(b) Extension. An extension is a continuation, agreed to by the lessor and the lessee, of an existing consumer lease beyond the originally scheduled end of the lease term, except when the continuation is the result of a renegotiation. An extension that exceeds six months requires new disclosures, except as provided in paragraph (d) of this section.

(c) Assumption. New disclosures are not required when a consumer lease is assumed by another person, whether or not the lessor charges an assumption fee.

(d) Exceptions. New disclosures are not required for the following, even if they meet the definition of a renegotiation or an extension:

(1) A reduction in the rent charge;

(2) The deferment of one or more payments, whether or not a fee is charged;

(3) The extension of a lease for not more than six months on a month-to-month basis or otherwise;

(4) A substitution of leased property with property that has a substantially equivalent or greater economic value, provided no other lease terms are changed;

(5) The addition, deletion, or substitution of leased property in a multiple-item lease, provided the average periodic payment does not change by more than 25 percent; or

(6) An agreement resulting from a court proceeding.

§ 1013.6 [Reserved].

§ 1013.7 Advertising.

(a) General rule. An advertisement for a consumer lease may state that a specific lease of property at specific amounts or terms is available only if the lessor usually and customarily leases or will lease the property at those amounts or terms.

(b) Clear and conspicuous standard. Disclosures required by this section shall be made clearly and conspicuously.

(1) **Amount due at lease signing or delivery.** Except for the statement of a periodic payment, any affirmative or negative reference to a charge that is a part of the disclosure required under paragraph (d)(2)(ii) of this section shall not be more prominent than that disclosure.

(2) **Advertisement of a lease rate.** If a lessor provides a percentage rate in an advertisement, the rate shall not be more prominent than any of the disclosures in § 1013.4, with the exception of the notice in § 1013.4(s) required to accompany the rate; and the lessor shall not use the term "annual percentage rate," "annual lease rate," or equivalent term.

(c) Catalogs or other multipage advertisements; electronic advertisements. A catalog or other multipage advertisement, or an electronic advertisement (such as an advertisement appearing on an Internet Web site), that provides a table or schedule of the required disclosures shall be considered a single advertisement if, for lease terms that appear without all the required disclosures, the advertisement refers to the page or pages on which the table or schedule appears.

(d) Advertisement of terms that require additional disclosure.

(1) **Triggering terms.** An advertisement that states any of the following items shall contain the disclosures required by paragraph (d)(2) of this section, except as provided in paragraphs (e) and (f) of this section:

(i) The amount of any payment; or

(ii) A statement of any capitalized cost reduction or other payment (or that no payment is required) prior to or at consummation or by delivery, if delivery occurs after consummation.

(2) **Additional terms.** An advertisement stating any item listed in paragraph (d)(1) of this section shall also state the following items:

(i) That the transaction advertised is a lease;

(ii) The total amount due prior to or at consummation or by delivery, if delivery occurs after consummation;

(iii) The number, amounts, and due dates or periods of scheduled payments under the lease;

(iv) A statement of whether or not a security deposit is required; and

(v) A statement that an extra charge may be imposed at the end of the lease term where the lessee's liability (if any) is based on the difference between the residual value of the leased property and its realized value at the end of the lease term.

(e) **Alternative disclosures—merchandise tags.** A merchandise tag stating any item listed in paragraph (d)(1) of this section may comply with paragraph (d)(2) of this section by referring to a sign or display prominently posted in the lessor's place of business that contains a table or schedule of the required disclosures.

(f) **Alternative disclosures—television or radio advertisements—**

(1) **Toll-free number or print advertisement.** An advertisement made through television or radio stating any item listed in paragraph (d)(1) of this section complies with paragraph (d)(2) of this section if the advertisement states the items listed in paragraphs (d)(2)(i) through (iii) of this section, and:

(i) Lists a toll-free telephone number along with a reference that such number may be used by consumers to obtain the information required by paragraph (d)(2) of this section; or

(ii) Directs the consumer to a written advertisement in a publication of general circulation in the community served by the media station, including the name and the date of the publication, with a statement that information required by paragraph (d)(2) of this section is included in the advertisement. The written advertisement shall be published beginning at least three days before and ending at least ten days after the broadcast.

(2) **Establishment of toll-free number.**

(i) The toll-free telephone number shall be available for no fewer than ten days, beginning on the date of the broadcast.

(ii) The lessor shall provide the information required by paragraph (d)(2) of this section orally, or in writing upon request.

§ 1013.8   Record retention.

A lessor shall retain evidence of compliance with the requirements imposed by this part, other than the advertising requirements under § 1013.7, for a period of not less than two years after the date the disclosures are required to be made or an action is required to be taken.

§ 1013.9   Relation to state laws.

(a) **Inconsistent state law.** A state law that is inconsistent with the requirements of the Act and this part is preempted to the extent of the inconsistency. If a lessor cannot comply with a state law without violating a provision of this part, the state law is inconsistent within the meaning of section 186(a) of the Act and is preempted, unless the state law gives greater protection and benefit to the consumer. A state, through an official having primary enforcement or interpretative responsibilities for the state consumer leasing law, may apply to the Bureau for a preemption determination.

(b) Exemptions.—

(1) Application. A state may apply to the Bureau for an exemption from the requirements of the Act and this part for any class of lease transactions within the state. The Bureau will grant such an exemption if the Bureau determines that:

    (i) The class of leasing transactions is subject to state law requirements substantially similar to the Act and this part or that lessees are afforded greater protection under state law; and

    (ii) There is adequate provision for state enforcement.

(2) Enforcement and liability. After an exemption has been granted, the requirements of the applicable state law (except for additional requirements not imposed by Federal law) will constitute the requirements of the Act and this part. No exemption will extend to the civil liability provisions of sections 130, 131, and 185 of the Act.

EQUAL CREDIT OPPORTUNITY
(REGULATION B)

12 C.F.R. Part 1002

Current through March 13, 2016; 81 F.R. 12795

For updates, see www.ecfr.gov

Note from West Advisory Board

This regulation is the Consumer Financial Protection Bureau's recodification of the Federal Reserve Board's Regulation M (12 C.F.R. Part 202), as mandated by the Dodd-Frank Wall Street Reform and Consumer Protection Act of 2010. The Federal Reserve Board's regulation still has the same applicability, primarily to auto dealers. The text of that regulation can be found at www.ecfr.gov.

§ 1002.1   Authority, scope and purpose.

   (a) **Authority and scope.** This part, known as Regulation B, is issued by the Consumer Credit Protection Bureau (Bureau) pursuant to title VII (Equal Credit Opportunity Act) of the Consumer Credit Protection Act, as amended (15 U.S.C. 1601 et seq.). Except as otherwise provided herein, this part applies to all persons who are creditors, as defined in § 1002.2(1), other than a person excluded from coverage of this part by section 1029 of the Consumer Financial Protection Act of 2010, Title X of the Dodd-Frank Wall Street Reform and Consumer Protection Act, Public Law 111–203, 124 Stat. 1376. Information collection requirements contained in this part have been approved by the Office of Management and Budget under the provisions of 44 U.S.C. 3501 et seq. and have been assigned OMB No. 3170–0013.

   (b) **Purpose.** The purpose of this part is to promote the availability of credit to all creditworthy applicants without regard to race, color, religion, national origin, sex, marital status, or age (provided the applicant has the capacity to contract); to the fact that all or part of the applicant's income derives from a public assistance program; or to the fact that the applicant has in good faith exercised any right under the Consumer Credit Protection Act. The regulation prohibits creditor practices that discriminate on the basis of any of these factors. The regulation also requires creditors to notify applicants of action taken on their applications; to report credit history in the names of both spouses on an account; to retain records of credit applications; to collect information about the applicant's race and other personal characteristics in applications for certain dwelling-related loans; and to provide applicants with copies of appraisal reports used in connection with credit transactions.

§ 1002.2   Definitions.

For the purposes of this part, unless the context indicates otherwise, the following definitions apply.

(a)   Account means an extension of credit. When employed in relation to an account, the word use refers only to open-end credit.

(b)   Act means the Equal Credit Opportunity Act (title VII of the Consumer Credit Protection Act).

(c)   Adverse action.

(1)   The term means:

(i)   A refusal to grant credit in substantially the amount or on substantially the terms requested in an application unless the creditor makes a counteroffer (to grant credit in a different amount or on other terms) and the applicant uses or expressly accepts the credit offered;

(ii)   A termination of an account or an unfavorable change in the terms of an account that does not affect all or substantially all of a class of the creditor's accounts; or

(iii)   A refusal to increase the amount of credit available to an applicant who has made an application for an increase.

(2)   The term does not include:

(i)   A change in the terms of an account expressly agreed to by an applicant.

(ii)   Any action or forbearance relating to an account taken in connection with inactivity, default, or delinquency as to that account;

(iii)   A refusal or failure to authorize an account transaction at point of sale or loan, except when the refusal is a termination or an unfavorable change in the terms of an account that does not affect all or substantially all of a class of the creditor's accounts, or when the refusal is a denial of an application for an increase in the amount of credit available under the account;

(iv)   A refusal to extend credit because applicable law prohibits the creditor from extending the credit requested; or

(v)   A refusal to extend credit because the creditor does not offer the type of credit or credit plan requested.

(3)   An action that falls within the definition of both paragraphs (c)(1) and (c)(2) of this section is governed by paragraph (c)(2) of this section.

(d)   Age refers only to the age of natural persons and means the number of fully elapsed years from the date of an applicant's birth.

(e)   Applicant means any person who requests or who has received an extension of credit from a creditor, and includes any person who is or may become contractually liable regarding an extension of credit. For purposes of § 1002.7(d), the term includes guarantors, sureties, endorsers, and similar parties.

(f)   Application means an oral or written request for an extension of credit that is made in accordance with procedures used by a creditor for the type of credit requested. The term application does not include the use of an account or line of credit to obtain an amount of credit that is within a previously established credit limit. A completed application means an application in connection with which a creditor has received all the information that the creditor regularly obtains and considers in evaluating applications for the amount and type of credit requested (including, but not limited to, credit reports, any additional information requested from the applicant, and any approvals or reports by governmental agencies or other persons that are necessary to guarantee, insure, or provide security for the credit or collateral). The creditor shall exercise reasonable diligence in obtaining such information.

(g) Business credit refers to extensions of credit primarily for business or commercial (including agricultural) purposes, but excluding extensions of credit of the types described in § 1002.3(a)–(d).

(h) Consumer credit means credit extended to a natural person primarily for personal, family, or household purposes.

(i) Contractually liable means expressly obligated to repay all debts arising on an account by reason of an agreement to that effect.

(j) Credit means the right granted by a creditor to an applicant to defer payment of a debt, incur debt and defer its payment, or purchase property or services and defer payment therefor.

(k) Credit card means any card, plate, coupon book, or other single credit device that may be used from time to time to obtain money, property, or services on credit.

(l) Creditor means a person who, in the ordinary course of business, regularly participates in a credit decision, including setting the terms of the credit. The term creditor includes a creditor's assignee, transferee, or subrogee who so participates. For purposes of § 1002.4(a) and (b), the term creditor also includes a person who, in the ordinary course of business, regularly refers applicants or prospective applicants to creditors, or selects or offers to select creditors to whom requests for credit may be made. A person is not a creditor regarding any violation of the Act or this part committed by another creditor unless the person knew or had reasonable notice of the act, policy, or practice that constituted the violation before becoming involved in the credit transaction. The term does not include a person whose only participation in a credit transaction involves honoring a credit card.

(m) Credit transaction means every aspect of an applicant's dealings with a creditor regarding an application for credit or an existing extension of credit (including, but not limited to, information requirements; investigation procedures; standards of creditworthiness; terms of credit; furnishing of credit information; revocation, alteration, or termination of credit; and collection procedures).

(n) Discriminate against an applicant means to treat an applicant less favorably than other applicants.

(o) Elderly means age 62 or older.

(p) Empirically derived and other credit scoring systems.

(1) A credit scoring system is a system that evaluates an applicant's creditworthiness mechanically, based on key attributes of the applicant and aspects of the transaction, and that determines, alone or in conjunction with an evaluation of additional information about the applicant, whether an applicant is deemed creditworthy. To qualify as an empirically derived, demonstrably and statistically sound, credit scoring system, the system must be:

    (i) Based on data that are derived from an empirical comparison of sample groups or the population of creditworthy and noncreditworthy applicants who applied for credit within a reasonable preceding period of time;

    (ii) Developed for the purpose of evaluating the creditworthiness of applicants with respect to the legitimate business interests of the creditor utilizing the system (including, but not limited to, minimizing bad debt losses and operating expenses in accordance with the creditor's business judgment);

    (iii) Developed and validated using accepted statistical principles and methodology; and

    (iv) Periodically revalidated by the use of appropriate statistical principles and methodology and adjusted as necessary to maintain predictive ability.

(2) A creditor may use an empirically derived, demonstrably and statistically sound, credit scoring system obtained from another person or may obtain credit experience from which to develop such a system. Any such system must satisfy the criteria set forth in paragraph (p)(1)(i) through (iv) of this section; if the creditor is unable during the development process to validate the system based on its own credit experience in accordance with paragraph (p)(1) of this section, the system must be validated when sufficient credit experience becomes available. A system that fails this validity test is no longer an empirically derived, demonstrably and statistically sound, credit scoring system for that creditor.

(q) Extend credit and extension of credit mean the granting of credit in any form (including, but not limited to, credit granted in addition to any existing credit or credit limit; credit granted pursuant to an open-end credit plan; the refinancing or other renewal of credit, including the issuance of a new credit card in place of an expiring credit card or in substitution for an existing credit card; the consolidation of two or more obligations; or the continuance of existing credit without any special effort to collect at or after maturity).

(r) Good faith means honesty in fact in the conduct or transaction.

(s) Inadvertent error means a mechanical, electronic, or clerical error that a creditor demonstrates was not intentional and occurred notwithstanding the maintenance of procedures reasonably adapted to avoid such errors.

(t) Judgmental system of evaluating applicants means any system for evaluating the creditworthiness of an applicant other than an empirically derived, demonstrably and statistically sound, credit scoring system.

(u) Marital status means the state of being unmarried, married, or separated, as defined by applicable state law. The term "unmarried" includes persons who are single, divorced, or widowed.

(v) Negative factor or value, in relation to the age of elderly applicants, means utilizing a factor, value, or weight that is less favorable regarding elderly applicants than the creditor's experience warrants or is less favorable than the factor, value, or weight assigned to the class of applicants that are not classified as elderly and are most favored by a creditor on the basis of age.

(w) Open-end credit means credit extended under a plan in which a creditor may permit an applicant to make purchases or obtain loans from time to time directly from the creditor or indirectly by use of a credit card, check, or other device.

(x) Person means a natural person, corporation, government or governmental subdivision or agency, trust, estate, partnership, cooperative, or association.

(y) Pertinent element of creditworthiness, in relation to a judgmental system of evaluating applicants, means any information about applicants that a creditor obtains and considers and that has a demonstrable relationship to a determination of creditworthiness.

(z) Prohibited basis means race, color, religion, national origin, sex, marital status, or age (provided that the applicant has the capacity to enter into a binding contract); the fact that all or part of the applicant's income derives from any public assistance program; or the fact that the applicant has in good faith exercised any right under the Consumer Credit Protection Act or any state law upon which an exemption has been granted by the Bureau.

(aa) State means any state, the District of Columbia, the Commonwealth of Puerto Rico, or any territory or possession of the United States.

§ 1002.3   Limited exceptions for certain classes of transactions.

(a) Public utilities credit.

(1) Definition. Public utilities credit refers to extensions of credit that involve public utility services provided through pipe, wire, or other connected facilities, or radio or similar transmission (including extensions of such facilities), if the charges for service, delayed payment, and any discount for prompt payment are filed with or regulated by a government unit.

(2) Exceptions. The following provisions of this regulation do not apply to public utilities credit:

    (i) Section 1002.5(d)(1) concerning information about marital status; and

    (ii) Section 1002.12(b) relating to record retention.

(b) Securities credit.

    (1) Definition. Securities credit refers to extensions of credit subject to regulation under section 7 of the Securities Exchange Act of 1934 or extensions of credit by a broker or dealer subject to regulation as a broker or dealer under the Securities Exchange Act of 1934.

    (2) Exceptions. The following provisions of this regulation do not apply to securities credit:

    (i) Section 1002.5(b) concerning information about the sex of an applicant;

    (ii) Section 1002.5(c) concerning information about a spouse or former spouse;

    (iii) Section 1002.5(d)(1) concerning information about marital status;

    (iv) Section 1002.7(b) relating to designation of name to the extent necessary to comply with rules regarding an account in which a broker or dealer has an interest, or rules regarding the aggregation of accounts of spouses to determine controlling interests, beneficial interests, beneficial ownership, or purchase limitations and restrictions;

    (v) Section 1002.7(c) relating to action concerning open-end accounts, to the extent the action taken is on the basis of a change of name or marital status;

    (vi) Section 1002.7(d) relating to the signature of a spouse or other person;

    (vii) Section 1002.10 relating to furnishing of credit information; and

    (viii) Section 1002.12(b) relating to record retention.

(c) Incidental credit—

    (1) Definition. Incidental credit refers to extensions of consumer credit other than the types described in paragraphs (a) and (b) of this section:

    (i) That are not made pursuant to the terms of a credit card account;

    (ii) That are not subject to a finance charge (as defined in Regulation Z, 12 CFR 1026.4); and

    (iii) That are not payable by agreement in more than four installments.

    (2) Exceptions. The following provisions of this regulation do not apply to incidental credit:

    (i) Section 1002.5(b) concerning information about the sex of an applicant, but only to the extent necessary for medical records or similar purposes;

    (ii) Section 1002.5(c) concerning information about a spouse or former spouse;

    (iii) Section 1002.5(d)(1) concerning information about marital status;

    (iv) Section 1002.5(d)(2) concerning information about income derived from alimony, child support, or separate maintenance payments;

    (v) Section 1002.7(d) relating to the signature of a spouse or other person;

    (vi) Section 1002.9 relating to notifications;

    (vii) Section 1002.10 relating to furnishing of credit information; and

    (viii) Section 1002.12(b) relating to record retention.

(d) Government credit—

    (1) Definition. Government credit refers to extensions of credit made to governments or governmental subdivisions, agencies, or instrumentalities.

(2) **Applicability of regulation.** Except for § 1002.4(a), the general rule against discrimination on a prohibited basis, the requirements of this regulation do not apply to government credit.

§ 1002.4   General rules.

(a) **Discrimination.** A creditor shall not discriminate against an applicant on a prohibited basis regarding any aspect of a credit transaction.

(b) **Discouragement.** A creditor shall not make any oral or written statement, in advertising or otherwise, to applicants or prospective applicants that would discourage on a prohibited basis a reasonable person from making or pursuing an application.

(c) **Written applications.** A creditor shall take written applications for the dwelling-related types of credit covered by § 1002.13(a).

(d) **Form of disclosures.**

(1) **General rule.** A creditor that provides in writing any disclosures or information required by this part must provide the disclosures in a clear and conspicuous manner and, except for the disclosures required by §§ 1002.5 and 1002.13, in a form the applicant may retain.

(2) **Disclosures in electronic form.** The disclosures required by this part that are required to be given in writing may be provided to the applicant in electronic form, subject to compliance with the consumer consent and other applicable provisions of the Electronic Signatures in Global and National Commerce Act (E-Sign Act) (15 U.S.C. 7001 et seq.). Where the disclosures under §§ 1002.5(b)(1), 1002.5(b)(2), 1002.5(d)(1), 1002.5(d)(2), 1002.13, and 1002.14(a)(2)(i) accompany an application accessed by the applicant in electronic form, these disclosures may be provided to the applicant in electronic form on or with the application form, without regard to the consumer consent or other provisions of the E-Sign Act.

(e) **Foreign-language disclosures.** Disclosures may be made in languages other than English, provided they are available in English upon request.

§ 1002.5   Rules concerning requests for information.

(a) **General rules.**

(1) **Requests for information.** Except as provided in paragraphs (b) through (d) of this section, a creditor may request any information in connection with a credit transaction. This paragraph does not limit or abrogate any Federal or state law regarding privacy, privileged information, credit reporting limitations, or similar restrictions on obtainable information.

(2) **Required collection of information.** Notwithstanding paragraphs (b) through (d) of this section, a creditor shall request information for monitoring purposes as required by § 1002.13 for credit secured by the applicant's dwelling. In addition, a creditor may obtain information required by a regulation, order, or agreement issued by, or entered into with, a court or an enforcement agency (including the Attorney General of the United States or a similar state official) to monitor or enforce compliance with the Act, this part, or other Federal or state statutes or regulations.

(3) **Special-purpose credit.** A creditor may obtain information that is otherwise restricted to determine eligibility for a special purpose credit program, as provided in § 1002.8(b), (c), and (d).

(b) **Limitation on information about race, color, religion, national origin, or sex.** A creditor shall not inquire about the race, color, religion, national origin, or sex of an applicant or any other person in connection with a credit transaction, except as provided in paragraphs (b)(1) and (b)(2) of this section.

(1) **Self-test.** A creditor may inquire about the race, color, religion, national origin, or sex of an applicant or any other person in connection with a credit transaction for the purpose of conducting a self-test that meets the requirements of § 1002.15. A creditor that makes such an inquiry shall disclose orally or in writing, at the time the information is requested, that:

(i) The applicant will not be required to provide the information;

(ii) The creditor is requesting the information to monitor its compliance with the federal Equal Credit Opportunity Act;

(iii) Federal law prohibits the creditor from discriminating on the basis of this information, or on the basis of an applicant's decision not to furnish the information; and

(iv) If applicable, certain information will be collected based on visual observation or surname if not provided by the applicant or other person.

(2) **Sex.** An applicant may be requested to designate a title on an application form (such as Ms., Miss, Mr., or Mrs.) if the form discloses that the designation of a title is optional. An application form shall otherwise use only terms that are neutral as to sex.

(c) **Information about a spouse or former spouse.**

(1) **General rule.** Except as permitted in this paragraph, a creditor may not request any information concerning the spouse or former spouse of an applicant.

(2) **Permissible inquiries.** A creditor may request any information concerning an applicant's spouse (or former spouse under paragraph (c)(2)(v) of this section) that may be requested about the applicant if:

(i) The spouse will be permitted to use the account;

(ii) The spouse will be contractually liable on the account;

(iii) The applicant is relying on the spouse's income as a basis for repayment of the credit requested;

(iv) The applicant resides in a community property state or is relying on property located in such a state as a basis for repayment of the credit requested; or

(v) The applicant is relying on alimony, child support, or separate maintenance payments from a spouse or former spouse as a basis for repayment of the credit requested.

(3) **Other accounts of the applicant.** A creditor may request that an applicant list any account on which the applicant is contractually liable and to provide the name and address of the person in whose name the account is held. A creditor may also ask an applicant to list the names in which the applicant has previously received credit.

(d) **Other limitations on information requests.**

(1) **Marital status.** If an applicant applies for individual unsecured credit, a creditor shall not inquire about the applicant's marital status unless the applicant resides in a community property state or is relying on property located in such a state as a basis for repayment of the credit requested. If an application is for other than individual unsecured credit, a creditor may inquire about the applicant's marital status, but shall use only the terms married, unmarried, and separated. A creditor may explain that the category unmarried includes single, divorced, and widowed persons.

(2) **Disclosure about income from alimony, child support, or separate maintenance.** A creditor shall not inquire whether income stated in an application is derived from alimony, child support, or separate maintenance payments unless the creditor discloses to the applicant that such income need not be revealed if the applicant does not want the creditor to consider it in determining the applicant's creditworthiness.

(3) **Childbearing, childrearing.** A creditor shall not inquire about birth control practices, intentions concerning the bearing or rearing of children, or capability to bear children. A creditor may inquire about the number and ages of an applicant's dependents or about dependent-related financial obligations or expenditures, provided such information is requested without regard to sex, marital status, or any other prohibited basis.

(e)   Permanent residency and immigration status. A creditor may inquire about the permanent residency and immigration status of an applicant or any other person in connection with a credit transaction.

§ 1002.6   Rules concerning evaluation of applications.

(a)   General rule concerning use of information. Except as otherwise provided in the Act and this part, a creditor may consider any information obtained, so long as the information is not used to discriminate against an applicant on a prohibited basis. The legislative history of the Act indicates that the Congress intended an "effects test" concept, as outlined in the employment field by the Supreme Court in the cases of Griggs v. Duke Power Co., 401 U.S. 424 (1971), and Albemarle Paper Co. v. Moody, 422 U.S. 405 (1975), to be applicable to a creditor's determination of creditworthiness.

(b)   Specific rules concerning use of information—

(1)   Except as provided in the Act and this part, a creditor shall not take a prohibited basis into account in any system of evaluating the creditworthiness of applicants.

(2)   Age, receipt of public assistance.

(i)   Except as permitted in this paragraph, a creditor shall not take into account an applicant's age (provided that the applicant has the capacity to enter into a binding contract) or whether an applicant's income derives from any public assistance program.

(ii)   In an empirically derived, demonstrably and statistically sound, credit scoring system, a creditor may use an applicant's age as a predictive variable, provided that the age of an elderly applicant is not assigned a negative factor or value.

(iii)   In a judgmental system of evaluating creditworthiness, a creditor may consider an applicant's age or whether an applicant's income derives from any public assistance program only for the purpose of determining a pertinent element of creditworthiness.

(iv)   In any system of evaluating creditworthiness, a creditor may consider the age of an elderly applicant when such age is used to favor the elderly applicant in extending credit.

(3)   Childbearing, childrearing. In evaluating creditworthiness, a creditor shall not make assumptions or use aggregate statistics relating to the likelihood that any category of persons will bear or rear children or will, for that reason, receive diminished or interrupted income in the future.

(4)   Telephone listing. A creditor shall not take into account whether there is a telephone listing in the name of an applicant for consumer credit but may take into account whether there is a telephone in the applicant's residence.

(5)   Income. A creditor shall not discount or exclude from consideration the income of an applicant or the spouse of an applicant because of a prohibited basis or because the income is derived from part-time employment or is an annuity, pension, or other retirement benefit; a creditor may consider the amount and probable continuance of any income in evaluating an applicant's creditworthiness. When an applicant relies on alimony, child support, or separate maintenance payments in applying for credit, the creditor shall consider such payments as income to the extent that they are likely to be consistently made.

(6)   Credit history. To the extent that a creditor considers credit history in evaluating the creditworthiness of similarly qualified applicants for a similar type and amount of credit, in evaluating an applicant's creditworthiness a creditor shall consider:

(i)   The credit history, when available, of accounts designated as accounts that the applicant and the applicant's spouse are permitted to use or for which both are contractually liable;

(ii)   On the applicant's request, any information the applicant may present that tends to indicate the credit history being considered by the creditor does not accurately reflect the applicant's creditworthiness; and

    (iii) On the applicant's request, the credit history, when available, of any account reported in the name of the applicant's spouse or former spouse that the applicant can demonstrate accurately reflects the applicant's creditworthiness.

    (7) Immigration status. A creditor may consider the applicant's immigration status or status as a permanent resident of the United States, and any additional information that may be necessary to ascertain the creditor's rights and remedies regarding repayment.

    (8) Marital status. Except as otherwise permitted or required by law, a creditor shall evaluate married and unmarried applicants by the same standards; and in evaluating joint applicants, a creditor shall not treat applicants differently based on the existence, absence, or likelihood of a marital relationship between the parties.

    (9) Race, color, religion, national origin, sex. Except as otherwise permitted or required by law, a creditor shall not consider race, color, religion, national origin, or sex (or an applicant's or other person's decision not to provide the information) in any aspect of a credit transaction.

    (c) State property laws. A creditor's consideration or application of state property laws directly or indirectly affecting creditworthiness does not constitute unlawful discrimination for the purposes of the Act or this part.

§ 1002.7   Rules concerning extensions of credit.

    (a) Individual accounts. A creditor shall not refuse to grant an individual account to a creditworthy applicant on the basis of sex, marital status, or any other prohibited basis.

    (b) Designation of name. A creditor shall not refuse to allow an applicant to open or maintain an account in a birth-given first name and a surname that is the applicant's birth-given surname, the spouse's surname, or a combined surname.

    (c) Action concerning existing open-end accounts.

    (1) Limitations. In the absence of evidence of the applicant's inability or unwillingness to repay, a creditor shall not take any of the following actions regarding an applicant who is contractually liable on an existing open-end account on the basis of the applicant's reaching a certain age or retiring or on the basis of a change in the applicant's name or marital status:

    (i) Require a reapplication, except as provided in paragraph (c)(2) of this section;

    (ii) Change the terms of the account; or

    (iii) Terminate the account.

    (2) Requiring reapplication. A creditor may require a reapplication for an open-end account on the basis of a change in the marital status of an applicant who is contractually liable if the credit granted was based in whole or in part on income of the applicant's spouse and if information available to the creditor indicates that the applicant's income may not support the amount of credit currently available.

    (d) Signature of spouse or other person.

    (1) Rule for qualified applicant. Except as provided in this paragraph, a creditor shall not require the signature of an applicant's spouse or other person, other than a joint applicant, on any credit instrument if the applicant qualifies under the creditor's standards of creditworthiness for the amount and terms of the credit requested. A creditor shall not deem the submission of a joint financial statement or other evidence of jointly held assets as an application for joint credit.

    (2) Unsecured credit. If an applicant requests unsecured credit and relies in part upon property that the applicant owns jointly with another person to satisfy the creditor's standards of creditworthiness, the creditor may require the signature of the other person only on the instrument(s) necessary, or reasonably believed by the creditor to be necessary, under the law of the state in which the property is located, to enable the creditor to reach the property being relied upon in the event of the death or default of the applicant.

(3)   Unsecured credit—community property states. If a married applicant requests unsecured credit and resides in a community property state, or if the applicant is relying on property located in such a state, a creditor may require the signature of the spouse on any instrument necessary, or reasonably believed by the creditor to be necessary, under applicable state law to make the community property available to satisfy the debt in the event of default if:

  (i)   Applicable state law denies the applicant power to manage or control sufficient community property to qualify for the credit requested under the creditor's standards of creditworthiness; and

  (ii)   The applicant does not have sufficient separate property to qualify for the credit requested without regard to community property.

(4)   Secured credit. If an applicant requests secured credit, a creditor may require the signature of the applicant's spouse or other person on any instrument necessary, or reasonably believed by the creditor to be necessary, under applicable state law to make the property being offered as security available to satisfy the debt in the event of default, for example, an instrument to create a valid lien, pass clear title, waive inchoate rights, or assign earnings.

(5)   Additional parties. If, under a creditor's standards of creditworthiness, the personal liability of an additional party is necessary to support the credit requested, a creditor may request a cosigner, guarantor, endorser, or similar party. The applicant's spouse may serve as an additional party, but the creditor shall not require that the spouse be the additional party.

(6)   Rights of additional parties. A creditor shall not impose requirements upon an additional party that the creditor is prohibited from imposing upon an applicant under this section.

(e)   Insurance. A creditor shall not refuse to extend credit and shall not terminate an account because credit life, health, accident, disability, or other credit-related insurance is not available on the basis of the applicant's age.

§ 1002.8   Special purpose credit programs.

(a)   Standards for programs. Subject to the provisions of paragraph (b) of this section, the Act and this part permit a creditor to extend special purpose credit to applicants who meet eligibility requirements under the following types of credit programs:

(1)   Any credit assistance program expressly authorized by federal or state law for the benefit of an economically disadvantaged class of persons;

(2)   Any credit assistance program offered by a not-for-profit organization, as defined under section 501(c) of the Internal Revenue Code of 1954, as amended, for the benefit of its members or for the benefit of an economically disadvantaged class of persons; or

(3)   Any special purpose credit program offered by a for-profit organization, or in which such an organization participates to meet special social needs, if:

  (i)   The program is established and administered pursuant to a written plan that identifies the class of persons that the program is designed to benefit and sets forth the procedures and standards for extending credit pursuant to the program; and

  (ii)   The program is established and administered to extend credit to a class of persons who, under the organization's customary standards of creditworthiness, probably would not receive such credit or would receive it on less favorable terms than are ordinarily available to other applicants applying to the organization for a similar type and amount of credit.

(b)   Rules in other sections.

(1)   General applicability. All the provisions of this part apply to each of the special purpose credit programs described in paragraph (a) of this section except as modified by this section.

(2)   Common characteristics. A program described in paragraph (a)(2) or (a)(3) of this section qualifies as a special purpose credit program only if it was established and is administered so as not to discriminate against an applicant on any prohibited basis; however, all program participants may be required to share one or more common characteristics (for example, race, national origin, or sex) so long as the program was not established and is not administered with the purpose of evading the requirements of the Act or this part.

(c) **Special rule concerning requests and use of information.** If participants in a special purpose credit program described in paragraph (a) of this section are required to possess one or more common characteristics (for example, race, national origin, or sex) and if the program otherwise satisfies the requirements of paragraph (a) of this section, a creditor may request and consider information regarding the common characteristic(s) in determining the applicant's eligibility for the program.

(d) **Special rule in the case of financial need.** If financial need is one of the criteria under a special purpose credit program described in paragraph (a) of this section, the creditor may request and consider, in determining an applicant's eligibility for the program, information regarding the applicant's marital status; alimony, child support, and separate maintenance income; and the spouse's financial resources. In addition, a creditor may obtain the signature of an applicant's spouse or other person on an application or credit instrument relating to a special purpose credit program if the signature is required by Federal or state law.

§1002.9 Notifications.

(a) **Notification of action taken, ECOA notice, and statement of specific reasons.**

(1) **When notification is required.** A creditor shall notify an applicant of action taken within:

(i) 30 days after receiving a completed application concerning the creditor's approval of, counteroffer to, or adverse action on the application;

(ii) 30 days after taking adverse action on an incomplete application, unless notice is provided in accordance with paragraph (c) of this section;

(iii) 30 days after taking adverse action on an existing account; or

(iv) 90 days after notifying the applicant of a counteroffer if the applicant does not expressly accept or use the credit offered.

(2) **Content of notification when adverse action is taken.** A notification given to an applicant when adverse action is taken shall be in writing and shall contain a statement of the action taken; the name and address of the creditor; a statement of the provisions of §701(a) of the Act; the name and address of the Federal agency that administers compliance with respect to the creditor; and either:

(i) A statement of specific reasons for the action taken; or

(ii) A disclosure of the applicant's right to a statement of specific reasons within 30 days, if the statement is requested within 60 days of the creditor's notification. The disclosure shall include the name, address, and telephone number of the person or office from which the statement of reasons can be obtained. If the creditor chooses to provide the reasons orally, the creditor shall also disclose the applicant's right to have them confirmed in writing within 30 days of receiving the applicant's written request for confirmation.

(3) **Notification to business credit applicants.** For business credit, a creditor shall comply with the notification requirements of this section in the following manner:

(i) With regard to a business that had gross revenues of $1 million or less in its preceding fiscal year (other than an extension of trade credit, credit incident to a factoring agreement, or other similar types of business credit), a creditor shall comply with paragraphs (a)(1) and (2) of this section, except that:

(A) The statement of the action taken may be given orally or in writing, when adverse action is taken;

(B) Disclosure of an applicant's right to a statement of reasons may be given at the time of application, instead of when adverse action is taken, provided the disclosure contains the information required by paragraph (a)(2)(ii) of this section and the ECOA notice specified in paragraph (b)(1) of this section;

(C) For an application made entirely by telephone, a creditor satisfies the requirements of paragraph (a)(3)(i) of this section by an oral statement of the action taken and of the applicant's right to a statement of reasons for adverse action.

(ii) With regard to a business that had gross revenues in excess of $1 million in its preceding fiscal year or an extension of trade credit, credit incident to a factoring agreement, or other similar types of business credit, a creditor shall:

(A) Notify the applicant, within a reasonable time, orally or in writing, of the action taken; and

(B) Provide a written statement of the reasons for adverse action and the ECOA notice specified in paragraph (b)(1) of this section if the applicant makes a written request for the reasons within 60 days of the creditor's notification.

(b) Form of ECOA notice and statement of specific reasons.

(1) **ECOA notice.** To satisfy the disclosure requirements of paragraph (a)(2) of this section regarding section 701(a) of the Act, the creditor shall provide a notice that is substantially similar to the following: The Federal Equal Credit Opportunity Act prohibits creditors from discriminating against credit applicants on the basis of race, color, religion, national origin, sex, marital status, age (provided the applicant has the capacity to enter into a binding contract); because all or part of the applicant's income derives from any public assistance program; or because the applicant has in good faith exercised any right under the Consumer Credit Protection Act. The Federal agency that administers compliance with this law concerning this creditor is [name and address as specified by the appropriate agency listed in appendix A of this regulation].

(2) **Statement of specific reasons.** The statement of reasons for adverse action required by paragraph (a)(2)(i) of this section must be specific and indicate the principal reason(s) for the adverse action. Statements that the adverse action was based on the creditor's internal standards or policies or that the applicant, joint applicant, or similar party failed to achieve a qualifying score on the creditor's credit scoring system are insufficient.

(c) Incomplete applications.

(1) **Notice alternatives.** Within 30 days after receiving an application that is incomplete regarding matters that an applicant can complete, the creditor shall notify the applicant either:

(i) Of action taken, in accordance with paragraph (a) of this section; or

(ii) Of the incompleteness, in accordance with paragraph (c)(2) of this section.

(2) **Notice of incompleteness.** If additional information is needed from an applicant, the creditor shall send a written notice to the applicant specifying the information needed, designating a reasonable period of time for the applicant to provide the information, and informing the applicant that failure to provide the information requested will result in no further consideration being given to the application. The creditor shall have no further obligation under this section if the applicant fails to respond within the designated time period. If the applicant supplies the requested information within the designated time period, the creditor shall take action on the application and notify the applicant in accordance with paragraph (a) of this section.

(3) **Oral request for information.** At its option, a creditor may inform the applicant orally of the need for additional information. If the application remains incomplete the creditor shall send a notice in accordance with paragraph (c)(1) of this section.

(d) Oral notifications by small-volume creditors. In the case of a creditor that did not receive more than 150 applications during the preceding calendar year, the requirements of this section (including statements of specific reasons) are satisfied by oral notifications.

(e) Withdrawal of approved application. When an applicant submits an application and the parties contemplate that the applicant will inquire about its status, if the creditor approves the application and the applicant has not inquired within 30 days after applying, the creditor may treat the application as withdrawn and need not comply with paragraph (a)(1) of this section.

(f) Multiple applicants. When an application involves more than one applicant, notification need only be given to one of them but must be given to the primary applicant where one is readily apparent.

(g) Applications submitted through a third party. When an application is made on behalf of an applicant to more than one creditor and the applicant expressly accepts or uses credit offered by one of the creditors, notification of action taken by any of the other creditors is not required. If no credit is offered or if the applicant does not expressly accept or use the credit offered, each creditor taking adverse action must comply with this section, directly or through a third party. A notice given by a third party shall disclose the identity of each creditor on whose behalf the notice is given.

§ 1002.10   Furnishing of credit information.

(a) Designation of accounts. A creditor that furnishes credit information shall designate:

(1) Any new account to reflect the participation of both spouses if the applicant's spouse is permitted to use or is contractually liable on the account (other than as a guarantor, surety, endorser, or similar party); and

(2) Any existing account to reflect such participation, within 90 days after receiving a written request to do so from one of the spouses.

(b) Routine reports to consumer reporting agency. If a creditor furnishes credit information to a consumer reporting agency concerning an account designated to reflect the participation of both spouses, the creditor shall furnish the information in a manner that will enable the agency to provide access to the information in the name of each spouse.

(c) Reporting in response to inquiry. If a creditor furnishes credit information in response to an inquiry, concerning an account designated to reflect the participation of both spouses, the creditor shall furnish the information in the name of the spouse about whom the information is requested.

§ 1002.11   Relation to state law.

(a) Inconsistent state laws. Except as otherwise provided in this section, this part alters, affects, or preempts only those state laws that are inconsistent with the Act and this part and then only to the extent of the inconsistency. A state law is not inconsistent if it is more protective of an applicant.

(b) Preempted provisions of state law.

(1) A state law is deemed to be inconsistent with the requirements of the Act and this part and less protective of an applicant within the meaning of section 705(f) of the Act to the extent that the law:

(i) Requires or permits a practice or act prohibited by the Act or this part;

(ii) Prohibits the individual extension of consumer credit to both parties to a marriage if each spouse individually and voluntarily applies for such credit;

(iii) Prohibits inquiries or collection of data required to comply with the Act or this part;

(iv) Prohibits asking about or considering age in an empirically derived, demonstrably and statistically sound, credit scoring system to determine a pertinent element of creditworthiness, or to favor an elderly applicant; or

(v) Prohibits inquiries necessary to establish or administer a special purpose credit program as defined by § 1002.8.

(2) A creditor, state, or other interested party may request that the Bureau determine whether a state law is inconsistent with the requirements of the Act and this part.

(c) **Laws on finance charges, loan ceilings.** If married applicants voluntarily apply for and obtain individual accounts with the same creditor, the accounts shall not be aggregated or otherwise combined for purposes of determining permissible finance charges or loan ceilings under any Federal or state law. Permissible loan ceiling laws shall be construed to permit each spouse to become individually liable up to the amount of the loan ceilings, less the amount for which the applicant is jointly liable.

(d) **State and Federal laws not affected.** This section does not alter or annul any provision of state property laws, laws relating to the disposition of decedents' estates, or Federal or state banking regulations directed only toward insuring the solvency of financial institutions.

(e) **Exemption for state-regulated transactions.**

(1) **Applications.** A state may apply to the Bureau for an exemption from the requirements of the Act and this part for any class of credit transactions within the state. The Bureau will grant such an exemption if the Bureau determines that:

(i) The class of credit transactions is subject to state law requirements substantially similar to those of the Act and this part or that applicants are afforded greater protection under state law; and

(ii) There is adequate provision for state enforcement.

(2) **Liability and enforcement.**

(i) No exemption will extend to the civil liability provisions of section 706 of the Act or the administrative enforcement provisions of section 704 of the Act.

(ii) After an exemption has been granted, the requirements of the applicable state law (except for additional requirements not imposed by Federal law) will constitute the requirements of the Act and this part.

§ 1002.12   Record retention.

(a) **Retention of prohibited information.** A creditor may retain in its files information that is prohibited by the Act or this part for use in evaluating applications, without violating the Act or this part, if the information was obtained:

(1) From any source prior to March 23, 1977;

(2) From consumer reporting agencies, an applicant, or others without the specific request of the creditor; or

(3) As required to monitor compliance with the Act and this part or other Federal or state statutes or regulations.

(b) **Preservation of records.**

(1) **Applications.** For 25 months (12 months for business credit, except as provided in paragraph (b)(5) of this section) after the date that a creditor notifies an applicant of action taken on an application or of incompleteness, the creditor shall retain in original form or a copy thereof:

(i) Any application that it receives, any information required to be obtained concerning characteristics of the applicant to monitor compliance with the Act and this part or other similar law, and any other written or recorded information used in evaluating the application and not returned to the applicant at the applicant's request;

(ii) A copy of the following documents if furnished to the applicant in written form (or, if furnished orally, any notation or memorandum made by the creditor):

(A) The notification of action taken; and

(B) The statement of specific reasons for adverse action; and

(iii) Any written statement submitted by the applicant alleging a violation of the Act or this part.

(2) Existing accounts. For 25 months (12 months for business credit, except as provided in paragraph (b)(5) of this section) after the date that a creditor notifies an applicant of adverse action regarding an existing account, the creditor shall retain as to that account, in original form or a copy thereof:

(i) Any written or recorded information concerning the adverse action; and

(ii) Any written statement submitted by the applicant alleging a violation of the Act or this part.

(3) Other applications. For 25 months (12 months for business credit, except as provided in paragraph (b)(5) of this section) after the date that a creditor receives an application for which the creditor is not required to comply with the notification requirements of § 1002.9, the creditor shall retain all written or recorded information in its possession concerning the applicant, including any notation of action taken.

(4) Enforcement proceedings and investigations. A creditor shall retain the information beyond 25 months (12 months for business credit, except as provided in paragraph (b)(5) of this section) if the creditor has actual notice that it is under investigation or is subject to an enforcement proceeding for an alleged violation of the Act or this part, by the Attorney General of the United States or by an enforcement agency charged with monitoring that creditor's compliance with the Act and this part, or if it has been served with notice of an action filed pursuant to section 706 of the Act and § 1002.17 of this regulation. The creditor shall retain the information until final disposition of the matter, unless an earlier time is allowed by order of the agency or court.

(5) Special rule for certain business credit applications. With regard to a business that had gross revenues in excess of $1 million in its preceding fiscal year, or an extension of trade credit, credit incident to a factoring agreement, or other similar types of business credit, the creditor shall retain records for at least 60 days after notifying the applicant of the action taken. If within that time period the applicant requests in writing the reasons for adverse action or that records be retained, the creditor shall retain records for 12 months.

(6) Self-tests. For 25 months after a self-test (as defined in § 1002.15) has been completed, the creditor shall retain all written or recorded information about the self-test. A creditor shall retain information beyond 25 months if it has actual notice that it is under investigation or is subject to an enforcement proceeding for an alleged violation, or if it has been served with notice of a civil action. In such cases, the creditor shall retain the information until final disposition of the matter, unless an earlier time is allowed by the appropriate agency or court order.

(7) Prescreened solicitations. For 25 months after the date on which an offer of credit is made to potential customers (12 months for business credit, except as provided in paragraph (b)(5) of this section), the creditor shall retain in original form or a copy thereof:

(i) The text of any prescreened solicitation;

(ii) The list of criteria the creditor used to select potential recipients of the solicitation; and

(iii) Any correspondence related to complaints (formal or informal) about the solicitation.

§ 1002.13 Information for monitoring purposes.

(a) Information to be requested.

(1) A creditor that receives application for credit primarily for the purchase or refinancing of a dwelling occupied or to be occupied by the applicant as a principal residence, where the extension of credit will be secured by the dwelling, shall request as part of the application the following information regarding the applicant(s):

    (i) Ethnicity, using the categories Hispanic or Latino, and not Hispanic or Latino; and race, using the categories American Indian or Alaska Native, Asian, Black or African American, Native Hawaiian or Other Pacific Islander, and White;

    (ii) Sex;

    (iii) Marital status, using the categories married, unmarried, and separated; and

    (iv) Age.

    (2) Dwelling means a residential structure that contains one to four units, whether or not that structure is attached to real property. The term includes, but is not limited to, an individual condominium or cooperative unit and a mobile or other manufactured home.

    (b) Obtaining information. Questions regarding ethnicity, race, sex, marital status, and age may be listed, at the creditor's option, on the application form or on a separate form that refers to the application. The applicant(s) shall be asked but not required to supply the requested information. If the applicant(s) chooses not to provide the information or any part of it, that fact shall be noted on the form. The creditor shall then also note on the form, to the extent possible, the ethnicity, race, and sex of the applicant(s) on the basis of visual observation or surname.

    (c) Disclosure to applicant(s). The creditor shall inform the applicant(s) that the information regarding ethnicity, race, sex, marital status, and age is being requested by the Federal Government for the purpose of monitoring compliance with Federal statutes that prohibit creditors from discriminating against applicants on those bases. The creditor shall also inform the applicant(s) that if the applicant(s) chooses not to provide the information, the creditor is required to note the ethnicity, race and sex on the basis of visual observation or surname.

    (d) Substitute monitoring program. A monitoring program required by an agency charged with administrative enforcement under section 704 of the Act may be substituted for the requirements contained in paragraphs (a), (b), and (c) of this section.

§ 1002.14 Rules on providing appraisal reports.

    (a) Providing appraisals. A creditor shall provide a copy of an appraisal report used in connection with an application for credit that is to be secured by a lien on a dwelling. A creditor shall comply with either paragraph (a)(1) or (a)(2) of this section.

    (1) Routine delivery. A creditor may routinely provide a copy of an appraisal report to an applicant (whether credit is granted or denied or the application is withdrawn).

    (2) Upon request. A creditor that does not routinely provide appraisal reports shall provide a copy upon an applicant's written request.

    (i) Notice. A creditor that provides appraisal reports only upon request shall notify an applicant in writing of the right to receive a copy of an appraisal report. The notice may be given at any time during the application process but no later than when the creditor provides notice of action taken under § 1002.9 of this part. The notice shall specify that the applicant's request must be in writing, give the creditor's mailing address, and state the time for making the request as provided in paragraph (a)(2)(ii) of this section.

    (ii) Delivery. A creditor shall mail or deliver a copy of the appraisal report promptly (generally within 30 days) after the creditor receives an applicant's request, receives the report, or receives reimbursement from the applicant for the report, whichever is last to occur. A creditor need not provide a copy when the applicant's request is received more than 90 days after the creditor has provided notice of action taken on the application under § 1002.9 of this part or 90 days after the application is withdrawn.

(b) Credit unions. A creditor that is subject to the regulations of the National Credit Union Administration on making copies of appraisal reports available is not subject to this section.

(c) Definitions. For purposes of paragraph (a) of this section, the term dwelling means a residential structure that contains one to four units whether or not that structure is attached to real property. The term includes, but is not limited to, an individual condominium or cooperative unit, and a mobile or other manufactured home. The term appraisal report means the document(s) relied upon by a creditor in evaluating the value of the dwelling.

§1002.15 Incentives for self-testing and self-correction.

(a) General rules.

(1) Voluntary self-testing and correction. The report or results of a self-test that a creditor voluntarily conducts (or authorizes) are privileged as provided in this section. Data collection required by law or by any governmental authority is not a voluntary self-test.

(2) Corrective action required. The privilege in this section applies only if the creditor has taken or is taking appropriate corrective action.

(3) Other privileges. The privilege created by this section does not preclude the assertion of any other privilege that may also apply.

(b) Self-test defined.

(1) Definition. A self-test is any program, practice, or study that:

(i) Is designed and used specifically to determine the extent or effectiveness of a creditor's compliance with the Act or this part; and

(ii) Creates data or factual information that is not available and cannot be derived from loan or application files or other records related to credit transactions.

(2) Types of information privileged. The privilege under this section applies to the report or results of the self-test, data or factual information created by the self-test, and any analysis, opinions, and conclusions pertaining to the self-test report or results. The privilege covers workpapers or draft documents as well as final documents.

(3) Types of information not privileged. The privilege under this section does not apply to:

(i) Information about whether a creditor conducted a self-test, the methodology used or the scope of the self-test, the time period covered by the self-test, or the dates it was conducted; or

(ii) Loan and application files or other business records related to credit transactions, and information derived from such files and records, even if the information has been aggregated, summarized, or reorganized to facilitate analysis.

(c) Appropriate corrective action.

(1) General requirement. For the privilege in this section to apply, appropriate corrective action is required when the self-test shows that it is more likely than not that a violation occurred, even though no violation has been formally adjudicated.

(2) Determining the scope of appropriate corrective action. A creditor must take corrective action that is reasonably likely to remedy the cause and effect of a likely violation by:

(i) Identifying the policies or practices that are the likely cause of the violation; and

(ii) Assessing the extent and scope of any violation.

(3) Types of relief. Appropriate corrective action may include both prospective and remedial relief, except that to establish a privilege under this section:

(i) A creditor is not required to provide remedial relief to a tester used in a self-test;

(ii) A creditor is only required to provide remedial relief to an applicant identified by the self-test as one whose rights were more likely than not violated; and

(iii) A creditor is not required to provide remedial relief to a particular applicant if the statute of limitations applicable to the violation expired before the creditor obtained the results of the self-test or the applicant is otherwise ineligible for such relief.

(4)   No admission of violation. Taking corrective action is not an admission that a violation occurred.

(d)   Scope of privilege.

(1)   General rule. The report or results of a privileged self-test may not be obtained or used:

(i) By a government agency in any examination or investigation relating to compliance with the Act or this part; or

(ii) By a government agency or an applicant (including a prospective applicant who alleges a violation of § 1002.4(b)) in any proceeding or civil action in which a violation of the Act or this part is alleged.

(2)   Loss of privilege. The report or results of a self-test are not privileged under paragraph (d)(1) of this section if the creditor or a person with lawful access to the report or results:

(i) Voluntarily discloses any part of the report or results, or any other information privileged under this section, to an applicant or government agency or to the public;

(ii) Discloses any part of the report or results, or any other information privileged under this section, as a defense to charges that the creditor has violated the Act or regulation; or

(iii) Fails or is unable to produce written or recorded information about the self-test that is required to be retained under § 1002.12(b)(6) when the information is needed to determine whether the privilege applies. This paragraph does not limit any other penalty or remedy that may be available for a violation of § 1002.12.

(3)   Limited use of privileged information. Notwithstanding paragraph (d)(1) of this section, the self-test report or results and any other information privileged under this section may be obtained and used by an applicant or government agency solely to determine a penalty or remedy after a violation of the Act or this part has been adjudicated or admitted. Disclosures for this limited purpose may be used only for the particular proceeding in which the adjudication or admission was made. Information disclosed under this paragraph (d)(3) remains privileged under paragraph (d)(1) of this section.

§ 1002.16   Enforcement, penalties and liabilities.

(a)   Administrative enforcement.

(1) As set forth more fully in section 704 of the Act, administrative enforcement of the Act and this part regarding certain creditors is assigned to the Comptroller of the Currency, Board of Governors of the Federal Reserve System, Board of Directors of the Federal Deposit Insurance Corporation, National Credit Union Administration, Surface Transportation Board, Civil Aeronautics Board, Secretary of Agriculture, Farm Credit Administration, Securities and Exchange Commission, Small Business Administration, Secretary of Transportation, and Bureau of Consumer Financial Protection.

(2) Except to the extent that administrative enforcement is specifically assigned to some government agency other than the Bureau, and subject to subtitle B of the Consumer Financial Protection Act of 2010, the Federal Trade Commission is authorized to enforce the requirements imposed under the Act and this part.

(b)   Penalties and liabilities.

(1) Sections 702(g) and 706(a) and (b) of the Act provide that any creditor that fails to comply with a requirement imposed by the Act or this part is subject to civil liability for actual and punitive damages in individual or class actions. Pursuant to sections 702(g) and 704(b), (c), and (d) of the Act, violations of the Act or this part also constitute violations of other Federal laws. Liability for punitive damages can apply only to nongovernmental entities and is limited to $10,000 in individual actions and the lesser of $500,000 or 1 percent of the creditor's net worth in class actions. Section 706(c) provides for equitable and declaratory relief and section 706(d) authorizes the awarding of costs and reasonable attorney's fees to an aggrieved applicant in a successful action.

(2) As provided in section 706(f) of the Act, a civil action under the Act or this part may be brought in the appropriate United States district court without regard to the amount in controversy or in any other court of competent jurisdiction within two years after the date of the occurrence of the violation, or within one year after the commencement of an administrative enforcement proceeding or of a civil action brought by the Attorney General of the United States within two years after the alleged violation.

(3) If an agency responsible for administrative enforcement is unable to obtain compliance with the Act or this part, it may refer the matter to the Attorney General of the United States. If the Bureau, the Comptroller of the Currency, the Federal Deposit Insurance Corporation, the Board of Governors of the Federal Reserve System, or the National Credit Union Administration has reason to believe that one or more creditors have engaged in a pattern or practice of discouraging or denying applications in violation of the Act or this part, the agency shall refer the matter to the Attorney General. If the agency has reason to believe that one or more creditors violated section 701(a) of the Act, the agency may refer a matter to the Attorney General.

(4) On referral, or whenever the Attorney General has reason to believe that one or more creditors have engaged in a pattern or practice in violation of the Act or this part, the Attorney General may bring a civil action for such relief as may be appropriate, including actual and punitive damages and injunctive relief.

(5) If the Comptroller of the Currency, the Federal Deposit Insurance Corporation, the Board of Governors of the Federal Reserve System, or the National Credit Union Administration has reason to believe (as a result of a consumer complaint, a consumer compliance examination, or some other basis) that a violation of the Act or this part has occurred which is also a violation of the Fair Housing Act, and the matter is not referred to the Attorney General, the agency shall:

(i) Notify the Secretary of Housing and Urban Development; and

(ii) Inform the applicant that the Secretary of Housing and Urban Development has been notified and that remedies may be available under the Fair Housing Act.

(c)   Failure of compliance. A creditor's failure to comply with §§ 1002.6(b)(6), 1002.9, 1002.10, 1002.12 or 1002.13 is not a violation if it results from an inadvertent error. On discovering an error under §§ 1002.9 and 1002.10, the creditor shall correct it as soon as possible. If a creditor inadvertently obtains the monitoring information regarding the ethnicity, race, and sex of the applicant in a dwelling-related transaction not covered by § 1002.13, the creditor may retain information and act on the application without violating the regulation.

AVAILABILITY OF FUNDS AND COLLECTION OF CHECKS (REGULATION CC)

---

12 C.F.R. Part 229

Current through March 13, 2016; 81 F.R. 12795

For updates, see www.ecfr.gov

SUBPART A—GENERAL

SUBPART B—AVAILABILITY OF FUNDS AND DISCLOSURE OF FUNDS AVAILABILITY POLICIES

SUBPART C—COLLECTION OF CHECKS

SUBPART D—SUBSTITUTE CHECKS

SUBPART A—GENERAL

§ 229.1   Authority and purpose; organization.

(a) **Authority and purpose.** This part is issued by the Board of Governors of the Federal Reserve System (Board) to implement the Expedited Funds Availability Act (12 U.S.C. 4001–4010) (the EFA Act) and the Check Clearing for the 21st Century Act (12 U.S.C. 5001–5018) (the Check 21 Act).

(b) **Organization.** This part is divided into subparts and appendices as follows—

(1) Subpart A contains general information. It sets forth—

(i)   The authority, purpose, and organization;

(ii) Definition of terms; and

(iii) Authority for administrative enforcement of this part's provisions.

(2) Subpart B of this part contains rules regarding the duty of banks to make funds deposited into accounts available for withdrawal, including availability schedules. Subpart B of this part also contains rules regarding exceptions to the schedules, disclosure of funds availability policies, payment of interest, liability of banks for failure to comply with Subpart B of this part, and other matters.

(3) Subpart C of this part contains rules to expedite the collection and return of checks by banks. These rules cover the direct return of checks, the manner in which the paying bank and returning banks must return checks to the depositary bank, notification of nonpayment by the paying bank, indorsement and presentment of checks, same-day settlement for certain checks, the liability of banks for failure to comply with subpart C of this part, and other matters.

(4) Subpart D of this part contains rules relating to substitute checks. These rules address the creation and legal status of substitute checks; the substitute check warranties and indemnity; expedited recredit procedures for resolving improper charges and warranty claims associated with substitute checks provided to consumers; and the disclosure and notices that banks must provide.

§ 229.2   Definitions.

As used in this part, and unless the context requires otherwise, the following terms have the meanings set forth in this section, and the terms not defined in this section have the meanings set forth in the Uniform Commercial Code:

(a) Account.

(1) Except as provided in paragraphs (a)(2) and (a)(3) of this section, account means a deposit as defined in 12 CFR 204.2(a)(1)(i) that is a transaction account as described in 12 CFR 204.2(e). As defined in these sections, account generally includes accounts at a bank from which the account holder is permitted to make transfers or withdrawals by negotiable or transferable instrument, payment order

of withdrawal, telephone transfer, electronic payment, or other similar means for the purpose of making payments or transfers to third persons or others. Account also includes accounts at a bank from which the account holder may make third party payments at an ATM, remote service unit, or other electronic device, including by debit card, but the term does not include savings deposits or accounts described in 12 CFR 204.2(d)(2) even though such accounts permit third party transfers. An account may be in the form of—

    (i) A demand deposit account,

    (ii) A negotiable order of withdrawal account,

    (iii) A share draft account,

    (iv) An automatic transfer account, or

    (v) Any other transaction account described in 12 CFR 204.2(e).

    (2) For purposes of subpart B of this part and, in connection therewith, this subpart A, account does not include an account where the account holder is a bank, where the account holder is an office of an institution described in paragraphs (e)(1) through (e)(6) of this section or an office of a "foreign bank" as defined in section 1(b) of the International Banking Act (12 U.S.C. 3101) that is located outside the United States, or where the direct or indirect account holder is the Treasury of the United States.

    (3) For purposes of subpart D of this part and, in connection therewith, this subpart A, account means any deposit, as defined in 12 CFR 204.2(a)(1)(i), at a bank, including a demand deposit or other transaction account and a savings deposit or other time deposit, as those terms are defined in 12 CFR 204.2.

(b) Automated clearinghouse or ACH means a facility that processes debit and credit transfers under rules established by a Federal Reserve Bank operating circular on automated clearinghouse items or under rules of an automated clearinghouse association.

(c) Automated teller machine or ATM means an electronic device at which a natural person may make deposits to an account by cash or check and perform other account transactions.

(d) Available for withdrawal with respect to funds deposited means available for all uses generally permitted to the customer for actually and finally collected funds under the bank's account agreement or policies, such as for payment of checks drawn on the account, certification of checks drawn on the account, electronic payments, withdrawals by cash, and transfers between accounts.

(e) Bank means—

    (1) An insured bank as defined in section 3 of the Federal Deposit Insurance Act (12 U.S.C. 18I3) or a bank that is eligible to apply to become an insured bank under section 5 of that Act (12 U.S.C. 1815);

    (2) A mutual savings bank as defined in section 3 of the Federal Deposit Insurance Act (12 U.S.C. 1813);

    (3) A savings bank as defined in section 3 of the Federal Deposit Insurance Act (12 U.S.C. 1813);

    (4) An insured credit union as defined in section 101 of the Federal Credit Union Act (12 U.S.C. 1752) or a credit union that is eligible to make application to become an insured credit union under section 201 of that Act (12 U.S.C. 1781);

    (5) A member as defined in section 2 of the Federal Home Loan Bank Act (12 U.S.C. 1422);

    (6) A savings association as defined in section 3 of the Federal Deposit Insurance Act (12 U.S.C. 1813) that is an insured depository institution as defined in section 3 of that Act (12 U.S.C. 1813(c)(2)) or that is eligible to apply to become an insured depository institution under section 5 of that Act (12 U.S.C. 1815); or

(7) An agency or a branch of a foreign bank as defined in section l(b) of the International Banking Act (12 U.S.C. 3101).

For purposes of subparts C and D of this part and, in connection therewith, this subpart A, the term bank also includes any person engaged in the business of banking, as well as a Federal Reserve Bank, a Federal Home Loan Bank, and a state or unit of general local government to the extent that the state or unit of general local government acts as a paying bank. Unless otherwise specified, the term bank includes all of a bank's offices in the United States, but not offices located outside the United States. Note: For purposes of subpart D of this part and, in connection therewith, this subpart A, bank also includes the Treasury of the United States or the United States Postal Service to the extent that the Treasury or the Postal Service acts as a paying bank.

(f) Banking day means that part of any business day on which an office of a bank is open to the public for carrying on substantially all of its banking functions.

(g) Business day means a calendar day other than a Saturday or a Sunday, January 1, the third Monday in January, the third Monday in February, the last Monday in May, July 4, the first Monday in September, the second Monday in October, November 11, the fourth Thursday in November, or December 25. If January 1, July 4, November 11, or December 25 fall on a Sunday, the next Monday is not a business day.

(h) Cash means United States coins and currency.

(i) Cashier's check means a check that is—

    (1) Drawn on a bank;

    (2) Signed by an officer or employee of the bank on behalf of the bank as drawer;

    (3) A direct obligation of the bank; and

    (4) Provided to a customer of the bank or acquired from the bank for remittance purposes.

(j) Certified check means a check with respect to which the drawee bank certifies by signature on the check of an officer or other authorized employee of the bank that—

    (1)(i) The signature of the drawer on the check is genuine; and

        (ii) The bank has set aside funds that—

            (A) Are equal to the amount of the check, and

            (B) Will be used to pay the check; or

    (2) The bank will pay the check upon presentment.

(k) Check means—

    (1) A negotiable demand draft drawn on or payable through or at an office of a bank;

    (2) A negotiable demand draft drawn on a Federal Reserve Bank or a Federal Home Loan Bank;

    (3) A negotiable demand draft drawn on the Treasury of the United States;

    (4) A demand draft drawn on a state government or unit of general local government that is not payable through or at a bank;

    (5) A United States Postal Service money order; or

    (6) A traveler's check drawn on or payable through or at a bank.

    (7) The term check includes an original check and a substitute check. Note: The term check does not include a noncash item or an item payable in a medium other than United States money. A draft may be a check even though it is described on its face by another term, such as money order. For purposes of subparts C and D, and in connection therewith, subpart A, of this part, the term check also includes a demand draft of the type described above that is nonnegotiable.

(l) [Reserved]

(m) Check processing region means the geographical area served by an office of a Federal Reserve Bank for purposes of its check processing activities.

(n) Consumer account means any account used primarily for personal, family, or household purposes.

(o) Depositary bank means the first bank to which a check is transferred even though it is also the paying bank or the payee. A check deposited in an account is deemed to be transferred to the bank holding the account into which the check is deposited, even though the check is physically received and indorsed first by another bank.

(p) Electronic payment means a wire transfer or an ACH credit transfer.

(q) Forward collection means the process by which a bank sends a check on a cash basis to a collecting bank for settlement or to the paying bank for payment.

(r) Local check means a check payable by or at a local paying bank, or a check payable by a nonbank payor and payable through a local paying bank.

(s) Local paying bank means a paying bank that is located in the same check-processing region as the physical location of the branch, contractual branch, or proprietary ATM of the depositary bank in which that check was deposited.

(t) Merger transaction means—

(1) A merger or consolidation of two or more banks; or

(2) The transfer of substantially all of the assets of one or more banks or branches to another bank in consideration of the assumption by the acquiring bank of substantially all of the liabilities of the transferring banks, including the deposit liabilities.

(u) Noncash item means an item that would otherwise be a check, except that—

(1) A passbook, certificate, or other document is attached;

(2) It is accompanied by special instructions, such as a request for special advice of payment or dishonor;

(3) It consists of more than a single thickness of paper, except a check that qualifies for handling by automated check processing equipment; or

(4) It has not been preprinted or post-encoded in magnetic ink with the routing number of the paying bank.

(v) Nonlocal check means a check payable by, through, or at a nonlocal paying bank.

(w) Nonlocal paying bank means a paying bank that is not a local paying bank with respect to the depositary bank.

(x) Nonproprietary ATM means an ATM that is not a proprietary ATM.

(y) [Reserved]

(z) Paying bank means—

(1) The bank by which a check is payable, unless the check is payable at another bank and is sent to the other bank for payment or collection;

(2) The bank at which a check is payable and to which it is sent for payment or collection;

(3) The Federal Reserve Bank or Federal Home Loan Bank by which a check is payable;

(4) The bank through which a check is payable and to which it is sent for payment or collection, if the check is not payable by a bank; or

(5) The state or unit of general local government on which a check is drawn and to which it is sent for payment or collection.

For purposes of subparts C and D, and in connection therewith, subpart A, paying bank includes the bank through which a check is payable and to which the check is sent for payment or collection, regardless of whether the check is payable by another bank, and the bank whose routing number appears on a check in fractional or magnetic form and to which the check is sent for payment or collection. Note: For purposes of subpart D of this part and, in connection therewith, this subpart A, paying bank also includes the Treasury of the United States or the United States Postal Service for a check that is payable by that entity and that is sent to that entity for payment or collection.

(aa) Proprietary ATM means an ATM that is—

(1) Owned or operated by, or operated exclusively for, the depositary bank;

(2) Located on the premises (including the outside wall) of the depositary bank; or

(3) Located within 50 feet of the premises of the depositary bank, and not identified as being owned or operated by another entity.

If more than one bank meets the owned or operated criterion of paragraph (aa)(1) of this section, the ATM is considered proprietary to the bank that operates it.

(bb) Qualified returned check means a returned check that is prepared for automated return to the depositary bank by placing the check in a carrier envelope or placing a strip on the check and encoding the strip or envelope in magnetic ink. A qualified returned check need not contain other elements of a check drawn on the depositary bank, such as the name of the depositary bank.

(cc) Returning bank means a bank (other than the paying or depositary bank) handling a returned check or notice in lieu of return. A returning bank is also a collecting bank for purposes of UCC 4–202(b).

(dd) Routing number means—

(1) The number printed on the face of a check in fractional form on in nine-digit form; or

(2) The number in a bank's indorsement in fractional or nine-digit form.

(ee) Similarly situated bank means a bank of similar size, located in the same community, and with similar check handling activities as the paying bank or returning bank.

(ff) State means a state, the District of Columbia, Puerto Rico, or the U.S. Virgin Islands. For purposes of subpart D of this part and, in connection therewith, this subpart A, state also means Guam, American Samoa, the Trust Territory of the Pacific Islands, the Northern Mariana Islands, and any other territory of the United States.

(gg) Teller's check means a check provided to a customer of a bank or acquired from a bank for remittance purposes, that is drawn by the bank, and drawn on another bank or payable through or at a bank.

(hh) Traveler's check means an instrument for the payment of money that—

(1) Is drawn on or payable through or at a bank;

(2) Is designated on its face by the term traveler's check or by any substantially similar term or is commonly known and marketed as a traveler's check by a corporation or bank that is an issuer of traveler's checks;

(3) Provides for a specimen signature of the purchaser to be completed at the time of purchase; and

(4) Provides for a countersignature of the purchaser to be completed at the time of negotiation.

(ii) Uniform Commercial Code, Code, or U.C.C. means the Uniform Commercial Code as adopted in a state.

(jj) United States means the states, including the District of Columbia, the U.S. Virgin Islands, and Puerto Rico.

(kk) Unit of general local government means any city, county, parish, town, township, village, or other general purpose political subdivision of a state. The term does not include special purpose units of government, such as school districts or water districts.

(ll) Wire transfer means an unconditional order to a bank to pay a fixed or determinable amount of money to a beneficiary upon receipt or on a day stated in the order, that is transmitted by electronic or other means through Fedwire, the Clearing House Interbank Payments System, other similar network, between banks, or on the books of a bank. Wire transfer does not include an electronic fund transfer as defined in section 903(6) of the Electronic Fund Transfer Act (15 U.S.C. 1693a(6)).

(mm) Fedwire has the same meaning as that set forth in § 210.26(e) of this chapter.

(nn) Good faith means honesty in fact and observance of reasonable commercial standards of fair dealing.

(oo) Interest compensation means an amount of money calculated at the average of the Federal Funds rates published by the Federal Reserve Bank of New York for each of the days for which interest compensation is payable, divided by 360. The Federal Funds rate for any day on which a published rate is not available is the same as the published rate for the last preceding day for which there is a published rate.

(pp) Contractual branch, with respect to a bank, means a branch of another bank that accepts a deposit on behalf of the first bank.

(qq) Claimant bank means a bank that submits a claim for a recredit for a substitute check to an indemnifying bank under § 229.55.

(rr) Collecting bank means any bank handling a check for forward collection, except the paying bank.

(ss) Consumer means a natural person who—

    (1) With respect to a check handled for forward collection, draws the check on a consumer account; or

    (2) With respect to a check handled for return, deposits the check into or cashes the check against a consumer account.

(tt) Customer means a person having an account with a bank.

(uu) Indemnifying bank means a bank that provides an indemnity under § 229.53 with respect to a substitute check.

(vv) Magnetic ink character recognition line and MICR line mean the numbers, which may include the routing number, account number, check number, check amount, and other information, that are printed near the bottom of a check in magnetic ink in accordance with American National Standard Specifications for Placement and Location of MICR Printing, X9.13 (hereinafter ANS X9.13) for an original check and American National Standard Specifications for an Image Replacement Document—IRD, X9.100–140 (hereinafter ANS X9.100–140) for a substitute check (unless the Board by rule or order determines that different standards apply).

(ww) Original check means the first paper check issued with respect to a particular payment transaction.

(xx) Paper or electronic representation of a substitute check means any copy of or information related to a substitute check that a bank handles for forward collection or return, charges to a customer's account, or provides to a person as a record of a check payment made by the person.

(yy) Person means a natural person, corporation, unincorporated company, partnership, government unit or instrumentality, trust, or any other entity or organization.

(zz) Reconverting bank means—

    (1) The bank that creates a substitute check; or

(2) With respect to a substitute check that was created by a person that is not a bank, the first bank that transfers, presents, or returns that substitute check or, in lieu thereof, the first paper or electronic representation of that substitute check.

(aaa) Substitute check means a paper reproduction of an original check that—

(1) Contains an image of the front and back of the original check;

(2) Bears a MICR line that, except as provided under ANS X9.100–140 (unless the Board by rule or order determines that a different standard applies), contains all the information appearing on the MICR line of the original check at the time that the original check was issued and any additional information that was encoded on the original check's MICR line before an image of the original check was captured;

(3) Conforms in paper stock, dimension, and otherwise with ANS X9.100–140 (unless the Board by rule or order determines that a different standard applies); and

(4) Is suitable for automated processing in the same manner as the original check.

(bbb) Sufficient copy and copy.

(1) A sufficient copy is a copy of an original check that accurately represents all of the information on the front and back of the original check as of the time the original check was truncated or is otherwise sufficient to determine whether or not a claim is valid.

(2) A copy of an original check means any paper reproduction of an original check, including a paper printout of an electronic image of the original check, a photocopy of the original check, or a substitute check.

(ccc) Transfer and consideration. The terms transfer and consideration have the meanings set forth in the Uniform Commercial Code and in addition, for purposes of subpart D—

(1) The term transfer with respect to a substitute check or a paper or electronic representation of a substitute check means delivery of the substitute check or other representation of the substitute check by a bank to a person other than a bank; and

(2) A bank that transfers a substitute check or a paper or electronic representation of a substitute check directly to a person other than a bank has received consideration for the substitute check or other paper or electronic representation of the substitute check if it has charged, or has the right to charge, the person's account or otherwise has received value for the original check, a substitute check, or a representation of the original check or substitute check.

(ddd) Truncate means to remove an original check from the forward collection or return process and send to a recipient, in lieu of such original check, a substitute check or, by agreement, information relating to the original check (including data taken from the MICR line of the original check or an electronic image of the original check), whether with or without the subsequent delivery of the original check.

(eee) Truncating bank means—

(1) The bank that truncates the original check; or

(2) If a person other than a bank truncates the original check, the first bank that transfers, presents, or returns, in lieu of such original check, a substitute check or, by agreement with the recipient, information relating to the original check (including data taken from the MICR line of the original check or an electronic image of the original check), whether with or without the subsequent delivery of the original check.

(fff) Remotely created check means a check that is not created by the paying bank and that does not bear a signature applied, or purported to be applied, by the person on whose account the check is drawn. For purposes of this definition, "account" means an account as defined in paragraph (a) of this section as well as a credit or other arrangement that allows a person to draw checks that are payable by, through, or at a bank.

§ 229.3   Administrative enforcement.

(a)   **Enforcement agencies.** Compliance with this part is enforced under—

(1)   Section 8 of the Federal Deposit Insurance Act (12 U.S.C. 1818 et seq.) in the case of—

(i)   National banks, and Federal branches and Federal agencies of foreign banks, by the Office of the Comptroller of the Currency;

(ii)   Member banks of the Federal Reserve System (other than national banks), and offices, branches, and agencies of foreign banks located in the United States (other than Federal branches, Federal agencies, and insured State branches of foreign banks), by the Board; and

(iii)   Banks insured by the Federal Deposit Insurance Corporation (other than members of the Federal Reserve System) and insured State branches of foreign banks, by the Board of Directors of the Federal Deposit Insurance Corporation;

(2)   Section 8 of the Federal Deposit Insurance Act, by the Director of the Office of Thrift Supervision in the case of savings associations the deposits of which are insured by the Federal Deposit Insurance Corporation; and

(3)   The Federal Credit Union Act (12 U.S.C. 1751 et seq.) by the National Credit Union Administration Board with respect to any federal credit union or credit union insured by the National Credit Union Share Insurance Fund.

The terms used in paragraph (a)(1) of this section that are not defined in this part or otherwise defined in section 3(s) of the Federal Deposit Insurance Act (12 U.S.C. 1813(s)) shall have the meaning given to them in section 1(b) of the International Banking Act of 1978 (12 U.S.C. 3101).

(b)   **Additional powers.**

(1)   For the purposes of the exercise by any agency referred to in paragraph (a) of this section of its powers under any statute referred to in that paragraph, a violation of any requirement imposed under the EFA Act is deemed to be a violation of a requirement imposed under that statute.

(2)   In addition to its powers under any provision of law specifically referred to in paragraph (a) of this section, each of the agencies referred to in that paragraph may exercise, for purposes of enforcing compliance with any requirement imposed under this part, any other authority conferred on it by law.

(c)   **Enforcement by the Board.**

(1)   Except to the extent that enforcement of the requirements imposed under this part is specifically committed to some other government agency, the Board shall enforce such requirements.

(2)   If the Board determines that—

(i)   Any bank that is not a bank described in paragraph (a) of this section; or

(ii)   Any other person subject to the authority of the Board under the EFA Act and this part,

has failed to comply with any requirement imposed by this part, the Board may issue an order prohibiting any bank, any Federal Reserve Bank, or any other person subject to the authority of the Board from engaging in any activity or transaction that directly or indirectly involves such noncomplying bank or person (including any activity or transaction involving the receipt, payment, collection, and clearing of checks, and any related function of the payment system with respect to checks).

SUBPART B—AVAILABILITY OF FUNDS AND DISCLOSURE OF FUNDS AVAILABILITY POLICIES

§ 229.10   Next-day availability.

(a)   **Cash deposits.**

(1)   A bank shall make funds deposited in an account by cash available for withdrawal not later than the business day after the banking day on which the cash is deposited, if the deposit is made in person to an employee of the depositary bank.

(2)   bank shall make funds deposited in an account by cash available for withdrawal not later than the second business day after the banking day on which the cash is deposited, if the deposit is not made in person to an employee of the depositary bank.

(b)   **Electronic payments—**

(1)   **In general.** A bank shall make funds received for deposit in an account by an electronic payment available for withdrawal not later than the business day after the banking day on which the bank received the electronic payment.

(2)   **When an electronic payment is received.** An electronic payment is received when the bank receiving the payment has received both—

(i)   Payment in actually and finally collected funds; and

(ii)   Information on the account and amount to be credited.

A bank receives an electronic payment only to the extent that the bank has received payment in actually and finally collected funds.

(c)   **Certain check deposits—**

(1)   **General rule.** A depositary bank shall make funds deposited in an account by check available for withdrawal not later than the business day after the banking day on which the funds are deposited, in the case of—

(i)   A check drawn on the Treasury of the United States and deposited in an account held by a payee of the check;

(ii)   A U.S. Postal Service money order deposited—

(A)   In an account held by a payee of the money order; and

(B)   In person to an employee of the depositary bank.

(iii)   A check drawn on a Federal Reserve Bank or Federal Home Loan Bank and deposited—

(A)   In an account held by a payee of the check; and

(B)   In person to an employee of the depositary bank;

(iv)   A check drawn by a state or a unit of general local government and deposited—

(A)   In an account held by a payee of the check;

(B)   In a depositary bank located in the state that issued the check, or the same state as the unit of general local government that issued the check;

(C)   In person to an employee of the depositary bank; and

(D)   With a special deposit slip or deposit envelope, if such slip or envelope is required by the depositary bank under paragraph (c)(3) of this section.

(v)   A cashier's, certified, or teller's check deposited—

(A)   In an account held by a payee of the check;

(B) In person to an employee of the depositary bank; and

(C) With a special deposit slip or deposit envelope, if such slip or envelope is required by the depositary bank under paragraph (c)(3) of this section.

(vi) A check deposited in a branch of the depositary bank and drawn on the same or another branch of the same bank if both branches are located in the same state or the same check processing region; and,

(vii) The lesser of—

(A) $100,[1] or

(B) The aggregate amount deposited on any one banking day to all accounts of the customer by check or checks not subject to next-day availability under paragraphs (c)(1)(i) through (vi) of this section.

(2) **Checks not deposited in person.** A depositary bank shall make funds deposited in an account by check or checks available for withdrawal not later than the second business day after the banking day on which funds are deposited, in the case of a check deposit described in and that meets the requirements of paragraphs (c)(1)(ii), (iii), (iv), and (v), of this section, except that it is not deposited in person to an employee of the depositary bank.

(3) **Special deposit slip.**

(i) As a condition to making the funds available for withdrawal in accordance with this section, a depositary bank may require that a state or local government check or a cashier's, certified, or teller's check be deposited with a special deposit slip or deposit envelope that identifies the type of check.

(ii) If a depositary bank requires the use of a special deposit slip or deposit envelope, the bank must either provide the special deposit slip or deposit envelope to its customers or inform its customers how the slip or envelope may be prepared or obtained and make the slip or envelope reasonably available.

§ 229.11 [Reserved].

§ 229.12 Availability schedule.

(a) **Effective date.** The availability schedule contained in this section is effective September 1, 1990.

(b) **Local checks and certain other checks.** Except as provided in paragraphs (d), (e), and (f) of this section, a depository bank shall make funds deposited in an account by a check available for withdrawal not later than the second business day following the banking day on which funds are deposited, in the case of—

(1) A local check;

(2) A check drawn on the Treasury of the United States that is not governed by the availability requirements of § 229.10(c);

(3) A U.S. Postal Service money order that is not governed by the availability requirements of § 229.10(c); and

(4) A check drawn on a Federal Reserve Bank or Federal Home Loan Bank; a check drawn by a state or unit of general local government; or a cashier's, certified, or teller's check; if any check referred to in this paragraph (b)(4) is a local check that is not governed by the availability requirements of § 229.10(c).

---

[1] *Note from West Advisory Panel: Should be $200. See 12 U.S.C.A. § 4002(a)(2)(D), included in this volume.*

(c) Nonlocal checks—

(1) In general. Except as provided in paragraphs (d), (e), and (f) of this section, a depositary bank shall make funds deposited in an account by a check available for withdrawal not later than the fifth business day following the banking day on which funds are deposited, in the case of—

(i) A nonlocal check; and

(ii) A check drawn on a Federal Reserve Bank or Federal Home Loan Bank; a check drawn by a state or unit of general local government; a cashier's, certified, or teller's check; or a check deposited in a branch of the depositary bank and drawn on the same or another branch of the same bank, if any check referred to in this paragraph (c)(1)(ii) is a nonlocal check that is not governed by the availability requirements of § 229.10(c).

(2) Nonlocal checks specified in Appendix B–2 to this part must be made available for withdrawal not later than the times prescribed in that Appendix.

(d) Time period adjustment for withdrawal by cash or similar means. A depositary bank may extend by one business day the time that funds deposited in an account by one or more checks subject to paragraphs (b), (c), or (f) of this section are available for withdrawal by cash or similar means. Similar means include electronic payment, issuance of a cashier's or teller's check, or certification of a check, or other irrevocable commitment to pay, but do not include the granting of credit to a bank, a Federal Reserve Bank, or a Federal Home Loan Bank that presents a check to the depositary bank for payment. A depositary bank shall, however, make $400 of these funds available for withdrawal by cash or similar means not later than 5:00 p.m. on the business day on which the funds are available under paragraphs (b), (c), or (f) of this section. This $400 is in addition to the $100[1] available under § 229.10(c)(1)(vii).

(e) Extension of schedule for certain deposits in Alaska, Hawaii, Puerto Rico, and the U.S. Virgin Islands. The depositary bank may extend the time periods set forth in this section by one business day in the case of any deposit, other than a deposit described in § 229.10, that is—

(1) Deposited in an account at a branch of a depositary bank if the branch is located in Alaska, Hawaii, Puerto Rico, or the U.S. Virgin Islands; and

(2) Deposited by a check drawn on or payable at or through a paying bank not located in the same state as the depositary bank.

(f) Deposits at nonproprietary ATMs. A depositary bank shall make funds deposited in an account at a nonproprietary ATM by cash or check available for withdrawal not later than the fifth business day following the banking day on which the funds are deposited.

§ 229.13 Exceptions.

(a) New accounts. For purposes of this paragraph, checks subject to § 229.10(c)(1)(v) include traveler's checks.

(1) A deposit in a new account—

(i) Is subject to the requirements of § 229.10(a) and (b) to make funds from deposits by cash and electronic payments available for withdrawal on the business day following the banking day of deposit or receipt;

(ii) Is subject to the requirements of § 229.10(c)(1)(i) through (v) and § 229.10(c)(2) only with respect to the first $5,000 of funds deposited on any one banking day; but the amount of the deposit in excess of $5,000 shall be available for withdrawal not later than the ninth business day following the banking day on which funds are deposited; and

(iii) Is not subject to the availability requirements of §§ 229.10(c)(1)(vi) and (vii) and 229.12.

(2) An account is considered a new account during the first 30 calendar days after the account is established. An account is not considered a new account if each customer on the account has had,

---

[1]   *Note from West Advisory Panel: Should be $200. See 12 U.S.C.A. § 4002(a)(2)(D), included in this volume.*

within 30 calendar days before the account is established, another account at the depositary bank for at least 30 calendar days.

(b) Large deposits. Sections 229.10(c) and 229.12 do not apply to the aggregate amount of deposits by one or more checks to the extent that the aggregate amount is in excess of $5,000 on any one banking. day. For customers that have multiple accounts at a depositary bank, the bank may apply this exception to the aggregate deposits to all accounts held by the customer, even if the customer is not the sole holder of the accounts and not all of the holders of the accounts are the same.

(c) Redeposited checks. Sections 229.10(c) and 229.12 do not apply to a check that has been returned unpaid and redeposited by the customer or the depositary bank. This exception does not apply—

(1) To a check that has been returned due to a missing indorsement and redeposited after the missing indorsement has been obtained, if the reason for return indication on the check states that it was returned due to a missing indorsement; or

(2) To a check that has been returned because it was post dated, if the reason for return indicated on the check states that it was returned because it was post dated, and if the check is no longer postdated when redeposited.

(d) Repeated overdrafts. If any account or combination of accounts of a depositary bank's customer has been repeatedly overdrawn, then for a period of six months after the last such overdraft, §§ 229.10(c) and 229.12 do not apply to any of the accounts. A depositary bank may consider a customer's account to be repeatedly overdrawn if—

(1) On six or more banking days within the preceding six months, the account balance is negative, or the account balance would have become negative if checks or other charges to the account had been paid; or

(2) On two or more banking days within the preceding six months, the account balance is negative, or the account balance would have become negative, in the amount of $5,000 or more, if checks or other charges to the account had been paid.

(e) Reasonable cause to doubt collectibility—

(1) In general. Sections 229.10(c) and 229.12 do not apply to a check deposited in an account at a depositary bank if the depositary bank has reasonable cause to believe that the check is uncollectible from the paying bank. Reasonable cause to believe a check is uncollectible requires the existence of facts that would cause a well-grounded belief in the mind of a reasonable person. Such belief shall not be based on the fact that the check is of a particular class or is deposited by a particular class of persons. The reason for the bank's belief that the check is uncollectible shall be included in the notice required under paragraph (g) of this section.

(2) Overdraft and returned check fees. A depositary bank that extends the time when funds will be available for withdrawal as described in paragraph (e)(1) of this section, and does not furnish the depositor with written notice at the time of deposit shall not assess any fees for any subsequent overdrafts (including use of a line of credit) or return of checks of other debits to the account, if—

(i) The overdraft or return of the check would not have occurred except for the fact that the deposited funds were delayed under paragraph (e)(1) of this section; and

(ii) The deposited check was paid by the paying bank.

Notwithstanding the foregoing, the depositary bank may assess an overdraft or returned check fee if it includes a notice concerning overdraft and returned check fees with the notice of exception required in paragraph (g) of this section and, when required, refunds any such fees upon the request of the customer. The notice must state that the customer may be entitled to a refund of overdraft or returned check fees that are assessed if the check subject to the exception is paid and how to obtain a refund.

(f) Emergency conditions. Sections 229.10(c) and 229.12 do not apply to funds deposited by check in a depositary bank in the case of—

(1) An interruption of communications or computer or other equipment facilities;

1841

(2) A suspension of payments by another bank;

(3) A war; or

(4) An emergency condition beyond the control of the depositary bank,

if the depositary bank exercises such diligence as the circumstances require.

(g) Notice of exception—

(1) In general. Subject to paragraphs (g)(2) and (g)(3) of this section, when a depositary bank extends the time when funds will be available for withdrawal based on the application of an exception contained in paragraphs (b) through (e) of this section, it must provide the depositor with a written notice.

(i) The notice shall include the following information—

(A) A number or code, which need not exceed four digits, that identifies the customer's account;

(B) The date of the deposit;

(C) The amount of the deposit that is being delayed;

(D) The reason the exception was invoked; and

(E) The time period within which the funds will be available for withdrawal.

(ii) Timing of notice. The notice shall be provided to the depositor at the time of the deposit, unless the deposit is not made in person to an employee of the depositary bank, or, if the facts upon which a determination to invoke one of the exceptions in paragraphs (b) through (e) of this section to delay a deposit only become known to the depositary bank after the time of the deposit. If the notice is not given at the time of the deposit, the depositary bank shall mail or deliver the notice to the customer as soon as practicable, but no later than the first business day following the day the facts become known to the depositary bank, or the deposit is made, whichever is later.

(2) One-time exception notice. In lieu of providing notice pursuant to paragraph (g)(1) of this section, a depositary bank that extends the time when the funds deposited in a nonconsumer account will be available for withdrawal based on an exception contained in paragraph (b) or (c) of this section may provide a single notice to the customer that includes the following information—

(i) The reason(s) the exception may be invoked; and

(ii) The time period within which deposits subject to the exception generally will be available for withdrawal.

This one-time notice shall be provided only if each type of exception cited in the notice will be invoked for most check deposits in the account to which the exception could apply. This notice shall be provided at or prior to the time notice must be provided under paragraph (g)(1)(ii) of this section.

(3) Notice of repeated overdrafts exception. In lieu of providing notice pursuant to paragraph (g)(1) of this section, a depositary bank that extends the time when funds deposited in an account will be available for withdrawal based on the exception contained in paragraph (d) of this section may provide a notice to the customer for each time period during which the exception will be in effect. The notice shall include the following information—

(i) The account number of the customer;

(ii) The fact that the availability of funds deposited in the customer's account will be delayed because the repeated overdrafts exception will be invoked;

(iii) The time period within which deposits subject to the exception generally will be available for withdrawal; and

(iv) The time period during which the exception will apply.

This notice shall be provided at or prior to the time notice must be provided under paragraph (g)(1)(ii) of this section and only if the exception cited in the notice will be invoked for most check deposits in the account.

(4) **Emergency conditions exception notice.** When a depositary bank extends the time when funds will be available for withdrawal based on the application of the emergency conditions exception contained in paragraph (f) of this section, it must provide the depositor with notice in a reasonable form and within a reasonable time given the circumstances. The notice shall include the reason the exception was invoked and the time period within which funds shall be made available for withdrawal, unless the depositary bank, in good faith, does not know at the time the notice is given the duration of the emergency and, consequently, when the funds must be made available. The depositary bank is not required to provide a notice if the funds subject to the exception become available before the notice must be sent.

(5) **Record retention.** A depositary bank shall retain a record, in accordance with § 229.21(g), of each notice provided pursuant to its application of the reasonable cause exception under paragraph (e) of this section, together with a brief statement of the facts giving rise to the bank's reason to doubt the collectibility of the check.

(h) Availability of deposits subject to exceptions.

(1) If an exception contained in paragraphs (b) through (f) of this section applies, the depositary bank may extend the time periods established under §§ 229.10(c) and 229.12 by a reasonable period of time.

(2) If a depositary bank invokes an exception contained in paragraphs (b) through (e) of this section with respect to a check described in § 229.10(c)(1)(i) through (v) or § 229.10(c)(2), it shall make the funds available for withdrawal not later than a reasonable period after the day the funds would have been required to be made available had the check been subject to 229.12.

(3) If a depositary bank invokes an exception under paragraph (f) of this section based on an emergency condition, the depositary bank shall make the funds available for withdrawal not later than a reasonable period after the emergency has ceased or the period established in §§ 229.10(c) and 229.12, whichever is later.

(4) For the purposes of this section, a "reasonable period" is an extension of up to one business day for checks described in § 229.10(c)(1)(vi), five business days for checks described in § 229.12(b)(1) through (4), and six business days for checks described in § 229.12(c)(1) and (2) or § 229.12(f). A longer extension may be reasonable, but the bank has the burden of so establishing.

§ 229.14 Payment of interest.

(a) **In general.** A depositary bank shall begin to accrue interest or dividends on funds deposited in an interest-bearing account not later than the business day on which the depositary bank receives credit for the funds. For the purposes of this section, the depositary bank may—

(1) Rely on the availability schedule of its Federal Reserve Bank, Federal Home Loan Bank, or correspondent bank to determine the time credit is actually received; and

(2) Accrue interest or dividends on funds deposited in interest-bearing accounts by checks that the depositary bank sends to paying banks or subsequent collecting banks for payment or collection based on the availability of funds the depositary bank receives from the paying or collecting banks.

(b) **Special rule for credit unions.** Paragraph (a) of this section does not apply to any account at a bank described in § 229.2(e)(4), if the bank—

(1) Begins the accrual of interest or dividends at a later date than the date described in paragraph (a) of this section with respect to all funds, including cash, deposited in the account; and

(2) Provides notice of its interest or dividend payment policy in the manner required under § 229.16(d).

(c)   Exception for checks returned unpaid. This subpart does not require a bank to pay interest or dividends on funds deposited by a check that is returned unpaid.

§ 229.15   General disclosure requirements.

(a)   Form of disclosures. A bank shall make the disclosures required by this subpart clearly and conspicuously in writing. Disclosures, other than those posted at locations where employees accept consumer deposits and ATMs and the notice on preprinted deposit slips, must be in a form that the customer may keep. The disclosures shall be grouped together and shall not contain any information not related to the disclosures required by this subpart. If contained in a document that sets forth other account terms, the disclosures shall be highlighted within the document by, for example, use of a separate heading.

(b)   Uniform reference to day of availability. In its disclosure, a bank shall describe funds as being available for withdrawal on "the _____ business day after" the day of deposit. In this calculation, the first business day is the business day following the banking day the deposit is received, and the last business day is the day on which the funds are made available.

(c)   Multiple accounts and multiple account holders. A bank need not give multiple disclosures to a customer that holds multiple accounts if the accounts are subject to the same availability policies. Similarly, a bank need not give separate disclosures to each customer on a jointly held account.

(d)   Dormant or inactive accounts. A bank need not give availability disclosures to a customer that holds a dormant or inactive account.

§ 229.16   Specific availability policy disclosure.

(a)   General. To meet the requirements of a specific availability policy disclosure under §§ 229.17 and 229.18(d), a bank shall provide a disclosure describing the bank's policy as to when funds deposited in an account are available for withdrawal. The disclosure must reflect the policy followed by the bank in most cases. A bank may impose longer delays on a case-by-case basis or by invoking one of the exceptions in § 229.13, provided this is reflected in the disclosure.

(b)   Content of specific availability policy disclosure. The specific availability policy disclosure shall contain the following, as applicable—

(1)   A summary of the bank's availability policy;

(2)   A description of any categories of deposits or checks used by the bank when it delays availability (such as local or nonlocal checks); how to determine the category to which a particular deposit or check belongs; and when each category will be available for withdrawal (including a description of the bank's business days and when a deposit is considered received);[1]

(3)   A description of any of the exceptions in § 229.13 that may be invoked by the bank, including the time following a deposit that funds generally will be available for withdrawal and a statement that the bank will notify the customer if the bank invokes one of the exceptions;

(4)   A description, as specified in paragraph (c)(1) of this section, of any case-by-case policy of delaying availability that may result in deposited funds being available for withdrawal later than the time periods stated in the bank's availability policy; and

---

[1]   A bank that distinguishes in its disclosure between local and nonlocal checks based on the routing number on the check must disclose that certain checks, such as some credit union share drafts that are payable by one bank but payable through another bank, will be treated as local or nonlocal checks based upon the location of the bank by which they are payable and not on the basis of the location of the bank whose routing number appears on the check. A bank that makes funds from nonlocal checks available for withdrawal within the time periods required for local checks under §§ 229.12 and 229.13 is not required to provide this disclosure on payable-through checks to its customers. The statement concerning payable-through checks must describe how the customer can determine whether these checks will be treated as local or nonlocal, or state that special rules apply to such checks and that the customer may ask about the availability of these checks.

(5) A description of how the customer can differentiate between a proprietary and a nonproprietary ATM, if the bank makes funds from deposits at nonproprietary ATMs available for withdrawal later than funds from deposits at proprietary ATMs.

(c) Longer delays on a case-by-case basis—

(1) Notice in specific policy disclosure. A bank that has a policy of making deposited funds available for withdrawal sooner than required by this subpart may extend the time when funds are available up to the time periods allowed under this subpart on a case-by-case basis, provided the bank includes the following in its specific policy disclosure—

(i) A statement that the time when deposited funds are available for withdrawal may be extended in some cases, and the latest time following a deposit that funds will be available for withdrawal;

(ii) A statement that the bank will notify the customer if funds deposited in the customer's account will not be available for withdrawal until later than the time periods stated in the bank's availability policy; and

(iii) A statement that customers should ask if they need to be sure about when a particular deposit will be available for withdrawal.

(2) Notice at time of case-by-case delay—

(i) In general. When a depositary bank extends the time when funds will be available for withdrawal on a case-by-case basis, it must provide the depositor with a written notice. The notice shall include the following information—

(A) A number or code, which need not exceed four digits, that identifies the customer's account.

(B) The date of the deposit;

(C) The amount of the deposit that is being delayed; and

(D) The day the funds will be available for withdrawal.

(ii) Timing of notice. The notice shall be provided to the depositor at the time of the deposit, unless the deposit is not made in person to an employee of the depositary bank or the decision to extend the time when the deposited funds will be available is made after the time of the deposit. If notice is not given at the time of the deposit, the depositary bank shall mail or deliver the notice to the customer not later than the first business day following the banking day the deposit is made.

(3) Overdraft and returned check fees. A depositary bank that extends the time when funds will be available for withdrawal on a case-by-case basis and does not furnish the depositor with written notice at the time of deposit shall not assess any fees for any subsequent overdrafts (including use of a line of credit) or return of checks or other debits to the account, if—

(i) The overdraft or return of the check or other debit would not have occurred except for the fact that the deposited funds were delayed under paragraph (c)(1) of this section; and

(ii) The deposited check was paid by the paying bank.

Notwithstanding the foregoing, the depositary bank may assess an overdraft or returned check fee if it includes a notice concerning overdraft and returned check fees with the notice required in paragraph (c)(2) of this section and, when required, refunds any such fees upon the request of the customer. The notice must state that the customer may be entitled to a refund of overdraft or returned check fees that are assessed if the check subject to the delay is paid and how to obtain a refund.

(d) Credit union notice of interest payment policy. If a bank described in § 229.2(e)(4) begins to accrue interest or dividends on all deposits made in an interest-bearing account, including cash deposits, at a later time than the day specified in § 229.14(a), the bank's specific policy disclosures shall contain an explanation of when interest or dividends on deposited funds begin to accrue.

§ 229.17   Initial disclosures.

Before opening a new account, a bank shall provide a potential customer with the applicable specific availability policy disclosure described in § 229.16.

§ 229.18   Additional disclosure requirements.

(a) **Deposit slips.** A bank shall include on all preprinted deposit slips furnished to its customers a notice that deposits may not be available for immediate withdrawal.

(b) **Locations where employees accept consumer deposits.** A bank shall post in a conspicuous place in each location where its employees receive deposits to consumer accounts a notice that sets forth the time periods applicable to the availability of funds deposited in a consumer account.

(c) **Automated teller machines.**

(1) A depository bank shall post or provide a notice at each ATM location that funds deposited in the ATM may not be available for immediate withdrawal.

(2) A depository bank that operates an off-premises ATM from which deposits are removed not more than two times each week, as described in § 229.19(a)(4), shall disclose at or on the ATM the days on which deposits made at the ATM will be considered received.

(d) **Upon request.** A bank shall provide to any person, upon oral or written request, a notice containing the applicable specific availability policy disclosure described in § 229.16.

(e) **Changes in policy.** A bank shall send a notice to holders of consumer accounts at least 30 days before implementing a change to the bank's availability policy regarding such accounts, except that a change that expedites the availability of funds may be disclosed not later than 30 days after implementation.

§ 229.19   Miscellaneous.

(a) **When funds are considered deposited.** For the purposes of this subpart—

(1) Funds deposited at a staffed facility, ATM, or contractual branch are considered deposited when they are received at the staffed facility, ATM, or contractual branch;

(2) Funds mailed to the depositary bank are considered deposited on the day they are received by the depositary bank;

(3) Funds deposited to a night depository, lock box, or similar facility are considered deposited on the day on which the deposit is removed from such facility and is available for processing by the depositary bank;

(4) Funds deposited at an ATM that is not on, or within 50 feet of, the premises of the depositary bank are considered deposited on the day the funds are removed from the ATM, if funds normally are removed from the ATM not more than two times each week; and

(5) Funds may be considered deposited on the next banking day, in the case of funds that are deposited—

(i)   On a day that is not a banking day for the depositary bank; or

(ii) After a cut-off hour set by the depositary bank for the receipt of deposits of 2:00 p.m. or later, or, for the receipt of deposits at ATMs, contractual branches, or off-premise facilities, of 12:00 noon or later. Different cut-off hours later than these times may be established for the receipt of different types of deposits, or receipt of deposits at different locations.

(b) **Availability at start of business day.** Except as otherwise provided in § 229.12(d), if any provision of this subpart requires that funds be made available for withdrawal on any business day, the funds shall be available for withdrawal by the later of—

(1)   9:00 a.m. (local time of the depositary bank); or

(2) The time the depositary bank's teller facilities (including ATMs) are available for customer account withdrawals.

(c)   **Effect on policies of depositary bank.** This part does not—

(1) Prohibit a depositary bank from making funds available to a customer for withdrawal in a shorter period of time than the time required by this subpart;

(2) Affect a depositary bank's right—

     (i) To accept or reject a check for deposit;

     (ii) To revoke any settlement made by the depositary bank with respect to a check accepted by the bank for deposit, to charge back the customer's account for the amount of a check based on the return of the check or receipt of a notice of nonpayment of the check, or to claim a refund of such credit; and

     (iii) To charge back funds made available to its customer for an electronic payment for which the bank has not received payment in actually and finally collected funds;

(3) Require a depositary bank to open or otherwise to make its facilities available for customer transactions on a given business day; or

(4) Supersede any policy of a depositary bank that limits the amount of cash a customer may withdraw from its account on any one day, if that policy—

     (i) Is not dependent on the time the funds have been deposited in the account, as long as the funds have been on deposit for the time period specified in §§ 229.10, 229.12, or 229.13; and

     (ii) In the case of withdrawals made in person to an employee of the depositary bank—

         (A) Is applied without discrimination to all customers of the bank; and

         (B) Is related to security, operating, or bonding requirements of the depositary bank.

(d)   **Use of calculated availability.** A depositary bank may provide availability to its nonconsumer accounts based on a sample of checks that represents the average composition of the customer's deposits, if the terms for availability based on the sample are equivalent to or more prompt than the availability requirements of this subpart.

(e)   **Holds on other funds.**

(1) A depositary bank that receives a check for deposit in an account may not place a hold on any funds of the customer at the bank, where—

     (i) The amount of funds that are held exceeds the amount of the check; or

     (ii) The funds are not made available for withdrawal within the times specified in §§ 229.10, 229.12, and 229.13.

(2) A depositary bank that cashes a check for a customer over the counter, other than a check drawn on the depositary bank, may not place a hold on funds in an account of the customer at the bank, if—

     (i) The amount of funds that are held exceeds the amount of the check; or

     (ii) The funds are not made available for withdrawal within the times specified in §§ 229.10, 229.12, and 229.13.

(f)   **Employee training and compliance.** Each bank shall establish procedures to ensure that the bank complies with the requirements of this subpart, and shall provide each employee who performs duties subject to the requirements of this subpart with a statement of the procedures applicable to that employee.

(g)   **Effect of merger transaction—**

(1)   **In general.** For purposes of this subpart, except for the purposes of the new accounts exception of § 229.13(a), and when funds are considered deposited under § 229.19(a), two or more banks that have engaged in a merger transaction may be considered to be separate banks for a period of one year following the consummation of the merger transaction.

(2) Merger transactions on or after July 1, 1998, and before March 1, 2000. If banks have consummated a merger transaction on or after July 1, 1998, and before March 1, 2000, the merged banks may be considered separate banks until March 1, 2001.

§ 229.20   Relation to state law.

(a) In general. Any provision of a law or regulation of any state in effect on or before September 1, 1989, that requires funds deposited in an account at a bank chartered by the state to be made available for withdrawal in a shorter time than the time provided in subpart B, and, in connection therewith, subpart A, shall—

(1) Supersede the provisions of the EFA Act and subpart B, and, in connection therewith, subpart A, to the extent the provisions relate to the time by which funds deposited or received for deposit in an account are available for withdrawal; and

(2) Apply to all federally insured banks located within the state.

No amendment to a state law or regulation governing the availability of funds that becomes effective after September 1, 1989, shall supersede the EFA Act and subpart B, and, in connection therewith, subpart A, but unamended provisions of state law shall remain in effect.

(b) Preemption of inconsistent law. Except as provided in paragraph (a), the EFA Act and subpart B, and, in connection therewith, subpart A, supersede any provision of inconsistent state law.

(c) Standards for preemption. A provision of a state law in effect on or before September 2, 1989, is not inconsistent with the EFA Act, or subpart B, or in connection therewith, subpart A, if it requires that funds shall be available in a shorter period of time than the time provided in this subpart. Inconsistency with the EFA Act and subpart B, and in connection therewith, subpart A, may exist when state law—

(1) Permits a depositary bank to make funds deposited in an account by cash, electronic payment, or check available for withdrawal in a longer period of time than the maximum period of time permitted under subpart B, and, in connection therewith, subpart A; or

(2) Provides for disclosures or notices concerning funds availability relating to accounts.

(d) Preemption determinations. The Board may determine, upon the request of any state, bank, or other interested party, whether the EFA Act and subpart B, and, in connection therewith, subpart A, preempt provisions of state laws relating to the availability of funds.

(e) Procedures for preemption determinations. A request for a preemption determination shall include the following—

(1) A copy of the full text of the state law in question, including any implementing regulations or judicial interpretations of that law; and

(2) A comparison of the provisions of state law with the corresponding provisions in the EFA Act and subparts A and B of this part, together with a discussion of the reasons why specific provisions of state law are either consistent or inconsistent with corresponding sections of the EFA Act and subparts A and B of this part.

A request for a preemption determination shall be addressed to the Secretary, Board of Governors of the Federal Reserve System.

§ 229.21   Civil liability.

(a) Civil liability. A bank that fails to comply with any requirement imposed under subpart B, and in connection therewith, subpart A, of this part or any provision of state law that supersedes any provision of subpart B, and in connection therewith, subpart A, with respect to any person is liable to that person in an amount equal to the sum of—

(1)   Any actual damage sustained by that person as a result of the failure;

(2)   Such additional amount as the court may allow, except that—

(i)   In the case of an individual action, liability under this paragraph shall not be less than $100 nor greater than $1,000; and

(ii)   In the case of a class action—

(A)   No minimum recovery shall be applicable to each member of the class; and

(B)   The total recovery under this paragraph in any class action or series of class actions arising out of the same failure to comply by the same depositary bank shall not be more than the lesser of $500,000 or 1 percent of the net worth of the bank involved; and

(3)   In the case of a successful action to enforce the foregoing liability, the costs of the action, together with a reasonable attorney's fee as determined by the court.

(b)   Class action awards. In determining the amount of any award in any class action, the court shall consider, among other relevant factors—

(1)   The amount of any damages awarded;

(2)   The frequency and persistence of failures of compliance;

(3)   The resources of the bank;

(4)   The number of persons adversely affected; and

(5)   The extent to which the failure of compliance was intentional.

(c)   Bona fide errors—

(1)   **General rule.** A bank is not liable in any action brought under this section for a violation of this subpart if the bank demonstrates by a preponderance of the evidence that the violation was not intentional and resulted from a bona fide error, notwithstanding the maintenance of procedures reasonably adapted to avoid any such error.

(2)   **Examples.** Examples of a bona fide error include clerical, calculation, computer malfunction and programming, and printing errors, except that an error of legal judgment with respect to the bank's obligation under this subpart is not a bona fide error.

(d)   Jurisdiction. Any action under this section may be brought in any United States district court or in any other court of competent jurisdiction, and shall be brought within one year after the date of the occurrence of the violation involved.

(e)   Reliance on Board rulings. No provision of this subpart imposing any liability shall apply to any act done or omitted in good faith in conformity with any rule, regulation, or interpretation thereof by the Board, regardless of whether such rule, regulation, or interpretation is amended, rescinded, or determined by judicial or other authority to be invalid for any reason after the act or omission has occurred.

(f)   Exclusions. This section does not apply to claims that arise under Subpart C of this part or to actions for wrongful dishonor.

(g)   Record retention.

(1)   A bank shall retain evidence of compliance with the requirements imposed by this subpart for not less than two years. Records may be stored by use of microfiche, microfilm, magnetic tape, or other methods capable of accurately retaining and reproducing information.

(2)   If a bank has actual notice that it is being investigated, or is subject to an enforcement proceeding by an agency charged with monitoring that bank's compliance with the EFA Act and this subpart, or has been served with notice of an action filed under this section, it shall retain the records pertaining to the action or proceeding pending final disposition of the matter, unless an earlier time is allowed by order of the agency or court.

SUBPART C—COLLECTION OF CHECKS

§ 229.30   Paying bank's responsibility for return of checks.

(a)   **Return of checks.** If a paying bank determines not to pay a check, it shall return the check in an expeditious manner as provided in either paragraph (a)(1) or (a)(2) of this section.

(1)   **Two-day/four-day test.** A paying bank returns a check in an expeditious manner if it sends the returned check in a manner such that the check would normally be received by the depositary bank not later than 4:00 p.m. (local time of the depositary bank) of—

(i)   The second business day following the banking day on which the check was presented to the paying bank, if the paying bank is located in the same check processing region as the depositary bank; or

(ii)   The fourth business day following the banking day on which the check was presented to the paying bank, if the paying bank is not located in the same check processing region as the depositary bank.

If the last business day on which the paying bank may deliver a returned check to the depositary bank is not a banking day for the depositary bank, the paying bank meets the two-day/four-day test if the returned check is received by the depositary bank on or before the depositary bank's next banking day.

(2)   **Forward collection test.** A paying bank also returns a check in an expeditious manner if it sends the returned check in a manner that a similarly situated bank would normally handle a check—

(i)   Of similar amount as the returned check;

(ii)   Drawn on the depositary bank; and

(iii)   Deposited for forward collection in the similarly situated bank by noon on the banking day following the banking day on which the check was presented to the paying bank.

Subject to the requirement for expeditious return, a paying bank may send a returned check to the depositary bank, or to any other bank agreeing to handle the returned check expeditiously under § 229.31(a). A paying bank may convert a check to a qualified returned check. A qualified returned check shall be encoded in magnetic ink with the routing number of the depositary bank, the amount of the returned check, and a "2" in the case of an original check (or a "5" in the case of a substitute check) in position 44 of the qualified return MICR line as a return identifier. A qualified returned original check shall be encoded in accordance with ANS X9.13, and a qualified returned substitute check shall be encoded in accordance with ANS X9.100–140. This paragraph does not affect a paying bank's responsibility to return a check within the deadlines required by the U.C.C., Regulation J (12 CFR Part 210), or § 229.30(c).

(b)   **Unidentifiable depositary bank.** A paying bank that is unable to identify the depositary bank with respect to a check may send the returned check to any bank that handled the check for forward collection even if that bank does not agree to handle the check expeditiously under § 229.31(a). A paying bank sending a returned check under this paragraph to a bank that handled the check for forward collection must advise the bank to which the check is sent that the paying bank is unable to identify the depositary bank. The expeditious return requirements in § 229.30(a) do not apply to the paying bank's return of a check under this paragraph.

(c)   **Extension of deadline.** The deadline for return or notice of nonpayment under the U.C.C. or Regulation J (12 CFR part 210), or § 229.36(f)(2) is extended to the time of dispatch of such return or notice of nonpayment where a paying bank uses a means of delivery that would ordinarily result in receipt by the bank to which it is sent—

(1)   On or before the receiving bank's next banking day following the otherwise applicable deadline by the earlier of the close of that banking day or a cutoff hour of 2 p.m. or later set by the receiving bank under U.C.C. 4–108, for all deadlines other than those described in paragraph (c)(2) of this section; this deadline is extended further if a paying bank uses a highly expeditious means of

transportation, even if this means of transportation would ordinarily result in delivery after the receiving bank's next cutoff hour or banking day referred to above; or

(2)   Prior to the cut-off hour for the next processing cycle (if sent to a returning bank), or on the next banking day (if sent to the depositary bank), for a deadline falling on a Saturday that is a banking day (as defined in the applicable U.C.C.) for the paying bank.

(d)   **Identification of returned check.** A paying bank returning a check shall clearly indicate on the front of the check that it is a returned check and the reason for return. If the check is a substitute check, the paying bank shall place this information within the image of the original check that appears on the front of the substitute check.

(e)   **Depositary bank without accounts.** The expeditious return requirements of paragraph (a) of this section do not apply to checks deposited in a depositary bank that does not maintain accounts.

(f)   **Notice in lieu of return.** If a check is unavailable for return, the paying bank may send in its place a copy of the front and back of the returned check, or, if no such copy is available, a written notice of nonpayment containing the information specified in § 229.33(b). The copy or notice shall clearly state that it constitutes a notice in lieu of return. A notice in lieu of return is considered a returned check subject to the expeditious return requirements of this section and to the other requirements of this subpart.

(g)   **Reliance on routing number.** A paying bank may return a returned check based on any routing number designating the depositary bank appearing on the returned check in the depositary bank's indorsement.

§ 229.31   Returning bank's responsibility for return of checks.

(a)   **Return of checks.** A returning bank shall return a returned check in an expeditious manner as provided in either paragraph (a)(1) or (a)(2) of this section.

(1)   **Two-day/four-day test.** A returning bank returns a check in an expeditious manner if it sends the returned check in a manner such that the check would normally be received by the depositary bank not later than 4:00 p.m. (local time) of—

(i)   The second business day following the banking day on which the check was presented to the paying bank if the paying bank is located in the same check processing region as the depositary bank; or

(ii)   The fourth business day following the banking day on which the check was presented to the paying bank if the paying bank is not located in the same check processing region as the depositary bank.

If the last business day on which the returning bank may deliver a returned check to the depositary bank is not a banking day for the depositary bank, the returning bank meets this requirement if the returned check is received by the depositary bank on or before the depositary bank's next banking day.

(2)   **Forward collection test.** A returning bank also returns a check in an expeditious manner if it sends the returned check in a manner that a similarly situated bank would normally handle a check—

(i)   Of similar amount as the returned check;

(ii)   Drawn on the depositary bank; and

(iii)   Received for forward collection by the similarly situated bank at the time the returning bank received the returned check, except that a returning bank may set a cut-off hour for the receipt of returned checks that is earlier than the similarly situated bank's cut-off hour for checks received for forward collection, if the cut-off hour is not earlier than 2:00 p.m.

Subject to the requirement for expeditious return, the returning bank may send the returned check to the depositary bank, or to any bank agreeing to handle the returned check expeditiously under § 229.31(a). The returning bank may convert the returned check to a qualified returned check. A qualified returned check shall be encoded in magnetic ink with the routing number of the depositary bank, the amount of the returned check, and a "2" in the case of an original check (or a "5" in the case of a substitute check) in position 44 of the qualified return MICR line as a return identifier. A qualified returned original check shall be encoded in accordance with ANS X9.13, and a qualified returned substitute check shall be encoded in accordance with ANS X9.100–140. The time for expeditious return under the forward collection test, and the deadline for return under the U.C.C. and Regulation J (12 CFR part 210), are extended by one business day if the returning bank converts a returned check to a qualified returned check. This extension does not apply to the two-day/four-day test specified in paragraph (a)(1) of this section or when a returning bank is returning a check directly to the depositary bank.

(b) **Unidentifiable depositary bank.** A returning bank that is unable to identify the depositary bank with respect to a returned check may send the returned check to—

(1) Any collecting bank that handled the check for forward collection if the returning bank was not a collecting bank with respect to the returned check; or

(2) A prior collecting bank, if the returning bank was a collecting bank with respect to the returned check;

even if that collecting bank does not agree to handle the returned check expeditiously under § 229.31(a). A returning bank sending a returned check under this paragraph must advise the bank to which the check is sent that the returning bank is unable to identify the depositary bank. The expeditious return requirements in paragraph (a) of this section do not apply to return of a check under this paragraph. A returning bank that receives a returned check from a paying bank under § 229.30(b), or from a returning bank under this paragraph, but that is able to identify the depositary bank, must thereafter return the check expeditiously to the depositary bank.

(c) **Settlement.** A returning bank shall settle with a bank sending a returned check to it for return by the same means that it settles or would settle with the sending bank for a check received for forward collection drawn on the depositary bank. This settlement is final when made.

(d) **Charges.** A returning bank may impose a charge on a bank sending a returned check for handling the returned check.

(e) **Depositary bank without accounts.** The expeditious return requirements of paragraph (a) of this section do not apply to checks deposited with a depositary bank that does not maintain accounts.

(f) **Notice in lieu of return.** If a check is unavailable for return, the returning bank may send in its place a copy of the front and back of the returned check, or, if no copy is available, a written notice of nonpayment containing the information specified in § 229.33(b). The copy or notice shall clearly state that it constitutes a notice in lieu of return. A notice in lieu of return is considered a returned check subject to the expeditious return requirements of this section and to the other requirements of this subpart.

(g) **Reliance on routing number.** A returning bank may return a returned check based on any routing number designating the depositary bank appearing on the returned check in the depositary bank's indorsement or in magnetic ink on a qualified returned check.

§ 229.32   Depositary bank's responsibility for returned checks.

(a) **Acceptance of returned checks.** A depositary bank shall accept returned checks and written notices of nonpayment

(1) At a location at which presentment of checks for forward collection is requested by the depositary bank; and

(2)(i) At a branch, head office, or other location consistent with the name and address of the bank in its indorsement on the check;

(ii) If no address appears in the indorsement, at a branch or head office associated with the routing number of the bank in its indorsement on the check;

(iii) If the address in the indorsement is not in the same check processing region as the address associated with the routing number of the bank in its indorsement on the check, at a location consistent with the address in the indorsement and at a branch or head office associated with the routing number in the bank's indorsement; or

    (iv) If no routing number or address appears in its indorsement on the check, at any branch or head office of the bank.

A depositary bank may require that returned checks be separated from forward collection checks.

    (b) **Payment.** A depositary bank shall pay the returning or paying bank returning the check to it for the amount of the check prior to the close of business on the banking day on which it received the check ("payment date") by—

    (1) Debit to an account of the depositary bank on the books of the returning or paying bank;

    (2) Cash;

    (3) Wire transfer; or

    (4) Any other form of payment acceptable to the returning or paying bank;

provided that the proceeds of the payment are available to the returning or paying bank in cash or by credit to an account of the returning or paying bank on or as of the payment date. If the payment date is not a banking day for the returning or paying bank or the depositary bank is unable to make the payment on the payment date, payment shall be made by the next day that is a banking day for the returning or paying bank. These payments are final when made.

    (c) **Misrouted returned checks and written notices of nonpayment.** If a bank receives a returned check or written notice of nonpayment on the basis that it is the depositary bank, and the bank determines that it is not the depositary bank with respect to the check or notice, it shall either promptly send the returned check or notice to the depositary bank directly or by means of a returning bank agreeing to handle the returned check expeditiously under § 229.31(a), or send the check or notice back to the bank from which it was received.

    (d) **Charges.** A depositary bank may not impose a charge for accepting and paying checks being returned to it.

§ 229.33   Notice of nonpayment.

    (a) **Requirement.** If a paying bank determines not to pay a check in the amount of $2,500 or more, it shall provide notice of nonpayment such that the notice is received by the depositary bank by 4:00 p.m. (local time) on the second business day following the banking day on which the check was presented to the paying bank. If the day the paying bank is required to provide notice is not a banking day for the depositary bank, receipt of notice on the depositary bank's next banking day constitutes timely notice. Notice may be provided by any reasonable means, including the returned check, a writing (including a copy of the check), telephone, Fedwire, telex, or other form of telegraph.

    (b) **Content of notice.** Notice must include the—

    (1) Name and routing number of the paying bank;

    (2) Name of the payee(s);

    (3) Amount;

    (4) Date of the indorsement of the depositary bank;

    (5) Account number of the customer(s) of the depositary bank;

    (6) Branch name or number of the depositary bank from its indorsement;

    (7) Trace number associated with the indorsement of the depositary bank; and

    (8) Reason for nonpayment.

The notice may include other information from the check that may be useful in identifying the check being returned and the customer, and, in the case of a written notice, must include the name and routing number of the depositary bank from its indorsement. If the paying bank is not sure of an item of information, it shall include the information required by this paragraph to the extent possible, and identify any item of information for which the bank is not sure of the accuracy.

(c) **Acceptance of notice.** The depositary bank shall accept notices during its banking day—

(1) Either at the telephone or telegraph number of its return check unit indicated in the indorsement, or, if no such number appears in the indorsement or if the number is illegible, at the general purpose telephone or telegraph number of its head office or the branch indicated in the indorsement; and

(2) At any other number held out by the bank for receipt of notice of nonpayment, and, in the case of written notice, as specified in § 229.32(a).

(d) **Notification to customer.** If the depositary bank receives a returned check or notice of nonpayment, it shall send or give notice to its customer of the facts by midnight of the banking day following the banking day on which it received the returned check or notice, or within a longer reasonable time.

(e) **Depositary bank without accounts.** The requirements of this section do not apply to checks deposited in a depositary bank that does not maintain accounts.

§ 229.34   Warranties.

(a) **Warranties.** Each paying bank or returning bank that transfers a returned check and receives a settlement or other consideration for it warrants to the transferee returning bank, to any subsequent returning bank, to the depositary bank, and to the owner of the check, that—

(1) The paying bank, or in the case of a check payable by a bank and payable through another bank, the bank by which the check is payable, returned the check within its deadline under the U.C.C., Regulation J (12 CFR Part 210), or § 229.30(c) of this part;

(2) It is authorized to return the check;

(3) The check has not been materially altered; and

(4) In the case of a notice in lieu of return, the original check has not and will not be returned.

These warranties are not made with respect to checks drawn on the Treasury of the United States, U.S. Postal Service money orders, or checks drawn on a state or a unit of general local government that are not payable through or at a bank.

(b) **Warranty of notice of nonpayment.** Each paying bank that gives a notice of nonpayment warrants to the transferee bank, to any subsequent transferee bank, to the depositary bank, and to the owner of the check that—

(1) The paying bank, or in the case of a check payable by a bank and payable through another bank, the bank by which the check is payable, returned or will return the check within its deadline under the U.C.C., Regulation J (12 CFR Part 210), or § 229.30(c) of this part;

(2) It is authorized to send the notice; and

(3) The check has not been materially altered.

These warranties are not made with respect to checks drawn on a state or a unit of general local government that are not payable through or at a bank.

(c) **Warranty of settlement amount, encoding, and offset.**

(1) Each bank that presents one or more checks to a paying bank and in return receives a settlement or other consideration warrants to the paying bank that the total amount of the checks presented is equal to the total amount of the settlement demanded by the presenting bank from the paying bank.

(2) Each bank that transfers one or more checks or returned checks to a collecting, returning, or depositary bank and in return receives a settlement or other consideration warrants to the

transferee bank that the accompanying information, if any, accurately indicates the total amount of the checks or returned checks transferred.

(3)   Each bank that presents or transfers a check or returned check warrants to any bank that subsequently handles it that, at the time of presentment or transfer, the information encoded after issue in magnetic ink on the check or returned check is correct. For purposes of this paragraph, the information encoded after issue on the check or returned check includes any information placed in the MICR line of a substitute check that represents that check or returned check.

(4)   If a bank settles with another bank for checks presented, or for returned checks for which it is the depositary bank, in amount exceeding the total amount of the checks, the settling bank may set off the excess settlement amount against subsequent settlements for checks presented, or for returned checks for which it is the depositary bank, that it receives from the other bank.

(d)   **Transfer and presentment warranties with respect to a remotely created check.**

(1)   A bank that transfers or presents a remotely created check and receives a settlement or other consideration warrants to the transferee bank, any subsequent collecting bank, and the paying bank that the person on whose account the remotely created check is drawn authorized the issuance of the check in the amount stated on the check and to the payee stated on the check. For purposes of this paragraph (d)(1), "account" includes an account as defined in § 229.2(a) as well as a credit or other arrangement that allows a person to draw checks that are payable by, through, or at a bank.

(2)   If a paying bank asserts a claim for breach of warranty under paragraph (d)(1) of this section, the warranting bank may defend by proving that the customer of the paying bank is precluded under U.C.C. 4–406, as applicable, from asserting against the paying bank the unauthorized issuance of the check.

(e)   **Damages.** Damages for breach of these warranties shall not exceed the consideration received by the bank that presents or transfers a check or returned check, plus interest compensation and expenses related to the check or returned check, if any.

(f)   **Tender of defense.** If a bank is sued for breach of a warranty under this section, it may give a prior bank in the collection or return chain written notice of the litigation, and the bank notified may then give similar notice to any other prior bank. If the notice states that the bank notified may come in and defend and that failure to do so will bind the bank notified in an action later brought by the bank giving the notice as to any determination of fact common to the two litigations, the bank notified is so bound unless after seasonable receipt of the notice the bank notified does come in and defend.

(g)   **Notice of claim.** Unless a claimant gives notice of a claim for breach of warranty under this section to the bank that made the warranty within 30 days after the claimant has reason to know of the breach and the identity of the warranting bank, the warranting bank is discharged to the extent of any loss caused by the delay in giving notice of the claim.

§ 229.35   Indorsements.

(a)   **Indorsement standards.** A bank (other than a paying bank) that handles a check during forward collection or a returned check shall indorse the check in a manner that permits a person to interpret the indorsement, in accordance with the indorsement standard set forth in appendix D of this part.

(b)   **Liability of bank handling check.** A bank that handles a check for forward collection or return is liable to any bank that subsequently handles the check to the extent that the subsequent bank does not receive payment for the check because of suspension of payments by another bank or otherwise. This paragraph applies whether or not a bank has placed its indorsement on the check. This liability is not affected by the failure of any bank to exercise ordinary care, but any bank failing to do so remains liable. A bank seeking recovery against a prior bank shall send notice to that prior bank reasonably promptly after it learns the facts entitling it to recover. A bank may recover from the bank with which it settled for the check by revoking the settlement, charging back any credit given to an account, or obtaining a refund. A bank may have the rights of a holder with respect to each check it handles.

(c) **Indorsement by a bank.** After a check has been indorsed by a bank, only a bank may acquire the rights of a holder—

(1) Until the check has been returned to the person initiating collection; or

(2) Until the check has been specially indorsed by a bank to a person who is not a bank.

(d) **Indorsement for depositary bank.** A depositary bank may arrange with another bank to apply the other bank's indorsement as the depositary bank indorsement, provided that any indorsement of the depositary bank on the check avoids the area reserved for the depositary bank indorsement as specified in Appendix D. The other bank indorsing as depositary bank is considered the depositary bank for purposes of Subpart C of this part.

§ 229.36 Presentment and issuance of checks.

(a) **Payable through and payable at checks.** A check payable at or through a paying bank is considered to be drawn on that bank for purposes of the expeditious return and notice of nonpayment requirements of this subpart.

(b) **Receipt at bank office or processing center.** A check is considered received by the paying bank when it is received:

(1) At a location to which delivery is requested by the paying bank;

(2) At an address of the bank associated with the routing number on the check, whether in magnetic ink or in fractional form;

(3) At any branch or head office, if the bank is identified on the check by name without address; or

(4) At a branch, head office, or other location consistent with the name and address of the bank on the check if the bank is identified on the check by name and address.

(c) **[Reserved]**

(d) **Liability of bank during forward collection.** Settlements between banks for the forward collection of a check are final when made; however, a collecting bank handling a check for forward collection may be liable to a prior collecting bank, including the depositary bank, and the depositary bank's customer.

(e) **Issuance of payable-through checks.**

(1) A bank that arranges for checks payable by it to be payable through another bank shall require that the following information be printed conspicuously on the face of each check:

(i) The name, location, and first four digits of the nine-digit routing number of the bank by which the check is payable; and

(ii) The words "payable through" followed by the name of the payable-through bank.

(2) A bank is responsible for damages under § 229.38 to the extent that a check payable by it and not payable through another bank is labelled as provided in this section.

(f) **Same-day settlement.**

(1) A check is considered presented, and a paying bank must settle for or return the check pursuant to paragraph (f)(2) of this section, if a presenting bank delivers the check in accordance with reasonable delivery requirements established by the paying bank and demands payment under this paragraph (f)—

(i) At a location designated by the paying bank for receipt of checks under this paragraph (f) that is in the check processing region consistent with the routing number encoded in magnetic ink on the check and at which the paying bank would be considered to have received the check under paragraph (b) of this section or, if no location is designated, at any location described in paragraph (b) of this section; and

(ii) By 8 a.m. on a business day (local time of the location described in paragraph (f)(1)(i) of this section).

A paying bank may require that checks presented for settlement pursuant to this paragraph (f)(1) be separated from other forward-collection checks or returned checks.

(2) If presentment of a check meets the requirements of paragraph (f)(1) of this section, the paying bank is accountable to the presenting bank for the amount of the check unless, by the close of Fedwire on the business day it receives the check, it either:

(i) Settles with the presenting bank for the amount of the check by credit to an account at a Federal Reserve Bank designated by the presenting bank; or

(ii) Returns the check.

(3) Notwithstanding paragraph (f)(2) of this section, if a paying bank closes on a business day and receives presentment of a check on that day in accordance with paragraph (f)(1) of this section, the paying bank is accountable to the presenting bank for the amount of the check unless, by the close of Fedwire on its next banking day, it either:

(i) Settles with the presenting bank for the amount of the check by credit to an account at a Federal Reserve Bank designated by the presenting bank; or

(ii) Returns the check.

If the closing is voluntary, unless the paying bank settles for or returns the check in accordance with paragraph (f)(2) of this section, it shall pay interest compensation to the presenting bank for each day after the business day on which the check was presented until the paying bank settles for the check, including the day of settlement.

§ 229.37   Variation by agreement.

The effect of the provisions of Subpart C may be varied by agreement, except that no agreement can disclaim the responsibility of a bank for its own lack of good faith or failure to exercise ordinary care, or can limit the measure of damages for such lack or failure; but the parties may determine by agreement the standards by which such responsibility is to be measured if such standards are not manifestly unreasonable.

§ 229.38   Liability.

(a) **Standard of care; liability; measure of damages.** A bank shall exercise ordinary care and act in good faith in complying with the requirements of this subpart. A bank that fails to exercise ordinary care or act in good faith under this subpart may be liable to the depositary bank, the depositary bank's customer, the owner of a check, or another party to the check. The measure of damages for failure to exercise ordinary care is the amount of the loss incurred, up to the amount of the check, reduced by the amount of the loss that party would have incurred even if the bank had exercised ordinary care. A bank that fails to act in good faith under this subpart may be liable for other damages, if any, suffered by the party as a proximate consequence. Subject to a bank's duty to exercise ordinary care or act in good faith in choosing the means of return or notice of nonpayment, the bank is not liable for the insolvency, neglect, misconduct, mistake, or default of another bank or person, or for loss or destruction of a check or notice of nonpayment in transit or in the possession of others. This section does not affect a paying bank's liability to its customer under the U.C.C. or other law.

(b) **Paying bank's failure to make timely return.** If a paying bank fails both to comply with § 229.30(a) and to comply with the deadline for return under the U.C.C., Regulation J (12 CFR Part 210), or § 229.30(c) in connection with a single nonpayment of a check, the paying bank shall be liable under either § 229.30(a) or such other provision, but not both.

(c) **Comparative negligence.** If a person, including a bank, fails to exercise ordinary care or act in good faith under this subpart in indorsing a check (§ 229.35), accepting a returned check or notice of nonpayment (§§ 229.32(a) and 229.33(c)), or otherwise, the damages incurred by that person under

§ 229.38(a) shall be diminished in proportion to the amount of negligence or bad faith attributable to that person.

(d) **Responsibility for certain aspects of checks—**

(1) A paying bank, or in the case of a check payable through the paying bank and payable by another bank, the bank by which the check is payable, is responsible for damages under paragraph (a) of this section to the extent that the condition of the check when issued by it or its customer adversely affects the ability of a bank to indorse the check legibly in accordance with § 229.35. A depositary bank is responsible for damages under paragraph (a) of this section to the extent that the condition of the back of a check arising after the issuance of the check and prior to acceptance of the check by it adversely affects the ability of a bank to indorse the check legibly in accordance with § 229.35. A reconverting bank is responsible for damages under paragraph (a) of this section to the extent that the condition of the back of a substitute check transferred, presented, or returned by it—

(i) Adversely affects the ability of a subsequent bank to indorse the check legibly in accordance with § 229.35; or

(ii) Causes an indorsement that previously was applied in accordance with § 229.35 to become illegible.

Note: Responsibility under this paragraph (d) shall be treated as negligence of the paying bank, depositary bank, or reconverting bank for purposes of paragraph (c) of this section.

(2) **Responsibility for payable through checks.** In the case of a check that is payable by a bank and payable through a paying bank located in a different check processing region than the bank by which the check is payable, the bank by which the check is payable is responsible for damages under paragraph (a) of this section, to the extent that the check is not returned to the depositary bank through the payable through bank as quickly as the check would have been required to be returned under § 229.30(a) had the bank by which the check is payable—

(i) Received the check as paying bank on the day the payable through bank received the check; and

(ii) Returned the check as paying bank in accordance with § 229.30(a)(1).

Responsibility under this paragraph shall be treated as negligence of the bank by which the check is payable for purposes of paragraph (c) of this section.

(e) **Timeliness of action.** If a bank is delayed in acting beyond the time limits set forth in this subpart because of interruption of communication or computer facilities, suspension of payments by a bank, war, emergency conditions, failure of equipment, or other circumstances beyond its control, its time for acting is extended for the time necessary to complete the action, if it exercises such diligence as the circumstances require.

(f) **Exclusion.** Section 229.21 of this part and section 611(a), (b), and (c) of the EFA Act (12 U.S.C. 4010(a), (b), and (c)) do not apply to this subpart.

(g) **Jurisdiction.** Any action under this subpart may be brought in any United States district court, or in any other court of competent jurisdiction, and shall be brought within one year after the date of the occurrence of the violation involved.

(h) **Reliance on Board rulings.** No provision of this subpart imposing any liability shall apply to any act done or omitted in good faith in conformity with any rule, regulation, or interpretation thereof by the Board, regardless of whether the rule, regulation, or interpretation is amended, rescinded, or determined by judicial or other authority to be invalid for any reason after the act or omission has occurred.

§ 229.39   Insolvency of bank.

(a) **Duty of receiver.** A check or returned check in, or coming into, the possession of a paying, collecting, depositary, or returning bank that suspends payment, and which is not paid, shall be returned by the receiver, trustee, or agent in charge of the closed bank to the bank or customer that transferred the check to the closed bank.

(b) Preference against paying or depositary bank. If a paying bank finally pays a check, or if a depositary bank becomes obligated to pay a returned check, and suspends payment without making a settlement for the check or returned check with the prior bank that is or becomes final, the prior bank has a preferred claim against the paying bank or the depositary bank.

(c) Preference against collecting, paying, or returning bank. If a collecting, paying, or returning bank receives settlement from a subsequent bank for a check or returned check, which settlement is or becomes final, and suspends payments without making a settlement for the check with the prior bank, which is or becomes final, the prior bank has a preferred claim against the collecting or returning bank.

(d) Preference against presenting bank. If a paying bank settles with a presenting bank for one or more checks, and if the presenting bank breaches a warranty specified in § 229.34(c)(1) or (3) with respect to those checks and suspends payments before satisfying the paying bank's warranty claim, the paying bank has a preferred claim against the presenting bank for the amount of the warranty claim.

(e) Finality of settlement. If a paying or depositary bank gives, or a collecting, paying, or returning bank gives or receives, a settlement for a check or returned check and thereafter suspends payment, the suspension does not prevent or interfere with the settlement becoming final if such finality occurs automatically upon the lapse of a certain time or the happening of certain events.

§ 229.40 Effect of merger transaction.

(a) In general. For purposes of this subpart, two or more banks that have engaged in a merger transaction may be considered to be separate banks for a period of one year following the consummation of the merger transaction.

(b) Merger transactions on or after July 1, 1998, and before March 1, 2000. If banks have consummated a merger transaction on or after July 1, 1998, and before March 1, 2000, the merged banks may be considered separate banks until March 1, 2001.

§ 229.41 Relation to state law.

The provisions of this subpart supersede any inconsistent provisions of the U.C.C. as adopted in any state, or of any other state law, but only to the extent of the inconsistency.

§ 229.42 Exclusions.

The expeditious-return (§§ 229.30(a) and 229.31(a)), notice-of-nonpayment (§ 229.33), and same-day settlement (§ 229.36(f)) requirements of this subpart do not apply to a check drawn upon the United States Treasury, to a U.S. Postal Service money order, or to a check drawn on a state or a unit of general local government that is not payable through or at a bank.

§ 229.43 Checks payable in Guam, American Samoa, and the Northern Mariana Islands.

(a) Definitions. The definitions in § 229.2 apply to this section, unless otherwise noted. In addition, for the purposes of this section—

(1) Pacific island bank means an office of an institution that would be a bank as defined in § 229.2(e) but for the fact that the office is located in Guam, American Samoa, or the Northern Mariana Islands;

(2) Pacific island check means a demand draft drawn on or payable through or at a Pacific island bank, which is not a check as defined in § 229.2(k).

(b) Rules applicable to Pacific island checks. To the extent a bank handles a Pacific island check as if it were a check defined in § 229.2(k), the bank is subject to the following sections of this part (and the word "check" in each such section is construed to include a Pacific island check)—

(1) § 229.31, except that the returning bank is not subject to the requirement to return a Pacific island check in an expeditious manner;

(2) § 229.32;

(3) § 229.34(c)(2), (c)(3), (d), (e), and (f);

(4) § 229.35; for purposes of § 229.35(c), the Pacific island bank is deemed to be a bank;

(5) § 229.36(d);

(6) § 229.37;

(7) § 229.38(a) and (c) through (h);

(8) § 229.39(a), (b), (c) and (e); and

(9) §§ 229.40 through 229.42.

SUBPART D—SUBSTITUTE CHECKS

§ 229.51 General provisions governing substitute checks.

(a) **Legal equivalence.** A substitute check for which a bank has provided the warranties described in § 229.52 is the legal equivalent of an original check for all persons and all purposes, including any provision of federal or state law, if the substitute check—

(1) Accurately represents all of the information on the front and back of the original check as of the time the original check was truncated; and

(2) Bears the legend, "This is a legal copy of your check. You can use it the same way you would use the original check."

(b) **Reconverting bank duties.** A bank shall ensure that a substitute check for which it is the reconverting bank—

(1) Bears all indorsements applied by parties that previously handled the check in any form (including the original check, a substitute check, or another paper or electronic representation of such original check or substitute check) for forward collection or return;

(2) Identifies the reconverting bank in a manner that preserves any previous reconverting bank identifications, in accordance with ANS X9.100–140 and appendix D of this part; and

(3) Identifies the bank that truncated the original check, in accordance with ANS X9.100–140 and appendix D of this part.

(c) **Applicable law.** A substitute check that is the legal equivalent of an original check under paragraph (a) of this section shall be subject to any provision, including any provision relating to the protection of customers, of this part, the U.C.C., and any other applicable federal or state law as if such substitute check were the original check, to the extent such provision of law is not inconsistent with the Check 21 Act or this subpart.

§ 229.52 Substitute check warranties.

(a) **Content and provision of substitute check warranties.** A bank that transfers, presents, or returns a substitute check (or a paper or electronic representation of a substitute check) for which it receives consideration warrants to the parties listed in paragraph (b) of this section that—

(1) The substitute check meets the requirements for legal equivalence described in § 229.51(a)(1)–(2); and

(2) No depositary bank, drawee, drawer, or indorser will receive presentment or return of, or otherwise be charged for, the substitute check, the original check, or a paper or electronic representation of the substitute check or original check such that that person will be asked to make a payment based on a check that it already has paid.

(b) Warranty recipients. A bank makes the warranties described in paragraph (a) of this section to the person to which the bank transfers, presents, or returns the substitute check or a paper or electronic representation of such substitute check and to any subsequent recipient, which could include a collecting or returning bank, the depositary bank, the drawer, the drawee, the payee, the depositor, and any indorser. These parties receive the warranties regardless of whether they received the substitute check or a paper or electronic representation of a substitute check.

§ 229.53   Substitute check indemnity.

(a) Scope of indemnity. A bank that transfers, presents, or returns a substitute check or a paper or electronic representation of a substitute check for which it receives consideration shall indemnify the recipient and any subsequent recipient (including a collecting or returning bank, the depositary bank, the drawer, the drawee, the payee, the depositor, and any indorser) for any loss incurred by any recipient of a substitute check if that loss occurred due to the receipt of a substitute check instead of the original check.

(b) Indemnity amount—

(1) In general. Unless otherwise indicated by paragraph (b)(2) or (b)(3) of this section, the amount of the indemnity under paragraph (a) of this section is as follows:

(i) If the loss resulted from a breach of a substitute check warranty provided under § 229.52, the amount of the indemnity shall be the amount of any loss (including interest, costs, reasonable attorney's fees, and other expenses of representation) proximately caused by the warranty breach.

(ii) If the loss did not result from a breach of a substitute check warranty provided under § 229.52, the amount of the indemnity shall be the sum of—

(A) The amount of the loss, up to the amount of the substitute check; and

(B) Interest and expenses (including costs and reasonable attorney's fees and other expenses of representation) related to the substitute check.

(2) Comparative negligence.

(i) If a loss described in paragraph (a) of this section results in whole or in part from the indemnified person's negligence or failure to act in good faith, then the indemnity amount described in paragraph (b)(1) of this section shall be reduced in proportion to the amount of negligence or bad faith attributable to the indemnified person.

(ii) Nothing in this paragraph (b)(2) reduces the rights of a consumer or any other person under the U.C.C. or other applicable provision of state or federal law.

(3) Effect of producing the original check or a sufficient copy—

(i) If an indemnifying bank produces the original check or a sufficient copy, the indemnifying bank shall—

(A) Be liable under this section only for losses that are incurred up to the time that the bank provides that original check or sufficient copy to the indemnified person; and

(B) Have a right to the return of any funds it has paid under this section in excess of those losses.

(ii) The production by the indemnifying bank of the original check or a sufficient copy under paragraph (b)(3)(i) of this section shall not absolve the indemnifying bank from any liability under any warranty that the bank has provided under § 229.52 or other applicable law.

(c) Subrogation of rights—

(1) In general. An indemnifying bank shall be subrogated to the rights of the person that it indemnifies to the extent of the indemnity it has provided and may attempt to recover from another person based on a warranty or other claim.

(2) Duty of indemnified person for subrogated claims. Each indemnified person shall have a duty to comply with all reasonable requests for assistance from an indemnifying bank in connection with any claim the indemnifying bank brings against a warrantor or other person related to a check that forms the basis for the indemnification.

§ 229.54   Expedited recredit for consumers.

(a) Circumstances giving rise to a claim. A consumer may make a claim under this section for a recredit with respect to a substitute check if the consumer asserts in good faith that—

(1) The bank holding the consumer's account charged that account for a substitute check that was provided to the consumer (although the consumer need not be in possession of that substitute check at the time he or she submits a claim);

(2) The substitute check was not properly charged to the consumer account or the consumer has a warranty claim with respect to the substitute check;

(3) The consumer suffered a resulting loss; and

(4) Production of the original check or a sufficient copy is necessary to determine whether or not the substitute check in fact was improperly charged or whether the consumer's warranty claim is valid.

(b) Procedures for making claims. A consumer shall make his or her claim for a recredit under this section with the bank that holds the consumer's account in accordance with the timing, content, and form requirements of this section.

(1) Timing of claim.

(i) The consumer shall submit his or her claim such that the bank receives the claim by the end of the 40th calendar day after the later of the calendar day on which the bank mailed or delivered, by a means agreed to by the consumer—

(A) The periodic account statement that contains information concerning the transaction giving rise to the claim; or

(B) The substitute check giving rise to the claim.

(ii) If the consumer cannot submit his or her claim by the time specified in paragraph (b)(1)(i) of this section because of extenuating circumstances, the bank shall extend the 40-calendar-day period by an additional reasonable amount of time.

(iii) If a consumer makes a claim orally and the bank requires the claim to be in writing, the consumer's claim is timely if the oral claim was received within the time described in paragraphs (b)(1)(i)–(ii) of this section and the written claim was received within the time described in paragraph (b)(3)(ii) of this section.

(2) Content of claim.

(i) The consumer's claim shall include the following information:

(A) A description of the consumer's claim, including the reason why the consumer believes his or her account was improperly charged for the substitute check or the nature of his or her warranty claim with respect to such check;

(B) A statement that the consumer suffered a loss and an estimate of the amount of that loss;

(C) The reason why production of the original check or a sufficient copy is necessary to determine whether or not the charge to the consumer's account was proper or the consumer's warranty claim is valid; and

(D) Sufficient information to allow the bank to identify the substitute check and investigate the claim.

(ii) If a consumer attempts to make a claim but fails to provide all the information in paragraph (b)(2)(i) of this section that is required to constitute a claim, the bank shall inform the consumer that the claim is not complete and identify the information that is missing.

(3) Form and submission of claim; computation of time for bank action. The bank holding the account that is the subject of the consumer's claim may, in its discretion, require the consumer to submit the information required by this section in writing. A bank that requires a written submission—

(i) May permit the consumer to submit the written claim electronically;

(ii) Shall inform a consumer who submits a claim orally of the written claim requirement at the time of the oral claim and may require such consumer to submit the written claim such that the bank receives the written claim by the 10th business day after the banking day on which the bank received the oral claim; and

(iii) Shall compute the time periods for acting on the consumer's claim described in paragraph (c) of this section from the date on which the bank received the written claim.

(c) **Action on claims.** A bank that receives a claim that meets the requirements of paragraph (b) of this section shall act as follows:

(1) **Valid consumer claim.** If the bank determines that the consumer's claim is valid, the bank shall—

(i) Recredit the consumer's account for the amount of the consumer's loss, up to the amount of the substitute check, plus interest if the account is an interest-bearing account, no later than the end of the business day after the banking day on which the bank makes that determination; and

(ii) Send to the consumer the notice required by paragraph (e)(1) of this section.

(2) **Invalid consumer claim.** If a bank determines that the consumer's claim is not valid, the bank shall send to the consumer the notice described in paragraph (e)(2) of this section.

(3) **Recredit pending investigation.** If the bank has not taken an action described in paragraph (c)(1) or (c)(2) of this section before the end of the 10th business day after the banking day on which the bank received the claim, the bank shall—

(i) By the end of that business day—

(A) Recredit the consumer's account for the amount of the consumer's loss, up to the lesser of the amount of the substitute check or $2,500, plus interest on that amount if the account is an interest-bearing account; and

(B) Send to the consumer the notice required by paragraph (e)(1) of this section; and

(ii) Recredit the consumer's account for the remaining amount of the consumer's loss, if any, up to the amount of the substitute check, plus interest if the account is an interest-bearing account, no later than the end of the 45th calendar day after the banking day on which the bank received the claim and send to the consumer the notice required by paragraph (e)(1) of this section, unless the bank prior to that time has determined that the consumer's claim is or is not valid in accordance with paragraph (c)(1) or (c)(2) of this section.

(4) Reversal of recredit. A bank may reverse a recredit that it has made to a consumer account under paragraph (c)(1) or (c)(3) of this section, plus interest that the bank has paid, if any, on that amount, if the bank—

(i) Determines that the consumer's claim was not valid; and

(ii) Notifies the consumer in accordance with paragraph (e)(3) of this section.

(d) **Availability of recredit—**

(1) **Next-day availability.** Except as provided in paragraph (d)(2) of this section, a bank shall make any amount that it recredits to a consumer account under this section available for withdrawal no later than the start of the business day after the banking day on which the bank provides the recredit.

(2) Safeguard exceptions. A bank may delay availability to a consumer of a recredit provided under paragraph (c)(3)(i) of this section until the start of the earlier of the business day after the banking day on which the bank determines the consumer's claim is valid or the 45th calendar day after the banking day on which the bank received the oral or written claim, as required by paragraph (b) of this section, if—

(i) The consumer submits the claim during the 30-calendar-day period beginning on the banking day on which the consumer account was established;

(ii) Without regard to the charge that gave rise to the recredit claim—

(A) On six or more business days during the six-month period ending on the calendar day on which the consumer submitted the claim, the balance in the consumer account was negative or would have become negative if checks or other charges to the account had been paid; or

(B) On two or more business days during such six-month period, the balance in the consumer account was negative or would have become negative in the amount of $5,000 or more if checks or other charges to the account had been paid; or

(iii) The bank has reasonable cause to believe that the claim is fraudulent, based on facts that would cause a well-grounded belief in the mind of a reasonable person that the claim is fraudulent. The fact that the check in question or the consumer is of a particular class may not be the basis for invoking this exception.

(3) Overdraft fees. A bank that delays availability as permitted in paragraph (d)(2) of this section may not impose an overdraft fee with respect to drafts drawn by the consumer on such recredited funds until the fifth calendar day after the calendar day on which the bank sent the notice required by paragraph (e)(1) of this section.

(e) Notices relating to consumer expedited recredit claims—

(1) Notice of recredit. A bank that recredits a consumer account under paragraph (c) of this section shall send notice to the consumer of the recredit no later than the business day after the banking day on which the bank recredits the consumer account. This notice shall describe—

(i) The amount of the recredit; and

(ii) The date on which the recredited funds will be available for withdrawal.

(2) Notice that the consumer's claim is not valid. If a bank determines that a substitute check for which a consumer made a claim under this section was in fact properly charged to the consumer account or that the consumer's warranty claim for that substitute check was not valid, the bank shall send notice to the consumer no later than the business day after the banking day on which the bank makes that determination. This notice shall—

(i) Include the original check or a sufficient copy, except as provided in § 229.58;

(ii) Demonstrate to the consumer that the substitute check was properly charged or the consumer's warranty claim is not valid; and

(iii) Include the information or documents (in addition to the original check or sufficient copy), if any, on which the bank relied in making its determination or a statement that the consumer may request copies of such information or documents.

(3) Notice of a reversal of recredit. A bank that reverses an amount it previously recredited to a consumer account shall send notice to the consumer no later than the business day after the banking day on which the bank made the reversal. This notice shall include the information listed in paragraph (e)(2) of this section and also describe—

(i) The amount of the reversal, including both the amount of the recredit (including the interest component, if any) and the amount of interest paid on the recredited amount, if any, being reversed; and

(ii) The date on which the bank made the reversal.

(f) **Other claims not affected.** Providing a recredit in accordance with this section shall not absolve the bank from liability for a claim made under any other provision of law, such as a claim for wrongful dishonor of a check under the U.C.C., or from liability for additional damages, such as damages under § 229.53 or § 229.56 of this subpart or U.C.C. 4–402.

§ 229.55 Expedited recredit for banks.

(a) **Circumstances giving rise to a claim.** A bank that has an indemnity claim under § 229.53 with respect to a substitute check may make an expedited recredit claim against an indemnifying bank if—

(1) The claimant bank or a bank that the claimant bank has indemnified—

(i) Has received a claim for expedited recredit from a consumer under § 229.54; or

(ii) Would have been subject to such a claim if the consumer account had been charged for the substitute check;

(2) The claimant bank is obligated to provide an expedited recredit with respect to such substitute check under § 229.54 or otherwise has suffered a resulting loss; and

(3) The production of the original check or a sufficient copy is necessary to determine the validity of the charge to the consumer account or the validity of any warranty claim connected with such substitute check.

(b) **Procedures for making claims.** A claimant bank shall send its claim to the indemnifying bank, subject to the timing, content, and form requirements of this section.

(1) **Timing of claim.** The claimant bank shall submit its claim such that the indemnifying bank receives the claim by the end of the 120th calendar day after the date of the transaction that gave rise to the claim.

(2) **Content of claim.** The claimant bank's claim shall include the following information—

(i) A description of the consumer's claim or the warranty claim related to the substitute check, including why the bank believes that the substitute check may not be properly charged to the consumer account;

(ii) A statement that the claimant bank is obligated to recredit a consumer account under § 229.54 or otherwise has suffered a loss and an estimate of the amount of that recredit or loss, including interest if applicable;

(iii) The reason why production of the original check or a sufficient copy is necessary to determine the validity of the charge to the consumer account or the warranty claim; and

(iv) Sufficient information to allow the indemnifying bank to identify the substitute check and investigate the claim.

(3) **Requirements relating to copies of substitute checks.** If the information submitted by a claimant bank under paragraph (b)(2) of this section includes a copy of any substitute check, the claimant bank shall take reasonable steps to ensure that the copy cannot be mistaken for the legal equivalent of the check under § 229.51(a) or sent or handled by any bank, including the indemnifying bank, for forward collection or return.

(4) **Form and submission of claim; computation of time.** The indemnifying bank may, in its discretion, require the claimant bank to submit the information required by this section in writing, including a copy of the paper or electronic claim submitted by the consumer, if any. An indemnifying bank that requires a written submission—

(i) May permit the claimant bank to submit the written claim electronically;

(ii) Shall inform a claimant bank that submits a claim orally of the written claim requirement at the time of the oral claim; and

(iii) Shall compute the 10-day time period for acting on the claim described in paragraph (c) of this section from the date on which the bank received the written claim.

(c) **Action on claims.** No later than the 10th business day after the banking day on which the indemnifying bank receives a claim that meets the requirements of paragraph (b) of this section, the indemnifying bank shall—

(1) Recredit the claimant bank for the amount of the claim, up to the amount of the substitute check, plus interest if applicable;

(2) Provide to the claimant bank the original check or a sufficient copy; or

(3) Provide information to the claimant bank regarding why the indemnifying bank is not obligated to comply with paragraph (c)(1) or (c)(2) of this section.

(d) **Recredit does not abrogate other liabilities.** Providing a recredit to a claimant bank under this section does not absolve the indemnifying bank from liability for claims brought under any other law or from additional damages under § 229.53 or § 229.56.

(e) **Indemnifying bank's right to a refund.**

(1) If a claimant bank reverses a recredit it previously made to a consumer account under § 229.54 or otherwise receives reimbursement for a substitute check that formed the basis of its claim under this section, the claimant bank shall provide a refund promptly to any indemnifying bank that previously advanced funds to the claimant bank. The amount of the refund to the indemnifying bank shall be the amount of the reversal or reimbursement obtained by the claimant bank, up to the amount previously advanced by the indemnifying bank.

(2) If the indemnifying bank provides the claimant bank with the original check or a sufficient copy under paragraph (c)(2) of this section, § 229.53(b)(3) governs the indemnifying bank's entitlement to repayment of any amount provided to the claimant bank that exceeds the amount of losses the claimant bank incurred up to that time.

§ 229.56   Liability.

(a) **Measure of damages—**

(1) **In general.** Except as provided in paragraph (a)(2) or (a)(3) of this section or § 229.53, any person that breaches a warranty described in § 229.52 or fails to comply with any requirement of this subpart with respect to any other person shall be liable to that person for an amount equal to the sum of—

(i) The amount of the loss suffered by the person as a result of the breach or failure, up to the amount of the substitute check; and

(ii) Interest and expenses (including costs and reasonable attorney's fees and other expenses of representation) related to the substitute check.

(2) **Offset of recredits.** The amount of damages a person receives under paragraph (a)(1) of this section shall be reduced by any amount that the person receives and retains as a recredit under § 229.54 or § 229.55.

(3) **Comparative negligence.**

(i) If a person incurs damages that resulted in whole or in part from that person's negligence or failure to act in good faith, then the amount of any damages due to that person under paragraph (a)(1) of this section shall be reduced in proportion to the amount of negligence or bad faith attributable to that person.

(ii) Nothing in this paragraph (a)(3) reduces the rights of a consumer or any other person under the U.C.C. or other applicable provision of federal or state law.

(b) Timeliness of action. Delay by a bank beyond any time limits prescribed or permitted by this subpart is excused if the delay is caused by interruption of communication or computer facilities, suspension of payments by another bank, war, emergency conditions, failure of equipment, or other circumstances beyond the control of the bank and if the bank uses such diligence as the circumstances require.

(c) Jurisdiction. A person may bring an action to enforce a claim under this subpart in any United States district court or in any other court of competent jurisdiction. Such claim shall be brought within one year of the date on which the person's cause of action accrues. For purposes of this paragraph, a cause of action accrues as of the date on which the injured person first learns, or by which such person reasonably should have learned, of the facts and circumstances giving rise to the cause of action, including the identity of the warranting or indemnifying bank against which the action is brought.

(d) Notice of claims. Except as otherwise provided in this paragraph (d), unless a person gives notice of a claim under this section to the warranting or indemnifying bank within 30 calendar days after the person has reason to know of both the claim and the identity of the warranting or indemnifying bank, the warranting or indemnifying bank is discharged from liability in an action to enforce a claim under this subpart to the extent of any loss caused by the delay in giving notice of the claim. A timely recredit claim by a consumer under § 229.54 constitutes timely notice under this paragraph.

§ 229.57   Consumer awareness.

(a) General disclosure requirement and content. Each bank shall provide, in accordance with paragraph (b) of this section, a brief disclosure to each of its consumer customers that describes—

(1) That a substitute check is the legal equivalent of an original check; and

(2) The consumer recredit rights that apply when a consumer in good faith believes that a substitute check was not properly charged to his or her account.

(b) Distribution—

(1) Disclosure to consumers who receive paid checks with periodic account statements. A bank shall provide the disclosure described in paragraph (a) of this section to a consumer customer who receives paid original checks or paid substitute checks with his or her periodic account statement—

(i) No later than the first regularly scheduled communication with the consumer after October 28, 2004, for each consumer who is a customer of the bank on that date; and

(ii) At the time the customer relationship is initiated, for each customer relationship established after October 28, 2004.

(2) Disclosure to consumers who receive substitute checks on an occasional basis—

(i) The bank shall provide the disclosure described in paragraph (a) of this section to a consumer customer of the bank who requests an original check or a copy of a check and receives a substitute check. If feasible, the bank shall provide this disclosure at the time of the consumer's request; otherwise, the bank shall provide this disclosure no later than the time at which the bank provides a substitute check in response to the consumer's request.

(ii) The bank shall provide the disclosure described in paragraph (a) of this section to a consumer customer of the bank who receives a returned substitute check, at the time the bank provides such substitute check.

(3) Multiple account holders. A bank need not give separate disclosures to each customer on a jointly held account.

§ 229.58   Mode of delivery of information.

A bank may deliver any notice or other information that it is required to provide under this subpart by United States mail or by any other means through which the recipient has agreed to receive account information. If a bank is required to provide an original check or a sufficient copy, the bank instead may provide an electronic image of the original check or sufficient copy if the recipient has agreed to receive that information electronically.

§ 229.59   Relation to other law.

The Check 21 Act and this subpart supersede any provision of federal or state law, including the Uniform Commercial Code, that is inconsistent with the Check 21 Act or this subpart, but only to the extent of the inconsistency.

§ 229.60   Variation by agreement.

Any provision of § 229.55 may be varied by agreement of the banks involved. No other provision of this subpart may be varied by agreement by any person or persons.

FEDERAL RESERVE COMMENTARY ON REGULATION CC

APPENDIX E to 12 C.F.R. Part 229—COMMENTARY

Current through March 13, 2016; 81 F.R. 12795

For updates, see www.ecfr.gov

I. Introduction

A. Background

1.   The Board interpretations, which are labeled "Commentary" and follow each section of Regulation CC (12 CFR Part 229), provide background material to explain the Board's intent in adopting a particular part of the regulation; the Commentary also provides examples to aid in understanding how a particular requirement is to work. Under section 611(e) of the Expedited Funds Availability Act (12 U.S.C. 4010(e)), no provision of section 611 imposing any liability shall apply to any act done or omitted in good faith conformity with any rule, regulation, or interpretation thereof by the Board of Governors of the Federal Reserve System, notwithstanding the fact that after such act or omission has occurred, such rule, regulation, or interpretation is amended, rescinded, or determined by judicial or other authority to be invalid for any reason. The Commentary is an "interpretation" of a regulation by the Board within the meaning of section 611.

II.   Section 229.2 Definitions

A.   Background

1.   Section 229.2 defines the terms used in the regulation. For the most part, terms are defined as they are in section 602 of the Expedited Funds Availability Act (12 U.S.C. 4001). The Board has made a number of changes for the sake of clarity, to conform the terminology to that which is familiar to the banking industry, to define terms that are not defined in the EFA Act, and to carry out the purposes of the EFA Act. The Board also has incorporated by reference the definitions of the Uniform Commercial Code where appropriate. Some of Regulation CC's definitions are self-explanatory and therefore are not discussed in this Commentary.

B.   229.2(a) Account

1.   The EFA Act defines account to mean "a demand deposit account or similar transaction account at a depository institution." The regulation defines account, for purposes other than subpart D, in terms of the definition of "transaction account" in the Board's Regulation D (12 CFR part 204). This definition of account, however, excludes certain deposits, such as nondocumentary obligations (see 12 CFR 204.2(a)(1)(vii)), that are covered under the definition of "transaction account" in Regulation D. The definition applies to accounts with general third party payment powers but does not cover time deposits or savings deposits, including money market deposit accounts, even though they may have limited third party payment powers. The Board believes that it is appropriate to exclude these accounts because of the reference to demand deposits in the EFA Act, which suggests that the EFA Act is intended to apply only to accounts that permit unlimited third party transfers.

2.   The term account also differs from the definition of transaction account in Regulation D because the term account refers to accounts held at banks. Under Subparts A and C, the term bank includes not only any depository institution, as defined in the EFA Act, but also any person engaged in the business of banking, such as a Federal Reserve Bank, a Federal Home Loan Bank, or a private banker that is not subject to Regulation D. Thus, accounts at these institutions benefit from the expeditious return requirements of Subpart C.

COMMENTARY ON REGULATION CC

3.   Interbank deposits, including accounts of offices of domestic banks or foreign banks located outside the United States, and direct and indirect accounts of the United States Treasury (including Treasury General Accounts and Treasury Tax and Loan deposits) are exempt from subpart B and, in connection therewith, subpart A. However, interbank deposits are included as accounts for purposes of subparts C and D and, in connection therewith, subpart A.

4.   The Check 21 Act defines account to mean any deposit account at a bank. Therefore, for purposes of subpart D and, in connection therewith, subpart A, account means any deposit, as that term is defined by § 204.2(a)(1)(i) of Regulation D, at a bank. Many deposits that are not accounts for purposes of the other subparts of Regulation CC, such as savings deposits, are accounts for purposes of subpart D.

C.   229.2(b) Automated Clearinghouse (ACH)

1.   The Board has defined automated clearinghouse as a facility that processes debit and credit transfers under rules established by a Federal Reserve Bank operating circular governing automated clearinghouse items or the rules of an ACH association. ACH credit transfers are included in the definition of electronic payment.

2.   The reference to "debit and credit transfers" does not refer to the corresponding debit and credit entries that are part of the same transaction, but to different kinds of ACH payments. In an ACH credit transfer, the originator orders that its account be debited and another account credited. In an ACH debit transfer, the originator, with prior authorization, orders another account to be debited and the originator's account to be credited.

3.   A facility that handles only wire transfers (defined elsewhere) is not an ACH.

D.   229.2(c) Automated Teller Machine (ATM)

1.   ATM is not defined in the EFA Act. The regulation defines an ATM as an electronic device at which a natural person may make deposits to an account by cash or check and perform other account transactions. Point-of-sale terminals, machines that only dispense cash, night depositories, and lobby deposit boxes are not ATMs within the meaning of the definition, either because they do not accept deposits of cash or checks (e.g., point-of-sale terminals and cash dispensers) or because they only accept deposits (e.g., night depositories and lobby boxes) and cannot perform other transactions. A lobby deposit box or similar receptacle in which written payment orders or deposits may be placed is not an ATM.

2.   A facility may be an ATM within this definition even if it is a branch under state or federal law, although an ATM is not a branch as that term is used in this regulation.

E.   229.2(d) Available for Withdrawal

1.   Under this definition, when funds become available for withdrawal, the funds may be put to all uses for which the customer may use actually and finally collected funds in the customer's account under the customer's account agreement with the bank. Examples of such uses include payment of checks drawn on the account, certification of checks, electronic payments, and cash withdrawals. Funds are available for these uses notwithstanding provisions of other law that may restrict the use of uncollected funds (e.g., 18 U.S.C. 1004; 12 U.S.C. 331).

2.   If a bank makes funds available to a customer for a specific purpose (such as paying checks that would otherwise overdraw the customer's account and be returned for insufficient funds) before the funds must be made available under the bank's policy or this regulation, it may nevertheless apply a hold consistent with this regulation to those funds for other purposes (such as cash withdrawals). For purposes of this regulation, funds are considered available for withdrawal even though they are being held by the bank to satisfy an obligation of the customer other than the customer's potential liability for the return of the check. For example, a bank does not violate its obligations under this subpart by holding funds to satisfy a garnishment, tax levy, or court order restricting disbursements from the account; or to satisfy the customer's liability arising from the certification of a check, sale of a cashier's or teller's check, guaranty or acceptance of a check, or similar transaction to be debited from the customer's account.

COMMENTARY ON REGULATION CC

F.   229.2(e) Bank

1.   The EFA Act uses the term depository institution, which it defines by reference to section 19(b)(1)(A)(i) through (vi) of the Federal Reserve Act (12 U.S.C. 461(b)(1)(A)(i) through (vi)). This regulation uses the term bank, a term that conforms to the usage the Board has previously adopted in Regulation J. Bank is also used in Articles 4 and 4A of the Uniform Commercial Code.

2.   Bank is defined to include depository institutions, such as commercial banks, savings banks, savings and loan associations, and credit unions as defined in the EFA Act, and U.S. branches and agencies of foreign banks. For purposes of Subpart B, the term does not include corporations organized under section 25A of the Federal Reserve Act, 12 U.S.C. 611–631 (Edge corporations) or corporations having an agreement or undertaking with the Board under section 25 of the Federal Reserve Act, 12 U.S.C. 601–604a (agreement corporations). For purposes of Subparts C and D, and in connection therewith, Subpart A, any Federal Reserve Bank, Federal Home Loan Bank, or any other person engaged in the business of banking is regarded as a bank. The phrase "any other person engaged in the business of banking" is derived from U.C.C. 1–201(4), and is intended to cover entities that handle checks for collection and payment, such as Edge and agreement corporations, commercial lending companies under 12 U.S.C. 3101, certain industrial banks, and private bankers, so that virtually all checks will be covered by the same rules for forward collection and return, even though they may not be covered by the requirements of Subpart B. For the purposes of Subparts C and D, and in connection therewith, Subpart A, the term also may include a state or a unit of general local government to the extent that it pays warrants or other drafts drawn directly on the state or local government itself, and the warrants or other drafts are sent to the state or local government for payment or collection.

3.   Unless otherwise specified, the term bank includes all of a bank's offices in the United States. The regulation does not cover foreign offices of U.S. banks.

4.   For purposes of subpart D and, in connection therewith, subpart A, the term bank also includes the Treasury of the United States and the United States Postal Service to the extent that they act as paying banks because the Check 21 Act includes these two entities in the definition of the term bank to the extent that they act as payors.

G.   229.2(f) Banking Day and (g) Business Day

1.   The EFA Act defines business day as any day excluding Saturdays, Sundays, and legal holidays. Legal holiday, however, is not defined, and the variety of local holidays, together with the practice of some banks to close midweek, makes the EFA Act's definition difficult to apply. The Board believes that two kinds of business days are relevant. First, when determining the day when funds are deposited or when a bank must perform certain actions (such as returning a check), the focus should be on a day that the bank is actually open for business. Second, when counting days for purposes of determining when funds must be available under the regulation or when notice of nonpayment must be received by the depositary bank, there would be confusion and uncertainty in trying to follow the schedule of a particular bank, and there is less need to identify a day when a particular bank is open. Most banks that act as intermediaries (large correspondents and Federal Reserve Banks) follow the same holiday schedule. Accordingly, the regulation has two definitions: Business day generally follows the standard Federal Reserve Bank holiday schedule (which is followed by most large banks), and banking day is defined to mean that part of a business day on which a bank is open for substantially all of its banking activities.

2.   The definition of banking day corresponds to the definition of banking day in U.C.C. 4–104(a)(3), except that a banking day is defined in terms of a business day. Thus, if a bank is open on Saturday, Saturday might be a banking day for purposes of the U.C.C., but it would not be a banking day for purposes of Regulation CC because Saturday is never a business day under the regulation.

3.   The definition of banking day is phrased in terms of when "an office of a bank is open" to indicate that a bank may observe a banking day on a per-branch basis. A deposit made at an ATM or off-premise facility (such as a remote depository or a lock box) is considered made at the branch holding the account into which the deposit is made for the purpose of determining the day of deposit. All other deposits are considered made at the branch at which the deposit is received. For example, under § 229.19(a)(1), funds deposited at an ATM are considered deposited at the time they are received at the ATM. On a calendar day that is a

banking day for the branch or other location of the depositary bank at which the account is maintained, a deposit received at an ATM before the ATM's cut-off hour is considered deposited on that banking day, and a deposit received at an ATM after the ATM's cut-off hour is considered deposited on the next banking day of the branch or other location where the account is maintained. On a calendar day that is not a banking day for the account-holding location, all ATM deposits are considered deposited on that location's next banking day. This rule for determining the day of deposit also would apply to a deposit to an off-premise facility, such as a night depository or lock box, which is considered deposited when removed from the facility and available for processing under § 229.19(a)(3). If an unstaffed facility, such as a night depository or lock box, is on branch premises, the day of deposit is determined by the banking day at the branch at which the deposit is received, whether or not it is the branch at which the account is maintained.

H.   229.2(h) Cash

1.   Cash means U.S. coins and currency. The phrase in the EFA Act "including Federal Reserve notes" has been deleted as unnecessary. (See 31 U.S.C. 5103.)

I.   229.2(i) Cashier's Check

1.   The regulation adds to the second item in the EFA Act's definition of cashier's check the phrase, "on behalf of the bank as drawer," to clarify that the term cashier's check is intended to cover only checks that a bank draws on itself. The definition of cashier's check includes checks provided to a customer of the bank in connection with customer deposit account activity, such as account disbursements and interest payments. The definition also includes checks acquired from a bank by noncustomers for remittance purposes, such as certain loan disbursement checks. Cashier's checks provided to customers or others are often labeled as "cashier's check," "officer's check," or "official check." The definition excludes checks that a bank draws on itself for other purposes, such as to pay employees and vendors, and checks issued by the bank in connection with a payment service, such as a payroll or a bill-paying service. Cashier's checks generally are sold by banks to substitute the bank's credit for the customer's credit and thereby enhance the collectibility of the checks. A check issued in connection with a payment service generally is provided as a convenience to the customer rather than as a guarantee of the check's collectibility. In addition, such checks are often more difficult to distinguish from other types of checks than are cashier's checks as defined by this regulation.

J.   229.2(j) Certified Check

1.   The EFA Act defines a certified check as one to which a bank has certified that the drawer's signature is genuine and that the bank has set aside funds to pay the check. Under the Uniform Commercial Code, certification of a check means the bank's signed agreement that it will honor the check as presented (U.C.C. 3–409). The regulation defines certified check to include both the EFA Act's and U.C.C.'s definitions.

K.   229.2(k) Check

1.   Check is defined in section 602(7) of the EFA Act as a negotiable demand draft drawn on or payable through an office of a depository institution located in the United States, excluding noncash items. The regulation includes six categories of instruments within the definition of check.

2.   The first category is negotiable demand drafts drawn on, or payable through or at, an office of a bank. As the definition of bank includes only offices located in the United States, this category is limited to checks drawn on, or payable through or at, a banking office located in the United States.

3.   The EFA Act treats drafts payable through a bank as checks, even though under the U.C.C. the payable-through bank is a collecting bank to make presentment and generally is not authorized to make payment (U.C.C. 4–106(a)). The EFA Act does not expressly address items that are payable at a bank. This regulation treats both payable-through and payable-at demand drafts as checks. The Board believes that treating demand drafts payable at a bank as checks will not have a substantial effect on the operations of payable-at banks—by far the largest proportion of payable-at items are not negotiable demand drafts, but time items, such as commercial paper, bonds, notes, bankers' acceptances, and securities. These time items are not covered by the requirements of the EFA Act or this regulation. (The treatment of payable-through drafts is discussed in greater detail in connection with the definitions of local check and paying bank.)

4.   The second category is checks drawn on Federal Reserve Banks and Federal Home Loan Banks. Principal and interest payments on federal debt instruments often are paid with checks drawn on a Federal Reserve Bank as fiscal agent of the United States, and these fiscal agency checks are indistinguishable from other checks drawn on Federal Reserve Banks. (See 31 CFR Part 355.) Federal Reserve Bank checks also are used by some banks as substitutes for cashier's or teller's checks. Similarly, savings and loan associations often use checks drawn on Federal Home Loan Banks as teller's checks. The definition of check includes checks drawn on Federal Home Loan Banks and Federal Reserve Banks because in many cases they are the functional equivalent of Treasury checks or teller's checks.

5.   The third and fourth categories of instrument included in the definition of check refer to government checks. The EFA Act refers to checks drawn on the U.S. Treasury, even though these instruments are not drawn on or payable through an office of a depository institution, and checks drawn by state and local governments. The EFA Act also gives the Board authority to define functionally equivalent instruments as depository checks.[1] Thus, the EFA Act is intended to apply to instruments other than those that meet the strict definition of check in section 602(7) of the EFA Act. Checks and warrants drawn by states and local governments often are used for the purposes of making unemployment compensation payments and other payments that are important to the recipients. Consequently, the Board has expressly defined check to include drafts drawn on the U.S. Treasury and drafts or warrants drawn by a state or a unit of general local government on itself.

6.   The fifth category of instrument included in the definition of check is U.S. Postal Service money orders. These instruments are defined as checks because they often are used as a substitute for checks by consumers, even though money orders are not negotiable under Postal Service regulations. The Board has not provided specific rules for other types of money orders; these instruments generally are drawn on or payable through or payable at banks and are treated as checks on that basis.

7.   The sixth and final category of instrument included in the definition of check is traveler's checks drawn on or payable through or at a bank. Traveler's check is defined in paragraph (hh) of this section.

8.   Finally, for the purposes of Subparts C and D, and in connection therewith, Subpart A, the definition of check includes nonnegotiable demand drafts because these instruments are often handled as cash items in the forward collection process.

9.   A substitute check as defined in § 229.2(aaa) is a check for purposes of Regulation CC and the U.C.C., even if that substitute check does not meet the requirements for legal equivalence set forth in § 229.51(a).

10.   The definition of check does not include an instrument payable in a foreign currency (i.e., other than in United States money as defined in 31 U.S.C. 5101) or a credit card draft (i.e., a sales draft used by a merchant or a draft generated by a bank as a result of a cash advance), or an ACH debit transfer. The definition of check includes a check that a bank may supply to a customer as a means of accessing a credit line without the use of a credit card.

L.   229.2(*l*) [Reserved]

M.   229.2(m) Check Processing Region

1.   The EFA Act defines this term as "the geographic area served by a Federal Reserve bank check processing center or such larger area as the Board may prescribe by regulations." The Board has defined check processing region as the territory served by one of the Federal Reserve head offices, branches, or regional check processing centers. Appendix A includes a list of routing numbers arranged by Federal Reserve Bank office. The definition of check processing region is key to determining whether a check is considered local or nonlocal.

N.   229.2(n) Consumer Account

1.   Consumer account is defined as an account used primarily for personal, family, or household purposes. An account that does not meet the definition of consumer account is a nonconsumer account. A

---

[1]   Section 602(11) of the EFA Act (12 U.S.C. 4001(11)) defines "depository check" as "any cashier's check, certified check, teller's check, and any other functionally equivalent instrument as determined by the Board."

clearing account maintained at a bank directly by a brokerage firm is not a consumer account, even if the account is used to pay checks drawn by consumers using the funds in that account. The bank's relationship is with the brokerage firm, and the account is used by the brokerage firm to facilitate the clearing of its customers' checks. Because for purposes of Regulation CC the term account includes only deposit accounts, a consumer's revolving credit relationship or other line of credit with a bank is not a consumer account, even if the consumer draws on such credit lines by using a check. Both consumer and nonconsumer accounts are subject to the requirements of this regulation, including the requirement that funds be made available according to specific schedules and that the bank make specified disclosures of its availability policies. Section 229.18(b) (notices at branch locations) and § 229.18(e) (notice of changes in policy) apply only to consumer accounts. Section 229.13(g)(2) (one-time exception notice) and § 229.19(d) (use of calculated availability) apply only to nonconsumer accounts.

O.   229.2(*o*) Depositary Bank

1.   The regulation uses the term depositary bank rather than the term receiving depository institution. Receiving depository institution is a term unique to the EFA Act, while depositary bank is the term used in Article 4 of the U.C.C. and Regulation J.

2.   A depositary bank includes the bank in which the check is first deposited. If a foreign office of a U.S. or foreign bank sends checks to its U.S. correspondent bank for forward collection, the U.S. correspondent is the depositary bank because foreign offices of banks are not included in the definition of bank.

3.   If a customer deposits a check in its account at a bank, the customer's bank is the depositary bank with respect to the check. For example, if a person deposits a check into an account at a nonproprietary ATM, the bank holding the account into which the check is deposited is the depositary bank even though another bank may service the nonproprietary ATM and send the check for collection. (Under § 229.35 the depositary bank may agree with the bank servicing the nonproprietary ATM to have the servicing bank place its own indorsement on the check as the depositary bank. For the purposes of Subpart C, the bank applying its indorsement as the depositary bank indorsement on the check is the depositary bank.)

4.   For purposes of Subpart B, a bank may act as both the depositary bank and the paying bank with respect to a check, if the check is payable by the bank in which it was deposited, or if the check is payable by a nonbank payor and payable through or at the bank in which it was deposited. A bank also is considered a depositary bank with respect to checks it receives as payee. For example, a bank is a depositary bank with respect to checks it receives for loan repayment, even though these checks are not deposited in an account at the bank. Because these checks would not be "deposited to accounts," they would not be subject to the availability or disclosure requirements of Subpart B.

P.   229.2(p) Electronic Payment

1.   Electronic payment is defined to mean a wire transfer as defined in § 229.2(11) or an ACH credit transfer. The EFA Act requires that funds deposited by wire transfer be made available for withdrawal on the business day following deposit but expressly leaves the definition of the term wire transfer to the Board. Because ACH credit transfers frequently involve important consumer payments, such as wages, the regulation requires that funds deposited by ACH credit transfers be available for withdrawal on the business day following deposit.

2.   ACH debit transfers, even though they may be transmitted electronically, are not defined as electronic payments because the receiver of an ACH debit transfer has the right to return the transfer, which would reverse the credit given to the originator. Thus, ACH debit transfers are more like checks than wire transfers. Further, bank customers that receive funds by originating ACH debit transfers are primarily large corporations, which generally would be able to negotiate with their banks for prompt availability.

3.   A point-of-sale transaction would not be considered an electronic payment unless the transaction was effected by means of an ACH credit transfer or wire transfer.

Q.   229.2(q) Forward Collection

1.   Forward collection is defined to mean the process by which a bank sends a check to the paying bank for collection, including sending the check to an intermediary collecting bank for settlement, as

distinguished from the process by which the check is returned unpaid. Noncash collections are not included in the term forward collection.

R.   229.2(r) Local Check

1.   Local check is defined as a check payable by or at a local paying bank, or, in the case of nonbank payors, payable through a local paying bank. A check payable by a local bank but payable through a nonlocal bank is a local check. Conversely, a check payable through a local bank but payable by a nonlocal bank is a nonlocal check. Where two banks are named on a check and neither is designated as a payable-through bank, the check is considered payable by either bank and may be considered local or nonlocal depending on the bank to which it is sent for payment. Generally, the depositary bank may rely on the routing number to determine whether a check is local or nonlocal. Appendix A includes a list of routing numbers arranged by Federal Reserve Bank Office to assist persons in determining whether or not such a check is local. If, however, a check is payable by one bank but payable through another bank, the routing number appearing on the check will be that of the payable-through bank, not the paying bank. Many credit union share drafts and certain other checks payable by banks are payable through other banks. In such cases, the routing number cannot be relied on to determine whether the check is local or nonlocal. For payable-through checks that meet the labeling requirements of § 229.36(e), the depositary bank may rely on the four-digit routing symbol of the paying bank that is printed on the face of the check as required by that section, e.g., in the title plate, but not on the first four digits of the payable-through bank's routing number printed in magnetic ink in the MICR line or in fractional form, to determine whether the check is local or nonlocal.

S.   229.2(s) Local Paying Bank

1.   "Local paying bank" is defined as a paying bank located in the same check-processing region as the branch, contractual branch, or proprietary ATM of the depositary bank. For example, a check deposited at a contractual branch would be deemed local or nonlocal based on the location of the contractual branch with respect to the location of the paying bank.

Examples.

a.   If a check that is payable by a bank that is located in the same check processing region as the depositary bank is payable through a bank located in another check processing region, the check is considered local or nonlocal depending on the location of the bank by which it is payable even if the check is sent to the nonlocal bank for collection.

b.   The location of the depositary bank is determined by the physical location of the branch or proprietary ATM at which a check is deposited, regardless of whether the deposit is made in person, by mail, or otherwise. For example, if a branch of the depositary bank located in one check-processing region sends a check that was deposited at that branch to the depositary bank's central facility in another check-processing region, and the central facility is in the same check-processing region as the paying bank, the check is still considered nonlocal. (See the commentary to the definition of "paying bank.")

c.   If a person deposits a check to an account by mailing or otherwise sending the check to a facility or office that is not a bank, the check is considered local or nonlocal depending on the location of the bank whose indorsement appears on the check as the depositary bank.

T.   229.2(t) Merger Transaction

1.   Merger transaction is a term used in Subparts B and C in connection with transition rules for merged banks. It encompasses mergers, consolidations, and purchase/assumption transactions of the type that usually must be approved under the Bank Merger Act (12 U.S.C. 1828(c)) or similar statutes; it does not encompass acquisitions of a bank under the Bank Holding Company Act (12 U.S.C. 1842) where an acquired bank maintains its separate corporate existence.

2.   Regulation CC adopts a one-year transition period for banks that are party to a merger transaction during which the merged banks will continue to be treated as separate entities. (See §§ 229.19(g) and 229.40.)

COMMENTARY ON REGULATION CC

U.   229.2(u) Noncash Item

1.   The EFA Act defines the term check to exclude noncash items, and defines noncash items to include checks to which another document is attached, checks accompanied by special instructions, or any similar item classified as a noncash item in the Board's regulation. To qualify as a noncash item, an item must be handled as such and may not be handled as a cash item by the depositary bank.

2.   The regulation's definition of noncash item also includes checks that consist of more than a single thickness of paper (except checks that qualify for handling by automated check processing equipment, e.g. those placed in carrier envelopes) and checks that have not been preprinted or post-encoded in magnetic ink with the paying bank's routing number, as well as checks with documents attached or accompanied by special instructions. (In the context of this definition, paying bank refers to the paying bank as defined for purposes of Subpart C.)

3.   A check that has been preprinted or post-encoded with a routing number that has been retired (e.g., because of a merger) for at least three years is a noncash item unless the current number is added for processing purposes by placing the check in an encoded carrier envelope or adding a strip to the check.

4.   Checks that are accompanied by special instructions are also noncash items. For example, a person concerned about whether a check will be paid may request the depositary bank to send a check for collection as a noncash item with an instruction to the paying bank to notify the depositary bank promptly when the check is paid or dishonored.

5.   For purposes of forward collection, a copy of a check is neither a check nor a noncash item, but may be treated as either. For purposes of return, a copy is generally a notice in lieu of return. (See §§ 229.30(f) and 229.31(f).)

V.   229.2(v) [Reserved]

W.   229.2(w) [Reserved]

X.   229.2(x) [Reserved]

Y.   229.2(y) [Reserved]

Z.   229.2(z) Paying Bank

1.   The regulation uses this term in lieu of the EFA Act's "originating depository institution." For purposes of all subparts of Regulation CC, the term paying bank includes the bank by which a check is payable, the payable-at bank to which a check is sent, or, if the check is payable by a nonbank payor, the bank through which the check is payable and to which it is sent for payment or collection. For purposes of subparts C and D, the term paying bank also includes the payable-through bank and the bank whose routing number appears on the check, regardless of whether the check is payable by a different bank, provided that the check is sent for payment or collection to the payable through bank or the bank whose routing number appears on the check.

2.   Under §§ 229.30 and 229.36(a), a bank designated as a payable-through bank or payable-at bank and to which the check is sent for payment or collection is responsible for the expedited return of checks and notice of nonpayment requirements of Subpart C. The payable-through or payable-at bank may contract with the payor with respect to its liability in discharging these responsibilities. The Board believes that the EFA Act makes a clear connection between availability and the time it takes for checks to be cleared and returned. Allowing the payable-through bank additional time to forward checks to the payor and await return or pay instructions from the payor would delay the return of these checks, increasing the risks to depositary banks. Subpart C places on payable-through and payable-at banks the requirements of expeditious return based on the time the payable-through or payable-at bank received the check for forward collection.

3.   If a check is sent for forward collection based on the routing number, the bank associated with the routing number is a paying bank for the purposes of Subparts C and D requirements, including notice of nonpayment, even if the check is not drawn by a customer of that bank or the check is fraudulent.

COMMENTARY ON REGULATION CC

4. The phrase "and to which [the check] is sent for payment or collection" includes sending not only the physical check, but information regarding the check under a truncation arrangement.

5. Federal Reserve Banks and Federal Home Loan Banks are also paying banks under all subparts of the regulation with respect to checks payable by them, even though such banks are not defined as banks for purposes of Subpart B.

6. In accordance with the Check 21 Act, for purposes of subpart D and, in connection therewith, subpart A, paying bank includes the Treasury of the United States or the United States Postal Service with respect to a check payable by that entity and sent to that entity for payment or collection, even though the Treasury and Postal Service are not defined as banks for purposes of subparts B and C. Because the Federal Reserve Banks act as fiscal agents for the Treasury and the U.S. Postal Service and in that capacity are designated as presentment locations for Treasury checks and U.S. Postal Service money orders, a Treasury check or U.S. Postal Service money order presented to a Federal Reserve Bank is considered to be presented to the Treasury or U.S. Postal Service, respectively.

AA. 229.2(aa) Proprietary ATM

1. All deposits at nonproprietary ATMs are treated as deposits of nonlocal checks, and deposits at proprietary ATMs generally are treated as deposits at banking offices. The Conference Report on the EFA Act indicates that the special availability rules for deposits received through nonproprietary ATMs are provided because "nonproprietary ATMs today do not distinguish among check deposits or between check and cash deposits" (H.R. Rep. No. 261, 100th Cong., 1st Sess. at 179 (1987)). Thus, a deposit of any combination of cash and checks at a nonproprietary ATM may be treated as if it were a deposit of nonlocal checks, because the depositary bank does not know the makeup of the deposit and consequently is unable to place different holds on cash, local check, and nonlocal check deposits made at the ATM.

2. A colloquy between Senators Proxmire and Dodd during the floor debate on the Competitive Equality Banking Act (133 Cong. Rec. S11289 (Aug. 4, 1987)) indicates that whether a bank operates the ATM is the primary criterion in determining whether the ATM is proprietary to that bank. Because a bank should be capable of ascertaining the composition of deposits made to an ATM operated by that bank, an exception to the availability schedules is not warranted for these deposits. If more than one bank meets the "owns or operates" criterion, the ATM is considered proprietary to the bank that operates it. For the purpose of this definition, the bank that operates an ATM is the bank that puts checks deposited into the ATM into the forward collection stream. An ATM owned by one or more banks, but operated by a nonbank servicer, is considered proprietary to the bank or banks that own it.

3. The EFA Act also includes location as a factor in determining whether an ATM that is either owned or operated by a bank is proprietary to that bank. The definition of proprietary ATM includes an ATM located on the premises of the bank, either inside the branch or on its outside wall, regardless of whether the ATM is owned or operated by that bank. Because the EFA Act also defines a proprietary ATM as one that is "in close proximity" to the bank, the regulation defines an ATM located within 50 feet of a bank to be proprietary to that bank unless it is identified as being owned or operated by another entity. The Board believes that the statutory proximity test was designed to apply to situations where it would appear to the depositor that the ATM is run by his or her bank, because of the proximity of the ATM to the bank. The Board believes that an ATM located within 50 feet of a banking office would be presumed proprietary to that bank unless it is clearly identified as being owned or operated by another entity.

BB. 229.2(bb) Qualified Returned Check

1. Subpart C requires the paying bank and returning bank(s) to return checks in an expeditious manner. The banks may meet this responsibility by returning a check to the depositary bank by the same general means used for forward collection of a check from the depositary bank to the paying bank. One way to speed the return process is to prepare the returned check for automated processing. Qualified returned checks are identified by placing a "2" in the case of an original check (or a "5" in the case of a substitute check) in position 44 of the qualified return MICR line as a return identifier in accordance with American National Standard Specifications for Placement and Location of MICR Printing, X9.13 (hereinafter "ANS X9.13") for original checks or American National Standard Specifications for an Image Replacement Document—IRD, X9.100–140 (hereinafter "ANS X9.100–140") for substitute checks.

2.   Generally, under the standard of care imposed by § 229.38, a paying or returning bank would be liable for any damages incurred due to misencoding of the routing number, the amount of the check, or return identifier on a qualified returned check unless the error was due to problems with the depositary bank's indorsement. (See also discussion of § 229.38(c).) A qualified returned check that contains an encoding error would still be a qualified returned check for purposes of the regulation.

3.   A qualified returned check need not contain the elements of a check drawn on the depositary bank, such as the name of the depositary bank. Because indorsements and other information on carrier envelopes or strips will not appear on a returned check itself, banks will wish to retain carrier envelopes and/or microfilm or other records of carrier envelopes or strips with their check records.

CC. 229.2(cc) Returning Bank

1.   Returning bank is defined to mean any bank (excluding the paying bank and the depositary bank) handling a returned check. A returning bank may or may not be a bank that handled the returned check in the forward collection process. A returning bank includes a bank that agrees to handle a returned check for expeditious return to the depositary bank under § 229.31(a). A returning bank is also a collecting bank for the purpose of a collecting bank's duty to exercise ordinary care under U.C.C. 4–202(b) and is analogous to a collecting bank for purposes of final settlement. (See Commentary to § 229.35(b).)

DD. 229.2(dd) Routing Number

1.   Each bank is assigned a routing number by an agent of the American Bankers Association, an agent of the American Bankers Association. The routing number takes two forms—a fractional form and a nine-digit form. A paying bank is identified by both the fractional form routing number (which normally appears in the upper right hand corner of the check) and the nine-digit form. The nine-digit routing number of the paying bank generally is printed in magnetic ink near the bottom of the check (the MICR strip; see ANSI X9.13–1983). Subpart C requires depositary banks and subsequent collecting banks to place their routing numbers in nine-digit form in their indorsements.

EE. 229.2(ee) [Reserved]

FF. 229.2(ff) [Reserved]

GG. 229.2(gg) Teller's Check

1.   Teller's check is defined in the EFA Act to mean a check issued by a depository institution and drawn on another depository institution. The definition in the regulation includes not only checks drawn by a bank on another bank, but also checks payable through or at a bank. This would include checks drawn on a nonbank, as long as the check is payable through or at a bank. The definition does not include checks that are drawn by a nonbank on a nonbank even if payable through or at a bank. The definition includes checks provided to a customer of the bank in connection with customer deposit account activity, such as account disbursements and interest payments. The definition also includes checks acquired from a bank by a noncustomer for remittance purposes, such as certain loan disbursement checks. The definition excludes checks used by the bank to pay employees or vendors and checks issued by the bank in connection with a payment service, such as a payroll or a bill-paying service. Teller's checks generally are sold by banks to substitute the bank's credit for the customer's credit and thereby enhance the collectibility of the checks. A check issued in connection with a payment service generally is provided as a convenience to the customer rather than as a guarantee of the check's collectibility. In addition, such checks are often more difficult to distinguish from other types of checks than are teller's checks as defined by this regulation.

HH. 229.2(hh) Traveler's Check

1.   The EFA Act and regulation require that traveler's checks be treated as cashier's, teller's, or certified checks when a new depositor opens an account. (See § 229.13(a); 12 U.S.C. 4003(a)(1)(C).) The EFA Act does not define traveler's check.

2.   One element of the definition states that a traveler's check is "drawn on or payable through or at a bank." Sometimes traveler's checks that are not issued by banks do not have any words on them identifying a bank as drawee or paying agent, but instead bear unique routing numbers with an 8000 prefix that identifies a bank as paying agent.

COMMENTARY ON REGULATION CC

3.   Because a traveler's check is payable by, at, or through a bank, it is also a check for purposes of this regulation. When not subject to the next-day availability requirement for new accounts, a traveler's check should be treated as a local or nonlocal check depending on the location of the paying bank. The depositary bank may rely on the designation of the paying bank by the routing number to determine whether local or nonlocal treatment is required.

II.   229.2(ii) Uniform Commercial Code

1.   Uniform Commercial Code is defined as the version of the Code adopted by the individual states. For purposes of uniform citation, all citations to the U.C.C. in this part refer to the Official Text as approved by the American Law Institute and the National Conference of Commissioners on Uniform State Laws.

JJ. 229.2(jj) [Reserved]

KK. 229.2(kk) Unit of General Local Government

1.   Unit of general local government is defined to include a city, county, parish, town, township, village, or other general purpose political subdivision of a state. The term does not include special purpose units, such as school districts, water districts, or Indian nations.

LL. 229.2(*ll*) Wire Transfer

1.   The EFA Act delegates to the Board the authority to define the term wire transfer. The regulation defines wire transfer as an unconditional order to a bank to pay a fixed or determinable amount of money to a beneficiary, upon receipt or on a day stated in the order, that is transmitted by electronic or other means over certain networks or on the books of banks and that is used primarily to transfer funds between commercial accounts. "Unconditional" means that no condition, such as presentation of documents, must be met before the bank receiving the order is to make payment. A wire transfer may be transmitted by electronic or other means. "Electronic means" include computer-to-computer links, on-line terminals, telegrams (including TWX, TELEX, or similar methods of communication), telephone calls, or other similar methods. Fedwire (the Federal Reserve's wire transfer network), CHIPS (Clearing House Interbank Payments System, operated by the New York Clearing House), and book transfers among banks or within one bank are covered by this definition. Credits for credit and debit card transactions are not wire transfers. The term wire transfer excludes electronic fund transfers as that term is defined by the Electronic Fund Transfer Act.

MM. 229.2(mm) [Reserved]

NN. 229.2(nn) Good Faith

1.   This definition of good faith derives from U.C.C. 3–103(a)(4).

OO. 229.2(*oo*) Interest Compensation

1.   This calculation of interest compensation derives from U.C.C. 4A–506(b). (See §§ 229.34(e) and 229.36(f).)

PP. 229.2(pp) Contractual Branch

1.   When one bank arranges for another bank to accept deposits on its behalf, the second bank is a contractual branch of the first bank. For further discussion of contractual branch deposits and related disclosures, see §§ 229.2(s) and 229.19(a) of the regulation and the commentary to §§ 229.2(s), 229.10(c), 229.14(a), 229.16(a), 229.18(b), and 229.19(a).

QQ. 229.2(qq) [Reserved]

RR. 229.2(rr) [Reserved]

SS. 229.2(ss) [Reserved]

TT. 229.2(tt) [Reserved]

UU. 229.2(uu) [Reserved]

COMMENTARY ON REGULATION CC

VV. 229.2(vv) MICR Line

1.   Information in the MICR line of a check must be printed in accordance with ANS X9.13 for original checks and ANS X9.100–140 for substitute checks. These standards could vary the requirements for printing the MICR line, such as by indicating circumstances under which the use of magnetic ink is not required.

WW. 229.2(ww) Original Check

1.   The definition of original check distinguishes the first paper check signed or otherwise authorized by the drawer to effect a particular payment transaction from a substitute check or other paper or electronic representation that is derived from an original check or substitute check. There is only one original check for any particular payment transaction. However, multiple substitute checks could be created to represent that original check at various points in the check collection and return process.

XX. 229.2(xx) Paper or Electronic Representation of a Substitute Check

1.   Receipt of a paper or electronic representation of a substitute check does not trigger indemnity or expedited recredit rights, although the recipient nonetheless could have a warranty claim or a claim under other check law with respect to that document or the underlying payment transaction. A paper or electronic representation of a substitute check would include a representation of a substitute check that was drawn on an account, as well as a representation of a substitute traveler's check, credit card check, or other item that meets the substitute check definition. The following examples illustrate the scope of the definition.

Examples.

a.   A bank receives electronic presentment of a substitute check that has been converted to electronic form and charges the customer's account for that electronic item. The periodic account statement that the bank provides to the customer includes information about the electronically-presented substitute check in a line-item list describing all the checks the bank charged to the customer's account during the previous month. The electronic file that the bank received for presentment and charged to the customer's account would be an electronic representation of a substitute check, and the line-item appearing on the customer's account statement would be a paper representation of a substitute check.

b.   A paying bank receives and settles for a substitute check and then realizes that its settlement was for the wrong amount. The paying bank sends an adjustment request to the presenting bank to correct the error. The adjustment request is not a paper or electronic representation of a substitute check under the definition because it is not being handled for collection or return as a check. Rather, it is a separate request that is related to a check. As a result, no substitute check warranty, indemnity, or expedited recredit rights attach to the adjustment.

YY. 229.2(yy) [Reserved]

ZZ. 229.2(zz) Reconverting Bank

1.   A substitute check is "created" when and where a paper reproduction of an original check that meets the requirements of § 229.2(aaa) is physically printed. A bank is a reconverting bank if it creates a substitute check directly or if another person by agreement creates a substitute check on the bank's behalf. A bank also is a reconverting bank if it is the first bank that receives a substitute check created by a nonbank and transfers, presents, or returns that substitute check or, in lieu thereof, the first paper or electronic representation of such substitute check.

Examples.

a.   Bank A, by agreement, sends an electronic check file for collection to Bank B. Bank B chooses to use that file to print a substitute check that meets the requirements of § 229.2(aaa). Bank B is the reconverting bank as of the time it prints the substitute check.

b.   Company A, which is not a bank, by agreement receives check information electronically from Bank A. Bank A becomes the reconverting bank when Company A prints a substitute check on behalf of Bank A in accordance with that agreement.

c.   A depositary bank's customer, which is a nonbank business, receives a check for payment, truncates that original check, and creates a substitute check to deposit with its bank. The depositary bank receives that substitute check from its customer and is the first bank to handle the substitute check. The depositary bank becomes the reconverting bank as of the time that it transfers or presents the substitute check (or in lieu thereof the first paper or electronic representation of the substitute check) for forward collection.

d.   A bank is the payable-through bank for checks that are drawn on a nonbank payor, which is the bank's customer. When the customer decides not to pay a check that is payable through the bank, the customer creates a substitute check for purposes of return. The payable-through bank becomes the reconverting bank when it returns the substitute check (or in lieu thereof the first paper or electronic representation of the substitute check) to a returning bank or the depositary bank.

e.   A paying bank returns a substitute check to the depositary bank, which in turn gives that substitute check back to its nonbank customer. That customer then redeposits the substitute check for collection at a different bank. Because the substitute check was already transferred by a bank, the second depositary bank does not become a reconverting bank when it transfers or presents that substitute check for collection.

2.   In some cases there will be one or more banks between the truncating bank and the reconverting bank.

Example.

A depositary bank truncates the original check and sends an electronic representation of the original check for collection to an intermediary bank. The intermediary bank sends the electronic representation of the original check to the presenting bank, which creates a substitute check to present to the paying bank. The presenting bank is the reconverting bank.

3.   A check could move from electronic form to substitute check form several times during the collection and return process. It therefore is possible that there could be multiple substitute checks, and thus multiple reconverting banks, with respect to the same underlying payment.

AAA.   229.2(aaa) Substitute Check

1.   "A paper reproduction of an original check" could include a reproduction created directly from the original check or a reproduction of the original check that is created from some other source that contains an image of the original check, such as an electronic representation of an original check or substitute check, or a previous substitute check.

2.   Because a substitute check must be a piece of paper, an electronic file or electronic check image that has not yet been printed in accordance with the substitute check definition is not a substitute check.

3.   Because a substitute check must be a representation of a check, a paper reproduction of something that is not a check cannot be a substitute check. For example, a savings bond or a check drawn on a non-U.S. branch of a foreign bank cannot be reconverted to a substitute check.

4.   As described in § 229.51(b) and the commentary thereto, a reconverting bank is required to ensure that a substitute check contains all indorsements applied by previous parties that handled the check in any form. Therefore, the image of the original check that appears on the back of a substitute check would include indorsements that were physically applied to the original check before an image of the original check was captured. An indorsement that was applied physically to the original check after an image of the original check was captured would be conveyed as an electronic indorsement (see paragraph 3 of the commentary to § 229.35(a)). The back of the substitute check would contain a physical representation of any indorsements that were applied electronically to the check after an image of the check was captured but before creation of the substitute check.

Example.

Bank A, which is the depositary bank, captures an image of an original check, indorses it electronically and, by agreement, transmits to Bank B an electronic image of the check accompanied by the electronic indorsement. Bank B then creates a substitute check to send to Bank C. The back of the substitute check created by Bank B must contain a representation of the indorsement previously applied electronically by Bank A and Bank B's own indorsement. (For more information on indorsement requirements, see § 229.35, appendix D, and the commentary thereto.)

5.   Some substitute checks will not be created directly from the original check, but rather will be created from a previous substitute check. The back of a subsequent substitute check will contain an image of the full length of the back of the previous substitute check. ANS X9.100–140 requires preservation of the full length of the back of the previous substitute check in order to preserve previous indorsements and reconverting bank identifications. By contrast, the front of a subsequent substitute check will not contain an image of the entire previous substitute check. Rather, the image field of the subsequent substitute check will contain the image of the front of the original check that appeared on the previous substitute check at the time the previous substitute check was converted to electronic form. The portions of the front of the subsequent substitute check other than the image field will contain information applied by the subsequent reconverting bank, such as its reconverting bank identification, the MICR line, the legal equivalence legend, and optional security information.

Examples.

a.   The back of a subsequent substitute check would contain the following indorsements, all of which would be preserved through the image of the back of the previous substitute check: (1) The indorsements that were applied physically to the original check before an image of the original check was captured; (2) a physical representation of indorsements that were applied electronically to the original check after an image of the original check was captured but before creation of the first substitute check; and (3) indorsements that were applied physically to the previous substitute check. In addition, the reconverting bank for the subsequent substitute check must overlay onto the back of that substitute check a physical representation of any indorsements that were applied electronically after the previous substitute check was converted to electronic form but before creation of the subsequent substitute check.

b.   Because information could have been physically added to the image of the front of the original check that appeared on the previous substitute check, the original check image that appears on the front of a subsequent substitute check could contain information in addition to that which appeared on the original check at the time it was truncated.

6.   The MICR line applied to a substitute check must contain information in all fields of the MICR line that were encoded on the original check at any time before an image of the original check was captured. This includes all the MICR-line information that was preprinted on the original check, plus any additional information that was added to the MICR line before the image of the original check was captured (for example, the amount of the check). The information in each field of the substitute check's MICR line must be the same information as in the corresponding field of the MICR line of the original check, except as provided by ANS X9.100–140 (unless the Board by rule or order determines that a different standard applies). Industry standards may not, however, vary the requirement that a substitute check at the time of its creation must bear a full-field MICR line.

7.   ANS X9.100–140, provides that a substitute check must have a "4" in position 44 and that a qualified returned substitute check must have a "4" in position 44 of the forward-collection MICR line as well as a "5" in position 44 of the qualified return MICR line. The "4" and "5" indicate that the document is a substitute check so that the size of the check image remains constant throughout the collection and return process, regardless of the number of substitute checks created that represent the same original check (see also §§ 229.30(a)(2) and 229.31(a)(2) and the commentary thereto regarding requirements for qualified returned substitute checks). An original check generally has a blank position 44 for forward collection. Because a reconverting bank must encode position 44 of a substitute check's forward collection MICR line with a "4," the reconverting bank must vary any character that appeared in position 44 of the forward-collection MICR line of the original check. A bank that misencodes or fails to encode position 44 at the time it attempts to create a substitute check has failed to create a substitute check. A bank that receives a properly-encoded substitute check may further encode that item but does so subject to the encoding warranties in Regulation CC and the U.C.C.

8.   A substitute check's MICR line could contain information in addition to the information required at the time the substitute check is created. For example, if the amount field of the original check was not

encoded and the substitute check therefore did not, when created, have an encoded amount field, the MICR line of the substitute check later could be amount-encoded.

9.   A bank may receive a substitute check that contains a MICR-line variation but nonetheless meets the MICR-line replication requirements of § 229.2(aaa)(2) because that variation is permitted by ANS X9.100–140. If such a substitute check contains a MICR-line error, a bank that receives it may, but is not required to, repair that error. Such a repair must be made in accordance with ANS X9.100–140 for repairing a MICR line, which generally allows a bank to correct an error by applying a strip that may or may not contain information in all fields encoded on the check's MICR line. A bank's repair of a MICR-line error on a substitute check is subject to the encoding warranties in Regulation CC and the U.C.C.

10.   A substitute check must conform to all the generally applicable industry standards for substitute checks set forth in ANS X9.100–140, which incorporates other industry standards by reference. Thus, multiple substitute check images contained on the same page of an account statement are not substitute checks.

BBB.   229.2(bbb) Sufficient Copy and Copy

1.   A copy must be a paper reproduction of a check. An electronic image therefore is not a copy or a sufficient copy. However, if a customer has agreed to receive such information electronically, a bank that is required to provide an original check or sufficient copy may satisfy that requirement by providing an electronic image in accordance with § 229.58 and the commentary thereto.

2.   A bank under § 229.53(b)(3) may limit its liability for an indemnity claim and under §§ 229.54(e)(2) and 229.55(c)(2) may respond to an expedited recredit claim by providing the claimant with a copy of a check that accurately represents all of the information on the front and back of the original check as of the time the original check was truncated or that otherwise is sufficient to determine the validity of the claim against the bank.

Examples.

a.   A copy of an original check that accurately represents all the information on the front and back of the original check as of the time of truncation would constitute a sufficient copy if that copy resolved the claim. For example, if resolution of the claim required accurate payment and indorsement information, an accurate copy of the front and back of a legible original check (including but not limited to a substitute check) would be a sufficient copy.

b.   A copy of the original check that does not accurately represent all the information on both the front and back of the original check also could be a sufficient copy if such copy contained all the information necessary to determine the validity of the relevant claim. For instance, if a consumer received a substitute check that contained a blurry image of a legible original check, the consumer might seek an expedited recredit because his or her account was charged for $1,000, but he or she believed that the check was written for only $100. If the amount that appeared on the front of the original check was legible, an accurate copy of only the front of the original check that showed the amount of the check would be sufficient to determine whether or not the consumer's claim regarding the amount of the check was valid.

CCC.   229.2(ccc) Transfer and Consideration

1.   Under §§ 229.52 and 229.53, a bank is responsible for the warranties and indemnity when it transfers, presents, or returns a substitute check (or a paper or electronic representation thereof) for consideration. Drawers and other nonbank persons that receive checks from a bank are not transferees that receive consideration as those terms are defined in the U.C.C. However, the Check 21 Act clearly contemplates that such nonbank persons that receive substitute checks (or representations thereof) from a bank will receive the warranties and indemnity from all previous banks that handled the check. To ensure that these parties are covered by the substitute check warranties and indemnity in the manner contemplated by the Check 21 Act, § 229.2(ccc) incorporates the U.C.C. definitions of the term transfer and consideration by reference and expands those definitions to cover a broader range of situations. Delivering a check to a nonbank that is acting on behalf of a bank (such as a third-party check processor or presentment point) is a transfer of the check to that bank.

COMMENTARY ON REGULATION CC

Examples.

a.   A paying bank pays a substitute check and then provides that paid substitute check (or a representation thereof) to a drawer with a periodic statement. Under the expanded definitions, the paying bank thereby transfers the substitute check (or representation thereof) to the drawer for consideration and makes the substitute check warranties described in § 229.52. A drawer that suffers a loss due to receipt of a substitute check may have warranty, indemnity, and, if the drawer is a consumer, expedited recredit rights under the Check 21 Act and subpart D. A drawer that suffers a loss due to receipt of a paper or electronic representation of a substitute check would receive the substitute check warranties but would not have indemnity or expedited recredit rights.

b.   The expanded definitions also operate such that a paying bank that pays an original check (or a representation thereof) and then creates a substitute check to provide to the drawer with a periodic statement transfers the substitute check for consideration and thereby provides the warranties and indemnity.

c.   The expanded definitions ensure that a bank that receives a returned check in any form and then provides a substitute check to the depositor gives the substitute check warranties and indemnity to the depositor.

d.   The expanded definitions apply to substitute checks representing original checks that are not drawn on deposit accounts, such as checks used to access a credit card or a home equity line of credit.

DDD.   229.2(ddd) Truncate

1.   Truncate means to remove the original check from the forward collection or return process and to send in lieu of the original check either a substitute check or, by agreement, information relating to the original check. Truncation does not include removal of a substitute check from the check collection or return process.

EEE.   229.2(eee) Truncating Bank

1.   A bank is a truncating bank if it truncates an original check or if it is the first bank to transfer, present, or return another form of an original check that was truncated by a person that is not a bank.

Example.

a.   A bank's customer that is a nonbank business receives a check for payment and deposits either a substitute check or an electronic representation of the original check with its depositary bank instead of the original check. That depositary bank is the truncating bank when it transfers, presents, or returns the substitute check or electronic representation in lieu of the original check. That bank also would be the reconverting bank if it were the first bank to transfer, present, or return a substitute check that it received from (or created from the information given by) its nonbank customer (see § 229.2(yy) and the commentary thereto).

2.   A truncating bank does not make the subpart D warranties and indemnity unless it also is the reconverting bank. Therefore, a bank that truncates the original check and sends an electronic file to a collecting bank does not provide subpart D protections to the recipient of that electronic item. However, a recipient of an electronic item may protect itself against losses associated with that item by agreement with the truncating bank.

FFF.   229.2(fff) Remotely Created Check

1.   A check authorized by a consumer over the telephone that is not created by the paying bank and bears a legend on the signature line, such as "Authorized by Drawer," is an example of a remotely created check. A check that bears the signature applied, or purported to be applied, by the person on whose account the check is drawn is not a remotely created check. A typical forged check, such as a stolen personal check fraudulently signed by a person other than the drawer, is not covered by the definition of a remotely created check.

2.   The term signature as used in this definition has the meaning set forth at U.C.C. 3–401. The term "applied by" refers to the physical act of placing the signature on the check.

3. The definition of a "remotely created check" differs from the definition of a "remotely created consumer item" under the U.C.C. A "remotely created check" may be drawn on an account held by a consumer, corporation, unincorporated company, partnership, government unit or instrumentality, trust, or any other entity or organization. A "remotely created consumer item" under the U.C.C., however, must be drawn on a consumer account.

4. Under Regulation CC (12 CFR part 229), the term "check" includes a negotiable demand draft drawn on or payable through or at an office of a bank. In the case of a "payable through" or "payable at" check, the signature of the person on whose account the check is drawn would include the signature of the payor institution or the signatures of the customers who are authorized to draw checks on that account, depending on the arrangements between the "payable through" or "payable at" bank, the payor institution, and the customers.

5. The definition of a remotely created check includes a remotely created check that has been reconverted to a substitute check.

III. Section 229.3 Administrative Enforcement) [Reserved]

IV. Section 229.10 Next-Day Availability

A. Business Days and Banking Days

1. This section, as well as other provisions of this subpart governing the availability of funds, provides that funds must be made available for withdrawal not later than a specified number of business days following the banking day on which the funds are deposited. Thus, a deposit is considered made only on a banking day, i.e., a day that the bank is open to the public for carrying on substantially all of its banking functions. For example, if a deposit is made at an ATM on a Saturday, Sunday, or other day on which the bank is closed to the public, the deposit is considered received on that bank's next banking day.

2. Nevertheless, business days are used to determine the number of days following the banking day of deposit that funds must be available for withdrawal. For example, if a deposit of a local check were made on a Monday, the availability schedule requires that funds be available for withdrawal on the second business day after deposit. Therefore, funds must be made available on Wednesday regardless of whether the bank was closed on Tuesday for other than a standard legal holiday as specified in the definition of business day.

B. 229.10(a) Cash Deposits

1. This paragraph implements the EFA Act's requirement for next-day availability for cash deposits to accounts at a depositary bank "staffed by individuals employed by such institution."[2] Under this paragraph, cash deposited in an account at a staffed teller station on a Monday must become available for withdrawal by the start of business on Tuesday. It must become available for withdrawal by the start of business on Wednesday if it is deposited by mail, at a proprietary ATM, or by other means other than at a staffed teller station.

C. 229.10(b) Electronic Payments

1. The EFA Act provides next-day availability for funds received for deposit by wire transfer. The regulation uses the term electronic payment, rather than wire transfer, to include both wire transfers and ACH credit transfers under the next-day availability requirement. (See discussion of definitions of automated clearinghouse, electronic payment, and wire transfer in § 229.2.)

2. The EFA Act requires that funds received by wire transfer be available for withdrawal not later than the business day following the day a wire transfer is received. This paragraph clarifies what constitutes receipt of an electronic payment. For the purposes of this paragraph, a bank receives an electronic payment when the bank receives both payment in finally collected funds and the payment instructions indicating the customer accounts to be credited and the amount to be credited to each account. For example, in the case of Fedwire, the bank receives finally collected funds at the time the payment is made. (See 12 CFR 210.31.)

---

[2] Nothing in the EFA Act or this regulation affects terms of account arrangements, such as negotiable order of withdrawal accounts, which may require prior notice of withdrawal. (See 12 CFR 204.2(e)(2).)

Finally collected funds generally are received for an ACH credit transfer when they are posted to the receiving bank's account on the settlement day. In certain cases, the bank receiving ACH credit payments will not receive the specific payment instructions indicating which accounts to credit until after settlement day. In these cases, the payments are not considered received until the information on the account and amount to be credited is received.

3.   This paragraph also establishes the extent to which an electronic payment is considered made. Thus, if a participant on a private network fails to settle and the receiving bank receives finally settled funds representing only a partial amount of the payment, it must make only the amount that it actually received available for withdrawal.

4.   The availability requirements of this regulation do not preempt or invalidate other rules, regulations, or agreements which require funds to be made available on a more prompt basis. For example, the next-day availability requirement for ACH credits in this section does not preempt ACH association rules and Treasury regulations (31 CFR part 210), which provide that the proceeds of these credit payments be available to the recipient for withdrawal on the day the bank receives the funds.

D.   229.10(c) Certain Check Deposits

1.   The EFA Act generally requires that funds be made available on the business day following the banking day of deposit for Treasury checks, state and local government checks, cashier's checks, certified checks, teller's checks, and "on us" checks, under specified conditions. (Treasury checks are checks drawn on the Treasury of the United States and have a routing number beginning with the digits "0000.") This section also requires next-day availability for additional types of checks not addressed in the EFA Act. Checks drawn on a Federal Reserve Bank or a Federal Home Loan Bank and U.S. Postal Service money orders also must be made available on the first business day following the day of deposit under specified conditions. For the purposes of this section, all checks drawn on a Federal Reserve Bank or a Federal Home Loan Bank that contain in the MICR line a routing number that is listed in Appendix A are subject to the next-day availability requirement if they are deposited in an account held by a payee of the check and in person to an employee of the depositary bank, regardless of the purposes for which the checks were issued. For all new accounts, even if the new account exception is not invoked, traveler's checks must be included in the $5,000 aggregation of checks deposited on any one banking day that are subject to the next-day availability requirement. (See § 229.13(a).)

2.   Deposit in Account of Payee. One statutory condition to receipt of next-day availability of Treasury checks, state and local government checks, cashier's checks, certified checks, and teller's checks is that the check must be "endorsed only by the person to whom it was issued." The EFA Act could be interpreted to include a check that has been indorsed in blank and deposited into an account of a third party that is not named as payee. The Board believes that such a check presents greater risks than a check deposited by the payee and that Congress did not intend to require next-day availability for such checks. The regulation, therefore, provides that funds must be available on the business day following deposit only if the check is deposited in an account held by a payee of the check. For the purposes of this section, payee does not include transferees other than named payees. The regulation also applies this condition to Postal Service money orders and checks drawn on Federal Reserve Banks and Federal Home Loan Banks.

3.   Deposits Made to an Employee of the Depositary Bank.

a.   In most cases, next-day availability of the proceeds of checks subject to this section is conditioned on the deposit of these checks in person to an employee of the depositary bank. If the deposit is not made to an employee of the depositary bank on the premises of such bank, the proceeds of the deposit must be made available for withdrawal by the start of business on the second business day after deposit, under paragraph (c)(2) of this section. For example, second-day availability rather than next-day availability would be allowed for deposits of checks subject to this section made at a proprietary ATM, night depository, through the mail or a lock box, or at a teller station staffed by a person who is not an employee of the depositary bank. Second-day availability also may be allowed for deposits picked up by an employee of the depositary bank at the customer's premises; such deposits would be considered made upon receipt at the branch or other location of the depositary bank. Employees of a contractual branch would not be considered employees of the depositary bank for the purposes of this regulation, and deposits at contractual branches would be treated

COMMENTARY ON REGULATION CC

the same as deposits to a proprietary ATM for the purposes of this regulation. (See also, Commentary to § 229.19(a).)

b.   In the case of Treasury checks, the EFA Act and regulation do not condition the receipt of next-day availability to deposits at staffed teller stations. Therefore, Treasury checks deposited at a proprietary ATM must be accorded next-day availability, if the check is deposited to an account of a payee of the check.

4.   "On Us" Checks. The EFA Act and regulation require next-day availability for "on us" checks, i.e., checks deposited in a branch of the depositary bank and drawn on the same or another branch of the same bank, if both branches are located in the same state or check processing region. Thus, checks deposited in one branch of a bank and drawn on another branch of the same bank must receive next-day availability even if the branch on which the checks are drawn is located in another check processing region but in the same state as the branch in which the check is deposited. For the purposes of this requirement, deposits at facilities that are not located on the premises of a brick-and-mortar branch of the bank, such as off-premise ATMs and remote depositories, are not considered deposits made at branches of the depositary bank.

5.   First $100.

a.   The EFA Act and regulation also require that up to $100 of the aggregate deposit by check or checks not subject to next-day availability on any one banking day be made available on the next business day. For example, if $70 were deposited in an account by check(s) on a Monday, the entire $70 must be available for withdrawal at the start of business on Tuesday. If $200 were deposited by check(s) on a Monday, this section requires that $100 of the funds be available for withdrawal at the start of business on Tuesday. The portion of the customer's deposit to which the $100 must be applied is at the discretion of the depositary bank, as long as it is not applied to any checks subject to next-day availability. The $100 next-day availability rule does not apply to deposits at nonproprietary ATMs.

b.   The $100 that must be made available under this rule is in addition to the amount that must be made available for withdrawal on the business day after deposit under other provisions of this section. For example, if a customer deposits a $1,000 Treasury check, and a $1,000 local check in its account on Monday, $1,100 must be made available for withdrawal on Tuesday—the proceeds of the $1,000 Treasury check, as well as the first $100 of the local check.

c.   A depositary bank may aggregate all local and nonlocal check deposits made by the customer on a given banking day for the purposes of the $100 next-day availability rule. Thus, if a customer has two accounts at the depositary bank, and on a particular banking day makes deposits to each account, $100 of the total deposited to the two accounts must be made available on the business day after deposit. Banks may aggregate deposits to individual and joint accounts for the purposes of this provision.

d.   If the customer deposits a $500 local check, and gets $100 cash back at the time of deposit, the bank need not make an additional $100 available for withdrawal on the following day. Similarly, if the customer depositing the local check has a negative book balance, or negative available balance in its account at the time of deposit, the $100 that must be available on the next business day may be made available by applying the $100 to the negative balance, rather than making the $100 available for withdrawal by cash or check on the following day.

6.   Special Deposit Slips.

a.   Under the EFA Act, a depositary bank may require the use of a special deposit slip as a condition to providing next-day availability for certain types of checks. This condition was included in the EFA Act because many banks determine the availability of their customers' check deposits in an automated manner by reading the MICR-encoded routing number on the deposited checks. Using these procedures, a bank can determine whether a check is a local or nonlocal check, a check drawn on the Treasury, a Federal Reserve Bank, a Federal Home Loan Bank, or a branch of the depositary bank, or a U.S. Postal Service money order. Appendix A includes the routing numbers of certain categories of checks that are subject to next-day availability. The bank cannot require a special deposit slip for these checks.

b.   A bank cannot distinguish whether the check is a state or local government check, cashier's check, certified check, or teller's check by reading the MICR-encoded routing number, because these checks bear the same routing number as other checks drawn on the same bank that are not accorded next-day availability. Therefore, a bank may require a special deposit slip for these checks.

c.   The regulation specifies that if a bank decides to require the use of a special deposit slip (or a special deposit envelope in the case of a deposit at an ATM or other unstaffed facility) as a condition to granting next-day availability under paragraphs (c)(1)(iv) or (c)(1)(v) of this section or second-day availability under paragraph (c)(2) of this section, and if the deposit slip that must be used is different from the bank's regular deposit slips, the bank must either provide the special slips to its customers or inform its customers how such slips may be obtained and make the slips reasonably available to the customers.

d.   A bank may meet this requirement by providing customers with an order form for the special deposit slips and allowing sufficient time for the customer to order and receive the slips before this condition is imposed. If a bank provides deposit slips in its branches for use by its customers, it also must provide the special deposit slips in the branches. If special deposit envelopes are required for deposits at an ATM, the bank must provide such envelopes at the ATM.

e.   Generally, a teller is not required to advise depositors of the availability of special deposit slips merely because checks requiring special deposit slips for next-day availability are deposited without such slips. If a bank provides the special deposit slips only upon the request of a depositor, however, the teller must advise the depositor of the availability of the special deposit slips, or the bank must post a notice advising customers that the slips are available upon request. Such notice need not be posted at each teller window, but the notice must be posted in a place where consumers seeking to make deposits are likely to see it before making their deposits. For example, the notice might be posted at the point where the line forms for teller service in the lobby. The notice is not required at any drive-through teller windows nor is it required at night depository locations, or at locations where consumer deposits are not accepted. If a bank prepares a deposit for a depositor, it must use a special deposit slip where appropriate. A bank may require the customer to segregate the checks subject to next-day availability for which special deposit slips could be required, and to indicate on a regular deposit slip that such checks are being deposited, if the bank so instructs its customers in its initial disclosure.

V.   Section 229.11 [Reserved]

VI.   Section 229.12 Availability Schedule

A.   229.12(a) Effective Date

1.   The availability schedule set forth in this section supersedes the temporary schedule that was effective September 1, 1988, through August 31, 1990.

B.   229.12(b) Local Checks and Certain Other Checks

1.   Local checks must be made available for withdrawal not later than the second business day following the banking day on which the checks were deposited.

2.   In addition, the proceeds of Treasury checks and U.S. Postal Service money orders not subject to next-day (or second-day) availability under § 229.10(c), checks drawn on Federal Reserve Banks and Federal Home Loan Banks, checks drawn by a state or unit of general local government, cashier's checks, certified checks, and teller's checks not subject to next-day (or second-day) availability under § 229.10(c) and payable in the same check processing region as the depositary bank, must be made available for withdrawal by the second business day following deposit.

3.   Exceptions are made for withdrawals by cash or similar means and for deposits in banks located outside the 48 contiguous states. Thus, the proceeds of a local check deposited on a Monday generally must be made available for withdrawal on Wednesday.

C.   229.12(c) Nonlocal Checks

1.   Nonlocal checks must be made available for withdrawal not later than the fifth business day following deposit, i.e., proceeds of a nonlocal check deposited on a Monday must be made available for withdrawal on the following Monday. In addition, a check described in § 229.10(c) that does not meet the conditions for next-day availability (or second-day availability) is treated as a nonlocal check, if the check is

drawn on or payable through or at a nonlocal paying bank. Adjustments are made to the schedule for withdrawals by cash or similar means and deposits in banks located outside the 48 contiguous states.

2.   Reduction in Schedules.

a.   Section 603(d)(1) of the EFA Act (12 U.S.C. 4002(d)(1)) requires the Board to reduce the statutory schedules for any category of checks where most of those checks would be returned in a shorter period of time than provided in the schedules. The conferees indicated that "if the new system makes it possible for two-thirds of the items of a category of checks to meet this test in a shorter period of time, then the Federal Reserve must shorten the schedules accordingly." H.R. Rep. No. 261, 100th Cong., 1st Sess. at 179 (1987).

b.   Reduced schedules are provided for certain nonlocal checks where significant improvements can be made to the EFA Act's schedules due to transportation arrangements or proximity between the check processing regions of the depositary bank and the paying bank, allowing for faster collection and return. Appendix B sets forth the specific reduction of schedules applicable to banks located in certain check processing regions.

c.   A reduction in schedules may apply even in those cases where the determination that the check is nonlocal cannot be made based on the routing number on the check. For example, a nonlocal credit union payable-through share draft may be subject to a reduction in schedules if the routing number of the payable-through bank that appears on the draft is included in Appendix B, even though the determination that the payable-through share draft is nonlocal is based on the location of the credit union and not the routing number on the draft.

D.   229.12(d) Time Period Adjustment for Withdrawal by Cash or Similar Means

1.   The EFA Act provides an adjustment to the availability rules for cash withdrawals. Funds from local and nonlocal checks need not be available for cash withdrawal until 5:00 p.m. on the day specified in the schedule. At 5:00 p.m., $400 of the deposit must be made available for cash withdrawal. This $400 is in addition to the first $100 of a day's deposit, which must be made available for withdrawal at the start of business on the first business day following the banking day of deposit. If the proceeds of local and nonlocal checks become available for withdrawal on the same business day, the $400 withdrawal limitation applies to the aggregate amount of the funds that became available for withdrawal on that day. The remainder of the funds must be available for cash withdrawal at the start of business on the business day following the business day specified in the schedule.

2.   The EFA Act recognizes that the $400 that must be provided on the day specified in the schedule may exceed a bank's daily ATM cash withdrawal limit, and explicitly provides that the EFA Act does not supersede the bank's policy in this regard. The Board believes that the rationale for accommodating a bank's ATM withdrawal limit also applies to other cash withdrawal limits established by that bank. Section 229.19(c)(4) of the regulation addresses the relation between a bank's cash withdrawal limit (for over-the-counter cash withdrawals as well as ATM cash withdrawals) and the requirements of this subpart.

3.   The Board believes that the Congress included this special cash withdrawal rule to provide a depositary bank with additional time to learn of the nonpayment of a check before it must make funds available to its customer. If a customer deposits a local check on a Monday, and that check is returned by the paying bank, the depositary bank may not receive the returned check until Thursday, the day after funds for a local check ordinarily must be made available for withdrawal. The intent of the special cash withdrawal rule is to minimize this risk to the depositary bank. For this rule to minimize the depositary bank's risk, it must apply not only to cash withdrawals, but also to withdrawals by other means that result in an irrevocable debit to the customer's account or commitment to pay by the bank on the customer's behalf during the day. Thus, the cash withdrawal rule also includes withdrawals by electronic payment, issuance of a cashier's or teller's check, certification of a check, or other irrevocable commitment to pay, such as authorization of an on-line point-of-sale debit. The rule also would apply to checks presented over the counter for payment on the day of presentment by the depositor or another person. Such checks could not be dishonored for insufficient funds if an amount sufficient to cover the check had became available for cash withdrawal under this rule; however, payment of such checks would be subject to the bank's cut-off hour

established under U.C.C. 4–108. The cash withdrawal rule does not apply to checks and other provisional debits presented to the bank for payment that the bank has the right to return.

E. 229.12(e) Extension of Schedule for Certain Deposits in Alaska, Hawaii, Puerto Rico, and the U.S. Virgin Islands

1. The EFA Act and regulation provide an extension of the availability schedules for check deposits at a branch of a bank if the branch is located in Alaska, Hawaii, Puerto Rico, or the U.S. Virgin Islands. The schedules for local checks, nonlocal checks (including nonlocal checks subject to the reduced schedules of Appendix B), and deposits at nonproprietary ATMs are extended by one business day for checks deposited to accounts in banks located in these jurisdictions that are drawn on or payable at or through a paying bank not located in the same jurisdiction as the depositary bank. For example, a check deposited in a bank in Hawaii and drawn on a San Francisco paying bank must be made available for withdrawal not later than the third business day following deposit. This extension does not apply to deposits that must be made available for withdrawal on the next business day.

2. The Congress did not provide this extension of the schedules to checks drawn on a paying bank located in Alaska, Hawaii, Puerto Rico, or the U.S. Virgin Islands and deposited in an account at a depositary bank in the 48 contiguous states. Therefore, a check deposited in a San Francisco bank drawn on a Hawaii paying bank must be made available for withdrawal not later than the second rather than the third business day following deposit.

F. 229.12(f) Deposits at Nonproprietary ATMs

1. The EFA Act and regulation provide a special rule for deposits made at nonproprietary ATMs. This paragraph does not apply to deposits made at proprietary ATMs. All deposits at a nonproprietary ATM must be made available for withdrawal by the fifth business day following the banking day of deposit. For example, a deposit made at a nonproprietary ATM on a Monday, including any deposit by cash or checks that would otherwise be subject to next-day (or second-day) availability, must be made available for withdrawal not later than Monday of the following week. The provisions of § 229.10(c)(1)(vii) requiring a depositary bank to make up to $100 of an aggregate daily deposit available for withdrawal on the first business day after the banking day of deposit do not apply to deposits at a nonproprietary ATM.

VII. Section 229.13 Exceptions

A. Introduction

1. While certain safeguard exceptions (such as those for new accounts and checks the bank has reasonable cause to believe are uncollectible) are established in the EFA Act, the Congress gave the Board the discretion to determine whether certain other exceptions should be included in its regulations. Specifically, the EFA Act gives the Board the authority to establish exceptions to the schedules for large or redeposited checks and for accounts that have been repeatedly overdrawn. These exceptions apply to local and nonlocal checks as well as to checks that must otherwise be accorded next-day (or second-day) availability under § 229.10(c).

2. Many checks will not be returned to the depositary bank by the time funds must be made available for withdrawal under the next-day (or second-day), local, and nonlocal schedules. In order to reduce risk to depositary banks, the Board has exercised its statutory authority to adopt these exceptions to the schedules in the regulation to allow the depositary bank to extend the time within which it is required to make funds available.

3. The EFA Act also gives the Board the authority to suspend the schedules for any classification of checks, if the schedules result in an unacceptable level of fraud losses. The Board will adopt regulations or issue orders to implement this statutory authority if and when circumstances requiring its implementation arise.

B. 229.13(a) New Accounts

1. Definition of New Account.

a. The EFA Act provides an exception to the availability schedule for new accounts. An account is defined as a new account during the first 30 calendar days after the account is opened. An account is opened when the first deposit is made to the account. An account is not considered a new account, however, if each customer on the account has a transaction account relationship with the depositary bank, including a dormant account, that is at least 30 calendar days old or if each customer has had an established transaction account with the depositary bank within the 30 calendar days prior to opening the second account.

b.　The following are examples of what constitutes, and does not constitute, a new account:

i.　If the customer has an established account with a bank and opens a second account with the bank, the second account is not subject to the new account exception.

ii.　If a customer's account were closed and another account opened as a successor to the original account (due, for example, to the theft of checks or a debit card used to access the original account), the successor account is not subject to the new account exception, assuming the previous account relationship is at least 30 days old. Similarly, if a customer closes an established account and opens a separate account within 30 days, the new account is not subject to the new account exception.

iii.　If a customer has a savings deposit or other deposit that is not an account (as that term is defined in § 229.2(a)) at the bank, and opens an account, the account is subject to the new account exception.

iv.　If a person that is authorized to sign on a corporate account (but has no other relationship with the bank) opens a personal account, the personal account is subject to the new account exception.

v.　If a customer has an established joint account at a bank, and subsequently opens an individual account with that bank, the individual account is not subject to the new account exception.

vi.　If two customers that each have an established individual account with the bank open a joint account, the joint account is not subject to the new account exception. If one of the customers on the account has no current or recent established account relationship with the bank, however, the joint account is subject to the new account exception, even if the other individual on the account has an established account relationship with the bank.

2.　Rules Applicable to New Accounts.

a.　During the new account exception period, the schedules for local and nonlocal checks do not apply, and, unlike the other exceptions provided in this section, the regulation provides no maximum time frames within which the proceeds of these deposits must be made available for withdrawal. Maximum times within which funds must be available for withdrawal during the new account period are provided, however, for certain other deposits. Deposits received by cash and electronic payments must be made available for withdrawal in accordance with § 229.10.

b.　Special rules also apply to deposits of Treasury checks, U.S. Postal Service money orders, checks drawn on Federal Reserve Banks and Federal Home Loan Banks, state and local government checks, cashier's checks, certified checks, teller's checks, and, for the purposes of the new account exception only, traveler's checks. The first $5,000 of funds deposited to a new account on any one banking day by these check deposits must be made available for withdrawal in accordance with § 229.10(c). Thus, the first $5,000 of the proceeds of these check deposits must be made available on the first business day following deposit, if the deposit is made in person to an employee of the depositary bank and the other conditions of next-day availability are met. Funds must be made available on the second business day after deposit for deposits that are not made over the counter, in accordance with § 229.10(c)(2). (Proceeds of Treasury check deposits must be made available on the first business day after deposit, even if the check is not deposited in person to an employee of the depositary bank.) Funds in excess of the first $5,000 deposited by these types of checks on a banking day must be available for withdrawal not later than the ninth business day following the banking day of deposit. The requirements of § 229.10(c)(1)(vi) and (vii) that "on us" checks and the first $100 of a day's deposit be made available for withdrawal on the next business day do not apply during the new account period.

3.　Representation by Customer. The depositary bank may rely on the representation of the customer that the customer has no established account relationship with the bank, and has not had any such account relationship within the past 30 days, to determine whether an account is subject to the new account exception.

COMMENTARY ON REGULATION CC

C. 229.13(b) Large Deposits

1.   Under the large deposit exception, a depositary bank may extend the hold placed on check deposits to the extent that the amount of the aggregate deposit on any banking day exceeds $5,000. This exception applies to local and nonlocal checks, as well as to checks that otherwise would be made available on the next (or second) business day after the day of deposit under § 229.10(c). Although the first $5,000 of a day's deposit is subject to the availability otherwise provided for checks, the amount in excess of $5,000 may be held for an additional period of time as provided in § 229.13(h). When the large deposit exception is applied to deposits composed of a mix of checks that would otherwise be subject to differing availability schedules, the depositary bank has the discretion to choose the portion of the deposit to which it applies the exception. Deposits by cash or electronic payment are not subject to this exception for large deposits.

2.   The following example illustrates the operation of the large deposit exception. If a customer deposits $2,000 in cash and a $9,000 local check on a Monday, $2,100 (the proceeds of the cash deposit and $100 from the local check deposit) must be made available for withdrawal on Tuesday. An additional $4,900 of the proceeds of the local check must be available for withdrawal on Wednesday in accordance with the local schedule, and the remaining $4,000 may be held for an additional period of time under the large deposit exception.

3.   Where a customer has multiple accounts with a depositary bank, the bank may apply the large deposit exception to the aggregate deposits to all of the customer's accounts, even if the customer is not the sole holder of the accounts and not all of the holders of the customer's accounts are the same. Thus, a depositary bank may aggregate the deposits made to two individual accounts in the same name, to an individual and a joint account with one common name, or to two joint accounts with at least one common name for the purpose of applying the large deposit exception. Aggregation of deposits to multiple accounts is permitted because the Board believes that the risk to the depositary bank associated with large deposits is similar regardless of how the deposits are allocated among the customer's accounts.

D. 229.13(c) Redeposited Checks

1.   The EFA Act gives the Board the authority to promulgate an exception to the schedule for checks that have been returned unpaid and redeposited. Section 229.13(c) provides such an exception for checks that have been returned unpaid and redeposited by the customer or the depositary bank. This exception applies to local and nonlocal checks, as well as to checks that would otherwise be made available on the next (or second) business day after the day of deposit under § 229.10(c).

2.   This exception addresses the increased risk to the depositary bank that checks that have been returned once will be uncollectible when they are presented to the paying bank a second time. The Board, however, does not believe that this increased risk is present for checks that have been returned due to a missing indorsement. Thus, the exception does not apply to checks returned unpaid due to missing indorsements and redeposited after the missing indorsement has been obtained, if the reason for return indicated on the check (see § 229.30(d)) states that it was returned due to a missing indorsement. For the same reason, this exception does not apply to a check returned because it was postdated (future dated), if the reason for return indicated on the check states that it was returned because it was postdated, and if it is no longer postdated when redeposited.

3.   To determine when funds must be made available for withdrawal, the banking day on which the check is redeposited is considered to be the day of deposit. A depositary bank that made $100 of a check available for withdrawal under § 229.10(c)(1)(vii) can charge back the full amount of the check, including the $100, if the check is returned unpaid, and the $100 need not be made available again if the check is redeposited.

E. 229.13(d) Repeated Overdrafts

1.   The EFA Act gives the Board the authority to establish an exception for "deposit accounts which have been overdrawn repeatedly." This paragraph provides two tests to determine what constitutes repeated overdrafts. Under the first test, a customer's accounts are considered repeatedly overdrawn if, on six banking days within the preceding six months, the available balance in any account held by the customer is negative, or the balance would have become negative if checks or other charges to the account had been paid, rather than returned. This test can be met based on separate occurrences (e.g., checks that are

1892

COMMENTARY ON REGULATION CC

returned for insufficient funds on six different days), or based on one occurrence (e.g., a negative balance that remains on the customer's account for six banking days). If the bank dishonors a check that otherwise would have created a negative balance, however, the incident is considered an overdraft only on that day.

2. The second test addresses substantial overdrafts. Such overdrafts increase the risk to the depositary bank of dealing with the repeated overdrafter. Under this test, a customer incurs repeated overdrafts if, on two banking days within the preceding six months, the available balance in any account held by the customer is negative in an amount of $5,000 or more, or would have become negative in an amount of $5,000 or more if checks or other charges to the account had been paid.

3. The exception relates not only to overdrafts caused by checks drawn on the account, but also overdrafts caused by other debit charges (e.g. ACH debits, point-of-sale transactions, returned checks, account fees, etc.). If the potential debit is in excess of available funds, the exception applies regardless of whether the items were paid or returned unpaid. An overdraft resulting from an error on the part of the depositary bank, or from the imposition of overdraft charges for which the customer is entitled to a refund under §§ 229.13(e) or 229.16(c), cannot be considered in determining whether the customer is a repeated overdrafter. The exception excludes accounts with overdraft lines of credit, unless the credit line has been exceeded or would have been exceeded if the checks or other charges to the account had been paid.

4. This exception applies to local and nonlocal checks, as well as to checks that otherwise would be made available on the next (or second) business day after the day of deposit under § 229.10(c). When a bank places or extends a hold under this exception, it need not make the first $100 of a deposit available for withdrawal on the next business day, as otherwise would be required by § 229.10(c)(1)(vii).

F. 229.13(e) Reasonable Cause To Doubt Collectibility

1. In the case of certain check deposits, if the bank has reasonable cause to believe the check is uncollectible, it may extend the time funds must be made available for withdrawal. This exception applies to local and nonlocal checks, as well as to checks that would otherwise be made available on the next (or second) business day after the day of deposit under § 229.10(c). When a bank places or extends a hold under this exception, it need not make the first $100 of a deposit available for withdrawal on the next business day, as otherwise would be required by § 229.10(c)(1)(vii). If the reasonable cause exception is invoked, the bank must include in the notice to its customer, required by § 229.13(g), the reason that the bank believes that the check is uncollectible.

2. The following are several examples of circumstances under which the reasonable cause exception may be invoked:

a. If a bank received a notice from the paying bank that a check was not paid and is being returned to the depositary bank, the depositary bank could place a hold on the check or extend a hold previously placed on that check, and notify the customer that the bank had received notice that the check is being returned. The exception could be invoked even if the notice were incomplete, if the bank had reasonable cause to believe that the notice applied to that particular check.

b. The depositary bank may have received information from the paying bank, prior to the presentment of the check, that gives the bank reasonable cause to believe that the check is uncollectible. For example, the paying bank may have indicated that payment has been stopped on the check, or that the drawer's account does not currently have sufficient funds to honor the check. Such information may provide sufficient basis to invoke this exception. In these cases, the depositary bank could invoke the exception and disclose as the reason the exception is being invoked the fact that information from the paying bank indicates that the check may not be paid.

c. The fact that a check is deposited more than six months after the date on the check (i.e. a stale check) is a reasonable indication that the check may be uncollectible, because under U.C.C. 4–404 a bank has no duty to its customer to pay a check that is more than six months old. Similarly, if a check being deposited is postdated (future dated), the bank may have a reasonable cause to believe the check is uncollectible, because the check may not be properly payable under U.C.C. 4–401. The bank, in its notice, should specify that the check is stale-dated or postdated.

d.   There are reasons that may cause a bank to believe that a check is uncollectible that are based on confidential information. For example, a bank could conclude that a check being deposited is uncollectible based on its reasonable belief that the depositor is engaging in kiting activity. Reasonable belief as to the insolvency or pending insolvency of the drawer of the check or the drawee bank and that the checks will not be paid also may justify invoking this exception. In these cases, the bank may indicate, as the reason it is invoking the exception, that the bank has confidential information that indicates that the check might not be paid.

3.   The Board has included a reasonable cause exception notice as a model notice in Appendix C (C–13). The model notice includes several reasons for which this exception may be invoked. The Board does not intend to provide a comprehensive list of reasons for which this exception may be invoked; another reason that does not appear on the model notice may be used as the basis for extending a hold, if the reason satisfies the conditions for invoking this exception. A depositary bank may invoke the reasonable cause exception based on a combination of factors that give rise to a reasonable cause to doubt the collectibility of a check. In these cases, the bank should disclose the primary reasons for which the exception was invoked in accordance with paragraph (g) of this section.

4.   The regulation provides that the determination that a check is uncollectible shall not be based on a class of checks or persons. For example, a depositary bank cannot invoke this exception simply because the check is drawn on a paying bank in a rural area and the depositary bank knows it will not have the opportunity to learn of nonpayment of that check before funds must be made available under the availability schedules. Similarly, a depositary bank cannot invoke the reasonable cause exception based on the race or national origin of the depositor.

5.   If a depositary bank invokes this exception with respect to a particular check and does not provide a written notice to the depositor at the time of deposit, the depositary bank may not assess any overdraft fee (such as an "NSF" charge) or charge interest for use of overdraft credit, if the check is paid by the paying bank and these charges would not have occurred had the exception not been invoked. A bank may assess an overdraft fee under these circumstances, however, if it provides notice to the customer, in the notice of exception required by paragraph (g) of this section, that the fee may be subject to refund, and refunds the charges upon the request of the customer. The notice must state that the customer may be entitled to a refund of any overdraft fees that are assessed if the check being held is paid, and indicate where such requests for a refund of overdraft fees should be directed.

G.   229.13(f) Emergency Conditions

1.   Certain emergency conditions may arise that delay the collection or return of checks, or delay the processing and updating of customer accounts. In the circumstances specified in this paragraph, the depositary bank may extend the holds that are placed on deposits of checks that are affected by such delays, if the bank exercises such diligence as the circumstances require. For example, if a bank learns that a check has been delayed in the process of collection due to severe weather conditions or other causes beyond its control, an emergency condition covered by this section may exist and the bank may place a hold on the check to reflect the delay. This exception applies to local and nonlocal checks, as well as checks that would otherwise be made available on the next (or second) business day after the day of deposit under § 229.10(c). When a bank places or extends a hold under this exception, it need not make the first $100 of a deposit available for withdrawal on the next business day, as otherwise would be required by § 229.10(c)(1)(vii). In cases where the emergency conditions exception does not apply, as in the case of deposits of cash or electronic payments under § 229.10 (a) and (b), the depositary bank may not be liable for a delay in making funds available for withdrawal if the delay is due to a bona fide error such as an unavoidable computer malfunction.

H.   229.13(g) Notice of Exception

1.   In general.

a.   If a depositary bank invokes any of the safeguard exceptions to the schedules listed above, other than the new account or emergency conditions exception, and extends the hold on a deposit beyond the time periods permitted in §§ 229.10(c) and 229.12, it must provide a notice to its customer. Except in the cases described in paragraphs (g)(2) and (g)(3) of this section, notices must be given each time an exception hold is invoked and must state the customer's account number, the date of deposit, the reason the exception was invoked, and the time period within which funds will be available for withdrawal. For a customer that is not a consumer, a depositary bank satisfies the written-notice requirement by sending an electronic notice that displays the text and is in a form that the customer may keep, if the customer agrees to such means of notice. Information is in a form that the customer may keep if, for example, it can be downloaded or printed. For a customer who is a consumer, a depositary bank satisfies the written-notice requirement by sending an electronic notice in compliance with the requirements of the Electronic Signatures in Global and National Commerce Act (12 U.S.C. 7001 et seq.), which include obtaining the consumer's affirmative consent to such means of notice.

b.   With respect to paragraph (g)(1), the requirement that the notice state the time period within which the funds shall be made available may be satisfied if the notice identifies the date the deposit is received and information sufficient to indicate when funds will be available and the amounts that will be available at those times. For example, for a deposit involving more than one check, the bank need not provide a notice that discloses when funds from each individual check in the deposit will be available for withdrawal; instead, the bank may provide a total dollar amount for each of the time periods when funds will be available, or provide the customer with an explanation of how to determine the amount of the deposit that will be held and when the funds will be available for deposit. Appendix C (C–12) contains a model notice.

c.   For deposits made in person to an employee of the depositary bank, the notice generally must be given to the person making the deposit, i.e., the "depositor", at the time of deposit. The depositor need not be the customer holding the account. For other deposits, such as deposits received at an ATM, lobby deposit box, night depository, or through the mail, notice must be mailed to the customer not later than the close of the business day following the banking day on which the deposit was made.

d.   Notice to the customer also may be provided at a later time, if the facts upon which the determination to invoke the exception do not become known to the depositary bank until after notice would otherwise have to be given. In these cases, the bank must mail the notice to the customer as soon as practicable, but not later than the business day following the day the facts become known. A bank is deemed to have knowledge when the facts are brought to the attention of the person or persons in the bank responsible for making the determination, or when the facts would have been brought to their attention if the bank had exercised due diligence.

e.   In those cases described in paragraphs (g)(2) and (g)(3), the depositary bank need not provide a notice every time an exception hold is applied to a deposit. When paragraph (g)(2) or (g)(3) requires disclosure of the time period within which deposits subject to the exception generally will be available for withdrawal, the requirement may be satisfied if the one-time notice states when "on us," local, and nonlocal checks will be available for withdrawal if an exception is invoked.

2.   One-time exception notice.

a.   Under paragraph (g)(2), if a nonconsumer account (see Commentary to § 229.2(n)) is subject to the large deposit or redeposited check exception, the depositary bank may give its customer a single notice at or prior to the time notice must be provided under paragraph (g)(1). Notices provided under paragraph (g)(2) must contain the reason the exception may be invoked and the time period within which deposits subject to the exception will be available for withdrawal (see Model Notice C–14). A depositary bank may provide a one-time notice to a nonconsumer customer under paragraph (g)(2) only if each exception cited in the notice (the large deposit and/or the redeposited check exception) will be invoked for most check deposits to the customer's account to which the exception could apply. A one-time notice may state that the depositary bank will apply exception holds to certain subsets of deposits to which the large deposit or redeposited check exception may apply, and the notice should identify such subsets. For example, the depositary bank may apply the redeposited check exception only to checks that were redeposited automatically by the depositary bank in accordance with an agreement with the customer, rather than to all redeposited checks. In lieu of sending the one-time notice, a depositary bank may send individual hold notices for each deposit subject to the large deposit or redeposited check exception in accordance with § 229.13(g)(1) (see Model Notice C–12).

b.   In the case of a deposit of multiple checks, the depositary bank has the discretion to place an exception hold on any combination of checks in excess of $5,000. The notice should enable a customer to determine the availability of the deposit in the case of a deposit of multiple checks. For example, if a customer deposits a $5,000 local check and a $5,000 nonlocal check, under the large deposit exception, the depositary bank may make funds available in the amount of (1) $100 on the first business day after deposit, $4,900 on the second business day after deposit (local check), and $5,000 on the eleventh business day after deposit (nonlocal check with 6-day exception hold), or (2) $100 on the first business day after deposit, $4,900 on the fifth business day after deposit (nonlocal check), and $5,000 on the seventh business day after deposit (local check with 5-day exception hold). The notice should reflect the bank's priorities in placing exception holds on next-day (or second-day), local, and nonlocal checks.

3.   Notice of repeated overdraft exception. Under paragraph (g)(3), if an account is subject to the repeated overdraft exception, the depositary bank may provide one notice to its customer for each time period during which the exception will apply. Notices sent pursuant to paragraph (g)(3) must state the customer's account number, the fact the exception was invoked under the repeated overdraft exception, the time period within which deposits subject to the exception will be made available for withdrawal, and the time period during which the exception will apply (see Model Notice C–15). A depositary bank may provide a one-time notice to a customer under paragraph (g)(3) only if the repeated overdraft exception will be invoked for most check deposits to the customer's account.

4.   Emergency conditions exception notice.

a.   If an account is subject to the emergency conditions exception under § 229.13(f), the depositary bank must provide notice in a reasonable form within a reasonable time, depending on the circumstances. For example, a depositary bank may learn of a weather emergency or a power outage that affects the paying bank's operations. Under these circumstances, it likely would be reasonable for the depositary bank to provide an emergency conditions exception notice in the same manner and within the same time as required for other exception notices. On the other hand, if a depositary bank experiences a weather or power outage emergency that affects its own operations, it may be reasonable for the depositary bank to provide a general notice to all depositors via postings at branches and ATMs, or through newspaper, television, or radio notices.

b.   If the depositary bank extends the hold placed on a deposit due to an emergency condition, the bank need not provide a notice if the funds would be available for withdrawal before the notice must be sent. For example, if on the last day of a hold period the depositary bank experiences a computer failure and customer accounts cannot be updated in a timely fashion to reflect the funds as available balances, notices are not required if the funds are made available before the notices must be sent.

5.   Record retention. A depositary bank must retain a record of each notice of a reasonable cause exception for a period of two years, or such longer time as provided in the record retention requirements of § 229.21. This record must contain a brief description of the facts on which the depositary bank based its judgment that there was reasonable cause to doubt the collectibility of a check. In many cases, such as where the exception was invoked on the basis of a notice of nonpayment received, the record requirement may be met by retaining a copy of the notice sent to the customer. In other cases, such as where the exception was invoked on the basis of confidential information, a further description to the facts, such as insolvency of drawer, should be included in the record.

I.   229.13(h) Availability of Deposits Subject to Exceptions

1.   If a depositary bank invokes any exception other than the new account exception, the bank may extend the time within which funds must be made available under the schedule by a reasonable period of time. This provision establishes that an extension of up to one business day for "on us" checks, five business days for local checks, and six business days for nonlocal checks and checks deposited in a nonproprietary ATM is reasonable. Under certain circumstances, however, a longer extension of the schedules may be reasonable. In these cases, the burden is placed on the depositary bank to establish that a longer period is reasonable.

2.   For example, assume a bank extended the hold on a local check deposit by five business days based on its reasonable cause to believe that the check is uncollectible. If, on the day before the extended hold is scheduled to expire, the bank receives a notification from the paying bank that the check is being returned unpaid, the bank may determine that a longer hold is warranted, if it decides not to charge back the customer's account based on the notification. If the bank decides to extend the hold, the bank must send

a second notice, in accordance with paragraph (g) of this section, indicating the new date that the funds will be available for withdrawal.

3.   With respect to Treasury checks, U.S. Postal Service money orders, checks drawn on Federal Reserve Banks or Federal Home Loan Banks, state and local government checks, cashier's checks, certified checks, and teller's checks subject to the next-day (or second-day) availability requirement, the depositary bank may extend the time funds must be made available for withdrawal under the large deposit, redeposited check, repeated overdraft, or reasonable cause exception by a reasonable period beyond the delay that would have been permitted under the regulation had the checks not been subject to the next-day (or second-day) availability requirement. The additional hold is added to the local or nonlocal schedule that would apply based on the location of the paying bank.

4.   One business day for "on us" checks, five business days for local checks, and six business days for nonlocal checks or checks deposited in a nonproprietary ATM, in addition to the time period provided in the schedule, should provide adequate time for the depositary bank to learn of the nonpayment of virtually all checks that are returned. For example, if a customer deposits a $7,000 cashier's check drawn on a nonlocal bank, and the depositary bank applies the large deposit exception to that check, $5,000 must be available for withdrawal on the first business day after the day of deposit and the remaining $2,000 must be available for withdrawal on the eleventh business day following the day of deposit (six business days added to the five-day schedule for nonlocal checks), unless the depositary bank establishes that a longer hold is reasonable.

5.   In the case of the application of the emergency conditions exception, the depositary bank may extend the hold placed on a check by not more than a reasonable period following the end of the emergency or the time funds must be available for withdrawal under §§ 229.10(c) or 229.12, whichever is later.

6.   This provision does not apply to holds imposed under the new account exception. Under that exception, the maximum time period within which funds must be made available for withdrawal is specified for deposits that generally must be accorded next-day availability under § 229.10. This subpart does not specify the maximum time period within which the proceeds of local and nonlocal checks must be made available for withdrawal during the new account period.

VIII.   Section 229.14 Payment of Interest

A.   229.14(a) In General

1.   This section requires that a depositary bank begin accruing interest on interest-bearing accounts not later than the day on which the depositary bank receives credit for the funds deposited.[3] A depositary bank generally receives credit on checks within one or two days following deposit. A bank receives credit on a cash deposit, an electronic payment, and the deposit of a check that is drawn on the depositary bank itself on the day the cash, electronic payment, or check is received. In the case of a deposit at a nonproprietary ATM, credit generally is received on the day the bank that operates the ATM credits the depositary bank for the amount of the deposit. In the case of a deposit at a contractual branch, credit is received on the day the depositary bank receives credit for the amount of the deposit, which may be different from the day the contractual branch receives credit for the deposit.

2.   Because account includes only transaction accounts, other interest-bearing accounts of the depositary bank, such as money market deposit accounts, savings deposits, and time deposits, are not subject to this requirement; however, a bank may accrue interest on such deposits in the same way that it

---

[3]   This section implements section 606 of the EFA Act (12 U.S.C. 4005). The EFA Act keys the requirement to pay interest to the time the depositary bank receives provisional credit for a check. Provisional credit is a term used in the U.C.C. that is derived from the Code's concept of provisional settlement. (See U.C.C. 4–214 and 4–215.) Provisional credit is credit that is subject to charge-back if the check is returned unpaid; once the check is finally paid, the right to charge back expires and the provisional credit becomes final. Under Subpart C, a paying bank no longer has an automatic right to charge back credits given in settlement of a check, and the concept of provisional settlement is no longer useful and has been eliminated by the regulation. Accordingly, this section uses the term credit rather than provisional credit, and this section applies regardless of whether a credit would be provisional or final under the U.C.C. Credit does not include a bookkeeping entry (sometimes referred to as deferred credit) that does not represent funds actually available for the bank's use.

accrues interest under this paragraph for simplicity of operation. The Board intends the term interest to refer to payments to or for the account of any customer as compensation for the use of funds, but to exclude the absorption of expenses incident to providing a normal banking function or a bank's forbearance from charging a fee in connection with such a service. (See 12 CFR 217.2(d).) Thus, earnings credits often applied to corporate accounts are not interest payments for the purposes of this section.

3. It may be difficult for a depositary bank to track which day the depositary bank receives credit for specific checks in order to accrue interest properly on the account to which the check is deposited. This difficulty may be pronounced if the bank uses different means of collecting checks based on the time of day the check is received, the dollar amount of the check, and/or the paying bank to which it must be sent. Thus, for the purpose of the interest accrual requirement, a bank may rely on an availability schedule from its Federal Reserve Bank, Federal Home Loan Bank, or correspondent to determine when the depositary bank receives credit. If availability is delayed beyond that specified in the availability schedule, a bank may charge back interest erroneously accrued or paid on the basis of that schedule.

4. This paragraph also permits a depositary bank to accrue interest on checks deposited to all of its interest-bearing accounts based on when the bank receives credit on all checks sent for payment or collection. For example, if a bank receives credit on 20 percent of the funds deposited in the bank by check as of the business day of deposit (e.g., "on us" checks), 70 percent as of the business day following deposit, and 10 percent on the second business day following deposit, the bank can apply these percentages to determine the day interest must begin to accrue on check deposits to all interest-bearing accounts, regardless of when the bank received credit on the funds deposited in any particular account. Thus, a bank may begin accruing interest on a uniform basis for all interest-bearing accounts, without the need to track the type of check deposited to each account.

5. This section is not intended to limit a policy of a depositary bank that provides that interest accrues only on balances that exceed a specified amount, or on the minimum balance maintained in the account during a given period, provided that the balance is determined based on the date that the depositary bank receives credit for the funds. This section also is not intended to limit any policy providing that interest accrues sooner than required by this paragraph.

B.   229.14(b) Special Rule for Credit Unions

1. This provision implements a requirement in section 606(b) of the EFA Act, and provides an exemption from the payment-of-interest requirements for credit unions that do not begin to accrue interest or dividends on their customer accounts until a later date than the day the credit union receives credit for those deposits, including cash deposits. These credit unions are exempt from the payment-of-interest requirements, as long as they provide notice of their interest accrual policies in accordance with § 229.16(d). For example, if a credit union has a policy of computing interest on all deposits received by the 10th of the month from the first of that month, and on all deposits received after the 10th of the month from the first of the next month, that policy is not superseded by this regulation, if the credit union provides proper disclosure of this policy to its customers.

2. The EFA Act limits this exemption to credit unions; other types of banks must comply with the payment-of-interest requirements. In addition, credit unions that compute interest from the day of deposit or day of credit should not change their existing practices in order to avoid compliance with the requirement that interest accrue from the day the credit union receives credit.

C.   229.14(c) Exception for Checks Returned Unpaid

1. This provision is based on section 606(c) of the EFA Act (12 U.S.C. 4005(c)) and provides that interest need not be paid on funds deposited in an interest-bearing account by check that has been returned unpaid, regardless of the reason for return.

IX.   Section 229.15 General Disclosure Requirements
A.   229.15(a) Form of Disclosures

1. This paragraph sets forth the general requirements for the disclosures required under Subpart B. All of the disclosures must be given in a clear and conspicuous manner, must be in writing, and, in most cases, must be in a form the customer may keep. A disclosure is in a form that the customer may keep if, for

example, it can be downloaded or printed. For a customer that is not a consumer, a depositary bank satisfies the written-disclosure requirement by sending an electronic disclosure that displays the text and is in a form that the customer may keep, if the customer agrees to such means of disclosure. For a customer who is a consumer, a depositary bank satisfies the written-notice requirement by sending an electronic notice in compliance with the requirements of the Electronic Signatures in Global and National Commerce Act (12 U.S.C. 7001 et seq.), which include obtaining the consumer's affirmative consent to such means of notice. Appendix C of the regulation contains model forms, clauses, and notices to assist banks in preparing disclosures.

2. Disclosures concerning availability must be grouped together and may not contain any information that is not related to the disclosures required by this subpart. Therefore, banks may not intersperse the required disclosures with other account disclosures, and may not include other account information that is not related to their availability policy within the text of the required disclosures. Banks may, however, include information that is related to their availability policies. For example, a bank may inform its customers that, even when the bank has already made funds available for withdrawal, the customer is responsible for any problem with the deposit, such as the return of a deposited check.

3. The regulation does not require that the disclosures be segregated from other account terms and conditions. For example, banks may include the disclosure of their specific availability policy in a booklet or pamphlet that sets out all of the terms and conditions of the bank's accounts. The required disclosures must, however, be grouped together and highlighted or identified in some manner, for example, by use of a separate heading for the disclosures, such as "When Deposits are Available for Withdrawal."

4. A bank may, by agreement or at the consumer's request, provide any disclosure or notice required by subpart B in a language other than English, provided that the bank makes a complete disclosure available in English at the customer's request.

B.   229.15(b) Uniform Reference to Day of Availability

1. This paragraph requires banks to disclose in a uniform manner when deposited funds will be available for withdrawal. Banks must disclose when deposited funds are available for withdrawal by stating the business day on which the customer may begin to withdraw funds. The business day funds will be available must be disclosed as "the _____ business day after" the day of deposit, or substantially similar language. The business day of availability is determined by counting the number of business days starting with the business day following the banking day on which the deposit is received, as determined under § 229.19(a), and ending with the business day on which the customer may begin to withdraw funds. For example, a bank that imposes delays of four intervening business days for nonlocal checks must describe those checks as being available on "the fifth business day after" the day of the deposit.

C.   229.15(c) Multiple Accounts and Multiple Account Holders

1. This paragraph clarifies that banks need not provide multiple disclosures under the regulation. A single disclosure to a customer that holds multiple accounts, or a single disclosure to one of the account holders of a jointly held account, satisfies the disclosure requirements of the regulation.

D.   229.15(d) Dormant or Inactive Accounts

1. This paragraph makes clear that banks need not provide disclosure of their specific availability policies to customers that hold accounts that are either dormant or inactive. The determination that certain accounts are dormant or inactive must be made by the bank. If a bank considers an account dormant or inactive for purposes other than this regulation and no longer provides statements and other mailings to an account for this reason, such an account is considered dormant or inactive for purposes of this regulation.

X.   Section 229.16 Specific Availability Policy Disclosure

A.   229.16(a) General

1. This section describes the information that must be disclosed by banks to comply with §§ 229.17 and 229.18(d), which require that banks furnish notices of their specific policy regarding availability of deposited funds. The disclosure provided by a bank must reflect the availability policy followed by the bank in most cases, even though a bank may in some cases make funds available sooner or impose a longer delay.

COMMENTARY ON REGULATION CC

2.   The disclosure must reflect the policy and practice of the bank regarding availability as to most accounts and most deposits into those accounts. In disclosing the availability policy that it follows in most cases, a bank may provide a single disclosure that reflects one policy to all its transaction account customers, even though some of its customers may receive faster availability than that reflected in the policy disclosure. Thus, a bank need not disclose to some customers that they receive faster availability than indicated in the disclosure. If, however, a bank has a policy of imposing delays in availability on any customers longer than those specified in its disclosure, those customers must receive disclosures that reflect the longer applicable availability periods. A bank may establish different availability policies for different groups of customers, such as customers in a particular geographic area or customers of a particular branch. For purposes of providing a specific availability policy, the bank may allocate customers among groups through good faith use of a reasonable method. A bank may also establish different availability policies for deposits at different locations, such as deposits at a contractual branch.

3.   A bank may disclose that funds are available for withdrawal on a given day notwithstanding the fact that the bank uses the funds to pay checks received before that day. For example, a bank may disclose that its policy is to make funds available from deposits of local checks on the second business day following the day of deposit, even though it may use the deposited funds to pay checks prior to the second business day; the funds used to pay checks in this example are not available for withdrawal until the second business day after deposit because the funds are not available for all uses until the second business day. (See the definition of available for withdrawal in § 229.2(d).)

B.   229.16(b) Content of Specific Policy Disclosure

1.   This paragraph sets forth the items that must be included, as applicable, in a bank's specific availability policy disclosure. The information that must be disclosed by a particular bank will vary considerably depending upon the bank's availability policy. For example, a bank that makes deposited funds available for withdrawal on the business day following the day of deposit need simply disclose that deposited funds will be available for withdrawal on the first business day after the day of deposit, the bank's business days, and when deposits are considered received.

2.   On the other hand, a bank that has a policy of routinely delaying on a blanket basis the time when deposited funds are available for withdrawal would have a more detailed disclosure. Such blanket hold policies might be for the maximum time allowed under the federal law or might be for shorter periods. These banks must disclose the types of deposits that will be subject to delays, how the customer can determine the type of deposit being made, and the day that funds from each type of deposit will be available for withdrawal.

3.   Some banks may have a combination of next-day availability and blanket delays. For example, a bank may provide next-day availability for all deposits except for one or two categories, such as deposits at nonproprietary ATMs and nonlocal personal checks over a specified dollar amount. The bank would describe the categories that are subject to delays in availability and tell the customer when each category would be available for withdrawal, and state that other deposits will be available for withdrawal on the first business day after the day of deposit. Similarly, a bank that provides availability on the second business day for most of its deposits would need to identify the categories of deposits which, under the regulation, are subject to next-day availability and state that all other deposits will be available on the second business day.

4.   Because many banks' availability policies may be complex, a bank must give a brief summary of its policy at the beginning of the disclosure. In addition, the bank must describe any circumstances when actual availability may be longer than the schedules disclosed. Such circumstances would arise, for example, when the bank invokes one of the exceptions set forth in § 229.13 of the regulation, or when the bank delays or extends the time when deposited funds are available for withdrawal up to the time periods allowed by the regulation on a case-by-case basis. Also, a bank that must make certain checks available faster under Appendix B (reduction of schedules for certain nonlocal checks) must state that some check deposits will be available for withdrawal sooner because of special rules and that a list of the pertinent routing numbers is available upon request.

5.   Generally, a bank that distinguishes in its disclosure between local and nonlocal checks based on the routing number on the check must disclose to its customers that certain checks, such as some credit union payable-through drafts, will be treated as local or nonlocal based on the location of the bank by which

1900

they are payable (e.g., the credit union), and not on the basis of the location of the bank whose routing number appears on the check. A bank is not required to provide this disclosure, however, if it makes the proceeds of both local and nonlocal checks available for withdrawal within the time periods required for local checks in §§ 229.12 and 229.13.

6.   The business day cut-off time used by the bank must be disclosed and if some locations have different cut-off times the bank must note this in the disclosure and state the earliest time that might apply. A bank need not list all of the different cut-off times that might apply. If a bank does not have a cut-off time prior to its closing time, the bank need not disclose a cut-off time.

7.   A bank taking advantage of the extended time period for making deposits at nonproprietary ATMs available for withdrawal under § 229.12(f) must explain this in the initial disclosure. In addition, the bank must provide a list (on or with the initial disclosure) of either the bank's proprietary ATMs or those ATMs that are nonproprietary at which customers may make deposits. As an alternative to providing such a list, the bank may label all of its proprietary ATMs with the bank's name and state in the initial disclosure that this has been done. Similarly, a bank taking advantage of the cash withdrawal limitations of § 229.12(d), or the provision in § 229.19(e) allowing holds to be placed on other deposits when a deposit is made or a check is cashed, must explain this in the initial disclosure.

8.   A bank that provides availability based on when the bank generally receives credit for deposited checks need not disclose the time when a check drawn on a specific bank will be available for withdrawal. Instead, the bank may disclose the categories of deposits that must be available on the first business day after the day of deposit (deposits subject to § 229.10) and state the other categories of deposits and the time periods that will be applicable to those deposits. For example, a bank might disclose the four-digit Federal Reserve routing symbol for local checks and indicate that such checks as well as certain nonlocal checks will be available for withdrawal on the first or second business day following the day of deposit, depending on the location of the particular bank on which the check is drawn, and disclose that funds from all other checks will be available on the second or third business day. The bank must also disclose that the customer may request a copy of the bank's detailed schedule that would enable the customer to determine the availability of any check and must provide such schedule upon request. A change in the bank's detailed schedule would not trigger the change in policy disclosure requirement of § 229.18(e).

C.   229.16(c) Longer Delays on a Case-by-Case Basis

1.   Notice in specific policy disclosure.

a.   Banks that make deposited funds available for withdrawal sooner than required by the regulation—for example, providing their customers with immediate or next-day availability for deposited funds—and delay the time when funds are available for withdrawal only from time to time determined on a case-by-case basis, must provide notice of this in their specific availability policy disclosure. This paragraph outlines the requirements for that notice.

b.   In addition to stating what their specific availability policy is in most cases, banks that may delay or extend the time when deposits are available on a case-by-case basis must: state that from time to time funds may be available for withdrawal later than the time periods in their specific policy disclosure, disclose the latest time that a customer may have to wait for deposited funds to be available for withdrawal when a case-by-case hold is placed, state that customers will be notified when availability of a deposit is delayed on a case-by-case basis, and advise customers to ask if they need to be sure of the availability of a particular deposit.

c.   A bank that imposes delays on a case-by-case basis is still subject to the availability requirements of this regulation. If the bank imposes a delay on a particular deposit that is not longer than the availability required by § 229.12 for local and nonlocal checks, the reason for the delay need not be based on the exceptions provided in § 229.13. If the delay exceeds the time periods permitted under § 229.12, however, then it must be based on an exception provided in § 229.13, and the bank must comply with the § 229.13 notice requirements. A bank that imposes delays on a case-by-case basis may avail itself of the one-time notice provisions in § 229.13(g)(2) and (3) for deposits to which those provisions apply.

2.   Notice at time of case-by-case delay.

a.   In addition to including the disclosures required by paragraph (c)(1) of this section in their specific availability policy disclosure, banks that delay or extend the time period when funds are available for withdrawal on a case-by-case basis must give customers a notice when availability of funds from a particular deposit will be delayed or extended beyond the time when deposited funds are generally available for withdrawal. The notice must state that a delay is being imposed and indicate when the funds will be available. In addition, the notice must include the account number, the date of the deposit, and the amount of the deposit being delayed.

b.   If notice of the delay was not given at the time the deposit was made and the bank assesses overdraft or returned check fees on accounts when a case-by-case hold has been placed, the case-by-case hold notice provided to the customer must include a notice concerning overdraft or returned check fees. The notice must state that the customer may be entitled to a refund of any overdraft or returned check fees that result from the deposited funds not being available if the check that was deposited was in fact paid by the payor bank, and explain how to request a refund of any fees. (See § 229.16(c)(3).)

c.   The requirement that the case-by-case hold notice state the day that funds will be made available for withdrawal may be met by stating the date or the number of business days after deposit that the funds will be made available. This requirement is satisfied if the notice provides information sufficient to indicate when funds will be available and the amounts that will be available at those times. For example, for a deposit involving more than one check, the bank need not provide a notice that discloses when funds from each individual item in the deposit will be available for withdrawal. Instead, the bank may provide a total dollar amount for each of the time periods when funds will be available, or provide the customer with an explanation of how to determine the amount of the deposit that will be held and when the held funds will be available for withdrawal.

d.   For deposits made in person to an employee of the depositary bank, the notice generally must be given at the time of the deposit. The notice at the time of the deposit must be given to the person making the deposit, that is, the "depositor." The depositor need not be the customer holding the account. For other deposits, such as deposits received at an ATM, lobby deposit box, night depository, through the mail, or by armored car, notice must be mailed to the customer not later than the close of the business day following the banking day on which the deposit was made. Notice to the customer also may be provided not later than the close of the business day following the banking day on which the deposit was made if the decision to delay availability is made after the time of the deposit.

3.   Overdraft and returned check fees. If a depositary bank delays or extends the time when funds from a deposited check are available for withdrawal on a case-by-case basis and does not provide a written notice to its depositor at the time of deposit, the depositary bank may not assess any overdraft or returned check fees (such as an insufficient funds charge) or charge interest for use of an overdraft line of credit, if the deposited check is paid by the paying bank and these fees would not have occurred had the additional case-by-case delay not been imposed. A bank may assess an overdraft or returned check fee under these circumstances, however, if it provides notice to the customer in the notice required by paragraph (c)(2) of this section that the fee may be subject to refund, and refunds the fee upon the request of the customer when required to do so. The notice must state that the customer may be entitled to a refund of any overdraft or returned check fees that are assessed if the deposited check is paid, and indicate where such requests for a refund of overdraft fees should be directed. Paragraph (c)(3) applies when a bank provides a case-by-case notice in accordance with paragraph (c)(2) and does not apply if the bank has provided an exception hold notice in accordance with § 229.13.

D.   229.16(d) Credit Union Notice of Interest Payment Policy

1.   This paragraph sets forth the special disclosure requirement for credit unions that delay accrual of interest or dividends for all cash and check deposits beyond the date of receiving provisional credit for checks being deposited. (The interest payment requirement is set forth in § 229.14(a).) Such credit unions are required to describe their policy with respect to accrual of interest or dividends on deposits in their specific availability policy disclosure.

COMMENTARY ON REGULATION CC

XI. Section 229.17 Initial Disclosures

A.   This paragraph requires banks to provide a notice of their availability policy to all potential customers prior to opening an account. The requirement of a notice prior to opening an account requires banks to provide disclosures prior to accepting a deposit to open an account. Disclosures must be given at the time the bank accepts an initial deposit regardless of whether the bank has opened the account yet for the customer. If a bank, however, receives a written request by mail from a person asking that an account be opened and the request includes an initial deposit, the bank may open the account with the deposit, provided the bank mails the required disclosures to the customer not later than the business day following the banking day on which the bank receives the deposit. Similarly, if a bank receives a telephone request from a customer asking that an account be opened with a transfer from a separate account of the customer's at the bank, the disclosure may be mailed not later than the business day following the banking day of the request.

XII. Section 229.18 Additional Disclosure Requirements

A.   229.18(a) Deposit Slips

1.   This paragraph requires banks to include a notice on all preprinted deposit slips. The deposit slip notice need only state, somewhere on the front of the deposit slip, that deposits may not be available for immediate withdrawal. The notice is required only on preprinted deposit slips—those printed with the customer's account number and name and furnished by the bank in response to a customer's order to the bank. A bank need not include the notice on deposit slips that are not preprinted and supplied to the customer—such as counter deposit slips—or on those special deposit slips provided to the customer under § 229.10(c). A bank is not responsible for ensuring that the notice appear on deposit slips that the customer does not obtain from or through the bank. This paragraph applies to preprinted deposit slips furnished to customers on or after September 1, 1988.

B.   229.18(b) Locations Where Employees Accept Consumer Deposits

1.   This paragraph describes the statutory requirement that a bank post in each location where its employees accept consumer deposits a notice of its availability policy pertaining to consumer accounts. The notice that is required must specifically state the availability periods for the various deposits that may be made to consumer accounts. The notice need not be posted at each teller window, but the notice must be posted in a place where consumers seeking to make deposits are likely to see it before making their deposits. For example, the notice might be posted at the point where the line forms for teller service in the lobby. The notice is not required at any drive-through teller windows nor is it required at night depository locations, or at locations where consumer deposits are not accepted. A bank that acts as a contractual branch at a particular location must include the availability policy that applies to its own customers but need not include the policy that applies to the customers of the bank for which it is acting as a contractual branch.

C.   229.18(c) Automated Teller Machines

1.   This paragraph sets forth the required notices for ATMs. Paragraph (c)(1) provides that the depositary bank is responsible for posting a notice on all ATMs at which deposits can be made to accounts at the depositary bank. The depositary bank may arrange for a third party, such as the owner or operator of the ATM, to post the notice and indemnify the depositary bank from liability if the depositary bank is liable under § 229.21 for the owner or operator failing to provide the required notice.

2.   The notice may be posted on a sign, shown on the screen, or included on deposit envelopes provided at the ATM. This disclosure must be given before the customer has made the deposit. Therefore, a notice provided on the customer's deposit receipt or appearing on the ATM's screen after the customer has made the deposit would not satisfy this requirement.

3.   Paragraph (c)(2) requires a depositary bank that operates an off-premise ATM from which deposits are removed not more than two times a week to make a disclosure of this fact on the off-premise ATM. The notice must disclose to the customer the days on which deposits made at the ATM will be considered received.

COMMENTARY ON REGULATION CC

D.   229.18(d) Upon Request

1.   This paragraph requires banks to provide written notice of their specific availability policy to any person upon that person's oral or written request. The notice must be sent within a reasonable period of time following receipt of the request.

E.   229.18(e) Changes in Policy

1.   This paragraph requires banks to send notices to their customers when the banks change their availability policies with regard to consumer accounts. A notice may be given in any form as long as it is clear and conspicuous. If the bank gives notice of a change by sending the customer a complete new availability disclosure, the bank must direct the customer to the changed terms in the disclosure by use of a letter or insert, or by highlighting the changed terms in the disclosure.

2.   Generally, a bank must send a notice at least 30 calendar days before implementing any change in its availability policy. If the change results in faster availability of deposits—for example, if the bank changes its availability for nonlocal checks from the fifth business day after deposit to the fourth business day after deposit—the bank need not send advance notice. The bank must, however, send notice of the change no later than 30 calendar days after the change is implemented. A bank is not required to give a notice when there is a change in Appendix B (reduction of schedules for certain nonlocal checks).

3.   A bank that has provided its customers with a list of ATMs under § 229.16(b)(5) shall provide its customers with an updated list of ATMs once a year if there are changes in the list of ATMs previously disclosed to the customers.

XIII.   Section 229.19 Miscellaneous

A.   229.19(a) When Funds Are Considered Deposited

1.   The time funds must be made available for withdrawal under this subpart is determined by the day the deposit is made. This paragraph provides rules to determine the day funds are considered deposited in various circumstances.

2.   Staffed facilities and ATMs. Funds received at a staffed teller station or ATM are considered deposited when received by the teller or placed in the ATM. Funds received at a contractual branch are considered deposited when received by a teller at the contractual branch or deposited into a proprietary ATM of the contractual branch. (See also, Commentary to § 229.10(c) on deposits made to an employee of the depositary bank.) Funds deposited to a deposit box in a bank lobby that is accessible to customers only during regular business hours generally are considered deposited when placed in the lobby box; a bank may, however, treat deposits to lobby boxes the same as deposits to night depositories (as provided in § 229.19(a)(3)), provided a notice appears on the lobby box informing the customer when such funds will be considered deposited.

3.   Mail. Funds mailed to the depositary bank are considered deposited on the banking day they are received by the depositary bank. The funds are received by the depositary bank at the time the mail is delivered to the bank, even if it is initially delivered to a mail room, rather than the check processing area.

4.   Other facilities.

a.   In addition to deposits at staffed facilities, at ATMs, and by mail, funds may be deposited at a facility such as a night depository or a lock box. A night depository is a receptacle for receipt of deposits, typically used by corporate depositors when the branch is closed. Funds deposited at a night depository are considered deposited on the banking day the deposit is removed, and the contents of the deposit are accessible to the depositary bank for processing. For example, some businesses deposit their funds in a locked bag at the night depository late in the evening, and return to the bank the following day to open the bag. Other depositors may have an agreement with their bank that the deposit bag must be opened under the dual control of the bank and the depositor. In these cases, the funds are considered deposited when the customer returns to the bank and opens the deposit bag.

b.   A lock box is a post office box used by a corporation for the collection of bill payments or other check receipts. The depositary bank generally assumes the responsibility for collecting the mail from the lock box, processing the checks, and crediting the corporation for the amount of the deposit. Funds deposited through a lock box arrangement are considered deposited on the day the deposit is removed from the lock box and are accessible to the depositary bank for processing.

5. Certain off-premise ATMs. A special provision is made for certain off-premise ATMs that are not serviced daily. Funds deposited at such an ATM are considered deposited on the day they are removed from the ATM, if the ATM is not serviced more than two times each week. This provision is intended to address the practices of some banks of servicing certain remote ATMs infrequently. If a depositary bank applies this provision with respect to an ATM, a notice must be posted at the ATM informing depositors that funds deposited at the ATM may not be considered deposited until a future day, in accordance with § 229.18.

6. Banking day of deposit.

a. This paragraph also provides that a deposit received on a day that the depositary bank is closed, or after the bank's cut-off hour, may be considered made on the next banking day. Generally, for purposes of the availability schedules of this subpart, a bank may establish a cut-off hour of 2 p.m. or later for receipt of deposits at its head office or branch offices. For receipt of deposits at ATMs, contractual branches, or other off-premise facilities, such as night depositories or lock boxes, the depositary bank may establish a cut-off hour of 12:00 noon or later (either local time of the branch or other location of the depositary bank at which the account is maintained or local time of the ATM, contractual branch, or other off-premise facility). The depositary bank must use the same timing method for establishing the cut-off hour for all ATMs, contractual branches, and other off-premise facilities used by its customers. The choice of cut-off hour must be reflected in the bank's internal procedures, and the bank must inform its customers of the cut-off hour upon request. This earlier cut-off for ATM, contractual branch, or other off-premise deposits is intended to provide greater flexibility in the servicing of these facilities.

b. Different cut-off hours may be established for different types of deposits. For example, a bank may establish a 2 p.m. cut-off for the receipt of check deposits, but a later cut-off for the receipt of wire transfers. Different cut-off hours also may be established for deposits received at different locations. For example, a different cut-off may be established for ATM deposits than for over-the-counter deposits, or for different teller stations at the same branch. With the exception of the 12 noon cut-off for deposits at ATMs and off-premise facilities, no cut-off hour for receipt of deposits for purposes of this subpart can be established earlier than 2 p.m.

c. A bank is not required to remain open until 2 p.m. If a bank closes before 2 p.m., deposits received after the closing may be considered deposited on the next banking day. Further, as § 229.2(f) defines the term banking day as the portion of a business day on which a bank is open to the public for substantially all of its banking functions, a day, or a portion of a day, is not necessarily a banking day merely because the bank is open for only limited functions, such as keeping drive-in or walk-up teller windows open, when the rest of the bank is closed to the public. For example, a banking office that usually provides a full range of banking services may close at 12 noon but leave a drive-in teller window open for the limited purpose of receiving deposits and making cash withdrawals. Under those circumstances, the bank is considered closed and may consider deposits received after 12 noon as having been received on the next banking day. The fact that a bank may reopen for substantially all of its banking functions after 2 p.m., or that it continues its back office operations throughout the day, would not affect this result. A bank may not, however, close individual teller stations and reopen them for next-day's business before 2 p.m. during a banking day.

B. 229.19(b) Availability at Start of Business Day

1. If funds must be made available for withdrawal on a business day, the funds must be available for withdrawal by the later of 9 a.m. or the time the depositary bank's teller facilities, including ATMs, are available for customer account withdrawals, except under the special rule for cash withdrawals set forth in § 229.12(d). Thus, if a bank has no ATMs and its branch facilities are available for customer transactions beginning at 10 a.m., funds must be available for customer withdrawal beginning at 10 a.m. If the bank has ATMs that are available 24 hours a day, rather than establishing 12:01 a.m. as the start of the business day, this paragraph sets 9 a.m. as the start of the day with respect to ATM withdrawals. The Board believes that this rule provides banks with sufficient time to update their accounting systems to reflect the available funds in customer accounts for that day.

COMMENTARY ON REGULATION CC

2.   The start of business is determined by the local time of the branch or other location of the depositary bank at which the account is maintained. For example, if funds in a customer's account at a west coast bank are first made available for withdrawal at the start of business on a given day, and the customer attempts to withdraw the funds at an east coast ATM, the depositary bank is not required to make the funds available until 9 a.m. west coast time (12 noon east coast time).

C.   229.19(c) Effect on Policies of Depositary Bank

1.   This subpart establishes the maximum hold that may be placed on customer deposits. A depositary bank may provide availability to its customers in a shorter time than prescribed in this subpart. A depositary bank also may adopt different funds availability policies for different segments of its customer base, as long as each policy meets the schedules in the regulation. For example, a bank may differentiate between its corporate and consumer customers, or may adopt different policies for its consumer customers based on whether a customer has an overdraft line of credit associated with the account.

2.   This regulation does not affect a depositary bank's right to accept or reject a check for deposit, to charge back the customer's account based on a returned check or notice of nonpayment, or to claim a refund for any credit provided to the customer. For example, even if a check is returned or a notice of nonpayment is received after the time by which funds must be made available for withdrawal in accordance with this regulation, the depositary bank may charge back the customer's account for the full amount of the check. (See § 229.33(d) and Commentary.)

3.   Nothing in the regulation requires a depositary bank to have facilities open for customers to make withdrawals at specified times or on specified days. For example, even though the special cash withdrawal rule set forth in § 229.12(d) states that a bank must make up to $400 available for cash withdrawals no later than 5 p.m. on specific business days, if a bank does not participate in an ATM system and does not have any teller windows open at or after 5 p.m., the bank need not join an ATM system or keep offices open. In this case, the bank complies with this rule if the funds that are required to be available for cash withdrawal at 5 p.m. on a particular day are available for withdrawal at the start of business on the following day. Similarly, if a depositary bank is closed for customer transactions, including ATMs, on a day funds must be made available for withdrawal, the regulation does not require the bank to open.

4.   The special cash withdrawal rule in the EFA Act recognizes that the $400 that must be made available for cash withdrawal by 5 p.m. on the day specified in the schedule may exceed a bank's daily ATM cash withdrawal limit and explicitly provides that the EFA Act does not supersede a bank's policy in this regard. As a result, if a bank has a policy of limiting cash withdrawals from automated teller machines to $250 per day, the regulation would not require that the bank dispense $400 of the proceeds of the customer's deposit that must be made available for cash withdrawal on that day.

5.   Even though the EFA Act clearly provides that the bank's ATM withdrawal limit is not superseded by the federal availability rules on the day funds must first be made available, the EFA Act does not specifically permit banks to limit cash withdrawals at ATMs on subsequent days when the entire amount of the deposit must be made available for withdrawal. The Board believes that the rationale behind the EFA Act's provision that a bank's ATM withdrawal limit is not superseded by the requirement that funds be made available for cash withdrawal applies on subsequent days. Nothing in the regulation prohibits a depositary bank from establishing ATM cash withdrawal limits that vary among customers of the bank, as long as the limit is not dependent on the length of time funds have been in the customer's account (provided that the permissible hold has expired).

6.   Some small banks, particularly credit unions, due to lack of secure facilities, keep no cash on their premises and hence offer no cash withdrawal capability to their customers. Other banks limit the amount of cash on their premises due to bonding requirements or cost factors, and consequently reserve the right to limit the amount of cash each customer can withdraw over-the-counter on a given day. For example, some banks require advance notice for large cash withdrawals in order to limit the amount of cash needed to be maintained on hand at any time.

7.   Nothing in the regulation is intended to prohibit a bank from limiting the amount of cash that may be withdrawn at a staffed teller station if the bank has a policy limiting the amount of cash that may be withdrawn, and if that policy is applied equally to all customers of the bank, is based on security,

operating, or bonding requirements, and is not dependent on the length of time the funds have been in the customer's account (as long as the permissible hold has expired). The regulation, however, does not authorize such policies if they are otherwise prohibited by statutory, regulatory, or common law.

D. 229.19(d) Use of Calculated Availability

1. A depositary bank may provide availability to its nonconsumer accounts on a calculated availability basis. Under calculated availability, a specified percentage of funds from check deposits may be made available to the customer on the next business day, with the remaining percentage deferred until subsequent days. The determination of the percentage of deposited funds that will be made available each day is based on the customer's typical deposit mix as determined by a sample of the customer's deposits. Use of calculated availability is permitted only if, on average, the availability terms that result from the sample are equivalent to or more prompt than the requirements of this subpart.

E. 229.19(e) Holds on Other Funds

1. Section 607(d) of the EFA Act (12 U.S.C. 4006(d)) provides that once funds are available for withdrawal under the EFA Act, such funds shall not be frozen solely due to the subsequent deposit of additional checks that are not yet available for withdrawal. This provision of the EFA Act is designed to prevent evasion of the EFA Act's availability requirements.

2. This paragraph clarifies that if a customer deposits a check in an account (as defined in § 229.2(a)), the bank may not place a hold on any of the customer's funds so that the funds that are held exceed the amount of the check deposited or the total amount of funds held are not made available for withdrawal within the times required in this subpart. For example, if a bank places a hold on funds in a customer's non transaction account, rather than a transaction account, for deposits made to the customer's transaction account, the bank may place such a hold only to the extent that the funds held do not exceed the amount of the deposit and the length of the hold does not exceed the time periods permitted by this regulation.

3. These restrictions also apply to holds placed on funds in a customer's account (as defined in § 229.2(a)) if a customer cashes a check at a bank (other than a check drawn on that bank) over the counter. The regulation does not prohibit holds that may be placed on other funds of the customer for checks cashed over the counter, to the extent that the transaction does not involve a deposit to an account. A bank may not, however, place a hold on any account when an "on us" check is cashed over the counter. "On us" checks are considered finally paid when cashed (see U.C.C. 4–215(a)(1)). When a customer cashes a check over the counter and the bank places a hold on an account of the customer, the bank must give whatever notice would have been required under §§ 229.13 or 229.16 had the check been deposited in the account.

F. 229.19(f) Employee Training and Compliance

1. The EFA Act requires banks to take such actions as may be necessary to inform fully each employee that performs duties subject to the EFA Act of the requirements of the EFA Act, and to establish and maintain procedures reasonably designed to assure and monitor employee compliance with such requirements.

2. This paragraph requires a bank to establish procedures to ensure compliance with these requirements and provide these procedures to the employees responsible for carrying them out.

G. 229.19(g) Effect of Merger Transaction

1. After banks merge, there is often a period of adjustment before their operations are consolidated. This paragraph accommodates this adjustment period by allowing merged banks to be treated as separate banks for purposes of this subpart for a period of up to one year after consummation of the merger transaction, except that a customer of any bank that is a party to the transaction that has an established account with that bank may not be treated as a new account holder for any other party to the transaction for purposes of the new account exception of § 229.13(a), and a deposit in any branch of the merged bank is considered deposited in the bank for purposes of the availability schedules in accordance with § 229.19(a).

COMMENTARY ON REGULATION CC

2.   This rule affects the status of the combined entity in several areas. For example, this rule would affect when an ATM is a proprietary ATM (§ 229.2(aa) and § 229.12(b)) and when a check is considered drawn on a branch of the depositary bank (§ 229.10(c)(1)(vi)).

3.   Merger transaction is defined in § 229.2(t).

XIV.   Section 229.20 Relation to State Law
A.   229.20(a) In General

1.   Several states have enacted laws that govern when banks in those states must make funds available to their customers. The EFA Act provides that any state law in effect on September 1, 1989, that provides that funds be made available in a shorter period of time than provided in this regulation, will supersede the time periods in the EFA Act and the regulation. The Conference Report on the EFA Act clarifies this provision by stating that any state law enacted on or before September 1, 1989, may supersede federal law to the extent that the law relates to the time funds must be made available for withdrawal. H.R. Rep. No. 261, 100th Cong. 1st Sess. at 182 (1987).

2.   Thus, if a state had wished to adopt a law governing funds availability, it had to have made that law effective on or before September 1, 1989. Laws adopted after that date do not supersede federal law, even if they provide for shorter availability periods than are provided under federal law. If a state that had a law governing funds availability in effect before September 1, 1989, amended its law after that date, the amendment would not supersede federal law, but an amendment deleting a state requirement would be effective.

3.   If a state provides for a shorter hold for a certain category of checks than is provided for under federal law, that state requirement will supersede the federal provision. For example, most state laws base some hold periods on whether the check being deposited is drawn on an in-state or out-of-state bank. If a state contains more than one check processing region, the state's hold period for in-state checks may be shorter than the federal maximum hold period for nonlocal checks. Thus, the state schedule would supersede the federal schedule to the extent that it applies to in-state, nonlocal checks.

4.   The EFA Act also provides that any state law that provides for availability in a shorter period of time than required by federal law is applicable to all federally insured institutions in that state, including federally chartered institutions. If a state law provides shorter availability only for deposits in accounts in certain categories of banks, such as commercial banks, the superseding state law continues to apply only to those categories of banks, rather than to all federally insured banks in the state.

B.   229.20(b) Preemption of Inconsistent Law

1.   This paragraph reflects the statutory provision that other provisions of state law that are inconsistent with federal law are preempted. Preemption does not require a determination by the Board to be effective.

C.   229.20(c) Standards for Preemption

1.   This section describes the standards the Board uses in making determinations on whether federal law will preempt state laws governing funds availability. A provision of state law is considered inconsistent with federal law if it permits a depositary bank to make funds available to a customer in a longer period of time than the maximum period permitted by the EFA Act and this regulation. For example, a state law that permits a hold of four business days or longer for local checks permits a hold that is longer than that permitted under the EFA Act and this regulation, and therefore is inconsistent and preempted. State availability schedules that provide for availability in a shorter period of time than required under Regulation CC supersede the federal schedule.

2.   Under a state law, some categories of deposits could be available for withdrawal sooner or later than the time required by this subpart, depending on the composition of the deposit. For example, the EFA Act and this regulation (§ 229.10(c)(1)(vii)) require next-day availability for the first $100 of the aggregate deposit of local or nonlocal checks on any day, and a state law could require next-day availability for any check of $100 or less that is deposited. Under the EFA Act and this regulation, if either one $150 check or three $50 checks are deposited on a given day, $100 must be made available for withdrawal on the next

business day, and $50 must be made available in accordance with the local or nonlocal schedule. Under the state law, however, the two deposits would be subject to different availability rules. In the first case, none of the proceeds of the deposit would be subject to next-day availability; in the second case, the entire proceeds of the deposit would be subject to next-day availability. In this example, because the state law would, in some situations, permit a hold longer than the maximum permitted by the EFA Act, this provision of state law is inconsistent and preempted in its entirety.

3. In addition to the differences between state and federal availability schedules, a number of state laws contain exceptions to the state availability schedules that are different from those provided under the EFA Act and this regulation. The state exceptions continue to apply only in those cases where the state schedule is shorter than or equal to the federal schedule, and then only up to the limit permitted by the Regulation CC schedule. Where a deposit is subject to a state exception under a state schedule that is not preempted by Regulation CC and is also subject to a federal exception, the hold on the deposit cannot exceed the hold permissible under the federal exception in accordance with Regulation CC. In such cases, only one exception notice is required, in accordance with § 229.13(g). This notice need only include the applicable federal exception as the reason the exception was invoked. For those categories of checks for which the state schedule is preempted by the federal schedule, only the federal exceptions may be used.

4. State laws that provide maximum availability periods for categories of deposits that are not covered by the EFA Act would not be preempted. Thus, state funds availability laws that apply to funds in time and savings deposits are not affected by the EFA Act or this regulation. In addition, the availability schedules of several states apply to "items" deposited to an account. The term items may encompass deposits, such as nonnegotiable instruments, that are not subject to the Regulation CC availability schedules. Deposits that are not covered by Regulation CC continue to be subject to the state availability schedules. State laws that provide maximum availability periods for categories of institutions that are not covered by the EFA Act also would not be preempted. For example, a state law that governs money market mutual funds would not be affected by the EFA Act or this regulation.

5. Generally, state rules governing the disclosure or notice of availability policies applicable to accounts also are preempted, if they are different from the federal rules. Nevertheless, a state law requiring disclosure of funds availability policies that apply to deposits other than "accounts," such as savings or time deposits, are not inconsistent with the EFA Act and this subpart. Banks in these states would have to follow the state disclosure rules for these deposits.

D. 229.20(d) Preemption Determinations

1. The Board may issue preemption determinations upon the request of an interested party in a state. The determinations will relate only to the provisions of Subparts A and B; generally the Board will not issue individual preemption determinations regarding the relation of state U.C.C. provisions to the requirements of Subpart C.

E. 229.20(e) Procedures for Preemption Determinations

1. This provision sets forth the information that must be included in a request by an interested party for a preemption determination by the Board.

XV. Section 229.21 Civil Liability

A. 229.21(a) Civil Liability

1. This paragraph sets forth the statutory penalties for failure to comply with the requirements of this subpart. These penalties apply to provisions of state law that supersede provisions of this regulation, such as requirements that funds deposited in accounts at banks be made available more promptly than required by this regulation, but they do not apply to other provisions of state law. (See Commentary to § 229.20.)

B. 229.21(b) Class Action Awards

1. This paragraph sets forth the provision in the EFA Act concerning the factors that should be considered by the court in establishing the amount of a class action award.

COMMENTARY ON REGULATION CC

C.   229.21(c) Bona Fide Errors

1.   A bank is shielded from liability under this section for a violation of a requirement of this subpart if it can demonstrate, by a preponderance of the evidence, that the violation resulted from a bona fide error and that it maintains procedures designed to avoid such errors. For example, a bank may make a bona fide error if it fails to give next-day availability on a check drawn on the Treasury because the bank's computer system malfunctions in a way that prevents the bank from updating its customer's account; or if it fails to identify whether a payable-through check is a local or nonlocal check despite procedures designed to make this determination accurately.

D.   229.21(d) Jurisdiction

1.   The EFA Act confers subject matter jurisdiction on courts of competent jurisdiction and provides a time limit for civil actions for violations of this subpart.

E.   229.21(e) Reliance on Board Rulings

1.   This provision shields banks from civil liability if they act in good faith in reliance on any rule, regulation, model form, notice, or clause (if the disclosure actually corresponds to the bank's availability policy), or interpretation of the Board, even if it were subsequently determined to be invalid. Banks may rely on this Commentary, which is issued as an official Board interpretation, as well as on the regulation itself.

F.   229.21(f) Exclusions

1.   This provision clarifies that liability under this section does not apply to violations of the requirements of Subpart C of this regulation, or to actions for wrongful dishonor of a check by a paying bank's customer.

G.   229.21(g) Record Retention

1.   Banks must keep records to show compliance with the requirements of this subpart for at least two years. This record retention period is extended in the case of civil actions and enforcement proceedings. Generally, a bank is not required to retain records showing that it actually has given disclosures or notices required by this subpart to each customer, but it must retain evidence demonstrating that its procedures reasonably ensure the customers' receipt of the required disclosures and notices. A bank must, however, retain a copy of each notice provided pursuant to its use of the reasonable cause exception under § 229.13(g) as well as a brief description of the facts giving rise to the availability of that exception.

XVI.   Section 229.30 Paying Bank's Responsibility for Return of Checks

A.   229.30(a) Return of Checks

1.   This section requires a paying bank (which, for purposes of Subpart C, may include a payable-through and payable-at bank; see § 229.2(z)) that determines not to pay a check to return the check expeditiously. Generally, a check is returned expeditiously if the return process is as fast as the forward collection process. This paragraph provides two standards for expeditious return, the "two-day/four-day" test, and the "forward collection" test.

2.   Under the "two-day/four-day" test, if a check is returned such that it would normally be received by the depositary bank two business days after presentment where both the paying and depositary banks are located in the same check processing region or four business days after presentment where the paying and depositary banks are not located in the same check processing region, the check is considered returned expeditiously. In certain limited cases, however, these times are shorter than the time it would normally take a forward collection check deposited in the paying bank and payable by the depositary bank to be collected. Therefore, the Board has included a "forward collection" test, whereby a check is nonetheless considered to be returned expeditiously if the paying bank uses transportation methods and banks for return comparable to those used for forward collection checks, even if the check is not received by the depositary banks within the two-day or four-day period.

COMMENTARY ON REGULATION CC

3.   Two-day/four-day test.

a.   Under the first test, a paying bank must return the check so that the check would normally be received by the depositary bank within specified times, depending on whether or not the paying and depositary banks are located in the same check processing region.

b.   Where both banks are located in the same check processing region, a check is returned expeditiously if it is returned to the depositary bank by 4:00 p.m. (local time of the depositary bank) of the second business day after the banking day on which the check was presented to the paying bank. For example, a check presented on Monday to a paying bank must be returned to a depositary bank located in the same check processing region by 4 p.m. on Wednesday. For a paying bank that is located in a different check processing region than the depositary bank, the deadline to complete return is 4 p.m. (local time of the depositary bank) of the fourth business day after the banking day on which the check was presented to the paying bank. For example, a check presented to such a paying bank on Monday must be returned to the depositary bank by 4:00 p.m. on Friday.

c.   This two-day/four-day test does not necessarily require actual receipt of the check by the depositary bank within these times. Rather, the paying bank must send the check so that the check would normally be received by the depositary bank within the specified time. Thus, the paying bank is not responsible for unforeseeable delays in the return of the check, such as transportation delays.

d.   Often, returned checks will be delivered to the depositary bank together with forward collection checks. Where the last day on which a check could be delivered to a depositary bank under this two-day/four-day test is not a banking day for the depositary bank, a returning bank might not schedule delivery of forward collection checks to the depositary bank on that day. Further, the depositary bank may not process checks on that day. Consequently, if the last day of the time limit is not a banking day for the depositary bank, the check may be delivered to the depositary bank before the close of the depositary bank's next banking day and the return will still be considered expeditious. Ordinarily, this extension of time will allow the returned checks to be delivered with the next shipment of forward collection checks destined for the depositary bank.

e.   The times specified in this two-day/four-day test are based on estimated forward collection times, but take into account the particular difficulties that may be encountered in handling returned checks. It is anticipated that the normal process for forward collection of a check coupled with these return requirements will frequently result in the return of checks before the proceeds of nonlocal checks, other than those covered by § 229.10(c), must be made available for withdrawal.

f.   Under this two-day/four-day test, no particular means of returning checks is required, thus providing flexibility to paying banks in selecting means of return. The Board anticipates that paying banks will often use returning banks (see § 229.31) as their agents to return checks to depositary banks. A paying bank may rely on the availability schedule of the returning bank it uses in determining whether the returned check would "normally" be returned within the required time under this two-day/four-day test, unless the paying bank has reason to believe that these schedules do not reflect the actual time for return of a check.

4.   Forward collection test.

a.   Under the second, "forward collection," test, a paying bank returns a check expeditiously if it returns a check by means as swift as the means similarly situated banks would use for the forward collection of a check drawn on the depositary bank.

b.   Generally, the paying bank would satisfy the "forward collection" test if it uses a transportation method and collection path for return comparable to that used for forward collection, provided that the returning bank selected to process the return agrees to handle the returned check under the standards for expeditious return for returning banks under § 229.31(a). This test allows many paying banks a simple means of expeditious return of checks and takes into account the longer time for return that will be required by banks that do not have ready access to direct courier transportation.

c.   The paying bank's normal method of sending a check for forward collection would not be expeditious, however, if it is materially slower than that of other banks of similar size and with similar check handling activity in its community.

d.   Under the "forward collection" test, a paying bank must handle, route, and transport a returned check in a manner designed to be at least as fast as a similarly situated bank would collect a forward collection check (1) of similar amount, (2) drawn on the depositary bank, and (3) received for deposit by a branch of the paying bank or a similarly situated bank by noon on the banking day following the banking day of presentment of the returned check.

e.   This test refers to similarly situated banks to indicate a general community standard. In the case of a paying bank (other than a Federal Reserve Bank), a similarly situated bank is a bank of similar asset size, in the same community, and with similar check handling activity as the paying bank. (See § 229.2(ee).) A paying bank has similar check handling activity to other banks that handle similar volumes of checks for collection.

f.   Under the forward collection test, banks that use means of handling returned checks that are less efficient than the means used by similarly situated banks must improve their procedures. On the other hand, a bank with highly efficient means of collecting checks drawn on a particular bank, such as a direct presentment of checks to a bank in a remote community, is not required to use that means for returned checks, i.e. direct return, if similarly situated banks do not present checks directly to that depositary bank.

5.   Examples.

a.   If a check is presented to a paying bank on Monday and the depositary bank and the paying bank are participants in the same clearinghouse, the paying bank should arrange to have the returned check received by the depositary bank by Wednesday. This would be the same day the paying bank would deliver a forward collection check to the depositary bank if the paying bank received the deposit by noon on Tuesday.

b.   i. If a check is presented to a paying bank on Monday and the paying bank would normally collect checks drawn on the depositary bank by sending them to a correspondent or a Federal Reserve Bank by courier, the paying bank could send the returned check to its correspondent or Federal Reserve Bank, provided that the correspondent has agreed to handle returned checks expeditiously under § 229.31(a). (All Federal Reserve Banks agree to handle returned checks expeditiously.)

ii.   The paying bank must deliver the returned check to the correspondent or Federal Reserve Bank by the correspondent's or Federal Reserve Bank's appropriate cut-off hour. The appropriate cut-off hour is the cut-off hour for returned checks that corresponds to the cut-off hour for forward collection checks drawn on the depositary bank that would normally be used by the paying bank or a similarly situated bank. A returned check cut-off hour corresponds to a forward collection cut-off hour if it provides for the same or faster availability for checks destined for the same depositary banks.

iii.   In this example, delivery to the correspondent or a Federal Reserve Bank by the appropriate cut-off hour satisfies the paying bank's duty, even if use of the correspondent or Federal Reserve Bank is not the most expeditious means of returning the check. Thus, a paying bank may send a local returned check to a correspondent instead of a Federal Reserve Bank, even if the correspondent then sends the returned check to a Federal Reserve Bank the following day as a qualified returned check. Where the paying bank delivers forward collection checks by courier to the correspondent or the Federal Reserve Bank, mailing returned checks to the correspondent or Federal Reserve Bank would not satisfy the forward collection test.

iv.   If a paying bank ordinarily mails its forward collection checks to its correspondent or Federal Reserve Bank in order to avoid the costs of a courier delivery, but similarly situated banks use a courier to deliver forward collection checks to their correspondent or Federal Reserve Bank, the paying bank must send its returned checks by courier to meet the forward collection test.

c.   If a paying bank normally sends its forward collection checks directly to the depositary bank, which is located in another community, but similarly situated banks send forward collection checks drawn on the depositary bank to a correspondent or a Federal Reserve Bank, the paying bank would not have to send returned checks directly to the depositary bank, but could send them to a correspondent or a Federal Reserve Bank.

d. The dollar amount of the returned check has a bearing on how it must be returned. If the paying bank and similarly situated banks present large-dollar checks drawn on the depositary bank directly to the depositary bank, but use a Federal Reserve Bank or a correspondent to collect small-dollar checks, generally the paying bank would be required to send its large-dollar returns directly to the depositary bank (or through a returning bank, if the checks are returned as quickly), but could use a Federal Reserve Bank or a correspondent for its small-dollar returns.

6. Choice of returning bank. In meeting the requirements of the forward collection test, the paying bank is responsible for its own actions, but not for those of the depositary bank or returning banks. (This is analogous to the responsibility of collecting banks under U.C.C. 4–202(c).) For example, if the paying bank starts the return of the check in a timely manner but return is delayed by a returning bank (including delay to create a qualified returned check), generally the paying bank has met its requirements. (See § 229.38.) If, however, the paying bank selects a returning bank that the paying bank should know is not capable of meeting its return requirements, the paying bank will not have met its obligation of exercising ordinary care in selecting intermediaries to return the check. The paying bank is free to use a method of return, other than its method of forward collection, as long as the alternate method results in delivery of the returned check to the depositary bank as quickly as the forward collection of a check drawn on the depositary bank or, where the returning bank takes a day to create a qualified returned check under § 229.31(a), one day later than the forward collection time. If a paying bank returns a check on its banking day of receipt without settling for the check, as permitted under U.C.C. 4–302(a), and receives settlement for the returned check from a returning bank, it must promptly pay the amount of the check to the collecting bank from which it received the check.

7. Qualified returned checks. Although paying banks may wish to prepare qualified returned checks because they will be handled at a lower cost by returning banks, the one business day extension provided to returning banks is not available to paying banks because of the longer time that a paying bank has to dispatch the check. Normally, paying banks will be able to convert a check to a qualified returned check at any time after the determination is made to return the check until late in the day following presentment, while a returning bank may receive returned checks late on one day and be expected to dispatch them early the next morning. A check that is converted to a qualified returned check must be encoded in accordance with ANS X9.13 for original checks or ANS X9.100–140 for substitute checks.

8. Routing of returned checks.

a. In effect, under either test, the paying bank acts as an agent or subagent of the depositary bank in selecting a means of return. Under § 229.30(a), a paying bank is authorized to route the returned check in a variety of ways:

i. It may send the returned check directly to the depositary bank by courier or other means of delivery, bypassing returning banks; or

ii. It may send the returned check to any returning bank agreeing to handle the returned check for expeditious return to the depositary bank under § 229.31(a), regardless of whether or not the returning bank handled the check for forward collection.

b. If the paying bank elects to return the check directly to the depositary bank, it is not necessarily required to return the check to the branch of first deposit. The check may be returned to the depositary bank at any location permitted under § 229.32(a).

9. Midnight deadline.

a. Except for the extension permitted by § 229.30(c), discussed below, this section does not relieve a paying bank from the requirement for timely return (i.e., midnight deadline) under U.C.C. 4–301 and 4–302, which continue to apply. Under U.C.C. 4–302, a paying bank is "accountable" for the amount of a demand item, other than a documentary draft, if it does not pay or return the item or send notice of dishonor by its midnight deadline. Under U.C.C. 3–418(c) and 4–215(a), late return constitutes payment and would be final in favor of a holder in due course or a person who has in good faith changed his position in reliance on the payment. Thus, retaining this requirement gives the paying bank an additional incentive to make a prompt return.

b.   The expeditious return requirement applies to a paying bank that determines not to pay a check. This requirement applies to a payable-through or a payable-at bank that is defined as a paying bank (see § 229.2(z)) and that returns a check. This requirement begins when the payable-through or payable-at bank receives the check during forward collection, not when the payor returns the check to the payable-through or payable-at bank. Nevertheless, a check sent for payment or collection to a payable-through or payable-at bank is not considered to be drawn on that bank for purposes of the midnight deadline provision of U.C.C. 4–301. (See discussion of § 229.36(a).)

c.   The liability section of this subpart (§ 229.38) provides that a paying bank is not subject to both "accountability" for missing the midnight deadline under the U.C.C. and liability for missing the timeliness requirements of this regulation. Also, a paying bank is not responsible for failure to make expeditious return to a party that has breached a presentment warranty under U.C.C. 4–208, notwithstanding that the paying bank has returned the check. (See Commentary to § 229.33(a).)

10.   U.C.C. provisions affected. This paragraph directly affects the following provisions of the U.C.C., and may affect other sections or provisions:

a.   Section 4–301(d), in that instead of returning a check through a clearinghouse or to the presenting bank, a paying bank may send a returned check to the depositary bank or to a returning bank.

b.   Section 4–301(a), in that time limits specified in that section may be affected by the additional requirement to make an expeditious return and in that settlement for returned checks is made under § 229.31(c), not by revocation of settlement.

B.   229.30(b) Unidentifiable Depositary Bank

1.   In some cases, a paying bank will be unable to identify the depositary bank through the use of ordinary care and good faith. The Board expects that these cases will be unusual as skilled return clerks will readily identify the depositary bank from the depositary bank indorsement required under § 229.35 and Appendix D. In cases where the paying bank is unable to identify the depositary bank, the paying bank may, in accordance with § 229.30(a), send the returned check to a returning bank that agrees to handle the returned check for expeditious return to the depositary bank under § 229.31(a). The returning bank may be better able to identify the depositary bank.

2.   In the alternative, the paying bank may send the check back up the path used for forward collection of the check. The presenting bank and prior collecting banks normally will be able to trace the collection path of the check through the use of their internal records in conjunction with the indorsements on the returned check. In these limited cases, the paying bank may send such a returned check to any bank that handled the check for forward collection, even if that bank does not agree to handle the returned check for expeditious return to the depositary bank under § 229.31(a). A paying bank returning a check under this paragraph to a bank that has not agreed to handle the check expeditiously must advise that bank that it is unable to identify the depositary bank. This advice must be conspicuous, such as a stamp on each check for which the depositary bank is unknown if such checks are commingled with other returned checks, or, if such checks are sent in a separate cash letter, by one notice on the cash letter. This information will warn the bank that this check will require special research and handling in accordance with § 229.31(b). The returned check may not be prepared for automated return. The return of a check to a bank that handled the check for forward collection is consistent with § 229.35(b), which requires a bank handling a check to take up the check it is has not been paid.

3.   The sending of a check to a bank that handled the check for forward collection under this paragraph is not subject to the requirements for expeditious return by the paying bank. Often, the paying bank will not have courier or other expeditious means of transportation to the collecting or presenting bank. Although the lack of a requirement of expeditious return will create risks for the depositary bank, in many cases the inability to identify the depositary bank will be due to the depositary bank's, or a collecting bank's, failure to use the indorsement required by § 229.35(a) and Appendix D. If the depositary bank failed to use the proper indorsement, it should bear the risks of less than expeditious return. Similarly, where the inability to identify the depositary bank is due to indorsements or other information placed on the back of the check by the depositary bank's customer or other prior indorser, the depositary bank should bear the risk that it cannot charge a returned check back to that customer. Where the inability to identify the

depositary bank is due to subsequent indorsements of collecting banks, these collecting banks may be liable for a loss incurred by the depositary bank due to less than expeditious return of a check; those banks therefore have an incentive to return checks sent to them under this paragraph quickly.

4.   This paragraph does not relieve a paying bank from the liability for the lack of expeditious return in cases where the paying bank is itself responsible for the inability to identify the depositary bank, such as when the paying bank's customer has used a check with printing or other material on the back in the area reserved for the depositary bank's indorsement, making the indorsement unreadable. (See § 229.38(d).)

5.   A paying bank's return under this paragraph is also subject to its midnight deadline under U.C.C. 4–301, Regulation J (if the check is returned through a Federal Reserve Bank), and the exception provided in § 229.30(c). A paying bank also may send a check to a prior collecting bank to make a claim against that bank under § 229.35(b) where the depositary bank is insolvent or in other cases as provided in § 229.35(b). Finally, a paying bank may make a claim against a prior collecting bank based on a breach of warranty under U.C.C. 4–208.

C.   229.30(c) Extension of Deadline

1.   This paragraph permits extension of the deadlines for returning a check for which the paying bank previously has settled (generally midnight of the banking day following the banking day on which the check is received by the paying bank) and for returning a check without settling for it (generally midnight of the banking day on which the check is received by the paying bank, or such other time provided by § 210.9 of Regulation J (12 CFR part 210) or § 229.36(f)(2) of this part), but not of the duty of expeditious return, in two circumstances:

a.   A paying bank may have a courier that leaves after midnight (or after any other applicable deadline) to deliver its forward-collection checks. This paragraph removes the constraint of the midnight deadline for returned checks if the returned check reaches the receiving bank on or before the receiving bank's next banking day following the otherwise applicable deadline by the earlier of the close of that banking day or a cutoff hour of 2 p.m. or later set by the receiving bank under U.C.C. 4–108. The extension also applies if the check reaches the bank to which it is sent later than the time described in the previous sentence if highly expeditious means of transportation are used. For example, a West Coast paying bank may use this further extension to ship a returned check by air courier directly to an East Coast returning bank even if the check arrives after the returning bank's cutoff hour. This paragraph applies to the extension of all midnight deadlines except Saturday midnight deadlines (see paragraph XVI.C.1.b of this appendix).

b.   A paying bank may observe a banking day, as defined in the applicable U.C.C., on a Saturday, which is not a business day and therefore not a banking day under Regulation CC. In such a case, the U.C.C. deadline for returning checks received and settled for on Friday, or for returning checks received on Saturday without settling for them, might require the bank to return the checks by midnight Saturday. However, the bank may not have couriers leaving on Saturday to carry returned checks, and even if it did, the returning or depositary bank to which the returned checks were sent might not be open until Sunday night or Monday morning to receive and process the checks. This paragraph extends the midnight deadline if the returned checks reach the returning bank by a cut-off hour (usually on Sunday night or Monday morning) that permits processing during its next processing cycle or reach the depositary bank by the cut-off hour on its next banking day following the Saturday midnight deadline. This paragraph applies exclusively to the extension of Saturday midnight deadlines.

2.   The time limits that are extended in each case are the paying bank's midnight deadline for returning a check for which it has already settled and the paying bank's deadline for returning a check without settling for it in U.C.C. 4–301 and 4–302, §§ 210.9 and 210.12 of Regulation J (12 CFR 210.9 and 210.12), and § 229.36(f)(2) of this part. As these extensions are designed to speed (§ 229.30(c)(1)), or at least not slow (§ 229.30(c)(2)), the overall return of checks, no modification or extension of the expeditious return requirements in § 229.30(a) is required.

3.   The paying bank satisfies its midnight or other return deadline by dispatching returned checks to another bank by courier, including a courier under contract with the paying bank, prior to expiration of the deadline.

COMMENTARY ON REGULATION CC

4.   This paragraph directly affects U.C.C. 4–301 and 4–302 and §§ 210.9 and 210.12 of Regulation J (12 CFR 210.9 and 210.12) to the extent that this paragraph applies by its terms, and may affect other provisions.

D.   229.30(d) Identification of Returned Check

1.   The reason for the return must be clearly indicated. A check is identified as a returned check if the front of that check indicates the reason for return, even though it does not specifically state that the check is a returned check. A reason such as "Refer to Maker" is permissible in appropriate cases. If the returned check is a substitute check, the reason for return must be placed within the image of the original check that appears on the front of the substitute check so that the information is retained on any subsequent substitute check. If the paying bank places the returned check in a carrier envelope, the carrier envelope should indicate that it is a returned check but need not repeat the reason for return stated on the check if it in fact appears on the check.

E.   229.30(e) Depositary Bank Without Accounts

1.   Subpart B of this regulation applies only to "checks" deposited in transaction-type "accounts." Thus, a depositary bank with only time or savings accounts need not comply with the availability requirements of Subpart B. Collecting banks will not have couriers delivering checks to these banks as paying banks, because no checks are drawn on them. Consequently, the costs of using a courier or other expedited means to deliver returned checks directly to such a depositary bank may not be justified. Thus, the expedited return requirement of § 229.30(a) and the notice of nonpayment requirement of § 229.33 do not apply to checks being returned to banks that do not hold accounts. The paying bank's midnight deadline in U.C.C. 4–301 and 4–302 and § 210.12 of Regulation J (12 CFR 210.12) would continue to apply to these checks. Returning banks also would be required to act on such checks within their midnight deadline. Further, in order to avoid complicating the process of returning checks generally, banks without accounts are required to use the standard indorsement, and their checks are returned by returning banks and paid for by the depositary bank under the same rules as checks deposited in other banks, with the exception of the expeditious return and notice of nonpayment requirements of §§ 229.30(a), 229.31(a), and 229.33.

2.   The expeditious return requirements also apply to a check deposited in a bank that is not a depository institution. Federal Reserve Banks, Federal Home Loan Banks, private bankers, and possibly certain industrial banks are not depository institutions within the meaning of the EFA Act, and therefore are not subject to the expedited availability and disclosure requirements of Subpart B. These banks do, however, maintain accounts as defined in § 229.2(a), and a paying bank returning a check to one of these banks would be required to return the check to the depositary bank, in accordance with the requirements of this section.

F.   229.30(f) Notice in Lieu of Return

1.   A check that is lost or otherwise unavailable for return may be returned by sending a legible copy of both sides of the check or, if such a copy is not available to the paying bank, a written notice of nonpayment containing the information specified in § 229.33(b). The copy or written notice must clearly indicate it is a notice in lieu of return and must be handled in the same manner as other returned checks. Notice by telephone, telegraph, or other electronic transmission, other than a legible facsimile or similar image transmission of both sides of the check, does not satisfy the requirements for a notice in lieu of return. The requirement for a writing and the indication that the notice is a substitute for the returned check is necessary so that the returning and depositary banks are informed that the notice carries value. Notice in lieu of return is permitted only when a bank does not have and cannot obtain possession of the check or must retain possession of the check for protest. A check is not unavailable for return if it is merely difficult to retrieve from a filing system or from storage by a keeper of checks in a truncation system. A notice in lieu of return may be used by a bank handling a returned check that has been lost or destroyed, including when the original returned check has been charged back as lost or destroyed as provided in § 229.35(b). A bank using a notice in lieu of return gives a warranty under § 229.34(a)(4) that the original check has not been and will not be returned.

2.   The requirement of this paragraph supersedes the requirement of U.C.C. 4–301(a) as to the form and information required of a notice of dishonor or nonpayment. Reference in the regulation and this commentary to a returned check includes a notice in lieu of return unless the context indicates otherwise.

3.   The notice in lieu of return is subject to the provisions of § 229.30 and is treated like a returned check for settlement purposes. If the original check is over $2,500, the notice of nonpayment under § 229.33 is still required, but may be satisfied by the notice in lieu of return if the notice in lieu meets the time and information requirements of § 229.33.

4.   If not all of the information required by § 229.33(b) is available, the paying bank may make a claim against any prior bank handling the check as provided in § 229.35(b).

G.   229.30(g) Reliance on Routing Number

1.   Although § 229.35 and Appendix D require that the depositary bank indorsement contain its nine-digit routing number, it is possible that a returned check will bear the routing number of the depositary bank in fractional, nine-digit, or other form. This paragraph permits a paying bank to rely on the routing number of the depositary bank as it appears on the check (in the depositary bank's indorsement) when it is received by the paying bank.

2.   If there are inconsistent routing numbers, the paying bank may rely on any routing number designating the depositary bank. The paying bank is not required to resolve the inconsistency prior to processing the check. The paying bank remains subject to the requirement to act in good faith and use ordinary care under § 229.38(a).

XVII. Section 229.31 Returning Bank's Responsibility for Return of Checks

A.   229.31(a) Return of Checks

1.   The standards for return of checks established by this section are similar to those for paying banks in § 229.30(a). This section requires a returning bank to return a returned check expeditiously if it agrees to handle the returned check for expeditious return under this paragraph. In effect, the returning bank is an agent or subagent of the paying bank and a subagent of the depositary bank for the purposes of returning the check.

2.   A returning bank agrees to handle a returned check for expeditious return to the depositary bank if it:

a.   Publishes or distributes availability schedules for the return of returned checks and accepts the returned check for return;

b.   Handles a returned check for return that it did not handle for forward collection; or

c.   Otherwise agrees to handle a returned check for expeditious return.

3.   Two-day/four-day test. As in the case of a paying bank, a returning bank's return of a returned check is expeditious if it meets either of two tests. Under the "two-day/four-day" test, the check must be returned so that it would normally be received by the depositary bank by 4:00 p.m. either two or four business days after the check was presented to the paying bank, depending on whether or not the paying bank is located in the same check processing region as the depositary bank. This is the same test as the two-day/four-day test applicable to paying banks. (See Commentary to § 229.30(a).) While a returning bank will not have first hand knowledge of the day on which a check was presented to the paying bank, returning banks may, by agreement, allocate with paying banks liability for late return based on the delays caused by each. In effect, the two-day/four day test protects all paying and returning banks that return checks from claims that they failed to return a check expeditiously, where the check is returned within the specified time following presentment to the paying bank, or a later time as would result from unforeseen delays.

4.   Forward collection test.

a.   The "forward collection" test is similar to the forward collection test for paying banks. Under this test, a returning bank must handle a returned check in the same manner that a similarly situated collecting bank would handle a check of similar size drawn on the depositary bank for forward collection. A similarly situated bank is a bank (other than a Federal Reserve Bank) that is of similar asset size and check handling activity in the same community. A bank has similar check handling activity if it handles a similar volume of checks for forward collection as the forward collection volume of the returning bank.

b.   Under the forward collection test, a returning bank must accept returned checks, including both qualified and other returned checks ("raw returns"), at approximately the same times and process them according to the same general schedules as checks handled for forward collection. Thus, a returning bank generally must process even raw returns on an overnight basis, unless its time limit is extended by one day to convert a raw return to a qualified returned check.

5.   Cut-off hours. A returning bank may establish earlier cut-off hours for receipt of returned checks than for receipt of forward collection checks, but the cut-off hour for returned checks may not be earlier than 2:00 p.m. The returning bank also may set different sorting requirements for returned checks than those applicable to other checks. Thus, a returning bank may allow itself more processing time for returns than for forward collection checks. All returned checks received by a cut-off hour for returned checks must be processed and dispatched by the returning bank by the time that it would dispatch forward collection checks received at a corresponding forward collection cut-off hour that provides for the same or faster availability for checks destined for the same depositary banks.

6.   Examples.

a.   If a returning bank receives a returned check by its cut-off hour for returned checks on Monday and the depositary bank and the returning bank are participants in the same clearinghouse, the returning bank should arrange to have the returned check received by the depositary bank by Tuesday. This would be the same day that it would deliver a forward collection check drawn on the depositary bank and received by the returning bank at a corresponding forward collection cut-off hour on Monday.

b.   i. If a returning bank receives a returned check, and the returning bank normally would collect a forward collection check drawn on the depositary bank by sending the forward collection check to a correspondent or a Federal Reserve Bank by courier, the returning bank could send the returned check in the same manner if the correspondent has agreed to handle returned checks expeditiously under § 229.31(a). The returning bank would have to deliver the check by the correspondent's or Federal Reserve Bank's cut-off hour for returned checks that corresponds to its cut-off hour for forward collection checks drawn on the depositary bank. A returning bank may take a day to convert a check to a qualified returned check. Where the forward collection checks are delivered by courier, mailing the returned checks would not meet the duty established by this section for returning banks.

ii.   A returning bank must return a check to the depositary bank by courier or other means as fast as a courier, if similarly situated returning banks use couriers to deliver their forward collection checks to the depositary bank.

iii.   For some depositary banks, no community practice exists as to delivery of checks. For example, a credit union whose customers use payable-through drafts normally does not have checks presented to it because the drafts are normally sent to the payable-through bank for collection. In these circumstances, the community standard is established by taking into account the dollar volume of the checks being sent to the depositary bank and the location of the depositary bank, and determining whether similarly situated banks normally would deliver forward collection checks to the depositary bank, taking into account the particular risks associated with returned checks. Where the community standard does not require courier delivery, other means of delivery, including mail, are acceptable.

7.   Qualified returned checks.

a.   The expeditious return requirement for a returning bank in this regulation is more stringent in many cases than the duty of a collecting bank to exercise ordinary care under U.C.C. 4–202 in returning a check. A returning bank is under a duty to act as expeditiously in returning a check as it would in the forward collection of a check. Notwithstanding its duty of expeditious return, its midnight deadline under U.C.C. 4–202 and § 210.12(a) of Regulation J (12 CFR 210.12(a)), under the forward collection test, a returning bank may take an extra day to qualify a returned check. A qualified returned check will be handled by subsequent returning banks more efficiently than a raw return. This paragraph gives a returning bank an extra business day beyond the time that would otherwise be required to return the returned check to convert a returned check to a qualified returned check. The qualified returned check must include the routing number of the depositary bank, the amount of the check, and a return identifier encoded on the check in magnetic ink. A check that is converted to a qualified returned check must be encoded in accordance with ANS X9.13 for original checks or ANS X9.100–140 for substitute checks.

b. If the returning bank is sending the returned check directly to the depositary bank, this extra day is not available because preparing a qualified returned check will not expedite handling by other banks. If the returning bank makes an encoding error in creating a qualified returned check, it may be liable under § 229.38 for losses caused by any negligence or under § 229.34(c)(3) for breach of an encoding warranty. The returning bank would not lose the one-day extension available to it for creating a qualified returned check because of an encoding error.

8. Routing of returned check.

a. Under § 229.31(a), the returning bank is authorized to route the returned check in a variety of ways:

i. It may send the returned check directly to the depositary bank by courier or other expeditious means of delivery; or

ii. It may send the returned check to any returning bank agreeing to handle the returned check for expeditious return to the depositary bank under this section regardless of whether or not the returning bank handled the check for forward collection.

b. If the returning bank elects to send the returned check directly to the depositary bank, it is not required to send the check to the branch of the depositary bank that first handled the check. The returned check may be sent to the depositary bank at any location permitted under § 229.32(a).

9. Responsibilities of returning bank. In meeting the requirements of this section, the returning bank is responsible for its own actions, but not those of the paying bank, other returning banks, or the depositary bank. (See U.C.C. 4–202(c) regarding the responsibility of collecting banks.) For example, if the paying bank has delayed the start of the return process, but the returning bank acts in a timely manner, the returning bank may satisfy the requirements of this section even if the delayed return results in a loss to the depositary bank. (See § 229.38.) A returning bank must handle a notice in lieu of return as expeditiously as a returned check.

10. U.C.C. sections affected. This paragraph directly affects the following provisions of the U.C.C., and may affect other sections or provisions:

a. Section 4–202(b), in that time limits required by that section may be affected by the additional requirement to make an expeditious return.

b. Section 4–214(a), in that settlement for returned checks is made under § 229.31(c) and not by charge-back of provisional credit, and in that the time limits may be affected by the additional requirement to make an expeditious return.

B. 229.31(b) Unidentifiable Depositary Bank

1. This section is similar to § 229.30(b), but applies to returning banks instead of paying banks. In some cases a returning bank will be unable to identify the depositary bank with respect to a check. Returning banks agreeing to handle checks for return to depositary banks under § 229.31(a) are expected to be expert in identifying depositary bank indorsements. In the limited cases where the returning bank cannot identify the depositary bank, the returning bank may send the returned check to a returning bank that agrees to handle the returned check for expeditious return under § 229.31(a), or it may send the returned check to a bank that handled the check for forward collection, even if that bank does not agree to handle the returned check expeditiously under § 229.31(a).

2. If the returning bank itself handled the check for forward collection, it may send the returned check to a collecting bank that was prior to it in the forward collection process, which will be better able to identify the depositary bank. If there are no prior collecting banks, the returning bank must research the collection of the check and identify the depositary bank. As in the case of paying banks under § 229.30(b), a returning bank's sending of a check to a bank that handled the check for forward collection under § 229.31(b) is not subject to the expeditious return requirements of § 229.31(a).

3.   The returning bank's return of a check under this paragraph is subject to the midnight deadline under U.C.C. 4–202(b). (See definition of returning bank in § 229.2(cc).)

4.   Where a returning bank receives a check that it does not agree to handle expeditiously under § 229.31(a), such as a check sent to it under § 229.30(b), but the returning bank is able to identify the depositary bank, the returning bank must thereafter return the check expeditiously to the depositary bank. The returning bank returns a check expeditiously under this paragraph if it returns the check by the same means it would use to return a check drawn on it to the depositary bank or by other reasonably prompt means.

5.   As in the case of a paying bank returning a check under § 229.30(b), a returning bank returning a check under this paragraph to a bank that has not agreed to handle the check expeditiously must advise that bank that it is unable to identify the depositary bank. This advice must be conspicuous, such as a stamp on each check for which the depositary bank is unknown if such checks are commingled with other returned checks, or, if such checks are sent in a separate cash letter, by one notice on the cash letter. The returned check may not be prepared for automated return.

C.   229.31(c) Settlement

1.   Under the U.C.C., a collecting bank receives settlement for a check when it is presented to the paying bank. The paying bank may recover the settlement when the paying bank returns the check to the presenting bank. Under this regulation, however, the paying bank may return the check directly to the depositary bank or through returning banks that did not handle the check for forward collection. On these more efficient return paths, the paying bank does not recover the settlement made to the presenting bank. Thus, this paragraph requires the returning bank to settle for a returned check (either with the paying bank or another returning bank) in the same way that it would settle for a similar check for forward collection. To achieve uniformity, this paragraph applies even if the returning bank handled the check for forward collection.

2.   Any returning bank, including one that handled the check for forward collection, may provide availability for returned checks pursuant to an availability schedule as it does for forward collection checks. These settlements by returning banks, as well as settlements between banks made during the forward collection of a check, are considered final when made subject to any deferment of availability. (See § 229.36(d) and Commentary to § 229.35(b).)

3.   A returning bank may vary the settlement method it uses by agreement with paying banks or other returning banks. Special rules apply in the case of insolvency of banks. (See § 229.39.) If payment cannot be obtained from a depositary or returning bank because of its insolvency or otherwise, recovery can be had by returning, paying, and collecting banks from prior banks on this basis of the liability of prior banks under § 229.35(b).

4.   This paragraph affects U.C.C. 4–214(a) in that a paying or collecting bank does not ordinarily have a right to charge back against the bank from which it received the returned check, although it is entitled to settlement if it returns the returned check to that bank, and may affect other sections or provisions. Under § 229.36(d), a bank collecting a check remains liable to prior collecting banks and the depositary bank's customer under the U.C.C.

D.   229.31(d) Charges

1.   This paragraph permits any returning bank, even one that handled the check for forward collection, to impose a fee on the paying bank or other returning bank for its service in handling a returned check. Where a claim is made under § 229.35(b), the bank on which the claim is made is not authorized by this paragraph to impose a charge for taking up a check. This paragraph preempts state laws to the extent that these laws prevent returning banks from charging fees for handling returned checks.

E.   229.31(e) Depositary Bank Without Accounts

1.   This paragraph is similar to § 229.30(e) and relieves a returning bank of its obligation to make expeditious return to a depositary bank that does not maintain any accounts. (See the Commentary to § 229.30(e).)

COMMENTARY ON REGULATION CC

F.   229.31(f) Notice in Lieu of Return

1.   This paragraph is similar to § 229.30(f) and authorizes a returning bank to originate a notice in lieu of return if the returned check is unavailable for return. Notice in lieu of return is permitted only when a bank does not have and cannot obtain possession of the check or must retain possession of the check for protest. A check is not unavailable for return if it is merely difficult to retrieve from a filing system or from storage by a keeper of checks in a truncation system. (See the Commentary to § 229.30(f).)

G.   229.31(g) Reliance on Routing Number

1.   This paragraph is similar to § 229.30(g) and permits a returning bank to rely on routing numbers appearing on a returned check such as routing numbers in the depositary bank's indorsement or on qualified returned checks. (See the Commentary to § 229.30(g).)

XVIII.   Section 229.32 Depositary Bank's Responsibility for Returned Checks

A.   229.32(a) Acceptance of Returned Checks

1.   This regulation seeks to encourage direct returns by paying and returning banks and may result in a number of banks sending checks to depositary banks with no preexisting arrangements as to where the returned checks should be delivered. This paragraph states where the depositary bank is required to accept returned checks and written notices of nonpayment under § 229.33. (These locations differ from locations at which a depositary bank must accept electronic notices.) It is derived from U.C.C. 3–111, which specifies that presentment for payment may be made at the place specified in the instrument or, if there is none, at the place of business of the party to pay. In the case of returned checks, the depositary bank does not print the check and can only specify the place of "payment" of the returned check in its indorsement.

2.   The paragraph specifies four locations at which the depositary bank must accept returned checks:

a.   The depositary bank must accept returned checks at any location at which it requests presentment of forward collection checks such as a processing center. A depositary bank does not request presentment of forward collection checks at a branch of the bank merely by paying checks presented over the counter.

b.   i. If the depositary bank indorsement states the name and address of the depositary bank, it must accept returned checks at the branch, head office, or other location, such as a processing center, indicated by the address. If the address is too general to identify a particular location, then the depositary bank must accept returned checks at any branch or head office consistent with the address. If, for example, the address is "New York, New York," each branch in New York City must accept returned checks.

ii.   If no address appears in the depositary bank's indorsement, the depositary bank must accept returned checks at any branch or head office associated with the depositary bank's routing number. The offices associated with the routing number of a bank are found in American Bankers Association Key to Routing Numbers, published by an agent of the American Bankers Association, which lists a city and state address for each routing number.

iii.   The depositary bank must accept returned checks at the address in its indorsement and at an address associated with its routing number in the indorsement if the written address in the indorsement and the address associated with the routing number in the indorsement are not in the same check processing region. Under §§ 229.30(g) and 229.31(g), a paying or returning bank may rely on the depositary bank's routing number in its indorsement in handling returned checks and is not required to send returned checks to an address in the depositary bank's indorsement that is not in the same check processing region as the address associated with the routing number in the indorsement.

iv.   If no routing number or address appears in its indorsement, the depositary bank must accept a returned check at any branch or head office of the bank. The indorsement requirement of § 229.35 and Appendix D requires that the indorsement contain a routing number, a name, and a location. Consequently, this provision, as well as paragraph (a)(2)(ii) of this section, only applies where the depositary bank has failed to comply with the indorsement requirement.

3.   For ease of processing, a depositary bank may require that returning or paying banks returning checks to it separate returned checks from forward collection checks being presented.

4.   Under § 229.33(d), a depositary bank receiving a returned check or notice of nonpayment must send notice to its customer by its midnight deadline or within a longer reasonable time.

B.   229.32(b) Payment

1.   As discussed in the commentary to § 229.31(c), under this regulation a paying or returning bank does not obtain credit for a returned check by charge-back but by, in effect, presenting the returned check to the depositary bank. This paragraph imposes an obligation to "pay" a returned check that is similar to the obligation to pay a forward collection check by a paying bank, except that the depositary bank may not return a returned check for which it is the depositary bank. Also, certain means of payment, such as remittance drafts, may be used only with the agreement of the returning bank.

2.   The depositary bank must pay for a returned check by the close of the banking day on which it received the returned check. The day on which a returned check is received is determined pursuant to U.C.C. 4–108, which permits the bank to establish a cut-off hour, generally not earlier than 2:00 p.m., and treat checks received after that hour as being received on the next banking day. If the depositary bank is unable to make payment to a returning or paying bank on the banking day that it receives the returned check, because the returning or paying bank is closed for a holiday or because the time when the depositary bank received the check is after the close of Fedwire, e.g., west coast banks with late cut-off hours, payment may be made on the next banking day of the bank receiving payment.

3.   Payment must be made so that the funds are available for use by the bank returning the check to the depositary bank on the day the check is received by the depositary bank. For example, a depositary bank meets this requirement if it sends a wire transfer of funds to the returning or paying bank on the day it receives the returned check, even if the returning or paying bank has closed for the day. A wire transfer should indicate the purpose of the payment.

4.   The depositary bank may use a net settlement arrangement to settle for a returned check. Banks with net settlement agreements could net the appropriate credits and debits for returned checks with the accounting entries for forward collection checks if they so desired. If, for purposes of establishing additional controls or for other reasons, the banks involved desired a separate settlement for returned checks, a separate net settlement agreement could be established.

5.   The bank sending the returned check to the depositary bank may agree to accept payment at a later date if, for example, it does not believe that the amount of the returned check or checks warrants the costs of same-day payment. Thus, a returning or paying bank may agree to accept payment through an ACH credit or debit transfer that settles the day after the returned check is received instead of a wire transfer that settles on the same day.

6.   This paragraph and this subpart do not affect the depositary bank's right to recover a provisional settlement with its nonbank customer for a check that is returned. (See also §§ 229.19(c)(2)(ii), 229.33(d) and 229.35(b).)

C.   229.32(c) Misrouted Returned Checks

1.   This paragraph permits a bank receiving a check on the basis that it is the depositary bank to send the misrouted returned check to the correct depositary bank, if it can identify the correct depositary bank, either directly or through a returning bank agreeing to handle the check expeditiously under § 229.30(a). In these cases, the bank receiving the check is acting as a returning bank. Alternatively, the bank receiving the misrouted returned check must send the check back to the bank from which it was received. In either case the bank to which the returned check was misrouted could receive settlement for the check. The depositary bank would be required to pay for the returned check under § 229.32(b), and any other bank to which the check is sent under this paragraph would be required to settle for the check as a returning bank under § 229.31(c). If the check was originally received "free," that is, without a charge for the check, the bank incorrectly receiving the check would have to return the check, without a charge, to the bank from which it came. The bank to which the returned check was misrouted is required to act promptly but is not required to meet the expeditious return requirements of § 229.31(a); however, it must act within its midnight deadline. This paragraph does not affect a bank's duties under § 229.35(b).

COMMENTARY ON REGULATION CC

D.   229.32(d) Charges

1.   This paragraph prohibits a depositary bank from charging the equivalent of a presentment fee for returned checks. A returning bank, however, may charge a fee for handling returned checks. If the returning bank receives a mixed cash letter of returned checks, which includes some checks for which the returning bank also is the depositary bank, the fee may be applied to all the returned checks in the cash letter. In the case of a sorted cash letter containing only returned checks for which the returning bank is the depositary bank, however, no fee may be charged.

XIX.   Section 229.33 Notice of Nonpayment

A.   229.33(a) Requirement

1.   Notice of nonpayment as required by this section and written notice in lieu of return as provided in §§ 229.30(f) and 229.31(f) serve different functions. The two kinds of notice, however, must meet the content requirements of this section. The paying bank must send a notice of nonpayment if it decides not to pay a check of $2,500 or more. A paying bank may rely on an amount encoded on the check in magnetic ink to determine whether the check is in the amount of $2,500 or more. The notice of nonpayment carries no value, and the check itself (or the notice in lieu of return) must be returned. The paying bank must ensure that the notice of nonpayment is received by the depositary bank by 4:00 p.m. local time on the second business day following presentment. A bank identified by routing number as the paying bank is considered the paying bank under this regulation and would be required to create a notice of nonpayment even though that bank determined that the check was not drawn by a customer of that bank. (See Commentary to the definition of paying bank in § 229.2(z).)

2.   The paying bank should not send a notice of nonpayment until it has finally determined not to pay the check. Under § 229.34(b), by sending the notice the paying bank warrants that it has returned or will return the check. If a paying bank sends a notice and subsequently decides to pay the check, the paying bank may mitigate its liability on this warranty by notifying the depositary bank that the check has been paid.

3.   Because the return of the check itself may serve as the required notice of nonpayment, in many cases no notice other than the return of the check will be necessary. For example, in many cases the return of a check through a clearinghouse to another participant of the clearinghouse will be made in time to meet the time requirements of this section. If the check normally will not be received by the depositary bank within the time limits for notice, the return of the check will not satisfy the notice requirement. In determining whether the returned check will satisfy the notice requirement, the paying bank may rely on the availability schedules of returning banks as the time that the returned check is expected to be delivered to the depositary bank, unless the paying bank has reason to know the availability schedules are inaccurate.

4.   Unless the returned check is used to satisfy the notice requirement, the requirement for notice is independent of and does not affect the requirements for timely and expeditious return of the check under § 229.30 and the U.C.C. (See § 229.30(a).) If a paying bank fails both to comply with this section and to comply with the requirements for timely and expeditious return under § 229.30 and the U.C.C. and Regulation J (12 CFR part 210), the paying bank shall be liable under either this section or such other requirements, but not both. (See § 229.38(b).) A paying bank is not responsible for failure to give notice of nonpayment to a party that has breached a presentment warranty under U.C.C. 4–208, notwithstanding that the paying bank may have returned the check. (See U.C.C. 4–208 and 4–302.)

B.   229.33(b) Content of Notices

1.   This paragraph provides that the notice must at a minimum contain eight elements which are specifically enumerated. In the case of written notices, the name and routing number of the depositary bank also are required.

2.   If the paying bank cannot identify the depositary bank from the check itself, it may wish to send the notice to the earliest collecting bank it can identify and indicate that the notice is not being sent to the depositary bank. The collecting bank may be able to identify the depositary bank and forward the notice, but is under no duty to do so. In addition, the collecting bank may actually be the depositary bank.

COMMENTARY ON REGULATION CC

3.   A bank must identify an item of information if the bank is uncertain as to that item's accuracy. A bank may make this identification by setting the item off with question marks, asterisks, or other symbols designated for this purpose by generally applicable industry standards.

C.   229.33(c) Acceptance of Notice

1.   In the case of a written notice, the depositary bank is required to accept notices at the locations specified in § 229.32(a). In the case of telephone notices, the bank may not refuse to accept notices at the telephone numbers identified in this section, but may transfer calls or use a recording device. Banks may vary by agreement the location and manner in which notices are received.

D.   229.33(d) Notification to Customer

1.   This paragraph requires a depositary bank to notify its customer of nonpayment upon receipt of a returned check or notice of nonpayment, regardless of the amount of the check or notice. This requirement is similar to the requirement under the U.C.C. as interpreted in Appliance Buyers Credit Corp. v. Prospect National Bank, 708 F.2d 290 (7th Cir. 1983), that a depositary bank may be liable for damages incurred by its customer for its failure to give its customer timely advice that it has received a notice of nonpayment. Notice also must be given if a depositary bank receives a notice of recovery under § 229.35(b). A bank that chooses to provide the notice required by § 229.33(d) in writing may send the notice by e-mail or facsimile if the bank sends the notice to the e-mail address or facsimile number specified by the customer for that purpose. The notice to the customer required under this paragraph also may satisfy the notice requirement of § 229.13(g) if the depositary bank invokes the reasonable-cause exception of § 229.13(e) due to the receipt of a notice of nonpayment, provided the notice meets all the requirements of § 229.13(g).

XX.   Section 229.34 Warranties

A.   229.34(a) Warranty of Returned Check

1.   This paragraph includes warranties that a returned check, including a notice in lieu of return, was returned by the paying bank, or in the case of a check payable by a bank and payable through another bank, the bank by which the check is payable, within the deadline under the U.C.C. (subject to any claims or defenses under the U.C.C., such as breach of a presentment warranty), Regulation J (12 CFR part 210), or § 229.30(c); that the paying or returning bank is authorized to return the check; that the returned check has not been materially altered; and that, in the case of a notice in lieu of return, the original check has not been and will not be returned for payment. (See the Commentary to § 229.30(f).) The warranty does not include a warranty that the bank complied with the expeditious return requirements of §§ 229.30(a) and 229.31(a). These warranties do not apply to checks drawn on the United States Treasury, to U.S. Postal Service money orders, or to checks drawn on a state or a unit of general local government that are not payable through or at a bank. (See § 229.42.)

B.   229.34(b) Warranty of Notice of Nonpayment

1.   This paragraph provides for warranties for notices of nonpayment. This warranty does not include a warranty that the notice is accurate and timely under § 229.33. The requirements of § 229.33 that are not covered by the warranty are subject to the liability provisions of § 229.38. These warranties are designed to give the depositary bank more confidence in relying on notices of nonpayment. This paragraph imposes liability on a paying bank that gives notice of nonpayment and then subsequently returns the check. (See Commentary on § 229.33(a).)

C.   229.34(c) Warranty of Settlement Amount, Encoding, and Offset

1.   Paragraph (c)(1) provides that a bank that presents and receives settlement for checks warrants to the paying bank that the settlement it demands (e.g., as noted on the cash letter) equals the total amount of the checks it presents. This paragraph gives the paying bank a warranty claim against the presenting bank for the amount of any excess settlement made on the basis of the amount demanded, plus expenses. If the amount demanded is understated, a paying bank discharges its settlement obligation under U.C.C. 4–301 by paying the amount demanded, but remains liable for the amount by which the demand is understated; the presenting bank is nevertheless liable for expenses in resolving the adjustment.

1924

COMMENTARY ON REGULATION CC

2.   When checks or returned checks are transferred to a collecting, returning, or depositary bank, the transferor bank is not required to demand settlement, as is required upon presentment to the paying bank. However, often the checks or returned checks will be accompanied by information (such as a cash letter listing) that will indicate the total of the checks or returned checks. Paragraph (c)(2) provides that if the transferor bank includes information indicating the total amount of checks or returned checks transferred, it warrants that the information is correct (i.e., equals the actual total of the items).

3.   Paragraph (c)(3) provides that a bank that presents or transfers a check or returned check warrants the accuracy of the magnetic ink encoding that was placed on the item after issue, and that exists at the time of presentment or transfer, to any bank that subsequently handles the check or returned check. Under U.C.C. 4–209(a), only the encoder (or the encoder and the depositary bank, if the encoder is a customer of the depositary bank) warrants the encoding accuracy, thus any claims on the warranty must be directed to the encoder. Paragraph (c)(3) expands on the U.C.C. by providing that all banks that transfer or present a check or returned check make the encoding warranty. In addition, under the U.C.C., the encoder makes the warranty to subsequent collecting banks and the paying bank, while paragraph (c)(3) provides that the warranty is made to banks in the return chain as well. Paragraph (c)(3) applies to all MICR-line encoding on a substitute check.

4.   A paying bank that settles for an overstated cash letter because of a misencoded check may make a warranty claim against the presenting bank under paragraph (c)(1) (which would require the paying bank to show that the check was part of the overstated cash letter) or an encoding warranty claim under paragraph (c)(3) against the presenting bank or any preceding bank that handled the misencoded check.

5.   Paragraph (c)(4) provides that a paying bank or a depositary bank may set off excess settlement paid to another bank against settlement owed to that bank for checks presented or returned checks received (for which it is the depositary bank) subsequent to the excess settlement.

D.   229.34(d) Transfer and Presentment Warranties

1.   A bank that transfers or presents a remotely created check and receives a settlement or other consideration warrants that the person on whose account the check is drawn authorized the issuance of the check in the amount stated on the check and to the payee stated on the check. The warranties are given only by banks and only to subsequent banks in the collection chain. The warranties ultimately shift liability for the loss created by an unauthorized remotely created check to the depositary bank. The depositary bank cannot assert the transfer and presentment warranties against a depositor. However, a depositary bank may, by agreement, allocate liability for such an item to the depositor and also may have a claim under other laws against that person.

2.   The transfer and presentment warranties for remotely created checks supplement the Federal Trade Commission's Telemarketing Sales Rule, which requires telemarketers that submit checks for payment to obtain the customer's "express verifiable authorization" (the authorization may be either in writing or tape recorded and must be made available upon request to the customer's bank). 16 CFR 310.3(a)(3). The transfer and presentment warranties shift liability to the depositary bank only when the remotely created check is unauthorized, and would not apply when the customer initially authorizes a check but then experiences "buyer's remorse" and subsequently tries to revoke the authorization by asserting a claim against the paying bank under U.C.C. 4–401. If the depositary bank suspects "buyer's remorse," it may obtain from its customer the express verifiable authorization of the check by the paying bank's customer, required under the Federal Trade Commission's Telemarketing Sales Rule, and use that authorization as a defense to the warranty claim.

3.   The scope of the transfer and presentment warranties for remotely created checks differs from that of the corresponding U.C.C. warranty provisions in two respects. The U.C.C. warranties differ from the § 229.34(d) warranties in that they are given by any person, including a nonbank depositor, that transfers a remotely created check and not just to a bank, as is the case under § 229.34(d). In addition, the U.C.C. warranties state that the person on whose account the item is drawn authorized the issuance of the item in the amount for which the item is drawn. The § 229.34(d) warranties specifically cover the amount as well as the payee stated on the check. Neither the U.C.C. warranties, nor the § 229.34(d) warranties apply to the date stated on the remotely created check.

4.   A bank making the § 229.34(d) warranties may defend a claim asserting violation of the warranties by proving that the customer of the paying bank is precluded by U.C.C. 4–406 from making a claim against the paying bank. This may be the case, for example, if the customer failed to discover the unauthorized remotely created check in a timely manner.

5.   The transfer and presentment warranties for a remotely created check apply to a remotely created check that has been reconverted to a substitute check.

E.   229.34(e) Damages

1.   This paragraph adopts for the warranties in § 229.34 (a), (b), and (c) the damages provided in U.C.C. 4–207(c) and 4A–506(b). (See definition of interest compensation in § 229.2(oo).)

F.   229.34(f) Tender of Defense

1.   This paragraph adopts for this regulation the vouching-in provisions of U.C.C. 3–119.

G.   229.34(g) Notice of Claim

1.   This paragraph adopts the notice provisions of U.C.C. sections 4–207(d) and 4–208(e). The time limit set forth in this paragraph applies to notices of claims for warranty breaches only. As provided in § 229.38(g), all actions under this section must be brought within one year after the date of the occurrence of the violation involved.

XXI.   Section 229.35 Indorsements

A.   229.35(a) Indorsement Standards

1.   This section and Appendix D require banks to use a standard form of indorsement when indorsing checks during the forward collection and return process. The standard provides for indorsements by all collecting and returning banks, plus a unique standard for depositary bank indorsements. It is designed to facilitate the identification of the depositary bank and the prompt return of checks. The regulation places a duty on banks to ensure that their indorsements can be interpreted by any person. The indorsement standard specifies the information each indorsement must contain and its location and ink color.

2.   Banks generally apply indorsements to a paper check in one of two ways: (1) banks print or "spray" indorsements onto a check when the check is processed through the banks' automated check sorters (regardless of whether the checks are original checks or substitute checks), and (2) reconverting banks print or "overlay" previously applied electronic indorsements and their own indorsements and identifications onto a substitute check at the time that the substitute check is created. If a subsequent substitute check is created in the course of collection or return, that substitute check will contain, in its image of the back of the previous substitute check, reproductions of indorsements that were sprayed or overlaid onto the previous item. For purposes of the indorsement standard set forth in appendix D, a reproduction of a previously applied sprayed or overlaid indorsement contained within an image of a check does not constitute "an indorsement that previously was applied electronically." To accommodate these two indorsement scenarios, the appendix includes two indorsement location specifications: one standard applies to banks spraying indorsements onto existing paper original checks and substitute checks, and another applies to reconverting banks overlaying indorsements that previously were applied electronically and their own indorsements onto substitute checks at the time the substitute checks are created.

3.   A bank might use check processing equipment that captures an image of a check prior to spraying an indorsement onto that item. If the bank truncates that item, it should ensure that it also applies an indorsement to the item electronically. A reconverting bank satisfies its obligation to preserve all previously applied indorsements by overlaying a bank's indorsement that previously was applied electronically onto a substitute check that the reconverting bank creates.

4.   The location of an indorsement applied to an original paper check in accordance with appendix D may shift if that check is truncated and later reconverted to a substitute check. If an indorsement applied to the original check in accordance with appendix D is overwritten by a subsequent indorsement applied to the substitute check in accordance with appendix D, then one or both of those indorsements could be rendered illegible. As explained in § 229.38(d) and the commentary thereto, a reconverting bank is liable for losses associated with indorsements that are rendered illegible as a result of check substitution.

COMMENTARY ON REGULATION CC

5.   To ensure that indorsements can be easily read and would remain legible after an image of a check is captured, the standard requires all indorsements applied to original checks and substitute checks to be printed in black ink as of January 1, 2006.

6.   The standard requires the depositary bank's indorsement to include (1) its nine-digit routing number set off by an arrow at each end of the routing number and, if the depositary bank is a reconverting bank with respect to the check, an asterisk outside the arrow at each end of the routing number to identify the bank as a reconverting bank; (2) the indorsement date; and (3) if the indorsement is applied physically, name or location information. The standard also permits but does not require the indorsement to include other identifying information. The standard requires a collecting bank's or returning bank's indorsement to include only (1) the bank's nine digit routing number (without arrows) and, if the collecting bank or returning bank is a reconverting bank with respect to the check, an asterisk at each end of the number to identify the bank as a reconverting bank, (2) the indorsement date, and (3) an optional trace or sequence number.

7.   Depositary banks should not include information that can be confused with required information. For example, a nine-digit zip code could be confused with the nine-digit routing number.

8.   A depositary bank may want to include an address in its indorsement in order to limit the number of locations at which it must receive returned checks. In instances where this address is not consistent with the routing number in the indorsement, the depositary bank is required to receive returned checks at a branch or head office consistent with the routing number. Banks should note, however, that § 229.32 requires a depositary bank to receive returned checks at the location(s) at which it receives forward-collection checks.

9.   In addition to indorsing a substitute check in accordance with appendix D, a reconverting bank must identify itself and the truncating bank by applying its routing number and the routing number of the truncating bank to the front of the check in accordance with appendix D and ANS X9.100–140. Further, if the reconverting bank is the paying bank, it also must identify itself by applying its routing number to the back of the check in accordance with appendix D. In these instances, the reconverting bank and truncating bank routing numbers are for identification purposes only and are not indorsements or acceptances.

10.   Under the U.C.C., a specific guarantee of prior indorsement is not necessary. (See U.C.C. 4–207(a) and 4–208(a).) Use of guarantee language in indorsements, such as "P.E.G." ("prior endorsements guaranteed"), may result in reducing the type size used in bank indorsements, thereby making them more difficult to read. Use of this language may make it more difficult for other banks to identify the depositary bank. Subsequent collecting bank indorsements may not include this language.

11.   If the bank maintaining the account into which a check is deposited agrees with another bank (a correspondent, ATM operator, or lock box operator) to have the other bank accept returns and notices of nonpayment for the bank of account, the indorsement placed on the check as the depositary bank indorsement may be the indorsement of the bank that acts as correspondent, ATM operator, or lock box operator as provided in paragraph (d) of this section.

12.   The backs of many checks bear pre-printed information or blacked out areas for various reasons. For example, some checks are printed with a carbon band across the back that allows the transfer of information from the check to a ledger with one writing. Also, contracts or loan agreements are printed on certain checks. Other checks that are mailed to recipients may contain areas on the back that are blacked out so that they may not be read through the mailer. On the deposit side, the payee of the check may place its indorsement or information identifying the drawer of the check in the area specified for the depositary bank indorsement, thus making the depositary bank indorsement unreadable.

13.   The indorsement standard does not prohibit the use of a carbon band or other printed or written matter on the backs of checks and does not require banks to avoid placing their indorsements in these areas. Nevertheless, checks will be handled more efficiently if depositary banks design indorsement stamps so that the nine-digit routing number avoids the carbon band area. Indorsing parties other than banks, e.g., corporations, will benefit from the faster return of checks if they protect the identifiability and legibility of the depositary bank indorsement by staying clear of the area reserved for the depositary bank indorsement.

14.   Section 229.38(d) allocates responsibility for loss resulting from a delay in return of a check due to indorsements that are unreadable because of material on the back of the check. The depositary bank is responsible for a loss resulting from a delay in return caused by the condition of the check arising after its issuance until its acceptance by the depositary bank that made the depositary bank's indorsement illegible. The paying bank is responsible for loss resulting from a delay in return caused by indorsements that are not readable because of other material on the back of the check at the time that it was issued. Depositary and paying banks may shift these risks to their customers by agreement.

15.   The standard does not require the paying bank to indorse the check; however, if a paying bank does indorse a check that is returned, it should follow the indorsement standard for collecting banks and returning banks. The standard requires collecting and returning banks to indorse the check for tracing purposes. With respect to the identification of a paying bank that is also a reconverting bank, see the commentary to § 229.51(b)(2).

B.   229.35(b) Liability of Bank Handling Check

1.   When a check is sent for forward collection, the collection process results in a chain of indorsements extending from the depositary bank through any subsequent collecting banks to the paying bank. This section extends the indorsement chain through the paying bank to the returning banks, and would permit each bank to recover from any prior indorser if the claimant bank does not receive payment for the check from a subsequent bank in the collection or return chain. For example, if a returning bank returned a check to an insolvent depositary bank, and did not receive the full amount of the check from the failed bank, the returning bank could obtain the unrecovered amount of the check from any bank prior to it in the collection and return chain including the paying bank. Because each bank in the collection and return chain could recover from a prior bank, any loss would fall on the first collecting bank that received the check from the depositary bank. To avoid circuity of actions, the returning bank could recover directly from the first collecting bank. Under the U.C.C., the first collecting bank might ultimately recover from the depositary bank's customer or from the other parties on the check.

2.   Where a check is returned through the same banks used for the forward collection of the check, priority during the forward collection process controls over priority in the return process for the purpose of determining prior and subsequent banks under this regulation.

3.   Where a returning bank is insolvent and fails to pay the paying bank or a prior returning bank for a returned check, § 229.39(a) requires the receiver of the failed bank to return the check to the bank that transferred the check to the failed bank. That bank then either could continue the return to the depositary bank or recover based on this paragraph. Where the paying bank is insolvent, and fails to pay the collecting bank, the collecting bank also could recover from a prior collecting bank under this paragraph, and the bank from which it recovered could in turn recover from its prior collecting bank until the loss settled on the depositary bank (which could recover from its customer).

4.   A bank is not required to make a claim against an insolvent bank before exercising its right to recovery under this paragraph. Recovery may be made by charge-back or by other means. This right of recovery also is permitted even where nonpayment of the check is the result of the claiming bank's negligence such as failure to make expeditious return, but the claiming bank remains liable for its negligence under § 229.38.

5.   This liability is imposed on a bank handling a check for collection or return regardless of whether the bank's indorsement appears on the check. Notice must be sent under this paragraph to a prior bank from which recovery is sought reasonably promptly after a bank learns that it did not receive payment from another bank, and learns the identity of the prior bank. Written notice reasonably identifying the check and the basis for recovery is sufficient if the check is not available. Receipt of notice by the bank against which the claim is made is not a precondition to recovery by charge-back or other means; however, a bank may be liable for negligence for failure to provide timely notice. A paying or returning bank also may recover from a prior collecting bank as provided in §§ 229.30(b) and 229.31(b). This provision is not a substitute for a paying or returning bank making expeditious return under §§ 229.30(a) or 229.31(b). This paragraph does not affect a paying bank's accountability for a check under U.C.C. 4–215(a) and 4–302. Nor does this paragraph affect a collecting bank's accountability under U.C.C. 4–213 and 4–215(d). A collecting bank becomes accountable upon receipt of final settlement as provided in the foregoing U.C.C. sections. The term

final settlement in §§ 229.31 (c), 229.32 (b), and 229.36(d) is intended to be consistent with the use of the term final settlement in the U.C.C. (e.g., U.C.C. 4–213, 4–214, and 4–215). (See also § 229.2(cc) and Commentary.)

6.   This paragraph also provides that a bank may have the rights of a holder based on the handling of the check for collection or return. A bank may become a holder or a holder in due course regardless of whether prior banks have complied with the indorsement standard in § 229.35(a) and Appendix D.

7.   This paragraph affects the following provisions of the U.C.C., and may affect other provisions:

a.   Section 4–214(a), in that the right to recovery is not based on provisional settlement, and recovery may be had from any prior bank. Section 4–214(a) would continue to permit a depositary bank to recover a provisional settlement from its customer. (See § 229.33(d).)

b.   Section 3–415 and related provisions (such as section 3–503), in that such provisions would not apply as between banks, or as between the depositary bank and its customer.

C.   229.35(c) Indorsement by Bank

1.   This section protects the rights of a customer depositing a check in a bank without requiring the words "pay any bank," as required by the U.C.C. (See U.C.C. 4–201(b).) Use of this language in a depositary bank's indorsement will make it more difficult for other banks to identify the depositary bank. The indorsement standard in Appendix D prohibits such material in subsequent collecting bank indorsements. The existence of a bank indorsement provides notice of the restrictive indorsement without any additional words.

D.   229.35(d) Indorsement for Depositary Bank

1.   This section permits a depositary bank to arrange with another bank to indorse checks. This practice may occur when a correspondent indorses for a respondent, or when the bank servicing an ATM or lock box indorses for the bank maintaining the account in which the check is deposited—i.e., the depositary bank. If the indorsing bank applies the depositary bank's indorsement, checks will be returned to the depositary bank. If the indorsing bank does not apply the depositary bank's indorsement, by agreement with the depositary bank it may apply its own indorsement as the depositary bank indorsement. In that case, the depositary bank's own indorsement on the check (if any) should avoid the location reserved for the depositary bank. The actual depositary bank remains responsible for the availability and other requirements of Subpart B, but the bank indorsing as depositary bank is considered the depositary bank for purposes of Subpart C. The check will be returned, and notice of nonpayment will be given, to the bank indorsing as depositary bank.

2.   Because the depositary bank for Subpart B purposes will desire prompt notice of nonpayment, its arrangement with the indorsing bank should provide for prompt notice of nonpayment. The bank indorsing as depositary bank may require the depositary bank to agree to take up the check if the check is not paid even if the depositary bank's indorsement does not appear on the check and it did not handle the check. The arrangement between the banks may constitute an agreement varying the effect of provisions of Subpart C under § 229.37.

XXII.   Section 229.36 Presentment and Issuance of Checks

A.   229.36(a) Payable Through and Payable at Checks

1.   For purposes of Subpart C, the regulation defines a payable-through or payable-at bank (which could be designated the collectible-through or collectible-at bank) as a paying bank. The requirements of § 229.30(a) and the notice of nonpayment requirements of § 229.33 are imposed on a payable-through or payable-at bank and are based on the time of receipt of the forward collection check by the payable-through or payable-at bank. This provision is intended to speed the return of checks that are payable through or at a bank to the depositary bank.

B.   229.36(b) Receipt at Bank Office or Processing Center

1.   This paragraph seeks to facilitate efficient presentment of checks to promote early return or notice of nonpayment to the depositary bank and clarifies the law as to the effect of presentment by routing

number. This paragraph differs from § 229.32(a) because presentment of checks differs from delivery of returned checks.

2.   The paragraph specifies four locations at which the paying bank must accept presentment of checks. Where the check is payable through a bank and the check is sent to that bank, the payable-through bank is the paying bank for purposes of this subpart, regardless of whether the paying bank must present the check to another bank or to a nonbank payor for payment.

a.   Delivery of checks may be made, and presentment is considered to occur, at a location (including a processing center) requested by the paying bank. This is the way most checks are presented by banks today. This provision adopts the common law rule of a number of legal decisions that the processing center acts as the agent of the paying bank to accept presentment and to begin the time for processing of the check. (See also U.C.C. 4–204(c).) If a bank designates different locations for the presentment of forward collection checks bearing different routing numbers, for purposes of this paragraph it requests presentment of checks bearing a particular routing number only at the location designated for receipt of forward collection checks bearing that routing number.

b.   i. Delivery may be made at an office of the bank associated with the routing number on the check. The office associated with the routing number of a bank is found in American Bankers Association Key to Routing Numbers, published by an agent of the American Bankers Association, which lists a city and state address for each routing number. Checks generally are handled by collecting banks on the basis of the nine-digit routing number encoded in magnetic ink (or on the basis of the fractional form routing number if the magnetic ink characters are obliterated) on the check, rather than the printed name or address. The definition of a paying bank in § 229.2(z) includes a bank designated by routing number, whether or not there is a name on the check, and whether or not any name is consistent with the routing number. Where a check is payable by one bank, but payable through another, the routing number is that of the payable-through bank, not that of the payor bank. As the payor bank has selected the payable-through bank as the point through which presentment is to be made, it is proper to treat the payable-through bank as the paying bank for purposes of this section.

ii.   There is no requirement in the regulation that the name and address on the check agree with the address associated with the routing number on the check. A bank generally may control the use of its routing number, just as it does the use of its name. The address associated with the routing number may be a processing center.

iii.   In some cases, a paying bank may have several offices in the city associated with the routing number. In such case, it would not be reasonable or efficient to require the presenting bank to sort the checks by more specific branch addresses that might be printed on the checks, and to deliver the checks to each branch. A collecting bank normally would deliver all checks to one location. In cases where checks are delivered to a branch other than the branch on which they may be drawn, computer and courier communication among branches should permit the paying bank to determine quickly whether to pay the check.

c.   If the check specifies the name of the paying bank but no address, the bank must accept delivery at any office. Where delivery is made by a person other than a bank, or where the routing number is not readable, delivery will be made based on the name and address of the paying bank on the check. If there is no address, delivery may be made at any office of the paying bank. This provision is consistent with U.C.C. 3–111, which states that presentment for payment may be made at the place specified in the instrument, or, if there is none, at the place of business of the party to pay. Thus, there is a trade-off for a paying bank between specifying a particular address on a check to limit locations of delivery, and simply stating the name of the bank to encourage wider currency for the check.

d.   If the check specifies the name and address of a branch or head office, or other location (such as a processing center), the check may be delivered by delivery to that office or other location. If the address is too general to identify a particular office, delivery may be made at any office consistent with the address. For example, if the address is "San Francisco, California," each office in San Francisco must accept presentment. The designation of an address on the check generally is in the control of the paying bank.

3.   This paragraph may affect U.C.C. 3–111 to the extent that the U.C.C. requires presentment to occur at a place specified in the instrument.

C.   [Reserved]

D.   229.36(d) Liability of Bank During Forward Collection

1.   This paragraph makes settlement between banks during forward collection final when made, subject to any deferment of credit, just as settlements between banks during the return of checks are final. In addition, this paragraph clarifies that this change does not affect the liability scheme under U.C.C. 4–201 during forward collection of a check. That U.C.C. section provides that, unless a contrary intent clearly appears, a bank is an agent or subagent of the owner of a check, but that Article 4 of the U.C.C. applies even though a bank may have purchased an item and is the owner of it. This paragraph preserves the liability of a collecting bank to prior collecting banks and the depositary bank's customer for negligence during the forward collection of a check under the U.C.C., even though this paragraph provides that settlement between banks during forward collection is final rather than provisional. Settlement by a paying bank is not considered to be final payment for the purposes of U.C.C. 4–215(a)(2) or (3), because a paying bank has the right to recover settlement from a returning or depositary bank to which it returns a check under this subpart. Other provisions of the U.C.C. not superseded by this subpart, such as section 4–202, also continue to apply to the forward collection of a check and may apply to the return of a check. (See definition of returning bank in § 229.2(cc).)

E.   229.36(e) Issuance of Payable Through Checks

1.   If a bank arranges for checks payable by it to be payable through another bank, it must require its customers to use checks that contain conspicuously on their face the name, location, and first four digits of the nine-digit routing number of the bank by which the check is payable and the legend "payable through" followed by the name of the payable-through bank. The first four digits of the nine-digit routing number and the location of the bank by which the check is payable must be associated with the same check processing region. (This section does not affect § 229.36(b).) The required information is deemed conspicuous if it is printed in a type size not smaller than six-point type and if it is contained in the title plate, which is located in the lower left quadrant of the check. The required information may be conspicuous if it is located elsewhere on the check.

2.   If a payable-through check does not meet the requirements of this paragraph, the bank by which the check is payable may be liable to the depositary bank or others as provided in § 229.38. For example, a bank by which a payable-through check is payable could be liable to a depositary bank that suffers a loss, such as lost interest or liability under Subpart B, that would not have occurred had the check met the requirements of this paragraph. Similarly, a bank may be liable under § 229.38 if a check payable by it that is not payable through another bank is labeled as provided in this section. For example, a bank that holds checking accounts and processes checks at a central location but has widely-dispersed branches may be liable under this section if it labels all of its checks as "payable through" a single branch and includes the name, address, and four-digit routing symbol of another branch. These checks would not be payable through another bank and should not be labeled as payable-through checks. (All of a bank's offices within the United States are considered part of the same bank; see § 229.2(e).) In this example, the bank by which the checks are payable could be liable to a depositary bank that suffers a loss, such as lost interest or liability under Subpart B, due to the mislabeled check. The bank by which the check is payable may be liable for additional damages if it fails to act in good faith.

F.   229.36(f) Same-Day Settlement

1.   This paragraph provides that, under certain conditions, a paying bank must settle with a presenting bank for a check on the same day the check is presented in order to avail itself of the ability to return the check on its next banking day under U.C.C. 4–301 and 4–302. This paragraph does not apply to checks presented for immediate payment over the counter. Settling for a check under this paragraph does not constitute final payment of the check under the U.C.C. This paragraph does not supersede or limit the rules governing collection and return of checks through Federal Reserve Banks that are contained in Subpart A of Regulation J (12 CFR part 210).

COMMENTARY ON REGULATION CC

2.   Presentment requirements.

a.   Location and time.

i.   For presented checks to qualify for mandatory same-day settlement, information accompanying the checks must indicate that presentment is being made under this paragraph—e.g. "these checks are being presented for same-day settlement"—and must include a demand for payment of the total amount of the checks together with appropriate payment instructions in order to enable the paying bank to discharge its settlement responsibilities under this paragraph. In addition, the check or checks must be presented at a location designated by the paying bank for receipt of checks for same-day settlement by 8:00 a.m. local time of that location. The designated presentment location must be a location at which the paying bank would be considered to have received a check under § 229.36(b). The paying bank may not designate a location solely for presentment of checks subject to settlement under this paragraph; by designating a location for the purposes of § 229.36(f), the paying bank agrees to accept checks at that location for the purposes of § 229.36(b).

ii.   The designated presentment location also must be within the check processing region consistent with the nine-digit routing number encoded in magnetic ink on the check. A paying bank that uses more than one routing number associated with a single check processing region may designate, for purposes of this paragraph, one or more locations in that check processing region at which checks will be accepted, but the paying bank must accept any checks with a routing number associated with that check processing region at each designated location. A paying bank may designate a presentment location for traveler's checks with an 8000-series routing number anywhere in the country because these traveler's checks are not associated with any check processing region. The paying bank, however, must accept at that presentment location any other checks for which it is paying bank that have a routing number consistent with the check processing region of that location.

iii.   If the paying bank does not designate a presentment location, it must accept presentment for same-day settlement at any location identified in § 229.36(b), i.e., at an address of the bank associated with the routing number on the check, at any branch or head office if the bank is identified on the check by name without address, or at a branch, head office, or other location consistent with the name and address of the bank on the check if the bank is identified on the check by name and address. A paying bank and a presenting bank may agree that checks will be accepted for same-day settlement at an alternative location (e.g., at an intercept processor located in a different check processing region) or that the cut-off time for same-day settlement be earlier or later than 8:00 a.m. local time.

iv.   In the case of a check payable through a bank but payable by another bank, this paragraph does not authorize direct presentment to the bank by which the check is payable. The requirements of same-day settlement under this paragraph would apply to a payable-through or payable-at bank to which the check is sent for payment or collection.

b.   Reasonable delivery requirements. A check is considered presented when it is delivered to and payment is demanded at a location specified in paragraph (f)(1). Ordinarily, a presenting bank will find it necessary to contact the paying bank to determine the appropriate presentment location and any delivery instructions. Further, because presentment might not take place during the paying bank's banking day, a paying bank may establish reasonable delivery requirements to safeguard the checks presented, such as use of a night depository. If a presenting bank fails to follow reasonable delivery requirements established by the paying bank, it runs the risk that it will not have presented the checks. However, if no reasonable delivery requirements are established or if the paying bank does not make provisions for accepting delivery of checks during its non-business hours, leaving the checks at the presentment location constitutes effective presentment.

c.   Sorting of checks. A paying bank may require that checks presented to it for same-day settlement be sorted separately from other forward collection checks it receives as a collecting bank or returned checks it receives as a returning or depositary bank. For example, if a bank provides correspondent check collection services and receives unsorted checks from a respondent bank that include checks for which it is the paying bank and that would otherwise meet the requirements for same-day settlement under this section, the collecting bank need not make settlement in accordance with paragraph (f)(2). If the collecting bank receives sorted checks from its respondent bank, consisting only of checks for which the collecting bank is the paying bank and that meet the requirements for same-day settlement under this paragraph, the collecting bank may not charge a fee for handling those checks and must make settlement in accordance with this paragraph.

3.   Settlement

a.   If a bank presents a check in accordance with the time and location requirements for presentment under paragraph (f)(1), the paying bank either must settle for the check on the business day it receives the check without charging a presentment fee or return the check prior to the time for settlement. (This return deadline is subject to extension under § 229.30(c).) The settlement must be in the form of a credit to an account designated by the presenting bank at a Federal Reserve Bank (e.g., a Fedwire transfer). The presenting bank may agree with the paying bank to accept settlement in another form (e.g., credit to an account of the presenting bank at the paying bank or debit to an account of the paying bank at the presenting bank). The settlement must occur by the close of Fedwire on the business day the check is received by the paying bank. Under the provisions of § 229.34(c), a settlement owed to a presenting bank may be set off by adjustments for previous settlements with the presenting bank. (See also § 229.39(d).)

b.   Checks that are presented after the 8 a.m. (local time) presentment deadline for same-day settlement and before the paying bank's cut-off hour are treated as if they were presented under other applicable law and settled for or returned accordingly. However, for purposes of settlement only, the presenting bank may require the paying bank to treat such checks as presented for same-day settlement on the next business day in lieu of accepting settlement by cash or other means on the business day the checks are presented to the paying bank. Checks presented after the paying bank's cut-off hour or on non-business days, but otherwise in accordance with this paragraph, are considered presented for same-day settlement on the next business day.

4.   Closed Paying Bank

a.   There may be certain business days that are not banking days for the paying bank. Some paying banks may continue to settle for checks presented on these days (e.g., by opening their back office operations or by using an intercept processor). In other cases, a paying bank may be unable to settle for checks presented on a day it is closed.

If the paying bank closes on a business day and checks are presented to the paying bank in accordance with paragraph (f)(1), the paying bank is accountable for the checks unless it settles for or returns the checks by the close of Fedwire on its next banking day. In addition, checks presented on a business day on which the paying bank is closed are considered received on the paying bank's next banking day for purposes of the U.C.C. midnight deadline (U.C.C. 4–301 and 4–302) and this regulation's expeditious return and notice of nonpayment provisions.

b.   If the paying bank is closed on a business day voluntarily, the paying bank must pay interest compensation, as defined in § 229.2(oo), to the presenting bank for the value of the float associated with the check from the day of the voluntary closing until the day of settlement. Interest compensation is not required in the case of an involuntary closing on a business day, such as a closing required by state law. In addition, if the paying bank is closed on a business day due to emergency conditions, settlement delays and interest compensation may be excused under § 229.38(e) or U.C.C. 4–109(b).

5.   Good faith. Under § 229.38(a), both presenting banks and paying banks are held to a standard of good faith, defined in § 229.2(nn) to mean honesty in fact and the observance of reasonable commercial standards of fair dealing. For example, designating a presentment location or changing presentment locations for the primary purpose of discouraging banks from presenting checks for same-day settlement might not be considered good faith on the part of the paying bank. Similarly, presenting a large volume of checks without prior notice could be viewed as not meeting reasonable commercial standards of fair dealing and therefore may not constitute presentment in good faith. In addition, if banks, in the general course of business, regularly agree to certain practices related to same-day settlement, it might not be considered consistent with reasonable commercial standards of fair dealing, and therefore might not be considered good faith, for a bank to refuse to agree to those practices if agreeing would not cause it harm.

6.   U.C.C. sections affected. This paragraph directly affects the following provisions of the U.C.C. and may affect other sections or provisions:

a.   Section 4–204(b)(1), in that a presenting bank may not send a check for same-day settlement directly to the paying bank, if the paying bank designates a different location in accordance with paragraph (f)(1).

b.   Section 4–213(a), in that the medium of settlement for checks presented under this paragraph is limited to a credit to an account at a Federal Reserve Bank and that, for checks presented after the deadline for same-day settlement and before the paying bank's cut-off hour, the presenting bank may require settlement on the next business day in accordance with this paragraph rather than accept settlement on the business day of presentment by cash.

c.   Section 4–301(a), in that, to preserve the ability to exercise deferred posting, the time limit specified in that section for settlement or return by a paying bank on the banking day a check is received is superseded by the requirement to settle for checks presented under this paragraph by the close of Fedwire.

d.   Section 4–302(a), in that, to avoid accountability, the time limit specified in that section for settlement or return by a paying bank on the banking day a check is received is superseded by the requirement to settle for checks presented under this paragraph by the close of Fedwire.

XXIII. Section 229.37 Variations by Agreement

A.   This section is similar to U.C.C. 4–103, and permits consistent treatment of agreements varying Article 4 or Subpart C, given the substantial interrelationship of the two documents. To achieve consistency, the official comment to U.C.C. 4–103(a) (which in turn follows U.C.C. 1–201(3)) should be followed in construing this section. For example, as stated in Official Comment 2 to section 4–103, owners of items and other interested parties are not affected by agreements under this section unless they are parties to the agreement or are bound by adoption, ratification, estoppel, or the like. In particular, agreements varying this subpart that delay the return of a check beyond the times required by this subpart may result in liability under § 229.38 to entities not party to the agreement.

B.   The Board has not followed U.C.C. 4–103(b), which permits Federal Reserve regulations and operating letters, clearinghouse rules, and the like to apply to parties that have not specifically assented. Nevertheless, this section does not affect the status of such agreements under the U.C.C.

C.   The following are examples of situations where variation by agreement is permissible, subject to the limitations of this section:

1.   A depositary bank may authorize another bank to apply the other bank's indorsement to a check as the depositary bank. (See § 229.35(d).)

2.   A depositary bank may authorize returning banks to commingle qualified returned checks with forward collection checks. (See § 229.32(a).)

3.   A depositary bank may limit its liability to its customer in connection with the late return of a deposited check where the lateness is caused by markings on the check by the depositary bank's customer or prior indorser in the area of the depositary bank indorsement. (See § 229.38(d).)

4.   A paying bank may require its customer to assume the paying bank's liability for delayed or missent checks where the delay or missending is caused by markings placed on the check by the paying bank's customer that obscured a properly placed indorsement of the depositary bank. (See § 229.38(d).)

5.   A collecting or paying bank may agree to accept forward collection checks without the indorsement of a prior collecting bank. (See § 229.35(a).)

6.   A bank may agree to accept returned checks without the indorsement of a prior bank. (See § 229.35(a).)

7.   A presenting bank may agree with a paying bank to present checks for same-day settlement at a location that is not in the check processing region consistent with the routing number on the checks. (See § 229.36(f)(1)(i).)

8.   A presenting bank may agree with a paying bank to present checks for same-day settlement by a deadline earlier or later than 8:00 a.m. (See § 229.36(f)(1)(ii).)

COMMENTARY ON REGULATION CC

9.   A presenting bank and a paying bank may agree that presentment takes place when the paying bank receives an electronic transmission of information describing the check rather than upon delivery of the physical check. (See § 229.36(b).)

10.   A depositary bank may agree with a paying or returning bank to accept an image or other notice in lieu of a returned check even when the check is available for return under this part. Except to the extent that other parties interested in the check assent to or are bound by the variation of the notice-in-lieu provisions of this part, banks entering into such an agreement may be responsible under this part or other applicable law to other interested parties for any losses caused by the handling of a returned check under the agreement. (See §§ 229.30(f), 229.31(f), 229.38(a).)

D.   The Board expects to review the types of variation by agreement that develop under this section and will consider whether it is necessary to limit certain variations.

XXIV. Section 229.38 Liability

A.   229.38(a) Standard of care; liability; measure of damages

1.   The standard of care established by this section applies to any bank covered by the requirements of Subpart C of the regulation. Thus, the standard of care applies to a paying bank under §§ 229.30 and 229.33, to a returning bank under § 229.31, to a depositary bank under §§ 229.32 and 229.33, to a bank erroneously receiving a returned check or written notice of nonpayment as depositary bank under § 229.32(d), and to a bank indorsing a check under § 229.35. The standard of care is similar to the standard imposed by U.C.C. 1–203 and 4–103(a) and includes a duty to act in good faith, as defined in § 229.2(nn) of this regulation.

2.   A bank not meeting this standard of care is liable to the depositary bank, the depositary bank's customer, the owner of the check, or another party to the check. The depositary bank's customer is usually a depositor of a check in the depositary bank (but see § 229.35(d)). The measure of damages provided in this section (loss incurred up to amount of check, less amount of loss party would have incurred even if bank had exercised ordinary care) is based on U.C.C. 4–103(e) (amount of the item reduced by an amount that could not have been realized by the exercise of ordinary care), as limited by 4–202(c) (bank is liable only for its own negligence and not for actions of subsequent banks in chain of collection). This subpart does not absolve a collecting bank of liability to prior collecting banks under U.C.C. 4–201.

3.   Under this measure of damages, a depositary bank or other person must show that the damage incurred results from the negligence proved. For example, the depositary bank may not simply claim that its customer will not accept a charge-back of a returned check, but must prove that it could not charge back when it received the returned check and could have charged back if no negligence had occurred, and must first attempt to collect from its customer. (See Marcoux v. Van Wyk, 572 F.2d 651 (8th Cir. 1978); Appliance Buyers Credit Corp. v. Prospect Nat'l Bank, 708 F.2d 290 (7th Cir. 1983).) Generally, a paying or returning bank's liability would not be reduced because the depositary bank did not place a hold on its customer's deposit before it learned of nonpayment of the check.

4.   This paragraph also states that it does not affect a paying bank's liability to its customer. Under U.C.C. 4–402, for example, a paying bank is liable to its customer for wrongful dishonor, which is different from failure to exercise ordinary care and has a different measure of damages.

B.   229.38(b) Paying Bank's Failure To Make Timely Return

1.   Section 229.30(a) imposes requirements on the paying bank for expeditious return of a check and leaves in place the U.C.C. deadlines (as they may be modified by § 229.30(c)), which may allow return at a different time. This paragraph clarifies that the paying bank could be liable for failure to meet either standard, but not for failure to meet both. The regulation intends to preserve the paying bank's accountability for missing its midnight or other deadline under the U.C.C., (e.g., sections 4–215 and 4–302), provisions that are not incorporated in this regulation, but may be useful in establishing the time of final payment by the paying bank.

COMMENTARY ON REGULATION CC

C.   229.38(c) Comparative negligence

1.   This paragraph establishes a "pure" comparative negligence standard for liability under Subpart C of this regulation. This comparative negligence rule may have particular application where a paying or returning bank delays in returning a check because of difficulty in identifying the depositary bank. Some examples will illustrate liability in such cases. In each example, it is assumed that the returned check is received by the depositary bank after it has made funds available to its customer, that it may no longer recover the funds from its customer, and that the inability to recover the funds from the customer is due to a delay in returning the check contrary to the standards established by §§ 229.30(a) or 229.31(a).

2.   Examples.

a.   If a depositary bank fails to use the indorsement required by this regulation, and this failure is caused by a failure to exercise ordinary care, and if a paying or returning bank is delayed in returning the check because additional time is required to identify the depositary bank or find its routing number, the paying or returning bank's liability to the depositary bank would be reduced or eliminated.

b.   If the depositary bank uses the standard indorsement, but that indorsement is obscured by a subsequent collecting bank's indorsement, and a paying or returning bank is delayed in returning the check because additional time was required to identify the depositary bank or find its routing number, the paying or returning bank may not be liable to the depositary bank because the delay was not due to its negligence. Nonetheless, the collecting bank may be liable to the depositary bank to the extent that its negligence in indorsing the check caused the paying or returning bank's delay.

c.   If a depositary bank accepts a check that has printing, a carbon band, or other material on the back of the check that existed at the time the check was issued, and the depositary bank's indorsement is obscured by the printing, carbon band, or other material, and a paying or returning bank is delayed in returning the check because additional time was required to identify the depositary bank, the returning bank may not be liable to the depositary bank because the delay was not due to its negligence. Nonetheless, the paying bank may be liable to the depositary bank to the extent that the printing, carbon band, or other material caused the delay.

D.   229.38(d) Responsibility for Certain Aspects of Checks

1.   Responsibility for back of check. The indorsement standard in § 229.35 is most effective if the back of the check remains clear of other matter that may obscure bank indorsements. Because bank indorsements are usually applied by automated equipment, it is not possible to avoid pre-existing matter on the back of the check. For example, bank indorsements are not required to avoid a carbon band or printed, stamped, or written terms or notations on the back of the check. Accordingly, this provision places responsibility on the paying bank, depositary bank, or reconverting bank, as appropriate, for keeping the back of the check clear for bank indorsements during forward collection and return.

2.   ANS X9.100–140 provides that an image of an original check must be reduced in size when placed on the first substitute check associated with that original check. (The image thereafter would be constant in size on any subsequent substitute check that might be created.) Because of this size reduction, the location of an indorsement, particularly a depositary bank indorsement, applied to an original paper check likely will change when the first reconverting bank creates a substitute check that contains that indorsement within the image of the original paper check. If the indorsement was applied to the original paper check in accordance with appendix D's location requirements for indorsements applied to existing paper checks, and if the size reduction of the image causes the placement of the indorsement to no longer be consistent with the appendix's requirements, then the reconverting bank bears the liability for any loss that results from the shift in the placement of the indorsement. Such a loss could result either because the original indorsement applied in accordance with appendix D is rendered illegible by a subsequent indorsement that later is applied to the substitute check in accordance with appendix D, or because the subsequent bank cannot apply its indorsement to the substitute check legibly in accordance with appendix D as a result of the shift in the previous indorsement.

COMMENTARY ON REGULATION CC

Example.

In accordance with appendix D's specifications, a depositary bank sprays its indorsement onto a business-sized original check between 3.0 inches from the leading edge of the check and 1.5 inches from the trailing edge of the check. The check's conversion to electronic form and subsequent reconversion to paper form causes the location of the depositary bank indorsement, now contained within the image of the original check, to change such that it is less than 3.0 inches from the leading edge of the substitute check. In accordance with appendix D's specifications, a subsequent collecting bank sprays its indorsement onto the substitute check between the leading edge of the check and 3.0 inches from the leading edge of the check and the indorsement happens to be on top of the shifted depositary bank indorsement. If the check is returned unpaid and the return is not expeditious because of the illegibility of the depositary bank indorsement, and the depositary bank incurs a loss that it would not have incurred had the return been expeditious, the reconverting bank bears the liability for that loss.

3. Responsibility for payable-through checks.

a. This paragraph provides that the bank by which a payable-through check is payable is liable for damages under paragraph (a) of this section to the extent that the check is not returned through the payable-through bank as quickly as would have been necessary to meet the requirements of § 229.30(a)(1) (the 2-day/4-day test) had the bank by which it is payable received the check as paying bank on the day the payable-through bank received it. The location of the bank by which a check is payable for purposes of the 2-day/4-day test may be determined from the location or the first four digits of the routing number of the bank by which the check is payable. This information should be stated on the check. (See § 229.36(e) and accompanying Commentary.) Responsibility under paragraph (d)(2) does not include responsibility for the time required for the forward collection of a check to the payable-through bank.

b. Generally, liability under paragraph (d)(2) will be limited in amount. Under § 229.33(a), a paying bank that returns a check in the amount of $2,500 or more must provide notice of nonpayment to the depositary bank by 4:00 p.m. on the second business day following the banking day on which the check is presented to the paying bank. Even if a payable-through check in the amount of $2,500 or more is not returned through the payable-through bank as quickly as would have been required had the check been received by the bank by which it is payable, the depositary bank should not suffer damages unless it has not received timely notice of nonpayment. Thus, ordinarily the bank by which a payable-through check is payable would be liable under paragraph (a) only for checks in amounts up to $2,500, and the paying bank would be responsible for notice of nonpayment for checks in the amount of $2,500 or more.

4. Responsibility under paragraphs (d)(1) and (d)(2) is treated as negligence for comparative negligence purposes, and the contribution to damages under paragraphs (d)(1) and (d)(2) is treated in the same way as the degree of negligence under paragraph (c) of this section.

E.   229.38(e) Timeliness of Action

1. This paragraph excuses certain delays. It adopts the standard of U.C.C. 4–109(b).

F.   229.38(f) Exclusion

1. This paragraph provides that the civil liability and class action provisions, particularly the punitive damage provisions of sections 611(a) and (b), and the bona fide error provision of 611(c) of the EFA Act (12 U.S.C. 4010(a), (b), and (c)) do not apply to regulatory provisions adopted to improve the efficiency of the payments mechanism. Allowing punitive damages for delays in the return of checks where no actual damages are incurred would only encourage litigation and provide little or no benefit to the check collection system. In view of the provisions of paragraph (a), which incorporate traditional bank collection standards based on negligence, the provision on bona fide error is not included in Subpart C.

G.   229.38(g) Jurisdiction

1. The EFA Act confers subject matter jurisdiction on courts of competent jurisdiction and provides a time limit for civil actions for violations of this subpart.

COMMENTARY ON REGULATION CC

H.   229.38(h) Reliance on Board Rulings

1.   This provision shields banks from civil liability if they act in good faith in reliance on any rule, regulation, or interpretation of the Board, even if it were subsequently determined to be invalid. Banks may rely on the Commentary to this regulation, which is issued as an official Board interpretation, as well as on the regulation itself.

XXV.   Section 229.39 Insolvency of Bank

A.   Introduction

1.   These provisions cover situations where a bank becomes insolvent during collection or return and are derived from U.C.C. 4–216. They are intended to apply to all banks.

B.   229.39(a) Duty of Receiver

1.   This paragraph requires a receiver of a closed bank to return a check to the prior bank if it does not pay for the check. This permits the prior bank, as holder, to pursue its claims against the closed bank or prior indorsers on the check.

C.   229.39(b) Preference Against Paying or Depositary Bank

1.   This paragraph gives a bank a preferred claim against a closed paying bank that finally pays a check without settling for it or a closed depositary bank that becomes obligated to pay a returned check without settling for it. If the bank with a preferred claim under this paragraph recovers from a prior bank or other party to the check, the prior bank or other party to the check is subrogated to the preferred claim.

D.   229.39(c) Preference Against Paying,
Collecting, or Depositary Bank

1.   This paragraph gives a bank a preferred claim against a closed collecting, paying, or returning bank that receives settlement but does not settle for a check. (See Commentary to § 229.35(b) for discussion of prior and subsequent banks.) As in the case of § 229.39(b), if the bank with a preferred claim under this paragraph recovers from a prior bank or other party to the check, the prior bank or other party to the check is subrogated to the preferred claim.

E.   229.39(d) Preference Against Presenting Bank

1.   This paragraph gives a paying bank a preferred claim against a closed presenting bank in the event that the presenting bank breaches an amount or encoding warranty as provided in § 229.34(c)(1) or (3) and does not reimburse the paying bank for adjustments for a settlement made by the paying bank in excess of the value of the checks presented. This preference is intended to have the effect of a perfected security interest and is intended to put the paying bank in the position of a secured creditor for purposes of the receivership provisions of the Federal Deposit Insurance Act and similar provisions of state law.

F.   229.39(e) Finality of Settlement

1.   This paragraph provides that insolvency does not interfere with the finality of a settlement, such as a settlement by a paying bank that becomes final by expiration of the midnight deadline.

XXVI.   Section 229.40 Effect on Merger Transaction

A.   When banks merge, there is normally a period of adjustment required before their operations are consolidated. To allow for this adjustment period, the regulation provides that the merged banks may be treated as separate banks for a period of up to one year after the consummation of the transaction. The term merger transaction is defined in § 229.2(t). This rule affects the status of the combined entity in a number of areas in this subpart. For example:

1.   The paying bank's responsibility for expeditious return (§ 229.30).

2.   The returning bank's responsibility for expeditious return (§ 229.31).

3.   Whether a returning bank is entitled to an extra day to qualify a return that will be delivered directly to a depositary bank that has merged with the returning bank (§ 229.31(a)).

COMMENTARY ON REGULATION CC

4. Where the depositary bank must accept returned checks (§ 229.32(a)).

5. Where the depositary bank must accept notice of nonpayment (§ 229.33(c)).

6. Where a paying bank must accept presentment of checks (§ 229.36(b)).

XXVII. Section 229.41 Relation to State Law

A. This section specifies that state law relating to the collection of checks is preempted only to the extent that it is inconsistent with this regulation. Thus, this regulation is not a complete replacement for state laws relating to the collection or return of checks.

XXVIII. Section 229.42 Exclusions

A. Checks drawn on the United States Treasury, U.S. Postal Service money orders, and checks drawn on states and units of general local government that are presented directly to the state or unit of general local government and that are not payable through or at a bank are excluded from the coverage of the expeditious-return, notice-of-nonpayment, and same-day settlement requirements of subpart C of this part. Other provisions of this subpart continue to apply to the checks. This exclusion does not apply to checks drawn by the U.S. government on banks.

XXIX. Section 229.43 Checks Payable in Guam, American Samoa, and the Northern Mariana Islands

A. 229.43(a) Definitions

1. Bank offices in Guam, American Samoa, and the Northern Mariana Islands (which Regulation CC defines as Pacific island banks) do not meet the definition of bank in § 229.2(e) because they are not located in the United States. Some checks drawn on Pacific island banks (defined as Pacific island checks) bear U.S. routing numbers and are collected and returned by banks in the same manner as checks payable in the U.S.

B. 229.43(b) Rules Applicable to Pacific Island Checks

1. When a bank handles a Pacific island check as if it were a check as defined in § 229.2(k), the bank is subject to certain provisions of Regulation CC, as provided in this section. Because the Pacific island bank is not a bank as defined in § 229.2(e), it is not a paying bank as defined in § 229.2(z) (unless otherwise noted in this section). Pacific island banks are not subject to the provisions of Regulation CC.

2. A bank may agree to handle a Pacific island check as a returned check under § 229.31 and may convert the returned Pacific island check to a qualified returned check. The returning bank is not, however, subject to the expeditious-return requirements of § 229.31. The returning bank may receive the Pacific island check directly from a Pacific island bank or from another returning bank. As a Pacific island bank is not a paying bank under Regulation CC, § 229.31(c) does not apply to a returning bank settling with the Pacific island bank.

3. A depositary bank that handles a Pacific island check is not subject to the provisions of subpart B of Regulation CC, including the availability, notice, and interest accrual requirements, with respect to that check. If, however, a bank accepts a Pacific island check for deposit (or otherwise accepts the check as transferee) and collects the Pacific island check in the same manner as other checks, the bank is subject to the provisions of § 229.32, including the provisions regarding time and manner of settlement for returned checks in § 229.32(b), in the event the Pacific island check is returned by a returning bank. If the depositary bank receives the returned Pacific island check directly from the Pacific island bank, however, the provisions of § 229.32(b) do not apply, because the Pacific island bank is not a paying bank under Regulation CC. The depositary bank is not subject to the notice of nonpayment provisions in § 229.33 for Pacific island checks.

4. Banks that handle Pacific island checks in the same manner as other checks are subject to the indorsement provisions of § 229.35. Section 229.35(c) eliminates the need for the restrictive indorsement "pay any bank." For purposes of § 229.35(c), the Pacific island bank is deemed to be a bank.

5. Pacific island checks will often be intermingled with other checks in a single cash letter. Therefore, a bank that handles Pacific island checks in the same manner as other checks is subject to the transfer warranty provision in § 229.34(c)(2) regarding accurate cash letter totals and the encoding

warranty in § 229.34(c)(3). A bank that acts as a returning bank for a Pacific island check is not subject to the warranties in § 229.34(a). Similarly, because the Pacific island bank is not a "bank" or a "paying bank" under Regulation CC, § 229.34(b), (c)(1), and (c)(4) do not apply. For the same reason, the provisions of § 229.36 governing paying bank responsibilities such as place of receipt and same-day settlement do not apply to checks presented to a Pacific island bank, and the liability provisions applicable to paying banks in § 229.38 do not apply to Pacific island banks. Section 229.36(d), regarding finality of settlement between banks during forward collection, applies to banks that handle Pacific island checks in the same manner as other checks, as do the liability provisions of § 229.38, to the extent the banks are subject to the requirements of Regulation CC as provided in this section, and §§ 229.37 and 229.39 through 229.42.

XXX. § 229.51 General provisions governing substitute checks

A. § 229.51(a) Legal Equivalence

1.   Section 229.51(a) states that a substitute check for which a bank has provided the substitute check warranties is the legal equivalent of the original check for all purposes and all persons if it meets the accuracy and legend requirements. Where the law (or a contract) requires production of the original check, production of a legally equivalent substitute check would satisfy that requirement. A person that receives a substitute check cannot be assessed costs associated with the creation of the substitute check, absent agreement to the contrary.

Examples.

a.   A presenting bank presents a substitute check that meets the legal equivalence requirements to a paying bank. The paying bank cannot refuse presentment of the substitute check on the basis that it is a substitute check, because the substitute check is the legal equivalent of the original check.

b.   A depositor's account agreement with a bank provides that the depositor is entitled to receive original cancelled checks back with his or her periodic account statement. The bank may honor that agreement by providing original checks, substitute checks, or a combination thereof. However, a bank may not honor such an agreement by providing something other than an original check or a substitute check.

c.   A mortgage company argues that a consumer missed a monthly mortgage payment that the consumer believes she made. A legally equivalent substitute check concerning that mortgage payment could be used in the same manner as the original check to prove the payment.

2.   A person other than a bank that creates a substitute check could transfer, present, or return that check only by agreement unless and until a bank provided the substitute check warranties.

3.   To be the legal equivalent of the original check, a substitute check must accurately represent all the information on the front and back of the check as of the time the original check was truncated. An accurate representation of information that was illegible on the original check would satisfy this requirement. The payment instructions placed on the check by, or as authorized by, the drawer, such as the amount of the check, the payee, and the drawer's signature, must be accurately represented, because that information is an essential element of a negotiable instrument. Other information that must be accurately represented includes (1) the information identifying the drawer and the paying bank that is preprinted on the check, including the MICR line; and (2) other information placed on the check prior to the time an image of the check is captured, such as any required identification written on the front of the check and any indorsements applied to the back of the check. A substitute check need not capture other characteristics of the check, such as watermarks, microprinting, or other physical security features that cannot survive the imaging process or decorative images, in order to meet the accuracy requirement. Conversely, some security features that are latent on the original check might become visible as a result of the check imaging process. For example, the original check might have a faint representation of the word "void" that will appear more clearly on a photocopied or electronic image of the check. Provided the inclusion of the clearer version of the word on the image used to create a substitute check did not obscure the required information listed above, a substitute check that contained such information could be the legal equivalent of an original check under § 229.51(a). However, if a person suffered a loss due to receipt of such a substitute check instead of the original check, that person could have an indemnity claim under § 229.53 and, in the case of a consumer, an expedited recredit claim under § 229.54.

4.   To be the legal equivalent of the original check, a substitute check must bear the legal equivalence legend described in § 229.51(a)(2). A bank may not vary the language of the legal equivalence legend and must place the legend on the substitute check as specified by generally applicable industry standards for substitute checks contained in ANS X9.100–140.

5.   In some cases, the original check used to create a substitute check could be forged or otherwise fraudulent. A substitute check created from a fraudulent original check would have the same status under Regulation CC and the U.C.C. as the original fraudulent check. For example, a substitute check of a fraudulent original check would not be properly payable under U.C.C. 4–401 and would be subject to the transfer and presentment warranties in U.C.C. 4–207 and 4–208.

B.   229.51(b) Reconverting Bank Duties

1.   As discussed in more detail in appendix D and the commentary to § 229.35, a reconverting bank must indorse (or, if it is a paying bank with respect to the check, identify itself on) the back of a substitute check in a manner that preserves all indorsements applied, whether physically or electronically, by persons that previously handled the check in any form for forward collection or return. Indorsements applied physically to the original check before an image of the check was captured would be preserved through the image of the back of the original check that a substitute check must contain. Indorsements applied physically to the original check after an image of the original check was captured would be conveyed as electronic indorsements (see paragraph 3 of the commentary to § 229.35(a)). If indorsements were applied electronically after an image of the original check was captured or were applied electronically after a previous substitute check was converted to electronic form, the reconverting bank must apply those indorsements physically to the substitute check. A reconverting bank is not responsible for obtaining indorsements that persons that previously handled the check should have applied but did not apply.

2.   A reconverting bank also must identify itself as such on the front and back of the substitute check and must preserve on the back of the substitute check the identifications of any previous reconverting banks in accordance with appendix D. The presence on the back of a substitute check of indorsements that were applied by previous reconverting banks and identified with asterisks in accordance with appendix D would satisfy the requirement that the reconverting bank preserve the identification of previous reconverting banks. As discussed in more detail in the commentary to § 229.35, the reconverting bank and truncating bank routing numbers on the front of a substitute check and, if the reconverting bank is the paying bank, the reconverting bank's routing number on the back of a substitute check are for identification only and are not indorsements or acceptances.

3.   The reconverting bank must place the routing number of the truncating bank surrounded by brackets on the front of the substitute check in accordance with appendix D and ANS X9.100–140.

Example.

A bank's customer, which is a nonbank business, receives checks for payment and by agreement deposits substitute checks instead of the original checks with its depositary bank. The depositary bank is the reconverting bank with respect to the substitute checks and the truncating bank with respect to the original checks. In accordance with appendix D and with ANS X9.100–140, the bank must therefore be identified on the front of the substitute checks as a reconverting bank and as the truncating bank, and on the back of the substitute checks as the depositary bank and a reconverting bank.

C.   229.51(c) Applicable Law

1.   A substitute check that meets the requirements for legal equivalence set forth in this section is subject to any provision of federal or state law that applies to original checks, except to the extent such provision is inconsistent with the Check 21 Act or subpart D. A legally equivalent substitute check is subject to all laws that are not preempted by the Check 21 Act in the same manner and to the same extent as is an original check. Thus, any person could satisfy a law that requires production of an original check by producing a substitute check that is derived from the relevant original check and that meets the legal equivalence requirements of § 229.51(a).

2.   A law is not inconsistent with the Check 21 Act or subpart D merely because it allows for the recovery of a greater amount of damages.

COMMENTARY ON REGULATION CC

Example.

A drawer that suffers a loss with respect to a substitute check that was improperly charged to its account and for which the drawer has an indemnity claim but not a warranty claim would be limited under the Check 21 Act to recovery of the amount of the substitute check plus interest and expenses. However, if the drawer also suffered damages that were proximately caused because the bank wrongfully dishonored subsequently presented checks as a result of the improper substitute check charge, the drawer could recover those losses under U.C.C. 4–402.

XXXI. § 229.52 Substitute Check Warranties

A. 229.52(a) Warranty Content and Provision

1.   The responsibility for providing the substitute check warranties begins with the reconverting bank. In the case of a substitute check created by a bank, the reconverting bank starts the flow of warranties when it transfers, presents, or returns a substitute check for which it receives consideration. A bank that receives a substitute check created by a nonbank starts the flow of warranties when it transfers, presents, or returns for consideration either the substitute check it received or an electronic or paper representation of that substitute check. To ensure that warranty protections flow all the way through to the ultimate recipient of a substitute check or paper or electronic representation thereof, any subsequent bank that transfers, presents, or returns for consideration either the substitute check or a paper or electronic representation of the substitute check is responsible to subsequent transferees for the warranties. Any warranty recipient could bring a claim for a breach of a substitute check warranty if it received either the actual substitute check or a paper or electronic representation of a substitute check.

2.   The substitute check warranties and indemnity are not given under §§ 229.52 and 229.53 by a bank that truncates the original check and by agreement transfers the original check electronically to a subsequent bank for consideration. However, parties may, by agreement, allocate liabilities associated with the exchange of electronic check information.

Example.

A bank that receives check information electronically and uses it to create substitute checks is the reconverting bank and, when it transfers, presents, or returns that substitute check, becomes the first warrantor. However, that bank may protect itself by including in its agreement with the sending bank provisions that specify the sending bank's warranties and responsibilities to the receiving bank, particularly with respect to the accuracy of the check image and check data transmitted under the agreement.

3.   A bank need not affirmatively make the warranties because they attach automatically when a bank transfers, presents, or returns the substitute check (or a representation thereof) for which it receives consideration. Because a substitute check transferred, presented, or returned for consideration is warranted to be the legal equivalent of the original check and thereby subject to existing laws as if it were the original check, all U.C.C. and other Regulation CC warranties that apply to the original check also apply to the substitute check.

4.   The legal equivalence warranty by definition must be linked to a particular substitute check. When an original check is truncated, the check may move from electronic form to substitute check form and then back again, such that there would be multiple substitute checks associated with one original check. When a check changes form multiple times in the collection or return process, the first reconverting bank and subsequent banks that transfer, present, or return the first substitute check (or a paper or electronic representation of the first substitute check) warrant the legal equivalence of only the first substitute check. If a bank receives an electronic representation of a substitute check and uses that representation to create a second substitute check, the second reconverting bank and subsequent transferees of the second substitute check (or a representation thereof) warrant the legal equivalence of both the first and second substitute checks. A reconverting bank would not be liable for a warranty breach under § 229.52 if the legal equivalence defect is the fault of a subsequent bank that handled the substitute check, either as a substitute check or in other paper or electronic form.

5.   The warranty in § 229.52(a)(2), which addresses multiple payment requests for the same check, is not linked to a particular substitute check but rather is given by each bank handling the substitute check,

1942

an electronic representation of a substitute check, or a subsequent substitute check created from an electronic representation of a substitute check. All banks that transfer, present, or return a substitute check (or a paper or electronic representation thereof) therefore provide the warranty regardless of whether the ultimate demand for double payment is based on the original check, the substitute check, or some other electronic or paper representation of the substitute or original check, and regardless of the order in which the duplicative payment requests occur. This warranty is given by the banks that transfer, present, or return a substitute check even if the demand for duplicative payment results from a fraudulent substitute check about which the warranting bank had no knowledge.

Example.

A nonbank depositor truncates a check and in lieu thereof sends an electronic version of that check to both Bank A and Bank B. Bank A and Bank B each uses the check information that it received electronically to create a substitute check, which it presents to Bank C for payment. Bank A and Bank B each is a reconverting bank that made the substitute check warranties when it presented a substitute check to and received payment from Bank C. Bank C could pursue a warranty claim for the loss it suffered as a result of the duplicative payment against either Bank A or Bank B.

B.   229.52(b) Warranty Recipients

1.   A reconverting bank makes the warranties to the person to which it transfers, presents, or returns the substitute check for consideration and to any subsequent recipient that receives either the substitute check or a paper or electronic representation derived from the substitute check. These subsequent recipients could include a subsequent collecting or returning bank, the depositary bank, the drawer, the drawee, the payee, the depositor, and any indorser. The paying bank would be included as a warranty recipient, for example because it would be the drawee of a check or a transferee of a check that is payable through it.

2.   The warranties flow with the substitute check to persons that receive a substitute check or a paper or electronic representation of a substitute check. The warranties do not flow to a person that receives only the original check or a representation of an original check that was not derived from a substitute check. However, a person that initially handled only the original check could become a warranty recipient if that person later receives a returned substitute check or a paper or electronic representation of a substitute check that was derived from that original check.

XXXII.   § 229.53 Substitute Check Indemnity

A.   229.53(a) Scope of Indemnity

1.   Each bank that for consideration transfers, presents, or returns a substitute check or a paper or electronic representation of a substitute check is responsible for providing the substitute check indemnity. The indemnity covers losses due to any subsequent recipient's receipt of the substitute check instead of the original check. The indemnity therefore covers the loss caused by receipt of the substitute check as well as the loss that a bank incurs because it pays an indemnity to another person. A bank that pays an indemnity would in turn have an indemnity claim regardless of whether it received the substitute check or a paper or electronic representation of the substitute check The indemnity would not apply to a person that handled only the original check or a paper or electronic version of the original check that was not derived from a substitute check.

Examples.

a.   A paying bank makes payment based on a substitute check that was derived from a fraudulent original cashier's check. The amount and other characteristics of the original cashier's check are such that, had the original check been presented instead, the paying bank would have inspected the original check for security features. The paying bank's fraud detection procedures were designed to detect the fraud in question and allow the bank to return the fraudulent check in a timely manner. However, the security features that the bank would have inspected were security features that did not survive the imaging process (see the commentary to § 229.51(a)). Under these circumstances, the paying bank could assert an indemnity claim against the bank that presented the substitute check.

b.   By contrast with the previous examples, the indemnity would not apply if the characteristics of the presented substitute check were such that the bank's security policies and procedures would not have detected the fraud even if the original had been presented. For example, if the check was under the threshold amount at which the bank subjects an item to its fraud detection procedures, the bank would not have inspected the item for security features regardless of the form of the item and accordingly would have suffered a loss even if it had received the original check.

c.   A paying bank makes an erroneous payment based on an electronic representation of a substitute check because the electronic cash letter accompanying the electronic item included the wrong amount to be charged. The paying bank would not have an indemnity claim associated with that payment because its loss did not result from receipt of an actual substitute check instead of the original check. However, the paying bank could protect itself from such losses through its agreement with the bank that sent the check to it electronically and may have rights under other law.

d.   A drawer has agreed with its bank that the drawer will not receive paid checks with periodic account statements. The drawer requested a copy of a paid check in order to prove payment and received a photocopy of a substitute check. The photocopy that the bank provided in response to this request was illegible, such that the drawer could not prove payment. Any loss that the drawer suffered as a result of receiving the blurry check image would not trigger an indemnity claim because the loss was not caused by the receipt of a substitute check. The drawer may, however, still have a warranty claim if he received a copy of a substitute check, and may also have rights under the U.C.C.

B.   229.53(b) Indemnity Amount

1.   If a recipient of a substitute check is making an indemnity claim because a bank has breached one of the substitute check warranties, the recipient can recover any losses proximately caused by that warranty breach.

Examples.

a.   A drawer discovers that its account has been charged for two different substitute checks that were provided to the drawer and that were associated with the same original check. As a result of this duplicative charge, the paying bank dishonored several subsequently-presented checks that it otherwise would have paid and charged the drawer returned check fees. The payees of the returned checks also charged the drawer returned check fees. The drawer would have a warranty claim against any of the warranting banks, including its bank, for breach of the warranty described in § 229.52(a)(2). The drawer also could assert an indemnity claim. Because there is only one original check for any payment transaction, if the collecting and presenting bank had collected the original check instead of using a substitute check the bank would have been asked to make only one payment. The drawer could assert its warranty and indemnity claims against the paying bank, because that is the bank with which the drawer has a customer relationship and the drawer has received an indemnity from that bank. The drawer could recover from the indemnifying bank the amount of the erroneous charge, as well as the amount of the returned check fees charged by both the paying bank and the payees of the returned checks. If the drawer's account were an interest-bearing account, the drawer also could recover any interest lost on the erroneously debited amount and the erroneous returned check fees. The drawer also could recover its expenditures for representation in connection with the claim. Finally, the drawer could recover any other losses that were proximately caused by the warranty breach.

b.   In the example above, the paying bank that received the duplicate substitute checks also would have a warranty claim against the previous transferor(s) of those substitute checks and could seek an indemnity from that bank (or either of those banks). The indemnifying bank would be responsible for compensating the paying bank for all the losses proximately caused by the warranty breach, including representation expenses and other costs incurred by the paying bank in settling the drawer's claim.

2.   If the recipient of the substitute check does not have a substitute check warranty claim with respect to the substitute check, the amount of the loss the recipient may recover under § 229.53 is limited to the amount of the substitute check, plus interest and expenses. However, the indemnified person might be entitled to additional damages under some other provision of law.

COMMENTARY ON REGULATION CC

Examples.

a.   A drawer received a substitute check that met all the legal equivalence requirements and for which the drawer was only charged once, but the drawer believed that the underlying original check was a forgery. If the drawer suffered a loss because it could not prove the forgery based on the substitute check, for example because proving the forgery required analysis of pen pressure that could be determined only from the original check, the drawer would have an indemnity claim. However, the drawer would not have a substitute check warranty claim because the substitute check was the legal equivalent of the original check and no person was asked to pay the substitute check more than once. In that case, the amount of the drawer's indemnity under § 229.53 would be limited to the amount of the substitute check, plus interest and expenses. However, the drawer could attempt to recover additional losses, if any, under other law.

b.   As described more fully in the commentary to § 229.53(a) regarding the scope of the indemnity, a paying bank could have an indemnity claim if it paid a legally equivalent substitute check that was created from a fraudulent cashier's check that the paying bank's fraud detection procedures would have caught and that the bank would have returned by its midnight deadline had it received the original check. However, if the substitute check was not subject to a warranty claim (because it met the legal equivalence requirements and there was only one payment request) the paying bank's indemnity would be limited to the amount of the substitute check plus interest and expenses.

3.   The amount of an indemnity would be reduced in proportion to the amount of any amount loss attributable to the indemnified person's negligence or bad faith. This comparative negligence standard is intended to allocate liability in the same manner as the comparative negligence provision of § 229.38(c).

4.   An indemnifying bank may limit the losses for which it is responsible under § 229.53 by producing the original check or a sufficient copy. However, production of the original check or a sufficient copy does not absolve the indemnifying bank from liability claims relating to a warranty the bank has provided under § 229.52 or any other law, including but not limited to subpart C of this part or the U.C.C.

C.   229.53(c) Subrogation of Rights

1.   A bank that pays an indemnity claim is subrogated to the rights of the person it indemnified, to the extent of the indemnity it provided, so that it may attempt to recover that amount from another person based on an indemnity, warranty, or other claim. The person that the bank indemnified must comply with reasonable requests from the indemnifying bank for assistance with respect to the subrogated claim.

Example.

A paying bank indemnifies a drawer for a substitute check that the drawer alleged was a forgery that would have been detected had the original check instead been presented. The bank that provided the indemnity could pursue its own indemnity claim against the bank that presented the substitute check, could attempt to recover from the forger, or could pursue any claim that it might have under other law. The bank also could request from the drawer any information that the drawer might possess regarding the possible identity of the forger.

XXXIII.   § 229.54 Expedited Recredit for Consumers

A.   229.54(a) Circumstances Giving Rise to a Claim

1.   A consumer may make a claim for expedited recredit under this section only for a substitute check that he or she has received and for which the bank charged his or her deposit account. As a result, checks used to access loans, such as credit card checks or home equity line of credit checks, that are reconverted to substitute checks would not give rise to an expedited recredit claim, unless such a check was returned unpaid and the bank charged the consumer's deposit account for the amount of the returned check. In addition, a consumer who received only a statement that contained images of multiple substitute checks per page would not be entitled to make an expedited recredit claim, although he or she could seek redress under other provisions of law, such as § 229.52 or U.C.C. 4–401. However, a consumer who originally received only a statement containing images of multiple substitute checks per page but later received a substitute check, such as in response to a request for a copy of a check shown in the statement, could bring a claim if the other expedited recredit criteria were met. Although a consumer must at some point have received a substitute

check to make an expedited recredit claim, the consumer need not be in possession of the substitute check at the time he or she submits the claim.

2.   A consumer must in good faith assert that the bank improperly charged the consumer's account for the substitute check or that the consumer has a warranty claim for the substitute check (or both). The warranty in question could be a substitute check warranty described in § 229.52 or any other warranty that a bank provides with respect to a check under other law. A consumer could, for example, have a warranty claim under § 229.34(b), which contains returned check warranties that are made to the owner of the check.

3.   A consumer's recovery under the expedited recredit section is limited to the amount of his or her loss, up to the amount of the substitute check subject to the claim, plus interest if the consumer's account is an interest-bearing account. The consumer's loss could include fees that resulted from the allegedly incorrect charge, such as bounced check fees that were imposed because the improper charge caused the bank to dishonor subsequently presented checks that it otherwise would have honored. A consumer who suffers a total loss greater than the amount of the substitute check plus interest could attempt to recover the remainder of that loss by bringing warranty, indemnity, or other claim under this subpart or other applicable law.

Examples.

a.   A consumer who received a substitute check believed that he or she wrote the check for $150, but the bank charged his or her account for $1,500. The amount on the substitute check the consumer received is illegible. If the substitute check contained a blurry image of what was a legible original check, the consumer could have a claim for a breach of the legal equivalence warranty in addition to an improper charge claim. Because the amount of the check cannot be determined from the substitute check provided to the consumer, the consumer, if acting in good faith, could assert that the production of the original check or a better copy of the original check is necessary to determine the validity of the claim. The consumer in this case could attempt to recover his or her losses by using the expedited recredit procedure. The consumer's losses recoverable under § 229.54 could include the $1,350 he or she believed was incorrectly charged plus any improperly charged fees associated with that charge, up to $150 (plus foregone interest on the amount of the consumer's loss if the account was an interest-bearing account). The consumer could recover any additional losses, if any, under other law, such as U.C.C. 4–401 and 4–402.

b.   A consumer received a substitute check for which his or her account was charged and believed that the original check from which the substitute was derived was a forgery. The forgery was good enough that analysis of the original check was necessary to verify whether the signature is that of the consumer. Under those circumstances, the consumer, if acting in good faith, could assert that the charge was improper, that he or she therefore had incurred a loss in the amount of the check (plus foregone interest if the account was an interest-bearing account), and that he or she needed the original check to determine the validity of the forgery claim. By contrast, if the signature on the substitute check obviously was forged (for example, if the forger signed a name other than that of the account holder) and there was no other defect with the substitute check, the consumer would not need the original check or a sufficient copy to determine the fact of the forgery and thus would not be able to make an expedited recredit claim under this section. However, the consumer would have a claim under U.C.C. 4–401 if the item was not properly payable.

B.   229.54(b) Procedures for Making Claims

1.   The consumer must submit his or her expedited recredit claim to the bank within 40 calendar days of the later of the day on which the bank mailed or delivered, by a means agreed to by the consumer, (1) the periodic account statement containing information concerning the transaction giving rise to the claim, or (2) the substitute check giving rise to the claim. The mailing or delivery of a substitute check could be in connection with a regular account statement, in response to a consumer's specific request for a copy of a check, or in connection with the return of a substitute check to the payee.

2.   Section 229.54(b) contemplates more than one possible means of delivering an account statement or a substitute check to the consumer. The time period for making a claim thus could be triggered by the mailed, in-person, or electronic delivery of an account statement or by the mailed or in-person delivery of a substitute check. In-person delivery would include, for example, making an account statement or substitute check available at the bank for the consumer's retrieval under an arrangement agreed to by the consumer.

In the case of a mailed statement or substitute check, the 40-day period should be calculated from the postmark on the envelope. In the case of in-person delivery, the 40-day period should be calculated from the earlier of the calendar day on which delivery occurred or the bank first made the statement or substitute check available for the consumer's retrieval.

3. A bank must extend the consumer's time for submitting a claim for a reasonable period if the consumer is prevented from submitting his or her claim within 40 days because of extenuating circumstances. Extenuating circumstances could include, for example, the extended travel or illness of the consumer.

4. For purposes of determining the timeliness of a consumer's actions, a consumer's claim is considered received on the banking day on which the consumer's bank receives a complete claim in person or by telephone or on the banking day on which the consumer's bank receives a letter or e-mail containing a complete claim. (But see paragraphs 9–11 of this section for a discussion of time periods related to oral claims that the bank requires to be put in writing.)

5. A consumer who makes an untimely claim would not be entitled to recover his or her losses using the expedited recredit procedure. However, he or she still could have rights under other law, such as a warranty or indemnity claim under subpart D, a claim for an improper charge to his or her account under U.C.C. 4–401, or a claim for wrongful dishonor under U.C.C. 4–402.

6. A consumer's claim must include the reason why the consumer believes that his or her account was charged improperly or why he or she has a warranty claim. A charge could be improper, for example, if the bank charged the consumer's account for an amount different than the consumer believes he or she authorized or charged the consumer more than once for the same check, or if the check in question was a forgery or otherwise fraudulent.

7. A consumer also must provide a reason why production of the original check or a sufficient copy is necessary to determine the validity of the claim identified by the consumer. For example, if the consumer believed that the bank charged his or her account for the wrong amount, the original check might be necessary to prove this claim if the amount of the substitute check were illegible. Similarly, if the consumer believed that his or her signature had been forged, the original check might be necessary to confirm the forgery if, for example, pen pressure or similar analysis were necessary to determine the genuineness of the signature.

8. The information that the consumer is required to provide under § 229.54(b)(2)(iv) to facilitate the bank's investigation of the claim could include, for example, a copy of the allegedly defective substitute check or information related to that check, such as the number, amount, and payee.

9. A bank may accept an expedited recredit claim in any form but could in its discretion require the consumer to submit the claim in writing. A bank that requires a recredit claim to be in writing must inform the consumer of that requirement and provide a location to which such a written claim should be sent. If the consumer attempts to make a claim orally, the bank must inform the consumer at that time of the written notice requirement. A bank that receives a timely oral claim and then requires the consumer to submit the claim in writing may require the consumer to submit the written claim within 10 business days of the bank's receipt of the timely oral claim. If the consumer's oral claim was timely and the consumer's written claim was received within the 10-day period for submitting the claim in writing, the consumer would satisfy the requirement of § 229.54(b)(1) to submit his or her claim within 40 days, even if the bank received the written claim after that 40-day period.

10. A bank may permit but may not require a consumer to submit a written claim electronically.

11. If a bank requires a consumer to submit a claim in writing, the bank may compute time periods for the bank's action on the claim from the date that the bank received the written claim. Thus, if a consumer called the bank to make an expedited recredit claim and the bank required the consumer to submit the claim in writing, the time at which the bank must take action on the claim would be determined based on the date on which the bank received the written claim, not the date on which the consumer made the oral claim.

12. Regardless of whether the consumer's communication with the bank is oral or written, a consumer complaint that does not contain all the elements described in § 229.54(b) is not a claim for purposes of

COMMENTARY ON REGULATION CC

§ 229.54. If the consumer attempts to submit a claim but does not provide all the required information, then the bank has a duty to inform the consumer that the complaint does not constitute a claim under § 229.54 and identify what information is missing.

C.   229.54(c) Action on Claims

1.   If the bank has not determined whether or not the consumer's claim is valid by the end of the 10th business day after the banking day on which the consumer submitted the claim, the bank must by that time recredit the consumer's account for the amount of the consumer's loss, up to the lesser of the amount of the substitute check or $2,500, plus interest if the account is an interest-bearing account. A bank must provide the recredit pending investigation for each substitute check for which the consumer submitted a claim, even if the consumer submitted multiple substitute check claims in the same communication.

2.   A bank that provides a recredit to the consumer, either provisionally or after determining that the consumer's claim is valid, may reverse the amount of the recredit if the bank later determines that the claim in fact was not valid. A bank that reverses a recredit also may reverse the amount of any interest that it has paid on the previously recredited amount. A bank's time for reversing a recredit may be limited by a statute of limitations.

D.   229.54(d) Availability of Recredit

1.   The availability of a recredit provided by a bank under § 229.54(c) is governed solely by § 229.54(d) and therefore is not subject to the availability provisions of subpart B. A bank generally must make a recredit available for withdrawal no later than the start of the business day after the banking day on which the bank provided the recredit. However, a bank may delay the availability of up to the first $2,500 that it provisionally recredits to a consumer account under § 229.54(c)(3)(i) if (1) the account is a new account, (2) without regard to the substitute check giving rise to the recredit claim, the account has been repeatedly overdrawn during the six month period ending on the date the bank received the claim, or (3) the bank has reasonable cause to believe that the claim is fraudulent. These first two exceptions are meant to operate in the same manner as the corresponding new account and repeated overdraft exceptions in subpart B, as described in § 229.13(a) and (d) and the commentary thereto regarding application of the exceptions. When a recredit amount for which a bank delays availability contains an interest component, that component also is subject to the delay because it is part of the amount recredited under § 229.54(c)(3)(i). However, interest continues to accrue during the hold period.

2.   Section 229.54(d)(2) describes the maximum period of time that a bank may delay availability of a recredit provided under § 229.54(c). The bank may delay availability under one of the three listed exceptions until the business day after the banking day on which the bank determines that the consumer's claim is valid or the 45th calendar day after the banking day on which the bank received the consumer's claim, whichever is earlier. The only portion of the recredit that is subject to delay under § 229.54(d)(2) is the amount that the bank recredits under § 229.54(c)(3)(i) (including the interest component, if any) pending its investigation of a claim.

E.   229.54(e) Notices Relating to Consumer Expedited Recredit Claims

1.   A bank must notify a consumer of its action regarding a recredit claim no later than the business day after the banking day that the bank makes a recredit, determines a claim is not valid, or reverses a recredit, as appropriate. As provided in § 229.58, a bank may provide any notice required by this section by U.S. mail or by any other means through which the consumer has agreed to receive account information.

2.   A bank that denies the consumer's recredit claim must demonstrate to the consumer that the substitute check was properly charged or that the warranty claim was not valid, such as by explaining the reason that the substitute check charge was proper or the consumer's warranty claim was not valid. For example, if a consumer has claimed that the bank charged its account for an improper amount, the bank denying that claim must explain why it determined that the charged amount was proper.

3.   A bank denying a recredit claim also must provide the original check or a sufficient copy, unless the bank is providing the claim denial notice electronically and the consumer has agreed to receive that type of information electronically. In that case, § 229.58 allows the bank instead to provide an image of the

original check or an image of the sufficient copy that the bank would have sent to the consumer had the bank provided the notice by mail.

4.   A bank that relies on information or documents in addition to the original check or sufficient copy when denying a consumer expedited recredit claim also must either provide such information or documents to the consumer or inform the consumer that he or she may request copies of such information or documents. This requirement does not apply to a bank that relies only on the original check or a sufficient copy to make its determination.

5.   Models C–22 through C–25 in appendix C contain model language for each of three notices described in § 229.54(e). A bank may, but is not required to, use the language listed in the appendix. The Check 21 Act does not provide banks that use these models with a safe harbor. However, the Board has published these models to aid banks' efforts to comply with § 229.54(e).

F.   229.54(f) Recredit Does Not Abrogate Other Liabilities

1.   The amount that a consumer may recover under § 229.54 is limited to the lesser of the amount of his or her loss or the amount of the substitute check, plus interest on that amount if his or her account earns interest. However, a consumer's total loss associated with the substitute check could exceed that amount, and the consumer could be entitled to additional damages under other law. For example, if a consumer's loss exceeded the amount of the substitute check plus interest and he or she had both a warranty and an indemnity claim with respect to the substitute check, he or she would be entitled to additional damages under § 229.53 of this subpart. Similarly, if a consumer was charged bounced check fees as a result of an improperly charged substitute check and could not recover all of those fees because of the § 229.54's limitation on recovery, he or she could attempt to recover additional amounts under U.C.C. 4–402.

XXXIV.   § 229.55 Expedited Recredit Procedures for Banks

A.   229.55(a) Circumstances Giving Rise to a Claim

1.   This section allows a bank to make an expedited recredit claim under two sets of circumstances: first, because it is obligated to provide a recredit, either to the consumer or to another bank that is obligated to provide a recredit in connection with the consumer's claim; and second, because the bank detected a problem with the substitute check that, if uncaught, could have given rise to a consumer claim.

2.   The loss giving rise to an interbank recredit claim could be the recredit that the claimant bank provided directly to its consumer customer under § 229.54 or a loss incurred because the claimant bank was required to indemnify another bank that provided an expedited recredit to either a consumer or a bank.

Examples.

a.   A paying bank charged a consumer's account based on a substitute check that contained a blurry image of a legible original check, and the consumer whose account was charged made an expedited recredit claim against the paying bank because the consumer suffered a loss and needed the original check or a sufficient copy to determine the validity of his or her claim. The paying bank would have a warranty claim against the presenting bank that transferred the defective substitute check to it and against any previous transferring bank(s) that handled that substitute check or another paper or electronic representation of the check. The paying bank therefore would meet each of the requirements necessary to bring an interbank expedited recredit claim.

b.   Continuing with the example in paragraph a, if the presenting bank determined that the paying bank's claim was valid and provided a recredit, the presenting bank would have suffered a loss in the amount of the recredit it provided and could, in turn, make an expedited recredit claim against the bank that transferred the defective substitute check to it.

B.   229.55(b) Procedures for Making Claims

1.   An interbank recredit claim under this section must be brought within 120 calendar days of the transaction giving rise to the claim. For purposes of computing this period, the transaction giving rise to the claim is the claimant bank's settlement for the substitute check in question.

2.   When estimating the amount of its loss, § 229.55(b)(2)(ii) states that the claimant bank should include "interest if applicable." The quoted phrase refers to any interest that the claimant bank or a bank that the claimant bank indemnified paid to a consumer who has an interest-bearing account in connection with an expedited recredit under § 229.54.

3.   The information that the claimant bank is required to provide under § 229.55(b)(2)(iv) to facilitate investigation of the claim could include, for example, a copy of any written claim that a consumer submitted under § 229.54 or any written record the bank may have of a claim the consumer submitted orally. The information also could include a copy of the defective substitute check or information relating to that check, such as the number, amount, and payee of the check. However, a claimant bank that provides a copy of the substitute check must take reasonable steps to ensure that the copy is not mistaken for a legal equivalent of the original check or handled for forward collection or return.

4.   The indemnifying bank's right to require a claimant bank to submit a claim in writing and the computation of time from the date of the written submission parallel the corresponding provision in the consumer recredit section (§ 229.54(b)(3)). However, the indemnifying bank also may require the claimant bank to submit a copy of the written or electronic claim submitted by the consumer under that section, if any.

C.   229.55(c) Action on Claims

1.   An indemnifying bank that responds to an interbank expedited recredit claim by providing the original check or a sufficient copy of the original check need not demonstrate why that claim or the underlying consumer expedited recredit claim is or is not valid.

XXXV. § 229.56 Liability

A.   229.56(a) Measure of Damages

1.   In general, a person's recovery under this section is limited to the amount of the loss up to the amount of the substitute check that is the subject of the claim, plus interest and expenses (including costs and reasonable attorney's fees and other expenses of representation) related to that substitute check. However, a person that is entitled to an indemnity under § 229.53 because of a breach of a substitute check warranty also may recover under § 229.53 any losses proximately caused by the warranty breach, including interest, costs, wrongfully-charged fees imposed as a result of the warranty breach, reasonable attorney's fees, and other expenses of representation.

2.   A reconverting bank also may be liable under § 229.38 for damages associated with the illegibility of indorsements applied to substitute checks if that illegibility results because the reduction of the original check image and its placement on the substitute check shifted a previously-applied indorsement that, when applied, complied with appendix D. For more detailed discussion of this topic, see § 229.38 and the accompanying commentary.

B.   229.56(b) Timeliness of Action

1.   A bank's delay beyond the time limits prescribed or permitted by any provision of subpart D is excused if the delay is caused by certain circumstances beyond the bank's control. This parallels the standard of U.C.C. 4–109(b).

C.   229.56(c) Jurisdiction

1.   The Check 21 Act confers subject matter jurisdiction on courts of competent jurisdiction and provides a time limit for civil actions for violations of subpart D.

D.   229.56(d) Notice of Claims

1.   This paragraph is designed to adopt the notice of claim provisions of U.C.C. 4–207(d) and 4–208(e), with an added provision that a timely § 229.54 expedited recredit claim satisfies the generally-applicable notice requirement. The time limit described in this paragraph applies only to notices of warranty and indemnity claims. As provided in § 229.56(c), all actions under § 229.56 must be brought within one year of the date that the cause of action accrues.

COMMENTARY ON REGULATION CC

XXXVI. Consumer Awareness

A. 229.57(a) General Disclosure Requirement and Content

1. A bank must provide the disclosure required by § 229.57 under two circumstances. First, each bank must provide the disclosure to each of its consumer customers who receives paid checks with his or her account statement. This requirement does not apply if the bank provides with the account statement something other than paid original checks, paid substitute checks, or a combination thereof. For example, this requirement would not apply if a bank provided with the account statement only a document that contained multiple check images per page. Second, a bank also must provide the disclosure when it (a) provides a substitute check to a consumer in response to that consumer's request for a check or check copy or (b) returns a substitute check to a consumer depositor. A bank must provide the disclosure each time it provides a substitute check to a consumer on an occasional basis, regardless of whether the bank previously provided the disclosure to that consumer.

2. A bank may, but is not required to, use the model disclosure in appendix C–5A to satisfy the disclosure content requirements of this section. A bank that uses the model language is deemed to comply with the disclosure content requirement(s) for which it uses the model language, provided the information in the disclosure accurately describes the bank's policies and practices. A bank also may include in its disclosure additional information relating to substitute checks that is not required by this section.

3. A bank may, by agreement or at the consumer's request, provide the disclosure required by this section in a language other than English, provided that the bank makes a complete English notice available at the consumer's request.

B. 229.57(b) Distribution

1. A consumer may request a check or a copy of a check on an occasional basis, such as to prove that he or she made a particular payment. A bank that responds to the consumer's request by providing a substitute check must provide the required disclosure at the time of the consumer's request if feasible. Otherwise, the bank must provide the disclosure no later than the time at which the bank provides a substitute check in response to the consumer's request. It would not be feasible for a bank to provide notice to the consumer at the time of the request if, for example, the bank did not know at the time of the request whether it would provide a substitute check in response to that request, regardless of the form of the consumer's request. It also would not be feasible for a bank to provide notice at the time of the request if the consumer's request was mailed to the bank or made by telephone, even if the bank knew when it received the request that it would provide a substitute check in response. A bank's provision to the consumer of something other a substitute check, such as a photocopy of a check or a statement containing images of multiple substitute checks per page, does not trigger the notice requirement.

2. A consumer who does not routinely receive paid checks might receive a returned substitute check. For example, a consumer deposits an original check that is payable to him or her into his or her deposit account. The paying bank returns the check unpaid and the depositary bank returns the check to the depositor in the form of a substitute check. A depositary bank that provides a returned substitute check to a consumer depositor must provide the substitute check disclosure at that time.

XXXVII. Variation by Agreement

Section 229.60 provides that banks involved in an interbank expedited recredit claim under § 229.55 may vary the terms of that section by agreement, but otherwise no person may vary the terms of subpart D by agreement. A bank's decision to provide more generous protections for consumers than this subpart requires, such as by providing consumers additional time to submit expedited claims under § 229.54 under non-exigent circumstances, would not be a variation prohibited by § 229.60.

COLLECTION OF CHECKS AND OTHER ITEMS BY FEDERAL RESERVE BANKS AND FUNDS TRANSFERS THROUGH FEDWIRE (REGULATION J)

12 C.F.R. Part 210

Current through March 13, 2016; 81 F.R. 12795

For updates, see www.ecfr.gov

SUBPART A—COLLECTION OF CHECKS AND OTHER ITEMS BY FEDERAL RESERVE BANKS

SUBPART B—FUNDS TRANSFERS THROUGH FEDWIRE

SUBPART A—COLLECTION OF CHECKS AND OTHER ITEMS BY FEDERAL RESERVE BANKS

§ 210.1   Authority, purpose, and scope.

The Board of Governors of the Federal Reserve System (Board) has issued this subpart pursuant to the Federal Reserve Act, sections 11(i) and (j) (12 U.S.C. 248(i) and (j)), section 13 (12 U.S.C. 342), section

1953

16 (12 U.S.C. 248(*o*) and 360), and section 19(f) (12 U.S.C. 464); the Expedited Funds Availability Act (12 U.S.C. 4001 et seq.); the Check Clearing for the 21st Century Act (12 U.S.C. 5001–5018) and other laws. This subpart governs the collection of checks and other cash and noncash items and the handling of returned checks by Federal Reserve Banks. Its purpose is to provide rules for collecting and returning items and settling balances.

§ 210.2   Definitions.

As used in this subpart, unless the context otherwise requires:

(a) Account means an account on the books of a Federal Reserve Bank. A subaccount is an informational record of a subset of transactions that affect an account and is not a separate account.

(b) Actually and finally collected funds means cash or any other form of payment that is, or has become, final and irrevocable.

(c) Administrative Reserve Bank with respect to an entity means the Reserve Bank in whose District the entity is located, as determined under the procedure described in § 204.3(g) of this chapter (Regulation D), even if the entity is not otherwise subject to that section.

(d) Bank means any person engaged in the business of banking. A branch or separate office of a bank is a separate bank to the extent provided in the Uniform Commercial Code.

(e) Bank draft means a check drawn by one bank on another bank.

(f) Banking day means the part of a day on which a bank is open to the public for carrying on substantially all of its banking functions.

(g) Cash item means—

(1) A check other than one classified as a noncash item under this section; or

(2) Any other item payable on demand and collectible at par that the Reserve Bank that receives the item is willing to accept as a cash item. Cash item does not include a returned check.

(h) Check means a draft, as defined in the Uniform Commercial Code, that is drawn on a bank and payable on demand. Check as defined in 12 CFR 229.2(k) means an item defined as a check in 12 CFR 229.2(k) for purposes of subparts C and D of part 229.

(i) Item and electronic item.

(1) Item means—

(i) An instrument or a promise or order to pay money, whether negotiable or not, that is—

(A) Payable in a Federal Reserve District[1] (District);

(B) Sent by a sender to a Reserve Bank for handling under this subpart; and

(C) Collectible in funds acceptable to the Reserve Bank of the District in which the instrument is payable; and

(ii) An electronic image of an item described in paragraph (i)(1)(i) of this section, and information describing that item, that a Reserve Bank agrees to handle as an item pursuant to an operating circular.

(2) Electronic item means an item described in paragraph (i)(1)(ii) of this section.

Note: Unless otherwise indicated, item includes both a cash and a noncash item, and includes a returned check sent by a paying or returning bank. Item does not include a check that cannot be collected at par, or a payment order as defined in § 210.26(i) and handled under subpart B of this part.

---

[1] For purposes of this subpart, the Virgin Islands and Puerto Rico are deemed to be in the Second District, and Guam, American Samoa, and the Northern Mariana Islands in the Twelfth District.

(j) Nonbank payor means a payor of an item, other than a bank.

(k) Noncash item means an item that a receiving Reserve Bank classifies in its operating circulars as requiring special handling. The term also means an item normally received as a cash item if a Reserve Bank decides that special conditions require that it handle the item as a noncash item.

(*l*) Paying bank means—

    (1) The bank by which an item is payable unless the item is payable or collectible at or through another bank and is sent to the other bank for payment or collection;

    (2) The bank at or through which an item is payable or collectible and to which it sent for payment or collection; or

    (3) The bank whose routing number appears on a check in the MICR line or in fractional form (or in the MICR-line information that accompanies an electronic item) and to which the check is sent for payment or collection.

(m) Returned check means a cash item or a check as defined in 12 CFR 229.2(k) returned by a paying bank, including a notice of nonpayment in lieu of a returned check, whether or not a Reserve Bank handled the check for collection.

(n) Sender means any of the following entities that sends an item to a Reserve Bank for forward collection—

    (1) A depository institution, as defined in section 19(b) of the Federal Reserve Act (12 U.S.C. 461(b));

    (2) A clearing institution, defined as—

        (i) An institution that is not a depository institution but that maintains with a Reserve Bank the balance referred to in the first paragraph of section 13 of the Federal Reserve Act (12 U.S.C. 342); or

        (ii) A corporation that maintains an account with a Reserve Bank in conformity with § 211.4 of this chapter (Regulation K);

    (3) Another Reserve Bank;

    (4) An international organization for which a Reserve Bank is empowered to act as depositary or fiscal agent and maintains an account;

    (5) A foreign correspondent, defined as any of the following entities for which a Reserve Bank maintains an account: a foreign bank or banker, a foreign state as defined in section 25(b) of the Federal Reserve Act (12 U.S.C. 632), or a foreign correspondent or agency referred to in section 14(e) of that act (12 U.S.C. 358); or

    (6) A branch or agency of a foreign bank maintaining reserves under section 7 of the International Banking Act of 1978 (12 U.S.C. 347d, 3105).

(o) State means a State of the United States, the District of Columbia, Puerto Rico, or a territory, possession, or dependency of the United States.

(p) Clock hour and clock half-hour.

    (1) Clock hour means a time that is on the hour, such as 1:00, 2:00, etc.

    (2) Clock half-hour means a time that is on the half-hour, such as 1:30, 2:30, etc.

(q) Fedwire has the same meaning as that set forth in § 210.26(e).

(r) Uniform Commercial Code and U.C.C. mean the Uniform Commercial Code as adopted in a state.

(s) Terms not defined in this section. Unless the context otherwise requires—

    (1) The terms not defined herein have the meanings set forth in § 229.2 of this chapter applicable to subpart C or subpart D of part 229 of this chapter, as appropriate; and

(2) The terms not defined herein or in § 229.2 of this chapter have the meanings set forth in the Uniform Commercial Code.

§ 210.3 General provisions.

(a) **General.** Each Reserve Bank shall receive and handle items in accordance with this subpart, and shall issue operating circulars governing the details of its handling of items and other matters deemed appropriate by the Reserve Bank. The circulars may, among other things, classify cash items and noncash items, require separate sorts and letters, provide different closing times for the receipt of different classes or types of items, provide for instructions by an administrative Reserve Bank to other Reserve Banks, set forth terms of services, and establish procedures for adjustments on a Reserve Bank's books, including amounts, waiver of expenses, and payment of compensation.

(b) **Binding effect.** This subpart, together with subparts C and D of Part 229 and the operating circulars of the Reserve Banks, are binding on all parties interested in an item handled by any Reserve Bank.

(c) **Government items.** As depositaries and fiscal agents of the United States, Reserve Banks handle certain items payable by the United States or certain Federal agencies as cash or noncash items. To the extent provided by regulations issued by, and arrangements made with, the United States Treasury Department and other Government departments and agencies, the handling of such items is governed by this subpart. The Reserve Banks shall include in their operating circulars such information regarding these regulations and arrangements as the Reserve Banks deem appropriate.

(d) **Government senders.** Except as otherwise provided by statutes of the United States, or regulations issued or arrangements made thereunder, this subpart and the operating circulars of the Reserve Banks apply to the following when acting as a sender: a department, agency, instrumentality, independent establishment, or office of the United States, or a wholly owned or controlled Government corporation, that maintains or uses an account with a Reserve Bank.

(e) **Foreign items.** A Reserve Bank also may receive and handle certain items payable outside a Federal Reserve District, as provided in its operating circulars. The handling of such items in a state is governed by this subpart, and the handling of such items outside a state is governed by the local law.

(f) **Relation to other law.** The provisions of this subpart supersede any inconsistent provisions of the Uniform Commercial Code, of any other state law, or of part 229 of this title, but only to the extent of the inconsistency.

§ 210.4 Sending items to Reserve Banks.

(a) **Sending of items.** A sender, other than a Reserve Bank, may send any item to any Reserve Bank, whether or not the item is payable within the Reserve Bank's District, unless the sender's administrative Reserve Bank directs the sender to send the item to a specific Reserve Bank.

(b) **Handling of items.**

(1) The following parties, in the following order, are deemed to have handled an item that is sent to a Reserve Bank for collection:

(i) The initial sender;

(ii) The initial sender's administrative Reserve Bank (which is deemed to have accepted deposit of the item from the initial sender);

(iii) The Reserve Bank that receives the item from the initial sender (if different from the initial sender's administrative Reserve Bank); and

(iv) Another Reserve Bank, if any, that receives the item from a Reserve Bank.

(2) A Reserve Bank that is not described in paragraph (b)(1) of this section is not a person that handles an item and is not a collecting bank with respect to an item.

(3) The identity and order of the parties under paragraph (b)(1) of this section determine the relationships and the rights and liabilities of the parties under this subpart, part 229 of this chapter (Regulation CC), section 13(1) and section 16(13) of the Federal Reserve Act, and the Uniform Commercial Code. An initial sender's administrative Reserve Bank that is deemed to accept an item for deposit or handle an item is also deemed to be a sender with respect to that item. The Reserve Banks that are deemed to handle an item are deemed to be agents or subagents of the owner of the item, as provided in section 210.6(a) of this subpart.

(c) Checks received at par. The Reserve Banks shall receive cash items and other checks at par.

§ 210.5 Sender's agreement; recovery by Reserve Bank.

(a) Sender's agreement. The warranties, authorizations, and agreements made pursuant to this paragraph may not be disclaimed and are made whether or not the item bears an indorsement of the sender. By sending an item to a Reserve Bank, the sender does all of the following.

(1) Authorization to handle item. The sender authorizes the sender's administrative Reserve Bank and any other Reserve Bank or collecting bank to which the item is sent to handle the item (and authorizes any Reserve Bank that handles settlement for the item to make accounting entries), subject to this subpart and to the Reserve Banks' operating circulars, and warrants its authority to give this authorization.

(2) Warranties for all items. The sender warrants to each Reserve Bank handling the item that—

(i) The sender is a person entitled to enforce the item or authorized to obtain payment of the item on behalf of a person entitled to enforce the item;

(ii) The item has not been altered; and

(iii) The item bears all indorsements applied by parties that previously handled the item, in paper or electronic form, for forward collection or return.

(3) Warranties for all electronic items. The sender makes all the warranties set forth in and subject to the terms of 4–207 of the U.C.C. for an electronic item as if it were an item subject to the U.C.C. and makes the warranties set forth in and subject to the terms of § 229.34(c) and (d) of this chapter for an electronic item as if it were a check subject to that section.

(4) Warranties for electronic items that are not representations of substitute checks. If an electronic item is not a representation of a substitute check, the sender of that item warrants to each Reserve Bank handling the item that—

(i) The electronic image portion of the item accurately represents all of the information on the front and back of the original check as of the time that the original check was truncated; the information portion of the item contains a record of all MICR-line information required for a substitute check under § 229.2(aaa) of this chapter; and the item conforms to the technical standards for an electronic item set forth in an operating circular; and

(ii) No person will receive a transfer, presentment, or return of, or otherwise be charged for, the electronic item, the original item, or a paper or electronic representation of the original item such that the person will be asked to make payment based on an item it already has paid.

(5) Sender's liability to Reserve Bank.

(i) Except as provided in paragraph (a)(5)(ii) of this section, the sender agrees to indemnify each Reserve Bank for any loss or expense sustained (including attorneys' fees and expenses of litigation) resulting from—

(A) The sender's lack of authority to make the warranty in paragraph (a)(1) of this section;

(B) Any action taken by the Reserve Bank within the scope of its authority in handling the item; or

(C) Any warranty or indemnity made by the Reserve Bank under § 210.6(b) of this subpart, part 229 of this chapter, or the U.C.C.

(ii) A sender's liability for warranties and indemnities that the Reserve Bank makes for a substitute check, a paper or electronic representation thereof, or any other electronic item is subject to the following conditions and limitations—

(A) A sender of an original check shall not be liable under paragraph (a)(5)(i) of this section for any amount that the Reserve Bank pays under subpart D of part 229 of this chapter or under § 210.6(b)(3) of this subpart, absent the sender's agreement to the contrary;

(B) Nothing in this subpart alters the liability of a sender of a substitute check or paper or electronic representation of a substitute check under subpart D of part 229 of this chapter; and

(C) A sender of an electronic item that is not a representation of a substitute check shall not be liable for any amount that the Reserve Bank pays under subpart D of part 229 of this chapter or § 210.6(b)(3)(ii) of this subpart that is attributable to the Reserve Bank's own lack of good faith or failure to exercise ordinary care.

(b) Sender's liability under other law. Nothing in paragraph (a) of this section limits any warranty or indemnity by a sender (or a person that handled an item prior to the sender) arising under state law or regulation (such as the U.C.C.), other federal law or regulation (such as part 229 of this chapter), or an agreement with a Reserve Bank.

(c) Recovery by Reserve Bank. If an action or proceeding is brought against (or if defense is tendered to) a Reserve Bank that has handled an item, based on:

(1) The alleged failure of the sender to have the authority to make the warranty and agreement in paragraph (a)(1) of this section;

(2) Any action by the Reserve Bank within the scope of its authority in handling the item; or

(3) Any warranty or indemnity made by the Reserve Bank under section 210.6(b) of this subpart, part 229 of this chapter, or the U.C.C.,[1] the Reserve Bank may, upon entry of a final judgment or decree, recover from the sender the amount of attorneys' fees and other expenses of litigation incurred, as well as any amount the Reserve Bank is required to pay because of the judgment or decree or the tender of defense, together with interest thereon.

(d) Methods of recovery.

(1) The Reserve Bank may recover the amount stated in paragraph (c) of this section by charging any account on its books that is maintained or used by the sender (or by charging a Reserve Bank sender), if—

(i) The Reserve Bank made seasonable written demand on the sender to assume defense of the action or proceeding; and

(ii) The sender has not made any other arrangement for payment that is acceptable to the Reserve Bank.

(2) The Reserve Bank is not responsible for defending the action or proceeding before using this method of recovery. A Reserve Bank that has been charged under this paragraph (c) may recover from its sender in the manner and under the circumstances set forth in this paragraph (c). A Reserve Bank's failure to avail itself of the remedy provided in this paragraph (c) does not prejudice its enforcement in any other manner of the indemnity agreement referred to in paragraph (a)(3) of this section.

---

[1]　See 69 FR 62553. The remainder of the paragraph following this point appears to have been inadvertently deleted from the amendment.

(e) Security interest. When a sender sends an item to a Reserve Bank, the sender and any prior collecting bank grant to the sender's Administrative Reserve Bank a security interest in all of their respective assets in the possession of, or held for the account of, any Reserve Bank to secure their respective obligations due or to become due to the Administrative Reserve Bank under this subpart or part 229 of this chapter (Regulation CC). The security interest attaches when a warranty is breached or any other obligation to the Reserve Bank is incurred. If the Reserve Bank, in its sole discretion, deems itself insecure and gives notice thereof to the sender or prior collecting bank, or if the sender or prior collecting bank suspends payments or is closed, the Reserve Bank may take any action authorized by law to recover the amount of an obligation, including, but not limited to, the exercise of rights of set off, the realization on any available collateral, and any other rights it may have as a creditor under applicable law.

§ 210.6 Status, warranties, and liability of Reserve Bank.

(a)(1) Status. A Reserve Bank that handles an item shall act as agent or subagent of the owner with respect to the item. This agency terminates when a Reserve Bank receives final payment for the item in actually and finally collected funds, a Reserve Bank makes the proceeds available for use by the sender, and the time for commencing all actions against the Reserve Bank has expired.

(2) Limitations on Reserve Bank liability. A Reserve Bank shall not have or assume any liability with respect to an item or its proceeds except—

(i) For the Reserve Bank's own lack of good faith or failure to exercise ordinary care;

(ii) As provided in paragraph (b) of this section; and

(iii) As provided in subparts C and D of Regulation CC.

(3) Reliance on routing designation appearing on item. A Reserve Bank may present or send an item based on the routing number or other designation of a paying bank or nonbank payor appearing in any form on the item when the Reserve Bank receives it. A Reserve Bank shall not be responsible for any delay resulting from its acting on any designation, whether inscribed by magnetic ink or by other means, and whether or not the designation acted on is consistent with any other designation appearing on the item.

(b) Warranties and liability. The following provisions apply when a Reserve Bank presents or sends an item.

(1) Warranties for all items. The Reserve Bank warrants to a subsequent collecting bank and to the paying bank and any other payor that—

(i) The Reserve Bank is a person entitled to enforce the item (or is authorized to obtain payment of the item on behalf of a person that is either entitled to enforce the item or authorized to obtain payment on behalf of a person entitled to enforce the item);

(ii) The item has not been altered; and

(iii) The item bears all indorsements applied by parties that previously handled the item, in paper or electronic form, for forward collection or return.

(2) Warranties for all electronic items. The Reserve Bank makes all the warranties set forth in and subject to the terms of 4–207 of the U.C.C. for an electronic item as if it were an item subject to the U.C.C. and makes the warranties set forth in and subject to the terms of § 229.34(c) and (d) of this chapter for an electronic item as if it were a check subject to that section.

(3) Warranties and indemnity for electronic items that are not representations of substitute checks.

(i) If the electronic item is not a representation of a substitute check, the Reserve Bank warrants to the bank to which it transfers or presents that item that—

(A) The electronic image portion of the item accurately represents all of the information on the front and back of the original check as of the time that the original check was truncated; the information portion of the item contains a record of all MICR-line information required for a substitute check under § 229.2(aaa) of this chapter; and the item conforms to the technical standards for an electronic item set forth in an operating circular; and

(B) No person will receive a transfer, presentment, or return of, or otherwise be charged for, the electronic item, the original item, or a paper or electronic representation of the original item such that the person will be asked to make payment based on an item it already has paid.

(ii) If the item is an electronic item that is not a representation of a substitute check—

(A) Except as provided in paragraph (b)(3)(ii)(B) of this section, the Reserve Bank agrees to indemnify the bank to which it transfers or presents the electronic item (the recipient bank) for the amount of any losses that the recipient bank incurs under subpart D of part 229 of this chapter for an indemnity that the recipient bank was required to make under subpart D of part 229 of this chapter in connection with a substitute check later created from the electronic item.

(B) The Reserve Bank shall not be liable under paragraph (b)(3)(ii)(A) of this section for any amount that the recipient bank pays under subpart D of part 229 of this chapter that is attributable to the lack of good faith or failure to exercise ordinary care of the recipient bank or a person that handled the item, in any form, after the recipient bank.

(c) **Limitation on liability.** A Reserve Bank shall not have or assume any liability to the paying bank or other payor, except as provided in paragraph (b) of this section, § 229.34(c) or subpart D of part 229 of this chapter, or for the Reserve Bank's own lack of good faith or failure to exercise ordinary care.

(d) **Time for commencing action against Reserve Bank.**

(1) A claim against a Reserve Bank for lack of good faith or failure to exercise ordinary care shall be barred unless the action on the claim is commenced within two years after the claim accrues. Such a claim accrues on the date when a Reserve Bank's alleged failure to exercise ordinary care or to act in good faith first results in damages to the claimant.

(2) A claim that arises under paragraph (b)(3) of this section shall be barred unless the action on the claim is commenced within one year after the claim accrues. Such a claim accrues as of the date on which the claimant first learns, or by which the claimant reasonably should have learned, of the facts and circumstances giving rise to the claim.

(3) This paragraph (d) does not alter the time limit for claims under section 229.38(g) of this chapter (which include claims for breach of warranty under § 229.34 of this chapter) or subpart D of part 229 of this chapter.

§ 210.7   Presenting items for payment.

(a) **Presenting or sending.** As provided under State law or as otherwise permitted by this section:

(1) A Reserve Bank or a subsequent collecting bank may present an item for payment or send the item for presentment and payment; and

(2) A Reserve Bank may send an item to a subsequent collecting bank with authority to present it for payment or to send it for presentment and payment.

(b) **Place of presentment.** A Reserve Bank or subsequent collecting bank may present an item—

(1) At a place requested by the paying bank;

(2) In the case of a check as defined in 12 CFR 229.2(k), in accordance with 12 CFR 229.36;

(3) At a place requested by the nonbank payor, if the item is payable by a nonbank payor other than through or at a paying bank;

(4) Under a special collection agreement consistent with this subpart; or

(5) Through a clearinghouse and subject to its rules and practices.

(c) Presenting or sending direct. A Reserve Bank or subsequent collecting bank may, with respect to an item that may be sent to the paying bank or nonbank payor in the Reserve Bank's District—

(1) Present or send the item direct to the paying bank, or to a place requested by the paying bank; or

(2) If the item is payable by a nonbank payor other than through a paying bank, present it direct to the nonbank payor. Documents, securities, or other papers accompanying a noncash item shall not be delivered to the nonbank payor before the item is paid unless the sender specifically authorizes delivery.

(d) Item sent to another district. A Reserve Bank receiving an item that may be sent to a paying bank or nonbank payor in another District ordinarily sends the item to the Reserve Bank of the other District, but with the agreement of the other Reserve Bank, may present or send the item as if it were sent to a paying bank or nonbank payor in its own District.

§ 210.8   Presenting noncash items for acceptance.

(a) A Reserve Bank or a subsequent collecting bank may, if instructed by the sender, present a noncash item for acceptance in any manner authorized by law if—

(1) The item provides that it must be presented for acceptance;

(2) The item may be presented elsewhere than at the residence or place of business of the payor; or

(3) The date of payment of the item depends on presentment for acceptance.

(b) Documents accompanying a noncash item shall not be delivered to the payor upon acceptance of the item unless the sender specifically authorizes delivery. A Reserve Bank shall not have or assume any other obligation to present or to send for presentment for acceptance any noncash item.

§ 210.9   Settlement and payment.

(a) Settlement through Administrative Reserve Bank. A paying bank shall settle for an item under this subpart with its Administrative Reserve Bank, whether or not the paying bank received the item from that Reserve Bank. A paying bank's settlement with its Administrative Reserve Bank is deemed to be settlement with the Reserve Bank from which the paying bank received the item. A paying bank may settle for an item using any account on a Reserve Bank's books by agreement with its Administrative Reserve Bank, any other Reserve Bank holding the settlement account, and the account-holder. The paying bank remains responsible for settlement if the Reserve Bank holding the settlement account does not, for any reason, obtain settlement in that account.

(b) Cash items—

(1) Settlement obligation. On the day a paying bank receives[2] a cash item from a Reserve Bank, it shall settle for the item such that the proceeds of the settlement are available to its Administrative Reserve Bank by the close of Fedwire on that day, or it shall return the item by the later of the close of its banking day or the close of Fedwire. If the paying bank fails to settle for or return a cash item in accordance with this paragraph (b)(1), it is accountable for the amount of the item as of the close of its banking day or the close of Fedwire on the day it receives the item, whichever is earlier.

---

[2]   A paying bank is deemed to receive a cash item on its next banking day if it receives the item—
(1) On a day other than a banking day for it; or
(2) On a banking day for it, but after a "cut-off hour" established by it in accordance with state law.

(2)　Time of settlement.

(i)　On the day a paying bank receives a cash item from a Reserve Bank, it shall settle for the item so that the proceeds of the settlement are available to its administrative Reserve Bank, or return the item, by the latest of—

(A)　The next clock hour or clock half-hour that is at least one half-hour after the paying bank receives the item;

(B)　8:30 a.m. eastern time; or

(C)　Such later time as provided in the Reserve Banks' operating circulars.

(ii)　If the paying bank fails to settle for or return a cash item in accordance with paragraph (b)(2)(i) of this section, it shall be subject to any applicable overdraft charges. Settlement under paragraph (b)(2)(i) of this section satisfies the settlement requirements of paragraph (b)(1) of this section.

(3)　Paying bank closes voluntarily.

(i)　If a paying bank closes voluntarily so that it does not receive a cash item on a day that is a banking day for a Reserve Bank, and the Reserve Bank makes a cash item available to the paying bank on that day, the paying bank shall either—

(A)　On that day, settle for the item so that the proceeds of the settlement are available to its administrative Reserve Bank, or return the item, by the latest of the next clock hour or clock half-hour that is at least one half-hour after it ordinarily would have received the item, 8:30 a.m. eastern time, or such later time as provided in the Reserve Banks' operating circulars; or

(B)　On the next day that is a banking day for both the paying bank and the Reserve Bank, settle for the item so that the proceeds of the settlement are available to its administrative Reserve Bank by 8:30 a.m. eastern time on that day or such later time as provided in the Reserve Banks' operating circulars; and compensate the Reserve Bank for the value of the float associated with the item in accordance with procedures provided in the Reserve Bank's operating circular.

(ii)　If a paying bank closes voluntarily so that it does not receive a cash item on a day that is a banking day for a Reserve Bank, and the Reserve Bank makes a cash item available to the paying bank on that day, the paying bank is not considered to have received the item until its next banking day, but it shall be subject to any applicable overdraft charges if it fails to settle for or return the item in accordance with paragraph (b)(3)(i) of this section. The settlement requirements of paragraphs (b)(1) and (b)(2) of this section do not apply to a paying bank that settles in accordance with paragraph (b)(3)(i) of this section.

(4)　Reserve Bank closed.

(i)　If a paying bank receives a cash item from a Reserve Bank on a banking day that is not a banking day for the Reserve Bank, the paying bank shall—

(A)　Settle for the item so that the proceeds of the settlement are available to its administrative Reserve Bank by the close of Fedwire on the Reserve Bank's next banking day, or return the item by midnight of the day it receives the item (if the paying bank fails to settle for or return a cash item in accordance with this paragraph (b)(4)(i)(A), it shall become accountable for the amount of the item as of the close of its banking day on the day it receives the item); and

(B)　Settle for the item so that the proceeds of the settlement are available to its administrative Reserve Bank by 8:30 a.m. eastern time on the Reserve Bank's next banking day or such later time as provided in the Reserve Bank's operating circular, or return the item by midnight of the day it receives the item. If the paying bank fails to settle for or return a cash item in accordance with this paragraph (b)(4)(i)(B), it shall be subject to any applicable overdraft charges. Settlement under this paragraph (b)(4)(i)(B) satisfies the settlement requirements of paragraph (b)(4)(i)(A) of this section.

(ii) The settlement requirements of paragraphs (b)(1) and (b)(2) of this section do not apply to a paying bank that settles in accordance with paragraph (b)(4)(i) of this section.

(5) **Manner of settlement.** Settlement with a Reserve Bank under paragraphs (b)(1) through (4) of this section shall be made by debit to an account on the Reserve Bank's books, cash, or other form of settlement to which the Reserve Bank agrees, except that the Reserve Bank may, in its discretion, obtain settlement by charging the paying bank's account. A paying bank may not set off against the amount of a settlement under this section the amount of a claim with respect to another cash item, cash letter, or other claim under § 229.34(c) and (d) of this chapter (Regulation CC) or other law.

(6) **Notice in lieu of return.** If a cash item is unavailable for return, the paying bank may send a notice in lieu of return as provided in § 229.30(f) of this chapter (Regulation CC).

(c) **Noncash items.** A Reserve Bank may require the paying or collecting bank to which it has presented or sent a noncash item to pay for the item in cash, but the Reserve Bank may permit payment by a debit to an account maintained or used by the paying or collecting bank on a Reserve Bank's books or by any of the following that is in a form acceptable to the collecting Reserve Bank: bank draft, transfer of funds or bank credit, or any other form of payment authorized by State law.

(d) **Nonbank payor.** A Reserve Bank may require a nonbank payor to which it has presented an item to pay for it in cash, but the Reserve Bank may permit payment in any of the following that is in a form acceptable to the Reserve Bank: cashier's check, certified check, or other bank draft or obligation.

(e) **Handling of payment.** A Reserve Bank may handle a bank draft or other form of payment it receives in payment of a cash item as a cash item. A Reserve Bank may handle a bank draft or other form of payment it receives in payment of a noncash item as either a cash item or a noncash item.

(f) **Liability of Reserve Bank.** Except as set forth in 12 CFR 229.35(b), a Reserve Bank shall not be liable for the failure of a collecting bank, paying bank, or nonbank payor to pay for an item, or for any loss resulting from the Reserve Bank's acceptance of any form of payment other than cash authorized in paragraphs (b), (c), and (d) of this section. A Reserve Bank that acts in good faith and exercises ordinary care shall not be liable for the nonpayment of, or failure to realize upon, a bank draft or other form of payment that it accepts under paragraphs (b), (c), and (d) of this section.

§ 210.10   Time schedule and availability of credits for cash items and returned checks.

(a) Each Reserve Bank shall include in its operating circulars a time schedule for each of its offices indicating when the amount of any cash item or returned check received by it is counted toward the balance maintained to satisfy a reserve balance requirement for purposes of part 204 of this chapter (Regulation D) and becomes available for use by the sender or paying or returning bank. The Reserve Bank that holds the settlement account shall give either immediate or deferred credit to a sender, a paying bank, or a returning bank (other than a foreign correspondent) in accordance with the time schedule of the receiving Reserve Bank. A Reserve Bank ordinarily gives credit to a foreign correspondent only when the Reserve Bank receives payment of the item in actually and finally collected funds, but, in its discretion, a Reserve Bank may give immediate or deferred credit in accordance with its time schedule.

(b) Notwithstanding its time schedule, a Reserve Bank may refuse at any time to permit the use of credit given by it for any cash item or returned check, and may defer availability after credit is received by the Reserve Bank for a period of time that is reasonable under the circumstances.

§ 210.11   Availability of proceeds of noncash items; time schedule.

(a) **Availability of credit.** A Reserve Bank shall give credit to the sender for the proceeds of a noncash item when it receives payment in actually and finally collected funds (or advice from another Reserve Bank of such payment to it). The amount of the item is counted toward the balance maintained to satisfy a reserve balance requirement for purposes of part 204 of this chapter (Regulation D) and becomes available for use by the sender when the Reserve Bank receives the payment or advice, except as provided in paragraph (b) of this section.

(b) **Time schedule.** A Reserve Bank may give credit for the proceeds of a noncash item subject to payment in actually and finally collected funds in accordance with a time schedule included in its operating circulars. The time schedule shall indicate when the proceeds of the noncash item will be counted toward the balance maintained to satisfy a reserve balance requirement for purposes of part 204 of this chapter (Regulation D) and become available for use by the sender. A Reserve Bank may, however, refuse at any time to permit the use of credit given by it for a noncash item for which the Reserve Bank has not yet received payment in actually and finally collected funds.

(c) **Handling of payment.** If a Reserve Bank receives, in payment for a noncash item, a bank draft of other form of payment that it elects to handle as a noncash item, the Reserve Bank shall neither count the proceeds toward the balance maintained to satisfy a reserve balance requirement for purposes of part 204 of this chapter (Regulation D) nor make the proceeds available for use until it receives payment in actually and finally collected funds.

§ 210.12   Return of cash items and handling of returned checks.

(a) **Return of items—**

(1) **Return of cash items handled by Reserve Banks.** A paying bank that receives a cash item from a Reserve Bank, other than for immediate payment over the counter, and that settles for the item as provided in § 210.9(b) of this subpart, may, before it has finally paid the item, return the item to any Reserve Bank (unless its Administrative Reserve Bank directs it to return the item to a specific Reserve Bank) in accordance with subpart C of part 229 of this chapter (Regulation CC), the Uniform Commercial Code, and the Reserve Banks' operating circulars. A paying bank that receives a cash item from a Reserve Bank also may return the item prior to settlement, in accordance with § 210.9(b) of this subpart and the Reserve Banks' operating circulars. The rules or practices of a clearinghouse through which the item was presented, or a special collection agreement under which the item was presented, may not extend these return times, but may provide for a shorter return time.

(2) **Return of checks not handled by Reserve Banks.** A paying bank that receives a check as defined in § 229.2(k) of this chapter (Regulation CC), other than from a Reserve Bank, and that determines not to pay the check, may send the returned check to any Reserve Bank (unless its Administrative Reserve Bank directs it to send the returned check to a specific Reserve Bank) in accordance with subpart C of part 229 of this chapter (Regulation CC), the Uniform Commercial Code, and the Reserve Banks' operating circulars. A returning bank may send a returned check to any Reserve Bank (unless its Administrative Reserve Bank directs it to send the returned check to a specific Reserve Bank) in accordance with subpart C of part 229 of this chapter (Regulation CC), the Uniform Commercial Code, and the Reserve Banks' operating circulars.

(b) **Handling of returned checks.**

(1) The following parties, in the following order, are deemed to have handled a returned check sent to a Reserve Bank under paragraph (a) of this section—

(i) The paying or returning bank;

(ii) The paying bank's or returning bank's Administrative Reserve Bank;

(iii) The Reserve Bank that receives the returned check from the paying or returning bank (if different from the paying bank's or returning bank's Administrative Reserve Bank); and

(iv) Another Reserve Bank, if any, that receives the returned check from a Reserve Bank.

(2) A Reserve Bank that is not described in paragraph (b)(1) of this section is not a person that handles a returned check and is not a returning bank with respect to a returned check.

(3)   The identity and order of the parties under paragraph (b)(1) of this section determine the relationships and the rights and liabilities of the parties under this subpart, part 229 of this chapter (Regulation CC), and the Uniform Commercial Code.

(c) **Paying bank's and returning bank's agreement.** The warranties, authorizations, and agreements made pursuant to this paragraph may not be disclaimed and are made whether or not the returned check bears an indorsement of the paying bank or returning bank. By sending a returned check to a Reserve Bank, the paying bank or returning bank does all of the following.

(1) **Authorization to handled returned check.** The paying bank or returning bank authorizes the paying bank's or returning bank's administrative Reserve Bank, and any other Reserve Bank or returning bank to which the returned check is sent, to handle the returned check (and authorizes any Reserve Bank that handles settlement for the returned check to make accounting entries) subject to this subpart and to the Reserve Banks' operating circulars.

(2) **Warranties for all returned checks.** The paying bank or returning bank warrants to each Reserve Bank handling a returned check that the returned check bears all indorsements applied by parties that previously handled the returned check, in paper or electronic form, for forward collection or return.

(3) **Warranties for all returned checks that are electronic items.** A paying bank or returning bank that sends a returned check that is an electronic item makes the returning bank warranties set forth in and subject to the terms of § 229.34 of this chapter for the electronic item as if it were a check subject to that section.

(4) **Warranties for returned checks that are electronic items that are not representations of substitute checks.** If the returned check is an electronic item that is not a representation of a substitute check, the paying bank or returning bank warrants to each Reserve Bank handling the returned check that—

(i)   The electronic image portion of the item accurately represents all of the information on the front and back of the original check as of the time that the original check was truncated; the information portion of the item contains a record of all MICR-line information required for a substitute check under § 229.2(aaa) of this chapter; and the item conforms to the technical standards for an electronic item set forth in an operating circular; and

(ii)   No person will receive a transfer, presentment, or return of, or otherwise be charged for, the electronic item, the original item, or a paper or electronic representation of the original item such that the person will be asked to make payment based on an item it already has paid.

(5) **Paying bank or returning bank's liability to Reserve Bank.**

(i)   Except as provided in paragraph (c)(5)(ii) of this section, a paying bank or returning bank agrees to indemnify each Reserve Bank for any loss or expense (including attorneys' fees and expenses of litigation) resulting from—

(A)   The paying or returning bank's lack of authority to give the authorization in paragraph (c)(1) of this section;

(B)   Any action taken by a Reserve Bank within the scope of its authority in handling the returned check; or

(C)   Any warranty or indemnity made by the Reserve Bank under paragraph (e) of this section or part 229 of this chapter.

(ii)   A paying bank's or returning bank's liability for warranties and indemnities that a Reserve Bank makes for a returned check that is a substitute check, a paper or electronic representation thereof, or any other electronic item is subject to the following conditions and limitations—

(A)   A paying bank or returning bank that sent an original check shall not be liable for any amount that a Reserve Bank pays under subpart D of part 229 of this chapter or under § 210.12(e)(1)(iii) of this subpart, absent the paying bank's or returning bank's agreement to the contrary;

(B) Nothing in this subpart alters the liability under subpart D of part 229 of this chapter of a paying bank or returning bank that sent a substitute check or a paper or electronic representation of a substitute check; and

(C) A paying bank or returning bank that sent an electronic item that is not a representation of a substitute check shall not be liable under paragraph (c)(5)(i) of this section for any amount that the Reserve Bank pays under subpart D of part 229 of this chapter or paragraph (e)(1)(iii) of this section that is attributable to the Reserve Bank's own lack of good faith or failure to exercise ordinary care.

(d) Preservation of other warranties and indemnities. Nothing in paragraph (c) of this section limits any warranty or indemnity by a returning bank or paying bank (or a person that handled an item prior to that bank) arising under state law or regulation (such as the U.C.C.), other federal law or regulation (such as part 229 of this chapter), or an agreement with a Reserve Bank.

(e) Warranties by and liability of Reserve Bank.

(1) The following provisions apply when a Reserve Bank handles a returned check under this subpart.

(i) Warranties for all items. The Reserve Bank warrants to the bank to which it sends the returned check that the returned check bears all indorsements applied by parties that previously handled the returned check, in paper or electronic form, for forward collection or return.

(ii) Warranties for all returned checks that are electronic items. A Reserve Bank that sends a returned check that is an electronic item makes the returning bank warranties set forth in and subject to the terms of § 229.34 of this chapter as if the electronic item were a check subject to that section.

(iii) Warranties and indemnity for returned checks that are electronic items that are not representations of substitute checks.

(A) If the returned check is an electronic item that is not a representation of a substitute check, the Reserve Bank warrants to the bank to which it sends the returned check that—

(1) The electronic image portion of the item accurately represents all of the information on the front and back of the original check as of the time that the original check was truncated; the information portion of the item contains a record of all MICR-line information required for a substitute check under § 229.2(aaa) of this chapter; and the item conforms with the technical standards for an electronic item set forth in an operating circular; and

(2) No person will receive a transfer, presentment, or return of, or otherwise be charged for, the electronic item, the original item, or a paper or electronic representation of the original item such that the person will be asked to make payment based on an item it already has paid.

(B) If the returned check is an electronic item that is not a representation of a substitute check—

(1) Except as provided in paragraph (e)(1)(iii)(B)(2) of this section, the Reserve Bank agrees to indemnify the bank to which it sends the returned check (the recipient bank) for the amount of any losses that the bank incurs under subpart D of part 229 of this chapter for an indemnity that the bank was required to make under subpart D of part 229 of this chapter in connection with a substitute check later created from the returned check.

(2) A Reserve Bank shall not be liable under paragraph (e)(1)(iii)(B)(1) of this section for any amount that the recipient bank pays under subpart D of part 229 of this chapter that is attributable to the lack of good faith or failure to exercise ordinary care of the recipient bank or a person that handled the item, in any form, after the recipient bank.

(2) A Reserve Bank shall not have or assume any other liability to any person except—

(i) As provided in paragraph (e)(1) of this section;

(ii) For the Reserve Bank's own lack of good faith or failure to exercise ordinary care as provided in subpart C of part 229 of this chapter; or

(iii) As provided in subpart D of part 229 of this chapter.

(f) **Recovery by Reserve Bank.** If an action or proceeding is brought against (or if defense is tendered to) a Reserve Bank that has handled a returned Check based on—

(1) The alleged failure of the paying or returning bank to have the authority to give the authorization in paragraph (c)(1) of this section;

(2) Any action by the Reserve Bank within the scope of its authority in handling the returned check; or

(3) Any warranty or indemnity made by the Reserve Bank under paragraph (e) of this section or part 229 of this chapter,

(g) **Methods of recovery.**

(1) The Reserve Bank may recover the amount stated in paragraph (e) of this section by charging any account on its books that is maintained or used by the paying or returning bank (or by charging another returning Reserve Bank), if—

(i) The Reserve Bank made seasonable written demand on the paying or returning bank to assume defense of the action or proceeding; and

(ii) The paying or returning bank has not made any other arrangement for payment that is acceptable to the Reserve Bank.

(2) The Reserve Bank is not responsible for defending the action or proceeding before using this method of recovery. A Reserve Bank that has been charged under this paragraph (g) may recover from the paying or returning bank in the manner and under the circumstances set forth in this paragraph (g). A Reserve Bank's failure to avail itself of the remedy provided in this paragraph (g) does not prejudice its enforcement in any other manner of the indemnity agreement referred to in paragraph (c)(5) of this section.

(h) **Reserve Bank's responsibility.** A Reserve Bank shall handle a returned check, or a notice of nonpayment, in accordance with Subpart C of Part 229 and its operating circular.

(i) **Settlement.** A subsequent returning bank or depositary bank shall settle with its Administrative Reserve Bank for returned checks in the same manner and by the same time as for cash items presented for payment under this subpart. Settlement with its Administrative Reserve Bank is deemed to be settlement with the Reserve Bank from which the returning bank or depositary bank received the item.

(j) **Security interest.** When a paying or returning bank sends a returned check to a Reserve Bank, the paying bank, returning bank, and any prior returning bank grant to the paying bank's or returning bank's Administrative Reserve Bank a security interest in all of their respective assets in the possession of, or held for the account of, any Reserve Bank, to secure their respective obligations due or to become due to the Administrative Reserve Bank under this subpart or subpart C of part 229 of this chapter (Regulation CC). The security interest attaches when a warranty is breached or any other obligation to the Reserve Bank is incurred. If the Reserve Bank, in its sole discretion, deems itself insecure and gives notice thereof to the paying bank, returning bank, or prior returning bank, or if the paying bank, returning bank, or prior returning bank suspends payments or is closed, the Reserve Bank may take any action authorized by law to recover the amount of an obligation, including, but not limited to, the exercise of rights of set off, the realization on any available collateral, and any other rights it may have as a creditor under applicable law.

§ 210.13   Unpaid items.

(a) **Right of recovery.** If a Reserve Bank does not receive payment in actually and finally collected funds for an item, the Reserve Bank shall recover by charge-back or otherwise the amount of the item from the sender, prior collecting bank, paying bank, or returning bank from or through which it was received, whether or not the item itself can be sent back. In the event of recovery from such a person, no person, including the owner or holder of the item, shall, for the purpose of obtaining payment of the amount of the item, have any interest in any reserve balance or other funds or property in the Reserve Bank's possession of the bank that failed to make payment in actually and finally collected funds.

(b) **Suspension or closing of bank.** A Reserve Bank shall not pay or act on a draft, authorization to charge (including a charge authorized by § 210.9(b)(5)), or other order on a reserve balance or other funds in its possession for the purpose of settling for items under § 210.9 or § 210.12 after it receives notice of suspension or closing of the bank making the settlement for that bank's own or another's account.

§ 210.14   Extension of time limits.

If a bank (including a Reserve Bank) or nonbank payor is delayed in acting on an item beyond applicable time limits because of interruption of communication or computer facilities, suspension of payments by a bank or nonbank payor, war, emergency conditions, failure of equipment, or other circumstances beyond its control, its time for acting is extended for the time necessary to complete the action, if it exercises such diligence as the circumstances require.

§ 210.15   Direct presentment of certain warrants.

If a Reserve Bank elects to present direct to the payor a bill, note, or warrant that is issued and payable by a State or a political subdivision and that is a cash item not payable or collectible through a bank: (a) Sections 210.9, 210.12, and 210.13 and the operating circulars of the Reserve Banks apply to the payor as if it were a paying bank; (b) § 210.14 applies to the payor as if it were a bank; and (c) under § 210.9 each day on which the payor is open for the regular conduct of its affairs or the accommodation of the public is considered a banking day.

SUBPART B—FUNDS TRANSFERS THROUGH FEDWIRE

§ 210.25   Authority, purpose, and scope.

(a) **Authority and purpose.** This subpart provides rules to govern funds transfers through Fedwire, and has been issued pursuant to the Federal Reserve Act—section 13 (12 U.S.C. 342), paragraph (f) of section 19 (12 U.S.C. 464), paragraph 14 of section 16 (12 U.S.C. 248(*o*)), and paragraphs (i) and (j) of section 11 (12 U.S.C. 248(i) and (j))—and other laws and has the force and effect of federal law. This Subpart is not a funds-transfer system rule as defined in Section 4A–501(b) of Article 4A.

(b) **Scope.**

(1) This subpart incorporates the provisions of article 4A set forth in appendix B to this subpart. In the event of an inconsistency between the provisions of the sections of this subpart and appendix B to this subpart, the provisions of the sections of this subpart shall prevail. In the event of an inconsistency between the provisions this subpart and section 919 of the Electronic Fund Transfer Act, section 919 of the Electronic Fund Transfer Act shall prevail.

(2) Except as otherwise provided in paragraphs (b)(3) and (b)(4) of this section, this Subpart governs the rights and obligations of:

(i) Federal Reserve Banks sending or receiving payment orders;

(ii) Senders that send payment orders directly to a Federal Reserve Bank;

(iii) Receiving banks that receive payment orders directly from a Federal Reserve Bank;

(iv) Beneficiaries that receive payment for payment orders sent to a Federal Reserve Bank by means of credit to an account maintained or used at a Federal Reserve Bank; and

(v) Other parties to a funds transfer any part of which is carried out through Fedwire to the same extent as if this subpart were considered a funds-transfer system rule under Article 4A.

(3) This subpart governs a funds transfer that is sent through Fedwire, as provided in paragraph (b)(2) of this section, even though a portion of the funds transfer is governed by the Electronic Fund Transfer Act, but the portion of such funds transfer that is governed by the Electronic Fund Transfer Act (other than section 919 governing remittance transfers) is not governed by this subpart.

(4) In the event that any portion of this Subpart establishes rights or obligations with respect to the availability of funds that are also governed by the Expedited Funds Availability Act or the Board's Regulation CC, Availability of Funds and Collection of Checks, those provisions of the Expedited Funds Availability Act or Regulation CC shall apply and the portion of this Subpart, including Article 4A as incorporated herein, shall not apply.

(c) Operating Circulars. Each Federal Reserve Bank shall issue an Operating Circular consistent with this Subpart that governs the details of its funds-transfer operations and other matters it deems appropriate. Among other things, the Operating Circular may: set cut-off hours and funds-transfer business days; address available security procedures; specify format and media requirements for payment orders; identify messages that are not payment orders; and impose charges for funds-transfer services.

(d) Government senders, receiving banks, and beneficiaries. Except as otherwise expressly provided by the statutes of the United States, the parties specified in paragraphs (b)(2)(ii) through (v) of this section include:

(1) A department, agency, instrumentality, independent establishment, or office of the United States, or a wholly-owned or controlled Government corporation;

(2) An international organization;

(3) A foreign central bank; and

(4) A department, agency, instrumentality, independent establishment, or office of a foreign government, or a wholly-owned or controlled corporation of a foreign government.

§ 210.26 Definitions.

As used in this subpart, the following definitions apply:

(a) Article 4A means article 4A of the Uniform Commercial Code as set forth in appendix B of this subpart.

(b) [Reserved].

(c) Automated clearing house transfer means any transfer designated as an automated clearing house transfer in a Federal Reserve Bank Operating Circular.

(d) Beneficiary's bank has the same meaning as in Article 4A, except that:

(1) A Federal Reserve Bank need not be identified in the payment order in order to be the beneficiary's bank; and

(2) The term includes a Federal Reserve Bank when that Federal Reserve Bank is the beneficiary of a payment order.

(e) Fedwire is the funds-transfer system owned and operated by the Federal Reserve Banks that is used primarily for the transmission and settlement of payment orders governed by this Subpart. Fedwire does not include the system for making automated clearing house transfers.

(f)   Interdistrict transfer means a funds transfer involving entries to accounts maintained at two Federal Reserve Banks.

(g)   Intradistrict transfer means a funds transfer involving entries to accounts maintained at one Federal Reserve Bank.

(h)   Off-line bank means a bank that transmits payment orders to and receives payment orders from a Federal Reserve Bank by telephone orally or by other means other than electronic data transmission.

(i)   Payment order has the same meaning as in Article 4A, except that the term does not include automated clearing house transfers or any communication designated in a Federal Reserve Bank Operating Circular issued under this Subpart as not being a payment order.

(j)   Sender's account, receiving bank's account, and beneficiary's account mean the reserve, clearing, or other funds deposit account at a Federal Reserve Bank maintained or used by the sender, receiving bank, or beneficiary, respectively.

(k)   Sender's Federal Reserve Bank and receiving bank's Federal Reserve Bank mean the Federal Reserve Bank at which the sender or receiving bank, respectively, maintains or uses an account.

§ 210.27   Reliance on identifying number.

(a)   Reliance by a Federal Reserve Bank on number to identify an intermediary bank or beneficiary's bank. A Federal Reserve Bank may rely on the number in a payment order that identifies the intermediary bank or beneficiary's bank, even if it identifies a bank different from the bank identified by name in the payment order, if the Federal Reserve Bank does not know of such an inconsistency in identification. A Federal Reserve Bank has no duty to detect any such inconsistency in identification.

(b)   Reliance by a Federal Reserve Bank on number to identify beneficiary. A Federal Reserve Bank, acting as a beneficiary's bank, may rely on the number in a payment order that identifies the beneficiary, even if it identifies a person different from the person identified by name in the payment order, if the Federal Reserve Bank does not know of such an inconsistency in identification. A Federal Reserve Bank has no duty to detect any such inconsistency in identification.

§ 210.28   Agreement of sender.

(a)   Payment of sender's obligation to a Federal Reserve Bank. A sender (other than a Federal Reserve Bank), by maintaining or using an account with a Federal Reserve Bank, authorizes the sender's Federal Reserve Bank to obtain payment for the sender's payment orders by debiting the amount of the payment order from the sender's account.

(b)   Overdrafts.

(1)   A sender does not have the right to an overdraft in the sender's account. In the event an overdraft is created, the overdraft shall be due and payable immediately without the need for a demand by the Federal Reserve Bank, at the earliest of the following times:

(i)   At the end of the funds-transfer business day;

(ii)   At the time the Federal Reserve Bank, in its sole discretion, deems itself insecure and gives notice thereof to the sender; or

(iii)   At the time the sender suspends payments or is closed.

(2)   The sender shall have in its account, at the time the overdraft is due and payable, a balance of actually and finally collected funds sufficient to cover the aggregate amount of all its obligations to the Federal Reserve Bank, whether the obligations result from the execution of a payment order or otherwise.

(3)   To secure any overdraft, as well as any other obligation due or to become due to its Federal Reserve Bank, each sender, by sending a payment order to a Federal Reserve Bank that is accepted by the Federal Reserve Bank, grants to the Federal Reserve Bank a security interest in all of the sender's assets in the possession of, or held for the account of, the Federal Reserve Bank. The security interest attaches when an overdraft, or any other obligation to the Federal Reserve Bank, becomes due and payable.

(4) A Federal Reserve Bank may take any action authorized by law to recover the amount of an overdraft that is due and payable, including, but not limited to, the exercise of rights of set off, the realization on any available collateral, and any other rights it may have as a creditor under applicable law.

(5) If a sender, other than a government sender described in § 210.25(d), incurs an overdraft in its account as a result of a debit to the account by a Federal Reserve Bank under paragraph (a) of this section, the account will be subject to any applicable overdraft charges, regardless of whether the overdraft has become due and payable. A Federal Reserve Bank may debit a sender's account under paragraph (a) of this section immediately on acceptance of the payment order.

(c) **Review of payment orders.** A sender, by sending a payment order to a Federal Reserve Bank, agrees that for the purposes of sections 4A–204(a) and 4A–304 of Article 4A, a reasonable time to notify a Federal Reserve Bank of the relevant facts concerning an unauthorized or erroneously executed payment order is within 30 calendar days after the sender receives notice that the payment order was accepted or executed, or that the sender's account was debited with respect to the payment order.

§ 210.29   Agreement of receiving bank.

(a) **Payment.** A receiving bank (other than a Federal Reserve Bank) that receives a payment order from its Federal Reserve Bank authorizes that Federal Reserve Bank to pay for the payment order by crediting the amount of the payment order to the receiving bank's account.

(b) **Off-line banks.** An off-line bank that does not expressly notify its Federal Reserve Bank in writing that it maintains an account for another bank warrants to that Federal Reserve Bank that the off-line bank does not act as an intermediary bank or a beneficiary's bank with respect to payment orders received through Fedwire for a beneficiary that is a bank.

§ 210.30   Payment orders.

(a) **Rejection.** A sender shall not send a payment order to a Federal Reserve Bank unless authorized to do so by the Federal Reserve Bank. A Federal Reserve Bank may reject, or impose conditions that must be satisfied before it will accept, a payment order for any reason.

(b) **Selection of an intermediary bank.** For an interdistrict transfer, a Federal Reserve Bank is authorized and directed to execute a payment order through another Federal Reserve Bank. A sender shall not send a payment order to a Federal Reserve Bank that requires the Federal Reserve Bank to issue a payment order to an intermediary bank (other than a Federal Reserve Bank) unless that intermediary bank is designated in the sender's payment order. A sender shall not send to a Federal Reserve Bank a payment order instructing use by a Federal Reserve Bank of a funds-transfer system or means of transmission other than Fedwire, unless the Federal Reserve Bank agrees with the sender in writing to follow such instructions.

(c) **Same-day execution.** A sender shall not issue a payment order that instructs a Federal Reserve Bank to execute the payment order on a funds-transfer business day that is later than the funds-transfer business day on which the order is received by the Federal Reserve Bank, unless the Federal Reserve Bank agrees with the sender in writing to follow such instructions.

§ 210.31   Payment by a Federal Reserve Bank to a receiving bank or beneficiary.

(a) **Payment to a receiving bank.** Payment of a Federal Reserve Bank's obligation to pay a receiving bank (other than a Federal Reserve Bank) occurs at the earlier of the time when the amount of the payment order is credited to the receiving bank's account or when the payment order is sent to the receiving bank.

(b) **Payment to a beneficiary.** Payment by a Federal Reserve Bank to a beneficiary of a payment order, where the Federal Reserve Bank is the beneficiary's bank, occurs at the earlier of the time when the amount of the payment order is credited to the beneficiary's account or when notice of the credit is sent to the beneficiary.

§ 210.32　　Federal Reserve Bank liability; payment of interest.

(a) **Damages.** In connection with its handling of a payment order under this subpart, a Federal Reserve Bank shall not be liable to a sender, receiving bank, beneficiary, or other Federal Reserve Bank, governed by this subpart, for any damages other than those payable under Article 4A. A Federal Reserve Bank shall not agree to be liable to a sender, receiving bank, beneficiary, or other Federal Reserve Bank for consequential damages under section 4A–305(d) of Article 4A.

(b) **Payment of interest.**

(1) A Federal Reserve Bank shall satisfy its obligation, or that of another Federal Reserve Bank, to pay compensation in the form of interest under article 4A by paying compensation in the form of interest to its sender, its receiving bank, its beneficiary, or another party to the funds transfer that is entitled to such payment, in an amount that is calculated in accordance with section 4A–506 of article 4A.

(2) If the sender or receiving bank that is the recipient of interest payment is not the party entitled to compensation under article 4A, the sender or receiving bank shall pass through the benefit of the interest payment by making an interest payment, as of the day the interest payment is effected, to the party entitled to compensation. The interest payment that is made to the party entitled to compensation shall not be less than the value of the interest payment that was provided by the Federal Reserve Bank to the sender or receiving bank. The party entitled to compensation may agree to accept compensation in a form other than a direct interest payment, provided that such an alternative form of compensation is not less than the value of the interest payment that otherwise would be made.

(c) **Nonwaiver of right of recovery.** Nothing in this subpart or any Operating Circular issued hereunder shall constitute, or be construed as constituting, a waiver by a Federal Reserve Bank of a cause of action for recovery under any applicable law of mistake and restitution.

ELECTRONIC FUND TRANSFERS
(REGULATION E)

12 C.F.R. Part 1005

Current through March 13, 2016; 81 F.R. 12795

For updates, see www.ecfr.gov

Note from West Advisory Board

This regulation is the Consumer Financial Protection Bureau's recodification of the Federal Reserve Board's Regulation E (12 C.F.R. Part 205), as mandated by the Dodd-Frank Wall Street Reform and Consumer Protection Act of 2010. The Federal Reserve Board's regulation still has some applicability, primarily to auto dealers. The text of that regulation can be found at www.ecfr.gov.

SUBPART A—GENERAL

§ 1005.1   Authority and purpose.

(a) Authority. The regulation in this part, known as Regulation E, is issued by the Bureau of Consumer Financial Protection (Bureau) pursuant to the Electronic Fund Transfer Act (15 U.S.C. 1693 et seq.). The information-collection requirements have been approved by the Office of Management and Budget under 44 U.S.C. 3501 et seq. and have been assigned OMB No. 3170–0014.

(b) Purpose. This part carries out the purposes of the Electronic Fund Transfer Act, which establishes the basic rights, liabilities, and responsibilities of consumers who use electronic fund transfer services and of financial institutions that offer these services. The primary objective of the Act and this part is the protection of individual consumers engaging in electronic fund transfers.

§ 1005.2   Definitions.

Except as otherwise provided in subpart B, for purposes of this part, the following definitions apply:

(a)(1) "Access device" means a card, code, or other means of access to a consumer's account, or any combination thereof, that may be used by the consumer to initiate electronic fund transfers.

(2) An access device becomes an "accepted access device" when the consumer:

(i) Requests and receives, or signs, or uses (or authorizes another to use) the access device to transfer money between accounts or to obtain money, property, or services;

(ii) Requests validation of an access device issued on an unsolicited basis; or

(iii) Receives an access device in renewal of, or in substitution for, an accepted access device from either the financial institution that initially issued the device or a successor.

(b)(1) "Account" means a demand deposit (checking), savings, or other consumer asset account (other than an occasional or incidental credit balance in a credit plan) held directly or indirectly by a financial institution and established primarily for personal, family, or household purposes.

(2) The term includes a "payroll card account" which is an account that is directly or indirectly established through an employer and to which electronic fund transfers of the consumer's wages, salary, or other employee compensation (such as commissions), are made on a recurring basis, whether the account is operated or managed by the employer, a third-party payroll processor, a depository institution or any other person. For rules governing payroll card accounts, see § 1005.18.

(3) The term does not include an account held by a financial institution under a bona fide trust agreement.

(c) "Act" means the Electronic Fund Transfer Act (Title IX of the Consumer Credit Protection Act, 15 U.S.C. 1693 et seq.).

(d) "Business day" means any day on which the offices of the consumer's financial institution are open to the public for carrying on substantially all business functions.

(e) "Consumer" means a natural person.

(f) "Credit" means the right granted by a financial institution to a consumer to defer payment of debt, incur debt and defer its payment, or purchase property or services and defer payment therefor.

(g) "Electronic fund transfer" is defined in 1105.3.

(h) "Electronic terminal" means an electronic device, other than a telephone operated by a consumer, through which a consumer may initiate an electronic fund transfer. The term includes, but is not limited to, point-of-sale terminals, automated teller machines (ATMs), and cash dispensing machines.

(i) "Financial institution" means a bank, savings association, credit union, or any other person that directly or indirectly holds an account belonging to a consumer, or that issues an access device and agrees with a consumer to provide electronic fund transfer services, other than a person excluded from coverage of this part by section 1029 of the Consumer Financial Protection Act of 2010, Title X of the Dodd-Frank Wall Street Reform and Consumer Protection Act, Public Law 111–203, 124 Stat. 1376.

(j) "Person" means a natural person or an organization, including a corporation, government agency, estate, trust, partnership, proprietorship, cooperative, or association.

(k) "Preauthorized electronic fund transfer" means an electronic fund transfer authorized in advance to recur at substantially regular intervals.

(*l*) "State" means any state, territory, or possession of the United States; the District of Columbia; the Commonwealth of Puerto Rico; or any political subdivision of the thereof in this paragraph (*l*).

(m) "Unauthorized electronic fund transfer" means an electronic fund transfer from a consumer's account initiated by a person other than the consumer without actual authority to initiate the transfer and from which the consumer receives no benefit. The term does not include an electronic fund transfer initiated:

(1) By a person who was furnished the access device to the consumer's account by the consumer, unless the consumer has notified the financial institution that transfers by that person are no longer authorized;

(2) With fraudulent intent by the consumer or any person acting in concert with the consumer; or

(3) By the financial institution or its employee.

§ 1005.3   Coverage.

(a) **General.** This part applies to any electronic fund transfer that authorizes a financial institution to debit or credit a consumer's account. Generally, this part applies to financial institutions. For purposes of §§ 1005.3(b)(2) and (3), 1005.10(b), (d), and (e), 1005.13, and 1005.20 this part applies to any person, other than a person excluded from coverage of this part by section 1029 of the Consumer Financial Protection Act of 2010, Title X of the Dodd-Frank Wall Street Reform and Consumer Protection Act, Public Law 111–203, 124 Stat. 1376. The requirements of subpart B apply to remittance transfer providers.

(b) **Electronic fund transfer.**

(1) **Definition.** The term "electronic fund transfer" means any transfer of funds that is initiated through an electronic terminal, telephone, computer, or magnetic tape for the purpose of ordering, instructing, or authorizing a financial institution to debit or credit a consumer's account. The term includes, but is not limited to:

(i)   Point-of-sale transfers;

(ii)   Automated teller machine transfers;

(iii) Direct deposits or withdrawals of funds;

(iv)   Transfers initiated by telephone; and

(v)   Transfers resulting from debit card transactions, whether or not initiated through an electronic terminal.

(2) **Electronic fund transfer using information from a check.**

(i)   This part applies where a check, draft, or similar paper instrument is used as a source of information to initiate a one-time electronic fund transfer from a consumer's account. The consumer must authorize the transfer.

(ii)   The person initiating an electronic fund transfer using the consumer's check as a source of information for the transfer must provide a notice that the transaction will or may be processed as an electronic fund transfer, and obtain a consumer's authorization for each transfer. A consumer authorizes a one-time electronic fund transfer (in providing a check to a merchant or other payee for the MICR encoding, that is, the routing number of the financial institution, the consumer's account number and the serial number) when the consumer receives notice and goes forward with the underlying transaction. For point-of-sale transfers, the notice must be posted in a prominent and conspicuous location, and a copy thereof, or a substantially similar notice, must be provided to the consumer at the time of the transaction.

(iii) A person may provide notices that are substantially similar to those set forth in Appendix A–6 to comply with the requirements of this paragraph (b)(2).

(3) Collection of returned item fees via electronic fund transfer.

(i) General. The person initiating an electronic fund transfer to collect a fee for the return of an electronic fund transfer or a check that is unpaid, including due to insufficient or uncollected funds in the consumer's account, must obtain the consumer's authorization for each transfer. A consumer authorizes a one-time electronic fund transfer from his or her account to pay the fee for the returned item or transfer if the person collecting the fee provides notice to the consumer stating that the person may electronically collect the fee, and the consumer goes forward with the underlying transaction. The notice must state that the fee will be collected by means of an electronic fund transfer from the consumer's account if the payment is returned unpaid and must disclose the dollar amount of the fee. If the fee may vary due to the amount of the transaction or due to other factors, then, except as otherwise provided in paragraph (b)(3)(ii) of this section, the person collecting the fee may disclose, in place of the dollar amount of the fee, an explanation of how the fee will be determined.

(ii) Point-of-sale transactions. If a fee for an electronic fund transfer or check returned unpaid may be collected electronically in connection with a point-of-sale transaction, the person initiating an electronic fund transfer to collect the fee must post the notice described in paragraph (b)(3)(i) of this section in a prominent and conspicuous location. The person also must either provide the consumer with a copy of the posted notice (or a substantially similar notice) at the time of the transaction, or mail the copy (or a substantially similar notice) to the consumer's address as soon as reasonably practicable after the person initiates the electronic fund transfer to collect the fee. If the amount of the fee may vary due to the amount of the transaction or due to other factors, the posted notice may explain how the fee will be determined, but the notice provided to the consumer must state the dollar amount of the fee if the amount can be calculated at the time the notice is provided or mailed to the consumer.

(c) Exclusions from coverage. The term "electronic fund transfer" does not include:

(1) Checks. Any transfer of funds originated by check, draft, or similar paper instrument; or any payment made by check, draft, or similar paper instrument at an electronic terminal.

(2) Check guarantee or authorization. Any transfer of funds that guarantees payment or authorizes acceptance of a check, draft, or similar paper instrument but that does not directly result in a debit or credit to a consumer's account.

(3) Wire or other similar transfers. Any transfer of funds through Fedwire or through a similar wire transfer system that is used primarily for transfers between financial institutions or between businesses.

(4) Securities and commodities transfers. Any transfer of funds the primary purpose of which is the purchase or sale of a security or commodity, if the security or commodity is:

(i) Regulated by the Securities and Exchange Commission or the Commodity Futures Trading Commission;

(ii) Purchased or sold through a broker-dealer regulated by the Securities and Exchange Commission or through a futures commission merchant regulated by the Commodity Futures Trading Commission; or

(iii) Held in book-entry form by a Federal Reserve Bank or Federal agency.

(5) Automatic transfers by account-holding institution. Any transfer of funds under an agreement between a consumer and a financial institution which provides that the institution will initiate individual transfers without a specific request from the consumer:

    (i) Between a consumer's accounts within the financial institution;

    (ii) From a consumer's account to an account of a member of the consumer's family held in the same financial institution; or

    (iii) Between a consumer's account and an account of the financial institution, except that these transfers remain subject to 1105.10(e) regarding compulsory use and sections 916 and 917 of the Act regarding civil and criminal liability.

    (6) Telephone-initiated transfers. Any transfer of funds that:

    (i) Is initiated by a telephone communication between a consumer and a financial institution making the transfer; and

    (ii) Does not take place under a telephone bill-payment or other written plan in which periodic or recurring transfers are contemplated.

    (7) Small institutions. Any preauthorized transfer to or from an account if the assets of the account-holding financial institution were $100 million or less on the preceding December 31. If assets of the account-holding institution subsequently exceed $100 million, the institution's exemption for preauthorized transfers terminates one year from the end of the calendar year in which the assets exceed $100 million. Preauthorized transfers exempt under this paragraph (c)(7) remain subject to 1105.10(e) regarding compulsory use and sections 916 and 917 of the Act regarding civil and criminal liability.

§ 1005.4   General disclosure requirements; jointly offered services.

    (a)(1) Form of disclosures. Disclosures required under this part shall be clear and readily understandable, in writing, and in a form the consumer may keep, except as otherwise provided in this part. The disclosures required by this part may be provided to the consumer in electronic form, subject to compliance with the consumer-consent and other applicable provisions of the Electronic Signatures in Global and National Commerce Act (E-Sign Act) (15 U.S.C. 7001 et seq.). A financial institution may use commonly accepted or readily understandable abbreviations in complying with the disclosure requirements of this part.

    (2) Foreign language disclosures. Disclosures required under this part may be made in a language other than English, provided that the disclosures are made available in English upon the consumer's request.

    (b) Additional information; disclosures required by other laws. A financial institution may include additional information and may combine disclosures required by other laws (such as the Truth in Lending Act 15 U.S.C. 1601 et seq.) or the Truth in Savings Act (12 U.S.C. 4301 et seq.) with the disclosures required by this part.

    (c) Multiple accounts and account holders.

    (1) Multiple accounts. A financial institution may combine the required disclosures into a single statement for a consumer who holds more than one account at the institution.

    (2) Multiple account holders. For joint accounts held by two or more consumers, a financial institution need provide only one set of the required disclosures and may provide them to any of the account holders.

    (d) Services offered jointly. Financial institutions that provide electronic fund transfer services jointly may contract among themselves to comply with the requirements that this part imposes on any or all of them. An institution need make only the disclosures required by §§ 1005.7 and 1005.8 that are within its knowledge and within the purview of its relationship with the consumer for whom it holds an account.

§ 1005.5   Issuance of access devices.

    (a) Solicited issuance. Except as provided in paragraph (b) of this section, a financial institution may issue an access device to a consumer only:

(1) In response to an oral or written request for the device; or

(2) As a renewal of, or in substitution for, an accepted access device whether issued by the institution or a successor.

(b) Unsolicited issuance. A financial institution may distribute an access device to a consumer on an unsolicited basis if the access device is:

(1) Not validated, meaning that the institution has not yet performed all the procedures that would enable a consumer to initiate an electronic fund transfer using the access device;

(2) Accompanied by a clear explanation that the access device is not validated and how the consumer may dispose of it if validation is not desired;

(3) Accompanied by the disclosures required by § 1005.7, of the consumer's rights and liabilities that will apply if the access device is validated; and

(4) Validated only in response to the consumer's oral or written request for validation, after the institution has verified the consumer's identity by a reasonable means.

§ 1005.6   Liability of consumer for unauthorized transfers.

(a) Conditions for liability. A consumer may be held liable, within the limitations described in paragraph (b) of this section, for an unauthorized electronic fund transfer involving the consumer's account only if the financial institution has provided the disclosures required by § 1005.7(b)(1), (2), and (3). If the unauthorized transfer involved an access device, it must be an accepted access device and the financial institution must have provided a means to identify the consumer to whom it was issued.

(b) Limitations on amount of liability. A consumer's liability for an unauthorized electronic fund transfer or a series of related unauthorized transfers shall be determined as follows:

(1) Timely notice given. If the consumer notifies the financial institution within two business days after learning of the loss or theft of the access device, the consumer's liability shall not exceed the lesser of $50 or the amount of unauthorized transfers that occur before notice to the financial institution.

(2) Timely notice not given. If the consumer fails to notify the financial institution within two business days after learning of the loss or theft of the access device, the consumer's liability shall not exceed the lesser of $500 or the sum of:

(i) $50 or the amount of unauthorized transfers that occur within the two business days, whichever is less; and

(ii) The amount of unauthorized transfers that occur after the close of two business days and before notice to the institution, provided the institution establishes that these transfers would not have occurred had the consumer notified the institution within that two-day period.

(3) Periodic statement; timely notice not given. A consumer must report an unauthorized electronic fund transfer that appears on a periodic statement within 60 days of the financial institution's transmittal of the statement to avoid liability for subsequent transfers. If the consumer fails to do so, the consumer's liability shall not exceed the amount of the unauthorized transfers that occur after the close of the 60 days and before notice to the institution, and that the institution establishes would not have occurred had the consumer notified the institution within the 60-day period. When an access device is involved in the unauthorized transfer, the consumer may be liable for other amounts set forth in paragraphs (b)(1) or (b)(2) of this section, as applicable.

(4) Extension of time limits. If the consumer's delay in notifying the financial institution was due to extenuating circumstances, the institution shall extend the times specified above to a reasonable period.

(5)   Notice to financial institution.

(i)   Notice to a financial institution is given when a consumer takes steps reasonably necessary to provide the institution with the pertinent information, whether or not a particular employee or agent of the institution actually receives the information.

(ii)   The consumer may notify the institution in person, by telephone, or in writing.

(iii)   Written notice is considered given at the time the consumer mails the notice or delivers it for transmission to the institution by any other usual means. Notice may be considered constructively given when the institution becomes aware of circumstances leading to the reasonable belief that an unauthorized transfer to or from the consumer's account has been or may be made.

(6)   Liability under state law or agreement. If state law or an agreement between the consumer and the financial institution imposes less liability than is provided by this section, the consumer's liability shall not exceed the amount imposed under the state law or agreement.

§ 1005.7   Initial disclosures.

(a)   Timing of disclosures. A financial institution shall make the disclosures required by this section at the time a consumer contracts for an electronic fund transfer service or before the first electronic fund transfer is made involving the consumer's account.

(b)   Content of disclosures. A financial institution shall provide the following disclosures, as applicable:

(1)   Liability of consumer. A summary of the consumer's liability, under 1005.6 or under state or other applicable law or agreement, for unauthorized electronic fund transfers.

(2)   Telephone number and address. The telephone number and address of the person or office to be notified when the consumer believes that an unauthorized electronic fund transfer has been or may be made.

(3)   Business days. The financial institution's business days.

(4)   Types of transfers; limitations. The type of electronic fund transfers that the consumer may make and any limitations on the frequency and dollar amount of transfers. Details of the limitations need not be disclosed if confidentiality is essential to maintain the security of the electronic fund transfer system.

(5)   Fees. Any fees imposed by the financial institution for electronic fund transfers or for the right to make transfers.

(6)   Documentation. A summary of the consumer's right to receipts and periodic statements, as provided in § 1005.9 of this part, and notices regarding preauthorized transfers as provided in § 1005.10(a) and (d).

(7)   Stop payment. A summary of the consumer's right to stop payment of a preauthorized electronic fund transfer and the procedure for placing a stop-payment order, as provided in § 1005.10(c).

(8)   Liability of institution. A summary of the financial institution's liability to the consumer under section 910 of the Act for failure to make or to stop certain transfers.

(9)   Confidentiality. The circumstances under which, in the ordinary course of business, the financial institution may provide information concerning the consumer's account to third parties.

(10)   Error resolution. A notice that is substantially similar to Model Form A–3 as set out in Appendix A of this part concerning error resolution.

(11) ATM fees. A notice that a fee may be imposed by an automated teller machine operator as defined in § 1005.16(a)(1), when the consumer initiates an electronic fund transfer or makes a balance inquiry, and by any network used to complete the transaction.

(c) Addition of electronic fund transfer services. If an electronic fund transfer service is added to a consumer's account and is subject to terms and conditions different from those described in the initial disclosures, disclosures for the new service are required.

§ 1005.8   Change in terms notice; error resolution notice.

(a) Change in terms notice.

(1) Prior notice required. A financial institution shall mail or deliver a written notice to the consumer, at least 21 days before the effective date, of any change in a term or condition required to be disclosed under § 1005.7(b) of this part if the change would result in:

    (i) Increased fees for the consumer;

    (ii) Increased liability for the consumer;

    (iii) Fewer types of available electronic fund transfers; or

    (iv) Stricter limitations on the frequency or dollar amount of transfers.

(2) Prior notice exception. A financial institution need not give prior notice if an immediate change in terms or conditions is necessary to maintain or restore the security of an account or an electronic fund transfer system. If the institution makes such a change permanent and disclosure would not jeopardize the security of the account or system, the institution shall notify the consumer in writing on or with the next regularly scheduled periodic statement or within 30 days of making the change permanent.

(b) Error resolution notice. For accounts to or from which electronic fund transfers can be made, a financial institution shall mail or deliver to the consumer, at least once each calendar year, an error resolution notice substantially similar to the model form set forth in Appendix A of this part (Model Form A–3). Alternatively, an institution may include an abbreviated notice substantially similar to the model form error resolution notice set forth in Appendix A of this part (Model Form A–3), on or with each periodic statement required by § 1005.9(b).

§ 1005.9   Receipts at electronic terminals; periodic statements.

(a) Receipts at electronic terminals—General. Except as provided in paragraph (e) of this section, a financial institution shall make a receipt available to a consumer at the time the consumer initiates an electronic fund transfer at an electronic terminal. The receipt shall set forth the following information, as applicable:

(1) Amount. The amount of the transfer. A transaction fee may be included in this amount, provided the amount of the fee is disclosed on the receipt and displayed on or at the terminal.

(2) Date. The date the consumer initiates the transfer.

(3) Type. The type of transfer and the type of the consumer's account(s) to or from which funds are transferred. The type of account may be omitted if the access device used is able to access only one account at that terminal.

(4) Identification. A number or code that identifies the consumer's account or accounts, or the access device used to initiate the transfer. The number or code need not exceed four digits or letters to comply with the requirements of this paragraph (a)(4).

(5) Terminal location. The location of the terminal where the transfer is initiated, or an identification such as a code or terminal number. Except in limited circumstances where all terminals are located in the same city or state, if the location is disclosed, it shall include the city and state or foreign country and one of the following:

(i)   The street address; or

(ii) A generally accepted name for the specific location; or

(iii) The name of the owner or operator of the terminal if other than the account-holding institution.

(6)   Third party transfer. The name of any third party to or from whom funds are transferred.

(b)   Periodic statements. For an account to or from which electronic fund transfers can be made, a financial institution shall send a periodic statement for each monthly cycle in which an electronic fund transfer has occurred; and shall send a periodic statement at least quarterly if no transfer has occurred. The statement shall set forth the following information, as applicable:

(1)   Transaction information. For each electronic fund transfer occurring during the cycle:

(i)   The amount of the transfer;

(ii) The date the transfer was credited or debited to the consumer's account;

(iii) The type of transfer and type of account to or from which funds were transferred;

(iv) For a transfer initiated by the consumer at an electronic terminal (except for a deposit of cash or a check, draft, or similar paper instrument), the terminal location described in paragraph (a)(5) of this section; and

(v)   The name of any third party to or from whom funds were transferred.

(2)   Account number. The number of the account.

(3)   Fees. The amount of any fees assessed against the account during the statement period for electronic fund transfers, the right to make transfers, or account maintenance.

(4)   Account balances. The balance in the account at the beginning and at the close of the statement period.

(5)   Address and telephone number for inquiries. The address and telephone number to be used for inquiries or notice of errors, preceded by "Direct inquiries to" or similar language. The address and telephone number provided on an error resolution notice under § 1005.8(b) given on or with the statement satisfies this requirement.

(6)   Telephone number for preauthorized transfers. A telephone number the consumer may call to ascertain whether preauthorized transfers to the consumer's account have occurred, if the financial institution uses the telephone-notice option under § 1005.10(a)(1)(iii).

(c)   Exceptions to the periodic statement requirement for certain accounts.

(1)   Preauthorized transfers to accounts. For accounts that may be accessed only by preauthorized transfers to the account the following rules apply:

(i)   **Passbook accounts.** For passbook accounts, the financial institution need not provide a periodic statement if the institution updates the passbook upon presentation or enters on a separate document the amount and date of each electronic fund transfer since the passbook was last presented.

(ii) **Other accounts.** For accounts other than passbook accounts, the financial institution must send a periodic statement at least quarterly.

(2)   Intra-institutional transfers. For an electronic fund transfer initiated by the consumer between two accounts of the consumer in the same institution, documenting the transfer on a periodic statement for one of the two accounts satisfies the periodic statement requirement.

(3)   Relationship between paragraphs (c)(1) and (2) of this section. An account that is accessed by preauthorized transfers to the account described in paragraph (c)(1) of this section and by intra-institutional transfers described in paragraph (c)(2) of this section, but by no other type of electronic fund transfers, qualifies for the exceptions provided by paragraph (c)(1) of this section.

(d) **Documentation for foreign-initiated transfers.** The failure by a financial institution to provide a terminal receipt for an electronic fund transfer or to document the transfer on a periodic statement does not violate this part if:

    (1) The transfer is not initiated within a state; and

    (2) The financial institution treats an inquiry for clarification or documentation as a notice of error in accordance with § 1005.11.

(e) **Exception for receipts in small-value transfers.** A financial institution is not subject to the requirement to make available a receipt under paragraph (a) of this section if the amount of the transfer is $15 or less.

§ 1005.10   Preauthorized transfers.

(a) **Preauthorized transfers to consumer's account.**

    (1) **Notice by financial institution.** When a person initiates preauthorized electronic fund transfers to a consumer's account at least once every 60 days, the account-holding financial institution shall provide notice to the consumer by:

        (i) **Positive notice.** Providing oral or written notice of the transfer within two business days after the transfer occurs; or

        (ii) **Negative notice.** Providing oral or written notice, within two business days after the date on which the transfer was scheduled to occur, that the transfer did not occur; or

        (iii) Readily-available telephone line. Providing a readily available telephone line that the consumer may call to determine whether the transfer occurred and disclosing the telephone number on the initial disclosure of account terms and on each periodic statement.

    (2) **Notice by payor.** A financial institution need not provide notice of a transfer if the payor gives the consumer positive notice that the transfer has been initiated.

    (3) **Crediting.** A financial institution that receives a preauthorized transfer of the type described in paragraph (a)(1) of this section shall credit the amount of the transfer as of the date the funds for the transfer are received.

(b) **Written authorization for preauthorized transfers from consumer's account.** Preauthorized electronic fund transfers from a consumer's account may be authorized only by a writing signed or similarly authenticated by the consumer. The person that obtains the authorization shall provide a copy to the consumer.

(c) **Consumer's right to stop payment.**

    (1) **Notice.** A consumer may stop payment of a preauthorized electronic fund transfer from the consumer's account by notifying the financial institution orally or in writing at least three business days before the scheduled date of the transfer.

    (2) **Written confirmation.** The financial institution may require the consumer to give written confirmation of a stop-payment order within 14 days of an oral notification. An institution that requires written confirmation shall inform the consumer of the requirement and provide the address where confirmation must be sent when the consumer gives the oral notification. An oral stop-payment order ceases to be binding after 14 days if the consumer fails to provide the required written confirmation.

(d) **Notice of transfers varying in amount.**

    (1) **Notice.** When a preauthorized electronic fund transfer from the consumer's account will vary in amount from the previous transfer under the same authorization or from the preauthorized amount, the designated payee or the financial institution shall send the consumer written notice of the amount and date of the transfer at least 10 days before the scheduled date of transfer.

    (2) **Range.** The designated payee or the institution shall inform the consumer of the right to receive notice of all varying transfers, but may give the consumer the option of receiving notice only when a transfer falls outside a specified range of amounts or only when a transfer differs from the most recent transfer by more than an agreed-upon amount.

(e) Compulsory use.

(1) **Credit.** No financial institution or other person may condition an extension of credit to a consumer on the consumer's repayment by preauthorized electronic fund transfers, except for credit extended under an overdraft credit plan or extended to maintain a specified minimum balance in the consumer's account.

(2) **Employment or government benefit.** No financial institution or other person may require a consumer to establish an account for receipt of electronic fund transfers with a particular institution as a condition of employment or receipt of a government benefit.

§ 1005.11 Procedures for resolving errors.

(a) Definition of error.

(1) **Types of transfers or inquiries covered.** The term "error" means:

(i) An unauthorized electronic fund transfer;

(ii) An incorrect electronic fund transfer to or from the consumer's account;

(iii) The omission of an electronic fund transfer from a periodic statement;

(iv) A computational or bookkeeping error made by the financial institution relating to an electronic fund transfer;

(v) The consumer's receipt of an incorrect amount of money from an electronic terminal;

(vi) An electronic fund transfer not identified in accordance with § 1005.9 or § 1005.10(a); or

(vii) The consumer's request for documentation required by § 1005.9 or § 1005.10(a) or for additional information or clarification concerning an electronic fund transfer, including a request the consumer makes to determine whether an error exists under paragraphs (a)(1)(i) through (vi) of this section.

(2) **Types of inquiries not covered.** The term "error" does not include:

(i) A routine inquiry about the consumer's account balance;

(ii) A request for information for tax or other recordkeeping purposes; or

(iii) A request for duplicate copies of documentation.

(b) Notice of error from consumer.

(1) **Timing; contents.** A financial institution shall comply with the requirements of this section with respect to any oral or written notice of error from the consumer that:

(i) Is received by the institution no later than 60 days after the institution sends the periodic statement or provides the passbook documentation, required by § 1005.9, on which the alleged error is first reflected;

(ii) Enables the institution to identify the consumer's name and account number; and

(iii) Indicates why the consumer believes an error exists and includes to the extent possible the type, date, and amount of the error, except for requests described in paragraph (a)(1)(vii) of this section.

(2) **Written confirmation.** A financial institution may require the consumer to give written confirmation of an error within 10 business days of an oral notice. An institution that requires written confirmation shall inform the consumer of the requirement and provide the address where confirmation must be sent when the consumer gives the oral notification.

(3) Request for documentation or clarifications. When a notice of error is based on documentation or clarification that the consumer requested under paragraph (a)(1)(vii) of this section, the consumer's notice of error is timely if received by the financial institution no later than 60 days after the institution sends the information requested.

(c) Time limits and extent of investigation.

(1) Ten-day period. A financial institution shall investigate promptly and, except as otherwise provided in this paragraph (c), shall determine whether an error occurred within 10 business days of receiving a notice of error. The institution shall report the results to the consumer within three business days after completing its investigation. The institution shall correct the error within one business day after determining that an error occurred.

(2) Forty-five day period. If the financial institution is unable to complete its investigation within 10 business days, the institution may take up to 45 days from receipt of a notice of error to investigate and determine whether an error occurred, provided the institution does the following:

    (i) Provisionally credits the consumer's account in the amount of the alleged error (including interest where applicable) within 10 business days of receiving the error notice. If the financial institution has a reasonable basis for believing that an unauthorized electronic fund transfer has occurred and the institution has satisfied the requirements of § 1005.6(a), the institution may withhold a maximum of $50 from the amount credited. An institution need not provisionally credit the consumer's account if:

        (A) The institution requires but does not receive written confirmation within 10 business days of an oral notice of error; or

        (B) The alleged error involves an account that is subject to Regulation T of the Board of Governors of the Federal Reserve System (Securities Credit by Brokers and Dealers, 12 CFR part 220);

    (ii) Informs the consumer, within two business days after the provisional crediting, of the amount and date of the provisional crediting and gives the consumer full use of the funds during the investigation;

    (iii) Corrects the error, if any, within one business day after determining that an error occurred; and

    (iv) Reports the results to the consumer within three business days after completing its investigation (including, if applicable, notice that a provisional credit has been made final).

(3) Extension of time periods. The time periods in paragraphs (c)(1) and (c)(2) of this section are extended as follows:

    (i) The applicable time is 20 business days in place of 10 business days under paragraphs (c)(1) and (2) of this section if the notice of error involves an electronic fund transfer to or from the account within 30 days after the first deposit to the account was made.

    (ii) The applicable time is 90 days in place of 45 days under paragraph (c)(2) of this section, for completing an investigation, if a notice of error involves an electronic fund transfer that:

        (A) Was not initiated within a state;

        (B) Resulted from a point-of-sale debit card transaction; or

        (C) Occurred within 30 days after the first deposit to the account was made.

(4) Investigation. With the exception of transfers covered by § 1005.14 of this part, a financial institution's review of its own records regarding an alleged error satisfies the requirements of this section if:

    (i) The alleged error concerns a transfer to or from a third party; and

(ii) There is no agreement between the institution and the third party for the type of electronic fund transfer involved.

(d) Procedures if financial institution determines no error or different error occurred. In addition to following the procedures specified in paragraph (c) of this section, the financial institution shall follow the procedures set forth in this paragraph (d) if it determines that no error occurred or that an error occurred in a manner or amount different from that described by the consumer:

(1) Written explanation. The institution's report of the results of its investigation shall include a written explanation of the institution's findings and shall note the consumer's right to request the documents that the institution relied on in making its determination. Upon request, the institution shall promptly provide copies of the documents.

(2) Debiting provisional credit. Upon debiting a provisionally credited amount, the financial institution shall:

(i) Notify the consumer of the date and amount of the debiting;

(ii) Notify the consumer that the institution will honor checks, drafts, or similar instruments payable to third parties and preauthorized transfers from the consumer's account (without charge to the consumer as a result of an overdraft) for five business days after the notification. The institution shall honor items as specified in the notice, but need honor only items that it would have paid if the provisionally credited funds had not been debited.

(e) Reassertion of error. A financial institution that has fully complied with the error resolution requirements has no further responsibilities under this section should the consumer later reassert the same error, except in the case of an error asserted by the consumer following receipt of information provided under paragraph (a)(1)(vii) of this section.

§ 1005.12 Relation to other laws.

(a) Relation to Truth in Lending.

(1) The Electronic Fund Transfer Act and this part govern:

(i) The addition to an accepted credit card, as defined in Regulation Z (12 CFR 1026.12, comment 12–2), of the capability to initiate electronic fund transfers;

(ii) The issuance of an access device that permits credit extensions (under a preexisting agreement between a consumer and a financial institution) only when the consumer's account is overdrawn or to maintain a specified minimum balance in the consumer's account, or under an overdraft service, as defined in § 1005.17(a) of this part;

(iii) The addition of an overdraft service, as defined in § 1005.17(a), to an accepted access device; and

(iv) A consumer's liability for an unauthorized electronic fund transfer and the investigation of errors involving an extension of credit that occurs under an agreement between the consumer and a financial institution to extend credit when the consumer's account is overdrawn or to maintain a specified minimum balance in the consumer's account, or under an overdraft service, as defined in § 1005.17(a).

(2) The Truth in Lending Act and Regulation Z (12 CFR part 1026), which prohibit the unsolicited issuance of credit cards, govern:

(i) The addition of a credit feature to an accepted access device; and

(ii) Except as provided in paragraph (a)(1)(ii) of this section, the issuance of a credit card that is also an access device.

(b) Preemption of inconsistent state laws.

(1) Inconsistent requirements. The Bureau shall determine, upon its own motion or upon the request of a state, financial institution, or other interested party, whether the Act and this part preempt state law relating to electronic fund transfers, or dormancy, inactivity, or service fees, or expiration dates in the case of gift certificates, store gift cards, or general-use prepaid cards.

(2) Standards for determination. State law is inconsistent with the requirements of the Act and this part if state law:

(i) Requires or permits a practice or act prohibited by the Federal law;

(ii) Provides for consumer liability for unauthorized electronic fund transfers that exceeds the limits imposed by the Federal law;

(iii) Allows longer time periods than the Federal law for investigating and correcting alleged errors, or does not require the financial institution to credit the consumer's account during an error investigation in accordance with § 1005.11(c)(2)(i) of this part; or

(iv) Requires initial disclosures, periodic statements, or receipts that are different in content from those required by the Federal law except to the extent that the disclosures relate to consumer rights granted by the state law and not by the Federal law.

(c) State exemptions

(1) General rule. Any state may apply for an exemption from the requirements of the Act or this part for any class of electronic fund transfers within the state. The Bureau shall grant an exemption if it determines that:

(i) Under state law the class of electronic fund transfers is subject to requirements substantially similar to those imposed by the Federal law; and

(ii) There is adequate provision for state enforcement.

(2) Exception. To assure that the Federal and state courts continue to have concurrent jurisdiction, and to aid in implementing the Act:

(i) No exemption shall extend to the civil liability provisions of section 916 of the Act; and

(ii) When the Bureau grants an exemption, the state law requirements shall constitute the requirements of the Federal law for purposes of section 916 of the Act, except for state law requirements not imposed by the Federal law.

§ 1005.13　Administrative enforcement; record retention.

(a) Enforcement by Federal agencies. Compliance with this part is enforced in accordance with section 918 of the Act.

(b) Record retention.

(1) Any person subject to the Act and this part shall retain evidence of compliance with the requirements imposed by the Act and this part for a period of not less than two years from the date disclosures are required to be made or action is required to be taken.

(2) Any person subject to the Act and this part having actual notice that it is the subject of an investigation or an enforcement proceeding by its enforcement agency, or having been served with notice of an action filed under sections 910, 916, or 917(a) of the Act, shall retain the records that pertain to the investigation, action, or proceeding until final disposition of the matter unless an earlier time is allowed by court or agency order.

§ 1005.14 Electronic fund transfer service provider not holding consumer's account.

(a) Provider of electronic fund transfer service. A person that provides an electronic fund transfer service to a consumer but that does not hold the consumer's account is subject to all requirements of this part if the person:

(1) Issues a debit card (or other access device) that the consumer can use to access the consumer's account held by a financial institution; and

(2) Has no agreement with the account-holding institution regarding such access.

(b) Compliance by service provider. In addition to the requirements generally applicable under this part, the service provider shall comply with the following special rules:

(1) **Disclosures and documentation.** The service provider shall give the disclosures and documentation required by §§ 1105.7, 1105.8, and 1105.9 of this part that are within the purview of its relationship with the consumer. The service provider need not furnish the periodic statement required by § 1105.9(b) if the following conditions are met:

(i) The debit card (or other access device) issued to the consumer bears the service provider's name and an address or telephone number for making inquiries or giving notice of error;

(ii) The consumer receives a notice concerning use of the debit card that is substantially similar to the notice contained in Appendix A of this part;

(iii) The consumer receives, on or with the receipts required by § 1105.9(a), the address and telephone number to be used for an inquiry, to give notice of an error, or to report the loss or theft of the debit card;

(iv) The service provider transmits to the account-holding institution the information specified in § 1005.9(b)(1), in the format prescribed by the automated clearinghouse (ACH) system used to clear the fund transfers;

(v) The service provider extends the time period for notice of loss or theft of a debit card, set forth in § 1005.6(b)(1) and (2), from two business days to four business days after the consumer learns of the loss or theft; and extends the time periods for reporting unauthorized transfers or errors, set forth in §§ 1005.6(b)(3) and 1005.11(b)(1)(i), from 60 days to 90 days following the transmittal of a periodic statement by the account-holding institution.

(2) **Error resolution.**

(i) The service provider shall extend by a reasonable time the period in which notice of an error must be received, specified in § 1005.11(b)(1)(i), if a delay resulted from an initial attempt by the consumer to notify the account-holding institution.

(ii) The service provider shall disclose to the consumer the date on which it initiates a transfer to effect a provisional credit in accordance with § 1005.11(c)(2)(ii).

(iii) If the service provider determines an error occurred, it shall transfer funds to or from the consumer's account, in the appropriate amount and within the applicable time period, in accordance with § 1005.11(c)(2)(i).

(iv) If funds were provisionally credited and the service provider determines no error occurred, it may reverse the credit. The service provider shall notify the account-holding institution of the period during which the account-holding institution must honor debits to the account in accordance with § 1005.11(d)(2)(ii). If an overdraft results, the service provider shall promptly reimburse the account-holding institution in the amount of the overdraft.

(c) Compliance by account-holding institution. The account-holding institution need not comply with the requirements of the Act and this part with respect to electronic fund transfers initiated through the service provider except as follows:

(1) Documentation. The account-holding institution shall provide a periodic statement that describes each electronic fund transfer initiated by the consumer with the access device issued by the service provider. The account-holding institution has no liability for the failure to comply with this requirement if the service provider did not provide the necessary information; and

(2) Error resolution. Upon request, the account-holding institution shall provide information or copies of documents needed by the service provider to investigate errors or to furnish copies of documents to the consumer. The account-holding institution shall also honor debits to the account in accordance with § 1005.11(d)(2)(ii).

§ 1005.15   Electronic fund transfer of government benefits.

(a)   Government agency subject to regulation.

(1)   A government agency is deemed to be a financial institution for purposes of the Act and this part if directly or indirectly it issues an access device to a consumer for use in initiating an electronic fund transfer of government benefits from an account, other than needs-tested benefits in a program established under state or local law or administered by a state or local agency. The agency shall comply with all applicable requirements of the Act and this part, except as provided in this section.

(2)   For purposes of this section, the term "account" means an account established by a government agency for distributing government benefits to a consumer electronically, such as through automated teller machines or point-of-sale terminals, but does not include an account for distributing needs-tested benefits in a program established under state or local law or administered by a state or local agency.

(b)   Issuance of access devices. For purposes of this section, a consumer is deemed to request an access device when the consumer applies for government benefits that the agency disburses or will disburse by means of an electronic fund transfer. The agency shall verify the identity of the consumer receiving the device by reasonable means before the device is activated.

(c)   Alternative to periodic statement. A government agency need not furnish the periodic statement required by § 1005.9(b) if the agency makes available to the consumer:

(1)   The consumer's account balance, through a readily available telephone line and at a terminal (such as by providing balance information at a balance-inquiry terminal or providing it, routinely or upon request, on a terminal receipt at the time of an electronic fund transfer); and

(2)   A written history of the consumer's account transactions that is provided promptly in response to an oral or written request and that covers at least 60 days preceding the date of a request by the consumer.

(d)   Modified requirements. A government agency that does not furnish periodic statements, in accordance with paragraph (c) of this section, shall comply with the following special rules:

(1)   Initial disclosures. The agency shall modify the disclosures under § 1005.7(b) by disclosing:

(i)   Account balance. The means by which the consumer may obtain information concerning the account balance, including a telephone number. The agency provides a notice substantially similar to the notice contained in paragraph A–5 in appendix A of this part.

(ii)   Written account history. A summary of the consumer's right to receive a written account history upon request, in place of the periodic statement required by § 1005.7(b)(6), and the telephone number to call to request an account history. This disclosure may be made by providing a notice substantially similar to the notice contained in paragraph A–5 in appendix A of this part.

(iii)   Error resolution. A notice concerning error resolution that is substantially similar to the notice contained in paragraph A–5 in appendix A of this part, in place of the notice required by § 1005.7(b)(10).

(2)   **Annual error resolution notice.** The agency shall provide an annual notice concerning error resolution that is substantially similar to the notice contained in paragraph A–5 in appendix A, in place of the notice required by § 1005.8(b).

(3)   **Limitations on liability.** For purposes of § 1005.6(b)(3), regarding a 60-day period for reporting any unauthorized transfer that appears on a periodic statement, the 60-day period shall begin with transmittal of a written account history or other account information provided to the consumer under paragraph (c) of this section.

(4)   **Error resolution.** The agency shall comply with the requirements of § 1005.11 of this part in response to an oral or written notice of an error from the consumer that is received no later than 60 days after the consumer obtains the written account history or other account information, under paragraph (c) of this section, in which the error is first reflected.

§ 1005.16   Disclosures at automated teller machines.

(a)   **Definition.** "Automated teller machine operator" means any person that operates an automated teller machine at which a consumer initiates an electronic fund transfer or a balance inquiry and that does not hold the account to or from which the transfer is made, or about which an inquiry is made.

(b)   **General.** An automated teller machine operator that imposes a fee on a consumer for initiating an electronic fund transfer or a balance inquiry must provide a notice that a fee will be imposed for providing electronic fund transfer services or a balance inquiry that discloses the amount of the fee.

(c)   **Notice requirement.** An automated teller machine operator must provide the notice required by paragraph (b) of this section either by showing it on the screen of the automated teller machine or by providing it on paper, before the consumer is committed to paying a fee.

(d)   **Imposition of fee.** An automated teller machine operator may impose a fee on a consumer for initiating an electronic fund transfer or a balance inquiry only if:

(1)   The consumer is provided the notice required under paragraph (c) of this section, and

(2)   The consumer elects to continue the transaction or inquiry after receiving such notice.

§ 1005.17   Requirements for overdraft services.

(a)   **Definition.** For purposes of this section, the term "overdraft service" means a service under which a financial institution assesses a fee or charge on a consumer's account held by the institution for paying a transaction (including a check or other item) when the consumer has insufficient or unavailable funds in the account. The term "overdraft service" does not include any payment of overdrafts pursuant to:

(1)   A line of credit subject to Regulation Z (12 CFR part 1026), including transfers from a credit card account, home equity line of credit, or overdraft line of credit;

(2)   A service that transfers funds from another account held individually or jointly by a consumer, such as a savings account; or

(3)   A line of credit or other transaction exempt from Regulation Z (12 CFR part 1026) pursuant to 12 CFR 1026.3(d).

(b)   **Opt-in requirement.**

(1)   **General.** Except as provided under paragraph (c) of this section, a financial institution holding a consumer's account shall not assess a fee or charge on a consumer's account for paying an ATM or one-time debit card transaction pursuant to the institution's overdraft service, unless the institution:

(i)   Provides the consumer with a notice in writing, or if the consumer agrees, electronically, segregated from all other information, describing the institution's overdraft service;

(ii) Provides a reasonable opportunity for the consumer to affirmatively consent, or opt in, to the service for ATM and one-time debit card transactions;

(iii) Obtains the consumer's affirmative consent, or opt-in, to the institution's payment of ATM or one-time debit card transactions; and

(iv) Provides the consumer with confirmation of the consumer's consent in writing, or if the consumer agrees, electronically, which includes a statement informing the consumer of the right to revoke such consent.

(2) Conditioning payment of other overdrafts on consumer's affirmative consent. A financial institution shall not:

(i) Condition the payment of any overdrafts for checks, ACH transactions, and other types of transactions on the consumer affirmatively consenting to the institution's payment of ATM and one-time debit card transactions pursuant to the institution's overdraft service; or

(ii) Decline to pay checks, ACH transactions, and other types of transactions that overdraw the consumer's account because the consumer has not affirmatively consented to the institution's overdraft service for ATM and one-time debit card transactions.

(3) Same account terms, conditions, and features. A financial institution shall provide to consumers who do not affirmatively consent to the institution's overdraft service for ATM and one-time debit card transactions the same account terms, conditions, and features that it provides to consumers who affirmatively consent, except for the overdraft service for ATM and one-time debit card transactions.

(c) Timing.

(1) Existing account holders. For accounts opened prior to July 1, 2010, the financial institution must not assess any fees or charges on a consumer's account on or after August 15, 2010, for paying an ATM or one-time debit card transaction pursuant to the overdraft service, unless the institution has complied with § 1005.17(b)(1) and obtained the consumer's affirmative consent.

(2) New account holders. For accounts opened on or after July 1, 2010, the financial institution must comply with § 1005.17(b)(1) and obtain the consumer's affirmative consent before the institution assesses any fee or charge on the consumer's account for paying an ATM or one-time debit card transaction pursuant to the institution's overdraft service.

(d) Content and format. The notice required by paragraph (b)(1)(i) of this section shall be substantially similar to Model Form A–9 set forth in Appendix A of this part, include all applicable items in this paragraph, and may not contain any information not specified in or otherwise permitted by this paragraph.

(1) Overdraft service. A brief description of the financial institution's overdraft service and the types of transactions for which a fee or charge for paying an overdraft may be imposed, including ATM and one-time debit card transactions.

(2) Fees imposed. The dollar amount of any fees or charges assessed by the financial institution for paying an ATM or one-time debit card transaction pursuant to the institution's overdraft service, including any daily or other overdraft fees. If the amount of the fee is determined on the basis of the number of times the consumer has overdrawn the account, the amount of the overdraft, or other factors, the institution must disclose the maximum fee that may be imposed.

(3) Limits on fees charged. The maximum number of overdraft fees or charges that may be assessed per day, or, if applicable, that there is no limit.

(4) Disclosure of opt-in right. An explanation of the consumer's right to affirmatively consent to the financial institution's payment of overdrafts for ATM and one-time debit card transactions pursuant to the institution's overdraft service, including the methods by which the consumer may consent to the service; and

(5)   Alternative plans for covering overdrafts. If the institution offers a line of credit subject to Regulation Z (12 CFR part 1026) or a service that transfers funds from another account of the consumer held at the institution to cover overdrafts, the institution must state that fact. An institution may, but is not required to, list additional alternatives for the payment of overdrafts.

(6)   Permitted modifications and additional content. If applicable, the institution may modify the content required by § 1005.17(d) to indicate that the consumer has the right to opt into, or opt out of, the payment of overdrafts under the institution's overdraft service for other types of transactions, such as checks, ACH transactions, or automatic bill payments; to provide a means for the consumer to exercise this choice; and to disclose the associated returned item fee and that additional merchant fees may apply. The institution may also disclose the consumer's right to revoke consent. For notices provided to consumers who have opened accounts prior to July 1, 2010, the financial institution may describe the institution's overdraft service with respect to ATM and one-time debit card transactions with a statement such as "After August 15, 2010, we will not authorize and pay overdrafts for the following types of transactions unless you ask us to (see below)."

(e)   Joint relationships. If two or more consumers jointly hold an account, the financial institution shall treat the affirmative consent of any of the joint consumers as affirmative consent for that account. Similarly, the financial institution shall treat a revocation of affirmative consent by any of the joint consumers as revocation of consent for that account.

(f)   Continuing right to opt in or to revoke the opt-in. A consumer may affirmatively consent to the financial institution's overdraft service at any time in the manner described in the notice required by paragraph (b)(1)(i) of this section. A consumer may also revoke consent at any time in the manner made available to the consumer for providing consent. A financial institution must implement a consumer's revocation of consent as soon as reasonably practicable.

(g)   Duration and revocation of opt-in. A consumer's affirmative consent to the institution's overdraft service is effective until revoked by the consumer, or unless the financial institution terminates the service.

§ 1005.18   Requirements for financial institutions offering payroll card accounts.

(a)   Coverage. A financial institution shall comply with all applicable requirements of the Act and this part with respect to payroll card accounts except as provided in this section.

(b)   Alternative to periodic statements.

(1)   A financial institution need not furnish periodic statements required by 1005.9(b) if the institution makes available to the consumer:

(i)   The consumer's account balance, through a readily available telephone line;

(ii)   An electronic history of the consumer's account transactions, such as through a Web site, that covers at least 60 days preceding the date the consumer electronically accesses the account; and

(iii)   A written history of the consumer's account transactions that is provided promptly in response to an oral or written request and that covers at least 60 days preceding the date the financial institution receives the consumer's request.

(2)   The history of account transactions provided under paragraphs (b)(1)(ii) and (iii) of this section must include the information set forth in § 1005.9(b).

(c)   Modified requirements. A financial institution that provides information under paragraph (b) of this section, shall comply with the following:

(1)   Initial disclosures. The financial institution shall modify the disclosures under § 1005.7(b) by disclosing:

(i)   Account information. A telephone number that the consumer may call to obtain the account balance, the means by which the consumer can obtain an electronic account history, such as the address of a Web site, and a summary of the consumer's right to receive a written account history upon request (in place of the summary of the right to receive a periodic statement required by § 1005.7(b)(6)), including a telephone number to call to request a history. The disclosure required by this paragraph (c)(1)(i) may be made by providing a notice substantially similar to the notice contained in paragraph A–7(a) in appendix A of this part.

　　　(ii)　**Error resolution.** A notice concerning error resolution that is substantially similar to the notice contained in paragraph A–7(b) in appendix A of this part, in place of the notice required by § 1005.7(b)(10).

　(2)　**Annual error resolution notice.** The financial institution shall provide an annual notice concerning error resolution that is substantially similar to the notice contained in paragraph A–7(b) in appendix A of this part, in place of the notice required by § 1005.8(b). Alternatively, a financial institution may include on or with each electronic and written history provided in accordance with § 1005.18(b)(1), a notice substantially similar to the abbreviated notice for periodic statements contained in paragraph A–3(b) in appendix A of this part, modified as necessary to reflect the error resolution provisions set forth in this section.

　(3)　**Limitations on liability.**

　　　(i)　For purposes of § 1005.6(b)(3), the 60-day period for reporting any unauthorized transfer shall begin on the earlier of:

　　　　　(A)　The date the consumer electronically accesses the consumer's account under paragraph (b)(1)(ii) of this section, provided that the electronic history made available to the consumer reflects the transfer; or

　　　　　(B)　The date the financial institution sends a written history of the consumer's account transactions requested by the consumer under paragraph (b)(1)(iii) of this section in which the unauthorized transfer is first reflected.

　　　(ii)　A financial institution may comply with paragraph (c)(3)(i) of this section by limiting the consumer's liability for an unauthorized transfer as provided under § 1005.6(b)(3) for any transfer reported by the consumer within 120 days after the transfer was credited or debited to the consumer's account.

　(4)　**Error resolution.**

　　　(i)　The financial institution shall comply with the requirements of § 1005.11 in response to an oral or written notice of an error from the consumer that is received by the earlier of:

　　　　　(A)　Sixty days after the date the consumer electronically accesses the consumer's account under paragraph (b)(1)(ii) of this section, provided that the electronic history made available to the consumer reflects the alleged error; or

　　　　　(B)　Sixty days after the date the financial institution sends a written history of the consumer's account transactions requested by the consumer under paragraph (b)(1)(iii) of this section in which the alleged error is first reflected.

　　　(ii)　In lieu of following the procedures in paragraph (c)(4)(i) of this section, a financial institution complies with the requirements for resolving errors in § 1005.11 if it investigates any oral or written notice of an error from the consumer that is received by the institution within 120 days after the transfer allegedly in error was credited or debited to the consumer's account.

§ 1005.19　　[Reserved].

§ 1005.20　　Requirements for gift cards and gift certificates.

　(a)　**Definitions.** For purposes of this section, except as excluded under paragraph (b), the following definitions apply:

　　　(1)　"Gift certificate" means a card, code, or other device that is:

(i) Issued on a prepaid basis primarily for personal, family, or household purposes to a consumer in a specified amount that may not be increased or reloaded in exchange for payment; and

(ii) Redeemable upon presentation at a single merchant or an affiliated group of merchants for goods or services.

(2) "Store gift card" means a card, code, or other device that is:

(i) Issued on a prepaid basis primarily for personal, family, or household purposes to a consumer in a specified amount, whether or not that amount may be increased or reloaded, in exchange for payment; and

(ii) Redeemable upon presentation at a single merchant or an affiliated group of merchants for goods or services.

(3) "General-use prepaid card" means a card, code, or other device that is:

(i) Issued on a prepaid basis primarily for personal, family, or household purposes to a consumer in a specified amount, whether or not that amount may be increased or reloaded, in exchange for payment; and

(ii) Redeemable upon presentation at multiple, unaffiliated merchants for goods or services, or usable at automated teller machines.

(4) "Loyalty, award, or promotional gift card" means a card, code, or other device that:

(i) Is issued on a prepaid basis primarily for personal, family, or household purposes to a consumer in connection with a loyalty, award, or promotional program;

(ii) Is redeemable upon presentation at one or more merchants for goods or services, or usable at automated teller machines; and

(iii) Sets forth the following disclosures, as applicable:

(A) A statement indicating that the card, code, or other device is issued for loyalty, award, or promotional purposes, which must be included on the front of the card, code, or other device;

(B) The expiration date for the underlying funds, which must be included on the front of the card, code, or other device;

(C) The amount of any fees that may be imposed in connection with the card, code, or other device, and the conditions under which they may be imposed, which must be provided on or with the card, code, or other device; and

(D) A toll-free telephone number and, if one is maintained, a Web site, that a consumer may use to obtain fee information, which must be included on the card, code, or other device.

(5) Dormancy or inactivity fee. The terms "dormancy fee" and "inactivity fee" mean a fee for non-use of or inactivity on a gift certificate, store gift card, or general-use prepaid card.

(6) Service fee. The term "service fee" means a periodic fee for holding or use of a gift certificate, store gift card, or general-use prepaid card. A periodic fee includes any fee that may be imposed on a gift certificate, store gift card, or general-use prepaid card from time to time for holding or using the certificate or card.

(7) Activity. The term "activity" means any action that results in an increase or decrease of the funds underlying a certificate or card, other than the imposition of a fee, or an adjustment due to an error or a reversal of a prior transaction.

(b) Exclusions. The terms "gift certificate," "store gift card," and "general-use prepaid card", as defined in paragraph (a) of this section, do not include any card, code, or other device that is:

(1) Useable solely for telephone services;

(2) Reloadable and not marketed or labeled as a gift card or gift certificate. For purposes of this paragraph (b)(2), the term "reloadable" includes a temporary non-reloadable card issued solely in connection with a reloadable card, code, or other device;

(3) A loyalty, award, or promotional gift card;

(4) Not marketed to the general public;

(5) Issued in paper form only; or

(6) Redeemable solely for admission to events or venues at a particular location or group of affiliated locations, or to obtain goods or services in conjunction with admission to such events or venues, either at the event or venue or at specific locations affiliated with and in geographic proximity to the event or venue.

(c) Form of disclosures

(1) Clear and conspicuous. Disclosures made under this section must be clear and conspicuous. The disclosures may contain commonly accepted or readily understandable abbreviations or symbols.

(2) Format. Disclosures made under this section generally must be provided to the consumer in written or electronic form. Except for the disclosures in paragraphs (c)(3) and (h)(2) of this section, written and electronic disclosures made under this section must be in a retainable form. Only disclosures provided under paragraphs (c)(3) and (h)(2) may be given orally.

(3) Disclosures prior to purchase. Before a gift certificate, store gift card, or general-use prepaid card is purchased, a person that issues or sells such certificate or card must disclose to the consumer the information required by paragraphs (d)(2), (e)(3), and (f)(1) of this section. The fees and terms and conditions of expiration that are required to be disclosed prior to purchase may not be changed after purchase.

(4) Disclosures on the certificate or card. Disclosures required by paragraphs (a)(4)(iii), (d)(2), (e)(3), and (f)(2) of this section must be made on the certificate or card, or in the case of a loyalty, award, or promotional gift card, on the card, code, or other device. A disclosure made in an accompanying terms and conditions document, on packaging surrounding a certificate or card, or on a sticker or other label affixed to the certificate or card does not constitute a disclosure on the certificate or card. For an electronic certificate or card, disclosures must be provided electronically on the certificate or card provided to the consumer. An issuer that provides a code or confirmation to a consumer orally must provide to the consumer a written or electronic copy of the code or confirmation promptly, and the applicable disclosures must be provided on the written copy of the code or confirmation.

(d) Prohibition on imposition of fees or charges. No person may impose a dormancy, inactivity, or service fee with respect to a gift certificate, store gift card, or general-use prepaid card, unless:

(1) There has been no activity with respect to the certificate or card, in the one-year period ending on the date on which the fee is imposed;

(2) The following are stated, as applicable, clearly and conspicuously on the gift certificate, store gift card, or general-use prepaid card:

(i) The amount of any dormancy, inactivity, or service fee that may be charged;

(ii) How often such fee may be assessed; and

(iii) That such fee may be assessed for inactivity; and

(3) Not more than one dormancy, inactivity, or service fee is imposed in any given calendar month.

(e)   Prohibition on sale of gift certificates or cards with expiration dates. No person may sell or issue a gift certificate, store gift card, or general-use prepaid card with an expiration date, unless:

(1)   The person has established policies and procedures to provide consumers with a reasonable opportunity to purchase a certificate or card with at least five years remaining until the certificate or card expiration date;

(2)   The expiration date for the underlying funds is at least the later of:

(i)   Five years after the date the gift certificate was initially issued, or the date on which funds were last loaded to a store gift card or general-use prepaid card; or

(ii)   The certificate or card expiration date, if any;

(3)   The following disclosures are provided on the certificate or card, as applicable:

(i)   The expiration date for the underlying funds or, if the underlying funds do not expire, that fact;

(ii)   A toll-free telephone number and, if one is maintained, a Web site that a consumer may use to obtain a replacement certificate or card after the certificate or card expires if the underlying funds may be available; and

(iii) Except where a non-reloadable certificate or card bears an expiration date that is at least seven years from the date of manufacture, a statement, disclosed with equal prominence and in close proximity to the certificate or card expiration date, that:

(A)   The certificate or card expires, but the underlying funds either do not expire or expire later than the certificate or card, and;

(B)   The consumer may contact the issuer for a replacement card; and

(4)   No fee or charge is imposed on the cardholder for replacing the gift certificate, store gift card, or general-use prepaid card or for providing the certificate or card holder with the remaining balance in some other manner prior to the funds expiration date, unless such certificate or card has been lost or stolen.

(f)   Additional disclosure requirements for gift certificates or cards. The following disclosures must be provided in connection with a gift certificate, store gift card, or general-use prepaid card, as applicable:

(1)   Fee disclosures. For each type of fee that may be imposed in connection with the certificate or card (other than a dormancy, inactivity, or service fee subject to the disclosure requirements under paragraph (d)(2) of this section), the following information must be provided on or with the certificate or card:

(i)   The type of fee;

(ii)   The amount of the fee (or an explanation of how the fee will be determined); and

(iii) The conditions under which the fee may be imposed.

(2)   Telephone number for fee information. A toll-free telephone number and, if one is maintained, a Web site, that a consumer may use to obtain information about fees described in paragraphs (d)(2) and (f)(1) of this section must be disclosed on the certificate or card.

(g)   Compliance dates.

(1)   Effective date for gift certificates, store gift cards, and general-use prepaid cards. Except as provided in paragraph (h) of this section, the requirements of this section apply to any gift certificate, store gift card, or general-use prepaid card sold to a consumer on or after August 22, 2010, or provided to a consumer as a replacement for such certificate or card.

(2)   Effective date for loyalty, award, or promotional gift cards. The requirements in paragraph (a)(4)(iii) of this section apply to any card, code, or other device provided to a consumer in connection with a loyalty, award, or promotional program if the period of eligibility for such program began on or after August 22, 2010.

(h) Temporary exemption.

(1) Delayed mandatory compliance date. For any gift certificate, store gift card, or general-use prepaid card produced prior to April 1, 2010, the mandatory compliance date of the requirements of paragraphs (c)(3), (d)(2), (e)(1), (e)(3), and (f) of this section is January 31, 2011, provided that an issuer of such certificate or card:

(i) Complies with all other provisions of this section;

(ii) Does not impose an expiration date with respect to the funds underlying such certificate or card;

(iii) At the consumer's request, replaces such certificate or card if it has funds remaining at no cost to the consumer; and

(iv) Satisfies the requirements of paragraph (h)(2) of this section.

(2) Additional disclosures. Issuers relying on the delayed effective date in § 1005.20(h)(1) must disclose through in-store signage, messages during customer service calls, Web sites, and general advertising, that:

(i) The underlying funds of such certificate or card do not expire;

(ii) Consumers holding such certificate or card have a right to a free replacement certificate or card, which must be accompanied by the packaging and materials typically associated with such certificate or card; and

(iii) Any dormancy, inactivity, or service fee for such certificate or card that might otherwise be charged will not be charged if such fees do not comply with section 916 of the Act.

(3) Expiration of additional disclosure requirements. The disclosures in paragraph (h)(2) of this section:

(i) Are not required to be provided on or after January 31, 2011, with respect to in-store signage and general advertising.

(ii) Are not required to be provided on or after January 31, 2013, with respect to messages during customer service calls and Web sites.

SUBPART B—REQUIREMENTS FOR REMITTANCE TRANSFERS

§ 1005.30   Remittance transfer definitions.

Except as otherwise provided, for purposes of the subpart, the following definitions apply:

(a) "Agent" means an agent, authorized delegate, or person affiliated with a remittance transfer provider, as defined under State or other applicable law, when such agent, authorized delegate, or affiliate acts for that remittance transfer provider.

(b) "Business day" means any day on which the offices of a remittance transfer provider are open to the public for carrying on substantially all business functions.

(c) "Designated recipient" means any person specified by the sender as the authorized recipient of a remittance transfer to be received at a location in a foreign country.

(d) "Preauthorized remittance transfer" means a remittance transfer authorized in advance to recur at substantially regular intervals.

(e) Remittance transfer—(1) General definition. A "remittance transfer" means the electronic transfer of funds requested by a sender to a designated recipient that is sent by a remittance transfer provider. The term applies regardless of whether the sender holds an account with the remittance transfer provider, and regardless of whether the transaction is also an electronic fund transfer, as defined in § 1005.3(b).

    (2)   **Exclusions from coverage.** The term "remittance transfer" does not include:

        (i)   **Small value transactions.** Transfer amounts, as described in § 1005.31(b)(1)(i), of $15 or less.

        (ii)   **Securities and commodities transfers.** Any transfer that is excluded from the definition of electronic fund transfer under § 1005.3(c)(4).

    (f)   **Remittance transfer provider—(1) General definition.** "Remittance transfer provider" or "provider" means any person that provides remittance transfers for a consumer in the normal course of its business, regardless of whether the consumer holds an account with such person.

    (2)   **Normal course of business—(i) Safe harbor.** For purposes of paragraph (f)(1) of this section, a person is deemed not to be providing remittance transfers for a consumer in the normal course of its business if the person:

        (A)   Provided 100 or fewer remittance transfers in the previous calendar year; and

        (B)   Provides 100 or fewer remittance transfers in the current calendar year.

        (ii)   **Transition period.** If a person that provided 100 or fewer remittance transfers in the previous calendar year provides more than 100 remittance transfers in the current calendar year, and if that person is then providing remittance transfers for a consumer in the normal course of its business pursuant to paragraph (f)(1) of this section, the person has a reasonable period of time, not to exceed six months, to begin complying with this subpart. Compliance with this subpart will not be required for any remittance transfers for which payment is made during that reasonable period of time.

    (g)   "Sender" means a consumer in a State who primarily for personal, family, or household purposes requests a remittance transfer provider to send a remittance transfer to a designated recipient.

    (h)   **Third-party fees. (1) "Covered third-party fees."** The term "covered third-party fees" means any fees imposed on the remittance transfer by a person other than the remittance transfer provider except for fees described in paragraph (h)(2) of this section.

    (2)   **"Non-covered third-party fees."** The term "non-covered third-party fees" means any fees imposed by the designated recipient's institution for receiving a remittance transfer into an account except if the institution acts as an agent of the remittance transfer provider.

§ 1005.31   Disclosures.

    (a)   **General form of disclosures—(1) Clear and conspicuous.** Disclosures required by this subpart or permitted by paragraph (b)(1)(viii) of this section or § 1005.33(h)(3) must be clear and conspicuous. Disclosures required by this subpart or permitted by paragraph (b)(1)(viii) of this section or § 1005.33(h)(3) may contain commonly accepted or readily understandable abbreviations or symbols.

    (2)   **Written and electronic disclosures.** Disclosures required by this subpart generally must be provided to the sender in writing. Disclosures required by paragraph (b)(1) of this section may be provided electronically, if the sender electronically requests the remittance transfer provider to send the remittance transfer. Written and electronic disclosures required by this subpart generally must be made in a retainable form. Disclosures provided via mobile application or text message, to the extent permitted by paragraph (a)(5) of this section, need not be retainable.

    (3)   **Disclosures for oral telephone transactions.** The information required by paragraph (b)(1) of this section may be disclosed orally if:

        (i)   The transaction is conducted orally and entirely by telephone;

(ii) The remittance transfer provider complies with the requirements of paragraph (g)(2) of this section;

(iii) The provider discloses orally a statement about the rights of the sender regarding cancellation required by paragraph (b)(2)(iv) of this section pursuant to the timing requirements in paragraph (e)(1) of this section; and

(iv) The provider discloses orally, as each is applicable, the information required by paragraph (b)(2)(vii) of this section and the information required by § 1005.36(d)(1)(i)(A), with respect to transfers subject to § 1005.36(d)(2)(ii), pursuant to the timing requirements in paragraph (e)(1) of this section.

(4) Oral disclosures for certain error resolution notices. The information required by § 1005.33(c)(1) may be disclosed orally if:

(i) The remittance transfer provider determines that an error occurred as described by the sender; and

(ii) The remittance transfer provider complies with the requirements of paragraph (g)(2) of this section.

(5) Disclosures for mobile application or text message transactions. The information required by paragraph (b)(1) of this section may be disclosed orally or via mobile application or text message if:

(i) The transaction is conducted entirely by telephone via mobile application or text message;

(ii) The remittance transfer provider complies with the requirements of paragraph (g)(2) of this section; and

(iii) The provider discloses orally or via mobile application or text message a statement about the rights of the sender regarding cancellation required by paragraph (b)(2)(iv) of this section pursuant to the timing requirements in paragraph (e)(1) of this section; and

(iv) The provider discloses orally or via mobile application or text message, as each is applicable, the information required by paragraph (b)(2)(vii) of this section and the information required by § 1005.36(d)(1)(i)(A), with respect to transfers subject to § 1005.36(d)(2)(ii), pursuant to the timing requirements in paragraph (e)(1) of this section.

(b) Disclosure requirements—(1) Pre-payment disclosure. A remittance transfer provider must disclose to a sender, as applicable:

(i) The amount that will be transferred to the designated recipient, in the currency in which the remittance transfer is funded, using the term "Transfer Amount" or a substantially similar term;

(ii) Any fees and any taxes collected on the remittance transfer by the provider, in the currency in which the remittance transfer is funded, using the terms "Transfer Fees" for fees and "Transfer Taxes" for taxes, or substantially similar terms;

(iii) The total amount of the transaction, which is the sum of paragraphs (b)(1)(i) and (ii) of this section, in the currency in which the remittance transfer is funded, using the term "Total" or a substantially similar term;

(iv) The exchange rate used by the provider for the remittance transfer, rounded consistently for each currency to no fewer than two decimal places and no more than four decimal places, using the term "Exchange Rate" or a substantially similar term;

(v) The amount in paragraph (b)(1)(i) of this section, in the currency in which the funds will be received by the designated recipient, but only if covered third-party fees are imposed under paragraph (b)(1)(vi) of this section, using the term "Transfer Amount" or a substantially similar term. The exchange rate used to calculate this amount is the exchange rate in paragraph (b)(1)(iv) of this section, including an estimated exchange rate to the extent permitted by § 1005.32, prior to any rounding of the exchange rate;

(vi) Any covered third-party fees, in the currency in which the funds will be received by the designated recipient, using the term "Other Fees," or a substantially similar term. The exchange rate used to calculate any covered third-party fees is the exchange rate in paragraph (b)(1)(iv) of this section, including an estimated exchange rate to the extent permitted by § 1005.32, prior to any rounding of the exchange rate;

(vii) The amount that will be received by the designated recipient, in the currency in which the funds will be received, using the term "Total to Recipient" or a substantially similar term except that this amount shall not include non-covered third party fees or taxes collected on the remittance transfer by a person other than the provider regardless of whether such fees or taxes are disclosed pursuant to paragraph (b)(1)(viii) of this section. The exchange rate used to calculate this amount is the exchange rate in paragraph (b)(1)(iv) of this section, including an estimated exchange rate to the extent permitted by § 1005.32, prior to any rounding of the exchange rate.

(viii) A statement indicating that non-covered third-party fees or taxes collected on the remittance transfer by a person other than the provider may apply to the remittance transfer and result in the designated recipient receiving less than the amount disclosed pursuant to paragraph (b)(1)(vii) of this section. A provider may only include this statement to the extent that such fees or taxes do or may apply to the transfer, using the language set forth in Model Forms A–30(a) through (c) of Appendix A to this part, as appropriate, or substantially similar language. In this statement, a provider also may, but is not required, to disclose any applicable non-covered third-party fees or taxes collected by a person other than the provider. Any such figure must be disclosed in the currency in which the funds will be received, using the language set forth in Model Forms A–30(b) through (d) of Appendix A to this part, as appropriate, or substantially similar language. The exchange rate used to calculate any disclosed non-covered third-party fees or taxes collected on the remittance transfer by a person other than the provider is the exchange rate in paragraph (b)(1)(iv) of this section, including an estimated exchange rate to the extent permitted by § 1005.32, prior to any rounding of the exchange rate;

(2) **Receipt.** A remittance transfer provider must disclose to a sender, as applicable:

(i) The disclosures described in paragraphs (b)(1)(i) through (viii) of this section;

(ii) The date in the foreign country on which funds will be available to the designated recipient, using the term "Date Available" or a substantially similar term. A provider may provide a statement that funds may be available to the designated recipient earlier than the date disclosed, using the term "may be available sooner" or a substantially similar term;

(iii) The name and, if provided by the sender, the telephone number and/or address of the designated recipient, using the term "Recipient" or a substantially similar term;

(iv) A statement about the rights of the sender regarding the resolution of errors and cancellation, using language set forth in Model Form A–37 of Appendix A to this part or substantially similar language. For any remittance transfer scheduled by the sender at least three business days before the date of the transfer, the statement about the rights of the sender regarding cancellation must instead reflect the requirements of § 1005.36(c);

(v) The name, telephone number(s), and Web site of the remittance transfer provider;

(vi) A statement that the sender can contact the State agency that licenses or charters the remittance transfer provider with respect to the remittance transfer and the Consumer Financial Protection Bureau for questions or complaints about the remittance transfer provider, using language set forth in Model Form A–37 of Appendix A to this part or substantially similar language. The disclosure must provide the name, telephone number(s), and Web site of the State agency that licenses or charters the remittance transfer provider with respect to the remittance transfer and the name, toll-free telephone number(s), and Web site of the Consumer Financial Protection Bureau; and

(vii) For any remittance transfer scheduled by the sender at least three business days before the date of the transfer, or the first transfer in a series of preauthorized remittance transfers, the date the remittance transfer provider will make or made the remittance transfer, using the term "Transfer Date," or a substantially similar term.

(3) Combined disclosure—(i) In general. As an alternative to providing the disclosures described in paragraph (b)(1) and (2) of this section, a remittance transfer provider may provide the disclosures described in paragraph (b)(2) of this section, as applicable, in a single disclosure pursuant to the timing requirements in paragraph (e)(1) of this section. Except as provided in paragraph (b)(3)(ii) of this section, if the remittance transfer provider provides the combined disclosure and the sender completes the transfer, the remittance transfer provider must provide the sender with proof of payment when payment is made for the remittance transfer. The proof of payment must be clear and conspicuous, provided in writing or electronically, and provided in a retainable form.

(ii) Transfers scheduled before the date of transfer. If the disclosure described in paragraph (b)(3)(i) of this section is provided in accordance with § 1005.36(a)(1)(i) and payment is not processed by the remittance transfer provider at the time the remittance transfer is scheduled, a remittance transfer provider may provide confirmation that the transaction has been scheduled in lieu of the proof of payment otherwise required by paragraph (b)(3)(i) of this section. The confirmation of scheduling must be clear and conspicuous, provided in writing or electronically, and provided in a retainable form.

(4) Long form error resolution and cancellation notice. Upon the sender's request, a remittance transfer provider must promptly provide to the sender a notice describing the sender's error resolution and cancellation rights, using language set forth in Model Form A–36 of Appendix A to this part or substantially similar language. For any remittance transfer scheduled by the sender at least three business days before the date of the transfer, the description of the rights of the sender regarding cancellation must instead reflect the requirements of § 1005.36(c).

(c) Specific format requirements—(1) Grouping. The information required by paragraphs (b)(1)(i), (ii), and (iii) of this section generally must be grouped together. The information required by paragraphs (b)(1)(v), (vi), (vii), and (viii) of this section generally must be grouped together. Disclosures provided via mobile application or text message, to the extent permitted by paragraph (a)(5) of this section, generally need not comply with the grouping requirements of this paragraph, however information required or permitted by paragraph (b)(1)(viii) of this section must be grouped with information required by paragraph (b)(1)(vii) of this section.

(2) Proximity. The information required by paragraph (b)(1)(iv) of this section generally must be disclosed in close proximity to the other information required by paragraph (b)(1) of this section. The information required by paragraph (b)(2)(iv) of this section generally must be disclosed in close proximity to the other information required by paragraph (b)(2) of this section. The information required or permitted by paragraph (b)(1)(viii) must be in close proximity to the information required by paragraph (b)(1)(vii) of this section. Disclosures provided via mobile application or text message, to the extent permitted by paragraph (a)(5) of this section, generally need not comply with the proximity requirements of this paragraph, however information required or permitted by paragraph (b)(1)(viii) of this section must follow the information required by paragraph (b)(1)(vii) of this section.

(3) Prominence and size. Written disclosures required by this subpart or permitted by paragraph (b)(1)(viii) of this section must be provided on the front of the page on which the disclosure is printed. Disclosures required by this subpart or permitted by paragraph (b)(1)(viii) of this section that are provided in writing or electronically must be in a minimum eight-point font, except for disclosures provided via mobile application or text message, to the extent permitted by paragraph (a)(5) of this section. Disclosures required by paragraph (b) of this section or permitted by paragraph (b)(1)(viii) of this section that are provided in writing or electronically must be in equal prominence to each other.

(4) Segregation. Except for disclosures provided via mobile application or text message, to the extent permitted by paragraph (a)(5) of this section, disclosures required by this subpart that are provided in writing or electronically must be segregated from everything else and must contain only information that is directly related to the disclosures required under this subpart.

(d) Estimates. Estimated disclosures may be provided to the extent permitted by § 1005.32. Estimated disclosures must be described using the term "Estimated" or a substantially similar term in close proximity to the estimated term or terms.

(e) Timing. (1) Except as provided in § 1005.36(a), a pre-payment disclosure required by paragraph (b)(1) of this section or a combined disclosure required by paragraph (b)(3) of this section must be provided to the sender when the sender requests the remittance transfer, but prior to payment for the transfer.

(2) Except as provided in § 1005.36(a), a receipt required by paragraph (b)(2) of this section generally must be provided to the sender when payment is made for the remittance transfer. If a transaction is conducted entirely by telephone, a receipt required by paragraph (b)(2) of this section may be mailed or delivered to the sender no later than one business day after the date on which payment is made for the remittance transfer. If a transaction is conducted entirely by telephone and involves the transfer of funds from the sender's account held by the provider, the receipt required by paragraph (b)(2) of this section may be provided on or with the next regularly scheduled periodic statement for that account or within 30 days after payment is made for the remittance transfer if a periodic statement is not provided. The statement about the rights of the sender regarding cancellation required by paragraph (b)(2)(iv) of this section may, but need not, be disclosed pursuant to the timing requirements of this paragraph if a provider discloses this information pursuant to paragraphs (a)(3)(iii) or (a)(5)(iii) of this section.

(f) Accurate when payment is made. Except as provided in § 1005.36(b), disclosures required by this section or permitted by paragraph (b)(1)(viii) of this section must be accurate when a sender makes payment for the remittance transfer, except to the extent estimates are permitted by § 1005.32.

(g) Foreign language disclosures—(1) General. Except as provided in paragraph (g)(2) of this section, disclosures required by this subpart or permitted by paragraph (b)(1)(viii) of this section or § 1005.33(h)(3) must be made in English and, if applicable, either in:

    (i) Each of the foreign languages principally used by the remittance transfer provider to advertise, solicit, or market remittance transfer services, either orally, in writing, or electronically, at the office in which a sender conducts a transaction or asserts an error; or

    (ii) The foreign language primarily used by the sender with the remittance transfer provider to conduct the transaction (or for written or electronic disclosures made pursuant to § 1005.33, in the foreign language primarily used by the sender with the remittance transfer provider to assert the error), provided that such foreign language is principally used by the remittance transfer provider to advertise, solicit, or market remittance transfer services, either orally, in writing, or electronically, at the office in which a sender conducts a transaction or asserts an error, respectively.

    (2) Oral, mobile application, or text message disclosures. Disclosures provided orally for transactions conducted orally and entirely by telephone under paragraph (a)(3) of this section or orally or via mobile application or text message for transactions conducted via mobile application or text message under paragraph (a)(5) of this section shall be made in the language primarily used by the sender with the remittance transfer provider to conduct the transaction. Disclosures provided orally under paragraph (a)(4) of this section for error resolution purposes shall be made in the language primarily used by the sender with the remittance transfer provider to assert the error.

§ 1005.32 Estimates.

(a) Temporary exception for insured institutions—(1) General. For disclosures described in §§ 1005.31(b)(1) through (3) and 1005.36(a)(1) and (2), estimates may be provided in accordance with paragraph (c) of this section for the amounts required to be disclosed under § 1005.31(b)(1)(iv) through (vii), if:

    (i) A remittance transfer provider cannot determine the exact amounts for reasons beyond its control;

    (ii) A remittance transfer provider is an insured institution; and

    (iii) The remittance transfer is sent from the sender's account with the institution.

  (2) **Sunset date.** Paragraph (a)(1) of this section expires on July 21, 2020.

  (3) **Insured institution.** For purposes of this section, the term "insured institution" means insured depository institutions (which includes uninsured U.S. branches and agencies of foreign depository institutions) as defined in section 3 of the Federal Deposit Insurance Act (12 U.S.C. 1813), and insured credit unions as defined in section 101 of the Federal Credit Union Act (12 U.S.C. 1752).

(b) **Permanent exceptions—(1) Permanent exception for transfers to certain countries.**

    (i) **General.** For disclosures described in §§ 1005.31(b)(1) through (b)(3) and 1005.36(a)(1) and (a)(2), estimates may be provided for transfers to certain countries in accordance with paragraph (c) of this section for the amounts required to be disclosed under § 1005.31(b)(1)(iv) through (b)(1)(vii), if a remittance transfer provider cannot determine the exact amounts when the disclosure is required because:

      (A) The laws of the recipient country do not permit such a determination, or

      (B) The method by which transactions are made in the recipient country does not permit such determination.

    (ii) **Safe harbor.** A remittance transfer provider may rely on the list of countries published by the Bureau to determine whether estimates may be provided under paragraph (b)(1) of this section, unless the provider has information that a country's laws or the method by which transactions are conducted in that country permits a determination of the exact disclosure amount.

  (2) **Permanent exception for transfers scheduled before the date of transfer. (i)** Except as provided in paragraph (b)(2)(ii) of this section, for disclosures described in §§ 1005.36(a)(1)(i) and (a)(2)(i), estimates may be provided in accordance with paragraph (d) of this section for the amounts to be disclosed under §§ 1005.31(b)(1)(iv) through (vii) if the remittance transfer is scheduled by a sender five or more business days before the date of the transfer. In addition, if, at the time the sender schedules such a transfer, the provider agrees to a sender's request to fix the amount to be transferred in the currency in which the remittance transfer will be received and not the currency in which it is funded, estimates may also be provided for the amounts to be disclosed under §§ 1005.31(b)(1)(i) through (iii), except as provided in paragraph (b)(2)(iii) of this section.

    (ii) Fees and taxes described in § 1005.31(b)(1)(vi) may be estimated under paragraph (b)(2)(i) of this section only if the exchange rate is also estimated under paragraph (b)(2)(i) and the estimated exchange rate affects the amount of such fees and taxes.

    (iii) Covered third-party fees described in § 1005.31(b)(1)(ii) may be estimated under paragraph (b)(2)(i) of this section only if the amount that will be transferred in the currency in which it is funded is also estimated under paragraph (b)(2)(i) of this section, and the estimated amount affects the amount of such fees.

  (3) **Permanent exception for optional disclosure of non-covered third-party fees and taxes collected by a person other than the provider.** For disclosures described in §§ 1005.31(b)(1) through (3) and 1005.36(a)(1) and (2), estimates may be provided for applicable non-covered third-party fees and taxes collected on the remittance transfer by a person other than the provider, which are permitted to be disclosed under § 1005.31(b)(1)(viii), provided such estimates are based on reasonable sources of information.

(c) **Bases for estimates generally.** Estimates provided pursuant to the exceptions in paragraph (a) or (b)(1) of this section must be based on the below-listed approach or approaches, except as otherwise permitted by this paragraph. If a remittance transfer provider bases an estimate on an approach that is not listed in this paragraph, the provider is deemed to be in compliance with this paragraph so long as the designated recipient receives the same, or greater, amount of funds than the remittance transfer provider disclosed under § 1005.31(b)(1)(vii).

(1) **Exchange rate.** In disclosing the exchange rate as required under 1005.31(b)(1)(iv), an estimate must be based on one of the following:

(i) For remittance transfers sent via international ACH that qualify for the exception in paragraph (b)(1)(ii) of this section, the most recent exchange rate set by the recipient country's central bank or other governmental authority and reported by a Federal Reserve Bank;

(ii) The most recent publicly available wholesale exchange rate and, if applicable, any spread that the remittance transfer provider or its correspondent typically applies to such a wholesale rate for remittance transfers for that currency; or

(iii) The most recent exchange rate offered or used by the person making funds available directly to the designated recipient or by the person setting the exchange rate.

(2) **Transfer amount in the currency in which the funds will be received by the designated recipient.** In disclosing the transfer amount in the currency in which the funds will be received by the designated recipient, as required under § 1005.31(b)(1)(v), an estimate must be based on the estimated exchange rate provided in accordance with paragraph (c)(1) of this section, prior to any rounding of the estimated exchange rate.

(3) **Other fees. (i) Imposed as percentage of amount transferred.** In disclosing covered third-party fees as required under § 1005.31(b)(1)(vi) that are a percentage of the amount transferred to the designated recipient, an estimated exchange rate must be based on the estimated exchange rate provided in accordance with paragraph (c)(1) of this section, prior to any rounding of the estimated exchange rate.

(ii) **Imposed by intermediary or final institution.** In disclosing covered third-party fees pursuant to § 1005.31(b)(1)(vi), an estimate must be based on one of the following:

(A) The remittance transfer provider's most recent remittance transfer to the designated recipient's institution, or

(B) A representative transmittal route identified by the remittance transfer provider.

(4) **Other taxes imposed in the recipient country.** In disclosing taxes imposed in the recipient country as required under § 1005.31(b)(1)(vi) that are a percentage of the amount transferred to the designated recipient, an estimate must be based on the estimated exchange rate provided in accordance with paragraph (c)(1) of this section, prior to any rounding of the estimated exchange rate, and the estimated fees provided in accordance with paragraph (c)(3) of this section.

(5) **Amount of currency that will be received by the designated recipient.** In disclosing the amount of currency that will be received by the designated recipient as required under § 1005.31(b)(1)(vii), an estimate must be based on the information provided in accordance with paragraphs (c)(1) through (3) of this section, as applicable.

(d) **Bases for estimates for transfers scheduled before the date of transfer.** Estimates provided pursuant to paragraph (b)(2) of this section must be based on the exchange rate or, where applicable, the estimated exchange rate based on an estimation methodology permitted under paragraph (c) of this section that the provider would have used or did use that day in providing disclosures to a sender requesting such a remittance transfer to be made on the same day. If, in accordance with this paragraph, a remittance transfer provider uses a basis described in paragraph (c) of this section but not listed in paragraph (c)(1) of this section, the provider is deemed to be in compliance with this paragraph regardless of the amount received by the designated recipient, so long as the estimation methodology is the same that the provider would have used or did use in providing disclosures to a sender requesting such a remittance transfer to be made on the same day.

§ 1005.33 Procedures for resolving errors.

(a) **Definition of error. (1) Types of transfers or inquiries covered.** For purposes of this section, the term error means:

(i) An incorrect amount paid by a sender in connection with a remittance transfer unless the disclosure stated an estimate of the amount paid by a sender in accordance with § 1005.32(b)(2) and the difference results from application of the actual exchange rate, fees, and taxes, rather than any estimated amount;

(ii) A computational or bookkeeping error made by the remittance transfer provider relating to a remittance transfer;

(iii) The failure to make available to a designated recipient the amount of currency disclosed pursuant to § 1005.31(b)(2) or (3) for the remittance transfer, unless:

(A) The disclosure stated an estimate of the amount to be received in accordance with § 1005.32(a), (b)(1), or (b)(2) and the difference results from application of the actual exchange rate, fees, and taxes, rather than any estimated amounts; or

(B) The failure resulted from extraordinary circumstances outside the remittance transfer provider's control that could not have been reasonably anticipated; or

(C) The difference results from the application of non-covered third-party fees or taxes collected on the remittance transfer by a person other than the provider and the provider provided the disclosure required by § 1005.31(b)(1)(viii).

(iv) The failure to make funds available to a designated recipient by the date of availability stated in the disclosure provided to the sender under § 1005.31(b)(2) or (3) for the remittance transfer, unless the failure to make the funds available resulted from:

(A) Extraordinary circumstances outside the remittance transfer provider's control that could not have been reasonably anticipated;

(B) Delays related to a necessary investigation or other special action by the remittance transfer provider or a third party as required by the provider's fraud screening procedures or in accordance with the Bank Secrecy Act, 31 U.S.C. 5311 et seq., Office of Foreign Assets Control requirements, or similar laws or requirements;

(C) The remittance transfer being made with fraudulent intent by the sender or any person acting in concert with the sender; or

(D) The sender having provided the remittance transfer provider an incorrect account number or recipient institution identifier for the designated recipient's account or institution, provided that the remittance transfer provider meets the conditions set forth in paragraph (h) of this section;

(v) The sender's request for documentation required by § 1005.31 or for additional information or clarification concerning a remittance transfer, including a request a sender makes to determine whether an error exists under paragraphs (a)(1)(i) through (iv) of this section.

(2) **Types of transfers or inquiries not covered.** The term error does not include:

(i) An inquiry about the status of a remittance transfer, except where the funds from the transfer were not made available to a designated recipient by the disclosed date of availability as described in paragraph (a)(1)(iv) of this section;

(ii) A request for information for tax or other recordkeeping purposes;

(iii) A change requested by the designated recipient; or

(iv) A change in the amount or type of currency received by the designated recipient from the amount or type of currency stated in the disclosure provided to the sender under

§1005.31(b)(2) or (3) if the remittance transfer provider relied on information provided by the sender as permitted under §1005.31 in making such disclosure.

(b) Notice of error from sender. (1) Timing; contents. A remittance transfer provider shall comply with the requirements of this section with respect to any oral or written notice of error from a sender that:

    (i) Is received by the remittance transfer provider no later than 180 days after the disclosed date of availability of the remittance transfer;

    (ii) Enables the provider to identify:

        (A) The sender's name and telephone number or address;

        (B) The recipient's name, and if known, the telephone number or address of the recipient; and

        (C) The remittance transfer to which the notice of error applies; and

    (iii) Indicates why the sender believes an error exists and includes to the extent possible the type, date, and amount of the error, except for requests for documentation, additional information, or clarification described in paragraph (a)(1)(v) of this section.

    (2) Request for documentation or clarification. When a notice of error is based on documentation, additional information, or clarification that the sender previously requested under paragraph (a)(1)(v) of this section, the sender's notice of error is timely if received by the remittance transfer provider the later of 180 days after the disclosed date of availability of the remittance transfer or 60 days after the provider sent the documentation, information, or clarification that had been requested.

(c) Time limits and extent of investigation. (1) Time limits for investigation and report to consumer of error. A remittance transfer provider shall investigate promptly and determine whether an error occurred within 90 days of receiving a notice of error. The remittance transfer provider shall report the results to the sender, including notice of any remedies available for correcting any error that the provider determines has occurred, within three business days after completing its investigation.

    (2) Remedies. Except as provided in paragraph (c)(2)(iii) of this section, if, following an assertion of an error by a sender, the remittance transfer provider determines an error occurred, the provider shall, within one business day of, or as soon as reasonably practicable after, receiving the sender's instructions regarding the appropriate remedy, correct the error as designated by the sender by:

    (i) In the case of any error under paragraphs (a)(1)(i) through (iii) of this section, as applicable, either:

        (A) Refunding to the sender the amount of funds provided by the sender in connection with a remittance transfer which was not properly transmitted, or the amount appropriate to resolve the error; or

        (B) Making available to the designated recipient, without additional cost to the sender or to the designated recipient, the amount appropriate to resolve the error;

    (ii) Except as provided in paragraph (c)(2)(iii), in the case of an error under paragraph (a)(1)(iv) of this section:

        (A) As applicable, either:

            (1) Refunding to the sender the amount of funds provided by the sender in connection with a remittance transfer which was not properly transmitted, or the amount appropriate to resolve the error; or

            (2) Making available to the designated recipient the amount appropriate to resolve the error. Such amount must be made available to the designated recipient without additional cost to the sender or to the designated recipient; and

(B) Refunding to the sender any fees imposed and, to the extent not prohibited by law, taxes collected on the remittance transfer;

(iii) In the case of an error under paragraph (a)(1)(iv) of this section that occurred because the sender provided incorrect or insufficient information in connection with the remittance transfer, the remittance transfer provider shall provide the remedies required by paragraphs (c)(2)(ii)(A)(1) and (c)(2)(ii)(B) of this section within three business days of providing the report required by paragraph (c)(1) or (d)(1) of this section except that the provider may agree to the sender's request, upon receiving the results of the error investigation, that the funds be applied towards a new remittance transfer, rather than be refunded, if the provider has not yet processed a refund. The provider may deduct from the amount refunded or applied towards a new transfer any fees actually imposed on or, to the extent not prohibited by law, taxes actually collected on the remittance transfer as part of the first unsuccessful remittance transfer attempt, except that the provider shall not deduct its own fee.

(d) Procedures if remittance transfer provider determines no error or different error occurred. In addition to following the procedures specified in paragraph (c) of this section, the remittance transfer provider shall follow the procedures set forth in this paragraph (d) if it determines that no error occurred or that an error occurred in a manner or amount different from that described by the sender.

(1) Explanation of results of investigation. The remittance transfer provider's report of the results of the investigation shall include a written explanation of the provider's findings and shall note the sender's right to request the documents on which the provider relied in making its determination. The explanation shall also address the specific complaint of the sender.

(2) Copies of documentation. Upon the sender's request, the remittance transfer provider shall promptly provide copies of the documents on which the provider relied in making its error determination.

(e) Reassertion of error. A remittance transfer provider that has fully complied with the error resolution requirements of this section has no further responsibilities under this section should the sender later reassert the same error, except in the case of an error asserted by the sender following receipt of information provided under paragraph (a)(1)(v) of this section.

(f) Relation to other laws—(1) Relation to Regulation E § 1005.11 for incorrect EFTs from a sender's account. If an alleged error involves an incorrect electronic fund transfer from a sender's account in connection with a remittance transfer, and the sender provides a notice of error to the account-holding institution, the account-holding institution shall comply with the requirements of § 1005.11 governing error resolution rather than the requirements of this section, provided that the account-holding institution is not also the remittance transfer provider. If the remittance transfer provider is also the financial institution that holds the consumer's account, then the error-resolution provisions of this section apply when the sender provides such notice of error.

(2) Relation to Truth in Lending Act and Regulation Z. If an alleged error involves an incorrect extension of credit in connection with a remittance transfer, an incorrect amount received by the designated recipient under paragraph (a)(1)(iii) of this section that is an extension of credit for property or services not delivered as agreed, or the failure to make funds available by the disclosed date of availability under paragraph (a)(1)(iv) of this section that is an extension of credit for property or services not delivered as agreed, and the sender provides a notice of error to the creditor extending the credit, the provisions of Regulation Z, 12 CFR 1026.13, governing error resolution apply to the creditor, rather than the requirements of this section, even if the creditor is the remittance transfer provider. However, if the creditor is the remittance transfer provider, paragraph (b) of this section will apply instead of 12 CFR 1026.13(b). If the sender instead provides a notice of error to the remittance transfer provider that is not also the creditor, then the error-resolution provisions of this section apply to the remittance transfer provider.

(3) Unauthorized remittance transfers. If an alleged error involves an unauthorized electronic fund transfer for payment in connection with a remittance transfer, §§ 1005.6 and 1005.11 apply with respect to the account-holding institution. If an alleged error involves an unauthorized use of a credit account for payment in connection with a remittance transfer, the provisions of Regulation Z, 12 CFR 1026.12(b), if applicable, and § 1026.13, apply with respect to the creditor.

(g) Error resolution standards and recordkeeping requirements—(1) Compliance program. A remittance transfer provider shall develop and maintain written policies and procedures that are designed to ensure compliance with the error resolution requirements applicable to remittance transfers under this section.

(2) Retention of error-related documentation. The remittance transfer provider's policies and procedures required under paragraph (g)(1) of this section shall include policies and procedures regarding the retention of documentation related to error investigations. Such policies and procedures must ensure, at a minimum, the retention of any notices of error submitted by a sender, documentation provided by the sender to the provider with respect to the alleged error, and the findings of the remittance transfer provider regarding the investigation of the alleged error. Remittance transfer providers are subject to the record retention requirements under § 1005.13.

(h) Incorrect account number or recipient institution identifier provided by the sender. The exception in paragraph (a)(1)(iv)(D) of this section applies if:

(1) The remittance transfer provider can demonstrate that the sender provided an incorrect account number or recipient institution identifier to the provider in connection with the remittance transfer;

(2) For any instance in which the sender provided the incorrect recipient institution identifier, prior to or when sending the transfer, the provider used reasonably available means to verify that the recipient institution identifier provided by the sender corresponded to the recipient institution name provided by the sender;

(3) The provider provided notice to the sender before the sender made payment for the remittance transfer that, in the event the sender provided an incorrect account number or recipient institution identifier, the sender could lose the transfer amount. For purposes of providing this disclosure, § 1005.31(a)(2) applies to this notice unless the notice is given at the same time as other disclosures required by this subpart for which information is permitted to be disclosed orally or via mobile application or text message, in which case this disclosure may be given in the same medium as those other disclosures;

(4) The incorrect account number or recipient institution identifier resulted in the deposit of the remittance transfer into a customer's account that is not the designated recipient's account; and

(5) The provider promptly used reasonable efforts to recover the amount that was to be received by the designated recipient.

§ 1005.34 Procedures for cancellation and refund of remittance transfers.

(a) Sender right of cancellation and refund. Except as provided in 1005.36(c), a remittance transfer provider shall comply with the requirements of this section with respect to any oral or written request to cancel a remittance transfer from the sender that is received by the provider no later than 30 minutes after the sender makes payment in connection with the remittance transfer if:

(1) The request to cancel enables the provider to identify the sender's name and address or telephone number and the particular transfer to be cancelled; and

(2) The transferred funds have not been picked up by the designated recipient or deposited into an account of the designated recipient.

(b) Time limits and refund requirements. A remittance transfer provider shall refund, at no additional cost to the sender, the total amount of funds provided by the sender in connection with a remittance transfer, including any fees and, to the extent not prohibited by law, taxes imposed in connection with the remittance transfer, within three business days of receiving a sender's request to cancel the remittance transfer.

§ 1005.35   Acts of agents.

A remittance transfer provider is liable for any violation of this subpart by an agent when such agent acts for the provider.

§ 1005.36   Transfers scheduled before the date of transfer.

(a)   **Timing.** (1) For a one-time transfer scheduled five or more business days before the date of transfer or for the first in a series of preauthorized remittance transfers, the remittance transfer provider must:

(i)   Provide either the pre-payment disclosure described in § 1005.31(b)(1) and the receipt described in § 1005.31(b)(2) or the combined disclosure described in § 1005.31(b)(3), in accordance with the timing requirements set forth in § 1005.31(e); and

(ii)   If any of the disclosures provided pursuant to paragraph (a)(1)(i) of this section contain estimates as permitted by § 1005.32(b)(2), mail or deliver to the sender an additional receipt meeting the requirements described in § 1005.31(b)(2) no later than one business day after the date of the transfer. If the transfer involves the transfer of funds from the sender's account held by the provider, the receipt required by this paragraph may be provided on or with the next periodic statement for that account, or within 30 days after the date of the transfer if a periodic statement is not provided.

(2)   For each subsequent preauthorized remittance transfer:

(i)   If any of the information on the most recent receipt provided pursuant to paragraph (a)(1)(i) of this section, or by this paragraph (a)(2)(i), other than the temporal disclosures required by § 1005.31(b)(2)(ii) and (b)(2)(vii), is no longer accurate with respect to a subsequent preauthorized remittance transfer for reasons other than as permitted by § 1005.32, then the remittance transfer provider must provide an updated receipt meeting the requirements described in § 1005.31(b)(2) to the sender. The provider must mail or deliver this receipt to the sender within a reasonable time prior to the scheduled date of the next subsequent preauthorized remittance transfer. Such receipt must clearly and conspicuously indicate that it contains updated disclosures.

(ii)   Unless a receipt was provided in accordance with paragraph (a)(2)(i) of this section that contained no estimates pursuant to § 1005.32, the remittance transfer provider must mail or deliver to the sender a receipt meeting the requirements described in § 1005.31(b)(2) no later than one business day after the date of the transfer. If the remittance transfer involves the transfer of funds from the sender's account held by the provider, the receipt required by this paragraph may be provided on or with the next periodic statement for that account, or within 30 days after the date of the transfer if a periodic statement is not provided.

(iii)   A remittance transfer provider must provide the disclosures required by paragraph (d) of this section in accordance with the timing requirements of that section.

(b)   **Accuracy.** (1) For a one-time transfer scheduled five or more business days in advance or for the first in a series of preauthorized remittance transfers, disclosures provided pursuant to paragraph (a)(1)(i) of this section must comply with § 1005.31(f) by being accurate when a sender makes payment except to the extent estimates are permitted by § 1005.32.

(2)   For each subsequent preauthorized remittance transfer, the most recent receipt provided pursuant to paragraph (a)(1)(i) or (a)(2)(i) of this section must be accurate as of when such transfer is made, except:

(i)   The temporal elements required by § 1005.31(b)(2)(ii) and (b)(2)(vii) must be accurate only if the transfer is the first transfer to occur after the disclosure was provided; and

(ii)   To the extent estimates are permitted by § 1005.32.

(3) Disclosures provided pursuant to paragraph (a)(1)(ii) or (a)(2)(ii) of this section must be accurate as of when the remittance transfer to which it pertains is made, except to the extent estimates are permitted by § 1005.32(a) or (b)(1).

(c) Cancellation. For any remittance transfer scheduled by the sender at least three business days before the date of the transfer, a remittance transfer provider shall comply with any oral or written request to cancel the remittance transfer from the sender if the request to cancel:

(1) Enables the provider to identify the sender's name and address or telephone number and the particular transfer to be cancelled; and

(2) Is received by the provider at least three business days before the scheduled date of the remittance transfer.

(d) Additional requirements for subsequent preauthorized remittance transfers—(1) Disclosure requirement. (i) For any subsequent transfer in a series of preauthorized remittance transfers, the remittance transfer provider must disclose to the sender:

(A) The date the provider will make the subsequent transfer, using the term "Future Transfer Date," or a substantially similar term;

(B) A statement about the rights of the sender regarding cancellation as described in § 1005.31(b)(2)(iv); and

(C) The name, telephone number(s), and Web site of the remittance transfer provider.

(ii) If the future date or dates of transfer are described as occurring in regular periodic intervals, e.g., the 15th of every month, rather than as a specific calendar date or dates, the remittance transfer provider must disclose any future date or dates of transfer that do not conform to the described interval.

(2) Notice requirements. (i) Except as described in paragraph (d)(2)(ii) of this section, the disclosures required by paragraph (d)(1) of this section must be received by the sender no more than 12 months, and no less than five business days prior to the date of any subsequent transfer to which it pertains. The disclosures required by paragraph (d)(1) of this section may be provided in a separate disclosure or may be provided on one or more disclosures required by this subpart related to the same series of preauthorized transfers, so long as the consumer receives the required information for each subsequent preauthorized remittance transfer in accordance with the timing requirements of this paragraph (d)(2)(i).

(ii) For any subsequent preauthorized remittance transfer for which the date of transfer is four or fewer business days after the date payment is made for that transfer, the information required by paragraph (d)(1) of this section must be provided on or with the receipt described in § 1005.31(b)(2), or disclosed as permitted by § 1005.31(a)(3) or (a)(5), for the initial transfer in that series in accordance with paragraph (a)(1)(i) of this section.

(3) Specific format requirement. The information required by paragraph (d)(1)(i)(A) of this section generally must be disclosed in close proximity to the other information required by paragraph (d)(1)(i)(B) of this section.

(4) Accuracy. Any disclosure required by paragraph (d)(1) of this section must be accurate as of the date the preauthorized remittance transfer to which it pertains is made.

OFFICIAL INTERPRETATIONS OF REGULATION E

---

12 C.F.R. Part 1005 Supplement I.—OFFICIAL INTERPRETATIONS

Current through March 13, 2016; 81 F.R. 12795

For updates, see www.ecfr.gov

SECTION 1005.2   DEFINITIONS

2(a) Access Device

1.   *Examples.* The term "access device" includes debit cards, personal identification numbers (PINs), telephone transfer and telephone bill payment codes, and other means that may be used by a consumer to initiate an electronic fund transfer (EFT) to or from a consumer account. The term does not include magnetic tape or other devices used internally by a financial institution to initiate electronic transfers.

2.   *Checks used to capture information.* The term "access device" does not include a check or draft used to capture the Magnetic Ink Character Recognition (MICR) encoding to initiate a one-time automated clearinghouse (ACH) debit. For example, if a consumer authorizes a one-time ACH debit from the consumer's account using a blank, partially completed, or fully completed and signed check for the merchant to capture the routing, account, and serial numbers to initiate the debit, the check is not an access device. (Although the check is not an access device under Regulation E, the transaction is nonetheless covered by the regulation. *See* comment 3(b)(1)–1.v.)

2(b) Account

1.   *Consumer asset account.* The term "consumer asset account" includes:

  i.   Club accounts, such as vacation clubs. In many cases, however, these accounts are exempt from the regulation under § 1005.3(c)(5) because all electronic transfers to or from the account have been preauthorized by the consumer and involve another account of the consumer at the same institution.

  ii.   A retail repurchase agreement (repo), which is a loan made to a financial institution by a consumer that is collateralized by government or government-insured securities.

2.   *Certain employment-related cards not covered.* The term "payroll card account" does not include a card used solely to disburse incentive-based payments (other than commissions which can represent the primary means through which a consumer is paid), such as bonuses, which are unlikely to be a consumer's primary source of salary or other compensation. The term also does not include a card used solely to make disbursements unrelated to compensation, such as petty cash reimbursements or travel per diem payments. Similarly, a payroll card account does not include a card that is used in isolated instances to which an employer typically does not make recurring payments, such as when providing final payments or in emergency situations when other payment methods are unavailable. However, all transactions involving the transfer of funds to or from a payroll card account are covered by the regulation, even if a particular transaction involves payment of a bonus, other incentive-based payment, or reimbursement, or the transaction does not represent a transfer of wages, salary, or other employee compensation.

3.   Examples of accounts not covered by Regulation E (12 CFR part 1005) include:

  i.   Profit-sharing and pension accounts established under a trust agreement, which are exempt under § 1005.2(b)(2).

  ii.   Escrow accounts, such as those established to ensure payment of items such as real estate taxes, insurance premiums, or completion of repairs or improvements.

  iii. Accounts for accumulating funds to purchase U.S. savings bonds.

OFFICIAL INTERPRETATIONS OF REGULATION E

Paragraph 2(b)(2)

1. *Bona fide trust agreements.* The term "bona fide trust agreement" is not defined by the Act or regulation; therefore, financial institutions must look to state or other applicable law for interpretation.

2. *Custodial agreements.* An account held under a custodial agreement that qualifies as a trust under the Internal Revenue Code, such as an individual retirement account, is considered to be held under a trust agreement for purposes of Regulation E.

2(d) Business Day

1. *Duration.* A business day includes the entire 24-hour period ending at midnight, and a notice required by the regulation is effective even if given outside normal business hours. The regulation does not require, however, that a financial institution make telephone lines available on a 24-hour basis.

2. *Substantially all business functions.* Substantially all business functions include both the public and the back-office operations of the institution. For example, if the offices of an institution are open on Saturdays for handling some consumer transactions (such as deposits, withdrawals, and other teller transactions), but not for performing internal functions (such as investigating account errors), then Saturday is not a business day for that institution. In this case, Saturday does not count toward the business-day standard set by the regulation for reporting lost or stolen access devices, resolving errors, *etc.*

3. *Short hours.* A financial institution may determine, at its election, whether an abbreviated day is a business day. For example, if an institution engages in substantially all business functions until noon on Saturdays instead of its usual 3 p.m. closing, it may consider Saturday a business day.

4. *Telephone line.* If a financial institution makes a telephone line available on Sundays for reporting the loss or theft of an access device, but performs no other business functions, Sunday is not a business day under the substantially all business functions standard.

2(h) Electronic Terminal

1. *Point-of-sale (POS) payments initiated by telephone.* Because the term "electronic terminal" excludes a telephone operated by a consumer, a financial institution need not provide a terminal receipt when:

    i.   A consumer uses a debit card at a public telephone to pay for the call.

    ii.   A consumer initiates a transfer by a means analogous in function to a telephone, such as by home banking equipment or a facsimile machine.

2. *POS terminals.* A POS terminal that captures data electronically, for debiting or crediting to a consumer's asset account, is an electronic terminal for purposes of Regulation E even if no access device is used to initiate the transaction. See § 1005.9 for receipt requirements.

3. *Teller-operated terminals.* A terminal or other computer equipment operated by an employee of a financial institution is not an electronic terminal for purposes of the regulation. However, transfers initiated at such terminals by means of a consumer's access device (using the consumer's PIN, for example) are EFTs and are subject to other requirements of the regulation. If an access device is used only for identification purposes or for determining the account balance, the transfers are not EFTs for purposes of the regulation.

2(k) Preauthorized Electronic Fund Transfer

1. *Advance authorization.* A preauthorized electronic fund transfer under Regulation E is one authorized by the consumer in advance of a transfer that will take place on a recurring basis, at substantially regular intervals, and will require no further action by the consumer to initiate the transfer. In a bill-payment system, for example, if the consumer authorizes a financial institution to make monthly payments to a payee by means of EFTs, and the payments take place without further action by the consumer, the payments are preauthorized EFTs. In contrast, if the consumer must take action each month to initiate a payment (such as by entering instructions on a touch-tone telephone or home computer), the payments are not preauthorized EFTs.

OFFICIAL INTERPRETATIONS OF REGULATION E

2(m) Unauthorized Electronic Fund Transfer

1. *Transfer by institution's employee.* A consumer has no liability for erroneous or fraudulent transfers initiated by an employee of a financial institution.

2. *Authority.* If a consumer furnishes an access device and grants authority to make transfers to a person (such as a family member or co-worker) who exceeds the authority given, the consumer is fully liable for the transfers unless the consumer has notified the financial institution that transfers by that person are no longer authorized.

3. *Access device obtained through robbery or fraud.* An unauthorized EFT includes a transfer initiated by a person who obtained the access device from the consumer through fraud or robbery.

4. *Forced initiation.* An EFT at an ATM is an unauthorized transfer if the consumer has been induced by force to initiate the transfer.

5. *Reversal of direct deposits.* The reversal of a direct deposit made in error is not an unauthorized EFT when it involves:

    i.   A credit made to the wrong consumer's account;

    ii. A duplicate credit made to a consumer's account; or

    iii. A credit in the wrong amount (for example, when the amount credited to the consumer's account differs from the amount in the transmittal instructions).

SECTION 1005.3 COVERAGE

3(a) General

1. *Accounts covered.* The requirements of the regulation apply only to an account for which an agreement for EFT services to or from the account has been entered into between:

    i.   The consumer and the financial institution (including an account for which an access device has been issued to the consumer, for example);

    ii. The consumer and a third party (for preauthorized debits or credits, for example), when the account-holding institution has received notice of the agreement and the fund transfers have begun.

2. *Automated clearing house (ACH) membership.* The fact that membership in an ACH requires a financial institution to accept EFTs to accounts at the institution does not make every account of that institution subject to the regulation.

3. *Foreign applicability.* Regulation E applies to all persons (including branches and other offices of foreign banks located in the United States) that offer EFT services to residents of any state, including resident aliens. It covers any account located in the United States through which EFTs are offered to a resident of a state. This is the case whether or not a particular transfer takes place in the United States and whether or not the financial institution is chartered in the United States or a foreign country. The regulation does not apply to a foreign branch of a U.S. bank unless the EFT services are offered in connection with an account in a state as defined in § 1005.2(l).

3(b) Electronic Fund Transfer

3(b)(1) Definition

1. *Fund transfers covered.* The term "electronic fund transfer" includes:

    i.   A deposit made at an ATM or other electronic terminal (including a deposit in cash or by check) provided a specific agreement exists between the financial institution and the consumer for EFTs to or from the account to which the deposit is made.

    ii. A transfer sent via ACH. For example, social security benefits under the U.S. Treasury's direct-deposit program are covered, even if the listing of payees and payment amounts reaches the account-holding institution by means of a computer printout from a correspondent bank.

iii.   A preauthorized transfer credited or debited to an account in accordance with instructions contained on magnetic tape, even if the financial institution holding the account sends or receives a composite check.

iv.   A transfer from the consumer's account resulting from a debit-card transaction at a merchant location, even if no electronic terminal is involved at the time of the transaction, if the consumer's asset account is subsequently debited for the amount of the transfer.

v.   A transfer via ACH where a consumer has provided a check to enable the merchant or other payee to capture the routing, account, and serial numbers to initiate the transfer, whether the check is blank, partially completed, or fully completed and signed; whether the check is presented at POS or is mailed to a merchant or other payee or lockbox and later converted to an EFT; or whether the check is retained by the consumer, the merchant or other payee, or the payee's financial institution.

vi.   A payment made by a bill payer under a bill-payment service available to a consumer via computer or other electronic means, unless the terms of the bill-payment service explicitly state that all payments, or all payments to a particular payee or payees, will be solely by check, draft, or similar paper instrument drawn on the consumer's account, and the payee or payees that will be paid in this manner are identified to the consumer.

2.   *Fund transfers not covered.* The term "electronic fund transfer" does not include:

i.   A payment that does not debit or credit a consumer asset account, such as a payroll allotment to a creditor to repay a credit extension (which is deducted from salary).

ii.   A payment made in currency by a consumer to another person at an electronic terminal.

iii.   A preauthorized check drawn by the financial institution on the consumer's account (such as an interest or other recurring payment to the consumer or another party), even if the check is computer-generated.

iv.   Transactions arising from the electronic collection, presentment, or return of checks through the check collection system, such as through transmission of electronic check images.

3(b)(2) Electronic Fund Transfer Using Information From a Check

1.   *Notice at POS not furnished due to inadvertent error.* If the copy of the notice under section 1005.3(b)(2)(ii) for electronic check conversion (ECK) transactions is not provided to the consumer at POS because of a bona fide unintentional error, such as when a terminal printing mechanism jams, no violation results if the payee maintains procedures reasonably adapted to avoid such occurrences.

2.   *Authorization to process a transaction as an EFT or as a check.* In order to process a transaction as an EFT, or alternatively as a check, the payee must obtain the consumer's authorization to do so. A payee may, at its option, specify the circumstances under which a check may not be converted to an EFT. *See* model clauses in appendix A–6.

3.   *Notice for each transfer.* Generally, a notice to authorize an electronic check conversion transaction must be provided for each transaction. For example, a consumer must receive a notice that the transaction will be processed as an EFT for each transaction at POS or each time a consumer mails a check in an accounts receivable (ARC) transaction to pay a bill, such as a utility bill, if the payee intends to convert a check received as payment. Similarly, the consumer must receive notice if the payee intends to collect a service fee for insufficient or uncollected funds via an EFT for each transaction whether at POS or if the consumer mails a check to pay a bill. The notice about when funds may be debited from a consumer's account and the non-return of consumer checks by the consumer's financial institution must also be provided for each transaction. However, if in an ARC transaction, a payee provides a coupon book to a consumer, for example, for mortgage loan payments, and the payment dates and amounts are set out in the coupon book, the payee may provide a single notice on the coupon book stating all of the required disclosures under paragraph (b)(2) of this section in order to obtain authorization for each conversion of a check and any debits via EFT to the consumer's account to collect any service fees imposed by the payee for insufficient or uncollected funds in the consumer's account. The notice must be placed on a conspicuous location of the coupon book that a consumer can retain—for example, on the first page, or inside the front cover.

OFFICIAL INTERPRETATIONS OF REGULATION E

4. *Multiple payments/multiple consumers.* If a merchant or other payee will use information from a consumer's check to initiate an EFT from the consumer's account, notice to a consumer listed on the billing account that a check provided as payment during a single billing cycle or after receiving an invoice or statement will be processed as a one-time EFT or as a check transaction constitutes notice for all checks provided in payment for the billing cycle or the invoice for which notice has been provided, whether the check(s) is submitted by the consumer or someone else. The notice applies to all checks provided in payment for the billing cycle or invoice until the provision of notice on or with the next invoice or statement. Thus, if a merchant or other payee receives a check as payment for the consumer listed on the billing account after providing notice that the check will be processed as a one-time EFT, the authorization from that consumer constitutes authorization to convert any other checks provided for that invoice or statement. Other notices required under this paragraph (b)(2) (for example, to collect a service fee for insufficient or uncollected funds via an EFT) provided to the consumer listed on the billing account also constitutes notice to any other consumer who may provide a check for the billing cycle or invoice.

5. *Additional disclosures about ECK transactions at POS.* When a payee initiates an EFT at POS using information from the consumer's check, and returns the check to the consumer at POS, the payee need not provide a notice to the consumer that the check will not be returned by the consumer's financial institution.

3(b)(3) Collection of Returned Item Fees via Electronic Fund Transfer

1. *Fees imposed by account-holding institution.* The requirement to obtain a consumer's authorization to collect a fee via EFT for the return of an EFT or check unpaid applies only to the person that intends to initiate an EFT to collect the returned item fee from the consumer's account. The authorization requirement does not apply to any fees assessed by the consumer's account-holding financial institution when it returns the unpaid underlying EFT or check or pays the amount of an overdraft.

2. *Accounts receivable transactions.* In an ARC transaction where a consumer sends in a payment for amounts owed (or makes an in-person payment at a biller's physical location, such as when a consumer makes a loan payment at a bank branch or places a payment in a drop box), a person seeking to electronically collect a fee for items returned unpaid must obtain the consumer's authorization to collect the fee in this manner. A consumer authorizes a person to electronically collect a returned item fee when the consumer receives notice, typically on an invoice or statement, that the person may collect the fee through an EFT to the consumer's account, and the consumer goes forward with the underlying transaction by providing payment. The notice must also state the dollar amount of the fee. However, an explanation of how that fee will be determined may be provided in place of the dollar amount of the fee if the fee may vary due to the amount of the transaction or due to other factors, such as the number of days the underlying transaction is left outstanding. For example, if a state law permits a maximum fee of $30 or 10% of the underlying transaction, whichever is greater, the person collecting the fee may explain how the fee is determined, rather than state a specific dollar amount for the fee.

3. *Disclosure of dollar amount of fee for POS transactions.* The notice provided to the consumer in connection with a POS transaction under § 1005.3(b)(3)(ii) must state the amount of the fee for a returned item if the dollar amount of the fee can be calculated at the time the notice is provided or mailed. For example, if notice is provided to the consumer at the time of the transaction, if the applicable state law sets a maximum fee that may be collected for a returned item based on the amount of the underlying transaction (such as where the amount of the fee is expressed as a percentage of the underlying transaction), the person collecting the fee must state the actual dollar amount of the fee on the notice provided to the consumer. Alternatively, if the amount of the fee to be collected cannot be calculated at the time of the transaction (for example, where the amount of the fee will depend on the number of days a debt continues to be owed), the person collecting the fee may provide a description of how the fee will be determined on both the posted notice as well as on the notice provided at the time of the transaction. However, if the person collecting the fee elects to send the consumer notice after the person has initiated an EFT to collect the fee, that notice must state the amount of the fee to be collected.

4. *Third party providing notice.* The person initiating an EFT to a consumer's account to electronically collect a fee for an item returned unpaid may obtain the authorization and provide the notices required under § 1005.3(b)(3) through third parties, such as merchants.

OFFICIAL INTERPRETATIONS OF REGULATION E

3(c) Exclusions From Coverage

3(c)(1) Checks

1.   *Re-presented checks.* The electronic re-presentment of a returned check is not covered by Regulation E because the transaction originated by check. Regulation E does apply, however, to any fee debited via an EFT from a consumer's account by the payee because the check was returned for insufficient or uncollected funds. The person debiting the fee electronically must obtain the consumer's authorization.

2.   *Check used to capture information for a one-time EFT. See* comment 3(b)(1)–1.v.

3(c)(2) Check Guarantee or Authorization

1.   *Memo posting.* Under a check guarantee or check authorization service, debiting of the consumer's account occurs when the check or draft is presented for payment. These services are exempt from coverage, even when a temporary hold on the account is memo-posted electronically at the time of authorization.

3(c)(3) Wire or Other Similar Transfers

1.   *Fedwire and ACH.* If a financial institution makes a fund transfer to a consumer's account after receiving funds through Fedwire or a similar network, the transfer by ACH is covered by the regulation even though the Fedwire or network transfer is exempt.

2.   *Article 4A.* Financial institutions that offer telephone-initiated Fedwire payments are subject to the requirements of UCC section 4A–202, which encourages verification of Fedwire payment orders pursuant to a security procedure established by agreement between the consumer and the receiving bank. These transfers are not subject to Regulation E and the agreement is not considered a telephone plan if the service is offered separately from a telephone bill-payment or other prearranged plan subject to Regulation E. Regulation J of the Board of Governors of the Federal Reserve System (12 CFR part 210) specifies the rules applicable to funds handled by Federal Reserve Banks. To ensure that the rules for all fund transfers through Fedwire are consistent, the Board of Governors used its preemptive authority under UCC section 4A–107 to determine that subpart B of the Board's Regulation J, including the provisions of Article 4A, applies to all fund transfers through Fedwire, even if a portion of the fund transfer is governed by the EFTA. The portion of the fund transfer that is governed by the EFTA is not governed by subpart B of the Board's Regulation J.

3.   *Similar fund transfer systems.* Fund transfer systems that are similar to Fedwire include the Clearing House Interbank Payments System (CHIPS), Society for Worldwide Interbank Financial Telecommunication (SWIFT), Telex, and transfers made on the books of correspondent banks.

3(c)(4) Securities and Commodities Transfers

1.   *Coverage.* The securities exemption applies to securities and commodities that may be sold by a registered broker-dealer or futures commission merchant, even when the security or commodity itself is not regulated by the Securities and Exchange Commission or the Commodity Futures Trading Commission.

2.   *Example of exempt transfer.* The exemption applies to a transfer involving a transfer initiated by a telephone order to a stockbroker to buy or sell securities or to exercise a margin call.

3.   *Examples of nonexempt transfers.* The exemption does not apply to a transfer involving:

   i.   A debit card or other access device that accesses a securities or commodities account such as a money market mutual fund and that the consumer uses for purchasing goods or services or for obtaining cash.

   ii.   A payment of interest or dividends into the consumer's account (for example, from a brokerage firm or from a Federal Reserve Bank for government securities).

OFFICIAL INTERPRETATIONS OF REGULATION E

3(c)(5) Automatic Transfers by Account-Holding Institution

1. *Automatic transfers exempted.* The exemption applies to:

    i.   Electronic debits or credits to consumer accounts for check charges, stop-payment charges, non-sufficient funds (NSF) charges, overdraft charges, provisional credits, error adjustments, and similar items that are initiated automatically on the occurrence of certain events.

    ii.   Debits to consumer accounts for group insurance available only through the financial institution and payable only by means of an aggregate payment from the institution to the insurer.

    iii. EFTs between a thrift institution and its paired commercial bank in the state of Rhode Island, which are deemed under state law to be intra-institutional.

    iv.   Automatic transfers between a consumer's accounts within the same financial institution, even if the account holders on the two accounts are not identical.

2. *Automatic transfers not exempted.* Transfers between accounts of the consumer at affiliated institutions (such as between a bank and its subsidiary or within a holding company) are not intra-institutional transfers, and thus do not qualify for the exemption.

3(c)(6) Telephone-Initiated Transfers

1. *Written plan or agreement.* A transfer that the consumer initiates by telephone is covered by Regulation E if the transfer is made under a written plan or agreement between the consumer and the financial institution making the transfer. A written statement available to the public or to account holders that describes a service allowing a consumer to initiate transfers by telephone constitutes a plan; for example, a brochure, or material included with periodic statements. The following, however, do not by themselves constitute a written plan or agreement:

    i.   A hold-harmless agreement on a signature card that protects the institution if the consumer requests a transfer.

    ii.   A legend on a signature card, periodic statement, or passbook that limits the number of telephone-initiated transfers the consumer can make from a savings account because of reserve requirements under Regulation D of the Board of Governors of the Federal Reserve System (12 CFR part 204).

    iii. An agreement permitting the consumer to approve by telephone the rollover of funds at the maturity of an instrument.

2. *Examples of covered transfers.* When a written plan or agreement has been entered into, a transfer initiated by a telephone call from a consumer is covered even though:

    i.   An employee of the financial institution completes the transfer manually (for example, by means of a debit memo or deposit slip).

    ii.   The consumer is required to make a separate request for each transfer.

    iii. The consumer uses the plan infrequently.

    iv.   The consumer initiates the transfer via a facsimile machine.

    v.   The consumer initiates the transfer using a financial institution's audio-response or voice-response telephone system.

3(c)(7) Small Institutions

1. *Coverage.* This exemption is limited to preauthorized transfers; institutions that offer other EFTs must comply with the applicable sections of the regulation as to such services. The preauthorized transfers remain subject to sections 913, 916, and 917 of the Act and § 1005.10(e), and are therefore exempt from UCC Article 4A.

OFFICIAL INTERPRETATIONS OF REGULATION E

SECTION 1005.4 GENERAL DISCLOSURE REQUIREMENTS; JOINTLY OFFERED SERVICES

4(a) Form of Disclosures

1. *General.* Although no particular rules govern type size, number of pages, or the relative conspicuousness of various terms, the disclosures must be in a clear and readily understandable written form that the consumer may retain. Numbers or codes are considered readily understandable if explained elsewhere on the disclosure form.

2. *Foreign language disclosures.* Disclosures may be made in languages other than English, provided they are available in English upon request.

SECTION 1005.5 ISSUANCE OF ACCESS DEVICES

1. *Coverage.* The provisions of this section limit the circumstances under which a financial institution may issue an access device to a consumer. Making an additional account accessible through an existing access device is equivalent to issuing an access device and is subject to the limitations of this section.

5(a) Solicited Issuance

Paragraph 5(a)(1)

1. *Joint account.* For a joint account, a financial institution may issue an access device to each account holder if the requesting holder specifically authorizes the issuance.

2. *Permissible forms of request.* The request for an access device may be written or oral (for example, in response to a telephone solicitation by a card issuer).

Paragraph 5(a)(2)

1. *One-for-one rule.* In issuing a renewal or substitute access device, only one renewal or substitute device may replace a previously issued device. For example, only one new card and PIN may replace a card and PIN previously issued. A financial institution may provide additional devices at the time it issues the renewal or substitute access device, however, provided the institution complies with § 1005.5(b). *See* comment 5(b)–5. If the replacement device or the additional device permits either fewer or additional types of electronic fund transfer services, a change-in-terms notice or new disclosures are required.

2. *Renewal or substitution by a successor institution.* A successor institution is an entity that replaces the original financial institution (for example, following a corporate merger or acquisition) or that acquires accounts or assumes the operation of an EFT system.

5(b) Unsolicited Issuance

1. *Compliance.* A financial institution may issue an unsolicited access device (such as the combination of a debit card and PIN) if the institution's ATM system has been programmed not to accept the access device until after the consumer requests and the institution validates the device. Merely instructing a consumer not to use an unsolicited debit card and PIN until after the institution verifies the consumer's identity does not comply with the regulation.

2. *PINs.* A financial institution may impose no liability on a consumer for unauthorized transfers involving an unsolicited access device until the device becomes an "accepted access device" under the regulation. A card and PIN combination may be treated as an accepted access device once the consumer has used it to make a transfer.

3. *Functions of PIN.* If an institution issues a PIN at the consumer's request, the issuance may constitute both a way of validating the debit card and the means to identify the consumer (required as a condition of imposing liability for unauthorized transfers).

4. *Verification of identity.* To verify the consumer's identity, a financial institution may use any reasonable means, such as a photograph, fingerprint, personal visit, signature comparison, or personal information about the consumer. However, even if reasonable means were used, if an institution fails to verify correctly the consumer's identity and an imposter succeeds in having the device validated, the consumer is not liable for any unauthorized transfers from the account.

5. *Additional access devices in a renewal or substitution.* A financial institution may issue more than one access device in connection with the renewal or substitution of a previously issued accepted access device, provided that any additional access device (beyond the device replacing the accepted access device) is not validated at the time it is issued, and the institution complies with the other requirements of § 1005.5(b). The institution may, if it chooses, set up the validation procedure such that both the device replacing the previously issued device and the additional device are not validated at the time they are issued, and validation will apply to both devices. If the institution sets up the validation procedure in this way, the institution should provide a clear and readily understandable disclosure to the consumer that both devices are unvalidated and that validation will apply to both devices.

SECTION 1005.6 LIABILITY OF CONSUMER FOR UNAUTHORIZED TRANSFERS

6(a) Conditions for Liability

1. *Means of identification.* A financial institution may use various means for identifying the consumer to whom the access device is issued, including but not limited to:

    i.   Electronic or mechanical confirmation (such as a PIN).

    ii.   Comparison of the consumer's signature, fingerprint, or photograph.

2. *Multiple users.* When more than one access device is issued for an account, the financial institution may, but need not, provide a separate means to identify each user of the account.

6(b) Limitations on Amount of Liability

1. *Application of liability provisions.* There are three possible tiers of consumer liability for unauthorized EFTs depending on the situation. A consumer may be liable for: (1) up to $50; (2) up to $500; or (3) an unlimited amount depending on when the unauthorized EFT occurs. More than one tier may apply to a given situation because each corresponds to a different (sometimes overlapping) time period or set of conditions.

2. *Consumer negligence.* Negligence by the consumer cannot be used as the basis for imposing greater liability than is permissible under Regulation E. Thus, consumer behavior that may constitute negligence under state law, such as writing the PIN on a debit card or on a piece of paper kept with the card, does not affect the consumer's liability for unauthorized transfers. (However, refer to comment 2(m)–2 regarding termination of the authority of given by the consumer to another person.)

3. *Limits on liability.* The extent of the consumer's liability is determined solely by the consumer's promptness in reporting the loss or theft of an access device. Similarly, no agreement between the consumer and an institution may impose greater liability on the consumer for an unauthorized transfer than the limits provided in Regulation E.

6(b)(1) Timely Notice Given

1. *$50 limit applies.* The basic liability limit is $50. For example, the consumer's card is lost or stolen on Monday and the consumer learns of the loss or theft on Wednesday. If the consumer notifies the financial institution within two business days of learning of the loss or theft (by midnight Friday), the consumer's liability is limited to $50 or the amount of the unauthorized transfers that occurred before notification, whichever is less.

2. *Knowledge of loss or theft of access device.* The fact that a consumer has received a periodic statement that reflects unauthorized transfers may be a factor in determining whether the consumer had knowledge of the loss or theft, but cannot be deemed to represent conclusive evidence that the consumer had such knowledge.

3. *Two business day rule.* The two business day period does not include the day the consumer learns of the loss or theft or any day that is not a business day. The rule is calculated based on two 24-hour periods, without regard to the financial institution's business hours or the time of day that the consumer learns of the loss or theft. For example, a consumer learns of the loss or theft at 6 p.m. on Friday. Assuming that

OFFICIAL INTERPRETATIONS OF REGULATION E

Saturday is a business day and Sunday is not, the two business day period begins on Saturday and expires at 11:59 p.m. on Monday, not at the end of the financial institution's business day on Monday.

6(b)(2) Timely Notice Not Given

1. *$500 limit applies.* The second tier of liability is $500. For example, the consumer's card is stolen on Monday and the consumer learns of the theft that same day. The consumer reports the theft on Friday. The $500 limit applies because the consumer failed to notify the financial institution within two business days of learning of the theft (which would have been by midnight Wednesday). How much the consumer is actually liable for, however, depends on when the unauthorized transfers take place. In this example, assume a $100 unauthorized transfer was made on Tuesday and a $600 unauthorized transfer on Thursday. Because the consumer is liable for the amount of the loss that occurs within the first two business days (but no more than $50), plus the amount of the unauthorized transfers that occurs after the first two business days and before the consumer gives notice, the consumer's total liability is $500 ($50 of the $100 transfer plus $450 of the $600 transfer, in this example). But if $600 was taken on Tuesday and $100 on Thursday, the consumer's maximum liability would be $150 ($50 of the $600 plus $100).

6(b)(3) Periodic Statement; Timely Notice Not Given

1. *Unlimited liability applies.* The standard of unlimited liability applies if unauthorized transfers appear on a periodic statement, and may apply in conjunction with the first two tiers of liability. If a periodic statement shows an unauthorized transfer made with a lost or stolen debit card, the consumer must notify the financial institution within 60 calendar days after the periodic statement was sent; otherwise, the consumer faces unlimited liability for all unauthorized transfers made after the 60-day period. The consumer's liability for unauthorized transfers before the statement is sent, and up to 60 days following, is determined based on the first two tiers of liability: up to $50 if the consumer notifies the financial institution within two business days of learning of the loss or theft of the card and up to $500 if the consumer notifies the institution after two business days of learning of the loss or theft.

2. *Transfers not involving access device.* The first two tiers of liability do not apply to unauthorized transfers from a consumer's account made without an access device. If, however, the consumer fails to report such unauthorized transfers within 60 calendar days of the financial institution's transmittal of the periodic statement, the consumer may be liable for any transfers occurring after the close of the 60 days and before notice is given to the institution. For example, a consumer's account is electronically debited for $200 without the consumer's authorization and by means other than the consumer's access device. If the consumer notifies the institution within 60 days of the transmittal of the periodic statement that shows the unauthorized transfer, the consumer has no liability. However, if in addition to the $200, the consumer's account is debited for a $400 unauthorized transfer on the 61st day and the consumer fails to notify the institution of the first unauthorized transfer until the 62nd day, the consumer may be liable for the full $400.

6(b)(4) Extension of Time Limits

1. *Extenuating circumstances.* Examples of circumstances that require extension of the notification periods under this section include the consumer's extended travel or hospitalization.

6(b)(5) Notice to Financial Institution

1. *Receipt of notice.* A financial institution is considered to have received notice for purposes of limiting the consumer's liability if notice is given in a reasonable manner, even if the consumer notifies the institution but uses an address or telephone number other than the one specified by the institution.

2. *Notice by third party.* Notice to a financial institution by a person acting on the consumer's behalf is considered valid under this section. For example, if a consumer is hospitalized and unable to report the loss or theft of an access device, notice is considered given when someone acting on the consumer's behalf notifies the bank of the loss or theft. A financial institution may require appropriate documentation from the person representing the consumer to establish that the person is acting on the consumer's behalf.

3. *Content of notice.* Notice to a financial institution is considered given when a consumer takes reasonable steps to provide the institution with the pertinent account information. Even when the consumer is unable to provide the account number or the card number in reporting a lost or stolen access device or an

unauthorized transfer, the notice effectively limits the consumer's liability if the consumer otherwise identifies sufficiently the account in question. For example, the consumer may identify the account by the name on the account and the type of account in question.

SECTION 1005.7 INITIAL DISCLOSURES
7(a) Timing of Disclosures

1. *Early disclosures.* Disclosures given by a financial institution earlier than the regulation requires (for example, when the consumer opens a checking account) need not be repeated when the consumer later enters into an agreement with a third party to initiate preauthorized transfers to or from the consumer's account, unless the terms and conditions differ from those that the institution previously disclosed. This interpretation also applies to any notice provided about one-time EFTs from a consumer's account initiated using information from the consumer's check. On the other hand, if an agreement for EFT services to be provided by an account-holding institution is directly between the consumer and the account-holding institution, disclosures must be given in close proximity to the event requiring disclosure, for example, when the consumer contracts for a new service.

2. *Lack of advance notice of a transfer.* Where a consumer authorizes a third party to debit or credit the consumer's account, an account-holding institution that has not received advance notice of the transfer or transfers must provide the required disclosures as soon as reasonably possible after the first debit or credit is made, unless the institution has previously given the disclosures.

3. *Addition of new accounts.* If a consumer opens a new account permitting EFTs at a financial institution, and the consumer already has received Regulation E disclosures for another account at that institution, the institution need only disclose terms and conditions that differ from those previously given.

4. *Addition of service in interchange systems.* If a financial institution joins an interchange or shared network system (which provides access to terminals operated by other institutions), disclosures are required for additional EFT services not previously available to consumers if the terms and conditions differ from those previously disclosed.

5. *Disclosures covering all EFT services offered.* An institution may provide disclosures covering all EFT services that it offers, even if some consumers have not arranged to use all services.

7(b) Content of Disclosures
7(b)(1) Liability of Consumer

1. *No liability imposed by financial institution.* If a financial institution chooses to impose zero liability for unauthorized EFTs, it need not provide the liability disclosures. If the institution later decides to impose liability, however, it must first provide the disclosures.

2. *Preauthorized transfers.* If the only EFTs from an account are preauthorized transfers, liability could arise if the consumer fails to report unauthorized transfers reflected on a periodic statement. To impose such liability on the consumer, the institution must have disclosed the potential liability and the telephone number and address for reporting unauthorized transfers.

3. *Additional information.* At the institution's option, the summary of the consumer's liability may include advice on promptly reporting unauthorized transfers or the loss or theft of the access device.

7(b)(2) Telephone Number and Address

1. *Disclosure of telephone numbers.* An institution may use the same or different telephone numbers in the disclosures for the purpose of:

    i.   Reporting the loss or theft of an access device or possible unauthorized transfers;

    ii. Inquiring about the receipt of a preauthorized credit;

    iii. Stopping payment of a preauthorized debit;

    iv. Giving notice of an error.

OFFICIAL INTERPRETATIONS OF REGULATION E

2.   *Location of telephone number.* The telephone number need not be incorporated into the text of the disclosure; for example, the institution may instead insert a reference to a telephone number that is readily available to the consumer, such as "Call your branch office. The number is shown on your periodic statement." However, an institution must provide a specific telephone number and address, on or with the disclosure statement, for reporting a lost or stolen access device or a possible unauthorized transfer.

7(b)(4) Types of Transfers; Limitations

1.   *Security limitations.* Information about limitations on the frequency and dollar amount of transfers generally must be disclosed in detail, even if related to security aspects of the system. If the confidentiality of certain details is essential to the security of an account or system, these details may be withheld (but the fact that limitations exist must still be disclosed). For example, an institution limits cash ATM withdrawals to $100 per day. The institution may disclose that daily withdrawal limitations apply and need not disclose that the limitations may not always be in force (such as during periods when its ATMs are off-line).

2.   *Restrictions on certain deposit accounts.* A limitation on account activity that restricts the consumer's ability to make EFTs must be disclosed even if the restriction also applies to transfers made by non-electronic means. For example, Regulation D of the Board of Governors of the Federal Reserve System (12 CFR part 204) restricts the number of payments to third parties that may be made from a money market deposit account; an institution that does not execute fund transfers in excess of those limits must disclose the restriction as a limitation on the frequency of EFTs.

3.   *Preauthorized transfers.* Financial institutions are not required to list preauthorized transfers among the types of transfers that a consumer can make.

4.   *One-time EFTs initiated using information from a check.* Financial institutions must disclose the fact that one-time EFTs initiated using information from a consumer's check are among the types of transfers that a consumer can make. *See* appendix A–2.

7(b)(5) Fees

1.   *Disclosure of EFT fees.* An institution is required to disclose all fees for EFTs or the right to make them. Others fees (for example, minimum-balance fees, stop-payment fees, or account overdrafts) may, but need not, be disclosed. *But see* Regulation DD, 12 CFR part 1030. An institution is not required to disclose fees for inquiries made at an ATM since no transfer of funds is involved.

2.   *Fees also applicable to non-EFT.* A per-item fee for EFTs must be disclosed even if the same fee is imposed on non-electronic transfers. If a per-item fee is imposed only under certain conditions, such as when the transactions in the cycle exceed a certain number, those conditions must be disclosed. Itemization of the various fees may be provided on the disclosure statement or on an accompanying document that is referenced in the statement.

3.   *Interchange system fees.* Fees paid by the account-holding institution to the operator of a shared or interchange ATM system need not be disclosed, unless they are imposed on the consumer by the account-holding institution. Fees for use of an ATM that are debited directly from the consumer's account by an institution other than the account-holding institution (for example, fees included in the transfer amount) need not be disclosed. *See* § 1005.7(b)(11) for the general notice requirement regarding fees that may be imposed by ATM operators and by a network used to complete the transfer.

7(b)(9) Confidentiality

1.   *Information provided to third parties.* An institution must describe the circumstances under which any information relating to an account to or from which EFTs are permitted will be made available to third parties, not just information concerning those EFTs. The term "third parties" includes affiliates such as other subsidiaries of the same holding company.

7(b)(10) Error Resolution

1.   *Substantially similar.* The error resolution notice must be substantially similar to the model form in appendix A of part 1005. An institution may use different wording so long as the substance of the notice remains the same, may delete inapplicable provisions (for example, the requirement for written

confirmation of an oral notification), and may substitute substantive state law requirements affording greater consumer protection than Regulation E.

2.   *Extended time-period for certain transactions.* To take advantage of the longer time periods for resolving errors under § 1005.11(c)(3) (for new accounts as defined in Regulation CC of the Board of Governors of the Federal Reserve System (12 CFR part 229), transfers initiated outside the United States, or transfers resulting from POS debit-card transactions), a financial institution must have disclosed these longer time periods. Similarly, an institution that relies on the exception from provisional crediting in § 1005.11(c)(2) for accounts subject to Regulation T of the Board of Governors of the Federal Reserve System (12 CFR part 220) must have disclosed accordingly.

7(c) Addition of Electronic Fund Transfer Services

1.   *Addition of electronic check conversion services.* One-time EFTs initiated using information from a consumer's check are a new type of transfer requiring new disclosures, as applicable. *See* appendix A–2.

SECTION 1005.8 CHANGE-IN-TERMS NOTICE; ERROR RESOLUTION NOTICE

8(a) Change-in-Terms Notice

1.   *Form of notice.* No specific form or wording is required for a change-in-terms notice. The notice may appear on a periodic statement, or may be given by sending a copy of a revised disclosure statement, provided attention is directed to the change (for example, in a cover letter referencing the changed term).

2.   *Changes not requiring notice.* The following changes do not require disclosure:

    i.   Closing some of an institution's ATMs;

    ii.   Cancellation of an access device.

3.   *Limitations on transfers.* When the initial disclosures omit details about limitations because secrecy is essential to the security of the account or system, a subsequent increase in those limitations need not be disclosed if secrecy is still essential. If, however, an institution had no limits in place when the initial disclosures were given and now wishes to impose limits for the first time, it must disclose at least the fact that limits have been adopted. *See also* § 1005.7(b)(4) and the related commentary.

4.   *Change in telephone number or address.* When a financial institution changes the telephone number or address used for reporting possible unauthorized transfers, a change-in-terms notice is required only if the institution will impose liability on the consumer for unauthorized transfers under § 1005.6. *See also* § 1005.6(a) and the related commentary.

8(b) Error Resolution Notice

1.   *Change between annual and periodic notice.* If an institution switches from an annual to a periodic notice, or vice versa, the first notice under the new method must be sent no later than 12 months after the last notice sent under the old method.

2.   *Exception for new accounts.* For new accounts, disclosure of the longer error resolution time periods under § 1005.11(c)(3) is not required in the annual error resolution notice or in the notice that may be provided with each periodic statement as an alternative to the annual notice.

SECTION 1005.9 RECEIPTS AT ELECTRONIC TERMINALS; PERIODIC STATEMENTS

9(a) Receipts at Electronic Terminals

1.   *Receipts furnished only on request.* The regulation requires that a receipt be "made available." A financial institution may program its electronic terminals to provide a receipt only to consumers who elect to receive one.

2.   *Third party providing receipt.* An account-holding institution may make terminal receipts available through third parties such as merchants or other financial institutions.

3.   *Inclusion of promotional material.* A financial institution may include promotional material on receipts if the required information is set forth clearly (for example, by separating it from the promotional material).

OFFICIAL INTERPRETATIONS OF REGULATION E

In addition, a consumer may not be required to surrender the receipt or that portion containing the required disclosures in order to take advantage of a promotion.

4. *Transfer not completed.* The receipt requirement does not apply to a transfer that is initiated but not completed (for example, if the ATM is out of currency or the consumer decides not to complete the transfer).

5. *Receipts not furnished due to inadvertent error.* If a receipt is not provided to the consumer because of a bona fide unintentional error, such as when a terminal runs out of paper or the mechanism jams, no violation results if the financial institution maintains procedures reasonably adapted to avoid such occurrences.

6. *Multiple transfers.* If the consumer makes multiple transfers at the same time, the financial institution may document them on a single or on separate receipts.

9(a)(1) Amount

1. *Disclosure of transaction fee.* The required display of a fee amount on or at the terminal may be accomplished by displaying the fee on a sign at the terminal or on the terminal screen for a reasonable duration. Displaying the fee on a screen provides adequate notice, as long as a consumer is given the option to cancel the transaction after receiving notice of a fee. *See* § 1005.16 for the notice requirements applicable to ATM operators that impose a fee for providing EFT services.

2. *Relationship between § 1005.9(a)(1) and § 1005.16.* The requirements of §§ 1005.9(a)(1) and 1005.16 are similar but not identical.

    i.   Section 1005.9(a)(1) requires that if the amount of the transfer as shown on the receipt will include the fee, then the fee must be disclosed either on a sign on or at the terminal, or on the terminal screen. Section 1005.16 requires disclosure both on a sign on or at the terminal (in a prominent and conspicuous location) and on the terminal screen. Section 1005.16 permits disclosure on a paper notice as an alternative to the on-screen disclosure.

    ii.   The disclosure of the fee on the receipt under § 1005.9(a)(1) cannot be used to comply with the alternative paper disclosure procedure under § 1005.16, if the receipt is provided at the completion of the transaction because, pursuant to the statute, the paper notice must be provided before the consumer is committed to paying the fee.

    iii.   Section 1005.9(a)(1) applies to any type of electronic terminal as defined in Regulation E (for example, to POS terminals as well as to ATMs), while § 1005.16 applies only to ATMs.

9(a)(2) Date

1. *Calendar date.* The receipt must disclose the calendar date on which the consumer uses the electronic terminal. An accounting or business date may be disclosed in addition if the dates are clearly distinguished.

9(a)(3) Type

1. *Identifying transfer and account.* Examples identifying the type of transfer and the type of the consumer's account include "withdrawal from checking," "transfer from savings to checking," or "payment from savings."

2. *Exception.* Identification of an account is not required when the consumer can access only one asset account at a particular time or terminal, even if the access device can normally be used to access more than one account. For example, the consumer may be able to access only one particular account at terminals not operated by the account-holding institution, or may be able to access only one particular account when the terminal is off-line. The exception is available even if, in addition to accessing one asset account, the consumer also can access a credit line.

3. *Access to multiple accounts.* If the consumer can use an access device to make transfers to or from different accounts of the same type, the terminal receipt must specify which account was accessed, such as "withdrawal from checking I" or "withdrawal from checking II." If only one account besides the primary checking account can be debited, the receipt can identify the account as "withdrawal from other account."

OFFICIAL INTERPRETATIONS OF REGULATION E

4. *Generic descriptions.* Generic descriptions may be used for accounts that are similar in function, such as share draft or NOW accounts and checking accounts. In a shared system, for example, when a credit union member initiates transfers to or from a share draft account at a terminal owned or operated by a bank, the receipt may identify a withdrawal from the account as a "withdrawal from checking."

5. *Point-of-sale transactions.* There is no prescribed terminology for identifying a transfer at a merchant's POS terminal. A transfer may be identified, for example, as a purchase, a sale of goods or services, or a payment to a third party. When a consumer obtains cash from a POS terminal in addition to purchasing goods, or obtains cash only, the documentation need not differentiate the transaction from one involving the purchase of goods.

9(a)(5) Terminal Location

1. *Options for identifying terminal.* The institution may provide either:

   i. The city, state or foreign country, and the information in § 1005.9(a)(5) (i), (ii), or (iii), or

   ii. A number or a code identifying the terminal. If the institution chooses the second option, the code or terminal number identifying the terminal where the transfer is initiated may be given as part of a transaction code.

2. *Omission of city name.* The city may be omitted if the generally accepted name (such as a branch name) contains the city name.

3. *Omission of a state.* A state may be omitted from the location information on the receipt if:

   i. All the terminals owned or operated by the financial institution providing the statement (or by the system in which it participates) are located in that state, or

   ii. All transfers occur at terminals located within 50 miles of the financial institution's main office.

4. *Omission of a city and state.* A city and state may be omitted if all the terminals owned or operated by the financial institution providing the statement (or by the system in which it participates) are located in the same city.

Paragraph 9(a)(5)(i)

1. *Street address.* The address should include number and street (or intersection); the number (or intersecting street) may be omitted if the street alone uniquely identifies the terminal location.

Paragraph 9(a)(5)(ii)

1. *Generally accepted name.* Examples of a generally accepted name for a specific location include a branch of the financial institution, a shopping center, or an airport.

Paragraph 9(a)(5)(iii)

1. *Name of owner or operator of terminal.* Examples of an owner or operator of a terminal are a financial institution or a retail merchant.

9(a)(6) Third Party Transfer

1. *Omission of third-party name.* The receipt need not disclose the third-party name if the name is provided by the consumer in a form that is not machine readable (for example, if the consumer indicates the payee by depositing a payment stub into the ATM). If, on the other hand, the consumer keys in the identity of the payee, the receipt must identify the payee by name or by using a code that is explained elsewhere on the receipt.

2. *Receipt as proof of payment.* Documentation required under the regulation constitutes prima facie proof of a payment to another person, except in the case of a terminal receipt documenting a deposit.

9(b) Periodic Statements

1. *Periodic cycles.* Periodic statements may be sent on a cycle that is shorter than monthly. The statements must correspond to periodic cycles that are reasonably equal, that is, do not vary by more than

four days from the regular cycle. The requirement of reasonably equal cycles does not apply when an institution changes cycles for operational or other reasons, such as to establish a new statement day or date.

2. *Interim statements.* Generally, a financial institution must provide periodic statements for each monthly cycle in which an EFT occurs, and at least quarterly if a transfer has not occurred. Where EFTs occur between regularly-scheduled cycles, interim statements must be provided. For example, if an institution issues quarterly statements at the end of March, June, September and December, and the consumer initiates an EFT in February, an interim statement for February must be provided. If an interim statement contains interest or rate information, the institution must comply with Regulation DD, 12 CFR 1030.6.

3. *Inactive accounts.* A financial institution need not send statements to consumers whose accounts are inactive as defined by the institution.

4. *Statement pickup.* A financial institution may permit, but may not require, consumers to pick up their periodic statements at the financial institution.

5. *Periodic statements limited to EFT activity.* A financial institution that uses a passbook as the primary means for displaying account activity, but also allows the account to be debited electronically, may provide a periodic statement requirement that reflects only the EFTs and other required disclosures (such as charges, account balances, and address and telephone number for inquiries). *See* § 1005.9(c)(1)(i) for the exception applicable to preauthorized transfers for passbook accounts.

6. *Codes and accompanying documents.* To meet the documentation requirements for periodic statements, a financial institution may:

   i.   Include copies of terminal receipts to reflect transfers initiated by the consumer at electronic terminals;

   ii. Enclose posting memos, deposit slips, and other documents that, together with the statement, disclose all the required information;

   iii. Use codes for names of third parties or terminal locations and explain the information to which the codes relate on an accompanying document.

9(b)(1) Transaction Information

1. *Information obtained from others.* While financial institutions must maintain reasonable procedures to ensure the integrity of data obtained from another institution, a merchant, or other third parties, verification of each transfer that appears on the periodic statement is not required.

Paragraph 9(b)(1)(i)

1. *Incorrect deposit amount.* If a financial institution determines that the amount actually deposited at an ATM is different from the amount entered by the consumer, the institution need not immediately notify the consumer of the discrepancy. The periodic statement reflecting the deposit may show either the correct amount of the deposit or the amount entered by the consumer along with the institution's adjustment.

Paragraph 9(b)(1)(iii)

1. *Type of transfer.* There is no prescribed terminology for describing a type of transfer. Placement of the amount of the transfer in the debit or the credit column is sufficient if other information on the statement, such as a terminal location or third-party name, enables the consumer to identify the type of transfer.

Paragraph 9(b)(1)(iv)

1. *Nonproprietary terminal in network.* An institution need not reflect on the periodic statement the street addresses, identification codes, or terminal numbers for transfers initiated in a shared or interchange system at a terminal operated by an institution other than the account-holding institution. The statement must, however, specify the entity that owns or operates the terminal, plus the city and state.

OFFICIAL INTERPRETATIONS OF REGULATION E

Paragraph 9(b)(1)(v)

1.   *Recurring payments by government agency.* The third-party name for recurring payments from Federal, state, or local governments need not list the particular agency. For example, "U.S. gov't" or "N.Y. sal" will suffice.

2.   *Consumer as third-party payee.* If a consumer makes an electronic fund transfer to another consumer, the financial institution must identify the recipient by name (not just by an account number, for example).

3.   *Terminal location/third party.* A single entry may be used to identify both the terminal location and the name of the third party to or from whom funds are transferred. For example, if a consumer purchases goods from a merchant, the name of the party to whom funds are transferred (the merchant) and the location of the terminal where the transfer is initiated will be satisfied by a disclosure such as "XYZ Store, Anytown, Ohio."

4.   *Account-holding institution as third party.* Transfers to the account-holding institution (by ATM, for example) must show the institution as the recipient, unless other information on the statement (such as, "loan payment from checking") clearly indicates that the payment was to the account-holding institution.

5.   *Consistency in third-party identity.* The periodic statement must disclose a third-party name as it appeared on the receipt, whether it was, for example, the "dba" (doing business as) name of the third party or the parent corporation's name.

6.   *Third-party identity on deposits at electronic terminal.* A financial institution need not identify third parties whose names appear on checks, drafts, or similar paper instruments deposited to the consumer's account at an electronic terminal.

9(b)(3) Fees

1.   *Disclosure of fees.* The fees disclosed may include fees for EFTs and for other non-electronic services, and both fixed fees and per-item fees; they may be given as a total or may be itemized in part or in full.

2.   *Fees in interchange system.* An account-holding institution must disclose any fees it imposes on the consumer for EFTs, including fees for ATM transactions in an interchange or shared ATM system. Fees for use of an ATM imposed on the consumer by an institution other than the account-holding institution and included in the amount of the transfer by the terminal-operating institution need not be separately disclosed on the periodic statement.

3.   *Finance charges.* The requirement to disclose any fees assessed against the account does not include a finance charge imposed on the account during the statement period.

9(b)(4) Account Balances

1.   *Opening and closing balances.* The opening and closing balances must reflect both EFTs and other account activity.

9(b)(5) Address and Telephone Number for Inquiries

1.   *Telephone number.* A single telephone number, preceded by the "direct inquiries to" language, will satisfy the requirements of §§ 1005.9(b)(5) and (6).

9(b)(6) Telephone Number for Preauthorized Transfers

1.   *Telephone number. See* comment 9(b)(5)–1.

9(c) Exceptions to the Periodic Statement Requirements for Certain Accounts

1.   *Transfers between accounts.* The regulation provides an exception from the periodic statement requirement for certain intra-institutional transfers between a consumer's accounts. The financial institution must still comply with the applicable periodic statement requirements for any other EFTs to or from the account. For example, a Regulation E statement must be provided quarterly for an account that also receives payroll deposits electronically, or for any month in which an account is also accessed by a withdrawal at an ATM.

OFFICIAL INTERPRETATIONS OF REGULATION E

9(c)(1) Preauthorized Transfers to Accounts

1. *Accounts that may be accessed only by preauthorized transfers to the account.* The exception for "accounts that may be accessed only by preauthorized transfers to the account" includes accounts that can be accessed by means other than EFTs, such as checks. If, however, an account may be accessed by any EFT other than preauthorized credits to the account, such as preauthorized debits or ATM transactions, the account does not qualify for the exception.

2. *Reversal of direct deposits.* For direct-deposit-only accounts, a financial institution must send a periodic statement at least quarterly. A reversal of a direct deposit to correct an error does not trigger the monthly statement requirement when the error represented a credit to the wrong consumer's account, a duplicate credit, or a credit in the wrong amount. *See also* comment 2(m)–5.

9(d) Documentation for Foreign-Initiated Transfers

1. *Foreign-initiated transfers.* An institution must make a good faith effort to provide all required information for foreign-initiated transfers. For example, even if the institution is not able to provide a specific terminal location, it should identify the country and city in which the transfer was initiated.

SECTION 1005.10 PREAUTHORIZED TRANSFERS

10(a) Preauthorized Transfers to Consumer's Account

10(a)(1) Notice by Financial Institution

1. *Content.* No specific language is required for notice regarding receipt of a preauthorized transfer. Identifying the deposit is sufficient; however, simply providing the current account balance is not.

2. *Notice of credit.* A financial institution may use different methods of notice for various types or series of preauthorized transfers, and the institution need not offer consumers a choice of notice methods.

3. *Positive notice.* A periodic statement sent within two business days of the scheduled transfer, showing the transfer, can serve as notice of receipt.

4. *Negative notice.* The absence of a deposit entry (on a periodic statement sent within two business days of the scheduled transfer date) will serve as negative notice.

5. *Telephone notice.* If a financial institution uses the telephone notice option, the institution should be able in most instances to verify during a consumer's initial call whether a transfer was received. The institution must respond within two business days to any inquiry not answered immediately.

6. *Phone number for passbook accounts.* The financial institution may use any reasonable means necessary to provide the telephone number to consumers with passbook accounts that can only be accessed by preauthorized credits and that do not receive periodic statements. For example, it may print the telephone number in the passbook, or include the number with the annual error resolution notice.

7. *Telephone line availability.* To satisfy the readily-available standard, the financial institution must provide enough telephone lines so that consumers get a reasonably prompt response. The institution need only provide telephone service during normal business hours. Within its primary service area, an institution must provide a local or toll-free telephone number. It need not provide a toll-free number or accept collect long-distance calls from outside the area where it normally conducts business.

10(b) Written Authorization for Preauthorized Transfers from Consumer's Account

1. *Preexisting authorizations.* The financial institution need not require a new authorization before changing from paper-based to electronic debiting when the existing authorization does not specify that debiting is to occur electronically or specifies that the debiting will occur by paper means. A new authorization also is not required when a successor institution begins collecting payments.

2. *Authorization obtained by third party.* The account-holding financial institution does not violate the regulation when a third-party payee fails to obtain the authorization in writing or fails to give a copy to the consumer; rather, it is the third-party payee that is in violation of the regulation.

OFFICIAL INTERPRETATIONS OF REGULATION E

3. *Written authorization for preauthorized transfers.* The requirement that preauthorized EFTs be authorized by the consumer "only by a writing" cannot be met by a payee's signing a written authorization on the consumer's behalf with only an oral authorization from the consumer.

4. *Use of a confirmation form.* A financial institution or designated payee may comply with the requirements of this section in various ways. For example, a payee may provide the consumer with two copies of a preauthorization form, and ask the consumer to sign and return one and to retain the second copy.

5. *Similarly authenticated.* The similarly authenticated standard permits signed, written authorizations to be provided electronically. The writing and signature requirements of this section are satisfied by complying with the Electronic Signatures in Global and National Commerce Act, 15 U.S.C. 7001 *et seq.,* which defines electronic records and electronic signatures. Examples of electronic signatures include, but are not limited to, digital signatures and security codes. A security code need not originate with the account-holding institution. The authorization process should evidence the consumer's identity and assent to the authorization. The person that obtains the authorization must provide a copy of the terms of the authorization to the consumer either electronically or in paper form. Only the consumer may authorize the transfer and not, for example, a third-party merchant on behalf of the consumer.

6. *Requirements of an authorization.* An authorization is valid if it is readily identifiable as such and the terms of the preauthorized transfer are clear and readily understandable.

7. *Bona fide error.* Consumers sometimes authorize third-party payees, by telephone or online, to submit recurring charges against a credit card account. If the consumer indicates use of a credit card account when in fact a debit card is being used, the payee does not violate the requirement to obtain a written authorization if the failure to obtain written authorization was not intentional and resulted from a bona fide error, and if the payee maintains procedures reasonably adapted to avoid any such error. Procedures reasonably adapted to avoid error will depend upon the circumstances. Generally, requesting the consumer to specify whether the card to be used for the authorization is a debit (or check) card or a credit card is a reasonable procedure. Where the consumer has indicated that the card is a credit card (or that the card is not a debit or check card), the payee may rely on the consumer's statement without seeking further information about the type of card. If the payee believes, at the time of the authorization, that a credit card is involved, and later finds that the card used is a debit card (for example, because the consumer later brings the matter to the payee's attention), the payee must obtain a written and signed or (where appropriate) a similarly authenticated authorization as soon as reasonably possible, or cease debiting the consumer's account.

10(c) Consumer's Right to Stop Payment

1. *Stop-payment order.* The financial institution must honor an oral stop-payment order made at least three business days before a scheduled debit. If the debit item is resubmitted, the institution must continue to honor the stop-payment order (for example, by suspending all subsequent payments to the payee-originator until the consumer notifies the institution that payments should resume).

2. *Revocation of authorization.* Once a financial institution has been notified that the consumer's authorization is no longer valid, it must block all future payments for the particular debit transmitted by the designated payee-originator. *But see* comment 10(c)–3. The institution may not wait for the payee-originator to terminate the automatic debits. The institution may confirm that the consumer has informed the payee-originator of the revocation (for example, by requiring a copy of the consumer's revocation as written confirmation to be provided within 14 days of an oral notification). If the institution does not receive the required written confirmation within the 14-day period, it may honor subsequent debits to the account.

3. *Alternative procedure for processing a stop-payment request.* If an institution does not have the capability to block a preauthorized debit from being posted to the consumer's account—as in the case of a preauthorized debit made through a debit card network or other system, for example—the institution may instead comply with the stop-payment requirements by using a third party to block the transfer(s), as long as the consumer's account is not debited for the payment.

OFFICIAL INTERPRETATIONS OF REGULATION E

10(d) Notice of Transfers Varying in Amount

10(d)(1) Notice

1. *Preexisting authorizations.* A financial institution holding the consumer's account does not violate the regulation if the designated payee fails to provide notice of varying amounts.

10(d)(2) Range

1. *Range.* A financial institution or designated payee that elects to offer the consumer a specified range of amounts for debiting (in lieu of providing the notice of transfers varying in amount) must provide an acceptable range that could be anticipated by the consumer. For example, if the transfer is for payment of a gas bill, an appropriate range might be based on the highest bill in winter and the lowest bill in summer.

2. *Transfers to an account of the consumer held at another institution.* A financial institution need not provide a consumer the option of receiving notice with each varying transfer, and may instead provide notice only when a debit to an account of the consumer falls outside a specified range or differs by more than a specified amount from the most recent transfer, if the funds are transferred and credited to an account of the consumer held at another financial institution. The specified range or amount, however, must be one that reasonably could be anticipated by the consumer, and the institution must notify the consumer of the range or amount at the time the consumer provides authorization for the preauthorized transfers. For example, if the transfer is for payment of interest for a fixed-rate certificate of deposit account, an appropriate range might be based on a month containing 28 days and a month containing 31 days.

10(e) Compulsory Use

10(e)(1) Credit

1. *Loan payments.* Creditors may not require repayment of loans by electronic means on a preauthorized, recurring basis. A creditor may offer a program with a reduced annual percentage rate or other cost-related incentive for an automatic repayment feature, provided the program with the automatic payment feature is not the only loan program offered by the creditor for the type of credit involved. Examples include:

    i.   Mortgages with graduated payments in which a pledged savings account is automatically debited during an initial period to supplement the monthly payments made by the borrower.

    ii.   Mortgage plans calling for preauthorized biweekly payments that are debited electronically to the consumer's account and produce a lower total finance charge.

2. *Overdraft.* A financial institution may require the automatic repayment of an overdraft credit plan even if the overdraft extension is charged to an open-end account that may be accessed by the consumer in ways other than by overdrafts.

10(e)(2) Employment or Government Benefit

1. *Payroll.* An employer (including a financial institution) may not require its employees to receive their salary by direct deposit to any particular institution. An employer may require direct deposit of salary by electronic means if employees are allowed to choose the institution that will receive the direct deposit. Alternatively, an employer may give employees the choice of having their salary deposited at a particular institution (designated by the employer) or receiving their salary by another means, such as by check or cash.

SECTION 1005.11 PROCEDURES FOR RESOLVING ERRORS

11(a) Definition of Error

1. *Terminal location.* With regard to deposits at an ATM, a consumer's request for the terminal location or other information triggers the error resolution procedures, but the financial institution need only provide the ATM location if it has captured that information.

2. *Verifying an account debit or credit.* If the consumer contacts the financial institution to ascertain whether a payment (for example, in a home-banking or bill-payment program) or any other type of EFT was debited to the account, or whether a deposit made via ATM, preauthorized transfer, or any other type of EFT was credited to the account, without asserting an error, the error resolution procedures do not apply.

3. *Loss or theft of access device.* A financial institution is required to comply with the error resolution procedures when a consumer reports the loss or theft of an access device if the consumer also alleges possible unauthorized use as a consequence of the loss or theft.

4. *Error asserted after account closed.* The financial institution must comply with the error resolution procedures when a consumer properly asserts an error, even if the account has been closed.

5. *Request for documentation or information.* A request for documentation or other information must be treated as an error unless it is clear that the consumer is requesting a duplicate copy for tax or other record-keeping purposes.

6. *Terminal receipts for transfers of $15 or less.* The fact that an institution does not make a terminal receipt available for a transfer of $15 or less in accordance with § 1005.9(e) is not an error for purposes of § 1005.11(a)(1)(vi) or (vii).

11(b) Notice of Error From Consumer

11(b)(1) Timing; Contents

1. *Content of error notice.* The notice of error is effective even if it does not contain the consumer's account number, so long as the financial institution is able to identify the account in question. For example, the consumer could provide a Social Security number or other unique means of identification.

2. *Investigation pending receipt of information.* While a financial institution may request a written, signed statement from the consumer relating to a notice of error, it may not delay initiating or completing an investigation pending receipt of the statement.

3. *Statement held for consumer.* When a consumer has arranged for periodic statements to be held until picked up, the statement for a particular cycle is deemed to have been transmitted on the date the financial institution first makes the statement available to the consumer.

4. *Failure to provide statement.* When a financial institution fails to provide the consumer with a periodic statement, a request for a copy is governed by this section if the consumer gives notice within 60 days from the date on which the statement should have been transmitted.

5. *Discovery of error by institution.* The error resolution procedures of this section apply when a notice of error is received from the consumer, and not when the financial institution itself discovers and corrects an error.

6. *Notice at particular phone number or address.* A financial institution may require the consumer to give notice only at the telephone number or address disclosed by the institution, provided the institution maintains reasonable procedures to refer the consumer to the specified telephone number or address if the consumer attempts to give notice to the institution in a different manner.

7. *Effect of late notice.* An institution is not required to comply with the requirements of this section for any notice of error from the consumer that is received by the institution later than 60 days from the date on which the periodic statement first reflecting the error is sent. Where the consumer's assertion of error involves an unauthorized EFT, however, the institution must comply with § 1005.6 before it may impose any liability on the consumer.

11(b)(2) Written Confirmation

1. *Written confirmation-of-error notice.* If the consumer sends a written confirmation of error to the wrong address, the financial institution must process the confirmation through normal procedures. But the institution need not provisionally credit the consumer's account if the written confirmation is delayed beyond 10 business days in getting to the right place because it was sent to the wrong address.

11(c) Time Limits and Extent of Investigation

1. *Notice to consumer.* Unless otherwise indicated in this section, the financial institution may provide the required notices to the consumer either orally or in writing.

2. *Written confirmation of oral notice.* A financial institution must begin its investigation promptly upon receipt of an oral notice. It may not delay until it has received a written confirmation.

OFFICIAL INTERPRETATIONS OF REGULATION E

3.   *Charges for error resolution.* If a billing error occurred, whether as alleged or in a different amount or manner, the financial institution may not impose a charge related to any aspect of the error-resolution process (including charges for documentation or investigation). Since the Act grants the consumer error-resolution rights, the institution should avoid any chilling effect on the good-faith assertion of errors that might result if charges are assessed when no billing error has occurred.

4.   *Correction without investigation.* A financial institution may make, without investigation, a final correction to a consumer's account in the amount or manner alleged by the consumer to be in error, but must comply with all other applicable requirements of § 1005.11.

5.   *Correction notice.* A financial institution may include the notice of correction on a periodic statement that is mailed or delivered within the 10-business-day or 45-calendar-day time limits and that clearly identifies the correction to the consumer's account. The institution must determine whether such a mailing will be prompt enough to satisfy the requirements of this section, taking into account the specific facts involved.

6.   *Correction of an error.* If the financial institution determines an error occurred, within either the 10-day or 45-day period, it must correct the error (subject to the liability provisions of §§ 1005.6(a) and (b)) including, where applicable, the crediting of interest and the refunding of any fees imposed by the institution. In a combined credit/EFT transaction, for example, the institution must refund any finance charges incurred as a result of the error. The institution need not refund fees that would have been imposed whether or not the error occurred.

7.   *Extent of required investigation.* A financial institution complies with its duty to investigate, correct, and report its determination regarding an error described in § 1005.11(a)(1)(vii) by transmitting the requested information, clarification, or documentation within the time limits set forth in § 1005.11(c). If the institution has provisionally credited the consumer's account in accordance with § 1005.11(c)(2), it may debit the amount upon transmitting the requested information, clarification, or documentation.

Paragraph 11(c)(2)(i)

1.   *Compliance with all requirements.* Financial institutions exempted from provisionally crediting a consumer's account under §§ 1005.11(c)(2)(i)(A) and (B) must still comply with all other requirements of § 1005.11.

11(c)(3) Extension of Time Periods

1.   *POS debit card transactions.* The extended deadlines for investigating errors resulting from POS debit card transactions apply to all debit card transactions, including those for cash only, at merchants' POS terminals, and also including mail and telephone orders. The deadlines do not apply to transactions at an ATM, however, even though the ATM may be in a merchant location.

11(c)(4) Investigation

1.   *Third parties.* When information or documentation requested by the consumer is in the possession of a third party with whom the financial institution does not have an agreement, the institution satisfies the error resolution requirement by so advising the consumer within the specified time period.

2.   *Scope of investigation.* When an alleged error involves a payment to a third party under the financial institution's telephone bill-payment plan, a review of the institution's own records is sufficient, assuming no agreement exists between the institution and the third party concerning the bill-payment service.

3.   *POS transfers.* When a consumer alleges an error involving a transfer to a merchant via a POS terminal, the institution must verify the information previously transmitted when executing the transfer. For example, the financial institution may request a copy of the sales receipt to verify that the amount of the transfer correctly corresponds to the amount of the consumer's purchase.

4.   *Agreement.* An agreement that a third party will honor an access device is an agreement for purposes of this paragraph. A financial institution does not have an agreement for purposes of § 1005.11(c)(4)(ii) solely because it participates in transactions that occur under the Federal recurring payments programs, or that are cleared through an ACH or similar arrangement for the clearing and settlement of fund transfers generally, or because the institution agrees to be bound by the rules of such an arrangement.

5. *No EFT agreement.* When there is no agreement between the institution and the third party for the type of EFT involved, the financial institution must review any relevant information within the institution's own records for the particular account to resolve the consumer's claim. The extent of the investigation required may vary depending on the facts and circumstances. However, a financial institution may not limit its investigation solely to the payment instructions where additional information within its own records pertaining to the particular account in question could help to resolve a consumer's claim. Information that may be reviewed as part of an investigation might include:

    i.   The ACH transaction records for the transfer;

    ii.   The transaction history of the particular account for a reasonable period of time immediately preceding the allegation of error;

    iii.   Whether the check number of the transaction in question is notably out-of-sequence;

    iv.   The location of either the transaction or the payee in question relative to the consumer's place of residence and habitual transaction area;

    v.   Information relative to the account in question within the control of the institution's third-party service providers if the financial institution reasonably believes that it may have records or other information that could be dispositive; or

    vi.   Any other information appropriate to resolve the claim.

11(d) Procedures if Financial Institution Determines No Error or Different Error Occurred

1. *Error different from that alleged.* When a financial institution determines that an error occurred in a manner or amount different from that described by the consumer, it must comply with the requirements of both §§ 1005.11(c) and (d), as relevant. The institution may give the notice of correction and the explanation separately or in a combined form.

11(d)(1) Written Explanation

1. *Request for documentation.* When a consumer requests copies of documents, the financial institution must provide the copies in an understandable form. If an institution relied on magnetic tape, it must convert the applicable data into readable form, for example, by printing it and explaining any codes.

11(d)(2) Debiting Provisional Credit

1. *Alternative procedure for debiting of credited funds.* The financial institution may comply with the requirements of this section by notifying the consumer that the consumer's account will be debited five business days from the transmittal of the notification, specifying the calendar date on which the debiting will occur.

2. *Fees for overdrafts.* The financial institution may not impose fees for items it is required to honor under § 1005.11. It may, however, impose any normal transaction or item fee that is unrelated to an overdraft resulting from the debiting. If the account is still overdrawn after five business days, the institution may impose the fees or finance charges to which it is entitled, if any, under an overdraft credit plan.

11(e) Reassertion of Error

1. *Withdrawal of error; right to reassert.* The financial institution has no further error resolution responsibilities if the consumer voluntarily withdraws the notice alleging an error. A consumer who has withdrawn an allegation of error has the right to reassert the allegation unless the financial institution had already complied with all of the error resolution requirements before the allegation was withdrawn. The consumer must do so, however, within the original 60-day period.

SECTION 1005.12 RELATION TO OTHER LAWS

12(a) Relation to Truth in Lending

1. *Determining applicable regulation.*

    i.   For transactions involving access devices that also function as credit cards, whether Regulation E or Regulation Z (12 CFR part 1026) applies depends on the nature of the transaction. For example, if the transaction solely involves an extension of credit, and does not include a debit to a checking account (or other consumer asset account), the liability limitations and error resolution requirements of Regulation Z apply. If the transaction debits a checking account only (with no credit extended), the provisions of Regulation E apply. If the transaction debits a checking account but also draws on an overdraft line of credit attached to the account, Regulation E's liability limitations apply, in addition to §§ 1026.13(d) and (g) of Regulation Z (which apply because of the extension of credit associated with the overdraft feature on the checking account). If a consumer's access device is also a credit card and the device is used to make unauthorized withdrawals from a checking account, but also is used to obtain unauthorized cash advances directly from a line of credit that is separate from the checking account, both Regulation E and Regulation Z apply.

ii.   The following examples illustrate these principles:

A.   A consumer has a card that can be used either as a credit card or a debit card. When used as a debit card, the card draws on the consumer's checking account. When used as a credit card, the card draws only on a separate line of credit. If the card is stolen and used as a credit card to make purchases or to get cash advances at an ATM from the line of credit, the liability limits and error resolution provisions of Regulation Z apply; Regulation E does not apply.

B.   In the same situation, if the card is stolen and is used as a debit card to make purchases or to get cash withdrawals at an ATM from the checking account, the liability limits and error resolution provisions of Regulation E apply; Regulation Z does not apply.

C.   In the same situation, assume the card is stolen and used both as a debit card and as a credit card; for example, the thief makes some purchases using the card as a debit card, and other purchases using the card as a credit card. Here, the liability limits and error resolution provisions of Regulation E apply to the unauthorized transactions in which the card was used as a debit card, and the corresponding provisions of Regulation Z apply to the unauthorized transactions in which the card was used as a credit card.

D.   Assume a somewhat different type of card, one that draws on the consumer's checking account and can also draw on an overdraft line of credit attached to the checking account. There is no separate line of credit, only the overdraft line, associated with the card. In this situation, if the card is stolen and used, the liability limits and the error resolution provisions of Regulation E apply. In addition, if the use of the card has resulted in accessing the overdraft line of credit, the error resolution provisions of §§ 1026.13(d) and (g) of Regulation Z also apply, but not the other error resolution provisions of Regulation Z.

2.   *Issuance rules.* For access devices that also constitute credit cards, the issuance rules of Regulation E apply if the only credit feature is a preexisting credit line attached to the asset account to cover overdrafts (or to maintain a specified minimum balance) or an overdraft service, as defined in § 1005.17(a). Regulation Z (12 CFR part 1026) rules apply if there is another type of credit feature; for example, one permitting direct extensions of credit that do not involve the asset account.

3.   *Overdraft service.* The addition of an overdraft service, as that term is defined in § 1005.17(a), to an accepted access device does not constitute the addition of a credit feature subject to Regulation Z. Instead, the provisions of Regulation E apply, including the liability limitations (§ 1005.6) and the requirement to obtain consumer consent to the service before any fees or charges for paying an overdraft may be assessed on the account (§ 1005.17).

12(b) Preemption of Inconsistent State Laws

1.   *Specific determinations.* The regulation prescribes standards for determining whether state laws that govern EFTs, and state laws regarding gift certificates, store gift cards, or general-use prepaid cards that govern dormancy, inactivity, or service fees, or expiration dates, are preempted by the Act and the regulation. A state law that is inconsistent may be preempted even if the Bureau has not issued a determination. However, nothing in § 1005.12(b) provides a financial institution with immunity for violations of state law if the institution chooses not to make state disclosures and the Bureau later determines that the state law is not preempted.

OFFICIAL INTERPRETATIONS OF REGULATION E

2. *Preemption determination.* The Bureau recognizes state law preemption determinations made by the Board of Governors of the Federal Reserve System prior to July 21, 2011, until and unless the Bureau makes and publishes any contrary determination. The Board of Governors determined that certain provisions in the state law of Michigan are preempted by the Federal law, effective March 30, 1981:

    i.   Definition of unauthorized use. Section 5(4) is preempted to the extent that it relates to the section of state law governing consumer liability for unauthorized use of an access device.

    ii.   Consumer liability for unauthorized use of an account. Section 14 is inconsistent with § 1005.6 and is less protective of the consumer than the Federal law. The state law places liability on the consumer for the unauthorized use of an account in cases involving the consumer's negligence. Under the Federal law, a consumer's liability for unauthorized use is not related to the consumer's negligence and depends instead on the consumer's promptness in reporting the loss or theft of the access device.

    iii.   Error resolution. Section 15 is preempted because it is inconsistent with § 1005.11 and is less protective of the consumer than the Federal law. The state law allows financial institutions up to 70 days to resolve errors, whereas the Federal law generally requires errors to be resolved within 45 days.

    iv.   Receipts and periodic statements. Sections 17 and 18 are preempted because they are inconsistent with § 1005.9. The state provisions require a different disclosure of information than does the Federal law. The receipt provision is also preempted because it allows the consumer to be charged for receiving a receipt if a machine cannot furnish one at the time of a transfer.

SECTION 1005.13 ADMINISTRATIVE ENFORCEMENT; RECORD RETENTION

13(b) Record Retention

1. *Requirements.* A financial institution need not retain records that it has given disclosures and documentation to each consumer; it need only retain evidence demonstrating that its procedures reasonably ensure the consumers' receipt of required disclosures and documentation.

SECTION 1005.14 ELECTRONIC FUND TRANSFER SERVICE PROVIDER NOT HOLDING CONSUMER'S ACCOUNT

14(a) Electronic Fund Transfer Service Providers Subject to Regulation

1. *Applicability.* This section applies only when a service provider issues an access device to a consumer for initiating transfers to or from the consumer's account at a financial institution and the two entities have no agreement regarding this EFT service. If the service provider does not issue an access device to the consumer for accessing an account held by another institution, it does not qualify for the treatment accorded by § 1005.14. For example, this section does not apply to an institution that initiates preauthorized payroll deposits to consumer accounts on behalf of an employer. By contrast, § 1005.14 can apply to an institution that issues a code for initiating telephone transfers to be carried out through the ACH from a consumer's account at another institution. This is the case even if the consumer has accounts at both institutions.

2. *ACH agreements.* The ACH rules generally do not constitute an agreement for purposes of this section. However, an ACH agreement under which members specifically agree to honor each other's debit cards is an "agreement," and thus this section does not apply.

14(b) Compliance by Electronic Fund Transfer Service Provider

1. *Liability.* The service provider is liable for unauthorized EFTs that exceed limits on the consumer's liability under § 1005.6.

14(b)(1) Disclosures and Documentation

1. *Periodic statements from electronic fund transfer service provider.* A service provider that meets the conditions set forth in this paragraph does not have to issue periodic statements. A service provider that does not meet the conditions need only include on periodic statements information about transfers initiated with the access device it has issued.

OFFICIAL INTERPRETATIONS OF REGULATION E

14(b)(2) Error Resolution

1. *Error resolution.* When a consumer notifies the service provider of an error, the EFT service provider must investigate and resolve the error in compliance with § 1005.11 as modified by § 1005.14(b)(2). If an error occurred, any fees or charges imposed as a result of the error, either by the service provider or by the account-holding institution (for example, overdraft or dishonor fees) must be reimbursed to the consumer by the service provider.

14(c) Compliance by Account-Holding Institution

14(c)(1) Documentation

1. *Periodic statements from account-holding institution.* The periodic statement provided by the account-holding institution need only contain the information required by § 1005.9(b)(1).

SECTION 1005.17 REQUIREMENTS FOR OVERDRAFT SERVICES

17(a) Definition

1. *Exempt securities- and commodities-related lines of credit.* The definition of "overdraft service" does not include the payment of transactions in a securities or commodities account pursuant to which credit is extended by a broker-dealer registered with the Securities and Exchange Commission or the Commodity Futures Trading Commission.

17(b) Opt-In Requirement

1. *Scope.*

    i. *Account-holding institutions.* Section 1005.17(b) applies to ATM and one-time debit card transactions made with a debit card issued by or on behalf of the account-holding institution. Section 1005.17(b) does not apply to ATM and one-time debit card transactions made with a debit card issued by or through a third party unless the debit card is issued on behalf of the account-holding institution.

    ii. *Coding of transactions.* A financial institution complies with the rule if it adapts its systems to identify debit card transactions as either one-time or recurring. If it does so, the financial institution may rely on the transaction's coding by merchants, other institutions, and other third parties as a one-time or a preauthorized or recurring debit card transaction.

    iii. *One-time debit card transactions.* The opt-in applies to any one-time debit card transaction, whether the card is used, for example, at a point-of-sale, in an online transaction, or in a telephone transaction.

    iv. *Application of fee prohibition.* The prohibition on assessing overdraft fees under § 1005.17(b)(1) applies to all institutions. For example, the prohibition applies to an institution that has a policy and practice of declining to authorize and pay any ATM or one-time debit card transactions when the institution has a reasonable belief at the time of the authorization request that the consumer does not have sufficient funds available to cover the transaction. However, the institution is not required to comply with §§ 1005.17(b)(1)(i)–(iv), including the notice and opt-in requirements, if it does not assess overdraft fees for paying ATM or one-time debit card transactions that overdraw the consumer's account. Assume an institution does not provide an opt-in notice, but authorizes an ATM or one-time debit card transaction on the reasonable belief that the consumer has sufficient funds in the account to cover the transaction. If, at settlement, the consumer has insufficient funds in the account (for example, due to intervening transactions that post to the consumer's account), the institution is not permitted to assess an overdraft fee or charge for paying that transaction.

2. *No affirmative consent.* A financial institution may pay overdrafts for ATM and one-time debit card transactions even if a consumer has not affirmatively consented or opted in to the institution's overdraft service. If the institution pays such an overdraft without the consumer's affirmative consent, however, it may not impose a fee or charge for doing so. These provisions do not limit the institution's ability to debit the consumer's account for the amount overdrawn if the institution is permitted to do so under applicable law.

OFFICIAL INTERPRETATIONS OF REGULATION E

3. *Overdraft transactions not required to be authorized or paid.* Section 1005.17 does not require a financial institution to authorize or pay an overdraft on an ATM or one-time debit card transaction even if the consumer has affirmatively consented to an institution's overdraft service for such transactions.

4. *Reasonable opportunity to provide affirmative consent.* A financial institution provides a consumer with a reasonable opportunity to provide affirmative consent when, among other things, it provides reasonable methods by which the consumer may affirmatively consent. A financial institution provides such reasonable methods, if:

   i. *By mail.* The institution provides a form for the consumer to fill out and mail to affirmatively consent to the service.

   ii. *By telephone.* The institution provides a readily-available telephone line that consumers may call to provide affirmative consent.

   iii. *By electronic means.* The institution provides an electronic means for the consumer to affirmatively consent. For example, the institution could provide a form that can be accessed and processed at its Web site, where the consumer may click on a check box to provide consent and confirm that choice by clicking on a button that affirms the consumer's consent.

   iv. *In person.* The institution provides a form for the consumer to complete and present at a branch or office to affirmatively consent to the service.

5. *Implementing opt-in at account-opening.* A financial institution may provide notice regarding the institution's overdraft service prior to or at account-opening. A financial institution may require a consumer, as a necessary step to opening an account, to choose whether or not to opt into the payment of ATM or one-time debit card transactions pursuant to the institution's overdraft service. For example, the institution could require the consumer, at account opening, to sign a signature line or check a box on a form (consistent with comment 17(b)–6) indicating whether or not the consumer affirmatively consents at account opening. If the consumer does not check any box or provide a signature, the institution must assume that the consumer does not opt in. Or, the institution could require the consumer to choose between an account that does not permit the payment of ATM or one-time debit card transactions pursuant to the institution's overdraft service and an account that permits the payment of such overdrafts, provided that the accounts comply with § 1005.17(b)(2) and § 1005.17(b)(3).

6. *Affirmative consent required.* A consumer's affirmative consent, or opt-in, to a financial institution's overdraft service must be obtained separately from other consents or acknowledgements obtained by the institution, including a consent to receive disclosures electronically. An institution may obtain a consumer's affirmative consent by providing a blank signature line or check box that the consumer could sign or select to affirmatively consent, provided that the signature line or check box is used solely for purposes of evidencing the consumer's choice whether or not to opt into the overdraft service and not for other purposes. An institution does not obtain a consumer's affirmative consent by including preprinted language about the overdraft service in an account disclosure provided with a signature card or contract that the consumer must sign to open the account and that acknowledges the consumer's acceptance of the account terms. Nor does an institution obtain a consumer's affirmative consent by providing a signature card that contains a pre-selected check box indicating that the consumer is requesting the service.

7. *Confirmation.* A financial institution may comply with the requirement in § 1005.17(b)(1)(iv) to provide confirmation of the consumer's affirmative consent by mailing or delivering to the consumer a copy of the consumer's completed opt-in notice, or by mailing or delivering a letter or notice to the consumer acknowledging that the consumer has elected to opt into the institution's service. The confirmation, which must be provided in writing, or electronically if the consumer agrees, must include a statement informing the consumer of the right to revoke the opt-in at any time. *See* § 1005.17(d)(6), which permits institutions to include the revocation statement on the initial opt-in notice. An institution complies with the confirmation requirement if it has adopted reasonable procedures designed to ensure that overdraft fees are assessed only in connection with transactions paid after the confirmation has been mailed or delivered to the consumer.

8. *Outstanding Negative Balance.* If a fee or charge is based on the amount of the outstanding negative balance, an institution is prohibited from assessing any such fee if the negative balance is solely attributable

to an ATM or one-time debit card transaction, unless the consumer has opted into the institution's overdraft service for ATM or one-time debit card transactions. However, the rule does not prohibit an institution from assessing such a fee if the negative balance is attributable in whole or in part to a check, ACH, or other type of transaction not subject to the prohibition on assessing overdraft fees in § 1005.17(b)(1).

9. *Daily or Sustained Overdraft, Negative Balance, or Similar Fee or Charge.*

i. *Daily or sustained overdraft, negative balance, or similar fees or charges.* If a consumer has not opted into the institution's overdraft service for ATM or one-time debit card transactions, the fee prohibition in § 1005.17(b)(1) applies to all overdraft fees or charges for paying those transactions, including but not limited to daily or sustained overdraft, negative balance, or similar fees or charges. Thus, where a consumer's negative balance is solely attributable to an ATM or one-time debit card transaction, the rule prohibits the assessment of such fees unless the consumer has opted in. However, the rule does not prohibit an institution from assessing daily or sustained overdraft, negative balance, or similar fees or charges if a negative balance is attributable in whole or in part to a check, ACH, or other type of transaction not subject to the fee prohibition. When the negative balance is attributable in part to an ATM or one-time debit card transaction, and in part to a check, ACH, or other type of transaction not subject to the fee prohibition, the date on which such a fee may be assessed is based on the date on which the check, ACH, or other type of transaction is paid into overdraft.

ii. *Examples.* The following examples illustrate how an institution complies with the fee prohibition. For each example, assume the following: (a) The consumer has not opted into the payment of ATM or one-time debit card overdrafts; (b) these transactions are paid into overdraft because the amount of the transaction at settlement exceeded the amount authorized or the amount was not submitted for authorization; (c) under the account agreement, the institution may charge a per-item fee of $20 for each overdraft, and a one-time sustained overdraft fee of $20 on the fifth consecutive day the consumer's account remains overdrawn; (d) the institution posts ATM and debit card transactions before other transactions; and (e) the institution allocates deposits to account debits in the same order in which it posts debits.

A. Assume that a consumer has a $50 account balance on March 1. That day, the institution posts a one-time debit card transaction of $60 and a check transaction of $40. The institution charges an overdraft fee of $20 for the check overdraft but cannot assess an overdraft fee for the debit card transaction. At the end of the day, the consumer has an account balance of negative $70. The consumer does not make any deposits to the account, and no other transactions occur between March 2 and March 6. Because the consumer's negative balance is attributable in part to the $40 check (and associated overdraft fee), the institution may charge a sustained overdraft fee on March 6 in connection with the check.

B. Same facts as in A., except that on March 3, the consumer deposits $40 in the account. The institution allocates the $40 to the debit card transaction first, consistent with its posting order policy. At the end of the day on March 3, the consumer has an account balance of negative $30, which is attributable to the check transaction (and associated overdraft fee). The consumer does not make any further deposits to the account, and no other transactions occur between March 4 and March 6. Because the remaining negative balance is attributable to the March 1 check transaction, the institution may charge a sustained overdraft fee on March 6 in connection with the check.

C. Assume that a consumer has a $50 account balance on March 1. That day, the institution posts a one-time debit card transaction of $60. At the end of that day, the consumer has an account balance of negative $10. The institution may not assess an overdraft fee for the debit card transaction. On March 3, the institution pays a check transaction of $100 and charges an overdraft fee of $20. At the end of that day, the consumer has an account balance of negative $130. The consumer does not make any deposits to the account, and no other transactions occur between March 4 and March 8. Because the consumer's negative balance is attributable in part to the check, the institution may assess a $20 sustained overdraft fee. However, because the check was paid on March 3, the institution must use March 3 as the start date for determining the date on which the sustained overdraft fee may be assessed. Thus, the institution may charge a $20 sustained overdraft fee on March 8.

iii.   *Alternative approach.* For a consumer who does not opt into the institution's overdraft service for ATM and one-time debit card transactions, an institution may also comply with the fee prohibition in § 1005.17(b)(1) by not assessing daily or sustained overdraft, negative balance, or similar fees or charges unless a consumer's negative balance is attributable solely to check, ACH or other types of transactions not subject to the fee prohibition while that negative balance remains outstanding. In such case, the institution would not have to determine how to allocate subsequent deposits that reduce but do not eliminate the negative balance. For example, if a consumer has a negative balance of $30, of which $10 is attributable to a one-time debit card transaction, an institution complies with the fee prohibition if it does not assess a sustained overdraft fee while that negative balance remains outstanding.

17(b)(2) Conditioning Payment of Other Overdrafts on Consumer's Affirmative Consent

1.   *Application of the same criteria.* The prohibitions on conditioning in § 1005.17(b)(2) generally require an institution to apply the same criteria for deciding when to pay overdrafts for checks, ACH transactions, and other types of transactions, whether or not the consumer has affirmatively consented to the institution's overdraft service with respect to ATM and one-time debit card overdrafts. For example, if an institution's internal criteria would lead the institution to pay a check overdraft if the consumer had affirmatively consented to the institution's overdraft service for ATM and one-time debit card transactions, it must also apply the same criteria in a consistent manner in determining whether to pay the check overdraft if the consumer has not opted in.

2.   *No requirement to pay overdrafts on checks, ACH transactions, or other types of transactions.* The prohibition on conditioning in § 1005.17(b)(2) does not require an institution to pay overdrafts on checks, ACH transactions, or other types of transactions in all circumstances. Rather, the rule simply prohibits institutions from considering the consumer's decision not to opt in when deciding whether to pay overdrafts for checks, ACH transactions, or other types of transactions.

17(b)(3) Same Account Terms, Conditions, and Features

1.   *Variations in terms, conditions, or features.* A financial institution may not vary the terms, conditions, or features of an account provided to a consumer who does not affirmatively consent to the payment of ATM or one-time debit card transactions pursuant to the institution's overdraft service. This includes, but is not limited to:

i.   Interest rates paid and fees assessed;

ii.   The type of ATM or debit card provided to the consumer. For instance, an institution may not provide consumers who do not opt in a PIN-only card while providing a debit card with both PIN and signature-debit functionality to consumers who opt in;

iii.   Minimum balance requirements; or

iv.   Account features such as online bill payment services.

2.   *Limited-feature bank accounts.* Section 1005.17(b)(3) does not prohibit institutions from offering deposit account products with limited features, provided that a consumer is not required to open such an account because the consumer did not opt in. For example, § 1005.17(b)(3) does not prohibit an institution from offering a checking account designed to comply with state basic banking laws, or designed for consumers who are not eligible for a checking account because of their credit or checking account history, which may include features limiting the payment of overdrafts. However, a consumer who applies, and is otherwise eligible, for a full-service or other particular deposit account product may not be provided instead with the account with more limited features because the consumer has declined to opt in.

17(c) Timing

1.   *Permitted fees or charges.* Fees or charges for ATM and one-time debit card overdrafts may be assessed only for overdrafts paid on or after the date the financial institution receives the consumer's affirmative consent to the institution's overdraft service. *See also* comment 17(b)–7.

OFFICIAL INTERPRETATIONS OF REGULATION E

17(d) Content and Format

1.   *Overdraft service.* The description of the institution's overdraft service should indicate that the consumer has the right to affirmatively consent, or opt into payment of overdrafts for ATM and one-time debit card transactions. The description should also disclose the institution's policies regarding the payment of overdrafts for other transactions, including checks, ACH transactions, and automatic bill payments, provided that this content is not more prominent than the description of the consumer's right to opt into payment of overdrafts for ATM and one-time debit card transactions. As applicable, the institution also should indicate that it pays overdrafts at its discretion, and should briefly explain that if the institution does not authorize and pay an overdraft, it may decline the transaction.

2.   *Maximum fee.* If the amount of a fee may vary from transaction to transaction, the financial institution may indicate that the consumer may be assessed a fee "up to" the maximum fee. The financial institution must disclose all applicable overdraft fees, including but not limited to:

   i.   Per item or per transaction fees;

   ii.   Daily overdraft fees;

   iii.   Sustained overdraft fees, where fees are assessed when the consumer has not repaid the amount of the overdraft after some period of time (for example, if an account remains overdrawn for five or more business days); or

   iv.   Negative balance fees.

3.   *Opt-in methods.* The opt-in notice must include the methods by which the consumer may consent to the overdraft service for ATM and one-time debit card transactions. Institutions may tailor Model Form A–9 to the methods offered to consumers for affirmatively consenting to the service. For example, an institution need not provide the tear-off portion of Model Form A–9 if it is only permitting consumers to opt-in telephonically or electronically. Institutions may, but are not required, to provide a signature line or check box where the consumer can indicate that he or she declines to opt in.

4.   *Identification of consumer's account.* An institution may use any reasonable method to identify the account for which the consumer submits the opt-in notice. For example, the institution may include a line for a printed name and an account number, as shown in Model Form A–9. Or, the institution may print a bar code or use other tracking information. *See also* comment 17(b)–6, which describes how an institution obtains a consumer's affirmative consent.

5.   *Alternative plans for covering overdrafts.* If the institution offers both a line of credit subject to Regulation Z (12 CFR part 1026) and a service that transfers funds from another account of the consumer held at the institution to cover overdrafts, the institution must state in its opt-in notice that both alternative plans are offered. For example, the notice might state "We also offer *overdraft protection plans,* such as a link to a savings account or to an overdraft line of credit, which may be less expensive than our standard overdraft practices." If the institution offers one, but not the other, it must state in its opt-in notice the alternative plan that it offers. If the institution does not offer either plan, it should omit the reference to the alternative plans.

17(f) Continuing Right To Opt-In or To Revoke the Opt-In

1.   *Fees or charges for overdrafts incurred prior to revocation.* Section 1005.17(f)(1) provides that a consumer may revoke his or her prior consent at any time. If a consumer does so, this provision does not require the financial institution to waive or reverse any overdraft fees assessed on the consumer's account prior to the institution's implementation of the consumer's revocation request.

17(g) Duration of Opt-In

1.   *Termination of overdraft service.* A financial institution may, for example, terminate the overdraft service when the consumer makes excessive use of the service.

OFFICIAL INTERPRETATIONS OF REGULATION E

SECTION 1005.18 REQUIREMENTS FOR FINANCIAL INSTITUTIONS OFFERING PAYROLL CARD ACCOUNTS

18(a) Coverage

1. *Issuance of access device.* Consistent with § 1005.5(a), a financial institution may issue an access device only in response to an oral or written request for the device, or as a renewal or substitute for an accepted access device. A consumer is deemed to request an access device for a payroll card account when the consumer chooses to receive salary or other compensation through a payroll card account.

2. *Application to employers and service providers.* Typically, employers and third-party service providers do not meet the definition of a "financial institution" subject to the regulation because they neither hold payroll card accounts nor issue payroll cards and agree with consumers to provide EFT services in connection with payroll card accounts. However, to the extent an employer or a service provider undertakes either of these functions, it would be deemed a financial institution under the regulation.

18(b) Alternative to Periodic Statements

1. *Posted transactions.* A history of transactions provided under §§ 1005.18(b)(1)(ii) and (iii) shall reflect transfers once they have been posted to the account. Thus, an institution does not need to include transactions that have been authorized, but that have not yet posted to the account.

2. *Electronic history.* The electronic history required under § 1005.18(b)(1)(ii) must be provided in a form that the consumer may keep, as required under § 1005.4(a)(1). Financial institutions may satisfy this requirement if they make the electronic history available in a format that is capable of being retained. For example, an institution satisfies the requirement if it provides a history at a Web site in a format that is capable of being printed or stored electronically using a web browser.

18(c) Modified Requirements

1. *Error resolution safe harbor provision.* Institutions that choose to investigate notices of error provided up to 120 days from the date a transaction has posted to a consumer's account may still disclose the error resolution time period required by the regulation (as set forth in the Model Form in appendix A–7). Specifically, an institution may disclose to payroll card account holders that the institution will investigate any notice of error provided within 60 days of the consumer electronically accessing an account or receiving a written history upon request that reflects the error, even if, for some or all transactions, the institution investigates any notice of error provided up to 120 days from the date that the transaction alleged to be in error has posted to the consumer's account. Similarly, an institution's summary of the consumer's liability (as required under § 1005.7(b)(1)) may disclose that liability is based on the consumer providing notice of error within 60 days of the consumer electronically accessing an account or receiving a written history reflecting the error, even if, for some or all transactions, the institution allows a consumer to assert a notice of error up to 120 days from the date of posting of the alleged error.

2. *Electronic access.* A consumer is deemed to have accessed a payroll card account electronically when the consumer enters a user identification code or password or otherwise complies with a security procedure used by an institution to verify the consumer's identity. An institution is not required to determine whether a consumer has in fact accessed information about specific transactions to trigger the beginning of the 60-day periods for liability limits and error resolution under §§ 1005.6 and 1005.11.

3. *Untimely notice of error.* An institution that provides a transaction history under § 1005.18(b)(1) is not required to comply with the requirements of § 1005.11 for any notice of error from the consumer pertaining to a transfer that occurred more than 60 days prior to the earlier of the date the consumer electronically accesses the account or the date the financial institution sends a written history upon the consumer's request. (Alternatively, as provided in § 1005.18(c)(4)(ii), an institution need not comply with the requirements of § 1005.11 with respect to any notice of error received from the consumer more than 120 days after the date of posting of the transfer allegedly in error.) Where the consumer's assertion of error involves an unauthorized EFT, however, the institution must comply with § 1005.6 before it may impose any liability on the consumer.

OFFICIAL INTERPRETATIONS OF REGULATION E

SECTION 1005.20 REQUIREMENTS FOR GIFT CARDS AND GIFT CERTIFICATES

20(a) Definitions

1.   *Form of card, code, or device.* Section 1005.20 applies to any card, code, or other device that meets one of the definitions in §§ 1005.20(a)(1) through (a)(3) (and is not otherwise excluded by § 1005.20(b)), even if it is not issued in card form. Section 1005.20 applies, for example, to an account number or bar code that can be used to access underlying funds. Similarly, § 1005.20 applies to a device with a chip or other embedded mechanism that links the device to stored funds, such as a mobile phone or sticker containing a contactless chip that enables the consumer to access the stored funds. A card, code, or other device that meets the definition in §§ 1005.20(a)(1) through (a)(3) includes an electronic promise (*see* comment 20(a)–2) as well as a promise that is not electronic. *See, however,* § 1005.20(b)(5). In addition, § 1005.20 applies if a merchant issues a code that entitles a consumer to redeem the code for goods or services, regardless of the medium in which the code is issued (*see, however,* § 1005.20(b)(5)), and whether or not it may be redeemed electronically or in the merchant's store. Thus, for example, if a merchant emails a code that a consumer may redeem in a specified amount either online or in the merchant's store, that code is covered under § 1005.20, unless one of the exclusions in § 1005.20(b) apply.

2.   *Electronic promise.* The term "electronic promise" as used in EFTA sections 915(a)(2)(B), (a)(2)(C), and (a)(2)(D) means a person's commitment or obligation communicated or stored in electronic form made to a consumer to provide payment for goods or services for transactions initiated by the consumer. The electronic promise is itself represented by a card, code or other device that is issued or honored by the person, reflecting the person's commitment or obligation to pay. For example, if a merchant issues a code that can be given as a gift and that entitles the recipient to redeem the code in an online transaction for goods or services, that code represents an electronic promise by the merchant and is a card, code, or other device covered by § 1005.20.

3.   *Cards, codes, or other devices redeemable for specific goods or services.* Certain cards, codes, or other devices may be redeemable upon presentation for a specific good or service, or "experience," such as a spa treatment, hotel stay, or airline flight. In other cases, a card, code, or other device may entitle the consumer to a certain percentage off the purchase of a good or service, such as 20% off of any purchase in a store. Such cards, codes, or other devices generally are not subject to the requirements of this section because they are not issued to a consumer "in a specified amount" as required under the definitions of "gift certificate," "store gift card," or "general-use prepaid card." However, if the card, code, or other device is issued in a specified or denominated amount that can be applied toward the purchase of a specific good or service, such as a certificate or card redeemable for a spa treatment up to $50, the card, code, or other device is subject to this section, unless one of the exceptions in § 1005.20(b) apply. *See, e.g.,* § 1005.20(b)(3). Similarly, if the card, code, or other device states a specific monetary value, such as "a $50 value," the card, code, or other device is subject to this section, unless an exclusion in § 1005.20(b) applies.

4.   *Issued primarily for personal, family, or household purposes.* Section 1005.20 only applies to cards, codes, or other devices that are sold or issued to a consumer primarily for personal, family, or household purposes. A card, code, or other device initially purchased by a business is subject to this section if the card, code, or other device is purchased for redistribution or resale to consumers primarily for personal, family, or household purposes. Moreover, the fact that a card, code, or other device may be primarily funded by a business, for example, in the case of certain rewards or incentive cards, does not mean the card, code, or other device is outside the scope of § 1005.20, if the card, code, or other device will be provided to a consumer primarily for personal, family, or household purposes. *But see* § 1005.20(b)(3). Whether a card, code, or other device is issued to a consumer primarily for personal, family, or household purposes will depend on the facts and circumstances. For example, if a program manager purchases store gift cards directly from an issuing merchant and sells those cards through the program manager's retail outlets, such gift cards are subject to the requirements of § 1005.20 because the store gift cards are sold to consumers primarily for personal, family, or household purposes. In contrast, a card, code, or other device generally would not be issued to consumers primarily for personal, family, or household purposes, and therefore would fall outside the scope of § 1005.20, if the purchaser of the card, code, or device is contractually prohibited from reselling or redistributing the card, code, or device to consumers primarily for personal, family, or household purposes, and reasonable policies and procedures are maintained to avoid such sale or distribution for such purposes.

However, if an entity that has purchased cards, codes, or other devices for business purposes sells or distributes such cards, codes, or other devices to consumers primarily for personal, family, or household purposes, that entity does not comply with § 1005.20 if it has not otherwise met the substantive and disclosure requirements of the rule or unless an exclusion in § 1005.20(b) applies.

5. *Examples of cards, codes, or other devices issued for business purposes.* Examples of cards, codes, or other devices that are issued and used for business purposes and therefore excluded from the definitions of "gift certificate," "store gift card," or "general-use prepaid card" include:

    i.   Cards, codes, or other devices to reimburse employees for travel or moving expenses.

    ii.   Cards, codes, or other devices for employees to use to purchase office supplies and other business-related items.

20(a)(2) Store Gift Card

1. *Relationship between "gift certificate" and "store gift card."* The term "store gift card" in § 1005.20(a)(2) includes "gift certificate" as defined in § 1005.20(a)(1). For example, a numeric or alphanumeric code representing a specified dollar amount or value that is electronically sent to a consumer as a gift which can be redeemed or exchanged by the recipient to obtain goods or services may be both a "gift certificate" and a "store gift card" if the specified amount or value cannot be increased.

2. *Affiliated group of merchants.* The term "affiliated group of merchants" means two or more affiliated merchants or other persons that are related by common ownership or common corporate control (*see, e.g.,* 12 CFR 227.3(b) and 12 CFR 223.2) and that share the same name, mark, or logo. For example, the term includes franchisees that are subject to a common set of corporate policies or practices under the terms of their franchise licenses. The term also applies to two or more merchants or other persons that agree among themselves, by contract or otherwise, to redeem cards, codes, or other devices bearing the same name, mark, or logo (other than the mark, logo, or brand of a payment network), for the purchase of goods or services solely at such merchants or persons. For example, assume a movie theatre chain and a restaurant chain jointly agree to issue cards that share the same "Flix and Food" logo that can be redeemed solely towards the purchase of movie tickets or concessions at any of the participating movie theatres, or towards the purchase of food or beverages at any of the participating restaurants. For purposes of § 1005.20, the movie theatre chain and the restaurant chain would be considered to be an affiliated group of merchants, and the cards are considered to be "store gift cards." However, merchants or other persons are not considered to be affiliated merely because they agree to accept a card that bears the mark, logo, or brand of a payment network.

3. *Mall gift cards. See* comment 20(a)(3)–2.

20(a)(3) General-Use Prepaid Card

1. *Redeemable upon presentation at multiple, unaffiliated merchants.* A card, code, or other device is redeemable upon presentation at multiple, unaffiliated merchants if, for example, such merchants agree to honor the card, code, or device if it bears the mark, logo, or brand of a payment network, pursuant to the rules of the payment network.

2. *Mall gift cards.* Mall gift cards that are intended to be used or redeemed for goods or services at participating retailers within a shopping mall may be considered store gift cards or general-use prepaid cards depending on the merchants with which the cards may be redeemed. For example, if a mall card may only be redeemed at merchants within the mall itself, the card is more likely to be redeemable at an affiliated group of merchants and considered a store gift card. However, certain mall cards also carry the brand of a payment network and can be used at any retailer that accepts that card brand, including retailers located outside of the mall. Such cards are considered general-use prepaid cards.

20(a)(4) Loyalty, Award, or Promotional Gift Card

1. *Examples of loyalty, award, or promotional programs.* Examples of loyalty, award, or promotional programs under § 1005.20(a)(4) include, but are not limited to:

OFFICIAL INTERPRETATIONS OF REGULATION E

i.   Consumer retention programs operated or administered by a merchant or other person that provide to consumers cards or coupons redeemable for or towards goods or services or other monetary value as a reward for purchases made or for visits to the participating merchant.

ii.   Sales promotions operated or administered by a merchant or product manufacturer that provide coupons or discounts redeemable for or towards goods or services or other monetary value.

iii. Rebate programs operated or administered by a merchant or product manufacturer that provide cards redeemable for or towards goods or services or other monetary value to consumers in connection with the consumer's purchase of a product or service and the consumer's completion of the rebate submission process.

iv.   Sweepstakes or contests that distribute cards redeemable for or towards goods or services or other monetary value to consumers as an invitation to enter into the promotion for a chance to win a prize.

v.   Referral programs that provide cards redeemable for or towards goods or services or other monetary value to consumers in exchange for referring other potential consumers to a merchant.

vi.   Incentive programs through which an employer provides cards redeemable for or towards goods or services or other monetary value to employees, for example, to recognize job performance, such as increased sales, or to encourage employee wellness and safety.

vii. Charitable or community relations programs through which a company provides cards redeemable for or towards goods or services or other monetary value to a charity or community group for their fundraising purposes, for example, as a reward for a donation or as a prize in a charitable event.

2.   *Issued for loyalty, award, or promotional purposes.* To indicate that a card, code, or other device is issued for loyalty, award, or promotional purposes as required by § 1005.20(a)(4)(iii), it is sufficient for the card, code, or other device to state on the front, for example, "Reward" or "Promotional."

3.   *Reference to toll-free number and Web site.* If a card, code, or other device issued in connection with a loyalty, award, or promotional program does not have any fees, the disclosure under § 1005.20(a)(4)(iii)(D) is not required on the card, code, or other device.

20(a)(6) Service Fee

1.   *Service fees.* Under § 1005.20(a)(6), a service fee includes a periodic fee for holding or use of a gift certificate, store gift card, or general-use prepaid card. A periodic fee includes any fee that may be imposed on a gift certificate, store gift card, or general-use prepaid card from time to time for holding or using the certificate or card, such as a monthly maintenance fee, a transaction fee, an ATM fee, a reload fee, a foreign currency transaction fee, or a balance inquiry fee, whether or not the fee is waived for a certain period of time or is only imposed after a certain period of time. A service fee does not include a one-time fee or a fee that is unlikely to be imposed more than once while the underlying funds are still valid, such as an initial issuance fee, a cash-out fee, a supplemental card fee, or a lost or stolen certificate or card replacement fee.

20(a)(7) Activity

1.   *Activity.* Under § 1005.20(a)(7), any action that results in an increase or decrease of the funds underlying a gift certificate, store gift card, or general-use prepaid card, other than the imposition of a fee, or an adjustment due to an error or a reversal of a prior transaction, constitutes activity for purposes of § 1005.20. For example, the purchase and activation of a certificate or card, the use of the certificate or card to purchase a good or service, or the reloading of funds onto a store gift card or general-use prepaid card constitutes activity. However, the imposition of a fee, the replacement of an expired, lost, or stolen certificate or card, and a balance inquiry do not constitute activity. In addition, if a consumer attempts to engage in a transaction with a gift certificate, store gift card, or general-use prepaid card, but the transaction cannot be completed due to technical or other reasons, such attempt does not constitute activity. Furthermore, if the funds underlying a gift certificate, store gift card, or general-use prepaid card are adjusted because there was an error or the consumer has returned a previously purchased good, the adjustment also does not constitute activity with respect to the certificate or card.

OFFICIAL INTERPRETATIONS OF REGULATION E

20(b) Exclusions

1. *Application of exclusion.* A card, code, or other device is excluded from the definition of "gift certificate," "store gift card," or "general-use prepaid card" if it meets any of the exclusions in § 1005.20(b). An excluded card, code, or other device generally is not subject to any of the requirements of this section. *See, however,* § 1005.20(a)(4)(iii), requiring certain disclosures for loyalty, award, or promotional gift cards.

2. *Eligibility for multiple exclusions.* A card, code, or other device may qualify for one or more exclusions. For example, a corporation may give its employees a gift card that is marketed solely to businesses for incentive-related purposes, such as to reward job performance or promote employee safety. In this case, the card may qualify for the exclusion for loyalty, award, or promotional gift cards under § 1005.20(b)(3), or for the exclusion for cards, codes, or other devices not marketed to the general public under § 1005.20(b)(4). In addition, as long as any one of the exclusions applies, a card, code, or other device is not covered by § 1005.20, even if other exclusions do not apply. In the above example, the corporation may give its employees a type of gift card that can also be purchased by a consumer directly from a merchant. Under these circumstances, while the card does not qualify for the exclusion for cards, codes, or other devices not marketed to the general public under § 1005.20(b)(4) because the card can also be obtained through retail channels, it is nevertheless exempt from the substantive requirements of § 1005.20 because it is a loyalty, award, or promotional gift card. *See, however,* § 1005.20(a)(4)(iii), requiring certain disclosures for loyalty, award, or promotional gift cards. Similarly, a person may market a reloadable card to teenagers for occasional expenses that enables parents to monitor spending. Although the card does not qualify for the exclusion for cards, codes, or other devices not marketed to the general public under § 1005.20(b)(4), it may nevertheless be exempt from the requirements of § 1005.20 under § 1005.20(b)(2) if it is reloadable and not marketed or labeled as a gift card or gift certificate.

Paragraph 20(b)(1)

1. *Examples of excluded products.* The exclusion for products usable solely for telephone services applies to prepaid cards for long-distance telephone service, prepaid cards for wireless telephone service and prepaid cards for other services that function similar to telephone services, such as prepaid cards for voice over Internet protocol (VoIP) access time.

Paragraph 20(b)(2)

1. *Reloadable.* A card, code, or other device is "reloadable" if the terms and conditions of the agreement permit funds to be added to the card, code, or other device after the initial purchase or issuance. A card, code, or other device is not "reloadable" merely because the issuer or processor is technically able to add functionality that would otherwise enable the card, code, or other device to be reloaded.

2. *Marketed or labeled as a gift card or gift certificate.* The term "marketed or labeled as a gift card or gift certificate" means directly or indirectly offering, advertising, or otherwise suggesting the potential use of a card, code or other device, as a gift for another person. Whether the exclusion applies generally does not depend on the type of entity that makes the promotional message. For example, a card may be marketed or labeled as a gift card or gift certificate if anyone (other than the purchaser of the card), including the issuer, the retailer, the program manager that may distribute the card, or the payment network on which a card is used, promotes the use of the card as a gift card or gift certificate. A card, code, or other device, including a general-purpose reloadable card, is marketed or labeled as a gift card or gift certificate even if it is only occasionally marketed as a gift card or gift certificate. For example, a network-branded general purpose reloadable card would be marketed or labeled as a gift card or gift certificate if the issuer principally advertises the card as a less costly alternative to a bank account but promotes the card in a television, radio, newspaper, or Internet advertisement, or on signage as "the perfect gift" during the holiday season. However, the mere mention of the availability of gift cards or gift certificates in an advertisement or on a sign that also indicates the availability of other excluded prepaid cards does not by itself cause the excluded prepaid cards to be marketed as a gift card or a gift certificate. For example, the posting of a sign in a store that refers to the availability of gift cards does not by itself constitute the marketing of otherwise excluded prepaid cards that may also be sold in the store as gift cards or gift certificates, provided that a consumer acting reasonably under the circumstances would not be led to believe that the sign applies to all prepaid cards sold in the store. *See, however,* comment 20(b)(2)–4.ii.

3. *Examples of marketed or labeled as a gift card or gift certificate.*

    i.   Examples of marketed or labeled as a gift card or gift certificate include:

    A.   Using the word "gift" or "present" on a card, certificate, or accompanying material, including documentation, packaging and promotional displays.

    B.   Representing or suggesting that a certificate or card can be given to another person, for example, as a "token of appreciation" or a "stocking stuffer," or displaying a congratulatory message on the card, certificate or accompanying material.

    C.   Incorporating gift-giving or celebratory imagery or motifs, such as a bow, ribbon, wrapped present, candle, or congratulatory message, on a card, certificate, accompanying documentation, or promotional material.

    ii.   The term does not include:

    A.   Representing that a card or certificate can be used as a substitute for a checking, savings, or deposit account.

    B.   Representing that a card or certificate can be used to pay for a consumer's health-related expenses—for example, a card tied to a health savings account.

    C.   Representing that a card or certificate can be used as a substitute for traveler's checks or cash.

    D.   Representing that a card or certificate can be used as a budgetary tool, for example, by teenagers, or to cover emergency expenses.

4. *Reasonable policies and procedures to avoid marketing as a gift card.* The exclusion for a card, code, or other device that is reloadable and not marketed or labeled as a gift card or gift certificate in § 1005.20(b)(2) applies if a reloadable card, code, or other device is not marketed or labeled as a gift card or gift certificate and if persons subject to the rule, including issuers, program managers, and retailers, maintain policies and procedures reasonably designed to avoid such marketing. Such policies and procedures may include contractual provisions prohibiting a reloadable card, code, or other device from being marketed or labeled as a gift card or gift certificate, merchandising guidelines or plans regarding how the product must be displayed in a retail outlet, and controls to regularly monitor or otherwise verify that the card, code or other device is not being marketed as a gift card. Whether a reloadable card, code, or other device has been marketed as a gift card or gift certificate will depend on the facts and circumstances, including whether a reasonable consumer would be led to believe that the card, code, or other device is a gift card or gift certificate. The following examples illustrate the application of § 1005.20(b)(2):

    i.   An issuer or program manager of prepaid cards agrees to sell general-purpose reloadable cards through a retailer. The contract between the issuer or program manager and the retailer establishes the terms and conditions under which the cards may be sold and marketed at the retailer. The terms and conditions prohibit the general-purpose reloadable cards from being marketed as a gift card or gift certificate, and require policies and procedures to regularly monitor or otherwise verify that the cards are not being marketed as such. The issuer or program manager sets up one promotional display at the retailer for gift cards and another physically separated display for excluded products under § 1005.20(b), including general-purpose reloadable cards and wireless telephone cards, such that a reasonable consumer would not believe that the excluded cards are gift cards. The exclusion in § 1005.20(b)(2) applies because policies and procedures reasonably designed to avoid the marketing of the general-purpose reloadable cards as gift cards or gift certificates are maintained, even if a retail clerk inadvertently stocks or a consumer inadvertently places a general-purpose reloadable card on the gift card display.

    ii.   Same facts as in i., except that the issuer or program manager sets up a single promotional display at the retailer on which a variety of prepaid cards are sold, including store gift cards and general-purpose reloadable cards. A sign stating "Gift Cards" appears prominently at the top of the display. The exclusion in § 1005.20(b)(2) does not apply with respect to the general-purpose reloadable cards because policies and procedures reasonably designed to avoid the marketing of excluded cards as gift cards or gift certificates are not maintained.

iii.   Same facts as in i., except that the issuer or program manager sets up a single promotional multi-sided display at the retailer on which a variety of prepaid card products, including store gift cards and general-purpose reloadable cards are sold. Gift cards are segregated from excluded cards, with gift cards on one side of the display and excluded cards on a different side of a display. Signs of equal prominence at the top of each side of the display clearly differentiate between gift cards and the other types of prepaid cards that are available for sale. The retailer does not use any more conspicuous signage suggesting the general availability of gift cards, such as a large sign stating "Gift Cards" at the top of the display or located near the display. The exclusion in § 1005.20(b)(2) applies because policies and procedures reasonably designed to avoid the marketing of the general-purpose reloadable cards as gift cards or gift certificates are maintained, even if a retail clerk inadvertently stocks or a consumer inadvertently places a general-purpose reloadable card on the gift card display.

iv.   Same facts as in i., except that the retailer sells a variety of prepaid card products, including store gift cards and general-purpose reloadable cards, arranged side-by-side in the same checkout lane. The retailer does not affirmatively indicate or represent that gift cards are available, such as by displaying any signage or other indicia at the checkout lane suggesting the general availability of gift cards. The exclusion in § 1005.20(b)(2) applies because policies and procedures reasonably designed to avoid marketing the general-purpose reloadable cards as gift cards or gift certificates are maintained.

5.   *Online sales of prepaid cards.* Some Web sites may prominently advertise or promote the availability of gift cards or gift certificates in a manner that suggests to a consumer that the Web site exclusively sells gift cards or gift certificates. For example, a Web site may display a banner advertisement or a graphic on the home page that prominently states "Gift Cards," "Gift Giving," or similar language without mention of other available products, or use a web address that includes only a reference to gift cards or gift certificates in the address. In such a case, a consumer acting reasonably under the circumstances could be led to believe that all prepaid products sold on the Web site are gift cards or gift certificates. Under these facts, the Web site has marketed all such products, including general-purpose reloadable cards, as gift cards or gift certificates, and the exclusion in § 1005.20(b)(2) does not apply.

6.   *Temporary non-reloadable cards issued in connection with a general-purpose reloadable card.* Certain general-purpose reloadable cards that are typically marketed as an account substitute initially may be sold or issued in the form of a temporary non-reloadable card. After the card is purchased, the cardholder is typically required to call the issuer to register the card and to provide identifying information in order to obtain a reloadable replacement card. In most cases, the temporary non-reloadable card can be used for purchases until the replacement reloadable card arrives and is activated by the cardholder. Because the temporary non-reloadable card may only be obtained in connection with the general-purpose reloadable card, the exclusion in § 1005.20(b)(2) applies so long as the card is not marketed as a gift card or gift certificate.

Paragraph 20(b)(4)

1.   *Marketed to the general public.* A card, code, or other device is marketed to the general public if the potential use of the card, code, or other device is directly or indirectly offered, advertised, or otherwise promoted to the general public. A card, code, or other device may be marketed to the general public through any advertising medium, including television, radio, newspaper, the Internet, or signage. However, the posting of a company policy that funds may be disbursed by prepaid card (such as a sign posted at a cash register or customer service center stating that store credit will be issued by prepaid card) does not constitute the marketing of a card, code, or other device to the general public. In addition, the method of distribution by itself is not dispositive in determining whether a card, code, or other device is marketed to the general public. Factors that may be considered in determining whether the exclusion applies to a particular card, code, or other device include the means or channel through which the card, code, or device may be obtained by a consumer, the subset of consumers that are eligible to obtain the card, code, or device, and whether the availability of the card, code, or device is advertised or otherwise promoted in the marketplace.

OFFICIAL INTERPRETATIONS OF REGULATION E

2. *Examples.* The following examples illustrate the application of the exclusion in § 1005.20(b)(4):

i. A merchant sells its gift cards at a discount to a business which may give them to employees or loyal consumers as incentives or rewards. In determining whether the gift card falls within the exclusion in § 1005.20(b)(4), the merchant must consider whether the card is of a type that is advertised or made available to consumers generally or can be obtained elsewhere. If the card can also be purchased through retail channels, the exclusion in § 1005.20(b)(4) does not apply, even if the consumer obtained the card from the business as an incentive or reward. *See, however,* § 1005.20(b)(3).

ii. A national retail chain decides to market its gift cards only to members of its frequent buyer program. Similarly, a bank may decide to sell gift cards only to its customers. If a member of the general public may become a member of the program or a customer of the bank, the card does not fall within the exclusion in § 1005.20(b)(4) because the general public has the ability to obtain the cards. *See, however,* § 1005.20(b)(3).

iii. A card issuer advertises a reloadable card to teenagers and their parents promoting the card for use by teenagers for occasional expenses, schoolbooks and emergencies and by parents to monitor spending. Because the card is marketed to and may be sold to any member of the general public, the exclusion in § 1005.20(b)(4) does not apply. *See, however,* § 1005.20(b)(2).

iv. An insurance company settles a policyholder's claim and distributes the insurance proceeds to the consumer by means of a prepaid card. Because the prepaid card is simply the means for providing the insurance proceeds to the consumer and the availability of the card is not advertised to the general public, the exclusion in § 1005.20(b)(4) applies.

v. A merchant provides store credit to a consumer following a merchandise return by issuing a prepaid card that clearly indicates that the card contains funds for store credit. Because the prepaid card is issued for the stated purpose of providing store credit to the consumer and the ability to receive refunds by a prepaid card is not advertised to the general public, the exclusion in § 1005.20(b)(4) applies.

vi. A tax preparation company elects to distribute tax refunds to its clients by issuing prepaid cards, but does not advertise or otherwise promote the ability to receive proceeds in this manner. Because the prepaid card is simply the mechanism for providing the tax refund to the consumer, and the tax preparer does not advertise the ability to obtain tax refunds by a prepaid card, the exclusion in § 1005.20(b)(4) applies. However, if the tax preparer promotes the ability to receive tax refund proceeds through a prepaid card as a way to obtain "faster" access to the proceeds, the exclusion in § 1005.20(b)(4) does not apply.

Paragraph 20(b)(5)

1. *Exclusion explained.* To qualify for the exclusion in § 1005.20(b)(5), the sole means of issuing the card, code, or other device must be in a paper form. Thus, the exclusion generally applies to certificates issued in paper form where solely the paper itself may be used to purchase goods or services. A card, code or other device is not issued solely in paper form simply because it may be reproduced or printed on paper. For example, a bar code, card or certificate number, or certificate or coupon electronically provided to a consumer and redeemable for goods and services is not issued in paper form, even if it may be reproduced or otherwise printed on paper by the consumer. In this circumstance, although the consumer might hold a paper facsimile of the card, code, or other device, the exclusion does not apply because the information necessary to redeem the value was initially issued in electronic form. A paper certificate is within the exclusion regardless of whether it may be redeemed electronically. For example, a paper certificate or receipt that bears a bar code, code, or account number falls within the exclusion in § 1005.20(b)(5) if the bar code, code, or account number is not issued in any form other than on the paper. In addition, the exclusion in § 1005.20(b)(5) continues to apply in circumstances where an issuer replaces a gift certificate that was initially issued in paper form with a card or electronic code (for example, to replace a lost paper certificate).

2. *Examples.* The following examples illustrate the application of the exclusion in § 1005.20(b)(5):

i. A merchant issues a paper gift certificate that entitles the bearer to a specified dollar amount that can be applied towards a future meal. The merchant fills in the certificate with the name of the certificate holder and the amount of the certificate. The certificate falls within the exclusion in § 1005.20(b)(5) because it is issued in paper form only.

ii.   A merchant allows a consumer to prepay for a good or service, such as a car wash or time at a parking meter, and issues a paper receipt bearing a numerical or bar code that the consumer may redeem to obtain the good or service. The exclusion in § 1005.20(b)(5) applies because the code is issued in paper form only.

iii.   A merchant issues a paper certificate or receipt bearing a bar code or certificate number that can later be scanned or entered into the merchant's system and redeemed by the certificate or receipt holder towards the purchase of goods or services. The bar code or certificate number is not issued by the merchant in any form other than paper. The exclusion in § 1005.20(b)(5) applies because the bar code or certificate number is issued in paper form only.

iv.   An online merchant electronically provides a bar code, card or certificate number, or certificate or coupon to a consumer that the consumer may print on a home printer and later redeem towards the purchase of goods or services. The exclusion in § 1005.20(b)(5) does not apply because the bar code or card or certificate number was issued to the consumer in electronic form, even though it can be reproduced or otherwise printed on paper by the consumer.

Paragraph 20(b)(6)

1.   *Exclusion explained.* The exclusion for cards, codes, or other devices that are redeemable solely for admission to events or venues at a particular location or group of affiliated locations generally applies to cards, codes, or other devices that are not redeemed for a specified monetary value, but rather solely for admission or entry to an event or venue. The exclusion also covers a card, code, or other device that is usable to purchase goods or services in addition to entry into the event or the venue, either at the event or venue or at an affiliated location or location in geographic proximity to the event or venue.

2.   *Examples.* The following examples illustrate the application of the exclusion in § 1005.20(b)(6):

i.   A consumer purchases a prepaid card that entitles the holder to a ticket for entry to an amusement park. The prepaid card may only be used for entry to the park. The card qualifies for the exclusion in § 1005.20(b)(6) because it is redeemable for admission or entry and for goods or services in conjunction with that admission. In addition, if the prepaid card does not have a monetary value, and therefore is not "issued in a specified amount," the card does not meet the definitions of "gift certificate," "store gift card," or "general-use prepaid card" in § 1005.20(a). *See* comment 20(a)–3.

ii.   Same facts as in i., except that the gift card also entitles the holder of the gift card to a dollar amount that can be applied towards the purchase of food and beverages or goods or services at the park or at nearby affiliated locations. The card qualifies for the exclusion in § 1005.20(b)(6) because it is redeemable for admission or entry and for goods or services in conjunction with that admission.

iii.   A consumer purchases a $25 gift card that the holder of the gift card can use to make purchases at a merchant, or, alternatively, can apply towards the cost of admission to the merchant's affiliated amusement park. The card is not eligible for the exclusion in § 1005.20(b)(6) because it is not redeemable solely for the admission or ticket itself (or for goods and services purchased in conjunction with such admission). The card meets the definition of "store gift card" and is therefore subject to § 1005.20, unless a different exclusion applies.

20(c) Form of Disclosures

20(c)(1) Clear and Conspicuous

1.   *Clear and conspicuous standard.* All disclosures required by this section must be clear and conspicuous. Disclosures are clear and conspicuous for purposes of this section if they are readily understandable and, in the case of written and electronic disclosures, the location and type size are readily noticeable to consumers. Disclosures need not be located on the front of the certificate or card, except where otherwise required, to be considered clear and conspicuous. Disclosures are clear and conspicuous for the purposes of this section if they are in a print that contrasts with and is otherwise not obstructed by the background on which they are printed. For example, disclosures on a card or computer screen are not likely to be conspicuous if

obscured by a logo printed in the background. Similarly, disclosures on the back of a card that are printed on top of indentations from embossed type on the front of the card are not likely to be conspicuous if the indentations obstruct the readability of the disclosures. To the extent permitted, oral disclosures meet the standard when they are given at a volume and speed sufficient for a consumer to hear and comprehend them.

2. *Abbreviations and symbols.* Disclosures may contain commonly accepted or readily understandable abbreviations or symbols, such as "mo." for month or a "/" to indicate "per." Under the clear and conspicuous standard, it is sufficient to state, for example, that a particular fee is charged "$2.50/mo. after 12 mos."

20(c)(2) Format

1. *Electronic disclosures.* Disclosures provided electronically pursuant to this section are not subject to compliance with the consumer consent and other applicable provisions of the Electronic Signatures in Global and National Commerce Act (E-Sign Act) (15 U.S.C. 7001 *et seq.*). Electronic disclosures must be in a retainable form. For example, a person may satisfy the requirement if it provides an online disclosure in a format that is capable of being printed. Electronic disclosures may not be provided through a hyperlink or in another manner by which the purchaser can bypass the disclosure. A person is not required to confirm that the consumer has read the electronic disclosures.

20(c)(3) Disclosure Prior to Purchase

1. *Method of purchase.* The disclosures required by this paragraph must be provided before a certificate or card is purchased regardless of whether the certificate or card is purchased in person, online, by telephone, or by other means.

2. *Electronic disclosures.* Section 1005.20(c)(3) provides that the disclosures required by this section must be provided to the consumer prior to purchase. For certificates or cards purchased electronically, disclosures made to the consumer after a consumer has initiated an online purchase of a certificate or card, but prior to completing the purchase of the certificate or card, would satisfy the prior-to-purchase requirement. However, electronic disclosures made available on a person's Web site that may or may not be accessed by the consumer are not provided to the consumer and therefore would not satisfy the prior-to-purchase requirement.

3. *Non-physical certificates and cards.* If no physical certificate or card is issued, the disclosures must be provided to the consumer before the certificate or card is purchased. For example, where a gift certificate or card is a code that is provided by telephone, the required disclosures may be provided orally prior to purchase. *See also* § 1005.20(c)(2).

20(c)(4) Disclosures on the Certificate or Card

1. *Non-physical certificates and cards.* If no physical certificate or card is issued, the disclosures required by this paragraph must be disclosed on the code, confirmation, or other written or electronic document provided to the consumer. For example, where a gift certificate or card is a code or confirmation that is provided to a consumer online or sent to a consumer's email address, the required disclosures may be provided electronically on the same document as the code or confirmation.2. *No disclosures on a certificate or card.* Disclosures required by § 1005.20(c)(4) need not be made on a certificate or card if it is accompanied by a certificate or card that complies with this section. For example, a person may issue or sell a supplemental gift card that is smaller than a standard size and that does not bear the applicable disclosures if it is accompanied by a fully compliant certificate or card. *See also* comment 20(c)(2)–2.

20(d) Prohibition on Imposition of Fees or Charges

1. *One-year period.* Section 1005.20(d) provides that a person may impose a dormancy, inactivity, or service fee only if there has been no activity with respect to a certificate or card for one year. The following examples illustrate this rule:

    i.   A certificate or card is purchased on January 15 of year one. If there has been no activity on the certificate or card since the certificate or card was purchased, a dormancy, inactivity, or service fee may be imposed on the certificate or card on January 15 of year two.

ii.   Same facts as i., and a fee was imposed on January 15 of year two. Because no more than one dormancy, inactivity, or service fee may be imposed in any given calendar month, the earliest date that another dormancy, inactivity, or service fee may be imposed, assuming there continues to be no activity on the certificate or card, is February 1 of year two. A dormancy, inactivity, or service fee is permitted to be imposed on February 1 of year two because there has been no activity on the certificate or card for the preceding year (February 1 of year one through January 31 of year two), and February is a new calendar month. The imposition of a fee on January 15 of year two is not activity for purposes of § 1005.20(d). *See* comment 20(a)(7)–1.

iii.   Same facts as i., and a fee was imposed on January 15 of year two. On January 31 of year two, the consumer uses the card to make a purchase. Another dormancy, inactivity, or service fee could not be imposed until January 31 of year three, assuming there has been no activity on the certificate or card since January 31 of year two.

2.   *Relationship between §§ 1005.20(d)(2) and (c)(3).* Sections 1005.20(d)(2) and (c)(3) contain similar, but not identical, disclosure requirements. Section 1005.20(d)(2) requires the disclosure of dormancy, inactivity, and service fees on a certificate or card. Section 1005.20(c)(3) requires that vendor person that issues or sells such certificate or card disclose to a consumer any dormancy, inactivity, and service fees associated with the certificate or card before such certificate or card may be purchased. Depending on the context, a single disclosure that meets the clear and conspicuous requirements of both §§ 1005.20(d)(2) and (c)(3) may be used to disclose a dormancy, inactivity, or service fee. For example, if the disclosures on a certificate or card, required by § 1005.20(d)(2), are visible to the consumer without having to remove packaging or other materials sold with the certificate or card, for a purchase made in person, the disclosures also meet the requirements of § 1005.20(c)(3). Otherwise, a dormancy, inactivity, or service fee may need to be disclosed multiple times to satisfy the requirements of §§ 1005.20(d)(2) and (c)(3). For example, if the disclosures on a certificate or card, required by § 1005.20(d)(2), are obstructed by packaging sold with the certificate or card, for a purchase made in person, they also must be disclosed on the packaging sold with the certificate or card to meet the requirements of § 1005.20(c)(3).

3.   *Relationship between §§ 1005.20(d)(2), (e)(3), and (f)(2).* In addition to any disclosures required under § 1005.20(d)(2), any applicable disclosures under §§ 1005.20(e)(3) and (f)(2) of this section must also be provided on the certificate or card.

4.   *One fee per month.* Under § 1005.20(d)(3), no more than one dormancy, inactivity, or service fee may be imposed in any given calendar month. For example, if a dormancy fee is imposed on January 1, following a year of inactivity, and a consumer makes a balance inquiry on January 15, a balance inquiry fee may not be imposed at that time because a dormancy fee was already imposed earlier that month and a balance inquiry fee is a type of service fee. If, however, the dormancy fee could be imposed on January 1, following a year of inactivity, and the consumer makes a balance inquiry on the same date, the person assessing the fees may choose whether to impose the dormancy fee or the balance inquiry fee on January 1. The restriction in § 1005.20(d)(3) does not apply to any fee that is not a dormancy, inactivity, or service fee. For example, assume a service fee is imposed on a general-use prepaid card on January 1, following a year of inactivity. If a consumer cashes out the remaining funds by check on January 15, a cash-out fee, to the extent such cash-out fee is permitted under § 1005.20(e)(4), may be imposed at that time because a cash-out fee is not a dormancy, inactivity, or service fee.

5.   *Accumulation of fees.* Section 1005.20(d) prohibits the accumulation of dormancy, inactivity, or service fees for previous periods into a single fee because such a practice would circumvent the limitation in § 1005.20(d)(3) that only one fee may be charged per month. For example, if a consumer purchases and activates a store gift card on January 1 but never uses the card, a monthly maintenance fee of $2.00 a month may not be accumulated such that a fee of $24 is imposed on January 1 the following year.

20(e) Prohibition on Sale of Gift Certificates or Cards With Expiration Dates

1.   *Reasonable opportunity.* Under § 1005.20(e)(1), no person may sell or issue a gift certificate, store gift card, or general-use prepaid card with an expiration date, unless there are policies and procedures in place to provide consumers with a reasonable opportunity to purchase a certificate or card with at least five years remaining until the certificate or card expiration date. Consumers are deemed to have a reasonable

opportunity to purchase a certificate or card with at least five years remaining until the certificate or card expiration date if:

    i.   There are policies and procedures established to prevent the sale of a certificate or card unless the certificate or card expiration date is at least five years after the date the certificate or card was sold or initially issued to a consumer; or

    ii.   A certificate or card is available to consumers to purchase five years and six months before the certificate or card expiration date.

2.   *Applicability to replacement certificates or cards.* Section 1005.20(e)(1) applies solely to the *purchase* of a certificate or card. Therefore, § 1005.20(e)(1) does not apply to the replacement of such certificates or cards. Certificates or cards issued as a replacement may bear a certificate or card expiration date of less than five years from the date of issuance of the replacement certificate or card. If the certificate or card expiration date for a replacement certificate or card is later than the date set forth in § 1005.20(e)(2)(i), then pursuant to § 1005.20(e)(2), the expiration date for the underlying funds at the time the replacement certificate or card is issued must be no earlier than the expiration date for the replacement certificate or card. For purposes of § 1005.20(e)(2), funds are not considered to be loaded to a store gift card or general-use prepaid card solely because a replacement card has been issued or activated for use.

3.   *Disclosure of funds expiration—date not required.* Section 1005.20(e)(3)(i) does not require disclosure of the precise date the funds will expire. It is sufficient to disclose, for example, "Funds expire 5 years from the date funds last loaded to the card."; "Funds can be used 5 years from the date money was last added to the card."; or "Funds do not expire."

4.   *Disclosure not required if no expiration date.* If the certificate or card and underlying funds do not expire, the disclosure required by § 1005.20(e)(3)(i) need not be stated on the certificate or card. If the certificate or card and underlying funds expire at the same time, only one expiration date need be disclosed on the certificate or card.

5.   *Reference to toll-free telephone number and Web site.* If a certificate or card does not expire, or if the underlying funds are not available after the certificate or card expires, the disclosure required by § 1005.20(e)(3)(ii) need not be stated on the certificate or card. *See, however,* § 1005.20(f)(2).

6.   *Relationship to § 226.20(f)(2).* The same toll-free telephone number and Web site may be used to comply with §§ 226.20(e)(3)(ii) and (f)(2). Neither a toll-free number nor a Web site must be maintained or disclosed if no fees are imposed in connection with a certificate or card, and the certificate or card and the underlying funds do not expire.

7.   *Distinguishing between certificate or card expiration and funds expiration.* If applicable, a disclosure must be made on the certificate or card that notifies a consumer that the certificate or card expires, but the funds either do not expire or expire later than the certificate or card, and that the consumer may contact the issuer for a replacement card. The disclosure must be made with equal prominence and in close proximity to the certificate or card expiration date. The close proximity requirement does not apply to oral disclosures. In the case of a certificate or card, close proximity means that the disclosure must be on the same side as the certificate or card expiration date. For example, if the disclosure is the same type size and is located immediately next to or directly above or below the certificate or card expiration date, without any intervening text or graphical displays, the disclosures would be deemed to be equally prominent and in close proximity. The disclosure need not be embossed on the certificate or card to be deemed equally prominent, even if the expiration date is embossed on the certificate or card. The disclosure may state on the front of the card, for example, "Funds expire after card. Call for replacement card." or "Funds do not expire. Call for new card after 09/2016." Disclosures made pursuant to § 1005.20(e)(3)(iii)(A) may also fulfill the requirements of § 1005.20(e)(3)(i). For example, making a disclosure that "Funds do not expire" to comply with § 1005.20(e)(3)(iii)(A) also fulfills the requirements of § 1005.20(e)(3)(i).

8.   *Expiration date safe harbor.* A non-reloadable certificate or card that bears an expiration date that is at least seven years from the date of manufacture need not state the disclosure required by § 1005.20(e)(3)(iii). However, § 1005.20(e)(1) still prohibits the sale or issuance of such certificate or card unless there are policies and procedures in place to provide a consumer with a reasonable opportunity to purchase the certificate or card with at least five years remaining until the certificate or card expiration

date. In addition, under § 1005.20(e)(2), the funds may not expire before the certificate or card expiration date, even if the expiration date of the certificate or card bears an expiration date that is more than five years from the date of purchase. For purposes of this safe harbor, the date of manufacture is the date on which the certificate or card expiration date is printed on the certificate or card.

9. *Relationship between §§ 1005.20(d)(2), (e)(3), and (f)(2).* In addition to any disclosures required to be made under § 1005.20(e)(3), any applicable disclosures under §§ 1005.20(d)(2) and (f)(2) must also be provided on the certificate or card.

10. *Replacement or remaining balance of an expired certificate or card.* When a certificate or card expires, but the underlying funds have not expired, an issuer, at its option in accordance with applicable state law, may provide either a replacement certificate or card or otherwise provide the certificate or card holder, for example, by check, with the remaining balance on the certificate or card. In either case, the issuer may not charge a fee for the service.

11. *Replacement of a lost or stolen certificate or card not required.* Section 1005.20(e)(4) does not require the replacement of a certificate or card that has been lost or stolen.

12. *Date of issuance or loading.* For purposes of § 1005.20(e)(2)(i), a certificate or card is not issued or loaded with funds until the certificate or card is activated for use.

13. *Application of expiration date provisions after redemption of certificate or card.* The requirement that funds underlying a certificate or card must not expire for at least five years from the date of issuance or date of last load ceases to apply once the certificate or card has been fully redeemed, even if the underlying funds are not used to contemporaneously purchase a specific good or service. For example, some certificates or cards can be used to purchase music, media, or virtual goods. Once redeemed by a consumer, the entire balance on the certificate or card is debited from the certificate or card and credited or transferred to another "account" established by the merchant of such goods or services. The consumer can then make purchases of songs, media, or virtual goods from the merchant using that "account" either at the time the value is transferred from the certificate or card or at a later time. Under these circumstances, once the card has been fully redeemed and the "account" credited with the amount of the underlying funds, the five-year minimum expiration term no longer applies to the underlying funds. However, if the consumer only partially redeems the value of the certificate or card, the five-year minimum expiration term requirement continues to apply to the funds remaining on the certificate or card.

20(f) Additional Disclosure Requirements for Gift Certificates or Cards

1. *Reference to toll-free telephone number and Web site.* If a certificate or card does not have any fees, the disclosure under § 1005.20(f)(2) is not required on the certificate or card. *See, however,* § 1005.20(e)(3)(ii).

2. *Relationship to § 226.20(e)(3)(ii).* The same toll-free telephone number and Web site may be used to comply with §§ 226.20(e)(3)(ii) and (f)(2). Neither a toll-free number nor a Web site must be maintained or disclosed if no fees are imposed in connection with a certificate or card, and both the certificate or card and underlying funds do not expire.

3. *Relationship between §§ 1005.20(d)(2), (e)(3), and (f)(2).* In addition to any disclosures required pursuant to § 1005.20(f)(2), any applicable disclosures under §§ 1005.20(d)(2) and (e)(3) must also be provided on the certificate or card.

20(g) Compliance Dates

1. *Period of eligibility for loyalty, award, or promotional programs.* For purposes of § 1005.20(g)(2), the period of eligibility is the time period during which a consumer must engage in a certain action or actions to meet the terms of eligibility for a loyalty, award, or promotional program and obtain the card, code, or other device. Under § 1005.20(g)(2), a gift card issued pursuant to a loyalty, award, or promotional program that began prior to August 22, 2010 need not state the disclosures in § 1005.20(a)(4)(iii) regardless of whether the consumer became eligible to receive the gift card prior to August 22, 2010, or after that date. For example, a product manufacturer may provide a $20 rebate card to a consumer if the consumer purchases a particular product and submits a fully completed entry between January 1, 2010 and December 31, 2010. Similarly, a merchant may provide a $20 gift card to a consumer if the consumer makes $200 worth of qualifying purchases between June 1, 2010 and October 30, 2010. Under both examples, gift cards

provided pursuant to these loyalty, award, or promotional programs need not state the disclosures in § 1005.20(a)(4)(iii) to qualify for the exclusion in § 1005.20(b)(3) for loyalty, award, or promotional gift cards because the period of eligibility for each program began prior to August 22, 2010.

20(h) Temporary Exemption

20(h)(1) Delayed Effective Date

1. *Application to certificates or cards produced prior to April 1, 2010.* Certificates or cards produced prior to April 1, 2010 may be sold to a consumer on or after August 22, 2010 without satisfying the requirements of §§ 1005.20(c)(3), (d)(2), (e)(1), (e)(3), and (f) through January 30, 2011, provided that issuers of such certificates or cards comply with the additional substantive and disclosure requirements of §§ 1005.20(h)(1)(i) through (iv). Issuers of certificates or cards produced prior to April 1, 2010 need not satisfy these additional requirements if the certificates or cards fully comply with the rule (§§ 1005.20(a) through (f)). For example, the in-store signage and other disclosures required by § 1005.20(h)(2) do not apply to gift cards produced prior to April 1, 2010 that do not have fees and do not expire, and which otherwise comply with the rule.

2. *Expiration of temporary exemption.* Certificates or cards produced prior to April 1, 2010 that do not fully comply with §§ 1005.20(a) through (f) may not be issued or sold to consumers on or after January 31, 2011.

20(h)(2) Additional Disclosures

1. *Disclosures through third parties.* Issuers may make the disclosures required by § 1005.20(h)(2) through a third party, such as a retailer or merchant. For example, an issuer may have a merchant install in-store signage with the disclosures required by § 1005.20(h)(2) on the issuer's behalf.

2. *General advertising disclosures.* Section 1005.20(h)(2) does not impose an obligation on the issuer to advertise gift certificates, store gift cards, or general-use prepaid cards.

SECTION 1005.30—REMITTANCE TRANSFER DEFINITIONS

1. *Applicability of definitions in subpart A.* Except as modified or limited by subpart B (which modifications or limitations apply only to subpart B), the definitions in § 1005.2 apply to all of Regulation E, including subpart B.

30(b) Business Day

1. *General.* A business day, as defined in § 1005.30(b), includes the entire 24-hour period ending at midnight, and a notice given pursuant to any section of subpart B is effective even if given outside of normal business hours. A remittance transfer provider is not required under subpart B to make telephone lines available on a 24-hour basis.

2. *Substantially all business functions.* "Substantially all business functions" include both the public and the back-office operations of the provider. For example, if the offices of a provider are open on Saturdays for customers to request remittance transfers, but not for performing internal functions (such as investigating errors), then Saturday is not a business day for that provider. In this case, Saturday does not count toward the business-day standard set by subpart B for resolving errors, processing refunds, etc.

3. *Short hours.* A provider may determine, at its election, whether an abbreviated day is a business day. For example, if a provider engages in substantially all business functions until noon on Saturdays instead of its usual 3 p.m. closing, it may consider Saturday a business day.

4. *Telephone line.* If a provider makes a telephone line available on Sundays for cancelling the transfer, but performs no other business functions, Sunday is not a business day under the "substantially all business functions" standard.

30(c) Designated Recipient

1. *Person.* A designated recipient can be either a natural person or an organization, such as a corporation. *See* § 1005.2(j) (definition of person). The designated recipient is identified by the name of the person

provided by the sender to the remittance transfer provider and disclosed by the provider to the sender pursuant to § 1005.31(b)(1)(iii).

2. *Location in a foreign country.*

i.   A remittance transfer is received at a location in a foreign country if funds are to be received at a location physically outside of any State, as defined in § 1005.2(l). A specific pick-up location need not be designated for funds to be received at a location in a foreign country. If it is specified that the funds will be transferred to a foreign country to be picked up by the designated recipient, the transfer will be received at a location in a foreign country, even though a specific pick-up location within that country has not been designated. If it is specified that the funds will be received at a location on a U.S. military installation that is physically located in a foreign country, the transfer will be received in a State.

ii.   For transfers to a designated recipient's account, whether funds are to be received at a location physically outside of any State depends on where the recipient's account is located. If the account is located in a State, the funds will not be received at a location in a foreign country. Accounts that are located on a U.S. military installation that is physically located in a foreign country are located in a State.

iii.   Where the sender does not specify information about a designated recipient's account, but instead provides information about the recipient, a remittance transfer provider may make the determination of whether the funds will be received at a location in a foreign country on information that is provided by the sender, and other information the provider may have, at the time the transfer is requested. For example, if a consumer in a State gives a provider the recipient's email address, and the provider has no other information about whether the funds will be received by the recipient at a location in a foreign country, then the provider may determine that funds are not to be received at a location in a foreign country. However, if the provider at the time the transfer is requested has additional information indicating that funds are to be received in a foreign country, such as if the recipient's email address is already registered with the provider and associated with a foreign account, then the provider has sufficient information to conclude that the remittance transfer will be received at a location in a foreign country. Similarly, if a consumer in a State purchases a prepaid card, and the provider mails or delivers the card directly to the consumer, the provider may conclude that funds are not to be received in a foreign country, because the provider does not know whether the consumer will subsequently send the prepaid card to a recipient in a foreign country. In contrast, the provider has sufficient information to conclude that the funds are to be received in a foreign country if the remittance transfer provider sends a prepaid card to a specified recipient in a foreign country, even if a person located in a State, including the sender, retains the ability to access funds on the prepaid card.

3. *Sender as designated recipient.* A "sender," as defined in § 1005.30(g), may also be a designated recipient if the sender meets the definition of "designated recipient" in § 1005.30(c). For example, a sender may request that a provider send an electronic transfer of funds from the sender's checking account in a State to the sender's checking account located in a foreign country. In this case, the sender would also be a designated recipient.

30(d) Preauthorized Remittance Transfer

1. *Advance authorization.* A preauthorized remittance transfer is a remittance transfer authorized in advance of a transfer that will take place on a recurring basis, at substantially regular intervals, and will require no further action by the consumer to initiate the transfer. In a bill-payment system, for example, if the consumer authorizes a remittance transfer provider to make monthly payments to a payee by means of a remittance transfer, and the payments take place without further action by the consumer, the payments are preauthorized remittance transfers. In contrast, if the consumer must take action each month to initiate a transfer (such as by entering instructions on a telephone or home computer), the payments are not preauthorized remittance transfers.

30(e) Remittance Transfer

1. *Electronic transfer of funds.* The definition of "remittance transfer" requires an electronic transfer of funds. The term electronic has the meaning given in section 106(2) of the Electronic Signatures in Global and National Commerce Act. There may be an electronic transfer of funds if a provider makes an electronic

book entry between different settlement accounts to effectuate the transfer. However, where a sender mails funds directly to a recipient, or provides funds to a courier for delivery to a foreign country, there is not an electronic transfer of funds. Similarly, generally, where a provider issues a check, draft, or other paper instrument to be mailed to a person abroad, there is not an electronic transfer of funds. Nonetheless, an electronic transfer of funds occurs for a payment made by a provider under a bill-payment service available to a consumer via computer or other electronic means, unless the terms of the bill-payment service explicitly state that all payments, or all payments to a particular payee or payees, will be solely by check, draft, or similar paper instrument drawn on the consumer's account to be mailed abroad, and the payee or payees that will be paid in this manner are identified to the consumer. With respect to such a bill-payment service, if a provider provides a check, draft or similar paper instrument drawn on a consumer's account to be mailed abroad for a payee that is not identified to the consumer as described above, this payment by check, draft or similar payment instrument will be an electronic transfer of funds.

2. *Sent by a remittance transfer provider.*

i. The definition of "remittance transfer" requires that a transfer be "sent by a remittance transfer provider." This means that there must be an intermediary that is directly engaged with the sender to send an electronic transfer of funds on behalf of the sender to a designated recipient.

ii. A payment card network or other third party payment service that is functionally similar to a payment card network does not send a remittance transfer when a consumer provides a debit, credit or prepaid card directly to a foreign merchant as payment for goods or services. In such a case, the payment card network or third party payment service is not directly engaged with the sender to send a transfer of funds to a person in a foreign country; rather, the network or third party payment service is merely providing contemporaneous third-party payment processing and settlement services on behalf of the merchant or the card issuer, rather than on behalf of the sender. In such a case, the card issuer also is not directly engaged with the sender to send an electronic transfer of funds to the foreign merchant when the card issuer provides payment to the merchant. Similarly, where a consumer provides a checking or other account number, or a debit, credit or prepaid card, directly to a foreign merchant as payment for goods or services, the merchant is not acting as an intermediary that sends a transfer of funds on behalf of the sender when it submits the payment information for processing.

iii. However, a card issuer or a payment network may offer a service to a sender where the card issuer or a payment network is an intermediary that is directly engaged with the sender to obtain funds using the sender's debit, prepaid or credit card and to send those funds to a recipient's checking account located in a foreign country. In this case, the card issuer or the payment network is an intermediary that is directly engaged with the sender to send an electronic transfer of funds on behalf of the sender, and this transfer of funds is a remittance transfer because it is made to a designated recipient. *See* comment 30(c)–2.ii.

3. *Examples of remittance transfers.*

i. Examples of remittance transfers include:

A. Transfers where the sender provides cash or another method of payment to a money transmitter or financial institution and requests that funds be sent to a specified location or account in a foreign country.

B. Consumer wire transfers, where a financial institution executes a payment order upon a sender's request to wire money from the sender's account to a designated recipient.

C. An addition of funds to a prepaid card by a participant in a prepaid card program, such as a prepaid card issuer or its agent, that is directly engaged with the sender to add these funds, where the prepaid card is sent or was previously sent by a participant in the prepaid card program to a person in a foreign country, even if a person located in a State (including a sender) retains the ability to withdraw such funds.

D. International ACH transactions sent by the sender's financial institution at the sender's request.

E. Online bill payments and other electronic transfers that a sender schedules in advance, including preauthorized remittance transfers, made by the sender's financial institution at the sender's request to a designated recipient.

ii. The term remittance transfer does not include, for example:

A. A consumer's provision of a debit, credit or prepaid card, directly to a foreign merchant as payment for goods or services because the issuer is not directly engaged with the sender to send an electronic transfer of funds to the foreign merchant when the issuer provides payment to the merchant. *See* comment 30(e)–2.

B. A consumer's deposit of funds to a checking or savings account located in a State, because there has not been a transfer of funds to a designated recipient. *See* comment 30(c)–2.ii.

C. Online bill payments and other electronic transfers that senders can schedule in advance, including preauthorized transfers, made through the Web site of a merchant located in a foreign country and via direct provision of a checking account, credit card, debit card or prepaid card number to the merchant, because the financial institution is not directly engaged with the sender to send an electronic transfer of funds to the foreign merchant when the institution provides payment to the merchant. *See* comment 30(e)–2.

30(f) Remittance Transfer Provider

1. *Agents.* A person is not deemed to be acting as a remittance transfer provider when it performs activities as an agent on behalf of a remittance transfer provider.

2. *Normal course of business.*

i. *General.* Whether a person provides remittance transfers in the normal course of business depends on the facts and circumstances, including the total number and frequency of remittance transfers sent by the provider. For example, if a financial institution generally does not make remittance transfers available to customers, but sends a couple of such transfers in a given year as an accommodation for a customer, the institution does not provide remittance transfers in the normal course of business. In contrast, if a financial institution makes remittance transfers generally available to customers (whether described in the institution's deposit account agreement, or in practice) and makes transfers many times per month, the institution provides remittance transfers in the normal course of business.

ii. *Safe harbor.* Under § 1005.30(f)(2)(i), a person that provided 100 or fewer remittance transfers in the previous calendar year and provides 100 or fewer remittance transfers in the current calendar year is deemed not to be providing remittance transfers in the normal course of its business. Accordingly, a person that qualifies for the safe harbor in § 1005.30(f)(2)(i) is not a "remittance transfer provider" and is not subject to the requirements of subpart B. For purposes of determining whether a person qualifies for the safe harbor under § 1005.30(f)(2)(i), the number of remittance transfers provided includes any transfers excluded from the definition of "remittance transfer" due simply to the safe harbor. In contrast, the number of remittance transfers provided does not include any transfers that are excluded from the definition of "remittance transfer" for reasons other than the safe harbor, such as small value transactions or securities and commodities transfers that are excluded from the definition of "remittance transfer" by § 1005.30(e)(2).

iii. *Transition period.* A person may cease to satisfy the requirements of the safe harbor described in § 1005.30(f)(2)(i) if the person provides in excess of 100 remittance transfers in a calendar year. For example, if a person that provided 100 or fewer remittance transfers in the previous calendar year provides more than 100 remittance transfers in the current calendar year, the safe harbor applies to the first 100 remittance transfers that the person provides in the current calendar year. For any additional remittance transfers provided in the current calendar year and for any remittance transfers provided in the subsequent calendar year, whether the person provides remittance transfers for a consumer in the normal course of its business, as defined in § 1005.30(f)(1), and is thus a remittance transfer provider for those additional transfers, depends on the facts and circumstances. Section 1005.30(f)(2)(ii) provides a reasonable period of time, not to exceed six months, for such a person to begin complying with subpart B, if that person is then providing remittance transfers in the normal course of its business. At the end of that reasonable period of time, such person would be required to comply with subpart B unless, based on the facts and circumstances, the person is not a remittance transfer provider.

iv.   *Example of safe harbor and transition period.* Assume that a person provided 90 remittance transfers in 2012 and 90 such transfers in 2013. The safe harbor will apply to the person's transfers in 2013, as well as the person's first 100 remittance transfers in 2014. However, if the person provides a 101st transfer on September 5, the facts and circumstances determine whether the person provides remittance transfers in the normal course of business and is thus a remittance transfer provider for the 101st and any subsequent remittance transfers that it provides in 2014. Furthermore, the person would not qualify for the safe harbor described in § 1005.30(f)(2)(i) in 2015 because the person did not provide 100 or fewer remittance transfers in 2014. However, for the 101st remittance transfer provided in 2014, as well as additional remittance transfers provided thereafter in 2014 and 2015, if that person is then providing remittance transfers for a consumer in the normal course of business, the person will have a reasonable period of time, not to exceed six months, to come into compliance with subpart B. Assume that in this case, a reasonable period of time is six months. Thus, compliance with subpart B is not required for remittance transfers made on or before March 5, 2015 (*i.e.,* six months after September 5, 2014). After March 5, 2015, the person is required to comply with subpart B if, based on the facts and circumstances, the person provides remittance transfers in the normal course of business and is thus a remittance transfer provider.

3.   *Multiple remittance transfer providers.* If the remittance transfer involves more than one remittance transfer provider, only one set of disclosures must be given, and the remittance transfer providers must agree among themselves which provider must take the actions necessary to comply with the requirements that subpart B imposes on any or all of them. Even though the providers must designate one provider to take the actions necessary to comply with the requirements that subpart B imposes on any or all of them, all remittance transfer providers involved in the remittance transfer remain responsible for compliance with the applicable provisions of the EFTA and Regulation E.

30(g) Sender

1.   *Determining whether a consumer is located in a State.* Under § 1005.30(g), the definition of "sender" means a consumer in a State who, primarily for personal, family, or household purposes, requests a remittance transfer provider to send a remittance transfer to a designated recipient. A sender located on a U.S. military installation that is physically located in a foreign country is located in a State. For transfers from a consumer's account, whether a consumer is located in a State depends on where the consumer's account is located. If the account is located in a State, the consumer will be located in a State for purposes of the definition of "sender" in § 1005.30(g), notwithstanding comment 3(a)–3. Accounts that are located on a U.S. military installation that is physically located in a foreign country are located in a State. Where a transfer is requested electronically or by telephone and the transfer is not from an account, the provider may make the determination of whether a consumer is located in a State based on information that is provided by the consumer and on any records associated with the consumer that the provider may have, such as an address provided by the consumer.

2.   *Personal, family, or household purposes.* Under § 1005.30(g), a consumer is a "sender" only where he or she requests a transfer primarily for personal, family, or household purposes. A consumer who requests a transfer primarily for other purposes, such as business or commercial purposes, is not a sender under § 1005.30(g). For transfers from an account that was established primarily for personal, family, or household purposes, a remittance transfer provider may generally deem that the transfer is requested primarily for personal, family, or household purposes and the consumer is therefore a "sender" under § 1005.30(g). But if the consumer indicates that he or she is requesting the transfer primarily for other purposes, such as business or commercial purposes, then the consumer is not a sender under § 1005.30(g), even if the consumer is requesting the transfer from an account that is used primarily for personal, family, or household purposes.

3.   *Non-consumer accounts.* A provider may deem that a transfer that is requested to be sent from an account that was not established primarily for personal, family, or household purposes, such as an account that was established as a business or commercial account or an account held by a business entity such as a

corporation, not-for-profit corporation, professional corporation, limited liability company, partnership, or sole proprietorship, as not being requested primarily for personal, family, or household purposes. A consumer requesting a transfer from such an account therefore is not a sender under § 1005.30(g). Additionally, a transfer that is requested to be sent from an account held by a financial institution under a *bona fide* trust agreement pursuant to § 1005.2(b)(3) is not requested primarily for personal, family, or household purposes, and a consumer requesting a transfer from such an account is therefore not a sender under § 1005.30(g).

30(h) Third-Party Fees

1. *Fees imposed on the remittance transfer.* Fees imposed on the remittance transfer by a person other than the remittance transfer provider include only those fees that are charged to the designated recipient and are specifically related to the remittance transfer. For example, overdraft fees that are imposed by a recipient's bank or funds that are garnished from the proceeds of a remittance transfer to satisfy an unrelated debt are not fees imposed on the remittance transfer because these charges are not specifically related to the remittance transfer. Account fees are also not specifically related to a remittance transfer if such fees are merely assessed based on general account activity and not for receiving transfers. Where an incoming remittance transfer results in a balance increase that triggers a monthly maintenance fee, that fee is not specifically related to a remittance transfer. Similarly, fees that banks charge one another for handling a remittance transfer or other fees that do not affect the total amount of the transaction or the amount that will be received by the designated recipient are not fees imposed on the remittance transfer. For example, an interchange fee that is charged to a provider when a sender uses a credit or debit card to pay for a remittance transfer is not a fee imposed upon the remittance transfer. Fees that specifically relate to a remittance transfer may be structured on a flat per-transaction basis, or may be conditioned on other factors (such as account status or the quantity of remittance transfers received) in addition to the remittance transfer itself. For example, where an institution charges an incoming transfer fee on most customers' accounts, but not on preferred accounts, such a fee is nonetheless specifically related to a remittance transfer. Similarly, if the institution assesses a fee for every transfer beyond the fifth received each month, such a fee would be specifically related to the remittance transfer regardless of how many remittance transfers preceded it that month.

2. *Covered third-party fees.*

   i. Under § 1005.30(h)(1), a covered third-party fee means any fee that is imposed on the remittance transfer by a person other than the remittance transfer provider that is not a non-covered third-party fee.

   ii. Examples of covered third-party fees include:

   A. Fees imposed on a remittance transfer by intermediary institutions in connection with a wire transfer (sometimes referred to as "lifting fees").

   B. Fees imposed on a remittance transfer by an agent of the provider at pick-up for receiving the transfer.

3. *Non-covered third-party fees.* Under § 1005.30(h)(2), a non-covered third-party fee means any fee imposed by the designated recipient's institution for receiving a remittance transfer into an account except if such institution acts as the agent of the remittance transfer provider. For example, a fee imposed by the designated recipient's institution for receiving an incoming transfer into an account is a non-covered third-party fee, provided such institution is not acting as the agent of the remittance transfer provider. *See also* comment 31(b)(1)(viii)–1. Furthermore, designated recipient's account in § 1005.30(h)(2) refers to an asset account, regardless of whether it is a consumer asset account, established for any purpose and held by a bank, savings association, credit union, or equivalent institution. A designated recipient's account does not, however, include a credit card, prepaid card, or a virtual account held by an Internet-based or mobile telephone company that is not a bank, savings association, credit union or equivalent institution.

OFFICIAL INTERPRETATIONS OF REGULATION E

SECTION 1005.31—DISCLOSURES
31(a) General Form of Disclosures
31(a)(1) Clear and Conspicuous

1. *Clear and conspicuous standard.* Disclosures are clear and conspicuous for purposes of subpart B if they are readily understandable and, in the case of written and electronic disclosures, the location and type size are readily noticeable to senders. Oral disclosures as permitted by § 1005.31(a)(3), (4), and (5) are clear and conspicuous when they are given at a volume and speed sufficient for a sender to hear and comprehend them.

2. *Abbreviations and symbols.* Disclosures may contain commonly accepted or readily understandable abbreviations or symbols, such as "USD" to indicate currency in U.S. dollars or "MXN" to indicate currency in Mexican pesos.

31(a)(2) Written and Electronic Disclosures

1. *E-Sign Act requirements.* If a sender electronically requests the remittance transfer provider to send a remittance transfer, the disclosures required by § 1005.31(b)(1) may be provided to the sender in electronic form without regard to the consumer consent and other applicable provisions of the Electronic Signatures in Global and National Commerce Act (E-Sign Act) (15 U.S.C. 7001 *et seq.*). If a sender electronically requests the provider to send a remittance transfer, the disclosures required by § 1005.31(b)(2) may be provided to the sender in electronic form, subject to compliance with the consumer consent and other applicable provisions of the E-Sign Act. *See* § 1005.4(a)(1).

2. *Paper size.* Written disclosures may be provided on any size paper, as long as the disclosures are clear and conspicuous. For example, disclosures may be provided on a register receipt or on an 8.5 inch by 11 inch sheet of paper.

3. *Retainable electronic disclosures.* A remittance transfer provider may satisfy the requirement to provide electronic disclosures in a retainable form if it provides an online disclosure in a format that is capable of being printed. Electronic disclosures may not be provided through a hyperlink or in another manner by which the sender can bypass the disclosure. A provider is not required to confirm that the sender has read the electronic disclosures.

4. *Pre-payment disclosures to a mobile telephone.* Disclosures provided via mobile application or text message, to the extent permitted by § 1005.31(a)(5), need not be retainable. However, disclosures provided electronically to a mobile telephone that are not provided via mobile application or text message must be retainable. For example, disclosures provided via email must be retainable, even if a sender accesses them by mobile telephone.

5. *Disclosures provided by fax.* For purposes of disclosures required to be provided pursuant to § 1005.31 or § 1005.36, disclosures provided by facsimile transmission (*i.e.,* fax) are considered to be provided in writing for purposes of providing disclosures in writing pursuant to subpart B and are not subject to the requirements for electronic disclosures set forth in § 1005.31(a)(2).

31(a)(3) Disclosures for Oral Telephone Transactions

1. *Transactions conducted partially by telephone.* Except as provided in comment 31(a)(3)–2, for transactions conducted partially by telephone, providing the information required by § 1005.31(b)(1) to a sender orally does not fulfill the requirement to provide the disclosures required by § 1005.31(b)(1). For example, a sender may begin a remittance transfer at a remittance transfer provider's dedicated telephone in a retail store, and then provide payment in person to a store clerk to complete the transaction. In such cases, all disclosures must be provided in writing. A provider complies with this requirement, for example, by providing the written pre-payment disclosure in person prior to the sender's payment for the transaction, and the written receipt when the sender pays for the transaction.

2. *Oral telephone transactions.* Section 1005.31(a)(3) applies to transactions conducted orally and entirely by telephone, such as transactions conducted orally on a landline or mobile telephone. A remittance transfer provider may treat a written or electronic communication as an inquiry when it believes that treating the communication as a request would be impractical. For example, if a sender physically located abroad

contacts a U.S. branch of the sender's financial institution and attempts to initiate a remittance transfer by first sending a mailed letter, further communication with the sender by letter may be impractical due to the physical distance and likely mail delays. In such circumstances, a provider may conduct the transaction orally and entirely by telephone pursuant to § 1005.31(a)(3) when the provider treats that initial communication as an inquiry and subsequently responds to the consumer's inquiry by calling the consumer on a telephone and orally gathering or confirming the information needed to identify and understand a request for a remittance transfer and otherwise conducts the transaction orally and entirely by telephone.

31(a)(5) Disclosures for Mobile Application or Text Message Transactions

1. *Mobile application and text message transactions.* A remittance transfer provider may provide the required pre-payment disclosures orally or via mobile application or text message if the transaction is conducted entirely by telephone via mobile application or text message, the remittance transfer provider complies with the requirements of § 1005.31(g)(2), and the provider discloses orally or via mobile application or text message a statement about the rights of the sender regarding cancellation required by § 1005.31(b)(2)(iv) pursuant to the timing requirements in § 1005.31(e)(1). For example, if a sender conducts a transaction via text message on a mobile telephone, the remittance transfer provider may call the sender and orally provide the required pre-payment disclosures. Alternatively, the provider may provide the required pre-payment disclosures via text message. Section 1005.31(a)(5) applies only to transactions conducted entirely by mobile telephone via mobile application or text message.

31(b) Disclosure Requirements

1. *Disclosures provided as applicable.* Disclosures required by § 1005.31(b) need only be provided to the extent applicable. A remittance transfer provider may choose to omit an item of information required by § 1005.31(b) if it is inapplicable to a particular transaction. Alternatively, for disclosures required by § 1005.31(b)(1)(i) through (vii), a provider may disclose a term and state that an amount or item is "not applicable," "N/A," or "None." For example, if fees or taxes are not imposed in connection with a particular transaction, the provider need not provide the disclosures about fees and taxes generally required by § 1005.31(b)(1)(ii), the disclosures about covered third-party fees generally required by § 1005.31(b)(1)(vi), or the disclaimers about non-covered third-party fees and taxes collected by a person other than the provider generally required by § 1005.31(b)(1)(viii). Similarly, a Web site need not be disclosed if the provider does not maintain a Web site. A provider need not provide the exchange rate disclosure required by § 1005.31(b)(1)(iv) if a recipient receives funds in the currency in which the remittance transfer is funded, or if funds are delivered into an account denominated in the currency in which the remittance transfer is funded. For example, if a sender in the United States sends funds from an account denominated in Euros to an account in France denominated in Euros, no exchange rate would need to be provided. Similarly, if a sender funds a remittance transfer in U.S. dollars and requests that a remittance transfer be delivered to the recipient in U.S. dollars, a provider need not disclose an exchange rate.

2. *Substantially similar terms, language, and notices.* Certain disclosures required by § 1005.31(b) must be described using the terms set forth in § 1005.31(b) or substantially similar terms. Terms may be more specific than those provided. For example, a remittance transfer provider sending funds may describe fees imposed by an agent at pick-up as "Pick-up Fees" in lieu of describing them as "Other Fees." Foreign language disclosures required under § 1005.31(g) must contain accurate translations of the terms, language, and notices required by § 1005.31(b) or permitted by § 1005.31(b)(1)(viii) and § 1005.33(h)(3).

31(b)(1) Pre-Payment Disclosures

1. *Fees and taxes.*

   i. Taxes collected on the remittance transfer by the remittance transfer provider include taxes collected on the remittance transfer by a State or other governmental body. A provider need only disclose fees imposed or taxes collected on the remittance transfer by the provider in § 1005.31(b)(1)(ii), as applicable. For example, if no transfer taxes are imposed on a remittance transfer, a provider would only disclose applicable transfer fees. *See* comment 31(b)–1. If both fees and taxes are imposed, the fees and taxes must be disclosed as separate, itemized disclosures. For example, a provider would disclose all transfer fees using the term "Transfer Fees" or a substantially similar term and would separately disclose all transfer taxes using the term "Transfer Taxes" or a substantially similar term.

ii.   The fees and taxes required to be disclosed by § 1005.31(b)(1)(ii) include all fees imposed and all taxes collected on the remittance transfer by the provider. For example, a provider must disclose any service fee, any fees imposed by an agent of the provider at the time of the transfer, and any State taxes collected on the remittance transfer at the time of the transfer. Fees imposed on the remittance transfer by the provider required to be disclosed under § 1005.31(b)(1)(ii) include only those fees that are charged to the sender and are specifically related to the remittance transfer. *See also* comment 30(h)–1. In contrast, the fees required to be disclosed by § 1005.31(b)(1)(vi) are any covered third-party fees as defined in § 1005.30(h)(1).

iii.   The term used to describe the fees imposed on the remittance transfer by the provider in § 1005.31(b)(1)(ii) and the term used to describe covered third-party fees under § 1005.31(b)(1)(vi) must differentiate between such fees. For example the terms used to describe fees disclosed under § 1005.31(b)(1)(ii) and (vi) may not both be described solely as "Fees."

2.   *Transfer amount.* Sections 1005.31(b)(1)(i) and (v) require two transfer amount disclosures. First, under § 1005.31(b)(1)(i), a provider must disclose the transfer amount in the currency in which the remittance transfer is funded to show the calculation of the total amount of the transaction. Typically, the remittance transfer is funded in U.S. dollars, so the transfer amount would be expressed in U.S. dollars. However, if the remittance transfer is funded, for example, from a Euro-denominated account, the transfer amount would be expressed in Euros. Second, under § 1005.31(b)(1)(v), a provider must disclose the transfer amount in the currency in which the funds will be made available to the designated recipient. For example, if the funds will be picked up by the designated recipient in Japanese yen, the transfer amount would be expressed in Japanese yen. However, this second transfer amount need not be disclosed if covered third-party fees as described under § 1005.31(b)(1)(vi) are not imposed on the remittance transfer. The terms used to describe each transfer amount should be the same.

3.   *Exchange rate for calculation.* The exchange rate used to calculate the transfer amount in § 1005.31(b)(1)(v), the covered third-party fees in § 1005.31(b)(1)(vi), the amount received in § 1005.31(b)(1)(vii), and the optional disclosures of non-covered third-party fees and other taxes permitted by § 1005.31(b)(1)(viii) is the exchange rate in § 1005.31(b)(1)(iv), including an estimated exchange rate to the extent permitted by § 1005.32, prior to any rounding of the exchange rate. For example, if one U.S. dollar exchanges for 11.9483779 Mexican pesos, a provider must calculate these disclosures using this rate, even though the provider may disclose pursuant to § 1005.31(b)(1)(iv) that the U.S. dollar exchanges for 11.9484 Mexican pesos. Similarly, if a provider estimates pursuant to § 1005.32 that one U.S. dollar exchanges for 11.9483 Mexican pesos, a provider must calculate these disclosures using this rate, even though the provider may disclose pursuant to § 1005.31(b)(1)(iv) that the U.S. dollar exchanges for 11.95 Mexican pesos (Estimated). If an exchange rate need not be rounded, a provider must use that exchange rate to calculate these disclosures. For example, if one U.S. dollar exchanges for exactly 11.9 Mexican pesos, a provider must calculate these disclosures using this exchange rate.

31(b)(1)(iv) Exchange Rate

1.   *Applicable exchange rate.* If the designated recipient will receive funds in a currency other than the currency in which the remittance transfer is funded, a remittance transfer provider must disclose the exchange rate to be used by the provider for the remittance transfer. An exchange rate that is estimated must be disclosed pursuant to the requirements of § 1005.32. A remittance transfer provider may not disclose, for example, that an exchange rate is "unknown," "floating," or "to be determined." If a provider does not have specific knowledge regarding the currency in which the funds will be received, the provider may rely on a sender's representation as to the currency in which funds will be received for purposes of determining whether an exchange rate is applied to the transfer. For example, if a sender requests that a remittance transfer be deposited into an account in U.S. dollars, the provider need not disclose an exchange rate, even if the account is actually denominated in Mexican pesos and the funds are converted prior to deposit into the account. If a sender does not know the currency in which funds will be received, the provider may assume that the currency in which funds will be received is the currency in which the remittance transfer is funded.

2.   *Rounding.* The exchange rate disclosed by the provider for the remittance transfer is required to be rounded. The provider may round to two, three, or four decimal places, at its option. For example, if one

OFFICIAL INTERPRETATIONS OF REGULATION E

U.S. dollar exchanges for 11.9483779 Mexican pesos, a provider may disclose that the U.S. dollar exchanges for 11.9484 Mexican pesos. The provider may alternatively disclose, for example, that the U.S. dollar exchanges for 11.948 pesos or 11.95 pesos. On the other hand, if one U.S. dollar exchanges for exactly 11.9 Mexican pesos, the provider may disclose that "US$1 = 11.9 MXN" in lieu of, for example, "US$1 = 11.90 MXN." The exchange rate disclosed for the remittance transfer must be rounded consistently for each currency. For example, a provider may not round to two decimal places for some transactions exchanged into Euros and round to four decimal places for other transactions exchanged into Euros.

3. *Exchange rate used.* The exchange rate used by the provider for the remittance transfer need not be set by that provider. For example, an exchange rate set by an intermediary institution and applied to the remittance transfer would be the exchange rate used for the remittance transfer and must be disclosed by the provider.

31(b)(1)(vi) Disclosure of Covered Third-Party Fees

1. *Fees disclosed in the currency in which the funds will be received.* Section 1005.31(b)(1)(vi) requires the disclosure of covered third-party fees in the currency in which the funds will be received by the designated recipient. A covered third-party fee described in § 1005.31(b)(1)(vi) may be imposed in one currency, but the funds may be received by the designated recipient in another currency. In such cases, the remittance transfer provider must calculate the fee to be disclosed under § 1005.31(b)(1)(vi) in the currency of receipt using the exchange rate in § 1005.31(b)(1)(iv), including an estimated exchange rate to the extent permitted by § 1005.32, prior to any rounding of the exchange rate. For example, an intermediary institution involved in sending an international wire transfer funded in U.S. dollars may impose a fee in U.S. dollars, but funds are ultimately deposited in the recipient's account in Euros. In this case, the provider would disclose the covered third-party fee to the sender expressed in Euros, calculated using the exchange rate disclosed under § 1005.31(b)(1)(iv), prior to any rounding of the exchange rate. For purposes of § 1005.31(b)(1)(v), (vi), and (vii), if a provider does not have specific knowledge regarding the currency in which the funds will be received, the provider may rely on a sender's representation as to the currency in which funds will be received. For example, if a sender requests that a remittance transfer be deposited into an account in U.S. dollars, the provider may provide the disclosures required in § 1005.31(b)(1)(v), (vi), and (vii) in U.S. dollars, even if the account is actually denominated in Mexican pesos and the funds are subsequently converted prior to deposit into the account. If a sender does not know the currency in which funds will be received, the provider may assume that the currency in which funds will be received is the currency in which the remittance transfer is funded.

31(b)(1)(vii) Amount Received

1. *Amount received.* The remittance transfer provider is required to disclose the amount that will be received by the designated recipient in the currency in which the funds will be received. The amount received must reflect the exchange rate, all fees imposed and all taxes collected on the remittance transfer by the remittance transfer provider, as well as any covered third-party fees required to be disclosed by § 1005.31(b)(1)(vi). The disclosed amount received must be reduced by the amount of any fee or tax—except for a non-covered third-party fee or tax collected on the remittance transfer by a person other than the provider—that is imposed on the remittance transfer that affects the amount received even if that amount is imposed or itemized separately from the transaction amount.

31(b)(1)(viii) Statement When Additional Fees and Taxes May Apply

1. *Required disclaimer when non-covered third-party fees and taxes collected by a person other than the provider may apply.* If non-covered third-party fees or taxes collected by a person other than the provider apply to a particular remittance transfer or if a provider does not know if such fees or taxes may apply to a particular remittance transfer, § 1005.31(b)(1)(viii) requires the provider to include the disclaimer with respect to such fees and taxes. Required disclosures under § 1005.31(b)(1)(viii) may only be provided to the extent applicable. For example, if the designated recipient's institution is an agent of the provider and thus, non-covered third-party fees cannot apply to the transfer, the provider must disclose all fees imposed on the remittance transfer and may not provide the disclaimer regarding non-covered third-party fees. In this scenario, the provider may only provide the disclaimer regarding taxes collected on the remittance transfer by a person other than the provider, as applicable. *See* Model Form A–30(c).

2. *Optional disclosure of non-covered third-party fees and taxes collected by a person other than the provider.* When a remittance transfer provider knows the non-covered third-party fees or taxes collected on the remittance transfer by a person other than the provider that will apply to a particular transaction, § 1005.31(b)(1)(viii) permits the provider to disclose the amount of such fees and taxes. Section 1005.32(b)(3)–1 additionally permits a provider to disclose an estimate of such fees and taxes, provided any estimates are based on reasonable source of information. *See* comment 32(b)(3). For example, a provider may know that the designated recipient's institution imposes an incoming wire fee for receiving a transfer. Alternatively, a provider may know that foreign taxes will be collected on the remittance transfer by a person other than the remittance transfer provider. In these examples, the provider may choose, at its option, to disclose the amounts of the relevant recipient institution fee and tax as part of the information disclosed pursuant to § 1005.31(b)(1)(viii). The provider must not include that fee or tax in the amount disclosed pursuant to § 1005.31(b)(1)(vi) or (b)(1)(vii). Fees and taxes disclosed under § 1005.31(b)(1)(viii) must be disclosed in the currency in which the funds will be received. *See* comment 31(b)(1)(vi)–1. Estimates of any non-covered third-party fees and any taxes collected on the remittance transfer by a person other than the provider must be disclosed in accordance with § 1005.32(b)(3).

31(b)(2) Receipt

1. *Date funds will be available.* A remittance transfer provider does not comply with the requirements of § 1005.31(b)(2)(ii) if it provides a range of dates that the remittance transfer may be available or an estimate of the date on which funds will be available. If a provider does not know the exact date on which funds will be available, the provider may disclose the latest date on which the funds will be available. For example, if funds may be available on January 3, but are not certain to be available until January 10, then a provider complies with § 1005.31(b)(2)(ii) if it discloses January 10 as the date funds will be available. However, a remittance transfer provider may also disclose that funds "may be available sooner" or use a substantially similar term to inform senders that funds may be available to the designated recipient on a date earlier than the date disclosed. For example, a provider may disclose "January 10 (may be available sooner)."

2. *Agencies required to be disclosed.* A remittance transfer provider must only disclose information about a State agency that licenses or charters the remittance transfer provider with respect to the remittance transfer as applicable. For example, if a financial institution is solely regulated by a Federal agency, and not licensed or chartered by a State agency, then the institution need not disclose information about a State agency. A remittance transfer provider must disclose information about the Consumer Financial Protection Bureau, whether or not the Consumer Financial Protection Bureau is the provider's primary Federal regulator.

3. *State agency that licenses or charters a provider.* A remittance transfer provider must only disclose information about one State agency that licenses or charters the remittance transfer provider with respect to the remittance transfer, even if other State agencies also regulate the remittance transfer provider. For example, a provider may disclose information about the State agency which granted its license. If a provider is licensed in multiple States, and the State agency that licenses the provider with respect to the remittance transfer is determined by a sender's location, a provider may make the determination as to the State in which the sender is located based on information that is provided by the sender and on any records associated with the sender. For example, if the State agency that licenses the provider with respect to an online remittance transfer is determined by a sender's location, a provider could rely on the sender's statement regarding the State in which the sender is located and disclose the State agency that licenses the provider in that State. A State-chartered bank must disclose information about the State agency that granted its charter, regardless of the location of the sender.

4. *Web site of the Consumer Financial Protection Bureau.* Section 1005.31(b)(2)(vi) requires a remittance transfer provider to disclose the name, toll-free telephone number(s), and Web site of the Consumer Financial Protection Bureau. Providers may satisfy this requirement by disclosing the Web site of the Consumer Financial Protection Bureau's homepage, *www.consumerfinance.gov,* as shown on Model Forms A–32, A–34, A–35, and A–39. Alternatively, providers may, but are not required to, disclose the Bureau's Web site as the address of a page on the Bureau's Web site that provides information for consumers about remittance transfers, currently, *consumerfinance.gov/sending-money,* as shown on Model Form A–31. In addition, providers making disclosures in a language other than English pursuant to § 1005.31(g) may, but are not required to, disclose the Bureau's Web site as a page on the Bureau's Web site that provides

information for consumers about remittance transfers in the relevant language, if such Web site exists. For example, a provider that is making disclosures in Spanish under § 1005.31(g) may, but is not required to, disclose the Bureau's Web site on Spanish-language disclosures as the page on the Bureau's Web site that provides information regarding remittance transfers in Spanish, currently *consumerfinance.gov/envios*. This optional disclosure is shown on Model A–40. The Bureau will publish a list of any other foreign language Web sites that provide information regarding remittance transfers.

5. *Date of transfer on receipt.* Where applicable, § 1005.31(b)(2)(vii) requires disclosure of the date of transfer for the remittance transfer that is the subject of a receipt required by § 1005.31(b)(2), including a receipt that is provided in accordance with the timing requirements in § 1005.36(a). For any subsequent preauthorized remittance transfer subject to § 1005.36(d)(2)(ii), the future date of transfer must be provided on any receipt provided for the initial transfer in that series of preauthorized remittance transfers, or where permitted, or disclosed as permitted by § 1005.31(a)(3) and (a)(5), in accordance with § 1005.36(a)(1)(i).

6. *Transfer date disclosures.* The following example demonstrates how the information required by § 1005.31(b)(2)(vii) and § 1005.36(d)(1) should be disclosed on receipts: On July 1, a sender instructs the provider to send a preauthorized remittance transfer of US$100 each week to a designated recipient. The sender requests that first transfer in the series be sent on July 15. On the receipt, the remittance transfer provider discloses an estimated exchange rate to the sender pursuant to § 1005.32(b)(2). In accordance with § 1005.31(b)(2)(vii), the provider should disclose the date of transfer for that particular transaction (*i.e.,* July 15) on the receipt provided when payment is made for the transfer pursuant to the timing requirements in § 1005.36(a)(1)(i). The second receipt, which § 1005.36(a)(1)(ii) requires to be provided within one business day after the date of the transfer or, for transfers from the sender's account held by the provider, on the next regularly scheduled periodic statement or within 30 days after payment is made if a periodic statement is not provided, is also required to include the date of transfer. If the provider discloses on either receipt the cancellation period applicable to and dates of subsequent preauthorized remittance transfers in accordance with § 1005.36(d)(2), the disclosure must be phrased and formatted in such a way that it is clear to the sender which cancellation period is applicable to any date of transfer on the receipt.

7. *Cancellation disclosure.* Remittance transfer providers that offer remittance transfers scheduled three or more business days before the date of the transfer, as well as remittance transfers scheduled fewer than three business days before the date of the transfer, may meet the cancellation disclosure requirements in § 1005.31(b)(2)(iv) by describing the three-business-day and 30-minute cancellation periods on the same disclosure and using a checkbox or other method to clearly designate the applicable cancellation period. The provider may use a number of methods to indicate which cancellation period applies to the transaction including, but not limited to, a statement to that effect, use of a checkbox, highlighting, circling, and the like. For transfers scheduled three business days before the date of the transfer, the cancellation disclosures provided pursuant to § 1005.31(b)(2)(iv) should be phrased and formatted in such a way that it is clear to the sender which cancellation period is applicable to the date of transfer disclosed on the receipt.

31(b)(3) Combined Disclosure

1. *Proof of payment.* If a sender initiating a remittance transfer receives a combined disclosure provided under § 1005.31(b)(3) and then completes the transaction, the remittance transfer provider must provide the sender with proof of payment. The proof of payment must be clear and conspicuous, provided in writing or electronically, and provided in a retainable form. The combined disclosure must be provided to the sender when the sender requests the remittance transfer, but prior to payment for the transfer, pursuant to § 1005.31(e)(1), and the proof of payment must be provided when payment is made for the remittance transfer. The proof of payment for the transaction may be provided on the same piece of paper as the combined disclosure or on a separate piece of paper. For example, a provider may feed a combined disclosure through a computer printer when payment is made to add the date and time of the transaction, a confirmation code, and an indication that the transfer was paid in full. A provider may also provide this additional information to a sender on a separate piece of paper when payment is made. A remittance transfer provider does not comply with the requirements of § 1005.31(b)(3) by providing a combined disclosure with no further indication that payment has been received.

2. *Confirmation of scheduling.* As discussed in comment 31(e)–2, payment is considered to be made when payment is authorized for purposes of various timing requirements in subpart B, including with regard to

OFFICIAL INTERPRETATIONS OF REGULATION E

the timing requirement for provision of the proof of payment described in § 1005.31(b)(3)(i). However, where a transfer (whether a one-time remittance transfer or the first in a series of preauthorized remittance transfers) is scheduled before the date of transfer and the provider does not intend to process payment until at or near the date of transfer, the provider may provide a confirmation of scheduling in lieu of the proof of payment required by § 1005.31(b)(3)(i). No further proof of payment is required when payment is later processed.

31(c) Specific Format Requirements

31(c)(1) Grouping

1. *Grouping.* Information is grouped together for purposes of subpart B if multiple disclosures are in close proximity to one another and a sender can reasonably calculate the total amount of the transaction and the amount that will be received by the designated recipient. Model Forms A–30(a)–(d) through A–35 in Appendix A illustrate how information may be grouped to comply with the rule, but a remittance transfer provider may group the information in another manner. For example, a provider could provide the grouped information as a horizontal, rather than a vertical, calculation. A provider could also send multiple text messages sequentially to provide the full disclosure.

31(c)(4) Segregation

1. *Segregation.* Disclosures may be segregated from other information in a variety of ways. For example, the disclosures may appear on a separate sheet of paper or may appear on the front of a page where other information appears on the back of that page. The disclosures may be set off from other information on a notice by outlining them in a box or series of boxes, with bold print dividing lines or a different color background, or by using other means.

2. *Directly related.* For purposes of § 1005.31(c)(4), the following is directly related information:

    i. The date and time of the transaction;

    ii. The sender's name and contact information;

    iii. The location at which the designated recipient may pick up the funds;

    iv. The confirmation or other identification code;

    v. A company name and logo;

    vi. An indication that a disclosure is or is not a receipt or other indicia of proof of payment;

    vii. A designated area for signatures or initials;

    viii. A statement that funds may be available sooner, as permitted by § 1005.31(b)(2)(ii);

    ix. Instructions regarding the retrieval of funds, such as the number of days the funds will be available to the recipient before they are returned to the sender; and

    x. A statement that the provider makes money from foreign currency exchange.

    xi. Disclosure of any non-covered third-party fees and any taxes collected by a person other than the provider pursuant to § 1005.31(b)(1)(viii).

31(d) Estimates

1. *Terms.* A remittance transfer provider may provide estimates of the amounts required by § 1005.31(b), to the extent permitted by § 1005.32. An estimate must be described using the term "Estimated" or a substantially similar term in close proximity to the term or terms described. For example, a remittance transfer provider could describe an estimated disclosure as "Estimated Transfer Amount," "Other Estimated Fees and Taxes," or "Total to Recipient (Est.)."

31(e) Timing

1. *Request to send a remittance transfer.* Except as provided in § 1005.36(a), pre-payment and combined disclosures are required to be provided to the sender when the sender requests the remittance transfer, but prior to payment for the transfer. Whether a consumer has requested a remittance transfer depends on the

facts and circumstances. A sender that asks a provider to send a remittance transfer, and provides transaction-specific information to the provider in order to send funds to a designated recipient, has requested a remittance transfer. A sender that has sent an email, fax, mailed letter, or similar written or electronic communication has not requested a remittance transfer if the provider believes that it is impractical for the provider to treat that communication as a request and if the provider treats the communication as an inquiry and subsequently responds to that inquiry by calling the consumer on a telephone and orally gathering or confirming the information needed to process a request for a remittance transfer. *See* comment 31(a)(3)–2. Likewise, a consumer who solely inquires about that day's rates and fees to send to Mexico has not requested the provider to send a remittance transfer. Conversely, a sender who asks the provider at an agent location to send money to a recipient in Mexico and provides the sender and recipient information to the provider has requested a remittance transfer.

2. *When payment is made.* Except as provided in § 1005.36(a), a receipt required by § 1005.31(b)(2) must be provided to the sender when payment is made for the remittance transfer. For example, a remittance transfer provider could give the sender the disclosures after the sender pays for the remittance transfer, but before the sender leaves the counter. A provider could also give the sender the disclosures immediately before the sender pays for the transaction. For purposes of subpart B, payment is made, for example, when a sender provides cash to the remittance transfer provider or when payment is authorized.

3. *Telephone transfer from an account.* A sender may transfer funds from his or her account, as defined by § 1005.2(b), that is held by the remittance transfer provider. For example, a financial institution may send an international wire transfer for a sender using funds from the sender's account with the institution. Except as provided in § 1005.36(a), if the sender conducts such a transfer entirely by telephone, the institution may provide a receipt required by § 1005.31(b)(2) on or with the sender's next regularly scheduled periodic statement for that account or within 30 days after payment is made for the remittance transfer if a periodic statement is not provided.

4. *Mobile application and text message transactions.* If a transaction is conducted entirely by telephone via mobile application or text message, a receipt required by § 1005.31(b)(2) may be mailed or delivered to the sender pursuant to the timing requirements in § 1005.31(e)(2). For example, if a sender conducts a transfer entirely by telephone via mobile application, a remittance transfer provider may mail or deliver the disclosures to a sender pursuant to the timing requirements in § 1005.31(e)(2).

5. *Statement about cancellation rights.* The statement about the rights of the sender regarding cancellation required by § 1005.31(b)(2)(iv) may, but need not, be disclosed pursuant to the timing requirements of § 1005.31(e)(2) if a provider discloses this information pursuant to § 1005.31(a)(3)(iii) or (a)(5)(iii). The statement about the rights of the sender regarding error resolution required by § 1005.31(b)(2)(iv), however, must be disclosed pursuant to the timing requirements of § 1005.31(e)(2).

31(f) Accurate When Payment Is Made

1. *No guarantee of disclosures provided before payment.* Except as provided in § 1005.36(b), disclosures required by § 1005.31(b) or permitted by § 1005.31(b)(1)(viii) must be accurate when a sender makes payment for the remittance transfer. A remittance transfer provider is not required to guarantee the terms of the remittance transfer in the disclosures required or permitted by § 1005.31(b) for any specific period of time. However, if any of the disclosures required by § 1005.31(b) or permitted by § 1005.31(b)(1)(viii) are not accurate when a sender makes payment for the remittance transfer, a provider must give new disclosures before accepting payment.

31(g) Foreign Language Disclosures

1. *Number of foreign languages used in written disclosure.* Section 1005.31(g)(1) does not limit the number of languages that may be used on a single document, but such disclosures must be clear and conspicuous pursuant to § 1005.31(a)(1). Under § 1005.31(g)(1), a remittance transfer provider may, but need not, provide the sender with a written or electronic disclosure that is in English and, if applicable, in each foreign language that the remittance transfer provider principally uses to advertise, solicit, or market either orally, in writing, or electronically, at the office in which a sender conducts a transaction or asserts an error, respectively. Alternatively, the remittance transfer provider may provide the disclosure solely in English and, if applicable, the foreign language primarily used by the sender with the remittance transfer provider

to conduct the transaction or assert an error, provided such language is principally used by the remittance transfer provider to advertise, solicit, or market either orally, in writing, or electronically, at the office in which the sender conducts the transaction or asserts the error, respectively. If the remittance transfer provider chooses the alternative method, it may provide disclosures in a single document with both languages or in two separate documents with one document in English and the other document in the applicable foreign language. The following examples illustrate this concept.

i.   A remittance transfer provider principally uses only Spanish and Vietnamese to advertise, solicit, or market remittance transfer services at a particular office. The remittance transfer provider may provide all senders with disclosures in English, Spanish, and Vietnamese, regardless of the language the sender uses with the remittance transfer provider to conduct the transaction or assert an error.

ii.   Same facts as i. If a sender primarily uses Spanish with the remittance transfer provider to conduct a transaction or assert an error, the remittance transfer provider may provide a written or electronic disclosure in English and Spanish, whether in a single document or two separate documents. If the sender primarily uses English with the remittance transfer provider to conduct the transaction or assert an error, the remittance transfer provider may provide a written or electronic disclosure solely in English. If the sender primarily uses a foreign language with the remittance transfer provider to conduct the transaction or assert an error that the remittance transfer provider does not use to advertise, solicit, or market either orally, in writing, or electronically, at the office in which the sender conducts the transaction or asserts the error, respectively, the remittance transfer provider may provide a written or electronic disclosure solely in English.

2.   *Primarily used.* The language primarily used by the sender with the remittance transfer provider to conduct the transaction is the primary language used by the sender with the remittance transfer provider to convey the information necessary to complete the transaction. Similarly, the language primarily used by the sender with the remittance transfer provider to assert the error is the primary language used by the sender with the remittance transfer provider to provide the information required by § 1005.33(b) to assert an error. For example:

i.   A sender initiates a conversation with a remittance transfer provider with a greeting in English and expresses interest in sending a remittance transfer to Mexico in English. If the remittance transfer provider thereafter communicates with the sender in Spanish and the sender conveys the other information needed to complete the transaction, including the designated recipient's information and the amount and funding source of the transfer, in Spanish, then Spanish is the language primarily used by the sender with the remittance transfer provider to conduct the transaction.

ii.   A sender initiates a conversation with the remittance transfer provider with a greeting in English and states in English that there was a problem with a prior remittance transfer to Vietnam. If the remittance transfer provider thereafter communicates with the sender in Vietnamese and the sender uses Vietnamese to convey the information required by § 1005.33(b) to assert an error, then Vietnamese is the language primarily used by the sender with the remittance transfer provider to assert the error.

iii.   A sender accesses the Web site of a remittance transfer provider that may be used by senders to conduct remittance transfers or assert errors. The Web site is offered in English and French. If the sender uses the French version of the Web site to conduct the remittance transfer, then French is the language primarily used by the sender with the remittance transfer provider to conduct the transaction.

31(g)(1) General

1.   *Principally used.*

i.   All relevant facts and circumstances determine whether a foreign language is principally used by the remittance transfer provider to advertise, solicit, or market under § 1005.31(g)(1). Generally, whether a foreign language is considered to be principally used by the remittance transfer provider to advertise, solicit, or market is based on:

A.   The frequency with which the foreign language is used in advertising, soliciting, or marketing of remittance transfer services at that office;

B.   The prominence of the advertising, soliciting, or marketing of remittance transfer services in that foreign language at that office; and

C.   The specific foreign language terms used in the advertising soliciting, or marketing of remittance transfer service at that office.

ii.   For example, if a remittance transfer provider posts several prominent advertisements in a foreign language for remittance transfer services, including rate and fee information, on a consistent basis in an office, the provider is creating an expectation that a consumer could receive information on remittance transfer services in the foreign language used in the advertisements. The foreign language used in such advertisements would be considered to be principally used at that office based on the frequency and prominence of the advertising. In contrast, an advertisement for remittance transfer services, including rate and fee information, that is featured prominently at an office and is entirely in English, except for a greeting in a foreign language, does not create an expectation that a consumer could receive information on remittance transfer services in the foreign language used for such greeting. The foreign language used in such an advertisement is not considered to be principally used at that office based on the incidental specific foreign language term used.

2.   *Advertise, solicit, or market.*

i.   Any commercial message in a foreign language, appearing in any medium, that promotes directly or indirectly the availability of remittance transfer services constitutes advertising, soliciting, or marketing in such foreign language for purposes of § 1005.31(g)(1). Examples illustrating when a foreign language is used to advertise, solicit, or market include:

A.   Messages in a foreign language in a leaflet or promotional flyer at an office.

B.   Announcements in a foreign language on a public address system at an office.

C.   On-line messages in a foreign language, such as on the internet.

D.   Printed material in a foreign language on any exterior or interior sign at an office.

E.   Point-of-sale displays in a foreign language at an office.

F.   Telephone solicitations in a foreign language.

ii.   Examples illustrating use of a foreign language for purposes other than to advertise, solicit, or market include:

A.   Communicating in a foreign language (whether by telephone, electronically, or otherwise) about remittance transfer services in response to a consumer-initiated inquiry.

B.   Making disclosures in a foreign language that are required by Federal or other applicable law.

3.   *Office.* An office includes any physical location, telephone number, or Web site of a remittance transfer provider where a sender may conduct a remittance transfer or assert an error for a remittance transfer. The location need not exclusively offer remittance transfer services. For example, if an agent of a remittance transfer provider is located in a grocery store, the grocery store is considered an office for purposes of § 1005.31(g)(1). Because a consumer must be located in a State in order to be considered a "sender" under § 1005.30(g), a Web site is not an office for purposes of § 1005.31(g)(1), even if the Web site can be accessed by consumers that are located in the United States, unless a sender may conduct a remittance transfer on the Web site or may assert an error for a remittance transfer on the Web site.

4.   *At the office.* Any advertisement, solicitation, or marketing is considered to be made at the office in which a sender conducts a transaction or asserts an error if such advertisement, solicitation, or marketing is posted, provided, or made: at a physical office of a remittance transfer provider; on a Web site of a remittance transfer provider that may be used by senders to conduct remittance transfers or assert errors; during a telephone call with a remittance transfer provider that may be used by senders to conduct

remittance transfers or assert errors; or via mobile application or text message by a remittance transfer provider if the mobile application or text message may be used by senders to conduct remittance transfers or assert errors. An advertisement, solicitation, or marketing that is considered to be made at an office does not include general advertisements, solicitations, or marketing that are not intended to be made at a particular office. For example, if an advertisement for remittance transfers in Chinese appears in a Chinese newspaper that is being distributed at a grocery store in which the agent of a remittance transfer provider is located, such advertisement would not be considered to be made at that office. For disclosures provided pursuant to § 1005.31, the relevant office is the office in which the sender conducts the transaction. For disclosures provided pursuant to § 1005.33 for error resolution purposes, the relevant office is the office in which the sender first asserts the error, not the office where the transaction was conducted.

SECTION 1005.32—ESTIMATES

1.   *Disclosures where estimates can be used.* Sections 1005.32(a) and (b)(1) permit estimates to be used in certain circumstances for disclosures described in §§ 1005.31(b)(1) through (3) and 1005.36(a)(1) and(2). To the extent permitted in § 1005.32(a) and (b)(1), estimates may be used in the pre-payment disclosure described in § 1005.31(b)(1), the receipt disclosure described in § 1005.31(b)(2), the combined disclosure described in § 1005.31(b)(3), and the pre-payment disclosures and receipt disclosures for both first and subsequent preauthorized remittance transfers described in § 1005.36(a)(1) and (a)(2). Section 1005.32(b)(2) permits estimates to be used for certain information if the remittance transfer is scheduled by a sender five or more business days before the date of the transfer, for disclosures described in § 1005.36(a)(1)(i) and (a)(2)(i).

32(a) Temporary Exception for Insured Institutions

32(a)(1) General

1.   *Control.* For purposes of this section, an insured institution cannot determine exact amounts "for reasons beyond its control" when a person other than the insured institution or with which the insured institution has no correspondent relationship sets the exchange rate required to be disclosed under § 1005.31(b)(1)(iv) or imposes a covered third-party fee required to be disclosed under § 1005.31(b)(1)(vi). For example, if an insured institution has a correspondent relationship with an intermediary financial institution in another country and that intermediary institution sets the exchange rate or imposes a fee for remittance transfers sent from the insured institution to the intermediary institution, then the insured institution must determine exact amounts for the disclosures required under § 1005.31(b)(1)(iv) or (vi), because the determination of those amounts are not beyond the insured institution's control.

2.   *Examples of scenarios that qualify for the temporary exception.* The following examples illustrate when an insured institution cannot determine an exact amount "for reasons beyond its control" and thus would qualify for the temporary exception.

   i.   *Exchange rate.* An insured institution cannot determine the exact exchange rate to disclose under § 1005.31(b)(1)(iv) for an international wire transfer if the insured institution does not set the exchange rate, and the rate is set when the funds are deposited into the recipient's account by the designated recipient's institution with which the insured institution does not have a correspondent relationship. The insured institution will not know the exchange rate that the recipient institution will apply when the funds are deposited into the recipient's account.

   ii.   *Covered third-party fees.* An insured institution cannot determine the exact covered third-party fees to disclose under § 1005.31(b)(1)(vi) if an intermediary institution with which the insured institution does not have a correspondent relationship, imposes a transfer or conversion fee.

3.   *Examples of scenarios that do not qualify for the temporary exception.* The following examples illustrate when an insured institution can determine exact amounts and thus would not qualify for the temporary exception.

   i.   *Exchange rate.* An insured institution can determine the exact exchange rate required to be disclosed under § 1005.31(b)(1)(iv) if it converts the funds into the local currency to be received by the designated recipient using an exchange rate that it sets. The determination of the exchange rate is in the insured institution's control even if there is no correspondent relationship with an intermediary institution in the transmittal route or the designated recipient's institution.

ii.   *Covered third-party fees.* An insured institution can determine the exact covered third-party fees required to be disclosed under § 1005.31(b)(1)(vi) if it has agreed upon the specific fees with an intermediary correspondent institution, and this correspondent institution is the only institution in the transmittal route to the designated recipient's institution.

32(b) Permanent Exceptions

32(b)(1) Permanent Exceptions for Transfers to Certain Countries

1.   *Laws of the recipient country.* The laws of the recipient country do not permit a remittance transfer provider to determine exact amounts required to be disclosed when a law or regulation of the recipient country requires the person making funds directly available to the designated recipient to apply an exchange rate that is:

i.   Set by the government of the recipient country after the remittance transfer provider sends the remittance transfer or

ii.   Set when the designated recipient receives the funds.

2.   *Example illustrating when exact amounts can and cannot be determined because of the laws of the recipient country.*

i.   The laws of the recipient country do not permit a remittance transfer provider to determine the exact exchange rate required to be disclosed under § 1005.31(b)(1)(iv) when, for example, the government of the recipient country, on a daily basis, sets the exchange rate that must, by law, apply to funds received and the funds are made available to the designated recipient in the local currency the day after the remittance transfer provider sends the remittance transfer.

ii.   In contrast, the laws of the recipient country permit a remittance transfer provider to determine the exact exchange rate required to be disclosed under § 1005.31(b)(1)(iv) when, for example, the government of the recipient country ties the value of its currency to the U.S. dollar.

3.   *Method by which transactions are made in the recipient country.* The method by which transactions are made in the recipient country does not permit a remittance transfer provider to determine exact amounts required to be disclosed when transactions are sent via international ACH on terms negotiated between the United States government and the recipient country's government, under which the exchange rate is a rate set by the recipient country's central bank or other governmental authority after the provider sends the remittance transfer.

4.   *Example illustrating when exact amounts can and cannot be determined because of the method by which transactions are made in the recipient country.*

i.   The method by which transactions are made in the recipient country does not permit a remittance transfer provider to determine the exact exchange rate required to be disclosed under § 1005.31(b)(1)(iv) when the provider sends a remittance transfer via international ACH on terms negotiated between the United States government and the recipient country's government, under which the exchange rate is a rate set by the recipient country's central bank on the business day after the provider has sent the remittance transfer.

ii. In contrast, a remittance transfer provider would not qualify for the § 1005.32(b)(1)(i)(B) methods exception if it sends a remittance transfer via international ACH on terms negotiated between the United States government and a private-sector entity or entities in the recipient country, under which the exchange rate is set by the institution acting as the entry point to the recipient country's payments system on the next business day. However, a remittance transfer provider sending a remittance transfer using such a method may qualify for the § 1005.32(a) temporary exception.

iii.   A remittance transfer provider would not qualify for the § 1005.32(b)(1)(i)(B) methods exception if, for example, it sends a remittance transfer via international ACH on terms negotiated between the United States government and the recipient country's government, under which the exchange rate is set by the recipient country's central bank or other governmental authority before the sender requests a transfer.

5. *Safe harbor list.* If a country is included on a safe harbor list published by the Bureau under § 1005.32(b)(1)(ii), a remittance transfer provider may provide estimates of the amounts to be disclosed under § 1005.31(b)(1)(iv) through (b)(1)(vii). If a country does not appear on the Bureau's list, a remittance transfer provider may provide estimates under § 1005.32(b)(1)(i) if the provider determines that the recipient country does not legally permit or method by which transactions are conducted in that country does not permit the provider to determine exact disclosure amounts.

6. *Reliance on Bureau list of countries.* A remittance transfer provider may rely on the list of countries published by the Bureau to determine whether the laws of a recipient country do not permit the remittance transfer provider to determine exact amounts required to be disclosed under § 1005.31(b)(1)(iv) through (vii). Thus, if a country is on the Bureau's list, the provider may give estimates under this section, unless a remittance transfer provider has information that a country on the Bureau's list legally permits the provider to determine exact disclosure amounts.

7. *Change in laws of recipient country.*

   i.   If the laws of a recipient country change such that a remittance transfer provider can determine exact amounts, the remittance transfer provider must begin providing exact amounts for the required disclosures as soon as reasonably practicable if the provider has information that the country legally permits the provider to determine exact disclosure amounts.

   ii.   If the laws of a recipient country change such that a remittance transfer provider cannot determine exact disclosure amounts, the remittance transfer provider may provide estimates under § 1005.32(b)(1)(i), even if that country does not appear on the list published by the Bureau.

32(b)(2) Permanent Exceptions for Transfers Scheduled Before the Date of Transfer

1. *Fixed amount of foreign currency.* The following is an example of when and how a remittance transfer provider may disclose estimates for remittance transfers scheduled five or more business days before the date of transfer where the provider agrees to the sender's request to fix the amount to be transferred in a currency in which the transfer will be received and not the currency in which it was funded. If on February 1, a sender schedules a 1000 Euro wire transfer to be sent from the sender's bank account denominated in U.S. dollars to a designated recipient on February 15, § 1005.32(b)(2) allows the provider to estimate the amount that will be transferred to the designated recipient (*i.e.,* the amount described in § 1005.31(b)(1)(i)), any fees imposed or taxes collected on the remittance transfer by the provider (if based on the amount transferred) (*i.e.,* the amount described in § 1005.31(b)(1)(ii)), and the total amount of the transaction (*i.e.,* the amount described in § 1005.31(b)(1)(iii)). The provider may also estimate any covered third-party fees if the exchange rate is also estimated and the estimated exchange rate affects the amount of fees (as allowed by § 1005.32(b)(2)(ii)).

2. *Relationship to § 1005.10(d).* To the extent § 1005.10(d) requires, for an electronic fund transfer that is also a remittance transfer, notice when a preauthorized electronic fund transfer from the consumer's account will vary in amount from the previous transfer under the same authorization or from the preauthorized amount, that provision applies even if subpart B would not otherwise require notice before the date of transfer. However, insofar as § 1005.10(d) does not specify the form of such notice, a notice sent pursuant to § 1005.36(a)(2)(i) will satisfy § 1005.10(d) as long as the timing requirements of § 1005.10(d) are satisfied.

32(b)(3) Permanent Exception for Optional Disclosure of Non-Covered Third-Party Fees and Taxes Collected on the Remittance Transfer by a Person Other Than the Provider

1. *Reasonable sources of information.* Pursuant to § 1005.32(b)(3) a remittance transfer provider may estimate applicable non-covered third-party fees and taxes collected on the remittance transfer by a person other than the provider using reasonable sources of information. Reasonable sources of information may include, for example: information obtained from recent transfers to the same institution or the same country or region; fee schedules from the recipient institution; fee schedules from the recipient institution's competitors; surveys of recipient institution fees in the same country or region as the recipient institution;

OFFICIAL INTERPRETATIONS OF REGULATION E

information provided or surveys of recipient institutions' regulators or taxing authorities; commercially or publicly available databases, services or sources; and information or resources developed by international nongovernmental organizations or intergovernmental organizations.

32(c) Bases for Estimates

32(c)(1) Exchange Rate

1. *Most recent exchange rate for qualifying international ACH transfers.* If the exchange rate for a remittance transfer sent via international ACH that qualifies for the § 1005.32(b)(1)(i)(B) exception is set the following business day, the most recent exchange rate available for a transfer is the exchange rate set for the day that the disclosure is provided, *i.e.,* the current business day's exchange rate.

2. *Publicly available.* Examples of publicly available sources of information containing the most recent wholesale exchange rate for a currency include U.S. news services, such as Bloomberg, the Wall Street Journal, and the New York Times; a recipient country's national news services, and a recipient country's central bank or other government agency.

3. *Spread.* An estimate for disclosing the exchange rate based on the most recent publicly available wholesale exchange rate must also reflect any spread the remittance transfer provider typically applies to the wholesale exchange rate for remittance transfers for a particular currency.

4. *Most recent.* For the purposes of § 1005.32(c)(1)(ii) and (iii), if the exchange rate with respect to a particular currency is published or provided multiple times throughout the day because the exchange rate fluctuates throughout the day, a remittance transfer provider may use any exchange rate available on that day to determine the most recent exchange rate.

32(c)(3) Covered Third-Party Fees

1. *Potential transmittal routes.* A remittance transfer from the sender's account at an insured institution to the designated recipient's institution may take several routes, depending on the correspondent relationships each institution in the transmittal route has with other institutions. In providing an estimate of the fees required to be disclosed under § 1005.31(b)(1)(vi) pursuant to the § 1005.32(a) temporary exception, an insured institution may rely upon the representations of the designated recipient's institution and the institutions that act as intermediaries in any one of the potential transmittal routes that it reasonably believes a requested remittance transfer may travel.

32(d) Bases for Estimates for Transfers Scheduled Before the Date of Transfer

1. *In general.* When providing an estimate pursuant to § 1005.32(b)(2), § 1005.32(d) requires that a remittance transfer provider's estimated exchange rate must be the exchange rate (or estimated exchange rate) that the remittance transfer provider would have used or did use that day in providing disclosures to a sender requesting such a remittance transfer to be made on the same day. If, for the same-day remittance transfer, the provider could utilize either of the other two exceptions permitting the provision of estimates in § 1005.32(a) or (b)(1), the provider may provide estimates based on a methodology permitted under § 1005.32(c). For example, if, on February 1, the sender schedules a remittance transfer to occur on February 10, the provider should disclose the exchange rate as if the sender was requesting the transfer be sent on February 1. However, if at the time payment is made for the requested transfer, the remittance transfer provider could not send any remittance transfer until the next day (for reasons such as the provider's deadline for the batching of transfers), the remittance transfer provider can use the rate (or estimated exchange rate) that the remittance transfer provider would have used or did use in providing disclosures that day with respect to a remittance transfer requested that day that could not be sent until the following day.

SECTION 1005.33—PROCEDURES FOR RESOLVING ERRORS

33(a) Definition of Error

1. *Incorrect amount of currency paid by sender.* Section 1005.33(a)(1)(i) covers circumstances in which a sender pays an amount that differs from the total amount of the transaction, including fees imposed in connection with the transfer, stated in the receipt or combined disclosure provided under § 1005.31(b)(2) or (3). Such error may be asserted by a sender regardless of the form or method of payment provided, including

when a debit, credit, or prepaid card is used to fund the transfer and an excess amount is paid. For example, if a remittance transfer provider incorrectly charged a sender's credit card account for US$150, and US$120 was sent, plus a transfer fee of US$10, the sender could assert an error with the remittance transfer provider for the incorrect charge under § 1005.33(a)(1)(i).

2. *Incorrect amount of currency received—coverage.* Section 1005.33(a)(1)(iii) covers circumstances in which the designated recipient receives an amount of currency that differs from the amount of currency identified on the disclosures provided to the sender, except where the disclosure stated an estimate of the amount of currency to be received in accordance with § 1005.32 and the difference results from application of the actual exchange rate, fees, and taxes, rather than any estimated amounts, or the failure was caused by circumstances outside the remittance transfer provider's control. A designated recipient may receive an amount of currency that differs from the amount of currency disclosed, for example, if an exchange rate other than the disclosed rate is applied to the remittance transfer, or if the provider fails to account for fees or taxes that may be imposed by the provider or a third party before the transfer is picked up by the designated recipient or deposited into the recipient's account in the foreign country. However, if the provider rounds the exchange rate used to calculate the amount received consistent with § 1005.31(b)(1)(iv) and comment 31(b)(1)(iv)–2 for the disclosed rate, there is no error if the designated recipient receives an amount of currency that results from applying the exchange rate used, prior to any rounding of the exchange rate, to calculate fees, taxes, or the amount received rather than the disclosed rate. Section 1005.33(a)(1)(iii) also covers circumstances in which the remittance transfer provider transmits an amount that differs from the amount requested by the sender.

3. *Incorrect amount of currency received—examples.* For purposes of the following examples illustrating the error for an incorrect amount of currency received under § 1005.33(a)(1)(iii), assume that none of the circumstances permitting an estimate under § 1005.32 apply (unless otherwise stated).

   i.   A consumer requests to send funds to a relative in Mexico to be received in local currency. Upon receiving the sender's payment, the remittance transfer provider provides a receipt indicating that the amount of currency that will be received by the designated recipient will be 1180 Mexican pesos, after fees and taxes are applied. However, when the relative picks up the transfer in Mexico a day later, he only receives 1150 Mexican pesos because the exchange rate applied by the recipient agent in Mexico was lower than the exchange rate used by the provider, prior to any rounding of the exchange rate, to disclose the amount of currency to be received by the designated recipient on the receipt. Because the designated recipient has received less than the amount of currency disclosed on the receipt, an error has occurred.

   ii. A consumer requests to send funds to a relative in Colombia to be received in local currency. The remittance transfer provider provides the sender a receipt stating an amount of currency that will be received by the designated recipient, which does not reflect the additional foreign taxes that will be collected in Colombia on the transfer but does include the statement required by § 1005.31(b)(1)(viii). If the designated recipient will receive less than the amount of currency disclosed on the receipt due solely to the additional foreign taxes that the provider was not required to disclose, no error has occurred.

   iii. Same facts as in ii., except that the receipt provided by the remittance transfer provider does not reflect additional fees that are imposed by the receiving agent in Colombia on the transfer. Because the designated recipient will receive less than the amount of currency disclosed in the receipt due to the additional covered third-party fees, an error has occurred.

   iv. A consumer requests to send US$250 to a relative in India to a U.S. dollar-denominated account held by the relative at an Indian bank. Instead of the US$250 disclosed on the receipt as the amount to be sent, the remittance transfer provider sends US$200, resulting in a smaller deposit to the designated recipient's account than was disclosed as the amount to be received after fees and taxes. Because the designated recipient received less than the amount of currency that was disclosed, an error has occurred.

   v.   A consumer requests to send US$100 to a relative in a foreign country to be received in local currency. The remittance transfer provider provides the sender a receipt that discloses an estimated exchange rate, other taxes, and amount of currency that will be received due to the law in the foreign country requiring that the exchange rate be set by the foreign country's central bank. When the relative picks up the remittance transfer, the relative receives less currency than the estimated amount disclosed to the sender on the receipt due to application of the actual exchange rate, fees, and taxes, rather than any estimated amounts. Because § 1005.32(b) permits the remittance transfer provider to disclose an estimate of the amount of currency to be received, no error has occurred unless the estimate was not based on an approach set forth under § 1005.32(c).

vi.   A sender requests that his bank send US$120 to a designated recipient's account at an institution in a foreign country. The foreign institution is not an agent of the provider. Only US$100 is deposited into the designated recipient's account because the recipient institution imposed a US$20 incoming wire fee and deducted the fee from the amount transferred. Because this fee is a non-covered third-party fee that the provider is not required to disclose under § 1005.31(b)(1)(vi), no error has occurred if the provider provided the disclosure required by § 1005.31(b)(1)(viii).

4.   *Incorrect amount of currency received—extraordinary circumstances.* Under § 1005.33(a)(1)(iii)(B), a remittance transfer provider's failure to make available to a designated recipient the amount of currency disclosed pursuant to § 1005.31(b)(1)(vii) and stated in the disclosure provided pursuant to § 1005.31(b)(2) or (3) for the remittance transfer is not an error if such failure was caused by extraordinary circumstances outside the remittance transfer provider's control that could not have been reasonably anticipated. Examples of extraordinary circumstances outside the remittance transfer provider's control that could not have been reasonably anticipated under § 1005.33(a)(1)(iii)(B) include circumstances such as war or civil unrest, natural disaster, garnishment or attachment of some of the funds after the transfer is sent, and government actions or restrictions that could not have been reasonably anticipated by the remittance transfer provider, such as the imposition of foreign currency controls or foreign taxes unknown at the time the receipt or combined disclosure is provided under § 1005.31(b)(2) or (3).

5.   *Failure to make funds available by disclosed date of availability—coverage.* Section 1005.33(a)(1)(iv) generally covers disputes about the failure to make funds available in connection with a remittance transfer to a designated recipient by the disclosed date of availability. If only a portion of the funds were made available by the disclosed date of availability, then § 1005.33(a)(1)(iv) does not apply, but § 1005.33(a)(1)(iii) may apply instead. The following are examples of errors for failure to make funds available by the disclosed date of availability (assuming that none of the exceptions in § 1005.33(a)(1)(iv)(A), (B), or (C) apply).

i.   Late or non-delivery of a remittance transfer;

ii.   Delivery of funds to the wrong account;

iii.   The fraudulent pick-up of a remittance transfer in a foreign country by a person other than the designated recipient;

iv.   The recipient agent or institution's retention of the remittance transfer, instead of making the funds available to the designated recipient.

6.   *Failure to make funds available by disclosed date of availability—extraordinary circumstances.* Under § 1005.33(a)(1)(iv)(A), a remittance transfer provider's failure to deliver or transmit a remittance transfer by the disclosed date of availability is not an error if such failure was caused by extraordinary circumstances outside the remittance transfer provider's control that could not have been reasonably anticipated. Examples of extraordinary circumstances outside the remittance transfer provider's control that could not have been reasonably anticipated under § 1005.33(a)(1)(iv)(A) include circumstances such as war or civil unrest, natural disaster, garnishment or attachment of funds after the transfer is sent, and government actions or restrictions that could not have been reasonably anticipated by the remittance transfer provider, such as the imposition of foreign currency controls.

7.   *Failure to make funds available by disclosed date of availability—fraud and other screening procedures.* Under § 1005.33(a)(1)(iv)(B), a remittance transfer provider's failure to deliver funds by the disclosed date of availability is not an error if such delay is related to the provider's or any third party's investigation necessary to address potentially suspicious, blocked or prohibited activity, and the provider did not and could not have reasonably foreseen the delay so as to enable it to timely disclose an accurate date of availability when providing the sender with a receipt or combined disclosure. For example, no error occurs if delivery of funds is delayed because, after the receipt is provided, the provider's fraud screening system

flags a remittance transfer because the designated recipient has a name similar to the name of a blocked person under a sanctions program and further investigation is needed to determine that the designated recipient is not actually a blocked person. Similarly, no error occurs where, after disclosing a date of availability to the sender, a remittance transfer provider receives specific law enforcement information indicating that the characteristics of a remittance transfer match a pattern of fraudulent activity, and as a result, the provider deems it necessary to delay delivery of the funds to allow for further investigation. However, if a delay could have been reasonably foreseen, the exception in § 1005.33(a)(1)(iv)(B) would not apply. For example, if a provider knows in time to make a disclosure that all remittance transfers to a certain geographic area must undergo screening procedures that routinely delay such transfers by two days, the provider's failure to include the additional two days in its disclosure of the date of availability constitutes an error if delivery of the funds is indeed delayed beyond the disclosed date of availability.

8. *Sender account number or recipient institution identifier error.* The exception in § 1005.33(a)(1)(iv)(D) applies where a sender gives the remittance transfer provider an incorrect account number or recipient institution identifier and all five conditions in § 1005.33(h) are satisfied. The exception does not apply, however, where the failure to make funds available is the result of a mistake by a provider or a third party or due to incorrect or insufficient information provided by the sender other than an incorrect account number or recipient institution identifier, such as an incorrect name of the recipient institution.

9. *Account number or recipient institution identifier.* For purposes of the exception in § 1005.33(a)(1)(iv)(D), the terms account number and recipient institution identifier refer to alphanumerical account or institution identifiers other than names or addresses, such as account numbers, routing numbers, Canadian transit numbers, International Bank Account Numbers (IBANs), Business Identifier Codes (BICs)) and other similar account or institution identifiers used to route a transaction. In addition and for purposes of this exception, the term designated recipient's account in § 1005.30(h)(2) refers to an asset account, regardless of whether it is a consumer asset account, established for any purpose and held by a bank, savings association, credit union, or equivalent institution. A designated recipient's account does not, however, include a credit card, prepaid card, or a virtual account held by an Internet-based or mobile telephone company that is not a bank, savings association, credit union or equivalent institution.

10. *Recipient-requested changes.* Under § 1005.33(a)(2)(iii), a change requested by the designated recipient that the remittance transfer provider or others involved in the remittance transfer decide to accommodate is not considered an error. The exception under § 1005.33(a)(2)(iii) is available only if the change is made solely because the designated recipient requested the change. For example, if a sender requests to send US$100 to a designated recipient at a designated location, but the designated recipient requests the amount in a different currency (either at the sender-designated location or another location requested by the recipient) and the remittance transfer provider accommodates the recipient's request, the change does not constitute an error.

11. *Change from disclosure made in reliance on sender information.* Under the commentary accompanying § 1005.31, the remittance transfer provider may rely on the sender's representations in making certain disclosures. *See, e.g.,* comments 31(b)(1)(iv)–1 and 31(b)(1)(vi)–1. For example, suppose a sender requests U.S. dollars to be deposited into an account of the designated recipient and represents that the account is U.S. dollar-denominated. If the designated recipient's account is actually denominated in local currency and the recipient account-holding institution must convert the remittance transfer into local currency in order to deposit the funds and complete the transfer, the change in currency does not constitute an error pursuant to § 1005.33(a)(2)(iv).

33(b) Notice of Error from Sender

1. *Person asserting or discovering error.* The error resolution procedures of this section apply only when a notice of error is received from the sender, and not when a notice of error is received from the designated recipient or when the remittance transfer provider itself discovers and corrects an error.

2. *Content of error notice.* The notice of error is effective so long as the remittance transfer provider is able to identify the elements in § 1005.33(b)(1)(ii). For example, the sender could provide the confirmation number or code that would be used by the designated recipient to pick up the transfer, or other identification number or code supplied by the remittance transfer provider in connection with the transfer, if such number or code is sufficient for the remittance transfer provider to identify the sender (and contact information),

designated recipient, and the transfer in question. For an account-based remittance transfer, the notice of error is effective even if it does not contain the sender's account number, so long as the remittance transfer provider is able to identify the account and the transfer in question.

3.   *Address on notice of error.* A remittance transfer provider may request, or a sender may provide, the sender's or designated recipient's email address, as applicable, instead of a physical address, on a notice of error.

4.   *Effect of late notice.* A remittance transfer provider is not required to comply with the requirements of this section for any notice of error from a sender that is received by the provider more than 180 days from the disclosed date of availability of the remittance transfer to which the notice of error applies or, if applicable, more than 60 days after a provider sent documentation, additional information, or clarification requested by the sender, provided such date is later than 180 days after the disclosed date of availability.

5.   *Notice of error provided to agent.* A notice of error provided by a sender to an agent of the remittance transfer provider is deemed to be received by the provider under § 1005.33(b)(1)(i) when received by the agent.

6.   *Consumer notice of error resolution rights.* Section 1005.31 requires a remittance transfer provider to include an abbreviated notice of the consumer's error resolution rights on the receipt or combined notice provided under § 1005.31(b)(2) or (3). In addition, the remittance transfer provider must make available to a sender upon request, a notice providing a full description of the sender's error resolution rights, using language set forth in Appendix A of this part (Model Form A–36) or substantially similar language.

33(c) Time Limits and Extent of Investigation

1.   *Notice to sender of finding of error.* If the remittance transfer provider determines during its investigation that an error occurred as described by the sender, the remittance provider may inform the sender of its findings either orally or in writing. However, if the provider determines that no error or a different error occurred, the provider must provide a written explanation of its findings under § 1005.33(d)(1).

2.   *Incorrect or insufficient information provided for transfer.* The remedy in § 1005.33(c)(2)(iii) applies if a remittance transfer provider's failure to make funds in connection with a remittance transfer available to a designated recipient by the disclosed date of availability occurred because the sender provided incorrect or insufficient information in connection with the transfer, such as by erroneously identifying the designated recipient's address or by providing insufficient information such that the entity distributing the funds cannot identify the correct designated recipient. A sender is not considered to have provided incorrect or insufficient information for purposes of § 1005.33(c)(2)(iii) if the provider discloses the incorrect location where the transfer may be picked up, gives the wrong confirmation number/code for the transfer, or otherwise miscommunicates information necessary for the designated recipient to pick-up the transfer. The remedies in § 1005.33(c)(2)(iii) do not apply if the sender provided an incorrect account number or recipient institution identifier and the provider has met the requirements of § 1005.33(h) because under § 1005.33(a)(1)(iv)(D) no error would have occurred. *See* § 1005.33(a)(1)(iv)(D) and comment 33(a)–7.

3.   *Designation of requested remedy.* Under § 1005.33(c)(2)(ii), the sender may generally choose to obtain a refund of funds that were not properly transmitted or delivered to the designated recipient or, request redelivery of the amount appropriate to correct the error at no additional cost unless the error is determined to have occurred because the sender provided incorrect or insufficient information. Upon receiving the sender's request, the remittance transfer provider shall correct the error within one business day, or as soon as reasonably practicable, applying the same exchange rate, fees, and taxes stated in the disclosure provided under § 1005.31(b)(2) or (3), if the sender requests delivery of the amount appropriate to correct the error and the error did not occur because the sender provided incorrect or insufficient information. The provider may also request that the sender indicate the preferred remedy at the time the sender provides notice of the error although if provider does so, it should indicate that the if the sender chooses a resend at the time, the remedy may be unavailable if the error occurred because the sender provided incorrect or insufficient information. However, if the sender does not indicate the desired remedy at the time of providing notice of error, the remittance transfer provider must notify the sender of any available remedies in the report provided under § 1005.33(c)(1) or (d)(1) if the provider determines an error occurred.

4. *Default remedy.* Unless the sender provided incorrect or insufficient information and § 1005.33(c)(2)(iii) applies, the remittance transfer provider may set a default remedy that the provider will provide if the sender does not designate a remedy within a reasonable time after the sender receives the report provided under § 1005.33(c)(1). A provider that permits a sender to designate a remedy within 10 days after the provider has sent the report provided under § 1005.33(c)(1) or (d)(1) before imposing the default remedy is deemed to have provided the sender with a reasonable time to designate a remedy. In the case a default remedy is provided, the provider must correct the error within one business day, or as soon as reasonably practicable, after the reasonable time for the sender to designate the remedy has passed, consistent with § 1005.33(c)(2).

5. *Amount appropriate to resolve the error.* For purposes of the remedies set forth in § 1005.33(c)(2)(i)(A), (c)(2)(i)(B), (c)(2)(ii)(A)(*1*), and (c)(2)(i)(A)(*2*) the amount appropriate to resolve the error is the specific amount of transferred funds that should have been received if the remittance transfer had been effected without error. The amount appropriate to resolve the error does not include consequential damages. For example, when the amount that was disclosed pursuant to § 1005.31(b)(1)(vii) was received by the designated recipient before the provider must determine the appropriate remedy for an error under § 1005.33(a)(1)(iv), no additional amounts are required to resolve the error after the remittance transfer provider refunds the appropriate fees and taxes paid by the sender pursuant to § 1005.33(c)(2)(ii)(B) or (c)(2)(iii), as applicable.

6. *Form of refund.* For a refund provided under § 1005.33(c)(2)(i)(A), (c)(2)(ii)(A)(*1*), (c)(2)(ii)(B), or (c)(2)(iii), a remittance transfer provider may generally, at its discretion, issue a refund either in cash or in the same form of payment that was initially provided by the sender for the remittance transfer. For example, if the sender originally provided a credit card as payment for the transfer, the remittance transfer provider may issue a credit to the sender's credit card account in the appropriate amount. However, if a sender initially provided cash for the remittance transfer, a provider may issue a refund by check. For example, if the sender originally provided cash as payment for the transfer, the provider may mail a check to the sender in the amount of the payment.

7. *Remedies for incorrect amount paid.* If an error under § 1005.33(a)(1)(i) occurred, the sender may request the remittance transfer provider refund the amount necessary to resolve the error under § 1005.33(c)(2)(i)(A) or that the remittance transfer provider make the amount necessary to resolve the error available to the designated recipient at no additional cost under § 1005.33(c)(2)(i)(B).

8. *Correction of an error if funds not available by disclosed date.* If the remittance transfer provider determines an error of failure to make funds available by the disclosed date occurred under § 1005.33(a)(1)(iv), it must correct the error in accordance with § 1005.33(c)(2)(ii)(A), as applicable, and refund any fees imposed for the transfer (unless the sender provided incorrect or insufficient information to the remittance transfer provider in connection with the remittance transfer), whether the fee was imposed by the provider or a third party involved in sending the transfer, such as an intermediary bank involved in sending a wire transfer or the institution from which the funds are picked up in accordance with § 1005.33(c)(2)(ii)(B).

9. *Charges for error resolution.* If an error occurred, whether as alleged or in a different amount or manner, the remittance transfer provider may not impose a charge related to any aspect of the error resolution process (including charges for documentation or investigation).

10. *Correction without investigation.* A remittance transfer provider may correct an error, without investigation, in the amount or manner alleged by the sender, or otherwise determined, to be in error, but must comply with all other applicable requirements of § 1005.33.

11. *Procedure for sending a new remittance transfer after a sender provides incorrect or insufficient information.* Section 1005.33(c)(2)(iii) generally requires a remittance transfer provider to refund the transfer amount to the sender even if the sender's previously designated remedy was a resend or if the provider's default remedy in other circumstances was a resend. However, if before the refund is processed, the sender receives notice pursuant to § 1005.33(c)(1) or (d)(1) that an error occurred because the sender provided incorrect or insufficient information and then requests that the provider send the remittance transfer again, and the provider agrees to that request, § 1005.33(c)(2)(iii) requires that the request be treated as a new remittance transfer and the provider must provide new disclosures in accordance with

§ 1005.31 and all other applicable provisions of subpart B. However, § 1005.33(c)(2)(iii) does not obligate the provider to agree to a sender's request to send a new remittance transfer.

12. *Determining amount of refund.* Section 1005.33(c)(2)(iii) permits the provider to deduct from the amount refunded, or applied towards a new transfer, any fees or taxes actually deducted from the transfer amount by a person other than the provider as part of the first unsuccessful remittance transfer attempt or that were deducted in the course of returning the transfer amount to the provider following a failed delivery. However, a provider may not deduct those fees and taxes that will ultimately be refunded to the provider. When the provider deducts fees or taxes from the amount refunded pursuant to § 1005.33(c)(2)(iii), the provider must inform the sender of the deduction as part of the notice required by either § 1005.33(c)(1) or (d)(1) and the reason for the deduction. The following examples illustrate these concepts.

i. A sender instructs a remittance transfer provider to send US$100 to a designated recipient in local currency, for which the provider charges a transfer fee of US$10 (and thus the sender pays the provider $110). The provider's correspondent imposes a fee of US$15 that it deducts from the amount of the transfer. The sender provides incorrect or insufficient information that results in non-delivery of the remittance transfer as requested. Once the provider determines that an error occurred because the sender provided incorrect or insufficient information, the provider must provide the report required by § 1005.33(c)(1) or (d)(1) and inform the sender, pursuant to § 1005.33(c)(1) or (d)(1), that it will refund US$95 to the sender within three business days, unless the sender chooses to apply the US$95 towards a new remittance transfer and the provider agrees. Of the $95 that is refunded to the sender, $10 reflects the refund of the provider's transfer fee, and $85 reflects the refund of the amount of funds provided by the sender in connection with the transfer which was not properly transmitted. The provider is not required to refund the US$15 fee imposed by the correspondent (unless the $15 will be refunded to the provider by the correspondent).

ii. A sender instructs a remittance transfer provider to send US$100 to a designated recipient in a foreign country, for which the provider charges a transfer fee of US$10 (and thus the sender pays the provider US$110) and an intermediary institution charges a lifting fee of US$5, such that the designated recipient is expected to receive only US$95, as indicated in the receipt. If an error occurs because the sender provides incorrect or insufficient information that results in non-delivery of the remittance transfer by the date of availability stated in the disclosure provided to the sender for the remittance transfer under § 1005.31(b)(2) or (3), the provider is required to refund, or reapply if requested and the provider agrees, $105 unless the intermediary institution refunds to the provider the US$5 fee. If the sender requests to have the transfer amount applied to a new remittance transfer pursuant to § 1005.33(c)(2)(iii) and provides the corrected or additional information, and the remittance transfer provider agrees to a resend remedy, the remittance transfer provider may charge the sender another transfer fee of US$10 to send the remittance transfer again with the corrected or additional information necessary to complete the transfer. Insofar as the resend is an entirely new remittance transfer, the provider must provide a prepayment disclosure and receipt or combined disclosure in accordance with, among other provisions, the timing requirements of § 1005.31(f) and the cancellation provision of § 1005.34(a).

iii. In connection with a remittance transfer, a provider imposes a $15 tax that it then remits to a State taxing authority. An error occurs because the sender provided incorrect or insufficient information that resulted in non-delivery of the transfer to the designated recipient. The provider may deduct $15 from the amount it refunds to the sender pursuant to § 1005.33(c)(2)(iii) unless the relevant tax law will result in the $15 tax being refunded to the provider by the State taxing authority because the transfer was not completed.

33(d) Procedures if Remittance Transfer Provider Determines
No Error or Different Error Occurred

1. *Error different from that alleged.* When a remittance transfer provider determines that an error occurred in a manner or amount different from that described by the sender, it must comply with the requirements of both § 1005.33(c) and (d), as applicable. The provider may give the notice of correction and the explanation separately or in a combined form.

OFFICIAL INTERPRETATIONS OF REGULATION E

33(e) Reassertion of Error

1.   *Withdrawal of error; right to reassert.* The remittance transfer provider has no further error resolution responsibilities if the sender voluntarily withdraws the notice alleging an error. A sender who has withdrawn an allegation of error has the right to reassert the allegation unless the remittance transfer provider had already complied with all of the error resolution requirements before the allegation was withdrawn. The sender must do so, however, within the original 180-day period from the disclosed date of availability or, if applicable, the 60-day period for a notice of error asserted pursuant to § 1005.33(b)(2).

33(f) Relation to Other Laws

1.   *Concurrent error obligations.* A financial institution that is also the remittance transfer provider may have error obligations under both §§ 1005.11 and 1005.33. For example, if a sender asserts an error under § 1005.11 with a remittance transfer provider that holds the sender's account, and the error is not also an error under § 1005.33 (such as the omission of an EFT on a periodic statement), then the error-resolution provisions of § 1005.11 exclusively apply to the error. However, if a sender asserts an error under § 1005.33 with a remittance transfer provider that holds the sender's account, and the error is also an error under § 1005.11 (such as when the amount the sender requested to be deducted from the sender's account and sent for the remittance transfer differs from the amount that was actually deducted from the account and sent), then the error-resolution provisions of § 1005.33 exclusively apply to the error.

2.   *Holder in due course.* Nothing in this section limits a sender's rights to assert claims and defenses against a card issuer concerning property or services purchased with a credit card under Regulation Z, 12 CFR 1026.12(c)(1), as applicable.

3.   *Assertion of same error with multiple parties.* If a sender receives credit to correct an error of an incorrect amount paid in connection with a remittance transfer from either the remittance transfer provider or account-holding institution (or creditor), and subsequently asserts the same error with another party, that party has no further responsibilities to investigate the error if the error has been corrected. For example, assume that a sender initially asserts an error with a remittance transfer provider with respect to a remittance transfer alleging that US$130 was debited from his checking account, but the sender only requested a remittance transfer for US$100, plus a US$10 transfer fee. If the remittance transfer provider refunds US$20 to the sender to correct the error, and the sender subsequently asserts the same error with his account-holding institution, the account-holding institution has no error resolution responsibilities under Regulation E because the error has been fully corrected. In addition, nothing in this section prevents an account-holding institution or creditor from reversing amounts it has previously credited to correct an error if a sender receives more than one credit to correct the same error. For example, assume that a sender concurrently asserts an error with his or her account-holding institution and remittance transfer provider for the same error, and the sender receives credit from the account-holding institution for the error within 45 days of the notice of error. If the remittance transfer provider subsequently provides a credit of the same amount to the sender for the same error, the account-holding institution may reverse the amounts it had previously credited to the consumer's account, even after the 45-day error resolution period under § 1005.11.

33(g) Error Resolution Standards and Recordkeeping Requirements

1.   *Record retention requirements.* As noted in § 1005.31(g)(2), remittance transfer providers are subject to the record retention requirements under § 1005.13. Therefore, remittance transfer providers must retain documentation, including documentation related to error investigations, for a period of not less than two years from the date a notice of error was submitted to the provider or action was required to be taken by the provider. A remittance transfer provider need not maintain records of individual disclosures that it has provided to each sender; it need only retain evidence demonstrating that its procedures reasonably ensure the sender's receipt of required disclosures and documentation.

33(h) Incorrect Account Number Supplied

1.   *Reasonable methods of verification.* When a sender provides an incorrect recipient institution identifier, § 1005.33(h)(2) limits the exception in § 1005.33(a)(1)(iv)(D) to situations where the provider used reasonably available means to verify that the recipient institution identifier provided by the sender did correspond to the recipient institution name provided by the sender. Reasonably available means may include accessing a directory of Business Identifier Codes and verifying that the code provided by the sender

matches the provided institution name, and, if possible, the specific branch or location provided by the sender. Providers may also rely on other commercially available databases or directories to check other recipient institution identifiers. If reasonable verification means fail to identify that the recipient institution identifier is incorrect, the exception in § 1005.33(a)(1)(iv)(D) will apply, assuming that the provider can satisfy the other conditions in § 1005.33(h). Similarly, if no reasonably available means exist to verify the accuracy of the recipient institution identifier, § 1005.33(h)(2) would be satisfied and thus the exception in § 1005.33(a)(1)(iv)(D) also will apply, again assuming the provider can satisfy the other conditions in § 1005.33(h). However, where a provider does not employ reasonably available means to verify a recipient institution identifier, § 1005.33(h)(2) is not satisfied and the exception in § 1005.33(a)(1)(iv)(D) will not apply.

2.   *Reasonable efforts.* Section 1005.33(h)(5) requires a remittance transfer provider to use reasonable efforts to recover the amount that was to be received by the designated recipient. Whether a provider has used reasonable efforts does not depend on whether the provider is ultimately successful in recovering the amount that was to be received by the designated recipient. Under § 1005.33(h)(5), if the remittance transfer provider is requested to provide documentation or other supporting information in order for the pertinent institution or authority to obtain the proper authorization for the return of the incorrectly credited amount, reasonable efforts to recover the amount include timely providing any such documentation to the extent that it is available and permissible under law. The following are examples of reasonable efforts:

i.   The remittance transfer provider promptly calls or otherwise contacts the institution that received the transfer, either directly or indirectly through any correspondent(s) or other intermediaries or service providers used for the particular transfer, to request that the amount that was to be received by the designated recipient be returned, and if required by law or contract, by requesting that the recipient institution obtain a debit authorization from the holder of the incorrectly credited account.

ii.   The remittance transfer provider promptly uses a messaging service through a funds transfer system to contact institution that received the transfer, either directly or indirectly through any correspondent(s) or other intermediaries or service providers used for the particular transfer, to request that the amount that was to be received by the designated recipient be returned, in accordance with the messaging service's rules and protocol, and if required by law or contract, by requesting that the recipient institution obtain a debit authorization from the holder of the incorrectly credited account.

3.   *Promptness of Reasonable Efforts.* Section 1005.33(h)(5) requires that a remittance transfer provider act promptly in using reasonable efforts to recover the amount that was to be received by the designated recipient. Whether a provider acts promptly to use reasonable efforts depends on the facts and circumstances. For example, if, before the date of availability disclosed pursuant to § 1005.31(b)(2)(ii), the sender informs the provider that the sender provided a mistaken account number, the provider will have acted promptly if it attempts to contact the recipient's institution before the date of availability.

SECTION 1005.34—PROCEDURES FOR CANCELLATION AND REFUND OF REMITTANCE TRANSFERS

34(a) Sender Right of Cancellation and Refund

1.   *Content of cancellation request.* A request to cancel a remittance transfer is valid so long as the remittance transfer provider is able to identify the remittance transfer in question. For example, the sender could provide the confirmation number or code that would be used by the designated recipient to pick up the transfer or other identification number or code supplied by the remittance transfer provider in connection with the transfer, if such number or code is sufficient for the remittance transfer provider to identify the transfer. A remittance transfer provider may also request, or the sender may provide, the sender's email address instead of a physical address, so long as the remittance transfer provider is able to identify the transfer to which the request to cancel applies.

2.   *Notice of cancellation right.* Section 1005.31 requires a remittance transfer provider to include an abbreviated notice of the sender's right to cancel a remittance transfer on the receipt or combined disclosure given under § 1005.31(b)(2) or (3). In addition, the remittance transfer provider must make available to a

sender upon request, a notice providing a full description of the right to cancel a remittance transfer using language that is set forth in Model Form A–36 of Appendix A to this part or substantially similar language.

3. *Thirty-minute cancellation right.* A remittance transfer provider must comply with the cancellation and refund requirements of § 1005.34 if the cancellation request is received by the provider no later than 30 minutes after the sender makes payment. The provider may, at its option, provide a longer time period for cancellation. A provider must provide the 30-minute cancellation right regardless of the provider's normal business hours. For example, if an agent closes less than 30 minutes after the sender makes payment, the provider could opt to take cancellation requests through the telephone number disclosed on the receipt. The provider could also set a cutoff time after which the provider will not accept requests to send a remittance transfer. For example, a financial institution that closes at 5:00 p.m. could stop accepting payment for remittance transfers after 4:30 p.m.

4. *Cancellation request provided to agent.* A cancellation request provided by a sender to an agent of the remittance transfer provider is deemed to be received by the provider under § 1005.34(a) when received by the agent.

5. *Payment made.* For purposes of subpart B, payment is made, for example, when a sender provides cash to the remittance transfer provider or when payment is authorized.

34(b) Time Limits and Refund Requirements

1. *Form of refund.* At its discretion, a remittance transfer provider generally may issue a refund either in cash or in the same form of payment that was initially provided by the sender for the remittance transfer. For example, if the sender originally provided a credit card as payment for the transfer, the remittance transfer provider may issue a credit to the sender's credit card account in the amount of the payment. However, if a sender initially provided cash for the remittance transfer, a provider may issue a refund by check. For example, if the sender originally provided cash as payment for the transfer, the provider may mail a check to the sender in the amount of the payment.

2. *Fees and taxes refunded.* If a sender provides a timely request to cancel a remittance transfer, a remittance transfer provider must refund all funds provided by the sender in connection with the remittance transfer, including any fees and, to the extent not prohibited by law, taxes that have been imposed for the transfer, whether the fee or tax was assessed by the provider or a third party, such as an intermediary institution, the agent or bank in the recipient country, or a State or other governmental body.

SECTION 1005.35—ACTS OF AGENTS

1. *General.* Remittance transfer providers must comply with the requirements of subpart B, including, but not limited to, providing the disclosures set forth in § 1005.31 and providing any remedies as set forth in § 1005.33, even if an agent or other person performs functions for the remittance transfer provider, and regardless of whether the provider has an agreement with a third party that transfers or otherwise makes funds available to a designated recipient.

SECTION 1005.36—TRANSFERS SCHEDULED IN ADVANCE

1. *Applicability of subpart B.* The requirements set forth in subpart B apply to remittance transfers subject to § 1005.36, to the extent that § 1005.36 does not modify those requirements. For example, the foreign language disclosure requirements in § 1005.31(g) and related commentary continue to apply to disclosures provided in accordance with § 1005.36(a)(2).

SECTION 1005.36—TRANSFERS SCHEDULED BEFORE THE DATE OF TRANSFER

36(a) Timing

36(a)(2) Subsequent Preauthorized Remittance Transfers

1. *Changes in Disclosures.* When a sender schedules a series of preauthorized remittance transfers, the provider is generally not required to provide a pre-payment disclosure prior to the date of each subsequent transfer. However, § 1005.36(a)(1)(i) requires the provider to provide a pre-payment disclosure and receipt for the first in the series of preauthorized remittance transfers in accordance with the timing requirements set forth in § 1005.31(e). While certain information in those disclosures is expressly permitted to be

estimated (see § 1005.32(b)(2)), other information is not permitted to be estimated, or is limited in how it may be estimated. When any of the information on the most recent receipt provided pursuant to § 1005.36(a)(1)(i) or (a)(2)(i), other than the temporal disclosures required by § 1005.31(b)(2)(ii) and (b)(2)(vii), is no longer accurate with respect to a subsequent preauthorized remittance transfer for reasons other than as permitted by § 1005.32, the provider must provide, within a reasonable time prior to the scheduled date of the next preauthorized remittance transfer, a receipt that complies with § 1005.31(b)(2) and which discloses, among the other disclosures required by § 1005.31(b)(2), the changed terms. For example, if the provider discloses in the pre-payment disclosure for the first in the series of preauthorized remittance transfers that its fee for each remittance transfer is $20 and, after six preauthorized remittance transfers, the provider increases its fee to $30 (to the extent permitted by contract law), the provider must provide the sender a receipt that complies with §§ 1005.31(b)(2) and 1005.36(b)(2) within a reasonable time prior to the seventh transfer. Barring a further change, this receipt will apply to transfers after the seventh transfer. Or, if, after the sixth transfer, a tax collected by the provider increases from 1.5% of the amount that will be transferred to the designated recipient to 2.0% of the amount that will be transferred to the designated recipient, the provider must provide the sender a receipt that complies with §§ 1005.31(b)(2) and 1005.36(b)(2) within a reasonable time prior to the seventh transfer. In contrast, § 1005.36(a)(2)(i) does not require an updated receipt where an exchange rate, estimated as permitted by § 1005.32(b)(2), changes.

2. *Clearly and conspicuously.* In order to indicate clearly and conspicuously that the provider's fee has changed as required by § 1005.36(a)(2)(i), the provider could, for example, state on the receipt: "Transfer Fees (UPDATED) * * * $30." To the extent that other figures on the receipt must be revised because of the new fee, the receipt should also indicate that those figures are updated.

3. *Reasonable time.* If a disclosure required by § 1005.36(a)(2)(i) or (d)(1) is mailed, the disclosure would be considered to be received by the sender five business days after it is posted in the mail. If hand delivered or provided electronically, the receipt would be considered to be received by the sender at the time of delivery. Thus, if the provider mails a disclosure required by § 1005.36(a)(2)(i) or (d)(1) not later than ten business days before the scheduled date of the transfer, or hand or electronically delivers a disclosure not later than five business days before the scheduled date of the transfer, the provider would be deemed to have provided the disclosure within a reasonable time prior to the scheduled date of the subsequent preauthorized remittance transfer.

36(b) Accuracy

1. *Use of estimates.* In providing the disclosures described in § 1005.36(a)(1)(i) or (a)(2)(i), remittance transfer providers may use estimates to the extent permitted by any of the exceptions in § 1005.32. When estimates are permitted, however, they must be disclosed in accordance with § 1005.31(d).

2. *Subsequent preauthorized remittance transfers.* For a subsequent transfer in a series of preauthorized remittance transfers, the receipt provided pursuant to § 1005.36(a)(1)(i), except for the temporal disclosures in that receipt required by § 1005.31(b)(2)(ii) (Date Available) and (b)(2)(vii) (Transfer Date), applies to each subsequent preauthorized remittance transfer unless and until it is superseded by a receipt provided pursuant to § 1005.36(a)(2)(i). For each subsequent preauthorized remittance transfer, only the most recent receipt provided pursuant to § 1005.36(a)(1)(i) or (a)(2)(i) must be accurate as of the date each subsequent transfer is made.

3. *Receipts.* A receipt required by § 1005.36(a)(1)(ii) or (a)(2)(ii) must accurately reflect the details of the transfer to which it pertains and may not contain estimates pursuant to § 1005.32(b)(2). However, the remittance transfer provider may continue to disclose estimates to the extent permitted by § 1005.32(a) or (b)(1). In providing receipts pursuant to § 1005.36(a)(1)(ii) or (a)(2)(ii), § 1005.36(b)(2) and (3) do not allow a remittance transfer provider to change figures previously disclosed on a receipt provided pursuant to § 1005.36(a)(1)(i) or (a)(2)(i), unless a figure was an estimate or based on an estimate disclosed pursuant to § 1005.32. Thus, for example, if a provider disclosed its fee as $10 in a receipt provided pursuant to § 1005.36(a)(1)(i) and that receipt contained an estimate of the exchange rate pursuant to § 1005.32(b)(2), the second receipt provided pursuant to § 1005.36(a)(1)(ii) must also disclose the fee as $10.

OFFICIAL INTERPRETATIONS OF REGULATION E

36(c) Cancellation

1. *Scheduled remittance transfer.* Section 1005.36(c) applies when a remittance transfer is scheduled by the sender at least three business days before the date of the transfer, whether the sender schedules a preauthorized remittance transfer or a one-time transfer. A remittance transfer is scheduled if it will require no further action by the sender to send the transfer after the sender requests the transfer. For example, a remittance transfer is scheduled at least three business days before the date of the transfer, and § 1005.36(c) applies, where a sender on March 1 requests a remittance transfer provider to send a wire transfer to pay a bill in a foreign country on March 15, if it will require no further action by the sender to send the transfer after the sender requests the transfer. A remittance transfer is not scheduled, and § 1005.36(c) does not apply, where a transfer occurs more than three days after the date the sender requests the transfer solely due to the provider's processing time. The following are examples of when a sender has not scheduled a remittance transfer at least three business days before the date of the remittance transfer, such that the cancellation rule in § 1005.34 applies.

   i.   A sender on March 1 requests a remittance transfer provider to send a wire transfer to pay a bill in a foreign country on March 3.

   ii. A sender on March 1 requests that a remittance transfer provider send a remittance transfer on March 15, but the provider requires the sender to confirm the request on March 14 in order to send the transfer.

   iii. A sender on March 1 requests that a remittance transfer provider send an ACH transfer, and that transfer is sent on March 2, but due to the time required for processing, funds will not be deducted from the sender's account until March 5.

2. *Cancelled preauthorized remittance transfers.* For preauthorized remittance transfers, the provider must assume the request to cancel applies to all future preauthorized remittance transfers, unless the sender specifically indicates that it should apply only to the next scheduled remittance transfer.

3. *Concurrent cancellation obligations.* A financial institution that is also a remittance transfer provider may have both stop payment obligations under § 1005.10 and cancellation obligations under § 1005.36. If a sender cancels a remittance transfer under § 1005.36 with a remittance transfer provider that holds the sender's account, and the transfer is a preauthorized transfer under § 1005.10, then the cancellation provisions of § 1005.36 exclusively apply.

36(d) Date of Transfer for Subsequent Preauthorized Remittance Transfers

1. *General.* Section 1005.36(d)(2)(i) permits remittance transfer providers some flexibility in determining how and when the disclosures required by § 1005.36(d)(1) may be provided to senders. The disclosure described in § 1005.36(d)(1) may be provided as a separate disclosure, or on or with any other disclosure required by this subpart B related to the same series of preauthorized remittance transfers, provided that the disclosure and timing requirements in § 1005.36(d)(2) and other applicable provisions in subpart B are satisfied. For example, the required disclosures may be made on or with a receipt provided pursuant to § 1005.36(a)(1)(i); a receipt provided pursuant to § 1005.36(a)(2); or in a separate disclosure created by the provider. Thus, for example, a remittance transfer provider complies with § 1005.36(d)(1) for a period of one year if it provides in the receipt provided to the sender when payment is made for the initial preauthorized remittance transfer, a schedule or summary of the dates of transfer of all the subsequent preauthorized remittance transfers in the series scheduled to occur over the next 12 months (and the applicable cancellation requirements and contact information).

2. *Delivery of disclosure.* Section 1005.36(d)(2)(i) requires that the sender receive disclosure of the date of transfer, applicable cancellation requirements, and the provider's contact information no more than 12 months, and no less than 5 business days prior to the date of transfer of the subsequent preauthorized remittance transfer. For purposes of determining when a disclosure required by § 1005.36(d)(1) is received by the sender, refer to comment 36(a)(2)–3.

3. *Disclosure of the date of transfer.* The date of transfer of a subsequent preauthorized remittance transfer may be disclosed as a specific date (*e.g.,* July 19, 2013) or by using a method that clearly permits identification of the date of the transfer, such as periodic intervals (*e.g.,* the third Monday of every month,

or the 15th of every month). If the future dates of transfer are disclosed as occurring periodically and there is a break in the sequence, or the date of transfer does not otherwise conform to the described period, *e.g.,* if a holiday or weekend causes the provider to deviate from the normal schedule, the remittance transfer provider should disclose the specific date of transfer for the affected transfer.

4. *Accuracy requirements.* Section 1005.36(d)(4) sets forth accuracy requirements for disclosures required for subsequent preauthorized remittance transfers under § 1005.36(d)(1). If any of the information provided in these disclosures change, the provider must provide an updated disclosure with the revised information that is accurate as of when the transfer is made, pursuant to § 1005.36(d)(2).

FEDERAL TRADE COMMISSION
CREDIT PRACTICES REGULATIONS

---

16 C.F.R. Part 444

Current through March 31, 2016; 80 F.R. 18737

For updates, see www.gpo.gov/fdsys

---

§ 444.1   Definitions.

(a) **Lender.** A person who engages in the business of lending money to consumers within the jurisdiction of the Federal Trade Commission.

(b) **Retail installment seller.** A person who sells goods or services to consumers on a deferred payment basis or pursuant to a lease-purchase arrangement within the jurisdiction of the Federal Trade Commission.

(c) **Person.** An individual, corporation, or other business organization.

(d) **Consumer.** A natural person who seeks or acquires goods, services, or money for personal, family, or household use.

(e) **Obligation.** An agreement between a consumer and a lender or retail installment seller.

(f) **Creditor.** A lender or a retail installment seller.

(g) **Debt.** Money that is due or alleged to be due from one to another.

(h) **Earnings.** Compensation paid or payable to an individual or for his or her account for personal services rendered or to be rendered by him or her, whether denominated as wages, salary, commission, bonus, or otherwise, including periodic payments pursuant to a pension, retirement, or disability program.

(i) **Household goods.** Clothing, furniture, appliances, one radio and one television, linens, china, crockery, kitchenware, and personal effects (including wedding rings) of the consumer and his or her dependents, provided that the following are not included within the scope of the term household goods:

    (1)   Works of art;

    (2)   Electronic entertainment equipment (except one television and one radio);

    (3)   Items acquired as antiques; and

    (4)   Jewelry (except wedding rings).

(j) **Antique.** Any item over one hundred years of age, including such items that have been repaired or renovated without changing their original form or character.

(k) **Cosigner.** A natural person who renders himself or herself liable for the obligation of another person without compensation. The term shall include any person whose signature is requested as a condition to granting credit to another person, or as a condition for forbearance on collection of another person's obligation that is in default. The term shall not include a spouse whose signature is required on a credit obligation to perfect a security interest pursuant to State law. A person who does not receive goods, services, or money in return for a credit obligation does not receive compensation within the meaning of this definition. A person is a cosigner within the meaning of this definition whether or not he or she is designated as such on a credit obligation.

§ 444.2   Unfair credit practices.

(a)   In connection with the extension of credit to consumers in or affecting commerce, as commerce is defined in the Federal Trade Commission Act, it is an unfair act or practice within the meaning of Section 5 of that Act for a lender or retail installment seller directly or indirectly to take or receive from a consumer an obligation that:

(1)   Constitutes or contains a cognovit or confession of judgment (for purposes other than executory process in the State of Louisiana), warrant of attorney, or other waiver of the right to notice and the opportunity to be heard in the event of suit or process thereon.

(2)   Constitutes or contains an executory waiver or a limitation of exemption from attachment, execution, or other process on real or personal property held, owned by, or due to the consumer, unless the waiver applies solely to property subject to a security interest executed in connection with the obligation.

(3)   Constitutes or contains an assignment of wages or other earnings unless:

(i)   The assignment by its terms is revocable at the will of the debtor, or

(ii)   The assignment is a payroll deduction plan or preauthorized payment plan, commencing at the time of the transaction, in which the consumer authorizes a series of wage deductions as a method of making each payment, or

(iii)   The assignment applies only to wages or other earnings already earned at the time of the assignment.

(4)   Constitutes or contains a nonpossessory security interest in household goods other than a purchase money security interest.

(b)   [Reserved]

§ 444.3   Unfair or deceptive cosigner practices.

(a)   In connection with the extension of credit to consumers in or affecting commerce, as commerce is defined in the Federal Trade Commission Act, it is:

(1)   A deceptive act or practice within the meaning of Section 5 of that Act for a lender or retail installment seller, directly or indirectly, to misrepresent the nature or extent of cosigner liability to any person.

(2)   An unfair act or practice within the meaning of Section 5 of that Act for a lender or retail installment seller, directly or indirectly, to obligate a cosigner unless the cosigner is informed prior to becoming obligated, which in the case of open end credit shall mean prior to the time that the agreement creating the cosigner's liability for future charges is executed, of the nature of his or her liability as cosigner.

(b)   Any lender or retail installment seller who complies with the preventive requirements in paragraph (c) of this section does not violate paragraph (a) of this section.

(c)   To prevent these unfair or deceptive acts or practices, a disclosure, consisting of a separate document that shall contain the following statement and no other, shall be given to the cosigner prior to becoming obligated, which in the case of open end credit shall mean prior to the time that the agreement creating the cosigner's liability for future charges is executed:

Notice to Cosigner

You are being asked to guarantee this debt. Think carefully before you do. If the borrower doesn't pay the debt, you will have to. Be sure you can afford to pay if you have to, and that you want to accept this responsibility.

You may have to pay up to the full amount of the debt if the borrower does not pay. You may also have to pay late fees or collection costs, which increase this amount.

The creditor can collect this debt from you without first trying to collect from the borrower. The creditor can use the same collection methods against you that can be used against the borrower, such as suing you, garnishing your wages, etc. If this debt is ever in default, that fact may become a part of your credit record.

This notice is not the contract that makes you liable for the debt.

§ 444.4   Late charges.

(a)   In connection with collecting a debt arising out of an extension of credit to a consumer in or affecting commerce, as commerce is defined in the Federal Trade Commission Act, it is an unfair act or practice within the meaning of section 5 of that Act for a creditor, directly or indirectly, to levy or collect any delinquency charge on a payment, which payment is otherwise a full payment for the applicable period and is paid on its due date or within an applicable grace period, when the only delinquency is attributable to late fee(s) or delinquency charge(s) assessed on earlier installment(s).

(b)   For purposes of this section, collecting a debt means any activity other than the use of judicial process that is intended to bring about or does bring about repayment of all or part of a consumer debt.

§ 444.5   State exemptions.

(a)   If, upon application to the Federal Trade Commission by an appropriate State agency, the Federal Trade Commission determines that:

(1)   There is a State requirement or prohibition in effect that applies to any transaction to which a provision of this rule applies; and

(2)   The State requirement or prohibition affords a level of protection to consumers that is substantially equivalent to, or greater than, the protection afforded by this rule;

Then that provision of the rule will not be in effect in that State to the extent specified by the Federal Trade Commission in its determination, for as long as the State administers and enforces the State requirement or prohibition effectively.

(b)   [Reserved]

FEDERAL TRADE COMMISSION
HOLDER-IN-DUE-COURSE REGULATIONS

---

16 C.F.R. Part 433

Current through March 31, 2016; 80 F.R. 18737

For updates, see www.gpo.gov/fdsys

---

§ 433.1   Definitions.

(a)   **Person.** An individual, corporation, or any other business organization.

(b)   **Consumer.** A natural person who seeks or acquires goods or services for personal, family, or household use.

(c)   **Creditor.** A person who, in the ordinary course of business, lends purchase money or finances the sale of goods or services to consumers on a deferred payment basis; Provided, such person is not acting, for the purposes of a particular transaction, in the capacity of a credit card issuer.

(d)   **Purchase money loan.** A cash advance which is received by a consumer in return for a "Finance Charge" within the meaning of the Truth in Lending Act and Regulation Z, which is applied, in whole or substantial part, to a purchase of goods or services from a seller who (1) refers consumers to the creditor or (2) is affiliated with the creditor by common control, contract, or business arrangement.

(e)   **Financing a sale.** Extending credit to a consumer in connection with a "Credit Sale" within the meaning of the Truth in Lending Act and Regulation Z.

(f)   **Contract.** Any oral or written agreement, formal or informal, between a creditor and a seller, which contemplates or provides for cooperative or concerted activity in connection with the sale of goods or services to consumers or the financing thereof.

(g)   **Business arrangement.** Any understanding, procedure, course of dealing, or arrangement, formal or informal, between a creditor and a seller, in connection with the sale of goods or services to consumers or the financing thereof.

(h)   **Credit card issuer.** A person who extends to cardholders the right to use a credit card in connection with purchases of goods or services.

(i)   **Consumer credit contract.** Any instrument which evidences or embodies a debt arising from a "Purchase Money Loan" transaction or a "financed sale" as defined in paragraphs (d) and (e) of this section.

(j)   **Seller.** A person who, in the ordinary course of business, sells or leases goods or services to consumers.

§ 433.2   Preservation of consumers' claims and defenses, unfair or deceptive acts or practices.

In connection with any sale or lease of goods or services to consumers, in or affecting commerce as "commerce" is defined in the Federal Trade Commission Act, it is an unfair or deceptive act or practice within the meaning of Section 5 of that Act for a seller, directly or indirectly, to:

(a)   Take or receive a consumer credit contract which fails to contain the following provision in at least ten point, bold face, type:

NOTICE

ANY HOLDER OF THIS CONSUMER CREDIT CONTRACT IS SUBJECT TO ALL CLAIMS AND DEFENSES WHICH THE DEBTOR COULD ASSERT AGAINST THE SELLER OF GOODS OR SERVICES OBTAINED PURSUANT HERETO OR WITH THE PROCEEDS HEREOF. RECOVERY HEREUNDER BY THE DEBTOR SHALL NOT EXCEED AMOUNTS PAID BY THE DEBTOR HEREUNDER.

or,

(b)   Accept, as full or partial payment for such sale or lease, the proceeds of any purchase money loan (as purchase money loan is defined herein), unless any consumer credit contract made in connection with such purchase money loan contains the following provision in at least ten point, bold face, type:

NOTICE

ANY HOLDER OF THIS CONSUMER CREDIT CONTRACT IS SUBJECT TO ALL CLAIMS AND DEFENSES WHICH THE DEBTOR COULD ASSERT AGAINST THE SELLER OF GOODS OR SERVICES OBTAINED WITH THE PROCEEDS HEREOF. RECOVERY HEREUNDER BY THE DEBTOR SHALL NOT EXCEED AMOUNTS PAID BY THE DEBTOR HEREUNDER.

§ 433.3   Exemption of sellers taking or receiving open end consumer credit contracts before November 1, 1977 from requirements of § 433.2(a).

(a)   Any seller who has taken or received an open end consumer credit contract before November 1, 1977, shall be exempt from the requirements of 16 CFR part 433 with respect to such contract provided the contract does not cut off consumers' claims and defenses.

(b)   **Definitions.** The following definitions apply to this exemption:

(1)   All pertinent definitions contained in 16 CFR 433.1.

(2)   **Open end consumer credit contract:** a consumer credit contract pursuant to which "open end credit" is extended.

(3)   **"Open end credit":** consumer credit extended on an account pursuant to a plan under which a creditor may permit an applicant to make purchases or make loans, from time to time, directly from the creditor or indirectly by use of a credit card, check, or other device, as the plan may provide. The term does not include negotiated advances under an open-end real estate mortgage or a letter of credit.

(4)   **Contract which does not cut off consumers' claims and defenses:** A consumer credit contract which does not constitute or contain a negotiable instrument, or contain any waiver, limitation, term, or condition which has the effect of limiting a consumer's right to assert against any holder of the contract all legally sufficient claims and defenses which the consumer could assert against the seller of goods or services purchased pursuant to the contract.

FEDERAL TAX LIEN STATUTE

INTERNAL REVENUE CODE

26 U.S.C. §§ 6321–6323

Current through March 30, 2016; P.L. 114–141

For updates, see http://uscode.house.gov

---

§ 6321.   Lien for taxes

If any person liable to pay any tax neglects or refuses to pay the same after demand, the amount (including any interest, additional amount, addition to tax, or assessable penalty, together with any costs that may accrue in addition thereto) shall be a lien in favor of the United States upon all property and rights to property, whether real or personal, belonging to such person.

(Aug. 16, 1954, c. 736, 68A Stat. 779.)

§ 6322.   Period of lien

Unless another date is specifically fixed by law, the lien imposed by section 6321 shall arise at the time the assessment is made and shall continue until the liability for the amount so assessed (or a judgment against the taxpayer arising out of such liability) is satisfied or becomes unenforceable by reason of lapse of time.

(Aug. 16, 1954, c. 736, 68A Stat. 779; Nov. 2, 1966, Pub.L. 89–719, Title I, § 113(a), 80 Stat. 1146.)

§ 6323.   Validity and priority against certain persons

(a) Purchasers, holders of security interests, mechanic's lienors, and judgment lien creditors.—The lien imposed by section 6321 shall not be valid as against any purchaser, holder of a security interest, mechanic's lienor, or judgment lien creditor until notice thereof which meets the requirements of subsection (f) has been filed by the Secretary.

(b) Protection for certain interests even though notice filed.—Even though notice of a lien imposed by section 6321 has been filed, such lien shall not be valid—

    (1) Securities.—With respect to a security (as defined in subsection (h)(4))—

        (A) as against a purchaser of such security who at the time of purchase did not have actual notice or knowledge of the existence of such lien; and

        (B) as against a holder of a security interest in such security who, at the time such interest came into existence, did not have actual notice or knowledge of the existence of such lien.

    (2) Motor vehicles.—With respect to a motor vehicle (as defined in subsection (h)(3)), as against a purchaser of such motor vehicle, if—

        (A) at the time of the purchase such purchaser did not have actual notice or knowledge of the existence of such lien, and

        (B) before the purchaser obtains such notice or knowledge, he has acquired possession of such motor vehicle and has not thereafter relinquished possession of such motor vehicle to the seller or his agent.

    (3) Personal property purchased at retail.—With respect to tangible personal property purchased at retail, as against a purchaser in the ordinary course of the seller's trade or business, unless at the time of such purchase such purchaser intends such purchase to (or knows such purchase will) hinder, evade, or defeat the collection of any tax under this title.

(4) Personal property purchased in casual sale.—With respect to household goods, personal effects, or other tangible personal property described in section 6334(a) purchased (not for resale) in a casual sale for less than $1,000, as against the purchaser, but only if such purchaser does not have actual notice or knowledge (A) of the existence of such lien, or (B) that this sale is one of a series of sales.

(5) Personal property subject to possessory lien.—With respect to tangible personal property subject to a lien under local law securing the reasonable price of the repair or improvement of such property, as against a holder of such a lien, if such holder is, and has been, continuously in possession of such property from the time such lien arose.

(6) Real property tax and special assessment liens.—With respect to real property, as against a holder of a lien upon such property, if such lien is entitled under local law to priority over security interests in such property which are prior in time, and such lien secures payment of—

    (A) a tax of general application levied by any taxing authority based upon the value of such property;

    (B) a special assessment imposed directly upon such property by any taxing authority, if such assessment is imposed for the purpose of defraying the cost of any public improvement; or

    (C) charges for utilities or public services furnished to such property by the United States, a State or political subdivision thereof, or an instrumentality of any one or more of the foregoing.

(7) Residential property subject to a mechanic's lien for certain repairs and improvements.—With respect to real property subject to a lien for repair or improvement of a personal residence (containing not more than four dwelling units) occupied by the owner of such residence, as against a mechanic's lienor, but only if the contract price on the contract with the owner is not more than $5,000.

(8) Attorneys' liens.—With respect to a judgment or other amount in settlement of a claim or of a cause of action, as against an attorney who, under local law, holds a lien upon or a contract enforceable against such judgment or amount, to the extent of his reasonable compensation for obtaining such judgment or procuring such settlement, except that this paragraph shall not apply to any judgment or amount in settlement of a claim or of a cause of action against the United States to the extent that the United States offsets such judgment or amount against any liability of the taxpayer to the United States.

(9) Certain insurance contracts.—With respect to a life insurance, endowment, or annuity contract, as against the organization which is the insurer under such contract, at any time—

    (A) before such organization had actual notice or knowledge of the existence of such lien;

    (B) after such organization had such notice or knowledge, with respect to advances required to be made automatically to maintain such contract in force under an agreement entered into before such organization had such notice or knowledge; or

    (C) after satisfaction of a levy pursuant to section 6332(b), unless and until the Secretary delivers to such organization a notice, executed after the date of such satisfaction, of the existence of such lien.

(10) Deposit-secured loans.—With respect to a savings deposit, share, or other account, with an institution described in section 581 or 591, to the extent of any loan made by such institution without actual notice or knowledge of the existence of such lien, as against such institution, if such loan is secured by such account.

(c) Protection for certain commercial transactions financing agreements, etc.—

(1) In general.—To the extent provided in this subsection, even though notice of a lien imposed by section 6321 has been filed, such lien shall not be valid with respect to a security interest which came into existence after tax lien filing but which—

(A) is in qualified property covered by the terms of a written agreement entered into before tax lien filing and constituting—

(i) a commercial transactions financing agreement,

(ii) a real property construction or improvement financing agreement, or

(iii) an obligatory disbursement agreement, and

(B) is protected under local law against a judgment lien arising, as of the time of tax lien filing, out of an unsecured obligation.

(2) Commercial transactions financing agreement.—For purposes of this subsection—

(A) Definition.—The term "commercial transactions financing agreement" means an agreement (entered into by a person in the course of his trade or business)—

(i) to make loans to the taxpayer to be secured by commercial financing security acquired by the taxpayer in the ordinary course of his trade or business, or

(ii) to purchase commercial financing security (other than inventory) acquired by the taxpayer in the ordinary course of his trade or business;

but such an agreement shall be treated as coming within the term only to the extent that such loan or purchase is made before the 46th day after the date of tax lien filing or (if earlier) before the lender or purchaser had actual notice or knowledge of such tax lien filing.

(B) Limitation on qualified property.—The term "qualified property", when used with respect to a commercial transactions financing agreement, includes only commercial financing security acquired by the taxpayer before the 46th day after the date of tax lien filing.

(C) Commercial financing security defined.—The term "commercial financing security" means (i) paper of a kind ordinarily arising in commercial transactions, (ii) accounts receivable, (iii) mortgages on real property, and (iv) inventory.

(D) Purchaser treated as acquiring security interest.—A person who satisfies subparagraph (A) by reason of clause (ii) thereof shall be treated as having acquired a security interest in commercial financing security.

(3) Real property construction or improvement financing agreement.—For purposes of this subsection—

(A) Definition.—The term "real property construction or improvement financing agreement" means an agreement to make cash disbursements to finance—

(i) the construction or improvement of real property,

(ii) a contract to construct or improve real property, or

(iii) the raising or harvesting of a farm crop or the raising of livestock or other animals.

For purposes of clause (iii), the furnishing of goods and services shall be treated as the disbursement of cash.

(B) Limitation on qualified property.—The term "qualified property", when used with respect to a real property construction or improvement financing agreement, includes only—

(i) in the case of subparagraph (A)(i), the real property with respect to which the construction or improvement has been or is to be made,

(ii) in the case of subparagraph (A)(ii), the proceeds of the contract described therein, and

(iii) in the case of subparagraph (A)(iii), property subject to the lien imposed by section 6321 at the time of tax lien filing and the crop or the livestock or other animals referred to in subparagraph (A)(iii).

(4) Obligatory disbursement agreement.—For purposes of this subsection—

(A) Definition.—The term "obligatory disbursement agreement" means an agreement (entered into by a person in the course of his trade or business) to make disbursements, but such an agreement shall be treated as coming within the term only to the extent of disbursements which are required to be made by reason of the intervention of the rights of a person other than the taxpayer.

(B) Limitation on qualified property.—The term "qualified property", when used with respect to an obligatory disbursement agreement, means property subject to the lien imposed by section 6321 at the time of tax lien filing and (to the extent that the acquisition is directly traceable to the disbursements referred to in subparagraph (A)) property acquired by the taxpayer after tax lien filing.

(C) Special rules for surety agreements.—Where the obligatory disbursement agreement is an agreement ensuring the performance of a contract between the taxpayer and another person—

(i) the term "qualified property" shall be treated as also including the proceeds of the contract the performance of which was ensured, and

(ii) if the contract the performance of which was ensured was a contract to construct or improve real property, to produce goods, or to furnish services, the term "qualified property" shall be treated as also including any tangible personal property used by the taxpayer in the performance of such ensured contract.

(d) 45-day period for making disbursements.—Even though notice of a lien imposed by section 6321 has been filed, such lien shall not be valid with respect to a security interest which came into existence after tax lien filing by reason of disbursements made before the 46th day after the date of tax lien filing, or (if earlier) before the person making such disbursements had actual notice or knowledge of tax lien filing, but only if such security interest—

(1) is in property (A) subject, at the time of tax lien filing, to the lien imposed by section 6321, and (B) covered by the terms of a written agreement entered into before tax lien filing, and

(2) is protected under local law against a judgment lien arising, as of the time of tax lien filing, out of an unsecured obligation.

(e) Priority of interest and expenses.—If the lien imposed by section 6321 is not valid as against a lien or security interest, the priority of such lien or security interest shall extend to—

(1) any interest or carrying charges upon the obligation secured,

(2) the reasonable charges and expenses of an indenture trustee or agent holding the security interest for the benefit of the holder of the security interest,

(3) the reasonable expenses, including reasonable compensation for attorneys, actually incurred in collecting or enforcing the obligation secured,

(4) the reasonable costs of insuring, preserving, or repairing the property to which the lien or security interest relates,

(5) the reasonable costs of insuring payment of the obligation secured, and

(6) amounts paid to satisfy any lien on the property to which the lien or security interest relates, but only if the lien so satisfied is entitled to priority over the lien imposed by section 6321, to the extent that, under local law, any such item has the same priority as the lien or security interest to which it relates.

(f) Place for filing notice; form.—

(1) Place for filing.—The notice referred to in subsection (a) shall be filed—

(A) Under State laws.—

(i) Real property.—In the case of real property, in one office within the State (or the county, or other governmental subdivision), as designated by the laws of such State, in which the property subject to the lien is situated; and

(ii) Personal property.—In the case of personal property, whether tangible or intangible, in one office within the State (or the county, or other governmental subdivision), as designated by the laws of such State, in which the property subject to the lien is situated, except that State law merely conforming to or reenacting Federal law establishing a national filing system does not constitute a second office for filing as designated by the laws of such State; or

(B) With clerk of district court.—In the office of the clerk of the United States district court for the judicial district in which the property subject to the lien is situated, whenever the State has not by law designated one office which meets the requirements of subparagraph (A); or

(C) With Recorder of Deeds of the District of Columbia.—In the office of the Recorder of Deeds of the District of Columbia, if the property subject to the lien is situated in the District of Columbia.

(2) Situs of property subject to lien.—For purposes of paragraphs (1) and (4), property shall be deemed to be situated—

(A) Real property.—In the case of real property, at its physical location; or

(B) Personal property.—In the case of personal property, whether tangible or intangible, at the residence of the taxpayer at the time the notice of lien is filed.

For purposes of paragraph (2)(B), the residence of a corporation or partnership shall be deemed to be the place at which the principal executive office of the business is located, and the residence of a taxpayer whose residence is without the United States shall be deemed to be in the District of Columbia.

(3) Form.—The form and content of the notice referred to in subsection (a) shall be prescribed by the Secretary. Such notice shall be valid notwithstanding any other provision of law regarding the form or content of a notice of lien.

(4) Indexing required with respect to certain real property.—In the case of real property, if—

(A) under the laws of the State in which the real property is located, a deed is not valid as against a purchaser of the property who (at the time of purchase) does not have actual notice or knowledge of the existence of such deed unless the fact of filing of such deed has been entered and recorded in a public index at the place of filing in such a manner that a reasonable inspection of the index will reveal the existence of the deed, and

(B) there is maintained (at the applicable office under paragraph (1)) an adequate system for the public indexing of Federal tax liens,

then the notice of lien referred to in subsection (a) shall not be treated as meeting the filing requirements under paragraph (1) unless the fact of filing is entered and recorded in the index referred to in subparagraph (B) in such a manner that a reasonable inspection of the index will reveal the existence of the lien.

(5)   National filing systems.—The filing of a notice of lien shall be governed solely by this title and shall not be subject to any other Federal law establishing a place or places for the filing of liens or encumbrances under a national filing system.

(g)   Refiling of notice.—For purposes of this section—

(1)   General rule.—Unless notice of lien is refiled in the manner prescribed in paragraph (2) during the required refiling period, such notice of lien shall be treated as filed on the date on which it is filed (in accordance with subsection (f)) after the expiration of such refiling period.

(2)   Place for filing.—A notice of lien refiled during the required refiling period shall be effective only—

   **(A)   if—

      (i)   such notice of lien is refiled in the office in which the prior notice of lien was filed, and

      (ii)   in the case of real property, the fact of refiling is entered and recorded in an index to the extent required by subsection (f)(4); and

   (B)   in any case in which, 90 days or more prior to the date of a refiling of notice of lien under subparagraph (A), the Secretary received written information (in the manner prescribed in regulations issued by the Secretary) concerning a change in the taxpayer's residence, if a notice of such lien is also filed in accordance with subsection (f) in the State in which such residence is located.

(3)   Required refiling period.—In the case of any notice of lien, the term "required refiling period" means—

   (A)   the one-year period ending 30 days after the expiration of 10 years after the date of the assessment of the tax, and

   (B)   the one-year period ending with the expiration of 10 years after the close of the preceding required refiling period for such notice of lien.

(4)   Transitional rule.—Notwithstanding paragraph (3), if the assessment of the tax was made before January 1, 1962, the first required refiling period shall be the calendar year 1967.

(h)   Definitions.—For purposes of this section and section 6324—

(1)   Security interest.—The term "security interest" means any interest in property acquired by contract for the purpose of securing payment or performance of an obligation or indemnifying against loss or liability. A security interest exists at any time (A) if, at such time, the property is in existence and the interest has become protected under local law against a subsequent judgment lien arising out of an unsecured obligation, and (B) to the extent that, at such time, the holder has parted with money or money's worth.

(2)   Mechanic's lienor.—The term "mechanic's lienor" means any person who under local law has a lien on real property (or on the proceeds of a contract relating to real property) for services, labor, or materials furnished in connection with the construction or improvement of such property. For purposes of the preceding sentence, a person has a lien on the earliest date such lien becomes valid under local law against subsequent purchasers without actual notice, but not before he begins to furnish the services, labor, or materials.

(3)   Motor vehicle.—The term "motor vehicle" means a self-propelled vehicle which is registered for highway use under the laws of any State or foreign country.

(4)   Security.—The term "security" means any bond, debenture, note, or certificate or other evidence of indebtedness, issued by a corporation or a government or political subdivision thereof, with interest coupons or in registered form, share of stock, voting trust certificate, or any certificate of interest or participation in, certificate of deposit or receipt for, temporary or interim certificate for, or warrant or right to subscribe to or purchase, any of the foregoing; negotiable instrument; or money.

(5) Tax lien filing.—The term "tax lien filing" means the filing of notice (referred to in subsection (a)) of the lien imposed by section 6321.

(6) Purchaser.—The term "purchaser" means a person who, for adequate and full consideration in money or money's worth, acquires an interest (other than a lien or security interest) in property which is valid under local law against subsequent purchasers without actual notice. In applying the preceding sentence for purposes of subsection (a) of this section, and for purposes of section 6324—

    (A) a lease of property,

    (B) a written executory contract to purchase or lease property,

    (C) an option to purchase or lease property or any interest therein, or

    (D) an option to renew or extend a lease of property,

which is not a lien or security interest shall be treated as an interest in property.

(i) Special rules.—

(1) Actual notice or knowledge.—For purposes of this subchapter, an organization shall be deemed for purposes of a particular transaction to have actual notice or knowledge of any fact from the time such fact is brought to the attention of the individual conducting such transaction, and in any event from the time such fact would have been brought to such individual's attention if the organization had exercised due diligence. An organization exercises due diligence if it maintains reasonable routines for communicating significant information to the person conducting the transaction and there is reasonable compliance with the routine. Due diligence does not require an individual acting for the organization to communicate information unless such communication is part of his regular duties or unless he has reason to know of the transaction and that the transaction would be materially affected by the information.

(2) Subrogation.—Where, under local law, one person is subrogated to the rights of another with respect to a lien or interest, such person shall be subrogated to such rights for purposes of any lien imposed by section 6321 or 6324.

(3) Forfeitures.—For purposes of this subchapter, a forfeiture under local law of property seized by a law enforcement agency of a State, county, or other local governmental subdivision shall relate back to the time of seizure, except that this paragraph shall not apply to the extent that under local law the holder of an intervening claim or interest would have priority over the interest of the State, county, or other local governmental subdivision in the property.

(4) Cost-of-living adjustment.—In the case of notices of liens imposed by section 6321 which are filed in any calendar year after 1998, each of the dollar amounts under paragraph (4) or (7) of subsection (b) shall be increased by an amount equal to.—

    (A) such dollar amount, multiplied by

    (B) the cost-of-living adjustment determined under section 1(f)(3) for the calendar year, determined by substituting "calendar year 1996" for "calendar year 1992" in subparagraph (B) thereof.

    If any amount as adjusted under the preceding sentence is not a multiple of $10, such amount shall be rounded to the nearest multiple of $10.

(j) Withdrawal of notice in certain circumstances.—

(1) In general.—The Secretary may withdraw a notice of a lien filed under this section and this chapter shall be applied as if the withdrawn notice had not been filed, if the Secretary determines that—

    (A) the filing of such notice was premature or otherwise not in accordance with administrative procedures of the Secretary,

(B) the taxpayer has entered into an agreement under section 6159 to satisfy the tax liability for which the lien was imposed by means of installment payments, unless such agreement provides otherwise,

(C) the withdrawal of such notice will facilitate the collection of the tax liability, or

(D) with the consent of the taxpayer or the National Taxpayer Advocate, the withdrawal of such notice would be in the best interests of the taxpayer (as determined by the National Taxpayer Advocate) and the United States.

Any such withdrawal shall be made by filing notice at the same office as the withdrawn notice. A copy of such notice of withdrawal shall be provided to the taxpayer.

(2) Notice to credit agencies, etc.—Upon written request by the taxpayer with respect to whom a notice of a lien was withdrawn under paragraph (1), the Secretary shall promptly make reasonable efforts to notify credit reporting agencies, and any financial institution or creditor whose name and address is specified in such request, of the withdrawal of such notice. Any such request shall be in such form as the Secretary may prescribe.

(Aug. 16, 1954, c. 736, 68A Stat. 779; Feb. 26, 1964, Pub.L. 88–272, Title II, § 236(a), (c)(1), 78 Stat. 127, 128; July 5, 1966, Pub.L. 89–493, § 17(a), 80 Stat. 266; Nov. 2, 1966, Pub.L. 89–719, Title I, § 101(a), 80 Stat. 1125; Oct. 4, 1976, Pub.L. 94–455, Title XII, § 1202(h)(2), Title XIX, § 1906(b)(13)(A), Title XX, § 2008(c), 90 Stat. 1688, 1834, 1892; Nov. 6, 1978, Pub.L. 95–600, Title VII, § 702(q)(1), (2), 92 Stat. 2937, 2938; Oct. 22, 1986, Pub.L. 99–514, Title XV, § 1659(a), 100 Stat. 2764; Nov. 10, 1988, Pub. 100–647, Title I, § 1015(s)(1), 102 Stat. 3573; Nov. 5, 1990, Pub.L. 101–508, Title XI, §§ 11317(b), 11704(a)(26), 104 Stat. 1388–458, 1388–519; July 30, 1996, Pub.L. 104–168, Title V, § 501(a), 110 Stat. 1460; July 22, 1998, Pub.L. 105–206, Title I, §§ 1102(d)(1)(A), Title III, 3435(a), (b), 112 Stat. 704, 760, 761.)

UNITED NATIONS CONVENTION ON CONTRACTS FOR THE INTERNATIONAL SALE OF GOODS (CISG)*

THE STATES PARTIES TO THIS CONVENTION

BEARING IN MIND the broad objectives in the resolutions adopted by the sixth special session of the General Assembly of the United Nations on the establishment of a New International Economic Order,

CONSIDERING that the development of international trade on the basis of equality and mutual benefit is an important element in promoting friendly relations among States,

BEING OF THE OPINION that the adoption of uniform rules which govern contracts for the international sale of goods and take into account the different social, economic and legal systems would

---

* This Convention (CISG) was issued by the United Nations Commission on International Trade Law (UNCITRAL) on April 11, 1980. Pursuant to Article 99, it entered into force on January 1, 1988, on the "first day of the month following the expiration of twelve months after the date of deposit of the tenth instrument of ratification, acceptance, approval of accession . . ." For each subsequent state, the CISG entered into force on the "first day of the month following the expiration of twelve months after the date of the deposit of its instrument of ratification, acceptance, approval or accession."

As of April 1, 2016, the CISG has been adopted by 84 countries. For a current list of countries, see www.uncitral.org.

contribute to the removal of legal barriers in international trade and promote the development of international trade,

HAVE AGREED as follows:

PART I. SPHERE OF APPLICATION AND GENERAL PROVISIONS

CHAPTER I. SPHERE OF APPLICATION

Article 1

(1)   This Convention applies to contracts of sale of goods between parties whose places of business are in different States:

    (a)   when the States are Contracting States; or

    (b)   when the rules of private international law lead to the application of the law of a Contracting State.

(2)   The fact that the parties have their places of business in different States is to be disregarded whenever this fact does not appear either from the contract or from any dealings between, or from information disclosed by, the parties at any time before or at the conclusion of the contract.

(3)   Neither the nationality of the parties nor the civil or commercial character of the parties or of the contract is to be taken into consideration in determining the application of this Convention.

[The United States has declared a reservation under Article 95, and therefore is not bound by Article 1(1)(b).]

Article 2

This Convention does not apply to sales:

    (a)   of goods bought for personal, family or household use, unless the seller, at any time before or at the conclusion of the contract, neither knew nor ought to have known that the goods were bought for any such use;

    (b)   by auction;

    (c)   on execution or otherwise by authority of law;

    (d)   of stocks, shares, investment securities, negotiable instruments or money;

    (e)   of ships, vessels, hovercraft or aircraft;

    (f)   of electricity.

Article 3

(1)   Contracts for the supply of goods to be manufactured or produced are to be considered sales unless the party who orders the goods undertakes to supply a substantial part of the materials necessary for such manufacture or production.

(2)   This Convention does not apply to contracts in which the preponderant part of the obligations of the party who furnishes the goods consists in the supply of labour or other services.

Article 4

This Convention governs only the formation of the contract of sale and the rights and obligations of the seller and the buyer arising from such a contract. In particular, except as otherwise expressly provided in this Convention, it is not concerned with:

    (a)   the validity of the contract or of any of its provisions or of any usage;

    (b)   the effect which the contract may have on the property in the goods sold.

Article 5

This Convention does not apply to the liability of the seller for death or personal injury caused by the goods to any person.

Article 6

The parties may exclude the application of this Convention or, subject to Article 12, derogate from or vary the effect of any of its provisions.

CHAPTER II.   GENERAL PROVISIONS

Article 7

(1)   In the interpretation of this Convention, regard is to be had to its international character and to the need to promote uniformity in its application and the observance of good faith in international trade.

(2)   Questions concerning matters governed by this Convention which are not expressly settled in it are to be settled in conformity with the general principles on which it is based or, in the absence of such principles, in conformity with the law applicable by virtue of the rules of private international law.

Article 8

(1)   For the purposes of this Convention statements made by and other conduct of a party are to be interpreted according to his intent where the other party knew or could not have been unaware what that intent was.

(2)   If the preceding paragraph is not applicable, statements made by and other conduct of a party are to be interpreted according to the understanding that a reasonable person of the same kind as the other party would have had in the same circumstances.

(3)   In determining the intent of a party or the understanding a reasonable person would have had, due consideration is to be given to all relevant circumstances of the case including the negotiations, any practices which the parties have established between themselves, usages and any subsequent conduct of the parties.

Article 9

(1)   The parties are bound by any usage to which they have agreed and by any practices which they have established between themselves.

(2)   The parties are considered, unless otherwise agreed, to have impliedly made applicable to their contract or its formation a usage of which the parties knew or ought to have known and which in international trade is widely known to, and regularly observed by, parties to contracts of the type involved in the particular trade concerned.

Article 10

For the purposes of this Convention:

(a)   if a party has more than one place of business, the place of business is that which has the closest relationship to the contract and its performance, having regard to the circumstances known to or contemplated by the parties at any time before or at the conclusion of the contract;

(b)   if a party does not have a place of business, reference is to be made to his habitual residence.

Article 11

A contract of sale need not be concluded in or evidenced by writing and is not subject to any other requirement as to form. It may be proved by any means, including witnesses.

Article 12

Any provision of article 11, article 29 or Part II of this Convention that allows a contract of sale or its modification or termination by agreement or any offer, acceptance or other indication of intention to be made in any form other than in writing does not apply where any party has his place of business in a Contracting State which has made a declaration under article 96 of this Convention. The parties may not derogate from or vary the effect of this article.

Article 13

For the purposes of this Convention "writing" includes telegram and telex.

PART II.   FORMATION OF THE CONTRACT

Article 14

(1)   A proposal for concluding a contract addressed to one or more specific persons constitutes an offer if it is sufficiently definite and indicates the intention of the offeror to be bound in case of acceptance. A proposal is sufficiently definite if it indicates the goods and expressly or implicitly fixes or makes provision for determining the quantity and the price.

(2)   A proposal other than one addressed to one or more specific persons is to be considered merely as an invitation to make offers, unless the contrary is clearly indicated by the person making the proposal.

Article 15

(1)   An offer becomes effective when it reaches the offeree.

(2)   An offer, even if it is irrevocable, may be withdrawn if the withdrawal reaches the offeree before or at the same time as the offer.

Article 16

(1)   Until a contract is concluded an offer may be revoked if the revocation reaches the offeree before he has dispatched an acceptance.

(2)   However, an offer cannot be revoked:

(a)   if it indicates, whether by stating a fixed time for acceptance or otherwise, that it is irrevocable; or

(b)   if it was reasonable for the offeree to rely on the offer as being irrevocable and the offeree has acted in reliance on the offer.

Article 17

An offer, even if it is irrevocable, is terminated when a rejection reaches the offeror.

Article 18

(1)   A statement made by or other conduct of the offeree indicating assent to an offer is an acceptance. Silence or inactivity does not in itself amount to acceptance.

(2)   An acceptance of an offer becomes effective at the moment the indication of assent reaches the offeror. An acceptance is not effective if the indication of assent does not reach the offeror within the time he has fixed or, if no time is fixed, within a reasonable time, due account being taken of the circumstances of the transaction, including the rapidity of the means of communication employed by the offeror. An oral offer must be accepted immediately unless the circumstances indicate otherwise.

(3)   However, if, by virtue of the offer or as a result of practices which the parties have established between themselves or of usage, the offeree may indicate assent by performing an act, such as one relating to the dispatch of the goods or payment of the price, without notice to the offeror, the acceptance is effective

at the moment the act is performed, provided that the act is performed within the period of time laid down in the preceding paragraph.

Article 19

(1) A reply to an offer which purports to be an acceptance but contains additions, limitations or other modifications is a rejection of the offer and constitutes a counter-offer.

(2) However, a reply to an offer which purports to be an acceptance but contains additional or different terms which do not materially alter the terms of the offer constitutes an acceptance, unless the offeror, without undue delay, objects orally to the discrepancy or dispatches a notice to that effect. If he does not so object, the terms of the contract are the terms of the offer with the modifications contained in the acceptance.

(3) Additional or different terms relating, among other things, to the price, payment, quality and quantity of the goods, place and time of delivery, extent of one party's liability to the other or the settlement of disputes are considered to alter the terms of the offer materially.

Article 20

(1) A period of time for acceptance fixed by the offeror in a telegram or a letter begins to run from the moment the telegram is handed in for dispatch or from the date shown on the letter or, if no such date is shown, from the date shown on the envelope. A period of time for acceptance fixed by the offeror by telephone, telex or other means of instantaneous communication, begins to run from the moment that the offer reaches the offeree.

(2) Official holidays or non-business days occurring during the period for acceptance are included in calculating the period. However, if a notice of acceptance cannot be delivered at the address of the offeror on the last day of the period because that day falls on an official holiday or a non-business day at the place of business of the offeror, the period is extended until the first business day which follows.

Article 21

(1) A late acceptance is nevertheless effective as an acceptance if without delay the offeror orally so informs the offeree or dispatches a notice to that effect.

(2) If a letter or other writing containing a late acceptance shows that it has been sent in such circumstances that if its transmission had been normal it would have reached the offeror in due time, the late acceptance is effective as an acceptance unless, without delay, the offeror orally informs the offeree that he considers his offer as having lapsed or dispatches a notice to that effect.

Article 22

An acceptance may be withdrawn if the withdrawal reaches the offeror before or at the same time as the acceptance would have become effective.

Article 23

A contract is concluded at the moment when an acceptance of an offer becomes effective in accordance with the provisions of this Convention.

Article 24

For the purposes of this Part of the Convention, an offer, declaration of acceptance or any other indication of intention "reaches" the addressee when it is made orally to him or delivered by any other means to him personally, to his place of business or mailing address or, if he does not have a place of business or mailing address, to his habitual residence.

UNITED NATIONS CONVENTION

PART III.   SALE OF GOODS

CHAPTER I.   GENERAL PROVISIONS

Article 25

A breach of contract committed by one of the parties is fundamental if it results in such detriment to the other party as substantially to deprive him of what he is entitled to expect under the contract, unless the party in breach did not foresee and a reasonable person of the same kind in the same circumstances would not have foreseen such a result.

Article 26

A declaration of avoidance of the contract is effective only if made by notice to the other party.

Article 27

Unless otherwise expressly provided in this Part of the Convention, if any notice, request or other communication is given or made by a party in accordance with this Part and by means appropriate in the circumstances, a delay or error in the transmission of the communication or its failure to arrive does not deprive that party of the right to rely on the communication.

Article 28

If, in accordance with the provisions of this Convention, one party is entitled to require performance of any obligation by the other party, a court is not bound to enter a judgment for specific performance unless the court would do so under its own law in respect of similar contracts of sale not governed by this Convention.

Article 29

(1)   A contract may be modified or terminated by the mere agreement of the parties.

(2)   A contract in writing which contains a provision requiring any modification or termination by agreement to be in writing may not be otherwise modified or terminated by agreement. However, a party may be precluded by his conduct from asserting such a provision to the extent that the other party has relied on that conduct.

CHAPTER II.   OBLIGATIONS OF THE SELLER

Article 30

The seller must deliver the goods, hand over any documents relating to them and transfer the property in the goods, as required by the contract and this Convention.

SECTION I.

DELIVERY OF THE GOODS AND HANDING OVER OF DOCUMENTS

Article 31

If the seller is not bound to deliver the goods at any other particular place, his obligation to deliver consists:

(a)   if the contract of sale involves carriage of the goods—in handing the goods over to the first carrier for transmission to the buyer;

(b)   if, in cases not within the preceding subparagraph, the contract relates to specific goods, or unidentified goods to be drawn from a specific stock or to be manufactured or produced, and at the time of the conclusion of the contract the parties knew that the goods were at, or were to be manufactured or produced at, a particular place—in placing the goods at the buyer's disposal at that place;

(c)   in other cases—in placing the goods at the buyer's disposal at the place where the seller had his place of business at the time of the conclusion of the contract.

Article 32

(1)   If the seller, in accordance with the contract or this Convention, hands the goods over to a carrier and if the goods are not clearly identified to the contract by markings on the goods, by shipping documents or otherwise, the seller must give the buyer notice of the consignment specifying the goods.

(2)   If the seller is bound to arrange for carriage of the goods, he must make such contracts as are necessary for carriage to the place fixed by means of transportation appropriate in the circumstances and according to the usual terms for such transportation.

(3)   If the seller is not bound to effect insurance in respect of the carriage of the goods, he must, at the buyer's request, provide him with all available information necessary to enable him to effect such insurance.

Article 33

The seller must deliver the goods:

(a)   if a date is fixed by or determinable from the contract, on that date;

(b)   if a period of time is fixed by or determinable from the contract, at any time within that period unless circumstances indicate that the buyer is to choose a date; or

(c)   in any other case, within a reasonable time after the conclusion of the contract.

Article 34

If the seller is bound to hand over documents relating to the goods, he must hand them over at the time and place and in the form required by the contract. If the seller has handed over documents before that time, he may, up to that time, cure any lack of conformity in the documents, if the exercise of this right does not cause the buyer unreasonable inconvenience or unreasonable expense. However, the buyer retains any right to claim damages as provided for in this Convention.

Section II.

Conformity of the Goods and Third Party Claims

Article 35

(1)   The seller must deliver goods which are of the quantity, quality and description required by the contract and which are contained or packaged in the manner required by the contract.

(2)   Except where the parties have agreed otherwise, the goods do not conform with the contract unless they;

(a)   are fit for the purposes for which goods of the same description would ordinarily be used;

(b)   are fit for any particular purpose expressly or impliedly made known to the seller at the time of the conclusion of the contract, except where the circumstances show that the buyer did not rely, or that it was unreasonable for him to rely, on the seller's skill and judgement;

(c)   possess the qualities of goods which the seller has held out to the buyer as a sample or model;

(d)   are contained or packaged in the manner usual for such goods or, where there is no such manner, in a manner adequate to preserve and protect the goods.

(3)   The seller is not liable under subparagraphs (a) to (d) of the preceding paragraph for any lack of conformity of the goods if at the time of the conclusion of the contract the buyer knew or could not have been unaware of such lack of conformity.

Article 36

(1)   The seller is liable in accordance with the contract and this Convention for any lack of conformity which exists at the time when the risk passes to the buyer, even though the lack of conformity becomes apparent only after that time.

(2)   The seller is also liable for any lack of conformity which occurs after the time indicated in the preceding paragraph and which is due to a breach of any of his obligations, including a breach of any guarantee that for a period of time the goods will remain fit for their ordinary purpose or for some particular purpose or will retain specified qualities or characteristics.

Article 37

If the seller has delivered goods before the date for delivery, he may, up to that date, deliver any missing part or make up any deficiency in the quantity of the goods delivered, or deliver goods in replacement of any non-conforming goods delivered or remedy any lack of conformity in the goods delivered, provided that the exercise of this right does not cause the buyer unreasonable inconvenience or unreasonable expense. However, the buyer retains any right to claim damages as provided for in this Convention.

Article 38

(1)   The buyer must examine the goods, or cause them to be examined, within as short a period as is practicable in the circumstances.

(2)   If the contract involves carriage of the goods, examination may be deferred until after the goods have arrived at their destination.

(3)   If the goods are redirected in transit or redispatched by the buyer without a reasonable opportunity for examination by him and at the time of the conclusion of the contract the seller knew or ought to have known of the possibility of such redirection or redispatch, examination may be deferred until after the goods have arrived at the new destination.

Article 39

(1)   The buyer loses the right to rely on a lack of conformity of the goods if he does not give notice to the seller specifying the nature of the lack of conformity within a reasonable time after he has discovered it or ought to have discovered it.

(2)   In any event, the buyer loses the right to rely on a lack of conformity of the goods if he does not give the seller notice thereof at the latest within a period of two years from the date on which the goods were actually handed over to the buyer, unless this time-limit is inconsistent with a contractual period of guarantee.

Article 40

The seller is not entitled to rely on the provisions of articles 38 and 39 if the lack of conformity relates to facts of which he knew or could not have been unaware and which he did not disclose to the buyer.

Article 41

The seller must deliver goods which are free from any right or claim of a third party, unless the buyer agreed to take the goods subject to that right or claim. However, if such right or claim is based on industrial property or other intellectual property, the seller's obligation is governed by article 42.

Article 42

(1)   The seller must deliver goods which are free from any right or claim of a third party based on industrial property or other intellectual property, of which at the time of the conclusion of the contract the seller knew or could not have been unaware, provided that the right or claim is based on industrial property or other intellectual property:

(a)   under the law of the State where the goods will be resold or otherwise used, if it was contemplated by the parties at the time of the conclusion of the contract that the goods would be resold or otherwise used in that State; or

(b)   in any other case, under the law of the State where the buyer has his place of business.

(2)   The obligation of the seller under the preceding paragraph does not extend to cases where:

(a)   at the time of the conclusion of the contract the buyer knew or could not have been unaware of the right or claim; or

(b)   the right or claim results from the seller's compliance with technical drawings, designs, formulae or other such specifications furnished by the buyer.

Article 43

(1)   The buyer loses the right to rely on the provisions of article 41 or article 42 if he does not give notice to the seller specifying the nature of the right or claim of the third party within a reasonable time after he has become aware or ought to have become aware of the right or claim.

(2)   The seller is not entitled to rely on the provisions of the preceding paragraph if he knew of the right or claim of the third party and the nature of it.

Article 44

Notwithstanding the provisions of paragraph (1) of article 39 and paragraph (1) of article 43, the buyer may reduce the price in accordance with article 50 or claim damages, except for loss of profit, if he has a reasonable excuse for his failure to give the required notice.

SECTION III.

REMEDIES FOR BREACH OF CONTRACT BY THE SELLER

Article 45

(1)   If the seller fails to perform any of his obligations under the contract or this Convention, the buyer may:

(a)   exercise the rights provided in articles 46 to 52;

(b)   claim damages as provided in articles 74 to 77.

(2)   The buyer is not deprived of any right he may have to claim damages by exercising his right to other remedies.

(3)   No period of grace may be granted to the seller by a court or arbitral tribunal when the buyer resorts to a remedy for breach of contract.

Article 46

(1)   The buyer may require performance by the seller of his obligations unless the buyer has resorted to a remedy which is inconsistent with this requirement.

(2)   If the goods do not conform with the contract, the buyer may require delivery of substitute goods only if the lack of conformity constitutes a fundamental breach of contract and a request for substitute goods is made either in conjunction with notice given under article 39 or within a reasonable time thereafter.

(3)   If the goods do not conform with the contract, the buyer may require the seller to remedy the lack of conformity by repair, unless this is unreasonable having regard to all the circumstances. A request for repair must be made either in conjunction with notice given under article 39 or within a reasonable time thereafter.

Article 47

(1)   The buyer may fix an additional period of time of reasonable length for performance by the seller of his obligations.

(2)   Unless the buyer has received notice from the seller that he will not perform within the period so fixed, the buyer may not, during that period, resort to any remedy for breach of contract. However, the buyer is not deprived thereby of any right he may have to claim damages for delay in performance.

Article 48

(1)   Subject to article 49, the seller may, even after the date for delivery, remedy at his own expense any failure to perform his obligations, if he can do so without unreasonable delay and without causing the buyer unreasonable inconvenience or uncertainty of reimbursement by the seller of expenses advanced by the buyer. However, the buyer retains any right to claim damages as provided for in this Convention.

(2)   If the seller requests the buyer to make known whether he will accept performance and the buyer does not comply with the request within a reasonable time, the seller may perform within the time indicated in his request. The buyer may not, during that period of time, resort to any remedy which is inconsistent with performance by the seller.

(3)   A notice by the seller that he will perform within a specified period of time is assumed to include a request, under the preceding paragraph, that the buyer make known his decision.

(4)   A request or notice by the seller under paragraph (2) or (3) of this article is not effective unless received by the buyer.

Article 49

(1)   The buyer may declare the contract avoided:

(a)   if the failure by the seller to perform any of his obligations under the contract or this Convention amounts to a fundamental breach of contract; or

(b)   in case of non-delivery, if the seller does not deliver the goods within the additional period of time fixed by the buyer in accordance with paragraph (1) of article 47 or declares that he will not deliver within the period so fixed.

(2)   However, in cases where the seller has delivered the goods, the buyer loses the right to declare the contract avoided unless he does so:

(a)   in respect of late delivery, within a reasonable time after he has become aware that delivery has been made;

(b)   in respect of any breach other than late delivery, within a reasonable time:

(i)   after he knew or ought to have known of the breach;

(ii)   after the expiration of any additional period of time fixed by the buyer in accordance with paragraph (1) of article 47, or after the seller has declared that he will not perform his obligations within such an additional period; or

(iii)   after the expiration of any additional period of time indicated by the seller in accordance with paragraph (2) of article 48, or after the buyer has declared that he will not accept performance.

Article 50

If the goods do not conform with the contract and whether or not the price has already been paid, the buyer may reduce the price in the same proportion as the value that the goods actually delivered had at the time of the delivery bears to the value that conforming goods would have had at that time. However, if the seller remedies any failure to perform his obligations in accordance with article 37 or article 48 or if the buyer refuses to accept performance by the seller in accordance with those articles, the buyer may not reduce the price.

Article 51

(1)   If the seller delivers only a part of the goods or if only a part of the goods delivered is in conformity with the contract, articles 46 to 50 apply in respect of the part which is missing or which does not conform.

(2)   The buyer may declare the contract avoided in its entirety only if the failure to make delivery completely or in conformity with the contract amounts to a fundamental breach of the contract.

Article 52

(1)   If the seller delivers the goods before the date fixed, the buyer may take delivery or refuse to take delivery.

(2)   If the seller delivers a quantity of goods greater than that provided for in the contract, the buyer may take delivery or refuse to take delivery of the excess quantity. If the buyer takes delivery of all or part of the excess quantity, he must pay for it at the contract rate.

CHAPTER III.   OBLIGATIONS OF THE BUYER

Article 53

The buyer must pay the price for the goods and take delivery of them as required by the contract and this Convention.

SECTION I.

PAYMENT OF THE PRICE

Article 54

The buyer's obligation to pay the price includes taking such steps and complying with such formalities as may be required under the contract or any laws and regulations to enable payment to be made.

Article 55

Where a contract has been validly concluded but does not expressly or implicitly fix or make provision for determining the price, the parties are considered, in the absence of any indication to the contrary, to have impliedly made reference to the price generally charged at the time of the conclusion of the contract for such goods sold under comparable circumstances in the trade concerned.

Article 56

If the price if fixed according to the weight of the goods, in case of doubt it is to be determined by the net weight.

Article 57

(1)   If the buyer is not bound to pay the price at any other particular place, he must pay it to the seller:

   (a)   at the seller's place of business; or

   (b)   if the payment is to be made against the handing over of the goods or of documents, at the place where the handing over takes place.

(2)   The seller must bear any increase in the expenses incidental to payment which is caused by a change in his place of business subsequent to the conclusion of the contract.

Article 58

(1)   If the buyer is not bound to pay the price at any other specific time, he must pay it when the seller places either the goods or documents controlling their disposition at the buyer's disposal in accordance with the contract and this Convention. The seller may make such payment a condition for handing over the goods or documents.

(2)   If the contract involves carriage of the goods, the seller may dispatch the goods on terms whereby the goods, or documents controlling their disposition, will not be handed over to the buyer except against payment of the price.

(3)   The buyer is not bound to pay the price until he has had an opportunity to examine the goods, unless the procedures for delivery or payment agreed upon by the parties are inconsistent with his having such an opportunity.

Article 59

The buyer must pay the price on the date fixed by or determinable from the contract and this Convention without the need for any request or compliance with any formality on the part of the seller.

SECTION II.
TAKING DELIVERY

Article 60

The buyer's obligation to take delivery consists:

(a)   in doing all the acts which could reasonably be expected of him in order to enable the seller to make delivery; and

(b)   in taking over the goods.

SECTION III.
REMEDIES FOR BREACH OF CONTRACT BY THE BUYER

Article 61

(1)   If the buyer fails to perform any of his obligations under the contract or this Convention, the seller may:

(a)   exercise the rights provided in articles 62 to 65;

(b)   claim damages as provided in articles 74 to 77.

(2)   The seller is not deprived of any right he may have to claim damages by exercising his right to other remedies.

(3)   No period of grace may be granted to the buyer by a court or arbitral tribunal when the seller resorts to a remedy for breach of contract.

Article 62

The seller may require the buyer to pay the price, take delivery or perform his other obligations, unless the seller has resorted to a remedy which is inconsistent with this requirement.

Article 63

(1)   The seller may fix an additional period of time of reasonable length for performance by the buyer of his obligations.

(2)   Unless the seller has received notice from the buyer that he will not perform within the period so fixed, the seller may not, during that period, resort to any remedy for breach of contract. However, the seller is not deprived thereby of any right he may have to claim damages for delay in performance.

Article 64

(1)   The seller may declare the contract avoided:

(a)   if the failure by the buyer to perform any of his obligations under the contract or this Convention amounts to a fundamental breach of contract; or

(b)   if the buyer does not, within the additional period of time fixed by the seller in accordance with paragraph (1) of article 63, perform his obligation to pay the price or take delivery of the goods, or if he declares that he will not do so within the period so fixed.

(2)   However, in cases where the buyer has paid the price, the seller loses the right to declare the contract avoided unless he does so:

(a)   in respect of late performance by the buyer, before the seller has become aware that performance has been rendered; or

(b)   in respect of any breach other than late performance by the buyer, within a reasonable time:

(i)   after the seller knew or ought to have known of the breach; or

(ii)   after the expiration of any additional period of time fixed by the seller in accordance with paragraph (1) of article 63, or after the buyer has declared that he will not perform his obligations within such an additional period.

Article 65

(1)   If under the contract the buyer is to specify the form, measurement or other features of the goods and he fails to make such specification either on the date agreed upon or within a reasonable time after receipt of a request from the seller, the seller may, without prejudice to any other rights he may have, make the specification himself in accordance with the requirements of the buyer that may be known to him.

(2)   If the seller makes the specification himself, he must inform the buyer of the details thereof and must fix a reasonable time within which the buyer may make a different specification. If, after receipt of such a communication, the buyer fails to do so within the time so fixed, the specification made by the seller is binding.

CHAPTER IV.   PASSING OF RISK

Article 66

Loss of or damage to the goods after the risk has passed to the buyer does not discharge him from his obligation to pay the price, unless the loss or damage is due to an act or omission of the seller.

Article 67

(1)   If the contract of sale involves carriage of the goods and the seller is not bound to hand them over at a particular place, the risk passes to the buyer when the goods are handed over to the first carrier for transmission to the buyer in accordance with the contract of sale. If the seller is bound to hand the goods over to a carrier at a particular place, the risk does not pass to the buyer until the goods are handed over to the carrier at that place. The fact that the seller is authorized to retain documents controlling the disposition of the goods does not affect the passage of the risk.

(2)   Nevertheless, the risk does not pass to the buyer until the goods are clearly identified to the contract, whether by markings on the goods, by shipping documents, by notice given to the buyer or otherwise.

Article 68

The risk in respect of goods sold in transit passes to the buyer from the time of the conclusion of the contract. However, if the circumstances so indicate, the risk is assumed by the buyer from the time the goods were handed over to the carrier who issued the documents embodying the contract of carriage. Nevertheless, if at the time of the conclusion of the contract of sale the seller knew or ought to have known that the goods had been lost or damaged and did not disclose this to the buyer, the loss or damage is at the risk of the seller.

Article 69

(1)   In cases not within articles 67 and 68, the risk passes to the buyer when he takes over the goods or, if he does not do so in due time, from the time when the goods are placed at his disposal and he commits a breach of contract by failing to take delivery.

(2)   However, if the buyer is bound to take over the goods at a place other than a place of business of the seller, the risk passes when delivery is due and the buyer is aware of the fact that the goods are placed at his disposal at that place.

(3)   If the contract relates to goods not then identified, the goods are considered not to be placed at the disposal of the buyer until they are clearly identified to the contract.

Article 70

If the seller had committed a fundamental breach of contract, articles 67, 68 and 69 do not impair the remedies available to the buyer on account of the breach.

CHAPTER V.   PROVISIONS COMMON TO THE OBLIGATIONS
OF THE SELLER AND OF THE BUYER

SECTION I.

ANTICIPATORY BREACH AND INSTALMENT CONTRACTS

Article 71

(1)   A party may suspend the performance of his obligations if, after the conclusion of the contract, it becomes apparent that the other party will not perform a substantial part of his obligations as a result of:

(a)   a serious deficiency in his ability to perform or in his creditworthiness; or

(b)   his conduct in preparing to perform or in performing the contract.

(2)   If the seller has already dispatched the goods before the grounds described in the preceding paragraph become evident, he may prevent the handing over of the goods to the buyer even though the buyer holds a document which entitles him to obtain them. The present paragraph relates only to the rights in the goods as between the buyer and the seller.

(3)   A party suspending performance, whether before or after dispatch of the goods, must immediately give notice of the suspension to the other party and must continue with performance if the other party provides adequate assurance of his performance.

Article 72

(1)   If prior to the date for performance of the contract it is clear that one of the parties will commit a fundamental breach of contract, the other party may declare the contract avoided.

(2)   If time allows, the party intending to declare the contract avoided must give reasonable notice to the other party in order to permit him to provide adequate assurance of his performance.

(3)   The requirements of the preceding paragraph do not apply if the other party has declared that he will not perform his obligations.

Article 73

(1)   In the case of a contract for delivery of goods by instalments, if the failure of one party to perform any of his obligations in respect of any instalment constitutes a fundamental breach of contract with respect to that instalment, the other party may declare the contract avoided with respect to that instalment.

(2)   If one party's failure to perform any of his obligations in respect of any instalment gives the other party good grounds to conclude that a fundamental breach of contract will occur with respect to future instalments, he may declare the contract avoided for the future, provided that he does so within a reasonable time.

(3)   A buyer who declares the contract avoided in respect of any delivery may, at the same time, declare it avoided in respect of deliveries already made or of future deliveries if, by reason of their interdependence, those deliveries could not be used for the purpose contemplated by the parties at the time of the conclusion of the contract.

SECTION II.

DAMAGES

Article 74

Damages for breach of contract by one party consist of a sum equal to the loss, including loss of profit, suffered by the other party as a consequence of the breach. Such damages may not exceed the loss which the party in breach foresaw or ought to have foreseen at the time of the conclusion of the contract, in the light of the facts and matters of which he then knew or ought to have known, as a possible consequence of the breach of contract.

Article 75

If the contract is avoided and if, in a reasonable manner and within a reasonable time after avoidance, the buyer has bought goods in replacement or the seller has resold the goods, the party claiming damages may recover the difference between the contract price and the price in the substitute transaction as well as any further damages recoverable under article 74.

Article 76

(1)   If the contract is avoided and there is a current price for the goods, the party claiming damages may, if he has not made a purchase or resale under article 75, recover the difference between the price fixed by the contract and the current price at the time of avoidance as well as any further damages recoverable under article 74. If, however, the party claiming damages has avoided the contract after taking over the goods, the current price at the time of such taking over shall be applied instead of the current price at the time of avoidance.

(2)   For the purpose of the preceding paragraph, the current price is the price prevailing at the place where delivery of the goods should have been made or, if there is no current price at that place, the price at such other place as serves as a reasonable substitute, making due allowance for differences in the cost of transporting the goods.

Article 77

A party who relies on a breach of contract must take such measures as are reasonable in the circumstances to mitigate the loss, including loss of profit, resulting from the breach. If he fails to take such measures, the party in breach may claim a reduction in the damages in the amount by which the loss should have been mitigated.

SECTION III.

INTEREST

Article 78

If a party fails to pay the price or any other sum that is in arrears, the other party is entitled to interest on it, without prejudice to any claim for damages recoverable under article 74.

SECTION IV.

EXEMPTIONS

Article 79

(1)   A party is not liable for a failure to perform any of his obligations if he proves that the failure was due to an impediment beyond his control and that he could not reasonably be expected to have taken the impediment into account at the time of the conclusion of the contract or to have avoided or overcome it or its consequences.

(2)   If the party's failure is due to the failure by a third person whom he has engaged to perform the whole or a part of the contract, that party is exempt from liability only if:

(a)   he is exempt under the preceding paragraph; and

(b)   the person whom he has so engaged would be so exempt if the provisions of that paragraph were applied to him.

(3)   The exemption provided by this article has effect for the period during which the impediment exists.

(4)   The party who fails to perform must give notice to the other party of the impediment and its effects on his ability to perform. If the notice is not received by the other party within a reasonable time after the party who fails to perform knew or ought to have known of the impediment, he is liable for damages resulting from such non-receipt.

(5)   Nothing in this article prevents either party from exercising any right other than to claim damages under this Convention.

Article 80

A party may not rely on a failure of the other party to perform, to the extent that such failure was caused by the first party's act or omission.

SECTION V.

EFFECTS OF AVOIDANCE

Article 81

(1)   Avoidance of the contract releases both parties from their obligations under it, subject to any damages which may be due. Avoidance does not affect any provision of the contract for the settlement of disputes or any other provision of the contract governing the rights and obligations of the parties consequent upon the avoidance of the contract.

(2)   A party who has performed the contract either wholly or in part may claim restitution from the other party of whatever the first party has supplied or paid under the contract. If both parties are bound to make restitution, they must do so concurrently.

Article 82

(1)   The buyer loses the right to declare the contract avoided or to require the seller to deliver substitute goods if it is impossible for him to make restitution of the goods substantially in the condition in which he received them.

(2)   The preceding paragraph does not apply:

(a)   if the impossibility of making restitution of the goods or of making restitution of the goods substantially in the condition in which the buyer received them is not due to his act or omission;

(b)   if the goods or part of the goods have perished or deteriorated as a result of the examination provided for in article 38; or

(c)   if the goods or part of the goods have been sold in the normal course of business or have been consumed or transformed by the buyer in the course of normal use before he discovered or ought to have discovered the lack of conformity.

Article 83

A buyer who has lost the right to declare the contract avoided or to require the seller to deliver substitute goods in accordance with article 82 retains all other remedies under the contract and this Convention.

Article 84

(1)   If the seller is bound to refund the price, he must also pay interest on it, from the date on which the price was paid.

(2)   The buyer must account to the seller for all benefits which he has derived from the goods or part of them:

(a)   if he must make restitution of the goods or part of them; or

(b)   if it is impossible for him to make restitution of all or part of the goods or to make restitution of all or part of the goods substantially in the condition in which he received them, but he has nevertheless declared the contract avoided or required the seller to deliver substitute goods.

SECTION VI.

PRESERVATION OF THE GOODS

Article 85

If the buyer is in delay in taking delivery of the goods or, where payment of the price and delivery of the goods are to be made concurrently, if he fails to pay the price, and the seller is either in possession of the goods or otherwise able to control their disposition, the seller must take such steps as are reasonable in the circumstances to preserve them. He is entitled to retain them until he has been reimbursed his reasonable expenses by the buyer.

Article 86

(1)   If the buyer has received the goods and intends to exercise any right under the contract or this Convention to reject them, he must take such steps to preserve them as are reasonable in the circumstances. He is entitled to retain them until he has been reimbursed his reasonable expenses by the seller.

(2)   If goods dispatched to the buyer have been placed at his disposal at their destination and he exercises the right to reject them, he must take possession of them on behalf of the seller, provided that this can be done without payment of the price and without unreasonable inconvenience or unreasonable expense. This provision does not apply if the seller or a person authorized to take charge of the goods on his behalf is present at the destination. If the buyer takes possession of the goods under this paragraph, his rights and obligations are governed by the preceding paragraph.

Article 87

A party who is bound to take steps to preserve the goods may deposit them in a warehouse of a third person at the expense of the other party provided that the expense incurred is not unreasonable.

Article 88

(1)   A party who is bound to preserve the goods in accordance with article 85 or 86 may sell them by any appropriate means if there has been an unreasonable delay by the other party in taking possession of the goods or in taking them back or in paying the price or the cost of preservation, provided that reasonable notice of the intention to sell has been given to the other party.

(2)   If the goods are subject to rapid deterioration or their preservation would involve unreasonable expense, a party who is bound to preserve the goods in accordance with article 85 or 86 must take reasonable measures to sell them. To the extent possible he must give notice to the other party of his intention to sell.

(3)   A party selling the goods has the right to retain out of the proceeds of sale an amount equal to the reasonable expenses of preserving the goods and of selling them. He must account to the other party for the balance.

PART IV.   FINAL PROVISIONS

Article 89

The Secretary-General of the United Nations is hereby designated as the depositary for this Convention.

Article 90

This Convention does not prevail over any international agreement which has already been or may be entered into and which contains provisions concerning the matters governed by this Convention, provided that the parties have their places of business in States parties to such agreement.

Article 91

(1)   This Convention is open for signature at the concluding meeting of the United Nations Conference on Contracts for the International Sale of Goods and will remain open for signature by all States at the Headquarters of the United Nations, New York until 30 September 1981.

(2)   This Convention is subject to ratification, acceptance or approval by the signatory States.

(3)   This Convention is open for accession by all States which are not signatory States as from the date it is open for signature.

(4)   Instruments of ratification, acceptance, approval and accession are to be deposited with the Secretary-General of the United Nations.

Article 92

(1)   A Contracting State may declare at the time of signature, ratification, acceptance, approval or accession that it will not be bound by Part II of this Convention or that it will not be bound by Part III of this Convention.

(2)   A Contracting State which makes a declaration in accordance with the preceding paragraph in respect of Part II or Part III of this Convention is not to be considered a Contracting State within paragraph (1) of article 1 of this Convention in respect of matters governed by the Part to which the declaration applies.

Article 93

(1)   If a Contracting State has two or more territorial units in which, according to its constitution, different systems of law are applicable in relation to the matters dealt with in this Convention, it may, at

the time of signature, ratification, acceptance, approval or accession, declare that this Convention is to extend to all its territorial units or only to one or more of them, and may amend its declaration by submitting another declaration at any time.

(2)   These declarations are to be notified to the depositary and are to state expressly the territorial units to which the Convention extends.

(3)   If, by virtue of a declaration under this article, this Convention extends to one or more but not all of the territorial units of a Contracting State, and if the place of business of a party is located in that State, this place of business, for the purposes of this Convention, is considered not to be in a Contracting State, unless it is in a territorial unit to which the Convention extends.

(4)   If a Contracting State makes no declaration under paragraph (1) of this article, the Convention is to extend to all territorial units of that State.

Article 94

(1)   Two or more Contracting States which have the same or closely related legal rules on matters governed by this Convention may at any time declare that the Convention is not to apply to contracts of sale or to their formation where the parties have their places of business in those States. Such declarations may be made jointly or by reciprocal unilateral declarations.

(2)   A Contracting State which has the same or closely related legal rules on matters governed by this Convention as one or more non-Contracting States may at any time declare that the Convention is not to apply to contracts of sale or to their formation where the parties have their places of business in those States.

(3)   If a State which is the object of a declaration under the preceding paragraph subsequently becomes a Contracting State, the declaration made will, as from the date on which the Convention enters into force in respect of the new Contracting State, have the effect of a declaration made under paragraph (1), provided that the new Contracting State joins in such declaration or makes a reciprocal unilateral declaration.

Article 95

Any State may declare at the time of the deposit of its instrument of ratification, acceptance, approval or accession that it will not be bound by subparagraph (1)(b) of article 1 of this Convention.

[The United States has declared a reservation to CISG under Article 95].

Article 96

A Contracting State whose legislation requires contracts of sale to be concluded in or evidenced by writing may at any time make a declaration in accordance with article 12 that any provision of article 11, article 29, or Part II of this Convention, that allows a contract of sale or its modification or termination by agreement or any offer, acceptance, or other indication of intention to be made in any form other than in writing, does not apply where any party has his place of business in that State.

Article 97

(1)   Declarations made under this Convention at the time of signature are subject to confirmation upon ratification, acceptance or approval.

(2)   Declarations and confirmations of declarations are to be in writing and be formally notified to the depositary.

(3)   A declaration takes effect simultaneously with the entry into force of this Convention in respect of the State concerned. However, a declaration of which the depositary receives formal notification after such entry into force takes effect on the first day of the month following the expiration of six months after the date of its receipt by the depositary. Reciprocal unilateral declarations under article 94 take effect on the first day of the month following the expiration of six months after the receipt of the latest declaration by the depositary.

(4)   Any State which makes a declaration under this Convention may withdraw it at any time by a formal notification in writing addressed to the depositary. Such withdrawal is to take effect on the first day of the month following the expiration of six months after the date of the receipt of the notification by the depositary.

(5)   A withdrawal of a declaration made under article 94 renders inoperative, as from the date on which the withdrawal takes effect, any reciprocal declaration made by another State under that article.

Article 98

No reservations are permitted except those expressly authorized in this Convention.

Article 99

(1)   This Convention enters into force, subject to the provisions of paragraph (6) of this article, on the first day of the month following the expiration of twelve months after the date of deposit of the tenth instrument of ratification, acceptance, approval or accession, including an instrument which contains a declaration made under article 92.

(2)   When a State ratifies, accepts, approves or accedes to this Convention after the deposit of the tenth instrument of ratification, acceptance, approval or accession, this Convention, with the exception of the Part excluded, enters into force in respect of that State, subject to the provisions of paragraph (6) of this article, on the first day of the month following the expiration of twelve months after the date of the deposit of its instrument of ratification, acceptance, approval or accession.

(3)   A State which ratifies, accepts, approves or accedes to this Convention and is a party to either or both the Convention relating to a Uniform Law on the Formation of Contracts for the International Sale of Goods done at The Hague on 1 July 1964 (1964 Hague Formation Convention) and the Convention relating to a Uniform Law on the International Sale of Goods done at The Hague on 1 July 1964 (1964 Hague Sales Convention) shall at the same time denounce, as the case may be, either or both the 1964 Hague Sales Convention and the 1964 Hague Formation Convention by notifying the Government of the Netherlands to that effect.

(4)   A State party to the 1964 Hague Sales Convention which ratifies, accepts, approves or accedes to the present Convention and declares or has declared under article 92 that it will not be bound by Part II of this Convention shall at the time of ratification, acceptance, approval or accession denounce the 1964 Hague Sales Convention by notifying the Government of the Netherlands to that effect.

(5)   A State party to the 1964 Hague Formation Convention which ratifies, accepts, approves or accedes to the present Convention and declares or has declared under article 92 that it will not be bound by Part III of this Convention shall at the time of ratification, acceptance, approval or accession denounce the 1964 Hague Formation Convention by notifying the Government of the Netherlands to that effect.

(6)   For the purpose of this article, ratifications, acceptances, approvals and accessions in respect of this Convention by States parties to the 1964 Hague Formation Convention or to the 1964 Hague Sales Convention shall not be effective until such denunciations as may be required on the part of those States in respect of the latter two Conventions have themselves become effective. The depositary of this Convention shall consult with the Government of the Netherlands, as the depositary of the 1964 Convention, so as to ensure necessary co-ordination in this respect.

Article 100

(1)   This Convention applies to the formation of a contract only when the proposal for concluding the contract is made on or after the date when the Convention enters into force in respect of the Contracting States referred to in subparagraph (1)(a) or the Contracting State referred to in subparagraph (1)(b) of article 1.

(2)   This Convention applies only to contracts concluded on or after the date when the Convention enters into force in respect of the Contracting States referred to in subparagraph (1)(a) or the Contracting State referred to in subparagraph (1)(b) of article 1.

Article 101

(1)   A Contracting State may denounce this Convention, or Part II or Part III of the Convention, by a formal notification in writing addressed to the depositary.

(2)   The denunciation takes effect on the first day of the month following the expiration of twelve months after the notification is received by the depositary. Where a longer period for the denunciation to take effect is specified in the notification, the denunciation takes effect upon the expiration of such longer period after the notification is received by the depositary.

BANKRUPTCY CODE

---

11 U.S.C.A. §§ 101–1530
Current through March 30, 2016; P.L. 114–141
For updates, see http://uscode.house.gov

CHAPTER 1—GENERAL PROVISIONS

§ 101. Definitions

In this title the following definitions shall apply:

(1) The term "accountant" means accountant authorized under applicable law to practice public accounting, and includes professional accounting association, corporation, or partnership, if so authorized.

(2) The term "affiliate" means—

(A) entity that directly or indirectly owns, controls, or holds with power to vote, 20 percent or more of the outstanding voting securities of the debtor, other than an entity that holds such securities—

    (i) in a fiduciary or agency capacity without sole discretionary power to vote such securities; or

    (ii) solely to secure a debt, if such entity has not in fact exercised such power to vote;

  (B) corporation 20 percent or more of whose outstanding voting securities are directly or indirectly owned, controlled, or held with power to vote, by the debtor, or by an entity that directly or indirectly owns, controls, or holds with power to vote, 20 percent or more of the outstanding voting securities of the debtor, other than an entity that holds such securities—

    (i) in a fiduciary or agency capacity without sole discretionary power to vote such securities; or

    (ii) solely to secure a debt, if such entity has not in fact exercised such power to vote;

  (C) person whose business is operated under a lease or operating agreement by a debtor, or person substantially all of whose property is operated under an operating agreement with the debtor; or

  (D) entity that operates the business or substantially all of the property of the debtor under a lease or operating agreement.

  (3) The term "assisted person" means any person whose debts consist primarily of consumer debts and the value of whose nonexempt property is less than $192,450.[*]

  (4) The term "attorney" means attorney, professional law association, corporation, or partnership, authorized under applicable law to practice law.

  (4A) The term "bankruptcy assistance" means any goods or services sold or otherwise provided to an assisted person with the express or implied purpose of providing information, advice, counsel, document preparation, or filing, or attendance at a creditors' meeting or appearing in a case or proceeding on behalf of another or providing legal representation with respect to a case or proceeding under this title.

  (5) The term "claim" means—

  (A) right to payment, whether or not such right is reduced to judgment, liquidated, unliquidated, fixed, contingent, matured, unmatured, disputed, undisputed, legal, equitable, secured, or unsecured; or

  (B) right to an equitable remedy for breach of performance if such breach gives rise to a right to payment, whether or not such right to an equitable remedy is reduced to judgment, fixed, contingent, matured, unmatured, disputed, undisputed, secured, or unsecured.

  (6) The term "commodity broker" means futures commission merchant, foreign futures commission merchant, clearing organization, leverage transaction merchant, or commodity options dealer, as defined in section 761 of this title, with respect to which there is a customer, as defined in section 761 of this title.

  (7) The term "community claim" means claim that arose before the commencement of the case concerning the debtor for which property of the kind specified in section 541(a)(2) of this title is liable, whether or not there is any such property at the time of the commencement of the case.

  (7A) The term "commercial fishing operation" means—

  (A) the catching or harvesting of fish, shrimp, lobsters, urchins, seaweed, shellfish, or other aquatic species or products of such species; or

  (B) for purposes of section 109 and chapter 12, aquaculture activities consisting of raising for market any species or product described in subparagraph (A).

---

  [*] *Note from West Advisory Panel: Dollar amounts adjusted pursuant to 11 U.S.C. § 104; 81 Fed. Reg. 8748 (Feb. 22, 2016).*

(7B) The term "commercial fishing vessel" means a vessel used by a family fisherman to carry out a commercial fishing operation.

(8) The term "consumer debt" means debt incurred by an individual primarily for a personal, family, or household purpose.

(9) The term "corporation"—

    (A) includes—

        (i) association having a power or privilege that a private corporation, but not an individual or a partnership, possesses;

        (ii) partnership association organized under a law that makes only the capital subscribed responsible for the debts of such association;

        (iii) joint-stock company;

        (iv) unincorporated company or association; or

        (v) business trust; but

    (B) does not include limited partnership.

(10) The term "creditor" means—

    (A) entity that has a claim against the debtor that arose at the time of or before the order for relief concerning the debtor;

    (B) entity that has a claim against the estate of a kind specified in section 348(d), 502(f), 502(g), 502(h) or 502(i) of this title; or

    (C) entity that has a community claim.

(10A) The term "current monthly income"—

    (A) means the average monthly income from all sources that the debtor receives (or in a joint case the debtor and the debtor's spouse receive) without regard to whether such income is taxable income, derived during the 6-month period ending on—

        (i) the last day of the calendar month immediately preceding the date of the commencement of the case if the debtor files the schedule of current income required by section 521(a)(1)(B)(ii); or

        (ii) the date on which current income is determined by the court for purposes of this title if the debtor does not file the schedule of current income required by section 521(a)(1)(B)(ii); and

    (B) includes any amount paid by any entity other than the debtor (or in a joint case the debtor and the debtor's spouse), on a regular basis for the household expenses of the debtor or the debtor's dependents (and in a joint case the debtor's spouse if not otherwise a dependent), but excludes benefits received under the Social Security Act, payments to victims of war crimes or crimes against humanity on account of their status as victims of such crimes, and payments to victims of international terrorism (as defined in section 2331 of title 18) or domestic terrorism (as defined in section 2331 of title 18) on account of their status as victims of such terrorism.

(11) The term "custodian" means—

    (A) receiver or trustee of any of the property of the debtor, appointed in a case or proceeding not under this title;

    (B) assignee under a general assignment for the benefit of the debtor's creditors; or

    (C) trustee, receiver, or agent under applicable law, or under a contract, that is appointed or authorized to take charge of property of the debtor for the purpose of enforcing a lien against such property, or for the purpose of general administration of such property for the benefit of the debtor's creditors.

(12) The term "debt" means liability on a claim.

(12A) The term "debt relief agency" means any person who provides any bankruptcy assistance to an assisted person in return for the payment of money or other valuable consideration, or who is a bankruptcy petition preparer under section 110, but does not include—

(A) any person who is an officer, director, employee, or agent of a person who provides such assistance or of the bankruptcy petition preparer;

(B) a nonprofit organization that is exempt from taxation under section 501(c)(3) of the Internal Revenue Code of 1986;

(C) a creditor of such assisted person, to the extent that the creditor is assisting such assisted person to restructure any debt owed by such assisted person to the creditor;

(D) a depository institution (as defined in section 3 of the Federal Deposit Insurance Act) or any Federal credit union or State credit union (as those terms are defined in section 101 of the Federal Credit Union Act), or any affiliate or subsidiary of such depository institution or credit union; or

(E) an author, publisher, distributor, or seller of works subject to copyright protection under title 17, when acting in such capacity.

(13) The term "debtor" means person or municipality concerning which a case under this title has been commenced.

(13A) The term "debtor's principal residence"—

(A) means a residential structure if used as the principal residence by the debtor, including incidental property, without regard to whether that structure is attached to real property; and

(B) includes an individual condominium or cooperative unit, a mobile or manufactured home, or trailer if used as the principal residence by the debtor.

(14) The term "disinterested person" means a person that—

(A) is not a creditor, an equity security holder, or an insider;

(B) is not and was not, within 2 years before the date of the filing of the petition, a director, officer, or employee of the debtor; and

(C) does not have an interest materially adverse to the interest of the estate or of any class of creditors or equity security holders, by reason of any direct or indirect relationship to, connection with, or interest in, the debtor, or for any other reason.

(14A) The term "domestic support obligation" means a debt that accrues before, on, or after the date of the order for relief in a case under this title, including interest that accrues on that debt as provided under applicable nonbankruptcy law notwithstanding any other provision of this title, that is—

(A) owed to or recoverable by—

(i) a spouse, former spouse, or child of the debtor or such child's parent, legal guardian, or responsible relative; or

(ii) a governmental unit;

(B) in the nature of alimony, maintenance, or support (including assistance provided by a governmental unit) of such spouse, former spouse, or child of the debtor or such child's parent, without regard to whether such debt is expressly so designated;

(C) established or subject to establishment before, on, or after the date of the order for relief in a case under this title, by reason of applicable provisions of—

(i)   a separation agreement, divorce decree, or property settlement agreement;

(ii) an order of a court of record; or

(iii) a determination made in accordance with applicable nonbankruptcy law by a governmental unit; and

(D)   not assigned to a nongovernmental entity, unless that obligation is assigned voluntarily by the spouse, former spouse, child of the debtor, or such child's parent, legal guardian, or responsible relative for the purpose of collecting the debt.

(15) The term "entity" includes person, estate, trust, governmental unit, and United States trustee.

(16) The term "equity security" means—

(A)   share in a corporation, whether or not transferable or denominated "stock", or similar security;

(B)   interest of a limited partner in a limited partnership; or

(C)   warrant or right, other than a right to convert, to purchase, sell, or subscribe to a share, security, or interest of a kind specified in subparagraph (A) or (B) of this paragraph.

(17) The term "equity security holder" means holder of an equity security of the debtor.

(18) The term "family farmer" means—

(A)   individual or individual and spouse engaged in a farming operation whose aggregate debts do not exceed $4,153,150* and not less than 50 percent of whose aggregate noncontingent, liquidated debts (excluding a debt for the principal residence of such individual or such individual and spouse unless such debt arises out of a farming operation), on the date the case is filed, arise out of a farming operation owned or operated by such individual or such individual and spouse, and such individual or such individual and spouse receive from such farming operation more than 50 percent of such individual's or such individual and spouse's gross income for—

(i)   the taxable year preceding; or

(ii) each of the 2d and 3d taxable years preceding;

the taxable year in which the case concerning such individual or such individual and spouse was filed; or

(B)   corporation or partnership in which more than 50 percent of the outstanding stock or equity is held by one family, or by one family and the relatives of the members of such family, and such family or such relatives conduct the farming operation, and

(i)   more than 80 percent of the value of its assets consists of assets related to the farming operation;

(ii) its aggregate debts do not exceed $4,153,150* and not less than 50 percent of its aggregate noncontingent, liquidated debts (excluding a debt for one dwelling which is owned by such corporation or partnership and which a shareholder or partner maintains as a principal residence, unless such debt arises out of a farming operation), on the date the case is filed, arise out of the farming operation owned or operated by such corporation or such partnership; and

(iii) if such corporation issues stock, such stock is not publicly traded.

(19) The term "family farmer with regular annual income" means family farmer whose annual income is sufficiently stable and regular to enable such family farmer to make payments under a plan under chapter 12 of this title.

---

*   *Note from West Advisory Panel: Dollar amounts adjusted pursuant to 11 U.S.C. § 104; 81 Fed. Reg. 8748 (Feb. 22, 2016).*

(19A) The term "family fisherman" means—

(A) an individual or individual and spouse engaged in a commercial fishing operation—

(i) whose aggregate debts do not exceed $1,924,550* and not less than 80 percent of whose aggregate noncontingent, liquidated debts (excluding a debt for the principal residence of such individual or such individual and spouse, unless such debt arises out of a commercial fishing operation), on the date the case is filed, arise out of a commercial fishing operation owned or operated by such individual or such individual and spouse; and

(ii) who receive from such commercial fishing operation more than 50 percent of such individual's or such individual's and spouse's gross income for the taxable year preceding the taxable year in which the case concerning such individual or such individual and spouse was filed; or

(B) a corporation or partnership—

(i) in which more than 50 percent of the outstanding stock or equity is held by—

(I) 1 family that conducts the commercial fishing operation; or

(II) 1 family and the relatives of the members of such family, and such family or such relatives conduct the commercial fishing operation; and

(ii)(I) more than 80 percent of the value of its assets consists of assets related to the commercial fishing operation;

(II) its aggregate debts do not exceed $1,924,550* and not less than 80 percent of its aggregate noncontingent, liquidated debts (excluding a debt for 1 dwelling which is owned by such corporation or partnership and which a shareholder or partner maintains as a principal residence, unless such debt arises out of a commercial fishing operation), on the date the case is filed, arise out of a commercial fishing operation owned or operated by such corporation or such partnership; and

(III) if such corporation issues stock, such stock is not publicly traded.

(19B) The term "family fisherman with regular annual income" means a family fisherman whose annual income is sufficiently stable and regular to enable such family fisherman to make payments under a plan under chapter 12 of this title.

(20) The term "farmer" means (except when such term appears in the term "family farmer") person that received more than 80 percent of such person's gross income during the taxable year of such person immediately preceding the taxable year of such person during which the case under this title concerning such person was commenced from a farming operation owned or operated by such person.

(21) The term "farming operation" includes farming, tillage of the soil, dairy farming, ranching, production or raising of crops, poultry, or livestock, and production of poultry or livestock products in an unmanufactured state.

(21A) The term "farmout agreement" means a written agreement in which—

(A) the owner of a right to drill, produce, or operate liquid or gaseous hydrocarbons on property agrees or has agreed to transfer or assign all or a part of such right to another entity; and

(B) such other entity (either directly or through its agents or its assigns), as consideration, agrees to perform drilling, reworking, recompleting, testing, or similar or related operations, to develop or produce liquid or gaseous hydrocarbons on the property.

(21B) The term "Federal depository institutions regulatory agency" means—

---

* *Note from West Advisory Panel: Dollar amounts adjusted pursuant to 11 U.S.C. § 104; 81 Fed. Reg. 8748 (Feb. 22, 2016).*

(A) with respect to an insured depository institution (as defined in section 3(c)(2) of the Federal Deposit Insurance Act) for which no conservator or receiver has been appointed, the appropriate Federal banking agency (as defined in section 3(q) of such Act);

(B) with respect to an insured credit union (including an insured credit union for which the National Credit Union Administration has been appointed conservator or liquidating agent), the National Credit Union Administration;

(C) with respect to any insured depository institution for which the Resolution Trust Corporation has been appointed conservator or receiver, the Resolution Trust Corporation; and

(D) with respect to any insured depository institution for which the Federal Deposit Insurance Corporation has been appointed conservator or receiver, the Federal Deposit Insurance Corporation.

(22) The term "financial institution" means—

(A) a Federal reserve bank, or an entity that is a commercial or savings bank, industrial savings bank, savings and loan association, trust company, federally-insured credit union, or receiver, liquidating agent, or conservator for such entity and, when any such Federal reserve bank, receiver, liquidating agent, conservator or entity is acting as agent or custodian for a customer (whether or not a "customer", as defined in section 741) in connection with a securities contract (as defined in section 741) such customer; or

(B) in connection with a securities contract (as defined in section 741) an investment company registered under the Investment Company Act of 1940.

(22A) The term "financial participant" means—

(A) an entity that, at the time it enters into a securities contract, commodity contract, swap agreement, repurchase agreement, or forward contract, or at the time of the date of the filing of the petition, has one or more agreements or transactions described in paragraph (1), (2), (3), (4), (5), or (6) of section 561(a) with the debtor or any other entity (other than an affiliate) of a total gross dollar value of not less than $1,000,000,000 in notional or actual principal amount outstanding (aggregated across counterparties) at such time or on any day during the 15-month period preceding the date of the filing of the petition, or has gross mark-to-market positions of not less than $100,000,000 (aggregated across counterparties) in one or more such agreements or transactions with the debtor or any other entity (other than an affiliate) at such time or on any day during the 15-month period preceding the date of the filing of the petition; or

(B) a clearing organization (as defined in section 402 of the Federal Deposit Insurance Corporation Improvement Act of 1991).

(23) The term "foreign proceeding" means a collective judicial or administrative proceeding in a foreign country, including an interim proceeding, under a law relating to insolvency or adjustment of debt in which proceeding the assets and affairs of the debtor are subject to control or supervision by a foreign court, for the purpose of reorganization or liquidation.

(24) The term "foreign representative" means a person or body, including a person or body appointed on an interim basis, authorized in a foreign proceeding to administer the reorganization or the liquidation of the debtor's assets or affairs or to act as a representative of such foreign proceeding.

(25) The term "forward contract" means—

(A) a contract (other than a commodity contract, as defined in section 761) for the purchase, sale, or transfer of a commodity, as defined in section 761(8) of this title, or any similar good, article, service, right, or interest which is presently or in the future becomes the subject of dealing in the forward contract trade, or product or byproduct thereof, with a maturity date more than two days after the date the contract is entered into, including, but not limited to, a repurchase or reverse repurchase transaction (whether or not such repurchase or reverse repurchase transaction is a "repurchase agreement", as defined in this section)[1] consignment, lease, swap, hedge transaction, deposit, loan, option, allocated transaction, unallocated transaction, or any other similar agreement;

    (B) any combination of agreements or transactions referred to in subparagraphs (A) and (C);

    (C) any option to enter into an agreement or transaction referred to in subparagraph (A) or (B);

    (D) a master agreement that provides for an agreement or transaction referred to in subparagraph (A), (B), or (C), together with all supplements to any such master agreement, without regard to whether such master agreement provides for an agreement or transaction that is not a forward contract under this paragraph, except that such master agreement shall be considered to be a forward contract under this paragraph only with respect to each agreement or transaction under such master agreement that is referred to in subparagraph (A), (B), or (C); or

    (E) any security agreement or arrangement, or other credit enhancement related to any agreement or transaction referred to in subparagraph (A), (B), (C), or (D), including any guarantee or reimbursement obligation by or to a forward contract merchant or financial participant in connection with any agreement or transaction referred to in any such subparagraph, but not to exceed the damages in connection with any such agreement or transaction, measured in accordance with section 562.

(26) The term "forward contract merchant" means a Federal reserve bank, or an entity the business of which consists in whole or in part of entering into forward contracts as or with merchants in a commodity (as defined in section 761) or any similar good, article, service, right, or interest which is presently or in the future becomes the subject of dealing in the forward contract trade.

(27) The term "governmental unit" means United States; State; Commonwealth; District; Territory; municipality; foreign state; department, agency, or instrumentality of the United States (but not a United States trustee while serving as a trustee in a case under this title), a State, a Commonwealth, a District, a Territory, a municipality, or a foreign state; or other foreign or domestic government.

(27A) The term "health care business"—

    (A) means any public or private entity (without regard to whether that entity is organized for profit or not for profit) that is primarily engaged in offering to the general public facilities and services for—

        (i) the diagnosis or treatment of injury, deformity, or disease; and

        (ii) surgical, drug treatment, psychiatric, or obstetric care; and

    (B) includes—

        (i) any—

            (I) general or specialized hospital;

            (II) ancillary ambulatory, emergency, or surgical treatment facility;

            (III) hospice;

            (IV) home health agency; and

            (V) other health care institution that is similar to an entity referred to in subclause (I), (II), (III), or (IV); and

        (ii) any long-term care facility, including any—

---

[1]   So in original. Probably should be followed by a comma.

    (I) skilled nursing facility;

    (II) intermediate care facility;

    (III) assisted living facility;

    (IV) home for the aged;

    (V) domiciliary care facility; and

    (VI) health care institution that is related to a facility referred to in subclause (I), (II), (III), (IV), or (V), if that institution is primarily engaged in offering room, board, laundry, or personal assistance with activities of daily living and incidentals to activities of daily living.

(27B) The term "incidental property" means, with respect to a debtor's principal residence—

    (A) property commonly conveyed with a principal residence in the area where the real property is located;

    (B) all easements, rights, appurtenances, fixtures, rents, royalties, mineral rights, oil or gas rights or profits, water rights, escrow funds, or insurance proceeds; and

    (C) all replacements or additions.

(28) The term "indenture" means mortgage, deed of trust, or indenture, under which there is outstanding a security, other than a voting-trust certificate, constituting a claim against the debtor, a claim secured by a lien on any of the debtor's property, or an equity security of the debtor.

(29) The term "indenture trustee" means trustee under an indenture.

(30) The term "individual with regular income" means individual whose income is sufficiently stable and regular to enable such individual to make payments under a plan under chapter 13 of this title, other than a stockbroker or a commodity broker.

(31) The term "insider" includes—

    (A) if the debtor is an individual—

        (i) relative of the debtor or of a general partner of the debtor;

        (ii) partnership in which the debtor is a general partner;

        (iii) general partner of the debtor; or

        (iv) corporation of which the debtor is a director, officer, or person in control;

    (B) if the debtor is a corporation—

        (i) director of the debtor;

        (ii) officer of the debtor;

        (iii) person in control of the debtor;

        (iv) partnership in which the debtor is a general partner;

        (v) general partner of the debtor; or

        (vi) relative of a general partner, director, officer, or person in control of the debtor;

    (C) if the debtor is a partnership—

        (i) general partner in the debtor;

        (ii) relative of a general partner in, general partner of, or person in control of the debtor;

        (iii) partnership in which the debtor is a general partner;

        (iv) general partner of the debtor; or

    (v)   person in control of the debtor;

    (D) if the debtor is a municipality, elected official of the debtor or relative of an elected official of the debtor;

    (E) affiliate, or insider of an affiliate as if such affiliate were the debtor; and

    (F) managing agent of the debtor.

(32) The term "insolvent" means—

    (A) with reference to an entity other than a partnership and a municipality, financial condition such that the sum of such entity's debts is greater than all of such entity's property, at a fair valuation, exclusive of—

        (i) property transferred, concealed, or removed with intent to hinder, delay, or defraud such entity's creditors; and

        (ii) property that may be exempted from property of the estate under section 522 of this title;

    (B) with reference to a partnership, financial condition such that the sum of such partnership's debts is greater than the aggregate of, at a fair valuation—

        (i) all of such partnership's property, exclusive of property of the kind specified in subparagraph (A)(i) of this paragraph; and

        (ii) the sum of the excess of the value of each general partner's nonpartnership property, exclusive of property of the kind specified in subparagraph (A) of this paragraph, over such partner's nonpartnership debts; and

    (C) with reference to a municipality, financial condition such that the municipality is—

        (i) generally not paying its debts as they become due unless such debts are the subject of a bona fide dispute; or

        (ii) unable to pay its debts as they become due.

(33) The term "institution-affiliated party"—

    (A) with respect to an insured depository institution (as defined in section 3(c)(2) of the Federal Deposit Insurance Act), has the meaning given it in section 3(u) of the Federal Deposit Insurance Act; and

    (B) with respect to an insured credit union, has the meaning given it in section 206(r) of the Federal Credit Union Act.

(34) The term "insured credit union" has the meaning given it in section 101(7) of the Federal Credit Union Act.

(35) The term "insured depository institution"—

    (A) has the meaning given it in section 3(c)(2) of the Federal Deposit Insurance Act; and

    (B) includes an insured credit union (except in the case of paragraphs (21B) and (33)(A) of this subsection).

(35A) The term "intellectual property" means—

    (A) trade secret;

    (B) invention, process, design, or plant protected under title 35;

    (C) patent application;

    (D) plant variety;

    (E) work of authorship protected under title 17; or

(F) mask work protected under chapter 9 of title 17;

to the extent protected by applicable nonbankruptcy law.

(36) The term "judicial lien" means lien obtained by judgment, levy, sequestration, or other legal or equitable process or proceeding.

(37) The term "lien" means charge against or interest in property to secure payment of a debt or performance of an obligation.

(38) The term "margin payment" means, for purposes of the forward contract provisions of this title, payment or deposit of cash, a security or other property, that is commonly known in the forward contract trade as original margin, initial margin, maintenance margin, or variation margin, including mark-to-market payments, or variation payments.

(38A) The term "master netting agreement"—

(A) means an agreement providing for the exercise of rights, including rights of netting, setoff, liquidation, termination, acceleration, or close out, under or in connection with one or more contracts that are described in any one or more of paragraphs (1) through (5) of section 561(a), or any security agreement or arrangement or other credit enhancement related to one or more of the foregoing, including any guarantee or reimbursement obligation related to 1 or more of the foregoing; and

(B) if the agreement contains provisions relating to agreements or transactions that are not contracts described in paragraphs (1) through (5) of section 561(a), shall be deemed to be a master netting agreement only with respect to those agreements or transactions that are described in any one or more of paragraphs (1) through (5) of section 561(a).

(38B) The term "master netting agreement participant" means an entity that, at any time before the date of the filing of the petition, is a party to an outstanding master netting agreement with the debtor.

(39) The term "mask work" has the meaning given it in section 901(a)(2) of title 17.

(39A) The term "median family income" means for any year—

(A) the median family income both calculated and reported by the Bureau of the Census in the then most recent year; and

(B) if not so calculated and reported in the then current year, adjusted annually after such most recent year until the next year in which median family income is both calculated and reported by the Bureau of the Census, to reflect the percentage change in the Consumer Price Index for All Urban Consumers during the period of years occurring after such most recent year and before such current year.

(40) The term "municipality" means political subdivision or public agency or instrumentality of a State.

(40A) The term "patient" means any individual who obtains or receives services from a health care business.

(40B) The term "patient records" means any record relating to a patient, including a written document or a record recorded in a magnetic, optical, or other form of electronic medium.

(41) The term "person" includes individual, partnership, and corporation, but does not include governmental unit, except that a governmental unit that—

(A) acquires an asset from a person—

(i) as a result of the operation of a loan guarantee agreement; or

(ii) as receiver or liquidating agent of a person;

(B) is a guarantor of a pension benefit payable by or on behalf of the debtor or an affiliate of the debtor; or

(C) is the legal or beneficial owner of an asset of—

(i) an employee pension benefit plan that is a governmental plan, as defined in section 414(d) of the Internal Revenue Code of 1986; or

(ii) an eligible deferred compensation plan, as defined in section 457(b) of the Internal Revenue Code of 1986;

shall be considered, for purposes of section 1102 of this title, to be a person with respect to such asset or such benefit.

(41A) The term "personally identifiable information" means—

(A) if provided by an individual to the debtor in connection with obtaining a product or a service from the debtor primarily for personal, family, or household purposes—

(i) the first name (or initial) and last name of such individual, whether given at birth or time of adoption, or resulting from a lawful change of name;

(ii) the geographical address of a physical place of residence of such individual;

(iii) an electronic address (including an e-mail address) of such individual;

(iv) a telephone number dedicated to contacting such individual at such physical place of residence;

(v) a social security account number issued to such individual; or

(vi) the account number of a credit card issued to such individual; or

(B) if identified in connection with 1 or more of the items of information specified in subparagraph (A)—

(i) a birth date, the number of a certificate of birth or adoption, or a place of birth; or

(ii) any other information concerning an identified individual that, if disclosed, will result in contacting or identifying such individual physically or electronically.

(42) The term "petition" means petition filed under section 301, 302, 303, and[2] 1504 of this title, as the case may be, commencing a case under this title.

(42A) The term "production payment" means a term overriding royalty satisfiable in cash or in kind—

(A) contingent on the production of a liquid or gaseous hydrocarbon from particular real property; and

(B) from a specified volume, or a specified value, from the liquid or gaseous hydrocarbon produced from such property, and determined without regard to production costs.

(43) The term "purchaser" means transferee of a voluntary transfer, and includes immediate or mediate transferee of such a transferee.

(44) The term "railroad" means common carrier by railroad engaged in the transportation of individuals or property or owner of trackage facilities leased by such a common carrier.

(45) The term "relative" means individual related by affinity or consanguinity within the third degree as determined by the common law, or individual in a step or adoptive relationship within such third degree.

(46) The term "repo participant" means an entity that, at any time before the filing of the petition, has an outstanding repurchase agreement with the debtor.

---

[2]   So in original. Probably should be "or".

(47) The term "repurchase agreement" (which definition also applies to a reverse repurchase agreement)—

    (A) means—

        (i) an agreement, including related terms, which provides for the transfer of one or more certificates of deposit, mortgage related securities (as defined in section 3 of the Securities Exchange Act of 1934), mortgage loans, interests in mortgage related securities or mortgage loans, eligible bankers' acceptances, qualified foreign government securities (defined as a security that is a direct obligation of, or that is fully guaranteed by, the central government of a member of the Organization for Economic Cooperation and Development), or securities that are direct obligations of, or that are fully guaranteed by, the United States or any agency of the United States against the transfer of funds by the transferee of such certificates of deposit, eligible bankers' acceptances, securities, mortgage loans, or interests, with a simultaneous agreement by such transferee to transfer to the transferor thereof certificates of deposit, eligible bankers' acceptance, securities, mortgage loans, or interests of the kind described in this clause, at a date certain not later than 1 year after such transfer or on demand, against the transfer of funds;

        (ii) any combination of agreements or transactions referred to in clauses (i) and (iii);

        (iii) an option to enter into an agreement or transaction referred to in clause (i) or (ii);

        (iv) a master agreement that provides for an agreement or transaction referred to in clause (i), (ii), or (iii), together with all supplements to any such master agreement, without regard to whether such master agreement provides for an agreement or transaction that is not a repurchase agreement under this paragraph, except that such master agreement shall be considered to be a repurchase agreement under this paragraph only with respect to each agreement or transaction under the master agreement that is referred to in clause (i), (ii), or (iii); or

        (v) any security agreement or arrangement or other credit enhancement related to any agreement or transaction referred to in clause (i), (ii), (iii), or (iv), including any guarantee or reimbursement obligation by or to a repo participant or financial participant in connection with any agreement or transaction referred to in any such clause, but not to exceed the damages in connection with any such agreement or transaction, measured in accordance with section 562 of this title; and

    (B) does not include a repurchase obligation under a participation in a commercial mortgage loan.

(48) The term "securities clearing agency" means person that is registered as a clearing agency under section 17A of the Securities Exchange Act of 1934, or exempt from such registration under such section pursuant to an order of the Securities and Exchange Commission, or whose business is confined to the performance of functions of a clearing agency with respect to exempted securities, as defined in section 3(a)(12) of such Act for the purposes of such section 17A.

(48A) The term "securities self regulatory organization" means either a securities association registered with the Securities and Exchange Commission under section 15A of the Securities Exchange Act of 1934 or a national securities exchange registered with the Securities and Exchange Commission under section 6 of the Securities Exchange Act of 1934.

(49) The term "security"—

    (A) includes—

        (i) note;

        (ii) stock;

        (iii) treasury stock;

        (iv) bond;

    (v)   debenture;

    (vi)   collateral trust certificate;

    (vii) pre-organization certificate or subscription;

    (viii) transferable share;

    (ix)   voting-trust certificate;

    (x)   certificate of deposit;

    (xi)   certificate of deposit for security;

    (xii) investment contract or certificate of interest or participation in a profit-sharing agreement or in an oil, gas, or mineral royalty or lease, if such contract or interest is required to be the subject of a registration statement filed with the Securities and Exchange Commission under the provisions of the Securities Act of 1933, or is exempt under section 3(b) of such Act from the requirement to file such a statement;

    (xiii) interest of a limited partner in a limited partnership;

    (xiv) other claim or interest commonly known as "security"; and

    (xv) certificate of interest or participation in, temporary or interim certificate for, receipt for, or warrant or right to subscribe to or purchase or sell, a security; but

(B)   does not include—

    (i)   currency, check, draft, bill of exchange, or bank letter of credit;

    (ii)   leverage transaction, as defined in section 761 of this title;

    (iii) commodity futures contract or forward contract;

    (iv) option, warrant, or right to subscribe to or purchase or sell a commodity futures contract;

    (v)   option to purchase or sell a commodity;

    (vi) contract or certificate of a kind specified in subparagraph (A)(xii) of this paragraph that is not required to be the subject of a registration statement filed with the Securities and Exchange Commission and is not exempt under section 3(b) of the Securities Act of 1933 from the requirement to file such a statement; or

    (vii) debt or evidence of indebtedness for goods sold and delivered or services rendered.

    (50) The term "security agreement" means agreement that creates or provides for a security interest.

    (51) The term "security interest" means lien created by an agreement.

    (51A) The term "settlement payment" means, for purposes of the forward contract provisions of this title, a preliminary settlement payment, a partial settlement payment, an interim settlement payment, a settlement payment on account, a final settlement payment, a net settlement payment, or any other similar payment commonly used in the forward contract trade.

    (51B) The term "single asset real estate" means real property constituting a single property or project, other than residential real property with fewer than 4 residential units, which generates substantially all of the gross income of a debtor who is not a family farmer and on which no substantial business is being conducted by a debtor other than the business of operating the real property and activities incidental thereto.

    (51C) The term "small business case" means a case filed under chapter 11 of this title in which the debtor is a small business debtor.

    (51D) The term "small business debtor"—

(A) subject to subparagraph (B), means a person engaged in commercial or business activities (including any affiliate of such person that is also a debtor under this title and excluding a person whose primary activity is the business of owning or operating real property or activities incidental thereto) that has aggregate noncontingent liquidated secured and unsecured debts as of the date of the filing of the petition or the date of the order for relief in an amount not more than $2,566,050* (excluding debts owed to 1 or more affiliates or insiders) for a case in which the United States trustee has not appointed under section 1102(a)(1) a committee of unsecured creditors or where the court has determined that the committee of unsecured creditors is not sufficiently active and representative to provide effective oversight of the debtor; and

(B) does not include any member of a group of affiliated debtors that has aggregate noncontingent liquidated secured and unsecured debts in an amount greater than $2,566,050* (excluding debt owed to 1 or more affiliates or insiders).

(52) The term "State" includes the District of Columbia and Puerto Rico, except for the purpose of defining who may be a debtor under chapter 9 of this title.

(53) The term "statutory lien" means lien arising solely by force of a statute on specified circumstances or conditions, or lien of distress for rent, whether or not statutory, but does not include security interest or judicial lien, whether or not such interest or lien is provided by or is dependent on a statute and whether or not such interest or lien is made fully effective by statute.

(53A) The term "stockbroker" means person—

(A) with respect to which there is a customer, as defined in section 741 of this title; and

(B) that is engaged in the business of effecting transactions in securities—

(i) for the account of others; or

(ii) with members of the general public, from or for such person's own account.

(53B) The term "swap agreement"—

(A) means—

(i) any agreement, including the terms and conditions incorporated by reference in such agreement, which is—

(I) an interest rate swap, option, future, or forward agreement, including a rate floor, rate cap, rate collar, cross-currency rate swap, and basis swap;

(II) a spot, same day-tomorrow, tomorrow-next, forward, or other foreign exchange, precious metals, or other commodity agreement;

(III) a currency swap, option, future, or forward agreement;

(IV) an equity index or equity swap, option, future, or forward agreement;

(V) a debt index or debt swap, option, future, or forward agreement;

(VI) a total return, credit spread or credit swap, option, future, or forward agreement;

(VII) a commodity index or a commodity swap, option, future, or forward agreement;

(VIII) a weather swap, option, future, or forward agreement;

(IX) an emissions swap, option, future, or forward agreement; or

(X) an inflation swap, option, future, or forward agreement;

---

* *Note from West Advisory Panel: Dollar amounts adjusted pursuant to 11 U.S.C. § 104; 81 Fed. Reg. 8748 (Feb. 22, 2016).*

      (ii) any agreement or transaction that is similar to any other agreement or transaction referred to in this paragraph and that—

          (I) is of a type that has been, is presently, or in the future becomes, the subject of recurrent dealings in the swap or other derivatives markets (including terms and conditions incorporated by reference therein); and

          (II) is a forward, swap, future, option, or spot transaction on one or more rates, currencies, commodities, equity securities, or other equity instruments, debt securities or other debt instruments, quantitative measures associated with an occurrence, extent of an occurrence, or contingency associated with a financial, commercial, or economic consequence, or economic or financial indices or measures of economic or financial risk or value;

      (iii) any combination of agreements or transactions referred to in this subparagraph;

      (iv) any option to enter into an agreement or transaction referred to in this subparagraph;

      (v) a master agreement that provides for an agreement or transaction referred to in clause (i), (ii), (iii), or (iv), together with all supplements to any such master agreement, and without regard to whether the master agreement contains an agreement or transaction that is not a swap agreement under this paragraph, except that the master agreement shall be considered to be a swap agreement under this paragraph only with respect to each agreement or transaction under the master agreement that is referred to in clause (i), (ii), (iii), or (iv); or

      (vi) any security agreement or arrangement or other credit enhancement related to any agreements or transactions referred to in clause (i) through (v), including any guarantee or reimbursement obligation by or to a swap participant or financial participant in connection with any agreement or transaction referred to in any such clause, but not to exceed the damages in connection with any such agreement or transaction, measured in accordance with section 562; and

    (B) is applicable for purposes of this title only, and shall not be construed or applied so as to challenge or affect the characterization, definition, or treatment of any swap agreement under any other statute, regulation, or rule, including the Gramm-Leach-Bliley Act, the Legal Certainty for Bank Products Act of 2000, the securities laws (as such term is defined in section 3(a)(47) of the Securities Exchange Act of 1934) and the Commodity Exchange Act.

  (53C) The term "swap participant" means an entity that, at any time before the filing of the petition, has an outstanding swap agreement with the debtor.

  (56A)[3] The term "term overriding royalty" means an interest in liquid or gaseous hydrocarbons in place or to be produced from particular real property that entitles the owner thereof to a share of production, or the value thereof, for a term limited by time, quantity, or value realized.

  (53D) The term "timeshare plan" means and shall include that interest purchased in any arrangement, plan, scheme, or similar device, but not including exchange programs, whether by membership, agreement, tenancy in common, sale, lease, deed, rental agreement, license, right to use agreement, or by any other means, whereby a purchaser, in exchange for consideration, receives a right to use accommodations, facilities, or recreational sites, whether improved or unimproved, for a specific period of time less than a full year during any given year, but not necessarily for consecutive years, and which extends for a period of more than three years. A "timeshare interest" is that interest purchased in a timeshare plan which grants the purchaser the right to use and occupy accommodations, facilities, or recreational sites, whether improved or unimproved, pursuant to a timeshare plan.

_____

[3]　So in original.

(54) The term "transfer" means—

    (A) the creation of a lien;

    (B) the retention of title as a security interest;

    (C) the foreclosure of a debtor's equity of redemption; or

    (D) each mode, direct or indirect, absolute or conditional, voluntary or involuntary, of disposing of or parting with—

        (i) property; or

        (ii) an interest in property.

(54A) The term "uninsured State member bank" means a State member bank (as defined in section 3 of the Federal Deposit Insurance Act) the deposits of which are not insured by the Federal Deposit Insurance Corporation.

(55) The term "United States", when used in a geographical sense, includes all locations where the judicial jurisdiction of the United States extends, including territories and possessions of the United States.

(Pub.L. 95–598, Nov. 6, 1978, 92 Stat. 2549; Pub.L. 97–222, § 1, July 27, 1982, 96 Stat. 235; Pub.L. 98–353, title III, §§ 391, 401, 421, July 10, 1984, 98 Stat. 364, 366, 367; Pub.L. 99–554, title II, §§ 201, 251, 283(a), Oct. 27, 1986, 100 Stat. 3097, 3104, 3116; Pub.L. 100–506, § 1(a), Oct. 18, 1988, 102 Stat. 2538; Pub.L. 100–597, § 1, Nov. 3, 1988, 102 Stat. 3028; Pub.L. 101–311, title I, § 101, title II, § 201, June 25, 1990, 104 Stat. 267, 268; Pub.L. 101–647, title XXV, § 2522(e), Nov. 29, 1990, 104 Stat. 4867; Pub.L. 102–486, title XXX, § 3017(a), Oct. 24, 1992, 106 Stat. 3130; Pub.L. 103–394, title I, § 106, title II, §§ 208(a), 215, 217(a), 218(a), title III, § 304(a), title V, § 501(a), (b)(1), (d)(1), Oct. 22, 1994, 108 Stat. 4111, 4124, 4126–4128, 4132, 4141–4143; Pub.L. 106–554, § 1(a)(5) [title I, § 112(c)(3), (4)], Dec. 21, 2000, 114 Stat. 2763, 2763A–393; Pub.L. 109–8, title I, § 102(b), (k), title II, §§ 211, 226(a), 231(b), title III, § 306(c), title IV, §§ 401(a), 414, 432(a), title VIII, § 802(b), title IX, § 907(a)(1), (b), (c), title X, §§ 1004, 1005, 1007(a), title XI, § 1101(a), (b), title XII, § 1201, Apr. 20, 2005, 119 Stat. 32, 35, 50, 66, 73, 80, 104, 107, 110, 145, 170, 175, 186, 187, 189, 192; Pub.L. 109–390, § 5(a)(1), Dec. 12, 2006, 120 Stat. 2695; Pub.L. 111–327, § 2(a)(1), Dec. 22, 2010, 124 Stat. 3557.)

§ 102. Rules of construction

In this title—

    (1) "after notice and a hearing", or a similar phrase—

    (A) means after such notice as is appropriate in the particular circumstances, and such opportunity for a hearing as is appropriate in the particular circumstances; but

    (B) authorizes an act without an actual hearing if such notice is given properly and if—

        (i) such a hearing is not requested timely by a party in interest; or

        (ii) there is insufficient time for a hearing to be commenced before such act must be done, and the court authorizes such act;

    (2) "claim against the debtor" includes claim against property of the debtor;

    (3) "includes" and "including" are not limiting;

    (4) "may not" is prohibitive, and not permissive;

    (5) "or" is not exclusive;

    (6) "order for relief" means entry of an order for relief;

    (7) the singular includes the plural;

    (8) a definition, contained in a section of this title that refers to another section of this title, does not, for the purpose of such reference, affect the meaning of a term used in such other section; and

(9) "United States trustee" includes a designee of the United States trustee.

(Pub.L. 95–598, Nov. 6, 1978, 92 Stat. 2554; Pub.L. 98–353, title III, § 422, July 10, 1984, 98 Stat. 369; Pub.L. 99–554, title II, § 202, Oct. 27, 1986, 100 Stat. 3097.)

§ 103. Applicability of chapters

(a) Except as provided in section 1161 of this title, chapters 1, 3, and 5 of this title apply in a case under chapter 7, 11, 12, or 13 of this title, and this chapter, sections 307, 362(*o*), 555 through 557, and 559 through 562 apply in a case under chapter 15.

(b) Subchapters I and II of chapter 7 of this title apply only in a case under such chapter.

(c) Subchapter III of chapter 7 of this title applies only in a case under such chapter concerning a stockbroker.

(d) Subchapter IV of chapter 7 of this title applies only in a case under such chapter concerning a commodity broker.

(e) Scope of Application.—Subchapter V of chapter 7 of this title shall apply only in a case under such chapter concerning the liquidation of an uninsured State member bank, or a corporation organized under section 25A of the Federal Reserve Act, which operates, or operates as, a multilateral clearing organization pursuant to section 409 of the Federal Deposit Insurance Corporation Improvement Act of 1991.

(f) Except as provided in section 901 of this title, only chapters 1 and 9 of this title apply in a case under such chapter 9.

(g) Except as provided in section 901 of this title, subchapters I, II, and III of chapter 11 of this title apply only in a case under such chapter.

(h) Subchapter IV of chapter 11 of this title applies only in a case under such chapter concerning a railroad.

(i) Chapter 13 of this title applies only in a case under such chapter.

(j) Chapter 12 of this title applies only in a case under such chapter.

(k) Chapter 15 applies only in a case under such chapter, except that—

    (1) sections 1505, 1513, and 1514 apply in all cases under this title; and

    (2) section 1509 applies whether or not a case under this title is pending.

(Pub.L. 95–598, Nov. 6, 1978, 92 Stat. 2555; Pub.L. 97–222, § 2, July 27, 1982, 96 Stat. 235; Pub.L. 98–353, title III, § 423, July 10, 1984, 98 Stat. 369; Pub.L. 99–554, title II, § 252, Oct. 27, 1986, 100 Stat. 3104; Pub.L. 106–554, § 1(a)(5) [title I, § 112(c)(5)(A)], Dec. 21, 2000, 114 Stat. 2763, 2763A–394; Pub.L. 109–8, title VIII, § 802(a), Apr. 20, 2005, 119 Stat. 145; Pub.L. 111–327, § 2(a)(2), Dec. 22, 2010, 124 Stat. 3557.)

§ 104. Adjustment of dollar amounts

(a) On April 1, 1998, and at each 3-year interval ending on April 1 thereafter, each dollar amount in effect under sections 101(3), 101(18), 101(19A), 101(51D), 109(e), 303(b), 507(a), 522(d), 522(f)(3) and 522(f)(4), 522(n), 522(p), 522(q), 523(a)(2)(C), 541(b), 547(c)(9), 707(b), 1322(d), 1325(b), and 1326(b)(3) of this title and section 1409(b) of title 28 immediately before such April 1 shall be adjusted—

    (1) to reflect the change in the Consumer Price Index for All Urban Consumers, published by the Department of Labor, for the most recent 3-year period ending immediately before January 1 preceding such April 1, and

    (2) to round to the nearest $25 the dollar amount that represents such change.

(b) Not later than March 1, 1998, and at each 3-year interval ending on March 1 thereafter, the Judicial Conference of the United States shall publish in the Federal Register the dollar amounts that will become effective on such April 1 under sections 101(3), 101(18), 101(19A), 101(51D), 109(e), 303(b), 507(a),

522(d), 522(f)(3) and 522(f)(4), 522(n), 522(p), 522(q), 523(a)(2)(C), 541(b), 547(c)(9), 707(b), 1322(d), 1325(b), and 1326(b)(3) of this title and section 1409(b) of title 28.

(c) Adjustments made in accordance with subsection (a) shall not apply with respect to cases commenced before the date of such adjustments.

(Pub.L. 95–598, Nov. 6, 1978, 92 Stat. 2555; Pub.L. 103–394, title I, § 108(e), Oct. 22, 1994, 108 Stat. 4112; Pub.L. 109–8, title I, § 102(j), title II, §§ 224(e)(2), 226(b), title III, § 322(b), title IV, § 432(c), title X, § 1002, title XII, § 1202, Apr. 20, 2005, 119 Stat. 35, 65, 67, 97, 110, 186, 193; Pub.L. 110–406, § 7, Oct. 13, 2008, 122 Stat. 4293.)

§ 105. Power of court

(a) The court may issue any order, process, or judgment that is necessary or appropriate to carry out the provisions of this title. No provision of this title providing for the raising of an issue by a party in interest shall be construed to preclude the court from, sua sponte, taking any action or making any determination necessary or appropriate to enforce or implement court orders or rules, or to prevent an abuse of process.

(b) Notwithstanding subsection (a) of this section, a court may not appoint a receiver in a case under this title.

(c) The ability of any district judge or other officer or employee of a district court to exercise any of the authority or responsibilities conferred upon the court under this title shall be determined by reference to the provisions relating to such judge, officer, or employee set forth in title 28. This subsection shall not be interpreted to exclude bankruptcy judges and other officers or employees appointed pursuant to chapter 6 of title 28 from its operation.

(d) The court, on its own motion or on the request of a party in interest—

(1) shall hold such status conferences as are necessary to further the expeditious and economical resolution of the case; and

(2) unless inconsistent with another provision of this title or with applicable Federal Rules of Bankruptcy Procedure, may issue an order at any such conference prescribing such limitations and conditions as the court deems appropriate to ensure that the case is handled expeditiously and economically, including an order that—

(A) sets the date by which the trustee must assume or reject an executory contract or unexpired lease; or

(B) in a case under chapter 11 of this title—

(i) sets a date by which the debtor, or trustee if one has been appointed, shall file a disclosure statement and plan;

(ii) sets a date by which the debtor, or trustee if one has been appointed, shall solicit acceptances of a plan;

(iii) sets the date by which a party in interest other than a debtor may file a plan;

(iv) sets a date by which a proponent of a plan, other than the debtor, shall solicit acceptances of such plan;

(v) fixes the scope and format of the notice to be provided regarding the hearing on approval of the disclosure statement; or

(vi) provides that the hearing on approval of the disclosure statement may be combined with the hearing on confirmation of the plan.

(Pub.L. 95–598, Nov. 6, 1978, 92 Stat. 2555; Pub.L. 98–353, title I, § 118, July 10, 1984, 98 Stat. 344; Pub.L. 99–554, title II, § 203, Oct. 27, 1986, 100 Stat. 3097; Pub.L. 103–394, title I, § 104(a), Oct. 22, 1994, 108 Stat. 4108; Pub.L. 109–8, title IV, § 440, Apr. 20, 2005, 119 Stat. 114; Pub.L. 111–327, § 2(a)(3), Dec. 22, 2010, 124 Stat. 3557.)

§ 106. Waiver of sovereign immunity

(a) Notwithstanding an assertion of sovereign immunity, sovereign immunity is abrogated as to a governmental unit to the extent set forth in this section with respect to the following:

(1) Sections 105, 106, 107, 108, 303, 346, 362, 363, 364, 365, 366, 502, 503, 505, 506, 510, 522, 523, 524, 525, 542, 543, 544, 545, 546, 547, 548, 549, 550, 551, 552, 553, 722, 724, 726, 744, 749, 764, 901, 922, 926, 928, 929, 944, 1107, 1141, 1142, 1143, 1146, 1201, 1203, 1205, 1206, 1227, 1231, 1301, 1303, 1305, and 1327 of this title.

(2) The court may hear and determine any issue arising with respect to the application of such sections to governmental units.

(3) The court may issue against a governmental unit an order, process, or judgment under such sections or the Federal Rules of Bankruptcy Procedure, including an order or judgment awarding a money recovery, but not including an award of punitive damages. Such order or judgment for costs or fees under this title or the Federal Rules of Bankruptcy Procedure against any governmental unit shall be consistent with the provisions and limitations of section 2412(d)(2)(A) of title 28.

(4) The enforcement of any such order, process, or judgment against any governmental unit shall be consistent with appropriate nonbankruptcy law applicable to such governmental unit and, in the case of a money judgment against the United States, shall be paid as if it is a judgment rendered by a district court of the United States.

(5) Nothing in this section shall create any substantive claim for relief or cause of action not otherwise existing under this title, the Federal Rules of Bankruptcy Procedure, or nonbankruptcy law.

(b) A governmental unit that has filed a proof of claim in the case is deemed to have waived sovereign immunity with respect to a claim against such governmental unit that is property of the estate and that arose out of the same transaction or occurrence out of which the claim of such governmental unit arose.

(c) Notwithstanding any assertion of sovereign immunity by a governmental unit, there shall be offset against a claim or interest of a governmental unit any claim against such governmental unit that is property of the estate.

(Pub.L. 95–598, Nov. 6, 1978, 92 Stat. 2555; Pub.L. 103–394, title I, § 113, Oct. 22, 1994, 108 Stat. 4117; Pub.L. 111–327, § 2(a)(4), Dec. 22, 2010, 124 Stat. 3557.)

§ 107. Public access to papers

(a) Except as provided in subsections (b) and (c) of this section and subject to section 112, a paper filed in a case under this title and the dockets of a bankruptcy court are public records and open to examination by an entity at reasonable times without charge.

(b) On request of a party in interest, the bankruptcy court shall, and on the bankruptcy court's own motion, the bankruptcy court may—

(1) protect an entity with respect to a trade secret or confidential research, development, or commercial information; or

(2) protect a person with respect to scandalous or defamatory matter contained in a paper filed in a case under this title.

(c)(1) The bankruptcy court, for cause, may protect an individual, with respect to the following types of information to the extent the court finds that disclosure of such information would create undue risk of identity theft or other unlawful injury to the individual or the individual's property:

(A) Any means of identification (as defined in section 1028(d) of title 18) contained in a paper filed, or to be filed, in a case under this title.

(B) Other information contained in a paper described in subparagraph (A).

(2) Upon ex parte application demonstrating cause, the court shall provide access to information protected pursuant to paragraph (1) to an entity acting pursuant to the police or regulatory power of a domestic governmental unit.

(3) The United States trustee, bankruptcy administrator, trustee, and any auditor serving under section 586(f) of title 28—

(A) shall have full access to all information contained in any paper filed or submitted in a case under this title; and

(B) shall not disclose information specifically protected by the court under this title.

(Pub.L. 95–598, Nov. 6, 1978, 92 Stat. 2556; Pub.L. 109–8, title II, §§ 233(c), 234(a), (c), Apr. 20, 2005, 119 Stat. 74, 75; Pub.L. 111–327, § 2(a)(5), Dec. 22, 2010, 124 Stat. 3557.)

§ 108. Extension of time

(a) If applicable nonbankruptcy law, an order entered in a nonbankruptcy proceeding, or an agreement fixes a period within which the debtor may commence an action, and such period has not expired before the date of the filing of the petition, the trustee may commence such action only before the later of—

(1) the end of such period, including any suspension of such period occurring on or after the commencement of the case; or

(2) two years after the order for relief.

(b) Except as provided in subsection (a) of this section, if applicable nonbankruptcy law, an order entered in a nonbankruptcy proceeding, or an agreement fixes a period within which the debtor or an individual protected under section 1201 or 1301 of this title may file any pleading, demand, notice, or proof of claim or loss, cure a default, or perform any other similar act, and such period has not expired before the date of the filing of the petition, the trustee may only file, cure, or perform, as the case may be, before the later of—

(1) the end of such period, including any suspension of such period occurring on or after the commencement of the case; or

(2) 60 days after the order for relief.

(c) Except as provided in section 524 of this title, if applicable nonbankruptcy law, an order entered in a nonbankruptcy proceeding, or an agreement fixes a period for commencing or continuing a civil action in a court other than a bankruptcy court on a claim against the debtor, or against an individual with respect to which such individual is protected under section 1201 or 1301 of this title, and such period has not expired before the date of the filing of the petition, then such period does not expire until the later of—

(1) the end of such period, including any suspension of such period occurring on or after the commencement of the case; or

(2) 30 days after notice of the termination or expiration of the stay under section 362, 922, 1201, or 1301 of this title, as the case may be, with respect to such claim.

(Pub.L. 95–598, Nov. 6, 1978, 92 Stat. 2556; Pub.L. 98–353, title III, § 424, July 10, 1984, 98 Stat. 369; Pub.L. 99–554, title II, § 257(b), Oct. 27, 1986, 100 Stat. 3114; Pub.L. 109–8, title XII, § 1203, Apr. 20, 2005, 119 Stat. 193.)

§ 109. Who may be a debtor

(a) Notwithstanding any other provision of this section, only a person that resides or has a domicile, a place of business, or property in the United States, or a municipality, may be a debtor under this title.

(b) A person may be a debtor under chapter 7 of this title only if such person is not—

(1) a railroad;

(2)   a domestic insurance company, bank, savings bank, cooperative bank, savings and loan association, building and loan association, homestead association, a New Markets Venture Capital company as defined in section 351 of the Small Business Investment Act of 1958, a small business investment company licensed by the Small Business Administration under section 301 of the Small Business Investment Act of 1958, credit union, or industrial bank or similar institution which is an insured bank as defined in section 3(h) of the Federal Deposit Insurance Act, except that an uninsured State member bank, or a corporation organized under section 25A of the Federal Reserve Act, which operates, or operates as, a multilateral clearing organization pursuant to section 409 of the Federal Deposit Insurance Corporation Improvement Act of 1991 may be a debtor if a petition is filed at the direction of the Board of Governors of the Federal Reserve System; or

(3)(A)   a foreign insurance company, engaged in such business in the United States; or

(B)   a foreign bank, savings bank, cooperative bank, savings and loan association, building and loan association, or credit union, that has a branch or agency (as defined in section 1(b) of the International Banking Act of 1978) in the United States.

(c)   An entity may be a debtor under chapter 9 of this title if and only if such entity—

(1)   is a municipality;

(2)   is specifically authorized, in its capacity as a municipality or by name, to be a debtor under such chapter by State law, or by a governmental officer or organization empowered by State law to authorize such entity to be a debtor under such chapter;

(3)   is insolvent;

(4)   desires to effect a plan to adjust such debts; and

(5)(A)   has obtained the agreement of creditors holding at least a majority in amount of the claims of each class that such entity intends to impair under a plan in a case under such chapter;

(B)   has negotiated in good faith with creditors and has failed to obtain the agreement of creditors holding at least a majority in amount of the claims of each class that such entity intends to impair under a plan in a case under such chapter;

(C)   is unable to negotiate with creditors because such negotiation is impracticable; or

(D)   reasonably believes that a creditor may attempt to obtain a transfer that is avoidable under section 547 of this title.

(d)   Only a railroad, a person that may be a debtor under chapter 7 of this title (except a stockbroker or a commodity broker), and an uninsured State member bank, or a corporation organized under section 25A of the Federal Reserve Act, which operates, or operates as, a multilateral clearing organization pursuant to section 409 of the Federal Deposit Insurance Corporation Improvement Act of 1991 may be a debtor under chapter 11 of this title.

(e)   Only an individual with regular income that owes, on the date of the filing of the petition, noncontingent, liquidated, unsecured debts of less than $394,725* and noncontingent, liquidated, secured debts of less than $1,184,200*, or an individual with regular income and such individual's spouse, except a stockbroker or a commodity broker, that owe, on the date of the filing of the petition, noncontingent, liquidated, unsecured debts that aggregate less than $394,725* and noncontingent, liquidated, secured debts of less than $1,184,200* may be a debtor under chapter 13 of this title.

(f)   Only a family farmer or family fisherman with regular annual income may be a debtor under chapter 12 of this title.

(g)   Notwithstanding any other provision of this section, no individual or family farmer may be a debtor under this title who has been a debtor in a case pending under this title at any time in the preceding 180 days if—

---

*   *Note from West Advisory Panel: Dollar amounts adjusted pursuant to 11 U.S.C. § 104; 81 Fed. Reg. 8748 (Feb. 22, 2016).*

(1) the case was dismissed by the court for willful failure of the debtor to abide by orders of the court, or to appear before the court in proper prosecution of the case; or

(2) the debtor requested and obtained the voluntary dismissal of the case following the filing of a request for relief from the automatic stay provided by section 362 of this title.

(h)(1) Subject to paragraphs (2) and (3), and notwithstanding any other provision of this section other than paragraph (4) of this subsection, an individual may not be a debtor under this title unless such individual has, during the 180-day period ending on the date of filing of the petition by such individual, received from an approved nonprofit budget and credit counseling agency described in section 111(a) an individual or group briefing (including a briefing conducted by telephone or on the Internet) that outlined the opportunities for available credit counseling and assisted such individual in performing a related budget analysis.

(2)(A) Paragraph (1) shall not apply with respect to a debtor who resides in a district for which the United States trustee (or the bankruptcy administrator, if any) determines that the approved nonprofit budget and credit counseling agencies for such district are not reasonably able to provide adequate services to the additional individuals who would otherwise seek credit counseling from such agencies by reason of the requirements of paragraph (1).

(B) The United States trustee (or the bankruptcy administrator, if any) who makes a determination described in subparagraph (A) shall review such determination not later than 1 year after the date of such determination, and not less frequently than annually thereafter. Notwithstanding the preceding sentence, a nonprofit budget and credit counseling agency may be disapproved by the United States trustee (or the bankruptcy administrator, if any) at any time.

(3)(A) Subject to subparagraph (B), the requirements of paragraph (1) shall not apply with respect to a debtor who submits to the court a certification that—

(i) describes exigent circumstances that merit a waiver of the requirements of paragraph (1);

(ii) states that the debtor requested credit counseling services from an approved nonprofit budget and credit counseling agency, but was unable to obtain the services referred to in paragraph (1) during the 7-day period beginning on the date on which the debtor made that request; and

(iii) is satisfactory to the court.

(B) With respect to a debtor, an exemption under subparagraph (A) shall cease to apply to that debtor on the date on which the debtor meets the requirements of paragraph (1), but in no case may the exemption apply to that debtor after the date that is 30 days after the debtor files a petition, except that the court, for cause, may order an additional 15 days.

(4) The requirements of paragraph (1) shall not apply with respect to a debtor whom the court determines, after notice and hearing, is unable to complete those requirements because of incapacity, disability, or active military duty in a military combat zone. For the purposes of this paragraph, incapacity means that the debtor is impaired by reason of mental illness or mental deficiency so that he is incapable of realizing and making rational decisions with respect to his financial responsibilities; and "disability" means that the debtor is so physically impaired as to be unable, after reasonable effort, to participate in an in person, telephone, or Internet briefing required under paragraph (1).

(Pub.L. 95–598, Nov. 6, 1978, 92 Stat. 2557; Pub.L. 97–320, title VII, § 703(d), Oct. 15, 1982, 96 Stat. 1539; Pub.L. 98–353, title III, §§ 301, 425, July 10, 1984, 98 Stat. 352, 369; Pub.L. 99–554, title II, § 253, Oct. 27, 1986, 100 Stat. 3105; Pub.L. 100–597, § 2, Nov. 3, 1988, 102 Stat. 3028; Pub.L. 103–394, title I, § 108(a), title II, § 220, title IV, § 402, title V, § 501(d)(2), Oct. 22, 1994, 108 Stat. 4111, 4129, 4141, 4143; Pub.L. 106–554, § 1(a)(5) [title I, § 112(c)(1), (2)], (8) [§ 1(e)], Dec. 21, 2000, 114 Stat. 2763, 2763A–393, 2763A–665; Pub.L. 109–8, title I, § 106(a), title VIII, § 802(d)(1), title X, § 1007(b), title XII, § 1204(1), Apr. 20, 2005, 119 Stat. 37, 146, 188, 193; Pub.L. 111–16, § 2(1), May 7, 2009, 123 Stat. 1607; Pub.L. 111–327, § 2(a)(6), Dec. 22, 2010, 124 Stat. 3557.)

§ 110.   Penalty for persons who negligently or fraudulently prepare bankruptcy petitions

(a)   In this section—

(1)   "bankruptcy petition preparer" means a person, other than an attorney for the debtor or an employee of such attorney under the direct supervision of such attorney, who prepares for compensation a document for filing; and

(2)   "document for filing" means a petition or any other document prepared for filing by a debtor in a United States bankruptcy court or a United States district court in connection with a case under this title.

(b)(1)   A bankruptcy petition preparer who prepares a document for filing shall sign the document and print on the document the preparer's name and address. If a bankruptcy petition preparer is not an individual, then an officer, principal, responsible person, or partner of the bankruptcy petition preparer shall be required to—

(A)   sign the document for filing; and

(B)   print on the document the name and address of that officer, principal, responsible person, or partner.

(2)(A)   Before preparing any document for filing or accepting any fees from or on behalf of a debtor, the bankruptcy petition preparer shall provide to the debtor a written notice which shall be on an official form prescribed by the Judicial Conference of the United States in accordance with rule 9009 of the Federal Rules of Bankruptcy Procedure.

(B)   The notice under subparagraph (A)—

(i)   shall inform the debtor in simple language that a bankruptcy petition preparer is not an attorney and may not practice law or give legal advice;

(ii)   may contain a description of examples of legal advice that a bankruptcy petition preparer is not authorized to give, in addition to any advice that the preparer may not give by reason of subsection (e)(2); and

(iii)   shall—

(I)   be signed by the debtor and, under penalty of perjury, by the bankruptcy petition preparer; and

(II)   be filed with any document for filing.

(c)(1)   A bankruptcy petition preparer who prepares a document for filing shall place on the document, after the preparer's signature, an identifying number that identifies individuals who prepared the document.

(2)(A)   Subject to subparagraph (B), for purposes of this section, the identifying number of a bankruptcy petition preparer shall be the Social Security account number of each individual who prepared the document or assisted in its preparation.

(B)   If a bankruptcy petition preparer is not an individual, the identifying number of the bankruptcy petition preparer shall be the Social Security account number of the officer, principal, responsible person, or partner of the bankruptcy petition preparer.

(d)   A bankruptcy petition preparer shall, not later than the time at which a document for filing is presented for the debtor's signature, furnish to the debtor a copy of the document.

(e)(1)   A bankruptcy petition preparer shall not execute any document on behalf of a debtor.

(2)(A)   A bankruptcy petition preparer may not offer a potential bankruptcy debtor any legal advice, including any legal advice described in subparagraph (B).

(B)   The legal advice referred to in subparagraph (A) includes advising the debtor—

(i)   whether—

(I)   to file a petition under this title; or

(II)   commencing a case under chapter 7, 11, 12, or 13 is appropriate;

(ii)   whether the debtor's debts will be discharged in a case under this title;

(iii)   whether the debtor will be able to retain the debtor's home, car, or other property after commencing a case under this title;

(iv)   concerning—

(I)   the tax consequences of a case brought under this title; or

(II)   the dischargeability of tax claims;

(v)   whether the debtor may or should promise to repay debts to a creditor or enter into a reaffirmation agreement with a creditor to reaffirm a debt;

(vi)   concerning how to characterize the nature of the debtor's interests in property or the debtor's debts; or

(vii)   concerning bankruptcy procedures and rights.

(f)   A bankruptcy petition preparer shall not use the word "legal" or any similar term in any advertisements, or advertise under any category that includes the word "legal" or any similar term.

(g)   A bankruptcy petition preparer shall not collect or receive any payment from the debtor or on behalf of the debtor for the court fees in connection with filing the petition.

(h)(1)   The Supreme Court may promulgate rules under section 2075 of title 28, or the Judicial Conference of the United States may prescribe guidelines, for setting a maximum allowable fee chargeable by a bankruptcy petition preparer. A bankruptcy petition preparer shall notify the debtor of any such maximum amount before preparing any document for filing for the debtor or accepting any fee from or on behalf of the debtor.

(2)   A declaration under penalty of perjury by the bankruptcy petition preparer shall be filed together with the petition, disclosing any fee received from or on behalf of the debtor within 12 months immediately prior to the filing of the case, and any unpaid fee charged to the debtor. If rules or guidelines setting a maximum fee for services have been promulgated or prescribed under paragraph (1), the declaration under this paragraph shall include a certification that the bankruptcy petition preparer complied with the notification requirement under paragraph (1).

(3)(A)   The court shall disallow and order the immediate turnover to the bankruptcy trustee any fee referred to in paragraph (2)—

(i)   found to be in excess of the value of any services rendered by the bankruptcy petition preparer during the 12-month period immediately preceding the date of the filing of the petition; or

(ii)   found to be in violation of any rule or guideline promulgated or prescribed under paragraph (1).

(B)   All fees charged by a bankruptcy petition preparer may be forfeited in any case in which the bankruptcy petition preparer fails to comply with this subsection or subsection (b), (c), (d), (e), (f), or (g).

(C)   An individual may exempt any funds recovered under this paragraph under section 522(b).

(4)   The debtor, the trustee, a creditor, the United States trustee (or the bankruptcy administrator, if any) or the court, on the initiative of the court, may file a motion for an order under paragraph (3).

(5)   A bankruptcy petition preparer shall be fined not more than $500 for each failure to comply with a court order to turn over funds within 30 days of service of such order.

(i)(1) If a bankruptcy petition preparer violates this section or commits any act that the court finds to be fraudulent, unfair, or deceptive, on the motion of the debtor, trustee, United States trustee (or the bankruptcy administrator, if any), and after notice and a hearing, the court shall order the bankruptcy petition preparer to pay to the debtor—

>   **(A)**   the debtor's actual damages;

>   **(B)**   the greater of—

>>   **(i)** $2,000; or

>>   **(ii)**   twice the amount paid by the debtor to the bankruptcy petition preparer for the preparer's services; and

>   **(C)**   reasonable attorneys' fees and costs in moving for damages under this subsection.

>   **(2)**   If the trustee or creditor moves for damages on behalf of the debtor under this subsection, the bankruptcy petition preparer shall be ordered to pay the movant the additional amount of $1,000 plus reasonable attorneys' fees and costs incurred.

(j)(1) A debtor for whom a bankruptcy petition preparer has prepared a document for filing, the trustee, a creditor, or the United States trustee in the district in which the bankruptcy petition preparer resides, has conducted business, or the United States trustee in any other district in which the debtor resides may bring a civil action to enjoin a bankruptcy petition preparer from engaging in any conduct in violation of this section or from further acting as a bankruptcy petition preparer.

>   **(2)(A)**   In an action under paragraph (1), if the court finds that—

>>   **(i)**   a bankruptcy petition preparer has—

>>>   **(I)**   engaged in conduct in violation of this section or of any provision of this title;

>>>   **(II)**   misrepresented the preparer's experience or education as a bankruptcy petition preparer; or

>>>   **(III)** engaged in any other fraudulent, unfair, or deceptive conduct; and

>>   **(ii)**   injunctive relief is appropriate to prevent the recurrence of such conduct,

the court may enjoin the bankruptcy petition preparer from engaging in such conduct.

>   **(B)**   If the court finds that a bankruptcy petition preparer has continually engaged in conduct described in subclause (I), (II), or (III) of clause (i) and that an injunction prohibiting such conduct would not be sufficient to prevent such person's interference with the proper administration of this title, has not paid a penalty imposed under this section, or failed to disgorge all fees ordered by the court the court may enjoin the person from acting as a bankruptcy petition preparer.

>   **(3)**   The court, as part of its contempt power, may enjoin a bankruptcy petition preparer that has failed to comply with a previous order issued under this section. The injunction under this paragraph may be issued on the motion of the court, the trustee, or the United States trustee (or the bankruptcy administrator, if any).

>   **(4)**   The court shall award to a debtor, trustee, or creditor that brings a successful action under this subsection reasonable attorneys' fees and costs of the action, to be paid by the bankruptcy petition preparer.

(k) Nothing in this section shall be construed to permit activities that are otherwise prohibited by law, including rules and laws that prohibit the unauthorized practice of law.

(*l*)(1) A bankruptcy petition preparer who fails to comply with any provision of subsection (b), (c), (d), (e), (f), (g), or (h) may be fined not more than $500 for each such failure.

>   **(2)**   The court shall triple the amount of a fine assessed under paragraph (1) in any case in which the court finds that a bankruptcy petition preparer—

(A) advised the debtor to exclude assets or income that should have been included on applicable schedules;

(B) advised the debtor to use a false Social Security account number;

(C) failed to inform the debtor that the debtor was filing for relief under this title; or

(D) prepared a document for filing in a manner that failed to disclose the identity of the bankruptcy petition preparer.

(3) A debtor, trustee, creditor, or United States trustee (or the bankruptcy administrator, if any) may file a motion for an order imposing a fine on the bankruptcy petition preparer for any violation of this section.

(4)(A) Fines imposed under this subsection in judicial districts served by United States trustees shall be paid to the United States trustees, who shall deposit an amount equal to such fines in the United States Trustee Fund.

(B) Fines imposed under this subsection in judicial districts served by bankruptcy administrators shall be deposited as offsetting receipts to the fund established under section 1931 of title 28, and shall remain available until expended to reimburse any appropriation for the amount paid out of such appropriation for expenses of the operation and maintenance of the courts of the United States.

(Added Pub.L. 103–394, title III, § 308(a), Oct. 22, 1994, 108 Stat. 4135, amended Pub.L. 109–8, title II, § 221, title XII, § 1205, Apr. 20, 2005, 119 Stat. 59, 194; Pub.L. 110–161, div. B, title II, § 212(b), Dec. 26, 2007, 121 Stat. 1914; Pub.L. 111–327, § 2(a)(7), Dec. 22, 2010, 124 Stat. 3558.)

§ 111. Nonprofit budget and credit counseling agencies; financial management instructional courses

(a) The clerk shall maintain a publicly available list of—

(1) nonprofit budget and credit counseling agencies that provide 1 or more services described in section 109(h) currently approved by the United States trustee (or the bankruptcy administrator, if any); and

(2) instructional courses concerning personal financial management currently approved by the United States trustee (or the bankruptcy administrator, if any), as applicable.

(b) The United States trustee (or bankruptcy administrator, if any) shall only approve a nonprofit budget and credit counseling agency or an instructional course concerning personal financial management as follows:

(1) The United States trustee (or bankruptcy administrator, if any) shall have thoroughly reviewed the qualifications of the nonprofit budget and credit counseling agency or of the provider of the instructional course under the standards set forth in this section, and the services or instructional courses that will be offered by such agency or such provider, and may require such agency or such provider that has sought approval to provide information with respect to such review.

(2) The United States trustee (or bankruptcy administrator, if any) shall have determined that such agency or such instructional course fully satisfies the applicable standards set forth in this section.

(3) If a nonprofit budget and credit counseling agency or instructional course did not appear on the approved list for the district under subsection (a) immediately before approval under this section, approval under this subsection of such agency or such instructional course shall be for a probationary period not to exceed 6 months.

(4) At the conclusion of the applicable probationary period under paragraph (3), the United States trustee (or bankruptcy administrator, if any) may only approve for an additional 1-year period, and for successive 1-year periods thereafter, an agency or instructional course that has demonstrated

during the probationary or applicable subsequent period of approval that such agency or instructional course—

    (A) has met the standards set forth under this section during such period; and

    (B) can satisfy such standards in the future.

    (5) Not later than 30 days after any final decision under paragraph (4), an interested person may seek judicial review of such decision in the appropriate district court of the United States.

(c)(1) The United States trustee (or the bankruptcy administrator, if any) shall only approve a nonprofit budget and credit counseling agency that demonstrates that it will provide qualified counselors, maintain adequate provision for safekeeping and payment of client funds, provide adequate counseling with respect to client credit problems, and deal responsibly and effectively with other matters relating to the quality, effectiveness, and financial security of the services it provides.

    (2) To be approved by the United States trustee (or the bankruptcy administrator, if any), a nonprofit budget and credit counseling agency shall, at a minimum—

    (A) have a board of directors the majority of which—

        (i) are not employed by such agency; and

        (ii) will not directly or indirectly benefit financially from the outcome of the counseling services provided by such agency;

    (B) if a fee is charged for counseling services, charge a reasonable fee, and provide services without regard to ability to pay the fee;

    (C) provide for safekeeping and payment of client funds, including an annual audit of the trust accounts and appropriate employee bonding;

    (D) provide full disclosures to a client, including funding sources, counselor qualifications, possible impact on credit reports, and any costs of such program that will be paid by such client and how such costs will be paid;

    (E) provide adequate counseling with respect to a client's credit problems that includes an analysis of such client's current financial condition, factors that caused such financial condition, and how such client can develop a plan to respond to the problems without incurring negative amortization of debt;

    (F) provide trained counselors who receive no commissions or bonuses based on the outcome of the counseling services provided by such agency, and who have adequate experience, and have been adequately trained to provide counseling services to individuals in financial difficulty, including the matters described in subparagraph (E);

    (G) demonstrate adequate experience and background in providing credit counseling; and

    (H) have adequate financial resources to provide continuing support services for budgeting plans over the life of any repayment plan.

(d) The United States trustee (or the bankruptcy administrator, if any) shall only approve an instructional course concerning personal financial management—

    (1) for an initial probationary period under subsection (b)(3) if the course will provide at a minimum—

    (A) trained personnel with adequate experience and training in providing effective instruction and services;

    (B) learning materials and teaching methodologies designed to assist debtors in understanding personal financial management and that are consistent with stated objectives directly related to the goals of such instructional course;

(C) adequate facilities situated in reasonably convenient locations at which such instructional course is offered, except that such facilities may include the provision of such instructional course by telephone or through the Internet, if such instructional course is effective;

(D) the preparation and retention of reasonable records (which shall include the debtor's bankruptcy case number) to permit evaluation of the effectiveness of such instructional course, including any evaluation of satisfaction of instructional course requirements for each debtor attending such instructional course, which shall be available for inspection and evaluation by the Executive Office for United States Trustees, the United States trustee (or the bankruptcy administrator, if any), or the chief bankruptcy judge for the district in which such instructional course is offered; and

(E) if a fee is charged for the instructional course, charge a reasonable fee, and provide services without regard to ability to pay the fee; and

(2) for any 1-year period if the provider thereof has demonstrated that the course meets the standards of paragraph (1) and, in addition—

(A) has been effective in assisting a substantial number of debtors to understand personal financial management; and

(B) is otherwise likely to increase substantially the debtor's understanding of personal financial management.

(e) The district court may, at any time, investigate the qualifications of a nonprofit budget and credit counseling agency referred to in subsection (a), and request production of documents to ensure the integrity and effectiveness of such agency. The district court may, at any time, remove from the approved list under subsection (a) a nonprofit budget and credit counseling agency upon finding such agency does not meet the qualifications of subsection (b).

(f) The United States trustee (or the bankruptcy administrator, if any) shall notify the clerk that a nonprofit budget and credit counseling agency or an instructional course is no longer approved, in which case the clerk shall remove it from the list maintained under subsection (a).

(g)(1) No nonprofit budget and credit counseling agency may provide to a credit reporting agency information concerning whether a debtor has received or sought instruction concerning personal financial management from such agency.

(2) A nonprofit budget and credit counseling agency that willfully or negligently fails to comply with any requirement under this title with respect to a debtor shall be liable for damages in an amount equal to the sum of—

(A) any actual damages sustained by the debtor as a result of the violation; and

(B) any court costs or reasonable attorneys' fees (as determined by the court) incurred in an action to recover those damages.

(Added Pub.L. 109–8, title I, § 106(e)(1), Apr. 20, 2005, 119 Stat. 39, amended Pub.L. 111–327, § 2(a)(8), Dec. 22, 2010, 124 Stat. 3558.)

§ 112. Prohibition on disclosure of name of minor children

The debtor may be required to provide information regarding a minor child involved in matters under this title but may not be required to disclose in the public records in the case the name of such minor child. The debtor may be required to disclose the name of such minor child in a nonpublic record that is maintained by the court and made available by the court for examination by the United States trustee, the trustee, and the auditor (if any) serving under section 586(f) of title 28, in the case. The court, the United States trustee, the trustee, and such auditor shall not disclose the name of such minor child maintained in such nonpublic record.

(Added Pub.L. 109–8, title II, § 233(a), Apr. 20, 2005, 119 Stat. 74.)

BANKRUPTCY CODE

CHAPTER 3—CASE ADMINISTRATION

SUBCHAPTER I—COMMENCEMENT OF A CASE

§ 301. Voluntary cases

(a) A voluntary case under a chapter of this title is commenced by the filing with the bankruptcy court of a petition under such chapter by an entity that may be a debtor under such chapter.

(b) The commencement of a voluntary case under a chapter of this title constitutes an order for relief under such chapter.

> (Pub.L. 95–598, Nov. 6, 1978, 92 Stat. 2558; Pub.L. 109–8, title V, § 501(b), Apr. 20, 2005, 119 Stat. 118.)

§ 302. Joint cases

(a) A joint case under a chapter of this title is commenced by the filing with the bankruptcy court of a single petition under such chapter by an individual that may be a debtor under such chapter and such individual's spouse. The commencement of a joint case under a chapter of this title constitutes an order for relief under such chapter.

(b) After the commencement of a joint case, the court shall determine the extent, if any, to which the debtors' estates shall be consolidated.

> (Pub.L. 95–598, Nov. 6, 1978, 92 Stat. 2558.)

§ 303. Involuntary cases

(a) An involuntary case may be commenced only under chapter 7 or 11 of this title, and only against a person, except a farmer, family farmer, or a corporation that is not a moneyed, business, or commercial corporation, that may be a debtor under the chapter under which such case is commenced.

(b) An involuntary case against a person is commenced by the filing with the bankruptcy court of a petition under chapter 7 or 11 of this title—

    (1) by three or more entities, each of which is either a holder of a claim against such person that is not contingent as to liability or the subject of a bona fide dispute as to liability or amount, or an indenture trustee representing such a holder, if such noncontingent, undisputed claims aggregate at least $15,775* more than the value of any lien on property of the debtor securing such claims held by the holders of such claims;

    (2) if there are fewer than 12 such holders, excluding any employee or insider of such person and any transferee of a transfer that is voidable under section 544, 545, 547, 548, 549, or 724(a) of this title, by one or more of such holders that hold in the aggregate at least $15,775* of such claims;

    (3) if such person is a partnership—

        (A) by fewer than all of the general partners in such partnership; or

        (B) if relief has been ordered under this title with respect to all of the general partners in such partnership, by a general partner in such partnership, the trustee of such a general partner, or a holder of a claim against such partnership; or

    (4) by a foreign representative of the estate in a foreign proceeding concerning such person.

(c) After the filing of a petition under this section but before the case is dismissed or relief is ordered, a creditor holding an unsecured claim that is not contingent, other than a creditor filing under subsection (b) of this section, may join in the petition with the same effect as if such joining creditor were a petitioning creditor under subsection (b) of this section.

---

*   *Note from West Advisory Panel: Dollar amounts adjusted pursuant to 11 U.S.C. § 104; 81 Fed. Reg. 8748 (Feb. 22, 2016).*

(d) The debtor, or a general partner in a partnership debtor that did not join in the petition, may file an answer to a petition under this section.

(e) After notice and a hearing, and for cause, the court may require the petitioners under this section to file a bond to indemnify the debtor for such amounts as the court may later allow under subsection (i) of this section.

(f) Notwithstanding section 363 of this title, except to the extent that the court orders otherwise, and until an order for relief in the case, any business of the debtor may continue to operate, and the debtor may continue to use, acquire, or dispose of property as if an involuntary case concerning the debtor had not been commenced.

(g) At any time after the commencement of an involuntary case under chapter 7 of this title but before an order for relief in the case, the court, on request of a party in interest, after notice to the debtor and a hearing, and if necessary to preserve the property of the estate or to prevent loss to the estate, may order the United States trustee to appoint an interim trustee under section 701 of this title to take possession of the property of the estate and to operate any business of the debtor. Before an order for relief, the debtor may regain possession of property in the possession of a trustee ordered appointed under this subsection if the debtor files such bond as the court requires, conditioned on the debtor's accounting for and delivering to the trustee, if there is an order for relief in the case, such property, or the value, as of the date the debtor regains possession, of such property.

(h) If the petition is not timely controverted, the court shall order relief against the debtor in an involuntary case under the chapter under which the petition was filed. Otherwise, after trial, the court shall order relief against the debtor in an involuntary case under the chapter under which the petition was filed, only if—

    (1) the debtor is generally not paying such debtor's debts as such debts become due unless such debts are the subject of a bona fide dispute as to liability or amount; or

    (2) within 120 days before the date of the filing of the petition, a custodian, other than a trustee, receiver, or agent appointed or authorized to take charge of less than substantially all of the property of the debtor for the purpose of enforcing a lien against such property, was appointed or took possession.

(i) If the court dismisses a petition under this section other than on consent of all petitioners and the debtor, and if the debtor does not waive the right to judgment under this subsection, the court may grant judgment—

    (1) against the petitioners and in favor of the debtor for—

        (A) costs; or

        (B) a reasonable attorney's fee; or

    (2) against any petitioner that filed the petition in bad faith, for—

        (A) any damages proximately caused by such filing; or

        (B) punitive damages.

(j) Only after notice to all creditors and a hearing may the court dismiss a petition filed under this section—

    (1) on the motion of a petitioner;

    (2) on consent of all petitioners and the debtor; or

    (3) for want of prosecution.

(k)(1) If—

    (A) the petition under this section is false or contains any materially false, fictitious, or fraudulent statement;

    (B) the debtor is an individual; and

(C) the court dismisses such petition,

the court, upon the motion of the debtor, shall seal all the records of the court relating to such petition, and all references to such petition.

(2) If the debtor is an individual and the court dismisses a petition under this section, the court may enter an order prohibiting all consumer reporting agencies (as defined in section 603(f) of the Fair Credit Reporting Act (15 U.S.C. 1681a(f))) from making any consumer report (as defined in section 603(d) of that Act) that contains any information relating to such petition or to the case commenced by the filing of such petition.

(3) Upon the expiration of the statute of limitations described in section 3282 of title 18, for a violation of section 152 or 157 of such title, the court, upon the motion of the debtor and for good cause, may expunge any records relating to a petition filed under this section.

(Pub.L. 95–598, Nov. 6, 1978, 92 Stat. 2559; Pub.L. 98–353, title III, §§ 426, 427, July 10, 1984, 98 Stat. 369; Pub.L. 99–554, title II, §§ 204, 254, 283(b), Oct. 27, 1986, 100 Stat. 3097, 3105, 3116; Pub.L. 103–394, title I, § 108(b), Oct. 22, 1994, 108 Stat. 4112; Pub.L. 109–8, title III, § 332(b), title VIII, § 802(d)(2), title XII, § 1234(a), Apr. 20, 2005, 119 Stat. 103, 146, 204; Pub.L. 111–327, § 2(a)(9), Dec. 22, 2010, 124 Stat. 3558.)

§ 304. [Repealed.]

(Pub.L. 95–598, Nov. 6, 1978, 92 Stat. 2560; Pub.L. 109–8, title VII, § 802(d)(3), Apr. 20, 2005, 119 Stat. 146.)

§ 305. Abstention

(a) The court, after notice and a hearing, may dismiss a case under this title, or may suspend all proceedings in a case under this title, at any time if—

(1) the interests of creditors and the debtor would be better served by such dismissal or suspension; or

(2)(A) a petition under section 1515 for recognition of a foreign proceeding has been granted; and

(B) the purposes of chapter 15 of this title would be best served by such dismissal or suspension.

(b) A foreign representative may seek dismissal or suspension under subsection (a)(2) of this section.

(c) An order under subsection (a) of this section dismissing a case or suspending all proceedings in a case, or a decision not so to dismiss or suspend, is not reviewable by appeal or otherwise by the court of appeals under section 158(d), 1291, or 1292 of title 28 or by the Supreme Court of the United States under section 1254 of title 28.

(Pub.L. 95–598, Nov. 6, 1978, 92 Stat. 2561; Pub.L. 101–650, title III, § 309(a), Dec. 1, 1990, 104 Stat. 5113; Pub.L. 102–198, § 5, Dec. 9, 1991, 105 Stat. 1623; Pub.L. 109–8, title VII, § 802(d)(6), Apr. 20, 2005, 119 Stat. 146.)

§ 306. Limited appearance

An appearance in a bankruptcy court by a foreign representative in connection with a petition or request under section 303 or 305 of this title does not submit such foreign representative to the jurisdiction of any court in the United States for any other purpose, but the bankruptcy court may condition any order under section 303 or 305 of this title on compliance by such foreign representative with the orders of such bankruptcy court.

(Pub.L. 95–598, Nov. 6, 1978, 92 Stat. 2561; Pub.L. 109–8, title VII, § 802(d)(7), Apr. 20, 2005, 119 Stat. 146.)

§ 307. United States trustee

The United States trustee may raise and may appear and be heard on any issue in any case or proceeding under this title but may not file a plan pursuant to section 1121(c) of this title.

(Added Pub.L. 99–554, title II, § 205(a), Oct. 27, 1986, 100 Stat. 3098.)

§ 308. Debtor reporting requirements

(a) For purposes of this section, the term "profitability" means, with respect to a debtor, the amount of money that the debtor has earned or lost during current and recent fiscal periods.

(b) A debtor in a small business case shall file periodic financial and other reports containing information including—

(1) the debtor's profitability;

(2) reasonable approximations of the debtor's projected cash receipts and cash disbursements over a reasonable period;

(3) comparisons of actual cash receipts and disbursements with projections in prior reports;

(4) whether the debtor is—

(A) in compliance in all material respects with postpetition requirements imposed by this title and the Federal Rules of Bankruptcy Procedure; and

(B) timely filing tax returns and other required government filings and paying taxes and other administrative expenses when due;

(5) if the debtor is not in compliance with the requirements referred to in paragraph (4)(A) or filing tax returns and other required government filings and making the payments referred to in paragraph (4)(B), what the failures are and how, at what cost, and when the debtor intends to remedy such failures; and

(6) such other matters as are in the best interests of the debtor and creditors, and in the public interest in fair and efficient procedures under chapter 11 of this title.

(Added Pub.L. 109–8, title IV, § 434(a)(1), Apr. 20, 2005, 119 Stat. 111, amended Pub.L. 111–327, § 2(a)(10), Dec. 22, 2010, 124 Stat. 3558.)

SUBCHAPTER II—OFFICERS

§ 321. Eligibility to serve as trustee

(a) A person may serve as trustee in a case under this title only if such person is—

(1) an individual that is competent to perform the duties of trustee and, in a case under chapter 7, 12, or 13 of this title, resides or has an office in the judicial district within which the case is pending, or in any judicial district adjacent to such district; or

(2) a corporation authorized by such corporation's charter or bylaws to act as trustee, and, in a case under chapter 7, 12, or 13 of this title, having an office in at least one of such districts.

(b) A person that has served as an examiner in the case may not serve as trustee in the case.

(c) The United States trustee for the judicial district in which the case is pending is eligible to serve as trustee in the case if necessary.

(Pub.L. 95–598, Nov. 6, 1978, 92 Stat. 2561; Pub.L. 98–353, title III, § 428, July 10, 1984, 98 Stat. 369; Pub.L. 99–554, title II, §§ 206, 257(c), Oct. 27, 1986, 100 Stat. 3098, 3114.)

§ 322. Qualification of trustee

(a) Except as provided in subsection (b)(1), a person selected under section 701, 702, 703, 1104, 1163, 1202, or 1302 of this title to serve as trustee in a case under this title qualifies if before seven days after such selection, and before beginning official duties, such person has filed with the court a bond in favor of the United States conditioned on the faithful performance of such official duties.

(b)(1) The United States trustee qualifies wherever such trustee serves as trustee in a case under this title.

(2) The United States trustee shall determine—

(A) the amount of a bond required to be filed under subsection (a) of this section; and

(B) the sufficiency of the surety on such bond.

(c) A trustee is not liable personally or on such trustee's bond in favor of the United States for any penalty or forfeiture incurred by the debtor.

(d) A proceeding on a trustee's bond may not be commenced after two years after the date on which such trustee was discharged.

(Pub.L. 95–598, Nov. 6, 1978, 92 Stat. 2562; Pub.L. 98–353, title III, § 429, July 10, 1984, 98 Stat. 369; Pub.L. 99–554, title II, §§ 207, 257(d), Oct. 27, 1986, 100 Stat. 3098, 3114; Pub.L. 103–394, title V, § 501(d)(3), Oct. 22, 1994, 108 Stat. 4143; Pub.L. 111–16, § 2(2), May 7, 2009, 123 Stat. 1607.)

§ 323. Role and capacity of trustee

(a) The trustee in a case under this title is the representative of the estate.

(b) The trustee in a case under this title has capacity to sue and be sued.

(Pub.L. 95–598, Nov. 6, 1978, 92 Stat. 2562.)

§ 324. Removal of trustee or examiner

(a) The court, after notice and a hearing, may remove a trustee, other than the United States trustee, or an examiner, for cause.

(b) Whenever the court removes a trustee or examiner under subsection (a) in a case under this title, such trustee or examiner shall thereby be removed in all other cases under this title in which such trustee or examiner is then serving unless the court orders otherwise.

(Pub.L. 95–598, Nov. 6, 1978, 92 Stat. 2562; Pub.L. 99–554, title II, § 208, Oct. 27, 1986, 100 Stat. 3098.)

§ 325. Effect of vacancy

A vacancy in the office of trustee during a case does not abate any pending action or proceeding, and the successor trustee shall be substituted as a party in such action or proceeding.

(Pub.L. 95–598, Nov. 6, 1978, 92 Stat. 2562.)

§ 326. Limitation on compensation of trustee

(a) In a case under chapter 7 or 11, the court may allow reasonable compensation under section 330 of this title of the trustee for the trustee's services, payable after the trustee renders such services, not to exceed 25 percent on the first $5,000 or less, 10 percent on any amount in excess of $5,000 but not in excess of $50,000, 5 percent on any amount in excess of $50,000 but not in excess of $1,000,000, and reasonable compensation not to exceed 3 percent of such moneys in excess of $1,000,000, upon all moneys disbursed or turned over in the case by the trustee to parties in interest, excluding the debtor, but including holders of secured claims.

(b) In a case under chapter 12 or 13 of this title, the court may not allow compensation for services or reimbursement of expenses of the United States trustee or of a standing trustee appointed under section

586(b) of title 28, but may allow reasonable compensation under section 330 of this title of a trustee appointed under section 1202(a) or 1302(a) of this title for the trustee's services, payable after the trustee renders such services, not to exceed five percent upon all payments under the plan.

    (c)   If more than one person serves as trustee in the case, the aggregate compensation of such persons for such service may not exceed the maximum compensation prescribed for a single trustee by subsection (a) or (b) of this section, as the case may be.

    (d)   The court may deny allowance of compensation for services or reimbursement of expenses of the trustee if the trustee failed to make diligent inquiry into facts that would permit denial of allowance under section 328(c) of this title or, with knowledge of such facts, employed a professional person under section 327 of this title.

    (Pub.L. 95–598, Nov. 6, 1978, 92 Stat. 2562; Pub.L. 98–353, title III, § 430(a), (b), July 10, 1984, 98 Stat. 369; Pub.L. 99–554, title II, § 209, Oct. 27, 1986, 100 Stat. 3098; Pub.L. 103–394, title I, § 107, Oct. 22, 1994, 108 Stat. 4111.)

§ 327. Employment of professional persons

    (a)   Except as otherwise provided in this section, the trustee, with the court's approval, may employ one or more attorneys, accountants, appraisers, auctioneers, or other professional persons, that do not hold or represent an interest adverse to the estate, and that are disinterested persons, to represent or assist the trustee in carrying out the trustee's duties under this title.

    (b)   If the trustee is authorized to operate the business of the debtor under section 721, 1202, or 1108 of this title, and if the debtor has regularly employed attorneys, accountants, or other professional persons on salary, the trustee may retain or replace such professional persons if necessary in the operation of such business.

    (c)   In a case under chapter 7, 12, or 11 of this title, a person is not disqualified for employment under this section solely because of such person's employment by or representation of a creditor, unless there is objection by another creditor or the United States trustee, in which case the court shall disapprove such employment if there is an actual conflict of interest.

    (d)   The court may authorize the trustee to act as attorney or accountant for the estate if such authorization is in the best interest of the estate.

    (e)   The trustee, with the court's approval, may employ, for a specified special purpose, other than to represent the trustee in conducting the case, an attorney that has represented the debtor, if in the best interest of the estate, and if such attorney does not represent or hold any interest adverse to the debtor or to the estate with respect to the matter on which such attorney is to be employed.

    (f)   The trustee may not employ a person that has served as an examiner in the case.

    (Pub.L. 95–598, Nov. 6, 1978, 92 Stat. 2563; Pub.L. 98–353, title III, § 430(c), July 10, 1984, 98 Stat. 370; Pub.L. 99–554, title II, §§ 210, 257(e), Oct. 27, 1986, 100 Stat. 3099, 3114.)

§ 328. Limitation on compensation of professional persons

    (a)   The trustee, or a committee appointed under section 1102 of this title, with the court's approval, may employ or authorize the employment of a professional person under section 327 or 1103 of this title, as the case may be, on any reasonable terms and conditions of employment, including on a retainer, on an hourly basis, on a fixed or percentage fee basis, or on a contingent fee basis. Notwithstanding such terms and conditions, the court may allow compensation different from the compensation provided under such terms and conditions after the conclusion of such employment, if such terms and conditions prove to have been improvident in light of developments not capable of being anticipated at the time of the fixing of such terms and conditions.

    (b)   If the court has authorized a trustee to serve as an attorney or accountant for the estate under section 327(d) of this title, the court may allow compensation for the trustee's services as such attorney or accountant only to the extent that the trustee performed services as attorney or accountant for the estate and not for performance of any of the trustee's duties that are generally performed by a trustee without the assistance of an attorney or accountant for the estate.

(c)   Except as provided in section 327(c), 327(e), or 1107(b) of this title, the court may deny allowance of compensation for services and reimbursement of expenses of a professional person employed under section 327 or 1103 of this title if, at any time during such professional person's employment under section 327 or 1103 of this title, such professional person is not a disinterested person, or represents or holds an interest adverse to the interest of the estate with respect to the matter on which such professional person is employed.

(Pub.L. 95–598, Nov. 6, 1978, 92 Stat. 2563; amended Pub.L. 98–353, title III, § 431, July 10, 1984, 98 Stat. 370; Pub.L. 109–8, title XII, § 1206, Apr. 20, 2005, 119 Stat. 194.)

§ 329.   Debtor's transactions with attorneys

(a)   Any attorney representing a debtor in a case under this title, or in connection with such a case, whether or not such attorney applies for compensation under this title, shall file with the court a statement of the compensation paid or agreed to be paid, if such payment or agreement was made after one year before the date of the filing of the petition, for services rendered or to be rendered in contemplation of or in connection with the case by such attorney, and the source of such compensation.

(b)   If such compensation exceeds the reasonable value of any such services, the court may cancel any such agreement, or order the return of any such payment, to the extent excessive, to—

(1)   the estate, if the property transferred—

(A)   would have been property of the estate; or

(B)   was to be paid by or on behalf of the debtor under a plan under chapter 11, 12, or 13 of this title; or

(2)   the entity that made such payment.

(Pub.L. 95–598, Nov. 6, 1978, 92 Stat. 2564; Pub.L. 98–353, title III, § 432, July 10, 1984, 98 Stat. 370; Pub.L. 99–554, title II, § 257(c), Oct. 27, 1986, 100 Stat. 3114.)

§ 330.   Compensation of officers

(a)(1)   After notice to the parties in interest and the United States Trustee and a hearing, and subject to sections 326, 328, and 329, the court may award to a trustee, a consumer privacy ombudsman appointed under section 332, an examiner, an ombudsman appointed under section 333, or a professional person employed under section 327 or 1103—

(A)   reasonable compensation for actual, necessary services rendered by the trustee, examiner, ombudsman, professional person, or attorney and by any paraprofessional person employed by any such person; and

(B)   reimbursement for actual, necessary expenses.

(2)   The court may, on its own motion or on the motion of the United States Trustee, the United States Trustee for the District or Region, the trustee for the estate, or any other party in interest, award compensation that is less than the amount of compensation that is requested.

(3)   In determining the amount of reasonable compensation to be awarded to an examiner, trustee under chapter 11, or professional person, the court shall consider the nature, the extent, and the value of such services, taking into account all relevant factors, including—

(A)   the time spent on such services;

(B)   the rates charged for such services;

(C)   whether the services were necessary to the administration of, or beneficial at the time at which the service was rendered toward the completion of, a case under this title;

(D) whether the services were performed within a reasonable amount of time commensurate with the complexity, importance, and nature of the problem, issue, or task addressed;

(E) with respect to a professional person, whether the person is board certified or otherwise has demonstrated skill and experience in the bankruptcy field; and

(F) whether the compensation is reasonable based on the customary compensation charged by comparably skilled practitioners in cases other than cases under this title.

(4)(A) Except as provided in subparagraph (B), the court shall not allow compensation for—

    (i) unnecessary duplication of services; or

    (ii) services that were not—

        (I) reasonably likely to benefit the debtor's estate; or

        (II) necessary to the administration of the case.

(B) In a chapter 12 or chapter 13 case in which the debtor is an individual, the court may allow reasonable compensation to the debtor's attorney for representing the interests of the debtor in connection with the bankruptcy case based on a consideration of the benefit and necessity of such services to the debtor and the other factors set forth in this section.

(5) The court shall reduce the amount of compensation awarded under this section by the amount of any interim compensation awarded under section 331, and, if the amount of such interim compensation exceeds the amount of compensation awarded under this section, may order the return of the excess to the estate.

(6) Any compensation awarded for the preparation of a fee application shall be based on the level and skill reasonably required to prepare the application.

(7) In determining the amount of reasonable compensation to be awarded to a trustee, the court shall treat such compensation as a commission, based on section 326.

(b)(1) There shall be paid from the filing fee in a case under chapter 7 of this title $45 to the trustee serving in such case, after such trustee's services are rendered.

(2) The Judicial Conference of the United States—

(A) shall prescribe additional fees of the same kind as prescribed under section 1914(b) of title 28; and

(B) may prescribe notice of appearance fees and fees charged against distributions in cases under this title;

to pay $15 to trustees serving in cases after such trustees' services are rendered. Beginning 1 year after the date of the enactment of the Bankruptcy Reform Act of 1994, such $15 shall be paid in addition to the amount paid under paragraph (1).

(c) Unless the court orders otherwise, in a case under chapter 12 or 13 of this title the compensation paid to the trustee serving in the case shall not be less than $5 per month from any distribution under the plan during the administration of the plan.

(d) In a case in which the United States trustee serves as trustee, the compensation of the trustee under this section shall be paid to the clerk of the bankruptcy court and deposited by the clerk into the United States Trustee System Fund established by section 589a of title 28.

(Pub.L. 95–598, Nov. 6, 1978, 92 Stat. 2564; Pub.L. 98–353, title III, §§ 433, 434, July 10, 1984, 98 Stat. 370; Pub.L. 99–554, title II, §§ 211, 257(f), Oct. 27, 1986, 100 Stat. 3099, 3114; Pub.L. 103–394, title I, § 117, title II, § 224(b), Oct. 22, 1994, 108 Stat. 4119, 4130; Pub.L. 109–8, title II, § 232(b), title IV, § 407, 415, title XI, § 1104(b), Apr. 20, 2005, 119 Stat. 74, 106, 107, 192.)

§ 331. Interim compensation

A trustee, an examiner, a debtor's attorney, or any professional person employed under section 327 or 1103 of this title may apply to the court not more than once every 120 days after an order for relief in a case under this title, or more often if the court permits, for such compensation for services rendered before the date of such an application or reimbursement for expenses incurred before such date as is provided under section 330 of this title. After notice and a hearing, the court may allow and disburse to such applicant such compensation or reimbursement.

(Pub.L. 95–598, Nov. 6, 1978, 92 Stat. 2564.)

§ 332. Consumer privacy ombudsman

(a) If a hearing is required under section 363(b)(1)(B), the court shall order the United States trustee to appoint, not later than 7 days before the commencement of the hearing, 1 disinterested person (other than the United States trustee) to serve as the consumer privacy ombudsman in the case and shall require that notice of such hearing be timely given to such ombudsman.

(b) The consumer privacy ombudsman may appear and be heard at such hearing and shall provide to the court information to assist the court in its consideration of the facts, circumstances, and conditions of the proposed sale or lease of personally identifiable information under section 363(b)(1)(B). Such information may include presentation of—

(1) the debtor's privacy policy;

(2) the potential losses or gains of privacy to consumers if such sale or such lease is approved by the court;

(3) the potential costs or benefits to consumers if such sale or such lease is approved by the court; and

(4) the potential alternatives that would mitigate potential privacy losses or potential costs to consumers.

(c) A consumer privacy ombudsman shall not disclose any personally identifiable information obtained by the ombudsman under this title.

(Added Pub.L. 109–8, title II, § 232(a), Apr. 20, 2005, 119 Stat. 73, and amended Pub.L. 111–16, § 2(3), May 7, 2009, 123 Stat. 1607.)

§ 333. Appointment of patient care ombudsman

(a)(1) If the debtor in a case under chapter 7, 9, or 11 is a health care business, the court shall order, not later than 30 days after the commencement of the case, the appointment of an ombudsman to monitor the quality of patient care and to represent the interests of the patients of the health care business unless the court finds that the appointment of such ombudsman is not necessary for the protection of patients under the specific facts of the case.

(2)(A) If the court orders the appointment of an ombudsman under paragraph (1), the United States trustee shall appoint 1 disinterested person (other than the United States trustee) to serve as such ombudsman.

(B) If the debtor is a health care business that provides long-term care, then the United States trustee may appoint the State Long-Term Care Ombudsman appointed under the Older Americans Act of 1965 for the State in which the case is pending to serve as the ombudsman required by paragraph (1).

(C) If the United States trustee does not appoint a State Long-Term Care Ombudsman under subparagraph (B), the court shall notify the State Long-Term Care Ombudsman appointed under the Older Americans Act of 1965 for the State in which the case is pending, of the name and address of the person who is appointed under subparagraph (A).

(b) An ombudsman appointed under subsection (a) shall—

    (1)   monitor the quality of patient care provided to patients of the debtor, to the extent necessary under the circumstances, including interviewing patients and physicians;

    (2)   not later than 60 days after the date of appointment, and not less frequently than at 60-day intervals thereafter, report to the court after notice to the parties in interest, at a hearing or in writing, regarding the quality of patient care provided to patients of the debtor; and

    (3)   if such ombudsman determines that the quality of patient care provided to patients of the debtor is declining significantly or is otherwise being materially compromised, file with the court a motion or a written report, with notice to the parties in interest immediately upon making such determination.

  (c)(1)   An ombudsman appointed under subsection (a) shall maintain any information obtained by such ombudsman under this section that relates to patients (including information relating to patient records) as confidential information. Such ombudsman may not review confidential patient records unless the court approves such review in advance and imposes restrictions on such ombudsman to protect the confidentiality of such records.

    (2)   An ombudsman appointed under subsection (a)(2)(B) shall have access to patient records consistent with authority of such ombudsman under the Older Americans Act of 1965 and under non-Federal laws governing the State Long-Term Care Ombudsman program.

    (Pub.L. 109–8, title XI, § 1104(a)(1), Apr. 20, 2005, 119 Stat. 191.)

SUBCHAPTER III—ADMINISTRATION

§ 341.   Meetings of creditors and equity security holders

  (a)   Within a reasonable time after the order for relief in a case under this title, the United States trustee shall convene and preside at a meeting of creditors.

  (b)   The United States trustee may convene a meeting of any equity security holders.

  (c)   The court may not preside at, and may not attend, any meeting under this section including any final meeting of creditors. Notwithstanding any local court rule, provision of a State constitution, any otherwise applicable nonbankruptcy law, or any other requirement that representation at the meeting of creditors under subsection (a) be by an attorney, a creditor holding a consumer debt or any representative of the creditor (which may include an entity or an employee of an entity and may be a representative for more than 1 creditor) shall be permitted to appear at and participate in the meeting of creditors in a case under chapter 7 or 13, either alone or in conjunction with an attorney for the creditor. Nothing in this subsection shall be construed to require any creditor to be represented by an attorney at any meeting of creditors.

  (d)   Prior to the conclusion of the meeting of creditors or equity security holders, the trustee shall orally examine the debtor to ensure that the debtor in a case under chapter 7 of this title is aware of—

    (1)   the potential consequences of seeking a discharge in bankruptcy, including the effects on credit history;

    (2)   the debtor's ability to file a petition under a different chapter of this title;

    (3)   the effect of receiving a discharge of debts under this title; and

    (4)   the effect of reaffirming a debt, including the debtor's knowledge of the provisions of section 524(d) of this title.

  (e)   Notwithstanding subsections (a) and (b), the court, on the request of a party in interest and after notice and a hearing, for cause may order that the United States trustee not convene a meeting of creditors or equity security holders if the debtor has filed a plan as to which the debtor solicited acceptances prior to the commencement of the case.

(Pub.L. 95–598, Nov. 6, 1978, 92 Stat. 2564; Pub.L. 99–554, title II, § 212, Oct. 27, 1986, 100 Stat. 3099; Pub.L. 103–394, title I, § 115, Oct. 22, 1994, 108 Stat. 4118; Pub.L. 109–8, title IV, §§ 402, 413, Apr. 20, 2005, 119 Stat. 104, 107.)

§ 342. Notice

(a) There shall be given such notice as is appropriate, including notice to any holder of a community claim, of an order for relief in a case under this title.

(b) Before the commencement of a case under this title by an individual whose debts are primarily consumer debts, the clerk shall give to such individual written notice containing—

(1) a brief description of—

(A) chapters 7, 11, 12, and 13 and the general purpose, benefits, and costs of proceeding under each of those chapters; and

(B) the types of services available from credit counseling agencies; and

(2) statements specifying that—

(A) a person who knowingly and fraudulently conceals assets or makes a false oath or statement under penalty of perjury in connection with a case under this title shall be subject to fine, imprisonment, or both; and

(B) all information supplied by a debtor in connection with a case under this title is subject to examination by the Attorney General.

(c)(1) If notice is required to be given by the debtor to a creditor under this title, any rule, any applicable law, or any order of the court, such notice shall contain the name, address, and last 4 digits of the taxpayer identification number of the debtor. If the notice concerns an amendment that adds a creditor to the schedules of assets and liabilities, the debtor shall include the full taxpayer identification number in the notice sent to that creditor, but the debtor shall include only the last 4 digits of the taxpayer identification number in the copy of the notice filed with the court.

(2)(A) If, within the 90 days before the commencement of a voluntary case, a creditor supplies the debtor in at least 2 communications sent to the debtor with the current account number of the debtor and the address at which such creditor requests to receive correspondence, then any notice required by this title to be sent by the debtor to such creditor shall be sent to such address and shall include such account number.

(B) If a creditor would be in violation of applicable nonbankruptcy law by sending any such communication within such 90-day period and if such creditor supplies the debtor in the last 2 communications with the current account number of the debtor and the address at which such creditor requests to receive correspondence, then any notice required by this title to be sent by the debtor to such creditor shall be sent to such address and shall include such account number.

(d) In a case under chapter 7 of this title in which the debtor is an individual and in which the presumption of abuse arises under section 707(b), the clerk shall give written notice to all creditors not later than 10 days after the date of the filing of the petition that the presumption of abuse has arisen.

(e)(1) In a case under chapter 7 or 13 of this title of a debtor who is an individual, a creditor at any time may both file with the court and serve on the debtor a notice of address to be used to provide notice in such case to such creditor.

(2) Any notice in such case required to be provided to such creditor by the debtor or the court later than 7 days after the court and the debtor receive such creditor's notice of address, shall be provided to such address.

(f)(1) An entity may file with any bankruptcy court a notice of address to be used by all the bankruptcy courts or by particular bankruptcy courts, as so specified by such entity at the time such notice is filed, to provide notice to such entity in all cases under chapters 7 and 13 pending in the courts with respect to which such notice is filed, in which such entity is a creditor.

(2)　In any case filed under chapter 7 or 13, any notice required to be provided by a court with respect to which a notice is filed under paragraph (1), to such entity later than 30 days after the filing of such notice under paragraph (1) shall be provided to such address unless with respect to a particular case a different address is specified in a notice filed and served in accordance with subsection (e).

(3)　A notice filed under paragraph (1) may be withdrawn by such entity.

(g)(1)　Notice provided to a creditor by the debtor or the court other than in accordance with this section (excluding this subsection) shall not be effective notice until such notice is brought to the attention of such creditor. If such creditor designates a person or an organizational subdivision of such creditor to be responsible for receiving notices under this title and establishes reasonable procedures so that such notices receivable by such creditor are to be delivered to such person or such subdivision, then a notice provided to such creditor other than in accordance with this section (excluding this subsection) shall not be considered to have been brought to the attention of such creditor until such notice is received by such person or such subdivision.

(2)　A monetary penalty may not be imposed on a creditor for a violation of a stay in effect under section 362(a) (including a monetary penalty imposed under section 362(k)) or for failure to comply with section 542 or 543 unless the conduct that is the basis of such violation or of such failure occurs after such creditor receives notice effective under this section of the order for relief.

(Pub.L. 95–598, Nov. 6, 1978, 92 Stat. 2565; Pub.L. 98–353, title III, §§ 302, 435, July 10, 1984, 98 Stat. 352, 370; Pub.L. 103–394, title II, § 225, Oct. 22, 1994, 108 Stat. 4131; Pub.L. 109–8, title I, § 102(d), 104, title II, § 234(b), title III, § 315(a), Apr. 20, 2005, 119 Stat. 33, 35, 75, 88; Pub.L. 111–16, § 2(4), May 7, 2009, 123 Stat. 1607.)

§ 343.　Examination of the debtor

The debtor shall appear and submit to examination under oath at the meeting of creditors under section 341(a) of this title. Creditors, any indenture trustee, any trustee or examiner in the case, or the United States trustee may examine the debtor. The United States trustee may administer the oath required under this section.

(Pub.L. 95–598, Nov. 6, 1978, 92 Stat. 2565; Pub.L. 98–353, title III, § 436, July 10, 1984, 98 Stat. 370; Pub.L. 99–554, title II, § 213, Oct. 27, 1986, 100 Stat. 3099.)

§ 344.　Self-incrimination; immunity

Immunity for persons required to submit to examination, to testify, or to provide information in a case under this title may be granted under part V of title 18.

(Pub.L. 95–598, Nov. 6, 1978, 92 Stat. 2565.)

§ 345.　Money of estates

(a)　A trustee in a case under this title may make such deposit or investment of the money of the estate for which such trustee serves as will yield the maximum reasonable net return on such money, taking into account the safety of such deposit or investment.

(b)　Except with respect to a deposit or investment that is insured or guaranteed by the United States or by a department, agency, or instrumentality of the United States or backed by the full faith and credit of the United States, the trustee shall require from an entity with which such money is deposited or invested—

(1)　a bond—

(A)　in favor of the United States;

(B)　secured by the undertaking of a corporate surety approved by the United States trustee for the district in which the case is pending; and

(C)　conditioned on—

(i) a proper accounting for all money so deposited or invested and for any return on such money;

(ii) prompt repayment of such money and return; and

(iii) faithful performance of duties as a depository; or

(2) the deposit of securities of the kind specified in section 9303 of title 31;

unless the court for cause orders otherwise.

(c) An entity with which such moneys are deposited or invested is authorized to deposit or invest such moneys as may be required under this section.

(Pub.L. 95–598, Nov. 6, 1978, 92 Stat. 2565; Pub.L. 97–258, § 3(c), Sept. 13, 1982, 96 Stat. 1064; Pub.L. 98–353, title III, § 437, July 10, 1984, 98 Stat. 370; Pub.L. 99–554, title II, § 214, Oct. 27, 1986, 100 Stat. 3099; Pub.L. 103–394, title II, § 210, Oct. 22, 1994, 108 Stat. 4125.)

§ 346. Special provisions related to the treatment of State and local taxes

(a) Whenever the Internal Revenue Code of 1986 provides that a separate taxable estate or entity is created in a case concerning a debtor under this title, and the income, gain, loss, deductions, and credits of such estate shall be taxed to or claimed by the estate, a separate taxable estate is also created for purposes of any State and local law imposing a tax on or measured by income and such income, gain, loss, deductions, and credits shall be taxed to or claimed by the estate and may not be taxed to or claimed by the debtor. The preceding sentence shall not apply if the case is dismissed. The trustee shall make tax returns of income required under any such State or local law.

(b) Whenever the Internal Revenue Code of 1986 provides that no separate taxable estate shall be created in a case concerning a debtor under this title, and the income, gain, loss, deductions, and credits of an estate shall be taxed to or claimed by the debtor, such income, gain, loss, deductions, and credits shall be taxed to or claimed by the debtor under a State or local law imposing a tax on or measured by income and may not be taxed to or claimed by the estate. The trustee shall make such tax returns of income of corporations and of partnerships as are required under any State or local law, but with respect to partnerships, shall make such returns only to the extent such returns are also required to be made under such Code. The estate shall be liable for any tax imposed on such corporation or partnership, but not for any tax imposed on partners or members.

(c) With respect to a partnership or any entity treated as a partnership under a State or local law imposing a tax on or measured by income that is a debtor in a case under this title, any gain or loss resulting from a distribution of property from such partnership, or any distributive share of any income, gain, loss, deduction, or credit of a partner or member that is distributed, or considered distributed, from such partnership, after the commencement of the case, is gain, loss, income, deduction, or credit, as the case may be, of the partner or member, and if such partner or member is a debtor in a case under this title, shall be subject to tax in accordance with subsection (a) or (b).

(d) For purposes of any State or local law imposing a tax on or measured by income, the taxable period of a debtor in a case under this title shall terminate only if and to the extent that the taxable period of such debtor terminates under the Internal Revenue Code of 1986.

(e) The estate in any case described in subsection (a) shall use the same accounting method as the debtor used immediately before the commencement of the case, if such method of accounting complies with applicable nonbankruptcy tax law.

(f) For purposes of any State or local law imposing a tax on or measured by income, a transfer of property from the debtor to the estate or from the estate to the debtor shall not be treated as a disposition for purposes of any provision assigning tax consequences to a disposition, except to the extent that such transfer is treated as a disposition under the Internal Revenue Code of 1986.

(g) Whenever a tax is imposed pursuant to a State or local law imposing a tax on or measured by income pursuant to subsection (a) or (b), such tax shall be imposed at rates generally applicable to the same types of entities under such State or local law.

(h) The trustee shall withhold from any payment of claims for wages, salaries, commissions, dividends, interest, or other payments, or collect, any amount required to be withheld or collected under applicable State or local tax law, and shall pay such withheld or collected amount to the appropriate governmental unit at the time and in the manner required by such tax law, and with the same priority as the claim from which such amount was withheld or collected was paid.

(i)(1) To the extent that any State or local law imposing a tax on or measured by income provides for the carryover of any tax attribute from one taxable period to a subsequent taxable period, the estate shall succeed to such tax attribute in any case in which such estate is subject to tax under subsection (a).

    (2) After such a case is closed or dismissed, the debtor shall succeed to any tax attribute to which the estate succeeded under paragraph (1) to the extent consistent with the Internal Revenue Code of 1986.

    (3) The estate may carry back any loss or tax attribute to a taxable period of the debtor that ended before the date of the order for relief under this title to the extent that—

        (A) applicable State or local tax law provides for a carryback in the case of the debtor; and

        (B) the same or a similar tax attribute may be carried back by the estate to such a taxable period of the debtor under the Internal Revenue Code of 1986.

(j)(1) For purposes of any State or local law imposing a tax on or measured by income, income is not realized by the estate, the debtor, or a successor to the debtor by reason of discharge of indebtedness in a case under this title, except to the extent, if any, that such income is subject to tax under the Internal Revenue Code of 1986.

    (2) Whenever the Internal Revenue Code of 1986 provides that the amount excluded from gross income in respect of the discharge of indebtedness in a case under this title shall be applied to reduce the tax attributes of the debtor or the estate, a similar reduction shall be made under any State or local law imposing a tax on or measured by income to the extent such State or local law recognizes such attributes. Such State or local law may also provide for the reduction of other attributes to the extent that the full amount of income from the discharge of indebtedness has not been applied.

(k)(1) Except as provided in this section and section 505, the time and manner of filing tax returns and the items of income, gain, loss, deduction, and credit of any taxpayer shall be determined under applicable nonbankruptcy law.

    (2) For Federal tax purposes, the provisions of this section are subject to the Internal Revenue Code of 1986 and other applicable Federal nonbankruptcy law.

    (Pub.L. 95–598, Nov. 6, 1978, 92 Stat. 2565; Pub.L. 98–353, title III, § 438, July 10, 1984, 98 Stat. 370; Pub.L. 99–554, title II, §§ 257(g), 283(c), Oct. 27, 1986, 100 Stat. 3114, 3116; Pub.L. 103–394, title V, § 501(d)(4), Oct. 22, 1994, 108 Stat. 4143; Pub.L. 109–8, title VII, § 719(a)(1), Apr. 20, 2005, 119 Stat. 131.)

§ 347. Unclaimed property

(a) Ninety days after the final distribution under section 726, 1226, or 1326 of this title in a case under chapter 7, 12, or 13 of this title, as the case may be, the trustee shall stop payment on any check remaining unpaid, and any remaining property of the estate shall be paid into the court and disposed of under chapter 129 of title 28.

(b) Any security, money, or other property remaining unclaimed at the expiration of the time allowed in a case under chapter 9, 11, or 12 of this title for the presentation of a security or the performance of any other act as a condition to participation in the distribution under any plan confirmed under section 943(b), 1129, 1173, or 1225 of this title, as the case may be, becomes the property of the debtor or of the entity acquiring the assets of the debtor under the plan, as the case may be.

    (Pub.L. 95–598, Nov. 6, 1978, 92 Stat. 2568; Pub.L. 99–554, title II, § 257(h), Oct. 27, 1986, 100 Stat. 3114.)

§ 348. Effect of conversion

(a) Conversion of a case from a case under one chapter of this title to a case under another chapter of this title constitutes an order for relief under the chapter to which the case is converted, but, except as provided in subsections (b) and (c) of this section, does not effect a change in the date of the filing of the petition, the commencement of the case, or the order for relief.

(b) Unless the court for cause orders otherwise, in sections 701(a), 727(a)(10), 727(b), 1102(a), 1110(a)(1), 1121(b), 1121(c), 1141(d)(4), 1201(a), 1221, 1228(a), 1301(a), and 1305(a) of this title, "the order for relief under this chapter" in a chapter to which a case has been converted under section 706, 1112, 1208, or 1307 of this title means the conversion of such case to such chapter.

(c) Sections 342 and 365(d) of this title apply in a case that has been converted under section 706, 1112, 1208, or 1307 of this title, as if the conversion order were the order for relief.

(d) A claim against the estate or the debtor that arises after the order for relief but before conversion in a case that is converted under section 1112, 1208, or 1307 of this title, other than a claim specified in section 503(b) of this title, shall be treated for all purposes as if such claim had arisen immediately before the date of the filing of the petition.

(e) Conversion of a case under section 706, 1112, 1208, or 1307 of this title terminates the service of any trustee or examiner that is serving in the case before such conversion.

(f)(1) Except as provided in paragraph (2), when a case under chapter 13 of this title is converted to a case under another chapter under this title—

> **(A)** property of the estate in the converted case shall consist of property of the estate, as of the date of filing of the petition, that remains in the possession of or is under the control of the debtor on the date of conversion;

> **(B)** valuations of property and of allowed secured claims in the chapter 13 case shall apply only in a case converted to a case under chapter 11 or 12, but not in a case converted to a case under chapter 7, with allowed secured claims in cases under chapters 11 and 12 reduced to the extent that they have been paid in accordance with the chapter 13 plan; and

> **(C)** with respect to cases converted from chapter 13—

>> **(i)** the claim of any creditor holding security as of the date of the filing of the petition shall continue to be secured by that security unless the full amount of such claim determined under applicable nonbankruptcy law has been paid in full as of the date of conversion, notwithstanding any valuation or determination of the amount of an allowed secured claim made for the purposes of the case under chapter 13; and

>> **(ii)** unless a prebankruptcy default has been fully cured under the plan at the time of conversion, in any proceeding under this title or otherwise, the default shall have the effect given under applicable nonbankruptcy law.

(2) If the debtor converts a case under chapter 13 of this title to a case under another chapter under this title in bad faith, the property of the estate in the converted case shall consist of the property of the estate as of the date of conversion.

(Pub.L. 95–598, Nov. 6, 1978, 92 Stat. 2568; Pub.L. 99–554, title II, § 257(i), Oct. 27, 1986, 100 Stat. 3115; Pub.L. 103–394, title III, § 311, title V, § 501(d)(5), Oct. 22, 1994, 108 Stat. 4138, 4144; Pub.L. 109–8, title III, § 309(a), title XII, § 1207, Apr. 20, 2005, 119 Stat. 82, 194; Pub.L. 111–327, § 2(a)(11), Dec. 22, 2010, 124 Stat. 3558.)

§ 349. Effect of dismissal

(a) Unless the court, for cause, orders otherwise, the dismissal of a case under this title does not bar the discharge, in a later case under this title, of debts that were dischargeable in the case dismissed; nor does the dismissal of a case under this title prejudice the debtor with regard to the filing of a subsequent petition under this title, except as provided in section 109(g) of this title.

(b) Unless the court, for cause, orders otherwise, a dismissal of a case other than under section 742 of this title—

    (1) reinstates—

        (A) any proceeding or custodianship superseded under section 543 of this title;

        (B) any transfer avoided under section 522, 544, 545, 547, 548, 549, or 724(a) of this title, or preserved under section 510(c)(2), 522(i)(2), or 551 of this title; and

        (C) any lien voided under section 506(d) of this title;

    (2) vacates any order, judgment, or transfer ordered, under section 522(i)(1), 542, 550, or 553 of this title; and

    (3) revests the property of the estate in the entity in which such property was vested immediately before the commencement of the case under this title.

(Pub.L. 95–598, Nov. 6, 1978, 92 Stat. 2569; Pub.L. 98–353, title III, § 303, July 10, 1984, 98 Stat. 352; Pub.L. 103–394, title V, § 501(d)(6), Oct. 22, 1994, 108 Stat. 4144.)

§ 350. Closing and reopening cases

(a) After an estate is fully administered and the court has discharged the trustee, the court shall close the case.

(b) A case may be reopened in the court in which such case was closed to administer assets, to accord relief to the debtor, or for other cause.

(Pub.L. 95–598, Nov. 6, 1978, 92 Stat. 2569; Pub.L. 98–353, title III, § 439, July 10, 1984, 98 Stat. 370.)

§ 351. Disposal of patient records

If a health care business commences a case under chapter 7, 9, or 11, and the trustee does not have a sufficient amount of funds to pay for the storage of patient records in the manner required under applicable Federal or State law, the following requirements shall apply:

    (1) The trustee shall—

        (A) promptly publish notice, in 1 or more appropriate newspapers, that if patient records are not claimed by the patient or an insurance provider (if applicable law permits the insurance provider to make that claim) by the date that is 365 days after the date of that notification, the trustee will destroy the patient records; and

        (B) during the first 180 days of the 365-day period described in subparagraph (A), promptly attempt to notify directly each patient that is the subject of the patient records and appropriate insurance carrier concerning the patient records by mailing to the most recent known address of that patient, or a family member or contact person for that patient, and to the appropriate insurance carrier an appropriate notice regarding the claiming or disposing of patient records.

    (2) If, after providing the notification under paragraph (1), patient records are not claimed during the 365-day period described under that paragraph, the trustee shall mail, by certified mail, at the end of such 365-day period a written request to each appropriate Federal agency to request permission from that agency to deposit the patient records with that agency, except that no Federal agency is required to accept patient records under this paragraph.

    (3) If, following the 365-day period described in paragraph (2) and after providing the notification under paragraph (1), patient records are not claimed by a patient or insurance provider, or request is not granted by a Federal agency to deposit such records with that agency, the trustee shall destroy those records by—

        (A) if the records are written, shredding or burning the records; or

(B) if the records are magnetic, optical, or other electronic records, by otherwise destroying those records so that those records cannot be retrieved.

(Added Pub.L. 109–8, title XI, § 1102(a), Apr. 20, 2005, 119 Stat. 189.)

SUBCHAPTER IV—ADMINISTRATIVE POWERS

§ 361. Adequate protection

When adequate protection is required under section 362, 363, or 364 of this title of an interest of an entity in property, such adequate protection may be provided by—

(1) requiring the trustee to make a cash payment or periodic cash payments to such entity, to the extent that the stay under section 362 of this title, use, sale, or lease under section 363 of this title, or any grant of a lien under section 364 of this title results in a decrease in the value of such entity's interest in such property;

(2) providing to such entity an additional or replacement lien to the extent that such stay, use, sale, lease, or grant results in a decrease in the value of such entity's interest in such property; or

(3) granting such other relief, other than entitling such entity to compensation allowable under section 503(b)(1) of this title as an administrative expense, as will result in the realization by such entity of the indubitable equivalent of such entity's interest in such property.

(Pub.L. 95–598, Nov. 6, 1978, 92 Stat. 2569; Pub.L. 98–353, title III, § 440, July 10, 1984, 98 Stat. 370.)

§ 362. Automatic stay

(a) Except as provided in subsection (b) of this section, a petition filed under section 301, 302, or 303 of this title, or an application filed under section 5(a)(3) of the Securities Investor Protection Act of 1970, operates as a stay, applicable to all entities, of—

(1) the commencement or continuation, including the issuance or employment of process, of a judicial, administrative, or other action or proceeding against the debtor that was or could have been commenced before the commencement of the case under this title, or to recover a claim against the debtor that arose before the commencement of the case under this title;

(2) the enforcement, against the debtor or against property of the estate, of a judgment obtained before the commencement of the case under this title;

(3) any act to obtain possession of property of the estate or of property from the estate or to exercise control over property of the estate;

(4) any act to create, perfect, or enforce any lien against property of the estate;

(5) any act to create, perfect, or enforce against property of the debtor any lien to the extent that such lien secures a claim that arose before the commencement of the case under this title;

(6) any act to collect, assess, or recover a claim against the debtor that arose before the commencement of the case under this title;

(7) the setoff of any debt owing to the debtor that arose before the commencement of the case under this title against any claim against the debtor; and

(8) the commencement or continuation of a proceeding before the United States Tax Court concerning a tax liability of a debtor that is a corporation for a taxable period the bankruptcy court may determine or concerning the tax liability of a debtor who is an individual for a taxable period ending before the date of the order for relief under this title.

(b) The filing of a petition under section 301, 302, or 303 of this title, or of an application under section 5(a)(3) of the Securities Investor Protection Act of 1970, does not operate as a stay—

(1) under subsection (a) of this section, of the commencement or continuation of a criminal action or proceeding against the debtor;

(2) under subsection (a)—

(A) of the commencement or continuation of a civil action or proceeding—

(i) for the establishment of paternity;

(ii) for the establishment or modification of an order for domestic support obligations;

(iii) concerning child custody or visitation;

(iv) for the dissolution of a marriage, except to the extent that such proceeding seeks to determine the division of property that is property of the estate; or

(v) regarding domestic violence;

(B) of the collection of a domestic support obligation from property that is not property of the estate;

(C) with respect to the withholding of income that is property of the estate or property of the debtor for payment of a domestic support obligation under a judicial or administrative order or a statute;

(D) of the withholding, suspension, or restriction of a driver's license, a professional or occupational license, or a recreational license, under State law, as specified in section 466(a)(16) of the Social Security Act;

(E) of the reporting of overdue support owed by a parent to any consumer reporting agency as specified in section 466(a)(7) of the Social Security Act;

(F) of the interception of a tax refund, as specified in sections 464 and 466(a)(3) of the Social Security Act or under an analogous State law; or

(G) of the enforcement of a medical obligation, as specified under title IV of the Social Security Act;

(3) under subsection (a) of this section, of any act to perfect, or to maintain or continue the perfection of, an interest in property to the extent that the trustee's rights and powers are subject to such perfection under section 546(b) of this title or to the extent that such act is accomplished within the period provided under section 547(e)(2)(A) of this title;

(4) under paragraph (1), (2), (3), or (6) of subsection (a) of this section, of the commencement or continuation of an action or proceeding by a governmental unit or any organization exercising authority under the Convention on the Prohibition of the Development, Production, Stockpiling and Use of Chemical Weapons and on Their Destruction, opened for signature on January 13, 1993, to enforce such governmental unit's or organization's police and regulatory power, including the enforcement of a judgment other than a money judgment, obtained in an action or proceeding by the governmental unit to enforce such governmental unit's or organization's police or regulatory power;

[(5) Repealed. Pub.L. 105–277, div. I, title VI, § 603(1), Oct. 21, 1998, 112 Stat. 2681–886;]

(6) under subsection (a) of this section, of the exercise by a commodity broker, forward contract merchant, stockbroker, financial institution, financial participant, or securities clearing agency of any contractual right (as defined in section 555 or 556) under any security agreement or arrangement or other credit enhancement forming a part of or related to any commodity contract, forward contract or securities contract, or of any contractual right (as defined in section 555 or 556) to offset or net out any termination value, payment amount, or other transfer obligation arising under or in connection with 1 or more such contracts, including any master agreement for such contracts;

(7) under subsection (a) of this section, of the exercise by a repo participant or financial participant of any contractual right (as defined in section 559) under any security agreement or arrangement or other credit enhancement forming a part of or related to any repurchase agreement, or of any contractual right (as defined in section 559) to offset or net out any termination value, payment amount, or other transfer obligation arising under or in connection with 1 or more such agreements, including any master agreement for such agreements;

(8) under subsection (a) of this section, of the commencement of any action by the Secretary of Housing and Urban Development to foreclose a mortgage or deed of trust in any case in which the mortgage or deed of trust held by the Secretary is insured or was formerly insured under the National Housing Act and covers property, or combinations of property, consisting of five or more living units;

(9) under subsection (a), of—

(A) an audit by a governmental unit to determine tax liability;

(B) the issuance to the debtor by a governmental unit of a notice of tax deficiency;

(C) a demand for tax returns; or

(D) the making of an assessment for any tax and issuance of a notice and demand for payment of such an assessment (but any tax lien that would otherwise attach to property of the estate by reason of such an assessment shall not take effect unless such tax is a debt of the debtor that will not be discharged in the case and such property or its proceeds are transferred out of the estate to, or otherwise revested in, the debtor).

(10) under subsection (a) of this section, of any act by a lessor to the debtor under a lease of nonresidential real property that has terminated by the expiration of the stated term of the lease before the commencement of or during a case under this title to obtain possession of such property;

(11) under subsection (a) of this section, of the presentment of a negotiable instrument and the giving of notice of and protesting dishonor of such an instrument;

(12) under subsection (a) of this section, after the date which is 90 days after the filing of such petition, of the commencement or continuation, and conclusion to the entry of final judgment, of an action which involves a debtor subject to reorganization pursuant to chapter 11 of this title and which was brought by the Secretary of Transportation under section 31325 of title 46 (including distribution of any proceeds of sale) to foreclose a preferred ship or fleet mortgage, or a security interest in or relating to a vessel or vessel under construction, held by the Secretary of Transportation under chapter 537 of title 46 or section 109(h) of title 49, or under applicable State law;

(13) under subsection (a) of this section, after the date which is 90 days after the filing of such petition, of the commencement or continuation, and conclusion to the entry of final judgment, of an action which involves a debtor subject to reorganization pursuant to chapter 11 of this title and which was brought by the Secretary of Commerce under section 31325 of title 46 (including distribution of any proceeds of sale) to foreclose a preferred ship or fleet mortgage in a vessel or a mortgage, deed of trust, or other security interest in a fishing facility held by the Secretary of Commerce under chapter 537 of title 46;

(14) under subsection (a) of this section, of any action by an accrediting agency regarding the accreditation status of the debtor as an educational institution;

(15) under subsection (a) of this section, of any action by a State licensing body regarding the licensure of the debtor as an educational institution;

(16) under subsection (a) of this section, of any action by a guaranty agency, as defined in section 435(j) of the Higher Education Act of 1965 or the Secretary of Education regarding the eligibility of the debtor to participate in programs authorized under such Act;

(17) under subsection (a) of this section, of the exercise by a swap participant or financial participant of any contractual right (as defined in section 560) under any security agreement or arrangement or other credit enhancement forming a part of or related to any swap agreement, or of any contractual right (as defined in section 560) to offset or net out any termination value, payment amount, or other transfer obligation arising under or in connection with 1 or more such agreements, including any master agreement for such agreements;

(18) under subsection (a) of the creation or perfection of a statutory lien for an ad valorem property tax, or a special tax or special assessment on real property whether or not ad valorem, imposed by a governmental unit, if such tax or assessment comes due after the date of the filing of the petition;

(19) under subsection (a), of withholding of income from a debtor's wages and collection of amounts withheld, under the debtor's agreement authorizing that withholding and collection for the benefit of a pension, profit-sharing, stock bonus, or other plan established under section 401, 403, 408, 408A, 414, 457, or 501(c) of the Internal Revenue Code of 1986, that is sponsored by the employer of the debtor, or an affiliate, successor, or predecessor of such employer—

    (A) to the extent that the amounts withheld and collected are used solely for payments relating to a loan from a plan under section 408(b)(1) of the Employee Retirement Income Security Act of 1974 or is subject to section 72(p) of the Internal Revenue Code of 1986; or

    (B) a loan from a thrift savings plan permitted under subchapter III of chapter 84 of title 5, that satisfies the requirements of section 8433(g) of such title;

but nothing in this paragraph may be construed to provide that any loan made under a governmental plan under section 414(d), or a contract or account under section 403(b), of the Internal Revenue Code of 1986 constitutes a claim or a debt under this title;

(20) under subsection (a), of any act to enforce any lien against or security interest in real property following entry of the order under subsection (d)(4) as to such real property in any prior case under this title, for a period of 2 years after the date of the entry of such an order, except that the debtor, in a subsequent case under this title, may move for relief from such order based upon changed circumstances or for other good cause shown, after notice and a hearing;

(21) under subsection (a), of any act to enforce any lien against or security interest in real property—

    (A) if the debtor is ineligible under section 109(g) to be a debtor in a case under this title; or

    (B) if the case under this title was filed in violation of a bankruptcy court order in a prior case under this title prohibiting the debtor from being a debtor in another case under this title;

(22) subject to subsection (*l*), under subsection (a)(3), of the continuation of any eviction, unlawful detainer action, or similar proceeding by a lessor against a debtor involving residential property in which the debtor resides as a tenant under a lease or rental agreement and with respect to which the lessor has obtained before the date of the filing of the bankruptcy petition, a judgment for possession of such property against the debtor;

(23) subject to subsection (m), under subsection (a)(3), of an eviction action that seeks possession of the residential property in which the debtor resides as a tenant under a lease or rental agreement based on endangerment of such property or the illegal use of controlled substances on such property, but only if the lessor files with the court, and serves upon the debtor, a certification under penalty of perjury that such an eviction action has been filed, or that the debtor, during the 30-day period preceding the date of the filing of the certification, has endangered property or illegally used or allowed to be used a controlled substance on the property;

(24) under subsection (a), of any transfer that is not avoidable under section 544 and that is not avoidable under section 549;

(25) under subsection (a), of—

    (A) the commencement or continuation of an investigation or action by a securities self regulatory organization to enforce such organization's regulatory power;

    (B) the enforcement of an order or decision, other than for monetary sanctions, obtained in an action by such securities self regulatory organization to enforce such organization's regulatory power; or

    (C) any act taken by such securities self regulatory organization to delist, delete, or refuse to permit quotation of any stock that does not meet applicable regulatory requirements;

(26) under subsection (a), of the setoff under applicable nonbankruptcy law of an income tax refund, by a governmental unit, with respect to a taxable period that ended before the date of the order for relief against an income tax liability for a taxable period that also ended before the date of the order for relief, except that in any case in which the setoff of an income tax refund is not permitted under applicable nonbankruptcy law because of a pending action to determine the amount or legality of a tax liability, the governmental unit may hold the refund pending the resolution of the action, unless the court, on the motion of the trustee and after notice and a hearing, grants the taxing authority adequate protection (within the meaning of section 361) for the secured claim of such authority in the setoff under section 506(a);

(27) under subsection (a) of this section, of the exercise by a master netting agreement participant of any contractual right (as defined in section 555, 556, 559, or 560) under any security agreement or arrangement or other credit enhancement forming a part of or related to any master netting agreement, or of any contractual right (as defined in section 555, 556, 559, or 560) to offset or net out any termination value, payment amount, or other transfer obligation arising under or in connection with 1 or more such master netting agreements to the extent that such participant is eligible to exercise such rights under paragraph (6), (7), or (17) for each individual contract covered by the master netting agreement in issue; and

(28) under subsection (a), of the exclusion by the Secretary of Health and Human Services of the debtor from participation in the medicare program or any other Federal health care program (as defined in section 1128B(f) of the Social Security Act pursuant to title XI or XVIII of such Act).

The provisions of paragraphs (12) and (13) of this subsection shall apply with respect to any such petition filed on or before December 31, 1989.

(c)   Except as provided in subsections (d), (e), (f), and (h) of this section—

(1)   the stay of an act against property of the estate under subsection (a) of this section continues until such property is no longer property of the estate;

(2)   the stay of any other act under subsection (a) of this section continues until the earliest of—

(A)   the time the case is closed;

(B)   the time the case is dismissed; or

(C)   if the case is a case under chapter 7 of this title concerning an individual or a case under chapter 9, 11, 12, or 13 of this title, the time a discharge is granted or denied;

(3)   if a single or joint case is filed by or against a debtor who is an individual in a case under chapter 7, 11, or 13, and if a single or joint case of the debtor was pending within the preceding 1-year period but was dismissed, other than a case refiled under a chapter other than chapter 7 after dismissal under section 707(b)—

(A)   the stay under subsection (a) with respect to any action taken with respect to a debt or property securing such debt or with respect to any lease shall terminate with respect to the debtor on the 30th day after the filing of the later case;

(B)   on the motion of a party in interest for continuation of the automatic stay and upon notice and a hearing, the court may extend the stay in particular cases as to any or all creditors (subject to such conditions or limitations as the court may then impose) after notice and a hearing completed before the expiration of the 30-day period only if the party in interest demonstrates that the filing of the later case is in good faith as to the creditors to be stayed; and

(C)   for purposes of subparagraph (B), a case is presumptively filed not in good faith (but such presumption may be rebutted by clear and convincing evidence to the contrary)—

(i)   as to all creditors, if—

(I)   more than 1 previous case under any of chapters 7, 11, and 13 in which the individual was a debtor was pending within the preceding 1-year period;

(II)   a previous case under any of chapters 7, 11, and 13 in which the individual was a debtor was dismissed within such 1-year period, after the debtor failed to—

(aa) file or amend the petition or other documents as required by this title or the court without substantial excuse (but mere inadvertence or negligence shall not be a substantial excuse unless the dismissal was caused by the negligence of the debtor's attorney);

(bb) provide adequate protection as ordered by the court; or

(cc) perform the terms of a plan confirmed by the court; or

(III) there has not been a substantial change in the financial or personal affairs of the debtor since the dismissal of the next most previous case under chapter 7, 11, or 13 or any other reason to conclude that the later case will be concluded—

(aa) if a case under chapter 7, with a discharge; or

(bb) if a case under chapter 11 or 13, with a confirmed plan that will be fully performed; and

(ii) as to any creditor that commenced an action under subsection (d) in a previous case in which the individual was a debtor if, as of the date of dismissal of such case, that action was still pending or had been resolved by terminating, conditioning, or limiting the stay as to actions of such creditor; and

(4)(A)(i) if a single or joint case is filed by or against a debtor who is an individual under this title, and if 2 or more single or joint cases of the debtor were pending within the previous year but were dismissed, other than a case refiled under a chapter other than Chapter 7 after dismissal under section 707(b), the stay under subsection (a) shall not go into effect upon the filing of the later case; and

(ii) on request of a party in interest, the court shall promptly enter an order confirming that no stay is in effect;

(B) if, within 30 days after the filing of the later case, a party in interest requests the court may order the stay to take effect in the case as to any or all creditors (subject to such conditions or limitations as the court may impose), after notice and a hearing, only if the party in interest demonstrates that the filing of the later case is in good faith as to the creditors to be stayed;

(C) a stay imposed under subparagraph (B) shall be effective on the date of the entry of the order allowing the stay to go into effect; and

(D) for purposes of subparagraph (B), a case is presumptively filed not in good faith (but such presumption may be rebutted by clear and convincing evidence to the contrary)—

(i) as to all creditors if—

(I) 2 or more previous cases under this title in which the individual was a debtor were pending within the 1-year period;

(II) a previous case under this title in which the individual was a debtor was dismissed within the time period stated in this paragraph after the debtor failed to file or amend the petition or other documents as required by this title or the court without substantial excuse (but mere inadvertence or negligence shall not be substantial excuse unless the dismissal was caused by the negligence of the debtor's attorney), failed to provide adequate protection as ordered by the court, or failed to perform the terms of a plan confirmed by the court; or

(III) there has not been a substantial change in the financial or personal affairs of the debtor since the dismissal of the next most previous case under this title, or any other reason to conclude that the later case will not be concluded, if a case under chapter 7, with a discharge, and if a case under chapter 11 or 13, with a confirmed plan that will be fully performed; or

(ii) as to any creditor that commenced an action under subsection (d) in a previous case in which the individual was a debtor if, as of the date of dismissal of such case, such action was still pending or had been resolved by terminating, conditioning, or limiting the stay as to such action of such creditor.

(d)   On request of a party in interest and after notice and a hearing, the court shall grant relief from the stay provided under subsection (a) of this section, such as by terminating, annulling, modifying, or conditioning such stay—

(1)   for cause, including the lack of adequate protection of an interest in property of such party in interest;

(2)   with respect to a stay of an act against property under subsection (a) of this section, if—

(A)   the debtor does not have an equity in such property; and

(B)   such property is not necessary to an effective reorganization;

(3)   with respect to a stay of an act against single asset real estate under subsection (a), by a creditor whose claim is secured by an interest in such real estate, unless, not later than the date that is 90 days after the entry of the order for relief (or such later date as the court may determine for cause by order entered within that 90-day period) or 30 days after the court determines that the debtor is subject to this paragraph, whichever is later—

(A)   the debtor has filed a plan of reorganization that has a reasonable possibility of being confirmed within a reasonable time; or

(B)   the debtor has commenced monthly payments that—

(i)   may, in the debtor's sole discretion, notwithstanding section 363(c)(2), be made from rents or other income generated before, on, or after the date of the commencement of the case by or from the property to each creditor whose claim is secured by such real estate (other than a claim secured by a judgment lien or by an unmatured statutory lien); and

(ii)   are in an amount equal to interest at the then applicable nondefault contract rate of interest on the value of the creditor's interest in the real estate; or

(4)   with respect to a stay of an act against real property under subsection (a), by a creditor whose claim is secured by an interest in such real property, if the court finds that the filing of the petition was part of a scheme to delay, hinder, or defraud creditors that involved either—

(A)   transfer of all or part ownership of, or other interest in, such real property without the consent of the secured creditor or court approval; or

(B)   multiple bankruptcy filings affecting such real property.

If recorded in compliance with applicable State laws governing notices of interests or liens in real property, an order entered under paragraph (4) shall be binding in any other case under this title purporting to affect such real property filed not later than 2 years after the date of the entry of such order by the court, except that a debtor in a subsequent case under this title may move for relief from such order based upon changed circumstances or for good cause shown, after notice and a hearing. Any Federal, State, or local governmental unit that accepts notices of interests or liens in real property shall accept any certified copy of an order described in this subsection for indexing and recording.

(e)(1)   Thirty days after a request under subsection (d) of this section for relief from the stay of any act against property of the estate under subsection (a) of this section, such stay is terminated with respect to the party in interest making such request, unless the court, after notice and a hearing, orders such stay continued in effect pending the conclusion of, or as a result of, a final hearing and determination under subsection (d) of this section. A hearing under this subsection may be a preliminary hearing, or may be consolidated with the final hearing under subsection (d) of this section. The court shall order such stay continued in effect pending the conclusion of the final hearing under subsection (d) of this section if there is a reasonable likelihood that the party opposing relief from such stay will prevail at the conclusion of such final hearing. If the hearing under this subsection is a preliminary hearing, then such final hearing shall be concluded not later than thirty days after the conclusion of such preliminary hearing, unless the 30-day period is extended with the consent of the parties in interest or for a specific time which the court finds is required by compelling circumstances.

(2)   Notwithstanding paragraph (1), in a case under chapter 7, 11, or 13 in which the debtor is an individual, the stay under subsection (a) shall terminate on the date that is 60 days after a request is made by a party in interest under subsection (d), unless—

(A)   a final decision is rendered by the court during the 60-day period beginning on the date of the request; or

(B)   such 60-day period is extended—

(i)   by agreement of all parties in interest; or

(ii)   by the court for such specific period of time as the court finds is required for good cause, as described in findings made by the court.

(f)   Upon request of a party in interest, the court, with or without a hearing, shall grant such relief from the stay provided under subsection (a) of this section as is necessary to prevent irreparable damage to the interest of an entity in property, if such interest will suffer such damage before there is an opportunity for notice and a hearing under subsection (d) or (e) of this section.

(g)   In any hearing under subsection (d) or (e) of this section concerning relief from the stay of any act under subsection (a) of this section—

(1)   the party requesting such relief has the burden of proof on the issue of the debtor's equity in property; and

(2)   the party opposing such relief has the burden of proof on all other issues.

(h)(1)   In a case in which the debtor is an individual, the stay provided by subsection (a) is terminated with respect to personal property of the estate or of the debtor securing in whole or in part a claim, or subject to an unexpired lease, and such personal property shall no longer be property of the estate if the debtor fails within the applicable time set by section 521(a)(2)—

(A)   to file timely any statement of intention required under section 521(a)(2) with respect to such personal property or to indicate in such statement that the debtor will either surrender such personal property or retain it and, if retaining such personal property, either redeem such personal property pursuant to section 722, enter into an agreement of the kind specified in section 524(c) applicable to the debt secured by such personal property, or assume such unexpired lease pursuant to section 365(p) if the trustee does not do so, as applicable; and

(B)   to take timely the action specified in such statement, as it may be amended before expiration of the period for taking action, unless such statement specifies the debtor's intention to reaffirm such debt on the original contract terms and the creditor refuses to agree to the reaffirmation on such terms.

(2)   Paragraph (1) does not apply if the court determines, on the motion of the trustee filed before the expiration of the applicable time set by section 521(a)(2), after notice and a hearing, that such personal property is of consequential value or benefit to the estate, and orders appropriate adequate protection of the creditor's interest, and orders the debtor to deliver any collateral in the debtor's possession to the trustee. If the court does not so determine, the stay provided by subsection (a) shall terminate upon the conclusion of the hearing on the motion.

(i)   If a case commenced under chapter 7, 11, or 13 is dismissed due to the creation of a debt repayment plan, for purposes of subsection (c)(3), any subsequent case commenced by the debtor under any such chapter shall not be presumed to be filed not in good faith.

(j)   On request of a party in interest, the court shall issue an order under subsection (c) confirming that the automatic stay has been terminated.

(k)(1) Except as provided in paragraph (2), an individual injured by any willful violation of a stay provided by this section shall recover actual damages, including costs and attorneys' fees, and, in appropriate circumstances, may recover punitive damages.

(2) If such violation is based on an action taken by an entity in the good faith belief that subsection (h) applies to the debtor, the recovery under paragraph (1) of this subsection against such entity shall be limited to actual damages.

(*l*)(1) Except as otherwise provided in this subsection, subsection (b)(22) shall apply on the date that is 30 days after the date on which the bankruptcy petition is filed, if the debtor files with the petition and serves upon the lessor a certification under penalty of perjury that—

　　(A) under nonbankruptcy law applicable in the jurisdiction, there are circumstances under which the debtor would be permitted to cure the entire monetary default that gave rise to the judgment for possession, after that judgment for possession was entered; and

　　(B) the debtor (or an adult dependent of the debtor) has deposited with the clerk of the court, any rent that would become due during the 30-day period after the filing of the bankruptcy petition.

(2) If, within the 30-day period after the filing of the bankruptcy petition, the debtor (or an adult dependent of the debtor) complies with paragraph (1) and files with the court and serves upon the lessor a further certification under penalty of perjury that the debtor (or an adult dependent of the debtor) has cured, under nonbankruptcy law applicable in the jurisdiction, the entire monetary default that gave rise to the judgment under which possession is sought by the lessor, subsection (b)(22) shall not apply, unless ordered to apply by the court under paragraph (3).

(3)(A) If the lessor files an objection to any certification filed by the debtor under paragraph (1) or (2), and serves such objection upon the debtor, the court shall hold a hearing within 10 days after the filing and service of such objection to determine if the certification filed by the debtor under paragraph (1) or (2) is true.

　　(B) If the court upholds the objection of the lessor filed under subparagraph (A)—

　　　　(i) subsection (b)(22) shall apply immediately and relief from the stay provided under subsection (a)(3) shall not be required to enable the lessor to complete the process to recover full possession of the property; and

　　　　(ii) the clerk of the court shall immediately serve upon the lessor and the debtor a certified copy of the court's order upholding the lessor's objection.

(4) If a debtor, in accordance with paragraph (5), indicates on the petition that there was a judgment for possession of the residential rental property in which the debtor resides and does not file a certification under paragraph (1) or (2)—

　　(A) subsection (b)(22) shall apply immediately upon failure to file such certification, and relief from the stay provided under subsection (a)(3) shall not be required to enable the lessor to complete the process to recover full possession of the property; and

　　(B) the clerk of the court shall immediately serve upon the lessor and the debtor a certified copy of the docket indicating the absence of a filed certification and the applicability of the exception to the stay under subsection (b)(22).

(5)(A) Where a judgment for possession of residential property in which the debtor resides as a tenant under a lease or rental agreement has been obtained by the lessor, the debtor shall so indicate on the bankruptcy petition and shall provide the name and address of the lessor that obtained that pre-petition judgment on the petition and on any certification filed under this subsection.

　　(B) The form of certification filed with the petition, as specified in this subsection, shall provide for the debtor to certify, and the debtor shall certify—

(i) whether a judgment for possession of residential rental housing in which the debtor resides has been obtained against the debtor before the date of the filing of the petition; and

(ii) whether the debtor is claiming under paragraph (1) that under nonbankruptcy law applicable in the jurisdiction, there are circumstances under which the debtor would be permitted to cure the entire monetary default that gave rise to the judgment for possession, after that judgment of possession was entered, and has made the appropriate deposit with the court.

(C) The standard forms (electronic and otherwise) used in a bankruptcy proceeding shall be amended to reflect the requirements of this subsection.

(D) The clerk of the court shall arrange for the prompt transmittal of the rent deposited in accordance with paragraph (1)(B) to the lessor.

(m)(1) Except as otherwise provided in this subsection, subsection (b)(23) shall apply on the date that is 15 days after the date on which the lessor files and serves a certification described in subsection (b)(23).

(2)(A) If the debtor files with the court an objection to the truth or legal sufficiency of the certification described in subsection (b)(23) and serves such objection upon the lessor, subsection (b)(23) shall not apply, unless ordered to apply by the court under this subsection.

(B) If the debtor files and serves the objection under subparagraph (A), the court shall hold a hearing within 10 days after the filing and service of such objection to determine if the situation giving rise to the lessor's certification under paragraph (1) existed or has been remedied.

(C) If the debtor can demonstrate to the satisfaction of the court that the situation giving rise to the lessor's certification under paragraph (1) did not exist or has been remedied, the stay provided under subsection (a)(3) shall remain in effect until the termination of the stay under this section.

(D) If the debtor cannot demonstrate to the satisfaction of the court that the situation giving rise to the lessor's certification under paragraph (1) did not exist or has been remedied—

(i) relief from the stay provided under subsection (a)(3) shall not be required to enable the lessor to proceed with the eviction; and

(ii) the clerk of the court shall immediately serve upon the lessor and the debtor a certified copy of the court's order upholding the lessor's certification.

(3) If the debtor fails to file, within 15 days, an objection under paragraph (2)(A)—

(A) subsection (b)(23) shall apply immediately upon such failure and relief from the stay provided under subsection (a)(3) shall not be required to enable the lessor to complete the process to recover full possession of the property; and

(B) the clerk of the court shall immediately serve upon the lessor and the debtor a certified copy of the docket indicating such failure.

(n)(1) Except as provided in paragraph (2), subsection (a) does not apply in a case in which the debtor—

(A) is a debtor in a small business case pending at the time the petition is filed;

(B) was a debtor in a small business case that was dismissed for any reason by an order that became final in the 2-year period ending on the date of the order for relief entered with respect to the petition;

(C) was a debtor in a small business case in which a plan was confirmed in the 2-year period ending on the date of the order for relief entered with respect to the petition; or

(D) is an entity that has acquired substantially all of the assets or business of a small business debtor described in subparagraph (A), (B), or (C), unless such entity establishes by a preponderance of the evidence that such entity acquired substantially all of the assets or business of such small business debtor in good faith and not for the purpose of evading this paragraph.

(2) Paragraph (1) does not apply—

(A) to an involuntary case involving no collusion by the debtor with creditors; or

(B) to the filing of a petition if—

(i) the debtor proves by a preponderance of the evidence that the filing of the petition resulted from circumstances beyond the control of the debtor not foreseeable at the time the case then pending was filed; and

(ii) it is more likely than not that the court will confirm a feasible plan, but not a liquidating plan, within a reasonable period of time.

(*o*) The exercise of rights not subject to the stay arising under subsection (a) pursuant to paragraph (6), (7), (17), or (27) of subsection (b) shall not be stayed by any order of a court or administrative agency in any proceeding under this title.

(Pub.L. 95–598, Nov. 6, 1978, 92 Stat. 2570; Pub.L. 97–222, § 3, July 27, 1982, 96 Stat. 235; Pub.L. 98–353, title III, §§ 304, 363(b), 392, 441, July 10, 1984, 98 Stat. 352, 363, 365, 371; Pub.L. 99–509, title V, § 5001(a), Oct. 21, 1986, 100 Stat. 1911; Pub.L. 99–554, title II, §§ 257(j), 283(d), Oct. 27, 1986, 100 Stat. 3115, 3116; Pub.L. 101–311, title I, § 102, title II, § 202, June 25, 1990, 104 Stat. 267, 269; Pub.L. 101–508, title III, § 3007(a)(1), Nov. 5, 1990, 104 Stat. 1388–28; Pub.L. 103–394, title I, §§ 101, 116, title II, §§ 204(a), 218(b), title III, § 304(b), title IV, § 401, title V, § 501(b)(2), (d)(7), Oct. 22, 1994, 108 Stat. 4107, 4119, 4122, 4128, 4132, 4141, 4142, 4144; Pub.L. 105–277, div. I, title VI, § 603, Oct. 21, 1998, 112 Stat. 2681–886; Pub.L. 109–8, title I, § 106(f), title II, §§ 214, 224(b), title III, §§ 302, 303, 305(1), 311, 320, title IV, §§ 401(b), 441, 444, title VII, §§ 709, 718, title IX, § 907(d), (*o*)(1), (2), title XI, § 1106, title XII, § 1225, Apr. 20, 2005, 119 Stat. 41, 54, 64, 75, 77, 79, 84, 94, 104, 114, 117, 127, 131, 176, 181, 182, 192, 199; Pub.L. 109–304, § 17(b)(1), Oct. 6, 2006, 120 Stat. 1706; Pub.L. 109–390, § 5(a)(2), Dec. 12, 2006, 120 Stat. 2696; Pub.L. 111–327, § 2(a)(12), Dec. 22, 2010, 124 Stat. 3558.)

§ 363. Use, sale, or lease of property

(a) In this section, "cash collateral" means cash, negotiable instruments, documents of title, securities, deposit accounts, or other cash equivalents whenever acquired in which the estate and an entity other than the estate have an interest and includes the proceeds, products, offspring, rents, or profits of property and the fees, charges, accounts or other payments for the use or occupancy of rooms and other public facilities in hotels, motels, or other lodging properties subject to a security interest as provided in section 552(b) of this title, whether existing before or after the commencement of a case under this title.

(b)(1) The trustee, after notice and a hearing, may use, sell, or lease, other than in the ordinary course of business, property of the estate, except that if the debtor in connection with offering a product or a service discloses to an individual a policy prohibiting the transfer of personally identifiable information about individuals to persons that are not affiliated with the debtor and if such policy is in effect on the date of the commencement of the case, then the trustee may not sell or lease personally identifiable information to any person unless—

(A) such sale or such lease is consistent with such policy; or

(B) after appointment of a consumer privacy ombudsman in accordance with section 332, and after notice and a hearing, the court approves such sale or such lease—

(i) giving due consideration to the facts, circumstances, and conditions of such sale or such lease; and

(ii) finding that no showing was made that such sale or such lease would violate applicable nonbankruptcy law.

(2) If notification is required under subsection (a) of section 7A of the Clayton Act in the case of a transaction under this subsection, then—

(A) notwithstanding subsection (a) of such section, the notification required by such subsection to be given by the debtor shall be given by the trustee; and

(B) notwithstanding subsection (b) of such section, the required waiting period shall end on the 15th day after the date of the receipt, by the Federal Trade Commission and the Assistant Attorney General in charge of the Antitrust Division of the Department of Justice, of the notification required under such subsection (a), unless such waiting period is extended—

(i) pursuant to subsection (e)(2) of such section, in the same manner as such subsection (e)(2) applies to a cash tender offer;

(ii) pursuant to subsection (g)(2) of such section; or

(iii) by the court after notice and a hearing.

(c)(1) If the business of the debtor is authorized to be operated under section 721, 1108, 1203, 1204, or 1304 of this title and unless the court orders otherwise, the trustee may enter into transactions, including the sale or lease of property of the estate, in the ordinary course of business, without notice or a hearing, and may use property of the estate in the ordinary course of business without notice or a hearing.

(2) The trustee may not use, sell, or lease cash collateral under paragraph (1) of this subsection unless—

(A) each entity that has an interest in such cash collateral consents; or

(B) the court, after notice and a hearing, authorizes such use, sale, or lease in accordance with the provisions of this section.

(3) Any hearing under paragraph (2)(B) of this subsection may be a preliminary hearing or may be consolidated with a hearing under subsection (e) of this section, but shall be scheduled in accordance with the needs of the debtor. If the hearing under paragraph (2)(B) of this subsection is a preliminary hearing, the court may authorize such use, sale, or lease only if there is a reasonable likelihood that the trustee will prevail at the final hearing under subsection (e) of this section. The court shall act promptly on any request for authorization under paragraph (2)(B) of this subsection.

(4) Except as provided in paragraph (2) of this subsection, the trustee shall segregate and account for any cash collateral in the trustee's possession, custody, or control.

(d) The trustee may use, sell, or lease property under subsection (b) or (c) of this section—

(1) In the case of a debtor that is a corporation or trust that is not a moneyed business, commercial corporation, or trust, only in accordance with nonbankruptcy law applicable to the transfer of property by a debtor that such a corporation or trust; and

(2) only to the extent not inconsistent with any relief granted under subsection (c), (d), (e), or (f) of section 362.

(e) Notwithstanding any other provision of this section, at any time, on request of an entity that has an interest in property used, sold, or leased, or proposed to be used, sold, or leased, by the trustee, the court, with or without a hearing, shall prohibit or condition such use, sale, or lease as is necessary to provide adequate protection of such interest. This subsection also applies to property that is subject to any unexpired lease of personal property (to the exclusion of such property being subject to an order to grant relief from the stay under section 362).

(f) The trustee may sell property under subsection (b) or (c) of this section free and clear of any interest in such property of an entity other than the estate, only if—

(1) applicable nonbankruptcy law permits sale of such property free and clear of such interest;

(2) such entity consents;

(3) such interest is a lien and the price at which such property is to be sold is greater than the aggregate value of all liens on such property;

(4) such interest is in bona fide dispute; or

(5) such entity could be compelled, in a legal or equitable proceeding, to accept a money satisfaction of such interest.

(g) Notwithstanding subsection (f) of this section, the trustee may sell property under subsection (b) or (c) of this section free and clear of any vested or contingent right in the nature of dower or curtesy.

(h) Notwithstanding subsection (f) of this section, the trustee may sell both the estate's interest, under subsection (b) or (c) of this section, and the interest of any co-owner in property in which the debtor had, at the time of the commencement of the case, an undivided interest as a tenant in common, joint tenant, or tenant by the entirety, only if—

(1) partition in kind of such property among the estate and such co-owners is impracticable;

(2) sale of the estate's undivided interest in such property would realize significantly less for the estate than sale of such property free of the interests of such co-owners;

(3) the benefit to the estate of a sale of such property free of the interests of co-owners outweighs the detriment, if any, to such co-owners; and

(4) such property is not used in the production, transmission, or distribution, for sale, of electric energy or of natural or synthetic gas for heat, light, or power.

(i) Before the consummation of a sale of property to which subsection (g) or (h) of this section applies, or of property of the estate that was community property of the debtor and the debtor's spouse immediately before the commencement of the case, the debtor's spouse, or a co-owner of such property, as the case may be, may purchase such property at the price at which such sale is to be consummated.

(j) After a sale of property to which subsection (g) or (h) of this section applies, the trustee shall distribute to the debtor's spouse or the co-owners of such property, as the case may be, and to the estate, the proceeds of such sale, less the costs and expenses, not including any compensation of the trustee, of such sale, according to the interests of such spouse or co-owners, and of the estate.

(k) At a sale under subsection (b) of this section of property that is subject to a lien that secures an allowed claim, unless the court for cause orders otherwise the holder of such claim may bid at such sale, and, if the holder of such claim purchases such property, such holder may offset such claim against the purchase price of such property.

(*l*) Subject to the provisions of section 365, the trustee may use, sell, or lease property under subsection (b) or (c) of this section, or a plan under chapter 11, 12, or 13 of this title may provide for the use, sale, or lease of property, notwithstanding any provision in a contract, a lease, or applicable law that is conditioned on the insolvency or financial condition of the debtor, on the commencement of a case under this title concerning the debtor, or on the appointment of or the taking possession by a trustee in a case under this title or a custodian, and that effects, or gives an option to effect, a forfeiture, modification, or termination of the debtor's interest in such property.

(m) The reversal or modification on appeal of an authorization under subsection (b) or (c) of this section of a sale or lease of property does not affect the validity of a sale or lease under such authorization to an entity that purchased or leased such property in good faith, whether or not such entity knew of the pendency of the appeal, unless such authorization and such sale or lease were stayed pending appeal.

(n) The trustee may avoid a sale under this section if the sale price was controlled by an agreement among potential bidders at such sale, or may recover from a party to such agreement any amount by which the value of the property sold exceeds the price at which such sale was consummated, and may recover any costs, attorneys' fees, or expenses incurred in avoiding such sale or recovering such amount. In addition to any recovery under the preceding sentence, the court may grant judgment for punitive damages in favor of the estate and against any such party that entered into such an agreement in willful disregard of this subsection.

(o) Notwithstanding subsection (f), if a person purchases any interest in a consumer credit transaction that is subject to the Truth in Lending Act or any interest in a consumer credit contract (as defined in section 433.1 of title 16 of the Code of Federal Regulations (January 1, 2004), as amended from time to time), and if such interest is purchased through a sale under this section, then such person shall remain subject to all claims and defenses that are related to such consumer credit transaction or such consumer credit contract, to the same extent as such person would be subject to such claims and defenses of the consumer had such interest been purchased at a sale not under this section.

(p)   In any hearing under this section—

(1)   the trustee has the burden of proof on the issue of adequate protection; and

(2)   the entity asserting an interest in property has the burden of proof on the issue of the validity, priority, or extent of such interest.

(Pub.L. 95–598, Nov. 6, 1978, 92 Stat. 2572; Pub.L. 98–353, title III, § 442, July 10, 1984, 98 Stat. 371; Pub.L. 99–554, title II, § 257(k), Oct. 27, 1986, 100 Stat. 3115; Pub.L. 103–394, title I, § 109, title II, §§ 214(b), 219(c), title V, § 501(d)(8), Oct. 22, 1994, 108 Stat. 4113, 4126, 4129, 4144; Pub.L. 109–8, title II, §§ 204, 231(a), title XII, § 1221(a), Apr. 20, 2005, 119 Stat. 49, 72, 195; Pub.L. 111–327, § 2(a)(13), Dec. 22, 2010, 124 Stat. 3559.)

§ 364.   Obtaining credit

(a)   If the trustee is authorized to operate the business of the debtor under section 721, 1108, 1203, 1204, or 1304 of this title, unless the court orders otherwise, the trustee may obtain unsecured credit and incur unsecured debt in the ordinary course of business allowable under section 503(b)(1) of this title as an administrative expense.

(b)   The court, after notice and a hearing, may authorize the trustee to obtain unsecured credit or to incur unsecured debt other than under subsection (a) of this section, allowable under section 503(b)(1) of this title as an administrative expense.

(c)   If the trustee is unable to obtain unsecured credit allowable under section 503(b)(1) of this title as an administrative expense, the court, after notice and a hearing, may authorize the obtaining of credit or the incurring of debt—

(1)   with priority over any or all administrative expenses of the kind specified in section 503(b) or 507(b) of this title;

(2)   secured by a lien on property of the estate that is not otherwise subject to a lien; or

(3)   secured by a junior lien on property of the estate that is subject to a lien.

(d)(1)   The court, after notice and a hearing, may authorize the obtaining of credit or the incurring of debt secured by a senior or equal lien on property of the estate that is subject to a lien only if—

(A)   the trustee is unable to obtain such credit otherwise; and

(B)   there is adequate protection of the interest of the holder of the lien on the property of the estate on which such senior or equal lien is proposed to be granted.

(2)   In any hearing under this subsection, the trustee has the burden of proof on the issue of adequate protection.

(e)   The reversal or modification on appeal of an authorization under this section to obtain credit or incur debt, or of a grant under this section of a priority or a lien, does not affect the validity of any debt so incurred, or any priority or lien so granted, to an entity that extended such credit in good faith, whether or not such entity knew of the pendency of the appeal, unless such authorization and the incurring of such debt, or the granting of such priority or lien, were stayed pending appeal.

(f)   Except with respect to an entity that is an underwriter as defined in section 1145(b) of this title, section 5 of the Securities Act of 1933, the Trust Indenture Act of 1939, and any State or local law requiring registration for offer or sale of a security or registration or licensing of an issuer of, underwriter of, or broker or dealer in, a security does not apply to the offer or sale under this section of a security that is not an equity security.

(Pub.L. 95–598, Nov. 6, 1978, 92 Stat. 2574; Pub.L. 99–554, title II, § 257(l), Oct. 27, 1986, 100 Stat. 3115; Pub.L. 103–394, title V, § 501(d)(9), Oct. 22, 1994, 108 Stat. 4144.)

§ 365. Executory contracts and unexpired leases

(a) Except as provided in sections 765 and 766 of this title and in subsections (b), (c), and (d) of this section, the trustee, subject to the court's approval, may assume or reject any executory contract or unexpired lease of the debtor.

(b)(1) If there has been a default in an executory contract or unexpired lease of the debtor, the trustee may not assume such contract or lease unless, at the time of assumption of such contract or lease, the trustee—

(A) cures, or provides adequate assurance that the trustee will promptly cure, such default other than a default that is a breach of a provision relating to the satisfaction of any provision (other than a penalty rate or penalty provision) relating to a default arising from any failure to perform nonmonetary obligations under an unexpired lease of real property, if it is impossible for the trustee to cure such default by performing nonmonetary acts at and after the time of assumption, except that if such default arises from a failure to operate in accordance with a nonresidential real property lease, then such default shall be cured by performance at and after the time of assumption in accordance with such lease, and pecuniary losses resulting from such default shall be compensated in accordance with the provisions of this paragraph;

(B) compensates, or provides adequate assurance that the trustee will promptly compensate, a party other than the debtor to such contract or lease, for any actual pecuniary loss to such party resulting from such default; and

(C) provides adequate assurance of future performance under such contract or lease.

(2) Paragraph (1) of this subsection does not apply to a default that is a breach of a provision relating to—

(A) the insolvency or financial condition of the debtor at any time before the closing of the case;

(B) the commencement of a case under this title;

(C) the appointment of or taking possession by a trustee in a case under this title or a custodian before such commencement; or

(D) the satisfaction of any penalty rate or penalty provision relating to a default arising from any failure by the debtor to perform nonmonetary obligations under the executory contract or unexpired lease.

(3) For the purposes of paragraph (1) of this subsection and paragraph (2)(B) of subsection (f), adequate assurance of future performance of a lease of real property in a shopping center includes adequate assurance—

(A) of the source of rent and other consideration due under such lease, and in the case of an assignment, that the financial condition and operating performance of the proposed assignee and its guarantors, if any, shall be similar to the financial condition and operating performance of the debtor and its guarantors, if any, as of the time the debtor became the lessee under the lease;

(B) that any percentage rent due under such lease will not decline substantially;

(C) that assumption or assignment of such lease is subject to all the provisions thereof, including (but not limited to) provisions such as a radius, location, use, or exclusivity provision, and will not breach any such provision contained in any other lease, financing agreement, or master agreement relating to such shopping center; and

(D) that assumption or assignment of such lease will not disrupt any tenant mix or balance in such shopping center.

(4) Notwithstanding any other provision of this section, if there has been a default in an unexpired lease of the debtor, other than a default of a kind specified in paragraph (2) of this subsection, the trustee may not require a lessor to provide services or supplies incidental to such lease before assumption of such lease unless the lessor is compensated under the terms of such lease for any services and supplies provided under such lease before assumption of such lease.

(c) The trustee may not assume or assign any executory contract or unexpired lease of the debtor, whether or not such contract or lease prohibits or restricts assignment of rights or delegation of duties, if—

    (1)(A) applicable law excuses a party, other than the debtor, to such contract or lease from accepting performance from or rendering performance to an entity other than the debtor or the debtor in possession, whether or not such contract or lease prohibits or restricts assignment of rights or delegation of duties; and

        (B) such party does not consent to such assumption or assignment; or

    (2) such contract is a contract to make a loan, or extend other debt financing or financial accommodations, to or for the benefit of the debtor, or to issue a security of the debtor; or

    (3) such lease is of nonresidential real property and has been terminated under applicable nonbankruptcy law prior to the order for relief.

    [(4) Repealed. Pub.L. 109–8, Title III, § 328(a)(2)(C), Apr. 20, 2005, 119 Stat. 100]

(d)(1) In a case under chapter 7 of this title, if the trustee does not assume or reject an executory contract or unexpired lease of residential real property or of personal property of the debtor within 60 days after the order for relief, or within such additional time as the court, for cause, within such 60-day period, fixes, then such contract or lease is deemed rejected.

    (2) In a case under chapter 9, 11, 12, or 13 of this title, the trustee may assume or reject an executory contract or unexpired lease of residential real property or of personal property of the debtor at any time before the confirmation of a plan but the court, on the request of any party to such contract or lease, may order the trustee to determine within a specified period of time whether to assume or reject such contract or lease.

    (3) The trustee shall timely perform all the obligations of the debtor, except those specified in section 365(b)(2), arising from and after the order for relief under any unexpired lease of nonresidential real property, until such lease is assumed or rejected, notwithstanding section 503(b)(1) of this title. The court may extend, for cause, the time for performance of any such obligation that arises within 60 days after the date of the order for relief, but the time for performance shall not be extended beyond such 60-day period. This subsection shall not be deemed to affect the trustee's obligations under the provisions of subsection (b) or (f) of this section. Acceptance of any such performance does not constitute waiver or relinquishment of the lessor's rights under such lease or under this title.

    (4)(A) Subject to subparagraph (B), an unexpired lease of nonresidential real property under which the debtor is the lessee shall be deemed rejected, and the trustee shall immediately surrender that nonresidential real property to the lessor, if the trustee does not assume or reject the unexpired lease by the earlier of—

        (i) the date that is 120 days after the date of the order for relief; or

        (ii) the date of the entry of an order confirming a plan.

    (B)(i) The court may extend the period determined under subparagraph (A), prior to the expiration of the 120-day period, for 90 days on the motion of the trustee or lessor for cause.

        (ii) If the court grants an extension under clause (i), the court may grant a subsequent extension only upon prior written consent of the lessor in each instance.

    (5) The trustee shall timely perform all of the obligations of the debtor, except those specified in section 365(b)(2), first arising from or after 60 days after the order for relief in a case under chapter 11 of this title under an unexpired lease of personal property (other than personal property leased to an individual primarily for personal, family, or household purposes), until such lease is assumed or rejected notwithstanding section 503(b)(1) of this title, unless the court, after notice and a hearing and based on the equities of the case, orders otherwise with respect to the obligations or timely performance thereof. This subsection shall not be deemed to affect the trustee's obligations under the provisions of subsection (b) or (f). Acceptance of any such performance does not constitute waiver or relinquishment of the lessor's rights under such lease or under this title.

[**(6) to (9)** Repealed. Pub.L. 109–8, Title III, § 328(a)(3)(A), Apr. 20, 2005, 119 Stat. 100]

[**(10)** Redesignated (5)]

(e)(1) Notwithstanding a provision in an executory contract or unexpired lease, or in applicable law, an executory contract or unexpired lease of the debtor may not be terminated or modified, and any right or obligation under such contract or lease may not be terminated or modified, at any time after the commencement of the case solely because of a provision in such contract or lease that is conditioned on—

   (A) the insolvency or financial condition of the debtor at any time before the closing of the case;

   (B) the commencement of a case under this title; or

   (C) the appointment of or taking possession by a trustee in a case under this title or a custodian before such commencement.

(2) Paragraph (1) of this subsection does not apply to an executory contract or unexpired lease of the debtor, whether or not such contract or lease prohibits or restricts assignment of rights or delegation of duties, if—

   (A)(i) applicable law excuses a party, other than the debtor, to such contract or lease from accepting performance from or rendering performance to the trustee or to an assignee of such contract or lease, whether or not such contract or lease prohibits or restricts assignment of rights or delegation of duties; and

   (ii) such party does not consent to such assumption or assignment; or

   (B) such contract is a contract to make a loan, or extend other debt financing or financial accommodations, to or for the benefit of the debtor, or to issue a security of the debtor.

(f)(1) Except as provided in subsections (b) and (c) of this section, notwithstanding a provision in an executory contract or unexpired lease of the debtor, or in applicable law, that prohibits, restricts, or conditions the assignment of such contract or lease, the trustee may assign such contract or lease under paragraph (2) of this subsection.

(2) The trustee may assign an executory contract or unexpired lease of the debtor only if—

   (A) the trustee assumes such contract or lease in accordance with the provisions of this section; and

   (B) adequate assurance of future performance by the assignee of such contract or lease is provided, whether or not there has been a default in such contract or lease.

(3) Notwithstanding a provision in an executory contract or unexpired lease of the debtor, or in applicable law that terminates or modifies, or permits a party other than the debtor to terminate or modify, such contract or lease or a right or obligation under such contract or lease on account of an assignment of such contract or lease, such contract, lease, right, or obligation may not be terminated or modified under such provision because of the assumption or assignment of such contract or lease by the trustee.

(g) Except as provided in subsections (h)(2) and (i)(2) of this section, the rejection of an executory contract or unexpired lease of the debtor constitutes a breach of such contract or lease—

   (1) if such contract or lease has not been assumed under this section or under a plan confirmed under chapter 9, 11, 12, or 13 of this title, immediately before the date of the filing of the petition; or

   (2) if such contract or lease has been assumed under this section or under a plan confirmed under chapter 9, 11, 12, or 13 of this title—

    (A) if before such rejection the case has not been converted under section 1112, 1208, or 1307 of this title, at the time of such rejection; or

    (B) if before such rejection the case has been converted under section 1112, 1208, or 1307 of this title—

        (i) immediately before the date of such conversion, if such contract or lease was assumed before such conversion; or

        (ii) at the time of such rejection, if such contract or lease was assumed after such conversion.

  (h)(1)(A) If the trustee rejects an unexpired lease of real property under which the debtor is the lessor and—

        (i) if the rejection by the trustee amounts to such a breach as would entitle the lessee to treat such lease as terminated by virtue of its terms, applicable nonbankruptcy law, or any agreement made by the lessee, then the lessee under such lease may treat such lease as terminated by the rejection; or

        (ii) if the term of such lease has commenced, the lessee may retain its rights under such lease (including rights such as those relating to the amount and timing of payment of rent and other amounts payable by the lessee and any right of use, possession, quiet enjoyment, subletting, assignment, or hypothecation) that are in or appurtenant to the real property for the balance of the term of such lease and for any renewal or extension of such rights to the extent that such rights are enforceable under applicable nonbankruptcy law.

    (B) If the lessee retains its rights under subparagraph (A)(ii), the lessee may offset against the rent reserved under such lease for the balance of the term after the date of the rejection of such lease and for the term of any renewal or extension of such lease, the value of any damage caused by the nonperformance after the date of such rejection, of any obligation of the debtor under such lease, but the lessee shall not have any other right against the estate or the debtor on account of any damage occurring after such date caused by such nonperformance.

    (C) The rejection of a lease of real property in a shopping center with respect to which the lessee elects to retain its rights under subparagraph (A)(ii) does not affect the enforceability under applicable nonbankruptcy law of any provision in the lease pertaining to radius, location, use, exclusivity, or tenant mix or balance.

    (D) In this paragraph, "lessee" includes any successor, assign, or mortgagee permitted under the terms of such lease.

  (2)(A) If the trustee rejects a timeshare interest under a timeshare plan under which the debtor is the timeshare interest seller and—

        (i) if the rejection amounts to such a breach as would entitle the timeshare interest purchaser to treat the timeshare plan as terminated under its terms, applicable nonbankruptcy law, or any agreement made by timeshare interest purchaser, the timeshare interest purchaser under the timeshare plan may treat the timeshare plan as terminated by such rejection; or

        (ii) if the term of such timeshare interest has commenced, then the timeshare interest purchaser may retain its rights in such timeshare interest for the balance of such term and for any term of renewal or extension of such timeshare interest to the extent that such rights are enforceable under applicable nonbankruptcy law.

    (B) If the timeshare interest purchaser retains its rights under subparagraph (A), such timeshare interest purchaser may offset against the moneys due for such timeshare interest for the balance of the term after the date of the rejection of such timeshare interest, and the term of any renewal or extension of such timeshare interest, the value of any damage caused by the nonperformance after the date of such rejection, of any obligation of the debtor under such timeshare plan, but the timeshare interest purchaser shall not have any right against the estate or the debtor on account of any damage occurring after such date caused by such nonperformance.

(i)(1) If the trustee rejects an executory contract of the debtor for the sale of real property or for the sale of a timeshare interest under a timeshare plan, under which the purchaser is in possession, such purchaser may treat such contract as terminated, or, in the alternative, may remain in possession of such real property or timeshare interest.

(2) If such purchaser remains in possession—

(A) such purchaser shall continue to make all payments due under such contract, but may,[*] offset against such payments any damages occurring after the date of the rejection of such contract caused by the nonperformance of any obligation of the debtor after such date, but such purchaser does not have any rights against the estate on account of any damages arising after such date from such rejection, other than such offset; and

(B) the trustee shall deliver title to such purchaser in accordance with the provisions of such contract, but is relieved of all other obligations to perform under such contract.

(j) A purchaser that treats an executory contract as terminated under subsection (i) of this section, or a party whose executory contract to purchase real property from the debtor is rejected and under which such party is not in possession, has a lien on the interest of the debtor in such property for the recovery of any portion of the purchase price that such purchaser or party has paid.

(k) Assignment by the trustee to an entity of a contract or lease assumed under this section relieves the trustee and the estate from any liability for any breach of such contract or lease occurring after such assignment.

(l) If an unexpired lease under which the debtor is the lessee is assigned pursuant to this section, the lessor of the property may require a deposit or other security for the performance of the debtor's obligations under the lease substantially the same as would have been required by the landlord upon the initial leasing to a similar tenant.

(m) For purposes of this section 365 and sections 541(b)(2) and 362(b)(10), leases of real property shall include any rental agreement to use real property.

(n)(1) If the trustee rejects an executory contract under which the debtor is a licensor of a right to intellectual property, the licensee under such contract may elect—

(A) to treat such contract as terminated by such rejection if such rejection by the trustee amounts to such a breach as would entitle the licensee to treat such contract as terminated by virtue of its own terms, applicable nonbankruptcy law, or an agreement made by the licensee with another entity; or

(B) to retain its rights (including a right to enforce any exclusivity provision of such contract, but excluding any other right under applicable nonbankruptcy law to specific performance of such contract) under such contract and under any agreement supplementary to such contract, to such intellectual property (including any embodiment of such intellectual property to the extent protected by applicable nonbankruptcy law), as such rights existed immediately before the case commenced, for—

(i) the duration of such contract; and

(ii) any period for which such contract may be extended by the licensee as of right under applicable nonbankruptcy law.

(2) If the licensee elects to retain its rights, as described in paragraph (1)(B) of this subsection, under such contract—

(A) the trustee shall allow the licensee to exercise such rights;

---

[*] So in original. The comma probably should not appear.

(B) the licensee shall make all royalty payments due under such contract for the duration of such contract and for any period described in paragraph (1)(B) of this subsection for which the licensee extends such contract; and

(C) the licensee shall be deemed to waive—

(i) any right of setoff it may have with respect to such contract under this title or applicable nonbankruptcy law; and

(ii) any claim allowable under section 503(b) of this title arising from the performance of such contract.

(3) If the licensee elects to retain its rights, as described in paragraph (1)(B) of this subsection, then on the written request of the licensee the trustee shall—

(A) to the extent provided in such contract, or any agreement supplementary to such contract, provide to the licensee any intellectual property (including such embodiment) held by the trustee; and

(B) not interfere with the rights of the licensee as provided in such contract, or any agreement supplementary to such contract, to such intellectual property (including such embodiment) including any right to obtain such intellectual property (or such embodiment) from another entity.

(4) Unless and until the trustee rejects such contract, on the written request of the licensee the trustee shall—

(A) to the extent provided in such contract or any agreement supplementary to such contract—

(i) perform such contract; or

(ii) provide to the licensee such intellectual property (including any embodiment of such intellectual property to the extent protected by applicable nonbankruptcy law) held by the trustee; and

(B) not interfere with the rights of the licensee as provided in such contract, or any agreement supplementary to such contract, to such intellectual property (including such embodiment), including any right to obtain such intellectual property (or such embodiment) from another entity.

(o) In a case under chapter 11 of this title, the trustee shall be deemed to have assumed (consistent with the debtor's other obligations under section 507), and shall immediately cure any deficit under, any commitment by the debtor to a Federal depository institutions regulatory agency (or predecessor to such agency) to maintain the capital of an insured depository institution, and any claim for a subsequent breach of the obligations thereunder shall be entitled to priority under section 507. This subsection shall not extend any commitment that would otherwise be terminated by any act of such an agency.

(p)(1) If a lease of personal property is rejected or not timely assumed by the trustee under subsection (d), the leased property is no longer property of the estate and the stay under section 362(a) is automatically terminated.

(2)(A) If the debtor in a case under chapter 7 is an individual, the debtor may notify the creditor in writing that the debtor desires to assume the lease. Upon being so notified, the creditor may, at its option, notify the debtor that it is willing to have the lease assumed by the debtor and may condition such assumption on cure of any outstanding default on terms set by the contract.

(B) If, not later than 30 days after notice is provided under subparagraph (A), the debtor notifies the lessor in writing that the lease is assumed, the liability under the lease will be assumed by the debtor and not by the estate.

(C) The stay under section 362 and the injunction under section 524(a) (2) shall not be violated by notification of the debtor and negotiation of cure under this subsection.

(3) In a case under chapter 11 in which the debtor is an individual and in a case under chapter 13, if the debtor is the lessee with respect to personal property and the lease is not assumed in the plan confirmed by the court, the lease is deemed rejected as of the conclusion of the hearing on confirmation. If the lease is rejected, the stay under section 362 and any stay under section 1301 is automatically terminated with respect to the property subject to the lease.

(Pub.L. 95–598, Nov. 6, 1978, 92 Stat. 2574; Pub.L. 98–353, title III, §§ 362, 402–404, July 10, 1984, 98 Stat. 361, 367; Pub.L. 99–554, title II, §§ 257(j), (m), 283(e), Oct. 27, 1986, 100 Stat. 3115, 3117; Pub.L. 100–506, § 1(b), Oct. 18, 1988, 102 Stat. 2538; Pub.L. 101–647, title XXV, § 2522(c), Nov. 29, 1990, 104 Stat. 4866; Pub.L. 102–365, § 19(b)–(e), Sept. 3, 1992, 106 Stat. 982–984; Pub.L. 103–394, title II, §§ 205(a), 219(a), (b), title V, § 501(d)(10), Oct. 22, 1994, 108 Stat. 4122, 4128, 4145; Pub.L. 103–429, § 1, Oct. 31, 1994, 108 Stat. 4377; Pub.L. 109–8, title III, §§ 309(b), 328(a), title IV, § 404, Apr. 20, 2005, 119 Stat. 82, 100, 104.)

§ 366. Utility service

(a) Except as provided in subsections (b) and (c) of this section, a utility may not alter, refuse, or discontinue service to, or discriminate against, the trustee or the debtor solely on the basis of the commencement of a case under this title or that a debt owed by the debtor to such utility for service rendered before the order for relief was not paid when due.

(b) Such utility may alter, refuse, or discontinue service if neither the trustee nor the debtor, within 20 days after the date of the order for relief, furnishes adequate assurance of payment, in the form of a deposit or other security, for service after such date. On request of a party in interest and after notice and a hearing, the court may order reasonable modification of the amount of the deposit or other security necessary to provide adequate assurance of payment.

(c)(1)(A) For purposes of this subsection, the term "assurance of payment" means—

    (i) a cash deposit;

    (ii) a letter of credit;

    (iii) a certificate of deposit;

    (iv) a surety bond;

    (v) a prepayment of utility consumption; or

    (vi) another form of security that is mutually agreed on between the utility and the debtor or the trustee.

    (B) For purposes of this subsection an administrative expense priority shall not constitute an assurance of payment.

(2) Subject to paragraphs (3) and (4), with respect to a case filed under chapter 11, a utility referred to in subsection (a) may alter, refuse, or discontinue utility service, if during the 30-day period beginning on the date of the filing of the petition, the utility does not receive from the debtor or the trustee adequate assurance of payment for utility service that is satisfactory to the utility.

(3)(A) On request of a party in interest and after notice and a hearing, the court may order modification of the amount of an assurance of payment under paragraph (2).

    (B) In making a determination under this paragraph whether an assurance of payment is adequate, the court may not consider—

        (i) the absence of security before the date of the filing of the petition;

        (ii) the payment by the debtor of charges for utility service in a timely manner before the date of the filing of the petition; or

        (iii) the availability of an administrative expense priority.

(4) Notwithstanding any other provision of law, with respect to a case subject to this subsection, a utility may recover or set off against a security deposit provided to the utility by the debtor before the date of the filing of the petition without notice or order of the court.

(Pub.L. 95–598, Nov. 6, 1978, 92 Stat. 2578; Pub.L. 98–353, title III, § 443, July 10, 1984, 98 Stat. 373; Pub.L. 109–8, title IV, § 417, Apr. 20, 2005, 119 Stat. 108.)

CHAPTER 5—CREDITORS, THE DEBTOR, AND THE ESTATE

SUBCHAPTER I—CREDITORS AND CLAIMS

SUBCHAPTER II—DEBTOR'S DUTIES AND BENEFITS

SUBCHAPTER III—THE ESTATE

561.   Contractual right to terminate, liquidate, accelerate, or offset under a master netting agreement and
        across contracts; proceedings under chapter 15.
562.   Timing of damage measurement in connection with swap agreements, securities contracts, forward
        contracts, commodity contracts, repurchase agreements, and master netting agreements.

SUBCHAPTER I—CREDITORS AND CLAIMS

§ 501.   Filing of proofs of claims or interests

(a)   A creditor or an indenture trustee may file a proof of claim. An equity security holder may file a proof of interest.

(b)   If a creditor does not timely file a proof of such creditor's claim, an entity that is liable to such creditor with the debtor, or that has secured such creditor, may file a proof of such claim.

(c)   If a creditor does not timely file a proof of such creditor's claim, the debtor or the trustee may file a proof of such claim.

(d)   A claim of a kind specified in section 502(e)(2), 502(f), 502(g), 502(h) or 502(i) of this title may be filed under subsection (a), (b), or (c) of this section the same as if such claim were a claim against the debtor and had arisen before the date of the filing of the petition.

(e)   A claim arising from the liability of a debtor for fuel use tax assessed consistent with the requirements of section 31705 of title 49 may be filed by the base jurisdiction designated pursuant to the International Fuel Tax Agreement (as defined in section 31701 of title 49) and, if so filed, shall be allowed as a single claim.

      (Pub.L. 95–598, Nov. 6, 1978, 92 Stat. 2578; Pub.L. 98–353, title III, § 444, July 10, 1984, 98 Stat. 373; Pub.L. 109–8, title VII, § 702, Apr. 20, 2005, 119 Stat. 125.)

§ 502.   Allowance of claims or interests

(a)   A claim or interest, proof of which is filed under section 501 of this title, is deemed allowed, unless a party in interest, including a creditor of a general partner in a partnership that is a debtor in a case under chapter 7 of this title, objects.

(b)   Except as provided in subsections (e)(2), (f), (g), (h) and (i) of this section, if such objection to a claim is made, the court, after notice and a hearing, shall determine the amount of such claim in lawful currency of the United States as of the date of the filing of the petition, and shall allow such claim in such amount, except to the extent that—

    (1)   such claim is unenforceable against the debtor and property of the debtor, under any agreement or applicable law for a reason other than because such claim is contingent or unmatured;

    (2)   such claim is for unmatured interest;

    (3)   if such claim is for a tax assessed against property of the estate, such claim exceeds the value of the interest of the estate in such property;

    (4)   if such claim is for services of an insider or attorney of the debtor, such claim exceeds the reasonable value of such services;

    (5)   such claim is for a debt that is unmatured on the date of the filing of the petition and that is excepted from discharge under section 523(a)(5) of this title;

    (6)   if such claim is the claim of a lessor for damages resulting from the termination of a lease of real property, such claim exceeds—

        (A)   the rent reserved by such lease, without acceleration, for the greater of one year, or 15 percent, not to exceed three years, of the remaining term of such lease, following the earlier of—

            (i)   the date of the filing of the petition; and

    (ii) the date on which such lessor repossessed, or the lessee surrendered, the leased property; plus

    (B) any unpaid rent due under such lease, without acceleration, on the earlier of such dates;

    (7) if such claim is the claim of an employee for damages resulting from the termination of an employment contract, such claim exceeds—

        (A) the compensation provided by such contract, without acceleration, for one year following the earlier of—

            (i) the date of the filing of the petition; or

            (ii) the date on which the employer directed the employee to terminate, or such employee terminated, performance under such contract; plus

        (B) any unpaid compensation due under such contract, without acceleration, on the earlier of such dates;

    (8) such claim results from a reduction, due to late payment, in the amount of an otherwise applicable credit available to the debtor in connection with an employment tax on wages, salaries, or commissions earned from the debtor; or

    (9) proof of such claim is not timely filed, except to the extent tardily filed as permitted under paragraph (1), (2), or (3) of section 726(a) of this title or under the Federal Rules of Bankruptcy Procedure, except that a claim of a governmental unit shall be timely filed if it is filed before 180 days after the date of the order for relief or such later time as the Federal Rules of Bankruptcy Procedure may provide, and except that in a case under chapter 13, a claim of a governmental unit for a tax with respect to a return filed under section 1308 shall be timely if the claim is filed on or before the date that is 60 days after the date on which such return was filed as required.

    (c) There shall be estimated for purpose of allowance under this section—

    (1) any contingent or unliquidated claim, the fixing or liquidation of which, as the case may be, would unduly delay the administration of the case; or

    (2) any right to payment arising from a right to an equitable remedy for breach of performance.

    (d) Notwithstanding subsections (a) and (b) of this section, the court shall disallow any claim of any entity from which property is recoverable under section 542, 543, 550, or 553 of this title or that is a transferee of a transfer avoidable under section 522(f), 522(h), 544, 545, 547, 548, 549, or 724(a) of this title, unless such entity or transferee has paid the amount, or turned over any such property, for which such entity or transferee is liable under section 522(i), 542, 543, 550, or 553 of this title.

    (e)(1) Notwithstanding subsections (a), (b), and (c) of this section and paragraph (2) of this subsection, the court shall disallow any claim for reimbursement or contribution of an entity that is liable with the debtor on or has secured the claim of a creditor, to the extent that—

    (A) such creditor's claim against the estate is disallowed;

    (B) such claim for reimbursement or contribution is contingent as of the time of allowance or disallowance of such claim for reimbursement or contribution; or

    (C) such entity asserts a right of subrogation to the rights of such creditor under section 509 of this title.

    (2) A claim for reimbursement or contribution of such an entity that becomes fixed after the commencement of the case shall be determined, and shall be allowed under subsection (a), (b), or (c) of this section, or disallowed under subsection (d) of this section, the same as if such claim had become fixed before the date of the filing of the petition.

    (f) In an involuntary case, a claim arising in the ordinary course of the debtor's business or financial affairs after the commencement of the case but before the earlier of the appointment of a trustee and the order for relief shall be determined as of the date such claim arises, and shall be allowed under subsection (a), (b), or (c) of this section or disallowed under subsection (d) or (e) of this section, the same as if such claim had arisen before the date of the filing of the petition.

(g)(1) A claim arising from the rejection, under section 365 of this title or under a plan under chapter 9, 11, 12, or 13 of this title, of an executory contract or unexpired lease of the debtor that has not been assumed shall be determined, and shall be allowed under subsection (a), (b), or (c) of this section or disallowed under subsection (d) or (e) of this section, the same as if such claim had arisen before the date of the filing of the petition.

(2) A claim for damages calculated in accordance with section 562 shall be allowed under subsection (a), (b), or (c), or disallowed under subsection (d) or (e), as if such claim had arisen before the date of the filing of the petition.

(h) A claim arising from the recovery of property under section 522, 550, or 553 of this title shall be determined, and shall be allowed under subsection (a), (b), or (c) of this section, or disallowed under subsection (d) or (e) of this section, the same as if such claim had arisen before the date of the filing of the petition.

(i) A claim that does not arise until after the commencement of the case for a tax entitled to priority under section 507(a)(8) of this title shall be determined, and shall be allowed under subsection (a), (b), or (c) of this section, or disallowed under subsection (d) or (e) of this section, the same as if such claim had arisen before the date of the filing of the petition.

(j) A claim that has been allowed or disallowed may be reconsidered for cause. A reconsidered claim may be allowed or disallowed according to the equities of the case. Reconsideration of a claim under this subsection does not affect the validity of any payment or transfer from the estate made to a holder of an allowed claim on account of such allowed claim that is not reconsidered, but if a reconsidered claim is allowed and is of the same class as such holder's claim, such holder may not receive any additional payment or transfer from the estate on account of such holder's allowed claim until the holder of such reconsidered and allowed claim receives payment on account of such claim proportionate in value to that already received by such other holder. This subsection does not alter or modify the trustee's right to recover from a creditor any excess payment or transfer made to such creditor.

(k)(1) The court, on the motion of the debtor and after a hearing, may reduce a claim filed under this section based in whole on an unsecured consumer debt by not more than 20 percent of the claim, if—

    (A) the claim was filed by a creditor who unreasonably refused to negotiate a reasonable alternative repayment schedule proposed on behalf of the debtor by an approved nonprofit budget and credit counseling agency described in section 111;

    (B) the offer of the debtor under subparagraph (A)—

        (i) was made at least 60 days before the date of the filing of the petition; and

        (ii) provided for payment of at least 60 percent of the amount of the debt over a period not to exceed the repayment period of the loan, or a reasonable extension thereof; and

    (C) no part of the debt under the alternative repayment schedule is nondischargeable.

(2) The debtor shall have the burden of proving, by clear and convincing evidence, that—

    (A) the creditor unreasonably refused to consider the debtor's proposal; and

    (B) the proposed alternative repayment schedule was made prior to expiration of the 60-day period specified in paragraph (1)(B)(i).

(Pub.L. 95–598, Nov. 6, 1978, 92 Stat. 2579; Pub.L. 98–353, title III, § 445, July 10, 1984, 98 Stat. 373; Pub.L. 99–554, title II, §§ 257(j), 283(f), Oct. 27, 1986, 100 Stat. 3115, 3117; Pub.L. 103–394, title II, § 213(a), title III, § 304(h)(1), Oct. 22, 1994, 108 Stat. 4125, 4134; Pub.L. 109–8, title II, § 201(a), title VII, § 716(d), title IX, § 910(b), Apr. 20, 2005, 119 Stat. 42, 130. 184.)

§ 503. Allowance of administrative expenses

(a)   An entity may timely file a request for payment of an administrative expense, or may tardily file such request if permitted by the court for cause.

(b)   After notice and a hearing, there shall be allowed administrative expenses, other than claims allowed under section 502(f) of this title, including—

(1)(A)   the actual, necessary costs and expenses of preserving the estate including—

(i)   wages, salaries, and commissions for services rendered after the commencement of the case; and

(ii)   wages and benefits awarded pursuant to a judicial proceeding or a proceeding of the National Labor Relations Board as back pay attributable to any period of time occurring after commencement of the case under this title, as a result of a violation of Federal or State law by the debtor, without regard to the time of the occurrence of unlawful conduct on which such award is based or to whether any services were rendered, if the court determines that payment of wages and benefits by reason of the operation of this clause will not substantially increase the probability of layoff or termination of current employees, or of nonpayment of domestic support obligations, during the case under this title;

(B)   any tax—

(i)   incurred by the estate, whether secured or unsecured, including property taxes for which liability is in rem, in personam, or both, except a tax of a kind specified in section 507(a)(8) of this title; or

(ii)   attributable to an excessive allowance of a tentative carryback adjustment that the estate received, whether the taxable year to which such adjustment relates ended before or after the commencement of the case;

(C)   any fine, penalty, or reduction in credit relating to a tax of a kind specified in subparagraph (B) of this paragraph; and

(D)   notwithstanding the requirements of subsection (a), a governmental unit shall not be required to file a request for the payment of an expense described in subparagraph (B) or (C), as a condition of its being an allowed administrative expense;

(2)   compensation and reimbursement awarded under section 330(a) of this title;

(3)   the actual, necessary expenses, other than compensation and reimbursement specified in paragraph (4) of this subsection, incurred by—

(A)   a creditor that files a petition under section 303 of this title;

(B)   a creditor that recovers, after the court's approval, for the benefit of the estate any property transferred or concealed by the debtor;

(C)   a creditor in connection with the prosecution of a criminal offense relating to the case or to the business or property of the debtor;

(D)   a creditor, an indenture trustee, an equity security holder, or a committee representing creditors or equity security holders other than a committee appointed under section 1102 of this title, in making a substantial contribution in a case under chapter 9 or 11 of this title;

(E)   a custodian superseded under section 543 of this title, and compensation for the services of such custodian; or

(F)   a member of a committee appointed under section 1102 of this title, if such expenses are incurred in the performance of the duties of such committee;

(4)   reasonable compensation for professional services rendered by an attorney or an accountant of an entity whose expense is allowable under subparagraph (A), (B), (C), (D), or (E) of paragraph (3)

of this subsection, based on the time, the nature, the extent, and the value of such services, and the cost of comparable services other than in a case under this title, and reimbursement for actual, necessary expenses incurred by such attorney or accountant;

(5) reasonable compensation for services rendered by an indenture trustee in making a substantial contribution in a case under chapter 9 or 11 of this title, based on the time, the nature, the extent, and the value of such services, and the cost of comparable services other than in a case under this title;

(6) the fees and mileage payable under chapter 119 of title 28;

(7) with respect to a nonresidential real property lease previously assumed under section 365, and subsequently rejected, a sum equal to all monetary obligations due, excluding those arising from or relating to a failure to operate or a penalty provision, for the period of 2 years following the later of the rejection date or the date of actual turnover of the premises, without reduction or setoff for any reason whatsoever except for sums actually received or to be received from an entity other than the debtor, and the claim for remaining sums due for the balance of the term of the lease shall be a claim under section 502(b)(6);

(8) the actual, necessary costs and expenses of closing a health care business incurred by a trustee or by a Federal agency (as defined in section 551(1) of title 5) or a department or agency of a State or political subdivision thereof, including any cost or expense incurred—

(A) in disposing of patient records in accordance with section 351; or

(B) in connection with transferring patients from the health care business that is in the process of being closed to another health care business; and

(9) the value of any goods received by the debtor within 20 days before the date of commencement of a case under this title in which the goods have been sold to the debtor in the ordinary course of such debtor's business.

(c) Notwithstanding subsection (b), there shall neither be allowed, nor paid—

(1) a transfer made to, or an obligation incurred for the benefit of, an insider of the debtor for the purpose of inducing such person to remain with the debtor's business, absent a finding by the court based on evidence in the record that—

(A) the transfer or obligation is essential to retention of the person because the individual has a bona fide job offer from another business at the same or greater rate of compensation;

(B) the services provided by the person are essential to the survival of the business; and

(C) either—

(i) the amount of the transfer made to, or obligation incurred for the benefit of, the person is not greater than an amount equal to 10 times the amount of the mean transfer or obligation of a similar kind given to nonmanagement employees for any purpose during the calendar year in which the transfer is made or the obligation is incurred; or

(ii) if no such similar transfers were made to, or obligations were incurred for the benefit of, such nonmanagement employees during such calendar year, the amount of the transfer or obligation is not greater than an amount equal to 25 percent of the amount of any similar transfer or obligation made to or incurred for the benefit of such insider for any purpose during the calendar year before the year in which such transfer is made or obligation is incurred;

(2) a severance payment to an insider of the debtor, unless—

(A) the payment is part of a program that is generally applicable to all full-time employees; and

(B) the amount of the payment is not greater than 10 times the amount of the mean severance pay given to nonmanagement employees during the calendar year in which the payment is made; or

(3) other transfers or obligations that are outside the ordinary course of business and not justified by the facts and circumstances of the case, including transfers made to, or obligations incurred for the benefit of, officers, managers, or consultants hired after the date of the filing of the petition.

(Pub.L. 95–598, Nov. 6, 1978, 92 Stat. 2581; Pub.L. 98–353, title III, § 446, July 10, 1984, 98 Stat. 374; Pub.L. 99–554, title II, § 283(g), Oct. 27, 1986, 100 Stat. 3117; Pub.L. 103–394, title I, § 110, title II, § 213(c), title III, § 304(h)(2), Oct. 22, 1994, 108 Stat. 4113, 4126, 4134; Pub.L. 109–8, title III, §§ 329, 331, title IV, § 445, title VII, § 712(b), (c), title XI, § 1103, title XII, §§ 1208, 1227(b), Apr. 20, 2005, 119 Stat. 101, 102, 117, 128, 190, 194, 200.)

§ 504. Sharing of compensation

(a) Except as provided in subsection (b) of this section, a person receiving compensation or reimbursement under section 503(b)(2) or 503(b)(4) of this title may not share or agree to share—

(1) any such compensation or reimbursement with another person; or

(2) any compensation or reimbursement received by another person under such sections.

(b)(1) A member, partner, or regular associate in a professional association, corporation, or partnership may share compensation or reimbursement received under section 503(b)(2) or 503(b)(4) of this title with another member, partner, or regular associate in such association, corporation, or partnership, and may share in any compensation or reimbursement received under such sections by another member, partner, or regular associate in such association, corporation, or partnership.

(2) An attorney for a creditor that files a petition under section 303 of this title may share compensation and reimbursement received under section 503(b)(4) of this title with any other attorney contributing to the services rendered or expenses incurred by such creditor's attorney.

(c) This section shall not apply with respect to sharing, or agreeing to share, compensation with a bona fide public service attorney referral program that operates in accordance with non-Federal law regulating attorney referral services and with rules of professional responsibility applicable to attorney acceptance of referrals.

(Pub.L. 95–598, Nov. 6, 1978, 92 Stat. 2582; Pub.L. 109–8, Title III, § 326, Apr. 20, 2005, 119 Stat. 99.)

§ 505. Determination of tax liability

(a)(1) Except as provided in paragraph (2) of this subsection, the court may determine the amount or legality of any tax, any fine or penalty relating to a tax, or any addition to tax, whether or not previously assessed, whether or not paid, and whether or not contested before and adjudicated by a judicial or administrative tribunal of competent jurisdiction.

(2) The court may not so determine—

(A) the amount or legality of a tax, fine, penalty, or addition to tax if such amount or legality was contested before and adjudicated by a judicial or administrative tribunal of competent jurisdiction before the commencement of the case under this title;

(B) any right of the estate to a tax refund, before the earlier of—

(i) 120 days after the trustee properly requests such refund from the governmental unit from which such refund is claimed; or

(ii) a determination by such governmental unit of such request; or

(C) the amount or legality of any amount arising in connection with an ad valorem tax on real or personal property of the estate, if the applicable period for contesting or redetermining that amount under applicable nonbankruptcy law has expired.

(b)(1)(A) The clerk shall maintain a list under which a Federal, State, or local governmental unit responsible for the collection of taxes within the district may—

(i) designate an address for service of requests under this subsection; and

(ii) describe where further information concerning additional requirements for filing such requests may be found.

(B) If such governmental unit does not designate an address and provide such address to the clerk under subparagraph (A), any request made under this subsection may be served at the address for the filing of a tax return or protest with the appropriate taxing authority of such governmental unit.

(2) A trustee may request a determination of any unpaid liability of the estate for any tax incurred during the administration of the case by submitting a tax return for such tax and a request for such a determination to the governmental unit charged with responsibility for collection or determination of such tax at the address and in the manner designated in paragraph (1). Unless such return is fraudulent, or contains a material misrepresentation, the estate, the trustee, the debtor, and any successor to the debtor are discharged from any liability for such tax—

(A) upon payment of the tax shown on such return, if—

(i) such governmental unit does not notify the trustee, within 60 days after such request, that such return has been selected for examination; or

(ii) such governmental unit does not complete such an examination and notify the trustee of any tax due, within 180 days after such request or within such additional time as the court, for cause, permits;

(B) upon payment of the tax determined by the court, after notice and a hearing, after completion by such governmental unit of such examination; or

(C) upon payment of the tax determined by such governmental unit to be due.

(c) Notwithstanding section 362 of this title, after determination by the court of a tax under this section, the governmental unit charged with responsibility for collection of such tax may assess such tax against the estate, the debtor, or a successor to the debtor, as the case may be, subject to any otherwise applicable law.

(Pub.L. 95–598, Nov. 6, 1978, 92 Stat. 2582; Pub.L. 98–353, title III, § 447, July 10, 1984, 98 Stat. 374; Pub.L. 109–8, title VII, §§ 701(b), 703, 715, Apr. 20, 2005, 119 Stat. 124, 125, 129; Pub.L. 111–327, § 2(a)(14), Dec. 22, 2010, 124 Stat. 3559.)

§ 506. Determination of secured status

(a)(1) An allowed claim of a creditor secured by a lien on property in which the estate has an interest, or that is subject to setoff under section 553 of this title, is a secured claim to the extent of the value of such creditor's interest in the estate's interest in such property, or to the extent of the amount subject to setoff, as the case may be, and is an unsecured claim to the extent that the value of such creditor's interest or the amount so subject to setoff is less than the amount of such allowed claim. Such value shall be determined in light of the purpose of the valuation and of the proposed disposition or use of such property, and in conjunction with any hearing on such disposition or use or on a plan affecting such creditor's interest.

(2) If the debtor is an individual in a case under chapter 7 or 13, such value with respect to personal property securing an allowed claim shall be determined based on the replacement value of such property as of the date of the filing of the petition without deduction for costs of sale or marketing. With respect to property acquired for personal, family, or household purposes, replacement value shall mean the price a retail merchant would charge for property of that kind considering the age and condition of the property at the time value is determined.

(b) To the extent that an allowed secured claim is secured by property the value of which, after any recovery under subsection (c) of this section, is greater than the amount of such claim, there shall be allowed to the holder of such claim, interest on such claim, and any reasonable fees, costs, or charges provided for under the agreement or State statute under which such claim arose.

(c)   The trustee may recover from property securing an allowed secured claim the reasonable, necessary costs and expenses of preserving, or disposing of, such property to the extent of any benefit to the holder of such claim, including the payment of all ad valorem property taxes with respect to the property.

(d)   To the extent that a lien secures a claim against the debtor that is not an allowed secured claim, such lien is void, unless—

(1)   such claim was disallowed only under section 502(b)(5) or 502(e) of this title; or

(2)   such claim is not an allowed secured claim due only to the failure of any entity to file a proof of such claim under section 501 of this title.

(Pub.L. 95–598, Nov. 6, 1978, 92 Stat. 2583; Pub.L. 98–353, title III, § 448, July 10, 1984, 98 Stat. 374; Pub.L. 109–8, title III, § 327, title VII, § 712(d), Apr. 20, 2005, 119 Stat. 99, 128.)

§ 507.   Priorities

(a)   The following expenses and claims have priority in the following order:

(1)   First:

(A)   Allowed unsecured claims for domestic support obligations that, as of the date of the filing of the petition in a case under this title, are owed to or recoverable by a spouse, former spouse, or child of the debtor, or such child's parent, legal guardian, or responsible relative, without regard to whether the claim is filed by such person or is filed by a governmental unit on behalf of such person, on the condition that funds received under this paragraph by a governmental unit under this title after the date of the filing of the petition shall be applied and distributed in accordance with applicable nonbankruptcy law.

(B)   Subject to claims under subparagraph (A), allowed unsecured claims for domestic support obligations that, as of the date of the filing of the petition, are assigned by a spouse, former spouse, child of the debtor, or such child's parent, legal guardian, or responsible relative to a governmental unit (unless such obligation is assigned voluntarily by the spouse, former spouse, child, parent, legal guardian, or responsible relative of the child for the purpose of collecting the debt) or are owed directly to or recoverable by a governmental unit under applicable nonbankruptcy law, on the condition that funds received under this paragraph by a governmental unit under this title after the date of the filing of the petition be applied and distributed in accordance with applicable nonbankruptcy law.

(C)   If a trustee is appointed or elected under section 701, 702, 703, 1104, 1202, or 1302, the administrative expenses of the trustee allowed under paragraphs (1)(A), (2), and (6) of section 503(b) shall be paid before payment of claims under subparagraphs (A) and (B), to the extent that the trustee administers assets that are otherwise available for the payment of such claims.

(2)   Second, administrative expenses allowed under section 503(b) of this title, unsecured claims of any Federal reserve bank related to loans made through programs or facilities authorized under section 13(3) of the Federal Reserve Act (12 U.S.C. 343), and any fees and charges assessed against the estate under chapter 123 of title 28.

(3)   Third, unsecured claims allowed under section 502(f) of this title.

(4)   Fourth, allowed unsecured claims, but only to the extent of $12,850* for each individual or corporation, as the case may be, earned within 180 days before the date of the filing of the petition or the date of the cessation of the debtor's business, whichever occurs first, for—

---

*   *Note from West Advisory Panel: Dollar amounts adjusted pursuant to 11 U.S.C. § 104; 81 Fed. Reg. 8748 (Feb. 22, 2016).*

    (A) wages, salaries, or commissions, including vacation, severance, and sick leave pay earned by an individual; or

    (B) sales commissions earned by an individual or by a corporation with only 1 employee, acting as an independent contractor in the sale of goods or services for the debtor in the ordinary course of the debtor's business if, and only if, during the 12 months preceding that date, at least 75 percent of the amount that the individual or corporation earned by acting as an independent contractor in the sale of goods or services was earned from the debtor.

    (5) Fifth, allowed unsecured claims for contributions to an employee benefit plan—

    (A) arising from services rendered within 180 days before the date of the filing of the petition or the date of the cessation of the debtor's business, whichever occurs first; but only

    (B) for each such plan, to the extent of—

        (i) the number of employees covered by each such plan multiplied by \$12,850*; less

        (ii) the aggregate amount paid to such employees under paragraph (4) of this subsection, plus the aggregate amount paid by the estate on behalf of such employees to any other employee benefit plan.

    (6) Sixth, allowed unsecured claims of persons—

    (A) engaged in the production or raising of grain, as defined in section 557(b) of this title, against a debtor who owns or operates a grain storage facility, as defined in section 557(b) of this title, for grain or the proceeds of grain, or

    (B) engaged as a United States fisherman against a debtor who has acquired fish or fish produce from a fisherman through a sale or conversion, and who is engaged in operating a fish produce storage or processing facility—

but only to the extent of \$6,325* for each such individual.

    (7) Seventh, allowed unsecured claims of individuals, to the extent of \$2,850* for each such individual, arising from the deposit, before the commencement of the case, of money in connection with the purchase, lease, or rental of property, or the purchase of services, for the personal, family, or household use of such individuals, that were not delivered or provided.

    (8) Eighth, allowed unsecured claims of governmental units, only to the extent that such claims are for—

    (A) a tax on or measured by income or gross receipts for a taxable year ending on or before the date of the filing of the petition—

        (i) for which a return, if required, is last due, including extensions, after three years before the date of the filing of the petition;

        (ii) assessed within 240 days before the date of the filing of the petition, exclusive of—

            (I) any time during which an offer in compromise with respect to that tax was pending or in effect during that 240-day period, plus 30 days; and

            (II) any time during which a stay of proceedings against collections was in effect in a prior case under this title during that 240-day period, plus 90 days; or

        (iii) other than a tax of a kind specified in section 523(a)(1)(B) or 523(a)(1)(C) of this title, not assessed before, but assessable, under applicable law or by agreement, after, the commencement of the case;

    (B) a property tax incurred before the commencement of the case and last payable without penalty after one year before the date of the filing of the petition;

---

    * *Note from West Advisory Panel: Dollar amounts adjusted pursuant to 11 U.S.C. § 104; 81 Fed. Reg. 8748 (Feb. 22, 2016).*

    (C) a tax required to be collected or withheld and for which the debtor is liable in whatever capacity;

    (D) an employment tax on a wage, salary, or commission of a kind specified in paragraph (4) of this subsection earned from the debtor before the date of the filing of the petition, whether or not actually paid before such date, for which a return is last due, under applicable law or under any extension, after three years before the date of the filing of the petition;

    (E) an excise tax on—

        (i) a transaction occurring before the date of the filing of the petition for which a return, if required, is last due, under applicable law or under any extension, after three years before the date of the filing of the petition; or

        (ii) if a return is not required, a transaction occurring during the three years immediately preceding the date of the filing of the petition;

    (F) a customs duty arising out of the importation of merchandise—

        (i) entered for consumption within one year before the date of the filing of the petition;

        (ii) covered by an entry liquidated or reliquidated within one year before the date of the filing of the petition; or

        (iii) entered for consumption within four years before the date of the filing of the petition but unliquidated on such date, if the Secretary of the Treasury certifies that failure to liquidate such entry was due to an investigation pending on such date into assessment of antidumping or countervailing duties or fraud, or if information needed for the proper appraisement or classification of such merchandise was not available to the appropriate customs officer before such date; or

    (G) a penalty related to a claim of a kind specified in this paragraph and in compensation for actual pecuniary loss.

An otherwise applicable time period specified in this paragraph shall be suspended for any period during which a governmental unit is prohibited under applicable nonbankruptcy law from collecting a tax as a result of a request by the debtor for a hearing and an appeal of any collection action taken or proposed against the debtor, plus 90 days; plus any time during which the stay of proceedings was in effect in a prior case under this title or during which collection was precluded by the existence of 1 or more confirmed plans under this title, plus 90 days.

    (9) Ninth, allowed unsecured claims based upon any commitment by the debtor to a Federal depository institutions regulatory agency (or predecessor to such agency) to maintain the capital of an insured depository institution.

    (10) Tenth, allowed claims for death or personal injury resulting from the operation of a motor vehicle or vessel if such operation was unlawful because the debtor was intoxicated from using alcohol, a drug, or another substance.

    (b) If the trustee, under section 362, 363, or 364 of this title, provides adequate protection of the interest of a holder of a claim secured by a lien on property of the debtor and if, notwithstanding such protection, such creditor has a claim allowable under subsection (a)(2) of this section arising from the stay of action against such property under section 362 of this title, from the use, sale, or lease of such property under section 363 of this title, or from the granting of a lien under section 364(d) of this title, then such creditor's claim under such subsection shall have priority over every other claim allowable under such subsection.

    (c) For the purpose of subsection (a) of this section, a claim of a governmental unit arising from an erroneous refund or credit of a tax has the same priority as a claim for the tax to which such refund or credit relates.

(d) An entity that is subrogated to the rights of a holder of a claim of a kind specified in subsection (a)(1), (a)(4), (a)(5), (a)(6), (a)(7), (a)(8), or (a)(9) of this section is not subrogated to the right of the holder of such claim to priority under such subsection.

(Pub.L. 95–598, Nov. 6, 1978, 92 Stat. 2583; Pub.L. 98–353, title III, §§ 350, 449, July 10, 1984, 98 Stat. 358, 374; Pub.L. 101–647, title XXV, § 2522(d), Nov. 29, 1990, 104 Stat. 4867; Pub.L. 103–394, title I, § 108(c), title II, § 207, title III, § 304(c), title V, § 501(b)(3), (d)(11), Oct. 22, 1994, 108 Stat. 4112, 4123, 4132, 4142, 4145; Pub.L. 109–8, title II, §§ 212, 223, title VII, §§ 705, 706, title XIV, § 1401, title XV, § 1502(a)(1), Apr. 20, 2005, 119 Stat. 51, 62, 126, 214, 216; Pub.L. 111–203, title XI, § 1101(b), July 21, 2010, 124 Stat. 2115; Pub.L. 111–327, § 2(a)(15), Dec. 22, 2010, 124 Stat. 3559.)

§ 508.   Effect of distribution other than under this title

If a creditor of a partnership debtor receives, from a general partner that is not a debtor in a case under chapter 7 of this title, payment of, or a transfer of property on account of, a claim that is allowed under this title and that is not secured by a lien on property of such partner, such creditor may not receive any payment under this title on account of such claim until each of the other holders of claims on account of which such holders are entitled to share equally with such creditor under this title has received payment under this title equal in value to the consideration received by such creditor from such general partner.

(Pub.L. 95–598, Nov. 6, 1978, 92 Stat. 2585; Pub.L. 109–8, title VIII, § 802(d)(7), Apr. 20, 2005, 119 Stat. 146.)

§ 509.   Claims of codebtors

(a) Except as provided in subsection (b) or (c) of this section, an entity that is liable with the debtor on, or that has secured, a claim of a creditor against the debtor, and that pays such claim, is subrogated to the rights of such creditor to the extent of such payment.

(b) Such entity is not subrogated to the rights of such creditor to the extent that—

   (1) a claim of such entity for reimbursement or contribution on account of such payment of such creditor's claim is—

   (A) allowed under section 502 of this title;

   (B) disallowed other than under section 502(e) of this title; or

   (C) subordinated under section 510 of this title; or

   (2) as between the debtor and such entity, such entity received the consideration for the claim held by such creditor.

(c) The court shall subordinate to the claim of a creditor and for the benefit of such creditor an allowed claim, by way of subrogation under this section, or for reimbursement or contribution, of an entity that is liable with the debtor on, or that has secured, such creditor's claim, until such creditor's claim is paid in full, either through payments under this title or otherwise.

(Pub.L. 95–598, Nov. 6, 1978, 92 Stat. 2585; Pub.L. 98–353, title III, § 450, July 10, 1984, 98 Stat. 375.)

§ 510.   Subordination

(a) A subordination agreement is enforceable in a case under this title to the same extent that such agreement is enforceable under applicable nonbankruptcy law.

(b) For the purpose of distribution under this title, a claim arising from rescission of a purchase or sale of a security of the debtor or of an affiliate of the debtor, for damages arising from the purchase or sale of such a security, or for reimbursement or contribution allowed under section 502 on account of such a claim, shall be subordinated to all claims or interests that are senior to or equal the claim or interest represented by such security, except that if such security is common stock, such claim has the same priority as common stock.

(c) Notwithstanding subsections (a) and (b) of this section, after notice and a hearing, the court may—

    (1) under principles of equitable subordination, subordinate for purposes of distribution all or part of an allowed claim to all or part of another allowed claim or all or part of an allowed interest to all or part of another allowed interest; or

    (2) order that any lien securing such a subordinated claim be transferred to the estate.

    (Pub.L. 95–598, Nov. 6, 1978, 92 Stat. 2586; Pub.L. 98–353, title III, § 451, July 10, 1984, 98 Stat. 375.)

§ 511. Rate of interest on tax claims

    (a) If any provision of this title requires the payment of interest on a tax claim or on an administrative expense tax, or the payment of interest to enable a creditor to receive the present value of the allowed amount of a tax claim, the rate of interest shall be the rate determined under applicable nonbankruptcy law.

    (b) In the case of taxes paid under a confirmed plan under this title, the rate of interest shall be determined as of the calendar month in which the plan is confirmed.

    (Added Pub.L. 109–8, title VII, § 704(a), Apr. 20, 2005, 119 Stat. 125.)

SUBCHAPTER II—DEBTOR'S DUTIES AND BENEFITS

§ 521. Debtor's duties

    (a) The debtor shall—

        (1) file—

            (A) a list of creditors; and

            (B) unless the court orders otherwise—

                (i) a schedule of assets and liabilities;

                (ii) a schedule of current income and current expenditures;

                (iii) a statement of the debtor's financial affairs and, if section 342(b) applies, a certificate—

                    (I) of an attorney whose name is indicated on the petition as the attorney for the debtor, or a bankruptcy petition preparer signing the petition under section 110(b)(1), indicating that such attorney or the bankruptcy petition preparer delivered to the debtor the notice required by section 342(b); or

                    (II) if no attorney is so indicated, and no bankruptcy petition preparer signed the petition, of the debtor that such notice was received and read by the debtor;

                (iv) copies of all payment advices or other evidence of payment received within 60 days before the date of the filing of the petition, by the debtor from any employer of the debtor;

                (v) a statement of the amount of monthly net income, itemized to show how the amount is calculated; and

                (vi) a statement disclosing any reasonably anticipated increase in income or expenditures over the 12-month period following the date of the filing of the petition;

        (2) if an individual debtor's schedule of assets and liabilities includes debts which are secured by property of the estate—

            (A) within thirty days after the date of the filing of a petition under chapter 7 of this title or on or before the date of the meeting of creditors, whichever is earlier, or within such additional time as the court, for cause, within such period fixes, file with the clerk a statement of his intention with respect to the retention or surrender of such property and, if applicable, specifying that such property is claimed as exempt, that the debtor intends to redeem such property, or that the debtor intends to reaffirm debts secured by such property; and

(B) within 30 days after the first date set for the meeting of creditors under section 341(a), or within such additional time as the court, for cause, within such 30-day period fixes, perform his intention with respect to such property, as specified by subparagraph (A) of this paragraph;

except that nothing in subparagraphs (A) and (B) of this paragraph shall alter the debtor's or the trustee's rights with regard to such property under this title, except as provided in section 362(h);

(3) if a trustee is serving in the case or an auditor is serving under section 586(f) of title 28, cooperate with the trustee as necessary to enable the trustee to perform the trustee's duties under this title;

(4) if a trustee is serving in the case or an auditor is serving under section 586(f) of title 28, surrender to the trustee all property of the estate and any recorded information, including books, documents, records, and papers, relating to property of the estate, whether or not immunity is granted under section 344 of this title;

(5) appear at the hearing required under section 524(d) of this title;

(6) in a case under chapter 7 of this title in which the debtor is an individual, not retain possession of personal property as to which a creditor has an allowed claim for the purchase price secured in whole or in part by an interest in such personal property unless the debtor, not later than 45 days after the first meeting of creditors under section 341(a), either—

(A) enters into an agreement with the creditor pursuant to section 524(c) with respect to the claim secured by such property; or

(B) redeems such property from the security interest pursuant to section 722; and

(7) unless a trustee is serving in the case, continue to perform the obligations required of the administrator (as defined in section 3 of the Employee Retirement Income Security Act of 1974) of an employee benefit plan if at the time of the commencement of the case the debtor (or any entity designated by the debtor) served as such administrator.

If the debtor fails to so act within the 45-day period referred to in paragraph (6), the stay under section 362(a) is terminated with respect to the personal property of the estate or of the debtor which is affected, such property shall no longer be property of the estate, and the creditor may take whatever action as to such property as is permitted by applicable nonbankruptcy law, unless the court determines on the motion of the trustee filed before the expiration of such 45-day period, and after notice and a hearing, that such property is of consequential value or benefit to the estate, orders appropriate adequate protection of the creditor's interest, and orders the debtor to deliver any collateral in the debtor's possession to the trustee.

(b) In addition to the requirements under subsection (a), a debtor who is an individual shall file with the court—

(1) a certificate from the approved nonprofit budget and credit counseling agency that provided the debtor services under section 109(h) describing the services provided to the debtor; and

(2) a copy of the debt repayment plan, if any, developed under section 109(h) through the approved nonprofit budget and credit counseling agency referred to in paragraph (1).

(c) In addition to meeting the requirements under subsection (a), a debtor shall file with the court a record of any interest that a debtor has in an education individual retirement account (as defined in section 530(b)(1) of the Internal Revenue Code of 1986), an interest in an account in a qualified ABLE program (as defined in section 529A(b) of such Code,[1] or under a qualified State tuition program (as defined in section 529(b)(1) of such Code).

(d)   If the debtor fails timely to take the action specified in subsection (a)(6) of this section, or in paragraphs (1) and (2) of section 362(h), with respect to property which a lessor or bailor owns and has leased, rented, or bailed to the debtor or as to which a creditor holds a security interest not otherwise voidable under section 522(f), 544, 545, 547, 548, or 549, nothing in this title shall prevent or limit the operation of a provision in the underlying lease or agreement that has the effect of placing the debtor in default under such lease or agreement by reason of the occurrence, pendency, or existence of a proceeding under this title or the insolvency of the debtor. Nothing in this subsection shall be deemed to justify limiting such a provision in any other circumstance.

(e)(1)   If the debtor in a case under chapter 7 or 13 is an individual and if a creditor files with the court at any time a request to receive a copy of the petition, schedules, and statement of financial affairs filed by the debtor, then the court shall make such petition, such schedules, and such statement available to such creditor.

> **(2)(A)**   The debtor shall provide—
>
> > **(i)**   not later than 7 days before the date first set for the first meeting of creditors, to the trustee a copy of the Federal income tax return required under applicable law (or at the election of the debtor, a transcript of such return) for the most recent tax year ending immediately before the commencement of the case and for which a Federal income tax return was filed; and
> >
> > **(ii)**   at the same time the debtor complies with clause (i), a copy of such return (or if elected under clause (i), such transcript) to any creditor that timely requests such copy.
>
> **(B)**   If the debtor fails to comply with clause (i) or (ii) of subparagraph (A), the court shall dismiss the case unless the debtor demonstrates that the failure to so comply is due to circumstances beyond the control of the debtor.
>
> **(C)**   If a creditor requests a copy of such tax return or such transcript and if the debtor fails to provide a copy of such tax return or such transcript to such creditor at the time the debtor provides such tax return or such transcript to the trustee, then the court shall dismiss the case unless the debtor demonstrates that the failure to provide a copy of such tax return or such transcript is due to circumstances beyond the control of the debtor.
>
> **(3)**   If a creditor in a case under chapter 13 files with the court at any time a request to receive a copy of the plan filed by the debtor, then the court shall make available to such creditor a copy of the plan—
>
> > **(A)**   at a reasonable cost; and
> >
> > **(B)**   not later than 7 days after such request is filed.

(f)   At the request of the court, the United States trustee, or any party in interest in a case under chapter 7, 11, or 13, a debtor who is an individual shall file with the court—

> **(1)**   at the same time filed with the taxing authority, a copy of each Federal income tax return required under applicable law (or at the election of the debtor, a transcript of such tax return) with respect to each tax year of the debtor ending while the case is pending under such chapter;
>
> **(2)**   at the same time filed with the taxing authority, each Federal income tax return required under applicable law (or at the election of the debtor, a transcript of such tax return) that had not been filed with such authority as of the date of the commencement of the case and that was subsequently filed for any tax year of the debtor ending in the 3-year period ending on the date of the commencement of the case;

---

[1]   So in original. A closing parenthesis probably should precede the comma.

(3) a copy of each amendment to any Federal income tax return or transcript filed with the court under paragraph (1) or (2); and

(4) in a case under chapter 13—

(A) on the date that is either 90 days after the end of such tax year or 1 year after the date of the commencement of the case, whichever is later, if a plan is not confirmed before such later date; and

(B) annually after the plan is confirmed and until the case is closed, not later than the date that is 45 days before the anniversary of the confirmation of the plan;

a statement, under penalty of perjury, of the income and expenditures of the debtor during the tax year of the debtor most recently concluded before such statement is filed under this paragraph, and of the monthly income of the debtor, that shows how income, expenditures, and monthly income are calculated.

(g)(1) A statement referred to in subsection (f)(4) shall disclose—

(A) the amount and sources of the income of the debtor;

(B) the identity of any person responsible with the debtor for the support of any dependent of the debtor; and

(C) the identity of any person who contributed, and the amount contributed, to the household in which the debtor resides.

(2) The tax returns, amendments, and statement of income and expenditures described in subsections (e)(2)(A) and (f) shall be available to the United States trustee (or the bankruptcy administrator, if any), the trustee, and any party in interest for inspection and copying, subject to the requirements of section 315(c) of the Bankruptcy Abuse Prevention and Consumer Protection Act of 2005.

(h) If requested by the United States trustee or by the trustee, the debtor shall provide—

(1) a document that establishes the identity of the debtor, including a driver's license, passport, or other document that contains a photograph of the debtor; or

(2) such other personal identifying information relating to the debtor that establishes the identity of the debtor.

(i)(1) Subject to paragraphs (2) and (4) and notwithstanding section 707(a), if an individual debtor in a voluntary case under chapter 7 or 13 fails to file all of the information required under subsection (a)(1) within 45 days after the date of the filing of the petition, the case shall be automatically dismissed effective on the 46th day after the date of the filing of the petition.

(2) Subject to paragraph (4) and with respect to a case described in paragraph (1), any party in interest may request the court to enter an order dismissing the case. If requested, the court shall enter an order of dismissal not later than 7 days after such request.

(3) Subject to paragraph (4) and upon request of the debtor made within 45 days after the date of the filing of the petition described in paragraph (1), the court may allow the debtor an additional period of not to exceed 45 days to file the information required under subsection (a)(1) if the court finds justification for extending the period for the filing.

(4) Notwithstanding any other provision of this subsection, on the motion of the trustee filed before the expiration of the applicable period of time specified in paragraph (1), (2), or (3), and after notice and a hearing, the court may decline to dismiss the case if the court finds that the debtor attempted in good faith to file all the information required by subsection (a)(1)(B)(iv) and that the best interests of creditors would be served by administration of the case.

(j)(1) Notwithstanding any other provision of this title, if the debtor fails to file a tax return that becomes due after the commencement of the case or to properly obtain an extension of the due date for filing such return, the taxing authority may request that the court enter an order converting or dismissing the case.

    (2) If the debtor does not file the required return or obtain the extension referred to in paragraph (1) within 90 days after a request is filed by the taxing authority under that paragraph, the court shall convert or dismiss the case, whichever is in the best interests of creditors and the estate.

    (Pub.L. 95–598, Nov. 6, 1978, 92 Stat. 2586; Pub.L. 98–353, title III, §§ 305, 452, July 10, 1984, 98 Stat. 352, 375; Pub.L. 99–554, title II, § 283(h), Oct. 27, 1986, 100 Stat. 3117; Pub.L. 109–8, title I, § 106(d), title II, § 225(b), title III, §§ 304(1), 305(2), 315(b), 316, title IV, § 446(a), title VI, § 603(c), title VII, § 720, Apr. 20, 2005, 119 Stat. 38, 66, 78, 80, 89, 90, 92, 118, 123, 133; Pub.L. 111–16, § 2(5), (6), May 7, 2009, 123 Stat. 1607; Pub.L. 111–327, § 2(a)(16), Dec. 22, 2010, 124 Stat. 3559; Pub.L. 113–295, div. B, title I, § 104(C), Dec. 19, 2014, 128 Stat. 4064.)

§ 522.　Exemptions

    (a) In this section—

        (1) "dependent" includes spouse, whether or not actually dependent; and

        (2) "value" means fair market value as of the date of the filing of the petition or, with respect to property that becomes property of the estate after such date, as of the date such property becomes property of the estate.

    (b)(1) Notwithstanding section 541 of this title, an individual debtor may exempt from property of the estate the property listed in either paragraph (2) or, in the alternative, paragraph (3) of this subsection. In joint cases filed under section 302 of this title and individual cases filed under section 301 or 303 of this title by or against debtors who are husband and wife, and whose estates are ordered to be jointly administered under Rule 1015(b) of the Federal Rules of Bankruptcy Procedure, one debtor may not elect to exempt property listed in paragraph (2) and the other debtor elect to exempt property listed in paragraph (3) of this subsection. If the parties cannot agree on the alternative to be elected, they shall be deemed to elect paragraph (2), where such election is permitted under the law of the jurisdiction where the case is filed.

        (2) Property listed in this paragraph is property that is specified under subsection (d), unless the State law that is applicable to the debtor under paragraph (3)(A) specifically does not so authorize.

        (3) Property listed in this paragraph is—

            (A) subject to subsections (*o*) and (p), any property that is exempt under Federal law, other than subsection (d) of this section, or State or local law that is applicable on the date of the filing of the petition to the place in which the debtor's domicile has been located for the 730 days immediately preceding the date of the filing of the petition or if the debtor's domicile has not been located in a single State for such 730-day period, the place in which the debtor's domicile was located for 180 days immediately preceding the 730-day period or for a longer portion of such 180-day period than in any other place;

            (B) any interest in property in which the debtor had, immediately before the commencement of the case, an interest as a tenant by the entirety or joint tenant to the extent that such interest as a tenant by the entirety or joint tenant is exempt from process under applicable nonbankruptcy law; and

            (C) retirement funds to the extent that those funds are in a fund or account that is exempt from taxation under section 401, 403, 408, 408A, 414, 457, or 501(a) of the Internal Revenue Code of 1986.

If the effect of the domiciliary requirement under subparagraph (A) is to render the debtor ineligible for any exemption, the debtor may elect to exempt property that is specified under subsection (d).

        (4) For purposes of paragraph (3)(C) and subsection (d)(12), the following shall apply:

            (A) If the retirement funds are in a retirement fund that has received a favorable determination under section 7805 of the Internal Revenue Code of 1986, and that determination is in effect as of the date of the filing of the petition in a case under this title, those funds shall be presumed to be exempt from the estate.

(B) If the retirement funds are in a retirement fund that has not received a favorable determination under such section 7805, those funds are exempt from the estate if the debtor demonstrates that—

(i) no prior determination to the contrary has been made by a court or the Internal Revenue Service; and

(ii)(I) the retirement fund is in substantial compliance with the applicable requirements of the Internal Revenue Code of 1986; or

(II) the retirement fund fails to be in substantial compliance with the applicable requirements of the Internal Revenue Code of 1986 and the debtor is not materially responsible for that failure.

(C) A direct transfer of retirement funds from 1 fund or account that is exempt from taxation under section 401, 403, 408, 408A, 414, 457, or 501(a) of the Internal Revenue Code of 1986, under section 401(a)(31) of the Internal Revenue Code of 1986, or otherwise, shall not cease to qualify for exemption under paragraph (3)(C) or subsection (d)(12) by reason of such direct transfer.

(D)(i) Any distribution that qualifies as an eligible rollover distribution within the meaning of section 402(c) of the Internal Revenue Code of 1986 or that is described in clause (ii) shall not cease to qualify for exemption under paragraph (3)(C) or subsection (d)(12) by reason of such distribution.

(ii) A distribution described in this clause is an amount that—

(I) has been distributed from a fund or account that is exempt from taxation under section 401, 403, 408, 408A, 414, 457, or 501(a) of the Internal Revenue Code of 1986; and

(II) to the extent allowed by law, is deposited in such a fund or account not later than 60 days after the distribution of such amount.

(c) Unless the case is dismissed, property exempted under this section is not liable during or after the case for any debt of the debtor that arose, or that is determined under section 502 of this title as if such debt had arisen, before the commencement of the case, except—

(1) a debt of a kind specified in paragraph (1) or (5) of section 523(a) (in which case, notwithstanding any provision of applicable nonbankruptcy law to the contrary, such property shall be liable for a debt of a kind specified in such paragraph);

(2) a debt secured by a lien that is—

(A)(i) not avoided under subsection (f) or (g) of this section or under section 544, 545, 547, 548, 549, or 724(a) of this title; and

(ii) not void under section 506(d) of this title; or

(B) a tax lien, notice of which is properly filed;

(3) a debt of a kind specified in section 523(a)(4) or 523(a)(6) of this title owed by an institution-affiliated party of an insured depository institution to a Federal depository institutions regulatory agency acting in its capacity as conservator, receiver, or liquidating agent for such institution; or

(4) a debt in connection with fraud in the obtaining or providing of any scholarship, grant, loan, tuition, discount, award, or other financial assistance for purposes of financing an education at an institution of higher education (as that term is defined in section 101 of the Higher Education Act of 1965 (20 U.S.C. 1001)).

(d) The following property may be exempted under subsection (b)(2) of this section:

(1)   The debtor's aggregate interest, not to exceed $23,675* in value, in real property or personal property that the debtor or a dependent of the debtor uses as a residence, in a cooperative that owns property that the debtor or a dependent of the debtor uses as a residence, or in a burial plot for the debtor or a dependent of the debtor.

(2)   The debtor's interest, not to exceed $3,775* in value, in one motor vehicle.

(3)   The debtor's interest, not to exceed $600* in value in any particular item or $12,625* in aggregate value, in household furnishings, household goods, wearing apparel, appliances, books, animals, crops, or musical instruments, that are held primarily for the personal, family, or household use of the debtor or a dependent of the debtor.

(4)   The debtor's aggregate interest, not to exceed $1,600* in value, in jewelry held primarily for the personal, family, or household use of the debtor or a dependent of the debtor.

(5)   The debtor's aggregate interest in any property, not to exceed in value $1,250* plus up to $11,850* of any unused amount of the exemption provided under paragraph (1) of this subsection.

(6)   The debtor's aggregate interest, not to exceed $2,375* in value, in any implements, professional books, or tools, of the trade of the debtor or the trade of a dependent of the debtor.

(7)   Any unmatured life insurance contract owned by the debtor, other than a credit life insurance contract.

(8)   The debtor's aggregate interest, not to exceed in value $12,625* less any amount of property of the estate transferred in the manner specified in section 542(d) of this title, in any accrued dividend or interest under, or loan value of, any unmatured life insurance contract owned by the debtor under which the insured is the debtor or an individual of whom the debtor is a dependent.

(9)   Professionally prescribed health aids for the debtor or a dependent of the debtor.

(10) The debtor's right to receive—

(A)   a social security benefit, unemployment compensation, or a local public assistance benefit;

(B)   a veterans' benefit;

(C)   a disability, illness, or unemployment benefit;

(D)   alimony, support, or separate maintenance, to the extent reasonably necessary for the support of the debtor and any dependent of the debtor;

(E)   a payment under a stock bonus, pension, profitsharing, annuity, or similar plan or contract on account of illness, disability, death, age, or length of service, to the extent reasonably necessary for the support of the debtor and any dependent of the debtor, unless—

(i)   such plan or contract was established by or under the auspices of an insider that employed the debtor at the time the debtor's rights under such plan or contract arose;

(ii)   such payment is on account of age or length of service; and

(iii)   such plan or contract does not qualify under section 401(a), 403(a), 403(b), or 408 of the Internal Revenue Code of 1986.

(11) The debtor's right to receive, or property that is traceable to—

(A)   an award under a crime victim's reparation law;

(B)   a payment on account of the wrongful death of an individual of whom the debtor was a dependent, to the extent reasonably necessary for the support of the debtor and any dependent of the debtor;

---

*   *Note from West Advisory Panel: Dollar amounts adjusted pursuant to 11 U.S.C. § 104; 81 Fed. Reg. 8748 (Feb. 22, 2016).*

(C) a payment under a life insurance contract that insured the life of an individual of whom the debtor was a dependent on the date of such individual's death, to the extent reasonably necessary for the support of the debtor and any dependent of the debtor;

(D) a payment, not to exceed $23,675*, on account of personal bodily injury, not including pain and suffering or compensation for actual pecuniary loss, of the debtor or an individual of whom the debtor is a dependent; or

(E) a payment in compensation of loss of future earnings of the debtor or an individual of whom the debtor is or was a dependent, to the extent reasonably necessary for the support of the debtor and any dependent of the debtor.

(12) Retirement funds to the extent that those funds are in a fund or account that is exempt from taxation under section 401, 403, 408, 408A, 414, 457, or 501(a) of the Internal Revenue Code of 1986.

(e) A waiver of an exemption executed in favor of a creditor that holds an unsecured claim against the debtor is unenforceable in a case under this title with respect to such claim against property that the debtor may exempt under subsection (b) of this section. A waiver by the debtor of a power under subsection (f) or (h) of this section to avoid a transfer, under subsection (g) or (i) of this section to exempt property, or under subsection (i) of this section to recover property or to preserve a transfer, is unenforceable in a case under this title.

(f)(1) Notwithstanding any waiver of exemptions but subject to paragraph (3), the debtor may avoid the fixing of a lien on an interest of the debtor in property to the extent that such lien impairs an exemption to which the debtor would have been entitled under subsection (b) of this section, if such lien is—

(A) a judicial lien, other than a judicial lien that secures a debt of a kind that is specified in section 523(a)(5); or

(B) a nonpossessory, nonpurchase-money security interest in any—

(i) household furnishings, household goods, wearing apparel, appliances, books, animals, crops, musical instruments, or jewelry that are held primarily for the personal, family, or household use of the debtor or a dependent of the debtor;

(ii) implements, professional books, or tools, of the trade of the debtor or the trade of a dependent of the debtor; or

(iii) professionally prescribed health aids for the debtor or a dependent of the debtor.

(2)(A) For the purposes of this subsection, a lien shall be considered to impair an exemption to the extent that the sum of—

(i) the lien;

(ii) all other liens on the property; and

(iii) the amount of the exemption that the debtor could claim if there were no liens on the property;

exceeds the value that the debtor's interest in the property would have in the absence of any liens.

(B) In the case of a property subject to more than 1 lien, a lien that has been avoided shall not be considered in making the calculation under subparagraph (A) with respect to other liens.

(C) This paragraph shall not apply with respect to a judgment arising out of a mortgage foreclosure.

(3) In a case in which State law that is applicable to the debtor—

(A) permits a person to voluntarily waive a right to claim exemptions under subsection (d) or prohibits a debtor from claiming exemptions under subsection (d); and

---

* *Note from West Advisory Panel: Dollar amounts adjusted pursuant to 11 U.S.C. § 104; 81 Fed. Reg. 8748 (Feb. 22, 2016).*

(B) either permits the debtor to claim exemptions under State law without limitation in amount, except to the extent that the debtor has permitted the fixing of a consensual lien on any property or prohibits avoidance of a consensual lien on property otherwise eligible to be claimed as exempt property;

the debtor may not avoid the fixing of a lien on an interest of the debtor or a dependent of the debtor in property if the lien is a nonpossessory, nonpurchase-money security interest in implements, professional books, or tools of the trade of the debtor or a dependent of the debtor or farm animals or crops of the debtor or a dependent of the debtor to the extent the value of such implements, professional books, tools of the trade, animals, and crops exceeds $6,425.*

(4)(A)   Subject to subparagraph (B), for purposes of paragraph (1)(B), the term "household goods" means—

    (i)   clothing;

    (ii)   furniture;

    (iii)   appliances;

    (iv)   1 radio;

    (v)   1 television;

    (vi)   1 VCR;

    (vii)   linens;

    (viii)   china;

    (ix)   crockery;

    (x)   kitchenware;

    (xi)   educational materials and educational equipment primarily for the use of minor dependent children of the debtor;

    (xii)   medical equipment and supplies;

    (xiii)   furniture exclusively for the use of minor children, or elderly or disabled dependents of the debtor;

    (xiv)   personal effects (including the toys and hobby equipment of minor dependent children and wedding rings) of the debtor and the dependents of the debtor; and

    (xv)   1 personal computer and related equipment.

(B)   The term "household goods" does not include—

    (i)   works of art (unless by or of the debtor, or any relative of the debtor);

    (ii)   electronic entertainment equipment with a fair market value of more than $675* in the aggregate (except 1 television, 1 radio, and 1 VCR);

    (iii)   items acquired as antiques with a fair market value of more than $675* in the aggregate;

    (iv)   jewelry with a fair market value of more than $675* in the aggregate (except wedding rings); and

    (v)   a computer (except as otherwise provided for in this section), motor vehicle (including a tractor or lawn tractor), boat, or a motorized recreational device, conveyance, vehicle, watercraft, or aircraft.

---

*   *Note from West Advisory Panel: Dollar amounts adjusted pursuant to 11 U.S.C. § 104; 81 Fed. Reg. 8748 (Feb. 22, 2016).*

(g) Notwithstanding sections 550 and 551 of this title, the debtor may exempt under subsection (b) of this section property that the trustee recovers under section 510(c)(2), 542, 543, 550, 551, or 553 of this title, to the extent that the debtor could have exempted such property under subsection (b) of this section if such property had not been transferred, if—

    (1)(A) such transfer was not a voluntary transfer of such property by the debtor; and

        (B) the debtor did not conceal such property; or

    (2) the debtor could have avoided such transfer under subsection (f)(1)(B) of this section.

(h) The debtor may avoid a transfer of property of the debtor or recover a setoff to the extent that the debtor could have exempted such property under subsection (g)(1) of this section if the trustee had avoided such transfer, if—

    (1) such transfer is avoidable by the trustee under section 544, 545, 547, 548, 549, or 724(a) of this title or recoverable by the trustee under section 553 of this title; and

    (2) the trustee does not attempt to avoid such transfer.

(i)(1) If the debtor avoids a transfer or recovers a setoff under subsection (f) or (h) of this section, the debtor may recover in the manner prescribed by, and subject to the limitations of, section 550 of this title, the same as if the trustee had avoided such transfer, and may exempt any property so recovered under subsection (b) of this section.

    (2) Notwithstanding section 551 of this title, a transfer avoided under section 544, 545, 547, 548, 549, or 724(a) of this title, under subsection (f) or (h) of this section, or property recovered under section 553 of this title, may be preserved for the benefit of the debtor to the extent that the debtor may exempt such property under subsection (g) of this section or paragraph (1) of this subsection.

(j) Notwithstanding subsections (g) and (i) of this section, the debtor may exempt a particular kind of property under subsections (g) and (i) of this section only to the extent that the debtor has exempted less property in value of such kind than that to which the debtor is entitled under subsection (b) of this section.

(k) Property that the debtor exempts under this section is not liable for payment of any administrative expense except—

    (1) the aliquot share of the costs and expenses of avoiding a transfer of property that the debtor exempts under subsection (g) of this section, or of recovery of such property, that is attributable to the value of the portion of such property exempted in relation to the value of the property recovered; and

    (2) any costs and expenses of avoiding a transfer under subsection (f) or (h) of this section, or of recovery of property under subsection (i)(1) of this section, that the debtor has not paid.

(l) The debtor shall file a list of property that the debtor claims as exempt under subsection (b) of this section. If the debtor does not file such a list, a dependent of the debtor may file such a list, or may claim property as exempt from property of the estate on behalf of the debtor. Unless a party in interest objects, the property claimed as exempt on such list is exempt.

(m) Subject to the limitation in subsection (b), this section shall apply separately with respect to each debtor in a joint case.

(n) For assets in individual retirement accounts described in section 408 or 408A of the Internal Revenue Code of 1986, other than a simplified employee pension under section 408(k) of such Code or a simple retirement account under section 408(p) of such Code, the aggregate value of such assets exempted under this section, without regard to amounts attributable to rollover contributions under section 402(c), 402(e)(6), 403(a)(4), 403(a)(5), and 403(b)(8) of the Internal Revenue Code of 1986, and earnings thereon, shall not exceed $1,283,025* in a case filed by a debtor who is an individual, except that such amount may be increased if the interests of justice so require.

---

    * *Note from West Advisory Panel: Dollar amounts adjusted pursuant to 11 U.S.C. § 104; 81 Fed. Reg. 8748 (Feb. 22, 2016).*

(o) For purposes of subsection (b)(3)(A), and notwithstanding subsection (a), the value of an interest in—

(1) real or personal property that the debtor or a dependent of the debtor uses as a residence;

(2) a cooperative that owns property that the debtor or a dependent of the debtor uses as a residence;

(3) a burial plot for the debtor or a dependent of the debtor; or

(4) real or personal property that the debtor or a dependent of the debtor claims as a homestead;

shall be reduced to the extent that such value is attributable to any portion of any property that the debtor disposed of in the 10-year period ending on the date of the filing of the petition with the intent to hinder, delay, or defraud a creditor and that the debtor could not exempt, or that portion that the debtor could not exempt, under subsection (b), if on such date the debtor had held the property so disposed of.

(p)(1) Except as provided in paragraph (2) of this subsection and sections 544 and 548, as a result of electing under subsection (b)(3)(A) to exempt property under State or local law, a debtor may not exempt any amount of interest that was acquired by the debtor during the 1215-day period preceding the date of the filing of the petition that exceeds in the aggregate $160,375* in value in—

(A) real or personal property that the debtor or a dependent of the debtor uses as a residence;

(B) a cooperative that owns property that the debtor or a dependent of the debtor uses as a residence;

(C) a burial plot for the debtor or a dependent of the debtor; or

(D) real or personal property that the debtor or dependent of the debtor claims as a homestead.

(2)(A) The limitation under paragraph (1) shall not apply to an exemption claimed under subsection (b)(3)(A) by a family farmer for the principal residence of such farmer.

(B) For purposes of paragraph (1), any amount of such interest does not include any interest transferred from a debtor's previous principal residence (which was acquired prior to the beginning of such 1215-day period) into the debtor's current principal residence, if the debtor's previous and current residences are located in the same State.

(q)(1) As a result of electing under subsection (b)(3)(A) to exempt property under State or local law, a debtor may not exempt any amount of an interest in property described in subparagraphs (A), (B), (C), and (D) of subsection (p)(1) which exceeds in the aggregate $160,375* if—

(A) the court determines, after notice and a hearing, that the debtor has been convicted of a felony (as defined in section 3156 of title 18), which under the circumstances, demonstrates that the filing of the case was an abuse of the provisions of this title; or

(B) the debtor owes a debt arising from—

(i) any violation of the Federal securities laws (as defined in section 3(a)(47) of the Securities Exchange Act of 1934), any State securities laws, or any regulation or order issued under Federal securities laws or State securities laws;

(ii) fraud, deceit, or manipulation in a fiduciary capacity or in connection with the purchase or sale of any security registered under section 12 or 15(d) of the Securities Exchange Act of 1934 or under section 6 of the Securities Act of 1933;

(iii) any civil remedy under section 1964 of title 18; or

(iv) any criminal act, intentional tort, or willful or reckless misconduct that caused serious physical injury or death to another individual in the preceding 5 years.

---

* *Note from West Advisory Panel: Dollar amounts adjusted pursuant to 11 U.S.C. § 104; 81 Fed. Reg. 8748 (Feb. 22, 2016).*

(2) Paragraph (1) shall not apply to the extent the amount of an interest in property described in subparagraphs (A), (B), (C), and (D) of subsection (p)(1) is reasonably necessary for the support of the debtor and any dependent of the debtor.

(Pub.L. 95–598, Nov. 6, 1978, 92 Stat. 2586; Pub.L. 98–353, title III, §§ 306, 453, July 10, 1984, 98 Stat. 353, 375; Pub.L. 99–554, title II, § 283(i), Oct. 27, 1986, 100 Stat. 3117; Pub.L. 101–647, title XXV, § 2522(b), Nov. 29, 1990, 104 Stat. 4866; Pub.L. 103–394, title I, § 108(d), title III, §§ 303, 304(d), 310, title V, § 501(d)(12), Oct. 22, 1994, 108 Stat. 4112, 4132, 4133, 4137, 4145; Pub.L. 106–420, § 4, Nov. 1, 2000, 114 Stat. 1868; Pub.L. 109–8, title II, §§ 216, 224(a), (e)(1), title III, §§ 307, 308, 313(a), 322(a), Apr. 20, 2005, 119 Stat. 55, 62, 65, 81, 87, 96; Pub.L. 111–327, § 2(a)(17), Dec. 22, 2010, 124 Stat. 3559.)

§ 523. Exceptions to discharge

(a) A discharge under section 727, 1141, 1228(a), 1228(b), or 1328(b) of this title does not discharge an individual debtor from any debt—

(1) for a tax or a customs duty—

(A) of the kind and for the periods specified in section 507(a)(3) or 507(a)(8) of this title, whether or not a claim for such tax was filed or allowed;

(B) with respect to which a return, or equivalent report or notice, if required—

(i) was not filed or given; or

(ii) was filed or given after the date on which such return, report, or notice was last due, under applicable law or under any extension, and after two years before the date of the filing of the petition; or

(C) with respect to which the debtor made a fraudulent return or willfully attempted in any manner to evade or defeat such tax;

(2) for money, property, services, or an extension, renewal, or refinancing of credit, to the extent obtained by—

(A) false pretenses, a false representation, or actual fraud, other than a statement respecting the debtor's or an insider's financial condition;

(B) use of a statement in writing—

(i) that is materially false;

(ii) respecting the debtor's or an insider's financial condition;

(iii) on which the creditor to whom the debtor is liable for such money, property, services, or credit reasonably relied; and

(iv) that the debtor caused to be made or published with intent to deceive; or

(C)(i) for purposes of subparagraph (A)—

(I) consumer debts owed to a single creditor and aggregating more than $675* for luxury goods or services incurred by an individual debtor on or within 90 days before the order for relief under this title are presumed to be nondischargeable; and

(II) cash advances aggregating more than $950* that are extensions of consumer credit under an open end credit plan obtained by an individual debtor on or within 70 days before the order for relief under this title, are presumed to be nondischargeable; and

(ii) for purposes of this subparagraph—

---

* *Note from West Advisory Panel: Dollar amounts adjusted pursuant to 11 U.S.C. § 104; 81 Fed. Reg. 8748 (Feb. 22, 2016).*

        (I)   the terms "consumer", "credit", and "open end credit plan" have the same meanings as in section 103 of the Truth in Lending Act; and

        (II)   the term "luxury goods or services" does not include goods or services reasonably necessary for the support or maintenance of the debtor or a dependent of the debtor;

  (3)   neither listed nor scheduled under section 521(a)(1) of this title, with the name, if known to the debtor, of the creditor to whom such debt is owed, in time to permit—

     (A)   if such debt is not of a kind specified in paragraph (2), (4), or (6) of this subsection, timely filing of a proof of claim, unless such creditor had notice or actual knowledge of the case in time for such timely filing; or

     (B)   if such debt is of a kind specified in paragraph (2), (4), or (6) of this subsection, timely filing of a proof of claim and timely request for a determination of dischargeability of such debt under one of such paragraphs, unless such creditor had notice or actual knowledge of the case in time for such timely filing and request;

  (4)   for fraud or defalcation while acting in a fiduciary capacity, embezzlement, or larceny;

  (5)   for a domestic support obligation;

  (6)   for willful and malicious injury by the debtor to another entity or to the property of another entity;

  (7)   to the extent such debt is for a fine, penalty, or forfeiture payable to and for the benefit of a governmental unit, and is not compensation for actual pecuniary loss, other than a tax penalty—

     (A)   relating to a tax of a kind not specified in paragraph (1) of this subsection; or

     (B)   imposed with respect to a transaction or event that occurred before three years before the date of the filing of the petition;

  (8)   unless excepting such debt from discharge under this paragraph would impose an undue hardship on the debtor and the debtor's dependents, for—

     (A)(i)   an educational benefit overpayment or loan made, insured, or guaranteed by a governmental unit, or made under any program funded in whole or in part by a governmental unit or nonprofit institution; or

       (ii)   an obligation to repay funds received as an educational benefit, scholarship, or stipend; or

     (B)   any other educational loan that is a qualified education loan, as defined in section 221(d)(1) of the Internal Revenue Code of 1986, incurred by a debtor who is an individual;

  (9)   for death or personal injury caused by the debtor's operation of a motor vehicle, vessel, or aircraft if such operation was unlawful because the debtor was intoxicated from using alcohol, a drug, or another substance;

  (10)   that was or could have been listed or scheduled by the debtor in a prior case concerning the debtor under this title or under the Bankruptcy Act in which the debtor waived discharge, or was denied a discharge under section 727(a)(2), (3), (4), (5), (6), or (7) of this title, or under section 14c(1), (2), (3), (4), (6), or (7) of such Act;

  (11)   provided in any final judgment, unreviewable order, or consent order or decree entered in any court of the United States or of any State, issued by a Federal depository institutions regulatory agency, or contained in any settlement agreement entered into by the debtor, arising from any act of fraud or defalcation while acting in a fiduciary capacity committed with respect to any depository institution or insured credit union;

  (12)   for malicious or reckless failure to fulfill any commitment by the debtor to a Federal depository institutions regulatory agency to maintain the capital of an insured depository institution, except that this paragraph shall not extend any such commitment which would otherwise be terminated due to any act of such agency;

(13) for any payment of an order of restitution issued under title 18, United States Code;

(14) incurred to pay a tax to the United States that would be nondischargeable pursuant to paragraph (1);

(14A) incurred to pay a tax to a governmental unit, other than the United States, that would be nondischargeable under paragraph (1);

(14B) incurred to pay fines or penalties imposed under Federal election law;

(15) to a spouse, former spouse, or child of the debtor and not of the kind described in paragraph (5) that is incurred by the debtor in the course of a divorce or separation or in connection with a separation agreement, divorce decree or other order of a court of record, or a determination made in accordance with State or territorial law by a governmental unit;

(16) for a fee or assessment that becomes due and payable after the order for relief to a membership association with respect to the debtor's interest in a unit that has condominium ownership, in a share of a cooperative corporation, or a lot in a homeowners association, for as long as the debtor or the trustee has a legal, equitable, or possessory ownership interest in such unit, such corporation, or such lot, but nothing in this paragraph shall except from discharge the debt of a debtor for a membership association fee or assessment for a period arising before entry of the order for relief in a pending or subsequent bankruptcy case;

(17) for a fee imposed on a prisoner by any court for the filing of a case, motion, complaint, or appeal, or for other costs and expenses assessed with respect to such filing, regardless of an assertion of poverty by the debtor under subsection (b) or (f)(2) of section 1915 of title 28 (or a similar non-Federal law), or the debtor's status as a prisoner, as defined in section 1915(h) of title 28 (or a similar non-Federal law);

(18) owed to a pension, profit-sharing, stock bonus, or other plan established under section 401, 403, 408, 408A, 414, 457, or 501(c) of the Internal Revenue Code of 1986, under—

    (A) a loan permitted under section 408(b)(1) of the Employee Retirement Income Security Act of 1974, or subject to section 72(p) of the Internal Revenue Code of 1986; or

    (B) a loan from a thrift savings plan permitted under subchapter III of chapter 84 of title 5, that satisfies the requirements of section 8433(g) of such title;

but nothing in this paragraph may be construed to provide that any loan made under a governmental plan under section 414(d), or a contract or account under section 403(b), of the Internal Revenue Code of 1986 constitutes a claim or a debt under this title; or

(19) that—

    (A) is for—

        (i) the violation of any of the Federal securities laws (as that term is defined in section 3(a)(47) of the Securities Exchange Act of 1934), any of the State securities laws, or any regulation or order issued under such Federal or State securities laws; or

        (ii) common law fraud, deceit, or manipulation in connection with the purchase or sale of any security; and

    (B) results, before, on, or after the date on which the petition was filed, from—

        (i) any judgment, order, consent order, or decree entered in any Federal or State judicial or administrative proceeding;

        (ii) any settlement agreement entered into by the debtor; or

(iii) any court or administrative order for any damages, fine, penalty, citation, restitutionary payment, disgorgement payment, attorney fee, cost, or other payment owed by the debtor.

For purposes of this subsection, the term "return" means a return that satisfies the requirements of applicable nonbankruptcy law (including applicable filing requirements). Such term includes a return prepared pursuant to section 6020(a) of the Internal Revenue Code of 1986, or similar State or local law, or a written stipulation to a judgment or a final order entered by a nonbankruptcy tribunal, but does not include a return made pursuant to section 6020(b) of the Internal Revenue Code of 1986, or a similar State or local law.

(b) Notwithstanding subsection (a) of this section, a debt that was excepted from discharge under subsection (a)(1), (a)(3), or (a)(8) of this section, under section 17a(1), 17a(3), or 17a(5) of the Bankruptcy Act, under section 439A of the Higher Education Act of 1965, or under section 733(g) of the Public Health Service Act in a prior case concerning the debtor under this title, or under the Bankruptcy Act, is dischargeable in a case under this title unless, by the terms of subsection (a) of this section, such debt is not dischargeable in the case under this title.

(c)(1) Except as provided in subsection (a)(3)(B) of this section, the debtor shall be discharged from a debt of a kind specified in paragraph (2), (4), or (6) of subsection (a) of this section, unless, on request of the creditor to whom such debt is owed, and after notice and a hearing, the court determines such debt to be excepted from discharge under paragraph (2), (4), or (6), as the case may be, of subsection (a) of this section.

(2) Paragraph (1) shall not apply in the case of a Federal depository institutions regulatory agency seeking, in its capacity as conservator, receiver, or liquidating agent for an insured depository institution, to recover a debt described in subsection (a)(2), (a)(4), (a)(6), or (a)(11) owed to such institution by an institution-affiliated party unless the receiver, conservator, or liquidating agent was appointed in time to reasonably comply, or for a Federal depository institutions regulatory agency acting in its corporate capacity as a successor to such receiver, conservator, or liquidating agent to reasonably comply, with subsection (a)(3)(B) as a creditor of such institution-affiliated party with respect to such debt.

(d) If a creditor requests a determination of dischargeability of a consumer debt under subsection (a)(2) of this section, and such debt is discharged, the court shall grant judgment in favor of the debtor for the costs of, and a reasonable attorney's fee for, the proceeding if the court finds that the position of the creditor was not substantially justified, except that the court shall not award such costs and fees if special circumstances would make the award unjust.

(e) Any institution-affiliated party of an insured depository institution shall be considered to be acting in a fiduciary capacity with respect to the purposes of subsection (a)(4) or (11).

(Pub.L. 95–598, Nov. 6, 1978, 92 Stat. 2590; Pub.L. 96–56, § 3, Aug. 14, 1979, 93 Stat. 387; Pub.L. 97–35, title XXIII, § 2334(b), Aug. 13, 1981, 95 Stat. 863; Pub.L. 98–353, title III, §§ 307, 371, 454, July 10, 1984, 98 Stat. 353, 364, 375; Pub.L. 99–554, title II, §§ 257(n), 281, 283(j), Oct. 27, 1986, 100 Stat. 3115 to 3117; Pub.L. 101–581, § 2(a), Nov. 15, 1990, 104 Stat. 2865; Pub.L. 101–647, title XXV, § 2522(a), title XXXI, § 3102(a), title XXXVI, § 3621, Nov. 29, 1990, 104 Stat. 4865, 4916, 4964; Pub.L. 103–322, title XXXII, § 320934, Sept. 13, 1994, 108 Stat. 2135; Pub.L. 103–394, title II, § 221, title III, §§ 304(e), (h)(3), 306, 309, title V, § 501(d)(13), Oct. 22, 1994, 108 Stat. 4129, 4133 to 4135, 4137, 4145; Pub.L. 104–134, title I, § 101[(a)][title VIII, § 804(b)], Apr. 26, 1996, 110 Stat. 1321–74; renumbered title I, Pub.L. 104–140, § 1(a), May 2, 1996, 110 Stat. 1327, Pub.L. 104–193, title III, § 374(a), Aug. 22, 1996, 110 Stat. 2255; Pub.L. 105–244, title IX, § 971(a), Oct. 7, 1998, 112 Stat. 1837; Pub.L. 107–204, title VIII, § 803, July 30, 2002, 116 Stat. 801; Pub.L. 109–8, title II, §§ 215, 220, 224(c), title III, §§ 301, 310, 314(a), title IV, § 412, title VII, § 714, title XII, §§ 1209, 1235, title XIV, § 1404(a), title XV, § 1502(a)(2), Apr. 20, 2005, 119 Stat. 54, 59, 64, 75, 84, 88, 107, 128, 194, 204, 215, 216; Pub.L. 111–327, § 2(a)(18), Dec. 22, 2010, 124 Stat. 3559.)

§ 524. Effect of discharge

(a) A discharge in a case under this title—

(1) voids any judgment at any time obtained, to the extent that such judgment is a determination of the personal liability of the debtor with respect to any debt discharged under section 727, 944, 1141, 1228, or 1328 of this title, whether or not discharge of such debt is waived;

(2) operates as an injunction against the commencement or continuation of an action, the employment of process, or an act, to collect, recover or offset any such debt as a personal liability of the debtor, whether or not discharge of such debt is waived; and

(3) operates as an injunction against the commencement or continuation of an action, the employment of process, or an act, to collect or recover from, or offset against, property of the debtor of the kind specified in section 541(a)(2) of this title that is acquired after the commencement of the case, on account of any allowable community claim, except a community claim that is excepted from discharge under section 523, 1228(a)(1), or 1328(a)(1), or that would be so excepted, determined in accordance with the provisions of sections 523(c) and 523(d) of this title, in a case concerning the debtor's spouse commenced on the date of the filing of the petition in the case concerning the debtor, whether or not discharge of the debt based on such community claim is waived.

(b) Subsection (a)(3) of this section does not apply if—

(1)(A) the debtor's spouse is a debtor in a case under this title, or a bankrupt or a debtor in a case under the Bankruptcy Act, commenced within six years of the date of the filing of the petition in the case concerning the debtor; and

(B) the court does not grant the debtor's spouse a discharge in such case concerning the debtor's spouse; or

(2)(A) the court would not grant the debtor's spouse a discharge in a case under chapter 7 of this title concerning such spouse commenced on the date of the filing of the petition in the case concerning the debtor; and

(B) a determination that the court would not so grant such discharge is made by the bankruptcy court within the time and in the manner provided for a determination under section 727 of this title of whether a debtor is granted a discharge.

(c) An agreement between a holder of a claim and the debtor, the consideration for which, in whole or in part, is based on a debt that is dischargeable in a case under this title is enforceable only to any extent enforceable under applicable nonbankruptcy law, whether or not discharge of such debt is waived, only if—

(1) such agreement was made before the granting of the discharge under section 727, 1141, 1228, or 1328 of this title;

(2) the debtor received the disclosures described in subsection (k) at or before the time at which the debtor signed the agreement;

(3) such agreement has been filed with the court and, if applicable, accompanied by a declaration or an affidavit of the attorney that represented the debtor during the course of negotiating an agreement under this subsection, which states that—

(A) such agreement represents a fully informed and voluntary agreement by the debtor;

(B) such agreement does not impose an undue hardship on the debtor or a dependent of the debtor; and

(C) the attorney fully advised the debtor of the legal effect and consequences of—

(i) an agreement of the kind specified in this subsection; and

(ii) any default under such an agreement;

(4) the debtor has not rescinded such agreement at any time prior to discharge or within sixty days after such agreement is filed with the court, whichever occurs later, by giving notice of rescission to the holder of such claim;

(5) the provisions of subsection (d) of this section have been complied with; and

(6)(A) in a case concerning an individual who was not represented by an attorney during the course of negotiating an agreement under this subsection, the court approves such agreement as—

    (i) not imposing an undue hardship on the debtor or a dependent of the debtor; and

    (ii) in the best interest of the debtor.

(B) Subparagraph (A) shall not apply to the extent that such debt is a consumer debt secured by real property.

(d) In a case concerning an individual, when the court has determined whether to grant or not to grant a discharge under section 727, 1141, 1228, or 1328 of this title, the court may hold a hearing at which the debtor shall appear in person. At any such hearing, the court shall inform the debtor that a discharge has been granted or the reason why a discharge has not been granted. If a discharge has been granted and if the debtor desires to make an agreement of the kind specified in subsection (c) of this section and was not represented by an attorney during the course of negotiating such agreement, then the court shall hold a hearing at which the debtor shall appear in person and at such hearing the court shall—

(1) inform the debtor—

    (A) that such an agreement is not required under this title, under nonbankruptcy law, or under any agreement not made in accordance with the provisions of subsection (c) of this section; and

    (B) of the legal effect and consequences of—

        (i) an agreement of the kind specified in subsection (c) of this section; and

        (ii) a default under such an agreement; and

(2) determine whether the agreement that the debtor desires to make complies with the requirements of subsection (c)(6) of this section, if the consideration for such agreement is based in whole or in part on a consumer debt that is not secured by real property of the debtor.

(e) Except as provided in subsection (a)(3) of this section, discharge of a debt of the debtor does not affect the liability of any other entity on, or the property of any other entity for, such debt.

(f) Nothing contained in subsection (c) or (d) of this section prevents a debtor from voluntarily repaying any debt.

(g)(1)(A) After notice and hearing, a court that enters an order confirming a plan of reorganization under chapter 11 may issue, in connection with such order, an injunction in accordance with this subsection to supplement the injunctive effect of a discharge under this section.

(B) An injunction may be issued under subparagraph (A) to enjoin entities from taking legal action for the purpose of directly or indirectly collecting, recovering, or receiving payment or recovery with respect to any claim or demand that, under a plan of reorganization, is to be paid in whole or in part by a trust described in paragraph (2)(B)(i), except such legal actions as are expressly allowed by the injunction, the confirmation order, or the plan of reorganization.

(2)(A) Subject to subsection (h), if the requirements of subparagraph (B) are met at the time an injunction described in paragraph (1) is entered, then after entry of such injunction, any proceeding that involves the validity, application, construction, or modification of such injunction, or of this subsection with respect to such injunction, may be commenced only in the district court in which such injunction was entered, and such court shall have exclusive jurisdiction over any such proceeding without regard to the amount in controversy.

(B) The requirements of this subparagraph are that—

    (i) the injunction is to be implemented in connection with a trust that, pursuant to the plan of reorganization—

        (I) is to assume the liabilities of a debtor which at the time of entry of the order for relief has been named as a defendant in personal injury, wrongful death, or property-damage actions seeking recovery for damages allegedly caused by the presence of, or exposure to, asbestos or asbestos-containing products;

(II) is to be funded in whole or in part by the securities of 1 or more debtors involved in such plan and by the obligation of such debtor or debtors to make future payments, including dividends;

(III) is to own, or by the exercise of rights granted under such plan would be entitled to own if specified contingencies occur, a majority of the voting shares of—

(aa) each such debtor;

(bb) the parent corporation of each such debtor; or

(cc) a subsidiary of each such debtor that is also a debtor; and

(IV) is to use its assets or income to pay claims and demands; and

(ii) subject to subsection (h), the court determines that—

(I) the debtor is likely to be subject to substantial future demands for payment arising out of the same or similar conduct or events that gave rise to the claims that are addressed by the injunction;

(II) the actual amounts, numbers, and timing of such future demands cannot be determined;

(III) pursuit of such demands outside the procedures prescribed by such plan is likely to threaten the plan's purpose to deal equitably with claims and future demands;

(IV) as part of the process of seeking confirmation of such plan—

(aa) the terms of the injunction proposed to be issued under paragraph (1)(A), including any provisions barring actions against third parties pursuant to paragraph (4)(A), are set out in such plan and in any disclosure statement supporting the plan; and

(bb) a separate class or classes of the claimants whose claims are to be addressed by a trust described in clause (i) is established and votes, by at least 75 percent of those voting, in favor of the plan; and

(V) subject to subsection (h), pursuant to court orders or otherwise, the trust will operate through mechanisms such as structured, periodic, or supplemental payments, pro rata distributions, matrices, or periodic review of estimates of the numbers and values of present claims and future demands, or other comparable mechanisms, that provide reasonable assurance that the trust will value, and be in a financial position to pay, present claims and future demands that involve similar claims in substantially the same manner.

(3)(A) If the requirements of paragraph (2)(B) are met and the order confirming the plan of reorganization was issued or affirmed by the district court that has jurisdiction over the reorganization case, then after the time for appeal of the order that issues or affirms the plan—

(i) the injunction shall be valid and enforceable and may not be revoked or modified by any court except through appeal in accordance with paragraph (6);

(ii) no entity that pursuant to such plan or thereafter becomes a direct or indirect transferee of, or successor to any assets of, a debtor or trust that is the subject of the injunction shall be liable with respect to any claim or demand made against such entity by reason of its becoming such a transferee or successor; and

(iii) no entity that pursuant to such plan or thereafter makes a loan to such a debtor or trust or to such a successor or transferee shall, by reason of making the loan, be liable with respect to any claim or demand made against such entity, nor shall any pledge of assets made in connection with such a loan be upset or impaired for that reason;

(B) Subparagraph (A) shall not be construed to—

(i) imply that an entity described in subparagraph (A)(ii) or (iii) would, if this paragraph were not applicable, necessarily be liable to any entity by reason of any of the acts described in subparagraph (A);

(ii) relieve any such entity of the duty to comply with, or of liability under, any Federal or State law regarding the making of a fraudulent conveyance in a transaction described in subparagraph (A)(ii) or (iii); or

(iii) relieve a debtor of the debtor's obligation to comply with the terms of the plan of reorganization, or affect the power of the court to exercise its authority under sections 1141 and 1142 to compel the debtor to do so.

(4)(A)(i) Subject to subparagraph (B), an injunction described in paragraph (1) shall be valid and enforceable against all entities that it addresses.

(ii) Notwithstanding the provisions of section 524(e), such an injunction may bar any action directed against a third party who is identifiable from the terms of such injunction (by name or as part of an identifiable group) and is alleged to be directly or indirectly liable for the conduct of, claims against, or demands on the debtor to the extent such alleged liability of such third party arises by reason of—

(I) the third party's ownership of a financial interest in the debtor, a past or present affiliate of the debtor, or a predecessor in interest of the debtor;

(II) the third party's involvement in the management of the debtor or a predecessor in interest of the debtor, or service as an officer, director or employee of the debtor or a related party;

(III) the third party's provision of insurance to the debtor or a related party; or

(IV) the third party's involvement in a transaction changing the corporate structure, or in a loan or other financial transaction affecting the financial condition, of the debtor or a related party, including but not limited to—

(aa) involvement in providing financing (debt or equity), or advice to an entity involved in such a transaction; or

(bb) acquiring or selling a financial interest in an entity as part of such a transaction.

(iii) As used in this subparagraph, the term "related party" means—

(I) a past or present affiliate of the debtor;

(II) a predecessor in interest of the debtor; or

(III) any entity that owned a financial interest in—

(aa) the debtor;

(bb) a past or present affiliate of the debtor; or

(cc) a predecessor in interest of the debtor.

(B) Subject to subsection (h), if, under a plan of reorganization, a kind of demand described in such plan is to be paid in whole or in part by a trust described in paragraph (2)(B)(i) in connection with which an injunction described in paragraph (1) is to be implemented, then such injunction shall be valid and enforceable with respect to a demand of such kind made, after such plan is confirmed, against the debtor or debtors involved, or against a third party described in subparagraph (A)(ii), if—

(i) as part of the proceedings leading to issuance of such injunction, the court appoints a legal representative for the purpose of protecting the rights of persons that might subsequently assert demands of such kind, and

(ii) the court determines, before entering the order confirming such plan, that identifying such debtor or debtors, or such third party (by name or as part of an identifiable group), in such injunction with respect to such demands for purposes of this subparagraph is fair and equitable with respect to the persons that might subsequently assert such demands, in light of the benefits provided, or to be provided, to such trust on behalf of such debtor or debtors or such third party.

(5) In this subsection, the term "demand" means a demand for payment, present or future, that—

(A) was not a claim during the proceedings leading to the confirmation of a plan of reorganization;

(B) arises out of the same or similar conduct or events that gave rise to the claims addressed by the injunction issued under paragraph (1); and

(C) pursuant to the plan, is to be paid by a trust described in paragraph (2)(B)(i).

(6) Paragraph (3)(A)(i) does not bar an action taken by or at the direction of an appellate court on appeal of an injunction issued under paragraph (1) or of the order of confirmation that relates to the injunction.

(7) This subsection does not affect the operation of section 1144 or the power of the district court to refer a proceeding under section 157 of title 28 or any reference of a proceeding made prior to the date of the enactment of this subsection.

(h) **Application to Existing Injunctions.**—For purposes of subsection (g)—

(1) subject to paragraph (2), if an injunction of the kind described in subsection (g)(1)(B) was issued before the date of the enactment of this Act, as part of a plan of reorganization confirmed by an order entered before such date, then the injunction shall be considered to meet the requirements of subsection (g)(2)(B) for purposes of subsection (g)(2)(A), and to satisfy subsection (g)(4)(A)(ii), if—

(A) the court determined at the time the plan was confirmed that the plan was fair and equitable in accordance with the requirements of section 1129(b);

(B) as part of the proceedings leading to issuance of such injunction and confirmation of such plan, the court had appointed a legal representative for the purpose of protecting the rights of persons that might subsequently assert demands described in subsection (g)(4)(B) with respect to such plan; and

(C) such legal representative did not object to confirmation of such plan or issuance of such injunction; and

(2) for purposes of paragraph (1), if a trust described in subsection (g)(2)(B)(i) is subject to a court order on the date of the enactment of this Act staying such trust from settling or paying further claims—

(A) the requirements of subsection (g)(2)(B)(ii)(V) shall not apply with respect to such trust until such stay is lifted or dissolved; and

(B) if such trust meets such requirements on the date such stay is lifted or dissolved, such trust shall be considered to have met such requirements continuously from the date of the enactment of this Act.

(i) The willful failure of a creditor to credit payments received under a plan confirmed under this title, unless the order confirming the plan is revoked, the plan is in default, or the creditor has not received payments required to be made under the plan in the manner required by the plan (including crediting the amounts required under the plan), shall constitute a violation of an injunction under subsection (a)(2) if the act of the creditor to collect and failure to credit payments in the manner required by the plan caused material injury to the debtor.

(j) Subsection (a)(2) does not operate as an injunction against an act by a creditor that is the holder of a secured claim, if—

(1) such creditor retains a security interest in real property that is the principal residence of the debtor;

(2) such act is in the ordinary course of business between the creditor and the debtor; and

(3) such act is limited to seeking or obtaining periodic payments associated with a valid security interest in lieu of pursuit of in rem relief to enforce the lien.

(k)(1) The disclosures required under subsection (c)(2) shall consist of the disclosure statement described in paragraph (3), completed as required in that paragraph, together with the agreement specified in subsection (c), statement, declaration, motion and order described, respectively, in paragraphs (4) through (8), and shall be the only disclosures required in connection with entering into such agreement.

(2) Disclosures made under paragraph (1) shall be made clearly and conspicuously and in writing. The terms "Amount Reaffirmed" and "Annual Percentage Rate" shall be disclosed more conspicuously than other terms, data or information provided in connection with this disclosure, except that the phrases "Before agreeing to reaffirm a debt, review these important disclosures" and "Summary of Reaffirmation Agreement" may be equally conspicuous. Disclosures may be made in a different order and may use terminology different from that set forth in paragraphs (2) through (8), except that the terms "Amount Reaffirmed" and "Annual Percentage Rate" must be used where indicated.

(3) The disclosure statement required under this paragraph shall consist of the following:

(A) The statement: "Part A: Before agreeing to reaffirm a debt, review these important disclosures:";

(B) Under the heading "Summary of Reaffirmation Agreement", the statement: "This Summary is made pursuant to the requirements of the Bankruptcy Code";

(C) The "Amount Reaffirmed", using that term, which shall be—

(i) the total amount of debt that the debtor agrees to reaffirm by entering into an agreement of the kind specified in subsection (c), and

(ii) the total of any fees and costs accrued as of the date of the disclosure statement, related to such total amount.

(D) In conjunction with the disclosure of the "Amount Reaffirmed", the statements—

(i) "The amount of debt you have agreed to reaffirm"; and

(ii) "Your credit agreement may obligate you to pay additional amounts which may come due after the date of this disclosure. Consult your credit agreement.".

(E) The "Annual Percentage Rate", using that term, which shall be disclosed as—

(i) if, at the time the petition is filed, the debt is an extension of credit under an open end credit plan, as the terms "credit" and "open end credit plan" are defined in section 103 of the Truth in Lending Act, then—

(I) the annual percentage rate determined under paragraphs (5) and (6) of section 127(b) of the Truth in Lending Act, as applicable, as disclosed to the debtor in the most recent periodic statement prior to entering into an agreement of the kind specified in subsection (c) or, if no such periodic statement has been given to the debtor during the prior 6 months, the annual percentage rate as it would have been so disclosed at the time the disclosure statement is given to the debtor, or to the extent this annual percentage rate is not readily available or not applicable, then

(II) the simple interest rate applicable to the amount reaffirmed as of the date the disclosure statement is given to the debtor, or if different simple interest rates apply to different balances, the simple interest rate applicable to each such balance, identifying the amount of each such balance included in the amount reaffirmed, or

(III) if the entity making the disclosure elects, to disclose the annual percentage rate under subclause (I) and the simple interest rate under subclause (II); or

(ii) if, at the time the petition is filed, the debt is an extension of credit other than under an open end credit plan, as the terms "credit" and "open end credit plan" are defined in section 103 of the Truth in Lending Act, then—

(I) the annual percentage rate under section 128(a)(4) of the Truth in Lending Act, as disclosed to the debtor in the most recent disclosure statement given to the debtor prior to the entering into an agreement of the kind specified in subsection (c) with respect to the debt, or, if no such disclosure statement was given to the debtor, the annual percentage rate as it would have been so disclosed at the time the disclosure statement is given to the debtor, or to the extent this annual percentage rate is not readily available or not applicable, then

(II) the simple interest rate applicable to the amount reaffirmed as of the date the disclosure statement is given to the debtor, or if different simple interest rates apply to different balances, the simple interest rate applicable to each such balance, identifying the amount of such balance included in the amount reaffirmed, or

(III) if the entity making the disclosure elects, to disclose the annual percentage rate under (I) and the simple interest rate under (II).

(F) If the underlying debt transaction was disclosed as a variable rate transaction on the most recent disclosure given under the Truth in Lending Act, by stating "The interest rate on your loan may be a variable interest rate which changes from time to time, so that the annual percentage rate disclosed here may be higher or lower."

(G) If the debt is secured by a security interest which has not been waived in whole or in part or determined to be void by a final order of the court at the time of the disclosure, by disclosing that a security interest or lien in goods or property is asserted over some or all of the debts the debtor is reaffirming and listing the items and their original purchase price that are subject to the asserted security interest, or if not a purchase-money security interest then listing by items or types and the original amount of the loan.

(H) At the election of the creditor, a statement of the repayment schedule using 1 or a combination of the following—

(i) by making the statement: "Your first payment in the amount of $___ is due on ___ but the future payment amount may be different. Consult your reaffirmation agreement or credit agreement, as applicable.", and stating the amount of the first payment and the due date of that payment in the places provided;

(ii) by making the statement: "Your payment schedule will be:", and describing the repayment schedule with the number, amount, and due dates or period of payments scheduled to repay the debts reaffirmed to the extent then known by the disclosing party; or

(iii) by describing the debtor's repayment obligations with reasonable specificity to the extent then known by the disclosing party.

(I) The following statement: "Note: When this disclosure refers to what a creditor 'may' do, it does not use the word 'may' to give the creditor specific permission. The word 'may' is used to tell you what might occur if the law permits the creditor to take the action. If you have questions about your reaffirming a debt or what the law requires, consult with the attorney who helped you negotiate this agreement reaffirming a debt. If you don't have an attorney helping you, the judge will explain the effect of your reaffirming a debt when the hearing on the reaffirmation agreement is held.".

(J)(i)　The following additional statements:

"Reaffirming a debt is a serious financial decision. The law requires you to take certain steps to make sure the decision is in your best interest. If these steps are not completed, the reaffirmation agreement is not effective, even though you have signed it.

"1.　Read the disclosures in this Part A carefully. Consider the decision to reaffirm carefully. Then, if you want to reaffirm, sign the reaffirmation agreement in Part B (or you may use a separate agreement you and your creditor agree on).

"2.　Complete and sign Part D and be sure you can afford to make the payments you are agreeing to make and have received a copy of the disclosure statement and a completed and signed reaffirmation agreement.

"3.　If you were represented by an attorney during the negotiation of your reaffirmation agreement, the attorney must have signed the certification in Part C.

"4.　If you were not represented by an attorney during the negotiation of your reaffirmation agreement, you must have completed and signed Part E.

"5.　The original of this disclosure must be filed with the court by you or your creditor. If a separate reaffirmation agreement (other than the one in Part B) has been signed, it must be attached.

"6.　If you were represented by an attorney during the negotiation of your reaffirmation agreement, your reaffirmation agreement becomes effective upon filing with the court unless the reaffirmation is presumed to be an undue hardship as explained in Part D.

"7.　If you were not represented by an attorney during the negotiation of your reaffirmation agreement, it will not be effective unless the court approves it. The court will notify you of the hearing on your reaffirmation agreement. You must attend this hearing in bankruptcy court where the judge will review your reaffirmation agreement. The bankruptcy court must approve your reaffirmation agreement as consistent with your best interests, except that no court approval is required if your reaffirmation agreement is for a consumer debt secured by a mortgage, deed of trust, security deed, or other lien on your real property, like your home.

"Your right to rescind (cancel) your reaffirmation agreement. You may rescind (cancel) your reaffirmation agreement at any time before the bankruptcy court enters a discharge order, or before the expiration of the 60-day period that begins on the date your reaffirmation agreement is filed with the court, whichever occurs later. To rescind (cancel) your reaffirmation agreement, you must notify the creditor that your reaffirmation agreement is rescinded (or canceled).

"What are your obligations if you reaffirm the debt? A reaffirmed debt remains your personal legal obligation. It is not discharged in your bankruptcy case. That means that if you default on your reaffirmed debt after your bankruptcy case is over, your creditor may be able to take your property or your wages. Otherwise, your obligations will be determined by the reaffirmation agreement which may have changed the terms of the original agreement. For example, if you are reaffirming an open end credit agreement, the creditor may be permitted by that agreement or applicable law to change the terms of that agreement in the future under certain conditions.

"Are you required to enter into a reaffirmation agreement by any law? No, you are not required to reaffirm a debt by any law. Only agree to reaffirm a debt if it is in your best interest. Be sure you can afford the payments you agree to make.

"What if your creditor has a security interest or lien? Your bankruptcy discharge does not eliminate any lien on your property. A 'lien' is often referred to as a security interest, deed of trust, mortgage or security deed. Even if you do not reaffirm and your personal liability on the debt is discharged, because of the lien your creditor may still have the right to take the property securing the lien if you do not pay the debt or default on it. If the lien is on an item of personal property that is exempt under your State's law or that the trustee has abandoned, you may be able to redeem the item rather than reaffirm the debt. To redeem, you must make a single payment to the creditor equal to the amount of the allowed secured claim, as agreed by the parties or determined by the court.".

        (ii) In the case of a reaffirmation under subsection (m)(2), numbered paragraph 6 in the disclosures required by clause (i) of this subparagraph shall read as follows:

        "6. If you were represented by an attorney during the negotiation of your reaffirmation agreement, your reaffirmation agreement becomes effective upon filing with the court.".

    (4) The form of such agreement required under this paragraph shall consist of the following:

"Part B: Reaffirmation Agreement. I (we) agree to reaffirm the debts arising under the credit agreement described below.

"Brief description of credit agreement:

"Description of any changes to the credit agreement made as part of this reaffirmation agreement:

"Signature: Date:

"Borrower:

"Co-borrower, if also reaffirming these debts:

"Accepted by creditor:

"Date of creditor acceptance:".

    (5) The declaration shall consist of the following:

        (A) The following certification:

"Part C: Certification by Debtor's Attorney (If Any).

"I hereby certify that (1) this agreement represents a fully informed and voluntary agreement by the debtor; (2) this agreement does not impose an undue hardship on the debtor or any dependent of the debtor; and (3) I have fully advised the debtor of the legal effect and consequences of this agreement and any default under this agreement.

"Signature of Debtor's Attorney: Date:".

        (B) If a presumption of undue hardship has been established with respect to such agreement, such certification shall state that, in the opinion of the attorney, the debtor is able to make the payment.

        (C) In the case of a reaffirmation agreement under subsection (m)(2), subparagraph (B) is not applicable.

    (6)(A) The statement in support of such agreement, which the debtor shall sign and date prior to filing with the court, shall consist of the following:

"Part D: Debtor's Statement in Support of Reaffirmation Agreement.

"1. I believe this reaffirmation agreement will not impose an undue hardship on my dependents or me. I can afford to make the payments on the reaffirmed debt because my monthly income (take home pay plus any other income received) is $___, and my actual current monthly expenses including monthly payments on post-bankruptcy debt and other reaffirmation agreements total $___, leaving $___ to make the required payments on this reaffirmed debt. I understand that if my income less my monthly expenses does not leave enough to make the payments, this reaffirmation agreement is presumed to be an undue hardship on me and must be reviewed by the court. However, this presumption may be overcome if I explain to the satisfaction of the court how I can afford to make the payments here: ___.

"2.   I received a copy of the Reaffirmation Disclosure Statement in Part A and a completed and signed reaffirmation agreement.".

    (B)   Where the debtor is represented by an attorney and is reaffirming a debt owed to a creditor defined in section 19(b)(1)(A)(iv) of the Federal Reserve Act, the statement of support of the reaffirmation agreement, which the debtor shall sign and date prior to filing with the court, shall consist of the following:

    "I believe this reaffirmation agreement is in my financial interest. I can afford to make the payments on the reaffirmed debt. I received a copy of the Reaffirmation Disclosure Statement in Part A and a completed and signed reaffirmation agreement.".

    (7)   The motion that may be used if approval of such agreement by the court is required in order for it to be effective, shall be signed and dated by the movant and shall consist of the following:

    "Part E: Motion for Court Approval (To be completed only if the debtor is not represented by an attorney.). I (we), the debtor(s), affirm the following to be true and correct:

    "I am not represented by an attorney in connection with this reaffirmation agreement.

    "I believe this reaffirmation agreement is in my best interest based on the income and expenses I have disclosed in my Statement in Support of this reaffirmation agreement, and because (provide any additional relevant reasons the court should consider):

    "Therefore, I ask the court for an order approving this reaffirmation agreement.".

    (8)   The court order, which may be used to approve such agreement, shall consist of the following:

    "Court Order: The court grants the debtor's motion and approves the reaffirmation agreement described above.".

(l)   Notwithstanding any other provision of this title the following shall apply:

    (1)   A creditor may accept payments from a debtor before and after the filing of an agreement of the kind specified in subsection (c) with the court.

    (2)   A creditor may accept payments from a debtor under such agreement that the creditor believes in good faith to be effective.

    (3)   The requirements of subsections (c)(2) and (k) shall be satisfied if disclosures required under those subsections are given in good faith.

(m)(1)   Until 60 days after an agreement of the kind specified in subsection (c) is filed with the court (or such additional period as the court, after notice and a hearing and for cause, orders before the expiration of such period), it shall be presumed that such agreement is an undue hardship on the debtor if the debtor's monthly income less the debtor's monthly expenses as shown on the debtor's completed and signed statement in support of such agreement required under subsection (k)(6)(A) is less than the scheduled payments on the reaffirmed debt. This presumption shall be reviewed by the court. The presumption may be rebutted in writing by the debtor if the statement includes an explanation that identifies additional sources of funds to make the payments as agreed upon under the terms of such agreement. If the presumption is not rebutted to the satisfaction of the court, the court may disapprove such agreement. No agreement shall be disapproved without notice and a hearing to the debtor and creditor, and such hearing shall be concluded before the entry of the debtor's discharge.

    (2)   This subsection does not apply to reaffirmation agreements where the creditor is a credit union, as defined in section 19(b)(1)(A)(iv) of the Federal Reserve Act.

    (Pub.L. 95–598, Nov. 6, 1978, 92 Stat. 2592; Pub.L. 98–353, title III, §§ 308, 455, July 10, 1984, 98 Stat. 354, 376; Pub.L. 99–554, title II, §§ 257(*o*), 282, 283(k), Oct. 27, 1986, 100 Stat. 3115–3117; Pub.L. 103–394, title I, §§ 103, 111(a), title V, § 501(d)(14), Oct. 22, 1994, 108 Stat. 4108, 4113, 4145; Pub.L. 109–8, title II, §§ 202, 203(a), title XII, § 1210, Apr. 20, 2005, 119 Stat. 43, 194; Pub.L. 111–327, § 2(a)(19), Dec. 22, 2010, 124 Stat. 3559.)

§ 525.   Protection against discriminatory treatment

(a)   Except as provided in the Perishable Agricultural Commodities Act, 1930, the Packers and Stockyards Act, 1921, and section 1 of the Act entitled "An Act making appropriations for the Department of Agriculture for the fiscal year ending June 30, 1944, and for other purposes," approved July 12, 1943, a governmental unit may not deny, revoke, suspend, or refuse to renew a license, permit, charter, franchise, or other similar grant to, condition such a grant to, discriminate with respect to such a grant against, deny employment to, terminate the employment of, or discriminate with respect to employment against, a person that is or has been a debtor under this title or a bankrupt or a debtor under the Bankruptcy Act, or another person with whom such bankrupt or debtor has been associated, solely because such bankrupt or debtor is or has been a debtor under this title or a bankrupt or debtor under the Bankruptcy Act, has been insolvent before the commencement of the case under this title, or during the case but before the debtor is granted or denied a discharge, or has not paid a debt that is dischargeable in the case under this title or that was discharged under the Bankruptcy Act.

(b)   No private employer may terminate the employment of, or discriminate with respect to employment against, an individual who is or has been a debtor under this title, a debtor or bankrupt under the Bankruptcy Act, or an individual associated with such debtor or bankrupt, solely because such debtor or bankrupt—

(1)   is or has been a debtor under this title or a debtor or bankrupt under the Bankruptcy Act;

(2)   has been insolvent before the commencement of a case under this title or during the case but before the grant or denial of a discharge; or

(3)   has not paid a debt that is dischargeable in a case under this title or that was discharged under the Bankruptcy Act.

(c)(1)   A governmental unit that operates a student grant or loan program and a person engaged in a business that includes the making of loans guaranteed or insured under a student loan program may not deny a student grant, loan, loan guarantee, or loan insurance to a person that is or has been a debtor under this title or a bankrupt or debtor under the Bankruptcy Act, or another person with whom the debtor or bankrupt has been associated, because the debtor or bankrupt is or has been a debtor under this title or a bankrupt or debtor under the Bankruptcy Act, has been insolvent before the commencement of a case under this title or during the pendency of the case but before the debtor is granted or denied a discharge, or has not paid a debt that is dischargeable in the case under this title or that was discharged under the Bankruptcy Act.

(2)   In this section, "student loan program" means any program operated under title IV of the Higher Education Act of 1965 or a similar program operated under State or local law.

(Pub.L. 95–598, Nov. 6, 1978, 92 Stat. 2593; Pub.L. 98–353, title III, § 309, July 10, 1984, 98 Stat. 354; Pub.L. 103–394, title III, § 313, title V, § 501(d)(15), Oct. 22, 1994, 108 Stat. 4140, 4145; Pub.L. 109–8, title XII, § 1211, Apr. 20, 2005, 119 Stat. 194.)

§ 526.   Restrictions on debt relief agencies

(a)   A debt relief agency shall not—

(1)   fail to perform any service that such agency informed an assisted person or prospective assisted person it would provide in connection with a case or proceeding under this title;

(2)   make any statement, or counsel or advise any assisted person or prospective assisted person to make a statement in a document filed in a case or proceeding under this title, that is untrue or misleading, or that upon the exercise of reasonable care, should have been known by such agency to be untrue or misleading;

(3)   misrepresent to any assisted person or prospective assisted person, directly or indirectly, affirmatively or by material omission, with respect to—

(A)   the services that such agency will provide to such person; or

(B) the benefits and risks that may result if such person becomes a debtor in a case under this title; or

(4) advise an assisted person or prospective assisted person to incur more debt in contemplation of such person filing a case under this title or to pay an attorney or bankruptcy petition preparer a fee or charge for services performed as part of preparing for or representing a debtor in a case under this title.

(b) Any waiver by any assisted person of any protection or right provided under this section shall not be enforceable against the debtor by any Federal or State court or any other person, but may be enforced against a debt relief agency.

(c)(1) Any contract for bankruptcy assistance between a debt relief agency and an assisted person that does not comply with the material requirements of this section, section 527, or section 528 shall be void and may not be enforced by any Federal or State court or by any other person, other than such assisted person.

(2) Any debt relief agency shall be liable to an assisted person in the amount of any fees or charges in connection with providing bankruptcy assistance to such person that such debt relief agency has received, for actual damages, and for reasonable attorneys' fees and costs if such agency is found, after notice and a hearing, to have—

(A) intentionally or negligently failed to comply with any provision of this section, section 527, or section 528 with respect to a case or proceeding under this title for such assisted person;

(B) provided bankruptcy assistance to an assisted person in a case or proceeding under this title that is dismissed or converted to a case under another chapter of this title because of such agency's intentional or negligent failure to file any required document including those specified in section 521; or

(C) intentionally or negligently disregarded the material requirements of this title or the Federal Rules of Bankruptcy Procedure applicable to such agency.

(3) In addition to such other remedies as are provided under State law, whenever the chief law enforcement officer of a State, or an official or agency designated by a State, has reason to believe that any person has violated or is violating this section, the State—

(A) may bring an action to enjoin such violation;

(B) may bring an action on behalf of its residents to recover the actual damages of assisted persons arising from such violation, including any liability under paragraph (2); and

(C) in the case of any successful action under subparagraph (A) or (B), shall be awarded the costs of the action and reasonable attorneys' fees as determined by the court.

(4) The district courts of the United States for districts located in the State shall have concurrent jurisdiction of any action under subparagraph (A) or (B) of paragraph (3).

(5) Notwithstanding any other provision of Federal law and in addition to any other remedy provided under Federal or State law, if the court, on its own motion or on the motion of the United States trustee or the debtor, finds that a person intentionally violated this section, or engaged in a clear and consistent pattern or practice of violating this section, the court may—

(A) enjoin the violation of such section; or

(B) impose an appropriate civil penalty against such person.

(d) No provision of this section, section 527, or section 528 shall—

(1) annul, alter, affect, or exempt any person subject to such sections from complying with any law of any State except to the extent that such law is inconsistent with those sections, and then only to the extent of the inconsistency; or

(2) be deemed to limit or curtail the authority or ability—

(A) of a State or subdivision or instrumentality thereof, to determine and enforce qualifications for the practice of law under the laws of that State; or

(B) of a Federal court to determine and enforce the qualifications for the practice of law before that court.

(Added Pub.L. 109–8, title II, § 227(a), Apr. 20, 2005, 119 Stat. 67; amended Pub.L. 111–327, § 2(a)(20), Dec. 22, 2010, 124 Stat. 3560.)

§ 527. Disclosures

(a) A debt relief agency providing bankruptcy assistance to an assisted person shall provide—

(1) the written notice required under section 342(b)(1); and

(2) to the extent not covered in the written notice described in paragraph (1), and not later than 3 business days after the first date on which a debt relief agency first offers to provide any bankruptcy assistance services to an assisted person, a clear and conspicuous written notice advising assisted persons that—

(A) all information that the assisted person is required to provide with a petition and thereafter during a case under this title is required to be complete, accurate, and truthful;

(B) all assets and all liabilities are required to be completely and accurately disclosed in the documents filed to commence the case, and the replacement value of each asset as defined in section 506 must be stated in those documents where requested after reasonable inquiry to establish such value;

(C) current monthly income, the amounts specified in section 707(b)(2), and, in a case under chapter 13 of this title, disposable income (determined in accordance with section 707(b)(2)), are required to be stated after reasonable inquiry; and

(D) information that an assisted person provides during their case may be audited pursuant to this title, and that failure to provide such information may result in dismissal of the case under this title or other sanction, including a criminal sanction.

(b) A debt relief agency providing bankruptcy assistance to an assisted person shall provide each assisted person at the same time as the notices required under subsection (a)(1) the following statement, to the extent applicable, or one substantially similar. The statement shall be clear and conspicuous and shall be in a single document separate from other documents or notices provided to the assisted person:

"IMPORTANT INFORMATION ABOUT BANKRUPTCY ASSISTANCE SERVICES FROM AN ATTORNEY OR BANKRUPTCY PETITION PREPARER.

"If you decide to seek bankruptcy relief, you can represent yourself, you can hire an attorney to represent you, or you can get help in some localities from a bankruptcy petition preparer who is not an attorney. THE LAW REQUIRES AN ATTORNEY OR BANKRUPTCY PETITION PREPARER TO GIVE YOU A WRITTEN CONTRACT SPECIFYING WHAT THE ATTORNEY OR BANKRUPTCY PETITION PREPARER WILL DO FOR YOU AND HOW MUCH IT WILL COST. Ask to see the contract before you hire anyone.

"The following information helps you understand what must be done in a routine bankruptcy case to help you evaluate how much service you need. Although bankruptcy can be complex, many cases are routine.

"Before filing a bankruptcy case, either you or your attorney should analyze your eligibility for different forms of debt relief available under the Bankruptcy Code and which form of relief is most likely to be beneficial for you. Be sure you understand the relief you can obtain and its limitations. To file a bankruptcy case, documents called a Petition, Schedules, and Statement of Financial Affairs, and in some cases a Statement of Intention, need to be prepared correctly and filed with the bankruptcy court. You will have to pay a filing fee to the bankruptcy court. Once your case starts, you will have to attend the required first meeting of creditors where you may be questioned by a court official called a 'trustee' and by creditors.

"If you choose to file a chapter 7 case, you may be asked by a creditor to reaffirm a debt. You may want help deciding whether to do so. A creditor is not permitted to coerce you into reaffirming your debts.

"If you choose to file a chapter 13 case in which you repay your creditors what you can afford over 3 to 5 years, you may also want help with preparing your chapter 13 plan and with the confirmation hearing on your plan which will be before a bankruptcy judge.

"If you select another type of relief under the Bankruptcy Code other than chapter 7 or chapter 13, you will want to find out what should be done from someone familiar with that type of relief.

"Your bankruptcy case may also involve litigation. You are generally permitted to represent yourself in litigation in bankruptcy court, but only attorneys, not bankruptcy petition preparers, can give you legal advice.".

(c) Except to the extent the debt relief agency provides the required information itself after reasonably diligent inquiry of the assisted person or others so as to obtain such information reasonably accurately for inclusion on the petition, schedules or statement of financial affairs, a debt relief agency providing bankruptcy assistance to an assisted person, to the extent permitted by nonbankruptcy law, shall provide each assisted person at the time required for the notice required under subsection (a)(1) reasonably sufficient information (which shall be provided in a clear and conspicuous writing) to the assisted person on how to provide all the information the assisted person is required to provide under this title pursuant to section 521, including—

    (1) how to value assets at replacement value, determine current monthly income, the amounts specified in section 707(b)(2) and, in a chapter 13 case, how to determine disposable income in accordance with section 707(b)(2) and related calculations;

    (2) how to complete the list of creditors, including how to determine what amount is owed and what address for the creditor should be shown; and

    (3) how to determine what property is exempt and how to value exempt property at replacement value as defined in section 506.

(d) A debt relief agency shall maintain a copy of the notices required under subsection (a) of this section for 2 years after the date on which the notice is given the assisted person.

(Added Pub.L. 109–8, title II, § 228(a), Apr. 20, 2005, 119 Stat. 69; amended Pub.L. 111–327, § 2(a)(21), Dec. 22, 2010, 124 Stat. 3560.)

§ 528.   Requirements for debt relief agencies

(a) A debt relief agency shall—

    (1) not later than 5 business days after the first date on which such agency provides any bankruptcy assistance services to an assisted person, but prior to such assisted person's petition under this title being filed, execute a written contract with such assisted person that explains clearly and conspicuously—

        (A) the services such agency will provide to such assisted person; and

        (B) the fees or charges for such services, and the terms of payment;

    (2) provide the assisted person with a copy of the fully executed and completed contract;

    (3) clearly and conspicuously disclose in any advertisement of bankruptcy assistance services or of the benefits of bankruptcy directed to the general public (whether in general media, seminars or specific mailings, telephonic or electronic messages, or otherwise) that the services or benefits are with respect to bankruptcy relief under this title; and

    (4) clearly and conspicuously use the following statement in such advertisement: "We are a debt relief agency. We help people file for bankruptcy relief under the Bankruptcy Code." or a substantially similar statement.

(b)(1)   An advertisement of bankruptcy assistance services or of the benefits of bankruptcy directed to the general public includes—

(A)   descriptions of bankruptcy assistance in connection with a chapter 13 plan whether or not chapter 13 is specifically mentioned in such advertisement; and

(B)   statements such as "federally supervised repayment plan" or "Federal debt restructuring help" or other similar statements that could lead a reasonable consumer to believe that debt counseling was being offered when in fact the services were directed to providing bankruptcy assistance with a chapter 13 plan or other form of bankruptcy relief under this title.

(2)   An advertisement, directed to the general public, indicating that the debt relief agency provides assistance with respect to credit defaults, mortgage foreclosures, eviction proceedings, excessive debt, debt collection pressure, or inability to pay any consumer debt shall—

(A)   disclose clearly and conspicuously in such advertisement that the assistance may involve bankruptcy relief under this title; and

(B)   include the following statement: "We are a debt relief agency. We help people file for bankruptcy relief under the Bankruptcy Code." or a substantially similar statement.

(Added Pub.L. 109–8, title II, § 229(a), Apr. 20, 2005, 119 Stat. 71.)

SUBCHAPTER III—THE ESTATE

§ 541.   Property of the estate

(a)   The commencement of a case under section 301, 302, or 303 of this title creates an estate. Such estate is comprised of all the following property, wherever located and by whomever held:

(1)   Except as provided in subsections (b) and (c)(2) of this section, all legal or equitable interests of the debtor in property as of the commencement of the case.

(2)   All interests of the debtor and the debtor's spouse in community property as of the commencement of the case that is—

(A)   under the sole, equal, or joint management and control of the debtor; or

(B)   liable for an allowable claim against the debtor, or for both an allowable claim against the debtor and an allowable claim against the debtor's spouse, to the extent that such interest is so liable.

(3)   Any interest in property that the trustee recovers under section 329(b), 363(n), 543, 550, 553, or 723 of this title.

(4)   Any interest in property preserved for the benefit of or ordered transferred to the estate under section 510(c) or 551 of this title.

(5)   Any interest in property that would have been property of the estate if such interest had been an interest of the debtor on the date of the filing of the petition, and that the debtor acquires or becomes entitled to acquire within 180 days after such date—

(A)   by bequest, devise, or inheritance;

(B)   as a result of a property settlement agreement with the debtor's spouse, or of an interlocutory or final divorce decree; or

(C)   as a beneficiary of a life insurance policy or of a death benefit plan.

(6)   Proceeds, product, offspring, rents, or profits of or from property of the estate, except such as are earnings from services performed by an individual debtor after the commencement of the case.

(7)   Any interest in property that the estate acquires after the commencement of the case.

(b)   Property of the estate does not include—

(1) any power that the debtor may exercise solely for the benefit of an entity other than the debtor;

(2) any interest of the debtor as a lessee under a lease of nonresidential real property that has terminated at the expiration of the stated term of such lease before the commencement of the case under this title, and ceases to include any interest of the debtor as a lessee under a lease of nonresidential real property that has terminated at the expiration of the stated term of such lease during the case;

(3) any eligibility of the debtor to participate in programs authorized under the Higher Education Act of 1965 (20 U.S.C. 1001 et seq.; 42 U.S.C. 2751 et seq.), or any accreditation status or State licensure of the debtor as an educational institution;

(4) any interest of the debtor in liquid or gaseous hydrocarbons to the extent that—

(A)(i) the debtor has transferred or has agreed to transfer such interest pursuant to a farmout agreement or any written agreement directly related to a farmout agreement; and

(ii) but for the operation of this paragraph, the estate could include the interest referred to in clause (i) only by virtue of section 365 or 544(a)(3) of this title; or

(B)(i) the debtor has transferred such interest pursuant to a written conveyance of a production payment to an entity that does not participate in the operation of the property from which such production payment is transferred; and

(ii) but for the operation of this paragraph, the estate could include the interest referred to in clause (i) only by virtue of section 365 or 542 of this title;

(5) funds placed in an education individual retirement account (as defined in section 530(b)(1) of the Internal Revenue Code of 1986) not later than 365 days before the date of the filing of the petition in a case under this title, but—

(A) only if the designated beneficiary of such account was a child, stepchild, grandchild, or stepgrandchild of the debtor for the taxable year for which funds were placed in such account;

(B) only to the extent that such funds—

(i) are not pledged or promised to any entity in connection with any extension of credit; and

(ii) are not excess contributions (as described in section 4973(e) of the Internal Revenue Code of 1986); and

(C) in the case of funds placed in all such accounts having the same designated beneficiary not earlier than 720 days nor later than 365 days before such date, only so much of such funds as does not exceed $6,425;*

(6) funds used to purchase a tuition credit or certificate or contributed to an account in accordance with section 529(b)(1)(A) of the Internal Revenue Code of 1986 under a qualified State tuition program (as defined in section 529(b)(1) of such Code) not later than 365 days before the date of the filing of the petition in a case under this title, but—

(A) only if the designated beneficiary of the amounts paid or contributed to such tuition program was a child, stepchild, grandchild, or stepgrandchild of the debtor for the taxable year for which funds were paid or contributed;

(B) with respect to the aggregate amount paid or contributed to such program having the same designated beneficiary, only so much of such amount as does not exceed the total contributions permitted under section 529(b)(6) of such Code with respect to such beneficiary, as adjusted beginning on the date of the filing of the petition in a case under this title by the annual

---

*   *Note from West Advisory Panel: Dollar amounts adjusted pursuant to 11 U.S.C. § 104; 81 Fed. Reg. 8748 (Feb. 22, 2016).*

increase or decrease (rounded to the nearest tenth of 1 percent) in the education expenditure category of the Consumer Price Index prepared by the Department of Labor; and

(C) in the case of funds paid or contributed to such program having the same designated beneficiary not earlier than 720 days nor later than 365 days before such date, only so much of such funds as does not exceed $6,425;[*]

(7) any amount—

(A) withheld by an employer from the wages of employees for payment as contributions—

(i) to—

(I) an employee benefit plan that is subject to title I of the Employee Retirement Income Security Act of 1974 or under an employee benefit plan which is a governmental plan under section 414(d) of the Internal Revenue Code of 1986;

(II) a deferred compensation plan under section 457 of the Internal Revenue Code of 1986; or

(III) a tax-deferred annuity under section 403(b) of the Internal Revenue Code of 1986;

except that such amount under this subparagraph shall not constitute disposable income as defined in section 1325(b)(2); or

(ii) to a health insurance plan regulated by State law whether or not subject to such title; or

(B) received by an employer from employees for payment as contributions—

(i) to—

(I) an employee benefit plan that is subject to title I of the Employee Retirement Income Security Act of 1974 or under an employee benefit plan which is a governmental plan under section 414(d) of the Internal Revenue Code of 1986;

(II) a deferred compensation plan under section 457 of the Internal Revenue Code of 1986; or

(III) a tax-deferred annuity under section 403(b) of the Internal Revenue Code of 1986;

except that such amount under this subparagraph shall not constitute disposable income, as defined in section 1325(b)(2); or

(ii) to a health insurance plan regulated by State law whether or not subject to such title;

(8) subject to subchapter III of chapter 5, any interest of the debtor in property where the debtor pledged or sold tangible personal property (other than securities or written or printed evidences of indebtedness or title) as collateral for a loan or advance of money given by a person licensed under law to make such loans or advances, where—

(A) the tangible personal property is in the possession of the pledgee or transferee;

(B) the debtor has no obligation to repay the money, redeem the collateral, or buy back the property at a stipulated price; and

(C) neither the debtor nor the trustee have exercised any right to redeem provided under the contract or State law, in a timely manner as provided under State law and section 108(b);

---

[*] *Note from West Advisory Panel: Dollar amounts adjusted pursuant to 11 U.S.C. § 104; 81 Fed. Reg. 8748 (Feb. 22, 2016).*

(9) any interest in cash or cash equivalents that constitute proceeds of a sale by the debtor of a money order that is made—

    (A) on or after the date that is 14 days prior to the date on which the petition is filed; and

    (B) under an agreement with a money order issuer that prohibits the commingling of such proceeds with property of the debtor (notwithstanding that, contrary to the agreement, the proceeds may have been commingled with property of the debtor),

unless the money order issuer had not taken action, prior to the filing of the petition, to require compliance with the prohibition; or

(10) funds placed in an account of a qualified ABLE program (as defined in section 529A(b) of the Internal Revenue Code of 1986) not later than 365 days before the date of the filing of the petition in a case under this title, but—

    (A) only if the designated beneficiary of such account was a child, stepchild, grandchild, or stepgrandchild of the debtor for the taxable year for which funds were placed in such account;

    (B) only to the extent that such funds—

        (i) are not pledged or promised to any entity in connection with any extension of credit; and

        (ii) are not excess contributions (as described in section 4973(h) of the Internal Revenue Code of 1986); and

    (C) in the case of funds placed in all such accounts having the same designated beneficiary not earlier than 720 days nor later than 365 days before such date, only so much of such funds as does not exceed $6,225.

Paragraph (4) shall not be construed to exclude from the estate any consideration the debtor retains, receives, or is entitled to receive for transferring an interest in liquid or gaseous hydrocarbons pursuant to a farmout agreement.

(c)(1) Except as provided in paragraph (2) of this subsection, an interest of the debtor in property becomes property of the estate under subsection (a)(1), (a)(2), or (a)(5) of this section notwithstanding any provision in an agreement, transfer instrument, or applicable nonbankruptcy law—

    (A) that restricts or conditions transfer of such interest by the debtor; or

    (B) that is conditioned on the insolvency or financial condition of the debtor, on the commencement of a case under this title, or on the appointment of or taking possession by a trustee in a case under this title or a custodian before such commencement, and that effects or gives an option to effect a forfeiture, modification, or termination of the debtor's interest in property.

    (2) A restriction on the transfer of a beneficial interest of the debtor in a trust that is enforceable under applicable nonbankruptcy law is enforceable in a case under this title.

(d) Property in which the debtor holds, as of the commencement of the case, only legal title and not an equitable interest, such as a mortgage secured by real property, or an interest in such a mortgage, sold by the debtor but as to which the debtor retains legal title to service or supervise the servicing of such mortgage or interest, becomes property of the estate under subsection (a)(1) or (2) of this section only to the extent of the debtor's legal title to such property, but not to the extent of any equitable interest in such property that the debtor does not hold.

(e) In determining whether any of the relationships specified in paragraph (5)(A) or (6)(A) of subsection (b) exists, a legally adopted child of an individual (and a child who is a member of an individual's household, if placed with such individual by an authorized placement agency for legal adoption by such individual), or a foster child of an individual (if such child has as the child's principal place of abode the home of the debtor and is a member of the debtor's household) shall be treated as a child of such individual by blood.

(f) Notwithstanding any other provision of this title, property that is held by a debtor that is a corporation described in section 501(c)(3) of the Internal Revenue Code of 1986 and exempt from tax under section 501(a) of such Code may be transferred to an entity that is not such a corporation, but only under the same conditions as would apply if the debtor had not filed a case under this title.

(Pub.L. 95–598, Nov. 6, 1978, 92 Stat. 2594; Pub.L. 98–353, title III, §§ 363(a), 456, July 10, 1984, 98 Stat. 363, 376; Pub.L. 101–508, title III, § 3007(a)(2), Nov. 5, 1990, 104 Stat. 1388–28; Pub.L. 102–486, title XXX, § 3017(b), Oct. 24, 1992, 106 Stat. 3130; Pub.L. 103–394, title II, §§ 208(b), 223, Oct. 22, 1994, 108 Stat. 4124, 4129; Pub.L. 109–8, title II, § 225(a), title III, § 323, title XII, §§ 1212, 1221(c), 1230, Apr. 20, 2005, 119 Stat. 65, 97, 194, 196, 201; Pub.L. 111–327, § 2(a)(22), Dec. 22, 2010, 124 Stat. 3560; Pub.L. 113–295, div. B, title I, § 104(a), Dec. 19, 2014, 128 Stat. 4063.)

§ 542. Turnover of property to the estate

(a) Except as provided in subsection (c) or (d) of this section, an entity, other than a custodian, in possession, custody, or control, during the case, of property that the trustee may use, sell, or lease under section 363 of this title, or that the debtor may exempt under section 522 of this title, shall deliver to the trustee, and account for, such property or the value of such property, unless such property is of inconsequential value or benefit to the estate.

(b) Except as provided in subsection (c) or (d) of this section, an entity that owes a debt that is property of the estate and that is matured, payable on demand, or payable on order, shall pay such debt to, or on the order of, the trustee, except to the extent that such debt may be offset under section 553 of this title against a claim against the debtor.

(c) Except as provided in section 362(a)(7) of this title, an entity that has neither actual notice nor actual knowledge of the commencement of the case concerning the debtor may transfer property of the estate, or pay a debt owing to the debtor, in good faith and other than in the manner specified in subsection (d) of this section, to an entity other than the trustee, with the same effect as to the entity making such transfer or payment as if the case under this title concerning the debtor had not been commenced.

(d) A life insurance company may transfer property of the estate or property of the debtor to such company in good faith, with the same effect with respect to such company as if the case under this title concerning the debtor had not been commenced, if such transfer is to pay a premium or to carry out a nonforfeiture insurance option, and is required to be made automatically, under a life insurance contract with such company that was entered into before the date of the filing of the petition and that is property of the estate.

(e) Subject to any applicable privilege, after notice and a hearing, the court may order an attorney, accountant, or other person that holds recorded information, including books, documents, records, and papers, relating to the debtor's property or financial affairs, to turn over or disclose such recorded information to the trustee.

(Pub.L. 95–598, Nov. 6, 1978, 92 Stat. 2595; Pub.L. 98–353, title III, § 457, July 10, 1984, 98 Stat. 376; Pub.L. 103–394, title V, § 501(d)(16), Oct. 22, 1994, 108 Stat. 4146.)

§ 543. Turnover of property by a custodian

(a) A custodian with knowledge of the commencement of a case under this title concerning the debtor may not make any disbursement from, or take any action in the administration of, property of the debtor, proceeds, product, offspring, rents, or profits of such property, or property of the estate, in the possession, custody, or control of such custodian, except such action as is necessary to preserve such property.

(b) A custodian shall—

(1) deliver to the trustee any property of the debtor held by or transferred to such custodian, or proceeds, product, offspring, rents, or profits of such property, that is in such custodian's possession, custody, or control on the date that such custodian acquires knowledge of the commencement of the case; and

(2) file an accounting of any property of the debtor, or proceeds, product, offspring, rents, or profits of such property, that, at any time, came into the possession, custody, or control of such custodian.

(c) The court, after notice and a hearing, shall—

(1) protect all entities to which a custodian has become obligated with respect to such property or proceeds, product, offspring, rents, or profits of such property;

(2) provide for the payment of reasonable compensation for services rendered and costs and expenses incurred by such custodian; and

(3) surcharge such custodian, other than an assignee for the benefit of the debtor's creditors that was appointed or took possession more than 120 days before the date of the filing of the petition, for any improper or excessive disbursement, other than a disbursement that has been made in accordance with applicable law or that has been approved, after notice and a hearing, by a court of competent jurisdiction before the commencement of the case under this title.

(d) After notice and hearing, the bankruptcy court—

(1) may excuse compliance with subsection (a), (b), or (c) of this section if the interests of creditors and, if the debtor is not insolvent, of equity security holders would be better served by permitting a custodian to continue in possession, custody, or control of such property, and

(2) shall excuse compliance with subsections (a) and (b)(1) of this section if the custodian is an assignee for the benefit of the debtor's creditors that was appointed or took possession more than 120 days before the date of the filing of the petition, unless compliance with such subsections is necessary to prevent fraud or injustice.

(Pub.L. 95–598, Nov. 6, 1978, 92 Stat. 2595; Pub.L. 98–353, title III, § 458, July 10, 1984, 98 Stat. 376; Pub.L. 103–394, title V, § 501(d)(17), Oct. 22, 1994, 108 Stat. 4146.)

§ 544. Trustee as lien creditor and as successor to certain creditors and purchasers

(a) The trustee shall have, as of the commencement of the case, and without regard to any knowledge of the trustee or of any creditor, the rights and powers of, or may avoid any transfer of property of the debtor or any obligation incurred by the debtor that is voidable by—

(1) a creditor that extends credit to the debtor at the time of the commencement of the case, and that obtains, at such time and with respect to such credit, a judicial lien on all property on which a creditor on a simple contract could have obtained such a judicial lien, whether or not such a creditor exists;

(2) a creditor that extends credit to the debtor at the time of the commencement of the case, and obtains, at such time and with respect to such credit, an execution against the debtor that is returned unsatisfied at such time, whether or not such a creditor exists; or

(3) a bona fide purchaser of real property, other than fixtures, from the debtor, against whom applicable law permits such transfer to be perfected, that obtains the status of a bona fide purchaser and has perfected such transfer at the time of the commencement of the case, whether or not such a purchaser exists.

(b)(1) Except as provided in paragraph (2), the trustee may avoid any transfer of an interest of the debtor in property or any obligation incurred by the debtor that is voidable under applicable law by a creditor holding an unsecured claim that is allowable under section 502 of this title or that is not allowable only under section 502(e) of this title.

(2) Paragraph (1) shall not apply to a transfer of a charitable contribution (as that term is defined in section 548(d)(3)) that is not covered under section 548(a)(1)(B), by reason of section 548(a)(2). Any claim by any person to recover a transferred contribution described in the preceding sentence under Federal or State law in a Federal or State court shall be preempted by the commencement of the case.

(Pub.L. 95–598, Nov. 6, 1978, 92 Stat. 2596; Pub.L. 98–353, title III, § 459, July 10, 1984, 98 Stat. 377; Pub.L. 105–183, § 3(b), June 19, 1998, 112 Stat. 518.)

§ 545. Statutory liens

The trustee may avoid the fixing of a statutory lien on property of the debtor to the extent that such lien—

(1) first becomes effective against the debtor—

(A) when a case under this title concerning the debtor is commenced;

(B) when an insolvency proceeding other than under this title concerning the debtor is commenced;

(C) when a custodian is appointed or authorized to take or takes possession;

(D) when the debtor becomes insolvent;

(E) when the debtor's financial condition fails to meet a specified standard; or

(F) at the time of an execution against property of the debtor levied at the instance of an entity other than the holder of such statutory lien;

(2) is not perfected or enforceable at the time of the commencement of the case against a bona fide purchaser that purchases such property at the time of the commencement of the case, whether or not such a purchaser exists, except in any case in which a purchaser is a purchaser described in section 6323 of the Internal Revenue Code of 1986, or in any other similar provision of State or local law;

(3) is for rent; or

(4) is a lien of distress for rent.

(Pub.L. 95–598, Nov. 6, 1978, 92 Stat. 2597; Pub.L. 98–353, title III, § 460, July 10, 1984, 98 Stat. 377; Pub.L. 109–8, title VII, § 711, Apr. 20, 2005, 119 Stat. 127.)

§ 546. Limitations on avoiding powers

(a) An action or proceeding under section 544, 545, 547, 548, or 553 of this title may not be commenced after the earlier of—

(1) the later of—

(A) 2 years after the entry of the order for relief; or

(B) 1 year after the appointment or election of the first trustee under section 702, 1104, 1163, 1202, or 1302 of this title if such appointment or such election occurs before the expiration of the period specified in subparagraph (A); or

(2) the time the case is closed or dismissed.

(b)(1) The rights and powers of a trustee under sections 544, 545, and 549 of this title are subject to any generally applicable law that—

(A) permits perfection of an interest in property to be effective against an entity that acquires rights in such property before the date of perfection; or

(B) provides for the maintenance or continuation of perfection of an interest in property to be effective against an entity that acquires rights in such property before the date on which action is taken to effect such maintenance or continuation.

(2) If—

(A) a law described in paragraph (1) requires seizure of such property or commencement of an action to accomplish such perfection, or maintenance or continuation of perfection of an interest in property; and

    (B) such property has not been seized or such an action has not been commenced before the date of the filing of the petition;

such interest in such property shall be perfected, or perfection of such interest shall be maintained or continued, by giving notice within the time fixed by such law for such seizure or such commencement.

    (c)(1) Except as provided in subsection (d) of this section and in section 507(c), and subject to the prior rights of a holder of a security interest in such goods or the proceeds thereof, the rights and powers of the trustee under sections 544(a), 545, 547, and 549 are subject to the right of a seller of goods that has sold goods to the debtor, in the ordinary course of such seller's business, to reclaim such goods if the debtor has received such goods while insolvent, within 45 days before the date of the commencement of a case under this title, but such seller may not reclaim such goods unless such seller demands in writing reclamation of such goods—

    (A) not later than 45 days after the date of receipt of such goods by the debtor; or

    (B) not later than 20 days after the date of commencement of the case, if the 45-day period expires after the commencement of the case.

    (2) If a seller of goods fails to provide notice in the manner described in paragraph (1), the seller still may assert the rights contained in section 503(b)(9).

    (d) In the case of a seller who is a producer of grain sold to a grain storage facility, owned or operated by the debtor, in the ordinary course of such seller's business (as such terms are defined in section 557 of this title) or in the case of a United States fisherman who has caught fish sold to a fish processing facility owned or operated by the debtor in the ordinary course of such fisherman's business, the rights and powers of the trustee under sections 544(a), 545, 547, and 549 of this title are subject to any statutory or common law right of such producer or fisherman to reclaim such grain or fish if the debtor has received such grain or fish while insolvent, but—

    (1) such producer or fisherman may not reclaim any grain or fish unless such producer or fisherman demands, in writing, reclamation of such grain or fish before ten days after receipt thereof by the debtor; and

    (2) the court may deny reclamation to such a producer or fisherman with a right of reclamation that has made such a demand only if the court secures such claim by a lien.

    (e) Notwithstanding sections 544, 545, 547, 548(a)(1)(B), and 548(b) of this title, the trustee may not avoid a transfer that is a margin payment, as defined in section 101, 741, or 761 of this title, or settlement payment, as defined in section 101 or 741 of this title, made by or to (or for the benefit of) a commodity broker, forward contract merchant, stockbroker, financial institution, financial participant, or securities clearing agency, or that is a transfer made by or to (or for the benefit of) a commodity broker, forward contract merchant, stockbroker, financial institution, financial participant, or securities clearing agency, in connection with a securities contract, as defined in section 741(7), commodity contract, as defined in section 761(4), or forward contract, that is made before the commencement of the case, except under section 548(a)(1)(A) of this title.

    (f) Notwithstanding sections 544, 545, 547, 548(a)(1)(B), and 548(b) of this title, the trustee may not avoid a transfer made by or to (or for the benefit of) a repo participant or financial participant, in connection with a repurchase agreement and that is made before the commencement of the case, except under section 548(a)(1)(A) of this title.

    (g) Notwithstanding sections 544, 545, 547, 548(a)(1)(B) and 548(b) of this title, the trustee may not avoid a transfer, made by or to (or for the benefit of) a swap participant or financial participant, under or in connection with any swap agreement and that is made before the commencement of the case, except under section 548(a)(1)(A) of this title.

    (h) Notwithstanding the rights and powers of a trustee under sections 544(a), 545, 547, 549, and 553, if the court determines on a motion by the trustee made not later than 120 days after the date of the order for relief in a case under chapter 11 of this title and after notice and a hearing, that a return is in the best interests of the estate, the debtor, with the consent of a creditor and subject to the prior rights of holders of security interests in such goods or the proceeds of such goods, may return goods shipped to the debtor by the creditor before the commencement of the case, and the creditor may offset the purchase price of such goods against any claim of the creditor against the debtor that arose before the commencement of the case.

(i)(1) Notwithstanding paragraphs (2) and (3) of section 545, the trustee may not avoid a warehouseman's lien for storage, transportation, or other costs incidental to the storage and handling of goods.

(2) The prohibition under paragraph (1) shall be applied in a manner consistent with any State statute applicable to such lien that is similar to section 7–209 of the Uniform Commercial Code, as in effect on the date of enactment of the Bankruptcy Abuse Prevention and Consumer Protection Act of 2005, or any successor to such section 7–209.

(j) Notwithstanding sections 544, 545, 547, 548(a)(1)(B), and 548(b) the trustee may not avoid a transfer made by or to (or for the benefit of) a master netting agreement participant under or in connection with any master netting agreement or any individual contract covered thereby that is made before the commencement of the case, except under section 548(a)(1)(A) and except to the extent that the trustee could otherwise avoid such a transfer made under an individual contract covered by such master netting agreement.

(Pub.L. 95–598, Nov. 6, 1978, 92 Stat. 2597; Pub.L. 97–222, § 4, July 27, 1982, 96 Stat. 236; Pub.L. 98–353, title III, §§ 351, 393, 461, July 10, 1984, 98 Stat. 358, 365, 377; Pub.L. 99–554, title II, §§ 257(d), 283(*l*), Oct. 27, 1986, 100 Stat. 3114, 3117; Pub.L. 101–311, title I, § 103, title II, § 203, June 25, 1990, 104 Stat. 268, 269; Pub.L. 103–394, title II, §§ 204(b), 209, 216, 222(a), title V, § 501(b)(4), Oct. 22, 1994, 108 Stat. 4122, 4125, 4126, 4129, 4142; Pub.L. 105–183, § 3(c), June 19, 1998, 112 Stat. 518; Pub.L. 109–8, title IV, § 406, title IX, §§ 907(e), (*o*)(2), (3), title XII, § 1227(a), Apr. 20, 2005, 119 Stat. 105, 177, 182, 199; Pub.L. 109–390, § 5(b), Dec. 12, 2006, 120 Stat. 2697.)

§ 547. Preferences

(a) In this section—

(1) "inventory" means personal property leased or furnished, held for sale or lease, or to be furnished under a contract for service, raw materials, work in process, or materials used or consumed in a business, including farm products such as crops or livestock, held for sale or lease;

(2) "new value" means money or money's worth in goods, services, or new credit, or release by a transferee of property previously transferred to such transferee in a transaction that is neither void nor voidable by the debtor or the trustee under any applicable law, including proceeds of such property, but does not include an obligation substituted for an existing obligation;

(3) "receivable" means right to payment, whether or not such right has been earned by performance; and

(4) a debt for a tax is incurred on the day when such tax is last payable without penalty, including any extension.

(b) Except as provided in subsections (c) and (i) of this section, the trustee may avoid any transfer of an interest of the debtor in property—

(1) to or for the benefit of a creditor;

(2) for or on account of an antecedent debt owed by the debtor before such transfer was made;

(3) made while the debtor was insolvent;

(4) made—

(A) on or within 90 days before the date of the filing of the petition; or

(B) between ninety days and one year before the date of the filing of the petition, if such creditor at the time of such transfer was an insider; and

(5) that enables such creditor to receive more than such creditor would receive if—

(A) the case were a case under chapter 7 of this title;

(B) the transfer had not been made; and

(C) such creditor received payment of such debt to the extent provided by the provisions of this title.

(c) The trustee may not avoid under this section a transfer—

(1) to the extent that such transfer was—

(A) intended by the debtor and the creditor to or for whose benefit such transfer was made to be a contemporaneous exchange for new value given to the debtor; and

(B) in fact a substantially contemporaneous exchange;

(2) to the extent that such transfer was in payment of a debt incurred by the debtor in the ordinary course of business or financial affairs of the debtor and the transferee, and such transfer was—

(A) made in the ordinary course of business or financial affairs of the debtor and the transferee; or

(B) made according to ordinary business terms;

(3) that creates a security interest in property acquired by the debtor—

(A) to the extent such security interest secures new value that was—

(i) given at or after the signing of a security agreement that contains a description of such property as collateral;

(ii) given by or on behalf of the secured party under such agreement;

(iii) given to enable the debtor to acquire such property; and

(iv) in fact used by the debtor to acquire such property; and

(B) that is perfected on or before 30 days after the debtor receives possession of such property;

(4) to or for the benefit of a creditor, to the extent that, after such transfer, such creditor gave new value to or for the benefit of the debtor—

(A) not secured by an otherwise unavoidable security interest; and

(B) on account of which new value the debtor did not make an otherwise unavoidable transfer to or for the benefit of such creditor;

(5) that creates a perfected security interest in inventory or a receivable or the proceeds of either, except to the extent that the aggregate of all such transfers to the transferee caused a reduction, as of the date of the filing of the petition and to the prejudice of other creditors holding unsecured claims, of any amount by which the debt secured by such security interest exceeded the value of all security interests for such debt on the later of—

(A)(i) with respect to a transfer to which subsection (b)(4)(A) of this section applies, 90 days before the date of the filing of the petition; or

(ii) with respect to a transfer to which subsection (b)(4)(B) of this section applies, one year before the date of the filing of the petition; or

(B) the date on which new value was first given under the security agreement creating such security interest;

(6) that is the fixing of a statutory lien that is not avoidable under section 545 of this title;

(7) to the extent such transfer was a bona fide payment of a debt for a domestic support obligation;

(8) if, in a case filed by an individual debtor whose debts are primarily consumer debts, the aggregate value of all property that constitutes or is affected by such transfer is less than $600; or

(9) if, in a case filed by a debtor whose debts are not primarily consumer debts, the aggregate value of all property that constitutes or is affected by such transfer is less than $6,425.*

(d) The trustee may avoid a transfer of an interest in property of the debtor transferred to or for the benefit of a surety to secure reimbursement of such a surety that furnished a bond or other obligation to dissolve a judicial lien that would have been avoidable by the trustee under subsection (b) of this section. The liability of such surety under such bond or obligation shall be discharged to the extent of the value of such property recovered by the trustee or the amount paid to the trustee.

(e)(1) For the purposes of this section—

(A) a transfer of real property other than fixtures, but including the interest of a seller or purchaser under a contract for the sale of real property, is perfected when a bona fide purchaser of such property from the debtor against whom applicable law permits such transfer to be perfected cannot acquire an interest that is superior to the interest of the transferee; and

(B) a transfer of a fixture or property other than real property is perfected when a creditor on a simple contract cannot acquire a judicial lien that is superior to the interest of the transferee.

(2) For the purposes of this section, except as provided in paragraph (3) of this subsection, a transfer is made—

(A) at the time such transfer takes effect between the transferor and the transferee, if such transfer is perfected at, or within 30 days after, such time, except as provided in subsection (c)(3)(B);

(B) at the time such transfer is perfected, if such transfer is perfected after such 30 days; or

(C) immediately before the date of the filing of the petition, if such transfer is not perfected at the later of—

(i) the commencement of the case; or

(ii) 30 days after such transfer takes effect between the transferor and the transferee.

(3) For the purposes of this section, a transfer is not made until the debtor has acquired rights in the property transferred.

(f) For the purposes of this section, the debtor is presumed to have been insolvent on and during the 90 days immediately preceding the date of the filing of the petition.

(g) For the purposes of this section, the trustee has the burden of proving the avoidability of a transfer under subsection (b) of this section, and the creditor or party in interest against whom recovery or avoidance is sought has the burden of proving the nonavoidability of a transfer under subsection (c) of this section.

(h) The trustee may not avoid a transfer if such transfer was made as a part of an alternative repayment schedule between the debtor and any creditor of the debtor created by an approved nonprofit budget and credit counseling agency.

(i) If the trustee avoids under subsection (b) a transfer made between 90 days and 1 year before the date of the filing of the petition, by the debtor to an entity that is not an insider for the benefit of a creditor that is an insider, such transfer shall be considered to be avoided under this section only with respect to the creditor that is an insider.

(Pub.L. 95–598, Nov. 6, 1978, 92 Stat. 2597; Pub.L. 98–353, title III, §§ 310, 462, July 10, 1984, 98 Stat. 355, 377; Pub.L. 99–554, title II, § 283(m), Oct. 27, 1986, 100 Stat. 3117; Pub.L. 103–394, title II, § 203, title

---

* *Note from West Advisory Panel: Dollar amounts adjusted pursuant to 11 U.S.C. § 104; 81 Fed. Reg. 8748 (Feb. 22, 2016).*

III, § 304(f), Oct. 22, 1994, 108 Stat. 4121, 4133; Pub.L. 109–8, title II, §§ 201(b), 217, title IV, §§ 403, 409, title XII, § 1213(a), 1222, Apr. 20, 2005, 119 Stat. 42, 55, 104, 106, 194, 196.)

§ 548.   Fraudulent transfers and obligations

    (a)(1)   The trustee may avoid any transfer (including any transfer to or for the benefit of an insider under an employment contract) of an interest of the debtor in property, or any obligation (including any obligation to or for the benefit of an insider under an employment contract) incurred by the debtor, that was made or incurred on or within 2 years before the date of the filing of the petition, if the debtor voluntarily or involuntarily—

        (A)   made such transfer or incurred such obligation with actual intent to hinder, delay, or defraud any entity to which the debtor was or became, on or after the date that such transfer was made or such obligation was incurred, indebted; or

        (B)(i)   received less than a reasonably equivalent value in exchange for such transfer or obligation; and

            (ii)(I)   was insolvent on the date that such transfer was made or such obligation was incurred, or became insolvent as a result of such transfer or obligation;

            (II)   was engaged in business or a transaction, or was about to engage in business or a transaction, for which any property remaining with the debtor was an unreasonably small capital;

            (III) intended to incur, or believed that the debtor would incur, debts that would be beyond the debtor's ability to pay as such debts matured; or

            (IV) made such transfer to or for the benefit of an insider, or incurred such obligation to or for the benefit of an insider, under an employment contract and not in the ordinary course of business.

    (2)   A transfer of a charitable contribution to a qualified religious or charitable entity or organization shall not be considered to be a transfer covered under paragraph (1)(B) in any case in which—

        (A)   the amount of that contribution does not exceed 15 percent of the gross annual income of the debtor for the year in which the transfer of the contribution is made; or

        (B)   the contribution made by a debtor exceeded the percentage amount of gross annual income specified in subparagraph (A), if the transfer was consistent with the practices of the debtor in making charitable contributions.

    (b)   The trustee of a partnership debtor may avoid any transfer of an interest of the debtor in property, or any obligation incurred by the debtor, that was made or incurred on or within 2 years before the date of the filing of the petition, to a general partner in the debtor, if the debtor was insolvent on the date such transfer was made or such obligation was incurred, or became insolvent as a result of such transfer or obligation.

    (c)   Except to the extent that a transfer or obligation voidable under this section is voidable under section 544, 545, or 547 of this title, a transferee or obligee of such a transfer or obligation that takes for value and in good faith has a lien on or may retain any interest transferred or may enforce any obligation incurred, as the case may be, to the extent that such transferee or obligee gave value to the debtor in exchange for such transfer or obligation.

    (d)(1)   For the purposes of this section, a transfer is made when such transfer is so perfected that a bona fide purchaser from the debtor against whom applicable law permits such transfer to be perfected cannot acquire an interest in the property transferred that is superior to the interest in such property of the transferee, but if such transfer is not so perfected before the commencement of the case, such transfer is made immediately before the date of the filing of the petition.

    (2)   In this section—

(A) "value" means property, or satisfaction or securing of a present or antecedent debt of the debtor, but does not include an unperformed promise to furnish support to the debtor or to a relative of the debtor;

(B) a commodity broker, forward contract merchant, stockbroker, financial institution, financial participant, or securities clearing agency that receives a margin payment, as defined in section 101, 741, or 761 of this title, or settlement payment, as defined in section 101 or 741 of this title, takes for value to the extent of such payment;

(C) a repo participant or financial participant that receives a margin payment, as defined in section 741 or 761 of this title, or settlement payment, as defined in section 741 of this title, in connection with a repurchase agreement, takes for value to the extent of such payment;

(D) a swap participant or financial participant that receives a transfer in connection with a swap agreement takes for value to the extent of such transfer; and

(E) a master netting agreement participant that receives a transfer in connection with a master netting agreement or any individual contract covered thereby takes for value to the extent of such transfer, except that, with respect to a transfer under any individual contract covered thereby, to the extent that such master netting agreement participant otherwise did not take (or is otherwise not deemed to have taken) such transfer for value.

(3) In this section, the term "charitable contribution" means a charitable contribution, as that term is defined in section 170(c) of the Internal Revenue Code of 1986, if that contribution—

(A) is made by a natural person; and

(B) consists of—

(i) a financial instrument (as that term is defined in section 731(c)(2)(C) of the Internal Revenue Code of 1986); or

(ii) cash.

(4) In this section, the term "qualified religious or charitable entity or organization" means—

(A) an entity described in section 170(c)(1) of the Internal Revenue Code of 1986; or

(B) an entity or organization described in section 170(c)(2) of the Internal Revenue Code of 1986.

(e)(1) In addition to any transfer that the trustee may otherwise avoid, the trustee may avoid any transfer of an interest of the debtor in property that was made on or within 10 years before the date of the filing of the petition, if—

(A) such transfer was made to a self-settled trust or similar device;

(B) such transfer was by the debtor;

(C) the debtor is a beneficiary of such trust or similar device; and

(D) the debtor made such transfer with actual intent to hinder, delay, or defraud any entity to which the debtor was or became, on or after the date that such transfer was made, indebted.

(2) For the purposes of this subsection, a transfer includes a transfer made in anticipation of any money judgment, settlement, civil penalty, equitable order, or criminal fine incurred by, or which the debtor believed would be incurred by—

(A) any violation of the securities laws (as defined in section 3(a)(47) of the Securities Exchange Act of 1934 (15 U.S.C. 78c(a)(47))), any State securities laws, or any regulation or order issued under Federal securities laws or State securities laws; or

(B) fraud, deceit, or manipulation in a fiduciary capacity or in connection with the purchase or sale of any security registered under section 12 or 15(d) of the Securities Exchange Act of 1934 (15 U.S.C. 78l and 78o(d)) or under section 6 of the Securities Act of 1933 (15 U.S.C. 77f).

(Pub.L. 95–598, Nov. 6, 1978, 92 Stat. 2600; Pub.L. 97–222, § 5, July 27, 1982, 96 Stat. 236; Pub.L. 98–353, title III, §§ 394, 463, July 10, 1984, 98 Stat. 365, 378; Pub.L. 99–554, title II, § 283(n), Oct. 27, 1986, 100 Stat. 3117; Pub.L. 101–311, title I, § 104, title II, § 204, June 25, 1990, 104 Stat. 268, 269; Pub.L. 103–394, title V, § 501(b)(5), Oct. 22, 1994, 108 Stat. 4142; Pub.L. 105–183, §§ 2, 3(a), June 19, 1998, 112 Stat. 517; Pub.L. 109–8, title IX, § 907(f), (o)(4) to (6), title XIV, § 1402, Apr. 20, 2005, 119 Stat. 177, 182, 214.)

§ 549. Postpetition transactions

(a)   Except as provided in subsection (b) or (c) of this section, the trustee may avoid a transfer of property of the estate—

> **(1)**   that occurs after the commencement of the case; and

> **(2)(A)**   that is authorized only under section 303(f) or 542(c) of this title; or

>> **(B)**   that is not authorized under this title or by the court.

(b)   In an involuntary case, the trustee may not avoid under subsection (a) of this section a transfer made after the commencement of such case but before the order for relief to the extent any value, including services, but not including satisfaction or securing of a debt that arose before the commencement of the case, is given after the commencement of the case in exchange for such transfer, notwithstanding any notice or knowledge of the case that the transferee has.

(c)   The trustee may not avoid under subsection (a) of this section a transfer of an interest in real property to a good faith purchaser without knowledge of the commencement of the case and for present fair equivalent value unless a copy or notice of the petition was filed, where a transfer of an interest in such real property may be recorded to perfect such transfer, before such transfer is so perfected that a bona fide purchaser of such real property, against whom applicable law permits such transfer to be perfected, could not acquire an interest that is superior to such interest of such good faith purchaser. A good faith purchaser without knowledge of the commencement of the case and for less than present fair equivalent value has a lien on the property transferred to the extent of any present value given, unless a copy or notice of the petition was so filed before such transfer was so perfected.

(d)   An action or proceeding under this section may not be commenced after the earlier of—

> **(1)**   two years after the date of the transfer sought to be avoided; or

> **(2)**   the time the case is closed or dismissed.

(Pub.L. 95–598, Nov. 6, 1978, 92 Stat. 2601; Pub.L. 98–353, title III, § 464, July 10, 1984, 98 Stat. 379; Pub.L. 99–554, title II, § 283(o), Oct. 27, 1986, 100 Stat. 3117; Pub.L. 103–394, title V, § 501(d)(18), Oct. 22, 1994, 108 Stat. 4146; Pub.L. 109–8, title XII, § 1214, Apr. 20, 2005, 119 Stat. 195.)

§ 550. Liability of transferee of avoided transfer

(a)   Except as otherwise provided in this section, to the extent that a transfer is avoided under section 544, 545, 547, 548, 549, 553(b), or 724(a) of this title, the trustee may recover, for the benefit of the estate, the property transferred, or, if the court so orders, the value of such property, from—

> **(1)**   the initial transferee of such transfer or the entity for whose benefit such transfer was made; or

> **(2)**   any immediate or mediate transferee of such initial transferee.

(b)   The trustee may not recover under section[1] (a)(2) of this section from—

> **(1)**   a transferee that takes for value, including satisfaction or securing of a present or antecedent debt, in good faith, and without knowledge of the voidability of the transfer avoided; or

> **(2)**   any immediate or mediate good faith transferee of such transferee.

(c)   If a transfer made between 90 days and one year before the filing of the petition—

---

[1]   So in original. Probably should be "subsection".

(1) is avoided under section 547(b) of this title; and

(2) was made for the benefit of a creditor that at the time of such transfer was an insider;

the trustee may not recover under subsection (a) from a transferee that is not an insider.

(d) The trustee is entitled to only a single satisfaction under subsection (a) of this section.

(e)(1) A good faith transferee from whom the trustee may recover under subsection (a) of this section has a lien on the property recovered to secure the lesser of—

(A) the cost, to such transferee, of any improvement made after the transfer, less the amount of any profit realized by or accruing to such transferee from such property; and

(B) any increase in the value of such property as a result of such improvement, of the property transferred.

(2) In this subsection, "improvement" includes—

(A) physical additions or changes to the property transferred;

(B) repairs to such property;

(C) payment of any tax on such property;

(D) payment of any debt secured by a lien on such property that is superior or equal to the rights of the trustee; and

(E) preservation of such property.

(f) An action or proceeding under this section may not be commenced after the earlier of—

(1) one year after the avoidance of the transfer on account of which recovery under this section is sought; or

(2) the time the case is closed or dismissed.

(Pub.L. 95–598, Nov. 6, 1978, 92 Stat. 2601; Pub.L. 98–353, title III, § 465, July 10, 1984, 98 Stat. 379; Pub.L. 103–394, title II, § 202, Oct. 22, 1994, 108 Stat. 4121.)

§ 551. Automatic preservation of avoided transfer

Any transfer avoided under section 522, 544, 545, 547, 548, 549, or 724(a) of this title, or any lien void under section 506(d) of this title, is preserved for the benefit of the estate but only with respect to property of the estate.

(Pub.L. 95–598, Nov. 6, 1978, 92 Stat. 2602.)

§ 552. Postpetition effect of security interest

(a) Except as provided in subsection (b) of this section, property acquired by the estate or by the debtor after the commencement of the case is not subject to any lien resulting from any security agreement entered into by the debtor before the commencement of the case.

(b)(1) Except as provided in sections 363, 506(c), 522, 544, 545, 547, and 548 of this title, if the debtor and an entity entered into a security agreement before the commencement of the case and if the security interest created by such security agreement extends to property of the debtor acquired before the commencement of the case and to proceeds, products, offspring, or profits of such property, then such security interest extends to such proceeds, products, offspring, or profits acquired by the estate after the commencement of the case to the extent provided by such security agreement and by applicable nonbankruptcy law, except to any extent that the court, after notice and a hearing and based on the equities of the case, orders otherwise.

(2) Except as provided in sections 363, 506(c), 522, 544, 545, 547, and 548 of this title, and notwithstanding section 546(b) of this title, if the debtor and an entity entered into a security agreement before the commencement of the case and if the security interest created by such security

2245

agreement extends to property of the debtor acquired before the commencement of the case and to amounts paid as rents of such property or the fees, charges, accounts, or other payments for the use or occupancy of rooms and other public facilities in hotels, motels, or other lodging properties, then such security interest extends to such rents and such fees, charges, accounts, or other payments acquired by the estate after the commencement of the case to the extent provided in such security agreement, except to any extent that the court, after notice and a hearing and based on the equities of the case, orders otherwise.

(Pub.L. 95–598, Nov. 6, 1978, 92 Stat. 2602; Pub.L. 98–353, title III, § 466, July 10, 1984, 98 Stat. 380; Pub.L. 103–394, title II, § 214(a), Oct. 22, 1994, 108 Stat. 4126; Pub.L. 109–8, title XII, § 1204(2), Apr. 20, 2005, 119 Stat. 194.)

§ 553. Setoff

(a) Except as otherwise provided in this section and in sections 362 and 363 of this title, this title does not affect any right of a creditor to offset a mutual debt owing by such creditor to the debtor that arose before the commencement of the case under this title against a claim of such creditor against the debtor that arose before the commencement of the case, except to the extent that—

(1) the claim of such creditor against the debtor is disallowed;

(2) such claim was transferred, by an entity other than the debtor, to such creditor—

(A) after the commencement of the case; or

(B)(i) after 90 days before the date of the filing of the petition; and

(ii) while the debtor was insolvent (except for a setoff of a kind described in section 362(b)(6), 362(b)(7), 362(b)(17), 362(b)(27), 555, 556, 559, 560, or 561); or

(3) the debt owed to the debtor by such creditor was incurred by such creditor—

(A) after 90 days before the date of the filing of the petition;

(B) while the debtor was insolvent; and

(C) for the purpose of obtaining a right of setoff against the debtor (except for a setoff of a kind described in section 362(b)(6), 362(b)(7), 362(b)(17), 362(b)(27), 555, 556, 559, 560, or 561).

(b)(1) Except with respect to a setoff of a kind described in section 362(b)(6), 362(b)(7), 362(b)(17), 362(b)(27), 555, 556, 559, 560, 561, 365(h), 546(h), or 365(i)(2) of this title, if a creditor offsets a mutual debt owing to the debtor against a claim against the debtor on or within 90 days before the date of the filing of the petition, then the trustee may recover from such creditor the amount so offset to the extent that any insufficiency on the date of such setoff is less than the insufficiency on the later of—

(A) 90 days before the date of the filing of the petition; and

(B) the first date during the 90 days immediately preceding the date of the filing of the petition on which there is an insufficiency.

(2) In this subsection, "insufficiency" means amount, if any, by which a claim against the debtor exceeds a mutual debt owing to the debtor by the holder of such claim.

(c) For the purposes of this section, the debtor is presumed to have been insolvent on and during the 90 days immediately preceding the date of the filing of the petition.

(Pub.L. 95–598, Nov. 6, 1978, 92 Stat. 2602; Pub.L. 98–353, title III, §§ 395, 467, July 10, 1984, 98 Stat. 365, 380; Pub.L. 101–311, title I, § 105, June 25, 1990, 104 Stat. 268; Pub.L. 103–394, title II, §§ 205(b), 222(b), title V, § 501(d)(19), Oct. 22, 1994, 108 Stat. 4123, 4129, 4146; Pub.L. 109–8, title IX, § 907(n), Apr. 20, 2005, 119 Stat. 181.)

§ 554. Abandonment of property of the estate

  (a) After notice and a hearing, the trustee may abandon any property of the estate that is burdensome to the estate or that is of inconsequential value and benefit to the estate.

  (b) On request of a party in interest and after notice and a hearing, the court may order the trustee to abandon any property of the estate that is burdensome to the estate or that is of inconsequential value and benefit to the estate.

  (c) Unless the court orders otherwise, any property scheduled under section 521(a)(1) of this title not otherwise administered at the time of the closing of a case is abandoned to the debtor and administered for purposes of section 350 of this title.

  (d) Unless the court orders otherwise, property of the estate that is not abandoned under this section and that is not administered in the case remains property of the estate.

  (Pub.L. 95–598, Nov. 6, 1978, 92 Stat. 2603; Pub.L. 98–353, title III, § 468, July 10, 1984, 98 Stat. 380; Pub.L. 99–554, title II, § 283(p), Oct. 27, 1986, 100 Stat. 3118; Pub.L. 111–327, § 2(a)(23), Dec. 22, 2010, 124 Stat. 3560.)

§ 555. Contractual right to liquidate, terminate, or accelerate a securities contract

  The exercise of a contractual right of a stockbroker, financial institution, financial participant, or securities clearing agency to cause the liquidation, termination, or acceleration of a securities contract, as defined in section 741 of this title, because of a condition of the kind specified in section 365(e)(1) of this title shall not be stayed, avoided, or otherwise limited by operation of any provision of this title or by order of a court or administrative agency in any proceeding under this title unless such order is authorized under the provisions of the Securities Investor Protection Act of 1970 or any statute administered by the Securities and Exchange Commission. As used in this section, the term "contractual right" includes a right set forth in a rule or bylaw of a derivatives clearing organization (as defined in the Commodity Exchange Act), a multilateral clearing organization (as defined in the Federal Deposit Insurance Corporation Improvement Act of 1991), a national securities exchange, a national securities association, a securities clearing agency, a contract market designated under the Commodity Exchange Act, a derivatives transaction execution facility registered under the Commodity Exchange Act, or a board of trade (as defined in the Commodity Exchange Act), or in a resolution of the governing board thereof, and a right, whether or not in writing, arising under common law, under law merchant, or by reason of normal business practice.

  (Added Pub.L. 97–222, § 6(a), July 27, 1982, 96 Stat. 236, amended Pub.L. 98–353, title III, § 469, July 10, 1984, 98 Stat. 380; Pub.L. 103–394, title V, § 501(b)(6), (d)(20), Oct. 22, 1994, 108 Stat. 4143, 4146; Pub.L. 109–8, title IX, § 907(g), (o)(7), Apr. 20, 2005, 119 Stat. 177, 182.)

§ 556. Contractual right to liquidate, terminate, or accelerate a commodities contract or forward contract

  The contractual right of a commodity broker, financial participant, or forward contract merchant to cause the liquidation, termination, or acceleration of a commodity contract, as defined in section 761 of this title, or forward contract because of a condition of the kind specified in section 365(e)(1) of this title, and the right to a variation or maintenance margin payment received from a trustee with respect to open commodity contracts or forward contracts, shall not be stayed, avoided, or otherwise limited by operation of any provision of this title or by the order of a court in any proceeding under this title. As used in this section, the term "contractual right" includes a right set forth in a rule or bylaw of a derivatives clearing organization (as defined in the Commodity Exchange Act), a multilateral clearing organization (as defined in the Federal Deposit Insurance Corporation Improvement Act of 1991), a national securities exchange, a national securities association, a securities clearing agency, a contract market designated under the Commodity Exchange Act, a derivatives transaction execution facility registered under the Commodity Exchange Act, or a board of trade (as defined in the Commodity Exchange Act) or in a resolution of the governing board thereof and a right, whether or not evidenced in writing, arising under common law, under law merchant or by reason of normal business practice.

(Added Pub.L. 97–222, § 6(a), July 27, 1982, 96 Stat. 236, amended Pub.L. 101–311, title II, § 205, June 25, 1990, 104 Stat. 270; Pub.L. 103–394, title V, § 501(b)(7), Oct. 22, 1994, 108 Stat. 4143; Pub.L. 109–8, title IX, § 907(h), (*o*)(8), Apr. 20, 2005, 119 Stat. 178, 182.)

§ 557. Expedited determination of interests in, and abandonment or other disposition of grain assets

(a) This section applies only in a case concerning a debtor that owns or operates a grain storage facility and only with respect to grain and the proceeds of grain. This section does not affect the application of any other section of this title to property other than grain and proceeds of grain.

(b) In this section—

(1) "grain" means wheat, corn, flaxseed, grain sorghum, barley, oats, rye, soybeans, other dry edible beans, or rice;

(2) "grain storage facility" means a site or physical structure regularly used to store grain for producers, or to store grain acquired from producers for resale; and

(3) "producer" means an entity which engages in the growing of grain.

(c)(1) Notwithstanding sections 362, 363, 365, and 554 of this title, on the court's own motion the court may, and on the request of the trustee or an entity that claims an interest in grain or the proceeds of grain the court shall, expedite the procedures for the determination of interests in and the disposition of grain and the proceeds of grain, by shortening to the greatest extent feasible such time periods as are otherwise applicable for such procedures and by establishing, by order, a timetable having a duration of not to exceed 120 days for the completion of the applicable procedure specified in subsection (d) of this section. Such time periods and such timetable may be modified by the court, for cause, in accordance with subsection (f) of this section.

(2) The court shall determine the extent to which such time periods shall be shortened, based upon—

(A) any need of an entity claiming an interest in such grain or the proceeds of grain for a prompt determination of such interest;

(B) any need of such entity for a prompt disposition of such grain;

(C) the market for such grain;

(D) the conditions under which such grain is stored;

(E) the costs of continued storage or disposition of such grain;

(F) the orderly administration of the estate;

(G) the appropriate opportunity for an entity to assert an interest in such grain; and

(H) such other considerations as are relevant to the need to expedite such procedures in the case.

(d) The procedures that may be expedited under subsection (c) of this section include—

(1) the filing of and response to—

(A) a claim of ownership;

(B) a proof of claim;

(C) a request for abandonment;

(D) a request for relief from the stay of action against property under section 362(a) of this title;

(E) a request for determination of secured status;

 (F) a request for determination of whether such grain or the proceeds of grain—

  (i) is property of the estate;

  (ii) must be turned over to the estate; or

  (iii) may be used, sold, or leased; and

 (G) any other request for determination of an interest in such grain or the proceeds of grain;

 (2) the disposition of such grain or the proceeds of grain, before or after determination of interests in such grain or the proceeds of grain, by way of—

  (A) sale of such grain;

  (B) abandonment;

  (C) distribution; or

  (D) such other method as is equitable in the case;

 (3) subject to sections 701, 702, 703, 1104, 1202, and 1302 of this title, the appointment of a trustee or examiner and the retention and compensation of any professional person required to assist with respect to matters relevant to the determination of interests in or disposition of such grain or the proceeds of grain; and

 (4) the determination of any dispute concerning a matter specified in paragraph (1), (2), or (3) of this subsection.

 (e)(1) Any governmental unit that has regulatory jurisdiction over the operation or liquidation of the debtor or the debtor's business shall be given notice of any request made or order entered under subsection (c) of this section.

 (2) Any such governmental unit may raise, and may appear and be heard on, any issue relating to grain or the proceeds of grain in a case in which a request is made, or an order is entered, under subsection (c) of this section.

 (3) The trustee shall consult with such governmental unit before taking any action relating to the disposition of grain in the possession, custody, or control of the debtor or the estate.

 (f) The court may extend the period for final disposition of grain or the proceeds of grain under this section beyond 120 days if the court finds that—

 (1) the interests of justice so require in light of the complexity of the case; and

 (2) the interests of those claimants entitled to distribution of grain or the proceeds of grain will not be materially injured by such additional delay.

 (g) Unless an order establishing an expedited procedure under subsection (c) of this section, or determining any interest in or approving any disposition of grain or the proceeds of grain, is stayed pending appeal—

 (1) the reversal or modification of such order on appeal does not affect the validity of any procedure, determination, or disposition that occurs before such reversal or modification, whether or not any entity knew of the pendency of the appeal; and

 (2) neither the court nor the trustee may delay, due to the appeal of such order, any proceeding in the case in which such order is issued.

 (h)(1) The trustee may recover from grain and the proceeds of grain the reasonable and necessary costs and expenses allowable under section 503(b) of this title attributable to preserving or disposing of grain or the proceeds of grain, but may not recover from such grain or the proceeds of grain any other costs or expenses.

 (2) Notwithstanding section 326(a) of this title, the dollar amounts of money specified in such section include the value, as of the date of disposition, of any grain that the trustee distributes in kind.

(i) In all cases where the quantity of a specific type of grain held by a debtor operating a grain storage facility exceeds ten thousand bushels, such grain shall be sold by the trustee and the assets thereof distributed in accordance with the provisions of this section.

(Added Pub.L. 98–353, title III, § 352(a), July 10, 1984, 98 Stat. 359, amended Pub.L. 99–554, title II, § 257(p), Oct. 27, 1986, 100 Stat. 3115.)

§ 558. Defenses of the estate

The estate shall have the benefit of any defense available to the debtor as against any entity other than the estate, including statutes of limitation, statutes of frauds, usury, and other personal defenses. A waiver of any such defense by the debtor after the commencement of the case does not bind the estate.

(Added Pub.L. 98–353, title III, § 470(a), July 10, 1984, 98 Stat. 380.)

§ 559. Contractual right to liquidate, terminate, or accelerate a repurchase agreement

The exercise of a contractual right of a repo participant or financial participant to cause the liquidation, termination, or acceleration of a repurchase agreement because of a condition of the kind specified in section 365(e)(1) of this title shall not be stayed, avoided, or otherwise limited by operation of any provision of this title or by order of a court or administrative agency in any proceeding under this title, unless, where the debtor is a stockbroker or securities clearing agency, such order is authorized under the provisions of the Securities Investor Protection Act of 1970 or any statute administered by the Securities and Exchange Commission. In the event that a repo participant or financial participant liquidates one or more repurchase agreements with a debtor and under the terms of one or more such agreements has agreed to deliver assets subject to repurchase agreements to the debtor, any excess of the market prices received on liquidation of such assets (or if any such assets are not disposed of on the date of liquidation of such repurchase agreements, at the prices available at the time of liquidation of such repurchase agreements from a generally recognized source or the most recent closing bid quotation from such a source) over the sum of the stated repurchase prices and all expenses in connection with the liquidation of such repurchase agreements shall be deemed property of the estate, subject to the available rights of setoff. As used in this section, the term "contractual right" includes a right set forth in a rule or bylaw of a derivatives clearing organization (as defined in the Commodity Exchange Act), a multilateral clearing organization (as defined in the Federal Deposit Insurance Corporation Improvement Act of 1991), a national securities exchange, a national securities association, a securities clearing agency, a contract market designated under the Commodity Exchange Act, a derivatives transaction execution facility registered under the Commodity Exchange Act, or a board of trade (as defined in the Commodity Exchange Act) or in a resolution of the governing board thereof and a right, whether or not evidenced in writing, arising under common law, under law merchant or by reason of normal business practice.

(Added Pub.L. 98–353, title III, § 396(a), July 10, 1984, 98 Stat. 366, amended Pub.L. 103–394, title V, § 501(d)(21), Oct. 22, 1994, 108 Stat. 4146; Pub.L. 109–8, title IX, § 907(i), (o)(9), Apr. 20, 2005, 119 Stat. 178, 182.)

§ 560. Contractual right to liquidate, terminate, or accelerate a swap agreement

The exercise of any contractual right of any swap participant or financial participant to cause the liquidation, termination, or acceleration of one or more swap agreements because of a condition of the kind specified in section 365(e)(1) of this title or to offset or net out any termination values or payment amounts arising under or in connection with the termination, liquidation, or acceleration of one or more swap agreements shall not be stayed, avoided, or otherwise limited by operation of any provision of this title or by order of a court or administrative agency in any proceeding under this title. As used in this section, the term "contractual right" includes a right set forth in a rule or bylaw of a derivatives clearing organization (as defined in the Commodity Exchange Act), a multilateral clearing organization (as defined in the Federal Deposit Insurance Corporation Improvement Act of 1991), a national securities exchange, a national securities association, a securities clearing agency, a contract market designated under the Commodity Exchange Act, a derivatives transaction execution facility registered under the Commodity Exchange Act, or a board of trade (as defined in the Commodity Exchange Act) or in a resolution of the governing board thereof and a right, whether or not evidenced in writing, arising under common law, under law merchant, or by reason of normal business practice.

(Added Pub.L. 101–311, title I, § 106(a), June 25, 1990, 104 Stat. 268, amended Pub.L. 109–8, title IX, § 907(j), (*o*)(10), Apr. 20, 2005, 119 Stat. 178, 182.)

§ 561. Contractual right to terminate, liquidate, accelerate, or offset under a master netting agreement and across contracts; proceedings under chapter 15

(a) Subject to subsection (b), the exercise of any contractual right, because of a condition of the kind specified in section 365(e)(1), to cause the termination, liquidation, or acceleration of or to offset or net termination values, payment amounts, or other transfer obligations arising under or in connection with one or more (or the termination, liquidation, or acceleration of one or more)—

    (1) securities contracts, as defined in section 741(7);

    (2) commodity contracts, as defined in section 761(4);

    (3) forward contracts;

    (4) repurchase agreements;

    (5) swap agreements; or

    (6) master netting agreements,

shall not be stayed, avoided, or otherwise limited by operation of any provision of this title or by any order of a court or administrative agency in any proceeding under this title.

(b)(1) A party may exercise a contractual right described in subsection (a) to terminate, liquidate, or accelerate only to the extent that such party could exercise such a right under section 555, 556, 559, or 560 for each individual contract covered by the master netting agreement in issue.

    (2) If a debtor is a commodity broker subject to subchapter IV of chapter 7—

        (A) a party may not net or offset an obligation to the debtor arising under, or in connection with, a commodity contract traded on or subject to the rules of a contract market designated under the Commodity Exchange Act or a derivatives transaction execution facility registered under the Commodity Exchange Act against any claim arising under, or in connection with, other instruments, contracts, or agreements listed in subsection (a) except to the extent that the party has positive net equity in the commodity accounts at the debtor, as calculated under such subchapter; and

        (B) another commodity broker may not net or offset an obligation to the debtor arising under, or in connection with, a commodity contract entered into or held on behalf of a customer of the debtor and traded on or subject to the rules of a contract market designated under the Commodity Exchange Act or a derivatives transaction execution facility registered under the Commodity Exchange Act against any claim arising under, or in connection with, other instruments, contracts, or agreements listed in subsection (a).

    (3) No provision of subparagraph (A) or (B) of paragraph (2) shall prohibit the offset of claims and obligations that arise under—

        (A) a cross-margining agreement or similar arrangement that has been approved by the Commodity Futures Trading Commission or submitted to the Commodity Futures Trading Commission under paragraph (1) or (2) of section 5c(c) of the Commodity Exchange Act and has not been abrogated or rendered ineffective by the Commodity Futures Trading Commission; or

        (B) any other netting agreement between a clearing organization (as defined in section 761) and another entity that has been approved by the Commodity Futures Trading Commission.

(c) As used in this section, the term "contractual right" includes a right set forth in a rule or bylaw of a derivatives clearing organization (as defined in the Commodity Exchange Act), a multilateral clearing organization (as defined in the Federal Deposit Insurance Corporation Improvement Act of 1991), a national securities exchange, a national securities association, a securities clearing agency, a contract market designated under the Commodity Exchange Act, a derivatives transaction execution facility registered under the Commodity Exchange Act, or a board of trade (as defined in the Commodity Exchange Act) or in a resolution of the governing board thereof, and a right, whether or not evidenced in writing, arising under common law, under law merchant, or by reason of normal business practice.

(d) Any provisions of this title relating to securities contracts, commodity contracts, forward contracts, repurchase agreements, swap agreements, or master netting agreements shall apply in a case under chapter 15, so that enforcement of contractual provisions of such contracts and agreements in accordance with their terms will not be stayed or otherwise limited by operation of any provision of this title or by order of a court in any case under this title, and to limit avoidance powers to the same extent as in a proceeding under chapter 7 or 11 of this title (such enforcement not to be limited based on the presence or absence of assets of the debtor in the United States).

(Added Pub.L. 109–8, title IX, § 907(k)(1), Apr. 20, 2005, 119 Stat. 179.)

§ 562. Timing of damage measurement in connection with swap agreements, securities contracts, forward contracts, commodity contracts, repurchase agreements, and master netting agreements

(a) If the trustee rejects a swap agreement, securities contract (as defined in section 741), forward contract, commodity contract (as defined in section 761), repurchase agreement, or master netting agreement pursuant to section 365(a), or if a forward contract merchant, stockbroker, financial institution, securities clearing agency, repo participant, financial participant, master netting agreement participant, or swap participant liquidates, terminates, or accelerates such contract or agreement, damages shall be measured as of the earlier of—

> **(1)** the date of such rejection; or

> **(2)** the date or dates of such liquidation, termination, or acceleration.

(b) If there are not any commercially reasonable determinants of value as of any date referred to in paragraph (1) or (2) of subsection (a), damages shall be measured as of the earliest subsequent date or dates on which there are commercially reasonable determinants of value.

(c) For the purposes of subsection (b), if damages are not measured as of the date or dates of rejection, liquidation, termination, or acceleration, and the forward contract merchant, stockbroker, financial institution, securities clearing agency, repo participant, financial participant, master netting agreement participant, or swap participant or the trustee objects to the timing of the measurement of damages—

> **(1)** the trustee, in the case of an objection by a forward contract merchant, stockbroker, financial institution, securities clearing agency, repo participant, financial participant, master netting agreement participant, or swap participant; or

> **(2)** the forward contract merchant, stockbroker, financial institution, securities clearing agency, repo participant, financial participant, master netting agreement participant, or swap participant, in the case of an objection by the trustee,

has the burden of proving that there were no commercially reasonable determinants of value as of such date or dates.

(Added Pub.L. 109–8, title IX, § 910(a)(1), Apr. 20, 2005, 119 Stat. 184.)

CHAPTER 7—LIQUIDATION

SUBCHAPTER I—OFFICERS AND ADMINISTRATION

LIQUIDATION

SUBCHAPTER I—OFFICERS AND ADMINISTRATION

§ 701. Interim trustee

(a)(1) Promptly after the order for relief under this chapter, the United States trustee shall appoint one disinterested person that is a member of the panel of private trustees established under section 586(a)(1) of title 28 or that is serving as trustee in the case immediately before the order for relief under this chapter to serve as interim trustee in the case.

(2) If none of the members of such panel is willing to serve as interim trustee in the case, then the United States trustee may serve as interim trustee in the case.

(b) The service of an interim trustee under this section terminates when a trustee elected or designated under section 702 of this title to serve as trustee in the case qualifies under section 322 of this title.

(c) An interim trustee serving under this section is a trustee in a case under this title.

(Pub.L. 95–598, Nov. 6, 1978, 92 Stat. 2604; Pub.L. 99–554, title II, § 215, Oct. 27, 1986, 100 Stat. 3100.)

§ 702. Election of trustee

(a) A creditor may vote for a candidate for trustee only if such creditor—

(1) holds an allowable, undisputed, fixed, liquidated, unsecured claim of a kind entitled to distribution under section 726(a)(2), 726(a)(3), 726(a)(4), 752(a), 766(h), or 766(i) of this title;

(2) does not have an interest materially adverse, other than an equity interest that is not substantial in relation to such creditor's interest as a creditor, to the interest of creditors entitled to such distribution; and

(3) is not an insider.

(b) At the meeting of creditors held under section 341 of this title, creditors may elect one person to serve as trustee in the case if election of a trustee is requested by creditors that may vote under subsection (a) of this section, and that hold at least 20 percent in amount of the claims specified in subsection (a)(1) of this section that are held by creditors that may vote under subsection (a) of this section.

(c) A candidate for trustee is elected trustee if—

(1) creditors holding at least 20 percent in amount of the claims of a kind specified in subsection (a)(1) of this section that are held by creditors that may vote under subsection (a) of this section vote; and

(2) such candidate receives the votes of creditors holding a majority in amount of claims specified in subsection (a)(1) of this section that are held by creditors that vote for a trustee.

(d) If a trustee is not elected under this section, then the interim trustee shall serve as trustee in the case.

(Pub.L. 95–598, Nov. 6, 1978, 92 Stat. 2604; Pub.L. 97–222, § 7, July 27, 1982, 96 Stat. 237; Pub.L. 98–353, title III, § 472, July 10, 1984, 98 Stat. 380.)

§ 703. Successor trustee

(a) If a trustee dies or resigns during a case, fails to qualify under section 322 of this title, or is removed under section 324 of this title, creditors may elect, in the manner specified in section 702 of this title, a person to fill the vacancy in the office of trustee.

(b) Pending election of a trustee under subsection (a) of this section, if necessary to preserve or prevent loss to the estate, the United States trustee may appoint an interim trustee in the manner specified in section 701(a).

(c) If creditors do not elect a successor trustee under subsection (a) of this section or if a trustee is needed in a case reopened under section 350 of this title, then the United States trustee—

(1) shall appoint one disinterested person that is a member of the panel of private trustees established under section 586(a)(1) of title 28 to serve as trustee in the case; or

(2) may, if none of the disinterested members of such panel is willing to serve as trustee, serve as trustee in the case.

(Pub.L. 95–598, Nov. 6, 1978, 92 Stat. 2605; Pub.L. 98–353, title III, § 473, July 10, 1984, 98 Stat. 381; Pub.L. 99–554, title II, § 216, Oct. 27, 1986, 100 Stat. 3100.)

§ 704. Duties of trustee

(a) The trustee shall—

(1) collect and reduce to money the property of the estate for which such trustee serves, and close such estate as expeditiously as is compatible with the best interests of parties in interest;

(2) be accountable for all property received;

(3) ensure that the debtor shall perform his intention as specified in section 521(a)(2)(B) of this title;

(4) investigate the financial affairs of the debtor;

(5) if a purpose would be served, examine proofs of claims and object to the allowance of any claim that is improper;

(6) if advisable, oppose the discharge of the debtor;

(7) unless the court orders otherwise, furnish such information concerning the estate and the estate's administration as is requested by a party in interest;

(8) if the business of the debtor is authorized to be operated, file with the court, with the United States trustee, and with any governmental unit charged with responsibility for collection or determination of any tax arising out of such operation, periodic reports and summaries of the operation of such business, including a statement of receipts and disbursements, and such other information as the United States trustee or the court requires;

(9) make a final report and file a final account of the administration of the estate with the court and with the United States trustee;

(10) if with respect to the debtor there is a claim for a domestic support obligation, provide the applicable notice specified in subsection (c);

(11) if, at the time of the commencement of the case, the debtor (or any entity designated by the debtor) served as the administrator (as defined in section 3 of the Employee Retirement Income Security Act of 1974) of an employee benefit plan, continue to perform the obligations required of the administrator; and

(12) use all reasonable and best efforts to transfer patients from a health care business that is in the process of being closed to an appropriate health care business that—

(A) is in the vicinity of the health care business that is closing;

(B) provides the patient with services that are substantially similar to those provided by the health care business that is in the process of being closed; and

(C) maintains a reasonable quality of care.

(b)(1) With respect to a debtor who is an individual in a case under this chapter—

(A) the United States trustee (or the bankruptcy administrator, if any) shall review all materials filed by the debtor and, not later than 10 days after the date of the first meeting of creditors, file with the court a statement as to whether the debtor's case would be presumed to be an abuse under section 707(b); and

(B) not later than 7 days after receiving a statement under subparagraph (A), the court shall provide a copy of the statement to all creditors.

(2) The United States trustee (or bankruptcy administrator, if any) shall, not later than 30 days after the date of filing a statement under paragraph (1), either file a motion to dismiss or convert under section 707(b) or file a statement setting forth the reasons the United States trustee (or the bankruptcy administrator, if any) does not consider such a motion to be appropriate, if the United States trustee (or the bankruptcy administrator, if any) determines that the debtor's case should be presumed to be an abuse under section 707(b) and the product of the debtor's current monthly income, multiplied by 12 is not less than—

(A) in the case of a debtor in a household of 1 person, the median family income of the applicable State for 1 earner; or

(B) in the case of a debtor in a household of 2 or more individuals, the highest median family income of the applicable State for a family of the same number or fewer individuals.

(c)(1) In a case described in subsection (a)(10) to which subsection (a)(10) applies, the trustee shall—

(A)(i) provide written notice to the holder of the claim described in subsection (a)(10) of such claim and of the right of such holder to use the services of the State child support enforcement agency established under sections 464 and 466 of the Social Security Act for the State in which such holder resides, for assistance in collecting child support during and after the case under this title;

(ii) include in the notice provided under clause (i) the address and telephone number of such State child support enforcement agency; and

(iii) include in the notice provided under clause (i) an explanation of the rights of such holder to payment of such claim under this chapter;

(B)(i) provide written notice to such State child support enforcement agency of such claim; and

(ii) include in the notice provided under clause (i) the name, address, and telephone number of such holder; and

(C) at such time as the debtor is granted a discharge under section 727, provide written notice to such holder and to such State child support enforcement agency of—

(i) the granting of the discharge;

(ii) the last recent known address of the debtor;

(iii) the last recent known name and address of the debtor's employer; and

(iv) the name of each creditor that holds a claim that—

(I) is not discharged under paragraph (2), (4), or (14A) of section 523(a); or

(II) was reaffirmed by the debtor under section 524(c).

(2)(A) The holder of a claim described in subsection (a)(10) or the State child support enforcement agency of the State in which such holder resides may request from a creditor described in paragraph (1)(C)(iv) the last known address of the debtor.

(B) Notwithstanding any other provision of law, a creditor that makes a disclosure of a last known address of a debtor in connection with a request made under subparagraph (A) shall not be liable by reason of making such disclosure.

(Pub.L. 95–598, Nov. 6, 1978, 92 Stat. 2605; Pub.L. 98–353, title III, §§ 311(a), 474, July 10, 1984, 98 Stat. 355, 381; Pub.L. 99–554, title II, § 217, Oct. 27, 1986, 100 Stat. 3100; Pub.L. 109–8, title I, § 102(c), title

II, § 219(a), title IV, § 446(b), title XI, § 1105(a), Apr. 20, 2005, 119 Stat. 32, 55, 118, 192; Pub.L. 111–16, § 2(7), May 7, 2009, 123 Stat. 1607; Pub.L. 111–327, § 2(a)(24), Dec. 22, 2010, 124 Stat. 3560.)

§ 705. Creditors' committee

(a) At the meeting under section 341(a) of this title, creditors that may vote for a trustee under section 702(a) of this title may elect a committee of not fewer than three, and not more than eleven, creditors, each of whom holds an allowable unsecured claim of a kind entitled to distribution under section 726(a)(2) of this title.

(b) A committee elected under subsection (a) of this section may consult with the trustee or the United States trustee in connection with the administration of the estate, make recommendations to the trustee or the United States trustee respecting the performance of the trustee's duties, and submit to the court or the United States trustee any question affecting the administration of the estate.

(Pub.L. 95–598, Nov. 6, 1978, 92 Stat. 2605; Pub.L. 99–554, title II, § 218, Oct. 27, 1986, 100 Stat. 3100.)

§ 706. Conversion

(a) The debtor may convert a case under this chapter to a case under chapter 11, 12, or 13 of this title at any time, if the case has not been converted under section 1112, 1208, or 1307 of this title. Any waiver of the right to convert a case under this subsection is unenforceable.

(b) On request of a party in interest and after notice and a hearing, the court may convert a case under this chapter to a case under chapter 11 of this title at any time.

(c) The court may not convert a case under this chapter to a case under chapter 12 or 13 of this title unless the debtor requests or consents to such conversion.

(d) Notwithstanding any other provision of this section, a case may not be converted to a case under another chapter of this title unless the debtor may be a debtor under such chapter.

(Pub.L. 95–598, Nov. 6, 1978, 92 Stat. 2606; Pub.L. 99–554, title II, § 257(q), Oct. 27, 1986, 100 Stat. 3115; Pub.L. 103–394, title V, § 501(d)(22), Oct. 22, 1994, 108 Stat. 4146; Pub.L. 109–8, title I, § 101, Apr. 20, 2005, 119 Stat. 27.)

§ 707. Dismissal of a case or conversion to a case under chapter 11 or 13

(a) The court may dismiss a case under this chapter only after notice and a hearing and only for cause, including—

(1) unreasonable delay by the debtor that is prejudicial to creditors;

(2) nonpayment of any fees or charges required under chapter 123 of title 28; and

(3) failure of the debtor in a voluntary case to file, within fifteen days or such additional time as the court may allow after the filing of the petition commencing such case, the information required by paragraph (1) of section 521(a), but only on a motion by the United States trustee.

(b)(1) After notice and a hearing, the court, on its own motion or on a motion by the United States trustee, trustee (or bankruptcy administrator, if any), or any party in interest, may dismiss a case filed by an individual debtor under this chapter whose debts are primarily consumer debts, or, with the debtor's consent, convert such a case to a case under chapter 11 or 13 of this title, if it finds that the granting of relief would be an abuse of the provisions of this chapter. In making a determination whether to dismiss a case under this section, the court may not take into consideration whether a debtor has made, or continues to make, charitable contributions (that meet the definition of "charitable contribution" under section 548(d)(3)) to any qualified religious or charitable entity or organization (as that term is defined in section 548(d)(4)).

(2)(A)(i) In considering under paragraph (1) whether the granting of relief would be an abuse of the provisions of this chapter, the court shall presume abuse exists if the debtor's current monthly income reduced by the amounts determined under clauses (ii), (iii), and (iv), and multiplied by 60 is not less than the lesser of—

(I) 25 percent of the debtor's nonpriority unsecured claims in the case, or $7,700[*], whichever is greater; or

(II) $12,850.[*]

(ii)(I) The debtor's monthly expenses shall be the debtor's applicable monthly expense amounts specified under the National Standards and Local Standards, and the debtor's actual monthly expenses for the categories specified as Other Necessary Expenses issued by the Internal Revenue Service for the area in which the debtor resides, as in effect on the date of the order for relief, for the debtor, the dependents of the debtor, and the spouse of the debtor in a joint case, if the spouse is not otherwise a dependent. Such expenses shall include reasonably necessary health insurance, disability insurance, and health savings account expenses for the debtor, the spouse of the debtor, or the dependents of the debtor. Notwithstanding any other provision of this clause, the monthly expenses of the debtor shall not include any payments for debts. In addition, the debtor's monthly expenses shall include the debtor's reasonably necessary expenses incurred to maintain the safety of the debtor and the family of the debtor from family violence as identified under section 302 of the Family Violence Prevention and Services Act, or other applicable Federal law. The expenses included in the debtor's monthly expenses described in the preceding sentence shall be kept confidential by the court. In addition, if it is demonstrated that it is reasonable and necessary, the debtor's monthly expenses may also include an additional allowance for food and clothing of up to 5 percent of the food and clothing categories as specified by the National Standards issued by the Internal Revenue Service.

(II) In addition, the debtor's monthly expenses may include, if applicable, the continuation of actual expenses paid by the debtor that are reasonable and necessary for care and support of an elderly, chronically ill, or disabled household member or member of the debtor's immediate family (including parents, grandparents, siblings, children, and grandchildren of the debtor, the dependents of the debtor, and the spouse of the debtor in a joint case who is not a dependent) and who is unable to pay for such reasonable and necessary expenses. Such monthly expenses may include, if applicable, contributions to an account of a qualified ABLE program to the extent such contributions are not excess contributions (as described in Section 4973(h) of the Internal Revenue Code of 1986) and if the designated beneficiary of each account is a child, stepchild, grandchild, or stepgrandchild of the debtor.

(III) In addition, for a debtor eligible for chapter 13, the debtor's monthly expenses may include the actual administrative expenses of administering a chapter 13 plan for the district in which the debtor resides, up to an amount of 10 percent of the projected plan payments, as determined under schedules issued by the Executive Office for United States Trustees.

(IV) In addition, the debtor's monthly expenses may include the actual expenses for each dependent child less than 18 years of age, not to exceed $1,925[*] per year per child, to attend a private or public elementary or secondary school if the debtor provides documentation of such expenses and a detailed explanation of why such expenses are reasonable and necessary, and why such expenses are not already accounted for in the National Standards, Local Standards, or Other Necessary Expenses referred to in subclause (I).

(V) In addition, the debtor's monthly expenses may include an allowance for housing and utilities, in excess of the allowance specified by the Local Standards for housing and utilities issued by the Internal Revenue Service, based on the actual expenses for home energy costs if the debtor provides documentation of such actual expenses and demonstrates that such actual expenses are reasonable and necessary.

---

[*]   *Note from West Advisory Panel: Dollar amounts adjusted pursuant to 11 U.S.C. § 104; 81 Fed. Reg. 8748 (Feb. 22, 2016).*

(iii) The debtor's average monthly payments on account of secured debts shall be calculated as the sum of—

(I) the total of all amounts scheduled as contractually due to secured creditors in each month of the 60 months following the date of the filing of the petition; and

(II) any additional payments to secured creditors necessary for the debtor, in filing a plan under chapter 13 of this title, to maintain possession of the debtor's primary residence, motor vehicle, or other property necessary for the support of the debtor and the debtor's dependents, that serves as collateral for secured debts;

divided by 60.

(iv) The debtor's expenses for payment of all priority claims (including priority child support and alimony claims) shall be calculated as the total amount of debts entitled to priority, divided by 60.

(B)(i) In any proceeding brought under this subsection, the presumption of abuse may only be rebutted by demonstrating special circumstances, such as a serious medical condition or a call or order to active duty in the Armed Forces, to the extent such special circumstances that justify additional expenses or adjustments of current monthly income for which there is no reasonable alternative.

(ii) In order to establish special circumstances, the debtor shall be required to itemize each additional expense or adjustment of income and to provide—

(I) documentation for such expense or adjustment to income; and

(II) a detailed explanation of the special circumstances that make such expenses or adjustment to income necessary and reasonable.

(iii) The debtor shall attest under oath to the accuracy of any information provided to demonstrate that additional expenses or adjustments to income are required.

(iv) The presumption of abuse may only be rebutted if the additional expenses or adjustments to income referred to in clause (i) cause the product of the debtor's current monthly income reduced by the amounts determined under clauses (ii), (iii), and (iv) of subparagraph (A) when multiplied by 60 to be less than the lesser of—

(I) 25 percent of the debtor's nonpriority unsecured claims, or $7,700,[*] whichever is greater; or

(II) $12,850.[*]

(C) As part of the schedule of current income and expenditures required under section 521, the debtor shall include a statement of the debtor's current monthly income, and the calculations that determine whether a presumption arises under subparagraph (A)(i), that show how each such amount is calculated.

(D) Subparagraphs (A) through (C) shall not apply, and the court may not dismiss or convert a case based on any form of means testing—

(i) if the debtor is a disabled veteran (as defined in section 3741(1) of title 38), and the indebtedness occurred primarily during a period during which he or she was—

(I) on active duty (as defined in section 101(d)(1) of title 10); or

(II) performing a homeland defense activity (as defined in section 901(1) of title 32); or

(ii) with respect to the debtor, while the debtor is—

---

[*] *Note from West Advisory Panel: Dollar amounts adjusted pursuant to 11 U.S.C. § 104; 81 Fed. Reg. 8748 (Feb. 22, 2016).*

(I) on, and during the 540-day period beginning immediately after the debtor is released from, a period of active duty (as defined in section 101(d)(1) of title 10) of not less than 90 days; or

(II) performing, and during the 540-day period beginning immediately after the debtor is no longer performing, a homeland defense activity (as defined in section 901(1) of title 32) performed for a period of not less than 90 days;

if after September 11, 2001, the debtor while a member of a reserve component of the Armed Forces or a member of the National Guard, was called to such active duty or performed such homeland defense activity.

(3) In considering under paragraph (1) whether the granting of relief would be an abuse of the provisions of this chapter in a case in which the presumption in paragraph (2)(A)(i) does not arise or is rebutted, the court shall consider—

(A) whether the debtor filed the petition in bad faith; or

(B) the totality of the circumstances (including whether the debtor seeks to reject a personal services contract and the financial need for such rejection as sought by the debtor) of the debtor's financial situation demonstrates abuse.

(4)(A) The court, on its own initiative or on the motion of a party in interest, in accordance with the procedures described in rule 9011 of the Federal Rules of Bankruptcy Procedure, may order the attorney for the debtor to reimburse the trustee for all reasonable costs in prosecuting a motion filed under section 707(b), including reasonable attorneys' fees, if—

(i) a trustee files a motion for dismissal or conversion under this subsection; and

(ii) the court—

(I) grants such motion; and

(II) finds that the action of the attorney for the debtor in filing a case under this chapter violated rule 9011 of the Federal Rules of Bankruptcy Procedure.

(B) If the court finds that the attorney for the debtor violated rule 9011 of the Federal Rules of Bankruptcy Procedure, the court, on its own initiative or on the motion of a party in interest, in accordance with such procedures, may order—

(i) the assessment of an appropriate civil penalty against the attorney for the debtor; and

(ii) the payment of such civil penalty to the trustee, the United States trustee (or the bankruptcy administrator, if any).

(C) The signature of an attorney on a petition, pleading, or written motion shall constitute a certification that the attorney has—

(i) performed a reasonable investigation into the circumstances that gave rise to the petition, pleading, or written motion; and

(ii) determined that the petition, pleading, or written motion—

(I) is well grounded in fact; and

(II) is warranted by existing law or a good faith argument for the extension, modification, or reversal of existing law and does not constitute an abuse under paragraph (1).

(D) The signature of an attorney on the petition shall constitute a certification that the attorney has no knowledge after an inquiry that the information in the schedules filed with such petition is incorrect.

(5)(A) Except as provided in subparagraph (B) and subject to paragraph (6), the court, on its own initiative or on the motion of a party in interest, in accordance with the procedures described in rule 9011 of the Federal Rules of Bankruptcy Procedure, may award a debtor all reasonable costs (including reasonable attorneys' fees) in contesting a motion filed by a party in interest (other than a trustee or United States trustee (or bankruptcy administrator, if any)) under this subsection if—

    (i) the court does not grant the motion; and

    (ii) the court finds that—

        (I) the position of the party that filed the motion violated rule 9011 of the Federal Rules of Bankruptcy Procedure; or

        (II) the attorney (if any) who filed the motion did not comply with the requirements of clauses (i) and (ii) of paragraph (4)(C), and the motion was made solely for the purpose of coercing a debtor into waiving a right guaranteed to the debtor under this title.

(B) A small business that has a claim of an aggregate amount less than $1,300* shall not be subject to subparagraph (A)(ii)(I).

(C) For purposes of this paragraph—

    (i) the term "small business" means an unincorporated business, partnership, corporation, association, or organization that—

        (I) has fewer than 25 full-time employees as determined on the date on which the motion is filed; and

        (II) is engaged in commercial or business activity; and

    (ii) the number of employees of a wholly owned subsidiary of a corporation includes the employees of—

        (I) a parent corporation; and

        (II) any other subsidiary corporation of the parent corporation.

(6) Only the judge or United States trustee (or bankruptcy administrator, if any) may file a motion under section 707(b), if the current monthly income of the debtor, or in a joint case, the debtor and the debtor's spouse, as of the date of the order for relief, when multiplied by 12, is equal to or less than—

    (A) in the case of a debtor in a household of 1 person, the median family income of the applicable State for 1 earner;

    (B) in the case of a debtor in a household of 2, 3, or 4 individuals, the highest median family income of the applicable State for a family of the same number or fewer individuals; or

    (C) in the case of a debtor in a household exceeding 4 individuals, the highest median family income of the applicable State for a family of 4 or fewer individuals, plus $700* per month for each individual in excess of 4.

(7)(A) No judge, United States trustee (or bankruptcy administrator, if any), trustee, or other party in interest may file a motion under paragraph (2) if the current monthly income of the debtor, including a veteran (as that term is defined in section 101 of title 38), and the debtor's spouse combined, as of the date of the order for relief when multiplied by 12, is equal to or less than—

    (i) in the case of a debtor in a household of 1 person, the median family income of the applicable State for 1 earner;

---

* *Note from West Advisory Panel: Dollar amounts adjusted pursuant to 11 U.S.C. § 104; 81 Fed. Reg. 8748 (Feb. 22, 2016).*

(ii) in the case of a debtor in a household of 2, 3, or 4 individuals, the highest median family income of the applicable State for a family of the same number or fewer individuals; or

(iii) in the case of a debtor in a household exceeding 4 individuals, the highest median family income of the applicable State for a family of 4 or fewer individuals, plus $700* per month for each individual in excess of 4.

(B) In a case that is not a joint case, current monthly income of the debtor's spouse shall not be considered for purposes of subparagraph (A) if—

(i)(I) the debtor and the debtor's spouse are separated under applicable nonbankruptcy law; or

(II) the debtor and the debtor's spouse are living separate and apart, other than for the purpose of evading subparagraph (A); and

(ii) the debtor files a statement under penalty of perjury—

(I) specifying that the debtor meets the requirement of subclause (I) or (II) of clause (i); and

(II) disclosing the aggregate, or best estimate of the aggregate, amount of any cash or money payments received from the debtor's spouse attributed to the debtor's current monthly income.

(c)(1) In this subsection—

(A) the term "crime of violence" has the meaning given such term in section 16 of title 18; and

(B) the term "drug trafficking crime" has the meaning given such term in section 924(c)(2) of title 18.

(2) Except as provided in paragraph (3), after notice and a hearing, the court, on a motion by the victim of a crime of violence or a drug trafficking crime, may when it is in the best interest of the victim dismiss a voluntary case filed under this chapter by a debtor who is an individual if such individual was convicted of such crime.

(3) The court may not dismiss a case under paragraph (2) if the debtor establishes by a preponderance of the evidence that the filing of a case under this chapter is necessary to satisfy a claim for a domestic support obligation.

(Pub.L. 95–598, Nov. 6, 1978, 92 Stat. 2606; Pub.L. 98–353, title III, §§ 312, 475, July 10, 1984, 98 Stat. 355, 381; Pub.L. 99–554, title II, § 219, Oct. 27, 1986, 100 Stat. 3100; Pub.L. 105–183, § 4(b), June 19, 1998, 112 Stat. 518; Pub.L. 109–8, title I, § 102(a), (f), Apr. 20, 2005, 119 Stat. 27, 33; Pub.L. 110–438, § 2, Oct. 20, 2008, 122 Stat. 5000; Pub.L. 111–320, title II, § 202(a), Dec. 20, 2010, 124 Stat. 3509; Pub.L. 111–327, § 2(a)(25), Dec. 22, 2010, 124 Stat. 3560; Pub.L. 113–295, div. B, title I, § 104(b), Dec. 19, 2014, 128 Stat. 4064.)

SUBCHAPTER II—COLLECTION, LIQUIDATION, AND DISTRIBUTION OF THE ESTATE

§ 721. Authorization to operate business

The court may authorize the trustee to operate the business of the debtor for a limited period, if such operation is in the best interest of the estate and consistent with the orderly liquidation of the estate.

(Pub.L. 95–598, Nov. 6, 1978, 92 Stat. 2606.)

---

* *Note from West Advisory Panel: Dollar amounts adjusted pursuant to 11 U.S.C. § 104; 81 Fed. Reg. 8748 (Feb. 22, 2016).*

§ 722. Redemption

An individual debtor may, whether or not the debtor has waived the right to redeem under this section, redeem tangible personal property intended primarily for personal, family, or household use, from a lien securing a dischargeable consumer debt, if such property is exempted under section 522 of this title or has been abandoned under section 554 of this title, by paying the holder of such lien the amount of the allowed secured claim of such holder that is secured by such lien in full at the time of redemption.

(Pub.L. 95–598, Nov. 6, 1978, 92 Stat. 2606; Pub.L. 109–8, title III, § 304(2), Apr. 20, 2005, 119 Stat. 79.)

§ 723. Rights of partnership trustee against general partners

(a) If there is a deficiency of property of the estate to pay in full all claims which are allowed in a case under this chapter concerning a partnership and with respect to which a general partner of the partnership is personally liable, the trustee shall have a claim against such general partner to the extent that under applicable nonbankruptcy law such general partner is personally liable for such deficiency.

(b) To the extent practicable, the trustee shall first seek recovery of such deficiency from any general partner in such partnership that is not a debtor in a case under this title. Pending determination of such deficiency, the court may order any such partner to provide the estate with indemnity for, or assurance of payment of, any deficiency recoverable from such partner, or not to dispose of property.

(c) The trustee has a claim against the estate of each general partner in such partnership that is a debtor in a case under this title for the full amount of all claims of creditors allowed in the case concerning such partnership. Notwithstanding section 502 of this title, there shall not be allowed in such partner's case a claim against such partner on which both such partner and such partnership are liable, except to any extent that such claim is secured only by property of such partner and not by property of such partnership. The claim of the trustee under this subsection is entitled to distribution in such partner's case under section 726(a) of this title the same as any other claim of a kind specified in such section.

(d) If the aggregate that the trustee recovers from the estates of general partners under subsection (c) of this section is greater than any deficiency not recovered under subsection (b) of this section, the court, after notice and a hearing, shall determine an equitable distribution of the surplus so recovered, and the trustee shall distribute such surplus to the estates of the general partners in such partnership according to such determination.

(Pub.L. 95–598, Nov. 6, 1978, 92 Stat. 2606; Pub.L. 98–353, title III, § 476, July 10, 1984, 98 Stat. 381; Pub.L. 103–394, title II, § 212, Oct. 22, 1994, 108 Stat. 4125; Pub.L. 111–327, § 2(a)(26), Dec. 22, 2010, 124 Stat. 3560.)

§ 724. Treatment of certain liens

(a) The trustee may avoid a lien that secures a claim of a kind specified in section 726(a)(4) of this title.

(b) Property in which the estate has an interest and that is subject to a lien that is not avoidable under this title (other than to the extent that there is a properly perfected unavoidable tax lien arising in connection with an ad valorem tax on real or personal property of the estate) and that secures an allowed claim for a tax, or proceeds of such property, shall be distributed—

(1) first, to any holder of an allowed claim secured by a lien on such property that is not avoidable under this title and that is senior to such tax lien;

(2) second, to any holder of a claim of a kind specified in section 507(a)(1)(C) or 507(a)(2) (except that such expenses under each such section, other than claims for wages, salaries, or commissions that arise after the date of the filing of the petition, shall be limited to expenses incurred under this chapter and shall not include expenses incurred under chapter 11 of this title), 507(a)(1)(A), 507(a)(1)(B), 507(a)(3), 507(a)(4), 507(a)(5), 507(a)(6), or 507(a)(7) of this title, to the extent of the amount of such allowed tax claim that is secured by such tax lien;

(3) third, to the holder of such tax lien, to any extent that such holder's allowed tax claim that is secured by such tax lien exceeds any amount distributed under paragraph (2) of this subsection;

(4) fourth, to any holder of an allowed claim secured by a lien on such property that is not avoidable under this title and that is junior to such tax lien;

(5) fifth, to the holder of such tax lien, to the extent that such holder's allowed claim secured by such tax lien is not paid under paragraph (3) of this subsection; and

(6) sixth, to the estate.

(c) If more than one holder of a claim is entitled to distribution under a particular paragraph of subsection (b) of this section, distribution to such holders under such paragraph shall be in the same order as distribution to such holders would have been other than under this section.

(d) A statutory lien the priority of which is determined in the same manner as the priority of a tax lien under section 6323 of the Internal Revenue Code of 1986 shall be treated under subsection (b) of this section the same as if such lien were a tax lien.

(e) Before subordinating a tax lien on real or personal property of the estate, the trustee shall—

(1) exhaust the unencumbered assets of the estate; and

(2) in a manner consistent with section 506(c), recover from property securing an allowed secured claim the reasonable, necessary costs and expenses of preserving or disposing of such property.

(f) Notwithstanding the exclusion of ad valorem tax liens under this section and subject to the requirements of subsection (e), the following may be paid from property of the estate which secures a tax lien, or the proceeds of such property:

(1) Claims for wages, salaries, and commissions that are entitled to priority under section 507(a)(4).

(2) Claims for contributions to an employee benefit plan entitled to priority under section 507(a)(5).

(Pub.L. 95–598, Nov. 6, 1978, 92 Stat. 2607; Pub.L. 98–353, title III, § 477, July 10, 1984, 98 Stat. 381; Pub.L. 99–554, title II, § 283(r), Oct. 27, 1986, 100 Stat. 3118; Pub.L. 103–394, title III, § 304(h)(4), title V, § 501(d)(23), Oct. 22, 1994, 108 Stat. 4134, 4146; Pub.L. 109–8, title VII, § 701(a), Apr. 20, 2005, 119 Stat. 124; Pub.L. 111–327, § 2(a)(27), Dec. 22, 2010, 124 Stat. 3560.)

§ 725. Disposition of certain property

After the commencement of a case under this chapter, but before final distribution of property of the estate under section 726 of this title, the trustee, after notice and a hearing, shall dispose of any property in which an entity other than the estate has an interest, such as a lien, and that has not been disposed of under another section of this title.

(Pub.L. 95–598, Nov. 6, 1978, 92 Stat. 2607; Pub.L. 98–353, title III, § 478, July 10, 1984, 98 Stat. 381.)

§ 726. Distribution of property of the estate

(a) Except as provided in section 510 of this title, property of the estate shall be distributed—

(1) first, in payment of claims of the kind specified in, and in the order specified in, section 507 of this title, proof of which is timely filed under section 501 of this title or tardily filed on or before the earlier of—

(A) the date that is 10 days after the mailing to creditors of the summary of the trustee's final report; or

(B) the date on which the trustee commences final distribution under this section;

(2) second, in payment of any allowed unsecured claim, other than a claim of a kind specified in paragraph (1), (3), or (4) of this subsection, proof of which is—

(A) timely filed under section 501(a) of this title;

(B) timely filed under section 501(b) or 501(c) of this title; or

(C) tardily filed under section 501(a) of this title, if—

(i) the creditor that holds such claim did not have notice or actual knowledge of the case in time for timely filing of a proof of such claim under section 501(a) of this title; and

(ii) proof of such claim is filed in time to permit payment of such claim;

(3) third, in payment of any allowed unsecured claim proof of which is tardily filed under section 501(a) of this title, other than a claim of the kind specified in paragraph (2)(C) of this subsection;

(4) fourth, in payment of any allowed claim, whether secured or unsecured, for any fine, penalty, or forfeiture, or for multiple, exemplary, or punitive damages, arising before the earlier of the order for relief or the appointment of a trustee, to the extent that such fine, penalty, forfeiture, or damages are not compensation for actual pecuniary loss suffered by the holder of such claim;

(5) fifth, in payment of interest at the legal rate from the date of the filing of the petition, on any claim paid under paragraph (1), (2), (3), or (4) of this subsection; and

(6) sixth, to the debtor.

(b) Payment on claims of a kind specified in paragraph (1), (2), (3), (4), (5), (6), (7), (8), (9), or (10) of section 507(a) of this title, or in paragraph (2), (3), (4), or (5) of subsection (a) of this section, shall be made pro rata among claims of the kind specified in each such particular paragraph, except that in a case that has been converted to this chapter under section 1112, 1208, or 1307 of this title, a claim allowed under section 503(b) of this title incurred under this chapter after such conversion has priority over a claim allowed under section 503(b) of this title incurred under any other chapter of this title or under this chapter before such conversion and over any expenses of a custodian superseded under section 543 of this title.

(c) Notwithstanding subsections (a) and (b) of this section, if there is property of the kind specified in section 541(a)(2) of this title, or proceeds of such property, in the estate, such property or proceeds shall be segregated from other property of the estate, and such property or proceeds and other property of the estate shall be distributed as follows:

(1) Claims allowed under section 503 of this title shall be paid either from property of the kind specified in section 541(a)(2) of this title, or from other property of the estate, as the interest of justice requires.

(2) Allowed claims, other than claims allowed under section 503 of this title, shall be paid in the order specified in subsection (a) of this section, and, with respect to claims of a kind specified in a particular paragraph of section 507 of this title or subsection (a) of this section, in the following order and manner:

(A) First, community claims against the debtor or the debtor's spouse shall be paid from property of the kind specified in section 541(a)(2) of this title, except to the extent that such property is solely liable for debts of the debtor.

(B) Second, to the extent that community claims against the debtor are not paid under subparagraph (A) of this paragraph, such community claims shall be paid from property of the kind specified in section 541(a)(2) of this title that is solely liable for debts of the debtor.

(C) Third, to the extent that all claims against the debtor including community claims against the debtor are not paid under subparagraph (A) or (B) of this paragraph such claims shall be paid from property of the estate other than property of the kind specified in section 541(a)(2) of this title.

(D) Fourth, to the extent that community claims against the debtor or the debtor's spouse are not paid under subparagraph (A), (B), or (C) of this paragraph, such claims shall be paid from all remaining property of the estate.

(Pub.L. 95–598, Nov. 6, 1978, 92 Stat. 2608; Pub.L. 98–353, title III, § 479, July 10, 1984, 98 Stat. 381; Pub.L. 99–554, title II, §§ 257(r), 283(s), Oct. 27, 1986, 100 Stat. 3115, 3118; Pub.L. 103–394, title II, § 213(b), title III, § 304(h)(5), title V, § 501(d)(24), Oct. 22, 1994, 108 Stat. 4126, 4134, 4146; Pub.L. 109–8, title VII, § 713, title XII, § 1215, Apr. 20, 2005, 119 Stat. 128, 195; Pub.L. 111–327, § 2(a)(28), Dec. 22, 2010, 124 Stat. 3560.)

§ 727.   Discharge

(a)   The court shall grant the debtor a discharge, unless—

     (1)   the debtor is not an individual;

     (2)   the debtor, with intent to hinder, delay, or defraud a creditor or an officer of the estate charged with custody of property under this title, has transferred, removed, destroyed, mutilated, or concealed, or has permitted to be transferred, removed, destroyed, mutilated, or concealed—

         (A)   property of the debtor, within one year before the date of the filing of the petition; or

         (B)   property of the estate, after the date of the filing of the petition;

     (3)   the debtor has concealed, destroyed, mutilated, falsified, or failed to keep or preserve any recorded information, including books, documents, records, and papers, from which the debtor's financial condition or business transactions might be ascertained, unless such act or failure to act was justified under all of the circumstances of the case;

     (4)   the debtor knowingly and fraudulently, in or in connection with the case—

         (A)   made a false oath or account;

         (B)   presented or used a false claim;

         (C)   gave, offered, received, or attempted to obtain money, property, or advantage, or a promise of money, property, or advantage, for acting or forbearing to act; or

         (D)   withheld from an officer of the estate entitled to possession under this title, any recorded information, including books, documents, records, and papers, relating to the debtor's property or financial affairs;

     (5)   the debtor has failed to explain satisfactorily, before determination of denial of discharge under this paragraph, any loss of assets or deficiency of assets to meet the debtor's liabilities;

     (6)   the debtor has refused, in the case—

         (A)   to obey any lawful order of the court, other than an order to respond to a material question or to testify;

         (B)   on the ground of privilege against self-incrimination, to respond to a material question approved by the court or to testify, after the debtor has been granted immunity with respect to the matter concerning which such privilege was invoked; or

         (C)   on a ground other than the properly invoked privilege against self-incrimination, to respond to a material question approved by the court or to testify;

     (7)   the debtor has committed any act specified in paragraph (2), (3), (4), (5), or (6) of this subsection, on or within one year before the date of the filing of the petition, or during the case, in connection with another case, under this title or under the Bankruptcy Act, concerning an insider;

     (8)   the debtor has been granted a discharge under this section, under section 1141 of this title, or under section 14, 371, or 476 of the Bankruptcy Act, in a case commenced within 8 years before the date of the filing of the petition;

     (9)   the debtor has been granted a discharge under section 1228 or 1328 of this title, or under section 660 or 661 of the Bankruptcy Act, in a case commenced within six years before the date of the filing of the petition, unless payments under the plan in such case totaled at least—

         (A)   100 percent of the allowed unsecured claims in such case; or

(B)(i) 70 percent of such claims; and

(ii) the plan was proposed by the debtor in good faith, and was the debtor's best effort;

(10) the court approves a written waiver of discharge executed by the debtor after the order for relief under this chapter;

(11) after filing the petition, the debtor failed to complete an instructional course concerning personal financial management described in section 111, except that this paragraph shall not apply with respect to a debtor who is a person described in section 109(h)(4) or who resides in a district for which the United States trustee (or the bankruptcy administrator, if any) determines that the approved instructional courses are not adequate to service the additional individuals who would otherwise be required to complete such instructional courses under this section (The United States trustee (or the bankruptcy administrator, if any) who makes a determination described in this paragraph shall review such determination not later than 1 year after the date of such determination, and not less frequently than annually thereafter.); or

(12) the court after notice and a hearing held not more than 10 days before the date of the entry of the order granting the discharge finds that there is reasonable cause to believe that—

(A) section 522(q)(1) may be applicable to the debtor; and

(B) there is pending any proceeding in which the debtor may be found guilty of a felony of the kind described in section 522(q)(1)(A) or liable for a debt of the kind described in section 522(q)(1)(B).

(b) Except as provided in section 523 of this title, a discharge under subsection (a) of this section discharges the debtor from all debts that arose before the date of the order for relief under this chapter, and any liability on a claim that is determined under section 502 of this title as if such claim had arisen before the commencement of the case, whether or not a proof of claim based on any such debt or liability is filed under section 501 of this title, and whether or not a claim based on any such debt or liability is allowed under section 502 of this title.

(c)(1) The trustee, a creditor, or the United States trustee may object to the granting of a discharge under subsection (a) of this section.

(2) On request of a party in interest, the court may order the trustee to examine the acts and conduct of the debtor to determine whether a ground exists for denial of discharge.

(d) On request of the trustee, a creditor, or the United States trustee, and after notice and a hearing, the court shall revoke a discharge granted under subsection (a) of this section if—

(1) such discharge was obtained through the fraud of the debtor, and the requesting party did not know of such fraud until after the granting of such discharge;

(2) the debtor acquired property that is property of the estate, or became entitled to acquire property that would be property of the estate, and knowingly and fraudulently failed to report the acquisition of or entitlement to such property, or to deliver or surrender such property to the trustee;

(3) the debtor committed an act specified in subsection (a)(6) of this section; or

(4) the debtor has failed to explain satisfactorily—

(A) a material misstatement in an audit referred to in section 586(f) of title 28; or

(B) a failure to make available for inspection all necessary accounts, papers, documents, financial records, files, and all other papers, things, or property belonging to the debtor that are requested for an audit referred to in section 586(f) of title 28.

(e) The trustee, a creditor, or the United States trustee may request a revocation of a discharge—

(1) under subsection (d)(1) of this section within one year after such discharge is granted; or

(2) under subsection (d)(2) or (d)(3) of this section before the later of—

(A) one year after the granting of such discharge; and

(B) the date the case is closed.

(Pub.L. 95–598, Nov. 6, 1978, 92 Stat. 2609; Pub.L. 98–353, title III, § 480, July 10, 1984, 98 Stat. 382; Pub.L. 99–554, title II, §§ 220, 257(s), Oct. 27, 1986, 100 Stat. 3101, 3116; Pub.L. 109–8, title I, § 106(b), title III, §§ 312(1), 330(a), title VI, § 603(d), Apr. 20, 2005, 119 Stat. 38, 86, 101, 123.)

§ 728.   [Repealed.]

(Pub.L. 95–598, Nov. 6, 1978, 92 Stat. 2611; Pub.L. 98–353, title III, § 481, July 10, 1984, 98 Stat. 382; Pub.L. 99–554, title II, § 257(t), Oct. 27, 1986, 100 Stat. 3116; Pub.L. 109–8, title VII, § 719(b)(1), Apr. 20, 2005, 119 Stat. 133.)

SUBCHAPTER III—STOCKBROKER LIQUIDATION

§ 741.   Definitions for this subchapter

In this subchapter—

(1) "Commission" means Securities and Exchange Commission;

(2) "customer" includes—

(A) entity with whom a person deals as principal or agent and that has a claim against such person on account of a security received, acquired, or held by such person in the ordinary course of such person's business as a stockbroker, from or for the securities account or accounts of such entity—

    (i) for safekeeping;

    (ii) with a view to sale;

    (iii) to cover a consummated sale;

    (iv) pursuant to a purchase;

    (v) as collateral under a security agreement; or

    (vi) for the purpose of effecting registration of transfer; and

(B) entity that has a claim against a person arising out of—

    (i) a sale or conversion of a security received, acquired, or held as specified in subparagraph (A) of this paragraph; or

    (ii) a deposit of cash, a security, or other property with such person for the purpose of purchasing or selling a security;

(3) "customer name security" means security—

(A) held for the account of a customer on the date of the filing of the petition by or on behalf of the debtor;

(B) registered in such customer's name on such date or in the process of being so registered under instructions from the debtor; and

(C) not in a form transferable by delivery on such date;

(4) "customer property" means cash, security, or other property, and proceeds of such cash, security, or property, received, acquired, or held by or for the account of the debtor, from or for the securities account of a customer—

(A) including—

    (i) property that was unlawfully converted from and that is the lawful property of the estate;

    (ii) a security held as property of the debtor to the extent such security is necessary to meet a net equity claim of a customer based on a security of the same class and series of an issuer;

    (iii) resources provided through the use or realization of a customer's debit cash balance or a debit item includible in the Formula for Determination of Reserve Requirement for Brokers and Dealers as promulgated by the Commission under the Securities Exchange Act of 1934; and

    (iv) other property of the debtor that any applicable law, rule, or regulation requires to be set aside or held for the benefit of a customer, unless including such property as customer property would not significantly increase customer property; but

  (B) not including—

    (i) a customer name security delivered to or reclaimed by a customer under section 751 of this title; or

    (ii) property to the extent that a customer does not have a claim against the debtor based on such property;

  (5) "margin payment" means payment or deposit of cash, a security, or other property, that is commonly known to the securities trade as original margin, initial margin, maintenance margin, or variation margin, or as a mark-to-market payment, or that secures an obligation of a participant in a securities clearing agency;

  (6) "net equity" means, with respect to all accounts of a customer that such customer has in the same capacity—

  (A)(i) aggregate dollar balance that would remain in such accounts after the liquidation, by sale or purchase, at the time of the filing of the petition, of all securities positions in all such accounts, except any customer name securities of such customer; minus

    (ii) any claim of the debtor against such customer in such capacity that would have been owing immediately after such liquidation; plus

  (B) any payment by such customer to the trustee, within 60 days after notice under section 342 of this title, of any business related claim of the debtor against such customer in such capacity;

  (7) "securities contract"—

  (A) means—

    (i) a contract for the purchase, sale, or loan of a security, a certificate of deposit, a mortgage loan, any interest in a mortgage loan, a group or index of securities, certificates of deposit, or mortgage loans or interests therein (including an interest therein or based on the value thereof), or option on any of the foregoing, including an option to purchase or sell any such security, certificate of deposit, mortgage loan, interest, group or index, or option, and including any repurchase or reverse repurchase transaction on any such security, certificate of deposit, mortgage loan, interest, group or index, or option (whether or not such repurchase or reverse repurchase transaction is a "repurchase agreement", as defined in section 101);

    (ii) any option entered into on a national securities exchange relating to foreign currencies;

    (iii) the guarantee (including by novation) by or to any securities clearing agency of a settlement of cash, securities, certificates of deposit, mortgage loans or interests therein, group or index of securities, or mortgage loans or interests therein (including any interest therein or based on the value thereof), or option on any of the foregoing, including an option to purchase or sell any such security, certificate of deposit, mortgage loan, interest, group or index, or option (whether or not such settlement is in connection with any agreement or transaction referred to in clauses (i) through (xi));

    (iv)   any margin loan;

    (v)   any extension of credit for the clearance or settlement of securities transactions;

    (vi)   any loan transaction coupled with a securities collar transaction, any prepaid forward securities transaction, or any total return swap transaction coupled with a securities sale transaction;

    (vii)   any other agreement or transaction that is similar to an agreement or transaction referred to in this subparagraph;

    (viii)   any combination of the agreements or transactions referred to in this subparagraph;

    (ix)   any option to enter into any agreement or transaction referred to in this subparagraph;

    (x)   a master agreement that provides for an agreement or transaction referred to in clause (i), (ii), (iii), (iv), (v), (vi), (vii), (viii), or (ix), together with all supplements to any such master agreement, without regard to whether the master agreement provides for an agreement or transaction that is not a securities contract under this subparagraph, except that such master agreement shall be considered to be a securities contract under this subparagraph only with respect to each agreement or transaction under such master agreement that is referred to in clause (i), (ii), (iii), (iv), (v), (vi), (vii), (viii), or (ix); or

    (xi)   any security agreement or arrangement or other credit enhancement related to any agreement or transaction referred to in this subparagraph, including any guarantee or reimbursement obligation by or to a stockbroker, securities clearing agency, financial institution, or financial participant in connection with any agreement or transaction referred to in this subparagraph, but not to exceed the damages in connection with any such agreement or transaction, measured in accordance with section 562; and

    (B)   does not include any purchase, sale, or repurchase obligation under a participation in a commercial mortgage loan;

  (8)   "settlement payment" means a preliminary settlement payment, a partial settlement payment, an interim settlement payment, a settlement payment on account, a final settlement payment, or any other similar payment commonly used in the securities trade; and

  (9)   "SIPC" means Securities Investor Protection Corporation.

    (Pub.L. 95–598, Nov. 6, 1978, 92 Stat. 2611; Pub.L. 97–222, § 8, July 27, 1982, 96 Stat. 237; Pub.L. 98–353, title III, § 482, July 10, 1984, 98 Stat. 382; Pub.L. 103–394, title V, § 501(d)(25), Oct. 22, 1994, 108 Stat. 4146; Pub.L. 109–8, title IX, § 907(a)(2), Apr. 20, 2005, 119 Stat. 173; Pub.L. 109–390, § 5(a)(3), Dec. 12, 2006, 120 Stat. 2697)

§ 742.   Effect of section 362 of this title in this subchapter

    Notwithstanding section 362 of this title, SIPC may file an application for a protective decree under the Securities Investor Protection Act of 1970. The filing of such application stays all proceedings in the case under this title unless and until such application is dismissed. If SIPC completes the liquidation of the debtor, then the court shall dismiss the case.

    (Pub.L. 95–598, Nov. 6, 1978, 92 Stat. 2613; Pub.L. 97–222, § 9, July 27, 1982, 96 Stat. 237; Pub.L. 103–394, title V, § 501(d)(26), Oct. 22, 1994, 108 Stat. 4146.)

§ 743.   Notice

    The clerk shall give the notice required by section 342 of this title to SIPC and to the Commission.

    (Pub.L. 95–598, Nov. 6, 1978, 92 Stat. 2613; Pub.L. 99–554, title II, § 283(t), Oct. 27, 1986, 100 Stat. 3118); Pub.L. 103–394, title V, § 501(d)(27), Oct. 22, 1994, 108 Stat. 4146.)

§ 744. Executory contracts

Notwithstanding section 365(d)(1) of this title, the trustee shall assume or reject, under section 365 of this title, any executory contract of the debtor for the purchase or sale of a security in the ordinary course of the debtor's business, within a reasonable time after the date of the order for relief, but not to exceed 30 days. If the trustee does not assume such a contract within such time, such contract is rejected.

(Pub.L. 95–598, Nov. 6, 1978, 92 Stat. 2613; Pub.L. 97–222, § 10, July 27, 1982, 96 Stat. 238.)

§ 745. Treatment of accounts

(a) Accounts held by the debtor for a particular customer in separate capacities shall be treated as accounts of separate customers.

(b) If a stockbroker or a bank holds a customer net equity claim against the debtor that arose out of a transaction for a customer of such stockbroker or bank, each such customer of such stockbroker or bank shall be treated as a separate customer of the debtor.

(c) Each trustee's account specified as such on the debtor's books, and supported by a trust deed filed with, and qualified as such by, the Internal Revenue Service, and under the Internal Revenue Code of 1986, shall be treated as a separate customer account for each beneficiary under such trustee account.

(Pub.L. 95–598, Nov. 6, 1978, 92 Stat. 2613; Pub.L. 97–222, § 11, July 27, 1982, 96 Stat. 238; Pub.L. 98–353, title III, § 483, July 10, 1984, 98 Stat. 383; Pub.L. 103–394, title V, § 501(d)(28), Oct. 22, 1994, 108 Stat. 4146.)

§ 746. Extent of customer claims

(a) If, after the date of the filing of the petition, an entity enters into a transaction with the debtor, in a manner that would have made such entity a customer had such transaction occurred before the date of the filing of the petition, and such transaction was entered into by such entity in good faith and before the qualification under section 322 of this title of a trustee, such entity shall be deemed a customer, and the date of such transaction shall be deemed to be the date of the filing of the petition for the purpose of determining such entity's net equity.

(b) An entity does not have a claim as a customer to the extent that such entity transferred to the debtor cash or a security that, by contract, agreement, understanding, or operation of law, is—

(1) part of the capital of the debtor; or

(2) subordinated to the claims of any or all creditors.

(Pub.L. 95–598, Nov. 6, 1978, 92 Stat. 2613; Pub.L. 97–222, § 12, July 27, 1982, 96 Stat. 238.)

§ 747. Subordination of certain customer claims

Except as provided in section 510 of this title, unless all other customer net equity claims have been paid in full, the trustee may not pay in full or pay in part, directly or indirectly, any net equity claim of a customer that was, on the date the transaction giving rise to such claim occurred—

(1) an insider;

(2) a beneficial owner of at least five percent of any class of equity securities of the debtor, other than—

(A) nonconvertible stock having fixed preferential dividend and liquidation rights; or

(B) interests of limited partners in a limited partnership;

(3) a limited partner with a participation of at least five percent in the net assets or net profits of the debtor; or

(4) an entity that, directly or indirectly, through agreement or otherwise, exercised or had the power to exercise control over the management or policies of the debtor.

(Pub.L. 95–598, Nov. 6, 1978, 92 Stat. 2613; Pub.L. 97–222, § 13, July 27, 1982, 96 Stat. 238.)

§ 748. Reduction of securities to money

As soon as practicable after the date of the order for relief, the trustee shall reduce to money, consistent with good market practice, all securities held as property of the estate, except for customer name securities delivered or reclaimed under section 751 of this title.

(Pub.L. 95–598, Nov. 6, 1978, 92 Stat. 2614.)

§ 749. Voidable transfers

(a) Except as otherwise provided in this section, any transfer of property that, but for such transfer, would have been customer property, may be avoided by the trustee, and such property shall be treated as customer property, if and to the extent that the trustee avoids such transfer under section 544, 545, 547, 548, or 549 of this title. For the purpose of such sections, the property so transferred shall be deemed to have been property of the debtor and, if such transfer was made to a customer or for a customer's benefit, such customer shall be deemed, for the purposes of this section, to have been a creditor.

(b) Notwithstanding sections 544, 545, 547, 548, and 549 of this title, the trustee may not avoid a transfer made before seven days after the order for relief if such transfer is approved by the Commission by rule or order, either before or after such transfer, and if such transfer is—

(1) a transfer of a securities contract entered into or carried by or through the debtor on behalf of a customer, and of any cash, security, or other property margining or securing such securities contract; or

(2) the liquidation of a securities contract entered into or carried by or through the debtor on behalf of a customer.

(Pub.L. 95–598, Nov. 6, 1978, 92 Stat. 2614; Pub.L. 97–222, § 14, July 27, 1982, 96 Stat. 238; Pub.L. 111–16, § 2(8), May 7, 2009, 123 Stat. 1607.)

§ 750. Distribution of securities

The trustee may not distribute a security except under section 751 of this title.

(Pub.L. 95–598, Nov. 6, 1978, 92 Stat. 2614.)

§ 751. Customer name securities

The trustee shall deliver any customer name security to or on behalf of the customer entitled to such security, unless such customer has a negative net equity. With the approval of the trustee, a customer may reclaim a customer name security after payment to the trustee, within such period as the trustee allows, of any claim of the debtor against such customer to the extent that such customer will not have a negative net equity after such payment.

(Pub.L. 95–598, Nov. 6, 1978, 92 Stat. 2614.)

§ 752. Customer property

(a) The trustee shall distribute customer property ratably to customers on the basis and to the extent of such customers' allowed net equity claims and in priority to all other claims, except claims of the kind specified in section 507(a)(2) of this title that are attributable to the administration of such customer property.

(b)(1) The trustee shall distribute customer property in excess of that distributed under subsection (a) of this section in accordance with section 726 of this title.

(2) Except as provided in section 510 of this title, if a customer is not paid the full amount of such customer's allowed net equity claim from customer property, the unpaid portion of such claim is a claim entitled to distribution under section 726 of this title.

(c)   Any cash or security remaining after the liquidation of a security interest created under a security agreement made by the debtor, excluding property excluded under section 741(4)(B) of this title, shall be apportioned between the general estate and customer property in the same proportion as the general estate of the debtor and customer property were subject to such security interest.

(Pub.L. 95–598, Nov. 6, 1978, 92 Stat. 2614; Pub.L. 97–222, § 15, July 27, 1982, 96 Stat. 238; Pub.L. 98–353, title III, § 484, July 10, 1984, 98 Stat. 383; Pub.L. 109–8, title XV, § 1502(a)(3), Apr. 20, 2005, 119 Stat. 216.)

§ 753. Stockbroker liquidation and forward contract merchants, commodity brokers, stockbrokers, financial institutions, financial participants, securities clearing agencies, swap participants, repo participants, and master netting agreement participants

Notwithstanding any other provision of this title, the exercise of rights by a forward contract merchant, commodity broker, stockbroker, financial institution, financial participant, securities clearing agency, swap participant, repo participant, or master netting agreement participant under this title shall not affect the priority of any unsecured claim it may have after the exercise of such rights.

(Added Pub.L. 109–8, title IX, § 907(m), Apr. 20, 2005, 119 Stat. 181.)

SUBCHAPTER IV—COMMODITY BROKER LIQUIDATION

§ 761. Definitions for this subchapter

In this subchapter—

(1)   "Act" means Commodity Exchange Act;

(2)   "clearing organization" means a derivatives clearing organization registered under the Act;

(3)   "Commission" means Commodity Futures Trading Commission;

(4)   "commodity contract" means—

(A)   with respect to a futures commission merchant, contract for the purchase or sale of a commodity for future delivery on, or subject to the rules of, a contract market or board of trade;

(B)   with respect to a foreign futures commission merchant, foreign future;

(C)   with respect to a leverage transaction merchant, leverage transaction;

(D)   with respect to a clearing organization, contract for the purchase or sale of a commodity for future delivery on, or subject to the rules of, a contract market or board of trade that is cleared by such clearing organization, or commodity option traded on, or subject to the rules of, a contract market or board of trade that is cleared by such clearing organization;

(E)   with respect to a commodity options dealer, commodity option;

(F)(i)   any other contract, option, agreement, or transaction that is similar to a contract, option, agreement, or transaction referred to in this paragraph; and

(ii)   with respect to a futures commission merchant or a clearing organization, any other contract, option, agreement, or transaction, in each case, that is cleared by a clearing organization;

(G)   any combination of the agreements or transactions referred to in this paragraph;

(H)   any option to enter into an agreement or transaction referred to in this paragraph;

(I)   a master agreement that provides for an agreement or transaction referred to in subparagraph (A), (B), (C), (D), (E), (F), (G), or (H), together with all supplements to such master agreement, without regard to whether the master agreement provides for an agreement or transaction that is not a commodity contract under this paragraph, except that the master agreement shall be considered to be a commodity contract under this paragraph only with respect to each agreement or transaction under the master agreement that is referred to in subparagraph (A), (B), (C), (D), (E), (F), (G), or (H); or

(J) any security agreement or arrangement or other credit enhancement related to any agreement or transaction referred to in this paragraph, including any guarantee or reimbursement obligation by or to a commodity broker or financial participant in connection with any agreement or transaction referred to in this paragraph, but not to exceed the damages in connection with any such agreement or transaction, measured in accordance with section 562;

(5) "commodity option" means agreement or transaction subject to regulation under section 4c(b) of the Act;

(6) "commodity options dealer" means person that extends credit to, or that accepts cash, a security, or other property from, a customer of such person for the purchase or sale of an interest in a commodity option;

(7) "contract market" means a registered entity;

(8) "contract of sale", "commodity", "derivatives clearing organization", "future delivery", "board of trade", "registered entity", and "futures commission merchant" have the meanings assigned to those terms in the Act;

(9) "customer" means—

(A) with respect to a futures commission merchant—

(i) entity for or with whom such futures commission merchant deals and that holds a claim against such futures commission merchant on account of a commodity contract made, received, acquired, or held by or through such futures commission merchant in the ordinary course of such futures commission merchant's business as a futures commission merchant from or for the commodity futures account of such entity; or

(ii) entity that holds a claim against such futures commission merchant arising out of—

(I) the making, liquidation, or change in the value of a commodity contract of a kind specified in clause (i) of this subparagraph;

(II) a deposit or payment of cash, a security, or other property with such futures commission merchant for the purpose of making or margining such a commodity contract; or

(III) the making or taking of delivery on such a commodity contract;

(B) with respect to a foreign futures commission merchant—

(i) entity for or with whom such foreign futures commission merchant deals and that holds a claim against such foreign futures commission merchant on account of a commodity contract made, received, acquired, or held by or through such foreign futures commission merchant in the ordinary course of such foreign futures commission merchant's business as a foreign futures commission merchant from or for the foreign futures account of such entity; or

(ii) entity that holds a claim against such foreign futures commission merchant arising out of—

(I) the making, liquidation, or change in value of a commodity contract of a kind specified in clause (i) of this subparagraph;

(II) a deposit or payment of cash, a security, or other property with such foreign futures commission merchant for the purpose of making or margining such a commodity contract; or

(III) the making or taking of delivery on such a commodity contract;

(C) with respect to a leverage transaction merchant—

(i) entity for or with whom such leverage transaction merchant deals and that holds a claim against such leverage transaction merchant on account of a commodity contract engaged in by or with such leverage transaction merchant in the ordinary course of such leverage transaction merchant's business as a leverage transaction merchant from or for the leverage account of such entity; or

(ii) entity that holds a claim against such leverage transaction merchant arising out of—

(I) the making, liquidation, or change in value of a commodity contract of a kind specified in clause (i) of this subparagraph;

(II) a deposit or payment of cash, a security, or other property with such leverage transaction merchant for the purpose of entering into or margining such a commodity contract; or

(III) the making or taking of delivery on such a commodity contract;

(D) with respect to a clearing organization, clearing member of such clearing organization with whom such clearing organization deals and that holds a claim against such clearing organization on account of cash, a security, or other property received by such clearing organization to margin, guarantee, or secure a commodity contract in such clearing member's proprietary account or customers' account; or

(E) with respect to a commodity options dealer—

(i) entity for or with whom such commodity options dealer deals and that holds a claim on account of a commodity contract made, received, acquired, or held by or through such commodity options dealer in the ordinary course of such commodity options dealer's business as a commodity options dealer from or for the commodity options account of such entity; or

(ii) entity that holds a claim against such commodity options dealer arising out of—

(I) the making of, liquidation of, exercise of, or a change in value of, a commodity contract of a kind specified in clause (i) of this subparagraph; or

(II) a deposit or payment of cash, a security, or other property with such commodity options dealer for the purpose of making, exercising, or margining such a commodity contract;

(10) "customer property" means cash, a security, or other property, or proceeds of such cash, security, or property, received, acquired, or held by or for the account of the debtor, from or for the account of a customer—

(A) including—

(i) property received, acquired, or held to margin, guarantee, secure, purchase, or sell a commodity contract;

(ii) profits or contractual or other rights accruing to a customer as a result of a commodity contract;

(iii) an open commodity contract;

(iv) specifically identifiable customer property;

(v) warehouse receipt or other document held by the debtor evidencing ownership of or title to property to be delivered to fulfill a commodity contract from or for the account of a customer;

(vi) cash, a security, or other property received by the debtor as payment for a commodity to be delivered to fulfill a commodity contract from or for the account of a customer;

(vii) a security held as property of the debtor to the extent such security is necessary to meet a net equity claim based on a security of the same class and series of an issuer;

(viii)　　property that was unlawfully converted from and that is the lawful property of the estate; and

(ix) other property of the debtor that any applicable law, rule, or regulation requires to be set aside or held for the benefit of a customer, unless including such property as customer property would not significantly increase customer property; but

(B) not including property to the extent that a customer does not have a claim against the debtor based on such property;

(11) "foreign future" means contract for the purchase or sale of a commodity for future delivery on, or subject to the rules of, a board of trade outside the United States;

(12) "foreign futures commission merchant" means entity engaged in soliciting or accepting orders for the purchase or sale of a foreign future or that, in connection with such a solicitation or acceptance, accepts cash, a security, or other property, or extends credit to margin, guarantee, or secure any trade or contract that results from such a solicitation or acceptance;

(13) "leverage transaction" means agreement that is subject to regulation under section 19 of the Commodity Exchange Act, and that is commonly known to the commodities trade as a margin account, margin contract, leverage account, or leverage contract;

(14) "leverage transaction merchant" means person in the business of engaging in leverage transactions;

(15) "margin payment" means payment or deposit of cash, a security, or other property, that is commonly known to the commodities trade as original margin, initial margin, maintenance margin, or variation margin, including mark-to-market payments, settlement payments, variation payments, daily settlement payments, and final settlement payments made as adjustments to settlement prices;

(16) "member property" means customer property received, acquired, or held by or for the account of a debtor that is a clearing organization, from or for the proprietary account of a customer that is a clearing member of the debtor; and

(17) "net equity" means, subject to such rules and regulations as the Commission promulgates under the Act, with respect to the aggregate of all of a customer's accounts that such customer has in the same capacity—

(A) the balance remaining in such customer's accounts immediately after—

(i) all commodity contracts of such customer have been transferred, liquidated, or become identified for delivery; and

(ii) all obligations of such customer in such capacity to the debtor have been offset; plus

(B) the value, as of the date of return under section 766 of this title, of any specifically identifiable customer property actually returned to such customer before the date specified in subparagraph (A) of this paragraph; plus

(C) the value, as of the date of transfer, of—

(i) any commodity contract to which such customer is entitled that is transferred to another person under section 766 of this title; and

(ii) any cash, security, or other property of such customer transferred to such other person under section 766 of this title to margin or secure such transferred commodity contract.

(Pub.L. 95–598, Nov. 6, 1978, 92 Stat. 2615; Pub.L. 97–222, § 16, July 27, 1982, 96 Stat. 238; Pub.L. 98–353, title III, § 485, July 10, 1984, 98 Stat. 383; Pub.L. 103–394, title V, § 501(d)(29), Oct. 22, 1994, 108 Stat. 4146; Pub.L. 106–554, § 1(a)(5) [title I, § 112(c)(6)], Dec. 21, 2000, 114 Stat. 2763, 2763A–395; Pub.L. 109–8, title IX, § 907(a)(3), Apr. 20, 2005, 119 Stat. 174; Pub.L. 111–203, title VII, § 724(b), July 21, 2010, 124 Stat. 1684.)

§ 762. Notice to the Commission and right to be heard

(a) The clerk shall give the notice required by section 342 of this title to the Commission.

(b) The Commission may raise and may appear and be heard on any issue in a case under this chapter.

(Pub.L. 95–598, Nov. 6, 1978, 92 Stat. 2618.)

§ 763. Treatment of accounts

(a) Accounts held by the debtor for a particular customer in separate capacities shall be treated as accounts of separate customers.

(b) A member of a clearing organization shall be deemed to hold such member's proprietary account in a separate capacity from such member's customers' account.

(c) The net equity in a customer's account may not be offset against the net equity in the account of any other customer.

(Pub.L. 95–598, Nov. 6, 1978, 92 Stat. 2618; Pub.L. 98–353, title III, § 486, July 10, 1984, 98 Stat. 383.)

§ 764. Voidable transfers

(a) Except as otherwise provided in this section, any transfer by the debtor of property that, but for such transfer, would have been customer property, may be avoided by the trustee, and such property shall be treated as customer property, if and to the extent that the trustee avoids such transfer under section 544, 545, 547, 548, 549, or 724(a) of this title. For the purpose of such sections, the property so transferred shall be deemed to have been property of the debtor, and, if such transfer was made to a customer or for a customer's benefit, such customer shall be deemed, for the purposes of this section, to have been a creditor.

(b) Notwithstanding sections 544, 545, 547, 548, 549, and 724(a) of this title, the trustee may not avoid a transfer made before seven days after the order for relief, if such transfer is approved by the Commission by rule or order, either before or after such transfer, and if such transfer is—

(1) a transfer of a commodity contract entered into or carried by or through the debtor on behalf of a customer, and of any cash, securities, or other property margining or securing such commodity contract; or

(2) the liquidation of a commodity contract entered into or carried by or through the debtor on behalf of a customer.

(Pub.L. 95–598, Nov. 6, 1978, 92 Stat. 2618; Pub.L. 97–222, § 17, July 27, 1982, 96 Stat. 240; Pub.L. 98–353, title III, § 487, July 10, 1984, 98 Stat. 383; Pub.L. 111–16, § 2(9), May 7, 2009, 123 Stat. 1607.)

§ 765. Customer instructions

(a) The notice required by section 342 of this title to customers shall instruct each customer—

(1) to file a proof of such customer's claim promptly, and to specify in such claim any specifically identifiable security, property, or commodity contract; and

(2) to instruct the trustee of such customer's desired disposition, including transfer under section 766 of this title or liquidation, of any commodity contract specifically identified to such customer.

(b) The trustee shall comply, to the extent practicable, with any instruction received from a customer regarding such customer's desired disposition of any commodity contract specifically identified to such customer. If the trustee has transferred, under section 766 of this title, such a commodity contract, the trustee shall transmit any such instruction to the commodity broker to whom such commodity contract was so transferred.

(Pub.L. 95–598, Nov. 6, 1978, 92 Stat. 2619; Pub.L. 97–222, § 18, July 27, 1982, 96 Stat. 240; Pub.L. 98–353, title III, § 488, July 10, 1984, 98 Stat. 383.)

§ 766.　Treatment of customer property

(a) The trustee shall answer all margin calls with respect to a specifically identifiable commodity contract of a customer until such time as the trustee returns or transfers such commodity contract, but the trustee may not make a margin payment that has the effect of a distribution to such customer of more than that to which such customer is entitled under subsection (h) or (i) of this section.

(b) The trustee shall prevent any open commodity contract from remaining open after the last day of trading in such commodity contract, or into the first day on which notice of intent to deliver on such commodity contract may be tendered, whichever occurs first. With respect to any commodity contract that has remained open after the last day of trading in such commodity contract or with respect to which delivery must be made or accepted under the rules of the contract market on which such commodity contract was made, the trustee may operate the business of the debtor for the purpose of—

(1) accepting or making tender of notice of intent to deliver the physical commodity underlying such commodity contract;

(2) facilitating delivery of such commodity; or

(3) disposing of such commodity if a party to such commodity contract defaults.

(c) The trustee shall return promptly to a customer any specifically identifiable security, property, or commodity contract to which such customer is entitled, or shall transfer, on such customer's behalf, such security, property, or commodity contract to a commodity broker that is not a debtor under this title, subject to such rules or regulations as the Commission may prescribe, to the extent that the value of such security, property, or commodity contract does not exceed the amount to which such customer would be entitled under subsection (h) or (i) of this section if such security, property, or commodity contract were not returned or transferred under this subsection.

(d) If the value of a specifically identifiable security, property, or commodity contract exceeds the amount to which the customer of the debtor is entitled under subsection (h) or (i) of this section, then such customer to whom such security, property, or commodity contract is specifically identified may deposit cash with the trustee equal to the difference between the value of such security, property, or commodity contract and such amount, and the trustee then shall—

(1) return promptly such security, property, or commodity contract to such customer; or

(2) transfer, on such customer's behalf, such security, property, or commodity contract to a commodity broker that is not a debtor under this title, subject to such rules or regulations as the Commission may prescribe.

(e) Subject to subsection (b) of this section, the trustee shall liquidate any commodity contract that—

(1) is identified to a particular customer and with respect to which such customer has not timely instructed the trustee as to the desired disposition of such commodity contract;

(2) cannot be transferred under subsection (c) of this section; or

(3) cannot be identified to a particular customer.

(f) As soon as practicable after the commencement of the case, the trustee shall reduce to money, consistent with good market practice, all securities and other property, other than commodity contracts, held as property of the estate, except for specifically identifiable securities or property distributable under subsection (h) or (i) of this section.

(g) The trustee may not distribute a security or other property except under subsection (h) or (i) of this section.

(h) Except as provided in subsection (b) of this section, the trustee shall distribute customer property ratably to customers on the basis and to the extent of such customers' allowed net equity claims, and in priority to all other claims, except claims of a kind specified in section 507(a)(2) of this title that are attributable to the administration of customer property. Such distribution shall be in the form of—

   (1) cash;

   (2) the return or transfer, under subsection (c) or (d) of this section, of specifically identifiable customer securities, property, or commodity contracts; or

   (3) payment of margin calls under subsection (a) of this section.

Notwithstanding any other provision of this subsection, a customer net equity claim based on a proprietary account, as defined by Commission rule, regulation, or order, may not be paid either in whole or in part, directly or indirectly, out of customer property unless all other customer net equity claims have been paid in full.

(i) If the debtor is a clearing organization, the trustee shall distribute—

   (1) customer property, other than member property, ratably to customers on the basis and to the extent of such customers' allowed net equity claims based on such customers' accounts other than proprietary accounts, and in priority to all other claims, except claims of a kind specified in section 507(a)(2) of this title that are attributable to the administration of such customer property; and

   (2) member property ratably to customers on the basis and to the extent of such customers' allowed net equity claims based on such customers' proprietary accounts, and in priority to all other claims, except claims of a kind specified in section 507(a)(2) of this title that are attributable to the administration of member property or customer property.

(j)(1) The trustee shall distribute customer property in excess of that distributed under subsection (h) or (i) of this section in accordance with section 726 of this title.

   (2) Except as provided in section 510 of this title, if a customer is not paid the full amount of such customer's allowed net equity claim from customer property, the unpaid portion of such claim is a claim entitled to distribution under section 726 of this title.

   (Pub.L. 95–598, Nov. 6, 1978, 92 Stat. 2619; Pub.L. 97–222, § 19, July 27, 1982, 96 Stat. 240; Pub.L. 98–353, title III, § 489, July 10, 1984, 98 Stat. 383; Pub.L. 109–8, title XV, § 1502(a)(4), Apr. 20, 2005, 119 Stat. 216.)

§ 767. Commodity broker liquidation and forward contract merchants, commodity brokers, stockbrokers, financial institutions, financial participants, securities clearing agencies, swap participants, repo participants, and master netting agreement participants

Notwithstanding any other provision of this title, the exercise of rights by a forward contract merchant, commodity broker, stockbroker, financial institution, financial participant, securities clearing agency, swap participant, repo participant, or master netting agreement participant under this title shall not affect the priority of any unsecured claim it may have after the exercise of such rights.

   (Added Pub.L. 109–8, title IX, § 907(*l*), Apr. 20, 2005, 119 Stat. 181.)

SUBCHAPTER V—CLEARING BANK LIQUIDATION

§ 781. Definitions

For purposes of this subchapter, the following definitions shall apply:

(1) Board.—The term "Board" means the Board of Governors of the Federal Reserve System.

(2) Depository Institution.—The term "depository institution" has the same meaning as in section 3 of the Federal Deposit Insurance Act.

(3) Clearing Bank.—The term "clearing bank" means an uninsured State member bank, or a corporation organized under section 25A of the Federal Reserve Act, which operates, or operates as, a multilateral clearing organization pursuant to section 409 of the Federal Deposit Insurance Corporation Improvement Act of 1991.

(Added Pub.L. 106–554, § 1(a)(5) [title I, § 112(c)(5)(B)], Dec. 21, 2000, 114 Stat. 2763, 2763A–394.)

§ 782. Selection of trustee

(a) In General.—

(1) Appointment.—Notwithstanding any other provision of this title, the conservator or receiver who files the petition shall be the trustee under this chapter, unless the Board designates an alternative trustee.

(2) Successor.—The Board may designate a successor trustee if required.

(b) Authority of Trustee.—Whenever the Board appoints or designates a trustee, chapter 3 and sections 704 and 705 of this title shall apply to the Board in the same way and to the same extent that they apply to a United States trustee.

(Added Pub.L. 106–554, § 1(a)(5) [title I, § 112(c)(5)(B)], Dec. 21, 2000, 114 Stat. 2763, 2763A–394.)

§ 783. Additional powers of trustee

(a) Distribution of Property Not of the Estate.—The trustee under this subchapter has power to distribute property not of the estate, including distributions to customers that are mandated by subchapters III and IV of this chapter.

(b) Disposition of Institution.—The trustee under this subchapter may, after notice and a hearing—

(1) sell the clearing bank to a depository institution or consortium of depository institutions (which consortium may agree on the allocation of the clearing bank among the consortium);

(2) merge the clearing bank with a depository institution;

(3) transfer contracts to the same extent as could a receiver for a depository institution under paragraphs (9) and (10) of section 11(e) of the Federal Deposit Insurance Act;

(4) transfer assets or liabilities to a depository institution; and

(5) transfer assets and liabilities to a bridge depository institution as provided in paragraphs (1), (3)(A), (5), and (6) of section 11(n) of the Federal Deposit Insurance Act, paragraphs (9) through (13) of such section, and subparagraphs (A) through (H) and subparagraph (K) of paragraph (4) of such section 11(n), except that—

(A) the bridge depository institution to which such assets or liabilities are transferred shall be treated as a clearing bank for the purpose of this subsection; and

(B) any references in any such provision of law to the Federal Deposit Insurance Corporation shall be construed to be references to the appointing agency and that references to deposit insurance shall be omitted.

(c) Certain Transfers Included.—Any reference in this section to transfers of liabilities includes a ratable transfer of liabilities within a priority class.

(Added Pub.L. 106–554, § 1(a)(5) [title I, § 112(c)(5)(B)], Dec. 21, 2000, 114 Stat. 2763, 2763A–395, amended Pub.L. 110–289, div. A, title VI, § 1604(b)(3), July 30, 2008, 122 Stat. 2829.)

§ 784. Right to be heard

The Board or a Federal reserve bank (in the case of a clearing bank that is a member of that bank) may raise and may appear and be heard on any issue in a case under this subchapter.

(Added Pub.L. 106–554, § 1(a)(5) [title I, § 112(c)(5)(B)], Dec. 21, 2000, 114 Stat. 2763, 2763A–395.)

CHAPTER 9—ADJUSTMENT OF DEBTS
OF A MUNICIPALITY

SUBCHAPTER I—GENERAL PROVISIONS

SUBCHAPTER II—ADMINISTRATION

SUBCHAPTER III—THE PLAN

SUBCHAPTER I—GENERAL PROVISIONS

§ 901. Applicability of other sections of this title

(a) Sections 301, 333, 344, 347(b), 349, 350(b), 351,,[1] 361, 362, 364(c), 364(d), 364(e), 364(f), 365, 366, 501, 502, 503, 504, 506, 507(a)(2), 509, 510, 524(a)(1), 524(a)(2), 544, 545, 546, 547, 548, 549(a), 549(c), 549(d), 550, 551, 552, 553, 555, 556, 557, 559, 560, 561, 562, 1102, 1103, 1109, 1111(b), 1122, 1123(a)(1), 1123(a)(2), 1123(a)(3), 1123(a)(4), 1123(a)(5), 1123(b), 1123(d), 1124, 1125, 1126(a), 1126(b), 1126(c), 1126(e),

---

[1] So in original.

1126(f), 1126(g), 1127(d), 1128, 1129(a)(2), 1129(a)(3), 1129(a)(6), 1129(a)(8), 1129(a)(10), 1129(b)(1), 1129(b)(2)(A), 1129(b)(2)(B), 1142(b), 1143, 1144, and 1145 of this title apply in a case under this chapter.

(b)   A term used in a section of this title made applicable in a case under this chapter by subsection (a) of this section or section 103(e) of this title has the meaning defined for such term for the purpose of such applicable section, unless such term is otherwise defined in section 902 of this title.

(c)   A section made applicable in a case under this chapter by subsection (a) of this section that is operative if the business of the debtor is authorized to be operated is operative in a case under this chapter.

(Pub.L. 95–598, Nov. 6, 1978, 92 Stat. 2621; Pub.L. 98–353, title III, §§ 353, 490, July 10, 1984, 98 Stat. 361, 383; Pub.L. 100–597, § 3, Nov. 3, 1988, 102 Stat. 3028; Pub.L. 109–8, title V, § 502, title XII, § 1216, title XV, § 1502(a)(5), Apr. 20, 2005, 119 Stat. 118, 195, 216; Pub.L. 111–327, § 2(a)(29), Dec. 22, 2010, 124 Stat. 3560.)

§ 902.   Definitions for this chapter

In this chapter—

(1)   "property of the estate", when used in a section that is made applicable in a case under this chapter by section 103(e) or 901 of this title, means property of the debtor;

(2)   "special revenues" means—

(A)   receipts derived from the ownership, operation, or disposition of projects or systems of the debtor that are primarily used or intended to be used primarily to provide transportation, utility, or other services, including the proceeds of borrowings to finance the projects or systems;

(B)   special excise taxes imposed on particular activities or transactions;

(C)   incremental tax receipts from the benefited area in the case of tax-increment financing;

(D)   other revenues or receipts derived from particular functions of the debtor, whether or not the debtor has other functions; or

(E)   taxes specifically levied to finance one or more projects or systems, excluding receipts from general property, sales, or income taxes (other than tax-increment financing) levied to finance the general purposes of the debtor;

(3)   "special tax payer" means record owner or holder of legal or equitable title to real property against which a special assessment or special tax has been levied the proceeds of which are the sole source of payment of an obligation issued by the debtor to defray the cost of an improvement relating to such real property;

(4)   "special tax payer affected by the plan" means special tax payer with respect to whose real property the plan proposes to increase the proportion of special assessments or special taxes referred to in paragraph (2) of this section assessed against such real property; and

(5)   "trustee", when used in a section that is made applicable in a case under this chapter by section 103(e) or 901 of this title, means debtor, except as provided in section 926 of this title.

(Pub.L. 95–598, Nov. 6, 1978, 92 Stat. 2622; Pub.L. 98–353, title III, § 491, July 10, 1984, 98 Stat. 383; Pub.L. 100–597, § 4, Nov. 3, 1988, 102 Stat. 3028.)

§ 903.   Reservation of State power to control municipalities

This chapter does not limit or impair the power of a State to control, by legislation or otherwise, a municipality of or in such State in the exercise of the political or governmental powers of such municipality, including expenditures for such exercise, but—

(1)   a State law prescribing a method of composition of indebtedness of such municipality may not bind any creditor that does not consent to such composition; and

(2) a judgment entered under such a law may not bind a creditor that does not consent to such composition.

(Pub.L. 95–598, Nov. 6, 1978, 92 Stat. 2622; Pub.L. 98–353, title III, § 492, July 10, 1984, 98 Stat. 383.)

§ 904. Limitation on jurisdiction and powers of court

Notwithstanding any power of the court, unless the debtor consents or the plan so provides, the court may not, by any stay, order, or decree, in the case or otherwise, interfere with—

(1) any of the political or governmental powers of the debtor;

(2) any of the property or revenues of the debtor; or

(3) the debtor's use or enjoyment of any income-producing property.

(Pub.L. 95–598, Nov. 6, 1978, 92 Stat. 2622.)

SUBCHAPTER II—ADMINISTRATION

§ 921. Petition and proceedings relating to petition

(a) Notwithstanding sections 109(d) and 301 of this title, a case under this chapter concerning an unincorporated tax or special assessment district that does not have such district's own officials is commenced by the filing under section 301 of this title of a petition under this chapter by such district's governing authority or the board or body having authority to levy taxes or assessments to meet the obligations of such district.

(b) The chief judge of the court of appeals for the circuit embracing the district in which the case is commenced shall designate the bankruptcy judge to conduct the case.

(c) After any objection to the petition, the court, after notice and a hearing, may dismiss the petition if the debtor did not file the petition in good faith or if the petition does not meet the requirements of this title.

(d) If the petition is not dismissed under subsection (c) of this section, the court shall order relief under this chapter notwithstanding section 301(b).

(e) The court may not, on account of an appeal from an order for relief, delay any proceeding under this chapter in the case in which the appeal is being taken; nor shall any court order a stay of such proceeding pending such appeal. The reversal on appeal of a finding of jurisdiction does not affect the validity of any debt incurred that is authorized by the court under section 364(c) or 364(d) of this title.

(Pub.L. 95–598, Nov. 6, 1978, 92 Stat. 2622; Pub.L. 98–353, title III, § 494, July 10, 1984, 98 Stat. 383; Pub.L. 109–8, title V, § 501(a), Apr. 20, 2005, 119 Stat. 118.)

§ 922. Automatic stay of enforcement of claims against the debtor

(a) A petition filed under this chapter operates as a stay, in addition to the stay provided by section 362 of this title, applicable to all entities, of—

(1) the commencement or continuation, including the issuance or employment of process, of a judicial, administrative, or other action or proceeding against an officer or inhabitant of the debtor that seeks to enforce a claim against the debtor; and

(2) the enforcement of a lien on or arising out of taxes or assessments owed to the debtor.

(b) Subsections (c), (d), (e), (f), and (g) of section 362 of this title apply to a stay under subsection (a) of this section the same as such subsections apply to a stay under section 362(a) of this title.

(c) If the debtor provides, under section 362, 364, or 922 of this title, adequate protection of the interest of the holder of a claim secured by a lien on property of the debtor and if, notwithstanding such protection such creditor has a claim arising from the stay of action against such property under section 362 or 922 of this title or from the granting of a lien under section 364(d) of this title, then such claim shall be allowable as an administrative expense under section 503(b) of this title.

   (d) Notwithstanding section 362 of this title and subsection (a) of this section, a petition filed under this chapter does not operate as a stay of application of pledged special revenues in a manner consistent with section 927 of this title to payment of indebtedness secured by such revenues.

   (Pub.L. 95–598, Nov. 6, 1978, 92 Stat. 2623; Pub.L. 98–353, title III, § 495, July 10, 1984, 98 Stat. 384; Pub.L. 100–597, § 5, Nov. 3, 1988, 102 Stat. 3029.)

§ 923. Notice

   There shall be given notice of the commencement of a case under this chapter, notice of an order for relief under this chapter, and notice of the dismissal of a case under this chapter. Such notice shall also be published at least once a week for three successive weeks in at least one newspaper of general circulation published within the district in which the case is commenced, and in such other newspaper having a general circulation among bond dealers and bondholders as the court designates.

   (Pub.L. 95–598, Nov. 6, 1978, 92 Stat. 2623.)

§ 924. List of creditors

   The debtor shall file a list of creditors.

   (Pub.L. 95–598, Nov. 6, 1978, 92 Stat. 2623.)

§ 925. Effect of list of claims

   A proof of claim is deemed filed under section 501 of this title for any claim that appears in the list filed under section 924 of this title, except a claim that is listed as disputed, contingent, or unliquidated.

   (Pub.L. 95–598, Nov. 6, 1978, 92 Stat. 2623.)

§ 926. Avoiding powers

   (a) If the debtor refuses to pursue a cause of action under section 544, 545, 547, 548, 549(a), or 550 of this title, then on request of a creditor, the court may appoint a trustee to pursue such cause of action.

   (b) A transfer of property of the debtor to or for the benefit of any holder of a bond or note, on account of such bond or note, may not be avoided under section 547 of this title.

   (Pub.L. 95–598, Nov. 6, 1978, 92 Stat. 2623; Pub.L. 100–597, § 6, Nov. 3, 1988, 102 Stat. 3029.)

§ 927. Limitation on recourse

   The holder of a claim payable solely from special revenues of the debtor under applicable nonbankruptcy law shall not be treated as having recourse against the debtor on account of such claim pursuant to section 1111(b) of this title.

   (Added Pub.L. 100–597, § 7(2), Nov. 3, 1988, 102 Stat. 3029.)

§ 928. Post petition effect of security interest

   (a) Notwithstanding section 552(a) of this title and subject to subsection (b) of this section, special revenues acquired by the debtor after the commencement of the case shall remain subject to any lien resulting from any security agreement entered into by the debtor before the commencement of the case.

   (b) Any such lien on special revenues, other than municipal betterment assessments, derived from a project or system shall be subject to the necessary operating expenses of such project or system, as the case may be.

   (Added Pub.L. 100–597, § 8, Nov. 3, 1988, 102 Stat. 3029.)

§ 929. Municipal leases

A lease to a municipality shall not be treated as an executory contract or unexpired lease for the purposes of section 365 or 502(b)(6) of this title solely by reason of its being subject to termination in the event the debtor fails to appropriate rent.

(Added Pub.L. 100–597, § 9, Nov. 3, 1988, 102 Stat. 3030.)

§ 930. Dismissal

(a) After notice and a hearing, the court may dismiss a case under this chapter for cause, including—

(1) want of prosecution;

(2) unreasonable delay by the debtor that is prejudicial to creditors;

(3) failure to propose a plan within the time fixed under section 941 of this title;

(4) if a plan is not accepted within any time fixed by the court;

(5) denial of confirmation of a plan under section 943(b) of this title and denial of additional time for filing another plan or a modification of a plan; or

(6) if the court has retained jurisdiction after confirmation of a plan—

(A) material default by the debtor with respect to a term of such plan; or

(B) termination of such plan by reason of the occurrence of a condition specified in such plan.

(b) The court shall dismiss a case under this chapter if confirmation of a plan under this chapter is refused.

(Pub.L. 95–598, Nov. 6, 1978, 92 Stat. 2623, § 927; Pub.L. 98–353, title III, § 496, July 10, 1984, 98 Stat. 384; renumbered § 930, Pub.L. 100–597, § 7(1), Nov. 3, 1988, 102 Stat. 3029.)

SUBCHAPTER III—THE PLAN

§ 941. Filing of plan

The debtor shall file a plan for the adjustment of the debtor's debts. If such a plan is not filed with the petition, the debtor shall file such a plan at such later time as the court fixes.

(Pub.L. 95–598, Nov. 6, 1978, 92 Stat. 2624.)

§ 942. Modification of plan

The debtor may modify the plan at any time before confirmation, but may not modify the plan so that the plan as modified fails to meet the requirements of this chapter. After the debtor files a modification, the plan as modified becomes the plan.

(Pub.L. 95–598, Nov. 6, 1978, 92 Stat. 2624.)

§ 943. Confirmation

(a) A special tax payer may object to confirmation of a plan.

(b) The court shall confirm the plan if—

(1) the plan complies with the provisions of this title made applicable by sections 103(e) and 901 of this title;

(2) the plan complies with the provisions of this chapter;

(3) all amounts to be paid by the debtor or by any person for services or expenses in the case or incident to the plan have been fully disclosed and are reasonable;

(4) the debtor is not prohibited by law from taking any action necessary to carry out the plan;

(5) except to the extent that the holder of a particular claim has agreed to a different treatment of such claim, the plan provides that on the effective date of the plan each holder of a claim of a kind specified in section 507(a)(2) of this title will receive on account of such claim cash equal to the allowed amount of such claim;

(6) any regulatory or electoral approval necessary under applicable nonbankruptcy law in order to carry out any provision of the plan has been obtained, or such provision is expressly conditioned on such approval; and

(7) the plan is in the best interests of creditors and is feasible.

(Pub.L. 95–598, Nov. 6, 1978, 92 Stat. 2624; Pub.L. 98–353, title III, § 497, July 10, 1984, 98 Stat. 384; Pub.L. 100–597, § 10, Nov. 3, 1988, 102 Stat. 3030; Pub.L. 109–8, title XV, § 1502(a)(6), Apr. 20, 2005, 119 Stat. 216.)

§ 944. Effect of confirmation

(a) The provisions of a confirmed plan bind the debtor and any creditor, whether or not—

(1) a proof of such creditor's claim is filed or deemed filed under section 501 of this title;

(2) such claim is allowed under section 502 of this title; or

(3) such creditor has accepted the plan.

(b) Except as provided in subsection (c) of this section, the debtor is discharged from all debts as of the time when—

(1) the plan is confirmed;

(2) the debtor deposits any consideration to be distributed under the plan with a disbursing agent appointed by the court; and

(3) the court has determined—

(A) that any security so deposited will constitute, after distribution, a valid legal obligation of the debtor; and

(B) that any provision made to pay or secure payment of such obligation is valid.

(c) The debtor is not discharged under subsection (b) of this section from any debt—

(1) excepted from discharge by the plan or order confirming the plan; or

(2) owed to an entity that, before confirmation of the plan, had neither notice nor actual knowledge of the case.

(Pub.L. 95–598, Nov. 6, 1978, 92 Stat. 2624.)

§ 945. Continuing jurisdiction and closing of the case

(a) The court may retain jurisdiction over the case for such period of time as is necessary for the successful implementation of the plan.

(b) Except as provided in subsection (a) of this section, the court shall close the case when administration of the case has been completed.

(Pub.L. 95–598, Nov. 6, 1978, 92 Stat. 2625; Pub.L. 98–353, title III, § 498, July 10, 1984, 98 Stat. 384.)

§ 946. Effect of exchange of securities before the date of the filing of the petition

The exchange of a new security under the plan for a claim covered by the plan, whether such exchange occurred before or after the date of the filing of the petition, does not limit or impair the effectiveness of the plan or of any provision of this chapter. The amount and number specified in section 1126(c) of this title include the amount and number of claims formerly held by a creditor that has participated in any such exchange.

(Pub.L. 95–598, Nov. 6, 1978, 92 Stat. 2625.)

CHAPTER 11—REORGANIZATION

SUBCHAPTER I—OFFICERS AND ADMINISTRATION

§ 1101.   Definitions for this chapter

In this chapter—

(1) "debtor in possession" means debtor except when a person that has qualified under section 322 of this title is serving as trustee in the case;

(2) "substantial consummation" means—

(A) transfer of all or substantially all of the property proposed by the plan to be transferred;

(B) assumption by the debtor or by the successor to the debtor under the plan of the business or of the management of all or substantially all of the property dealt with by the plan; and

(C) commencement of distribution under the plan.

(Pub.L. 95–598, Nov. 6, 1978, 92 Stat. 2626.)

§ 1102.   Creditors' and equity security holders' committees

(a)(1) Except as provided in paragraph (3), as soon as practicable after the order for relief under chapter 11 of this title, the United States trustee shall appoint a committee of creditors holding unsecured claims and may appoint additional committees of creditors or of equity security holders as the United States trustee deems appropriate.

(2) On request of a party in interest, the court may order the appointment of additional committees of creditors or of equity security holders if necessary to assure adequate representation of creditors or of equity security holders. The United States trustee shall appoint any such committee.

(3) On request of a party in interest in a case in which the debtor is a small business debtor and for cause, the court may order that a committee of creditors not be appointed.

(4) On request of a party in interest and after notice and a hearing, the court may order the United States trustee to change the membership of a committee appointed under this subsection, if the court determines that the change is necessary to ensure adequate representation of creditors or equity security holders. The court may order the United States trustee to increase the number of members of a committee to include a creditor that is a small business concern (as described in section 3(a)(1) of the Small Business Act), if the court determines that the creditor holds claims (of the kind represented by the committee) the aggregate amount of which, in comparison to the annual gross revenue of that creditor, is disproportionately large.

(b)(1) A committee of creditors appointed under subsection (a) of this section shall ordinarily consist of the persons, willing to serve, that hold the seven largest claims against the debtor of the kinds represented on such committee, or of the members of a committee organized by creditors before the commencement of the case under this chapter, if such committee was fairly chosen and is representative of the different kinds of claims to be represented.

(2) A committee of equity security holders appointed under subsection (a)(2) of this section shall ordinarily consist of the persons, willing to serve, that hold the seven largest amounts of equity securities of the debtor of the kinds represented on such committee.

(3) A committee appointed under subsection (a) shall—

    (A) provide access to information for creditors who—

        (i) hold claims of the kind represented by that committee; and

        (ii) are not appointed to the committee;

    (B) solicit and receive comments from the creditors described in subparagraph (A); and

    (C) be subject to a court order that compels any additional report or disclosure to be made to the creditors described in subparagraph (A).

(Pub.L. 95–598, Nov. 6, 1978, 92 Stat. 2626; Pub.L. 98–353, title III, § 499, July 10, 1984, 98 Stat. 384; Pub.L. 99–554, title II, § 221, Oct. 27, 1986, 100 Stat. 3101; Pub.L. 103–394, title II, § 217(b), Oct. 22, 1994, 108 Stat. 4127; Pub.L. 109–8, title IV, §§ 405, 432(b), Apr. 20, 2005, 119 Stat. 105, 110.)

§ 1103. Powers and duties of committees

(a) At a scheduled meeting of a committee appointed under section 1102 of this title, at which a majority of the members of such committee are present, and with the court's approval, such committee may select and authorize the employment by such committee of one or more attorneys, accountants, or other agents, to represent or perform services for such committee.

(b) An attorney or accountant employed to represent a committee appointed under section 1102 of this title may not, while employed by such committee, represent any other entity having an adverse interest in connection with the case. Representation of one or more creditors of the same class as represented by the committee shall not per se constitute the representation of an adverse interest.

(c) A committee appointed under section 1102 of this title may—

    (1) consult with the trustee or debtor in possession concerning the administration of the case;

    (2) investigate the acts, conduct, assets, liabilities, and financial condition of the debtor, the operation of the debtor's business and the desirability of the continuance of such business, and any other matter relevant to the case or to the formulation of a plan;

    (3) participate in the formulation of a plan, advise those represented by such committee of such committee's determinations as to any plan formulated, and collect and file with the court acceptances or rejections of a plan;

    (4) request the appointment of a trustee or examiner under section 1104 of this title; and

    (5) perform such other services as are in the interest of those represented.

(d) As soon as practicable after the appointment of a committee under section 1102 of this title, the trustee shall meet with such committee to transact such business as may be necessary and proper.

(Pub.L. 95–598, Nov. 6, 1978, 92 Stat. 2627; Pub.L. 98–353, title III, §§ 324, 500, July 10, 1984, 98 Stat. 358, 384.)

§ 1104. Appointment of trustee or examiner

(a) At any time after the commencement of the case but before confirmation of a plan, on request of a party in interest or the United States trustee, and after notice and a hearing, the court shall order the appointment of a trustee—

    (1) for cause, including fraud, dishonesty, incompetence, or gross mismanagement of the affairs of the debtor by current management, either before or after the commencement of the case, or similar cause, but not including the number of holders of securities of the debtor or the amount of assets or liabilities of the debtor; or

(2)   if such appointment is in the interests of creditors, any equity security holders, and other interests of the estate, without regard to the number of holders of securities of the debtor or the amount of assets or liabilities of the debtor.

(b)(1)   Except as provided in section 1163 of this title, on the request of a party in interest made not later than 30 days after the court orders the appointment of a trustee under subsection (a), the United States trustee shall convene a meeting of creditors for the purpose of electing one disinterested person to serve as trustee in the case. The election of a trustee shall be conducted in the manner provided in subsections (a), (b), and (c) of section 702 of this title.

(2)(A)   If an eligible, disinterested trustee is elected at a meeting of creditors under paragraph (1), the United States trustee shall file a report certifying that election.

(B)   Upon the filing of a report under subparagraph (A)—

(i)   the trustee elected under paragraph (1) shall be considered to have been selected and appointed for purposes of this section; and

(ii)   the service of any trustee appointed under subsection (a) shall terminate.

(C)   The court shall resolve any dispute arising out of an election described in subparagraph (A).

(c)   If the court does not order the appointment of a trustee under this section, then at any time before the confirmation of a plan, on request of a party in interest or the United States trustee, and after notice and a hearing, the court shall order the appointment of an examiner to conduct such an investigation of the debtor as is appropriate, including an investigation of any allegations of fraud, dishonesty, incompetence, misconduct, mismanagement, or irregularity in the management of the affairs of the debtor of or by current or former management of the debtor, if—

(1)   such appointment is in the interests of creditors, any equity security holders, and other interests of the estate; or

(2)   the debtor's fixed, liquidated, unsecured debts, other than debts for goods, services, or taxes, or owing to an insider, exceed $5,000,000.

(d)   If the court orders the appointment of a trustee or an examiner, if a trustee or an examiner dies or resigns during the case or is removed under section 324 of this title, or if a trustee fails to qualify under section 322 of this title, then the United States trustee, after consultation with parties in interest, shall appoint, subject to the court's approval, one disinterested person other than the United States trustee to serve as trustee or examiner, as the case may be, in the case.

(e)   The United States trustee shall move for the appointment of a trustee under subsection (a) if there are reasonable grounds to suspect that current members of the governing body of the debtor, the debtor's chief executive or chief financial officer, or members of the governing body who selected the debtor's chief executive or chief financial officer, participated in actual fraud, dishonesty, or criminal conduct in the management of the debtor or the debtor's public financial reporting.

(Pub.L. 95–598, Nov. 6, 1978, 92 Stat. 2627; Pub.L. 99–554, title II, § 222, Oct. 27, 1986, 100 Stat. 3102; Pub.L. 103–394, title II, § 211(a), title V, § 501(d)(30), Oct. 22, 1994, 108 Stat. 4125, 4146; Pub.L. 109–8, title IV, §§ 416, 442(b), title XIV, § 1405, Apr. 20, 2005, 119 Stat. 107, 116, 215; Pub.L. 111–327, § 2(a)(30), Dec. 22, 2010, 124 Stat. 3560.)

§ 1105.   Termination of trustee's appointment

At any time before confirmation of a plan, on request of a party in interest or the United States trustee, and after notice and a hearing, the court may terminate the trustee's appointment and restore the debtor to possession and management of the property of the estate and of the operation of the debtor's business.

(Pub.L. 95–598, Nov. 6, 1978, 92 Stat. 2628; Pub.L. 98–353, title III, § 501, July 10, 1984, 98 Stat. 384; Pub.L. 99–554, title II, § 223, Oct. 27, 1986, 100 Stat. 3102.)

§ 1106.   Duties of trustee and examiner

(a)   A trustee shall—

(1)   perform the duties of the trustee, as specified in paragraphs (2), (5), (7), (8), (9), (10), (11), and (12) of section 704(a);

(2)   if the debtor has not done so, file the list, schedule, and statement required under section 521(a)(1) of this title;

(3)   except to the extent that the court orders otherwise, investigate the acts, conduct, assets, liabilities, and financial condition of the debtor, the operation of the debtor's business and the desirability of the continuance of such business, and any other matter relevant to the case or to the formulation of a plan;

(4)   as soon as practicable—

(A)   file a statement of any investigation conducted under paragraph (3) of this subsection, including any fact ascertained pertaining to fraud, dishonesty, incompetence, misconduct, mismanagement, or irregularity in the management of the affairs of the debtor, or to a cause of action available to the estate; and

(B)   transmit a copy or a summary of any such statement to any creditors' committee or equity security holders' committee, to any indenture trustee, and to such other entity as the court designates;

(5)   as soon as practicable, file a plan under section 1121 of this title, file a report of why the trustee will not file a plan, or recommend conversion of the case to a case under chapter 7, 12, or 13 of this title or dismissal of the case;

(6)   for any year for which the debtor has not filed a tax return required by law, furnish, without personal liability, such information as may be required by the governmental unit with which such tax return was to be filed, in light of the condition of the debtor's books and records and the availability of such information;

(7)   after confirmation of a plan, file such reports as are necessary or as the court orders; and

(8)   if with respect to the debtor there is a claim for a domestic support obligation, provide the applicable notice specified in subsection (c).

(b)   An examiner appointed under section 1104(d) of this title shall perform the duties specified in paragraphs (3) and (4) of subsection (a) of this section, and, except to the extent that the court orders otherwise, any other duties of the trustee that the court orders the debtor in possession not to perform.

(c)(1)   In a case described in subsection (a)(8) to which subsection (a)(8) applies, the trustee shall—

(A)(i)   provide written notice to the holder of the claim described in subsection (a)(8) of such claim and of the right of such holder to use the services of the State child support enforcement agency established under sections 464 and 466 of the Social Security Act for the State in which such holder resides, for assistance in collecting child support during and after the case under this title; and

(ii)   include in the notice required by clause (i) the address and telephone number of such State child support enforcement agency;

(B)(i)   provide written notice to such State child support enforcement agency of such claim; and

(ii)   include in the notice required by clause (i) the name, address, and telephone number of such holder; and

(C)   at such time as the debtor is granted a discharge under section 1141, provide written notice to such holder and to such State child support enforcement agency of—

(i)   the granting of the discharge;

    (ii)　the last recent known address of the debtor;

    (iii)　the last recent known name and address of the debtor's employer; and

    (iv)　the name of each creditor that holds a claim that—

      (I)　is not discharged under paragraph (2), (4), or (14A) of section 523(a); or

      (II)　was reaffirmed by the debtor under section 524(c).

(2)(A)　The holder of a claim described in subsection (a)(8) or the State child enforcement support agency of the State in which such holder resides may request from a creditor described in paragraph (1)(C)(iv) the last known address of the debtor.

    (B)　Notwithstanding any other provision of law, a creditor that makes a disclosure of a last known address of a debtor in connection with a request made under subparagraph (A) shall not be liable by reason of making such disclosure.

(Pub.L. 95–598, Nov. 6, 1978, 92 Stat. 2628; Pub.L. 98–353, title III, §§ 311(b)(1), 502, July 10, 1984, 98 Stat. 355, 384; Pub.L. 99–554, title II, § 257(c), Oct. 27, 1986, 100 Stat. 3114; Pub.L. 103–394, title II, § 211(b), Oct. 22, 1994, 108 Stat. 4125; Pub.L. 109–8, title II, § 219(b), title IV, § 446(c), title XI, § 1105(b), Apr. 20, 2005, 119 Stat. 56, 118, 192; Pub.L. 111–327, § 2(a)(31), Dec. 22, 2010, 124 Stat. 3560.)

§ 1107.　　Rights, powers, and duties of debtor in possession

(a)　Subject to any limitations on a trustee serving in a case under this chapter, and to such limitations or conditions as the court prescribes, a debtor in possession shall have all the rights, other than the right to compensation under section 330 of this title, and powers, and shall perform all the functions and duties, except the duties specified in sections 1106(a)(2), (3), and (4) of this title, of a trustee serving in a case under this chapter.

(b)　Notwithstanding section 327(a) of this title, a person is not disqualified for employment under section 327 of this title by a debtor in possession solely because of such person's employment by or representation of the debtor before the commencement of the case.

(Pub.L. 95–598, Nov. 6, 1978, 92 Stat. 2628; Pub.L. 98–353, title III, § 503, July 10, 1984, 98 Stat. 384.)

§ 1108.　　Authorization to operate business

Unless the court, on request of a party in interest and after notice and a hearing, orders otherwise, the trustee may operate the debtor's business.

(Pub.L. 95–598, Nov. 6, 1978, 92 Stat. 2629; Pub.L. 98–353, title III, § 504, July 10, 1984, 98 Stat. 384.)

§ 1109.　　Right to be heard

(a)　The Securities and Exchange Commission may raise and may appear and be heard on any issue in a case under this chapter, but the Securities and Exchange Commission may not appeal from any judgment, order, or decree entered in the case.

(b)　A party in interest, including the debtor, the trustee, a creditors' committee, an equity security holders' committee, a creditor, an equity security holder, or any indenture trustee, may raise and may appear and be heard on any issue in a case under this chapter.

(Pub.L. 95–598, Nov. 6, 1978, 92 Stat. 2629.)

§ 1110.　　Aircraft equipment and vessels

(a)(1)　Except as provided in paragraph (2) and subject to subsection (b), the right of a secured party with a security interest in equipment described in paragraph (3), or of a lessor or conditional vendor of such equipment, to take possession of such equipment in compliance with a security agreement, lease, or conditional sale contract, and to enforce any of its other rights or remedies, under such security agreement, lease, or conditional sale contract, to sell, lease, or otherwise retain or dispose of such equipment, is not limited or otherwise affected by any other provision of this title or by any power of the court.

(2)   The right to take possession and to enforce the other rights and remedies described in paragraph (1) shall be subject to section 362 if—

(A)   before the date that is 60 days after the date of the order for relief under this chapter, the trustee, subject to the approval of the court, agrees to perform all obligations of the debtor under such security agreement, lease, or conditional sale contract; and

(B)   any default, other than a default of a kind specified in section 365(b)(2), under such security agreement, lease, or conditional sale contract—

(i)   that occurs before the date of the order is cured before the expiration of such 60-day period;

(ii)   that occurs after the date of the order and before the expiration of such 60-day period is cured before the later of—

(I)   the date that is 30 days after the date of the default; or

(II)   the expiration of such 60-day period; and

(iii)   that occurs on or after the expiration of such 60-day period is cured in compliance with the terms of such security agreement, lease, or conditional sale contract, if a cure is permitted under that agreement, lease, or contract.

(3)   The equipment described in this paragraph—

(A)   is—

(i)   an aircraft, aircraft engine, propeller, appliance, or spare part (as defined in section 40102 of title 49) that is subject to a security interest granted by, leased to, or conditionally sold to a debtor that, at the time such transaction is entered into, holds an air carrier operating certificate issued pursuant to chapter 447 of title 49 for aircraft capable of carrying 10 or more individuals or 6,000 pounds or more of cargo; or

(ii)   a vessel documented under chapter 121 of title 46 that is subject to a security interest granted by, leased to, or conditionally sold to a debtor that is a water carrier that, at the time such transaction is entered into, holds a certificate of public convenience and necessity or permit issued by the Department of Transportation; and

(B)   includes all records and documents relating to such equipment that are required, under the terms of the security agreement, lease, or conditional sale contract, to be surrendered or returned by the debtor in connection with the surrender or return of such equipment.

(4)   Paragraph (1) applies to a secured party, lessor, or conditional vendor acting in its own behalf or acting as trustee or otherwise in behalf of another party.

(b)   The trustee and the secured party, lessor, or conditional vendor whose right to take possession is protected under subsection (a) may agree, subject to the approval of the court, to extend the 60-day period specified in subsection (a)(1).

(c)(1)   In any case under this chapter, the trustee shall immediately surrender and return to a secured party, lessor, or conditional vendor, described in subsection (a)(1), equipment described in subsection (a)(3), if at any time after the date of the order for relief under this chapter such secured party, lessor, or conditional vendor is entitled pursuant to subsection (a)(1) to take possession of such equipment and makes a written demand for such possession to the trustee.

(2)   At such time as the trustee is required under paragraph (1) to surrender and return equipment described in subsection (a)(3), any lease of such equipment, and any security agreement or conditional sale contract relating to such equipment, if such security agreement or conditional sale contract is an executory contract, shall be deemed rejected.

(d) With respect to equipment first placed in service on or before October 22, 1994, for purposes of this section—

(1) the term "lease" includes any written agreement with respect to which the lessor and the debtor, as lessee, have expressed in the agreement or in a substantially contemporaneous writing that the agreement is to be treated as a lease for Federal income tax purposes; and

(2) the term "security interest" means a purchase-money equipment security interest.

(Pub.L. 95–598, Nov. 6, 1978, 92 Stat. 2629; Pub.L. 103–272, § 5(c), July 5, 1994, 108 Stat. 1373; Pub.L. 103–394, title II, § 201(a), Oct. 22, 1994, 108 Stat. 4119; Pub.L. 106–181, title VII, § 744(b), Apr. 5, 2000, 114 Stat. 177; Pub.L. 109–304, § 17(b)(2), Oct. 6, 2006, 120 Stat. 1707.)

§ 1111.   Claims and interests

(a) A proof of claim or interest is deemed filed under section 501 of this title for any claim or interest that appears in the schedules filed under section 521(a)(1) or 1106(a)(2) of this title, except a claim or interest that is scheduled as disputed, contingent, or unliquidated.

(b)(1)(A) A claim secured by a lien on property of the estate shall be allowed or disallowed under section 502 of this title the same as if the holder of such claim had recourse against the debtor on account of such claim, whether or not such holder has such recourse, unless—

(i) the class of which such claim is a part elects, by at least two-thirds in amount and more than half in number of allowed claims of such class, application of paragraph (2) of this subsection; or

(ii) such holder does not have such recourse and such property is sold under section 363 of this title or is to be sold under the plan.

(B) A class of claims may not elect application of paragraph (2) of this subsection if—

(i) the interest on account of such claims of the holders of such claims in such property is of inconsequential value; or

(ii) the holder of a claim of such class has recourse against the debtor on account of such claim and such property is sold under section 363 of this title or is to be sold under the plan.

(2) If such an election is made, then notwithstanding section 506(a) of this title, such claim is a secured claim to the extent that such claim is allowed.

(Pub.L. 95–598, Nov. 6, 1978, 92 Stat. 2630; Pub.L. 111–327, § 2(a)(32), Dec. 22, 2010, 124 Stat. 3561.)

§ 1112.   Conversion or dismissal

(a) The debtor may convert a case under this chapter to a case under chapter 7 of this title unless—

(1) the debtor is not a debtor in possession;

(2) the case originally was commenced as an involuntary case under this chapter; or

(3) the case was converted to a case under this chapter other than on the debtor's request.

(b)(1) Except as provided in paragraph (2) and subsection (c), on request of a party in interest, and after notice and a hearing, the court shall convert a case under this chapter to a case under chapter 7 or dismiss a case under this chapter, whichever is in the best interests of creditors and the estate, for cause unless the court determines that the appointment under section 1104(a) of a trustee or an examiner is in the best interests of creditors and the estate.

(2) The court may not convert a case under this chapter to a case under chapter 7 or dismiss a case under this chapter if the court finds and specifically identifies unusual circumstances establishing that converting or dismissing the case is not in the best interests of creditors and the estate, and the debtor or any other party in interest establishes that—

(A) there is a reasonable likelihood that a plan will be confirmed within the timeframes established in sections 1121(e) and 1129(e) of this title, or if such sections do not apply, within a reasonable period of time; and

(B) the grounds for converting or dismissing the case include an act or omission of the debtor other than under paragraph (4)(A)—

 (i) for which there exists a reasonable justification for the act or omission; and

 (ii) that will be cured within a reasonable period of time fixed by the court.

(3) The court shall commence the hearing on a motion under this subsection not later than 30 days after filing of the motion, and shall decide the motion not later than 15 days after commencement of such hearing, unless the movant expressly consents to a continuance for a specific period of time or compelling circumstances prevent the court from meeting the time limits established by this paragraph.

(4) For purposes of this subsection, the term "cause" includes—

(A) substantial or continuing loss to or diminution of the estate and the absence of a reasonable likelihood of rehabilitation;

(B) gross mismanagement of the estate;

(C) failure to maintain appropriate insurance that poses a risk to the estate or to the public;

(D) unauthorized use of cash collateral substantially harmful to 1 or more creditors;

(E) failure to comply with an order of the court;

(F) unexcused failure to satisfy timely any filing or reporting requirement established by this title or by any rule applicable to a case under this chapter;

(G) failure to attend the meeting of creditors convened under section 341(a) or an examination ordered under rule 2004 of the Federal Rules of Bankruptcy Procedure without good cause shown by the debtor;

(H) failure timely to provide information or attend meetings reasonably requested by the United States trustee (or the bankruptcy administrator, if any);

(I) failure timely to pay taxes owed after the date of the order for relief or to file tax returns due after the date of the order for relief;

(J) failure to file a disclosure statement, or to file or confirm a plan, within the time fixed by this title or by order of the court;

(K) failure to pay any fees or charges required under chapter 123 of title 28;

(L) revocation of an order of confirmation under section 1144;

(M) inability to effectuate substantial consummation of a confirmed plan;

(N) material default by the debtor with respect to a confirmed plan;

(O) termination of a confirmed plan by reason of the occurrence of a condition specified in the plan; and

(P) failure of the debtor to pay any domestic support obligation that first becomes payable after the date of the filing of the petition.

(c) The court may not convert a case under this chapter to a case under chapter 7 of this title if the debtor is a farmer or a corporation that is not a moneyed, business, or commercial corporation, unless the debtor requests such conversion.

(d) The court may convert a case under this chapter to a case under chapter 12 or 13 of this title only if—

(1)   the debtor requests such conversion;

(2)   the debtor has not been discharged under section 1141(d) of this title; and

(3)   if the debtor requests conversion to chapter 12 of this title, such conversion is equitable.

(e)   Except as provided in subsections (c) and (f), the court, on request of the United States trustee, may convert a case under this chapter to a case under chapter 7 of this title or may dismiss a case under this chapter, whichever is in the best interest of creditors and the estate if the debtor in a voluntary case fails to file, within fifteen days after the filing of the petition commencing such case or such additional time as the court may allow, the information required by paragraph (1) of section 521(a), including a list containing the names and addresses of the holders of the twenty largest unsecured claims (or of all unsecured claims if there are fewer than twenty unsecured claims), and the approximate dollar amounts of each of such claims.

(f)   Notwithstanding any other provision of this section, a case may not be converted to a case under another chapter of this title unless the debtor may be a debtor under such chapter.

(Pub.L. 95–598, Nov. 6, 1978, 92 Stat. 2630; Pub.L. 98–353, title III, § 505, July 10, 1984, 98 Stat. 384; Pub.L. 99–554, title II, §§ 224, 256, Oct. 27, 1986, 100 Stat. 3102, 3114; Pub.L. 103–394, title II, § 217(c), Oct. 22, 1994, 108 Stat. 4127; Pub.L. 109–8, title IV, § 442(a), Apr. 20, 2005, 119 Stat. 115; Pub.L. 111–327, § 2(a)(33), Dec. 22, 2010, 124 Stat. 3561.)

§ 1113.   Rejection of collective bargaining agreements

(a)   The debtor in possession, or the trustee if one has been appointed under the provisions of this chapter, other than a trustee in a case covered by subchapter IV of this chapter and by title I of the Railway Labor Act, may assume or reject a collective bargaining agreement only in accordance with the provisions of this section.

(b)(1)   Subsequent to filing a petition and prior to filing an application seeking rejection of a collective bargaining agreement, the debtor in possession or trustee (hereinafter in this section "trustee" shall include a debtor in possession), shall—

(A)   make a proposal to the authorized representative of the employees covered by such agreement, based on the most complete and reliable information available at the time of such proposal, which provides for those necessary modifications in the employees benefits and protections that are necessary to permit the reorganization of the debtor and assures that all creditors, the debtor and all of the affected parties are treated fairly and equitably; and

(B)   provide, subject to subsection (d)(3), the representative of the employees with such relevant information as is necessary to evaluate the proposal.

(2)   During the period beginning on the date of the making of a proposal provided for in paragraph (1) and ending on the date of the hearing provided for in subsection (d)(1), the trustee shall meet, at reasonable times, with the authorized representative to confer in good faith in attempting to reach mutually satisfactory modifications of such agreement.

(c)   The court shall approve an application for rejection of a collective bargaining agreement only if the court finds that—

(1)   the trustee has, prior to the hearing, made a proposal that fulfills the requirements of subsection (b)(1);

(2)   the authorized representative of the employees has refused to accept such proposal without good cause; and

(3)   the balance of the equities clearly favors rejection of such agreement.

(d)(1)   Upon the filing of an application for rejection the court shall schedule a hearing to be held not later than fourteen days after the date of the filing of such application. All interested parties may appear and be heard at such hearing. Adequate notice shall be provided to such parties at least ten days before the date of such hearing. The court may extend the time for the commencement of such hearing for a period not exceeding seven days where the circumstances of the case, and the interests of justice require such extension, or for additional periods of time to which the trustee and representative agree.

(2)   The court shall rule on such application for rejection within thirty days after the date of the commencement of the hearing. In the interests of justice, the court may extend such time for ruling for such additional period as the trustee and the employees' representative may agree to. If the court does not rule on such application within thirty days after the date of the commencement of the hearing, or within such additional time as the trustee and the employees' representative may agree to, the trustee may terminate or alter any provisions of the collective bargaining agreement pending the ruling of the court on such application.

(3)   The court may enter such protective orders, consistent with the need of the authorized representative of the employee to evaluate the trustee's proposal and the application for rejection, as may be necessary to prevent disclosure of information provided to such representative where such disclosure could compromise the position of the debtor with respect to its competitors in the industry in which it is engaged.

(e)   If during a period when the collective bargaining agreement continues in effect, and if essential to the continuation of the debtor's business, or in order to avoid irreparable damage to the estate, the court, after notice and a hearing, may authorize the trustee to implement interim changes in the terms, conditions, wages, benefits, or work rules provided by a collective bargaining agreement. Any hearing under this paragraph shall be scheduled in accordance with the needs of the trustee. The implementation of such interim changes shall not render the application for rejection moot.

(f)   No provision of this title shall be construed to permit a trustee to unilaterally terminate or alter any provisions of a collective bargaining agreement prior to compliance with the provisions of this section.

(Added Pub.L. 98–353, title III, § 541(a), July 10, 1984, 98 Stat. 390.)

§ 1114.   Payment of insurance benefits to retired employees

(a)   For purposes of this section, the term "retiree benefits" means payments to any entity or person for the purpose of providing or reimbursing payments for retired employees and their spouses and dependents, for medical, surgical, or hospital care benefits, or benefits in the event of sickness, accident, disability, or death under any plan, fund, or program (through the purchase of insurance or otherwise) maintained or established in whole or in part by the debtor prior to filing a petition commencing a case under this title.

(b)(1)   For purposes of this section, the term "authorized representative" means the authorized representative designated pursuant to subsection (c) for persons receiving any retiree benefits covered by a collective bargaining agreement or subsection (d) in the case of persons receiving retiree benefits not covered by such an agreement.

(2)   Committees of retired employees appointed by the court pursuant to this section shall have the same rights, powers, and duties as committees appointed under sections 1102 and 1103 of this title for the purpose of carrying out the purposes of sections 1114 and 1129(a)(13) and, as permitted by the court, shall have the power to enforce the rights of persons under this title as they relate to retiree benefits.

(c)(1)   A labor organization shall be, for purposes of this section, the authorized representative of those persons receiving any retiree benefits covered by any collective bargaining agreement to which that labor organization is signatory, unless (A) such labor organization elects not to serve as the authorized representative of such persons, or (B) the court, upon a motion by any party in interest, after notice and hearing, determines that different representation of such persons is appropriate.

(2)   In cases where the labor organization referred to in paragraph (1) elects not to serve as the authorized representative of those persons receiving any retiree benefits covered by any collective bargaining agreement to which that labor organization is signatory, or in cases where the court, pursuant to paragraph (1) finds different representation of such persons appropriate, the court, upon a motion by any party in interest, and after notice and a hearing, shall appoint a committee of retired

employees if the debtor seeks to modify or not pay the retiree benefits or if the court otherwise determines that it is appropriate, from among such persons, to serve as the authorized representative of such persons under this section.

(d) The court, upon a motion by any party in interest, and after notice and a hearing, shall order the appointment of a committee of retired employees if the debtor seeks to modify or not pay the retiree benefits or if the court otherwise determines that it is appropriate, to serve as the authorized representative, under this section, of those persons receiving any retiree benefits not covered by a collective bargaining agreement. The United States trustee shall appoint any such committee.

(e)(1) Notwithstanding any other provision of this title, the debtor in possession, or the trustee if one has been appointed under the provisions of this chapter (hereinafter in this section "trustee" shall include a debtor in possession), shall timely pay and shall not modify any retiree benefits, except that—

    (A) the court, on motion of the trustee or authorized representative, and after notice and a hearing, may order modification of such payments, pursuant to the provisions of subsections (g) and (h) of this section, or

    (B) the trustee and the authorized representative of the recipients of those benefits may agree to modification of such payments,

after which such benefits as modified shall continue to be paid by the trustee.

(2) Any payment for retiree benefits required to be made before a plan confirmed under section 1129 of this title is effective has the status of an allowed administrative expense as provided in section 503 of this title.

(f)(1) Subsequent to filing a petition and prior to filing an application seeking modification of the retiree benefits, the trustee shall—

    (A) make a proposal to the authorized representative of the retirees, based on the most complete and reliable information available at the time of such proposal, which provides for those necessary modifications in the retiree benefits that are necessary to permit the reorganization of the debtor and assures that all creditors, the debtor and all of the affected parties are treated fairly and equitably; and

    (B) provide, subject to subsection (k)(3), the representative of the retirees with such relevant information as is necessary to evaluate the proposal.

(2) During the period beginning on the date of the making of a proposal provided for in paragraph (1), and ending on the date of the hearing provided for in subsection (k)(1), the trustee shall meet, at reasonable times, with the authorized representative to confer in good faith in attempting to reach mutually satisfactory modifications of such retiree benefits.

(g) The court shall enter an order providing for modification in the payment of retiree benefits if the court finds that—

    (1) the trustee has, prior to the hearing, made a proposal that fulfills the requirements of subsection (f);

    (2) the authorized representative of the retirees has refused to accept such proposal without good cause; and

    (3) such modification is necessary to permit the reorganization of the debtor and assures that all creditors, the debtor, and all of the affected parties are treated fairly and equitably, and is clearly favored by the balance of the equities;

except that in no case shall the court enter an order providing for such modification which provides for a modification to a level lower than that proposed by the trustee in the proposal found by the court to have complied with the requirements of this subsection and subsection (f): *Provided, however,* That at any time after an order is entered providing for modification in the payment of retiree benefits, or at any time after an agreement modifying such benefits is made between the trustee and the authorized representative of the recipients of such benefits, the authorized representative may apply to the court for an order increasing those benefits which order shall be granted if the increase in retiree benefits sought is consistent with the standard set forth in paragraph (3): *Provided further,* That neither the trustee nor the authorized representative is precluded from making more than one motion for a modification order governed by this subsection.

(h)(1) Prior to a court issuing a final order under subsection (g) of this section, if essential to the continuation of the debtor's business, or in order to avoid irreparable damage to the estate, the court, after notice and a hearing, may authorize the trustee to implement interim modifications in retiree benefits.

(2) Any hearing under this subsection shall be scheduled in accordance with the needs of the trustee.

(3) The implementation of such interim changes does not render the motion for modification moot.

(i) No retiree benefits paid between the filing of the petition and the time a plan confirmed under section 1129 of this title becomes effective shall be deducted or offset from the amounts allowed as claims for any benefits which remain unpaid, or from the amounts to be paid under the plan with respect to such claims for unpaid benefits, whether such claims for unpaid benefits are based upon or arise from a right to future unpaid benefits or from any benefits not paid as a result of modifications allowed pursuant to this section.

(j) No claim for retiree benefits shall be limited by section 502(b)(7) of this title.

(k)(1) Upon the filing of an application for modifying retiree benefits, the court shall schedule a hearing to be held not later than fourteen days after the date of the filing of such application. All interested parties may appear and be heard at such hearing. Adequate notice shall be provided to such parties at least ten days before the date of such hearing. The court may extend the time for the commencement of such hearing for a period not exceeding seven days where the circumstances of the case, and the interests of justice require such extension, or for additional periods of time to which the trustee and the authorized representative agree.

(2) The court shall rule on such application for modification within ninety days after the date of the commencement of the hearing. In the interests of justice, the court may extend such time for ruling for such additional period as the trustee and the authorized representative may agree to. If the court does not rule on such application within ninety days after the date of the commencement of the hearing, or within such additional time as the trustee and the authorized representative may agree to, the trustee may implement the proposed modifications pending the ruling of the court on such application.

(3) The court may enter such protective orders, consistent with the need of the authorized representative of the retirees to evaluate the trustee's proposal and the application for modification, as may be necessary to prevent disclosure of information provided to such representative where such disclosure could compromise the position of the debtor with respect to its competitors in the industry in which it is engaged.

(*l*) If the debtor, during the 180-day period ending on the date of the filing of the petition—

(1) modified retiree benefits; and

(2) was insolvent on the date such benefits were modified;

the court, on motion of a party in interest, and after notice and a hearing, shall issue an order reinstating as of the date the modification was made, such benefits as in effect immediately before such date unless the court finds that the balance of the equities clearly favors such modification.

(m) This section shall not apply to any retiree, or the spouse or dependents of such retiree, if such retiree's gross income for the twelve months preceding the filing of the bankruptcy petition equals or exceeds $250,000, unless such retiree can demonstrate to the satisfaction of the court that he is unable to obtain health, medical, life, and disability coverage for himself, his spouse, and his dependents who would otherwise be covered by the employer's insurance plan, comparable to the coverage provided by the employer on the day before the filing of a petition under this title.

(Added Pub.L. 100–334, § 2(a), June 16, 1988, 102 Stat. 610, amended Pub.L. 109–8, title IV, § 447, title XIV, § 1403, Apr. 20, 2005, 119 Stat. 118, 215.)

§ 1115.   Property of the estate

(a) In a case in which the debtor is an individual, property of the estate includes, in addition to the property specified in section 541—

(1) all property of the kind specified in section 541 that the debtor acquires after the commencement of the case but before the case is closed, dismissed, or converted to a case under chapter 7, 12, or 13, whichever occurs first; and

(2) earnings from services performed by the debtor after the commencement of the case but before the case is closed, dismissed, or converted to a case under chapter 7, 12, or 13, whichever occurs first.

(b) Except as provided in section 1104 or a confirmed plan or order confirming a plan, the debtor shall remain in possession of all property of the estate.

(Added Pub.L. 109–8, title III, § 321(a)(1), Apr. 20, 2005, 119 Stat. 94.)

§ 1116.   Duties of trustee or debtor in possession in small business cases

In a small business case, a trustee or the debtor in possession, in addition to the duties provided in this title and as otherwise required by law, shall—

(1) append to the voluntary petition or, in an involuntary case, file not later than 7 days after the date of the order for relief—

(A) its most recent balance sheet, statement of operations, cash-flow statement, and Federal income tax return; or

(B) a statement made under penalty of perjury that no balance sheet, statement of operations, or cash-flow statement has been prepared and no Federal tax return has been filed;

(2) attend, through its senior management personnel and counsel, meetings scheduled by the court or the United States trustee, including initial debtor interviews, scheduling conferences, and meetings of creditors convened under section 341 unless the court, after notice and a hearing, waives that requirement upon a finding of extraordinary and compelling circumstances;

(3) timely file all schedules and statements of financial affairs, unless the court, after notice and a hearing, grants an extension, which shall not extend such time period to a date later than 30 days after the date of the order for relief, absent extraordinary and compelling circumstances;

(4) file all postpetition financial and other reports required by the Federal Rules of Bankruptcy Procedure or by local rule of the district court;

(5) subject to section 363(c)(2), maintain insurance customary and appropriate to the industry;

(6)(A) timely file tax returns and other required government filings; and

(B) subject to section 363(c)(2), timely pay all taxes entitled to administrative expense priority except those being contested by appropriate proceedings being diligently prosecuted; and

(7) allow the United States trustee, or a designated representative of the United States trustee, to inspect the debtor's business premises, books, and records at reasonable times, after reasonable prior written notice, unless notice is waived by the debtor.

(Added Pub.L. 109–8, title IV, § 436(a), Apr. 20, 2005, 119 Stat. 112.)

SUBCHAPTER II—THE PLAN

§ 1121.   Who may file a plan

(a) The debtor may file a plan with a petition commencing a voluntary case, or at any time in a voluntary case or an involuntary case.

(b) Except as otherwise provided in this section, only the debtor may file a plan until after 120 days after the date of the order for relief under this chapter.

(c) Any party in interest, including the debtor, the trustee, a creditors' committee, an equity security holders' committee, a creditor, an equity security holder, or any indenture trustee, may file a plan if and only if—

(1) a trustee has been appointed under this chapter;

(2) the debtor has not filed a plan before 120 days after the date of the order for relief under this chapter; or

(3) the debtor has not filed a plan that has been accepted, before 180 days after the date of the order for relief under this chapter, by each class of claims or interests that is impaired under the plan.

(d)(1) Subject to paragraph (2), on request of a party in interest made within the respective periods specified in subsections (b) and (c) of this section and after notice and a hearing, the court may for cause reduce or increase the 120-day period or the 180-day period referred to in this section.

(2)(A) The 120-day period specified in paragraph (1) may not be extended beyond a date that is 18 months after the date of the order for relief under this chapter.

(B) The 180-day period specified in paragraph (1) may not be extended beyond a date that is 20 months after the date of the order for relief under this chapter.

(e) In a small business case—

(1) only the debtor may file a plan until after 180 days after the date of the order for relief, unless that period is—

(A) extended as provided by this subsection, after notice and a hearing; or

(B) the court, for cause, orders otherwise;

(2) the plan and a disclosure statement (if any) shall be filed not later than 300 days after the date of the order for relief; and

(3) the time periods specified in paragraphs (1) and (2), and the time fixed in section 1129(e) within which the plan shall be confirmed, may be extended only if—

(A) the debtor, after providing notice to parties in interest (including the United States trustee), demonstrates by a preponderance of the evidence that it is more likely than not that the court will confirm a plan within a reasonable period of time;

(B) a new deadline is imposed at the time the extension is granted; and

(C) the order extending time is signed before the existing deadline has expired.

(Pub.L. 95–598, Nov. 6, 1978, 92 Stat. 2631; Pub.L. 98–353, title III, § 506, July 10, 1984, 98 Stat. 385; Pub.L. 99–554, title II, § 283(u), Oct. 27, 1986, 100 Stat. 3118; Pub.L. 103–394, title II, § 217(d), Oct. 22, 1994, 108 Stat. 4127; Pub.L. 109–8, title IV, §§ 411, 437, Apr. 20, 2005, 119 Stat. 106, 113.)

§ 1122.   Classification of claims or interests

(a) Except as provided in subsection (b) of this section, a plan may place a claim or an interest in a particular class only if such claim or interest is substantially similar to the other claims or interests of such class.

(b)   A plan may designate a separate class of claims consisting only of every unsecured claim that is less than or reduced to an amount that the court approves as reasonable and necessary for administrative convenience.

(Pub.L. 95–598, Nov. 6, 1978, 92 Stat. 2631.)

§ 1123.   Contents of plan

(a)   Notwithstanding any otherwise applicable nonbankruptcy law, a plan shall—

(1)   designate, subject to section 1122 of this title, classes of claims, other than claims of a kind specified in section 507(a)(2), 507(a)(3), or 507(a)(8) of this title, and classes of interests;

(2)   specify any class of claims or interests that is not impaired under the plan;

(3)   specify the treatment of any class of claims or interests that is impaired under the plan;

(4)   provide the same treatment for each claim or interest of a particular class, unless the holder of a particular claim or interest agrees to a less favorable treatment of such particular claim or interest;

(5)   provide adequate means for the plan's implementation, such as—

(A)   retention by the debtor of all or any part of the property of the estate;

(B)   transfer of all or any part of the property of the estate to one or more entities, whether organized before or after the confirmation of such plan;

(C)   merger or consolidation of the debtor with one or more persons;

(D)   sale of all or any part of the property of the estate, either subject to or free of any lien, or the distribution of all or any part of the property of the estate among those having an interest in such property of the estate;

(E)   satisfaction or modification of any lien;

(F)   cancellation or modification of any indenture or similar instrument;

(G)   curing or waiving of any default;

(H)   extension of a maturity date or a change in an interest rate or other term of outstanding securities;

(I)   amendment of the debtor's charter; or

(J)   issuance of securities of the debtor, or of any entity referred to in subparagraph (B) or (C) of this paragraph, for cash, for property, for existing securities, or in exchange for claims or interests, or for any other appropriate purpose;

(6)   provide for the inclusion in the charter of the debtor, if the debtor is a corporation, or of any corporation referred to in paragraph (5)(B) or (5)(C) of this subsection, of a provision prohibiting the issuance of nonvoting equity securities, and providing, as to the several classes of securities possessing voting power, an appropriate distribution of such power among such classes, including, in the case of any class of equity securities having a preference over another class of equity securities with respect to dividends, adequate provisions for the election of directors representing such preferred class in the event of default in the payment of such dividends;

(7)   contain only provisions that are consistent with the interests of creditors and equity security holders and with public policy with respect to the manner of selection of any officer, director, or trustee under the plan and any successor to such officer, director, or trustee; and

(8)   in a case in which the debtor is an individual, provide for the payment to creditors under the plan of all or such portion of earnings from personal services performed by the debtor after the commencement of the case or other future income of the debtor as is necessary for the execution of the plan.

(b)   Subject to subsection (a) of this section, a plan may—

(1) impair or leave unimpaired any class of claims, secured or unsecured, or of interests;

(2) subject to section 365 of this title, provide for the assumption, rejection, or assignment of any executory contract or unexpired lease of the debtor not previously rejected under such section;

(3) provide for—

(A) the settlement or adjustment of any claim or interest belonging to the debtor or to the estate; or

(B) the retention and enforcement by the debtor, by the trustee, or by a representative of the estate appointed for such purpose, of any such claim or interest;

(4) provide for the sale of all or substantially all of the property of the estate, and the distribution of the proceeds of such sale among holders of claims or interests;

(5) modify the rights of holders of secured claims, other than a claim secured only by a security interest in real property that is the debtor's principal residence, or of holders of unsecured claims, or leave unaffected the rights of holders of any class of claims; and

(6) include any other appropriate provision not inconsistent with the applicable provisions of this title.

(c) In a case concerning an individual, a plan proposed by an entity other than the debtor may not provide for the use, sale, or lease of property exempted under section 522 of this title, unless the debtor consents to such use, sale, or lease.

(d) Notwithstanding subsection (a) of this section and sections 506(b), 1129(a)(7), and 1129(b) of this title, if it is proposed in a plan to cure a default the amount necessary to cure the default shall be determined in accordance with the underlying agreement and applicable nonbankruptcy law.

(Pub.L. 95–598, Nov. 6, 1978, 92 Stat. 2631; Pub.L. 98–353, title III, § 507, July 10, 1984, 98 Stat. 385; Pub.L. 103–394, title II, § 206, title III, §§ 304(h)(6), 305(a), title V, § 501(d)(31), Oct. 22, 1994, 108 Stat. 4123, 4134, 4146; Pub.L. 109–8, title III, § 321(b), title XV, § 1502(a)(7), Apr. 20, 2005, 119 Stat. 95, 216.)

§ 1124. Impairment of claims or interests

Except as provided in section 1123(a)(4) of this title, a class of claims or interests is impaired under a plan unless, with respect to each claim or interest of such class, the plan—

(1) leaves unaltered the legal, equitable, and contractual rights to which such claim or interest entitles the holder of such claim or interest; or

(2) notwithstanding any contractual provision or applicable law that entitles the holder of such claim or interest to demand or receive accelerated payment of such claim or interest after the occurrence of a default—

(A) cures any such default that occurred before or after the commencement of the case under this title, other than a default of a kind specified in section 365(b)(2) of this title or of a kind that section 365(b)(2) expressly does not require to be cured;

(B) reinstates the maturity of such claim or interest as such maturity existed before such default;

(C) compensates the holder of such claim or interest for any damages incurred as a result of any reasonable reliance by such holder on such contractual provision or such applicable law;

(D) if such claim or such interest arises from any failure to perform a nonmonetary obligation, other than a default arising from failure to operate a nonresidential real property lease subject to section 365(b)(1)(A), compensates the holder of such claim or such interest (other than the debtor or an insider) for any actual pecuniary loss incurred by such holder as a result of such failure; and

(E) does not otherwise alter the legal, equitable, or contractual rights to which such claim or interest entitles the holder of such claim or interest.

(Pub.L. 95–598, Nov. 6, 1978, 92 Stat. 2633; Pub.L. 98–353, title III, § 508, July 10, 1984, 98 Stat. 385; Pub.L. 103–394, title II, § 213(d), Oct. 22, 1994, 108 Stat. 4126; Pub.L. 109–8, title III, § 328(b), Apr. 20, 2005, 119 Stat. 100.)

§ 1125.　　Postpetition disclosure and solicitation

(a) In this section—

(1) "adequate information" means information of a kind, and in sufficient detail, as far as is reasonably practicable in light of the nature and history of the debtor and the condition of the debtor's books and records, including a discussion of the potential material Federal tax consequences of the plan to the debtor, any successor to the debtor, and a hypothetical investor typical of the holders of claims or interests in the case, that would enable such a hypothetical investor of the relevant class to make an informed judgment about the plan, but adequate information need not include such information about any other possible or proposed plan and in determining whether a disclosure statement provides adequate information, the court shall consider the complexity of the case, the benefit of additional information to creditors and other parties in interest, and the cost of providing additional information; and

(2) "investor typical of holders of claims or interests of the relevant class" means investor having—

(A) a claim or interest of the relevant class;

(B) such a relationship with the debtor as the holders of other claims or interests of such class generally have; and

(C) such ability to obtain such information from sources other than the disclosure required by this section as holders of claims or interests in such class generally have.

(b) An acceptance or rejection of a plan may not be solicited after the commencement of the case under this title from a holder of a claim or interest with respect to such claim or interest, unless, at the time of or before such solicitation, there is transmitted to such holder the plan or a summary of the plan, and a written disclosure statement approved, after notice and a hearing, by the court as containing adequate information. The court may approve a disclosure statement without a valuation of the debtor or an appraisal of the debtor's assets.

(c) The same disclosure statement shall be transmitted to each holder of a claim or interest of a particular class, but there may be transmitted different disclosure statements, differing in amount, detail, or kind of information, as between classes.

(d) Whether a disclosure statement required under subsection (b) of this section contains adequate information is not governed by any otherwise applicable nonbankruptcy law, rule, or regulation, but an agency or official whose duty is to administer or enforce such a law, rule, or regulation may be heard on the issue of whether a disclosure statement contains adequate information. Such an agency or official may not appeal from, or otherwise seek review of, an order approving a disclosure statement.

(e) A person that solicits acceptance or rejection of a plan, in good faith and in compliance with the applicable provisions of this title, or that participates, in good faith and in compliance with the applicable provisions of this title, in the offer, issuance, sale, or purchase of a security, offered or sold under the plan, of the debtor, of an affiliate participating in a joint plan with the debtor, or of a newly organized successor to the debtor under the plan, is not liable, on account of such solicitation or participation, for violation of any applicable law, rule, or regulation governing solicitation of acceptance or rejection of a plan or the offer, issuance, sale, or purchase of securities.

(f) Notwithstanding subsection (b), in a small business case—

(1) the court may determine that the plan itself provides adequate information and that a separate disclosure statement is not necessary;

(2) the court may approve a disclosure statement submitted on standard forms approved by the court or adopted under section 2075 of title 28; and

(3)(A) the court may conditionally approve a disclosure statement subject to final approval after notice and a hearing;

(B) acceptances and rejections of a plan may be solicited based on a conditionally approved disclosure statement if the debtor provides adequate information to each holder of a claim or interest that is solicited, but a conditionally approved disclosure statement shall be mailed not later than 25 days before the date of the hearing on confirmation of the plan; and

(C) the hearing on the disclosure statement may be combined with the hearing on confirmation of a plan.

(g) Notwithstanding subsection (b), an acceptance or rejection of the plan may be solicited from a holder of a claim or interest if such solicitation complies with applicable nonbankruptcy law and if such holder was solicited before the commencement of the case in a manner complying with applicable nonbankruptcy law.

(Pub.L. 95–598, Nov. 6, 1978, 92 Stat. 2633; Pub.L. 98–353, title III, § 509, July 10, 1984, 98 Stat. 385; Pub.L. 103–394, title II, § 217(e), Oct. 22, 1994, 108 Stat. 4127; Pub.L. 109–8, title IV, §§ 408, 431, title VII, § 717, Apr. 20, 2005, 119 Stat. 106, 109, 131.)

§ 1126.   Acceptance of plan

(a) The holder of a claim or interest allowed under section 502 of this title may accept or reject a plan. If the United States is a creditor or equity security holder, the Secretary of the Treasury may accept or reject the plan on behalf of the United States.

(b) For the purposes of subsections (c) and (d) of this section, a holder of a claim or interest that has accepted or rejected the plan before the commencement of the case under this title is deemed to have accepted or rejected such plan, as the case may be, if—

(1) the solicitation of such acceptance or rejection was in compliance with any applicable nonbankruptcy law, rule, or regulation governing the adequacy of disclosure in connection with such solicitation; or

(2) if there is not any such law, rule, or regulation, such acceptance or rejection was solicited after disclosure to such holder of adequate information, as defined in section 1125(a) of this title.

(c) A class of claims has accepted a plan if such plan has been accepted by creditors, other than any entity designated under subsection (e) of this section, that hold at least two-thirds in amount and more than one-half in number of the allowed claims of such class held by creditors, other than any entity designated under subsection (e) of this section, that have accepted or rejected such plan.

(d) A class of interests has accepted a plan if such plan has been accepted by holders of such interests, other than any entity designated under subsection (e) of this section, that hold at least two-thirds in amount of the allowed interests of such class held by holders of such interests, other than any entity designated under subsection (e) of this section, that have accepted or rejected such plan.

(e) On request of a party in interest, and after notice and a hearing, the court may designate any entity whose acceptance or rejection of such plan was not in good faith, or was not solicited or procured in good faith or in accordance with the provisions of this title.

(f) Notwithstanding any other provision of this section, a class that is not impaired under a plan, and each holder of a claim or interest of such class, are conclusively presumed to have accepted the plan, and solicitation of acceptances with respect to such class from the holders of claims or interests of such class is not required.

(g) Notwithstanding any other provision of this section, a class is deemed not to have accepted a plan if such plan provides that the claims or interests of such class do not entitle the holders of such claims or interests to receive or retain any property under the plan on account of such claims or interests.

(Pub.L. 95–598, Nov. 6, 1978, 92 Stat. 2634; Pub.L. 98–353, title III, § 510, July 10, 1984, 98 Stat. 386.)

§ 1127.   Modification of plan

(a) The proponent of a plan may modify such plan at any time before confirmation, but may not modify such plan so that such plan as modified fails to meet the requirements of sections 1122 and 1123 of this title. After the proponent of a plan files a modification of such plan with the court, the plan as modified becomes the plan.

(b) The proponent of a plan or the reorganized debtor may modify such plan at any time after confirmation of such plan and before substantial consummation of such plan, but may not modify such plan so that such plan as modified fails to meet the requirements of sections 1122 and 1123 of this title. Such plan as modified under this subsection becomes the plan only if circumstances warrant such modification and the court, after notice and a hearing, confirms such plan as modified, under section 1129 of this title.

(c) The proponent of a modification shall comply with section 1125 of this title with respect to the plan as modified.

(d) Any holder of a claim or interest that has accepted or rejected a plan is deemed to have accepted or rejected, as the case may be, such plan as modified, unless, within the time fixed by the court, such holder changes such holder's previous acceptance or rejection.

(e) If the debtor is an individual, the plan may be modified at any time after confirmation of the plan but before the completion of payments under the plan, whether or not the plan has been substantially consummated, upon request of the debtor, the trustee, the United States trustee, or the holder of an allowed unsecured claim, to—

     (1) increase or reduce the amount of payments on claims of a particular class provided for by the plan;

     (2) extend or reduce the time period for such payments; or

     (3) alter the amount of the distribution to a creditor whose claim is provided for by the plan to the extent necessary to take account of any payment of such claim made other than under the plan.

(f)(1) Sections 1121 through 1128 and the requirements of section 1129 apply to any modification under subsection (e).

     (2) The plan, as modified, shall become the plan only after there has been disclosure under section 1125 as the court may direct, notice and a hearing, and such modification is approved.

(Pub.L. 95–598, Nov. 6, 1978, 92 Stat. 2635; Pub.L. 98–353, title III, § 511, July 10, 1984, 98 Stat. 386; Pub.L. 109–8, title III, § 321(e), Apr. 20, 2005, 119 Stat. 96; Pub.L. 111–327, § 2(a)(34), Dec. 22, 2010, 124 Stat. 3561.)

§ 1128.   Confirmation hearing

(a) After notice, the court shall hold a hearing on confirmation of a plan.

(b) A party in interest may object to confirmation of a plan.

(Pub.L. 95–598, Nov. 6, 1978, 92 Stat. 2635.)

§ 1129.   Confirmation of plan

(a) The court shall confirm a plan only if all of the following requirements are met:

     (1) The plan complies with the applicable provisions of this title.

     (2) The proponent of the plan complies with the applicable provisions of this title.

     (3) The plan has been proposed in good faith and not by any means forbidden by law.

     (4) Any payment made or to be made by the proponent, by the debtor, or by a person issuing securities or acquiring property under the plan, for services or for costs and expenses in or in connection with the case, or in connection with the plan and incident to the case, has been approved by, or is subject to the approval of, the court as reasonable.

(5)(A)(i) The proponent of the plan has disclosed the identity and affiliations of any individual proposed to serve, after confirmation of the plan, as a director, officer, or voting trustee of the debtor, an affiliate of the debtor participating in a joint plan with the debtor, or a successor to the debtor under the plan; and

      (ii) the appointment to, or continuance in, such office of such individual, is consistent with the interests of creditors and equity security holders and with public policy; and

(B) the proponent of the plan has disclosed the identity of any insider that will be employed or retained by the reorganized debtor, and the nature of any compensation for such insider.

(6) Any governmental regulatory commission with jurisdiction, after confirmation of the plan, over the rates of the debtor has approved any rate change provided for in the plan, or such rate change is expressly conditioned on such approval.

(7) With respect to each impaired class of claims or interests—

(A) each holder of a claim or interest of such class—

      (i) has accepted the plan; or

      (ii) will receive or retain under the plan on account of such claim or interest property of a value, as of the effective date of the plan, that is not less than the amount that such holder would so receive or retain if the debtor were liquidated under chapter 7 of this title on such date; or

(B) if section 1111(b)(2) of this title applies to the claims of such class, each holder of a claim of such class will receive or retain under the plan on account of such claim property of a value, as of the effective date of the plan, that is not less than the value of such holder's interest in the estate's interest in the property that secures such claims.

(8) With respect to each class of claims or interests—

(A) such class has accepted the plan; or

(B) such class is not impaired under the plan.

(9) Except to the extent that the holder of a particular claim has agreed to a different treatment of such claim, the plan provides that—

(A) with respect to a claim of a kind specified in section 507(a)(2) or 507(a)(3) of this title, on the effective date of the plan, the holder of such claim will receive on account of such claim cash equal to the allowed amount of such claim;

(B) with respect to a class of claims of a kind specified in section 507(a)(1), 507(a)(4), 507(a)(5), 507(a)(6), or 507(a)(7) of this title, each holder of a claim of such class will receive—

      (i) if such class has accepted the plan, deferred cash payments of a value, as of the effective date of the plan, equal to the allowed amount of such claim; or

      (ii) if such class has not accepted the plan, cash on the effective date of the plan equal to the allowed amount of such claim;

(C) with respect to a claim of a kind specified in section 507(a)(8) of this title, the holder of such claim will receive on account of such claim regular installment payments in cash—

      (i) of a total value, as of the effective date of the plan, equal to the allowed amount of such claim;

      (ii) over a period ending not later than 5 years after the date of the order for relief under section 301, 302, or 303; and

       (iii) in a manner not less favorable than the most favored nonpriority unsecured claim provided for by the plan (other than cash payments made to a class of creditors under section 1122(b)); and

       (D) with respect to a secured claim which would otherwise meet the description of an unsecured claim of a governmental unit under section 507(a)(8), but for the secured status of that claim, the holder of that claim will receive on account of that claim, cash payments, in the same manner and over the same period, as prescribed in subparagraph (C).

    (10) If a class of claims is impaired under the plan, at least one class of claims that is impaired under the plan has accepted the plan, determined without including any acceptance of the plan by any insider.

    (11) Confirmation of the plan is not likely to be followed by the liquidation, or the need for further financial reorganization, of the debtor or any successor to the debtor under the plan, unless such liquidation or reorganization is proposed in the plan.

    (12) All fees payable under section 1930 of title 28, as determined by the court at the hearing on confirmation of the plan, have been paid or the plan provides for the payment of all such fees on the effective date of the plan.

    (13) The plan provides for the continuation after its effective date of payment of all retiree benefits, as that term is defined in section 1114 of this title, at the level established pursuant to subsection (e)(1)(B) or (g) of section 1114 of this title, at any time prior to confirmation of the plan, for the duration of the period the debtor has obligated itself to provide such benefits.

    (14) If the debtor is required by a judicial or administrative order, or by statute, to pay a domestic support obligation, the debtor has paid all amounts payable under such order or such statute for such obligation that first become payable after the date of the filing of the petition.

    (15) In a case in which the debtor is an individual and in which the holder of an allowed unsecured claim objects to the confirmation of the plan—

       (A) the value, as of the effective date of the plan, of the property to be distributed under the plan on account of such claim is not less than the amount of such claim; or

       (B) the value of the property to be distributed under the plan is not less than the projected disposable income of the debtor (as defined in section 1325(b)(2)) to be received during the 5-year period beginning on the date that the first payment is due under the plan, or during the period for which the plan provides payments, whichever is longer.

    (16) All transfers of property under the plan shall be made in accordance with any applicable provisions of nonbankruptcy law that govern the transfer of property by a corporation or trust that is not a moneyed, business, or commercial corporation or trust.

  (b)(1) Notwithstanding section 510(a) of this title, if all of the applicable requirements of subsection (a) of this section other than paragraph (8) are met with respect to a plan, the court, on request of the proponent of the plan, shall confirm the plan notwithstanding the requirements of such paragraph if the plan does not discriminate unfairly, and is fair and equitable, with respect to each class of claims or interests that is impaired under, and has not accepted, the plan.

    (2) For the purpose of this subsection, the condition that a plan be fair and equitable with respect to a class includes the following requirements:

       (A) With respect to a class of secured claims, the plan provides—

         (i)(I) that the holders of such claims retain the liens securing such claims, whether the property subject to such liens is retained by the debtor or transferred to another entity, to the extent of the allowed amount of such claims; and

         (II) that each holder of a claim of such class receive on account of such claim deferred cash payments totaling at least the allowed amount of such claim, of a value, as of the effective date of the plan, of at least the value of such holder's interest in the estate's interest in such property;

    (ii) for the sale, subject to section 363(k) of this title, of any property that is subject to the liens securing such claims, free and clear of such liens, with such liens to attach to the proceeds of such sale, and the treatment of such liens on proceeds under clause (i) or (iii) of this subparagraph; or

    (iii) for the realization by such holders of the indubitable equivalent of such claims.

  (B) With respect to a class of unsecured claims—

    (i) the plan provides that each holder of a claim of such class receive or retain on account of such claim property of a value, as of the effective date of the plan, equal to the allowed amount of such claim; or

    (ii) the holder of any claim or interest that is junior to the claims of such class will not receive or retain under the plan on account of such junior claim or interest any property, except that in a case in which the debtor is an individual, the debtor may retain property included in the estate under section 1115, subject to the requirements of subsection (a)(14) of this section.

  (C) With respect to a class of interests—

    (i) the plan provides that each holder of an interest of such class receive or retain on account of such interest property of a value, as of the effective date of the plan, equal to the greatest of the allowed amount of any fixed liquidation preference to which such holder is entitled, any fixed redemption price to which such holder is entitled, or the value of such interest; or

    (ii) the holder of any interest that is junior to the interests of such class will not receive or retain under the plan on account of such junior interest any property.

  (c) Notwithstanding subsections (a) and (b) of this section and except as provided in section 1127(b) of this title, the court may confirm only one plan, unless the order of confirmation in the case has been revoked under section 1144 of this title. If the requirements of subsections (a) and (b) of this section are met with respect to more than one plan, the court shall consider the preferences of creditors and equity security holders in determining which plan to confirm.

  (d) Notwithstanding any other provision of this section, on request of a party in interest that is a governmental unit, the court may not confirm a plan if the principal purpose of the plan is the avoidance of taxes or the avoidance of the application of section 5 of the Securities Act of 1933. In any hearing under this subsection, the governmental unit has the burden of proof on the issue of avoidance.

  (e) In a small business case, the court shall confirm a plan that complies with the applicable provisions of this title and that is filed in accordance with section 1121(e) not later than 45 days after the plan is filed unless the time for confirmation is extended in accordance with section 1121(e)(3).

    (Pub.L. 95–598, Nov. 6, 1978, 92 Stat. 2635; Pub.L. 98–353, title III, § 512, July 10, 1984, 98 Stat. 386; Pub.L. 99–554, title II, §§ 225, 283(v), Oct. 27, 1986, 100 Stat. 3102, 3118; Pub.L. 100–334, § 2(b), June 16, 1988, 102 Stat. 613; Pub.L. 103–394, title III, § 304(h)(7), title V, § 501(d)(32), Oct. 22, 1994, 108 Stat. 4134, 4146; Pub.L. 109–8, title II, § 213(1), title III, § 321(c), title IV, § 438, title VII, § 710, title XII, § 1221(b), title XV, § 1502(a)(8), Apr. 20, 2005, 119 Stat. 52, 95, 113, 127, 196, 216; Pub.L. 111–327, § 2(a)(35), Dec. 22, 2010, 124 Stat. 3561.)

SUBCHAPTER III—POSTCONFIRMATION MATTERS

§ 1141.   Effect of confirmation

  (a) Except as provided in subsections (d)(2) and (d)(3) of this section, the provisions of a confirmed plan bind the debtor, any entity issuing securities under the plan, any entity acquiring property under the plan, and any creditor, equity security holder, or general partner in the debtor, whether or not the claim or interest of such creditor, equity security holder, or general partner is impaired under the plan and whether or not such creditor, equity security holder, or general partner has accepted the plan.

(b)   Except as otherwise provided in the plan or the order confirming the plan, the confirmation of a plan vests all of the property of the estate in the debtor.

(c)   Except as provided in subsections (d)(2) and (d)(3) of this section and except as otherwise provided in the plan or in the order confirming the plan, after confirmation of a plan, the property dealt with by the plan is free and clear of all claims and interests of creditors, equity security holders, and of general partners in the debtor.

(d)(1)   Except as otherwise provided in this subsection, in the plan, or in the order confirming the plan, the confirmation of a plan—

     (A)   discharges the debtor from any debt that arose before the date of such confirmation, and any debt of a kind specified in section 502(g), 502(h), or 502(i) of this title, whether or not—

         (i)   a proof of the claim based on such debt is filed or deemed filed under section 501 of this title;

         (ii)   such claim is allowed under section 502 of this title; or

         (iii)   the holder of such claim has accepted the plan; and

     (B)   terminates all rights and interests of equity security holders and general partners provided for by the plan.

(2)   A discharge under this chapter does not discharge a debtor who is an individual from any debt excepted from discharge under section 523 of this title.

(3)   The confirmation of a plan does not discharge a debtor if—

     (A)   the plan provides for the liquidation of all or substantially all of the property of the estate;

     (B)   the debtor does not engage in business after consummation of the plan; and

     (C)   the debtor would be denied a discharge under section 727(a) of this title if the case were a case under chapter 7 of this title.

(4)   The court may approve a written waiver of discharge executed by the debtor after the order for relief under this chapter.

(5)   In a case in which the debtor is an individual—

     (A)   unless after notice and a hearing the court orders otherwise for cause, confirmation of the plan does not discharge any debt provided for in the plan until the court grants a discharge on completion of all payments under the plan;

     (B)   at any time after the confirmation of the plan, and after notice and a hearing, the court may grant a discharge to the debtor who has not completed payments under the plan if—

         (i)   the value, as of the effective date of the plan, of property actually distributed under the plan on account of each allowed unsecured claim is not less than the amount that would have been paid on such claim if the estate of the debtor had been liquidated under chapter 7 on such date;

         (ii)   modification of the plan under section 1127 is not practicable; and

         (iii)   subparagraph (C) permits the court to grant a discharge; and

     (C)   the court may grant a discharge if, after notice and a hearing held not more than 10 days before the date of the entry of the order granting the discharge, the court finds that there is no reasonable cause to believe that—

         (i)   section 522(q)(1) may be applicable to the debtor; and

(ii) there is pending any proceeding in which the debtor may be found guilty of a felony of the kind described in section 522(q)(1)(A) or liable for a debt of the kind described in section 522(q)(1)(B);

and if the requirements of subparagraph (A) or (B) are met.

(6) Notwithstanding paragraph (1), the confirmation of a plan does not discharge a debtor that is a corporation from any debt—

(A) of a kind specified in paragraph (2)(A) or (2)(B) of section 523(a) that is owed to a domestic governmental unit, or owed to a person as the result of an action filed under subchapter III of chapter 37 of title 31 or any similar State statute; or

(B) for a tax or customs duty with respect to which the debtor—

(i) made a fraudulent return; or

(ii) willfully attempted in any manner to evade or to defeat such tax or such customs duty.

(Pub.L. 95–598, Nov. 6, 1978, 92 Stat. 2638; Pub.L. 98–353, title III, § 513, July 10, 1984, 98 Stat. 387; Pub.L. 109–8, title III, §§ 321(d), 330(b), title VII, § 708, Apr. 20, 2005, 119 Stat. 95, 101, 126; Pub.L. 111–327, § 2(a)(36) Dec. 22, 2010, 124 Stat. 3561.)

§ 1142. Implementation of plan

(a) Notwithstanding any otherwise applicable nonbankruptcy law, rule, or regulation relating to financial condition, the debtor and any entity organized or to be organized for the purpose of carrying out the plan shall carry out the plan and shall comply with any orders of the court.

(b) The court may direct the debtor and any other necessary party to execute or deliver or to join in the execution or delivery of any instrument required to effect a transfer of property dealt with by a confirmed plan, and to perform any other act, including the satisfaction of any lien, that is necessary for the consummation of the plan.

(Pub.L. 95–598, Nov. 6, 1978, 92 Stat. 2639; Pub.L. 98–353, title III, § 514(a), (c), (d), July 10, 1984, 98 Stat. 387.)

§ 1143. Distribution

If a plan requires presentment or surrender of a security or the performance of any other act as a condition to participation in distribution under the plan, such action shall be taken not later than five years after the date of the entry of the order of confirmation. Any entity that has not within such time presented or surrendered such entity's security or taken any such other action that the plan requires may not participate in distribution under the plan.

(Pub.L. 95–598, Nov. 6, 1978, 92 Stat. 2639.)

§ 1144. Revocation of an order of confirmation

On request of a party in interest at any time before 180 days after the date of the entry of the order of confirmation, and after notice and a hearing, the court may revoke such order if and only if such order was procured by fraud. An order under this section revoking an order of confirmation shall—

(1) contain such provisions as are necessary to protect any entity acquiring rights in good faith reliance on the order of confirmation; and

(2) revoke the discharge of the debtor.

(Pub.L. 95–598, Nov. 6, 1978, 92 Stat. 2639; Pub.L. 98–353, title III, § 515, July 10, 1984, 98 Stat. 387.)

§ 1145.   Exemption from securities laws

(a) Except with respect to an entity that is an underwriter as defined in subsection (b) of this section, section 5 of the Securities Act of 1933 and any State or local law requiring registration for offer or sale of a security or registration or licensing of an issuer of, underwriter of, or broker or dealer in, a security do not apply to—

    (1) the offer or sale under a plan of a security of the debtor, of an affiliate participating in a joint plan with the debtor, or of a successor to the debtor under the plan—

        (A) in exchange for a claim against, an interest in, or a claim for an administrative expense in the case concerning, the debtor or such affiliate; or

        (B) principally in such exchange and partly for cash or property;

    (2) the offer of a security through any warrant, option, right to subscribe, or conversion privilege that was sold in the manner specified in paragraph (1) of this subsection, or the sale of a security upon the exercise of such a warrant, option, right, or privilege;

    (3) the offer or sale, other than under a plan, of a security of an issuer other than the debtor or an affiliate, if—

        (A) such security was owned by the debtor on the date of the filing of the petition;

        (B) the issuer of such security is—

            (i) required to file reports under section 13 or 15(d) of the Securities Exchange Act of 1934; and

            (ii) in compliance with the disclosure and reporting provision of such applicable section; and

        (C) such offer or sale is of securities that do not exceed—

            (i) during the two-year period immediately following the date of the filing of the petition, four percent of the securities of such class outstanding on such date; and

            (ii) during any 180-day period following such two-year period, one percent of the securities outstanding at the beginning of such 180-day period; or

    (4) a transaction by a stockbroker in a security that is executed after a transaction of a kind specified in paragraph (1) or (2) of this subsection in such security and before the expiration of 40 days after the first date on which such security was bona fide offered to the public by the issuer or by or through an underwriter, if such stockbroker provides, at the time of or before such transaction by such stockbroker, a disclosure statement approved under section 1125 of this title, and, if the court orders, information supplementing such disclosure statement.

(b)(1) Except as provided in paragraph (2) of this subsection and except with respect to ordinary trading transactions of an entity that is not an issuer, an entity is an underwriter under section 2(a)(11) of the Securities Act of 1933, if such entity—

        (A) purchases a claim against, interest in, or claim for an administrative expense in the case concerning, the debtor, if such purchase is with a view to distribution of any security received or to be received in exchange for such a claim or interest;

        (B) offers to sell securities offered or sold under the plan for the holders of such securities;

        (C) offers to buy securities offered or sold under the plan from the holders of such securities, if such offer to buy is—

            (i) with a view to distribution of such securities; and

            (ii) under an agreement made in connection with the plan, with the consummation of the plan, or with the offer or sale of securities under the plan; or

        (D) is an issuer, as used in such section 2(a)(11), with respect to such securities.

(2) An entity is not an underwriter under section 2(a)(11) of the Securities Act of 1933 or under paragraph (1) of this subsection with respect to an agreement that provides only for—

(A)(i) the matching or combining of fractional interests in securities offered or sold under the plan into whole interests; or

(ii) the purchase or sale of such fractional interests from or to entities receiving such fractional interests under the plan; or

(B) the purchase or sale for such entities of such fractional or whole interests as are necessary to adjust for any remaining fractional interests after such matching.

(3) An entity other than an entity of the kind specified in paragraph (1) of this subsection is not an underwriter under section 2(a)(11) of the Securities Act of 1933 with respect to any securities offered or sold to such entity in the manner specified in subsection (a)(1) of this section.

(c) An offer or sale of securities of the kind and in the manner specified under subsection (a)(1) of this section is deemed to be a public offering.

(d) The Trust Indenture Act of 1939 does not apply to a note issued under the plan that matures not later than one year after the effective date of the plan.

(Pub.L. 95–598, Nov. 6, 1978, 92 Stat. 2639; Pub.L. 98–353, title III, § 516, July 10, 1984, 98 Stat. 387; Pub.L. 103–394, title V, § 501(d)(33), Oct. 22, 1994, 108 Stat. 4146; Pub.L. 111–327, § 2(a)(37), Dec. 22, 2010, 124 Stat. 3561.)

§ 1146.   Special tax provisions

(a) The issuance, transfer, or exchange of a security, or the making or delivery of an instrument of transfer under a plan confirmed under section 1129 of this title, may not be taxed under any law imposing a stamp tax or similar tax.

(b) The court may authorize the proponent of a plan to request a determination, limited to questions of law, by a State or local governmental unit charged with responsibility for collection or determination of a tax on or measured by income, of the tax effects, under section 346 of this title and under the law imposing such tax, of the plan. In the event of an actual controversy, the court may declare such effects after the earlier of—

(1) the date on which such governmental unit responds to the request under this subsection; or

(2) 270 days after such request.

(Pub.L. 95–598, Nov. 6, 1978, 92 Stat. 2641; Pub.L. 98–353, title III, § 517, July 10, 1984, 98 Stat. 388; Pub.L. 109–8, title VII, § 719(b)(3), Apr. 20, 2005, 119 Stat. 133.)

SUBCHAPTER IV—RAILROAD REORGANIZATION

§ 1161.   Inapplicability of other sections

Sections 341, 343, 1102(a)(1), 1104, 1105, 1107, 1129(a)(7), and 1129(c) of this title do not apply in a case concerning a railroad.

(Pub.L. 95–598, Nov. 6, 1978, 92 Stat. 2641.)

§ 1162.   Definition

In this subchapter, "Board" means the "Surface Transportation Board".

(Added Pub.L. 104–88, title III, § 302(1), Dec. 29, 1995, 109 Stat. 943.)

§ 1163.   Appointment of trustee

As soon as practicable after the order for relief the Secretary of Transportation shall submit a list of five disinterested persons that are qualified and willing to serve as trustees in the case. The United States trustee shall appoint one of such persons to serve as trustee in the case.

(Pub.L. 95–598, Nov. 6, 1978, 92 Stat. 2641; Pub.L. 99–554, title II, § 226, Oct. 27, 1986, 100 Stat. 3102.)

§ 1164.   Right to be heard

The Board, the Department of Transportation, and any State or local commission having regulatory jurisdiction over the debtor may raise and may appear and be heard on any issue in a case under this chapter, but may not appeal from any judgment, order, or decree entered in the case.

(Pub.L. 95–598, Nov. 6, 1978, 92 Stat. 2641; Pub.L. 104–88, title III, § 302(2), Dec. 29, 1995, 109 Stat. 943.)

§ 1165.   Protection of the public interest

In applying sections 1166, 1167, 1169, 1170, 1171, 1172, 1173, and 1174 of this title, the court and the trustee shall consider the public interest in addition to the interests of the debtor, creditors, and equity security holders.

(Pub.L. 95–598, Nov. 6, 1978, 92 Stat. 2641.)

§ 1166.   Effect of subtitle IV of title 49 and of Federal, State, or local regulations

Except with respect to abandonment under section 1170 of this title, or merger, modification of the financial structure of the debtor, or issuance or sale of securities under a plan, the trustee and the debtor are subject to the provisions of subtitle IV of title 49 that are applicable to railroads, and the trustee is subject to orders of any Federal, State, or local regulatory body to the same extent as the debtor would be if a petition commencing the case under this chapter had not been filed, but—

(1)   any such order that would require the expenditure, or the incurring of an obligation for the expenditure, of money from the estate is not effective unless approved by the court; and

(2)   the provisions of this chapter are subject to section 601(b) of the Regional Rail Reorganization Act of 1973.

(Pub.L. 95–598, Nov. 6, 1978, 92 Stat. 2642; Pub.L. 97–449, § 5(a)(2), Jan. 12, 1983, 96 Stat. 2442; Pub.L. 98–353, title III, § 518, July 10, 1984, 98 Stat. 388; Pub.L. 103–394, title V, § 501(d)(34), Oct. 22, 1994, 108 Stat. 4146.)

§ 1167.   Collective bargaining agreements

Notwithstanding section 365 of this title, neither the court nor the trustee may change the wages or working conditions of employees of the debtor established by a collective bargaining agreement that is subject to the Railway Labor Act except in accordance with section 6 of such Act.

(Pub.L. 95–598, Nov. 6, 1978, 92 Stat. 2642; Pub.L. 103–394, title V, § 501(d)(35), Oct. 22, 1994, 108 Stat. 4146.)

§ 1168.   Rolling stock equipment

(a)(1)   The right of a secured party with a security interest in or of a lessor or conditional vendor of equipment described in paragraph (2) to take possession of such equipment in compliance with an equipment security agreement, lease, or conditional sale contract, and to enforce any of its other rights or remedies under such security agreement, lease, or conditional sale contract, to sell, lease, or otherwise retain or dispose of such equipment, is not limited or otherwise affected by any other provision of this title or by any power of the court, except that right to take possession and enforce those other rights and remedies shall be subject to section 362, if—

(A) before the date that is 60 days after the date of commencement of a case under this chapter, the trustee, subject to the court's approval, agrees to perform all obligations of the debtor under such security agreement, lease, or conditional sale contract; and

(B) any default, other than a default of a kind described in section 365(b)(2), under such security agreement, lease, or conditional sale contract—

(i) that occurs before the date of commencement of the case and is an event of default therewith is cured before the expiration of such 60-day period;

(ii) that occurs or becomes an event of default after the date of commencement of the case and before the expiration of such 60-day period is cured before the later of—

(I) the date that is 30 days after the date of the default or event of the default; or

(II) the expiration of such 60-day period; and

(iii) that occurs on or after the expiration of such 60-day period is cured in accordance with the terms of such security agreement, lease, or conditional sale contract, if cure is permitted under that agreement, lease, or conditional sale contract.

(2) The equipment described in this paragraph—

(A) is rolling stock equipment or accessories used on rolling stock equipment, including superstructures or racks, that is subject to a security interest granted by, leased to, or conditionally sold to a debtor; and

(B) includes all records and documents relating to such equipment that are required, under the terms of the security agreement, lease, or conditional sale contract, that is to be surrendered or returned by the debtor in connection with the surrender or return of such equipment.

(3) Paragraph (1) applies to a secured party, lessor, or conditional vendor acting in its own behalf or acting as trustee or otherwise in behalf of another party.

(b) The trustee and the secured party, lessor, or conditional vendor whose right to take possession is protected under subsection (a) may agree, subject to the court's approval, to extend the 60-day period specified in subsection (a)(1).

(c)(1) In any case under this chapter, the trustee shall immediately surrender and return to a secured party, lessor, or conditional vendor, described in subsection (a)(1), equipment described in subsection (a)(2), if at any time after the date of commencement of the case under this chapter such secured party, lessor, or conditional vendor is entitled pursuant to subsection (a)(1) to take possession of such equipment and makes a written demand for such possession of the trustee.

(2) At such time as the trustee is required under paragraph (1) to surrender and return equipment described in subsection (a)(2), any lease of such equipment, and any security agreement or conditional sale contract relating to such equipment, if such security agreement or conditional sale contract is an executory contract, shall be deemed rejected.

(d) With respect to equipment first placed in service on or prior to October 22, 1994, for purposes of this section—

(1) the term "lease" includes any written agreement with respect to which the lessor and the debtor, as lessee, have expressed in the agreement or in a substantially contemporaneous writing that the agreement is to be treated as a lease for Federal income tax purposes; and

(2) the term "security interest" means a purchase-money equipment security interest.

(e) With respect to equipment first placed in service after October 22, 1994, for purposes of this section, the term "rolling stock equipment" includes rolling stock equipment that is substantially rebuilt and accessories used on such equipment.

(Pub.L. 95–598, Nov. 6, 1978, 92 Stat. 2642; Pub.L. 98–353, title III, § 519, July 10, 1984, 98 Stat. 388; Pub.L. 103–394, title II, § 201(b), Oct. 22, 1994, 108 Stat. 4120; Pub.L. 106–181, title VII, § 744(a), Apr. 5, 2000, 114 Stat. 175.)

§ 1169.　　Effect of rejection of lease of railroad line

(a)　Except as provided in subsection (b) of this section, if a lease of a line of railroad under which the debtor is the lessee is rejected under section 365 of this title, and if the trustee, within such time as the court fixes, and with the court's approval, elects not to operate the leased line, the lessor under such lease, after such approval, shall operate the line.

(b)　If operation of such line by such lessor is impracticable or contrary to the public interest, the court, on request of such lessor, and after notice and a hearing, shall order the trustee to continue operation of such line for the account of such lessor until abandonment is ordered under section 1170 of this title, or until such operation is otherwise lawfully terminated, whichever occurs first.

(c)　During any such operation, such lessor is deemed a carrier subject to the provisions of subtitle IV of title 49 that are applicable to railroads.

(Pub.L. 95–598, Nov. 6, 1978, 92 Stat. 2643; Pub.L. 97–449, § 5(a)(3), Jan. 12, 1983, 96 Stat. 2442; Pub.L. 98–353, title III, § 520, July 10, 1984, 98 Stat. 388.)

§ 1170.　　Abandonment of railroad line

(a)　The court, after notice and a hearing, may authorize the abandonment of all or a portion of a railroad line if such abandonment is—

(1)(A)　in the best interest of the estate; or

(B)　essential to the formulation of a plan; and

(2)　consistent with the public interest.

(b)　If, except for the pendency of the case under this chapter, such abandonment would require approval by the Board under a law of the United States, the trustee shall initiate an appropriate application for such abandonment with the Board. The court may fix a time within which the Board shall report to the court on such application.

(c)　After the court receives the report of the Board, or the expiration of the time fixed under subsection (b) of this section, whichever occurs first, the court may authorize such abandonment, after notice to the Board, the Secretary of Transportation, the trustee, any party in interest that has requested notice, any affected shipper or community, and any other entity prescribed by the court, and a hearing.

(d)(1)　Enforcement of an order authorizing such abandonment shall be stayed until the time for taking an appeal has expired, or, if an appeal is timely taken, until such order has become final.

(2)　If an order authorizing such abandonment is appealed, the court, on request of a party in interest, may authorize suspension of service on a line or a portion of a line pending the determination of such appeal, after notice to the Board, the Secretary of Transportation, the trustee, any party in interest that has requested notice, any affected shipper or community, and any other entity prescribed by the court, and a hearing. An appellant may not obtain a stay of the enforcement of an order authorizing such suspension by the giving of a supersedeas bond or otherwise, during the pendency of such appeal.

(e)(1)　In authorizing any abandonment of a railroad line under this section, the court shall require the rail carrier to provide a fair arrangement at least as protective of the interests of employees as that established under section 11326(a) of title 49.

(2)　Nothing in this subsection shall be deemed to affect the priorities or timing of payment of employee protection which might have existed in the absence of this subsection.

(Pub.L. 95–598, Nov. 6, 1978, 92 Stat. 2643; Pub.L. 96–448, title II, § 227(a), Oct. 14, 1980, 94 Stat. 1931; Pub.L. 98–353, title III, § 521, July 10, 1984, 98 Stat. 388; Pub.L. 104–88, title III, § 302(2), Dec. 29, 1995, 109 Stat. 943; Pub.L. 109–8, title XII, § 1217, Apr. 20, 2005, 119 Stat. 195.)

§ 1171.   Priority claims

(a)   There shall be paid as an administrative expense any claim of an individual or of the personal representative of a deceased individual against the debtor or the estate, for personal injury to or death of such individual arising out of the operation of the debtor or the estate, whether such claim arose before or after the commencement of the case.

(b)   Any unsecured claim against the debtor that would have been entitled to priority if a receiver in equity of the property of the debtor had been appointed by a Federal court on the date of the order for relief under this title shall be entitled to the same priority in the case under this chapter.

(Pub.L. 95–598, Nov. 6, 1978, 92 Stat. 2643; Pub.L. 98–353, title III, § 522, July 10, 1984, 98 Stat. 388.)

§ 1172.   Contents of plan

(a)   In addition to the provisions required or permitted under section 1123 of this title, a plan—

(1)   shall specify the extent to and the means by which the debtor's rail service is proposed to be continued, and the extent to which any of the debtor's rail service is proposed to be terminated; and

(2)   may include a provision for—

(A)   the transfer of any or all of the operating railroad lines of the debtor to another operating railroad; or

(B)   abandonment of any railroad line in accordance with section 1170 of this title.

(b)   If, except for the pendency of the case under this chapter, transfer of, or operation of or over, any of the debtor's rail lines by an entity other than the debtor or a successor to the debtor under the plan would require approval by the Board under a law of the United States, then a plan may not propose such a transfer or such operation unless the proponent of the plan initiates an appropriate application for such a transfer or such operation with the Board and, within such time as the court may fix, not exceeding 180 days, the Board, with or without a hearing, as the Board may determine, and with or without modification or condition, approves such application, or does not act on such application. Any action or order of the Board approving, modifying, conditioning, or disapproving such application is subject to review by the court only under sections 706(2)(A), 706(2)(B), 706(2)(C), and 706(2)(D) of title 5.

(c)(1)   In approving an application under subsection (b) of this section, the Board shall require the rail carrier to provide a fair arrangement at least as protective of the interests of employees as that established under section 11326(a) of title 49.

(2)   Nothing in this subsection shall be deemed to affect the priorities or timing of payment of employee protection which might have existed in the absence of this subsection.

(Pub.L. 95–598, Nov. 6, 1978, 92 Stat. 2644; Pub.L. 96–448, title II, § 227(b), Oct. 14, 1980, 94 Stat. 1931; Pub.L. 104–88, title III, § 302(2), Dec. 29, 1995, 109 Stat. 943; Pub.L. 109–8, title XII, § 1218, Apr. 20, 2005, 119 Stat. 195.)

§ 1173.   Confirmation of plan

(a)   The court shall confirm a plan if—

(1)   the applicable requirements of section 1129 of this title have been met;

(2)   each creditor or equity security holder will receive or retain under the plan property of a value, as of the effective date of the plan, that is not less than the value of property that each such creditor or equity security holder would so receive or retain if all of the operating railroad lines of the debtor were sold, and the proceeds of such sale, and the other property of the estate, were distributed under chapter 7 of this title on such date;

    (3) in light of the debtor's past earnings and the probable prospective earnings of the reorganized debtor, there will be adequate coverage by such prospective earnings of any fixed charges, such as interest on debt, amortization of funded debt, and rent for leased railroads, provided for by the plan; and

    (4) the plan is consistent with the public interest.

  (b) If the requirements of subsection (a) of this section are met with respect to more than one plan, the court shall confirm the plan that is most likely to maintain adequate rail service in the public interest.

    (Pub.L. 95–598, Nov. 6, 1978, 92 Stat. 2644; Pub.L. 98–353, title III, § 523, July 10, 1984, 98 Stat. 388.)

§ 1174.   Liquidation

  On request of a party in interest and after notice and a hearing, the court may, or, if a plan has not been confirmed under section 1173 of this title before five years after the date of the order for relief, the court shall, order the trustee to cease the debtor's operation and to collect and reduce to money all of the property of the estate in the same manner as if the case were a case under chapter 7 of this title.

    (Pub.L. 95–598, Nov. 6, 1978, 92 Stat. 2644.)

CHAPTER 12—ADJUSTMENT OF DEBTS OF A FAMILY FARMER OR FISHERMAN WITH REGULAR ANNUAL INCOME

SUBCHAPTER I—OFFICERS, ADMINISTRATION, AND THE ESTATE

SUBCHAPTER II—THE PLAN

SUBCHAPTER I—OFFICERS, ADMINISTRATION, AND THE ESTATE

§ 1201.   Stay of action against codebtor

  (a) Except as provided in subsections (b) and (c) of this section, after the order for relief under this chapter, a creditor may not act, or commence or continue any civil action, to collect all or any part of a consumer debt of the debtor from any individual that is liable on such debt with the debtor, or that secured such debt, unless—

   (1)   such individual became liable on or secured such debt in the ordinary course of such individual's business; or

   (2)   the case is closed, dismissed, or converted to a case under chapter 7 of this title.

   (b)   A creditor may present a negotiable instrument, and may give notice of dishonor of such an instrument.

   (c)   On request of a party in interest and after notice and a hearing, the court shall grant relief from the stay provided by subsection (a) of this section with respect to a creditor, to the extent that—

   (1)   as between the debtor and the individual protected under subsection (a) of this section, such individual received the consideration for the claim held by such creditor;

   (2)   the plan filed by the debtor proposes not to pay such claim; or

   (3)   such creditor's interest would be irreparably harmed by continuation of such stay.

   (d)   Twenty days after the filing of a request under subsection (c)(2) of this section for relief from the stay provided by subsection (a) of this section, such stay is terminated with respect to the party in interest making such request, unless the debtor or any individual that is liable on such debt with the debtor files and serves upon such party in interest a written objection to the taking of the proposed action.

   (Added and amended Pub.L. 99–554, Title II, § 255, title III, § 302(f), Oct. 27, 1986, 100 Stat. 3105, 3124; Pub.L. 103–65, § 1, Aug. 6, 1993, 107 Stat. 311; Pub.L. 105–277, div. C, title I, § 149(a), Oct. 21, 1998, 112 Stat. 2681–610; Pub.L. 106–5, § 1(1),(2), Mar. 30, 1999, 113 Stat. 9; Pub.L. 106–70, § 1, Oct. 9, 1999, 113 Stat. 1031; Pub.L. 107–8, § 1, May 11, 2001, 115 Stat. 10; Pub.L. 107–17, § 1, June 26, 2001, 115 Stat. 151; Pub.L. 107–170, § 1, May 7, 2002, 116 Stat. 133; Pub.L. 107–171, title X, § 10814(a), May 13, 2002, 116 Stat. 532; Pub.L. 107–377, § 2(a), Dec. 19, 2002, 116 Stat. 3115; Pub.L. 108–73, § 2(a), Aug. 15, 2003, 117 Stat. 891; Pub.L. 108–369, § 2(a), Oct. 25, 2004, 118 Stat. 1749; Pub.L. 109–8, title X, § 1001(a)(1), Apr. 20, 2005, 119 Stat. 185, 186.)

§ 1202.   Trustee

   (a)   If the United States trustee has appointed an individual under section 586(b) of title 28 to serve as standing trustee in cases under this chapter and if such individual qualifies as a trustee under section 322 of this title, then such individual shall serve as trustee in any case filed under this chapter. Otherwise, the United States trustee shall appoint one disinterested person to serve as trustee in the case or the United States trustee may serve as trustee in the case if necessary.

   (b)   The trustee shall—

   (1)   perform the duties specified in sections 704(a)(2), 704(a)(3), 704(a)(5), 704(a)(6), 704(a)(7), and 704(a)(9) of this title;

   (2)   perform the duties specified in section 1106(a)(3) and 1106(a)(4) of this title if the court, for cause and on request of a party in interest, the trustee, or the United States trustee, so orders;

   (3)   appear and be heard at any hearing that concerns—

   (A)   the value of property subject to a lien;

   (B)   confirmation of a plan;

   (C)   modification of the plan after confirmation; or

   (D)   the sale of property of the estate;

   (4)   ensure that the debtor commences making timely payments required by a confirmed plan;

   (5)   if the debtor ceases to be a debtor in possession, perform the duties specified in sections 704(a)(8), 1106(a)(1), 1106(a)(2), 1106(a)(6), 1106(a)(7), and 1203; and

(6)   if with respect to the debtor there is a claim for a domestic support obligation, provide the applicable notice specified in subsection (c).

(c)(1)   In a case described in subsection (b)(6) to which subsection (b)(6) applies, the trustee shall—

(A)(i)   provide written notice to the holder of the claim described in subsection (b)(6) of such claim and of the right of such holder to use the services of the State child support enforcement agency established under sections 464 and 466 of the Social Security Act for the State in which such holder resides, for assistance in collecting child support during and after the case under this title; and

(ii)   include in the notice provided under clause (i) the address and telephone number of such State child support enforcement agency;

(B)(i)   provide written notice to such State child support enforcement agency of such claim; and

(ii)   include in the notice provided under clause (i) the name, address, and telephone number of such holder; and

(C)   at such time as the debtor is granted a discharge under section 1228, provide written notice to such holder and to such State child support enforcement agency of—

(i)   the granting of the discharge;

(ii)   the last recent known address of the debtor;

(iii)   the last recent known name and address of the debtor's employer; and

(iv)   the name of each creditor that holds a claim that—

(I)   is not discharged under paragraph (2), (4), or (14A) of section 523(a); or

(II)   was reaffirmed by the debtor under section 524(c).

(2)(A)   The holder of a claim described in subsection (b)(6) or the State child support enforcement agency of the State in which such holder resides may request from a creditor described in paragraph (1)(C)(iv) the last known address of the debtor.

(B)   Notwithstanding any other provision of law, a creditor that makes a disclosure of a last known address of a debtor in connection with a request made under subparagraph (A) shall not be liable by reason of making that disclosure.

(Added and amended Pub.L. 99–554, title II, §§ 227, 255, title III, § 302(f), Oct. 27, 1986, 100 Stat. 3103, 3106, 3124; Pub.L. 103–65, § 1, Aug. 6, 1993, 107 Stat. 311; Pub.L. 105–277, div. C, title I, § 149(a), Oct. 21, 1998, 112 Stat. 2681–610; Pub.L. 106–5, §§ 1(1), (2), Mar. 30, 1999, 113 Stat. 9; Pub.L. 106–70, § 1, Oct. 9, 1999, 113 Stat. 1031; Pub.L. 107–8, § 1, May 11, 2001, 115 Stat. 10; Pub.L. 107–17, § 1, June 26, 2001, 115 Stat. 151; Pub.L. 107–170, § 1, May 7, 2002, 116 Stat. 133; Pub.L. 107–171, title X, § 10814(a), May 13, 2002, 116 Stat. 532; Pub.L. 107–377, § 2(a), Dec. 19, 2002, 116 Stat. 3115; Pub.L. 108–73, § 2(a), Aug. 15, 2003, 117 Stat. 891; Pub.L. 108–369, § 2(a), Oct. 25, 2004, 118 Stat. 1749; Pub.L. 109–8, title II, § 219(c), title X, § 1001(a)(1), Apr. 20, 2005, 119 Stat. 57, 185; Pub.L. 111–327, § 2(a)(38), Dec. 22, 2010, 124 Stat. 3561.)

§ 1203.   Rights and powers of debtor

Subject to such limitations as the court may prescribe, a debtor in possession shall have all the rights, other than the right to compensation under section 330, and powers, and shall perform all the functions and duties, except the duties specified in paragraphs (3) and (4) of section 1106(a), of a trustee serving in a case under chapter 11, including operating the debtor's farm or commercial fishing operation.

(Added and amended Pub.L. 99–554, title II, § 255, title III, § 302(f), Oct. 27, 1986, 100 Stat. 3107, 3124; Pub.L. 103–65, § 1, Aug. 6, 1993, 107 Stat. 311; Pub.L. 105–277, div. C, title I, § 149(a), Oct. 21, 1998, 112 Stat. 2681–610; Pub.L. 106–5, § 1(1), (2), Mar. 30, 1999, 113 Stat. 9; Pub.L. 106–70, § 1, Oct. 9, 1999, 113 Stat. 1031; Pub.L. 107–8, § 1, May 11, 2001, 115 Stat. 10; Pub.L. 107–17, § 1, June 26, 2001, 115 Stat. 151; Pub.L. 107–170, § 1, May 7, 2002, 116 Stat. 133; Pub.L. 107–171, title X, § 10814(a), May 13, 2002, 116

Stat. 532; Pub.L. 107–377, § 2(a), Dec. 19, 2002, 116 Stat. 3115; Pub.L. 108–73, § 2(a), Aug. 15, 2003, 117 Stat. 891; Pub.L. 108–369, § 2(a), Oct. 25, 2004, 118 Stat. 1749; Pub.L. 109–8, title X, §§ 1001(a)(1), (c), 1007(c)(2), Apr. 20, 2005, 119 Stat. 185, 186, 188.)

§ 1204.   Removal of debtor as debtor in possession

(a)   On request of a party in interest, and after notice and a hearing, the court shall order that the debtor shall not be a debtor in possession for cause, including fraud, dishonesty, incompetence, or gross mismanagement of the affairs of the debtor, either before or after the commencement of the case.

(b)   On request of a party in interest, and after notice and a hearing, the court may reinstate the debtor in possession.

(Added and amended Pub.L. 99–554, title II, § 255, title III, § 302(f), Oct. 27, 1986, 100 Stat. 3107, 3124; Pub.L. 103–65, § 1, Aug. 6, 1993, 107 Stat. 311; Pub.L. 105–277, div. C, title I, § 149(a), Oct. 21, 1998, 112 Stat. 2681–610; Pub.L. 106–5, § 1(1), (2), Mar. 30, 1999, 113 Stat. 9; Pub.L. 106–70, § 1, Oct. 9, 1999, 113 Stat. 1031; Pub.L. 107–8, § 1, May 11, 2001, 115 Stat. 10; Pub.L. 107–17, § 1, June 26, 2001, 115 Stat. 151; Pub.L. 107–170, § 1, May 7, 2002, 116 Stat. 133; Pub.L. 107–171, title X, § 10814(a), May 13, 2002, 116 Stat. 532; Pub.L. 107–377, § 2(a), Dec. 19, 2002, 116 Stat. 3115; Pub.L. 108–73, § 2(a), Aug. 15, 2003, 117 Stat. 891; Pub.L. 108–369, § 2(a), Oct. 25, 2004, 118 Stat. 1749; Pub.L. 109–8, title X, § 1001(a)(1), (c), Apr. 20, 2005, 119 Stat. 185, 186.)

§ 1205.   Adequate protection

(a)   Section 361 does not apply in a case under this chapter.

(b)   In a case under this chapter, when adequate protection is required under section 362, 363, or 364 of this title of an interest of an entity in property, such adequate protection may be provided by—

(1)   requiring the trustee to make a cash payment or periodic cash payments to such entity, to the extent that the stay under section 362 of this title, use, sale, or lease under section 363 of this title, or any grant of a lien under section 364 of this title results in a decrease in the value of property securing a claim or of an entity's ownership interest in property;

(2)   providing to such entity an additional or replacement lien to the extent that such stay, use, sale, lease, or grant results in a decrease in the value of property securing a claim or of an entity's ownership interest in property;

(3)   paying to such entity for the use of farmland the reasonable rent customary in the community where the property is located, based upon the rental value, net income, and earning capacity of the property; or

(4)   granting such other relief, other than entitling such entity to compensation allowable under section 503(b)(1) of this title as an administrative expense, as will adequately protect the value of property securing a claim or of such entity's ownership interest in property.

(Added and amended Pub.L. 99–554, title II, § 255, title III, § 302(f), Oct. 27, 1986, 100 Stat. 3107, 3124; Pub.L. 103–65, § 1, Aug. 6, 1993, 107 Stat. 311; Pub.L. 105–277, div. C, title I, § 149(a), Oct. 21, 1998, 112 Stat. 2681–610; Pub.L. 106–5, § 1(1), (2), Mar. 30, 1999, 113 Stat. 9; Pub.L. 106–70, § 1, Oct. 9, 1999, 113 Stat. 1031; Pub.L. 107–8, § 1, May 11, 2001, 115 Stat. 10; Pub.L. 107–17, § 1, June 26, 2001, 115 Stat. 151; Pub.L. 107–170, § 1, May 7, 2002, 116 Stat. 133; Pub.L. 107–171, title X, § 10814(a), May 13, 2002, 116 Stat. 532; Pub.L. 107–377, § 2(a), Dec. 19, 2002, 116 Stat. 3115; Pub.L. 108–73, § 2(a), Aug. 15, 2003, 117 Stat. 891; Pub.L. 108–369, § 2(a), Oct. 25, 2004, 118 Stat. 1749; Pub.L. 109–8, title X, § 1001(a)(1), (c), Apr. 20, 2005, 119 Stat. 185, 186.)

§ 1206.   Sales free of interests

After notice and a hearing, in addition to the authorization contained in section 363(f), the trustee in a case under this chapter may sell property under section 363(b) and (c) free and clear of any interest in such property of an entity other than the estate if the property is farmland, farm equipment, or property used to carry out a commercial fishing operation (including a commercial fishing vessel), except that the proceeds of such sale shall be subject to such interest.

(Added and amended Pub.L. 99–554, title II, § 255, title III, § 302(f), Oct. 27, 1986, 100 Stat. 3108, 3124; Pub.L. 103–65, § 1, Aug. 6, 1993, 107 Stat. 311; Pub.L. 105–277, div. C, title I, § 149(a), Oct. 21, 1998, 112 Stat. 2681–610; Pub.L. 106–5, § 1(1), (2), Mar. 30, 1999, 113 Stat. 9; Pub.L. 106–70, § 1, Oct. 9, 1999, 113 Stat. 1031; Pub.L. 107–8, § 1, May 11, 2001, 115 Stat. 10; Pub.L. 107–17, § 1, June 26, 2001, 115 Stat. 151; Pub.L. 107–170, § 1, May 7, 2002, 116 Stat. 133; Pub.L. 107–171, title X, § 10814(a), May 13, 2002, 116 Stat. 532; Pub.L. 107–377, § 2(a), Dec. 19, 2002, 116 Stat. 3115; Pub.L. 108–73, § 2(a), Aug. 15, 2003, 117 Stat. 891; Pub.L. 108–369, § 2(a), Oct. 25, 2004, 118 Stat. 1749; Pub.L. 109–8, title X, §§ 1001(a)(1), (c), 1007(c)(3), Apr. 20, 2005, 119 Stat. 185, 186, 188.)

§ 1207.   Property of the estate

(a) Property of the estate includes, in addition to the property specified in section 541 of this title—

(1) all property of the kind specified in such section that the debtor acquires after the commencement of the case but before the case is closed, dismissed, or converted to a case under chapter 7 of this title, whichever occurs first; and

(2) earnings from services performed by the debtor after the commencement of the case but before the case is closed, dismissed, or converted to a case under chapter 7 of this title, whichever occurs first.

(b) Except as provided in section 1204, a confirmed plan, or an order confirming a plan, the debtor shall remain in possession of all property of the estate.

(Added and amended Pub.L. 99–554, title II, § 255, title III, § 302(f), Oct. 27, 1986, 100 Stat. 3108, 3124; Pub.L. 103–65, § 1, Aug. 6, 1993, 107 Stat. 311; Pub.L. 105–277, div. C, title I, § 149(a), Oct. 21, 1998, 112 Stat. 2681–610; Pub.L. 106–5, § 1(1), (2), Mar. 30, 1999, 113 Stat. 9; Pub.L. 106–70, § 1, Oct. 9, 1999, 113 Stat. 1031; Pub.L. 107–8, § 1, May 11, 2001, 115 Stat. 10; Pub.L. 107–17, § 1, June 26, 2001, 115 Stat. 151; Pub.L. 107–170, § 1, May 7, 2002, 116 Stat. 133; Pub.L. 107–171, title X, § 10814(a), May 13, 2002, 116 Stat. 532; Pub.L. 107–377, § 2(a), Dec. 19, 2002, 116 Stat. 3115; Pub.L. 108–73, § 2(a), Aug. 15, 2003, 117 Stat. 891; Pub.L. 108–369, § 2(a), Oct. 25, 2004, 118 Stat. 1749; Pub.L. 109–8, title X, § 1001(a)(1), (c), Apr. 20, 2005, 119 Stat. 185, 186.)

§ 1208.   Conversion or dismissal

(a) The debtor may convert a case under this chapter to a case under chapter 7 of this title at any time. Any waiver of the right to convert under this subsection is unenforceable.

(b) On request of the debtor at any time, if the case has not been converted under section 706 or 1112 of this title, the court shall dismiss a case under this chapter. Any waiver of the right to dismiss under this subsection is unenforceable.

(c) On request of a party in interest, and after notice and a hearing, the court may dismiss a case under this chapter for cause, including—

(1) unreasonable delay, or gross mismanagement, by the debtor that is prejudicial to creditors;

(2) nonpayment of any fees and charges required under chapter 123 of title 28;

(3) failure to file a plan timely under section 1221 of this title;

(4) failure to commence making timely payments required by a confirmed plan;

(5) denial of confirmation of a plan under section 1225 of this title and denial of a request made for additional time for filing another plan or a modification of a plan;

(6) material default by the debtor with respect to a term of a confirmed plan;

(7) revocation of the order of confirmation under section 1230 of this title, and denial of confirmation of a modified plan under section 1229 of this title;

(8) termination of a confirmed plan by reason of the occurrence of a condition specified in the plan;

(9) continuing loss to or diminution of the estate and absence of a reasonable likelihood of rehabilitation; and

(10) failure of the debtor to pay any domestic support obligation that first becomes payable after the date of the filing of the petition.

(d) On request of a party in interest, and after notice and a hearing, the court may dismiss a case under this chapter or convert a case under this chapter to a case under chapter 7 of this title upon a showing that the debtor has committed fraud in connection with the case.

(e) Notwithstanding any other provision of this section, a case may not be converted to a case under another chapter of this title unless the debtor may be a debtor under such chapter.

(Added and amended Pub.L. 99–554, title II, § 255, title III, § 302(f), Oct. 27, 1986, 100 Stat. 3108, 3124; Pub.L. 103–65, § 1, Aug. 6, 1993, 107 Stat. 311; Pub.L. 105–277, div. C, title I, § 149(a), Oct. 21, 1998, 112 Stat. 2681–610; Pub.L. 106–5, § 1(1), (2), Mar. 30, 1999, 113 Stat. 9; Pub.L. 106–70, § 1, Oct. 9, 1999, 113 Stat. 1031; Pub.L. 107–8, § 1, May 11, 2001, 115 Stat. 10; Pub.L. 107–17, § 1, June 26, 2001, 115 Stat. 151; Pub.L. 107–170, § 1, May 7, 2002, 116 Stat. 133; Pub.L. 107–171, title X, § 10814(a), May 13, 2002, 116 Stat. 532; Pub.L. 107–377, § 2(a), Dec. 19, 2002, 116 Stat. 3115; Pub.L. 108–73, § 2(a), Aug. 15, 2003, 117 Stat. 891; Pub.L. 108–369, § 2(a), Oct. 25, 2004, 118 Stat. 1749; Pub.L. 109–8, title II, § 213(2), title X, § 1001(a)(1), (c), Apr. 20, 2005, 119 Stat. 52, 185, 186.)

SUBCHAPTER II—THE PLAN

§ 1221. Filing of plan

The debtor shall file a plan not later than 90 days after the order for relief under this chapter, except that the court may extend such period if the need for an extension is attributable to circumstances for which the debtor should not justly be held accountable.

(Added and amended Pub.L. 99–554, title II, § 255, title III, § 302(f), Oct. 27, 1986, 100 Stat. 3109, 3124; Pub.L. 103–65, §§ 1, 2, Aug. 6, 1993, 107 Stat. 311; Pub.L. 105–277, div. C, title I, § 149(a), Oct. 21, 1998, 112 Stat. 2681–610; Pub.L. 106–5, § 1(1), (2), Mar. 30, 1999, 113 Stat. 9; Pub.L. 106–70, § 1, Oct. 9, 1999, 113 Stat. 1031; Pub.L. 107–8, § 1, May 11, 2001, 115 Stat. 10; Pub.L. 107–17, § 1, June 26, 2001, 115 Stat. 151; Pub.L. 107–170, § 1, May 7, 2002, 116 Stat. 133; Pub.L. 107–171, title X, § 10814(a), May 13, 2002, 116 Stat. 532; Pub.L. 107–377, § 2(a), Dec. 19, 2002, 116 Stat. 3115; Pub.L. 108–73, § 2(a), Aug. 15, 2003, 117 Stat. 891; Pub.L. 108–369, § 2(a), Oct. 25, 2004, 118 Stat. 1749; Pub.L. 109–8, title X, § 1001(a)(1), (c), Apr. 20, 2005, 119 Stat. 185, 186.)

§ 1222. Contents of plan

(a) The plan shall—

(1) provide for the submission of all or such portion of future earnings or other future income of the debtor to the supervision and control of the trustee as is necessary for the execution of the plan;

(2) provide for the full payment, in deferred cash payments, of all claims entitled to priority under section 507, unless—

(A) the claim is a claim owed to a governmental unit that arises as a result of the sale, transfer, exchange, or other disposition of any farm asset used in the debtor's farming operation, in which case the claim shall be treated as an unsecured claim that is not entitled to priority under section 507, but the debt shall be treated in such manner only if the debtor receives a discharge; or

(B) the holder of a particular claim agrees to a different treatment of that claim;

(3) if the plan classifies claims and interests, provide the same treatment for each claim or interest within a particular class unless the holder of a particular claim or interest agrees to less favorable treatment; and

(4) notwithstanding any other provision of this section, a plan may provide for less than full payment of all amounts owed for a claim entitled to priority under section 507(a)(1)(B) only if the plan provides that all of the debtor's projected disposable income for a 5-year period beginning on the date that the first payment is due under the plan will be applied to make payments under the plan.

(b) Subject to subsections (a) and (c) of this section, the plan may—

(1) designate a class or classes of unsecured claims, as provided in section 1122 of this title, but may not discriminate unfairly against any class so designated; however, such plan may treat claims for a consumer debt of the debtor if an individual is liable on such consumer debt with the debtor differently than other unsecured claims;

(2) modify the rights of holders of secured claims, or of holders of unsecured claims, or leave unaffected the rights of holders of any class of claims;

(3) provide for the curing or waiving of any default;

(4) provide for payments on any unsecured claim to be made concurrently with payments on any secured claim or any other unsecured claim;

(5) provide for the curing of any default within a reasonable time and maintenance of payments while the case is pending on any unsecured claim or secured claim on which the last payment is due after the date on which the final payment under the plan is due;

(6) subject to section 365 of this title, provide for the assumption, rejection, or assignment of any executory contract or unexpired lease of the debtor not previously rejected under such section;

(7) provide for the payment of all or part of a claim against the debtor from property of the estate or property of the debtor;

(8) provide for the sale of all or any part of the property of the estate or the distribution of all or any part of the property of the estate among those having an interest in such property;

(9) provide for payment of allowed secured claims consistent with section 1225(a)(5) of this title, over a period exceeding the period permitted under section 1222(c);

(10) provide for the vesting of property of the estate, on confirmation of the plan or at a later time, in the debtor or in any other entity;

(11) provide for the payment of interest accruing after the date of the filing of the petition on unsecured claims that are nondischargeable under section 1228(a), except that such interest may be paid only to the extent that the debtor has disposable income available to pay such interest after making provision for full payment of all allowed claims; and

(12) include any other appropriate provision not inconsistent with this title.

(c) Except as provided in subsections (b)(5) and (b)(9), the plan may not provide for payments over a period that is longer than three years unless the court for cause approves a longer period, but the court may not approve a period that is longer than five years.

(d) Notwithstanding subsection (b)(2) of this section and sections 506(b) and 1225(a)(5) of this title, if it is proposed in a plan to cure a default, the amount necessary to cure the default, shall be determined in accordance with the underlying agreement and applicable nonbankruptcy law.

(Added and amended Pub.L. 99–554, title II, § 255, title III, § 302(f), Oct. 27, 1986, 100 Stat. 3109, 3124; Pub.L. 103–65, § 1, Aug. 6, 1993, 107 Stat. 311; Pub.L. 103–394, title III, § 305(b), Oct. 22, 1994, 108 Stat. 4134; Pub.L. 105–277, div. C, title I, § 149(a), Oct. 21, 1998, 112 Stat. 2681–610; Pub.L. 106–5, § 1(1), (2), Mar. 30, 1999, 113 Stat. 9; Pub.L. 106–70, § 1, Oct. 9, 1999, 113 Stat. 1031; Pub.L. 107–8, § 1, May 11, 2001, 115 Stat. 10; Pub.L. 107–17, § 1, June 26, 2001, 115 Stat. 151; Pub.L. 107–170, § 1, May 7, 2002, 116 Stat. 133; Pub.L. 107–171, title X, § 10814(a), May 13, 2002 116 Stat. 532; Pub.L. 107–377, § 2(a), Dec. 19,

2002, 116 Stat. 3115; Pub.L. 108–73, § 2(a), Aug. 15, 2003, 117 Stat. 891; Pub.L. 108–369, § 2(a), Oct. 25, 2004, 118 Stat. 1749; Pub.L. 109–8, title II, § 213(3), (4) title X, §§ 1001(a)(1), (c), 1003(a), Apr. 20, 2005, 119 Stat. 52, 185, 186.)

§ 1223. Modification of plan before confirmation

(a) The debtor may modify the plan at any time before confirmation, but may not modify the plan so that the plan as modified fails to meet the requirements of section 1222 of this title.

(b) After the debtor files a modification under this section, the plan as modified becomes the plan.

(c) Any holder of a secured claim that has accepted or rejected the plan is deemed to have accepted or rejected, as the case may be, the plan as modified, unless the modification provides for a change in the rights of such holder from what such rights were under the plan before modification, and such holder changes such holder's previous acceptance or rejection.

(Added and amended Pub.L. 99–554, title II, § 255, title III, § 302(f), Oct. 27, 1986, 100 Stat. 3110, 3124; Pub.L. 103–65, § 1, Aug. 6, 1993, 107 Stat. 311; Pub.L. 105–277, div. C, title I, § 149(a), Oct. 21, 1998, 112 Stat. 2681–610; Pub.L. 106–5, § 1(1), (2), Mar. 30, 1999, 113 Stat. 9; Pub.L. 106–70, § 1, Oct. 9, 1999, 113 Stat. 1031; Pub.L. 107–8, § 1, May 11, 2001, 115 Stat. 10; Pub.L. 107–17, § 1, June 26, 2001, 115 Stat. 151; Pub.L. 107–170, § 1, May 7, 2002, 116 Stat. 133; Pub.L. 107–171, title X, § 10814(a), May 13, 2002, 116 Stat. 532; Pub.L. 107–377, § 2(a), Dec. 19, 2002, 116 Stat. 3115; Pub.L. 108–73, § 2(a), Aug. 15, 2003, 117 Stat. 891; Pub.L. 108–369, § 2(a), Oct. 25, 2004, 118 Stat. 1749; Pub.L. 109–8, title X, § 1001(a)(1), (c), Apr. 20, 2005, 119 Stat. 185, 186.)

§ 1224. Confirmation hearing

After expedited notice, the court shall hold a hearing on confirmation of the plan. A party in interest, the trustee, or the United States trustee may object to the confirmation of the plan. Except for cause, the hearing shall be concluded not later than 45 days after the filing of the plan.

(Added and amended Pub.L. 99–554, title II, § 255, title III, § 302(f), Oct. 27, 1986, 100 Stat. 3110, 3124; Pub.L. 103–65, § 1, Aug. 6, 1993, 107 Stat. 311; Pub.L. 105–277, div. C, title I, § 149(a), Oct. 21, 1998, 112 Stat. 2681–610; Pub.L. 106–5, § 1(1), (2), Mar. 30, 1999, 113 Stat. 9; Pub.L. 106–70, § 1, Oct. 9, 1999, 113 Stat. 1031; Pub.L. 107–8, § 1, May 11, 2001, 115 Stat. 10; Pub.L. 107–17, § 1, June 26, 2001, 115 Stat. 151; Pub.L. 107–170, § 1, May 7, 2002, 116 Stat. 133; Pub.L. 107–171, title X, § 10814(a), May 13, 2002, 116 Stat. 532; Pub.L. 107–377, § 2(a), Dec. 19, 2002, 16 Stat. 3115; Pub.L. 108–73, § 2(a), Aug. 15, 2003, 117 Stat. 891; Pub.L. 108–369, § 2(a), Oct. 25, 2004, 118 Stat. 1749; Pub.L. 109–8, title X, § 1001(a)(1), (c), Apr. 20, 2005, 119 Stat. 185, 186.)

§ 1225. Confirmation of plan

(a) Except as provided in subsection (b), the court shall confirm a plan if—

(1) the plan complies with the provisions of this chapter and with the other applicable provisions of this title;

(2) any fee, charge, or amount required under chapter 123 of title 28, or by the plan, to be paid before confirmation, has been paid;

(3) the plan has been proposed in good faith and not by any means forbidden by law;

(4) the value, as of the effective date of the plan, of property to be distributed under the plan on account of each allowed unsecured claim is not less than the amount that would be paid on such claim if the estate of the debtor were liquidated under chapter 7 of this title on such date;

(5) with respect to each allowed secured claim provided for by the plan—

(A) the holder of such claim has accepted the plan;

(B)(i) the plan provides that the holder of such claim retain the lien securing such claim; and

       (ii) the value, as of the effective date of the plan, of property to be distributed by the trustee or the debtor under the plan on account of such claim is not less than the allowed amount of such claim; or

       (C) the debtor surrenders the property securing such claim to such holder;

    (6) the debtor will be able to make all payments under the plan and to comply with the plan; and

    (7) the debtor has paid all amounts that are required to be paid under a domestic support obligation and that first become payable after the date of the filing of the petition if the debtor is required by a judicial or administrative order, or by statute, to pay such domestic support obligation.

  (b)(1) If the trustee or the holder of an allowed unsecured claim objects to the confirmation of the plan, then the court may not approve the plan unless, as of the effective date of the plan—

    (A) the value of the property to be distributed under the plan on account of such claim is not less than the amount of such claim;

    (B) the plan provides that all of the debtor's projected disposable income to be received in the three-year period, or such longer period as the court may approve under section 1222(c), beginning on the date that the first payment is due under the plan will be applied to make payments under the plan; or

    (C) the value of the property to be distributed under the plan in the 3-year period, or such longer period as the court may approve under section 1222(c), beginning on the date that the first distribution is due under the plan is not less than the debtor's projected disposable income for such period.

  (2) For purposes of this subsection, "disposable income" means income which is received by the debtor and which is not reasonably necessary to be expended—

    (A) for the maintenance or support of the debtor or a dependent of the debtor or for a domestic support obligation that first becomes payable after the date of the filing of the petition; or

    (B) for the payment of expenditures necessary for the continuation, preservation, and operation of the debtor's business.

  (c) After confirmation of a plan, the court may order any entity from whom the debtor receives income to pay all or any part of such income to the trustee.

  (Added and amended Pub.L. 99–554, title II, § 255, title III, § 302(f), Oct. 27, 1986, 100 Stat. 3110, 3124; Pub.L. 103–65, § 1, Aug. 6, 1993, 107 Stat. 311; Pub.L. 105–277, div. C, title I, § 149(a), Oct. 21, 1998, 112 Stat. 2681–610; Pub.L. 106–5, § 1(1), (2), Mar. 30, 1999, 113 Stat. 9; Pub.L. 106–70, § 1, Oct. 9, 1999, 113 Stat. 1031; Pub.L. 107–8, § 1, May 11, 2001, 115 Stat. 10; Pub.L. 107–17, § 1, June 26, 2001, 115 Stat. 151; Pub.L. 107–170, § 1, May 7, 2002, 116 Stat. 133; Pub.L. 107–171, title X, § 10814(a), May 13, 2002, 116 Stat. 532; Pub.L. 107–377, § 2(a), Dec. 19, 2002, 116 Stat. 3115; Pub.L. 108–73, § 2(a), Aug. 15, 2003, 117 Stat. 891; Pub.L. 108–369, § 2(a), Oct. 25, 2004, 118 Stat. 1749; Pub.L. 109–8, title II, §§ 213(5), 218, title X, §§ 1001(a)(1), (c), 1006(a), Apr. 20, 2005, 119 Stat. 52, 55, 185–187.)

§ 1226.   Payments

  (a) Payments and funds received by the trustee shall be retained by the trustee until confirmation or denial of confirmation of a plan. If a plan is confirmed, the trustee shall distribute any such payment in accordance with the plan. If a plan is not confirmed, the trustee shall return any such payments to the debtor, after deducting—

    (1) any unpaid claim allowed under section 503(b) of this title; and

    (2) if a standing trustee is serving in the case, the percentage fee fixed for such standing trustee.

  (b) Before or at the time of each payment to creditors under the plan, there shall be paid—

(1) any unpaid claim of the kind specified in section 507(a)(2) of this title; and

(2) if a standing trustee appointed under section 1202(c) of this title is serving in the case, the percentage fee fixed for such standing trustee under section 1202(d) of this title.

(c) Except as otherwise provided in the plan or in the order confirming the plan, the trustee shall make payments to creditors under the plan.

> (Added and amended Pub.L. 99–554, title II, § 255, title III, § 302(f), Oct. 27, 1986, 100 Stat. 3111, 3124; Pub.L. 103–65, § 1, Aug. 6, 1993, 107 Stat. 311; Pub.L. 103–394, title V, § 501(d)(36), Oct. 22, 1994, 108 Stat. 4147; Pub.L. 105–277, div. C, title I, § 149(a), Oct. 21, 1998, 112 Stat. 2681–610; Pub.L. 106–5, § 1(1), (2), Mar. 30, 1999, 113 Stat. 9; Pub.L. 106–70, § 1, Oct. 9, 1999, 113 Stat. 1031; Pub.L. 107–8, § 1, May 11, 2001, 115 Stat. 10; Pub.L. 107–17, § 1, June 26, 2001, 115 Stat. 151; Pub.L. 107–170, § 1, May 7, 2002, 116 Stat. 133; Pub.L. 107–171, title X, § 10814(a), May 13, 2002, 116 Stat. 532; Pub.L. 107–377, § 2(a), Dec. 19, 2002, 116 Stat. 3115; Pub.L. 108–73, § 2(a), Aug. 15, 2003, 117 Stat. 891; Pub.L. 108–369, § 2(a), Oct. 25, 2004, 118 Stat. 1749; Pub.L. 109–8, title X, § 1001(a)(1), (c), title XV, § 1502(a)(9), Apr. 20, 2005, 119 Stat. 185, 186, 217.)

§ 1227. Effect of confirmation

(a) Except as provided in section 1228(a) of this title, the provisions of a confirmed plan bind the debtor, each creditor, each equity security holder, and each general partner in the debtor, whether or not the claim of such creditor, such equity security holder, or such general partner in the debtor is provided for by the plan, and whether or not such creditor, such equity security holder, or such general partner in the debtor has objected to, has accepted, or has rejected the plan.

(b) Except as otherwise provided in the plan or the order confirming the plan, the confirmation of a plan vests all of the property of the estate in the debtor.

(c) Except as provided in section 1228(a) of this title and except as otherwise provided in the plan or in the order confirming the plan, the property vesting in the debtor under subsection (b) of this section is free and clear of any claim or interest of any creditor provided for by the plan.

> (Added and amended Pub.L. 99–554, title II, § 255, title III, § 302(f), Oct. 27, 1986, 100 Stat. 3112, 3124; Pub.L. 103–65, § 1, Aug. 6, 1993, 107 Stat. 311; Pub.L. 105–277, div. C, title I, § 149(a), Oct. 21, 1998, 112 Stat. 2681–610; Pub.L. 106–5, § 1(1), (2), Mar. 30, 1999, 113 Stat. 9; Pub.L. 106–70, § 1, Oct. 9, 1999, 113 Stat. 1031; Pub.L. 107–8, § 1, May 11, 2001, 115 Stat. 10; Pub.L. 107–17, § 1, June 26, 2001, 115 Stat. 151; Pub.L. 107–170, § 1, May 7, 2002, 116 Stat. 133; Pub.L. 107–171, title X, § 10814(a), May 13, 2002, 116 Stat. 532; Pub.L. 107–377, § 2(a), Dec. 19, 2002, 116 Stat. 3115; Pub.L. 108–73, § 2(a), Aug. 15, 2003, 117 Stat. 891; Pub.L. 108–369, § 2(a), Oct. 25, 2004, 118 Stat. 1749; Pub.L. 109–8, title X, § 1001(a)(1), (c), Apr. 20, 2005, 119 Stat. 185, 186.)

§ 1228. Discharge

(a) Subject to subsection (d), as soon as practicable after completion by the debtor of all payments under the plan, and in the case of a debtor who is required by a judicial or administrative order, or by statute, to pay a domestic support obligation, after such debtor certifies that all amounts payable under such order or such statute that are due on or before the date of the certification (including amounts due before the petition was filed, but only to the extent provided for by the plan) have been paid, other than payments to holders of allowed claims provided for under section 1222(b)(5) or 1222(b)(9) of this title, unless the court approves a written waiver of discharge executed by the debtor after the order for relief under this chapter, the court shall grant the debtor a discharge of all debts provided for by the plan allowed under section 503 of this title or disallowed under section 502 of this title, except any debt—

(1) provided for under section 1222(b)(5) or 1222(b)(9) of this title; or

(2) of the kind specified in section 523(a) of this title.

(b) Subject to subsection (d), at any time after the confirmation of the plan and after notice and a hearing, the court may grant a discharge to a debtor that has not completed payments under the plan only if—

    (1)   the debtor's failure to complete such payments is due to circumstances for which the debtor should not justly be held accountable;

    (2)   the value, as of the effective date of the plan, of property actually distributed under the plan on account of each allowed unsecured claim is not less than the amount that would have been paid on such claim if the estate of the debtor had been liquidated under chapter 7 of this title on such date; and

    (3)   modification of the plan under section 1229 of this title is not practicable.

  (c)   A discharge granted under subsection (b) of this section discharges the debtor from all unsecured debts provided for by the plan or disallowed under section 502 of this title, except any debt—

    (1)   provided for under section 1222(b)(5) or 1222(b)(9) of this title; or

    (2)   of a kind specified in section 523(a) of this title.

  (d)   On request of a party in interest before one year after a discharge under this section is granted, and after notice and a hearing, the court may revoke such discharge only if—

    (1)   such discharge was obtained by the debtor through fraud; and

    (2)   the requesting party did not know of such fraud until after such discharge was granted.

  (e)   After the debtor is granted a discharge, the court shall terminate the services of any trustee serving in the case.

  (f)   The court may not grant a discharge under this chapter unless the court after notice and a hearing held not more than 10 days before the date of the entry of the order granting the discharge finds that there is no reasonable cause to believe that—

    (1)   section 522(q)(1) may be applicable to the debtor; and

    (2)   there is pending any proceeding in which the debtor may be found guilty of a felony of the kind described in section 522(q)(1)(A) or liable for a debt of the kind described in section 522(q)(1)(B).

  (Added and amended Pub.L. 99–554, title II, § 255, title III, § 302(f), Oct. 27, 1986, 100 Stat. 3112, 3124; Pub.L. 103–65, § 1, Aug. 6, 1993, 107 Stat. 311; Pub.L. 105–277, div. C, title I, § 149(a), Oct. 21, 1998, 112 Stat. 2681–610; Pub.L. 106–5, § 1(1), (2), Mar. 30, 1999, 113 Stat. 9; Pub.L. 106–70, § 1, Oct. 9, 1999, 113 Stat. 1031; Pub.L. 106–518, title II, § 208, Nov. 13, 2000, 114 Stat. 2415; Pub.L. 107–8, § 1, May 11, 2001, 115 Stat. 10; Pub.L. 107–17, § 1, June 26, 2001, 115 Stat. 151; Pub.L. 107–170, § 1, May 7, 2002, 116 Stat. 133; Pub.L. 107–171, title X, § 10814(a), May 13, 2002, 116 Stat. 532; Pub.L. 107–377, § 2(a), Dec. 19, 2002, 116 Stat. 3115; Pub.L. 108–73, § 2(a), Aug. 15, 2003, 117 Stat. 891; Pub.L. 108–369, § 2(a), Oct. 25, 2004, 118 Stat. 1749; Pub.L. 109–8, title II, § 213(6), title III, § 330(c), title X, § 1001(a)(1), (c), Apr. 20, 2005, 119 Stat. 53, 101, 185, 186.)

§ 1229.   Modification of plan after confirmation

  (a)   At any time after confirmation of the plan but before the completion of payments under such plan, the plan may be modified, on request of the debtor, the trustee, or the holder of an allowed unsecured claim, to—

    (1)   increase or reduce the amount of payments on claims of a particular class provided for by the plan;

    (2)   extend or reduce the time for such payments; or

    (3)   alter the amount of the distribution to a creditor whose claim is provided for by the plan to the extent necessary to take account of any payment of such claim other than under the plan.

  (b)(1)   Sections 1222(a), 1222(b), and 1223(c) of this title and the requirements of section 1225(a) of this title apply to any modification under subsection (a) of this section.

    (2)   The plan as modified becomes the plan unless, after notice and a hearing, such modification is disapproved.

(c) A plan modified under this section may not provide for payments over a period that expires after three years after the time that the first payment under the original confirmed plan was due, unless the court, for cause, approves a longer period, but the court may not approve a period that expires after five years after such time.

(d) A plan may not be modified under this section—

(1) to increase the amount of any payment due before the plan as modified becomes the plan;

(2) by anyone except the debtor, based on an increase in the debtor's disposable income, to increase the amount of payments to unsecured creditors required for a particular month so that the aggregate of such payments exceeds the debtor's disposable income for such month; or

(3) in the last year of the plan by anyone except the debtor, to require payments that would leave the debtor with insufficient funds to carry on the farming operation after the plan is completed.

(Added and amended Pub.L. 99–554, title II, § 255, title III, § 302(f), Oct. 27, 1986, 100 Stat. 3113, 3124; Pub.L. 103–65, § 1, Aug. 6, 1993, 107 Stat. 311; Pub.L. 105–277, div. C, title I, § 149(a), Oct. 21, 1998, 112 Stat. 2681–610; Pub.L. 106–5, § 1(1), (2), Mar. 30, 1999, 113 Stat. 9; Pub.L. 106–70, § 1, Oct. 9, 1999, 113 Stat. 1031; Pub.L. 107–8, § 1, May 11, 2001, 115 Stat. 10; Pub.L. 107–17, § 1, June 26, 2001, 115 Stat. 151; Pub.L. 107–170, § 1, May 7, 2002, 116 Stat. 133; Pub.L. 107–171, title X, § 10814(a), May 13, 2002, 116 Stat. 532; Pub.L. 107–377, § 2(a), Dec. 19, 2002, 116 Stat. 3115; Pub.L. 108–73, § 2(a), Aug. 15, 2003, 117 Stat. 891; Pub.L. 108–369, § 2(a), Oct. 25, 2004, 118 Stat. 1749; Pub.L. 109–8, title X, §§ 1001(a)(1), (c), 1006(b), Apr. 20, 2005, 199 Stat. 185–187.)

§ 1230. Revocation of an order of confirmation

(a) On request of a party in interest at any time within 180 days after the date of the entry of an order of confirmation under section 1225 of this title, and after notice and a hearing, the court may revoke such order if such order was procured by fraud.

(b) If the court revokes an order of confirmation under subsection (a) of this section, the court shall dispose of the case under section 1207 of this title, unless, within the time fixed by the court, the debtor proposes and the court confirms a modification of the plan under section 1229 of this title.

(Added and amended Pub.L. 99–554, title II, § 255, title III, § 302(f), Oct. 27, 1986, 100 Stat. 3113, 3124; Pub.L. 103–65, § 1, Aug. 6, 1993, 107 Stat. 311; Pub.L. 105–277, div. C, title I, § 149(a), Oct. 21, 1998, 112 Stat. 2681–610; Pub.L. 106–5, § 1(1), (2), Mar. 30, 1999, 113 Stat. 9; Pub.L. 106–70, § 1, Oct. 9, 1999, 113 Stat. 1031; Pub.L. 107–8, § 1, May 11, 2001, 115 Stat. 10; Pub.L. 107–17, § 1, June 26, 2001, 115 Stat. 151; Pub.L. 107–170, § 1, May 7, 2002, 116 Stat. 133; Pub.L. 107–171, title X, § 10814(a), May 13, 2002, 116 Stat. 532; Pub.L. 107–377, § 2(a), Dec. 19, 2002, 116 Stat. 3115; Pub.L. 108–73, § 2(a), Aug. 15, 2003, 117 Stat. 891; Pub.L. 108–369, § 2(a), Oct. 25, 2004, 118 Stat. 1749; Pub.L. 109–8, title X, § 1001(a)(1), (c), Apr. 20, 2005, 119 Stat. 185, 186.)

§ 1231. Special tax provisions

(a) The issuance, transfer, or exchange of a security, or the making or delivery of an instrument of transfer under a plan confirmed under section 1225 of this title, may not be taxed under any law imposing a stamp tax or similar tax.

(b) The court may authorize the proponent of a plan to request a determination, limited to questions of law, by any governmental unit charged with responsibility for collection or determination of a tax on or measured by income, of the tax effects, under section 346 of this title and under the law imposing such tax, of the plan. In the event of an actual controversy, the court may declare such effects after the earlier of—

(1) the date on which such governmental unit responds to the request under this subsection; or

(2) 270 days after such request.

(Added and amended Pub.L. 99–554, title II, § 255, title III, § 302(f), Oct. 27, 1986, 100 Stat. 3113, 3124; Pub.L. 103–65, § 1, Aug. 6, 1993, 107 Stat. 311; Pub.L. 105–277, div. C, title I, § 149(a), Oct. 21, 1998, 112 Stat. 2681–610; Pub.L. 106–5, § 1(1), (2), Mar. 30, 1999, 113 Stat. 9; Pub.L. 106–70, § 1, Oct. 9, 1999,

113 Stat. 1031; Pub.L. 107–8, § 1, May 11, 2001, 115 Stat. 10; Pub.L. 107–17, § 1, June 26, 2001, 115 Stat. 151; Pub.L. 107–170, § 1, May 7, 2002, 116 Stat. 133; Pub.L. 107–171, title X, § 10814(a), May 13, 2002, 116 Stat. 532; Pub.L. 107–377, § 2(a), Dec. 19, 2002, 116 Stat. 3115; Pub.L. 108–73, § 2(a), Aug. 15, 2003, 117 Stat. 891; Pub.L. 108–369, § 2(a), Oct. 25, 2004, 118 Stat. 1749; Pub.L. 109–8, title VII, § 719(b)(4), title X, §§ 1001(a)(1), (c), 1003(b), Apr. 20, 2005, 119 Stat. 133, 185, 186.)

CHAPTER 13—ADJUSTMENT OF DEBTS OF AN INDIVIDUAL WITH REGULAR INCOME

SUBCHAPTER I—OFFICERS, ADMINISTRATION, AND THE ESTATE

SUBCHAPTER II—THE PLAN

SUBCHAPTER I—OFFICERS, ADMINISTRATION, AND THE ESTATE

§ 1301.   Stay of action against codebtor

(a) Except as provided in subsections (b) and (c) of this section, after the order for relief under this chapter, a creditor may not act, or commence or continue any civil action, to collect all or any part of a consumer debt of the debtor from any individual that is liable on such debt with the debtor, or that secured such debt, unless—

    (1) such individual became liable on or secured such debt in the ordinary course of such individual's business; or

    (2) the case is closed, dismissed, or converted to a case under chapter 7 or 11 of this title.

(b) A creditor may present a negotiable instrument, and may give notice of dishonor of such an instrument.

(c) On request of a party in interest and after notice and a hearing, the court shall grant relief from the stay provided by subsection (a) of this section with respect to a creditor, to the extent that—

    (1) as between the debtor and the individual protected under subsection (a) of this section, such individual received the consideration for the claim held by such creditor;

    (2) the plan filed by the debtor proposes not to pay such claim; or

(3) such creditor's interest would be irreparably harmed by continuation of such stay.

(d) Twenty days after the filing of a request under subsection (c)(2) of this section for relief from the stay provided by subsection (a) of this section, such stay is terminated with respect to the party in interest making such request, unless the debtor or any individual that is liable on such debt with the debtor files and serves upon such party in interest a written objection to the taking of the proposed action.

(Pub.L. 95–598, Nov. 6, 1978, 92 Stat. 2645; Pub.L. 98–353, title III, §§ 313, 524, July 10, 1984, 98 Stat. 355, 388.)

§ 1302.   Trustee

(a) If the United States trustee appoints an individual under section 586(b) of title 28 to serve as standing trustee in cases under this chapter and if such individual qualifies under section 322 of this title, then such individual shall serve as trustee in the case. Otherwise, the United States trustee shall appoint one disinterested person to serve as trustee in the case or the United States trustee may serve as a trustee in the case.

(b) The trustee shall—

(1) perform the duties specified in sections 704(a)(2), 704(a)(3), 704(a)(4), 704(a)(5), 704(a)(6), 704(a)(7), and 704(a)(9) of this title;

(2) appear and be heard at any hearing that concerns—

(A) the value of property subject to a lien;

(B) confirmation of a plan; or

(C) modification of the plan after confirmation;

(3) dispose of, under regulations issued by the Director of the Administrative Office of the United States Courts, moneys received or to be received in a case under chapter XIII of the Bankruptcy Act;

(4) advise, other than on legal matters, and assist the debtor in performance under the plan;

(5) ensure that the debtor commences making timely payments under section 1326 of this title; and

(6) if with respect to the debtor there is a claim for a domestic support obligation, provide the applicable notice specified in subsection (d).

(c) If the debtor is engaged in business, then in addition to the duties specified in subsection (b) of this section, the trustee shall perform the duties specified in sections 1106(a)(3) and 1106(a)(4) of this title.

(d)(1) In a case described in subsection (b)(6) to which subsection (b)(6) applies, the trustee shall—

(A)(i) provide written notice to the holder of the claim described in subsection (b)(6) of such claim and of the right of such holder to use the services of the State child support enforcement agency established under sections 464 and 466 of the Social Security Act for the State in which such holder resides, for assistance in collecting child support during and after the case under this title; and

(ii) include in the notice provided under clause (i) the address and telephone number of such State child support enforcement agency;

(B)(i) provide written notice to such State child support enforcement agency of such claim; and

(ii) include in the notice provided under clause (i) the name, address, and telephone number of such holder; and

(C) at such time as the debtor is granted a discharge under section 1328, provide written notice to such holder and to such State child support enforcement agency of—

(i) the granting of the discharge;

    (ii) the last recent known address of the debtor;

    (iii) the last recent known name and address of the debtor's employer; and

    (iv) the name of each creditor that holds a claim that—

        (I) is not discharged under paragraph (2) or (4) of section 523(a); or

        (II) was reaffirmed by the debtor under section 524(c).

  (2)(A) The holder of a claim described in subsection (b)(6) or the State child support enforcement agency of the State in which such holder resides may request from a creditor described in paragraph (1)(C)(iv) the last known address of the debtor.

  (B) Notwithstanding any other provision of law, a creditor that makes a disclosure of a last known address of a debtor in connection with a request made under subparagraph (A) shall not be liable by reason of making that disclosure.

  (Pub.L. 95–598, Nov. 6, 1978, 92 Stat. 2645; Pub.L. 98–353, title III, §§ 314, 525, July 10, 1984, 98 Stat. 356, 388; Pub.L. 99–554, title II, §§ 228, 283(w), Oct. 27, 1986, 100 Stat. 3103, 3118; Pub.L. 103–394, title V, § 501(d)(37), Oct. 22, 1994, 108 Stat. 4147; Pub.L. 109–8, title II, § 219(d), Apr. 20, 2005, 119 Stat. 58; Pub.L. 111–327, § 2(a)(39), Dec. 22, 2010, 124 Stat. 3561.)

§ 1303.   Rights and powers of debtor

  Subject to any limitations on a trustee under this chapter, the debtor shall have, exclusive of the trustee, the rights and powers of a trustee under sections 363(b), 363(d), 363(e), 363(f), and 363(*l*), of this title.

  (Pub.L. 95–598, Nov. 6, 1978, 92 Stat. 2646.)

§ 1304.   Debtor engaged in business

  (a) A debtor that is self-employed and incurs trade credit in the production of income from such employment is engaged in business.

  (b) Unless the court orders otherwise, a debtor engaged in business may operate the business of the debtor and, subject to any limitations on a trustee under sections 363(c) and 364 of this title and to such limitations or conditions as the court prescribes, shall have, exclusive of the trustee, the rights and powers of the trustee under such sections.

  (c) A debtor engaged in business shall perform the duties of the trustee specified in section 704(a)(8) of this title.

  (Pub.L. 95–598, Nov. 6, 1978, 92 Stat. 2646; Pub.L. 98–353, title III, §§ 311(b)(2), 526, July 10, 1984, 98 Stat. 355, 389; Pub.L. 111–327, § 2(a)(40), Dec. 22, 2010, 124 Stat. 3562.)

§ 1305.   Filing and allowance of postpetition claims

  (a) A proof of claim may be filed by any entity that holds a claim against the debtor—

  (1) for taxes that become payable to a governmental unit while the case is pending; or

  (2) that is a consumer debt, that arises after the date of the order for relief under this chapter, and that is for property or services necessary for the debtor's performance under the plan.

  (b) Except as provided in subsection (c) of this section, a claim filed under subsection (a) of this section shall be allowed or disallowed under section 502 of this title, but shall be determined as of the date such claim arises, and shall be allowed under section 502(a), 502(b), or 502(c) of this title, or disallowed under section 502(d) or 502(e) of this title, the same as if such claim had arisen before the date of the filing of the petition.

(c) A claim filed under subsection (a)(2) of this section shall be disallowed if the holder of such claim knew or should have known that prior approval by the trustee of the debtor's incurring the obligation was practicable and was not obtained.

(Pub.L. 95–598, Nov. 6, 1978, 92 Stat. 2647.)

§ 1306.   Property of the estate

(a) Property of the estate includes, in addition to the property specified in section 541 of this title—

(1) all property of the kind specified in such section that the debtor acquires after the commencement of the case but before the case is closed, dismissed, or converted to a case under chapter 7, 11, or 12 of this title, whichever occurs first; and

(2) earnings from services performed by the debtor after the commencement of the case but before the case is closed, dismissed, or converted to a case under chapter 7, 11, or 12 of this title, whichever occurs first.

(b) Except as provided in a confirmed plan or order confirming a plan, the debtor shall remain in possession of all property of the estate.

(Pub.L. 95–598, Nov. 6, 1978, 92 Stat. 2647; Pub.L. 99–554, title II, § 257(u), Oct. 27, 1986, 100 Stat. 3116.)

§ 1307.   Conversion or dismissal

(a) The debtor may convert a case under this chapter to a case under chapter 7 of this title at any time. Any waiver of the right to convert under this subsection is unenforceable.

(b) On request of the debtor at any time, if the case has not been converted under section 706, 1112, or 1208 of this title, the court shall dismiss a case under this chapter. Any waiver of the right to dismiss under this subsection is unenforceable.

(c) Except as provided in subsection (f) of this section, on request of a party in interest or the United States trustee and after notice and a hearing, the court may convert a case under this chapter to a case under chapter 7 of this title, or may dismiss a case under this chapter, whichever is in the best interests of creditors and the estate, for cause, including—

(1) unreasonable delay by the debtor that is prejudicial to creditors;

(2) nonpayment of any fees and charges required under chapter 123 of title 28;

(3) failure to file a plan timely under section 1321 of this title;

(4) failure to commence making timely payments under section 1326 of this title;

(5) denial of confirmation of a plan under section 1325 of this title and denial of a request made for additional time for filing another plan or a modification of a plan;

(6) material default by the debtor with respect to a term of a confirmed plan;

(7) revocation of the order of confirmation under section 1330 of this title, and denial of confirmation of a modified plan under section 1329 of this title;

(8) termination of a confirmed plan by reason of the occurrence of a condition specified in the plan other than completion of payments under the plan;

(9) only on request of the United States trustee, failure of the debtor to file, within fifteen days, or such additional time as the court may allow, after the filing of the petition commencing such case, the information required by paragraph (1) of section 521(a);

(10) only on request of the United States trustee, failure to timely file the information required by paragraph (2) of section 521(a); or

(11) failure of the debtor to pay any domestic support obligation that first becomes payable after the date of the filing of the petition.

(d)   Except as provided in subsection (f) of this section, at any time before the confirmation of a plan under section 1325 of this title, on request of a party in interest or the United States trustee and after notice and a hearing, the court may convert a case under this chapter to a case under chapter 11 or 12 of this title.

(e)   Upon the failure of the debtor to file a tax return under section 1308, on request of a party in interest or the United States trustee and after notice and a hearing, the court shall dismiss a case or convert a case under this chapter to a case under chapter 7 of this title, whichever is in the best interest of the creditors and the estate.

(f)   The court may not convert a case under this chapter to a case under chapter 7, 11, or 12 of this title if the debtor is a farmer, unless the debtor requests such conversion.

(g)   Notwithstanding any other provision of this section, a case may not be converted to a case under another chapter of this title unless the debtor may be a debtor under such chapter.

(Pub.L. 95–598, Nov. 6, 1978, 92 Stat. 2647; Pub.L. 98–353, title III, §§ 315, 527, July 10, 1984, 98 Stat. 356, 389; Pub.L. 99–554, title II, §§ 229, 257(v), Oct. 27, 1986, 100 Stat. 3103, 3116; Pub.L. 109–8, title II, § 213(7), title VII, § 716(c), Apr. 20, 2005, 119 Stat. 53, 130; Pub.L. 111–327, § 2(a)(41), Dec. 22, 2010, 124 Stat. 3562.)

§ 1308.   Filing of prepetition tax returns

(a)   Not later than the day before the date on which the meeting of the creditors is first scheduled to be held under section 341(a), if the debtor was required to file a tax return under applicable nonbankruptcy law, the debtor shall file with appropriate tax authorities all tax returns for all taxable periods ending during the 4-year period ending on the date of the filing of the petition.

(b)(1)   Subject to paragraph (2), if the tax returns required by subsection (a) have not been filed by the date on which the meeting of creditors is first scheduled to be held under section 341(a), the trustee may hold open that meeting for a reasonable period of time to allow the debtor an additional period of time to file any unfiled returns, but such additional period of time shall not extend beyond—

(A)   for any return that is past due as of the date of the filing of the petition, the date that is 120 days after the date of that meeting; or

(B)   for any return that is not past due as of the date of the filing of the petition, the later of—

(i)   the date that is 120 days after the date of that meeting; or

(ii)   the date on which the return is due under the last automatic extension of time for filing that return to which the debtor is entitled, and for which request is timely made, in accordance with applicable nonbankruptcy law.

(2)   After notice and a hearing, and order entered before the tolling of any applicable filing period determined under paragraph (1), if the debtor demonstrates by a preponderance of the evidence that the failure to file a return as required under paragraph (1) is attributable to circumstances beyond the control of the debtor, the court may extend the filing period established by the trustee under paragraph (1) for—

(A)   a period of not more than 30 days for returns described in paragraph (1)(A); and

(B)   a period not to extend after the applicable extended due date for a return described in paragraph (1)(B).

(c)   For purposes of this section, the term "return" includes a return prepared pursuant to subsection (a) or (b) of section 6020 of the Internal Revenue Code of 1986, or a similar State or local law, or a written stipulation to a judgment or a final order entered by a nonbankruptcy tribunal.

(Added Pub.L. 109–8, title VII, § 716(b)(1), Apr. 20, 2005, 119 Stat. 129, amended Pub.L. 111–327, § 2(a)(42), Dec. 22, 2010, 124 Stat. 3562.)

SUBCHAPTER II—THE PLAN

§ 1321. Filing of plan

The debtor shall file a plan.

(Pub.L. 95–598, Nov. 6, 1978, 92 Stat. 2648.)

§ 1322. Contents of plan

(a) The plan—

(1) shall provide for the submission of all or such portion of future earnings or other future income of the debtor to the supervision and control of the trustee as is necessary for the execution of the plan;

(2) shall provide for the full payment, in deferred cash payments, of all claims entitled to priority under section 507 of this title, unless the holder of a particular claim agrees to a different treatment of such claim;

(3) if the plan classifies claims, shall provide the same treatment for each claim within a particular class; and.

(4) notwithstanding any other provision of this section, may provide for less than full payment of all amounts owed for a claim entitled to priority under section 507(a)(1)(B) only if the plan provides that all of the debtor's projected disposable income for a 5-year period beginning on the date that the first payment is due under the plan will be applied to make payments under the plan.

(b) Subject to subsections (a) and (c) of this section, the plan may—

(1) designate a class or classes of unsecured claims, as provided in section 1122 of this title, but may not discriminate unfairly against any class so designated; however, such plan may treat claims for a consumer debt of the debtor if an individual is liable on such consumer debt with the debtor differently than other unsecured claims;

(2) modify the rights of holders of secured claims, other than a claim secured only by a security interest in real property that is the debtor's principal residence, or of holders of unsecured claims, or leave unaffected the rights of holders of any class of claims;

(3) provide for the curing or waiving of any default;

(4) provide for payments on any unsecured claim to be made concurrently with payments on any secured claim or any other unsecured claim;

(5) notwithstanding paragraph (2) of this subsection, provide for the curing of any default within a reasonable time and maintenance of payments while the case is pending on any unsecured claim or secured claim on which the last payment is due after the date on which the final payment under the plan is due;

(6) provide for the payment of all or any part of any claim allowed under section 1305 of this title;

(7) subject to section 365 of this title, provide for the assumption, rejection, or assignment of any executory contract or unexpired lease of the debtor not previously rejected under such section;

(8) provide for the payment of all or part of a claim against the debtor from property of the estate or property of the debtor;

(9) provide for the vesting of property of the estate, on confirmation of the plan or at a later time, in the debtor or in any other entity;

(10) provide for the payment of interest accruing after the date of the filing of the petition on unsecured claims that are nondischargeable under section 1328(a), except that such interest may be paid only to the extent that the debtor has disposable income available to pay such interest after making provision for full payment of all allowed claims; and

(11) include any other appropriate provision not inconsistent with this title.

(c) Notwithstanding subsection (b)(2) and applicable nonbankruptcy law—

(1) a default with respect to, or that gave rise to, a lien on the debtor's principal residence may be cured under paragraph (3) or (5) of subsection (b) until such residence is sold at a foreclosure sale that is conducted in accordance with applicable nonbankruptcy law; and

(2) in a case in which the last payment on the original payment schedule for a claim secured only by a security interest in real property that is the debtor's principal residence is due before the date on which the final payment under the plan is due, the plan may provide for the payment of the claim as modified pursuant to section 1325(a)(5) of this title.

(d)(1) If the current monthly income of the debtor and the debtor's spouse combined, when multiplied by 12, is not less than—

(A) in the case of a debtor in a household of 1 person, the median family income of the applicable State for 1 earner;

(B) in the case of a debtor in a household of 2, 3, or 4 individuals, the highest median family income of the applicable State for a family of the same number or fewer individuals; or

(C) in the case of a debtor in a household exceeding 4 individuals, the highest median family income of the applicable State for a family of 4 or fewer individuals, plus $700* per month for each individual in excess of 4,

the plan may not provide for payments over a period that is longer than 5 years.

(2) If the current monthly income of the debtor and the debtor's spouse combined, when multiplied by 12, is less than—

(A) in the case of a debtor in a household of 1 person, the median family income of the applicable State for 1 earner;

(B) in the case of a debtor in a household of 2, 3, or 4 individuals, the highest median family income of the applicable State for a family of the same number or fewer individuals; or

(C) in the case of a debtor in a household exceeding 4 individuals, the highest median family income of the applicable State for a family of 4 or fewer individuals, plus $700* per month for each individual in excess of 4,

the plan may not provide for payments over a period that is longer than 3 years, unless the court, for cause, approves a longer period, but the court may not approve a period that is longer than 5 years.

(e) Notwithstanding subsection (b)(2) of this section and sections 506(b) and 1325(a)(5) of this title, if it is proposed in a plan to cure a default, the amount necessary to cure the default, shall be determined in accordance with the underlying agreement and applicable nonbankruptcy law.

(f) A plan may not materially alter the terms of a loan described in section 362(b)(19) and any amounts required to repay such loan shall not constitute "disposable income" under section 1325.

(Pub.L. 95–598, Nov. 6, 1978, 92 Stat. 2648; Pub.L. 98–353, title III, §§ 316, 528, July 10, 1984, 98 Stat. 356, 389; Pub.L. 103–394, title III, §§ 301, 305(c), Oct. 22, 1994, 108 Stat. 4131, 4134; Pub.L. 109–8, title II, §§ 213(8), (9), 224(d), title III, § 318(1), Apr. 20, 2005, 119 Stat. 53, 65, 93; Pub.L. 111–327, § 2(a)(43), Dec. 22, 2010, 124 Stat. 3562.)

---

*   *Note from West Advisory Panel: Dollar amounts adjusted pursuant to 11 U.S.C. § 104; 81 Fed. Reg. 8748 (Feb. 22, 2016).*

§ 1323. Modification of plan before confirmation

(a) The debtor may modify the plan at any time before confirmation, but may not modify the plan so that the plan as modified fails to meet the requirements of section 1322 of this title.

(b) After the debtor files a modification under this section, the plan as modified becomes the plan.

(c) Any holder of a secured claim that has accepted or rejected the plan is deemed to have accepted or rejected, as the case may be, the plan as modified, unless the modification provides for a change in the rights of such holder from what such rights were under the plan before modification, and such holder changes such holder's previous acceptance or rejection.

(Pub.L. 95–598, Nov. 6, 1978, 92 Stat. 2649.)

§ 1324. Confirmation hearing

(a) Except as provided in subsection (b) and after notice, the court shall hold a hearing on confirmation of the plan. A party in interest may object to confirmation of the plan.

(b) The hearing on confirmation of the plan may be held not earlier than 20 days and not later than 45 days after the date of the meeting of creditors under section 341(a), unless the court determines that it would be in the best interests of the creditors and the estate to hold such hearing at an earlier date and there is no objection to such earlier date.

(Pub.L. 95–598, Nov. 6, 1978, 92 Stat. 2649; Pub.L. 98–353, title III, § 529, July 10, 1984, 98 Stat. 389; Pub.L. 99–554, title II, § 283(x), Oct. 27, 1986, 100 Stat. 3118; Pub.L. 109–8, title III, § 317, Apr. 20, 2005, 119 Stat. 92.)

§ 1325. Confirmation of plan

(a) Except as provided in subsection (b), the court shall confirm a plan if—

(1) the plan complies with the provisions of this chapter and with the other applicable provisions of this title;

(2) any fee, charge, or amount required under chapter 123 of title 28, or by the plan, to be paid before confirmation, has been paid;

(3) the plan has been proposed in good faith and not by any means forbidden by law;

(4) the value, as of the effective date of the plan, of property to be distributed under the plan on account of each allowed unsecured claim is not less than the amount that would be paid on such claim if the estate of the debtor were liquidated under chapter 7 of this title on such date;

(5) with respect to each allowed secured claim provided for by the plan—

(A) the holder of such claim has accepted the plan;

(B)(i) the plan provides that—

(I) the holder of such claim retain the lien securing such claim until the earlier of—

(aa) the payment of the underlying debt determined under nonbankruptcy law; or

(bb) discharge under section 1328; and

(II) if the case under this chapter is dismissed or converted without completion of the plan, such lien shall also be retained by such holder to the extent recognized by applicable nonbankruptcy law;

(ii) the value, as of the effective date of the plan, of property to be distributed under the plan on account of such claim is not less than the allowed amount of such claim; and

(iii) if—

(I)　property to be distributed pursuant to this subsection is in the form of periodic payments, such payments shall be in equal monthly amounts; and

(II)　the holder of the claim is secured by personal property, the amount of such payments shall not be less than an amount sufficient to provide to the holder of such claim adequate protection during the period of the plan; or

(C)　the debtor surrenders the property securing such claim to such holder;

(6)　the debtor will be able to make all payments under the plan and to comply with the plan;

(7)　the action of the debtor in filing the petition was in good faith;

(8)　the debtor has paid all amounts that are required to be paid under a domestic support obligation and that first become payable after the date of the filing of the petition if the debtor is required by a judicial or administrative order, or by statute, to pay such domestic support obligation; and

(9)　the debtor has filed all applicable Federal, State, and local tax returns as required by section 1308.

For purposes of paragraph (5), section 506 shall not apply to a claim described in that paragraph if the creditor has a purchase money security interest securing the debt that is the subject of the claim, the debt was incurred within the 910-day period preceding the date of the filing of the petition, and the collateral for that debt consists of a motor vehicle (as defined in section 30102 of title 49) acquired for the personal use of the debtor, or if collateral for that debt consists of any other thing of value, if the debt was incurred during the 1-year period preceding that filing.

(b)(1)　If the trustee or the holder of an allowed unsecured claim objects to the confirmation of the plan, then the court may not approve the plan unless, as of the effective date of the plan—

(A)　the value of the property to be distributed under the plan on account of such claim is not less than the amount of such claim; or

(B)　the plan provides that all of the debtor's projected disposable income to be received in the applicable commitment period beginning on the date that the first payment is due under the plan will be applied to make payments to unsecured creditors under the plan.

(2)　For purposes of this subsection, the term "disposable income" means current monthly income received by the debtor (other than child support payments, foster care payments, or disability payments for a dependent child made in accordance with applicable nonbankruptcy law to the extent reasonably necessary to be expended for such child) less amounts reasonably necessary to be expended—

(A)(i)　for the maintenance or support of the debtor or a dependent of the debtor, or for a domestic support obligation, that first becomes payable after the date the petition is filed; and

(ii)　for charitable contributions (that meet the definition of "charitable contribution" under section 548(d)(3)) to a qualified religious or charitable entity or organization (as defined in section 548(d)(4)) in an amount not to exceed 15 percent of gross income of the debtor for the year in which the contributions are made; and

(B)　if the debtor is engaged in business, for the payment of expenditures necessary for the continuation, preservation, and operation of such business.

(3)　Amounts reasonably necessary to be expended under paragraph (2), other than subparagraph (A)(ii) of paragraph (2), shall be determined in accordance with subparagraphs (A) and (B) of section 707(b)(2), if the debtor has current monthly income, when multiplied by 12, greater than—

(A)　in the case of a debtor in a household of 1 person, the median family income of the applicable State for 1 earner;

(B) in the case of a debtor in a household of 2, 3, or 4 individuals, the highest median family income of the applicable State for a family of the same number or fewer individuals; or

(C) in the case of a debtor in a household exceeding 4 individuals, the highest median family income of the applicable State for a family of 4 or fewer individuals, plus $700* per month for each individual in excess of 4.

(4) For purposes of this subsection, the "applicable commitment period"—

    (A) subject to subparagraph (B), shall be—

        (i) 3 years; or

        (ii) not less than 5 years, if the current monthly income of the debtor and the debtor's spouse combined, when multiplied by 12, is not less than—

            (I) in the case of a debtor in a household of 1 person, the median family income of the applicable State for 1 earner;

            (II) in the case of a debtor in a household of 2, 3, or 4 individuals, the highest median family income of the applicable State for a family of the same number or fewer individuals; or

            (III) in the case of a debtor in a household exceeding 4 individuals, the highest median family income of the applicable State for a family of 4 or fewer individuals, plus $700* per month for each individual in excess of 4; and

    (B) may be less than 3 or 5 years, whichever is applicable under subparagraph (A), but only if the plan provides for payment in full of all allowed unsecured claims over a shorter period.

(c) After confirmation of a plan, the court may order any entity from whom the debtor receives income to pay all or any part of such income to the trustee.

    (Pub.L. 95–598, Nov. 6, 1978, 92 Stat. 2649; Pub.L. 98–353, title III, §§ 317, 530, July 10, 1984, 98 Stat. 356, 389; Pub.L. 99–554, title II, § 283(y), Oct. 27, 1986, 100 Stat. 3118; Pub.L. 105–183, § 4(a), June 19, 1998, 112 Stat. 518; Pub.L. 109–8, title I, § 102(g), (h), title II, § 213(10), title III, §§ 306(a), (b), 309(c)(1), 318(2), (3), title VII, § 716(a), Apr. 20, 2005, 119 Stat. 33, 53, 80, 83, 93 129; Pub.L. 109–439, § 2, Dec. 20, 2006, 120 Stat. 3285; Pub.L. 111–327, § 2(a)(44), Dec. 22, 2010, 124 Stat. 3562.)

§ 1326.   Payments

(a)(1) Unless the court orders otherwise, the debtor shall commence making payments not later than 30 days after the date of the filing of the plan or the order for relief, whichever is earlier, in the amount—

    (A) proposed by the plan to the trustee;

    (B) scheduled in a lease of personal property directly to the lessor for that portion of the obligation that becomes due after the order for relief, reducing the payments under subparagraph (A) by the amount so paid and providing the trustee with evidence of such payment, including the amount and date of payment; and

    (C) that provides adequate protection directly to a creditor holding an allowed claim secured by personal property to the extent the claim is attributable to the purchase of such property by the debtor for that portion of the obligation that becomes due after the order for relief, reducing the payments under subparagraph (A) by the amount so paid and providing the trustee with evidence of such payment, including the amount and date of payment.

(2) A payment made under paragraph (1)(A) shall be retained by the trustee until confirmation or denial of confirmation. If a plan is confirmed, the trustee shall distribute any such payment in accordance with the plan as soon as is practicable. If a plan is not confirmed, the trustee shall return

---

* *Note from West Advisory Panel: Dollar amounts adjusted pursuant to 11 U.S.C. § 104; 81 Fed. Reg. 8748 (Feb. 22, 2016).*

any such payments not previously paid and not yet due and owing to creditors pursuant to paragraph (3) to the debtor, after deducting any unpaid claim allowed under section 503(b).

(3)   Subject to section 363, the court may, upon notice and a hearing, modify, increase, or reduce the payments required under this subsection pending confirmation of a plan.

(4)   Not later than 60 days after the date of filing of a case under this chapter, a debtor retaining possession of personal property subject to a lease or securing a claim attributable in whole or in part to the purchase price of such property shall provide the lessor or secured creditor reasonable evidence of the maintenance of any required insurance coverage with respect to the use or ownership of such property and continue to do so for so long as the debtor retains possession of such property.

(b)   Before or at the time of each payment to creditors under the plan, there shall be paid—

(1)   any unpaid claim of the kind specified in section 507(a)(2) of this title;

(2)   if a standing trustee appointed under section 586(b) of title 28 is serving in the case, the percentage fee fixed for such standing trustee under section 586(e)(1)(B) of title 28; and

(3)   if a chapter 7 trustee has been allowed compensation due to the conversion or dismissal of the debtor's prior case pursuant to section 707(b), and some portion of that compensation remains unpaid in a case converted to this chapter or in the case dismissed under section 707(b) and refiled under this chapter, the amount of any such unpaid compensation, which shall be paid monthly—

(A)   by prorating such amount over the remaining duration of the plan; and

(B)   by monthly payments not to exceed the greater of—

(i) $25;* or

(ii)   the amount payable to unsecured nonpriority creditors, as provided by the plan, multiplied by 5 percent, and the result divided by the number of months in the plan.

(c)   Except as otherwise provided in the plan or in the order confirming the plan, the trustee shall make payments to creditors under the plan.

(d)   Notwithstanding any other provision of this title—

(1)   compensation referred to in subsection (b)(3) is payable and may be collected by the trustee under that paragraph, even if such amount has been discharged in a prior case under this title; and

(2)   such compensation is payable in a case under this chapter only to the extent permitted by subsection (b)(3).

(Pub.L. 95–598, Nov. 6, 1978, 92 Stat. 2650; Pub.L. 98–353, title III, §§ 318(a), 531, July 10, 1984, 98 Stat. 357, 389; Pub.L. 99–554, title II, §§ 230, 283(z), Oct. 27, 1986, 100 Stat. 3103, 3118; Pub.L. 103–394, title III, § 307, Oct. 22, 1994, 108 Stat. 4135; Pub.L. 109–8, title III, § 309(c)(2), title XII, § 1224, title XV, § 1502(a)(10), Apr. 20, 2005, 119 Stat. 83, 199, 217.)

§ 1327.   Effect of confirmation

(a)   The provisions of a confirmed plan bind the debtor and each creditor, whether or not the claim of such creditor is provided for by the plan, and whether or not such creditor has objected to, has accepted, or has rejected the plan.

(b)   Except as otherwise provided in the plan or the order confirming the plan, the confirmation of a plan vests all of the property of the estate in the debtor.

(c)   Except as otherwise provided in the plan or in the order confirming the plan, the property vesting in the debtor under subsection (b) of this section is free and clear of any claim or interest of any creditor provided for by the plan.

---

*   *Note from West Advisory Panel: Dollar amounts adjusted pursuant to 11 U.S.C. § 104; 81 Fed. Reg. 8748 (Feb. 22, 2016).*

(Pub.L. 95–598, Nov. 6, 1978, 92 Stat. 2650.)

§ 1328. Discharge

(a) Subject to subsection (d), as soon as practicable after completion by the debtor of all payments under the plan, and in the case of a debtor who is required by a judicial or administrative order, or by statute, to pay a domestic support obligation, after such debtor certifies that all amounts payable under such order or such statute that are due on or before the date of the certification (including amounts due before the petition was filed, but only to the extent provided for by the plan) have been paid, unless the court approves a written waiver of discharge executed by the debtor after the order for relief under this chapter, the court shall grant the debtor a discharge of all debts provided for by the plan or disallowed under section 502 of this title, except any debt—

(1) provided for under section 1322(b)(5);

(2) of the kind specified in section 507(a)(8)(C) or in paragraph (1)(B), (1)(C), (2), (3), (4), (5), (8), or (9) of section 523(a);

(3) for restitution, or a criminal fine, included in a sentence on the debtor's conviction of a crime; or

(4) for restitution, or damages, awarded in a civil action against the debtor as a result of willful or malicious injury by the debtor that caused personal injury to an individual or the death of an individual.

(b) Subject to subsection (d), at any time after the confirmation of the plan and after notice and a hearing, the court may grant a discharge to a debtor that has not completed payments under the plan only if—

(1) the debtor's failure to complete such payments is due to circumstances for which the debtor should not justly be held accountable;

(2) the value, as of the effective date of the plan, of property actually distributed under the plan on account of each allowed unsecured claim is not less than the amount that would have been paid on such claim if the estate of the debtor had been liquidated under chapter 7 of this title on such date; and

(3) modification of the plan under section 1329 of this title is not practicable.

(c) A discharge granted under subsection (b) of this section discharges the debtor from all unsecured debts provided for by the plan or disallowed under section 502 of this title, except any debt—

(1) provided for under section 1322(b)(5) of this title; or

(2) of a kind specified in section 523(a) of this title.

(d) Notwithstanding any other provision of this section, a discharge granted under this section does not discharge the debtor from any debt based on an allowed claim filed under section 1305(a)(2) of this title if prior approval by the trustee of the debtor's incurring such debt was practicable and was not obtained.

(e) On request of a party in interest before one year after a discharge under this section is granted, and after notice and a hearing, the court may revoke such discharge only if—

(1) such discharge was obtained by the debtor through fraud; and

(2) the requesting party did not know of such fraud until after such discharge was granted.

(f) Notwithstanding subsections (a) and (b), the court shall not grant a discharge of all debts provided for in the plan or disallowed under section 502, if the debtor has received a discharge—

(1) in a case filed under chapter 7, 11, or 12 of this title during the 4-year period preceding the date of the order for relief under this chapter, or

(2) in a case filed under chapter 13 of this title during the 2-year period preceding the date of such order.

(g)(1) The court shall not grant a discharge under this section to a debtor unless after filing a petition the debtor has completed an instructional course concerning personal financial management described in section 111.

(2) Paragraph (1) shall not apply with respect to a debtor who is a person described in section 109(h)(4) or who resides in a district for which the United States trustee (or the bankruptcy administrator, if any) determines that the approved instructional courses are not adequate to service the additional individuals who would otherwise be required to complete such instructional course by reason of the requirements of paragraph (1).

(3) The United States trustee (or the bankruptcy administrator, if any) who makes a determination described in paragraph (2) shall review such determination not later than 1 year after the date of such determination, and not less frequently than annually thereafter.

(h) The court may not grant a discharge under this chapter unless the court after notice and a hearing held not more than 10 days before the date of the entry of the order granting the discharge finds that there is no reasonable cause to believe that—

(1) section 522(q)(1) may be applicable to the debtor; and

(2) there is pending any proceeding in which the debtor may be found guilty of a felony of the kind described in section 522(q)(1)(A) or liable for a debt of the kind described in section 522(q)(1)(B).

(Pub.L. 95–598, Nov. 6, 1978, 92 Stat. 2650; Pub.L. 98–353, title III, § 532, July 10, 1984, 98 Stat. 389; Pub.L. 101–508, title III, § 3007(b)(1), Nov. 5, 1990, 104 Stat. 1388–28; Pub.L. 101–581, §§ 2(b), 3, Nov. 15, 1990, 104 Stat. 2865; Pub.L. 101–647, title XXXI, §§ 3102(b), 3103, Nov. 29, 1990, 104 Stat. 4916; Pub.L. 103–394, title III, § 302, title V, § 501(d)(38), Oct. 22, 1994, 108 Stat. 4132, 4147; Pub.L. 109–8, title I, § 106(c), title II, § 213(11), title III, §§ 312(2), 314(b), 330(d), title VII, § 707, Apr. 20, 2005, 119 Stat. 38, 53, 87, 88, 102, 126.)

§ 1329.   Modification of plan after confirmation

(a) At any time after confirmation of the plan but before the completion of payments under such plan, the plan may be modified, upon request of the debtor, the trustee, or the holder of an allowed unsecured claim, to—

(1) increase or reduce the amount of payments on claims of a particular class provided for by the plan;

(2) extend or reduce the time for such payments;

(3) alter the amount of the distribution to a creditor whose claim is provided for by the plan to the extent necessary to take account of any payment of such claim other than under the plan; or

(4) reduce amounts to be paid under the plan by the actual amount expended by the debtor to purchase health insurance for the debtor (and for any dependent of the debtor if such dependent does not otherwise have health insurance coverage) if the debtor documents the cost of such insurance and demonstrates that—

(A) such expenses are reasonable and necessary;

(B)(i) if the debtor previously paid for health insurance, the amount is not materially larger than the cost the debtor previously paid or the cost necessary to maintain the lapsed policy; or

(ii) if the debtor did not have health insurance, the amount is not materially larger than the reasonable cost that would be incurred by a debtor who purchases health insurance, who has similar income, expenses, age, and health status, and who lives in the same geographical location with the same number of dependents who do not otherwise have health insurance coverage; and

(C) the amount is not otherwise allowed for purposes of determining disposable income under section 1325(b) of this title;

and upon request of any party in interest, files proof that a health insurance policy was purchased.

(b)(1)   Sections 1322(a), 1322(b), and 1323(c) of this title and the requirements of section 1325(a) of this title apply to any modification under subsection (a) of this section.

(2)   The plan as modified becomes the plan unless, after notice and a hearing, such modification is disapproved.

(c)   A plan modified under this section may not provide for payments over a period that expires after the applicable commitment period under section 1325(b)(1)(B) after the time that the first payment under the original confirmed plan was due, unless the court, for cause, approves a longer period, but the court may not approve a period that expires after five years after such time.

(Pub.L. 95–598, Nov. 6, 1978, 92 Stat. 2651; Pub.L. 98–353, title III, §§ 319, 533, July 10, 1984, 98 Stat. 357, 389; Pub.L. 109–8, title I, § 102(i), title III, § 318(4), Apr. 20, 2005, 119 Stat. 34, 94.)

§ 1330.   Revocation of an order of confirmation

(a)   On request of a party in interest at any time within 180 days after the date of the entry of an order of confirmation under section 1325 of this title, and after notice and a hearing, the court may revoke such order if such order was procured by fraud.

(b)   If the court revokes an order of confirmation under subsection (a) of this section, the court shall dispose of the case under section 1307 of this title, unless, within the time fixed by the court, the debtor proposes and the court confirms a modification of the plan under section 1329 of this title.

(Pub.L. 95–598, Nov. 6, 1978, 92 Stat. 2651.)

CHAPTER 15—ANCILLARY AND OTHER CROSS-BORDER CASES

---

§ 1501.   Purpose and scope of application

(a)   The purpose of this chapter is to incorporate the Model Law on Cross-Border Insolvency so as to provide effective mechanisms for dealing with cases of cross-border insolvency with the objectives of—

(1)   cooperation between—

(A)   courts of the United States, United States trustees, trustees, examiners, debtors, and debtors in possession; and

(B)   the courts and other competent authorities of foreign countries involved in cross-border insolvency cases;

(2)   greater legal certainty for trade and investment;

(3)   fair and efficient administration of cross-border insolvencies that protects the interests of all creditors, and other interested entities, including the debtor;

(4)   protection and maximization of the value of the debtor's assets; and

(5)   facilitation of the rescue of financially troubled businesses, thereby protecting investment and preserving employment.

(b)   This chapter applies where—

(1)   assistance is sought in the United States by a foreign court or a foreign representative in connection with a foreign proceeding;

(2)   assistance is sought in a foreign country in connection with a case under this title;

(3)   a foreign proceeding and a case under this title with respect to the same debtor are pending concurrently; or

(4)   creditors or other interested persons in a foreign country have an interest in requesting the commencement of, or participating in, a case or proceeding under this title.

(c)   This chapter does not apply to—

(1) a proceeding concerning an entity, other than a foreign insurance company, identified by exclusion in section 109(b);

(2) an individual, or to an individual and such individual's spouse, who have debts within the limits specified in section 109(e) and who are citizens of the United States or aliens lawfully admitted for permanent residence in the United States; or

(3) an entity subject to a proceeding under the Securities Investor Protection Act of 1970, a stockbroker subject to subchapter III of chapter 7 of this title, or a commodity broker subject to subchapter IV of chapter 7 of this title.

(d) The court may not grant relief under this chapter with respect to any deposit, escrow, trust fund, or other security required or permitted under any applicable State insurance law or regulation for the benefit of claim holders in the United States.

(Added Pub.L. 109–8, title VIII, § 801(a), Apr. 20, 2005, 119 Stat. 135.)

SUBCHAPTER I—GENERAL PROVISIONS

§ 1502. Definitions

For the purposes of this chapter, the term—

(1) "debtor" means an entity that is the subject of a foreign proceeding;

(2) "establishment" means any place of operations where the debtor carries out a nontransitory economic activity;

(3) "foreign court" means a judicial or other authority competent to control or supervise a foreign proceeding;

(4) "foreign main proceeding" means a foreign proceeding pending in the country where the debtor has the center of its main interests;

(5) "foreign nonmain proceeding" means a foreign proceeding, other than a foreign main proceeding, pending in a country where the debtor has an establishment;

(6) "trustee" includes a trustee, a debtor in possession in a case under any chapter of this title, or a debtor under chapter 9 of this title;

(7) "recognition" means the entry of an order granting recognition of a foreign main proceeding or foreign nonmain proceeding under this chapter; and

(8) "within the territorial jurisdiction of the United States", when used with reference to property of a debtor, refers to tangible property located within the territory of the United States and intangible property deemed under applicable nonbankruptcy law to be located within that territory, including any property subject to attachment or garnishment that may properly be seized or garnished by an action in a Federal or State court in the United States.

(Added Pub.L. 109–8, title VIII, § 801(a), Apr. 20, 2005, 119 Stat. 135.)

§ 1503. International obligations of the United States

To the extent that this chapter conflicts with an obligation of the United States arising out of any treaty or other form of agreement to which it is a party with one or more other countries, the requirements of the treaty or agreement prevail.

(Added Pub.L. 109–8, title VIII, § 801(a), Apr. 20, 2005, 119 Stat. 136.)

§ 1504. Commencement of ancillary case

A case under this chapter is commenced by the filing of a petition for recognition of a foreign proceeding under section 1515.

(Added Pub.L. 109–8, title VIII, § 801(a), Apr. 20, 2005, 119 Stat. 136.)

§ 1505.   Authorization to act in a foreign country

A trustee or another entity (including an examiner) may be authorized by the court to act in a foreign country on behalf of an estate created under section 541. An entity authorized to act under this section may act in any way permitted by the applicable foreign law.

(Added Pub.L. 109–8, title VIII, § 801(a), Apr. 20, 2005, 119 Stat. 136.)

§ 1506.   Public policy exception

Nothing in this chapter prevents the court from refusing to take an action governed by this chapter if the action would be manifestly contrary to the public policy of the United States.

(Added Pub.L. 109–8, title VIII, § 801(a), Apr. 20, 2005, 119 Stat. 136.)

§ 1507.   Additional assistance

(a) Subject to the specific limitations stated elsewhere in this chapter the court, if recognition is granted, may provide additional assistance to a foreign representative under this title or under other laws of the United States.

(b) In determining whether to provide additional assistance under this title or under other laws of the United States, the court shall consider whether such additional assistance, consistent with the principles of comity, will reasonably assure—

(1) just treatment of all holders of claims against or interests in the debtor's property;

(2) protection of claim holders in the United States against prejudice and inconvenience in the processing of claims in such foreign proceeding;

(3) prevention of preferential or fraudulent dispositions of property of the debtor;

(4) distribution of proceeds of the debtor's property substantially in accordance with the order prescribed by this title; and

(5) if appropriate, the provision of an opportunity for a fresh start for the individual that such foreign proceeding concerns.

(Added Pub.L. 109–8, title VIII, § 801(a), Apr. 20, 2005, 119 Stat. 136.)

§ 1508.   Interpretation

In interpreting this chapter, the court shall consider its international origin, and the need to promote an application of this chapter that is consistent with the application of similar statutes adopted by foreign jurisdictions.

(Added Pub.L. 109–8, title VIII, § 801(a), Apr. 20, 2005, 119 Stat. 137.)

SUBCHAPTER II—ACCESS OF FOREIGN REPRESENTATIVES AND CREDITORS TO THE COURT

§ 1509.   Right of direct access

(a) A foreign representative may commence a case under section 1504 by filing directly with the court a petition for recognition of a foreign proceeding under section 1515.

(b) If the court grants recognition under section 1517, and subject to any limitations that the court may impose consistent with the policy of this chapter—

(1) the foreign representative has the capacity to sue and be sued in a court in the United States;

(2)   the foreign representative may apply directly to a court in the United States for appropriate relief in that court; and

(3)   a court in the United States shall grant comity or cooperation to the foreign representative.

(c)   A request for comity or cooperation by a foreign representative in a court in the United States other than the court which granted recognition shall be accompanied by a certified copy of an order granting recognition under section 1517.

(d)   If the court denies recognition under this chapter, the court may issue any appropriate order necessary to prevent the foreign representative from obtaining comity or cooperation from courts in the United States.

(e)   Whether or not the court grants recognition, and subject to sections 306 and 1510, a foreign representative is subject to applicable nonbankruptcy law.

(f)   Notwithstanding any other provision of this section, the failure of a foreign representative to commence a case or to obtain recognition under this chapter does not affect any right the foreign representative may have to sue in a court in the United States to collect or recover a claim which is the property of the debtor.

(Added Pub.L. 109–8, title VIII, § 801(a), Apr. 20, 2005, 119 Stat. 137.)

§ 1510.   Limited jurisdiction

The sole fact that a foreign representative files a petition under section 1515 does not subject the foreign representative to the jurisdiction of any court in the United States for any other purpose.

(Added Pub.L. 109–8, title VIII, § 801(a), Apr. 20, 2005, 119 Stat. 138.)

§ 1511.   Commencement of case under section 301, 302, or 303

(a)   Upon recognition, a foreign representative may commence—

(1)   an involuntary case under section 303; or

(2)   a voluntary case under section 301 or 302, if the foreign proceeding is a foreign main proceeding.

(b)   The petition commencing a case under subsection (a) must be accompanied by a certified copy of an order granting recognition. The court where the petition for recognition has been filed must be advised of the foreign representative's intent to commence a case under subsection (a) prior to such commencement.

(Added Pub.L. 109–8, title VIII, § 801(a), Apr. 20, 2005, 119 Stat. 138; Pub.L. 111–327, § 2(a)(45), Dec. 22, 2010, 124 Stat. 3562.)

§ 1512.   Participation of a foreign representative in a case under this title

Upon recognition of a foreign proceeding, the foreign representative in the recognized proceeding is entitled to participate as a party in interest in a case regarding the debtor under this title.

(Added Pub.L. 109–8, title VIII, § 801(a), Apr. 20, 2005, 119 Stat. 138.)

§ 1513.   Access of foreign creditors to a case under this title

(a)   Foreign creditors have the same rights regarding the commencement of, and participation in, a case under this title as domestic creditors.

(b)(1)   Subsection (a) does not change or codify present law as to the priority of claims under section 507 or 726, except that the claim of a foreign creditor under those sections shall not be given a lower priority than that of general unsecured claims without priority solely because the holder of such claim is a foreign creditor.

(2)(A) Subsection (a) and paragraph (1) do not change or codify present law as to the allowability of foreign revenue claims or other foreign public law claims in a proceeding under this title.

(B) Allowance and priority as to a foreign tax claim or other foreign public law claim shall be governed by any applicable tax treaty of the United States, under the conditions and circumstances specified therein.

(Added Pub.L. 109–8, title VIII, § 801(a), Apr. 20, 2005, 119 Stat. 138.)

§ 1514.   Notification to foreign creditors concerning a case under this title

(a) Whenever in a case under this title notice is to be given to creditors generally or to any class or category of creditors, such notice shall also be given to the known creditors generally, or to creditors in the notified class or category, that do not have addresses in the United States. The court may order that appropriate steps be taken with a view to notifying any creditor whose address is not yet known.

(b) Such notification to creditors with foreign addresses described in subsection (a) shall be given individually, unless the court considers that, under the circumstances, some other form of notification would be more appropriate. No letter or other formality is required.

(c) When a notification of commencement of a case is to be given to foreign creditors, such notification shall—

(1) indicate the time period for filing proofs of claim and specify the place for filing such proofs of claim;

(2) indicate whether secured creditors need to file proofs of claim; and

(3) contain any other information required to be included in such notification to creditors under this title and the orders of the court.

(d) Any rule of procedure or order of the court as to notice or the filing of a proof of claim shall provide such additional time to creditors with foreign addresses as is reasonable under the circumstances.

(Added Pub.L. 109–8, title VIII, § 801(a), Apr. 20, 2005, 119 Stat. 138.)

SUBCHAPTER III—RECOGNITION OF A FOREIGN PROCEEDING AND RELIEF

§ 1515.   Application for recognition

(a) A foreign representative applies to the court for recognition of a foreign proceeding in which the foreign representative has been appointed by filing a petition for recognition.

(b) A petition for recognition shall be accompanied by—

(1) a certified copy of the decision commencing such foreign proceeding and appointing the foreign representative;

(2) a certificate from the foreign court affirming the existence of such foreign proceeding and of the appointment of the foreign representative; or

(3) in the absence of evidence referred to in paragraphs (1) and (2), any other evidence acceptable to the court of the existence of such foreign proceeding and of the appointment of the foreign representative.

(c) A petition for recognition shall also be accompanied by a statement identifying all foreign proceedings with respect to the debtor that are known to the foreign representative.

(d) The documents referred to in paragraphs (1) and (2) of subsection (b) shall be translated into English. The court may require a translation into English of additional documents.

(Added Pub.L. 109–8, title VIII, § 801(a), Apr. 20, 2005, 119 Stat. 139.)

§ 1516. Presumptions concerning recognition

(a) If the decision or certificate referred to in section 1515(b) indicates that the foreign proceeding is a foreign proceeding and that the person or body is a foreign representative, the court is entitled to so presume.

(b) The court is entitled to presume that documents submitted in support of the petition for recognition are authentic, whether or not they have been legalized.

(c) In the absence of evidence to the contrary, the debtor's registered office, or habitual residence in the case of an individual, is presumed to be the center of the debtor's main interests.

(Added Pub.L. 109–8, title VIII, § 801(a), Apr. 20, 2005, 119 Stat. 139.)

§ 1517. Order granting recognition

(a) Subject to section 1506, after notice and a hearing, an order recognizing a foreign proceeding shall be entered if—

(1) such foreign proceeding for which recognition is sought is a foreign main proceeding or foreign nonmain proceeding within the meaning of section 1502;

(2) the foreign representative applying for recognition is a person or body; and

(3) the petition meets the requirements of section 1515.

(b) Such foreign proceeding shall be recognized—

(1) as a foreign main proceeding if it is pending in the country where the debtor has the center of its main interests; or

(2) as a foreign nonmain proceeding if the debtor has an establishment within the meaning of section 1502 in the foreign country where the proceeding is pending.

(c) A petition for recognition of a foreign proceeding shall be decided upon at the earliest possible time. Entry of an order recognizing a foreign proceeding constitutes recognition under this chapter.

(d) The provisions of this subchapter do not prevent modification or termination of recognition if it is shown that the grounds for granting it were fully or partially lacking or have ceased to exist, but in considering such action the court shall give due weight to possible prejudice to parties that have relied upon the order granting recognition. A case under this chapter may be closed in the manner prescribed under section 350.

(Added Pub.L. 109–8, title VIII, § 801(a), Apr. 20, 2005, 119 Stat. 139.)

§ 1518. Subsequent information

From the time of filing the petition for recognition of a foreign proceeding, the foreign representative shall file with the court promptly a notice of change of status concerning—

(1) any substantial change in the status of such foreign proceeding or the status of the foreign representative's appointment; and

(2) any other foreign proceeding regarding the debtor that becomes known to the foreign representative.

(Added Pub.L. 109–8, title VIII, § 801(a), Apr. 20, 2005, 119 Stat. 140.)

§ 1519. Relief that may be granted upon filing petition for recognition

(a) From the time of filing a petition for recognition until the court rules on the petition, the court may, at the request of the foreign representative, where relief is urgently needed to protect the assets of the debtor or the interests of the creditors, grant relief of a provisional nature, including—

(1) staying execution against the debtor's assets;

(2)   entrusting the administration or realization of all or part of the debtor's assets located in the United States to the foreign representative or another person authorized by the court, including an examiner, in order to protect and preserve the value of assets that, by their nature or because of other circumstances, are perishable, susceptible to devaluation or otherwise in jeopardy; and

(3)   any relief referred to in paragraph (3), (4), or (7) of section 1521(a).

(b)   Unless extended under section 1521(a)(6), the relief granted under this section terminates when the petition for recognition is granted.

(c)   It is a ground for denial of relief under this section that such relief would interfere with the administration of a foreign main proceeding.

(d)   The court may not enjoin a police or regulatory act of a governmental unit, including a criminal action or proceeding, under this section.

(e)   The standards, procedures, and limitations applicable to an injunction shall apply to relief under this section.

(f)   The exercise of rights not subject to the stay arising under section 362(a) pursuant to paragraph (6), (7), (17), or (27) of section 362(b) or pursuant to section 362(*o*) shall not be stayed by any order of a court or administrative agency in any proceeding under this chapter.

(Added Pub.L. 109–8, title VIII, § 801(a), Apr. 20, 2005, 119 Stat. 140, amended Pub.L. 111–327, § 2(a)(46), Dec. 22, 2010, 124 Stat. 3562.)

§ 1520.   Effects of recognition of a foreign main proceeding

(a)   Upon recognition of a foreign proceeding that is a foreign main proceeding—

(1)   sections 361 and 362 apply with respect to the debtor and the property of the debtor that is within the territorial jurisdiction of the United States;

(2)   sections 363, 549, and 552 apply to a transfer of an interest of the debtor in property that is within the territorial jurisdiction of the United States to the same extent that the sections would apply to property of an estate;

(3)   unless the court orders otherwise, the foreign representative may operate the debtor's business and may exercise the rights and powers of a trustee under and to the extent provided by sections 363 and 552; and

(4)   section 552 applies to property of the debtor that is within the territorial jurisdiction of the United States.

(b)   Subsection (a) does not affect the right to commence an individual action or proceeding in a foreign country to the extent necessary to preserve a claim against the debtor.

(c)   Subsection (a) does not affect the right of a foreign representative or an entity to file a petition commencing a case under this title or the right of any party to file claims or take other proper actions in such a case.

(Added Pub.L. 109–8, title VIII, § 801(a), Apr. 20, 2005, 119 Stat. 141.)

§ 1521.   Relief that may be granted upon recognition

(a)   Upon recognition of a foreign proceeding, whether main or nonmain, where necessary to effectuate the purpose of this chapter and to protect the assets of the debtor or the interests of the creditors, the court may, at the request of the foreign representative, grant any appropriate relief, including—

(1)   staying the commencement or continuation of an individual action or proceeding concerning the debtor's assets, rights, obligations or liabilities to the extent they have not been stayed under section 1520(a);

(2)   staying execution against the debtor's assets to the extent it has not been stayed under section 1520(a);

(3)   suspending the right to transfer, encumber or otherwise dispose of any assets of the debtor to the extent this right has not been suspended under section 1520(a);

(4)   providing for the examination of witnesses, the taking of evidence or the delivery of information concerning the debtor's assets, affairs, rights, obligations or liabilities;

(5)   entrusting the administration or realization of all or part of the debtor's assets within the territorial jurisdiction of the United States to the foreign representative or another person, including an examiner, authorized by the court;

(6)   extending relief granted under section 1519(a); and

(7)   granting any additional relief that may be available to a trustee, except for relief available under sections 522, 544, 545, 547, 548, 550, and 724(a).

(b)   Upon recognition of a foreign proceeding, whether main or nonmain, the court may, at the request of the foreign representative, entrust the distribution of all or part of the debtor's assets located in the United States to the foreign representative or another person, including an examiner, authorized by the court, provided that the court is satisfied that the interests of creditors in the United States are sufficiently protected.

(c)   In granting relief under this section to a representative of a foreign nonmain proceeding, the court must be satisfied that the relief relates to assets that, under the law of the United States, should be administered in the foreign nonmain proceeding or concerns information required in that proceeding.

(d)   The court may not enjoin a police or regulatory act of a governmental unit, including a criminal action or proceeding, under this section.

(e)   The standards, procedures, and limitations applicable to an injunction shall apply to relief under paragraphs (1), (2), (3), and (6) of subsection (a).

(f)   The exercise of rights not subject to the stay arising under section 362(a) pursuant to paragraph (6), (7), (17), or (27) of section 362(b) or pursuant to section 362(o) shall not be stayed by any order of a court or administrative agency in any proceeding under this chapter.

(Added Pub.L. 109–8, title VIII, § 801(a), Apr. 20, 2005, 119 Stat. 141, amended Pub.L. 111–327, § 2(a)(47), Dec. 22, 2010, 124 Stat. 3562.)

§ 1522.   Protection of creditors and other interested persons

(a)   The court may grant relief under section 1519 or 1521, or may modify or terminate relief under subsection (c), only if the interests of the creditors and other interested entities, including the debtor, are sufficiently protected.

(b)   The court may subject relief granted under section 1519 or 1521, or the operation of the debtor's business under section 1520(a)(3), to conditions it considers appropriate, including the giving of security or the filing of a bond.

(c)   The court may, at the request of the foreign representative or an entity affected by relief granted under section 1519 or 1521, or at its own motion, modify or terminate such relief.

(d)   Section 1104(d) shall apply to the appointment of an examiner under this chapter. Any examiner shall comply with the qualification requirements imposed on a trustee by section 322.

(Added Pub.L. 109–8, title VIII, § 801(a), Apr. 20, 2005, 119 Stat. 142.)

§ 1523.   Actions to avoid acts detrimental to creditors

(a)   Upon recognition of a foreign proceeding, the foreign representative has standing in a case concerning the debtor pending under another chapter of this title to initiate actions under sections 522, 544, 545, 547, 548, 550, 553, and 724(a).

(b)　When a foreign proceeding is a foreign nonmain proceeding, the court must be satisfied that an action under subsection (a) relates to assets that, under United States law, should be administered in the foreign nonmain proceeding.

(Added Pub.L. 109–8, title VIII, § 801(a), Apr. 20, 2005, 119 Stat. 142.)

§ 1524.　　　Intervention by a foreign representative

Upon recognition of a foreign proceeding, the foreign representative may intervene in any proceedings in a State or Federal court in the United States in which the debtor is a party.

(Added Pub.L. 109–8, title VIII, § 801(a), Apr. 20, 2005, 119 Stat. 142.)

SUBCHAPTER IV—COOPERATION WITH FOREIGN COURTS AND FOREIGN REPRESENTATIVES

§ 1525.　　　Cooperation and direct communication between the court and foreign courts or foreign representatives

(a)　Consistent with section 1501, the court shall cooperate to the maximum extent possible with a foreign court or a foreign representative, either directly or through the trustee.

(b)　The court is entitled to communicate directly with, or to request information or assistance directly from, a foreign court or a foreign representative, subject to the rights of a party in interest to notice and participation.

(Added Pub.L. 109–8, title VIII, § 801(a), Apr. 20, 2005, 119 Stat. 143.)

§ 1526.　　　Cooperation and direct communication between the trustee and foreign courts or foreign representatives

(a)　Consistent with section 1501, the trustee or other person, including an examiner, authorized by the court, shall, subject to the supervision of the court, cooperate to the maximum extent possible with a foreign court or a foreign representative.

(b)　The trustee or other person, including an examiner, authorized by the court is entitled, subject to the supervision of the court, to communicate directly with a foreign court or a foreign representative.

(Added Pub.L. 109–8, title VIII, § 801(a), Apr. 20, 2005, 119 Stat. 143.)

§ 1527.　　　Forms of cooperation

Cooperation referred to in sections 1525 and 1526 may be implemented by any appropriate means, including—

(1)　appointment of a person or body, including an examiner, to act at the direction of the court;

(2)　communication of information by any means considered appropriate by the court;

(3)　coordination of the administration and supervision of the debtor's assets and affairs;

(4)　approval or implementation of agreements concerning the coordination of proceedings; and

(5)　coordination of concurrent proceedings regarding the same debtor.

(Added Pub.L. 109–8, title VIII, § 801(a), Apr. 20, 2005, 119 Stat. 143.)

SUBCHAPTER V—CONCURRENT PROCEEDINGS

§ 1528. Commencement of a case under this title after recognition of a foreign main proceeding

After recognition of a foreign main proceeding, a case under another chapter of this title may be commenced only if the debtor has assets in the United States. The effects of such case shall be restricted to the assets of the debtor that are within the territorial jurisdiction of the United States and, to the extent necessary to implement cooperation and coordination under sections 1525, 1526, and 1527, to other assets of the debtor that are within the jurisdiction of the court under sections 541(a) of this title, and 1334(e) of title 28, to the extent that such other assets are not subject to the jurisdiction and control of a foreign proceeding that has been recognized under this chapter.

(Added Pub.L. 109–8, title VIII, § 801(a), Apr. 20, 2005, 119 Stat. 143.)

§ 1529. Coordination of a case under this title and a foreign proceeding

If a foreign proceeding and a case under another chapter of this title are pending concurrently regarding the same debtor, the court shall seek cooperation and coordination under sections 1525, 1526, and 1527, and the following shall apply:

(1) If the case in the United States is pending at the time the petition for recognition of such foreign proceeding is filed—

(A) any relief granted under section 1519 or 1521 must be consistent with the relief granted in the case in the United States; and

(B) section 1520 does not apply even if such foreign proceeding is recognized as a foreign main proceeding.

(2) If a case in the United States under this title commences after recognition, or after the date of the filing of the petition for recognition, of such foreign proceeding—

(A) any relief in effect under section 1519 or 1521 shall be reviewed by the court and shall be modified or terminated if inconsistent with the case in the United States; and

(B) if such foreign proceeding is a foreign main proceeding, the stay and suspension referred to in section 1520(a) shall be modified or terminated if inconsistent with the relief granted in the case in the United States.

(3) In granting, extending, or modifying relief granted to a representative of a foreign nonmain proceeding, the court must be satisfied that the relief relates to assets that, under the laws of the United States, should be administered in the foreign nonmain proceeding or concerns information required in that proceeding.

(4) In achieving cooperation and coordination under sections 1528 and 1529, the court may grant any of the relief authorized under section 305.

(Added Pub.L. 109–8, title VIII, § 801(a), Apr. 20, 2005, 119 Stat. 144, amended Pub.L. 111–327, § 2(a)(48), Dec. 22, 2010, 124 Stat. 3562.)

§ 1530. Coordination of more than 1 foreign proceeding

In matters referred to in section 1501, with respect to more than 1 foreign proceeding regarding the debtor, the court shall seek cooperation and coordination under sections 1525, 1526, and 1527, and the following shall apply:

(1) Any relief granted under section 1519 or 1521 to a representative of a foreign nonmain proceeding after recognition of a foreign main proceeding must be consistent with the foreign main proceeding.

(2) If a foreign main proceeding is recognized after recognition, or after the filing of a petition for recognition, of a foreign nonmain proceeding, any relief in effect under section 1519 or 1521 shall

be reviewed by the court and shall be modified or terminated if inconsistent with the foreign main proceeding.

    (3)   If, after recognition of a foreign nonmain proceeding, another foreign nonmain proceeding is recognized, the court shall grant, modify, or terminate relief for the purpose of facilitating coordination of the proceedings.

(Added Pub.L. 109–8, title VIII, § 801(a), Apr. 20, 2005, 119 Stat. 144.)

§ 1531.   Presumption of insolvency based on recognition of a foreign main proceeding

In the absence of evidence to the contrary, recognition of a foreign main proceeding is, for the purpose of commencing a proceeding under section 303, proof that the debtor is generally not paying its debts as such debts become due.

(Added Pub.L. 109–8, title VIII, § 801(a), Apr. 20, 2005, 119 Stat. 144.)

§ 1532.   Rule of payment in concurrent proceedings

Without prejudice to secured claims or rights in rem, a creditor who has received payment with respect to its claim in a foreign proceeding pursuant to a law relating to insolvency may not receive a payment for the same claim in a case under any other chapter of this title regarding the debtor, so long as the payment to other creditors of the same class is proportionately less than the payment the creditor has already received.

(Added Pub.L. 109–8, title VIII, § 801(a), Apr. 20, 2005, 119 Stat. 145.)

SELECTED BANKRUPTCY-RELATED PROVISIONS

TITLE 18. CRIMES AND CRIMINAL PROCEDURE

18 U.S.C.A. §§ 151–158

Current through March 30, 2016; P.L. 114–141

§ 151. Definition

As used in this chapter, the term "debtor" means a debtor concerning whom a petition has been filed under title 11.

(June 25, 1948, ch. 645, 62 Stat. 689; Pub.L. 95–598, title III, § 314(b)(1), Nov. 6, 1978, 92 Stat. 2676; Pub.L. 103–322, title XXXIII, § 330008(5), Sept. 13, 1994, 108 Stat. 2143.)

§ 152. Concealment of assets; false oaths and claims; bribery

A person who—

(1)   knowingly and fraudulently conceals from a custodian, trustee, marshal, or other officer of the court charged with the control or custody of property, or, in connection with a case under title 11, from creditors or the United States Trustee, any property belonging to the estate of a debtor;

(2)   knowingly and fraudulently makes a false oath or account in or in relation to any case under title 11;

(3)   knowingly and fraudulently makes a false declaration, certificate, verification, or statement under penalty of perjury as permitted under section 1746 of title 28, in or in relation to any case under title 11;

2355

(4)   knowingly and fraudulently presents any false claim for proof against the estate of a debtor, or uses any such claim in any case under title 11, in a personal capacity or as or through an agent, proxy, or attorney;

(5)   knowingly and fraudulently receives any material amount of property from a debtor after the filing of a case under title 11, with intent to defeat the provisions of title 11;

(6)   knowingly and fraudulently gives, offers, receives, or attempts to obtain any money or property, remuneration, compensation, reward, advantage, or promise thereof for acting or forbearing to act in any case under title 11;

(7)   in a personal capacity or as an agent or officer of any person or corporation, in contemplation of a case under title 11 by or against the person or any other person or corporation, or with intent to defeat the provisions of title 11, knowingly and fraudulently transfers or conceals any of his property or the property of such other person or corporation;

(8)   after the filing of a case under title 11 or in contemplation thereof, knowingly and fraudulently conceals, destroys, mutilates, falsifies, or makes a false entry in any recorded information (including books, documents, records, and papers) relating to the property or financial affairs of a debtor; or

(9)   after the filing of a case under title 11, knowingly and fraudulently withholds from a custodian, trustee, marshal, or other officer of the court or a United States Trustee entitled to its possession, any recorded information (including books, documents, records, and papers) relating to the property or financial affairs of a debtor,

shall be fined under this title, imprisoned not more than 5 years, or both.

(June 25, 1948, ch. 645, 62 Stat. 689; Pub.L. 86–519, § 2, June 12, 1960, 74 Stat. 217; Pub.L. 86–701, Sept. 2, 1960, 74 Stat. 753; Pub.L. 94–550, § 4, Oct. 18, 1976, 90 Stat. 2535; Pub.L. 95–598, title III, § 314(a), (c), Nov. 6, 1978, 92 Stat. 2676, 2677; Pub.L. 100–690, title VII, § 7017, Nov. 18, 1988, 102 Stat. 4395; Pub.L. 103–322, title XXXIII, § 330016(1)(K), Sept. 13, 1994, 108 Stat. 2147; Pub.L. 103–394, title III, § 312(a)(1)(A), Oct. 22, 1994, 108 Stat. 4138; Pub.L. 104–294, title VI, § 601(a)(1), Oct. 11, 1996, 110 Stat. 3497.)

§ 153.   Embezzlement against estate

(a)   Offense.—A person described in subsection (b) who knowingly and fraudulently appropriates to the person's own use, embezzles, spends, or transfers any property or secretes or destroys any document belonging to the estate of a debtor shall be fined under this title, imprisoned not more than 5 years, or both.

(b)   Person to Whom Section Applies.—A person described in this subsection is one who has access to property or documents belonging to an estate by virtue of the person's participation in the administration of the estate as a trustee, custodian, marshal, attorney, or other officer of the court or as an agent, employee, or other person engaged by such an officer to perform a service with respect to the estate.

(June 25, 1948, ch. 645, 62 Stat. 690; Pub.L. 95–598, title III, § 314(a)(1), (d)(1), (2), Nov. 6, 1978, 92 Stat. 2676, 2677; Pub.L. 103–322, title XXXIII, § 330016(1)(K), Sept. 13, 1994, 108 Stat. 2147; Pub.L. 103–394, title III, § 312(a)(1)(A), Oct. 22, 1994, 108 Stat. 4139; Pub.L. 104–294, title VI, § 601(a)(1), Oct. 11, 1996, 110 Stat. 3497.)

§ 154.   Adverse interest and conduct of officers

A person who, being a custodian, trustee, marshal, or other officer of the court—

(1)   knowingly purchases, directly or indirectly, any property of the estate of which the person is such an officer in a case under title 11;

(2)   knowingly refuses to permit a reasonable opportunity for the inspection by parties in interest of the documents and accounts relating to the affairs of estates in the person's charge by parties when directed by the court to do so; or

(3)   knowingly refuses to permit a reasonable opportunity for the inspection by the United States Trustee of the documents and accounts relating to the affairs of an estate in the person's charge,

shall be fined under this title and shall forfeit the person's office, which shall thereupon become vacant.

(June 25, 1948, ch. 645, 62 Stat. 690; Pub.L. 95–598, title III, § 314(a)(2), (e)(1), (2), Nov. 6, 1978, 92 Stat. 2676, 2677; Pub.L. 103–322, title XXXIII, § 330016(1)(G), Sept. 13, 1994, 108 Stat. 2147; Pub.L. 103–394, title III, § 312(a)(1)(A), Oct. 22, 1994, 108 Stat. 4139; Pub.L. 104–294, title VI, § 601(a)(1), Oct. 11, 1996, 110 Stat. 3497.)

§ 155.   Fee agreements in cases under title 11 and receiverships

Whoever, being a party in interest, whether as a debtor, creditor, receiver, trustee or representative of any of them, or attorney for any such party in interest, in any receivership or case under title 11 in any United States court or under its supervision, knowingly and fraudulently enters into any agreement, express or implied, with another such party in interest or attorney for another such party in interest, for the purpose of fixing the fees or other compensation to be paid to any party in interest or to any attorney for any party in interest for services rendered in connection therewith, from the assets of the estate, shall be fined under this title or imprisoned not more than one year, or both.

(June 25, 1948, ch. 645, 62 Stat. 690; May 24, 1949, ch. 139, § 4, 63 Stat. 90; Pub.L. 95–598, title III, § 314(f)(1), (2), Nov. 6, 1978, 92 Stat. 2677; Pub.L. 103–322, title XXXIII, § 330016(1)(K), Sept. 13, 1994, 108 Stat. 2147.)

§ 156.   Knowing disregard of bankruptcy law or rule

(a)   Definitions.—In this section—

(1)   the term "bankruptcy petition preparer" means a person, other than the debtor's attorney or an employee of such an attorney, who prepares for compensation a document for filing; and

(2)   the term "document for filing" means a petition or any other document prepared for filing by a debtor in a United States bankruptcy court or a United States district court in connection with a case under title 11.

(b)   Offense.—If a bankruptcy case or related proceeding is dismissed because of a knowing attempt by a bankruptcy petition preparer in any manner to disregard the requirements of title 11, United States Code, or the Federal Rules of Bankruptcy Procedure, the bankruptcy petition preparer shall be fined under this title, imprisoned not more than 1 year, or both.

(Added Pub.L. 103–394, title III, § 312(a)(1)(B), Oct. 22, 1994, 108 Stat. 4140; amended Pub.L. 109–8, title XII, § 1220, Apr. 20, 2005, 119 Stat. 195.)

§ 157.   Bankruptcy fraud

A person who, having devised or intending to devise a scheme or artifice to defraud and for the purpose of executing or concealing such a scheme or artifice or attempting to do so—

(1)   files a petition under title 11, including a fraudulent involuntary petition under section 303 of such title;

(2)   files a document in a proceeding under title 11; or

(3)   makes a false or fraudulent representation, claim, or promise concerning or in relation to a proceeding under title 11, at any time before or after the filing of the petition, or in relation to a proceeding falsely asserted to be pending under such title,

shall be fined under this title, imprisoned not more than 5 years, or both.

(Added Pub.L. 103–394, title III, § 312(a)(1)(B), Oct. 22, 1994, 108 Stat. 4140; amended Pub.L. 109–8, title III, § 332(c), Apr. 20, 2005, 119 Stat. 103; Pub.L. 111–327, § 2(b), Dec. 22, 2010, 124 Stat. 3562.)

§ 158.   Designation of United States attorneys and agents of the Federal Bureau of Investigation to address abusive reaffirmations of debt and materially fraudulent statements in bankruptcy schedules

(a)   In General.—The Attorney General of the United States shall designate the individuals described in subsection (b) to have primary responsibility in carrying out enforcement activities in addressing violations of section 152 or 157 relating to abusive reaffirmations of debt. In addition to addressing the violations referred to in the preceding sentence, the individuals described under subsection (b) shall address violations of section 152 or 157 relating to materially fraudulent statements in bankruptcy schedules that are intentionally false or intentionally misleading.

(b)   United States Attorneys and Agents of the Federal Bureau of Investigation.—The individuals referred to in subsection (a) are—

(1)   the United States attorney for each judicial district of the United States; and

(2)   an agent of the Federal Bureau of Investigation for each field office of the Federal Bureau of Investigation.

(c)   Bankruptcy Investigations.—Each United States attorney designated under this section shall, in addition to any other responsibilities, have primary responsibility for carrying out the duties of a United States attorney under section 3057.

(d)   Bankruptcy Procedures.—The bankruptcy courts shall establish procedures for referring any case that may contain a materially fraudulent statement in a bankruptcy schedule to the individuals designated under this section.

(Added Pub.L. 109–8, title II, § 203(b)(1), Apr. 20, 2005, 119 Stat. 49.)

* * *

§ 1032.   Concealment of assets from conservator, receiver, or liquidating agent

Whoever—

(1)   knowingly conceals or endeavors to conceal an asset or property from the Federal Deposit Insurance Corporation, acting as conservator or receiver or in the Corporation's corporate capacity with respect to any asset acquired or liability assumed by the Corporation under section 11, 12, or 13 of the Federal Deposit Insurance Act, any conservator appointed by the Comptroller of the Currency, the Federal Deposit Insurance Corporation acting as receiver for a covered financial company, in accordance with title II of the Dodd-Frank Wall Street Reform and Consumer Protection Act, or the National Credit Union Administration Board, acting as conservator or liquidating agent;

(2)   corruptly impedes or endeavors to impede the functions of such Corporation, Board, or conservator; or

(3)   corruptly places or endeavors to place an asset or property beyond the reach of such Corporation, Board, or conservator,

shall be fined under this title or imprisoned not more than 5 years, or both.

(Added Pub.L. 101–647, title XXV, § 2501(a), Nov. 29, 1990, 104 Stat. 4859; amended Pub.L. 107–273, div. B, title IV, § 4002(b)(13), Nov. 2, 2002, 116 Stat. 1808; Pub.L. 111–203, title II, § 211(a), (b), title III, § 377(7), July 21, 2010, 124 Stat. 1514, 1569.)

* * *

§ 1519.   Destruction, alteration, or falsification of records in Federal investigations and bankruptcy

Whoever knowingly alters, destroys, mutilates, conceals, covers up, falsifies, or makes a false entry in any record, document, or tangible object with the intent to impede, obstruct, or influence the investigation or proper administration of any matter within the jurisdiction of any department or agency of the United States or any case filed under title 11, or in relation to or contemplation of any such matter or case, shall be fined under this title, imprisoned not more than 20 years, or both.

(Added Pub.L. 107–204, title VIII, § 802(a), July 30, 2002, 116 Stat. 800.)

* * *

§ 3057.   Bankruptcy investigations

(a)   Any judge, receiver, or trustee having reasonable grounds for believing that any violation under chapter 9 of this title or other laws of the United States relating to insolvent debtors, receiverships or reorganization plans has been committed, or that an investigation should be had in connection therewith, shall report to the appropriate United States attorney all the facts and circumstances of the case, the names of the witnesses and the offense or offenses believed to have been committed. Where one of such officers has made such report, the others need not do so.

(b)   The United States attorney thereupon shall inquire into the facts and report thereon to the judge, and if it appears probable that any such offense has been committed, shall without delay, present the matter to the grand jury, unless upon inquiry and examination he decides that the ends of public justice do not require investigation or prosecution, in which case he shall report the facts to the Attorney General for his direction.

(June 25, 1948, ch. 645, 62 Stat. 818; May 24, 1949, ch. 139, § 48, 63 Stat. 96; Pub.L. 95–598, title III, § 314(i), Nov. 6, 1978, 92 Stat. 2677.)

* * *

§ 3284.   Concealment of bankrupt's assets

The concealment of assets of a debtor in a case under title 11 shall be deemed to be a continuing offense until the debtor shall have been finally discharged or a discharge denied, and the period of limitations shall not begin to run until such final discharge or denial of discharge.

(June 25, 1948, ch. 645, 62 Stat. 828; Pub.L. 95–598, title III, § 314(k), Nov. 6, 1978, 92 Stat. 2678.)

TITLE 28. JUDICIARY AND JUDICIAL PROCEDURE

28 U.S.C.A. §§ 151–158

Current through March 30, 2016; P.L. 114–141

CH. 6.   BANKRUPTCY JUDGES

CH. 39.   UNITED STATES TRUSTEES

* * *

OTHER TITLE 28 PROVISIONS

* * *

§ 151.   Designation of bankruptcy courts

In each judicial district, the bankruptcy judges in regular active service shall constitute a unit of the district court to be known as the bankruptcy court for that district. Each bankruptcy judge, as a judicial officer of the district court, may exercise the authority conferred under this chapter with respect to any action, suit, or proceeding and may preside alone and hold a regular or special session of the court, except as otherwise provided by law or by rule or order of the district court.

(Added Pub.L. 98–353, title I, § 104(a), July 10, 1984, 98 Stat. 336.)

§ 152.   Appointment of bankruptcy judges

(a)(1)   Each bankruptcy judge to be appointed for a judicial district, as provided in paragraph (2), shall be appointed by the court of appeals of the United States for the circuit in which such district is located. Such appointments shall be made after considering the recommendations of the Judicial Conference submitted pursuant to subsection (b). Each bankruptcy judge shall be appointed for a term of fourteen years, subject to the provisions of subsection (e). However, upon the expiration of the term, a bankruptcy judge may, with the approval of the judicial council of the circuit, continue to perform the duties of the office until the earlier of the date which is 180 days after the expiration of the term or the date of the appointment of a successor. Bankruptcy judges shall serve as judicial officers of the United States district court established under Article III of the Constitution.

* * * *

(Added Pub.L. 98–353, title I, § 104(a), July 10, 1984, 98 Stat. 336; amended Pub.L. 99–554, title I, § 101, Oct. 27, 1986, 100 Stat. 3088; Pub.L. 100–587, Nov. 3, 1988, 102 Stat. 2982; Pub.L. 101–650, title III, § 304, Dec. 1, 1990, 104 Stat. 5105; Pub.L. 102–361, §§ 2, 4, Aug. 26, 1992, 106 Stat. 965, 966; Pub.L. 109–8, title XII, § 1223(d), Apr. 20, 2005, 119 Stat. 198; Pub.L. 109–63,§ 2(c), Sept. 9, 2005, 119 Stat. 1994.)

§ 153.   Salaries; character of service

(a)   Each bankruptcy judge shall serve on a full-time basis and shall receive as full compensation for his services, a salary at an annual rate that is equal to 92 percent of the salary of a judge of the district court of the United States as determined pursuant to section 135, to be paid at such times as the Judicial Conference of the United States determines.

* * * *

(Added Pub.L. 98–353, title I, § 104(a), July 10, 1984, 98 Stat. 338; amended Pub.L. 100–202, § 101(a), [title IV, § 408(a)], Dec. 22, 1987, 101 Stat. 1329, 1329–26; Pub.L. 100–702, title X, § 1003(a)(1), Nov. 19, 1988, 102 Stat. 4665.)

§ 157.   Procedures

(a)   Each district court may provide that any or all cases under title 11 and any or all proceedings arising under title 11 or arising in or related to a case under title 11 shall be referred to the bankruptcy judges for the district.

(b)(1)   Bankruptcy judges may hear and determine all cases under title 11 and all core proceedings arising under title 11, or arising in a case under title 11, referred under subsection (a) of this section, and may enter appropriate orders and judgments, subject to review under section 158 of this title.

(2)   Core proceedings include, but are not limited to—

(A)   matters concerning the administration of the estate;

(B)   allowance or disallowance of claims against the estate or exemptions from property of the estate, and estimation of claims or interests for the purposes of confirming a plan under chapter 11, 12, or 13 of title 11 but not the liquidation or estimation of contingent or unliquidated personal injury tort or wrongful death claims against the estate for purposes of distribution in a case under title 11;

(C)   counterclaims by the estate against persons filing claims against the estate;

(D)   orders in respect to obtaining credit;

(E)   orders to turn over property of the estate;

(F)   proceedings to determine, avoid, or recover preferences;

(G)   motions to terminate, annul, or modify the automatic stay;

(H)   proceedings to determine, avoid, or recover fraudulent conveyances;

(I)   determinations as to the dischargeability of particular debts;

(J)   objections to discharges;

(K)   determinations of the validity, extent, or priority of liens;

(L)   confirmations of plans;

(M)   orders approving the use or lease of property, including the use of cash collateral;

(N)   orders approving the sale of property other than property resulting from claims brought by the estate against persons who have not filed claims against the estate;

(O)   other proceedings affecting the liquidation of the assets of the estate or the adjustment of the debtor-creditor or the equity security holder relationship, except personal injury tort or wrongful death claims; and

(P)   recognition of foreign proceedings and other matters under chapter 15 of title 11.

(3)   The bankruptcy judge shall determine, on the judge's own motion or on timely motion of a party, whether a proceeding is a core proceeding under this subsection or is a proceeding that is otherwise related to a case under title 11. A determination that a proceeding is not a core proceeding shall not be made solely on the basis that its resolution may be affected by State law.

(4)   Non-core proceedings under section 157(b)(2)(B) of title 28, United States Code, shall not be subject to the mandatory abstention provisions of section 1334(c)(2).

(5)   The district court shall order that personal injury tort and wrongful death claims shall be tried in the district court in which the bankruptcy case is pending, or in the district court in the district in which the claim arose, as determined by the district court in which the bankruptcy case is pending.

(c)(1)   A bankruptcy judge may hear a proceeding that is not a core proceeding but that is otherwise related to a case under title 11. In such proceeding, the bankruptcy judge shall submit proposed findings of fact and conclusions of law to the district court, and any final order or judgment shall be entered by the district judge after considering the bankruptcy judge's proposed findings and conclusions and after reviewing de novo those matters to which any party has timely and specifically objected.

(2)   Notwithstanding the provisions of paragraph (1) of this subsection, the district court, with the consent of all the parties to the proceeding, may refer a proceeding related to a case under title 11 to a bankruptcy judge to hear and determine and to enter appropriate orders and judgments, subject to review under section 158 of this title.

(d)   The district court may withdraw, in whole or in part, any case or proceeding referred under this section, on its own motion or on timely motion of any party, for cause shown. The district court shall, on timely motion of a party, so withdraw a proceeding if the court determines that resolution of the proceeding requires consideration of both title 11 and other laws of the United States regulating organizations or activities affecting interstate commerce.

(e)   If the right to a jury trial applies in a proceeding that may be heard under this section by a bankruptcy judge, the bankruptcy judge may conduct the jury trial if specially designated to exercise such jurisdiction by the district court and with the express consent of all the parties.

(Added Pub.L. 98–353, title I, § 104(a), July 10, 1984, 98 Stat. 340; amended Pub.L. 99–554, title I, §§ 143, 144(b), Oct. 27, 1986, 100 Stat. 3096; Pub.L. 103–394, title I, § 112, Oct. 22, 1994, 108 Stat. 4117; Pub.L. 109–8, title VIII, § 802(c)(1), Apr. 20, 2005, 119 Stat. 145.)

§ 158. Appeals

(a)   The district courts of the United States shall have jurisdiction to hear appeals[1]

(1)   from final judgments, orders, and decrees;

(2)   from interlocutory orders and decrees issued under section 1121(d) of title 11 increasing or reducing the time periods referred to in section 1121 of such title; and

(3)   with leave of the court, from other interlocutory orders and decrees;

and, with leave of the court, from interlocutory orders and decrees, of bankruptcy judges entered in cases and proceedings referred to the bankruptcy judges under section 157 of this title. An appeal under this subsection shall be taken only to the district court for the judicial district in which the bankruptcy judge is serving.

(b)(1)   The judicial council of a circuit shall establish a bankruptcy appellate panel service composed of bankruptcy judges of the districts in the circuit who are appointed by the judicial council in accordance with paragraph (3), to hear and determine, with the consent of all the parties, appeals under subsection (a) unless the judicial council finds that—

(A)   there are insufficient judicial resources available in the circuit; or

(B)   establishment of such service would result in undue delay or increased cost to parties in cases under title 11.

Not later than 90 days after making the finding, the judicial council shall submit to the Judicial Conference of the United States a report containing the factual basis of such finding.

(2)(A)   A judicial council may reconsider, at any time, the finding described in paragraph (1).

(B)   On the request of a majority of the district judges in a circuit for which a bankruptcy appellate panel service is established under paragraph (1), made after the expiration of the 1-year period beginning on the date such service is established, the judicial council of the circuit shall determine whether a circumstance specified in subparagraph (A) or (B) of such paragraph exists.

(C)   On its own motion, after the expiration of the 3-year period beginning on the date a bankruptcy appellate panel service is established under paragraph (1), the judicial council of the circuit may determine whether a circumstance specified in subparagraph (A) or (B) of such paragraph exists.

(D)   If the judicial council finds that either of such circumstances exists, the judicial council may provide for the completion of the appeals then pending before such service and the orderly termination of such service.

(3)   Bankruptcy judges appointed under paragraph (1) shall be appointed and may be reappointed under such paragraph.

(4)   If authorized by the Judicial Conference of the United States, the judicial councils of 2 or more circuits may establish a joint bankruptcy appellate panel comprised of bankruptcy judges from the districts within the circuits for which such panel is established, to hear and determine, upon the consent of all the parties, appeals under subsection (a) of this section.

(5)   An appeal to be heard under this subsection shall be heard by a panel of 3 members of the bankruptcy appellate panel service, except that a member of such service may not hear an appeal originating in the district for which such member is appointed or designated under section 152 of this title.

---

[1]   So in original. Probably should be followed by a dash.

(6) Appeals may not be heard under this subsection by a panel of the bankruptcy appellate panel service unless the district judges for the district in which the appeals occur, by majority vote, have authorized such service to hear and determine appeals originating in such district.

(c)(1) Subject to subsections (b) and (d)(2), each appeal under subsection (a) shall be heard by a 3-judge panel of the bankruptcy appellate panel service established under subsection (b)(1) unless—

(A) the appellant elects at the time of filing the appeal; or

(B) any other party elects, not later than 30 days after service of notice of the appeal; to have such appeal heard by the district court.

(2) An appeal under subsections (a) and (b) of this section shall be taken in the same manner as appeals in civil proceedings generally are taken to the courts of appeals from the district courts and in the time provided by Rule 8002 of the Bankruptcy Rules.

(d)(1) The courts of appeals shall have jurisdiction of appeals from all final decisions, judgments, orders, and decrees entered under subsections (a) and (b) of this section.

(2)(A) The appropriate court of appeals shall have jurisdiction of appeals described in the first sentence of subsection (a) if the bankruptcy court, the district court, or the bankruptcy appellate panel involved, acting on its own motion or on the request of a party to the judgment, order, or decree described in such first sentence, or all the appellants and appellees (if any) acting jointly, certify that—

(i) the judgment, order, or decree involves a question of law as to which there is no controlling decision of the court of appeals for the circuit or of the Supreme Court of the United States, or involves a matter of public importance;

(ii) the judgment, order, or decree involves a question of law requiring resolution of conflicting decisions; or

(iii) an immediate appeal from the judgment, order, or decree may materially advance the progress of the case or proceeding in which the appeal is taken;

and if the court of appeals authorizes the direct appeal of the judgment, order, or decree.

(B) If the bankruptcy court, the district court, or the bankruptcy appellate panel—

(i) on its own motion or on the request of a party, determines that a circumstance specified in clause (i), (ii), or (iii) of subparagraph (A) exists; or

(ii) receives a request made by a majority of the appellants and a majority of appellees (if any) to make the certification described in subparagraph (A);

then the bankruptcy court, the district court, or the bankruptcy appellate panel shall make the certification described in subparagraph (A).

(C) The parties may supplement the certification with a short statement of the basis for the certification.

(D) An appeal under this paragraph does not stay any proceeding of the bankruptcy court, the district court, or the bankruptcy appellate panel from which the appeal is taken, unless the respective bankruptcy court, district court, or bankruptcy appellate panel, or the court of appeals in which the appeal is pending, issues a stay of such proceeding pending the appeal.

(E) Any request under subparagraph (B) for certification shall be made not later than 60 days after the entry of the judgment, order, or decree.

(Added Pub.L. 98–353, title I, § 104(a), July 10, 1984, 98 Stat. 341; amended Pub.L. 101–650, title III, § 305, Dec. 1, 1990, 104 Stat. 5105; Pub.L. 103–394, title I, §§ 102, 104(c), (d), Oct. 22, 1994, 108 Stat. 4108–4110; Pub.L. 109–8, title XII, § 1233(a), Apr. 20, 2005, 119 Stat. 202; Pub.L. 111–327, § 2(c)(1), Dec. 22, 2010, 124 Stat. 3562.)

* * *

§ 581. United States trustees

(a) The Attorney General shall appoint one United States trustee for each of the following regions composed of Federal judicial districts . . .

       * * *

(b) Each United States trustee shall be appointed for a term of five years. On the expiration of his term, a United States trustee shall continue to perform the duties of his office until his successor is appointed and qualifies.

(c) Each United States trustee is subject to removal by the Attorney General.

    (Added Pub.L. 95–598, title II, § 224(a), Nov. 6, 1978, 92 Stat. 2662; amended Pub.L. 99–554, title I, § 111(a)–(c), Oct. 27, 1986, 100 Stat. 3090, 3091.)

* * *

§ 586. Duties; supervision by Attorney General

(a) Each United States trustee, within the region for which such United States trustee is appointed, shall—

(1) establish, maintain, and supervise a panel of private trustees that are eligible and available to serve as trustees in cases under chapter 7 of title 11;

(2) serve as and perform the duties of a trustee in a case under title 11 when required under title 11 to serve as trustee in such a case;

(3) supervise the administration of cases and trustees in cases under chapter 7, 11, 12, 13, or 15 of title 11 by, whenever the United States trustee considers it to be appropriate—

(A)(i) reviewing, in accordance with procedural guidelines adopted by the Executive Office of the United States Trustee (which guidelines shall be applied uniformly by the United States trustee except when circumstances warrant different treatment), applications filed for compensation and reimbursement under section 330 of title 11; and

(ii) filing with the court comments with respect to such application and, if the United States Trustee considers it to be appropriate, objections to such application;

(B) monitoring plans and disclosure statements filed in cases under chapter 11 of title 11 and filing with the court, in connection with hearings under sections 1125 and 1128 of such title, comments with respect to such plans and disclosure statements;

(C) monitoring plans filed under chapters 12 and 13 of title 11 and filing with the court, in connection with hearings under sections 1224, 1229, 1324, and 1329 of such title, comments with respect to such plans;

(D) taking such action as the United States trustee deems to be appropriate to ensure that all reports, schedules, and fees required to be filed under title 11 and this title by the debtor are properly and timely filed;

(E) monitoring creditors' committees appointed under title 11;

(F) notifying the appropriate United States attorney of matters which relate to the occurrence of any action which may constitute a crime under the laws of the United States and, on the request of the United States attorney, assisting the United States attorney in carrying out prosecutions based on such action;

(G) monitoring the progress of cases under title 11 and taking such actions as the United States trustee deems to be appropriate to prevent undue delay in such progress;

(H) in small business cases (as defined in section 101 of title 11), performing the additional duties specified in title 11 pertaining to such cases; and

2366

(I)   monitoring applications filed under section 327 of title 11 and, whenever the United States trustee deems it to be appropriate, filing with the court comments with respect to the approval of such applications;

(4)   deposit or invest under section 345 of title 11 money received as trustee in cases under title 11;

(5)   perform the duties prescribed for the United States trustee under title 11 and this title, and such duties consistent with title 11 and this title as the Attorney General may prescribe;

(6)   make such reports as the Attorney General directs, including the results of audits performed under section 603(a) of the Bankruptcy Abuse Prevention and Consumer Protection Act of 2005;

(7)   in each of such small business cases—

(A)   conduct an initial debtor interview as soon as practicable after the date of the order for relief but before the first meeting scheduled under section 341(a) of title 11, at which time the United States trustee shall—

(i)   begin to investigate the debtor's viability;

(ii)   inquire about the debtor's business plan;

(iii)   explain the debtor's obligations to file monthly operating reports and other required reports;

(iv)   attempt to develop an agreed scheduling order; and

(v)   inform the debtor of other obligations;

(B)   if determined to be appropriate and advisable, visit the appropriate business premises of the debtor, ascertain the state of the debtor's books and records, and verify that the debtor has filed its tax returns; and

(C)   review and monitor diligently the debtor's activities, to determine as promptly as possible whether the debtor will be unable to confirm a plan; and

(8)   in any case in which the United States trustee finds material grounds for any relief under section 1112 of title 11, apply promptly after making that finding to the court for relief.

(b)   If the number of cases under chapter 12 or 13 of title 11 commenced in a particular region so warrants, the United States trustee for such region may, subject to the approval of the Attorney General, appoint one or more individuals to serve as standing trustee, or designate one or more assistant United States trustees to serve in cases under such chapter. The United States trustee for such region shall supervise any such individual appointed as standing trustee in the performance of the duties of standing trustee.

(c)   Each United States trustee shall be under the general supervision of the Attorney General, who shall provide general coordination and assistance to the United States trustees.

(d)(1)   The Attorney General shall prescribe by rule qualifications for membership on the panels established by United States trustees under paragraph (a)(1) of this section, and qualifications for appointment under subsection (b) of this section to serve as standing trustee in cases under chapter 12 or 13 of title 11. The Attorney General may not require that an individual be an attorney in order to qualify for appointment under subsection (b) of this section to serve as standing trustee in cases under chapter 12 or 13 of title 11.

(2)   A trustee whose appointment under subsection (a)(1) or under subsection (b) is terminated or who ceases to be assigned to cases filed under title 11, United States Code, may obtain judicial review of the final agency decision by commencing an action in the district court of the United States for the district for which the panel to which the trustee is appointed under subsection (a)(1), or in the district court of the United States for the district in which the trustee is appointed under subsection (b) resides, after first exhausting all available administrative remedies, which if the trustee so elects, shall also include an administrative hearing on the record. Unless the trustee elects to have an

administrative hearing on the record, the trustee shall be deemed to have exhausted all administrative remedies for purposes of this paragraph if the agency fails to make a final agency decision within 90 days after the trustee requests administrative remedies. The Attorney General shall prescribe procedures to implement this paragraph. The decision of the agency shall be affirmed by the district court unless it is unreasonable and without cause based on the administrative record before the agency.

(e)(1)   The Attorney General, after consultation with a United States trustee that has appointed an individual under subsection (b) of this section to serve as standing trustee in cases under chapter 12 or 13 of title 11, shall fix—

   (A)   a maximum annual compensation for such individual consisting of—

      (i)   an amount not to exceed the highest annual rate of basic pay in effect for level V of the Executive Schedule; and

      (ii)   the cash value of employment benefits comparable to the employment benefits provided by the United States to individuals who are employed by the United States at the same rate of basic pay to perform similar services during the same period of time; and

   (B)   a percentage fee not to exceed—

      (i)   in the case of a debtor who is not a family farmer, ten percent; or

      (ii)   in the case of a debtor who is a family farmer, the sum of—

         (I)   not to exceed ten percent of the payments made under the plan of such debtor, with respect to payments in an aggregate amount not to exceed $450,000; and

         (II)   three percent of payments made under the plan of such debtor, with respect to payments made after the aggregate amount of payments made under the plan exceeds $450,000;

based on such maximum annual compensation and the actual, necessary expenses incurred by such individual as standing trustee.

   (2)   Such individual shall collect such percentage fee from all payments received by such individual under plans in the cases under chapter 12 or 13 of title 11 for which such individual serves as standing trustee. Such individual shall pay to the United States trustee, and the United States trustee shall deposit in the United States Trustee System Fund—

   (A)   any amount by which the actual compensation of such individual exceeds 5 per centum upon all payments received under plans in cases under chapter 12 or 13 of title 11 for which such individual serves as standing trustee; and

   (B)   any amount by which the percentage for all such cases exceeds—

      (i)   such individual's actual compensation for such cases, as adjusted under subparagraph (A) of paragraph (1); plus

      (ii)   the actual, necessary expenses incurred by such individual as standing trustee in such cases. Subject to the approval of the Attorney General, any or all of the interest earned from the deposit of payments under plans by such individual may be utilized to pay actual, necessary expenses without regard to the percentage limitation contained in subparagraph (d)(1)(B) of this section.

   (3)   After first exhausting all available administrative remedies, an individual appointed under subsection (b) may obtain judicial review of final agency action to deny a claim of actual, necessary expenses under this subsection by commencing an action in the district court of the United States for the district where the individual resides. The decision of the agency shall be affirmed by the district court unless it is unreasonable and without cause based upon the administrative record before the agency.

   (4)   The Attorney General shall prescribe procedures to implement this subsection.

(f)(1) The United States trustee for each district is authorized to contract with auditors to perform audits in cases designated by the United States trustee, in accordance with the procedures established under section 603(a) of the Bankruptcy Abuse Prevention and Consumer Protection Act of 2005.

(2)(A) The report of each audit referred to in paragraph (1) shall be filed with the court and transmitted to the United States trustee. Each report shall clearly and conspicuously specify any material misstatement of income or expenditures or of assets identified by the person performing the audit. In any case in which a material misstatement of income or expenditures or of assets has been reported, the clerk of the district court (or the clerk of the bankruptcy court if one is certified under section 156(b) of this title) shall give notice of the misstatement to the creditors in the case.

(B) If a material misstatement of income or expenditures or of assets is reported, the United States trustee shall—

(i) report the material misstatement, if appropriate, to the United States Attorney pursuant to section 3057 of title 18; and

(ii) if advisable, take appropriate action, including but not limited to commencing an adversary proceeding to revoke the debtor's discharge pursuant to section 727(d) of title 11.

(Added Pub.L. 95–598, title II, § 224(a), Nov. 6, 1978, 92 Stat. 2663; amended Pub.L. 99–554, title I, § 113, Oct. 27, 1986, 100 Stat. 3091; Pub.L. 101–509, title V, § 529 [title I, § 110(a)], Nov. 5, 1990, 104 Stat. 1427, 1452; Pub.L. 103–394, title II, § 224(a), title V, § 502, Oct. 22, 1994, 108 Stat. 4130, 4147; Pub.L. 109–8, title IV, § 439, title VI, § 603(b), title VIII, § 802(c)(3), title XII, § 1231, Apr. 20, 2005, 119 Stat. 113, 122, 146, 201; Pub.L. 111–327, § 2(c)(3), Dec. 22, 2010, 124 Stat. 3563.)

* * *

§ 959. Trustees and receivers suable; management; State laws

(a) Trustees, receivers or managers of any property, including debtors in possession, may be sued, without leave of the court appointing them, with respect to any of their acts or transactions in carrying on business connected with such property. Such actions shall be subject to the general equity power of such court so far as the same may be necessary to the ends of justice, but this shall not deprive a litigant of his right to trial by jury.

(b) Except as provided in section 1166 of title 11, a trustee, receiver or manager appointed in any cause pending in any court of the United States, including a debtor in possession, shall manage and operate the property in his possession as such trustee, receiver or manager according to the requirements of the valid laws of the State in which such property is situated, in the same manner that the owner or possessor thereof would be bound to do if in possession thereof.

(June 25, 1948, ch. 646, 62 Stat. 926; Pub.L. 95–598, title II, § 235, Nov. 6, 1978, 92 Stat. 2667.)

§ 960. Tax liability

(a) Any officers and agents conducting any business under authority of a United States court shall be subject to all Federal, State and local taxes applicable to such business to the same extent as if it were conducted by an individual or corporation.

(b) A tax under subsection (a) shall be paid on or before the due date of the tax under applicable nonbankruptcy law, unless—

(1) the tax is a property tax secured by a lien against property that is abandoned under section 554 of title 11, within a reasonable period of time after the lien attaches, by the trustee in a case under title 11; or

(2) payment of the tax is excused under a specific provision of title 11.

(c) In a case pending under chapter 7 of title 11, payment of a tax may be deferred until final distribution is made under section 726 of title 11, if—

(1)   the tax was not incurred by a trustee duly appointed or elected under chapter 7 of title 11; or

(2)   before the due date of the tax, an order of the court makes a finding of probable insufficiency of funds of the estate to pay in full the administrative expenses allowed under section 503(b) of title 11 that have the same priority in distribution under section 726(b) of title 11 as the priority of that tax.

(June 25, 1948, ch. 646, 62 Stat. 927; Pub.L. 109–8, title VII, § 712(a), Apr. 20, 2005, 119 Stat. 127.)

* * *

§ 1291.   Final decisions of district courts

The courts of appeals (other than the United States Court of Appeals for the Federal Circuit) shall have jurisdiction of appeals from all final decisions of the district courts of the United States, the United States District Court for the District of the Canal Zone, the District Court of Guam, and the District Court of the Virgin Islands, except where a direct review may be had in the Supreme Court. The jurisdiction of the United States Court of Appeals for the Federal Circuit shall be limited to the jurisdiction described in sections 1292(c) and (d) and 1295 of this title.

(June 25, 1948, ch. 646, 62 Stat. 929; Oct. 31, 1951, ch. 655, § 48, 65 Stat. 726; Pub.L. 85–508, § 12(e), July 7, 1958, 72 Stat. 348; Pub.L. 97–164, title I, § 124, Apr. 2, 1982, 96 Stat. 36.)

§ 1292.   Interlocutory decisions

(a)   Except as provided in subsections (c) and (d) of this section, the courts of appeals shall have jurisdiction of appeals from:

(1)   Interlocutory orders of the district courts of the United States, the United States District Court for the District of the Canal Zone, the District Court of Guam, and the District Court of the Virgin Islands, or of the judges thereof, granting, continuing, modifying, refusing or dissolving injunctions, or refusing to dissolve or modify injunctions, except where a direct review may be had in the Supreme Court;

(2)   Interlocutory orders appointing receivers, or refusing orders to wind up receiverships or to take steps to accomplish the purposes thereof, such as directing sales or other disposals of property;

(3)   Interlocutory decrees of such district courts or the judges thereof determining the rights and liabilities of the parties to admiralty cases in which appeals from final decrees are allowed.

(b)   When a district judge, in making in a civil action an order not otherwise appealable under this section, shall be of the opinion that such order involves a controlling question of law as to which there is substantial ground for difference of opinion and that an immediate appeal from the order may materially advance the ultimate termination of the litigation, he shall so state in writing in such order. The Court of Appeals which would have jurisdiction of an appeal of such action may thereupon, in its discretion, permit an appeal to be taken from such order, if application is made to it within ten days after the entry of the order: *Provided, however*, That application for an appeal hereunder shall not stay proceedings in the district court unless the district judge or the Court of Appeals or a judge thereof shall so order.

(c)   The United States Court of Appeals for the Federal Circuit shall have exclusive jurisdiction—

(1)   of an appeal from an interlocutory order or decree described in subsection (a) or (b) of this section in any case over which the court would have jurisdiction of an appeal under section 1295 of this title; and

(2)   of an appeal from a judgment in a civil action for patent infringement which would otherwise be appealable to the United States Court of Appeals for the Federal Circuit and is final except for an accounting.

(d)(1)   When the chief judge of the Court of International Trade issues an order under the provisions of section 256(b) of this title, or when any judge of the Court of International Trade, in issuing any other interlocutory order, includes in the order a statement that a controlling question of law is involved with respect to which there is a substantial ground for difference of opinion and that an immediate appeal from that order may materially advance the ultimate termination of the litigation, the United States Court of Appeals for the Federal Circuit may, in its discretion, permit an appeal to be taken from such order, if application is made to that Court within ten days after the entry of such order.

(2)　When the chief judge of the United States Court of Federal Claims issues an order under section 798(b) of this title, or when any judge of the United States Court of Federal Claims, in issuing an interlocutory order, includes in the order a statement that a controlling question of law is involved with respect to which there is a substantial ground for difference of opinion and that an immediate appeal from that order may materially advance the ultimate termination of the litigation, the United States Court of Appeals for the Federal Circuit may, in its discretion, permit an appeal to be taken from such order, if application is made to that Court within ten days after the entry of such order.

(3)　Neither the application for nor the granting of an appeal under this subsection shall stay proceedings in the Court of International Trade or in the Court of Federal Claims, as the case may be, unless a stay is ordered by a judge of the Court of International Trade or of the Court of Federal Claims or by the United States Court of Appeals for the Federal Circuit or a judge of that court.

(4)(A)　The United States Court of Appeals for the Federal Circuit shall have exclusive jurisdiction of an appeal from an interlocutory order of a district court of the United States, the District Court of Guam, the District Court of the Virgin Islands, or the District Court for the Northern Mariana Islands, granting or denying, in whole or in part, a motion to transfer an action to the United States Court of Federal Claims under section 1631 of this title.

(B)　When a motion to transfer an action to the Court of Federal Claims is filed in a district court, no further proceedings shall be taken in the district court until 60 days after the court has ruled upon the motion. If an appeal is taken from the district court's grant or denial of the motion, proceedings shall be further stayed until the appeal has been decided by the Court of Appeals for the Federal Circuit. The stay of proceedings in the district court shall not bar the granting of preliminary or injunctive relief, where appropriate and where expedition is reasonably necessary. However, during the period in which proceedings are stayed as provided in this subparagraph, no transfer to the Court of Federal Claims pursuant to the motion shall be carried out.

(e)　The Supreme Court may prescribe rules, in accordance with section 2072 of this title, to provide for an appeal of an interlocutory decision to the courts of appeals that is not otherwise provided for under subsection (a), (b), (c), or (d).

(June 25, 1948, ch. 646, 62 Stat. 929; Oct. 31, 1951, ch. 655, § 49, 65 Stat. 726; Pub.L. 85–508, § 12(e), July 7, 1958, 72 Stat. 348; Pub.L. 85–919, Sept. 2, 1958, 72 Stat. 1770; Pub.L. 97–164,§ 125, Apr. 2, 1982, 96 Stat. 36; Pub.L. 98–620, title IV, § 412, Nov. 8, 1984, 98 Stat. 3362; Pub.L. 100–702, title V, § 501, Nov. 19, 1988, 102 Stat. 4652; Pub.L. 102–572, title I, § 101, title IX, §§ 902(b), 906(c), Oct. 29, 1992, 106 Stat. 4506, 4516, 4518.)

* * *

§ 1334.　Bankruptcy cases and proceedings

(a)　Except as provided in subsection (b) of this section, the district courts shall have original and exclusive jurisdiction of all cases under title 11.

(b)　Except as provided in subsection (e)(2), and notwithstanding any Act of Congress that confers exclusive jurisdiction on a court or courts other than the district courts, the district courts shall have original but not exclusive jurisdiction of all civil proceedings arising under title 11, or arising in or related to cases under title 11.

(c)(1)Except with respect to a case under chapter 15 of title 11, nothing in this section prevents a district court in the interest of justice, or in the interest of comity with State courts or respect for State law, from abstaining from hearing a particular proceeding arising under title 11 or arising in or related to a case under title 11.

(2)   Upon timely motion of a party in a proceeding based upon a State law claim or State law cause of action, related to a case under title 11 but not arising under title 11 or arising in a case under title 11, with respect to which an action could not have been commenced in a court of the United States absent jurisdiction under this section, the district court shall abstain from hearing such proceeding if an action is commenced, and can be timely adjudicated, in a State forum of appropriate jurisdiction.

(d)   Any decision to abstain or not to abstain made under subsection (c) (other than a decision not to abstain in a proceeding described in subsection (c)(2)) is not reviewable by appeal or otherwise by the court of appeals under section 158(d), 1291, or 1292 of this title or by the Supreme Court of the United States under section 1254 of this title. Subsection (c) and this subsection shall not be construed to limit the applicability of the stay provided for by section 362 of title 11, United States Code, as such section applies to an action affecting the property of the estate in bankruptcy.

(e)   The district court in which a case under title 11 is commenced or is pending shall have exclusive jurisdiction—

(1)   of all the property, wherever located, of the debtor as of the commencement of such case, and of property of the estate; and

(2)   over all claims or causes of action that involve construction of section 327 of title 11, United States Code, or rules relating to disclosure requirements under section 327.

(June 25, 1948, ch. 646, 62 Stat. 931; Pub.L. 95–598, title II, § 238(a), Nov. 6, 1978, 92 Stat. 2667; Pub.L. 98–353, title I, § 101(a), July 10, 1984, 98 Stat. 333; Pub.L. 99–554, title I, § 144(e), Oct. 27, 1986, 100 Stat. 3096; Pub.L. 101–650, title III, § 309(b), Dec. 1, 1990, 104 Stat. 5113; Pub.L. 103–394, title I, § 104(b), Oct. 22, 1994, 108 Stat. 4109; Pub.L. 109–8, title III, § 324(a), title VIII, § 802(c)(2), title XII, § 1219, Apr. 20, 2005, 119 Stat. 98, 145, 195.)

* * *

§ 1408.   Venue of cases under title 11

Except as provided in section 1410 of this title, a case under title 11 may be commenced in the district court for the district—

(1)   in which the domicile, residence, principal place of business in the United States, or principal assets in the United States, of the person or entity that is the subject of such case have been located for the one hundred and eighty days immediately preceding such commencement, or for a longer portion of such one-hundred-and-eighty-day period than the domicile, residence, or principal place of business, in the United States, or principal assets in the United States, of such person were located in any other district; or

(2)   in which there is pending a case under title 11 concerning such person's affiliate, general partner, or partnership.

(Added Pub.L. 98–353, title I, § 102(a), July 10, 1984, 98 Stat. 334.)

§ 1409.   Venue of proceedings arising under title 11 or arising in or related to cases under title 11

(a)   Except as otherwise provided in subsections (b) and (d), a proceeding arising under title 11 or arising in or related to a case under title 11 may be commenced in the district court in which such case is pending.

(b)   Except as provided in subsection (d) of this section, a trustee in a case under title 11 may commence a proceeding arising in or related to such case to recover a money judgment of or property worth less than $1,300 or a consumer debt of less than $19,250, or a debt (excluding a consumer debt) against a noninsider of less than $12,850, only in the district court for the district in which the defendant resides.

(c)   Except as provided in subsection (b) of this section, a trustee in a case under title 11 may commence a proceeding arising in or related to such case as statutory successor to the debtor or creditors under section 541 or 544(b) of title 11 in the district court for the district where the State or Federal court sits in which, under applicable nonbankruptcy venue provisions, the debtor or creditors, as the case may be, may have commenced an action on which such proceeding is based if the case under title 11 had not been commenced.

(d)   A trustee may commence a proceeding arising under title 11 or arising in or related to a case under title 11 based on a claim arising after the commencement of such case from the operation of the business of the debtor only in the district court for the district where a State or Federal court sits in which, under applicable nonbankruptcy venue provisions, an action on such claim may have been brought.

(e)   A proceeding arising under title 11 or arising in or related to a case under title 11, based on a claim arising after the commencement of such case from the operation of the business of the debtor, may be commenced against the representative of the estate in such case in the district court for the district where the State or Federal court sits in which the party commencing such proceeding may, under applicable nonbankruptcy venue provisions, have brought an action on such claim, or in the district court in which such case is pending.

(Added Pub.L. 98–353, title I, § 102(a), July 10, 1984, 98 Stat. 334; amended Pub.L. 109–8, title IV, § 410, Apr. 20, 2005, 119 Stat. 106.)

§ 1410.   Venue of cases ancillary to foreign proceedings

A case under chapter 15 of title 11 may be commenced in the district court of the United States for the district—

(1)   in which the debtor has its principal place of business or principal assets in the United States;

(2)   if the debtor does not have a place of business or assets in the United States, in which there is pending against the debtor an action or proceeding in a Federal or State court; or

(3)   in a case other than those specified in paragraph (1) or (2), in which venue will be consistent with the interests of justice and the convenience of the parties, having regard to the relief sought by the foreign representative.

(Added Pub.L. 98–353, title I, § 102(a), July 10, 1984, 98 Stat. 335; amended Pub.L. 109–8, title VIII, § 802(c)(4), Apr. 20, 2005, 119 Stat. 146.)

§ 1411.   Jury trials

(a)   Except as provided in subsection (b) of this section, this chapter and title 11 do not affect any right to trial by jury that an individual has under applicable nonbankruptcy law with regard to a personal injury or wrongful death tort claim.

(b)   The district court may order the issues arising under section 303 of title 11 to be tried without a jury.

(Added Pub.L. 98–353, title I, § 102(a), July 10, 1984, 98 Stat. 335.)

§ 1412.   Change of venue

A district court may transfer a case or proceeding under title 11 to a district court for another district, in the interest of justice or for the convenience of the parties.

(Added Pub.L. 98–353, title I, § 102(a), July 10, 1984, 98 Stat. 335.)

* * *

§ 1452.   Removal of claims related to bankruptcy cases

(a)   A party may remove any claim or cause of action in a civil action other than a proceeding before the United States Tax Court or a civil action by a governmental unit to enforce such governmental unit's police or regulatory power, to the district court for the district where such civil action is pending, if such district court has jurisdiction of such claim or cause of action under section 1334 of this title.

(b)   The court to which such claim or cause of action is removed may remand such claim or cause of action on any equitable ground. An order entered under this subsection remanding a claim or cause of action, or a decision to not remand, is not reviewable by appeal or otherwise by the court of appeals under section 158(d), 1291, or 1292 of this title or by the Supreme Court of the United States under section 1254 of this title.

(Added Pub.L. 98–353, title I, § 103(a), July 10, 1984, 98 Stat. 335; amended Pub.L. 101–650, title III, § 309(c), Dec. 1, 1990, 104 Stat. 5113.)

* * *

§ 1930.   Bankruptcy fees

(a)   The parties commencing a case under title 11 shall pay to the clerk of the district court or the clerk of the bankruptcy court, if one has been certified pursuant to section 156(b) of this title, the following filing fees:

(1)   For a case commenced under—

(A)   chapter 7 of title 11, $245, and

(B)   chapter 13 of title 11, $235.

(2)   For a case commenced under chapter 9 of title 11, equal to the fee specified in paragraph (3) for filing a case under chapter 11 of title 11. The amount by which the fee payable under this paragraph exceeds $300 shall be deposited in the fund established under section 1931 of this title.

(3)   For a case commenced under chapter 11 of title 11 that does not concern a railroad, as defined in section 101 of title 11, $1,167.

(4)   For a case commenced under chapter 11 of title 11 concerning a railroad, as so defined, $1,000.

(5)   For a case commenced under chapter 12 of title 11, $200.

(6)   In addition to the filing fee paid to the clerk, a quarterly fee shall be paid to the United States trustee, for deposit in the Treasury, in each case under chapter 11 of title 11 for each quarter (including any fraction thereof) until the case is converted or dismissed, whichever occurs first. The fee shall be $325 for each quarter in which disbursements total less than $15,000; $650 for each quarter in which disbursements total $15,000 or more but less than $75,000; $975 for each quarter in which disbursements total $75,000 or more but less than $150,000; $1,625 for each quarter in which disbursements total $150,000 or more but less than $225,000; $1,950 for each quarter in which disbursements total $225,000 or more but less than $300,000; $4,875 for each quarter in which disbursements total $300,000 or more but less than $1,000,000; $6,500 for each quarter in which disbursements total $1,000,000 or more but less than $2,000,000; $9,750 for each quarter in which disbursements total $2,000,000 or more but less than $3,000,000; $10,400 for each quarter in which disbursements total $3,000,000 or more but less than $5,000,000; $13,000 for each quarter in which disbursements total $5,000,000 or more but less than $15,000,000; $20,000 for each quarter in which disbursements total $15,000,000 or more but less than $30,000,000; $30,000 for each quarter in which disbursements total more than $30,000,000. The fee shall be payable on the last day of the calendar month following the calendar quarter for which the fee is owed.

(7)   In districts that are not part of a United States trustee region as defined in section 581 of this title, the Judicial Conference of the United States may require the debtor in a case under chapter 11 of title 11 to pay fees equal to those imposed by paragraph (6) of this subsection. Such fees shall be deposited as offsetting receipts to the fund established under section 1931 of this title and shall remain available until expended.

An individual commencing a voluntary case or a joint case under title 11 may pay such fee in installments. For converting, on request of the debtor, a case under chapter 7, or 13 of title 11, to a case under chapter 11 of title 11, the debtor shall pay to the clerk of the district court or the clerk of the bankruptcy court, if one has been certified pursuant to section 156(b) of this title, a fee of the amount equal to the difference between the fee specified in paragraph (3) and the fee specified in paragraph (1).

(b)   The Judicial Conference of the United States may prescribe additional fees in cases under title 11 of the same kind as the Judicial Conference prescribes under section 1914(b) of this title.

(c)   Upon the filing of any separate or joint notice of appeal or application for appeal or upon the receipt of any order allowing, or notice of the allowance of, an appeal or a writ of certiorari $5 shall be paid to the clerk of the court, by the appellant or petitioner.

(d)   Whenever any case or proceeding is dismissed in any bankruptcy court for want of jurisdiction, such court may order the payment of just costs.

(e)   The clerk of the court may collect only the fees prescribed under this section.

(f)(1)   Under the procedures prescribed by the Judicial Conference of the United States, the district court or the bankruptcy court may waive the filing fee in a case under chapter 7 of title 11 for an individual if the court determines that such individual has income less than 150 percent of the income official poverty line (as defined by the Office of Management and Budget, and revised annually in accordance with section 673(2) of the Omnibus Budget Reconciliation Act of 1981) applicable to a family of the size involved and is unable to pay that fee in installments. For purposes of this paragraph, the term "filing fee" means the filing fee required by subsection (a), or any other fee prescribed by the Judicial Conference under subsections (b) and (c) that is payable to the clerk upon the commencement of a case under chapter 7.

(2)   The district court or the bankruptcy court may waive for such debtors other fees prescribed under subsections (b) and (c).

(3)   This subsection does not restrict the district court or the bankruptcy court from waiving, in accordance with Judicial Conference policy, fees prescribed under this section for other debtors and creditors.

(Added Pub.L. 95–598, title II, § 246(a), Nov. 6, 1978, 92 Stat. 2671; amended Pub.L. 98–353, title I, § 111(a), (b), July 10, 1984, 98 Stat. 342; Pub.L. 99–500, § 101(b) [title IV, § 407(b)], Oct. 18, 1986, 100 Stat. 1783–39, 1783–64, and Pub.L. 99–591, § 101(b) [title IV, § 407(b)], Oct. 30, 1986, 100 Stat. 3341–39, 3341–64; Pub.L. 99–554, title I, §§ 117, 144(f), Oct. 27, 1986, 100 Stat. 3095, 3097; Pub.L. 101–162, title IV, § 406(a), Nov. 21, 1989, 103 Stat. 1016; Pub.L. 102–140, title I, § 111(a), Oct. 28, 1991, 105 Stat. 795; Pub.L. 103–121, title I, § 111(a)(1), (b)(1), Oct. 27, 1993, 107 Stat. 1164; Pub.L. 104–91, title I, § 101(a), Jan. 6, 1996, 110 Stat. 11, amended Pub.L. 104–99, title II, § 211, Jan. 26, 1996, 110 Stat. 37; Pub.L. 104–208, div. A, title I, § 101(a) [title I, § 109(a)], Sept. 30, 1996, 110 Stat. 3009, 3009–18; Pub.L. 106–113, div. B, § 1000(a)(1) [title I, § 113], Nov. 29, 1999, 113 Stat. 1535, 1501A–20; Pub.L. 106–518, title I, §§ 103–105, Nov. 13, 2000, 114 Stat. 2411, 2412; Pub.L. 109–8, title III, § 325(a), title IV, § 418, Apr. 20, 2005, 119 Stat. 98, 108; Pub.L. 109–13, div. A, title VI, § 6058(a), May 11, 2005, 119 Stat. 297; Pub.L. 109–171, title X, § 10101(a), Feb. 8, 2006, 120 Stat. 184; Pub.L. 110–161, div. B, title II, § 213(a), Dec. 26, 2007, 121 Stat. 1914; Pub.L. 112–121, § 3(a), May 25, 2012, 126 Stat. 348.)

Effective December 1, 2015

Bankruptcy Court Miscellaneous Fee Schedule

The fees included in the Bankruptcy Court Miscellaneous Fee Schedule are to be charged for services provided by the bankruptcy courts.

* * *

(8)   Administrative fee:

- For filing a petition under Chapter 7, 12, or 13, $75.

- For filing a petition under Chapter 9, 11, or 15, $550.

- When a motion to divide a joint case under Chapter 7, 12, or 13 is filed, $75.

- When a motion to divide a joint case under Chapter 11 is filed, $550.

(9) For payment to trustees pursuant to 11 U.S.C. § 330(b)(2), a $15 fee applies in the following circumstances:

- For filing a petition under Chapter 7

* * *

§ 2075.   Bankruptcy rules

The Supreme Court shall have the power to prescribe by general rules, the forms of process, writs, pleadings, and motions, and the practice and procedure in cases under title 11.

Such rules shall not abridge, enlarge, or modify any substantive right.

The Supreme Court shall transmit to Congress not later than May 1 of the year in which a rule prescribed under this section is to become effective a copy of the proposed rule. The rule shall take effect no earlier than December 1 of the year in which it is transmitted to Congress unless otherwise provided by law.

The bankruptcy rules promulgated under this section shall prescribe a form for the statement required under section 707(b)(2)(C) of title 11 and may provide general rules on the content of such statement.

(Added Pub.L. 88–623, § 1, Oct. 3, 1964, 78 Stat. 1001; amended Pub.L. 95–598, title II, § 247, Nov. 6, 1978, 92 Stat. 2672; Pub.L. 103–394, title I, § 104(f), Oct. 22, 1994, 108 Stat. 4110; Pub.L. 109–8, title XII, § 1232, Apr. 20, 2005, 119 Stat. 202.)

FEDERAL RULES OF BANKRUPTCY PROCEDURE

For updates, see www.selectedcommercialstatutes.com

Rule 1001. Scope of Rules and Forms; Short Title

The Bankruptcy Rules and Forms govern procedure in cases under title 11 of the United States Code. The rules shall be cited as the Federal Rules of Bankruptcy Procedure and the forms as the Official Bankruptcy Forms. These rules shall be construed to secure the just, speedy, and inexpensive determination of every case and proceeding.

(As amended Mar. 30, 1987, eff. Aug. 1, 1987; Apr. 30, 1991, eff. Aug. 1, 1991.)

PART I

COMMENCEMENT OF CASE: PROCEEDINGS RELATING TO PETITION AND ORDER FOR RELIEF

Rule 1002. Commencement of Case

(a) Petition.

A petition commencing a case under the Code shall be filed with the clerk.

(b) Transmission to United States Trustee.

The clerk shall forthwith transmit to the United States trustee a copy of the petition filed pursuant to subdivision (a) of this rule.

(As amended Mar. 30, 1987, eff. Aug. 1, 1987; Apr. 30, 1991, eff. Aug. 1, 1991.)

Rule 1003.   Involuntary Petition

(a) Transferor or Transferee of Claim.

A transferor or transferee of a claim shall annex to the original and each copy of the petition a copy of all documents evidencing the transfer, whether transferred unconditionally, for security, or otherwise, and a signed statement that the claim was not transferred for the purpose of commencing the case and setting forth the consideration for and terms of the transfer. An entity that has transferred or acquired a claim for the purpose of commencing a case for liquidation under chapter 7 or for reorganization under chapter 11 shall not be a qualified petitioner.

(b) Joinder of Petitioners After Filing.

If the answer to an involuntary petition filed by fewer than three creditors avers the existence of 12 or more creditors, the debtor shall file with the answer a list of all creditors with their addresses, a brief statement of the nature of their claims, and the amounts thereof. If it appears that there are 12 or more creditors as provided in § 303(b) of the Code, the court shall afford a reasonable opportunity for other creditors to join in the petition before a hearing is held thereon.

(As amended Mar. 30, 1987, eff. Aug. 1, 1987.)

Rule 1004.   Involuntary Petition Against a Partnership

After filing of an involuntary petition under § 303(b)(3) of the Code, (1) the petitioning partners or other petitioners shall promptly send to or serve on each general partner who is not a petitioner a copy of the petition; and (2) the clerk shall promptly issue a summons for service on each general partner who is not a petitioner. Rule 1010 applies to the form and service of the summons.

(As amended Apr. 29, 2002, eff. Dec. 1, 2002.)

Rule 1004.1.   Petition for an Infant or Incompetent Person

If an infant or incompetent person has a representative, including a general guardian, committee, conservator, or similar fiduciary, the representative may file a voluntary petition on behalf of the infant or incompetent person. An infant or incompetent person who does not have a duly appointed representative may file a voluntary petition by next friend or guardian ad litem. The court shall appoint a guardian ad litem for an infant or incompetent person who is a debtor and is not otherwise represented or shall make any other order to protect the infant or incompetent debtor.

(Added Apr. 29, 2002, eff. Dec. 1, 2002.)

Rule 1004.2.   Petition in Chapter 15 Cases

(a) Designating Center of Main Interests.

A petition for recognition of a foreign proceeding under chapter 15 of the Code shall state the country where the debtor has its center of main interests. The petition shall also identify each country in which a foreign proceeding by, regarding, or against the debtor is pending.

(b) Challenging Designation.

The United States trustee or a party in interest may file a motion for a determination that the debtor's center of main interests is other than as stated in the petition for recognition commencing the chapter 15 case. Unless the court orders otherwise, the motion shall be filed no later than seven days before the date set for the hearing on the petition. The motion shall be transmitted to the United States trustee and served on the debtor, all persons or bodies authorized to administer foreign proceedings of the debtor, all entities against whom provisional relief is being sought under § 1519 of the Code, all parties to litigation pending in the United States in which the debtor was a party as of the time the petition was filed, and such other entities as the court may direct.

(Adopted Apr. 26, 2011, eff. Dec. 1, 2011.)

Rule 1005.   Caption of Petition

The caption of a petition commencing a case under the Code shall contain the name of the court, the title of the case, and the docket number. The title of the case shall include the following information about the debtor: name, employer identification number, last four digits of the social-security number or individual debtor's taxpayer-identification number, any other federal taxpayer-identification number, and all other names used within eight years before filing the petition. If the petition is not filed by the debtor, it shall include all names used by the debtor which are known to the petitioners.

(As amended Mar. 30, 1987, eff. Aug. 1, 1987; Mar. 27, 2003, eff. Dec. 1, 2003; Apr. 23, 2008, eff. Dec. 1, 2008.)

Rule 1006.   Filing Fee

(a) General Requirement.

Every petition shall be accompanied by the filing fee except as provided in subdivisions (b) and (c) of this rule. For the purpose of this rule, "filing fee" means the filing fee prescribed by 28 U.S.C. § 1930(a)(1)–(a)(5) and any other fee prescribed by the Judicial Conference of the United States under 28 U.S.C. § 1930(b) that is payable to the clerk upon the commencement of a case under the Code.

(b) Payment of Filing Fee in Installments.

(1) Application to Pay Filing Fee in Installments.

A voluntary petition by an individual shall be accepted for filing if accompanied by the debtor's signed application, prepared as prescribed by the appropriate Official Form, stating that the debtor is unable to pay the filing fee except in installments.

(2) Action on Application.

Prior to the meeting of creditors, the court may order the filing fee paid to the clerk or grant leave to pay in installments and fix the number, amount and dates of payment. The number of installments shall not exceed four, and the final installment shall be payable not later than 120 days after filing the petition. For cause shown, the court may extend the time of any installment, provided the last installment is paid not later than 180 days after filing the petition.

(3) Postponement of Attorney's Fees.

All installments of the filing fee must be paid in full before the debtor or chapter 13 trustee may make further payments to an attorney or any other person who renders services to the debtor in connection with the case.

(c) Waiver of Filing Fee.

A voluntary chapter 7 petition filed by an individual shall be accepted for filing if accompanied by the debtor's application requesting a waiver under 28 U.S.C. § 1930(f), prepared as prescribed by the appropriate Official Form.

(As amended Mar. 30, 1987, eff. Aug. 1, 1987; Apr. 23, 1996, eff. Dec. 1, 1996; Apr. 23, 2008, eff. Dec. 1, 2008.)

Rule 1007.   Lists, Schedules, Statements, and Other Documents; Time Limits

(a) Corporate Ownership Statement, List of Creditors and Equity Security Holders, and Other Lists.

(1) Voluntary Case.

In a voluntary case, the debtor shall file with the petition a list containing the name and address of each entity included or to be included on Schedules D, E/F, G, and H as prescribed by the Official Forms. If the debtor is a corporation, other than a governmental unit, the debtor shall file with the petition a corporate ownership statement containing the information described in Rule 7007.1. The debtor shall file a supplemental statement promptly upon any change in circumstances that renders the corporate ownership statement inaccurate.

(2) Involuntary Case.

In an involuntary case, the debtor shall file, within seven days after entry of the order for relief, a list containing the name and address of each entity included or to be included on Schedules D, E/F, G, and H as prescribed by the Official Forms.

(3) Equity Security Holders.

In a chapter 11 reorganization case, unless the court orders otherwise, the debtor shall file within 14 days after entry of the order for relief a list of the debtor's equity security holders of each class showing the number and kind of interests registered in the name of each holder, and the last known address or place of business of each holder.

(4) Chapter 15 Case.

In addition to the documents required under § 1515 of the Code, a foreign representative filing a petition for recognition under chapter 15 shall file with the petition: (A) a corporate ownership statement containing the information described in Rule 7007.1; and (B) unless the court orders otherwise, a list containing the names and addresses of all persons or bodies authorized to administer foreign proceedings of the debtor, all parties to litigation pending in the United States in which the debtor is a party at the time of the filing of the petition, and all entities against whom provisional relief is being sought under § 1519 of the Code.

(5) Extension of Time.

Any extension of time for the filing of the lists required by this subdivision may be granted only on motion for cause shown and on notice to the United States trustee and to any trustee, committee elected under § 705 or appointed under § 1102 of the Code, or other party as the court may direct.

(b) Schedules, Statements, and Other Documents Required.

(1) Except in a chapter 9 municipality case, the debtor, unless the court orders otherwise, shall file the following schedules, statements, and other documents, prepared as prescribed by the appropriate Official Forms, if any:

(A) schedules of assets and liabilities;

(B) a schedule of current income and expenditures;

(C) a schedule of executory contracts and unexpired leases;

(D) a statement of financial affairs;

(E) copies of all payment advices or other evidence of payment, if any, received by the debtor from an employer within 60 days before the filing of the petition, with redaction of all but the last four digits of the debtor's social-security number or individual taxpayer-identification number; and

(F) a record of any interest that the debtor has in an account or program of the type specified in § 521(c) of the Code.

(2) An individual debtor in a chapter 7 case shall file a statement of intention as required by § 521(a) of the Code, prepared as prescribed by the appropriate Official Form. A copy of the statement of intention shall be served on the trustee and the creditors named in the statement on or before the filing of the statement.

(3) Unless the United States trustee has determined that the credit counseling requirement of § 109(h) does not apply in the district, an individual debtor must file a statement of compliance with the credit counseling requirement, prepared as prescribed by the appropriate Official Form which must include one of the following:

(A) an attached certificate and debt repayment plan, if any, required by § 521(b);

(B) a statement that the debtor has received the credit counseling briefing required by § 109(h)(1) but does not have the certificate required by § 521(b);

(C) a certification under § 109(h)(3); or

(D) a request for a determination by the court under § 109(h)(4).

(4) Unless § 707(b)(2)(D) applies, an individual debtor in a chapter 7 case shall file a statement of current monthly income prepared as prescribed by the appropriate Official Form, and, if the current monthly income exceeds the median family income for the applicable state and household size, the information, including calculations, required by § 707(b), prepared as prescribed by the appropriate Official Form.

(5) An individual debtor in a chapter 11 case shall file a statement of current monthly income, prepared as prescribed by the appropriate Official Form.

(6) A debtor in a chapter 13 case shall file a statement of current monthly income, prepared as prescribed by the appropriate Official Form, and, if the current monthly income exceeds the median family income for the applicable state and household size, a calculation of disposable income made in accordance with § 1325(b)(3), prepared as prescribed by the appropriate Official Form.

(7) Unless an approved provider of an instructional course concerning personal financial management has notified the court that a debtor has completed the course after filing the petition:

(A) An individual debtor in a chapter 7 or chapter 13 case shall file a statement of completion of the course, prepared as prescribed by the appropriate Official Form; and

(B) An individual debtor in a chapter 11 case shall file the statement if § 1141(d)(3) applies.

(8) If an individual debtor in a chapter 11, 12, or 13 case has claimed an exemption under § 522(b)(3)(A) in property of the kind described in § 522(p)(1) with a value in excess of the amount set out in § 522(q)(1), the debtor shall file a statement as to whether there is any proceeding pending in which the debtor may be found guilty of a felony of a kind described in § 522(q)(1)(A) or found liable for a debt of the kind described in § 522(q)(1)(B).

(c) **Time Limits.**

In a voluntary case, the schedules, statements, and other documents required by subdivision (b)(1), (4), (5), and (6) shall be filed with the petition or within 14 days thereafter, except as otherwise provided in subdivisions (d), (e), (f), and (h) of this rule. In an involuntary case, the schedules, statements, and other documents required by subdivision (b)(1) shall be filed by the debtor within 14 days of the entry of the order for relief. In a voluntary case, the documents required by paragraphs (A), (C), and (D) of subdivision (b)(3) shall be filed with the petition. Unless the court orders otherwise, a debtor who has filed a statement under subdivision (b)(3)(B), shall file the documents required by subdivision (b)(3)(A) within 14 days of the order for relief. In a chapter 7 case, the debtor shall file the statement required by subdivision (b)(7) within 60 days after the first date set for the meeting of creditors under § 341 of the Code, and in a chapter 11 or 13 case no later than the date when the last payment was made by the debtor as required by the plan or the filing of a motion for a discharge under § 1141(d)(5)(B) or § 1328(b) of the Code. The court may, at any time and in its discretion, enlarge the time to file the statement required by subdivision (b)(7). The debtor shall file the statement required by subdivision (b)(8) no earlier than the date of the last payment made under the plan or the date of the filing of a motion for a discharge under §§ 1141(d)(5)(B), 1228(b), or 1328(b) of the Code. Lists, schedules, statements, and other documents filed prior to the conversion of a case to another chapter shall be deemed filed in the converted case unless the court directs otherwise. Except as provided in § 1116(3), any extension of time to file schedules, statements, and other documents required under this rule may be granted only on motion for cause shown and on notice to the United States trustee, any committee elected under § 705 or appointed under § 1102 of the Code, trustee, examiner, or other party as the court may direct. Notice of an extension shall be given to the United States trustee and to any committee, trustee, or other party as the court may direct.

(d) List of 20 Largest Creditors in Chapter 9 Municipality Case or Chapter 11 Reorganization Case.

In addition to the list required by subdivision (a) of this rule, a debtor in a chapter 9 municipality case or a debtor in a voluntary chapter 11 reorganization case shall file with the petition a list containing the name, address and claim of the creditors that hold the 20 largest unsecured claims, excluding insiders, as prescribed by the appropriate Official Form. In an involuntary chapter 11 reorganization case, such list shall be filed by the debtor within 2 days after entry of the order for relief under § 303(h) of the Code.

(e) List in Chapter 9 Municipality Cases.

The list required by subdivision (a) of this rule shall be filed by the debtor in a chapter 9 municipality case within such time as the court shall fix. If a proposed plan requires a revision of assessments so that the proportion of special assessments or special taxes to be assessed against some real property will be different from the proportion in effect at the date the petition is filed, the debtor shall also file a list showing the name and address of each known holder of title, legal or equitable, to real property adversely affected. On motion for cause shown, the court may modify the requirements of this subdivision and subdivision (a) of this rule.

(f) Statement of Social Security Number.

An individual debtor shall submit a verified statement that sets out the debtor's social security number, or states that the debtor does not have a social security number. In a voluntary case, the debtor shall submit the statement with the petition. In an involuntary case, the debtor shall submit the statement within 14 days after the entry of the order for relief.

(g) Partnership and Partners.

The general partners of a debtor partnership shall prepare and file the list required under subdivision (a), the schedules of the assets and liabilities, schedule of current income and expenditures, schedule of executory contracts and unexpired leases, and statement of financial affairs of the partnership. The court may order any general partner to file a statement of personal assets and liabilities within such time as the court may fix.

(h) Interests Acquired or Arising After Petition.

If, as provided by § 541(a)(5) of the Code, the debtor acquires or becomes entitled to acquire any interest in property, the debtor shall within 14 days after the information comes to the debtor's knowledge or within such further time the court may allow, file a supplemental schedule in the chapter 7 liquidation case, chapter 11 reorganization case, chapter 12 family farmer's debt adjustment case, or chapter 13 individual debt adjustment case. If any of the property required to be reported under this subdivision is claimed by the debtor as exempt, the debtor shall claim the exemptions in the supplemental schedule. The duty to file a supplemental schedule in accordance with this subdivision continues notwithstanding the closing of the case, except that the schedule need not be filed in a chapter 11, chapter 12, or chapter 13 case with respect to property acquired after entry of the order confirming a chapter 11 plan or discharging the debtor in a chapter 12 or chapter 13 case.

(i) Disclosure of List of Security Holders.

After notice and hearing and for cause shown, the court may direct an entity other than the debtor or trustee to disclose any list of security holders of the debtor in its possession or under its control, indicating the name, address and security held by any of them. The entity possessing this list may be required either to produce the list or a true copy thereof, or permit inspection or copying, or otherwise disclose the information contained on the list.

(j)   Impounding of Lists.

On motion of a party in interest and for cause shown the court may direct the impounding of the lists filed under this rule, and may refuse to permit inspection by any entity. The court may permit inspection or use of the lists, however, by any party in interest on terms prescribed by the court.

(k)   Preparation of List, Schedules, or Statements on Default of Debtor.

If a list, schedule, or statement, other than a statement of intention, is not prepared and filed as required by this rule, the court may order the trustee, a petitioning creditor, committee, or other party to prepare and file any of these papers within a time fixed by the court. The court may approve reimbursement of the cost incurred in complying with such an order as an administrative expense.

(l)   Transmission to United States Trustee.

The clerk shall forthwith transmit to the United States trustee a copy of every list, schedule, and statement filed pursuant to subdivision (a)(1), (a)(2), (b), (d), or (h) of this rule.

(m)   Infants and Incompetent Persons.

If the debtor knows that a person on the list of creditors or schedules is an infant or incompetent person, the debtor also shall include the name, address, and legal relationship of any person upon whom process would be served in an adversary proceeding against the infant or incompetent person in accordance with Rule 7004(b)(2).

> (As amended Mar. 30, 1987, eff. Aug. 1, 1987; Apr. 30, 1991, eff. Aug. 1, 1991; Apr. 23, 1996, eff. Dec. 1, 1996; Apr. 23, 2001, eff. Dec. 1, 2001; Mar. 27, 2003, eff. Dec. 1, 2003; Apr. 25, 2005, eff. Dec. 1, 2005; Apr. 23, 2008, eff. Dec. 1, 2008; Mar. 26, 2009, eff. Dec. 1, 2009; Apr. 28, 2010, eff. Dec. 1, 2010; Apr. 23, 2012, eff. Dec. 1, 2012; Apr. 16, 2013, eff. Dec. 1, 2013; Apr. 29, 2015, eff. Dec. 1, 2015.)

Rule 1008.   Verification of Petitions and Accompanying Papers

All petitions, lists, schedules, statements and amendments thereto shall be verified or contain an unsworn declaration as provided in 28 U.S.C. § 1746.

> (As amended Apr. 30, 1991, eff. Aug. 1, 1991.)

Rule 1009.   Amendments of Voluntary Petitions, Lists, Schedules and Statements

(a)   General Right to Amend.

A voluntary petition, list, schedule, or statement may be amended by the debtor as a matter of course at any time before the case is closed. The debtor shall give notice of the amendment to the trustee and to any entity affected thereby. On motion of a party in interest, after notice and a hearing, the court may order any voluntary petition, list, schedule, or statement to be amended and the clerk shall give notice of the amendment to entities designated by the court.

(b)   Statement of Intention.

The statement of intention may be amended by the debtor at any time before the expiration of the period provided in § 521(a) of the Code. The debtor shall give notice of the amendment to the trustee and to any entity affected thereby.

(c)   Statement of Social Security Number.

If a debtor becomes aware that the statement of social security number submitted under Rule 1007(f) is incorrect, the debtor shall promptly submit an amended verified statement setting forth the correct social security number. The debtor shall give notice of the amendment to all of the entities required to be included on the list filed under Rule 1007(a)(1) or (a)(2).

(d) Transmission to United States Trustee.

The clerk shall promptly transmit to the United States trustee a copy of every amendment filed or submitted under subdivision (a), (b), or (c) of this rule.

(As amended Mar. 30, 1987, eff. Aug. 1, 1987; Apr. 30, 1991, eff. Aug. 1, 1991; Apr. 12, 2006, eff. Dec. 1, 2006; Apr. 23, 2008, eff. Dec. 1, 2008.)

Rule 1010.   Service of Involuntary Petition and Summons; Petition for Recognition of a Foreign Nonmain Proceeding

(a) Service of Involuntary Petition and Summons; Service of Petition for Recognition of Foreign Nonmain Proceeding.

On the filing of an involuntary petition or a petition for recognition of a foreign nonmain proceeding, the clerk shall forthwith issue a summons for service. When an involuntary petition is filed, service shall be made on the debtor. When a petition for recognition of a foreign nonmain proceeding is filed, service shall be made on the debtor, any entity against whom provisional relief is sought under § 1519 of the Code, and on any other party as the court may direct. The summons shall be served with a copy of the petition in the manner provided for service of a summons and complaint by Rule 7004(a) or (b). If service cannot be so made, the court may order that the summons and petition be served by mailing copies to the party's last known address, and by at least one publication in a manner and form directed by the court. The summons and petition may be served on the party anywhere. Rule 7004(e) and Rule 4(*l*) F.R.Civ.P. apply when service is made or attempted under this rule.

(b) Corporate Ownership Statement.

Each petitioner that is a corporation shall file with the involuntary petition a corporate ownership statement containing the information described in Rule 7007.1.

(As amended Mar. 30, 1987, eff. Aug. 1, 1987; Apr. 30, 1991, eff. Aug. 1, 1991; Apr. 22, 1993, eff. Aug. 1, 1993; Apr. 11, 1997, eff. Dec. 1, 1997; Apr. 23, 2008, eff. Dec. 1, 2008.)

Rule 1011.   Responsive Pleading or Motion in Involuntary and Cross-Border Cases

(a) Who May Contest Petition.

The debtor named in an involuntary petition, or a party in interest to a petition for recognition of a foreign proceeding, may contest the petition. In the case of a petition against a partnership under Rule 1004, a nonpetitioning general partner, or a person who is alleged to be a general partner but denies the allegation, may contest the petition.

(b) Defenses and Objections; When Presented.

Defenses and objections to the petition shall be presented in the manner prescribed by Rule 12 F.R.Civ.P. and shall be filed and served within 21 days after service of the summons, except that if service is made by publication on a party or partner not residing or found within the state in which the court sits, the court shall prescribe the time for filing and serving the response.

(c) Effect of Motion.

Service of a motion under Rule 12(b) F.R.Civ.P. shall extend the time for filing and serving a responsive pleading as permitted by Rule 12(a) F.R.Civ.P.

(d) Claims Against Petitioners.

A claim against a petitioning creditor may not be asserted in the answer except for the purpose of defeating the petition.

(e) Other Pleadings.

No other pleadings shall be permitted, except that the court may order a reply to an answer and prescribe the time for filing and service.

(f)   Corporate Ownership Statement.

If the entity responding to the involuntary petition or the petition for recognition of a foreign proceeding is a corporation, the entity shall file with its first appearance, pleading, motion, response, or other request addressed to the court a corporate ownership statement containing the information described in Rule 7007.1.

(As amended Mar. 30, 1987, eff. Aug. 1, 1987; Apr. 26, 2004, eff. Dec. 1, 2004; Apr. 23, 2008, eff. Dec. 1, 2008; Mar. 26, 2009, eff. Dec. 1, 2009.)

Rule 1012.   [Abrogated Mar. 30, 1987, eff. Aug. 1, 1987]

Rule 1013.   Hearing and Disposition of a Petition in an Involuntary Case

(a)   Contested Petition.

The court shall determine the issues of a contested petition at the earliest practicable time and forthwith enter an order for relief, dismiss the petition, or enter any other appropriate order.

(b)   Default.

If no pleading or other defense to a petition is filed within the time provided by Rule 1011, the court, on the next day, or as soon thereafter as practicable, shall enter an order for the relief requested in the petition.

(c)   [Abrogated]

(As amended Apr. 30, 1991, eff. Aug. 1, 1991; Apr. 22, 1993, eff. Aug. 1, 1993.)

Rule 1014.   Dismissal and Change of Venue

(a)   Dismissal and Transfer of Cases.

(1)   Cases Filed in Proper District.

If a petition is filed in the proper district, the court, on the timely motion of a party in interest or on its own motion, and after hearing on notice to the petitioners, the United States trustee, and other entities as directed by the court, may transfer the case to any other district if the court determines that the transfer is in the interest of justice or for the convenience of the parties.

(2)   Cases Filed in Improper District.

If a petition is filed in an improper district, the court, on the timely motion of a party in interest or on its own motion, and after hearing on notice to the petitioners, the United States trustee, and other entities as directed by the court, may dismiss the case or transfer it to any other district if the court determines that transfer is in the interest of justice or for the convenience of the parties.

(b)   Procedure When Petitions Involving the Same Debtor or Related Debtors are Filed in Different Courts.

If petitions commencing cases under the Code or seeking recognition under chapter 15 are filed in different districts by, regarding, or against (1) the same debtor, (2) a partnership and one or more of its general partners, (3) two or more general partners, or (4) a debtor and an affiliate, the court in the district in which the first-filed petition is pending may determine, in the interest of justice or for the convenience of the parties, the district or districts in which any of the cases should proceed. The court may so determine on motion and after a hearing, with notice to the following entities in the affected cases: the United States trustee, entities entitled to notice under Rule 2002(a), and other entities as the court directs. The court may order the parties to the later-filed cases not to proceed further until it makes the determination.

(As amended Mar. 30, 1987, eff. Aug. 1, 1987; Apr. 30, 1991, eff. Aug. 1, 1991; Apr. 30, 2007, eff. Dec. 1, 2007; Apr. 28, 2010, eff. Dec. 1, 2010; Apr. 25, 2014, eff. Dec. 1, 2014.)

Rule 1015.   Consolidation or Joint Administration of Cases Pending in Same Court

(a)   Cases Involving Same Debtor.

If two or more petitions by, regarding, or against the same debtor are pending in the same court, the court may order consolidation of the cases.

(b)   Cases Involving Two or More Related Debtors.

If a joint petition or two or more petitions are pending in the same court by or against (1) a husband and wife, or (2) a partnership and one or more of its general partners, or (3) two or more general partners, or (4) a debtor and an affiliate, the court may order a joint administration of the estates. Prior to entering an order the court shall give consideration to protecting creditors of different estates against potential conflicts of interest. An order directing joint administration of individual cases of a husband and wife shall, if one spouse has elected the exemptions under § 522(b)(2) of the Code and the other has elected the exemptions under § 522(b)(3), fix a reasonable time within which either may amend the election so that both shall have elected the same exemptions. The order shall notify the debtors that unless they elect the same exemptions within the time fixed by the court, they will be deemed to have elected the exemptions provided by § 522(b)(2).

(c)   Expediting and Protective Orders.

When an order for consolidation or joint administration of a joint case or two or more cases is entered pursuant to this rule, while protecting the rights of the parties under the Code, the court may enter orders as may tend to avoid unnecessary costs and delay.

(As amended Mar. 30, 1987, eff. Aug. 1, 1987; Apr. 23, 2008, eff. Dec. 1, 2008; Apr. 28, 2010, eff. Dec. 1, 2010.)

Rule 1016.   Death or Incompetency of Debtor

Death or incompetency of the debtor shall not abate a liquidation case under chapter 7 of the Code. In such event the estate shall be administered and the case concluded in the same manner, so far as possible, as though the death or incompetency had not occurred. If a reorganization, family farmer's debt adjustment, or individual's debt adjustment case is pending under chapter 11, chapter 12, or chapter 13, the case may be dismissed; or if further administration is possible and in the best interest of the parties, the case may proceed and be concluded in the same manner, so far as possible, as though the death or incompetency had not occurred.

(As amended Apr. 30, 1991, eff. Aug. 1, 1991.)

Rule 1017.   Dismissal or Conversion of Case; Suspension

(a)   Voluntary Dismissal; Dismissal for Want of Prosecution or Other Cause.

Except as provided in §§ 707(a)(3), 707(b), 1208(b), and 1307(b) of the Code, and in Rule 1017(b), (c), and (e), a case shall not be dismissed on motion of the petitioner, for want of prosecution or other cause, or by consent of the parties, before a hearing on notice as provided in Rule 2002. For the purpose of the notice, the debtor shall file a list of creditors with their addresses within the time fixed by the court unless the list was previously filed. If the debtor fails to file the list, the court may order the debtor or another entity to prepare and file it.

(b)   Dismissal for Failure to Pay Filing Fee.

(1)   If any installment of the filing fee has not been paid, the court may, after a hearing on notice to the debtor and the trustee, dismiss the case.

(2)   If the case is dismissed or closed without full payment of the filing fee, the installments collected shall be distributed in the same manner and proportions as if the filing fee had been paid in full.

(c)   Dismissal of Voluntary Chapter 7 or Chapter 13 Case for Failure to Timely File List of Creditors, Schedules, and Statement of Financial Affairs.

The court may dismiss a voluntary chapter 7 or chapter 13 case under § 707(a)(3) or § 1307(c)(9) after a hearing on notice served by the United States trustee on the debtor, the trustee, and any other entities as the court directs.

(d)   Suspension.

The court shall not dismiss a case or suspend proceedings under § 305 before a hearing on notice as provided in Rule 2002(a).

(e)   Dismissal of an Individual Debtor's Chapter 7 case, or Conversion to a Case Under Chapter 11 or 13, for Abuse.

The court may dismiss or, with the debtor's consent, convert an individual debtor's case for abuse under § 707(b) only on motion and after a hearing on notice to the debtor, the trustee, the United States trustee, and any other entity as the court directs.

(1)   Except as otherwise provided in § 704(b)(2), a motion to dismiss a case for abuse under § 707(b) or (c) may be filed only within 60 days after the first date set for the meeting of creditors under § 341(a), unless, on request filed before the time has expired, the court for cause extends the time for filing the motion to dismiss. The party filing the motion shall set forth in the motion all matters to be considered at the hearing. In addition, a motion to dismiss under § 707(b)(1) and (3) shall state with particularity the circumstances alleged to constitute abuse.

(2)   If the hearing is set on the court's own motion, notice of the hearing shall be served on the debtor no later than 60 days after the first date set for the meeting of creditors under § 341(a). The notice shall set forth all matters to be considered by the court at the hearing.

(f)   Procedure for Dismissal, Conversion, or Suspension.

(1)   Rule 9014 governs a proceeding to dismiss or suspend a case, or to convert a case to another chapter, except under §§ 706(a), 1112(a), 1208(a) or (b), or 1307(a) or (b).

(2)   Conversion or dismissal under §§ 706(a), 1112(a), 1208(b), or 1307(b) shall be on motion filed and served as required by Rule 9013.

(3)   A chapter 12 or chapter 13 case shall be converted without court order when the debtor files a notice of conversion under §§ 1208(a) or 1307(a). The filing date of the notice becomes the date of the conversion order for the purposes of applying § 348(c) and Rule 1019. The clerk shall promptly transmit a copy of the notice to the United States trustee.

(As amended Mar. 30, 1987, eff. Aug. 1, 1987; Apr. 30, 1991, eff. Aug. 1, 1991; Apr. 22, 1993, eff. Aug. 1, 1993; Apr. 29, 1999, eff. Dec. 1, 1999; Apr. 17, 2000, eff. Dec. 1, 2000; Apr. 23, 2008, eff. Dec. 1, 2008.)

Rule 1018.   Contested Involuntary Petitions; Contested Petitions Commencing Chapter 15 Cases; Proceedings to Vacate Order for Relief; Applicability of Rules in Part VII Governing Adversary Proceedings

Unless the court otherwise directs and except as otherwise prescribed in Part I of these rules, the following rules in Part VII apply to all proceedings contesting an involuntary petition or a chapter 15 petition for recognition, and to all proceedings to vacate an order for relief: Rules 7005, 7008–7010, 7015, 7016, 7024–7026, 7028–7037, 7052, 7054, 7056, and 7062. The court may direct that other rules in Part VII shall also apply. For the purposes of this rule a reference in the Part VII rules to adversary proceedings shall be read as a reference to proceedings contesting an involuntary petition or a chapter 15 petition for recognition, or proceedings to vacate an order for relief. Reference in the Federal Rules of Civil Procedure to the complaint shall be read as a reference to the petition.

(As amended Mar. 30, 1987, eff. Aug. 1, 1987; Apr. 28, 2010, eff. Dec. 1, 2010.)

Rule 1019.   Conversion of a Chapter 11 Reorganization Case, Chapter 12 Family Farmer's Debt Adjustment Case, or Chapter 13 Individual's Debt Adjustment Case to a Chapter 7 Liquidation Case

When a chapter 11, chapter 12, or chapter 13 case has been converted or reconverted to a chapter 7 case:

(1)   Filing of Lists, Inventories, Schedules, Statements.

(A)   Lists, inventories, schedules, and statements of financial affairs theretofore filed shall be deemed to be filed in the chapter 7 case, unless the court directs otherwise. If they have not been previously filed, the debtor shall comply with Rule 1007 as if an order for relief had been entered on an involuntary petition on the date of the entry of the order directing that the case continue under chapter 7.

(B)   If a statement of intention is required, it shall be filed within 30 days after entry of the order of conversion or before the first date set for the meeting of creditors, whichever is earlier. The court may grant an extension of time for cause only on written motion filed, or oral request made during a hearing, before the time has expired. Notice of an extension shall be given to the United States trustee and to any committee, trustee, or other party as the court may direct.

(2)   New Filing Periods.

(A)   A new time period for filing a motion under § 707(b) or (c), a claim, a complaint objecting to discharge, or a complaint to obtain a determination of dischargeability of any debt shall commence under Rules 1017, 3002, 4004, or 4007, but a new time period shall not commence if a chapter 7 case had been converted to a chapter 11, 12, or 13 case and thereafter reconverted to a chapter 7 case and the time for filing a motion under § 707(b) or (c), a claim, a complaint objecting to discharge, or a complaint to obtain a determination of the dischargeability of any debt, or any extension thereof, expired in the original chapter 7 case.

(B)   A new time period for filing an objection to a claim of exemptions shall commence under Rule 4003(b) after conversion of a case to chapter 7 unless:

(i)   the case was converted to chapter 7 more than one year after the entry of the first order confirming a plan under chapter 11, 12, or 13; or

(ii)   the case was previously pending in chapter 7 and the time to object to a claimed exemption had expired in the original chapter 7 case.

(3)   Claims Filed Before Conversion.

All claims actually filed by a creditor before conversion of the case are deemed filed in the chapter 7 case.

(4)   Turnover of Records and Property.

After qualification of, or assumption of duties by the chapter 7 trustee, any debtor in possession or trustee previously acting in the chapter 11, 12, or 13 case shall, forthwith, unless otherwise ordered, turn over to the chapter 7 trustee all records and property of the estate in the possession or control of the debtor in possession or trustee.

(5)   Filing Final Report and Schedule of Postpetition Debts.

(A)   Conversion of Chapter 11 or Chapter 12 Case.

Unless the court directs otherwise, if a chapter 11 or chapter 12 case is converted to chapter 7, the debtor in possession or, if the debtor is not a debtor in possession, the trustee serving at the time of conversion, shall:

(i)   not later than 14 days after conversion of the case, file a schedule of unpaid debts incurred after the filing of the petition and before conversion of the case, including the name and address of each holder of a claim; and

(ii)   not later than 30 days after conversion of the case, file and transmit to the United States trustee a final report and account;

(B)   Conversion of Chapter 13 Case.

Unless the court directs otherwise, if a chapter 13 case is converted to chapter 7,

(i)   the debtor, not later than 14 days after conversion of the case, shall file a schedule of unpaid debts incurred after the filing of the petition and before conversion of the case, including the name and address of each holder of a claim; and

(ii)   the trustee, not later than 30 days after conversion of the case, shall file and transmit to the United States trustee a final report and account;

(C)   Conversion After Confirmation of a Plan.

Unless the court orders otherwise, if a chapter 11, chapter 12, or chapter 13 case is converted to chapter 7 after confirmation of a plan, the debtor shall file:

(i)   a schedule of property not listed in the final report and account acquired after the filing of the petition but before conversion, except if the case is converted from chapter 13 to chapter 7 and § 348(f)(2) does not apply;

(ii)   a schedule of unpaid debts not listed in the final report and account incurred after confirmation but before the conversion; and

(iii)   a schedule of executory contracts and unexpired leases entered into or assumed after the filing of the petition but before conversion.

(D)   Transmission to United States Trustee.

The clerk shall forthwith transmit to the United States trustee a copy of every schedule filed pursuant to Rule 1019(5).

(6)   Postpetition Claims; Preconversion Administrative Expenses; Notice.

A request for payment of an administrative expense incurred before conversion of the case is timely filed under § 503(a) of the Code if it is filed before conversion or a time fixed by the court. If the request is filed by a governmental unit, it is timely if it is filed before conversion or within the later of a time fixed by the court or 180 days after the date of the conversion. A claim of a kind specified in § 348(d) may be filed in accordance with Rules 3001(a)–(d) and 3002. Upon the filing of the schedule of unpaid debts incurred after commencement of the case and before conversion, the clerk, or some other person as the court may direct, shall give notice to those entities listed on the schedule of the time for filing a request for payment of an administrative expense and, unless a notice of insufficient assets to pay a dividend is mailed in accordance with Rule 2002(e), the time for filing a claim of a kind specified in § 348(d).

(7)   [Abrogated]

(As amended Mar. 30, 1987, eff. Aug. 1, 1987; Apr. 30, 1991, eff. Aug. 1, 1991; Apr. 23, 1996, eff. Dec. 1, 1996; Apr. 11, 1997, eff. Dec. 1, 1997; Apr. 29, 1999, eff. Dec. 1, 1999; Apr. 23, 2008, eff. Dec. 1, 2008; Mar. 26, 2009, eff. Dec. 1, 2009; Apr. 28, 2010, eff. Dec. 1, 2010.)

Rule 1020.   Small Business Chapter 11 Reorganization Case

(a)   Small Business Debtor Designation.

In a voluntary chapter 11 case, the debtor shall state in the petition whether the debtor is a small business debtor. In an involuntary chapter 11 case, the debtor shall file within 14 days after entry of the order for relief a statement as to whether the debtor is a small business debtor. Except as provided in subdivision (c), the status of the case as a small business case shall be in accordance with the debtor's statement under this subdivision, unless and until the court enters an order finding that the debtor's statement is incorrect.

(b) Objecting to Designation.

Except as provided in subdivision (c), the United States trustee or a party in interest may file an objection to the debtor's statement under subdivision (a) no later than 30 days after the conclusion of the meeting of creditors held under § 341(a) of the Code, or within 30 days after any amendment to the statement, whichever is later.

(c) Appointment of Committee of Unsecured Creditors.

If a committee of unsecured creditors has been appointed under § 1102(a)(1), the case shall proceed as a small business case only if, and from the time when, the court enters an order determining that the committee has not been sufficiently active and representative to provide effective oversight of the debtor and that the debtor satisfies all the other requirements for being a small business. A request for a determination under this subdivision may be filed by the United States trustee or a party in interest only within a reasonable time after the failure of the committee to be sufficiently active and representative. The debtor may file a request for a determination at any time as to whether the committee has been sufficiently active and representative.

(d) Procedure for Objection or Determination.

Any objection or request for a determination under this rule shall be governed by Rule 9014 and served on: the debtor; the debtor's attorney; the United States trustee; the trustee; any committee appointed under § 1102 or its authorized agent, or, if no committee of unsecured creditors has been appointed under § 1102, the creditors included on the list filed under Rule 1007(d); and any other entity as the court directs.

(Added Apr. 11, 1997, eff. Dec. 1, 1997, and amended Apr. 23, 2008, eff. Dec. 1, 2008; Mar, 26, 2009, eff. Dec. 1, 2009.)

Rule 1021.   Health Care Business Case

(a) Health Care Business Designation.

Unless the court orders otherwise, if a petition in a case under Chapter 7, chapter 9, or chapter 11 states that the debtor is a health care business, the case shall proceed as a case in which the debtor is a health care business.

(b) Motion.

The United States trustee or a party in interest may file a motion to determine whether the debtor is a health care business. The motion shall be transmitted to the United States trustee and served on: the debtor; the trustee; any committee elected under § 705 or appointed under § 1102 of the Code or its authorized agent, or, if the case is a chapter 9 municipality case or a chapter 11 reorganization case and no committee of unsecured creditors has been appointed under § 1102, the creditors included on the list filed under Rule 1007(d); and any other entity as the court directs. The motion shall be governed by Rule 9014.

(Added Apr. 23, 2008, eff. Dec. 1, 2008.)

PART II

OFFICERS AND ADMINISTRATION; NOTICES; MEETINGS; EXAMINATIONS; ELECTIONS; ATTORNEYS AND ACCOUNTANTS

Rule 2001.   Appointment of Interim Trustee Before Order for Relief in a Chapter 7 Liquidation Case

(a) Appointment.

At any time following the commencement of an involuntary liquidation case and before an order for relief, the court on written motion of a party in interest may order the appointment of an interim trustee under § 303(g) of the Code. The motion shall set forth the necessity for the appointment and may be granted only after hearing on notice to the debtor, the petitioning creditors, the United States trustee, and other parties in interest as the court may designate.

(b) Bond of Movant.

An interim trustee may not be appointed under this rule unless the movant furnishes a bond in an amount approved by the court, conditioned to indemnify the debtor for costs, attorney's fee, expenses, and damages allowable under § 303(i) of the Code.

(c) Order of Appointment.

The order directing the appointment of an interim trustee shall state the reason the appointment is necessary and shall specify the trustee's duties.

(d) Turnover and Report.

Following qualification of the trustee selected under § 702 of the Code, the interim trustee, unless otherwise ordered, shall (1) forthwith deliver to the trustee all the records and property of the estate in possession or subject to control of the interim trustee and, (2) within 30 days thereafter file a final report and account.

(As amended Mar. 30, 1987, eff. Aug. 1, 1987; Apr. 30, 1991, eff. Aug. 1, 1991.)

Rule 2002.   Notices to Creditors, Equity Security Holders, Administrators in Foreign Proceedings, Persons Against Whom Provisional Relief is Sought in Ancillary and Other Cross-Border Cases, United States, and United States Trustee

(a)   Twenty-One-Day Notices to Parties in Interest.

Except as provided in subdivisions (h), (i), (*l*), (p), and (q) of this rule, the clerk, or some other person as the court may direct, shall give the debtor, the trustee, all creditors and indenture trustees at least 21 days' notice by mail of:

(1)   the meeting of creditors under § 341 or § 1104(b) of the Code, which notice, unless the court orders otherwise, shall include the debtor's employer identification number, social security number, and any other federal taxpayer identification number;

(2)   a proposed use, sale, or lease of property of the estate other than in the ordinary course of business, unless the court for cause shown shortens the time or directs another method of giving notice;

(3)   the hearing on approval of a compromise or settlement of a controversy other than approval of an agreement pursuant to Rule 4001(d), unless the court for cause shown directs that notice not be sent;

(4)   in a chapter 7 liquidation, a chapter 11 reorganization case, or a chapter 12 family farmer debt adjustment case, the hearing on the dismissal of the case or the conversion of the case to another chapter, unless the hearing is under § 707(a)(3) or § 707(b) or is on dismissal of the case for failure to pay the filing fee;

(5)   the time fixed to accept or reject a proposed modification of a plan;

(6)   a hearing on any entity's request for compensation or reimbursement of expenses if the request exceeds $1,000;

(7)   the time fixed for filing proofs of claims pursuant to Rule 3003(c); and

(8)   the time fixed for filing objections and the hearing to consider confirmation of a chapter 12 plan.

(b)   Twenty-Eight-Day Notices to Parties in Interest.

Except as provided in subdivision (*l*) of this rule, the clerk, or some other person as the court may direct, shall give the debtor, the trustee, all creditors and indenture trustees not less than 28 days' notice by mail of the time fixed (1) for filing objections and the hearing to consider approval of a disclosure statement or, under § 1125(f), to make a final determination whether the plan provides adequate information so that a separate disclosure statement is not necessary; and (2) for filing objections and the hearing to consider confirmation of a chapter 9, chapter 11, or chapter 13 plan.

(c)   Content of Notice.

(1)   Proposed Use, Sale, or Lease of Property.

Subject to Rule 6004, the notice of a proposed use, sale, or lease of property required by subdivision (a)(2) of this rule shall include the time and place of any public sale, the terms and conditions of any private sale and the time fixed for filing objections. The notice of a proposed use, sale, or lease of property, including real estate, is sufficient if it generally describes the property. The notice of a proposed sale or lease of personally identifiable information under § 363(b)(1) of the Code shall state whether the sale is consistent with any policy prohibiting the transfer of the information.

(2)   Notice of Hearing on Compensation.

The notice of a hearing on an application for compensation or reimbursement of expenses required by subdivision (a)(6) of this rule shall identify the applicant and the amounts requested.

(3)   Notice of Hearing on Confirmation When Plan Provides for an Injunction.

If a plan provides for an injunction against conduct not otherwise enjoined under the Code, the notice required under Rule 2002(b)(2) shall:

    (A) include in conspicuous language (bold, italic, or underlined text) a statement that the plan proposes an injunction;

    (B) describe briefly the nature of the injunction; and

    (C) identify the entities that would be subject to the injunction.

(d) Notice to Equity Security Holders.

In a chapter 11 reorganization case, unless otherwise ordered by the court, the clerk, or some other person as the court may direct, shall in the manner and form directed by the court give notice to all equity security holders of (1) the order for relief; (2) any meeting of equity security holders held pursuant to § 341 of the Code; (3) the hearing on the proposed sale of all or substantially all of the debtor's assets; (4) the hearing on the dismissal or conversion of a case to another chapter; (5) the time fixed for filing objections to and the hearing to consider approval of a disclosure statement; (6) the time fixed for filing objections to and the hearing to consider confirmation of a plan; and (7) the time fixed to accept or reject a proposed modification of a plan.

(e) Notice of No Dividend.

In a chapter 7 liquidation case, if it appears from the schedules that there are no assets from which a dividend can be paid, the notice of the meeting of creditors may include a statement to that effect; that it is unnecessary to file claims; and that if sufficient assets become available for the payment of a dividend, further notice will be given for the filing of claims.

(f) Other Notices.

Except as provided in subdivision (*l*) of this rule, the clerk, or some other person as the court may direct, shall give the debtor, all creditors, and indenture trustees notice by mail of:

    (1) the order for relief;

    (2) the dismissal or the conversion of the case to another chapter, or the suspension of proceedings under § 305;

    (3) the time allowed for filing claims pursuant to Rule 3002;

    (4) the time fixed for filing a complaint objecting to the debtor's discharge pursuant to § 727 of the Code as provided in Rule 4004;

    (5) the time fixed for filing a complaint to determine the dischargeability of a debt pursuant to § 523 of the Code as provided in Rule 4007;

    (6) the waiver, denial, or revocation of a discharge as provided in Rule 4006;

    (7) entry of an order confirming a chapter 9, 11, or 12 plan;

    (8) a summary of the trustee's final report in a chapter 7 case if the net proceeds realized exceed $1,500;

    (9) a notice under Rule 5008 regarding the presumption of abuse;

    (10) a statement under § 704(b)(1) as to whether the debtor's case would be presumed to be an abuse under § 707(b); and

    (11) the time to request a delay in the entry of the discharge under §§ 1141(d)(5)(C), 1228(f), and 1328(h). Notice of the time fixed for accepting or rejecting a plan pursuant to Rule 3017(c) shall be given in accordance with Rule 3017(d).

(g) Addressing Notices.

    (1) Notices required to be mailed under Rule 2002 to a creditor, indenture trustee, or equity security holder shall be addressed as such entity or an authorized agent has directed in its last request filed in the particular case. For the purposes of this subdivision—

(A) a proof of claim filed by a creditor or indenture trustee that designates a mailing address constitutes a filed request to mail notices to that address, unless a notice of no dividend has been given under Rule 2002(e) and a later notice of possible dividend under Rule 3002(c)(5) has not been given; and

(B) a proof of interest filed by an equity security holder that designates a mailing address constitutes a filed request to mail notices to that address.

(2) Except as provided in § 342(f) of the Code, if a creditor or indenture trustee has not filed a request designating a mailing address under Rule 2002(g)(1) or Rule 5003(e), the notices shall be mailed to the address shown on the list of creditors or schedule of liabilities, whichever is filed later. If an equity security holder has not filed a request designating a mailing address under Rule 2002(g)(1) or Rule 5003(e), the notices shall be mailed to the address shown on the list of equity security holders.

(3) If a list or schedule filed under Rule 1007 includes the name and address of a legal representative of an infant or incompetent person, and a person other than that representative files a request or proof of claim designating a name and mailing address that differs from the name and address of the representative included in the list or schedule, unless the court orders otherwise, notices under Rule 2002 shall be mailed to the representative included in the list or schedules and to the name and address designated in the request or proof of claim.

(4) Notwithstanding Rule 2002(g)(1)–(3), an entity and a notice provider may agree that when the notice provider is directed by the court to give a notice, the notice provider shall give the notice to the entity in the manner agreed to and at the address or addresses the entity supplies to the notice provider. That address is conclusively presumed to be a proper address for the notice. The notice provider's failure to use the supplied address does not invalidate any notice that is otherwise effective under applicable law.

(5) A creditor may treat a notice as not having been brought to the creditor's attention under § 342(g)(1) only if, prior to issuance of the notice, the creditor has filed a statement that designates the name and address of the person or organizational subdivision of the creditor responsible for receiving notices under the Code, and that describes the procedures established by the creditor to cause such notices to be delivered to the designated person or subdivision.

(h) Notices to Creditors Whose Claims are Filed.

In a chapter 7 case, after 90 days following the first date set for the meeting of creditors under § 341 of the Code, the court may direct that all notices required by subdivision (a) of this rule be mailed only to the debtor, the trustee, all indenture trustees, creditors that hold claims for which proofs of claim have been filed, and creditors, if any, that are still permitted to file claims by reason of an extension granted pursuant to Rule 3002(c)(1) or (c)(2). In a case where notice of insufficient assets to pay a dividend has been given to creditors pursuant to subdivision (e) of this rule, after 90 days following the mailing of a notice of the time for filing claims pursuant to Rule 3002(c)(5), the court may direct that notices be mailed only to the entities specified in the preceding sentence.

(i) Notices to Committees.

Copies of all notices required to be mailed pursuant to this rule shall be mailed to the committees elected under § 705 or appointed under § 1102 of the Code or to their authorized agents. Notwithstanding the foregoing subdivisions, the court may order that notices required by subdivision (a)(2), (3) and (6) of this rule be transmitted to the United States trustee and be mailed only to the committees elected under § 705 or appointed under § 1102 of the Code or to their authorized agents and to the creditors and equity security holders who serve on the trustee or debtor in possession and file a request that all notices be mailed to them. A committee appointed under § 1114 shall receive copies of all notices required by subdivisions (a)(1), (a)(5), (b), (f)(2), and (f)(7), and such other notices as the court may direct.

(j) Notices to the United States.

Copies of notices required to be mailed to all creditors under this rule shall be mailed (1) in a chapter 11 reorganization case, to the Securities and Exchange Commission at any place the Commission designates, if the Commission has filed either a notice of appearance in the case or a written request to receive notices;

(2) in a commodity broker case, to the Commodity Futures Trading Commission at Washington, D.C.; (3) in a chapter 11 case, to the Internal Revenue Service at its address set out in the register maintained under Rule 5003(e) for the district in which the case is pending; (4) if the papers in the case disclose a debt to the United States other than for taxes, to the United States attorney for the district in which the case is pending and to the department, agency, or instrumentality of the United States through which the debtor became indebted; or (5) if the filed papers disclose a stock interest of the United States, to the Secretary of the Treasury at Washington, D.C.

(k) Notices to United States Trustee.

Unless the case is a chapter 9 municipality case or unless the United States trustee requests otherwise, the clerk, or some other person as the court may direct, shall transmit to the United States trustee notice of the matters described in subdivisions (a)(2), (a)(3), (a)(4), (a)(8), (b), (f)(1), (f)(2), (f)(4), (f)(6), (f)(7), (f)(8), and (q) of this rule and notice of hearings on all applications for compensation or reimbursement of expenses. Notices to the United States trustee shall be transmitted within the time prescribed in subdivision (a) or (b) of this rule. The United States trustee shall also receive notice of any other matter if such notice is requested by the United States trustee or ordered by the court. Nothing in these rules requires the clerk or any other person to transmit to the United States trustee any notice, schedule, report, application or other document in a case under the Securities Investor Protection Act, 15 U.S.C. § 78aaa et.[1] seq.

(*l*) Notice by Publication.

The court may order notice by publication if it finds that notice by mail is impracticable or that it is desirable to supplement the notice.

(m) Orders Designating Matter of Notices.

The court may from time to time enter orders designating the matters in respect to which, the entity to whom, and the form and manner in which notices shall be sent except as otherwise provided by these rules.

(n) Caption.

The caption of every notice given under this rule shall comply with Rule 1005. The caption of every notice required to be given by the debtor to a creditor shall include the information required to be in the notice by § 342(c) of the Code.

(*o*) Notice of Order for Relief in Consumer Case.

In a voluntary case commenced by an individual debtor whose debts are primarily consumer debts, the clerk or some other person as the court may direct shall give the trustee and all creditors notice by mail of the order for relief within 21 days from the date thereof.

(p) Notice to a Creditor With a Foreign Address.

(1) If, at the request of the United States trustee or a party in interest, or on its own initiative, the court finds that a notice mailed within the time prescribed by these rules would not be sufficient to give a creditor with a foreign address to which notices under these rules are mailed reasonable notice under the circumstances, the court may order that the notice be supplemented with notice by other means or that the time prescribed for the notice by mail be enlarged.

(2) Unless the court for cause orders otherwise, a creditor with a foreign address to which notices under this rule are mailed shall be given at least 30 days' notice of the time fixed for filing a proof of claim under Rule 3002(c) or Rule 3003(c).

(3) Unless the court for cause orders otherwise, the mailing address of a creditor with a foreign address shall be determined under Rule 2002(g).

(q) Notice of Petition for Recognition of Foreign Proceeding and of Court's Intention to Communicate With Foreign Courts and Foreign Representatives.

---

[1] So in original. Period probably should not appear.

(1) Notice of Petition for Recognition.

The clerk, or some other person as the court may direct, shall forthwith give the debtor, all persons or bodies authorized to administer foreign proceedings of the debtor, all entities against whom provisional relief is being sought under § 1519 of the Code, all parties to litigation pending in the United States in which the debtor is a party at the time of the filing of the petition, and such other entities as the court may direct, at least 21 days' notice by mail of the hearing on the petition for recognition of a foreign proceeding. The notice shall state whether the petition seeks recognition as a foreign main proceeding or foreign nonmain proceeding.

(2) Notice of Court's Intention to Communicate with Foreign Courts and Foreign Representatives.

The clerk, or some other person as the court may direct, shall give the debtor, all persons or bodies authorized to administer foreign proceedings of the debtor, all entities against whom provisional relief is being sought under § 1519 of the Code, all parties to litigation pending in the United States in which the debtor is a party at the time of the filing of the petition, and such other entities as the court may direct, notice by mail of the court's intention to communicate with a foreign court or foreign representative.

(As amended Pub.L. 98–91, § 2(a), Aug. 30, 1983, 97 Stat. 607; Pub.L. 98–353, Title III, § 321, July 10, 1984, 98 Stat. 357; Mar. 30, 1987, eff. Aug. 1, 1987; Apr. 30, 1991, eff. Aug. 1, 1991; Apr. 22, 1993, eff. Aug. 1, 1993; Apr. 23, 1996, eff. Dec. 1, 1996; Apr. 11, 1997, eff. Dec. 1, 1997; Apr. 29, 1999, eff. Dec. 1, 1999; Apr. 17, 2000, eff. Dec. 1, 2000; Apr. 23, 2001, eff. Dec. 1, 2001; Mar. 27, 2003, eff. Dec. 1, 2003; Apr. 26, 2004, eff. Dec. 1, 2004; Apr. 25, 2005, eff. Dec. 1, 2005; Apr. 23, 2008, eff. Dec. 1, 2008; Mar. 26, 2009, eff. Dec. 1, 2009.)

Rule 2003.   Meeting of Creditors or Equity Security Holders

(a) Date and Place.

Except as otherwise provided in § 341(e) of the Code, in a chapter 7 liquidation or a chapter 11 reorganization case, the United States trustee shall call a meeting of creditors to be held no fewer than 21 and no more than 40 days after the order for relief. In a chapter 12 family farmer debt adjustment case, the United States trustee shall call a meeting of creditors to be held no fewer than 21 and no more than 35 days after the order for relief. In a chapter 13 individual's debt adjustment case, the United States trustee shall call a meeting of creditors to be held no fewer than 21 and no more than 50 days after the order for relief. If there is an appeal from or a motion to vacate the order for relief, or if there is a motion to dismiss the case, the United States trustee may set a later date for the meeting. The meeting may be held at a regular place for holding court or at any other place designated by the United States trustee within the district convenient for the parties in interest. If the United States trustee designates a place for the meeting which is not regularly staffed by the United States trustee or an assistant who may preside at the meeting, the meeting may be held not more than 60 days after the order for relief.

(b) Order of Meeting.

(1) Meeting of Creditors.

The United States trustee shall preside at the meeting of creditors. The business of the meeting shall include the examination of the debtor under oath and, in a chapter 7 liquidation case, may include the election of a creditors' committee and, if the case is not under subchapter V of chapter 7, the election of a trustee. The presiding officer shall have the authority to administer oaths.

(2) Meeting of Equity Security Holders.

If the United States trustee convenes a meeting of equity security holders pursuant to § 341(b) of the Code, the United States trustee shall fix a date for the meeting and shall preside.

(3) Right to Vote.

In a chapter 7 liquidation case, a creditor is entitled to vote at a meeting if, at or before the meeting, the creditor has filed a proof of claim or a writing setting forth facts evidencing a right to vote pursuant to § 702(a) of the Code unless objection is made to the claim or the proof of claim is insufficient on its face. A creditor of a partnership may file a proof of claim or writing evidencing a right to vote for the trustee for the estate of a general partner notwithstanding that a trustee for the estate of the partnership has previously qualified. In the event of an objection to the amount or allowability of a claim for the purpose of voting, unless the court orders otherwise, the United States trustee shall tabulate the votes for each alternative presented by the dispute and, if resolution of such dispute is necessary to determine the result of the election, the tabulations for each alternative shall be reported to the court.

(c)   Record of Meeting.

Any examination under oath at the meeting of creditors held pursuant to § 341(a) of the Code shall be recorded verbatim by the United States trustee using electronic sound recording equipment or other means of recording, and such record shall be preserved by the United States trustee and available for public access until two years after the conclusion of the meeting of creditors. Upon request of any entity, the United States trustee shall certify and provide a copy or transcript of such recording at the entity's expense.

(d)   Report of Election and Resolution of Disputes in a Chapter 7 Case.

(1)   Report of Undisputed Election.

In a chapter 7 case, if the election of a trustee or a member of a creditors' committee is not disputed, the United States trustee shall promptly file a report of the election, including the name and address of the person or entity elected and a statement that the election is undisputed.

(2)   Disputed Election.

If the election is disputed, the United States trustee shall promptly file a report stating that the election is disputed, informing the court of the nature of the dispute, and listing the name and address of any candidate elected under any alternative presented by the dispute. No later than the date on which the report is filed, the United States trustee shall mail a copy of the report to any party in interest that has made a request to receive a copy of the report. Pending disposition by the court of a disputed election for trustee, the interim trustee shall continue in office. Unless a motion for the resolution of the dispute is filed no later than 14 days after the United States trustee files a report of a disputed election for trustee, the interim trustee shall serve as trustee in the case.

(e)   Adjournment.

The meeting may be adjourned from time to time by announcement at the meeting of the adjourned date and time. The presiding official shall promptly file a statement specifying the date and time to which the meeting is adjourned.

(f)   Special Meetings.

The United States trustee may call a special meeting of creditors on request of a party in interest or on the United States trustee's own initiative.

(g)   Final Meeting.

If the United States trustee calls a final meeting of creditors in a case in which the net proceeds realized exceed $1,500, the clerk shall mail a summary of the trustee's final account to the creditors with a notice of the meeting, together with a statement of the amount of the claims allowed. The trustee shall attend the final meeting and shall, if requested, report on the administration of the estate.

(As amended Mar. 30, 1987, eff. Aug. 1, 1987; Apr. 30, 1991, eff. Aug. 1, 1991; Apr. 22, 1993, eff. Aug. 1, 1993; Apr. 29, 1999, eff. Dec. 1, 1999; Mar. 27, 2003, eff. Dec. 1, 2003; Apr. 23, 2008, eff. Dec. 1, 2008; Mar. 26, 2009, eff. Dec. 1, 2009; Apr. 26, 2011, eff. Dec. 1, 2011.)

Rule 2004.   Examination

(a)   Examination on Motion.

On motion of any party in interest, the court may order the examination of any entity.

(b)   Scope of Examination.

The examination of an entity under this rule or of the debtor under § 343 of the Code may relate only to the acts, conduct, or property or to the liabilities and financial condition of the debtor, or to any matter which may affect the administration of the debtor's estate, or to the debtor's right to a discharge. In a family farmer's debt adjustment case under chapter 12, an individual's debt adjustment case under chapter 13, or a reorganization case under chapter 11 of the Code, other than for the reorganization of a railroad, the examination may also relate to the operation of any business and the desirability of its continuance, the source of any money or property acquired or to be acquired by the debtor for purposes of consummating a plan and the consideration given or offered therefor, and any other matter relevant to the case or to the formulation of a plan.

(c)   Compelling Attendance and Production of Documents.

The attendance of an entity for examination and for the production of documents, whether the examination is to be conducted within or without the district in which the case is pending, may be compelled as provided in Rule 9016 for the attendance of a witness at a hearing or trial. As an officer of the court, an attorney may issue and sign a subpoena on behalf of the court for the district in which the examination is to be held if the attorney is admitted to practice in that court or in the court in which the case is pending.

(d)   Time and Place of Examination of Debtor.

The court may for cause shown and on terms as it may impose order the debtor to be examined under this rule at any time or place it designates, whether within or without the district wherein the case is pending.

(e)   Mileage.

An entity other than a debtor shall not be required to attend as a witness unless lawful mileage and witness fee for one day's attendance shall be first tendered. If the debtor resides more than 100 miles from the place of examination when required to appear for an examination under this rule, the mileage allowed by law to a witness shall be tendered for any distance more than 100 miles from the debtor's residence at the date of the filing of the first petition commencing a case under the Code or the residence at the time the debtor is required to appear for the examination, whichever is the lesser.

(As amended Mar. 30, 1987, eff. Aug. 1, 1987; Apr. 30, 1991, eff. Aug. 1, 1991; Apr. 29, 2002, eff. Dec. 1, 2002.)

Rule 2005.   Apprehension and Removal of Debtor to Compel Attendance for Examination

(a)   Order to Compel Attendance for Examination.

On motion of any party in interest supported by an affidavit alleging (1) that the examination of the debtor is necessary for the proper administration of the estate and that there is reasonable cause to believe that the debtor is about to leave or has left the debtor's residence or principal place of business to avoid examination, or (2) that the debtor has evaded service of a subpoena or of an order to attend for examination, or (3) that the debtor has willfully disobeyed a subpoena or order to attend for examination, duly served, the court may issue to the marshal, or some other officer authorized by law, an order directing the officer to bring the debtor before the court without unnecessary delay. If, after hearing, the court finds the allegations to be true, the court shall thereupon cause the debtor to be examined forthwith. If necessary, the court shall fix conditions for further examination and for the debtor's obedience to all orders made in reference thereto.

(b)   Removal.

Whenever any order to bring the debtor before the court is issued under this rule and the debtor is found in a district other than that of the court issuing the order, the debtor may be taken into custody under the order and removed in accordance with the following rules:

(1)   If the debtor is taken into custody under the order at a place less than 100 miles from the place of issue of the order, the debtor shall be brought forthwith before the court that issued the order.

(2) If the debtor is taken into custody under the order at a place 100 miles or more from the place of issue of the order, the debtor shall be brought without unnecessary delay before the nearest available United States magistrate judge, bankruptcy judge, or district judge. If, after hearing, the magistrate judge, bankruptcy judge, or district judge finds that an order has issued under this rule and that the person in custody is the debtor, or if the person in custody waives a hearing, the magistrate judge, bankruptcy judge, or district judge shall order removal, and the person in custody shall be released on conditions ensuring prompt appearance before the court that issued the order to compel the attendance.

(c) Conditions of Release.

In determining what conditions will reasonably assure attendance or obedience under subdivision (a) of this rule or appearance under subdivision (b) of this rule, the court shall be governed by the provisions and policies of title 18, U.S.C., § 3146(a) and (b).

(As amended Mar. 30, 1987, eff. Aug. 1, 1987; Apr. 22, 1993, eff. Aug. 1, 1993.)

Rule 2006.   Solicitation and Voting of Proxies in Chapter 7 Liquidation Cases

(a) Applicability.

This rule applies only in a liquidation case pending under chapter 7 of the Code.

(b) Definitions.

(1) Proxy.

A proxy is a written power of attorney authorizing any entity to vote the claim or otherwise act as the owner's attorney in fact in connection with the administration of the estate.

(2) Solicitation of Proxy.

The solicitation of a proxy is any communication, other than one from an attorney to a regular client who owns a claim or from an attorney to the owner of a claim who has requested the attorney to represent the owner, by which a creditor is asked, directly or indirectly, to give a proxy after or in contemplation of the filing of a petition by or against the debtor.

(c) Authorized Solicitation.

(1) A proxy may be solicited only by (A) a creditor owning an allowable unsecured claim against the estate on the date of the filing of the petition; (B) a committee elected pursuant to § 705 of the Code; (C) a committee of creditors selected by a majority in number and amount of claims of creditors (i) whose claims are not contingent or unliquidated, (ii) who are not disqualified from voting under § 702(a) of the Code and (iii) who were present or represented at a meeting of which all creditors having claims of over $500 or the 100 creditors having the largest claims had at least seven days' notice in writing and of which meeting written minutes were kept and are available reporting the names of the creditors present or represented and voting and the amounts of their claims; or (D) a bona fide trade or credit association, but such association may solicit only creditors who were its members or subscribers in good standing and had allowable unsecured claims on the date of the filing of the petition.

(2) A proxy may be solicited only in writing.

(d) Solicitation Not Authorized.

This rule does not permit solicitation (1) in any interest other than that of general creditors; (2) by or on behalf of any custodian; (3) by the interim trustee or by or on behalf of any entity not qualified to vote under § 702(a) of the Code; (4) by or on behalf of an attorney at law; or (5) by or on behalf of a transferee of a claim for collection only.

(e) Data Required From Holders of Multiple Proxies.

At any time before the voting commences at any meeting of creditors pursuant to § 341(a) of the Code, or at any other time as the court may direct, a holder of two or more proxies shall file and transmit to the

United States trustee a verified list of the proxies to be voted and a verified statement of the pertinent facts and circumstances in connection with the execution and delivery of each proxy, including:

    (1)   a copy of the solicitation;

    (2)   identification of the solicitor, the forwarder, if the forwarder is neither the solicitor nor the owner of the claim, and the proxyholder, including their connections with the debtor and with each other. If the solicitor, forwarder, or proxyholder is an association, there shall also be included a statement that the creditors whose claims have been solicited and the creditors whose claims are to be voted were members or subscribers in good standing and had allowable unsecured claims on the date of the filing of the petition. If the solicitor, forwarder, or proxyholder is a committee of creditors, the statement shall also set forth the date and place the committee was organized, that the committee was organized in accordance with clause (B) or (C) of paragraph (c)(1) of this rule, the members of the committee, the amounts of their claims, when the claims were acquired, the amounts paid therefor, and the extent to which the claims of the committee members are secured or entitled to priority;

    (3)   a statement that no consideration has been paid or promised by the proxyholder for the proxy;

    (4)   a statement as to whether there is any agreement and, if so, the particulars thereof, between the proxyholder and any other entity for the payment of any consideration in connection with voting the proxy, or for the sharing of compensation with any entity, other than a member or regular associate of the proxyholder's law firm, which may be allowed the trustee or any entity for services rendered in the case, or for the employment of any person as attorney, accountant, appraiser, auctioneer, or other employee for the estate;

    (5)   if the proxy was solicited by an entity other than the proxyholder, or forwarded to the holder by an entity who is neither a solicitor of the proxy nor the owner of the claim, a statement signed and verified by the solicitor or forwarder that no consideration has been paid or promised for the proxy, and whether there is any agreement, and, if so, the particulars thereof, between the solicitor or forwarder and any other entity for the payment of any consideration in connection with voting the proxy, or for sharing compensation with any entity, other than a member or regular associate of the solicitor's or forwarder's law firm which may be allowed the trustee or any entity for services rendered in the case, or for the employment of any person as attorney, accountant, appraiser, auctioneer, or other employee for the estate;

    (6)   if the solicitor, forwarder, or proxyholder is a committee, a statement signed and verified by each member as to the amount and source of any consideration paid or to be paid to such member in connection with the case other than by way of dividend on the member's claim.

(f)   **Enforcement of Restrictions on Solicitation.**

On motion of any party in interest or on its own initiative, the court may determine whether there has been a failure to comply with the provisions of this rule or any other impropriety in connection with the solicitation or voting of a proxy. After notice and a hearing the court may reject any proxy for cause, vacate any order entered in consequence of the voting of any proxy which should have been rejected, or take any other appropriate action.

    (As amended Mar. 30, 1987, eff. Aug. 1, 1987; Apr. 30, 1991, eff. Aug. 1, 1991; Mar. 26, 2009, eff. Dec. 1, 2009.)

Rule 2007.   Review of Appointment of Creditors' Committee Organized Before Commencement of the Case

(a)   **Motion To Review Appointment.**

If a committee appointed by the United States trustee pursuant to § 1102(a) of the Code consists of the members of a committee organized by creditors before the commencement of a chapter 9 or chapter 11 case, on motion of a party in interest and after a hearing on notice to the United States trustee and other entities as the court may direct, the court may determine whether the appointment of the committee satisfies the requirements of § 1102(b)(1) of the Code.

(b)   Selection of Members of Committee.

The court may find that a committee organized by unsecured creditors before the commencement of a chapter 9 or chapter 11 case was fairly chosen if:

(1)   it was selected by a majority in number and amount of claims of unsecured creditors who may vote under § 702(a) of the Code and were present in person or represented at a meeting of which all creditors having unsecured claims of over $1,000 or the 100 unsecured creditors having the largest claims had at least seven days' notice in writing, and of which meeting written minutes reporting the names of the creditors present or represented and voting and the amounts of their claims were kept and are available for inspection;

(2)   all proxies voted at the meeting for the elected committee were solicited pursuant to Rule 2006 and the lists and statements required by subdivision (e) thereof have been transmitted to the United States trustee; and

(3)   the organization of the committee was in all other respects fair and proper.

(c)   Failure To Comply With Requirements for Appointment.

After a hearing on notice pursuant to subdivision (a) of this rule, the court shall direct the United States trustee to vacate the appointment of the committee and may order other appropriate action if the court finds that such appointment failed to satisfy the requirements of § 1102(b)(1) of the Code.

(As amended Mar. 30, 1987, eff. Aug. 1, 1987; Apr. 30, 1991, eff. Aug. 1, 1991; Mar. 26, 2009, eff. Dec. 1, 2009.)

Rule 2007.1.   Appointment of Trustee or Examiner in a Chapter 11 Reorganization Case

(a)   Order To Appoint Trustee or Examiner.

In a chapter 11 reorganization case, a motion for an order to appoint a trustee or an examiner under § 1104(a) or § 1104(c) of the Code shall be made in accordance with Rule 9014.

(b)   Election of Trustee.

(1)   Request for an Election.

A request to convene a meeting of creditors for the purpose of electing a trustee in a chapter 11 reorganization case shall be filed and transmitted to the United States trustee in accordance with Rule 5005 within the time prescribed by § 1104(b) of the Code. Pending court approval of the person elected, any person appointed by the United States trustee under § 1104(d) and approved in accordance with subdivision (c) of this rule shall serve as trustee.

(2)   Manner of Election and Notice.

An election of a trustee under § 1104(b) of the Code shall be conducted in the manner provided in Rules 2003(b)(3) and 2006. Notice of the meeting of creditors convened under § 1104(b) shall be given as provided in Rule 2002. The United States trustee shall preside at the meeting. A proxy for the purpose of voting in the election may be solicited only by a committee of creditors appointed under § 1102 of the Code or by any other party entitled to solicit a proxy pursuant to Rule 2006.

(3)   Report of Election and Resolution of Disputes.

(A)   Report of Undisputed Election.

If no dispute arises out of the election, the United States trustee shall promptly file a report certifying the election, including the name and address of the person elected and a statement that the election is undisputed. The report shall be accompanied by a verified statement of the person elected setting forth that person's connections with the debtor, creditors, any other party in interest, their respective attorneys and accountants, the United States trustee, or any person employed in the office of the United States trustee.

(B) Dispute Arising Out of an Election.

If a dispute arises out of an election, the United States trustee shall promptly file a report stating that the election is disputed, informing the court of the nature of the dispute, and listing the name and address of any candidate elected under any alternative presented by the dispute. The report shall be accompanied by a verified statement by each candidate elected under each alternative presented by the dispute, setting forth the person's connections with the debtor, creditors, any other party in interest, their respective attorneys and accountants, the United States trustee, or any person employed in the office of the United States trustee. Not later than the date on which the report of the disputed election is filed, the United States trustee shall mail a copy of the report and each verified statement to any party in interest that has made a request to convene a meeting under § 1104(b) or to receive a copy of the report, and to any committee appointed under § 1102 of the Code.

(c) Approval of Appointment.

An order approving the appointment of a trustee or an examiner under § 1104(d) of the Code shall be made on application of the United States trustee. The application shall state the name of the person appointed and, to the best of the applicant's knowledge, all the person's connections with the debtor, creditors, any other parties in interest, their respective attorneys and accountants, the United States trustee, or persons employed in the office of the United States trustee. The application shall state the names of the parties in interest with whom the United States trustee consulted regarding the appointment. The application shall be accompanied by a verified statement of the person appointed setting forth the person's connections with the debtor, creditors, any other party in interest, their respective attorneys and accountants, the United States trustee, or any person employed in the office of the United States trustee.

(Added Apr. 30, 1991, eff. Aug. 1, 1991; amended Apr. 11, 1997, eff. Dec. 1, 1997; Apr. 23, 2008, eff. Dec. 1, 2008.)

Rule 2007.2.   Appointment of Patient Care Ombudsman in a Health Care Business Case

(a) Order to Appoint Patient Care Ombudsman.

In a chapter 7, chapter 9, or chapter 11 case in which the debtor is a health care business, the court shall order the appointment of a patient care ombudsman under § 333 of the Code, unless the court, on motion of the United States trustee or a party in interest filed no later than 21 days after the commencement of the case or within another time fixed by the court, finds that the appointment of a patient care ombudsman is not necessary under the specific circumstances of the case for the protection of patients.

(b) Motion for Order To Appoint Ombudsman.

If the court has found that the appointment of an ombudsman is not necessary, or has terminated the appointment, the court, on motion of the United States trustee or a party in interest, may order the appointment at a later time if it finds that the appointment has become necessary to protect patients.

(c) Notice of Appointment.

If a patient care ombudsman is appointed under § 333, the United States trustee shall promptly file a notice of the appointment, including the name and address of the person appointed. Unless the person appointed is a State Long-Term Care Ombudsman, the notice shall be accompanied by a verified statement of the person appointed setting forth the person's connections with the debtor, creditors, patients, any other party in interest, their respective attorneys and accountants, the United States trustee, and any person employed in the office of the United States trustee.

(d) Termination of Appointment.

On motion of the United States trustee or a party in interest, the court may terminate the appointment of a patient care ombudsman if the court finds that the appointment is not necessary to protect patients.

(e)   Motion.

A motion under this rule shall be governed by Rule 9014. The motion shall be transmitted to the United States trustee and served on: the debtor; the trustee; any committee elected under § 705 or appointed under § 1102 of the Code or its authorized agent, or, if the case is a chapter 9 municipality case or a chapter 11 reorganization case and no committee of unsecured creditors has been appointed under § 1102, on the creditors included on the list filed under Rule 1007(d); and such other entities as the court may direct.

(Added Apr. 23, 2008, eff. Dec. 1, 2008. As amended Mar. 26, 2009, eff. Dec. 1, 2009.)

Rule 2008.   Notice to Trustee of Selection

The United States trustee shall immediately notify the person selected as trustee how to qualify and, if applicable, the amount of the trustee's bond. A trustee that has filed a blanket bond pursuant to Rule 2010 and has been selected as trustee in a chapter 7, 12, or chapter 13 case that does not notify the court and the United States trustee in writing of rejection of the office within seven days after receipt of notice of selection shall be deemed to have accepted the office. Any other person selected as trustee shall notify the court and the United States trustee in writing of acceptance of the office within seven days after receipt of notice of selection or shall be deemed to have rejected the office.

(As amended Mar. 30, 1987, eff. Aug. 1, 1987; Apr. 30, 1991, eff. Aug. 1, 1991; Mar. 26, 2009, eff. Dec. 1, 2009.)

Rule 2009.   Trustees for Estates When Joint Administration Ordered

(a)   Election of Single Trustee for Estates Being Jointly Administered.

If the court orders a joint administration of two or more estates under Rule 1015(b), creditors may elect a single trustee for the estates being jointly administered, unless the case is under subchapter V of chapter 7 of the Code.

(b)   Right of Creditors To Elect Separate Trustee.

Notwithstanding entry of an order for joint administration under Rule 1015(b), the creditors of any debtor may elect a separate trustee for the estate of the debtor as provided in § 702 of the Code, unless the case is under subchapter V of chapter 7.

(c)   Appointment of Trustees for Estates Being Jointly Administered.

(1)   Chapter 7 Liquidation Cases.

Except in a case governed by subchapter V of chapter 7, the United States trustee may appoint one or more interim trustees for estates being jointly administered in chapter 7 cases.

(2)   Chapter 11 Reorganization Cases.

If the appointment of a trustee is ordered, the United States trustee may appoint one or more trustees for estates being jointly administered in chapter 11 cases.

(3)   Chapter 12 Family Farmer's Debt Adjustment Cases.

The United States trustee may appoint one or more trustees for estates being jointly administered in chapter 12 cases.

(4)   Chapter 13 Individual's Debt Adjustment Cases.

The United States trustee may appoint one or more trustees for estates being jointly administered in chapter 13 cases.

(d)   Potential Conflicts of Interest.

On a showing that creditors or equity security holders of the different estates will be prejudiced by conflicts of interest of a common trustee who has been elected or appointed, the court shall order the selection of separate trustees for estates being jointly administered.

(e) Separate Accounts.

The trustee or trustees of estates being jointly administered shall keep separate accounts of the property and distribution of each estate.

(As amended Mar. 30, 1987, eff. Aug. 1, 1987; Apr. 30, 1991, eff. Aug. 1, 1991; Mar. 27, 2003, eff. Dec. 1, 2003.)

Rule 2010.   Qualification by Trustee; Proceeding on Bond

(a) Blanket Bond.

The United States trustee may authorize a blanket bond in favor of the United States conditioned on the faithful performance of official duties by the trustee or trustees to cover (1) a person who qualifies as trustee in a number of cases, and (2) a number of trustees each of whom qualifies in a different case.

(b) Proceeding on Bond.

A proceeding on the trustee's bond may be brought by any party in interest in the name of the United States for the use of the entity injured by the breach of the condition.

(As amended Mar. 30, 1987, eff. Aug. 1, 1987; Apr. 30, 1991, eff. Aug. 1, 1991.)

Rule 2011.   Evidence of Debtor in Possession or Qualification of Trustee

(a) Whenever evidence is required that a debtor is a debtor in possession or that a trustee has qualified, the clerk may so certify and the certificate shall constitute conclusive evidence of that fact.

(b) If a person elected or appointed as trustee does not qualify within the time prescribed by § 322(a) of the Code, the clerk shall so notify the court and the United States trustee.

(As amended Apr. 30, 1991, eff. Aug. 1, 1991.)

Rule 2012.   Substitution of Trustee or Successor Trustee; Accounting

(a) Trustee.

If a trustee is appointed in a chapter 11 case or the debtor is removed as debtor in possession in a chapter 12 case, the trustee is substituted automatically for the debtor in possession as a party in any pending action, proceeding, or matter.

(b) Successor Trustee.

When a trustee dies, resigns, is removed, or otherwise ceases to hold office during the pendency of a case under the Code (1) the successor is automatically substituted as a party in any pending action, proceeding, or matter; and (2) the successor trustee shall prepare, file, and transmit to the United States trustee an accounting of the prior administration of the estate.

(As amended Mar. 30, 1987, eff. Aug. 1, 1987; Apr. 30, 1991, eff. Aug. 1, 1991.)

Rule 2013.   Public Record of Compensation Awarded to Trustees, Examiners, and Professionals

(a) Record To Be Kept.

The clerk shall maintain a public record listing fees awarded by the court (1) to trustees and attorneys, accountants, appraisers, auctioneers and other professionals employed by trustees, and (2) to examiners. The record shall include the name and docket number of the case, the name of the individual or firm receiving the fee and the amount of the fee awarded. The record shall be maintained chronologically and shall be kept current and open to examination by the public without charge. "Trustees," as used in this rule, does not include debtors in possession.

(b)   Summary of Record.

At the close of each annual period, the clerk shall prepare a summary of the public record by individual or firm name, to reflect total fees awarded during the preceding year. The summary shall be open to examination by the public without charge. The clerk shall transmit a copy of the summary to the United States trustee.

(As amended Mar. 30, 1987, eff. Aug. 1, 1987; Apr. 30, 1991, eff. Aug. 1, 1991.)

Rule 2014.   Employment of Professional Persons

(a)   Application for and Order of Employment.

An order approving the employment of attorneys, accountants, appraisers, auctioneers, agents, or other professionals pursuant to § 327, § 1103, or § 1114 of the Code shall be made only on application of the trustee or committee. The application shall be filed and, unless the case is a chapter 9 municipality case, a copy of the application shall be transmitted by the applicant to the United States trustee. The application shall state the specific facts showing the necessity for the employment, the name of the person to be employed, the reasons for the selection, the professional services to be rendered, any proposed arrangement for compensation, and, to the best of the applicant's knowledge, all of the person's connections with the debtor, creditors, any other party in interest, their respective attorneys and accountants, the United States trustee, or any person employed in the office of the United States trustee. The application shall be accompanied by a verified statement of the person to be employed setting forth the person's connections with the debtor, creditors, any other party in interest, their respective attorneys and accountants, the United States trustee, or any person employed in the office of the United States trustee.

(b)   Services Rendered by Member or Associate of Firm of Attorneys or Accountants.

If, under the Code and this rule, a law partnership or corporation is employed as an attorney, or an accounting partnership or corporation is employed as an accountant, or if a named attorney or accountant is employed, any partner, member, or regular associate of the partnership, corporation or individual may act as attorney or accountant so employed, without further order of the court.

(As amended Mar. 30, 1987, eff. Aug. 1, 1987; Apr. 30, 1991, eff. Aug. 1, 1991.)

Rule 2015.   Duty to Keep Records, Make Reports, and Give Notice of Case or Change of Status

(a)   Trustee or Debtor in Possession.

A trustee or debtor in possession shall:

(1)   in a chapter 7 liquidation case and, if the court directs, in a chapter 11 reorganization case file and transmit to the United States trustee a complete inventory of the property of the debtor within 30 days after qualifying as a trustee or debtor in possession, unless such an inventory has already been filed;

(2)   keep a record of receipts and the disposition of money and property received;

(3)   file the reports and summaries required by § 704(a)(8) of the Code, which shall include a statement, if payments are made to employees, of the amounts of deductions for all taxes required to be withheld or paid for and in behalf of employees and the place where these amounts are deposited;

(4)   as soon as possible after the commencement of the case, give notice of the case to every entity known to be holding money or property subject to withdrawal or order of the debtor, including every bank, savings or building and loan association, public utility company, and landlord with whom the debtor has a deposit, and to every insurance company which has issued a policy having a cash surrender value payable to the debtor, except that notice need not be given to any entity who has knowledge or has previously been notified of the case;

(5)   in a chapter 11 reorganization case, on or before the last day of the month after each calendar quarter during which there is a duty to pay fees under 28 U.S.C. § 1930(a)(6), file and transmit to the

United States trustee a statement of any disbursements made during that quarter and of any fees payable under 28 U.S.C. § 1930(a)(6) for that quarter; and

    (6) in a chapter 11 small business case, unless the court, for cause, sets another reporting interval, file and transmit to the United States trustee for each calendar month after the order for relief, on the appropriate Official Form, the report required by § 308. If the order for relief is within the first 15 days of a calendar month, a report shall be filed for the portion of the month that follows the order for relief. If the order for relief is after the 15th day of a calendar month, the period for the remainder of the month shall be included in the report for the next calendar month. Each report shall be filed no later than 21 days after the last day of the calendar month following the month covered by the report. The obligation to file reports under this subparagraph terminates on the effective date of the plan, or conversion or dismissal of the case.

(b) Chapter 12 Trustee and Debtor in Possession.

In a chapter 12 family farmer's debt adjustment case, the debtor in possession shall perform the duties prescribed in clauses (2)–(4) of subdivision (a) of this rule and, if the court directs, shall file and transmit to the United States trustee a complete inventory of the property of the debtor within the time fixed by the court. If the debtor is removed as debtor in possession, the trustee shall perform the duties of the debtor in possession prescribed in this paragraph.

(c) Chapter 13 Trustee and Debtor.

    (1) Business Cases.

    In a chapter 13 individual's debt adjustment case, when the debtor is engaged in business, the debtor shall perform the duties prescribed by clauses (2)–(4) of subdivision (a) of this rule and, if the court directs, shall file and transmit to the United States trustee a complete inventory of the property of the debtor within the time fixed by the court.

    (2) Nonbusiness Cases.

    In a chapter 13 individual's debt adjustment case, when the debtor is not engaged in business, the trustee shall perform the duties prescribed by clause (2) of subdivision (a) of this rule.

(d) Foreign Representative.

In a case in which the court has granted recognition of a foreign proceeding under chapter 15, the foreign representative shall file any notice required under § 1518 of the Code within 14 days after the date when the representative becomes aware of the subsequent information.

(e) Transmission of Reports.

In a chapter 11 case the court may direct that copies or summaries of annual reports and copies or summaries of other reports shall be mailed to the creditors, equity security holders, and indenture trustees. The court may also direct the publication of summaries of any such reports. A copy of every report or summary mailed or published pursuant to this subdivision shall be transmitted to the United States trustee.

    (As amended Mar. 30, 1987, eff. Aug. 1, 1987; Apr. 30, 1991, eff. Aug. 1, 1991; Apr. 23, 1996, eff. Dec. 1, 1996; Apr. 29, 2002, eff. Dec. 1, 2002; Apr. 23, 2008, eff. Dec. 1, 2008; Mar. 26, 2009, eff. Dec. 1, 2009; Apr. 23, 2012, eff. Dec. 1, 2012.)

Rule 2015.1.   Patient Care Ombudsman

(a) Reports.

A patient care ombudsman, at least 14 days before making a report under § 333(b)(2) of the Code, shall give notice that the report will be made to the court, unless the court orders otherwise. The notice shall be transmitted to the United States trustee, posted conspicuously at the health care facility that is the subject of the report, and served on: the debtor; the trustee; all patients; and any committee elected under § 705 or appointed under § 1102 of the Code or its authorized agent, or, if the case is a chapter 9 municipality case or a chapter 11 reorganization case and no committee of unsecured creditors has been appointed under § 1102, on the creditors included on the list filed under Rule 1007(d); and such other entities as the court may direct. The notice shall state the date and time when the report will be made, the manner in which the report will be made, and, if the report is in writing, the name, address, telephone number, email address, and website, if any, of the person from whom a copy of the report may be obtained at the debtor's expense.

(b) Authorization to Review Confidential Patient Records.

A motion by a patient care ombudsman under § 333(c) to review confidential patient records shall be governed by Rule 9014, served on the patient and any family member or other contact person whose name and address have been given to the trustee or the debtor for the purpose of providing information regarding the patient's health care, and transmitted to the United States trustee subject to applicable nonbankruptcy law relating to patient privacy. Unless the court orders otherwise, a hearing on the motion may not be commenced earlier than 14 days after service of the motion.

(Added Apr. 23, 2008, eff. Dec. 1, 2008, and amended Mar. 26, 2009, eff. Dec. 1, 2009.)

Rule 2015.2.   Transfer of Patient in Health Care Business Case

Unless the court orders otherwise, if the debtor is a health care business, the trustee may not transfer a patient to another health care business under § 704(a)(12) of the Code unless the trustee gives at least 14 days' notice of the transfer to the patient care ombudsman, if any, the patient, and any family member or other contact person whose name and address has been given to the trustee or the debtor for the purpose of providing information regarding the patient's health care. The notice is subject to applicable nonbankruptcy law relating to patient privacy.

(Added Apr. 23, 2008, eff. Dec. 1, 2008, and amended Mar. 26, 2009, eff. Dec. 1, 2009.)

Rule 2015.3.   Reports of Financial Information on Entities in Which a Chapter 11 Estate Holds a Controlling or Substantial Interest

(a) Reporting Requirement.

In a chapter 11 case, the trustee or debtor in possession shall file periodic financial reports of the value, operations, and profitability of each entity that is not a publicly traded corporation or a debtor in a case under title 11, and in which the estate holds a substantial or controlling interest. The reports shall be prepared as prescribed by the appropriate Official Form, and shall be based upon the most recent information reasonably available to the trustee or debtor in possession.

(b) Time for Filing; Service.

The first report required by this rule shall be filed no later than seven days before the first date set for the meeting of creditors under § 341 of the Code. Subsequent reports shall be filed no less frequently than every six months thereafter, until the effective date of a plan or the case is dismissed or converted. Copies of the report shall be served on the United States trustee, any committee appointed under § 1102 of the Code, and any other party in interest that has filed a request therefor.

(c) Presumption of Substantial or Controlling Interest; Judicial Determination.

For purposes of this rule, an entity of which the estate controls or owns at least a 20 percent interest, shall be presumed to be an entity in which the estate has a substantial or controlling interest. An entity in which the estate controls or owns less than a 20 percent interest shall be presumed not to be an entity in which the estate has a substantial or controlling interest. Upon motion, the entity, any holder of an interest therein, the United States trustee, or any other party in interest may seek to rebut either presumption, and the court shall, after notice and a hearing, determine whether the estate's interest in the entity is substantial or controlling.

(d) Modification of Reporting Requirement.

The court may, after notice and a hearing, vary the reporting requirement established by subdivision (a) of this rule for cause, including that the trustee or debtor in possession is not able, after a good faith effort, to comply with those reporting requirements, or that the information required by subdivision (a) is publicly available.

(e)   Notice and Protective Orders.

No later than 14 days before filing the first report required by this rule, the trustee or debtor in possession shall send notice to the entity in which the estate has a substantial or controlling interest, and to all holders—known to the trustee or debtor in possession—of an interest in that entity, that the trustee or debtor in possession expects to file and serve financial information relating to the entity in accordance with this rule. The entity in which the estate has a substantial or controlling interest, or a person holding an interest in that entity, may request protection of the information under § 107 of the Code.

(f)   Effect of Request.

Unless the court orders otherwise, the pendency of a request under subdivisions (c), (d), or (e) of this rule shall not alter or stay the requirements of subdivision (a).

(Added Apr. 23, 2008, eff. Dec. 1, 2008, and amended Mar. 26, 2009, eff. Dec. 1, 2009.)

Rule 2016.   Compensation for Services Rendered and Reimbursement of Expenses

(a)   Application for Compensation or Reimbursement.

An entity seeking interim or final compensation for services, or reimbursement of necessary expenses, from the estate shall file an application setting forth a detailed statement of (1) the services rendered, time expended and expenses incurred, and (2) the amounts requested. An application for compensation shall include a statement as to what payments have theretofore been made or promised to the applicant for services rendered or to be rendered in any capacity whatsoever in connection with the case, the source of the compensation so paid or promised, whether any compensation previously received has been shared and whether an agreement or understanding exists between the applicant and any other entity for the sharing of compensation received or to be received for services rendered in or in connection with the case, and the particulars of any sharing of compensation or agreement or understanding therefor, except that details of any agreement by the applicant for the sharing of compensation as a member or regular associate of a firm of lawyers or accountants shall not be required. The requirements of this subdivision shall apply to an application for compensation for services rendered by an attorney or accountant even though the application is filed by a creditor or other entity. Unless the case is a chapter 9 municipality case, the applicant shall transmit to the United States trustee a copy of the application.

(b)   Disclosure of Compensation Paid or Promised to Attorney for Debtor.

Every attorney for a debtor, whether or not the attorney applies for compensation, shall file and transmit to the United States trustee within 14 days after the order for relief, or at another time as the court may direct, the statement required by § 329 of the Code including whether the attorney has shared or agreed to share the compensation with any other entity. The statement shall include the particulars of any such sharing or agreement to share by the attorney, but the details of any agreement for the sharing of the compensation with a member or regular associate of the attorney's law firm shall not be required. A supplemental statement shall be filed and transmitted to the United States trustee within 14 days after any payment or agreement not previously disclosed.

(c)   Disclosure of Compensation Paid or Promised to Bankruptcy Petition Preparer.

Before a petition is filed, every bankruptcy petition preparer for a debtor shall deliver to the debtor, the declaration under penalty of perjury required by § 110(h)(2). The declaration shall disclose any fee, and the source of any fee, received from or on behalf of the debtor within 12 months of the filing of the case and all unpaid fees charged to the debtor. The declaration shall also describe the services performed and documents prepared or caused to be prepared by the bankruptcy petition preparer. The declaration shall be filed with the petition. The petition preparer shall file a supplemental statement within 14 days after any payment or agreement not previously disclosed.

(As amended Mar. 30, 1987, eff. Aug. 1, 1987; Apr. 30, 1991, eff. Aug. 1, 1991; Mar. 27, 2003, eff. Dec. 1, 2003; Mar. 26, 2009, eff. Dec. 1, 2009.)

Rule 2017.   Examination of Debtor's Transactions with Debtor's Attorney

(a)   Payment or Transfer to Attorney Before Order for Relief.

On motion by any party in interest or on the court's own initiative, the court after notice and a hearing may determine whether any payment of money or any transfer of property by the debtor, made directly or indirectly and in contemplation of the filing of a petition under the Code by or against the debtor or before entry of the order for relief in an involuntary case, to an attorney for services rendered or to be rendered is excessive.

(b)   Payment or Transfer to Attorney After Order for Relief.

On motion by the debtor, the United States trustee, or on the court's own initiative, the court after notice and a hearing may determine whether any payment of money or any transfer of property, or any agreement therefor, by the debtor to an attorney after entry of an order for relief in a case under the Code is excessive, whether the payment or transfer is made or is to be made directly or indirectly, if the payment, transfer, or agreement therefor is for services in any way related to the case.

(As amended Mar. 30, 1987, eff. Aug. 1, 1987; Apr. 30, 1991, eff. Aug. 1, 1991.)

Rule 2018.   Intervention; Right to Be Heard

(a)   Permissive Intervention.

In a case under the Code, after hearing on such notice as the court directs and for cause shown, the court may permit any interested entity to intervene generally or with respect to any specified matter.

(b)   Intervention by Attorney General of a State.

In a chapter 7, 11, 12, or 13 case, the Attorney General of a State may appear and be heard on behalf of consumer creditors if the court determines the appearance is in the public interest, but the Attorney General may not appeal from any judgment, order, or decree in the case.

(c)   Chapter 9 Municipality Case.

The Secretary of the Treasury of the United States may, or if requested by the court shall, intervene in a chapter 9 case. Representatives of the state in which the debtor is located may intervene in a chapter 9 case with respect to matters specified by the court.

(d)   Labor Unions.

In a chapter 9, 11, or 12 case, a labor union or employees' association, representative of employees of the debtor, shall have the right to be heard on the economic soundness of a plan affecting the interests of the employees. A labor union or employees' association which exercises its right to be heard under this subdivision shall not be entitled to appeal any judgment, order, or decree relating to the plan, unless otherwise permitted by law.

(e)   Service on Entities Covered by This Rule.

The court may enter orders governing the service of notice and papers on entities permitted to intervene or be heard pursuant to this rule.

(As amended Mar. 30, 1987, eff. Aug. 1, 1987; Apr. 30, 1991, eff. Aug. 1, 1991.)

Rule 2019.   Disclosure Regarding Creditors and Equity Security Holders in Chapter 9 and Chapter 11 Cases

(a)   Definitions.

In this rule the following terms have the meanings indicated:

(1)   "Disclosable economic interest" means any claim, interest, pledge, lien, option, participation, derivative instrument, or any other right or derivative right granting the holder an economic interest that is affected by the value, acquisition, or disposition of a claim or interest.

(2) "Represent" or "represents" means to take a position before the court or to solicit votes regarding the confirmation of a plan on behalf of another.

(b)   Disclosure by Groups, Committees, and Entities.

(1)   In a chapter 9 or 11 case, a verified statement setting forth the information specified in subdivision (c) of this rule shall be filed by every group or committee that consists of or represents, and every entity that represents, multiple creditors or equity security holders that are (A) acting in concert to advance their common interests, and (B) not composed entirely of affiliates or insiders of one another.

(2)   Unless the court orders otherwise, an entity is not required to file the verified statement described in paragraph (1) of this subdivision solely because of its status as:

(A)   an indenture trustee;

(B)   an agent for one or more other entities under an agreement for the extension of credit;

(C)   a class action representative; or

(D)   a governmental unit that is not a person.

(c)   Information Required.

The verified statement shall include:

(1)   the pertinent facts and circumstances concerning:

(A)   with respect to a group or committee, other than a committee appointed under § 1102 or § 1114 of the Code, the formation of the group or committee, including the name of each entity at whose instance the group or committee was formed or for whom the group or committee has agreed to act; or

(B)   with respect to an entity, the employment of the entity, including the name of each creditor or equity security holder at whose instance the employment was arranged;

(2)   if not disclosed under subdivision (c)(1), with respect to an entity, and with respect to each member of a group or committee:

(A)   name and address;

(B)   the nature and amount of each disclosable economic interest held in relation to the debtor as of the date the entity was employed or the group or committee was formed; and

(C)   with respect to each member of a group or committee that claims to represent any entity in addition to the members of the group or committee, other than a committee appointed under § 1102 or § 1114 of the Code, the date of acquisition by quarter and year of each disclosable economic interest, unless acquired more than one year before the petition was filed;

(3)   if not disclosed under subdivision (c)(1) or (c)(2), with respect to each creditor or equity security holder represented by an entity, group, or committee, other than a committee appointed under § 1102 or § 1114 of the Code:

(A)   name and address; and

(B)   the nature and amount of each disclosable economic interest held in relation to the debtor as of the date of the statement; and

(4)   a copy of the instrument, if any, authorizing the entity, group, or committee to act on behalf of creditors or equity security holders.

(d)   Supplemental Statements.

If any fact disclosed in its most recently filed statement has changed materially, an entity, group, or committee shall file a verified supplemental statement whenever it takes a position before the court or solicits votes on the confirmation of a plan. The supplemental statement shall set forth the material changes in the facts required by subdivision (c) to be disclosed.

(e)   Determination of Failure to Comply; Sanctions.

(1)   On motion of any party in interest, or on its own motion, the court may determine whether there has been a failure to comply with any provision of this rule.

(2)   If the court finds such a failure to comply, it may:

(A)   refuse to permit the entity, group, or committee to be heard or to intervene in the case;

(B)   hold invalid any authority, acceptance, rejection, or objection given, procured, or received by the entity, group, or committee; or

(C)   grant other appropriate relief.

(As amended Mar. 30, 1987, eff. Aug. 1, 1987; Apr. 30, 1991, eff. Aug. 1, 1991; Apr. 26, 2011, eff. Dec. 1, 2011.)

Rule 2020.   Review of Acts by United States Trustee

A proceeding to contest any act or failure to act by the United States trustee is governed by Rule 9014.

(Added Apr. 30, 1991, eff. Aug. 1, 1991.)

PART III

CLAIMS AND DISTRIBUTION TO CREDITORS AND EQUITY INTEREST HOLDERS; PLANS

Rule 3001.　　Proof of Claim

(a)　Form and Content.

A proof of claim is a written statement setting forth a creditor's claim. A proof of claim shall conform substantially to the appropriate Official Form.

(b)　Who May Execute.

A proof of claim shall be executed by the creditor or the creditor's authorized agent except as provided in Rules 3004 and 3005.

(c)　Supporting Information.

(1)　Claim Based on a Writing.

Except for a claim governed by paragraph (3) of this subdivision, when a claim, or an interest in property of the debtor securing the claim, is based on a writing, a copy of the writing shall be filed with the proof of claim. If the writing has been lost or destroyed, a statement of the circumstances of the loss or destruction shall be filed with the claim.

(2)　Additional Requirements in an Individual Debtor Case; Sanctions for Failure to Comply.

In a case in which the debtor is an individual:

(A)　If, in addition to its principal amount, a claim includes interest, fees, expenses, or other charges incurred before the petition was filed, an itemized statement of the interest, fees, expenses, or charges shall be filed with the proof of claim.

(B)　If a security interest is claimed in the debtor's property, a statement of the amount necessary to cure any default as of the date of the petition shall be filed with the proof of claim.

(C)　If a security interest is claimed in property that is the debtor's principal residence, the attachment prescribed by the appropriate Official Form shall be filed with the proof of claim. If an escrow account has been established in connection with the claim, an escrow account statement prepared as of the date the petition was filed and in a form consistent with applicable nonbankruptcy law shall be filed with the attachment to the proof of claim.

(D)　If the holder of a claim fails to provide any information required by this subdivision (c), the court may, after notice and hearing, take either or both of the following actions:

(i)　preclude the holder from presenting the omitted information, in any form, as evidence in any contested matter or adversary proceeding in the case, unless the court determines that the failure was substantially justified or is harmless; or

(ii)　award other appropriate relief, including reasonable expenses and attorney's fees caused by the failure.

(3)　Claim Based on an Open-End or Revolving Consumer Credit Agreement.

(A)　When a claim is based on an open-end or revolving consumer credit agreement—except one for which a security interest is claimed in the debtor's real property—a statement shall be filed with the proof of claim, including all of the following information that applies to the account:

(i)　the name of the entity from whom the creditor purchased the account;

2412

(ii) the name of the entity to whom the debt was owed at the time of an account holder's last transaction on the account;

(iii) the date of an account holder's last transaction;

(iv) the date of the last payment on the account; and

(v) the date on which the account was charged to profit and loss.

(B) On written request by a party in interest, the holder of a claim based on an open-end or revolving consumer credit agreement shall, within 30 days after the request is sent, provide the requesting party a copy of the writing specified in paragraph (1) of this subdivision.

(d) Evidence of Perfection of Security Interest.

If a security interest in property of the debtor is claimed, the proof of claim shall be accompanied by evidence that the security interest has been perfected.

(e) Transferred Claim.

(1) Transfer of Claim Other Than for Security Before Proof Filed.

If a claim has been transferred other than for security before proof of the claim has been filed, the proof of claim may be filed only by the transferee or an indenture trustee.

(2) Transfer of Claim Other Than for Security After Proof Filed.

If a claim other than one based on a publicly traded note, bond, or debenture has been transferred other than for security after the proof of claim has been filed, evidence of the transfer shall be filed by the transferee. The clerk shall immediately notify the alleged transferor by mail of the filing of the evidence of transfer and that objection thereto, if any, must be filed within 21 days of the mailing of the notice or within any additional time allowed by the court. If the alleged transferor files a timely objection and the court finds, after notice and a hearing, that the claim has been transferred other than for security, it shall enter an order substituting the transferee for the transferor. If a timely objection is not filed by the alleged transferor, the transferee shall be substituted for the transferor.

(3) Transfer of Claim for Security Before Proof Filed.

If a claim other than one based on a publicly traded note, bond, or debenture has been transferred for security before proof of the claim has been filed, the transferor or transferee or both may file a proof of claim for the full amount. The proof shall be supported by a statement setting forth the terms of the transfer. If either the transferor or the transferee files a proof of claim, the clerk shall immediately notify the other by mail of the right to join in the filed claim. If both transferor and transferee file proofs of the same claim, the proofs shall be consolidated. If the transferor or transferee does not file an agreement regarding its relative rights respecting voting of the claim, payment of dividends thereon, or participation in the administration of the estate, on motion by a party in interest and after notice and a hearing, the court shall enter such orders respecting these matters as may be appropriate.

(4) Transfer of Claim for Security after Proof Filed.

If a claim other than one based on a publicly traded note, bond, or debenture has been transferred for security after the proof of claim has been filed, evidence of the terms of the transfer shall be filed by the transferee. The clerk shall immediately notify the alleged transferor by mail of the filing of the evidence of transfer and that objection thereto, if any, must be filed within 21 days of the mailing of the notice or within any additional time allowed by the court. If a timely objection is filed by the alleged transferor, the court, after notice and a hearing, shall determine whether the claim has been transferred for security. If the transferor or transferee does not file an agreement regarding its relative rights respecting voting of the claim, payment of dividends thereon, or participation in the administration of the estate, on motion by a party in interest and after notice and a hearing, the court shall enter such orders respecting these matters as may be appropriate.

(5)   Service of Objection or Motion; Notice of Hearing.

A copy of an objection filed pursuant to paragraph (2) or (4) or a motion filed pursuant to paragraph (3) or (4) of this subdivision together with a notice of a hearing shall be mailed or otherwise delivered to the transferor or transferee, whichever is appropriate, at least 30 days prior to the hearing.

(f)   Evidentiary Effect.

A proof of claim executed and filed in accordance with these rules shall constitute prima facie evidence of the validity and amount of the claim.

(g)[1] To the extent not inconsistent with the United States Warehouse Act or applicable State law, a warehouse receipt, scale ticket, or similar document of the type routinely issued as evidence of title by a grain storage facility, as defined in section 557 of title 11, shall constitute prima facie evidence of the validity and amount of a claim of ownership of a quantity of grain.

(As amended Pub.L. 98–353, Title III, § 354, July 10, 1984, 98 Stat. 361; Apr. 30, 1991, eff. Aug. 1, 1991; Mar. 26, 2009, eff. Dec. 1, 2009; Apr. 26, 2011, eff. Dec. 1, 2011; Apr. 23, 2012, eff. Dec. 1, 2012.)

Rule 3002.   Filing Proof of Claim or Interest

(a)   Necessity for Filing.

An unsecured creditor or an equity security holder must file a proof of claim or interest for the claim or interest to be allowed, except as provided in Rules 1019(3), 3003, 3004, and 3005.

(b)   Place of Filing.

A proof of claim or interest shall be filed in accordance with Rule 5005.

(c)   Time for Filing.

In a chapter 7 liquidation, chapter 12 family farmer's debt adjustment, or chapter 13 individual's debt adjustment case, a proof of claim is timely filed if it is filed not later than 90 days after the first date set for the meeting of creditors called under § 341(a) of the Code, except as follows:

(1)   A proof of claim filed by a governmental unit, other than for a claim resulting from a tax return filed under § 1308, is timely filed if it is filed not later than 180 days after the date of the order for relief. A proof of claim filed by a governmental unit for a claim resulting from a tax return filed under § 1308 is timely filed if it is filed no later than 180 days after the date of the order for relief or 60 days after the date of the filing of the tax return. The court may, for cause, enlarge the time for a governmental unit to file a proof of claim only upon motion of the governmental unit made before expiration of the period for filing a timely proof of claim.

(2)   In the interest of justice and if it will not unduly delay the administration of the case, the court may extend the time for filing a proof of claim by an infant or incompetent person or the representative of either.

(3)   An unsecured claim which arises in favor of an entity or becomes allowable as a result of a judgment may be filed within 30 days after the judgment becomes final if the judgment is for the recovery of money or property from that entity or denies or avoids the entity's interest in property. If the judgment imposes a liability which is not satisfied, or a duty which is not performed within such period or such further time as the court may permit, the claim shall not be allowed.

(4)   A claim arising from the rejection of an executory contract or unexpired lease of the debtor may be filed within such time as the court may direct.

(5)   If notice of insufficient assets to pay a dividend was given to creditors under Rule 2002(e), and subsequently the trustee notifies the court that payment of a dividend appears possible, the clerk shall give at least 90 days' notice by mail to creditors of that fact and of the date by which proofs of claim must be filed.

---

[1]   So in original. Subsec. (g) enacted without a catchline.

(6)   If notice of the time to file a proof of claim has been mailed to a creditor at a foreign address, on motion filed by the creditor before or after the expiration of the time, the court may extend the time by not more than 60 days if the court finds that the notice was insufficient under the circumstances to give the creditor a reasonable time to file a proof of claim.

(As amended Mar. 30, 1987, eff. Aug. 1, 1987; Apr. 30, 1991, eff. Aug. 1, 1991; Apr. 23, 1996, eff. Dec. 1, 1996; Apr. 23, 2008, eff. Dec. 1, 2008.)

Rule 3002.1.   Notice Relating to Claims Secured by Security Interest in the Debtor's Principal Residence

(a)   In General.

This rule applies in a chapter 13 case to claims that are (1) secured by a security interest in the debtor's principal residence, and (2) provided for under § 1322(b)(5) of the Code in the debtor's plan.

(b)   Notice of Payment Changes.

The holder of the claim shall file and serve on the debtor, debtor's counsel, and the trustee a notice of any change in the payment amount, including any change that results from an interest rate or escrow account adjustment, no later than 21 days before a payment in the new amount is due.

(c)   Notice of Fees, Expenses, and Charges.

The holder of the claim shall file and serve on the debtor, debtor's counsel, and the trustee a notice itemizing all fees, expenses, or charges (1) that were incurred in connection with the claim after the bankruptcy case was filed, and (2) that the holder asserts are recoverable against the debtor or against the debtor's principal residence. The notice shall be served within 180 days after the date on which the fees, expenses, or charges are incurred.

(d)   Form and Content.

A notice filed and served under subdivision (b) or (c) of this rule shall be prepared as prescribed by the appropriate Official Form, and filed as a supplement to the holder's proof of claim. The notice is not subject to Rule 3001(f).

(e)   Determination of Fees, Expenses, or Charges.

On motion of the debtor or trustee filed within one year after service of a notice under subdivision (c) of this rule, the court shall, after notice and hearing, determine whether payment of any claimed fee, expense, or charge is required by the underlying agreement and applicable nonbankruptcy law to cure a default or maintain payments in accordance with § 1322(b)(5) of the Code.

(f)   Notice of Final Cure Payment.

Within 30 days after the debtor completes all payments under the plan, the trustee shall file and serve on the holder of the claim, the debtor, and debtor's counsel a notice stating that the debtor has paid in full the amount required to cure any default on the claim. The notice shall also inform the holder of its obligation to file and serve a response under subdivision (g). If the debtor contends that final cure payment has been made and all plan payments have been completed, and the trustee does not timely file and serve the notice required by this subdivision, the debtor may file and serve the notice.

(g)   Response to Notice of Final Cure Payment.

Within 21 days after service of the notice under subdivision (f) of this rule, the holder shall file and serve on the debtor, debtor's counsel, and the trustee a statement indicating (1) whether it agrees that the debtor has paid in full the amount required to cure the default on the claim, and (2) whether the debtor is otherwise current on all payments consistent with § 1322(b)(5) of the Code. The statement shall itemize the required cure or postpetition amounts, if any, that the holder contends remain unpaid as of the date of the statement. The statement shall be filed as a supplement to the holder's proof of claim and is not subject to Rule 3001(f).

(h)   Determination of Final Cure and Payment.

On motion of the debtor or trustee filed within 21 days after service of the statement under subdivision (g) of this rule, the court shall, after notice and hearing, determine whether the debtor has cured the default and paid all required postpetition amounts.

(i)   Failure to Notify.

If the holder of a claim fails to provide any information as required by subdivision (b), (c), or (g) of this rule, the court may, after notice and hearing, take either or both of the following actions:

> **(1)**   preclude the holder from presenting the omitted information, in any form, as evidence in any contested matter or adversary proceeding in the case, unless the court determines that the failure was substantially justified or is harmless; or

> **(2)**   award other appropriate relief, including reasonable expenses and attorney's fees caused by the failure.

(Adopted Apr. 26, 2011, eff. Dec. 1, 2011.)

Rule 3003.   Filing Proof of Claim or Equity Security Interest in Chapter 9 Municipality or Chapter 11 Reorganization Cases

(a)   Applicability of Rule.

This rule applies in chapter 9 and 11 cases.

(b)   Schedule of Liabilities and List of Equity Security Holders.

(1)   Schedule of Liabilities.

The schedule of liabilities filed pursuant to § 521(1) of the Code shall constitute prima facie evidence of the validity and amount of the claims of creditors, unless they are scheduled as disputed, contingent, or unliquidated. It shall not be necessary for a creditor or equity security holder to file a proof of claim or interest except as provided in subdivision (c)(2) of this rule.

(2)   List of Equity Security Holders.

The list of equity security holders filed pursuant to Rule 1007(a)(3) shall constitute prima facie evidence of the validity and amount of the equity security interests and it shall not be necessary for the holders of such interests to file a proof of interest.

(c)   Filing Proof of Claim.

(1)   Who May File.

Any creditor or indenture trustee may file a proof of claim within the time prescribed by subdivision (c)(3) of this rule.

(2)   Who Must File.

Any creditor or equity security holder whose claim or interest is not scheduled or scheduled as disputed, contingent, or unliquidated shall file a proof of claim or interest within the time prescribed by subdivision (c)(3) of this rule; any creditor who fails to do so shall not be treated as a creditor with respect to such claim for the purposes of voting and distribution.

(3)   Time for Filing.

The court shall fix and for cause shown may extend the time within which proofs of claim or interest may be filed. Notwithstanding the expiration of such time, a proof of claim may be filed to the extent and under the conditions stated in Rule 3002(c)(2), (c)(3), (c)(4), and (c)(6).

(4)   Effect of Filing Claim or Interest.

A proof of claim or interest executed and filed in accordance with this subdivision shall supersede any scheduling of that claim or interest pursuant to § 521(a)(1) of the Code.

(5)   Filing by Indenture Trustee.

An indenture trustee may file a claim on behalf of all known or unknown holders of securities issued pursuant to the trust instrument under which it is trustee.

(d)   Proof of Right to Record Status.

For the purposes of Rules 3017, 3018 and 3021 and for receiving notices, an entity who is not the record holder of a security may file a statement setting forth facts which entitle that entity to be treated as the record holder. An objection to the statement may be filed by any party in interest.

(As amended Mar. 30, 1987, eff. Aug. 1, 1987; Apr. 30, 1991, eff. Aug. 1, 1991; Apr. 23, 2008, eff. Dec. 1, 2008.)

Rule 3004.   Filing of Claims by Debtor or Trustee

If a creditor does not timely file a proof of claim under Rule 3002(c) or 3003(c), the debtor or trustee may file a proof of the claim within 30 days after the expiration of the time for filing claims prescribed by Rule 3002(c) or 3003(c), whichever is applicable. The clerk shall forthwith give notice of the filing to the creditor, the debtor and the trustee.

(As amended Mar. 30, 1987, eff. Aug. 1, 1987; Apr. 25, 2005, eff. Dec. 1, 2005.)

Rule 3005.   Filing of Claim, Acceptance, or Rejection By Guarantor, Surety, Indorser, or Other Codebtor

(a)   Filing of Claim.

If a creditor does not timely file a proof of claim under Rule 3002(c) or 3003(c), any entity that is or may be liable with the debtor to that creditor, or who has secured that creditor, may file a proof of the claim within 30 days after the expiration of the time for filing claims prescribed by Rule 3002(c) or Rule 3003(c) whichever is applicable. No distribution shall be made on the claim except on satisfactory proof that the original debt will be diminished by the amount of distribution.

(b)   Filing of Acceptance or Rejection; Substitution of Creditor.

An entity which has filed a claim pursuant to the first sentence of subdivision (a) of this rule may file an acceptance or rejection of a plan in the name of the creditor, if known, or if unknown, in the entity's own name but if the creditor files a proof of claim within the time permitted by Rule 3003(c) or files a notice prior to confirmation of a plan of the creditor's intention to act in the creditor's own behalf, the creditor shall be substituted for the obligor with respect to that claim.

(As amended Mar. 30, 1987, eff. Aug. 1, 1987; Apr. 30, 1991, eff. Aug. 1, 1991; Apr. 25, 2005, eff. Dec. 1, 2005.)

Rule 3006.   Withdrawal of Claim; Effect on Acceptance or Rejection of Plan

A creditor may withdraw a claim as of right by filing a notice of withdrawal, except as provided in this rule. If after a creditor has filed a proof of claim an objection is filed thereto or a complaint is filed against that creditor in an adversary proceeding, or the creditor has accepted or rejected the plan or otherwise has participated significantly in the case, the creditor may not withdraw the claim except on order of the court after a hearing on notice to the trustee or debtor in possession, and any creditors' committee elected pursuant to § 705(a) or appointed pursuant to § 1102 of the Code. The order of the court shall contain such terms and conditions as the court deems proper. Unless the court orders otherwise, an authorized withdrawal of a claim shall constitute withdrawal of any related acceptance or rejection of a plan.

(As amended Apr. 30, 1991, eff. Aug. 1, 1991.)

Rule 3007.   Objections to Claims

(a)   Objections to Claims.

An objection to the allowance of a claim shall be in writing and filed. A copy of the objection with notice of the hearing thereon shall be mailed or otherwise delivered to the claimant, the debtor or debtor in possession, and the trustee at least 30 days prior to the hearing.

(b)   Demand for Relief Requiring an Adversary Proceeding.

A party in interest shall not include a demand for relief of a kind specified in Rule 7001 in an objection to the allowance of a claim, but may include the objection in an adversary proceeding.

(c)   Limitation on Joinder of Claims Objections.

Unless otherwise ordered by the court or permitted by subdivision (d), objections to more than one claim shall not be joined in a single objection.

(d)   Omnibus Objection.

Subject to subdivision (e), objections to more than one claim may be joined in an omnibus objection if all the claims were filed by the same entity, or the objections are based solely on the grounds that the claims should be disallowed, in whole or in part, because:

(1)   they duplicate other claims;

(2)   they have been filed in the wrong case;

(3)   they have been amended by subsequently filed proofs of claim;

(4)   they were not timely filed;

(5)   they have been satisfied or released during the case in accordance with the Code, applicable rules, or a court order;

(6)   they were presented in a form that does not comply with applicable rules, and the objection states that the objector is unable to determine the validity of the claim because of the noncompliance;

(7)   they are interests, rather than claims; or

(8)   they assert priority in an amount that exceeds the maximum amount under § 507 of the Code.

(e)   Requirements For Omnibus Objection.

An omnibus objection shall:

(1)   state in a conspicuous place that claimants receiving the objection should locate their names and claims in the objection;

(2)   list claimants alphabetically, provide a cross-reference to claim numbers, and, if appropriate, list claimants by category of claims;

(3)   state the grounds of the objection to each claim and provide a cross-reference to the pages in the omnibus objection pertinent to the stated grounds;

(4)   state in the title the identity of the objector and the grounds for the objections;

(5)   be numbered consecutively with other omnibus objections filed by the same objector; and

(6)   contain objections to no more than 100 claims.

(f)   Finality of Objection.

The finality of any order regarding a claim objection included in an omnibus objection shall be determined as though the claim had been subject to an individual objection.

(As amended Apr. 30, 1991, eff. Aug. 1, 1991; Apr. 30, 2007, eff. Dec. 1, 2007.)

Rule 3008.   Reconsideration of Claims

A party in interest may move for reconsideration of an order allowing or disallowing a claim against the estate. The court after a hearing on notice shall enter an appropriate order.

Rule 3009.   Declaration and Payment of Dividends in a Chapter 7 Liquidation Case

In a chapter 7 case, dividends to creditors shall be paid as promptly as practicable. Dividend checks shall be made payable to and mailed to each creditor whose claim has been allowed, unless a power of attorney authorizing another entity to receive dividends has been executed and filed in accordance with Rule 9010. In that event, dividend checks shall be made payable to the creditor and to the other entity and shall be mailed to the other entity.

(As amended Mar. 30, 1987, eff. Aug. 1, 1987; Apr. 22, 1993, eff. Aug. 1, 1993.)

Rule 3010.   Small Dividends and Payments in Chapter 7 Liquidation, Chapter 12 Family Farmer's Debt Adjustment, and Chapter 13 Individual's Debt Adjustment Cases

(a)   Chapter 7 Cases.

In a chapter 7 case no dividend in an amount less than $5 shall be distributed by the trustee to any creditor unless authorized by local rule or order of the court. Any dividend not distributed to a creditor shall be treated in the same manner as unclaimed funds as provided in § 347 of the Code.

(b)   Chapter 12 and Chapter 13 Cases.

In a chapter 12 or chapter 13 case no payment in an amount less than $15 shall be distributed by the trustee to any creditor unless authorized by local rule or order of the court. Funds not distributed because of this subdivision shall accumulate and shall be paid whenever the accumulation aggregates $15. Any funds remaining shall be distributed with the final payment.

(As amended Mar. 30, 1987, eff. Aug. 1, 1987; Apr. 30, 1991, eff. Aug. 1, 1991.)

Rule 3011.   Unclaimed Funds in Chapter 7 Liquidation, Chapter 12 Family Farmer's Debt Adjustment, and Chapter 13 Individual's Debt Adjustment Cases

The trustee shall file a list of all known names and addresses of the entities and the amounts which they are entitled to be paid from remaining property of the estate that is paid into court pursuant to § 347(a) of the Code.

(As amended Mar. 30, 1987, eff. Aug. 1, 1987; Apr. 30, 1991, eff. Aug. 1, 1991.)

Rule 3012.   Valuation of Security

The court may determine the value of a claim secured by a lien on property in which the estate has an interest on motion of any party in interest and after a hearing on notice to the holder of the secured claim and any other entity as the court may direct.

(As amended Mar. 30, 1987, eff. Aug. 1, 1987.)

Rule 3013.   Classification of Claims and Interests

For the purposes of the plan and its acceptance, the court may, on motion after hearing on notice as the court may direct, determine classes of creditors and equity security holders pursuant to §§ 1122, 1222(b)(1), and 1322(b)(1) of the Code.

(As amended Apr. 30, 1991, eff. Aug. 1, 1991.)

Rule 3014.   Election Under § 1111(b) by Secured Creditor in Chapter 9 Municipality or Chapter 11 Reorganization Case

An election of application of § 1111(b)(2) of the Code by a class of secured creditors in a chapter 9 or 11 case may be made at any time prior to the conclusion of the hearing on the disclosure statement or within such later time as the court may fix. If the disclosure statement is conditionally approved pursuant to Rule 3017.1, and a final hearing on the disclosure statement is not held, the election of application of § 1111(b)(2) may be made not later than the date fixed pursuant to Rule 3017.1(a)(2) or another date the court may fix. The election shall be in writing and signed unless made at the hearing on the disclosure statement. The election, if made by the majorities required by § 1111(b)(1)(A)(i), shall be binding on all members of the class with respect to the plan.

(As amended Apr. 11, 1997, eff. Dec. 1, 1997)

Rule 3015.   Filing, Objection to Confirmation, and Modification of a Plan in a Chapter 12 Family Farmer's Debt Adjustment or a Chapter 13 Individual's Debt Adjustment Case

(a)   Chapter 12 Plan.

The debtor may file a chapter 12 plan with the petition. If a plan is not filed with the petition, it shall be filed within the time prescribed by § 1221 of the Code.

(b)   Chapter 13 Plan.

The debtor may file a chapter 13 plan with the petition. If a plan is not filed with the petition, it shall be filed within 14 days thereafter, and such time may not be further extended except for cause shown and on notice as the court may direct. If a case is converted to chapter 13, a plan shall be filed within 14 days thereafter, and such time may not be further extended except for cause shown and on notice as the court may direct.

(c)   Dating.

Every proposed plan and any modification thereof shall be dated.

(d)   Notice and Copies.

The plan or a summary of the plan shall be included with each notice of the hearing on confirmation mailed pursuant to Rule 2002. If required by the court, the debtor shall furnish a sufficient number of copies to enable the clerk to include a copy of the plan with the notice of the hearing.

(e)   Transmission to United States Trustee.

The clerk shall forthwith transmit to the United States trustee a copy of the plan and any modification thereof filed pursuant to subdivision (a) or (b) of this rule.

(f)   Objection to Confirmation; Determination of Good Faith in the Absence of an Objection.

An objection to confirmation of a plan shall be filed and served on the debtor, the trustee, and any other entity designated by the court, and shall be transmitted to the United States trustee, before confirmation of the plan. An objection to confirmation is governed by Rule 9014. If no objection is timely filed, the court may determine that the plan has been proposed in good faith and not by any means forbidden by law without receiving evidence on such issues.

(g)   Modification of Plan After Confirmation.

A request to modify a plan pursuant to § 1229 or § 1329 of the Code shall identify the proponent and shall be filed together with the proposed modification. The clerk, or some other person as the court may direct, shall give the debtor, the trustee, and all creditors not less than 21 days' notice by mail of the time fixed for filing objections and, if an objection is filed, the hearing to consider the proposed modification, unless the court orders otherwise with respect to creditors who are not affected by the proposed modification. A copy of the notice shall be transmitted to the United States trustee. A copy of the proposed modification, or a summary thereof, shall be included with the notice. If required by the court, the proponent shall furnish a sufficient number of copies of the proposed modification, or a summary thereof, to enable the clerk to include a copy with each notice. Any objection to the proposed modification shall be filed and served on the debtor, the trustee, and any other entity designated by the court, and shall be transmitted to the United States trustee. An objection to a proposed modification is governed by Rule 9014.

(As amended Apr. 30, 1991, eff. Aug. 1, 1991; Apr. 22, 1993, eff. Aug. 1, 1993; Mar. 26, 2009, eff. Dec. 1, 2009.)

Rule 3016.   Filing of Plan and Disclosure Statement in a Chapter 9 Municipality or Chapter 11 Reorganization Case

(a)   Identification of Plan.

Every proposed plan and any modification thereof shall be dated and, in a chapter 11 case, identified with the name of the entity or entities submitting or filing it.

(b)   Disclosure Statement.

In a chapter 9 or 11 case, a disclosure statement under § 1125 of the Code or evidence showing compliance with § 1126(b) shall be filed with the plan or within a time fixed by the court, unless the plan is intended to provide adequate information under § 1125(f)(1). If the plan is intended to provide adequate information under § 1125(f)(1), it shall be so designated and Rule 3017.1 shall apply as if the plan is a disclosure statement.

(c)   Injunction Under a Plan.

If a plan provides for an injunction against conduct not otherwise enjoined under the Code, the plan and disclosure statement shall describe in specific and conspicuous language (bold, italic, or underlined text) all acts to be enjoined and identify the entities that would be subject to the injunction.

(d)   Standard Form Small Business Disclosure Statement and Plan.

In a small business case, the court may approve a disclosure statement and may confirm a plan that conform substantially to the appropriate Official Forms or other standard forms approved by the court.

(As amended Mar. 30, 1987, eff. Aug. 1, 1987; Apr. 30, 1991, eff. Aug. 1, 1991; Apr. 23, 1996, eff. Dec. 1, 1996; Apr. 23, 2001, eff. Dec. 1, 2001; Apr. 23, 2008, eff. Dec. 1, 2008.)

Rule 3017.   Court Consideration of Disclosure Statement in a Chapter 9 Municipality or Chapter 11 Reorganization Case

(a)   Hearing on Disclosure Statement and Objections.

Except as provided in Rule 3017.1, after a disclosure statement is filed in accordance with Rule 3016(b), the court shall hold a hearing on at least 28 days' notice to the debtor, creditors, equity security holders and other parties in interest as provided in Rule 2002 to consider the disclosure statement and any objections or modifications thereto. The plan and the disclosure statement shall be mailed with the notice of the hearing only to the debtor, any trustee or committee appointed under the Code, the Securities and Exchange Commission and any party in interest who requests in writing a copy of the statement or plan. Objections to the disclosure statement shall be filed and served on the debtor, the trustee, any committee appointed under the Code, and any other entity designated by the court, at any time before the disclosure statement is approved or by an earlier date as the court may fix. In a chapter 11 reorganization case, every notice, plan, disclosure statement, and objection required to be served or mailed pursuant to this subdivision shall be transmitted to the United States trustee within the time provided in this subdivision.

(b)   Determination on Disclosure Statement.

Following the hearing the court shall determine whether the disclosure statement should be approved.

(c)   Dates Fixed for Voting on Plan and Confirmation.

On or before approval of the disclosure statement, the court shall fix a time within which the holders of claims and interests may accept or reject the plan and may fix a date for the hearing on confirmation.

(d)   Transmission and Notice to United States Trustee, Creditors and Equity Security Holders.

Upon approval of a disclosure statement,—[1] except to the extent that the court orders otherwise with respect to one or more unimpaired classes of creditors or equity security holders—the debtor in possession, trustee, proponent of the plan, or clerk as the court orders shall mail to all creditors and equity security holders, and in a chapter 11 reorganization case shall transmit to the United States trustee,

(1)   the plan or a court-approved summary of the plan;

(2)   the disclosure statement approved by the court;

(3)   notice of the time within which acceptances and rejections of the plan may be filed; and

(4)   any other information as the court may direct, including any court opinion approving the disclosure statement or a court-approved summary of the opinion.

In addition, notice of the time fixed for filing objections and the hearing on confirmation shall be mailed to all creditors and equity security holders in accordance with Rule 2002(b), and a form of ballot conforming to the appropriate Official Form shall be mailed to creditors and equity security holders entitled to vote on the plan. If the court opinion is not transmitted or only a summary of the plan is transmitted, the court opinion or the plan shall be provided on request of a party in interest at the plan proponent's expense. If the court orders that the disclosure statement and the plan or a summary of the plan shall not be mailed to any unimpaired class, notice that the class is designated in the plan as unimpaired and notice of the name and address of the person from whom the plan or summary of the plan and disclosure statement may be obtained upon request and at the plan proponent's expense, shall be mailed to members of the unimpaired class together with the notice of the time fixed for filing objections to and the hearing on confirmation. For the purposes of this subdivision, creditors and equity security holders shall include holders of stock, bonds, debentures, notes, and other securities of record on the date the order approving the disclosure statement is entered or another date fixed by the court, for cause, after notice and a hearing.

(e)   Transmission to Beneficial Holders of Securities.

At the hearing held pursuant to subdivision (a) of this rule, the court shall consider the procedures for transmitting the documents and information required by subdivision (d) of this rule to beneficial holders of stock, bonds, debentures, notes, and other securities, determine the adequacy of the procedures, and enter any orders the court deems appropriate.

(f)   Notice and Transmission of Documents to Entities Subject to an Injunction Under a Plan.

If a plan provides for an injunction against conduct not otherwise enjoined under the Code and an entity that would be subject to the injunction is not a creditor or equity security holder, at the hearing held under Rule 3017(a), the court shall consider procedures for providing the entity with:

(1)   at least 28 days' notice of the time fixed for filing objections and the hearing on confirmation of the plan containing the information described in Rule 2002(c)(3); and

(2)   to the extent feasible, a copy of the plan and disclosure statement.

(As amended Mar. 30, 1987, eff. Aug. 1, 1987; Apr. 30, 1991, eff. Aug. 1, 1991; Apr. 11, 1997, eff. Dec. 1, 1997; Apr. 23, 2001, eff. Dec. 1, 2001; Mar. 26, 2009, eff. Dec. 1, 2009.)

---

[1]   So in original. The comma probably should not appear.

Rule 3017.1.   Court Consideration of Disclosure Statement in a Small Business Case

(a)   Conditional Approval of Disclosure Statement.

In a small business case, the court may, on application of the plan proponent or on its own initiative, conditionally approve a disclosure statement filed in accordance with Rule 3016. On or before conditional approval of the disclosure statement, the court shall:

(1)   fix a time within which the holders of claims and interests may accept or reject the plan;

(2)   fix a time for filing objections to the disclosure statement;

(3)   fix a date for the hearing on final approval of the disclosure statement to be held if a timely objection is filed; and

(4)   fix a date for the hearing on confirmation.

(b)   Application of Rule 3017.

Rule 3017(a), (b), (c), and (e) do not apply to a conditionally approved disclosure statement. Rule 3017(d) applies to a conditionally approved disclosure statement, except that conditional approval is considered approval of the disclosure statement for the purpose of applying Rule 3017(d).

(c)   Final Approval.

(1)   Notice.

Notice of the time fixed for filing objections and the hearing to consider final approval of the disclosure statement shall be given in accordance with Rule 2002 and may be combined with notice of the hearing on confirmation of the plan.

(2)   Objections.

Objections to the disclosure statement shall be filed, transmitted to the United States trustee, and served on the debtor, the trustee, any committee appointed under the Code and any other entity designated by the court at any time before final approval of the disclosure statement or by an earlier date as the court may fix.

(3)   Hearing.

If a timely objection to the disclosure statement is filed, the court shall hold a hearing to consider final approval before or combined with the hearing on confirmation of the plan.

(Added Apr. 11, 1997, eff. Dec. 1, 1997; amended Apr. 23, 2008, eff. Dec. 1, 2008.)

Rule 3018.   Acceptance or Rejection of Plan in a Chapter 9 Municipality or a Chapter 11 Reorganization Case

(a)   Entities Entitled to Accept or Reject Plan; Time for Acceptance or Rejection.

A plan may be accepted or rejected in accordance with § 1126 of the Code within the time fixed by the court pursuant to Rule 3017. Subject to subdivision (b) of this rule, an equity security holder or creditor whose claim is based on a security of record shall not be entitled to accept or reject a plan unless the equity security holder or creditor is the holder of record of the security on the date the order approving the disclosure statement is entered or on another date fixed by the court, for cause, after notice and a hearing. For cause shown, the court after notice and hearing may permit a creditor or equity security holder to change or withdraw an acceptance or rejection. Notwithstanding objection to a claim or interest, the court after notice and hearing may temporarily allow the claim or interest in an amount which the court deems proper for the purpose of accepting or rejecting a plan.

(b)   Acceptances or Rejections Obtained Before Petition.

An equity security holder or creditor whose claim is based on a security of record who accepted or rejected the plan before the commencement of the case shall not be deemed to have accepted or rejected the plan pursuant to § 1126(b) of the Code unless the equity security holder or creditor was the holder of record of the security on the date specified in the solicitation of such acceptance or rejection for the purposes of such solicitation. A holder of a claim or interest who has accepted or rejected a plan before the commencement of the case under the Code shall not be deemed to have accepted or rejected the plan if the court finds after notice and hearing that the plan was not transmitted to substantially all creditors and equity security holders of the same class, that an unreasonably short time was prescribed for such creditors and equity security holders to accept or reject the plan, or that the solicitation was not in compliance with § 1126(b) of the Code.

(c) Form of Acceptance or Rejection.

An acceptance or rejection shall be in writing, identify the plan or plans accepted or rejected, be signed by the creditor or equity security holder or an authorized agent, and conform to the appropriate Official Form. If more than one plan is transmitted pursuant to Rule 3017, an acceptance or rejection may be filed by each creditor or equity security holder for any number of plans transmitted and if acceptances are filed for more than one plan, the creditor or equity security holder may indicate a preference or preferences among the plans so accepted.

(d) Acceptance or Rejection by Partially Secured Creditor.

A creditor whose claim has been allowed in part as a secured claim and in part as an unsecured claim shall be entitled to accept or reject a plan in both capacities.

(As amended Mar. 30, 1987, eff. Aug. 1, 1987; Apr. 30, 1991, eff. Aug. 1, 1991; Apr. 22, 1993, eff. Aug. 1, 1993; Apr. 11, 1997, eff. Dec. 1, 1997.)

Rule 3019.   Modification of Accepted Plan in a Chapter 9 Municipality or a Chapter 11 Reorganization Case

(a) Modification of Plan Before Confirmation.

In a chapter 9 or chapter 11 case, after a plan has been accepted and before its confirmation, the proponent may file a modification of the plan. If the court finds after hearing on notice to the trustee, any committee appointed under the Code, and any other entity designated by the court that the proposed modification does not adversely change the treatment of the claim of any creditor or the interest of any equity security holder who has not accepted in writing the modification, it shall be deemed accepted by all creditors and equity security holders who have previously accepted the plan.

(b) Modification of Plan After Confirmation in Individual Debtor Case.

If the debtor is an individual, a request to modify the plan under § 1127(e) of the Code is governed by Rule 9014. The request shall identify the proponent and shall be filed together with the proposed modification. The clerk, or some other person as the court may direct, shall give the debtor, the trustee, and all creditors not less than 21 days' notice by mail of the time fixed to file objections and, if an objection is filed, the hearing to consider the proposed modification, unless the court orders otherwise with respect to creditors who are not affected by the proposed modification. A copy of the notice shall be transmitted to the United States trustee, together with a copy of the proposed modification. Any objection to the proposed modification shall be filed and served on the debtor, the proponent of the modification, the trustee, and any other entity designated by the court, and shall be transmitted to the United States trustee.

(As amended Mar. 30, 1987, eff. Aug. 1, 1987; Apr. 22, 1993, eff. Aug. 1, 1993; Apr. 23, 2008, eff. Dec. 1, 2008; Mar. 26, 2009, eff. Dec. 1, 2009.)

Rule 3020.   Deposit; Confirmation of Plan in a Chapter 9 Municipality or Chapter 11 Reorganization Case

(a) Deposit.

In a chapter 11 case, prior to entry of the order confirming the plan, the court may order the deposit with the trustee or debtor in possession of the consideration required by the plan to be distributed on confirmation. Any money deposited shall be kept in a special account established for the exclusive purpose of making the distribution.

(b)   Objection to and Hearing on Confirmation in a Chapter 9 or Chapter 11 Case.

   (1)   Objection.

   An objection to confirmation of the plan shall be filed and served on the debtor, the trustee, the proponent of the plan, any committee appointed under the Code, and any other entity designated by the court, within a time fixed by the court. Unless the case is a chapter 9 municipality case, a copy of every objection to confirmation shall be transmitted by the objecting party to the United States trustee within the time fixed for filing objections. An objection to confirmation is governed by Rule 9014.

   (2)   Hearing.

   The court shall rule on confirmation of the plan after notice and hearing as provided in Rule 2002. If no objection is timely filed, the court may determine that the plan has been proposed in good faith and not by any means forbidden by law without receiving evidence on such issues.

(c)   Order of Confirmation.

   (1)   The order of confirmation shall conform to the appropriate Official Form. If the plan provides for an injunction against conduct not otherwise enjoined under the Code, the order of confirmation shall (1) describe in reasonable detail all acts enjoined; (2) be specific in its terms regarding the injunction; and (3) identify the entities subject to the injunction.

   (2)   Notice of entry of the order of confirmation shall be mailed promptly to the debtor, the trustee, creditors, equity security holders, other parties in interest, and, if known, to any identified entity subject to an injunction provided for in the plan against conduct not otherwise enjoined under the Code.

   (3)   Except in a chapter 9 municipality case, notice of entry of the order of confirmation shall be transmitted to the United States trustee as provided in Rule 2002(k).

(d)   Retained Power.

   Notwithstanding the entry of the order of confirmation, the court may issue any other order necessary to administer the estate.

(e)   Stay of Confirmation Order.

   An order confirming a plan is stayed until the expiration of 14 days after the entry of the order, unless the court orders otherwise.

   (As amended Mar. 30, 1987, eff. Aug. 1, 1987; Apr. 30, 1991, eff. Aug. 1, 1991; Apr. 22, 1993, eff. Aug. 1, 1993; Apr. 29, 1999, eff. Dec. 1, 1999; Apr. 23, 2001, eff. Dec. 1, 2001; Mar. 26, 2009, eff. Dec. 1, 2009.)

Rule 3021.   Distribution Under Plan

Except as provided in Rule 3020(e), after a plan is confirmed, distribution shall be made to creditors whose claims have been allowed, to interest holders whose interests have not been disallowed, and to indenture trustees who have filed claims under Rule 3003(c)(5) that have been allowed. For purposes of this rule, creditors include holders of bonds, debentures, notes, and other debt securities, and interest holders include the holders of stock and other equity securities, of record at the time of commencement of distribution, unless a different time is fixed by the plan or the order confirming the plan.

   (As amended Apr. 11, 1997, eff. Dec. 1, 1997; Apr. 29, 1999, eff. Dec. 1, 1999.)

Rule 3022.   Final Decree in Chapter 11 Reorganization Case

After an estate is fully administered in a chapter 11 reorganization case, the court, on its own motion or on motion of a party in interest, shall enter a final decree closing the case.

   (As amended Mar. 30, 1987, eff. Aug. 1, 1987; Apr. 30, 1991, eff. Aug. 1, 1991.)

PART IV

THE DEBTOR: DUTIES AND BENEFITS

Rule 4001.   Relief From Automatic Stay; Prohibiting or Conditioning the Use, Sale, or Lease of Property; Use of Cash Collateral; Obtaining Credit; Agreements

(a)   Relief From Stay; Prohibiting or Conditioning the Use, Sale, or Lease of Property.

(1)   Motion.

A motion for relief from an automatic stay provided by the Code or a motion to prohibit or condition the use, sale, or lease of property pursuant to § 363(e) shall be made in accordance with Rule 9014 and shall be served on any committee elected pursuant to § 705 or appointed pursuant to § 1102 of the Code or its authorized agent, or, if the case is a chapter 9 municipality case or a chapter 11 reorganization case and no committee of unsecured creditors has been appointed pursuant to § 1102, on the creditors included on the list filed pursuant to Rule 1007(d), and on such other entities as the court may direct.

(2)   Ex Parte Relief.

Relief from a stay under § 362(a) or a request to prohibit or condition the use, sale, or lease of property pursuant to § 363(e) may be granted without prior notice only if (A) it clearly appears from specific facts shown by affidavit or by a verified motion that immediate and irreparable injury, loss, or damage will result to the movant before the adverse party or the attorney for the adverse party can be heard in opposition, and (B) the movant's attorney certifies to the court in writing the efforts, if any, which have been made to give notice and the reasons why notice should not be required. The party obtaining relief under this subdivision and § 362(f) or § 363(e) shall immediately give oral notice thereof to the trustee or debtor in possession and to the debtor and forthwith mail or otherwise transmit to such adverse party or parties a copy of the order granting relief. On two days notice to the party who obtained relief from the stay without notice or on shorter notice to that party as the court may prescribe, the adverse party may appear and move reinstatement of the stay or reconsideration of the order prohibiting or conditioning the use, sale, or lease of property. In that event, the court shall proceed expeditiously to hear and determine the motion.

(3)   Stay of Order.

An order granting a motion for relief from an automatic stay made in accordance with Rule 4001(a)(1) is stayed until the expiration of 14 days after the entry of the order, unless the court orders otherwise.

(b)   Use of Cash Collateral.

(1)   Motion; Service.

(A)   Motion.

A motion for authority to use cash collateral shall be made in accordance with Rule 9014 and shall be accompanied by a proposed form of order.

(B) Contents.

The motion shall consist of or (if the motion is more than five pages in length) begin with a concise statement of the relief requested, not to exceed five pages, that lists or summarizes, and sets out the location within the relevant documents of, all material provisions, including:

    (i) the name of each entity with an interest in the cash collateral;

    (ii) the purposes for the use of the cash collateral;

    (iii) the material terms, including duration, of the use of the cash collateral; and

    (iv) any liens, cash payments, or other adequate protection that will be provided to each entity with an interest in the cash collateral or, if no additional adequate protection is proposed, an explanation of why each entity's interest is adequately protected.

(C) Service.

The motion shall be served on: (1) any entity with an interest in the cash collateral; (2) any committee elected under § 705 or appointed under § 1102 of the Code, or its authorized agent, or, if the case is a chapter 9 municipality case or a chapter 11 reorganization case and no committee of unsecured creditors has been appointed under § 1102, the creditors included on the list filed under Rule 1007(d); and (3) any other entity that the court directs.

(2) Hearing.

The court may commence a final hearing on a motion for authorization to use cash collateral no earlier than 14 days after service of the motion. If the motion so requests, the court may conduct a preliminary hearing before such 14-day period expires, but the court may authorize the use of only that amount of cash collateral as is necessary to avoid immediate and irreparable harm to the estate pending a final hearing.

(3) Notice.

Notice of hearing pursuant to this subdivision shall be given to the parties on whom service of the motion is required by paragraph (1) of this subdivision and to such other entities as the court may direct.

(c) Obtaining Credit.

(1) Motion; Service.

(A) Motion.

A motion for authority to obtain credit shall be made in accordance with Rule 9014 and shall be accompanied by a copy of the credit agreement and a proposed form of order.

(B) Contents.

The motion shall consist of or (if the motion is more than five pages in length) begin with a concise statement of the relief requested, not to exceed five pages, that lists or summarizes, and sets out the location within the relevant documents of, all material provisions of the proposed credit agreement and form of order, including interest rate, maturity, events of default, liens, borrowing limits, and borrowing conditions. If the proposed credit agreement or form of order includes any of the provisions listed below, the concise statement shall also: briefly list or summarize each one; identify its specific location in the proposed agreement and form of order; and identify any such provision that is proposed to remain in effect if interim approval is granted, but final relief is denied, as provided under Rule 4001(c)(2). In addition, the motion shall describe the nature and extent of each provision listed below:

    (i) a grant of priority or a lien on property of the estate under § 364(c) or (d);

    (ii) the providing of adequate protection or priority for a claim that arose before the commencement of the case, including the granting of a lien on property of the estate to secure the claim, or the use of property of the estate or credit obtained under § 364 to make cash payments on account of the claim;

    (iii) a determination of the validity, enforceability, priority, or amount of a claim that arose before the commencement of the case, or of any lien securing the claim;

    (iv) a waiver or modification of Code provisions or applicable rules relating to the automatic stay;

    (v) a waiver or modification of any entity's authority or right to file a plan, seek an extension of time in which the debtor has the exclusive right to file a plan, request the use of cash collateral under § 363(c), or request authority to obtain credit under § 364;

    (vi) the establishment of deadlines for filing a plan of reorganization, for approval of a disclosure statement, for a hearing on confirmation, or for entry of a confirmation order;

    (vii) a waiver or modification of the applicability of nonbankruptcy law relating to the perfection of a lien on property of the estate, or on the foreclosure or other enforcement of the lien;

    (viii) a release, waiver, or limitation on any claim or other cause of action belonging to the estate or the trustee, including any modification of the statute of limitations or other deadline to commence an action;

    (ix) the indemnification of any entity;

    (x) a release, waiver, or limitation of any right under § 506(c); or

    (xi) the granting of a lien on any claim or cause of action arising under §§ 544, 545, 547, 548, 549, 553(b), 723(a), or 724(a).

    (C) Service.

The motion shall be served on: (1) any committee elected under § 705 or appointed under § 1102 of the Code, or its authorized agent, or, if the case is a chapter 9 municipality case or a chapter 11 reorganization case and no committee of unsecured creditors has been appointed under § 1102, on the creditors included on the list filed under Rule 1007(d); and (2) on any other entity that the court directs.

    (2) Hearing.

The court may commence a final hearing on a motion for authority to obtain credit no earlier than 14 days after service of the motion. If the motion so requests, the court may conduct a hearing before such 14-day period expires, but the court may authorize the obtaining of credit only to the extent necessary to avoid immediate and irreparable harm to the estate pending a final hearing.

    (3) Notice.

Notice of hearing pursuant to this subdivision shall be given to the parties on whom service of the motion is required by paragraph (1) of this subdivision and to such other entities as the court may direct.

    (d) Agreement Relating to Relief From the Automatic Stay, Prohibiting or Conditioning the Use, Sale, or Lease of Property, Providing Adequate Protection, Use of Cash Collateral, and Obtaining Credit.

    (1) Motion; Service.

    (A) Motion.

A motion for approval of any of the following shall be accompanied by a copy of the agreement and a proposed form of order:

(i) an agreement to provide adequate protection;

(ii) an agreement to prohibit or condition the use, sale, or lease of property;

(iii) an agreement to modify or terminate the stay provided for in § 362;

(iv) an agreement to use cash collateral; or

(v) an agreement between the debtor and an entity that has a lien or interest in property of the estate pursuant to which the entity consents to the creation of a lien senior or equal to the entity's lien or interest in such property.

(B) Contents.

The motion shall consist of or (if the motion is more than five pages in length) begin with a concise statement of the relief requested, not to exceed five pages, that lists or summarizes, and sets out the location within the relevant documents of, all material provisions of the agreement. In addition, the concise statement shall briefly list or summarize, and identify the specific location of, each provision in the proposed form of order, agreement, or other document of the type listed in subdivision (c)(1)(B). The motion shall also describe the nature and extent of each such provision.

(C) Service.

The motion shall be served on: (1) any committee elected under § 705 or appointed under § 1102 of the Code, or its authorized agent, or, if the case is a chapter 9 municipality case or a chapter 11 reorganization case and no committee of unsecured creditors has been appointed under § 1102, on the creditors included on the list filed under Rule 1007(d); and (2) on any other entity the court directs.

(2) Objection.

Notice of the motion and the time within which objections may be filed and served on the debtor in possession or trustee shall be mailed to the parties on whom service is required by paragraph (1) of this subdivision and to such other entities as the court may direct. Unless the court fixes a different time, objections may be filed within 14 days of the mailing of notice.

(3) Disposition; Hearing.

If no objection is filed, the court may enter an order approving or disapproving the agreement without conducting a hearing. If an objection is filed or if the court determines a hearing is appropriate, the court shall hold a hearing on no less than seven days' notice to the objector, the movant, the parties on whom service is required by paragraph (1) of this subdivision and such other entities as the court may direct.

(4) Agreement in Settlement of Motion.

The court may direct that the procedures prescribed in paragraphs (1), (2), and (3) of this subdivision shall not apply and the agreement may be approved without further notice if the court determines that a motion made pursuant to subdivisions (a), (b), or (c) of this rule was sufficient to afford reasonable notice of the material provisions of the agreement and opportunity for a hearing.

(As amended Mar. 30, 1987, eff. Aug. 1, 1987; Apr. 30, 1991, eff. Aug. 1, 1991; Apr. 29, 1999, eff. Dec. 1, 1999; Apr. 30, 2007, eff. Dec. 1, 2007; Mar. 26, 2009, eff. Dec. 1, 2009; Apr. 28, 2010, eff. Dec. 1, 2010.)

Rule 4002.   Duties of Debtor

(a) In General.

In addition to performing other duties prescribed by the Code and rules, the debtor shall:

(1) attend and submit to an examination at the times ordered by the court;

(2) attend the hearing on a complaint objecting to discharge and testify, if called as a witness;

(3) inform the trustee immediately in writing as to the location of real property in which the debtor has an interest and the name and address of every person holding money or property subject to the debtor's withdrawal or order if a schedule of property has not yet been filed pursuant to Rule 1007;

(4) cooperate with the trustee in the preparation of an inventory, the examination of proofs of claim, and the administration of the estate; and

(5) file a statement of any change of the debtor's address.

(b) Individual Debtor's Duty to Provide Documentation.

(1) Personal Identification.

Every individual debtor shall bring to the meeting of creditors under § 341:

(A) a picture identification issued by a governmental unit, or other personal identifying information that establishes the debtor's identity; and

(B) evidence of social-security number(s), or a written statement that such documentation does not exist.

(2) Financial Information.

Every individual debtor shall bring to the meeting of creditors under § 341, and make available to the trustee, the following documents or copies of them, or provide a written statement that the documentation does not exist or is not in the debtor's possession:

(A) evidence of current income such as the most recent payment advice;

(B) unless the trustee or the United States trustee instructs otherwise, statements for each of the debtor's depository and investment accounts, including checking, savings, and money market accounts, mutual funds and brokerage accounts for the time period that includes the date of the filing of the petition; and

(C) documentation of monthly expenses claimed by the debtor if required by § 707(b)(2)(A) or (B).

(3) Tax Return.

At least 7 days before the first date set for the meeting of creditors under § 341, the debtor shall provide to the trustee a copy of the debtor's federal income tax return for the most recent tax year ending immediately before the commencement of the case and for which a return was filed, including any attachments, or a transcript of the tax return, or provide a written statement that the documentation does not exist.

(4) Tax Returns Provided to Creditors.

If a creditor, at least 14 days before the first date set for the meeting of creditors under § 341, requests a copy of the debtor's tax return that is to be provided to the trustee under subdivision (b)(3), the debtor, at least 7 days before the first date set for the meeting of creditors under § 341, shall provide to the requesting creditor a copy of the return, including any attachments, or a transcript of the tax return, or provide a written statement that the documentation does not exist.

(5) Confidentiality of Tax Information.

The debtor's obligation to provide tax returns under Rule 4002(b)(3) and (b)(4) is subject to procedures for safeguarding the confidentiality of tax information established by the Director of the Administrative Office of the United States Courts.

(As amended Mar. 30, 1987, eff. Aug. 1, 1987; Apr. 23, 2008, eff. Dec. 1, 2008; Mar. 26, 2009, eff. Dec. 1, 2009.)

Rule 4003.   Exemptions

(a)   Claim of Exemptions.

A debtor shall list the property claimed as exempt under § 522 of the Code on the schedule of assets required to be filed by Rule 1007. If the debtor fails to claim exemptions or file the schedule within the time specified in Rule 1007, a dependent of the debtor may file the list within 30 days thereafter.

(b)   Objecting to a Claim of Exemptions.

(1)   Except as provided in paragraphs (2) and (3), a party in interest may file an objection to the list of property claimed as exempt within 30 days after the meeting of creditors held under § 341(a) is concluded or within 30 days after any amendment to the list or supplemental schedules is filed, whichever is later. The court may, for cause, extend the time for filing objections if, before the time to object expires, a party in interest files a request for an extension.

(2)   The trustee may file an objection to a claim of exemption at any time prior to one year after the closing of the case if the debtor fraudulently asserted the claim of exemption. The trustee shall deliver or mail the objection to the debtor and the debtor's attorney, and to any person filing the list of exempt property and that person's attorney.

(3)   An objection to a claim of exemption based on § 522(q) shall be filed before the closing of the case. If an exemption is first claimed after a case is reopened, an objection shall be filed before the reopened case is closed.

(4)   A copy of any objection shall be delivered or mailed to the trustee, the debtor and the debtor's attorney, and the person filing the list and that person's attorney.

(c)   Burden of Proof.

In any hearing under this rule, the objecting party has the burden of proving that the exemptions are not properly claimed. After hearing on notice, the court shall determine the issues presented by the objections.

(d)   Avoidance by Debtor of Transfers of Exempt Property.

A proceeding by the debtor to avoid a lien or other transfer of property exempt under § 522(f) of the Code shall be by motion in accordance with Rule 9014. Notwithstanding the provisions of subdivision (b), a creditor may object to a motion filed under § 522(f) by challenging the validity of the exemption asserted to be impaired by the lien.

> (As amended Mar. 30, 1987, eff. Aug. 1, 1987; Apr. 30, 1991, eff. Aug. 1, 1991; Apr. 17, 2000, eff. Dec. 1, 2000; Apr. 23, 2008, eff. Dec. 1, 2008.)

Rule 4004.   Grant or Denial of Discharge

(a)   Time for Objecting to Discharge; Notice of Time Fixed.

In a chapter 7 case, a complaint, or a motion under § 727(a)(8) or (a)(9) of the Code, objecting to the debtor's discharge shall be filed no later than 60 days after the first date set for the meeting of creditors under § 341(a). In a chapter 11 case, the complaint shall be filed no later than the first date set for the hearing on confirmation. In a chapter 13 case, a motion objecting to the debtor's discharge under § 1328(f) shall be filed no later than 60 days after the first date set for the meeting of creditors under § 341(a). At least 28 days' notice of the time so fixed shall be given to the United States trustee and all creditors as provided in Rule 2002(f) and (k) and to the trustee and the trustee's attorney.

(b)   Extension of Time.

(1)   On motion of any party in interest, after notice and hearing, the court may for cause extend the time to object to discharge. Except as provided in subdivision (b)(2), the motion shall be filed before the time has expired.

(2)   A motion to extend the time to object to discharge may be filed after the time for objection has expired and before discharge is granted if (A) the objection is based on facts that, if learned after the discharge, would provide a basis for revocation under § 727(d) of the Code, and (B) the movant did not have knowledge of those facts in time to permit an objection. The motion shall be filed promptly after the movant discovers the facts on which the objection is based.

(c)   Grant of Discharge.

(1)   In a chapter 7 case, on expiration of the times fixed for objecting to discharge and for filing a motion to dismiss the case under Rule 1017(e), the court shall forthwith grant the discharge, except that the court shall not grant the discharge if:

(A)   the debtor is not an individual;

(B)   a complaint, or a motion under § 727(a)(8) or (a)(9), objecting to the discharge has been filed and not decided in the debtor's favor;

(C)   the debtor has filed a waiver under § 727(a)(10);

(D)   a motion to dismiss the case under § 707 is pending;

(E)   a motion to extend the time for filing a complaint objecting to the discharge is pending;

(F)   a motion to extend the time for filing a motion to dismiss the case under Rule 1017(e)(1) is pending;

(G)   the debtor has not paid in full the filing fee prescribed by 28 U.S.C. § 1930(a) and any other fee prescribed by the Judicial Conference of the United States under 28 U.S.C. § 1930(b) that is payable to the clerk upon the commencement of a case under the Code, unless the court has waived the fees under 28 U.S.C. § 1930(f);

(H)   the debtor has not filed with the court a statement of completion of a course concerning personal financial management if required by Rule 1007(b)(7);

(I)   a motion to delay or postpone discharge under § 727(a)(12) is pending;

(J)   a motion to enlarge the time to file a reaffirmation agreement under Rule 4008(a) is pending;

(K)   a presumption is in effect under § 524(m) that a reaffirmation agreement is an undue hardship and the court has not concluded a hearing on the presumption; or

(L)   a motion is pending to delay discharge because the debtor has not filed with the court all tax documents required to be filed under § 521(f).

(2)   Notwithstanding Rule 4004(c)(1), on motion of the debtor, the court may defer the entry of an order granting a discharge for 30 days and, on motion within that period, the court may defer entry of the order to a date certain.

(3)   If the debtor is required to file a statement under Rule 1007(b)(8), the court shall not grant a discharge earlier than 30 days after the statement is filed.

(4)   In a chapter 11 case in which the debtor is an individual, or a chapter 13 case, the court shall not grant a discharge if the debtor has not filed any statement required by Rule 1007(b)(7).

(d)   Applicability of Rules in Part VII and Rule 9014.

An objection to discharge is governed by Part VII of these rules, except that an objection to discharge under §§ 727(a)(8), (a)(9), or 1328(f) is commenced by motion and governed by Rule 9014.

(e)   Order of Discharge.

An order of discharge shall conform to the appropriate Official Form.

(f)   Registration in Other Districts.

An order of discharge that has become final may be registered in any other district by filing a certified copy of the order in the office of the clerk of that district. When so registered the order of discharge shall have the same effect as an order of the court of the district where registered.

(g) Notice of Discharge.

The clerk shall promptly mail a copy of the final order of discharge to those specified in subdivision (a) of this rule.

(As amended Mar. 30, 1987, eff. Aug. 1, 1987; Apr. 30, 1991, eff. Aug. 1, 1991; Apr. 23, 1996, eff. Dec. 1, 1996; Apr. 29, 1999, eff. Dec. 1, 1999; Apr. 17, 2000, eff. Dec. 1, 2000; Apr. 29, 2002, eff. Dec. 1, 2002; Apr. 23, 2008, eff. Dec. 1, 2008; Mar. 26, 2009, eff. Dec. 1, 2009; Apr. 28, 2010, eff. Dec. 1, 2010; Apr. 26, 2011, eff. Dec. 1, 2011; Apr. 16, 2013, eff. Dec. 1, 2013.)

Rule 4005.   Burden of Proof in Objecting to Discharge

At the trial on a complaint objecting to a discharge, the plaintiff has the burden of proving the objection.

(As amended Mar. 30, 1987, eff. Aug. 1, 1987.)

Rule 4006.   Notice of No Discharge

If an order is entered: denying a discharge; revoking a discharge; approving a waiver of discharge; or, in the case of an individual debtor, closing the case without the entry of a discharge, the clerk shall promptly notify all parties in interest in the manner provided by Rule 2002.

(As amended Mar. 30, 1987, eff. Aug. 1, 1987; Apr. 23, 2008, eff. Dec. 1, 2008.)

Rule 4007.   Determination of Dischargeability of a Debt

(a) Persons Entitled to File Complaint.

A debtor or any creditor may file a complaint to obtain a determination of the dischargeability of any debt.

(b) Time for Commencing Proceeding Other Than Under § 523(c) of the Code.

A complaint other than under § 523(c) may be filed at any time. A case may be reopened without payment of an additional filing fee for the purpose of filing a complaint to obtain a determination under this rule.

(c) Time for Filing Complaint Under § 523(c) in a Chapter 7 Liquidation, Chapter 11 Reorganization, Chapter 12 Family Farmer's Debt Adjustment Case, or Chapter 13 Individual's Debt Adjustment Case; Notice of Time Fixed.

Except as otherwise provided in subdivision (d), a complaint to determine the dischargeability of a debt under § 523(c) shall be filed no later than 60 days after the first date set for the meeting of creditors under § 341(a). The court shall give all creditors no less than 30 days' notice of the time so fixed in the manner provided in Rule 2002. On motion of a party in interest, after hearing on notice, the court may for cause extend the time fixed under this subdivision. The motion shall be filed before the time has expired.

(d) Time for Filing Complaint Under § 523(a)(6) in a Chapter 13 Individual's Debt Adjustment Case; Notice of Time Fixed.

On motion by a debtor for a discharge under § 1328(b), the court shall enter an order fixing the time to file a complaint to determine the dischargeability of any debt under § 523(a)(6) and shall give no less than 30 days' notice of the time fixed to all creditors in the manner provided in Rule 2002. On motion of any party in interest, after hearing on notice, the court may for cause extend the time fixed under this subdivision. The motion shall be filed before the time has expired.

(e) Applicability of Rules in Part VII.

A proceeding commenced by a complaint filed under this rule is governed by Part VII of these rules.

(As amended Mar. 30, 1987, eff. Aug. 1, 1987; Apr. 30, 1991, eff. Aug. 1, 1991; Apr. 29, 1999, eff. Dec. 1, 1999; Apr. 23, 2008, eff. Dec. 1, 2008.)

Rule 4008. Filing of Reaffirmation Agreement; Statement in Support of Reaffirmation Agreement

(a) Filing of Reaffirmation Agreement.

A reaffirmation agreement shall be filed no later than 60 days after the first date set for the meeting of creditors under § 341(a) of the Code. The reaffirmation agreement shall be accompanied by a cover sheet, prepared as prescribed by the appropriate Official Form. The court may, at any time and in its discretion, enlarge the time to file a reaffirmation agreement.

(b) Statement in Support of Reaffirmation Agreement.

The debtor's statement required under § 524(k)(6)(A) of the Code shall be accompanied by a statement of the total income and expenses stated on schedules I and J. If there is a difference between the total income and expenses stated on those schedules and the statement required under § 524(k)(6)(A), the statement required by this subdivision shall include an explanation of the difference.

(As amended Apr. 30, 1991, eff. Aug. 1, 1991; Apr. 23, 2008, eff. Dec. 1, 2008; Mar. 26, 2009, eff. Dec. 1, 2009.)

PART V

COURTS AND CLERKS

5001.	Courts and Clerks' Offices.
5002.	Restrictions on Approval of Appointments.
5003.	Records Kept By the Clerk.
5004.	Disqualification.
5005.	Filing and Transmittal of Papers.
5006.	Certification of Copies of Papers.
5007.	Record of Proceedings and Transcripts.
5008.	Notice Regarding Presumption of Abuse in Chapter 7 Cases of Individual Debtors.
5009.	Closing Chapter 7 Liquidation, Chapter 12 Family Farmer's Debt Adjustment, Chapter 13 Individual's Debt Adjustment, and Chapter 15 Ancillary and Cross-Border Cases.
5010.	Reopening Cases.
5011.	Withdrawal and Abstention from Hearing a Proceeding.
5012.	Agreements Concerning Coordination of Proceedings in Chapter 15 Cases.

Rule 5001. Courts and Clerks' Offices

(a) Courts Always Open.

The courts shall be deemed always open for the purpose of filing any pleading or other proper paper, issuing and returning process, and filing, making, or entering motions, orders and rules.

(b) Trials and Hearings; Orders in Chambers.

All trials and hearings shall be conducted in open court and so far as convenient in a regular court room. Except as otherwise provided in 28 U.S.C. § 152(c), all other acts or proceedings may be done or conducted by a judge in chambers and at any place either within or without the district; but no hearing, other than one ex parte, shall be conducted outside the district without the consent of all parties affected thereby.

(c) Clerk's Office.

The clerk's office with the clerk or a deputy in attendance shall be open during business hours on all days except Saturdays, Sundays and the legal holidays listed in Rule 9006(a).

(As amended Mar. 30, 1987, eff. Aug. 1, 1987; Apr. 30, 1991, eff. Aug. 1, 1991; Apr. 23, 2008, eff. Dec. 1, 2008.)

Rule 5002.   Restrictions on Approval of Appointments

(a) Approval of Appointment of Relatives Prohibited.

The appointment of an individual as a trustee or examiner pursuant to § 1104 of the Code shall not be approved by the court if the individual is a relative of the bankruptcy judge approving the appointment or the United States trustee in the region in which the case is pending. The employment of an individual as attorney, accountant, appraiser, auctioneer, or other professional person pursuant to §§ 327, 1103, or 1114 shall not be approved by the court if the individual is a relative of the bankruptcy judge approving the employment. The employment of an individual as attorney, accountant, appraiser, auctioneer, or other professional person pursuant to §§ 327, 1103, or 1114 may be approved by the court if the individual is a relative of the United States trustee in the region in which the case is pending, unless the court finds that the relationship with the United States trustee renders the employment improper under the circumstances of the case. Whenever under this subdivision an individual may not be approved for appointment or employment, the individual's firm, partnership, corporation, or any other form of business association or relationship, and all members, associates and professional employees thereof also may not be approved for appointment or employment.

(b) Judicial Determination That Approval of Appointment or Employment Is Improper.

A bankruptcy judge may not approve the appointment of a person as a trustee or examiner pursuant to § 1104 of the Code or approve the employment of a person as an attorney, accountant, appraiser, auctioneer, or other professional person pursuant to §§ 327, 1103, or 1114 of the Code if that person is or has been so connected with such judge or the United States trustee as to render the appointment or employment improper.

(As amended Apr. 29, 1985, eff. Aug. 1, 1985; Apr. 30, 1991, eff. Aug. 1, 1991.)

Rule 5003.   Records Kept By the Clerk

(a) Bankruptcy Dockets.

The clerk shall keep a docket in each case under the Code and shall enter thereon each judgment, order, and activity in that case as prescribed by the Director of the Administrative Office of the United States Courts. The entry of a judgment or order in a docket shall show the date the entry is made.

(b) Claims Register.

The clerk shall keep in a claims register a list of claims filed in a case when it appears that there will be a distribution to unsecured creditors.

(c) Judgments and Orders.

The clerk shall keep, in the form and manner as the Director of the Administrative Office of the United States Courts may prescribe, a correct copy of every final judgment or order affecting title to or lien on real property or for the recovery of money or property, and any other order which the court may direct to be kept. On request of the prevailing party, a correct copy of every judgment or order affecting title to or lien upon real or personal property or for the recovery of money or property shall be kept and indexed with the civil judgments of the district court.

(d) Index of Cases; Certificate of Search.

The clerk shall keep indices of all cases and adversary proceedings as prescribed by the Director of the Administrative Office of the United States Courts. On request, the clerk shall make a search of any index and papers in the clerk's custody and certify whether a case or proceeding has been filed in or transferred to the court or if a discharge has been entered in its records.

(e)   Register of Mailing Addresses of Federal and State Governmental Units and Certain Taxing Authorities.

The United States or the state or territory in which the court is located may file a statement designating its mailing address. The United States, state, territory, or local governmental unit responsible for collecting taxes within the district in which the case is pending may also file a statement designating an address for service of requests under § 505(b) of the Code, and the designation shall describe where further information concerning additional requirements for filing such requests may be found. The clerk shall keep, in the form and manner as the Director of the Administrative Office of the United States Courts may prescribe, a register that includes the mailing addresses designated under the first sentence of this subdivision, and a separate register of the addresses designated for the service of requests under § 505(b) of the Code. The clerk is not required to include in any single register more than one mailing address for each department, agency, or instrumentality of the United States or the state or territory. If more than one address for a department, agency, or instrumentality is included in the register, the clerk shall also include information that would enable a user of the register to determine the circumstances when each address is applicable, and mailing notice to only one applicable address is sufficient to provide effective notice. The clerk shall update the register annually, effective January 2 of each year. The mailing address in the register is conclusively presumed to be a proper address for the governmental unit, but the failure to use that mailing address does not invalidate any notice that is otherwise effective under applicable law.

(f)   Other Books and Records of the Clerk.

The clerk shall keep any other books and records required by the Director of the Administrative Office of the United States Courts.

(As amended Mar. 30, 1987, eff. Aug. 1, 1987; Apr. 17, 2000, Dec. 1, 2000; Apr. 23, 2008, eff. Dec. 1, 2008.)

Rule 5004.   Disqualification

(a)   Disqualification of Judge.

A bankruptcy judge shall be governed by 28 U.S.C. § 455, and disqualified from presiding over the proceeding or contested matter in which the disqualifying circumstances[1] arises or, if appropriate, shall be disqualified from presiding over the case.

(b)   Disqualification of Judge from Allowing Compensation.

A bankruptcy judge shall be disqualified from allowing compensation to a person who is a relative of the bankruptcy judge or with whom the judge is so connected as to render it improper for the judge to authorize such compensation.

(As amended Apr. 29, 1985, eff. Aug. 1, 1985; Mar. 30, 1987, eff. Aug. 1, 1987.)

Rule 5005.   Filing and Transmittal of Papers

(a)   Filing.

(1)   Place of Filing.

The lists, schedules, statements, proofs of claim or interest, complaints, motions, applications, objections and other papers required to be filed by these rules, except as provided in 28 U.S.C. § 1409, shall be filed with the clerk in the district where the case under the Code is pending. The judge of that court may permit the papers to be filed with the judge, in which event the filing date shall be noted thereon, and they shall be forthwith transmitted to the clerk. The clerk shall not refuse to accept for filing any petition or other paper presented for the purpose of filing solely because it is not presented in proper form as required by these rules or any local rules or practices.

---

[1]   So in original. Probably should be "circumstance".

(2)   Filing by Electronic Means.

A court may by local rule permit or require documents to be filed, signed, or verified by electronic means that are consistent with technical standards, if any, that the Judicial Conference of the United States establishes. A local rule may require filing by electronic means only if reasonable exceptions are allowed. A document filed by electronic means in compliance with a local rule constitutes a written paper for the purpose of applying these rules, the Federal Rules of Civil Procedure made applicable by these rules, and § 107 of the Code.

(b)   Transmittal to the United States Trustee.

(1)   The complaints, motions, applications, objections and other papers required to be transmitted to the United States trustee by these rules shall be mailed or delivered to an office of the United States trustee, or to another place designated by the United States trustee, in the district where the case under the Code is pending.

(2)   The entity, other than the clerk, transmitting a paper to the United States trustee shall promptly file as proof of such transmittal a verified statement identifying the paper and stating the date on which it was transmitted to the United States trustee.

(3)   Nothing in these rules shall require the clerk to transmit any paper to the United States trustee if the United States trustee requests in writing that the paper not be transmitted.

(c)   Error in Filing or Transmittal.

A paper intended to be filed with the clerk but erroneously delivered to the United States trustee, the trustee, the attorney for the trustee, a bankruptcy judge, a district judge, the clerk of the bankruptcy appellate panel, or the clerk of the district court shall, after the date of its receipt has been noted thereon, be transmitted forthwith to the clerk of the bankruptcy court. A paper intended to be transmitted to the United States trustee but erroneously delivered to the clerk, the trustee, the attorney for the trustee, a bankruptcy judge, a district judge, the clerk of the bankruptcy appellate panel, or the clerk of the district court shall, after the date of its receipt has been noted thereon, be transmitted forthwith to the United States trustee. In the interest of justice, the court may order that a paper erroneously delivered shall be deemed filed with the clerk or transmitted to the United States trustee as of the date of its original delivery.

(As amended Mar. 30, 1987, eff. Aug. 1, 1987; Apr. 30, 1991, eff. Aug. 1, 1991; Apr. 22, 1993, eff. Aug. 1, 1993; Apr. 23, 1996, eff. Dec. 1, 1996; Apr. 12, 2006, eff. Dec. 1, 2006.)

Rule 5006.   Certification of Copies of Papers

The clerk shall issue a certified copy of the record of any proceeding in a case under the Code or of any paper filed with the clerk on payment of any prescribed fee.

(As amended Apr. 30, 1991, eff. Aug. 1, 1991.)

Rule 5007.   Record of Proceedings and Transcripts

(a)   Filing of Record or Transcript.

The reporter or operator of a recording device shall certify the original notes of testimony, tape recording, or other original record of the proceeding and promptly file them with the clerk. The person preparing any transcript shall promptly file a certified copy.

(b)   Transcript Fees.

The fees for copies of transcripts shall be charged at rates prescribed by the Judicial Conference of the United States. No fee may be charged for the certified copy filed with the clerk.

(c)   Admissibility of Record in Evidence.

A certified sound recording or a transcript of a proceeding shall be admissible as prima facie evidence to establish the record.

(As amended Mar. 30, 1987, eff. Aug. 1, 1987; Apr. 30, 1991, eff. Aug. 1, 1991.)

Rule 5008. **Notice Regarding Presumption of Abuse in Chapter 7 Cases of Individual Debtors**

If a presumption of abuse has arisen under § 707(b) in a chapter 7 case of an individual with primarily consumer debts, the clerk shall within 10 days after the date of the filing of the petition notify creditors of the presumption of abuse in accordance with Rule 2002. If the debtor has not filed a statement indicating whether a presumption of abuse has arisen, the clerk shall within 10 days after the date of the filing of the petition notify creditors that the debtor has not filed the statement and that further notice will be given if a later filed statement indicates that a presumption of abuse has arisen. If a debtor later files a statement indicating that a presumption of abuse has arisen, the clerk shall notify creditors of the presumption of abuse as promptly as practicable.

(Added Apr. 23, 2008, eff. Dec. 1, 2008.)

Rule 5009. **Closing Chapter 7 Liquidation, Chapter 12 Family Farmer's Debt Adjustment, and Chapter 13 Individual's Debt Adjustment, and Chapter 15 Ancillary and Cross-Border Cases**

(a)   Cases under Chapters 7, 12, and 13.

If in a chapter 7, chapter 12, or chapter 13 case the trustee has filed a final report and final account and has certified that the estate has been fully administered, and if within 30 days no objection has been filed by the United States trustee or a party in interest, there shall be a presumption that the estate has been fully administered.

(b)   Notice of Failure to File Rule 1007(b)(7) Statement.

If an individual debtor in a chapter 7 or 13 case is required to file a statement under Rule 1007(b)(7) and fails to do so within 45 days after the first date set for the meeting of creditors under § 341(a) of the Code, the clerk shall promptly notify the debtor that the case will be closed without entry of a discharge unless the required statement is filed within the applicable time limit under Rule 1007(c).

(c)   Cases under Chapter 15.

A foreign representative in a proceeding recognized under § 1517 of the Code shall file a final report when the purpose of the representative's appearance in the court is completed. The report shall describe the nature and results of the representative's activities in the court. The foreign representative shall transmit the report to the United States trustee, and give notice of its filing to the debtor, all persons or bodies authorized to administer foreign proceedings of the debtor, all parties to litigation pending in the United States in which the debtor was a party at the time of the filing of the petition, and such other entities as the court may direct. The foreign representative shall file a certificate with the court that notice has been given. If no objection has been filed by the United States trustee or a party in interest within 30 days after the certificate is filed, there shall be a presumption that the case has been fully administered.

(As amended Apr. 30, 1991, eff. Aug. 1, 1991; Apr. 28, 2010, eff. Dec. 1, 2010; Apr. 16, 2013, eff. Dec. 1, 2013.)

Rule 5010. **Reopening Cases**

A case may be reopened on motion of the debtor or other party in interest pursuant to § 350(b) of the Code. In a chapter 7, 12, or 13 case a trustee shall not be appointed by the United States trustee unless the court determines that a trustee is necessary to protect the interests of creditors and the debtor or to insure efficient administration of the case.

(As amended Mar. 30, 1987, eff. Aug. 1, 1987; Apr. 30, 1991, eff. Aug. 1, 1991.)

Rule 5011. **Withdrawal and Abstention from Hearing a Proceeding**

(a)   Withdrawal.

A motion for withdrawal of a case or proceeding shall be heard by a district judge.

(b) Abstention from Hearing a Proceeding.

A motion for abstention pursuant to 28 U.S.C. § 1334(c) shall be governed by Rule 9014 and shall be served on the parties to the proceeding.

(c) Effect of Filing of Motion for Withdrawal or Abstention.

The filing of a motion for withdrawal of a case or proceeding or for abstention pursuant to 28 U.S.C. § 1334(c) shall not stay the administration of the case or any proceeding therein before the bankruptcy judge except that the bankruptcy judge may stay, on such terms and conditions as are proper, proceedings pending disposition of the motion. A motion for a stay ordinarily shall be presented first to the bankruptcy judge. A motion for a stay or relief from a stay filed in the district court shall state why it has not been presented to or obtained from the bankruptcy judge. Relief granted by the district judge shall be on such terms and conditions as the judge deems proper.

(Added Mar. 30, 1987, eff. Aug. 1, 1987 and amended Apr. 30, 1991, eff. Aug. 1, 1991.)

Rule 5012.   **Agreements Concerning Coordination of Proceedings in Chapter 15 Cases**

Approval of an agreement under § 1527(4) of the Code shall be sought by motion. The movant shall attach to the motion a copy of the proposed agreement or protocol and, unless the court directs otherwise, give at least 30 days' notice of any hearing on the motion by transmitting the motion to the United States trustee, and serving it on the debtor, all persons or bodies authorized to administer foreign proceedings of the debtor, all entities against whom provisional relief is being sought under § 1519, all parties to litigation pending in the United States in which the debtor was a party at the time of the filing of the petition, and such other entities as the court may direct.

(Added Apr. 28, 2010, eff. Dec. 1, 2010.)

PART VI

COLLECTION AND LIQUIDATION OF THE ESTATE

6001.   Burden of Proof as to Validity of Postpetition Transfer.
6002.   Accounting by Prior Custodian of Property of the Estate.
6003.   Interim and Final Relief Immediately Following the Commencement of the Case—Applications for Employment; Motions for Use, Sale, or Lease of Property; and Motions for Assumption or Assignment of Executory Contracts.
6004.   Use, Sale, or Lease of Property.
6005.   Appraisers and Auctioneers.
6006.   Assumption, Rejection or Assignment of an Executory Contract or Unexpired Lease.
6007.   Abandonment or Disposition of Property.
6008.   Redemption of Property from Lien or Sale.
6009.   Prosecution and Defense of Proceedings by Trustee or Debtor in Possession.
6010.   Proceeding to Avoid Indemnifying Lien or Transfer to Surety.
6011.   Disposal of Patient Records in Health Care Business Case.

Rule 6001.   **Burden of Proof as to Validity of Postpetition Transfer**

Any entity asserting the validity of a transfer under § 549 of the Code shall have the burden of proof.

Rule 6002.   Accounting by Prior Custodian of Property of the Estate

(a) Accounting Required.

Any custodian required by the Code to deliver property in the custodian's possession or control to the trustee shall promptly file and transmit to the United States trustee a report and account with respect to the property of the estate and the administration thereof.

(b) Examination of Administration.

On the filing and transmittal of the report and account required by subdivision (a) of this rule and after an examination has been made into the superseded administration, after notice and a hearing, the court shall determine the propriety of the administration, including the reasonableness of all disbursements.

(As amended Mar. 30, 1987, eff. Aug. 1, 1987; Apr. 30, 1991, eff. Aug. 1, 1991; Apr. 22, 1993, eff. Aug. 1, 1993.)

Rule 6003.   Interim and Final Relief Immediately Following the Commencement of the Case—Applications for Employment; Motions for Use, Sale, or Lease of Property; and Motions for Assumption or Assignment of Executory Contracts

Except to the extent that relief is necessary to avoid immediate and irreparable harm, the court shall not, within 21 days after the filing of the petition, issue an order granting the following:

(a) an application under Rule 2014;

(b) a motion to use, sell, lease, or otherwise incur an obligation regarding property of the estate, including a motion to pay all or part of a claim that arose before the filing of the petition, but not a motion under Rule 4001; or

(c) a motion to assume or assign an executory contract or unexpired lease in accordance with § 365.

(Added Apr. 30, 2007, eff. Dec. 1, 2007, and amended Mar. 26, 2009, eff. Dec. 1, 2009; Apr. 26, 2011, eff. Dec. 1, 2011.)

Rule 6004.   Use, Sale, or Lease of Property

(a) Notice of Proposed Use, Sale, or Lease of Property.

Notice of a proposed use, sale, or lease of property, other than cash collateral, not in the ordinary course of business shall be given pursuant to Rule 2002(a)(2), (c)(1), (i), and (k) and, if applicable, in accordance with § 363(b)(2) of the Code.

(b) Objection to Proposal.

Except as provided in subdivisions (c) and (d) of this rule, an objection to a proposed use, sale, or lease of property shall be filed and served not less than seven days before the date set for the proposed action or within the time fixed by the court. An objection to the proposed use, sale, or lease of property is governed by Rule 9014.

(c) Sale Free and Clear of Liens and Other Interests.

A motion for authority to sell property free and clear of liens or other interests shall be made in accordance with Rule 9014 and shall be served on the parties who have liens or other interests in the property to be sold. The notice required by subdivision (a) of this rule shall include the date of the hearing on the motion and the time within which objections may be filed and served on the debtor in possession or trustee.

(d) Sale of Property Under $2,500.

Notwithstanding subdivision (a) of this rule, when all of the nonexempt property of the estate has an aggregate gross value less than $2,500, it shall be sufficient to give a general notice of intent to sell such property other than in the ordinary course of business to all creditors, indenture trustees, committees appointed or elected pursuant to the Code, the United States trustee and other persons as the court may direct. An objection to any such sale may be filed and served by a party in interest within 14 days of the mailing of the notice, or within the time fixed by the court. An objection is governed by Rule 9014.

(e) Hearing.

If a timely objection is made pursuant to subdivision (b) or (d) of this rule, the date of the hearing thereon may be set in the notice given pursuant to subdivision (a) of this rule.

(f) Conduct of Sale Not in the Ordinary Course of Business.

(1) Public or Private Sale.

All sales not in the ordinary course of business may be by private sale or by public auction. Unless it is impracticable, an itemized statement of the property sold, the name of each purchaser, and the price received for each item or lot or for the property as a whole if sold in bulk shall be filed on completion of a sale. If the property is sold by an auctioneer, the auctioneer shall file the statement, transmit a copy thereof to the United States trustee, and furnish a copy to the trustee, debtor in possession, or chapter 13 debtor. If the property is not sold by an auctioneer, the trustee, debtor in possession, or chapter 13 debtor shall file the statement and transmit a copy thereof to the United States trustee.

(2) Execution of Instruments.

After a sale in accordance with this rule the debtor, the trustee, or debtor in possession, as the case may be, shall execute any instrument necessary or ordered by the court to effectuate the transfer to the purchaser.

(g) Sale of Personally Identifiable Information.

(1) Motion.

A motion for authority to sell or lease personally identifiable information under § 363(b)(1)(B) shall include a request for an order directing the United States trustee to appoint a consumer privacy ombudsman under § 332. Rule 9014 governs the motion which shall be served on: any committee elected under § 705 or appointed under § 1102 of the Code, or if the case is a chapter 11 reorganization case and no committee of unsecured creditors has been appointed under § 1102, on the creditors included on the list of creditors filed under Rule 1007(d); and on such other entities as the court may direct. The motion shall be transmitted to the United States trustee.

(2) Appointment.

If a consumer privacy ombudsman is appointed under § 332, no later than seven days before the hearing on the motion under § 363(b)(1)(B), the United States trustee shall file a notice of the appointment, including the name and address of the person appointed. The United States trustee's notice shall be accompanied by a verified statement of the person appointed setting forth the person's connections with the debtor, creditors, any other party in interest, their respective attorneys and accountants, the United States trustee, or any person employed in the office of the United States trustee.

(h) Stay of Order Authorizing Use, Sale, or Lease of Property.

An order authorizing the use, sale, or lease of property other than cash collateral is stayed until the expiration of 14 days after entry of the order, unless the court orders otherwise.

(As amended Mar. 30, 1987, eff. Aug. 1, 1987; Apr. 30, 1991, eff. Aug. 1, 1991; Apr. 29, 1999, eff. Dec. 1, 1999; Apr. 23, 2008, eff. Dec. 1, 2008; Mar. 26, 2009, eff. Dec. 1, 2009.)

Rule 6005.   Appraisers and Auctioneers

The order of the court approving the employment of an appraiser or auctioneer shall fix the amount or rate of compensation. No officer or employee of the Judicial Branch of the United States or the United States

Department of Justice shall be eligible to act as appraiser or auctioneer. No residence or licensing requirement shall disqualify an appraiser or auctioneer from employment.

(As amended Mar. 30, 1987, eff. Aug. 1, 1987; Apr. 30, 1991, eff. Aug. 1, 1991.)

Rule 6006.   Assumption, Rejection or Assignment of an Executory Contract or Unexpired Lease

(a)   Proceeding to Assume, Reject, or Assign.

A proceeding to assume, reject, or assign an executory contract or unexpired lease, other than as part of a plan, is governed by Rule 9014.

(b)   Proceeding to Require Trustee to Act.

A proceeding by a party to an executory contract or unexpired lease in a chapter 9 municipality case, chapter 11 reorganization case, chapter 12 family farmer's debt adjustment case, or chapter 13 individual's debt adjustment case, to require the trustee, debtor in possession, or debtor to determine whether to assume or reject the contract or lease is governed by Rule 9014.

(c)   Notice

Notice of a motion made pursuant to subdivision (a) or (b) of this rule shall be given to the other party to the contract or lease, to other parties in interest as the court may direct, and, except in a chapter 9 municipality case, to the United States trustee.

(d)   Stay of Order Authorizing Assignment.

An order authorizing the trustee to assign an executory contract or unexpired lease under § 365(f) is stayed until the expiration of 14 days after the entry of the order, unless the court orders otherwise.

(e)   Limitations.

The trustee shall not seek authority to assume or assign multiple executory contracts or unexpired leases in one motion unless: (1) all executory contracts or unexpired leases to be assumed or assigned are between the same parties or are to be assigned to the same assignee; (2) the trustee seeks to assume, but not assign to more than one assignee, unexpired leases of real property; or (3) the court otherwise authorizes the motion to be filed. Subject to subdivision (f), the trustee may join requests for authority to reject multiple executory contracts or unexpired leases in one motion.

(f)   Omnibus Motions.

A motion to reject or, if permitted under subdivision (e), a motion to assume or assign multiple executory contracts or unexpired leases that are not between the same parties shall:

(1)   state in a conspicuous place that parties receiving the omnibus motion should locate their names and their contracts or leases listed in the motion;

(2)   list parties alphabetically and identify the corresponding contract or lease;

(3)   specify the terms, including the curing of defaults, for each requested assumption or assignment;

(4)   specify the terms, including the identity of each assignee and the adequate assurance of future performance by each assignee, for each requested assignment;

(5)   be numbered consecutively with other omnibus motions to assume, assign, or reject executory contracts or unexpired leases; and

(6)   be limited to no more than 100 executory contracts or unexpired leases.

(g)   Finality of Determination.

The finality of any order respecting an executory contract or unexpired lease included in an omnibus motion shall be determined as though such contract or lease had been the subject of a separate motion.

(As amended Mar. 30, 1987, eff. Aug. 1, 1987; Apr. 30, 1991, eff. Aug. 1, 1991; Apr. 22, 1993, eff. Aug. 1, 1993; Apr. 29, 1999, eff. Dec. 1, 1999; Apr. 30, 2007, eff. Dec. 1, 2007; Mar. 26, 2009, eff. Dec. 1, 2009.)

Rule 6007.   Abandonment or Disposition of Property

(a)   Notice of Proposed Abandonment or Disposition; Objections; Hearing.

Unless otherwise directed by the court, the trustee or debtor in possession shall give notice of a proposed abandonment or disposition of property to the United States trustee, all creditors, indenture trustees, and committees elected pursuant to § 705 or appointed pursuant to § 1102 of the Code. A party in interest may file and serve an objection within 14 days of the mailing of the notice, or within the time fixed by the court. If a timely objection is made, the court shall set a hearing on notice to the United States trustee and to other entities as the court may direct.

(b)   Motion by Party in Interest.

A party in interest may file and serve a motion requiring the trustee or debtor in possession to abandon property of the estate.

[(c)   Hearing] (Abrogated Apr. 22, 1993, eff. Aug. 1, 1993)

(As amended Mar. 30, 1987, eff. Aug. 1, 1987; Apr. 30, 1991, eff. Aug. 1, 1991; Apr. 22, 1993, eff. Aug. 1, 1993; Mar. 26, 2009, eff. Dec. 1, 2009.)

Rule 6008.   Redemption of Property from Lien or Sale

On motion by the debtor, trustee, or debtor in possession and after hearing on notice as the court may direct, the court may authorize the redemption of property from a lien or from a sale to enforce a lien in accordance with applicable law.

Rule 6009.   Prosecution and Defense of Proceedings by Trustee or Debtor in Possession

With or without court approval, the trustee or debtor in possession may prosecute or may enter an appearance and defend any pending action or proceeding by or against the debtor, or commence and prosecute any action or proceeding in behalf of the estate before any tribunal.

Rule 6010.   Proceeding to Avoid Indemnifying Lien or Transfer to Surety

If a lien voidable under § 547 of the Code has been dissolved by the furnishing of a bond or other obligation and the surety thereon has been indemnified by the transfer of, or the creation of a lien upon, nonexempt property of the debtor, the surety shall be joined as a defendant in any proceeding to avoid the indemnifying transfer or lien. Such proceeding is governed by the rules in Part VII.

(As amended Apr. 30, 1991, eff. Aug. 1, 1991.)

Rule 6011.   Disposal of Patient Records in Health Care Business Case

(a)   Notice by Publication Under § 351(1)(A).

A notice regarding the claiming or disposing of patient records under § 351(1)(A) shall not identify any patient by name or other identifying information, but shall:

(1)   identify with particularity the health care facility whose patient records the trustee proposes to destroy;

(2)   state the name, address, telephone number, email address, and website, if any, of a person from whom information about the patient records may be obtained;

(3)   state how to claim the patient records; and

(4)   state the date by which patient records must be claimed, and that if they are not so claimed the records will be destroyed.

(b)   Notice by Mail Under § 351(1)(B).

Subject to applicable nonbankruptcy law relating to patient privacy, a notice regarding the claiming or disposing of patient records under § 351(1)(B) shall, in addition to including the information in subdivision (a), direct that a patient's family member or other representative who receives the notice inform the patient of the notice. Any notice under this subdivision shall be mailed to the patient and any family member or other contact person whose name and address have been given to the trustee or the debtor for the purpose of providing information regarding the patient's health care, to the Attorney General of the State where the health care facility is located, and to any insurance company known to have provided health care insurance to the patient.

(c)   Proof of Compliance With Notice Requirement.

Unless the court orders the trustee to file proof of compliance with § 351(1)(B) under seal, the trustee shall not file, but shall maintain, the proof of compliance for a reasonable time.

(d)   Report of Destruction of Records.

The trustee shall file, no later than 30 days after the destruction of patient records under § 351(3), a report certifying that the unclaimed records have been destroyed and explaining the method used to effect the destruction. The report shall not identify any patient by name or other identifying information.

(Added Apr. 23, 2008, eff. Dec. 1, 2008.)

PART VII
ADVERSARY PROCEEDINGS

Rule 7001.   Scope of Rules of Part VII

An adversary proceeding is governed by the rules of this Part VII. The following are adversary proceedings:

(1)   a proceeding to recover money or property, other than a proceeding to compel the debtor to deliver property to the trustee, or a proceeding under § 554(b) or § 725 of the Code, Rule 2017, or Rule 6002;

(2)   a proceeding to determine the validity, priority, or extent of a lien or other interest in property, other than a proceeding under Rule 4003(d);

(3)   a proceeding to obtain approval under § 363(h) for the sale of both the interest of the estate and of a co-owner in property;

(4)   a proceeding to object to or revoke a discharge other than an objection to discharge under §§ 727(a)(8), (a)(9), or 1328(f);

(5)   a proceeding to revoke an order of confirmation of a chapter 11, chapter 12, or chapter 13 plan;

(6)   a proceeding to determine the dischargeability of a debt;

(7)   a proceeding to obtain an injunction or other equitable relief, except when a chapter 9, chapter 11, chapter 12, or chapter 13 plan provides for the relief;

(8)   a proceeding to subordinate any allowed claim or interest, except when a chapter 9, chapter 11, chapter 12, or chapter 13 plan provides for subordination;

(9)   a proceeding to obtain a declaratory judgment relating to any of the foregoing; or

(10)   a proceeding to determine a claim or cause of action removed under 28 U.S.C. § 1452.

(As amended Mar. 30, 1987, eff. Aug. 1, 1987; Apr. 30, 1991, eff. Aug. 1, 1991; Apr. 29, 1999, eff. Dec. 1, 1999; Apr. 28, 2010, eff. Dec. 1, 2010.)

Rule 7002.   References to Federal Rules of Civil Procedure

Whenever a Federal Rule of Civil Procedure applicable to adversary proceedings makes reference to another Federal Rule of Civil Procedure, the reference shall be read as a reference to the Federal Rule of Civil Procedure as modified in this Part VII.

Rule 7003.   Commencement of Adversary Proceeding

Rule 3 F.R.Civ.P. applies in adversary proceedings.

Rule 7004.   Process; Service of Summons, Complaint

(a)   Summons; Service; Proof of Service.

(1)   Except as provided in Rule 7004(a)(2), Rule 4(a), (b), (c)(1), (d)(1), (e)–(j), (*l*), and (m) F.R.Civ.P. applies in adversary proceedings. Personal service under Rule 4(e)–(j) F.R.Civ.P. may be made by any person at least 18 years of age who is not a party, and the summons may be delivered by the clerk to any such person.

(2)   The clerk may sign, seal, and issue a summons electronically by putting an "s/" before the clerk's name and including the court's seal on the summons.

(b)   Service by First Class Mail.

Except as provided in subdivision (h), in addition to the methods of service authorized by Rule 4(e)–(j) F.R.Civ.P., service may be made within the United States by first class mail postage prepaid as follows:

(1)   Upon an individual other than an infant or incompetent, by mailing a copy of the summons and complaint to the individual's dwelling house or usual place of abode or to the place where the individual regularly conducts a business or profession.

(2)   Upon an infant or an incompetent person, by mailing a copy of the summons and complaint to the person upon whom process is prescribed to be served by the law of the state in which service is made when an action is brought against such a defendant in the courts of general jurisdiction of that state. The summons and complaint in that case shall be addressed to the person required to be served at that person's dwelling house or usual place of abode or at the place where the person regularly conducts a business or profession.

(3)   Upon a domestic or foreign corporation or upon a partnership or other unincorporated association, by mailing a copy of the summons and complaint to the attention of an officer, a managing or general agent, or to any other agent authorized by appointment or by law to receive service of process and, if the agent is one authorized by statute to receive service and the statute so requires, by also mailing a copy to the defendant.

(4)   Upon the United States, by mailing a copy of the summons and complaint addressed to the civil process clerk at the office of the United States attorney for the district in which the action is brought and by mailing a copy of the summons and complaint to the Attorney General of the United States at Washington, District of Columbia, and in any action attacking the validity of an order of an officer or an agency of the United States not made a party, by also mailing a copy of the summons and complaint to that officer or agency. The court shall allow a reasonable time for service pursuant to this subdivision for the purpose of curing the failure to mail a copy of the summons and complaint to multiple officers, agencies, or corporations of the United States if the plaintiff has mailed a copy of the

summons and complaint either to the civil process clerk at the office of the United States attorney or to the Attorney General of the United States.

(5) Upon any officer or agency of the United States, by mailing a copy of the summons and complaint to the United States as prescribed in paragraph (4) of this subdivision and also to the officer or agency. If the agency is a corporation, the mailing shall be as prescribed in paragraph (3) of this subdivision of this rule. The court shall allow a reasonable time for service pursuant to this subdivision for the purpose of curing the failure to mail a copy of the summons and complaint to multiple officers, agencies, or corporations of the United States if the plaintiff has mailed a copy of the summons and complaint either to the civil process clerk at the office of the United States attorney or to the Attorney General of the United States. If the United States trustee is the trustee in the case and service is made upon the United States trustee solely as trustee, service may be made as prescribed in paragraph (10) of this subdivision of this rule.

(6) Upon a state or municipal corporation or other governmental organization thereof subject to suit, by mailing a copy of the summons and complaint to the person or office upon whom process is prescribed to be served by the law of the state in which service is made when an action is brought against such a defendant in the courts of general jurisdiction of that state, or in the absence of the designation of any such person or office by state law, then to the chief executive officer thereof.

(7) Upon a defendant of any class referred to in paragraph (1) or (3) of this subdivision of this rule, it is also sufficient if a copy of the summons and complaint is mailed to the entity upon whom service is prescribed to be served by any statute of the United States or by the law of the state in which service is made when an action is brought against such a defendant in the court of general jurisdiction of that state.

(8) Upon any defendant, it is also sufficient if a copy of the summons and complaint is mailed to an agent of such defendant authorized by appointment or by law to receive service of process, at the agent's dwelling house or usual place of abode or at the place where the agent regularly carries on a business or profession and, if the authorization so requires, by mailing also a copy of the summons and complaint to the defendant as provided in this subdivision.

(9) Upon the debtor, after a petition has been filed by or served upon the debtor and until the case is dismissed or closed, by mailing a copy of the summons and complaint to the debtor at the address shown in the petition or to such other address as the debtor may designate in a filed writing.

(10) Upon the United States trustee, when the United States trustee is the trustee in the case and service is made upon the United States trustee solely as trustee, by mailing a copy of the summons and complaint to an office of the United States trustee or another place designated by the United States trustee in the district where the case under the Code is pending.

(c) Service by Publication.

If a party to an adversary proceeding to determine or protect rights in property in the custody of the court cannot be served as provided in Rule 4(e)–(j) F.R.Civ.P. or subdivision (b) of this rule, the court may order the summons and complaint to be served by mailing copies thereof by first class mail, postage prepaid, to the party's last known address, and by at least one publication in such manner and form as the court may direct.

(d) Nationwide Service of Process.

The summons and complaint and all other process except a subpoena may be served anywhere in the United States.

(e) Summons: Time Limit for Service Within the United States.

Service made under Rule 4(e), (g), (h)(1), (i), or (j)(2) F. R. Civ. P. shall be by delivery of the summons and complaint within 7 days after the summons is issued. If service is by any authorized form of mail, the summons and complaint shall be deposited in the mail within 7 days after the summons is issued. If a summons is not timely delivered or mailed, another summons shall be issued and served. This subdivision does not apply to service in a foreign country.

(f)   Personal Jurisdiction.

If the exercise of jurisdiction is consistent with the Constitution and laws of the United States, serving a summons or filing a waiver of service in accordance with this rule or the subdivisions of Rule 4 F.R.Civ.P. made applicable by these rules is effective to establish personal jurisdiction over the person of any defendant with respect to a case under the Code or a civil proceeding arising under the Code, or arising in or related to a case under the Code.

(g)   Service on Debtor's Attorney.

If the debtor is represented by an attorney, whenever service is made upon the debtor under this Rule, service shall also be made upon the debtor's attorney by any means authorized under Rule 5(b) F. R. Civ. P.

(h)   Service of Process on an Insured Depository Institution.

Service on an insured depository institution (as defined in section 3 of the Federal Deposit Insurance Act) in a contested matter or adversary proceeding shall be made by certified mail addressed to an officer of the institution unless—

(1)   the institution has appeared by its attorney, in which case the attorney shall be served by first class mail;

(2)   the court orders otherwise after service upon the institution by certified mail of notice of an application to permit service on the institution by first class mail sent to an officer of the institution designated by the institution; or

(3)   the institution has waived in writing its entitlement to service by certified mail by designating an officer to receive service.

(As amended Mar. 30, 1987, eff. Aug. 1, 1987; Apr. 30, 1991, eff. Aug. 1, 1991; Oct. 22, 1994, Pub.L. 103–394, Title I, § 114, 108 Stat. 4118; Apr. 23, 1996, eff. Dec. 1, 1996; Apr. 29, 1999, eff. Dec. 1, 1999; Apr. 25, 2005, eff. Dec. 1, 2005; Apr. 12, 2006, eff. Dec. 1, 2006; Mar. 26, 2009, eff. Dec. 1, 2009; Apr. 25, 2014, eff. Dec. 1, 2014.)

Rule 7005.   Service and Filing of Pleadings and Other Papers

Rule 5 F.R.Civ.P. applies in adversary proceedings.

Rule 7007.   Pleadings Allowed

Rule 7 F.R.Civ.P. applies in adversary proceedings.

Rule 7007.1.   Corporate Ownership Statement

(a)   Required Disclosure.

Any corporation that is a party to an adversary proceeding, other than the debtor or a governmental unit, shall file two copies of a statement that identifies any corporation, other than a governmental unit, that directly or indirectly owns 10% or more of any class of the corporation's equity interests, or states that there are no entities to report under this subdivision.

(b)   Time for Filing.

A party shall file the statement required under Rule 7007.1(a) with its first appearance, pleading, motion, response, or other request addressed to the court. A party shall file a supplemental statement promptly upon any change in circumstances that this rule requires the party to identify or disclose.

(Added Mar. 27, 2003, eff. Dec. 1, 2003. As amended Apr. 30, 2007, eff. Dec. 1, 2007.)

Rule 7008.   General Rules of Pleading

Rule 8 F.R.Civ.P. applies in adversary proceedings. The allegation of jurisdiction required by Rule 8(a) shall also contain a reference to the name, number, and chapter of the case under the Code to which the adversary proceeding relates and to the district and division where the case under the Code is pending. In an adversary proceeding before a bankruptcy judge, the complaint, counterclaim, cross-claim, or third-party complaint shall contain a statement that the proceeding is core or non-core and, if non-core, that the pleader does or does not consent to entry of final orders or judgment by the bankruptcy judge.

(As amended Mar. 30, 1987, eff. Aug. 1, 1987; Apr. 25, 2014, eff. Dec. 1, 2014.)

Rule 7009.   Pleading Special Matters

Rule 9 F.R.Civ.P. applies in adversary proceedings.

Rule 7010.   Form of Pleadings

Rule 10 F.R.Civ.P. applies in adversary proceedings, except that the caption of each pleading in such a proceeding shall conform substantially to the appropriate Official Form.

(As amended Apr. 30, 1991, eff. Aug. 1, 1991.)

Rule 7012.   Defenses and Objections—When and How Presented—By Pleading or Motion—Motion for Judgment on the Pleadings

(a)   When Presented.

If a complaint is duly served, the defendant shall serve an answer within 30 days after the issuance of the summons, except when a different time is prescribed by the court. The court shall prescribe the time for service of the answer when service of a complaint is made by publication or upon a party in a foreign country. A party served with a pleading stating a cross-claim shall serve an answer thereto within 21 days after service. The plaintiff shall serve a reply to a counterclaim in the answer within 21 days after service of the answer or, if a reply is ordered by the court, within 21 days after service of the order, unless the order otherwise directs. The United States or an officer or agency thereof shall serve an answer to a complaint within 35 days after the issuance of the summons, and shall serve an answer to a cross-claim, or a reply to a counterclaim, within 35 days after service upon the United States attorney of the pleading in which the claim is asserted. The service of a motion permitted under this rule alters these periods of time as follows, unless a different time is fixed by order of the court: (1) if the court denies the motion or postpones its disposition until the trial on the merits, the responsive pleading shall be served within 14 days after notice of the court's action; (2) if the court grants a motion for a more definite statement, the responsive pleading shall be served within 14 days after the service of a more definite statement.

(b)   Applicability of Rule 12(b)–(i) F.R.Civ.P.

Rule 12(b)–(i) F.R.Civ.P. applies in adversary proceedings. A responsive pleading shall admit or deny an allegation that the proceeding is core or non-core. If the response is that the proceeding is non-core, it shall include a statement that the party does or does not consent to entry of final orders or judgment by the bankruptcy judge. In non-core proceedings final orders and judgments shall not be entered on the bankruptcy judge's order except with the express consent of the parties.

(As amended Mar. 30, 1987, eff. Aug. 1, 1987; Apr. 23, 2008, eff. Dec. 1, 2008; Mar. 26, 2009, eff. Dec. 1, 2009.)

Rule 7013.   Counterclaim and Cross-Claim

Rule 13 F.R.Civ.P. applies in adversary proceedings, except that a party sued by a trustee or debtor in possession need not state as a counterclaim any claim that the party has against the debtor, the debtor's property, or the estate, unless the claim arose after the entry of an order for relief. A trustee or debtor in possession who fails to plead a counterclaim through oversight, inadvertence, or excusable neglect, or when justice so requires, may by leave of court amend the pleading, or commence a new adversary proceeding or separate action.

(As amended Mar. 30, 1987, eff. Aug. 1, 1987.)

Rule 7014.   Third-Party Practice

Rule 14 F.R.Civ.P. applies in adversary proceedings.

Rule 7015.   Amended and Supplemental Pleadings

Rule 15 F.R.Civ.P. applies in adversary proceedings.

Rule 7016.   Pre-Trial Procedure; Formulating Issues

Rule 16 F.R.Civ.P. applies in adversary proceedings.

Rule 7017.   Parties Plaintiff and Defendant; Capacity

Rule 17 F.R.Civ.P. applies in adversary proceedings, except as provided in Rule 2010(b).

(As amended Apr. 30, 1991, eff. Aug. 1, 1991.)

Rule 7018.   Joinder of Claims and Remedies

Rule 18 F.R.Civ.P. applies in adversary proceedings.

Rule 7019.   Joinder of Persons Needed for Just Determination

Rule 19 F.R.Civ.P. applies in adversary proceedings, except that (1) if an entity joined as a party raises the defense that the court lacks jurisdiction over the subject matter and the defense is sustained, the court shall dismiss such entity from the adversary proceeding and (2) if an entity joined as a party properly and timely raises the defense of improper venue, the court shall determine, as provided in 28 U.S.C. § 1412, whether that part of the proceeding involving the joined party shall be transferred to another district, or whether the entire adversary proceeding shall be transferred to another district.

(As amended Mar. 30, 1987, eff. Aug. 1, 1987.)

Rule 7020.   Permissive Joinder of Parties

Rule 20 F.R.Civ.P. applies in adversary proceedings.

Rule 7021.   Misjoinder and Non-Joinder of Parties

Rule 21 F.R.Civ.P. applies in adversary proceedings.

Rule 7022.   Interpleader

Rule 22(a) F.R.Civ.P. applies in adversary proceedings. This rule supplements—and does not limit— the joinder of parties allowed by Rule 7020.

(As amended Apr. 23, 2008, eff. Dec. 1, 2008.)

Rule 7023.   Class Proceedings

Rule 23 F.R.Civ.P. applies in adversary proceedings.

Rule 7023.1.   Derivative Actions

Rule 23.1 F.R.Civ.P. applies in adversary proceedings.

(As amended Apr. 23, 2008, eff. Dec. 1,2008.)

Rule 7023.2.   Adversary Proceedings Relating to Unincorporated Associations

Rule 23.2 F.R.Civ.P. applies in adversary proceedings.

Rule 7024.   Intervention

Rule 24 F.R.Civ.P. applies in adversary proceedings.

Rule 7025.   Substitution of Parties

Subject to the provisions of Rule 2012, Rule 25 F.R.Civ.P. applies in adversary proceedings.

Rule 7026.   General Provisions Governing Discovery

Rule 26 F.R.Civ.P. applies in adversary proceedings.

Rule 7027.   Depositions Before Adversary Proceedings or Pending Appeal

Rule 27 F.R.Civ.P. applies to adversary proceedings.

Rule 7028.   Persons Before Whom Depositions May be Taken

Rule 28 F.R.Civ.P. applies in adversary proceedings.

Rule 7029.   Stipulations Regarding Discovery Procedure

Rule 29 F.R.Civ.P. applies in adversary proceedings.

Rule 7030.   Depositions Upon Oral Examination

Rule 30 F.R.Civ.P. applies in adversary proceedings.

Rule 7031.   Deposition Upon Written Questions

Rule 31 F.R.Civ.P. applies in adversary proceedings.

Rule 7032.   Use of Depositions in Adversary Proceedings

Rule 32 F.R.Civ.P. applies in adversary proceedings.

Rule 7033.   Interrogatories to Parties

Rule 33 F.R.Civ.P. applies in adversary proceedings.

Rule 7034.   Production of Documents and Things and Entry Upon Land for Inspection and Other Purposes

Rule 34 F.R.Civ.P. applies in adversary proceedings.

Rule 7035.   Physical and Mental Examination of Persons

Rule 35 F.R.Civ.P. applies in adversary proceedings.

Rule 7036.   Requests for Admission

Rule 36 F.R.Civ.P. applies in adversary proceedings.

Rule 7037.   Failure to Make Discovery: Sanctions

Rule 37 F.R.Civ.P. applies in adversary proceedings.

Rule 7040.   Assignment of Cases for Trial

Rule 40 F.R.Civ.P. applies in adversary proceedings.

Rule 7041.　　　Dismissal of Adversary Proceedings

Rule 41 F.R.Civ.P. applies in adversary proceedings, except that a complaint objecting to the debtor's discharge shall not be dismissed at the plaintiff's instance without notice to the trustee, the United States trustee, and such other persons as the court may direct, and only on order of the court containing terms and conditions which the court deems proper.

(As amended Apr. 30, 1991, eff. Aug. 1, 1991.)

Rule 7042.　　　Consolidation of Adversary Proceedings; Separate Trials

Rule 42 F.R.Civ.P. applies in adversary proceedings.

Rule 7052.　　　Findings by the Court

Rule 52 F. R. Civ. P. applies in adversary proceedings, except that any motion under subdivision (b) of that rule for amended or additional findings shall be filed no later than 14 days after entry of judgment. In these proceedings, the reference in Rule 52 F.R.Civ.P. to the entry of judgment under Rule 58 F.R.Civ.P. shall be read as a reference to the entry of a judgment or order under Rule 5003(a).

(As amended Mar. 26, 2009, eff. Dec. 1, 2009.)

Rule 7054.　　　Judgments; Costs

(a)　Judgments.

Rule 54(a)–(c) F.R.Civ.P. applies in adversary proceedings.

(b)　Costs; Attorney's Fees.

(1)　Costs Other Than Attorney's Fees. The court may allow costs to the prevailing party except when a statute of the United States or these rules otherwise provides. Costs against the United States, its officers and agencies shall be imposed only to the extent permitted by law. Costs may be taxed by the clerk on 14 days' notice; on motion served within seven days thereafter, the action of the clerk may be reviewed by the court.

(2)　Attorney's Fees.

(A)　Rule 54(d)(2)(A)–(C) and (E) F.R.Civ.P. applies in adversary proceedings except for the reference in Rule 54(d)(2)(C) to Rule 78.

(B)　By local rule, the court may establish special procedures to resolve fee-related issues without extensive evidentiary hearings.

(As amended Apr. 23, 2012, eff. Dec. 1, 2012; Apr. 25, 2014, eff. Dec. 1, 2014.)

Rule 7055.　　　Default

Rule 55 F.R.Civ.P. applies in adversary proceedings.

Rule 7056.　　　Summary Judgment

Rule 56 F.R.Civ.P. applies in adversary proceedings, except that any motion for summary judgment must be made at least 30 days before the initial date set for an evidentiary hearing on any issue for which summary judgment is sought, unless a different time is set by local rule or the court orders otherwise.

(As amended Apr. 23, 2012, eff. Dec. 1, 2012.)

Rule 7058.　　　Entering Judgment in Adversary Proceeding

Rule 58 F.R.Civ.P. applies in adversary proceedings. In these proceedings, the reference in Rule 58 F.R.Civ.P. to the civil docket shall be read as a reference to the docket maintained by the clerk under Rule 5003(a).

(Added Mar. 26, 2009, eff. Dec. 1, 2009.)

Rule 7062.   Stay of Proceedings to Enforce a Judgment

Rule 62 F.R.Civ.P. applies in adversary proceedings.

   (As amended Apr. 30, 1991, eff. Aug. 1, 1991; Apr. 29, 1999, eff. Dec. 1, 1999.)

Rule 7064.   Seizure of Person or Property

Rule 64 F.R.Civ.P. applies in adversary proceedings.

Rule 7065.   Injunctions

Rule 65 F.R.Civ.P. applies in adversary proceedings, except that a temporary restraining order or preliminary injunction may be issued on application of a debtor, trustee, or debtor in possession without compliance with Rule 65(c).

Rule 7067.   Deposit in Court

Rule 67 F.R.Civ.P. applies in adversary proceedings.

Rule 7068.   Offer of Judgment

Rule 68 F.R.Civ.P. applies in adversary proceedings.

Rule 7069.   Execution

Rule 69 F.R.Civ.P. applies in adversary proceedings.

Rule 7070.   Judgment for Specific Acts; Vesting Title

Rule 70 F.R.Civ.P. applies in adversary proceedings and the court may enter a judgment divesting the title of any party and vesting title in others whenever the real or personal property involved is within the jurisdiction of the court.

   (As amended Mar. 30, 1987, eff. Aug. 1, 1987.)

Rule 7071.   Process in Behalf of and Against Persons Not Parties

Rule 71 F.R.Civ.P. applies in adversary proceedings.

Rule 7087.   Transfer of Adversary Proceeding

On motion and after a hearing, the court may transfer an adversary proceeding or any part thereof to another district pursuant to 28 U.S.C. § 1412, except as provided in Rule 7019(2).

   (As amended Mar. 30, 1987, eff. Aug. 1, 1987.)

PART VIII[1]

APPEALS TO DISTRICT COURT OR BANKRUPTCY APPELLATE PANEL

---

   [1] The 2014 amendments to Part VIII of the Bankruptcy Rules are comprehensive. Proposed amendment of the heading, "Part VIII. Bankruptcy Appeals", was not transmitted for Congressional review.

Rule 8001.   Scope of Part VIII Rules; Definition of "BAP"; Method of Transmission

(a) General Scope.

These Part VIII rules govern the procedure in a United States district court and a bankruptcy appellate panel on appeal from a judgment, order, or decree of a bankruptcy court. They also govern certain procedures on appeal to a United States court of appeals under 28 U.S.C. § 158(d).

(b) Definition of "BAP."

"BAP" means a bankruptcy appellate panel established by a circuit's judicial council and authorized to hear appeals from a bankruptcy court under 28 U.S.C. § 158.

(c) Method of Transmitting Documents.

A document must be sent electronically under these Part VIII rules, unless it is being sent by or to an individual who is not represented by counsel or the court's governing rules permit or require mailing or other means of delivery.

(Added Apr. 25, 2014, eff. Dec. 1, 2014.)

Rule 8002.   Time for Filing Notice of Appeal

(a) In General.

(1) **Fourteen-Day Period.** Except as provided in subdivisions (b) and (c), a notice of appeal must be filed with the bankruptcy clerk within 14 days after entry of the judgment, order, or decree being appealed.

(2) Filing Before the Entry of Judgment. A notice of appeal filed after the bankruptcy court announces a decision or order—but before entry of the judgment, order, or decree—is treated as filed on the date of and after the entry.

(3) Multiple Appeals. If one party files a timely notice of appeal, any other party may file a notice of appeal within 14 days after the date when the first notice was filed, or within the time otherwise allowed by this rule, whichever period ends later.

(4) Mistaken Filing in Another Court. If a notice of appeal is mistakenly filed in a district court, BAP, or court of appeals, the clerk of that court must state on the notice the date on which it was received and transmit it to the bankruptcy clerk. The notice of appeal is then considered filed in the bankruptcy court on the date so stated.

(b) Effect of a Motion on the Time to Appeal.

(1) In General. If a party timely files in the bankruptcy court any of the following motions, the time to file an appeal runs for all parties from the entry of the order disposing of the last such remaining motion:

(A) to amend or make additional findings under Rule 7052, whether or not granting the motion would alter the judgment;

(B) to alter or amend the judgment under Rule 9023;

(C) for a new trial under Rule 9023; or

(D) for relief under Rule 9024 if the motion is filed within 14 days after the judgment is entered.

(2) Filing an Appeal Before the Motion is Decided. If a party files a notice of appeal after the court announces or enters a judgment, order, or decree—but before it disposes of any motion listed in subdivision (b)(1)—the notice becomes effective when the order disposing of the last such remaining motion is entered.

(3) Appealing the Ruling on the Motion. If a party intends to challenge an order disposing of any motion listed in subdivision (b)(1)—or the alteration or amendment of a judgment, order, or decree upon the motion—the party must file a notice of appeal or an amended notice of appeal. The notice or amended notice must comply with Rule 8003 or 8004 and be filed within the time prescribed by this rule, measured from the entry of the order disposing of the last such remaining motion.

(4) No Additional Fee. No additional fee is required to file an amended notice of appeal.

(c) Appeal by an Inmate Confined in an Institution.

(1) In General. If an inmate confined in an institution files a notice of appeal from a judgment, order, or decree of a bankruptcy court, the notice is timely if it is deposited in the institution's internal mail system on or before the last day for filing. If the institution has a system designed for legal mail, the inmate must use that system to receive the benefit of this rule. Timely filing may be shown by a declaration in compliance with 28 U.S.C. § 1746 or by a notarized statement, either of which must set forth the date of deposit and state that first-class postage has been prepaid.

(2) Multiple Appeals. If an inmate files under this subdivision the first notice of appeal, the 14-day period provided in subdivision (a)(3) for another party to file a notice of appeal runs from the date when the bankruptcy clerk dockets the first notice.

(d) Extending the Time to Appeal.

(1) When the Time May be Extended. Except as provided in subdivision (d)(2), the bankruptcy court may extend the time to file a notice of appeal upon a party's motion that is filed:

(A) within the time prescribed by this rule; or

(B) within 21 days after that time, if the party shows excusable neglect.

(2) When the Time May Not be Extended. The bankruptcy court may not extend the time to file a notice of appeal if the judgment, order, or decree appealed from:

    (A) grants relief from an automatic stay under § 362, 922, 1201, or 1301 of the Code;

    (B) the sale or lease of property or the use of cash collateral under § 363 of the Code;

    (C) authorizes the obtaining of credit under § 364 of the Code;

    (D) authorizes the assumption or assignment of an executory contract or unexpired lease under § 365 of the Code;

    (E) approves a disclosure statement under § 1125 of the Code; or

    (F) confirms a plan under § 943, 1129, 1225, or 1325 of the Code.

(3) Time Limits on an Extension. No extension of time may exceed 21 days after the time prescribed by this rule, or 14 days after the order granting the motion to extend time is entered, whichever is later.

(Added Apr. 25, 2014, eff. Dec. 1, 2014.)

Rule 8003.   Appeal as of Right—How Taken; Docketing the Appeal

(a) Filing the Notice of Appeal.

(1) In General. An appeal from a judgment, order, or decree of a bankruptcy court to a district court or BAP under 28 U.S.C. § 158(a)(1) or (a)(2) may be taken only by filing a notice of appeal with the bankruptcy clerk within the time allowed by Rule 8002.

(2) Effect of Not Taking Other Steps. An appellant's failure to take any step other than the timely filing of a notice of appeal does not affect the validity of the appeal, but is ground only for the district court or BAP to act as it considers appropriate, including dismissing the appeal.

(3) Contents. The notice of appeal must:

    (A) conform substantially to the appropriate Official Form;

    (B) be accompanied by the judgment, order, or decree, or the part of it, being appealed; and

    (C) be accompanied by the prescribed fee.

(4) Additional Copies. If requested to do so, the appellant must furnish the bankruptcy clerk with enough copies of the notice to enable the clerk to comply with subdivision (c).

(b) Joint or Consolidated Appeals.

(1) Joint Notice of Appeal. When two or more parties are entitled to appeal from a judgment, order, or decree of a bankruptcy court and their interests make joinder practicable, they may file a joint notice of appeal. They may then proceed on appeal as a single appellant.

(2) Consolidating Appeals. When parties have separately filed timely notices of appeal, the district court or BAP may join or consolidate the appeals.

(c) Serving the Notice of Appeal.

(1) Serving Parties and Transmitting to the United States Trustee. The bankruptcy clerk must serve the notice of appeal on counsel of record for each party to the appeal, excluding the appellant, and transmit it to the United States trustee. If a party is proceeding pro se, the clerk must send the notice of appeal to the party's last known address. The clerk must note, on each copy, the date when the notice of appeal was filed.

(2) Effect of Failing to Serve or Transmit Notice. The bankruptcy clerk's failure to serve notice on a party or transmit notice to the United States trustee does not affect the validity of the appeal.

(3)   **Noting Service on the Docket.** The clerk must note on the docket the names of the parties served and the date and method of the service.

(d)   **Transmitting the Notice of Appeal to the District Court or BAP; Docketing the Appeal.**

(1)   **Transmitting the Notice.** The bankruptcy clerk must promptly transmit the notice of appeal to the BAP clerk if a BAP has been established for appeals from that district and the appellant has not elected to have the district court hear the appeal. Otherwise, the bankruptcy clerk must promptly transmit the notice to the district clerk.

(2)   **Docketing in the District Court or BAP.** Upon receiving the notice of appeal, the district or BAP clerk must docket the appeal under the title of the bankruptcy case and the title of any adversary proceeding, and must identify the appellant, adding the appellant's name if necessary.

(Added Apr. 25, 2014, eff. Dec. 1, 2014.)

Rule 8004.   Appeal by Leave—How Taken; Docketing the Appeal

(a)   **Notice of Appeal and Motion for Leave to Appeal.**

To appeal from an interlocutory order or decree of a bankruptcy court under 28 U.S.C. § 158(a)(3), a party must file with the bankruptcy clerk a notice of appeal as prescribed by Rule 8003(a). The notice must:

(1)   be filed within the time allowed by Rule 8002;

(2)   be accompanied by a motion for leave to appeal prepared in accordance with subdivision (b); and

(3)   unless served electronically using the court's transmission equipment, include proof of service in accordance with Rule 8011(d).

(b)   **Contents of the Motion; Response.**

(1)   **Contents.** A motion for leave to appeal under 28 U.S.C. § 158(a)(3) must include the following:

(A)   the facts necessary to understand the question presented;

(B)   the question itself;

(C)   the relief sought;

(D)   the reasons why leave to appeal should be granted; and

(E)   a copy of the interlocutory order or decree and any related opinion or memorandum.

(2)   **Response.** A party may file with the district or BAP clerk a response in opposition or a cross-motion within 14 days after the motion is served.

(c)   **Transmitting the Notice of Appeal and the Motion; Docketing the Appeal; Determining the Motion.**

(1)   **Transmitting to the District Court or BAP.** The bankruptcy clerk must promptly transmit the notice of appeal and the motion for leave to the BAP clerk if a BAP has been established for appeals from that district and the appellant has not elected to have the district court hear the appeal. Otherwise, the bankruptcy clerk must promptly transmit the notice and motion to the district clerk.

(2)   **Docketing in the District Court or BAP.** Upon receiving the notice and motion, the district or BAP clerk must docket the appeal under the title of the bankruptcy case and the title of any adversary proceeding, and must identify the appellant, adding the appellant's name if necessary.

(3)   **Oral Argument Not Required.** The motion and any response or cross-motion are submitted without oral argument unless the district court or BAP orders otherwise.

(d) Failure to File a Motion With a Notice of Appeal. If an appellant timely files a notice of appeal under this rule but does not include a motion for leave, the district court or BAP may order the appellant to file a motion for leave, or treat the notice of appeal as a motion for leave and either grant or deny it. If the court orders that a motion for leave be filed, the appellant must do so within 14 days after the order is entered, unless the order provides otherwise.

(e) Direct Appeal to a Court of Appeals. If leave to appeal an interlocutory order or decree is required under 28 U.S.C. § 158(a)(3), an authorization of a direct appeal by the court of appeals under 28 U.S.C. § 158(d)(2) satisfies the requirement.

(Added Apr. 25, 2014, eff. Dec. 1, 2014.)

Rule 8005.   Election to Have an Appeal Heard by the District Court Instead of the BAP

(a) Filing of a Statement of Election.

To elect to have an appeal heard by the district court, a party must:

> **(1)** file a statement of election that conforms substantially to the appropriate Official Form; and

> **(2)** do so within the time prescribed by 28 U.S.C. § 158(c)(1).

(b) Transmitting the Documents Related to the Appeal.

Upon receiving an appellant's timely statement of election, the bankruptcy clerk must transmit to the district clerk all documents related to the appeal. Upon receiving a timely statement of election by a party other than the appellant, the BAP clerk must transmit to the district clerk all documents related to the appeal and notify the bankruptcy clerk of the transmission.

(c) Determining the Validity of an Election.

A party seeking a determination of the validity of an election must file a motion in the court where the appeal is then pending. The motion must be filed within 14 days after the statement of election is filed.

(d) Motion for Leave Without a Notice of Appeal—Effect on the Timing of an Election.

If an appellant moves for leave to appeal under Rule 8004 but fails to file a separate notice of appeal with the motion, the motion must be treated as a notice of appeal for purposes of determining the timeliness of a statement of election.

(Added Apr. 25, 2014, eff. Dec. 1, 2014.)

Rule 8006.   Certifying a Direct Appeal to the Court of Appeals

(a) Effective Date of a Certification.

A certification of a judgment, order, or decree of a bankruptcy court for direct review in a court of appeals under 28 U.S.C. § 158(d)(2) is effective when:

> **(1)** the certification has been filed;

> **(2)** a timely appeal has been taken under Rule 8003 or 8004; and

> **(3)** the notice of appeal has become effective under Rule 8002.

(b) Filing the Certification.

The certification must be filed with the clerk of the court where the matter is pending. For purposes of this rule, a matter remains pending in the bankruptcy court for 30 days after the effective date under Rule 8002 of the first notice of appeal from the judgment, order, or decree for which direct review is sought. A matter is pending in the district court or BAP thereafter.

(c)   Joint Certification by All Appellants and Appellees.

A joint certification by all the appellants and appellees under 28 U.S.C. § 158(d)(2)(A) must be made by using the appropriate Official Form. The parties may supplement the certification with a short statement of the basis for the certification, which may include the information listed in subdivision (f)(2).

(d)   The Court That May Make the Certification.

Only the court where the matter is pending, as provided in subdivision (b), may certify a direct review on request of parties or on its own motion.

(e)   Certification on the Court's own Motion.

    (1)   How Accomplished. A certification on the court's own motion must be set forth in a separate document. The clerk of the certifying court must serve it on the parties to the appeal in the manner required for service of a notice of appeal under Rule 8003(c)(1). The certification must be accompanied by an opinion or memorandum that contains the information required by subdivision (f)(2)(A)–(D).

    (2)   Supplemental Statement by a Party. Within 14 days after the court's certification, a party may file with the clerk of the certifying court a short supplemental statement regarding the merits of certification.

(f)   Certification by the Court on Request.

    (1)   How Requested. A request by a party for certification that a circumstance specified in 28 U.S.C. § 158(d)(2)(A)(i)–(iii) applies—or a request by a majority of the appellants and a majority of the appellees—must be filed with the clerk of the court where the matter is pending within 60 days after the entry of the judgment, order, or decree.

    (2)   Service and Contents. The request must be served on all parties to the appeal in the manner required for service of a notice of appeal under Rule 8003(c)(1), and it must include the following:

        (A)   the facts necessary to understand the question presented;

        (B)   the question itself;

        (C)   the relief sought;

        (D)   the reasons why the direct appeal should be allowed, including which circumstance specified in 28 U.S.C. § 158(d)(2)(A)(i)–(iii) applies; and

        (E)   a copy of the judgment, order, or decree and any related opinion or memorandum.

    (3)   Time to File a Response or a Cross-Request. A party may file a response to the request within 14 days after the request is served, or such other time as the court where the matter is pending allows. A party may file a cross-request for certification within 14 days after the request is served, or within 60 days after the entry of the judgment, order, or decree, whichever occurs first.

    (4)   Oral Argument Not Required. The request, cross-request, and any response are submitted without oral argument unless the court where the matter is pending orders otherwise.

    (5)   Form and Service of the Certification. If the court certifies a direct appeal in response to the request, it must do so in a separate document. The certification must be served on the parties to the appeal in the manner required for service of a notice of appeal under Rule 8003(c)(1).

(g)   Proceeding in the Court of Appeals Following a Certification. Within 30 days after the date the certification becomes effective under subdivision (a), a request for permission to take a direct appeal to the court of appeals must be filed with the circuit clerk in accordance with F.R.App.P. 6(c).

(Added Apr. 25, 2014, eff. Dec. 1, 2014.)

Rule 8007.   Stay Pending Appeal; Bonds; Suspension of Proceedings

(a) **Initial Motion in the Bankruptcy Court.**

(1) **In General.** Ordinarily, a party must move first in the bankruptcy court for the following relief:

(A) a stay of a judgment, order, or decree of the bankruptcy court pending appeal;

(B) the approval of a supersedeas bond;

(C) an order suspending, modifying, restoring, or granting an injunction while an appeal is pending; or

(D) the suspension or continuation of proceedings in a case or other relief permitted by subdivision (e).

(2) **Time to File.** The motion may be made either before or after the notice of appeal is filed.

(b) **Motion in the District Court, the BAP, or the Court of Appeals on Direct Appeal.**

(1) **Request for Relief.** A motion for the relief specified in subdivision (a)(1)—or to vacate or modify a bankruptcy court's order granting such relief—may be made in the court where the appeal is pending.

(2) **Showing or Statement Required.** The motion must:

(A) show that moving first in the bankruptcy court would be impracticable; or

(B) if a motion was made in the bankruptcy court, either state that the court has not yet ruled on the motion, or state that the court has ruled and set out any reasons given for the ruling.

(3) **Additional Content.** The motion must also include:

(A) the reasons for granting the relief requested and the facts relied upon;

(B) affidavits or other sworn statements supporting facts subject to dispute; and

(C) relevant parts of the record.

(4) **Serving Notice.** The movant must give reasonable notice of the motion to all parties.

(c) **Filing a Bond or Other Security.**

The district court, BAP, or court of appeals may condition relief on filing a bond or other appropriate security with the bankruptcy court.

(d) **Bond for a Trustee or the United States.**

The court may require a trustee to file a bond or other appropriate security when the trustee appeals. A bond or other security is not required when an appeal is taken by the United States, its officer, or its agency or by direction of any department of the federal government.

(e) **Continuation of Proceedings in the Bankruptcy Court.**

Despite Rule 7062 and subject to the authority of the district court, BAP, or court of appeals, the bankruptcy court may:

(1) suspend or order the continuation of other proceedings in the case; or

(2) issue any other appropriate orders during the pendency of an appeal to protect the rights of all parties in interest.

(Added Apr. 25, 2014, eff. Dec. 1, 2014.)

Rule 8008.   Indicative Rulings

(a)   Relief Pending Appeal.

If a party files a timely motion in the bankruptcy court for relief that the court lacks authority to grant because of an appeal that has been docketed and is pending, the bankruptcy court may:

    (1)   defer considering the motion;

    (2)   deny the motion; or

    (3)   state that the court would grant the motion if the court where the appeal is pending remands for that purpose, or state that the motion raises a substantial issue.

(b)   Notice to the Court Where the Appeal Is Pending.

The movant must promptly notify the clerk of the court where the appeal is pending if the bankruptcy court states that it would grant the motion or that the motion raises a substantial issue.

(c)   Remand After an Indicative Ruling.

If the bankruptcy court states that it would grant the motion or that the motion raises a substantial issue, the district court or BAP may remand for further proceedings, but it retains jurisdiction unless it expressly dismisses the appeal. If the district court or BAP remands but retains jurisdiction, the parties must promptly notify the clerk of that court when the bankruptcy court has decided the motion on remand.

    (Added Apr. 25, 2014, eff. Dec. 1, 2014.)

Rule 8009.   Record on Appeal; Sealed Documents

(a) Designating the Record on Appeal; Statement of the Issues.

    (1) Appellant.

        (A) The appellant must file with the bankruptcy clerk and serve on the appellee a designation of the items to be included in the record on appeal and a statement of the issues to be presented.

        (B) The appellant must file and serve the designation and statement within 14 days after:

            (i)   the appellant's notice of appeal as of right becomes effective under Rule 8002; or

            (ii)   an order granting leave to appeal is entered.

        A designation and statement served prematurely must be treated as served on the first day on which filing is timely.

    (2)   Appellee and Cross-Appellant. Within 14 days after being served, the appellee may file with the bankruptcy clerk and serve on the appellant a designation of additional items to be included in the record. An appellee who files a cross-appeal must file and serve a designation of additional items to be included in the record and a statement of the issues to be presented on the cross-appeal.

    (3)   Cross-Appellee. Within 14 days after service of the cross-appellant's designation and statement, a cross-appellee may file with the bankruptcy clerk and serve on the cross-appellant a designation of additional items to be included in the record.

    (4)   Record on Appeal. The record on appeal must include the following:

       •   docket entries kept by the bankruptcy clerk;

       •   items designated by the parties;

       •   the notice of appeal;

       •   the judgment, order, or decree being appealed;

       •   any order granting leave to appeal;

- any certification required for a direct appeal to the court of appeals;

- any opinion, findings of fact, and conclusions of law relating to the issues on appeal, including transcripts of all oral rulings;

- any transcript ordered under subdivision (b);

- any statement required by subdivision (c); and

- any additional items from the record that the court where the appeal is pending orders.

(5)   Copies for the Bankruptcy Clerk. If paper copies are needed, a party filing a designation of items must provide a copy of any of those items that the bankruptcy clerk requests. If the party fails to do so, the bankruptcy clerk must prepare the copy at the party's expense.

(b)   Transcript of Proceedings.

(1)   Appellant's Duty to Order. Within the time period prescribed by subdivision (a)(1), the appellant must:

(A)   order in writing from the reporter, as defined in Rule 8010(a)(1), a transcript of such parts of the proceedings not already on file as the appellant considers necessary for the appeal, and file a copy of the order with the bankruptcy clerk; or

(B)   file with the bankruptcy clerk a certificate stating that the appellant is not ordering a transcript.

(2)   Cross-Appellant's Duty to Order. Within 14 days after the appellant files a copy of the transcript order or a certificate of not ordering a transcript, the appellee as cross-appellant must:

(A)   order in writing from the reporter, as defined in Rule 8010(a)(1), a transcript of such additional parts of the proceedings as the cross-appellant considers necessary for the appeal, and file a copy of the order with the bankruptcy clerk; or

(B)   file with the bankruptcy clerk a certificate stating that the cross-appellant is not ordering a transcript.

(3)   Appellee's or Cross-Appellee's Right to Order. Within 14 days after the appellant or cross-appellant files a copy of a transcript order or certificate of not ordering a transcript, the appellee or cross-appellee may order in writing from the reporter a transcript of such additional parts of the proceedings as the appellee or cross-appellee considers necessary for the appeal. A copy of the order must be filed with the bankruptcy clerk.

(4)   Payment. At the time of ordering, a party must make satisfactory arrangements with the reporter for paying the cost of the transcript.

(5)   Unsupported Finding or Conclusion. If the appellant intends to argue on appeal that a finding or conclusion is unsupported by the evidence or is contrary to the evidence, the appellant must include in the record a transcript of all relevant testimony and copies of all relevant exhibits.

(c)   Statement of the Evidence When a Transcript is Unavailable.

If a transcript of a hearing or trial is unavailable, the appellant may prepare a statement of the evidence or proceedings from the best available means, including the appellant's recollection. The statement must be filed within the time prescribed by subdivision (a)(1) and served on the appellee, who may serve objections or proposed amendments within 14 days after being served. The statement and any objections or proposed amendments must then be submitted to the bankruptcy court for settlement and approval. As settled and approved, the statement must be included by the bankruptcy clerk in the record on appeal.

(d)   Agreed Statement as the Record on Appeal.

Instead of the record on appeal as defined in subdivision (a), the parties may prepare, sign, and submit to the bankruptcy court a statement of the case showing how the issues presented by the appeal arose and were decided in the bankruptcy court. The statement must set forth only those facts alleged and proved or sought to be proved that are essential to the court's resolution of the issues. If the statement is accurate, it—together with any additions that the bankruptcy court may consider necessary to a full presentation of the issues on appeal—must be approved by the bankruptcy court and must then be certified to the court where the appeal is pending as the record on appeal. The bankruptcy clerk must then transmit it to the clerk of that court within the time provided by Rule 8010. A copy of the agreed statement may be filed in place of the appendix required by Rule 8018(b) or, in the case of a direct appeal to the court of appeals, by F.R.App.P. 30.

(e) Correcting or Modifying the Record.

(1) Submitting to the Bankruptcy Court. If any difference arises about whether the record accurately discloses what occurred in the bankruptcy court, the difference must be submitted to and settled by the bankruptcy court and the record conformed accordingly. If an item has been improperly designated as part of the record on appeal, a party may move to strike that item.

(2) Correcting in Other Ways. If anything material to either party is omitted from or misstated in the record by error or accident, the omission or misstatement may be corrected, and a supplemental record may be certified and transmitted:

(A) on stipulation of the parties;

(B) by the bankruptcy court before or after the record has been forwarded; or

(C) by the court where the appeal is pending.

(3) Remaining Questions. All other questions as to the form and content of the record must be presented to the court where the appeal is pending.

(f) Sealed Documents.

A document placed under seal by the bankruptcy court may be designated as part of the record on appeal. In doing so, a party must identify it without revealing confidential or secret information, but the bankruptcy clerk must not transmit it to the clerk of the court where the appeal is pending as part of the record. Instead, a party must file a motion with the court where the appeal is pending to accept the document under seal. If the motion is granted, the movant must notify the bankruptcy court of the ruling, and the bankruptcy clerk must promptly transmit the sealed document to the clerk of the court where the appeal is pending.

(g) Other Necessary Actions.

All parties to an appeal must take any other action necessary to enable the bankruptcy clerk to assemble and transmit the record.

(Added Apr. 25, 2014, eff. Dec. 1, 2014.)

Rule 8010.   Completing and Transmitting the Record

(a) Reporter's Duties.

(1) Proceedings Recorded Without a Reporter Present. If proceedings were recorded without a reporter being present, the person or service selected under bankruptcy court procedures to transcribe the recording is the reporter for purposes of this rule.

(2) Preparing and Filing the Transcript. The reporter must prepare and file a transcript as follows:

(A) Upon receiving an order for a transcript in accordance with Rule 8009(b), the reporter must file in the bankruptcy court an acknowledgment of the request that shows when it was received, and when the reporter expects to have the transcript completed.

(B) After completing the transcript, the reporter must file it with the bankruptcy clerk, who will notify the district, BAP, or circuit clerk of its filing.

(C) If the transcript cannot be completed within 30 days after receiving the order, the reporter must request an extension of time from the bankruptcy clerk. The clerk must enter on the docket and notify the parties whether the extension is granted.

(D) If the reporter does not file the transcript on time, the bankruptcy clerk must notify the bankruptcy judge.

(b) Clerk's Duties.

(1) Transmitting the Record—In General. Subject to Rule 8009(f) and subdivision (b)(5) of this rule, when the record is complete, the bankruptcy clerk must transmit to the clerk of the court where the appeal is pending either the record or a notice that the record is available electronically.

(2) Multiple Appeals. If there are multiple appeals from a judgment, order, or decree, the bankruptcy clerk must transmit a single record.

(3) Receiving the Record. Upon receiving the record or notice that it is available electronically, the district, BAP, or circuit clerk must enter that information on the docket and promptly notify all parties to the appeal.

(4) If Paper Copies Are Ordered. If the court where the appeal is pending directs that paper copies of the record be provided, the clerk of that court must so notify the appellant. If the appellant fails to provide them, the bankruptcy clerk must prepare them at the appellant's expense.

(5) When Leave to Appeal is Requested. Subject to subdivision (c), if a motion for leave to appeal has been filed under Rule 8004, the bankruptcy clerk must prepare and transmit the record only after the district court, BAP, or court of appeals grants leave.

(c) Record for a Preliminary Motion in the District Court, BAP, or Court of Appeals.

This subdivision (c) applies if, before the record is transmitted, a party moves in the district court, BAP, or court of appeals for any of the following relief:

- leave to appeal;
- dismissal;
- a stay pending appeal;
- approval of a supersedeas bond, or additional security on a bond or undertaking on appeal; or
- any other intermediate order.

The bankruptcy clerk must then transmit to the clerk of the court where the relief is sought any parts of the record designated by a party to the appeal or a notice that those parts are available electronically.

(Added Apr. 25, 2014, eff. Dec. 1, 2014.)

Rule 8011.   Filing and Service; Signature

(a) Filing.

(1) With the Clerk. A document required or permitted to be filed in a district court or BAP must be filed with the clerk of that court.

(2) Method and Timeliness.

(A) In General. Filing may be accomplished by transmission to the clerk of the district court or BAP. Except as provided in subdivision (a)(2)(B) and (C), filing is timely only if the clerk receives the document within the time fixed for filing.

(B) Brief or Appendix. A brief or appendix is also timely filed if, on or before the last day for filing, it is:

    (i) mailed to the clerk by first-class mail—or other class of mail that is at least as expeditious—postage prepaid, if the district court's or BAP's procedures permit or require a brief or appendix to be filed by mailing; or

    (ii) dispatched to a third-party commercial carrier for delivery within 3 days to the clerk, if the court's procedures so permit or require.

    (C) **Inmate Filing.** A document filed by an inmate confined in an institution is timely if deposited in the institution's internal mailing system on or before the last day for filing. If the institution has a system designed for legal mail, the inmate must use that system to receive the benefit of this rule. Timely filing may be shown by a declaration in compliance with 28 U.S.C. § 1746 or by a notarized statement, either of which must set forth the date of deposit and state that first-class postage has been prepaid.

    (D) **Copies.** If a document is filed electronically, no paper copy is required. If a document is filed by mail or delivery to the district court or BAP, no additional copies are required. But the district court or BAP may require by local rule or by order in a particular case the filing or furnishing of a specified number of paper copies.

    (3) **Clerk's Refusal of Documents.** The court's clerk must not refuse to accept for filing any document transmitted for that purpose solely because it is not presented in proper form as required by these rules or by any local rule or practice.

(b)   **Service of all Documents Required.**

    Unless a rule requires service by the clerk, a party must, at or before the time of the filing of a document, serve it on the other parties to the appeal. Service on a party represented by counsel must be made on the party's counsel.

(c)   **Manner of Service.**

    (1) **Methods.** Service must be made electronically, unless it is being made by or on an individual who is not represented by counsel or the court's governing rules permit or require service by mail or other means of delivery. Service may be made by or on an unrepresented party by any of the following methods:

    (A) personal delivery;

    (B) mail; or

    (C) third-party commercial carrier for delivery within 3 days.

    (2) **When Service is Complete.** Service by electronic means is complete on transmission, unless the party making service receives notice that the document was not transmitted successfully. Service by mail or by commercial carrier is complete on mailing or delivery to the carrier.

(d)   **Proof of Service.**

    (1) **What is Required.** A document presented for filing must contain either:

    (A) an acknowledgment of service by the person served; or

    (B) proof of service consisting of a statement by the person who made service certifying:

        (i) the date and manner of service;

        (ii) the names of the persons served; and

        (iii) the mail or electronic address, the fax number, or the address of the place of delivery, as appropriate for the manner of service, for each person served.

    (2) **Delayed Proof.** The district or BAP clerk may permit documents to be filed without acknowledgment or proof of service, but must require the acknowledgment or proof to be filed promptly thereafter.

(3) **Brief or Appendix.** When a brief or appendix is filed, the proof of service must also state the date and manner by which it was filed.

(e) Signature.

Every document filed electronically must include the electronic signature of the person filing it or, if the person is represented, the electronic signature of counsel. The electronic signature must be provided by electronic means that are consistent with any technical standards that the Judicial Conference of the United States establishes. Every document filed in paper form must be signed by the person filing the document or, if the person is represented, by counsel.

(Added Apr. 25, 2014, eff. Dec. 1, 2014.)

Rule 8012.   Corporate Disclosure Statement

(a) Who Must File.

Any nongovernmental corporate party appearing in the district court or BAP must file a statement that identifies any parent corporation and any publicly held corporation that owns 10% or more of its stock or states that there is no such corporation.

(b) Time to File; Supplemental Filing.

A party must file the statement with its principal brief or upon filing a motion, response, petition, or answer in the district court or BAP, whichever occurs first, unless a local rule requires earlier filing. Even if the statement has already been filed, the party's principal brief must include a statement before the table of contents. A party must supplement its statement whenever the required information changes.

(Added Apr. 25, 2014, eff. Dec. 1, 2014.)

Rule 8013.   Motions; Intervention

(a) Contents of a Motion; Response; Reply.

(1) **Request for Relief.** A request for an order or other relief is made by filing a motion with the district or BAP clerk, with proof of service on the other parties to the appeal.

(2) **Contents of a Motion.**

(A) **Grounds and the Relief Sought.** A motion must state with particularity the grounds for the motion, the relief sought, and the legal argument necessary to support it.

(B) **Motion to Expedite an Appeal.** A motion to expedite an appeal must explain what justifies considering the appeal ahead of other matters. If the district court or BAP grants the motion, it may accelerate the time to transmit the record, the deadline for filing briefs and other documents, oral argument, and the resolution of the appeal. A motion to expedite an appeal may be filed as an emergency motion under subdivision (d).

(C) **Accompanying Documents.**

(i) Any affidavit or other document necessary to support a motion must be served and filed with the motion.

(ii) An affidavit must contain only factual information, not legal argument.

(iii) A motion seeking substantive relief must include a copy of the bankruptcy court's judgment, order, or decree, and any accompanying opinion as a separate exhibit.

(D) **Documents Barred or Not Required.**

(i) A separate brief supporting or responding to a motion must not be filed.

(ii) Unless the court orders otherwise, a notice of motion or a proposed order is not required.

(3) **Response and Reply; Time to File.** Unless the district court or BAP orders otherwise,

    (A) any party to the appeal may file a response to the motion within 7 days after service of the motion; and

    (B) the movant may file a reply to a response within 7 days after service of the response, but may only address matters raised in the response.

(b) **Disposition of a Motion for a Procedural Order.**

The district court or BAP may rule on a motion for a procedural order—including a motion under Rule 9006(b) or (c)—at any time without awaiting a response. A party adversely affected by the ruling may move to reconsider, vacate, or modify it within 7 days after the procedural order is served.

(c) **Oral Argument.**

A motion will be decided without oral argument unless the district court or BAP orders otherwise.

(d) **Emergency Motion.**

    (1) **Noting the Emergency.** When a movant requests expedited action on a motion because irreparable harm would occur during the time needed to consider a response, the movant must insert the word "Emergency" before the title of the motion.

    (2) **Contents of the Motion.** The emergency motion must

        (A) be accompanied by an affidavit setting out the nature of the emergency;

        (B) state whether all grounds for it were submitted to the bankruptcy court and, if not, why the motion should not be remanded for the bankruptcy court to consider;

        (C) include the e-mail addresses, office addresses, and telephone numbers of moving counsel and, when known, of opposing counsel and any unrepresented parties to the appeal; and

        (D) be served as prescribed by Rule 8011.

    (3) **Notifying Opposing Parties.** Before filing an emergency motion, the movant must make every practicable effort to notify opposing counsel and any unrepresented parties in time for them to respond. The affidavit accompanying the emergency motion must state when and how notice was given or state why giving it was impracticable.

(e) **Power of a Single BAP Judge to Entertain a Motion.**

    (1) **Single Judge's Authority.** A BAP judge may act alone on any motion, but may not dismiss or otherwise determine an appeal, deny a motion for leave to appeal, or deny a motion for a stay pending appeal if denial would make the appeal moot.

    (2) **Reviewing a Single Judge's Action.** The BAP may review a single judge's action, either on its own motion or on a party's motion.

(f) **Form of Documents; Page Limits; Number of Copies.**

    (1) **Format of a Paper Document.** Rule 27(d)(1) F.R.App.P. applies in the district court or BAP to a paper version of a motion, response, or reply.

    (2) **Format of an Electronically Filed Document.** A motion, response, or reply filed electronically must comply with the requirements for a paper version regarding covers, line spacing, margins, typeface, and type style. It must also comply with the page limits under paragraph (3).

    (3) **Page Limits.** Unless the district court or BAP orders otherwise:

        (A) a motion or a response to a motion must not exceed 20 pages, exclusive of the corporate disclosure statement and accompanying documents authorized by subdivision (a)(2)(C); and

        (B) a reply to a response must not exceed 10 pages.

(4) Paper Copies. Paper copies must be provided only if required by local rule or by an order in a particular case.

(g) Intervening in an Appeal.

Unless a statute provides otherwise, an entity that seeks to intervene in an appeal pending in the district court or BAP must move for leave to intervene and serve a copy of the motion on the parties to the appeal. The motion or other notice of intervention authorized by statute must be filed within 30 days after the appeal is docketed. It must concisely state the movant's interest, the grounds for intervention, whether intervention was sought in the bankruptcy court, why intervention is being sought at this stage of the proceeding, and why participating as an amicus curiae would not be adequate.

(Added Apr. 25, 2014, eff. Dec. 1, 2014.)

Rule 8014.   Briefs

(a) Appellant's Brief.

The appellant's brief must contain the following under appropriate headings and in the order indicated:

(1) a corporate disclosure statement, if required by Rule 8012;

(2) a table of contents, with page references;

(3) a table of authorities—cases (alphabetically arranged), statutes, and other authorities— with references to the pages of the brief where they are cited;

(4) a jurisdictional statement, including:

(A) the basis for the bankruptcy court's subject-matter jurisdiction, with citations to applicable statutory provisions and stating relevant facts establishing jurisdiction;

(B) the basis for the district court's or BAP's jurisdiction, with citations to applicable statutory provisions and stating relevant facts establishing jurisdiction;

(C) the filing dates establishing the timeliness of the appeal; and

(D) an assertion that the appeal is from a final judgment, order, or decree, or information establishing the district court's or BAP's jurisdiction on another basis;

(5) a statement of the issues presented and, for each one, a concise statement of the applicable standard of appellate review;

(6) a concise statement of the case setting out the facts relevant to the issues submitted for review, describing the relevant procedural history, and identifying the rulings presented for review, with appropriate references to the record;

(7) a summary of the argument, which must contain a succinct, clear, and accurate statement of the arguments made in the body of the brief, and which must not merely repeat the argument headings;

(8) the argument, which must contain the appellant's contentions and the reasons for them, with citations to the authorities and parts of the record on which the appellant relies;

(9) a short conclusion stating the precise relief sought; and

(10) the certificate of compliance, if required by Rule 8015(a)(7) or (b).

(b) Appellee's Brief.

The appellee's brief must conform to the requirements of subdivision (a)(1)–(8) and (10), except that none of the following need appear unless the appellee is dissatisfied with the appellant's statement:

(1) the jurisdictional statement;

(2) the statement of the issues and the applicable standard of appellate review; and

(3) the statement of the case.

(c) Reply Brief.

The appellant may file a brief in reply to the appellee's brief. A reply brief must comply with the requirements of subdivision (a)(2)–(3).

(d) Statutes, Rules, Regulations, or Similar Authority.

If the court's determination of the issues presented requires the study of the Code or other statutes, rules, regulations, or similar authority, the relevant parts must be set out in the brief or in an addendum.

(e) Briefs in a Case Involving Multiple Appellants or Appellees.

In a case involving more than one appellant or appellee, including consolidated cases, any number of appellants or appellees may join in a brief, and any party may adopt by reference a part of another's brief. Parties may also join in reply briefs.

(f) Citation of Supplemental Authorities.

If pertinent and significant authorities come to a party's attention after the party's brief has been filed—or after oral argument but before a decision—a party may promptly advise the district or BAP clerk by a signed submission setting forth the citations. The submission, which must be served on the other parties to the appeal, must state the reasons for the supplemental citations, referring either to the pertinent page of a brief or to a point argued orally. The body of the submission must not exceed 350 words. Any response must be made within 7 days after the party is served, unless the court orders otherwise, and must be similarly limited.

(Added Apr. 25, 2014, eff. Dec. 1, 2014.)

Rule 8015.   Form and Length of Briefs; Form of Appendices and Other Papers

(a) Paper Copies of a Brief.

If a paper copy of a brief may or must be filed, the following provisions apply:

(1) Reproduction.

(A) A brief may be reproduced by any process that yields a clear black image on light paper. The paper must be opaque and unglazed. Only one side of the paper may be used.

(B) Text must be reproduced with a clarity that equals or exceeds the output of a laser printer.

(C) Photographs, illustrations, and tables may be reproduced by any method that results in a good copy of the original. A glossy finish is acceptable if the original is glossy.

(2) Cover. The front cover of a brief must contain:

(A) the number of the case centered at the top;

(B) the name of the court;

(C) the title of the case as prescribed by Rule 8003(d)(2) or 8004(c)(2);

(D) the nature of the proceeding and the name of the court below;

(E) the title of the brief, identifying the party or parties for whom the brief is filed; and

(F) the name, office address, telephone number, and e-mail address of counsel representing the party for whom the brief is filed.

(3) Binding. The brief must be bound in any manner that is secure, does not obscure the text, and permits the brief to lie reasonably flat when open.

(4) Paper Size, Line Spacing, and Margins. The brief must be on 8½-by-11 inch paper. The text must be double-spaced, but quotations more than two lines long may be indented and single-spaced. Headings and footnotes may be single-spaced. Margins must be at least one inch on all four sides. Page numbers may be placed in the margins, but no text may appear there.

(5) Typeface. Either a proportionally spaced or monospaced face may be used.

(A) A proportionally spaced face must include serifs, but sans-serif type may be used in headings and captions. A proportionally spaced face must be 14-point or larger.

(B) A monospaced face may not contain more than 10½ characters per inch.

(6) Type Styles. A brief must be set in plain, roman style, although italics or boldface may be used for emphasis. Case names must be italicized or underlined.

(7) Length.

(A) Page limitation. A principal brief must not exceed 30 pages, or a reply brief 15 pages, unless it complies with (B) and (C).

(B) Type-volume limitation.

(i) A principal brief is acceptable if:

- it contains no more than 14,000 words; or
- it uses a monospaced face and contains no more than 1,300 lines of text.

(ii) A reply brief is acceptable if it contains no more than half of the type volume specified in item (i).

(iii) Headings, footnotes, and quotations count toward the word and line limitations. The corporate disclosure statement, table of contents, table of citations, statement with respect to oral argument, any addendum containing statutes, rules, or regulations, and any certificates of counsel do not count toward the limitation.

(C) Certificate of Compliance.

(i) A brief submitted under subdivision (a)(7)(B) must include a certificate signed by the attorney, or an unrepresented party, that the brief complies with the type-volume limitation. The person preparing the certificate may rely on the word or line count of the word-processing system used to prepare the brief. The certificate must state either:

- the number of words in the brief; or
- the number of lines of monospaced type in the brief.

(ii) The certification requirement is satisfied by a certificate of compliance that conforms substantially to the appropriate Official Form.

(b) Electronically Filed Briefs.

A brief filed electronically must comply with subdivision (a), except for (a)(1), (a)(3), and the paper requirement of (a)(4).

(c) Paper Copies of Appendices.

A paper copy of an appendix must comply with subdivision (a)(1), (2), (3), and (4), with the following exceptions:

(1) An appendix may include a legible photocopy of any document found in the record or of a printed decision.

(2) When necessary to facilitate inclusion of odd-sized documents such as technical drawings, an appendix may be a size other than 8½-by-11 inches, and need not lie reasonably flat when opened.

(d) Electronically Filed Appendices.

An appendix filed electronically must comply with subdivision (a)(2) and (4), except for the paper requirement of (a)(4).

(e)   **Other Documents.**

    (1)   **Motion.** Rule 8013(f) governs the form of a motion, response, or reply.

    (2)   **Paper Copies of Other Documents.** A paper copy of any other document, other than a submission under Rule 8014(f), must comply with subdivision (a), with the following exceptions:

       (A)   A cover is not necessary if the caption and signature page together contain the information required by subdivision (a)(2).

       (B)   Subdivision (a)(7) does not apply.

    (3)   **Other Documents Filed Electronically.** Any other document filed electronically, other than a submission under Rule 8014(f), must comply with the appearance requirements of paragraph (2).

(f)   **Local Variation.**

A district court or BAP must accept documents that comply with the applicable requirements of this rule. By local rule, a district court or BAP may accept documents that do not meet all of the requirements of this rule.

    (Added Apr. 25, 2014, eff. Dec. 1, 2014.)

Rule 8016.   Cross-Appeals

(a)   **Applicability.**

This rule applies to a case in which a cross-appeal is filed. Rules 8014(a)–(c), 8015(a)(7)(A)–(B), and 8018(a)(1)–(3) do not apply to such a case, except as otherwise provided in this rule.

(b)   **Designation of Appellant.**

The party who files a notice of appeal first is the appellant for purposes of this rule and Rule 8018(a)(4) and (b) and Rule 8019. If notices are filed on the same day, the plaintiff, petitioner, applicant, or movant in the proceeding below is the appellant. These designations may be modified by the parties' agreement or by court order.

(c)   **Briefs.**

In a case involving a cross-appeal:

    (1)   **Appellant's Principal Brief.** The appellant must file a principal brief in the appeal. That brief must comply with Rule 8014(a).

    (2)   **Appellee's Principal and Response Brief.** The appellee must file a principal brief in the cross-appeal and must, in the same brief, respond to the principal brief in the appeal. That brief must comply with Rule 8014(a), except that the brief need not include a statement of the case unless the appellee is dissatisfied with the appellant's statement.

    (3)   **Appellant's Response and Reply Brief.** The appellant must file a brief that responds to the principal brief in the cross-appeal and may, in the same brief, reply to the response in the appeal. That brief must comply with Rule 8014(a)(2)–(8) and (10), except that none of the following need appear unless the appellant is dissatisfied with the appellee's statement in the cross-appeal:

       (A)   the jurisdictional statement;

       (B)   the statement of the issues and the applicable standard of appellate review; and

       (C)   the statement of the case.

    (4)   **Appellee's Reply Brief.** The appellee may file a brief in reply to the response in the cross-appeal. That brief must comply with Rule 8014(a)(2)–(3) and (10) and must be limited to the issues presented by the cross-appeal.

(d) Length.

(1) Page Limitation. Unless it complies with paragraphs (2) and (3), the appellant's principal brief must not exceed 30 pages; the appellee's principal and response brief, 35 pages; the appellant's response and reply brief, 30 pages; and the appellee's reply brief, 15 pages.

(2) Type-Volume Limitation.

(A) The appellant's principal brief or the appellant's response and reply brief is acceptable if:

(i) it contains no more than 14,000 words; or

(ii) it uses a monospaced face and contains no more than 1,300 lines of text.

(B) The appellee's principal and response brief is acceptable if:

(i) it contains no more than 16,500 words; or

(ii) it uses a monospaced face and contains no more than 1,500 lines of text.

(C) The appellee's reply brief is acceptable if it contains no more than half of the type volume specified in subparagraph (A).

(D) Headings, footnotes, and quotations count toward the word and line limitations. The corporate disclosure statement, table of contents, table of citations, statement with respect to oral argument, any addendum containing statutes, rules, or regulations, and any certificates of counsel do not count toward the limitation.

(3) Certificate of Compliance. A brief submitted either electronically or in paper form under paragraph (2) must comply with Rule 8015(a)(7)(C).

(e) Time to Serve and File a Brief.

Briefs must be served and filed as follows, unless the district court or BAP by order in a particular case excuses the filing of briefs or specifies different time limits:

(1) the appellant's principal brief, within 30 days after the docketing of notice that the record has been transmitted or is available electronically;

(2) the appellee's principal and response brief, within 30 days after the appellant's principal brief is served;

(3) the appellant's response and reply brief, within 30 days after the appellee's principal and response brief is served; and

(4) the appellee's reply brief, within 14 days after the appellant's response and reply brief is served, but at least 7 days before scheduled argument unless the district court or BAP, for good cause, allows a later filing.

(Added Apr. 25, 2014, eff. Dec. 1, 2014.)

Rule 8017.   Brief of an Amicus Curiae

(a) When Permitted.

The United States or its officer or agency or a state may file an amicus-curiae brief without the consent of the parties or leave of court. Any other amicus curiae may file a brief only by leave of court or if the brief states that all parties have consented to its filing. On its own motion, and with notice to all parties to an appeal, the district court or BAP may request a brief by an amicus curiae.

(b) Motion for Leave to File.

The motion must be accompanied by the proposed brief and state:

(1) the movant's interest; and

(2) the reason why an amicus brief is desirable and why the matters asserted are relevant to the disposition of the appeal.

(c) Contents and Form.

An amicus brief must comply with Rule 8015. In addition to the requirements of Rule 8015, the cover must identify the party or parties supported and indicate whether the brief supports affirmance or reversal. If an amicus curiae is a corporation, the brief must include a disclosure statement like that required of parties by Rule 8012. An amicus brief need not comply with Rule 8014, but must include the following:

(1) a table of contents, with page references;

(2) a table of authorities—cases (alphabetically arranged), statutes, and other authorities— with references to the pages of the brief where they are cited;

(3) a concise statement of the identity of the amicus curiae, its interest in the case, and the source of its authority to file;

(4) unless the amicus curiae is one listed in the first sentence of subdivision (a), a statement that indicates whether:

(A) a party's counsel authored the brief in whole or in part;

(B) a party or a party's counsel contributed money that was intended to fund preparing or submitting the brief; and

(C) a person—other than the amicus curiae, its members, or its counsel—contributed money that was intended to fund preparing or submitting the brief and, if so, identifies each such person;

(5) an argument, which may be preceded by a summary and need not include a statement of the applicable standard of review; and

(6) a certificate of compliance, if required by Rule 8015(a)(7)(C) or 8015(b).

(d) Length.

Except by the district court's or BAP's permission, an amicus brief must be no more than one-half the maximum length authorized by these rules for a party's principal brief. If the court grants a party permission to file a longer brief, that extension does not affect the length of an amicus brief.

(e) Time for Filing.

An amicus curiae must file its brief, accompanied by a motion for filing when necessary, no later than 7 days after the principal brief of the party being supported is filed. An amicus curiae that does not support either party must file its brief no later than 7 days after the appellant's principal brief is filed. The district court or BAP may grant leave for later filing, specifying the time within which an opposing party may answer.

(f) Reply Brief.

Except by the district court's or BAP's permission, an amicus curiae may not file a reply brief.

(g) Oral Argument.

An amicus curiae may participate in oral argument only with the district court's or BAP's permission.

(Added Apr. 25, 2014, eff. Dec. 1, 2014.)

Rule 8018.   Serving and Filing Briefs; Appendices

(a) Time to Serve and File a Brief.

The following rules apply unless the district court or BAP by order in a particular case excuses the filing of briefs or specifies different time limits:

(1) The appellant must serve and file a brief within 30 days after the docketing of notice that the record has been transmitted or is available electronically.

(2) The appellee must serve and file a brief within 30 days after service of the appellant's brief.

(3) The appellant may serve and file a reply brief within 14 days after service of the appellee's brief, but a reply brief must be filed at least 7 days before scheduled argument unless the district court or BAP, for good cause, allows a later filing.

(4) If an appellant fails to file a brief on time or within an extended time authorized by the district court or BAP, an appellee may move to dismiss the appeal—or the district court or BAP, after notice, may dismiss the appeal on its own motion. An appellee who fails to file a brief will not be heard at oral argument unless the district court or BAP grants permission.

(b) Duty to Serve and File an Appendix to the Brief.

(1) **Appellant.** Subject to subdivision (e) and Rule 8009(d), the appellant must serve and file with its principal brief excerpts of the record as an appendix. It must contain the following:

(A) the relevant entries in the bankruptcy docket;

(B) the complaint and answer, or other equivalent filings;

(C) the judgment, order, or decree from which the appeal is taken;

(D) any other orders, pleadings, jury instructions, findings, conclusions, or opinions relevant to the appeal;

(E) the notice of appeal; and

(F) any relevant transcript or portion of it.

(2) **Appellee.** The appellee may also serve and file with its brief an appendix that contains material required to be included by the appellant or relevant to the appeal or cross-appeal, but omitted by the appellant.

(3) **Cross-Appellee.** The appellant as cross-appellee may also serve and file with its response an appendix that contains material relevant to matters raised initially by the principal brief in the cross-appeal, but omitted by the cross-appellant.

(c) Format of the Appendix.

The appendix must begin with a table of contents identifying the page at which each part begins. The relevant docket entries must follow the table of contents. Other parts of the record must follow chronologically. When pages from the transcript of proceedings are placed in the appendix, the transcript page numbers must be shown in brackets immediately before the included pages. Omissions in the text of documents or of the transcript must be indicated by asterisks. Immaterial formal matters (captions, subscriptions, acknowledgments, and the like) should be omitted.

(d) Exhibits.

Exhibits designated for inclusion in the appendix may be reproduced in a separate volume or volumes, suitably indexed.

(e) Appeal on the Original Record Without an Appendix.

The district court or BAP may, either by rule for all cases or classes of cases or by order in a particular case, dispense with the appendix and permit an appeal to proceed on the original record, with the submission of any relevant parts of the record that the district court or BAP orders the parties to file.

(Added Apr. 25, 2014, eff. Dec. 1, 2014.)

Rule 8019.   Oral Argument

(a) Party's Statement.

Any party may file, or a district court or BAP may require, a statement explaining why oral argument should, or need not, be permitted.

(b) Resumption of Oral Argument and Exceptions.

Oral argument must be allowed in every case unless the district judge—or all the BAP judges assigned to hear the appeal—examine the briefs and record and determine that oral argument is unnecessary because

> **(1)** the appeal is frivolous;
>
> **(2)** the dispositive issue or issues have been authoritatively decided; or
>
> **(3)** the facts and legal arguments are adequately presented in the briefs and record, and the decisional process would not be significantly aided by oral argument.

(c) Notice of Argument; Postponement.

The district court or BAP must advise all parties of the date, time, and place for oral argument, and the time allowed for each side. A motion to postpone the argument or to allow longer argument must be filed reasonably in advance of the hearing date.

(d) Order and Contents of Argument.

The appellant opens and concludes the argument. Counsel must not read at length from briefs, the record, or authorities.

(e) Cross-appeals and Separate Appeals.

If there is a cross-appeal, Rule 8016(b) determines which party is the appellant and which is the appellee for the purposes of oral argument. Unless the district court or BAP directs otherwise, a cross-appeal or separate appeal must be argued when the initial appeal is argued. Separate parties should avoid duplicative argument.

(f) Nonappearance of a Party.

If the appellee fails to appear for argument, the district court or BAP may hear the appellant's argument. If the appellant fails to appear for argument, the district court or BAP may hear the appellee's argument. If neither party appears, the case will be decided on the briefs unless the district court or BAP orders otherwise.

(g) Submission on Briefs.

The parties may agree to submit a case for decision on the briefs, but the district court or BAP may direct that the case be argued.

(h) Use of Physical Exhibits at Argument; Removal.

Counsel intending to use physical exhibits other than documents at the argument must arrange to place them in the courtroom on the day of the argument before the court convenes. After the argument, counsel must remove the exhibits from the courtroom unless the district court or BAP directs otherwise. The clerk may destroy or dispose of the exhibits if counsel does not reclaim them within a reasonable time after the clerk gives notice to remove them.

(Added Apr. 25, 2014, eff. Dec. 1, 2014.)

Rule 8020.   Frivolous Appeal and Other Misconduct

(a) Frivolous Appeal—Damages and Costs.

If the district court or BAP determines that an appeal is frivolous, it may, after a separately filed motion or notice from the court and reasonable opportunity to respond, award just damages and single or double costs to the appellee.

(b)   Other Misconduct.

The district court or BAP may discipline or sanction an attorney or party appearing before it for other misconduct, including failure to comply with any court order. First, however, the court must afford the attorney or party reasonable notice, an opportunity to show cause to the contrary, and, if requested, a hearing.

(Added Apr. 25, 2014, eff. Dec. 1, 2014.)

Rule 8021.   Costs

(a)   Against Whom Assessed.

The following rules apply unless the law provides or the district court or BAP orders otherwise:

(1)   if an appeal is dismissed, costs are taxed against the appellant, unless the parties agree otherwise;

(2)   if a judgment, order, or decree is affirmed, costs are taxed against the appellant;

(3)   if a judgment, order, or decree is reversed, costs are taxed against the appellee;

(4)   if a judgment, order, or decree is affirmed or reversed in part, modified, or vacated, costs are taxed only as the district court or BAP orders.

(b)   Costs For and Against the United States.

Costs for or against the United States, its agency, or its officer may be assessed under subdivision (a) only if authorized by law.

(c)   Costs on Appeal Taxable in the Bankruptcy Court.

The following costs on appeal are taxable in the bankruptcy court for the benefit of the party entitled to costs under this rule:

(1)   the production of any required copies of a brief, appendix, exhibit, or the record;

(2)   the preparation and transmission of the record;

(3)   the reporter's transcript, if needed to determine the appeal;

(4)   premiums paid for a supersedeas bond or other bonds to preserve rights pending appeal; and

(5)   the fee for filing the notice of appeal.

(d)   Bill of Costs; Objections.

A party who wants costs taxed must, within 14 days after entry of judgment on appeal, file with the bankruptcy clerk, with proof of service, an itemized and verified bill of costs. Objections must be filed within 14 days after service of the bill of costs, unless the bankruptcy court extends the time.

(Added Apr. 25, 2014, eff. Dec. 1, 2014.)

Rule 8022.   Motion for Rehearing

(a)   Time to File; Contents; Response; Action by the District Court or BAP if Granted.

(1)   **Time.** Unless the time is shortened or extended by order or local rule, any motion for rehearing by the district court or BAP must be filed within 14 days after entry of judgment on appeal.

(2)   **Contents.** The motion must state with particularity each point of law or fact that the movant believes the district court or BAP has overlooked or misapprehended and must argue in support of the motion. Oral argument is not permitted.

(3)   **Response.** Unless the district court or BAP requests, no response to a motion for rehearing is permitted. But ordinarily, rehearing will not be granted in the absence of such a request.

(4) **Action by the District Court or BAP.** If a motion for rehearing is granted, the district court or BAP may do any of the following:

(A) make a final disposition of the appeal without reargument;

(B) restore the case to the calendar for reargument or resubmission; or

(C) issue any other appropriate order.

(b) **Form of the Motion; Length.**

The motion must comply in form with Rule 8013(f)(1) and (2). Copies must be served and filed as provided by Rule 8011. Unless the district court or BAP orders otherwise, a motion for rehearing must not exceed 15 pages.

(Added Apr. 25, 2014, eff. Dec. 1, 2014.)

Rule 8023.   Voluntary Dismissal

The clerk of the district court or BAP must dismiss an appeal if the parties file a signed dismissal agreement specifying how costs are to be paid and pay any fees that are due. An appeal may be dismissed on the appellant's motion on terms agreed to by the parties or fixed by the district court or BAP.

(Added Apr. 25, 2014, eff. Dec. 1, 2014.)

Rule 8024.   Clerk's Duties on Disposition of the Appeal

(a) **Judgment on Appeal.**

The district or BAP clerk must prepare, sign, and enter the judgment after receiving the court's opinion or, if there is no opinion, as the court instructs. Noting the judgment on the docket constitutes entry of judgment.

(b) **Notice of a Judgment.**

Immediately upon the entry of a judgment, the district or BAP clerk must:

(1) transmit a notice of the entry to each party to the appeal, to the United States trustee, and to the bankruptcy clerk, together with a copy of any opinion; and

(2) note the date of the transmission on the docket.

(c) **Returning Physical Items.**

If any physical items were transmitted as the record on appeal, they must be returned to the bankruptcy clerk on disposition of the appeal.

(Added Apr. 25, 2014, eff. Dec. 1, 2014.)

Rule 8025.   Stay of a District Court or BAP Judgment

(a) **Automatic Stay of Judgment on Appeal.**

Unless the district court or BAP orders otherwise, its judgment is stayed for 14 days after entry.

(b) **Stay Pending Appeal to the Court of Appeals.**

(1) **In General.** On a party's motion and notice to all other parties to the appeal, the district court or BAP may stay its judgment pending an appeal to the court of appeals.

(2) **Time Limit.** The stay must not exceed 30 days after the judgment is entered, except for cause shown.

(3) **Stay Continued.** If, before a stay expires, the party who obtained the stay appeals to the court of appeals, the stay continues until final disposition by the court of appeals.

(4) Bond or Other Security. A bond or other security may be required as a condition for granting or continuing a stay of the judgment. A bond or other security may be required if a trustee obtains a stay, but not if a stay is obtained by the United States or its officer or agency or at the direction of any department of the United States government.

(c) Automatic Stay of an Order, Judgment, or Decree of a Bankruptcy Court.

If the district court or BAP enters a judgment affirming an order, judgment, or decree of the bankruptcy court, a stay of the district court's or BAP's judgment automatically stays the bankruptcy court's order, judgment, or decree for the duration of the appellate stay.

(d) Power of a Court of Appeals Not Limited.

This rule does not limit the power of a court of appeals or any of its judges to do the following:

    (1) stay a judgment pending appeal;

    (2) stay proceedings while an appeal is pending;

    (3) suspend, modify, restore, vacate, or grant a stay or an injunction while an appeal is pending; or

    (4) issue any order appropriate to preserve the status quo or the effectiveness of any judgment to be entered.

(Added Apr. 25, 2014, eff. Dec. 1, 2014.)

Rule 8026. Rules by Circuit Councils and District Courts; Procedure When There is No Controlling Law

(a) Local Rules by Circuit Councils and District Courts.

    (1) Adopting Local Rules. A circuit council that has authorized a BAP under 28 U.S.C. § 158(b) may make and amend rules governing the practice and procedure on appeal from a judgment, order, or decree of a bankruptcy court to the BAP. A district court may make and amend rules governing the practice and procedure on appeal from a judgment, order, or decree of a bankruptcy court to the district court. Local rules must be consistent with, but not duplicative of, Acts of Congress and these Part VIII rules. Rule 83 F.R.Civ.P. governs the procedure for making and amending rules to govern appeals.

    (2) Numbering. Local rules must conform to any uniform numbering system prescribed by the Judicial Conference of the United States.

    (3) Limitation on Imposing Requirements of Form. A local rule imposing a requirement of form must not be enforced in a way that causes a party to lose any right because of a nonwillful failure to comply.

(b) Procedure When There Is No Controlling law.

    (1) In General. A district court or BAP may regulate practice in any manner consistent with federal law, applicable federal rules, the Official Forms, and local rules.

    (2) Limitation on Sanctions. No sanction or other disadvantage may be imposed for noncompliance with any requirement not in federal law, applicable federal rules, the Official Forms, or local rules unless the alleged violator has been furnished in the particular case with actual notice of the requirement.

(Added Apr. 25, 2014, eff. Dec. 1, 2014.)

Rule 8027. Notice of a Mediation Procedure

If the district court or BAP has a mediation procedure applicable to bankruptcy appeals, the clerk must notify the parties promptly after docketing the appeal of:

(a) the requirements of the mediation procedure; and

(b)   any effect the mediation procedure has on the time to file briefs.

(Added Apr. 25, 2014, eff. Dec. 1, 2014.)

Rule 8028.   Suspension of Rules in Part VIII

In the interest of expediting decision or for other cause in a particular case, the district court or BAP, or where appropriate the court of appeals, may suspend the requirements or provisions of the rules in Part VIII, except Rules 8001, 8002, 8003, 8004, 8005, 8006, 8007, 8012, 8020, 8024, 8025, 8026, and 8028.

(Added Apr. 25, 2014, eff. Dec. 1, 2014.)

PART IX

GENERAL PROVISIONS

9037.   Privacy Protection For Filings Made with the Court.

Rule 9001.   General Definitions

The definitions of words and phrases in §§ 101, 902, 1101, and 1502 of the Code, and the rules of construction in § 102, govern their use in these rules. In addition, the following words and phrases used in these rules have the meanings indicated:

     (1)   "Bankruptcy clerk" means a clerk appointed pursuant to 28 U.S.C. § 156(b).

     (2)   "Bankruptcy Code" or "Code" means title 11 of the United States Code.

     (3)   "Clerk" means bankruptcy clerk, if one has been appointed, otherwise clerk of the district court.

     (4)   "Court" or "judge" means the judicial officer before whom a case or proceeding is pending.

     (5)   "Debtor." When any act is required by these rules to be performed by a debtor or when it is necessary to compel attendance of a debtor for examination and the debtor is not a natural person: (A) if the debtor is a corporation, "debtor" includes, if designated by the court, any or all of its officers, members of its board of directors or trustees or of a similar controlling body, a controlling stockholder or member, or any other person in control; (B) if the debtor is a partnership, "debtor" includes any or all of its general partners or, if designated by the court, any other person in control.

     (6)   "Firm" includes a partnership or professional corporation of attorneys or accountants.

     (7)   "Judgment" means any appealable order.

     (8)   "Mail" means first class, postage prepaid.

     (9)   "Notice provider" means any entity approved by the Administrative Office of the United States Courts to give notice to creditors under Rule 2002(g)(4).

     (10)   "Regular associate" means any attorney regularly employed by, associated with, or counsel to an individual or firm.

     (11)   "Trustee" includes a debtor in possession in a chapter 11 case.

     (12)   "United States trustee" includes an assistant United States trustee and any designee of the United States trustee.

     (As amended Mar. 30, 1987, eff. Aug. 1, 1987; Apr. 30, 1991, eff. Aug. 1, 1991; Apr. 25, 2005, eff. Dec. 1, 2005; Apr. 28, 2010, eff. Dec. 1, 2010.)

Rule 9002.   Meanings of Words in the Federal Rules of Civil Procedure When Applicable to Cases Under the Code

The following words and phrases used in the Federal Rules of Civil Procedure made applicable to cases under the Code by these rules have the meanings indicated unless they are inconsistent with the context:

     (1)   "Action" or "civil action" means an adversary proceeding or, when appropriate, a contested petition, or proceedings to vacate an order for relief or to determine any other contested matter.

     (2)   "Appeal" means an appeal as provided by 28 U.S.C. § 158.

     (3)   "Clerk" or "clerk of the district court" means the court officer responsible for the bankruptcy records in the district.

     (4)   "District court," "trial court," "court," "district judge," or "judge" means bankruptcy judge if the case or proceeding is pending before a bankruptcy judge.

     (5)   "Judgment" includes any order appealable to an appellate court.

     (As amended Mar. 30, 1987, eff. Aug. 1, 1987; Apr. 22, 1993, eff. Aug. 1, 1993.)

Rule 9003.   Prohibition of Ex Parte Contacts

(a) General Prohibition.

Except as otherwise permitted by applicable law, any examiner, any party in interest, and any attorney, accountant, or employee of a party in interest shall refrain from ex parte meetings and communications with the court concerning matters affecting a particular case or proceeding.

(b) United States Trustee.

Except as otherwise permitted by applicable law, the United States trustee and assistants to and employees or agents of the United States trustee shall refrain from ex parte meetings and communications with the court concerning matters affecting a particular case or proceeding. This rule does not preclude communications with the court to discuss general problems of administration and improvement of bankruptcy administration, including the operation of the United States trustee system.

(As amended Mar. 30, 1987, eff. Aug. 1, 1987; Apr. 30, 1991, eff. Aug. 1, 1991.)

Rule 9004.   General Requirements of Form

(a) Legibility; Abbreviations.

All petitions, pleadings, schedules and other papers shall be clearly legible. Abbreviations in common use in the English language may be used.

(b) Caption.

Each paper filed shall contain a caption setting forth the name of the court, the title of the case, the bankruptcy docket number, and a brief designation of the character of the paper.

Rule 9005.   Harmless Error

Rule 61 F.R.Civ.P. applies in cases under the Code. When appropriate, the court may order the correction of any error or defect or the cure of any omission which does not affect substantial rights.

Rule 9005.1.   Constitutional Challenge to a Statute—Notice, Certification, and Intervention

Rule 5.1 F.R.Civ.P. applies in cases under the Code.

(Added Apr. 30, 2007, eff. Dec. 1, 2007.)

Rule 9006.   Computing and Extending Time; Time for Motion Papers

(a) Computing Time.

The following rules apply in computing any time period specified in these rules, in the Federal Rules of Civil Procedure, in any local rule or court order, or in any statute that does not specify a method of computing time.

(1) Period Stated in Days or a Longer Unit.

When the period is stated in days or a longer unit of time:

    (A) exclude the day of the event that triggers the period;

    (B) count every day, including intermediate Saturdays, Sundays, and legal holidays; and

    (C) include the last day of the period, but if the last day is a Saturday, Sunday, or legal holiday, the period continues to run until the end of the next day that is not a Saturday, Sunday, or legal holiday.

(2) Period Stated in Hours.

When the period is stated in hours:

(A) begin counting immediately on the occurrence of the event that triggers the period;

(B) count every hour, including hours during intermediate Saturdays, Sundays, and legal holidays; and

(C) if the period would end on a Saturday, Sunday, or legal holiday, then continue the period until the same time on the next day that is not a Saturday, Sunday, or legal holiday.

(3) Inaccessibility of Clerk's Office.

Unless the court orders otherwise, if the clerk's office is inaccessible:

(A) on the last day for filing under Rule 9006(a)(1), then the time for filing is extended to the first accessible day that is not a Saturday, Sunday, or legal holiday; or

(B) during the last hour for filing under Rule 9006(a)(2), then the time for filing is extended to the same time on the first accessible day that is not a Saturday, Sunday, or legal holiday.

(4) "Last day" Defined.

Unless a different time is set by a statute, local rule, or order in the case, the last day ends:

(A) for electronic filing, at midnight in the court's time zone; and

(B) for filing by other means, when the clerk's office is scheduled to close.

(5) "Next Day" Defined.

The "next day" is determined by continuing to count forward when the period is measured after an event and backward when measured before an event.

(6) "Legal Holiday" Defined.

"Legal holiday" means:

(A) the day set aside by statute for observing New Year's Day, Martin Luther King Jr.'s Birthday, Washington's Birthday, Memorial Day, Independence Day, Labor Day, Columbus Day, Veterans' Day, Thanksgiving Day, or Christmas Day;

(B) any day declared a holiday by the President or Congress; and

(C) for periods that are measured after an event, any other day declared a holiday by the state where the district court is located. (In this rule, "state" includes the District of Columbia and any United States commonwealth or territory.)

(b) Enlargement.

(1) In General.

Except as provided in paragraphs (2) and (3) of this subdivision, when an act is required or allowed to be done at or within a specified period by these rules or by a notice given thereunder or by order of court, the court for cause shown may at any time in its discretion (1) with or without motion or notice order the period enlarged if the request therefor is made before the expiration of the period originally prescribed or as extended by a previous order or (2) on motion made after the expiration of the specified period permit the act to be done where the failure to act was the result of excusable neglect.

(2) Enlargement Not Permitted.

The court may not enlarge the time for taking action under Rules 1007(d), 2003(a) and (d), 7052, 9023, and 9024.

(3) Enlargement Governed By Other Rules.

The court may enlarge the time for taking action under Rules 1006(b)(2), 1017(e), 3002(c), 4003(b), 4004(a), 4007(c), 4008(a), 8002, and 9033, only to the extent and under the conditions stated in those rules. In addition, the court may enlarge the time to file the statement required under Rule 1007(b)(7), and to file schedules and statements in a small business case under § 1116(3) of the Code, only to the extent and under the conditions stated in Rule 1007(c).

(c)   Reduction.

(1)   In General.

Except as provided in paragraph (2) of this subdivision, when an act is required or allowed to be done at or within a specified time by these rules or by a notice given thereunder or by order of court, the court for cause shown may in its discretion with or without motion or notice order the period reduced.

(2)   Reduction Not Permitted.

The court may not reduce the time for taking action under Rules 2002(a)(7), 2003(a), 3002(c), 3014, 3015, 4001(b)(2), (c)(2), 4003(a), 4004(a), 4007(c), 4008(a), 8002, and 9033(b). In addition, the court may not reduce the time under Rule 1007(c) to file the statement required by Rule 1007(b)(7).

(d)   Motion Papers.

A written motion, other than one which may be heard ex parte, and notice of any hearing shall be served not later than seven days before the time specified for such hearing, unless a different period is fixed by these rules or by order of the court. Such an order may for cause shown be made on ex parte application. When a motion is supported by affidavit, the affidavit shall be served with the motion. Except as otherwise provided in Rule 9023, any written response shall be served not later than one day before the hearing, unless the court permits otherwise.

(e)   Time of Service.

Service of process and service of any paper other than process or of notice by mail is complete on mailing.

(f)   Additional Time After Service by Mail or Under Rule 5(b)(2)(D), (E), or (F) F.R.Civ.P.

When there is a right or requirement to act or undertake some proceedings within a prescribed period after service and that service is by mail or under Rule 5(b)(2)(D), (E), or (F) F.R.Civ.P., three days are added after the prescribed period would otherwise expire under Rule 9006(a).

(g)   Grain Storage Facility Cases.

This rule shall not limit the court's authority under § 557 of the Code to enter orders governing procedures in cases in which the debtor is an owner or operator of a grain storage facility.

(As amended Mar. 30, 1987, eff. Aug. 1, 1987; Apr. 25, 1989, eff. Aug. 1, 1989; Apr. 30, 1991, eff. Aug. 1, 1991; Apr. 23, 1996, eff. Dec. 1, 1996; Apr. 29, 1999, eff. Dec. 1, 1999; Apr. 23, 2001, eff. Dec. 1, 2001; Apr. 25, 2005, eff. Dec. 1, 2005; Apr. 23, 2008, eff. Dec. 1, 2008; Mar. 26, 2009, eff. Dec. 1, 2009; Apr. 16, 2013, eff. Dec. 1, 2013.)

Rule 9007.   General Authority to Regulate Notices

When notice is to be given under these rules, the court shall designate, if not otherwise specified herein, the time within which, the entities to whom, and the form and manner in which the notice shall be given. When feasible, the court may order any notices under these rules to be combined.

(As amended Mar. 30, 1987, eff. Aug. 1, 1987.)

Rule 9008.   Service or Notice by Publication

Whenever these rules require or authorize service or notice by publication, the court shall, to the extent not otherwise specified in these rules, determine the form and manner thereof, including the newspaper or other medium to be used and the number of publications.

Rule 9009.   Forms

Except as otherwise provided in Rule 3016(d), the Official Forms prescribed by the Judicial Conference of the United States shall be observed and used with alterations as may be appropriate. Forms may be combined and their contents rearranged to permit economies in their use. The Director of the Administrative Office of the United States Courts may issue additional forms for use under the Code. The forms shall be construed to be consistent with these rules and the Code.

(As amended Apr. 30, 1991, eff. Aug. 1, 1991; Apr. 23, 2008, eff. Dec. 1, 2008.)

Rule 9010.   Representation and Appearances; Powers of Attorney

(a) Authority to Act Personally or by Attorney.

A debtor, creditor, equity security holder, indenture trustee, committee or other party may (1) appear in a case under the Code and act either in the entity's own behalf or by an attorney authorized to practice in the court, and (2) perform any act not constituting the practice of law, by an authorized agent, attorney in fact, or proxy.

(b) Notice of Appearance.

An attorney appearing for a party in a case under the Code shall file a notice of appearance with the attorney's name, office address and telephone number, unless the attorney's appearance is otherwise noted in the record.

(c) Power of Attorney.

The authority of any agent, attorney in fact, or proxy to represent a creditor for any purpose other than the execution and filing of a proof of claim or the acceptance or rejection of a plan shall be evidenced by a power of attorney conforming substantially to the appropriate Official Form. The execution of any such power of attorney shall be acknowledged before one of the officers enumerated in 28 U.S.C. § 459, § 953, Rule 9012, or a person authorized to administer oaths under the laws of the state where the oath is administered.

(As amended Mar. 30, 1987, eff. Aug. 1, 1987; Apr. 30, 1991, eff. Aug. 1, 1991.)

Rule 9011.   Signing of Papers; Representations to the Court; Sanctions; Verification and Copies of Papers

(a) Signature.

Every petition, pleading, written motion, and other paper, except a list, schedule, or statement, or amendments thereto, shall be signed by at least one attorney of record in the attorney's individual name. A party who is not represented by an attorney shall sign all papers. Each paper shall state the signer's address and telephone number, if any. An unsigned paper shall be stricken unless omission of the signature is corrected promptly after being called to the attention of the attorney or party.

(b) Representations to the Court.

By presenting to the court (whether by signing, filing, submitting, or later advocating) a petition, pleading, written motion, or other paper, an attorney or unrepresented party is certifying that to the best of the person's knowledge, information, and belief, formed after an inquiry reasonable under the circumstances,—[1]

(1) it is not being presented for any improper purpose, such as to harass or to cause unnecessary delay or needless increase in the cost of litigation;

---

[1] So in original. The comma probably should not appear.

(2) the claims, defenses, and other legal contentions therein are warranted by existing law or by a nonfrivolous argument for the extension, modification, or reversal of existing law or the establishment of new law;

(3) the allegations and other factual contentions have evidentiary support or, if specifically so identified, are likely to have evidentiary support after a reasonable opportunity for further investigation or discovery; and

(4) the denials of factual contentions are warranted on the evidence or, if specifically so identified, are reasonably based on a lack of information or belief.

(c) Sanctions.

If, after notice and a reasonable opportunity to respond, the court determines that subdivision (b) has been violated, the court may, subject to the conditions stated below, impose an appropriate sanction upon the attorneys, law firms, or parties that have violated subdivision (b) or are responsible for the violation.

(1) How Initiated.

(A) By Motion.

A motion for sanctions under this rule shall be made separately from other motions or requests and shall describe the specific conduct alleged to violate subdivision (b). It shall be served as provided in Rule 7004. The motion for sanctions may not be filed with or presented to the court unless, within 21 days after service of the motion (or such other period as the court may prescribe), the challenged paper, claim, defense, contention, allegation, or denial is not withdrawn or appropriately corrected, except that this limitation shall not apply if the conduct alleged is the filing of a petition in violation of subdivision (b). If warranted, the court may award to the party prevailing on the motion the reasonable expenses and attorney's fees incurred in presenting or opposing the motion. Absent exceptional circumstances, a law firm shall be held jointly responsible for violations committed by its partners, associates, and employees.

(B) On Court's Initiative.

On its own initiative, the court may enter an order describing the specific conduct that appears to violate subdivision (b) and directing an attorney, law firm, or party to show cause why it has not violated subdivision (b) with respect thereto.

(2) Nature of Sanction; Limitations.

A sanction imposed for violation of this rule shall be limited to what is sufficient to deter repetition of such conduct or comparable conduct by others similarly situated. Subject to the limitations in subparagraphs (A) and (B), the sanction may consist of, or include, directives of a nonmonetary nature, an order to pay a penalty into court, or, if imposed on motion and warranted for effective deterrence, an order directing payment to the movant of some or all of the reasonable attorneys' fees and other expenses incurred as a direct result of the violation.

(A) Monetary sanctions may not be awarded against a represented party for a violation of subdivision (b)(2).

(B) Monetary sanctions may not be awarded on the court's initiative unless the court issues its order to show cause before a voluntary dismissal or settlement of the claims made by or against the party which is, or whose attorneys are, to be sanctioned.

(3) Order.

When imposing sanctions, the court shall describe the conduct determined to constitute a violation of this rule and explain the basis for the sanction imposed.

(d) Inapplicability To Discovery.

Subdivisions (a) through (c) of this rule do not apply to disclosures and discovery requests, responses, objections, and motions that are subject to the provisions of Rules 7026 through 7037.

(e)   Verification.

Except as otherwise specifically provided by these rules, papers filed in a case under the Code need not be verified. Whenever verification is required by these rules, an unsworn declaration as provided in 28 U.S.C. § 1746 satisfies the requirement of verification.

(f)   Copies of Signed or Verified Papers.

When these rules require copies of a signed or verified paper, it shall suffice if the original is signed or verified and the copies are conformed to the original.

(As amended Mar. 30, 1987, eff. Aug. 1, 1987; Apr. 30, 1991, eff. Aug. 1, 1991; Apr. 11, 1997, eff. Dec. 1, 1997.)

Rule 9012.   Oaths and Affirmations

(a)   Persons Authorized To Administer Oaths.

The following persons may administer oaths and affirmations and take acknowledgments: a bankruptcy judge, clerk, deputy clerk, United States trustee, officer authorized to administer oaths in proceedings before the courts of the United States or under the laws of the state where the oath is to be taken, or a diplomatic or consular officer of the United States in any foreign country.

(b)   Affirmation in Lieu of Oath.

When in a case under the Code an oath is required to be taken a solemn affirmation may be accepted in lieu thereof.

(As amended Mar. 30, 1987, eff. Aug. 1, 1987; Apr. 30, 1991, eff. Aug. 1, 1991.)

Rule 9013.   Motions: Form and Service

A request for an order, except when an application is authorized by the rules, shall be by written motion, unless made during a hearing. The motion shall state with particularity the grounds therefor, and shall set forth the relief or order sought. Every written motion, other than one which may be considered ex parte, shall be served by the moving party within the time determined under Rule 9006(d). The moving party shall serve the motion on:

(a)   the trustee or debtor in possession and on those entities specified by these rules; or

(b)   the entities the court directs if these rules do not require service or specify the entities to be served.

(As amended Mar. 30, 1987, eff. Aug. 1, 1987; Apr. 16, 2013, eff. Dec. 1, 2013.)

Rule 9014.   Contested Matters

(a)   Motion. In a contested matter not otherwise governed by these rules, relief shall be requested by motion, and reasonable notice and opportunity for hearing shall be afforded the party against whom relief is sought. No response is required under this rule unless the court directs otherwise.

(b)   Service. The motion shall be served in the manner provided for service of a summons and complaint by Rule 7004 and within the time determined under Rule 9006(d). Any written response to the motion shall be served within the time determined under Rule 9006(d). Any paper served after the motion shall be served in the manner provided by Rule 5(b) F.R.Civ.P.

(c)   Application of Part VII Rules. Except as otherwise provided in this rule, and unless the court directs otherwise, the following rules shall apply: 7009, 7017, 7021, 7025, 7026, 7028–7037, 7041, 7042, 7052, 7054–7056, 7064, 7069, and 7071. The following subdivisions of Fed. R. Civ. P. 26, as incorporated by Rule 7026, shall not apply in a contested matter unless the court directs otherwise: 26(a)(1) (mandatory disclosure), 26(a)(2) (disclosures regarding expert testimony) and 26(a)(3) (additional pre-trial disclosure), and 26(f) (mandatory meeting before scheduling conference/ discovery plan). An entity that desires to perpetuate testimony may proceed in the same manner as provided in Rule 7027 for the taking of a deposition before an adversary proceeding. The court may at any stage in a particular matter direct that one or more of the other rules in Part VII shall apply. The court shall give the parties notice of any order issued under this paragraph to afford them a reasonable opportunity to comply with the procedures prescribed by the order.

(d) Testimony of Witnesses. Testimony of witnesses with respect to disputed material factual issues shall be taken in the same manner as testimony in an adversary proceeding.

(e) Attendance of Witnesses. The court shall provide procedures that enable parties to ascertain at a reasonable time before any scheduled hearing whether the hearing will be an evidentiary hearing at which witnesses may testify.

(As amended Mar. 30, 1987, eff. Aug. 1, 1987; Apr. 29, 1999, eff. Dec. 1, 1999; Apr. 29, 2002, eff. Dec. 1, 2002; Apr. 26, 2004, eff. Dec. 1, 2004; Apr. 16, 2013, eff. Dec. 1, 2013.)

Rule 9015.   Jury Trials

(a) Applicability of Certain Federal Rules of Civil Procedure.

Rules 38, 39, 47–49, and 51, F.R.Civ.P., and Rule 81(c) F.R.Civ.P. insofar as it applies to jury trials, apply in cases and proceedings, except that a demand made under Rule 38(b) F.R.Civ.P. shall be filed in accordance with Rule 5005.

(b) Consent to Have Trial Conducted by Bankruptcy Judge.

If the right to a jury trial applies, a timely demand has been filed pursuant to Rule 38(b) F.R.Civ.P., and the bankruptcy judge has been specially designated to conduct the jury trial, the parties may consent to have a jury trial conducted by a bankruptcy judge under 28 U.S.C. § 157(e) by jointly or separately filing a statement of consent within any applicable time limits specified by local rule.

(c) Applicability of Rule 50 F.R.Civ.P.

Rule 50 F.R.Civ.P. applies in cases and proceedings, except that any renewed motion for judgment or request for a new trial shall be filed no later than 14 days after the entry of judgment.

(Added Apr. 11, 1997, eff. Dec. 1, 1997, and amended Mar. 26, 2009, eff. Dec. 1, 2009.)

Rule 9016.   Subpoena

Rule 45 F.R.Civ.P. applies in cases under the Code.

(As amended Mar. 30, 1987, eff. Aug. 1, 1987.)

Rule 9017.   Evidence

The Federal Rules of Evidence and Rules 43, 44 and 44.1 F.R.Civ.P. apply in cases under the Code.

Rule 9018.   Secret Confidential, Scandalous, or Defamatory Matter

On motion or on its own initiative, with or without notice, the court may make any order which justice requires (1) to protect the estate or any entity in respect of a trade secret or other confidential research, development, or commercial information, (2) to protect any entity against scandalous or defamatory matter contained in any paper filed in a case under the Code, or (3) to protect governmental matters that are made confidential by statute or regulation. If an order is entered under this rule without notice, any entity affected thereby may move to vacate or modify the order, and after a hearing on notice the court shall determine the motion.

(As amended Mar. 30, 1987, eff. Aug. 1, 1987.)

Rule 9019.   Compromise and Arbitration

(a) Compromise.

On motion by the trustee and after notice and a hearing, the court may approve a compromise or settlement. Notice shall be given to creditors, the United States trustee, the debtor, and indenture trustees as provided in Rule 2002 and to any other entity as the court may direct.

(b) Authority to Compromise or Settle Controversies Within Classes.

After a hearing on such notice as the court may direct, the court may fix a class or classes of controversies and authorize the trustee to compromise or settle controversies within such class or classes without further hearing or notice.

(c) Arbitration.

On stipulation of the parties to any controversy affecting the estate the court may authorize the matter to be submitted to final and binding arbitration.

(As amended Mar. 30, 1987, eff. Aug. 1, 1987; Apr. 30, 1991, eff. Aug. 1, 1991; Apr. 22, 1993, eff. Aug. 1, 1993.)

Rule 9020.   Contempt Proceedings

Rule 9014 governs a motion for an order of contempt made by the United States trustee or a party in interest.

(As amended Mar. 30, 1987, eff. Aug. 1, 1987; Apr. 30, 1991, eff. 1, 1991; Apr. 23, 2001, eff. Dec. 1, 2001.)

Rule 9021.   Entry of Judgment

A judgment or order is effective when entered under Rule 5003.

(As amended Mar. 30, 1987, eff. Aug. 1, 1987; Mar. 26, 2009, eff. Dec. 1, 2009.)

Rule 9022.   Notice of Judgment or Order

(a) Judgment or Order of Bankruptcy Judge.

Immediately on the entry of a judgment or order the clerk shall serve a notice of entry in the manner provided in Rule 5(b) F.R.Civ.P. on the contesting parties and on other entities as the court directs. Unless the case is a chapter 9 municipality case, the clerk shall forthwith transmit to the United States trustee a copy of the judgment or order. Service of the notice shall be noted in the docket. Lack of notice of the entry does not affect the time to appeal or relieve or authorize the court to relieve a party for failure to appeal within the time allowed, except as permitted in Rule 8002.

(b) Judgment or Order of District Judge.

Notice of a judgment or order entered by a district judge is governed by Rule 77(d) F.R.Civ.P. Unless the case is a chapter 9 municipality case, the clerk shall forthwith transmit to the United States trustee a copy of a judgment or order entered by a district judge.

(As amended Mar. 30, 1987, eff. Aug. 1, 1987; Apr. 30, 1991, eff. Aug. 1, 1991; Apr. 23, 2001, eff. Dec. 1, 2001.)

Rule 9023.   New Trials; Amendment of Judgments

Except as provided in this rule and Rule 3008, Rule 59 F.R.Civ.P. applies in cases under the Code. A motion for a new trial or to alter or amend a judgment shall be filed, and a court may on its own order a new trial, no later than 14 days after entry of judgment. In some circumstances, Rule 8008 governs post-judgment motion practice after an appeal has been docketed and is pending.

(As amended Mar. 26, 2009, eff. Dec. 1, 2009; Apr. 25, 2014, eff. Dec. 1, 2014.)

Rule 9024.   Relief from Judgment or Order

Rule 60 F.R.Civ.P. applies in cases under the Code except that (1) a motion to reopen a case under the Code or for the reconsideration of an order allowing or disallowing a claim against the estate entered without a contest is not subject to the one year limitation prescribed in Rule 60(c), (2) a complaint to revoke a discharge in a chapter 7 liquidation case may be filed only within the time allowed by § 727(e) of the Code, and (3) a complaint to revoke an order confirming a plan may be filed only within the time allowed by § 1144, § 1230, or § 1330. In some circumstances, Rule 8008 governs past-judgment motion practice after an appeal has been docketed and is pending.

(As amended Apr. 30, 1991, eff. Aug. 1, 1991; Apr. 23, 2008, eff. Dec. 1, 2008; Apr. 25, 2014, eff. Dec. 1, 2014.)

Rule 9025.   Security: Proceedings Against Sureties

Whenever the Code or these rules require or permit the giving of security by a party, and security is given in the form of a bond or stipulation or other undertaking with one or more sureties, each surety submits to the jurisdiction of the court, and liability may be determined in an adversary proceeding governed by the rules in Part VII.

Rule 9026.   Exceptions Unnecessary

Rule 46 F.R.Civ.P. applies in cases under the Code.

Rule 9027.   Removal

(a)   Notice of Removal.

(1)   Where Filed; Form and Content.

A notice of removal shall be filed with the clerk for the district and division within which is located the state or federal court where the civil action is pending. The notice shall be signed pursuant to Rule 9011 and contain a short and plain statement of the facts which entitle the party filing the notice to remove, contain a statement that upon removal of the claim or cause of action the proceeding is core or non-core and, if non-core, that the party filing the notice does or does not consent to entry of final orders or judgment by the bankruptcy judge, and be accompanied by a copy of all process and pleadings.

(2)   Time for Filing; Civil Action Initiated Before Commencement of the Case Under the Code.

If the claim or cause of action in a civil action is pending when a case under the Code is commenced, a notice of removal may be filed only within the longest of (A) 90 days after the order for relief in the case under the Code, (B) 30 days after entry of an order terminating a stay, if the claim or cause of action in a civil action has been stayed under § 362 of the Code, or (C) 30 days after a trustee qualifies in a chapter 11 reorganization case but not later than 180 days after the order for relief.

(3)   Time for Filing; Civil Action Initiated After Commencement of the Case Under the Code.

If a claim or cause of action is asserted in another court after the commencement of a case under the Code, a notice of removal may be filed with the clerk only within the shorter of (A) 30 days after receipt, through service or otherwise, of a copy of the initial pleading setting forth the claim or cause of action sought to be removed, or (B) 30 days after receipt of the summons if the initial pleading has been filed with the court but not served with the summons.

(b)   Notice.

Promptly after filing the notice of removal, the party filing the notice shall serve a copy of it on all parties to the removed claim or cause of action.

(c)　Filing in Non-Bankruptcy Court.

Promptly after filing the notice of removal, the party filing the notice shall file a copy of it with the clerk of the court from which the claim or cause of action is removed. Removal of the claim or cause of action is effected on such filing of a copy of the notice of removal. The parties shall proceed no further in that court unless and until the claim or cause of action is remanded.

(d)　Remand.

A motion for remand of the removed claim or cause of action shall be governed by Rule 9014 and served on the parties to the removed claim or cause of action.

(e)　Procedure After Removal.

(1)　After removal of a claim or cause of action to a district court the district court or, if the case under the Code has been referred to a bankruptcy judge of the district, the bankruptcy judge, may issue all necessary orders and process to bring before it all proper parties whether served by process issued by the court from which the claim or cause of action was removed or otherwise.

(2)　The district court or, if the case under the Code has been referred to a bankruptcy judge of the district, the bankruptcy judge, may require the party filing the notice of removal to file with the clerk copies of all records and proceedings relating to the claim or cause of action in the court from which the claim or cause of action was removed.

(3)　Any party who has filed a pleading in connection with the removed claim or cause of action, other than the party filing the notice of removal, shall file a statement admitting or denying any allegation in the notice of removal that upon removal of the claim or cause of action the proceeding is core or non-core. If the statement alleges that the proceeding is non-core, it shall state that the party does or does not consent to entry of final orders or judgment by the bankruptcy judge. A statement required by this paragraph shall be signed pursuant to Rule 9011 and shall be filed not later than 14 days after the filing of the notice of removal. Any party who files a statement pursuant to this paragraph shall mail a copy to every other party to the removed claim or cause of action.

(f)　Process After Removal.

If one or more of the defendants has not been served with process, the service has not been perfected prior to removal, or the process served proves to be defective, such process or service may be completed or new process issued pursuant to Part VII of these rules. This subdivision shall not deprive any defendant on whom process is served after removal of the defendant's right to move to remand the case.

(g)　Applicability of Part VII.

The rules of Part VII apply to a claim or cause of action removed to a district court from a federal or state court and govern procedure after removal. Repleading is not necessary unless the court so orders. In a removed action in which the defendant has not answered, the defendant shall answer or present the other defenses or objections available under the rules of Part VII within 21 days following the receipt through service or otherwise of a copy of the initial pleading setting forth the claim for relief on which the action or proceeding is based, or within 21 days following the service of summons on such initial pleading, or within seven days following the filing of the notice of removal, whichever period is longest.

(h)　Record Supplied.

When a party is entitled to copies of the records and proceedings in any civil action or proceeding in a federal or a state court, to be used in the removed civil action or proceeding, and the clerk of the federal or state court, on demand accompanied by payment or tender of the lawful fees, fails to deliver certified copies, the court may, on affidavit reciting the facts, direct such record to be supplied by affidavit or otherwise. Thereupon the proceedings, trial and judgment may be had in the court, and all process awarded, as if certified copies had been filed.

(i)　Attachment or Sequestration; Securities.

When a claim or cause of action is removed to a district court, any attachment or sequestration of property in the court from which the claim or cause of action was removed shall hold the property to answer the final judgment or decree in the same manner as the property would have been held to answer final judgment or decree had it been rendered by the court from which the claim or cause of action was removed. All bonds, undertakings, or security given by either party to the claim or cause of action prior to its removal shall remain valid and effectual notwithstanding such removal. All injunctions issued, orders entered and other proceedings had prior to removal shall remain in full force and effect until dissolved or modified by the court.

(As amended Mar. 30, 1987, eff. Aug. 1, 1987; Apr. 30, 1991, eff. Aug. 1, 1991; Apr. 29, 2002, eff. Dec. 1, 2002; Mar. 26, 2009, eff. Dec. 1, 2009.)

Rule 9028.   Disability of a Judge

Rule 63 F.R.Civ.P. applies in cases under the Code.

(As amended Mar. 30, 1987, eff. Aug. 1, 1987.)

Rule 9029.   Local Bankruptcy Rules; Procedure When There is No Controlling Law

(a) Local Bankruptcy Rules.

(1) Each district court acting by a majority of its district judges may make and amend rules governing practice and procedure in all cases and proceedings within the district court's bankruptcy jurisdiction which are consistent with—but not duplicative of—Acts of Congress and these rules and which do not prohibit or limit the use of the Official Forms. Rule 83 F.R.Civ.P. governs the procedure for making local rules. A district court may authorize the bankruptcy judges of the district, subject to any limitation or condition it may prescribe and the requirements of 83 F.R.Civ.P., to make and amend rules of practice and procedure which are consistent with—but not duplicative of—Acts of Congress and these rules and which do not prohibit or limit the use of the Official Forms. Local rules shall conform to any uniform numbering system prescribed by the Judicial Conference of the United States.

(2) A local rule imposing a requirement of form shall not be enforced in a manner that causes a party to lose rights because of a nonwillful failure to comply with the requirement.

(b) Procedure When There is No Controlling Law. A judge may regulate practice in any manner consistent with federal law, these rules, Official Forms, and local rules of the district. No sanction or other disadvantage may be imposed for noncompliance with any requirement not in federal law, federal rules, Official Forms, or the local rules of the district unless the alleged violator has been furnished in the particular case with actual notice of the requirement.

(As amended Mar. 30, 1987, eff. Aug. 1, 1987; Apr. 30, 1991, eff. Aug. 1, 1991; Apr. 27, 1995, eff. Dec. 1, 1995.)

Rule 9030.   Jurisdiction and Venue Unaffected

These rules shall not be construed to extend or limit the jurisdiction of the courts or the venue of any matters therein.

(As amended Mar. 30, 1987, eff. Aug. 1, 1987.)

Rule 9031.   Masters Not Authorized

Rule 53 F.R.Civ.P. does not apply in cases under the Code.

Rule 9032.   Effect of Amendment of Federal Rules of Civil Procedure

The Federal Rules of Civil Procedure which are incorporated by reference and made applicable by these rules shall be the Federal Rules of Civil Procedure in effect on the effective date of these rules and as thereafter amended, unless otherwise provided by such amendment or by these rules.

(As amended Apr. 30, 1991, eff. Aug. 1, 1991.)

Rule 9033.   Review of Proposed Findings of Fact and Conclusions of Law in Non-Core Proceedings

(a) Service.

In non-core proceedings heard pursuant to 28 U.S.C. § 157(c)(1), the bankruptcy judge shall file proposed findings of fact and conclusions of law. The clerk shall serve forthwith copies on all parties by mail and note the date of mailing on the docket.

(b) Objections: Time for Filing.

Within 14 days after being served with a copy of the proposed findings of fact and conclusions of law a party may serve and file with the clerk written objections which identify the specific proposed findings or conclusions objected to and state the grounds for such objection. A party may respond to another party's objections within 14 days after being served with a copy thereof. A party objecting to the bankruptcy judge's proposed findings or conclusions shall arrange promptly for the transcription of the record, or such portions of it as all parties may agree upon or the bankruptcy judge deems sufficient, unless the district judge otherwise directs.

(c) Extension of Time.

The bankruptcy judge may for cause extend the time for filing objections by any party for a period not to exceed 21 days from the expiration of the time otherwise prescribed by this rule. A request to extend the time for filing objections must be made before the time for filing objections has expired, except that a request made no more than 21 days after the expiration of the time for filing objections may be granted upon a showing of excusable neglect.

(d) Standard of Review.

The district judge shall make a de novo review upon the record or, after additional evidence, of any portion of the bankruptcy judge's findings of fact or conclusions of law to which specific written objection has been made in accordance with this rule. The district judge may accept, reject, or modify the proposed findings of fact or conclusions of law, receive further evidence, or recommit the matter to the bankruptcy judge with instructions.

(Added Mar. 30, 1987, eff. Aug. 1, 1987, and amended Mar. 26, 2009, eff. Dec. 1, 2009.)

Rule 9034.   Transmittal of Pleadings, Motion Papers, Objections, and Other Papers to the United States Trustee

Unless the United States trustee requests otherwise or the case is a chapter 9 municipality case, any entity that files a pleading, motion, objection, or similar paper relating to any of the following matters shall transmit a copy thereof to the United States trustee within the time required by these rules for service of the paper:

(a) a proposed use, sale, or lease of property of the estate other than in the ordinary course of business;

(b) the approval of a compromise or settlement of a controversy;

(c) the dismissal or conversion of a case to another chapter;

(d) the employment of professional persons;

(e) an application for compensation or reimbursement of expenses;

(f) a motion for, or approval of an agreement relating to, the use of cash collateral or authority to obtain credit;

(g) the appointment of a trustee or examiner in a chapter 11 reorganization case;

(h) the approval of a disclosure statement;

(i) the confirmation of a plan;

(j)   an objection to, or waiver or revocation of, the debtor's discharge;

(k)   any other matter in which the United States trustee requests copies of filed papers or the court orders copies transmitted to the United States trustee.

(Added Apr. 30, 1991, eff. Aug. 1, 1991.)

Rule 9035.   Applicability of Rules in Judicial Districts in Alabama and North Carolina

In any case under the Code that is filed in or transferred to a district in the State of Alabama or the State of North Carolina and in which a United States trustee is not authorized to act, these rules apply to the extent that they are not inconsistent with any federal statute effective in the case.

(Added Apr. 30, 1991, eff. Aug. 1, 1991; amended Apr. 11, 1997, eff. Dec. 1, 1997.)

Rule 9036.   Notice by Electronic Transmission

Whenever the clerk or some other person as directed by the court is required to send notice by mail and the entity entitled to receive the notice requests in writing that, instead of notice by mail, all or part of the information required to be contained in the notice be sent by a specified type of electronic transmission, the court may direct the clerk or other person to send the information by such electronic transmission. Notice by electronic means is complete on transmission.

(Added Apr. 22, 1993, eff. Aug. 1, 1993; amended Apr. 25, 2005, eff. Dec. 1, 2005.)

Rule 9037.   Privacy Protection For Filings Made with the Court

(a)   Redacted Filings.

Unless the court orders otherwise, in an electronic or paper filing made with the court that contains an individual's social-security number, taxpayer-identification number, or birth date, the name of an individual, other than the debtor, known to be and identified as a minor, or a financial-account number, a party or nonparty making the filing may include only:

(1)   the last four digits of the social-security number and taxpayer-identification number;

(2)   the year of the individual's birth;

(3)   the minor's initials; and

(4)   the last four digits of the financial-account number.

(b)   Exemptions From the Redaction Requirement.

The redaction requirement does not apply to the following:

(1)   a financial-account number that identifies the property allegedly subject to forfeiture in a forfeiture proceeding;

(2)   the record of an administrative or agency proceeding unless filed with a proof of claim;

(3)   the official record of a state-court proceeding;

(4)   the record of a court or tribunal, if that record was not subject to the redaction requirement when originally filed;

(5)   a filing covered by subdivision (c) of this rule; and

(6)   a filing that is subject to § 110 of the Code.

(c)   Filings Made Under Seal.

The court may order that a filing be made under seal without redaction. The court may later unseal the filing or order the entity that made the filing to file a redacted version for the public record.

(d) Protective Orders.

For cause, the court may by order in a case under the Code:

    (1) require redaction of additional information; or

    (2) limit or prohibit a nonparty's remote electronic access to a document filed with the court.

(e) Option for Additional Unredacted Filing Under Seal.

An entity making a redacted filing may also file an unredacted copy under seal. The court must retain the unredacted copy as part of the record.

(f) Option for Filing a Reference List.

A filing that contains redacted information may be filed together with a reference list that identifies each item of redacted information and specifies an appropriate identifier that uniquely corresponds to each item listed. The list must be filed under seal and may be amended as of right. Any reference in the case to a listed identifier will be construed to refer to the corresponding item of information.

(g) Waiver of Protection of Identifiers.

An entity waives the protection of subdivision (a) as to the entity's own information by filing it without redaction and not under seal.

    (Added Apr. 30, 2007, eff. Dec. 1, 2007.)

OFFICIAL BANKRUPTCY FORMS

––––––––––

For the current version of the Official Bankruptcy Forms, go to http://www.uscourts.gov/forms/ bankruptcy-forms, where the forms can be filled in electronically and either saved or printed. The forms are updated annually to reflect changes in the statute and bankruptcy rules.